W9-AQW-125

READERS' GUIDE TO PERIODICAL LITERATURE

AN AUTHOR AND SUBJECT INDEX

MARCH 1963—FEBRUARY 1965

EDITED BY
ZADA LIMERICK

INDEXERS
ANNE W. FURNESS
LINDA LACK HOY
LOVISA J. JENKINS
VALERIE F. OLDLAND
JOSEPHINE SAMUDIO

THE H. W. WILSON COMPANY
NEW YORK 1965

PRINTED IN THE UNITED STATES OF AMERICA

Library of Congress Catalog Card No. (6-8232)

List of Periodicals Indexed

All data as of latest issue received

ALA Bulletin—available only to members. m (bi-m Jl-Ag) American Library Association, 50 E Huron St, Chicago 60611

America—$8. w (bi-w year-end issue) America Press, 106 W 56th St, New York 10019

The American Academy of Political and Social Science Annals—$10. free to members. bi-m American Academy of Political and Social Science, 3937 Chestnut St, Philadelphia 19104

American Artist—$7. m (S-Je) American Artist, 2160 Patterson St, Cincinnati, Ohio 45214

The American City—$7. m Buttenheim Pub. Corp, 757 3d Av, New York 10017

American Forests—$6. m American Forestry Association, 919 17th St, NW, Washington, D.C. 20006

***American Heritage**—$15. bi-m American Heritage, 383 W Center St, Marion, Ohio 43301

The American Historical Review—$10. free to members of the American Historical Association, q The Macmillan Co, 60 5th Av, New York 10011

The American Home—$3. m (bi-m Ja, Jl) The American Home, Independence Sq, Philadelphia 19105

The American Record Guide—$4.50. m American Record Guide, P.O. Box 319, Radio City Station, New York 10019

Américas—$4. m Pan American Union, Washington, D.C. 20006

Antiques—$10.50. m Straight Enterprises, Inc, 601 5th Av, New York 10017

Architectural Forum—$7. m Architectural Forum, 540 N Michigan Av, Chicago 60611
Discontinued publication Ag-S '64

Architectural Record—$5.50. m (semi-m My) Architectural Record, P.O. Box 430, Hightstown, N.J. 08520

Art News—$11.50. m (q Je-Ag) The Art Foundation Press, Inc, 4 E 53d St, New York 10022

***The Atlantic**—$8.50. m Atlantic Monthly Co, 8 Arlington St, Boston 02116

Audubon Magazine—$7. bi-m National Audubon Society, 1130 5th Av, New York 10028

Aviation Week & Space Technology—$8. w Aviation Week, P.O. Box 430, Hightstown, N.J. 08520

Better Homes and Gardens—$3. m Better Homes and Gardens, 1716 Locust St, Des Moines, Ia. 50303

Bulletin of the Atomic Scientists—$6. m (S-Je) Bulletin of the Atomic Scientists, 935 E 60th St, Chicago 60637

Business Week—$7. w Business Week, P.O. Box 430, Hightstown, N.J. 08520

The Catholic World—$6. m Catholic World, Harristown Road, Glen Rock, N.J. 07452

***Changing Times**—$6. m Kiplinger Washington Editors, Inc, Editors Park, Md. 20782

The Christian Century—$7.50. w Christian Century Foundation, 407 S Dearborn St, Chicago 60605

Commentary—$7. m American Jewish Committee, 165 E 56th St, New York 10022

The Commonweal—$8. w (bi-w year-end issue, mid-Jl-mid-S) Commonweal Pub. Co, Inc, 232 Madison Av, New York 10016

Congressional Digest—$10. m (S-Je) Congressional Digest Corp, 3231 P St, NW, Washington, D.C. 20007

Consumer Bulletin—$5. m Consumers' Research, Inc, Washington, N.J. 07882

Consumer Reports—$6. m Consumers Union of U.S, Inc, 256 Washington St, Mount Vernon, N.Y. 10550

Craft Horizons—$8. bi-m American Craftsmen's Council, 44 W 53d St, New York 10019

Current History—$8. m Current History, Inc, 1822 Ludlow St, Philadelphia 19103

Dance Magazine—$7. m Dance Magazine, 268 W 47th St, New York 10036

The Department of State Bulletin—$10. w Department of State Bulletin, Superintendent of Documents, U.S. Government Printing Office, Washington, D.C. 20402

Design—$4.50. bi-m (S-Je) Design Magazine, 1100 Waterway Blvd, Indianapolis, Ind. 46207

Dun's Review and Modern Industry—$5. m Dun & Bradstreet Pub. Corp, 99 Church St, New York 10008

Ebony—$5. m Johnson Pub. Co, 1820 S Michigan Av, Chicago 60616

Electronics World—$5. m Electronics World, Portland Pl, Boulder, Colo. 80301

Esquire—$6.50. m Esquire, Portland Pl, Boulder, Colo. 80301

Farm Journal (Eastern edition)—$1. m Farm Journal, Inc, 230 W Washington Sq, Philadelphia 19105

Field & Stream—$4. m Holt, Rinehart and Winston, Inc, 383 Madison Av, New York 10017

Flower Grower, The Home Garden Magazine—$3.50. m Flower Grower, Albany, N.Y. 12201

Flying—$5. m Flying, 434 S Wabash Av, Chicago 60605

15243

Focus—$1.25. m (S-Je) American Geographical Society, Broadway at 156th St, New York 10032

*__Foreign Affairs__—$6. q Council on Foreign Relations, Inc, 58 E 68th St, New York 10021

Fortune—$12. m Fortune, 540 N Michigan Av, Chicago 60611

*__Good Housekeeping__—$4. m Good Housekeeping, 250 W 55th St, New York 10019

*__Harper's Magazine__—$7. m Harper's Magazine, 381 W Center St, Marion, Ohio 43301

Harvard Business Review—$10. bi-m Harvard Business Review, Soldier's Field Station, Boston 02163

High Fidelity—$7. m High Fidelity, 2160 Patterson St, Cincinnati, Ohio 45214

Hobbies—$4. m Lightner Pub. Corp, 1006 S Michigan Av, Chicago 60605

*__Holiday__—$5.95. m Holiday, Independence Sq, Philadelphia 19105

*__Horizon__—$16. q Horizon, 379 W Center St, Marion, Ohio 43301

The Horn Book Magazine—$5. bi-m Horn Book, Inc, 585 Boylston St, Boston 02116

Horticulture—$4. m Horticulture, 300 Massachusetts Av, Boston 02115

Hot Rod—$5. m Petersen Pub. Co, 5959 Hollywood Blvd, Los Angeles 90028

House & Garden incorporating Living for Young Homemakers—$6. m House & Garden, Boulder, Colo. 80301

House Beautiful—$6. m House Beautiful, 250 W 55th St, New York 10019

International Conciliation—$2.25. 5 times a yr (S-My) Carnegie Endowment for International Peace, United Nations Plaza at 46th St, New York 10017

*__Ladies' Home Journal__—$3. m (bi-m Ja, Jl) Ladies' Home Journal, Independence Sq, Philadelphia 19105

Library Journal—$10. semi-m (m Jl-Ag) R. R. Bowker Co, 3d & Hunting Park Av, Philadelphia 19140

Life—$7.75. w (except one issue at year-end) Life, 540 N Michigan Av, Chicago 60611

The Living Wilderness—$5. q The Wilderness Society, 2144 P St, NW, Washington, D.C. 20037

Look (Middle Atlantic edition)—$4. bi-w Look, Look Bldg, Des Moines, Ia. 50304

McCall's—$3. m McCall's, McCall St, Dayton, Ohio 45401

Mademoiselle—$5. m Mademoiselle, Boulder, Colo. 80301

Missiles and Rockets—$5. w (bi-w year-end issue) American Aviation Pub, 1001 Vermont Av, NW, Washington, D.C. 20005

Modern Photography—$5. m Modern Photography, 2160 Patterson St, Cincinnati, Ohio 45214

Monthly Labor Review—$7.50. m Superintendent of Documents, U.S. Government Printing Office, Washington, D.C. 20402

Motor Boating—$6. m Motor Boating, 250 W 55th St, New York 10019

Motor Trend—$5. m Petersen Pub. Co, 5959 Hollywood Blvd, Los Angeles 90028

Musical America—$7. m (bi-m My-Jl) Musical America, 111 W 57th St, New York 10019
Discontinued publication D '64

NEA Journal—available only to members. m (S-My) National Education Association of the United States, 1201 16th St, NW, Washington, D.C. 20036

The Nation—$10. w (bi-w Jl-Ag) Nation Associates, Inc, 333 6th Av, New York 10014

*__The National Geographic Magazine__—$8. m The Secretary, National Geographic Society, Washington, D.C. 20036

National Parks Magazine—$5. m National Parks Association, 1300 New Hampshire Av, Washington, D.C. 20036

National Review—$9. bi-w (36p issue) National Review, 150 E 35th St, New York 10016

Nation's Business—$19.75. (3 yrs) m Chamber of Commerce of the U.S, 1615 H St, NW, Washington, D.C. 20006

Natural History incorporating Nature Magazine—$5. m (bi-m Je-S) American Museum of Natural History, Central Park W at 79th St, New York 10024

The Negro History Bulletin—$2. m (O-My) Association for the Study of Negro Life and History, Inc, 1538 9th St, NW, Washington, D.C. 20001

The New Republic—$8. w (bi-w Jl-Ag) New Republic, 381 W Center St, Marion, Ohio 43301

The New York Times Magazine—$28.50. w (complete Sunday ed; not sold separately) New York Times, Times Bldg, 229 W 43d St, New York 10036

The New Yorker—$8. w New Yorker Magazine, Inc, 25 W 43d St, New York 10036

*__Newsweek__—$8. w Newsweek, 117 E 3d St, Dayton, Ohio 45402

Opera News—$7. w (24 issues S 26-My 1) The Metropolitan Opera Guild, 1425 Broadway, New York 10018

Outdoor Life—$4. m Outdoor Life, Boulder, Colo. 80313

The PTA Magazine—$1.50. m (S-Je) The PTA Magazine, 700 N Rush St, Chicago 60611

Parents' Magazine & Better Homemaking—$4. m Parents' Magazine, Bergenfield, N.J. 07621

Plays—$6. m (O-My) Plays, Inc, 8 Arlington St, Boston 02116

Poetry—$6. m (bi-m Ap-My) Modern Poetry Association, 1018 N State St, Chicago 60610

Popular Electronics—$4. m Popular Electronics, Portland Pl, Boulder, Colo. 80301

Popular Gardening & Living Outdoors—$3.50. m (bi-m My-D) Holt, Rinehart & Winston, Inc, 383 Madison Av, New York 10017

Popular Mechanics—$4. m Popular Mechanics, 250 W 55th St, New York 10019

Popular Photography—$5. m Popular Photography, Portland Pl, Boulder, Colo. 80301

Popular Science Monthly—$4. m Popular Science, P.O. Box 1083, Boulder, Colo. 80313

Publishers' Weekly—$15. w (bi-w year-end issue) R. R. Bowker Co, 3d & Hunting Park Av, Philadelphia 19140

*__Reader's Digest (Great Lakes edition)__—$2.97. m Reader's Digest Association, Inc, Pleasantville, N.Y. 10570

Enlarged type edition available from Xerox Corp, P.O. Box 3300, Grand Central Station, New York, N.Y. $4.50 a month or $25.65 for six months.

Recreation—$5. m (S-Je) National Recreation Association, 8 W 8th St, New York 10011

Redbook—$3. m Redbook, McCall St, Dayton, Ohio 45401

The Reporter—$7. bi-w (2 summer issues omitted) The Reporter, 660 Madison Av, New York 10021

The Saturday Evening Post—$3.95. 26 issues per year Saturday Evening Post, Independence Sq, Philadelphia 19105

Saturday Review—$8. w Saturday Review, Inc, 380 Madison Av, New York 10017

School and Society—$8.50. bi-w (O-My, including summer annual) Society for the Advancement of Education, Inc, 1834 Broadway, New York 10023

School Arts—$7. m (S-Je) School Arts, Printers Bldg, Worcester, Mass. 01608

School Life—$1.75. 9 times a year School Life, Superintendent of Documents, U.S. Government Printing Office, Washington, D.C. 20402

Discontinued publication D '64

Science—$8.50. w American Association for the Advancement of Science, 1515 Massachusetts Av, NW, Washington, D.C. 20005

Science Digest—$4. m Science Digest, 250 W 55th St, New York 10019

Science News Letter—$5.50. w Science Service, Inc, 1719 N St, NW, Washington, D.C. 20036

Scientific American—$6. m Scientific American, 415 Madison Av, New York 10017

Senior Scholastic (Teacher edition)—$4.50. w (S-My) Senior Scholastic, 900 Sylvan Av, Englewood Cliffs, N.J. 07632

Seventeen—$6. m Seventeen, Radnor, Pa. 19088

Sky and Telescope—$6. m Sky Pub. Corp, Harvard College Observatory, Cambridge, Mass. 02138

*__Sports Illustrated__—$7.50. w Sports Illustrated, 540 N Michigan Av, Chicago 60611

Successful Farming (Eastern edition)—$1. m Successful Farming, 1716 Locust St, Des Moines, Ia. 50303

Sunset (Central edition)—$3. in Calif, Ore, Wash, Idaho, Ariz, Nev, Utah, Hawaii. $4 in other states m Sunset Magazine, Menlo Park, Calif. 94025

Theatre Arts—$7.50. m Theatre Arts, 104 E 40th St, New York 10016

Discontinued publication Ja '64

Time—$9. w Time, 540 N Michigan Av, Chicago 60611

Today's Health—$4. m Today's Health, 535 N Dearborn St, Chicago 60610

Travel—$6. m Travel, Travel Bldg, Floral Park, N.Y. 11001

UN Monthly Chronicle—$6. m (except in Ag) UN Monthly Chronicle, Publishing Service, United Nations, N.Y. 10027

UNESCO Courier—$5. m (bi-m Jl-Ag) UNESCO Pub. Center, 317 E 34th St, Department WS, New York 10016

United Nations Review—$6. m United Nations Review, Publishing Service, United Nations, N.Y. 10027

Discontinued publication Ap '64

U.S. Camera & Travel—$5. m U.S. Camera Pub. Corp, 9 E 40th St, New York 10016

U.S. News & World Report—$8. w U.S. News & World Report, 435 Parker Av, Dayton, Ohio 45401

Vital Speeches of the Day—$8. semi-m City News Pub. Co, Inc, 1 Wolf's Lane, Pelham, N.Y. 10803

Vogue—$10. semi-m (m My-Jl, D) Vogue, Boulder, Colo. 80301

Wilson Library Bulletin—$4. m (S-Je) The H. W. Wilson Co, 950 University Av, Bronx, N.Y. 10452

The Writer—$5. m The Writer, Inc, 8 Arlington St, Boston 02116

Yachting—$6. m Yachting Pub. Corp, 50 W 44th St, New York 10036

The Yale Review—$5. q Yale Review, 92-A Yale Station, New Haven, Conn. 06511

* Available for blind readers on talking books, in braille, or on magnetic tape. For information address Division for the Blind, Library of Congress, Washington, D.C. 20540

Abbreviations of Periodicals Indexed

March 1963—February 1965

For full information, consult pages v–vii

ALA Bul—ALA Bulletin
Am Artist—American Artist
Am City—American City
Am For—American Forests
*Am Heritage—American Heritage
Am Hist R—American Historical Review
Am Home—American Home
Am Rec G—American Record Guide
America—America
Américas—Américas
Ann Am Acad—Annals of the American Academy of Political and Social Science
Antiques—Antiques
Arch Forum—Architectural Forum
Discontinued publication Ag-S '64
Arch Rec—Architectural Record
Art N—Art News
*Atlan—Atlantic
Audubon Mag—Audubon Magazine
Aviation W—Aviation Week & Space Technology

Bet Hom & Gard—Better Homes and Gardens
Bsns W—Business Week
Bul Atomic Sci—Bulletin of the Atomic Scientists

Cath World—Catholic World
*Changing T—Changing Times
Christian Cent—Christian Century
Commentary—Commentary
Commonweal—Commonweal
Cong Digest—Congressional Digest
Consumer Bul—Consumer Bulletin
Consumer Rep—Consumer Reports
Craft Horiz—Craft Horizons
Cur Hist—Current History

Dance Mag—Dance Magazine
Dept State Bul—Department of State Bulletin
Design—Design
Duns R—Dun's Review and Modern Industry

Ebony—Ebony
Electr World—Electronics World
Esquire—Esquire

Farm J—Farm Journal (Eastern edition)
Field & S—Field & Stream
Flower Grower—Flower Grower, The Home Garden Magazine
Flying—Flying
Focus—Focus
*For Affairs—Foreign Affairs
Fortune—Fortune

*Good H—Good Housekeeping

*Harper—Harper's Magazine
Harvard Bsns R—Harvard Business Review
Hi Fi—High Fidelity
Hobbies—Hobbies
*Holiday—Holiday
*Horizon—Horizon
Horn Bk—Horn Book Magazine
Horticulture—Horticulture
Hot Rod—Hot Rod
House & Gard—House & Garden incorporating Living for Young Homemakers
House B—House Beautiful

Int Concil—International Conciliation

*Ladies Home J—Ladies' Home Journal
Library J—Library Journal
Life—Life
Liv Wildn—Living Wilderness
Look—Look (Middle Atlantic edition)

McCalls—McCall's
Miss & Roc—Missiles and Rockets
Mlle—Mademoiselle
Mo Labor R—Monthly Labor Review

Mod Phot—Modern Photography
Motor B—Motor Boating
Motor T—Motor Trend
Mus Am—Musical America
Discontinued publication D '64

NEA J—NEA Journal
N Y Times Mag—New York Times Magazine
*Nat Geog Mag—National Geographic Magazine
Nat Parks Mag—National Parks Magazine
Nat R—National Review (36p issue only. pub. in alternate weeks)
Nation—Nation
Nations Bsns—Nation's Business
Natur Hist—Natural History incorporating Nature Magazine
Negro Hist Bul—Negro History Bulletin
New Repub—New Republic
New Yorker—New Yorker
*Newsweek—Newsweek

Opera N—Opera News
Outdoor Life—Outdoor Life

PTA Mag—PTA Magazine
Parents Mag—Parents' Magazine & Better Homemaking
Plays—Plays
Poetry—Poetry
Pop Electr—Popular Electronics
Pop Gard—Popular Gardening & Living Outdoors
Pop Mech—Popular Mechanics
Pop Phot—Popular Photography
Pop Sci—Popular Science Monthly
Pub W—Publishers' Weekly

*Read Digest—Reader's Digest (Great Lakes edition)
Recreation—Recreation
Redbook—Redbook
Reporter—The Reporter

Sat Eve Post—Saturday Evening Post
Sat R—Saturday Review
Sch & Soc—School and Society
Sch Arts—School Arts
Sch Life—School Life
Discontinued publication D '64
Sci Am—Scientific American
Sci Digest—Science Digest
Sci N L—Science News Letter
Science—Science
Seventeen—Seventeen
Sky & Tel—Sky and Telescope
*Sports Illus—Sports Illustrated
Sr Schol—Senior Scholastic (Teacher edition)
Suc Farm—Successful Farming (Eastern edition)
Sunset—Sunset (Central edition)

Theatre Arts—Theatre Arts
Discontinued publication Ja '64
Time—Time
Todays Health—Today's Health
Travel—Travel

UN Mo Chron—UN Monthly Chronicle
U N Rev—United Nations Review
Discontinued publication Ap '64
UNESCO Courier—UNESCO Courier
U S Camera—U.S. Camera & Travel
U S News—U.S. News & World Report

Vital Speeches—Vital Speeches of the Day
Vogue—Vogue

Wilson Lib Bul—Wilson Library Bulletin
Writer—Writer

Yachting—Yachting
Yale R—Yale Review

* Available for blind readers on talking books, in braille, or on magnetic tape. For information address Division for the Blind, Library of Congress, Washington, D.C. 20540

Key to Abbreviations

+	continued on later pages of same issue
abp	archbishop
abr	abridged
Ag	August
Ap	April
arch	architect
arr	arranged
assn	association
av	avenue
bart	baronet
bibliog	bibliography
bibliog f	bibliographical footnotes
bi-m	bimonthly
bi-w	biweekly
bldg	building
bp	bishop
bros	brothers
co	company
comp	compiled, compiler
cond	condensed
cont	continued
corp	corporation
D	December
dept	department
ed	edited, edition, editor
F	February
Hon	Honorable
il	illustrated, illustration, ilustrator
inc	incorporated
introd	introduction, introductory
Ja	January
Je	June
Jl	July
jr	junior
jt auth	joint author
ltd	limited
m	monthly
Mr	March
My	May
N	November
no	number
O	October
por	portrait
pseud	pseudonym
pt	part
pub	published, publisher, publishing
q	quarterly
rev	revised
S	September
semi-m	semimonthly
soc	society
sq	square
sr	senior
st	street
Sum	Summer
sup	supplement
supt	superintendent
tr	translated, translation, translator
v	volume
w	weekly
Wint	Winter
yr	year

Sample entry: **WEASELS**
Wonderful white weasel. R. Beck. il Outdoor Life 135:48-9+ Ja '65

Explanation: An illustrated article on the subject **WEASELS** entitled "Wonderful white weasel," by R. Beck, will be found in volume 135 of Outdoor Life, pages 48-9 (continued on later pages of the same issue) the January 1965 number

RG 3/63-2/65

READERS' GUIDE TO PERIODICAL LITERATURE

March 1963—February 1965

AA. See Alcoholics anonymous
AAAS. See American association for the advancement of science—Meetings, 1964
AACTE. See American association of colleges of teacher education
AALL. See American association of law libraries
AARP. See American association of retired persons
AASA. See American association of school administrators
AASHO. See American association of state highway officials
AASL. See American association of school librarians
AAU. See Amateur athletic union of the United States
AAUP. See American association of university professors; Association of American university presses
A and P company. See Great Atlantic and Pacific tea company
ABA. See American bar association; American booksellers association
ABAA. See Antiquarian booksellers association of America
ABC. See American broadcasting company
A. B. C, pseud.
Half-life begins at thirty. Atlan 214:109 Ag '64
ABC-Paramount. See American broadcasting-Paramount theaters, incorporated
ABCC. See Atomic bomb casualty commission
ABPC. See American book publishers council
ABS. See Benzenesulfonates
AC generators. See Electric generators, Alternating current
AC motors. See Electric motors, Alternating current
A. C. Nielsen company. See Nielsen, A. C, company
AC spark plugs division. See General motors corporation—AC spark plugs division
ACA. See Americans for constitutional action
ACCC. See American council of Christian churches
ACDA. See United States—Arms control and disarmament agency
ACE. See American council on education
ACEI. See Association for childhood education international
ACEP. See American council for emigrés in the professions
ACLU. See American civil liberties union
ACP. See Associated church press (organization)
ACRL. See Association of college and research libraries
ACS. See American chemical soicety
ACTH
ACTH molecule. C. H. Li. il Sci Am 209:46-53 Jl '63
Biochemical advance in total synthesis of ACTH. Sci N L 84:56 Jl 27 '63
Total synthesis of ACTH. Sci Am 209:57 O '63
ADA. See American dairy association; American dental association; Americans for democratic action
ADA (automatic data acquisition) See Electronic data processing
ADC (aid to dependent children) See Child welfare—United States
ADI. See American documentation institute
ADL. See B'nai b'rith—Anti-defamation league
ADP (automatic data processing) See Electronic data processing
AEA. See Adult education association of the U.S.A.
AEC. See United States—Atomic energy commission
AEW. See American education week
AFA. See Air force association; American forestry association
AFBF. See American farm bureau federation
AFCEA. See Armed forces communications and electronics association
AFDC (aid to families with dependent children) See Child welfare—United States
AFL. See American football league
AFLC. See United States—Air force—Logistics command
AFL-CIO. See American federation of labor and Congress of industrial organizations
AFS. See American field service
AFSCME. See American federation of state, county and municipal employees
AFT. See American federation of teachers
AFTRA. See American federation of television and radio artists
A-frames. See Framing (building)
AGMA. See American guild of musical artists
A. G. Spalding and brothers. See Spalding, A. G. and brothers, incorporated
AGVA. See American guild of variety artists
AHIL. See Association of hospital and institution libraries
AI. See Artificial insemination
AIA. See American institute of architects
AIA-Sunset Western home awards. See Western home awards
AIBS. See American institute of biological sciences
AICPA. See American institute of certified public accountants
AID. See United States—Agency for international development
AIGA. See American institute of graphic arts
AIMR. See American institute of motivation research
AJC. See American Jewish committee
ALA. See American library association
ALA bulletin
Apogees and perigees in library education; issue for June 1964, letter. S. R. Reed. ALA Bul 58:589-90 Jl '64
Some thoughts about publishing: June 1964 issue. ALA Bul 58:439 Je '64
ALA cataloging rules. See Cataloging
ALA filing rules. See Files and filing (documents, etc)
ALTA. See American library trustee association
AMA. See American management association; American medical association
AMA-ERF loan program. See American medical association
AMC. See American motors corporation
AMF. See American machine and foundry company
ANC (all-number calling) See Telephone, Dial
ANTA. See American national theatre and academy
AP. See Associated press
A. P. Smith manufacturing company. See Smith, A. P, manufacturing company
APA. See Association of producing artists
APBA. See American power boat association
APGA. See American personnel and guidance association
APHA. See American public health association

APRA (Alianza popular revolucionaria americana) See Political parties—Peru
APRO. See American publishers' representatives organization
APWA. See American public works association
ARA. See American relief administration; United States—Area redevelopment administration
ARINC. See Aeronautical radio incorporated
ARL. See Association of research libraries
ARPA. See United States—Defense, Department of—Advanced research projects agency
ARS. See American recreation society
A-SA spray-away respirator. See Respiratory apparatus
ASCAP. See American society of composers, authors and publishers
ASCD. See Association for supervision and curriculum development
ASCE. See American society of civil engineers
ASD. See American library association—Adult services division
ASE. See American stock exchange
ASFTA. See American Shakespeare festival theatre and academy, Stratford, Conn.
ASNLH. See Association for the study of Negro life and history
ASPAU. See African scholarship program of American universities
ASPCA. See American society for the prevention of cruelty to animals
ASSET (aerothermodynamic/elastic structural systems environmental tests) See Space vehicles—Atmospheric entry
ASTEC (advanced solar turbo electric concept) See Space vehicles—Power supply
ASTRA. See Air space transportation (proposed)
ASW (anti-submarine warfare) See Submarine warfare
AT and T. See American telephone and telegraph company
ATA. See American teachers association
ATE (air turbo-exchanger) See Rocket engines
ATLA. See American theological library association
ATPI. See American textbook publishers institute
ATS (advanced technology satellite) See Artificial satellites—Use in research
AUTEC (Atlantic undersea test and evaluation center) See Navy yards and naval stations
AALTO, Alvar
Aalto: Finland's greatest architect. il por Arch Forum 118:120-5 Mr '63
Alvar Aalto. Review
Nation 198:19-20 Ja 4 '64. W. McQuade
Alvar Aalto today. F. Gutheim. il por Arch Rec 133:135-50 Ap '63
Alvar Aalto wins 1963 A.I.A. gold medal. Arch Rec 133:26 Mr '63
Room of his own. il Time 84:84+ D 11 '64
AANNESTAD, Elling. See Lippincott, E. jt. auth.
AARHUS conference. See World conference on faith and order
AARON, Benjamin
Individual's legal rights as an employee. Mo Labor R 86:666-73 Je '63
AARON, Jonathan
Warsaw to Paris; poem. Poetry 104:234 Jl '64
ABALONES
See also
Cookery—Fish
ABANDONED children. See Foundlings
ABANDONED farms. See Farms, Worn-out
ABANDONED towns
Along New Mexico's haunted highway; ghost towns San Pedro, Golden, Madrid, and Cerrillos. il Sunset 133:58 N '64
Deerfield, a Negro ghost town in Weld County, Colorado; Dearfield colony. A. Harris. Negro Hist Bul 27:38 N '63
Gold rush on the Kootenay; Fort Steele, British Columbia. il Sunset 130:61-2 Ap '63
ABARBANEL, Albert
What's in a yawn? Todays Health 42:30-1+ My '64
ABBADO, Claudio
Music to my ears; assistant conductors of the Philharmonic. I. Kolodin. Sat R 47:34+ F 15 '64
Musical events; concert of New York philharmonic. W. Sargeant. New Yorker 39: 110+ F 8 '64
Triumphant trio. por Time 81:62 Ap 12 '63
ABBE, George
Judge; poem. New Repub 148:20 My 18 '63
ABBE, Katherine
Summer action, kids. il U S Camera 26:54-7 Ag '63
ABBEYS
Maria Laach revisited. H. A. Reinhold. Commonweal 78:497-500 Ag 23 '63
Whitby abbey. M. E. Bry. il U S Camera 27:45 Ap '64
ABBOTT, D. T.
Facts and fancies about propellers. Yachting 115:90-1+ Ja '64
ABBOTT, George
Funny thing happened on the way to the printer; excerpts from Mister Abbott. por Time 82:84 D 6 '63
Mister Abbott; excerpts. por Theatre Arts 48:26-8 Ja '64

about

Call him Mister. por Newsweek 62:91 D 9 '63
Round-up for Abbott; with report by T. Prideaux. il pors Life 55:112-14+ D 13 '63
ABBOTT, Harold
Win or sink! J. Martenhoff. il por Motor B 113:26+ Je '64
ABBOTT, Reginald H. See McKay, M. P. jt. auth.
ABBOTT, Walter M.
Cardinal of unity. America 108:484 Ap 13 '63
Cardinal Suenens in America. America 110:701 My 23 '64
Computers and scripture. America 109:696 N 30 '63
Future role of bishops. America 110:6 Ja 4 '64
Greeks, Romans and others. America 110: 108-10 Ja 18 '64
Sacredness of life. America 108:328 Mr 9 '63
Strange songs of Spain find friends. America 108:216 F 16 '63
(ed) See Cushing, R. J. Cardinal Cushing
(ed) See Cushing, R. J. Cushing wants church laws liberalized
(ed) See Doepfner, J. Cardinal Doepfner's views
(ed) See Florit, E. Archbishop Florit and the laity
(ed) See Koenig, F. Austria's Cardinal at the council
(ed) See Léger, P. E. Cardinal Léger
(ed) See Liénart, A. Visit with Cardinal Liénart
(ed) See Siri, G. Truth first and always
(ed) See Suenens, L. J. Cardinal Suenens on the church
ABBOTT laboratories
Chemical man exhibit tells life story. il(p241) Sci N L 84:244 O 19 '63
New in pathology: a giant jigsaw puzzle. il Todays Health 41:74 Ag '63
Pill to fight mental depression; Eutonyl. Bsns W p76+ Ap 13 '63
ABBREVIATIONS
Dictionary of modern acronyms and abbreviations, comp. by M. Goldstein. Review
Sci Digest 54:40 N '63. B. H. Frisch
ABBS, J. K.
Plan a year-round picture window garden. Pop Gard 16:29-30 Ja '65
ABD-el-Krim
By the will of Allah. Newsweek 61:48-9 F 18 '63
Warrior's rest. por Time 81:37 F 15 '63
ABDOMINAL surgery. See Surgery
ABDUCTION. See Kidnaping
ABDULLAH, Mohammed
Lion on the loose. por Newsweek 63:57 Ap 20 '64
Return of the lion. Time 83:34 Ap 10 '64
ABDUL-RAZIK, Taher
Art education in Egypt. Sch Arts 63:34-8 F '64
ABDUL Reza Pahlevi, prince of Iran
Royal trophy winner. W. Page. il por Field & S 67:74-5 F '63
ABE Lincoln in Illinois; drama. See Sherwood, R. E.
ABEDI, Z. H. and Miller, M. J.
Tsetse fly puparia: a new collecting technique. Science 141:264 Jl 19 '63
ABEL, Elie
(ed) See Rusk, D. Divided world of communism
ABEL, I. W.
Fight inside union; will it affect steel prices, wages? por U S News 57:80-1 N 23 '64
Rebellion in steel. R. W. Gibbons. Commonweal 81:540-2 Ja 22 '65
Union's price for peace in steel. il por U S News 57:81-3 D 14 '64
ABEL, John H. jr. See Ellis, R. A. jt. auth.
ABEL, Lionel
Cummings' Daisy. Nation 197:420-1 D 14 '63
Ethics on the couch. Nation 199:438-40 D 7 '64

ABEL, Lionel—*Continued*
Is there a tragic sense of life? Commentary 38:35-40 D '64
Theatre. Nation 198:249-50 Mr 9 '64
Theatre of politics: the Negro. Nation 196: 351-4 Ap 27 '63
ABEL, Reuben
One man's guide to England. Sat R 47:72 Ja 4 '64
Philosophers choose sides. Sat R 46:28 Je 15 '63
ABEL, Robert, and O'Neill, Patrick
By the sea. Sch Arts 63:24-7 N '63
ABEL, Rudolf Ivanovich
American example. por Newsweek 63:75-6 Mr 30 '64
Strangers on a bridge, by J. B. Donovan. Review
America 110:772 My 30 '64. D. L. Flaherty
Life 56:12+ Ap 17 '64. P. Mandel
Time il por 83:100+ My 1 '64
Strangers on a bridge; excerpt. J. B. Donovan. il pors Sat Eve Post 237:30-2+ Mr 28 '64
ABELES, Sigmund
Etchings of Sigmund Abeles. S. Hurwitz. il por Am Artist 28:58-63+ S '64
ABELL, George O.
Local group of galaxies; reprint. Sky & Tel 27:21 Ja '64
ABELL, Theodore L. See Schult, V. jt. auth.
ABELSON, John
Transfer of genetic information. Science 139: 774-6 F 22 '63
ABELSON, Philip Hauge
Only one side of the question. Science 145: 347 Jl 24 '64; Same with title Exorbitant cost of dissent. Sat R 47:62 O 3 '64
Proper public accounting for science. por Sat R 46:51-2 F 2 '63
Trends in scientific research; excerpts from address, November 6, 1963. Science 143:218-23 Ja 17 '64
about
Science, the humanities, and education. W. W. Brickman. Sch & Soc 91:159 Ap 6 '63
ABER, Mina E.
Rankin house. Negro Hist Bul 26:253 My '63
ABERCROMBIE, Thomas J.
Behind the veil of troubled Yemen. il Nat Geog Mag 125:402-45 Mr '64
Cambodia: Indochina's neutral corner. il Nat Geog Mag 126:514-51 O '64
Venezuela builds on oil. il Nat Geog Mag 123:344-87 Mr '63
ABERCROMBIE and Fitch company
Friendly president. New Yorker 39:24 Je 1 '63
ABERDEEN, S.D.
Medical team was ready; Fischer quints in St Luke's hospital. S. M. Spencer. Sat Eve Post 236:37 N 16 '63
Our town is on the map! quint boom. T. Armbrister. il Sat Eve Post 236:40 N 16 '63
Quintuplets and other news from Aberdeen. H. Jones. il Redbook 122:42-3+ Ja '64
Town reaction: wow! T. Armbrister. il Ladies Home J 80:74 D '63
ABERDEEN, Scotland
Ghost city; typhoid epidemic. il Newsweek 63: 52 Je 15 '64
ABERDEEN proving grounds. See Proving grounds
ABERLE, John W.
Merry-go-round calf feeder. Farm J 87:58R Ap '63
ABERNETHY, Roy
Still preaching compact gospel. il por Bsns W p86-8+ Ap 11 '64
ABERRATION (optics)
Discovery of stellar aberration. A. B. Stewart. il Sci Am 210:100-8 bibliog(p 152) Mr '64
ABIDJAN
Ivory Coast: Hôtel Relais Aériens de Cocody. il Arch Forum 118:116-17 Je '63
ABILITY
Keep your mind alive. il Changing T 18:15-18 F '64
Scholastic ability of school dropouts; with tables. O. R. Warner. bibliog Sch Life 47: 21-2 O '64
Tireless brain. Time 82:83-4 O 11 '63
See also
College students, Mentally superior
Genius
Intelligence
Success
ABILITY, Influence of age on
Delayed independence. D. Wolfle. Science 143: 103 Ja 10 '64
New look at readiness; excerpt from Democracy and excellence in American secondary education. H. S. Broudy and others. bibliog Sch & Soc 91:424-30 D 28 '63
ABILITY grouping in education
Grouping and human values; excerpt from address. J. W. Gordon. il Sch Life 45:10-15 Jl '63
Grouping children for instruction, a conference points the way; symposium. Sch Life 45:5-12+ Je '63
Grouping of children. C. M. Long. Sch Life 46:17-19 D '63
Viewpoint on school readiness; excerpt from School readiness: behavior tests used at the Gesell institute. F. L. Ilg and L. B. Ames. il Sch & Soc 92:397-402 D 26 '64
ABILITY tests
Perceptual quotient devised for children. Sci N L 86:302 N 7 '64
See also
Intelligence tests
ABINGTON, Pa.
Bike pike; Alverthorpe Park. J. C. Dittmar. il Recreation 57:495+ D '64
Park provides a living monument; Alverthorpe park. B. R. Goldberg. il Recreation 56:313-14 S '63
ABINGTON library society, Jenkintown, Pa.
Public library bookstore. E. J. Humeston, jr. il Wilson Lib Bul 37:563-4+ Mr '63
ABLATION shielding. See Shielding (heat)
ABNORMALITIES (animals)
Acquired chromosomal anomalies induced in mice by injection of a teratogen in pregnancy. T. H. Ingalls and others. bibliog il Science 141:810-12 Ag 30 '63
Nature's creepiest freaks. J. Sydney. il Sci Digest 55:5-7 My '64
Teratogenic effect of 5-hydroxytryptamine in mice. E. Poulson and others. bibliog il Science 141:717 Ag 23 '63
See also
Polydactylism
ABNORMALITIES (man) See Deformities
ABNORMALITIES (plants)
See also
Burls
ABOLITIONISTS
Abolitionists, by L. Ruchames. Review
Commentary 36:406-8 N '63. H. Swados
Little known abolitionist; J. M. Forbes. Negro Hist Bul 26:210-11 Ap '63
Myth and reality; book reviews. H. N. Meyer. Negro Hist Bul 27:178-9 Ap '64
Pioneers in protest. L. Bennett, jr. See issues of Ebony beginning March 1964
ABOOD, L. G. and Koyama, I.
Phosphate incorporation in desheathed nerves: effects of potassium and calcium ions. bibliog Science 141:1277-8 S 27 '63
ABORTION
Abortion, legal & illegal. Time 84:53 D 25 '64
Candle in a dark world; West German Protestant consultation centers to check abortions. America 109:445 O 19 '63
Chromosomes and miscarriage. Sci Am 210:59 Je '64
Deadly favor. M. Davidson. Ladies Home J 80:53-7 N '63; Same abr. with title Abortion, the deadly favor. Read Digest 84: 189-92 F '64
Grounds for abortion. Sci N L 84:75 Ag 3 '63
Legal abortion safer. F. Marley. Sci N L 83: 134 Mr 2 '63
Need new abortion laws. Sci N L 86:397 D 19 '64
New ways to prevent miscarriage. M. Pines. il Redbook 120:66-7+ Ap '63
One million abortions. J. Ridgeway. New Repub 148:14-17 F 9 '63; Reply. J. L. Titchener. 148:39 Mr 2 '63
Soldiers of humanity. America 108:790 Je 1 '63
What about therapeutic abortion? L. Kinsolving. Christian Cent 81:632-5 My 13 '64; Reply. D. S. Hamilton. 81:935 Jl 22 '64
Why did you do it? France's biggest postwar mass abortion trial. Newsweek 61:54+ Je 10 '63
ABOSCH, Heinz
Adenauer years. Nation 197:28-31 Jl 13 '63
ABOUCHAR, Joan
New York state council on the arts in its 2nd year. Dance Mag 37:22-3+ Ap '63
ABRAHAM, Henry H. L.
Alienation in Ingmar Bergman. Commonweal 80:290-2 My 29 '64
ABRAHAM, Willard
Children are people too! Todays Health 43: 28-9+ Ja '65
How important are your child's friends? Todays Health 42:6-7+ Mr '64
Making memories together. PTA Mag 57:27-9 bibliog(p35) My '63
ABRAHAMS, Peter
Real Jamaica. Holiday 33:96-105+ Mr '63
ABRAHAMSEN, David
But why do they do it? Life 55:36-7 S 20 '63

ABRAMOV, Fedor
Ah, poor Anany; excerpts from Round and about. Time 81:30-1 Ap 12 '63
New life: story, tr. by G. Reavey. Reporter 28:36-8 Je 20 '63
ABRAMS, Charles
California: going, going. Arch Forum 119: 104-7 S '63
Housing order & its limits. Commentary 35: 10-14 Ja '63
ABRAMS, Creighton W.
Three top soldiers. por Time 84:16 Jl 3 '64
ABRAMS, Daniel
Look at the future. por Mus Am 83:9 Jl '63
ABRAMS, W. Amos
Mahomet goes to the hill. NEA J 52:49 N '63
ABRAMS planetarium. See Planetariums
ABRAMSON, Martin
Box 100. N Y Times Mag p72+ S 15 '63
ABRASIVE belts. See Belting
ABRASIVE wheels. See Grinding wheels
ABRASIVES
It's no longer just grind, grind at Norton. il Fortune 68:118-23+ Ag '63
ABRIDGED books. See Books, Condensed
ABRUS precatorius. See Crabs eye vine
ABSCISSION (botany)
Abscisin II, an abscission-accelerating substance from young cotton fruit. K. Ohkuma and others. il Science 142:1592-3 D 20 '63
ABSENCE, Leave of. See Leave of absence
ABSENCE of a cello; drama. See Wallach, I.
ABSENTEEISM
Busy social life of germs. T. J. Fleming. Life 55:19-20 D 13 '63
Managing your manpower; absenteeism & profits. T. R. Brooks. Duns R 82:55 Jl '63
ABSORPTION spectra
Infrared emission spectra of organic solids from 5 to 6.6 microns. W. A. Hovis, jr. il Science 143:587-8 F 7 '64
Pressure distribution measurements in fixed-anvil high-pressure cells. E. R. Lippincott and H. C. Duecker. bibliog il Science 144: 1119-21 My 29 '64
Solid-solid interaction studies by spectral reflectance. H. Zeitlin and others. bibliog il Science 141:423-4 Ag 2 '63
ABSTINENCE. See Fasting; Temperance
ABSTRACT art. See Art, Abstract
ABSTRACT literature. See Literature
ABSTRACTION
Of order, abstraction, and language. S. Burckhardt. Yale R 53:533-50 Je '64
ABT, Helmut A.
Rotation of stars; with biographical sketch. Sci Am 208:32, 46-53 bibliog(p 184) F '63
ABU DHABI
O Long of Life drinks camel milk and runs on oil. T. Green. il Life 54:50+ My 3 '63
Sheik jackpot. il Time 81:36 My 3 '63
Sheik of Abu Dhabi; world's richest man? il U S News 57:54-6 Jl 6 '64
ABU SIMBEL, Temples of
Above, below & everywhere; monuments to be assembled on a higher location. il Time 83:84 Ja 17 '64
Abu Simbel. il UN Mo Chron 1:70-6 Ag '64
Abu Simbel: legacy of a pharaoh. T. L. Christie. il Sat R 47:80-1+ O 10 '64
Dam the Nile, full speed astern; with photographs by D. Steffan. A. Chamberlin. Sat Eve Post 237:73-7 Je 6 '64
Dying, Egypt, dying; U.S. declines contribution to the saving of the Abu Simbel temples. F. Getlein. New Repub 150:26-8 My 30 '64
Engineers to archaeology's aid. il Sci Digest 56:67 D '64
Fate of Egyptian temples still being decided. Sci N L 83:155 Mr 9 '63
House denies funds to save Nile temples. il Arch Forum 120:7 Je '64
Huge excavation operation will relocate temples at Abu Simbel. il Arch Rec 137:244 Ja '65
No U.S. funds for Nile temples? il U S News 56:10 My 18 '64
Pharaoh & the flood. il Time 81:68 Ap 12 '63
Plan accepted for preservation of temples of Abu Simbel. Dept State Bul 49:18 Jl 1 '63
Salvation for Abu Simbel. Time 81:51 Je 21 '63
Sunlight creates an Egyptian god. J. K. Van der Haagen. il Sci Digest 53:48-58 Mr '63
Threatened treasures of the Nile. G. Gerster. il Nat Geog Mag 124:586-621 O '63
U.S. aids international campaign to preserve Nubian monuments. Dept State Bul 51: 645 N 2 '64
ABU ZABI. See Abu Dhabi
La ABUELA: story. See Troy, G.
ABUNDANCE. See Prosperity
ABUNDANCES of elements. See Chemical elements
ABUNDANT dreamer; story. See Brodkey, H.
ABUTILON. See Flowering maples
ABYSSINIA. See Ethiopia
ACACIAS
Bull-horn acacia; Mexican ant acacia. V. N. Argo. il Natur Hist 74:22-7 Ja '65
Wonderful wattle tree. M. Buttner. il Am For 70:30-1 Jl '64
ACACIAS; story. See Stewart, N.
ACADEMIC costume
Rite of spring; Columbia's new doctoral dress. il Time 81:83-5 Je 14 '63
ACADEMIC degrees. See Degrees, Academic
ACADEMIC dissertations. See Dissertations, Academic
ACADEMIC evaluation. See Grading and marking (students)
ACADEMIC freedom
Academic freedom and Catholic dissent. L. Dewart. Commonweal 80:33-6 Ap 3 '64
Academic freedom at Grove City. J. P. Park. Christian Cent 80:928-9 Jl 24 '63
Academic freedom; how much is there? A. Hacker. il N Y Times Mag p25+ Je 7 '64
Academic freedom in the age of conflict; address, May 1, 1963. J. Kalvoda. Vital Speeches 29:526-31 Je 15 '63
AEC; energetic bargaining brings agreement on university contract clauses on security, information. J. Walsh. Science 140:38-9 Ap 5 '63
Conservatives, too, have tenure; G. V. Drake vs Wisconsin state college, Oshkosh. R. Kirk. Nat R 16:729 Ag 25 '64
Counterattack at Colorado; liberals vs. conservatives, college newspapers vs. B. Goldwater. W. H. Carroll. Nat R 14:494-5 Je 18 '63
Freedom to learn but not to riot; demonstrations at the Berkeley campus of the University of California. S. Hook. il N Y Times Mag p8-9+ Ja 3 '65
Freedom to teach and to learn. E. Gordon. il PTA Mag 58:4-7 O '63
Fresh wind in Illinois. D. Young and R. Auler. Nat R 14:495 Je 18 '63
From the academy; concerning C. Luckman's commencement address at San Diego state college. R. Kirk. Nat R 16:650 Jl 28 '64
Hell breaks loose in paradise. il Life 54:73-82+ Ap 26 '63
Incident at a college; dismissal of Austin J. Shelton, jr. from Mercy college. F. E. Kearns. Commonweal 79:215 N 15 '63; Reply with rejoinder. C. E. Schuetzinger. 79:430-1 Ja 10 '64
Incident at Boston college; dismissal of Dr Paul M. Michaud. M. J. Bennett. Commonweal 80:284-5 My 29 '64; Reply with rejoinder. R. F. Drinan. 80:420-3 Je 26 '64
Intellectual freedom; raising hell with the Legionnaires. E. T. Moore. ALA Bul 57: 224-6 Mr '63
Inviting Communists to speak at colleges; address, 1962. W. F. Buckley, jr. il Nat R 15:343-5+ O 22 '63
Is freedom an academic question? H. S. Commager. il Sat R 47:54-6 Je 20 '64
Kearns case. J. Leo. Commonweal 81:562-6 Ja 29 '65
Life among the libs (Hunter college division) S. Buck. Nat R 16:275-7+ Ap 7 '64; Discussion. 16:329 Ap 21 '64
Marxmanship at Illinois; case of R. P. Oliver. Time 83:56 Mr 27 '64
More of same; banning of speakers at Catholic colleges. Commonweal 79:681-2 Mr 6 '64
New name on the list; unsatisfactory educational conditions, Pleasantville, Ia. D. Janson. il Sr Schol 84:1T-2T Ap 10 '64
North Carolina's gag law; H.B. 1395, Act to regulate visiting speakers at state-supported colleges and universities. A. W. Stewart. Christian Cent 81:1336-8 O 28 '64
Statement by the Board of regents of the University of Minnesota on freedom and the university. Sch & Soc 92:108-9 Mr 7 '64
Student academic freedom and communist speakers on campus. S. Jacobson. Sch & Soc 92:336-7 N 14 '64
Uhuru for students. America 110:404-5 Mr 28 '64
University trustee reflects on freedom; excerpts from address, October 10, 1962. S. M. Linowitz. Sch & Soc 91:168-9 Ap 6 '63
What Johnny doesn't know; week as visiting resident, at University of Texas. W. F. Buckley, jr. Nat R 16:14+ Ja 14 '64

ACADEMIC freedom—*Continued*
What, where, when, how? ideas presented at annual meeting of the American association of university professors in San Francisco. il Time 81:72-4 My 10 '63

Anecdotes, facetiae, satire, etc.

Out, out . . .! D. Martin. Sat R 47:59 Ap 18 '64

ACADEMIC performance. See Student achievements

ACADEMIC tenure. See College professors and instructors—Tenure

ACADEMICALLY talented students. See High school students, Mentally superior

L'ACADÉMIE Maxim's. See Private schools

ACADEMY awards (moving pictures)
Emperor. il Time 81:67-8 Ap 19 '63
1963 Oscarace; nominations. Time 81:63 Mr 8 '63
Who's there? il Time 83:52 Ap 24 '64

ACADEMY of medicine, New York. See New York academy of medicine

ACADEMY of motion picture arts and sciences
See also
Academy awards (moving pictures)

ACADEMY of religion and mental health
Dialogue on the moral crisis. S. J. Roland, jr. Christian Cent 81:705 My 27 '64
Religion and mental health. S. J. Rowland, jr. Christian Cent 80:684 My 22 '63

ACADEMY of television arts and sciences
Emmy the outcast; withdrawal of ABC and CBS. Newsweek 63:70 My 25 '64
Night of the mutiny; Emmy awards. il Newsweek 63:70 Je 8 '64
Poor Emmy. Time 83:48 My 22 '64

ACADIA NATIONAL PARK
Acquaintance with Acadia. F. Tilden. il Nat Parks Mag 37:4-7 Jl '63

ACAPULCO, Mexico
Two Acapulcos. J. Cerruti. il Nat Geog Mag 126:848-78 D '64

ACARTIA tonsa. See Copepods

ACAULOPAGE pectospora. See Fungi

ACCELERATION in education. See Educational acceleration

ACCELERATORS (electrons, etc)
Atomic ghost tracked; resonances of certain nuclei. Sci N L 86:307 N 14 '64
Atomic scientists build cannon two miles long; linear accelerator. il Pop Sci 185:54-5 D '64
High-energy physics: major fight brewing as midwestern legislators take stand on MURA accelerator. D. S. Greenberg. Science 142:208-10 O 11 '63
MURA accelerator: compromise for the Mid-West. D. S. Greenberg. bibliog Science 143:450-2 Ja 31 '64; Reply. D. W. Kerst. 143:1274 Mr 20 '64
New atomic accelerator. il(p369) Sci N L 84:372 D 14 '63
New industrial hazard in cathode-ray machines. Sci N L 83:345 Je 1 '63
One trillion electron volts; proton accelerators. Sci Am 209:64-5 Jl '63
Particle accelerators at CERN. V. K. McElheny. il Science 144:983-6 My 22 '64
Program for particles. Time 81:60 Je 7 '63
Ripping up the campus for an atom gun; Stanford linear accelerator center. il Bsns W p24-5 F 1 '64
SLAC: Stanford-AEC accelerator is coming along on schedule, but creating some high tension. J. Walsh. Science 143:1419-21 Mr 27 '64
Storage rings. G. K. O'Neill. bibliog il Science 141:679-86 Ag 23 '63
Super atom smasher. Sci N L 83:358 Je 8 '63
U.S. plans mile-wide atom-smashing machine. Sci N L 84:143 Ag 31 '63
See also
Bevatron

ACCELEROMETERS
Low-G accelerometers await new ground and flight test developments. il Miss & Roc 15:32-5 D 7 '64
Thiokol monitors propellant behavior. il Miss & Roc 13:42, 45 Ag 26 '63
Turbulence studies investigate pilot aids. J. R. Ashlock. Aviation W 80:47 Ap 20 '64

ACCESS control of highways. See Roads—Intersections

ACCIDENT insurance. See Insurance, Accident

ACCIDENT law
See also
Damages
Personal injuries

ACCIDENT; novel. See Janeway, E.

ACCIDENTAL war. See Atomic weapons—Accidents

ACCIDENTS
Accident research: methods and approaches, by W. Haddon, jr. Review
Reporter 31:32+ D 31 '64. D. P. Moynihan
Accidents aren't accidental. G. Hechinger. il N Y Times Mag p52 Je 2 '63
Accidents don't just happen. H. H. Gibney. il Parents Mag 38:88-9+ O '63
Dangerous season; summertime death and injury. il Newsweek 62:76-7 Ag 12 '63
Deaths in refrigerators much increased in 1962. Sci N L 83:152 Mr 9 '63
First aid for childhood emergencies. J. A. Matz. il Parents Mag 39:42-3+ Ag '64
Foreign body in air passage. C. J. Potthoff. Todays Health 41:70 D '63
How not to go looking for owlets. M. Byers. il Life 56:33 My 15 '64
How to fall off a building. il Sci Digest 55:59-60 Ja '64
How to make yourself fall-safe. H. Higdon. il Todays Health 42:72-6 Ap '64
Left for dead; ed. by D. French. M. Jack. il Outdoor Life 134:36-7+ O '64
Nightmare ride. J. B. Wilwand. il Outdoor Life 134:50-1 Ag '64
Safety last. S. Blum. il Redbook 121:56-7+ S '63
They all fall down. M. R. Weisbord. il Parents Mag 38:54-5+ Mr '63
Why children have accidents. R. O'Brien. il Ladies Home J 81:46+ Mr '64
See also
Burns and scalds
Explosions
First aid in illness and injury
Mine accidents and explosions
Rescue work
Shipwrecks
Traffic accidents
also subhead Accidents or Accidents and injuries under various subjects, e.g. Sports—Accidents and injuries

Prevention

How to avoid glass-door dangers. Good H 156:142 Mr '63
How to protect children against accidental poisoning. Good H 158:161-3 Je '64
If there's trouble on a car trip; driving emergencies and how to handle them. il Changing T 18:25-9 Ag '64
Little ways to play it safe. Changing T 19:36 Ja '65
Reducing the hazard from slippery stairsteps, bathtubs, and showers. il Consumer Bul 47:13 O '64
Watch it, that's a door! Am Home 68:91 Ja '65
We are interested in Johnny, too. L. W. Larson. il Todays Health 41:82-4 O '63
See also
Safety devices and measures
Safety education
Safety engineering
also subhead Safety devices and measures under various subjects, e.g. Aviation—Safety devices and measures

Statistics

About: accidents. S. Blum. il N Y Times Mag p29-30+ My 17 '64
45,000 lose lives in non-car accidents. Sci N L 83:136 Mr 2 '63

ACCIDENTS, Industrial
Man with a lower back injury. Mo Labor R 87:III-IV S '64

Statistics

Preliminary estimates of work injuries in 1962-1963. F. W. Schmidt, jr. il Mo Labor R 86:418-20; 87:530-1 Ap '63, My '64
Work injuries; tables. See issues of Monthly labor review

ACCIDENTS, Liability for. See Liability (law); Municipal liability

ACCION (Americans for community cooperation in other nations) See Volunteer service, International

ACCO. See Anderson, Clayton and company

ACCORSI, William
William Accorsi's toy sculpture. il Craft Horiz 23:24-5 N '63

ACCOUNT books, Family
See also
Family records

ACCOUNTABILITY. See Responsibility

ACCOUNTABILITY (law)
See also
Criminal liability

ACCOUNTANTS
CPAs churn new rules; Accounting principles board. Bsns W p70 N 23 '63
How to rate your tax help. V. R. Houghaboom. Farm J 88:641 F '64

ACCOUNTANTS—*Continued*
Matter of principle splits CPAs: Accounting principles board. il Bsns W p50+ Ja 26 '63
ACCOUNTING
Case against capitalizing leases. D. C. Cook. bibliog f Harvard Bsns R 41:145-50+ Ja '63
How to use accounting. J. B. Kobak. il Pub W 183:26-7 My 20 '63
Showdown on accounting principles. R. N. Anthony. Harvard Bsns R 41:99-106 My '63
See also
Billing
Calculating machines
Cost accounting
Financial statements
Municipal accounting
also subhead Accounting under various subjects, e.g. Schools—Accounting
Mechanical aids
Machine accounting; Watkins Glen, N.Y. G. F. Scaptura. il Am City 79:103 Ap '64
See also
Calculating machines—Business applications
ACCOUNTING, Household. See Budget, Household; Domestic finance
ACCOUNTING office, General. See United States—General accounting office
ACCOUNTING principles board. See American institute of certified public accountants
ACCREDITATION, College. See Colleges and universities—Accreditation
ACCREDITATION of library schools. See Library schools and education
ACCREDITING, National commission on. See National commission on accrediting
ACCULTURATION
Catholics as immigrants. J. H. Smylie. Christian Cent 80:1396-9 N 13 '63
Exporting the American idea; Quaker technology among the Senecas. A. Wallace. Sat R 46:54-6 Ap 6 '63
Influence of Africans on American culture. J. A. Davis. bibliog f Ann Am Acad 354:75-83 Jl '64
ACCUTRON electronic watches. See Watches
ACE, Goodman
How to get by on $10,000 a week. Sat R 47:18 F 8 '64
Top of my head. See issues of Saturday review beginning February 29, 1964
about
Caesar or Como, the laughs are by Ace. R. P. Hunt. il pors N Y Times Mag p42+ S 15 '63
ACES (aviators) See Air pilots
ACETABULARIA
Endogenous circadian rhythm in cytoplasm of acetabularia: influence of the nucleus. E. Schweiger and others. bibliog il Science 146:658-9 O 30 '64
ACETIC acid
Experimental differentiation between phototaxis and motility in chlamydomonas snowiae. N. Stahl and A. M. Mayer. bibliog il Science 141:1282-4 S 27 '63
ACETO, Vincent J.
Panacea or Pandora's box? por Library J 89:322-4+ Ja 15 '64
ACETOPHENAZINE
Acetophenazine and fighting behavior in mice. W. R. Knight and others. bibliog il Science 141:830-1 Ag 30 '63
ACETYLCHOLINE
Acetylcholine and cholinacetylase content of synaptic vesicles. E. De Robertis and others. bibliog il Science 140:300-1 Ap 19 '63
Acetylcholine-like activity in sciatic nerve. E. A. Carlini and J. P. Green. bibliog il Science 141:901-2 S 6 '63
Atrophy of skeletal muscle in chick embryos treated with botulinum toxin. D. B. Drachman. bibliog il Science 145:719-21 Ag 14 '64
Cholinergic substance in the caudal neurosecretory storage organ of fish. H. Kobayashi and others. bibliog il Science 141:714-16 Ag 23 '63
Identification of acetylcholine in sympathetic ganglia by chemical and physical methods. A. J. D. Friesen and others. bibliog il Science 145:157-9 Jl 10 '64
Midbrain hemisection: effect on cortical acetylcholine in the cat. G. Pepeu and P. Mantegazzini. bibliog il Science 145:1069-70 S 4 '64
ACETYLENE compounds
Acetylene ester from aster spinosus. J. C. Spitzer and C. Steelink. bibliog Science 146:1460-1 D 11 '64
ACETYLSALICYLIC acid. See Aspirin
ACHESON, Dean Gooderham
Acheson's idea: get hardheaded abroad; excerpts from address, December 9, 1964. por U S News 57:14 D 21 '64; Newsweek 64:18 D 21 '64; Time 84:22-3 D 18 '64
Dean Acheson speaks out again: target is President de Gaulle; summaries of addresses. por U S News 55:15 S 30 '63
Practice of partnership. For Affairs 41:247-60 Ja '63
Withdrawal from Europe? an illusion. N Y Times Mag p7+ D 15 '63
about
Dealing with de Gaulle; Dean Acheson tells how. U S News 54:22 Mr 25 '63
ACHEY, Phillip M. See Pollard, E. C. jt. auth.
ACHIEVEMENTS, Student. See Student achievements
ACHIMENES
Achimenes on the terrace. J. B. Buerger. il Horticulture 41:321 Je '63
ACHKAR, Marof
Young power in diplomacy. por Vogue 143:90 Ap 15 '64
ACID phosphatases. See Phosphatases
ACID soils. See Soil acidity
ACIDITY of the stomach. See Stomach—Acidity
ACIDS
See also
Amino acids
Nucleic acids
ACIDS, Fatty
Albumin replacement by fatty acids in clonal growth of mammalian cells. R. G. Ham. bibliog il Science 140:802-3 My 17 '63
Autonomic mediation of the effect of raised arterial glucose upon free fatty acids. C. J. Goodner and W. A. Tustison. biblicg il Science 146:770-2 N 6 '64
Biosynthesis of unsaturated fatty acids in microorganisms. J. Erwin and K. Bloch. bibliog il Science 143:1006-12 Mr 6 '64
Fatty acid synthesis by subcellular fractions of lung tissue. E. G. Tombropoulos. bibliog il Science 146:1180-1 N 27 '64
Fatty acids: in vivo synthesis by the green peach aphid, myzus persicae (Sulzer) F. E. Strong. bibliog il Science 140:983-4 My 31 '63
Structure of lipoproteins: covalently bound fatty acids. W. R. Fisher and S. Gurin. bibliog il Science 143:362-3 Ja 24 '64
Synthesis of α-linolenic acid by leishmania enriettii. E. D. Korn and C. L. Greenblatt. bibliog il Science 142:1301-3 D 6 '63
ACKERLY, Nancy
WLB biography. Wilson Lib Bul 38:81 S '63
ACKERMAN, James L. See Proffit, W. R. jt. auth.
ACKERMANN, B. J.
Coming about, sorry! story. Atlan 212:75-80 Jl '63
ACKERSON, Cornelius
Build a greenhouse that runs itself. Pop Gard 15:36-7 Ja '64
ACKLEY, Gardner
Automation: threat and promise. N Y Times Mag p 16+ Mr 22 '64
LBJ's new economic adviser: his views. por U S News 57:20 N 30 '64
Old reliable team. por Newsweek 64:84 N 30 '64
ACME steel company
Acme steel's three years of hell. il Bsns W p 140+ Jl 11 '64
ACNE
Acne problem calls for doctor's care, AMA says. Sci N L 86:233 O 10 '64
What medical science can do about acne. B. H. Frisch. Sci Digest 57:61-4 Ja '65
ACOCA, Miguel
Agonized siege above a roomful of dynamite. Life 56:64-6 Ja 3 '64
Historic birth. Life 55:38B-39 S 20 '63
Luck with your locks, young John. Life 54:16 My 24 '63
Papa to midwife: keep this secret! Life 55:80+ D 13 '63
—and others
I guess I started this whole thing. Life 56:30-1 Ja 24 '64
ACONCAGUA, MOUNT
Awesome challenge of Mt Aconcagua. L. Stowe. il Read Digest 84:106-11 Mr '64
ACONITES, Winter. See Winter aconites
ACOSTA, Enrique
Green thumb that paid off. L. Zalamea. il por Américas 15:29-33 F '63
ACOSTA, Gilbert
Lions beat them all; ed. by S. P. English, jr. pors Outdoor Life 131:64-7+ My '63

ACOSTA, Maruja
Green thumb that paid off. L. Zalamea. il por Américas 15:29-33 F '63

ACOUSTIC transducers. See Transducers

ACOUSTICS. See Music—Acoustics and physics

ACOUSTICS, Architectural
Acoustics in-the-round at the Berlin philharmonic. R. S. Lanier. il Arch Forum 120: 98-105 My '64
Acoustics; what happened at Philharmonic Hall? R. S. Lanier. il Arch Forum 119:118-23 D '63
Architectural acoustics. V. O. Knudsen. il Sci Am 209:78-92 bibliog(p 187) N '63
FHA joins the tenants' war against noise. il Arch Forum 120:96-7 Mr '64
Listening room is an important part of your music system. R. Freas. il Am Home 66:4+ My '63
Lo-fi science of acoustics. il Sci Digest 54:61 Jl '63
Patterned titles; the new faces of silence. il House & Gard 123:202-3 Ap '63
Room acoustics for stereo. D. P. Eisenman. il Hi Fi 13:50-3+ F '63
Sound of words; deficiency in the bass frequencies. il Newsweek 61:92 Ap 15 '63
Where is science taking us? reprint. R. B. Newman. Sat R 46:48-9 S 7 '63

ACQUISITIONS, Library. See Libraries—Acquisitions

ACQUISITIONS, School library. See School libraries—Acquisitions

ACROBATS and acrobatism
Circus brings message; State Peking acrobatic troupe in Tokyo. il Bsns W p72-3 Mr 2 '63
Cookie! the wonder boy; Great Arturo family on the high wire. D. R. Maxey. il Look 27: 116-18+ D 3 '63
Ladeez and gentlemen, the sensational new aerial artiste, La Toria; with report by R. Oulahan, jr. il Life 54:49-50B Ap 19 '63
Ouch! Ringling bros. hairborne Chrystine Holt. il Time 83:81 My 1 '64
They flip for Joe Price; acrobatic dance. D. Duncan. il Dance Mag 38:10-12 Ag '64
Up, up, by the hair she goes. il Life 56:89-90 Ap 17 '64
War of nerves on the highwire. B. Ballantine. il Sat Eve Post 237:73-7 F 15 '64
See also
Circus performers

ACRONYMS
Dictionary of modern acronyms and abbreviations, comp. by M. Goldstein. Review
Sci Digest 54:40 N '63. B. H. Frisch

ACRYLAMIDE
Antiserums prepared with acrylamide gel used as adjuvant. M. Weintraub and S. Raymond. bibliog il Science 142:1677-8 D 27 '63

ACT of reparation; story. See Warner, S. T.

ACTING
Acting for dancers. il Dance Mag 37:47+ Ag '63 (to be cont)
Dramatic accent: singing-actor. A. Williamson. il Hi Fi 14:53-5+ Mr '64
I've lost my English accent; ed. by E. Miller. J. Haworth. il Seventeen 24:68-9+ Ja '65
Leaves from Stanislavsky's notebooks; excerpts. K. S. Stanislavskii. il UNESCO Courier 16:20-2 N '63
Mr Novak cuts class; ed. by E. Miller. J. Franciscus. il Seventeen 23:140-1+ S '64
My life in art; excerpts. K. S. Stanislavskii. il UNESCO Courier 16:15+ N '63
On unperfect actors. E. Capouya. Sat R 46: 40-1 D 14 '63
Redbook dialogue. A. Bancroft; P. Strasberg. il Redbook 121:56-7+ Jl '63
Stanislavsky; revolutionary of the modern theatre. G. Kristi. il UNESCO Courier 16: 12-14 N '63
Therapeutic theater; Group theater workshop, New York city. il Newsweek 65:75 F 1 '65
See also
Actors and actresses
Commedia dell' arte
Moving picture acting

Study and teaching

Actors can be teachers. L. Sutton. il Theatre Arts 47:64-5 Ag '63
There's a method in British acting. H. Clurman. il N Y Times Mag p 18-19+ Ja 12 '64
We work toward freedom; interview, ed. by W. Sorell. A. Sokolow. il Dance Mag 38:52-3+ Ja '64

ACTINOMYCIN
Actinomycin and puromycin: effects on sequential gene activation by ecdysone. U. Clever. bibliog il Science 146:794-5 N 6 '64
Actinomycin: correlation of structure and function of its complexes with purines and DNA. E. Reich. bibliog il Science 143:684-9 F 14 '64
Actinomycin D: an effect on rat liver homogenates unrelated to its action on RNA synthesis. M. Revel and others. bibliog il Science 146:1311-13 D 4 '64
Actinomycin D and the response to parathyroid hormone. H. Rasmussen and others. bibliog il Science 144:1019-21 My 22 '64
Actinomycin D as a probe for nucleic acid secondary structure. R. Haselkorn. bibliog il Science 143:682-4 F 14 '64
Actinomycin D: effect on the immune response. C. J. Wust and others. bibliog il Science 143:1041-3 Mr 6 '64
Actinomycin D effects in frog embryos: evidence for sequential synthesis of DNA-dependent RNA. R. A. Flickinger. bibliog il Science 141:1063-4 S 13 '63
Actinomycin D: its effect on antibody formation in vitro. J. W. Uhr. bibliog il Science 142:1476-7 D 13 '63
Actinomycin D: specific inhibitory effects on the explanted chick embryo. N. W. Klein and L. J. Pierro. bibliog il Science 142: 967-9 N 15 '63
Actinomycin D: suppression of recovery in X-irradiated mammalian cells. M. M. Elkind and others. bibliog il Science 143:1454-7 Mr 27 '64
Actinomycin: inhibition of cortisone-induced synthesis of hepatic gluconeogenic enzymes. G. Weber and others. bibliog il Science 142:390-2 O 18 '63
Actinomycin resistance in bacillus subtilis. I. J. Slotnick and B. H. Sells. bibliog il Science 146:407-8 O 16 '64
Breakdown of rat-liver ergosomes in vivo after actinomycin inhibition of messenger RNA synthesis. T. Staehelin and others. bibliog il Science 140:180-3 Ap 12 '63
Control of synthesis of RNA and protein in diapausing and injured cecropia pupae. S. J. Berry and others. bibliog il Science 146: 938-40 N 13 '64
Immunologically determined and competent cells are affected differentially by actinomycin D. E. Weiler. bibliog il Science 144: 846-9 My 15 '64; Reply with rejoinder. D. W. Talmage. 145:1073-4 S 4 '64
Incorporation of uridine-H^3 into nuclei of virus-infected tobacco. S. H. Smith and D. E. Schlegel. bibliog il Science 145:1058-9 S 4 '64
Induction of several adaptive enzymes by actinomycin D. F. Rosen and others. bibliog il Science 146:661-3 O 30 '64
Insulin action in alloxan diabetes modified by actinomycin D. A. Gellhorn and W. Benjamin. bibliog il Science 146:1166-8 N 27 '64
Intestinal phosphatase activity; acceleration of increase by puromycin and actinomycin. F. Moog. bibliog il Science 144:414-16 Ap 24 '64
Mitosis and differentiation in roots treated with actinomycin. A. K. Bal and P. R. Gross. bibliog il Science 139:584-6 F 15 '63
Ribonucleic acid synthesis in protoplasts of escherichia coli: inhibition by actinomycin D. B. Mach and E. L. Tatum. bibliog il Science 139:1051-2 Mr 15 '63
Skin tumorigenesis by 7,12-dimethylbenza(a) anthracene: inhibition by actinomycin D. H. V. Gelboin and M. Klein. bibliog il Science 145:1321-2 S 18 '64
Vitamin K induced prothrombin formation: antagonism by actinomycin D. R. E. Olson. bibliog il Science 145:926-8 Ag 28 '64; Correction. 147:66 Ja 1 '65

ACTION française
Action française, by E. Weber. Review
America 108:378 Mr 16 '63. F. Canavan
Sat R il 46:43-4 Je 22 '63. J. S. Schapiro

ACTION in art
Movement & light in today's art. F. Popper. il UNESCO Courier 16:12-17+ S '63
Perpetual motion. F. Getlein. New Repub 151:33-4+ O 3 '64

ACTION painting. See Art, Abstract

ACTION photography. See Photography of moving objects

ACTIONS and defenses
Climbing toll for the price-fixers. il Bsns W p96-8+ Ag 29 '64
Goldfarb case fought by anti-censorship forces. Pub W 187:105-6 Ja 18 '65
Goldfarb vs. Notre Dame. Newsweek 64:53 D 28 '64
Importance of an image; Notre Dame injunction against Twentieth century-Fox movie. il Time 84:69 D 18 '64
Notre Dame's Irish dander rises over a movie; case against Twentieth century-Fox. il Life 57:68+ D 18 '64

ACTIONS and defenses—*Continued*
Winchell v. Sugar Ray. Time 85:48 Ja 1 '65
See also
Libel and slander

Anecdotes, facetiae, satire, etc.
Lawsuit pursuit. Christian Cent 81:655 My 13 '64

ACTIVATION analysis. See Radioactivation analysis
ACTIVITIES, Playground. See Playground activities
ACTIVITIES, Student. See Student activities
ACTORS and actresses
Actors are people, too. D. Monsey. il Theatre Arts 47:25-6+ N '63
Audacious new swimsuits; Las Vegas show girls turn out in fashions for the beach. il Life 58:46-55+ Ja 8 '65
Bowling; tournament and teams run by Broadway show league. il New Yorker 39:21-2 Ja 11 '64
Britain's new actors: rougher, tougher, angrier. C. Barnes. il N Y Times Mag p44-5+ O 6 '63
Celebrities' choice. il McCalls 91:142-7+ O '63
English look. L. Lerman. il Mlle 56:142-5 Ap '63
Getting into the act; actors' children. il N Y Times Mag p80+ S 20 '64
Guess who's playing Santa! il Good H 157:100-1+ D '63
Let me entertain you; audition for To Broadway with love. M. Davidson. il Sat Eve Post 237:72-3 My 16 '64
Love letters of a tough critic; eulogies of four stars. W. Kerr. il Life 56:113-14 Je 19 '64
Men, women and children; Hamlets all. G. Eells. il Theatre Arts 48:18-21+ Ja '64
Promise! what a lovely word. J. Harris. Seventeen 22:138+ O '63
Ten favorites from Shakespeare; photographs. T. Guthrie. N Y Times Mag p 18-19 Mr 15 '64
Ten top Shakespeareans; photographs. S. Peck. N Y Times Mag p26-7 My 10 '64
There's a method in British acting. H. Clurman. il N Y Times Mag p 18-19+ Ja 12 '64
To be a Bernhardt. H. Butler. Harper 227:56-61 Ag '63
Working marriages; actors sharing the spotlight. il N Y Times Mag p88 Ap 21 '63
See also
Acting
Barrymore family
Children as actors
Comedians
Kemble family
Moving picture actors and actresses
Rehearsal club, New York
Stage fright
Theatrical agencies
ACTORS and actresses, Negro. See Negro actors and actresses
ACTORS' equity association
Actors' new boss. il Ebony 19:58-60+ Je '64
ACTOR'S workshop. See San Francisco— Theater
ACTRESSES. See Actors and actresses; Moving picture actors and actresses
ACUPUNCTURE
Acupuncture. B. Inglis. il Vogue 143:134+ Je '64
AD hoc committee on the triple revolution
Bread without sweat. Christian Cent 81:451-2 Ap 8 '64
Guaranteed income. New Repub 150:4-5 Ap 4 '64
If the machine wants our jobs, let's buy it. Life 57:4 Ag 14 '64
Triple revolution. G. W. Johnson. New Repub 150:38-9 Ap 11 '64
Triple revolution. J. Riha. America 112:162-4 Ja 30 '65
Triple revolution; concerning report of the Ad hoc committee on the triple revolution. J. O'Gara. Commonweal 80:78 Ap 10 '64
ADABUNU, Eunice
Togo woman leader. il pors Ebony 18:44+ Mr '63
ADAM, Robert
Robert Adam's Grand tour. D. Stillman. il Antiques 83:670-4 Je '63
ADAM and Eve in art
Adam and Eve in the decorative arts. L. E. Hawes. il Antiques 84:278-82 S '63
ADAMANTANAMINE
Antiviral activity of 1-adamantanamine (amantadine) W. L. Davies and others. il Science 144:862-3 My 15 '64
Rubella virus: inhibition in vitro by amantadine hydrochloride. H. F. Maassab and K. W. Cochran. bibliog il Science 145:1443-4 S 25 '64

ADAMJEE, Gul Mohamed
Jute King. il por Time 84:108 D 4 '64
ADAMS, Abigail (Smith)
Abigail Adams, integrator. Life 55:4 Jl 5 '63
John Adams and his wife, Abigail. L. Baritz. Nation 197:54-5 Jl 27 '63
Magic mail of John and Abigail. M. L. Coit. il Sat R 46:24-5 Ag 10 '63
ADAMS, Alexander B.
Conservation and progress: two inseparables. il Nat Parks Mag 37:4-8 N '63
ADAMS, Alice
Kate Auerbach's stitchery. Craft Horiz 23:32-3 Jl '63
Marianne Strengell. Craft Horiz 23:34-6+ Ja '63
ADAMS, Andrew
Haiti and the CIA: case of Andrew Adams. Nation 200:22-3 Ja 11 '65
ADAMS, Ansel
Ansel Adams. P. Caulfield. il Mod Phot 28:55-65+ Ap '64
Eloquent light: Ansel Adams' giant West Coast exhibit. P. Caulfield. il Mod Phot 28:12-13 F '64
Eloquent light; exhibition at the M. H. de Young memorial museum, San Francisco. B. Newhall; G. A. Allen. il Pop Phot 54:74-5+ Mr '64
How Ansel Adams makes an exposure. B. Newhall. il Pop Phot 52:40-3 F '63
Images of endless moments. il N Y Times Mag p 134-6 N 8 '64
John Muir awards; conservation achievement awards. por Liv Wildn 83:31 Spring '63
Light is the leitmotif. M. R. Weiss. il Sat R 47:30-2 Ja 25 '64
35mm techniques; exhibition at San Francisco's De Young museum. P. Stackpole. U S Camera 27:12 Mr '64
ADAMS, Armenta
Look at the future. por Mus Am 83:10 Jl '63
ADAMS, Augusta
(tr) See Meinecke, I. Klaus Schultze
ADAMS, Bert K. and Perkins, J. A. jr
Needed, better school financial accounting. Sch Life 45:11-12 My '63
ADAMS, Brooks
Brooks Adams and American nationalism. C. Hirschfeld. bibliog f Am Hist R 69:371-92 Ja '64
ADAMS, Charles Francis
Growing up distinguished. il por Time 84:112 O 9 '64
Iron hand and a soft heart. G. W. Allen. por Sat R 47:28 N 21 '64
ADAMS, Donald K.
Proposal for centers for development education. Sch & Soc 91:282-3 O 5 '63
ADAMS, Edie
Celebrity register. C. Amory. por McCalls 90:122 Je '63
Edie wins a big one. P. Bunzel. il pors Life 54:95-6+ Ap 5 '63
Tax missionary. por Time 81:46-7 Mr 1 '63
Year in the life of Edie Adams. R. W. Lewis. il pors Sat Eve Post 236:24-7 Ap 13 '63
ADAMS, Elijah. See Singh, R. M. M. jt. auth.
ADAMS, Eva
Celebrity register. C. Amory. por McCalls 90:152 Je '63
ADAMS, Frederick B. jr
New president. New Yorker 39:17-18 Jl 13 '63
ADAMS, Hank
Trailer for yard tracs. Pop Mech 119:156-8 My '63
ADAMS, Harriet
Yachting interviews; ed. by M. Wiley. por Yachting 115:66-7+ Je '64
ADAMS, Henry
Henry Adams, by E. Samuels. Review
Time il por 84:120+ N 27 '64
Posthumous Adams. K. S. Lynn. il Reporter 31:33-4 D 17 '64
ADAMS, Henry E. See Lewis, D. J. jt. auth.
ADAMS, J. Donald
Dilemma of success. Sat R 48:19+ Ja 30 '65
Dividing line. il por Newsweek 64:106 N 9 '64
Magic and mystery of words; adaptation. Sat R 46:8-12 Ag 31 '63

about
Celebrity register. C. Amory. por McCalls 90:168 Je '63
ADAMS, James N. and Bradley, S. G.
Recombination events in the bacterial genus nocardia. bibliog Science 140:1392-4 Je 28 '63
ADAMS, Jane
Corn husk dolls. Hobbies 68:40 F '64
ADAMS, Jane Hanover
Love, O love, O careful love. America 109:481-4; 110:149 O 26 '63, F 1 '64

ADAMS, John
John Adams and his wife, Abigail. L. Baritz. Nation 197:54-5 Jl 27 '63
John Adams, second President 1797-1801. F. Freidel. il pors Nat Geog Mag 126:658-63 N '64
Magic mail of John and Abigail. M. L. Coit. il Sat R 46:24-5 Ag 10 '63
Marbury v. Madison: case of the missing commissions. J. A. Garraty. il Am Heritage 14:6-9+ Je '63
Perspective on the founders. V. Miller. por Nat R 14:117-19 F 12 '63
ADAMS, John A. S. and Lowder, W. M.
Radiation in the natural environment. Science 141:365-6 Jl 26 '63
ADAMS, John Quincy
John Quincy Adams, sixth President 1825-1829. F. Freidel. il pors Nat Geog Mag 126:684-7 N '64
ADAMS, Leason H. See Davis, B. L. jt. auth.
ADAMS, Leon D.
What wine primers don't tell. Am Home 67:19+ N '64
ADAMS, Molly
House for Jenny-wren. Flower Grower 50:49 Je '63
ADAMS, Nathan
Malindi: a place of deep water. Sports Illus 18:78-84+ Je 17 '63
ADAMS, Neal Monroe
Northern Negrophobia during the Civil war as reported by the London Times. Negro Hist Bul 28:7-8 O '64
ADAMS, Paul DeWitt
General Adams: toughest of the tough. il por Time 83:40 Ap 17 '64
ADAMS, Phoebe Lou
Potpourri. See issues of Atlantic
Rough map of Greece. il Atlan 211:27-33 Ja; 73-7 Mr; 66-71 My; 212:54-8 Jl '63; 213:73-8 Ap; 57-62 My; 214:56-60 Jl; 71-4 Ag '64
ADAMS, Richard A.
Immunity and susceptibility toward cheek-pouch transplants of a mouse leukemia. bibliog Science 146:944-5 N 13 '64
ADAMS, Robert
Books. Esquire 60:26+ O '63; 61:38+ F '64
Pomp and circumstance: C. P. Snow. Atlan 214:95-8 N '64
ADAMS, Robert H.
Movies. Christian Cent 81:1144-5 S 16 '64
ADAMS, Scott
Medical libraries are in trouble: address, October 1962. bibliog por Library J 88:2615-21 Jl '63
ADAMS, Stan
College boy counsels on boy problems. por Seventeen 23:98 Ja '64
ADAMS, Taylor
Recognizing Peking. New Repub 151:36+ N 14 '64
ADAMS, Thomas
Hypothalamic temperature in the cat during feeding and sleep. bibliog Science 139:609-10 F 15 '63
ADAMS, Thomas B.
Adams papers. Atlan 214:95-8 O '64
ADAMS, Thomas C.
Salt migration to the northwest body of Great Salt Lake, Utah. bibliog Science 143:1027-9 Mr 6 '64
ADAMS, Velma A.
Rise of the trade relations director. Duns R 84:35-6+ D '64
ADAMS, W. R. and Kraft, L. M.
Epizootic diarrhea of infant mice: identification of the etiologic agent. bibliog Science 141:359-60 Jl 26 '63
ADAMS, Yates
Enter Adams' army. Sports Illus 21:8 Jl 27 '64
ADAMS family
Adams papers. T. B. Adams. il Atlan 214:95-8 O '64
ADAMS unexpected refuge, N.J. See Wildlife sanctuaries
ADAPTATION (biology)
Evolution of sparrows in North America. Sci N L 85:377 Je 13 '64
Evolutionary and population genetics. T. Dobzhansky. bibliog Science 142:1131-5 N 29 '63
Excretion of hypertonic urine by a teleost. J. G. Stanley and W. R. Fleming. bibliog il Science 144:63-4 Ap 3 '64
Hominid bipedalism: independent evidence for the food-carrying theory. G. W. Hewes. bibliog Science 146:416-18 O 16 '64
House sparrows: rapid evolution of races in North America. R. F. Johnston and R. K. Selander. bibliog il Science 144:548-50 My 1 '64
Must tomorrow's man look like this? from address. T. Freedman and G. S. Lindner. il Pop Sci 183:77-80+ N '63
That astounding creator, nature. J. George. il Read Digest 84:96-9 Ja '64
Thermoperiodism in sea-run cutthroat trout (salmo clarki clarki) W. G. Heath. bibliog il Science 142:486-8 O 25 '63
Visual experience in infants: decreased attention to familiar patterns relative to novel ones. R. L. Fantz. bibliog il Science 146:668-70 O 30 '64
See also
Ecology
Evolution
ADAPTATION, Literary. See Drama—Technique
ADAPTATION, Social. See Adjustment, Social
ADAPTATION, Visual. See Eye—Accommodation and refraction
ADAPTERS, Radio. See Radio apparatus
ADCOCK, Cynthia. See Adcock, J. jt. auth.
ADCOCK, Evelyn B.
New Jersey's tercentenary. Hobbies 69:116-17 D '64
Post card album. il Hobbies 68:118-19 Ap '63
ADCOCK, Joe, and Adcock, Cynthia
Smell of charity. Nation 200:5-8 Ja 4 '65
ADDAMS, Charles
TV's year of the monster. il Life 57:54B-57 Ag 21 '64
ADDAMS, Jane
Social workers and the Progressive party, 1912-1916. A. F. Davis. bibliog f Am Hist R 69:671-88 Ap '64
ADDICTS, Drug. See Narcotic habit
ADDING machines
Adding machines loom as mama's new helper. il Bsns W p34 Je 6 '64
ADDINGTON, S. K. See West, M. L. jt. auth.
ADDIS ABABA
Architecture
Africa Hall, an inspiring symbol; Addis Ababa. il U N Rev 10:40-2 F '63
ADDIS ABABA conference. See Pan-African conference, Addis Ababa, 1963
ADDISON, Adele
Adele Addison: American in Moscow. por Mus Am 83:19 My '63
ADDISS, Steve
Folk-singing ambassadors. il pors Sr Schol 83:17 S 27 '63
Hootenanny under fire; State-department-sponsored tour of the Far East and Africa. il por Time 85:48-9 Ja 8 '65
Long trail a-winding. il por Newsweek 61:53 Ap 29 '63
ADDITIONS, House. See Houses, Remodeled
ADDITIVE color. See Photography—Films
ADDITIVES. See Gasoline—Additives; Lubrication and lubricants—Additives
ADEBO, S. O.
African chief explains tribalism. por N Y Times Mag p26-7+ Mr 1 '64
ADELA. See Atlantic community development group for Latin America (proposed)
ADELBERG, Edward A.
DNA replication and recombination. Science 146:1193-5 N 27 '64
ADÉLIE penguins. See Penguins
ADELMAN, Bob
Birth of a voter. Ebony 19:88-90+ F '64
Unforgettable. A. Brodovitch. il Pop Phot 54:84-5 Je '64
ADELPHI college, Garden City, N.Y.
Adelphi's accent on grace; Leon A. Swirbul library. D. N. Gallagher. il Library J 88:4558-61 D 1 '63
Centerpiece of a library: Leon A. Swirbul library; excerpts from address, October 10, 1964. R. J. Neutra. il Library J 89:4695-9 D 1 '64
ADEN
Britain has a war on its hands, too. il U S News 56:48-9 Je 1 '64
It's no Eden; attacks from Yemen. Time 83:44 My 15 '64
Red Devils vs. Red Wolves. il Newsweek 63:43-4 My 18 '64
Remnants of empire. New Repub 150:5-6 Je 13 '64
Subcommittee on Aden says United Nations action urgently necessary. U N Rev 10:38 Jl '63
Time of troubles. il Newsweek 63:34+ My 4 '64
Too true; decapitated British soldiers. Newsweek 63:51 My 25 '64
Winds of change in the Garden of Aden. J. Contini. il Reporter 29:28-30 Jl 4 '63
See also
United Nations—Aden

ADENAUER, Konrad
Adenauer sizes up de Gaulle; interview. ed. by K. Lachmann. por U S News 54:31 F 11 '63
Adenauer talks about Johnson; interview, ed. by K. Lachmann. pors U S News 55: 44-7 D 16 '63
Old warrior looks back; ed. by D. Schorr. pors Sat Eve Post 236:96-9 O 19 '63
On nazism, de Gaulle, Russia, the future; interview. ed. by O. Schisgall. pors Look 27:27-9 D 17 '63

about

Adenauer, by C. Wighton. Review
Sat R por 47:64 Ap 11 '64. W. H. Chamberlin
Adenauer era: events and the man; photographs. A. J. Olsen. N Y Times Mag p 16-17 O 13 '63
Adenauer: still a major figure in world affairs. por U S News 57:19 N 23 '64
Adenauer years. H. Abosch. por Nation 197: 28-31 Jl 13 '63
Adenauer's adieu. Newsweek 61:38 Ap 22 '63
Adenaullism. Time 84:32 Jl 17 '64
Atlantic report. Atlan 213:32+ F '64
Back-seat driver. il por Newsweek 62:67-8 O 21 '63
Change at the top in West Germany. il por U S News 55:22 O 14 '63
Dream comes true for two old rivals. il por U S News 54:19 F 4 '63
Duty done. il por Time 82:36-7 O 18 '63
End of the Adenauer era. C. G. Anthon. il Cur Hist 44:193-201 Ap '63
Erhard finally moves toward the summit. A. J. Olsen. il por N Y Times Mag p20+ My 5 '63
Farewell to Der Alte. A. Horne. por Nat R 15:350-1 O 22 '63
From Adenauer to Erhard; changeover in West Germany. il por Sr Schol 83:12-15+ N 15 '63
Gaullist Adenauer challenges Erhard. A. J. Olsen. il por N Y Times Mag p 11+ Jl 26 '64
Germany: the Adenauer era ends. il pors Newsweek 61:48-9+ My 6 '63
Germany without Adenauer: what it will be like. il por U S News 55:80-1 O 21 '63
Germany's Erhard: ready to take over, but. . . por U S News 54:19 F 18 '63
Great legacy from Adenauer. Life 55:4 O 25 '63
Leader of the opposition. Newsweek 64:48+ N 16 '64
Mongoose and cobra. Newsweek 61:33-4 F 25 '63
Old man won't let go. T. Prittie. New Repub 148:9-10 Ap 27 '63
Old wolf Adenauer sits at bay. J. Bell. il pors Life 54:36-7 Ap 26 '63
Oldest grad. il por Time 82:28+ Jl 26 '63
Paris-Bonn axis. T. Prittie. New Repub 148: 8-9 F 9 '63
President and Secretary Rusk pay tribute to Chancellor Adenauer; letters, October 10 and October 15, 1963. J. F. Kennedy; D. Rusk. Dept State Bul 49:697 N 4 '63
Shadows on the success of Der Alte. D. Schorr. por Reporter 28:27-8 F 28 '63
Time of the sphinx. il por Time 82:27 S 27 '63
West loses two statesmen: editorial. Sat Eve Post 236:82 N 9 '63
Who's next? por Time 81:43 Mr 15 '63
Will Germany now edge closer to U.S? Kennedy and the Germans. il U S News 54: 62-3 Je 24 '63

ADENINE
Chemical of life created. Sci N L 83:323 My 25 '63
Primordial adenine. Sci Am 209:52 Ag '63
Re-creating the pre-life earth. il Time 81:59 Je 7 '63

ADENOSINE diphosphate-glucose. See Glucose

ADENOSINE phosphates
2,4-dinitrophenol: lack of interaction with high-energy intermediates of oxidative phosphorylation. R. H. Eisenhardt and O. Rosenthal. bibliog il Science 143:476 Ja 31 '64

ADENOSINE triphosphate
Adenosine triphosphate: changes in muscles doing negative work. A. A. Infante and others. bibliog il Science 144:1577-8 Je 26 '64
Calcium-activated adenosine triphosphatase localization in cultured beating heart cells. H. Lewis and I. Harary. bibliog il Science 141:47-8 Jl 5 '63
Contraction-band formation in barnacle myofibrils. R. J. Baskin and G. M. Wiese. bibliog il Science 143:134-6 Ja 10 '64
Electrophorus adenosine triphosphatase: sodium-activated exchange after N-ethyl maleimide treatment. S. Fahn and others. bibliog il Science 145:283-4 Jl 17 '64
Feeding response in aedes aegypti: stimulation by adenosine triphosphate. R. Galun and others. bibliog il Science 142:1674-5 D 27 '63
How food finally produces power; the energy factor. il Life 54:48-59+ Mr 29 '63
Mitochondrion. D. E. Green. il Sci Am 210: 63-6+ bibliog(p 152) Ja '64
Shot in the head. il Newsweek 61:56 Mr 4 '63

ADENOVIRUSES. See Viruses

ADER, Robert
Gastric erosions in the rat: effects of immobilization at different points in the activity cycle. bibliog Science 145:406-7 Jl 24 '64
—and Conklin, P. M.
Handling of pregnant rats: effects on emotionality of their offspring. Science 142:411-12 O 18 '63

ADES, Harlow. See Webb, W. B. jt. auth.

ADEY, W. Ross, and others
Sleep: cortical and subcortical recordings in the chimpanzee. bibliog Science 141:932-3 S 6 '63

ADHESION
Sticky issue. Newsweek 61:83 Ap 29 '63

ADHESIVE tape
Cellophane tapes. il Consumer Rep 28:545-6 N '63
New tapes for old jobs; self-stick tapes. il House B 106:131+ F '64

ADHESIVES
Gluing isn't what it used to be; with chart. D. X. Manners. House B 105:98-9+ Jl '63
Houses will soon stick together without nails. Sci N L 87:9 Ja 2 '65
They don't make fountain pens, or library paste, or hardly anything that way any more. R. P. Smith. il McCalls 90:194+ S '63
Useful sealants & adhesives. B. Cobb, jr. Yachting 115:178-9 Je '64
Wonder industrial adhesives. H. E. Klein. il Duns R 84:53-4+ O '64
See also
Cements, Adhesive
Epoxy adhesives
Paste

ADIE, A. D.
Trial and triumph of training. Recreation 57:240-1 My '64

ADIPOSE tissue. See Fat

ADIRONDACK MOUNTAINS
Beautiful, bedeviled Adirondacks. S. Birmingham. il Holiday 36:42-7+ Ag '64; Reply with rejoinder. T. A. Frankel. 36:6+ N '64
Bird finding in the Adirondacks. O. S. Pettingill. il Audubon Mag 65:138-41 My '63
Case of the Adirondacks. W. B. Conroy. il Recreation 58:15-16 Ja '65

ADISESHIAH, Malcolm S.
Results of Unesco's 12th general conference. Sch & Soc 91:198-9 Ap 20 '63

ADJUSTMENT (biology) See Adaptation (biology)

ADJUSTMENT, Social
Can Americans adjust? W. Wingo. il Sci N L 84:346 N 30 '63
Dealing with the disagreeable. M. B. Hoover. il Redbook 120:40 F '63
Emotional life of the teen-ager; with study-discussion program. by E. M. Duvall. J. R. Gallagher. bibliog il PTA Mag 58:26-8, 36-7 F '64
Guide for parents: your child's mental health. W. W. Wattenberg. bibliog il NEA J 53:35-50 F '64
Help for a shy child. L. Marett. il Parents Mag 39:52-3+ O '64
Help your child like himself; with study-discussion program. by C. W. Mattuck. S. Blau. il Parents Mag 38:37-8, 62-3+ D '63
Holiday cure for bored teen-agers. A. Gillette. il UNESCO Courier 16:24-7 Ap '63
I always feel like a stranger; questions and answers. A. Wood. il Seventeen 23:122-3+ Mr '64
I believe; ed. by A. Armstrong. E. J. Kohler. Seventeen 23:166 Je '64
Mothers must keep on growing, too; with group discussion program, ed. by M. R. Sherwin. E. G. Neisser. il Parents Mag 39: 20+, 52-3+ Je '64
Older man; questions and answers. A. Wood. il Seventeen 23:224-5+ Ag '64
Outsiders, studies in the sociology of deviance, by H. S. Becker. Review
Commentary 36:410-12 N '63. H. Dienstfrey; Reply with rejoinder. E. M. Schur. 37:16 Mr '64

ADJUSTMENT, Social—*Continued*
Slowing down the social pace. G. Hechinger. il N Y Times Mag p99 Ap 14 '63
Social graces and disgraces; with study-discussion program, by C. Smallenburg and H. Smallenburg. M. W. Piers. bibliog il PTA Mag 59:7-9, 35-6 D '64
Trials of families on the move. D. C. Disney. Ladies Home J 81:16+ My '64
Wanted: strong parents. J. B. Scofield. Parents Mag 38:53+ Je '63
Way we feel. Seventeen 22:143 Je '63
What teens gripe about. il Seventeen 22:138-9+ F '63
What's behind those teen-age masks? M. Sklansky and E. G. Neisser. il Parents Mag 39:64-5+ Ap '64
Who's afraid of the big, bad teen-agers? R. Bennett. il Parents Mag 38:62-3+ Mr '63
Why kids rebel. J. B. Scofield. Read Digest 82:130-3 Je '63
See also
Conformity
Individual and society
Maturity
Normality
Security and insecurity (psychology)
also subhead Adjustment under classes of people, e.g. School children—Adjustment

Anecdotes, facetiae, satire, etc.

Guilty party is Art Buchwald. A. Buchwald. McCalls 90:54 My '63

ADKINSON, Burton W.
Primary scientific publication and the federal government. bibliog Science 140:613-17 My 10 '63

ADKISSON, Perry L. See Bell, R. A; Cole, C. L. jt. auths.

ADLER, George
Cross-linking of polymers by radiation. bibliog Science 141:321-8 Jl 26 '63

ADLER, Hans
Auschwitz: fall 1964; poem. Christian Cent 81:1328 O 28 '64

ADLER, Irving
Fool your friends with numbers tricks; excerpt from Magic house of numbers. Sci Digest 53:59-60 Je '63

ADLER, Kurt Herbert
Competition in Bulgaria. por Opera N 28:6-7 O 19 '63
about
Coming of age in San Francisco. por Time 82:64 S 27 '63

ADLER, Lucile
Desert almanach; Whisper for K; While you sleep; Women looking out; poems. Poetry 102:12-16 Ap '63

ADLER, Morris
What is a Jew? Harper 228:41-5 Ja '64

ADLER, Myles
From slide to B&W print without a negative. U S Camera 26:26+ O '63
How wide can you get? U S Camera 26:58-9+ S '63

ADLER, Paula
Craftsmen of the northeastern states. Craft Horiz 23:37+ N '63
Five designers, five approaches. Craft Horiz 24:42-8 Mr '64

ADLER, Renata
Books. New Yorker 39:234-8+ N 9 '63; 40:181-5 My 2; 203-4 My 16; 60-8+ Jl 4 '64

ADLER, Richard
Presidentical man. il Newsweek 63:88 Je 8 '64

ADLER, Selig
Operation on President McKinley; with biographical sketch. Sci Am 208:34, 118-30 Mr '63

ADMINISTERED prices. See Price maintenance by industry

ADMINISTRATION, Public
See also
Bureaucracy
Government spending policy

ADMINISTRATION of justice. See Justice, Administration of

ADMINISTRATIVE ability. See Executive ability

ADMINISTRATIVE and political divisions
See also
Apportionment (election law)

ADMINISTRATIVE assistants to the president. See Public officers

ADMINISTRATIVE communication. See Communication in management

ADMINISTRATIVE counsel. See Administrative remedies

ADMINISTRATIVE procedure. See Administrative remedies

ADMINISTRATIVE remedies
Declaring a war on injustice. R. Goldfarb. New Repub 152:15-17 Ja 16 '65
New Zealand Ombudsman. D. P. O'Neill. America 112:166-8 Ja 30 '65
Ombudsman for America; Scandinavian-style grievance man to investigate complaints about the work of bureaucrats. H. S. Reuss. N Y Times Mag p30+ S 13 '64
Sweden's remedy for police brutality; Ombudsman. M. K. Sanders. Harper 229:132+ N '64
They fight city hall, and win; the ombudsman in Scandinavia. G. Kent. Read Digest 83:29-30+ Jl '63

ADMINISTRATORS, College. See College officials

ADMINISTRATORS, Government. See Public officers

ADMIRALTY ISLAND, Alaska
Last chance for Admiralty; island ruined for Japanese-owned pulpwood mill. R. W. Young. il Field & S 69:10-12+ My '64

ADOBE buildings. See Building, Adobe

ADOLESCENCE
Another epidemic of teen-age VD? C. S. Deschin. Ladies Home J 80:30+ Ja '63
Are teen-agers people? M. J. E. Senn. il McCalls 90:74+ S '63
Awkward age. D. Beckmann. PTA Mag 58:23 S '63
Boys and girls together; excerpt from Moving into manhood. W. W. Bauer. il Todays Health 41:54-5+ S '63
Ease them into the teens. C. Chilman. il Parents Mag 39:38-9+ Ag '64
Education of a modern girl; with study-discussion program, by E. M. Duvall. H. Taylor. bibliog il PTA Mag 58:4-6, 36 S '63
Health plan for young teens. E. F. Kraft. il Parents Mag 39:60-1+ N '64
How serious are your problems? G. Mayer and M. Hoover. il Seventeen 22:116-17+ S '63
How to win arguments with your parents. J. Hawkes. Seventeen 22:120-1+ N '63
Is disrespect inevitable? with study-discussion program, by E. M. Duvall. R. M. Butler. bibliog il PTA Mag 57:24-6, 36 Mr '63
It's tough to be a teen-ager; ed. by R. L. Smith. J. F. Phelan, jr. Read Digest 82:31-2+ Mr '63
On the fringe of a golden era: the U.S. student. il Time 85:56-57A+ Ja 29 '65
Personal business; troubled teenager. Bsns W p 173-4 O 17 '64
Problems on the path to manhood; excerpts from Moving into manhood. W. W. Bauer. il Todays Health 41:60-1+ O '63
Sensible way to understand teenagers. R. D. Cutter. il Parents Mag 40:46-7+ Ja '65
Teen-age tyranny, by G. Hechinger and F. Hechinger. Review
Sat R 46:72-3 Mr 23 '63. P. Woodring
Teens want to help. J. R. Gaver. il Parents Mag 38:60+ O '63; Same abr. with title To Claudia with love. Read Digest 83:215-16 O '63
Uneasy days before college. P. Chizcott. il Parents Mag 38:40-1+ Jl '63
What did you want most at seventeen? symposium, ed. by A. Ebert. il Seventeen 22:130-3 S '63
What happened when my school banned going steady. J. A. Carey. McCalls 90:69+ Je '63
What I've learned by twenty-six (that I wish I mad known at sixteen) B. Rollins. il Farm J 87:72+ My '63
What teen-agers don't know about sex. S. H. Fraiberg. Parents Mag 38:35+ Jl '63
Who's afraid of the big, bad teen-agers? R. Bennett. il Parents Mag 38:62-3+ Mr '63
Young moderns' marriage dreams; with study-discussion program. E. M. Duvall. bibliog il PTA Mag 57:4-7, 36 Ap '63
See also
Boys
Girls
Puberty
Youth

Anecdotes, facetiae, satire, etc.

Labors of love. B. Friel. Atlan 211:130-2 Ap '63

ADOLESCENTS. See Adolescence; Youth

ADOPTION
Adopting Negro children. E. Shepherd. New Repub 150:10-12 Je 20 '64
Adoption agencies grow up. J. Viorst. il Sci N L 86:362-3 D 5 '64
Adoption: the created family. C. Schoenberg. bibliog f Ann Am Acad 355:69-74 S '64
Are interracial homes bad for children? il Ebony 18:131-2+ Mr '63

ADOPTION—*Continued*
Babies without homes. W. Trombley. il Sat Eve Post 236:15-21 F 16 '63
Child is waiting for you. Christian Cent 81:1453-4 N 25 '64
Children for adoption, by P. S. Buck. Review
Sat R il 48:25-6 Ja 16 '65. C. C. Risen
Children who need adoption; a radical view. R. J. Isaac. Atlan 212:45-50 N '63; Discussion. 213:30+ Ja; 40+ F '64
Family for Freddie. A. Blair. il Read Digest 85:49-52 D '64
Fifteen years later; Moral adoption program; concerning article in the Asahi picture news of Tokyo. B. W. Fuson. Sat R 48:23 Ja 2 '65
If you're thinking of adoption. A. Blair. il Parents Mag 39:52-3+ Ag '64
It's easier to adopt a baby. P. Streit. il N Y Times Mag p48+ Ag 23 '64
Orphans and the maidens; report from Hiroshima. N. Cousins. il Sat R 47:20-2 Ap 25 '64
They cared enough to give the most. W. Trombley. il Ladies Home J 81:32+ Ap '64
Whose child? the parents' child. America 109: 376 O 5 '63
Why did my mother give me away? P. Streit. il N Y Times Mag p53+ Ja 24 '65

ADOPTION of cities. See Intercommunity cooperation

ADOULA, Cyrille
Adoula and peace with Belgium; address, February 27, 1963. Negro Hist Bul 26:247-8 My '63
Letter dated 22 August 1963 addressed to the Secretary-General, U Thant. U N Rev 10:47 O '63

about

Adoula tries to bind up the wounds. L. Garrison. il pors N Y Times Mag p25+ My 12 '63
Atlantic report. Atlan 212:16+ S '63
Clamping down. Newsweek 62:52+ N 4 '63
Mr Kennedy goes to war. J. Burnham. Nat R 15:59 Jl 30 '63

ADRENAL glands
See also
ACTH

ADRENALECTOMY
Electroconvulsive threshold elevation: from daily stimulation of adrenalectomized animals. C. F. Essig and others. bibliog il Science 140:828-9 My 17 '63

ADRENALIN
Enzymatic formation of adrenaline and other catechols from monophenols. J. Axelrod. bibliog il Science 140:499-500 My 3 '63
Potentiation by adrenaline of a proteolytic activity associated with purified myosin. P. Gordon and R. Zak. bibliog il Science 140: 294-5 Ap 19 '63

ADRENOCORTICOTROPIC hormones. See ACTH

ADRIAN, Mich.
Court scheme gives church an inward focus: Christ Episcopal church. il Arch Rec 134: 136-9 Jl '63

ADRIANA Lecouvreur; opera. See Cilea, F.

ADRIATIC SEA ISLANDS. See Islands of the Adriatic Sea

ADSORPTION
Elastic membrane: effect of increasing tension on the absorptive capacity. J. H. Lunseth. bibliog il Science 141:438 Ag 2 '63
Potential theory of adsorption; authority in science. M. Polanyi. bibliog Science 141: 1010-13 S 13 '63; Reply. G. A. Louis. 142: 1257 D 6 '63

ADULT-child relationship. See Child-adult relationship

ADULT education
Acquisition and distribution of instructional materials; symposium. il Pub W 185:39-43 My 4 '64
Adult education, dimensions and necessities; excerpt from address, February 15, 1963. F. E. Engleman. Sch Life 45:8-13 F '63
Adult education in an urban age. H. Stillwell. Sch & Soc 91:46-7 Ja 26 '63
Continuing your education, by C. O. Houle. Review
Sat R 47:66 Ag 15 '64. E. Strainchamps
Dangers of adult illiteracy. Sch & Soc 92:95+ Mr 7 '64
Educational change tomorrow. Sch & Soc 92:284-5 O 17 '64
Federal aid for the illiterate; address, April 8, 1964. R. B. Minnis. il Wilson Lib Bul 38:844+ Je '64
For adults only; Columbia university's School of general studies. il Time 83:44 My 8 '64
Future of adult education; excerpt from Adult education movement in the United States. M. S. Knowles; reply. P. R. Pierce. Sch & Soc 91:183 Ap 20 '63
Helping Cook County's culturally deprived adults. D. J. Brooks, jr. NEA J 52:29-30 Ap '63
High school diploma at seventy-two; D. D. Elmore. il Ebony 19:125-6+ Ag '64
House designed to please seventy-five women. J. Chapman. il House B 105:168-78 My '63
Housewife becomes literate in Communist China; testimony, tr. by D. C. Chu. L. Y. Wang. Sch & Soc 91:379-80 N 30 '63
Impact. il NEA J 53:22-4 D '64
It takes only two; literacy programs in New York state. T. L. Conklin. Christian Cent 81:1474 N 25 '64
It's what's up top that counts. G. Dapper. il Sat R 46:48-9+ D 21 '63
Lifetime of education. N. W. Chamberlain. NEA J 53:11 Ja '64
Massive attack on illiteracy: Cook County experience; excerpts from address, July 13, 1963. R. M. Hilliard. il ALA Bul 57:1034-8 D '63
No room at the bottom. il NEA J 53:44 My '64
Photography at Tucson high. R. Arnold. U S Camera 27:51+ Mr '64
Renewal of the professional man; address, November 7, 1963. C. C. Furnas. Vital Speeches 30:144-6 D 15 '63
School dropout and adult education. W. W. Brickman. Sch & Soc 92:179 Ap 18 '64
Teacher-opinion poll; adults and out-of-school youth. il NEA J 53:77 F '64
War on poverty; book publishing's role in adult education, job retraining; symposium; with editorial comment. il Pub W 185: 38-50, 57 F 17 '64
See also
Education of prisoners
Service men, Discharged—Education
Television in education
United States—Army—Education

Great books program

Great ideas today, by M. J. Adler and R. Hutchins. Review
Nat R 14:233-5 Mr 26 '63. J. Leonard

Library participation

College graduate as a lifetime reader; excerpts from address. J. S. Diekhoff. ALA Bul 58:995-7+ D '64
Cuba: public libraries and popular adult education. H. C. Campbell; reply. L. Deyá. Library J 88:1492+ Ap 1 '63
Libraries: active agents in adult reading improvement. H. A. Robinson. bibliog f il ALA Bul 57:416-20 My '63
Library adult education activities in public libraries of Germany, Denmark, and England; report. G. T. Stevenson. il ALA Bul 57:643-54 Jl '63
More fruitful use of knowledge. J. M. Chancellor. ALA Bul 57:326-9 Ap '63
Wanted: new adult materials; Adult services, New York public library. K. L. O'Brien. Sr Schol 85:24T O 7 '64
Way through the web. E. Johnson. il Library J 89:3246-8 S 15 '64

ADULT education association of the U.S.A. Meeting, 1962. Sch & Soc 91:46-7 Ja 26 '63

ADULT music study. See Music—Instruction and study

ADULT reading. See Books and reading

ADULTERY
Accommodation, Italian style; Elsa Martinelli and Willy Rizzo. G. Talese. il Esquire 59:88-93+ F '63

ADULTHOOD. See Maturity

ADVANCE (periodical)
Birds and the beasts were there; dinner to benefit liberal Republicans' magazine Advance. G. F. Hobart. Nat R 14:485 Je 18 '63

ADVANCED management courses. See Executives—Training

ADVANCED research projects agency. See United States—Defense, Department of—Advanced research projects agency

ADVANCED solar turbo electric concept. See Space vehicles—Power supply

ADVANCED technology, incorporated (proposed)
New space corporation forming in Hub City. Miss & Roc 12:16 Mr 18 '63

ADVANCED technology satellite. See Artificial satellites—Use in research

ADVENT
Advent season. Christian Cent 80:1535 D 11 '63

ADVENT—*Continued*
Glowing prelude to Christmas. il Good H 157:224 D '63
Word. C. P. McCorry. America 109:754-5; 111:724 D 7 '63, N 28 '64
ADVENT calendars. See Calendars
ADVENTURE
Today's adventurelands. L. Thomas. il Travel 121:44-6 Ja '64
ADVENTURE (periodical)
New look in Adventure. A. Norton. Writer 77:26-7 F '64
ADVENTURE stories
See also
Fiction in periodicals and newspapers
ADVENTURE; story. See Borgese, E. M.
ADVENTURERS
Overreachers; portfolio. G. Talese. Esquire 60:152-7 D '63
ADVENTURERS' club of Denmark. See Clubs
ADVENTURES, Joint. See Joint adventures
ADVENTURES of a people buff; story. See De Vries, P.
ADVERTISEMENTS. See Advertising
ADVERTISEMENTS, Personal. See Newspapers —Personal advertisements
ADVERTISING
Advertising: a public servant; address, November 19, 1964. V. E. Boyd. Vital Speeches 31:153-5 D 15 '64
Advertising needs standards to prove claims. Consumer Bul 46:6-7 S '63
Annals of business; soaps and synthetic detergents. T. Whiteside. New Yorker 40:44-6+ D 19 '64
Burning bright; ads giving up sex for tigers. il Time 84:88 S 25 '64
Chicago school of advertising. G. Lazarus. Sat R 47:60+ Jl 11 '64
Chicago: second city in advertising. G. Lazarus. il Sat R 47:60-1 Je 13 '64
Confessions of an advertising man, by D. Ogilvy. Review
Commonweal 79:223-4 N 15 '63. W. Sheed
New Repub 149:27+ N 2 '63. M. Mayer
Reporter 29:54+ N 7 '63. R. Bingham
Confidential; Gallagher report. il Newsweek 63:74-5 My 25 '64
Hard sell and the soft sell. J. Brooks. Consumer Rep 28:402-3 Ag '63
How to criticize advertising. H. C. Groome, jr. Sat R 46:54 O 12 '63; Discussion. 46:54-5 D 14 '63
Industrial marketing's new voice. L. Morse. il Duns R 81:31-2+ Mr '63
Larceny is good for you; curious ad. il Newsweek 62:54 Jl 1 '63
Madison avenue; economic repercussions. P. B. Bart. il Sat R 47:52+ F 8 '64; Reply. M. J. Grayson. 47:122-3 Mr 14 '64
Madison avenue: new view, old street. L. Valenstein. Sat R 46:72-3 Ap 13 '63
Mating on Madison avenue; the tie-in ad. Time 84:75 Jl 17 '64
Moppet market; aiming at the child as consumer. A. F. Gonzalez. Reporter 30:40+ Je 18 '64
New frontier for religion; advertisement of Stage coach manufacturing co. Christian Cent 81:1287 O 14 '64
News behind the ads. See issues of Changing times
Q & Advertising; questions and answers, ed. by B. Williams. See issues of McCall's
Right to choose. L. H. Hodges. Sat R 46:18+ Ap 13 '63
Should advertising be abolished? excerpts from Confessions of an advertising man. D. Ogilvy. Read Digest 84:67-70 F '64
Soap wars: a strategic analysis. S. Klaw. il Fortune 67:122-5+ Je '63
Tuning up tuna. Newsweek 62:60-1 Ag 5 '63
Who shall bell the cat? Nation 200:23 Ja 11 '65
Year of the tiger. il Newsweek 64:72 S 28 '64
See also
Bank advertising
Photography in advertising
Posters—Exhibitions
Public relations
Radio advertising
School publicity
Television advertising
also subhead Advertising under various subjects, e.g. Cigarettes—Advertising

Anecdotes, facetiae, satire, etc.

Bearded lions: Hoffritz shaving equipment. Christian Cent 81:751 Je 3 '64
Day the ads stopped. G. G. Kirstein. il Nation 198:555-7 Je 1 '64
First of the month. C. Amory. Sat R 47:6 O 3 '64
Hello, central, give me that jolly old pelf. S. J. Perelman. New Yorker 39:27-9 D 21 '63
No laughing matter. P. Bart. Sat R 47:78 Ja 11 '64
Trade winds. J. G. Fuller. Sat R 47:6 Jl 25 '64

Bibliography

Books in communications. J. F. Fixx. See second issue of each month of Saturday review

Costs

Bringing home the duck; advertising expenditures reach $13.1 billion. il Time 84:98 S 11 '64
Madison avenue crisis in creativity. il Duns R 84:36-7+ Jl '64
Moneymen of marketing. L. Morse. Duns R 81:41-2 Mr '63

International aspects

That local touch. il Time 82:93 S 20 '63

Laws and regulations

Policing the advertiser; U.S. department of commerce report on self-regulation in American advertising. R. L. Tobin. Sat R 47:49-50 Jl 11 '64; Discussion. 47:38+ Ag 8, 54 S 12 '64

Moral aspects

See Advertising ethics

Psychology

Battle of the sexes on Madison avenue. Consumer Rep 28:103 Mr '63
Image revolution. N. P. Hurley. il America 110:137-9 Ja 25 '64
Is advertising psychology outdated? Sci Digest 55:73 F '64
Mirrors of advertising. J. P. Sisk. il Commonweal 79:707-10 Mr 13 '64
Moppets and money. P. Korenvaes. Duns R 82:55 D '63

Social aspects

Mirrors of advertising. J. P. Sisk. il Commonweal 79:707-10 Mr 13 '64

Study and teaching

Madison avenue methods: teaching ideas that work; Harlem, N.Y. junior high school. S. R. Selby. il Sr Schol 85:7T O 14 '64

Testimonials

Ask the man who: use of unwitting presidential endorsements by admen. R. Cowley. il Am Heritage 15:24-7 Ag '64

Brazil

Master of his market; Cicero Leuenroth's Standard propaganda. il Time 84:104 O 30 '64

Europe, Western

Belated rise of advertising. D. Seligman. il Fortune 69:120-3+ Mr '64

France

Visual haymakers; Savignac posters. il Newsweek 63:76+ Ap 13 '64

Great Britain

Britain edges out of the ice age; advertising campaign for central-heating systems. A. Carthew. il N Y Times Mag p60+ D 13 '64

Japan

This is the new Japan. V. Packard. il Sat Eve Post 236:28-34+ Ap 20 '63
ADVERTISING, Cooperative
Can co-op ads survive FTC's broadside? Robinson-Patman act. Bsns W p86+ F 23 '63
ADVERTISING, Direct mail
About: mailing lists; direct-mail industry under fire. T. Irwin. N Y Times Mag p96-7 Mr 22 '64
Mailbox magnates. P. B. Bart. Sat R 46: 64-5 My 11 '63
ADVERTISING, Electric. See Electric signs
ADVERTISING, Fraudulent
Advertising at the bar; Regimen case. America 110:181 F 8 '64
FTC charges Rodale with making false ad claims. Pub W 185:40 My 18 '64
FTC presents: the great sandpaper shave; a real-life story of truth in advertising. D. Seligman. il Fortune 70:130-3+ D '64
Health claims: a new approach: Regimen case. Consumer Rep 29:156 Ap '64
Land frauds: look before you buy. T. Armbrister. il Sat Eve Post 236:17-23 Ap 27 '63
Mail-order gyps. il Consumer Bul 47:34-7 Ap '64

ADVERTISING, Fraudulent—*Continued*
Objectionable advertising of foods and beverages. A. Mullins. il Consumer Bul 46:35-7 N '63
Science of a dynamic advertisement. Consumer Bul 47:16-17 My '64
Shopping made easy, its says here. Consumer Rep 28:205 My '63
Traffic builders and confidence destroyers; bait advertisement in Reader's digest. Consumer Rep 29:269-70 Je '64

ADVERTISING, Outdoor
Goodbye Burma-Shave. W. K. Zinsser. il Sat Eve Post 237:65-6 S 5 '64
See also
Billboards
Electric signs

ADVERTISING, Political
Adman in politics. P. Bart. Sat R 47:81 Ap 11 '64
Bumper crop; Feinstein's Aldine printing co. il Newsweek 64:72 S 14 '64
Necessity in politics. J. Kaselow. Sat R 47:106 O 10 '64; Reply. R. W. Cooley. 47:77 N 14 '64
Proposition fourteen. K. M. Ruppenthal. Nation 199:inside cover N 23 '64
When the client is a candidate; five TV commercials for the Democrats. P. Hamill. il N Y Times Mag p30-1+ O 25 '64
Who's for whom; advertising agencies in politics for pay. Time 84:97-8 S 11 '64
See also
Political campaigns

ADVERTISING, Public service
SR's eleventh-twelfth annual advertising awards. W. D. Patterson. il Sat R 46:62-7 Ap 13 '63; 47:73-6+ Ap 11 '64; Discussion of Ap 11 issue. 47:60 My 9 '64

ADVERTISING, Radio. See Radio advertising

ADVERTISING agencies
$500 million whale. Newsweek 62:86+ O 21 '63
Health claims: a new approach; responsibility for ads. Consumer Rep 29:156 Ap '64
Mavericks on Madison avenue. P. B. Bart. Sat R 46:60+ D 14 '63
Pinning down adman's job. Bsns W p69 N 14 '64
Status seekers in advertising. P. Bart. Sat R 46:58 Mr 9 '63
This is the new Japan. V. Packard. il Sat Eve Post 236:28-34+ Ap 20 '63
Wheeling and dealing on the coast; Los Angeles agencies. G. Lazarus. Sat R 48:71+ Ja 9 '65
See also names of advertising agencies, e.g. Interpublic group of companies, incorporated

Securities

How Madison avenue views its own big sell; public stock ownership. il Bsns W p72-6+ My 2 '64

ADVERTISING art
Ads & posters. il Design 64:202-3 Je '63
Advertising designs of Jack Kabat. R. Day. il Am Artist 28:56-60+ Ja '64
Artist's biggest market; department stores and specialty shops. H. Greenwald. il Design 64:162-6+ Mr '63

ADVERTISING as a profession
Status seekers in advertising. P. Bart. Sat R 46:58 Mr 9 '63

ADVERTISING cards
Dancing commercials: 1880. il Dance Mag 38:37-9 Jl '64

ADVERTISING characters
Bear that almost made me infamous; Smokey Bear's living symbol. K. D. Flock. il Am For 70:20-1+ D '64
Flap; Aunt Jemima. il Newsweek 61:30 Mr 4 '63
Smokey comes up roses. D. K. Porter. il Am For 70:4+ Mr '64

ADVERTISING columns. See Newspapers—Sections, columns, etc.

ADVERTISING ethics
Ad-versions; New York world's fair advertising on license plates. il Newsweek 62:53 D 30 '63
Advertising at the bar; Regimen case. America 110:81 F 8 '64
Advertising ethics; tobacco industry. America 110:131-2 Ja 25 '64
. . . And slow death. Read Digest 82:49-53 F '63
Frankenstein in ad alley. J. Kaselow. Sat R 47:46-7 Ag 8 '64; Discussion. 47:54 S 12 '64
Honesty in advertising. P. Bart; discussion. Sat R 46:62 F 9 '63
Little station that won't; KWUN's refusal of cigarette commercials. R. L. Shayon. Sat R 47:24 F 8 '64
Pills and promises. Newsweek 63:65-6 F 3 '64
Weathervane. R. G. Miner. Flower Grower 50:6 Mr '63
What ads do you run. New Repub 148:4 Mr 16 '63
See also
Advertising—Testimonials
Advertising, Fraudulent

ADVERTISING in politics. See Advertising, Political

ADVERTISING mediums
Not so silent salesmen; point-of-purchase displays. il Bsns W p 130+ N 21 '64
Search for new media. P. Bart. Sat R 46:78 N 9 '63

Match books

Matches with messages. J. B. Weiner. Duns R 82:68+ O '63

Newspapers

Education in newspaper advertisements. G. Gerbner. Sch & Soc 92:363-5 N 28 '64
5.9 per cent rise in newspaper ads indicated by book firms. il Pub W 186:36-7 D 14 '64; Correction. 187:68 Ja 11 '65
Plum in the valley; Ridder newspaper group. il Time 83:48 My 8 '64
Strike's impact; New York and Cleveland newspaper strikes. il Time 81:76 F 8 '63

Packaging

Critical one-fifth of a second. J. F. Olesky. il Duns R 84:102-4+ D '64

Paperback books

Hard sell in soft cover. il Bsns W p30+ Jl 4 '64

Periodicals

Admen urge promotion curbs; free copies. Bsns W p28 Mr 28 '64
Fundamental issue: limitation of advertising. Nation 196:518 Je 22 '63
Image builders go back to print; ads in magazines again. il Bsns W p70 O 31 '64
Measuring up to predictions; best financial year ever. Time 85:45 Ja 22 '65
Reader total in doubt? free magazines distort figures. Bsns W p 151 D 14 '63
When magazines fight together. T. Peterson. Sat R 47:74 D 12 '64

Telephone

Asterisks, anyone? complaint against phone hucksters. il Time 84:59 Ag 28 '64
Electronic privacy. Nation 199:2 Jl 13 '64

ADVERTISING men
How Madison avenue views its own big sell; public stock ownership. il Bsns W p72-6+ My 2 '64
Image maker's image. Newsweek 61:71 My 6 '63
Media man. P. Bart. Sat R 47:126-7 Mr 14 '64

ADVERTISING models. See Models (persons)

ADVERTISING research
Can advertising be measured? Duns R 84:43-4+ S '64
Mating behavioral science and simulation. R. A. Bauer and R. D. Buzzell. il Harvard Bsns R 42:116-24 S '64

ADVERTISING signs. See Electric signs

ADVICE columns. See Newspapers—Advice columns

ADVISORY committee on the arts. See United States—State, Department of—Advisory committee on the arts

ADVISORY council on the arts. See United States—National council on the arts

ADVISORY councils, Government. See United States—Executive departments

ADVOCATE; drama. See Noah, R.

ADZHUBEI, Alekseĭ Ivanovich
Adzhubei and Italy today. M. Painelle. America 108:405-6 Mr 23 '63
Coexistence: the fasionable disease. Time 81:58 Je 28 '63
Fiat lux; private meeting between Pope John and Khrushchev's son-in-law. Time 82:53 S 6 '63
Mission accomplished. Newsweek 64:40 Ag 10 '64
Paris loves Moscow? por Newsweek 63:41-2 Ap 13 '64
Pope and atheist. Newsweek 61:52 Mr 18 '63
Pope meets Communist. il por Time 81:53 Mr 15 '63
Pope's bombshell. G. D. Kumlien. Commonweal 78:71-2 Ap 12 '63
Turning point in Kremlin-Vatican relations? il por U S News 54:21 Mr 18 '63
Uncharted waters; private audience with the Pope. America 108:393-4 Mr 23 '63

AEDES aegypti. See Mosquitoes

AEGEAN ISLANDS
In the light of the Aegean. J. Knowles. il Horizon 6:98-104 Spr '64
Serene isles. il Life 54:54-71+ Je 14 '63
See also
Cyclades (islands)
Hydra (island)
Syros (island)

AEGEAN SEA
Chartering in the Greek isles. W. Wolf. il Motor B 113:50-1+ Ap '64

AERATION of soils. See Soil aeration

AERIAL cableways. See Cableways

AERIAL cameras. See Cameras

AERIAL forest fire patrol. See Forest fire patrol, Aerial

AERIAL mapping. See Mapping, Aerial

AERIAL medical service. See Airplanes in medical service

AERIAL photography. See Photography, Aerial

AERIAL platforms. See Fire apparatus, Motor

AERIAL reconnaissance
Aerial reconnaissance R&D boost urged; excerpts from address. G. W. Goddard. Aviation W 80:85-91 Ja 6 '64; Discussion. 80:98 F 3; 86 Mr 9 '64
Alaskan air commander disputes official version of Soviet flights. L. Booda. Aviation W 78:30 Ap 1 '63
Cuba: overflight dispute. Sr Schol 84:12 My 15 '64
Film process may speed reconnaissance; Bimat film. B. Miller. il Aviation W 81:48-50 D 28 '64
First aerial photos of reds in Laos. il Life 56:42-3 Je 19 '64
How U.S. knows so much about Communist defenses; cameras in reconnaissance satellites. il U S News 57:70 N 30 '64
I spied on Castro's Cuba; Capt. Hennagan. il Ebony 18:114-16+ Ap '63
I spy, you spy, it's alright. R. D. Senter. New Repub 150:7-8 Je 13 '64
Laos; escalation in the air. il Time 83:22-3 Je 19 '64
Off-course planes; RB-66 New Repub 150:4-5 Ap 11 '64
Overflights; U-2 flights over Cuba. Commonweal 80:351 Je 12 '64
Raising the ante in Laos. il Newsweek 63:39 Je 22 '64
Real-time reconnaissance tests planned; Project see fast testing multi-sensor system. B. Miller. il Aviation W 81:73-4+ O 12 '64
Rockets with beards; Castro's complaint of U-2 flights. il Time 83:36 My 1 '64
Rotating prism panoramic camera adds new dimension to photo-recon technique. W. Wright. il Aviation W 78:112-13+ F 25 '63
Senate group says Cuban data unreliable. K. Johnsen. Aviation W 78:119+ My 20 '63
Soviet Badger two-plane team shadows carrier. il Aviation W 78:28-9 My 27 '63
Soviet planes spy on U.S. ships. il U S News 54:8 Mr 11 '63
Soviets flying electronic ferret missions. L. Booda. Aviation W 78:22-3 Mr 25 '63
TU-95 overhead. il Newsweek 61:24 Mr 11 '63
U.S. denies A-11 reconnaissance flights. Aviation W 80:306 Mr 16 '64
U.S. policy on flights over Cuba remains unchanged; statements, April 20 and April 21, 1964. R. I. Phillips and L. B. Johnson. Dept State Bul 50:744 My 11 '64
U.S. reconnaissance flights over Laos. Dept State Bul 50:994-5 Je 29 '64

AERIAL reconnaissance cameras. See Cameras

AERIAL routes. See Airways

AERIAL spraying. See Airplanes in insect control

AERIAL surveying. See Surveying, Aerial

AERIAL tramways. See Cableways

AERIAL warfare. See European war, 1914-1918 —Aerial operations; World war, 1939-1945— —Aerial operations

AERIALISTS. See Acrobats and acrobatism

AERO COMMANDER, incorporated
Aero Commander expects billings to reach $100 million in 1966. Aviation W 81:21 O 5 '64
Aero Commander plans to market full single-engine aircraft line. Aviation W 80:36 Mr 2 '64
Jet Commander purchase plan detailed. D. A. Brown. Aviation W 78:82-3+ Mr 4 '63
Pilot report; Commander's jet. R. Bach. il Flying 75:28-31+ Jl '64

AERO industries, incorporated
Production of Omega BS-12-D3S awaits court merger approval. Aviation W 79:108 N 11 '63

AERO spacelines, incorporated
Aero spacelines seeking options to buy Saunders-Roe flying boats. Aviation W 80: 34 Ja 20 '64

AEROBATICS. See Aviation—Stunt flying

AEROBIC bacteria. See Bacteria, Aerobic

AERODYNAMICS
Amateur scientist; aerodynamics of air-supported vehicles. R. W. Moffat. il Sci Am 210:135-8 Ja '64
Amateur scientist; dynamics of a golf club. L. A. Graham. il Sci Am 210:131-3+ Ja '64
When air began to flow. M. Lamm. il Motor T 16:40-3 My '64
See also
Boundary layer

AERODYNAMICS, Supersonic
ASSET to test hypersonic theory. il Miss & Roc 12:28 My 27 '63

AEROFLOT (airline). See Airlines—Russia

AEROHYDROFOIL. See Hydrofoils

AEROJET-General corporation
Aerojet dedicates big booster plant. il Miss & Roc 14:16 Je 1 '64
Aerojet gambles on future of solids at Florida plant. J. Judge. il Miss & Roc 13: 29-31 D 2 '63
Aerojet methods help boost Polaris range. Miss & Roc 12:35 F 25 '63
Aerojet moves into basic glass. J. F. Judge. il Miss & Roc 12:34-5 Mr 18 '63
Aerojet's Miami facility nears completion. G. Alexander. il Aviation W 78:54+ Ap 29 '63
Flight of M-1 delayed three years. H. Taylor. il Miss & Roc 12:16-17 Ap 22 '63
Gambling on finding a customer. il Bsns W p 128-30+ My 23 '64
How to spin a rocket. il Life 56:33-5 Mr 13 '64
Hybrid rockets. il Miss & Roc 15:42-5 N 9 '64
Notes for a gazetteer; Sacramento, Calif. P. Hamburger. New Yorker 38:81-2+ F 2 '63
Solid rocket thrust vectored by jet tabs. I. Stone. il Aviation W 78:57 F 4 '63
Still propelling itself into the space age. il Bsns W p86-8+ Jl 11 '64
Two new labs to sharpen Aerojet's solid, liquid capabilities. W. E. Wilks. il Miss & Roc 14:18+ Mr 23 '64

AEROLOGY. See Meteorology

AERONAUTIC associations. See Aviation associations

AERONAUTIC charts
Charting the future with Jeppesen. R. B. Weeghman. il Flying 74:42-3+ Ja '64

AERONAUTIC instruments
After the revolution, a King; navcom equipment. W. J. Kendall. il Flying 74:42-3+ My '64
Airborne turbulence sensors under test. P. J. Klass. Aviation W 81:26-8 Ag 31 '64
Automatic altitude encoder developed. il Aviation W 81:61 Jl 27 '64
British all-weather landing goal may be too severe, data shows; pros and cons of triple-redundancy avionics equipment. P. J. Klass. Aviation W 81:62-3 Jl 27 '64
Crab-oriented gyro produced for Athena. B. Miller. il Aviation W 79:85-9 D 16 '63
Design evolution gains maximum utility. il Aviation W 81:106-7+ S 7 '64
Diaries of destruction; flight recorders. F. A. Tinker. il Pop Mech 120:108-12+ Jl '63
Feedback system advances meter utility; Servometric technique improving D'Arsonval meter movement. P. J. Klass. il Aviation W 81:65-7 Jl 13 '64
Fluid sensors open way to many systems. P. J. Klass. il Aviation W 81:52-3+ D 7 '64
Gravitational field sensor studied by Hughes to measure asteroids. Aviation W 82:73 Ja 25 '65
Helicopter speed system accurate to ½ kt. W. Wright. il Aviation W 79:95+ Jl 1 '63
Navy helicopter avionics system concepts producing spillover benefit. B. Miller. il Aviation W 81:42-3+ Ag 10 '64
Navy may buy minimum helicopter navaid; basic advanced integrated navigation system. B. Miller. il Aviation W 81:79+ O 5 '64
Navy to deploy A-6A squadron next year. D. A. Brown. il Aviation W 81:46-7+ Ag 17 '64
New horizon sensors planned for Agena D. B. Miller. il Aviation W 79:82-3+ S 30 '63
New IR space sensors add to reliability. B. Miller. il Aviation W 81:68-71 Ag 31 '64

AERONAUTIC instruments—*Continued*
Packaging concept promotes versatility. B. Miller. il Aviation W 81:85-7+ D 14 '64
Real-time reconnaissance tests planned; Project see fast testing multi-sensor system. B. Miller. il Aviation W 81:73-4+ O 12 '64
SCAT. D. Kuhn. il Flying 74:54 My '64
Wide-range attack angle indicator shown. D. A. Brown. il Aviation W 79:105+ S 9 '63
See also
Accelerometers
Altimeters
Automatic pilot (airplanes)
Inertial guidance systems
Radio apparatus on aircraft
Space vehicles—Instrument boards

AERONAUTIC laboratories
See also
Cornell aeronautical laboratory

AERONAUTIC meteorology. See Meteorology, Aeronautic

AERONAUTIC museums
See also
Smithsonian institution—National air museum

AERONAUTIC research
Farnborough pushing Concorde research. H. J. Coleman. il Aviation W 79:40-1 D 23 '63
FAA funds cut threatens ATC research. P. J. Klass. Aviation W 80:45 Je 15 '64
NASA focuses on three aircraft areas. E. H. Kolcum. il Aviation W 79:58-60 Ag 5 '63
Peruvians study rotating-cylinder flap. D. A. Brown. il Aviation W 81:70-1 D 7 '64
See also
Shock tubes

AERONAUTICAL radio incorporated
Jet transport communications. R. L. Conhaim. il Electr World 70:27-30+ N '63

AERONAUTICS
See also
Balloon ascensions
Flight

Charts

See Aeronautic charts

History

Airman's almanac. A. Trammell. il Flying 75:68+ Ag; 58 S '64
Antique aircraft; symposium. il Flying 74:23-32+ Ja '64
Coast to coast in twelve crashes. S. Harris. il Am Heritage 15:46-9+ O '64
First round-the-world flight. W. S. Griswold. il Pop Sci 185:60-3 S '64
Flying circus; duplicate of Fokker DR-1 triplane. New Yorker 40:20-2 Ag 29 '64
Flying dinosaur; Brabazon, England's super transport. E. A. Phillips. il Flying 74:44-5+ Mr '64
How the Wright brothers learned to fly; with quotations from Papers of Wilbur and Orville Wright. G. Soule. il Pop Sci 183:51-7 D '63
New Nieuport; replica of famous French fighter built from photos, drawings, and old articles. il Flying 74:71 Ja '64
Science milestone; Lawrence Hargrave, Australian aviation pioneer. J. Rhea. il Sci Digest 53:79-86 F '63
Tin goose relives its days of glory; early Ford tri-motor flights. il Bsns W p33 Je 22 '63
Transatlantic jubilee. R. Hotz. Aviation W 81:21 S 14 '64
When the 20th century got off the ground. J. Hamilton. il Look 29:44-9 Ja 12 '65
Where did Charles Lindbergh go? W. Ross. Esquire 60:85-8+ O '63; Same abr. with title What became of Charles Lindbergh? Read Digest 84:91-6 F '64

Safety devices and measures

See Aviation—Safety devices and measures

AERONAUTICS, Commercial
New air transport. Sci N L 83:116 F 23 '63
Outlook for 1965. R. Hotz. Aviation W 82:11 Ja 4 '65
See also
Air freight service
Air travel
Airplanes, Freight

International aspects

See Aviation—International aspects

Russia

See also
Airlines—Russia

United States

Outlook and trends in civil aviation employment. S. H. Luskin. il Mo Labor R 86:1290-6 N '63
See also
Airlines—United States
Airplane industry and trade—United States

AERONAUTICS, Military
See also
Air maneuvers
Air pilots
Aircraft carriers
Airplanes, Military
Helicopters—Military applications
Semi-automatic ground environment system
World war, 1939-1945—Aerial operations

Canada

Canadian defense policy shift looms after voting. D. E. Fink. il Aviation W 78:288-9+ Mr 11 '63

China (People's Republic)

Burning fuse. R. Hotz. Aviation W 81:11 Jl 27 '64

Europe, Western

France and Britain prepare to strike out into space on own. W. Beller. il Miss & Roc 12:15-17 Je 17 '63

France

See also
Airplanes, Military—France

Germany (Federal Republic)

West Germany seeks shift in NATO role. C. Brownlow. Aviation W 78:32-3 F 4 '63

Great Britain

British emphasize integration of services. H. J. Coleman. Aviation W 78:38-9 Ja 21 '63
British planning Blue Steel replacement. H. J. Coleman. Aviation W 78:29 F 25 '63
British to reorganize Fighter Command. H. J. Coleman. Aviation W 78:32 Mr 18 '63

Japan

Japan embarks on defense modernization. il Aviation W 78:296-8 Mr 11 '63
Japanese select Hughes system. Aviation W 79:24 Jl 8 '63

Russia

Cost of Soviet AMSA defense appraised by USAF at $21 billion. Aviation W 82:26 Ja 18 '65
Soviets press technical modernization of military services. il Aviation W 78:92-5 Mr 11 '63

United Arab Republic

UAR building independent military force. il Aviation W 80:297-9+ Mr 16 '64

United States

Air assault development. W. Wright. il Aviation W 80:54-5+ F 17; 61-3+ F 24 '64
Army AAFSS proposals due Nov. 23. C. M. Plattner. Aviation W 81:92-4 N 9 '64
Army prepares to expand pilot training. L. Booda. Aviation W 78:35-6 F 4 '63
Army, USAF testing air support roles. C. Brownlow. il Aviation W 81:77+ S 21 '64
Combat vs. computers; testimony before the House defense appropriations subcommittee. C. E. LeMay. Aviation W 80:11 My 4 '64
Congress seen key to military space role. Aviation W 78:26-7 Mr 4 '63
Decision near on expanding Viet air war. C. Brownlow. Aviation W 81:17-18 D 7 '64
Flights replace hours as measuring unit. L. Booda. Aviation W 79:23 D 30 '63
Goldwater and the bomber-gap. R. D. Senter. New Repub 150:10-12 Ja 25 '64
GOP to capitalize on LeMay's charges; with excerpts from testimony before the House defense appropriation subcommittee. G. C. Wilson. Aviation W 80:26-7 Ap 20 '64
I was shot down by an American jet. C. P. Gilmore. il Pop Mech 121:108-13+ Mr '64
Johnson stress on military space seen. Aviation W 79:26-8 D 2 '63
Johnson weighing N. Vietnam air strikes. C. Brownlow. il Aviation W 81:22-3 N 30 '64
McNamara views strategic aircraft role; excerpt from testimony presented to the House armed services committee, January 30, 1963. R. S. McNamara. Aviation W 78:67+ F 11 '63
Mixed strategic force; address. T. S. Power. Aviation W 81:17 N 16 '64
New Mach 2 carrier plane. il Sci Digest 56:32-5 Ag '64
Next war: massed helicopters? il U S News 56:62-3 Ap 20 '64

AERONAUTICS, Military—United States—*Continued*
Nuclear delivery: theory vs. practice; excerpts from address. T. S. Power. Aviation W 79:21 S 23 '63
Remote-area conflict research sought. il Aviation W 79:26-7 N 25 '63
USAF girds for counterblow in Vietnam. il Aviation W 81:16-18 Ag 10 '64
USAF wages space, weapon fund battles. L. Booda. il Aviation W 78:76-9 Mr 11 '63
U.S. 90 per cent confident of capability to destroy vital enemy targets; excerpts from address. T. S. Power. Aviation W 79:39 S 23 '63
We've got the planes, what about the men? F. V. Drake. Read Digest 82:110-14 F '63
See also
Space flight—Military applications
United States—Air force
United States—Air force, Army

Viet Nam (Republic)

B-26, T-28, L-19 furnish air cover over Vietnam. il Aviation W 79:50-1 Jl 29 '63
Burning fuse. R. Hotz. Aviation W 81:11 Jl 27 '64
Operation backfire. il Time 84:37 N 27 '64
Quang Long battle typifies aircraft use. Aviation W 80:103 Ap 13 '64
Quiet escalation; U.S. air strikes in Laos. il Time 85:22 Ja 22 '65
UH-1Bs attack Viet Cong; aircraft buildup shown. il Aviation W 81:78-9 Ag 31 '64
USAF pushes Vietnamese pilot training. L. Booda. il Aviation W 80:94-5+ Ap 20 '64

AERONOMY. See Atmosphere, Upper
AEROSOL paint. See Paint
AEROSOLS
Don't get killed by a can! il Consumer Bul 47:43+ Je '64
How to find your way among the aerosols. D. X. Manners. il House B 105:140+ Je '63
Multicolor paints. il Consumer Rep 28:494-5 O '63
Not with a bang but a sssss. il Time 84:43 Ag 28 '64
Old sol and pressure cans. Consumer Rep 28: 461 O '63
Pushbutton can takes off on its own. il Bsns W p 102+ Ap 11 '64
Put safety first when using aerosol cans. il Good H 158:163 F '64
Spray cans: red arrow points the way. il Consumer Bul 46:17 D '63
Those handy aerosols can be dangerous. R. Dempewolff. il Pop Mech 121:85-9+ Mr '64; Same abr. with title Be careful with those aerosol sprays! Read Digest 84:130-3 Ap '64
Useful gadget for aerosol cans; Alfco handle. il Consumer Rep 29:212 My '64

AEROSPACE (term)
Air force coins a word. D. Burnham. Reporter 28:32-3 Je 6 '63

AEROSPACE corporation
Aerospace corp. steerable antenna seeking accuracy of twenty arc seconds. R. Pay. il Miss & Roc 13:26-7 D 23 '63

AEROSPACE industries

Employees

Aerospace employment dips in past year. Aviation W 80:20-1 Je 29 '64
Firms stress quality in technical hiring. il Aviation W 81:103+ S 21 '64
That manpower shortage. W. J. Coughlin. Miss & Roc 15:46 Jl 13 '64
Why aerospace needs flexible men. il Bsns W p44+ Je 22 '63

Exhibitions

Paris air show stresses surge by French aerospace industry; with editorial comment. C. Brownlow. il Aviation W 78:21, 26-9 Je 10 '63

Finance

Aerospace industry financial results, 1962-1963. Aviation W 78:109 Je 17 '63; 81:94-5+ Ag 17 '64
Aerospace interim financial results. Aviation W 81:29 N 16 '64
Firms' reports show sales, earnings gain. Aviation W 79:81-2 D 2 '63
How to survive in space business. il Bsns W p 102-4+ Ja 16 '65
Industry encounters snags in investing. W. H. Gregory. il Aviation W 80:19-20 Mr 30 '64
Industry results reflect wide variation; with tables. W. H. Gregory. Aviation W 81:87+ Ag 17 '64
Report cites industry reliance on leasing. W. H. Gregory. il Aviation W 78:113+ Je 17 '63
Wall Street expert sees steady level of spending but warns of profit drop. M. Getler. Miss & Roc 15:15 Jl 20 '64

Quality control

MA know-how may be boom for future. R. Hawkes. Miss & Roc 13:15 Jl 22 '63
New reliability goals; excerpts from address. H. M. Estes. Aviation W 80:21 Ja 13 '64

Salaries

Aerospace companies report on salaries (title varies) Aviation W 79:59+ Ag 26; 89-90 S 2; 107-8+ S 9; 92+ N 11; 95+ D 2 '63
Three firms report officer compensation. Aviation W 79:51+ D 30 '63

Securities

Aerospace stocks regaining strength. M. Getler. il Miss & Roc 14:31-3 Ap 20 '64
Experts say rise in ComSat stock due to scarcity, shortsightedness. M. Getler. Miss & Roc 15:18-19 S 14 '64
Fairchild reveals Republic stock buy. Miss & Roc 14:17 Je 29 '64

Statistics

Aerospace sales, earnings increase. Aviation W 78:29 Mr 25 '63

Canada

Canadian aerospace companies, contracts. Aviation W 81:225 Jl 6 '64

Egypt

Israel calls on Bonn to restrict its weapons scientists in Egypt. Aviation W 80:33 My 11 '64

Europe, Western

European market: will it blast off? il Bsns W p22 Jl 4 '64
How to do missile/space business in Europe. W. Beller. il Miss & Roc 13:22-5 Jl 22 '63
See also
Eurospace

France

French nuclear, space work moves toward major goals. R. E. Farrell. il Aviation W 80:270-2+ Mr 16 '64

Germany (Federal Republic)

German satellite contract due soon. W. Beller. il Miss & Roc 13:24-5 Ag 5 '63
West German industry exhibits resurgence. Aviation W 80:37 Ap 27 '64

Great Britain

Amery orders review of U.K. contracting. H. J. Coleman. Aviation W 80:111-13 My 18 '64
Blunting the spearhead. R. Hotz. Aviation W 81:17 N 23 '64
British facing shifting defense policy. H. J. Coleman. il Aviation W 80:263-7+ Mr 16 '64
Drive mounts to avert U.K. defense cuts. H. J. Coleman. Aviation W 82:22-3 Ja 18 '65
Ferranti will return $11 million in wake of Bloodhound report. H. J. Coleman. Aviation W 81:26 Ag 3 '64
Stabilized industry faces new unknowns; with editorial comment. H. J. Coleman. il Aviation W 81:21, 26-9 S 7 '64

Russia

New Soviet problem. R. Hotz. Aviation W 80:21 F 17 '64
USSR blends diplomatic, military goals. il Aviation W 80:101 Mr 16 '64

United States

Aerospace budget. R. Hotz. Aviation W 80:21 Ja 20 '64
Aerospace employment dips in past year. Aviation W 80:20-1 Je 29 '64
Aerospace firms chafe at government control. Miss & Roc 12:21 Je 10 '63
Aerospace industry leads R&D spending. W. Wright. Aviation W 78:187-9 Je 10 '63
Aerospace leaders to continue in Senate. G. C. Wilson. Aviation W 81:26 S 21 '64
Aerospace sales, earnings to continue climbing in 1963. R. Hotz. il Aviation W 78:68-70 Mr 11 '63
California: aerospace industry has meant a second gold rush; climate and education get credit. J. Walsh. Science 143:1151-3 Mr 13 '64
California firms study contract warnings. H. D. Watkins. il Aviation W 79:74-7 Jl 29 '63
Capitol outlook. R. Hotz. Aviation W 80:11 Je 1 '64

AEROSPACE industries—United States—*Continued*
Cost-cutting set as major industry factor. G. C. Wilson. il Aviation W 81:17-18 Jl 13 '64
Cost of cost reduction. W. J. Coughlin. Miss & Roc 14:58 F 24 '64
Dark clouds in space; fourth national symposium. il Bsns W p 116+ My 9 '64
DOD official urges industry to consider non-defense markets. R. Hawkes. Miss & Roc 13:16-17 D 23 '63
Economical year. R. Hotz. Aviation W 80:21 Ja 6 '64
Fewer new projects will follow chronic slippage, Seamans warns. Aviation W 81:32 O 19 '64
Firms must anticipate future needs. Miss & Roc 12:63 Mr 25 '63
Firms stress quality in technical hiring. il Aviation W 81:103+ S 21 '64
Fubini decries industry gloom; with editorial comment. Aviation W 81:9, 19 Jl 13 '64
Goose and the golden egg. W. J. Coughlin. Miss & Roc 13:46 N 18 '63
GOP unit seeks renegotiation phase-out. K. Johnsen. Aviation W 80:33-4 Ap 27 '64
Group urged to study application of technology to spur economy. K. Johnsen. Aviation W 79:35 D 16 '63
How to do missile/space business in Europe. W. Beller. il Miss & Roc 13:22-5 Jl 22 '63
Industry cautious in approach to manned spaceflight systems. C. D. LaFond and R. Pay. Miss & Roc 15:43+ O 5 '64
Industry encounters snags in investing. W. H. Gregory. il Aviation W 80:19-20 Mr 30 '64
Industry population mushrooms as MSC spawns new markets. Aviation W 81:66-7 N 16 '64
Industry results reflect wide variation; with tables. W. H. Gregory. Aviation W 81:87+ Ag 17 '64
Industry's growth problems; excerpts from address. R. I. McKenzie. Aviation W 79:13 S 2 '63
Is there a job for you in aerospace? J. M. Liston. il Pop Sci 184:53-7+ Mr '64
Laurels for 1963-1964. R. Hotz. Aviation W 79:15 D 30 '63; 81:9 D 28 '64
Lean year, or permanent cutback? il Bsns W p76-7 Ja 2 '65
Letter from the editor. W. J. Coughlin. Miss & Roc 13:52 D 23 '63; 15:46 D 21 '64
Lockheed chairman says industry has problems but remains sound. C. S. Gross. Aviation W 79:113-14+ N 11 '63
Lockheed chairman sees decline, resumption of industry growth. Aviation W 80:107 Ap 20 '64
Major aerospace decisions face Johnson. G. C. Wilson. Aviation W 81:22 N 9 '64
Management tightens its aerospace reins; stress on cost reduction, quality control, and delivery time. il Bsns W p96+ S 14 '63
MA know-how may be boon for future. R. Hawkes. Miss & Roc 13:15 Jl 22 '63
Message to company presidents. W. J. Coughlin. Miss & Roc 13:46 Jl 15 '63
Mid-course budget. R. Hotz. Aviation W 78:21 Ja 21 '63
Moon industry; how big it is now. il U S News 57:60-3 O 5 '64
More aerospace growth forecast. Aviation W 81:27 Ag 17 '64
Much ado about Little. W. J. Coughlin. Miss & Roc 16:46 Ja 25 '65
New aerospace products. See issues of Aviation week & space technology
1964 aerospace market levels at near-record peak. R. Hotz. Aviation W 80:68-9 Mr 16 '64
Outlook for 1965. R. Hotz. Aviation W 82:11 Ja 4 '65
Phasing out the long-range missiles. il Bsns W p 196-8+ Ap 20 '63
Preference urged for established firms in military spending cuts. K. Johnsen. Aviation W 79:31 D 23 '63
P.D. quick. Aviation W 78:106 Mr 4 '63
Prescription for stability proposed. il Miss & Roc 16:17-18 Ja 18 '65
Profile of an industry; with editorial comment. W. Beller. il Miss & Roc 13:22+. 70 O 28; 24-6 D 2; 30-2 D 16 '63
Pure gold in space work. il Bsns W p 129-30+ S 12 '64
Representative Karth urges U.S. sell boosters; interview, ed. by W. Beller; with editorial comment. J. E. Karth. Miss & Roc 13:21-2, 60 Ag 26 '63
Requirements merry-go-round: must need precede development? J. T. Ramey. Bul Atomic Sci 20:12-15 N '64
Revolution: changes in U.S. military policy and military organization. W. J. Coughlin. Miss & Roc 14:148 Mr 30; 54 Ap 6; 46 Ap 13 '64
SAE aerospace gathering covers broad spectrum. Miss & Roc 13:27+ S 30 '63
Space. il Life 57:79-91+ S 25; 74-81+ O 2 '64
Space agency nears decision on adopting parts qualification list. Miss & Roc 14:17 Ap 20 '64
Space and defense, a big industry with problems. il U S News 54:48-51 Mr 11 '63
Space billions, now a boom? What's happening in five states. il U S News 57:64-9 Jl 20 '64
Survival of the fittest. W. J. Coughlin. Miss & Roc 14:46 Je 29 '64
Technical talent utilization shifts urged. P. J. Klass. Aviation W 81:20 Jl 20 '64
Too many generals at work on contracts? concerning report by Stanford research institute. il Bsns W p91 Je 15 '63
U.S. industry faces sales test in Europe. C. Brownlow. il Aviation W 79:64-5+ Jl 29 '63
U.S. industry to profit from progress abroad. il Miss & Roc 15:106-7 N 30 '64
Wall Street experts sees steady level of spending but warns of profit drop. M. Getler. Miss & Roc 15:15 Jl 20 '64
Welcome aboard. Nation 196:217 Mr 16 '63
White House opposes legislation on industry conversion groups. Aviation W 80:28 My 25 '64
Zuckert gives views on aerospace issues; interview. E. M. Zuckert. Aviation W 80:72-3 Mr 2 '64
See also
United aircraft corporation

AEROSPACE industries association of America, incorporated
Relationship. W. J. Coughlin. Miss & Roc 13:46 Jl 8 '63

AEROSPACE medical division. See United States—Air force—Systems command

AEROSPACE telemetry. See Space telemetry

AEROTHERMODYNAMICS. See Thermodynamics

AESCHYLUS
Note on Aeschylus. R. Kirk. Nat R 15:62 Jl 30 '63

AESCHYNANTHUS. See Blush worts

AESCULAPE snakes. See Snakes

AESOP, man of fables; drama. See Phillips, E.

AESTHETIC values. See Worth

AESTHETICS
Accounting for taste. R. Park. Seventeen 23:114+ D '64
Artistic transaction, and essays on theory of literature, by E. Vivas. Review
Nat R il 16:500-2 Je 16 '64. G. Wills; Reply with rejoinder. E. Vivas. 16:695-6 Ag 11 '64
Bad bad word? E. Goble. Arch Rec 134:9 O '63
Descending spiral of ugliness. A. Heckscher. il Recreation 56:315-16+ S '63
Economics and the quality of life; adaptation of address, December 27, 1963. J. K. Galbraith. bibliog Science 145:117-23 Jl 10 '64; Discussion. 145:876 Ag 28 '64
Editor's notebook. M. S. Fenner. NEA J 53:84 F '64
Field, philosophy, & esthetics. E. R. Fagan. il Sch Arts 63:24-8 My '64
Identifying the role of the arts in education. M. Bryce. il Sch Arts 62:29 Ap '63
Sacred and profane beauty; the holy in art, by G. van der Leeuw. Review
Commonweal 78:513-14 Ag 23 '63. L. F. X. Mayhew
See also
Art—Philosophy
Romanticism

AFETINAN, Afet
Ataturk & the emancipation of women. UNESCO Courier 16:20-5 D '63

AFFAIR: drama. See Millar, R.

AFFECTION. See Love

AFGHANISTAN
Fight for the land of Hindu Kush; with report by J. Burke. il Life 55:18-27 Ag 9 '63
King of Afghanistan visits United States; joint communique, September 7, 1963. J. F. Kennedy and Mohammed Zaher. Dept State Bul 49:535 O 7 '63
Trade routes to the West. New Repub 148:10 Je 15 '63
See also
Economic assistance in Afghanistan

AFGHANISTAN—*Continued*

Antiquities

Prehistoric archeological surveys and excavations in Afghanistan: 1959-1960 and 1961-1963. L. Dupree. bibliog il Science 146: 638-40 O 30 '64

AFLAK, Michel

Danger: professor at work. il por Time 82: 28-9 N 22 '63

AFLATOXIN. See Fungi

AFRICA

Africa: birth of a continent. A. J. Toynbee. Sat R 47:27-9+ D 5 '64

Africa in motion; symposium, ed. by J. C. Charlesworth. bibliog f il Ann Am Acad 354: 1-152 Jl '64

Emerging Africa. W. P. Jones. bibliog il NEA J 52:38-41 My '63

Importance of being black; an Asian looks at Africa. F. Moraes. For Affairs 43:99-111 O '64

Myths about Africa and the reality. C. Bowles. il N Y Times Mag p8+ Je 16 '63

Nations growing up overnight. R. A. Manners. Sat R 47:48 Ap 18 '64

Weathering the wind of change. C. Miller. Sat R 47:33-4+ Je 13 '64

See also

Airlines—Africa
Americans in Africa
Asians in Africa
Aviation—Africa
Banks and banking—Africa
Children—Africa
Colonies in Africa
Communism—Africa
Economic assistance in Africa
Education—Africa
Europeans in Africa
Hunting—Africa
Investments, Foreign (in Africa)
Jazz music—Africa
Medicine—Africa
Mental illness—Africa
Paleontology—Africa
Public health—Africa
Publishers and publishing—Africa
Socialism—Africa
Technical assistance in Africa
Trade unions—Africa
United Nations—Africa
Women—Africa
Zanzibar
Zoology—Africa

Antiquities

African Bushman art treasures. A. Friendly. il Nat Geog Mag 123:848-65 Je '63

Africa's golden past. W. L. Hansberry and E. H. Johnson. il Ebony 20:30-2+ N '64; 86-92 Ja '65

Bibliography

Books about Africa. C. A. Kamundia. Horn Bk 39:79-80 F '63

Native son rises. J. Hughes. Sat R 46:40-1 Je 15 '63

Civilization

Africa: the face behind the mask; with editorial comment. B. Davidson. il Horizon 5:38-59, 105-6 Mr '63

African notebook; new methods, new manners, and new art forms. J. M. Fitch. il Horizon 6:48-59 Autumn '64

Fabric of African cultures. E. Mphahlele. For Affairs 42:614-27 Jl '64

Influence of Africans on American culture. J. A. Davis. bibliog f Ann Am Acad 354: 75-83 Jl '64

We may be rich but they are happy; transforming of prescientific communities. B. Ward. il N Y Times Mag p22-3+ My 5 '63

Commerce

International markets; significance of Africa to the European economic community. A. O. Stanley. Duns R 81:59-62 F '63

International trade and African trade problems; text of statement. P. de Seynes. U N Rev 10:9-13 Mr '63

Defenses

Army: problem for Africa. il N Y Times Mag p8-9 F 2 '64

Description and travel

Africa: the new grand tour. M. R. Henry. il Vogue 12:56-63+ Jl '63

Flight over Africa. G. Parks. Vogue 144:8 Jl '64

Impressions of Africa. I. Chase. Travel 121: 30-2 Je '64

Economic conditions

African development; statement, February 22, 1963. W. M. Kotschnig. Dept State Bul 48: 625-8 Ap 22 '63

Freedom and development; address, September 25, 1964. D. Rusk. Dept State Bul 51: 498-503 O 12 '64

International markets; significance of Africa to the European economic community. A. O. Stanley. Duns R 81:59-62 F '63

Recent economic growth in Africa. A. M. Kamarck. Ann Am Acad 354:46-53 Jl '64

True story of black Africa and its future; interview. G. H. T. Kimble. il U S News 54:72-9 F 11 '63

What's wrong in Africa: a new report. U S News 54:10 Mr 18 '63

See also

United Nations—Economic commission for Africa

Economic policy

Africa vis-à-vis the western powers; address, April 10, 1964; with questions and answers. C. Guellal. Ann Am Acad 354:9-21 Jl '64

Foreign relations

Africa's problems and progress; address, March 1, 1964. G. M. Williams. Dept State Bul 50:501-6 Mr 30 '64

China as the trump in the African pack. R. W. Howe. New Repub 151:16 S 5 '64

Long spoon of Peking. E. Huxley. Nat R 16: 868-9 O 6 '64

Momentary eclipse; wave of anti-Americanism. il Newsweek 65:33-4 F 1 '65

Tinderbox nations: Republic of the Congo; South Africa; Southern Rhodesia; Angola. il Sr Schol 85:20-1 O 7 '64

History

Africa: an African evaluation; address, April 11, 1964. J. D. Rubadiri. bibliog f Ann Am Acad 354:84-90 Jl '64

Africa's golden past. W. L. Hansberry and E. H. Johnson. il Ebony 20:30-2+ N '64; 86-92 Ja '65

In-service education of the teacher of African history; address, 1964. W. S. Robinson. bibliog Negro Hist Bul 28:33-4+ N '64

Bibliography

Articles and other books received; comp. by D. E. Gardinier. Am Hist R 70:304-5 O '64

Teaching of African history. bibliog f Am Hist R 69:47-63 O '63

Maps

Cartography in Africa; United Nations regional cartographic conference for Africa, Nairobi, Kenya, July 1-13, 1963. G. E. Pearcy. Dept State Bul 49:1014-18 D 30 '63

Map of Africa (cont) Sr Schol 83:31 O 4 '63; 85:35 O 7 '64

Nile: problem and promise. il Nat Geog Mag 124:622-3, sup(folded map) O '63

Nationalism

Africa and the world: problems of today and tomorrow; address, August 24, 1963. G. M. Williams. Dept State Bul 49:432-6 S 16 '63

African slaughter. Commonweal 79:616 F 21 '64

Hopes & realities. il Time 83:20 Ja 24 '64

Livingstone, the tourist. New Repub 148:9 My 25 '63

Nations in the making in Africa; address, October 23, 1963. J. W. Fredericks. Dept State Bul 49:783-6 N 18 '63

Racism at the United Nations. New Repub 151:9-10 D 26 '64

Rising Afro-Asian nations. U. A. Johnson Dept State Bul 48:449-56 Mr 25 '63

Sweep of nationalism in Africa; address, April 11, 1964; with questions and answers. T. P. Melady. Ann Am Acad 354:91-6 Jl '64

That's Africa: troubles worse than teething. Life 56:4 F 14 '64

U.S. of Africa? not very likely. G. H. T. Kimble. il N Y Times Mag p 10+ Mr 29 '64

Who is safe? il Time 83:30-4+ Mr 13 '64

Native races

African chief explains tribalism. S. O. Adebo. il N Y Times Mag p26-7+ Mr 1 '64

Bushmen of the Kalahari. E. M. Thomas. il Nat Geog Mag 123:866-88 Je '63

Just a click apart. J. Morris. il U S Camera 26:62-5 D '63

One tribe of Africa's 700; Bororo, the nomads of Africa; photographs. N Y Times Mag p24-5 S 27 '64

AFRICA—Native races—*Continued*
Plight of the Bushmen. il Newsweek 62:55 Ag 12 '63
Racialism is an African sickness, too. G. T. Kimble. il N Y Times Mag p38-9+ O 11 '64
See also
Negroes in Africa
Somalis

Politics

Africa: an African evaluation; address, April 11, 1964. J. D. Rubadiri. bibliog f Ann Am Acad 354:84-90 Jl '64
Africa: looking for a Lenin. il New Repub 150:8-9 F 1 '64
Africa south of the equator; address, June 18, 1964. G. M. Williams. Dept State Bul 51:51-4 Jl 13 '64
Africa: the mutinous armies. D. Hapgood. il Nation 198:209-12 Mr 2 '64
African specter: racial Armageddon. G. M. Williams. il Nations Bsns 51:72+ D '63
Africa's new elites. D. Hapgood. Harper 227:43-9 D '63; Reply with rejoinder. E. J. Murphy. 228:11 Mr '64
Africa's problems and progress; address, March 1, 1964. G. M. Williams. Dept State Bul 50:501-6 Mr 20 '64
American policy in Africa; address, July 7, 1964. J. W. Fredericks. Dept State Bul 51:197-203 Ag 10 '64
Democracy and the emerging nations of Africa; address, March 14, 1963. G. M. Williams. Dept State Bul 48:541-5 Ap 8 '63
Democracy on trial in Africa. S. Drake. bibliog f Ann Am Acad 354:110-21 Jl '64
Ferment in Africa. H. Foot. Christian Cent 81:1491-3 D 2 '64
Fixing Humpty Dumpty; OAU meeting in Dar es Salaam. Newsweek 63:46+ F 24 '64
Focus on Africa. il Sr Schol 83:36-7 O 4 '63
Frank exchange; private conference of high officials of African nations at Corning, N.Y. New Yorker 40:20-2 Jl 18 '64
Freedom and development; address, September 25, 1964. D. Rusk. Dept State Bul 51: 498-503 O 12 '64
How much unity for Africa? E. J. Schuster. Cath World 198:215-22 Ja '64
Last revolution; community and nation in Africa; address, April 10, 1964; with questions and answers. D. E. Ashford. bibliog f Ann Am Acad 354:33-45 Jl '64
Meanwhile in Africa. Nat R 15:224-5 S 24 '63
More growing pains. Newsweek 63:42 Mr 2 '64
Nations in the making in Africa; address, October 23, 1963. J. W. Fredericks. Dept State Bul 49:783-6 N 18 '63
Our policy toward Africa; address, July 18, 1963. J. W. Fredericks. Dept State Bul 49: 284-90 Ag 19 '63; Same. Vital Speeches 29: 699-702 S 1 '63
Ouster & death. il Time 85:23-4 Ja 22 '65
Political stability in the new African states; address, April 11, 1964; with questions and answers. H. J. Spiro. Ann Am Acad 354: 97-109 Jl '64
Promising trends in Africa; address, February 15, 1964. G. M. Williams. Dept State Bul 50:370-3 Mr 9 '64
Rash of violence: mutiny is contagious. il Newsweek 63:35 F 3 '64
Splintering of Africa. R. W. Howe. New Repub 152:9-10 Ja 30 '65
Stormy continent. Sr Schol 84:16-17 Mr 13 '64
Surprising Africa. America 108:662-3 My 11 '63
That's Africa: troubles worse than teething. Life 56:4 F 14 '64
Third thoughts on Africa. H. P. Van Dusen. Christian Cent 81:855-8 Jl 1 '64
Tinderbox nations: Republic of the Congo; South Africa; Southern Rhodesia; Angola. il Sr Schol 85:20-1 O 7 '64
True story of black Africa and its future; interview. G. H. T. Kimble. il U S News 54:72-9 F 11 '63
Two Africas. Commonweal 80:383 Je 19 '64
United Nations and the new Africa; address, March 29, 1963. G. M. Williams. Dept State Bul 48:602-5 Ap 22 '63
U.S. of Africa? not very likely. G. H. T. Kimble. il N Y Times Mag p 10+ Mr 29 '64
Violence in Africa: developments in Togo, Brazzaville and Dahomey. T. P. Melady. America 109:734-5 D 7 '63
What kind of radicalism for Africa? C. Legum. For Affairs 43:237-50 Ja '65
Who is safe? il Time 83:30-4+ Mr 13 '64
See also
Organization of African unity
Pan-Africanism

Race problems

African issues at the United Nations; address, April 18, 1964. G. M. Williams. Dept State Bul 50:751-5 My 11 '64
African specter: racial Armageddon. G. M. Williams. il Nations Bsns 51:72+ D '63
As the white man fights back in Africa. il U S News 54:77-9 Mr 18 '63
Civil rights for whites. J. S. Nye, jr. New Repub 151:5-6 O 24 '64
Do white men have a future in Africa? T. J. Mboya. il N Y Times Mag p24-5+ D 8 '63
Ferment in Africa. H. Foot. Christian Cent 81:1491-3 D 2 '64
Nations in the making in Africa; address, October 23, 1963. J. W. Fredericks. Dept State Bul 49:783-6 N 18 '63
Racism at the United Nations. New Repub 151:9-10 D 26 '64
Racism in Africa. R. Howe. New Repub 149: 18-20 O 5 '63
South West Africa; timetable for freedom. P. Duncan. il Nation 198:265-7 Mr 16 '64
Stormy continent. Sr Schol 84:16-17 Mr 13 '64
See also subhead Race problems under names of African countries, e.g. South Africa—Race problems

Religious institutions and affairs

Africa's prophet movements. R. C. Mitchell. Christian Cent 81:1427-9 N 18 '64
Christian polygamy? America 112:155 Ja 30 '65
Christianity in Africa, by C. Northcott. Review
Christian Cent 80:1210 O 2 '63. D. Kitagawa
Ferment in Africa. H. Foot. Christian Cent 81:1491-3 D 2 '64
See also
Catholic church in Africa
Christians in Africa
Church of England in Africa
Missions—Africa

Social conditions

Africa south of the equator; address, June 18, 1964. G. M. Williams. Dept State Bul 51:51-4 Jl 13 '64
Africa's uphill struggle for maturity; ed. by A. Eisenberg and H. Eisenberg. Mrs G. M. Williams. il Ladies Home J 80:38+ O '63
Place for all things; African markets. P. Bohannan. il Natur Hist 73:54-61 O '64
Promising trends in Africa; address, February 15, 1964. G. M. Williams. Dept State Bul 50:370-3 Mr 9 '64

Study and teaching

In-service education of the teacher of African history; address, 1964. W. S. Robinson. bibliog Negro Hist Bul 28:33-4+ N '64
St Paul's social studies institute. J. Engh. il Sr Schol 85:10T-11T Ja 14 '65

Union (proposed)

How much unity for Africa? E. J. Schuster. Cath World 198:215-22 Ja '64
Situation remains fluid. J. Burnham. Nat R 14:530 Jl 2 '63
Toward unity in Africa. C. Sanger. For Affairs 42:269-81 Ja '64
See also
Pan-African conference, Addis Ababa, 1963

AFRICA, CENTRAL
See also
Burundi
Chad
Malawi
Rhodesia and Nyasaland (Federation)
Rwanda
Zoology—Africa, Central

Politics

Central Africa: go down, Moses. New Repub 149:13 Jl 20 '63

AFRICA, EAST
Africa is poised on the razor's edge. W. A. Nielsen. il N Y Times Mag p 11+ F 9 '64
British answer an SOS and nip a mutiny. il Life 56:44-44C F 7 '64
Dream and reality. Newsweek 63:34+ F 3 '64
East Africa: a new federation. New Repub 148:10 Je 29 '63
East Africa, 1964; symposium. bibliog f il Cur Hist 46:129-74+ Mr '64
On the mend. il Time 83:32+ F 7 '64
Revolts rock East Africa. il Sr Schol 84:6 F 14 '64
Rise of the Rifles; army mutinies in Tanganyika, Uganda and Kenya. il Time 83:23-4 Ja 31 '64
Soldiers' pay. il Newsweek 63:38 F 10 '64

AFRICA, EAST—*Continued*
With forks and hope, by E. Huxley. Review
Nat R 16:826-7 S 22 '64. T. Molnar
Sat R 47:32-3 Ag 8 '64. C. Miller
See also
Communism—Africa, East
East African Federation (proposed)
Hunting—Africa, East
Railroads—Africa, East
Somalia
Tanganyika
Zoology—Africa, East

Description and travel

African holiday. I. Chase. Vogue 141:53+ Ap 1 '63
Express to the Mountains of the Moon. D. Reed. il Read Digest 85:234-40 S '64

Industries

Confident kinsmen. Time 82:94 S 20 '63

Politics

Red threat in black Africa? R. K. Massie. il Sat Eve Post 237:80-5 Ap 18 '64

AFRICA, NORTH
See also
Sahara Desert

Politics

North African unity derailed. New Repub 148:7 F 9 '63
Sahara, bridge or barrier? I. W. Zartman. bibliog il Int Concil 541:3-62 Ja '63

AFRICA, SOUTH. See South Africa
AFRICA, SOUTHEAST
See also
Swaziland
AFRICA, SOUTHWEST. See Southwest Africa
AFRICA, SUB-SAHARAN

Religious institutions and affairs

God, Allah and Ju Ju, by J. Mendelsohn. Review
Christian Cent 80:648-9 My 15 '63. F. D. Lueking

AFRICA, WEST
West Africa, 1963; symposium. bibliog f Cur Hist 45:321-65 D '63
West African diary. J. Mander. Commentary 36:453-9 D '63
See also
Angola
Dahomey
French West Africa
Ivory Coast
Nigeria
Portuguese Guinea
Sierra Leone
Togo

Antiquities

Vanished cities of West Africa. H. G. Lawrence. il Negro Hist Bul 27:117-19 F '64

Climate

Life under 150 inches of rain. A. V. Barwood. il Sci Digest 54:18-21 O '63

Commerce

African metamorphosis. E. A. K. Kalitsi. il UNESCO Courier 16:44-9 Jl '63

Politics

Black Africa: a critical appraisal. il U S News 57:43 D 7 '64
Togo: the lesson for Africa. J. K. Sale. Nation 196:135-7 F 16 '63

Religious institutions and affairs

Christianity and Islam in West Africa. K. Hughes. Christian Cent 81:264-7, 298-302 F 26- Mr 4 '64

Social conditions

Black Africa: a critical appraisal. il U S News 57:43 D 7 '64

AFRICA and China. See China and Africa
AFRICA and Germany (Federal Republic)
Germany's role in modern Africa; address, May 18, 1963. G. M. Williams. Dept State Bul 48:901-5 Je 10 '63
AFRICA and Russia. See Russia and Africa
AFRICA and the United States
America's image in Africa; address, November 7, 1964. G. M. Williams. Dept State Bul 51:730-5 N 23 '64
Cultural exchange program in Africa: a path to peace; address, December 18, 1962. G. M. Williams. Dept State Bul 48:67-70 Ja 14 '63
Germany's role in modern Africa; address, May 18, 1963. G. M. Williams. Dept State Bul 48:901-5 Je 10 '63
President sends message to conference of African leaders at Addis Ababa, May 22, 1963. J. F. Kennedy. Dept State Bul 48: 902 Je 10 '63
AFRICAN antelopes. See Antelopes
AFRICAN art. See Art, African
AFRICAN berries. See Berries
AFRICAN boxwood
Tolerant is the word for it. il Sunset 133:176 D '64
AFRICAN bronzes. See Bronzes
AFRICAN buffaloes. See Buffaloes
AFRICAN chameleons. See Chameleons
AFRICAN dancing. See Dancing, African
AFRICAN drama
Ghana's young theatre. A. Zeitlin. il Theatre Arts 47:65-7+ N '63
AFRICAN Methodist Episcopal church
A.M.E. church in conference. F. Stauffer. Christian Cent 81:808 Je 17 '64
Negro Methodists consider union. V. E. Lowder. Christian Cent 81:250+ F 19 '64
Richard Allen. L. Bennett, jr. il Ebony 19: 142-4+ My '64
AFRICAN Methodist Episcopal Zion church
Negro Methodists consider union. V. E. Lowder. Christian Cent 81:250+ F 19 '64
AFRICAN poetry
Where God is black; excerpts from Poems from black Africa, ed. by L. Hughes. Time 82:22-3 S 6 '63
AFRICAN scholarship program of American universities
Reporter at large. K. T. Kinkead. New Yorker 40:51-2+ My 23 '64
AFRICAN scientists. See Scientists, African
AFRICAN sculpture. See Sculpture, African
AFRICAN shrikes. See Shrikes
AFRICAN students
African lesson for the Russians. Life 56:4 Ja 3 '64
African students at iron curtain schools flee a hateful epithet: *cherni maimuni*. J. Bonfante. Life 54:19 Mr 15 '63
Competition for Africa's students. D. Hapgood. Reporter 29:41-2 S 12 '63; Discussion. 29:10+ O 10 '63
Wandering African intellectuals. W. Dillion. New Repub 148:17-19 Mr 9 '63
AFRICAN students in China (People's Republic) See Foreign students in China (People's Republic)
AFRICAN students in Communist countries. See Foreign students in Communist countries
AFRICAN students in Russia. See Foreign students in Russia
AFRICAN studies. See Area studies
AFRICAN teachers in the United States. See Foreign teachers in the United States
AFRICAN violets
African violet grower's primer. il Horticulture 42:37+ F '64
African violets are sheer delight. H. V. Wilson. il Flower Grower 51:22-3 O '64
African violets new for 1963. il Pop Gard 14: 29 Ap '63
How to grow African violets. il Good H 157: 152 S '63
More light on African-violets. B. Black. il Flower Grower 50:28-9+ S '63
Shopper's guide to African violets. il Sunset 130:188 F '63
AFRICANS
Clues to the African personality. E. Huxley. il N Y Times Mag p 18+ My 31 '64
Dark faces in the UN. A. Morrison. il Ebony 18:23-6+ F '63
Tribalism and social evolution in Africa; address, April 10, 1964; with questions and answers. C. M. Turnbull. bibliog f il Ann Am Acad 354:22-32 Jl '64
Very best intentions; a friendship in Ghana. M. Laurence. Holiday 36:107-8+ N '64
AFRICANS in the United States
When African envoys house-hunt in capital. U S News 55:11 Jl 1 '63
AFRO-ASIAN people's solidarity conference, Algiers, 1964
Chinese laundry. New Repub 150:9 Ap 18 '64
AFRO-ASIAN people's solidarity conference, Moshi, Tanganyika, 1963
In mouth only; with report by J. R. Nugent. Newsweek 61:46+ F 18 '63
Mishmash at Moshi. Time 81:38 F 15 '63
AFTER images
Afterimages. G. S. Brindley. il Sci Am 209: 84-90+ O '63
Cover; test pattern. il Sci Am 209:4 O '63
Disappearance of luminous designs. J. P. McKinney. bibliog il Science 140:403-4 Ap 26 '63; Discussion. 144:1359-60 Je 12 '64

AFTER images—*Continued*
Moon illusion; an event in imaginary space. H. E. Gruber and others. bibliog il Science 139:750-2 F 22 '63
Role of afterimages in dark adaptation. H. B. Barlow and J. M. B. Sparrock. bibliog il Science 144:1309-14 Je 12 '64
Single-unit activity in the cat's visual cortex; modification after an intense light flash. A. D. J. Robertson and C. R. Evans. bibliog il Science 147:303-4 Ja 15 '65
See also
Phosphenes
AFTER the fall; drama. See Miller, A.
AFTER the wedding; story. See Cave, H.
AFTER thirty, what indeed? story. See Jordan, E. H.
AFTERBURNERS. See Rocket engines
AFTEREFFECTS, Figural. See Figural aftereffects
AFTERIMAGES. See After images
AFTERNOON teas
At home from four to six. il Ladies Home J 81:145-6+ Ja '64
Here's a plan for a small, informal tea. il Sunset 132:174 Ap '64
AGA Khan IV
Prince Karim Aga Khan. P. E. Ress. il pors Sports Illus 21:58-67 Ag 10 '64
What became of the Aga Khan? S. de Gramont. il pors Sat Eve Post 237:30-2 D 5 '64
AGAMMAGLOBULINEMIA
Agammaglobulinemia: the fundamental defect. H. H. Fudenberg and K. Hirschhorn. bibliog il Science 145:611-12 Ag 7 '64
AGAPE
Theology is not American. N. F. S. Ferré; discussion. Christian Cent 80:244 F 20 '63
AGAR
Plaque formation in agar by single antibody-producing cells. N. K. Jerne and A. A. Nordin. il Science 140:405 Ap 26 '63
AGASSIZ, Louis
For the increase and diffusion of knowledge among men. Hobbies 68:123 N '63
AGATE FOSSIL BEDS NATIONAL MONUMENT (proposed) See National monuments
AGATES
Fortification agate. H. D. Brown. il Hobbies 69:127 Je '64
AGATHA; story. See O'Hara, J.
AGE
Just as smart at 50. Sci Digest 54:73 D '63
See also
Aging
Longevity
Middle age
AGE (plants)
Ethylene production in fading vanda orchid blossoms. E. K. Akamine. bibliog il Science 140:1217-18 Je 14 '63
Growth, maturation, and senescence in fruits. J. B. Biale.. bibliog il Science 146:880-8 N 13 '64
See also
Trees, Age of
AGE (psychology)
Older man; questions and answers. A. Wood. il Seventeen 23:224-5+ Ag '64
AGE, Voting. See Suffrage—United States
AGE and ability. See Ability, Influence of age on
AGE and employment
First findings of the 1963 survey of the aged; Work experience and earnings of the aged in 1962. E. Palmore. il Mo Labor R 87:1173-6 O '64
Job performance of federal mail sorters by age. J. F. Walker. bibliog f il Mo Labor R 87:296-300 Mr '64
Labor market experience of unemployed older workers. W. H. Franke. Mo Labor R 86:282-4 Mr '63
Older workers' performance in industrial retraining programs. E. Weinberg. bibliog f il Mo Labor R 86:935-9 Ag '63
Overqualified. R. A. Saunders. New Repub 151:22 Ag 22 '64
Table of working life for men, 1960. S. Garfinkle. il Mo Labor R 86:820-3 Jl '63
Too old at forty-five? J. Ridgeway. New Repub 151:22 Ag 22 '64
See also
Retirement from business, etc.
AGE determination by radioactivity. See Radioactive dating
AGE for marrying. See Marriage
AGE of the earth. See Earth—Age
AGE of the universe. See Universe—Age
AGE of trees. See Trees, Age of
AGED
Aging differently in the space age; excerpts from address. M. Mead. Recreation 57:219+ My '64
Brightening old age in Houston; Sheltering arms program. H. Whitman. il Todays Health 41:52-3+ S '63
Can three generations live together? B. M. Silverman. Parents Mag 38:43+ Ap '63
Carmel's key to happy retirement: help, not a handout. G. S. Bush. il Todays Health 42:58-9+ Ja '64
Does life end at sixty? A. Métraux. il UNESCO Courier 16:20-3 Ap '63
Fears of older Americans. F. Marley. Sci N L 83:339 Je 1 '63
Frauds against the aged. Consumer Rep 28:131 Mr '63
Growing old in America: frauds quackery, swindle the aged and compound their troubles. E. Langer. Science 140:470-2 My 3 '63; Reply. B. C. Hendricks. 141:1131-2 S 20 '63
Health of older people: a social survey, by E. Shanas. Review
Sat R 46:32 My 4 '63. A. Lindsey
How to be a happy, healthy oldster; furniture requirements of older people. House & Gard 124:112+ S '63
Key senator urges better help for the aging. G. A. Smathers. il Nations Bsns 52:36-7+ Jl '64
Old age brings honor to those who serve. F. Morley. il Nations Bsns 51:27-8 Je '63
Old age in America. America 108:328-9 Mr 9 '63
Old folks at home, and out of it; letter. D. Ewing. Ladies Home J 80:8 My '63
One thousand pages of research. A. Yezierska. Commentary 36:60-3 Jl '63; Discussion. 37:16+ Ja '64
Over sixty-five: beyond the merely bearable. H. H. Miller. il New Repub 151:65-8+ N 7 '64
Still going strong at ninety-one. il Todays Health 42:20 Je '64
Third Sunday in May; Senior citizen Sunday. W. D. Pfost. Recreation 57:236-7 My '64
See also
Aging
Church work with the aged
Libraries—Work with the aged
Old age

Adjustment

Growing old in America. M. Decter. Commentary 35:22-7 Ja '63; Discussion. 35:444-5 My '63
My father and the big camellia. G. B. Freeman. il Redbook 122:6+ Ap '64
Positive view of aging asks much of education. H. L. Dunn. il Sch Life 46:30-4 Ja '64
Sam Winter retires from old age; Senior service corps of National council of Jewish women. J. Shepherd. il Look 27:49-52 Ag 13 '63
When old folks become a problem. M. Parton. Ladies Home J 80:57+ Mr '63

Care and hygiene

Care of the aged, a responsible approach; adapted from address. E. R. Annis. Todays Health 41:88 D '63
Here's how they help out mother and dad; Earlham, Ia. R. C. Davids. il Farm J 88:58B-58C N '64
See also
Aged—Housing
Aged—Medical care
Nursing homes

Clubs

See Recreation for the aged

Employment

See Age and employment

Housing

Churches enter the housing business. L. E. Schaller. Christian Cent 80:1263-5 O 16 '63; Discussion. 80:1548 D 11 '63
Community for senior citizens; Leisure Village, Lakewood, N.J. il Am City 79:102 Ap '64
Decatur pinpoints the problems of the aged. Am City 78:138+ My '63
Earth being so good, would heaven seem best? homes for retired teachers. E. Warren. il NEA J 53:8-10+ Mr '64
Housing the aged. America 110:621 My 9 '64
Living it up; retirement hotels. il Newsweek 64:112A-112B O 12 '64
Maiden ladies; housing for unmarried daughters of the aristocracy in Germany and Denmark. N. S. Hazelton. New Yorker 39:162+ S 21 '63

AGED—Housing—*Continued*
New concept in housing and nursing spaces. il Arch Rec 135:189-91 Ap '64
Old folks at home? Rossmoor leisure world. il Newsweek 61:84 F 25 '63
Profits and problems from the golden years; Seal Beach Leisure World, Calif. il Bsns W p 132-3+ Ap 11 '64
Retirement city; haven or ghetto? il Bsns W p128-30 Ap 11 '64
Retirement hotels. N. D. Ford. il Travel 119: 36-40 Ap '63
Senior-citizen housing; Townsend towers; Dearborn, Mich. il Am City 79:79-80 Jl '64
Should your parents move to a retirement village? T. Irwin. il Am Home 66:8+ Ja '63
Thistles in paradise: truth about retirement housing. B. Davidson. il Sat Eve Post 238:19-25 Ja 16 '65
Vest-pocket renewal holds new hope for the elderly; Washington Heights, New York city. il Am City 79:105 My '64
Widening world of retirement towns; Leisure world development. il Life 55:93-8+ N 8 '63
See also
Old age homes
Sun City, Ariz.

Medical care

AMA alternative; war against medicare. America 112:97 Ja 23 '65
Elderly and medical care. P. Portz. America 110:256-8 F 22 '64; Reply. R. C. Brown. 110:574-5 Ap 25 '64
Ex-Cabinet member opposes health care plan; interview. J. E. Day. Nations Bsns 51:42-3+ D '63
False promise of Medicare. R. Cubbedge. Read Digest 84:137-41 Ap '64
Federal health estimates, 300 per cent wrong. B. S. Sanders. il Nations Bsns 52:31-3+ N '64; Reply. R. J. Myers. 53:10 Ja '65
Focus on aged; Kerr-Mills act. America 108: 658 My 11 '63
For Medicare: a new plan and a new outlook. U S News 57:77 Ag 31 '64
Health care for the aged: here are two plans. il U S News 56:46-8 F 24 '64
Here's JFK's plan for old folks: how good are its chances? il U S News 54:76-7 Mr 4 '63
How medicare was lost this year. M. Viorst. New Repub 151:6-7 O 17 '64
How to pay the hospital. M. B. Folsom. il Atlan 211:79-82 Je '63
Hurricane warning: next round on medicare. G. Richards. America 111:768 D 12 '64
Is this the year for Medicare? P. Duke and S. Meisler. il Reporter 30:23-6 Ap 23 '64
Justice for the aged. America 112:66 Ja 16 '65
Kerr-Mills in Kentucky. New Repub 152:4 Ja 9 '65
LBJ fills in his design; with editorial comment. il Bsns W p25-6, 132 Ja 16 '65
Medical care and pensions: what the Senate voted. il U S News 57:8 S 14 '64
Medical care for the aged. W. J. Cohen. bibliog f il Cur Hist 45:98-103+ Ag '63
Medical care for the aged, what young families should know. B. Spock. Redbook 123:34+ My '64
Medicare; address, January 11, 1963. E. R Annis. Vital Speeches 29:309-11 Mr 1 '63
Medicare revised: King-Anderson bill. Newsweek 62:72 N 25 '63
Medicare set for the next round; showdown between Mills and Johnson. Bsns W p32 O 31 '64
Medicare, the cure that could cause a setback. H. B. Meyers. il Fortune 67:131-3+ My '63
Mental health: slash in funds for staffing raises problems; House begins Medicare hearings. E. Langer. Science 142:1045-6 N 22 '63
New insurance battle. America 108:848 Je 15 '63
New plans to take care of the old folks. il U S News 56:85-6 Je 1 '64
New U.S. health-care plan in brief. U S News 57:43 S 21 '64
Old familiar; Medicare plan. Time 81:20 Mr 1 '63
President's message about the aged. E. T. Folliard. America 108:327 Mr 9 '63
Problem of medical costs, what can be done about it; with interview with R. E. Brown. il U S News 56:72-5 My 25 '64
Senior citizens; President Kennedy's message to Congress. Commonweal 77:609 Mr 8 '63
Speaking out; case against federalized medicine. G. M. Fister. Sat Eve Post 236:8+ F 23 '63
This month's feature: proposals to expand Medicare for aged. Cong Digest 42:193-224 Ag '63
Those medical plans. Nat R 17:52+ Ja 26 '65
Who pays for the care of the aged? controversy over government vs. private health insurance. Bsns W p68-9 N 23 '63
Who will be helped by medicare. il U S News 57:52-5 D 14 '64
Why we need medicare. M. H. Alderman. New Repub 151:17-20 D 26 '64
Will medicare alter private plans? il Bsns W p 100+ D 5 '64
See also
Insurance, Health—United States

Nutrition

Diets related to aging. Sci N L 84:279 N 2 '63
Good eating for all ages. H. L. Sipple. Todays Health 42:64-5+ F '64

Quotations, maxims, etc.

Old (?) age; comp. by E. C. Wood. il N Y Times Mag p 103 Ap 5 '64

Recreation

See Recreation for the aged

AGED, Homes for the. See Old age homes
AGEE, James
James Agee, by himself. por Esquire 60:149+ D '63
James Agee; with excerpts from Death in the family; photographs by E. Haas and report by R. Oulahan. il pors Life 55:57-67+ N 1 '63
AGEE, John F.
Fouled spark plug detector. Pop Electr 20:82 Ja '64
AGEMIAN, Charles A.
Look before you leap into computers. por Bsns W p 156+ O 17 '64
AGENCIES, Advertising. See Advertising agencies
AGENCIES, Federal. See United States—Executive departments
AGENCIES, Regulatory. See Independent regulatory commissions
AGENCIES, Travel. See Travel agencies
AGENCY for International development. See United States—Agency for international development
AGENCY shops. See Open and closed shop
AGENTS. See Literary agents
AGENTS, Real estate. See Real estate agents
AGENTS, Tax. See Tax consultants
AGENTS of foreign principals in the United States. See Foreign propagandists in the United States
AGGLUTINATION
Brucella-agglutinating antibodies: relation of mercaptoethanol stability to complement fixation. R. K. Anderson and others. bibliog il Science 143:1334-5 Mr 20 '64
AGGLUTININS
See also
Hemagglutinin
AGGREGATE spreaders. See Paving machines
AGGREGATES (building materials)
Cement-stabilized aggregate wins; Grandview, Mo. L. W. Weller. il Am City 78:75-7 N '63
AGHAJANIAN, G. K.
Microsome fraction of brain: structural changes induced by ascorbic acid. bibliog Science 141:628-30 Ag 16 '63
AGHNIDES, Thanassis
General assembly praises Chairman Aghnides. por U N Rev 10:41-2 D '63
AGING
Aging differently in the space age; excerpts from address. M. Mead. Recreation 57:219+ My '64
Antibody production and development of contact skin sensitivity in guinea pigs of various ages. H. Baer and R. T. Bowser. bibliog il Science 140:1211-12 Je 14 '63
Biological mechanisms underlying the aging process. H. J. Curtis. bibliog il Science 141: 686-94 Ag 23 '63; Discussion. 142:540, 1261; 144:11 N 1, D 6 '63; Ap 3 '64
Cause of aging diseases one of cell study aims. Sci N L 85:132 F 29 '64
Enzyme changes in flight muscle correlated with aging and flight ability in the male housefly. M. Rockstein and K. F. Brandt. bibliog il Science 139:1049-51 Mr 15 '63
Femoral expansion in aging women: implications for osteoporosis and fractures. R. W. Smith, jr. and R. R. Walker. bibliog il Science 145:156-7 Jl 10 '64
Glow of youth; experiments with cytoplasm. il Newsweek 62:98 D 2 '63

AGING—*Continued*
Positive view of aging asks much of education. H. L. Dunn. il Sch Life 46:30-4 Ja '64
Redundancy and biological aging. H. A. Johnson. bibliog il Science 141:910-12 S 6 '63
Ten basic concepts of aging; reprint. Recreation 56:67 F '63
Why do we grow old? A. J. Snider. Todays Health 41:18-20 Jl '63
You may be younger than you think. Read Digest 83:71-4 Jl '63
Youthful science of aging; gerontology. R. E. Knutti. il Todays Health 42:16-19+ Je '64

AGING head; story. See Warner, S. T.

AGING of plants. See Age (plants)

AGLE, Janet
How to live with a husband. Good H 156:62+ Ap '63

AGLER, Raymond B.
Problem books revisited; excerpts from report on survey of small public library's book selection practices in controversial areas. por Library J 89:2019-30 My 15 '64

AGNES, Sister
Elegy for Sister Angèle. America 109:456 O 19 '63
In memory of Flannery O'Connor; poem. America 111:455 O 17 '64
Mind is its own shape; poem. America 112: 165 Ja 30 '65
To Christ, Our Lord: a nun remembers her bridal day; poem. Commonweal 78:93 Ap 19 '63

AGNEW, Rea
Outdoor recreation policies: some differences. Am For 69:34-5+ Je '63

AGNEW, Ruth
Discipline? follow the yellow brick road. NEA J 53:52-4 O '64

AGNEW, Seth M.
Children's book show. Pub W 183:60-8 Ap 8 '63

AGNOSTICISM
See also
Atheism

AGOGINO, George A. and others
Early man in the New World. Science 143: 1350-2 Mr 20 '64

AGONY columns. See Newspapers—Personal advertisements

AGOSTINI, Peter
Is sculpture a step-child? a colloquy. por Art N 63:40-2+ S '64

about

Agostini: high-speed plaster. il Art N 62: 29+ Sum '63
Plaster cornucopia. il por Time 84:96+ N 13 '64
Riding the whirlwind; plaster sculpture. il por Newsweek 61:96 Ap 22 '63

AGRANOFF, Bernard W. and Klinger, P. D.
Puromycin effect on memory fixation in the goldfish. bibliog Science 146:952-3 N 13 '64

AGRAWAL, D. P.
Harappa culture: new evidence for a shorter chronology. bibliog Science 143:950-2 F 28 '64

AGREEMENTS, International. See Treaties

AGREEMENTS, Trade. See Trade agreements

AGRICULTURAL administration
Earth's yield. il Fortune 69:136-41 Mr '64
Economic development: some lessons of a common experience; address, August 19, 1963. W. W. Rostow. Dept State Bul 49: 422-30 S 16 '63; Same. Vital Speeches 29: 712-17 S 15 '63
It's an international farm mess now. M. A. Heilperin and R. Lubar. il Fortune 67:134-7+ My '63
Some lessons of economic development since the war; address, October 7, 1964. W. W. Rostow. Dept State Bul 51:664-9 N 9 '64
Transforming traditional agriculture. by T. W. Schultz. Review
New Repub 150:21-3 F 22 '64. A. Byrnes

Asia

Agrarian reform in Asia. W. Ladejinsky. For Affairs 42:445-60 Ap '64

China (People's Republic)

How Communist economics failed in China. S. Karnow. il Fortune 68:154-7+ Jl '63
Trends in Chinese agriculture. T. Herman. bibliog f Cur Hist 45:165-72 S '63

France

French new deal. V. E. Mares. bibliog f Cur Hist 45:276-82+ N '63

Germany (Federal Republic)

Politics of German wheat. D. Schoenbaum. Nation 197:447-9 D 28 '63

Russia

Khrushchev eats his words. A. Werth. Nation 198:64-6 Ja 20 '64
Rapid turnover on the farm. Time 81:43-4 Mr 15 '63
This is the absolute end; excerpts from address, September 17, 1963. N. Khrushchev. Fortune 68:122 N '63
Trends in the Soviet economy. M. T. Florinsky. Cur Hist 47:266-71 N '64

United States

Abundance aborted. Nation 196:497-8 Je 15 '63
Across the editor's desk; summary of letter. ed. by D. Hanson. O. B. Jesness. Suc Farm 61:12 F '63
Against the grain? referendum on wheat controls. Newsweek 61:32+ My 20 '63
Archival product of a century of federal assistance to agriculture. H. T. Pinkett. bibliog f Am Hist R 69:689-706 Ap '64
As a key vote nears on federal controls; wheat plan. U S News 54:11 My 13 '63
Backdown on the farm; Goldwater's farm subsidy program. Time 84:33 O 30 '64
Blue eagle, RIP; wheat referendum. Nat R 14:438 Je 4 '63
Cleaning up the farm mess. Fortune 68:132+ Jl '63
Conservative tide sets in. Farm J 88:142 F '64
Controlling farm surpluses. New Repub 148:5 F 16 '63
Controls rejected; wheat farmers. Commonweal 78:293 Je 7 '63
Crisis forces showdown on farm subsidies. il Nations Bsns 52:56-8+ F '64
Cross fire. by E. T. Benson. Review
New Repub 148:21-2 F 2 '63. A. Brynes
Day at the polls. M. L. Frichtel. New Repub 148:9 Je 15 '63
Department supports extension of Public law 480; statement, February 28, 1964. W. A. Harriman. Dept State Bul 50:507-9 Mr 30 '64
Does this fit your ASC committee? C. W. Gifford. Farm J 87:38+ F '63
Doing something for the farmer again. Bsns W p 160 D 14 '63
Don't pack ASC, farmers say, three to one. il Farm J 87:31 Mr '63
Double your money; annual farm-program battle. Time 81:19 F 8 '63
Farewell to the small farm; excerpt from Farms and farming in an urban age. E. Higbee. il Read Digest 84:176-80 Mr '64
Farm fix; attack on subsidies by president of the American farm bureau federation. Time 84:24-5 D 18 '64
Farm program fiasco. H. Hazlitt. Newsweek 62:108 O 14 '63
Farmers face their toughest choice. J. Bird. il Sat Eve Post 236:74-6 My 18 '63
Farmers say no; wheat referendums. New Repub 148:6 Je 1 '63
Farmers slap down wheat plan; secret-ballot referendum. il Bsns W p29 My 25 '63
Farmers vote for freedom; wheat referendum. J. Strohm. Read Digest 83:95-9 S '63
Farms and farmers in an urban age. by E. Higbee. Review
Time il 82:21 Jl 19 '63
Fear of free markets. H. Hazlitt. Newsweek 61:88 Je 10 '63
Feed grain program. F. Bailey, jr. Suc Farm 61:45 Ap '63
Government keeps food prices high. il Nations Bsns 52:38-9+ Je '64
Hard row to hoe. il Time 81:21-5 Ap 5 '63
How much wheat will we plant? Farm J 87:29+ S '63
How new wheat plan hits small growers. Farm J 87:27-8 Ap '63
How now, brown cow? A. Brynes. New Repub 148:8 Ap 20 '63
How the farmers get what they want. T. Lowi. il Reporter 30:34-7 My 21 '64
How to get soil bank acres back in corn. Farm J 88:45 Ap '64
King Cotton's road to ruin. Life 57:4 Jl 24 '64
Land coming out of soil bank? W. D. Pardee. Suc Farm 62:44-5 Ja '64
Last minute report straight from Washington. See issues of Farm journal
Let's invest in people not land; with editorial comment. T. W. Schultz. Suc Farm 61:6. 33 Jl '63
LBJ and the farmers. A. Byrnes. New Repub 150:15-16 F 15 '64
New rules for 1964 feed grain program F. Bailey, jr. Suc Farm 62:32-3 F '64
New wheat program ahead? B. Brantley and F. Bailey, jr. Suc Farm 62:40-1+ F '64
New worry for politicians: dollar wheat and '64 vote. il U S News 55:86-8 S 16 '63

AGRICULTURAL administration — United States—*Continued*
1963 feed grain program. F. Bailey, jr. and B. Brantley. il Suc Farm 61:69+ F '63
Nos have it; wheat farmers reject controls. Newsweek 61:21 Je 3 '63
Now, a hope of farm sanity. Life 54:4 Je 7 '63
Now the non-farmer asks for parity. E. Higbee. il N Y Times Mag p 15+ Je 2 '63
Paying the farmers; Feed grain act of 1963. New Repub 148:7 My 18 '63
Rules for handling diverted acres. Suc Farm 61:123 F '63
Should you divert feed grain acres? B. Brantley. il Suc Farm 62:36 Mr '64
Should you plow back to within allotment? Suc Farm 62:122 Ap '64
Social services for farmers. D. Hanson. Suc Farm 62:10 Ap '64
Spotlight on the farm subsidy. Bsns W p204 O 19 '63
Successful farming interviews Secretary Freeman. O. L. Freeman. Suc Farm 61:63+ F '63
Those annoying farmers: impossible but not really serious. J. Heinz. Harper 227:61-4+ Jl '63; Discussion. 227:12+ S '63
To him that hath. A. Brynes. New Repub 148: 9 Mr 30 '63
Too much government? D. Hanson. Suc Farm 62:8 Ag '64
Two lasting benefits. Farm J 87:90 Jl '63
We may have passed the high tide of government control of the production and pricing of farm products. D. Paarlberg. Suc Farm 61:31 Je '63
What farmers can expect from LBJ. C. E. Ball and C. W. Gifford. il Farm J 88: 35+ Ja '64
What farmers think of their future; present farm program; address, June 11, 1963. C. P. Streeter. Vital Speeches 29:600-2 Jl 15 '63
What now for wheat? C. W. Gifford. Farm J 87:26-7 Jl '63
What to plant this spring; feed grain program. L. M. Palmer. Farm J 88:34-5 Ap '64
What we are for; Farm journal platform. C. P. Streeter. Farm J 87:150 Ap '63
Wheat controls: yes or else? Life 54:4 My 10 '63
Wheat farmers' revolt: the reason and the result; What the growers said. il U S News 54:40-2 Je 3 '63
Wheat problem: back at White House. il U S News 55:39 D 30 '63
Wheat vote; against Freeman's program. il Time 81:13-14 My 31 '63
Wheat vote; historic farm election. F. Bailey, jr. Suc Farm 61:45 My '63
Where I stand on farming; questions and answers; with editorial comment. L. B. Johnson; B. M. Goldwater. il Farm J 88:5, 32-3+ O '64
Which is better for wheat growers? wheat certificate program for 1964; with editorial comment. J. G. Patton; C. B. Shuman. Farm J 87:32-3+, 142 Mr '63
Who's in the stew? Time 82:11-12 D 20 '63
See also
Farm produce—Prices
Surplus products, Agricultural
United States—Agriculture, Department of
AGRICULTURAL airplanes. See Airplanes in agriculture
AGRICULTURAL aviation academy, Minden, Nev. See Aviation schools
AGRICULTURAL chemicals
Follow directions or fail. D. Hanson. Suc Farm 62:8 S '64
No one fully understands; dangers of pollution. New Repub 148:5-6 Je 15 '63
Senator Ribicoff would end protest registration of insecticides. J. Prokop. il Am For 69:7+ O '63
Spring brings science to garden. A. Clarke. il Sci N L 83:170-1 Mr 16 '63
Will you be next? il Farm J 88:54A Ap '64
See also
Herbicides
Weeds—Chemical control
AGRICULTURAL clubs
See also
Future farmers of America
AGRICULTURAL colleges
Take a new look at AG colleges. Suc Farm 61:98+ Ap '63
See also
Land grant colleges
AGRICULTURAL credit
See also
Farm finance
AGRICULTURAL economics. See Agriculture—Economic aspects
AGRICULTURAL education
Coming, better agricultural jobs without college! training programs in technical agriculture. R. E. Geyer. Suc Farm 62:88 Ap '64
Training for future farmers; OAS Inter-American rural youth program. G. Meek. il Américas 16:32-4 O '64
See also
Agriculture—Study and teaching
AGRICULTURAL engineering
See also
Irrigation
AGRICULTURAL exhibitions
Our man in Amsterdam; U.S. food and agriculture exhibition. New Yorker 39:24-6 D 21 '63
AGRICULTURAL extension work
It's extension's move. Farm J 88:82 Jl '64
See also
United States—Federal extension service
AGRICULTURAL forecasts
Farmcast for the eastern states. See issues of Farm journal
How 1964 shapes up now. C. W. Gifford. Farm J 87:29+ D '63
1965: what's ahead for you? C. W. Gifford. Farm J 88:25+ D '64
AGRICULTURAL hand implements. See Farm tools
AGRICULTURAL index. See Biological and agricultural index
AGRICULTURAL insurance. See Insurance, Agricultural
AGRICULTURAL labor. See Farm labor
AGRICULTURAL laws and legislation
As Congress pushed for a farm bill. U S News 56:12 Mr 16 '64
Foot in the door; Munn v. Illinois. C. P. Magrath. il Am Heritage 15:44-8+ F '64
1964 wheat rules. F. Bailey, jr. Suc Farm 61:16 My '63
Plant inspection change. Sci N L 83:349 Je 1 '63
Taking care of farmers, whoever they are. P. R. Wieck. New Repub 150:9-10 Mr 28 '64
Wheat-cotton-food-stamp bill. Cato. Nat R 16:349 My 5 '64
Which is better for wheat growers? wheat certificate program for 1964; with editorial comment. J. G. Patton; C. B. Shuman. Farm J 87:32-3+, 142 Mr '63
AGRICULTURAL machinery
Be a smart buyer. L. H. Larson. il Suc Farm 62:72 Ja '64
Beats calendar with big machinery. il Suc Farm 62:36 My '64
Big-power farming is coming fast. R. J. Reiman. Suc Farm 63:46-7 Ja '65
Cut machinery tax costs. F. Bailey, jr. il Suc Farm 62:70 Ja '64
Farm lights and shadows. il Fortune 70:32+ S '64
Farm sees a new revolution. il Bsns W p 166-8+ O 24 '64
How much machinery do I need? D. O. Hull. il Suc Farm 62:82-3 Ja '64
How to save taxes when you trade machinery. Farm J 88:46F O '64
In a national emergency: what you should know about farm machinery. F. Bailey, jr. Suc Farm 61:44 Mr '63
Machinery management for 1964. il Suc Farm 62:46-7 Mr '64
Machinery parade; photographs. See issues of Farm journal
Machinery parade preview for '64; photographs. Farm J 88:40-5 Ja '64
Machinery parade preview for 1965; photographs. Farm J 89:28-33 Ja '65
New machines mix weed killers with soil; trifluralin weed killer. il Farm J 88:38-9+ Mr '64
Phrenological pickers & such. il Time 84:111C O 2 '64
Power farming news; photographs. See issues of Farm journal
Rube Goldberg on the farm. Time 82:37 Ag 16 '63
Using augers and elevators. il Suc Farm 62:47 O '64
What's new. See issues of Successful farming
See also
Corn planters
Feed grinders and grinding
Feed handling
Fertilizer spreaders
Harvesting machinery
Hay making machinery
Motor trucks
Planters (farm machines)
Plows
Silage handling
Tractors

AGRICULTURAL machinery—*Continued*

Care

Common-sense engine care. W. J. Fletcher. il Suc Farm 62:43 Ag '64
Do all your machines earn their keep? J. Dyer. Farm J 88:43 N '64
How to choose a service dealer. il Suc Farm 62:66-7 Ja '64
Plan your farm service center; with tool list. O. A. Kimmel. il Suc Farm 63:45+ Ja '65

Exhibitions

Tractors pull 'em in; Heart of America farm power show. il Bsns W p 136-7 S 28 '63

Prices

Do all your machines earn their keep? J. Dyer. Farm J 88:43 N '64

Renting

Buy, lease, or hire it done? machinery tax management. J. D. Keast. Farm J 88:22+ F '64
It pays us to lease machinery. D. K. O'Brien. il Farm J 87:50 D '63

Storage

Plan a machinery service center. J. H. Pederson and F. W. Roth. il Suc Farm 62:64-5 Ja '64

AGRICULTURAL machinery industry and trade
Farm sees a new revolution. il Bsns W p 166-8+ O 24 '64
Farmers' store goes to town; Tractor supply co. now Town suburban & country. Bsns W p44+ F 29 '64
How to choose a service dealer. il Suc Farm 62:66-7 Ja '64
U.S. tractors plow some global fields. il Bsns W p 174+ O 24 '64
See also
Deere and company
International harvester company
Tractor industry and trade

AGRICULTURAL pests
See also
Deer

AGRICULTURAL poisons. See Agricultural chemicals

AGRICULTURAL production. See Production, Agricultural

AGRICULTURAL products. See Farm produce

AGRICULTURAL research
Space-age agriculture geared to benefit man. Sci N L 85:72 F 1 '64
Spring brings science to garden. A. Clarke. il Sci N L 83:170-1 Mr 16 '63
See also
Field experiments (agriculture)
Inter-American institute of agricultural sciences
Midwest research institute

AGRICULTURAL research service. See United States—Agricultural research service

AGRICULTURAL societies
Contract that makes money for flock owners; Central cooperative turkey producers assn. il Farm J 88:42H N '64
See also
Farmers' educational and co-operative union of America
National farmers organization

AGRICULTURAL subsidies. See Agricultural administration—United States

AGRICULTURAL surplus products. See Surplus products, Agricultural

AGRICULTURAL terraces. See Terraces (agriculture)

AGRICULTURAL tractors. See Tractors

AGRICULTURAL use of airplanes. See Airplanes in agriculture

AGRICULTURAL workers. See Farm labor

AGRICULTURE
News from the world of farming. Read Digest 83:37-8 Jl '63
See also
Agricultural administration—United States
Airplanes in agriculture
Farmers
Food supply
Irrigation
Land utilization
Poultry industry and trade
also headings beginning Agricultural; Farm; Soil

Economic aspects

Across the editor's desk. D. Hanson. Suc Farm 63:8 Ja '65
Affluent farmer. il Fortune 68:48+ S '63
Agricultural meteorology; report on sixth national conference on agricultural meteorology of the American meteorological society. R. F. Dale. Science 146:1601-2 D 18 '64
Can you farm without debt today? R. E. Geyer. Suc Farm 62:74 My '64
Candidates' views on farm programs. D. Hanson. Suc Farm 62:7 N '64
Crop cost-cutting ideas that really work. P. R. Robbins. il Suc Farm 62:34-5 D '64
Do you plan your farm changes backward? C. E. French and R. B. Wilson. il Suc Farm 61:70D S '63
Farm business. See issues of Farm journal
Farm lights and shadows. il Fortune 70:32+ S '64
Farmcast for the eastern states. See issues of Farm journal
Farmers face their toughest choice. J. Bird. il Sat Eve Post 236:74-6 My 18 '63
Farmers' plight deepens. Christian Cent 80: 573-4 My 1 '63
Farmers: the real surplus. P. Dorner. il Nation 196:115-17+ F 9 '63
Five ways to cut grain losses. L. E. Zeman and W. H. Johnson. Suc Farm 61:30 Jl '63
How common stocks fit our savings program. J. H. Fithian. il Suc Farm 62:71+ Ag '64
How to be money smart. il Suc Farm 62: 39+ Je; 38+ Jl; 39+ Ag; 54+ S; 52+ O; 52+ N '64
How to be money smart. il B. Brantley and A. G. Mueller. Suc Farm 62:48-9+ Mr; 48+ Ap '64
How to be money smart. Suc Farm 62:39+ Je; 38+ Jl; 39+ Ag; 54+ S; 52+ O '64
How you can make more profit this year. Suc Farm 62:39+ F '64
It's an international farm mess now. M. A. Heilperin and R. Lubar. il Fortune 67:134-7+ My '63
Nationalization of takeoff; address, May 2, 1963. W. W. Rostow. Dept State Bul 48: 824-9 My 27 '63
Plan, to survive. D. Hanson. Suc Farm 62:8 Jl '64
They get two family incomes from 580 crop acres. P. B. Jones and R. L. Maddex. il Suc Farm 62:28-9 D '64
Transforming traditional agriculture, by T. W. Schultz. Review
New Repub 150:21-3 F 22 '64. A. Byrnes
We can get more bargaining power; ideas from R. L. Kohls of Purdue. Suc Farm 62:33 Jl '64
What's new in money management. See issues of Successful farming
When farmers go on strike. J. Bird. il Sat Eve Post 237:30+ N 21 '64
Who is raising what? interregional competition. D. Hanson. Suc Farm 61:28 S '63
See also
Agricultural laws and legislation
Farm produce—Prices
Farm tenancy
Land tenure
Production, Agricultural

Exhibitions

See Agricultural exhibitions

Federal aid

See Agricultural administration—United States

History

Origins of New World civilization. R. S. MacNeish. il Sci Am 211:29-37 bibliog(p 154) N '64

International aspects

Farming and foreign policy. il Newsweek 63: 38+ Ja 20 '64
Improving the effectiveness of U.S. assistance to international rural development; addresses, July 27, 1964. D. E. Bell; O. L. Freeman. Dept State Bul 51:376-88 S 14 '64
It's an international farm mess now. M. A. Heilperin and R. Lubar. il Fortune 67:134-7+ My '63
Policy problems in international trade of agricultural products; address, February 6, 1964. C. W. Nichols. Dept State Bul 50:416-23 Mr 16 '64
Requisites of abundance; address, March 9, 1964. H. Cleveland. Dept State Bul 50:550-5 Ap 6 '64
Role of agriculture in trade expansion; address, March 30, 1964. C. A. Herter. bibliog f Dept State Bul 50:671-5 Ap 27 '64
U.S. and Poland sign agricultural commodities agreements; Department announcement, with texts of agreements, February 3 and February 4, 1964. il Dept State Bul 50:308-12 F 24 '64

AGRICULTURE—International aspects—*Cont.*
United States-Polish agricultural commodities agreement. il Cur Hist 44:305-6 My '63
Vice President's address at Amsterdam, November 7, 1963. L. B. Johnson. Dept State Bul 49:851-2 D 2 '63

Periodicals

See also
Farm journal
Successful farming (periodical)

Public relations

Farm-city dinner. il Farm J 87:20+ N '63

Statistics

See also
Cattle, Beef—Statistics

Study and teaching

Can VO-AG answer its critics? with editorial comment. J. D. Boyd. il Farm J 87:4, 33+ N '63
My husband, the ag teacher. Mrs R. Duvall. Farm J 88:58E My '64
See also
Agricultural education

Brazil

Rich wasteland; Brazil's untapped campos cerrados. J. R. Camp. il Américas 15:11-14 Jl '63

California

California: what help for the harvest? discredited bracero program. il Newsweek 64:77 N 2 '64
California's half-million-acre greenhouse. J. N. Miller. il Read Digest 83:182-4+ Ag '63

China (People's Republic)

See also
Communes (China)

Colombia

Farmer, city founder, and poet; founding and construction of San Martín de Porres. L. Zalamea. il Américas 15:35-9 N '63

Communist countries

Food, the Achilles Heel of communism. J. Strohm and E. Lyons. Read Digest 84:246-7+ My '64
Polish miracle. R. H. S. Crossman. Commentary 35:210-19 Mr '63
Reds' crop outlook, it's still not enough. U S News 57:14 S 28 '64

Cuba

Five years of Castro's Cuba. T. Draper. bibliog f Commentary 37:25-37 Ja '64; Discussion. 37:8+ My '64

Europe, Western

Europe's farm problem, bad news for U.S. il U S News 55:68-9 Jl 22 '63

France

French paysan is angry. E. Higbee. il N Y Times Mag p20+ O 27 '63
Fresh out; dairy farmers strike. Newsweek 64:57 O 12 '64
Grapes of wrath; wine surplus angers French farmers. Time 82:83 S 6 '63
Peasant protest. il Newsweek 62:45-6 Jl 15 '63
Protests by the workers. New Repub 149:7-8 Ag 3 '63

Great Britain

Ideas from Britain on how you can make low-cost beef. D. Seim. il Farm J 88:40-2+ F '64

Greece, Modern

New Garden of Eden? American farmer looks at Greece. J. Stuart. il Am For 69:14-17+ S '63
New Garden of Eden? American farmer looks at Greece. J. Stuart. il Am For 69:14-17+ S '63; Reply. B. M. Lansdale. 70:6-7 Ja '64

Illinois

They accepted Successful farming's corn growing challenge. L. E. Zeman. il Suc Farm 61:58-9+ Ap '63

India

Farmer, key man of India; photographs. N Y Times Mag p8-9 S 6 '64
India's agricultural problems. A. Taylor and S. R. Ahsan. bibliog il Focus 14:1-6 S '63

Iowa

Where farming still pays; Burt farm, Clarion, Ia. il U S News 54:65-70 Je 10 '63

Latin America

Agricultural inventory. Américas 15:45 Je '63
Facts and figures of the Americas. il Américas 15:42-3 Je '63; 16:47 N '64
Technology is not enough. N. Ras. il Américas 17:10-15 Ja '65
Training for future farmers; OAS Inter-American rural youth program. G. Meek. il Américas 16:32-4 O '64
United fruit's experiment in international partnership; Associate producers program. P. Deutschman. il Read Digest 85:146-50 O '64
See also
Agriculture—Tropics

Mexico

See also
Chinampas

Nigeria

Big chickens of James and Samuel. P. Conklin. Reporter 28:30-1 Je 20 '63

Poland

Polish miracle. R. H. S. Crossman. Commentary 35:210-19 Mr '63

Russia

Agricultural products; the 1962 Soviet report. il Bul Atomic Sci 20:13 Ja '64
Agriculture, the principal trouble spot. il Life 55:56+ S 13 '63
Barnyard view of Soviet agriculture. A. B. Ballard, jr. il Reporter 28:38-40 My 23 '63
Farmer frustrates Khrushchev; would rather work for himself than the state. E. Crankshaw. il N Y Times Mag p 17+ S 20 '64
Food failure. Newsweek 62:37 S 30 '63
Food, the Achilles Heel of communism. J. Strohm and E. Lyons. Read Digest 84:246-7+ My '64
Last laugh; failure of gamble in Siberia and Kazakhstan. Time 83:32+ Mr 20 '64
Planting new ideas; a report on a visit to Soviet farms. O. L. Freeman. Bul Atomic Sci 19:44-5 D '63
Russia's greatest failure. R. Wilson. il Look 28:88+ F 25 '64
Russia's latest plan: confession of a failure. il U S News 55:44-5 D 23 '63
Russia's new bosses reshape its industry. il Bsns W p 104+ O 31 '64
Shades of Lenin; Central committee of the Soviet Communist party, discuss Russia's farm crisis. Newsweek 63:40+ F 24 '64
Something for the soil. il Time 82:35 D 13 '63
Soviet agriculture. D. G. Johnson. il Bul Atomic Sci 20:8-12 Ja; 35-6 Je '64
Tomorrow is three suits. il Time 83:28-33 F 21 '64; Same abr. with title Khrushchev's monumental economic mess. Read Digest 84:69-73 Je '64
Trouble by the ton. Time 82:32 S 27 '63
Trouble for Moscow: another poor crop. U S News 55:6 S 23 '63
U.S.S.R. resources: agriculture. C. D. Harris. bibliog f il Focus 13:1-6 Ja '63
Why Russia needs the wheat. Bsns W p27 S 28 '63

Southern states

Development of the U.S. South. A. Goldschmidt. il Sci Am 209:224-30+ bibliog(p310) S '63

Tropics

Underdeveloped tropics can blossom despite climate. Sci N L 84:184 S 21 '63

Underdeveloped areas

Agricultural planning for undeveloped nations. Sci N L 84:184 S 21 '63
Can a poor nation grow on an empty stomach? il Bsns W p56-7 D 26 '64
Food. N. S. Scrimshaw. il Sci Am 209:72-80 S '63

United States

Abundance, threat or promise? R. Theobald. Nation 196:387-412 My 11 '63; Discussion. 196:inside cover Je 15 '63
Agricultural revolution; excerpt from New manifesto on rural life. J. L. Vizzard. America 111:772-5 D 12 '64
As farming goes, so goes the country; still true? il U S News 56:94 Je 15 '64
Candidates' views on farm programs. D. Hanson. Suc Farm 62:7 N '64
Case of the disappearing farmer. il Sr Schol 83:16-18+ S 20 '63; Reply. H. Mitchell. 84:18 Ap 24 '64
Down on the farm. Christian Cent 81:661-2 My 20 '64
Down on the farm. Newsweek 62:74 D 2 '63
Down on the farm. M. Polnar. il Commonweal 78:164-5 My 3 '63

AGRICULTURE—United States—*Continued*
Farmcast for the eastern states. See issues of Farm journal
Farmers: the real surplus. P. Dorner. il Nation 196:115-17+ F 9 '63
Farms and farmers in an urban age, by E. Higbee. Review
New Repub 149:24-6 Jl 13 '63. A. Brynes
How 1964 shapes up now. C. W. Gifford. Farm J 87:29+ D '63
Industry. D. Teetor and B. DeRemer. il Flying 74:27+ My '64
Last minute report straight from Washington. See issues of Farm journal
New farm year begins! Farm J 87:136 F '63
1965: what's ahead for you? C. W. Gifford. Farm J 88:25+ D '64
Our day with President Johnson. il Suc Farm 62:41-3+ Mr '64
Rising worry: hard times on the farm. il U S News 56:106 My 18 '64
Supermarket to the world; U.S. farm exports. il Time 84:102 S 18 '64
23,000,000 jobs! J. B. Craig. Am For 70:64 S '64
What's new in Washington. See issues of Successful farming
Wheat shortage ahead? K. Hobson. Farm J 88:16 Ja '64
Who gets to farm? Farm J 88:106 Ja '64
Why the drive to raise cattle prices failed. R. T. Cooper. New Repub 151:7-8 O 3 '64
See also
Agricultural administration—United States
Agriculture—Economic aspects
Dairy industry and trade
Farm labor
United States—Agriculture, Department of

Western states

Big western feed lots, what you can learn from them. J. I. Sprague. il Suc Farm 61:64-5+ F '63

AGRICULTURE and climate. See Plants, Effect of climate on
AGRICULTURE and state. See Agricultural administration
AGRICULTURE as a profession
23,000,000 jobs! J. B. Craig. Am For 70:64 S '64
AGRICULTURISTS. See Agriculture as a profession
AGRIPPA VON NETTESHEIM, Heinrich Cornelius
Champion for the witch. por Todays Health 41:73 Ap '63
AGRON, P. A, and others
Xenon difluoride and the nature of the xenon-fluorine bond. bibliog Science 139:842-4 Mr 1 '63
AGRONOMISTS. See Agriculture as a profession
AGRONSKY, Martin
(ed) See Harriman, W. A. Mr Rusk and Mr Harriman discuss nuclear test ban treaty
(ed) See Rusk, D. Mr Rusk and Mr Harriman discuss nuclear test ban treaty
AGUILAR, Francis J.
Case of the earmarked executives; excerpt from European problems in general management, by E. P. Learned and others. Harvard Bsns R 41:6-8+ N '63
AGUIRRE, Hank
New Tiger rag! H. L. Masin. por Sr Schol 82:30 My 15 '63
AGUIRRE, Lope de
Ephemeral Amazon kingdom. R. J. Sender. il por Américas 15:28-32 My '63; Reply. A. B. Mason. 15:48 S '63
AGUNG, MOUNT. See Volcanoes
AHAMED brothers, incorporated
Saks of safaris. il Newsweek 62:91 O 21 '63
AHEARN, John L.
D-day plus twenty years; one who survived; ed. by C. Brossard. por Look 28:22-3 Je 16 '64
AHIDJO, Ahmadou
Summary of address, October 17, 1963. por U N Rev 10:8-9 D '63
AHLENDER, Leslie Judd
For young artists. Américas 17:36-8 Ja '65
AHLSTROM, Carl Gustaf, and others
Rous sarcoma in Chinese hamsters. bibliog Science 144:1232-3 Je 5 '64
AHMADJIAN, Vernon
Fungi of lichens. Sci Am 208:122-30+ F '63
AHMED, Hocine Ait. See Ait Ahmed, H.
AHN, Philip. See Caster, W. O. jt. auth.
AHSAN, S. Reza. See Taylor, A. jt. auth.
AID to dependent children (program) See Child welfare—United States
AID to families with dependent children (program) See Child welfare—United States
AÏDA; opera. See Verdi, G.
AIDES, Teachers. See Teachers aides
AIDMAN, Charles
Spoon River; dramatization of Spoon River anthology, by E. L. Masters. Criticism
America 109:496 O 26 '63
Nation 197:268 O 26 '63
N Y Times Mag il pors p 109-10 S 8 '63
Newsweek 62:72 O 14 '63
Sat R 46:30 O 19 '63
Theatre Arts il 47:12-13 D '63
Time 82:77 O 11 '63
AIDS to navigation. See Navigation aids
AIELLO, Edward, and Guideri, Giancarlo
Nervous control of ciliary activity. bibliog Science 146:1692-3 D 25 '64
AIKEN, Conrad
Poetry and the mind of modern man. Atlan 214:79-81 N '64
Red petals; poem. Ladies Home J 82:92 Ja '65
Seizure of limericks. Horizon 5:100-1 N '63
T. S. Eliot. Life 58:92-3 Ja 15 '65
about
Aiken as a novelist. H. Leibowitz. New Repub 150:24+ My 2 '64
Exotic side of everyman. G. Hicks. Sat R 47:53-4 Ja 11 '64
Heart for the gods. H. Carruth. Nation 198:171-2 F 17 '64
Language of the brain. J. Dickey. Poetry 103:187-90 D '63
AIKEN, Henry David
American pragmatism reconsidered. Commentary 34:120-30, 238-46, 334-44; 35:163-4 Ag-O '62, F '63
Free will, again. Commentary 37:79-82 F '64
Revolt against ideology. Commentary 37:29-39 Ap; 38:16+ S; 73-6 O '64
AIKEN, Joyce. See Laury, J. jt. auth.
AIKMAN, Lonnelle
Under the dome of freedom. Nat Geog Mag 125:4-59 Ja '64
AILEY, Alvin
Style, essence, allusion; interview, ed. by W. Sorell. por Dance Mag 37:47+ Ag '63
about
Alvin Ailey dance theatre; Clark center for the performing arts. J. Maskey. Dance Mag 38:54 Ag '64
Alvin Ailey dance theater, Delacorte theatre. M. Marks. Dance Mag 38:71 O '64
AIME, Frank
Amateur scientist. Sci Am 209:120-2+ Ag '63
AIMS in education. See Education—Aims and objectives
AINSWORTH, Ed
Small town in the big town; On the move, column in the Los Angeles times. il por Time 81:55-6 My 10 '63
AINSWORTH, Norma Ruedi
Can your reader identify? Writer 77:22-4 My '64
New kind of fiction. Writer 78:26-9 Ja '65
AINSWORTH, W. A.
Electrolytic growth of silver dendrites. bibliog Science 146:1294-5 D 4 '64
AIR
Air your knowledge; questions and answers. J. Daugherty and M. Daugherty. il Sci Digest 55:45-7 Ja '64
See also
Atmosphere
Atmosphere, Upper
Humidity
Ozone
AIR bases
Air force picks three sites for space landings; Edwards, Holloman, Wendover. il Miss & Roc 12:34 Je 10 '63
America's top ten targets. J. H. Winchester. il Sci Digest 54:54-8 N '63
Close call in Silo ten; Dyess air force base. J. Joseph. il Pop Sci 185:85-8+ N '64
Defense dept.'s base curtailments affect fifty-one aerospace installations. Aviation W 81:65+ N 30 '64
F-105D's limited-war capability boosted; Bitburg and Spangdehlem bases, West Germany. C. Brownlow. il Aviation W 78:105+ F 25 '63
How the modern Minuteman guards the peace; Malmstrom air force base. J. Atwater. il Sat Eve Post 236:65-9 F 9 '63
New Agena D checkout system in at Vandenberg. il Miss & Roc 13:42+ O 28 '63
Our about-face on African policy; bases on the Azores. G. M. Houser. Christian Cent 80:675-6 My 22 '63
Recovery site selection debated; Edwards AFB, Calif, Holloman AFB, N.Mex, and Wendover AFB, Utah. F. G. McGuire. Miss & Roc 13:14-15 Jl 8 '63

AIR bases—*Continued*
Signals off; Gem state utilities co. Idaho, cuts off service to Mountain home air force base. Newsweek 63:30 F 10 '64
SAC units bear closing brunt. Aviation W 81:34 N 23 '64
Trimming the fat. R. Hotz. Aviation W 81:11 N 30 '64
When a military base closes; what happens to a city? naval air station at New Iberia, La. il U S News 56:43-4 My 11 '64
AIR bearings. See Bearings (machinery)
AIR boats. See Airboats
AIR cargo dropping. See Airdrop
AIR commandos. See United States—Air force —Air commando groups
AIR compressors
Compressor for less than $10. R. G. Vaughn. il Pop Sci 184:152-4 Ap '64
AIR conditioning
Air conditioning helps if you use it right. Sci N L 84:34 Jl 20 '63
Budget-wise approach to air conditioning. R. Charles. il Parents Mag 39:68-9+ My '64
House kept too cold collapses in Texas. Sci N L 84:25 Jl 13 '63
How to gain new comfort at home with conditioned climate. il House & Gard 127:132-5 Ja '65
Personal business; central cooling systems. Bsns W p 169 Ap 11 '64
Shopping for an air conditioned house. il Am Home 66:36-7+ Je '63
See also subhead Air conditioning under various subjects, e.g. Automobiles—Air conditioning
AIR conditioning, Industrial
Structure delivers air and controls light. il Arch Rec 136:180-4 Jl '64
Utilities set on the roof of Phoenix shopping center. il Arch Rec 134:136-8 D '63
AIR conditioning equipment
Air conditioners and fans. il Consumer Bul 46:33-5 Je '63
Air conditioners with a furniture look. il House & Gard 123:196-7 Ap '63
Come out of your household smog. A. M. Watkins. Am Home 66:33 S '63
Filters for room air conditioners. il Consumer Rep 28:338-9 Jl '63
Guide to buying air conditioners. il Good H 156:168 My '63
Hot on the trail of room air conditioners. Am Home 67:128-9 Jl '64
Now; central air conditioning is cheaper and better. il Bet Hom & Gard 41:98+ Je '63
Portable air conditioner. Consumer Rep 28: 364 Ag '63
Room air conditioners. il Consumer Bul 47: 6-9 Jl '64
Thirteen steps to cooler, cheaper air conditioning. Bet Hom & Gard 42:114+ My '64
See also
Humidifiers
Testing
Room air conditioners. il Consumer Rep 28: 284-91 Je '63
AIR conditioning from central stations
Central heating and cooling of college campuses. il Arch Rec 134:162-4 Ag '63
AIR conditioning industry and trade
Cool age. il Time 82:60 Ag 2 '63
Room coolers run hot; doubling of last year's sales rate. Bsns W p29 Jl 18 '64
Working it cool; air conditioning in southeast Asia. il Time 84:99-100 N 6 '64
AIR cushion vehicles. See Ground effect machines
AIR defense. See Aeronautics, Military
AIR embolism. See Embolism
AIR filters
Fallout filters; Oak Harbor, Wash. J. Buckner. il Am City 78:107-8 Je '63
AIR filters, Automobile
Engine filters: how important? Motor T 16: 58-9 Mr '64
AIR force academy. See United States air force academy
AIR force association
Air force candidate Goldwater. R. D. Senter. New Repub 151:8 S 5 '64
Zuckert attacks AFA on test ban stand. Aviation W 79:31 S 16 '63
AIR force bases. See Air bases
AIR force eastern test range. See Proving grounds
AIR force families. See Service mens families
AIR force logistics command. See United States —Air force—Logistics command
AIR force missile test center. See Proving grounds
AIR force museum, Dayton, Ohio. See Dayton, Ohio—Galleries and museums
AIR force survival and special training school. See United States—Air force—Education
AIR force systems command. See United States—Air force—Systems command
AIR France. See Airlines—France
AIR freight service
Air cargo marketing, sales stress due. R. H. Cook. Aviation W 80:26-7 Je 8 '64
Air cargo: transportation's growing fledgling. il Duns R 83:pt2 128-31+ Je '64
Air cargo's new flight pattern. T. O'Hanlon. il Duns R 82:45-6+ N '63
Airway tide in transportation. D. W. Rentzel. Ann Am Acad 345:73-80 Ja '63
All-cargo jet increases pressure for rate reduction. il Aviation W 79:54-5+ O 7 '63
American cargo jet starts daily flights. Aviation W 80:36 Ja 13 '64
Big dogs, little dogs, and the air cargo bone. S. Freedgood. il Fortune 70:122-9+ O '64
Boyd favors all-cargo airline protection. J. R. Ashlock. Aviation W 80:180-1 Mr 16 '64
Boyd warns of sterner CAB fare policy. J. R. Ashlock. Aviation W 80:42-3 Ja 27 '64
By jet: lobsters, drugs, lions, cars. il Newsweek 64:62-5 Ag 3 '64
Carriers begin first move into jet cargo. J. R. Ashlock. il Aviation W 78:170-1+ Mr 11 '63
CAB cargo ruling sparks court appeal. J. W. Carter. Aviation W 81:29-30 Ag 17 '64
Coming boom in air freight; coast to coast in five hours. il U S News 56:108-10 Ap 13 '64
Court grants trunkline petitions, orders stay of CAB cargo policy. J. W. Carter. Aviation W 81:35-6 Ag 24 '64
Domestic all-jet cargo race starting. il Aviation W 79:37-8 D 2 '63
Drive to bolster all-cargo carriers slows. L. L. Doty. Aviation W 80:26-7 Mr 30 '64
Forwarders press for airline cooperation. J. W. Carter. Aviation W 81:32 N 30 '64
Freight in the sky. il Time 83:61-2 Ja 31 '64
International air cargo: the battle ahead. J. Thackray. il Duns R 83:pt2 132-5+ Je '64
Italy hinders TWA all-cargo jet effort. R. H. Cook. Aviation W 80:49-50 Ja 20 '64
Jet planes turn into cattle cars; ferrying calves to Italy. il Bsns W p 121-2 S 19 '64
Long steady rise of air freight. J. J. Friedman. il Duns R 81:pt2 S120-1+ Je '63
Monroney supports all-cargo carriers. Aviation W 81:29 Jl 13 '64
Pan Am to begin $7-million cargo facility. Aviation W 81:41 O 19 '64
Who will fly the cargo? CAB vs big trunk lines. il Bsns W p 102+ Ag 15 '64
See also
Airplanes, Freight
Flying Tiger line, incorporated
Riddle airlines
Rates
Pan Am to seek IATA freight rate trials for all-jet service. Aviation W 79:42 Jl 1 '63
AIR freight terminals. See Airport buildings
AIR glow. See Airglow
AIR guns
Litle old BB gun; air and gas pistols. H. Bradshaw. il Pop Sci 185:86-9+ D '64
AIR inter (airline) See Airlines—France
AIR lanes. See Airways
AIR-launched missiles. See Guided missiles—Launching from airplanes
AIR layering of plants. See Plant propagation
AIR line pilots association, International
ALPA adopts diplomatic bargaining. J. R. Ashlock. Aviation W 79:49 S 23 '63
ALPA challenges finding by CAB that crew erred in DC-7 accident. Aviation W 79:52 O 21 '63
ALPA may reject pact with American. J. R. Ashlock. Aviation W 78:42 F 25 '63
ALPA threatens to expel four at American. Aviation W 78:41 Mr 18 '63
American pact with new union reduces flying time requirement. Aviation W 79:39 Jl 15 '63
American pilots union seeks recognition. J. R. Ashlock. Aviation W 78:39 Ap 29 '63
Engineer meeting delays American pact. J. R. Ashlock. Aviation W 78:35 Mr 4 '63
Mediator appointed for new pilot's union. Aviation W 78:37 Je 3 '63
Pan Am pilots polled on split with ALPA. Aviation W 79:46 S 16 '63
AIR liquide (Industrial company) See France—Industries

AIR lubricated bearings. See Bearings (machinery)

AIR mail service
Airlines, CAB study reduction in subsidy. Aviation W 80:33 Je 29 '64
Alaska subsidy shift to post office urged. L. L. Doty. Aviation W 80:52 F 17 '64
American opposes mail rate cut. Aviation W 80:40 Ap 27 '64
Cargo carriers seek slash in mail rates. L. L. Doty. Aviation W 80:43 Ap 13 '64
Cargo lines want in; demand a share of mail business. il Bsns W p 120+ Ap 25 '64
Major changes facing airline mail trade. R. H. Cook. Aviation W 81:27-8 Jl 13 '64
No protests foreseen on mail rate cuts. Aviation W 81:35 N 9 '64
Token mail rate cut expected; post office criteria questioned. R. H. Cook. Aviation W 80:30 My 4 '64

AIR maneuvers
Strike command to test air support plan. C. Brownlow. il Aviation W 81:63-4+ O 26 '64
TAC evaluates ground support capability in maneuvers. E. J. Bulban. il Aviation W 81:62-4 Ag 17 '64
TAC evaluates new hardware concepts; Indian River exercise. C. Brownlow. il Aviation W 81:68-9+ O 5 '64
USAF will test ground support concepts. E. J. Bulban. Aviation W 80:23 Je 1 '64

AIR masks. See Respiratory apparatus

AIR mattresses. See Camping outfits

AIR national guard (United States) See United States—Air national guard

AIR pilot shortage. See Air pilots—Supply and demand

AIR pilots
Bush pilot's deadly, daily game. D. Moser. il Life 57:112-14+ N 27 '64
Busiest pilot in the bush. L. Elliott. il Read Digest 82:255-7+ My '63
Hell's angels fly again; National air races, Reno, Nev. J. N. Bell. il Sat Eve Post 237: 28-31 N 7 '64
Image. D. Kuhn. Flying 74:54 Ja '64
Sky-high courage; test pilot, R. White. D. Markinko. il Ladies Home J 80:62-3+ Ja '63
Small speedster; H. O. Fisher. New Yorker 38:23-4 F 2 '63
Tales of famous aces; World war I. J. Mills. il Life 56:78+ Mr 20 '64
See also
Airplane crews
Airplanes—Piloting
Negro air pilots
Women as air pilots

Diseases
Death in the cockpit; Royal Canadian air force's ECG program. Time 83:72 F 21 '64

Licenses
Four-way birthday; sixteen-year old Gregory Potter qualifies to drive planes and helicopters. il Time 84:68 S 25 '64

Physical examinations
Death in the cockpit; Royal Canadian air force's ECG program. Time 83:72 F 21 '64

Qualifications
Carriers changing pilot qualifications. J. R. Ashlock. Aviation W 80:29-31 Ap 6 '64
Project longlook. D. B. Kuhn. Flying 75:68 Jl '64

Salaries, pensions, etc.
Higher pay proposed to lure new pilots. Aviation W 81:34 O 5 '64
Low wages cited in investigation of airline manpower shortage. Aviation W 81:32 Jl 13 '64

Supply and demand
Carriers changing pilot qualifications. J. R. Ashlock. Aviation W 80:29-31 Ap 6 '64
Drought hits the pilot pool. Bsns W p 110 F 15 '64
FAA leads search for solution to civil air manpower shortage. J. R. Ashlock. Aviation W 81:35 O 12 '64
Low wages cited in investigation of airline manpower shortage. Aviation W 81:32 Jl 13 '64
Pilot shortage. il Time 83:80 Je 26 '64

Training
Animated light displays portray Boeing 727 systems for training. il Aviation W 80:80 Ja 6 '64
DOD relents; air force seeks pilots. Aviation W 79:27 N 18 '63
FAA using revised light-twin training program for inspectors. il Aviation W 78:102-3 Ap 8 '63
Flier's spending companion. J. Bergman. Esquire 61:85+ Je '64
Instructor flunks a test. M. W. Horowitz. Flying 75:24-7 S '64
Learn to fly go 'round. R. B. Parke. Flying 75:22 S '64
Let's check the check ride. J. Cushman. il Flying 74:46-7+ Ap '64
Pilots of Japan. D. H. Hickler. il Flying 75:80 Ag '64
Teaching airline pilots their ABCs; United air lines Denver training center. il Ebony 19:33-4+ Jl '64
United recruits private pilots. Aviation W 80:41 Je 15 '64
USAF plans civilian pilot training role. E. J. Bulban. Aviation W 81:23-4 Ag 3 '64
VC.10 training builds pilot confidence. il Aviation W 81:53+ S 7 '64
See also
Aviation schools
Flight simulators

AIR pistols. See Air guns

AIR plants
Strangler fig, native epiphyte. V. N. Argo. il Natur Hist 73:26-31 N '64

AIR pollution
Air around us. C. W. Griffin, jr. il Reporter 31:39-43 S 10 '64
Air pollution and health; report on 7th annual Air pollution medical research conference. J. R. Goldsmith. Science 145:184-6 Jl 10 '64
Air pollution and medical research; report of annual air-pollution medical research conference. J. R. Goldsmith. Science 141: 832-4 Ag 30 '63
Air pollution control notes (title varies) See issues of American city
Air pollution: no hazard now. Bsns W p 112 N 7 '64
Air pollution; report on symposium at the AAAS annual meeting. J. P. Dixon. Science 143:1349-50 Mr 20 '64; Reply. E. L. Tatum. 144:616 My 8 '64
Banishing auto fumes; anti-smog devices mandatory on 1966 cars. Bsns W p29 Je 20 '64
Building blocks of the clouds. J. A. Day. il Natur Hist 74:36-43 Ja '65
Cars and smog. New Repub 150:6 Je 13 '64
Cities with the cleanest air. il Am City 78: 96 N '63
Citizen-government group fights dirty air; New York state. Am City 79:168+ O '64
Coming struggle to breathe. T. O. Thackrey. Sat R 47:23-5+ O 10 '64
Contamination of the environment; address, January 28, 1963. P. D. Kilburn. Vital Speeches 29:475-8 My 15 '63
Cooperating to clear the air; California. Nat Parks Mag 38:17 S '64
Depleted uranium draws pollutants from exhausts. Sci N L 84:91 Ag 10 '63
Fight against smog: GM shows it's leading the band; exhaust control devices on '66 cars. il Bsns W p24-5 Ag 22 '64
Filth we breathe; symposium. il Sci Digest 53:4-11 My '63
Fumes from street tars seen as cancer threat. Sci N L 86:162 S 12 '64
How polluted is the air around us? W. Langewiesche. Read Digest 83:117-22 S '63
If your town smells, stop breathing; case of Lewiston, Idaho, and Clarkston, Wash. P. Hirsch. New Repub 150:7-8 Mr 14 '64
Is our environment poisoning us? R. Brecher and E. Brecher. il Parents Mag 38:72-3+ O '63
Leaf-burning pollutes air. Sci N L 84:203 S 28 '63
Meteorology of air pollution. D. H. Pack. bibliog il Science 146:1119-28 N 27 '64
Multibillion-dollar fight against pollution. il Duns R 81:pt2 S113-14+ Mr '63
Nassau County attacks automotive air pollution. K. Kowald. il Am City 78:109 O '63
Ozone formation in air exposed to cobalt-60 gamma radiation. Z. I. Kertesz and G. F. Parsons. bibliog il Science 142:1289-90 D 6 '63
Poison fills the silent sky. B. Tufty. il(p 17) Sci N L 86:26-7 Jl 11 '64
Politics of air pollution. C. Schaeffer. Nation 196:421-3 My 18 '63
Pollution of U.S. air and water: how serious? interview. L. L. Terry. il U S News 55: 98-101 S 16 '63
Pollution stunts plants. Sci N L 86:188 S 19 '64

AIR pollution—*Continued*
Refuse collection and disposal: air-pollution control; excerpts from panel discussion. W. S. Foster. Am City 78:7 Ap '63
Role of the allergist in the battle against air pollution; address, March 1963. F. L. Rosen. Consumer Bul 46:36-8 S '63
Sewers in the sky. Newsweek 62:96 S 23 '63
Sitting on a volcano! J. B. Craig. Am For 70: 11 S '64
Sky-high pollution; exhaust gases from rockets. Newsweek 61:48 F 4 '63
Sulfate particulates: size distribution in Pittsburgh air. M. Corn and L. DeMaio. bibliog il Science 143:803-4 F 21 '64
That hellish and dismal cloud. G. H. T. Kimble. il N Y Times Mag p26+ Ap 21 '63
Toward better air. Nat Parks Mag 38:18 Ag '64
Upper-air pollution. Sci Am 208:74 Mr '63
We are poisoning the air. A. Ribicoff. il Look 27:131-2+ O 22 '63
See also
Air filters
Plants, Effect of smog on
Smog
also subhead Air pollution under names of cities, e.g. Los Angeles—Air pollution

AIR proving grounds. See Proving grounds

AIR pumps
Air mattress inflator bag. il Consumer Rep 28:365 Ag '63

AIR purifiers
Air in coal-burning areas purified by new method. Sci N L 85:376 Je 13 '64
How to clean your house by cleaning the air. il House B 106:153+ Mr '64

AIR races. See Airplane racing

AIR raid alarms
See also
Conelrad warning system

AIR raid drills. See Air raids—Protective measures

AIR raid shelters
House in Wonderland. Nation 197:210-11 O 12 '63
Notes and comment; Underground world home at Worlds fair. New Yorker 40:19 Jl 18 '64
Shelters again; incentive program. New Repub 148:6 My 25 '63
See also
Atomic bomb shelters

AIR raid warning systems
They thought the war was on. L. Dickert. il McCalls 90:96-7+ Ap '63
Wanted: an electronic Paul Revere; CONELRAD; NEAR. E. Nanas. il Pop Electr 18:41-3+ F '63

AIR raids
See also
London—Air raids
World war, 1939-1945—Aerial operations

Protective measures

Cases of conscience. J. Ciardi. Sat R 46:10-11 F 2 '63
See also
Air raid shelters
Radar defense network
Semi-automatic ground environment system

AIR records. See Aviation records

AIR reduction company
Deepest freeze; liquid nitrogen to snap-freeze foods. Bsns W p92 Ag 15 '64

AIR rescue service. See United States—Air force—Air rescue service

AIR routes. See Airways

AIR ships. See Airships

AIR shows. See Aviation—Exhibitions

AIR space transportation (proposed)
Wiltshire boulevard to Broadway in sixty minutes; ASTRA system. W. Boyne. il Sci Digest 53:66-8 Je '63

AIR speed indicators. See Aeronautic instruments

AIR stewardesses. See Airlines—Hostesses

AIR taxi service
Heliport quandary. W. J. Kendall. il Flying 74:26-9+ F '64
New York airways, Sikorsky sign conditional pact for S-61N sale. Aviation W 80:37 F 10 '64
N.Y. fair helicopter agreement approved. Aviation W 80:43 Ja 27 '64
Pan Am may buy Sikorsky S-61Ns for World's fair sightseeing. Aviation W 79:45 D 16 '63
Weight limit curtails helicopters at fair. J. R. Ashlock. Aviation W 80:40-1 My 18 '64

AIR tickets. See Airlines—Tickets

AIR tides. See Atmospheric tides

AIR traffic control
ARTC. D. B. Kuhn. Flying 75:85 Ag '64
Air traffic control blueprint. P. J. Klass. il Aviation W 80:52-4+ Ja 20; 90-1+ Ja 27; 87-91+ F 3 '64
Bringing air safety into the jet age; Project horizon and Project beacon. il Bsns W p70-2 My 4 '63
FAA, Eastern test silent clearance plan. J. R. Ashlock. Aviation W 79:38-9 S 9 '63
FAA, military evaluate HF grid antenna. B. Miller. il Aviation W 79:80-1+ S 2 '63
Gonzalez renews fight with FAA on Texas traffic control center. R. H. Cook. Aviation W 79:42 O 7 '63
Jet transport communications. R. L. Conhaim. il Electr World 70:27-30+ N '63
No-notice checks recommended for curbing cockpit violations. W. Wright. Aviation W 79:40 Jl 1 '63
Northeast decision sets no precedents. L. L. Doty. Aviation W 79:38 Ag 26 '63
RTCA seeks simplified system in examining ATC problems. Aviation W 80:28 Je 22 '64
SST control needs. Aviation W 79:94 D 2 '63
Small Hawaiian carrier defies FAA, CAB in jurisdiction dispute. Aviation W 78:43 Je 10 '63
Technicians score FAA on traffic control. Aviation W 79:36-7 Jl 15 '63
TV in the cockpit: the control of landing aircraft. M. Lodeesen. il Atlan 212:83-6 N '63
Toll booth in the sky; Canada charges airlines for flying over. il Bsns W p 138 F 16 '63
Traffic control is focus of FAA budget; Project beacon. R. H. Cook. Aviation W 80: 52 Ja 27 '64
See also
Airports—Traffic control

AIR traffic control, Military
TSQ-47 traffic system undergoes test; Air force communications service. P. J. Klass. il Aviation W 79:69+ N 11 '63

AIR traffic controllers (persons)
ATCA, Halaby clash on control problems. Aviation W 79:41 O 21 '63
Study reports acute shortage of experienced air controllers. Aviation W 79:54+ D 16 '63

AIR training command. See United States—Air force—Air training command

AIR transport association of America
ATA told to submit to scrutiny by CAB. Aviation W 80:37 F 10 '64
CAB demands sweeping changes in air transport assn. activities. Aviation W 78:41 F 11 '63

AIR travel
Bad-weather day. Newsweek 63:70 F 3 '64
Biggest trek to Europe yet. il Bsns W p34 Mr 23 '63
Era of the seven-league sell; businessman and the jet. il Time 84:76-7 D 18 '64
It's progress, but is it necessary? symposium of industry's leaders. il Bsns W p54-6 My 25 '63
Minister's private experiment in parishioner tourism expanding. il Aviation W 80:42 Mr 2 '64
Supersonic airliner coming; is U.S. losing out to Europe? interview. J. Stack. il U S News 54:50-2 Je 24 '63
Travel notes. R. Joseph. Esquire 60:88-92 D '63
Washington to Moscow: nonstop in less than nine hours now. il U S News 54:14 Je 3 '63
What jet travel does to your metabolic clock. S. W. Bryant. il Fortune 68:160-3+ N '63
Why Johnny won't fly. H. Sutton. Sat R 47: 32-3 N 7 '64
Wiltshire boulevard to Broadway in sixty minutes. W. Boyne. il Sci Digest 53:66-8 Je '63
Wings of the future. E. Hall. il Sci N L 85: 298-9 My 9 '64

Brazil

Life on the fly. il Time 82:27 Ag 30 '63
Travel notes; flying down to Rio. R. Joseph. Esquire 60:91-2 D '63

Caribbean Region

Tourists boost Caribbean airline market. il Aviation W 79:143+ O 7 '63

Latin America

Lifeline in the air. il Time 84:33 Jl 31 '64
Think edit as you country-hop. L. Barry. il Pop Phot 52:24+ Ja '63

United States

Airlines' golden age. il Bsns W p52-3+ Mr 28 '64

AIR travel—United States—*Continued*
Airlines report record Florida traffic. J. W. Carter. Aviation W 80:38-9 Mr 2 '64
Flying holiday suggestions. il Flying 74:28-32+ Je; 75:38-49+ Jl; 42-4+ Ag; 34-6+ S '64
Flying on the cuff. il Bsns W p 115-16 Je 27 '64
Heavy eastern seaboard fog cuts Yule airline operations, revenues. J. R. Ashlock. Aviation W 82:27 Ja 4 '65
Lecture circuit (airborne division) J. Ciardi. Sat R 47:14-15 Je 6 '64
When the fog rolled in; pre-holiday weekend delays. il Bsns W p 18 Ja 2 '65

AIR travel with children. See Travel with children

AIR turbo-exchanger. See Rocket engines

AIRBOATS
Everglades skimmers; riding an airboat over Florida's river of grass. P. Redford. il Motor B 112:44-5+ D '63

AIRBORNE organisms. See Microorganisms, Pathogenic

AIRCARS. See Ground effect machines

AIRCRAFT
See also
Airships

AIRCRAFT carriers
Attack carrier force reduction planned. Aviation W 80:23 F 3 '64
Common sense about uncommon carriers. Sat Eve Post 236:96 N 23 '63
Fight for survival of the supercarrier; fleet admirals vs Secretary McNamara. R. K. Massie. il Sat Eve Post 236:17-25 N 2 '63
Folly of building an obsolescent supercarrier. Sat Eve Post 237:74 F 8 '64
Future navy might lack large carriers. Aviation W 78:35 F 11 '63
Navy building helicopter-attack vessels. W. Wright. il Aviation W 79:114-16 Ag 5 '63
Pulling the carriers' plug. il Time 81:16 Mr 29 '63

AIRCRAFT carriers, Atomic powered
Carrier task force shows nuclear range capabilities; Enterprise. D. E. Fink. il Aviation W 81:94-5+ N 16 '64
Incorrect, illogical, etc; concerning congressional committee report. il Time 83:31 Ja 3 '64
Intuitive nuclear carrier study rejected. Aviation W 78:35 My 6 '63
McNamara shifts policy, seeks nuclear power for large ships. Aviation W 78:37 Ap 15 '63
Mighty Enterprise. N. T. Kenney. il Nat Geog Mag 123:430-48 Mr '63

AIRCRAFT industry. See Airplane industry and trade

AIRCRAFT nuclear propulsion program. See Airplanes. Atomic powered

AIRDOMES. See Domes

AIRDROP
Flex wing tested in Thailand. il Aviation W 80:68 F 24 '64

AIREDALE terriers
Hunting airedale. J. Stetson. il Field & S 68:130-2 F '64

AIRGLOW
Above the green veil; airglow. il Time 82:54 Ag 23 '63
Airglow and the physics of upper atmospheres. J. W. Chamberlain. bibliog il Science 142:921-4 N 15 '63
Night airglow observations from orbiting spacecraft compared with measurements from rockets. M. J. Koomen and others. bibliog il Science 140:1087-9 Je 7 '63

AIRLINE hostesses. See Airlines—Hostesses

AIRLINE mergers. See Airlines—Consolidations and mergers

AIRLINE pilots association. See Air line pilots association. International

AIRLINES
See also
Air travel
Helicopter airlines

Advertising

Notes and comment; concerning advertisement: Thoughts on first class travel of American airlines. il New Yorker 40:33 Mr 14 '64
United tries spice in promotion efforts. J. W. Carter. Aviation W 81:28-9 O 5 '64

Consolidations and mergers

Airline economics distorted, Delta claims. Aviation W 78:45 F 4 '63
Airlines split over mergers, fare goals. L. L. Doty. il Aviation W 78:159-63 Mr 11 '63
Blocking air mergers. Time 81:74+ Je 28 '63
Blow to Eastern; merger with American turned down. Newsweek 62:56 Jl 1 '63
BEA chairman urges Parliament to reject BOAC merger idea. Aviation W 79:47 Ag 19 '63
CAB bureau criticizes Toolco agreement. R. G. O'Lone. Aviation W 81:40 O 26 '64
Court voids CAB order on Toolco-TWA. J. W. Carter. Aviation W 81:30-1 D 14 '64
Downbeat on mergers. Time 81:94+ Mr 15 '63
Explanation of merger rejection awaited: American-Eastern merger. Aviation W 79:38-9 Jl 1 '63
Garrett opposes Curtiss offer. Aviation W 79:39 S 16 '63
Grabbing again for TWA controls. il Bsns W p 168+ My 16 '64
How to survive without merging; CAB foils American, Eastern merger. Bsns W p30-1 Je 29 '63
Insurance firm probe may stall merger. Aviation W 78:41 Ap 1 '63
Merger seen as competitive tool. Aviation W 79:39 Ag 12 '63
Mergers: a new look by the New frontier. U S News 54:11 Mr 18 '64
Northeast, Hughes file trust agreement; step toward regaining Trans World airlines. J. W. Carter. Aviation W 81:34-5 O 12 '64
Pan Am-Panagra move opposed. Aviation W 78:37 Ap 29 '63
Pan Am, TWA seek early merger action. Aviation W 78:45 Mr 18 '63
Pan American's bid for chosen instrument status. L. L. Doty. Aviation W 78:38-9+ Mr 25; 41+ Ap 1; 42-3 Ap 8 '63
Seaboard president attacks case for Pan American-TWA merger; summary of address. R. M. Jackson. Aviation W 78:44 Ja 21 '63
Three groups formed by Hawker Siddeley. Aviation W 78:93-4 My 27 '63
Total Pan Am-Panagra merger is proposed. Aviation W 79:30 D 30 '63
Tough line on rail, air mergers; from intergovernmental committee. Bsns W p 140 Mr 16 '63
TWA enthusiasm for merger is wavering. L. L. Doty. Aviation W 78:33 Mr 4 '63
Trans World, Continental discuss merger. L. L. Doty. Aviation W 79:34-5 O 28 '63

Cooperative ownership

Cooperative flying boat hauls cargo. W. Wright. il Aviation W 80:38-9 Ja 6 '64

Credit cards

See Credit cards

Employees

Airline vote halted in fight with NMB. Bsns W p46 My 11 '63
BOAC staff cut scored by Labor party. H. J. Coleman. Aviation W 81:36 O 12 '64
CAB demands sweeping changes in air transport assn. activities. Aviation W 78:41 F 11 '63
Low wages cited in investigation of airline manpower shortage. Aviation W 81:32 Jl 13 '64
Outlook and trends in civil aviation employment. S. H. Luskin. il Mo Labor R 86:1290-6 N '63

Fares

Air fare down, confusion up; with editorial comment. il Bsns W p 116+, 164 Mr 16 '63
Air fares, and how they grew so jumbled. il Consumer Rep 29:448-9 S '64
Air fares are a mess. il Changing T 18:41-6 Jl '64
Air fares are coming down to earth. W. Langewiesche. il Read Digest 85:63-7 Ag '64
Air fares will drop. il Bsns W p 121-2+ S 7 '63
Airlines are bystanders in fare dispute. L. L. Doty. Aviation W 78:34-5 My 27 '63
Atlantic air fares. America 108:732 My 25 '63
Atlantic fare battle. R. Hotz. Aviation W 78:17 My 27 '63
Bid to extend three-class fare opposed. J. R. Ashlock. Aviation W 78:36 Ja 28 '63
Board rebuffs planned reductions to ease West Coast fare battle. Aviation W 81:37 O 12 '64
Board unit proposes fare policy. Aviation W 81:41 S 14 '64
Boyd warns of sterner CAB fare policy. J. R. Ashlock. Aviation W 80:42-3 Ja 27 '64
British say: raise air fares, or else. Bsns W p34 My 4 '63
Carriers flock to credit card bandwagon. J. W. Carter. Aviation W 81:30-1 Ag 31 '64
Changes in the air. il Time 81:75-6 F 8 '63

AIRLINES—Fares—*Continued*

CAB approves Pan Am-Qantas joint fare. Aviation W 79:31 S 2 '63
CAB asked to review economy fare ruling. Aviation W 82:29 Ja 11 '65
CAB nears economy fares case decision. R. G. O'Lone. Aviation W 81:38-9 O 19 '64
CAB seeking accurate reduced fare analyses. Aviation W 79:46 N 11 '63
CAB seeks to end domestic fare chaos. L. L. Doty. Aviation W 80:34-6 Ja 13 '64
Class struggle. Newsweek 61:72-4 F 4 '63
Confusion clouds international air travel. L. L. Doty. Aviation W 78:40-1 Ap 8 '63
Cutting transatlantic fares. R. Hotz. Aviation W 79:21 Jl 1 '63
Declassé; United air lines one-class service. Newsweek 64:62 Jl 6 '64
DOD regulation seeks first-class fare curb. Aviation W 79:96+ S 16 '63
El Al will seek changes in group fare. J. W. Carter. Aviation W 81:39 S 14 '64
Europeans flood in. il Bsns W p92 Je 6 '64
Fairer fares. Time 83:68 Ja 10 '64
Family fare plan producing shift to first class as traffic climbs. Aviation W 79:39 Ag 19 '63
Family fight over family fares; airlines fight over family fares. Bsns W p36 S 28 '63
Fare is foul, foul is fare for overseas air customers. il Newsweek 61:75 My 27 '63
Fares down, passengers up. Time 83:86 Mr 27 '64
First-class revenue drop spurs support for single-class service. Aviation W 78:44 F 18 '63
Great air-fare snare. M. Elfin. Reporter 30: 36-8 Mr 12 '64
Hildred urges new lures for IATA market; Bogota meeting. J. R. Ashlock. Aviation W 81:38-9 S 14 '64
How to fix prices. Nat R 14:439 Je 4 '63
Impact of reduced fares felt in Pacific. H. D. Watkins. il Aviation W 79:156-7+ O 7 '63
Industry wary of Eastern fare revisions. R. G. O'Lone. Aviation W 82:27-8 Ja 11 '65
IATA delegates seek end to fare battle; with editorial comment. L. L. Doty. Aviation W 79:21, 26-8 O 7 '63
IATA fares chaos could force governments to negotiate rates. Aviation W 78:41 Ap 22 '63
IATA fares dispute aids U.S. airlines. L. L. Doty. Aviation W 78:36 Je 3 '63
IATA traffic meeting recesses; early fare solution is unlikely. Aviation W 79:45 N 4 '63
Key Athens issues include credit, fares. J. W. Carter. Aviation W 81:36 S 21 '64
Knuckling under; international air fares. Time 81:94 My 24 '63
Legislation is key to Pacific fares. R. G. O'Lone. Aviation W 81:29 D 21 '64
Legislators cool to CAB foreign rate plea. J. R. Ashlock. Aviation W 80:28-9 Je 8 '64
London and back for $320? Bsns W p31 Je 29 '63
Lots of class; United air lines three-class service. il Time 84:79 Jl 3 '64
Lower cost Trippe. Time 82:84 Jl 5 '63
Major fare changes seen unlikely to follow IATA traffic session. L. L. Doty. Aviation W 81:39-40 O 19 '64
Nassau pact; IATA agree on new schedule of transatlantic fares. Newsweek 62:61 D 23 '63
Nations agree to retain IATA fares role. L. L. Doty. Aviation W 79:28-9 Jl 29 '63
New U.S. policy backfires in rate fight. L. L. Doty. Aviation W 78:39-40 My 20 '63
North Atlantic carriers bypass IATA, initiate Nassau fare plan. Aviation W 80:36 Ja 13 '64
One-class fare gets competition from reduced first-class ticket. J. W. Carter. Aviation W 80:31 Ap 6 '64
One-class fare stems shift from coach. L. L. Doty. Aviation W 79:43 S 16 '63
One-up-in-the-airmanship. M. T. Bloom. il N Y Times Mag p28+ Ja 10 '65
Other carriers likely to oppose Continental economy fare ruling. Aviation W 81:34 D 21 '64
Pace of Athens meeting slowed by infighting over group fares. Aviation W 81:39 O 26 '64
PSA slashes fares in West Coast battle. Aviation W 82:34 Ja 11 '65
Pan Am acts to cut fares to Caribbean. Bsns W p89 D 5 '64
Pan Am's ploy; suggested new thrift class. Newsweek 62:68 Jl 8 '63
Passengers never had it so good. il Bsns W p 124+ O 17 '64
Power play; international air fares. Newsweek 61:75 My 6 '63
Protests flood in as air fare dam breaks. Bsns W p34 My 18 '63
Renewal of three-class service expected. J. R. Ashlock. il Aviation W 79:40-2 S 16 '63
Restriction on fare veto asked at Bogota. J. R. Ashlock. Aviation W 81:35 S 21 '64
Santa goes to war; airlines cut fares on San Francisco to Los Angeles route. il Time 85:65 Ja 1 '65
Scramble for LA-SF traffic intensifies; new fares and services. il Aviation W 81:43+ S 14 '64
Senate group hears CAB plan for widespread fare reductions. R. H. Cook. Aviation W 80:39 Ap 27 '64
Storm over the Atlantic. il Time 81:95 My 3 '63
Swissair seeks simplified Atlantic fares. Aviation W 80:41 Je 15 '64
Three carriers indicate general approval of Pan Am fare proposal. Aviation W 79:30 Jl 8 '63
Tours de force. Newsweek 61:85 F 25 '63
Traffic boost seen in twenty-one day winter fare. J. W. Carter. il Aviation W 81:37-8 O 26 '64
Transatlantic air fares. New Repub 148:5 My 25 '63
Travel notes. R. Joseph. Esquire 62:16 Jl '64
Trunklines resist Eastern fare package. R. G. O'Lone. il Aviation W 82:34-5 Ja 18 '65
United gives up on one class. Bsns W p36 Je 27 '64
United single-class fare causes concern. J. R. Ashlock. Aviation W 78:45+ Ap 8 '63
U.S. draws a bead on IATA; international air fares. Bsns W p30-1 My 25 '63
U.S.-European air transport rift widens. L. L. Doty. Aviation W 79:28-9 S 2 '63
U.S. views on international air rate policy; statement, July 18, 1963. A. S. Boyd. Dept State Bul 49:247-8 Ag 12 '63
West Coast fare cuts trigger new proposals. Aviation W 81:38 S 21 '64
What's the air fare? well, it depends . . . il U S News 55:84-6 Jl 22 '63
Who pays the fare? New Repub 149:6 Jl 13 '63
Wide gap separates carriers on fare cut. L. L. Doty. Aviation W 79:38-9 S 30 '63

Anecdotes, facetiae, satire, etc.

Alitalia twits carriers on fares muddle; reprint. il Aviation W 78:47+ Je 24 '63

Federal aid

Board proposes $1-million subsidy cut. R. G. O'Lone. Aviation W 81:42 S 7 '64

Feeder airlines

See Local service airlines

Finance

Airline business soars to new high altitude. Bsns W p44 S 26 '64
Airline economics distorted, Delta claims. Aviation W 78:45 F 4 '63
Airline income and expenses; tables. See occasional issues of Aviation week & space technology
Airline net to top $200 million in 1964; with editorial comment. J. R. Ashlock. Aviation W 81:11, 28 D 21 '64
Airlines fear tax cut may bring U.S. airways user charge system. R. H. Cook. Aviation W 78:45 F 25 '63
Airlines pull over the hump. il Bsns W p 130+ S 7 '63
Airlines split over mergers, fare goals. L. L. Doty. il Aviation W 78:159-63 Mr 11 '63
American, Northwest, United earnings rise. Aviation W 80:43 Mr 2 '64
Atlantic carriers foresee higher earnings. il Aviation W 80:174-9 Mr 16 '64
BOAC, BEA revenue increases spur renewed British optimism. Aviation W 79:49+ O 7 '63
Capital funds up to $50 million provided by joint financing plan; for long-term lease or purchase of aircraft. Aviation W 80:21 Mr 30 '64
Competition stirs transcontinental traffic. J. W. Carter. Aviation W 80:26-7 Je 29 '64
Domestic trunks near reasonable return. R. G. O'Lone. Aviation W 82:26-7 Ja 4 '65
Financial plight is major obstacle confronting new BOAC chairman. H. J. Coleman. Aviation W 79:39-40 D 2 '63
First reports indicate substantial six-month profit for trunklines. Aviation W 79:47 Ag 12 '63
Four carriers report higher 1962 earnings. Aviation W 78:47 Ap 1 '63
Good times come to the airlines. il U S News 58:80 Ja 4 '65
Government files $1.2-million tax claim against Umbaugh aircraft. D. A. Brown. Aviation W 78:32 Ap 22 '63

AIRLINES—Finance—*Continued*
Heavy eastern seaboard fog cuts Yule airline operations, revenues. J. R. Ashlock. Aviation W 82:27 Ja 4 '65
Hughes makes new pass at TWA. Bsns W p32 O 10 '64
Increases in airline operating revenues; table. Aviation W 78:45 My 6; 79:77 O 7 '63
Indian airlines faces equipment shortage. J. R. Ashlock. il Aviation W 79:42-3 D 2 '63
Jets decrease all-cargo operating losses. R. G. O'Lone. Aviation W 81:35-6 N 23 '64
Long-term airline prospects seen bright. Aviation W 81:39 N 16 '64
MacIntyre gives view on Northeast finances. Aviation W 79:32 S 2 '63
1963 trunk profit may pass $100 million. L. L. Doty. Aviation W 79:29-30 D 30 '63
North American sales set industry record. Aviation W 81:29 N 16 '64
Northwest president sees twelve per cent gain in 1965 operating revenue. Aviation W 81:48 S 21 '64
Pan Am, TWA have record earnings. Aviation W 81:30 Ag 3 '64
Record trunkline profits seen for 1963. L. L. Doty. Aviation W 79:44 N 11 '63
Seven trunks list record profits as air travel boom continues. Aviation W 81:28 N 2 '64
TWA, Pan American report record profits. Aviation W 79:45 N 4 '63
Trunkline financial status dispute flares during merger hearings. Aviation W 78:43+ F 25 '63
Trunkline 1962 profit may top $25 million. Aviation W 78:42-3 F 18 '63
Turbine aircraft, 1962 operating costs, cents per mile; table. Aviation W 78:47 My 20 '63
Turbine powered aircraft 1962 operating expense; dollars per total aircraft hour. Aviation W 78:42-3 My 13 '63
U.S. airline assets and liabilities; tables. Aviation W 78:41 Ap 29; 79:79 O 7 '63; 80:46 My 25; 81:41 S 21 '64
U.S. airline operating revenues and expenses, 1962; table. Aviation W 78:46-7 My 6 '63
U.S. trunklines head for record earnings. L. L. Doty. Aviation W 80:33 My 25 '64
World airlines operating revenues, expenses, 1957-1962; table. Aviation W 79:84 O 7 '63

Freight service

See Air freight service; Airplanes, Freight

Hostesses

Aeroflot maintenance, hostess training shown. il Aviation W 81:30-1 Ag 10 '64
Flying sisters; Catlin sisters of Northwest airlines. il Ebony 20:81-2+ N '64
Guinea airline hostesses train in Canada. il Ebony 18:71-2+ F '63
Hard-selling stewardesses. L. Morse. Duns R 84:49-50 Jl '64
Kiwi at thirty-two. il Time 81:84 Ap 26 '63
Mrs Air France; married hostesses. Newsweek 61:76+ My 13 '63
Open skies for Negro girls. il Ebony 18:43-6+ Je '63
Thirty-two skiddoo. il Newsweek 61:56 Ap 8 '63
Travel notes; Cloud college, United air lines stewardess school. R. Joseph. Esquire 62: 19-20+ Ag '64

Anecdotes, facetiae, satire, etc.

Notes and comment; proper age. New Yorker 39:33 My 4 '63

International aspects

See Aviation—International aspects

Maintenance and repair

Airlines off course? D. Teetor. il Flying 75: 64-6 S '64
TWA develops vane straightener. Aviation W 79:30 S 2 '63

Management

Airline takes the marginal route; Continental air lines. il Bsns W p 111-12+ Ap 20 '63
Rosier horizons. R. Hotz. Aviation W 79:21 N 18 '63
Trunklines face management transition. L. L. Doty. il Aviation W 80:161-3 Mr 16 '64

Passenger service

ARCH to the rescue: Airline baggage recovery clearing house. Time 83:77 My 15 '64
ATC studies baggage rate plan. Aviation W 81:37 N 9 '64
Air shuttle soaring. il Bsns W p 130 Ap 27 '63
American credit plan includes car rentals. Aviation W 81:36 D 21 '64
Better passenger service. R. Hotz. Aviation W 81:11 D 14 '64
Changes in the air. il Time 81:75-6 F 8 '63
CAB grants carriers permission for further baggage discussions. Aviation W 81:36 D 21 '64
Class warfare. il Time 82:75-6 S 6 '63
Coffee, tea or Doris Day; introduction on inflight entertainment. il Time 84:103-4 O 16 '64
Convention challenge met by air services. Aviation W 81:19-20 Ag 31 '64
High see; movies in the air. il Time 84:87 Jl 10 '64
Industry, CAB scrutinize baggage charges. R. G. O'Lone. Aviation W 81:41+ O 12 '64
Inflight entertainment spread expected. J. W. Carter. Aviation W 81:28-9 D 7 '64
In-flight movies slated on United in November. Aviation W 81:42 O 26 '64
Little problem that wasn't there: no-show problem Consumer Rep 28:100 Mr '63
Meat and movies up there; dispensations from law of abstinence. America 111:683 N 28 '64
Northeast leases jet equipment, plans eighteen daily flights to Florida. Aviation W 79:40 N 18 '63
One-class fare stems shift from coach. L. L. Doty. Aviation W 79:43 S 16 '63
Pan Am adopts films; rate cut remote. J. W. Carter. Aviation W 82:36 Ja 18 '65
Passengers never had it so good. il Bsns W p 124+ O 17 '64
Scramble for LA-SF traffic intensifies; new fares and services. il Aviation W 81:43+ S 14 '64
Short flight; demonstration of Astrovision by American airlines. New Yorker 40:47 D 5 '64
Show biz in the sky. Newsweek 64:77-8 O 19 '64
United tries spice in promotion efforts: inflight entertainment. J. W. Carter. Aviation W 81:28-9 O 5 '64

Anecdotes, facetiae, satire, etc.

Expense-account economy: a traveler's hardships. Fortune 67:106+ My '63

Passenger traffic

See Airlines—Traffic

Purchasing

TWA goes on the road to get suppliers. il Bsns W p 138+ Ja 26 '63

Rates

See Airlines—Fares

Regulations

See Aviation—Laws and regulations

Reservation systems

SABRE, a $30-million application. il Fortune 69:142-5+ Ap '64

Routes

See Airways

Safety devices and measures

See Aviation—Safety devices and measures

Salaries

Airlines report officer salaries, holdings (title varies) See occasional issues of Aviation week & space technology to August 12, 1963
Low wages cited in investigation of airline manpower shortage. Aviation W 81:32 Jl 13 '64
Three airlines report officers' remuneration. Aviation W 78:104-5 My 6 '63

Securities

Stock answer; airline stocks rising. Newsweek 63:73-4 Ap 13 '64

Shops

See Airlines—Maintenance and repair

Statistics

Airline traffic. See issues of Aviation week & space technology
Daily average turbine aircraft utilizations by U.S. scheduled airlines; table. Aviation W 79:84 O 7 '63
International airline traffic results, 1962; table. Aviation W 79:69 O 7 '63
North Atlantic air passengers and load factors; table. Aviation W 81:48-9 S 14 '64
Passenger-mile revenue declines. il Aviation W 80:40 Je 15 '64
Passengers enplaned by U.S. flag carriers in Latin America; table. Aviation W 79:133 O 7 '63

AIRLINES—Statistics—*Continued*
Turbine aircraft load factors in scheduled service; table. Aviation W 79:75 O 7 '63; 81:57 S 14 '64
Turbine aircraft operating expenses, dollars per revenue hour; table. Aviation W 79:73 O 7 '63
U.S. airline scheduled service traffic growth first six months, 1963 over 1962; table. Aviation W 79:45 Ag 26 '63
U.S. airline scheduled service traffic growth; table. Aviation W 81:72 S 14 '64
U.S. scheduled service load factors. Jan.-June, 1963; table. Aviation W 79:44 Ag 26 '63
U.S. scheduled service load factors. Jan.-June, 1964; tables. Aviation W 81:77 S 14 '64

Taxation

Budget to include airways user tax plan. J. R. Ashlock. Aviation W 81:24 D 28 '64

Ticket offices

Pan Am ticket office; an airy sweep of sculptured space. il Arch Forum 119:98-101 Ag '63
Ticket offices in New York and Houston. il Arch Forum 119:102-5 N '63

Tickets

Air tickets brew a dogfight. il Bsns W p53-4 N 7 '64
Airline statement lists guidelines for safeguarding of ticket stock. Aviation W 80:47 Je 15 '64
Airlines planning ticket swindle defense. J. W. Carter. Aviation W 80:26-8 Mr 23 '64
Carrier concern mounting over rising ticket frauds and thefts. Aviation W 80:41 My 11 '64
Fly now, pay never; stolen airlines tickets. Newsweek 63:80+ Mr 16 '64
Old shell game takes to the air; cashing in phony airline tickets. il Bsns W p 132+ Je 13 '64
Single ticket form extended to thirteen states. Aviation W 81:32 D 14 '64
Ticket theft ring suspected in New York. W. H. Gregory. Aviation W 81:37+ N 23 '64
Tighter security for ticket stock urged. J. W. Carter. Aviation W 80:42 My 18 '64

Traffic

Airlines report record Florida traffic. J. W. Carter. Aviation W 80:38-9 Mr 2 '64
Airlines split over mergers, fare goals. L. L Doty. il Aviation W 78:159-63 Mr 11 '63
April trunk traffic rise brings load factor to nine-month high. Aviation W 78:40-1 My 20 '63
Atlantic carriers foresee higher earnings. il Aviation W 80:174-9 Mr 16 '64
Atlantic traffic surging toward record. J. W. Carter. Aviation W 81:26-7 Jl 20 '64
Canadian transatlantic traffic increases. D. A. Brown. Aviation W 81:32 D 21 '64
Delta April traffic increases 25 per cent; general gain seen for carriers. J. R. Ashlock. Aviation W 78:39+ My 6 '63
Domestic airline traffic results indicate record for six months. Aviation W 81:28 Jl 27 '64
Family fare plan producing shift to first class as traffic climbs. Aviation W 79:39 Ag 19 '63
Florida traffic reflects January pickup. J. R. Ashlock. Aviation W 78:38-9 F 4 '63
Foreign carrier concern growing as tourists shift to U.S. airlines. J. R. Ashlock. Aviation W 78:41 Je 10 '63
Four airlines achieve single-day traffic records as holidays end. Aviation W 82:29 Ja 11 '65
Frontier airlines pushes sales campaign. il Aviation W 78:43 My 20 '63
Last-half gain spurs domestic trunk traffic to 14 per cent rise in 1963. Aviation W 80:39 Ja 20 '64
Locals show heavy February gains, but trunkline figures vary widely. Aviation W 78:47 Ap 8 '63
Record transatlantic business expected. J. W. Carter. Aviation W 80:40-1 Ap 20 '64
Renewal of three-class service expected. J. R. Ashlock. il Aviation W 79:40-2 S 16 '63
Substantial rise in Florida market seen. R. G. O'Lone. Aviation W 82:33-4 Ja 25 '65
Traffic boost seen in twenty-one day winter fare. J. W. Carter. il Aviation W 81:37-8 O 26 '64
Trunkline 1962 profit may top $25 million. Aviation W 78:42-3 F 18 '63
Trunklines face management transition. L. L. Doty. il Aviation W 80:161-3 Mr 16 '64
U.S. lines brace for record Yule traffic. J. R. Ashlock. Aviation W 81:30 D 7 '64
See also
Aviation—Transatlantic flights

Africa

Africa sees air transport key to growth. R. H. Cook. Aviation W 79:152+ O 7 '63
Airline grows despite federation unrest. R. H. Cook. il Aviation W 78:42-3 F 11 '63
Independence of four territories may give East African airways new problems. R. H. Cook. il Aviation W 78:40-1+ F 4 '63

Alaska

Airlines in major Alaskan recovery role. R. G. O'Lone. il Aviation W 80:38-40 Ap 13 '64
Alaskan carriers eye Skyvan, Nord 262. R. G. O'Lone. Aviation W 80:43 Ap 20 '64

Argentina

Cooperative flying boat hauls cargo. W. Wright. il Aviation W 80:38-9 Ja 6 '64

Australia

Grim determination in the air. il Time 84:85 Ag 7 '64

Austria

Austrian airlines plans first domestic service. Aviation W 78:43 F 4 '63
Caravelle 6Rs boost AUA growth rate. E. Walford. il Aviation W 82:45-6 Ja 25 '65

Belgium

Sabena president sees chance for profit. J. W. Carter. il Aviation W 80:46-7 Je 15 '64

Bulgaria

Tabso seeks turbojets to boost traffic. E. Walford. il Aviation W 78:42-3 Ap 22 '63

Canada

Canadian transatlantic traffic increases. D. A. Brown. Aviation W 81:32 D 21 '64
Quebec airline achieves 12,000-hr. TBO. D. A. Brown. il Aviation W 81:53-4 D 28 '64
Support concept cuts surveying costs; Quebec Labrador airways. D. A. Brown. il Aviation W 81:103-5 N 9 '64

China (People's Republic)

Red Chinese carrier seeks new aircraft. W. H. Gregory. il Aviation W 80:43+ F 17 '64

Czechoslovakia

Czech carrier stresses route extension. E. Walford. il Aviation W 81:28-30 D 28 '64

Denmark

Minister's private experiment in parishioner tourism expanding. il Aviation W 80:42 Mr 2 '64

Egypt

Egypt seeks long-range jets, U.S. rights; United Arab airlines. R. H. Cook. il Aviation W 78:42-3+ Ja 28 '63
Egyptian carrier buys DC-6Bs. Aviation W 80:42 F 17 '64
Equipment gap faces Egyptian airline. C. Brownlow. il Aviation W 79:87+ O 7 '63

Ethiopia

Ethiopian carrier faces jet competition. R. H. Cook. il Aviation W 78:45+ Ja 21 '63

Europe, Eastern

East Europe airlines renew bids to West. E. Walford. il Aviation W 79:108-9+ O 7 '63

Europe, Western

European airlines report gains in domestic, intraeuropean yield. L. L. Doty. Aviation W 81:29 Jl 20 '64
Tax-free sales boost European carriers. E. Walford. il Aviation W 79:46-7 S 30 '63

Far East

Far East's lively little airline; Cathay Pacific. il Bsns W p 120+ S 14 '63

Finland

Finnair concentrates on route expansion. E. Walford. il Aviation W 81:50-1+ N 9 '64

France

Air France adopts BOAC show us attitude on supersonic transport. H. J. Coleman. Aviation W 78:39 Ja 28 '63
Air France African routes reduced. Aviation W 79:46 N 11 '63
Expanding Air inter plans foreign route. E. Walford. il Aviation W 80:31-2 Mr 23 '64

AIRLINES—France—*Continued*
Veterans D-day tour planned by Air France. Aviation W 80:47 Mr 2 '64

Germany (Democratic Republic)

East Germany reincorporated flag carrier; name is changed. Aviation W 79:51 S 9 '63

Germany (Federal Republic)

Lufthansa hopes break-even point near. E. Walford. il Aviation W 79:32-3 D 30 '63
Lufthansa is seeking short-range jets. E. Walford. Aviation W 78:45 Mr 4 '63
Lufthansa's $25,000 profit first in history. Aviation W 80:43 Je 15 '64

Great Britain

British Eagle appeals decision. Aviation W 79:43 D 23 '63
BEA chairman urges Parliament to reject BOAC merger idea. Aviation W 79:47 Ag 19 '63
BOAC, BEA revenue increases spur renewed British optimism. Aviation W 79:49+ O 7 '63
BOAC, BEA view with independents. Aviation W 78:40 Ap 22 '63
See also
British European airways corporation
British overseas airways corporation

Greece, Modern

Greek flag carrier seeking route to U.S. il Aviation W 81:36-7 D 7 '64

Guinea

Guinea airline hostesses train in Canada. il Ebony 18:71-2+ F '63

Hawaii

BAC 111 operation would reverse losses, Hawaiian airlines claims. L. L. Doty. Aviation W 78:37 Ja 28 '63
Lone DC-4 plays short-haul role in Island airlines-FAA struggle. Aviation W 79:39 Jl 15 '63
Overseas flight, or local hop? CAB in jurisdiction dispute. il Bsns W p31-2 D 26 '64
Small Hawaiian carrier defies FAA, CAB in jurisdiction dispute. Aviation W 78:43 Je 10 '63

Iceland

Airborne David v. Goliath; Icelandic airlines. Time 83:101 F 28 '64
Icelandic buys two CL-44 transports. Aviation W 80:47 F 24 '64

India

Air-India pushes route, fleet expansion. J. R. Ashlock. il Aviation W 79:41+ N 18 '63
Indian airlines faces equipment shortage. J. R. Ashlock. il Aviation W 79:42-3 D 2 '63

Ireland

Over the sea, ethnically. il Time 82:100 O 25 '63

Israel

El Al will seek changes in group fare. J. W. Carter. Aviation W 81:39 S 14 '64
Over the sea, ethnically. il Time 82:100 O 25 '63
Present El Al jet fleet may be expanded. C. Brownlow. il Aviation W 80:30-2 Je 8 '64

Jamaica

British carriers to form Jamaican airline. J. R. Ashlock. Aviation W 78:40 Mr 18 '63

Japan

Japan renews bid for SF-London route. L. Booda. Aviation W 80:45+ My 18 '64

Kenya

African operation handling varied tasks. R. H. Cook. il Aviation W 78:113-14 My 6 '63

Latin America

Competition stiffening in South America. W. Wright. il Aviation W 79:128-9+ O 7 '63
Lower-fare jet service challenges IATA. W. Wright. il Aviation W 79:40-1 D 2 '63

Lebanon

Flying shiek; privately owned Middle East airlines. il Time 84:96+ S 4 '64
Lebanese airways seeking jets to maintain competitive status. il Aviation W 79:47+ O 14 '63
Lebanese study route to South America. il Aviation W 79:99+ O 7 '63

Malaysia

Malaysian airways prefers leasing plan. J. R. Ashlock. il Aviation W 80:50-2 Ja 6 '64

Mexico

Mexicana will expand service, seat capacity. Aviation W 78:47 Ap 8 '63

Netherlands

Financial woes, internal strife face KLM. C. Brownlow. Aviation W 79:41 N 25 '63
Government ponders KLM board shuffle. C. Brownlow. Aviation W 79:50 D 16 '63
KLM optimistic on financial prospects. J. W. Carter. il Aviation W 80:38-9+ My 11 '64
Why KLM is in trouble. Bsns W p34 Ja 19 '63

Pakistan

Choppers over Pakistan; helicopter service of Pakistan international airlines. il Time 82:92 D 13 '63
In Pakistan, flooded rails give helicopters a boost; helicopter operations of PIA. il Bsns W p88+ D 14 '63
Major overhauls, economics cause Pakistan transatlantic suspension. Aviation W 79:49 S 30 '63
Pakistan airlines plans to resume transatlantic route after 1966. J. W. Carter. Aviation W 80:27 Je 8 '64
Pakistan route could link U.S, Russia. L. L. Doty. Aviation W 79:43 O 21 '63
Pakistan seeks more Russia, China routes. Aviation W 80:50 Ja 20 '64
Pakistani carrier obtains access agreement from Communist China. Aviation W 78:40 Je 24 '63

Philippines

Problems slow Philippine air expansion. L. Booda. il Aviation W 80:31-2 My 4 '64

Poland

Polish carrier plans start of jet service. E. Walford. il Aviation W 79:32-3 Jl 8 '63

Rumania

Romanian carrier plans Tu-124 purchase; Tarom Romanian air transport. E. Walford. il Aviation W 79:47+ D 9 '63

Russia

Aeroflot falls short of traffic objective. il Aviation W 80:182-3+ Mr 16 '64
Aeroflot introducing An-24 on local routes. Aviation W 79:43 Ag 5 '63
Aeroflot maintenance, hostess training shown. il Aviation W 81:30-1 Ag 10 '64
Aeroflot may be resuming rapid growth. il Aviation W 79:121+ O 7 '63
Excess capacity tempers Aeroflot growth; traffic falls short of goal. il Aviation W 78:178-82 Mr 11 '63
Halaby remark draws stiff Soviet reply. Aviation W 78:36 Mr 25 '63
New York-Moscow route decision due. L. L. Doty. il Aviation W 80:34+ Ja 6 '64
Nonstop to Moscow; report of flight from Havana. E. Stevens. il Time 81:23 Mr 22 '63
Peek beneath Aeroflot's veil. il Bsns W p62-4 D 21 '63
Rails curtailed in move to boost Aeroflot. Aviation W 79:41 Jl 1 '63
Regular U.S.-Russia flights now unlikely; with editorial comment. L. L. Doty. Aviation W 80:21, 38-9 F 24 '64
Russia's total airline; Aeroflot. A. Chamberlin. il Sat Eve Post 237:63-4 N 28 '64

Scandinavia

See also
Scandinavian airlines system

South Africa

Blockade in the air; banning of South African aircraft from airports and airspace. il Time 82:23 S 6 '63

South America

See Airlines—Latin America

Spain

Management shift spurs Iberia expansion. L. L. Doty. Aviation W 78:49 F 25 '63

Switzerland

Swiss charter carrier reflects continuing growth, pushes equipment expansion plans. E. Walford. il Aviation W 80:36-8 Je 22 '64
Swiss charter expanding turboprop fleet; Globe air ag. E. Walford. il Aviation W 81:34+ Ag 31 '64
Tiny airline with a sharp riposte; Swissair. il Bsns W p 108-10 Ja 11 '64

United States

Airline net to top $200 million in 1964; with editorial comment. J. R. Ashlock. Aviation W 81:11, 28 D 21 '64

AIRLINES—United States—*Continued*
Airlines' golden age. il Bsns W p52-3+ Mr 28 '64
Airlines split over mergers, fare goals. L. L. Doty. il Aviation W 78:159-63 Mr 11 '63
Boyd favors quality competition instead of quantity in some areas. Aviation W 79:31 S 2 '63
Change of pilots. Time 84:81 Jl 17 '64
Da Kine way to travel; Walton Wood and his comic-opera Island airlines. Newsweek 62:65+ Jl 15 '63
Domestic airline traffic results indicate record for six months. Aviation W 81:28 Jl 27 '64
Domestic trunks near reasonable return. R. G. O'Lone. Aviation W 82:26-7 Ja 4 '65
Forecast. R. Hotz. il Aviation W 78:68-70 Mr 11 '63
Good times come to the airlines. il U S News 58:80 Ja 4 '65
Long-term airline prospects seen bright. Aviation W 81:39 N 16 '64
Monroney supports all-cargo carriers. Aviation W 81:29 Jl 13 '64
Northeast decision seen aimed at Hughes. R. H. Cook. Aviation W 78:38-9 Ap 22 '63
Substantial rise in Florida market seen. R. G. O'Lone. Aviation W 82:33-4 Ja 25 '65
Trunklines resist Eastern fare package. R. G. O'Lone. il Aviation W 82:34-5 Ja 18 '65
Trunks support extension of SST study. J. R. Ashlock. Aviation W 81:28 D 14 '64
U.S. lines brace for record Yule traffic. J. R. Ashlock. Aviation W 81:30 D 7 '64
When the fog rolled in; pre-holiday weekend delays. il Bsns W p 18 Ja 2 '65
Who will fly the charters? nonscheduled, supplemental carriers. il Bsns W p47-8+ Ja 16 '65
See also
Local service airlines
Strikes—United States—Airlines
also names of airlines, e.g. American airlines, incorporated

Yugoslavia

Yugoslav carrier reflects steady growth. E. Walford. il Aviation W 81:32-3 Jl 20 '64

AIRLINES, Local service. See Local service airlines
AIRMEN. See Air pilots
AIRPLANE accidents. See Aviation—Accidents
AIRPLANE auctions. See Auctions
AIRPLANE brakes. See Brakes, Airplane
AIRPLANE building. See Airplanes—Manufacture
AIRPLANE carriers. See Aircraft carriers
AIRPLANE cockpits
FAA to test simplified cockpit layout; Project little guy. D. A. Brown. Aviation W 78:115+ F 18 '63
AIRPLANE collisions. See Aviation—Accidents
AIRPLANE construction. See Airplanes—Manufacture
AIRPLANE crews
ALPA threatens to expel four at American. Aviation W 78:41 Mr 18 '63
Engineer meeting delays American pact. J. R. Ashlock. Aviation W 78:35 Mr 4 '63
New airline labor fight looms over FAA's proposed crew cut. R. H. Cook. Aviation W 80:35 My 11 '64

Training

American designs and builds crew training aids. il Aviation W 80:35 Mr 9 '64
American engineers still ask pilot rating. Aviation W 79:47 S 9 '63

AIRPLANE engines
Convair will proceed with Dart refit kits. Aviation W 81:43 N 9 '64
More emphasis on V/STOL engines urged. Aviation W 82:27 Ja 18 '65
Rolls expands range of V/STOL engine development efforts. W. C. Wetmore. il Aviation W 81:78-80+ S 7 '64
Snecma TF-106 engine may be cut by French. Aviation W 80:31 F 17 '64
240 airframe bolstered for Dart engine. D. A. Brown. il Aviation W 81:41+ S 28 '64
UAC chairman says SST engine problems being underestimated. Aviation W 80:47 Ap 27 '64
U.S. reciprocating engines: specifications (cont) Aviation W 78:201 Mr 11 '63; 80:202 Mr 16 '64
See also
Gas turbines, Aircraft
Jet airplane engines

Fuel

Airlines trying anti-static fuel additive. M. L. Yaffee. Aviation W 81:26-7 N 30 '64

Fuel feeding

Hot start. G. Schlaeger. il Flying 75:52-4 S '64

Lubrication

AFSC cites lubrication research needs. E. J. Bulban. Aviation W 78:71+ My 6 '63
See also
Jet airplane engines—Lubrication

Maintenance and equipment

American, TWA to swap engine overhaul. Aviation W 79:41 Ag 19 '63

Materials

B. F. Goodrich building largest segmented case. il Miss & Roc 13:31-2 Ag 12 '63

Starting devices

See also
Jet airplane engines—Starting devices

Testing

Heat stressed in Concorde engine tests. il Aviation W 78:61+ Je 10 '63
See also
Gas turbines, Aircraft—Testing

AIRPLANE fares. See Airlines—Fares
AIRPLANE hostesses. See Airlines—Hostesses
AIRPLANE industry and trade
Take-off for the business jet. il Bsns W p 139-40+ S 28 '63

Consolidations and mergers

Douglas rejects merger offer. il Aviation W 78:28 Ap 1 '63
Douglas voids McDonnell merger. Aviation W 78:30 Ap 22 '63
Fairchild-Stratos acquires Hiller for cash. Aviation W 80:28 My 11 '64

Finance

Cessna, Piper, Beech report sales boosts. Aviation W 79:58 S 2 '63
Companies assured of technical ability; plan SST risk-sharing. E. H. Kolcum. Aviation W 79:41-3 S 30 '63
Congress awaits solution of SST dispute. R. H. Cook. Aviation W 79:40-1 N 4 '63
Private turbulence of Eastern air lines. I. Ross. il Fortune 70:172-4+ Jl '64
U.S. business & utility plane shipments. il Aviation W 79:79 Ag 12 '63

International aspects

Industry sales problems. R. Hotz. Aviation W 79:21 Ag 5 '63
NASARR problems hampering F-104G. C. Brownlow. il Aviation W 78:63-4 Mr 4 '63
PAA sees profit in Mystere 20 service. J. R. Ashlock. Aviation W 79:41+ Ag 12 '63

Statistics

U.S. business & utility aircraft shipments; tables (title varies) Aviation W 78:111 My 6; 79:79 Ag 12; 112 Ag 26; 104 S 23; 123 N 18 '63; 80:94 Ja 6; 97 Ja 20; 111 F 10; 86 Mr 2; 255 Mr 16; 71 Mr 30; 53 My 4; 110 Je 15; 81:71 Ag 3; 77 Ag 31; 89 O 5; 103 O 26; 59 D 28 '64; 82:77 Ja 4; 87 Ja 18 '65

Wages and hours

Wage chronology: Lockheed aircraft corp, California company. il Mo Labor R 87:680-5 Je '64
Wage chronology: North American aviation, inc. il Mo Labor R 87:556-60 My '64
Wage chronology: the Boeing co. Washington plants 1962-65. il Mo Labor R 87:900-3 Ag '64

Argentina

Argentine Guarani aimed at world market. W. Wright. il Aviation W 79:42-3+ D 30 '63

Canada

Canadian DC-9 delay raises political issue. Aviation W 79:39 N 25 '63
See also
Canadair, limited

Czechoslovakia

Czech industry drives for sales to West. E. Walford. il Aviation W 81:106-7+ O 19 '64
Czechs seeking foreign outlets for L-29. il Aviation W 78:89 Ap 22 '63
Markets in West sought for Czech Z-37. W. C. Wetmore. il Aviation W 80:105-6+ Ja 27 '64

Europe, Western

European manufacturers trimming costs. il Aviation W 80:258-60 Mr 16 '64
NASARR problems hampering F-104G. C. Brownlow. il Aviation W 78:63-4 Mr 4 '63

AIRPLANE industry and trade—Europe, Western—*Continued*
Smaller nations seek consortiums: Swedes forging modern air force. Aviation W 80: 285+ Mr 16 '64

France

French nuclear, space work moves toward major goals. R. E. Farrell. il Aviation W 80:270-2+ Mr 16 '64
French reach for technology in nuclear, Mach 2 transport programs. R. E. Farrell. il Aviation W 78:280-3 Mr 11 '63
French seek to extend aviation markets. C. Brownlow Aviation W 78:31-3 Je 24 '63
Modifications improve Mystere 20 stall. H. J. Coleman. il Aviation W 80:100-4 F 10 '64
SIPA seeks military orders for Antilope. H. J. Coleman. il Aviation W 78:96-7+ Je 24 '63
Special report on French industry; symposium. il Aviation W 78:56-7+ Je 10 '63

Germany (Federal Republic)

Delay expected in German VTOL decision. C. Brownlow. Aviation W 80:59+ Ap 6 '64
Dornier schedules Do. 31 V/STOL tests. W. C. Wetmore. il Aviation W 80:30-2 Mr 30 '64
German firms take step toward merger. Aviation W 81:24 Ag 24 '64
Germans fly again; Dornier werke. il Bsns W p 196+ N 16 '63
Looking for a lift. il Time 83:91 F 14 '64
Major Do.28D sales planned for Africa. il Aviation W 80:34 Ap 6 '64
Phoenix. il Newsweek 61:47 My 27 '63
U.S, Germany debating V/STOL needs. C. Brownlow. Aviation W 81:12-13 D 28 '64

Great Britain

Argument continues over Belfast future. H. J. Coleman. il Aviation W 79:80-1+ S 9 '63
British facing shifting defense policy. H. J. Coleman. il Aviation W 80:263-7+ Mr 16 '64
British seek to hold technological base. H. J. Coleman. il Aviation W 78:275-9 Mr 11 '63
Move to force U.K. cutback debate fails. H. J. Coleman. il Aviation W 82:26-7 Ja 25 '65
New subsonic jet generation forecast. Aviation W 81:36-7 S 7 '64
Problem legacy; proposal to cancel the TSR-2. il Newsweek 65:36+ Ja 25 '65
Sentence of death? threatened cancellation of Britain's all-purpose TSR-2 bomber. il Time 85:24 Ja 22 '65
Transports dominate Farnborough show. H. J. Coleman. il Aviation W 81:26-30 S 14 '64
Two independents turn to diversification. il Aviation W 81:141-3 S 7 '64
See also
Bristol aeroplane company
British aircraft corporation
Vickers-Armstrongs, limited

Israel

Israel aircraft planning major reshuffle. C. Brownlow. il Aviation W 80:104-5+ Je 15 '64
Stratocruiser to drop Israeli paratroops; conversion of Boeing 377 by Israel aircraft industries, ltd. W. C. Wetmore. il Aviation W 82:101+ Ja 18 '65

Japan

Japan embarks on defense modernization. il Aviation W 78:296-8 Mr 11 '63
Japan seeks markets for new projects. L. Booda. il Aviation W 80:276-8+ Mr 16 '64
Mitsubishi MU-2 business plane detailed. il Aviation W 78:34 Ap 1 '63
Mitsubishi seeking U.S. sales penetration. il Aviation W 79:98-9+ Ag 26 '63

Mexico

Mexican Cuauhtemoc built under license. Aviation W 80:95+ Je 8 '64

Netherlands

Fokker F.28 sales campaign opens in U.S. J. W. Carter. il Aviation W 80:41 My 25 '64
Government pledges F.28 program funds. Aviation W 80:47 F 24 '64

United States

Beech, Piper undecided on contest of demands in anti-trust suits. Aviation W 80: 34 Ap 13 '64
Big boost for the U.S. supersonic jet. il Newsweek 62:73 O 28 '63
Business aircraft manufacturers' reports indicate sales increases. il Aviation W 78:97 Ja 21 '63
Executive jet production lines grow as Aero Commander, Lear jet ready for first deliveries. il Aviation W 81:100-1 O 19 '64
French moves threaten U.S. jet exports. L. L. Doty. Aviation W 80:36 F 10 '64
Lear jet names ten distributors, state firm order backlog is seventy-two. Aviation W 81:33 Ag 24 '64
Out of the jet stream. il Time 81:84 F 15 '63
Pounding it out; TFX fighter-plane contract. il Newsweek 62:53-4 Ag 5 '63
Squabble to be first; U.S. supersonic jetliner program. il Time 82:93 O 25 '63
Uneasy crown; planemaker to the world. il Time 82:68 Ag 16 '63
U.S, Germany consider joint V/STOL; close-support jet fighter. C. Brownlow. Aviation W 81:22-3 N 23 '64
U.S, Germany debating V/STOL needs. C. Brownlow. Aviation W 81:12-13 D 28 '64
Who'll bear the supersonic risk? Bsns W p88+ N 9 '63
See also names of airplane manufacturing companies, e.g. Lockheed aircraft corporation

AIRPLANE instruments. See Aeronautic instruments

AIRPLANE models
Airborne antics. H. McDougall. il U S Camera 26:76-7 Je '63
Douglas, Convair unveil COIN mockups. D. E. Fink. il Aviation W 80:29-30 My 25 '64
Fastest way to build a model plane; using Styrofoam. R. L. Clough. il Pop Sci 182: 137-9 Mr '63
Hoopskirt; flying barrel. R. L. Clough, jr. il Pop Mech 119:155-7+ Ap '63
Seasonal reflections on the recent past, illustrating, in three stages. il Esquire 60: 164-7 D '63
Strictly a beep fleeter. il Am For 69:4-5 My '63

Radio control

Model airplanes fly for fun. F. Davis. il Sci N L 83:362-3 Je 8 '63
R/C model airplanes revisited. W. Hutchison. il Pop Electr 20:43-7+ My '64

AIRPLANE parts
Beech parts, supplies distribution grows. E. J. Bulban. il Aviation W 78:96 Ap 1 '63

AIRPLANE pilots. See Air pilots

AIRPLANE postal service. See Air mail service

AIRPLANE racing
Hell's angels fly again; National air races, Reno, Nev. J. N. Bell. il Sat Eve Post 237:28-31 N 7 '64
Just a dry run; National championship air races. il Time 84:81 O 2 '64
Memo from the publisher. E. D. Muhlfeld. il Flying 75:6 S '64
Powder for the powder puff. G. R. Wilson. Flying 74:20 Ja '64
Reno races; National championship air races. il Flying 75:60 S '64

AIRPLANE seats. See Airplanes—Seats

AIRPLANE shops. See Airlines—Maintenance and repair

AIRPLANE transportation of animals. See Animals—Transportation

AIRPLANE travel. See Air travel

AIRPLANE wings
Aerohydroski uses lift from skis, wings. M. L. Yaffee. il Aviation W 81:72-3+ O 26 '64
Fresh flock of fold-wing planes. J. Cushman and M. Dowd. il Pop Mech 119:90-5+ F '63
Modified XV-5A to incorporate new wing. C. M. Plattner. il Aviation W 81:38-9+ D 14 '64
NASA testifies that Rogallo wing is probably dead in Gemini program; Rogallo wing paraglider. H. M. David. Miss & Roc 14: 21 F 24 '64
Pilot report; high stepping high-wing. G. J. Schlaeger. il Flying 74:42-3+ Ap '64
Plane's wing breathes to boost its range. W. S. Griswold. il Pop Sci 182:96-7 Ap '63
Slots in the wings; Laminar flow control. il Newsweek 62:66 Jl 1 '63
Slotted for smoothness. il Time 81:43 Mr 29 '63
Swept-wing F-111 to use fuselage lift. E. J. Bulban. Aviation W 79:32 D 23 '63
Twin screw shafts operate F-111 wings. il Aviation W 81:33-4 O 26 '64
Wing sweep brings first F-111A bonus. il Aviation W 82:19 Ja 11 '65
Wing that breathes; laminar flow wings. J. Ball. il Flying 74:39-41+ Ap '64

AIRPLANE wings—*Continued*

Testing

Air-inhaling wing flies. il(p337) Sci N L 83:340 Je 1 '63
X-21 tests laminar flow control theory. C. M. Plattner. il Aviation W 78:52-3+ Je 24 '63

AIRPLANES

Flying dinosaur; Brabazon, England's super transport. E. A. Phillips. il Flying 74:44-5+ Mr '64
Leading international aircraft: specifications. Aviation W 78:218-21 Mr 11 '63; 80:218-21 Mr 16 '64
New Nieuport; replica of famous French fighter built from photos, drawings, and old articles. il Flying 74:71 Ja '64
U.S. airlines' transport fleet; specifications. il Aviation W 78:203 Mr 11 '63
U.S. commercial transports; specifications. Aviation W 80:216 Mr 16 '64
Westward the, what kind of airplane is that, anyway? open-cockpit biplane. R. Bach. il Flying 75:50-1+ Jl '64

See also
Autogiros
Seaplanes

Accidents

See Aviation—Accidents

Airworthiness

See Airplanes—Standards

Automobile combinations

See Airplanes, Light—Automobile combinations

Bird collisions

See Aviation—Bird hazards

Brakes

See Brakes, Airplane

Caricatures and cartoons

How to build & fly your own 1909 Bleriot. R. Green. Esquire 61:66-8 F '64

Chartering

American flyers plans piston phaseout. E. J. Bulban. il Aviation W 78:45+ Ap 22 '63
Buy and fly; dispute over CAB regulations governing charter flights. Newsweek 65:48 F 1 '65
Canadian mining boom boosts charter work. Aviation W 80:37 Je 1 '64
CAB hears complaints by Miami Beach hotels; illegal airline charters. Aviation W 79:45 D 16 '63
Extension of new supplemental charter rights to Pacific asked. L. L. Doty. Aviation W 80:30 Mr 23 '64
One-up-in-the-airmanship. M. T. Bloom. il N Y Times Mag p28+ Ja 10 '65
Supplementals get Atlantic charter rights. R. H. Cook. Aviation W 80:31 Mr 9 '64
Who will fly the charters? nonscheduled, supplemental carriers. il Bsns W p47-8+ Ja 16 '65

Cockpits

See Airplane cockpits

Collectors and collecting

Antique aircraft; symposium. il Flying 74:23-32+ Ja '64
Memo from the publisher. E. D. Muhlfeld. Flying 74:4 Ja '64
Open-cockpit thrills; with photographs by J. Zimmerman. Sat Eve Post 236:20-5 My 18 '63

Construction

See Airplanes—Manufacture

Control

See also
Automatic pilot (airplanes)

Corrosion

See Corrosion and anticorrosives

Cost

See Airplanes—Prices

Cost of operation

Boom restrictions may swell SST costs. il Aviation W 81:38-9+ Ag 3 '64
Comparative direct operating costs, domestic trunklines. Aviation W 80:162 Mr 16 '64

Crews

See Airplane crews

Design

DC-9 design, performance projections shown. il Aviation W 78:42-3 My 27 '63
Douglas to build DC-9 despite order lack. il Aviation W 78:40-2 Ap 15 '63
Payloads are increased by 21 per cent on BAC 111 series 300, 400. il Aviation W 80:43 Je 15 '64
Sud Caravelle Super A undergoes flight tests with new powerplants. il Aviation W 78:48-9 Je 10 '63
Wagner W-18 will use high lift devices. H. D. Watkins. il Aviation W 81:66-8+ Jl 27 '64

See also
Helicopters—Design

Ditching

Crash spurs ditching recommendations; Flying Tiger flight, September 23, 1962. Aviation W 80:96-105+ Ja 6 '64
When you must ditch at sea; reprint. E. J. Long. il Sci Digest 56:38-42 O '64

Electronic equipment

Arinc tests prove auto-checkout value. P. J. Klass. Aviation W 78:69-70+ Ja 28 '63
Defense plan lists avionic guidelines. P. J. Klass. il Aviation W 78:227-9 Mr 11 '63
E-2A compatible with carrier operations. L. Booda. il Aviation W 78:68-9+ Mr 4 '63
FAA, ATA shown anti-collision system. il Aviation W 78:105+ Ap 15 '63
FAA evaluating lightplane transponders. B. Miller. il Aviation W 79:107-11 Ag 26 '63
Litton developing VAX inertial navigator. B. Miller. il Aviation W 78:76-7+ Ap 29 '63
Microwave amplifier advances described. Aviation W 79:91-3+ N 4 '63
Military transponder plans implemented. Aviation W 81:60-2 Jl 27 '64
New avionic products. See issues of Aviation week & space technology
Optimizer programs best angle of attack. B. Miller. il Aviation W 79:95+ Ag 12 '63
Panel appraises outlook for microcircuits. P. J. Klass. il Aviation W 80:79+ Ap 6 '64
Tests verify navy microcircuit reliability. il Aviation W 80:89 Je 29 '64
Transponders are coming. W. J. Kendall. il Flying 75:49+ Ag '64
Tubes clue to air crashes. P. Halliday. Electr World 71:83 Ja '64
USAF seeking improved reconnaissance aids to conduct demanding new missions. W. Wright. il Aviation W 80:88-9+ Ap 6 '64

See also
Airplanes, Military—Electronic equipment
Automatic pilot (airplanes)

Emergency landing

See Airplanes—Landing

Equipment

United plans Caravelle-727 integration. J. R. Ashlock. il Aviation W 78:45+ Ap 15 '63

See also
Aeronautic instruments

Escape devices

Explosives will shear pilot pod from fuselage in F-111 escape. il Aviation W 79:34 Ag 12 '63
F-111 emergency escape system tests are scheduled at El Centro. Aviation W 79:33 D 23 '63
Rocket ejection improvement need cited. E. J. Bulban. il Aviation W 81:87+ Ag 3 '64

Exhibitions

See Aviation—Exhibitions

Flaps

See Flaps, Airplane

Fuel

See Airplane engines—Fuel

Fuel tank gages

See Gages

Gages

See Gages

History

See Aeronautics—History

Hydraulic equipment

Changes recommended in 727 hydraulics. R. D. Hibben. Aviation W 81:43+ N 23 '64

Ice protection

Crash probe spurs 1958 finding review. Aviation W 80:29 Je 22 '64
United's winterizing cuts flight delay; new methods of de-icing. J. W. Carter. il Aviation W 81:29-30 Jl 27 '64

AIRPLANES—*Continued*

Inspection

Engine inspectors use radioactive isotopes. Aviation W 80:65 Je 22 '64
Misunderstanding cited in Electra alarm. J. R. Ashlock. Aviation W 81:28-9 Ag 3 '64

Instruments

See Aeronautic instruments

Landing

All-weather landing progress reported. P. J. Klass. il Aviation W 79:165+ O 7 '63
All-weather landing proposals requested. P. J. Klass. Aviation W 78:70-1+ Ap 29 '63
British all-weather landing goal may be too severe, data shows. P. J. Klass. Aviation W 81:62-3 Jl 27 '64
Building safety into blind landings; electronic devices. il Bsns W p96+ D 19 '64
Economy ILS aids readied for evaluation at two airports. P. J. Klass. il Aviation W 80:68-9+ Mr 2 '64
FAA all-weather landing system office urged by pilot's report. Aviation W 78:44 Mr 18 '63
FAA selects integrated landing system. P. J. Klass. il Aviation W 79:78-9+ Jl 29 '63
Happy landing; emergency of Cessna 180 at Wyoming's Minuteman missile site. il Time 81:19 F 8 '63
How to come in blind. il Time 83:90+ My 15 '64
I learned about flying from that! down in the desert. B. R. Cobb. il Flying 74:50+ Mr '64
Lear Siegler pushes autoland time-lead. P. J. Klass. il Aviation W 82:59-62 Ja 18 '65
Mayday from Charlie Foxtrot. M. Conrad. il Flying 74:52-3+ Je '64
NASA wants manual blind landing system. C. Brownlow. Aviation W 78:89 My 20 '63
No-hands landing. il Newsweek 61:94+ Mr 18 '63
Off-airport landing. R. Bach. il Flying 74:30-2+ Mr '64
Piece of cake; emergency landing after pilot's death. Newsweek 61:36+ F 11 '63
Pilot, autopilot share approach duties. P. J. Klass. il Aviation W 81:93+ O 19 '64
Pilot drops dead, you can't fly; but you must. il Life 54:48 F 8 '63
SCAT. D. Kuhn. il Flying 74:54 My '64
Tailwheel techniques. R. G. Clarke. il Flying 74:46-7+ Ap '64
Triple slither. il Time 83:76 Ap 17 '64
U.K, U.S. disagree on blind-landing plans. C. Brownlow. Aviation W 78:45+ My 13 '63
See also
Airplanes, Jet propelled—Landing
Airports—Lighting
Automatic pilot (airplanes)
Seaplanes—Landing

Landing gear

See also
Airplanes—Wheels

Leasing

Capital funds up to $50 million provided by joint financing plan; for long-term lease or purchase of aircraft. Aviation W 80:21 Mr 30 '64

Lightning hazards

See Aviation—Lightning hazards

Lubrication

New jet oils beat heat. Sci N L 86:181 S 19 '64

Maintenance and repair

See also
Airlines—Maintenance and repair

Manufacture

Airplane in the basement; homemade airplanes. il Time 85:30-1 Ja 8 '65

Materials

ASSET to test hypersonic theory. il Miss & Roc 12:28 My 27 '63
Concorde alloy has high creep strength; hiduminium RR.58 il Aviation W 81:133+ S 7 '64
Titanium's future. M. L. Yaffee. il Aviation W 79:48-9+ D 2; 98-9+ D 9 '63
See also
Airplanes, Supersonic—Materials

Noise

Airport unit warns of SST noise level. Aviation W 80:28-9 Mr 30 '64
Hempstead versus jets; Idlewild airport. il Bsns W p93-4 D 7 '63
Program to soundproof houses near London-Heathrow rejected. Aviation W 79:41 Jl 15 '63
Report recommends tightened noise procedures at Heathrow. Aviation W 80:41 Ja 13 '64
Sonic boom town; Oklahoma City. R. Burkhardt. New Repub 151:5-6 Ag 22 '64
Special lighted traffic pattern planned to reduce Idlewild noise. Aviation W 79:29 Jl 8 '63

Parts

See Airplane parts

Passenger service

See Airlines—Passenger service

Piloting

Bush pilot's deadly, daily game. D. Moser. il Life 57:112-14+ N 27 '64
Fighter pilot. R. Bach. il Harper 227:39-45 Jl '63
Flights replace hours as measuring unit. L. Booda. Aviation W 79:23 D 30 '63
I learned about flying from that! See issues of Flying
Men in training to fly Dyna-Soar; six pilots whose mission may abort. A. Rosenfeld. il Life 54:100A-100B+ F 22 '63
No cause for alarm. Todays Health 42:48+ D '64
Pilot in command. D. B. Kuhn. Flying 74:58 Je '64
What to do when the pilot dies. il Time 82:54 O 18 '63

Power supply

Perils of Pluto. W. J. Coughlin. Miss & Roc 14:46 Je 22 '64

Prices

New plane breaks price barrier. K. V. Brown. il Pop Mech 121:100-4+ F '64

Private ownership

Last of the red hot cats; Grumman's Bearcat. N. R. Hanson. il Flying 74:46-7+ F '64
Personal business; private planes. Bsns W p85 Ag 3 '63
See also
Private flying

Purchasing

Buy and fly; own-your-own-airliner travel clubs. Newsweek 65:48 F 1 '65
Trading up. il Esquire 61:86-7 Je '64

Racing

See Airplane racing

Radio equipment

See Radio apparatus on aircraft

Refueling

Air guard tankers to use surplus J47s. E. J. Bulban. il Aviation W 81:42-3 D 28 '64

Safety devices and measures

Air-filled bags reduce injuries in plane crashes. Sci N L 86:24 Jl 11 '64
Crash brings Lear jet design modification. Aviation W 80:28 Je 15 '64
Delightful destruction. il Time 83:94 My 1 '64
Evacuation tests could affect high-density aircraft seating. L. L. Doty. Aviation W 80:41-2 Ap 20 '64
FAA plans wide recorder requirements. R. H. Cook. Aviation W 78:43 Mr 25 '63
Opposition may kill aircraft lighting plan. Aviation W 79:33 S 2 '63
Plane crash on purpose. il Life 56:123-5+ Je 12 '64
Sniffer may detect bombs on aircraft. P. J. Klass. il Aviation W 81:42+ N 16 '64
USAF drops bright markings on aircraft. Aviation W 79:77 N 25 '63
We have crashed; test of escape procedures. il Newsweek 63:87 Ap 20 '64
See also
Airplanes—Ice protection
Aviation—Safety devices and measures

Seats

Evacuation tests could affect high-density aircraft seating. L. L. Doty. Aviation W 80:41-2 Ap 20 '64

Speed

See also
Airplanes, Supersonic

Standards

Misunderstanding cited in Electra alarm. J. R. Ashlock. Aviation W 81:28-9 Ag 3 '64

Storm hazards

See Aviation—Storm hazards

AIRPLANES—*Continued*

Submarine combination

See Submarine boats—Airplane combination

Take off

See also
Airplanes, Vertical take-off and landing

Wheels

Tailwheel techniques. R. G. Clarke. il Flying 74:46-7+ Ap '64

Wings

See Airplane wings

AIRPLANES, Amphibious
Old ironsides; Seabee. R. B. Weeghman. il Flying 75:65-7 Ag '64
World record flight. il Ebony 18:85-6 Ag '63

AIRPLANES, Atomic powered
Reorientations hampered ANP program. K. Johnsen. il Aviation W 78:81-7 Ap 1 '63
R&D; ill-starred nuclear plane project is subject of hard look by General accounting office. J. Walsh. Science 140:37-8 Ap 5 '63

AIRPLANES, Business
Aero Commander plans to market full single-engine aircraft line. Aviation W 80:36 Mr 2 '64
As more and more businessmen take to the airways; executive jets. il U S News 55: 60-1 N 4 '63
Aztec C features major modifications. il Aviation W 80:111+ Ap 20 '64
Beech 18 conversion fitted with PT6-A6s. il Aviation W 81:93 N 16 '64
Beech reports fifteen firm King Air orders. E. J. Bulban. Aviation W 79:34 S 30 '63
Beech surveys high-density twin market; executive transport. il Aviation W 81:99+ O 12 '64
Business plane sales curve edges higher. E. J. Bulban. il Aviation W 78:265-7+ Mr 11 '63
Cessna acts to widen twin-engine sales; foresees industry growth: summary of address. D. L. Wallace. Aviation W 78:76+ Mr 18 '63
Corporate planes: flying for profit. il Newsweek 63:82-3 F 17 '64
Europe steps up small jet competition. il Aviation W 78:270-2 Mr 11 '63
European manufacturers trimming costs. il Aviation W 80:258-60 Mr 16 '64
Executive jet production lines grow as Aero Commander, Lear jet ready for first deliveries. il Aviation W 81:100-1 O 19 '64
Executive jets warm up for big sales takeoff. il Bsns W p60-2 N 21 '64
Executive plane with pull, also push: Cessna's Skymaster. il Bsns W p50 Mr 23 '63
GE seeks company pilot views in defining CF700 engine loan, overhaul programs. D. A. Brown. il Aviation W 80:98-9+ Ap 6 '64
Grand Commander features lengthened fuselage. il Aviation W 78:93 F 11 '63
Gulfstream 2 decision expected by March; turbofan executive transport. il Aviation W 81:39-40 N 9 '64
Jet Commander FAA certification begins. il Aviation W 80:29 Ja 6 '64
Jet Commander purchase plan detailed. D. A. Brown. Aviation W 78:82-3+ Mr 4 '63
Jets aim for place in business fleets. E. J. Bulban. il Aviation W 80:253-7 Mr 16 '64
Jets top business plane display at Paris. H. J. Coleman. il Aviation W 79:54-5+ Jl 8 '63
King Air displays advanced performance. D. A. Brown. il Aviation W 81:70-3 Jl 13 '64
Lear jet certification expected this week; Commander in August. Aviation W 81:20 Jl 27 '64
Lear jet handling resembles light twin; executive turbojet. D. A. Brown. il Aviation W 80:72-8 Mr 9 '64
Lear jet phases modifications into line. D. A. Brown. il Aviation W 82:87+ Ja 25 '65
Lear takes the controls; Lear jet corp. il Bsns W p 108-11 Mr 7 '64
Lear's jet. R. Bach. il Flying 74:34-7+ Ap '64
Markets in West sought for Czech Z-37. W. C. Wetmore. il Aviation W 80:105-6+ Ja 27 '64
Modifications improve Mystere 20 stall. H. J. Coleman. il Aviation W 80:100-4 F 10 '64
Mooney sales may top $12 million in 1965 with Mark 22. E. J. Bulban. il Aviation W 81:86-7+ O 12 '64
New series of small aircraft is planned. H. D. Watkins. il Aviation W 81:85 Jl 20 '64
140 retains traits of heavier Cherokees. D. A. Brown. il Aviation W 80:64-5+ Mr 30 '64
Pan Am considers Jet Commander. Aviation W 78:27 My 27 '63
Pilot report; production Beagle 206. J. Fricker. il Flying 74:42-3+ Mr '64
Piper plans enlarged Cherokee, new twin. G. Alexander. Aviation W 81:34 O 19 '64
Piper will add two-place Cherokee 140. il Aviation W 80:117-18 F 17 '64
Record smashing Sabreliner; ed. by W. B. Wentz. E. J. Brandreth, jr. il Flying 74: 48+ My '64
Reluctant executive; corporate jets. il Time 81:74 Mr 1 '63
S35 Bonanza speed, useful load boosted. D. A. Brown. il Aviation W 80:90-1+ F 24 '64
Sales of HS-125 expected in America; British twin-jet executive aircraft. il Aviation W 81:149 S 7 '64
Size, power increased on Beagle 206Y. H. J. Coleman. il Aviation W 80:90-1+ Je 29 '64
Small jets for big business. il Time 83:88 My 1 '64
SIPA seeks military orders for Antilope. H. J. Coleman. il Aviation W 78:96-7+ Je 24 '63
Super Skywagon broadens Cessna market. E. J. Bulban. il Aviation W 79:85+ D 9 '63
Take-off for the business jet. il Bsns W p 139-40+ S 28 '63
$10.8-million backlog reported by Beech for turboprop King Air. il Aviation W 79:34-5 N 25 '63
Twin-engine Jet Commander begins flight test program. E. J. Bulban. il Aviation W 78: 90-1 F 4 '63
U.S. personal and business aircraft: specifications (title varies) (cont) Aviation W 78:207 Mr 11 '63; 80:217 Mr 16 '64
See also
Airplanes in business

Design

Building boom in foreign bizjets. J. Fricker. il Flying 74:38-9+ Je '64
Corporate turbojet and turboprop sales plans aim at future executive markets. D. A. Brown. il Aviation W 79:102-4+ S 23 '63
DH-1725 stresses operational simplicity. H. J. Coleman. il Aviation W 79:52-3+ S 2 '63
Jet Commander provides solid handling. D. A. Brown. il Aviation W 80:98-103 My 11 '64
Lear jet prototype nears October flight date. il Aviation W 79:88-9 S 16 '63
Mitsubishi MU-2 business plane detailed. il Aviation W 78:34 Ap 1 '63
New Cherokee features payload increase. il Aviation W 79:57-8 S 2 '63

AIRPLANES, Drone
Firebee; pilotless plane shot down by Chinese. il Time 84:30 N 27 '64
Is U.S. using pilotless planes in Asia? U S News 57:11 N 30 '64
L-T-V to buy, operate Jindivik target drone. Aviation W 80:29 Ja 13 '64
Powers-less flight; Ryan Firebee. il Newsweek 64:90 N 30 '64
U.S. drones and target missiles: specifications. Aviation W 80:209 Mr 16 '64
U.S. drones; specifications (cont) Aviation W 78:209 Mr 11 '63

AIRPLANES, Experimental
A-11 proven in reconnaissance missions; with editorial comment. il Aviation W 80:11, 16-18 Mr 9 '64
Aerospaceplane may be two-stage vehicle. il Aviation W 79:245+ Jl 22 '63
AF seeks renewed X-15 interest. R. Hawkes. Miss & Roc 13:39-40 D 16 '63
AF sees manned Dyna-Soar flight by mid-1966. C. Butler. Miss & Roc 13:16-17 Ag 19 '63
Chances appear good for more pilot control in Dyna-Soar flight. Miss & Roc 13:15 O 21 '63
Coming up, though you may never hear it, a big roar over Dyna-Soar; with report by A. Rosenfeld. il Life 54:97-9+ F 22 '63
Contractors pressing for advanced XV-5A; fan-in-wing VTOL. il Aviation W 81:32-3 N 23 '64
Crash only speeded it up; X-15. il Bsns W p46 Mr 14 '64
Defense may ease impact of X-20 loss. E. H. Kolcum. Aviation W 78:31 Mr 18 '63
Douglas to build DC-9 despite order lack. il Aviation W 78:40-2 Ap 15 '63
Engine changes proposed for X-15A-2. il Aviation W 80:24 Mr 23 '64
Eulogy to a Dyna-Soar. W. J. Coughlin. Miss & Roc 12:50 Mr 11 '63
Flight research center, AF press for Hypersonic research vehicle. R. Hawkes. Miss & Roc 14:29-30 F 10 '64

AIRPLANES, Experimental—*Continued*

Flight tests of XV-5A scheduled to start this summer. D. A. Anderton. il Aviation W 78:64-5+ Ja 21 '63
Flying bathtub; M-2 glider. W. Cloud. il Pop Sci 183:64-5 N '63
GETOL plane uses air bubble for landing gear. W. S. Griswold. il Pop Sci 184:80-1 Ja '64
Getting a no, and a go; air force loses Dyna-Soar project, gets MOL. il Bsns W p 76+ D 14 '63
Gilpatric cites knowledge of X-22A firms. G. C. Wilson. Aviation W 78:36-7 Je 24 '63
Go or no go. W. J. Coughlin. Miss & Roc 12:46 Ap 8 '63
Hybrid spacecraft flies with no wings. il Bsns W p26-7 S 14 '63
Incredible X-15. W. S. Griswold. il Pop Sci 182:78-82+ F '63
Locals define transport aircraft needs. Aviation W 78:45 My 20 '63
Long-endurance, subsonic aircraft studies are revived by air force; Dromedary project. L. Booda. Aviation W 78:40 F 18 '63
Man in a tub; the M-2. il Newsweek 62:80 S 16 '63
Manual X-20A boost control simulated. E. J. Bulban. Aviation W 78:59+ F 18 '63
Modified XV-5A to incorporate new wing; army lift-fan research airplane. C. M. Plattner. il Aviation W 81:38-9+ D 14 '64
Modified X-15 may carry ramjet. il Miss & Roc 14:18 Mr 2 '64
New life; X-15 used for scientific experiments. il Newsweek 61:82 My 6 '63
Off we go; Dyna-Soar project abandoned. il Newsweek 62:54 D 23 '63
Official confirms cutback of Dyna-Soar. Miss & Roc 12:14 Mr 11 '63
Plane and fancy; TFX (Tactical fighter experimental) variable-wing F-111A. il Newsweek 64:99 O 26 '64
Rebirth; Second X-15. il Newsweek 63:58 Mr 9 '64
Report favors prototype development. B. H. Klein and others. il Aviation W 78:135+ Je 10 '63
Saenger's final interview with M/R; ed. by W. Beller. E. Saenger. Miss & Roc 14:35+ F 24 '64
Sky-high courage; test pilot. R. White. D. Markinko. il Ladies Home J 80:62-3+ Ja '63
Solid-state system to track X-20. il Miss & Roc 13:39-40 O 28 '63
Strange shapes of things to fly; with photographs by L. Schiller. Sat Eve Post 236:16-21 S 14 '63
Sunnyvale center preparing for Dyna-Soar control assignment. R. Lindsey. Miss & Roc 13:15 Jl 8 '63
USAF, NASA planning hypersonic research aircraft. E. H. Kolcum. il Aviation W 78:26-7 F 11 '63
USAF sees X-20 cancellation or cutback. E. H. Kolcum. Aviation W 78:26 F 25 '63
USAF to propose long-endurance aircraft. Aviation W 78:33-4 My 6 '63
Walker sets altitude record with X-15. Aviation W 79:24 Jl 29 '63
Wing that breathes; X-21. J. Ball. il Flying 74:39-41+ Ap '64
Winged spacemen; X-15 plane. L. Haynes. il Sat Eve Post 236:24+ Je 22 '63
Wingless orbit craft; M-2. W. Siegrist. il(p 145) Sci N L 83:147 Mr 9 '63
X-15 use planned in ramjet evaluations. I. Stone. il Aviation W 81:57+ Ag 31 '64
X-20 contract for $358 million does not assure glider's future. Aviation W 78:36 Ap 1 '63
X-20 decision may have come earlier. F. G. McGuire. Miss & Roc 12:14 Mr 18 '63
X-20 energy display system described. M. Getler. Miss & Roc 12:16 Ap 1 '63
X-20 will probe piloted lifting re-entry; Dyna-Soar. il Aviation W 79:230-3+ Jl 22 '63
X-20A guidance system completes flight-testing series. C. D. LaFond. il Miss & Roc 13:16-18 Ag 19 '63
X-21 tests laminar flow control theory. C. M. Plattner. il Aviation W 78:52-3+ Je 24 '63
X-22 report is rebuff to DOD civilians. R. G. O'Lone. Aviation W 80:32-3 F 17 '64
XB-70A's research role will contribute Mach 3 flight data for SST development. C. M. Plattner. il Aviation W 80:26-30 My 18 '64

Anecdotes, facetiae, satire, etc.

Raven; poem. A. Oberta. Miss & Roc 14:6 Ja 27 '64

Testing

Edwards extends data network for high-speed aircraft testing. C. M. Plattner. Aviation W 79:29 D 9 '63

AIRPLANES, Freight

Air cargo gets a lift; automating and expanding facilities. il Bsns W p 131-2 O 31 '64
All-cargo air carriers ask CAB to ease competition from trunks. Aviation W 79:51 S 16 '63
All-cargo jet increases pressure for rate reduction. il Aviation W 79:54-5+ O 7 '63
Belfast makes successful maiden flight; turboprop freighter. il Aviation W 80:39 Ja 13 '64
Cargo plane delivers truck while flying at 100 m.p.h. il Pop Sci 184:113 Ap '64
Carriers begin first move into jet cargo. J. R. Ashlock. il Aviation W 78:170-1+ Mr 11 '63
Carvair ferry proves sturdy, easy to fly. H. J. Coleman. il Aviation W 79:114-15+ S 23 '63
CAB plans cargo airline aid. Aviation W 80:41 F 3 '64
Conditional order placed by Slick for four Lockheed L-300B jets. Aviation W 80:34 My 4 '64
Flying Tiger is second carrier to order L-300Bs from Lockheed. Aviation W 80:43 My 18 '64
Heat posing major SST design problems. J. R. Ashlock. il Aviation W 79:74-5 Jl 8 '63
I rode the jet freight to Shannon. E. D. Fales, jr. il Pop Sci 185:52-5+ Jl '64
Jets decrease all-cargo operating losses. R. G. O'Lone. Aviation W 81:35-6 N 23 '64
Jets push the trade winds. il Sci N L 86:218-19 O 3 '64
Pan Am to seek IATA freight rate trials for all-jet service. Aviation W 79:42 Jl 1 '63
Vickers studying VC.10 tail cone extension as drag reduction move. H. J. Coleman. Aviation W 78:40 Ap 1 '63
Who'll fly the freight? il Bsns W p58+ O 12 '63

See also

Air freight service
Airplanes, Military transport

Design

Can jet freighters make air cargo pay? Bsns W p60-2+ Je 22 '63

AIRPLANES, Government

Flying White House. F. Knebel. il Look 28:86-92+ Je 2 '64
Now, for JFK: ten copters, four jets, two yachts, big cars. il U S News 55:60-1 Jl 22 '63
Travel fleets of two presidents. il U S News 55:65 S 16 '63

See also

Airplanes in government

AIRPLANES, Jet propelled

Airline outlook. R. Hotz. Aviation W 80:11 Je 8 '64
American cargo jet starts daily flights. Aviation W 80:36 Ja 13 '64
Automation, safety emphasized in Trident; British three-jet transport. H. J. Coleman. il Aviation W 81:83+ S 14 '64
Battling for new jet trade; Douglas DC-9 to counter Britain's BAC-111. il Bsns W p52+ Mr 23 '63
Boeing weighs plans for 707 successors. H. D. Watkins. Aviation W 82:36-7 Ja 25 '65
British aircraft corp. develops two new versions of BAC 111. H. J. Coleman. Aviation W 78:41 My 20 '63
BAC 111 maintainability concept formed. Aviation W 80:51 Mr 23 '64
British jet out in front; short-range jet field. il Bsns W p26 Jl 27 '63
CX-HLS studied as commercial transport. J. R. Ashlock. Aviation W 81:27 N 2 '64
Chance for 100 new DC-9 orders seen. il Aviation W 80:44-5+ My 4 '64
DC-9 enters the short-range jet race. il Newsweek 65:64-6 Ja 18 '65
Domestic all-jet cargo race starting. il Aviation W 79:37-8 D 2 '63
French moves threaten U.S. jet exports. L. L. Doty. Aviation W 80:36 F 10 '64
Gamble at Douglas; DC-9 and the BAC one-eleven short-range jetliners. il Time 81:104 Ap 19 '63
Is this today's best airliner? VC-10 jetliner. D. Scott. il Pop Sci 185:86-7 Jl '64
Italy hinders TWA all-cargo jet effort. R. H. Cook. Aviation W 80:49-50 Ja 20 '64
Jet fighters; short range planes. il Newsweek 61:72+ Ap 22 '63
Jets decrease all-cargo operating losses. R. G. O'Lone. Aviation W 81:35-6 N 23 '64
Jets for the short haul: DC-9. il Time 85:80+ Ja 15 '65
Jets push the trade winds. il Sci N L 86:218-19 O 3 '64
Lear liner specifications, costs detailed. D. A. Brown. il Aviation W 80:29-30 Je 29 '64

AIRPLANES, Jet propelled—*Continued*
Lebanese airways seeking jets to maintain competitive status. il Aviation W 79:47+ O 14 '63
Lockheed studies 10,000-mi. transport. J. W. Carter. Aviation W 80:47 Ap 13 '64
Mohawk predicts BAC 111 buy will help cut subsidy in 1966; short-haul jets. Aviation W 78:34 Mr 4 '63
NASA task may boost ramjet efforts. M. L. Yaffee. Aviation W 81:21-2 Ag 3 '64
New BAC 111 version proposed; production rate increases. il Aviation W 81:38-41 S 7 '64
New subsonic jet generation forecast. Aviation W 81:36-7 S 7 '64
Northeast leases jet equipment, plans eighteen daily flights to Florida. Aviation W 79: 40 N 18 '63
Out of the jet stream. il Time 81:84 F 15 '63
Pilot report; Commander's jet. R. Bach. il Flying 75:28-31+ Jl '64
Romanian carrier plans Tu-124 purchase; Tarom Romanian air transport. D. Walford. il Aviation W 79:47+ D 9 '63
Rosier horizons. R. Hotz. Aviation W 79:21 N 18 '63
Subsonic jets still booming. il Bsns W p63 Jl 25 '64
TWA keys domestic gain hopes to introduction of 727 service. Aviation W 80:29 Mr 23 '64
Tu-134 range, size increased over Tu-124; Russia's new twin-jet Tupolev. il Aviation W 81:43+ O 12 '64
United plans Caravelle-727 integration. J. R. Ashlock. il Aviation W 78:45+ Ap 15 '63
U.S. airlines' transport fleet; specifications. il Aviation W 78:203 Mr 11 '63
U.S. manufacturers' rejections led to American's BAC 111 order. Aviation W 79:29-30 Jl 29 '63
VC.10 training builds pilot confidence. il Aviation W 81:53+ S 7 '64
See also
Airplanes, Business

Design

Argument continues over Belfast future. H. J. Coleman. il Aviation W 79:80-1+ S 9 '63
Boeing defers decision on 737 go-ahead. il Aviation W 81:29 N 2 '64
Corporate turbojet and turboprop sales plans aim at future executive markets. D. A. Brown. il Aviation W 79:102-4+ S 23 '63
DC-9 unveiled early despite tail change. C. M. Plattner. il Aviation W 82:30-3 Ja 18 '65
Dassault studies turbofan for Mystere 20. il Aviation W 78:90-1+ Je 10 '63
Exterior, cockpit details of Il-62 shown; Soviet jet transport. il Aviation W 81:32-3 Ag 17 '64
HFB.320 modified to boost performance. W. C. Wetmore. il Aviation W 78:99+ Je 17 '63
Jet boundary layer flap doubles 707 lift. G. C. Wilson. il Aviation W 80:36-7 My 25 '64
Modifications improve Mystere 20 stall. H. J. Coleman. il Aviation W 80:100-4 F 10 '64
NAC-100 design altered to ease loading; Centuryliner short-haul jet transport. C. Brownlow. il Aviation W 81:43+ O 19 '64
Production appears near for Boeing 737. H. D. Watkins. il Aviation W 81:28-9 N 30 '64
727 program entering production phase at Boeing plant. C. M. Plattner. il Aviation W 79:50-5+ N 4 '63
Spey-25 bypass turbojet engine has additional compressor stage. il Aviation W 78: 64 Je 3 '63
Trident construction shown; new versions planned. il Aviation W 78:41 Je 3 '63
Turboprop use pushed for Canadian North. D. A. Brown. il Aviation W 80:80-1+ Je 22 '64
200 orders promised in Transall program. il Aviation W 78:78-9+ Je 10 '63

Fuel

See Jet airplane engines—Fuel

Instrument flying

See Aviation—Instrument flying

Landing

All-weather aircraft landing; ILS and PAR approach systems. F. B. Brady. il Sci Am 210:25-35 Mr '64
Blown flaps for slow landings. il Time 83: 57 Je 5 '64
Flying the beam when the fog rolls in. C. Leedham. il N Y Times Mag p22+ My 24 '64
Giant airfields for jets may soon be outmoded; testing boundary layer control. il Sci N L 85:358 Je 6 '64
Landing a jet without looking; Great Britain's blind landing experimental unit. L. Lader. il Sat Eve Post 237:64-5 F 15 '64
No hands landing; all-weather landing system. J. Eberhart. il Sci N L 86:386 D 19 '64

Lubrication

See Airplanes—Lubrication

Noise

See Airplanes—Noise

Piloting

Boyd sees jet turbulence ban unneeded. J. R. Ashlock. Aviation W 80:37-8 Ja 13 '64
Jet procedures in turbulence changed. R. H. Cook. Aviation W 79:43-4 D 16 '63
Jet turbulence problems. J. R. Ashlock. il Aviation W 80:38-41 F 17; 45-6 F 24 '64
Turbulence studies investigate pilot aids. J. R. Ashlock. Aviation W 80:47 Ap 20 '64

Testing

British aircraft corp. still aims at initial BAC 111 delivery dates. Aviation W 79:45 N 11 '63
Jet Commander size increased. Aviation W 79:29 Ag 5 '63
United asks FAA safety tests before adding extra jet seats. Aviation W 80:43 Ja 27 '64
X-15 modified for hypersonic research. il Aviation W 79:38 N 4 '63

AIRPLANES, Light
Aero Commander plans to market full single-engine aircraft line. Aviation W 80:36 Mr 2 '64
Bede BD-1 low cost lightplane scheduled to make flight in March. il Aviation W 78:95 F 11 '63
Cessna acts to widen twin-engine sales; foresees industry growth; summary of address. D. L. Wallace. Aviation W 78:76+ Mr 18 '63
Cessna seeking twin-engine leadership. E. J. Bulban. il Aviation W 80:105+ F 10 '64
Cuauhtemoc M-1 built for rugged Mexican use. il Aviation W 80:91 My 4 '64
Czechs seeking foreign outlets for L-29. il Aviation W 78:89 Ap 22 '63
Detachable sprayer converts all Piper Cherokee aircraft; from passenger to agricultural work. il Aviation W 80:89 Mr 2 '64
Fairchild plans to increase F-27 capacity in new sales program. Aviation W 79:49 N 11 '63
FAA seeks U.S. short-haul transport aid. Aviation W 79:49 S 16 '63
Flying the Montana missile line. K. W. Anderson. il Flying 74:38-40+ Mr '64
Lady's day in the Comanche 400; ed. by R. Beatty. M. Link. il Flying 75:49-51 S '64
Locals define transport aircraft needs. Aviation W 78:45 My 20 '63
Modified A-26 used for African surveys. C. Brownlow. il Aviation W 82:85-7 Ja 18 '65
New plane breaks price barrier. K. V. Brown. il Pop Mech 121:100-4+ F '64
140 retains traits of heavier Cherokees. D. A. Brown. il Aviation W 80:64-5+ Mr 30 '64
Pilot report; Bölkow Junior. R. Bach. il Flying 74:36-7+ F '64
Pilot report; Champion Lancer. G. J. Schlaeger. il Flying 74:45+ Ja '64
Pilot report; high stepping high-wing; Cessna model 210D Centurion. G. J. Schlaeger. il Flying 74:42-3+ Ap '64
Pilot report; production Beagle 206. J. Fricker. il Flying 74:42-3+ Mr '64
Pilot report; sweet sixteen plus two. G. J. Schlaeger. il Flying 74:40-1+ My '64
Piper plans enlarged Cherokee, new twin. G. Alexander. Aviation W 81:34 O 19 '64
Piper studying standardized parts plan. il Aviation W 79:99 O 28 '63
Queen's heir, King Air. R. B. Weeghman. il Flying 75:36 Jl '64
SIPA seeks military orders for Antilope. H. J. Coleman. il Aviation W 78:96-7+ Je 24 '63
Sud aviation begins GY-80 Horizon production. il Aviation W 78:85 My 27 '63
Takeoff at thirty; Cessna with modifications. K. Brown. il Pop Mech 120:94-7+ S '63
Tandem-engine Cessna Skymaster offers flying ease, simplified pilot transitioning; pilot report. D. A. Brown. il Aviation W 78:88-9+ Mr 18 '63
Testing causes changes in Turbo Skyvan. il Aviation W 81:146-9 S 7 '64

AIRPLANES, Light—*Continued*
Three for the fun of it. R. B. Weeghman. il Flying 74:33 F '64
Turbine power adds to Beaver capability. D. A. Brown. il Aviation W 82:84-5+ Ja 11 '65
Turbo-Porter displays exceptional STOL performance. D. A. Brown. il Aviation W 81: 84-9 O 5 '64
Twin Otter boosts hot climate capability; light STOL utility transport. D. A. Brown. il Aviation W 82:72-4 Ja 4 '65
U.S. personal and business aircraft: specifications (title varies) (cont) Aviation W 78:207 Mr 11 '63; 80:217 Mr 16 '64
Used aircraft pilot report; Beech Staggerwing. G. J. Schlaeger. il Flying 74:26-7+ Mr '64
Used aircraft pilot report; Ercoupe. C. Wolfe. il Flying 74:48-9+ Ap '64
See also
Airplanes, Business

Automobile combinations

Whirlaway way; Bensen's gyrocopter. il Newsweek 63:68-9 Mr 30 '64

Design

Control features boost Wren 460 STOL performance. D. A. Brown. il Aviation W 78: 116-19+ Ap 15 '63
Fine art of design improvement. G. J. Schlaeger. il Flying 74:46-7+ Ja '64
Found FBA-2C designed for bush service. D. A. Brown. il Aviation W 80:98-9+ Je 15 '64
Fresh flock of fold-wing planes. J. Cushman and M. Dowd. il Pop Mech 119:90-5+ F '63
Navy evaluates light attack aircraft bids. L. Booda. Aviation W 79:26-7 Ag 12 '63
1964 Cessna has control, style changes. il Aviation W 79:111+ O 14 '63
PAC receives certification for Tradewind. C. M. Plattner. il Aviation W 78:95+ Ap 29 '63
Pilot report; Bede BD-1. G. J. Schlaeger. il Flying 74:34-5+ F '64
Piper speeds Twin Comanche production. D. A. Brown. il Aviation W 78:106-7+ My 6 '63
Siebelwerke building prototype of Siat 223 aerobatic trainer. il Aviation W 78:133 Je 17 '63

Electronic equipment

See Airplanes—Electronic equipment

Landing

See Airplanes—Landing

Prices

See Airplanes—Prices

AIRPLANES, Military
Disarmament police aircraft planned. K. Johnsen. Aviation W 79:36-7 O 14 '63
Italy, Germany team on V/STOL; lightweight strike fighter. Aviation W 80:31 Ap 13 '64
Navy calls for integrated VAX avionics. P. J. Klass. Aviation W 78:89 Ap 1 '63
New plane cuts the red tape; C-141 StarLifter. il Bsns W p52-3 D 26 '64
U.S. military services to increase participation in Paris air show. Aviation W 78:36 My 13 '63
See also
Airplanes, Vertical take-off and landing
McDonnell aircraft corporation

Accidents

See Aviation—Accidents

Anecdotes, facetiae, satire, etc.

Onward, upward, backward, forward, and sideways with the RX-550. M. J. Arlen. New Yorker 39:37-8 My 11 '63

Armaments

F-111 navaid performs multiple functions. il Aviation W 81:77+ Ag 17 '64
Fire control system applies laser radar. B. Miller. il Aviation W 81:69-70 Ag 17 '64
See also
Helicopters—Armaments

Control

F-111 navaid performs multiple functions. il Aviation W 81:77+ Ag 17 '64
Fire control system applies laser radar. B. Miller. il Aviation W 81:69-70 Ag 17 '64

Design

A-7A contract defines scale of penalties. E. J. Bulban. Aviation W 80:109-10+ Je 15 '64
Admiral viewed Boeing TFX as one plane. Aviation W 78:28-9 Ap 8 '63
Air force minimized engineering changes on StarLifter. J. R. Ashlock. il Aviation W 79: 68-9+ S 2 '63
Airborne; XB-70. il Newsweek 64:108+ O 5 '64
Assembly of XB-70 prototype completed. Aviation W 79:85-6 Ag 12 '63
Beech, Douglas counter-insurgency design details shown. il Aviation W 80:88-9 Je 8 '64
Boeing reconsiders stretched 707 version. il Aviation W 81:24-5 N 30 '64
CL-41A designed for COIN, recon flights. D. E. Fink. il Aviation W 78:61+ Mr 25 '63
COIN design by Lockheed carries weapons, troops. H. D. Watkins. il Aviation W 80: 74-6+ My 25 '64
Convair COIN entry is tailored for primary attack mission. D. E. Fink. il Aviation W 80:74-5+ Je 1 '64
Details of F-111A inlet, radome, nose gear shown. il Aviation W 81:40-1 N 2 '64
F-111, B-58 techniques used on RB-57F. E. J. Bulban. il Aviation W 81:51+ Jl 20 '64
F-111 engineering inspection under way. Aviation W 79:24 S 2 '63
F-111A program posts several aeronautical and political firsts. G. C. Wilson. il Aviation W 81:27-9 O 19 '64
French navy crusaders will have boundary layer control on flaps. Aviation W 79:37 Ag 12 '63
Garrett uprates T76 engine to 660 shp. for COIN aircraft. C. M. Plattner. il Aviation W 81:92-3+ Ag 24 '64
Goodyear proposes plastic COIN aircraft. D. E. Fink. il Aviation W 80:31-2 Je 15 '64
Martin COIN design has inverted V-tail. D. E. Fink. il Aviation W 80:82-3+ Ap 13 '64
Modified Helio U-5 proposed for COIN. D. A. Brown. il Aviation W 80:20-1 Je 22 '64
Old before it's born; Mach 3 bomber, the B-70. il Bsns W p28-9 My 16 '64
Refinements reduce F-111A weight, drag. E. J. Bulban. il Aviation W 81:26-7 O 19 '64
Rollout due for second Mirage 3V program testbed. il Aviation W 78:100-2 Je 10 '63
Thrust reversers now considered for TFX. Aviation W 78:26 Ap 8 '63
YF-12A performance in F-108 category. C. M. Plattner. il Aviation W 81:54-8+ O 19 '64

Electronic equipment

See Airplanes—Electronic equipment

Equipment

New concepts sought for aging hardware. C. Brownlow. il Aviation W 81:65+ O 19 '64
U-2s gathering data on missile exhausts. il Aviation W 79:53+ N 18 '63
USAF seeking improved reconnaissance aids to conduct demanding new missions. W. Wright. il Aviation W 80:88-9+ Ap 6 '64

Escape devices

See Airplanes—Escape devices

Maintenance and repair

L-T-V must attain A-7A maintenance aims. G. C. Wilson. Aviation W 80:16-17 Mr 30 '64

Materials

Navy to allow plastic, glass fiber in constuction of COIN aircraft. Aviation W 79:43 N 11 '63

Piloting

See Airplanes—Piloting

Refueling

See Airplanes—Refueling

Safety devices and measures

See Airplanes—Safety devices and measures

Testing

C-141 flight tests continue on schedule. J. R. Ashlock. il Aviation W 81:38-41+ Ag 31 '64
Contractors gear to beat F-111 test dates. E. J. Bulban. il Aviation W 81:30-3 O 26 '64
Excellent data, malfunctions mark initial XB-70 flight. il Aviation W 81:24-6 S 28 '64
F-5B capability spans wide speed range. H. J. Coleman. il Aviation W 81:48-9+ O 12 '64
First look at the XB-70: for two planes, 1.3 billion dollars. il U S News 56:4 My 18 '64
Flight tests of C-2A are geared to 1966 fleet service. D. A. Brown. il Aviation W 81: 20-2 D 7 '64

AIRPLANES, Military—Testing—*Continued*
Malfunction shortens first flight of F-111. E. J. Bulban. il Aviation W 81:18-19 D 28 '64
Mission variety demonstrated by F-104G; pilot report. C. M. Plattner. il Aviation W 78:72-3+ F 11 '63
Photo sequences follow first XB-70A flight. il Aviation W 81:64-5+ O 5 '64
Trying its wings first time. il Bsns W p50 O 3 '64
Two aircraft scheduled for use in Belfast flight test program. il Aviation W 79:45 O 21 '63
Two worlds of speed; testing the wing control mechanism of the F-111. il Time 85: 56 Ja 15 '65
X-15 modified for hypersonic research. il Aviation W 79:38 N 4 '63

Australia

Controversial Australian order for F-111 to total $125 million. H. J. Coleman. Aviation W 79:34 N 18 '63

Canada

Canada details defense equipment needs. Aviation W 82:24 Ja 4 '65

Europe, Western

NASARR problems hampering F-104G. C. Brownlow. il Aviation W 78:63-4 Mr 4 '63

Finland

First MiG-21s are delivered to Finnish air force. il Aviation W 78:32-3 My 20 '63

France

Balzac may be rebuilt after crash; VTOL fighter. Aviation W 80:34 Ja 20 '64
Etendard 4M planned for nuclear mission. il Aviation W 78:106-7 Ja 28 '63
French reach for technology in nuclear. Mach 2 transport programs. R. E. Farrell. il Aviation W 78:280-3 Mr 11 '63
Mirage 3V VTOL flight delayed. Aviation W 79:42 D 16 '63
Rollout due for second Mirage 3V program testbed. il Aviation W 78:100-2 Je 10 '63
Snecma TF-106 engine may be cut by French. Aviation W 80:31 F 17 '64

Germany

Pilot report illustrated; Fokker E III. F. Tallman. il Flying 74:36-9+ My '64

Germany (Federal Republic)

Delay expected in German VTOL decision. C. Brownlow. Aviation W 80:59+ Ap 6 '64
German defense minister orders plans to buy TF-104Gs shelved. Aviation W 79:32 N 11 '63
Germans renew talks on TF-104G order. Aviation W 80:33 Ja 13 '64
Germany moves to retain design teams. il Aviation W 80:289+ Mr 16 '64
Perils of pushing; Lockheed's hard sell in West Germany. il Time 82:88 N 22 '63
Rolls expands range of V/STOL engine development efforts. W. C. Wetmore. il Aviation W 81:78-80+ S 7 '64
West Germans seek industry unification. il Aviation W 78:293-5 Mr 11 '63
West Germany seeks shift in NATO role. C. Brownlow. Aviation W 78:32-3 F 4 '63

Great Britain

AW-681 Pegasus, RB.162 engine placement shown; models. il Aviation W 78:57 Ap 1 '63
BS.100 VTOL powerplant readied for bench testing; turbofan engine. il Aviation W 81: 86-9 S 7 '64
Britain's manned missile. W. Cloud. il Pop Sci 184:68 Ja '64
British seek to hold technological base. H. J. Coleman. il Aviation W 78:275-9 Mr 11 '63
British select AW-681 STOL for RAF. H. J. Coleman. Aviation W 78:303 Mr 11 '63
Design demands by British navy cloud future of P.1154 program. Aviation W 79:30 N 25 '63
First RAF bomber unit equipped with Blue Steel now operational. il Aviation W 78:78-9 Mr 4 '63
Gnat trainer demonstrates reliability, maneuverability. H. J. Coleman. il Aviation W 79:58-60 D 23 '63
Problem legacy; proposal to cancel the TSR-2. il Newsweek 65:36+ Ja 25 '65
RAF issues order for twenty Beagle 206 Ys. Aviation W 78:35 My 13 '63
RAF plans P.1154 V/STOL fighter order. il Aviation W 81:72-3+ S 7 '64
Sentence of death? threatened cancellation of Britain's all-purpose TSR-2 bomber. il Time 85:24 Ja 22 '65
TSR.2 in advanced stage of construction. H. J. Coleman. il Aviation W 79:30-2 N 4 '63
Two aircraft scheduled for use in Belfast flight test program. il Aviation W 79:45 O 21 '63
U.K. will build aircraft carrier for P.1154 fighter operations. Aviation W 79:39 Ag 5 '63

India

India's experience reveals MiG problems. J. R. Ashlock. Aviation W 79:33-4 N 4 '63
Military missions begin study of India's air defense requirements. Aviation W 78:283+ Mr 11 '63

Israel

Stratocruiser to drop Israeli paratroops. W. C. Wetmore. il Aviation W 82:101+ Ja 18 '65

Italy

Italy screening military aircraft for five-year production effort; to meet NATO commitments. L. L. Doty. Aviation W 81:18-19 D 7 '64

Russia

USSR military and civil aircraft; specifications. Aviation W 78:211 Mr 11 '63; 80:222 Mr 16 '64

Sweden

Saab to push 105 military export sales. il Aviation W 80:83 Mr 23 '64
Smaller nations seek consortiums; Swedes forging modern air force. Aviation W 80: 285+ Mr 16 '64
Sweden seeking $320 million for Viggen. il Aviation W 80:77 My 11 '64
Viggen to be core of Swedish air force. W. C. Wetmore. il Aviation W 79:57-61 O 21 '63

Switzerland

Economy influences Swiss Mirage cutback. L. L. Doty. Aviation W 81:54+ O 12 '64

United States

A-11 proven in reconnaissance missions; with editorial comment. il Aviation W 80:11, 16-18 Mr 9 '64
A-11 shows way for hotter airliners. il Bsns W p26-7 Mr 7 '64
A-11, world's hottest jet. W. Cloud. il Pop Sci 184:68-9 My '64
Air force minimized engineering changes on StarLifter. J. R. Ashlock. il Aviation W 79: 68-9+ S 2 '63
Air force seeks funds to begin work on new strategic aircraft. Aviation W 79:30 D 23 '63
Air force shows off first triplesonic planes; XB-70A and YF-12A. W. S. Griswold. il Pop Sci 185:64-5 D '64
Aluminum barrier broken. il Sci N L 85:162 Mr 14 '64
Angel from the Skunk works; details of the U-2's birth. il Time 82:31 S 20 '63
Assembly of XB-70 prototype completed. Aviation W 79:85-6 Ag 12 '63
B-70 unveiled at last to fly this month. il Pop Sci 185:48-9 Ag '64
B-26K photo reconnaissance system shown. il Aviation W 81:43 N 2 '64
Barry's bomber gap. R. D. Senter. il New Repub 151:9-10 S 12 '64
Battle grows over new U.S. jet bomber; concerning replacement of B-52s and B-58s. il U S News 56:6 F 24 '64
Beech COIN designed for low-time pilot. D. A. Brown. il Aviation W 80:19-20 Je 1 '64
Blackburn memo criticizes TFX decision. A. W. Blackburn. Aviation W 78:79-83 Je 3 '63
Boeing reconsiders stretched 707 version. il Aviation W 81:24-5 N 30 '64
Bomb carrier nobody can stop; Convair B-58 Hustler. F. V. Drake. il Read Digest 84: 153-4+ Ap '64
Bombers vs. missiles: a new round in an old fight. U S News 56:4 Mr 2 '64
Bombs or bishops; light-armed reconnaissance airplane known as COIN. il Newsweek 64:48 Ag 31 '64
Bright new COIN; Convair's Charger. il Time 84:104 O 9 '64
C-141 completes successful first flight. R. H. Cook. il Aviation W 79:42-3 D 23 '63
C-141 flight tests continue on schedule. J. R. Ashlock. il Aviation W 81:38-41+ Ag 31 '64
CX-HLS phase 1 award expected in June. C. M. Plattner. Aviation W 80:22-3 My 11 '64
CX-HLS raises C-141 funding questions. il Aviation W 81:82+ Ag 3 '64

AIRPLANES, Military—United States—*Cont.*
CX-HLS studied as commercial transport. J. R. Ashlock. Aviation W 81:27 N 2 '64
Cessna YAT-37D nears final air force tests; gross weight increased. il Aviation W 81:36-7 Jl 13 '64
Confederate air force flies at last; World war II fighter planes. D. Jenkins. il Sports Illus 19:58-63 Ag 12 '63
Configurations of F-111A, B unveiled. E. H. Kolcum. il Aviation W 80:21-2 Je 1 '64
Contractors gear to beat F-111 test dates. E. J. Bulban. il Aviation W 81:30-3 O 26 '64
Contractors pressing for advanced XV-5A; fan-in-wing VTOL. il Aviation W 81:32-3 N 23 '64
Controversial B-70; military monster or supersonic transport? T. E. Stimson. il Pop Mech 119:67-71+ Je '63
Convair COIN rollout scheduled this week; photographs. Aviation W 81:22-3 S 28 '64
COIN aircraft proposal request is expected before end of year. Aviation W 79:33 O 7 '63
COIN decision spurs Pentagon debate. D. E. Fink. Aviation W 81:21 Ag 17 '64
COIN design by Lockheed carries weapons, troops. H. D. Watkins. il Aviation W 80:74-6+ My 25 '64
COIN evaluation nearly finished; purchase of 507 aircraft planned. Aviation W 80:23 Je 29 '64
COIN report withdrawn at session after review process bogs down. il Aviation W 80:18-19 Je 1 '64
Crewmen fly B-52 damaged in turbulence. il Aviation W 80:27 Mr 9 '64
Cruise fan engine effort pushed by GE; for proposed CX-HLS. J. R. Ashlock. il Aviation W 80:70-1+ My 11 '64
Death of the B-47. il U S News 55:66 O 21 '63
Defense interest in prototypes renewed. Aviation W 78:31 Ap 22 '63
DOD presses program to develop CX-HLS. Aviation W 80:29 Je 15 '64
Details of F-111A inlet, radome, nose gear shown. il Aviation W 81:40-1 N 2 '64
Double debut; YF12A and XB70. il Sci Digest 56:17 D '64
Douglas, Convair unveil COIN mockups. D. E. Fink. il Aviation W 80:29-30 My 25 '64
E-2A compatible with carrier operations. L. Booda. il Aviation W 78:68-9+ Mr 4 '63
Effort spurred to find C-133 loss cause. C. Brownlow. Aviation W 82:25 Ja 18 '65
End of the manned bomber. R. D. Senter. New Repub 148:19-20 F 9 '63
Excellent data, malfunctions mark initial XB-70 flight. il Aviation W 81:24-6 S 28 '64
Expanded X-15 program planned; hypersonic, higher flights sought. Aviation W 78:38 Je 10 '63
Experts rebut McNamara; back Boeing's use of titanium for F-111. G. C. Wilson. Aviation W 79:36 Jl 1 '63
F-111 gives and takes; supersonic fighter. J. Eberhart. il(p273) Sci N L 86:279 O 31 '64
F-111, B-58 techniques used on RB-57F. E. J. Bulban. il Aviation W 81:51+ Jl 20 '64
F-111, in model form, spreads its switch-blade wings; TFX plane. il Bsns W p27 My 30 '64
F-111 weight, drag increases alarm navy. G. C. Wilson. Aviation W 80:16-17 Mr 23 '64
F-111A program posts several aeronautical and political firsts. G. C. Wilson. il Aviation W 81:27-9 O 19 '64
F-105D's limited-war capability boosted; Bitburg and Spangdehlem bases. West Germany. C. Brownlow. il Aviation W 78:105+ F 25 '63
Facts about McNamara's folly; TFX. J. H. Winchester. il Sci Digest 54:14-18 Jl '63
Fighter for all speeds; TFX or F-111. il Time 84:52 O 23 '64
Fighter pilot. R. Bach. il Harper 227:39-45 Jl '63
Final reports due next month on initial studies for CX-HLS. Aviation W 81:26 Ag 10 '64
Firebee; pilotless plane shot down by Chinese. il Time 84:30 N 27 '64
First B-26K delivery planned next month. Aviation W 80:96-7 My 18 '64
First C-141 rolled out; production rate of seven planes monthly planned by 1966. J. R. Ashlock il Aviation W 79:30-3 Ag 26 '63
First look at the controversial TFX. il U S News 56:8 Je 8 '64
Flight tests of C-2A are geared to 1966 fleet service. D. A. Brown. il Aviation W 81:20-2 D 7 '64
Flying jeep; OV-10A, also referred to as LARA or COIN. H. Shuldiner. il Pop Sci 185:45-7+ D '64
Flying patent factory; B-70. il Sci Digest 56:74 Jl '64
Former key TFX official attacks choice. G. C. Wilson. Aviation W 78:32-3 My 27 '63
Garrett uprates T76 engine to 660 shp. for COIN aircraft. C. M. Plattner. il Aviation W 81:92-3+ Ag 24 '64
General dynamics defends F-111 design. Aviation W 78:104+ My 20 '63
General dynamics rejects plan for TFX flying prototype contest. G. C. Wilson. Aviation W 78:27-9 My 13 '63
General LeMay's case for new strategic aircraft; excerpts from statement before House defense appropriations subcommittee, February 26, 1964. C. E. LeMay. Aviation W 80:21 Ap 20 '64
Good news emphasis ordered in F-111 information policy shift. Aviation W 80:31 Ap 27 '64
Great A-11 deception. J. Atwater. il Sat Eve Post 237:15-17 My 2 '64
Grumman's variable sweep wing work cited. il Aviation W 78:105 My 20 '63
Happy landing; maiden flight of the F-111. il Time 85:30 Ja 1 '65
Heavy SST financial role seen for DOD. R. H. Cook. Aviation W 80:28-9 Ap 6 '64
Hot COIN; ingenious proposals for counter-insurgency aircraft. il Time 83:39 Je 12 '64
Humiliating triumph; B-70 project. il Newsweek 63:90 My 18 '64
I flew with TAC's top gun. K. V. Brown. il Pop Mech 120:118-22+ O '63
Invisible A-11. Nation 198:282-3 Mr 23 '64
Is U.S. using pilotless planes in Asia? U S News 57:11 N 30 '64
Jeep to fly missions; twin-engine LARA Light armed reconnaissance aircraft. Sci N L 86:132 Ag 29 '64
Jet scout for missiles; SR-71. il Bsns W p20 Ag 1 '64
Jet starter development effort growing. M. L. Yaffee. Aviation W 82:49+ Ja 25 '65
Korth defends TFX choice, hears charge he used raw judgment. G. C. Wilson. il Aviation W 79:19-21 Jl 8 '63
Large-scale COIN buy remains in doubt. G. C. Wilson. Aviation W 81:23-4 Ag 24 '64
Last of the red hot cats; Grumman's Bearcat. N. R. Hanson. il Flying 74:46-7+ F '64
Last stand of the big bomber; debate between McNamara and LeMay. J. Atwater. il Sat Eve Post 237:13-17 Je 20 '64
LeMay seeks two new aircraft. Aviation W 80:34 F 10 '64
Lockheed, Boeing study concepts for 700-800,000-lb. CX-HLS. J. R. Ashlock. Aviation W 80:17 My 4 '64
Lockheed YF-12A flight demonstration reveals design details. il Aviation W 81:30-3 O 12 '64
A look at the air force's 2,000-mph interceptor; YF-12A. il U S News 57:14 O 12 '64
McClellan claims $1 billion waste on TFX. G. C. Wilson. Aviation W 79:18-19 Jl 29 '63
McNamara clouds future of COIN effort. D. E. Fink. Aviation W 81:16 Jl 20 '64
McNamara, Congress differ on A-11 role. G. C. Wilson. Aviation W 80:18-19 Mr 9 '64
McNamara cool toward COIN proposals; navy counter-insurgency aircraft program. G. C. Wilson. Aviation W 80:16-17 Je 1 '64
McNamara details defense buying, R&D; summary of testimony before House armed services committee. R. S. McNamara. Aviation W 78:27-30 F 4 '63
McNamara doubts AMSA future; says budget to hold present level. C. Brownlow. Aviation W 81:23-4 N 16 '64
McNamara gives report on assets. il U S News 54:95-6 Ap 1 '63
McNamara tries to steer TFX questions. G. C. Wilson. Aviation W 78:26-8 Ap 1 '63
McNamara used rough judgement on TFX. G. C. Wilson. Aviation W 78:24-5 My 6 '63
McNamara's $1-billion TFX saving hypothetical. Aviation W 78:32 My 27 '63
Malfunction shortens first flight of F-111. E. J. Bulban. il Aviation W 81:18-19 D 28 '64
Manner of speaking; concerning a report of Laurence Barrett in the Herald tribune. J. Ciardi. Sat R 47:15 Je 13 '64; Reply. L. Barrett. 47:16 Jl 25 '64
Martin COIN design has inverted V-tail. D. E. Fink. il Aviation W 80:82-3+ Ap 13 '64

AIRPLANES, Military—United States—*Cont.*
Modified XV-5A to incorporate new wing; army lift-fan research airplane. C. M. Plattner. il Aviation W 81:38-9+ D 14 '64
NASA, GE study VTOL fighter with lift fans similar to XV-5A. Aviation W 78:28 Ja 28 '63
Navy calls manned aircraft indispensable. G. C. Wilson. Aviation W 78:40-1 F 25 '63
Navy evaluates light attack aircraft bids. L. Booda. Aviation W 79:26-7 Ag 12 '63
Navy scores DOD civilians' X-22A role. G. C. Wilson. Aviation W 78:32-3 Je 17 '63
Navy to deploy A-6A squadron next year. D. A. Brown. il Aviation W 81:46-7+ Ag 17 '64
Navy VAL contract may total $1 billion. G. C. Wilson. il Aviation W 80:27-8 F 17 '64
New bomber funds win early approval. K. Johnsen. Aviation W 80:26-7 F 24 '64
New bomber money authorized in $17-billion defense measure. Aviation W 80:307 Mr 16 '64
New bomber money prospect improves. Aviation W 80:29 Mr 2 '64
New Mach 2 carrier plane. il Sci Digest 56:32-5 Ag '64
New 12,000-mi. cargo aircraft is sought. L. Booda. Aviation W 79:26-7 N 18 '63
North American COIN competition entry incorporates twin tail, central fuselage. D. E. Fink. il Aviation W 81:38-9+ Jl 13 '64
Northrop X-21 to make first flight in March; photographs. Aviation W 78:80-1 F 11 '63
Now you see it, now . .; the A-11. il Newsweek 63:64+ Mr 16 '64
Old before it's born; Mach 3 bomber, the B-70. il Bsns W p28-9 My 16 '64
Our watchdog at the edge of space; YF-12A interceptor. J. Bergman. il Read Digest 85:56-50 D '64
Performance edge stressed in TFX quiz. G. C. Wilson. Aviation W 78:28-30 Ap 15 '63
Phasing out the air force? contract for TFX. Nat R 14:223-4 Mr 26 '63
Photo sequences follow first XB-70A flight. il Aviation W 81:64-5+ O 5 '64
Pilot report; Boeing P-12: 1928 fighter. F. Tallman. il Flying 75:54-6+ Ag '64
Plane and fancy; TFX (Tactical fighter experimental) variable-wing F-111A. il Newsweek 64:99 O 26 '64
Planes over Saigon: wings tear off. D. F. Ford il Nation 199:3-5 Jl 13 '64
PS reporter previews the F-111. F. Harvey. il Pop Sci 186:64-5 Ja '65
Power increase planned for COIN T-37. il Aviation W 79:57-9 Jl 1 '63
Powers-less flight; Ryan Firebee. il Newsweek 64:90 N 30 '64
President affirms A-11 surveillance role; with editorial comment. il Aviation W 81:11, 16-17 Ag 3 '64
President discloses development of SR-71 Mach 3 reconnaissance plane. Miss & Roc 15:11 Ag 3 '64
President's role in TFX award disclosed. E. H. Kolcum. Aviation W 79:34-6 Ag 26 '63
Probers told navy seeks more F-111s. G. C. Wilson. Aviation W 79:324 Jl 22 '63
Probers told of navy's qualms about bi-service TFX program. Aviation W 79:21-2 Jl 8 '63
Quang Long battle typifies aircraft use. Aviation W 80:103 Ap 13 '64
RB-57F built for varied special missions. E. J. Bulban. il Aviation W 81:22-4 Jl 13 '64
Refinements reduce F-111A weight, drag. E. J. Bulban. il Aviation W 81:26-7 O 19 '64
Report favors prototype development. B. H. Klein and others. il Aviation W 78:135+ Je 10 '63
Republicans plan Vietnam visit to stir COIN as political issue. D. E. Fink. Aviation W 81:18 Jl 27 '64
Rift may affect TFX role, configuration. L. Booda. Aviation W 79:26 S 9 '63
Russell scores abandonment of bombers. G. C. Wilson. Aviation W 79:28-9 S 23 '63
Search for new plane. il Bsns W p34 My 23 '64
Secret life of the A-11. D. Cater. Reporter 30:16-17 Ap 23 '64
Senate votes $363.7 million extra for RS-70. Aviation W 78:26 Ap 22 '63
$7-billion contract that changed the rules. R. A. Smith. il Fortune 67:96-101+ Mr; 110-11+ Ap '63
Story of the A-11. il Sci Digest 55:20-1 My '64
SAC seeking to maintain force mixture. W. H. Gregory. il Aviation W 80:80-1+ Ap 27 '64
SAC U-2s modified for fallout sampling. C. M. Plattner. il Aviation W 79:72-3+ Ag 12 '63
Swept-wing F-111 to use fuselage lift. E. J. Bulban. Aviation W 79:32 D 23 '63
Swift black bird; A-11 publicity shown and flown. il Time 84:104 O 9 '64
Systems tests begin XB-70A checkout for first flight. C. M. Plattner. il Aviation W 80:84-5+ Je 1 '64
TFX; a feud boils up; with editorial comment. il Bsns W p 19-20, 116 My 11 '63
TFX board selected Boeing four times; investigation of General dynamics-Grumman contract by Senate investigations subcommittee, with excerpts from hearing. G. C. Wilson. Aviation W 78:22-4 Mr 4 '63
TFX chief would drop thrust reversers. D. E. Fink. Aviation W 79:38 Ag 5 '63
TFX confrontation due this year. Aviation W 80:75 Mr 16 '64
TFX: Congress fumes and fusses but seems to recognize that the decision wasn't a bad one. D. S. Greenberg. Science 139:1271-2 Mr 29 '63
TFX flies but questions remain. il U S News 58:6+ Ja 4 '65
TFX plane controversy. Sci N L 84:7 Jl 6 '63
TFX plane: what the fight is about. il U S News 54:61-3 Mr 25 '63
TFX probe to focus on possible conflict in Gilpatric, Korth roles. G. C. Wilson. Aviation W 79:27-8 S 9 '63
Text of President's A-11 statements. L. B. Johnson. Aviation W 81:17 Ag 3 '64
That mysterious A-11. W. E. Boggs. New Repub 150:14-15 Mr 14 '64
Transition from VTOL to horizontal flight mode demonstrated by XV-4A Hummingbird turbojet. il Aviation W 79:82-3 D 16 '63
Turbine-powered Buffalo built for short, rough fields. D. A. Brown. il Aviation W 80:84-6+ My 25 '64
USAF, army differ on aircraft types and mission assignments. Aviation W 78:37 F 11 '63
USAF C-141 enters flight test phase. il Aviation W 80:78-9 Ja 13 '64
USAF seeking improved reconnaissance aids to conduct demanding new missions. W. Wright. il Aviation W 80:88-9+ Ap 6 '64
USAF stresses manned aircraft needs. L. Booda. Aviation W 79:38-9 S 23 '63
USAF stresses YF-12A interceptor role. il Aviation W 81:16-17 O 5 '64
USAF stronger in latest aircraft fight. G. C. Wilson. Aviation W 80:28 F 24 '64
U.S. denies A-11 reconnaissance flights. Aviation W 80:306 Mr 16 '64
U.S. military aircraft; specifications (cont) Aviation W 78:185-6 Mr 11 '63; 80:189-90 Mr 16 '64
U.S. Soviet strengths detailed; with editorial comment. J. Trainor. Miss & Roc 14:14, 46 Ap 20 '64
What goes there? the YF-12A. il Newsweek 64:80 O 12 '64
Why the TFX plane is still under fire; now known as the F-111. il U S News 57:8 O 26 '64
Wing sweep brings first F-111 bonus. il Aviation W 82:19 Ja 11 '65
Witnesses challenge McNamara on TFX. G. C. Wilson. Aviation W 78:26-7 Ap 8 '63
XB70 bomber makes costly research plane. Sci N L 86:217 O 3 '64
XB-70; building the world's weirdest airplane. K. Wheeler. il Life 58:74-80+ Ja 15 '65
XB-70A's research role will contribute Mach 3 flight data for SST development. C. M. Plattner. il Aviation W 80:26-30 My 18 '64
YB-26K delivered to air force for tests as COIN interim plane. Aviation W 78:32 Mr 4 '63
YB-26K interim counter-insurgency plane shown. il Aviation W 78:66 Mr 18 '63
YF-12A performance in F-108 category. C. M. Plattner. il Aviation W 81:54-8+ O 19 '64
Zuckert discusses TFX, follow-on aircraft. E. M. Zuckert. Aviation W 79:18 S 2 '63
Zuckert, LeMay agree B-70 effort is pushing technology to limits. Aviation W 80:29 F 24 '64
Zuckert TFK rough judgment charged. D. E. Fink. Aviation W 79:29-30 Ag 12 '63

AIRPLANES, Military transport
Big hopes ride on a big, big transport. Bsns W p28 D 19 '64
CX-4 concept has swing-nose, aft ramp. C. M. Plattner. il Aviation W 79:33-4 O 21 '63
CX-HLS phase 1 award expected in June. C. M. Plattner. Aviation W 80:22-3 My 11 '64
CX-HLS raises C-141 funding questions. il Aviation W 81:82+ Ag 3 '64
CX-HLS studied as commercial transport. J. R. Ashlock. Aviation W 81:27 N 2 '64

AIRPLANES, Military transport—*Continued*
COIN design by Lockheed carries weapons, troops. H. D. Watkins. il Aviation W 80: 74-6+ My 25 '64
Cruise fan engine effort pushed by GE; for proposed CX-HLS. J. R. Ashlock. il Aviation W 80:70-1+ My 11 '64
DC-9 cargo version proposed for Logair. il Aviation W 82:30-1 Ja 4 '65
Douglas proposes an intercontinental ballistic transport for 1,200 troops. W. E. Wilks. il Miss & Roc 14:35 F 17 '64
Final reports due next month on initial studies for CX-HLS. Aviation W 81:26 Ag 10 '64
550-seat airliner? CX-HLS (Cargo experimental-heavy logistics system) Newsweek 64:66 N 2 '64
Helio's Stallion designed for light military transport use. R. D. Hibben. il Aviation W 80:92-3+ Je 1 '64
India's experience reveals MiG problems. J. R. Ashlock. Aviation W 79:33-4 N 4 '63
Lockheed, Boeing study concepts for 700-800,000-lb. CX-HLS. J. R. Ashlock. Aviation W 80:17 My 4 '64
North American COIN competition entry incorporates twin tail, central fuselage. D. E. Fink. il Aviation W 81:38-9+ Jl 13 '64
Soon: planes carrying 700 passengers: C-5A. il U S News 58:6 Ja 4 '65
TAC center tests fast delivery concepts. C. Brownlow. il Aviation W 81:65+ O 12 '64
Turbine-powered Buffalo built for short, rough fields. D. A. Brown. il Aviation W 80:84-6+ My 25 '64

AIRPLANES, Model. *See* **Airplane models**

AIRPLANES, Old

Collectors and collecting

See Airplanes—Collectors and collecting

AIRPLANES, Short take-off and landing
Breguet 941 features stability, safety. H. J. Coleman. il Aviation W 79:42-4 Jl 29 '63
Canadair completes CL-84 VTOL design. D. E. Fink. il Aviation W 79:70-1+ N 25 '63
Caribou reverse thrust for STOL studied. D. E. Fink. il Aviation W 78:67+ F 18 '63
Control features boost Wren 460 STOL performance. D. A. Brown. il Aviation W 78: 116-19+ Ap 15 '63
Dornier schedules Do. 31 V/STOL tests. W. C. Wetmore. il Aviation W 80:30-2 Mr 30 '64
Foreign interest revived in Breguet 941. W. C. Wetmore. il Aviation W 79:73+ Jl 15 '63
Found FBA-2C designed for bush service. D. A. Brown. il Aviation W 80:98-9+ Je 15 '64
Helio changes improve cruise, climb rate. D. A. Brown. il Aviation W 81:74-5+ Ag 31 '64
Modified Helio U-5 proposed for COIN. D. A. Brown. il Aviation W 80:20-1 Je 22 '64
Power increase planned for COIN T-37. il Aviation W 79:57-9 Jl 1 '63
Takeoff at thirty; airplane in STOL category. K. Brown. il Pop Mech 120:94-7+ S '63
Twin Otter boosts hot climate capability; light STOL utility transport. D. A. Brown. il Aviation W 82:72-4 Ja 4 '65

AIRPLANES, Supersonic
A-11: new U.S. jet is fastest and highest. J. Hannifin. il Life 56:26-7 Mr 13 '64
A-11 shows way for hotter airliner. il Bsns W p26-7 Mr 7 '64
A-11, world's hottest jet. W. Cloud. il Pop Sci 184:68-9 My '64
Aid from rivals; BOAC and Air France place orders for the American SST. Time 83:88 F 14 '64
Air force shows off first triplesonic planes; XB-70A and YF-12A. W. S. Griswold. il Pop Sci 185:64-5 D '64
Air France adopts BOAC show us attitude on supersonic transport. H. J. Coleman. Aviation W 78:39 Ja 28 '63
Airborne; XB-70. il Newsweek 64:108+ O 5 '64
Airline insurance: advance orders for the Anglo-French Concorde. Newsweek 62:68 Ag 12 '63
Airlines suggest two SST prototypes for evaluation. Aviation W 80:27 Mr 23 '64
Airport unit warns of SST noise level. Aviation W 80:28-9 Mr 30 '64
Aluminum barrier broken. il Sci N L 85:162 Mr 14 '64
America's goal now: a Mach 3 plane by 1970. il U S News 55:14 Jl 1 '63
America's secret jet plane; the inside story: A-11 project. il U S News 56:36-7 Mr 16 '64
Anatomy of speed; Lockheed's A-11. il Time 83:58 Mr 20 '64
Another second for U.S? Europe leads in race. il U S News 54:94 Je 17 '63
B-70 unveiled at last to fly this month. il Pop Sci 185:48-9 Ag '64
Blunting the spearhead. R. Hotz. Aviation W 81:17 N 23 '64
Boom in a ghost town. Bsns W p29 D 12 '64
Boom restrictions may swell SST costs. il Aviation W 81:38-9+ Ag 3 '64
Boom town will keep tests; Oklahoma City. Bsns W p27 Mr 7 '64
BEA chief engineer criticizes SST plans. Aviation W 79:52 O 7 '63
British move for Concorde compromise seen. Aviation W 81:29 D 7 '64
Can we build a 2,000-m.p.h. airliner? W. Cloud. il Pop Sci 184:67-70+ Ap '64
Carriers may protest SST delivery policy. L. L. Doty. Aviation W 79:43 N 4 '63
Clouds over the Concorde; Lockheed's A-11. il Time 83:96 Mr 13 '64
Committed to a supersonic. Time 81:90 Je 14 '63
Concorde alloy has high creep strength. il Aviation W 81:133+ S 7 '64
Concorde discussions remain at standstill. H. J. Coleman. Aviation W 82:32 Ja 11 '65
Concorde, or an American supersonic? il Newsweek 61:73 Je 17 '63
Concorde order spurs U.S. SST action. L. L. Doty. Aviation W 78:40 Je 10 '63
Concorde tests at U.S. facility approved. L. L. Doty. Aviation W 79:38 Jl 15 '63
Congress awaits solution of SST dispute. R. H. Cook. Aviation W 79:40-1 N 4 '63
Cost barrier has not been broken. il Time 84:84 Jl 24 '64
Council drops boom protest. il Aviation W 80:34 Mr 9 '64
Demi-accord on Concorde. Newsweek 65:57 F 1 '65
Double debut; YF12A and XB70. il Sci Digest 56:17 D '64
Farnborough pushing Concorde research. H. J. Coleman. il Aviation W 79:40-1 D 23 '63
FAA-NASA pact aims to block creation of new SST authority. Aviation W 80:41 F 17 '64
Financing is prime factor in SST delay. G. C. Wilson. Aviation W 80:28-9 My 4 '64
Flight forum participants believe U.S. will develop Mach 2 SST. Aviation W 78:35 My 27 '63
Flight of the sea serpent; North American's XB-70A. il Time 84:98 O 2 '64
Flight research center, AF press for Hypersonic research vehicle. R. Hawkes. Miss & Roc 14:29-30 F 10 '64
Foreign competition is accelerating U.S. development of a supersonic transport. E. H. Kolcum. il Aviation W 78:58-61+ Ap 1 '63
France studies building Concorde alone. Aviation W 81:38 N 9 '64
Groping through the sound barrier. il Newsweek 62:77 S 23 '63
Heat posing major SST design problems. J. R. Ashlock. il Aviation W 79:74-5 Jl 8 '63
Heavy SST financial role seen for DOD. R. H. Cook. Aviation W 80:28-9 Ap 6 '64
Industry urges U.S. to revise SST plan. R. H. Cook. Aviation W 79:37+ O 28 '63
Inertial systems favored as SST navaid. P. J. Klass. Aviation W 80:27-8 Je 22 '64
Is the SST a must? Nation 197:149 S 21 '63
It's progress, but is it necessary? symposium of industry's leaders. il Bsns W p54-6 My 25 '63
Kennedy asks for supplemental funds to spur U.S. SST program. Aviation W 79:39 Jl 1 '63
Kennedy calls for risk sharing on SST. R. H. Cook. Aviation W 78:39 Je 24 '63
Kennedy memo maintains SST timetable. Aviation W 78:38 Ja 28 '63
Kennedy names Black as advisor on supersonic transport program. Aviation W 79:37 Ag 19 '63
Larger U.S. SST, bigger payloads to be proposed. Aviation W 80:35 Ja 13 '64
Late take-off on the SST. il Time 81:106 My 17 '63
Lead time gets longer for SST. Bsns W p58 Jl 25 '64
London-N.Y. in three hours via supersonic transport. Sci N L 84:175 S 14 '63
Maytag urges Mach 2 SST development. Aviation W 79:40 Jl 15 '63; Reply. H. A. Hutchinson. 79:126 Ag 26 '63
Medium-range Concorde may be dropped. C. Brownlow. Aviation W 79:40-1 S 30 '63
Meeting of worriers: International air transport association. Time 84:92+ S 25 '64
More supersonics. R. Hotz. Aviation W 79:21 Jl 15 '63

AIRPLANES, Supersonic—*Continued*
NASA task may boost ramjet efforts; hypersonic ramjet experiment. M. L. Yaffee. Aviation W 81:21-2 Ag 3 '64
New light on SST problems. R. Hotz. Aviation W 79:21 N 11 '63
Notes and comment; hazards of supersonic flight. New Yorker 40:19-20 Ag 8 '64
Now you see it, now . . ; the A-11. il Newsweek 63:64+ Mr 16 '64
On your Mach; technical problems. il Newsweek 62:57 Jl 8 '63
Orders pour in for a plane that isn't; commercial supersonic jet. U S News 55:6 O 28 '63
Our watchdog at the edge of space; YF-12A interceptor. J. Bergman. il Read Digest 85:56-60 D '64
Pan Am, TWA lay it on line; order of supersonic airplanes. Bsns W p 132 O 19 '63
Perils of Pluto. W. J. Coughlin. Miss & Roc 14:46 Je 22 '64
Pilots group maps SST operations policy. H. J. Coleman. Aviation W 79:47+ N 25 '63
Plane in a poke. W. E. Boggs. New Repub 149:7 N 2 '63
Plane nobody wants. W. E. Boggs. New Repub 149:12-14 S 14 '63
President affirms A-11 surveillance role; with editorial comment. il Aviation W 81:11, 16-17 Ag 3 '64
Prospect of SST shift to Pentagon grows. L. L. Doty. Aviation W 80:38 Ap 27 '64
Public affair of the SST; Supersonic transport. W. Langewiesche. il Read Digest 85: 141-5 O '64
RM-8 detail design pushed by Flygmotor; to power Sweden's next manned weapons system. W. C. Wetmore. il Aviation W 79:48-9+ N 18 '63
Racing to be first with the fastest; Mach 2, Concorde. il Bsns W p 146+ S 21 '63
Round one for Boeing. il Time 83:93 Ap 10 '64
Senate unit approves SST funds. Aviation W 79:40 N 18 '63
Six firms to enter SST contest. Aviation W 79:49 S 16 '63
Six sees economy in joint SST programs. Aviation W 79:43 O 7 '63
Size, speed, safety of SST are debated. Aviation W 80:29 Je 1 '64
Sonic boom reaction tests set. Aviation W 80:50 Ja 20 '64
Sonic bust? problems of financing British-French Concorde and others. il Newsweek 63:66+ Ap 6 '64
Squabble to be first; U.S. supersonic jetliner program. il Time 82:93 O 25 '63
Story of the A-11. il Sci Digest 55:20-1 My '64
Study finds supersonic transport will reduce terminal operations. Aviation W 81:29 O 5 '64
Supersonic advice: call off the race. Newsweek 63:77 F 17 '64
Supersonic airliner coming; is U.S. losing out to Europe? interview. J. Stack. il U S News 54:50-2 Je 24 '63
Supersonic cobra; XB-70A. il Time 83:56+ My 22 '64
Supersonic jet: is it worth it? E. T. Chase. Commonweal 80:9-12 Mr 27 '64
Supersonic pace. R. Hotz. Aviation W 80:21 Ap 13 '64
Supersonic race is on. il Bsns W p32 Je 8 '63
Supersonic race slows to a crawl. il Bsns W p92+ N 14 '64
SSScramble; contract to build a supersonic transport. il Time 82:90+ S 20 '63
Supersonic transport. D. Kuhn. Flying 74:54 Mr '64
Supersonic transport delivery priorities. Aviation W 79:44 D 23 '63
Supersonic transport progress stalled. J. R. Ashlock. Aviation W 78:40 Ja 21 '63
Supersonic transports. Sci Am 209:48-9 Ag '63
Supersonic transports: new race in the sky? pro and con discussion. il Sr Schol 82:14-15 Mr 13 '63
SST, aviation's leap in the dark. J. H. Winchester. il Sci Digest 55:23-9 F '64
SST control needs. Aviation W 79:94 D 2 '63
SST economics worry IATA conferees. J. R. Ashlock. il Aviation W 81:29-30 S 28 '64
SST may cause route competition curb. H. D. Watkins. il Aviation W 81:30-2 N 2 '64
SST: no music to airport men's ears. il Bsns W p60+ O 26 '63
SST program advances as FAA awards $22 million in contracts. Aviation W 80:34 Je 8 '64
SStart; design competition to built a U.S. supersonic transport. il Time 83:62 Ja 24 '64
SStart; faltering U.S. supersonic jet transport project. Newsweek 63:62+ Je 1 '64
Swift black bird; A-11 publicly shown and flown. il Time 84:104 O 9 '64
Take-off to the future: A-11. il Time 83:15 Mr 6 '64
Text of President's A-11 statements. L. B. Johnson. Aviation W 81:17 Ag 3 '64
That mysterious A-11. W. E. Boggs. New Repub 150:14-15 Mr 14 '64
Tillinghast criticizes government SST plan, asks drastic overhaul. Aviation W 80:43 Mr 2 '64
Timetable for supersonic plane. Bsns W p97 Je 29 '63
Titan III program reappraised; proposed AF-NASA manned hypersonic spacecraft. il Miss & Roc 12:12-13 F 25 '63
Titanium producers seeking major role in development of SST as market increases. M. L. Yaffee. il Aviation W 79:48-9+ D 2 '63
TWA official examines SST economics; address. R. W. Rummel. il Aviation W 82:59-60+ Ja 4 '65
TWA orders eight more SSTs. Aviation W 79:39 N 18 '63
Travel at 1,800 miles an hour? why? when? interview. N. E. Halaby. il U S News 55: 52-8 D 23 '63; Same abr. Read Digest 84: 88-91 Mr '64
Trunks support extension of SST study. J. R. Ashlock. Aviation W 81:28 D 14 '64
2,000-mph airliner runs into a slowdown; U.S. program. U S News 56:10 Je 1 '64
Uneasy crown; planemaker to the world. il Time 82:68 Ag 16 '63
UAC chairman says SST engine problems being underestimated. Aviation W 80:47 Ap 27 '64
U.K. treasury criticized on Concorde role. H. J. Coleman. Aviation W 80:45+ Ja 27 '64
U.S. carriers support SST development; with editorial comment. R. H. Cook. Aviation W 79:21, 38-9 O 21 '63
U.S. flag carriers receive SST priority. R. H. Cook. Aviation W 79:38-9 N 25 '63
U.S. officials believe SST race profitless. Aviation W 81:40 S 14 '64
U.S. participation in Concorde proposed. L. L. Doty. Aviation W 78:40 Je 17 '63
U.S. shuns bid to enter Concorde effort; with editorial comment. L. L. Doty. Aviation W 79:13, 28-9 Jl 8 '63
U.S. supersonic transport effort stalled. L. L. Doty. Aviation W 80:29-30 Mr 9 '64
Up goes B-70 at last. il Life 57:129-30 O 2 '64
We're losing the supersonic transport race. J. Hannifin and C. J. V. Murphy. il Fortune 69:118-22+ F '64
When the traveler gets ahead of sound; SST, the Concorde, capable of 1,450 miles an hour. A. Hano. il N Y Times Mag p21+ My 17 '64
White House study urges U.S. to pay 90 per cent of SST costs. L. L. Doty. il Aviation W 80:36-9 F 3 '64
Who will win the supersonic race? C. Leedham. il N Y Times Mag p38+ Ag 23 '64
Who'll bear the supersonic risk? Bsns W p88+ N 9 '63
XB-70; building the world's weirdest airplane. K. Wheeler. il Life 58:74-80+ Ja 15 '65

Cost of operation

See Airplanes—Cost of operation

Design

Boeing shows details of supersonic transport. il Aviation W 80:40-1 Mr 2 '64
Cabin, exterior design of NAC-60 revealed. il Aviation W 80:38-9 F 10 '64
Choice of SST winners may offer first details to foreign buyers. J. R. Ashlock. Aviation W 80:27-8 Mr 30 '64
Companies assured of technical ability; plan SST risk-sharing. E. H. Kolcum. Aviation W 79:41-3 S 30 '63
Concorde delivery slips to 1971; production details listed. H. J. Coleman. il Aviation W 80:40-3 F 24 '64
Concorde design stretched to carry 118. il Aviation W 80:3 My 11 '64
Concorde on schedule despite problems in coordination. L. L. Doty. il Aviation W 81: 60-1+ S 7 '64
Design demands heavy. il(p353) Sci N L 85: 358 Je 6 '64
FAA labels SCAT designs impractical. R. H. Cook. Aviation W 79:38 O 14 '63

AIRPLANES, Supersonic—Design—*Continued*
Four firms picked under new SST plan; with editorial comment. R. H. Cook. il Aviation W 80:17, 22-3 My 25 '64
Halaby denies rift on SST configuration. Aviation W 79:49 S 30 '63
Latest Ames, Langley SST configurations tested; photographs. Aviation W 78:40-1 Ja 28 '63
Latest SST designs show payload gains. J. R. Ashlock. il Aviation W 81:36-7 N 9 '64
Lockheed compares SST, subsonic costs. il Aviation W 80:30-2 Je 1 '64
Lockheed SST features double-delta wing, drooped nose. H. D. Watkins. il Aviation W 80:38-9+ Mr 23 '64
NASA favors two SCAT configurations. E. H. Kolcum. Aviation W 79:26 S 23 '63
Range/weight ratio of Concorde studied. il Aviation W 78:56-7 Je 10 '63
Start of detailed SST design contest due. R. H. Cook. Aviation W 80:39 My 18 '64
Supersonic hot seat. B. Kocivar. il Look 28: 93-5+ My 5 '64
Supersonic transport. R. L. Bisplinghoff. il Sci Am 210:25-35 Je '64
SST model wind tunnel tests due Nov. 1. Aviation W 80:26-7 Je 1 '64
U.S. supersonic transport clears first big congressional hurdle. G. C. Wilson. Aviation W 79:39-40 O 14 '63
Variable-sweep wing keynotes Boeing 733 SST proposal. C. M. Plattner. il Aviation W 80:36-9+ My 4 '64

Fuel

See Jet airplane engines—Fuel

Materials

Aluminum barrier broken. il Sci N L 85:162 Mr 14 '64
German scientists investigate materials resisting supersonic rain-erosion damage. W. C. Wetmore. il Aviation W 80:110-11+ Ap 27 '64

AIRPLANES, Tank. See Tank airplanes

AIRPLANES, Training
CL-41A designed for COIN, recon flights. D. E. Fink. il Aviation W 78:61+ Mr 25 '63
FAA using revised light-twin training program for inspectors. il Aviation W 78:102-3 Ap 8 '63
Gnat trainer demonstrates reliability, maneuverability. H. J. Coleman. il Aviation W 79:58-60 D 23 '63
Pappy checks the Cherokee. A. H. Sanfelici. il Flying 74:48-9+ Je '64
Politics cloud future of Miles student. H. J. Coleman. il Aviation W 79:95+ Ag 5 '63

AIRPLANES, Used
IBM in used airplanes. P. Korenvaes. Duns R 82:55-6 D '63
Used aircraft pilot report; Beech Staggerwing. G. J. Schlaeger. il Flying 74:26-7+ Mr '64
Used aircraft pilot report; Ercoupe. C. Wolfe. il Flying 74:48-9+ Ap '64
Used aircraft pilot report; Mooney Mite. C. Wolfe. il Flying 74:38+ F '64
Used aircraft pilot report; Stinson. V. M. Draper. il Flying 75:71-2+ S '64

AIRPLANES, Vertical take-off and landing
Avian gyroplane; VTOL. H. McDougall. il Flying 74:44-5+ Ap '64
Balzac VTOL shown in vertical, hover and lateral flight modes. il Aviation W 79:38-41 Jl 29 '63
Canadair completes CL-84 VTOL design. D. E. Fink. il Aviation W 79:70-1+ N 25 '63
Contractors pressing for advanced XV-5A; fan-in-wing VTOL. il Aviation W 81:32-3 N 23 '64
Delay expected in German VTOL decision. C. Brownlow. Aviation W 80:59+ Ap 6 '64
Design demands by British navy cloud future of P.1154 program. Aviation W 79:30 N 25 '63
Dornier schedules Do. 31 V/STOL tests. W. C. Wetmore. il Aviation W 80:30-2 Mr 30 '64
French Balzac VTOL testbed takes off vertically, translates to horizontal flight in demonstration. il Aviation W 78:68-9 Je 24 '63
Helicopter, where now? N. D. Ham. il Flying 74:32+ F '64
Helicopters facing V/STOL competition. D. A. Anderton. il Aviation W 78:255-7 Mr 11 '63
Lockheed studies 10,000-mi. transport. J. W. Carter. Aviation W 80:47 Ap 13 '64
Modification of Sikorsky S-61F helicopter proposed for stowed-rotor V/STOL study. D. A. Brown. il Aviation W 82:50-1+ Ja 18 '65
More emphasis on V/STOL engines urged. Aviation W 82:27 Ja 18 '65
NASA, GE study VTOL fighter with lift fans similar to XV-5A. Aviation W 78:28 Ja 28 '63
New aircraft designed with rotors, jet speed. Sci N L 86:47 Jl 18 '64
New era of air travel in the '70s? the XC-142A plane. il U S News 56:13 Je 29 '64
On the way, straight up; Curtiss-Wright's X-19. il Bsns W p 116+ Ag 17 '63
Pivot wing up to take off; level for full speed ahead; LTV's XC-142A. il Bsns W p34 Je 20 '64
Rolls expands range of V/STOL engine development efforts. W. C. Wetmore. il Aviation W 81:78-80+ S 7 '64
RAF plans P.1154 V/STOL fighter order. il Aviation W 81:72-3+ S 7 '64
Salute to Igor Sikorsky. R. Hotz. Aviation W 81:11 O 5 '64
Tilting plus swiveling makes agile aircraft; the XC-142A. il Time 83:63-4 Je 26 '64
Transition from VTOL to horizontal flight mode demonstrated by XV-4A Hummingbird turbojet. il Aviation W 79:82-3 D 16 '63
U.S. and German V/STOL teams discuss requirements for fighter. W. C. Wetmore. Aviation W 81:19 D 21 '64
U.S, Germany consider joint V/STOL; close-support jet fighter. C. Brownlow. Aviation W 81:22-3 N 23 '64
U.S. VTOL aircraft; specifications. Aviation W 78:199 Mr 11 '63; 80:204 Mr 16 '64
Up and at 'em; XC-142A. il Newsweek 63:86 Je 29 '64
Vee-Stol: airplane of the future? C. Leedham. il N Y Times Mag p66+ O 6 '63
VJ-101C effort is directed to possible Mach 2 version. il Aviation W 78:70-1+ My 27 '63
VJ-101C flight tested. Aviation W 78:38 My 20 '63
VTOL research seeks gains for combat. D. Brown. il Aviation W 80:243-7+ Mr 16 '64
XC-142A expected to define military role for V/STOLs. E. J. Bulban. il Aviation W 80: 16-19 Je 22 '64

AIRPLANES in agriculture
Ag-flying; symposium. il Flying 74:26-35+ My '64
Agplane features internal spray system. D. A. Brown. il Aviation W 81:131+ S 14 '64
Agricultural aircraft. D. A. Brown. il Aviation W 79:116-19+ N 18; 112-13+ N 25 '63
New way to apply fertilizer: by air; interview. P. J. Stangel. il Suc Farm 62:38+ Je '64
Old bombers strafe a pesky target. il Bsns W p 120-2 N 7 '64
Work horses in the sky. O. L. Freeman. Flying 74:24 My '64
See also
Airplanes in insect control

AIRPLANES in business
For love and money. T. Baxter. Flying 75:14 S '64

AIRPLANES in fishing. See Airplanes in hunting and fishing

AIRPLANES in forest fire protection. See Forest fire patrol, Aerial

AIRPLANES in government
JFK and Air force one. J. H. Winchester. Read Digest 82:189-90+ F '63
Montana's top Bonanza. K. W. Anderson. il Flying 75:37+ Jl '64

AIRPLANES in hunting and fishing
Fifty-six minutes to paradise; southern New England. W. R. Miller. il Flying 75:42-4 Ag '64
Get the game, grab the jet. B. East. il Outdoor Life 131:13-15+ Ja '63; Discussion. 131:34-5+ My '63
Go West; flying to fishing and hunting areas. J. Gartner. il Flying 75:38-49+ Jl '64
Hidden lakes; airplane trip. D. Hill. Flying 75:47+ Jl '64
Kodiak bear war. J. Rearden. il Outdoor Life 134:17-19+ Ag '64
Oregon. T. Bacon. il Flying 75:43-4+ Jl '64
Planes vs. fair chase. E. Zern. il Field & S 68:10-11+ Ag '63

AIRPLANES in insect control
Detachable sprayer converts all Piper Cherokee aircraft; from passenger to agricultural work. il Aviation W 80:89 Mr 2 '64
Operation budworm: Washington. T. Burrier. il Am For 69:28-9 S '63
Problems. F. A. Tinker. il Flying 74:28+ My '64
Spraying program uses new techniques; controlling outbreak of spruce budworms, New Brunswick. D. A. Brown. il Aviation W 80:88-9+ My 18 '64
You can control soil insects in the winter. H. B. Petty. il Suc Farm 61:74-5+ F '63

AIRPLANES in medical service
Where rural patients get air-age care. H. G. Earl. il Todays Health 42:14-16 My '64
AIRPLANES in meteorology
Aircraft follow hurricane from Genesis. G. Alexander. il Aviation W 81:80-1+ O 19 '64
Ordeal of Snowcloud one; flight into the eye of hurricane Cleo. E. D. Fales, jr. il Pop Sci 185:56-61+ D '64
Tornado hunters. il Newsweek 61:97 Je 10 '63
Wind, weather and waldorf salad. A. Erxleben. il Pop Electr 21:36-7 Jl '64
AIRPLANES in patrol work
Atlantic surmounts nationalism barriers. il Aviation W 78:72-3+ Je 10 '63
See also
Forest fire patrol, Aerial
AIRPLANES in political campaigns
Goldwater air campaign nears 70,000 mi. il Aviation W 81:67+ N 2 '64
AIRPLANES in rescue work
Air lift to flood area gains momentum. il Aviation W 82:20+ Ja 11 '65
Alaska aviation reacts rapidly to quake. R. G. O'Lone. il Aviation W 80:25-6 Ap 6 '64
Civil air operators active in flood area. H. D. Watkins. il Aviation W 82:94-5+ Ja 18 '65
Helicopters, fixed-wing aircraft supplying flood-bound areas in West. il Aviation W 82:22-4 Ja 4 '65
Mercy mission to McMurdo. il Time 84:43 Jl 3 '64
Operation Skyhook. il Time 84:51 D 4 '64
Weather, mud, slush challenge airlift crews. H. D. Watkins. Aviation W 82:21 Ja 11 '65
AIRPLANES in surveying. See Surveying, Aerial
AIRPORT buildings
Jet-age airport helps its neighbors; Washington, D.C. Dulles airport. B. A. Roth. il Am City 79:92-3 D '64
Pan Am to begin $7-million cargo facility; Kennedy international airport. Aviation W 81:41 O 19 '64
Rome airport displeases Alitalia, others. R. H. Cook. il Aviation W 80:46-8 F 3 '64
Sheremetyevo terminal designed to handle 1,600 passengers hourly. il Aviation W 81: 38-40 Ag 24 '64
AIRPORTS
Word is soar. il Time 81:67 Mr 29 '63
See also
Heliports
also subhead Airports under names of cities, e.g. New York (city)—Airports

Buildings

See Airport buildings

Control towers

New tower to grace airports. il Arch Forum 119:112-14 N '63

Federal aid

Airport aid stresses small fields. Aviation W 79:41 Ag 26 '63
How to build an airport; Willits, Calif. L. Mahan. il Flying 75:37-8+ Ag '64

Finance

Airports: our newest billion-dollar business. F. J. Taylor. il Read Digest 85:192-4+ D '64
High cost of landing. R. B. Parke. Flying 75: 22 Ag '64
Landing fee boost seen for NY airports. Aviation W 81:34 Ag 17 '64

Lighting

Economy ILS aids readied for evaluation at two airports. P. J. Klass. il Aviation W 80:68-9+ Mr 2 '64
No-glare lighting for Phoenix airport. W. Ralston. il Am City 79:111 Ja '64
Pulsed lights developed for small fields. D. A. Brown. il Aviation W 80:84-5 Mr 2 '64
Runway lights that aren't really there; microvision. il Sci Digest 56:63-4 O '64
USAF develops portable lighting. Aviation W 81:79-80 Ag 24 '64

Traffic control

Crash brings revision of fix reporting rules. Aviation W 81:37 Ag 24 '64
Flying into the big-city airport. A. H. Sanfelici. il Flying 74:26-9+ Mr '64
Ground facilities cited in airline delays. R. H. Cook. il Aviation W 80:37-8 Ja 6 '64
Surveillance, approach functions combined in traffic control radar. il Aviation W 79:91+ N 18 '63
See also
Air traffic controllers (persons)

Water supply

Airport water works requires more systems; O'Hare international airport, Chicago. M. Callahan. il Am City 79:93-4 Mr '64

Alaska

Anchorage receiving international flights. Aviation W 80:42 Ap 13 '64

California

How to build an airport; Willits, Calif. L. Mahan. il Flying 75:37-8+ Ag '64
Taming southern Cal's airport jungle. L. C. Philmus. il Flying 75:30-3+ Ag '64

Denmark

See also
Copenhagen—Airports

Germany (Federal Republic)

Rhein-Main airport expansion continues. E. Walford. il Aviation W 80:41 Ja 6 '64

Great Britain

Major British airport charges revised. Aviation W 79:41 O 7 '63

Haiti

U.S. suspends action on airport construction agreement with Haiti; press release, July 3, 1963. Dept State Bul 49:144 Jl 22 '63

Ireland

Tourism, expansion build Shannon traffic. J. W. Carter. il Aviation W 82:46+ Ja 18 '65

Italy

See also
Rome (city)—Airports

Netherlands

KLM optimistic on financial prospects; Schiphol airport modernization. J. W. Carter. il Aviation W 80:38-9+ My 11 '64

New Jersey

World's fair airports. A. Dawydoff. il Flying 74:28-30+ Ap '64

New York (state)

World's fair airports. A. Dawydoff. il Flying 74:28-30+ Ap '64

Russia

See also
Moscow—Airports

Saudi Arabia

See also
Dhahran, Saudi Arabia—Airports

Switzerland

Swiss town planning international airport. Aviation W 79:43 S 30 '63

United States

CAB regional airport plan faces delay. R. H. Cook. Aviation W 80:45 Ap 20 '64
Gone flying to Minnesota. V. M. Draper. il Flying 74:28-32+ Je '64
Major U.S. airports. R. H. Cook. il Aviation W 78:45-6 Je 17; 41+ Je 24; 79:43-4 Jl 1; 40-1 Jl 8; 45+ Jl 15; 33-4+ Jl 29; 47+ Ag 5; 40-1 Ag 26 '63
SST: no music to airport men's ears. il Bsns W p60+ O 26 '63
See also subhead Airports under names of cities, e.g. Washington, D.C.—Airports
AIRSHIPS
Airship studied as booster carrier. F. G. McGuire. Miss & Roc 12:16 Mr 4 '63
Blimp covers boat race, goes joyriding in its PR role. il Bsns W p40 Ap 20 '63
Triple blimp; Aeron. il Sci Digest 55:90 Ap '64
AIRSTREAM, incorporated
Modern wagon train on a worldwide ramble. il Bsns W p56-8 D 19 '64
AIRWAYS
American, Northwest granted new routes. J. R. Ashlock. Aviation W 81:29 Ag 10 '64
Bid to reverse Northeast ruling seen. Aviation W 79:42 Ag 5 '63
BOAC to drop NY-San Francisco route after review of services. J. W. Carter. Aviation W 81:32 S 28 '64
CAB feels wind from Northeast; refusal to renew Northeast airlines' Florida certificate. il Bsns W p45-6+ O 5 '63
CAB rejects Northeast renewal in 3-2 decision on Florida route. J. R. Ashlock. Aviation W 79:43 O 14 '63
CAB South American case bogged. Aviation W 79:129 O 7 '63

AIRWAYS—*Continued*
CAB starts studying Western area routes. Aviation W 81:37 Ag 24 '64
Further financial aid depends on Florida rights, Northeast says. Aviation W 78:37 Je 3 '63
N. Atlantic area concept urged. Aviation W 79:32 S 2 '63
Northeast case pressure seen as threat. L. L. Doty. Aviation W 79:40-1 S 9 '63
Northeast decision seen aimed at Hughes. R. H. Cook. Aviation W 78:38-9 Ap 22 '63
Northeast retention on aircraft proposed. J. R. Ashlock. Aviation W 79:37-8 Jl 1 '63
Piloting BOAC out of the storm; revising route structure. il Bsns W p 124+ S 19 '64
Southern route thrives on space industry. L. L. Doty. Aviation W 78:42-3 My 6 '63
Why Northeast faces its worst crisis yet; half local service feeder line, half long-haul trunk carrier. il Bsns W p48-51 Ja 9 '65

Traffic control
See Air traffic control

AIRWAYS, International. See Aviation—International aspects

AIRY, Sir George Biddell
Airy regime at Greenwich. J. Ashbrook. il por Sky & Tel 27:342-3 Je '64

AISHER, Owen
Agreement to hate. Yachting 116:45+ S '64

AIT AHMED, Hocine
Ben Bella balked. il por Newsweek 62:42 O 14 '63

AITA, John A.
It brings the close in closer. U S Camera 26:68-9 D '63

AITKEN, Russell B.
Goose that carries a knife. Field & S 69: 10-13 D '64

AITKEN, William Maxwell, 1st baron Beaverbrook. See Beaverbrook, W. M. A.

AIX-EN-PROVENCE festival. See Music festivals—France

AJACCIO, Corsica
Napoleonic dandy; paintings in the municipal museum. il Time 84:84 S 18 '64

AJANTA cave temples. See Cave temples

AJEMIAN, Robert
He did more than just get well. Life 58:35 Ja 15 '65
His style rallies the moderates, but his real job is to lure away the Goldwater fans. Life 56:32-3 Je 26 '64
Man's week to reckon. Life 57:24-31 Jl 3 '64
Salinger swings for Senate, there's bedlam in California. Life 56:43 Ap 3 '64
Senator finds the trail is icy. Life 56:31-3 Mr 6 '64
There the dam stood, proud and beautiful and then. . . Life 55:30-41 O 25 '63
Trio of G.O.P. stars fighting hard not to be buried with Barry. Life 57:32-7 O 30 '64
Two big fights start shaping up. Life 56:22 Mr 27 '64
Two Kennedys sweep two states; old man Young topples Taft. Life 57:38-9 N 13 '64
about
Reunion of two classmates. G. P. Hunt. il por Life 57:3 Jl 3 '64

AKADEMGORODOK, Siberia
Russia's hidden science city. A. Parry. il Sci Digest 53:22-8 My '63

AKAMINE, Ernest K.
Ethylene production in fading vanda orchid blossoms. bibliog Science 140:1217-18 Je 14 '63

AKE, Robert
Plan for political action; address. por Wilson Lib Bul 39:316-19 D '64; Summary. 39:181+ O '64
Scanty information on student use. por Library J 88:4707-8 D 15 '63

AKER, Suzanne
To carol is to dance. Dance Mag 38:40-1 D '64

AKHMATOVA, Anna
Poems; tr. by R. Lowell. Atlan 214:60-5 O '64
about
Biographical sketch. O. A. Carlisle. Atlan 214:60-1 O '64

AKIN, Stuart
On the edge of the Everglades. Travel 122: 32-4 O '64

AKIN, William
Lost heroes of touring. R. Cantwell. il Sports Illus 20:60-2+ Je 22 '64

AKOSUA, pseud.
Piper's village. Reporter 29:38-42 S 26 '63

AKRON, Ohio
Forums are successful in Akron. il Am City 78:136+ Mr '63

Courts
Automation anticipates $165,000 saving on alimony checks. F. P. Yacobucci. il Am City 79:106-7 O '64

Industries
Akron moonlighters: a special breed. il Bsns W p68+ D 5 '64

Parks and playgrounds
Radiators for frozen skaters. A. T. Wilcox. il Am City 78:36 Mr '63

AKRON, Ohio, public library
Common fine. J. H. Rebenack. Library J 89:4868-70 D 15 '64

AKS, Harold
Pitch memory. New Yorker 39:42-3 Mr 16 '63

AKSENOV, Evgeny P. and others
Countdown for space flight. UNESCO Courier 17:24-7 Ja '64

ALABAMA
Two-yacht governors; lavish spending of Alabama governors. il Time 81:25 F 22 '63
See also
Education—Alabama
Gardens—Alabama
Hunting—Alabama
Liquor laws and regulations—Alabama
Paleontology—Alabama

Legislature
Reconstruction legislators in Alabama. C. A. Brown. bibliog Negro Hist Bul 26:198-200 Mr '63

Politics and government
Aftermath in Alabama. R. Cleghorn. Reporter 31:34-5 D 3 '64
Birmingham, Alabama; a city in fear. J. D. Brown. il Sat Eve Post 236:11-19 Mr 2 '63
Wallace and the future of Dixie. R. G. Sherrill. Nation 199:266-72 O 26 '64
Wallace in Alabama. Nation 198:498 My 18 '64

Race problems
Alabama bombers kill four Negro girls. Christian Cent 80:1160 S 25 '63
Alabama's defiant leader Governor Wallace vs. JFK; against racial integration. U S News 54:23 My 27 '63
Collision course: Negro enrollment in Alabama university. il Newsweek 61:29 My 6 '63
Off the streets; race conflict. il Time 81:16 My 31 '63
Old times there are not forgiven. R. Dugger. Nation 198:659-60 Je 29 '64
President vs. a governor: another school showdown. il U S News 55:42-3 S 23 '63
Registration in Alabama. H. Zinn. New Repub 149:11-12 O 26 '63
Southerner goes North. W. B. Huie. New Repub 150:8 Ap 25 '64
Where the stars fall. il Time 82:17-21 S 27 '63
See also
Birmingham, Ala.—Negroes

Religious institutions and affairs
News of the Christian world. Christian Cent 80:188-90 F 6 '63

Social conditions
More on the Johnson fortune: Lady Bird's pine lands and her tenants. il U S News 56:43-5 My 4 '64

ALABAMA. University, Tuscaloosa
Alabama quality. il Time 81:80+ Je 14 '63
Bargain with the devil; Negro applicants at the University of Alabama. il Newsweek 61:30 Je 10 '63
Long march; Negro students. il Time 81:13-17 Je 21 '63
Nation's crisis crowds in on one man; with report by D. Nevin. il Life 54:77-8+ Je 14 '63
Next stand; court order to enroll Vivian Malone. il Time 81:19 Je 7 '63
Schoolhouse door: admission of Negro students. il Newsweek 61:30-2 Je 24 '63
Task force tusk. Newsweek 62:17 D 30 '63

ALADDIN and his wonderful lamp; drama. See Thane, A

ALADJEM, Frederick, and Fudenberg, H. H.
Heterogeneity of antibodies. Science 145:614-16 Ag 7 '64

ALAM, Assadollah
Grand vizier. il por Time 82:40 N 1 '63

ALAN, Ray
Franco's Spain and the new Europe. Commentary 34:231-7; 35:165 S '62, F '63
Spanish anti-Semitism today. Commentary 38:64-6 Ag '64; 39:8+ Ja '65

ALAN Wood steel company. See Wood, Alan, steel company
ALARM clocks. Electric. See Clocks, Electric
ALARM satellites. See Artificial satellites—Military applications
ALARMS
Portable eye spots intruders. Bsns W p 104 Ap 13 '63
See also
Fire alarms
ALARMS, Electric. See Electric alarms
ALASKA
New route to Alaska; Marine highway. il Travel 119:64 Ap '63
Now a new "highway" to Alaska by sea; Marine highway. K. M. Chrysler. il U S News 54:70-2 Je 24 '63
Road to reconstruction. T. R. Paden. Christian Cent 82:24 Ja 6 '65
To Alaska by outboard. il Yachting 114:42-3 D '63
See also
Admiralty Island
Airlines—Alaska
Airports—Alaska
Aleutian Islands
Aviation—Alaska
Botany—Alaska
Courts—Alaska
Dams—Alaska
Earthquakes—Alaska
Education—Alaska
Fishing—Alaska
Food supply—Alaska
Forests and forestry—Alaska
Geology—Alaska
Hunting—Alaska
Kobuk River
Libraries—Alaska
Mount McKinley National Park
Pribilof Islands
Public health—Alaska
Tourist trade—Alaska
Transportation—Alaska
Wages—Alaska
Waterways—Alaska
Zoology—Alaska

Caricatures and cartoons

Mush, mush, a brisk look at the Snowshoe state. R. Searle. Holiday 34:44-53 Jl '63

Defenses

Elegant white elephant; Port of Whittier declared surplus property. il Time 83:27 F 21 '64

Description and travel

Alaska offers new ski thrills. C. McClain. il Todays Health 42:18-20+ Ja '64
Arctic honeymoon; excerpt from Two in the Far North (cont) M. E. Murie. il Audubon Mag 65:16-19+ Ja '63
Arctic trail. W. O. Pruitt, jr. il Harper 226: 44-50 Je '63
On the river ice; excerpt from Two in the Far North. M. E. Murie. il Liv Wildn 82: 3-8 Winter '62
Runes of the Far North; excerpts. S. F. Olson. il Am For 69:26-7+ Je '63
This summer, why not Alaska? H. E. McLean. il Motor B 113:26-7+ My '64

Economic conditions

Alaska, a shattered giant picks up the pieces. il Sr Schol 84:6-8 Ap 24 '64
Alaska: can it survive as a state? R. Schulman. il Sat Eve Post 236:78+ O 12 '63
Five years of statehood; new look at Alaska. il U S News 55:96-8 O 28 '63

Reconstruction

Alaska rebuilds: you've got to start. il Newsweek 64:70-4 Jl 13 '64
How a stricken state met chaos. B. Lindeman. il Sat Eve Post 237:24-31 My 9 '64

Relief work

Alaska starts on way back; no outright federal grants to victims. il Bsns W p 162 Ap 11 '64
Long, hard road to recovery. T. R. Paden. Christian Cent 81:710+ My 27 '64

Religious institutions and affairs

News of the Christian world. Christian Cent 80:1248, 1616 O 9, D 25 '63
ALASKA highway
Alaska bound? C. Lane. il Travel 120:6 Ag '63
ALASKA science conference
Meeting, 1964. C. R. Kolb. Science 147:71-3 Ja 1 '65
ALASKAN brown bear hunting. See Bear hunting
ALASKAN brown bears. See Bears
ALASKAN cookery. See Cookery, American
ALASKANS
Alaska after the big quake: shaky jokes and too many cooks. D. Moser. il Life 56:21 My 29 '64
Alaska: can it survive as a state? R. Schulman. il Sat Eve Post 236:78+ O 12 '63
How a stricken state met chaos. B. Lindeman. il Sat Eve Post 237:24-31 My 9 '64
ALAUPOVIC, P. See Skinner, W. A. jt. auth.
ALBA, Maria
Ballet espanol Alba, Reyes, 92nd street Y. J. Maskey. Dance Mag 38:64 Je '64
ALBA, Victor
Alliance for progress is dead. New Repub 151: 17-18 S 5 '64
Latin America's future leaders. New Repub 149:12-13 S 21 '63
Why Bosch fell. New Repub 149:12-14 O 12 '63
ALBACORE fishing
Boil! R. S. Mikkelsen. il Outdoor Life 34: 46-7+ Jl '64
ALBACORES
See also
Cookery—Fish
ALBANESE, Licia
Essential Albanese. E. Del Gaudio. pors Opera N 28:30-1 Ja 11 '64
ALBANIA
Albania: the last Marxist paradise. J. Cameron. Atlan 211:41-50 Je '63
See also
United Nations—Albania

Foreign relations

Albanian-Soviet rift. W. S. Vucinich. Cur Hist 44:299-304+ My '63
Gnat that grabbed. il Time 83:30 Mr 6 '64
Independent dummy. Time 84:46 D 11 '64
ALBANY, Ga.

Libraries

Albany, Ga. public library reopens on vertical integration basis. Library J 88:1638 Ap 15 '63
Postscript on the Albany matter. ALA Bul 57:307 Ap '63
Still no decision in Albany. E. T. Moore. ALA Bul 57:111-16 F '63

Negroes

Albany cases. Nation 198:387 Ap 20 '64
Epilogue in Albany; were the mass marches worthwhile? R. Cleghorn. New Repub 149: 15-18 Jl 20 '63
Integration: officially unofficial. il Newsweek 61:30 Mr 25 '63
ALBANY, N.Y.

City planning

Albany: big new complex in a capital. il Arch Forum 118:9 Je '63
Capitol improvement. Time 81:75 My 3 '63
Most beautiful state capital; South mall redevelopment. il Am City 79:116 Ap '64

Public buildings

Most beautiful state capital; South mall redevelopment. il Am City 79:116 Ap '64
ALBATROSSES
Albatrosses of Midway. C. W. Buchheister. il Audubon Mag 66:84-5 Mr '64
Gooney birds of Midway. J. W. Aldrich. il Nat Geog Mag 125:838-51 Je '64
Midway islands: man and birds in conflict. O. S. Pettingill, jr. il Audubon Mag 66: 154-9 My '64
ALBEE, Edward
Novel beginning; excerpt from first novel. por Esquire 60:59-60 Jl '63
about
Albee: odd man in on Broadway. il pors Newsweek 61:49-52 F 4 '63
Albee revisited. New Yorker 40:31-3 D 19 '64
American dream. Criticism
America 108:891-2 Je 22 '63
Ballad of the sad café; dramatization of novel by C. McCullers. Criticism
America 110:26 Ja 4 '64
Cath World 198:264 Ja '64
Commonweal 79:256 N 22 '63
Nat R 16:34-5 Ja 14 '64
Nation 197:353-4 N 23 '63
New Repub 149:28-9 N 16 '63
New Yorker 39:95 N 9 '63
Newsweek il 62:76 N 11 '63
Sat R 46:54 N 16 '63
Time il 82:67 N 8 '63
Vogue 143:20 Ja 1 '64

ALBEE, Edward—about—*Continued*
Broadway's hottest playwright. Edward Albee. J. Skow. pors Sat Eve Post 237:32-3 Ja 18 '64
Edward Albee: red herrings & white whales. A. Chester. Commentary 35:296-301 Ap '63; Discussion. 36:272+ O '63
Psychiatrist looks at Tiny Alice. A. N. Franzblau. Sat R 48:39 Ja 30 '65
Tiny Alice. Criticism
Commonweal 81:543 Ja 22 '65
Life 58:14 Ja 29 '65
Nation 200:65 Ja 18 '65
New Repub 152:33-4+ Ja 23 '65
New Yorker 40:84 Ja 9 '65
Newsweek 65:75 Ja 11 '65
Reporter 32:53-4 Ja 28 '65
Sat R 48:40 Ja 16 '65
Sat R il(p 1) por 48:38-9+ Ja 30 '65
Time il por 85:32 Ja 8 '65
Time il 85:68+ Ja 15 '65
What's the matter with Edward Albee? T. F. Driver. Reporter 30:38-9 Ja 2 '64; Discussion. 30:10+ Ja 30 '64
Who's afraid of success? il por Newsweek 65:51 Ja 4 '65
Who's afraid of Virginia Woolf? Criticism
Atlan 213:122+ Ap '64
Commentary 35:296-301 Ap '63
Commentary 36:272+ O '63
Esquire 60:69+ D '63
Reporter 28:48 Ap 25 '63
Who's afraid of Virginia Woolf? not Columbia. S. Potter. il por Am Rec G 29:924-7 Ag '63
Zoo story. Criticism
America 108:891-2 Je 22 '63

ALBEE, George Sumner
Angels of Jean Pierre; story. McCalls 90:86-7 Je '63
Give her love on a cloudy day; story. McCalls 91:78-9 Jl '64
My big sister's romance; story. Ladies Home J 80:70-1 Ap '63
Streets along the way; story. McCalls 91:118-19 Ap '64

ALBEMARLE paper manufacturing company
Private route to new capital; direct placements. J. Ross-Skinner. il Duns R 81:35-6+ Ja '63

ALBENDA, Pauline
Oil painting. Sch Arts 62:18-19 Ap '63

ALBERS, Josef
Interaction of color; excerpts. il por Art N 62:32-5+ Mr '63
Josef Albers on tour; Smithsonian's traveling exhibition service. F. Getlein. New Repub 149:34-6 S 21 '63

ALBERT, Carl
Excerpt from address, April 2, 1963. Cong Digest 42:151+ My '63

about

Adequate number of Democrats. il pors Time 85:16-20 Ja 15 '65
Boy from Bug Tussle. por Bsns W p30-1 Mr 23 '63

ALBERT, Janie
She's our smasher for Wimbledon. il pors Life 54:87-9 Je 21 '63

ALBERT, Leo
What management expects of production. Pub W 183:76+ My 6 '63

ALBERT, Luke S. See Wallenstein, A. jt. auth.

ALBERT Lasker awards
Cite work on mental illness and cancer. Sci N L 86:344 N 28 '64
Lift from depression. il Time 84:106 N 27 '64
1963 Lasker awards. il Sci N L 84:246 O 19 '63
Second first; Dr N. S. Kline receives second award. Newsweek 64:101 N 23 '64
Separating the inseparable; 1963 award for basic medical research. il Time 82:62+ O 18 '63
Two congressmen win Lasker awards of $2,500; Oren Harris and Melvin R. Laird. Sci N L 85:329 My 23 '64

ALBERTA

Climate

Snow eaters of Alberta. D. Bodington. il Natur Hist 73:60-1 F '64

Description and travel

Along Alberta's dinosaur trail. il Sunset 133:39+ Jl '64

ALBERTA. University, Edmonton

Libraries

Alberta builds three; Rutherford and Education libraries, at Edmonton and new library at Calgary. B. Peel. il Library J 88:4582-5 D 1 '63

ALBERTO-Culver company
Scalping the competition; Alberto-Culver products. il Time 82:88 Jl 12 '63

ALBERTS, Robert C.
Fantastic adventures of Captain Stobo. Am Heritage 14:65-77 Ag '63

ALBERTSON, James
Churches and the bomb. America 111:692-3 N 28 '64

ALBINO rats. See Rats

ALBINOS and albinism
Albinism and water escape performance in the mouse. H. D. Winston and G. Lindzey. bibliog il Science 144:189-91 Ap 10 '64; Reply with rejoinder. G. W. Meier and D. P. Foshee. 147:307-8 Ja 15 '65
Meet the ghost kangaroo. il Sci Digest 55:48-9 Ap '64
Sex-linked albinism in the Japanese quail. J. K. Lauber. bibliog il Science 146:948-50 N 13 '64

ALBJERG, Victor
Truman and Eisenhower: their administrations and campaigns. Cur Hist 47:221-8 O '64

ALBRIGHT, Horace M.
S. 4 urged. Liv Wildn 83:30 Spring '63

ALBRIGHT, Ivan
Albright: humanist of decay. J. Kind. il por Art N 63:43-5+ N '64
Grandeur in decay. il por Time 84:82 D 18 '64
Growth and death. pors Newsweek 64:105 N 23 '64

ALBRIGHT, J. L. See Fryman, L. R. jt. auth.

ALBRIGHT, James F.
What to tell the neophyte: bookselling is a good career. por Pub W 185:47-9 Mr 30 '64

ALBRIGHT, William F.
Law that bound Israel. Life 57:55-6 D 25 '64

ALBRIGHT-Knox art gallery, Buffalo, N.Y.
In the right hands; C. Still's gift to gallery. Time 83:60 My 29 '64

ALBUMIN
Albumin replacement by fatty acids in clonal growth of mammalian cells. R. G. Ham. bibliog il Science 140:802-3 My 17 '63
See also
Blood—Proteins

ALBUMS
See also
Phonograph record albums
Photographic albums

ALBUQUERQUE, N.Mex.
Computer that earns a profit. J. L. Guggino. il Am City 79:102-3 Mr '64

Parks and playgrounds

How to have plenty of parks. R. L. Burgan. il Am City 78:118-19 Je '63

ALCAIDE, Tomas
Tomas Alcaide. A. Favia-Artsay. pors Hobbies 68:30-1 Ag '63

ALCAN. See Aluminum company of Canada

ALCATRAZ (Island)
Photographic team witnesses the end of Alcatraz. P. Stackpole. U S Camera 26:12-13 Jl '63
Rock on the block. il Newsweek 61:28-9 Ap 1 '63

ALCHEMIST; drama. See Jonson, B.

ALCHEMY
Ancient art of alchemy. D. Pramer. il Natur Hist 72:40-5 Ag '63
State and science five centuries ago. T. H. Stevenson. Bul Atomic Sci 21:28-9 Ja '65

ALCINDOR, Lewis
Big Lew's message to scouts shh! I'm busy. W. Bradbury. il pors Life 58:53-4 Ja 29 '65
Jack and his beanstalk. H. L. Masin. il por Sr Schol 82:24 Mr 13 '63
Wooing of a seven-foot wonder. G. Walsh. il pors Sat Eve Post 237:70-1 Mr 14 '64

ALCOA. See Aluminum company of America

ALCOCK, John
Flight into the unknown. J. Stewart-Gordon. il por Read Digest 82:120-5 Mr '63

ALCOCK, Norman Zinkan
One man's war on war. J. Robbins and J. Robbins. il pors Redbook 123:54-5+ My '64

ALCOHOL
Grain alcohol in gasoline? Sci N L 84:178 S 21 '63
Stupid questions about alcohol. R. Gannon. il Pop Sci 184:70-3+ Mr '64
Subject unknown: civilization and alcohol. J. Ciardi. Sat R 46:8 Je 1 '63
See also
Liquor traffic—United States

Physiological effects

Alcohol. R. D. Russell. NEA J 53:66-7 Mr '64

ALCOHOL—Physiological effects—*Continued*
Alcohol & barbiturates: deadly combination. il Time 83:48 Ja 3 '64
Alcohol and caffeine: effect on inferred visual dreaming. S. C. Gresham and others. bibliog il Science 140:1226-7 Je 14 '63
Alcohol consumption in rats: effects of intracranial injections of ethanol. R. D. Myers. bibliog il Science 142:240-1 O 11 '63
Booze and you; excerpt from Ann Landers talks to teen-agers about sex. A. Landers. Read Digest 84:133-4+ Mr '64
Drinking dinner brings neurological damage. Sci N L 84:101 Ag 17 '63
Juvenile hormone activity: effects of isoprenoid and straight-chain alcohols on insects. W. S. Bowers and M. J. Thompson. bibliog il Science 142:1469-70 D 13 '63
Liquor and love. Sci Digest 54:57 Jl '63
Science looks at liquor. J. E. Gibson. il Todays Health 41:84-6 F '63
What alcohol means to man. Sci Digest 54:41 S '63
See also
Alcoholism

ALCOHOL, Wood. See Methanol

ALCOHOL as fuel
Have you tried alcohol? C. Conley. il Field & S 68:113-14 Je '63

ALCOHOLIC drinks. See Liquors

ALCOHOLICS. See Alcoholism

ALCOHOLICS anonymous
Alcoholics anonymous: cult or cure? A. H. Cain. bibliog f Harper 226:48-52 F '63; Discussion. 226:6 Ap '63
Alcoholics anonymous; dangers of success. J. Ellison. Nation 198:212-14 Mr 2 '64
Law of unselfishness. F. Oursler. Read Digest 84:24C F '64
Speaking out; alcoholics can be cured, despite A.A. A. H. Cain. Sat Eve Post 237:6+ S 19 '64

ALCOHOLISM
Alcoholism controversy; normal drinking in recovered alcohol addicts. S. Katz. il Sci Digest 55:31-6 My '64
Alcoholism hard to face. Sci N L 86:183 S 19 '64
Bright light on the alcoholic. G. Littman. il N Y Times Mag p30+ Ap 5 '64
Dreyfus of drunks; alternatives to the practice of treating alcoholics like criminals. Time 84:52+ N 27 '64
Driving the alcoholic to drink. il Sci Digest 53:42-3 Je '63
Drunk on the 6:11. il Newsweek 63:101-2+ Mr 16 '64
Helping ministers help alcoholics. Christian Cent 80:1262 O 16 '63
How nations drink: the puzzle of alcoholism. M. E. Chafetz. il Nation 199:401-4 N 30 '64
If there's an alcoholic in the family. M. A. Block. il Parents Mag 39:52-3+ N '64
Many see alcoholics as only morally weak; survey. Sci N L 85:402 Je 27 '64
My problem is my parents! questions and answers. A. Wood. il Seventeen 23:168-9+ Ap '64
No cure as yet. A. Black. il America 110:712-14 My 23 '64
Normal social drinking by alcoholics challenged. Sci N L 83:216 Ap 6 '63
One man's triumph; H. Hughes, governor of Iowa. F. Knebel. il Look 28:97-8+ O 6 '64
Psychiatrist gives rules to prevent alcoholism. Sci N L 85:168 Mr 14 '64
Speaking out; alcoholics can be cured, despite A.A. A. H. Cain. Sat Eve Post 237:6+ S 19 '64
Test constitutionality of cases against alcoholics. Christian Cent 81:1260-1 O 14 '64
Tomorrow's alcoholic. A. Ogle. America 108:468-9 Ap 6 '63
When drinking's a disease. il Bsns W p 136-8+ S 21 '63
See also
Alcohol—Physiological effects
Liquor problem
Temperance

Therapy

If there's an alcoholic in the family. M. A. Block. il Parents Mag 39:52-3+ N '64
In search of a cure for the alcoholic; Chicago alcoholic treatment center. G. Samuels. il N Y Times Mag p51+ O 27 '63
See also
Alcoholics anonymous

ALCOHOLS
See also
Isopropyl alcohol
Phenethyl alcohol

ALCORN, John Wagner
John Alcorn: artist-designer with a sense of humor. P. A. Bennett. il por Pub W 185:76-8 Je 1 '64
Semper Fi. Newsweek 61:90 Je 10 '63

ALCOTT, Bronson
Mama, they've begun again! B. Bliven. il pors Am Heritage 16:12-16+ D '64

ALCOTT, Louisa May
Mama, they've begun again! B. Bliven. il por Am Heritage 16:12-16+ D '64

ALDA, Frances
Gatti's first lady. G. M. Eby. il por Opera N 27:14-15 My 4 '63

ALDAN, Daisy
Women at windows; poem. Poetry 104:232 Jl '64

ALDEBURGH festival. See Music festivals—England

ALDEHYDES
Atmospheric aldehydes related to petunia leaf damage. E. G. Brennan and others. bibliog il Science 143:818-20 F 21 '64
Plant damage caused by irradiation of aldehydes. I. J. Hindawi and A. P. Altshuller. bibliog il Science 146:540-2 O 23 '64

ALDEN, Harold Lee
Obituary
Sky & Tel por 27:203 Ap '64

ALDEN, Marion
Lady in a glass house. il por Newsweek 64:101 O 19 '64

ALDEN, Robert
Where the ins go out. N Y Times Mag p 12-13 D 27 '64

ALDEN, Vernon R.
Art of raiding. por Life 58:70-2 Ja 15 '65
What kind of excellence? Sat R 47:52-3 Jl 18 '64
about
President under the gun. il pors Life 58:58-68 Ja 15 '65

ALDER
Alder and its catkins. il Sunset 131:197 D '63

ALDERMAN, Michael H.
Why we need medicare. New Repub 151:17-20 D 26 '64

ALDERTON, Eileen
Apple tree; story. Redbook 123:38-9 Ag '64

ALDERTON, Gordon, and others
Heat adaptation and ion exchange in bacillus megaterium spores. Science 143:141-3 Ja 10 '64

ALDOSTERONE
Angiotensin pressor inhibition by aldosterone in the rabbit. Y. J. Katz and others. bibliog il Science 141:725 Ag 23 '63

ALDRICH, Daniel G.
Irvine campus. Arch Rec 136:186-8 N '64

ALDRICH, John W.
Gooney birds of Midway. Nat Geog Mag 125:838-51 Je '64

ALDRICH, Richard S.
Elephants in Tammanyland; seventeenth congressional district, Manhattan. B. Carter. il Reporter 29:41-3 N 21 '63
Kinfolk; backing by N. A. Rockefeller. por Newsweek 61:39 Je 24 '63

ALDRICH, Robert A.
Vital new chapter in medical research is being written. J. Raymond. il Parents Mag 38:69+ O '63

ALEATORIC music. See Music

ALEGRIA, Ciro
Ciro Alegría's worlds. A. Escobar. il por Américas 15:7-10 F '63

ALEGRIA, Fernando
Picture window on the arts. Américas 15:27-30 Mr '63

ALEKSEI, patriarch
Distinguished visitor. G. Murray. Christian Cent 81:1411-12 N 11 '64

ALENCAR ARRAES, Francisco de
April fool's day in Brazil. Commonweal 80:192-3 My 8 '64

ALERCES
Sequoia of South America. E. J. Wilhelm, jr. il Nat Parks Mag 37:8-10 D '63

ALEUTIAN ISLANDS
See also
Ethnology—Aleutian Islands
Geology—Aleutian Islands

Antiquities

Anangula: a geologic interpretation of the oldest archeologic site in the Aleutians. R. F. Black and W. S. Laughlin. bibliog il Science 143:1321-2 Mr 20 '64

Description and travel

Runes of the Far North; excerpts. S. F. Olson. il Am For 69:26-7+ Je '63
Where the williwaws blow. E. B. Roberts. il Américas 16:22-7 O '64

ALEUTIAN ISLANDS—*Continued*

History

Where the williwaws blow. E. B. Roberts. il Américas 16:22-7 O '64

ALEXANDER the Great, king of Macedonia

Godlike conqueror; with report by E. Kern. il Life 54:62-77 My 3 '63

Great confrontations: Diogenes and Alexander. G. Highet. il por Horizon 5:10-13 Mr '63

Great confrontations: Napoleon and Alexander. J. C. Herold. il por Horizon 5:28-32 S '63

ALEXANDER, A. L.

Thermal control in space vehicles. bibliog Science 143:654-60 F 14 '64

ALEXANDER, Archibald S.

Problem and the opportunity. Bul Atomic Sci 20:8-10 Ap '64

ALEXANDER, Dorothy

As of today; interview, ed. by D. Hering. Dance Mag 38:48-9+ O '64

ALEXANDER, Earla M.

Rubbings. Sch Arts 62:27-8 My '63

ALEXANDER, Edgar

Rolf Hochhuth: equivocal Deputy. America 109:416-18+, 519-20, 691 O 12, N 2, 30 '63

Serious charge, lightly tossed. R. A. Graham. America 110:859 Je 27 '64; Discussion. 111: 24+, 118 Jl 11, Ag 8 '64

ALEXANDER, Elenora

IMS merger. por Library J 89:4107-9 O 15 '64

ALEXANDER, G. and Williams, D.

Maternal facilitation of sucking drive in newborn lambs. bibliog Science 146:665-6 O 30 '64

ALEXANDER, Henry C.

Man in management; address, January 15, 1963. Vital Speeches 29:312-14 Mr 1 '63

ALEXANDER, Holmes, and Alexander, Hunter

Bulwark of sovereignty. Nat R 14:463 Je 4 '63

ALEXANDER, Hunter. See Alexander, Holmes, jt. auth

ALEXANDER, J. Herbert

Lilacs. Pop Gard 15:55+ S '64

ALEXANDER, Jean

TV teacher to Philly tots. il pors Ebony 19:147-50 O '64

ALEXANDER, John

Canning sunstuff beneath the plains. Sat R 46:61 O 5 '63

Chain reaction; interview, ed. by F. Stevenson. por Opera N 28:29 F 15 '64

ALEXANDER, Lloyd

Fifty years in the monkey house. McCalls 91:110-11+ F '64

ALEXANDER, M.

Applied microbiology in developing countries. Science 145:613-14 Ag 7 '64

ALEXANDER, Nancy. See Beck, S. D. jt. auth.

ALEXANDER, R. W.

Graduates; story. Redbook 121:20-1 Ag '63

Keep a place for me; story. Good H 158:82-3 Je '64

ALEXANDER, Raymond Pace

Study of Negro blasts racial myths; comments on textbooks. por(p 1) Negro Hist Bul 28:3-6 O '64

about

After forty years: a kiss and a cake. il pors Ebony 19:73-4+ F '64

ALEXANDER, Richard

Hell of Haiti. Nation 196:98-9 F 2 '63

ALEXANDER, Robert J.

Latin America and the Communist bloc. Cur Hist 44:73-7+ F '63

ALEXANDER, Ronald

Life theater review. Life 57:19 N 20 '64

Nobody loves an albatross. Criticism

America 110:147 Ja 25 '64
Commonweal 79:461 Ja 17 '64
New Repub 150:24 Ja 11 '64
New Yorker 39:58 Ja 4 '64
Newsweek il 62:58 D 30 '63
Sat R 47:52 Ja 11 '64
Time il 82:39 D 27 '63

ALEXANDER, Shana

Barbra. Life 56:51-2+ My 22 '64; Same abr. with title Barbra Streisand, funny girl. Read Digest 85:51-5 Ag '64

Congratulations, whispered Jackie, and thanks for my birthday letter. Life 57:30-1 S 4 '64

Decision to die. Life 56:74-6+ My 29 '64

Fashion's best joke on itself in years. Life 57:56-7 Jl 10 '64

Feminine eye. Life 57:29 O 23; 33 N 6; 31 N 20; 30 D 4 '64; 58:27 Ja 15; 23 Ja 29 '65

Fight promoter for the battle of the sexes. Life 54:102-4+ My 17 '63

High I.Q. frat. Life 55:11+ Ag 16 '63

His fears of nonexistence very nearly came true. Life 57:28+ Jl 31 '64

Parish priest accuses his cardinal on civil rights. Life 56:41 Je 26 '64

Singular girl's success. Life 54:60+ Mr 1 '63

T-shirted beer-lover as the suave spy. Life 56:55-6 Ap 3 '64

Will the real Burt please stand up? Life 55: 80-5 S 6 '63

Zero calorie diet. Life 55:105-8+ O 11 '63

about

How Nell J. picked out an author. G. P. Hunt. Life 56:3 My 29 '64

Shana talks about Shana. G. P. Hunt. il por Life 55:3 O 11 '63

ALEXANDER, Sidney

From the Tuscan. Reporter 31:60+ S 24 '64

Last aesthete? Reporter 29:55-6 Jl 18 '63

ALEXANDER, Susanna

Public library gains support, cooperation and 400 borrowers. Library J 88:1102-4 Mr 15 '63

ALEXANDER, Tom

Man to the moon. Pop Sci 185:60-5 Ag '64

Man in the moon suit. Esquire 60:104-5+ N '63

Wild birds find a corporate roost. Fortune 70:130-4+ Ag '64

ALEXANDER, W. Boyd

Farewell, groves of academe. por Time 82:80 Jl 12 '63

ALEXANDER, Will Winton

Seeds of southern change: the life of Will Alexander, by W. Dykeman and J. Stokely. Review

Christian Cent 80:174 F 6 '63. K. Haselden

ALEXANDER, William M. and Heffernan, Helen

Current curriculum developments. NEA J 52: 47-8 N '63

ALEXANDRA, princess of Great Britain

Alexandra's wedding. il por Newsweek 61:46 My 6 '63

Bra', bonny bride and a fortune fair. il por Time 81:28 My 3 '63

ALFALFA

Does dehy cause blood spots? G. Lorang. Farm J 88:61 Mr '64

Feed alfalfa pellets to dairy cows? B. Hardy. Farm J 87:40F Jl '63

First-year alfalfa makes three tons of hay. Farm J 87:48 F '63

He makes alfalfa his high-profit crop. J. C. Everly. il Suc Farm 62:42-3 Jl '64

How to establish late summer seedlings. Suc Farm 61:35 Ag '63

Moisture release from cut alfalfa. G. L. Byers and others. bibliog il Science 143: 1183 Mr 13 '64

Sure way to start alfalfa in corn. Farm J 88:32 Ag '64

What variety of alfalfa? Suc Farm 61:56 Mr '63

Diseases and pests

How to control alfalfa and clover diseases. M. Shurtleff and J. J. Fieght. il Suc Farm 62:52-3+ My '64

Hybrids

Hybrid alfalfa's here, how good is it? R. Davis. il Suc Farm 63:72-3 Ja '65

ALFALFA weevils

Can we stop the alfalfa weevil? G. W. Wormley. il Farm J 88:36-7+ O '64

ALFIE! drama. See Naughton, B.

ALFRED L. Boerner botanical gardens, Wisconsin. See Botanical gardens

ALFRED P. Sloan foundation

Foundation grants M.I.T. $5 million for advanced engineering study center. Arch Rec 133:29 Je '63

ALFVÉN, Hannes

Capture of the moon. por Time 81:81 My 24 '63

Moon captured by earth. W. Davis. Sci N L 83:291 My 11 '63

ALGAE

Airborne algae: their abundance and heterogeneity. R. M. Brown, jr. and others. bibliog il Science 143:583-5 F 7 '64

Algae farm tested; Richmond, Calif. il Sci N L 84:370 D 14 '63

Algae: nitrogen fixation by Antarctic species. O. Holm-Hansen. il Science 139:1059-60 Mr 15 '63

Algae studied on islands; Chesapeake Bay. Sci N L 84:119 Ag 24 '63

Coding ambiguity in cell-free extracts of chlamydomonas. R. Sager and others. bibliog il Science 140:304-6 Ap 19 '63

ALGAE—*Continued*
Cytochromes of a blue-green alga: extraction of a c-type with a strongly negative redox potential. R. W. Holton and J. Myers. bibliog il Science 142:234-5 O 11 '63
Experimental differentiation between phototaxis and motility in chlamydomonas snowiae. N. Stahl and A. M. Mayer. bibliog il Science 141:1282-4 S 27 '63
Extend algae life. Sci N L 83:274 My 4 '63
Extracellular polysaccharides of algae: effects on life-support systems. B. G. Moore and R. G. Tischer. bibliog il Science 145:586-7 Ag 7 '64
Fluorescence and absorption changes in chlorella exposed to strong light: the red band. D. Rubinstein and E. Rabinowitch. bibliog il Science 142:681-2 N 8 '63
Fluoroacetate inhibition of amino acids during photosynthesis of chlamydomonas reinhardti. J. R. Kates and R. F. Jones. bibliog il Science 143:145-6 Ja 10 '64
Fully deuterated euglena gracilis. S. E. Mandeville and others. bibliog il Science 146:769 N 6 '64
Home ponds create a problem for public water supplies; algae infestations. Am City 79:172 O '64
How to keep algae out of your pool. B. B. Paine. il Flower Grower 50:42-4 S '63
Molecular heterogeneity of enzymes: malate dehydrogenase of euglena. J. Chancellor-Maddison and C. R. Noll, jr. bibliog il Science 142:60-1 O 4 '63
Space food harvest may be speeded up. Sci N L 83:169 Mr 16 '63
Strontium and calcium uptake by the green alga, oocystis eremosphaeria. N. R. Kevern. bibliog il Science 145:1445-6 S 25 '64; Reply with rejoinder. L. G. Williams. 146:1488 D 11 '64
Symbiosis: on the role of algae symbiotic with hydra. L. Muscatine and H. M. Lenhoff. bibliog il Science 142:956-8 N 15 '63
Ultraviolet inactivation of chloroplast formation in synchronously dividing euglena gracilis. S. F. Petropulos. bibliog il Science 145:392-3 Jl 24 '64
Zoospores in scenedesmus obliquus. F. R. Trainor. bibliog il Science 142:1673-4 D 27 '63
See also
Lichens
Zooxanthella

ALGAL viruses. See Viruses

ALGARVE, Portugal
Europe's best travel bargain; with report by M. Leatherbee. il Life 57:62-71+ O 23 '64
Portugal's sunny shore. D. Dodge. il Holiday 33:40+ Mr '63

ALGEBRA
Algebra. W. W. Sawyer. il Sci Am 211:70-8 bibliog(p269) S '64

ALGEBRA, Boolean
Binary numbers & Boolean algebra. W. S. Andariese. il Electr World 69:72-3 Mr '63

ALGER, Bruce
Excerpt from address, April 2, 1963. Cong Digest 42:177+ Je '63
Excerpt from address, February 8, 1964. Cong Digest 43:85+ Mr '64
Excerpt from debate, April 7, 1964. Cong Digest 43:183+ Je '64
Excerpt from debate, January 30, 1962. Cong Digest 42:57+ F '63

ALGER, Horatio, 1832-1899
Forgettable centenary: Horatio Alger's. T. Meehan. il por N Y Times Mag p22-3+ Je 28 '64
Horatio Alger revisited; excerpt from From rags to riches, Horatio Alger, jr. and the American dream. J. Tebbel. il Pub W 183:121-5 F 18 '63

ALGERIA
At least not chaos. il Time 82:22-3 Ag 16 '63
Haven for exiles. Newsweek 61:49-50 My 20 '63
Hottening up; fighting on two new fronts. Newsweek 62:60+ O 21 '63
Secretary-General visits three African countries. U N Rev 11:12-13+ Mr '64
See also
Communism—Algeria
Elections—Algeria
Guerrillas—Algeria
Jews in Algeria
Petroleum industry and trade—Algeria

Boundaries

Another border, another war. New Repub 149:8 O 26 '63
Brief interlude. il Newsweek 62:56+ N 11 '63
Buzz saw; border war. il Newsweek 62:46 N 4 '63
Clash in the Sahara. il Sr Schol 83:6-9+ N 22 '63
Fight now, fly later; Algerian-Moroccan border clash. il Time 82:39-40 O 25 '63
Minuscule war; Moroccan-Algerian border clash. il Newsweek 62:44 O 28 '63
More than five-minute truce? border war between Morocco and Algeria. Time 82:35-6 N 8 '63
Reflections on the Barbary Coast. R. Kirk. Nat R 15:442 N 19 '63
They war over a wasteland. il Life 55:38-9 N 8 '63
Unwelcome are the peacemakers. il Time 82:36 N 1 '63
War in Africa: MIG jets on both sides; two outposts on Sahara Desert border between Algeria and Morocco. il U S News 55:6 O 28 '63

Description and travel

Notebooks, by A. Camus. Review
New Yorker 39:128+ F 8 '64. A. J. Liebling

Economic conditions

Algerians on their own. J. K. Cooley. Reporter 28:37-40 F 28 '63
Atlantic report. Atlan 213:14+ Ap '64
Back from development. Time 83:32+ Je 26 '64
Faith without works. New Repub 150:10-11 Mr 14 '64
Poverty & playthings. Time 83:24+ Ja 17 '64
Report from an Algerian village. P. Huston. il N Y Times Mag p20-1+ O 13 '63
Year of independence and rising troubles. F. C. Painton. il U S News 55:92-4 Ag 5 '63

Foreign relations

Man who came to dinner. il Time 81:27-8 Mr 22 '63

History

Rebellion, 1954-1962

See also
Secret army organization (Organisation de l'armée secréte)

Politics and government

After a year, it's Ben Bella's Algeria. P. Braestrup. il N Y Times Mag p31+ S 29 '63
Algeria going the way of Cuba? il U S News 55:62 O 14 '63
Algeria: year I of independence. R. Bosc. America 108:362-5 Mr 16 '63
Algerian crisis. A. Werth. il Nation 197:341-4 N 23 '63
Algerian strong man; Ben Bella gets more power; also FLN. U S News 55:26 S 23 '63
Algerians on their own. J. K. Cooley. Reporter 28:37-40 F 28 '63
Atlantic report. Atlan 213:14+ Ap '64
Ben Bella and Castro. J. Daniel. New Repub 149:9-11 O 5 '63
Ben Bella balked. il Newsweek 62:42 O 14 '63
Ben Bella's approach misfires in Algeria. Bsns W p65+ O 19 '63
Ben Bella's triumph. J. Daniel. New Repub 149:18-20 Jl 6 '63
Ben Castro? il Newsweek 62:51 S 23 '63
Can de Gaulle call a halt? nationalization of French-owned property. Time 82:50 O 4 '63
Clean sweep; political purge. Newsweek 64:40 Jl 20 '64
Double trouble in Algeria. Sr Schol 83:16 N 1 '63
Evian treaty; Ben Bella laughing at de Gaulle? G. Laffly. il Nat R 15:392-5 N 5 '63
First revolt. il Time 82:42 O 11 '63
Hex? Nasser's visit to Algeria. il Time 81:39 My 17 '63
Man on the mountain; Colonel Mohammed Chaabani. il Time 84:35 Jl 10 '64
Mystique without typists. il Newsweek 63:39 My 4 '64
Nation in transition. Newsweek 61:50-2 My 13 '63
Nationalization craze. il Time 82:34 S 27 '63
One-man rule in Algeria. C. Sterling. il Reporter 29:32+ O 10 '63
Rivals; capture of guerrilla leader Hocine Ait-Ahmed. il Newsweek 64:54 N 2 '64
Road to Cuba. E. Weintal. il Newsweek 62:38+ S 30 '63
Still in the saddle; short-lived revolt of Colonel Mohammed Chaabani. Time 84:32 Jl 17 '64
Supreme guide. Time 82:36 S 20 '63
Unhappy birthday. Newsweek 64:40 Jl 13 '64
Unrest in the Kabylia. il Time 83:36 Mr 20 '64

ALGERIA—*Continued*

Population

New dilemmas for the *pieds noirs.* P. Braestrup. il N Y Times Mag p28+ My 26 '63

Riots

Socialist regime where troubles grow. U S News 56:9 Ja 20 '64

ALGERIAN refugees. See Refugees, Algerian

ALGERIANS

Notebooks, by A. Camus. Review
New Yorker 39:128+ F 8 '64. A. J. Liebling

Report from an Algerian village. P. Huston. il N Y Times Mag p20-1+ O 13 '63

ALGERIANS in France

Algerian aftermath. H. Giniger. il N Y Times Mag p32+ Mr 22 '64

ALGOL. See Stars, Variable

ALGONQUIN PROVINCIAL PARK. See Ontario—Parks and reserves

ALGREN, Nelson

Donkeyman by twilight. Nation 198:509-12 My 18 '64

Ginger man who couldn't. Nation 198:351-2 Ap 6 '64

Moon of the arfy darfy; story. Sat Eve Post 237:44-5 S 26 '64

Nelson Algren at fifty-five; interview, ed. by H. E. F. Donohue. por Atlan 214:79-80+ O '64

Radical innocent. Nation 199:142-3 S 21 '64

Un-American idea: sex can be funny. Life 56:8 My 8 '64

Who's who at the lost & found. Nation 198: 560-1 Je 1 '64

about

Big bite. N. Mailer. Esquire 60:16+ S '63

He never left home. H. Kramer. Reporter 28:46-7 Je 20 '63

I ain't Abelard. por Newsweek 64:58-9 D 28 '64

Intellectual as ape man. por Time 81:88 My 31 '63

Question of fidelity; excerpts from Force of circumstance, tr. by R. Howard. S. de Beauvoir. Harper 229:111-14+ D '64

Talker. por Newsweek 64:119A+ O 26 '64

ALHAMBRA

Romantic realities. F. P. Keyes. il Travel 121:48-50 Ap '64

ALI, M. A. See Hanyu, I. jt. auth.

ALI BAIG, Tara

In the hands of the Mahatmas. Sat R 47: 35-6 My 30 '64

ALIANZA popular revolucionaria americana. See Political parties—Peru

ALIBIS. See Excuses

ALICE Blaine; story. See Randal, V.

ALICE Carlene, Sister

Dear Mother Superior. America 110:488-9 Ap 4 '64

ALICE Lloyd college, Pippa Passes, Ky.

College education for $40 a year. H. Ehrlich. il Look 28:134+ O 20 '64

ALIEN property

See also
World war, 1939-1945—Confiscations and contributions

ALIENS

See also
Expatriation
Naturalization

ALIENS; story. See Jhabvala, R. R.

ALIMONY

Speaking out; let's abolish alimony. A. Eliot. Sat Eve Post 237:12+ Ag 22 '64

ALINSKY, David

This is war; attack against poverty, misery, delinquency, disease and injustice. H. Black. il pors Sat Eve Post 237:60-3 Ja 25 '64

ALINSKY, Saul D.

Up from apathy, the Woodlawn experiment; excerpts from Crisis in black and white. C. E. Silberman. Commentary 37:51-8 My '64; Discussion. 38:14+ O '64

ALIVE; story. See Saroyan, W.

ALKALI soils. See Soils, Alkali

ALKALINE phosphatases. See Phosphatases

ALKAN, Charles Henri Valentin

Berlioz of the piano. R. Lewenthal. por Mus Am 84:44 F '64

ALKEMA, Chester Jay

Non-scientific insect mobiles. Sch Arts 64:10-13 N '64

Papier-mâché animals. Sch Arts 63:16-17 Mr '64

ALKYL benzene sulfonate. See Benzenesulfonates; Cleaning compositions

ALKYLATION

Alkylation of synthetic polynucleotides. D. B. Ludlum and others. bibliog Science 145: 397-9 Jl 24 '64

ALL-Africa Christian youth assembly

Young African Christians speak. R. French. Christian Cent 80:242-3 F 20 '63

ALL-Africa conference of churches. See Religious conferences

ALL America baseball team. See Baseball players

ALL-America cities

All America cities (cont) il Look 27:94-6+ Ap 23 '63; 28:93-6+ Ap 21 '64

All-America cities for 1962-1963. Am City 78:170+ My '63; 79:136+ My '64

ALL America selections. See Plants—All America selections

ALL-American tour; drama. See Newman, D.

ALL-Arabian horse show, Scottsdale, Ariz. See Horse shows

ALL-channel receiver. See Television receiving apparatus

ALL-city high school orchestra. See School orchestras

ALL creatures great and small; story. See Stein, G.

ALL-day school programs. See School day

ALL-England fishing championship. See Fishing—Competitions

ALL-expense tours. See Travel

ALL my beautiful darlings; story. See Sanders, G.

ALL my own; story. See Shyer, M. F.

ALL-number calling. See Telephone, Dial

ALL risk personal property insurance. See Insurance—All risk policies

ALL the blood within me; story. See Amis, K.

ALL the happy endings; story. See Reed, K.

ALL the pretty little horses; story. See Proulx, E. A.

ALL the summer's promise; story. See Robinson, B.

ALL things bright and beautiful; story. See Carter, M.

ALL this and Alan, too; drama. See Allred, J.

ALL tied up; story. See O'Hara, J.

ALL-woman transcontinental air race. See Airplane racing

ALLAGASH RIVER

Maine asks for a chance on the Allagash; editorial. J. B. Craig. Am For 69:10-11 O '63

New threat to the Allagash. Audubon Mag 65:211 Jl '63

Showdown on the Allagash. S. Carter, 3d. il Read Digest 85:178-82+ O '64

Waters of the Allagash. H. Clepper. il Am For 70:14-18+ N '64

Why we must save the Allagash. W. O. Douglas. il Field & S 68:24-9+ Jl '63

ALLAN, Donald A.

Santo Domingo: the empty showcase. Reporter 29:28-31 D 5 '63

—and Sherman, George

Panama: distrust and delay. Reporter 30:28-9 F 27 '64

ALLAN, Nelly

Beach glass and bric-a-brac. Design 65:12-14 S '63

ALLAN, Robert M. jr

Honolulu preview. Yachting 113:79-81+ Ap '63

Who will win the Honolulu race? Yachting 113:38-9+ Je '63

ALLAND, Mitchel

Out of darkness. New Yorker 40:178+ Ap 25 '64

ALLDREDGE, Melvin W.

New crowd minds store for the tea company. il pors Bsns W p88-90+ Je 13 '64

ALLEGHANY corporation

Gladder to get out than sorry to lose out. il Time 81:107 Ap 19 '63

Kirby comes home the winner. il Bsns W p 110-11 Jl 13 '63

Kirby's comeback. il Newsweek 61:80 Ap 22 '63

Kirby's last laugh. Newsweek 62:63-4 Jl 15 '63

Winner by a knockout. Time 82:88 Jl 12 '63

ALLEGHENY airlines

Allegheny plans fare, operations changes. J. W. Carter. il Aviation W 81:35+ Ag 10 '64

ALLEGHENY national forest. See National forest

ALLEGHENY reservoir project. See Dams

ALLEGHENY RIVER

Lake of Perfidity; Allegheny reservoir. New Repub 150:5 Ap 18 '64

ALLEGIANCE, Oaths of. See Loyalty, Oaths of

ALLEGORIES
See also
Parables
ALLELES. See Allelomorphism
ALLELOMORPHISM
Abnormalities associated with a chromosome region in the mouse. L. C. Dunn; D. Bennett. bibliog il Science 144:260-7 Ap 17 '64
Acid phosphatases of human red cells: predicted phenotype conforms to a genetic hypothesis. L. Lai and others. bibliog il Science 145:1187-8 S 11 '64
Allelic mapping in yeast by X-ray-induced mitotic reversion. T. R. Manney and R. K. Mortimer. bibliog il Science 143:581-3 F 7 '64
Hemoblobin loci: mice classified for their Hb and Sol alleles. R. A. Popp. bibliog il Science 140:893-4 My 24 '63
Independent action of allele-specific suppressor mutations. S. Brody and C. Yanofsky. bibliog il Science 145:399-400 Jl 24 '64
Lethal alleles in mus musculus: local distribution and evidence for isolation of demes. P. K. Anderson. bibliog il Science 145:177-8 Jl 10 '64
ALLEN, Arnold
Oils in one hour. il por Design 64:129-31 Ja '63
ALLEN, Arthur
Ambassador of birdlife. R. B. Fischer. il pors Audubon Mag 67:26-31 Ja '65
Obituary
Audubon Mag por 66:143 My '64
ALLEN, Casey
Landscapes. U S Camera 27:46-7+ Ja '64
ALLEN, Charles
Try camping for summer fun. Ebony 18:127-8+ Je '63
ALLEN, Charles, 1903-
Charlie's profit instinct. por Time 82:103 N 15 '63
ALLEN, Donald M.
(tr) See Ionesco, E. Bald soprano
(tr) See Ionesco, E. Lesson
ALLEN, Donna
Who gains from the fringes? Nation 199:379-81 N 23 '64
ALLEN, Douglass M.
Help wanted: a U.S. vice president. Read Digest 84:73-7 Mr '64
Washington's greatest spoof: the Gridiron dinner. Read Digest 84:51-2+ Ap '64
ALLEN, Durward L.
Costly and needless war on predators; condensation of address, November 12, 1962. Audubon Mag 65:85-9+ Mr '63
Count in the weatherman. Field & S 68:40-2+ Je '63
Drawdown for better fishing. Field & S 67:52-3+ Mr '63
Growing antagonism to hunting. Field & S 68:12-16 S '63
Isle Royale: predator vs. prey. Field & S 68:21-3 Ja '64
Musquash of the marshes. Field & S 68:35+ Jl '63
Seaside freeloader. Field & S 68:49+ Ap '64
—and Mech, L. D.
Wolves versus moose on Isle Royale. il pors Nat Geog Mag 123:200-19 F '63
ALLEN, Dwight W.
Eight-to-five schooling? Sr Schol 83:1T-2T O 11 '63; Discussion. 83:4T N 1; 4T N 15 '63
—See Gross, R. E. jt. auth.
ALLEN, E. Jerry
Water insurance pays dividends. Am City 79:100-2 My '64
ALLEN, Elizabeth
Loser; story. Seventeen 22:114-15 Mr; 146-7 Ap '63
ALLEN, Eric
Autumn in the Ozarks. Holiday 36:30+ N '64
ALLEN, Ethan
In the name of the great Jehovah and the Continental congress! K. S. Davis. il pors Am Heritage 14:65-77 O '63
ALLEN, Everett S.
Sailors on wheels. Motor B 113:148-51 Mr '64
What ever happened to the rotor ship? Motor B 111:116+ F '63
ALLEN, Fergus
Is there life on Venus? poem. Atlan 213:120 F '64
ALLEN, Frances H. See Allen, J. E. jt. auth.
ALLEN, Gay Wilson
Above the traffic of his times. Sat R 46:40-1 N 16 '63
Iron hand and a soft heart. Sat R 47:28 N 21 '64
Thistledown personality. Sat R 47:25+ S 5 '64
ALLEN, George V.
World laws for a war of words. Sat R 47:42 Ap 4 '64
ALLEN, Gracie
Celebrity register. C. Amory. por McCalls 90:136 My '63
ALLEN, James C. and Kunkel, H. G.
Antibodies to genetic types of gamma globulin after multiple transfusions. bibliog Science 139:418 F 1 '63
ALLEN, James E.
Doctor James E. Allen; Harlem YMCA man of the year. por Negro Hist Bul 27:161 Ap '64
School integration and civil rights; letter. Sch & Soc 92:342 N 14 '64
ALLEN, John Alexander
Bugler, whoever he is; poem. Reporter 30:33 Je 4 '64
Pismire agonistes; poem. Atlan 214:104 S '64
ALLEN, John E. and Allen, F. H.
Big, bad fears of childhood. Parents Mag 39:62-3+ Mr '64
ALLEN, Kenneth. See Brush, A. H. jt. auth.
ALLEN, Leland C.
Basic research: capabilities of universities and other research organizations. Science 141:674 Ag 23 '63
ALLEN, Linda
(ed) The look you like; questions and answers. See issues of Today's health
ALLEN, Louis
Life in Liberty. Nation 198:254 Mr 16 '64
ALLEN, Louis A.
How to run a growing company. Nations Bsns 53:68-70+ Ja '65
ALLEN, Marguerite
Look, the parade is coming. Sch Arts 63:13 D '63
ALLEN, Mary Louise
What can we do about America's unwed teen-age mothers; interview, ed. by E. Harris. McCalls 91:40+ N '63
ALLEN, Mel
Celebrity register. C. Amory. por McCalls 90:169 My '63
How about that? Sports Illus 21:17 O 19 '64
Skyrocket. il por Time 84:64 O 16 '64
ALLEN, Patricia Hunt
Current children's paperbacks. bibliog Library J 89:2156-8 My 15 '64
Melody lingers on a sour note. Library J 89:3403 S 15 '64
On beyond Notable. por Library J 88:2063-5 My 15 '63
—See Davis, E. L. jt. ed.
ALLEN, Paul E.
Never drop your guard. pors Outdoor Life 131:44-7+ F '63
ALLEN, R. C.
September is daffodil planting time. Horticulture 42:34-7+ S '64
Two dozen roses. Horticulture 42:18-19+ Ap '64
ALLEN, Richard, bp
Richard Allen. L. Bennett, jr. il pors Ebony 19:142-4+ My '64
ALLEN, Richard V.
Extrapolating the zig. Nat R 16:361 My 5 '64
Lenin the ideologist. Nat R 16:1024-6 N 17 '64
ALLEN, Richie
Rookie from Wampum, Pa. W. Leggett. il por Sports Illus 20:28-9 Ap 20 '64
ALLEN, Rita
Miscellany of playing cards of England. Hobbies 68:120-1 My '63
ALLEN, Robert D. and others
Shuttle-streaming: synchronization with heat production in slime mold. bibliog Science 142:1485-7 D 13 '63
ALLEN, Robert Porter
Our only native stork, the wood ibis. Nat Geog Mag 125:294-306 F '64
Obituary
Audubon Mag por 65:307 S '63
ALLEN, Robert Thomas
Next: automated people. Sci Digest 53:39-41 My '63
Women have no sense of humor. Read Digest 84:134-6 Ap '64
ALLEN, Robert V.
(comp) Articles and other books received; Soviet Union. See issues of American historical review
ALLEN, Ross
American kids can take it! ed. by K. Vining. Pop Sci 182:106-9+ F '63
ALLEN, Scott
Bashful barber and a worldly kid from Smoke Rise. H. Horn. il por Sports Illus 20:20-1 F 17 '64
Flips, loops, Lutzes. por Newsweek 63:76 Ja 27 '64

ALLEN, Steve
How to attack a liberal. Nat R 14:149-52 F 26 '63
about
Celebrity register. C. Amory. por McCalls 90: 182 My '63

ALLEN, Walter
Her Ladyship goes left. New Repub 150:27-8+ Je 13 '64
Love and the lyricist. New Repub 149:21-3 N 30 '63

ALLEN, William
Training and education of architects; excerpts from paper. Arch Rec 133:173-6 Ap '63

ALLEN, William W.
Total managerial failure. Fortune 69:62+ My '64

ALLEN, Woody
Bright new comic clowns toward success: Woody Allen. W. K. Zinsser. il pors Sat Eve Post 236:26-7 S 21 '63
His own Boswell. Time 81:78 F 15 '63
Loser on top. E. Kolowrat. por Sr Schol 83: 23 N 22 '63
Man with an ant on a leash. il pors Life 57:75-8 Ag 21 '64
On stage. C. L. Mee, jr. il por Horizon 5:46-7 My '63
Six quitters. por Esquire 62:102 S '64
Uptown expression. por Newsweek 63:102 Ap 27 '64
Verbal cartoons. J. Stang. pors N Y Times Mag p 120+ N 3 '63

ALLENTOWN, Pa.
Telephones give split-second emergency response. G. M. Monahan. il Am City 79:111 S '64

Education

Educating for industry; Allentown's vocational program. J. T. Shuman. Atlan 214: 90-4 D '64

ALLENTOWN, Pa, free library
Controversy in Allentown, Pa. as school board takes over P.L. Library J 88:3181-2 S 15 '63
Jackets in the library, please. E. K. Sanders. Library J 88:4108 N 1 '63

ALLER, Diane Lee. See Aller, Doris, jt. auth.

ALLER, Doris, and Aller, D. L.
Fun of doing mosaic-craft. Design 65:84-6 N '63

ALLERAND, C. Dominique, and Yahr, M. D.
Gamma globulin affinity for normal human tissue of the central nervous system. bibliog Science 144:1141-2 My 29 '64

ALLERGIC rhinitis. See Rhinitis

ALLERGY
Allergy test for penicillin. Bsns W p 146 Ap 25 '64
Antigenic histamine release from passively sensitized human leukocytes. P. P. Van-Arsdel, jr. and C. J. Sells. bibliog il Science 141:1190-1 S 20 '63
Canine antiserums analogous to human allergic and blocking antiserums. J. I. Tennenbaum and others. bibliog Science 142: 589-90 N 1 '63
Cosmetic allergies. L. D. Kirk. il Parents Mag 38:130 Ap '63
Delayed hypersensitivity in man: transfer by lymphocyte preparations of peripheral blood. R. G. Slavin and J. E. Garvin. bibliog il Science 145:52-3 Jl 3 '64
Extract for the allergic; whole insect extract. F. Marley. Sci N L 83:277 My 4 '63
Feeding the allergic child; with recipes. A. Yenne. il Parents Mag 39:57-8+ My '64
Help seen for allergy of ragweed-sensitive dogs. Sci N L 84:313 N 16 '63
How to control allergy. J. P. McGovern. il Parents Mag 39:95-6+ Jl '64
How to recognize an allergy, and what to do about it. C. Schwalberg. il Redbook 120: 20+ Mr '63
Hypersensitivity to a synthetic polypeptide: induction of a delayed reaction. S. Ben-Efraim and others. bibliog il Science 139: 1222-3 Mr 22 '63
Ills due to self allergy. Sci N L 86:196 S 26 '64
Meal planning for children allergic to wheat, milk and eggs; with recipes. R. Noonan. il Parents Mag 39:59+ My '64
Photosensitization in solids; report on international conference on photosensitization in solids. L. I. Grossweiner. Science 146: 88-90 O 2 '64
Role of the allergist in the battle against air pollution; address, March 1963. F. L. Rosen. Consumer Bul 46:36-8 S '63
Tuberculin hypersensitivity: studies with radioactive antigen and mononuclear cells. K. Kay and W. O. Rieke. bibliog il Science 139:487-9 F 8 '63
Where medicine stands on allergies. G. C. Greer. Bet Hom & Gard 42:12+ Ag '64
See also
Anaphylaxis
Hay fever

ALLERS, Franz
I'm floating. por Newsweek 63:72 Ja 13 '64

ALLEY, Jean
(ed) See Cuffey, I. I believe

ALLEY, John W. See Muul, I. jt. auth.

ALLEY theatre, Houston. See Houston, Tex.—Theater

ALLIANCE, Ohio
See also
Rodman public library, Alliance, Ohio

ALLIANCE for progress
Advice for the Alliance; private industry's needs. Newsweek 61:68+ My 6 '63
Aid for AID; cooperation of National academy of sciences. Newsweek 62:56-7 Jl 8 '63
Ali, ali, anza free-o! Tiresias. Nat R 14:113-14+ F 12 '63
Alianza: aid, trade, trouble. il Newsweek 62: 61-2 N 25 '63
Alliance for progress. L. Guernsey and A. Taylor. bibliog il Focus 14:1-6 Ap '64
Alliance for progress: a challenge and an opportunity; address, September 23, 1964. T. C. Mann. Dept State Bul 51:593-7 O 26 '64
Alliance for progress; address, December 12, 1962. H. W. Balgooyen. Vital Speeches 29: 325-32 Mr 15 '63
Alliance for progress; address, January 20, 1964. H. H. Humphrey. Vital Speeches 30: 307-11 Mr 1 '64
Alliance for progress; address, March 10, 1964. W. W. Rostow. Dept State Bul 50: 496-500 Mr 30 '64
Alliance for progress; address, May 11, 1964. L. B. Johnson. Vital Speeches 30:482-3 Je 1 '64
Alliance for progress; address, May 13, 1964. T. C. Mann. Dept State Bul 50:857-63 Je 1 '64
Alliance for progress: aims, distortions, obstacles. A. Lleras Camargo. For Affairs 42: 25-37 O '63
Alliance for progress: August 1964; address, August 7, 1964. W. W. Rostow. Dept State Bul 51:306-11 Ag 31 '64
Alliance for progress exhibits open at Pan American union; remarks, August 12, 1964. T. C. Mann. Dept State Bul 51:305 Ag 31 '64
Alliance for progress future doubtful. Christian Cent 80:876-7 Jl 10 '63
Alliance for progress in historical perspective. E. R. May. bibliog f For Affairs 41: 757-74 Jl '63
Alliance for progress is dead. V. Alba. New Repub 151:17-18 S 5 '64
Alliance for progress marks second anniversary. J. F. Kennedy; L. B. Johnson. Dept State Bul 49:401-3 S 9 '63
Alliance for progress notes. Américas 16:46 Je; 46 Ag; 47 S; 46 O; 46 N; 42 D '64; 17: 46 Ja '65
Alliance for progress seminars. Américas 15:46 Je '63
Alliance for progress: two-year review. N. A. Haverstock. il Américas 15:2-9 Ag '63
Alliance in danger. Time 81:29 F 15 '63
Alliance languishes. America 109:413-14 O 12 '63
Alliance that is making little progress. il U S News 54:40+ F 25 '63
Anniversary of the Alliance. M. Seoane. Américas 15:1 Ag '63
Are we ignoring Latin America? A. A. Berle. il N Y Times Mag p26+ N 24 '63
Atlantic report. Atlan 214:8+ Ag '64
Back to the drawing board. Nat R 15:334-5 O 22 '63
Battle for progress with freedom in the western hemisphere; address, November 18, 1963. J. F. Kennedy. Dept State Bul 49: 900-4 D 9 '63
Building on quicksand. S. Lens. Commonweal 79:159-61 N 1 '63
Can LBJ help Latin America solve its problems? il U S News 55:32-3 D 30 '63
Can the Alliance for progress succeed? W. F. Barber. bibliog f Ann Am Acad 351:81-91 Ja '64
Caribbean: our sea of troubles. J. Benitez. Sat R 46:11-13+ Jl 13 '63
Charter of Punta del Este; text. il Cur Hist 46:38-46 Ja '64
Culture comes into its own. M. I. Anderson. il Américas 15:2-6 N '63
Cut when it hurts. Time 82:42+ S 20 '63
Dean Rusk analyzes Alliance science progress; excerpts of remarks, October 5, 1964. D. Rusk. Sci N L 86:258+ O 24 '64

ALLIANCE for progress—*Continued*
Declaration of Cundinamarca; Inter-American conference of ministers of labor. il Américas 15:44-5 Jl '63
Development financing and the Alliance for progress. D. Dillon; P. Glaessner; W. A. Harriman. Dept State Bul 51:878-87 D 21 '64
Dissatisfaction down south. il Time 81:22-3 Mr 22 '63
Economic progress and Brazilian nationalism. D. Goulet. Cath World 198:314-19 F '64
Education: backbone of the Alliance for progress. G. Betancur-Mejia. il Américas 15:2-7 S '63
Farmer, city founder, and poet; founding and construction of San Martín de Porres. L. Zalamea. il Américas 15:38-9 N '63
First aid for an ailing Alliance; meeting of Latin American economic & social council. il Bsns W p47-8+ N 9 '63
Focus on Latin America. il Sr Schol 83:38-9 O 4 '63
Foreign aid: Latin-American science board set up to help with Alliance for progress. D. S. Greenberg. Science 141:28 Jl 5 '63
Formula for prosperity. D. Rockefeller. Sat R 46:28 O 12 '63
Free-world defense and assistance programs; message to Congress, April 2, 1963. J. F. Kennedy. Dept State Bul 48:591-9 Ap 22 '63
Frustrating monologue; concerning reports of Juscelino Kubitschek and Alberto Lleras Camargo. il Time 81:21 Je 28 '63
Going the wrong way. il Time 82:36+ N 22 '63
Great challenge of Latin America; address, May 23, 1963. J. P. Grace. Vital Speeches 29:613-16 Ag 1 '63
Great fear, by J. Gerassi. Review
Sat R 46:23-4 Jl 20 '63. W. O'Dwyer
Guarded optimism. Time 84:34+ D 18 '64
Health and social progress in Latin America; address, October 10, 1964. M. W. Williams. Dept State Bul 51:747-51 N 23 '64
Honest intervention. Christian Cent 80:731-2 Je 5 '63
How much progress in the Alliance for progress? il U S News 55:88-90+ O 7 '63
I have faith in the new man. R. Squirru. Américas 15:1 Je '63
Inter-American economic and social council reviews Alliance for progress; statement, December 8, 1964. T. C. Mann. Dept State Bul 51:898-901 D 28 '64
Interdependence and the principles of self-determination and nonintervention; address, April 16, 1963. E. M. Martin. Dept State Bul 48:710-15 My 6 '63
J.F.K. co-stars in a new Common market; Latinos have a hit; with report by L. Hall. il Life 54:26-35 Mr 29 '63
Labor and the Alliance. S. Romualdi. il Américas 15:18-21 Ag '63
Labor and the Alliance for progress. V. Andrade. America 108:850 Je 15 '63
Labor ministers' conference on the Alliance for progress; excerpts from address. W. W. Wirtz. Mo Labor R 86:789-93 Jl '63
Latin America bites U.S. again; dispute over oil development rights. Bsns W p26-7 N 16 '63
Latin America; necessity for politicial democracy and stability; address, November 18, 1963. J. F. Kennedy. Vital Speeches 30: 102-5 D 1 '63
Latin America progress report. G. J. Mangone. America 111:12-14 Jl 4 '64
Latin America's true voice. A. A. Berle. Sat R 46:14+ Jl 13 '63
Latin sky is brighter. Life 55:4 Ag 16 '63
Latin touch needed? Newsweek 62:50 S 2 '63
Let us have faith in the Alliance; excerpts from the two ex-presidents' reports. J. Kubitschek; A. Lleras Camargo. Américas 15:48 Ag '63
Let's stop financing socialism in Latin America. J. G. Tower. Read Digest 84:121-4 Ja '64
LBJ brand. Time 83:29 Mr 27 '64
Matter of tone; resignation of T. Moscoso, as special adviser and U.S. representative to the Inter-American committee. Time 83: 48 My 15 '64
Mexico: no aid for the competent. New Repub 149:9 N 2 '63
Misconceptions regarding Latin America; address, February 21, 1963. P. R. Nehemkis, jr. bibliog Vital Speeches 29:445-8 My 1 '63
Mr Moscoso named representative to Inter-American economic units. Dept State Bul 50:89 Ja 20 '64
My Mr Latin America. il Newsweek 63:39 Ja 6 '64
New approach to Latin America? W. V. Shannon. Commonweal 80:31-2 Ap 3 '64
New era for the Alliance: Inter-American committee on the Alliance for progress. M. I. Anderson. il Américas 16:1-7 Je '64
New look. Newsweek 63:54 My 25 '64
New office to spur Alliance investment. Bsns W p85-6 Mr 30 '63
New world of Latin America. T. Moscoso. il Sat R 46:23-7+ O 12 '63
Now U.S. is exporting union ideas to Latin America. A. W. Robinson. il U S News 54: 86+ My 20 '63
One Mann & twenty problems. il Time 83:15-18 Ja 31 '64
Organizing for progress in Latin America; address, September 17, 1964. T. C. Mann. Dept State Bul 51:479-82 O 5 '64
Parliamentary government and the Alliance for progress; address, February 5, 1964. D. Rusk. Dept State Bul 50:305-7 F 24 '64
President Johnson pledges redoubled efforts to Alliance for progress; remarks, May 11, 1964. L. B. Johnson. Dept State Bul 50:854-7 Je 1 '64
President Kennedy and General Clay urge restoration of aid funds; interview, August 30, 1963. J. F. Kennedy; L. D. Clay. Dept State Bul 49:476-8 S 23 '63
President reaffirms pledge to Latin America; address, November 26, 1963. L. B. Johnson. Dept State Bul 49:912-13 D 16 '63
President reaffirms U.S. support for Alliance for progress; statement, November 13, 1964. L. B. Johnson. Dept State Bul 51:804 D 7 '64
President sends message to Bogotá conference of labor ministers; text of message, May 7, 1963. J. F. Kennedy. Dept State Bul 48:884-5 Je 3 '63
Presidents' meeting at San José; statements, addresses and remarks, March 18-21, 1963; with Declaration of Central America. J. F. Kennedy. Dept State Bul 48:511-20 Ap 8 '63
Progress of the Alliance. W. Velloso. il Américas 16:10-13 Ja '64
Re-evaluation; excerpts from addresses, December 14, 1962. A. Lleras Camargo; J. Kubitschek. il Américas 15:44-5 F '63
Senate must save Alianza. Life 55:8 S 27 '63
Seven presidents. Newsweek 61:54+ Mr 25 '63
Social security and the Alliance for progress; seventh Inter-American conference on social security, Asunción, Paraguay, May 31-June 5, 1964. I. C. Merriam. Dept State Bul 51:320-1 Ag 31 '64
Soul for the Alliance; Third inter-American education ministers meeting, Bogotá, Colombia. R. C. Schroeder. il Américas 15: 2-6 O '63
Spirit of San Jose. Nation 196:258 Mr 30 '63
Strengthening the Alliance for progress; statement, November 13, 1963. W. A. Harriman. Dept State Bul 49:937-45 D 16 '63
Third anniversary of the Alliance for progress; address, March 16, 1964. L. B. Johnson. Dept State Bul 50:535-8 Ap 6 '64
This month's feature: U.S. and the Alliance for progress. Cong Digest 42:67-77+ Mr '63
Thomas Mann's report. Commonweal 81:216-17 N 13 '64
To salvage or to save; reflections on America's most pressing revolutions; address, May 9, 1963. J. Benitez. Vital Speeches 29: 535-7 Je 15 '63
Top man in the clearinghouse; Carlos Sanz de Santamaria. Time 83:38 F 7 '64
Trade union movement and social progress in the western hemisphere; address, November 23, 1964. D. Rusk. Dept State Bul 51:851-2 D 14 '64
Troubles & remedies. Time 81:26 My 3 '63
United in spirit and in arms; Rendezvous with destiny; addresses, March 18 and March 21, 1963. J. F. Kennedy. Vital Speeches 29:386-9 Ap 15 '63
U.S. policy in Latin America. H. H. Humphrey. For Affairs 42:585-601 Jl '64; Reply. Commonweal 80:439-40 Jl 3 '64
U.S. policy regarding military governments in Latin America; statement, October 6, 1963. E. M. Martin. Dept State Bul 49:698-700 N 4 '63
U.S. reports on success of Alliance for progress; remarks, with report, October 27 and October 30. L. B. Johnson; T. C. Mann. Dept State Bul 51:705-7 N 16 '64
U.S. still a bogeyman to Latin Americans. il Bsns W p27-8 D 7 '63
Useful booklet; explaining how to formulate requests for help. America 109:620 N 16 '63
What is progress? J. A. Mora. Américas 15: 1 S '63
What's wrong with the Alianza? J. H. Street. il Reporter 28:25-9 F 14 '63
Where reds may take over next in Latin America. il U S News 54:50 Mr 18 '63

ALLIANCE for progress—*Continued*
Why can't we save Latin America? R. Armstrong. il Sat Eve Post 236:34-6 N 30 '63
Why the Alianza may fail. E. Gruening. New Repub 148:11 Mr 30 '63
Wine is bitter, by M. S. Eisenhower. Review Sat R 46:22-3 Jl 20 '63. H. Lavine
Wrecking the Alliance? Newsweek 62:54+ O 14 '63
Zippity-do-dah! twice as much action, twice as much accomplishment next year. Time 83:27 My 22 '64
See also
Commerce committee on the Alliance for progress

ALLIANCE of Reformed churches throughout the world holding the Presbyterian system
Security checks threaten freedom. Christian Cent 80:164 F 6 '63
World alliance of reformed churches. D. Macleod. Christian Cent 80:1083-4 S 4 '63

ALLIANCES
American commonwealth? A. Buchan. Harper 226:95-101 Je '63
American policy in international affairs; address, February 17, 1964. U. A. Johnson. Dept State Bul 50:364-9 Mr 9 '64
Atlantic partnership; address, Jaunary 15, 1964. A. Segni. Vital Speeches 30:258-60 F 15 '64
Cold war alliances (cont) Sr Schol 83:33 O 4 '63; 85:37 O 7 '64
New world of loosening alliances. Life 56:4 Mr 13 '64
Reflections on the Pacific community; address, March 28, 1963. H. Cleveland. Dept State Bul 48:613-16 Ap 22 '63
Security and freedom: a free world responsibility: address, February 26, 1963. D. Rusk. Dept State Bul 48:383-8 Mr 18 '63
See also
North Atlantic treaty organization

ALLIED chemical and dye corporation
New look at old Allied. il Newsweek 63:68 My 4 '64

ALLIED crude vegetable oil refining corporation
Annals of finance; Ira Haupt & co. affair. J. Brooks. New Yorker 40:160+ N 14 '64
Boiling in oil. Time 82:87A D 13 '63
Commodities: soybeans and salad oil; the greatest scandal in the history of Wall Street is still going on. P. Vanderwicken. il Esquire 61:91-3+ Ap '64
Commodities: the troubled markets. il Newsweek 63:51-4 Ja 6 '64
$46.5 million bail. Newsweek 63:28+ Ja 27 '64
Future of American express. E. K. Faltermayer. Fortune 69:158-9+ Ap '64
In wake of Haupt failure; second thoughts on commodities dealing. Bsns W p 128 D 7 '63
Justice steps in. Time 83:75 Ja 3 '64
Lessons from the Haupt affair. Fortune 69:74+ Ja '64
Mystique of paper. Nation 197:426-7 D 21 '63
$150 million in oil, all gone! soybean oil swindle. P. Mandel. il Life 56:90-2+ Ap 3 '64
100-million-dollar mystery? attempt to aid Ira Haupt and co. by New York stock exchange. il U S News 55:109-10 D 16 '63
Salad oil deal still a mystery. Bsns W p54 Ja 25 '64
Scandal in salad oil gets bigger every day; with editorial comment. il Bsns W p32+, 160 D 14 '63
Tino's bottomless tanks of oil; salad oil swindle. N. C. Miller. il Sat Eve Post 237-20-5 Ap 25 '64
Where genius went wrong; crude oil scandal. il Bsns W p 164-6+ Ap 18 '64
Where's the oil? il Newsweek 62:65-6 D 16 '63

ALLIED invasion, June 6, 1944. See World war, 1939-1945—Campaigns and battles—Western

ALLIED maintenance corporation
Cleaner cleans up. il Time 84:78 Jl 3 '64
Unisphere begins to show a bit of a strain; high maintenance bills, poor service. il Bsns W p 100+ Je 27 '64

ALLIED pilots association
Court upholds Allied pilots pact. Aviation W 79:41 Ag 19 '63
Mediator appointed for new pilot's union. Aviation W 78:37 Je 3 '63
Pan Am pilots polled on split with ALPA. Aviation W 79:46 S 16 '63

ALLIGATOR hunting
Last stand of the alligators? A. E. Ayotte. il Audubon Mag 66:237-41 Jl '64

ALLIGATOR snapping turtles. See Turtles

ALLIGATORS
Last stand of the alligators? A. E. Ayotte. il Audubon Mag 66:237-41 Jl '64
Nature note. Sci N L 86:334 N 21 '64
Tender regard and a seat belt for Trudy. il Life 54:103-4 My 24 '63

ALLINGHAM, Margery
Party of one. Holiday 34:11-15 S '63

ALLIS-Chalmers manufacturing company
New pump test center; Allis-Chalmers Norwood works. il Am City 78:90 D '63

ALLISON, Don, and others
Insecticides: effects on cutthroat trout of repeated exposure to DDT. bibliog Science 142:958-61 N 15 '63

ALLISON, Eaves
Old man McGurkin. Field & S 68:38-9+ Je '63

ALLISON, John M.
Causes of a current event. Sat R 47:33-4 Je 20 '64
When policy resorts to power. Sat R 47:31-2 My 2 '64

ALLISON, Milton J. and others
Ethanol accumulation in the rumen after overfeeding with readily fermentable carbohydrate. bibliog Science 144:54-5 Ap 3 '64

ALLISON, Patricia Van Burgh. See Iffland, D. W. jt. auth.

ALLISON division. See General motors corporation—Allison division

ALLIUMS
Alliums for show and seasoning. D. W. Dial. il Horticulture 42:18-19 F '64
Ancient flavors for foods of the present, edible alliums. V. M. Quist. il Horticulture 41:272-3 My '63

ALLMAN, David B.
Are medical costs too high? interview. por Todays Health 42:8-10+ S '64

ALLOOCIMENE
Alloocimene: absence in cigarette smoke. J. D. Mold and others. bibliog il Science 144:1572-3 Je 26 '64

ALLOTROPY
Allotropy in some rare-earth metals at high pressures. G. J. Piermarini and C. E. Weir. bibliog il Science 144:69-71 Ap 3 '64

ALLOTT, Gordon A.
U.N. invites Republic of Korea to take part in debate; statement, December 11, 1962. Dept State Bul 48:70-4 Ja 14 '63
White House vs. Congress; is power balance shifting? excerpts from address, April 3, 1963. por U S News 54:95-6 Ap 15 '63

ALLOWANCES, Childrens. See Childrens allowances

ALLOWANCES, Duty free. See Duty free importation

ALLOWANCES, Family. See Family allowances

ALLOWAY, Lawrence
Betty Parsons, diary of an art dealer; excerpts from An American gallery. Vogue 142:156-7+ O 1 '63
Francis Bacon. Vogue 142:136-9 N 1 '63
Seven U.S. painters. Américas 16:39-41 Jl '64

ALLOXAN
Insulin action in alloxan diabetes modified by actinomycin D. A. Gellhorn and W. Benjamin. bibliog il Science 146:1166-8 N 27 '64

ALLOYS
Paktong; an Oriental alloy (cont) G. Kaler. il Hobbies 67:42+ F '63
Predictable alloys. Sci Am 211:40 Ag '64
See also
Aluminum alloys
Steel alloys

ALLOYS, Heat resistant. See Heat resistant alloys

ALLRED, Joan
All this and Alan, too; drama. Plays 23:37-44 Ap '64

ALLSTATE enterprises, incorporated
Allstate's catchall companion. il Bsns W p47-8+ S 7 '63
Sears is set to enter the mutual fund race. il Bsns W p 112+ F 15 '64

ALM, Richard S.
Books for you and the librarians' vote. Library J 89:4604-5+ N 15 '64

ALMANACS
Almanacs. R. J. Walker. Hobbies 68:122+ Ja '64
Old librarian and his almanack. H. A. Sullivan. Library J 89:1188-92 Mr 15 '64

ALMANACS, Chinese
Warning to Mao, it's the year of the dragon. R. Hughes. il N Y Times Mag p24-5+ Mr 1 '64

ALMANZA, Mirtha Margarita Borras y. See Borras y Almanza, M. M.

ALMASY, Paul
Stained glass; 400 years in one family. UNESCO Courier 16:17-20 My '63
University town built by a country doctor. il UNESCO Courier 16:37-40 Jl '63
ALMEIDA, June D. and others
Virus-like particles in blood of two acute leukemia patients. bibliog Science 142:1487-9 D 13 '63
ALMONDS
See also
Cookery—Nuts
ALMULLA, Bader
Where the money is. il pors Time 81:96 My 24 '63
ALOES
Ever hear of the first-aid plant? G. B. Foster. il House B 105:100+ Jl '63
ALONG the Yellow River; story. See Shen J. C. Y.
ALONSO, Alicia
Alicia Alonso and the National ballet of Cuba. T. De Gámez. il pors Dance Mag 38:30-5 Jl '64
ALONSO, Juan M.
(tr) See Xirau, R. Variety and contrast
ALONSO, Marcelo
Nuclear power for peace. Américas 15:2-8 Je '63
ALOPECIA. See Baldness
ALOU, Jesus
Player of the week; San Francisco Giant. por Sports Illus 21:61 Jl 20 '64
ALOUETTE (artificial satellite) See Artificial satellites, Canadian
ALOYSIUS GONZAGA, Saint
Love: meditations of Saint Aloysius Gonzaga (1591-1926) A. J. Álvarez. il pors Américas 16:22-6 F '64
ALPERN, Robert
Sidewalk cafés. New Yorker 40:30-2 Je 13 '64
ALPERT, Hollis
Cinema's ins and outs. Sat R 47:166-9 Ag 29 '64
Cleopatra: critics vs customers. McCalls 91: 136-7 O '63
From 1½ through 8½. N Y Times Mag p20-1 Jl 21 '63
Movies and the critics. Sat R 47:10-12+ D 26 '64
Movies that carry the freight. Sat R 47:69-70+ D 12 '64
Now the earlier, earlier show. N Y Times Mag p22-3+ Ag 11 '63
One man's festival. Sat R 46:18-19+ O 5 '63
SR goes to the movies. See issues of Saturday review
So deeply obscure, so widely discussed. N Y Times Mag p68-9+ Ap 21 '63
(ed) See Foreman, C. Something worth fighting for
ALPERT, Richard
Dangerous magic of LSD. J. Kobler. il por Sat Eve Post 236:30-2+ N 2 '63
Getting alienated with the right crowd at Harvard. M. Mayer. Esquire 60:73+ S '63; Reply with rejoinder. R. Alpert and T. Leary. 61:42+ Je '64
Hallucinogenic drug cult. N. Gordon. il Reporter 29:35-43 Ag 15 '63
LSD and all that. il por Time 81:72+ Mr 29 '63
No illusions; psilocybin tests at Harvard. por Newsweek 61:92-3 Je 10 '63
Straight scene. por Newsweek 64:74 Jl 27 '64
Strange case of the Harvard drug scandal. A. T. Weil. il Look 27:38+ N 5 '63
ALPHA 66. See Anti-Communist movements—Cuba
ALPHABET
Art of writing. M. Cohen. il UNESCO Courier 17:4-7+ Mr '64
Bizarre alphabet teaches Johnny to read. G. Riemer. il Ladies Home J 81:70-1+ O '64
Cracking the groen-ups' coed; Initial teaching alphabet. M. Gunther. il Sat Eve Post 237: 34-5 Je 20 '64
Easier way to learn to read: i/t/a; Initial teaching alphabet. W. D. Boutwell. il PTA Mag 59:11-13 S '64
Forms of sounds as shown on oscilloscope by roulette figures. G. W. Barton, jr. and S. H. Barton. il Science 142:1455-6 D 13 '63; Reply. B. O. Pyron and F. R. Williamson, jr. 145:72-3 Jl 3 '64
How Europe began to write. Phoenician alphabet. il UNESCO Courier 17:20-1 Mr '64
How Johnny can be taught to read, a new alphabet; Initial teaching alphabet. il U S News 56:76-7 My 18 '64
Janus face of reading; Initial teaching alphabet (i/t/a) C. Timm. il Wilson Lib Bul 39:160-3 O '64
New international phonetic alphabet; use in radio communications. Electr World 69:79 Ap '63
Notes and comment. New Yorker 39:23 Je 1 '63
Pitman forms subsidiary to introduce new alphabet. Pub W 183:58 Je 17 '63
Reading all of a sudden; Initial teaching alphabet. il Life 55:45-6+ N 1 '63
Reading scene; Initial teaching alphabet, or Augmented Roman. E. Geller. il Library J 89:4123-5 O 15 '64
Scripts shrouded in mystery. il UNESCO Courier 17:26-8 Mr '64
Teaching; Britain's initial teaching alphabet. il Time 83:52 Ap 3 '64
Teaching with i/t/a spreads through U.S. il Pub W 186:74-6 Ag 24 '64
Value of ITA; Initial teaching alphabet. J. Downing; I. Rose; W. G. Cutts. il NEA J 53:20-2 S '64
What forty-four letters can do; Initial teaching alphabet. N. Larrick. il Sat R 47:66-7 S 19 '64; Discussion. 47:56-7 N 21 '64
Wuns upon a tiem; Initial teaching alphabet, or ITA. Wilson Lib Bul 38:109 O '63
See also
Chinese language—Alphabet
Cyrillic alphabet
Hebrew language—Alphabet
Lettering
Phoenician language—Alphabet
Russian language—Alphabet
ALPHABETS. See Alphabet
ALPHAND, Hervé
Decisions of France; address, February 24, 1964. Vital Speeches 30:328-31 Mr 15 '64
Detente and French policy; address, October 22, 1963. Vital Speeches 30:55-7 N 1 '63
ALPHAND, Nicole Merenda (Bunau-Varilla)
Party line. il pors Time 82:21-5 N 22 '63
ALPINE flora
Flowers that bloom above the clouds. E. S. Clements. il Audubon Mag 66:180-1 My '64
Small plants for special uses. A. Sutcliffe. il Horticulture 42:30-5 Mr '64
ALPINE strawberries. See Strawberries
ALPINE tunnels. See Tunnels and tunneling
ALPS
Germany's high point offers a great Alps view; Garmisch-Partenkirchen. il Sunset 132:27-8+ Je '64
Snow of Courchevel. il Holiday 34:98-103 D '63
Snowy, snowy Alps. I. Shaw. Mlle 58:154+ N '63
See also
Dolomites
ALQUIT-BLUM, B.
Three poems: I drew you out of that particular night; Is there a darkness then which was not once light? Since I scarcely know what to do with you; tr. by E. Blum. Poetry 104: 88-90 My '64
ALSEBROOK, H. B.
Hummingbirds by the dozen. Audubon Mag 65:246-7 Jl '63
ALSOP, Joseph
Case of McNamara and the joint chiefs. Read Digest 83:102-3 Jl '63
How red China shook the Kremlin. Read Digest 83:129-30 O '63
Legacy of John F. Kennedy. Sat Eve Post 237:15-19 N 21 '64
One problem, two solutions. por Time 85:48 Ja 1 '65
Vacation from dreariness. por Time 84:42 S 25 '64
ALSOP, Stewart
Affairs of state. See issues of Saturday evening post
Campaign: what does it all add up to? Sat Eve Post 237:71-3 O 31 '64
Can Goldwater win in 64? Sat Eve Post 236: 19-25 Ag 24 '63
Can Goldwater win? Sat Eve Post 237:13-15 Ag 8 '64
CIA: battle for secret power. Sat Eve Post 236:17-21 Jl 27 '63; Same abr. with title Intelligence business; secret battle for power. Read Digest 83:114-20 O '63
Collapse of Kennedy's grand design. Sat Eve Post 236:78-81 Ap 6 '63
Crisis at the Cow palace. Sat Eve Post 237: 17-21 Jl 11 '64
Fruits of Castro's plotting. Sat Eve Post 236:75-9 Mr 16 '63
Johnson takes over: the untold story. Sat Eve Post 237:17-23 F 15 '64
—and Quayle, Oliver
What northerners really think of Negroes. pors Sat Eve Post 236:17-21 S 7 '63
—and Stevens, Edmund
What really happened to Khrushchev? Sat Eve Post 237:81-5 N 7 '64; Same abr. Read Digest 86:90-4 Ja '65
ALSTON, Annie May, and Wilcox, Earl
Freshman term paper. Wilson Lib Bul 37: 858-9 Je '63

ALSTON, Elizabeth
Egg cook book. House & Gard 123:151+ Mr '63

ALSTON, R. E. and others
Perspectives in chemotaxonomy. bibliog Science 142:545-52 N 1 '63

ALSTON, Walter Emmons
Alston winds up for two in a row. il pors Life 56:88A-88B+ Mr 20 '64
Speed and a strong leader. W. Leggett. il por Sports Illus 19:10-13 S 2 '63
Trouble with Walter. R. Creamer. il por Sports Illus 18:54+ My 13 '63
Walt Alston: manager with a hair shirt. M. Durslag. il por Look 27:64+ Jl 30 '63

ALSTROEMERIAS
For bright color all summer. il Sunset 131: 166-7 Jl '63

ALT, Fred
Instrumentation for biomedical sciences. Science 142:249-52 O 11 '63

ALTADENA, Calif.
Dressing up for Christmas; reprint. J. Q. Copeland. il Recreation 56:452 D '63

ALTAIC languages
Uralic and Altaic: the neglected area. D. Sinor. Ann Am Acad 356:86-92 N '64
See also
Ural-Altaic languages

ALTAR triptychs. See Triptychs

ALTARPIECES
Enduring to dazzle; 14th century Hungarian altarpiece acquired by The Cloisters. il Time 82:66-7 Jl 12 '63

ALTBACH, Philip G.
Catholic congress in Bombay. Christian Cent 82:116+ Ja 27 '65

ALTER, Robert
Few old Jews. Commentary 35:262-4 Mr '63
Maurice Samuel & Jewish letters. Commentary 37:50-4 Mr '64

ALTERMAN, Loraine
Looking and listening. Sr Schol 85:53 O 7 '64

ALTERNATING current motors. See Electric motors, Alternating current

ALTERNATORS. See Electric generators, Alternating current

ALTIERI, John
Boar for the Bronx; ed. by L. Miracle. Outdoor Life 131:48-51+ Je '63

ALTIMETERS
FM/CW radar altimeter is flight tested. B. Miller. il Aviation W 80:55-6 Mr 30 '64
No hands landing; all-weather landing system. J. Eberhart. il Sci N L 86:386 D 19 '64
Plane to aid spacecraft; radioaltimeter. Sci N L 87:29 Ja 9 '65
Pulse altimeter shows extreme accuracy. P. J. Klass. il Aviation W 78:127+ Je 10 '63

ALTITUDE, Influence of
Altitude will slow runners in 1968 Olympics. Sci N L 86:377 D 12 '64
Fitness in high places. il Bsns W p 188-90+ S 19 '64
Thin air affects brain. Sci N L 83:286 My 4 '63

ALTMAN, George T.
Tax-cut mirage. Nation 196:137-8 F 16; inside cover Mr 16 '63

ALTMAN, Harold A.
Five figures. Sch Arts 62:24-5 Je '63

ALTO ADIGE. See Tyrol

ALTON, G. A.
Pirate's eye view of boating. Yachting 116: 50-1+ Jl '64

ALTRINCHAM, John Edward Poynder Grigg, 2d baron. See Grigg, J. E. P.

ALTRUISM
Bias against man. H. M. Schulweis. Christian Cent 81:361-4 Mr 18 '64
Sweet, spontaneous humanity. H. Bowser. Sat R 46:24 Ap 27 '63

ALTSCHUL, A. M. See Yatsu, L. jt. auth.

ALTSCHUL, Frank
Appraising a position of power. Sat R 47:40-1 O 10 '64
Blueprint for global progress. Sat R 47:78-9 Ja 4 '64
Defense for no defense. Sat R 47:24-5 Jl 4 '64
Several sides of defense. Sat R 46:90 Mr 16 '63
Time and the political tide. Sat R 47:36+ Ap 25 '64

ALTSCHULER, Z. S. and others
Transformation of montmorillonite to kaolinite during weathering. bibliog Science 141:148-52 Jl 12 '63

ALTSHULLER, A. P. See Hindawi, I. J. jt. auth.

ALUM

Storage

How to store liquid alum for water treatment. il Am City 79:99 Mr '64

ALUMINAUT (submarine boat) See Submarine boats

ALUMINIUM limited (of Canada) See Aluminum company of Canada

ALUMINUM
Aluminum; light, white, versatile. G. E. Herrman. il Motor T 15:108-11 N '63
Aluminum; use as a structural material for boats. G. Carr. il Motor B 114:28-33 D '64
Crystal structures at high pressures of metallic modifications of compounds of indium, gallium, and aluminum. J. C. Jamieson. bibliog il Science 139:845-7 Mr 1 '63

Prices

Alcoa goes along on price rise; boost of ingot prices. Bsns W p28-9 Je 13 '64
Aluminum tries to hold prices. il Bsns W p29 F 2 '63
Aluminum's paradox in prices. Bsns W p21 F 1 '64
Trying to untangle a price snarl. Bsns W p81-2 D 7 '63

Protection

How to anodize aluminum. H. Stockert. il Pop Sci 182:144-6 F '63

ALUMINUM, Structural
Showcase for aluminum; fairground pavilion, Hanover, Germany. il Arch Forum 119: 106-7 Jl '63
Third force in urban renewal. H. Kay. il Fortune 70:130-3+ O '64

ALUMINUM alloys
Concorde alloy has high creep strength; hiduminium RR.58. il Aviation W 81:133+ S 7 '64

ALUMINUM cans
Thin tin gets rolling; battle between tin plate and aluminum. il Bsns W p66+ My 11 '63

ALUMINUM coated mirrors. See Mirrors for telescopes

ALUMINUM company of America
Aluminum's paradox in prices. Bsns W p21 F 1 '64
Antitrust law hits aluminum; Alcoa to divest itself of Rome cable corp. Bsns W p98 Je 6 '64
Third force in urban renewal. H. Kay. il Fortune 70:130-3+ O '64
Trying to untangle a price snarl. Bsns W p81-2 D 7 '63

ALUMINUM company of Canada
Alcan invades the U.S. Bsns W p27 O 17 '64

ALUMINUM compounds
See also
Alum

ALUMINUM foil
Aluminum maskmaking. P. Danielson. il Design 65:195 My '64
Cooking with foil. il House & Gard 125:186-8 Mr '64
Food wraps. il Consumer Rep 28:423-6 S '63
Party bravura: the gleam of Christmas gold. il House & Gard 126:154-5 D '64
Tricks with aluminum foil. H. G. Tapply. il Field & S 68:46 Ag '63

ALUMINUM industry and trade
Aluminum sees sales at new high. il Bsns W p98-9 Je 29 '63
See also
Kaiser aluminum and chemical corporation

Australia

Aluminum rush. il Fortune 70:71-2 Ag '64

Canada

Aluminium unlimited. il Time 81:90+ Mr 22 '63
See also
Aluminum company of Canada

United States

Aluminum stays nailed in its profits box; production and shipments high, earnings aren't. il Bsns W p 156 S 14 '63
Aluminum tries to hold prices. il Bsns W p29 F 2 '63
Back to glamour. il Time 82:88 D 13 '63
Half penny a pound. il Newsweek 63:64+ Je 22 '64
Stockpiled aluminum up for sale. Bsns W p34 Ap 13 '63
See also
Aluminum company of America
Reynolds metals company

ALUMINUM ingots
Aluminum stays nailed in its profits box; production and shipments high, earnings aren't. il Bsns W p 156 S 14 '63

ALUMINUM sheetmaking. See Sheet metal work

ALUMINUM silicates
Aluminum silicate system: experimental determination of the triple point. P. M. Bell. bibliog il Science 139:1055-6 Mr 15 '63

ALUMINUM silicates—*Continued*
Metastable rubidium aluminum silicate with a hexagonal sheet structure. C. A. Sorrell and T. Negas. bibliog il Science 141:917 S 6 '63
ALUMINUM storm doors. See Doors
ALUMINUM storm windows. See Windows
ALUMINUM work
Building better mouse traps; unique designs in aluminum by students. il Design 65:16-18 S '63
ALUMNI. See College graduates
ALUMNI funds. See Colleges and universities—Gifts, legacies, etc.
ALUMNI magazines. See Colleges and universities—Publications
ALVA, Luigi
Tenor from Peru; interview. ed. by F. Stevenson. por Opera N 28:16 Mr 21 '64
ALVARADO, Jerónimo
Old man of the selva. Américas 15:28-32 Ap '63
ALVAREZ, A.
Literature of the holocaust. Commentary 38: 65-9 N '64
Lost; Hunt; Spring fever; poems. Poetry 102:228-30 Jl '63
Opinion, please from London. Mlle 58:99-100 N '63; 92+ Ap '64
ALVAREZ, Arturo Jacinto
Love. Américas 16:22-6 F '64
ALVAREZ, Everett, jr
Prize prisoner for the reds; American flier shot down over Vietnam. por U S News 57: 15 Ag 24 '64
ALVORD, Ellsworth C. jr. See Kies, M. W. jt. auth.
AMABILE, George
Honeymoon: Lake Washburn, Minn; poem. Poetry 101:331-2 F '63
Retrospect: falling out of love; poem. Harper 229:120 D '64
AMADON, Dean
Familiar shore birds in Japan. Natur Hist 72:48-51 Ap '63
AMAHS. See Household employees
AMAHUACA Indians. See Indians of South America—Peru
AMALGAMATED bank of New York. See Banks and banking, Trade union
AMALGAMATED clothing workers of America
Amalgamated at fifty. il Newsweek 63:94 My 18 '64
Pressing the Chinese to join a union; organizing Chinese laundry workers. il Bsns W p 102 Je 8 '63
Security with liberty. Nation 198:471 My 11 '64
When a big union gets into big business. il U S News 56:91-3 My 18 '64
AMALGAMATED meat cutters and butcher workmen of North America
Four days on, four off; Bridgford packing co. Bsns W p 120 F 23 '63
When pickets are used to scare away customers. il U S News 54:74-5 F 4 '63
AMALGAMATION, Racial. See Intermarriage of races
AMANITAS. See Mushrooms
AMANN, Peter
Changing outlines of 1848. bibliog f Am Hist R 68:938-53 Jl '63
AMANTADINE. See Adamantanamine
AMARAL, Anthony A.
Struggle in Owens Valley. Am For 70:26-7+ Ag '64
AMARAL, José Vázquez
Nueva York. por Américas 16:6-11 Jl '64
AMARYLLIDACEAE. See Zephyr lilies
AMARYLLIS
Amaryllis. E. F. Steffek. Horticulture 43:16 Ja '65
Give a potted amaryllis. il Sunset 133:165 D '64
Make mine amaryllis. J. T. Weisner. il Flower Grower 50:22-3+ N '63
See also
Lycoris
AMATEUR astronomers. See Astronomers, Amateur
AMATEUR athletic union of the United States
Four wild days and nights at Yale; AAU championships. R. Lardner. il Sports Illus 18:67 Ap 1 '63
Joyful theme at the AAU: younger, higher and faster. G. S. Brown. il Sports Illus 21: 22-5 Jl 6 '64
Track and field development. J. B. Sharpless. il Recreation 57:230-1 My '64
Track's cold war heats up. Sports Illus 18:11 Ap 1 '63
AMATEUR bands. See Bands (music)
AMATEUR circus. See Circus, Amateur
AMATEUR moving pictures. See Moving pictures, Amateur
AMATEUR photography. See Photography
AMATEUR radio operators. See Radio operators, Amateur
AMATEUR radio stations. See Radio stations, Amateur
AMATEUR rocketry. See Rockets—Amateur experiments
AMATEUR sailors. See Seamen
AMATEUR scientists. See Scientists, Amateur
AMATEUR seamen. See Seamen
AMATEUR tennis. See Tennis
AMATEUR theatricals
Therapeutic theater; Group theater workshop, New York city. il Newsweek 65:75 F 1 '65

Anecdotes, facetiae, satire, etc.

Clean rural comedy. R. Jarman. il Harper 226: 43-7 My '63
AMATEUR trapshooting association
Biggest, loudest show in U.S. sport; Grand American trapshoot. V. Kraft. il Sports Illus 19:26-8+ S 9 '63
AMATEURISM (sports)
Bold proposal for American sport. R. F. Kennedy. il Sports Illus 21:12-15 Jl 27 '64
Laugh off $11 million? Columbia broadcasting system buys New York Yankee baseball club. J. R. Tunis. New Repub 152:11-12 Ja 2 '65
Olympics: myth of the amateur. D Cort. il Nation 199:157-9 S 28 '64
Question of honor; amateurs for Olympics. R. Creamer. il Sports Illus 20:58-61 Ja 27 '64
Women of the world, rejoice! Federation cup in tennis. J. Lovesey. Sports Illus 18:54+ Je 17 '63
AMATI violin. See Violin
AMATO, Joseph
I made this. Sch Arts 63:17-20 Ap '64
AMAUROTIC family idiocy
Doomed to an early death; Tay-Sachs disease. J. Atwater. il Sat Eve Post 237: 66-8 O 31 '64
AMAYA, Carmen
To Carmen Amaya; tribute. V. Romero. por Dance Mag 38:47 Ja '64
AMAZON RIVER
Amazon's rate of flow; data gathered by United States-Brazilian hydrologic field party. L. C. Davis, jr. il Natur Hist 73: 14-19 Je '64
Colossus of rivers: the Amazon. D. Reed. il Read Digest 83:210-14+ S '63
Ephemeral Amazon kingdom; dark deeds of Lope de Aguirre. R. J. Sender. il Américas 15:28-32 My '63; Reply. A. B. Mason. 15:48 S '63
On the Peruvian Amazon; photographs. M. Bernheim and E. Bernheim. Travel 119: 41-3 F '63
Out of the jungle. il Newsweek 63:90 F 24 '64
See also
Marajo (island)
AMBASSADORS
Ambassador in motion: S. Farland. il Time 82:31 S 6 '63
Dean of the corps; Nicaragua's ambassador, Sevilla-Sacasa. il Time 82:20 Jl 19 '63
Help wanted by our ambassadors. H. M. Jackson. il N Y Times Mag p36+ O 11 '64
Mr Ambassador. J. Kraft. Harper 227:101+ D '63
Rhubarb à la Mona Lisa. Newsweek 61:25 F 18 '63
Speaking out; waste in the world of diplomacy. E. O. Briggs. Sat Eve Post 236:10+ F 2 '63
See also
Negro ambassadors
United States—Diplomatic and consular service
AMBASSADORS wives
Ambassador's wife is an ambassador, too. P. Durdin. il N Y Times Mag p21+ O 4 '64
Busy life of the ambassador's wife. il Look 27:54-6+ Ag 13 '63
Washington: the women of the world. il Holiday 35:76-81 Mr '64
AMBATIELOS, Betty
No midsummer dream; mob disturbances on visit to London of King Paul and Queen Frederika of Greece. il por Newsweek 62:39 Jl 22 '63
AMBEDKAR, Bhimrao Ramji
Reporter at large. H. R. Isaacs. il New Yorker 40:60-4+ D 12; 75-6+ D 19 '64
AMBERG, Richard H.
Improvement of the human character; address, November 6, 1964. Vital Speeches 31: 121-3 D 1 '64

AMBERJACK fishing
Chaos in heaven. W. Blassingame. il Field & S 68:38-9+ Ja '64
AMBIDEXTERITY. See Left- and right-handedness
AMBLER, Eric
Ambler case. Reporter 30:6+ F 13 '64
AMBROSE, E. R.
Heat conservation in the electrically-heated house. Arch Rec 135:7+ mid-My '64
AMBROSE, Frank
Small but powerful snow fighters. Am City 78:145 D '63
AMBROSE his mark; story. See Barth, J.
AMBROSINI, Maria Luisa Boggeri
(ed) See Borghese, G. Horrors of Bomarzo
AMBRUS, Clara
Double life of the Drs Ambrus; with photographs. Sci Digest 54:48-55 D '63
AMBRUS, Julian
Double life of the Drs Ambrus; with photographs. Sci Digest 54:48-55 D '63
AMDUR, Harry
Case for custom processing. U S Camera 26:58-9+ D '63
AMEBA
Amoeba proteus: studying the contractile vacuole by micropuncture. B. Schmidt-Nielsen and C. R. Schrauger. bibliog il Science 139:606-7 F 15 '63
AMELAND (island)
Risking piles of money in the great gas race; beneath the North Sea. il Bsns W p 118-20+ Jl 11 '64
AMELIA goes to the ball; opera. See Menotti, G. C.
AMELUNG, John Frederick
Newly discovered Amelung tumbler at Corning museum. il Hobbies 69:76 S '64
Search for New Bremen and the glass of John Frederick Amelung. I. N. Hume. il Antiques 85:310-13 Mr '64
AMEN, Grover
Escape. New Yorker 39:138-9+ Ap 20 '63
AMENDMENTS to the Constitution. See United States—Constitution—Amendments
AMER, Mordechai
Yoke of the Torah; excerpts from memoirs, tr. by J. Sloan. Commentary 38:40-6 Ag '64
AMERICA
Achievable utopia; New World. A. Morales-Carrión. Américas 16:1 Ap '64
Our faith in tomorrow: New world man; excerpts from address, 1963. M. L. Pérez Marchand. Américas 16:2-4 Ag '64
See also
United States

Antiquities

Did the Romans discover America? R. B. Dunlop. il Pop Mech 120:70-4+ Jl '63
Holiday handbook; digging for America's past. A. Karlen. bibliog il Holiday 36:103-6 S '64

Discovery and exploration

America, the navigator's error. J. Lear. il Sat R 46:86-8 O 12 '63
Columbus wasn't first; Viking ruins L'Anse aux Meadows, Newfoundland. il Sci Digest 55:77-80 F '64
Did the Romans discover America? R. B. Dunlop. il Pop Mech 120:70-4+ Jl '63
Did Vikings get here first, after all? il U S News 55:10 N 18 '63
Littorina littorea: an indicator of Norse settlement in North America? N. Spjeldnaes and K. E. Henningsmoen. bibliog Science 141:275-6, Jl 19 '63; Discussion. 141:762; 142:1022 Ag 30, N 22 '63
Others than Columbus. C. Miles. il Hobbies 68:112+ F '64
Tragic dream of Jean Ribaut; flag of France on America's South Atlantic coast. S. Harris. il Am Heritage 14:8-15+ O '63
Viking settlement in America. Sci Am 210:56 Ja '64
Vinland ruins prove Vikings found the New World. H. Ingstad. il Nat Geog Mag 126:708-34 N '64
What's in a name? name-coining incidents. W. A. Naughton. il Américas 16:27-31 D '64
See also
Vikings
West Indies—Discovery and exploration
AMERICA (periodical)
America associates; 55th anniversary list. America 110:550-1 Ap 18 '64
America house; special report. il America 111:435-42 O 17 '64
Baltimore story. America 109:256 S 14 '63
Editorial announcement, April 17, 1909. America 110:527 Ap 18 '64
Notes and asides. Nat R 14:270 Ap 9 '63
AMERICA (ship) See Ocean liners
AMERICA is a song; drama. See Nolan, P. T.

AMERICAN academy of arts and letters
American academy gives first traveling fellowship. Pub W 183:39 My 27 '63
AMERICAN academy of arts and science
AAAS affiliate. R. W. Burhoe. Science 139:1226+ Mr 22 '63
AMERICAN academy of political and social science, Philadelphia
Report of the board of directors to the members of the American academy of political and social science for the years 1962-1963. il Ann Am Acad 347:129-34 My '63; 353:131-6 My '64
AMERICAN airlines, incorporated
ALPA may reject pact with American. J. R. Ashlock. Aviation W 78:42 F 25 '63
American airlines; history on the wing. G. J. Schlaeger. il Flying 74:40-1+ Ja '64
American airlines pessimistic over increased 1963 industry profits. Aviation W 78:49 Ap 8 '63
American cargo jet starts daily flights. Aviation W 80:36 Ja 13 '64
American engineers cancel strike vote following mediation request. Aviation W 79:45 S 16 '63
American engineers still ask pilot rating. Aviation W 79:47 S 9 '63
American, flight engineers agree in principle on proposed contract. Aviation W 81:42 O 26 '64
American, Northwest granted new routes. J. R. Ashlock. Aviation W 81:29 Ag 10 '64
American offers installment credit plan. J. W. Carter. Aviation W 80:34 Mr 30 '64
American pact with new union reduces flying time requirement. Aviation W 79:39 Jl 15 '63
American pilots union seeks recognition. J. R. Ashlock. Aviation W 78:39 Ap 29 '63
American, TWA to swap engine overhaul. Aviation W 79:41 Ag 19 '63
Court upholds Allied pilots pact. Aviation W 79:41 Ag 19 '63
Engineer meeting delays American pact. J. R. Ashlock. Aviation W 78:35 Mr 4 '63
Fasten executive belts; return of M. Sadler. il Time 84:100 O 23 '64
FEIA seeks injunction against America airlines in dues dispute. Aviation W 78:41 My 13 '63
Frustrated president. Time 84:98 O 9 '64
Notes and comment. il New Yorker 40:33 Mr 14 '64
SABRE, a $30-million application. il Fortune 69:142-5+ Ap '64
Sadler's back. Newsweek 64:92 O 26 '64
Short flight; demonstration of Astrovision. New Yorker 40:47 D 5 '64
Trouble at the top. Newsweek 64:91 O 12 '64
AMERICAN airlines-Eastern air lines merger. See Airlines—Consolidations and mergers
AMERICAN and foreign power company
How to survive foreign expropriation. il Bsns W p86+ Je 1 '63
AMERICAN arbitration association
Arbitrators: either too young or too old. il Bsns W p45-6 Ag 10 '63
Staying out of court. il Time 83:75 F 14 '64
AMERICAN architecture. See Architecture, American
AMERICAN art. See Art, American
AMERICAN art biennial of Córdoba. See Art—Exhibitions
AMERICAN artists. See Artists, American
AMERICAN association for the advancement of science
AAAS deplores integrity erosion from pressures of space program. D. E. Fink. Aviation W 82:18 Ja 4 '65
AAAS finances: report for 1963. D. Wolfle. il Science 145:953-4 Ag 28 '64
AAAS meeting and the press; letter. R. A. Bruner. Science 143:763 F 21 '64; Reply. S. Lambert. 144:486 My 1 '64
AAAS officers, committees, and representatives for 1964. Science 143:831-5 F 21 '64
R&D, and the relations of science and government; statement before a congressional subcommittee; with editorial comment. P. M. Gross. Science 142:625, 645-50 N 8 '63
Science and the race problem; report of the AAAS committee on science in the promotion of human welfare. bibliog Science 142:558-61 N 1 '63; Discussion. 142:1419; 143:306-8, 913-15; 144:365 D 13 '63, Ja 24, F 28, Ap 24 '64
Scientists urge a broader view. Bsns W p96-7 Ja 9 '65
Space program: results of poll of AAAS members. il Science 145:368 Jl 24 '64; Discussion. 145:539, 989; 146:342 Ag 7, S 4, O 16 '64

AMERICAN association for the advancement of science—*Continued*

Meetings, 1962

Association affairs. il Science 139:614-38+ F 15 '63
Election of AAAS officers. il Science 141: 1288-94 S 27 '63

Meetings, 1963

AAAS council meeting, 1963. D. Wolfle. il Science 143:829-31 F 21 '64
Bright future foreseen. A. Ewing. Sci N L 85:23 Ja 11 '64
Cleveland; 130th AAAS meeting, 26-30 December, 1963. il Science 142:1194-5 N 29 '63
Cleveland: 130th meeting; with program. il Science 142:1323-46+ D 6 '63
Report of the seventh Cleveland meeting. R. L. Taylor. il Science 143:835-42 F 21 '64
Science worries about the world. il Bsns W p24-5 Ja 4 '64
Science youth activities part of AAAS meeting. Sci N L 84:345 N 30 '63
Sciences in Japan; special symposium at the AAAS annual meeting, December 26-30, 1963. Science 142:604-5 N 1 '63
Seventh Cleveland meeting. R. L. Taylor. il Science 141:279-81 Jl 19 '63
Seventh Cleveland meeting; preliminary announcement. R. L. Taylor. il Science 140: 907-12+ My 24 '63

Meetings, 1964

AAAS: Southwestern and Rocky Mountain division 40th annual meeting; report. M. G. Anderson. Science 144:1599-600 Je 26 '64
Election of AAAS officers. il Science 145:1462-6 S 25 '64
Environmental variables in disease. il Science 146:954-5 N 13 '64
Exploring the universe; AAAS annual meeting, 26-31 December, 1964, Montreal. D. Wolfle. il Science 146:1190-2 N 27 '64
4.5 billion years of protein molecules: what do we know now about how they are made? AAAS annual meeting, 26-31 December, Montreal. il Science 146:1076-7 N 20 '64
Meeting, 1964. W. Davis. Sci N L 87:19-20 Ja 9 '65
131st AAAS annual meeting Montreal, Canada, 26-31 December 1964. il Science 146:436-7 O 16 '64
131st AAAS annual meeting; program. il Science 146:1331-58+ D 4 '64
Pest control symposium, 131st AAAS annual meeting, Montreal, 26-31 December, 1964. il Science 146:672-3 O 30 '64
Social nature of man; programs at AAAS Montreal meeting, 26-31 December 1964. il Science 146:801-3 N 6 '64
Third Montreal meeting. R. L. Taylor. il Science 144:1032-42; 145:297-9 My 22, Jl 17 '64

Committee on cooperation among scientists

Ethical problems: an invitation. D. Wolfle. Science 143:435 Ja 31 '64; Discussion. 145: 873 Ag 28 '64

School science library program

Science books and the young reader. C. B. Grannis. Pub W 185:62 Ap 20 '64

AMERICAN association for the United Nations
All human beings have a common stake in progress and prosperity, as they have in peace and survival; address, November 11, 1963. Thant. U N Rev 10:5-7 D '63

AMERICAN association of advertising agencies
Admen shed their worries; annual meeting. il Bsns W p58-61 My 4 '63

AMERICAN association of blood banks
Lurking risks of transfusion. K. Wheeler. il Life 54:70-2+ F 15 '63

AMERICAN association of colleges of teacher education
Conant report; is enlightened debate possible? account of the Chicago meetings of the American association of colleges of teacher education and the National society of college teachers of education, Feb. 19-22, 1964. H. D. Gideonse. Sat R 47:56-7+ S 19 '64
International orientation for college administrators. L. J. Stiles. Sch & Soc 91:356-8 N 16 '63

AMERICAN association of collegiate schools of business
Deans' club peps up. il Bsns W p 116-18 My 16 '64

AMERICAN association of fund-raising counsel
Art of fund-raising. L. L. L. Golden. Sat R 47:45 Ag 8 '64
Charity solicitations; under state control. Am City 79:150+ Mr '64

AMERICAN association of law libraries
Convention diary; annual meeting. E. J. Bander. Library J 89:2962-5 Ag '64
Law librarians at Mackinac; AALL annual meeting. F. R. McMaster. il Library J 88: 3033-4 S 1 '63

AMERICAN association of museums
Cooper union; committee to study proposals concerning museum's future. Nation 197: 379 D 7 '63

AMERICAN association of pastoral counselors
Minister as therapist. Newsweek 61:62 My 6 '63

AMERICAN association of physical anthropologists
American association of physical anthropologists; report on 33rd annual meeting. G. W. Lasker. Science 146:289 O 9 '64
Meeting, 1963. T. D. Stewart. Science 141: 177-8 Jl 12 '63

AMERICAN association of physics teachers
Scientists galore; joint meeting with American physical society. New Yorker 38:24-5 F 16 '63

AMERICAN association of retired persons
Dynamic retirement is their goal. J. L. Block. Read Digest 84:195-6+ Ja '64

AMERICAN association of school administrators
Closed circuit TV at AASA. NEA J 52:35 Mr '63
Educational statesmanship. P. Woodring. Sat R 46:55 Mr 23 '63; Discussion. 46:60 Ap 20 '63
Meeting, 1963. il Sr Schol 82:4T-7T Mr 13 '63
Meeting, 1964. Sr Schol 84:2T+ Mr 13 '64
On the beach; annual convention. il Newsweek 61:48 Mr 4 '63
Our schools: battleground of conflicting interests; adapted from address, February 18, 1964. J. H. Fischer. il Sat R 47:66-7+ Mr 21 '64
U.S. office of education: an inside view. S. M. McMurrin. il Sat R 46:78-81 F 16 '63

AMERICAN association of school librarians
AASL at the White House. ALA Bul 58:701 S '64
AASL urges organized and wide use of trade book examination centers. Library J 88:1308 Mr 15 '63
ALA highlights. E. Rudin. il Library J 88: 3268-9 S 15 '63
ALA, 1964. Library J 89:3391-3 S 15 '64
Knapp-sack of progress; visits to two schools selected for Knapp school libraries project. P. Sullivan. il Wilson Lib Bul 39:392-6 Ja '65
Librarian's dream come true; Knapp school libraries project, Marcus Whitman elementary school, Richland, Wash. P. Sullivan. il NEA J 53:46-7 S '64
Library service for the teacher. S. I. Fenwick and L. L. Batchelor. ALA Bul 57:129-30 F '63
Underway: the Knapp project's first year. P. Sullivan. Library J 89:2143-5 My 15 '64

AMERICAN association of state highway officials
How big should a truck get? il Bsns W p94-5 Ag 31 '63

AMERICAN association of state libraries
States and standards; pre-conference meeting. E. Moon. Library J 88:3023-4 S 1 '63

AMERICAN association of university professors
For freedom. Newsweek 61:86 My 6 '63
Incident at a college; dismissal of Austin J. Shelton, jr. from Mercy college. F. E. Kearns. Commonweal 79:215 N 15 '63; Reply with rejoinder. C. E. Schuetzinger. 79:430-1 Ja 10 '64
We will not put. America 108:700 My 18 '63; Reply. J. R. Price. 108:873 Je 22 '63
What, where, when, how? ideas presented at annual meeting. il Time 81:72-4 My 10 '63

AMERICAN association of variable star observers
AAVSO meets in St Louis. R. E. Cox. il Sky & Tel 27:352 Je '64
Fall meeting of the AAVSO. W. E. Shawcross. il Sky & Tel 28:357 D '64

AMERICAN association of zoological parks and aquariums
Reporter at large; meeting. E. Hahn. New Yorker 40:131-2+ S 19 '64

AMERICAN astronomical society
American astronomers report; highlights of some papers (cont) il Sky & Tel 25:143-5; 26:20-2, 82-4, 196-9; 27:147-9, 213-16; 28: 131-3, 201-3 Mr, Jl-Ag, O '63, Mr-Ap, S-O '64
Astronomers assemble in Arizona. il Sky & Tel 25:312-15 Je '63
Astronomers visit Alaska. J. B. Irwin. il Sky & Tel 26:120-5 S '63
Meeting, 1963. A. B. Meinel. Science 141:178+ Jl 12 '63

AMERICAN astronomical society—*Continued*
Physics of solar flares dissected at symposium. W. Beller. Miss & Roc 13:17 N 4 '63

AMERICAN athletes. See Athletes

AMERICAN Austin car company. See American Bantam car company

AMERICAN authors. See Authors, American

AMERICAN ballads. See Ballads, American

AMERICAN ballet. See Ballet

AMERICAN ballet theatre
Ambassadors of the dance; third Latin American tour. A. Todd. il Américas 16:6-11 O '64
Ballet theatre workshop at Hunter college playhouse. D. Hering. Dance Mag 38:30+ F; 29 Jl '64
Melissa Hayden, on stage and off; excerpts. M. Hayden. il Dance Mag 37:48-51 D '63
Summer snow. D. Hering. il Dance Mag 37: 48-9+ Mr '63

AMERICAN bank note company
Making money. il Time 81:86 Mr 22 '63

AMERICAN bankers association
Can we make more jobs without inflation? symposium on employment; with editorial comment. il Bsns W p26-7, 132 F 29 '64
Control the comptroller? il Newsweek 62:85 O 21 '63
Inflation spiral over the Continent; eleventh annual monetary conference. il Newsweek 63:59-61 Je 1 '64
Two more plans for aid to dollar. U S News 55:103 Ag 5 '63

AMERICAN Bantam car company
Special-interest cars; American Austin-Bantam. L. Spindler. il Motor T 16:75 N '64

AMERICAN Baptist convention. See Baptists in the United States

AMERICAN bar association
And so to court. Time 84:62 Jl 31 '64
Bar's side of Canon 35. J. H. Yauch. Sat R 46:61-2 Mr 9 '63
Eighty-seven years old & getting younger. il Time 84:65 Ag 21 '64
Reports to the ABA meetings; Labor relations law committee analyses. Mo Labor R 87: 1177-80 O '64
Right track. Time 82:52-3 O 18 '63
When newsmen become newsmakers; problem of publicity before and during a trial. E. N. Griswold. Sat R 47:21-3 O 24 '64

AMERICAN Bible society
American Bible society to build new center. Pub W 186:47-8 N 9 '64
Spreading the word. Time 82:51 N 29 '63

AMERICAN bison. See Buffaloes

AMERICAN black walnut trees. See Walnut trees

AMERICAN book publishers council
ABPC-ATPI position paper on copyright revision. Pub W 187:275 Ja 25 '65
ABPC: copyright, world trade, home markets, legislation and financial trends viewed at annual meeting; symposium. il Pub W 185:30-55 Je 15 '64
ABPC hits Conn. plan for censorship commission. Pub W 183:67 Ap 15 '63
ABPC meeting: educational market, overseas ties, copyright revision explored; symposium. il Pub W 183:22-38 Je 3 '63
ABPC: proposals to expand the prime market; with editorial comment. il Pub W 185:52-8, 73 Je 22 '64
ABPC: religious publishers consider ecumenical books, general reviews. Pub W 183: 22-4 My 27 '63
ABPC seminar: tax implications for book publishers. Pub W 186:27-30 N 23 '64; Reply. R. S. Helstein. 187:213 Ja 25 '65
ABPC statistical survey shows 1961-1962 trends in sales. il Pub W 184:13-15 D 16 '63
ABPC statistical survey shows 1962-1963 trends in sales. il Pub W 186:25-7 S 14 '64
ABPC votes opposition to manufacturing clause; annual meeting in Skytop, Pa. Pub W 185:34 Je 1 '64
Copyright: how the procedure operates for books. il Pub W 183:29-31 F 25 '63
New proposals for NBA. C. B. Grannis. Pub W 183:49 Mr 25 '63
1963-64 in review. Pub W 185:89-90 Ja 20 '64; 187:87-8 Ja 18 '65
Publishers sales well up according to ABPC survey. Library J 89:215-16 Ja 15 '64
RPG elects Wolfe, discusses paperback problems; symposium. il Pub W 185:49-52 Je 15 '64
RPG: how to integrate the promotion program; symposium. Pub W 183:16-21 My 6 '63
RPG topic: how to reach denominational markets. Pub W 184:26-7 O 28 '63
RPG workshop; profit or loss in religious book publishing. Pub W 185:24-8 Ap 13 '64
War on poverty: conference sponsored by American book publishers council and the American textbook publishers institute; with editorial comment. il Pub W 185:32-43, 52 My 4 '64
When in doubt, leave the safety on. D. Dempsey. Sat R 46:33-4+ Mr 23 '63

AMERICAN book-Stratford press, incorporated
American book-Stratford opens new special division. il Pub W 184:86-7 O 14 '63
AB-SP now operating huge new distribution center. Pub W 185:41 Mr 9 '64
American book-Stratford states copyright position; on proposed changes in the copyright law. Pub W 186:43-4 D 28 '64
Important break in copyright discussions. C. B. Grannis. Pub W 187:41 Ja 4 '65

AMERICAN booksellers association
ABA announces three October regional meetings. Pub W 184:29-30 S 30 '63
ABA booksellers examine the tools and skills of management; annual convention. il Pub W 184:24-9 Jl 1 '63
ABA disputes cut-price deal by wholesaler, insurance co. Pub W 183:31 Mr 18 '63
ABA expanding sales through effective bookstore promotion; symposium. il Pub W 185:35-45 Je 29 '64
ABA highlights of the 63rd booksellers' convention; symposium; with editorial comment. il Pub W 183:28-35, 52 Je 24 '63
ABA: highlights of the 64th booksellers convention; symposium. il Pub W 185:41-58 Je 22 '64
ABA model bookstore goes traveling. il Pub W 184:59-61 S 9 '63
ABA regional meetings: Denver, Dallas, New Orleans: summaries of panel discussions and addresses. il Pub W 184:18-40 N 18 '63
ABA regionals: Boston and Cleveland meetings; summaries of panel discussions and addresses. il Pub W 186:30-43 N 9 '64
ABA section. See issues of Publishers' weekly beginning January 6, 1964
Convention forcast: the ABA 1964. J. A. Duffy. Pub W 185:45-6 My 11 '64
Eisenhower to be guest at ABA international evening. Pub W 183:36 My 20 '63
More than 2000 attend ABA's 63rd annual meeting; Eisenhower, Allen Dulles speak at exhibit. il Pub W 183:54-5 Je 17 '63
1963-64 in review. Pub W 185:93 Ja 20 '64; 187:91 Ja 18 '65
Registration of 2250 for ABA's 64th annual meeting. Pub W 185:56-8 Je 15 '64
Short history of the ABA book buyer's handbook. G. Jennings. Pub W 186:57-8 N 2 '64
Trade winds; account of annual convention. J. Beatty, jr. Sat R 47:10-11 Je 27 '64
See also
Publisher of the year award

AMERICAN Bosch Arma corporation
Arma div. faces toughest decision. M. Getler. Miss & Roc 15:22 N 2 '64

AMERICAN broadcasting company
Soapy; ABC season. il Newsweek 64:65 S 28 '64

AMERICAN broadcasting-Paramount theaters, incorporated
Double thrust at ABC-Paramount; two challengers attack Goldenson regime. il Bsns W p 156+ Ap 11 '64

AMERICAN business men. See Business men

AMERICAN can company
Canco tightens up. il Bsns W p 174+ N 7 '64
Growth comes in many packages. il Bsns W p68+ My 9 '64

AMERICAN cancer society
America warns its youth. E. Scovell. America 108:451 Ap 6 '63
Hazards of teen-age smoking; excerpts from Smoke screen: tobacco and the public welfare. M. B. Neuberger. il Parents Mag 39:51+ Ja '64
To smoke or not to smoke; questions and answers; Tobacco institute replies. Sci N L 83:263+ Ap 27 '63

AMERICAN Catholic sociological society
Sociological mainstream. America 111:246 S 12 '64

AMERICAN Catholicism. See Catholic church in the United States

AMERICAN Catholics. See Catholics in the United States

AMERICAN chemical society
Chemists; annual fall meeting. New Yorker 39:33-5 S 28 '63
Division of chemical literature of the American chemical society. B. H. Heil. Science 143:1236-7 Mr 13 '64

AMERICAN chestnut trees. See Chestnut trees

AMERICAN children. See Children—United States
AMERICAN Chinese. See Chinese Americans
AMERICAN church in Paris. See Paris—Churches
AMERICAN citizenship. See Citizenship
AMERICAN city (periodical)
Ten cities, one county win merit certificates. il Am City 80:73-5 Ja '65
Twenty-two cities win certificates of merit. Am City 79:7+ F '64
AMERICAN civil liberties union
A.C.L.U. denies attack on chaplaincy. Christian Cent 81:630 My 13 '64
ACLU guide combats pressures on schools and libraries; excerpts from Combatting undemocratic pressures on schools and libraries. Library J 89:2052 My 15 '64
ACLU hits extremism; summary of pamphlet, Combatting undemocratic pressures on schools and libraries. Sr Schol 84:4T Ap 17 '64
A.C.L.U. opens southern regional office; in Atlanta. Christian Cent 81:1357 N 4 '64
Birchers lose; Goldmark case. P. Jacobs. New Repub 150:5 F 8 '64
Of social importance; Ohio anti-obscenity law. America 108:430, 526 Mr 30, Ap 20 '63
Roger Baldwin. W. Morris. New Repub 150:8-10 Ja 25 '64
Teachers' strike issue. Sr Schol 83:1T-2T N 1 '63
AMERICAN coins. See Coins
AMERICAN college students. See College students
AMERICAN committee for liberation
Traveling with Charley to the USSR. D. Dempsey. Sat R 46:40-1 N 9 '63
AMERICAN Communist party. See Communist party (United States)
AMERICAN composers. See Composers, American
AMERICAN conservatism. See Conservatism
AMERICAN contract bridge league
Captain is back on deck. C. Goren. il Sports Illus 21:63 Ag 31 '64
AMERICAN cookery. See Cookery, American
AMERICAN council for emigrés in the professions
Else Staudinger's 100-million-dollar gift to Uncle Sam. M. T. Bloom. Read Digest 85: 189-90+ Ag '64
AMERICAN council of Christian churches
Dissidents confounded; movement protesting the visit of Russian churchmen to Austin. H. Kilpatrick. Christian Cent 80:466-8 Ap 10 '63
AMERICAN council of independent laboratories
Industrial R&D: competition from universities, non-profits, alarms independent laboratories. E. Langer. Science 144:273-4 Ap 17 '64
AMERICAN council of learned societies
See also
Commission on the humanities
Joint committee on contemporary China of the American council of learned societies and the Social science research council
AMERICAN council on education
American council on education; conference designed to illuminate the ins and outs of grantsmanship. J. Walsh. Science 140:1383 Je 28 '63
Faculty pay: salary-charging practices on federal grants is subject of A.C.E. panel's advice. J. Walsh. Science 140:284+ Ap 19 '63
Higher education as a national resource: a proposed federal program; text of document, January 17, 1963. Sch & Soc 91:218-21 My 4 '63
Scholarships: a new study on who gets them and who needs them by American council on education. J. Walsh. Science 141:413-14 Ag 2 '63
AMERICAN craftsmen's council
American craftsmen's council, 1964: international era. A. O. Webb. Craft Horiz 24:9 My '64
Crafts reborn. D. Cort. il Nation 198:628-9 Je 22 '64
International crafts conference in 1964. A. O. Webb. Craft Horiz 23:11 Ja '63
Traveler's acknowledgments. M. Patch. Craft Horiz 23:4 Ja '63
AMERICAN cultural center, Japan. See United States—Cultural relations
AMERICAN cyanamid company
Moving house at American cyanamid. il Duns R 83:pt2 103 Mr '64
See also
Lederle laboratories
AMERICAN dairy association
$1 million to find if promotion pays. Farm J 87:10 Ap '63
AMERICAN dairy science association
Four good new ideas. il Farm J 87:34 Ag '63
AMERICAN dance festival. See Dance festivals
AMERICAN dance theater. See Dance companies
AMERICAN dental association
Annals of business; Crest toothpaste. B. Bliven, jr. New Yorker 39:83-4+Mr 23 '63
Fourteen questions on dental health answered. Todays Health 41:39+ Ap '63
AMERICAN design. See Design
AMERICAN documentation institute
Meeting, 1963. T. C. Hines. Library J 88:4336-8 N 15 '63
New York chapters of ADI and SLA hold joint meeting to honor Luhn. Library J 90:80-1 Ja 1 '65
SLA-ADI venture to implement technology information availability. Library J 88:2858 Ag '63
AMERICAN drama
Half-world of American drama. M. Mannes. Reporter 28:48-50 Ap 25 '63
AMERICAN dream; drama. See Albee, E.
AMERICAN dream; novel. See Mailer, N.
AMERICAN Eagle (yacht) See Yachts and yachting
AMERICAN economic assistance. See Economic assistance, American
AMERICAN economic association
Adding up the cost of economic swindling. il Bsns W p50-2 Ja 4 '64
AMERICAN education week
American education week. il NEA J 52:60 S '63
American education week pays dividends. il NEA J 53:64 S '64
Hand in hand with parents. NEA J 52:13 D '63
PTA standards and stand on public education. M. E. Jenkins. il PTA Mag 58:2-3 N '63
AMERICAN electric power company
Cooking with electricity. il Time 84:100 S 11 '64
We're the most enterprising utility in this country. H. Kay. il Fortune 69:138-41+ My '64
AMERICAN elk. See Elk
AMERICAN emblems. See Emblems, National
AMERICAN export and Isbrandtsen lines
Admiral and the opera; sponsorship of the Metropolitan's opening-night Aïda. Q Eaton. il Opera N 28:16 D 7 '63
Sponsor; Metropolitan's new production of Aïda. New Yorker 39:45-6 N 23 '63
AMERICAN express cards. See Credit cards
AMERICAN express company
Checks that never bounce. F. Sondern, jr. il Read Digest 83:205-8 Ag '63
Future of American express. E. K. Faltermayer. Fortune 69:158-9+ Ap '64
AMERICAN express field warehousing corporation
Future of American express. E. K. Faltermayer. Fortune 69:158-9+ Ap '64
AMERICAN farm bureau federation
Battle in the furrows; wheat referendum on price supports. il Bsns W p36 My 18 '63
Can farmers control food chains? Bsns W p25 D 19 '64
Farm bureau asks for... C. W. Gifford. Farm J 88:54-5 Ja '64
Now the non-farmer asks for parity. E. Higbee. il N Y Times Mag p 15+ Je 2 '63
Wheat vote: historic farm election. F. Bailey, jr. Suc Farm 61:45 My '63
AMERICAN farmers' educational and cooperative union. See Farmers' educational and co-operative union of America
AMERICAN fashion critics award
Jacques hits the jackpot. il Life 57:69-70 O 2 '64
AMERICAN federation of government employees
American federation of government employees; biennial convention in Dallas. M. F. Riche. Mo Labor R 87:1256-7 N '64
Government workers getting organized. il Bsns W p72 F 9 '63
AMERICAN federation of labor and Congress of industrial organizations
AFL-CIO: a confederation or federation? which road for the future? A. H. Raskin. Ann Am Acad 350:36-45 N '63
AFL-CIO aid for Democrats. U S News 57: 84 S 14 '64
AFL-CIO forecast: tax cut, or dip in '64. Bsns W p51 Ag 24 '63
AFL-CIO showdown: Meany wins. U S News 55:116 O 21 '63
AFL-CIO's election-year demands. U S News 57:82 Jl 20 '64
As labor sees LBJ now. U S News 58:90-1 Ja 25 '65

AMERICAN federation of labor and Congress of industrial organizations—*Continued*
Better day for brother Randolph. T. R. Brooks. Reporter 29:23 D 5 '63
Decline of labor; unions within unions. S. Lens. Commonweal 80:391-4 Je 19 '64
Fifth biennial convention of the AFL-CIO. J. W. Bloch. Mo Labor R 87:140-2 F '64
Hard times; executive council meeting at Miami Beach. il Time 81:13-17 Mr 1 '63
High policy vs. rank and file. Bsns W p38 Ag 8 '64
Hoffa beats back dissidents; locals reject bid to rejoin AFL-CIO. il Bsns W p47 My 4 '63
Hoffa: new strong man of U.S. labor. U S News 54:46 My 13 '63
Hoffa on the AFL-CIO; interview, ed. by R. Vermillion. J. R. Hoffa. Newsweek 62:87 N 25 '63
Hoffa wins again. T. Brooks. Reporter 28: 34-5 My 23 '63
I don't request; executive council meeting in Bal Harbour, Fla. il Newsweek 63:62 Mr 2 '64
Labor: a partner in American foreign policy. J. P. Windmuller. Ann Am Acad 350:104-14 N '63
Labor: a target for NLW? S. L. Simon. il Library J 88:1109-11 Mr 15 '63
Labor assembly: what unions want. U S News 55:96 D 2 '63
Labor: challenge of the new. Nat R 15:469-71 D 3 '63
Labor dilemmas, automation and image. il Newsweek 61:61 Mr 4 '63
Labor ducks the future. B. J. Widick. il Nation 197:389-90 D 7 '63
Labor flexes its muscle for the new Congress. il Bsns W p56 N 14 '64
Labor: how big a backlash vote? Newsweek 64:61 Ag 17 '64
Labor shudders at leisure. D. Wakefield. Nation 196:325-7 Ap 20 '63
Labor tries a comeback. H. Bernstein. Nation 197:107-9 S 7 '63
Labor union of today; address, November 14, 1963. G. Meany. Vital Speeches 30:176-81 Ja 1 '64
Labor's next demand: bigger pay raises. il U S News 55:107-9 N 25 '63
Labor's price tag for election; it's up to LBJ. il U S News 57:85-6 D 7 '64
LBJ and unions: what he tells them, what they want. il U S News 55:106-7 D 16 '63
Meany's two targets: automation and his critics. il U S News 55:16 N 25 '63
Meddling in Latin America. S. Meisler. il Nation 198:133-8 F 10 '64. Reply C. Jagan. 198:516 My 25 '64
Mr Meany's curse; automation. A. H. Raskin. Reporter 29:20-2 D 5 '63
New investment plan for unions. U S News 56:91 Mr 9 '64
New union drive for thirty-five hour week. U S News 54:97 Mr 11 '63
Nowhere to go but to Johnson; oppose archfoe Goldwater. Bsns W p47-8 Jl 25 '64
Organized labor and the city boss. L. L. Friedland. bibliog f Ann Am Acad 353:40-51 My '64
Passing the collective hat; money for community and charitable services. Bsns W p92 My 2 '64
Power but no push; AFL-CIO convention in New York. il Bsns W p25-7 N 23 '63
Rhetoric of Walter Reuther. S. Levey. Reporter 28:26-8 Mr 14 '63
Right to work battles planned. U S News 54:88-9 Mr 4 '63
Russia's grain is last straw; ILA boycott. il Bsns W p 106-7 F 22 '64
Staking the claims; executive council meeting in Washington. Time 84:23 D 4 '64
Union-financed houses rise in Latin America; AFL-CIO's Latin American investment program. il Bsns W p 128 N 28 '64
Union problem: imports vs. jobs; changes demanded in Trade expansion act of 1962. U S News 55:95 S 16 '63
Unions get a White House nod; repeal right-to-work laws. Bsns W p80 Ja 9 '65
Unions need public acceptance, too. L. L. L. Golden. Sat R 46:63-4 D 14 '63; Reply. H. C. Fleisher. 47:47+ F 8 '64
Unions open new attack on conservatives; in South. il Nations Bsns 51:80-4 Mr '63
Unions spend millions on foreign aid program. Bsns W p46+ Ag 24 '63
Unions' war on Goldwater; AFL-CIO plans its strategy. il U S News 57:73-4 Ag 17 '64
U.S. labor: affluence vs. influence; fifth biennial convention. il Newsweek 62:85-8 N 25 '63
Why labor lost the intellectuals. H. Harris. Harper 228:79-80+ Je '64
Wider split in the AFL-CIO? U S News 54: 91 F 11 '63

Committee on political education

On rewarding friends. Nation 198:177 F 24 '64
Unions' political machine builds more strength; Committee on political education. il Nations Bsns 51:36-7+ N '63
What unions did to help the Democrats. il U S News 57:102-4 N 9 '64

Industrial union department

Reuther's nursing home. M. Kempton. New Repub 149:6-7 N 23 '63
Unions' new strategy for bigger bites; coordinated bargaining. Bsns W p 112 Je 13 '64

AMERICAN federation of musicians
Discord in the discotheque; musicians protest against accompanying phonograph records. il Bsns W p 156+ My 23 '64

AMERICAN federation of state, county and municipal employees
Union discards its president; AFSCME votes out Zander. Bsns W p52 My 9 '64

AMERICAN federation of teachers
AFT elects Cogen. Sr Schol 85:1T+ S 23 '64
Big little man; C. Cogen elected president. Newsweek 64:71 Ag 31 '64
Big little man; Charles Cogen. Newsweek 62:71 S 2 '63
Church and state: AFT vs. NEA over federal aid to parochial schools. Sr Schol 85: 6T D 2 '64
Labor trouble ahead for schools? U S News 57:75 S 7 '64
New militants. il Time 82:45 Ag 16 '63
1964 convention of the teachers union. L. E. Lunden. Mo Labor R 87:1138-42 O '64
Scholastic teacher interview: ed. by H. Langer. C. Cogen. Sr Schol 85:7T-8T N 4 '64
Scholastic teacher interviews: Carl J. Megel; ed. by H. Langer. C. J. Megel. Sr Schol 83:24T-26T O 4 '63; Discussion. 83:6T D 6 '63
Strikes, sanctions, and the schools. J. Scanlon. il Sat R 46:51-5+ O 19 '63
Toward labor monopoly in teaching? NEA, AFT and UFT. R. Kirk. Nat R 15:241 S 24 '63
Union or guild? organizing the teachers. S. Elam. il Nation 198:651-3 Je 29 '64

AMERICAN federation of television and radio artists
Clear channels ahead; labor contract between NET and AFTRA. Sr Schol 85:7T O 7 '64

AMERICAN festival ballet company
American festival ballet, Fashion institute. M. Marks. Dance Mag 38:31+ Ap '64
American festival ballet, February 29, 1964. J. Maskey. Dance Mag 38:66+ Ap '64

AMERICAN fiction
Catholic novels & American culture. T. F. Curley. Commentary 36:34-42 Jl '63
Death of the reader. W. Morris. Nation 198: 53-4 Ja 13 '64
Fathers and sons in American fiction. E. Rovit. Yale R 53:248-57 D '63
Gift of fiction: 1964. G. Hicks. Sat R 47: 23-4 D 26 '64
Literary horizons; The thirties: a reappraisal. G. Hicks. Sat R 46:27-8 My 4 '63
Novel school for life. G. Hicks. Sat R 48: 23-4 Ja 16 '65
OK novelists today. A. Shulenberger. Nat R 16:115-16 F 11 '64
Onward and upward with the arts; can the rich write? G. T. Hellman. New Yorker 39: 46-8+ Je 8 '63
Post and fiction. Sat Eve Post 236:70 Mr 2 '63
Recent prose. R. J. Mills, jr. Poetry 102:269-73 Jl '63
Signatures to the significance of the self. G. Hicks. il Sat R 47:67-70+ Ag 29 '64
Works in progress, 1963. il Esquire 60:50-62+ Jl '63

See also
Short stories

AMERICAN field service
Americanization of Axel. R. Starnes. Field & S 69:10-11+ Ja '65
President speaks to American field service students; remarks, July 20, 1964. L. B. Johnson. Dept State Bul 51:189 Ag 10 '64
Pursuit of peace; address, August 2, 1964. D. Rusk. Dept State Bul 51:214-18 Ag 17 '64
Teen-age ambassadors of understanding. L. T. Henderson. Read Digest 83:181-4 S '63

AMERICAN film festival. See Moving picture festivals

AMERICAN fisheries society
American fisheries society. E. A. Seaman. Science 143:1237-40 Mr 13 '64

AMERICAN flyers airline corporation
American flyers plans piston phaseout. E. J. Bulban. il Aviation W 78:45+ Ap 22 '63

AMERICAN folk art. See Folk art
AMERICAN folk songs. See Folk songs, American
AMERICAN football league
AFL could win the world series. D. Jenkins. Sports Illus 19:26 D 16 '63
Coming of age. Newsweek 65:40 Ja 4 '65
Foggy feast for Buffalo's faithful; Bills won AFL title. E. Shrake. il Sports Illus 22:14-19 Ja 4 '65
How the West has won; West vs. East. E. Shrake. il Sports Illus 21:38+ N 23 '64
I don't need money, I need points; Al Davis, coach of Oakland Raiders. W. Bingham. il Sports Illus 19:27-9 N 4 '63
In the AFL, guile and go should win for the Chargers; San Diego Chargers. E. Shrake. il Sports Illus 21:26-7 D 21 '64
Pro football 1964. T. Maule. il Sports Illus 21:70-5 S 7 '64
Pro football scouting reports. T. Brody. il Sports Illus 19:64-8 S 9 '63
Run to a title; San Diego Chargers vs Boston Patriots in AFL championship. G. Rogin. il Sports Illus 20:8-11 Ja 13 '64
AMERICAN forest congress
AFA calls fifth American forest congress. Am For 69:10-11+ My '63
AFA pushes land reform. il Am For 69:4-5 O '63
Changing perspectives; address. S. T. Dana. il Am For 69:32-5 D '63
Fifth American forest congress. J. B. Craig. il Am For 69:30-1 D '63
Platform for American conservation. Am For 69:33-44 My; 30-1 Je '63
Timber! Forest congress. il Am For 69:6-7+ S '63
What the people said. il Am For 69:36-40+ D '63
AMERICAN forest products industries, incorporated
AFPI meeting; land ownership examined. Am For 70:42-4 D '64
AMERICAN forestry association
AFA calls fifth American forest congress. Am For 69:10-11+ My '63
AFA honors two solid citizens. il Am For 69:34-5 O '63
Annual meeting. Am For 70:38-40+ D '64
Call to action; AFA program. Am For 70:23 F '64
Calling all AFA members. il Am For 69:10 Je '63
Changing perspectives; address. S. T. Dana. il Am For 69:32-5 D '63
Conservation platform for American forestry; text. Am For 70:3-16 F '64
Cradle of forestry. il Am For 70:18-20 My '64
Dana named by the American forestry association to review and evaluate proposals for redwoods preservation. Am For 70:12 D '64
89th and 54th; joint annual meetings of North Carolina and American forestry associations. il Am For 70:15 O '64
Foot that rocks the cradle. il Am For 70:18-19 O '64
Laurance Rockefeller receives AFA award. il Am For 69:4 D '63
Needed, a who's who for shrubs. W. B. Morse. il Am For 70:30-1+ My '64
Presidents of the American forestry association. il Am For 71:8 Ja '65
Salute to two services; departments of Interior and Agriculture. il Am For 69:23 Ag '63
What AFA members think! conservation platform for American forestry. K. B. Pomeroy. Am For 70:6+ My '64
See also
Trail riders of the wilderness
AMERICAN foundation for the blind
Study of blind readers. E. Josephson. bibliog f ALA Bul 58:543-7 Je '64
AMERICAN friends service committee
Let the churches help Cubans. Christian Cent 80:1393-4 N 13 '63
AMERICAN furniture. See Furniture, American
AMERICAN glass. See Glassware
AMERICAN guild of musical artists
Opera: U.S; list of opera producing groups. Mus Am 83:325-6 D '63
Year-round employment. A. A. Bliss. il Opera N 29:8-11 O 17 '64
AMERICAN guild of variety artists
Labor union accused of white slave activities. U S News 55:11 Jl 8 '63
AMERICAN hardware corporation
American hardware marries for love. il Bsns W p 144+ My 16 '64
AMERICAN heart association
How to predict the next heart attack. Bsns W p34 O 26 '63
AMERICAN hemerocallis society
Daylily splendor. il Pop Gard 14:14+ Mr '63
AMERICAN historical association
Chicago meeting, 1962. B. A. Weisberger. Am Hist R 68:880-3 Ap '63
Historians honor Alfred A. Knopf. il Pub W 187:277-8 Ja 25 '65
Modest proposal to meet an urgent need: proposals for a national center for historical scholarship; address. J. P. Boyd. bibliog f Am Hist R 70:329-49 Ja '65
Philadelphia meeting, 1963. H. Conroy. Am Hist R 69:910-14 Ap '64
AMERICAN home products corporation
Pushbutton can takes off on its own. il Bsns W p 102+ Ap 11 '64
AMERICAN hospital association
Computer-aided hospital planning. il Arch Rec 135:90-1+ Mr '64
AMERICAN hotels. See Hotels, taverns, etc.
AMERICAN house decoration. See House decoration, American
AMERICAN humor. See Humor, American
AMERICAN institute for free labor development
Trade union movement and social progress in the western hemisphere; address, November 23, 1964. D. Rusk. Dept State Bul 51:849-52 D 14 '64
AMERICAN institute of aeronautics and astronautics
AIAA expects 5,000 registrants, seventy-five exhibitors at first meeting. il Miss & Roc 14:21 Je 29 '64
AIAA meeting sets future format. Miss & Roc 15:21 Jl 13 '64
Apollo use in military programs proposed. Aviation W 81:27-9 N 9 '64
Institute urged to sell space. il Miss & Roc 15:12-17 Jl 6 '64
Nova decision may be far away. R. Hawkes. il Miss & Roc 12:16-17 Ap 29 '63
AMERICAN institute of architects
Alvar Aalto wins 1963 A.I.A. gold medal; awards include first presidential citation. Arch Rec 133:26 Mr '63
A.I.A. aids information retrieval quest. Arch Rec 134:10 O '63
A.I.A. announces theme of 1964 convention: The city, visible and invisible. Arch Rec 134:23 O '63
A.I.A. award program for 1963 honors thirteen buildings. il Arch Rec 133:12-15 Mr '63
AIA holds competition for headquarters. il Arch Rec 135:20 Ap '64
A.I.A. holds 1963 convention in Miami. Arch Rec 133:23 My '63
A.I.A. in St Louis adopts new standards of practice. il Arch Rec 136:10+ Ag '64
AIA looks at invisibles; convention. il Arch Forum 121:7-8 Jl '64
A.I.A. looks forward and back and has a great time at Miami. il Arch Rec 133:10+ Je '63
A.I.A. names fifty-nine for rank of fellowship. Arch Rec 135:23 Je '64
A.I.A. plans a new kind of convention. Arch Rec 133:10 Ja '63
California buildings receive honor awards. il Arch Rec 135:14-15 Je '64
Computer-aided hospital planning. il Arch Rec 135:90-1+ Mr '64
Four city projects win architect merit awards. il Am City 79:83 Ag '64
Kennedy receives AIA citation for policies on architecture, art. il Arch Rec 134:33 Ag '63
1963 Pan Pacific citation awarded to Japan's Kikutake. il Arch Rec 135:14-15 Mr '64
1964 A.I.A. awards honor sixteen projects. il Arch Rec 136:10+ Jl '64
Quest for quality in architecture is theme for A.I.A. Miami convention; names thirty-five members for fellowship. Arch Rec 133:10 Ap '63
Sky-hooks available; seminar. C. J. McNaspy. America 110:378-9 Mr 21 '64
Three department heads named to A.I.A. national headquarters staff. Arch Rec 134:23 S '63
Two are named to top staff posts. Arch Rec 133:23 Mr '63
AMERICAN institute of biological sciences
American institute of biological sciences accused of misuse of NSF grant funds. D. S. Greenberg. il Science 139:317-21 Ja 25 '63; Discussion. 142:150+; 143:7-8, 430 O 11 '63, Ja 3, 31 '64
AIBS: bill for 1959-61 less than NSF original estimate. D. S. Greenberg. Science 139:1039 Mr 15 '63
AIBS: happy ending in prospect, but case adds to congressional skepticism on support for science. D. S. Greenberg. Science 139:814-15 Mr 1 '63
Biologists' choice. D. Wolfe. Science 139:459 F 8 '63

AMERICAN institute of biological sciences—*Continued*
Biology on the cuff, is AIBS worth saving? open letter from the Institute's president. J. D. Ebert. Science 139:321-2 Ja 25 '63
Emergency meeting of board. D. S. Greenberg. Science 139:392 F 1 '63
Morality in science: report on a crisis. J. Lear. il Sat R 46:49-54 Mr 2 '63; Discussion. 46:51-2 My 4; 37-8 Je 1; 46 Ag 3 '63

AMERICAN institute of certified public accountants
CPAs churn new rules; Accounting principles board. Bsns W p70 N 23 '63
Matter of principle splits CPAs; Accounting principles board. il Bsns W p50+ Ja 26 '63
Showdown on accounting principles. R. N. Anthony. Harvard Bsns R 41:99-106 My '63

AMERICAN institute of graphic arts
AIGA's Fifty books: a review of the 1963 show. R. F. Neale. bibliog il Pub W 183: 56+ My 6 '63
Children's book show: 1961-2 choices of AIGA. S. M. Agnew. il Pub W 183:60-8 Ap 8 '63
Design or content? AIGA 1961-1962 show of children's books. A. Dalgliesh. Sat R 46:44 My 11 '63
For eloquence and precision; award of medal to S. Steinberg. Pub W 183:71 Je 3 '63
Foreign sales, foreign services, reviewed at AIGA clinic. Pub W 183:92-4 F 4 '63
Printing for commerce and Fifty advertisements AIGA, 1962. Pub W 183:83 F 4 '63
Production man's role: combating confusion between publisher and manufacturer. L. Albert; F. Kleeberg. il Pub W 183:76+ My 6 '63
Reducing the confusion between publishers and manufacturers. Pub W 183:68+ Ap 8 '63
Singapore to Istanbul: printing design and production from seven countries; with report by M. Glick and E. H. Glick. il Pub W 183:84-6+ Mr 4 '63
See also
Textbook clinic
Trade book clinic

AMERICAN institute of Indian studies
Grant awarded to American institute of Indian studies. Dept State Bul 49:99-100 Jl 15 '63

AMERICAN institute of interior designers
Eclectic look; Elsie de Wolfe award. G. O'Brien. il N Y Times Mag p58-9 Mr 1 '64

AMERICAN institute of iron and steel. See American iron and steel institute

AMERICAN institute of motivation research
Phrenology updated; concerning the A.I.M.R. Special research report CP-64. Christian Cent 81:503 Ap 15 '64

AMERICAN institute of planners
Careers in planning; problems of city growth, traffic, land use. il Changing T 17:31-3 F '63

AMERICAN institute of steel construction
Nine buildings receive A.I.S.C. awards. il Arch Rec 134:14-15 S '63
Twelve buildings get A.I.S.C. awards. il Arch Rec 136:14-15 S '64

AMERICAN intellectuals. See Intellectuals

AMERICAN international music fund, incorporated
Koussevitzky recording awards. R. Jacobson. Mus Am 83:46 My '63

AMERICAN investments abroad. See Investments, Foreign

AMERICAN iris society
Iris society awards. Pop Gard 14:8 My '63

AMERICAN IRISH. See Irish Americans

AMERICAN iron and steel institute
Architects and engineers win awards of design in steel. il Arch Rec 133:82+ Ap '63
Good old days are back again. il Bsns W p29 Je 6 '64

AMERICAN Jewish committee
End of anti-Semitism? Newsweek 62:71 Ag 19 '63
No room at the top; discrimination against Jews. E. C. Parker. Christian Cent 81:152-4 Ja 29 '64
On the roots of bias; American Jewish committee report on textbooks used in Roman Catholic parochial schools. T. Cooper. Christian Cent 81:770-1 Je 10 '64

AMERICAN Jews. See Jews in the United States

AMERICAN judicature society
For a better bench; campaign against the election of judges. Time 83:52 F 7 '64

AMERICAN kennel club
Smart dogs keep on the right track. V. Kraft. il Sports Illus 18:99-100+ Ap 8 '63

AMERICAN landmarks week. See Special days, weeks and months

AMERICAN language. See English language

AMERICAN law institute
Pathfinders. Time 83:57-8 My 29 '64

AMERICAN legion
American legion; address, January 6, 1964. D. F. Foley. Vital Speeches 30:311-13 Mr 1 '64
American legion of today; address, November 9, 1963. D. F. Foley. Vital Speeches 30: 121-2 D 1 '63
Goal of the American legion; address, September 24, 1964. D. E. Johnson. Vital Speeches 31:48-50 N 1 '64
Independence day 1964; address, July 4, 1964. D. F. Foley. Vital Speeches 30:634-6 Ag 1 '64
Intellectual freedom; raising hell with the Legionnaires; disturbances in Ringwood, N.J. and Paradise, Calif. E. T. Moore. ALA Bul 57:222-6 Mr '63

AMERICAN liberalism. See Liberalism

AMERICAN libraries abroad
American library services in France. I. F. Fraser. Wilson Lib Bul 39:415+ Ja '65
Around the world, reds burn U.S. books. il U S News 57:62-3 D 21 '64
Secretary deplores book burning and damage to U.S. embassies; statement, December 9, 1964. D. Rusk. Dept State Bul 51:905 D 28 '64
Those-do-it-yourself spontaneous riots; anti-American demonstrations. il Time 84:27-8 D 18 '64
Three USIS libraries attacked in Cairo, Jakarta, and Surabaya. Library J 90:80 Ja 1 '65
To fill the reading gap; Books USA. E. R. Murrow. il Sat R 46:32-3 Ap 27 '63
USIA: building bridges of peace in a changing world; address, December 8, 1964. C. T. Rowan. Dept State Bul 51:906-12 D 28 '64
USIA overseas libraries 1964. C. T. Rowan. il Wilson Lib Bul 39:40-3+ S '64

AMERICAN library association
Access study; symposium. il Library J 88: 4685-709 D 15 '63; Discussion. 88:4710-12; 89:976+ D 15 '63, Mr 1 '64
American adults read more fiction. Wilson Lib Bul 38:441+ F '64
American library association and civil rights; excerpts from report, July 1963. J. E. Bryan. ALA Bul 57:747 S '63
ALA awards and citations for 1963. il Library J 88:3018-20 S 1 '63
ALA awards, citations, and scholarships for 1964-1965. Library J 88:4184-6; 89:4494-6 N 1 '63, N 15 '64
ALA establishes project to coordinate statistics. Library J 88:3184 S 15 '63
ALA go home! Library J 89:4128+ O 15 '64
ALA headquarters operations divided into seven departments. Library J 89:1928-9 My 1 '64
ALA invites application now for 1964 awards, scholarships. Library J 88:4834-6 D 15 '63
ALA invites nominations for awards and scholarships. Library J 89:4619-20 N 15 '64
ALA issues its annual list, Notable children's books. Pub W 183:29-30 Ap 1 '63
ALA makes administrative changes. Wilson Lib Bul 38:728 My '64
ALA organization and information, 1963-65. ALA Bul 57:885-6+; 58:845-8+ N '63, N '64
Coordination of library statistics. Wilson Lib Bul 38:121 O '63
Current foundation, industry, and government grants, 1962-63. il ALA Bul 57:430-1 My '63
Dewey abroad; survey. Wilson Lib Bul 37: 524+ Mr '63
Effect of ALA dues increase on membership and income. il ALA Bul 57:396 My '63
Field study of DDC abroad gets under way this spring. Library J 89:1704+ Ap 15 '64
Fleas come with the dog. D. H. Clift. Library J 88:1423 Ap 1 '63
Libraries for an affluent society with frayed edges; address, July 3, 1964. E. Castagna. ALA Bul 58:635-8 Jl '64
Library 21 report. Wilson Lib Bul 37:830 Je '63
Manuscript catalog, research manual aided by Council on library resources, Library of Congress and the American library association's Library technology project, respectively. Library J 89:829 F 15 '64
Medium sized P.L.'s report circulation increase in fiction. Library J 89:586+ F 1 '64
Nation's reading interests outlined in ALA report. Library J 88:530-1 F 1 '63
Needs of libraries and what ALA is doing about them. J. E. Bryan. ALA Bul 57:319-21 Ap '63
News from the divisions. See issues of ALA bulletin
1963 ALA awards winners. R. Austin. il ALA Bul 57:768-71 S '63
1964 ALA awards winners. il ALA Bul 58: 725-8 S '64

AMERICAN library association—*Continued*
Notable children's books of 1963 listed by ALA. Pub W 185:61-2 Ap 27 '64
Obligations to the future; address, July 19, 1963. F. H. Wagman. ALA Bul 57:761-6 S '63
President's report to council. F. H. Wagman. ALA Bul 58:627-9 Jl '64
Proposed amendments to ALA constitution and bylaws. ALA Bul 57:595 Je '63
Publications perspective. E. Moon; reply. C. R. Carner. Library J 88:896 Mr 1 '63
Underdeveloped areas to outer space: three new publications from ALA. Library J 88: 2224 Je 1 '63
Use of DDC abroad to be studied. Library J 88:980-1 Mr 1 '63
View from the plateau, fiscal year 1961-62. A. Yabroff. ALA Bul 57:249 Mr '63
What the young librarian thinks of his professional associations. R. Y. Weinbrecht. il Library J 88:1417-20 Ap 1 '63; Discussion. 88:1421-3, 1920+, 2952 Ap 1, My 15, S 1 '63
Where does ALA leadership come from? G. T. Stevenson. ALA Bul 57:105 F '63
See also
American association of school librarians
American association of state libraries
Booklist (periodical)

Meetings, 1963

ALA announces program for conference within a conference; student use of libraries. Library J 88:1844+ My 1 '63
ALA conference roundup. il Wilson Lib Bul 38:5+ S '63
ALA highlights; report of the conference activities for school, YA and children's librarians. E. Rudin. il Library J 88:3261-9 S 15 '63
ALA midwinter report. Wilson Lib Bul 37: 562+ Mr '63
ALA midwinter report; open meetings. E. Rudin. il Library J 88:1301-4 Mr 15 '63
ALA: student needs, library access were dominant conference topics. il Pub W 184: 28-32 Ag 12 '63
Bastille day and after. E. Moon. il Library J 88:3004-17 S 1 '63
Chicago conference; symposium. il ALA Bul 57:725-73 S '63
Enjoy your stay at ALA. B. Fast. ALA Bul 57:413+ My '63
Explosion-. Wilson Lib Bul 38:43 S '63
Figure in the carpet; report on the ALA conference within a conference. K. Molz. il Wilson Lib Bul 38:44-9 S '63
For the early birds; pre-conference meetings. il Library J 88:3021-8 S 1 '63
Highlights of the Chicago conference program. il ALA Bul 57:401-2 My '63
Highlights of the midwinter meeting. il ALA Bul 57:231-40+ Mr '63
JMRT plans Chicago program for young/new librarians; Junior members round table. Library J 88:1968 My 15 '63
Moments at midwinter. E. Moon. il Library J 88:967-72 Mr 1 '63
Plans set for first-time ALA conference within a conference; Inquiry into the needs of students. Library J 88:2091-2 My 15 '63
Problem, no! opportunity, yes! ALA's conference within a conference looks at library service to students. E. Rubin and E. Moon. il Library J 88:2829-36 Ag '63
Reading conclave? Sr Schol 83:1T-3T S 13 '63
Students and libraries. J. E. Bryan. ALA Bul 57:213 Mr '63
Two kinds of access; concerning the report, Access to public libraries, of International research associates. E. Moon. Library J 88:2849 Ag '63
Underprivileged reader; report on Access to public libraries survey, conducted by International research associates. E. Geller. Wilson Lib Bul 38:65-7 S '63
Zeal and apathy. E. Moon. Library J 88:973 Mr 1 '63; Discussion. 88:1564+ Ap 15 '63

Meetings, 1964

ALA annual conference to open in St Louis, June 28. Pub W 185:30 My 11 '64
ALA conference: news and events. Wilson Lib Bul 39:24-6 S '64
ALA conference notes. Library J 89:1931 My 1 '64
ALA midwinter meeting 1964; tentative program. ALA Bul 58:32 Ja '64
ALA midwinter report. K. Molz. Wilson Lib Bul 38:558-9+ Mr '64
ALA midwinter report; open meetings. E. Rudin. il Library J 89:925-6 F 15 '64
ALA, 1964; report of the conference activities for school, YA and children's librarians. il Library J 89:3390-403 S 15 '64
ALA report: St Louis, Mo, June 28-July 4. K. Molz. il Wilson Lib Bul 39:67-70 S '64
Bulletin board; ALA St Louis conference programs of direct interest to libraries in academic institutions. ALA Bul 58:336 My '64
From apathy to empathy; more notes from midwinter meeting. E. Moon. Library J 89: 1033-5 Mr 1 '64
Heat and/or light at the ALA conference: symposium. Pub W 186:16-22 Ag 3 '64
Highlights of the midwinter meeting; with report by F. H. Wagman. il ALA Bul 58: 191-6+ Mr '64
Highlights of the St Louis conference. il ALA Bul 58:607-32+ Jl '64
Pre-conference quartet. il Library J 89:2944-5 Ag '64
Reflections on the ALA conference in St Louis. E. Moon. il Library J 89:2919-28 Ag '64; Discussion. 89:2902, 3218, 4240 Ag, S 15, N 1 '64
St Louis conference program planning. ALA Bul 58:215-18 Mr '64
Silent giant; report on some highlights of the council sessions at midwinter meeting. E. Moon. il Library J 89:812-16 F 15 '64; Correction. 89:1482 Ap 1 '64
Tentative program of the 83d annual ALA conference; St Louis, Mo, June 28-July 4, 1964. ALA Bul 58:387-402 My '64
Year of the reactors; around the division meetings at ALA in St Louis. E. Moon. il Library J 89:2929-36 Ag '64

Meetings, 1965

ALA conference to present library resources inventory. Pub W 186:91-2 S 28 '64
ALA midwinter meeting 1965; tentative program. ALA Bul 59:13 Ja '65
Practical measures to combat censors topic of ALA invitational conference. Library J 90:217 Ja 15 '65

Adult services division

Adult services division. ALA Bul 59:68 Ja '65
ALA, 1964: ASD-YASD panel; with report by P. Allen. il Library J 89:3397-400, 3403 S 15 '64; Discussion. 89:4578+ N 15 '64
ALA to publish five more Age of change booklets. Library J 88:4009 O 15 '63
Notability and permanence; concerning notable books of 1963 of Notable books council. E. Moon. Library J 89:1201+ Mr 15 '64; Discussion. 89:1890+ My 1 '64
Reading improvement institute to be held in Chicago. Library J 88:1851 My 1 '63
Reading skills; pre-conference Institute on reading improvement for adults. R. R. McClarren. Library J 88:3026 S 1 '63

Children's services division

ALA highlights. E. Rudin. il Library J 88: 3266-8 S 15 '63
ALA, 1964. il Library J 89:3394-6 S 15 '64
Good reading for youth show opens in four pilot states. Library J 89:340 Ja 15 '64

Commission on a national plan for library education

Commission on a national plan for library education. ALA Bul 58:481 Je '64

Constitution and bylaws committee

Report of the committee on constitution and bylaws. ALA Bul 58:372-4 My '64

Finance

Treasurer's report; excerpt. A. Yabroff. ALA Bul 58:631-2 Jl '64

Headquarters

Look at the new headquarters. S. Smith. il ALA Bul 57:655-8 Jl '63
New ALA headquarters a symbol of accomplishment; address, July 14, 1963. R. Munn. il ALA Bul 57:729-33 S '63
People and places of the Milam era; excerpts from address, 1964. E. O. Fontaine. il ALA Bul 58:363-71 My '64

Intellectual freedom committee

ALA as amicus curiae: Tropic of Cancer before the U.S. Supreme court; excerpts from brief. bibliog f ALA Bul 58:290-8 Ap '64
Intellectual committee minutes reported in I.F. Newsletter. Library J 88:3566 O 1 '63
It is later than you think: an action program against censorship. L. B. Archer. Library J 88:3552-4 O 1 '63

AMERICAN library association—*Continued*

International relations committee

ALA at work in other countries; excerpts from memorandum. ALA Bul 58:138-40 F '64
As much to learn as to teach. L. Asheim. il Library J 89:4465-8 N 15 '64; Reply. P. Bixler. 90:4 Ja 1 '65

International relations office

ALA at work in other countries; excertps from memorandum. ALA Bul 58:138-40 F '64
As much to learn as to teach. L. Asheim. il Library J 89:4465-8 N 15 '64; Reply. P. Bixler. 90:4 Ja 1 '65

Library administration division

Everett Moore on dissent; concerning report at midwinter meeting; letter to the editor. E. T. Moore. ALA Bul 58:167 Mr '64
Library administration division, culprit or victim? ALA Bul 57:585-90 Je '63
LAD pre-conference institute to study building problems. Library J 88:2223-4 Je 1 '63
Local organization for recruitment; pattern and framework by Office for recruitment. A. Geddes. ALA Bul 58:825-6 O '64
Origin and development of the Library administration division. K. Laich. ALA Bul 57:346-50 Ap '63
Reading the lessons; standing of Access study now? E. Moon. Library J 89:817 F 15 '64
Report on the study of access to public libraries. ALA Bul 58:299-304 Ap '64
Shortcomings of LAD; letter to the editor. R. E. Ellsworth. ALA Bul 57:692-3 S '63; Reply. H. S. Hacker. 57:1001 D '63; Rejoinder. 58:9 Ja '64
Silent giant; concerning LAD report on Access study as presented at midwinter meeting. E. Moon. il Library J 89:814-16 F 15 '64

Library education division

ALA's library education commission holds first meeting in Chicago. Library J 88:1130 Mr 15 '63
LED is for librarians. V. L. Jones. Library J 88:739+ F 15 '63
Logsdon to head ALA commission on national plan for library education. Library J 88:744 F 15 '63
National plan for library education. Wilson Lib Bul 37:522+ Mr '63
Thoughts for the commission; ALA's commission on a national plan for library education. J. L. Wheeler. Library J 88:4170-1 N 1 '63

Library technology project

Book labeling system marketed: Se-Lin; product of LTP's first major project. G. T. Piez. ALA Bul 58:410-11 My '64
Book marking analysis; concerning program by LTP. N. H. Gaber. il Library J 89:1503-7 Ap 1 '64; Discussion. 89:2000+ My 15 '64
CLR awards $265,000 in grants, contract. Pub W 186:35-6 S 14 '64
Data processing equipment in libraries. J. Becker. il ALA Bul 58:227-30, 557-60, 714-18, 822-4, 1007-10 Mr, Je, S-O, D '64
Development and testing of a new book marking system; Se-Lin, by LTP and Battelle memorial institute. N. H. Gaber. il Library J 89:1911-13 My 1 '64
Film coatings; concerning program of LTP. G. T. Piez. ALA Bul 58:237 Mr '64
LTP book labeling system goes to market; Se-Lin. G. T. Piez. il ALA Bul 58:554-6 Je '64
New pricing policies. G. T. Piez. ALA Bul 59:69 Ja '65
Resources in library technology. E. N. Salmon. Library J 89:1495-502 Ap 1 '64

Membership

Geographical bigotry? letter to the editor. W. Brace. Library J 89:4238 N 1 '64
Keep talking; with editorial comment. W. Jones. Library J 89:2966-7 Ag '64
Membership in ALA. R. Land. ALA Bul 57:809-10 O '63
Memo to members; concerning statement on requirements of chapter status in ALA. E. Castagna. ALA Bul 58:670-1 S '64
Sermon on an obligation. R. G. Vosper. ALA Bul 58:757 O '64
Two stars from Georgia; reflections on the ALA conference in St. Louis. E. Moon. il Library J 89:2919-28 Ag '64

Notable books council

See American library association—Adult services division

Office for recruitment

See American library associaton—Library administration division

Program evaluation and budget committee

Begun, progressing, completed; activities and projects. ALA Bul 57:423-30 My '63
Needs of libraries; and what ALA can do to help meet them; report. ALA Bul 58:531-8 Je '64

Public library association

Planning for the long haul toward meeting standards; Standards committee. R. P. Tubby. ALA Bul 58:499+ Je '64

Publishing department

ALA publishing focus. Library J 88:1972 My 15 '63
New ALA publications. Wilson Lib Bul 38:23 S '63
Report of the committee on ALA publishing to the council. C. J. Frarey. ALA Bul 58:630-1 Jl '64

Reference services division

Prospecting in the West; Western Americana institute sponsored by the ACRL rare books section and RSD history section. G. D. McDonald. Library J 88:3021-2 S 1 '63

Small libraries project

Evaluating the small libraries project. G. K. Schenk. Wilson Lib Bul 39:346 D '64

Statistics coordinating project

International standardization of library statistics. F. L. Schick. ALA Bul 58:1011-13 D '64
Statistics coordinating project holds four regional meetings. Library J 89:1707 Ap 15 '64
Status report on the Statistics coordinating project. J. Williams. ALA Bul 58:551-3 Je '64

Young adult services division

ALA highlights. E. Rudin. il Library J 88:3265-6 S 15 '63
ALA, 1964. il Library J 89:3396-7 S 15 '64
ALA's young adult services division; list of interesting adult books for young people, 1962. Wilson Lib Bul 37:730+ My '63
Significant adult books for young people, 1963. Wilson Lib Bul 38:597-8 Ap '64
YASD committee chooses interesting adult books for young people, 1962. Library J 88:1743-4 Ap 15 '63
YASD picks thirty adult books of 1963 as good reading for US teenagers. Library J 89:1398 Mr 15 '64

AMERICAN library trustee association

Letter series that works: a report from the ALTA-NLW committee. R. A. Young and J. L. Love. Wilson Lib Bul 37:577 Mr '63
M.A. in trusteeship; First national meeting as a division of ALA. il Library J 89:2944-5 Ag '64
Thoughts for trustees about total service; annual pre-conference institute. G. Gordon. il Library J 88:3024-6 S 1 '63

AMERICAN literature

Books. E. Wilson. New Yorker 39:174-80 Mr 23 '63
Literary sampler; excerpts from new and forthcoming books. Sat R 47:44-5+ O 3 '64
New frontiers in American literature; excerpts from address, April 24, 1964. I. Hassan. Wilson Lib Bul 39:248-52 N '64
Soviet attitudes toward American writing, by D. Brown. Review
Nation 196:182-3 Mr 2 '63. H. Muchnic
Special issue on the American literary scene; symposium. il Esquire 60:27-35 Jl '63
Structure of the American literary establishment. L. R. Hills. Esquire 60:41 Jl '63; Reply. A. Marple. Writer 76:5-6 S '63
Waiting for the end, by L. A. Fiedler. Review
Nat R 16:654-6 Jl 28 '64. H. Kenner
While they waited for Lefty; proletarian writing. M. Cowley. il Sat R 47:16-19+ Je 6 '64
Year that was. il Newsweek 62:76+ D 23 '63

See also
American fiction
American poetry
Negro literature

Bibliography

Books for the Lincoln bedroom; Blair House. il House & Gard 127:148 Ja '65

Jewish authors

Breakthrough? D. Daiches. Commentary 38:61-4 Ag '64; Reply. I. Stark. 38:8+ D '64

AMERICAN literature—Jewish authors—*Cont.*
Jewish camp. T. Solotaroff. Commentary 37: 76-8 Mr '64
Radical innocent. N. Algren. Nation 199:142-3 S 21 '64

Illinois

Revival in Chicago. il Newsweek 62:94+ D 9 '63

Western states

Born a square; the westerners' dilemma. W. Stegner. il Atlan 213:46-50 Ja '64; Discussion. 213:40+ Mr '64

AMERICAN lithographs. See Lithographs

AMERICAN Lutheran church
Meeting the community; Faith in life dialogue experiment. il Time 84:91 O 16 '64
Taming the tongues; Rev. A. Herbert Mjorud, promoter of glossolalia. Time 84:64+ Jl 10 '64

AMERICAN machine and foundry company
AMF expects its R&D to yield new divisions. il Bsns W p 134-6+ My 4 '63
AMF study cites solids handling needs. Miss & Roc 13:28 Ag 5 '63
AMF tracking mount on job at PMR. W. Beller. il Miss & Roc 13:26 S 9 '63

AMERICAN management association
AMA getting set to spread its wings. il Bsns W p 144+ F 16 '63
AMA rings school bell. Bsns W p 110 Jl 6 '63
Teenage look at business. il Bsns W p 152-4 Je 27 '64

AMERICAN marketing association
AMA beats the drum for innovation; annual conference. il Bsns W p88+ Je 22 '63

AMERICAN medical association
AMA alternative; war against medicare. America 112:97 Ja 23 '65
AMA: convention accents positive by announcing research institute, reshaping scientific sections. J. Walsh. Science 140: 1382-3 Je 28 '63
AMA image; annual meeting. Newsweek 62:61 Jl 1 '63
AMA statistics. Commonweal 79:448 Ja 17 '64
AMA, the FDA and quacks. J. Ridgeway. New Repub 149:31-3 N 9 '63
AMA: vested reaction. F. P. Becker. New Repub 152:12 Ja 23 '65
AMA: voice of American medicine, by J. G. Burrow. Review
Christian Cent 81:179 F 5 '64. P. H. Smith
Barber of the battlefield; Ambroise Paré. il Todays Health 41:88 N '63
Call from Cousin. Newsweek 63:54 Ja 27 '64
Can the doctor do better? il Bsns W p 103-4+ S 26 '64
Cancer contribution. New Repub 150:5 Mr 7 '64
Doctor Koch and the boiled potato. il Todays Health 41:77 D '63
Hazards of judging. Newsweek 61:94 Mr 25 '63
Incredible story behind a cancer cure; krebiozen. S. Blum. il Redbook 123:40-1+ Je '64
Loan program that helps you become a doctor; Education and research foundation loan guarantee program. H. Earle. il Todays Health 41:36-41 Jl '63
Making of a president. il Time 84:67 D 11 '64
Medicare by Easter? redefinition of policy. Newsweek 65:52 Ja 25 '65
Medics in Miami; annual winter meeting. il Newsweek 64:50 D 14 '64
New deal and national health. R. Lubove. bibliog f Cur Hist 45:77-86+ Ag '63
New discoveries about your health; meeting. il U S News 57:14 D 14 '64
No time for silence; question of integration. America 109:2 Jl 6 '63; Reply. D. N. Kelly. 109:125 Ag 10 '63
Non-physician scientist to receive AMA award; Scientific achievement award. Sci N L 83:360 Je 8 '63
San Francisco smoke; AMA 113th annual meeting in San Francisco. Newsweek 64: 56-7 Jl 6 '64
Self-interest and the A.M.A. Commonweal 81:405 D 18 '64
Social change and medical organization in the United States; a sociological perspective. T. Parsons. bibliog f Ann Am Acad 346:30-3 Mr '63
Speaking out; case against federalized medicine. G. M. Fister. Sat Eve Post 236: 8+ F 23 '63
Time has not come; AMA opposition to extension of medical care from public sources. New Repub 149:26-8 N 9 '63
When AMA doctors met. Sci N L 83:402 Je 29 '63
Why are doctors out of step? L. Lasagna. New Repub 152:13-15 Ja 2 '65
Why we need medicare. M. H. Alderman. New Repub 151:17-20 D 26 '64
Writing an Rx on quacks; AMA and FDA national conference on quackery in medicine. il Bsns W p32-3 N 2 '63
You may be younger than you think. Read Digest 83:71-4 Jl '63

Woman's auxiliary

Doctor's wives tackle the suicide problem. M. Benson. il Todays Health 42:60-3 My '64

AMERICAN merchant marine. See Merchant marine—United States

AMERICAN meteorological society
Scientists galore; annual convention. New Yorker 38:25 F 16 '63

AMERICAN military assistance. See Military assistance, American

AMERICAN minorities. See Minorities

AMERICAN motors corporation
American's troubles. il Time 83:102+ My 15 '64
Bigger melon, smaller slices; AMC for UAW. Bsns W p32 N 23 '63
Introduction to the '65 cars. il Motor T 16:38-41 N '64
Off stride. Newsweek 63:68 Ja 27 '64
Profit sharing for workers: troubles of a noble experiment. il U S News 57:117+ O 26 '64
Profit-sharing issue raises hob. Bsns W p48+ O 17 '64
Profit sharing: what union won. U S News 57:72 N 2 '64
R in every month; Rambler sales. Bsns W p34 S 28 '63
Rambler history. il Motor T 15:34-9 F '63
Second look at profit sharing. U S News 56:78-9 Je 22 '64
'64 cars. il Motor T 15:52-4 N '63
Squeeze in American motors' road. E. K. Faltermayer. il Fortune 70:154-7+ S '64
Still preaching compact gospel. il Bsns W p86-8+ Ap 11 '64
What's new at American motors. J. Whipple. il Pop Sci 185:90-1 O '64

AMERICAN museum of natural history, New York
Admiral Peary and all that. il Sci Digest 54:28-33 N '63
Behind New York's window on nature; American museum of natural history. J. A. Oliver. il Nat Geog Mag 123:220-59 F '63
Bird hall; opening of Frank M. Chapman memorial hall of North American birds. New Yorker 40:21-2 Je 27 '64
Ebb and flow; visit to world's only marine tidal aquarium, in Living foraminifera laboratory at Museum of natural history. New Yorker 39:43-4 O 12 '63
Great gem caper; theft of gems. il Newsweek 64:38+ N 16 '64
Museum jewel robbery. il Time 84:23 N 6 '64
Museum memo. A. M. White. Natur Hist 73: 3 Mr '64
New exhibit offers sights of rare birds. il(p401) Sci N L 85:409 Je 27 '64
Night they stole the Star of India. il Life 57:77-80 N 13 '64
Open locker 0911; clues to recovery of gems taken from New York city's American museum of natural history. il Time 85:23 Ja 15 '65
Partners; exhibition marking seventy-fifth anniversary of National geographic society. New Yorker 39:22 Ag 17 '63
Termites. New Yorker 39:23 Ja 18 '64
$350,000 loot in a 25¢ locker. M. Acoca. il Life 58:30-3 Ja 22 '65
Worm lizards; pair of two-footed amphisbaenids, at Museum of natural history. New Yorker 40:33-4 Ap 4 '64

Expeditions

Onward and upward with the sciences. G. T. Hellman. il New Yorker 40:97-8+ D 5 '64
Science in action; launching an expedition. R. G. Van Gelder. il Natur Hist 73:64-7 Ap '64

Hayden planetarium

See Planetariums

AMERICAN music. See Music, American

AMERICAN musicians. See Musicians, American

AMERICAN national theatre and academy
Ask me later; what does ANTA do? S. Young. Sat R 47:33 F 22 '64

AMERICAN Negroes. See Negroes in the United States

AMERICAN Negroes in Africa. See Americans in Africa

AMERICAN newspaper guild
Dilemma of a guild reporter. M. Bracker; discussion. Reporter 28:10+ F 14 '63
For newspapers, new roadblocks; New York. U S News 54:124 Mr 25 '63
Money & other things; biggest obstacle to a settlement. Time 81:63-4 Mr 22 '63
New look at the New York newspaper strike. il U S News 54:50-2 Mr 4 '63
Score on strikes at newspapers; in Cleveland and New York. U S News 54:95-6 F 25 '63
Strikers oppose a union shop; Cleveland. U S News 54:86 F 18 '63
Too much power for labor? excerpts from address, February 12, 1963; with excerpts from letter by members of American newspaper guild. L. B. Seltzer. U S News 54:97 F 25 '63

AMERICAN newspaper publishers association
Celler and the first; concentration of news media ownership. Newsweek 61:72 Mr 25 '63

AMERICAN newspapers. See Newspapers—United States

AMERICAN novelists. See Novelists, American

AMERICAN novels. See American fiction

AMERICAN nursing home association
Accreditation: coming soon? Consumer Rep 29:86 F '64

AMERICAN opera. See Opera, American

AMERICAN opera society
Dr Faust; presentation in New York. F. Merkling. Opera N 29:31 Ja 2 '65
Faustian firsts. Newsweek 64:82+ D 14 '64
Live wire; interview, ed. by F. Stevenson. A. S. Oxenburg. il Opera N 28:30-1 F 22 '64
Music to my ears; Bellini's Capuletti. I. Kolodin. Sat R 47:35 My 16 '64
Music to my ears; Sutherland in concert version of Semiramide. I. Kolodin. Sat R 47:25 Mr 7 '64
Musical events; concert performance of Busoni's Doktor Faust. W. Sargeant. New Yorker 40:201 D 12 '64
Musical events; concert performance of Handel's Alcina. W. Sargeant. New Yorker 40: 115-16 Ja 16 '65
Musical events; concert performance of Massenet's Hérodiade, in Carnegie Hall. W. Sargeant. New Yorker 39:64+ D 21 '63
Musical events; concert performance of Poulenc's Dialogues des Carmélites, in Carnegie Hall. W. Sargeant. New Yorker 39:94-6 Ja 25 '64
Musical events; concert performance of Rossini's Semiramide. New Yorker 40:125-6 F 29 '64
Musical events; performance of Bellini's I Puritani. W. Sargeant. New Yorker 39:98 Ap 27 '63
Musical events; performance of Kálmán's Gräfin Mariza. W. Sargeant. New Yorker 39:116-17 Ap 6 '63
Opera for the ears alone; concert performances. A. Rich. il Mus Am 84:10-11+ N '64
Post-season New York. O. Eaton. il Opera N 28:24-5 S 28 '63
Vespers and dialogues; performance of Poulenc's Dialogues of the Carmélites at Carnegie Hall. J. W. Freeman. Opera N 28:33 F 15 '64

AMERICAN ordnance association
McNamara firm on conduct code; with editorial comment. Miss & Roc 15:13, 46 N 2 '64

AMERICAN overseas libraries. See American libraries abroad

AMERICAN overseas petroleum, limited
Exploring the big bubble; quest for natural gas. il Time 85:66 Ja 1 '65

AMERICAN painting. See Painting, American

AMERICAN personnel and guidance association
Meeting. N. Buchheimer. Sr Schol 84:1T-2T Ap 17 '64

AMERICAN pewter. See Pewter

AMERICAN pharmaceutical association
Profession of pharmacy in the United States; address, February 8, 1963. G. F. Archambault. Vital Speeches 29:349-52 Mr 15 '63

AMERICAN philosophical society
Preparing a manuscripts guide for a learned society; reprint. M. D. Smith. Hobbies 69: 110-11+ My '64

AMERICAN philosophy. See Philosophy, American

AMERICAN physical society
Scientists galore; joint meeting with American association of physics teachers. New Yorker 38:24-5 F 16 '63

AMERICAN place theatre. See New York (city)—Theater

AMERICAN poetry
Audience swam for their lives; excerpts from YM-YWHA-sponsored symposium on The state of American poetry today, ed. by J. Scully. G. Corso; J. Gilbert. Nation 198:244-5+ Mr 9 '64
Cadence for our time. C. Walsh. il Sat R 48:28-30 Ja 2 '65
Catalogue of nine. F. Stefanile. Poetry 103: 324-9 F '64
Celebration of flesh: poetry in Christian life, by A. C. McGill. Review
Christian Cent 82:80-2 Ja 20 '65. S. J. Rowland, jr
For summer, a wave of new verse. J. Jerome. Sat R 46:30-2 Jl 6 '63
Homer and the dragon: U.S. poetry before and after the beats. L. Holland. il Américas 16:28-32 Ja '64
Legacy of three poets. J. Jacobsen. Commonweal 78:189-92 My 10 '63
Miscellany. C. Tomlinson. Poetry 102:341-5 Ag '63
Muse is always gay. R. Pack. Sat R 47:60-3 N 14 '64
Of poetry and power, ed. by E. A. Glikes and P. Schwaber. Review
New Repub 151:17-19 N 21 '64. R. Whittemore
Poetry and the mind of modern man. C. Aiken. Atlan 214:79-81 N '64
Poetry chronicle. R. Howard. Poetry 102:250-9 Jl '63
Poetry in three dimensions; Poetry in crystal exhibition at Steuben's. J. Ciardi. il Sat R 46:22-5 Ap 20 '63
Poetry of three women. M. Swenson. Nation 196:164-6 F 23 '63
Poets without prophecy. H. Carruth. Nation 196:354-7 Ap 27 '63
Seven poets: the creation of images to delight. Commonweal 80:212-13 My 8 '64
Sky of late summer, by H. Rago. Review
Nation 198:126 F 3 '64. D. Levertov
Voice, the poet, and the poem. D. Geiger. Poetry 101:275-8 Ja '63
See also
Poets, American

Bibliography

Let us praise poets. A. P. Klausler. Christian Cent 80:369-70 Mr 20 '63

AMERICAN poets. See Poets, American

AMERICAN popular revolutionary alliance. See Political parties—Peru

AMERICAN potash and chemical corporation
Who owns what's in your head? W. Bowen. il Fortune 70:175-8+ Jl '64

AMERICAN pottery. See Pottery, American

AMERICAN power boat association
Benefits of predicted logging; symposium. il Motor B 111:45-50+ Ap '63
Drama at Detroit. C. D. Strang. il Motor B 114:48-9+ S '64
More power to you. M. Crook. See issues of Yachting
Racing and the A.P.B.A. C. D. Strang. il Motor B 115:112-13+ Ja '65
Wiget's winning year. C. D. Strang. Motor B 111:122-3 F '63

AMERICAN propaganda. See Propaganda

AMERICAN psychiatric association
Kennedy round. il Time 83:64 My 15 '64

AMERICAN public health association
Flu needle. il Newsweek 62:72 N 25 '63

AMERICAN public opinion. See Public opinion—United States

AMERICAN public works association
Apply imagination to urban problems; conferees told at Public works congress and equipment show in Atlantic City, N.J. Am City 79:86-8+ D '64
Snow conference expands coverage. Am City 78:162+ Je '63

AMERICAN publishers' representatives organization
American publishers' group formed in the Philippines. il Pub W 186:33-4 N 23 '64

AMERICAN radio relay league
K7UGA will get the ham vote. A. Whitman. il N Y Times Mag p64+ S 13 '64

AMERICAN railway progress exposition. See Railroads—Exhibitions

AMERICAN record guide (periodical)
ARG and how she grew. P. L. Miller. il Am Rec G 30:748-9 My '64
From the editor. J. Lyons. Am Rec G 30:935 Je '64
From this milestone, the future. G. R. Marek. Am Rec G 30:777 My '64
Good old days? G. Lieberson. Am Rec G 30:752 My '64

AMERICAN recreation society
Historical background of the relationship of NRA and ARS. il Recreation 56:170-3+ Ap '63
Progress report. Recreation 56:464+ D '63
AMERICAN Red cross. See Red cross—United States
AMERICAN relief administration
Memoir of a mission; ARA and Herbert Hoover in the USSR, 1921-23. H. C. Wolfe. Sat R 47:21+ Je 13 '64
AMERICAN reporters. See Reporters and reporting
AMERICAN research and development corporation
Profit-minded professor. Time 81:88+ Mr 8 '63
AMERICAN revolution. See United States—History—Revolution
AMERICAN revolutionary popular alliance. See Political parties—Peru
AMERICAN rhododendron society
Two hybridizers honored by American rhododendron society. il Flower Grower 50:8 S '63
AMERICAN RIVER
How the American River was saved; community action in the West. il Sunset 133:30-2+ O '64
AMERICAN rocket society. See American institute of areonautics and astronautics
AMERICAN SAMOA
Growing up in Samoa; whole school system turned over to television. il Time 84:90-1 D 4 '64
Puka Bill's gift to Samoa; validity of U.S. law. Time 84:64 S 4 '64
Sunday in the South Pacific. H. Sutton. il Sat R 47:26-8 Je 6 '64
35mm techniques. P. Stackpole. U S Camera 26:16-17 D '63
AMERICAN scene in literature. See United States in literature
AMERICAN schools abroad
American schools abroad. New Repub 150:7 Ja 25 '64
From Kent to Rome; St Stephen's coed school in Rome. il Newsweek 64:117A-117B+ O 5 '64
Industry rings the school bell; U.S. companies abroad running schools for staff members' children. il Bsns W p38-9 Jl 4 '64
See also
Military post schools, American
AMERICAN scientists. See Scientists, American
AMERICAN sculpture. See Sculpture, American
AMERICAN Shakespeare festival theatre and academy, Stratford, Conn.
All's well. Newsweek 61:102 Je 24 '63
Black intelligence. il Newsweek 63:80 Je 29 '64
Broadway postscript; good company. H. Hewes. Sat R 46:21-2 Je 29 '63
Conn. men. H. Hewes. Sat R 47:49 Je 27 '64
Everyman's disasters; Connecticut's triumph. Time 82:44 Ag 16 '63
Stratford, Connecticut; productions, 1963 season. A. Pryce-Jones. il(p 12) Theatre Arts 47:14+ Ag '63
Stratford's first decade. J. McLaughlin. America 111:152 Ag 15 '64
AMERICAN silverware. See Silverware
AMERICAN slang. See Slang
AMERICAN society for the prevention of cruelty to animals
Fifty years in the monkey house. L. Alexander. il McCalls 91:110-11+ F '64
AMERICAN society of civil engineers
Glen Canyon Dam complex receives award from A.S.C.E. il Arch Rec 135:53 Ap '64
Glen Canyon recommended for ASCE award. il Am City 79:116 Mr '64
AMERICAN society of clinical hypnosis
AAAS affiliate. W. T. Heron. Science 140:321+ Ap 19 '63
AMERICAN society of composers, authors and publishers
Fifty years of ASCAP. J. Molleson. Mus Am 84:7+ F '64
AMERICAN society of papyrologists
Papyri; meeting. New Yorker 40:22-4 S 5 '64
AMERICAN society of range management
Needed, a who's who for shrubs. W. B. Morse. il Am For 70:30-1+ My '64
AMERICAN soldiers. See United States—Army
AMERICAN songs. See Songs, American
AMERICAN standard Bible
New Testament
See Bible—New Testament—Versions
AMERICAN standards association
Binary computer codes and ASCII; American standard code for information interchange. E. Bukstein. il Electr World 72:28-9 Jl '64
New American standard approved for periodical title abbreviations. Library J 89:83 Ja 1 '64
Transliteration of modern Russian. J. Orne. il Library J 88:4157-60 N 1 '63
AMERICAN stock exchange
Amex: a new face and form. il Bsns W p91-2+ Je 8 '63
Fire brigade; new administrative team. Newsweek 61:75-6 Mr 11 '63
Young Ted Etherington's Amex. T. A. Wise. il Fortune 71:166-70+ Ja '65
AMERICAN strategy. See Strategy
AMERICAN students. See College students
AMERICAN students in foreign countries
College students and faculty abroad. R. M. Walker. il Sch Life 45:12 My '63
Free trade in ideas; excerpts from address. R. F. Kennedy. Sat R 46:43-4 F 16 '63
Our globetrotting students. J. Daniel. il Read Digest 85:106-10 Ag '64
Three American college girls on their junior year abroad; Paris. il Esquire 62:93-6 S '64
See also
Foreign study
AMERICAN students in France; in Russia; etc. See Foreign students in France; Foreign students in Russia; etc.
AMERICAN studies. See Area studies
AMERICAN symphony orchestra
Musical events. W. Sargeant. New Yorker 39:137-8 F 23; 117-18 Ap 6; 203 O 19 '63; 112-13 F 8 '64
Stokowski conducts a new life. E. Coleman. N Y Times Mag p72+ D 6 '64
AMERICAN symphony orchestra league
Lists: international reference guide. Mus Am 83:306-20 D '63
AMERICAN teachers association
American teachers association. Negro Hist Bul 27:26+ N '63
American teachers association pushes activity in two vital areas. Negro Hist Bul 27:149-52 Mr '64
ATA will merge, if. Sr Schol 85:6T-7T S 23 '64
Scholastic teacher interview; ed. by H. Langer. C. J. Duckworth. Sr Schol 85:9T-10T+ O 21 '64
AMERICAN teachers in foreign countries
America's first Peace corps; teachers in the Philippines between 1901 and 1933. W. P. Porter. Sat R 46:45 Jl 20 '63
College students and faculty abroad. R. M. Walker. il Sch Life 45:12 My '63
Every morning in Cairo; teaching creative writing at American university. J. Stuart. il Sr Schol 84:9T-10T My 8 '64
Teachers in the Peace corps. M. Edwards. il Sat R 46:42-4+ Jl 20 '63
AMERICAN technical assistance. See Technical assistance, American
AMERICAN telephone and telegraph company
AT&T splits two-one, and stocks jump. il Bsns W p 114 N 23 '63
AT&T's billion-dollar bargain scramble. il Newsweek 63:67 F 24 '64
Bell grows two billion dollars bigger; A.T.&T. and its affiliates. H. B. Jacobs. il N Y Times Mag p29+ Mr 1 '64
Bell is ringing. il Time 83:74-8 My 29 '64
COMSAT: Europeans wary of U.S. plan for American-dominated commercial satellite enterprise. E. Langer. Science 142:1637-40 D 27 '63
Cutting in on the line; A.T.& T. refused permission to transmit printed as well as spoken communications through its transatlantic cables. il Time 83:83 Mr 27 '64
Dial 2122428180. W. Marx. il Nation 197:344-5 N 23 '63
Does the FCC have AT&T's number? D. Gottlieb and D. Gottlieb. New Repub 148:17-19 Ap 6 '63
Firms oversubscribe Comsat stock issue. K. Johnsen. Aviation W 80:24 Je 1 '64
$500 million mistake; regulating AT&T the world's biggest business. A. Brynes. New Repub 151:11-14 S 26 '64
For the Bell system, all phones are ringing. il Bsns W p64-8 Ja 9 '65
ITT gets a dead line in buzz with AT&T; attempt to get into domestic telephone business. il Bsns W p70 Ap 25 '64
Latest AT&T station in sky; Telstar II. il Bsns W p92 My 11 '63
Mother Bell goes it alone as usual; largest stock offering in history. il Bsns W p 118+ Mr 7 '64
Mother Bell's children; stock split. Newsweek 64:68 Ag 24 '64
Mother Bell's Christmas present. il Time 82:89-90 N 29 '63

AMERICAN telephone and telegraph company —*Continued*
Mother Bell's record. Newsweek 63:63 Ja 13 '64
People, vitality and AT&T. T. R. Brooks. il Duns R 81:53-5+ Ap '63
Regulating AT&T. A. Brynes. New Repub 151:11-14 O 3 '64
Stock split by AT&T: meaning for shareholders. U S News 55:98-9 D 2 '63
Wrong numbers for A.T.&T; reduction in long-distance telephone rates. Time 84:105 D 4 '64
See also
Bell telephone laboratories

AMERICAN textbook publishers institute
ABPC-ATPI position paper on copyright revision. Pub W 187:275 Ja 25 '65
ATPI annual meeting. il Pub W 183:16-28 My 13 '63; 185:20-32 My 18 '64
ATPI resolves: eliminate the manufacturing clause. Pub W 185:27-8 My 11 '64
Copyright: how the procedure operates for books. il Pub W 183:29-31 F 25 '63
Federal, state, local economic developments; effect on schools and educational publishing; symposium at 1964 industry conference. il Pub W 185:14-24 Ap 6 '64
New era for textbooks: roles of government, foundations and industry in education; symposium at 1963 industry conference. il Pub W 183:16-25 Ap 8 '63
1963-64 in review. Pub W 185:90-1 Ja 20 '64; 187:88-90 Ja 18 '65
Textbooks and trapped idealists; excerpt from American reading public. F. G. Jennings. il Sat R 47:57-9+ Ja 18 '64
Treatment of minority groups in textbooks; adaptation of address, October 2, 1964. A. J. McCaffrey. Pub W 186:22-7 O 12 '64
War on poverty: conference sponsored by American book publishers council and the American textbook publishers institute; with editorial comment. il Pub W 185:32-43, 52 My 4 '64

AMERICAN theatre wing
Wing and the Tony. il Theatre Arts 47:30-2 My '63

AMERICAN theological library association
Salinger and John the Baptist; ATLA annual conference. N. H. Sonne. Library J 88:3031-3 S 1 '63
Theological library boom; annual conference. Library J 89:2965 Ag '64

AMERICAN tobacco company
Carlton's tar and nicotine. il Consumer Rep 29:114-15 Mr '64
Cigarette tar derby may be on again; tar, nicotine content on pack. il Bsns W p24-5 Ja 11 '64
Smoking and liability. Newsweek 61:86 Je 17 '63
Tobacco's bout with cancer. Time 81:89 Je 14 '63

AMERICAN transit association
New era in urban transportation. Am City 79:99 Ja '64

AMERICAN university, Washington, D.C.
Way to finish earlier; advanced placement students. Time 84:41 Jl 31 '64

AMERICAN university of Beirut
Our best investment in the Arab world. R. Littell. il Read Digest 82:240-1+ F '63

AMERICAN veterans of World war II
Africa and the world: problems of today and tomorrow; address, August 24, 1963. G. M. Williams. Dept State Bul 49:432-6 S 16 '63

AMERICAN viscose corporation
Antitrusters suffer a setback; FMC corp. merger with Avisco. Bsns W p88 Ag 10 '63
Giant that makes almost anything; FMC corp. to absorb American viscose. il Bsns W p58+ Mr 9 '63
Wage chronology: American viscose division, FMC corp; 1959-63. il Mo Labor R 86:1302-6 N '63

AMERICAN visitors in Mexico; in Russia; etc. See Foreign visitors in Mexico; Foreign visitors in Russia; etc.

AMERICAN walnut manufacturers association
World run on walnut. G. L'Allemand. il Am For 69:12-15+ Ag '63

AMERICAN water works association
Meeting, 1963. il Am City 78:123-4+ Jl '63
Quarterly report on improving your water service (cont) il Am City 78:151-4 Mr; 171-4 Je; 155-8 S; 139-42 D '63
Water-works men agree on needs, differ on methods. il Am City 79:120+ Jl '64
William D. Hurst; the generalist. Am City 78:150-1 My '63

AMERICAN way; drama. See Martens, A. C.

AMERICAN weekly
Vanishing American. il Newsweek 61:94 My 13 '63

AMERICAN wind symphony orchestra
It takes push to float a concert; orchestra on Ohio River barge. il Bsns W p30-1 Jl 11 '64

AMERICAN wines. See Wine

AMERICAN women. See Women—United States

AMERICAN writers. See Authors, American

AMERICAN youth hostels. See Youth hostels

AMERICAN Zionist council
Israel lobby. Newsweek 62:24 Ag 12 '63

AMERICANA (antiques) See Antiques

AMERICANISM
Hard kind of patriotism. A. E. Stevenson. Harper 227:31-4 Jl '63
National pharisaism. Nation 196:433 My 25 '63
See also
Patriotism

L'AMERICANO; story. See Murray, W.

AMERICANS
Ambiguous American; man of paradox. H. S. Commager. il N Y Times Mag p 16+ My 3 '64
America follows the middle of the road. A. Hacker. il N Y Times Mag p21+ My 5 '63
American character; address, December 5, 1963. J. W. Fulbright. Vital Speeches 30: 164-7 Ja 1 '64
American personality; excerpt from American aspects. D. W. Brogan. Sat R 48:34-5 Ja 2 '65
American resistance. E. Perényi. il Esquire 59:90-1+ Mr '63
Americans, by O. Handlin. Review
Newsweek 62:77 Ag 26 '63
Americans in my mind. V. S. Pritchett. il Holiday 34:28-41+ Jl '63
Are Americans human; Englishman's reflections. B. Leeming. il America 109:76-9 Jl 20 '63
Changing mood of America; what a nationwide survey shows. il U S News 55:36-45 Jl 29 '63
Coonskins and culture. Hobbies 67:49 F '63
Creed for a time of danger; excerpts from address. J. A. Farley. Read Digest 83:49-52 Jl '63
Deep analysis of the American mind. Lord Taylor. il N Y Times Mag p9+ F 23 '64
Diagnosing the American dream. M. W. Fishwick. il Sat R 46:8-11 D 21 '63
Fear or courage? the question that comes before politics. M. Mannes. Vogue 144:106-7 Ag 15 '64
Future that young people will face in America. il U S News 57:50-2+ Ag 17 '64
Have we learned our lessons? Kennedy's assassination. Christian Cent 80:1567-8 D 18 '63
How America lives. il Ladies Home J 80: 62-3+ Ja; 24+ Ap; 66-7+ Je; 147-51 Jl '63
How we live; symposium. il Look 28:13-28+ Ja 14 '64
Kind word for drink; American drinking habits. J. D. Brown. il Sat Eve Post 236: 64-6 My 25 '63
Mood now: urgent concern. il Bsns W p28-30 S 7 '63
Mood of America in election year; what a national survey shows. il U S News 56:68-73 Mr 30 '64
Mood of the land. il Time 82:9-10 D 20 '63
New breed of cat. J. Cogley. Commonweal 77:609-11 Mr 8 '63
1964: a chance to look at ourselves. M. Ways. il Fortune 70:102-5+ O '64
Opinion, please; from Boston. L. Kronenberger. Mlle 58:16-17+ Ja '64
Quietmouth American. D. Lloyd. Harper 227: 101-2+ S '63
Restless temper. G. W. Pierson. bibliog f Am Hist R 69:969-89 Jl '64
Speaking out; our way of life makes us miserable. E. Fromm. Sat Eve Post 237:8+ Jl 25 '64
Speaking out; stay home and don't vote. J. Keats. Sat Eve Post 236:8+ O 26 '63
U.S.A. revisited. J. Dos Passos. Atlan 213: 47-54 Ap '64
U.S, then and now; statistical portrait. A. Austin. il N Y Times Mag p54+ My 3 '64
Way people live today. il U S News 55:56-61 N 11 '63
Welcome, we need you; to the class of '64. A. Gordon. Read Digest 84:167-8 Je '64
What are Americans like? European school childrens observations. J. Robbins. il Redbook 122:56-7+ D '63
What kind of nation are we? American character. A. Hacker. il N Y Times Mag p23+ D 8 '63
What's right with America; as observers abroad see it. il U S News 57:44-50 S 14 '64

AMERICANS—*Continued*
Who'll take the hi-road? C. Fadiman. Read Digest 82:78-80 Ap '63
See also
New Englanders
Texans
United States
Westerners

Quotations, maxims, etc.

Just average; comp. by H. Helfer. il N Y Times Mag p46 O 18 '64

AMERICANS abroad. See Americans in foreign countries

AMERICANS for community co-operation in other nations. See Volunteer service, International

AMERICANS for constitutional action
How can you rate your congressman? D. G. M. Coxe. Nat R 14:525-8 Jl 2 '63
Right to be wrong; address, Novmber 22, 1963. B. Moreell. Vital Speeches 30:158-60 D 15 '63

AMERICANS for democratic action
Coming ADA government? J. Burnham. Nat R 16:954-9 N 3 '64
Does ADA run the New frontier? J. Burnham. il Nat R 14:355-62 My 7 '63
First ADA president? Nat R 16:801 S 22 '64
GOP renovation of Americans for democratic action. il Newsweek 64:30 S 28 '64
How can you rate your congressman? D. G. M. Coxe. Nat R 14:525-8 Jl 2 '63

AMERICANS in Africa
Our far-flung correspondents; visit of American Negro to Conakry, Guinea. H. Fuller. New Yorker 39:35-6+ Ja 4 '64

AMERICANS in Bolivia
Assistance offered to Bolivia in effort to free U.S. officials; White House statement, December 8, 1963. Dept State Bul 49:998 D 30 '63
Captives in the hills. il Time 82:26-7 D 20 '63
Four American hostages released by Bolivian miners; Department statement, December 16, 1963. Dept State Bul 50:9 Ja 6 '64
Free at last; American hostages. il Time 82:29 D 27 '63
Hostages of a mob of miners; with report by M. Acoca. il Life 56:62-6 Ja 3 '64
Walking out; release of hostages. Newsweek 62:31 D 30 '63

AMERICANS in Cuba
I was Castro's prisoner; ed. by B. Lindeman. G. Shamma. il Sat Eve Post 236:78-81 My 18 '63

AMERICANS in England
Basketball and beefeaters. J. McPhee. New Yorker 39:186-90+ Mr 16 '63
Busy life of the ambassador's wife. il Look 27:54-6+ Ag 13 '63
Freeze; personal view of Britain's coldest winter. N. Mostert. Reporter 28:39-40 Mr 14 '63
Great idea town; New York herald tribune columnist in London. il Newsweek 62:96 N 4 '63
Invitation: to young American librarians to work for a few years in British libraries. R. Stokes. Library J 88:4168 N 1 '63

AMERICANS in Europe
New faces in the expatriate colony. E. Gilbert. il N Y Times Mag p30+ D 8 '63

AMERICANS in Finland
Ambassador; American ambassador to Finland. New Yorker 39:45-6 D 7 '63

AMERICANS in foreign countries
Airborne V.I.P.s swarm; advice for church travelers from some of their hosts; reprint. Christian Cent 81:727-8 Je 3 '64
Ambassador's wife is an ambassador, too. P. Durdin. il N Y Times Mag p21+ O 4 '64
American librarians abroad. M. M. Jackson. Wilson Lib Bul 39:51+ S '64
Government jobs overseas. il Changing T 18:34-5 Ja '64
Pioneers of 1963; address, February 11, 1963. H. C. Jacobs. Vital Speeches 29:347-9 Mr 15 '63
Ugly American revisited. E. Burdick and W. Lederer. il Sat Eve Post 236:78-81 My 4 '63
Young Americans abroad, ed. by R. H. Klein. Review
Commonweal 79:440-1 Ja 10 '64. C. Robins
See also
American students in foreign countries
American teachers in foreign countries
United States—Armed forces—Forces in foreign countries

AMERICANS in France
Americans in Paris. il Newsweek 63:60 Ja 6 '64
Importance of being Malin. T. Foote. Esquire 60:109 O '63
Negroes in Paris. il Newsweek 64:54 S 21 '64
That summer in Paris, by M. Callaghan. Review
New Repub 148:26-8 F 9 '63. W. Saroyan
Time il 81:106 Mr 15 '63

AMERICANS in Gabon
Mrs Ambassador; interview, ed. by A. M. Lingg. A. B. Darlington. il Opera N 28:6 D 14 '63

AMERICANS in Germany
See also
United States—Armed forces—Forces in Europe

AMERICANS in India
I believe. J. Fritsche. Seventeen 22:67 Mr '63

AMERICANS in Israel
Jerusalem, my home. B. S. Vester. il Nat Geog Mag 126:826-47 D '64

AMERICANS in Japan
Letter from Sendagaya. J. M. Flagler. il New Yorker 40:58+ Jl 25; 86+ Ag 15 '64
Meeting with the West; first American residents pictured by Japanese artists. C. H. Boehringer. il Am Heritage 14:16-31 Ag '63
U.S. executive in Japan. il Bsns W p 142-4+ Je 13 '64
Yankee Barbarian at the Shogun's court. E. Hahn. il Am Heritage 15:60-3+ Je '64

AMERICANS in Latin America
Volunteers for progress; Peace corps in Latin America. N. A. Haverstock. il Américas 15:2-10 Jl '63

AMERICANS in Mexico
American in a Mexican death cell; Dykes Askew Simmons, jr. J. R. Phelan. il Sat Eve Post 236:81-5 S 21 '63
Hush-hush resort. W. W. Johnson. il Sat Eve Post 236:24-7 F 16 '63

AMERICANS in Morocco
Tangier: footnotes to a survey of the American socio-intellectual enclave; colored photographs by R. Fréson. W. Burroughs. il Esquire 62:114-19 S '64

AMERICANS in Nigeria
Doers, not do-gooders, the Peace corps in Nigeria. H. L. Callaway. il Mile 57:126-9+ Je '63

AMERICANS in Panama
Children who caused a crisis. J. Robbins. il Redbook 123:50-1+ Ag '64
Panama: the third force. Nation 198:225-6 Mr 9 '64

AMERICANS in Paris. See Americans in France

AMERICANS in Russia
Sasha's creed: Russia right or wrong. G. Feifer. il N Y Times Mag p9+ Ap 28 '63

AMERICANS in Saigon. See Americans in Viet Nam

AMERICANS in Spain
Why Spain is home. R. Ruark. il Sat Eve Post 237:28-33 Ap 4 '64

AMERICANS in Sweden
Sweden helps U.S. unemployed; fifty jobless auto workers to be sent to Scania-Vabis. Bsns W p50 Ap 4 '64

AMERICANS in Tahiti
Stop, august friend, and read carefully: letter to Richard Joseph. H. H. Kelley. il Esquire 62:66-7 Ag '64

AMERICANS in the Far East
This way to the great Pacific-Orient getaway. R. Joseph. il Esquire 62:68-78 Ag '64

AMERICANS in the Korean war. See Korean war, 1950-1953—American participation

AMERICANS in the Middle East
Middle East squiggle; J. Ferren, America's first artist-in-residence abroad. il Newsweek 63:56 Ap 13 '64

AMERICANS in the Philippines
Reporter at large; Peace corps in the Philippines. R. Shaplen. New Yorker 39:50-2+ S 28 '63

AMERICANS in Venezuela
Jungle captive. J. Liedloff and R. Massie. il Sat Eve Post 236:85-9 Ag 10 '63

AMERICANS in Viet Nam
Letter from Saigon. Nation 197:205-7 O 5 '63
Now it's a war against Americans in Vietnam il U S News 56:35 Mr 2 '64
Ordinary life of Americans in Saigon. P. Grose. il N Y Times Mag p26-7+ S 27 '64
Target: Americans. il Time 83:26 F 28 '64
Terror in Saigon: target, Americans. il Newsweek 63:31 Mr 2 '64

AMERICAS. See America

AMERICA'S cup race. See Yacht racing

AMERICAS essay contest. See Essays—Competitions

AMERICUS, Ga.
Americus rejects Americanism. Christian Cent 80:1261 O 16 '63

AMERINE, Maynard A.
Do you know the uniquely American wine Zinfandel? House B 105:236-7+ N '63
Wine; with biographical sketch. Sci Am 211: 10, 46-56 bibliog(p 116) Ag '64
AMERINGER, Charles D.
Panama Canal lobby of Philippe Bunau-Varilla and William Nelson Cromwell. Am Hist R 68:346-63 Ja '63
AMERY, Julian
Amery refuses to quit under labor fire. H. J. Coleman. Aviation W 81:25-6 Ag 10 '64
AMES, Amyas
Basic principle of the free world; address, November 29, 1962. Vital Speeches 29: 248-50 F 1 '63
AMES, B. Charles
Payoff from product management. Harvard Bsns R 41:141-52 N '63
AMES, Francis H.
Deer in the dunes. Outdoor Life 134:48-9+ Ag '64
Hog-wild chinooks. Outdoor Life 132:50-2+ D '63
Strong-arm steelheads. Outdoor Life 135:34-5+ Ja '65
Tall tule bass. Outdoor Life 133:40-1+ Ja '64
AMES, Louise Bates, and Ilg, F. L.
Twenty questions about children's eating. Am Home 67:32+ S '64
—See Ilg, F. L. jt. auth.
AMES, Nancy
That was the deb that was. il pors Life 56: 83-4+ Je 26 '64
AMES, Ia.
Everybody gets into the act; insect-control program. R. W. Mohri. il Am City 78:106-7 My '63
How we reduced electric rates. W. Schlagel. il Am City 78:136+ N '63
AMES research center. See United States—National aeronautics and space administration—Ames research center
AMESTOY, Joseph L.
Architectural *aggiornamento*. Cath World 199: 279-85 Ag '64
AMETHYSTS
Amethyst: optical properties and paramagnetic resonance. T. I. Barry and W. J. Moore. il Science 144:289-90 Ap 17 '64
AMEX. See American express company; American stock exchange
AMHERST college. Amherst, Mass.
Frost's personal library goes to NYU, not to library named in his honor. Library J 89: 594 F 1 '64
Kennedy speaks at Frost library dedication; summary of address, October 26, 1963. J. F. Kennedy. il Wilson Lib Bul 38:317 D '63
AMIDES
See also
Potassium amide
AMIDINES
Radioprotection by pressor amidines. W. E. Rothe and others. il Science 141:160 Jl 12 '63
AMIDON school. See Washington, D.C.—Education
AMIET, Pierre
Great Luristan mystery. Art N 62:24-6+ Ap '63
AMINES
See also
Phenethylamine
AMINO acid acylases
Aminoacyl position in aminoacyl sRNA. C. S. McLaughlin and V. M. Ingram. bibliog il Science 145:942-3 Ag 28 '64
AMINO acids
Amino acid code in alcaligenes faecalis. J. J. Protass and others. il Science 143:1174-6 Mr 13 '64
Amino acid composition of hemerythrin in relation to subunit structure. W. R. Groskopf and others. bibliog il Science 141:166-7 Jl 12 '63
Amino acid composition of univalent fragments of rabbit antibody. W. J. Mandy and others. bibliog il Science 140:901-3 My 24 '63
Amino acids in the proteins from aragonite and calcite in the shells of mytilus californianus. P. E. Hare. bibliog il Science 139:216-17 Ja 18 '63
Amino acids: incorporation into α-and β-chains of hemoglobin by normal and thalassemic reticulocytes. J. D. Heywood and others. bibliog il Science 146:530-1 O 23 '64
2-Aminoethylphosphonic acid in insoluble protein of the sea anemone metridium dianthus. L. D. Quin. bibliog il Science 144:1133-4 My 29 '64
Coding ambiguity in cell-free extracts of chlamydomonas. R. Sager and others. bibliog il Science 140:304-6 Ap 19 '63
Diet that might wipe out malnutrition. il Time 82:62 N 22 '63
Differences in the amino acid composition of a third rabbit antibody. M. E. Koshland and others. bibliog il Science 143:1330-1 Mr 20 '64
Endogenous metabolic factor in schizophrenic behavior. H. H. Berlet and others. bibliog il Science 144:311-13 Ap 17 '64
Fluoroacetate inhibition of amino acids during photosynthesis of chlamydomonas reinhardti. J. R. Kates and R. F. Jones. bibliog il Science 143:145-6 Ja 10 '64
Gamma irradiation of polypeptides: transformation of amino acids. F. Friedberg and G. A. Hayden. bibliog il Science 140:825-6 My 17 '63
Guanine: formation during the thermal polymerization of amino acids. C. Ponnamperuma and others. bibliog il Science 143: 1449-50 Mr 27 '64
Homocitrulline and homoarginine synthesis from lysine. W. L. Ryan and I. C. Wells. bibliog il Science 144:1122+ My 29 '64
Hypotheses confirmed. Sci Am 210:54-6 Mr '64
Life from a lava bed? Sci Am 210:64 Ap '64
Molecular model for protein synthesis. G. Zubay. bibliog il Science 140:1092-5 Je 7 '63
On biochemical variability and innovation; text of paper presented at a symposium on the general physiology of specialized cells. S. S. Cohen. bibliog il Science 139: 1017-26 Mr 15 '63
Protein structure relationships revealed by mutational analysis. C. Yanofsky and others. bibliog il Science 146:1593-4 D 18 '64
Rationale for a universal genetic code. R. T. Hinegardner and J. Engelberg. il Science 142:1083-5 N 22 '63
Reticulocyte protein synthesis: response of ribosome fractions to polyuridylic acid. I. B. Weinstein and others. bibliog il Science 140:314-16 Ap 19 '63
Steric factors in the chemistry of polypeptides, poly-α-amino acids and proteins. R. E. Whitfield. bibliog il Science 142:577-9 N 1 '63
See also
Phenylalanine
Tryptophan
Valine
AMINOACYL. See Amino acid acylases
AMINOHYDROXYBUTYRIC acid
Succinic ester and amide of homoserine: some spontaneous and enzymatic reactions. M. Flavin and others. bibliog il Science 143: 50-2 Ja 3 '64
AMINOPURINE. See Adenine
AMINOURACIL. See Uracil
AMIS, Kingsley
All the blood within me; story. Sat Eve Post 236:40-4 Ap 6 '63
Amis in London. por Newsweek 63:87 Mr 2 '64
AMISH Mennonites. See Mennonites
AMMETERS
Clip-on D.C. current probe. A. Bergh and others. il Electr World 72:41-3+ S '64
AMMONIA
Ammonia for speedy preservation of fish. Sci N L 84:265 O 26 '63
Ammonia: possible use for preserving fish. V. Subrahmanyan and others. bibliog il Science 142:233-4 O 11 '63
Ammonia rediscovered. il Changing T 18:47 Jl '64
Reversibility of reaction of potassium with liquid ammonia. E. J. Kirschke and W. L. Jolly. bibliog il Science 147:45-6 Ja 1 '65
AMMONIA in the body
Psychological changes associated with induced hyperammonemia. M. Eichler. bibliog il Science 144:886-8 My 15 '64
AMMONIUM compounds
Phase composition of commercial ammonium carbonate. C. B. Sclar and L. C. Carrison. bibliog il Science 140:1205-7 Je 14 '63
AMMONIUM nitrate
Smoke that calms bees shortens their lives. Sci N L 85:137 F 29 '64
Top-dressing pays on wheatgrass. Suc Farm 61:70C S '63
AMMONS, A. R.
Expressions of sea level; Catalyst; poems. Poetry 102:169-73 Je '63
Ginsberg's new poems. Poetry 104:186-7 Je '64
Note on prosody. Poetry 102:202-3 Je '63
Portrait; poem. Nation 199:310 N 2 '64
Street song; Connection; Dark song; World; poems. Poetry 104:352-4 S '64
about
Antennae to knowledge. W. Berry. Nation 198:304-6 Mr 23 '64
Five poets. J. Jacobsen. Poetry 105:205-6 D '64

AMMUNITION
See also
Cartridges
AMNESIA
Electroconvulsive shock, retroactive amnesia, and the single-shock method. D. J. Leonard and A. Zavala. bibliog il Science 146:1073-4 N 20 '64
Retrograde amnesia from conditioned competing responses; electroconvulsive shock. D. J. Lewis and H. E. Adams. Science 141: 516-17 Ag 9 '63; Reply. C. J. Dye. bibliog 143:973 F 28 '64
Strange case of Lee Lawrence. T. Congdon. il Sat Eve Post 236:85-9 Ap 20 '63
AMNESTY
See also
Political prisoners
AMNESTY international (organization)
Rescuing the forgotten prisoners. I. Ross. Sat R 48:17-18+ Ja 16 '65
AMOEBA. See Ameba
AMOORE, John E. and others
Stereochemical theory of odor; with biographical sketches. Sci Am 210:28, 42-9 bibliog(p 152) F '64
AMOR, Inéz
Dealer's view; tr. by E. Flint. Atlan 213:129-31 Mr '64
AMORE dei tre re; opera. See Montemezzi, I.
AMOROSE, Joseph D.
Interference stopper for AM sets. Electr World 69:73 Je '63
AMOROSO LIMA, Alceu
Catholicism in Brazil. America 110:766-7 My 30 '64
AMOROUS flea; musical comedy. See Musical comedies, revues, etc.—Criticisms, plots, etc.
AMORTIZATION deductions
Cut machinery tax costs. F. Bailey, jr. il Suc Farm 62:70 Ja '64
How city men cut taxes by farming. C. E. Ball. Farm J 87:26 O '63
How to save taxes when you trade machinery. Farm J 88:46F O '64
Tax changes replenish the till. il Bsns W p64 F 9 '63
Tax credit gets to work at last. Bsns W p60+ Ja 19 '63
Tax management tips for machinery and equipment. J. D. Keast. Farm J 87:50B D '63
AMORY, Cleveland
Bostonian unique; Miss Sears. Vogue 141:80-3 F 15 '63
Celebrity register. McCalls 90:132, 146, 188 Mr; 122, 152, 168 Je; 144 Jl; 158 Ag; 91: 188 O '63; 62 F; 166 Mr '64
First of the month. See issues of Saturday review
God, Nell, ain't it grand? excerpts from American heritage cookbook. Horizon 6:14-15 Sum '64
Jamaica's Old Boy with the new ideas. Sat R 47:56-8 O 10 '64
Millionaire as president. Vogue 144:96-7+ Ag 1 '64
Mrs Payson's ball park. Vogue 144:144-5+ S 15 '64
100 tons of bronze, son. por Yachting 116: 60-1+ S '64
Phenomenon of My fair lady. Vogue 144:152-5+ N 1 '64
Philip Johnson. Vogue 143:184-92+ My '64
Speaking out. por Sat Eve Post 236:10+ Ap 6; 10+ Jl 27 '63
Sunset Boulevardier. Esquire 62:116-17+ O '64
Who's afraid of Elsie De Wolfe? Vogue 141: 116-23+ Je '63
AMOS W. Shepard house. See Architecture, Colonial
AMOURY, Gloria
Background as plus-value. Writer 76:19-20+ S '63
AMPEX corporation
Electron beam readout shows potential. B. Miller. il Aviation W 80:107-10 Ap 13 '64
AMPHETAMINES
Eserine and amphetamine: interactive effects on sleeping time in mice. C. D. Barnes and F. H. Meyers. bibliog il Science 144:1221-2 Je 5 '64
Growing menace of nice drugs. J. Phipps and R. Robinson. il Good H 157:70-1+ S '63; Same abr. with title Sleeping pills and pep pills; handle with extreme caution. Read Digest 83:103-7 N '63
Pep pills believed to impair judgment. Sci N L 86:153 S 5 '64
Your guide to mind drugs. R. Mines. il Sci Digest 55:69-70 Ja '64
AMPHIBIA
See also
Color of amphibia
Salamanders

Development

Chemistry of amphibian metamorphosis. E. Frieden. il Sci Am 209:110-18 bibliog(p 187) N '63
Hemoglobin: molecular changes during anuran metamorphosis. C. D. Trader and others. bibliog il Science 139:918-19 Mr 8 '63
Metamorphosis-activating system of the frog. W. Etkin. bibliog il Science 139:810-14 Mr 1 '63
AMPHIBIOUS airplanes. See Airplanes, Amphibious
AMPHIBIOUS automobiles. See Automobiles, Amphibious
AMPHIBIOUS helicopters. See Helicopters, Amphibious
AMPHICAR. See Automobiles, Amphibious
AMPHISBAENIDAE. See Lizards
AMPHITHEATERS
Theater in the garden; Greenfield gardens, Wilmington, N.C. L. Lamica. il Recreation 56:474-5 D '63
AMPLIFIERS
Amplifier power: how much is enough? A. Sterling. il Hi Fi 13:54-7+ N '63
Amplifier quiz. R. P. Balin. il Pop Electr 20: 63+ F; 64+ Mr '64
Amplifiers that run on liquid diet. il Bsns W p 130+ N 7 '64
Assemble a phone-boost. L. Garner. il Pop Electr 19:55-6+ N '63
Audio-compression preamplifier. J. C. Wright. il Electr World 72:32-3+ N '64
Bargain page amplifier. D. Meyer. il Pop Electr 21:69-72 O '64
Boost box. A. Trauffer. il Pop Electr 18:58-9 My '63
Constant-voltage sound-distribution systems. A. B. Cohen. il Electr World 70:29-32 Jl '63
Design of a high-quality transistor power amplifier. R. E. Furst. il Electr World 71: 34-5+ F '64
Distortion; the eternal enigma. A. Sterling. il Hi Fi 14:50-3+ S '64
Distributed-amplifier techniques. S. L. Silver. il Electr World 73:38-40 Ja '65
Double CB talk power; compression amplifier. W. H. Minor. il Pop Electr 20:54-7 Ap '64
Easily built FM-TV booster. L. E. Garner, jr. il Pop Electr 21:41-4 N '64
Extreme reliability vacuum tubes; use in submarine cable system. il Electr World 73:41 Ja '65
Fluid control devices; fluid amplifiers. S. W. Angrist. il Sci Am 211:80-8 D '64
14-watt transistor hi-fi amplifier. D. F. Rehberger. il Electr World 69:46-7+ My '63
Hi-fi shutoff; time-delay switch. R. Wilensky. il Pop Electr 18:50-1+ Je '63
High fidelity. H. Fantel. Opera N 28:35 F 8; 36 Mr 7 '64
High fidelity equipment reports. il Hi Fi 13:69-73 S '63
High-gain low-hum module. H. Reed. il Pop Electr 18:54 My '63
Integrated amplifier-speaker. K. Gilmore. il Electr World 71:32-5+ Mr '64
Loudness control. R. A. Jacobs, jr. il Electr World 70:34-5+ D '63
Loudspeakers for transistor amplifiers. V. Brociner. il Electr World 71:42-4+ Ja '64
Mid-frequency amplifier-gain nomogram. K. W. James. il Electr World 71:31+ Je '64
More switched outlets for hi-fi. R. L. Conhaim. il Pop Electr 19:67 O '63
New high-quality transistor amplifier. F. L. Mergner. il Electr World 71:42-5+ My '64
New transistor stereo amp kit. C. P. Gilmore. il Pop Sci 182:174 F '63
9-watt transistorized hi-fi amplifier. S. E. Bammel. il Electr World 69:46-7+ Mr '63
Noise performance of transistors in audio circuits. W. A. Rheinfelder. il Electr World 73:31-3 Ja '65
Operational amplifier. J. E. Frecker. il Electr World 70:52-4+ Jl; 48-9+ Ag '63
Pros and cons of wideband response. N. Eisenberg. il Hi Fi 14:39-42+ My '64
Punch for portables; add-on amplifier and speaker. A. Kennedy. il Pop Mech 121:196-8 Ja '64
R.F. pickup in audio amplifiers. il Electr World 72:65 Jl '64
Self-protecting transistor hi-fi amplifier. N. Kramer and R. Japenga. il Electr World 71:32-3+ Je '64

AMPLIFIERS—*Continued*
Simple hum-bucking circuit. G. R. Gilbert. il Electr World 70:77 Ag '63
Simplified audio impedance matching. J. E. Pugh, jr. il Electr World 69:50-1+ Ap '63
6 meter 7 and 2 preamp. J. Tartas. il Pop Electr 21:53-4 Ag '64
Sound ideas. L. Zide. il Am Rec G 31:465-6 Ja '65
Sound ideas. M. Rotbard. il Am Rec G 30: 1130-1 Ag '64
Tape-deck preamp. D. M. Wherry. il Electr World 69:90-1 F '63
This homemade, battery-powered loud hailer talks big. R. Benrey. il Pop Sci 184:134-8 Ap '64
Transistor Williamson stereo power amplifier. K. H. Sueker. il Electr World 72: 42-6 O '64
Transistors for hi-fi, panacea or pandemonium? D. R. Von Recklinghausen and others. il Electr World 70:37-40+ S; 38-40+ O '63
Transistors for hi-fi: promise of progress. M. R. Myers, jr and M. D. Kahn. il Electr World 71:42-3+ Ap '64
Transistors for music; hi-fi amplifiers. R. E. Furst and L. Zide. il Electr World 71:48-50 Mr '64
Transistors vs tubes for hi-fi. E. S. Miller and others. il Electr World 70:48-9 N '63
Transistors vs tubes for hi-fi. F. L. Mergner. Electr World 71:45+ Ja '64
Transistors vs tubes for hi-fi. R. S. Burwen. Electr World 70:85 D '63
Transistors vs tubes for hi-fi. W. W. Chou. Electr World 71:36+ F '64
Utiliamp, an all-purpose audio amplifier. E. G. Louis. il Pop Electr 21:68 D '64
Variable electronic gain control. J. P. Shields. il Electr World 70:101 O '63
See also
Light amplifiers
Masers
Transistors
Traveling wave tubes
Tunnel diodes

Testing

Audio output power meter. K. Berry. il Electr World 70:48-9 O '63
Resistive load for hi-fi test. W. Temcor. il Pop Electr 19:54-5 S '63
Transistorized audio sweep generator. R. H. Douglas. il Electr World 72:71-4 Ag '64

AMPUTEES
Legless Frank Ellis can walk, run, climb and swim: he fights for a chance to fly. D. Martin. il Life 55:55-6+ O 25 '63

AMRINE, Michael
Scientists and Jesuits, gypsies and Jews; letter. Science 142:913 N 15 '63

AMSTER, L. J.
Center of gravity; story. Sat Eve Post 237: 52-3 Mr 14 '64

AMSTERDAM, Netherlands

Airports

Amsterdam airport modernization scheduled for completion in 1967: Schiphol. il Aviation W 78:47 Mr 18 '63

Description

Cruising Amsterdam's canals. il Sunset 130: 56+ Ap '63
Film flows freely on old canals. L. Barry. il Pop Phot 53:28+ O '63

Music

Notes from our correspondents (cont of) Notes from abroad. J. de Kruijff. Hi Fi 13: 34 Mr '63; 14:26 S; 16+ D '64
Wagner in Amsterdam. J. Mindszenthy. il Opera N 28:33 D 28 '63

AMSTERDAM, N.Y.
℞ for a sick bridge. A. Lichtenstein. il Am City 79:104-6 S '64

AMSTERDAM concertgebouw orchestra
Musical events; concert at Carnegie Hall. W. Sargeant. New Yorker 40:148 My 9 '64

AMSTUTZ, David E. and Neshyba, Steve
Location of an aircraft impact from gravity waves. Science 145:921-3 Ag 28 '64

AMUNDSON, Robert H.
No more second-class citizens. America 110: 847-8 Je 20 '64

AMUSEMENT parks
Mammon and monuments: Freedomland, USA; excerpts from Independent historical societies. W. M. Whitehill. il Am Heritage 14:110-11 Ag '63
Taking them for a ride. il Time 82:56-7 Jl 5 '63
See also
Disneyland park, Anaheim, Calif.

AMUSEMENT tax
Beauty and the tax collector. Sports Illus 18:8 Ap 22 '63

AMUSEMENTS
Amusements; exhibition at New York city's Museum of contemporary crafts; with editorial comment. P. Smith. il Craft Horiz 24:8-19 N '64
Season's reasons. L. Lerman. il Mlle 58:128-31 N '63
See also
Games
Hobbies
Play
Recreation

AMVETS. See American veterans of World war II

AMY Loveman national award
Amy Loveman award 1963. H. Bowser. il Sat R 46:22 Je 8 '63
Bookstores and blizzards; 1964 Amy Loveman award. J. F. Fixx. il Sat R 47:27 Je 13 '64

AMY; story. See Heinemann, A.

AMYGDALA. See Cerebellum

AMYLASE
Chromatographic heterogeneity of rabbit serum amylase. J. E. Berk and others. bibliog il Science 141:1182-3 S 20 '63

AMYOTROPIC lateral sclerosis. See Sclerosis

ANABIOSIS
Old lizards never die. Newsweek 61:43 Mr 11 '63

ANABLE, Anthony
Yacht club's year. Yachting 114:46-9+ D '63

ANACAPA ISLAND, Calif. See Santa Barbara Islands, Calif.

ANAEMIA. See Anemia

ANAEROBIC bacteria. See Bacteria, Anaerobic

ANAGRAMS
Enthusiasts; League of anagram enthusiasts. New Yorker 39:31-2 Mr 23 '63

ANAHEIM, Calif.
See also
Disneyland park

ANALGESICS
What to take for pain. B. H. Frisch. il Sci Digest 54:22-6 D '63

ANALOG computers. See Calculating machines —Analog computers

ANALYSIS (philosophy)
Linguistic analysis: a way for some to affirm their faith. Time 84:64 Jl 10 '64

ANALYSIS, Linguistic. See Analysis (philosophy)

ANALYSIS of soils. See Soils—Analysis

ANALYTICAL chemistry. See Chemistry, Analytic

ANANGULA. See Aleutian Islands—Antiquities

ANAPHYLAXIS
Histamine: differences in amount available for release in lungs of guinea pigs susceptible and resistant to acute anaphylaxis. S. H. Stone and others. bibliog il Science 146:1061-2 N 20 '64
Passive cutaneous anaphylaxis with antibody fragments. Z. Ovary and A. Taranta. bibliog il Science 140:193-5 Ap 12 '63

ANARCHISM and anarchists
Anarchists; excerpts. B. W. Tuchman. il Atlan 211:91-2+ My '63

ANASTASIA, grand duchess of Russia
Case of a new Anastasia; E. Smith. il pors Life 55:104A-112 O 18 '63

ANATI, Emmanuel
Rulers in the East. Natur Hist 72:18-27 Ag '63

ANATOLIA. See Asia Minor

ANATOMY
See also
Cadavers
Ear
Pelvis
Skeleton

Study and teaching

First encounter. il Newsweek 62:83 S 30 '63
Reappraisal of anatomical study. N. C. Hale. il Am Artist 29:48-53+ F '65

ANCESTRY. See Genealogy

ANCHEL, H. See Heron, W. jt. auth.

ANCHEL, Marjorie. See Takeshita, H. jt. auth.

ANCHOR Bible. See Bible—Versions

ANCHORAGE, Alaska
Alaska aviation reacts rapidly to quake. R. G. O'Lone. il Aviation W 80:25-6 Ap 6 '64
Anchorage fights back. L. L. Woodman. il Am City 79:118-20 S; 119-21 O '64
Earthquake! W. P. E. Graves. il Nat Geog Mag 126:112-39 Jl '64
Five utilities on one bill. J. P. Bell. il Am City 78:91-2 D '63

ANCHORAGE, Alaska—*Continued*
Hell on Good Friday; Alaskan quake. il Newsweek 63:19 Ap 6 '64
Largest sewer photo inspection. C. E. Cannon. il Am City 80:98-9 Ja '65
Seven severe sickening minutes. L. L. Woodman. il Am City 79:98-9+ My '64
Summer of surprises; playground program. L. S. Wulf. il Recreation 57:168-71 Ap '64

Hospitals

Alaska designs for a complex community. il Arch Rec 134:174-7 N '63
ANCHORAGE international airport. See Airports—Alaska
ANCHORING. See Boats—Mooring
ANCHORS
ABCs of anchoring. G. P. Manning. il Pop Mech 119:142-6 My '63
Anchoring tips. W. Britton. il Motor B 112: 132 Jl; 111 Ag; 125 S; 115 O '63; 113:256 Ja '64
Anchors and anchoring: basic principles. W. Britton. il Motor B 111:48-9+ My '63
Development of the anchor and rudder. il Nat Geog Mag 123:523 Ap '63
Drift sock. D. Mathesius. il Pop Mech 119: 146 Je '63
Electronic anchors. J. Joseph. il Pop Mech 121:141 Ja '64
No-snag anchor for your boat. M. Banister. il Pop Mech 121:155 Mr '64
Steady anchoring in two miles of water; freefall anchor system. il Pop Sci 184:92-3 Mr '64
Three thousand bucks and a brick. R. P. Kingett. il Motor B 11:46-7+ My '63
ANCHOVIES
See also
Cookery—Fish
ANCIENT Arabic order of the nobles of the mystic shrine. See Freemasonry
ANCIENT art. See Art, Ancient
ANCIENT civilization. See Civilization, Ancient
ANCIENT glassware. See Glassware, Ancient
AND baby makes three; story. See Frank, H. jr
ANDA, Geza
Music to my ears; recital in Philharmonic hall. I. Kolodin. Sat R 47:52 N 14 '64
Notes from our correspondents. S. Fleming. il por Hi Fi 15:22+ Ja '65
ANDARIESE, Walter S.
Binary numbers & Boolean algebra. Electr World 69:72-3 Mr '63
ANDEAN art. See Art, Pre-Columbian
ANDEAN Indians. See Indians of South America
ANDERBERG, Bengt
Limits of tolerance. Newsweek 63:30 Ja 13 '64
ANDERS, Edward, and others
Contaminated meteorite. bibliog Science 146: 1157-61 N 27 '64
—See Fitch, F. W. jt. auth.
ANDERS, Lon
Be my host. Harper 227:43-6 N '63
ANDERSEN, Christian A.
Silicon oxynitride: a meteoritic mineral. bibliog Science 146:256-7 O 9 '64
ANDERSEN, Elmer L.
Long recount. por Newsweek 61:27-8 Mr 11 '63
ANDERSEN, Hans Christian
Especially for Christmas. Am Rec G 31:373 D '64
To travel is to live. M. Gough. il House B 106:144+ My '64
ANDERSEN, Niels J.
Proposition fourteen and the liturgy. America 111:658+ N 21 '64
ANDERSEN, Stig Bryde, and Bierring, Franz
Lymphoid organs and normal gamma-globulin in the rat. bibliog Science 144:1219-20 Je 5 '64
ANDERSON, Arnold N.
Water-spray humidifier for a warm-air furnace. Pop Sci 186:156-7 Ja '65
ANDERSON, Arthur B.
Act of folly. Pub W 184:20-1 Jl 22 '63
ANDERSON, Augustus E. jr, and others
Emphysema in lung macrosections correlated with smoking habits. bibliog Science 144: 1025-6 My 22 '64
ANDERSON, Bill
Tragedy on the lake; Cleveland yachting club races. Sports Illus 19:5 Ag 26 '63
ANDERSON, Charles
Grandfather to half a million kids. R. C. Davids. il por Farm J 88:28-9+ Jl '64
ANDERSON, Charles B.
Paperbacks in Larchmont. Pub W 185:86-7 Ap 27 '64
Rental library: a report. Pub W 183:146-7 Je 10 '63
ANDERSON, Charles R.
Robert Frost, 1874-1963. Sat R 46:16-20 F 23 '63
ANDERSON, Clifton
Hammarskjold: the last haiku. New Repub 151:23-4 N 14 '64
ANDERSON, Clinton Presba
Case for a landing by 1970; excerpts from address, May 27, 1963. por U S News 54:91 Je 10 '63
Excerpt from address, February 21, 1963. Cong Digest 42:202+ Ag '63
Scientific advice for Congress; excerpts from address, November 20, 1963. Science 144: 29-32 Ap 3 '64
This we hold dear. pors Am For 69:24-5 Jl '63
Why we need the Land and water conservation fund bill. por Am For 70:24-7+ Mr '64

about

Congress: Senator Anderson brings activist record, some definite views, to space committee helm. J. Walsh. por Science 139: 1036-8 Mr 15 '63
Senator Anderson honored; National conservation award. il pors Liv Wildn 83:25-8 Spring '63
ANDERSON, Curtiss
World we want. Ladies Home J 80:49 Ja '63
ANDERSON, Dave
Final whistle. Sat Eve Post 236:34-5 Mr 16 '63
Hockey. Sports Illus 22:50-1 Ja 18 '65
Howie Young: hockey's abominable iceman. Sat Eve Post 237:30-1 F 22 '64
(ed) See Garagiola, J. They led the league in gags
(ed) See Garagiola, J. Yogi of the Yankees
—and Hewlett, R. S.
Officiating mess in the National hockey league. Sports Illus 18:26-8+ Ap 8 '63
ANDERSON, Don N.
Making history on the playgrounds; reprint. Recreation 57:172-4 Ap '64
ANDERSON, Donald Jack
Up the little finger. Field & S 69:24-6+ Ja '65
Wisdom of whitetails. Field & S 69:62-4+ O '64
ANDERSON, Donald Louis
Time is now. Commonweal 79:347-8 D 13 '63
ANDERSON, Duwayne M. and others
Volume changes of a thixotropic, sodium bentonite suspension during sol-gel-sol transition. bibliog Science 141:1040-1 S 13 '63
ANDERSON, Eddie
Advice from the doctor. il por Newsweek 64: 86 D 7 '64
ANDERSON, Edward J.
How we made the change-over. por Life 54:86 Mr 22 '63
ANDERSON, Erica
God bless all living beings. Ladies Home J 80:26-8 D '63
ANDERSON, Ernie
What catches the teen-age mind. por Time 82:55 S 27 '63
ANDERSON, Eugenie
Minister Eugenie Anderson speaks on Bulgarian television and radio; July 3, 1963. Dept State Bul 49:141 Jl 22 '63
Minister to Bulgaria opens Plastics-USA exhibit in Sofia; address, July 6, 1963. Dept State Bul 49:142 Jl 22 '63
Mrs Anderson addresses Bulgarian people on U.S. Independence day. Dept State Bul 51:78 Jl 20 '64
United States and eastern Europe; address, June 14, 1963. Dept State Bul 49:87-92 Jl 15 '63
ANDERSON, Florence
New publication tells story of Carnegie library program. Library J 88:3040 S 1 '63
ANDERSON, Frank J.
Library key club. por Library J 89:1918-21 My 1 '64
ANDERSON, G. M. See Keith, M. L. jt. auth.
ANDERSON, George W. 1906-
Our nuclear navy. por Nat Geog Mag 123:449-50 Mr '63
Pentagon imbalance; address, September 4, 1963. Vital Speeches 29:743-6 O 1 '63; Excerpts. Aviation W 79:21, 30 S 9 '63; Summary. por U S News 55:24 S 16 '63

about

Adamant Admiral. il Time 81:19 Je 21 '63
Admiral's epilogue. por Time 82:24 S 13 '63

ANDERSON, George W.—about—*Continued*
Bossing the brass. por Newsweek 61:36+ My 20 '63
Guys who get in their way. il por Time 81:28 My 17 '63
Hot spot jobs for two admirals. por U S News 55:9 Ag 12 '63
McNamara-Anderson rifts led to ouster. Aviation W 78:26-7 My 13 '63
McNamara's human problem. Life 55:4 S 20 '63
Travel orders. Time 81:19 My 31 '63
Vital factor; civilian v. military control. por Newsweek 62:28+ S 16 '63

ANDERSON, Gerald H
Asian studies in church history. Christian Cent 80:1306 O 23 '63

ANDERSON, Gerald Martin
Air force murder case; Nancy Johnson and her son. J. Foisie. Nation 196:285-7 Ap 6 '63
Innocent's grim ordeal; murder of wife of airman Alec Johnson, Mountain Home air force base, Idaho. J. R. Phelan. il pors Sat Eve Post 236:62-7 F 2 '63

ANDERSON, Herbert
Macro-micro man. W. Jonathan. por Sat R 47:46-7 Mr 7 '64

ANDERSON, J. Maxwell
Lingual vein injection in the rat. Science 140:195 Ap 12 '63

ANDERSON, J. W.
Brand new city for Maryland. Harper 229:100-2+ N '64
No home rule for D.C. New Repub 148:6-7 F 9 '63
That new-fangled thing called voting. New Repub 150:8 Mr 28 '64

ANDERSON, Jack
Bert Lahr and the beauties. Dance Mag 38:24-5 S '64
Big company in a small country. Dance Mag 38:18-19 Jl '64
Cultural empire in the Empire state. Dance Mag 38:52-4 D '64
Dancer's bookshelf. Dance Mag 38:147 D '64
Fabulous career of Bronislava Nijinska. Dance Mag 37:40-6 Ag '63
Manifold implications. Dance Mag 37:44-7 Ap '63
More interested in new than in old. Dance Mag 37:44-7 Je '63
(ed) See Moya, M. Introducing yoga

ANDERSON, Jack, 1923?-
Where Johnny gets his gun. Read Digest 83:138-40 Jl '63

about

Splasher. Newsweek 61:94 My 13 '63
Testimony that Congress didn't hear; House administration committee. U S News 54:10 Ap 22 '63

ANDERSON, Jane McDill
My mother, a stranger; story. McCalls 91:114-15 N '63

ANDERSON, Jean
Teen-age marriage craze. Ladies Home J 80:66-7+ Mr '63

ANDERSON, Jerome P.
Federal legislation for land acquisition; excerpts from address. Recreation 58:22-3 Ja '65

ANDERSON, Jervis
Record of injustice. Commentary 38:84-6 S '64

ANDERSON, John
Portfolio of stereo décor. Hi Fi 14:38-45 F '64

ANDERSON, John, 1917-
Can the state live on crumbs? Sat R 48:31-2+ Ja 9 '65

ANDERSON, John, 1st viscount Waverley. See Waverley, J. A.

ANDERSON, John F. See Horsfall, W. R. jt. auth.

ANDERSON, John Firth
Dust-off in the desert; reprint. por Library J 89:4705-8 D 1 '64

ANDERSON, John W.
Commodore leaves the sea. I. Taves. il pors Look 28:38-40+ Ap 21 '64
Tugs are a convenience. il por Newsweek 63:77-8 F 17 '64

ANDERSON, Joseph G.
Physical fitness pilot project. Recreation 56:276-7+ Je '63

ANDERSON, K. W.
Flying the Montana missile line. Flying 74:38-40+ Mr '64
Montana's top banana. Flying 75:37+ Jl '64

ANDERSON, Kristine
Curl up and read. Seventeen 23:40 D '64
Pill bug affair. Seventeen 23:58 My '64

ANDERSON, Lee
Saturday as usual; poem. Poetry 101:402-3 Mr '63

ANDERSON, Mabry I.
Case for pesticides. Field & S 69:12-14+ S '64

ANDERSON, Margaret
After integration, higher horizons. N Y Times Mag p 10+ Ap 21 '63
Negro child asks: why? N Y Times Mag p32+ D 1 '63
Plea to twelve Negro children; address. N Y Times Mag p7+ Je 14 '64

ANDERSON, Margaret I.
Culture comes into its own. Américas 15:2-6 N '63
New era for the Alliance. Américas 16:1-7 Je '64

ANDERSON, Marian
Marian Anderson says farewell. W. Hawkins. il pors Mus Am 84:8-11 S '64

ANDERSON, Marlowe G.
AAAS: Southwestern and Rocky Mountain division 40th annual meeting. Science 144:1599-600 Je 26 '64

ANDERSON, Martin
Fiasco of urban renewal. Harvard Bsns R 43:6-8+ Ja '65
Truth about urban renewal; interview. Nations Bsns 53:31+ Ja '65

about

Storm warnings fly for urban renewal. por Bsns W p51-2 D 19 '64

ANDERSON, Myron S.
Here's how to improve your problem soil. Am Home 67:82-3 My '64

ANDERSON, Niels J.
Strangers in God's family. America 108:300-2 Mr 2 '63

ANDERSON, Norman G. See James, T. W. jt. auth.

ANDERSON, Odin W.
Nation's health. Cur Hist 45:65-70+ Ag '63

ANDERSON, Osborne Perry
Five brave Negroes with John Brown at Harpers Ferry. por Negro Hist Bul 27:164-9 Ap '64

ANDERSON, P. W.
Superconductivity; a theoretical approach. bibliog Science 144:373-8 Ap 24 '64

ANDERSON, Patricia
It's a matter of salesmanship. Pub W 183:48-50 Mr 18 '63

ANDERSON, Paul K.
Lethal alleles in mus musculus: local distribution and evidence for isolation of demes. bibliog Science 145:177-8 Jl 10 '64

ANDERSON, R. K. and others
Brucella-agglutinating antibodies: relation of mercaptoethanol stability to complement fixation. bibliog Science 143:1334-5 Mr 20 '64

ANDERSON, Ray
Earlier crop, more income from tomatoes on trellises. Farm J 88:72-3 F '64

ANDERSON, Reba
NEA and the hill. NEA J 52:36-9 Ap '63

ANDERSON, Robert A.
Gold mine at Jeremiah Flats; drama. Plays 23:17-30 O '63

ANDERSON, Robert B.
LBJ's advisers: ins+outs=middle. il por Newsweek 64:65-6 Jl 13 '64

ANDERSON, Robert O.
Biggest cattle baron. T. G. Harris. il pors Look 27:62+ O 8 '63

ANDERSON, Robert O, Aspen award. See Aspen institute for humanistic studies

ANDERSON, Ron
Little digger. Pop Mech 119:144-7 F '63

ANDERSON, Sydney
Return of the beaver. Natur Hist 73:38-43 O '64

ANDERSON, Thom
Controversial search for value. Sat R 47:18-19+ D 26 '64

ANDERSON, Thomas F.
Biophysics. Science 147:186+ Ja 8 '65

ANDERSON, W. E.
(ed) See Longoria, S. New world record polar bear

ANDERSON, W. R.
Selecting arc-welding equipment. Suc Farm 62:82 O '64

ANDERSON, Walter A.
Shared time. NEA J 53:28+ Mr '64

ANDERSON, Wayne W.
Inner space: the campus and the mind. Sch & Soc 91:177 Ap 6 '63
State of liberal education. Sch & Soc 92:208-9 My 2 '64

ANDERSON, William Ashley
When the Wise man appeared. Read Digest 86:99-101 Ja '65

ANDERSON, William R.
Excerpt from testimony before subcommittee on the National service corps, June 6, 1963. Cong Digest 43:26+ Ja '64

ANDERSON, Clayton and company
Cotton's king tills new fields; pushing diversification. il Bsns W p 138+ Ja 23 '65
ANDERSSON, Theodore
From school to college in foreign languages. NEA J 53:35-6 Ap '64
ANDERTON, David A.
Minimal design changes appear in first all-metal mockup of LEM. Miss & Roc 15:21 O 19 '64
ANDERTON, Piers
Indian's front lines in the high Himalayas. Reporter 30:38-40 Ja 16 '64
ANDES MOUNTAINS
See also
Aconcagua, Mount
ANDORRA; drama. See Frisch, M.
ANDOVER, Me.
Project Telstar; Earth station. il Arch Rec 133:152-4 Ja '63
ANDRADE, Francisco de
Kurz, d'Andrade, Santley, Van Rooy. A. Favia-Artsay. por Hobbies 68:30-1 My '63
ANDRADE, Jorge Carrera
Official poster of green; poem. tr. by D. M. Pettinella. Nation 198:102 Ja 27 '64
ANDRADE, Mário Pinto de
Our far-flung correspondents. T. Sterling. New Yorker 39:167-8+ N 16 '63
ANDRADE, Mário Raul de Morais. See Morais Andrade, M. R. de
ANDRADE, Vicente
Labor and the Alliance for progress. America 108:850 Je 15 '63
Labor in Latin America. America 110:142-4 Ja 25 '64
World resounds: Bogotá. America 109:769-70 D 14 '63
ANDREA Chénier; opera. See Giordano, U.
ANDRESS, Ursula
Ursula Andress: success story of a lazy beauty. J. Hamilton. il pors Look 27:54-7+ N 5 '63
Ursula major. por Newsweek 64:79B-80 Jl 20 '64
ANDREW, prince of Great Britain
England's merry Prince Andrew. il pors Ladies Home J 80:60-1 Mr '63
ANDREW, Frank. See Shove, G. jt. auth.
ANDREW, John H. Jr
Lagenarias are unusual. il Horticulture 41:230-1 Ap '63
ANDREW, R. J.
Evolution of facial expression. bibliog Science 142:1034-41 N 22 '63
ANDREWES, Christopher Howard
Complex epidemiology of respiratory virus infections. bibliog Science 146:1274-7 D 4 '64
ANDREWS, Austin K. See Kallman, B. J. jt. auth.
ANDREWS, Charles R.
Jesus in Harlem. Christian Cent 81:400 Mr 25 '64
Repenting and rejoicing. Christian Cent 81:209 F 12 '64
ANDREWS, Hank
My no. 1 fishing spot. Outdoor Life 132:24-7+ Jl '63
ANDREWS, Henry N.
Early seed plants. bibliog Science 142:925-31 N 15 '63
ANDREWS, John J.
Automobile industry accentuates trends in industrial design. Arch Rec 136:172+ Jl '64
ANDREWS, Julie
At last Hollywood discovers the toast of Broadway: Julie. D. Zeitlin. il pors Life 57:117-18+ N 13 '64
Julie Andrews goes to Hollywood. S. Gordon. il pors Look 27:123-6 N 19 '63
Julie Andrews's star rises higher with The sound of music. J. Poppy. il pors Look 29:38-42+ Ja 26 '65
Julie for Emily. il por Newsweek 64:96-7 N 2 '64
My fair Julie. P. Hamill. il pors Sat Eve Post 236:68-9 D 21 '63
My friend Julie Andrews; ed. by H. Markel. C. Burnett. il pors Good H 157:34+ N '63
Once & future queen. por Time 84:42+ O 9 '64
ANDREWS, L. V.
Acid cleaning, inboard engines. Motor B 113:44+ Mr '64
ANDREWS, Lucia M.
Far flung family. Flower Grower 50:44-5+ Ag '63
Press plants for permanence. Horticulture 41:577 N '63
ANDREWS, Lynn H.
Sunshine at night. Am City 78:111 Ag '63
ANDREWS, Michael F.
Experience of being & becoming. Sch Arts 62:5-9 Mr; 22-4 Ap; 5-7 My '63 (to be cont)
Sculpture. bibliog NEA J 53:58-61 S '64
ANDREWS, Miriam Wise
For Rachel Carson; poem. Am For 70:16 S '64
Spruce tree; poem. Am For 71:41 Ja '65
ANDREWS, Phillip
Big trends in travel books. Pub W 183:32-41 Mr 4; 25-7 Mr 11 '63
Photo books are good sellers: are book sellers in the picture? Pub W 183:21-5 Mr 11 '63
ANDREWS, Ralph
Staff relations. Recreation 56:70 F '63
State recreation services. por Recreation 56:404-5 N '63
ANDREWS, Stanley
Inside story of in-betweens. Pop Phot 55:172+ N '64
ANDREWS, Victor L.
Captive finance companies. Harvard Bsns R 42:80-92 Jl '64
ANDREWS, Wayne
Uses of space. Sat R 48:32-3+ Ja 23 '65
ANDREWS, William G.
Don't blame the American voter. N Y Times Mag p42-3+ O 18 '64
ANDREWS, Win
Rope tangle. Yachting 113:76-8+ Ap '63
Will your rope let you down? Yachting 115:64-6+ My '64
ANDREWS, Tex.
Flexible environment for learning. il Arch Rec 133:168-73 My '63
ANDRIC, Ivo
Tea with Ivo Andric. J. Hitrec. Reporter 28:47-9 My 23 '63
ANDROCLES & the librarian; story. See Jensen, E.
ANDROFORM industries, incorporated
Androforming process comes of age. J. F. Judge. il Miss & Roc 12:22-3 F 4 '63
ANDROMEDA
Evergreen for coldest areas. M. E. Speeter. il Flower Grower 50:40 D '63
ANDROS ISLAND, Bahama Islands
Navy chafes to get up undersea test range. il Bsns W p84+ Ap 27 '63
ANDRUS, Ethel Percy
Dynamic retirement is their goal. J. L. Block. Read Digest 84:195-6+ Ja '64
ANECDOTES
Gentlemen: about that cocktail shaker. P. Paine. il Read Digest 85:127-9 S '64
ANEMIA
Amino acids; incorporation into α- and β-chains of hemoglobin by normal and thalassemic reticulocytes. J. D. Heywood and others. bibliog il Science 146:530-1 O 23 '64
Cooley's anemia can cause heart disease. Sci N L 85:41 Ja 18 '64
Erythroid homeostasis in normal and genetically anemic mice: reaction to induced polycythemia. R. L. Niece and others. bibliog il Science 142:1468-9 D 13 '63
Genetic control of hemoglobin synthesis. W. E. Nance. bibliog il Science 141:123-30 Jl 12 '63
Hemoglobin polymorphism: its relation to sickling of erythrocytes in white-tailed deer. H. Kitchen and others. bibliog il Science 144:1237-9 Je 5 '64
Hemoglobins A and F: formation in thalassemia and other hemolytic anemias. P. A. Marks and E. R. Burka. bibliog il Science 144:552-3 My 1 '64
Potent new Swiss drug used for iron poisoning; ferrous sulfate poisoning in anemia patients. Sci N L 84:57 Jl 27 '63
Radioactive isotopes diagnose anemia. Sci N L 86:25 Jl 11 '64
Risk of life; aplastic anemia. il Good H 158:12+ Je '64
Severe childhood disease treated with folic acid; Cooley's anemia. Sci N L 85:73 F 1 '64
Space test volunteers all develop anemia. Sci N L 83:296 My 11 '63
Spleen-colony formation in anemic mice of genotype WW^v. E. A. McCulloch and others. bibliog il Science 144:844-6 My 15 '64
What you should know about anemia. E. T. Wilkes. Parents Mag 38:163-4 S '63
ANESTHESIA
Anesthesia for the bottlenose dolphin, tursiops truncatus. E. L. Nagel and others. bibliog il Science 146:1591-3 D 18 '64
Differential estimation of gamma-butyrolactone and gamma-hydroxybutyric acid in rat blood and brain. N. J. Giarman and R. H. Roth. bibliog il Science 145:583-4 Ag 7 '64
Examination of diurnal variation in lethally irradiated rats. R. L. Straube. il Science 142:1062 N 22 '63

ANESTHESIA—*Continued*
Gamma hydroxybutyrate and gamma butyrolactone: concentration in rat tissues during anesthesia. S. P. Bessman and S. J. Skolnik. bibliog il Science 143:1045-7 Mr 6 '64
Temperature dependence of anesthesia in goldfish. A. Cherkin and J. F. Catchpool. bibliog il Science 144:1460-2 Je 19 '64
See also
Anesthetics
ANESTHESIA, Electronic. See Electronic anesthesia
ANESTHETICS
Is any anesthetic safe? C. Marwick. il Sci Digest 54:77-81 Ag '63
Local anesthetic drugs: penetration from the spinal extradural space into the neuraxis. P. R. Bromage and others. bibliog il Science 140:392-4 Ap 26 '63
See also
Chloroform
Halothane
ANEUPLOIDY. See Chromosomes
ANEURYSMS
Horse hair shot into brain to treat dangerous malady. Sci Digest 53:30 My '63
Patching brain blowouts; operation for cranial aneurysm. Sci Digest 56:20-1 D '64
L'ANGE de feu; opera. See Prokof'ev, S. S.
ANGEL of fire; opera. See Prokof'ev, S. S.
ANGELAKOS, E. T.
Histochemical demonstration of uptake of exogenous norepinephrine by adrenergic fibers in vitro. bibliog Science 145:503-4 Jl 31 '64
ANGELES, Victoria de los
Victoria de los Angeles on three new recordings from Angel: Barber of Seville, Cavalleria rusticana, and Mélodies de France. il por Am Rec G 30:184-7 N '63
ANGELES NATIONAL FOREST. See National forests
ANGELL, George W.
Do we need a National board of education? Sch & Soc 91:238-9 Sum '63
ANGELL, James W.
Dollar and the international monetary system. bibliog Science 138:1071-7; 140:1146+ D 7 '62, Je 7 '63
ANGELL, Roger
Adeste Brentano's! New Yorker 40:53 N 28 '64
L'après-midi d'un fan. New Yorker 40:48-50+ O 17 '64
More film fun. New Yorker 40:42-3 S 26 '64
Sporting scene (cont) New Yorker 39:132+ My 25; 91-5 Jl 27; 184+ O 26 '63; 40:96+ My 30; 185-8+ S 12; 224-8+ O 24 '64
Three more hats. New Yorker 40:29-31 F 29 '64
ANGELLI, Gianni
Fiat: the big wheel in Italy's traffic. il por Newsweek 63:68-70 Ja 20 '64
ANGELS (theater) See Theater—Finance
ANGELS of Jean Pierre; story. See Albee, G. S.
ANGEL'S trumpet. See Datura
ANGER, Hal O. and Van Dyke, D. C.
Human bone marrow distribution shown in vivo by iron-52 and the positron scintillation camera. bibliog Science 144:1587-9 Je 26 '64
ANGER
Everyone needs to get mad sometimes. K. Parkes. il Parents Mag 38:72-3+ S '63
Mommies are to be mad at. T. D. Topping. il Redbook 121:12 Ag '63
Turn anger into an asset. H. Levinson. il Nations Bsns 52:82-4+ My '64
Unsound and the fury. H. A. Smith. Sat Eve Post 236:62 Mr 9 '63
See also
Temper
ANGERS, W. P. and others
Characteristics of entering freshmen in a teachers college. Sch & Soc 91:68-9 F 9 '63
ANGINA pectoris. See Heart—Diseases
ANGIOTENSIN
Angiotensin pressor inhibition by aldosterone in the rabbit. Y. J. Katz and others. bibliog il Science 141:725 Ag 23 '63
Angiotensin II: its effects on corticoid production by chicken adrenals in vitro. R. DeRoos and C. C. DeRoos. bibliog il Science 141:1284 S 27 '63
Angiotensinase with a high degree of specificity in plasma and red cells. P. A. Khairallah and others. bibliog il Science 140:672-4 My 10 '63
Antibodies to bradykinin and angiotensin: a use of carbodiimides in immunology. T. L. Goodfriend and others. bibliog il Science 144:1344-6 Je 12 '64
Neurogenic component of chronic renal hypertension. J. W. McCubbin and I. H. Page. il Science 139:210+ Ja 18 '63
ANGLE, Paul M.
My father's grocery store. por Am Heritage 14:34-7+ Ag '63
ANGLICAN church. See Church of England; Protestant Episcopal church
ANGLICAN communion
Anglican imbalance; Toronto meeting. il Newsweek 62:69 Ag 26 '62
Anglican reappraisal; concerning the closing manifesto at the third World congress of the Anglican communion. America 109:204 Ag 31 '63
Episcopal dichotomy; 61st General convention of the Episcopal church. M. Frakes. Christian Cent 81:1390-2 N 11 '64
Is Anglicanism Protestant? excerpt from World Protestantism. W. H. Van De Pol. Cath World 200:95-9+ N '64
New Anglican horizons. C. Northcott. Christian Cent 81:134-5 Ja 29 '64
One big family; Anglican congress in Toronto. il Time 82:49 Ag 23 '63
Rebirth of a church? Toronto plan. C. Northcott. Christian Cent 80:1071 S 4 '63
Second chance for Anglicanism; manifesto issued at Third world congress. Christian Cent 80:1045 Ag 28 '63
Test of our discipleship; concerning manifesto, Mutual responsibility and interdependence. Time 82:45 Ag 30 '63
ANGLIN, Eleanor M. and King, J. H.
FTA summer experience. NEA J 53:31 My '64
ANGLO-AMERICAN relations. See England and the United States
ANGLO-CATHOLICISM
Quest for Catholicity: the development of high church Anglicanism, by G. Tavard. Review
Commonweal 80:487-8 Jl 10 '64. D. L. Clark
ANGLO IRISH. See Irish
ANGLO-SAXON (term)
Portrait of de Gaulle's Anglo-Saxons. G. Gorer. il N Y Times Mag p28+ My 12 '63
ANGLUND, Joan Walsh
Joan Walsh Anglund and her books. il por Pub W 184:104-6 Jl 8 '63
ANGOFF, Allan
Librarians view publishers' promotion and advertising; summary of address. Pub W 184:33-5 D 2 '63
ANGOFF, Charles
Atheist; poem. Christian Cent 81:77 Ja 15 '64
George Jean Nathan: superlative dandy. New Repub 150:17-20 Ja 4 '64
Mencken: prejudices and prophecies. Sat R 46:44-5 Ag 10 '63
No answer; poem. Christian Cent 82:7 Ja 6 '65
Secret metaphysics; poem. Christian Cent 80:1127 S 18 '63
ANGOLA
Angola: a non-self-governing territory. K. Irvine. bibliog f Cur Hist 45:321-8 D '63
Angola, arena of struggle. il N Y Times Mag p 18-19 N 3 '63
Angola: unfinished duel. F. F. Clairmonte. Yale R 53:1-10 O '63
Bond of blood. il Time 81:29 My 31 '63
Massacre at Quitexe. B. Teixeira. Nat R 16:822-3 S 22 '64
Now Angola: study of a rebel. L. Garrison. il N Y Times Mag p 12-13+ F 16 '64
Our far-flung correspondents. T. Sterling. il New Yorker 39:162+ N 16 '63
Portuguese way in Africa. H. Kay. il Fortune 69:112-15+ Ja '64
Truth about Angola. T. Molnar. Nat R 16:280 Ap 7 '64
See also
Hunting—Angola
Justice, Administration of—Angola
United Nations—Angola
ANGRIST, Stanley W.
Fluid control devices. Sci Am 211:80-8 D '64
ANGRY is the morning; story. See Butler, D. E.
ANGUISH, Mental. See Suffering
ANGUS, Robert
Earphones for stereo? Mod Phot 27:90+ S '63
Sound advice. Mod Phot 27:18-19 Mr; 34+ My; 18+ Je; 32-3+ Ag; 93+ S; 109+ N '63; 28:98+ Ja; 90+ F; 48+ Mr; 86 Ap; 46+ Ag '64
Tape recorder breakthrough: cross field head. Mod Phot 28:93+ S '64
ANHEUSER-Busch, incorporated
Africa's wild veldt moves in on Florida; Busch gardens, in Tampa. il Bsns W p 180-2 N 7 '64
Promotional flair keeps Busch on top. il Bsns W p 112-14+ Ap 13 '63

el-ANI, Arif S.
Self-sterile auxotrophs and their relation to heterothallism in sordaria fimicola. bibliog Science 145:1067-8 S 4 '64

ANIMAL actors. See Animals in the theater

ANIMAL behavior. See Animals—Habits and behavior

ANIMAL calling
How to call crows, coyotes, dogs, children, etc. T. Trueblood. il Field & S 69:24+ S '64
How to call moose. il Outdoor Life 132:42-3 Jl '63
They come a-running. F. R. Martin. il Outdoor Life 133:32-3+ Ja '64

ANIMAL camouflage. See Mimicry (biology)

ANIMAL ecology. See Zoology—Ecology

ANIMAL electricity. See Electrophysiology

ANIMAL experimentation
Animal experiments: regulatory measure in the Senate presents hazards to the public. M. B. Visscher. Science 139:871 Mr 8 '63
Animal surgeon. il Ebony 19:168-70 N '63
Antivivisection for high schools? S.P.C.A. action in New Jersey. Sci Am 211:58 O '64
Better than guinea pigs; experiments on baboons. il Bsns W p68-70+ N 16 '63
Chemical stimulation of the brain. A. E. Fisher. il Sci Am 210:60-8 Je '64
Congenital anomalies induced in hamster embryos with H-1 virus. V. H. Ferm and L. Kilham. bibliog il Science 145:510-11 Jl 31 '64
Early experience and emotional development. V. H. Denenberg. il Sci Am 208:138-40+ Je '63
Egghead of the animal astronauts; excerpts from Animal astronauts; they opened the way to the stars. C. R. Bergwin and W. T. Coleman. il Todays Health 42:32-5+ Ja '64
Electronic dog aids in heart research. il Todays Health 41:60 Ap '63
Escape and avoidance learning in newly hatched domestic chicks. H. James and C. Binks. bibliog il Science 139:1293-4 Mr 29 '63
Experimental animals; proposals to regulate use bring clash of scientists and humane societies. E. Langer. Science 139:1275 Mr 29 '63
Experimental narcotic addiction. J. R. Weeks. il Sci Am 210:46-52 Mr '64
Genotype and sex drive in intact and in castrated male mice. T. E. McGill and G. R. Tucker. bibliog il Science 145:514-15 Jl 31 '64
Habitat selection. S. C. Wecker. il Sci Am 211:109-16 O '64
Lamb experiment may help save human babies; alive in an artificial womb. il Life 57:37-8 Ag 28 '64
Laws for humane treatment of animals proposed. Christian Cent 80:1194 O 2 '63; Discussion. 80:1473 N 27 '63
Lingual vein injection in the rat. J. M. Anderson. Science 140:195 Ap 12 '63
Maisie's operation may help blue babies. il Todays Health 41:69 Ag '63
Medical progress depends on animal research. H. E. Essex. Todays Health 42:18+ N '64
Medical progress requires animal research. R. A. Rohweder. Todays Health 41:88 S '63
Monkey business in Oregon. J. B. Kemmerer. il Pop Sci 183:60-3 S '63
Monkeys stand in for humans. F. Marley. il Sci N L 84:218-19 O 5 '63
Seek humane treatment of animals; Clark-Neuberger bill in U.S. Senate. Christian Cent 80:230 F 20 '63; Discussion. 80:496 Ap 17 '63
Synthesis of chicken antibodies of high and low molecular weight. A. A. Benedict and others. bibliog il Science 139:1302-3 Mr 29 '63
Thalidomide: effect upon pregnancy in the rhesus monkey. J. F. Lucey and R. E. Behrman. bibliog il Science 139:1295-6 Mr 29 '63
Thalidomide remembered; research into effects of drugs on embryonic opossums. Time 84:81 S 25 '64
Veterinary medicine advances human medicine; excerpts from address. W. H. Feldman. Todays Health 41:12+ N '63
Water-breathing rodents. Sci Am 208:83-4 Ap '63
See also
Laboratory animals
Maze tests
Neuroses, Experimental
Stimulus and response
Vivisection

ANIMAL fat. See Fat

ANIMAL fighting. See Dog fighting

ANIMAL habitations. See Animals—Habitations

ANIMAL heat. See Temperature, Animal and human

ANIMAL intelligence
Albinism and water escape performance in the mouse. H. D. Winston and G. Lindzey. bibliog il Science 144:189-91 Ap 10 '64; Reply with rejoinder. G. W. Meier and D. P. Foshee. 147:307-8 Ja 15 '65
Evolution of intelligence. M. E. Bitterman. il Sci Am 212:92-100 Ja '65
Learn from animals. Sci N L 87:19-20 Ja 9 '65
Putting on the dog. Newsweek 64:46 Ag 3 '64
Vocal mimicry in tursiops: ability to match numbers and durations of human vocal bursts. J. C. Lilly. bibliog il Science 147:300-1 Ja 15 '65
See also
Animals—Habits and behavior
Animals—Language

ANIMAL locomotion
Locomotion in pinnipeds. C. Ray. il Natur Hist 72:10-21 Mr '63
Man of the woods; chimpanzee. V. Reynolds. il Natur Hist 73:44-51 Ja '64
Nutating annular cage for measuring motor activity. J. W. Kissel. il Science 139:1224-5 Mr 22 '63
Record holders of the animal world; speed; jump. A. W. Eckert. il Pop Sci 184:98-9 Ap '64

ANIMAL lore
Animal life and lore, by O. R. Breland. Review
Sci Digest il 55:90 Ja '64. D. Cohen

ANIMAL medical centers. See Veterinary medicine

ANIMAL moving pictures. See Moving pictures—Animal films

ANIMAL pests. See Animals, Predatory

ANIMAL pets. See Pets

ANIMAL populations
Animal dispersion in relation to social behaviour, by V. C. Wynne-Edwards. Review
Nation 197:326-7+ N 16 '63. D. Cort
Can animals survive in a fast-changing world? excerpt from Animal worlds. M. Bates. il Audubon Mag 65:276-9, 370-2 S-N '63
Endocrines, behavior, and population. J. J. Christian and D. E. Davis. bibliog il Science 146:1550-60 D 18 '64
Lethal alleles in mus musculus: local distribution and evidence for isolation of demes. P. K. Anderson. bibliog il Science 145:177-8 Jl 10 '64
Math killing to animals. Sci N L 84:166 S 14 '63
Population control in animals. V. C. Wynne-Edwards. il Sci Am 211:68-74 Ag '64
Real deer sleeper. P. Czura. il Field & S 68:104-6+ N '63
U.S. wildlife on the danger list. il U S News 57:16 Jl 20 '64
Varying sensitivity of C57BL/Crgl mice to grouping. D. D. Thiessen. bibliog il Science 141:827-8 Ag 30 '63
See also
Bird populations

Control

Africa's animals in peril; photographs by L. Dean; with report by M. A. Edey. Life 55:72-7+ O 25 '63
Are we wasting our best hunting? B. East. il Outdoor Life 131:32-5+ Mr '63
Costly and needless war on predators; condensation of address, November 12, 1962. D. L. Allen. il Audubon Mag 65:85-9+ Mr '63
Cybernetics of population control. H. Hoagland. Bul Atomic Sci 20:2-6 F '64
Deer war. B. East. il Outdoor Life 132:17-19+ D '63
Giving the predators a break. Nation 198:110 F 3 '64
Kodiak bear war. J. Rearden. il Outdoor Life 134:17-19+ Ag '64
My first doe. H. Stilwell. il Field & S 68:36-7+ O '63
Northern Yellowstone elk reduction goal achieved; with editorial comment. il Nat Parks Mag 37:2, 16 Mr '63
One more look at poisons. P. M. Tilden. Natur Hist 72:66-7 D '63
Overcrowding animals keeps population down. Sci N L 83:345 Je 1 '63
Population control in animals by overloading resources with sterile animals. bibliog il Science 140:496-7 My 3 '63
War on America's wildlife. A. S. Leopold and others. il Audubon Mag 66:228-33, 306-11 Jl-S '64

ANIMAL populations—Control—*Continued*
Wildlife management in the national parks. S. A. Cain and others. il Liv Wildn 83:11-19 Spring '63
Wolves and congressmen. D. Cort. il Nation 197:216-18 O 12 '63
ANIMAL repellents
Half ounce of prevention. C. Conley. il Field & S 68:83 Jl '63
ANIMAL sculpture
Animal kingdom of Anne Arnold. L. Campbell. il Art N 63:32-3+ D '64
Bob Scriver: western sculptor. M. Strachan. il Am Artist 28:50-2+ S '64
Bronze menagerie; exhibition at Manhattan's Bernard Black gallery. il Time 83:72 Mr 6 '64
Zoo puts on a mammoth match-up; elephants carved from a solid block of granite. il Life 54:40B+ Je 7 '63
ANIMAL sounds. See Sound production by animals
ANIMAL tagging
Biggest black bear ever caught. D. Mech. il Sci Digest 54:5-9 N '63
ANIMAL talent scouts, incorporated. See Animals in the theater
ANIMAL temperature. See Temperature, Animal and human
ANIMAL toys. See Toys
ANIMAL tracks and trails
Animals are hiding but they do leave tracks. il Sunset 130:30+ My '63
Can you match these tracks? il Suc Farm 61:92 O '63
Can you read the signs? D. Mech. il Outdoor Life 135:50-1+ Ja '65
Who dined here? D. Mech. il Outdoor Life 131:10-11 Ja '63
Wilderness whodunit; photographs. T. Eberhard. Outdoor Life 133:10+ Mr '64
ANIMAL training. See Animals—Training
ANIMAL trials and punishment. See Animals, Prosecution and punishment of
ANIMALPORT. See New York (city)—Airports
ANIMALS
Nature's weirdest inventions. J. Sidney. il Sci Digest 43:12-16 My '63
See also
Contraceptives (animals)
Hybridization
Mammals
Pets
Photography of animals
Society for indecency to naked animals
also names of animals and classes of animals, e.g. Kangaroos; *also* headings beginning Animal

Anecdotes, facetiae, satire, etc.

Bears and other commuters; if you can't lick 'em join 'em. R. Cantwell. il Sports Illus 19:47-8+ S 30 '63
Wild wisdom; comp. by M. Devoe. Read Digest 85:24C+ O '64

Capture

Fifty years in the monkey house. L. Alexander. il McCalls 91:110-11+ F '64
How to catch a giraffe. il Sci Digest 55:20-2 F '64
Needle for Felix. S. W. Taylor. il Field & S 67:58-61 Mr '63
Wild pigs' wild ride. il Life 54:51-2 Je 28 '63

Collisions with automobiles

See Automobile driving—Animal hazards

Diseases and pests

Heart disease common in dogs but not cats. Sci N L 85:328 My 23 '64
Wasting disease induced in young mice by administration of cortisol acetate. M. Schlesinger and R. Mark. bibliog il Science 143:965-6 F 28 '64
Zoo population increase affects animals' hearts. Sci N L 83:296 My 11 '63
See also
Communicable diseases in animals
Domestic animals—Diseases and pests

Drama

Mouse that soared. H. L. Miller. Plays 23:61-6, 95 O '63
Three little kittens. H. L. Miller. Plays 23:69-72, 96 Ap '64

Eyes

See Eye (animals)

Food

Bonanza in pet foods. T. J. Murray. Duns R 84:66+ N '64
Or they perish. J. Stuart. il Am For 69:18-20 D '63
What to serve under the table. il Redbook 121:48-9 Jl '63
Who dined here? D. Mech. il Outdoor Life 131:10-11 Ja '63
See also
Feeding and feeding stuffs

Footprints

See Animal tracks and trails

Habitations

Just out from under a rock. J. Terres. il Sports Illus 20:50-1+ My 4 '64
Who lives here? D. Mech. il Outdoor Life 132:14-15+ D '63

Habits and behavior

Acoustic activity recorder for burrowing animals. C. Gans and J. J. Bonin. bibliog il Science 140:398 Ap 26 '63
Animals can tell time, but how? A. Hills. il Life 54:41-2+ My 31 '63
Bears and other commuters; if you can't lick 'em, join 'em. R. Cantwell. il Sports Illus 19:47-8+ S 30 '63
Bionics: a new science looks at nature's secrets. J. R. Thomson. il Todays Health 42:44-9+ Ja '64
Critical periods in behavioral development. J. P. Scott; discussion. Science 139:673-4, 1110+ F 15, Mr 15 '63
Cycle of living. W. O. Pruitt, jr. il Holiday 33:32+ F '63
Endocrines, behavior, and population. J. J. Christian and D. E. Davis. bibliog il Science 146:1550-60 D 18 '64
Forest family of Mrs Helen Hoover; excerpts from Long-shadowed forest. H. Hoover. il Sat R 47:52-4 Ap 4 '64
Infant handling; effects on avoidance learning, brain weight, and cholinesterase activity. J. T. Tapp and H. Markowitz. bibliog il Science 140:486-7 My 3 '63
Inheritance of avoidance conditioning in mice: a diallel study. R. L. Collins. bibliog il Science 143:1188-90 Mr 13 '64
Isle Royale: predator vs. prey. D. L. Allen. il Field & S 68:21-3 Ja '64
Leadership in macaque societies; letter. J. P. Scott. Science 144:1179 Je 5 '64
Man not only toolmaker. N. Lawson. il Sci N L 85:191 Mr 21 '64
Mice reared with rats: modification of behavior by early experience with another species. V. H. Denenberg and others. bibliog il Science 143:380-1 Ja 24 '64
Microtus: a simple method of recording time spent in the nest. R. W. Barbour. il Science 141:41 Jl 5 '63
Opossum as a player; feigning death. Sci Am 211:64 D '64
Population control in animals. V. C. Wynne-Edwards. il Sci Am 211:68-74 Ag '64
Protopsychology; behavior in primitive worm. J. B. Best. il Sci Am 208:54-62 bibliog(p 184) F '63
Snakes are interesting; hognosed snakes. W. F. Heald. il Audubon Mag 65:218-21 Jl '63
Social life of Japanese monkeys; excerpts from paper. D. Miyadi. il Science 143:783-6 F 21 '64
Strange animals of Australia. D. Fleay. il Nat Geog Mag 124:388-411 S '63
Toolmaking chimpanzees. Sci Am 211:48 Jl '64
Varying sensitivity of C57BL/Crgl mice to grouping. D. D. Thiessen. bibliog il Science 141:827-8 Ag 30 '63
Visiting in periodicticus. U. M. Cowgill. il Science 146:1183 N 27 '64
When an elephant sleeps. J. Sidney. il Sci Digest 54:19-22 S '63
See also
Hibernation
Nature study
Periodicity
Sex behavior

Language

Can animals talk? P. J. Fournier. il Field & S 69:52-4+ Je '64
Chicken talk. il Time 83:50-1 Ja 24 '64
Monkey talk dictionary. Sci N L 85:6 Ja 4 '64
When a monkey says kwaa he means let's go. M. Bates. il N Y Times Mag p 14-15+ Mr 29 '64

Memory

See Memory

Migration

Journeys into autumn. B. Tufty. il Sci N L 86:186-7 S 19 '64
Satellites track animals. B. Tufty. Sci N L 83:130 Mr 2 '63

ANIMALS—Migration—*Continued*
Space tracks; bioelectronics extends its frontiers. D. W. Warner. il Natur Hist 72:8-15 F '63
See also
Animal tagging
Lemmings

Photographs

Animals on camera; excerpt from Animals of East Africa. C. A. Spinage. N Y Times Mag p 174-5 Ap 7 '63
Cats in our lives. A. Suehsdorf. il Nat Geog Mag 125:508-41 Ap '64
Come on in, the water's freezing; young polar bears. Look 28:40-1 Je 30 '64
Echo of western hoofbeats. J. Launois. Sat Eve Post 236:20-7 My 4 '63
How to weigh a baby gorilla. P. Steinemann. Look 27:74b+ Jl 30 '63
Lion learns to roar. K. Heyman. N Y Times Mag p 132 O 6 '63
Pet parade; Princeton, N.J. U S Camera 26:51-3 Jl '63
Pygmy goats. R. Hewett. Look 27:68-70 Jl 16 '63
Siamese twins. Look 27:114+ Je 18 '63
Snow leopard likes it. S. Falk. N Y Times Mag p22-3 F 16 '64
Taking a liberty with a leopard. Life 56:47-8 Je 26 '64
Top show dogs. N. Leen. Life 56:56-62 F 7 '64
Two for the swing. Look 27:86 Ag 13 '63
Zoo's who. J. Cooke. Sat Eve Post 236:28-31 Ag 10 '63

Protection

Golden plains of Tanganyika. P. Brooks. il Horizon 7:80-9 Wint '65
Growing antagonism to hunting. D. L. Allen. il Field & S 68:12-16 S '63
Operation Gwamba to rescue the animals: moving animals from flooded area in Dutch Guiana. il Life 58:24-9 Ja 22 '65
Our rare and extinct animals. B. Tufty. il Sci N L 84:154-5 S 7 '63
See also
American society for the prevention of cruelty to animals
Game protection

Protective equipment

See Defense mechanisms (biology)

Reproduction

See Reproduction

Sight

See Sight (animals)

Speed

Record holders of the animal world; speed; jump. A. W. Eckert. il Pop Sci 184:98-9 Ap '64

Stories

See also
Bears—Stories

Training

Cat man; C. Beatty. il Newsweek 61:92 F 18 '63
Gamboling dolphin in a new role; my pal Flipper. il Life 54:61-4+ Je 7 '63
How to live with animals. R. Osk. Am Home 66:90 N '63
Wavelength generalization after discrimination learning with and without errors. H. S. Terrace. bibliog il Science 144:78-80 Ap 3 '64

Transportation

Up in the air with the animal kingdom. D. Wharton. il Read Digest 85:31-4+ S '64

Treatment

Experimental animals; proposals to regulate use bring clash of scientists and humane societies. E. Langer. Science 139:1275 Mr 29 '63
Speaking out; science is needlessly cruel to animals. C. Amory. Sat Eve Post 236:10+ Jl 27 '63; Discussion. 236:4+ Ag 24; 88 S 7 '63
See also
Animal experimentation
Hunting—Ethical aspects
Vivisection

ANIMALS (quintet) See Singers

ANIMALS, Abnormalities. See Abnormalities (animals)

ANIMALS, Aquatic. See Marine fauna

ANIMALS, Color of. See Color of animals

ANIMALS, Domestication of. See Domestication

ANIMALS, Effect of light on. See Light—Physiological effects

ANIMALS, Effect of radiation on. See Radiation—Physiological effects

ANIMALS, Effect of temperature on. See Temperature—Physiological effects

ANIMALS, Experiments on. See Animal experimentation

ANIMALS, Extinct
Can animals survive in a fast-changing world? excerpt from Animal worlds. M. Bates. il Audubon Mag 65:276-9, 370-2 S-N '63
Our rare and extinct animals. B. Tufty. il Sci N L 84:154-5 S 7 '63
Reviews; three books on the fauna survival problem. T. D. Carter. il Natur Hist 73:4+ Ja '64
See also
Paleontology

ANIMALS, Germ free. See Germ free animals

ANIMALS, Infancy of
Age of weaning in two subspecies of deer mice. J. A. King and others. bibliog il Science 139:483-4 F 8 '63
Artificial feeding of neonatal rats. S. A. Miller and H. A. Dymsza. bibliog il Science 141:517-18 Ag 9 '63
Behavior of adult rats is modified by the experiences their mothers had as infants. V. H. Denenberg and A. E. Whimbey. bibliog il Science 142:1192-3 N 29 '63
Behavior of infant monkeys; differences attributable to mode of birth. G. W. Meier. bibliog il Science 143:968-70 F 28 '64
Choice behavior in rhesus monkeys: effect of stimulation during the first month of life. G. P. Sackett and others. bibliog il Science 147:304-6 Ja 15 '65
Depth perception in sheep: effects of interrupting the mother-neonate bond. W. B. Lemmon and G. H. Patterson. bibliog il Science 145:835-6 Ag 21 '64; Reply with rejoinder. E. Klinghammer. 146:1189 N 27 '64
Febrile convulsions in infant rats, and later behavior. J. Werboff and J. Havlena. bibliog il Science 142:684-5 N 8 '63
Infant handling; effects on avoidance learning, brain weight, and cholinesterase activity. J. T. Tapp and H. Markowitz. bibliog il Science 140:486-7 My 3 '63
Jambo, first gorilla raised by its mother in captivity. E. M. Lang. il Nat Geog Mag 125:446-53 Mr '64
Maternal deprivation: its influence on visual exploration in infant monkeys. P. C. Green and M. Gordon. il Science 145:292-4 Jl 17 '64
Maternal facilitation of sucking drive in newborn lambs. G. Alexander and D. Williams. bibliog il Science 146:665-6 O 30 '64
Out-of-pocket kangaroo. il Sci Digest 55:inside back cover Ja '64
Polar babies. il Look 27:78-9 Jl 2 '63

ANIMALS, Laboratory. See Laboratory animals

ANIMALS, Mythical
Crossing species produces strange life forms. L. Ehrman. il Sci Digest 53:70-6 Mr '63

ANIMALS, Performing. See Animals—Training

ANIMALS, Predatory
Costly and needless war on predators; condensation of address, November 12, 1962. D. L. Allen. il Audubon Mag 65:85-9+ Mr '63
Dog gods wept. C. E. Gillham. il Field & S 68:58-60 Je '63
Giving the predators a break. Nation 198:110 F 3 '64
Wolves and congressmen. D. Cort. il Nation 197:216-18 O 12 '63
See also
Coyotes
Turtles
Wolves

Bounties

It's time for mutiny on the bounties. H. C. Laun. il Audubon Mag 65:146-9, 232-5 My-Jl '63
Wolves and congressmen. D. Cort. il Nation 197:216-18 O 12 '63

ANIMALS, Prosecution and punishment of
Just like old times. Time 81:23-4 My 3 '63

ANIMALS, Rescue of. See Animals—Protection

ANIMALS, Respiration of. See Respiration

ANIMALS in art
Pompeii. W. Jashemski. il Natur Hist 73:30-41 D '64
Wild beasts of Chinese art. il Art N 62:32-3+ D '63
See also
Animal sculpture

ANIMALS in captivity. See Zoological gardens

ANIMALS in opera. See Animals in the theater

ANIMALS in the theater
Backstage bestiary; Mrs D'Essen's Animal talent scouts, inc. F. Stevenson. il Opera N 29:6-7 Ja 30 '65

ANIMALS on television programs
Lassie's future. New Yorker 40:36-7 Mr 14 '64
Saga of Lassie. V. Scott. il Sat Eve Post 237:24-7 O 3 '64

ANIMATED cartoons. See Moving pictures—Animated cartoons

ANIMATION, Suspended. See Anabiosis

ANIMATION rig. See Photography—Apparatus and supplies

ANISFIELD-Wolf awards
SR Anisfield-Wolf awards, 1963. A. Montagu. il Sat R 46:22-3 Ap 13 '63
SR-Anisfield-Wolf awards, 1964; Winning authors. A. Montagu. il Sat R 47:19 Ap 25 '64

ANKA, Paul
Paul in Poland; ed. by E. Miller. il pors Seventeen 23:160-1+ Ap '64

ANKARA
Our far-flung correspondents. C. Frankel. il New Yorker p40:136+ Je 6 '64

ANLIKER, James
Variations in alpha voltage of the electroencephalogram and time perception. bibliog Science 140:1307-9 Je 21 '63

ANN ARBOR, Mich.
City hall sets the pace for downtown growth. G. C. Larcom, jr. il Am City 79:93-4 Ja '64

ANN ARBOR May festival. See Music festivals—Michigan

ANN-MARGRET
Ann-Margret. D. Jennings. il pors Sat Eve Post 236:70-3 My 4 '63
Ann-Margret tries new hair styles. il pors Seventeen 22:156-7 Ap '63
Sight and sound; on location of Viva Las Vegas. il pors McCalls 91:12+ N '63

ANNAND, H. H.
Hands across the seas! J. Walsh. il pors Hobbies 69:32-4 S; 32-4 O; 32-5 N; 32-5+ D '64; 33-4+ Ja '65

ANNAPOLIS, Md.

City planning

American landmarks story; Annapolis raiders. M. G. Warren. il Am For 70:36-8+ O '64

Historic houses, etc.

American landmarks story; Annapolis raiders. M. G. Warren. il Am For 70:36-8+ O '64

ANNAPOLIS naval academy. See United States naval academy, Annapolis

ANNAPOLIS-to-Newport race. See Yacht racing

ANNE, princess of Great Britain
Princess Anne grows older. C. Plimmer and D. Plimmer. il pors Redbook 120:58-9+ Ap '63
Student princess. il por N Y Times Mag p74 S 8 '63
Teen-age princes and princesses. G. Fisher and H. Fisher. il por Seventeen 23:122-3+ Je '64

ANNE Marie, consort of Constantine II, king of the Hellenes
Lovely gift to the Greeks. H. Moffett. il pors Life 57:48-50 O 9 '64
Royal wedding. il por Newsweek 64:52+ S 28 '64
Storm over a royal love affair. C. Plimmer and D. Plimmer. il por Redbook 121:60-1+ O '63
Suddenly a queen. il por Seventeen 23:28 Je '64
Vogue's notebook; royal wedding in Athens. il Vogue 144:98-101 N 1 '64

ANNELIDS
See also
Marine worms

ANNIS, Edward Roland
Care of the aged, a responsible approach; adaptation of address. Todays Health 41:88 D '63
Excerpt from address, November 9, 1962. Cong Digest 42:213+ Ag '63
Government health care: first the aged, then everyone. bibliog f Cur Hist 45:104-9+ Ag '63
Medicare; address, January 11, 1963. Vital Speeches 29:309-11 Mr 1 '63

ANNISQUAM, Mass.
Crickets and katydids, long ago. M. Wallace. il Sat R 46:40-1+ Ap 13 '63

ANNIVERSARIES
See also
Celebrations
Fourth of July

ANNOTATIONS

Anecdotes, facetiae, satire, etc.

Epistle of Paul to the pedants; against the long discursive footnote. J. Shera. Wilson Lib Bul 38:485 F '64

ANNOUNCERS, Television. See Television broadcasting—Announcing

ANNUAL meetings, Stockholders. See Stockholders meetings

ANNUAL reports. See Reports

ANNUALS (plants)
Annuals. P. F. Frese. il Pop Gard 15:24-5 My '64
Annuals for quick garden joy. il Flower Grower 50:37-43 My '63
Annuals in a brand-new garden. il Sunset 130:284 Ap '63
Annuals, perennials, summer bulbs for 1964. H. Mason. il Bet Hom & Gard 42:58-63 Mr '64
Fall-sown annuals hide ripened bulb foliage in spring. M. Costigan. il Flower Grower 50:18-20 O '63
Here are twenty outstanding annuals. il Sunset 132:264-5 My '64
How to use annuals. il Pop Gard 15:51 Ja '64
It's easy to grow annuals from seed. R. C. Hands. il Horticulture 41:144-5 Mr '63
New annuals for 1964. P. F. Frese. il Pop Gard 15:52-4 Ja '64
See also
Browallia

ANNUITIES
Ruling on variable annuities. U S News 54:85 F 4 '63
Should you buy an annuity? variable annuities. il Changing T 18:17-20 Jl '64
Variable annuities get a go sign. U S News 56:112 Ap 27 '64
What young families should know about annuities. il Good H 156:172 Ap '63

ANNULMENT of marriage. See Marriage—Annulment

ANNUNZIO, Gabriele d'
Ascetic in Rome; interview, ed. by M. J. Matz. I. Pizzetti. il Opera N 28:14-16 Ja 18 '64

ANODIZING of aluminum. See Aluminum—Protection

ANOKA COUNTY library, Spring Lake Park, Minn.
Nickel-a-day addiction. J. Chaliman. Library J 89:4866-7 D 15 '64

ANON, Sister Mary. See Mary Anon, Sister

ANORGANIC bone. See Bone

ANOTHER country, another time; story. See Williams, T.

ANOTHER day; story. See Jacobson, D.

ANOUILH, Jean
Cynicism uncongealed. por Time 82:66 D 13 '63
Poor Bitos. Criticism
Nation 199:415-17 N 30 '64
New Repub 151:20-1 D 12 '64
Newsweek 64:92 N 30 '64
Sat R 47:43 D 5 '64
Time 84:104 N 27 '64
Rehearsal; tr. by P. H. Johnson and K. Black. Criticism
Commonweal 79:194 N 8 '63
Nat R 15:406-7 N 5 '63
Nation 197:245 O 19 '63
New Yorker 39:133-4 O 5 '63
Newsweek 62:96 O 7 '63
Sat R 46:30 O 12 '63
Theatre Arts il 47:10-11 D '63
Time 82:63 O 4 '63
Traveller without luggage; tr. by L. Hill. Criticism
Commonweal 81:73 O 9 '64
Nation 199:202 O 5 '64
Newsweek 64:90-1 S 28 '64
Sat R 47:28 O 3 '64
Time il 84:96 S 25 '64
Vogue 144:66 N 1 '64

ANOXEMIA
Anoxia: tolerance in reptiles. D. A. Belkin. bibliog il Science 139:492-3 F 8 '63
Excess lactate: an index of reversibility of shock in human patients. G. Broder and M. H. Weil. bibliog il Science 143:1457-9 Mr 27 '64
Heart defects caused by diminished oxygen. Sci N L 85:377 Je 13 '64
Hypoxia: effects on heart rate and respiration in the snapping turtle. D. R. Boyer. bibliog il Science 140:813-14 My 17 '63
Oxygen lack kills fish. Sci N L 85:365 Je 6 '64

ANQUETIL, Jacques
Another for the accountant. il por Time 82:62 Jl 26 '63

ANSCHLUSS (economics) See Austro-German customs union (proposed)
ANSELM, Saint
Anselm: fides quaerens intellectum, by K. Barth. Review
New Yorker 39:203-6+ O 12 '63. J. Updike
ANSELMO, Annette
Awake through a brain operation. Read Digest 85:53-7 Jl '64
ANSETT, Reginald Miles
Grim determination in the air. il por Time 84:85 Ag 7 '64
ANSHUTZ, Thomas
In turkey-chawed country. il Time 81:72 Mr 22 '63
ANSKY, S. pseud. See Rappoport, S.
ANSLEY, H. R. See Black, M. M. jt. auth.
ANSONIA clock company
Another Ansonia find. L. W. Slaughter. il Hobbies 68:52-3+ D '63
ANSONIA hotel. See New York (city)—Hotels, restaurants, etc.
ANSTRUTHER, Ian
When knighthood's flower wilted; excerpt from The knight and the umbrella. Sports Illus 20:88-90+ My 18 '64
ANSTRUTHER, James
As cheaply as one; poem. Ladies Home J 80:136 Je '63
ANSWER depends; story. See O'Hara, J.
ANSWERS to questions. See Questions and answers
ANT venom. See Venom
ANTA. See American national theatre and academy
ANTA theater. See New York (city)—Theater
ANTARCTIC REGIONS
Antarctica: colonization ends era of exploration, emphasis shifts to organized polar science program. J. Walsh. Science 139:578+ F 15 '63
Antarctica; the international laboratory. A. P. Crary. il Bul Atomic Sci 20:27-30 Ja '64
Breaking the ice in Antarctica. J. Lear. il Sat R 46:43-5 N 2 '63
Distribution of narrow-width magnetic anomalies in Antarctica. J. C. Behrendt. bibliog il Science 144:993-4+ My 22 '64
Ice movement of valley glaciers flowing into the Ross Ice Shelf, Antarctica. C. W. Swithinbank. bibliog il Science 141:523-4 Ag 9 '63
Mental strains of Antarctic solitude. P. Law. il UNESCO Courier 16:26-30 Je '63
New era in the loneliest continent. D. M. Tyree. il Nat Geog Mag 123:260-96 F '63
Reporter at large. A. Moorehead. il New Yorker 40:39-40+ Je 27 '64
Secrets from cold storage. W. J. Cromie. il Natur Hist 72:20-7 O '63
Times change in Antarctica; photographs. N Y Times Mag p68 D 1 '63
Unlocking the icebox. il Time 83:41 Ja 3 '64
See also
Geology—Antarctic Regions
Ice—Polar Regions
Zoology—Antarctic Regions
Maps
Filling in Antarctica's blank spaces. il Nat Geog Mag 123:296-7, sup(folded map) F '63
ANTARCTIC research. See Polar research
ANTARCTIC treaty, 1959
Antarctic inspection. Sci Am 209:65 N '63
Arctic disarmament. A. Rich and A. P. Vinogradov. Bul Atomic Sci 20:22-3 N '64
Secretary appoints observers for Antarctic inspection. Dept State Bul 49:932 D 16 '63
United States policy and international cooperation in Antarctica; excerpts from President's report to Congress; with letters of transmittal. L. B. Johnson; D. Rusk. bibliog f Dept State Bul 51:402-7 S 21 '64
U.S. to conduct inspection in Antarctica; Department statement, September 13, 1963. Dept State Bul 49:513 S 30 '63
ANTEATER association
Filet of hippo, anyone? A. Chamberlin. il Sat Eve Post 238:78+ Ja 30 '65
ANTEK, Samuel
This was Toscanini. Opera N 28:26-7 N 16 '63
ANTELOPE brush. See Bitterbrush
ANTELOPE hunting
Born smart, and suspicious. J. O'Connor. il Outdoor Life 132:32-3 D '63
Elusive Mrs Gray. F. C. Hibben. il Field & S 67:66-7+ Ap '63
Marsh walker. W. Page. il Field & S 68:40-1+ Ja '64
Where the antelope play; paintings by B. Shields; with account by D. Barnes. Sports Illus 21:46-54 O 12 '64
See also
Pronghorn hunting
ANTELOPES
Elusive Mrs Gray. F. C. Hibben. il Field & S 67:66-7+ Ap '63
Kingdom for the oryx; Arabian oryxes in Phoenix Maytag zoo. il Time 82:52 Jl 12 '63
Lo, the vanishing oryx makes tiny comeback. il Life 55:59-60 D 13 '63
ANTELOPES, American. See Pronghorns
ANTENNAS (electronics)
Aerospace corp. steerable antenna seeking accuracy of twenty arc seconds. R. Pay. il Miss & Roc 13:26-7 D 23 '63
Electronic antenna; pros and cons; symposium, ed. by C. S. Tepfer. Electr World 69:41-4+ F '63
Huge antenna to direct spacecraft. C. D. LaFond. il Miss & Roc 12:37 Mr 11 '63
Ionospheric satellites aiding design of long antenna systems. M. Getler. Miss & Roc 16:34-7 Ja 4 '65
Langley okays multiple-array concept. il Miss & Roc 14:18 Je 1 '64
S-band system subcontractors to Collins to be named this month. C. D. LaFond. il Miss & Roc 15:36-7 Ag 3 '64
Spacecraft antenna unfolds after launching. il(p 209) Sci N L 86:217 O 3 '64
Titan II sites pop-up antennas. M. Getler. il Miss & Roc 12:18+ Mr 11 '63
Your leisure. Consumer Rep 28:369-73 D '63
See also
Radar—Antenna and scanning mechanisms
Radio antennas
Television antennas
Testing
One way to do it. il Time 81:80+ Ap 26 '63
ANTHELMINTICS
What you need to know about beef cattle internal parasites. G. C. Shelton. Suc Farm 62:106 F '64
ANTHEMS
See also
Hymns
ANTHOCYANIDINS
Conversion of leucoanthocyanins into the corresponding anthocyanidins. M. A. Joslyn and J. L. Goldstein. bibliog il Science 143:954-5 F 28 '64
ANTHOLOGIES
Use of anthologies. D. Galler. Poetry 103:261-5 Ja '64
ANTHON, Carl G.
End of the Adenauer era. Cur Hist 44:193-201 Ap '63
Stalinist rule in East Germany. Cur Hist 44:265-72+ My '63
ANTHONY, Donald C.
Caring for your manuscripts and related material. Hobbies 68:110-11+ Ja '64
ANTHONY, George
Christmas in Vermont; poem. Atlan 212:60 D '63
Summer; poem. Nation 199:38 Jl 27 '64
ANTHONY, H. M.
Great way to spend the day, calibrate your rdf. Motor B 112:30-1 Ag '63
Request assistance! my estimated position is. Motor B 112:32-3 Ag '63
ANTHONY, Irvin
Dwellers and voyagers. Yachting 116:43+ D '64
ANTHONY, Mother Mary. See Mary Anthony, Mother
ANTHONY, Mark. See Antonius, M.
ANTHONY, Sir Mobolaji Bank-. See Bank-Anthony, M.
ANTHONY, Robert N.
Showdown on accounting principles. Harvard Bsns R 41:99-106 My '63
ANTHONY, Susan B.
Editor's notebook. M. S. Fenner. NEA J 53:92 Mr '64
ANTHRACENE
Skin tumorigenesis by 7,12-dimethylbenz(a)anthracene: inhibition by actinomycin D. H. V. Gelboin and M. Klein. bibliog il Science 145:1321-2 S 18 '64
ANTHROPOLOGY
Anthropology. G. D. Spindler. bibliog il NEA J 52:28-31 S '63
First Americans. il Newsweek 61:56-7 F 11 '63
In the beginnings: early man and his gods, by H. R. Hays. Review
Sat R il 46:54 D 7 '63. B. J. Siegel
Men with their faces on. G. P. Elliott. Nation 199:201 O 5 '64
Pygmy progenitor? il Time 83:68 Ap 24 '64

ANTHROPOLOGY—*Continued*
Rousseau, father of anthropology; summary of address. C. Levi-Strauss. il UNESCO Courier 16:10-15 Mr '63
Social anthropology; models, political systems, religion, and urbanization; report of joint Anglo-American meeting of the British Commonwealth association of social anthropology. F. Eggan. Science 141:1204-6 S 20 '63
See also
Culture
Ethnology
Man
Man, Prehistoric

Study and teaching

Grasping the drama of a culture. H. W. Hertzberg. il NEA J 52:44-6 F '63
ANTHURIUM scherzerianum. See Flamingo flowers
ANTHURIUMS
Anthuriums. K. Berggrav. il Horticulture 42: 22-3+ S '64
ANTI-AMERICANISM. See Public opinion
ANTIBACTERIAL drugs. See Drugs
ANTIBES
Eden on the rocks; Hôtel du Cap. H. Sutton. il Sat R 47:21-2+ Ag 1 '64

Hotels, restaurants, etc.

Small, proud, cream-colored hotel; Hotel du Cap. J. Bryan, 3d. Holiday 34:62-3+ S '63
ANTIBIOTIC feed supplements
Beef additives. W. Burroughs and S. A. Ewing. il Suc Farm 61:100 N '63
Scientist warns of curbs on additives; livestock feed. Farm J 87:43 N '63
ANTIBIOTICS
Antibiotics barred for colds. Sci N L 84:130 Ag 31 '63
Antibiotics: experts question value in treating colds; FDA issues ban on use in compounds. E. Langer. Science 141:791 Ag 30 '63
Antibiotics may help stop tooth troubles. Sci N L 87:56 Ja 23 '65
Antibody formation in vitro separated spleen cells: inhibition by actinomycin or chloramphenicol. S. E. Svehag. bibliog il Science 146:659-61 O 30 '64
Antimicrobial agents and chemotherapy; report on 3rd interscience conference on antimicrobial agents and chemotherapy. D. Perlman. Science 144:322-3 Ap 17 '64
Antimicrobial substances from aspen tissue grown in vitro. M. C. Mathes. bibliog il Science 140:1101-2 Je 7 '63
Capreomycin: activity against experimental infection with mycobacterium leprae. C. C. Shepard. bibliog il Science 146:403-4 O 16 '64
Chloramphenicol in blood: simple chemical estimations in patients receiving multiple antibiotics. D. W. O. Hughes and L. K. Diamond. bibliog il Science 144:296-7 Ap 17 '64
Coenzyme Q: reversal of inhibition of succinate cytochrome c reductase by lipophilic compounds. S. Takemori and T. E. King. bibliog il Science 14:852-3 My 15 '64
Cycloheximide: aspects of inhibition of protein synthesis in mammalian cells. H. L. Ennis and M. Lubin. bibliog il Science 146: 1474-6 D 11 '64
Ethylation: biological formation of an S-ethyl homolog of lincomycin. E. L. Patterson and others bibliog il Science 146: 1691-2 D 25 '64
History lesson. J. Lear. Sat R 46:50 S 7 '63
Italian antibiotic inhibits cancer, staph; daunomycin. Sci N L 85:134 F 29 '64
Mitomycins and porfiromycin: chemical mechanism of activation and cross-linking of DNA. V. N. Iyer and W. Szybalski. bibliog il Science 145:55-8 Jl 3 '64
New controls for antibiotics. Consumer Rep 28:463 O '63
New healer for the burn victim. Bsns W p 124+ N 21 '64
Phenethyl alcohol synergism with mitomycin C, porfiromycin, and streptonigrin. J. R. White and H. L. White. bibliog il Science 145:1312-13 S 18 '64
Stubborn germs killed by new antibiotic; gentamicin. Sci N L 85:8 Ja 4 '64
What those wonder drugs can and cannot do. Good H 158:121-2 Ja '64
See also
Actinomycin
Erythromycin
Penicillin
Puromycin
Streptomycin
Tetracyclines
Tomatin
ANTIBODIES. See Antigens and antibodies
ANTIBODIES, Fluorescent
Malaria parasites: fluorescent antibody technique for tissue stage study. R. L. Ingram and R. K. Carver. bibliog il Science 139: 405-6 F 1 '63
ANTICHOLINESTERASES
Anticholinesterase agents; report of symposium at meetings of the Federation of American societies for experimental biology. G. B. Koelle and others. Science 141: 63:5 Jl 5 '63
ANTICLERICALISM
On slaying clerical dragons. America 111:282 S 19 '64
ANTICOAGULANTS (medicine)
Better drugs foreseen; for protection against strokes and heart attacks. Sci N L 86:163 S 12 '64
Embolism rise requires anticoagulant drugs. Sci N L 84:248 O 19 '63
Too much spinach bad if taking anticoagulants. Sci N L 85:56 Ja 25 '64
ANTI-COLONIALISM. See Colonies
ANTI-COMMUNIST measures. See Communism—Anti-Communist measures
ANTI-COMMUNIST measures in the United States. See Communism—United States—Anti-Communist measures; United States—Foreign relations—Anti-Communist measures
ANTI-COMMUNIST movements
Captive nations. Cato. Nat R 16:649 Jl 28 '64

Cuba

Alpha 66. C. T. Sheldon. Nat R 14:172 F 26 '63
Anti-anti-Castro policy. Time 81:29 Ap 12 '63
Can't anyone here play this game? Time 83: 48 Je 12 '64
Cuban exiles: the mirage of Havana: Revolutionary recovery movement. A. Burt. Nation 200:76-9 Ja 25 '65
Evidence is mounting. il U S News 54:16 My 20 '63
Guerra! still the word in Miami. T. Szulc. il N Y Times Mag p9+ Jl 5 '64
How the war of nerves is going inside Cuba. U S News 56:8 Je 15 '64
Playing for high stakes. il Newsweek 63:40 Je 1 '64
Something is moving; exile activity. il Time 83:26 My 22 '64
To Ivan in Cuba: now hear this! broadcasts by anti-Communist Russians. Life 54:4 Ap 12 '63
Vamos! the buccaneers attack the Soviet prey. A. St George. il Life 54:18-25 Ap 12 '63
War of nerves; exile campaign. Time 83: 33 My 29 '64
War of nerves opens against Castro. U S News 56:40 Je 1 '64
What war? il Newsweek 63:52 My 25 '64

Latin America

Latin America, where military is moving to stop the reds. il U S News 54:49-50 Ap 15 '63

United States

Rightist binge in Omaha. L. McKie. Christian Cent 80:1270-1 O 16 '63
ANTI-COMMUNIST propaganda. See Propaganda
ANTICOSTI ISLAND
Legacy of a French Noah; whitetail deer to Anticosti Island. J. Olsen. il Sports Illus 19:62-4+ O 7 '63
ANTI-DEFAMATION league. See B'nai b'rith—Anti-defamation league
ANTI-DEPRESSANTS. See Depression, Mental
ANTI-DEPRESSION measures. See United States—Economic policy
ANTI-DUMPING. See Dumping (commercial policy)
ANTI-EARTHQUAKE building. See Earthquakes and building
ANTI-FOG preparations. See Glass—Fogging
ANTI-FREEZE solutions
Anti freeze. il Consumer Bul 46:25-7 S '63; 47:2+ N '64
ANTIFUNGAL drugs. See Drugs
ANTIGENS and antibodies
Actinomycin D: effect on the immune response. C. J. Wust and others. bibliog il Science 143:1041-3 Mr 6 '64

ANTIGENS and antibodies—*Continued*
Actinomycin D: its effect on antibody formation in vitro. J. W. Uhr. bibliog il Science 142:1476-7 D 13 '63
Agammaglobulinemia: the fundametal defect. H. H. Fudenberg and K. Hirschhorn. bibliog il Science 145:611-12 Ag 7 '64
Allergic encephalomyelitis: rapid induction without the aid of adjuvants. S. Levine and E. J. Wenk. bibliog il Science 141:529-30 Ag 9 '63
Amino acid composition of univalent fragments of rabbit antibody. W. J. Mandy and others. bibliog il Science 140:901-3 My 24 '63
Antibodies blueprinted. Sci N L 83:178 Mr 23 '63
Antibodies to bradykinin and angiotensin: a use of carbodiimides in immunology. T. L. Goodfriend and others. bibliog il Science 144:1344-6 Je 12 '64
Antibodies to genetic types of gamma globulin after multiple transfusions. J. C. Allen and H. G. Kunkel. bibliog il Science 139:418 F 1 '63
Antibody activity in six classes of human immunoglobulins. J. L. Fahey and H. Goodman. bibliog il Science 143:588-90 F 7 '64
Antibody combining site: the B polypeptide chain. O. A. Roholt and others. bibliog il Science 141:726-7 Ag 23 '63
Antibody formation in embryos. M. F. La Via and others. bibliog il Science 140:1219-20 Je 14 '63
Antibody formation in vitro by separated spleen cells: inhibition by actinomycin or chloramphenicol. S. E. Svehag. bibliog il Science 146:659-61 O 30 '64
Antibody plaque formation by normal mouse spleen cell cultures exposed in vitro to RNA from immune mice. H. Friedman. bibliog il Science 146:934-6 N 13 '64
Antibody production and development of contact skin sensitivity in guinea pigs of various ages. H. Baer and R. T. Bowser. bibliog il Science 140:1211-12 Je 14 '63
Antibody production by nonimmune spleen cells incubated with RNA from immunized mice. E. P. Cohen and J. J. Parks. bibliog il Science 144:1012-13 My 22 '64
Antibody quality after sequential immunization with related antigens. R. V. Gilden and S. Tokuda. bibliog il Science 140:405-6 Ap 26 '63
Antibody response to immunization by different routes. S. Shulman and others. bibliog il Science 145:815-17 Ag 21 '64
Antibody suppression by antigen heavily labeled with iodine-131. M. M. Webber. bibliog il Science 143:132-3 Ja 10 '64
Antibody synthesizing cells: appearance after secondary antigenic stimulation in vitro. M. Richardson and R. W. Dutton. bibliog il Science 146:655-6 O 30 '64
Antibody to hereditary human gamma-globulin (Gm) factor resulting from maternal-fetal incompatibility. H. H. Fudenberg and B. R. Fudenberg. bibliog il Science 145:170-1 Jl 10 '64
Antibody to rat kidney: in vivo effects of univalent and divalent fragments. J. H. Baxter and P. A. Small, jr. bibliog il Science 140:1406-7 Je 28 '63
Antigen-binding activity of 6S subunits of β_2-macroglobulin antibody. K. Onoue and others. bibliog il Science 146:404-5 O 16 '64
Antigenic behavior of Moloney lymphomas: independence of virus release and immunosensitivity. G. Klein and E. Klein. bibliog il Science 145:1316-17 S 18 '64
Antigenic determinants in fragments of gamma globulin from rabbit serum. J. W. Goodman. bibliog il Science 139:1292-3 Mr 29 '63
Antigenic histamine release from passively sensitized human leukocytes. P. P. VanArsdel, jr. and C. J. Sells. bibliog il Science 141:1190-1 S 20 '63
Antigenic material; persistence in hypersensitive cells. R. S. Speirs. bibliog il Science 140:71-2 Ap 5 '63
Antigenicity of polypeptides: immunological unresponsiveness to copolymers of α-amino acids. P. H. Maurer and others. bibliog il Science 139:1061-2 Mr 15 '63
Antigens and enzymes made insoluble by entrapping them into lattices of synthetic polymers. P. Bernfeld and J. Wan. bibliog il Science 142:678-9 N 8 '63
Antigens associated with a tumor virus: rejection of isogenic skin grafts from leukemic mice. E. J. Breyere and L. B. Williams. bibliog il Science 146:1055-6 N 20 '64
Antigens in insulin determinants of specificity of porcine insulin in man. S. A. Berson and R. S. Yalow. bibliog il Science 139:844-5 Mr 1 '63
Antigens; report of conference of scientists from Asia, Canada, Europe, South America, and the United States at Warrenton, Va. M. L. Robbins. Science 141:443-4 Ag 2 '63
Antiserums prepared with acrylamide gel used as adjuvant. M. Weintraub and S. Raymond. bibliog il Science 142:1677-8 D 27 '63
Autoantibodies may cause myasthenia gravis. Sci Digest 53:69 Mr '63
Binding capacity of reductively fragmented antibodies to the 2,4-dinitrophenyl group. H. Metzger and S. J. Singer. bibliog il Science 142:674-5 N 8 '63
Brucella-agglutinating antibodies: relation of mercaptoethanol stability to complement fixation. R. K. Anderson and others. bibliog il Science 143:1334-5 Mr 20 '64
Circulating small lymphocytes: immunologically competent cells with limited reactivities. D. L. Vredevoe and W. H. Hildemann. bibliog il Science 141:1272-4 S 27 '63
Complement-fixing antigens in tissue cultures of avian leucosis viruses. D. Armstrong and others. bibliog il Science 144:1584 Je 26 '64
Complement-fixing properties of pepsin-treated rabbit and sheep antibodies. P. H. Schur and E. L. Becker. bibliog il Science 141:360-2 Jl 26 '63
Conglutination: specific inhibition by carbohydrates. M. A. Leon and R. Yokohari. bibliog il Science 143:1327-8 Mr 20 '64
Cytoplasmic interaction between macrophages and lymphocytic cells in antibody synthesis. M. D. Schoenberg and others. bibliog il Science 143:964-5 F 28 '64
Dependence of a Gm(b) antigen on the quaternary structure of human gamma globulin. S. H. Polmar and A. G. Steinberg. bibliog il Science 145:928-9 Ag 28 '64
Differences in the amino acid composition of a third rabbit antibody. M. E. Kostland and others. bibliog il Science 143:1330-1 Mr 20 '64
Diphtheria antitoxin: antigen-combining and toxin-neutralizing properties of papain fragments. J. J. Cohen and others. bibliog il Science 144:1585-6 Je 26 '64
Electrophoretic and immunological studies of squid axoplasm proteins. F. Huneeus-Cox. bibliog il Science 143:1036-7 Mr 6 '64
Fixation of complement to fragments of antibody. A. M. Reiss and O. J. Plescia. bibliog il Science 141:812-13 Ag 30 '63
Fluorescent, electron microscopic, and immunoelectrophoretic studies of labeled antibodies. K. C. Hsu and others. bibliog il Science 142:1471-3 D 13 '63
Galactosidase action on human blood group B active escherichia coli and ox red cell substances. G. F. Springer and others. bibliog il Science 146:946-7 N 13 '64
Gamma globulin affinity for normal human tissue of the central nervous system. C. D. Allerand and M. D. Yahr. bibliog il Science 144:1141-2 My 29 '64
Gamma globulin antigenic types defined by heavy chain determinants. R. E. Ballieux and others. bibliog il Science 145:168-70 Jl 10 '64
Gamma globulin: unmasking of hidden antigenic sites on light chains. R. L. Nachman and R. L. Engle, jr. bibliog il Science 145:167-8 Jl 10 '64
Genetic differences in antibody production to determinant groups on insulin. E. R. Arquilla and J. Finn. bibliog il Science 142:400-1 O 18 '63
Growth inhibition of sarcoma and carcinoma cells of homozygous origin. K. E. Hellström. bibliog Science 143:477-8 Ja 31 '64
Hereditary globulin factors and immune tolerance in man. A. G. Steinberg and J. A. Wilson. bibliog il Science 140:303-4 Ap 19 '63
Heterogeneity of antibodies; report of third annual midwinter conference of immunologists. F. Aladjem and H. Fudenberg. Science 145:614-16 Ag 7 '64
Heterogeneity of the immune response. J. W. Uhr. bibliog il Science 145:457-64 Jl 31 '64
Homograft rejection in the fetal lamb: the role of circulating antibody. A. M. Silverstein and others. bibliog Science 142:1172-3 N 29 '63
Homograft target cells: specific destruction in vitro by contact interaction with immune macrophages. G. A. Granger and R. S. Weiser. bibliog il Science 145:1427-9 S 25 '64

ANTIGENS and antibodies—*Continued*
How antibody is made. il Time 85:29 Ja 8 '65
How cells attack antigens. R. S. Speirs. il Sci Am 210:58-64 bibliog(p 152) F '64
How cells make antibodies. G. J. V. Nossal. il Sci Am 211:106-15 D '64
How man becomes allergic to parts of himself; autoimmune diseases. il Time 83:55-6 My 1 '64
Human wart virus: in vitro cultivation. S. Oroszlan and M. A. Rich. bibliog il Science 146:531-3 O 23 '64
Humoral thymic factor in mice: further evidence. L. W. Law and others. bibliog il Science 143:1049-51 Mr 6 '64
Hypersensitivity to a synthetic polypeptide: induction of a delayed reaction. S. Ben-Efraim and others. bibliog il Science 139:1222-3 Mr 22 '63
Immune response and mitosis of human peripheral blood lymphocytes in vitro. K. Hirschhorn and others. bibliog il Science 142:1185-7 N 29 '63
Immune to sperm. il Newsweek 62:80 O 21 '63
Immunologic phenomena: cold-blooded vertebrates; report of meeting of the Federation of the American society for experimental microbiology. M. M. Sigel. Science 141:543+ Ag 9 '63
Immunologically determined and competent cells are affected differentially by actinomycin D. E. Weller. bibliog il Science 144:846-9 My 15 '64; Reply with rejoinder. D. W. Talmage. 145:1073-4 S 4 '64
Individual antigenic specificity of isolated antibodies. H. G. Kunkel and others. bibliog il Science 140:1218-19 Je 14 '63
Inhibition of antibody plaque formation by sensitized lymphoid cells: rapid indicator of transplantation immunity. H. Friedman. bibliog il Science 145:607-9 Ag 7 '64
Inhibition of antibody synthesis by L-phenylalanine. W. L. Ryan and M. J. Carver. bibliog il Science 143:479-80 Ja 31 '64
Inhibition of 19S antibody synthesis by 7S antibody. K. Sahiar and R. S. Schwartz. bibliog il Science 145:395-7 Jl 24 '64
Inhibition of specific binding of antibody to the Rh_0(D) factor of red cells in antibody excess. S. P. Masouredis and others. bibliog il Science 145:1197-9 S 11 '64
Killing of cultured rabbit fibroblasts with isoimmune serum. D. A. Pious and S. E. Mills. bibliog il Science 142:52-3 O 4 '63
Lymphoid organs and normal gammaglobulin in the rat. S. B. Andersen and F. Bierring. bibliog il Science 144:1219-20 Je 5 '64
Molecular and submolecular localization of two isoantigens of mouse immunoglobulins. R. I. Mishell and J. L. Fahey. bibliog il Science 143:1440-2 Mr 27 '64
Mosquitoes; comparative serology of four species of aedes (ochlerotatus) A. E. R. Downe. bibliog il Science 139:1286-7 Mr 29 '63
Ontogeny of the immune response. A. M. Silverstein. bibliog Science 144:1423-8 Je 19 '64
Passive cutaneous anaphylaxis with antibody fragments. Z. Ovary and A. Taranta. bibliog il Science 140:193-5 Ap 12 '63
Phytohemagglutinin elicitation of specific anamnestic immune response in vitro. T. W. Tao. bibliog il Science 146:247-8 O 9 '64
Plaque formation in agar by single antibody-producing cells. N. K. Jerne and A. A. Nordin. il Science 140:405 Ap 26 '63
Poliovirus type I: neutralization by papain-digested antibodies. A. Vogt and others. bibliog il Science 145:1447-8 S 25 '64
Possible cytoplasmic change in an immunologically competent tissue of the chicken. B. Glick. il Science 142:485-6 O 25 '63
Precipitins in the rabbit produced by protein polysaccharide from bovine nasal cartilage. N. Di Ferrante. bibliog il Science 143:250-2 Ja 17 '64
Purine- and pyrimidine-specific antibodies: effect on the fertilized sea urchin egg. H. S. Rosenkranz and others. bibliog il Science 145:282-3 Jl 17 '64
Reaction of lymphocytes with purified protein derivative conjugated with fluorescein. T. A. Witten and others. bibliog il Science 142:596-8 N 1 '63
Reovirus and wound-tumor virus; serological cross reactivity. G. Streissle and K. Maramorosch. bibliog Science 140:996-7 My 31 '63
Reticuloendothelial function and the immune response. W. R. Wooles and N. R. Di Luzio. bibliog il Science 142:1078-80 N 22 '63
Rubella antibodies in human serum: detection by the indirect fluorescent-antibody technique. G. C. Brown and others. bibliog il Science 145:943-5 Ag 28 '64
Rubella virus: neutralizing antibody in commercial gamma globulin. G. M. Schiff and others. bibliog il Science 142:58-60 O 4 '63
Serologic typing of human lymphocytes with immune serum obtained after homografting. R. L. Walford and others. bibliog il Science 144:868-70 My 15 '64
Shots that save. P. M. Stimson. il Parents Mag 39:47+ N '64
Specific immunologic unresponsiveness to synthetic polypeptide antigens. M. Sela and others. bibliog il Science 139:342-3 Ja 25 '63
Specific inhibition of antibody formation by passively administered 19S and 7S antibody. M. S. Finkelstein and J. W. Uhr. bibliog il Science 146:67-9 O 2 '64
Spontaneous autoimmunity in mice: antibodies to nucleoprotein in strain A/J. G. J. Friou and P. O. Teague. bibliog il Science 143:1333-4 Mr 20 '64
Synthesis of chicken antibodies of high and low molecular weight. A. A. Benedict and others. bibliog il Science 139:1302-3 Mr 29 '63
Thymectomy: prolongation of immunological tolerance in the adult mouse. H. N. Claman and D. W. Talmage. bibliog il Science 141:1193-4 S 20 '63
Thymus hormone. R. H. Levey. il Sci Am 211:66-71+ bibliog(p 142) Jl '64
Transplantation tolerance induced in adult mice by protein overloading of donors. P. Liacopoulos and J. H. Goode. bibliog il Science 146:1305-7 D 4 '64
Valence and affinity of equine nonprecipitating antibody to a haptenic group. N. R. Klinman and others. bibliog il Science 146:401-3 O 16 '64
See also
Agammaglobulinemia
Rh factors

ANTIGUA (Island)
Antigua incidentals; places and pleasures. Vogue 141:72+ My '63
Sullenness under the sun. N. T. di Giovanni. Nation 196:287-9 Ap 6 '63

ANTIHISTAMINES
Isolation of an antihistaminic principle resembling tomatine from crown gall tumors. B. A. Kovacs and others. bibliog il Science 144:295-6 Ap 17 '64; Reply with rejoinder. P. R. White. 146:670 O 30 '64
Teratogenic effects of meclizine hydrochloride on the rat. C. T. G. King. bibliog il Science 141:353-5 Jl 26 '63

ANTI-INFLATION measures. See Inflation (finance)

ANTI-KNOCK gasoline. See Gasoline—Anti-knock and anti-knock mixtures

ANTILLES. See West Indies

ANTIMICROBIAL substances. See Antibiotics

ANTI-MISSILE missile programs. See Guided missiles—Defenses

ANTI-NEGRO prejudice. See Race prejudice

ANTIOCH college, Yellow Springs, Ohio
Antioch college: ivory tower on a muddy road. M. A. Guitar. il Mlle 56:154-7+ Ap '63

ANTIOCHUS I, king of Commagene
Lost civilization. il Sci Digest 53:47-9 My '63

ANTIOXIDANTS
New food preservative isolated in oats. Sci N L 85:313 My 16 '64

ANTI-PARTICLES. See Particles (nuclear physics)

ANTIPATHIES. See Likes and dislikes

ANTI-POVERTY program. See Economic assistance, Domestic

ANTIQUARIAN book center. See Antiquarian booksellers association of America

ANTIQUARIAN book fairs. See Book fairs

ANTIQUARIAN booksellers association of America
Antiquarian book center opens in New York city. il Pub W 184:45 N 18 '63

ANTIQUE airplane association
See also
Airplanes—Collectors and collecting

ANTIQUE airplanes. See Aeronautics—History

ANTIQUE airplanes

Collectors and collecting

See Airplanes—Collectors and collecting

ANTIQUE automobiles. See Automobiles—Collectors and collecting

ANTIQUE automobiles in art. See Automobiles in art

ANTIQUE boat and yacht club. See Boat clubs
ANTIQUE boats. See Boats—Collectors and collecting
ANTIQUE dealers
Some practices in the antiques business; buying and selling by mail. A. G. Peterson. il Hobbies 68:82-3 S '63
Treasure hunting up North; Aberfoyle flea market. il Bsns W p 126-7 S 7 '63
See also
Parke-Bernet galleries, incorporated
ANTIQUE dealers fair and exhibition, London. See Antiques—Exhibitions
ANTIQUES
Antiques and the tariff. W. H. Van Hoesen. Antiques 85:328+ Mr '64
Antiques; questions and answers. T. H. Ormsbee. See issues of House & garden
Collectors' notes. E. Gaines. il Antiques 84: 304-5 S '63
Harlem's antique collector. il Ebony 18:105-6+ Ap '63
How a diversified harvest of antiques was united by a background. il House & Gard 123:162-5 My '63
How Jackie restyled the White House; paintings, antiques and historic objects. Sat Eve Post 236:42-51 O 26 '63
Living with antiques. J. A. H. Sweeney. il Antiques 85:542-7 My '64
Living with antiques; Casa Soberanes, the California home of Mrs William M. O'Donnell. il Antiques 83:190-3 F '63
Living with antiques; collector's choice in the plains states. B. Utley. il Antiques 84: 165-7 Ag '63
Living with antiques; Colorado ranch of Mr and Mrs Royal B. Hassrick. E. Gaines. il Antiques 84:162-4 Ag '63
Living with antiques: East meets West on Long Island. R. G. Gerry. il Antiques 87: 80-4 Ja '65
Living with antiques; Hacienda, Florida residence of H. R. Sharp. J. A. L. Hyde. il Antiques 85:76-9 Ja '64
Living with antiques; New York apartment. P. Warren. il Antiques 83:326-9 Mr '63
Living with antiques; Pagoda House in Newport, Rhode Island. J. A. L. Hyde. il Antiques 84:158-61 Ag '63
Living with antiques; Pennsylvania home of Mr and Mrs Andrew Wyeth. A. Winchester. il Antiques 86:592-7 N '64
Living with antiques; Shirley, Charles City County, Va. B. Snow. il Antiques 83:542-7 My '63
Living with antiques; the Brick House, Dover, N. H. J. C. Giffen. il Antiques 86:72-6 Jl '64
Living with antiques; Toddsbury, a seventeenth-century house in Virginia. G. M. Moore. il Antiques 85:686-9 Je '64
Living with antiques: Walnut Hill. G. Z. Thomas. il Antiques 86:707-11 D '64
Living with antiques; West St Marys Manor, Maryland home of Lieutenant Colonel and Mrs Miodrag Blagojevich. H. Comstock. il Antiques 83:186-9 F '63
Miscellaneous antiques. See issues of Hobbies to December 1963
New old; rise of junk. il Time 84:78 S 11 '64
On compiling a record for an antique. L. F. Reals. Hobbies 69:28+ O '64
Our home fits our way of living. V. T. Habeeb. il Am Home 66:26-9 N '63
Shop talk. R. Davidson. See issues of Antiques
Sources of the empire style. R. H. Randall, jr. il Antiques 83:452-3 Ap '63
Treasury of kitchen antiques. il McCalls 91: 118-23 O '63
Up-to-date way to use antiques. House & Gard 123:133 My '63
Wethersfield: living with antiques. il Antiques 86:462-7 O '64
See also
Chests
Heirlooms
Samplers
Shelburne museum, Shelburne, Vt.

Bibliography

Books about antiques. See issues of Antiques

Exhibitions

American art from American collections. J. Biddle. il Antiques 83:309-16 Mr '63
Antiques abroad. W. De Sager. il Antiques 84:312+ S '63
Antiques; American art from American collections. A. Winchester. il(cover) Antiques 83:299 Mr '63
Antiques show; East Side house settlement's winter antiques show. New Yorker 39:22 F 1 '64
At the show; East Side house winter antiques show. R. Davidson. il Antiques 85: 35-6+ Ja '64
Calendar of shows. See issues of Antiques
East Side house is grateful to Antiques magazine. C. F. Smithers. il Antiques 85: 34 Ja '64; 87:50 Ja '65
Ellis memorial antiques show. il Antiques 84: 394+ O '63
Hospital of the University of Pennsylvania in Philadelphia; Second annual antiques show and sale. il Antiques 83:408+ Ap '63
Lake Forest antiques show. il Antiques 83: 654 Je '63
League exhibition. R. Davidson. il Antiques 86:376+ O '64
London goes to the fair; Antique dealers fair and exhibition. il Art N 63:46+ My '64
Miniaturia department of the spring show; Antiques exposition and hobby fair at the Conrad Hilton. J. H. Gray. Hobbies 69:59 Ag '64
Special events. R. Davidson. il Antiques 83: 224, 334+, 468+, 574+; 85:336 F-My '63, Mr '64
ANTIQUES, Reproductions of
Redbook's guide to eighteenth century furniture. J. Macurdy. il Redbook 122:82-90 N '63
ANTIQUES dealers. See Antique dealers
ANTIQUITIES. See Archeology
ANTIQUITY of man. See Man—Origin and antiquity
ANTI-SATELLITE weapons systems. See Weapons systems
ANTISEGREGATION demonstrations. See Civil rights demonstrations
ANTI-SEMITISM
Anti-Semitism, by J. Parkes. Review
Christian Cent 81:437 Ap 1 '64. W. J. McCutcheon
Commentary 38:84-7 O '64. B. Halpern
Commonweal 81:19 S 25 '64. M. D. Zeik
Anti-Semitism continues in Soviet Union. Christian Cent 80:1457 N 27 '63
Anti-Semitism in Russia. America 110:565 Ap 25 '64
Bigotry's shifting patterns. Christian Cent 81:1196 S 30 '64
Bullyboys; Argentina's Tacuara. Newsweek 63:53-4 Mr 23 '64
Catholics and Jews. J. O'Gara. Commonweal 80:286 My 29 '64
Christian anti-Semitism. J. O'Gara. Commonweal 80:252 My 22 '64
Christians and Jews: a new rapprochement; excerpt from America is different. S. E. Rosenberg. Christian Cent 81:295-8 Mr 4 '64; Reply. A. T. K. Zadig. 81:801-3 Je 17 '64
Christians should repent of crime against Jews. Christian Cent 81:1326 O 28 '64
Communist anti-Semitism. America 109:546 N 9 '63
Council, reform and reunion, by H. Küng. Review
Christian Cent 80:709-10 My 29 '63. A. J. Wolf; Discussion. 80:829, 864-5 Je 26-Jl 3 '63
End of anti-Semitism? Newsweek 62:71 Ag 19 '63
Learning bigotry; anti-Semitism in books for children. C. H. Bishop. Commonweal 80:264-6 My 22 '64
Polls: their use and abuse; newspapers stress opinions of minority. America 111:432 O 17 '64
Pot and kettle dialogue. Christian Cent 80: 972 Ag 7 '63
Rector resigns under pressure; Scarsdale, N.Y. Christian Cent 80:165 F 6 '63; Discussion. 80:406 Mr 27 '63
Rising tide of Negro-Jewish tensions. R. C. Hertz. il Ebony 20:117-18+ D '64
Rolf Hochhuth: equivocal Deputy. E. Alexander. il America 109:416-18+ O 12 '63; Discussion. 109:518-20, 691 N 2, 30 '63
Russian anti-Semitism. Time 83:84 Ap 17 '64
Russian art & anti-Semitism; with introd. by M. Decter. E. A. Evtushenko; N. S. Khrushchev; M. Romm. Commentary 36: 433-7 D '63
Soviet anti-Semitism exposed. Christian Cent 81:508 Ap 22 '64
Soviet regime persecutes Russian Jews. Christian Cent 80:1358 N 6 '63
Soviet Union seeks to strangle Judaism. Christian Cent 80:485 Ap 17 '63
Spanish anti-Semitism today. R. Alan. Commentary 38:64-6 Ag '64; Discussion. 39:6+ Ja '65
State of Soviet Jewry. M. Friedberg. Commentary 39:38-43 Ja '65

ANTI-SEMITISM—*Continued*
Teaching of contempt, by J. Isaac. Review
Christian Cent 81:805 Je 17 '64. L. D. Streiker
Commonweal 80:372-3 Je 12 '64. G. Baum
Who killed Jesus of Nazareth? Christian Cent 81:262 F 26 '64
ANTI-SLAVERY amendment. See United States—Constitution—Amendments
ANTI-SLAVERY movement. See Slavery—United States
ANTI-SMOG devices. See Automobile engines—Exhaust
ANTI-SMOKING clinics. See Smoking
ANTI-SMOKING laws. See Smoking
ANTI-SUBMARINE warfare. See Submarine warfare
ANTI-SUBMARINE warfare trainer. See Simulators
ANTITANK missiles
Army gets antitank go-ahead. J. Trainor. Miss & Roc 15:14 S 7 '64
Army presses for tank killer. J. Trainor. Miss & Roc 15:10 Ag 3 '64
Low-cost missile has dual capability. W. S. Beller. il Miss & Roc 15:34-5 D 14 '64
Output of antitank Mosquito climbs. il Miss & Roc 12:40+ Ap 15 '63
ANTITOXINS. See Toxins and antitoxins
ANTITRUST division. See United States—Justice, Department of—Antitrust division
ANTITRUST legislation. See Trusts, Industrial—Law
ANTIVIRUS vaccines. See Vaccines
ANTIVIVISECTION. See Vivisection
ANTI-WRINKLE lotions. See Cosmetics
ANTI-XI-ZERO. See Particles (nuclear physics)
ANTOINETTE Perry awards. See American theatre wing
ANTONINUS, Brother
Poet from the West. T. P. McDonnell. Commonweal 78:13-14 Mr 29 '63
Think what's got away. . . R. Creeley. Poetry 102:42-4 Ap '63
ANTONIO
Cousins. il por Newsweek 64:88-9 S 28 '64
Music to my ears; Antonio-Rosario. I. Kolodin. Sat R 47:32 O 3 '64
ANTONIONI, Michelangelo
Hollywood myth has fallen! tr. by R. J. Moore. Pop Phot 93:94-7+ Jl '63
Most controversial director. M. S. Davis. il pors N Y Times Mag p34-5+ N 15 '64
Two on the aisle. P. V. Beckley. il por Sat R 47:36-7 F 8 '64
ANTONIUS, Marcus
Then Antony met Cleopatra. R. Payne. il por N Y Times Mag p26-7+ Je 2 '63
ANTONOV, O. K.
Khrushchev hits Soviet industry planning; excerpts from Izvestia articles. Aviation W 78:105 Ja 21 '63
ANTONY and Cleopatra; drama. See Shakespeare, W.—Plays
ANTOS, Joseph
Color slides. R. Miller. il por U S Camera 27:30-1+ My '64
ANTREASIAN, Garo
Mosaic mural. il Design 66:28-30 S '64
ANTROBUS, Ernest J.
Franklin Pursuit Phaeton. Motor T 15:56-9 Jl '63
ANTROBUS, John, and Milligan, Spike
Bed sitting room. Criticism
New Yorker 39:151-2 My 25 '63
ANTS
Animal husbandry in the animal kingdom; how and why carpenter ants protect caterpillars. il Time 82:98 D 6 '63
Determined ant. G. Laycock. il Field & S 68:61+ My '63
Trail marking substance of the Texas leaf-cutting ant: source and potency. J. C. Moser and M. S. Blum. il Science 140:1228 Je 14 '63
ANTS, White. See Termites
ANUSZKIEWICZ, Richard
Simple form, simple color; exhibition at Manhattan's Museum of modern art. il por Time 82:56-7+ Jl 19 '63
ANWAR, Chairil
Americans and others. J. M. Morrison. Poetry 104:117 My '64
Arena where we fight. D. Levertov. Nation 197:440-1 D 21 '63
ANXIETY
Big bite. N. Mailer. Esquire 60:50 O '63
Can love survive indifference? il Good H 156:14+ Je '63
Crowding brings anxiety. Sci N L 86:158 S 5 '64
Highest anxiety level found among newsmen. Sci N L 85:233 Ap 11 '64
Let's stop scaring our children. M. J. E. Senn. McCalls 92:74+ O '64
Nature and measurement of anxiety. R. B. Cattell. il Sci Am 208:96-104 Mr '63
Six ways to handle your anxiety. J. B. K. Smith and R. Mines. il Sci Digest 54:19-24 N '63
Student anxiety; excerpt from Anxiety as related to thinking and forgetting. F. F. Lighthall. il NEA J 53:26-8 D '64
What's your defense against anxiety? J. Brothers. Good H 158:40+ Ap '64
See also
Fear
Worry
ANY Wednesday; drama. See Resnik, M.
ANZJON, Otto
Race against death. F. Miller. il por Read Digest 83:140-6 O '63
ANZUS council
ANZUS council meets in New Zealand; final communique, June 6, 1963; U.S. delegation. Dept State Bul 48:967-9 Je 24 '63
ANZUS council to meet at Washington. Dept State Bul 51:43 Jl 13 '64
ANZUS reviews areas of mutual interest in Asia and Pacific; communique of the 13th ANZUS council meeting. Dept State Bul 51:146-7 Ag 3 '64
Shadow and substance of the ANZUS pact. D. Warner. il Reporter 30:21-3 Je 4 '64
U.S, New Zealand, and Australia reaffirm ties of friendship; remarks, July 17, 1964. D. Rusk; K. J. Holyoake; P. Hasluck. Dept State Bul 51:194-7 Ag 10 '64
AORTA
Heart stopper; dislocated aortic valve. Newsweek 61:59 F 4 '63
Vascular smooth muscle: dual effect of calcium. D. F. Bohr. bibliog il Science 139:597-9 F 15 '63
Surgery
See Blood vessels—Surgery
AORTICO-pulmonary glomus tissue. See Tissues
AOUDADS. See Mountain sheep
AOYAGI, Yoko
Yoko is her name. il pors Seventeen 23:140-1 Ap '64
APACHE Indian reservation. See Indians of North America—Reservations
APACHE Indians
Apaches have high blood pressure, few coronaries. Sci N L 85:11 Ja 4 '64
Arizona: booming youngster of the West. R. De Roos. il Nat Geog Mag 123:299-343 Mr '63
Hon dah (be my guest) J. Cook. il Am For 69:26-7+ Ap '63
APACHE JUNCTION, Ariz.
Land of the nonbreaking curve ball; spring training at Geronimo park. M. Herskowitz. il Sports Illus 18:59-61 Mr 11 '63
APARTHEID. See South Africa—Race problems
APARTMENT hotels
Music palace; Ansonia hotel, New York. M. J. Matz. il Opera N 27:30-3 F 9 '63
APARTMENT houses
Aalto; Finland's greatest architect. il Arch Forum 118:124-5 Mr '63
All this & country too. il Time 84:59 O 23 '64
Apartment boom. il Arch Forum 118:82-105 Ap '63
Apartment building: regional trends. H. C. F. Arnold. il Arch Rec 134:18 S '63
Apartments in Belvedere: bold forms sit at anchor. il Arch Forum 119:114-15 Jl '63
Apartments: what next? il Arch Forum 120:70-97 Mr '64
Brick bearing walls emerge in a new form. il Arch Rec 134:186-91 N '63
Building a base for prosperity; apartment and home building. il Bsns W p20-1 D 21 '63
Building types study (cont) il Arch Rec 133:127-46 Ja; 134:193 S '63; 135:143-62 Ja; 136:103-28 Ag '64
Cutting impact noise in apartment buildings. il Arch Rec 133:210-15 Ap '63
Elevatoring high-rise apartment buildings. G. R. Strakosch. il Arch Rec 135:191-2+ Je '64
Great Dakota, Manhattan's first luxury apartment building. C. Baiter. il Look 28:93-8 Jl 28 '64
High life on upper Fifth. il Newsweek 61:77 My 20 '63
High living; luxury-apartment gimmicks. il Newsweek 62:55 Jl 15 '63

APARTMENT houses—*Continued*
High-rise apartment structures of steel. R. M. Gensert. il Arch Rec 136:206-9 N '64
House the janitors built; Marina City, Chicago. G. Cross. il Read Digest 82:201-4 F '63
Instant neighborhoods. I. Mothner. il Look 27:41-3 Mr 26 '63
Life in the round; Marina City. il Ebony 20:106-8+ N '64
Marina City. J. M. Liston. il Pop Sci 182: 82-5+ Ap '63
Move to apartments. D. Seligman. il Fortune 67:98-101+ Ap '63
New work of Mies van der Rohe: Chicago. il Arch Forum 119:90-1 S '63
New work of Mies van der Rohe; Detroit. il Arch Forum 119:88-9 S '63
Park a boat at your doorstep. il Sports Illus 21:14-17 Ag 3 '64
Surveys show mixed market for apartments. G. A. Christie. Arch Rec 136:18 Ag '64
Versatile structures for apartment framing; notes on wind-resistant behavior of various concrete wall and column arrangements. R. M. Gensert. il Arch Rec 135:178-9 Je; 136:185-8 Jl '64 (to be cont)
Where there's life, there's business. il Bsns W p 16 Jl 4 '64
See also
Row houses

Condominium plan ownership

Co-ops & condominiums. il Time 83:76 Ap 17 '64
Like owning a house. il Bsns W p 108+ Ag 29 '64
Only place we can go is up. il Am Home 66: 46-7+ S '63
What condominium may mean to you. M. Colean. House B 105:226+ O '63

Cooperative ownership

Quality co-op in Manhattan; Butterfield house. il Arch Forum 118:86-9 Ap '63

Garden apartments

Mews type plan for Texas development. il Arch Rec 135:148-9 Ja '64

Heating and ventilation

Apartment heating costs cut by multiple-boiler system. il Arch Rec 134:144 D '63

Noise

Good gracious! living in the Decibel arms. M. A. Guitar. il N Y Times Mag p55-6+ D 1 '63
Hi-fi snore; Brooklyn criminal court case. il Time 83:38 Ja 31 '64
Other voices, other rooms. Time 82:52-3 D 20 '63

APARTMENT leases. See Leases

APARTMENT mates. See Roommates

APARTMENTS
Apartment that grew. G. O'Brien. il N Y Times Mag p 112-13 N 8 '64
Apartment where change is the rule. il House & Gard 123:146-51 Ap '63
Artful apartment. G. O'Brien. il N Y Times Mag p62-3 Ja 17 '65
Beautiful, budgetwise three-room apartment. il Good H 157:122-9 N '63
Breaking a rule with profit. G. O'Brien. il N Y Times Mag p 110-11 O 25 '64
Bright-on-a-budget; furniture with a long future; furnishing a one-room apartment. il House & Gard 124:208-9 O '63
Cheaper to buy or to rent? il U S News 54: 62-4 Je 10 '63
Checklist for apartment hunters. il Changing T 18:15-16 Ja '64
City apartment unified by the snap of black and white. il House & Gard 125:90-3 Ja '64
Crisp design with steel components. il Arch Forum 118:118-19 Mr '63
Epoch preserved; J. C. Levi's apartment. G. O'Brien. il N Y Times Mag p84-5 Ap 12 '64
Finnish accent. G. O'Brien. il N Y Times Mag p54-5 Ag 30 '64
Garden duplex, abridged edition. G. O'Brien. il N Y Times Mag p72-3 Ag 18 '63
How a diversified harvest of antiques was united by a background. il House & Gard 123:162-5 My '63
How to give an average apartment a made-to-order look. M. Gough. il House B 105: 102-5+ F '63
How to take the boxiness out of a box. il House B 105:238-41+ N '63
Livability plus looks. G. O'Brien. il N Y Times Mag p94-5 Ap 26 '64
Living room unlimited. G. O'Brien. il N Y Times Mag p 102-3 Je 7 '64
Living with antiques; New York apartment. P. Warren. il Antiques 83:326-9 Mr '63
Man's idea of comfort married to a woman's idea of beauty; Gardner Cowles' New York city apartment. il House & Gard 124:70-5 Jl '63
New apartment; Color is pepper; Manhattan pied-à-terre. il House & Gard 125:148-55 My '64
New lease on an old co-op. G. O'Brien. il N Y Times Mag p86-7 D 6 '64
Oasis of originality; New York apartment of Mr and Mrs John Barry Ryan, III. il Vogue 141:110-17+ Ap 15 '63
Penthouses: the boom at the top. il Life 51:82-6 N 20 '64
Personal business. Bsns W p 153 O 26 '63
Personal taste, the great blender. il House & Gard 124:218-23 N '63
Smart way to pick an apartment. il Changing T 18:27-31 O '64
Students count the pennies. G. O'Brien. il N Y Times Mag p90-1 Ap 5 '64
Very personal taste of a jockey turned art dealer. il House B 105:146 Ap '63
View of the future; modern apartment in tower of New York's Dakota. G. O'Brien. il N Y Times Mag p 116-19 O 18 '64
Well-traveled couple who bring the world back home. il House B 105:152 Ap '63
When a small room leads a big life. G. O'Brien. il N Y Times Mag p 104-5 S 15 '63

APARTMENTS, Remodeled
Entertaining in a small apartment. il Am Home 67:54-5 N '64

APATHY
Study of the sickness called apathy; concerning Catherine Genovese's murder. A. M. Rosenthal. il N Y Times Mag p24+ My 3 '64
Without portfolio; public apathy toward criminal acts. C. B. Luce. McCalls 91:18+ S '64

APATITE
Apatite: origin of blue color. P. D. Johnson and others. bibliog il Science 141:1179-80 S 20 '63

APÉRITIFS. See Liquors

APES
Blood groups in anthropoid apes and baboons. A. S. Wiener and J. Moor-Jankowski. bibliog il Science 142:67-9 O 4 '63; Reply. G. B. Rabb. 142:1261 D 6 '63
See also
Chimpanzees
Gibbons
Gorillas
Orangutans

APFEL, Adele
Closed-circuit TV in the school library. ALA Bul 57:259-60 Mr '63

APGAR, Virginia
How your unborn baby is nourished. Redbook 124:24-5+ Ja '65

APHASIA
Art classes for aphasic children. J. B. Helms. il Sch Arts 63:35-6 Ja '64
Boy who tuned out; Stanford's Institute for childhood aphasia. il Newsweek 63:90 Ap 13 '64
Speech defect needs nonverbal treatment. Sci N L 84:377 D 14 '63

APHIDS. See Plant lice

APHORISMS and apothegms
Aphorisms. L. Kronenberger. Vogue 143:138 Mr 1 '64
World of Eliana Simón; humorist in Chilean El Mercurio. R. S. Castro. il Américas 15: 40-1 Jl '63

APHRODISIAS
Atelier to the empire. il Horizon 5:96-101 Mr '63

APITHY, Sourou-Migan
Colored rulers. G. C. Turner. Negro Hist Bul 28:36-7 N '64

APLASTIC anemia. See Anemia

APOLLINAIRE, Guillaume
Apollinaire: poet among the painters, by F. Steegmuller. Review
Nation 197:370-1 N 30 '63. A. S. Mayor
Reporter 30:44+ Ja 2 '64. H. Kramer
Sat R 46:21 N 2 '63. J. T. Soby
Time 82:106 N 29 '63
Four poets and two dramatists. W. Fowlie. Poetry 104:188-9 Je '64
Multiple man. Newsweek 61:93-4 Ap 29 '63

APOLLO project. See Space flight to the moon

APOLOGETICS
Apologetics and the biblical Christ, by A. Dulles. Review
Cath World 198:122-3 N '63. C. L. Palms
Man the believer. S. H. Miller. Christian Cent 81:1167-8 S 23 '64

APOLOGETICS—*Continued*
Religionless religion. G. Foley. Christian Cent 80:1096-9 S 11 '63; Discussion. 80:1277-8, 1341-2, 1472 O 16, 30, N 27 '63
APOPLEXY. See Cerebral hemorrhage
APOSTLES
See also
Peter, Saint
APOSTOL, John N.
Drama at San Quentin. Recreation 56:366-7 O '63
APOTHECARY shops. See Drugstores
APPA RAO, M. V. K.
Estimate of neutron albedo on the moon's surface resulting from cosmic radiation. bibliog Science 141:530-1 Ag 9 '63
APPALACHIAN MOUNTAINS
See also
Great Smoky Mountains
APPALACHIAN REGION
Antipoverty plan for Appalachia. il U S News 57:38 Ag 24 '64
Appalachia; paradise regained or hell with the fires out? R. Starnes. il Field & S 69:30-3 Jl '64
Applalachia: the path from disaster. H. Caudill. il Nation 198:239-41 Mr 9 '64
Association opposes big dams as panaceas. Nat Parks Mag 38:19 F '64
Change in the mountains. B. Smith, jr. il Sat Eve Post 237:60-2 Mr 28 '64
Church keeps hospitals open. Christian Cent 80:1022 Ag 21 '63
College education for $40 a year; Alice Lloyd college, Pippa Passes, Ky. H. Ehrlich. il Look 28:134+ O 20 '64
Mountains of poverty; photographs. M. Hunter. N Y Times Mag p 12-13 My 17 '64
Night comes to the Cumberlands: a biography of a depressed area, by H. M. Caudill. Review
Sat R il 46:23 Ag 31 '63
Planning to push Appalachia; aid to poverty-stricken area. il Bsns W p44+ D 7 '63
Poverty laboratory: the cost, four billions; with interview with H. M. Caudill. il U S News 56:66-71 My 11 '64
Poverty U.S.A. Appalachia. il Newsweek 63:30-2 F 17 '64
Self-help in Appalachia. H. Gunther. il Sr Schol 85:11T O 21 '64
Statistical gaps in the war on poverty; improved statistics for Appalachia; excerpt from address. H. P. Miller. Mo Labor R 87:887-8 Ag '64
This month's feature; Congress and the Appalachia program. il Cong Digest 43:289-314 D '64
Tragedy of Appalachia. R. Armstrong. il Sat Eve Post 237:34-6+ Ag 22 '64
Trees of Appalachia. New Repub 150:5 My 2 '64
Valley of poverty; with report by M. Murphy and photographs by J. Dominis. Life 56: 54-65 Ja 31 '64
APPALACHIAN trail
Danger down the trail! E. J. Long. il Am For 70:20-3+ O '64
Long, long trail rewound. L. E. Foote. il Am For 70:38-41 My '64
Miniature hotels in the sky. B. Hackett. il Recreation 56:269-70 Je '63
APPALOOSAS in art. See Horses in art
APPARATUS for the blind. See Blind, Apparatus for the
APPEAL. See Appellate procedure
APPEASEMENT. See International relations
APPEL, Benjamin
Me and the Texas loyalty oath. Pub W 186: 28-30 S 7 '64
APPEL, Fredric C.
Intellectual mammal. Sat Eve Post 237:30+ Ja 4 '64
Their house was haunted by atomic ghosts. Sat Eve Post 237:72-3 S 26 '64
APPEL, James B.
Punishment and shock intensity. bibliog Science 141:528-9 Ag 9 '63
APPEL, James Ziegler
Making of a president. il por Time 84:67 D 11 '64
APPELLATE procedure
Fascinating & frenetic Fifth; Deep South's Fifth circuit court of appeals. il Time 84: 46+ D 4 '64
See also
Administrative remedies
APPENDICITIS
Appendicitis, the forgotten killer. T. Berland. il Todays Health 42:22-3+ My '64
APPERSON, Bob
Converting meter scales. Electr World 71: 74 Mr '64
APPERSON, R. C. Jr
Car battery saver. Pop Electr 20:33-6 Ap '64
Direct-reading audio-frequency meter. Electr World 73:88-9 Ja '65
Plumbing the microwave circuit. Electr World 71:23-5 Je '64
APPETITE, Abnormal. See Pica
APPETIZERS
Appetizers. il Redbook 122:86-7+ Ap '64
Appetizers assorted. C. Claiborne. il N Y Times Mag p92+ O 20 '63
Bon appetit; with recipes. C. Claiborne. il N Y Times Mag p 102 Ap 14 '63
Entertaining tidbits. C. Claiborne. il N Y Times Mag p90 D 13 '64
From China, Japan, Indonesia, and the Philippines; appetizer ideas for New Year's. il Sunset 134:92-3 Ja '65
Grand opening; with recipes. il McCalls 90: 110-11+ F '63
Hors d'oeuvres idea. P. Peck. il House B 105: 86-7+ Jl '63
Hot hors d'oeuvre cook book. E. Ross. il House & Gard 124:225+ O '63
Nibblers. il Good H 157:86-7+ D '63
Perfect hors d'oeuvres. il Esquire 61:104-5 Ja '64
Sausage for hors d'oeuvres, snacks, picnics. il House & Gard 123:182 Ap '63
These appetizers are all taste surprises. Sunset 132:105 Ja '64
Very merry snacking! il Bet Hom & Gard 42:77-8 D '64
APPLAUSE
Ignoble Romans; history of claque. F. Stevenson. il Opera N 28:8-12 O 19 '63
Notes and comment. New Yorker 40:23 Je 20 '64
APPLE, R. W. Jr
Chief policeman talks about his beat. N Y Times Mag p 10+ Je 21 '64
Ivy-league integrationists. Reporter 28:32-4 F 14 '63
125,000 New Yorkers work the whole night through. N Y Times Mag p53+ Ap 5 '64
Who's who updated. N Y Times Mag p94+ My 3 '64
(ed) See Bessie, M. Book publishing today
APPLE, Russell A.
On the beach at Honaunau. Ladies Home J 80:66-7+ Je '63
APPLE cider. See Cider
APPLE of contentment; drama. See Thane, A.
APPLE RIVER CANYON STATE PARK. See Illinois—Parks and reserves
APPLE tarts. See Tarts
APPLE tree; story. See Alderton, E.
APPLE trees
Starks unveil new apple tree. Farm J 87: 60D N '63
APPLE worms. See Codling moths
APPLEGATE, B. M.
Disobedience; poem. Christian Cent 81:1454 N 25 '64
APPLEGATE, Richard
Did Lloyd Miller kill Janice May? Sat Eve Post 237:75-9 Ja 25 '64
APPLEMAN, Daniel E. See Clark, J. R. jt. auth.
APPLEMAN, Philip
What the population explosion means to you. Ladies Home J 80:59+ Je '63
APPLES
All about apples. il Redbook 120:76-7+F '63
Last apple. F. Russell. Nat R 15:494-6 D 3 '63
See also
Cookery—Fruit

Handling

Apples direct: from tree to customer. il Farm J 88:58F N '64

Marketing

Get the big bite with your own vender; Fruit-o-matic. B. Hardy. il Farm J 88: 36-7 Ap '64

Picking

Two ways to make orchards pay more. B. Hardy. il Farm J 88:44B+ D '64

Storage

Fruit storage for half the cost. B. Hardy. il Farm J 87:21+ Ag '63
Now: longer life for CA produce; Tectrol process. G. Lorang. il Farm J 87:68 Ap '63
Stored lime can save your fruit. B. Hardy. il Farm J 87:36+ N '63
APPLETON, Sally
Season of fire; (to Père Teilhard de Chardin) poem. America 108:361 Mr 16 '63

APPLEYARD, Donald, and others
View from the road: a highway redesigned for the drama of driving; excerpts from View from the road. il Arch Forum 119:74-7 O '63

APPLIANCE buyers credit corporation
How long a rope for captives? il Bsns W p93-4 Jl 13 '63
Whirlpool; case of noncollectable bad paper. Time 82:78 Jl 5 '63

APPLIANCE warranties. See Warranty

APPLICATIONS for admission to colleges. See Student selection

APPLICATIONS for positions
Big job of job hunting. il Sr Schol 85:23-4 N 11 '64
How to apply for a teaching position. NEA J 52:42 Mr '63
How to get a job. A. Poinsett. il Ebony 19:79-80+ My '64
How to prepare a professional portfolio; suggestions for young artists. F. Johnson. il Am Artist 28:36+ Je '64
Job résumé: write it right. il Changing T 18:18 S '64
Personal business; resumé for the relocating executive. Bsns W p 133-4 S 21 '63

APPLIED art. See Art and industry; Arts and crafts; Design, Industrial

APPLING, Luke
Luke's in. Newsweek 63:50 Mr 2 '64

APPLIQUÉ work
Appliqué for impatient fingers. Sister Mary Philip. il Sch Arts 62:10 Ap '63
Appliqué pillows to make yourself. il House & Gard 126:94-5 Jl '64
Appliqué with felt. C. Ward. il Sch Arts 62:17 Ap '63
Art on a sewing machine; Applique decorating with paste and a felt pen; adapted from Decorative wall hangings. D. B. Van Dommelen. il Design 64:113-15+ Ja '63
Caricatured in burlap; cloth scraps become a colorful table linen animal kingdom. A. Hoopes. il Design 65:58-9 N '63
Cheerful pillows display children's art. il Sunset 134:88+ Ja '65

APPORTIONMENT (election law)
After redistricting decision: where states may see changes in taxes, welfare, highways. il U S News 57:34-6 Jl 6 '64
Agony all over. Newsweek 64:30+ N 30 '64
Art of compromise; Mansfield's proposal. Newsweek 64:71 O 5 '64
Battle over state reapportionment; pro and con discussion. Sr Schol 85:12-13+ O 28 '64
Breaking the rural strangle hold. W. Maslow. Nation 196:282-5 Ap 6 '63
Confusion and chaos in Illinois balloting. il U S News 57:16 D 7 '64
Counterattack; Congress reacts to Supreme court decision. Newsweek 64:27 Ag 24 '64
Court backs voter equity. Sr Schol 84:21-2 Mr 6 '64
Court challenges the Congress; Georgia case on apportionment of congressional districts. F. S. Meyer. Nat R 16:233 Mr 24 '64
Court intervenes; with table showing congressional representation. A. M. Bickel. New Repub 150:5-6 F 29 '64
Court says all votes must weigh the same; reapportionment of congressional districts. Bsns W p27 F 22 '64
Crusader: WMCA and Supreme court decision for reapportionment. New Yorker 40:24-6 Je 27 '64
Democracy and the Court. W. D. Burnham. il Commonweal 80:499-503 Jl 24 '64
Dirksen breather; opposition to Supreme court decision on reapportionment. Time 84:37 S 18 '64
District revamping poses new GOP woe. Bsns W p20+ D 26 '64
Equality in representation: congressional districts. Christian Cent 81:291-2 Mr 4 '64
Equality theory insults the uncommon man. F. Morley. Nations Bsns 52:27-8 Ap '64
Fair challenge to redistricting. Life 57:4 Ag 21 '64
Georgia redraws its political map; congressional districts. Bsns W p34 F 29 '64
How Congress is trying to cut the Supreme court's power. U S News 57:8 Ag 31 '64
How reapportionment threatens business. il Nations Bsns 52:94-7 D '64
Illegal Congress? effect of Supreme court decision; with excerpts of statements by H. L. Black and J. M. Harlan. il U S News 56:31-4 Mr 2 '64
Illinois: chaos at the polls. J. L. McDowell. Reporter 30:30-2 Mr 26 '64
Is your vote equal? M. Nord. il PTA Mag 58:16-18 D '63
Landmark I: equal votes. Life 56:4 Je 26 '64
Longer view. Nation 198:641-2 Je 29 '64
New charter for state legislatures. il Time 83:22-3 Je 26 '64
Non rule in America. D. T. Bazelon. bibliog f Commentary 36:438-45 D '63
Non-violent revolution; Court's decision. Nat R 16:519 Je 30 '64
One man, one vote. Commonweal 80:441 Jl 3 '64
One man, one vote; the Dirksen rider. New Repub 151:3-4 S 26 '64
One man, one vote: what it means. il U S News 57:62-4 O 19 '64
One man, one vote, yes or no? A. Hacker. il N Y Times Mag p31+ N 8 '64
One voter, one vote. W. D. Burnham. Commonweal 80:12-15 Mr 27 '64
Political backlash hits Supreme court; Congress moves to curb Court's power. Bsns W p26 Ag 22 '64
Quiet revolution in state government; reapportionment and redistricting; with chart Sr Schol 83:13-15+ N 22 '63
Reapportionment. D. Grunewald; A. M. Bickel. New Repub 151:10-11 D 26 '64
Reapportionment & liberal myths. A. M Bickel. Commentary 35:483-91 Je '63; Discussion. 36:342+ N '63
Reapportionment and the courts. A. M. Bickel. New Repub 150:7 Je 27 '64
Reapportionment and the courts. M. E. Jewell. New Repub 148:17-19 F 2 '63
Reapportionment, big issue for the 60's. I. Starr. il Sr Schol 85:6T-7T S 30 '64
Reapportionment: rhubarb in the political thicket; with chart. Sr Schol 85:8-11+ O 14 '64
Reapportionment riddle. J. E. Clayton. il Reporter 30:34-7 F 27 '64
Reapportionment rider. New Repub 151:5 O 10 '64
Reapportionment: what the Court didn't do. R. G. Dixon, jr. Reporter 31:39-41 O 8 '64
Redistricting order; redrawing of Texas congressional district boundaries by Supreme court. Sr Schol 84:18 Mr 20 '64
Redrawing the lines; Georgia's congressional districts. il Time 83:19-20 F 28 '64
Robert Moses warns against mob rule. R. Moses. Nations Bsns 52:100-2 D '64
Saved again; reaction to Supreme court decision. K. Crawford. Newsweek 64:29 S 14 '64
Setbacks for LBJ; congressional action. Newsweek 64:29+ S 28 '64
Seventeen states vote to destroy democracy as we know it. T. B Morgan. il Look 27:76+ D 3 '63
Shakeup in states; Supreme court decision. Sr Schol 85:21+ S 16 '64
Ship of state; Georgia congressional districting case. Nation 198:206 Mr 2 '64
Showdown on reapportionment. W. Maslow. Nation 197:314-16 N 16 '63
Speaking out; the Supreme court is defying the people. E. M. Dirksen. Sat Eve Post 237:10+ S 12 '64
Squeeze on both their houses. il Time 84:17 Ag 21 '64
Sticky questions. Newsweek 62:34 N 25 '63
Supreme court and the Republic; decisions on reapportionment. F. Morley. Fortune 70:102+ Ag '64
Supreme court draws the line; Wesberry vs. Sanders; Georgia redistricting case. il Newsweek 63:15-16 Mr 2 '64
Sweeping decision. Newsweek 63:22+ Je 29 '64
This month's feature: Congress & the apportionment decisions. Cong Digest 44:1-32 Ja '65
To reapportion or not. Cato. Nat R 16:762 S 8 '64
Tough act to follow; filibuster aimed at Dirksen's amendment. Newsweek 64:35 S 21 '64
Uhuru; redrawing of district lines. Nat R 16:182-3 Mr 10 '64
U.S. voting map: a year of change. il Newsweek 61:28-30 Mr 25 '63
Upheaval in state capitols; how redistricting hits the states. Bsns W p94-6+ Ag 22 '64
Watch out for the subverters! L. B. Bozell. Nat R 14:398 My 21 '63
What can happen when courts step into state elections; reapportionment in Illinois. il U S News 57:39 S 21 '64
What the courts are ordering states to do. il U S News 57:40-1 Ag 24 '64
What the Supreme court did to your vote; with editorial comments. C. W. Gifford. Farm J 88:3, 19+, 70 Ag '64
Who represents what? R. Moley. Newsweek 63:88 Mr 9 '64

APPRAISAL. See Valuation
APPRAISAL of art works. See Art—Valuation
APPRAISAL of books. See Book reviews
APPRAISAL of phonograph records. See Phonograph record reviews
APPRECIATION of art. See Art—Appreciation
APPRECIATION of literature. See Literature—Appreciation and interpretation
APPRECIATION of music. See Music—Appreciation
APPRECIATION of nature. See Nature
APPRECIATION of opera. See Music—Appreciation
APPRENTICES
Apprenticeship and skill training, a trial balance; excerpts from testimony before subcommittee on employment and manpower, October 24, 1963. F. F. Foltman. bibliog f Mo Labor R 87:28-35 Ja '64
National apprenticeship program: unfinished business. D. E. Christian. bibliog f il Mo Labor R 87:625-32 Je '64
Public policies and programs. M. F. Riche. bibliog f Mo Labor R 87:143-8 F '64
Statistics on apprenticeship and their limitations. P. Groom. bibliog f il Mo Labor R 87:391-5 Ap '64
Up from medievalism; German apprentices. il Time 81:105 My 3 '63
APPROACH lights, Airport. See Airports—Lighting
APRA. See Political parties—Peru
APRAHAMIAN, Felix
Notes from our correspondents. Hi Fi 14:14+ Jl; 24+ Ag; 12+ S; 29+ N '64
APRICOTS
See also
Cookery—Fruit
APRIL
In April; few of the dates, memorable and not so, coming up next month (title varies) (cont) N Y Times Mag p53 Mr 29 '64
What to do in April. Horticulture 42:16 Ap '64
APRISON, M. H. See Hingtgen, J. N. jt. auth.
APRONS
Aprons Americana made to appeal. il Good H 158:132 Ap '64
APTHEKER, Herbert
To travel freely. Bul Atomic Sci 20:25 Mr '64
APTITUDE. See Ability
APTITUDE tests
Aptitude tests: under a cloud; Motorola, inc. U S News 57:83-4 D 14 '64
College entrance exams. C. Jencks. New Repub 148:7 Ap 20 '63
Test your science aptitude. il Sci N L 85:87 F 8 '64
Tests that can cinch a better job; ed. by J. Joseph. F. Greene. il Pop Sci 185:66-7+ Jl '64
True or false? tests tell the story; with study-discussion program by D. Harris and E. Harris. E. S. Bordin. il PTA Mag 59:4-6, 35-6 Ja '65
What makes a good salesman. D. Mayer and H. M. Greenberg. il Harvard Bsns R 42:119-25 Jl '64
AQUALUNG. See Diving apparatus
AQUAPLANE
Build yourself a jet-drive aquaplane. J. Rogers. il Pop Sci 184:88-92 Je '64
AQUARIUMS
Fish watching is fun. il Sunset 133:151+ O '64
Guppy break. il Newsweek 61:94 Mr 11 '63
Marineland; southern California. il Sunset 132:94-7 Mr '64
New modern aquarium; National fisheries center and aquarium. B. Tufty. il(p97) Sci N L 85:101 F 15 '64
Olaf, the front man. B. H. Frisch. il Sci Digest 56:6-10 S '64
Reporter at large; meeting of American association of zoological parks and aquariums. E. Hahn. New Yorker 40:131-2+ S 19 '64
Victoria's new undersea gardens. il Sunset 132:92 My '64
AQUATIC animals. See Marine fauna
AQUATIC biology. See Marine biology
AQUATIC birds. See Water birds
AQUATIC insects. See Insects, Aquatic
AQUATIC life. See Fresh water fauna; Marine biology
AQUATIC plants
See also
Algae
Water hyacinths
Water lilies
AQUATIC safety. See Safety education
AQUATIC shows
Bend's nighttime water pageant. Sunset 131:29 Jl '63
AQUATIC sports
Adventure Cove; water-sports center. il Travel 119:8 F '63
Genial landfall; Bermuda. R. Joseph. il Esquire 61:68-71 Ap '64
Lifesaving with a realistic touch. F. A. Lindeburg and F. D. Lewis. il Recreation 57:134-5 Mr '64
Small watershed projects. H. R. Williams. il Recreation 57:276-8 Je '64
Some inner tubes for Thais; floating down the river on Princess Chumbhot's estate. il Sports Illus 22:22-5 Ja 4 '65
See also
Boats and boating
Diving
Motor boat racing
Surf riding
Swimming
Water skis and skiing
AQUEDUCT race track. See Race tracks
AQUILEGIA. See Columbines
AQUIN, Sister Mary. See Mary Aquin, Sister
AQUINAS, Thomas, Saint. See Thomas Aquinas, Saint
ARAB bank, limited. See Banks and banking—Middle East
ARAB-Jewish relations. See Jewish-Arab relations
ARAB league. See Arab states
ARAB refugees. See Refugees, Arab
ARAB states
Arab threat forces British lord to resign. Christian Cent 80:1601 D 25 '63; Reply. P. M. Schroeder. 81:180 F 5 '64
Five on the desert. C. Issawi. Nation 199:36-7 Jl 27 '64
Moderation in Cairo; Arab leaders conference. il Newsweek 63:35 Ja 27 '64
Somewhat secret pressure; conference of Arab premiers. il Time 85:29 Ja 22 '65
Troubled waters; rage at Israel. Newsweek 63:30-1 Ja 6 '64
See also
Communism—Arab states
Finance—Arab states
United Arab Republic
United Nations—Arab states

Commerce

That Arab boycott. Time 84:32+ Jl 24 '64

Foreign relations

Euphoria on the Nile. il Time 83:23 Ja 24 '64

Politics

Al Baath challenges Nasser; political party that rules Syria and Iraq. D. A. Schmidt. il N Y Times Mag p42+ O 6 '63
Arab against Arab. P. Seale. New Repub 149:11-13 D 14 '63
Arab unity evaporating. P. Seale. New Repub 149:11-12 Jl 13 '63
Arab world in ferment: the scorpion and the frog. G. Gersh. Commonweal 79:217-20 N 15 '63
Back to normal; second Arab summit conference. il Newsweek 64:41 S 14 '64
Cairo confidential. Newsweek 62:40 Jl 8 '63
Case of love-hate. il Time 82:21-2 Ag 2 '63
Emergence of the Ba'ath. P. Seale. New Repub 148:7-8 Mr 23 '63
Late, late fuse; another summit meeting. il Time 84:42+ S 18 '64
Nasser's dream comes a cropper; resistance from Socialist resurrection party. il Bsns W p46-8+ Ag 31 '63
Nasser's kaleidoscope. New Repub 150:9 F 22 '64
Shifting fortunes. il Time 81:31 My 10 '63
Syria in flux. P. Seale. New Repub 149:9-10 S 14 '63
Syria: test of Arab unity. G. LeCompte and L. Hamalian. Nation 196:375-6+ My 4 '63
Tremors in the Near East. D. Stewart. il Nation 198:23-5 Ja 6 '64
Unanimous discord; Arab summit conference. Newsweek 64:50+ S 21 '64
Unlove feast; second Arab summit conference. Time 84:42+ S 11 '64
Violent and vital world of Nasser: interview, ed. by R. Sherrod. G. A. Nasser. il Sat Eve Post 236:17-23 My 25 '63
Will Nasser's dream come true? il Newsweek 61:46-9 My 20 '63
ARABIA
See also
Aden

Antiquities

See also
Petra, Jordan

ARABIA in literature
Sheik justice. J. L. Barton. Read Digest 82: 132E-132F+ My '63

ARABIAN American oil company
Obliging Goliath. il Time 82:103 S 13 '63

ARABIAN cookery. See Cookery, Arabian

ARABIAN horses. See Horses

ARABIC language

Study and teaching

Language study and the Middle East. C. A. Ferguson. Ann Am Acad 356:76-85 N '64

ARABIDOPSIS
Somatic instability caused by a cysteine-sensitive gene in arabidopsis. G. P. Rédei. bibliog il Science 139:767-9 F 22 '63

ARABS
Five on the desert. C. Issawi. Nation 199:36-7 Jl 27 '64
Real Arabs. K. Williams. il Harper 226:64-6+ F '63
See also
Arab states
Jewish-Arab relations
Moors (people)

History

Great Arab conquests, by J. B. Glubb. Review
New Repub 150:19-21 F 22 '64. J. Thomson
Sat R 47:48-9 F 15 '64. M. Khadduri

ARABS in Israel
Eshkol in Nazareth. New Repub 150:10 Ap 4 '64

ARACEAE. See Arums

ARACHNIDS
Arachnid behavior; report on symposium. C. J. Goodnight. Science 144:82 Ap 3 '64
See also
Scorpions

ARAGON, Louis
Power of the king... Picasso; tr. by A. Foulke. Vogue 145:78-9+ Ja 15 '65

ARAGON ballroom, Chicago. See Dance halls

ARAGONITE
Calcite-aragonite equilibrium. G. Simmons and P. Bell. bibliog il Science 139:1197-8 Mr 22 '63; Reply. W. A. Crawford and W. S. Fyfe. 144:1569-70 Je 26 '64
Cave trophies; aragonite specimens. H. D. Brown. il Hobbies 69:123 Mr '64
Oysters: composition of the larval shell. H. B. Stenzel. bibliog il Science 145:155-6 Jl 10 '64
Sea water: saturation with apatites and carbonates. J. R. Kramer. bibliog il Science 146:637-8 O 30 '64

ARAL SEA
Shore of exile. R. Caillois. il UNESCO Courier 17:14-15 Je '64

ARALIAS
Two lives of the false aralia. il Sunset 132: 239+ Je '64

ARAMCO. See Arabian American oil company

ARAMINE. See Norephedrine

ARANGO, Gonzalo
Nadaísta poetry of Colombia. por Américas 15:28-31 N '63

ARANGO brothers
Forward's march. il Time 81:83 F 8 '63

ARANSAS national wildlife refuge. See Wildlife sanctuaries

ARANTES DE NASCIMENTO, Edison
Pay-lay! il por Time 81:55 Ap 12 '63
Pelé; king of the booters. A. Netto and C. Mello e Souza. il Read Digest 85:203-5+ O '64
World's highest-paid athlete. il pors Ebony 18:62-4+ F '63

ARAUCARIA
Family of sophisticated evergreens. O. K. Moore. House B 105:289-90+ N '63

ARAUCARIA excelsa. See Norfolk Island pine

ARAYA, Enrique
Condolences; story. Américas 16:29-31 Jl '64

ARBITAL, Samuel
Paperbacks and the election. Sr Schol 85: 10T-11T S 30 '64

ARBITRATION, Commercial
Staying out of court. il Time 83:75 F 14 '64

ARBITRATION, Industrial
How much ground can arbitrators cover? Bsns W p52+ O 26 '63
Managing your manpower; arbitration opinions stir controversy. T. R. Brooks. Duns R 84:49 S '64
Off the rails; railroad settlement. New Repub 149:6 D 28 '63
See also
Industrial relations

Anecdotes, facetiae, satire, etc.

Clock runs out at Sturbridge watch & clock. M. J. Arlen. New Yorker 39:39-40 My 4 '63

Canada

Canada's labor umpire faces first rhubarb. Bsns W p 100+ O 24 '64

Great Britain

Who does what? at Esso's Fawley refinery in England. T. R. Brooks. Duns R 82:84+ O '63

United States

American engineers cancel strike vote following mediation request. Aviation W 79: 45 S 16 '63
Arbitrator criticized. T. R. Brooks. Duns R 83:78+ Ja '64
Arbitrators: either too young or too old. il Bsns W p45-6 Ag 10 '63
Automation is for peacemakers, too; federal peacemaking role in labor-management relations. Bsns W p 108 F 22 '64
Big mediator is watching you. H. T. Ludlow. America 110:789-90 Je 6 '64; Reply. L. C. Brown. 111:696-7 N 28 '64
Deciding on the featherbed; railroad featherbedding fight. il Bsns W p67 S 28 '63
Dictated settlement. H. Hazlitt. Newsweek 61:82 F 11 '63
Dock dispute goes back to the umpires; walkout over size of work gangs on piers. il Bsns W p34 Ag 8 '64
End in sight for Railway labor act? U S News 55:93-4 Jl 22 '63
He fights the toughest battles; labor-management battles. Bsns W p 126+ Ja 16 '65
Heart of the matter. Nation 197:122 S 14 '63
History of a law. H. Hazlitt. Newsweek 62:75 S 16 '63
How to stop strikes before they start. il Bsns W p43-4 Ag 24 '63
Informed neutrals score a triumph; special mediators to reinforce collective bargaining. il Bsns W p43-4+ My 9 '64
Johnson's first labor crisis: threat of a railroad strike. U S News 56:104 F 17 '64
Kept on the track; rail strike barred. Bsns W p 19 Ag 31 '63
Labor experts urge new policies; interviews. G. D. Reilly; G. Farmer. il Nations Bsns 51:66-8+ Ap '63
Let's arbitrate communications strikes. Sat R 46:47-8 F 9 '63; Discussion. 46:50-1 Mr 9 '63
LBJ and big strikes; is rail fight a pattern? il U S News 56:99-101 Ap 27 '64
Managing your manpower; automation dilemma. T. R. Brooks. Duns R 81:65-6+ F '63
Master strategist of the railroad settlement. M. H. Zim. il Fortune 70:164-6+ Jl '64
Matter of necessity: independent tribunal to adjudicate labor disputes; address, April 2, 1964. A. F. Arpaia. Vital Speeches 30:477-80 My 15 '64
New look at arbitration. L. Stessin. il N Y Times Mag p26+ N 17 '63
New threat of rail strike as union lose another round. il U S News 55:110-11 D 9 '63
New trouble on rail work rules. U S News 55:123 O 7 '63
Now Cole takes on automation. A. H. Raskin. il N Y Times Mag p26+ Ap 5 '64
Now that the railroads have compulsory arbitration. U S News 55:95-6 S 9 '63
Protect your freedom to subcontract: Issues & arbitrators. M. L. Joseph. Harvard Bsns R 41:98-102 Ja '63
Rail bill: does it solve anything? il Newsweek 62:67 S 9 '63
Rail mediators throw a switch; rap bargaining methods of both sides. Bsns W p92 O 31 '64
Rail ruling points a way for others. Bsns W p 132+ D 7 '63
Rail strike? not right away. U S News 56: 85 F 3 '64
Railroad dispute: Johnson swings a red lantern; with editorial comment. il Bsns W p25-6, 202 Ap 18 '64
Railroad strike: what are the chances? il U S News 54:43-4 My 27 '63
Railroads' views on arbitration. U S News 54:106 Ap 22 '63
Railway bargaining. New Repub 150:5 Ap 25 '64
Role of the arbitrator. T. R. Brooks. Duns R 82:56+ N '63

ARBITRATION, Industrial—United States—*Continued*
Showdown over featherbedding. il Sr Schol 83:14-16+ S 27 '63
Solution that pleased nobody; forestalling of a national railway strike. Time 82:16 S 6 '63
Strike deadlocks go critical. Bsns W p34 F 9 '63
Theodore Kheel: master mediator. T. J. Murray. Duns R 83:37-8+ Je '64
They have no Hoffa; concerning settlement of rail crisis. Reporter 30:20+ Ja 30 '64
Three who will settle the work-rules dispute; problem of U.S. railroads. il U S News 55:22 S 16 '63
Union friends dominate federal labor panels. il Nations Bsns 51:56-8+ F '63
Until July 29; no railroad strike. il Newsweek 62:66 Jl 22 '63
What railroads want from LBJ now. il U S News 56:95-6 My 11 '64
When LBJ tackled threat of walkout; strike against the railroads. il U S News 56:77 Ap 20 '64
Will it be compulsory arbitration on the railroads? il U S News 55:78-80 Jl 1 '63
Working on the railroads as featherbedding goes. il U S News 55:82-3 Jl 15 '63
See also
Trade agreements
United States—Federal mediation and conciliation service
United States—National labor relations board

ARBITRATION, International
Aviation dispute with France settled by arbitration. Dept State Bul 50:506 Mr 30 '64
OAS council moves to assist in solving U.S.-Panama dispute; statements, January 31 and February 4, 1964; with resolutions. E. Bunker. bibliog f Dept State Bul 50:300-4 F 24 '64
President Johnson calls upon Soviet Union for concrete actions to promote peace; exchange of letters. L. B. Johnson; N. Khrushchev. Dept State Bul 50:157-63 F 3 '64
Prisoners of context. N. Cousins. Sat R 46:14+ Je 1 '63
See also
Disarmament
International court of arbitration, The Hague
International law
Peace

ARBITRATION, Judicial. See Procedure (law)

ARBITRATION association, American. See American arbitration association

ARBMAN, Holger
Bronze age seen in granite. Natur Hist 73:36-43 N '64

ARBOR day
Arbor day, America's magic holiday. J. Prokop. il Am For 70:24-6+ Ap '64
Arbor day; little bits of green. J. Prokop. Am For 70:9 Ap '64
Arbor day observances. Am For 70:55 Ap '64
Arbor day, our loveliest holiday. A. M. Sowder. il Am For 70:27+ Ap '64
Arbor day; the last Friday in April. H. J. Banker. il Am For 69:31+ Ap '63
Spot survey of Arbor day celebrations. Am For 70:26 Ap '64

Drama

Trouble in tree-land. C. Boiko. Plays 23:83-6, 108 My '64

ARBORETUMS
Dream for our schools. F. Lape. il Am For 70:8-11+ Ag '64
See also
Los Angeles state and county arboretum
New York state university—Agricultural and technical institute at Farmingdale, Long Island
Washington, D.C.—National arboretum

ARBORS
Build-it-yourself projects. il Pop Gard 15:35 F '64
Leafy arbors. il Sunset 132:98-103 Ap '64

ARBORVITAE
Cedar and the backyard living boom. W. J. Duchaine. il Am For 69:40-3 O '63

ARBUCKLE, Ernest C.
How companies will win success; interview. por Nations Bsns 52:26-7+ Ja '64

ARBUTUS menziesi. See Madronas

ARC, Electric. See Electric arc

ARC welders. See Welders

ARC welding. See Electric welding

ARC welding equipment. See Electric welding equipment

ARCADI, John A.
Glycogen-containing cells of estrogen-induced renal tumors of the hamster. bibliog Science 142:592-3 N 1 '63

ARCADIA, Calif. public library
City in torment over Kazantzakis. E. T. Moore. ALA Bul 57:305-6 Ap '63

ARCATA redwood company
World's tallest tree farm; follow-up for the future. E. A. Hofsted. il Am For 70:22-5+ S '64

ARCHAEOLOGY. See Archeology

ARCHAMBAULT, George F.
Profession of pharmacy in the United States; address, February 8, 1963. Vital Speeches 29:349-52 Mr 15 '63

ARCHDIOCESE of Los Angeles. See Catholic church—Dioceses

ARCHED bridges. See Bridges, Arched

ARCHEOLOGICAL expeditions
Teen with a trowel; expedition to Petra, Jordan, sponsored by Princeton theological seminary. C. Sayre. il Seventeen 22:118-19+ N '63

ARCHEOLOGICAL research
1963-1964 science review. il Sci N L 84:389; 86:389 D 21 '63, D 19 '64

ARCHEOLOGICAL smuggling. See Smuggling

ARCHEOLOGISTS, Amateur. See Scientists, Amateur

ARCHEOLOGY
Archeology as anthropology: a case study, Pueblos. W. A. Longacre. bibliog Science 144:1454-5 Je 19 '64
Atlantic report. Atlan 212:26 O '63
Eight riddles of mankind. il N Y Times Mag p20-1 S 6 '64
Holiday handbook; digging for America's past. A. Karlen. bibliog il Holiday 36:103-6 S '64
Re-uses of the past. J. Johnson. il Horizon 6:4-15 Autumn '64
Selected aspects of archaeology, 1958 to 1963. R. H. Dyson, jr. Ann Am Acad 351:181-93 Ja '64
Shards of history. il Time 82:50-60 D 13 '63
Uranium contents of ancient man-made glass. R. L. Fleischer and P. B. Price. bibliog il Science 144:841-2 My 15 '64
See also
Anthropology
Bible—Antiquities
Bronze age
Cliff dwellers and cliff dwellings
Coins
Earthworks (archeology)
Excavations (archeology)
Man—Origin and antiquity
Stone age
also subhead Antiquities under names of continents, countries, states, etc. e.g. Latin America—Antiquities

Bibliography

In the beginning was the artifact. L. Eiseley. Sat R 46:52 D 7 '63
Reviews; scholarly archeological works. E. Porada. Natur Hist 72:4-11 N '63

ARCHEOLOGY, Submarine
British explore sea for ancient treasure. Sci N L 87:41 Ja 16 '65
Bronze-age ship; excerpt from Lost ships. P. Throckmorton. il Atlan 213:96-7+ Je '64
First two-man sub to study ancient wrecks. Sci N L 85:89 F 8 '64
Relics from the rapids. S. F. Olson. il Nat Geog Mag 124:412-35 S '63
Sea level changes in the past 6000 years: possible archeological significance. F. P. Shepard. bibliog il Science 143:574-6 F 7 '64
Ships of Homer's time are there to be explored. il Time 81:47 Mr 22 '63
Underwater archeology: key to history's warehouse. G. F. Bass. il Nat Geog Mag 124:138-56 Jl '63
Wacky search for gold. L. H. Lapham. il Sat Eve Post 236:66-71 D 14 '63

ARCHER, Leonard B.
It is later than you think: an action program against censorship. por Library J 88:3552-4 O 1 '63

ARCHER, Marguerite P.
Behind the boom in books. Sr Schol 85:17T O 7 '64

ARCHER, R. K. See Hubbard, O. L. jt. auth.

ARCHER, Vern B.
Central Washington state college. NEA J 53:20-2 My '64

ARCHER, William Kay
Sense of subdued ecstasy. Am Rec G 30:790-7+ My '64

ARCHERFISH
Archer fish. K. H. Lüling. il Sci Am 209:100-4+ bibliog (p 171) Jl '63

ARCHERY
Archery. V. Kraft. il Sports Illus 19:40-2 Ag 5 '63

ARCHERY—*Continued*
Basics of bowhunting. G. H. Gillelan. il Outdoor Life 134:114+ S '64
Bows and arrows for boys and girls. G. H. Gillelan. il Outdoor Life 134:86+ N '64
Field vs. target archery. G. H. Gillelan. il Outdoor Life 134:78-9+ Jl '64
How to shoot a bow. G. H. Gillelan. il Outdoor Life 133:78-9+ Ja '64
Indoor lanes. G. H. Gillelan. il Outdoor Life 133:100-2 F '64
See also
Fishing with bow and arrow
Hunting with bow and arrow

Bibliography

Books for bowmen; comp. by G. H. Gillelan. Outdoor Life 135:16+ F '65

Equipment

Christmas gifts for archers. G. H. Gillelan. il Outdoor Life 132:90-1+ N '63
Hunting quiver. G. H. Gillelan. il Outdoor Life 132:8+ O '63
What's new in archery. G. H. Gillelan. il Outdoor Life 135:100-1+ Ja '65

ARCHES
Engineering of Saarinen's arch; Jefferson national expansion memorial. il Arch Rec 133:188-91 My '63
Incredible Gateway arch. C. B. Hicks. il Pop Mech 120:86-90+ D '63; Same abr. Read Digest 84:169-70+ Mr '64

ARCHES, Natural
Arches and bridges of stone; Utah. W. Luce. il Natur Hist 73:42-7 Ag '64

ARCHES NATIONAL MONUMENT
From Delicate Arch to the Devil's Garden and the Parade of Elephants. il Sunset 131:26-8 O '63

ARCHIPENKO, Alexander
Landmarks of modern art. K. Kuh. il Sat R 46:54 Ap 20 '63

ARCHITECTS
Architects of the Record houses of 1963. il Arch Rec 133:130 mid-My '63
Architecture and the moon age; summary of address. S. Moholy-Nagy. il Arch Forum 118:90-2 F '63; Discussion. 118:92-3 F; 17 Ap '63
Buildings in the vernacular. A. Temko. il Sat R 48:24-7+ Ja 23 '65
Civil defense official describes architect's role. R. Berne. Arch Rec 135:50+ Mr '64
Designers of the Record houses of 1964. il Arch Rec 135:127 mid-My '64
How architects practice interior design; summary of interviews. W. B. Foxhall. il Arch Rec 136:89+ N '64
How to pick an architect D. Canty. il Arch Forum 119:84-7 Jl '63
Library building consultant; address, July, 1963. K. D. Metcalf. ALA Bul 57:1043-7 D '63
Peace corps needs more architects. Arch Rec 135:284 Mr '64
President Johnson and public architecture: convictions on architect's role recalled. Arch Rec 135:10 Ja '64
What architects do and how to pay them. D. Canty. il Arch Forum 119:92-5 S '63
What's to become of architecture? R. Lynes. Harper 228:16+ Je '64
Yale's School of art and architecture; the architect. il Arch Forum 120:84-5 F '64
See also names of architects, e.g. J. C. Warnecke

Licenses and registration

In restraint of architectural practice. Arch Forum 120:77 My '64

Training

See also
Architectural education

ARCHITECTS, Landscape. See Landscape gardening

ARCHITECTURAL acoustics See Acoustics, Architectural

ARCHITECTURAL competitions. See Architecture—Competitions

ARCHITECTURAL conferences
A.I.A. plans a new kind of convention. Arch Rec 133:10 Ja '63
Canadian architects convene in Ontario. Arch Rec 134:24 Ag '63
On the calendar. See issues of Architectural record
Pacific rim conference meets in Mexico city. Arch Rec 135:68 Ja '64
Three A.I.A. western regional conferences. E. K. Thompson. il Arch Rec 133:26 Ja '63
Western regions hold annual conventions. E. K. Thompson. il Arch Rec 137:10 Ja '65

ARCHITECTURAL criticism
Time for dissent. E. Globe. Arch Rec 134:9 N '63
Yale's School of art and architecture; the measure. S. Moholy-Nagy. il Arch Forum 120:76-9 F '64

ARCHITECTURAL decoration. See Decoration and ornament, Architectural

ARCHITECTURAL designs. See Architecture, Domestic—Designs and plans

ARCHITECTURAL details. See Architecture—Details

ARCHITECTURAL drawing
Architectural drawing for printing by halftone. M. F. Schmertz. il Arch Rec 133:133-40 Je '63
Architectural drawing for printing processes. M. F. Schmertz. il Arch Rec 133:137-44 F '63
See also
Draftsmen

ARCHITECTURAL education
Accrediting board issues revised list of schools. Arch Rec 134:88 Ag '63
Architecture and the moon age; summary of address. S. Moholy-Nagy. il Arch Forum 118:90-2 F '63; Discussion. 118:92-3 F; 17 Ap '63
A.C.S.A. endorses A.I.A education report calling for major re-examination of curricula. Arch Rec 134:26 Jl '63
Education and architecture. Arch Forum 120:63 Ja '64
Go back to school? E. Goble. Arch Rec 134:9 S '63; Discussion. 135:9 F '64
Hard world department. E. Goble. Arch Rec 134:9 D '63
N.A.A.B. gives accreditation to fifty-three schools. Arch Rec 136:344 N '64
Training and education of architects; excerpts from paper. W. Allen. Arch Rec 133:173-6 Ap '63

ARCHITECTURAL firms
Control system for architects' office costs. G. R. Keane. il Arch Rec 134:125-6 Jl '63
Corporate architectural practice. D. Hunt, jr. Arch Rec 133:163-6 My '63
100 largest architectural firms in the U.S. il Arch Forum 118:110-12 Ap '63; 120:14-16 Ap '64
Organization for efficient practice; Eliot Noyes & associates. il Arch Rec 133:163-70 Mr '63
Organization for efficient practice; Nolen-Swinburne and associates. H. H. Swinburne. il Arch Rec 133:155-8 F '63
Publisher's note. J. C. Hazen, jr. Arch Forum 120:1 Ap '64
See also
Caudill, Rowlett and Scott (firm)
Roth, Emery, and sons
Silling, C. E. and associates
Skidmore, Owings and Merrill (firm)
Smith, Hinchman and Grylls associates, incorporated

ARCHITECTURAL forum (periodical)
Forum renascent. Time 84:62 D 11 '64
Forum roundtable takes a look at tomorrow's office; symposium. il Arch Forum 120:110-17 Ja '64
Publisher's note. J. C. Hagen, jr. Arch Forum 120:1 Ap '64
Publisher's note, the future of Forum. J. C. Hazen, jr. Arch Forum 121:1+ Jl '64
Time, inc. suspends Architectural forum. E. Goble. Arch Rec 136:9 Jl '64
Time inc.'s Architectural forum: 1932-1964. J. C. Hazen, jr. il Arch Forum 121:1+ Ag '64
Tributes to Forum. Arch Forum 121:21-3+ Ag '64

ARCHITECTURAL league of New York
Architectural league seeks new focus on role of building arts. Arch Rec 134:100 N '63

ARCHITECTURAL models
How structural models are used in practice. J. R. Janney. il Arch Rec 133:206-9 Ap '63
Merits of two model testing techniques. D. P. Billington and others. il Arch Rec 134:225-8 S '63

ARCHITECTURAL photography. See Photography of buildings and structures

ARCHITECTURAL plans. See Architecture, Domestic—Designs and plans

ARCHITECTURAL record (periodical)
Hero is not made. E. Goble. Arch Rec 135:9 Ja '64
Record houses of 1963-1964; with introd. by H. L. Smith, jr. il Arch Rec 133:49-129 mid-My '63; 135:47-128 mid-My '64

ARCHITECTURAL schools. See Architectural education

ARCHITECTURAL societies
N.C.A.R.B. approves regional district concept and authorizes bylaw changes to support it. Arch Rec 134:26 Jl '63

ARCHITECTURAL space. See Space (architecture)

ARCHITECTURE
Abroad. See issues of Architectural forum to May 1964
Architect Ed Barnes: toward simpler details, simpler forms, and greater unity. il Arch Forum 119:74-9 Ag '63
Architects panel selects sixteen best buildings of 1964. il Arch Forum 121:9 Jl '64
Architecture. W. Von Eckardt. New Repub 150:32-4 F 15; 35-6 Je 13; 151:26+ Jl 4 '64
Are most cities too ugly to save? interview. E. D. Stone. il U S News 57:82-8 N 30 '64
Building in the news. See issues of Architectural forum to April 1964
Buildings in the news. See issues of Architectural record
City as a single structure. il Arch Forum 121:200-9 Ag '64
Does the present measure up to the past in design? il Fortune 71:192 Ja '65
Earthbound feet of Antaeus. D. Haskell. il Arch Forum 120:132 Ap '64
Guide to games. D. Haskell. il Arch Forum 118:136 Ap '63
Home is what you make it; folk architecture. il Horizon 6:114-20 Autumn '64
How to look at architecture. E. Kaufmann, jr. il Harper 230:120-4 Ja '65
Love of life, and its opposite. D. Haskell. il Arch Forum 120:126 Mr '64
Muscles, mirrors, and wire. D. Haskell. il Arch Forum 120:118 Ja '64
New building abroad. il Arch Forum 118:94-121 Je '63
Projects. See issues of Architectural forum to July 1964
Prospect for mankind; necessity for scientific redesign. B. Fuller. Sat R 47:26-7 S 19 '64
Rudolph calls students to task of urban design. il Arch Rec 135:23+ My '64
Structure & design; ed. by W. McQuade. il Fortune 70:177-8+ O; 205-6+ N; 176-8+ D '64
Unity in architecture and how it is achieved. A. B. Parker. il House B 105:108-13 F '63
Wavy line versus the cube; reprint. L. Mumford. il Arch Rec 135:111-16 Ja '64
What's to become of architecture? R. Lynes. Harper 228:16+ Je '64
See also
Airlines—Ticket offices
Capitols
Church architecture
City planning
Clubhouses
College architecture
Concrete construction
Domes
Foundations
Industrial buildings
Library architecture
Naval architecture
Office buildings
Photography of buildings and structures
Railroads—Stations
School buildings
Skyscrapers
Theater buildings
also subhead Architecture under names of cities, e.g. Paris—Architecture

Appreciation

Man in space. B. Mumaw. il Dance Mag 38:44-5 Jl '64

Bibliography

Book list for White House includes architecture. Arch Rec 134:29+ D '63
Books. See issues of Architectural forum to July 1964
Required reading. See issues of Architectural record
Style and chaos. W. H. Jordy. Art N 62:44+ O '63
Use of space. W. Andrews. il Sat R 48:32-3+ Ja 23 '65

Competitions

AIA holds competition for headquarters. il Arch Rec 135:20 Ap '64
Anshen and Allen win closed competition: University of California's Lawrence hall of science. il Arch Rec 133:12-13 F '63
Award for best sanctuary. America 110:753-4 My 30 '64
Boston architectural center design chosen. il Arch Rec 135:14-15 Ap '64
Breger group wins Allegheny competition. il Arch Rec 135:20 Je '64
Chicago architects win R.P.I. contest. il Arch Forum 118:11 Mr '63
Competitions and public relations. E. Goble. Arch Rec 137:9 Ja '65
Competitions invite entrants. Arch Rec 133:315 Ap '63
Current competitions. Arch Rec 134:206-7 D '63; 135:23 F; 70+ Ap '64
Current competitions; library design awards. Arch Rec 134:206-7 D '63
Design for mechanical learning; architectural competition held by Rensselaer polytechnic institute. il Arch Rec 135:178-92 My '64
FHA awards recognize architectural merit. il Arch Rec 135:14-15 Ja '64
FHA honors awards for residential design. il Arch Rec 135:154-62 Ja '64
Four city projects win architect merit awards. il Am City 79:83 Ag '64
New patterns for city housing; competition for scheme in East Harlem. A. L. Huxtable. il N Y Times Mag p 12-13 Ag 25 '63
1964 A.I.A. awards honor sixteen projects. il Arch Rec 136:10+ Jl '64
Portfolio of seven award winning homes. R. Charles. il Parents Mag 38:77+ Mr '63
Ruberoid competition gives New York ideas for urban renewal. il Arch Rec 134:14-15 O '63
$25,000 Ruberoid competition uses Manhattan urban renewal project. Arch Rec 133:23 F '63
Winners in our 1962 home improvement contest. il Bet Hom & Gard 41:41-2+ O '63

Composition, proportion, etc.

Proportion, the role it plays in architecture. A. B. Parker. il House B 105:154-6+ Mr '63

Conservation and restoration

Charming folly restored; Goodspeed opera house, East Haddam, Conn. il Arch Forum 119:102-7 Ag '63
Civilization wins a round; Watts towers, Los Angeles. il Arch Forum 118:81 Ap '63
Destroying the American past. R. Kirk. Nat R 16:913 O 20 '64
Heritage homes are worth saving. J. B. Young. il Am Home 67:23-4 My '64
How to be serious about preservation. D. Haskell. il Arch Forum 120:130 My '64
Instinct for preservation. Arch Forum 118:75 Mr '63
Machu Picchu in danger; letter to the editor. C. E. Zavaleta. il Américas 16:48 O '64
Modernization and ruination; Perth, Scotland and Palma de Mallorca, Spain. R. Kirk. Nat R 15:352 O 22 '63
Parnell House in Galena. il Hobbies 68:55 S '63
Preservation and urban renewal: is coexistence possible? symposium, ed. by B. Snow. il Antiques 84:442-53 O '63
Strawbery Banke, Portsmouth, N.H. D. M. Vaughan. il Antiques 86:100-1 Jl '64
Wrecker, stop that ball. il Newsweek 65:54-5 Ja 25 '65
See also
Houses, Restored

Designs and plans

Basic necessities of store design. L. J. Israel. il Arch Rec 135:157-65 Je '64
Concrete abstract. G. O'Brien. il N Y Times Mag p96-7 Ap 28 '63
How to turn a problem into a set of plans. D. Canty. il Arch Forum 119:94-7 D '63
Structure plays leading role in latest Yamasaki designs. il Arch Rec 134:103-10 D '63
See also
Architecture, Domestic—Designs and plans

Details

Architectural details. il Arch Rec 134:150-64 O '63; 135:121-36 F; 137-52 Ap; 136:169-84 S '64
School component designs, costs revealed; California's program. il Arch Rec 135:166-72 F '64
See also
Doors
Facades

Exhibitions

Anonymous architecture. A. L. Huxtable. il N Y Times Mag p92-3 N 8 '64
Arts; architecture without architects at the Museum of modern art, New York. C. J. McNaspy. America 111:759-60 D 5 '64

ARCHITECTURE—Exhibitions—*Continued*
Corbu show in Chicago. P. Gardner. Christian Cent 80:832 Je 26 '63
Eight get awards in Boston arts festival. il Arch Rec 136:12-13 O '64
One major 1964 exhibition empowers architecture to reflect goals of program; Swiss national exhibition in Lausanne. il Arch Rec 135:14-15 My '64
Traveling shows: Smithsonian offers two more. Arch Rec 134:17 O '63

History

Forty story job. D. Haskell. il Arch Forum 120:118 F '64
Seventy-five years of change, mostly unpredicted. D. Haskell. il Arch Forum 121:72-80 Ag '64
World architecture, an illustrated history. Review
Arch Rec il 135:165-8 Mr '64. J. Barnett

Periodicals

See also
Architectural forum (periodical)

Philosophy

Criticism of criticism. E. Goble. Arch Rec 133:9 Je '63
Eloquent simplicity in architecture; address, March 1963. P. Belluschi. il Arch Rec 134:131-5 Jl '63
Give 'em hell. E. Goble. Arch Rec 134:9 Ag '63
People involvement, research, planning teams, economy and regionalism dictate the designs of Caudill, Rowlett and Scott. Arch Rec 137:111-12 Ja '65
Report to the President; excerpts. A. Heckscher. Arch Forum 119:55 Ag '63
Spirit of man. E. Goble. Arch Rec 135:9 My '64
They can afford architecture. E. Goble. Arch Rec 136:9 S '64
Tradition and continuity in architecture; address. W. Gropius. il Arch Rec 135:131-6 My; 133-40 Je; 136:151-6 Jl '64
Ulrich Franzen: architecture in transition. il Arch Forum 118:139-45 My '63
Why good design? E. Goble. Arch Rec 135:9 Je '64

Scholarships and fellowships

A.I.A. names fifty-nine for rank of fellowship. Arch Rec 135:23 Je '64
Architectural awards and fellowships are announced. Arch Rec 133:92 Je '63
Fellowships and awards (title varies) Arch Rec 134:128 O; 286 N '63
Scholarships and awards invite entrants. Arch Rec 133:92+ Mr '63

Social aspects

Architecture as total community: the challenge ahead. A. Mayer. bibliog f il Arch Rec 135:137-44 Mr; 169-78 Ap; 145-52 My; 141-6 Je; 136:157-62 Jl; 129-38 Ag; 197-205 S; 139-48 O '64; Reply to O issue. E. Goble. 136:9 D '64
Architecture in a social context. S. Markelius. Arch Rec 135:153 Ap '64

Study and teaching

Main St; resource of architectural appreciation. C. E. Hiller. il Sch Arts 64:25-8 S '64
What to teach about architecture. B. Foerster. il Sch Arts 62:24-6 My '63
See also
Architectural education

California

Buildings in the vernacular. A. Temko. il Sat R 48:24-7+ Ja 23 '65
California buildings receive honor awards. il Arch Rec 135:14-15 Je '64
Resent work of William Wilson Wurster. il Arch Rec 133:107-15 Ja '63

Connecticut

Architecture; Wethersfield. J. C. Willard. il Antiques 86:452-6 O '64

Cuba

New architecture of Castro's Cuba. D. Rowntree. il Arch Forum 120:122-5 Ap '64

Czechoslovakia

New architecture of Communist Europe. il Arch Forum 118:107 Mr '63

England

On from antiquity; St Catherine's college at Oxford; Churchill college at Cambridge. il Time 84:114-16 O 2 '64
See also
London—Architecture

Ethiopia

See also
Addis Ababa—Architecture

Europe, Eastern

New architecture of Communist Europe. il Arch Forum 118:104-9 Mr '63

Finland

Alvar Aalto. Review
Nation 198:19-20 Ja 4 '64. W. McQuade
Alvar Aalto today. F. Gutheim. il Arch Rec 133:135-50 Ap '63

France

See also
Paris—Architecture

Germany (Democratic Republic)

New architecure of Communist Europe. il Arch Forum 118:108-9 Mr '63

Germany (Federal Republic)

Aalto; Finland's greatest architect. il Arch Forum 118:120-5 Mr '63
New German theaters and concert halls; views from the audience. G. E. K. Smith. il Arch Rec 134:179-94 O '63

Hawaii

Hanging gardens on the rocks in Hawaii; Sheraton Maui hotel. il Arch Rec 135:149-54 Mr '64

Hong Kong

Hong Kong: new city hall. il Arch Forum 118:114-15 Je '63

Hungary

New architecture of Communist Europe. il Arch Forum 118:108 Mr '63

India

Tropical climate control techniques. B. Polk. il Arch Rec 135:208-10 Ap '64

Italy

Changing and changeless. D. Haskell. il Arch Forum 119:126 Jl '63
New building abroad; remodeled boutique, Genoa. il Arch Forum 118:102-3 Je '63

Japan

Japanese show off structural skills. il Arch Forum 118:114-15 Mr '63
See also
Earthquakes and building
Tokyo—Architecture

Mexico

Hanging a building in air sets new style. W. I. Fischman. il Pop Sci 183:62 D '63
Letter from Mexico City. R. Rosen. Nation 198:200-3 F 24 '64
Prisoner of geometry. il Time 81:60 Je 28 '63

Middle western states

Catch up with. L. Lerman. il Mlle 57:94+ My '63

New Mexico

Geometry in New Mexico; private chapel. il Arch Forum 121:154-5 Ag '64

Russia

New architecture of Communist Europe. il Arch Forum 118:104-5 Mr '63

Scandinavia

Impressions of Scandinavia. N. Kent. il Am Artist 28:40-7+ Ap '64

Sweden

Buildings that control environment. il Arch Rec 135:154-5 Ap '64

Switzerland

See also
Basel, Switzerland—Architecture

Taiwan

Shells soar in Formosa; Luce memorial chapel at Tunghai university. il Arch Forum 121:136-9 Ag '64

United States

America's heritage of great architecture is doomed. il Life 55:52-60 Jl 5 '63

ARCHITECTURE—United States—*Continued*
Architecture and the moon age; summary of address. S. Moholy-Nagy. il Arch Forum 118:90-2 F '63; Discussion. 118:92-3 F; 17 Ap '63
Architecture, I'm for it, Yasko says: challenges architects of fifty states to make architecture of U.S. buildings; excerpts from address. K. Yasko. Arch Rec 133:23+ Ap '63
Bold and innovative and egocentric. E. Goble. Arch Rec 134:9 Jl '63
Buildings in the news. See issues of Architectural record
Cosmetic architecture. il Time 81:44+ Je 7 '63
Foreign builders get a beachhead; newest look on U.S. skyline. il Bsns W p84-6+ My 11 '63
Light, form, and power: new work of Louis Kahn. V. Scully. il Arch Forum 121:162-70 Ag '64
New architecture of U.S. cities: symposium. il Sat R 48:15-33 Ja 23 '65
Projects. See issues of Architectural forum to July 1964
Recent work of Edward Durell Stone; with introductory statement by Stone. il Arch Rec 136:149-60 O '64
Report to the President; excerpts. A. Heckscher. Arch Forum 119:55 Ag '63
Secret scrapbook of an architectural scavenger. P. Blake. il Arch Forum 121:81-114 Ag '64
Ten buildings that point the future. il Fortune 70:134-9 O '64
There is no there there. W. Von Eckardt. New Repub 149:17-20 S 21 '63
Ulrich Franzen: architecture in transition. il Arch Forum 118:139-45 My '63
Vanishing glory in business buildings; portfolio of drawings by Nicholas Solovioff. Fortune 68:119-26 S '63
See also
American institute of architects
Architecture, American
Architecture, Domestic—United States
Skyscrapers
also subhead Architecture under names of cities i.e. Chicago—Architecture

History

History in towns: Mobile, Alabama. M. R. Ingate. il Antiques 85:294-309 Mr '64

Yugoslavia

New architecture of Communist Europe. il Arch Forum 118:106 Mr '63

ARCHITECTURE, American
Architecture and man at Yale. V. Scully. il Sat R 47:26-9 My 23 '64
Plague; or, Contemporary traditional architecture in America. H. H. Reed, jr. and H. S. Bryant, jr. il Arch Forum 119:112-15 S '63
Viable vernacular. E. Goble. Arch Rec 135:9 Mr '64
See also
Architecture, Domestic—United States

ARCHITECTURE, Buddhist
See also
Borobudur, Java

ARCHITECTURE, Colonial
Connecticut colonial; Amos W. Shepard house. G. O'Brien. il N Y Times Mag p36-7 D 20 '64

ARCHITECTURE, Domestic
Atrium house. il House B 105:57-79 Ag '63
Atrium way. il Time 84:66 Jl 3 '64
Closed-door policy. il Newsweek 64:78 Jl 20 '64
Colonial barn is transformed into a country estate. il Am Home 67:98+ My '64
Double the living in a two-story house. il Good H 156:102-13+ Je '63
How architecture can affect the way we live at home; excerpts from You and architecture. A. B. Parker. il House B 105:178-81+ Ap; 182-5+ My '63
How to lick the limitations of a narrow lot. D. X. Manners. il House B 105:90-5 Ag '63
Living and dining around a garden court. il Sunset 131:82-3 Jl '63
Living it up way down; underground dreamhouse in Texas. il Life 56:51+ Ap 24 '64
New highs in livability. il House & Gard 126:180-93+ O '64
See also
Apartment houses
Balconies
Beach architecture
Building, Adobe
Cabins
Ceilings
Concrete houses
Cottages
Country houses
Courtyards
Doorways
Farmhouses
Garages
Guest houses
Hillside architecture
Houses
Houses, Prefabricated
Houses, Remodeled
Housing
Orientation (architecture)
Porches
Ranch houses
Roofs
Row houses
Soundproofing
Summer homes

Anecdotes, facetiae, satire, etc.

Problem in architecture. A. Bendiner. Atlan 213:161-3 Mr '64

Competitions

See Architecture—Competitions

Designs and plans

Add-on house. il Ladies Home J 80:55-61+ My '63
Architect's trend-setting home for the fair. J. Peter. il Look 28:42-4 F 11 '64
Best ready-to-buy houses of 1964! editors choice. il Bet Hom & Gard 42:46-53+ My '64
Bold roof line creates an exciting house inside and out. A. Borg. il Am Home 66:6 Ja '63
Builder's house of the month. See occasional issues of American home, May 1963 to March 1964
Casual simplicity for a small country house. il Arch Rec 133:175-8 Mr '63
Designed for privacy. G. O'Brien. il N Y Times Mag p 116-17+ S 13 '64
Do you know all the advantages of a good split-entry? J. D. Bloodgood. il Bet Hom & Gard 42:58-61 O '64
Don't spend dollars for plan mistakes. il Bet Hom & Gard 41:133-5 O '63
Economy and excellence in a small house. J. D. Bloodgood. il Bet Hom & Gard 42:60-3 Jl '64
Exceptional floor plan in 1,400 square feet! J. D. Bloodgood. il Bet Hom & Gard 41:72-3 Ap '63
Fine house that can be built for $11,000. J. D. Bloodgood. il Bet Home & Gard 41:56-7 F '63
Five inexpensive but excellent houses. il House B 106:97-121+ Je '64
French colonial with remarkable space. J. D. Bloodgood. il Bet Hom & Gard 42:108 D '64
Good start for big ideas. il Bet Hom & Gard 42:16 My '64
Here is a very good small split level. J. D. Bloodgood. il Bet Hom & Gard 41:84-5 O '63
Here's a house that's practically maintenance-free! J. D. Bloodgood. il Bet Hom & Gard 42:66-7 N '64
Here's a very up-to-date traditional house. J. D. Bloodgood. il Bet Hom & Gard 42:66-9 S '64
Honeycomb house for all seasons. il Sports Illus 20:40-5 Mr 23 '64
House designed to please seventy-five women. J. Chapman. il House B 105:168-78 My '63
House for all seasons; with report by E. Noyes. il Life 54:48-60 F 15 '63
House that grew. G. O'Brien. il N Y Times Mag p32-3 S 1 '63
House that makes big space seem even bigger. il Bet Hom & Gard 41:52-3 Ag '63
House that proves you can afford good design. il Bet Hom & Gard 41:58-9 Jl '63
House with character and spaciousness! J. D. Bloodgood. il Bet Hom & Gard 42:70-3 F '64
How architecture can affect the way we live at home; excerpts from You and architecture. A. B. Parker. il House B 105:178-81+ Ap '63
How good an architect are you? use of space. il Bet Hom & Gard 42:111 Je '64
How to choose a good one-level house. J. D. Bloodgood. il Bet Hom & Gard 41:70-1+ My '63
How to make a little house feel big. il House & Gard 126:80-3 Jl '64
Ideal house for happy weekends at home. il Am Home 67:42-5 Je '64
Ideas for space in a budget house. il Arch Rec 133:171-4 Mr '63

ARCHITECTURE, Domestic—Designs and plans —*Continued*

If you're looking for a good two-story, this is it! J. D. Bloodgood. il Bet Hom & Gard 42:62-5 Je '64
Indoors and out-of-doors come together in Hawaii. il Sunset 130:108-13 My '63
Like the prow of a ship. il House & Gard 123: 122-9+ Mr '63
Lot of living space on a precipitous site. il Arch Rec 133:177-80 Ap '63
Lovely colonial copy with plans you can buy. J. Ingersoll. il Am Home 66:40-1+ Ja '63
McCall's certified house. See issues of McCall's
MacNeils tackle another house. H. Stark. il Bet Hom & Gard 41:54-7 My '63
Make your next home expandable. il Parents Mag 39:73+ N '64
New breed of ready-built houses. il House & Gard 123:86-97 F '63
New houses by Edward Larrabee Barnes. il Arch Rec 136:139-52 N '64
New version of an old favorite; colonial American design. il Am Home 67:60-1+ O '64
One house in a million. il House & Gard 123:124-35 Ap '63
One of our guys builds a house. J. D. Bloodgood. il Bet Hom & Gard 41:52-5 N '63
Parent's magazine's 14th expandable home. il Parents Mag 38:55-8+ Jl '63
Parents' magazine's special award home for families with children. il Parents Mag 38: 87+ S '63
Portfolio of seven award winning homes. R. Charles. il Parents Mag 38:77+ Mr '63
Problems. il Am Home 66:28-37 My '63
Rare house from everyday materials. il Am Home 67:48-51 N '64
Record houses of 1963-1964; with introd. by H. L. Smith, jr. il Arch Rec 133:49-129 mid-My '63; 135:47-128 mid-My '64
Remarkable split-entry house. il Bet Hom & Gard 41:68-9 S '63
Roomy steel-framed house prices under $30,000. il House & Gard 124:202-7 O '63
Seven new houses by Ulrich Franzen. il Arch Rec 134:127-42 N '63
Simple river house for simple pleasures. il House B 105:178-80 Mr '63
Space, privacy, and a plan for city living. il Am Home 67:54-5+ O '64
Split-level that doesn't look split. J. D. Bloodgood. il Bet Hom & Gard 42:54-7 Ag '64
Their house is in order. R. Martens. il Farm J 88:102-3 Mr '64
There's so much house here on one floor! J. D. Bloodgood. il Bet Hom & Gard 41:66-7 S '63
This H-shaped house is for people who believe in privacy. J. D. Bloodgood. il Bet Hom & Gard 41:56-7 Jl '63
This house invites the outdoors in. J. Parkison. il Bet Hom & Gard 43:23 Ja '65
This house keeps up with you. J. D. Bloodgood. il Bet Home & Gard 42:40-3 Ja '64
This house stretches the living all over the lot. il Bet Hom & Gard 41:86-7 O '63
This is a great house! J. D. Bloodgood. il Bet Home & Gard 41:62-5 Mr '63
This is how a split level should be! J. D. Bloodgood. il Bet Hom & Gard 41:68-9+ Je '63
This plan makes good use of every building dollar. J. D. Bloodgood. il Bet Hom & Gard 41:50-1 Ag '63
This two-level can take it! N. Seney. il Bet Hom & Gard 42:76-7 N '64
Three complete floors of good living. J. D. Bloodgood. il Bet Hom & Gard 43:58-61 Ja '65
Three-part house. G. O'Brien. il N Y Times Mag p46-8 Ag 9 '64
Three World's fair houses! P. Lindberg. il Bet Hom & Gard 42:48-65 S '64
Traditional & timeless: an old New England home was rebuilt piece by piece. il Am Home 68:48-51 Ja '65
Truly hospitable houses. il House & Gard 126:252-61+ N '64
Two floors of really comfortable living. il Bet Hom & Gard 41:72-3 My '63
Two-story plan with a new twist. il Bet Hom & Gard 42:116-17 Mr '64
Vacation houses. il Sunset 132:106-13 My '64
Vacation houses: fun for all seasons. A. C. Borg. il Am Home 66:22-33 Je '63
Very good example of a small traditional house. il Bet Hom & Gard 41:70-1+ Je '63
What makes a floor plan good? il Changing T 17:34-6 D '63
Winter-summer vacation house. il House B 105:86-99+ F '63
World's fair house. il Good H 158:100-13+ My '64
Wrapped up in itself. il House & Gard 123: 156-61+ My '63
You can buy plans for this lovely traditional home. B. Colvin. il Am Home 66:74-6 S '63
Your second home: design and material selection. il Am Home 67:20+ Ap '64

Exhibitions

Architect's trend-setting home for the fair. J. Peter. il Look 28:42-4 F 11 '64

Social aspects

How architecture can affect the way we live at home; excerpts from You and architecture. A. B. Parker. il House B 105:178-81+ Ap '63

Alabama

Sophisticated rusticity for country house. il Arch Rec 135:88-91 mid-My '64

Arizona

In the open desert near Tucson. il Sunset 131:94-5 N '63
McCall's certified house. il McCalls 91:120 Je '64
McCall's certified house $14,990 in Arizona. il McCalls 90:182 Ap '63

Arkansas

House that turns existing into living. il House B 105:176-81+ O '63
Magnificent space on a magnificent site. il House B 106:56-63+ Jl '64

Australia

House and garden both with wall of glass. il Sunset 133:56-7 Ag '64

Bahama Islands

Every room can be a breezeway. il House B 106:82-7 Ja '64

Barbados

Claudette Colbert's other home in the sun. il House B 106:98-101 Ja '64
How to answer the three tropical challenges: sun, wind, and rain. il House B 106:70-5 Ja '64
Successful Palladian transplant to Barbados. il House B 106:60-3+ Ja '64

California

Atrium expands builder house living area. il Arch Rec 135:108-11 mid-My '64
Brightest little house in the West. R. W. Houseman. il Am Home 66:43-5 S '63
California house is a real cliff-hanger. il Pop Sci 185:50-1 Jl '64
California, what a way to live! il McCalls 90:56-61 Jl '63
Clearing a jungle produced a better house. il House B 105:174-5+ S '63
Cliff-climbing house. il House & Gard 127: 102-9 Ja '65
Crisp design outside; soaring space inside; house of architect Donald Goodhue. A. C. Borg. il Am Home 66:29-32 S '63
Cross-shaped hilltop house provides wide variety of outlook. il Arch Rec 135:179-82 Ap '64
Decorated with a spirit of independence. R. W. Houseman. il Am Home 66:36-9 N '63
Elegant small house doubles its apparent space by a semi-enclosed court. il Arch Rec 133:122-5 mid-My '63
Expansive ranch house forms its own oasis. il Arch Rec 135:76-9 mid-My '64
Family home planned in three distinct units; La Jolla, Calif. il Arch Rec 136:217-20 S '64
Four linked pavilions form builder house. il Arch Rec 135:92-5 mid-My '64
Handsome adobe hacienda in the West. il Am Home 67:52-3 Jl '64
Hillside house for an artist. il Arch Rec 134: 195-8 O '63
House a wife built to please her husband. il House & Gard 124:80-3 Jl '63
H&G's house of ideas for 1964. il House & Gard 126:73-107, 138-9 Ag '64
House built with children in mind. il Am Home 67:46-9 S '64
House with restraint in the vastness of nature. C. Besinger. il House B 105:182-91+ O '63
How to have your own space platform. C. Besinger. il House B 105:128-31+ Je '63
Individualism in California. il House & Gard 123:92-7 F '63
Instead: simple trio of buildings, main house, bedrooms and cabaña patio. il House & Gard 125:104-11 Je '64
Like the prow of a ship. il House & Gard 123:122-9+ Mr '63
Lot of living space on a precipitous site. il Arch Rec 133:177-80 Ap '63

ARCHITECTURE, Domestic—California—*Cont.*
McCall's certified house: $21,950 in California. il McCalls 90:140 Mr '63
Modern & timeless. il Am Home 68:52-5 Ja '65
Natural materials and landscape blend in open-plan house. il Arch Rec 133:110-13 mid-My '63
New way to create a wide-open house. il House B 106:82-7 Jl '64
Pin-wheel plan provides privacy without fences. il Arch Rec 135:153-6 Je '64
Recent work of William Wilson Wurster. il Arch Rec 133:107-15 Ja '63
Remodel or move? the vote was remodel. il Sunset 130:102-15 Ap '63
Rhythm and symmetry in a steel-framed house. il Arch Rec 135:48-53 mid-My '64
Rugged elegance keynotes model development house. il Arch Rec 133:58-61 mid-My '63
Small wonder on a mountain. il House & Gard 125:118-21 Ap '64
Solution for suburbia. J. Peter. il Look 28: M7-M8 Jl 14 '64
Sometimes two houses can work better than one. il House B 105:206-15+ N '63
Stylishness of the new rustic life. il House B 106:88-91 Jl '64
Timeless quality of good design. A. C. Borg. il Am Home 66:42-7 O '63
Town house and a country house by Wurster, Bernardi and Emmons. il Arch Rec 135: 139-42 Ja '64
Willie Mays' new home. L. Robinson. il Ebony 18:88-92+ Ag '63

Connecticut

All this and children too. il Am Home 67: 36-9 S '64
Architecture; Wethersfield. J. C. Willard. il Antiques 86:452-6 O '64
Charm of an authentic 18th-century Colonial in a three-year-old home in the East. il Am Home 67:50-1 Jl '64
Exceptional floor plan in 1,400 square feet! J. D. Bloodgood. il Bet Hom & Gard 41: 72-3 Ap '63
House for all seasons; with report by E. Noyes. il Life 54:48-60 F 15 '63
House you will want to build. B. Colvin. il Am Home 66:30-1+ O '63
Lovely colonial copy with plans you can buy. J. Ingersoll. il Am Home 66:40-1+ Ja '63
Multi-level house for a rocky hilltop. il Arch Rec 135:100-3 mid-My '64
Sophisticated simplicity on a hilltop. il Am Home 67:37-41 My '64
Under one roof diversity. G. O'Brien. il N Y Times Mag p76-7 My 26 '63
Wondrous house, formerly a Baptist church. V. Lawford. il Vogue 143:164-73+ F 1 '64
Zoned, flexible house for a gently sloping site. il Arch Rec 133:159-62 My '63

England

My two houses; two lives, two different designs. C. Beaton. il Vogue 141:130-7+ Mr 15 '63

Finland

Inside view. G. O'Brien. il N Y Times Mag p50-1 Ja 26 '64

Florida

Breeze-conditioned and private. il Am Home 66:34-5 Jl '63
Concrete abstract. G. O'Brien. il N Y Times Mag p96-7 Ap 28 '63
Development house expresses the character of concrete. il Arch Rec 135:72-5 mid-My '64
House a man built to please himself. il House & Gard 124:76-9 Jl '63
How an atrium can increase summer comfort. il House B 105:84-9 Ag '63
McCall's certified house. $24,500 in Florida. il McCalls 90:142 Je '63
Open minded house with a world of warmth. P. Clapp. il Am Home 66:36-9 Mr '63
Problem: climate, insects, privacy from neighbors il Am Home 66:32-3 My '63
Raise the house and get all the breezes. il House B 106:88-91+ Ja '64
Retirement house that tenants help pay for. il House B 105:152-7+ My '63
Sculptured house of concrete block. il Arch Rec 133:70-3 mid-My '63
Simple, well-designed house for $15,867. il Arch Rec 133:94-7 mid-My '63
Simplicity cuts costs for a seaside house. il Arch Rec 136:147-50 Ag '64
What the Bermudian house has to offer us. C. Besinger. il House B 106:156-61+ Mr '64
When the only way to go is up. il House B 105:184-5+ S '63

Georgia

Living on three levels. il Good H 157:115-24 S '63

Hawaii

Four houses in Hawaii. il Arch Rec 136:161-4 O '64
From cultural traditions come new ways of building, and living. C. Besinger. il House B 106:92-7+ Ja '64
House of convertible pavilions adapts to climate and function. il Arch Rec 133:54-7 mid-My '63
House that welcomes every breeze. il House & Gard 126:70-7 Jl '64
How to keep dry in a moist, hot climate. il House B 106:64-9+ Ja '64
Indoors and out-of-doors come together in Hawaii. il Sunset 130:108-13 My '63
Inward-turning house gives a great sense of shelter. il Sunset 133:70-1 S '64
Plan your shadows to foil the heat of the sun. il House B 106:108-10 Ja '64
Urbanity in the lush Nuanu Valley. il House B 106:104-7 Ja '64
Your talent for living. il House & Gard 126: 51+ Jl '64

Illinois

Classic elegance in sturdy materials. il Arch Rec 133:106-9 mid-My '63
Crescent house to encompass a lake view. il Arch Rec 133:98-101 mid-My '63
Family room addition improves looks of the whole house. B. Colvin. il Am Home 67:95 Mr '64
House for all seasons. il House & Gard 125: 98-109+ F '64
Lakeside house combines traditional atmosphere with contemporary design. il Arch Rec 135:120-3 mid-My '64
New house takes root in an old setting. il House & Gard 125:158-63 Mr '64

Indiana

$12,075 in Indiana. il McCalls 91:158 Ap '64
Wrapped up in itself. il House & Gard 123: 156-61+ My '63

Iowa

Castle in the woods. il Life 58:86-91 Ja 15 '65
Simply designed home makes use of standard materials for maximum economy. il Arch Rec 135:96-9 mid-My '64

Italy

Arab-Venetian: a pleasure dome; the dune villa of Count Giovanni Volpi di Misurata. F. Sarazani. il Vogue 142:186-91 S 15 '63
Leisure-time living. G. O'Brien. il N Y Times Mag p92-3 N 3 '63

Japan

Japanese house, its interior and exterior, by K. Ishimoto and T. Ishimoto. Review Sunset il 131:74 Ag '63
Letter from Sendagaya. J. M. Flagler. il New Yorker 40:58+ Jl 25 '64

Long Island, N.Y.

Could this be your new home? Lloyds Neck. il Am Home 67:90+ S '64
Imaginative house that faces the facts of life. il House B 105:192-200+ O '63
Seashore house. il House & Gard 125:144-7 My '64

Louisiana

Logic and simplicity give livability on a budget. il Arch Rec 134:141-4 Ag '63
Patios and pavilions are combined for a walled-in city house for a large family. il Arch Rec 135:116-19 mid-My '64

Maryland

Feeling of space. G. O'Brien. il N Y Times Mag p 122-3 N 22 '64
Formal house planned for a river view. il Arch Rec 135:64-7 mid-My '64
Sunny house for a wooded site. il Arch Rec 135:169-72 Mr '64

Massachusetts

Better homes for all America! J. D. Bloodgood. il Bet Hom & Gard 42:40-3 Mr '64
Excitement at Cape Cod. il House & Gard 123:86-91 F '63
Home on the waterfront. G. O'Brien. il N Y Times Mag p 110-11+ N 17 '63
Raised basement adds space to neat development house. il Arch Rec 135:124-6 mid-My '64
Traditional & timeless: an old New England home was rebuilt piece by piece. il Am Home 68:48-51 Ja '65

Mexico

No translation needed. G. O'Brien. il N Y Times Mag p48-9+ F 9 '64
Yankee hacienda. G. O'Brien. il N Y Times Mag p60-1 Ja 10 '65

ARCHITECTURE, Domestic—*Continued*

Michigan

Palladio updated. il House & Gard 124:260-3+ N '63
What can you do with an old house? N. Seney and P. Lindberg. il Bet Hom & Gard 41:70-1 Ap '63
See also
Cabins

Minnesota

Gabled house for a small city lot. il Arch Rec 134:127-30 Jl '63
Receding walls give privacy to restricted site. il Arch Rec 135:84-7 mid-My '64

Missouri

Like brick? here's the house to build. B. Colvin. il Am Home 66:74-5 D '63
Staggered walls exploit site irregularities. il Arch Rec 135:112-15 mid-My '64

Mykonos (island)

My beautiful Greek house, handmade for $2,000. P. Glanville-Hicks. il Vogue 141:14+ Ap 1 '63

New England

Early New England homes with 20th-century owners. R. W. Houseman. il Am Home 66:26-31 Mr '63
New addition can change a whole house. C. C. Calkins. il House B 105:146-51+ S '63

New Hampshire

Compact saddle-roofed house that exploits a difficult site. il Arch Rec 135:157-60 My '64

New Jersey

Living in an art form. G. O'Brien. il N Y Times Mag p94-5 Mr 22 '64
Neo-classic builder house in concrete block. il Arch Rec 133:114-17 mid-My '63
One-story house has bold living spaces and light effects. il Arch Rec 135:68-71 mid-My '64
Place in the country. G. O'Brien. il N Y Times Mag p98-9 O 4 '64
Soaring laminated arches create dramatic interiors for a hilltop house. il Arch Rec 133:78-81 mid-My '63

New Mexico

Austerity of the desert pervades her home and her work. L. Gilpin. il House B 105: 144-5+ Ap '63

New York (state)

Adaptable house dramatizes use of steel. il Arch Rec 135:58-61 mid-My '64
Add the outdoors to an old house. il House B 105:152-3 S '63
Architect's home is development prototype. il Arch Rec 133:102-5 mid-My '63
Case for apartness. il House & Gard 124:254-9+ N '63
Casual simplicity for a small country house. il Arch Rec 133:175-8 Mr '63
First private house remodeled under urban renewal laws. il House B 105:158-9+ S '63
Five pavilions linked by a service spine. il Arch Rec 135:104-7 mid-My '64
Ideas for space in a budget house. il Arch Rec 133:171-4 Mr '63
Miracle on a mountain; weird junkpile or a masterpiece? D. L. Goodrich. il Sat Eve Post 237:22-7 S 12 '64
Modern house echoes tradition. il Arch Rec 134:111-14 D '63
Robert Motherwells who live in a brownstone with art of many periods. R. Motherwell. il Vogue 143:88-91+ Ja 15 '64
Two faced house. il Am Home 67:36-7 Ap '64
Two for the beach; Fire Island pines. G. O'Brien. il N Y Times Mag p70-1 My 12 '63
Yacht in a meadow; the Long Island house of Mrs De Menocal Simpson. il Vogue 141: 178-81 My '63
See also
Architecture, Domestic—Long Island, N.Y.

North Carolina

McCalls certified house; $15,000 in North Carolina. il McCalls 90:142 My '63

Oklahoma

Living is way out in Oklahoma. J. Peter and M. Kaytor. il Look 27:58-61 O 8 '63
One house in a million. il House & Gard 123:124-35 Ap '63

Oregon

House of ideas in the Northwest. il Am Home 66:89 O '63

Pennsylvania

Bold expression in brick and concrete. il Arch Rec 135:80-3 mid-My '64
Century-old house opened to a garden. il House & Gard 125:174-7 My '64
Dramatic living space on two levels. il Arch Rec 136:167-70 D '64
Purposefully regional architecture: country house by Winston Elting in the Pennsylvania countryside. il Arch Rec 137:135-42 Ja '65

Russia

Little red house; replica of Russian prize-winning one-family home. il Bsns W p78 N 23 '63

Texas

Come into the house, into the sun, and stay cool. il House B 106:114-23+ F '64
Formal house that exploits a sloping site. il Arch Rec 134:169-72 S '63
Green brick front, green woods behind. il House & Gard 123:142-7+ My '63
H&G's house of ideas for 1963. il House & Gard 124:81-117 Ag '63
House with a built-in landscape. il House & Gard 125:170-3 My '64
Neat town house for $20,000; home of architect, Ralph Anderson. il Arch Rec 133:151-4 F '63
Open plan for a family home. il Arch Rec 135:173-6 Mr '64
Past-and-present house. G. O'Brien. il N Y Times Mag p 126-7 O 6 '63
Walled-in privacy for a Houston town house. il Arch Rec 133:62-5 mid-My '63

Tunisia

Star of Venus; house in Tunisia owned by Edwina and Leo D'Erlanger. L. Blanch. il pors Vogue 144:194-201+ N 1 '64

United States

Adventure for the adventurous. il House & Gard 125:84-9 Ja '64
Custom look. il Time 82:78 O 11 '63
FHA awards recognize architectural merit. il Arch Rec 135:14-15 Ja '64
FHA honors awards for residential design. il Arch Rec 135:154-62 Ja '64
House you'll build from four boxes. B. Smallman. il Pop Sci 183:102-4 D '63
Houses will be different. Changing T 18:6 S '64
Ideas in houses. il Life 58:85-91 Ja 15 '65
Interesting people have the most interesting homes. il House B 105:131-55+ Ap '63
Natural houses of Frank Lloyd Wright; photographs. A. L. Huxtable. N Y Times Mag p78-9 N 17 '63
Speaking out; the suburbs are a mess; excerpt from God's own junkyard. P. Blake. Sat Eve Post 236:14+ O 5 '63
Three great new houses; what they have that you should aim for. House B 105:201 O '63

History

History in towns: Mobile, Alabama. M. R. Ingate. il Antiques 85:294-309 Mr '64
Legacy in danger; future of Frank Lloyd Wright houses. il Newsweek 62:105 O 7 '63

Virginia

House that easily converts into a duplex. il Arch Rec 133:147-50 Je '63
McCall's certified house, $27,490 in Virginia. il McCalls 91:190 Mr '64
You can have what you want, if you want it enough. il House B 105:60-71+ Jl '63

Washington, D.C.

Contemporary town house uses vaulted roofs. il Arch Rec 135:54-7 mid-My '64
Country house in the city. il House & Gard 124:186-91 O '63
Twice the size but still in character. il House B 105:154-7+ S '63

Washington (state)

Attractive development house for $5,995. il Arch Rec 135:62-3 mid-My '64
Maybe drastic changes aren't needed. C. Besinger. il House B 105:136-41+ S '63
Two-story court forms hub of house for a large family. il Arch Rec 133:74-7 mid-My '63

Western states

See also
Western home awards

ARCHITECTURE, Domestic and climate. See Architecture and climate

ARCHITECTURE, Ecclesiastical. See Church architecture

ARCHITECTURE, English
See also
Architecture, Domestic—England
ARCHITECTURE, Hillside. See Hillside architecture
ARCHITECTURE, Indian (East Indian)
See also
Architecture, Mogul
ARCHITECTURE, Islamic
Castle in the casbah; Moorish York castle, Tangier, Morocco. S. Kirtland and others. il Look 28:51-8 Ja 28 '64
ARCHITECTURE, Italian
Palladio updated. il House & Gard 124:260-3+ N '63
Successful Palladian transplant to Barbados. il House B 106:60-3+ Ja '64
ARCHITECTURE, Japanese
See also
Architecture, Domestic—Japan
ARCHITECTURE, Landscape. See Landscape gardening
ARCHITECTURE, Latin American
Art in Latin American architecture. P. Damaz. il Craft Horiz 23:12-39+ S '63
ARCHITECTURE, Modern
Aalto; Finland's greatest architect. il Arch Forum 118:120-5 Mr '63
Adventure for the adventurous. il House & Gard 125:84-9 Ja '64
Architecture at the New York world's fair. M. F. Schmertz. il Arch Rec 136:143-50 Jl '64
Art in modern architecture. P. Damaz. il Craft Horiz 23:36-9+ S '63
Big bite. N. Mailer. Esquire 59:37+ My; 60: 16+ Ag '63; Reply with rejoinder. V. J. Scully, jr. il Arch Forum 120:96-7 Ap '64
Changing the human habitat. W. Von Eckardt. New Repub 150:22+ F 1 '64
Death of the gargoyle; new architecture at Yale. il Time 82:80-5 N 15 '63
Epitaph for the international style. M. Ueland. Nat R 16:120-2 F 11 '64
Fortunate beauties. il Newsweek 64:60 Jl 13 '64
Give 'em hell. E. Goble. Arch Rec 134:9 Ag '63
Guide to modern architecture. by R. Banham. Review
Arch Forum il 118:145 Mr '63. S. Chermayeff
He adds elegance to modern architecture: P. Johnson. A. L. Huxtable. il N Y Times Mag p 18-19+ My 24 '64
Modern architecture. E. D. Stone. bibliog il NEA J 53:54-7 F '64
Modern house echoes tradition. il Arch Rec 134:111-14 D '63
New ways in architecture. H. Kramer. Reporter 29:58-60+ D 5 '63
Philip Johnson. C. Amory. il Vogue 143:184-92+ My '64
Pop architecture? E. Goble. Arch Rec 136:9 Ag '64
Seven new houses by Ulrich Franzen. il Arch Rec 134:127-42 N '63
Village of foetuses; housing development for millionaires on the slopes of the Maritime Alps. il Time 82:57 N 22 '63
ARCHITECTURE, Mogul
Fatehpur Sikri. il Arch Forum 119:118-23 N '63
ARCHITECTURE, Moorish. See Architecture, Islamic
ARCHITECTURE, Naval. See Naval architecture
ARCHITECTURE, Renaissance
Metropolitan's new marble hall. H. La Farge. il Art N 63:40-1 D '64
ARCHITECTURE, Roman
See also
Tivoli, Italy—Hadrian's villa
ARCHITECTURE, Romanesque
Romanesque runaround. A. C. Schmidt. il Reporter 32:36-8 Ja 14 '65
ARCHITECTURE, School. See School buildings
ARCHITECTURE, Victorian
America's Victorian homes. C. Carmer. Am Home 67:86-7 Mr '64
Why people live in Victorian houses. il Am Home 67:40-5 Mr '64
ARCHITECTURE and climate
Climate-balanced house design. V. Olgyay. il Arch Rec 133:7+ mid-My '63
Designed for sun and trade winds: Queen Emma gardens, Honolulu. il Arch Rec 136: 126-8 Ag '64
House for all seasons. il House & Gard 125: 98-109+ F '64
How to live happily ever after in a warm, sunny climate; symposium. il House B 106: 59-110+ Ja '64
Sensible way to control climate, with introduction. C. Besinger. il House B 106:67-75 Ag '64
Tropical climate control techniques. B. Polk. il Arch Rec 135:208-10 Ap '64
What the Bermudian house has to offer us. C. Besinger. il House B 106:156-61+ Mr '64
ARCHITECTURE and state. See Art and state
ARCHITECTURE as a profession. See Architects
ARCHITECTURE in art
Stately mansions of the imagination. J. Maass. il Horizon 5:10-27 S '63
ARCHIVES
See also
Documents

United States

Archival product of a century of federal assistance to agriculture. H. T. Pinkett. bibliog f Am Hist R 69:689-706 Ap '64
Current market values of presidential papers (cont) M. A. Benjamin. Hobbies 68:110-12 Ap '63
Preserving the secrets of the White House. H. F. Graft. il N Y Times Mag p9+ D 29 '63
See also
Harry S. Truman library, Independence, Mo.
United States—National archives
United States—National historical publications commission
ARCHIVISTS
Archivist and the historian; address. W. K. Lamb. Am Hist R 68:385-91 Ja '63
ARCINIEGAS, German
Culture and freedom; excerpt from Freedom and culture, comp. by UNESCO. UNESCO Courier 16:26-32 D '63
ARCTANDER, Erik H.
I drove a jeep on the moon. Pop Sci 182: 90-2+ My '63
PS tests H-D's spirited new Sprint. Pop Sci 183:142-4+ O '63
ARCTIC char. See Char
ARCTIC clothing. See Clothing, Cold weather
ARCTIC exploration
Ahdoolo! condensation. F. Miller. il Read Digest 82:263-9+ F '63
1,000 days in frozen space. E. D. Fales, jr. il Pop Sci 182:42-4 Je '63
ARCTIC OCEAN
Arctic waves flow over not one ocean but four. il Sci Digest 53:55-7 F '63
Ocean covers four seas. Sci N L 85:23 Ja 11 '64
ARCTIC REGIONS
Flesh freezes solid in thirty seconds. C. Mydans. il Life 54:26-7 Mr 1 '63
New perspective on the North. T. Lloyd. il For Affairs 42:293-308 Ja '64
See also
Aleutian Islands
Antarctic Regions
Banks Island (Arctic Ocean)
Disarmament—Arctic Regions
Fishing—Arctic Regions
Geology—Arctic Regions
Greenland
Ice—Polar Regions
Lapland
Svalbard

Climate

Arctic cold 14,000 years. Sci N L 86:134 Ag 29 '64

Description and travel

Flash: the Arctic. J. Cowan. il Vogue 144: 136-41+ N 1 '64
ARDAYNE, Julia Collins
Old-time garden; poem. McCalls 90:135 Jl '63
ARDEN house. See Columbia university
ARDENNES, Battle of the, 1944-1945
After twenty years: the GI's war fades away. W. C. Heinz. il Sat Eve Post 237:22-30+ D 12 '64
General said nuts! NBC documentary on Battle of the bulge. il Newsweek 64:51 D 14 '64
Way it was in the Bulge. L. Simpson. il N Y Times Mag p27-9+ D 6 '64
ARDOIN, John
Callas today. Mus Am 84:30-1 D '64
Echoes of the golden age. Mus Am 83:14-15+ N '63
Festival by accident. Mus Am 83:10-11 Je '63
Galli-Curci, 1883-1963. Mus Am 84:72 Ja '64
Great adventure. Mus Am 84:15-17 Ap '64
Lincoln Center: progress report. il Mus Am 84:10-13 My '64
Look at 1963. Mus Am 83:28-9+ D '63
1962 a backward look. Mus Am 83:26-7 Ja '63

ARDOIN, John—*Continued*
Opera abroad. Mus Am 84:12-15 S '64
Radio-TV (cont) Mus Am 83:212 Ja '63
Rarities for Rococo. Mus Am 84:50-1 My '64
Special report: imports and reissues. Mus Am 83:33 O '63
Tape (cont) Mus Am 83:131 Ja; 40 F; 20-1 Ag; 50-1 S '63
Truth into beauty. Mus Am 84:48-9 Mr '64
Welte heritage. Mus Am 84:46+ F '64

ARE you ready for Egyptland? story. See Fineman, M.

ARE you woman or wren? story. See Mercier, J.

AREA redevelopment administration. See United States—Area redevelopment administration

AREA studies
Africa, images and realities; summer Social studies institute program. J. Mather. il NEA J 52:33-5 Mr '63
American studies in Japan. M. B. Jansen. bibliog f Am Hist R 70:413-17 Ja '65
Diagnosing the American dream. M. W. Fishwick. il Sat R 46:8-11 D 21 '63
Foreign area studies in New York schools and colleges. W. Morehouse. Sch & Soc 91:280-2 O 5 '63
Leadership and world society; LAWS program at Emma Willard boarding school for girls. A. L. Homan. il Sr Schol 83:11T S 27 '63
Non-western world in higher education; symposium, ed. by D. N. Bigelow and L. H. Legters. bibliog f il Ann Am Acad 356:1-167 N '64
Wisconsin: Latin America's neighbor. W. P. Glade. il Américas 15:34-7 Jl '63

ARÉCHAGA, Eduardo Jiménez de. See Jiménez de Aréchaga, E.

ARECIBO ionospheric observatory. See Astronomical observatories—Puerto Rico

ARECIBO telescope. See Radio telescope

AREF, Abdul Salam
Baghdad between revolutions. L. Hamalian. il Nation 199:423-5 D 7 '64
Baghdad: coup by consent. D. Holden. il Reporter 29:30-2 D 19 '63
Shifting sands of Arab union. Sr Schol 83:10-11 Ja 17 '64
What's in store for Iraq. S. Huck. il Nat R 14:193-4 Mr 12 '63

ARENA stage. See Washington, D.C.—Theater

ARENAS, Sports. See Stadiums

ARENDS, Leslie Cornelius
Switch and fight. por Newsweek 65:24 Ja 25 '65
Triumph for a veteran: Arends re-elected as whip. por U S News 58:22 Ja 25 '65

ARENDS, Tulio, and Gallango, M. L.
Transferrins in Venezuelan Indians: high frequency of a slow-moving variant. bibliog Science 143:367-8 Ja 24 '64
—See Schön, M. A. jt. auth.

ARENDT, Hannah
Reporter at large. New Yorker 38:40-2+ F 16; 39:40-2+ F 23; 40-2+ Mr 2; 48-50+ Mr 9; 58-60+ Mr 16 '63

about

Hannah Arendt and her critics. M. Geltman. il Nat R 16:1007-12 N 17 '64; Discussion. 16:1130+ D 29 '64
Hannah Arendt on Eichmann. N. Podhoretz. Commentary 36:201-8 S '63; Discussion. 37: 6+ F; 16+ My '64
New Yorker & Hannah Arendt. I. Howe. Commentary 36:318-19 O '63; Discussion. 38:12+ S '64
Notes and comment; concerning review of Eichmann in Jerusalem. New Yorker 39:17 Jl 20 '63

ARÉVALO, Juan José
Where reds may take over next in Latin America. il por U S News 54:48-50 Mr 18 '63

ARGALI
Mystery ram of Dead Mountain; Nevada. C. E. Gillham. il Field & S 67:14+ Ap '63

ARGENTINA
Argentina: a study in self-contempt. L. Gross. il Look 28:74-7 Je 2 '64
See also
Airlines— Argentina
Airplane industry and trade—Argentina
Elections—Argentina
Fishing—Argentina
Iguassú Falls
Labor and laboring classes—Argentina
Opera—Argentina
Patagonia
Petroleum—Argentina
Petroleum industry and trade—Argentina
Railroads—Argentina
Space research—Argentina
Tierra del Fuego
Trade unions—Argentina

Economic conditions

Argentina; the depressed cork. il Fortune 67:65-6+ F '63
Argentina's problems. H. Hazlitt. Newsweek 63:84 My 11 '64
Atlantic report. Atlan 212:12+ O '63
Healing peace. Time 83:25 Ap 24 '64
New bread on the pampas. il Time 84:28 Ag 21 '64
New deal now in Argentina? U S News 55: 51 Jl 22 '63
See also
Argentina—Industries

Economic policy

Argentina gets off political treadmill. il Bsns W p39-40 Jl 27 '63
Argentina: struggle for recovery. A. P. Whitaker. Cur Hist 48:16-20+ Ja '65
Argentina; the depressed cork. il Fortune 67:65-6+ F '63

Foreign population

Italian way. il Time 82:54 N 15 '63

History

José Artigas: father of Uruguay; formation of Argentine nationality. H. E. Davis. bibliog il Américas 16:1-5 O '64
Powder keg politics in the land of the Pampa. il Sr Schol 82:10-13+ Ap 24 '63

Industries

Argentina: inflation in the midst of a recession. il Bsns W p54 My 2 '64
Argentina's nimble giant; SIAM Di Tella, ltda. Time 81:108+ Ap 19 '63
Peronist sword cuts two ways; plant seizures by unions. Bsns W p52 Je 27 '64
Stocks in the boondocks; Argentina's Deltec organization. il Time 83:85 Ja 17 '64

Politics and government

Argentina: a fragmented society. A. P. Whitaker. Cur Hist 46:15-18+ Ja '64
Argentina gets off political treadmill. il Bsns W p39-40 Jl 27 '63
Argentina: struggle for recovery. A. P. Whitaker. Cur Hist 48:16-20+ Ja '65
Atlantic report. Atlan 212:12+ O '63
Calling doctor Illia. il Newsweek 62:56 O 14 '63
Doctor in the casa; A. Illia, president-elect. Newsweek 62:45 Ag 12 '63
Freedom to maneuver. Time 81:36 Mr 15 '63
Left and right extremism in Argentina. A. P. Whitaker. Cur Hist 44:84-8+ F '63
Look of chaos. Time 81:33 My 17 '63
Mocking the turtle. Time 84:32-3 Jl 31 '64
Nation again. il Time 82:31 Ag 9 '63
Navy lost. il Newsweek 61:54 Ap 15 '63
New peronismo. il Time 84:48 S 4 '64
Nos. fifty-four through fifty-six. Time 81:40 My 24 '63
Peace by tranquilizer. il Newsweek 63:44-5 My 4 '64
Perón: this is the year. Time 84:30 N 6 '64
Political confusion. Newsweek 61:38 Je 10 '63
Powder keg politics in the land of the Pampa. il Sr Schol 82:10-13+ Ap 24 '63
President again. il Time 82:33 O 18 '63
Promise from Madrid. il Newsweek 64:44 Ag 31 '64
Shadowy anniversary; Perón's mass support. il Newsweek 64:58 S 28 '64
Slightly tarnished; De Gaulle visit marred by Peronista demonstration. Newsweek 64: 61 O 19 '64
Sure, you can vote. New Repub 148:11-12 Ap 20 '63
War & peace. il Time 81:28 Ap 12 '63
What is Illia? New Repub 149:8 Ag 17 '63
See also
Fascism—Argentina

Social conditions

Look to the heartland; charcoal production in Argentina. M. Belloni. il Américas 16: 36-9 Ja '64

ARGENTINA and Italy. See Italy and Argentina

ARGENTINE dancing. See Dancing, Argentine

ARGENTINE literature
Letter from Buenos Aires. A. Neish. Nation 196:272-4 Mr 30 '63

ARGENTINE poetry
Seven Argentine poets; with poems. M. Grinberg; J. C. Martelli. il Américas 16:16-21 O '64

ARGENTINE poetry—*Continued*
Translations into English
Robot; tr. by R. Connally. L. Marechal. il Américas 15:23-9 D '63
ARGININE
Neurospora mutant lacking an arginine-specific carbamyl phosphokinase. R. H. Davis. bibliog Science 142:1652-4 D 27 '63
ARGO, Virgil N.
Bull-horn acacia. Natur Hist 74:22-7 Ja '65
Index to next spring's growth. Natur Hist 73:52-6 Ja '64
Insect-trapping plants. Natur Hist 73:28-33 Mr '64
Root growth claims soil from sea. Natur Hist 72:52-5 Ap '63
Strangler fig, native epiphyte. Natur Hist 73:26-31 N '64
ARGONNE, Battle of the, 1918. See European war, 1914-1918—Campaigns and battles
ARGONNE national laboratory
Laboratory designed in fiber glass and plastics. il(p209) Sci N L 83:210 Ap 6 '63
Midwest: new arrangement for Argonne holds promise of greater federal financial aid for region. D. S. Greenberg. Science 146:749-51 N 6 '64
Reactor keeps itself going. Bsns W p76 N 16 '63
Smashing war. Newsweek 63:41 Ja 13 '64
ARGOUD, Antoine
L'affaire Argoud. il por Time 81:33 Mr 8 '63
Kidnaped. por Nat R 15:15-16 Jl 16 '63
Man in the middle. Time 83:29 Ja 10 '64
Model of stability. il Newsweek 63:32 Ja 13 '64
Package of treason. por Newsweek 61:40+ Mr 11 '63
ARGYLL, Ian Douglas Campbell, 11th duke of
High cost of adultery; Argyll divorce. il por Newsweek 61:45-6 My 20 '63
Remember Mrs Sweeny? por Time 81:39 My 17 '63
ARGYLL, Margaret (Whigham) duchess of
Remember Mrs Sweeny? por Time 81:39 My 17 '63
ARGYRIS, Chris
T-groups for organizational effectiveness. bibliog f Harvard Bsns R 42:60-74 Mr '64
ARIADNE auf Naxos; opera. See Strauss, R.
ARIAS, Arnulfo
Someone to love. por Time 83:39 My 1 '64
ARIAS, Mortimer
Latin American student conference. Christian Cent 81:1188-90 S 23 '64
ARIAS, Robert Emilio
Another payoff; Arias shot. il por Time 83: 30 Je 19 '64
Pistol-packing politics. il por Newsweek 63: 48-9 Je 22 '64
ARIAS DE AVILA, Pedro. See Pedrarias
ARID regions
Arid lands: environmental physiology and psychology; report of a symposium sponsored by UNESCO and the Central drug research institute of India. D. H. K. Lee. Science 140:1002-3+ My 31 '63
Management of water in arid lands. G. H. Davis. il Natur Hist 73:26-33 Ag '64
Ravelling watershed; grazing lands must be restored. C. L. Forsling. il Am For 69:12-14+ F '63
ARIDJIS, Homero
Month of June; poem. tr. by J. F. Nims. Atlan 213:105 Mr '64
ARIES, Robert Sancier
Who stole the formula? J. Kobler. il por Sat Eve Post 236:82+ Je 29 '63
ARINC research corporation
Technique predicts reliability of avionics before initial system design work begins. P. J. Klass. il Aviation W 80:76-7+ Ja 6 '64
ARISAEMA triphyllum. See Jack-in-the-pulpits
ARISTOCRACY
Maiden ladies; housing for unmarried daughters of the aristocracy in Germany and Denmark. N. S. Hazelton. New Yorker 39:162+ S 21 '63
See also
Upper classes
ARISTOPHANES
Aristophanes in American. X. J. Kennedy. Poetry 102:56-60 Ap '63
ARITHMETIC
Quick and easy math; condensation. I. Asimov. Pop Sci 185:77-83 D '64
ARIZIN, Paul
Still a star. Sports Illus 20:16 Ap 20 '64
ARIZONA
See also
Architecture, Domestic—Arizona
Chiricahua National Monument
Fishing—Arizona
Irrigation—Arizona
Navajo National Monument
Roads—Arizona
Water supply—Arizona
Antiquities
See Indians of North America—Antiquities—Arizona
Description and travel
Arizona: booming youngster of the West. R. De Roos. il Nat Geog Mag 123:299-343 Mr '63
Chevelon Canyon lures backpacking vacationers. R. B. Whitaker. il Todays Health 42: 24-7 F '64
Desert strip; airplane trip. J. Sanderson. il Flying 75:45 Jl '64
Personal business: desert oasis for wintering businessman. Bsns W p 129 Ja 23 '65
Snow-shunning in Arizona. B. Ballantine. il Holiday 36:36+ D '64
History
Spaniards came here 212 years ago. il Sunset 132:69+ Mr '64
Parks and reserves
Night life on the desert. J. J. Stophlet. il Nat Parks Mag 38:12-15 Mr '64
ARIZONA biochemical company
Coming struggle to breathe. T. O. Thackrey. Sat R 47:24-5+ O 10 '64
Questions and answers on composting. il Am City 78:119 S '63
ARIZONA journal. See Phoenix, Ariz.—Newspapers
ARIZONA-Sonora desert museum. See Natural history museums
ARIZONA star. See Tucson, Arizona—Newspapers
ARIZONA state library association
Intellectual freedom committee
Arizona LA adopts policy statement for Intellectual freedom committee. Library J 88:4338 N 15 '63
ARIZONA. University, Tucson
Lunar and planetary laboratory. G. P. Kuiper. il Sky & Tel 27:4-7, 88-92 Ja-F '64
ARKANSAS
Fresh look at Arkansas. B. Keating. il Holiday 34:52-5 S '63
See also
Architecture, Domestic—Arkansas
Courts—Arkansas
Education—Arkansas
Fishing—Arkansas
Politics and government
Arkansas: squire vs. demagogue; governor's race. T. Dearmore. il Reporter 31:38-42 O 22 '64
Can Win win? il Time 84:38 O 16 '64
Coming up: a two-party fight in Arkansas. il U S News 56:20 My 4 '64
How to lynch a newspaper. R. Reed. Atlan 214:59-63 N '64
Showdown in Arkansas: Win Rockefeller vs. Orval Faubus. B. H. Bagdikian. il Sat Eve Post 237:75-7 S 19 '64
ARKANSAS industrial development commission
Squire of Petit Jean. il Time 81:27 Mr 8 '63
ARKANSAS RIVER
Seaports for Oklahoma. il U S News 54:66-9 F 11 '63
ARKHIPOVA, Irina
Music to my ears; appearance at Carnegie Hall. I. Kolodin. Sat R 47:34+ D 12 '64
ARKIN, Frieda
Husband's tale; story. Yale R 54:51-8 O '64
ARKIN, Juki
Juki Arkin in An evening in pantomime at Judson Hall. D. Hering. il Dance Mag 37: 12-13 Ag '63
ARKING, Albert
Latitudinal distribution of cloud cover from Tiros III photographs. bibliog Science 143: 569-72 F 7 '64
ARLEN, M. J.
Clock runs out at Sturbridge watch & clock. New Yorker 39:39-40 My 4 '63
How to tell a novel by its cover. Life 57:11 Ag 21 '64
Onward, upward, backward, forward, and sideways with the RX-550. New Yorker 39:37-8 My 11 '63
Tips on tipping and tippees. N Y Times Mag p20+ My 31 '64
ARLINGTON, Mass.
Blowers boost loading, drop costs. F. N. O'Hara. il Am City 79:109-10 S '64

ARLINGTON, Va.
See also
Pentagon building

National cemetery

Burial plot in Arlington for the Kennedys. il U S News 55:8 D 16 '63
Walk through Arlington, and history. P. Streit. il N Y Times Mag p9+ D 22 '63
See also
Kennedy, J. F.—Tomb

ARLINGTON national cemetery. See Arlington, Va.—National cemetery

ARLINGTON SPRINGS man. See Man, Prehistoric

ARM grafting. See Transplantation of organs, tissues, etc.

ARMAGEDDON; story. See Uris, L.

ARMALITE rifle. See Rifles

ARMAMENTS
Arms race or disarmament? J. J. Stone. Bul Atomic Sci 20:20-4 S '64; Reply with rejoinder. D. K. Lewis. 21:29-31 Ja '65
Conventional weapons control. C. W. Tarr, jr. bibliog f Cur Hist 47:25-30 Jl '64
Free world split will widen. E. Stillman. il Nations Bsns 52:34-5+ Ap '64
Goldwater on the gap. New Repub 149:5-6 D 21 '63
World expenditure on arms 120,000 million dollars a year. il UNESCO Courier 17:4-5 N '64
See also
Disarmament
Militarism
Munitions

ARMBRISTER, Trevor
Is there any hope for Haiti? Sat Eve Post 236:78-81 Je 15 '63
Land frauds: look before you buy. Sat Eve Post 236:17-23 Ap 27 '63
Odd saga of the big Bahamas spenders. Sat Eve Post 237:30+ Ag 8 '64
O'Toole of Arabia. Sat Eve Post 236:22-6+ Mr 9 '63
Our town is on the map! Sat Eve Post 236:40 N 16 '63
Panama: why they hate us. Sat Eve Post 237:75-9 Mr 7 '64
Portrait of an extremist. Sat Eve Post 237:80-3 Ag 22 '64
Price of getting involved. Sat Eve Post 237:81-5 S 26 '64
Railroad that defies the unions. Sat Eve Post 237:84-9 F 22 '64
Sky is falling. Sat Eve Post 237:20-5 Ap 11 '64
Town reaction: wow! Ladies Home J 80:74 D '63
Village beyond despair. Sat Eve Post 236:66-9 N 9 '63
Will Chile go Communist? Sat Eve Post 237:69-73 S 5 '64

ARMCHAIRS. See Chairs

ARMED forces
Weapons and men, 1964. A. S. Nanes. bibliog f Cur Hist 47:12-17+ Jl '64

Officers, Retired

See Retired military officers

ARMED forces communications and electronics association
Super global complex being built. C. D. LaFond. il Miss & Roc 12:32+ Je 17 '63

ARMED forces day and week
Salute to 2,700,000: photographs. N Y Times Mag p 16-17 My 10 '64

ARMED forces of national liberation. See Political parties—Venezuela

ARMED forces strike command. See United States—Strike command

ARMED services committee, Senate. See United States—Congress—Senate—Committees

ARMENIA
Yankee fans in Yerevan. L. Gottlieb and G. Feifer. Reporter 30:36-7 Ja 16 '64

ARMENIAN church
Armenian church and ecumenism. C. S. Calian. Christian Cent 81:1007-8 Ag 12 '64
Interview with the Armenian observer at the council; ed. by E. M. Jung. A. K. Sarkissian. Cath World 197:258-63 Jl '63

ARMENIAN SOVIET REPUBLIC. See Armenia

ARMENIANS in the United States
Shout Armenia wherever you go. W. Saroyan. il Sat Eve Post 237:74+ N 21 '64

ARMIES
See also
Militarism
also subhead Army under names of countries, e.g. Congo (capital Leopoldville)—Army

Officers

See also
Generals
Germany—Army—Officers

ARMILLARIA mellea. See Fungi, Pathogenic

ARMILLAS, Pedro
Hydraulic civilizations. UNESCO Courier 17:60-3 Jl '64

ARMISTEAD, W. H. and Stookey, S. D.
Photochromic silicate glasses sensitized by silver halides. bibliog Science 144:150-4 Ap 10 '64

ARMISTICE, Korean. See Korean war, 1950-1953—Peace and mediation

ARMKNECHT, Richard F.
In planning stage; poem. Good H 156:236 Mr '63
On the meeting of lips; poem. Ladies Home J 80:108 Ja '63

ARMONK, N.Y.
International chef; Rob Roy restaurant. il Travel 119:65 Ap '63

ARMORED vessels. See Warships

ARMORY show. See Art—Exhibitions

ARMOUR, Allan A.
Magnetic stripe on film. U S Camera 26:20 S '63

ARMOUR, Richard
Constant reader; poem. McCalls 92:181 N '64
Drawn and quartered; poem. McCalls 90:52 Mr '63
Dust; poem. McCalls 91:118 Je '64
Fat chance; poem. McCalls 90:154 Ag '63
High, there! poem. McCalls 91:208 Ap '64
It all started with my mother and father. Writer 77:12-13 O '64
Mind over mattress; poem. McCalls 92:167 O '64
Room service; poem. McCalls 92:153 D '64
Shear nonsense; poem. McCalls 91:169 My '64
Variety is the spice of writing. Writer 76:18-19 N '63
What's the percentage? poem. McCalls 91:160 O '63

ARMOUR and company
Armour cuts the meat in its diet. il Bsns W p54+ My 9 '64
Fort Worth project of the Armour automation committee; excerpt of report. G. P. Shultz. il Mo Labor R 87:53-7 Ja '64
Packing it away. il Time 83:82 Ja 17 '64
Packing up an Armour packing plant, Sioux City. Bsns W p80+ Jl 20 '63
Quick-cook bacon; Brown 'n serve. Consumer Rep 28:215 My '63
Wage chronology: Armour and co. 1961-63. il Mo Labor R 86:399-408 Ap '63
When job retraining helps. Bsns W p50 N 16 '63

ARMOUR research foundation, Chicago
Learning to control runaway fires. il Todays Health 41:51 F '63

ARMS, Coats of. See Heraldry

ARMS and armor
See also
Pistols
Swords

ARMS control. See Disarmament

ARMS control and disarmament agency. See United States—Arms control and disarmament agency

ARMSEY, James W.
B.M.O.C: special program in education. por Newsweek 63:45 Ja 6 '64

ARMSTEAD, Edward, Jr
Image of the student in basic education. Negro Hist Bul 26:174-5 F '63

ARMSTRONG, Annabelle
(ed) See Falk, E. I believe
(ed) See Kohler, E. J. I believe
(ed) See Veach, L. I believe

ARMSTRONG, Barbara
Wethersfield: historic houses. Antiques 86:457-61 O '64

ARMSTRONG, Christa
Birth of a nation in Asia. il N Y Times Mag p30-1 S 15 '63
Communique from India's mountain front. il N Y Times Mag p 10-11+ Jl 7 '63

ARMSTRONG, Donald, and others
Complement-fixing antigens in tissue cultures of avian leucosis viruses. bibliog Science 144:1584 Je 26 '64

ARMSTRONG, George T.
Calorimetry. Science 143:158-60+ Ja 10 '64

ARMSTRONG, Hamilton Fish
This war in Borneo: whose side are we on? Reporter 30:16-20 Je 4 '64
Troubled birth of Malaysia. For Affairs 41:673-93 Jl '63

ARMSTRONG, Louis
Armstrong before Dolly. M. Williams. Sat R 47:77+ O 17 '64

ARMSTRONG, Louis—*Continued*
Louis Armstrong, the reluctant millionaire. C. L. Sanders. il pors Ebony 20:136-8+ N '64
Up among the Beatles. por Newsweek 63:103-4 Ap 27 '64
ARMSTRONG, Neal E. and Odum, H. T.
Photoelectric ecosystem. bibliog Science 143: 256-8 Ja 17 '64
ARMSTRONG, Neil
Australian odyssey. Flying 74:42-4+ Je '64
I decided to get aboard. Life 55:84 S 27 '63
Weird astronaut machines. il por Life 57: 137-40 S 25 '64
ARMSTRONG, Richard
Automakers and their mighty works. Sat Eve Post 237:15-27 S 19 '64
Crisis for capitalism. Sat Eve Post 237:17-29 Mr 21 '64
How the Communists plan to win Latin America. Sat Eve Post 236:19-34 Je 29 '63; Same abr. with title What the Communists plan for Latin America. Read Digest 83: 205-9+ O '63
Tragedy of Appalachia. Sat Eve Post 237: 34-6+ Ag 22 '64
Viva el candidato! Sat Eve Post 237:73-7 Je 20 '64
Why can't we save Latin America? Sat Eve Post 236:34-6 N 30 '63
ARMSTRONG, Ronald. See Gray, M. jt. auth.
ARMSTRONG, William H.
How to make words say something. Bet Hom & Gard 41:108-9 Mr '63
ARMSTRONG-JONES, Antony Charles Robert, 1st earl of Snowdon. See Snowdon, A. C. R. A.-J.
ARMSTRONG-JONES, David Albert Charles, viscount Linley. See Linley, D. A. C. A.-J.
ARMSTRONG cork company
Armstrong cork co.'s switch-hitting team. il Bsns W p 118+ S 12 '64
Keeping the product exclusive: Armstrong's Luminaire ceilings. il Bsns W p44+ Ja 25 '64
Natural cork providing ablative protection for Minuteman, Polaris, Scout. J. F. Judge. il Miss & Roc 13:32-3+ O 28 '63
To live and die for Armstrong. H. Kay. il Fortune 69:124-9+ Mr '64
ARMY
Missile command
See United States—Army—Missile command
ARMY (football) See Football
ARMY, International. See International police
ARMY air force. See United States—Air force, Army
ARMY ants. See Ants
ARMY around the world flight, 1924. See Aviation—World flights
ARMY education program. See United States—Army—Education
ARMY engineers. See United States—Army—Corps of engineers
ARMY food. See United States—Army—Commissariat
ARMY insignia. See United States—Army—Insignia
ARMY language school. See United States—Army—Education
ARMY rifles. See Rifles
ARNALDI, Jean
Small in the eyes of a tiger; story. Mlle 59:150-1 My '64
ARNAUD, Charles E.
How to make a light-tight window shield. Pop Phot 54:82-3 My '64
ARNAULT, Genevieve
Arabian nights tale launches 1,001 fights. il pors Life 54:42 Mr 22 '63
ARNEZ, Nancy Levi
Land of the free; poem. Negro Hist Bul 27: 37 N '63
What deeper sin? poem. Negro Hist Bul 26: 162 F '63
ARNO, Sig
Strength of innocence; poem. Ladies Home J 80:43 Je '63
ARNOLD, A. See Merola, A. J. jt. auth.
ARNOLD, Anne
Animal kingdom of Anne Arnold. L. Campbell. il por Art N 63:32-3+ D '64
Anne Arnold's wood menagerie. E. Dugmore. il por Craft Horiz 24:20-3 Jl '64
ARNOLD, Christian K.
Higher education: fourth branch of government? Sat R 47:60-1+ Ja 18 '64
ARNOLD, Francis A. Jr
Far worse than an aching tooth. Todays Health 42:56-9+ F '64
ARNOLD, Grace
All bugs are not bad. Horticulture 41:406 Ag '63
ARNOLD, Henry C. F.
Current trends in construction. See issues of Architectural record
Religious buildings: stability after the boom. Arch Rec 134:18 Jl '63
ARNOLD, James R. See Honda, M. jt. auth.
ARNOLD, Joseph F.
Crusade for rangeland restoration. Am For 69:28-32 My '63
ARNOLD, M. H.
Roses are rubra, violets are coerulea. Horticulture 41:364-5 Jl '63
ARNOLD, Margaret Long
Den mother to the clubwomen. B. Fancher. il pors Sat Eve Post 236:60-1 Mr 9 '63
ARNOLD, Matthew
D for disinterested. por Time 81:122 My 17 '63
ARNOLD, Paula
Spring of winter arrives in Israel. Audubon Mag 65:386-7 N '63
ARNOLD, Russ
Leisurely journey through Bayou country. U S Camera 26:14+ S '63
Photography at Tucson high. U S Camera 27:51+ Mr '64
ARNOLD, Stanley
Sales & distribution. J. B. Weiner. Duns R 82:45-6+ S '63
ARNOLD, Thurman
In contempt of justice. New Repub 150:32-3 Mr 7 '64
ARNOLD W. E.
Future of natural law theory. Commonweal 79:111 O 18 '63
Religion on campus. Commonweal 79:438-9 Ja 10 '64
ARNOLD, William E.
Is team teaching the answer? bibliog f Sch & Soc 91:407-9 D 14 '63
ARNOLD Stone; story. See O'Hara, J.
ARNOLDSON, Sigrid
Sigrid Arnoldson. A. Favia-Artsay. il por Hobbies 68:28-9 S '63
ARNON, Ruth
Something to talk about on campus. Mlle 59: 320-2 Ag '64
ARNSTEIN, George E.
Mixed blessings of automation. bibliog f Sch & Soc 92:311-13 O 31 '64
ARNSTEIN, Helene S.
Parent and child. N Y Times Mag p 119-20 O 6 '63
Why they never stick to anything. Parents Mag 39:52-3+ D '64
AROIDS. See Arums
AROMATIC compounds
Aromatic biosynthesis and metabolism; report of symposium. A. J. Finlayson. Science 142:981-2 N 15 '63
AROMATIC shrubs. See Shrubs
ARON, Kalman
Kalman Aron, draughtsman. J. Lovoos. il Am Artist 28:30-5+ Mr '64
ARON, Raymond
Coexistence and the class struggle. New Repub 149:10-11 S 28 '63
Demands of power. New Repub 148:12-13 Mr 30 '63
Europe & the United States; tr. by R. McInerny. Commentary 38:54-60 Ag '64
Government by disdain. New Repub 148:7-8 F 2; 31 F 23 '63
On putting detente to good use. New Repub 149:12-13 N 23 '63
Placing General de Gaulle. New Repub 148: 8-9 Mr 16 '63
Rationality of modern society. Bul Atomic Sci 20:23-4 Ja '64
Reading de Gaulle's mind. New Repub 148: 12-13 My 4 '63
Size-up of de Gaulle; interview, ed. by A. J. Meyers. por U S News 54:68-72 Ap 22 '63; Same abr. with title Frenchman explains de Gaulle. Read Digest 83:79-82 Jl '63
Spread of nuclear weapons; excerpt from Great debate. Atlan 215:44-50 Ja '65
Today's impasse, tomorrow's solution. New Repub 148:13-14 Je 1 '63
What of the grand design? New Repub 148: 8-9 F 16 '63
Why Europe fears us; excerpt from Great debate. tr. by E. Pawel. Atlan 214:47-52 D '64
ARONOWITZ, Alfred
Dominic Tucci slept here. Sat Eve Post 237: 20-1 Jl 25 '64
Dumb sound. Sat Eve Post 236:88, 91-5 O 5 '63
Lady Jane. Sat Eve Post 236:22-5 Mr 23 '63

ARONOWITZ, Alfred—*Continued*
Maccabees ride again. Sat Eve Post 237:32+ Je 27 '64
Play that rocked Europe. Sat Eve Post 237: 36, 39+ F 29 '64
Return of the Beatles. Sat Eve Post 237: 22-9 Ag 8 '64
Swinging nuns. Sat Eve Post 237:66-7 Ja 4 '64
They call me Tiger Lil. Sat Eve Post 236:28+ O 26 '63
What's so great about Ray Charles? Sat Eve Post 236:74-6 Ag 24 '63
Yeah! yeah! yeah! music's gold bugs: the Beatles. Sat Eve Post 237:30-5 Mr 21 '64
—and Blonsky, Marshall
Three's company: Peter, Paul and Mary. Sat Eve Post 237:30+ My 30 '64
ARONSON, David
Coats of many colors. il por Time 82:72-3 N 22 '63
ARONSON, Irene
Technique of the color lithograph. il por Am Artist 27:30-5+ O '63
ARONSON, Jason
Positive role of mental crisis. Sat R 47: 82-4 D 5 '64
AROSEMENA, Carlos Julio
Ecuador's socio-political mosaic. E. S. Urbanski. bibliog f Cur Hist 46:19-25 Ja '64
One for the road. il por Time 82:22-3 Jl 19 '63
Progress after a coup. por Time 81:29-30 Mr 8 '63
Toppled tippler. por Newsweek 62:49 Jl 22 '63
AROUND the world flight, Army, 1924. See Aviation—World flights
AROUND the world flights. See Aviation—World flights
AROUND the world in eighty days; musical comedy. See Musical comedies, revues, etc. —Criticisms, plots, etc.
ARPAIA, Anthony F.
Matter of necessity; independent tribunal to adjudicate labor disputes; address, April 2, 1964. Vital Speeches 30:477-80 My 15 '64
ARPINO, Giovanni
Peacock; story. Esquire 62:102 N '64
ARQUILLA, Edward R. and Finn, Jack
Genetic differences in antibody production to determinant groups on insulin. bibliog Science 142:400-1 O 18 '63
ARRAES, Francisco de Alencar. See Alencar Arraes, F. de
ARRAES, Miguel
Joe nobody. por Newsweek 63:34+ F 24 '64
ARRAN, Arthur Kattendyke Strange David Archibald Gore, 8th earl of
Plastered peer; Earl of Arran's column in London evening news. por Time 81:62+ F 8 '63
ARRANGEMENT of flowers. See Flowers, Arrangement of
ARRANGEMENT of furniture. See Furniture, Arrangement of
ARRANGING of pictures. See Pictures, Hanging of
ARRAU, Claudio
Arrau at sixty. T. F. Johnson. il Mus Am 83:27 Mr '63
ARRAU. See Turtles
ARREOLA, Juan José
Two sketches; tr. by L. Kemp. Atlan 213:127-8 Mr '64
ARREST
Do it yourself; citizen's arrest. Time 84:55-6 Ag 7 '64
ARRHENIUS, G. and others
Origin of oceanic manganese minerals. bibliog Science 144:170-3 Ap 10 '64
ARRIETA Y CORRERA, Pascual Juan Emilio
New Marina in stereo. J. Maclain. il Am Rec G 30:572-3 Mr '64
ARRINGTON, G. Austin
Shortia galacifolia. Horticulture 42:48-9 Ja '64
ARROW points. See Arrowheads
ARROW poisons. See Poisons
ARROWHEADS
Latest in arrowheads. G. H. Gillelan. il Outdoor Life 131:98-9+ Mr '63
Projectile point types. C. Miles. il Hobbies 69:113-15+ Ap '64
Small-game arrowheads. G. H. Gillelan. il Outdoor Life 133:14+ My '64
Wall of gem points. C. Miles. il Hobbies 69: 112+ S '64
ARROWS, Poisoned
Deadly point; poisoned darts. G. Vincent. il N Y Times Mag p62+ Mr 15 '64
ARROWSMITH, William
Aristophanes in American. X. J. Kennedy. Poetry 102:56-60 Ap '63
ARROYO, Martina
Look at the future. por Mus Am 83:9 Jl '63
ARSENIC
Lung cancer, arsenic linked in British study. Sci N L 84:89 Ag 10 '63
ARSENIC compounds
Arsenates; effect on fecundity in some diptera. A. D. Pickett and N. A. Patterson. bibliog il Science 140:493-4 My 3 '63
ARSENIC poisoning
What killed Napoleon? Sci N L 84:84 Ag 10 '63
ARSON
Thread of evidence. P. Hutchinson. il Am For 69:30-1+ Jl '63
War on the fire felons; address. B. Holleman. Am For 70:29+ F '64
Why children set fires. Sci Digest 57:21 Ja '65
ART
Art's voyage of discovery. K. Kuh. il Sat R 47:149-51+ Ag 29 '64
Goodbye Paris, hello New York; gradual shift of world art centers. il Time 84:58 Jl 17 '64
Next revolution in art. A. Reinhardt. Art N 62:48-9 F '64
Sense of wonder; preface to Faure's History of art. H. Miller. Vogue 144:216-17 D '64
See also
Advertising art
Aesthetics
Animals in art
Childrens art
Circus in art
Composition (art)
Cubism
Design
Expressionism (art)
Graphic arts
Impressionism (art)
Jesus Christ—Art
Light in art
Mothers in art
Nude in art
Prints
Realism in art
Sculpture
Surrealism (art)
Texture

Anecdotes, facetiae, satire, etc.

What's art, pop? il Time 84:74-5 S 11 '64

Appreciation

Approach to design. P. Johnson. il Sch Arts 62:16-20 Mr '63
Art as education. H. Wilson. il Sch Arts 63: 30-2 D '63
Is kindness killing the arts? R. Lynes. Harper 227:68-71+ N '63
Is sculpture a step-child? a colloquy. P. Agostini; R. Mallary; M. Friedman. il Art N 63:40-2+ S '64
Misunderstandings denying the appreciation of modern art. J. Schinneller. il Sch Arts 62:25-8 Ap; 21-3 My '63
Smart money in art. L. Lerman. il Mlle 59: 64-8 Je '64
See also
Art criticism

Bibliography

Art books. il Newsweek 62:61-3 D 30 '63
Art books of 1963. M. Kozloff. Nation 197: 459-62 D 28 '63
Art books of 1964. L. Kirstein. Nation 199: 470-2, 502-3, 519-22 D 14-28 '64
Arts and humanities; paperbacks. D. Zamchick. Sr Schol 85:23T D 2 '64
Backward glance: art books, books on art, and picture books. P. Pickrel. Harper 228: 101-6 Ja '64
Book list for White House includes architecture. Arch Rec 134:29+ D '63
Book notes. See issues of American artist
Book review section. See issues of Design
Books. See issues of School arts
Holiday for fine arts. G. H. Hamilton. il Sat R 46:45-6+ D 7 '63
Holiday package of paintings in print. G. H. Hamilton. il Sat R 47:56-62 D 5 '64
Some choice art books. C. J. McNaspy. America 109:716-17 N 30 '63
Summer bookshelf. il Art N 63:32-3+ Sum '64

Casting

See Casting (sculpture)

Collections

See Art—Private collections

Competitions

Competitions and awards. See issues of American artist
Córdoba biennial; second American art biennial. il Américas 16:37 D '64
Córdoba's biennial comes to Washington. J. Gómez-Sicre. il Américas 15:16-19 F '63

ART—Competitions—*Continued*
1964 Scholastic magazines art awards. il Sr Schol 84:18-19 My 15 '64
Olympics for painters; Guggenheim museum. J. Canaday. il N Y Times Mag p54 Ja 12 '64
Painting contests; Guggenheim international award and Pennsylvania academy awards. il Time 83:74-5 F 7 '64

Copyright

See Copyright—Art

Criticism

See Art criticism

Education

See Art education

Exhibitions

Again the Village Picassos emerge Washington square art exhibit. V. Raynor. il N Y Times Mag p26-7+ My 17 '64
American artist travelogue. il Am Artist 27: 65-9 Ap '63; 28:59-64 Ap '64
American panorama; Four centuries of American art at the Minneapolis institute of art. il Newsweek 62:91 D 2 '63
Antiques abroad; last decade's acquisitions by London's National gallery. W. De Sager. il Antiques 84:184+ Ag '63
Anything goes at the Carnegie; Pittsburgh international exhibition of contemporary painting and sculpture. K. Levin. il Art N 63:34-6+ D '64
Architect of peace; São Paulo biennial. R. Squirru. il Américas 16:2-4 Ap '64
Armory disarmed. F. Getlein. New Repub 148:33+ My 4 '63
Armory show. B. Kaufman. Commonweal 78:174-5 My 3 '63
Armory show; pictures and sculptures from Show of 1913. New Yorker 39:35-6 Mr 30 '63
Armory show: revolution reenacted. H. Rosenberg. New Yorker 39:99-100+ Ap 6 '63
Art. H. Kramer. See issues of Nation to June 22, 1963
Art. M. Kozloff. See occasional issues of Nation
Art galleries. H. Rosenberg. See issues of New Yorker to November 2, 1963
Art galleries. R. M. Coates. See issues of New Yorker
Art in church; St James' church, New York. New Yorker 39:34-6 My 4 '63
Art news from London; The Dunn international; exhibition of modern painting at the Tate gallery, London. J. Russell. Art N 62: 48 Ja '64
Art pops in; R. Rauschenberg, winner of Venice Biennale; with account by R. Constable. il Life 57:65-6+ Jl 10 '64
Art rite, opening night; New York galleries and museums. G. Glueck. il N Y Times Mag p44-5 D 13 '64
Arts and a man; 200 years of American art at St. Louis' art museum. C. J. McNaspy. America 110:775-6 My 30 '64
Before your very eyes; with colored reproductions. il Time 81:58-71 My 10 '63
Bienal's best; São Paulo bienal in Brazil. il Time 82:90 O 4 '63
Biennale: how evil is pop art? T. Zevi. New Repub 151:32-4 S 19 '64
Big collecting in a small democracy; Swiss private collections at the Lausanne fair. A. Frankfurter. il Art N 63:20-3+ S '64
Bologna-Rome-France: the classic ideal. A. Frankfurter. il Art N 61:35-7+ F '63
Bulletin board. See issues of American artist
Byzantium gloriously re-emerges in Athens; Council of Europe exhibition. K. Weitzmann. il Art N 63:28-31+ Sum '64
Carnegie's 43rd. il Time 84:78 N 6 '64
Carnival in Venice; 32nd Biennale. il Newsweek 64:74-5 Jl 6 '64
Choice's dealer; exhibition in honor of C. Valentin. T. B. Hess. il Art N 62:26-7+ D '63
Coming soon, 1964-1965 art exhibits. Design 66:6 S; 4 N '64
Continuity of Pierre Bonnard; exhibition at the Museum of modern art. M. Benedikt. il Art N 63:20-3+ O '64
Contrast in São Paulo; seventh São Paulo biennial. J. Gómez-Sicre. il Américas 15:18-22 D '63
Córdoba biennial; second American art biennial. il Américas 16:37 D '64
Córdoba's biennial comes to Washington. J. Gómez-Sicre. il Américas 15:16-19 F '63
Creative casting; exhibition at New York's Museum of contemporary crafts. L. Campbell. il Craft Horiz 23:10-17+ N '63
Day of the browser; opening of gallery season in Manhattan. il Time 82:86 O 18 '63
Designed by Eugene Berman. il Theatre Arts 47:13 Mr '63
Dutch focus on Italy; University of Michigan's exhibition. il Art N 63:38+ Sum '64
Familiar spirits; offbeat show at University of St Thomas, Houston. il Newsweek 64: 97-8 N 30 '64
First in the Nation, and six years later; Mile of art, exhibit at Eastgate shopping center, Indianapolis. il Design 66:30-2 N '64
Glorious affair; Armory show of 1913. il Time 81:58-67 Ap 5 '63
Goings on about town. See issues of New Yorker
Goya; exhibition at Royal academy, London. il Newsweek 62:72-3 D 23 '63
Hugger-mugger in the giardini; Venice biennale. M. Gendel. il Art N 63:32-5+ S '64
Illustrators '63. il Am Artist 27:36-42+ O '63
In the galleries. R. Davidson. il Antiques 86:622 N '64
Jane streeters; Jane street group at Knoedler's, New York. il Newsweek 62:100 S 23 '63
Kiesler and Mondrian, art into life. K. Levin. il Art N 63:38-41+ My '64
Letter from London; exhibition of paintings and sculptures of decade 1954 to 1964 at Tate gallery. M. Panter-Downes. New Yorker 40:98+ Je 13 '64
Letter from London; exhibition: Royal children at Owen's gallery at Buckingham palace. M. Panter-Downes. New Yorker 39: 208 N 30 '63
Letter from London; Goya exhibition at Burlington House. M. Panter-Downes. New Yorker 39:66-7 Ja 25 '64
Letter from Paris; exhibition at Right bank galerie creuze, devoted exclusively to the Virgin. Genêt. New Yorker 40:121-3 Je 13 '64
Letter from Paris; third Biennale at the Musée d'art moderne de la ville de Paris. Genêt. New Yorker 39:147-8 N 16 '63
Life guide. See issues of Life
Lively answer; Dunn international. il Time 82:74 S 20 '63
Lucid Spanish interspace; exhibition of Spanish still-life painting at the Newark museum. il Art N 63:37+ Ja '65
Meeting in Madrid: joint exhibit of Spanish and New World artists. J. Gómez-Sicre. il Américas 15:30-9 S '63
Mesopotamian legacy; 7000 years of Iranian art. F. Getlein. New Repub 151:27-8 S 12 '64
Museum calendar. See issues of American artist
1954-1964: painting and sculpture of a decade at the Tate gallery, London. J. Russell. il Art N 63:35-7+ My '64
1914; Baltimore museum's fiftieth-anniversary show. H. Rosenberg. il Art N 63:38-41 O '64
Notes of a peripatetic gallerygoer. K. Kuh. il Sat R 47:27+ Ap 25 '64
Opus anglicanum; English embroiderers loan exhibition at the Victoria & Albert museum, London. A. Frankfurter. il Art N 62:22-5+ D '63
Painters; exhibition by members of Hamilton-Madison's Golden age club. New Yorker 39:16-18 Je 29 '63
Paintings for sale: profits for performers. il Dance Mag 37:44-5 Mr '63
Peaceable in Pittsburgh. F. Getlein. New Repub 151:25-6 D 12 '64
Pleasant cataclysm; 1914, exhibition at Baltimore museum of art. F. Getlein. New Repub 151:34-5 N 14 '64
Pop goes the Biennale. il Time 84:54 Jl 3 '64
Portrait of Maine; exhibition at the Colby college art museum. il Newsweek 61:97 My 27 '63
Presentation matters. N. Kent. Am Artist 28:3+ D '64
Pride of Fredericton; Dunn international exhibition. Newsweek 62:100-1 S 23 '63
Reconstructing the Whirlwind of 26th street; Amory show. S. Sachs, 2d. il Art N 61: 26-9+ F '63
Retrospectives and more. C. J. McNaspy. America 111:570-1 N 7 '64
Reviews and previews. See issues of Art news
Rosetta stone at Kassel; Dokumenta III. il Time 84:70 Jl 10 '64
Seven new shows. il Newsweek 61:64-5 F 18 '63
7,000 years of Iranian art; showing at the National gallery of art, Washington, D.C. J. Eagle. il Craft Horiz 24:34-9+ N '64

ART—Exhibitions—*Continued*

Show that shook America; International exhibition of modern art, 1913, reconstituted at the Munson-Williams-Proctor institute in Utica, N.Y. il Newsweek 61:80-1 Mr 4 '63

Show's the thing. il Time 81:74 F 15 '63

Split worlds of Max Beckmann; retrospective at Modern museum, New York. M. Roskill. il Art N 63:46-8+ D '64

Story behind a great art event; Armory show. B. B. Perlman. il Am Artist 27:26-9+ F '63

Success story of American art; Sixty years of American painting, at Whitney museum. B. O'Doherty. il N Y Times Mag p66-7 S 15 '63

Summer exhibitions in Paris. R. C. Smith; R. Davidson. il Antiques 86:194-5 Ag '64

Three craftsmen. B. Kaufman. Commonweal 81:246-7 N 13 '64

Toronto treasures, universal and university; Royal Ontario museum draws a 50th anniversary show. J. S. Boggs. il Art N 61:32-4+ F '63

Tour of the galleries; seven New York shows. M. Kozloff. Nation 200:17-20 Ja 4 '65

Venice: the biennale. J. Guth and F. Guth. il Craft Horiz 24:48 S '64

View of her own; Americans 1963, at the Museum of modern art. il Newsweek 61: 90 Je 10 '63

Way, way out; Armory show. C. J. McNaspy. America 108:692-4 My 11 '63

What's happened to art? interview on present consequences of New York's 1913 Armory show; ed. by W. Seitz. M. Duchamp. il Vogue 141:110-13+ F 15 '63

Where and when to exhibit; exhibition calendar. See issues of Art news

See also

Childrens art—Exhibitions

Drawings—Exhibitions

Exhibitions, Traveling

Pottery—Exhibitions

Prints—Exhibitions

Expertising

Critique of connoisseurship. E. Wind. bibliog il Art N 63:26-9+ Mr '64

Missing Michelangelo? discovery of painted wood crucifix. il Life 56:45-6+ F 21 '64

Unburied cross; Romanesque cross recently acquired by Manhattan's Metropolitan museum of art. il Time 83:68-9+ Je 19 '64

Galleries and museums

Art for the man on foot. R. Joseph. il Esquire 60:90-3 S '63

Dealer's choice; A. Maeght museum in Saint-Paul-de-Vence. il Newsweek 64:61 Ag 10 '64

Great American museums. C. J. McNaspy. America 110:832-3 Je 13 '64

Imaginable museums; artists homes and studios in France and America. A. Frankfurter. Art N 63:25 N '64

In the museums. R. Davidson. See issues of Antiques

Maeghts' glorious adventure in art. P. Schneider. il Vogue 144:186-9+ O 15 '64

Maeghts' museum. M. Cournot. il Vogue 144: 190-1+ O 15 '64

Museum evaluations. A. Frankfurter. il Art N 63:26-9+ D '64; 24-7+ Ja '65

Museum in the sun; Fondation Marguerite et Aimé Maeght at Saint-Paul-de-Vence. il N Y Times Mag p36-7+ S 27 '64

Museums, press agents and art historians. A. Frankfurter. Art N 63:25 D '64

New Mexico Spanish colonial art for Britain. A. C. Vedder. il Antiques 83:553-6 My '63

New splendor on the Riviera; Fondation Maeght. A. Frankfurter. il Art N 63:40-1 N '64

Notes of a peripatetic gallerygoer. K. Kuh. il Sat R 47:27+ Ap 25 '64

Place on the Riviera; museum of art dealer, Aimé Maeght. il Time 84:64 Ag 7 '64

Rebuilding: three galleries. il Arch Forum 120:114-17 Mr '64

Role of art museums. N. Kent. Am Artist 27:3+ My '63

Sert on the Riviera. il Time 82:54 Ag 16 '63

Six ways to see art. J. Canaday. il N Y Times Mag p72-3 Mr 15 '64

Something of value; guided tours. il Newsweek 61:92+ My 6 '63

Travel notes; museum for every man, even one who doesn't like galleries. R. Joseph. Esquire 60:58-60+ S '63

Treasures on campus: pop goes Brandeis! Rose art museum. L. Lerman. il Mlle 58: 74-5+ D '63

See also

Art—Exhibitions

Art dealers

also subhead Galleries and museums under names of cities i.e. New York (city) —Galleries and museums

also names of museums, e.g. Louvre, Paris

Acquisitions

Entering public domain. il Art N 62:40-1+ N '63; 34-5+ F '64

Gifts, legacies, etc.

Furniture from the Rotch bequest to the Victoria and Albert museum. J. F. Hayward. il Antiques 83:560-3 My '63

In the right hands; gift to Buffalo's Albright-Knox art gallery. Time 83:60 My 29 '64

History

Eternal present: the beginnings of art, by S. Giedion. Review
Art N il 62:44-5+ O '63. O. H. Prufer

Evolution in the arts, by T. Munro. Review
Art N 62:42+ O '63. S. C. Pepper

1914; Baltimore museum's fiftieth-anniversary show. H. Rosenberg. il Art N 63:38-41 O '64

See also

Art nouveau (movement)

International aspects

Art galleries; exhibition at Lefebre gallery, and American federation of arts gallery's presentation of Retrospective art show of Educational alliance. H. Rosenberg. New Yorker 39:166-72 My 4 '63

Philosophy

Art galleries; short life of a work of art. H. Rosenberg. New Yorker 39:76-81 Ag 10 '63

Art galleries; the new as value. H. Rosenberg. New Yorker 39:136+ S 7 '63

Artist & teacher. C. Everts. il Sch Arts 62:21-3 Je '63

Charles B. Rogers pleads for the spirit in art. C. B. Rogers. il Am Artist 27:42-3+ S '63

Environmental sculpture; excerpt from The endless search. F. Kiesler. il Arch Forum 121:118 Jl '64

Gropius addresses convocation at Williams; excerpts from address. W. Gropius. Arch Rec 134:10 N '63

Identifying the role of the arts in education. M. Bryce. il Sch Arts 62:29 Ap '63

Pop extremists. A. Frankfurter. Art N 63: 19+ S '64

Solitude, modernity & art education. J. A. Richardson. il Sch Arts 63:34-7 S '63

Statement on the concept of art. N. Vergette. il Sch Arts 64:24-5 D '64

See also

Aesthetics

Prices

American painter as a blue chip. M. Elkoff. il Esquire 63:36-42+ Ja '65

As Europe sees art business now. il U S News 56:69 Ja 27 '64

Economics of taste: the rise and fall of the picture market, 1760-1960, by G. Reitlinger. Review
Nation 199:465-6 D 14 '64. J. Carter

Framed dollar; picture market. J. Carter. il Harper 227:22+ Jl '63

Investing in art: the latest boom. il U S News 56:66-9 Ja 27 '64

Testing the moderns; prices at auction of Ira Haupt's collection. Time 85:55 Ja 22 '65

Private collections

Abstract businessman; N. Simon's collection. il Time 83:90-5 Je 5 '64

America, America; collection of Lawrence and Barbara Fleischman of Detroit. F. Getlein. New Repub 150:25-6 Mr 14 '64

American art from American collections. J. Biddle. il Antiques 83:309-16 Mr '63

American painting collection of Henry Melville Fuller. W. H. Gerdts. il Antiques 86: 66-71 Jl '64

American painting in the collection of James H. Ricau. W. H. Gerdts. il Antiques 86: 578-82 N '64

American sculpture: the collection of James H. Ricau. il Antiques 86:291-8 S '64

Art and the ready-made artists. K. Kuh. Sat R 46:44 D 14 '63

Art gets its own mutual fund; joint purchase of art works by Houston collector-investors. il Bsns W p30-1 O 31 '64

ART—Private collections—*Continued*
Art is the core; the Robert Scull collection. A. Talmey. il Vogue 144:116-23+ Jl '64
Art of acquisition. il Newsweek 62:106 D 2 '63
Art of collecting; five private American collections shown on NBC. K. Kuh. il Sat R 47:37-52 Ja 18 '64
Art of collecting; Hahnlosers' post-impressionists. il Time 83:74-7 Mr 13 '64
At home with Henry; R. C. Scull's collection of pop art. il Time 83:68-71 F 21 '64
Big collecting in a small democracy; Swiss private collections at the Lausanne fair. A. Frankfurter. il Art N 63:20-3+ S '64
Can this be art? pop art collection of Mr & Mrs Robert C. Scull. E. Genauer. il Ladies Home J 81:151-5 Mr '64
Chester Dale: collector. N. MacNeil. il McCalls 91:120-7+ N '63
Collectors' choice from the collection of Mr and Mrs Lawrence A. Fleischman. il Antiques 86:572-7 N '64
Collector's double takes. il Life 54:68A-68B+ Ap 26 '63
Eighteenth-century porcelain in Seattle. il Antiques 85:80-5 Ja '64
English conquest in the Old Dominion; English paintings, 1700-1850, collection of Mr and Mrs Paul Mellon. C. Connolly. il Art N 62:30-3+ Sum '63
Fabulous hoard in a tiny realm; Liechtenstein art treasures. il Life 55:44-51+ Ag 30 '63
Genius defined; Paul Mellon collection. il Time 82:58-63 Jl 5 '63
Gracious way of life and art; another great Mellon collection. il Life 55:48-55 Ag 9 '63
Great gesture: just masterpieces; Wrightsman collection. il Vogue 143:162-3 Ap 1 '64
Interim collection; paintings of Mr and Mrs James M. Brown, 3d. E. Gaines. il Antiques 84:592-5 N '63
Jewel case for pre-Columbian gems; Bliss collection in Dumbarton Oaks. K. E. Meyer. il Art N 62:36-9+ F '64
Jones collection and the American club in London. W. J. Sainsbury. il Antiques 85: 185-9 F '64
Letter from Paris; exhibition of Besson collection in Louvre. Genêt. New Yorker 40: 106+ Ja 9 '65
Lived with; R. Fribourg collection. New Yorker 39:29-30 My 25 '63
Living frame for sculpture; Joseph H. Hirshhorn's magnificient collection. J. J. Sweeney. il House & Gard 126:110-15+ Ag '64
Mrs Guggenheim collection; on exhibition at Tate gallery. S. Price. il N Y Times Mag p 16-17+ Ja 17 '65
Monsieur Georges; illuminated miniatures from Wildenstein collection at Manhattan's Cloisters. il Time 81:56-9 Mr 1 '63
Paintings and antiques; New York apartment of E. A. Bragaline. R. Davidson. il Antiques 84:556-61 N '63
People are talking about Paul Mellon and collection. il Vogue 141:130-1 My '63
Picassos for New York; Justin K. Thannhauser gift to Guggenheim museum. il N Y Times Mag p72-3 N 10 '63
Pictures on the wall; art collection of A. Liberman. G. O'Brien. il N Y Times Mag p28-9 Jl 7 '63
Poetry in porcelain; some figures in the collection of Mrs Lesley G. Sheafer. il Antiques 84:302-3 S '63
Poor Peg's treasure; P. Guggenheim's collection. il Time 85:52-5 Ja 22 '65
Private lives with art; three special collections in New York. il Vogue 143:86-95+ Ja 15 '64
Queen's pictures. O. Millar. il Horizon 5:92-107 Jl '63
Question of the private museum. A. Frankfurter. Art N 63:25 Mr '64
Royal patrimony; the British royal collection now on public view. il Time 85:58-60 Ja 1 '65
Sale of the century; René Fribourg collection. il Newsweek 62:58 Jl 8 '63
Some aspects of English landscape painting; collection of Mr and Mrs Paul Mellon. J. Baskett. il Antiques 84:581-5 N '63
Town house revisited; tour of John Hay Whitney collection. New Yorker 39:24-5 Ja 18 '64
Treasures in English silver from the Morrison collection. M. D. Schwartz. il Antiques 85:570-4 My '64
Tudor, Stuart and Early Georgian pictures in the collection of H.M. the Queen, by O. Millar. Review
Art N il 62:44-5+ D '63. J. Russell
Tyson collection: a painter's eye on masterworks. H. H. F. Jayne. il Art N 63:28-30+ S '64
Versailles in Manhattan; R. Fribourg collection. il Time 81:72 Mr 8 '63
Wild beasts of Chinese art; collection of Mr and Mrs R. W. Finlayson. il Art N 62:32-3+ D '63
Yeasty surroundings of a fertile imagination. il House B 105:148-9+ Ap '63
See also
Art in the home
Barnes foundation. Merion, Pa.

Psychology

See also
Art therapy

Scholarships and fellowships

Competitions and awards. See issues of American artist
Competitions, scholarships. See issues of Art news
Guggenheim, Rome academy and Ford fellowships for 1964. Art N 63:9 My '64

Societies

See Art societies

Study and teaching

Art & craft in the British primary school. J. R. Milsome. il Sch Arts 64:16-17 Ja '65
Art and the student teacher. L. B. Kennon and T. Markle. il Sch Arts 63:5-10 Ap '63
Art education in Egypt. T. Abdul-Razik. il Sch Arts 63:34-8 F '64
Art enrichment; Ralph R. Smith elementary school, Hyde Park, N.Y. M. Sheridan. il Sch Arts 63:19-20 My '64
Art experiences in camping. R. E. Dodson. Recreation 56:135+ Mr '63
Art for enjoyment's sake. D. Shaw. il Recreation 58:31 Ja '65
Art for the pre-schooler. M. Nicolaysen. il Design 65:142-5 Mr '64
Art in the sun. D. Carlson. il Sch Arts 63:5-9 F '64
Art is a growing thing. R. L. Bloch. il Sat R 47:62-3 O 17 '64
Art with broken chalk. L. E. De Rosa. il Design 65:76-7 N '63
Artist & teacher. W. P. Daley. il Sch Arts 62:13-15 Mr '63
Beginning teacher. J. Schwartz. il Sch Arts 63:46 S '63
Beginning teacher; identifying what to teach in art. J. Schwartz. il Sch Arts 63:48 My '64
Case for individual latitude; junior high schools. A. Whitson. il Sch Arts 63:36-8 My '64
Community sources for art education. M. A. McKibben. il Sch Arts 62:17-19 My '63
Depth's four dimensions. R. C. Burkhart. Sch Arts 62:30-1 Ap '63
Elementary art to develop visual sensitivity. G. S. Wright, jr. il Sch Arts 63:19-20 N '63
Every surface has pattern or texture. R. Ferragallo. il Sch Arts 63:8-11 Je '64
Exceptional children's art; symposium, ed. by G. Barlow. il Sch Arts 63:2-38 Ja '64
Experience of being & becoming. M. F. Andrews. il Sch Arts 62:22-4 Ap '63
High school dumping grounds. M. Venable. il Sch Arts 63:32-4 My '64
Left bank, midwest style. il Design 66:16-17 S '64
Main St; resource of architectural appreciation. C. E. Hiller. il Sch Arts 64:25-8 S '64
Motivation/new ways of seeing. M. Pappas. il Sch Arts 63:8-11 S '63
New stereotype. L. H. Chapman. il Sch Arts 62:10-11 Mr '63
Paradox & prospect. E. Ziegfeld. il Sch Arts 62:36-7 F '63
Programmed instruction: challenge or threat to art education? D. W. Ecker. bibliog il Sch Arts 63:3-6 O; 12-14 N; 8-10 D '63
Proposal concerning art education at the elementary level. B. Chernow. il Sch Arts 63:30 S '63
Questions you ask. A. Baumgarner. See issues of School arts
Reaching students through the arts; Latin American students, in Brownsville, Tex. Mrs D. Morris. il Sr Schol 84:9T Ap 24 '64
Role of the art consultant; Downtown community school. P. Greenberg. il Sch Arts 63:21-3 Ap '64
Subject matter of art. G. S. Wright, jr. il Sch Arts 62:24 F '63
Teaching art to the gifted in a New York high school. A. C. Hollingsworth. il Am Artist 28:68-73+ Je '64
Team teaching & art teaching. H. Hoffa; T. Fawcett. il Sch Arts 62:18-20 F '63

ART—Study and teaching—*Continued*
There is a place for programmed instruction in the teaching of the visual arts. L. M. Quirke. il Sch Arts 63:31-3 Mr '64
Thoughts on teaching art in the elementary school. E. P. Cohen. il Sch Arts 62:33-5 F '63
Urban art program; Downtown community school, New York city. P. Greenberg. il Sch Arts 64:7-9 N '64
Vergette on teaching art. N. Vergette. il Sch Arts 64:26 D '64
What makes a good art teacher? M. K. Gerstman. il Sch Arts 64:31-2 S '64
Why I want to teach art; statements by art students, ed. by T. K. Kurzband. il Sch Arts 63:5-7 N '63
See also
Art education
Art schools
Barnes foundation, Merion, Pa.
Color
Institute of modern art, New York
Painting—Study and teaching

Materials

Art made in a kitchen; cornstarch clay creates realistic sculpture. il Design 65:192-3 My '64
Art on styrofoam. P. Arthurs. il Design 65:156-7 Mr '64
Batik on paper. F. M. Major. il Design 64:102-3+ Ja '63
Box full of boxes. R. P. Marxhausen. il Sch Arts 62:32 F '63
Buyer's guide. Sch Arts 62:38-43 F '63; 63:46-51 F '64
Children of all ages create in a variety of media. E. Madsen. il Sch Arts 62:8-11 My '63
Cloth assemblage, new dimensions in fabric. M. Pappas. il Sch Arts 64:14-16 O '64
Drawing on film. G. Manupelli. il Sch Arts 63:10-11 F '64
Fire with enthusiasm. D. Dubler. il Sch Arts 62:21 Mr '63
Flower painting. A. Ehrlich. il Sch Arts 63:5-7 D '63
Foam rubber fun. R. Von Hoorn. il Design 66:10-12 S '64
I made this; planning and making a cement tile mural. J. Amato. il Sch Arts 63:17-20 Ap '64
Made with toothpicks. M. Hoffhine. il Design 65:212-13 My '64
Plaster & burlap. R. Carboni. il Sch Arts 63:16-17 S '63
Printmakers delight; paperlike art fabric offers tactile surface. il Design 65:196-9 My '64
Refill mosaics. D. P. Malone and W. Karre. il Sch Arts 62:14 F '63
Straw and burlap creations. R. Fridenstine. il Design 65:194 My '64
Visual materials. D. Irving. il Sch Arts 63:28-9 D '63
See also
Arts and crafts—Study and teaching—Materials

Projects

Art project: burlap hangings. R. Emrich. il Sch Arts 64:33 D '64
Bas-relief mural; second grade. R. Moore. il Sch Arts 64:23 N '64
Book project. W. Bock. il Sch Arts 64:17-18 N '64
Centrifugal casting in the high school. H. F. Schlindwein. il Sch Arts 64:36-8 S '64
Colorful classroom project: animated films. R. E. Wright. il Sch Arts 64:10-13 O '64
Crayon-cement prints; fourth graders. D. Beringer. il Sch Arts 63:39-40 My '64
Creative project; Dalton public schools. W. Bell. il Sch Arts 63:24-5 Ap '64
Fire with enthusiasm. D. Dubler. il Sch Arts 62:21 Mr '63
Flags for space. P. Zich. il Sch Arts 63:43 N '63
Gyotaku Japanese fish printing. P. Greenberg. il Sch Arts 63:21-2 Je '64
How to make a monster. F. De Wys. il Design 65:19-21 S '63
Japanese technique on pellon; project by young Texans. N. Kitsinger. il Design 64:104-5 Ja '63
Jewelry making. J. A. Carey. il Sch Arts 63:31-2 F '64
John fights the Civil war. B. Hanson. il Sch Arts 62:7-10 Je '63
Joy of a pinata. J. Love. il Design 66:14-15 N '64
Mosaic mural for your school; History of Huntingdon, in the Huntingdon junior high-school, Huntingdon, Pa. M. L. Miller. bibliog il Sch Arts 64:10-15 D '64
Mosaic wall of N.Y.C. P. Greenberg. il Sch Arts 63:5-7 S '63
Our neighborhood as inspiration. T. Prentise. il Sch Arts 63:21 Mr '64
Our new school. J. O. Mitchell. il Sch Arts 63:10-11 N '63
People and the second grade. P. Greenberg. il Sch Arts 64:17-21 S '64
Printing experience; fifth graders. C. T. McCarthy. il Sch Arts 64:7-13 S '64
Roads make history. B. Zimo. il Sch Arts 63:18-20 Mr '64
Sequential program to develop textural sensitivity. P. A. Sisk. il Sch Arts 63:21-6 Ja '64
Story & color on film. Sister Mary Laurus. il Sch Arts 63:17-18 N '63
They made an animated film; high school art class creates a full color-and-sound cartoon. J. Lorr. il Design 65:78-9 N '63
Three-cornered achievement. D. A. Paul il Sch Arts 63:18-19 F '64
Wood and clay pots. R. W. Tormey. il Sch Arts 64:20 Ja '65
See also
Collage
Glass painting and staining
Masks (for the face)
Paper work
Wire sculpture

Taxation

See Taxation of works of art

Themes

Architectural paintings of John Lentine. J. Lovoos. il Am Artist 27:18-23 N '63
Art that inspires travel. il Sat R 46:46 Ap 13 '63
Familiar spirits; offbeat show at University of St Thomas, Houston. il Newsweek 64:97-8 N 30 '64
John Singer Sargent and decoration. D. F. Hoopes. il Antiques 86:588-91 N '64
Leonard Baskin; art for life's sake. A. Werner. il Am Artist 28:40-5+ N '64
Master art and opera. R. Rushmore. il Opera N 28:28-9 Ja 4; 28-9 Ap 4 '64
Notes for a gazetteer; Sunday morning in the mines. P. Hamburger. New Yorker 38:86-7 F 2 '63
Revival of the throb and sob; theme of trysts and troubled hearts. il Life 54:33-6 F 15 '63
Richard Whorf: painter of Americana. J. Lovoos. il Am Artist 28:32-7+ Ap '64
See also
Adam and Eve in art
Dancing in art
European war in art
Flowers in art
Latin America in art

Therapeutic use

See Art therapy

Valuation

Baroness' income tax; using art to get dubious tax deductions. il Time 81:59 Mr 1 '63

California

West Coast art: vital pathology. M. Kozloff. Nation 199:76-9 Ag 24 '64

Ceylon

See also
Art, Sinhalese

Corsica

Napoleonic dandy; paintings in the municipal museum. il Time 84:84 S 18 '64

Cuba

Position of the artist in Cuba today. T. de Gàmez. il Art N 63:36-9+ S '64

Dahomey

Tribal art from Africa. C. M. Turnbull. il Natur Hist 73:46-53 Mr '64

Dominican Republic

Baroque in Santo Domingo. D. Suro. il Américas 16:15-21 Je '64

Italy

Italy: pre-, pro- and post-Roman. M. Gendel. il Art N 63:34-6+ Ja '65
See also
Florence—Art

Japan

See also
Arts and crafts—Japan

Latin America

Architect of peace; São Paulo biennial. R. Squirru. il Américas 16:2-4 Ap '64

ART—*Continued*

Mexico

See also
Art, Mexican

New York (state)

New York state: the Hudson heritage. K. Kuh. il Sat R 46:29-30 Ap 27 '63

Russia

Art for Marx' sake. G. Feifer. il N Y Times Mag p 12-13+ D 20 '64
Art in the Soviet Union. K. Kuh. il Sat R 46:17-26 Ag 24 '63
Critic surveys the party line in art. J. Canaday. il N Y Times Mag p 18-19+ Ja 5 '64
If you'll pardon the expression. . ; remarks at exhibition of Soviet art. N. S. Khrushchev. Newsweek 61:34-5 Ap 1 '63
Khrushchev faces a Khrushchevian dilemma. M. Frankland. il N Y Times Mag p21+ My 12 '63
Mr K's turn toward Stalinism. E. Griffiths. il Sat Eve Post 236:70-3 Je 1 '63
Russian art & anti-Semitism; with introd. by M. Decter. E. A. Evtushenko; N. S. Khruschev; M. Romm. Commentary 36:433-7 D '63
Tempest in a gallery; Khrushchev's denunciation of abstract art. A. Brumberg. New Repub 148:17-20 F 16 '63
See also
Painting, Russian

United States

Art establishment. H. Rosenberg. Esquire 63:43-6+ Ja '65
Should the artist become a man of the world? with editorial comment. A. Kaprow. Art N 63:19, 34-7+ O '64
See also
Art, American
Federal art project
Painting, American
Provincetown art association
also subhead Art under names of cities, e.g. New York (city)—Art

Yugoslavia

Arts in Yugoslavia. A. Karlen. Nation 199:499-502 D 21 '64

ART, Abstract
Adolph Gottlieb: private symbols in public statements. M. Friedman. il Art N 62:32-5 My '63
Anxious object: art today and its audience, by H. Rosenberg. Review
Sat R il 48:48-9 Ja 23 '65
Art. F. Getlein. New Repub 148:26-8 F 16 '63
Art; Clyfford Still exhibition. M. Kozloff. Nation 198:39-40 Ja 6 '64
Art debased. N. Kent. Am Artist 27:3 N '63
Art galleries; exhibitions of pop art, and abstract expressionism at Janis, Pace and De Nagy galleries. R. M. Coates. New Yorker 39:107-10 Ja 18 '64
Art galleries; memorial exhibition at Sidney Janis gallery for F. Kline. R. M. Coates. New Yorker 39:70-2 D 21 '63
Attempt at abstracts. G. Haddad. il Sch Arts 62:20 My '63
Blue riders. il Art N 62:45+ Mr '63
Invisible world; International business machines corp. exhibition of paintings, commissioned for International science and technology magazine. Newsweek 62:72 Ag 12 '63
James Brooks and the abstract inscape. I. H. Sandler. il Art N 61:30-1+ F '63
Kandinsky: last of the heresiarchs. J. Kroll. il Art N 61:38-41+ F '63
Second-generation abstraction; exhibition at Manhattan's Jewish museum. il Time 81:78-9 My 24 '63
State of the market; Manhattan's art galleries. il Time 81:62 Je 21 '63
What do you think of modern art? E. W. Watson. Am Artist 27:3+ F '63

ART, African
Detroit branch, ASNLH, launches $50,000 African art drive. A. D. Coar. il Negro Hist Bul 27:99-102 F '64
Out of Africa; Museum of African art, Washington, D.C. F. Getlein. New Repub 150:34+ Je 27 '64
Playing the art market; May stores. il Bsns W p28-9 Ja 11 '64
Wall: painted clay. M. Cable. il Craft Horiz 23:27-31+ My '63
See also
Art—Dahomey

ART, American
American panorama; Four centuries of American art at the Minneapolis institute of art. il Newsweek 62:91 D 2 '63
Americans in Paris. il Newsweek 63:60 Ja 6 '64
Khouri memorial collection; Norfolk museum of arts & sciences. W. Caxton, jr. il Am Artist 28:24-9 F '64
New Mexico Spanish colonial art for Britain. A. C. Vedder. il Antiques 83:553-6 My '63
Paintings to think about; exhibition of contemporary painting and sculpture at Wadsworth atheneum, Hartford, Conn. S. J. Wagstaff, jr. il Art N 62:38+ Ja '64
Phony crisis in American art. T. B. Hess. il Art N 62:24-8+ Sum '63
Pleasant cataclysm; 1914, exhibition at Baltimore museum of art. F. Getlein. New Repub 151:34-5 N 14 '64
West Coast art: vital pathology. M. Kozloff. Nation 199:76-9 Ag 24 '64
See also
Art, Pre-Columbian
Painting, American
Whitney museum of American art, New York

ART, Ancient
Lost civilization emerges from the past: Hittites. E. Laroche. il UNESCO Courier 16:14-20 F '63
See also
Archeology
Art, Greek
Art, Roman

ART, Applied. See Arts and crafts; Design, Industrial

ART, Asian
History of Far Eastern art, by S. E. Lee. Review
Sat R il 47:45 D 12 '64. J. Cahill

ART, Australian
Australian visit, Australian UNESCO seminar on art education. S. Black. il Sch Arts 64:31-4 O '64

ART, Australian (aboriginal)
Aboriginal art and mythology; bark paintings. S. Scougall and P. C. Gifford. il Natur Hist 74:46-53 bibliog(p70) F '65

ART, Baroque
Baroque in Santo Domingo. D. Suro. il Américas 16:15-21 Je '64

ART, British
See also
Painting, British

ART, Buddhist
See also
Sculpture, Buddhist

ART, Byzantine
Artifice of eternity; exhibition of Byzantine art in Athens. il Newsweek 63:74 Ap 27 '64
Arts of Byzantium. D. Smith. il Craft Horiz 23:34-7+ My '63
Byzantium gloriously re-emerges in Athens; Council of Europe exhibition. K. Weitzmann. il Art N 63:28-31+ Sum '64
Cyprus: Byzantine frescoes and mosaics; excerpts. il UNESCO Courier 17:30-2 F '64
Mount Sinai's holy treasures. K. Weitzmann. il Nat Geog Mag 125:107-27 Ja '64

ART, Canadian
Art in Canada. A. Jarvis. il Atlan 214:124-34 N '64

ART, Chinese
Cache at Stone-fortress-hill. J. F. Haskins. il Natur Hist 72:30-9 F '63
Camel, Chinese; late Wei to North Chi, 255-577 A.D. C. B. Johnson. il Sch Arts 63:20 Ja '64
Wild beasts of Chinese art. il Art N 62:32-3+ D '63
See also
Painting, Chinese

ART, Colombian
For young artists: series of national salons begins in Bogotá; cultural program sponsored by International petroleum company. L. J. Ahlender. il Américas 17:36-8 Ja '65

ART, Commercial
Art director and you. Design 64:212+ Je '63
Artist's biggest market; department stores and specialty shops. H. Greenwald. il Design 64:162-6+ Mr '63
Dollars and sense of commercial art. il Design 64:170-2 Mr '63
Leslie Saalburg, illustrator of mode. F. Whitaker. il Am Artist 27:20-5+ F '63
Let's understand photo-engraving. il Design 64:214-15 Je '63
Morton Goldsholl, art director of the year. E. M. Ettenberg. il Am Artist 28:22-7+ S '64
See also
Advertising art
Design, Industrial

ART, Commercial—*Continued*
Terminology
Talking the language of commercial art. Design 64:156 Mr '63
ART, Coptic
Christians on the Nile. il Time 82:54-5 Ag 16 '63
Coptic and Byzantine. C. J. McNaspy. America 111:161-3 Ag 15 '64
Coptic eclectics: the vital mixture. P. Verdier. il Art N 62:34-9+ S '63
ART, Decorative. See Design, Decorative
ART, Dutch
See also
Painting, Dutch
ART, Egyptian
Bust of a man, stone fragment from the 18th-19th dynasty, 1555-1375 B.C. C. B. Johnson. il Sch Arts 63:40 N '63
See also
Art, Coptic
ART, Eskimo. See Eskimos—Art
ART, Ethiopian
Art of Ethiopia a folk tradition centuries old. O. A. Jager. il UNESCO Courier 17:18-23 O '64
ART, French
Aesthetics of failure. M. Kozloff. Nation 197:202-3 O 5 '63
Jones collection and the American club in London. W. J. Sainsbury. il Antiques 85:185-9 F '64
See also
Dadaism
Painting, French
ART, German
Shadow of the Bridge; beginnings of modern German art. il Time 82:44 Ag 2 '63
ART, Gothic
Prophetic prophet from Gothic Italy. H. A. La Farge. il Art N 62:42-3+ D '63
ART, Greek
Double-axes to grind. N. Calas. Art N 63:52-3 O '64
See also
Sculpture, Greek
ART, Hawaiian
Four ceramists of Hawaii. J. Lovoos. il Am Artist 27:66-73+ Je '63
ART, Indian (East Indian)
See also
Art, Nepalese
ART, Indonesian
Indonesian decorative design. G. Kaler. il Hobbies 69:44+ N; 42-4 D '64; 42-4 Ja '65
ART, Influence of. See Art therapy
ART, Italian
Antiques abroad. W. De Sager. il Antiques 84:312+ S '63
Venice, the eternal fantasy; drawings on loan from Venice's Correr museum. J. Canaday. il N Y Times Mag p70-1 O 27 '63
See also
Painting, Italian
ART, Japanese
Past marvelously preserved; colored photographs by B. Smith from Japan, a history in art. Life 57:50-8 S 11 '64
See also
Gardens, Japanese
ART, Jewish
Twenty-six Israeli artists. A. Werner. Reporter 32:42+ Ja 14 '65
ART, Latin American
Art. il Américas 16:38 Ap; 40 My; 40-1 Je; 42 S; 42 O; 41 N; 37 D '64; 17:39 Ja '65
Art in Latin American architecture. P. Damaz. il Craft Horiz 23:12-39+ S '63
Contrast in São Paulo: seventh São Paulo biennial. J. Gómez-Sicre. il Américas 15:18-22 D '63
Pop art or the art of things. R. Squirru. il Américas 15:15-21 Jl '63
See also
Art, Pre-Columbian
Painting, Latin American
ART, Medieval
See also
Art, Byzantine
Christian art and symbolism
Metropolitan museum of art. New York—Cloisters
ART, Mexican
Art in church: St James' church, New York. New Yorker 39:34-6 My 4 '63
Art in Mexico. I. Amor; A. Brenner. il Atlan 213:129-41 Mr '64
Letter from Mexico City. R. Rosen. Nation 198:200-3 F 24 '64
Thirty-five centuries of Mexican art. il Time 82:78-80 O 25 '63
See also
Arts and crafts—Mexico
Painting, Mexican

ART, Modern. See Modernism (art)
ART, Mogul
Great Mughals. il Newsweek 63:53 Ja 27 '64
See also
Painting, Mogul
ART, Mythology in. See Mythology in art
ART, Negro
Jacob's dream. il Newsweek 61:100 Ap 15 '63
Leading Negro artists. il Ebony 18:131-2+ S '63
ART, Nepalese
Art of Nepal; exhibition at Asia house. il N Y Times Mag p74 My 3 '64
Way to nirvana. il Time 83:72-5 My 1 '64
ART, Nigerian
New art of the new Africa. M. Bernheim and E. Bernheim. il N Y Times Mag p22-3 O 4 '64
ART, Persian
Iran: light vs. darkness; traveling show of Persian art. J. Brzostoski. il Art N 63:39-41+ Sum '64
Mesopotamian legacy; 7000 years of Iranian art. F. Getlein. New Repub 151:27-8 S 12 '64
Pulse of culture; exhibition at National gallery of art in Washington, D.C. il Newsweek 63:80 Je 22 '64
Seven millenniums under one roof. il Time 84:58-60 Jl 17 '64
7,000 years of Iranian art; showing National gallery of art, Washington, D.C. J. Eagle. il Craft Horiz 24:34-9+ N '64
See also
Pottery, Persian
ART, Peruvian
Art of a lost world; 300 ceramics in the Metropolitan museum. il N Y Times Mag p 126-7 S 20 '64
Golden art of ancient Peru; photographs. J. Canaday. N Y Times Mag p50 Ap 21 '63
ART, Polish
Medieval, modern, and macabre. K. Kuh. il Sat R 46:40-1 S 28 '63
ART, Pre-Columbian
Jewel case for pre-Columbian gems; Bliss collection in Dumbarton Oaks. K. E. Meyer. il Art N 62:36-9+ F '64
Pre-Columbian heritage. P. Damaz. il Craft Horiz 23:23-9 S '63
Sun-colored metal; new collection of pre-Columbian art at World's fair. il Time 83:76-7 Je 12 '64
Treasures of ancient American art. il Horizon 6:88-92 Sum '64
ART, Prehistoric. See Art, Primitive
ART, Primitive
Dawn of art; excerpt from History of mankind. J. Hawkes. il UNESCO Courier 16:11-13 Je '63
See also
Art, Australian (aboriginal)
Art, Pre-Columbian
Cave drawings and paintings
Petroglyphs
ART, Religious. See Christian art and symbolism
ART, Rococo
Curve of the sea shell. il Time 84:74 S 11 '64
ART, Roman
Rome becomes a system of roads; exhibition of Roman art in the western provinces. P. Schneider. il Art N 62:50-1+ S '63
ART, Russian
From Russia for cash; commercial exhibition at London's Grosvenor gallery. il Newsweek 63:81 Je 22 '64
Nightingale crows; Soviet Union's exhibit of graphic art. Newsweek 63:76 F 3 '64
See also
Icons
Painting, Russian
ART, Sinhalese
Sinhalese decorative art. G. Kaler. bibliog il Hobbies 68:42-3+ Jl; 42+ Ag; 41-2 S; 41-2+ O; 41-2 N; 42+ D '63; 42+ Ja; 42+ F '64
ART, Spanish
Iberian resurgence; with colored photographs. il Time 84:84-9 Ag 28 '64
See also
Painting, Spanish
Prado museum
ART, Yugoslav
Peasant painters of Yugoslavia. il Life 56:79-83 Ja 10 '64
ART and industry
Art and public relations. L. L. L. Golden. Sat R 46:60 Mr 9 '63
Business and the arts; address, November 11, 1963. D. C. Josephs. Mus Am 83:159-60 D '63
Chase Manhattan bank, a patron of art & artists. N. Lansdale. il Am Artist 29:32-7+ Ja '65

ART and industry—*Continued*
Culture, inc; corporations sponsor culture. il Time 83:85 F 21 '64
Should business support the arts? excerpt from Corporate support of the performing arts. R. Eells. Mus Am 84:8-9 O '64
Steel company in the world of culture; Italy's Italsider. il Fortune 68:138-41 O '63
See also
Design, Industrial
ART and libraries. See Libraries and art
ART and literature
Poetry of art. C. R. Rose. il Sch Arts 62:12 Mr '63
ART and music
See also
Music in art
ART and photography
Most durable panel topic. J. Deschin. Pop Phot 54:16 F '64
Viewpoints; photographs or graphics? J. Deschin. Pop Phot 53:24+ D '63
ART and politics
Art galleries. H. Rosenberg. New Yorker 39:60+ My 25 '63
Art; Weimar-Nürnberg-Bonn exhibition of German posters from 1919-1961. H. Kramer. Nation 196:513-15 Je 15 '63
Dream of culture. Reporter 28:20 Ap 25 '63
Posters as weapons; German posters at New school for social research. N Y Times Mag p 19 Ap 28 '63
ART and religion
Art and religion. N. Kent. Am Artist 27:3+ D '63
Art and sacrament; symbolism found in contemporary artistic creation. F. Eversole. Christian Cent 81:393-6 Mr 25 '64
Art and the liturgy. S. Hazo. il Cath World 199:286-92 Ag '64
Art and the religious community. W. Kliewer. Christian Cent 80:1605-7 D 25 '63; Discussion. 81:182 F 5 '64
Art and the sacred. C. J. McNaspy. America 109:179-80 Ag 17 '63
Mass of the artists. C. J. McNaspy. America 108:209 F 9 '63
New Orpheus, ed. by N. A. Scott, jr. Review
Commonweal 80:239-41 My 15 '64. G. Greene
Patron of the living arts. B. Bettinson. America 109:93-5 Jl 27 '63; Discussion. 109:356-8, 381, 648 S 28-O 5, N 23 '63
Pope and artists. America 110:704 My 23 '64
Pope strikes back. F. Getlein. New Repub 150:22-4 My 23 '64
Priest as patron. T. F. Mathews. America 110:794-5 Je 6 '64
Sacred and profane beauty: the holy in art, by G. van der Leeuw. Review
Christian Cent 81:19 Ja 1 '64. C. H. Long
Commonweal 78:513-14 Ag 23 '63. L. F. X. Mayhew
Vatican II and art. C. J. McNaspy. America 110:126-7 Ja 18 '64
ART and science
Abacus and the rose; a dialogue after Galileo. J. Bronowski. il Nation 198:4-17 Ja 4 '64
Art, science, and reality. G. R. Walker. Bul Atomic Sci 20:9-12 S '64
Artist and the scientist; excerpt from The artist in the modern world (cont) J. Langsner. Craft Horiz 23:37-8 Ja '63
Field, philosophy, & esthetics. E. R. Fagan. il Sch Arts 63:24-8 My '64
Long battle between art and the machine; excerpt from Art and anarchy. E. Wind. Harper 228:65-8+ F '64
Malina: artist-scientist of the space age. il UNESCO Courier 16:18-19 S '63
ART and society
Art & the new environment. G. Pappas. il Sch Arts 62:17 F '63
Art in orbit; excerpts from Kiesler's journals. F. Kiesler. Nation 198:486-8 My 11 '64
Artists and the rat-race. T. B. Hess. Art N 63:23 Ja '65
Arts as a national resource. S. L. Udall. Sat R 47:14-16 Mr 28 '64
Bohemian versus bourgeois, French society and the French man of letters in the nineteenth century, by C. Graña. Review
Commentary 38:88-90 S '64. J. G. Weightman
Creative dilemma. J. Baldwin; J. W. Krutch. Sat R 47:14-17+ F 8 '64
Culture consumers, by A. Toffler. Review
Nation 199:466-7 D 14 '64. H. Dienstfrey
Is kindness killing the arts? R. Lynes. Harper 227:68-71+ N '63
Late President's last reflections on the arts; excerpt from Creative America. J. F. Kennedy. Sat R 47:16-17 Mr 28 '64
Letter from London; the Happening movement. C. Marowitz. Nation 199:99-100 S 7 '64
Manhattan school symposium. A. M. Lingg. Opera N 28:35 Ja 11 '64
Manner of speaking; artist and society. J. Ciardi. Sat R 46:14-15 N 23 '63
Mondrian is a paper napkin. V. Goldberg. il Horizon 5:90-1 My '63
Obscene & indescent. il Time 81:76-7 Ap 19 '63
Quality of life in this technological age; symposium sponsored by the Manhattan school of music. il Mus Am 83:147-62 D '63
Stalling on the arts; plans for John F. Kennedy library. W. Von Eckardt. New Repub 150:8 Mr 21 '64
Them damn pictures. T. B. Hess. il Art N 62:23 My '63
ART and state
Art in politics. Newsweek 61:85 Je 17 '63
Art, non-art: the curse of official culture. R. Brustein. il New Repub 151:85-8+ N 7 '64
Critic surveys the party line in art. J. Canaday. il N Y Times Mag p 18-19+ Ja 5 '64
Federal architectural policy: will it be worthy of the great society? Arch Rec 136:10 O '64
Fuzz's progress; harassment of the arts. D. Di Prima. Nation 198:463-5 My 4 '64
Government as patron of the arts; dangers in official sponsorship and uncritical goodwill. M. Harris. il N Y Times Mag p35+ S 13 '64
Government in art. F. Getlein. New Repub 150:36-7 F 15 '64
Heckscher report. New Repub 148:8 Je 29 '63
Heckscher urges President to carry out Kennedy's program for advisory arts panel. Arch Rec 135:10 Ap '64
Honors and availabilities; award of Medal of freedom. F. Getlein. New Repub 150:25-6 Ja 11 '64
Housing design policies of unconfused accountants. E. Goble. Arch Rec 136:9 O '64
Interest revived in government arts role. Pub W 185:44 Mr 2 '64
Johnson inherits cultural leadership. il Arch Forum 120:5 Ja '64
Kennedy pro arte, et sequitur? A. Frankfurter. il Art N 62:23+ Ja '64
Late President's last reflections on the arts; excerpt from Creative America. J. F. Kennedy. Sat R 47:16-17 Mr 28 '64
New patron; proposed national foundation of the arts. Nation 200:42 Ja 18 '65
President Kennedy receives Heckscher report on art and government. Arch Rec 134:10 Ag '63
President's arts adviser speaks at annual meeting of book committee; excerpts from address, December 10, 1964. R. L. Stevens. Library J 90:210 Ja 15 '65
Stalling on the arts; plans for John F. Kennedy library. W. Von Eckardt. New Repub 150:8 Mr 21 '64
To divorce art from money-making. K. Tynan. il N Y Times Mag p35+ D 1 '63
Who serves must stand and wait: possible presidential appointment of a council of fine arts. N. Kent. Am Artist 27:3+ S '63
See also
State encouragement of science, literature and art
ART appreciation. See Art—Appreciation
ART as a profession
Art representative and you. Design 64:213 Je '63
Start in art. D. Holden. il Design 65:168-70+ Mr '64
ART as recreation. See Recreation—Activities
ART buildings, College. See College architecture
ART center school, Los Angeles
Motor trend design competition winners; scholarships to Art center school. il Motor T 16:50-5 Jl '64
Motor trend's search for stylists. il Motor T 16:34-6 Ja '64
School for stylists. il Motor T 15:76-8 D '63
ART centers
Arts in our colleges. W. Schuman. Mus Am 83:5 Je '63
Creative tank town; Rocky Mount arts and crafts center. W. A. Rawls, jr. il Recreation 56:380-1 O '63
New Corvallis arts center. il Sunset 132:54 Je '64
Puerto Rico's art centers. Am Artist 27:76-7 Je '63
ART collecting. See Art—Private collections
ART colonies. See Artists colonies

ART conferences
See also
International design conference
World congress of craftsmen
ART consultants. See Art teachers
ART criticism
Art. M. Kozloff. Nation 198:77-80 Ja 20 '64
Epoch and artist, by D. M. Jones. Review
New Yorker 40:114-18+ Ag 22 '64. H. Rosenberg
Meditations on a hobby horse and other essays on the theory of art, by E. H. Gombrich. Review
Sat R il 47:33-4 Ap 25 '64. H. Rosenberg
Museums, press agents and art historians. A. Frankfurter. Art N 63:25 D '64
New Year's resolutions. K. Kuh. il Sat R 47:32-3 D 26 '64
ART critics
Isadora Bennett. Dance Mag 37:33 Ap '63
Modest proposal; concerning the blackout of daily news of art. A. Frankfurter. Art N 62:21+ Mr '63
ART dealers
Art at Sears. F. Getlein. New Repub 148:27-8 Ap 20 '63
Auction! excerpt. J. Brough. McCalls 90: 112-13+ Ap '63
Be advised. N. Kent. Am Artist 28:3+ S '64
Betty Parsons, diary of an art dealer; excerpts from An American gallery, with editorial comment. L. Alloway. il Vogue 142: 156-7+ O 1 '63
Between two Castros; a questionable Modigliani sold by Knoedler company. Newsweek 62:66 Jl 1 '63
Choice's dealer; exhibition in honor of C. Valentin. T. B. Hess. il Art N 62:26-7+ D '63
Exit Lord Pengo. il Newsweek 63:61 My 4 '64
Fine art of art dealing; Marlborough-Gerson, Saidenberg, and Willard galleries. K. Kuh. Sat R 46:31 D 28 '63
Goodbye Paris, hello New York; gradual shift of world art centers. il Time 84:58 Jl 17 '64
Graphic centennial; Kornfeld & Klipstein, Berne. il Art N 63:31 S '64
Investing in art: the latest boom. il U S News 56:66-9 Ja 27 '64
Last customer; Manhattan's Duveen brothers. Time 83:75 My 1 '64
Marlborough country. il Newsweek 62:74-5 N 25 '63
On gallery hanging fees. J. Deschin. Pop Phot 54:22+ Mr '64
Palm Beach school. il Newsweek 61:96 Mr 11 '63
Rebuilding: three galleries. il Arch Forum 120:114-17 Mr '64
State of the market; Manhattan's art galleries. il Time 81:62 Je 21 '63
See also
Antique dealers
Marlborough fine art, limited
ART education
Art as education. H. Wilson. il Sch Arts 63: 30-2 D '63
Art, design: search for a new image. G. Pappas. il Sch Arts 63:19-20 O '63
Art for learning's sake. M. Q. Dix. il Sch Arts 63:36-7 Ap '64
Australian visit, Australian UNESCO seminar on art education. S. Black. il Sch Arts 64: 31-4 O '64
Conditions increasing self-reflective learning in art; research report. R. C. Burkhart. il Sch Arts 64:23-30 O '64
Creative art education workshop. V. D'Amico. il Sch Arts 62:32-4 Ap '63
Critics criticized. S. Black. Sch Arts 63:2 My '64
Educationist's influence on the teaching of art; excerpts from Educationists and the evisceration of the visual arts. D. Manzella. Craft Horiz 23:6-8 N '63
Is art education threatened? R. Beelke. Sch Arts 62:15-16 F '63
Letters. A. G. DeFurio. Sch Arts 64:46 N '64
Motivation/new ways of seeing. M. Pappas. il Sch Arts 63:8-11 S '63
Paradigm for teaching the visual arts. E. Eisner. il Sch Arts 63:29-31 My '64
President views art education. P. Bulger. il Sch Arts 63:36-8 Mr '64
Solitude, modernity & art education. J. A. Richardson. il Sch Arts 63:34-7 S '63
Strike him sharply with some hard object; excerpts from Educationists and the evisceration of the visual arts. D. Manzella. il Sch Arts 63:35 Mr '64
Subject matter of art. G. S. Wright, jr. il Sch Arts 64:37-8 D '64
Teen-agers on an art binge; visit to National gallery of art in Washington, D.C. B. Leavitt. il Look 27:M13-14+ S 24 '63
To act as an artist. R. Haberer. il Sch Arts 64:17-19 O '64
Training talent in the arts. D. Boroff. il Parents Mag 39:76-7+ F '64
Two faces of research. H. E. Hoffa. Sch Arts 63:20 Je '64
What part art? A. Christ-Janer. Sch Arts 62:28-31 F '63
Whatever happened to the arts in education? H. D. Cater. Sch Arts 63:20 F '64; Reply. P. Frankle. 64:40 S '64
Why art in education? K. M. Scollon. il Sat R 47:70-2+ F 15 '64
See also
Art—Study and teaching
Art schools
International society for education through art
National art education association
Yale university—School of art and architecture
ART exhibitions. See Art—Exhibitions
ART exhibitions, Traveling. See Exhibitions, Traveling
ART films. See Moving pictures—Art films
ART forgeries. See Forgery of works of art
ART galleries, Commercial. See Art dealers
ART galleries and museums. See Art—Galleries and museums
ART glass. See Glass, Ornamental
ART hoaxes. See Hoaxes
ART in commercial buildings
New York courts uphold tax on quality. il Arch Forum 118:5+ My '63
ART in industry. See Art and industry
ART in the home
Art for the home. bibliog il Changing T 17: 34-6 My '63
Diverse tastes of a stage director. il House B 105:150-1+ Ap '63
Fine paintings for your home. R. Martens. il Farm J 87:74-5 N '63
Flowers into art. il McCalls 91:80-5 Ag '64
Here art imitates nature, or is it vice versa? il House B 105:147 Ap '63
Living gallery; collection of Sterling Holloway. il Holiday 35:92-3 Mr '64
New wing, a new way of life. il House & Gard 125:72-7 Ja '64
Pictures on the wall; art collection of A. Liberman. G. O'Brien. il N Y Times Mag p28-9 Jl 7 '63
Private exhibits. G. O'Brien. il N Y Times Mag p96-7+ My 19 '63
Under the influence of art. G. O'Brien. il N Y Times Mag pt2 p 16-19 S 29 '63
See also
Antiques
Art—Private collections
ART investments, limited. See Joint adventures
ART juries. See Juries, Art
ART literature
See also
Publishers and publishing—Art literature
ART loans
Art notes, or why my wife did not go to New York for her thirty seconds' worth of the Mona Lisa. J. Ciardi. Sat R 46:14 Mr 30 '63
Art on the move. C. J. McNaspy. America 108:314-16 Mr 2 '63
Editorial; Mona Lisa. J. W. Cataldo. il Sch Arts 62:48 My '63
Escorting Mona Lisa to America. E. T. Folliard. il Nat Geog Mag 123:838-47 Je '63
Exhibitionship. E. H. Gombrich. il Atlan 213: 77-8 F '64
Historic journey of the Pietà. il Life 56:83-5+ Ap 17 '64
Is this trip necessary? Leonardo's Mona Lisa. K. Kuh. il Sat R 46:17 F 2 '63; Discussion. 46:25 F 23 '63
Keep the Pietà in Rome! Christian Cent 81: 102 Ja 22 '64
Mona Lisa. J. Skow. il Sat Eve Post 236: 22-3 F 16 '63
Mona Lisa; painting at the Metropolitan museum of art. New Yorker 38:23-4 F 9 '63
On making the world safe for art; Michelangelo's Pietà to be exhibited at the New York world's fair. A. Frankfurter. Art N 62:23 F '64
Outcry over Pietà. il Life 56:55-6 Je 5 '64
Pieta: masterpiece at the fair. C. McCarry. il Sat Eve Post 237:24-9 Mr 28 '64
Priceless peripatetics. il Time 83:82 Ap 10 '64
Russian work lent to U.S; seven key paintings by Vasily Kandinsky sent from Moscow. Am Artist 27:6+ Mr '63

ART loans—*Continued*
Sea connects the shores; new two-way artistic exchange between Latin America and Anglo-Saxon America. G. de Zéndegui. Américas 16:inside cover Jl '64
Vulnerable voyagers. il Newsweek 63:84 Ap 6 '64
ART metal work
Calder, B. Chernow. il Sch Arts 63:24-7 D '63
Creative casting. L. Campbell. il Craft Horiz 23:10-17+ N '63
Forged metal in Germany; excerpts from Neue schmiedeformen, tr. by H. Wegener. E. Roth. il Craft Horiz 24:12-17+ Ja '64
Metals. il Craft Horiz 24:85-91 My '64
Sinhalese decorative art. G. Kaler. il Hobbies 68:42-3+ Jl; 42+ Ag; 41-2 S; 41-2+ O; 41-2 N; 42+ D '63; 42+ Ja '64 (to be cont)
Workshop: electrofabrication of metals. S. Lechtzin. bibliog il Craft Horiz 24:40-3 N '64
See also
Tôle
Wire sculpture
ART museums. See Art—Galleries and museums
ART nouveau (movement)
New look at art nouveau. il Time 84:62 Ag 21 '64
ART objects
Collectors' notes. E. Gaines. il Antiques 84:304-5 S '63
Infinite riches in a little room. il Esquire 62:125-31 D '64
Profitable pleasure of a longed-for luxury. il House & Gard 124:184-5+ O '63
Shop talk. R. Davidson. See issues of Antiques
See also
Antiques
Souvenirs
Collectors and collecting
Comfortable clutter of an actor in love with the arts. il House B 105:153 Ap '63
Conservation and restoration
Preservation notes. B. Snow. il Antiques 85: 226, 460; 86:100 F, Ap, Jl '64
Copyright
See Copyright—Art
Taxation
See Taxation of works of art
Transportation
See Transportation of works of art
ART objects, Russian
England, Russia, and Virginia; seventeenth-century ties in wood and silver. C. Oman. il Antiques 83:317-19 Mr '63
ART of living. See Conduct of life
ART patronage
Culture, inc; corporations sponsor culture. il Time 83:85 F 21 '64
Every artist needs a hard boiled patron; excerpt from Art and anarchy. E. Wind. Harper 228:98-9+ Mr '64
Priest as patron. T. F. Mathews. America 110:794-5 Je 6 '64
ART prices. See Art—Prices
ART project, Federal. See Federal art project
ART sales
Antiques abroad: London auction notes. W. De Sager. il Antiques 84:456-7 O '63
Auction! excerpt. J. Brough. McCalls 90:112-13+ Ap '63
Coming auctions. See issues of Art news
Framed dollar; picture market. J. Carter. il Harper 227:22+ Jl '63
London captures a great Cézanne; Les grandes baigneuses. il Art N 63:48+ Ja '65
Party's over; sale in Venice's 17th century Palazzo Labia. il Time 83:114 Ap 17 '64
Record price for abstracts; Guggenheim museum sells some Kandinskys. Time 84:70 Jl 10 '64
Sale of the century; René Fribourg collection. il Newsweek 62:58 Jl 8 '63
Sold out art. il Life 55:125-9 S 20 '63
Testing the moderns; prices at auction of Ira Haupt's collection. Time 85:55 Ja 22 '65
Thumbs under the hammer; clearance sale of modern masters at Parke-Bernet galleries in Manhattan. Time 83:75 My 22 '64
See also
Parke-Bernet galleries, incorporated
Sotheby and company
ART schools
Art school directory, 1964. Am Artist 28:75-90 Mr '64
Scuola di Severino; a new home. M. D. Campell. il Sch Arts 62:12-16 My '63
Travel and study. Craft Horiz 23:38-9 My '63
What's wrong with U.S. art schools? with discussion. M. Matter. il Art N 62:40-2+ S '63
See also
Idyllwild school of music and the arts
ART smuggling. See Smuggling
ART societies
See also
Provincetown art association
Society of illustrators
ART studios. See Artists studios
ART teachers
Craftsman & teacher. N. Griner. il Sch Arts 63:28-9 S '63
Creative art education workshop. V. D'Amico. il Sch Arts 62:32-4 Ap '63
George Pappas, artist & teacher; interview. G. Pappas. il Sch Arts 63:12-15 Je '64
Personal challenge of teaching drawing. B. Carter. il Sch Arts 62:30-3 Je '63
Problems 1963: malaise in wonderland; address. J. Heller. Sch Arts 62:25-7 Mr '63
Reader survey, highlights & insights. H. E. Hoffa. il Sch Arts 63:33-4 D '63
Role of the art consultant; Downtown community school. P. Greenberg. il Sch Arts 63:21-3 Ap '64
Sir Herbert Read on the teaching of art. J. S. Keel. bibliog Sch Arts 63:19-21 D '63
Student teacher (title varies) G. Barlow. See issues of School arts
What makes a good art teacher? M. K. Gerstman. il Sch Arts 64:31-2 S '64
Why I want to teach art; statements by art students. ed. by T. K. Kurzband. il Sch Arts 63:5-7 N '63
ART thefts
Big dig for the lost earring; Boston museum of fine arts discovers stolen treasure. J. Howard. il Life 56:75-6+ My 1 '64
Lucrative paradise for grave robbers. D. J. Hamblin. il Life 57:118-20+ N 20 '64
Now the crime of art-napping. P. E. Schneider. il N Y Times Mag p36-7+ Ap 7 '63
Theft of a Boston goddess. il Life 55:88+ O 11 '63
To rob a museum. S. Peterson. il Atlan 213: 81-5 Je '64
ART therapy
Art cart brightens stay for patients in Chicago hospital. il Todays Health 42:70 S '64
Creative education & the special student. G. Barlow. il Sch Arts 63:29-34 Ja '64
Stitchery & the retarded child. B. McMillin. il Sch Arts 63:18-19 Ja '64
ART tours
Art tours (title varies) il Am Artist 27:70-1 Ap '63; 28:64-9 Ap '64
ART trade
Imports and the craftsman. N. Nelson. Craft Horiz 23:27+ Jl '63
Merchandising: the big store; W. R. Valentiner memorial exhibition at J. L. Hudson gallery, Detroit. F. Getlein. New Repub 149:24-6 D 21 '63
See also
Art dealers
ART vandalism. See Vandalism
ARTERENOL
Biosynthesis of norepinephrine in isolated canine heart. C. A. Chidsey and others. bibliog il Science 139:828-9 Mr 1 '63
Histochemical demonstration of uptake of exogenous norepinephrine by adrenergic fibers in vitro. E. T. Angelakos. bibliog il Science 145:503-4 Jl 31 '64
Norepinephrine and 3,4-dihydroxyphenethylamine turnover in guinea pig brain in vivo. S. Udenfriend and P. Zaltzman-Nirenberg. bibliog il Science 142:394-6 O 18 '63
Reduction of cardiac stores of norepinephrine in experimental heart failure. J. F. Spann, jr. and others. bibliog il Science 145:1439-41 S 25 '64
ARTERIES
Elastic membrane: effect of increasing tension on the absorptive capacity. J. H. Lunseth. bibliog il Science 141:438 Ag 2 '63
See also
Aorta
Surgery
See Blood vessels—Surgery
ARTERIOSCLEROSIS
Artery hardening clue. F. Marley. Sci N L 83:163 Mr 16 '63

ARTERIOSCLEROSIS—*Continued*
Atherosclerosis; report on conference on comparative atherosclerosis. O. J. Pollak. Science 145:1075-6 S 4 '64
Calcium and atherosclerosis. il Sci Digest 56:56 N '64
Cigarette smoking and arteriosclerosis. S. L. Wilens and C. M. Plair; discussion. il Science 139:1096+ Mr 15 '63
Clearing an artery; new technique. il Life 57:43-4+ Ag 14 '64
Should you or shouldn't you show preference for polyunsaturated fats? Consumer Bul 47: 19-20 S '64
Sudden death; coronary atherosclerosis. P. D. White. Atlan 212:75-8 O '63
ARTERIOSCLEROSIS research
Artery hardening cause. Sci N L 83:260 Ap 27 '63
Artery hardening cure? Sci N L 86:358 D 5 '64
Avian atherosclerosis: retardation by pectin. H. Fisher and others. bibliog il Science 146: 1063-4 N 20 '64
Four fats in the blood: which cause heart attacks? il Time 83:66-7 Je 19 '64
Lipoprotein movement through canine aortic wall. L. E. Duncan, jr. and others. bibliog il Science 142:972-3 N 15 '63
ARTESIAN wells
Fresh-water gushers in the Sahara; underground lake supplying artesian wells. il Pop Sci 185:98-9 O '64
ARTHRITIS
Arthritis hits millions. Sci N L 86:194 S 26 '64
Children with arthritis crave physical exercise. Sci N L 86:24 Jl 11 '64
New facts about arthritis. R. L. Cecil. Parents Mag 39:103-5 Ja '64
Scientists track disease by stinging mosquitoes; polyarthritis. Sci N L 86:312 N 14 '64
What doctors are learning about arthritis; questions and answers, ed. by H. G. Earl. J. J. Bunim. il Todays Health 42:38-9+ Ag '64
See also
Chloroquine
Therapy
Aspirin heals, kills pain. Sci N L 86:13 Jl 4 '64
Hucksters of pain; Ball clinic, Excelsior Springs, Mo. R. L. Smith. il Sat Eve Post 236:83-7 Ag 24 '63
Physical therapy restressed in arthritis treatment. il Sci Digest 53:44-5 Mr '63
Recreation project for arthritics. M. Thompson. Recreation 57:37 Ja '64
ARTHUR, Gloria
Episcias; African violet cousins. Horticulture 42:24 Ja '64
ARTHUR, Jay
Hydrostatic drive. Pop Mech 120:112-15 Ag '63
ARTHUR, King (romances, etc)
Quest for King Arthur. G. Thomas. il Holiday 36:34-9+ Ag '64
ARTHUR Curtiss James foundation
Mum money; James foundation dissolves itself. Time 84:36 Ag 14 '64
ARTHUR D. Little, incorporated. See Little, Arthur D, incorporated
ARTHURS, Polly
Art on styrofoam. il Design 65:156-7 Mr '64
ARTICHOKES
See also
Cookery—Vegetables
ARTICLES for periodicals. See Periodical literature
ARTICLES of confederation
Birth pangs of our Constitution. H. G. Earl. il Todays Health 42:30-1+ Jl '64
ARTIFACTS. See Implements, utensils, etc.
ARTIFACTS, Indian. See Indians of North America—Implements
ARTIFICIAL body parts. See Prosthesis
ARTIFICIAL cornea; Artificial diamonds; etc. See Cornea, Artificial; Diamonds, Artificial; etc.
ARTIFICIAL gill. See Respiratory apparatus
ARTIFICIAL heart valves. See Heart—Surgery
ARTIFICIAL insemination
Are you using the right dairy bull? questions and answers. C. E. Meadows. il Suc Farm 61:42-3 O '63
Commercial hog AI gets start. D. Hagen. il Farm J 87:44 O '63
Dairymen to get better sires. Farm J 87: 8 Je '63
New beef AI center started. O. Bay. Farm J 87:50 F '63
$21 more per cow with AI. J. Bickers. il Farm J 87:58-9 O '63
$2,000 bull for a five-cow herd! C. E. Ball. il Farm J 87:62L Mr '63
ARTIFICIAL insemination, Human
Babies from frozen sperm healthy, normal. Sci N L 85:374 Je 13 '64
Interventions in nature. W. J. Gibbons. Cath World 197:2-3 Ap '63
Science's touchiest subject. B. H. Frisch. il Sci Digest 54:34-9 N '63
ARTIFICIAL islands
Farewell to the iron bastards; Texas towers await the wreckers. E. M. Wylie. il Life 55:7+ Jl 26 '63
Incident I'll never forget; seeing is believing; Texas tower being towed. A. W. Moffat. il Yachting 115:47+ Mr '64
ARTIFICIAL limbs
Giving hope. il Time 84:54 S 4 '64
Helping hand for Carol. C. Mallison. il Parents Mag 39:66+ Mr '64
New hope for amputees; hydra-cadence prosthesis. Sci Digest 55:77-8 Je '64
New limbs for old. F. Marley. il Sci N L 85: 42-3 Ja 18 '64
ARTIFICIAL organs. See Prosthesis
ARTIFICIAL satellites
American patrol; Project 823. Newsweek 62: 62 O 28 '63
Eavesdropping on satellites. T. Lamb. il Pop Electr 18:52-3+ F '63
Engineering technology satellite among four new OART flight programs. Miss & Roc 15: 101-2+ N 30 '64
First five years of the space age. Sky & Tel 25:148-50 Mr '63
Going up in 1964: a skyful of space machines. il U S News 56:76 Ja 13 '64
Kennedy report reveals USAF launched thirty-three satellites in 1962. Aviation W 78:31 F 4 '63
Major international satellite programs. Aviation W 81:72-3 Jl 6 '64
Missiles and rockets astrolog; current status of U.S. missile and space programs. See occasional issues of Missiles and rockets
Missiles and rockets' world missile/space encyclopedia, 1963-1964. il Miss & Roc 13: 35-7+ Jl 29 '63; 15:39-46+ Jl 27 '64
NASA report shows 327 objects orbiting earth, sun; 312 are U.S. Aviation W 78:37 My 13 '63
Oddballs in orbit; eccentricities of spacecraft. Newsweek 62:80 S 16 '63
Rescue-aid satellites? SAFE (satellites for emergencies) Sci N L 86:219 O 3 '64
Roster of recent space successes. R. N. Watts, jr. il Sky & Tel 27:29-30 Ja '64
Roster of space activity. R. N. Watts, jr. Sky & Tel 29:28-9 Ja '65
Satellites in space. M. J. Vaccaro. il Electr World 71:51-3 Je '64
Satellites: manned and unmanned; report of conference at Virginia polytechnic institute. Science 142:1089+ N 22 '63
Satellites on patrol. il Time 84:50 Jl 31 '64
Satellites on the air (cont) il Pop Electr 18:106 F '63
Satellites track animals. B. Tufty. Sci N L 83:130 Mr 2 '63
Satellites will test advanced avionics. B. Miller. il Aviation W 81:60-3+ Jl 20 '64
SERT I shot is key step in ion engine development effort. il Miss & Roc 15:17 Jl 13 '64
Shut up, already. il Newsweek 63:50 Ja 27 '64
Space tracks; bioelectronics extends its frontiers. D. W. Warner. il Natur Hist 72:8-15 F '63
Space vehicle log. Aviation W 80:64 Ja 13; 135 Mr 16; 81:51 Jl 27 '64; 82:85 Ja 25 '65
U.S. delegate reports on space radio communication conference; statement, November 8, 1963. J. McConnell. Dept State Bul 49:835-7 N 25 '63
See also
Space vehicles
Astronomical applications
Ames satellite program pace accelerated. Aviation W 78:37 Ap 22 '63
Bad luck for OGO. Bsns W p88 S 12 '64
F-1 troubles won't delay Saturn V; new series of interplanetary monitoring satellites. H. Taylor il Miss & Roc 12:16 Mr 11 '63
GEP to alter all astronomy; second Orbiting astronomical observatory. W. Beller. il Miss & Roc 12:22-3 Mr 4 '63
Graduate education: navy program in rocket astronomy opens new horizons to university scientists. J. Walsh. il Science 141: 788-90 Ag 30 '63
Half-ton geophysical satellite; orbiting geophysical observatory. R. N. Watts, jr. il Sky & Tel 28:275-7 N '64
Helios to relay more accurate solar data. W. C. Wetmore. il Aviation W 78:48-9+ Mr 4 '63

ARTIFICIAL satellites—Astronomical applications—*Continued*
Looking afar, from afar; orbiting observatories. J. Eberhart. il Sci N L 87:10-11 Ja 2 '65
Mercury capsule conversion seen feasible for recoverable telescope; orbiting astronomical observatory. il Aviation W 82:23 Ja 11 '65
More about the OAO. R. N. Watts, jr. il Sky & Tel 28:78-9 Ag '64
Observatories in space. W. Von Braun. il Pop Sci 182:14+ My '63
Observatories in space; orbiting astronomical observatories. A. I. Berman. il Sci Am 209:28-37 bibliog(p 140) Ag '63
Observatories in the sky. D. F. Nolan. il Sci N L 85:74-5 F 1 '64
Observatory in space; OGO (Orbiting geophysical observatory) il Sci Digest 56:2 N '64
On predicting space weather; OSO I. H. Simon. il Sat R 46:52 Ap 6 '63
OAO control system tests advance. M. Getler. il Miss & Roc 12:28-9 Ap 15 '63
OAO experiment unit delivered to NASA. R. D. Hibben. il Aviation W 80:55-6 Je 29 '64
OGO-A to carry twenty experiments. H. Taylor. il Miss & Roc 15:12 Ag 31 '64
OGO seen achieving most goals. Aviation W 81:23 S 21 '64
OGO strangest-looking object circling earth. Sci N L 86:184 S 19 '64
OGO tests function despite boom failure. Aviation W 81:37 S 14 '64
OSO 2 instruments will scan solar disk. B. Miller. il Aviation W 80:52-3+ Ja 13 '64
Radio astronomy explorer program approval regarded as imminent. Miss & Roc 15:92-3 N 30 '64
Radio astronomy observatory expected to get development nod. H. Taylor. Miss & Roc 15:15 O 5 '64
Rich data from space reduced to meaning. R. D. Hibben. il Aviation W 80:54-5+ Ja 27 '64
Scientific satellite projects hit by cuts in FY '64 budget. il Miss & Roc 13:133-4+ N 25 '63
Second OSO flight scheduled next week. W. J. Normyle. Aviation W 82:77+ Ja 25 '65
Six-month lifetime predicted for Pioneer. I. Stone. il Aviation W 80:69+ Ja 27 '64
Space sciences challenge R. D. Hibben. il Aviation W 80:54-5+ Ja 27; 91-3+ F 17 '64
Storm warning: Orbiting solar observatory spots microflares. il Newsweek 61:98 Mr 25 '63
Streetcar satellite to study particles; Orbiting geophysical observatory. Sci N L 86: 232 O 10 '64
Sun-scanning satellite; OSO-B. A. Ewing. Sci N L 85:247 Ap 18 '64
Telescope will orbit; proposed radio astronomy satellite. A. Ewing. Sci N L 86:231 O 10 '64

Communication applications

See Communications satellites

Control systems

See Space vehicles—Control systems

Design

See Space vehicles—Design

Electronic equipment

See Space vehicles—Electronic equipment

Equipment

See Space vehicles—Equipment

Launching

See Space vehicles—Launching

Launching sites

See Space vehicles—Launching sites

Mapping applications

Army considering expansion of SECOR satellite mapping program. Miss & Roc 15:12 N 2 '64
Better maps with satellites; geodetic satellites. J. Dobbin. il Sci N L 85:253 Ap 18 '64
Geodesy by satellite. R. R. Newton. bibliog il Science 144:803-8 My 15 '64
Geodetic balloon satellite readied; Geos. H. Taylor. Miss & Roc 15:13 S 28 '64
Geodetic satellite pinpoints positions; Secor. Aviation W 80:33 F 24 '64
Surveillance promises civil spin-off. Miss & Roc 14:44+ Je 1 '64

Meteorological applications

Accord on new weather satellite awaited; future applications studied. il Miss & Roc 13:127-30 N 25 '63
Advanced research for meteorological satellites. E. A. Neil. il Electr World 71:61 Je '64
Advanced technology series, possible Navaid program highlight future R&D. il Miss & Roc 15:94-6 N 30 '64
Advanced weather satellite ready for launching; Nimbus. il Sci Digest 53:45-7 Ap '63
Avionics changes included in Tiros wheel. K. J. Stein. il Aviation W 81:44-5+ Ag 3 '64
Best eye yet; Nimbus. il Time 84:77 S 4 '64
Bureau buying three Tiros-type satellites. Miss & Roc 14:21 Ja 27 '64
ComSats, weather stressed; NASA plans. Miss & Roc 12:18 F 18 '63
Doing something about weather. Bsns W p68 Ag 24 '63
Eye for the weather; Tiros satellites. Newsweek 63:86 F 24 '64
Future Tiros launches to include elliptical and near-polar orbits. G. Alexander. Aviation W 78:38 Je 24 '63
Global distribution of the net energy balance of the atmosphere from Tiros radiation data. S. I. Rasool. bibliog il Science 143: 567-9 F 7 '64; Reply. R. Wexler and W. K. Widger, jr. 145:1206 S 11 '64
Ground facilities ready for Nimbus data. Aviation W 81:24 Ag 31 '64
Infrared emissivity of the Sahara from Tiros data. K. J. K. Buettner and C. D. Kern. bibliog Science 142:671-2 N 8 '63
Interim weather satellite plan ready; National operational meteorological satellite system. Miss & Roc 14:15 F 10 '64
Latitudinal distribution of cloud cover from Tiros III photographs. A. Arking. bibliog il Science 143:569-72 F 7 '64; Reply. R. Wexler and W. K. Widger, jr. 145:1206 S 11 '64
Meteorological satellites; report on 3rd western national meeting of the American geophysical union. C. O. Erickson. Science 143:612-13 F 7 '64
New Tiros wheel design studied. M. Getler. il Miss & Roc 12:17 Je 3 '63
Nimbus C undergoes final design changes. Aviation W 82:41+ Ja 11 '65
Nimbus I pictures cover U.S, Asia, Mediterranean. il Aviation W 81:32-3 S 14 '64
Nimbus IR, TV photos show Britain, Russia il Aviation W 81:34 S 7 '64
Nimbus launch is two years late. il Miss & Roc 15:15 Ag 3 '64
Nimbus program may be scrapped. Miss & Roc 13:15 S 23 '63
Nimbus suffers from elliptical orbit. il Miss & Roc 15:15 S 7 '64
Nimbus systems undergo rigid checking at GE. il Aviation W 80:75 Ja 6 '64
Nimbus views weather; automatic picture transmission. A. Ewing. il Sci N L 86:165 S 12 '64
Observation in space; address, April 13, 1963. L. C. Meeker. Dept State Bul 48:746-51 My 13 '63
Portrait of two continents; photos taken by Nimbus I. Sci Digest 56:inside back cover N '64
Receiving kits may widen Tiros data use. G. Alexander. Aviation W 79:26 D 30 '63
Relay box problem forces Nimbus delay. H. D. Watkins. il Aviation W 81:24-5 Ag 17 '64
S-6 satellite will probe upper atmosphere. Sci N L 83:185 Mr 23 '63
Satellites' greatest gift. Sci N L 83:78 F 2 '63
Saturn SA-5, Tiros 8 readied for flights. Aviation W 79:39 D 16 '63
Seventh successful Tiros. R. N. Watts, jr. Sky & Tel 26:76 Ag '63
Shooting the breeze; Nimbus. Newsweek 64: 57 S 7 '64
Sky watchers in schools gather satellite data. Sci N L 84:281 N 2 '63
Snap happy; computer for analyzing Tiros's pictures. Newsweek 62:62 Jl 8 '63
Space meteorology and communications: a challenge to science and diplomacy; address, April 19, 1963. R. N. Gardner. Dept State Bul 48:740-6 My 13 '63
Space sciences challenge. R. D. Hibben. il Aviation W 80:68-9+ F 10 '64
SMS flight program funding now expected no earlier than fiscal '66; Synchronous meteorological satellite and Nimbus program. Miss & Roc 13:20 Jl 1 '63
SMS satellite program under way. M. Getler. Miss & Roc 12:27 F 25 '63
Tiros 8 in operation. R. N. Watts, jr. Sky & Tel 27:93-4 F '64
Tiros 8's APT system already aids Cape Kennedy weather prediction. C. Butler. Miss & Roc 14:16 Ja 6 '64

ARTIFICIAL satellites—Meteorological applications—*Continued*
Tiros 5 and 6. Sky & Tel 26:23 Jl '63
Tiros launches to be moved to WTR. H. Taylor. Miss & Roc 16:15 Ja 25 '65
Tiros selected for weather net. Aviation W 80:27 F 10 '64
Tiros VII an improved storm-spotter. Miss & Roc 12:21 Je 17 '63
Tiros view of the storms: map of what went wrong. il Life 54:32-3 F 8 '63
TOS up; Tiros 9. Newsweek 65:52 F 1 '65
Trading weather data; U.S-Soviet space cooperation. il Bsns W p77 Je 13 '64
250,000 U.S. photos from space; now another success for Tiros. il U S News 55:68-9 Jl 1 '63
U.S.-USSR space plan covers direct exchange of weather data. Aviation W 78:36 Ap 1 '63
Volcano warning system; information by weather satellites. Sci N L 85:293 My 9 '64
Watching the world's weather; Tiros VIII. Time 83:50 Ja 3 '64
Weather bureau prepares to buy Tiros-type craft. Miss & Roc 14:14 Mr 16 '64
Weather bureau rejects Nimbus for operational satellite program. Aviation W 79:31 O 7 '63
Weather bureau; special report. il Miss & Roc 15:151-4+ N 30 '64
Weather by facsimile; Tiros-8 scheduled for launching. Bsns W p84 D 21 '63
Weather eye that never blinks. W. S. Griswold. il Pop Sci 183:70-3+ N '63
Weather vans promise better local forecasts. Sci N L 85:39 Ja 18 '64
World's largest weather satellite; Nimbus-A. il Sci Digest 56:inside cover O '64

Military applications

Accuracy, payload cost favor ground-based anti-satellite systems. M. Getler. Miss & Roc 13:19 O 28 '63
Air force launched fifty-six payloads last year. il Aviation W 80:53 F 10 '64
Destroying enemy satellites. A. Parry. il Sci Digest 53:35-41 Mr '63
Half of Midas spending viewed as waste. Aviation W 78:38 Je 17 '63
I spy, you spy, it's alright. R. D. Senter. New Repub 150:7-8 Je 13 '64
K's statement sticky for Pentagon. Miss & Roc 14:15 Je 8 '64
Letter to the Colonel; reply to an article in Red star. W. J. Coughlin. Miss & Roc 12:84 Je 24 '63
Military Comsat tests to start in 1966. P. J. Klass. Aviation W 81:19 Ag 17 '64
Military sees promise in new adaptive space array. M. Getler. il Miss & Roc 13:34 S 23 '63
Military space program; address, February 5, 1964. A. C. Hall. Vital Speeches 30:361-5 Ap 1 '64; Excerpts. Aviation W 80:17 F 10 '64
MIDAS concept showing promise. H. M. David. Miss & Roc 14:19 F 3 '64
New missile warning satellite succeeds; alarm satellites. D. E. Fink. Aviation W 80:33 F 3 '64
Non-nuclear anti-satellite system in making. J. Trainor. Miss & Roc 14:12-13 My 11 '64
Observation in space; address, April 13, 1963. L. C. Meeker. Dept State Bul 48:746-51 My 13 '63
Operational satellite killers need non-nuclear destruct device. Miss & Roc 15:10-11 S 28 '64
Satellite inspection study proposals asked. Aviation W 78:33 Je 3 '63
Sensor tests delay Vela hotel launch. G. Alexander. Aviation W 81:24 Jl 20 '64
Sentries in orbit; Atlas-Agena. Time 82:70 O 25 '63
Snap-9A isotope generator powers navy transit navigation satellite. Aviation W 79:37 O 7 '63
Space parts specifications are prepared. B. Miller. Aviation W 79:111 Ag 5 '63
SSD plans space test of unified avionics. B. Miller. il Aviation W 81:42+ N 30 '64
USAF pushes interim Comsat capability. il Aviation W 81:87+ N 23 '64
U.S. prepared to detect atomic explosions. Sci N L 86:233 O 10 '64

Navigational applications

Advanced technology series, possible Navaid program highlight future R&D. il Miss & Roc 15:94-6 N 30 '64
Clampdown; navy's Transit navigation satellite. Newsweek 61:67 Ap 22 '63
DOD declares Transit operational. il Miss & Roc 16:14 Ja 18 '65
GE designs navigation satellite network. D. E. Fink. il Aviation W 80:49+ Mr 30 '64
Instant navigation. il Sci Digest 55:inside cover My '64
NASA seeks establishment of Navsat study committee in a month. Miss & Roc 14:17 Je 22 '64
Navigation satellite system board urged. Aviation W 80:17 Mr 30 '64
Services delay satellite disclosure. Aviation W 79:25 Jl 29 '63
Single-satellite Navsat net being studied. P. J. Klass. il Aviation W 80:69+ My 4 '64

Orbits

Dynamical model for demonstrating satellite motions. L. Blitzer. il Sky & Tel 29:16-18 Ja '65
Future Tiros launches to include elliptical and near-polar orbits. G. Alexander. Aviation W 78:38 Je 24 '63
Nimbus suffers from elliptical orbit. il Miss & Roc 15:15 S 7 '64
Only six NASA payloads orbited in 1963. A. P. Alibrando. Aviation W 79:30-1 N 18 '63
STL may make $1-million bonus on Vela Hotel incentive contract. Aviation W 79:28 O 28 '63
Why a satellite stays up. W. Von Braun. il Pop Sci 183:16+ O '63

Power supply

See Space vehicles—Power supply

Shielding (radiation)

Method found to shield satellites; magnetic shield that could operate for 300 hours. Sci N L 86:136 Ag 29 '64

Stability and stabilizers

See Space vehicles—Stability and stabilizers

Testing

Large space science satellites get customized test facilities at Goddard. W. Beller. il Miss & Roc 14:33+ My 25 '64
NASA announces no further SERT flights are necessary. Miss & Roc 15:15 O 19 '6
No further SERT-type tests needed. Miss & Roc 15:32 S 7 '64

Tracking

Accuracy, payload, cost favor ground-based anti-satellite systems. M. Getler. Miss & Roc 13:19 O 28 '63
Air force dedicates second ARIS. C. D. LaFond. il Miss & Roc 13:34-5 Jl 22 '63
AF studying laser navigation sensors. M. Getler. il Miss & Roc 12:24-5 F 18 '63
Bendix star and planet tracker program locks on new detector device. M. Getler. il Miss & Roc 13:24-5 O 21 '63
Expansion of NASA tracking net planned. Aviation W 78:34 F 18 '63
Fused silica reflectors in laser test. W. Beller. il Miss & Roc 13:29+ O 21 '63
GE designs navigation satellite network. D. E. Fink. il Aviation W 80:49+ Mr 30 '64
Haystack will advance radar precision. P. J. Klass. il Aviation W 78:80-2 F 4 '63
Huge antenna to direct spacecraft. C. D. LaFond. il Miss & Roc 12:37 Mr 11 '63
NASA laser communications, tracking effort to double in FY '64. M. Getler. il Miss & Roc 13:22-3 N 18 '63
NASA testing laser satellite techniques. D. E. Fink. Aviation W 81:55+ N 2 '64
Observatory aircraft proposed for better satellite inspection. R. Pay. Miss & Roc 15:36-7 N 16 '64
100 eyes to the sky; JPL command center. il Pop Electr 21:56 O '64
Outside track at Standard oil co. of Ohio research laboratory. Newsweek 61:81 Ap 8 '63
Prototype laser system combines high information rate with tracking accuracy. R. Pay. il Miss & Roc 14:24-5 My 18 '64
RCA system pinpoints satellite size, shape, orbital characteristics. R. Pay. Miss & Roc 15:37 N 2 '64
S-66 may be first space test of laser. il Miss & Roc 13:21 Ag 5 '63
Satellite eavesdropper in an attic. S. Iker. il Pop Mech 121:102-3 Ap '64
Satellite tracker keeps sky vigil. Sci N L 86 265 O 24 '64
Single-satellite Navsat net being studied. P. J. Klass. il Aviation W 80:69+ My 4 '64
Sohio Project moonbeam. R. W. Burhans. il Sky & Tel 25:128-31 Mr '63
SSD plans space test of unified avionics. B. Miller. il Aviation W 81:42+ N 30 '64
Spadats network relies on varied sensors. P. J. Klass. il Aviation W 78:89+ F 18 '63
Syncom found by new R&RR tracking system. C. D. LaFond. Miss & Roc 12:36+ Mr 18 '63

ARTIFICIAL satellites—Tracking—*Continued*
$349 million bolsters system; NASA plans. il Miss & Roc 12:16 F 18 '63
Unique monopulse antenna developed. C. D LaFond. il Miss & Roc 12:35 Mr 11 '63
See also
Communications satellites—Tracking

Use in research

Anna. R. N. Watts. il Sky & Tel 25:212 Ap '63
Another air-density explorer balloon. R. N. Watts, jr. il Sky & Tel 27:93 F '64
Beacon Explorer surveys ionosphere. Aviation W 81:35 O 19 '64
Big lift; IMP. il Newsweek 62:72 D 9 '63
Biosatellite experiments chosen. Aviation W 79:68-9+ O 21 '63
Biosatellite experiments selected. Aviation W 80:37 F 24 '64
Canadian satellite: the topside sounder Alouette; report of United States-Canadian meeting of Union radio scientifique internationale. J. O. Thomas. il Science 139:229-32 Ja 18 '63
Encoder malfunction silences Explorer 14. Aviation W 78:32 Ja 28 '63
Explore pathway to moon; Interplanetary monitoring platform. il Sci N L 84:371 D 14 '63
Explorer 17 analyzes the atmosphere. il Sky & Tel 25:261-2 My '63
Explorer 17 returning high-quality data. G. Alexander. Aviation W 78:34+ Ap 8 '63
Explorer 20 launch succeeds. Aviation W 81:25 Ag 31 '64
Explorer 22. R. N. Watts, jr. il Sky & Tel 28:354-5 D '64
Explorer 23 furnishing data for Pegasus. D. E. Fink. Aviation W 81:53+ N 30 '64
Forty miles of information every day from space. L. Lessing. il Fortune 69:116-22+ Ja '64
Fourteen experiments on first biosatellite. Miss & Roc 14:17 F 24 '64
Fused silica reflectors in laser test; S-66 satellite. W. Beller. il Miss & Roc 13:29+ O 21 '63
GD/A satellite to study space phenomena; SATAR. I. Stone. il Aviation W 79:69 Jl 15 '63
GD/A's SATAR will serve as space probe, re-entry vehicle or satellite. W. E. Wilks. il Miss & Roc 14:24-7 Je 15 '64
GE gravity gradient design in final stage. D. E. Fink. il Aviation W 81:34+ D 28 '64
General electric wins biosatellite contract. Aviation W 79:33 Ag 26 '63
Geodesy by satellite. R. R. Newton. bibliog il Science 144:803-8 My 15 '64; Correction. 145:659-60 Ag 14 '64
Geodetic balloon satellite readied; Beacon Explorer. H. Taylor. Miss & Roc 15:13 S 28 '64
Giant bird satellites patrol for meteoroids. il(p 129) Sci N L 85:141 F 29 '64
Giant detector for meteoroids. il Sky & Tel 27:210-11 Ap '64
Hughes wins technology satellite. Aviation W 80:26 Mr 9 '64
Interplanetary monitoring platform. R. N. Watts, jr. il Sky & Tel 27:27-8 Ja '64
IMP discovers new radiation belt. W. Beller. il Miss & Roc 14:22-3 Mr 23 '64
IMP finds magnetosphere shock wave. Aviation W 80:23 Mr 23 '64
IMP will warn of dangerous solar flares. R. D. Hibben. il Aviation W 79:28-9 N 4 '63
Ionosphere beacon fails to orbit. Sky & Tel 27:289 My '64
Ionosphere Beacon fails to orbit. Sky & Tel Sky & Tel 26:255 N '63
Ionosphere Explorer I satellite: first observations from the fixed-frequency topside sounder. W. Calvert and others. bibliog il Science 146:391-5 O 16 '64
Ionosphere Explorer launch postponed. Aviation W 80:23 Mr 23 '64
Ionosphere Explorer to complement density data supplied by Alouette. L. J. Curran. il Miss & Roc 14:31-2 F 10 '64
Ionospheric beacon fails to reach orbit. Aviation W 80:25 Mr 23 '64
Ionospheric satellites aiding design of long antenna systems. M. Getler. Miss & Roc 16:34-7 Ja 4 '65
Lunar IMP experiments to be selected. D. E. Fink. il Aviation W 80:71+ My 18 '64
Map interplanetary field; IMP-I. Sci N L 86:279 O 31 '64
Meteoroid detection satellite mock-up shown. C. D LeFond. il Miss & Roc 12:32-3 Je 24 '63
Meteoroid satellite passes crucial test on way to mid-64 flight. C. D. LaFond. il Miss & Roc 14:22-3 F 17 '64
Mission growth planned for biosatellite. E. H. Kolcum. il Aviation W 79:20-1 D 30 '63
NASA and western Europe agree on scientific satellite project: NASA announcement, July 21, 1964, with text of agreement. Dept State Bul 51:203-5 Ag 10 '64
NASA laser communications, tracking effort to double in FY '64; S-66 satellite. M. Getler. Miss & Roc 13:22-3 N 18 '63
NASA plans new technological satellite. E. H. Kolcum. Aviation W 80:26 F 17 '64
NASA satellites to make detailed ionosphere study; Topside sounder, Ionosphere. il Miss & Roc 14:13 Mr 16 '64
NASA schedules October launch for ionospheric beacon, IMP B. Aviation W 81:30 S 21 '64
NASA set to launch second interplanetary monitoring platform. il Miss & Roc 15:18 O 5 '64
NASA testing laser satellite techniques; Beacon Explorer satellite. D. E. Fink. Aviation W 81:55+ N 2 '64
New booster raises biosatellite payload. D. C. Fink. il Aviation W 82:38-9 Ja 11 '65
Off-the-shelf Injun IV set to go in early '64. W. Beller. il Miss & Roc 14:22-3 Ja 6 '64
Pegasus circumlunar mission under study; meteoroid detection satellite. W. J. Normyle. il Aviation W 81:24-5 D 14 '64
Picture of earth's magnetosphere altered by data from IMP satellite. W. J. Normyle. Aviation W 81:25 D 21 '64
Piggyback explorers will study radiation. Miss & Roc 13:14 Ag 12 '63
Polka-dotted Explorer-19 only faintly visible. il(p 1) Sci N L 85:9 Ja 4 '64
Radiation bulge detected. Sci N L 85:179 Mr 21 '64
Radio astronomy explorer program approval regarded as imminent. Miss & Roc 15:92-3 N 30 '64
Rich data from space reduced to meaning. R. D. Hibben. il Aviation W 80:54-5+ Ja 27 '64
S-6 to study particles, drag effects. il Miss & Roc 12:21 Ap 1 '63
S-66 may be first space test of laser. il Miss & Roc 13:21 Ag 5 '63
S-66 to measure electron density profile. il Aviation W 79:82-3 Ag 5 '63
San Marco satellite to probe air density. W. C. Wetmore. il Aviation W 79:76-7+ Ag 26 '63
Satellite laser test. A. Ewing. Sci N L 85:3 Ja 4 '64
Satellite readied to probe radiation belt energetic particles; energetic particles Explorer D. il Miss & Roc 15:15 D 14 '64
Satellite to study mirror; S-66. W. Wingo. il Sci N L 84:85 Ag 10 '63
Satellites: scientific mission and design; concerning a special astronautics symposium at the AAAS Philadelphia meeting. J. G. Stephenson. Science 139:776+ F 22 '63
Scientists plan missions to comets. W. Beller. il Miss & Roc 12:22-3 My 6 '63
Second Ariel in orbit. il Sky & Tel 27:288-9 My '64
Solar flare warning system for astronauts considered possible. Aviation W 80:75 F 24 '64
Space mirror investigated; inspections of the ionosphere. W. Wingo. il Sci N L 85:194 Mr 28 '64
Space sciences challenge. R. D. Hibben. il Aviation W 80:54-5+ Ja 27; 68-9+ F 10; 91-3+ F 17 '64
Sputnik plus seven. Newsweek 64:80-1 O 12 '64
UK-2 to measure galactic noise, ozone, particles. il Miss & Roc 14:15 Mr 23 '64
UK3 satellite to carry five experiments. H. J. Coleman. il Aviation W 79:67+ Ag 12 '63
U.S, Canada to launch four satellites; Alouette and ISIS. Miss & Roc 14:16 Ja 20 '64
Wiesner, Charyk ordered Starad secrecy. L. Booda. Aviation W 78:26-7 Ap 15 '63

ARTIFICIAL satellites, British
U.K. orders ELDO Comsat study. Aviation W 78:38 Ap 8 '63
UK-2 to measure galactic noise, ozone, particles. il Miss & Roc 14:15 Mr 23 '64

ARTIFICIAL satellites, Canadian
Canadian satellite: the topside sounder Alouette; report of United States-Canadian meeting of Union radio scientifique internationale. J. O. Thomas. il Science 139:229-32 Ja 18 '63
Giant detector for meteoroids; Alouette. il Sky & Tel 27:210-11 Ap '64
Ionosphere Explorer to complement density data supplied by Alouette. L. J. Curran. il Miss & Roc 14:31-2 F 10 '64

ARTIFICIAL satellites, Canadian—*Continued*
Ionospheric satellites aiding design of long antenna systems. M. Getler. Miss & Roc 16:34-7 Ja 4 '65
U.S., Canada to launch four satellites; Alouette and ISIS. Miss & Roc 14:16 Ja 20 '64

ARTIFICIAL satellites, Egyptian
Egypt plans satellite launch within year. C. Brownlow. il Aviation W 79:32-3 S 9 '63

ARTIFICIAL satellites, German
German satellite contract due soon. W. Beller. il Miss & Roc 13:24-5 Ag 5 '63

ARTIFICIAL satellites, Russian
Cosmos may have photographed U.S. Miss & Roc 12:18 Ap 1 '63
New Russian satellite. R. N. Watts, jr. Sky & Tel 26:328 D '63
Polyot maneuvering claim questioned. Aviation W 79:28-9 N 11 '63
Radioactive Sputnik fragments. C. J. Matyas. il Sci Digest 53:35-41 F '63
Scientific Cosmos flights resumed. Aviation W 79:33 Ag 12 '63
Soviets describe equipment for Elektron. W. C. Wetmore. il Aviation W 80:49-50 Je 8 '64
Soviets may be using two Cosmos types. E. Clark. Aviation W 78:22-3 Ap 29 '63
USSR launches 21st in Cosmos program. Aviation W 79:33 N 18 '63

ARTIGAS, José
Artigas and the Americas. G. de Zéndegui. por Américas 16:inside cover, 1 Ag '64
José Artigas day; excerpts from eulogies. il Américas 16:43-4 Ag '64
José Artigas: father of Uruguay. H. E. Davis. bibliog il por Américas 16:1-5 O '64

ARTIGAS, Llorens
Miró, Artigas; their new ceramics. D. Ashton. il por Craft Horiz 24:24-33+ Ja '64

ARTISTIC ability. See Creation (literary, artistic, etc)

ARTISTIC photography. See Photography, Artistic

ARTISTS
Creative dilemma. J. Baldwin; J. W. Krutch. Sat R 47:14-17+ F 8 '64
For the benefit of? conditions under which artists should donate their work. T. B. Hess. Art N 62:23 Ap '63
It could happen to you; ways of setting up a contingency fund. N. Kent. Am Artist 29:3+ F '65
Problems 1963: malaise in wonderland; address. J. Heller. Sch Arts 62:25-7 Mr '63
Reviews and previews: new names this month. See issues of Art news
See also
Art as a profession
Cartoonists
Illustrators

Bibliography

Art and personalities. C. J. McNaspy. America 109:468 O 19 '63
They know they're monsters: some recent books on art. P. Pickrel. Harper 229:124+ D '64

ARTISTS, American
American painter as a blue chip. M. Elkoff. il Esquire 64:36-42+ Ja '65
Nineteenth-century still-life painting in New Jersey. W. H. Gerdts. il Antiques 86:718-21 D '64
Quiet realists; Lawrence Campbell, Rudy Burckhardt, and John Button. Newsweek 63:80-1 Je 22 '64
Should the artist become a man of the world? with editorial comment. A. Kaprow. Art N 63:19, 34-7+ O '64
Vanity fair: the New York art scene. il Newsweek 65:54-6+ Ja 4 '65
See also
Artists, Negro
Bearden, R.
Brumidi, C.
Franck, F.
Goldsholl, M.
Painting, American
Peterdi, G.
Saul, P.
Sculpture, American
Sheets, M.

ARTISTS, British
See also
Hogarth, P.

ARTISTS, Chinese
Painters: exhibition by members of Hamilton-Madison's Golden age club. New Yorker 39:16-18 Je 29 '63

ARTISTS, German
See also
Kollwitz, K.

ARTISTS, Israeli
Ein Hod, an artists' village in Israel. J. Lieber. il Am Artist 27:58-63+ Ap '63

ARTISTS, Japanese
See also
Munakata, S.

ARTISTS, Latin American
Looking at Latin America; group of juries assembles exhibits for forthcoming exhibition in Washington. F. Getlein. New Repub 152:28-30 Ja 30 '65
Meeting in Madrid: joint exhibit of Spanish and New World artists. J. Gómez-Sicre. il Américas 15:30-9 S '63

ARTISTS, Latvian
See also
Aron, K.

ARTISTS, Negro
Negro artist in America today. H. L. Smith. Negro Hist Bul 27:111-12 F '64

ARTISTS, Russian
Critic surveys the party line in art. J. Canaday. il N Y Times Mag p 18-19+ Ja 5 '64

ARTISTS, Spanish
Meeting in Madrid: joint exhibit of Spanish and New World artists. J. Gómez-Sicre. il Américas 15:30-9 S '63

ARTISTS, Uruguayan
See also
Frasconi, A.

ARTISTS colonies
Summer place. il Time 84:46 Ag 14 '64
See also
MacDowell memorial colony, Peterboro, N.H.

ARTISTS easels. See Easels

ARTISTS materials
Air of art is poisoned; with comment by L. J. Goldwater. R. Mallary. il Art N 62:34-7+ O '63
Art mart. See issues of American artist
Marisol's mannequins. il Horizon 5:102-4 Mr '63
Ninth-tenth annual buyer's guide of artists' materials. il Am Artist 28:81-96 Ja '64; 29:85-100 Ja '65
Printmaker into watercolorist. R. Weidenaar. il Am Artist 28:36-9+ N '64
Ralph Mayer's technical question & answer page. R. Mayer. See issues of American artist
Respect for tools. N. Kent. Am Artist 29:3+ Ja '65
See also
Paint

ARTISTS studios
Cover. il Am Artist 29:4 Ja '65

ARTS and crafts
Art, creativity and the home fires. M. White. il Ladies Home J 81:66-8 Je '64
How to remember the things you do this summer. il Am Home 67:114+ Jl '64
International crafts conference in 1964. A. O. Webb. Craft Horiz 23:11 Ja '63
See also
Appliqué work
Hairwork
Handicraft
Mosaics
Needlework
Paper work
Weaving
Wood carving
Woodworking
World congress of craftsmen

Bibliography

Book review section. See issues of Design
Books (cont) Craft Horiz 23:47 Ja; 49 Jl; 49 S; 46-7 N '63; 24:57 N '64

Competitions

First annual western craft competition. L. Harrington. il Craft Horiz 24:12-19 Jl '64

Exhibitions

Amusements; exhibition at New York city's Museum of contemporary crafts; with editorial comment. P. Smith. il Craft Horiz 24:8-19 N '64
Calendar; Where to show. See issues of Craft horizons
Craftsmen of the Northeast and Southeast. P. Adler; J. Hall. il Craft Horiz 23:36-9+ N '63
Designed for production: the craftsman's approach; exhibition at Museum of contemporary crafts, New York. il Craft Horiz 24:13-68 Mr '64
Exhibitions. See issues of Craft horizons
Munich: International handcrafts fair. J. Guth and F. Guth. il Craft Horiz 24:20-4 S '64

ARTS and crafts—*Continued*

Study and teaching

Art education and the crafts. F. Schwartz. Craft Horiz 24:8 Jl '64
Attend a crafts school this summer. House B 105:92 My '63
Crafts in education. K. Beittel and R. Burkhart. Craft Horiz 23:8-9 S '63
Education of the craftsman, its changing role. C. Sawyer. il Craft Horiz 23:10-13+ My '63
Experience of being & becoming. M. F. Andrews. il Sch Arts 62:5-9 Mr '63
Shoe box decorations. il Design 66:40-1 N '64
See also
Embroidery—Study and teaching

Materials

Arts & crafts corner. Recreation 56:138 Mr '63
Beach glass and bric-a-brac. N. Allan. il Design 65:12-14 S '63
Clown with a secret. il Design 64:101 Ja '63
Coat hanger chandelier. W. Floyd. il Design 65:154 Mr '64
Gifts from the sea. il Design 64:116-17+ Ja '63
Jewels of the sea: beach glass. N. Zyla. il Design 65:10-11+ S '63
Made of toothpicks. il Design 65:102-3 Ja '64
Made with macaroni. F. Jones. il Design 64: 98-9+ Ja '63
Made with popsicle sticks; novel baskets. T. Lau. il Design 65:100-1 Ja '64
New faces for common places; everyday household objects lead double lives. P. Sanders. il Design 65:61 N '63
Sketching with seeds. F. Major. il Design 65: 150-1 Mr '64
Stocking faces. F. Major. il Design 65:186-7 My '64
Tin can rooster. il Design 65:155 Mr '64
Towel bunny. il Design 65:149 Mr '64
Toys made of towels. il Design 65:110-12 Ja '64

Japan

Myth of Japanese good taste. B. White. Craft Horiz 23:21 N '63

Mexico

Mexican crafts. N. Cotton. il Sch Arts 62: 14-16 Ap '63
Shopping for Mexico's folk art and homewares. il Sunset 133:80-7 N '64

New England

Personal business. D. B. Warnick. il Travel 122:44-7 S '64

Nigeria

Narrow band weaving among the Yoruba of Nigeria. R. Boyer. il Craft Horiz 24:28-9+ N '64

Peru

Every shred of evidence; rediscovering ancient Peruvian weavers' craft. I. VanStan. il Américas 15:30-4 D '63

Puerto Rico

Crafts from Puerto Rico. House & Gard 123: 191 Ap '63

Scandinavia

Going places, finding things in Scandinavia. B. Pepis. il House & Gard 123:36+ Mr '63
Impressions of Scandinavia. N. Kent. il Am Artist 28:40-7+ Ap '64

United States

American craftsman, 1964. R. Slivka. Craft Horiz 24:10-11+ My '64
Christmas shopper. il Craft Horiz 23:22-3 N '63
Crafts in a technocracy & education. J. W. Cataldo. il Sch Arts 63:29-33 Ap '64
Crafts reborn. D. Cort. il Nation 198:628-9 Je 22 '64
Craftsmen of the Northeast and Southeast. P. Adler; J. Hall. il Craft Horiz 23:36-9+ N '63
Happy life and dutiful death of the Midwest designer-craftsmen. M. Higgins. Craft Horiz 23:52-3 Mr '63
In the heart of the Tarheel country; a flourishing center for American handcrafts. il House & Gard 123:206-9 My '63
Studio craftsman observed. il Craft Horiz 24: 94-103 My '64
See also
American craftsmen's council

ARTS and crafts, Indian. See Indians of South America—Industries
ARTS and crafts centers. See Art centers
ARTS and crafts trade. See Art trade
ARTSAY, Alda Favia-. See Favia-Artsay, A.
ARTURO Ui; drama. See Brecht, B.
ARTZ, Robert M.
Building a park and recreation department. por Recreation 57:442-5+ N '64
Summer pool dons a winter coat. Am City 79:94-6 Ag '64
ARUBA (island)
Aruba's one-man resources department. M. Frome. il Am For 70:24-6+ Jl '64
Editor's report: Aruba. M. M. Davis. il Travel 122:52-5 Ag '64
Island in sun adds industry to beaches; Aruba chemical industries. il Bsns W p36-7+ Ja 4 '64
ARUMS
Far flung family. L. M. Andrews. il Flower Grower 50:44-5+ Ag '63
See also
Sauromatum
ARVESON, Beth
No separate communism course: study in historical context. Sr Schol 83:19T O 18 '63
ARVIN, Newton
Critic to remember. G. Hicks. Sat R 46:21-2 Jl 13 '63
ASAKAMA Hiroshi. See Turner, C. D. jt. auth.
ASARINA
Plant that twists. G. R. Robinson. il Pop Gard 15:15 Mr '64
ASBELL, Bernard
Cape Kennedy's high school for sky-high learning. PTA Mag 58:14-16 Ja '64
Cuban doctor's decision. Redbook 120:46-7+ Mr '63
Housewives on campus: I feel alive again! McCalls 91:136-7+ N '63
Illiteracy: the key to poverty! McCalls 91: 96-7+ F '64
A man ain't nothin' but a man. Am Heritage 14:34-7+ O '63
Not like other children. Redbook 121:64-5+ O '63
What are Americans like? what are Russians like? Redbook 123:52-3+ O '64
Where can we go? what can we do? Redbook 122:52-3+ Mr '64
Where the jobs are. Ladies Home J 81:78+ Je '64
Wife, six children and no job. Redbook 121: 46-7+ Ag '63
ASBESTOS
Dangerous dust? Sci Am 211:64 D '64
ASBESTOSIS. See Diseases, Industrial
ASBRAND, Karin
Gold in your garden; drama. Plays 22:77-80 Mr '63
ASBURY, Beverly Allen
Minister. Nation 199:509-12 D 28 '64
ASBURY PARK, N.J.
Multi-purpose pavilion-bandstand. K. H. Lee. il Am City 78:157-8 Mr '63
ASBURY school of dancing, Houston. See Dance schools
ASCENSION ISLAND
Isotopic composition of lead and strontium from Ascension and Gough Islands. P. W. Gast and others. bibliog il Science 145:1181-5 S 11 '64
ASCH, Nathan
My father and I. Commentary 39:55-64 Ja '65
ASCH, Sholem
My father and I. M. Asch. Commentary 39: 55-64 Ja '65
ASCHER, Marcia
Computers in science fiction. bibliog f Harvard Bsns R 41:40-2+ N '63
—See Ascher, R. jt. auth.
ASCHER, Robert, and Ascher, Marcia
Recognizing the emergence of man. bibliog Science 147:243-50 Ja 15 '65
ASCHERSON, Neal
Young Germans. Holiday 36:78-83+ O '64
ASCLEPIAS curassavica. See Milkweed
ASCOLI, Max
Editorial. See issues of The reporter
This liberal magazine, 1964. Reporter 30: 12-14 My 7 '64
ASCORBIC acid. See Vitamins—Vitamin C
ASEPSIS and antisepsis
Germ-free isolators. P. C. Trexler. il Sci Am 211:78-80+ Jl '64
ASEPTIC surgery. See Surgery, Aseptic and antiseptic
ASEYEV, Yuri Alexeyevitch
Ordeal by defection. Newsweek 63:44+ Ap 20 '64
ASH, Lee
Opening the chambered nautilus. por Library J 89:2040-3 My 15 '64
Question of definition. por Library J 88:1617-20 Ap 15 '63

ASH, Lee—*Continued*
WLB biography (cont) Wilson Lib Bul 37: 598; 38:203, 410+, 875+; 39:268+, 422 Mr, O '63, Ja, Je, N '64, Ja '65
ASH, Michael
Fallout lollipops; A doctor tries to lick radiation. il pors Life 54:53-4+ F 8 '63
ASH, Roy
Appetite for the future. il por Time 82:104-8+ O 4 '63
ASH (tree)
How to prune your modesto ash. il Sunset 130:294 Ap '63
ASH, Volcanic. See Volcanic ash, tuff, etc.
ASH Wednesday
Value of ashes. Christian Cent 81:195 F 12 '64
ASHBAUGH, Byron L.
Welcome to another new center. Audubon Mag 66:15 Ja '64
ASHBERY, John
Art news from Paris. Art N 63:50-1 S; 48 N '64
Blessing in disguise; If the birds knew; Last month; Recent past; Civilization and its discontents; poems. Poetry 102:141-6 Je '63
ASHBROOK, John Milan
Not one word; Education and labor committee. por Time 81:26-7 Mr 8 '63
ASHBROOK, Joseph
Astronomical scrapbook. See issues of Sky and telescope
ASHBY, Eric
University presidency: what it takes. Sat R 47:58-9+ N 21 '64
ASHBY, Neal
New York's unrecognized park lands. Am For 69:12-15 Jl '63
Our smallest national forest. Am For 69: 30-1+ S '63
ASHBY, Philip H.
Pro-Sikh. Christian Cent 81:242 F 19 '64
ASHDOD
Original Philistines. il Horizon 6:40-1 Autumn '64
ASHE, Arthur, Jr
First Negro Davis cupper. il pors Ebony 18:151-2+ O '63
I'm simply me. il por Newsweek 64:53 S 7 '64
ASHEIM, Lester
As much to learn as to teach. por Library J 89:4465-8 N 15 '64
ASHER, Harry
They split my personality. Sat R 46:39-43 Je 1 '63
ASHES
See also
Volcanoes
ASHEVILLE, N.C.
Do-it-yourself program is best. G. Johnson. il Am City 78:103-4 Mr '63
ASHFORD, Douglas E.
Last revolution: community and nation in Africa; address, April 10, 1964; with questions and answers. bibliog f Ann Am Acad 354:33-45 Jl '64
ASHFORTH, Albert
Spokesman for Darwin, and for science. N Y Times Mag p64+ Ap 7 '63
When Pickwick went to Vanity fair. N Y Times Mag p8+ D 22 '63
ASHKENAZY, Vladimir
Family man. il por Newsweek 61:52 Ap 29 '63
Missing man. Newsweek 62:64 Jl 1 '63
Noted Soviet pianist to stay in West. Sr Schol 82:23-4 My 15 '63
Oh, Vladimir! oh, Malcolm! il por Time 81:46 Je 21 '63
Soviet virtuoso savors exile. il pors Life 54:71-2 My 17 '63
ASHLAND oil and refining company
Three-way oil deal waits on tax ruling; ABC deal. Bsns W p94+ F 9 '63
ASHLEY, Elizabeth
Elizabeth Ashley. il Vogue 143:158-61 F 1 '64
Star at odds with her career. il pors Life 57:87-8+ D 4 '64
Two in the center. il por Time 83:64-5 Mr 6 '64
ASHLEY, Roberta
My 365 most embarrassing moments. Redbook 121:28 My '63
ASHLEY, William Henry
Reading, writing, and history. B. Catton. Am Heritage 15:81-3 Je '64
ASHLOCK, Jules
Terror in the Cassiars. pors Outdoor Life 131: 52-5+ Ap '63
ASHMAN, R. F. and others
Intercellular electrical coupling at a forming membrane junction in a dividing cell. bibliog Science 145:604-5 Ag 7 '64
ASHMEAD, John
Man with only one suit; story. Harper 226: 65-72 Ap '63
ASHMORE, Harry Scott
Coming showdown in the race crisis. Look 27:62-7 Jl 16 '63
Desegregation decision. Sat R 47:68-70+ My 16 '64
Our footloose correspondents. J. Bainbridge. il New Yorker 39:105-6+ N 9 '63
ASHMORE, Robert Thomas
Ashmore seeks to label Court. Christian Cent 80:1458 N 27 '63
ASHTON, Dore
Miró Artigas; their new ceramics. Craft Horiz 24:24-33+ Ja '64
ASHTON, Enrico
Maddalena & Enrico; interview, ed. by F. Stevenson. por Opera N 29:16 D 12 '64
ASHTON-WARNER, Sylvia
In the beginning there is a key word. L. S. Mitchell. il por Sat R 46:45 O 5 '63
Putting life into learning. il por Time 82: 42+ S 6 '63
ASIA
See also
Agricultural administration—Asia
Cities and towns—Asia
Communism—Asia
Economic assistance in Asia
Education—Asia
Hindu Kush
Land tenure—Asia
Libraries—Asia
Opium trade
Publishers and publishing—Asia
Roads—Asia
Trade unions—Asia
United Nations—Asia
United Nations—Economic commission for Asia and the Far East
Women—Asia

Bibliography

Materials for teaching about Asia. S. Fersh. il Sr Schol 83:14T S 27 '63

Civilization

We may be rich but they are happy; transforming of prescientific communities. B. Ward. il N Y Times Mag p22-3+ My 5 '63

Description and travel

Asia A to Z, by R. S. Kane. Review
Travel il 121:53 Ja '64. K. Gardner

Economic conditions

Asian productivity development. Mo Labor R 86:302-4 Mr '63
Focus on Asia. il Sr Schol 83:40-1 O 4 '63
Hard struggle; United Nations report on non-Communist Asia. Time 84:80+ Ag 28 '64
Investment opportunities in Asia; address, September 29, 1964. D. E. Bell. Vital Speeches 31:61-4 N 1 '64
See also
Colombo plan

Economic policy

Economic progress in Asia; address, December 5, 1962. K. Okazaki. Vital Speeches 29:240-2 F 1 '63

Foreign relations

Australia's strategic position; address, January 25, 1964. R. Hilsman. Dept State Bul 50:243-50 F 17 '64

History

See also
Jenghiz Khan

Bibliography

Articles and other books received; east Asia, comp. by H. Conroy. See issues of American historical review
Articles and other books received; south Asia, comp. by C. Hobbs. See issues of American historical review

Maps

Map of Asia (cont) Sr Schol 83:32 O 4 '63; 85:36 O 7 '64

Nationalism

Rising Afro-Asian nations. U. A. Johnson. Dept State Bul 48:449-56 Mr 25 '63

Politics

Australia's strategic position; address, January 25, 1964. R. Hilsman. Dept State Bul 50:243-50 F 17 '64

ASIA—Politics—*Continued*
Challenge to freedom in Asia; address, June 14, 1963. R. W. Hilsman. Dept State Bul 49:43-50 Jl 8 '63
Focus on Asia. il Sr Schol 83:40-1 O 4 '63
Moscow, Peking and the Communist parties of Asia. R. A. Scalapino. For Affairs 41: 323-43 Ja '63
New Chinese adventuring threatens Asia. R. Hilsman, jr. il Nations Bsns 51:66-8 D '63
Progress and problems in east Asia: an American viewpoint; address, September 29, 1964. W. P. Bundy. Dept State Bul 51: 534-42 O 19 '64

Population

Asian population conference. F. C. Madigan. America 110:188-90 F 8 '64; Correction. 111: 202 Ag 29 '64

Religious institutions and affairs

See also
Church of England in Asia

ASIA, CENTRAL
See also
Afganistan

Description and travel

On ancient central Asian tracks, by A. Stein. Review
Sat R il 47:59 N 14 '64. W. O. Douglas

ASIA, SOUTHEASTERN
And now Maphilindo. Newsweek 61:63 Je 24 '63
Battle of time and the river. il Newsweek 62:36-8+ Jl 15 '63
Scrutable East, by R. Trumbull. Review
Sat R il 47:33-4 Je 20 '64. J. M. Allison
Secretary Rusk interviewed on Voice of America; ed. by R. L. Redeen. D. Rusk. Dept State Bul 50:330-6 Mr 2 '64
Situation remains fluid. J. Burnham. Nat R 14:530 Jl 2 '63
South and southeast Asia; symposium. bibliog f il Cur Hist 46:65-111+ F '64
Southeast Asian cockpit. J. Gange. Ann Am Acad 351:58-71 Ja '64
Year of the dragon. V. S. Kearney. America 110:226 F 15 '64
See also
Chinese in southeastern Asia
Communism—Asia, Southeastern
Food supply—Asia, Southeastern
Guerillas—Asia, Southeastern
Mekong River
United Nations—Asia, Southeastern
Water supply—Asia, Southeastern

Anecdotes, facetiae, satire, etc.

Who's who in Asia; certain verbal esprit de corps is discernible. J. A. Rose. New Repub 150:13-15 Ap 4 '64

Defenses

Drawing the line in southeast Asia. D. Warner. il Reporter 31:33-6 S 10 '64

Foreign relations

As the war in Asia gets hotter. il U S News 56:12 Je 29 '64
France's stake in South Asia. il U S News 56:64 Je 29 '64
Our stake in southeast Asia. P. Salinger. il Look 28:44+ O 20 '64
United States and southeast Asia; address, April 8, 1963. U. A. Johnson. Dept State Bul 48:635-41 Ap 29 '63

Maps

American special forces in action in Viet Nam. H. Sochurek. il Nat Geog Mag 127: 38-65, sup(folded map) Ja '65

Neutrality

De Gaulle on Vietnam. R. Steel. Commonweal 80:141-3 Ap 24 '64
If the war in Vietnam can't be won is neutralization an answer? il Newsweek 63: 44-5 F 17 '64
Listening to Sihanouk; neutralism. Newsweek 62:43-4 D 16 '63
Major crisis for Johnson: southeast Asia falling apart. il U S News 55:42-3 D 23 '63
Neutralists balloons. America 110:216-17 F 15 '64
Neutralization. Commonweal 79:584-5 F 14 '64

Politics

Circuses without bread. W. T. Thomas. Christian Cent 80:823 Je 26 '63
Eighth meeting of SEATO council of ministers; statement, April 8, 1963; with communique. D. Rusk. Dept State Bul 48:641-4 Ap 29 '63
Grave concern: holding the line in Asia. il Newsweek 63:39 Ap 27 '64
Indonesia: another Cuba? il Bsns W p59-60+ Ap 27 '63
Kennedy touch. Newsweek 63:36+ F 3 '64
Malaysia; a game of footsy in southeast Asia. D. Warner. New Repub 148:11-12 Mr 16 '63
Squeeze play on U.S. in Asia: the Mao-Sukarno axis. il U S News 56:72-4 My 18 '64
Stakes in southeast Asia; photographs. N Y Times Mag p 10-11 My 24 '64
Talking it over; Asian solutions to Asian problems. Newsweek 63:46 F 24 '64
Unfinished business: a neutral zone in southeastern Asia? D. Warner. New Repub 149: 17-20 D 7 '63
War in Asia. il Newsweek 63:24-30+ Je 8 '64
Which road for southeast Asia? T. Khoman. For Affairs 42:628-39 Jl '64
See also
Communism—Asia, Southeastern

ASIA, SOUTHERN
Religious strife: tear gas and daggers. il Newsweek 61:40 Je 17 '63
See also
Book industries and trade—Asia, Southern

ASIA, SOUTHWESTERN

Maps

Changing face of southwest Asia. Nat Geog Mag 123:662-3, sup(folded map) My '63

ASIA and the United States
Embattled neutralist on the Plaine des Jarres. C. J. V. Murphy. Fortune 69:160 My '64

ASIA MINOR
See also
Cappadocia

Antiquities

Assyrian trading outpost; Kanesh in Anatolia. T. Özgüç. il Sci Am 208:96-102+ bibliog (p 185) F '63
See also
Aphrodisias

History

See also
Hittites

ASIAD (games)
Politics makes strange sport; Jakarta games. Sports Illus 19:16 N 25 '63
Sukarno's lavish ganefo was mostly snafu. T. P. Ross. il Sports Illus 19:28-31 D 2 '63

ASIAN art. See Art, Asian

ASIAN flu. See Influenza

ASIAN games. See Asiad (games)

ASIAN writing. See Oriental languages—Writing

ASIANS
See also
Tankas

ASIANS in Africa
Asians in their midst. Time 81:44-5 Mr 15 '63
Exodus, 1963; Kenya's Asians and white settlers leaving. Newsweek 62:50 N 18 '63

ASIMOV, Isaac
Hello, CTA-21, is anyone there? N Y Times Mag p52+ N 29 '64
Quick and easy math; condensation. Pop Sci 185:77-83 D '64
Sword of Achilles. Bul Atomic Sci 19:17-18 N '63; Same with title SF: clue to creativity. Library J 89:914-17 F 15 '64
Views on science books. See issues of Horn book magazine
Visit to the World's fair of 2014. N Y Times Mag p20+ Ag 16 '64

ASIMOW, Morris
Backland's capitalism. por Time 84:66 Ag 14 '64

ASINOF, Eliot
Gambler's world series. Sat Eve Post 236: 72-4 N 30 '63

ASKARI, Amir
Erythrocytes: 5′-adenylic acid deaminase requirement for ammonia or monovalent metal ion. bibliog Science 141:44-5 Jl 5 '63

ASKE, Gladys
Tricks with ivy. Flower Grower 51:29 N '64

ASKEW, Richard Burton Marlowe
Fashion plates of Anaïs Toudouze. Antiques 85:575-7 My '64

ASKLIPIOS, pseud.
President's heart. Esquire 62:89-92 Ag '64

ASNIS, Al
Negative positive. See issues of U.S. camera to December 1963

ASOLO theatre comedy festival. See Drama festivals

ASPARAGUS
Some asparagus are just good looking. il Sunset 132:264+ Ap '64
See also
Cookery—Vegetables

ASPEN
Antimicrobial substances from aspen tissue grown in vitro. M. C. Mathes. bibliog il Science 140:1101-2 Je 7 '63

ASPEN, Colo.
Aspen's new silver lode. il Bsns W p30-1 Ja 25 '64

ASPEN airways
Skiers, tourists boost operations of third-level Colorado carrier. il Aviation W 78:45 F 11 '63

ASPEN award. See Aspen institute for humanistic studies

ASPEN festival of music and art. See Music festivals—Colorado

ASPEN film conference. See Moving picture industry—United States

ASPEN institute for humanistic studies
Aspen: a new day for the humanities. J. Scanlon. il Sat R 46:40-1+ D 21 '63; Reply. H. B. Rouse. 47:56 Ja 18 '64
Aspen summit conference. W. Von Eckardt. New Repub 151:31-2 Jl 25 '64
Bundle for Britten; Aspen award. A. Young. il Mus Am 84:18-19 S '64
High honor for a shy genius. T. Green. il Life 57:41-2 Ag 7 '64
On winning the first Aspen award; address. B. Britten. il Sat R 47:37-9+ Ag 22 '64
Rival for Nobel; Aspen award. Time 82:79 N 29 '63
Sunshine seminars; Institute for humanistic studies in Aspen, Colo. il Newsweek 64:48 Jl 27 '64

ASPEN international design conference. See International design conference

ASPEN music festival. See Music festivals—Colorado

ASPERGILLUS
Toxin from aspergillus flavus: production on food materials of a substance causing tremors in mice. B. J. Wilson and C. H. Wilson. bibliog Science 144:177-8 Ap 10 '64
Toxin-producing aspergillus isolated from domestic peanuts. U. L. Diener and others. bibliog il Science 142:1491-2 D 13 '63

ASPHALT
Asphalt eating bacteria help balance nature. Sci Digest 53:30 Mr '63
Weather control: use of asphalt coatings to tap solar energy. J. F. Black. il Science 139:226-7 Ja 18 '63

ASPHALT mulch. See Mulching

ASPHALT pavements. See Pavements, Asphalt

ASPHYXIA
Bilirubin: acute effects in newborn rhesus monkeys. R. E. Behrman and E. Hibbard. bibliog il Science 144:545-6 My 1 '64
Hypothermia, asphyxia, and cardiac glycogen in guinea pigs. J. A. Miller, jr. and others. bibliog il Science 144:1226-7 Je 5 '64
Neuropathology of certain forms of mental retardation; address, February 12, 1963. W. F. Windle. bibliog Science 140:1186-9 Je 14 '63

ASPHYXIATING gases. See Gases, Asphyxiating and poisonous

ASPINALL, Wayne Norviel
Congressman Aspinall vs. the people of the United States. P. Brooks. Harper 226:60-3 Mr '63
Should the outdoors be free? address. por Am For 70:32-4+ Ap '64

ASPINWALL, Alice
Trapped; poem. Christian Cent 80:1202 O 2 '63

ASPIRATION level
Study of aspirations. H. Cantril. il Sci Am 208:41-5 bibliog(p 184) F '63

ASPIRIN
Advertisers and the government missed the boat on the validity of aspirin advertising. Consumer Bul 46:36 My '63
Another note on children's aspirin. Consumer Rep 29:364 Ag '64
Aspirin. H. O. J. Collier. Sci Am 209:96-104+ bibliog(p 187) N '63
Aspirin heals, kills pain. Sci N L 86:13 Jl 4 '64
Candy aspirin; cause of child poisonings. Consumer Rep 29:121 Mr '64
Cause of bleeding due to aspirin discovered. Sci N L 84:281 N 2 '63
Rx: aspirin for Johnny; Bayer's aspirin for children. M. B. Keiser. il Parents Mag 39:12+ D '64
World's best is also the cheapest. il Time 83:68+ Ap 10 '64

ASPLENIUM nidus. See Bird's-nest ferns

ASPREY, L. B. and Penneman, R. A.
Protactinium fluorides, the new class, $MPaF_8$. bibliog Science 145:924 Ag 28 '64

ASROC (guided missile) See Guided missiles—Launching from ships

ASSASSINATION
After the party; murder of Q. Pholsena. Time 81:34 Ap 12 '63
Deed, by G. Frank. Review
Commentary 36:90-2 Jl '63. W. J. Dannhauser; Discussion. 37:6+ Ja '64
Flower potshot; third known attempt on de Gaulle's life. Newsweek 64:36+ S 14 '64
Imitators; post-Kennedy assassination threats of magnicide. il Newsweek 62:27 D 23 '63
Life & death in Jackson; M. Evers. il Time 81:17-18 Je 21 '63
Murder in Shangri-La; Prime Minister of Bhutan shot. Newsweek 63:58 Ap 20 '64
Perfect plan to kill de Gaulle. C. Plimmer and D. Plimmer. il Read Digest 82:101-6 Je '63
Target of assassin: strong man Nkrumah. U S News 56:19 Ja 13 '64
True or false? attempted assassination. il Newsweek 63:35 Ja 13 '64
See also
Kennedy, J. F.—Assassination
Presidents—United States—Assassinations

ASSATEAGUE ISLAND
Assateague Island National Seashore proposal. Nat Parks Mag 37:21 S '63
Assateague Island: our next national seashore? J. Martineau. il Am For 69:16-19+ Ag '63

ASSEMBLAGE. See Pictures

ASSEMBLY, Right of
Peaceably to assemble and petition; marches on the capital. il Newsweek 62:19 S 2 '63

ASSEMBLY line methods
Automation on the assembly line. H. E. Klein. il Duns R 84:37-8+ D '64
New power in automation. Time 83:65 Ja 31 '64
Squeezing ships out of an assembly plant; Gotaverken shipyard, Sweden. il Bsns W p60-2 F 8 '64
Versatile production line. il Duns R 83:pt2 119-20+ Mr '64
See also
Automation

ASSETS, Liquid. See Liquidity (economics)

ASSIMILATION (physiology) See Metabolism

ASSINIBOINE, MOUNT
Assiniboine pack trip. E. A. Bauer. il Field & S 68:29-31 F '64

ASSIUT university. See Colleges and universities—Egypt

ASSOCIATED booksellers of Great Britain and Ireland. See Booksellers association

ASSOCIATED church press (organization)
A.C.P. meets in Washington. Christian Cent 81:597 My 6 '64
New precedent. W. A. Geier. Christian Cent 80:594+ My 1 '63

ASSOCIATED colleges at Claremont
See also
Pitzer college

ASSOCIATED press
A.P.'s cliché hunt. Time 84:76 D 4 '64
Hail to the cliche; Associated press computer assesses use of clichés. R. L. Tobin. Sat R 48:65-6 Ja 9 '65
Quarterbacking a nation's news. J. F. Fixx. il Sat R 46:48-9 Ag 10 '63

ASSOCIATED testing laboratories, incorporated
Facility tests solids in environmental conditions. Miss & Roc 16:31 Ja 18 '65

ASSOCIATED transport, incorporated
You can make money at trucking. il Bsns W p 134+ F 16 '63

ASSOCIATES investment company
Where the money is. il Bsns W p56+ Ag 8 '64

ASSOCIATION and associations. See Associations

ASSOCIATION for childhood education international
Meeting. Sr Schol 82:1T+ My 15 '63
Meeting, 1964. il Sr Schol 84:1T+ My 1 '64

ASSOCIATION for school, college, and university staffing
Want a job? ASCUS. L. A. Eason. NEA J 52:53-4 D '63

ASSOCIATION for supervision and curriculum development
ASCD report. Sr Schol 83:2T D 6 '63
Current curriculum developments; with list of books. W. M. Alexander and H. Heffernan. NEA J 52:47-8 N '63
Meeting, 1963. il Sr Schol 82:1T-4T Ap 3 '63

ASSOCIATION for supervision and curriculum development—*Continued*
Meeting, 1964. Sr Schol 84:1T-2T My 1 '64
Statement on values; concerning document, Some intergroup factors influencing the teaching of American social values. Sr Schol 84:1T-2T My 8 '64
ASSOCIATION for the study of Negro life and history
Carter G. Woodson clubs; with list of institutional members. A. N. D. Brooks. Negro Hist Bul 26:180+ F '63
Detroit branch, ASNLH, launches $50,000 African art drive. A. D. Coar. il Negro Hist Bul 27:99-102 F '64
History and significance of Negro history week. M. Jackson. Negro Hist Bul 27:72+ D '63
History scholars at Petersburg; program of annual meeting. Negro Hist Bul 27:1-13 O '63
Negro historians convene in Detroit. Negro Hist Bul 28:21-2 O '64
Reflections: annual meeting. C. W. Thomas. il Negro Hist Bul 28:27-8 N '64
Why Negro history association? A. N. D. Brooks. Negro Hist Bul 27:189 My '64
ASSOCIATION of American colleges
Meetings, 1963-1964. W. W. Anderson. Sch & Soc 91:177 Ap 6 '63; 92:208-9, My 2 '64
ASSOCIATION of American railroads
New life on the tracks; American railway progress exposition. il Bsns W p 120-2+ O 19 '63
ASSOCIATION of American university presses
AAUP; new international moves, internal reorganization; symposium with editorial comment. il Pub W 186:26-47, 66 Jl 6 '64
AAUP; press management and world-wide interests are topics of meeting. il Pub W 184:30-54+ Jl 15 '63
AAUP production facts and figures needed for wise management. R. Kinney; W. C. Becker; W. Sloane. il Pub W 184:68-9+ Jl 1 '63
AAUP session scans problems of short-run scholarly books. il Pub W 184:76+ Jl 1 '63
AAUP trips to Asia and Africa to view scholarly publishing needs. Pub W 186:42-50 Jl 20 '64
Awareness of quality is theme of AAUP production discussions. il Pub W 186:110-12 Jl 6 '64
1963-64 in review. Pub W 185:91 Ja 20 '64; 187:90 Ja 18 '65
World opens up for scholarly publishing. C. Kerr. il Sat R 47:28-9 My 30 '64
ASSOCIATION of college admissions counselors
Admissions parley; 20th annual convention. Sr Schol 85:1T-2T O 28 '64
ASSOCIATION of college and research libraries
ACRL awards sixty-seven grants. Library J 89:829 F 15 '64
Negro college libraries and ACRL standards. E. J. Josey. bibliog il Library J 88:2989-96 S 1 '63
Prospecting in the West; Western Americana institute sponsored by the ACRL rare books section and RSD history section. G. D. McDonald. Library J 88:3021-2 S 1 '63
Richard K. Gardner to edit ALA-ACRL book selection journal. Library J 88:2653-4 Jl '63
Shortcomings of LAD; letter to the editor. R. E. Ellsworth. ALA Bul 57:692-3 S '63; Reply. H. S. Hacker. 57:1001 D '63; Rejoinder. 58:9 Ja '64

Rare books section

Strawberries & Linnaeus; institute on rare books in natural history, fifth annual conference of the rare book section of ACRL. W. J. Smith. Library J 89:2945-7 Ag '64; Reply. T. R. Buckman. 89:3898+ O 15 '64
ASSOCIATION of college representatives. See Association of college admissions counselors
ASSOCIATION of council secretaries
Association of council secretaries; annual conference. W. B. Cate. Christian Cent 80: 914-16 Jl 17 '63
ASSOCIATION of hospital and institution libraries
Bibliotherapy for mental health: subject of AHIL conference workshop. Library J 89:214 Ja 15 '64
ASSOCIATION of law schools
CLR grant to aid study of law school libraries. Library J 89:2306 Je 1 '64
ASSOCIATION of mental hospital chaplains
Healing community. Christian Cent 80:1043-4 Ag 28 '63
ASSOCIATION of producing artists
After the fall; Manhattan's Lincoln Center repertory theater. il Time 84:36 D 25 '64
APA at the Phoenix. R. Gilman. Commonweal 80:18 Mr 27 '64
Professional theatre at Ann Arbor. L. Cook. il Theatre Arts 47:29-31 Ag '63
ASSOCIATION of research libraries
Another chance for centralized cataloging; reprint. R. E. Ellsworth. il Library J 89:3105-7 S 1 '64
Association of research concentrates on centralized cataloging. J. Skipper. Library J 89:2953 Ag '64
Association of research libraries considers off-campus research needs. Library J 88: 3028-9 S 1 '63
Association of research libraries expands. ALA Bul 57:266 Mr '63
From the Library of Congress: union catalog of microfilms. E. Hamer and A. McCormick. ALA Bul 57:1017-19 D '63
LC and ARL announce plans for register of microfilms. Library J 88:4599-600 D 1 '63
National organization or a private club? E. Moon. Library J 88:1429 Ap 1 '63
New Farmington plan director appointed. Pub W 183:94 F 11 '63
Program for shared cataloging to be developed by ARL; committee, with Library of Congress. Library J 89:1046 Mr 1 '64
Sharing the cataloging load; planning committee of ARL with LC. Wilson Lib Bul 38:525+ Mr '64
ASSOCIATION of state foresters
None to go; identification of founders. il Am For 69:40 Mr '63
ASSOCIATION of the United States army
Sprint shape shown at AUSA meeting. J. Trainor. il Miss & Roc 15:11-12 N 23 '64
ASSOCIATION of urban universities
Meeting, 1962. N. P. Auburn. Sch & Soc 91: 73 F 9 '63
ASSOCIATION of western pulp and paper workers
First rebels on the labor front. W. S. Ellis. il Nation 200:8-10 Ja 4 '65; Reply with rejoinder. G. Derrickson. 200:inside cover+ Ja 25 '65
ASSOCIATIONS
Documentation activities of associations. M. F. Tauber. bibliog il Wilson Lib Bul 38:768-72 My '64
For inter-American understanding; Pan American societies in the United States. G. Meek. il Américas 15:27-34 Ag '63
Free to join and to meet. W. W. Van Alstyne. il PTA Mag 58:10-12 Ja '64
My struggle to be myself. il Good H 157: 10+ S '63
Unnecessary research institutes. D. Wolfle. Science 139:563 F 15 '63; Discussion. 140: 424+ Ap 26 '63
See also
Societies
Trade associations
ASSYRIAN antiquities. See Mesopotamia—Antiquities
ASSYRO-BABYLONIAN astronomy. See Astronomy, Assyro-Babylonian
ASTAXANTHIN. See Pigments (biology)
ASTER spinosus. See Asters
ASTEROIDS
Asteroid came close to earth during May; Betulia. il Sci N L 83:375 Je 15 '63
Asteroid due to make near-miss of earth. Sci N L 86:88 Ag 8 '64
Asteroids stir growing interest. D. M. Cole. il Miss & Roc 12:43+ F 25 '63
Kirkwood's gaps. il Sky & Tel 26:11 Jl '63
Near-miss by an asteroid; 1948 OA. Sky & Tel 28:70 Ag '64
New minor planet named Armisticia. Sci N L 84:313 N 16 '63
Newly named asteroids. Sky & Tel 26:323 D '63
Secular perturbations of asteroid Pallas. Sky & Tel 28:139 S '64
Three pygmy planets receive Yugoslav names. Sci N L 85:169 Mr 14 '64
Vesta is back. il Sky & Tel 28:48 Jl '64
Waiting for Betulia. New Yorker 39:29-30 My 18 '63
ASTERS
Acetylene ester from aster spinosus. J. C. Spitzer and C. Steelink. bibliog Science 146: 1460-1 D 11 '64
Asters; the prettiest of fall's flowers. M. J. Dietz. il Flower Grower 50:39 S '63
In many shades, fall asters. R. C. Hands. il Horticulture 41:558-9 N '63
Star performers in late summer garden: annual asters. P. H. Morris. il Horticulture 41:134-5 Mr '63
ASTHMA
Mary Beth and her road back; Children's asthma institute, Denver. V. Kelly. il Look 28:67-70 Ja 28 '64

ASTIER, Mary
Three sumac leaves; poem. Christian Cent 81:1302 O 21 '64
ASTILBES
Plumes that please. R. G. Miner. il Flower Grower 50:34-5 My '63
ASTIN, Alexander W.
Identification, motivation, and training of talented students; report. Sch & Soc 92:186-9 Ap 18 '64
Undergraduate institutions and the production of scientists. bibliog Science 141:334-8 Jl 26 '63
Weights and measures. Science 143:974+ F 28 '64
ASTOR, Brooke
No organized fun. Vogue 145:114-15+ Ja 15 '65
ASTOR, John Jacob, 1763-1848
Furs by Astor, by J. U. Terrell. Review
Time por 83:81+ Ja 3 '64
ASTOR, Nancy Witcher (Langhorne) viscountess
Ginger woman. pors Time 83:35 My 8 '64
My most unforgettable character. Attlee. il por Read Digest 85:81-5 O '64
Nancy: 1879-1964. por Newsweek 63:66 My 11 '64
ASTOR family
Britain's Cliveden set: back in the headlines. il U S News 55:64-5 Jl 15 '63
ASTOR torpedo. See Torpedoes
ASTRACHAN, Anthony
Visit to Dimeh. Reporter 31:37-8+ D 3 '64
ASTRAL body of a U.S. mail truck; story. See Herlihy, J. L.
ASTRO (space vehicle) See Space vehicles
ASTRO-ELECTRONICS division of RCA. See Radio corporation of America—Astro-Electronics division
ASTROLOGY
Astrology, by L. MacNeice. Review
Vogue 145:67 Ja 1 '65. J. Stafford
Fraud in your future? popularity of astrology in France. il Newsweek 64:56 S 14 '64
Onward and upward with the arts. H. Suyin. il New Yorker 39:38-40+ D 28 '63
Planets, palms, and numbers. H. Stackpole. il Mlle 60:50-1+ Ja '65
Quel est votre signe? French astrologers. il Time 85:32 Ja 15 '65
ASTRONAUTICS. See Space flight
ASTRONAUTS
America's astronauts on the moon by 1970? il U S News 56:15 Ap 27 '64
Astronaut and investor; Alan Shepard turns banker. U S News 55:16 N 4 '63
Astronauts may become artists. R. Hawkes. Miss & Roc 13:21 Jl 8 '63
Astronauts may include scientists. Miss & Roc 12:20 Ap 29 '63
Ayes and ears; two astronauts afflicted with inner ear troubles. il Newsweek 63:94-5 Ap 27 '64
Can an astronaut bail out and live? W. Von Braun. il Pop Sci 183:14+ S '63
Collier trophy award; astronauts in Project Mercury. B. Kocivar. il Look 27:141-4+ O 22 '63
Cult of the astronaut. Nation 196:499 Je 15 '63
First Negro astronaut candidate. L. Robinson. il Ebony 18:71+ Jl '63
Fourteen more astronauts: new and different. il Life 55:40 N 1 '63
Further on ethics. W. J. Coughlin. Miss & Roc 12:46 Je 10 '63
Good old days of space. L. Wainwright. Life 57:39 O 2 '64
Grissom, Young selected for Gemini crew. W. J. Normyle. Aviation W 80:38-9 Ap 20 '64
Long wait; with report by I. Goodwin. il Newsweek 62:54-5 S 2 '63
Mercury showed value of pilot in space. il Aviation W 79:197-204 Jl 22 '63
More honors for America's first spacemen. il U S News 55:8 O 21 '63
NASA seeks scientist-astronauts. Miss & Roc 15:21 O 26 '64
NASA space pilots assigned specialties. Aviation W 78:36 F 4 '63
Navy-NASA program may yield scientist astronauts. H. M. David. Miss & Roc 12:18 My 27 '63
New astronauts show strong academic backgrounds. W. Burkett. Miss & Roc 13:20 O 28 '63
New astronauts to provide manpower for three lunar landings. W. Burkett. Miss & Roc 13:32 S 30 '63
New astronauts will fly second Gemini. Aviation W 81:24 Ag 3 '64
New boys and old. il Newsweek 61:50-1 Mr 4 '63
New breed. il Newsweek 62:62 O 28 '63
Six astronauts picked for MOL; assignment to specialties planned. Aviation W 81:25 N 23 '64
Their families and own stories; symposium. il pors Life 55:39+ S 27 '63
Twenty-seven astronauts monitor specialized fields. Aviation W 81:51 N 23 '64
Two more Soviet astronauts. R. N. Watts, jr. Sky & Tel 26:76 Ag '63
USAF astronauts given ten-part physical. Aviation W 81:80 N 23 '64
U.S. seeks scientist-astronauts. Aviation W 81:29 O 26 '64
See also
Bykovskii, V. F.
Cooper, G.
Space flight—Manned flights
Women as astronauts

Clothing

Air-conditioned suit; SCAPE suit. il Sci Digest 56:inside back cover Ag '64
Annals of business; trade secrets in development of space suits issue in Goodrich vs D. W. Wohlgemuth case. J. Brooks. New Yorker 39:37-8+ Ja 11 '64
Coverall seen as best thermal protector. il Aviation W 81:72-3 N 23 '64
Eight Gemini astronaut suits begun. W. Burkett. Miss & Roc 14:31 My 25 '64
First photos show Gemini, Apollo space suit details. il Aviation W 78:54 Ja 21 '63
Hamilton standard starting manned tests of advanced Apollo suit design prototypes. D. E. Fink. il Aviation W 79:48-9+ O 28 '63
Man in the moon suit. T. Alexander. il Esquire 60:104-5+ N '63
MSC begins testing reliability of water-cooled Apollo space suit. W. Burkett. Miss & Roc 14:28 Je 22 '64
More armor suggested for moon spacesuits. Sci N L 85:99 F 15 '64
Myoelectric servo control is developed. B. Miller. il Aviation W 78:69-70+ Mr 25 '63
NASA considering Litton-developed hard-shell suit for explorations. H. M. David. il Miss & Roc 15:22-3 Ag 24 '64
New type of spacesuit may be needed for MOL astronauts. H. M. David. Miss & Roc 15:22 D 7 '64
Soviets reported improving space suits. C. Brownlow. Aviation W 79:33 O 14 '63
Spacesuit air is thinner than atop Mt Everest. Sci N L 86:376 D 12 '64
Suit cooling system cuts sweat rate. H. M. David. Miss & Roc 15:28 N 2 '64
Suited for a vacuum. il Time 83:51 Ja 24 '64
Tests of Gemini suits conducted by army. il Aviation W 81:79 N 23 '64
Unique lava tests show need for Apollo suit changes. Miss & Roc 15:19 S 14 '64
U.S. astronauts could fly without space suits. Sci N L 86:259 O 24 '64
Water-cooled underwear designed for Apollo crew. il Aviation W 81:71 Jl 20 '64

Testing

Device will test space suit performance. W. Wright. il Aviation W 78:104-5 Mr 18 '63

Publicity

Astronauts' million-dollar deal; with interview with J. H. Glenn. il U S News 55:76-8 S 30 '63
Fame and wealth for astronauts? pro and con discussion. il Sr Schol 83:10-11 N 15 '63
Fringe benefit from space. Time 82:40 S 27 '63
New astronauts to provide manpower for three lunar landings. W. Burkett. Miss & Roc 13:32 S 30 '63
New firms seek astronaut story rights. A. P. Alibrando. Aviation W 79:28-9 Jl 15 '63
Publisher drops offer for astronauts' stories. Pub W 184:28 Jl 22 '63
Scrubbed on the pad; concerning publicizing personal stories of astronauts. Time 82:40 Jl 19 '63

Salaries

Fame and wealth for astronauts? pro and con discussion. il Sr Schol 83:10-11 N 15 '63
U.S. astronauts: too much money, or not enough? il U S News 54:22 Je 10 '63

Training

Air force investigating cardiovascular effects of zero-g. H. David. Miss & Roc 14:21 Mr 2 '64
AF pilots far exceed expected performance in military experiment; at GE Valley Forge space station simulation facility. H. M. David. Miss & Roc 15:26+ S 7 '64

ASTRONAUTS—Training—*Continued*
Astronaut man of vision. L. Levy. Sci N L 83:101 F 16 '63
Astronaut proficiency plan proposed. Miss & Roc 13:35-6 S 9 '63
Astronauts trained in Gemini water egress. il Aviation W 80:39 Mr 9 '64
Astronauts trained to be more than pilots. il Aviation W 79:263-5+ Jl 22 '63
Crew-monitoring to have station priority. W. J. Normyle. Aviation W 81:71+ D 21 '64
Head over heels for what's out there; with photographs by R. Morse. Life 55:30-8 S 27 '63
MOL test subjects experience mild bends. Aviation W 80:21 Mr 30 '64
Making of an astronaut. R. R. Gilruth. il Nat Geog Mag 127:122-44 Ja '65
NASA plans boot camp; training programs for scientist-astronauts. Sci N L 85:309 My 16 '64
Russians using devil's chair in training for space missions. Aviation W 80:37 Mr 2 '64
Scientists, engineers seek roles in space. il Aviation W 81:48-9+ N 23 '64
Scientists walk on walls. il Sci N L 85:213 Ap 4 '64
Space test volunteers all develop anemia. Sci N L 83:296 My 11 '63
Trainer to simulate Gemini mission. W. Beller. il Miss & Roc 12:24-5 Ap 1 '63
USAF modifies astronaut training. Aviation W 78:65 Ap 8 '63
USAF school trains future space pilots; Aerospace research pilot school. il Aviation W 79:253+ Jl 22 '63

ASTRONAUTS ejection seats, capsules, etc. See Space vehicles—Escape devices

ASTRONOMERS
Serendipity in astronomy. J. B. Irwin. il Sky & Tel 28:192-5 O '64
Spiral galaxy of astronomers. O. Gingerich. il Sky & Tel 25:132-4 Mr '63

ASTRONOMERS, Amateur
Amateur astronomers. See issues of Sky and telescope
Amateur astronomy at Sacramento. N. Leonard and M. C. Rohrke. il Sky & Tel 25:82+ F '63
Gleanings for ATM's: ed. by R. Cox. See issues of Sky and telescope
Hawaiian amateur in the Arctic. M. J. Morrow. il Sky & Tel 26:88-9 Ag '63
Here and there with amateurs (cont) Sky & Tel 26:208-13; 28:220-5 O '63, O '64
Popular astronomy in Germany. G. D. Roth. il Sky & Tel 27:8-11 Ja '64
Seven amateur observatories. il Sky & Tel 28:134-7 S '64
See also
National amateur astronomers convention

ASTRONOMICAL clocks
Spilhaus space clock. L. W. Slaughter. il Hobbies 69:50-1+ Ag '64

ASTRONOMICAL conferences
Dallas conference on super radio sources. L. C. Green. il Sky & Tel 27:80-4 F '64
Solar symposium at Sydney. M. Minnaert. il Sky & Tel 27:151-3 Mr '64

ASTRONOMICAL distances
Astronomical constants; studies of working group of the International astronomical union. il Sky & Tel 29:19-21 Ja '65
See also
Stars—Distance

ASTRONOMICAL globes. See Globes, Astronomical

ASTRONOMICAL instruments
Exhibit notes from Hamburg; IAU exhibit. il Sky & Tel 28:272-3 N '64
Optical astronomy's instrumental needs. Sky & Tel 25:67 F '63
Star's size measured; dimensions of Vega. A. Ewing. Sci N L 85:195 Mr 28 '64
See also
Coronagraph
Interferometers
Radio telescope
Spectrograph
Telescope

ASTRONOMICAL league
Astronomical league convention is great success; Orono, Me. il Sky & Tel 26:144-6 S '63

ASTRONOMICAL measurements
Astronomical constants; studies of working group of the International astronomical union. il Sky & Tel 29:19-21 Ja '65
Most accurate measurement of Mercury. Time 81:59 Je 7 '63
New dimensions for the stars. il Time 83:48 Ap 3 '64
Star's size measured; dimensions of Vega. A. Ewing. Sci N L 85:195 Mr 28 '64
Vega's angular size measured. Sky & Tel 27:348 Je '64

ASTRONOMICAL models
See also
Globes. Astronomical
Planetariums

ASTRONOMICAL observations. See Astronomy—Observations

ASTRONOMICAL observatories
Astronomers assemble in Arizona. il Sky & Tel 25:312-15 Je '63
California's new Stony Ridge observatory. J. J. Terlep. il Sky & Tel 26:248-50 N '63
Large radio telescope of Ohio state university. J. D. Kraus. il Sky & Tel 26:12-16 Jl '63
Lindheimer astronomical research center. J. A. Hynek. il Sky & Tel 28:216-18 O '64
On top of Arizona's Kitt Peak. il Sunset 130:87 Ap '63
Schoonover public observatory; Lima, Ohio. E. E. Lhamon. il Sky & Tel 28:356-7 D '64
Seven amateur observatories. il Sky & Tel 28:134-7 S '64
Summer at Maria Mitchell observatory. D. Hoffleit. il Sky & Tel 27:274-5 My '64

Australia

International discussion of Milky way research; Mount Stromlo observatory. B. J. Bok. il Sky & Tel 26:4-7 Jl '63
Stellar interferometer at Narrabri observatory. R. H. Brown. il Sky & Tel 28:64-9 Ag '64

Chile

European southern observatory. Sky & Tel 28:259+ N '64

Estonia

Crucial years of Wilhelm Struve; Dorpat observatory. J. Ashbrook. il Sky & Tel 25:326-7 Je '63

France

First lady of French astronomy; Juvisy observatory. F. Baldet. il Sky & Tel 25:77 F '63

Germany (Democratic Republic)

Visiting Germany's largest telescope; Karl Schwarzschild observatory. S. Van Den Bergh. il Sky & Tel 27:268-72 My '64

Germany (Federal Republic)

Bamburg search for bright variable stars. W. Strohmeier. il Sky & Tel 26:264-5 N '63

Great Britain

Airy regime at Greenwich. J. Ashbrook. il Sky & Tel 27:342-3 Je '64

India

Astronomy's past preserved at Jaipur. D. J. de S. Price. il Natur Hist 73:48-53 Je '64
Great observatory at Delhi. il Sunset 133:48+ S '64

Puerto Rico

Arecibo ionospheric observatory. W. E. Gordon. bibliog il Science 146:26-30 O 2 '64
Arecibo observatory in Puerto Rico. il(p313) Sky & Tel 26:315+ D '63
Giant radio probe is sizing up Venus; Arecibo ionospheric observatory. il Bsns W p48+ Mr 14 '64
Observatory in Puerto Rico will far surpass existing big dishes; Arecibo ionospheric observatory. C. L. LaFond. il Miss & Roc 13:24-5 N 11 '63
Some current programs at Arecibo. C. A. Federer. il Sky & Tel 28:4-8, 73-7 Jl-Ag '64
Space explorers build their dream telescope; radio-radar telescope at Arecibo. il Fortune 70:127-9 Ag '64

ASTRONOMICAL photography
Astronomical photography with the new XR film. W. P. Boquist. il Sky & Tel 27:12-14 Ja '64
Automatic measurement of star photographs. il Sky & Tel 27:286 My '64
Balloon observations during the July eclipse. E. P. Ney. il Sky & Tel 26:251-4 N '63
Cameras to monitor entries of meteors. Aviation W 78:61 Ja 21 '63
Catch a falling star? B. Hering. il Pop Sci 183:118-21+ N '63
Color in astrophotography. G. T. Keene. il Sky & Tel 26:74-6 Ag '63
Easy ways to photograph the moon. M. Banister. il Sky & Tel 27:122-3 F '64
Eclipse films and slides available. Sky & Tel 26:247+ N '63
Eclipse outside totality. il Sky & Tel 26:140-3 S '63
Eclipse talk, air and ground. L. J. Robinson. il Sky & Tel 26:200-3 O '63
Experiences with cooled color emulsions. A. A. Hoag. il Sky & Tel 28:332-4 D '64

ASTRONOMICAL photography—*Continued*
High-resolution photography. T. Pope and T. Osypowski. il Sky & Tel 29:52-6 Ja '65
Huge galactic explosion; photographing of M-82. il(p209) Sci N L 84:215 O 5 '63
Image orthicon astronomy. J. A. Hynek and J. R. Dunlap. il Sky & Tel 28:126-30 S '64
Measuring the earth's shadow. J. Ashbrook. il Sky & Tel 27:156-60 Mr '64
Monochromatic photographs of the Orion nebula. W. A. Feibelman. il Sky & Tel 27:154-5 Mr '64
New look in eclipses. H. Keppler. il Mod Phot 27:93 N '63
Photographic record of Venus. G. A. T. Heillegger. il Sky & Tel 25:99 F '63
Photographing July's solar eclipse. P. A. Leavens. il Sky & Tel 25:216-19 Ap '63
Remarkable eclipse of the moon. il Sky & Tel 27:142-6 Mr '64
Reminiscences of E. C. Slipher. R. S. Richardson. il Sky & Tel 28:208-9 O '64
Sharper moon photographs. il Sky & Tel 26:196 O '63
Shoot the solar eclipse! P. A. Leavens. il U S Camera 26:42-3 Jl '63
Speedy film to explore fine details on moon. Sci N L 84:72 Ag 3 '63
Star-field photography with a stationary camera. S. A. Walther. il Sky & Tel 28:314-16 N '64
Stratoscope II: sky-high and starry-eyed. R. Gannon. il Pop Sci 182:86-90+ F '63
Sunspot and granulation photography at Sacramento Peak. P. S. McIntosh. il Sky & Tel 27:280-2 My '64
Unusual lunar halo photograph. il Sky & Tel 27:335 Je '64
Venus diameter. il Sky & Tel 26:199 O '63
See also
Coronagraph

ASTRONOMICAL photometry. See Photometry, Astronomical

ASTRONOMICAL research
B stars and galactic exploration. R. M. Petrie. il Sky & Tel 26:330-4 D '63
Ground-based astronomy: a ten-year program; summary of report. Science 146:1641-8 D 25 '64
1963-1964 science review. il(p385) Sci N L 84:389; 86:389-90 D 21 '63, D 19 '64
Soviet aims in astronomy and space research; reprint. B. Lovell. Bul Atomic Sci 19:36-9 O '63
West Ford dipole belt: optical detection at Palomar. A. Sandage and C. Kowal. il Science 141:797-8 Ag 30 '63
West Ford dipole belt: photometric observations. W. G. Tifft and others. il Science 141:798-9 Ag 30 '63
See also
Artificial satellites—Astronomical applications

ASTRONOMICAL societies
See also names of astronomical societies, e.g. International astronomical union

ASTRONOMY
Astronomy. See issues of Science news letter
Decade astronomy plan. A. Ewing. Sci N L 86:357 D 5 '64
Give them something to hold onto; star gazing for children. E. F. Hunter. il Parents Mag 39:36-7+ D '64
Ground-based astronomy: a ten-year program; summary of report. Science 146:1641-8 D 25 '64
Long-range planning for American astronomy. il Sky & Tel 29:3+ Ja '65
Serendipity in astronomy. J. B. Irwin. il Sky & Tel 28:192-5 O '64
Space astronomy; summary of address. L. Goldberg. il Sky & Tel 28:264-6 N '64
Triennial review of astronomy; report on twelfth general assembly of the International astronomical union. V. K. McElheny. bibliog il Science 146:627-30 O 30 '64
See also
Comets
Eclipses, Solar
Ether (of space)
Galactic systems
Life on other planets
Meteors
Nebulae
Occulations
Planets
Radar in astronomy
Radio astronomy
Spectrum analysis
Tides
Universe

Bibliography

Books and the sky. See issues of Sky and telescope
Books in review; oldest science updated. J. S. Pickering. Natur Hist 74:6+ Ja '65

Charts, diagrams, etc.

Sky reporter. S. D. Gossner. See issues of Natural history incorporating Nature magazine to December 1963
Sky reporter. T. D. Nicholson. See issues of Natural history incorporating Nature magazine beginning January 1964
Southern stars. See issues of Sky and telescope
Star charts of former days. G. Lovi. il Sky & Tel 27:222-5 Ap '64
Stars for [the month] See issues of Sky and telescope
Understanding the main-sequence stars; Hertzsprung-Russell diagram. S. S. Huang. il Sky & Tel 25:136-8 Mr '63

Exhibitions

Exhibit notes from Hamburg; IAU exhibit. il Sky & Tel 28:272-3 N '64

History

Astronomy of the 20th century. by O. Struve and V. Zebergs. Review
Natur Hist 72:4-6 Ag '63. T. D. Nicholson
Double stars of Christian Mayer. J. Ashbrook. il Sky & Tel 25:75-6 F '63
Galileo Galilei; a new vision of the universe. C. Maccagni. il UNESCO Courier 17:24-5+ My '64
Galileo Galilei, 1564-1642. C. A. Ronan. il Sky & Tel 27:72-8 F '64
Phoenix of astronomers: T. Brahe. C. A. Ronan. il Natur Hist 74:52-7 Ja '65
Recent findings about early solar system history. S. S. Huang. il Sky & Tel 28:13-15 Jl '64
Serendipity in astronomy. J. B. Irwin. il Sky & Tel 28:192-5 O '64
Some astronomical anniversaries. Sky & Tel 29:15 Ja '65
Spiral galaxy of astronomers. O. Gingerich. il Sky & Tel 25:132-4 Mr '63

Observations

Astronomical constants; studies of working group of the International astronomical union. il Sky & Tel 29:19-21 Ja '65
Coleridge's star within the moon. J. Ashbrook. Sky & Tel 28:335 D '64
Tape-recorder timing of astronomical observations. C. D. Geilker. il Sky & Tel 27:314-15 My '64
See also
Planets—Observations

Study and teaching

Laboratory exercises in astronomy, spectral classification; Henry Draper catalogue. O. Gingerich. il Sky & Tel 28:80-2 Ag '64
Summer at Maria Mitchell observatory. D. Hoffleit. il Sky & Tel 27:274-5 My '64
See also
Planetariums

Tables, etc.

Graphic time table of the heavens, 1964-1965. Sky & Tel 27:32-5; 29:33-5 Ja '64, Ja '65

ASTRONOMY, Assyro-Babylonian
First astronomers of China & Babylon; excerpt from History of mankind. L. Woolley. il UNESCO Courier 16:16-17 Je '63

ASTRONOMY, Chinese
First astronomers of China & Babylon; excerpt from History of mankind. L. Woolley. il UNESCO Courier 16:16-17 Je '63

ASTRONOMY, Spherical and practical
See also
Aberration (optics)

ASTRONOMY as a profession

Anecdotes, facetiae, satire, etc.

Littlest astronomer. B. T. Lynds; F. D. Drake. Science 141:594, 861 Ag 16, S 6 '63

ASTROPHOTOGRAPHY. See Astronomical photography

ASTROPHYSICS
See also
Magnetic field (cosmic physics)

ASTROROBOTS. See Automatons

ASTURIAS, Miguel Angel
Poetry of protest. J. Yglesias. Nation 198:376-7 Ap 13 '64

ASWAN HIGH DAM
Atlantic report. Atlan 211:36+ My '63
Dam the Nile, full speed astern; with photographs by D. Steffan. A. Chamberlin. Sat Eve Post 237:73-7 Je 6 '64

ASWAN HIGH DAM—*Continued*
Exodus from Nubia. il Time 82:22+ D 20 '63
Gods, men & the river. il Time 83:30-40 My 22 '64
Harnessing the flow of centuries; with report by H. Moffett. il Life 56:32-40D My 22 '64
Hero of Aswan. il Fortune 70:61+ Ag '64
New Nile. il UNESCO Courier 17:34-5 Jl '64
No U.S. funds for Nile temples? il U S News 56:10 My 18 '64
Pharaoh & the flood. il Time 81:68 Ap 12 '63
Russian job that's on schedule; Nasser's High Dam. J. Law. il U S News 56:82-5 Mr 23 '64
Threatened treasures of the Nile. G. Gerster. il Nat Geog Mag 124:586-621 O '63
Why the Aswan Dam may dry up the Nile. W. Cloud. Pop Sci 185:19 S '64

ASYLUM, Right of
Asylum, too, is a human right. Nat R 15:93 Ag 13 '63
Deported first. Sr Schol 83:7 S 20 '63
Men who came to dinner; Cardoso brothers in Buenos Aires. il Time 82:43 Jl 12 '63

AT a bar in Charlotte Amalie; story. See Updike, J.

AT Lake Lugano; story. See Michal, M.

AT the marketplace; story. See Gippner, E.

AT the Sea-Vue arms; story. See Rogin, G.

AT the table cookery. See Cookery

AT the window; story. See O'Hara, J.

ATACAMA DESERT
Oases in the Atacama Desert. S. Reyes. il Américas 15:10-16 S '63

ATATURK, Mustafa Kemal. See Kemal Ataturk, M.

ATCHAFALAYA RIVER
Death on the Atchafalaya. J. Ridgeway. New Repub 150:13-14 Ap 25 '64

ATCHESON, Richard
Can a chipmunk teach the new math on TV? Sat Eve Post 238:26-7 Ja 16 '65
Steve Lawrence, a guy from Brooklyn. Sat Eve Post 237:30-1 Je 27 '64

ATGET, Eugène
Paris, past perfect; photographs. N Y Times Mag p54-5 N 29 '64

about

Paris, past perfect. por N Y Times Mag p54-5 N 29 '64
Some Atget Paris pictures. R. Hattersley. Pop Phot 55:24+ O '64
Steichen, Atget. il Newsweek 62:100-1 N 4 '63

ATHABASCA oil sands. See Bituminous sand

ATHANAS, Verne
Twice-blessed family; story. Good H 156:74-5 Ap '63

ATHAY, R. Grant
Challenge of chromospheric physics. bibliog Science 143:1129-38 Mr 13 '64

ATHEISM
Atheism in our time, by I. Lepp. Review Time 82:60 Jl 19 '63
Charles Bradlaugh and the secularists. W. S. Smith. Christian Cent 80:331-4 Mr 13 '63
Christmas and the world. J. V. Schall. Commonweal 79:389-92 D 27 '63
Church and atheists. I. Lepp. il Commonweal 81:88-90 O 16 '64
Freedom of atheism. America 110:355 Mr 21 '64
Most hated woman in America: M. Murray. J. Howard. il Life 56:91-2+ Je 19 '64
New dimension in scientific atheism. R. H. Marshall, jr. il Cath World 199:238-44 Jl '64
Soviet atheist's Sputnik; Atheist's companion. D. A. Lowrie. Christian Cent 80:177-9 F 6 '63

ATHENAGORAS I, patriarch
Descendant of St Andrew. il por Time 83:39 Ja 10 '64
Kiss of peace. il por Newsweek 63:76 Ja 20 '64
Ordeal in the Phanar. B. Thompson. Christian Cent 82:72 Ja 20 '65
Pope meets Patriarch. il Time 83:58 Ja 3 '64
Seed planted. il Time 83:36-41 Ja 17 '64

ATHENS, Ga.

Recreation

Dedicated to youth. D. L. Dugan. Recreation 57:190 Ap '64

ATHENS, Greece
Golden age of Athens. il Life 54:60-73 Mr 8 '63
Rough map of Greece: Athens by moonlight. P. L. Adams. il Atlan 214:71-4 Ag '64; Reply. L. Turnbull. 214:50 N '64
See also
Parthenon

Art

Athens; her golden past still lights the world. K. F. Weaver. il Nat Geog Mag 124:100-37 Jl '63

Description

Athens; her golden past still lights the world. K. F. Weaver. il Nat Geog Mag 124:100-37 Jl '63
Travel notes. R. Joseph. Esquire 61:29-30+ Je '64

Hotels, restaurants, etc.

Athens Hilton: a study in vandalism. V. Scully. il Arch Forum 119:100-3 Jl '63
Let's travel to Europe; Hilton hotel. il Mlle 57:156-8 O '63

ATHEROSCLEROSIS. See Arteriosclerosis

ATHILL, Diana
On the edge of oasis. Sat R 46:43 Mr 23 '63

ATHLETES
Athletes get help from hypnotists. D. Moser. il Life 54:71-2+ Je 7 '63
Champions who gave the year its flavor; photographs. Sports Illus 20:30-40 Ja 6 '64
Cold meet; U.S.—U.S.S.R. track and field meet. il Newsweek 64:52 Ag 3 '64
Do professional sports set a good example for our kids? T. B. Quigley. Todays Health 42:16+ O '64
Flat-out to make the U.S. team for Tokyo. il Life 57:34D-34F Jl 17 '64
Four wild days and nights at Yale; AAU championships. R. Lardner. il Sports Illus 18:67 Ap 1 '63
From faraway places; XVIII Olympic games. il Sports Illus 21:42-55 O 5 '64
How they row in Ratzeburg. R. Lardner. il Sports Illus 18:56+ My 20 '63
International ski scandal; with editorial comment. J. Lovesey. il Sports Illus 19:9, 16-17+ D 16 '63
Life guide; Olympic hopefuls and where to see them. il Life 56:17 F 21 '64
Lonely champions quest for Olympic gold; America's Olympic torchbearers. R. Daley. il Sat Eve Post 237:66-73 O 10 '64
Most phenomenal athletes in history. I. Wolfert. Read Digest 85:151-4 O '64
On to Tokyo; American Olympic candidates. il Newsweek 63:58-9 Mr 23 '64
Over the first big hurdle on a golden trail; US Olympic team. J. Underwood. il Sports Illus 21:16-19 Jl 13 '64
Predictable glories and grand surprises; 1964 athletic drama. il Sports Illus 21:30-1 D 21 '64
Raves for the young; US vs USSR track meet in Los Angeles. J. Underwood. il Sports Illus 21:8-13 Ag 3 '64
Rhythm: transocean and land; affect on athletes. Sports Illus 19:20+ N 25 '63
Slight blow for extremism in sport's cold war; U.S. vs Russia in Los Angeles. D. Bank. il Sports Illus 21:46-7 Jl 27 '64
Tokyo games; Orient's first Olympiad. J. Underwood. il Sports Illus 21:34-6+ O 5 '64
Tokyo, Tokyo, Tokyo; American Olympic team. il Newsweek 64:80 Jl 13 '64
We win the five and ten. J. Underwood. il Sports Illus 21:20-31 O 26 '64
Well-fed men not soft. Sci N L 83:388 Je 22 '63
What makes the athlete run? excerpt from address. R. G. Bannister. il UNESCO Courier 17:10-19 Ja '64
Wild world of European sports. R. Daley. il Sat Eve Post 236:60-1 F 16 '63
Yang of China is world's best athlete. T. Maule. il Sports Illus 18:26-7+ My 6 '63
See also
Amateurism (sports)
Basketball players
Football players

Recruiting

Catch a rising star. il Newsweek 61:64 My 20 '63
High-heeled recruiter and a mama's boy. M. Stuhldreher. il Sports Illus 19:72-6 S 23 '63
Mr Big of the bonus baby war. il Life 58:56D-57 Ja 15 '65
Mossie Murphy's crusade. M. Cope. il Sports Illus 18:18-20+ Ja 28 '63
Why scandals afflict sport; Purdue and Indiana accused of illegal recruiting practices. Sports Illus 18:8 Ap 29 '63
See also
Basketball players—Recruiting

Salaries

Burden of proof; Del Shofner gets $175,000, possibly the biggest bonus ever paid to a baseball rookie. il Time 84:70-1 Jl 3 '64

ATHLETES—Salaries—*Continued*
200 grand kid; R. Reichardt. il Life 57:85-7 Jl 10 '64
Training
All-out agony at Indiana U. il Life 56:94-6 Ap 10 '64
Dingy, sprightly home of the good ones; Fifth street gym in Miami Beach. T. Maule. il Sports Illus 20:70-2+ Ap 6 '64
ATHLETES, Negro. See Negro athletes
ATHLETES, Women. See Women as athletes
ATHLETIC clubs
Payoff in Detroit; Detroit athletic club annual election. Newsweek 65:58+ F 1 '65
ATHLETIC scholarships and fellowships. See Scholarships and fellowships
ATHLETICS
Most phenomenal athletes in history. L Wolfert. Read Digest 85:151-4 O '64
Old frontier sets an athletic pace; Britain's bankers athletics programs. il Bsns W p30-1 Ap 6 '63
See also
Athletes
Gymnastics
Olympic games
Sports
Sportsmanship
Track athletics
Winter sports
ATHLONE, Ireland
Very heart of Ireland. il Sunset 134:22+ Ja '65
ATHOS, MOUNT
Hiking the Holy Mountain. D. M. Doren. il Sat R 47:44-6+ Mr 14 '64
Orthodoxy; state of the faith. il Time 82:40-9 Jl 5 '63
World without women. W. J. Granberg. il Travel 122:36-9 Jl '64
ATKESON, Ray
Pacific Northwest. U S Camera 27:70-1+ My '64
ATKIN, John
Great American sailboats; Island Princess. il Motor B 112:28-9+ Ag '63
Little Maid of Kent, in steel! Motor B 113: 35-6 Mr '64
Yum Yum; an inboard utility boat. il Motor B 114:52-3+ O '64
ATKINS, C. E.
Latest advances in touch control. Electr World 69:34-7+ My '63
Novel electrometer tube. Electr World 70: 44-5 O '63
ATKINS, Elisha, and others
Endogenous pyrogen release from rabbit blood cells incubated in vitro with parainfluenza virus. bibliog Science 146: 1469-70 D 11 '64
ATKINS, Ollie
Queen wins the heart of New Zealand. il Sat Eve Post 236:26-9 Ap 27 '63
(ed) See Salinger, P. Photography in the White House
ATKINS, Thomas V.
Unfreedom of Polish writers. New Repub 151: 6-7 O 31 '64
ATKINSON, Alex
By rocking chair across Spain. Holiday 34: 70-4+ S '63
ATKINSON, J. H. See Kadlec, J. E. jt. auth.
ATKINSON, James D.
Dimensions of war. Nat R 14:324-5 Ap 23 '63
ATKINSON, Robert E.
Bonsai in one day. Flower Grower 50:50-4 O '63
California poppies; new unusual colors. Horticulture 42:30 F '64
Dwarf citrus. Flower Grower 51:16-17 D '64
Rex begonias. Horticulture 41:623 D '63
West Coast pointers. See issues of Flower grower
ATKINSON, William C.
Sky during totality. Sky & Tel 25:205 Ap '63
ATL, Dr. See Murillo, G.
ATLANTA
Too busy to hate. K. Haselden. Christian Cent 80:392-3 Mr 27 '63
Airports
Atlanta, Miami share concepts, problems. R. H. Cook. il Aviation W 79:47+ Ag 5 '63
Architecture
Circular bank for a traffic island. il Arch Rec 135:120-1 Ja '64
Crisp steel and brick in Georgia. il Arch Forum 119:102-3 O '63
Offices for narrow urban site; Northwestern mutual insurance building. il Arch Rec 136: 158-9 D '64
Churches
Votes to admit Negroes; First Baptist church of Atlanta, Ga. Christian Cent 81:229 F 19 '64
Description
Atlanta has its own blend. il Bsns W p54-5+ S 7 '63
Scarlett O'Hara's millions. F. Knebel. il Look 27:39-40+ D 3 '63
Economic conditions
Atlanta has its own blend. il Bsns W p54-5+ S 7 '63
Education
Faith & prejudice in Georgia; Lovett school's whites-only admission policy. il Time 82:94 N 15 '63
In Atlanta schools. J. W. Letson. il NEA J 52:46-7 D '63
Hospitals
Progressive patient care, all five elements in one hospital. il Arch Rec 133:193-5 Mr '63
Hotels, restaurants, etc.
Beyond a doubt; Heart of Atlanta motel desegregated. il Time 84:13-14 D 25 '64
Pickrick capers; test of public accomodations title of Civil rights act. il Time 84:62 Jl 31 '64
Negroes
Atlanta: fruits of tokenism. P. Watters. il Nation 198:162-5 F 17 '64
Back on the home front. il Time 82:17 D 27 '63
Contemporary situation of: the Negro in Atlanta. G. Sisk. Negro Hist Bul 27:174-5 Ap '64
Economic condition of the Negro in Atlanta. G. Sisk. bibliog Negro Hist Bul 27:87-90 Ja '64
Negro in Atlanta politics (1870-1962) G. Sisk. bibliog Negro Hist Bul 28:17-18 O '64
Race trouble in a model city. il U S News 56:78 F 10 '64
Ruining a reputation; riots in Atlanta. il Time 83:24-5 F 7 '64
South learns to live with the civil-rights law. P. Watters. il Reporter 31:44-6 Ag 13 '64
Too busy to hate. K. Haselden. Christian Cent 80:392-3 Mr 27 '63
Newspapers
Another voice in Atlanta: Atlanta times. il Time 83:36+ Je 19 '64
Right face in Atlanta; new Atlanta times. il Newsweek 63:58-9 Je 22 '64
Politics and government
Negro in Atlanta politics (1870-1962) G. Sisk. bibliog Negro Hist Bul 28:17-18 O '64
Prisons and reformatories
Four and a half days in Atlanta's jails. G. W. Bishop. Atlan 214:68-70 Jl '64
Public health
Negro health in Atlanta. G. Sisk. bibliog Negro Hist Bul 27:65-6 D '63
Religious institutions and affairs
Should whites integrate Negro churches? Christian Cent 81:262 F 26 '64
Riots
Race trouble in a model city. il U S News 56:78 F 10 '64
Social life and customs
Atlanta adventure; the new southern society. P. Mesta. il McCalls 90:24+ Ap '63
Atlanta: aftermath of a tragedy. J. Blank. il Redbook 121:52-3+ Je '63
Water supply
Ready to move. il Am City 78:116-17 S '63
ATLANTA civic ballet (organization)
Tickets for the bug man. D. Hering. il Dance Mag 37:52-3 F '63
ATLANTA times. See Atlanta—Newspapers
ATLANTIC (periodical)
Insurance against lapidity. il Time 84:71+ O 9 '64
ATLANTIC alliance. See Atlantic community
ATLANTIC and Pacific tea company. See Great Atlantic and Pacific tea company
ATLANTIC cables. See Cables, Submarine
ATLANTIC cement company. See Cement industry and trade
ATLANTIC CITY
Democrats hit the beach. il Life 57:80-5 Ag 28 '64

ATLANTIC CITY—*Continued*
Gay life. il Time 84:22-9 S 4 '64
Polishing the playground. Reporter 31:22+ Ag 13 '64
Popcorn playpen. il Time 84:52-3 S 4 '64

Description

Boardwalk goes all out. il Bsns W p28-9 Ag 15 '64
Musical bagels, etc. il Newsweek 64:19 Ag 31 '64
Vacation by the sea. F. Somers. Redbook 123: 24 Ag '64

ATLANTIC community
After Brussels. E. Taylor. Reporter 28:29-32 F 14 '63
America's brightest opportunities. D. Rusk. Nations Bsns 51:76-8+ Je '63
Atlantic agenda; address, March 16, 1964. W. W. Rostow. bibliog f Dept State Bul 50: 578-87 Ap 13 '64
Atlantic alliance; address, April 7, 1964. D. Rusk. bibliog f Dept State Bul 50: 650-5 Ap 27 '64
Atlantic alliance: constant objectives in a context of change; address, April 27, 1964. W. R. Tyler. Dept State Bul 50:776-83 My 18 '64
Atlantic alliance; United States and Europe; address, October 21, 1963. J. R. Schaetzel. Vital Speeches 30:78-81 N 15 '63
Atlantic and European unity; address, May 9, 1964. D. Rusk. Dept State Bul 50:810-15 My 25 '64
Atlantic community: an American view; address, May 9, 1963. W. W. Rostow. Dept States Bul 48:855-60 Je 3 '63
Atlantic community: common hopes and objectives; address, December 3, 1964. L. B. Johnson. Dept State Bul 51:866-9 D 21 '64
Atlantic future: Europe's choice. F. Church. Harper 227:18+ N '63
Atlantic partnership: a vital force in motion; address, April 28, 1963. G. C. McGhee. Dept State Bul 48:771-5 My 20 '63
Atlantic partnership as viewed from the U.S.A; address, October 21, 1963. J. R. Schaetzel. Dept State Bul 49:731-6 N 11 '63
Atlantica. C. A. Herter. For Affairs 41:299-309 Ja '63
Can de Gaulle shape Europe to his mold? Bsns W p82-3+ Ja 26 '63
Clarence Streit may yet be right. A. Gingrich. Esquire 59:6+ F '63; Reply. C. Streit. 59:19-20+ Ap '63
Coalition diplomacy in a nuclear age. H. A. Kissinger. For Affairs 42:525-45 Jl '64
Crisis in the western alliance; American and British views. H. J. Morgenthau; G. Hutton. Commentary 35:185-98 Mr '63
Current look at NATO; address, January 15, 1964. G. C. McGhee. Dept State Bul 50: 338-44 Mr 2 '64
Dealing with a new Europe; with editorial comment. il Bsns W p46-54, 88 Jl 4 '64
De Gaulle charts a collision course. il Bsns W p 130+ N 14 '64
Detente and French policy; address, October 22, 1963. M. H. Alphand. Vital Speeches 30: 55-7 N 1 '63
Europe and the Atlantic alliances; address, June 24, 1964. W. W. Rostow. Dept State Bul 51:38-43 Jl 13 '64; Same. Vital Speeches 30:617-20 Ag 1 '64
Europe & the United States; tr. by R. McInerny. R. Aron. Commentary 38:54-60 Ag '64
For an Atlantic future. T. Sommer. For Affairs 43:112-25 O '64
Frank talk on NATO; McCloy blames no one, but: excerpts from address, 1963. J. J. McCloy. U S News 55:12 D 23 '63
Free world split will widen. E. Stillman. il Nations Bsns 52:34-5+ Ap '64
Germany and the Atlantic partnership; address, November 15, 1964. G. W. Ball. Dept State Bul 51:773-4 N 30 '64
Labor party's defense and foreign policy. P. C. G. Walker. For Affairs 42:391-8 Ap '64
New Britain and the Atlantic community; address, March 3, 1964. H. Wilson. Vital Speeches 30:436-9 My 1 '64
New social order; address, June 25, 1963. J. F. Kennedy. Vital Speeches 29:578-81 Jl 15 '63
New start for the Alliance. E. V. Rostow. il Reporter 28:23-9 Ap 25 '63
Next steps toward peace: some notes on the two-legged process; address, September 30, 1963. M. Bundy. Dept State Bul 49:625-30 O 21 '63
Our foreign policy: what is it? address, March 3, 1964. N. A. Rockefeller. Vital Speeches 30:402-6 Ap 15 '64
Parallel roles of business and diplomacy in an era of expanding frontiers; address, May 19, 1964. G. C. McGhee. Dept State Bul 51:20-5 Jl 6 '64
President Kennedy visits Europe; texts of joint communiques released at Bonn, Birch Grove house, Sussex, and Rome, with major addresses and remarks, June 23-July 2, 1963. J. F. Kennedy. Dept State Bul 49:114-28 Jl 22 '63
Realities underlying the Atlantic alliance; statement, January 24, 1963. J. F. Kennedy. Dept State Bul 48:197 F 11 '63
Rift in West: how serious. il U S News 54: 29-30 F 11 '63
Role of Germany in the evolution of world politics; address, September 18, 1963. W. W. Rostow. Dept State Bul 49:536-42 O 7 '63
Shaping the future; address, January 9, 1964. W. W. Rostow. Dept State Bul 50:177-83 F 3 '64
Strains on the Alliance. H. A. Kissinger. For Affairs 41:261-85 Ja '63
Tides of change; address, February 12, 1963. J. R. Schaetzel. Dept State Bul 48:322-8 Mr 4 '63
Toward a new dimension in the Atlantic partnership; address, October 27, 1963. D. Rusk. Dept State Bul 49:726-31 N 11 '63
Toward an Atlantic community; address, February 8, 1963. G. Kirk. Vital Speeches 29:293-5 Mr 1 '63
Trade and the Atlantic partnership; address, November 16, 1964. D. Rusk. Dept State Bul 51:766-71 N 30 '64
United States and a changing Europe; address, March 17, 1964. W. R. Tyler. Dept State Bul 50:587-90 Ap 13 '64
United States in the Atlantic community. L. B. Tennyson. Cur Hist 45:264-70+ N '63
United States of America and the Atlantic partnership; address, November 21, 1963. G. C. McGhee. Dept State Bul 49:954-9 D 23 '63
U.S. reaffirms its commitment to the Atlantic community; statement, November 28, 1964. L. B. Johnson. Dept State Bul 51:846-7 D 14 '64
Vice President Johnson visits Benelux countries; statement, November 4, and addresses, November 7 and 8, 1963. L. B. Johnson. Dept State Bul 49:850-4 D 2 '63
Vision of order. America 109:9 Jl 6 '63

ATLANTIC community development group for Latin America (proposed)
Debut for ADELA. Time 83:66 Ja 24 '64
Pool for ventures; joint U.S.-European effort. Bsns W p93 S 28 '63

ATLANTIC fault. See Faults (geology)

ATLANTIC green turtles. See Turtles, Green

ATLANTIC missile range. See Proving grounds

ATLANTIC OCEAN
Composition of basalts from the Mid-Atlantic Ridge. A. E. J. Engel and C. G. Engel. bibliog il Science 144:1330-3 Je 12 '64
See also
Ascension Island
Gough Island
Gulf Stream
Sargasso Sea

ATLANTIC research corporation
ARC hard at work on development of beryllium powder. il Miss & Roc 12:27 My 27 '63

ATLANTIC states

Politics

Campaign report from the East: if the people were voting for president now. il U S News 57:37-8 S 21 '64

ATLANTIC undersea test and evaluation center. See Navy yards and naval stations

ATLANTIS II (ship) See Ships, Research

ATLAS, Charles
Atlas was right all along. il pors Life 56:47-8 Ap 17 '64

ATLAS (launching vehicle) See Space vehicles—Propulsion systems

ATLASES
National geographic atlas of the world! M. B. Grosvenor. il Nat Geog Mag 123: 832-7 Je '63

ATMOSPHERE
Atmospheric photochemical reactions inhibited by iodine. E. R. Stephens and others; reply. L. G. Wayne. Science 139:251-3 Ja 18 '63
Atmospheric sciences. T. F. Malone. bibliog il NEA J 53:61-4 O '64
Building blocks of the clouds. J. A. Day. il Natur Hist 74:36-43 Ja '65
Possible lava source. Sci N L 86:5 Jl 4 '64

ATMOSPHERE—*Continued*
Thermodynamic equilibria in prebiological atmospheres. M. O. Dayhoff and others. bibliog il Science 146:1461-4 D 11 '64
See also
Atmospheric tides
Sun—Atmosphere

ATMOSPHERE, Upper
Aeronomy. J. W. Chamberlain. Science 142: 414-15 O 18 '63
Airglow and the physics of upper atmospheres. J. W. Chamberlain. bibliog il Science 142:921-4 N 15 '63
Circulation of the upper atmosphere. R. E. Newell. il Sci Am 210:62-72+ bibliog(p 152) Mr '64
Creation of the ionosphere. Sky & Tel 26:24 Jl '63
High-altitude grenade explosions furnished data for X-20 program. Aviation W 78:29 Ja 28 '63
IMP finds magnetosphere shock wave. Aviation W 80:23 Mr 23 '64
Ionosphere Explorer I satellite: first observations from the fixed-frequency topside sounder. W. Calvert and others. bibliog il Science 146:391-5 O 16 '64
Magnetopause: a new frontier in space. C. O. Hines. bibliog il Science 141:130-6 Jl 12 '63
Mapping the air by sound. Time 82:52 Ag 30 '63
Measuring plasma density of the magnetosphere. K. L. Bowles. bibliog il Science 139: 389-91 F 1 '63
Metallic emissions from the upper atmosphere. D. M. Hunten. bibliog il Science 145:26-31 Jl 3 '64
Moon's magnetic teardrop; magnetosphere. Sci N L 85:195 Mr 28 '64
Never so high and dry that clouds do not form: stratosphere. Sci N L 83:217 Ap 6 '63
Picture of earth's magnetosphere altered by data from IMP satellite. W. J. Normyle. Aviation W 81:25 D 21 '64
Radiation belts. B. J. O'Brien. il Sci Am 208:84-96 My '63; Reply with rejoinder. S. F. Singer. 209:8+ Jl '63
Satellite to study mirror; S-66. W. Wingo. il Sci N L 84:85 Ag 10 '63
Scientists measure drift of ionospheric clouds. Sci N L 83:168 Mr 16 '63
Space vehicles in an ionized medium. S. F. Singer. Science 147:74-6 Ja 1 '65
Strange air in space. Sci N L 87:6 Ja 2 '65
Stratospheric cloud over northern Arizona. J. E. McDonald. bibliog il Science 140:292-4 Ap 19 '63
Super-cooled paddles used in high altitude air sampler. C. M. Plattner. il Aviation W 82:44-5+ Ja 11 '65
Weather in space; reprint. J. S. Butz, jr. il Sci Digest 55:67-72 Je '64
Where is science taking us? C. Y. Johnson. il Sat R 46:59-60 Mr 2 '63
See also
Atmospheric temperature
Rockets—Use in research

ATMOSPHERIC aldehydes. See Aldehydes

ATMOSPHERIC dust. See Dust

ATMOSPHERIC entry problems. See Space vehicles—Atmospheric entry

ATMOSPHERIC humidity. See Humidity

ATMOSPHERIC nucleation
See also
Cloud physics

ATMOSPHERIC pollution. See Air pollution

ATMOSPHERIC pressure
Hyperbaric exposure of mice to pressures of 60 to 90 atmospheres. J. H. Membery and E. A. Link. bibliog il Science 144:1241-2 Je 5 '64

ATMOSPHERIC temperature
Lowest temperature in atmosphere recorded. Sci N L 84:326 N 23 '63

ATMOSPHERIC tides
Atmospheric tides. B. Haurwitz. bibliog il Science 144:1415-22 Je 19 '64

ATMOSPHERIC turbulence
Airborne turbulence sensors under test. P. J. Klass. Aviation W 81:26-8 Ag 31 '64
Crewmen fly B-52 damaged in turbulence. il Aviation W 80:27 Mr 9 '64
I learned about flying from that. G. Edwards. il Flying 74:56+ F '64
I learned about flying from that. H. A. Shanklin. il Flying 75:54+ Jl '64
Invisible CAT pilots dread. P. C. Geraci. il Pop Mech 121:104-7+ Ap '64
Jet turbulence problems. J. R. Ashlock. il Aviation W 80:38-41 F 17; 45-6 F 24 '64
Propagation of air waves from nuclear explosions. W. L. Donn and others. bibliog il Science 139:307-17 Ja 25 '63
Signs in a clear sky; clear air turbulence. il Time 82:97 D 6 '63
Turbulence: hidden giant in the sky. W. R. Young. il Life 57:86-8+ D 18 '64
Turbulence studies investigate pilot aids. J. R. Ashlock. Aviation W 80:47 Ap 20 '64
Unknown factor in jet crashes; clear air turbulence. il Bsns W p65-6+ Ja 18 '64
Way found to detect clear air turbulence. Sci N L 85:153 Mr 7 '64
Would you fly in a storm? J. H. Winchester. Sci Digest 55:85-90 Je '64

ATOM smashing apparatus. See Accelerators (electron, etc)

ATOMEDIC hospital, Montgomery, Ala. See Montgomery, Ala.—Hospitals

ATOMIC age
Age of nuclear power; excerpts from statement. G. T. Seaborg. il Sci N L 86:178 S 19 '64
Atomic era: twenty-five years old. W. Davis. Sci N L 85:85 F 8 '64
Living with the bomb. Sci Am 208:70+ F '63
Morgenthau on nuclear war. P. Ramsey. Commonweal 78:554-7 S 20 '63
Return of the native. N. Cousins. Sat R 47: 14 Jl 4 '64
Successor to democracy; warning against science. S. A. Coblentz. Christian Cent 81: 78-80 Ja 15 '64
Two worlds. S. Chase. Bul Atomic Sci 19:18-20 Je '63

ATOMIC blasting
Another Panama Canal: A-blasts may do the job. il U S News 54:74-5 Je 10 '63
Atomic blast to help build a U.S. canal? Tennessee-Tombigbee project. il U S News 54:14 My 20 '63
Bang-up way to dig a new canal. il Life 56:55+ Mr 6 '64
Dig ditches with atoms; Project plowshare. A. Ewing. Sci N L 83:95 F 9 '63
Dig with atomic energy; Project plowshare. Sci N L 86:149 S 5 '64
Dig with nuclear energy; new Panama Canal. A. Ewing. il(p 1) Sci N L 87:3 Ja 2 '65
Digging with H-bombs; Project sedan. il Bsns W p 154+ My 18 '63
H-blasted crater twelve million tons deep makes a lab for AEC men. il Life 54:47-50 Je 21 '63
Instant canals. il Time 81:59 F 8 '63
Man's first atomic cave. il Life 54:55+ Mr 15 '63
New canal, dug by atom bombs. L. Galton. il N Y Times Mag p24-5+ S 20 '64
Notes and comment; question of Plowshare project for Panama Canal. New Yorker 39:15 Jl 13 '63
Nuclear ditch-digging; AEC's Project carryall. il Bsns W p84-5 D 21 '63
Nuclear experiment may unleash oil reserves; Plowshare program. Sci N L 86: 331 N 21 '64
Ploughshare canals. il Time 83:36 Ja 31 '64
Project plowshare: AEC program for peaceful nuclear explosives slowed down by test ban treaty. E. Langer. Science 143:1153-5 Mr 13 '64
Second canal? projects Plowshare and Sedan. J. W. Finney. il New Repub 150:21-4 Mr 28 '64; Same abr. with title Biggest building job of all time. Sci Digest 56:33-7 Jl '64; Discussion. New Repub 150:30 Ap 18 '64
Slight hitch; problems over new canal in Latin America. Newsweek 65:45 Ja 18 '65

ATOMIC bomb casualty commission
Atomic bomb casualty commission: the first fifteen years. R. K. Cannan. Bul Atomic Sci 19:45-8 O '63
Hiroshima 1964. N. Cousins. il Sat R 47:24-7 Ap 18 '64

ATOMIC bomb shelters
Adequate shelters and quick reaction to warning: a key to civil defense. F. X. Lynch. il Science 142:665-7 N 8 '63
Chain reaction. il Newsweek 61:34 Je 10 '63
Civil defense: housing reverses direction and approves fallout shelter program, sequel pending. J. Walsh. Science 141:1264-5+ S 27 '63
Civil defense in a balanced national security. S. L. Pittman. Bul Atomic Sci 20:24-6 Je '64
Civil defense: make haste slowly is watchword of current strategy on fallout shelter program. E. Langer. Science 141:340-1 Jl 26 '63
Civil defense official describes architect's role. R. Berne. Arch Rec 135:50+ Mr '64
Do we want fallout shelters? S. Chapman. Bul Atomic Sci 19:24-6 F '63
Favored few; civil-defense center, Pomona, Calif. il Newsweek 63:58 Mr 9 '64

ATOMIC bomb shelters—*Continued*
More shelters? Newsweek 62:56 Jl 22 '63
Reflections on protection. C. Newman. Yale R 52:404-11 Mr '63
Revival of survival; federal fallout-shelter program. il Time 82:21 S 27 '63
Rice university conference develops five factory projects. S. L. Pittman. il Arch Rec 134:115-20 D '63
Shelter owners pro-war. Sci N L 83:246 Ap 20 '63
Sheltered life; no market for shelters. il Newsweek 64:75 Jl 27 '64
Some reflections on civil defense. M. E. Rozen. Bul Atomic Sci 20:21-4 Je '64
Survival of the fewest; with editorial comment. D. Oberdorfer. il Sat Eve Post 236: 17-21, 84 Mr 23 '63
Winners named in competition for school shelters. il Arch Rec 135:26+ F '64

ATOMIC bombs
Another finger on the button. Christian Cent 81:1259 O 14 '64
Atomic arsenal; concerning testimony of Secretary McNamara on nuclear test ban treaty before the Senate foreign relations, Senate armed forces and Joint atomic energy committees. il Time 82:11-15 Ag 23 '63; Same abr. with title Our awesome atomic arsenal. Read Digest 83:67-71 N '63
A-bombs for all? it's getting closer. il U S News 57:36 D 7 '64
Bipartisan proposal? how to eliminate Chinese bomb. W. F. Buckley, jr. Nat R 16:1143 D 29 '64
Bomb on a bullock cart; India debating whether to build A-bombs of its own. Time 84:29 N 6 '64
Children of the A-bomb, comp. by A. Osada; tr. by J. Dan and R. Sieben-Morgen. Review
Christian Cent 80:1108-9 S 11 '63. S. Klein
China and the bomb. Sci Digest 56:37 D '64
Chinese A-bomb. P. H. Abelson. Science 146: 601 O 30 '64
Fifth-nation problem. Sci Am 211:60-2 D '64
From Washington: the bomb in China. H. Margolis. Bul Atomic Sci 20:36-9 D '64
Greatest plot in history: how the reds stole the A-bomb, by R. De Toledano. Review
Bul Atomic Sci 20:29-30 F '64. H. P. Green
Hiroshima revisited. Christian Cent 80:971 Ag 7 '63
Number five; Chinese nuclear explosion. Nation 199:289 N 2 '64
Power of prediction, and example. R. G. Sachs. Bul Atomic Sci 20:20-1 D '64
Should we bomb red China's bomb? Nat R 17:8-10 Ja 12 '65
Spread of nuclear weapons; excerpt from Great debate. R. Aron. il Atlan 215:44-50 Ja '65
With red China getting the bomb. il U S News 57:38-9 O 12 '64

Accidents

Could this happen? Fail-safe. Sci Digest 56: 47 D '64

Detection

See Atomic bombs—Testing, Detection of

High altitude explosions

Facts about the 1962 space bomb. J. Lear. il Sat R 46:45-8 Ap 6 '63; Reply with rejoinder. S. F. Singer. 46:50-1 My 4 '63
Radiation belt intensity dispute grows; summary of study presented at meeting of the American physical society; ed. by W. C. Wetmore. W. L. Brown. il Aviation W 78: 60-1+ F 4 '63
Recent nuclear blasts boost space radiation hazard; Starfish test. il Sci Digest 53:56-63 Ap '63

History

Did Stalin understand? Newsweek 64:58 D 14 '64
Einstein letter that started it all. R. E. Lapp. il N Y Times Mag p 13+ Ag 2 '64
Fight over the A-bomb; secret revealed after eighteen years. F. Knebel and C. W. Bailey. Look 27:19-23 Ag 13 '63; Reply. A. K. Smith. But Atomic Sci 19:33 O '63
Teller urges strong nuclear management; excerpt from Science, technology, and management. E. Teller. Aviation W 78:92+ Ap 22 '63

International control

See Atomic power—International control

Manufacture

China's Manhattan project. C. Johnson. il N Y Times Mag p23+ O 25 '64
Fight over the A-bomb; Manhattan project F. Knebel and C. W. Bailey. Look 27:19-23 Ag 13 '63; Reply. A. K. Smith. Bul Atomic Sci 19:33 O '63
[Growth of the atom bomb project] E. Rabinowitch. il Bul Atomic Sci 20:16-20 O '64
Making nuclear bomb easier all the time. Sci N L 86:281 O 31 '64
Not-so-backward China. il Sci Digest 57:10 Ja '65
Nuclear detective looks at China's atom bomb. W. Cloud. Pop Sci 186:19-20+ Ja '65
One great question: whether to permit uncontrolled spread of nuclear weapons. S. Alsop. il Sat Eve Post 237:18 N 14 '64
Three-kiloton fizzle; French *force de frappe*. il Newsweek 64:30+ D 14 '64
Tilting the balance of A-power; red China's progress in nuclear technology. il Bsns W p74+ O 31 '64

Physiological effects

See Radioactivity—Physological effects

Testing

And now there are five; Communist China explodes its first atomic device. Newsweek 64:54 O 26 '64
Announced nuclear tests, July 16, 1945 to September 24, 1963. il Bul Atomic Sci 19: 44 N '63
Any number can play nuclear chicken. L. J. Halle. il N Y Times Mag p33+ N 8 '64
Arrogant dragon becomes atomic. D. Chu. il Sr Schol 85:13-16+ N 18 '64
Asia's atomic cloud. Sr Schol 85:23 O 28 '64
Blast at Lop Nor; first Chinese atomic test. il Time 84:66 O 30 '64
China's Manhattan project. C. Johnson. il N Y Times Mag p23+ O 25 '64
China's shot tells a startling story. il Bsns W p 144+ O 24 '64
Chinese bomb. J. Burnham. Nat R 16:910 O 20 '64
Chinese bomb menace. T. G. Harris. il Look 28:28-9 D 1 '64
Chinese Communists conduct nuclear test; statement, October 16, 1964. L. B. Johnson. Dept State Bul 51:612 N 2 '64
Dangers of hairsplitting; France as a nonsignatory of the test-ban treaty. Nation 199:506 D 28 '64
De Gaulle in Oceania; test site in French Polynesia. Nation 199:22-3 Jl 27 '64
Discouraging. Newsweek 61:30+ My 27 '63
Fateful firecracker; Chinese explosion of nuclear device. Time 84:36 O 23 '64
From Devil's Island to Cape de Gaulle. il Time 85:25 Ja 8 '65
McNamara minimizes red China atom test. Aviation W 81:29 O 26 '64
Mr Rusk and Mr Bundy interviewed on red China's nuclear testing, October 16, 1964. D. Rusk; W. Bundy. Dept State Bul 51:614-17 N 2 '64
Nature rises from the ashes; Bikini and Eniwetok atolls. il Bsns W p 116-18 O 10 '64
Nuclear club. Commonweal 81:148 O 30 '64
Nuclear politics. Sci Am 208:72 Mr '63
Nuclear tests affected by treaty. Aviation W 79:29 S 30 '63
On guard. Newsweek 62:72 Ag 19 '63
Peking joins the club. Nat R 16:942 N 3 '64
Preview of tomorrow's nuclear terror. W. J. Perkinson. Sci Digest 54:50-3 Ag '63
Propagation of air waves from nuclear explosions. W. L. Donn and others. bibliog il Science 139:307-17 Ja 25 '63
Red China gets ready to fire its A-bomb. il Bsns W p32+ Ag 1 '64
Red China's bomb: how it alters things in the world. il U S News 57:48-50 O 26 '64
Red Chinese test expected. Sr Schol 85:15 O 14 '64
Russia, China and England: our basic policy remains unchanged; address, October 18, 1964. L. B. Johnson. Vital Speeches 31:34-6 N 1 '64; Same with title President reports on change in Soviet leadership, Chinese nuclear test, and new British government. Dept State Bul 51:610-14 N 2 '64
Sovereign remedy. Nation 197:231 O 19 '63
Start of the chain; Peking's nuclear firecracker. il Time 84:38-9 O 30 '64
Test site in Tahiti. Newsweek 62:35-6 Ag 5 '63
Truth about red China's bomb; interview. C. Y. Cheng. il U S News 57:28-32 D 28 '64
U.S. comments on Peiping's nuclear capacity; statement, September 29, 1964. D. Rusk. Dept State Bul 51:542 O 19 '64

ATOMIC bombs—Testing—*Continued*
U.S. plans air fleet for nuclear testing. K. Johnsen. Aviation W 79:16 Jl 29 '63
What is enough? New Repub 148:6-7 Ap 27 '63
See also
Radioactive fallout

Testing, Detection of

Aim of inspection. New Repub 148:6 Mr 23 '63
Back to the table. New Repub 148:4-5 F 2 '63
Bomb detectors in space; Project Vela Hotel. R. N. Watts, jr. Sky & Tel 26:328 D '63
Conversations with the committee; excerpts from hearings before U.S. Senate subcommittee on disarmament, August, 1962. Bul Atomic Sci 19:15-18 Mr '63
Disadvantages of reliable inspection. T. C. O'Sullivan, jr. Bul Atomic Sci 19:18-19 Mr '63
Explosion seismology. E. W. Carpenter. bibliog il Science 147:363-73 Ja 22 '65
Fingering nuclear test cheats; detecting and locating underground nuclear blasts. Bsns W p46-7 F 2 '63
How we're policing the A-test ban. A. P. Armagnac. il Pop Sci 183:88-9 D '63
Inside the black box: telltale squiggles. H. Simmons. il Newsweek 61:14 F 4 '63
Loran-C tested as atomic blast detector. P. J. Klass. il Aviation W 79:105+ O 14 '63
Modular payload developed for probe. W. Beller. il Miss & Roc 15:24-5 N 23 '64
Network detects nuclear tests in atomosphere. Sci N L 83:392 Je 22 '63
Nevada blast begins test detection effort. Aviation W 79:119 N 11 '63
No major advance seen in U.S. nuclear test detection capability. K. Johnsen. Aviation W 78:302 Mr 11 '63
No pain for business; bomb research and monitoring devices. Bsns W p21-2 Ag 3 '63
Nuclear blast detection satellite flight testing to begin this fall. K. Johnsen. Aviation W 78:36 Mr 18 '63
Nuclear test ban and arms control; address, February 28, 1963. J. D. Beam. Dept State Bul 48:489-93 Ap 1 '63
Nuclear test ban issue; statement, February 12, 1963. W. C. Foster. Dept State Bul 48:398-402 Mr 18 '63
Numbers game. New Repub 148:4-5 Mr 9 '63
Numbers game. Newsweek 61:60 Mr 18 '63
Playing the numbers; on-site inspection. Nat R 14:220-1 Mr 26 '63
Policing the big beat. il Time 82:70 Ag 9 '63
Riddle of the black boxes. S. D. Pursglove. il Pop Mech 120:86-91+ Ag '63
Satellites on patrol. il Time 84:50 Jl 31 '64
Secretary Rusk's news conference of March 8, 1963. D. Rusk. Dept State Bul 48:432-9 Mr 25 '63
Sensor tests delay Vela hotel launch. G. Alexander. Aviation W 81:24 Jl 20 '64
Sentries in orbit; Atlas-Agena. Time 82:70 O 25 '63
Shaking a salt dome to help spot A-blasts. il Bsns W p 113-14 O 10 '64
Space blast detection system considered. K. Johnsen. Aviation W 79:26-7 Ag 5 '63
Test ban: choice between risks. il Bul Atomic Sci 19:37-44 My '63
Test ban: optimism on Project Vela; report. R. Preston. il Bul Atomic Sci 19:33-7 Je '63
Undersea sensors planted near USSR. M Getler. Miss & Roc 15:17 S 7 '64
USAF launches two Vela Hotel satellites. Aviation W 79:30 O 21 '63
U.S. plans air fleet for nuclear testing. K. Johnsen. Aviation W 79:16 Jl 29 '63
U.S. prepared to detect atomic explosions. Sci N L 86:233 O 10 '64
U.S. presses Vela hotel program. D. C. Breasted. Miss & Roc 13:14 Ag 19 '63
Was it a blast, or a quake? Project Vela. il Bsns W p94+ N 2 '63
Watching over nuclear tests; jet planes to monitor tests. il Bsns W p 139-40+ S 26 '64

Testing, Suspension of

At the brink of a test ban. J. Maddox. Commentary 35:461-6 Je '63; Reply with rejoinder. R. D. Levine. 36:190+ S '63
Avalanche begins; Hosmer committee. Nation 196:170 Mr 2 '63
Behind test ban talks. il Bsns W p26-7 Jl 13 '63
Beyond the test ban. Sci Am 209:64 N '63
Black boxes, etc. Commonweal 77:584 Mr 1 '63
Case against a test ban. Senator Dodd speaks out. U S News 54:22 Mr 18 '63
Choice. Commonweal 78:85-6 Ap 19 '63
Cold war thaw? several signs in recent months suggest that East-West relations are improving. D. S. Greenberg. Science 141:251-3 Jl 19 '63
Crack in the door. Nation 197:42 Jl 27 '63
FAS endorses test ban; backs policy with facts. Sci N L 84:104 Ag 17 '63
Genie and the dinosaur. N. Cousins. Sat R 46:22 My 25 '63
Good college try; President Kennedy's idea for a peace offensive. Newsweek 61:28 Je 24 '63
Immense task. Commonweal 78:179-80 My 10 '63; Discussion. 78:377-9 Je 28 '63
Letter to Moscow. Newsweek 61:34+ Je 10 '63
Monitoring a test ban. M. Sands. Bul Atomic Sci 19:12-15 Mr '63
National security and the nuclear-test ban. J. B. Wiesner and H. F. York. il Sci Am 211:27-35 bibliog(p 142) O '64; Reply. E. P. Wigner. 211:8+ D '64
Negotiating with Communists: a test case; excerpts from address, February 21, 1963. T. J. Dodd. Nat R 14:184 Mr 12 '63
New hope for nuclear test-ban? il Sr Schol 82:20 F 6 '63
New temperature; nuclear test ban treaty conference, Moscow. il Time 82:15-20 Ag 2 '63
No deal? Newsweek 61:36 F 25 '63
North America, the open continent; address, June 16, 1963. W. R. Tyler. Dept State Bul 49:93-7 Jl 15 '63
Nuclear ambush: the test-ban trap, by E. H. Voss. Review
Nat R 15:242-3 S 24 '63. J. H. Morse
U S News 55:75 Jl 29 '63
Nuclear test ban and arms control; address, February 28, 1963. J. D. Beam. Dept State Bul 48:489-93 Ap 1 '63
Nuclear test ban issue; statement, February 12, 1963. W. C. Foster. Dept State Bul 48: 398-402 Mr 18 '63
Of hope & skepticism. il Time 82:11 Jl 26 '63
One-in-twenty chance. New Repub 149:4-5 Jl 6 '63
Politics of courage. K. Crawford. Newsweek 61:41 Je 24 '63
Primary test; the people's decision. N. Cousins. Sat R 46:28-9+ Mr 30 '63
Reaching the Russians; concerning President's speech at American university. New Repub 148:7 Je 22 '63
Secretary Rusk addresses Advertising council; remarks, March 12, 1963; with questions and answers. D. Rusk. Dept State Bul 48:467-75 Ap 1 '63
Secretary Rusk's news conference of February 1, 1963. D. Rusk. Dept State Bul 48:235-43 F 18 '63
Secretary Rusk's news conference of May 29, 1963; with excerpts from remarks on discrimination and U.S. foreign policy, May 27, 1963. D. Rusk. Dept State Bul 48:931-8 Je 17 '63
Senate test ploy. K. Crawford. Newsweek 62: 28 Jl 22 '63
Senate unit collects evidence to challenge nuclear test ban. K. Johnsen. Aviation W 79:23 Jl 8 '63
Step toward steps; summary of address. J. F. Kennedy. il Time 82:9 Ag 2 '63
Strategy of peace: first, a test ban? Newsweek 62:17 Jl 15 '63
Sweet talk from Moscow, again. Bsns W p 116 Jl 20 '63
Test ban: a rosy glow on the horizon. il Newsweek 62:45 Jl 29 '63
Test ban and overkill. Sci Am 209:48 Ag '63
Test ban: choice between risks. il Bul Atomic Sci 19:37-44 My '63
Test ban chronology; December 1946—July 1963. Time 82:22-3 Jl 26 '63
Test-ban confusion. Commonweal 78:365 Je 28 '63
Test-ban hesitations. Commonweal 78:317-18 Je 14 '63
Test ban: Kennedy-Khrushchev exchange. J. F. Kennedy; N. Khrushchev. Bul Atomic Sci 19:32-7 Mr '63
Test-ban negotiations: implications for the future. H. K. Jacobson. bibliog f Ann Am Acad 351:92-101 Ja '64
Test ban now. E. Rabinowitch. Bul Atomic Sci 19:2 Ap '63
Test ban: prospects for agreement may be dim, but in Cuban aftermath they appear brighter. D. S. Greenberg. Science 139:739-41 F 22 '63

ATOMIC bombs—Testing, Suspension of—*Cont.*
Test ban talks raise hopes for peace. Christian Cent 80:948-9 Jl 31 '63
Thin but important opening. N. Cousins. Sat R 46:26-7 Mr 2 '63
Three-test ban; cancellation of scheduled May tests. Time 81:31 My 24 '63
To Moscow, with caution. Time 82:24 Jl 19 '63
To slow down the nuclear race. L. Beaton. il N Y Times Mag p 15+ Mr 8 '64
U.S. affirms willingness to work for test ban agreement; text of statement by the U.S. Arms control and disarmament agency. Dept State Bul 48:403 Mr 18 '63
U.S. and U.S.S.R. exchange views on nuclear test ban; exchange of letters; with Department statement of January 20, 1963. N. Khrushchev; J. F. Kennedy. Dept State Bul 48:198-202 F 11 '63
U.S. drafts new test ban plan calling for policing by principals. Aviation W 78:103 Mr 25 '63
U.S. efforts to achieve safeguarded test ban treaty; statement, March 11, 1963. D. Rusk. Dept State Bul 48:485-9 Ap 1 '63
U.S. tries again to get an A-test ban; new talks set in Moscow. il Bsns W p26-7 Je 15 '63
What goes on here? Nation 196:189 Mr 9 '63
Will the Senator yield? Nat R 14:483 Je 18 '63; Reply. T. J. Dodd. 15:75 Jl 30 '63
Winds of change, East and West. Newsweek 61:13-15 F 4 '63
See also
Conference on the discontinuance of nuclear weapons tests, Geneva, 1958-1961
Nuclear test ban treaty, 1963

Testing, Underground

DOD prepares for nuclear effects tests. K. Johnsen. Aviation W 80:24 Mr 30 '64
Explosion seismology. E. W. Carpenter. bibliog il Science 147:363-73 Ja 22 '65
Finding new ways to test A-weapons; scientists improve test techniques. il Bsns W p86+ O 5 '63
Fingering nuclear test cheats; detecting and locating underground nuclear blasts. Bsns W p46-7 F 2 '63
Iodine-131 fallout from underground tests. E. A. Martell. bibliog il Science 143:126-9 Ja 10 '64
No hot peril in tests. W. Wingo. Sci N L 84:133 Ag 31 '63
Nuclear explosions: some geologic effects of the Gnome shot. L. M. Gard. il Science 139:911-14 Mr 8 '63
Rumble in a salt mine; Salmon test shot in Tatum Salt Dome. il Bsns W p76 O 31 '64
Tritium distribution in ground water around large underground fusion explosions. F. W. Stead. bibliog il Science 142:1163-5 N 29 '63
Underground bomb tests awkward, but effective. Sci N L 84:73 Ag 3 '63
Underground test hazards. Sci N L 85:54 Ja 25 '64
U.S, U.K. test low-yield nuclear device underground in Nevada; joint U.S.-U.K. announcement, July 18, 1964. Dept State Bul 51:193 Ag 10 '64
Was it a blast, or a quake? Project Vela. il Bsns W p94+ N 2 '63

ATOMIC bombs and building. See Building, Bombproof

ATOMIC clocks. See Clocks—Atomic control

ATOMIC detectors. See Detectors

ATOMIC energy. See Atomic power

ATOMIC energy agency. See International atomic energy agency

ATOMIC energy commission. See United States—Atomic energy commission

ATOMIC frequency standards. See Frequency standards

ATOMIC nuclei
Atomic ghost tracked; resonances of certain nuclei. Sci N L 86:307 N 14 '64
Leptons and baryons. Newsweek 61:69 Je 24 '63
Shell model; address, December 12, 1963. M. G. Mayer. bibliog il Science 145:999-1006 S 4 '64
See also
Nuclear physics

Fusion

See Nuclear fusion

ATOMIC piles. See Nuclear reactors

ATOMIC power
Atomic power. il Sci Digest 53:69-70 My '63
Atomic power; the fear and the promise. C. Dreher. il Nation 198:289-93 Mr 23 '64
Civilian nuclear power. P. H. Abelson; discussion. Science 139:1117-18+ Mr 15 '63
Coming of nuclear age. Sci Am 211:56 N '64
Greatest plot in history, by R. De Toledano. Review
Nat R 15:200-1 S 10 '63. W. A. Rusher
Requirements merry-go-round: must need precede development? J. T. Ramey. Bul Atomic Sci 20:12-15 N '64
See also
Nuclear reactors

Economic aspects

Atom at work for peace; summary of views presented at third United Nations international conference on the peaceful uses of atomic energy. UN Mo Chron 1:59-66 O '64
Atomic power and disarmament. V. Emelyanov. Bul Atomic Sci 19:16-20 O '63
Atoms-for-peace: hope deferred. H. L. Nieburg. Bul Atomic Sci 20:35-40 Ja '64
Atoms for peace; photographs. UN Mo Chron 1:87-94 Jl '64
Big atom; solving the water shortage. C. Dreher. il Nation 197:451-4 D 28 '63; Same abr. with title A-power can end the water shortage. Sci Digest 56:57-60 Ag '64
Change, hope and the bomb, by D. E. Lilienthal. Review
Bsns W p200+ O 19 '63
Coming big industry? atomic power grows up. il U S News 54:52-4 Mr 18 '63
Economics of atomic power. S. H. Schurr. il Bul Atomic Sci 21:22-5 Ja '65
Electric power from atom. W. Davis. il Sci N L 86:147-8 S 5 '64
Growing market for nuclear kw. il Fortune 68:172-6+ Jl '63
H-bomb for power seen in new research. Sci N L 83:281 My 4 '63
Memorandum on cooperation signed in Moscow, May 21, 1963. Bul Atomic Sci 19:26-7 S '63
New try at caging atom fusion; Astron program. il Bsns W p 138+ Ag 22 '64
Nuclear power for peace; facts and opinions presented at a Conference on radiation and social ethics, University of Chicago. M. Alonso. il Américas 15:2-8 Je '63
Nuclear power in private hands. J. Ridgeway. New Repub 150:9-10 Ap 18 '64
Peaceful uses for military energy. R. Calder. il UNESCO Courier 17:29-32 N '64
Political fuel. Newsweek 61:51 Mr 4 '63
Private nuclear fuels. Sci Am 211:57-8 O '64
Promise of nuclear energy. H. J. Bhabha. il UNESCO Courier 16:14-17 Jl '63
Reducing nuclear materials production. L. B. Johnson; N. S. Khrushchev. Cur Hist 47:47-8 Jl '64
Two views of nuclear power: AEC, industry. P. Fozzy. Bul Atomic Sci 19:37-8 Je '63
U.S., USSR cooperate; peaceful uses of atomic energy. W. Davis. il Sci N L 83:373 Je 15 '63
Whatever happened to the peaceful atom? excerpts from Change, hope and the bomb. D. E. Lilienthal. Harper 227:41-6 O '63; Reply. W. B. Cottrell. 227:14+ N '63
See also
Atomic blasting
Atomic power plants
International conference on the peaceful uses of atomic energy, 3d, Geneva, 1964
Nuclear reactors

Ethical aspects

Radiation and social ethics; conference of nuclear scientists and theologians, University of Chicago. A. P. Klausler. Christian Cent 80:199-200 F 13 '63
Radiation and social ethics; conference of nuclear scientists and theologians, University of Chicago. W. A. Wallace. America 108:880-3 Je 22 '63

Industrial aspects

See Atomic power—Economic aspects

International aspects

Atomic bomb countries. W. Davis. Sci N L 83:359 Je 8 '63
Atomic energy exchanges: more now authorized, but U.S.-U.S.S.R. visits difficult to arrange. E. Langer. Science 140:963 My 31 '63
Atomic powers bid for civilian market. Bsns W p98+ Jl 13 '63
Battlefield A-bomb: should generals control it? M. S. Johnson. il U S News 57:44-5 Ag 24 '64
Chance for revaluation. Nation 197:309-10 N 16 '63

ATOMIC power—International aspects—*Cont.*
China's shot tells a startling story. il Bsns W p 144+ O 24 '64
Coming: A-bomb cheap enough for everybody? U S News 57:12 Jl 27 '64
Coming: nuclear bombs for all nations? il U S News 57:48-51 Ag 10 '64
Hands across the sea. Nation 199:150 S 28 '64
How to lose a war. D. Lawrence. U S News 57:92 Ag 31 '64
International atom; address, October 27, 1964. G. T. Seaborg. bibliog f Dept State Bul 51:779-86 N 30 '64
Memorandum on cooperation signed in Moscow, May 21, 1963. Bul Atomic Sci 19:26-7 S '63
New strategy for survival. il Newsweek 61:20-4 F 11 '63
Nuclear politics. Sci Am 208:72 Mr '63
Power politics and nuclear power. Sci Am 208:80 Ap '63
Spread of nuclear weapons, by L. Beaton and J. Maddox. Review
New Repub 148:22-3+ F 16 '63. R. E. Osgood
U.S. and Euratom to cooperate on fast neutron reactors; Department announcement, May 27, 1964. Dept State Bul 50:941-3 Je 15 '64
United States and India sign atomic energy agreement; text of the agreement, August 9, 1963. Dept State Bul 49:340-5 Ag 26 '63
United States and NATO members sign new agreement for cooperation in exchange of atomic information; message to Congress, June 30, 1964; with accompanying documents and text of agreement. L. B. Johnson. Dept State Bul 51:93-8 Jl 20 '64
U.S. USSR cooperate. W. Davis. il Sci N L 83:373 Je 15 '63
World atom agency; negotiations on Indian reactor hold promise of brighter future for IAEA. D. S. Greenberg. Science 140:163 Ap 12 '63
World of nuclear plenty. G. H. Evans. il Bul Atomic Sci 19:26-30 F '63
See also
International atomic energy agency

International control

A-bombs for all? it's getting closer. il U S News 57:36 D 7 '64
Authority over nuclear weapons; address, January 17, 1963. L. Norstad. Vital Speeches 29:258-60 F 15 '63
Behind the headlines. R. Stern. Sat R 47:38 N 14 '64
Dispersion of nuclear weapons, ed. by R. N. Rosecrance. Review
Science 144:677-8+ My 8 '64. H. Bull
McNamara vs. Goldwater. W. V. Kennedy. America 111:259 S 12 '64; Reply. J. D. Hayes. 111:394 O 10 '64
Nuclear containment. Christian Cent 80:259-60 F 27 '63
Nuclear weapons control. J. E. Dougherty. bibliog f Cur Hist 47:31-8+ Jl '64
On disarmament issues: the Polish plan. B. G. Lall. Bul Atomic Sci 20:41-3 Je '64
Preventing the spread of nuclear weapons. M. Kalkstein. Bul Atomic Sci 20:18-19 D '64
Pugwash XII; official statement. Bul Atomic Sci 20:45-8 Je '64
United States favors extension of IAEA safeguards system; statement, September 27, 1963. H. D. Smyth. Dept State Bul 49:1019-21 D 30 '63
U.S. makes proposals for safeguards for peaceful nuclear activities and for bomber destruction; statements, March 5 and March 19, 1964. A. S. Fisher. bibliog f Dept State Bul 50:641-5 Ap 20 '64
Universal nuclear deterrent force. S. Brown. Bul Atomic Sci 19:20-4 Ap '63
Who should control nuclear weapons; interview. L. Norstad. U S News 57:47-8 O 5 '64

Medical applications

See Radiology, Medical

Social aspects

Brain, morals, and politics. A. Szent-Györgyi. Bul Atomic Sci 20:2-3 My '64
See also
Atomic age

China (People's Republic)

Any number can play nuclear chicken. L. J. Halle. il N Y Times Mag p33+ N 8 '64
China's Manhattan project. C. Johnson. il N Y Times Mag p23+ O 25 '64
Now red China makes the bomb: what it means: U.S. view: no need to panic. il U S News 55:38-40 Jl 15 '63
Nuclear cutoff. Newsweek 62:45 Ag 26 '63
One great question: whether to permit uncontrolled spread of nuclear weapons. S. Alsop. il Sat Eve Post 237:18 N 14 '64
Polyot and Peking. Newsweek 62:73 N 11 '63
Tilting the balance of A-power. il Bsns W p74+ O 31 '64

France

Debate on the force de frappe takes shape. P. F. Palmedo. Bul Atomic Sci 20:29-30 Je '64
French bomb: how much technical fallout? V. K. McElheny. il Science 147:35-6 Ja 1 '65

India

U.S. and India complete negotiations on nuclear power station agreement; joint statement, June 29, 1963. Dept State Bul 49:143-4 Jl 22 '63
United States and India sign atomic energy agreement; text of the agreement, August 9, 1963. Dept State Bul 49:340-5 Ag 26 '63
World atom agency: Indian reactor accord, agreement on Japan point to more significant role for IAEA. D. S. Greenberg. Science 141:29 Jl 5 '63

Russia

Red carpet out for Seaborg; findings on visit to Russia. Bsns W p 100-2+ Je 15 '63

Spain

Who gets off first in nuclear fuel race? Bsns W p 128+ Ap 20 '63

Sweden

Atomic power in Sweden. E. G. Malmlöw. Bul Atomic Sci 19:44-6 F '63

United States

See Atomic power

ATOMIC power and meteorology
Severe winter not result of nuclear explosions. Sci N L 83:89 F 9 '63

ATOMIC power industry
Conventional versus nuclear power. P. H. Abelson. Science 146:721 N 6 '64
Nuclear energy for the benefit of man; statement, September 15, 1964. G. T. Seaborg. Dept State Bul 51:519-24 O 12 '64

ATOMIC power plants
Atlantic report. Atlan 213:22+ Mr '64
A-bomb on New York's doorstep; Ravenswood power plant. B. H. Frisch. il Sci Digest 54:29-35 O '63
A-power: creeping giant. S. D. Pursglove. il Pop Mech 119:100-4+ Je '63
Atomic dangers overrated. Sci N L 86:149 S 5 '64
AEC to aid water project; nuclear power plant for pumping water. Bsns W p98 Ja 9 '65
Atomic jitters; proposed new station at Corral Canyon, Los Angeles. il Newsweek 62:73 N 25 '63
Atomic plants seen for power, freshwater. Sci N L 85:233 Ap 11 '64
Atomic power plants and cities: fission or fusion? pro and con discussion. il Sr Schol 83:16-17 O 18 '63
Atomic power: the fear and the promise. C. Dreher. il Nation 198:289-93 Mr 23 '64
Atomic question for the city; proposed nuclear power plant in Queens. R. P. Hunt. il N Y Times Mag p46+ O 6 '63
Atoms downtown; question of a nuclear plant in New York city. il Time 82:42 Jl 26 '63
Bodega: symbol of a national crisis. K. S. Roe. il Am For 69:22-5 D '63
Boiling point; how atom can draw water and power from the seas. il Newsweek 63:68 Mr 16 '64
Breeder reactor gets its fuel; Enrico Fermi atomic power plant. il Bsns W p 144-5+ My 18 '63
Build the first one in Washington. Christian Cent 80:1491 D 4 '63
California atom controversy; Bodega Head, Sonoma County. P. M. Tilden. Natur Hist 72:64-5 D '63
Con Ed's atom. Newsweek 63:71 Ja 20 '64
Dig they must . . . nuclear plant in New York city. il Bsns W p82-4+ S 14 '63
Growing market for nuclear kw. il Fortune 68:172-6+ Jl '63
No rush to nuclear plants. il Bsns W p 100+ F 8 '64
Nuclear power, A.D. 2000. Sci N L 86:149 S 5 '64
Nuclear power for Piquads; Piqua, Ohio. J. P. Gallagher. il Am City 79:71-2 Jl '64
Power reactor makers launch business drive. Bsns W p43-4+ Mr 14 '64

ATOMIC power plants—*Continued*
Radioactivity in the atmospheric effluents of power plants that use fossil fuels. M. Eisenbud and H. G. Petrow. bibliog il Science 144:288-9 Ap 17 '64
Turning the corner. il Time 82:85 Jl 12 '63
U.S. and India complete negotiations on nuclear power station agreement; joint statement, June 29, 1963. Dept State Bul 49:143-4 Jl 22 '63
United States and India sign atomic energy agreement; text of the agreement, August 9, 1963. Dept State Bul 49:340-5 Ag 26 '63
Whatever happened to the peaceful atom? excerpts from Change, hope, and the bomb. D. E. Lilienthal. Harper 227:41-6 O '63; Reply. W. B. Cottrell. 227:14+ N '63
When the atom moves next door; excerpt from Change, hope, and the bomb. D. E. Lilienthal. McCalls 91:52+ O '63
Who gets off first in nuclear fuel race? Bsns W p 128+ Ap 20 '63
Would you want an atomic power plant near you? S. Grafton. McCalls 91:228-9 O '63

ATOMIC power plants (space vehicles) See Space vehicles—Atomic power plants

ATOMIC power plants, Portable. See Guided missiles—Atomic power plants; Space vehicles—Atomic power plants

ATOMIC powered aircraft carriers; Atomic powered rockets; etc. See Aircraft carriers, Atomic powered; Rockets, Atomic powered; etc.

ATOMIC research
Analytical chemistry in nuclear technology; report on 7th conference on analytical chemistry in nuclear technology. M. T. Kelley and others. Science 144:570-2 My 1 '64
Exploring atom structure. Sci N L 85:83 F 8 '64
Looking back. L. Meitner. Bul Atomic Sci 20:2-7 N '64
Merry-go-round. W. J. Coughlin. Miss & Roc 16:46 Ja 18 '65
New merry-go-round; excerpts from address. J. T. Ramey. Aviation W 82:11 Ja 11 '65
Requirements merry-go-round; excerpts from remarks. J. T. Ramey. Aviation W 80:21 My 18 '64
Requirements merry-go-round: must need precede development? J. T. Ramey. Bul Atomic Sci 20:12-15 N '64

Europe, Western

See also
European organization for nuclear research

Russia

Big race. il Newsweek 61:66 Je 17 '63
Red carpet out for Seaborg; findings on visit to Russia. Bsns W p 100-2+ Je 15 '63
Soviets leading in fusion research. W. Burkett. Miss & Roc 16:14 Ja 25 '65

United States

See Atomic research

ATOMIC research laboratories
Nuclear facilities; symposium. il Arch Rec 134:181-92 S '63
See also
Argonne national laboratory
Brookhaven national laboratory
Hanford laboratories, Richland, Wash.
Oak Ridge national laboratory

Equipment

'A' train. il N Y Times Mag p98-9 Ap 5 '64

ATOMIC standard. See Time—Systems and standards

ATOMIC test ban treaty. See Nuclear test ban treaty, 1963

ATOMIC warfare
Atomic age, ed. by M. Grodzins and E. Rabinowitch. Review
New Yorker 40:136-41 Je 13 '64. J. Bernstein
Bertrand Russell on the sinful Americans; exchange of letters. B. Russell; J. Fischer. Harper 226:20+ Je '63; Discussion. 227:8+ Ag '63
Bomb carrier nobody can stop; Convair B-58 Hustler. F. V. Drake. il Read Digest 84:153-4+ Ap '64
Conflict in space, by M. N. Golovine. Review
Bul Atomic Sci 19:32-3 My '63. R. P. Schuster
Confrontation with reality. Nation 196:129 F 16 '63
Direction and control of nuclear power; address, September 16, 1964. L. B. Johnson. Dept State Bul 51:458-60 O 5 '64
Fail-safe fallacy, by S. Hook. Review
Nat R 15:444-5 N 19 '63. J. G. Campaigne, jr
Fear & the facts; control of nuclear weaponry; attitudes of presidential candidates. il Time 84:15-19 S 25 '64
Foretaste of a new kind of war. Sr Schol 84:3 F 21 '64
Fortress America. R. Steel. Commentary 36:119-24 Ag '63
Need for total disarmament under enforceable world law. G. Clark. Cur Hist 47:93-6+ Ag '64
Nuclear abolitionism. P. Kecskemeti. Commentary 36:43-8 Jl '63; Reply with rejoinder. A. L. Waskow. 36:394-8 N '63
October, 1962 the Cuba crisis: nuclear war was hours away. il Newsweek 62:24-6 O 28 '63
100 million lives, by R. Fryklund. Review
Atlan 210:65-7 N '62. B. Russell; Discussion. 211:42 F '63
Peacemonger answers some questions. A. Etzioni. il N Y Times Mag p 14+ Ap 21 '63
Power of prediction, and example. R. G. Sachs. Bul Atomic Sci 20:20-1 D '64
Prospects for war and peace; interview. H. Kahn. Nations Bsns 52:34-5+ Jl '64
Russia's plans for the next war. M. S. Johnson. il U S News 54:52-5 Ap 8 '63
Soviet military strategy, ed. by V. D. Sokolovsky. Review
Newsweek 61:30 My 6 '63
Straight from the horse's mouth; Soviet military strategy and thermonuclear war. W. D. Jacobs. il Nat R 15:68-70 Jl 30 '63
Surviving fire effects of nuclear detonations. A. Broido. Bul Atomic Sci 19:20-3 Mr '63
U.S. pushes idea of multi-lateral force. G. C. Wilson. Aviation W 78:28-30 F 11 '63
U.S.-Soviet agreement possible on war definition, Enthoven says; summary of address. A. Enthoven. Aviation W 78:39 F 18 '63
What is left to hope for? M. Born. Bul Atomic Sci 20:2-5 Ap '64
See also
Atomic weapons
Civil defense

Defenses

America's top ten targets. J. H. Winchester. il Sci Digest 54:54-8 N '63
Atlantic future: Europe's choice. F. Church. Harper 227:18+ N '63
Battlefield A-bomb: should generals control it? M. S. Johnson. il U S News 57:44-5 Ag 24 '64
Big debate over arms. U S News 57:48 Ag 31 '64
Both sides of test ban; debate in the Senate. U S News 55:74-5 S 30 '63
Britain and the new Europe; address, April 5, 1963; with questions and answers. D. O. Gore. Ann Am Acad 348:1-14 Jl '63
China and the bomb. New Repub 151:3-4 O 10 '64
China and the bomb. N. Cousins. Sat R 47:18+ N 28 '64
Control of nuclear strategy. J. Slessor. For Affairs 42:96-106 O '63
Could this happen? Fail-safe. Sci Digest 56:47 D '64
Defense against ballistic missiles. F. J. Dyson. Bul Atomic Sci 20:12-18 Je '64
Defenses and security. Commonweal 81:316 N 27 '64
Detailed test and detection plans readied to back nuclear treaty. K. Johnsen. Aviation W 79:28-9 Ag 26 '63
Europe and the Atlantic alliance; address, June 24, 1964. W. W. Rostow. Dept State Bul 51:41-3 Jl 13 '64; Same. Vital Speeches 30:619-20 Ag 1 '64
Fate of counterforce. W. V. O'Brien. Commonweal 78:216-18 My 17 '63
How safe is Fail-safe? D. Robinson. Read Digest 82:91-4 My '63
Military power and money. S. Melman. il Sat R 46:10-12 My 4 '63
More light on who does control the bomb; with report by the Republican national committee. il U S News 57:46-9 O 19 '64
More talks with the Russians; American and Soviet leaders of public opinion meet in Leningrad. N. Cousins. Sat R 47:30 S 26; 30-1 O 10 '64
Moscow and the M.L.R: hostility and ambivalence. Z. Brzezinski. For Affairs 43:126-34 O '64
New strategy for survival. il Newsweek 61:20-4 F 11 '63
Nonproliferation of nuclear weapons. B. T. Feld. il Bul Atomic Sci 20:2-6 D '64
NATO's nuclear dilemma. H. A. Kissinger. il Reporter 28:22-33+ Mr 28 '63; Discussion. 28:6+ Ap 25; 8+ My 9 '63

ATOMIC warfare—Defenses—*Continued*
Nuclear blast detectors ring nation's capital; NUDETS. Sci N L 284:404 D 28 '63
Nuclear deterrent and the Atlantic alliance; address, April 26, 1963. G. W. Ball. Dept State Bul 48:736-9 My 13 '63
NUDETS, the paradox of horror. S. Alsop. il Sat Eve Post 236:18 D 7 '63
Pro and con of test-ban treaty; symposium. il U S News 55:54-67 Ag 26 '63
Projected European union and American military responsibilities; address, April 6, 1963; with questions and answers. W. R. Kintner. Ann Am Acad 348:121-31 Jl '63
Reason, morality and defense policy. A. C. Enthoven. America 108:461-5, 494-7 Ap 6-13 '63; Correction. 108:597-8 Ap 27 '63
Reflections on protection. C. Newman. Yale R 52:404-11 Mr '63
Reporter at large; inquiry into enoughness. D. Lang. il New Yorker 40:100+ O 10 '64
S.S. Lunatic. S. King-Hall. Nation 196:298 Ap 13 '63
Stockpiling to survive a nuclear attack. A. W. Bellamy; reply with rejoinder. T. E. Phipps, jr. Science 139:674-5 F 15 '63
Strategy of overkill. R. E. Lapp. Bul Atomic Sci 19:4-11 Ap '63
Sure way to prevent nuclear war? interview. T. S. Power. il U S News 58:72-6 Ja 25 '65
Taking stock of Europe's nuclear defenses. H. W. Baldwin. il Reporter 28:29-34 Ap 25 '63
Test ban: the military argument; excerpts from the testimony before the Senate foreign relations committee, August 13, 1963. R. S. McNamara. Bul Atomic Sci 19:42-3 O '63
Test ban treaty; the military considerations; address, September 9, 1963. L. Saltonstall. Vital Speeches 29:750-2 O 1 '63
U.S. and U.K. sign agreement on sale of Polaris missiles; announcement, letter from Secretary Rusk, and text of agreement, April 6 and April 9, 1963. Dept State Bul 48:759-64 My 13 '63
What kind of NATO nuclear force? R. H. Dawson. bibliog f Ann Am Acad 351:30-9 Ja '64
What price conventional capabilities in Europe? B. Brodie. il Reporter 28:25-9+ My 23 '63
Why Russia and China now fear U.S. il U S News 57:66-70 N 30 '64
Wrangle over strategy. L. J. Halle. New Repub 150:19-21 Ja 18 '64
See also
North Atlantic treaty organization—Multilateral force (proposed)

Economic aspects

Military power and money. S. Melman. il Sat R 46:10-12 My 4 '63

Ethical aspects

Christian and war. J. O'Gara. Commonweal 80:171 My 1 '64
Christian ethics and nuclear warfare, ed. by U. S. Allers and W. V. O'Brien. Review
Commonweal 80:214-16 My 8 '64. J. G. Lawler
Christians and the bomb. J. O'Gara. Commonweal 77:612 Mr 8 '63
Churches and the bomb. J. Albertson. il America 111:692-3 N 28 '64
Ecumenical war games. Nation 199:366-7 N 23 '64
Hostilities and belligerents. N. Cousins. Sat R 46:16-17 F 2 '63
Journals of David E. Lilienthal. Review
New Repub 151:24-5+ O 17 '64. J. W. Finney
Morality of American nuclear policy. W. V. Kennedy. Cath World 199:363-70 S '64
More on the bomb. J. O'Gara. Commonweal 78:66 Ap 12 '63
Nuclear morality and eschatological realism. J. W. Douglass. Cath World 198:177-84 D '63
Pacem in terris. Commonweal 78:123-4 Ap 26 '63
Pacem in terris: for all humanity; with excerpts. il Newsweek 61:21-2 Ap 22 '63
Peace and morality. Commonweal 81:435 D 25 '64
What we are for; summary of new encyclical on world peace. John XXIII. il Time 81:60+ Ap 19 '63
See also
War and children

International control

Limited war and American defense policy, by J. Deitchman. Review
U S News 57:128 O 5 '64. D. Lawrence

Protests, demonstrations, etc, against

End of Aldermaston? British peace movement. New Repub 148:7-8 Ap 27 '63; Reply. P. Noel-Baker. 148:36+ Je 15 '63
France's ban-the-bombers. S. Gervis. Nation 197:91-3 Ag 24 '63
Peace marchers, help or hindrance to peace? pro and con discussion. il Sr Schol 82:10-11 F 13 '63
See also
Committee for non-violent action

Social aspects

Responsibility: an escape and an approach. W. E. Olson. Bul Atomic Sci 19:2-6 Mr '63; Discussion. 19:29-30 Je '63

Terminology

Nuclear war of the words. il Newsweek 61:23 F 11 '63

ATOMIC warfare, Prevention of. See War, Prevention of

ATOMIC warfare and children. See War and children

ATOMIC warfare in literature
Children of the a-bomb: the testament of the boys and girls of Hiroshima, comp. by A. Osada. Review
Sat R 46:91 Mr 16 '63. R. Falk
Nuclear age parables. P. Deasy. Commonweal 77:616-18 Mr 8 '63
Speak up, Mr Critic; Fail-safe and Triumph. Nation 196:110-11 F 9 '63

ATOMIC waste. See Radioactive waste disposal

ATOMIC weapons
A-arms cutback; U.S. and U.S.S.R. Sr Schol 84:21-2 My 8 '64
After the test ban; letter. B. Russell. Nation 197:inside cover, 241 O 19 '63
Agreeing again with Russians; plan for keeping nuclear arms out of orbits in space. Bsns W p28 O 12 '63
Antic semantics; Anglo-American plan for an interallied nuclear force. Newsweek 61:42+ My 20 '63
Arms race: what LBJ faces. il U S News 57:71 N 23 '64
Atomic arsenal; concerning testimony of Secretary McNamara on nuclear test ban treaty before the Senate foreign relations, Senate armed forces and Joint atomic energy committees. il Time 82:11-15 Ag 23 '63; Same abr. with title Our awesome atomic arsenal. Read Digest 83:67-71 N '63
Atomic arsenal that set off the big argument; 1964 political campaign. il U S News 57:49-50 O 5 '64
Atomic bombs for everyone; Egypt, Indonesia, the Congo. B. H. Bagdikian. il Sat Eve Post 236:66-9 Mr 2 '63
AEC reports nuclear weapons expenditures topping $5 billion. Aviation W 81:56 N 30 '64
Big debate over arms. U S News 57:48 Ag 31 '64
Bomarc for Canada. M. Halperin. New Repub 148:6-7 Mr 2 '63
Britain and Europe: the lesson of Skybolt. R. Steel. Commonweal 77:507-9 F 8 '63
Canada explodes over nuclear warheads. il Bsns W p28-9 F 9 '63
Canada's option. Commonweal 77:505 F 8 '63
Confrontation with reality. Nation 196:129 F 16 '63
Conventional nuclear weapons. J. Burnham. Nat R 16:808 S 22 '64
Cutback in overkill? Newsweek 62:54 Jl 15 '63
David and the Goliath; White House control of nuclear weapons. il Newsweek 64:64 O 19 '64
End of overkill? size of the U.S. nuclear arsenal. Sci Am 210:66 F '64
Excerpt from address, February 6, 1963. W. Young. Bul Atomic Sci 19:11 Ap '63
Fear & the facts; control of nuclear weaponry; attitudes of presidential candidates. il Time 84:15-19 S 25 '64
Fortress America. R. Steel. Commentary 36:119-24 Ag '63
France earmarks $5.4 billion for nuclear force development. Aviation W 81:31 N 23 '64
France's nuclear sword; nuclear-armed supersonic bombers. il Bsns W p34+ F 23 '63
French logic vs. computers. T. D. White. Newsweek 61:24 F 11 '63
Goldwater and the bomb: wrong questions, wrong answers. H. A. Kissinger. Reporter 31:27-8 N 5 '64
Goldwater statement on nuclear weapons. Aviation W 81:27 Ag 24 '64
Gomulka proposals; freezing nuclear and thermonuclear armaments in central Europe. il Cur Hist 47:107-8 Ag '64

ATOMIC weapons—*Continued*
Great Britain: the bomb again. New Repub 150:8-9 F 22 '64
How new atomic shell builds U.S. strength. il U S News 55:8 D 23 '63
Is Khrushchev Dr Strangelove? U S News 57:51 O 5 '64
Is red China a paper tiger? il U S News 57:76-7 O 19 '64
Is Russia outstripping us in weapons of mass destruction? address, December 7, 1962. C. H. Coggins. Vital Speeches 29:263-6 F 15 '63
Khrushchev on overkill; excerpt from address, January 16, 1963. N. S. Khrushchev. Bul Atomic Sci 19:7 Ap '63
Labor party's defense and foreign policy. P. C. G. Walker. For Affairs 42:391-8 Ap '64
Love and power in today's setting. A. J. Muste. Christian Cent 80:639-42 My 15 '63
McNamara details nuclear yields; average tactical nuclear weapon in western Europe. R. S. McNamara. Miss & Roc 15:12 S 28 '64
McNamara discusses retaliatory forces; text of testimony before House armed services committee. R. S. McNamara. Aviation W 80:74-5+ Mr 2 '64
McNamara outlines nuclear force policy. Aviation W 78:106-9 Ap 22 '63
Major national security problems confronting the United States; address, November 18, 1963. R. S. McNamara. Dept State Bul 49:914-21 D 16 '63
Mathematics of destruction. F. Oppenheimer. Sat R 48:20 Ja 16 '65
Meeting de Gaulle's nuclear moves; multilateral deterrent under NATO. Bsns W p34 F 16 '63
Melman: Overkill critic finds a welcome reception in capital, but the reasons are complicated. D. S. Greenberg. Science 144: 271-3 Ap 17 '64; Reply with rejoinder. S. Melman. 145:232-3 Jl 17 '64
More light on who does control the bomb; with report by the Republican national committee. il U S News 57:46-9 O 19 '64
Multibafflement. Time 81:33 Ap 5 '63
Multilateral force: Germany's finger on the atom. A. Etzioni. il Nation 199:208-11 O 12 '64
Multilateral muddle. Nation 199:319-20 N 9 '64
N for nothing? French quest for an H-bomb. il Newsweek 61:67 Ap 22 '63
National security and the nuclear-test ban. J. B. Wiesner and H. F. York. il Sci Am 211:27-35 bibliog(p 142) O '64; Reply. E. P. Wigner. 211:8+ D '64
New hopes in the race for peace. Bsns W p26-7 Ja 25 '64
New stalemate and new strategy; Secretary McNamara's testimony before the House armed services committee. Bsns W p28 F 2 '63
New strategy for survival. il Newsweek 61: 20-4 F 11 '63
Nonproliferation of nuclear weapons. B. T. Feld. il Bul Atomic Sci 20:2-6 D '64
NATO shaping inter-allied force with air, sea nuclear capability. D. E. Fink. Aviation W 78:27 My 27 '63
NATO to share in SAC nuclear planning. Aviation W 78:25-7 Je 3 '63
NATO with an atomic punch? Sr Schol 82: 16+ F 13 '63
Nth country problem; adaptation of conference report, January 17 to 20, 1963. J. Phelps and M. Kalkstein. Bul Atomic Sci 19:50-1 D '63
Nuclear containment. Christian Cent 80:259-60 F 27 '63
Nuclear issue may cause Canadian elections. Aviation W 78:37 F 4 '63
Nuclear pickle; Goldwater's effort to make campaign issue of nuclear-weapons control. il Newsweek 64:32-3 O 19 '64
Nuclear policy and French intransigence. M. W. Hoag. For Affairs 41:286-98 Ja '63
Nuclear stockpile: data suggest that in absence of clear policy reserves just growed and growed. E. Langer. Science 144:660-2 My 8 '64
On the way: secret a-weapon for Britain: projectile. U S News 54:8 Mr 4 '63
Overkill of Melman. Nation 198:359 Ap 13 '64
Pause: the armaments race. Nation 199:505 D 28 '64
Peace in our time? nuclear weapons as a stabilizer. L. J. Halle. New Repub 149:16-19 D 28 '63
Plan to share the weapons. Time 84:18 S 25 '64
Poor man's nuclear bomb; Egyptian rocket program. Nation 198:594-5 Je 15 '64
Preventing the spread of nuclear weapons. M. Kalkstein. Bul Atomic Sci 20:18-19 D '64
Preview of tomorrow's nuclear terror. W. J. Perkinson. Sci Digest 54:50-3 Ag '63
Real and unreal: new weapons systems in U.S. and Russia. Sr Schol 85:24 S 30 '64
Reporter at large; inquiry into enoughness. D. Lang. il New Yorker 40:100+ O 10 '64
Revolt of Europe; with editorial comment. E. Griffiths. il Sat Eve Post 236:13-21, 76 Mr 9 '63
Sandia development tops IEEE hardware; memory elements for use with nuclear weapon systems. C. D. LaFond. Miss & Roc 14:44+ Ap 6 '64
Short fuse on a long crisis; NATO meeting at Ottawa. il Bsns W p30-2 My 18 '63
Sino-Soviet nuclear dialogue: 1963. A. L. Hsieh. bibliog Bul Atomic Sci 21:16-21 Ja '65
Spread of nuclear weapons, by L. Beaton and J. Maddox. Review
New Repub 148:22-3+ F 16 '63. R. E. Osgood
Spread of nuclear weapons; excerpt from Great debate. R. Aron. il Atlan 215:44-50 Ja '65
Stockpile still increasing. Sci N L 85:38 Ja 18 '64
Teller urges strong nuclear management; excerpt from Science, technology, and management. E. Teller. Aviation W 78:92+ Ap 22 '63
Terror's stable balance. S. Alsop. Sat Eve Post 237:12 My 30 '64
To slow down the nuclear race. L. Beaton. il N Y Times Mag p 15+ Mr 8 '64
U.S. and Canadian negotiations regarding nuclear weapons; Department statement, January 30, 1963. Dept State Bul 48:243-4 F 18 '63
U.S. calls for exploration of freeze concept; statement, January 31, 1964. W. C. Foster. Dept State Bul 50:350-2 Mr 2 '64
U.S. proposes curb on spread of nuclear weapons; statement, February 6, 1964. W. C. Foster. Dept State Bul 50:376-9 Mr 9 '64
U.S. pushes idea of multi-lateral force. G. C. Wilson. Aviation W 78:28-30 F 11 '63
U.S.-Soviet agreement possible on war definition, Enthoven says; summary of address. A. Enthoven. Aviation W 78:39 F 18 '63
Weapon to kill everybody; or just cold-war bluster? U S News 57:8 S 28 '64
Where we stand on defense; excerpts from address, November 28, 1963. R. S. McNamara. il Duns R 83:53-4+ F '64; Same. Bul Atomic Sci 20:35-9 Mr '64
Who's ahead in the age of overkill? il Newsweek 62:42 N 18 '63
Why Europe fears us; excerpt from Great debate, tr. by E. Pawel. R. Aron. Atlan 214:47-52 D '64
Words and weapons. Newsweek 64:87 S 28 '64

Accidents

Politics of destruction. H. Wheeler and E. Burdick. il Sat R 46:25-7+ N 9 '63
Very real risk, war by accident; technical mistake or fault, and miscalculation or error of judgment. C. N. Barclay. il N Y Times Mag p 17+ My 5 '63

International control

See Atomic power—International control

Testing

Atomic retaliation jeopardized; EMP effects. W. Davis. Sci N L 84:293+ N 9 '63
Latest nuclear weapons; test series Operation Dominic. Sci N L 85:111 F 15 '64
Release of EMP data urged. H. M. David. Miss & Roc 13:23-4 S 30 '63
Sovereign remedy. Nation 197:231 O 19 '63
Soviets may have ultimate ABM; possibility of de-activating U.S. missiles in silos. Miss & Roc 13:14-15 S 16 '63; Discussion. 13: 54 S 16; 9 S 30; 9 O 7 '63; Pop Sci 183:19 D '63
Testing those missiles. New Repub 149:4-5 S 21 '63
Treaty debate underscores lack of electromagnetic data. Miss & Roc 13:19 S 23 '63

ATOMIC weapons and disarmament
Alternatives to overkill: dream and reality. P. Green. Bul Atomic Sci 19:23-6 N '63
Arms control and disarmament; transcript of the television program, State department briefing: disarmament, first broadcast, January 14, 1963. Dept State Bul 48: 115-27 Ja 28 '63
Atom: slave or master? Christian Cent 81: 979-80 Ag 5 '64
Atomic power and disarmament. V. Emelyanov. Bul Atomic Sci 19:16-20 O '63

ATOMIC weapons and disarmament—*Cont.*
Breaking the impasse. A. B. Sabin. Bul Atomic Sci 19:36 O '63
Change, hope and the bomb. by D. E. Lilienthal. Review
Bsns W p200+ O 19 '63
Collapse of disarmament conference seen; United Nations conference on nuclear disarmament. L. L. Doty. Aviation W 81:16-17 Ag 31 '64
Congress and disarmament. J. S. Clark. Bul Atomic Sci 19:3-8 S '63; Reply. S. Gottlieb. 19:40-1 D '63
Day he dies. W. J. Coughlin. Miss & Roc 14:50 My 4 '64
De Gaulle's reasons. A. Werth. Nation 199: 422 D 7 '64
Deterrence, arms control, and disarmament. by J. D. Singer. Review
Bul Atomic Sci 19:25 Je '63. M. Raskin
Disarmament at the U.N: discussions in detente. H. A. Jack. Bul Atomic Sci 20:33-6 F '64
Economics and politics of arms reduction; symposium. Bul Atomic Sci 20:6-23 Ap '64
Gradual arms reduction. A. Etzioni. Bul Atomic Sci 19:30-3 O '63
Immediate steps toward disarmament. F. A. Long. Bul Atomic Sci 20:7-10 F '64
Information in arms control verification. B. G. Lall. Bul Atomic Sci 20:43-5 O '64
Minimal deterrent vs. saturation parity. L. Szilard. Bul Atomic Sci 20:6-12 Mr '64
Mutual deterrence. Commonweal 81:28-9 O 2 '64
Mythology of the atom; summary of addresses. D. E. Lilienthal. Bul Atomic Sci 19:21-4 O '63; Discussion. 19:37-8 D '63; 20: 25-6 F '64
North America, the open continent; address, June 16, 1963. W. R. Tyler. Dept State Bul 49:93-7 Jl 15 '63
Nato-Warsaw detente? B. G. Lall. Bul Atomic Sci 20:37-9 N '64
Nuclear abolitionism. P. Kecskemeti. Commentary 36:43-8 Jl '63; Reply with rejoinder. A. L. Waskow. 36:394-8 N '63
Nuclear controls. Commonweal 81:532-3 Ja 22 '65
Nuclear-free zone in Latin America; United Nations resolution. U N Rev 11:14-16+ F '64
Nuclear slow-down. Commonweal 80:187 My 8 '64
Nuclear weapons control. J. E. Dougherty. bibliog f Cur Hist 47:31-8+ Jl '64
Orbital bomb. N. Cousins. Sat R 46:24+ My 11 '63
Peaceful use of terror. W. H. Honan. New Repub 148:19-22 Ap 27 '63
Questions and answers on the U.S. production freeze proposal. B. G. Lall. Bul Atomic Sci 20:30-4 D '64
Risk and security in the age of nuclear weapons: address, December 15, 1962. W. C. Foster. Dept State Bul 48:128-34 Ja 28 '63
Safeguarded zonal disarmament. J. Orear. il Bul Atomic Sci 19:18-21 F '63
Secretary Rusk discusses world developments on Issues and answers, October 18, 1964. D. Rusk. Dept State Bul 51:654-60 N 9 '64
Should nuclear weapons be placed under international control? pro and con discussion. Sr Schol 85:8-9 N 18 '64
Soviet scientist looks at disarmament. Y. Sheinin. Bul Atomic Sci 20:19-22 Ja '64
Step-by-step disarmament. D. R. Inglis. Cur Hist 47:88-92+ Ag '64
Substantial reductions in strategic delivery vehicles. B. G. Lall. il Bul Atomic Sci 21: 45-8 Ja '65
Sure way to prevent nuclear war? interview. T. S. Power. il U S News 58:72-6 Ja 25 '65
This month's feature: U.S. & international control of arms. Cong Digest 43:193-224 Ag '64
U-turn; cut back in production of materials for nuclear weapons. il Newsweek 63:85 My 4 '64
U.S. China policy and disarmament. F. W. Neal. Bul Atomic Sci 19:5-8 N '63
U.S. discusses freeze proposal in disarmament committee; statement, April 16, 1964. A. S. Fisher. bibliog f Dept State Bul 50:756-9 My 11 '64
U.S. makes proposals for safeguards for peaceful nuclear activities and for bomber destruction; statements, March 5 and March 19, 1964. A. S. Fisher. bibliog f Dept State Bul 50:641-5 Ap 20 '64
U.S. outlines cutoff and verification provisions to halt production of fissionable materials for nuclear weapons use; statements, June 18 and June 25, 1964. W. C. Foster. Dept State Bul 51:123-7 Jl 27 '64
U.S. outlines verification measures to assure compliance with proposed freeze of strategic nuclear vehicles; statement, August 27, 1964. C. R. Timberlake. Dept State Bul 51:413-17 S 21 '64
Why Russia rejects U.S. plan to freeze arms. U S News 56:9 F 3 '64
See also
Atomic bombs—Testing, Suspension of

ATOMIC workers
Scientific and technical personnel in atomic energy. H. S. Liebling and A. Katz. il Mo Labor R 87:633-8 Je '64

ATOMS
Atoms and molecules; reprint. il Sci Digest 53:66-9 My '63
Biography of an atom and the universe. J. Bronowski. il N Y Times Mag p 19+ O 13 '63; Same abr. with title Amazing biography of an atom. Read Digest 84:133-6 Ja '64
Dislocation movements in metals. D. Kuhlmann-Wilsdorf and H. G. F. Wilsdorf. bibliog il Science 144:17-25 Ap 3 '64
Distribution of atoms in high chalcocite, Cu_2S. M. J. Buerger and B. J. Wuensch. bibliog il Science 141:276-7 Jl 19 '63
Optical pumping. T. R. Carver. bibliog il Science 141:599-608 Ag 16 '63
Optical studies at high pressures. L. S. Whatley and others. bibliog il Science 144: 968-76 My 22 '64
X-raying atoms. M. Mann. il Pop Mech 120: 112-15 D '63
See also
Atomic nuclei
Atomic research
Neutrinos
Protons
Quantum theory

ATOMS for peace awards
Smashing prize. Newsweek 62:75 Ag 12 '63

ATOMS-for-peace conference. See International conference on the peaceful uses of atomic energy, 3d, Geneva, 1964

ATONAL music. See Music

ATONEMENT
Outside the camp: excerpt from Passion. K. A. Olsson. Christian Cent 80:264-7 F 27 '63

ATRIUM houses. See Architecture, Domestic

ATROCITIES
Christmas crucible, 1963; portfolio. Esquire 60:133-7 D '63
Dominican Republic: the goons again. N. Gall. il Nation 198:159-61 F 17 '64

ATROMID S
New drug lowers fats in blood stream. Sci N L 85:40 Ja 18 '64

ATROPA belladonna. See Nightshade, Black

ATROPHIC rhinitis. See Rhinitis

ATROPINE
Deadly nightshade. Sci N L 86:204 S 26 '64

ATTACHED houses. See Row houses

ATTACK on Pearl Harbor, 1941. See Pearl Harbor, Attack on, 1941

ATTENDANCE (in industry) See Absenteeism

ATTENDANCE (school) See School attendance

ATTENTION
Attention, vigilance, and cortical evoked-potentials in humans. M. Haider and others. bibliog il Science 145:180-2 Jl 10 '64
Eye fixation aspect of attention to visual stimuli in infant chimpanzees. G. Berkson and F. L. Fitz-Gerald. bibliog il Science 139:586-7 F 15 '63
How to train pupils to listen. J. Mersand. Sr Schol 85:9T N 4 '64
See also
Observation (psychology)

ATTENUATORS, Radio. See Radio attenuators

ATTERBURY, Cathy
I believe. M. Woodward. por Seventeen 22: 168 F '63

ATTIC treasure; drama. See Miller, H. L.

ATTICS
Big idea: live in the whole attic. H. M. King. il Pop Sci 183:120-1 S '63
Exploit the true shape of an attic. il House B 105:186-7 S '63
Grand prize winner third-floor attic finished as a remarkable playroom. il Bet Hom & Gard 41:60-1 O '63
How to carve a shapely room out of a peaked attic. il House & Gard 125:190-1 My '64
How to transform your attic into an inviting room. il House & Gard 123:168-71 My '63
Increase your living space. il Ladies Home J 80:110 Mr '63

ATTILA, king of the Huns
Great confrontations: Leo the Great and Attila the Hun. C. V. Wedgwood. il Horizon 5:76-80 My '63

ATTITUDE gyro. See Gyroscope

ATTITUDES
Attitude statements as positive and negative reinforcements. C. Golightly and D. Byrne. il Science 146:798-9 N 6 '64
Attitudes toward desegregation. H. H. Hyman and P. B. Sheatsley. il Sci Am 211:16-23 bibliog(p 142) Jl '64
Creators and destroyers; polar attitudes toward life and death. E. Fromm. Sat R 47:22-5 Ja 4 '64; Discussion. 47:23 F 1 '64
Danger beyond smoking. N. Cousins. Sat R 47:22 Ja 25 '64; Same abr. Read Digest 84:41-2 My '64; Discussion. Sat R 47:31-2 F 15 '64
Economics and the quality of life; adaptation of address, December 27, 1963. J. K. Galbraith. bibliog Science 145:117-23 Jl 10 '64; Discussion. 145:876 Ag 28 '64
Fear or courage? the question that comes before politics. M. Mannes. Vogue 144:106-7 Ag 15 '64
Fearmongers; with report by B. Bettelheim. il Life 56:71-8+ F 7 '64
Fundamentals for survival; with program for discussion group, by E. G. Neisser. R. Brecher and E. Brecher. Parents Mag 38:35-6+, 45+ Je '63
Get off Johnny's back! L. M. Magill. il Sat R 47:64-6 F 15 '64; Discussion. 47:62-3 Mr 21 '64
Health, society, and social science. R. Straus and J. A. Clausen. bibliog f Ann Am Acad 346:1-8 Mr '63
Mailbag: the underwritten generation. J. Ciardi. Sat R 46:15-16 Mr 16 '63
Manner of speaking; circles: biographical approach to ideas. J. Ciardi. Sat R 46:29 Ag 24 '63
Manner of speaking; to be sure. J. Ciardi. Sat R 46:10-11 Ap 13 '63
Negro: why whites fear him. S. Hirsh. il Sci Digest 54:12-15 O '63
New parties. N. Cousins. Sat R 46:14 Ag 3 '63
Psychological puzzler; white boxes look bigger to whites. il Sci Digest 55:82-3 Ja '64
'63; best college class in history. Life 54:4 Je 21 '63
Ten most trusted whites. A. Poinsett. il Ebony 19:36-8+ Ap '64
Views, influence linked. Sci N L 86:198 S 26 '64
White is bigger to whites. E. Mirel. Sci N L 84:229 O 12 '63
Who are your child's heroes? with program for discussion group, by E. G. Neisser. D. B. Harris and M. R. Weisbord. il Parents Mag 38:35-6+, 50-2+ Je '63
See also
Optimism
Political attitudes
Political thought
Public opinion
Stereotype (psychology)
Value (psychology)

ATTITUDES, Professional. See Professionalism

ATTLEE, Clement Richard Attlee, 1st earl
My most unforgettable character. Read Digest 85:81-5 O '64

ATTORNEY General (United States) See United States—Justice, Department of

ATTORNEYS. See Lawyers

ATTRACTANTS, Insect. See Insect sex attractants

ATTWATER prairie chickens. See Prairie chickens

ATTWOOD, William
In memory of John F. Kennedy. Look 27:11-13 D 31 '63
We face a new kind of world. por Look 27:25-7 N 5 '63
Young power in diplomacy. por Vogue 143:90 Ap 15 '64

ATWATER, James
Crocodiles in the cellar. Sat Eve Post 237:32-3 S 26 '64
Detroit vs. the Mafia; a city fights back. Sat Eve Post 237:69-73 My 30 '64
Do they really hate us in Canada? Sat Eve Post 236:15-21 Ap 6 '63
Doomed to an early death. Sat Eve Post 237:66-8 O 31 '64
Great A-11 deception. Sat Eve Post 237:15-17 My 2 '64
Houseful of helpers awake at the switch. Sat Eve Post 237:15-21 D 5 '64
How the modern Minuteman guards the peace. Sat Eve Post 236:65-9 F 9 '63
If we can crack Mississippi. . . Sat Eve Post 237:15-19 Jl 25 '64
Last stand of the big bomber. Sat Eve Post 237:13-17 Je 20 '64
Spanish gold two fathoms deep. Sat Eve Post 237:66-71 D 12 '64

—and Vaughan, Roger
Room at the bottom of the sea. Sat Eve Post 237:18-25 S 5 '64

ATWATER, Maxine
Southern India. Travel 123:38-40 Ja '65

ATWATER, Richard
(tr) See Procopius. Emperor's vices

ATWATER, Ronald C.
Colombia: Señor Ron; with report by M. J. Kubic. por Newsweek 61:48 Je 3 '63

ATWOOD, Ellis D.
All aboard for happy land. E. L. Barcella. il Todays Health 41:62-3+ N '63

ATWOOD, John Leland
How 300,000 work for three moon men. il por Newsweek 64:61-5 D 21 '64

ATWOOD, Sanford Soverhill
New broom for Emory. por Time 82:36+ Jl 19 '63

AUBREY, James T. Jr
Great adventure. NEA J 52:33-48 O '63
No. 1 supplier of TV viewers. il pors Bsns W p90-1+ Ap 25 '64

AUBURN, Norman Paul
Free world vs. communism, as viewed around the world; address, September 25, 1964. Vital Speeches 31:57-61 N 1 '64
Problems of urban universities. Sch & Soc 91:73 F 9 '63

AUBUSSON tapestries. See Tapestry

AUCHINCLOSS, Douglas
Bishop of Woolwich speaks for the growing edge of Christian thought in America as well as Europe. Horizon 5:8-9 S '63

AUCHINCLOSS, Eve
Space-age guide for social astronauts. Mlle 56:173+ Ap '63
(ed) See Baldwin, J. Disturber of the peace

AUCHINCLOSS, Louis
Best man, vintage 361 A.D. Life 56:19+ Je 12 '64
Deductible yacht; story. Harper 226:42-7 F '63
Landmarker; story. Sat Eve Post 237:50-3 My 23 '64
Power in trust; story. Sat Eve Post 236:56-62 My 4 '63
Power of appointment; story. Sat Eve Post 236:34-5 Mr 9 '63

AUCLAIR, Jacques L. and Cartier, J. J.
Pea aphid: rearing on a chemically defined diet. bibliog Science 142:1068-9 N 22 '63

AUCOIN, Clifford
Banker to his own flesh and blood. New Yorker 40:125-6+ Ap 18 '64

AUCTIONS
Auction. T. B. Pratt, jr. il Flying 74:24-5+ Mr '64
Centuries-old pleasure of auctions. N. A. Hecht. Am Home 67:94 My '64
Nostalgia lifts the bids; Hal Roach studios. il Bsns W p30-1 Ag 10 '63
Report: selling by teletype; Integrated data auction. Suc Farm 61:132 Ap '63
What am I bid? Am Home 66:93 My '63
See also
Parke-Bernet galleries, incorporated

AUCTIONS, Art. See Art sales

AUDEN, Wynstan Hugh
Books. New Yorker 39:155-62+ Mr 9 '63
On the circuit; poem. New Yorker 40:36 Jl 4 '64
Thanksgiving for a habitat; poem. New Yorker 39:30 Ag 17 '63
(tr) See Hammarskjöld, D. Markings; Poems from Markings

about

Auden's sacred awe. R. M. Ohmann. Commonweal 78:279-81 My 31 '63
Books: power of perspective. D. Malcolm. New Yorker 39:185-90 My 4 '63
Poetry of W. H. Auden, by M. K. Spears. Review
Commonweal 79:437-8 Ja 10 '64. R. M. Ohmann
Recent criticism. H. Strickhausen. Poetry 104:265-6 Jl '64
Words, words, words. H. Tracy. New Repub 148:22-3 Mr 16 '63

AUDIENCES
Audiences are too acquiescent; excerpts from Gaily, gaily. B. Hecht. Theatre Arts 47:14-15+ Jl '63
Habit of opera. A. Vanderbilt. il Opera N 27:8-11 Mr 16 '63
Hollywood's teen-age gold mine. H. Ehrlich. il Look 28:60-4+ N 3 '64

AUDIENCES—*Continued*
Night at the opera; caustic opera audience at Parma's Royal theater. il Newsweek 65: 77-8 Ja 11 '65
Opinion, please, from New York: what's wrong with the theatre? J. Simon. Mlle 59: 48+ My '64
Pertussin instruments; coughs and wheezes. Newsweek 61:60 F 18 '63
See also
Applause

AUDIENCES, Papal. See Papal audiences

AUDIO amplifiers. See Amplifiers

AUDIO fairs
Audio in the '60s; this year's New York high fidelity music show. I. Berger. il Sat R 47: 55-7+ S 26 '64
Audio trends in Britain; International audio fair, London. P. Halliday. il Electr World 70:64+ D '63
High fidelity newsfronts (cont) N. Eisenberg. Hi Fi 13:23 Jl '63; 14:31-2 Je '64
High fidelity newsfronts; N.Y. high fidelity show. N. Eisenberg. Hi Fi 14:31 D '64
New York hi-fi show. W. A. Stocklin. Electr World 70:12 N '63; 72:6 D '64
New York high-fidelity music show. M. Rotbard. Am Rec G 30:250-1 N '63
1964 audio show. P. Davies. Mus Am 84:52 N '64
1963 hi-fi show. E. Salzman. Mus Am 83:35+ O '63
Notes from our correspondents; Festival du son in Paris. R. McMullen. Hi Fi 14:24+ Je '64
Other side; 1964 audio fair in London. T. Heinitz. Sat R 47:63-4 Ap 25 '64
See now, hear later; New York high fidelity music show. I. Berger. Sat R 46:122 O 12 '63
Shown at the show; New York high fidelity show. I. B. Berger. Sat R 47:73 O 31 '64
'63 hi-fi show: with directory. I. Berger. Sat R 46:56-7+ S 14 '63
Sound advice; N.Y. high fidelity show. R. N. Angus. Mod Phot 28:98+ Ja; 90+ F '64
Sound; highlights of the New York high fidelity show. J. Wesson. U S Camera 27: 38-9 Ja '64
Sound; transistors at N.Y. trade show. J. Wesson. U S Camera 28:32+ Ja '65
Tuning in to the ladies; High fidelity music show, New York. il Bsns W p 128 S 21 '63

AUDIO frequency. See Radio frequency

AUDIO frequency meters. See Radio instruments

AUDIO oscillators. See Oscillators

AUDIO-visual aids
Audiovisual materials. See issues of NEA journal to May 1964
Learning resources de luxe! S. Solomon. il Sr Schol 83:13T-14T S 20 '63
Misuse of audiovisual materials. NEA J 53:11 D '64
New sights and sounds in the classroom. A. Darnborough. il UNESCO Courier 17:12-14 F '64
School with teacherless classrooms. W. Hartley and E. Hartley. il Pop Mech 120:128-30 O '63
Special issue on A-V instruction; symposium, ed. by R. Burgert. il Sr Schol 85:8T-10T+ Ja 21 '65
What's happening in education? W. D. Boutwell. PTA Mag 58:15-16 Je '64
What's in a name? D. P. Ely. il NEA J 53:57-8 D '64
See also
Educational media index
Instructional materials centers
Libraries and audio-visual materials
Magnetic recorders and recording—Educational applications
Tape recordings

AUDIO-visual instruction
Special issue on A-V instruction; symposium, ed. by R. Burgert. il Sr Schol 85:8T-10T+ Ja 21 '65
Visual materials. D. Irving. il Sch Arts 63: 28-9 D '63
See also
Libraries and audio-visual materials
Television in education

AUDIOGENIC seizures. See Neuroses, Experimental

AUDIT bureau of circulations
Audit bureau of circulations at fifty. R. L. Tobin. Sat R 47:75-6 N 14 '64

AUDITING
Civil war among the auditors. J. Thackray. il Duns R 83:42-4+ Ap '64

AUDITIONS, Metropolitan. See Singing—Competitions

AUDITORIUM theater, Chicago. See Chicago—Auditorium theater

AUDITORIUMS
Again, they are readying the convention halls; excerpts from Two party system. R. Harrity. il Look 28:22-30+ Jl 14 '64
Building types study. il Arch Rec 136:115-42 D '64
Cleveland's $2-million mall covers a $17-million hall. il Bsns W p33 S 12 '64
Form defined by use. il Arch Rec 135:159-61 Ap '64
Giant Illinois dome nears completion. il Arch Forum 118:117 Mr '63
Illinois' flying saucer; spectacular assembly hall; reprint. il Recreation 57:340-1 S '64
Lift-dome auditorium; Brownwood, Tex. J. Clary. il Am City 78:100-1 O '63
Prestressed units form inverted dome. il Arch Rec 136:198-201 O '64
Thoughtful design; multipurpose auditorium. il Am City 79:94-5 My '64
Typhoon-proof louvers screen tropical sun; Philippine American life insurance office building, Manila. il Arch Rec 134:139-41 D '63
University of Illinois spectacular. il Arch Rec 134:111-16 Jl '63

Air conditioning

Air conditioning of auditorium-type buildings. A. Greenberg. bibliog il Arch Rec 135:205-8 Mr '64

AUDITORY nerves. See Nerves

AUDITORY sensations. See Hearing

AUDUBON, John James
Audubon mystery. Audubon Mag 66:91 Mr '64
Audubon, the artist. E. H. Dwight. il Audubon Mag 65:20-3 Ja '63
Audubon treasury. il N Y Times Mag p80 O 6 '63
John James Audubon, by A. Ford. Review Time il por 84:66-7 D 25 '64

AUDUBON medal
Greatest honor, says Justice Douglas of Audubon medal. il Audubon Mag 65:113 Mr '63
Rachel Carson receives Audubon medal; with acceptance address. J. Vosburgh. il Audubon Mag 66:98-9 Mr '64

AUDUBON nature camps
Our Maine camp. J. Vosburgh. bibliog f il Audubon Mag 65:90-7 Mr '63

AUDUBON nature centers
Aullwood farm produces a bumper crop of visitors; with dedication address, by H. H. Mills. il Audubon Mag 65:82-4 Mr '63
Goal: 2000 nature centers by the year 2000. J. J. Shomon. Audubon Mag 66:148-9 My '64
Nature centers are spreading fast. J. J. Shomon. il Audubon Mag 65:295 S '63
Nature centers gaining momentum. J. J. Shomon. il Audubon Mag 65:44-5 Ja '63
Welcome to another new center; Chet Ager bird and wildlife study center, Lincoln, Neb. B. L. Ashbaugh. il Audubon Mag 66: 15 Ja '64

AUDUBON prints. See Birds in art

AUDUBON societies
See also
National Audubon society

AUER, Bernhard M.
Letter from the publisher. Time 83:15 Ap 24 '64
Letter from the publisher; Time sponsors news tour of Europe for U.S. businessmen. Time 82:28-9 N 15 '63

AUERBACH, Arnold. See Auerbach, Red

AUERBACH, Kate
Kate Auerbach's stitchery. A. Adams. il Craft Horiz 23:32-3 Jl '63

AUERBACH, Red
Big Red. il por Time 81:55 F 15 '63

AUERBACH, Robert
Thymus: its role in lymphoid recovery after irradiation. bibliog Science 139:1061 Mr 15 '63

AUERBACH, Sylvia
Jobs in the money. Mlle 59:128-31+ S '64

AUERT, Edward
Examination of conscience; poem. Nation 198: 584 Je 8 '64

AUGSPURGER, George L.
Column loudspeaker systems. Electr World 69:25-7+ Je '63
Thin loudspeaker systems. Electr World 70: 30-2 S '63

AUGUST, Bob
Team on trial. Sat Eve Post 236:86-8 N 23 '63
—See Davis, E. jt. auth.

AUGUST, Kendall
Industrial packaging: the key word is merchandising. Duns R 84:92-3+ D '64
Office technology; the big leap forward. Duns R 84:pt2 118-19+ S '64

AUGUST
August bounty; excerpt from Sundial of the seasons. H. Borland. il Read Digest 85:29-30+ Ag '64
Dog days; quotations, comp. by E. F. Murphy. il N Y Times Mag p46 Ag 4 '63
In August; list of anniversaries, events and other notable dates coming up next month (title varies) (cont) il N Y Times Mag p 14 Jl 28 '63; 16 Ag 2 '64
AUGUSTA national golf club course. See Golf courses
AUGUSTUS, emperor of Rome
Year one. M. I. Finley.il por Horizon 6:4-17 Wint '64
AUKS
Birds of the sea. A. Sprunt, 4th. il Motor B 112:29+ O '63
AUL, Henry
Garden of many moods. Flower Grower 50:20-1 My '63
AULAIRE, Ingri Parin d'
Miss Moore in Brooklyn: a reminiscence. il Horn Bk 40:473-4 O '64
AULER, Robert. See Young, D. jt. auth.
AULETTA, Richard
Colorado conversion. Travel 121:58-9 My '64
AULL, Mrs John W.
Aullwood farm produces a bumper crop of visitors; with dedication address, by H. H. Mills. il por Audubon Mag 65:82-4 Mr '63
AULLWOOD Audubon center, Ohio. See Audubon nature centers
AULLWOOD children's farm, Ohio. See Audubon nature centers
AUNT Anna; story. See O'Hara, J.
AUNT Fran; story. See O'Hara, J.
AUNT Jemima. See Advertising characters
AURIANNE award
Emil Liers wins Aurianne award for his book A black bear's story. Library J 89:1396+ Mr 15 '64
AURIC, Georges
Auric's Wozzeck. Newsweek 62:61 D 16 '63
Right in the heart of Paris. il por Time 83:71-2 Je 26 '64
Second fame: good food. N. Lyon. por Vogue 145:116-18 Ja 15 '65
AURIOL, Jacqueline (Douet)
Sweet explosion in the air. P. Ress. il por Sports Illus 19:16-17 Jl 8 '63
AURORAS
Auroras in September. L. J. Robinson. il Sky & Tel 26:256-7 N '63
Brilliant August aurora. il Sky & Tel 26:217 O '63
September aurora sequel. il Sky & Tel 26:322 D '63
See also
Magnetic storms
AUSCHWITZ atrocities. See World war, 1939-1945—Atrocities
AUSCHWITZ concentration camp. See Concentration camps—Poland
AUSFORM process. See Steel metallurgy
AUSLANDER, Joseph
It is spring again! poem. McCalls 91:154 My '64
Next stop South; poem. McCalls 91:190 O '63
Women bear witness; poem. McCalls 90:198 Ap '63
AUST, R. B. and Drickamer, H. G.
Carbon: a new crystalline phase. bibliog Science 140:817-19 My 17 '63
AUSTEN, Jane
Our great favourite, Miss Austen. J. C. Herold. il Horizon 6:41-8 Spr '64
AUSTIN, Anthony
Honorifics. N Y Times Mag p 15-16 Ag 11 '63
Seventy-five years ago. N Y Times Mag p51+ Je 9 '63
U.S, then and now. N Y Times Mag p54+ My 3 '64
AUSTIN, J. E.
Fog-proof system. Am City 79:113-14 Mr '64
AUSTIN, J. Paul
New force for peace; address, June 10, 1964. Vital Speeches 30:605-8 Jl 15 '64
about
Coke tries new ways to refresh. il por Bsns W p 100-1+ Ag 24 '63
Kvass vs. Coke. New Yorker 40:33-4 Je 6 '64
AUSTIN, Rosemary
Reader's choice. Travel 120:6 N '63
AUSTIN, Roxanna
1963 ALA awards winners. ALA Bul 57:768-71 S '63
AUSTIN, Minn.
6.4 footcandles downtown. H. J. Lamon. il Am City 79:118 Ag '64
AUSTIN, Tex.
Hotels, restaurants, etc.
Driskill. il Newsweek 65:71 Ja 11 '65
Recreation
Guide for joint use of facilities: school and recreation facilities. Recreation 56:322-3+ S '63
Street traffic
Electronics de-irritate an intersection. W. H. Klapproth. il Am City 78:86-7 Jl '63
AUSTIN car company. See American Bantam car company
AUSTING, Ronald
Adventures with hummingbirds. il Audubon Mag 66:252-6 Jl '64
Caught in midair; excerpts from I went to the woods. il N Y Times Mag p 106-7 Ap 12 '64
AUSTRAL oil company, incorporated
Oil after the tax cut. Fortune 70:78+ D '64
AUSTRALIA
Australia's strategic position; address, January 25, 1964. R. Hilsman. Dept State Bul 50:243-50 F 17 '64
New pulse of Australia. J. Morris. il Sat Eve Post 236:20-3 Mr 2 '63
They're thinking big down under. F. Drake and K. Drake. il Read Digest 85:106-12 O '64
See also
Airlines—Australia
Airplanes, Military—Australia
Aluminum industry and trade—Australia
Architecture, Domestic—Australia
Astronomical observatories—Australia
Botany—Australia
Church unity—Australia
Crime and criminals—Australia
Elections—Australia
Festivals—Australia
Forests and forestry—Australia
Geology—Australia
Immigration and emigration—Australia
Labor and laboring classes—Australia
Melville Island
National parks and reserves—Australia
Petroleum—Australia
Political campaigns—Australia
Private schools—Australia
Publishers and publishing—Australia
Space research—Australia
Sports—Australia
Strikes—Australia
Trade unions—Australia
Yachts and yachting—Australia
Zoology—Australia
Commerce
Hustlers; surge in exports to Asia. Time 84:94 Jl 10 '64
Commercial treaties and agreements
U.S. concludes meat agreement with Australia; announcement, with Australian note, February 17, 1964, and United States reply. Dept State Bul 50:381 Mr 9 '64
Defenses
Australia plans air arm modernization. Aviation W 81:23 N 23 '64
Belated shape-up. Time 84:37 N 20 '64
Now Australia finds she's in the line of fire. il U S News 58:25-7 Ja 11 '65
Poor military posture. il Time 83:27 My 29 '64
Description and travel
Australia. A. Villiers. il Nat Geog Mag 124:309-85 S '63
Australia: everything is different. J. Betjemen. Vogue 142:182-3 D '63
Australia, where surf-riding is flying on wings of foam. R. Cameron. Vogue 143:119-20+ My '64
Australia's unknown islands. H. E. Mercer. il Travel 120:28-31+ N '63
Back of beyond. J. Sidney. il Travel 119:44-7 Ap '63
Dining adventures in Australia. S. Spitzer. il Holiday 36:94-5+ N '64
Just south of Sydney. H. E. Mercer. il Travel 122:47-51 Ag '64
Letter from Australia. A. Moorehead. il New Yorker 40:216+ O 10 '64
New good move for travellers: Australia. Vogue 143:75+ My '64
Discovery and exploration
Cooper's Creek. by A. Moorehead. Review
Newsweek 63:113A+ Mr 16 '64
Reporter 30:52-4 Mr 12 '64. G. Paulding
Sat R il 47:47-8 F 15 '64. L. E. Rorabacher
Time il 83:96 F 14 '64

AUSTRALIA—Discovery and exploration—*Cont.*
Ghastly blank; first exploration of Australia; excerpt from Cooper's Creek. A. Moorehead. il Atlan 213:100-14 F '64

Economic conditions

American invasion of Australia. il Newsweek 64:53-6 Ag 10 '64
Big rise hits down under. il Bsns W p92-3+ D 21 '63
Skyline rises in Sydney. il Bsns W p72+ N 21 '64
See also
Labor and laboring classes—Australia

Foreign relations

Australia: white island in a brown sea. D. Warner. il Reporter 28:25-9 My 9 '63
Shadow and substance of the ANZUS pact. D. Warner. il Reporter 30:21-3 Je 4 '64

Asia, Southeastern

Australia and southeast Asia. P. Hasluck. For Affairs 43:51-63 O '64

Indonesia

How Australia is rearming against threats of war. il U S News 57:10 N 23 '64

New Zealand

Tasman Sea: a moat between allies. New Repub 149:12 Jl 20 '63

Maps

Australia on maps, old and new. il Nat Geog Mag 124:386-7, sup(folded map) S '63

Native races

Civil rights for aborigines. Time 83:33 Je 5 '64

Politics and government

Australia: white island in a brown sea. D. Warner. il Reporter 28:25-9 My 9 '63
Turn on the water. New Repub 149:7-8 N 30 '63

Religious institutions and affairs

Doctor Wednesday; preacher at St Stephen's Presbyterian church in downtown Sydney. il Time 84:100 N 13 '64
News of the Christian world (cont) Christian Cent 80:788, 987-8, 1558-9; 81:156, 776-8, 1124-6, 1476-8 Je 12, Ag 7, D 11 '63, Ja 29, Je 10, S 9, N 25 '64
See also
Church of England in Australia
Methodist church in Australia

AUSTRALIA, New Zealand, and United States treaty council. See ANZUS council
AUSTRALIAN art. See Art, Australian (aboriginal)
AUSTRALIAN ballet company
Year of accomplishment. B. Dean. il Dance Mag 37:16-17 Ag '63
AUSTRALIAN fruit bats. See Bats
AUSTRALIAN netting spider. See Spiders
AUSTRALIAN NEW GUINEA. See New Guinea, Territory of
AUSTRALIAN songs. See Songs, Australian
AUSTRALIAN students
Civil rights now; students of Sydney university protest racial segregation in the United States. Newsweek 63:43 My 18 '64
AUSTRALIANS
Letter from Australia. A. Moorehead. il New Yorker 40:216+ O 10 '64
New pulse of Australia. J. Morris. il Sat Eve Post 236:20-3 Mr 2 '63
AUSTRALITES. See Tektites
AUSTRIA
See also
Airlines—Austria
Ballet—Austria
Danube River
Ferlach
Foreign visitors in Austria
Hunting—Austria
Innsbruck
Obergurgl
Space research—Austria
Television broadcasting—Austria
Tyrol

Commerce

One world or many? H. Hazlitt. Newsweek 62:95 O 7 '63

Description and travel

Reader's choice; Jenbach and environs. E. Hewitt. Travel 121:26 F '64
Winter Olympics; Innsbruck 1964. F. R. Smith. Sports Illus 19:52 Ag 12 '63

Economic conditions

Is Austria here to stay? G. Bailey. Reporter 29:45-8 O 24 '63

Foreign relations

Germany

See also
Austro-German customs union (proposed)

History

Booked for travel; rambles through the centuries. H. Sutton. il Sat R 46:48+ S 14 '63
Fall of the House of Habsburg, by E. Crankshaw. Review
Reporter 29:46+ D 19 '63. S. Elmerl

Bibliography

Articles and other books received; Germany, Austria, and Switzerland, comp. by A. H. Price. See issues of American historical review

Industries

See also
Firearms industry and trade

Politics and government

Austrian revival. H. C. Wolfe. America 108: 297-9 Mr 2 '63
Herr Doktor; way cleared for Archduke Otto's return to his homeland. il Time 81:34 Je 14 '63
Otto ante portas. E. von Kuehnelt-Leddihn. Nat R 15:184 S 10 '63
See also
Political parties—Austria

AUSTRIAN airlines. See Airlines—Austria
AUSTRIAN cookery. See Cookery, Austrian
AUSTRIAN refugees. See Refugees, Austrian
AUSTRIAN TYROL. See Tyrol
AUSTRO-GERMAN customs union (proposed)
Anschluss, by G. Brook-Shepherd. Review
Sat R 46:23-4 S 7 '63. J. Remak
AUTHORITY (religion)
Protestantism and authority. R. M. Brown. Commonweal 81:69-71 O 9 '64; Reply with rejoinder. P. E. Meehl. 81:329-31 N 27 '64
Religious authority & mysticism; excerpts from On the Kabbalah and its symbolism. G. Scholem. Commentary 38:31-9 N '64
See also
Catholic church—Infallibility
Tradition (theology)
AUTHORS
Author as fiction. W. Sheed. Commonweal 78:535-6 S 6 '63
Big money writers; books turned into movies. R. Schickel. il Life 57:58-60+ Jl 31 '64
Camera focuses on a famous fall lineup; photographs. Sat R 46:30-1 O 5 '63
Freewheelers; world of the travel writer. il Newsweek 63:72 Je 1 '64
Grave collector; visiting authors graves. S. Black. il Harper 228:26+ Je '64
Honorable profession; writing for children. M. Stolz. il Sat R 47:45-6 N 7 '64
It's me, O Lord! W. Saroyan. Sat Eve Post 237:75-6 Ap 18 '64
Life is the raw material. R. Standish. Writer 77:20-1+ Jl '64
Multiple authorship trends in scientific papers. B. L. Clarke. bibliog il Science 143: 822-4 F 21 '64; Discussion. 144:798 My 15 '64
Opinion, please, New York. A. Pryce-Jones. Mlle 57:40-1 O '63
Poet, actor, painter: cabbie; New York cab drivers. E. T. Ewen. il N Y Times Mag p36+ O 27 '63
Prose pace-setters invade the poet's season; portraits. Sat R 47:39-41 Ap 18 '64
So you want to write a book; excerpt from The writing and selling of nonfiction. P. R. Reynolds. Sat R 46:48-50 Jl 13 '63; Reply. D. B. Sanborn. 46:43 Ag 10 '63
There is only you. W. C. Gault. Writer 76: 25 O '63
When the writer comes of age. B. J. Chute. Writer 76:10-14 My '63
Who'll kill the mockingbirds? D. C. Davis. Horn Bk 39:265-71 Je '63
Writers at work: second series. Review
Commentary 36:408-10 N '63. E. Wensberg
Sat R 46:23-4 My 18 '63. G. Hicks
Writer's social security. D. Malcolmson. Writer 77:30-1 Ja '64
You can't tell an author by his cover. L. D'Angelo. Sat R 47:18-19 Ag 15 '64
See also
Authorship
Dramatists
Editors and editing
Historians
Humorists
Prisoners as authors
Women as authors

AUTHORS—*Continued*

Bibliography

Writers are people. K. G. Jackson. Harper 227:133-6 N '63

Homes and haunts

See Literary landmarks

AUTHORS, American

Awards to the new tale-tellers. R. Hughes. Sat R 46:27 Jl 20 '63

Born a square; the westerners' dilemma. W. Stegner. il Atlan 213:46-50 Ja '64; Discussion. 213:40+ Mr '64

Cultural desert for writers? Chicago. B. Katz. il Library J 88:2430-4 Je 15 '63

Fifty-two characters who found authors. C. H. Goren. il McCalls 91:34+ F '64

Guide write! N. A. Touge. il Travel 120:50-2 O '63

Party of one; American writers. N. Gordimer. Holiday 34:12+ Jl '63

Quotable notables; excerpts from Celebrity register, ed. by C. Amory. il Sat R 46:16-17 D 14 '63

Research on the searching. G. Hicks. Sat R 46:23 Je 15 '63

Shelf of St Louis writers. R. P. Collins. Wilson Lib Bul 38:865-6 Je '64

Special issue on the American literary scene; symposium. il Esquire 60:27-35 Jl '63

Structure of the American literary establishment. L. R. Hills. Esquire 60:41 Jl '63; Reply. A. Marple. Writer 76:5-6 S '63

That summer in Paris, by M. Callaghan. Review

New Repub 148:26-8 F 9 '63. W. Saroyan

Writer as moralist. S. Bellow. Atlan 211:58-62 Mr '63

See also

American literature
Bishop, J.
Bodenheim, M.
Clemens, S. L.
Dahlberg, E.
Dramatists, American
Fitzgerald, F. S. K.
Gehman, R.
Hughes, L.
James, H.
Kerr, J.
Kriegel, L.
Mailer, N.
Markfield, W.
Neville, E. C.
Nock, A. J.
Novelists, American
Parkman, F.
Podhoretz, N.
Poets, American
Purdy, J.
Rokeach, M.
Thompson, D.

AUTHORS, Argentine

See also

Cortázar, J.
Mallea, E.

AUTHORS, Brazilian

See also

Morais Andrade, M. R. de

AUTHORS, Canadian

Dilemma of the Canadian author. D. V. LePan. il Atlan 214:160-4 N '64

Look northward! books by Canadian and about Canada, for American children and young adults. S. A. Egoff and R. A. Hagler. Library J 88:4421-8 N 15 '63

Northern muse. R. Davies. Holiday 35:10+ Ap '64

AUTHORS, Catholic. See Catholic authors

AUTHORS, Colombian

See also

Novelists, Colombian

AUTHORS, Ecuadorian

See also

Icaza, J.
Novelists, Equadorian

AUTHORS, Egyptian

See also

Cossery, A.

AUTHORS, English

Literature and English Lakeland. G. Bott. il Sr Schol 85:12T Ja 7 '65

See also

Bacon, F.
Golding, W.
Poets, English
Waterhouse, K.
Wells, H. G.
Wilde, C.
Zangwill, I.

AUTHORS, European

Critique in brief; series of Columbia essays on modern writers. G. Hicks. Sat R 47:19-20 D 19 '64

AUTHORS, French

French books for children. S. B. Vogel. Library J 88:4428-33 N 15 '63

Gates of horn: a study of five French realists, by H. Levin. Review

Reporter 28:42+ Je 20 '63. J. O'Brien

See also

Apollinaire, G.
Cocteau, J.
French literature
Genêt, J.
Proust, M.
Sainte-Beuve, C. A.
Sartre, J. P.

AUTHORS, German

Voice from the future. K. Boyle. il Holiday 36:12+ O '64

Writers in Berlin. W. Höllerer; G. Grass; W. Hasenclever. Atlan 212:110-13 D '63

AUTHORS, Indian (East Indian)

Fiction in India. R. White. bibliog il Reporter 28:54+ F 14 '63; Reply with rejoinder. Z. L. Kaul. 28:12+ Mr 14 '63

AUTHORS, Italian

See also

Lampedusa, G. di

AUTHORS, Jewish

Jewish. M. Liben. Commentary 38:74-8 S '64

See also

American literature—Jewish authors
English literature—Jewish authors
Samuel, M.
Swados, H.

AUTHORS, Latin American

Indian in Latin American fiction. E. S. Urbanski. il Américas 15:20-4 My '63

AUTHORS, Negro. See Negro authors

AUTHORS, Russian

Contraband collection; gift of unpublished letters of 20th century Russian writers to Yale university library. Wilson Lib Bul 37:822 Je '63

Dissonant voices in Soviet literature, ed. by P. Blake and M. Hayward. Review

Reporter 28:49-50+ F 28 '63. R. W. Mathewson, jr

Mr K's turn toward Stalinism. E. Griffiths. il Sat Eve Post 236:70-3 Je 1 '63

New men of the Soviet sixties. P. Johnson. il Reporter 28:16-21 My 9 '63

Russia's writers: after silence, human voices. il Time 82:82-3+ D 20 '63

Screws are tightened again. A. Brumberg. il Reporter 28:21-4+ My 9 '63

See also

Chekhov, A. P.
Nekrasov, V. P.
Paustovsky, K.
Pushkin, A. S.
Serge, V.

AUTHORS, Scottish

See also

Scott, W.

AUTHORS, Spanish

See also

Unamuno y Jugo, M. de

AUTHORS, Venezuelan

See also

Bello, A.

AUTHORS, Yugoslav

See also

Andric, I.

AUTHORS agents. See Literary agents

AUTHORS and libraries. See Libraries and authors

AUTHORS and publishers

Imaginary correspondence; B. Potter and a present day children's book editor. R. Godden. Horn Bk 39:369-75 Ag '63

Scholar as author: indoctrinating the academics; symposium. il Pub W 184:37-42 Jl 15 '63

Skirmishes with a publisher; excerpts from Owl among colophons: a survey of American book publishing. C. A. Madison. il Sat R 46:24-5 N 16 '63

See also

Literary agents
Royalties

AUTHORS colonies

Yaddo. A. Vivante. Writer 77:28-9 Ag '64

See also

MacDowell memorial colony, Peterboro, N.H.

AUTHORS conferences

Ambler case. E. Ambler. Reporter 30:6+ F 13 '64

Author's purpose; Authors' colloquium in Buenos Aires, October 1962. H. Grossi. il Américas 15:37-8 F '63

Letter from San Juan. G. G. Kirstein. Nation 197:400-2 D 7 '63

AUTHORS conferences—*Continued*
My summer with writers; waiter-student at writers' conference, Bread Loaf Mountain, Vt. D. Wiedenman. il Seventeen 23:124-5+ My '64
Opinion, please; from Bread Loaf, Vt. D. Wakefield. il Mlle 60:70+ N '64
Play's the thing; Edinburgh conference. M. Zavada. America 109:511-12 N 2 '63
Poets' encounter; with excerpts from message by T. Merton. R. Connally. il Américas 16: 28-30 Ap '64
Summer festivals; Bread Loaf writers' conference. J. Ciardi. Sat R 46:12+ O 19 '63
Workshops for writers; with list. G. Munson. Sat R 46:45-7+ Ap 27 '63
Writers' conferences 1963-1964. Writer 76:26-30 Ap '63; 77:27-31 Ap '64
Writers' workshops; with list of conferences. G. Munson. il Sat R 47:43-5+ Ap 25 '64
See also
Authors league of America

AUTHORS guild of America. See Authors league of America—Authors guild

AUTHORS league of America
Authors and dramatists split within League. Pub W 186:88-9 S 28 '64
Authors league backs JFK, asking fairer tax treatment for writers. R. Stout. Pub W 183:27-9 Mr 11 '63
Authors league condemns loyalty oaths. Pub W 186:31 O 12 '64

Authors guild

Authors ask new policy on royalties and reprints. Pub W 186:36-8 Jl 27 '64

AUTHORSHIP
American way of success. J. Mitford. il Ladies Home J 81:22+ Je '64
Article ideas: from manuscript to magazine. J. P. Fried and H. I. Kurtz. Writer 77:16-19+ D '64
Confessions of an unpublished writer. B. Blaushild. Sat R 46:21 Mr 9 '63
Conversation with Sir Herbert Read; ed. by M. Y. Bassiouny. Sch Arts 64:24-6 N '64
Creating books; condensation of address, May 1963. L. Lenski. il Library J 88:3987-90+ O 15 '63
Editor's advice on article sales. C. Peterson, jr. Writer 77:14-17 O '64
Greeting card market today. C. Goeller. Writer 76:28-30 Mr '63
Helping hand for a literary upstart. J. Fischer. Harper 227:20+ S '63; Discussion. 227:10+ N '63
High cost of writing; Stern and Beinecke funds. J. F. Fixx. Sat R 47:53+ Je 13 '64
How to succeed at writing by trying very hard. J. Masters. Harper 226:54-9 Mr '63
If you really want to sell. D. Hill. Writer 76:23-4 Je '63
Know your markets. E. M. Dean. Writer 77: 28-30 F '64
Let the would-be writer beware. D. Dempsey. Sat R 46:22-3 Jl 13 '63
Letter to a young article writer. R. Gehman. Writer 76:15-17 N '63
Marketing of poetry. Writer 76:19-21+ Mr '63
Non-fiction that reads like a novel; Coin of contraband. G. Roark. Writer 78:16-18 Ja '65
Of writing and writers. J. Ciardi. Sat R 47: 23 Ap 18 '64
Off the cuff. A. Marple. See issues of Writer
On becoming a writer; excerpt from Shadow and act. R. Ellison. Commentary 38:57-60 O '64
On writing: interview; ed. by R. Diers. S. O'Faolain. Mlle 56:151+ Mr '63
Party of one; American writers. N. Gordimer. Holiday 34:12+ Jl '63
Party of one; how to live happily with a split personality. C. D. Lewis. il Holiday 33:32+ Mr '63
Professional attitude. K. Nelson. Writer 76: 9-11+ D '63
Question of fidelity; excerpts from Force of circumstance, tr. by R. Howard. S. de Beauvoir. Harper 229:57-64 N; 111-14+ D '64
Read your paper with scissors. J. C. Kennedy. Writer 78:30-1 Ja '65
Riddle. A. Camus. Atlan 211:83-5 Je '63
Salt crystals, spider webs, and words. P. Engle. Sat R 47:10-13 Mr 14 '64
Second harvest. M. Lodeesen. Writer 77:7-9+ Mr '64
Should I try to be a writer? L. T. Henderson. Writer 77:21-3 Ap '64
So it's all been done before. H. Rezatto. Writer 77:27-8+ N '64
Story behind the book; interview. J. J. Fahey. Writer 76:17-18 S '63
Successful query letters. C. W. Casewit. Writer 76:15-17 D '63
Time to write. V. Fifield. Writer 77:28-9 O '64
Tusitala. J. R. Ullman. Writer 76:10-12 Jl '63
Two writers talk it over. J. Jones; W. Styron. il Esquire 60:57-9 Jl '63
Way it isn't done; notes on the distress of Norman Mailer. Esquire 60:306-8 D '63
What beginning writers want to know. J. Reach. Writer 76:10-12 O '63
What makes a good sentimental greeting? D. K. Quinn. Writer 77:21-4+ O '64
Where to sell manuscripts. See issues of Writer
Would-be writer industry. A. Levy. Reporter 29:48+ O 24 '63; Discussion. 29:6+ N 21 '63; 30:6+ F 13 '64
Writers at work: the Paris review interviews. Review
Time il 82:86 Jl 5 '63
Writers, writing & the written; symposium. il Bul Atomic Sci 19:13-28 N; 19-33 D '63
Writing the nonfiction narrative. R. White. Writer 76:10-12 Ag '63
You asked for it. W. Macken. Writer 76:20-1 Jl '63
See also
Authors
Biography
Fiction—Technique
Journalism
Literary research
Moving picture authorship
Plagiarism
Plots (drama, novel, etc)
Poetics
Poetry—Authorship
Short stories
Style, Literary
Television authorship

Anecdotes, facetiae, satire, etc.

Coat hanger; symbol of every man's dilemma. House & Gard 124:68-9+ Jl '63
Confession. M. Mannes. Reporter 28:37-8 Je 6 '63
Do anything else, but lay off the quill. S. J. Perelman. Seventeen 23:148+ Je '64
Ordeal of Lash Calhoun. N. Hartshorne. Harper 228:43-4 My '64
Why don't you try the piano instead? R. Fontaine. il Atlan 214:124+ O '64

Bibliography

Writer's library. See issues of Writer

Collaboration

Busy ghosts. P. Bart. Sat R 46:78 S 14 '63; Reply. R. Gross. 46:49 O 12 '63
Goldwater's staff. R. Moley. Newsweek 64: 80 Ag 31 '64
Minds of Barry Goldwater. R. H. Rovere. Harper 229:37-42 S '64
Some perils of authorship. I. H. Page. Science 144:139 Ap 10 '64; Discussion. 144:952, 1294-5; 145:232 My 22, Je 12, Jl 17 '64
Vast ghostland of Washington. D. Oberdorfer. il N Y Times Mag p24+ Ap 26 '64

Competitions

See Literature—Competitions

Copy preparation

Expand or contract? E. Lee. Writer 76:18-20+ D '63

Quotations, maxims, etc.

Topic: writing; sayings of famous authors, comp. by E. F. Murphy. il N Y Times Mag p26 O 27 '63

AUTO radios. See Automobiles—Radio equipment

AUTO sirens. See Whistles

AUTOBIOGRAPHY
Is it confidential, or is it history? E. J. Hughes. il N Y Times Mag p24+ My 12 '63
Wayward reader. J. O'Hara. Holiday 36:31-4 D '64
See also
Biography

AUTOBIOGRAPHY; story. See Gallant, M.

AUTOGIROS
Avian gyroplane. H. McDougall. il Flying 74:44-5+ Ap '64
U-18 production plan approval expected; gyroplane. D. A. Brown. Aviation W 80:32 Ja 13 '64

AUTOGRAPHING parties. See Booksellers and bookselling—Publicity

AUTOGRAPHS
Current market values of presidential papers (cont) M. A. Benjamin. Hobbies 68:110-12 Ap '63
London collector goes for world celebrities. K. V. Hostick. il Hobbies 69:110 Je '64
Name catching. il Newsweek 63:84-5 F 10 '64
Stage door brigade. D. Sanders. il Dance Mag 37:22+ S '63
AUTOIMMUNE diseases. See Diseases
AUTOLAND. See Airplanes—Landing
AUTOMATED teaching aids. See Teaching—Aids and devices
AUTOMATIC alarms. See Electric alarms
AUTOMATIC bookcharging machines. See Libraries—Charging systems
AUTOMATIC canteen company of America. See Concessions (food, etc)
AUTOMATIC control
Control theory; feedback control. R. Bellman. il Sci Am 211:186-90+ S '64
New electronic control begins to take hold. il Bsns W p68+ O 24 '64
Robots help world's work. W. Davis. il Sci N L 85:346-7 My 30 '64
Watcher watched; alertors. Newsweek 62:59 S 30 '63
See also
Automation
Cybernetics
Hydraulic control
Inertial guidance systems
Machine tools—Control
Machinery, Automatic
AUTOMATIC data processing. See Electronic data processing
AUTOMATIVE direction finders. See Radio in navigation
AUTOMATIC elevators. See Elevators
AUTOMATIC exposure cameras. See Cameras
AUTOMATIC machinery. See Machinery, Automatic
AUTOMATIC mail handling. See Mail handling
AUTOMATIC parking machines. See Automobile parking
AUTOMATIC perspective translator. See Drawing instruments
AUTOMATIC pilot (airplanes)
Autopilot gains as lower minimum choice. P. J. Klass. Aviation W 82:28-9 Ja 4 '65
Building safety into blind landings; electronic devices. il Bsns W p96+ D 19 '64
Flying the Atlantic without a navigator. R. E. Smallman. il Pop Sci 182:86-8+ Ap '63
Lear Siegler pushes autoland time-lead. P. J. Klass. il Aviation W 82:59-62 Ja 18 '65
More profound gyro. W. Cloud. il Pop Sci 182:30+ Ap '63
Pilot, autopilot share approach duties. P. J. Klass. il Aviation W 81:93+ O 19 '64
Thumb thing new in trimming. R. B. Weeghman. il Flying 75:62 S '64
AUTOMATIC pilot (boats)
Self-servicing the automatic pilot. R. C. Beard. il Motor B 113:374-5 Ja '64
AUTOMATIC train control. See Railroads—Automatic train control
AUTOMATIC transmission. See Automobiles—Transmission
AUTOMATIC trim control. See Automatic pilot (airplanes)
AUTOMATION
Abundance, threat or promise? R. Theobald. Nation 196:387-412 My 11 '63; Discussion. 196:inside cover Je 15 '63
Automatic electronic testing. K. Gilmore. il Electr World 71:25-8+ Ja '64
Automation. V. M. Rogers. bibliog il NEA J 52:50-2+ O '63
Automation (cont) Sr Schol 83:12-13+ N 8 '63; 85:14-16+ N 11 '64
Automation affects more shop than office jobs. Sci N L 86:168 S 12 '64
Automation & the state. B. B. Seligman. Commentary 37:49-54 Je '64; Discussion. 38:23-4 D '64
Automation changes jobs. W. Wingo. il Sci N L 84:326 N 23 '63
Automation; end or a new day in unionism? J. L. Stern. bibliog f Ann Am Acad 350:25-35 N '63
Automation in railroads. W. Wingo. Sci N L 84:54 Jl 27 '63
Automation: its benefits and its slag heap. Life 56:4 Ja 10 '64
Automation of knowledge; address, April 19, 1964. L. Mumford. Vital Speeches 30:441-6 My 1 '64
Automation: problems and potentials in education. Pub W 183:21-2 Ap 8 '63
Automation: road to lifetime jobs? A. H. Raskin. Sat R 47:14-16+ N 28 '64
Automation speeds mail. Sci N L 85:198 Mr 28 '64
Automation surge. W. Wingo. il Sci N L 84:294 N 9 '63
Automation: threat and promise. G. Ackley; J. I. Snyder, jr. il N Y Times Mag p 16+ Mr 22 '64
Automation; we can handle it. T. G. Harris. il Look 29:58-62 Ja 12 '65
Automation will make more jobs. il Nations Bsns 51:38-9+ Je '63
Automation's challenge to education and human values; excerpts from Automation, education, and human values, ed. by William W. Brickman and Stanley Lehrer. bibliog f Sch & Soc 92:303-15 O 31 '64
Automation's impact. W. Wingo. il Sci N L 84:278 N 2 '63
Big step toward automation; Minneapolis. B. Corlett. il Am City 78:104-5 O '63
Can Americans adjust? W. Wingo. il Sci N L 84:346 N 30 '63
Challenge of automation. il Newsweek 65:73-8+ Ja 25 '65
Challenge of change; address, November 18, 1963. L. H. Hodges. Vital Speeches 30:107-11 D 1 '63
Does automation call for new solutions? V. M. Rogers. il PTA Mag 58:7-9 Je '64
Fallacies and facts about automation. V. R. Fuchs. il N Y Times Mag p27+ Ap 7 '63
Food, jobs and human rights; address, September 21, 1963. R. Theobald. Vital Speeches 30:61-4 N 1 '63
Galloping automation. W. Wingo. il Sci N L 84:310 N 16 '63
Great unemployment fallacy. E. L. Dale, jr. New Repub 151:10-12 S 5 '64; Discussion. 151:37-8 S 19; 27-30 S 26 '64
Hail automation, hail peace. N. Cousins. Sat R 47:20 Ja 18 '64
Help wanted, 1964. V. M. Rogers. il NEA J 53:53 F '64
In automation, a British empire. il Bsns W p82+ Jl 25 '64
Industry and the technological revolution; address, June 4, 1964. E. B. Fitzgerald. Vital Speeches 30:659-62 Ag 15 '64
Intermingled revolutions; the Negro and automation; address, July 20, 1964. W. M. Young, jr. Vital Speeches 30:692-4 S 1 '64
Is there a crisis in the labor movement? no. P. Taft. Ann Am Acad 350:10-15 N '63
Labor; the enigma of the unions. T. R. Brooks. il Duns R 81:pt2 S135-6+ Je '63
Longshoremen boxed-in. W. McCann. Sci N L 86:246 O 17 '64
Managing your manpower; effects of automation. T. R. Brooks. Duns R 83:71-2+ My '64
Managing your manpower; white collar employees. T. R. Brooks. Duns R 82:74A D '63
Manpower revolution; call for debate. G. G. Kirstein. il Nation 198:140-4 F 10 '64
Missing links in automation. H. E. Klein. il Duns R 81:38-41 F '63
New horizons in economics. R. L. Heilbroner. Sat R 47:34 Ag 29 '64
Our new automated world. D. Gray. il Recreation 56:401-2 N '63
Real news about automation. C. E. Silberman. il Fortune 71:124-6+ Ja '65
Reconversion and automation; proposed commissions. Nation 197:191 O 5 '63
Scranton on automation. Sci N L 86:35 Jl 18 '64
Stupid questions about automation. M. Mann. il Pop Sci 184:100-3+ My '64
That empty chair by the featherbed. L. Velie. Read Digest 82:97-102 Ap '63
What future managers will need; symposium. il Nations Bsns 51:69-73 Jl '63
When automation comes and workers stay on; Southern Pacific railway. U S News 54:88-9 Ap 1 '63
When will your husband be obsolete? interview, ed. by P. L. Cahn. J. Diebold. il McCalls 90:64-5+ Jl '63
White-collar automation. T. O'Toole. il Reporter 29:24-7 D 5 '63
Will there be jobs for our children? E. Cohen and S. Fremon. il Parents Mag 38:58-9+ N '63
See also
Assembly line methods
Automatic control
Calculating machines—Industrial applications
College libraries—Automation
Electronic data processing
Libraries—Automation
Machinery, Automatic
School libraries—Automation
Shipping—Automation
Unemployment, Technological

AUTOMATION—*Continued*

Anecdotes, facetiae, satire, etc.

Sad state of the Department of state: the hog-wild machine. M. Epernay. Esquire 60:102-3+ S '63

AUTOMATONS

Beast hears like bat. il(p81) Sci N L 86:87 Ag 8 '64

Eight planet-probe robots. B. Tufty. il (p225) Sci N L 84:227 O 12 '63

Gulliver, ambassador to the microbes of Mars. C. P. Gilmore. il Pop Sci 183:60-1 D '63

Her master's voice; synthetic intelligence machine, Cynthia. Sci Digest 55:47 Ja '64

Machine that plugs itself in. il Sci Digest 56: 61-2 Ag '64

Machine thinks for itself; Beast. E. Hall. il Sci N L 85:170 Mr 4 '64

March of the robots. T. R. Brooks. il Duns R 81:40-1+ Ja '63

Our heartless friends, the robots. D. S. Halacy, jr. il Pop Electr 18:39-44+ My '63

Out of this world life detectors; Gulliver, astrorobot. S. D. Pursglove. il Pop Mech 119:72-5 Je '63

Painstaking robot; excerpt from Minds of robots. J. T. Culbertson. il Sat R 47:54-5 Ap 4 '64

Robots help world's work. W. Davis. il Sci N L 85:346-7 My 30 '64

See also

Manipulators

AUTOMOBILE accessories. See Automobiles—Equipment

AUTOMOBILE accidents. See Traffic accidents

AUTOMOBILE air filters. See Air filters, Automobile

AUTOMOBILE batteries. See Storage batteries

AUTOMOBILE boat trailer camps. See Automobile trailer camps

AUTOMOBILE boat trailers

Better ways to trail your boat. V. L. Oertle. il Yachting 117:116-17+ Ja '65

Boating on the highway. il Consumer Bul 47:6-9 Ap '64

C'mon, try boat-camping. il Motor B 114:25-7 Jl '64

Compact cruising. F. M. Paulson. il Field & S 68:64-8 Jl '63

How to build a fold-up hinged boat. J. Payne. il Pop Sci 184:116-19 My '64

Let's trail'er right. S. Owen. il Yachting 115: 112-14+ Ja '64

My trailer does more than haul a boat. B. I. Buller. il Pop Sci 182:134-6+ F '63

New trailers. il Outdoor Life 131:60-1 F '63; 133:62-3 F '64

New trailers for 1965. J. A. Emmett. il Outdoor Life 135:60-1 Ja '65

Pack up and go. E. Robbins. il Pop Sci 184: 145+ F '64

Some ships of the desert on a long, long safari; the Waterdogs of Albuquerque. il Sports Illus 21:22-3 D 14 '64

Tips for safe and carefree boat trailering. il Suc Farm 61:86 My '63

Trailer the big ones down. A. Meske. il Motor B 112:28-9+ S '63

Trailers 64-65. il Motor B 113:162-3 Ja '64; 115:154-5 Ja '65

Trouble-free trailering. F. M. Paulson. il Field & S 68:102-3 My '63

AUTOMOBILE bodies. See Automobiles—Bodies

AUTOMOBILE brakes. See Brakes, Automobile

AUTOMOBILE buying. See Automobiles—Purchasing

AUTOMOBILE campers. See Campers and coaches, Truck

AUTOMOBILE camping. See Camping

AUTOMOBILE clubs

California, Washington, Pennsylvania and Florida; first four charter clubs of International car club association. il Hot Rod 16:82-3 Jl '63

Chrysler's ramblin' rallywagons; Sports car club of America. B. Greene. il Hot Rod 17: 78-81 Mr '64

Club safety check. L. Smith. il Hot Rod 17: 76-7 Mr '64

Day of the duners; Pismo Beach, Calif. G. Fauman. il Motor T 15:64-7 O '63

Drive to nowhere. L. Smith. il Hot Rod 17: 106-7 F '64

Franklin club homecoming trek. il Motor T 16:92-3 D '64

HRM salutes the Ram Rods of Silver Springs, Maryland. il Hot Rod 16:90-1 F '63

HRM salutes the Road Knights of Evansville, Ind. il Hot Rod 16:90-1 Mr '63

HRM salutes the Slo-Poks of Vancouver, Wash. il Hot Rod 16:80 Ap '63

HRM salutes the Stags of Ogden, Utah. il Hot Rod 16:88 N '63

ICCA, Canada. il Hot Rod 16:92-3 D '63

Roadsters, ho! L. Smith. il Hot Rod 16:48-51+ O '63

Sport of the speed demons; Trotters hot rod club. il Ebony 19:113-14+ N '63

Ten special-interest cars; symposium. il Motor T 16:73-83 N '64

Top ten. L. Smith. il Hot Rod 16:84-5 Mr '63; 17:42-3 Ja '64

AUTOMOBILE dealers

Round for GM. Newsweek 61:83 Mr 25 '63

Wide-open throttle for new-car sales. il Bsns W p28 Ap 25 '64

AUTOMOBILE decoration

Customizers. il Time 83:54 Ap 10 '64

AUTOMOBILE drivers

And now he (she) drives. B. Lang. il N Y Times Mag p 110+ N 8 '64

Can we get the sick drivers off the road? G. G. Greer. Bet Hom & Gard 42:21-2+ O '64

Can you predict which boy will drive you home safely? D. Klein. il Seventeen 23:134-5+ Mr '64

1410 is watching; National driver register service. Time 82:53 Ag 23 '63

Good driver drives smoothly, alertly. Sci N L 85:279 My 2 '64

Honk! biff! bam! pugnacity of French drivers. Time 85:26 Ja 22 '65

Liberty and junior's driving license. P. Jones. il PTA Mag 59:21-2 O '64

Look fast, think pink. K. W. Purdy. il Sat Eve Post 237:60-1 O 31 '64

1964 models: cars & dolls. A. Rothenberg. il Look 27:85-98 O 22 '63

1964 stock racing preview; leading race figures tell what's in store. M. Muhleman. il Motor T 16:44-7 Ja '64

Open road for women. K. D. Fishman. Mlle 59:110-11+ Je '64

Roman roulette & other games. il Time 84: 47 S 4 '64

Safe drivers cut costs, create goodwill; Little Rock, Ark. A. M. Douthit. Am City 78: 138 Je '63

Search; suspect of hit-and-run death in Celina, Tenn, 1944. Newsweek 62:24+ Jl 22 '63

Serious epidemic of automania. G. Hechinger and F. M. Hechinger. il N Y Times Mag p 18+ Ag 11 '63

Slow drivers can kill you. M. Mann. il Pop Sci 182:77-9+ Ap '63

Stop and go signals for teen-age drivers. P. Jones. il PTA Mag 57:4-6 Mr '63

There's hope for teen-age drivers! S. S. Jacobs. il Todays Health 41:18-21+ Mr '63

Traffic toll and the teen-ager; forum discussion. il Sr Schol 83:20 S 27 '63; Discussion. 83:12-14 Ja 17 '64

Warning on drugs and driving. Consumer Rep 28:150 Ap '63

What makes a safe driver safe; survey of safe-driving habits. F. J. Cook. il N Y Times Mag p79+ Ap 7 '63

When your teen-ager starts to drive. D. Klein. Ladies Home J 81:25+ My '64

You can't scare a bad driver. il Sci Digest 54:40-1 S '63

You, too, can be a race driver. R. P. Crossley. il Pop Sci 184:75 F '64

See also

Drinking and traffic accidents

Anecdotes, facetiae, satire, etc.

How to spot driving nuts. M. Lamm. il Motor T 15:48-9 S '63

Why economy run drivers get grey. W. Thoms. il Motor T 16:66-7 Ap '64

Licenses

Anecdotes, facetiae, satire, etc.

Not valid in Macao; international driving permit. H. F. Ellis. New Yorker 40:218+ O 31 '64

Psychological examinations

Why; driver's emotional and mental states prior to, and at moment of accident. New Yorker 40:20-1 Ag 8 '64

AUTOMOBILE driving

Any dope could drive a Model T. E. H. Ortner. il Pop Sci 183:73-4+ Jl '63

Avoid these fatal driving sins. Good H 158: 168 Ap '64

Brake debate. Time 83:43 My 8 '64

Do cars and school studies mix? il Good H 157:150-1 S '63

Experts discuss twelve driving emergencies. H. E. Dark. il Todays Health 42:38-42 Mr '64

AUTOMOBILE driving—*Continued*
For greater safety, flash those lights! turn-signal lights. L. F. Cortina. il Pop Electr 20:75-6+ Mr '64
Good advice for the summer driver. Good H 158:169 Je '64
Good ways to save on gasoline costs. il Good H 158:159 Mr '64
How to avoid night-driving dangers. Good H 157:164 O '63
How to be a slick driver; winter driving. il Bet Hom & Gard 43:6+ Ja '65
How to drive and stay alive. A. Rothenberg. il Look 27:64 My 21 '63
How to know what the driver ahead will do. Bet Hom & Gard 42:40+ N '64
How to lick the hazards of foul-weather driving. P. W. Kearney. il Read Digest 83:58-60 D '63
If there's trouble on a car trip; driving emergencies and how to handle them. il Changing T 18:25-9 Ag '64
More strain on driver than astronaut in orbit. il Sci Digest 53:23-5 F '63
Most drivers don't know how to drive safely on a freeway, do you? Bet Hom & Gard 42:131 My '64
New science of driving; freeway driving. A. Hamilton. il Sci Digest 55:86-90 F '64
Save money while you drive. il Changing T 17:35-6 Ag '63
Six driving crises and how to handle them. W. S. Griswold. il Pop Sci 185:43-5+ S '64
Strange highway forces that louse up your driving; report from Purdue university. E. D. Fales, jr. il Pop Sci 184:94-7+ My '64
What truck drivers say about your driving; tips from pros. il Changing T 18:37-40 N '64
See also
Automobile drivers

Anecdotes, facetiae, satire, etc.

They don't make drivers like they used to. F. Sparks. il Read Digest 84:21-2+ Je '64

Animal hazards

Deer mirrors: nine states test them to cut road kill. G. H. Gillelan. il Outdoor Life 135:24-6+ F '65

Laws and regulations

See Automobile laws and regulations

Study and teaching

And now he (she) drives. B. Lang. il N Y Times Mag p 110+ N 8 '64
Detroit's Mickey Mouse: the driver education myth. E. A. Tenney. il Nation 198:395-7 Ap 20 '64
Driver education pays off. P. W. Kearney. Parents Mag 39:64+ O '64; Same with title Why driver education is a must. il Read Digest 85:129-32 O '64
Elderly driver; geriatric driver training at Indiana university. il Time 84:57 Ag 14 '64
Fine art of fast driving; course run by the British school of motoring. D. Scott. il Pop Sci 183:60-4+ Ag '63
How's your driver education program? criteria for evaluation. G. E. Warneking. il NEA J 53:41 My '64
Need for driver education. A. E. Neyhart. il Motor T 16:102-5 N '64
Teen-age driving skill. il Hot Rod 17:90-1+ Jl '64
There's hope for teen-age drivers! S. S. Jacobs. il Todays Health 41:18-21+ Mr '63

Stunt driving

Daredevil auto stunt man. il Ebony 19:91-2+ D '63

AUTOMOBILE driving simulators. See Simulators

AUTOMOBILE engines
Backdrop for a mill; firewall. L. Smith. il Hot Rod 17:82-3 Ag '64
Big (?) inches for a BMW. J. O'Donnell. il Hot Rod 16:86-8 Mr '63
Big screen in Daytona; Chevrolet engines. K. Rudeen. Sports Illus 18:36-8 Mr 4 '63
Bigger engines for compacts in '64. R. Huntington. il Motor T 15:50-3 Ag '63
Boat engine, car engine; horse of a different color. N. A. Newman. il Motor B 113:95-6 Ja '64
Bolt on eighty horsepower. L. Smith. il Hot Rod 16:78-81 O '63
Can Detroit move in on Indy? H. B. Comstock. il Pop Sci 182:75-8+ My '63
Chevrolet's 427 mystery V8. R. Brock. il Hot Rod 16:40-3+ My '63
Chevys in the Indy lineup. D. Francisco. il Hot Rod 16:34-9+ O '63
Chrysler Hemi-Head V-8. J. Wright. il Motor T 16:38-9 My '64
Chrysler's 426, second stage. R. Brock. il Hot Rod 16:36-9+ Jl '63
Chrysler's new V8 tailored for a compact. R. Brock. il Hot Rod 16:36-9+ D '63
Corvair; customizing a flat six. J. Wright. il Motor T 15:40-3 S; 62-3+ O '63
Do your own tune-up. R. E. Jennings. il Motor T 17:66-8 Ja '65
Does Ford have a secret racing engine? il Motor T 15:64-5 Mr '63
Dream motor steps out; rotary piston engine. il Bsns W p48+ O 12 '63
Driving Ford's experimental OHC V-8. G. Moore. il Motor T 16:60-1 O '64
Driving the latest NSU-Wankel. G. Molter. il Motor T 15:64-5 F '63
Engines: five new ones. Consumer Rep 28:154 Ap '63
Ford with a hemi hummer. E. Rickman. il Hot Rod 17:48-9 Ja '64
Ford's ninety-day wonder. E. Dahlquist. il Hot Rod 18:30-6 Ja '65
Ford's 64 Indy V8. R. Brock. il Hot Rod 17:26-33+ Mr '64
Future of performance. R. Huntington. il Motor T 15:26-9 D '63
Go get 'em Corvair. D. Francisco. il Hot Rod 16:32-5+ S '63
Healey with V8 punch. R. Brock. il Hot Rod 16:34-7 Ag '63
Horsefeathers. E. Dahlquist. il Hot Rod 17:30-3 S '64
Horsepower race breaks out again. il Bsns W p30-1 Mr 9 '63
How about a heavy wheel? R. Huntington. il Hot Rod 16:46-7+ F '63
How to pick a power pack. R. Huntington. il Motor T 16:28-31+ Mr '64
Indianapolis 500; V-8 threat. J. Wright. il Motor T 15:64-9 Ag '63
Its four cylinders act like sixteen. D. Scott. il Pop Sci 184:80-3 F '64
Jet; a short-fused bomb? L. Smith. il Hot Rod 16:84-5+ Ag '63
Jet engine on wheels. il Sci Digest 57:inside back cover Ja '65
Lotus Ford at Indy: the little engine that almost did. D. Francis. il Pop Sci 183:38-9+ Ag '63
Make your Corvair go. E. Rickman. il Hot Rod 16:52-3+ F '63
Modern hemi from Chrysler. R. Brock. il Hot Rod 17:44-7 Ap '64
More oats for the Mustangs. E. Dahlquist. il Hot Rod 17:46-9 O; 84-6 N '64
MT road test; Comet S-22 V-8. B. McVay. il Motor T 15:44-9 Ag '63
MT road test; Valiant with a V-8. J. Wright. il Motor T 16:32-7 Mr '64
NSU Spider is powered by Wankel rotary engine. il Pop Sci 183:58 D '63
New breed of Bird, with 427 Thunder. E. Rickman. il Hot Rod 16:70-3 S '63
New thunder for an old bird; Pontiac engine in 1957 T-Bird. D. Francisco. il Hot Rod 16:42-5+ F '63
New V-8 for the F-85. R. Huntington. il Motor T 15:68-70 D '63
New variables: camshaft & compression. R. Huntington. il Motor T 16:50-1+ My '64
1964 Chrysler corp. engineering. J. Wright. il Motor T 15:28-31 S '63
Performance Pontiac for '63. R. Brock. il Hot Rod 16:28-31+ Mr '63
Pontiacs on a diet. R. Huntington. il Hot Rod 16:32-5 My '63
Power without pistons; Wankel engines. D. Scott. il Pop Sci 186:60-3 Ja '65
Precision combustion timing for faster track time. K. V. Nelson. il Hot Rod 17:40-1 F '64
Preview of Dodge & Plymouth engineering for 1965. J. Wright. il Motor T 16:28-31 S '64
Rocket, stage two. R. Huntington. il Hot Rod 17:54-9 N '64
Sharpen your Falcon's claws. D. Naef. il Hot Rod 16:102-3 O '63
Special section: 1965 engines. R. Huntington. il Motor T 16:36-47 D '64
Stiff lower lip; main bearing cluster for engine safety. L. Wineland. il Hot Rod 17:94-5 Ag '64
Stock swaps for more stuff. R. Huntington. il Hot Rod 16:90-2+ N '63; 17:78-81+ F; 76-9 Je '64
They said it couldn't be done! Chevy V8 in a Corvair. il Hot Rod 17:38-41 O '64
350HP Fairlane, Ford's racing V8. R. Brock. il Hot Rod 16:26-33+ Jl '63
326 inch V8 for Tempest. R. Brock. il Hot Rod 16:32-5+ F '63
Tune-up tips: Ford's 427. D. Francisco. il Hot Rod 16:71-5 Ag '63

AUTOMOBILE engines—*Continued*
289 Cobra Ford; performance unlimited. L. Smith. il Hot Rod 16:44-5+ D '63
Two stroke stuff. T. Medley. il Hot Rod 17:102 Mr '64
Where do all the horses go? A. Robertson. il Pop Sci 185:48-9+ Jl '64
See also
Anti-freeze solutions
Automobiles—Cams
Carburetors
Cranks and crankshafts
Diesel engines, Automotive
Gas turbines, Automotive
Indicators for gas and oil engines
Motor truck engines
Tachometers

Bearings

Roll 'em. R. Huntington. il Hot Rod 18:48-9 Ja '65
Tips on bearings. W. E. Thill. il Hot Rod 16:102-3 Jl '63

Care

Inside your engine. K. V. Nelson. il Hot Rod 16:76-9+ Mr '63
Snap starting in winter. G. F. Stillwell. il Suc Farm 61:149 F '63
When your engine misfires. E. F. Lindsley. il Pop Sci 185:88-91 Ag '64

Cooling

Automotive milestones; the Corvair's granddaddy; copper-cooled Chevrolet of 1922-23. M. King. il Motor T 16:84-5 Ag '64
How to keep your engine cool. V. L. Oertle. il Pop Sci 183:156-8 Jl '63
Know your car's cooling system. M. J. Schultz. il Pop Mech 119:170-3+ Ap; 166-71 My '63

Exhaust

Anti-smog kit. T. E. Stimson. il Pop Mech 120:125-7+ N '63
Banishing auto fumes; anti-smog devices mandatory on 1966 cars. Bsns W p29 Je 20 '64
Cars and smog. New Repub 150:6 Je 13 '64
Clearing the air; exhaust control systems. Time 84:81 Ag 21 '64
Cooperating to clear the air; California. Nat Parks Mag 38:17 S '64
Detroit's smog-shrouded mystery. P. Hillary. il Motor T 71:62-5 Ja '65
Fight against smog; GM shows it's leading the band; exhaust control devices on '66 cars. il Bsns W p24-5 Ag 22 '64
Out in the smog; smog neutralizers. Newsweek 64:62+ Ag 24 '64
Plumbing for horsepower. G. Blair. il Hot Rod 17:78-80 Ag '64
Smelly cars. New Repub 151:5 O 31 '64
Smog battle gets hot. C. N. Barnard. il Sat Eve Post 237:78+ Ap 25 '64
Smog devices tested by dynamometer system. Sci N L 85:152 Mr 7 '64
Truth about ram tuning. G. Blair. il Hot Rod 17:78-81 Jl '64
See also
Carbon monoxide

Filters

See Air filters, Automobile

Fuel

Full story on fuels. E. Dahlquist. il Hot Rod 17:40-3 D '64
Select your own fuel. il Motor T 15:52-3 Je '63
See also
Gasoline

Fuel consumption

Chevy tops the trials; Pure oil performance trials. M. Muhleman. il Motor T 16:86-9 Ap '64
Economy runs; Mobil economy run. J. Whipple. il Pop Mech 120:65-9+ Jl '63
Gas mileage engineering. R. Huntington. il Motor T 15:72-3+ Mr '63
How good are those gas-saving gadgets? H. Luckett. il Pop Sci 185:37-41 Ag '64
How I learned to be a teen-age gas saver; Mobil economy run. E. Schilling. il Pop Sci 184:58-61+ Je '64
ICCA-Dodge Econability run. D. Wells. il Hot Rod 17:70-3+ Ag '64
Let's have cars that will stop! Pure oil performance trials. H. Luckett. il Pop Sci 184:59-64 Ap '64
Teen-age driving skill; 1964 Mobil economy run. il Hot Rod 17:90-1+ Jl '64

Fuel feeding

See also
Fuel pumps

Ignition

All about transistorized ignition. M. J. Schultz. il Pop Mech 120:172-7+ S '63
Build Simplex transistorized ignition. E. P. Nawracaj. il Pop Electr 20:45-8+ F '64
Delcotronic transistor ignition system. J. C. Norris. il Electr World 70:39-41 Jl '63
Electronic pulse ignition. J. Whipple. il Pop Mech 120:92-5 D '63
Fireworks for flyers. L. Smith. il Hot Rod 17:52-3+ S '64
Ford transistor ignition system. J. Oldham. Electr World 69:46-7+ Ap '63
High-performance transistor ignition system. M. R. Mayfield. il Electr World 69:30-1+ Je '63
Latest word on transistor ignitions. R. E. Jennings. il Motor T 16:84-9 N '64
Look, pa, no points! H. Luckett. il Pop Sci 184:74-6 Je '64
More transistor ignition circuits. il Pop Electr 21:56 Jl '64
Operation pickup; transistorized project ignition converter keeping useful parts. C. E. Ruoff. il Pop Electr 18:33+ Je; 19:47-8+ O '63
Positive-ground transistor ignition system. W. H. Thornton. il Electr World 71:85 Ja '64
Relay switching for transistor ignitions. J. Molnar. il Pop Electr 20:90 My '64
SCR automotive ignition system. B. Ward. il Electr World 72:44-5+ N '64
Transistor ignition; make your own for less than $8. D. A. Gattis. il Pop Sci 184:106-9+ Mr '64
Transistor ignition systems. il Consumer Bul 47:19-21 Mr; 39-40 S '64
Transistor ignition; with list of manufacturers of transistor ignition systems. B. Ward. il Pop Electr 20:33-44+ Je '64
Updated transistor ignition system. B. N. Saatjian. il Electr World 71:51+ My '64
What you should know about engine timing. F. L. Greenwald. il Pop Sci 186:124-7 Ja '65
What's the story on transistor ignitions? il Hot Rod 16:32-5+ Je '63
Your ignition system. S. F. Wilder. Pop Electr 18:34 Je '63
See also
Spark plugs

Lubrication

See Automobiles—Lubrication

Noise

Sure cure for ham, CB mobile noise; ignition noise. J. D. Lenk. il Pop Electr 19:65-6 O '63

Repairing

Shop talk. D. Clark. See issues of Hot rod

Shielding

Horsepower havoc! E. Rickman. il Hot Rod 16:76-9+ Ag '63

Starting

See Automobiles—Starting

Superchargers

Blower drives. L. Smith. il Hot Rod 17:34-7 Mr '64
Dodge chargers. W. Thoms. il Hot Rod 17:48-51 Jl '64
How good are those gas-saving gadgets? H. Luckett. il Pop Sci 185:37-41 Ag '64
Puff, puff for magic draggin'. L. Smith. il Hot Rod 17:42-5+ F '64
Super turbocharging the F-85. R. Huntington. il Motor T 15:34-7+ Ap '63
Turbocharger for non-spyders. R. Brock. il Hot Rod 17:40-3 Ap '64

Temperature

Engine temperature indicator. W. T. Davis. il Electr World 71:36+ Ap '64

Testing

Allstate endurance test. D. Wells. il Hot Rod 17:92-3 D '64
Cam-dwell meter for quick, sure auto tuneup B. Ward. il Pop Mech 121:196-8 F '64
Horsepower from FoMoCo. A. Miller. il Hot Rod 17:74-7 Ap '64
100,000-mile durability run. il Hot Rod 17:44-5 Mr '64
Valiant V-8 vs. Comet Caliente, which is hotter? A. Markovich. il Pop Sci 184:78-81 Ap '64
See also
Dynamometers

Valves

Keep those lifters quiet! hydraulic valve lifters and mechanical lifters. F. Greenwald. il Pop Sci 185:90-3 S '64

AUTOMOBILE engines—Valves—*Continued*
Three minute valves. E. Danquist. il Hot Rod 17:76-7+ S '64
Valve nobody knows; heat control valve. M. J. Schultz. il Pop Mech 120:178-81 O '63

AUTOMOBILE equipment. See Automobiles—Equipment

AUTOMOBILE exhibitions. See Automobiles—Exhibitions

AUTOMOBILE factories
Automobile industry accentuates trends in industrial design. J. J. Andrews. il Arch Rec 136:172+ Jl '64
See also
Ford motor company

Employees

Day on an auto assembly line. il Newsweek 64:58 Ag 10 '64
Five months after the Studebaker shutdown. il Mo Labor R 87:899 Ag '64
Interplant transfers in the automobile industry. P. Taft. Mo Labor R 86:276-8 Mr '63
Learning new jobs before old ones fade; United auto workers. il Bsns W p 114+ Ap 11 '64
Modern times today: man vs. machine. il Newsweek 63:59 Mr 30 '64
This is the way an American factory worker lives now. il U S News 57:47 S 21 '64
Will there be a rush for early retirement? il U S News 57:106-8 S 28 '64
See also
Automobile industry and trade—Wages and hours

AUTOMOBILE filling stations. See Automobile service stations

AUTOMOBILE financing. See Instalment plan

AUTOMOBILE fire apparatus. See Fire apparatus, Motor

AUTOMOBILE graveyards
Billboards, slobs and cemeteries. R. Starnes. Field & S 68:10+ Jl '63
This is a junkyard; color it green. J. Prokop. il Am For 71:14-17+ Ja '65

AUTOMOBILE headlights. See Automobiles—Lighting

AUTOMOBILE horns
Automatic horn honker; Car-Finder. C. Conley. il Field & S 69:107 S '64

AUTOMOBILE industry and trade
Auto trade heads for open road: unified market for US-Canadian cars. il Bsns W p32+ Ja 23 '65
Car importers face the facts. il Bsns W p 136-8+ Ap 20 '63
Detroit: proving ground for new technology. H. E .Klein. il Duns R 83:49-50+ Ap '64
How the '64 autos fared. il Time 84:81 Jl 17 '64
Talking free trade on autos; U.S. and Canada negotiate. Bsns W p24 O 10 '64
Will foreign cars share in the U.S. boom? il U S News 57:125-6 O 19 '64
See also
Automobile factories
Automobiles—Manufacture

Advertising

Appeal to youth; Ford's concentrating on youth market. il Time 83:74-5 Ja 3 '64
F.O.B. Detroit. Time 82:34+ Ag 23 '63
Ford soups up its youth drive; folk-jazz wing dings at colleges. il Bsns W p32-4 Ja 4 '64
Horsepower race breaks out again. il Bsns W p30-1 Mr 9 '63
Those service-free cars. il Changing T 17: 19-20 My '63

Consolidations and mergers

German auto equation; cooperation between Volkswagen and Daimler-Benz. il Bsns W p29 O 31 '64

Employees

See Automobile factories—Employees

History

Automobile under the Blue Eagle, by S. Fine. Review
Newsweek il 62:94-5 D 16 '63

International aspects

How U.S. firms are sharing in the auto boom abroad. il U S News 56:100-2 Ap 20 '64

Used cars

Greenbacked year on the dusty lots. il Time 81:105-6 My 17 '63
Old cars never die. H. Manchester. Read Digest 82:107-10 My '63

Wages and hours

Auto makers vs. double-time pay. U S News 56:90 Mr 9 '64
Auto talks open amid hope, worries. il Bsns W p64-6 Jl 4 '64
Autos: will strikes cut off the boom? with address by H. Ford. il U S News 57:71-3, 77-8 Jl 6 '64
Breaking the logjam. il Bsns W p23-4 O 10 '64
Challenge from Ford. Newsweek 63:68 Je 29 '64
Chrysler settles: what price peace? il Newsweek 64:87-90 S 21 '64
Contracts a la mode; U.A.M. obtains concessions. il Time 84:87 S 25 '64
Detroit talkathon: UAW contract time. il Newsweek 64:61-2 Jl 6 '64
Detroit tries to level employment swings; system of scheduling to avoid layoffs. Bsns W p43-4 Mr 2 '63
Effects of pay raises in autos: an employer gives his view; excerpts from letter. U S News 58:66 Ja 4 '65
Facing UAW and a long, hot summer. il Bsns W p 150-1+ My 23 '64
Formula is set. il Bsns W p 154+ S 26 '64
Is the lid coming off bigger pay increases? il U S News 57:95-7 O 19 '64
Now that the auto industry knows what Reuther wants. il U S News 57:75-6 Jl 13 '64
Of cars and steel and tottering guideposts T. R. Brooks. il Reporter 31:23-5 D 17 '64
Pay tops UAW's 1964 shopping list. Bsns W p80-1 D 21 '63
Real issue in autos, as industry sees it. il U S News 56:83-5 Ap 13 '64
Sort of ending; United auto workers reach a national agreement with General motors. Time 84:104 O 16 '64
Union problem: what is there to strike about? il U S News 57:80-1 Jl 20 '64
UAW; countdown to a strike? il Newsweek 64:59 Ag 31 '64
UAW guns for more of the same. Bsns W p 144+ S 19 '64
UAW's collision course; lines drawn for bitter bargaining. il Bsns W p26-7 Mr 28 '64
UAW's push in Canada. Bsns W p90 O 31 '64
Victory on wages is labor's 1964 goal; also job security and shorter week. il Bsns W p88+ D 28 '63
Wage chronology: Chrysler corp; 1961-64. il Mo Labor R 87:904-15 Ag '64
Wage chronology: Ford motor co; 1959-64. H. West. il Mo Labor R 87:1039-50 S '64
Wage chronology; General motors corp, 1961-63. il Mo Labor R 86:1170-83 O '63
Wages in motor vehicle and parts plants, April 1963. L. E. Lewis and F. L. Bauer. il Mo Labor R 87:161-7 F '64
Wages or fringes? UAW weighs the odds. il Bsns W p60+ F 15 '64
What Reuther wants now from the auto industry. il U S News 56:87-8 Ap 6 '64
When a union tries to break the U.S. wage barrier. il U S News 56:85-6 Mr 30 '64
Year of the coffee break. il Time 83:79-80 Je 26 '64

Belgium

Volga car man. Newsweek 62:76-7 S 9 '63

Canada

Canadian carmaking has its own problems. Bsns W p 130+ Ja 26 '63

Czechoslovakia

Little red wagon heads west. il Bsns W p49-50+ S 19 '64

Europe, Western

Almost like Detroit. il Time 83:104+ Je 12 '64
Auto growing pains. il Time 84:99 N 6 '64
Bumper-to-bumper. il Newsweek 62:66 S 16 '63
European report. See issues of Motor trend
Europe's amazing auto boom. B. F. Phlegar. il U S News 56:57-61 Ap 6 '64
Is Europe's auto boom running out of gas? il U S News 57:71-2 Ag 31 '64
Low gear; auto sales. il Newsweek 64:67 Ag 17 '64
Onrushing auto makers. R. A. Smith. il Fortune 68:96-8+ Ag '63

France

Chrysler move rouses France. Bsns W p 100 Ja 26 '63
Philosophers of the auto. il Time 81:95 Je 14 '63

Germany (Federal Republic)

G.M. v. everybody; Opel's challenge. il Time 83:98 Mr 13 '64

AUTOMOBILE industry and trade—Germany (Federal Republic)—*Continued*
German auto equation; cooperation between Volkswagen and Daimler-Benz. il Bsns W p29 O 31 '64
Growing old richly; Stuttgart's Daimler-Benz. il Time 85:67 Ja 1 '65
New luxury on wheels; Grand Mercedes. Bsns W p36 S 21 '63
Road gets rougher for the Beetle; VW 1200. il Bsns W p47-8+ Ap 18 '64
Run for German market's money; GM's Opel vs VW. il Bsns W p34 Mr 7 '64
To prevent slipping, keep going; Volkswagen. il Time 82:80 S 27 '63

Great Britain

In high gear; record auto output. Newsweek 63:94 My 18 '64
Princess R; Vanden Plas Princess 4-litre R. il Newsweek 64:61 Ag 31 '64
Who's afraid of the BRM? K. Rudeen. il Sports Illus 18:47+ F 25 '63
See also
British motor corporation
Ford motor company, limited, Dagenham, England
Rootes motors, limited
Rover company

Italy

Ferrari built for two. il Time 81:94+ My 24 '63
Fiat: the big wheel in Italy's traffic. il Newsweek 63:68-70 Ja 20 '64
Foreign car boom explodes in Italy. il Bsns W p 136+ S 14 '63
Turin with a car thrown in. R. Joseph. il Esquire 60:110-13 O '63
Who's afraid of the BRM? K. Rudeen. il Sports Illus 18:47+ F 25 '63

Japan

Collision coming for Japanese cars; Toyota motor co. il Bsns W p70+ Je 27 '64
Nissan's new plant heralds auto age. il Bsns W p72-5+ D 19 '64
Profitable toy; small truck of Hiroshima's Toyo Kogyo co. Time 81:90 Mr 29 '63

Latin America

Too many auto plants. Time 81:105 My 3 '63

Mexico

Mexico's hope for growth: autos. Bsns W p92 F 9 '63

Sweden

Sweden helps U.S. unemployed; fifty jobless auto workers to be sent to Scania-Vabis. Bsns W p50 Ap 4 '64

United States

Another big year ahead. il Bsns W p23-4 S 14 '63
Another run for the record; sales figures for 1964 models. il Time 83:81 Ja 17 '64
As the auto boom goes on. il U S News 54:37 Je 3 '63
Auto outlook: boom to go on. il U S News 57:66 D 28 '64
Auto outlook: sales records to be broken. U S News 54:8 My 27 '63
Auto sales building to a record. il Bsns W p25-6 Jl 11 '64
Auto sales drive to higher peaks. il Bsns W p30-1 Ap 27 '63
Automakers and their mighty works. R. Armstrong. il Sat Eve Post 237:15-27 S 19 '64
Autos lead the way: big sales and a turn to luxury. il U S News 54:42-4 Mr 25 '63
Autos top all records. il Bsns W p 19 Ag 3 '63
Beginning of a new automobile era. A. Rothenberg. il Look 28:58 O 6 '64
Bending the guidelines; U.A.W.-Chrysler settlement. il Time 84:29-30 S 18 '64
Boom in city that autos built; how Detroit made a comeback. il U S News 57:64-7 Jl 27 '64
Bread-and-butter issues as Reuther reviews them; summary of address. W. Reuther. Newsweek 62:87 N 18 '63
Bumper-to-bumper crop. il Time 84:57 D 25 '64
Buoyant UAW likes the odds. Bsns W p 124 Mr 14 '64
Can automobiles be humanized? Christian Cent 81:899 Jl 15 '64
Cloak & camera in Detroit. il Time 84:61-2 Ag 14 '64
Detroit bets on a banner '65. il Bsns W p28-9 D 12 '64
Detroit dreams of millennium. il Bsns W p23-4 F 15 '64
Detroit launches greatest expansion. Bsns W p28 Mr 21 '64
Detroit listening post. J. Whipple. See issues of Popular mechanics
Detroit plays for four-of-a-kind. il Bsns W p62-4+ S 19 '64
Detroit still the bellwether. Bsns W p26 My 18 '63
Detroit's fast start. il Time 82:97 N 1 '63
Detroit's strategy: a new look for the '65s. il Bsns W p 23-4 My 16 '64
Eight million year? Newsweek 63:80 Mr 16 '64
Ford's young one; Mustang. il Time 83:92-102 Ap 17 '64
Full speed ahead. il Time 81:83 F 15 '63
Glee and gloom. Newsweek 64:83 O 19 '64
Good times in auto business: no letdown in sight. il U S News 55:66-8 S 30 '63
Handwriting on the wall. Nation 197:446 D 28 '63
Horse trading starts; Big three auto companies vs UAW. il Bsns W p23-4 Ag 22 '64
How Henry Ford II sees the outlook in autos; interview. H. Ford, 2d. il U S News 55:72-5 Ag 19 '63
How the new cars are selling. il U S News 55:46-8 O 21 '63
In autos: where the sixties are soaring. il U S News 56:98-9 Ja 13 '64
Look ahead to the auto negotiations. T. R. Brooks. il Reporter 30:27-9 My 21 '64
New auto year begins—. il U S News 57:94 Ag 17 '64
New car explosion. il Bsns W p29-30 N 9 '63
New-model cars keep coming: a record year in sight. il U S News 57:88-90 S 28 '64
1963: a banner year for auto sales? U S News 54:10 Ap 22 '63
1964 autos: off to best start on record. Bsns W p33 O 19 '63
1964 models: cars & dolls. A. Rothenberg. il Look 27:85-98 O 22 '63
Now, a shortage of new cars? il U S News 55:31 Jl 29 '63
Now it looks like an eight-million-car year. il U S News 56:38-9 Mr 16 '64
Production box score; 1963 versus 1962. Pop Mech 121:103 Ja '64
Profits, polemics & politics. Time 84:73 Ag 28 '64
Prospect for autos amazes even Detroit. il Bsns W p 19 D 28 '63
Routine marvel; 7 million cars a year. il Newsweek 62:55 Ag 26 '63
Selling them big and bigger. il Time 81:103-4+ Ap 19 '63
7.7 million sales. Newsweek 63:63 Ja 13 '64
Stock talk. M. Muhleman. See issues of Motor trend
They're off to a racing start. il Bsns W p25 O 10 '64
What Detroit didn't do for 1965. J. Whipple. il Pop Sci 185:92-6 O '64
When they buy a rolling status symbol. J. Keating. il N Y Times Mag p28+ S 27 '64
Yule logjam for car dealers. il Bsns W p27-8 N 21 '64
See also
Automobile dealers
Automobiles—Prices
Strikes—United States—Automobile industry and trade
United automobile, aircraft and agricultural implement workers of America
also names of automobile manufacturing companies, e.g. Chrysler corporation
AUTOMOBILE industry strikes. See Strikes—United States—Automobile industry and trade
AUTOMOBILE inspection. See Automobiles—Inspection
AUTOMOBILE insurance. See Insurance, Automobile
AUTOMOBILE jacks. See Jacks
AUTOMOBILE junk dealer. See Junk dealers
AUTOMOBILE laws and regulations
Mixed-up driving laws can kill you. D. B. Warnick. il Travel 121:45-7 Ap '64
Snow job. Nation 198:227 Mr 9 '64
See also
Automobiles—Inspection
AUTOMOBILE license plates. See Automobiles—License plates
AUTOMOBILE locks and keys
Don't let this happen! Twistlok rated not acceptable. Consumer Rep 28:460-1 O '63
AUTOMOBILE mechanics (persons)
College of mechanical knowledge. A. Markovich. il Pop Sci 184:76-8 Mr '64
Gasoline alley. E. Rickman. il Hot Rod 17:72-5+ S '64
Sput. . .pop. . .clank. . .varoom! Chrysler-Plymouth national troubleshooting contest. C. N. Barnard. il Sat Eve Post 237:66-8 N 14 '64

AUTOMOBILE mechanics (persons)—*Continued*
Trouble shooters; Plymouth's inter-scholastic automotive program. B. Greene. il Hot Rod 16:36-9 S '63
Will mechanics make the difference at Daytona? il Pop Sci 184:76-9+ F '64

AUTOMOBILE models
AMT builds XR-6 model; experimental roadster. L. Smith. il Hot Rod 17:105 F '64
Big little ones. il Hot Rod 16:96 My '63
Hot rod in a shoebox. D. Wells. il Hot Rod 16:86 D '63
Matchbox millions; Lesney's matchbox motors. il Newsweek 61:79 Ap 29 '63
Model car champs; winners of annual 1963 Fisher body craftsman's guild model car competition. il Sr Schol 83:31 O 18 '63
Projexions. S. MacMinn. il Motor T 15:76-9 O '63

Racing

In the groove; slot car racing. il Newsweek 63:54 Je 29 '64
Want to drive 600 m.p.h? scale speed, that is. H. B. Comstock. il Pop Sci 185:124-6+ D '64

Radio control

Fido's whistle-controlled flivvers. H. B. Smith. il Pop Electr 21:47-51+ O '64

AUTOMOBILE ownership. See Automobiles—Purchasing

AUTOMOBILE parking
Better plowing with parking bans; Lawrence, Kan. G. Williams. il Am City 79:44 F '64
Can U learn at drive-in U? problem of campus parking. il Time 83:68 Mr 13 '64
Downtown store with indoor parking; Dayton company department store, St Paul, Minn. il Arch Rec 135:170-2 Je '64
Five ways to give your home a lot of parking. J. B. Brimer. il Pop Sci 185:108-11 S '64
From farmers' market to parking ramp; La Crosse, Wis. M. R. Birnbaum. il Am City 78:128+ Mr '63
Make your drive and motor court interesting. il House B 105:166-7+ My '63
New shape parking ramps at Macy's new store in Elmhurst, L.I. il Time 83:54 Ap 10 '64
Off-street parking program; Greeley, Colo. B. H. Cruce. il Am City 79:113-14 F '64
Off-street parking; very good answers to a very tough problem. R. O'Harra. il Bet Hom & Gard 42:72-5 N '64
Parking by computer. Time 83:94 My 22 '64
Parking decks combined with Florida store. il Arch Rec 133:170-1 Je '63
Parking-lot program that leaves the motorist smiling; Santa Monica, Calif. E. N. Mobley. il Am City 78:147 Je '63
Parking: the crisis is downtown. il Arch Forum 118:100-9 F '63
Pffft! Rio de Janeiro's parking problem. il Time 83:35 Je 26 '64
Pittsburgh expands its parking program. M. A. Neale. il Am City 80:109 Ja '65
Read before you park. il House & Gard 124: 84-5 Jl '63
Shopper's park; Grand Junction, Colo. J. M. Lacy. il Am City 78:73-5 D '63
Shopping park shrinks accidents by 80 per cent; Grand Junction, Colo. J. M. Lacy. il Am City 79:142 O '64
Where auto meets garden. il Sunset 130:94-9 Je '63
See also
Garages
Garages, Municipal
Parking meters

AUTOMOBILE parts
Buy 'em by the piece. C. E. Nerpel. il Motor T 16:76-7 D '64
Ford road takes a surprise turn; merger with Electric autolite co. il Bsns W p 152+ S 14 '63
Monopoly is embarrassing; Joseph Lucas industries, ltd. il Fortune 68:80+ S '63
Radius rods for under $15. L. Smith. il Hot Rod 16:82-3 My '63
See also
Gulf and Western industries, incorporated

AUTOMOBILE periodicals. See Automobiles—Periodicals

AUTOMOBILE phonographs. See Phonograph, Automobile

AUTOMOBILE polishes. See Polishing materials

AUTOMOBILE racing
All stations are go! L. Smith. il Hot Rod 16: 102-3 D '63
America's uphill classic: Pikes Peak. R. Brock. il Hot Rod 16:46-51+ S '63
Another for the monster; Grand prix of endurance, Sebring, Fla. il Time 81:68 Ap 5 '63
Apperson Jack Rabbit; America's first sports car. J. L. Beardsley. il Motor T 16:54-7 Je '64
Are drag racers really crazy? D. Francis. il Pop Sci 183:72-5+ D '63
At the Daytona speedway derby; stockcar racing. il Newsweek 63:75-8 F 24 '64
Atlanta 500. M. Muhleman. il Motor T 15: 66-71 Je '63; 16:74-7 Jl '64
Auto racing on ice; photographs. Travel 120: 41-3 N '63
Automobile classic: the 1907 race from Peking to Paris by car; excerpts. L. Barzini. il Vogue 144:123-9 N 15 '64
Automotive milestones; Paige 6-66, up and over. J. L. Beardsley. il Motor T 15:62-3+ S '63
Automotive milestones; Ralph DePalma, Peter De Paolo, Indianapolis, 1920. il Motor T 15:76-7+ Ag '63
Automotive milestones; the Peugeot that outran time, Indianapolis, 1913. J. L. Beardsley. il Motor T 15:68-71+ O '63
Awful auto ride; Monte Carlo rally. K. Rudeen. il Sports Illus 18:12-15+ F 4 '63
Bakersfield showdown! D. Wells. il Hot Rod 17:44-7 My '64
Beetle bomb; Volkswagen race in Nassau. il Time 82:64 D 20 '63
Best thing since Napoleon; tour of Corsica. P. E. Ress. il Sports Illus 19:52-3 N 11 '63
Beware the blue Cobra; Sebring race. il Time 83:80+ Ap 3 '64
Big, big, big go! D. Wells. il Hot Rod 17:42-5+ S '64
Big day for Clarkhunters at the Glen; Watkins Glen, N.Y. K. Rudeen. il Sports Illus 19:26-8 O 14 '63
Big go '64; National championship drag races. D. Wells. il Hot Rod 17:72-81+ N '64
Big $$$ in the fast draft. T. Flaherty. il Life 54:15 Mr 22 '63
Bluebird to happiness; D. Campbell at Lake Eyre, South Australia. il Time 84:58 Jl 24 '64
Bonneville nationals; wind, water & speed. C. E. Nerpel. il Motor T 16:56-61 D '64
Bonneville '64; rough, windy and wet. E. Dahlquist. il Hot Rod 17:36-45 N '64
Bonneville speed week. C. Nerpel. il Motor T 15:62-7 D '63
Bonneville wrap-up. D. Francisco. il Hot Rod 17:80-6+ Ja '64
Bravery is not enough. J. Skow. il Sat Eve Post 236:78-80 Ag 10 '63
Can Detroit move in on Indy? H. B. Comstock. il Pop Sci 182:75-8+ My '63
Canadian winter rally. il Motor T 15:76-9 My '63
Canadian winter rally. B. Cummins. il Motor T 16:80-1 Je '64
Cashing in on speed; Daytona 500. il Bsns W p30-1 F 29 '64
Charlotte national 400. M. Muhleman. il Motor T 16:72-5 Ja '64; 17:70-3 Ja '65
Charlotte national 400. R. Brock. il Hot Rod 16:80-1+ D '63
Charlotte World 600. M. Muhleman. il Motor T 15:80-5 Ag '63
Chevy takes a 400. M. Muhleman. il Hot Rod 16:80-1 F '63
Comets on safari. B. McVay. il Motor T 16:78-9 Je '64
Comets on safari. R. Brock. il Hot Rod 17:26-31+ My '64
Cool fireball named Roberts. B. Heilman. il Sports Illus 20:31-4+ F 10 '64
Cool win in a crowded glen; U.S. Grand prix at Watkins Glen. B. Ottum. il Sports Illus 21:28-9 O 12 '64
Darlington Southern 500. M. Muhleman. il Motor T 16:66-9 D '64
Day for survivors; Indianapolis 500. il Time 83:70 Je 5 '64
Daytona 500. M. Muhleman. il Motor T 15: 28-33 My '63; 16:70-3 My '64
Daytona surprise party. R. Brock. il Hot Rod 17:36-9+ My '64
Death takes no holiday; seven-car crash at the Indianapolis 500. il Newsweek 63:86 Je 8 '64
Detroit goes back to the races. K. Vining. il Pop Sci 182:74-6+ F '63
Dixie 400. M. Muhleman. il Motor T 15:60-3 F; 74-9 S '63
Drag race is born; Riverside international raceway. B. Greene. il Hot Rod 17:77-8 My '64
Drive with devils behind you; Russians at Monte Carlo rally. C. N. Barnard. il Sat Eve Post 237:64-5 Mr 7 '64
Driver in a tight corner; Indianapolis 500-mile race. B. Ottum. il Sports Illus 20:78-80+ Je 1 '64
East African safari. R. Brock. il Hot Rod 17:34-41+ Je '64

AUTOMOBILE racing—*Continued*
End of an era at Indy; Indianapolis 500-mile race. K. W. Purdy. il Sat Eve Post 237:60-2 My 30 '64
Falcon and Valiant invade Europe; Monte Carlo rally. C. Nerpel. il Motor T 16:74-7 Ap '64
Fame and terror at 200 MPH drag racing. M. Kram. il Sports Illus 21:26-8+ Ag 31 '64
Fast Fords and a great Scot; Indianapolis 500-mile race. B. Ottum. il Sports Illus 20:32-5 My 25 '64
Fast 'n' fancy. D. Wells. il Hot Rod 17:88-9 D '64
Fast, wet, and almost dead; 526 mph speed record at Bonneville Salt Flats. H. Gorey. il Sports Illus 21:72-4 O 26 '64
Fastest 500. R. Brock. il Hot Rod 17:36-45+ Ag '64
Firecracker 400. M. Muhleman. il Motor T 15:68-73 S '63; 16:70-5 S '64
First annual British international drag festival. B. Foley. il Hot Rod 18:50-6 Ja '65
500 under attack; race at Indianapolis. K. Rudeen. il Sports Illus 18:18-21 My 27 '63
For Ferrari, some fast company at last; Fords at Le Mans race. P. E. Ress. il Sports Illus 20:51-2 Je 29 '64
Ford on the pole; qualification trials for Indianapolis 500. il Time 83:65 My 29 '64
Ford vs. Chevy at the Indianapolis 500. J. Whipple. il Pop Mech 119:69-73+ My '63
Ford wins again Atlanta 500. R. Brock. il Hot Rod 16:96-8 Je '63
Fords sweep Daytona 500. R. Brock. il Hot Rod 16:26-31+ My '63
Ford's up, Jaguar's on deck, Mercedes aims to play. G. Grant. Sports Illus 20:65-6+ My 11 '64
Forecast: the biggest big go; National championship drag races. D. Wells. il Hot Rod 16:84-5+ S '63
14th Southern 500; Darlington, S.C. R. Brock. il Hot Rod 16:46-50 N '63
From a wild race in Mexico: a surprise champion; J. Surtees, world champion driver for 1964. S. Moss. il Sports Illus 21:60-2 N 2 '64
Furious fun of Pinkie and Pat; Marlboro, Md. endurance race. B. H. LaFontaine. il Sports Illus 21:20-1 Ag 24 '64
Golden state 400. J. Wright. il Motor T 16:64-7 F '64
Golden state 400. R. Brock. il Hot Rod 17:44-7+ Ja '64
Green BRM; Grand prix de Monaco. il Newsweek 63:98 My 25 '64
Grudge match at Trenton; U.S. auto club's race. il Time 82:66 O 4 '63
Hard, lonely life of a champion driver. B. Libby. il Sat Eve Post 236:42-3 N 2 '63
Heat's on in drag racing! D. Wells. il Hot Rod 17:50-3 O '64
High & fast; 41 annual Pikes Peak auto hill climb. il Motor T 15:58-61 O '63
Hot rod magazine championship drag races. D. Wells. il Hot Rod 17:52-3+ Je '64
Hot rod's first annual championship drags. D. Wells. il Hot Rod 17:26-35+ Ag '64
How many chapters? Salt Flats at Bonneville? Sports Illus 19:14 O 28 '63
How stock is stock? NASCAR rules. il Motor T 15:26-7 Mr '63
How to build a brute; East African safari rally. il Pop Sci 184:84-6 My '64
How to drive a champion drag stocker. A. Eckstrand. il Hot Rod 16:46-7+ Je '63
How to drive and survive; ed. by K. W. Purdy. S. Moss. il Bet Hom & Gard 42:6+ Ja '64
How to win in Belgium by not really coasting; Jimmy Clark wins Belgian grand prix. il Time 83:45 Je 26 '64
I have a hunch the U.S. will be shocked. S. Moss. il Life 54:93-4+ My 24 '63
If you can't beat them, get them to join you; Ford wins at Milwaukee. B. Ottum. Sports Illus 21:88+ S 7 '64
I'll take horsepower; A. J. Foyt wins 250-mile American challenge cup race at Daytona. il Time 83:102-3 F 28 '64
Indianapolis 500; V-8 threat. J. Wright. il Motor T 15:64-9 Ag '63
Indianapolis, 1963. il Motor T 15:30-3 Je '63
Indianapolis '63. R. Brock. il Hot Rod 16:26-33+ Ag '63
Indy diary. G. Moore. il Motor T 16:55-7 Ap '64
Indy 500. J. Wright. il Motor T 16:28-33+ Ag '64
Indy 500 diary. B. Crower. il Hot Rod 16:90-2+ S '63
It was snakebite day at Sebring. H. Whall. il Sports Illus 20:20-3 Mr 30 '64
Japan zeroes in on world racing; first Oriental entrant of Grand prix competition. J. Lovesey. il Sports Illus 21:70-1 Ag 17 '64
Jeep derby, crisis on wheels. T. E. Stimson. il Pop Mech 119:123-5+ F '63
Jimmy's year; Europe's Grand prix circuit. il Time 82:60+ Jl 12 '63
Karting's Grand nationals; Windsor raceway, Rockford, Ill. il Hot Rod 16:104 D '63
Killer. Nation 198:545 Je 1 '64
Le Mans: twenty-four hours of what? R. Bensted-Smith. il Atlan 211:110-12 Je '63
Little engine that could; Chrysler vs. Ford. B. Ottum. il Sports Illus 20:106-7 Ap 13 '64
Little Le Mans on ice. R. F. Dempewolff. il Pop Mech 121:132-5+ F '64
Longhorn Enduro, IKF Kart Enduro national championship. T. Medley. il Hot Rod 17:88-9 Ja '64
Look fast, think pink. K. W. Purdy. il Sat Eve Post 237:60-1 O 31 '64
Los Angeles' times grand prix. J. Wright. il Motor T 16:56-9 Ja '64
Los Angeles times Grand prix; Riverside, Calif. B. McVay. il Motor T 17:44-5 Ja '65
Magnificent and the macabre; Indianapolis 500. B. Ottum. il Sports Illus 20:24-9 Je 8 '64
Man, what a drag! il Life 55:115-16+ S 20 '63
Mickey-go-round. D. Francisco. il Hot Rod 16:108-10 F '63
Mile high 250 miler; Continental Divide raceway. R. Brock. il Hot Rod 17:17 S '64
Mobil economy run; winners. il Motor T 15:80 Je '63
Money man; F. Lorenzen. Sports Illus 19:14 S 9 '63
Motor sports (cont) il Sport Illus 18:47+ F 25; 36-8 Mr 4; 68-9+ Ap 1; 72-3 Ap 15 '63
Motor trend Riverside 500. il Motor T 16:48-9 Ja '64
Motor trend's Riverside 500. il Motor T 15:26-33 Ap '63
Motor trend's 2nd annual Riverside 500. J. Wright. il Motor T 16:34-40 Ap '64
National scene. See issues of Hot rod
New race produces an old Ferrari story; Cobra-Ferrari race, Daytona Beach. B. Ottum. il Sports Illus 20:52+ F 24 '64
Nice place for a picnic; East African safari. il Time 81:44 Ap 26 '63
1964 Winternationals. D. Wells. il Hot Rod 17:26-33+ Ap '64
1964 world series; drag racing, Cordova dragway. D. Wells. il Hot Rod 17:50-2 N '64
1963 drag racing rules. J. Hart. il Hot Rod 16:76-9 F '63
Ninth annual Nationals. L. Smith and D. Wells. il Hot Rod 16:26-37+ N '63
No racing for GM. Newsweek 63:90+ My 25 '64
None so swift as wee Jimmy; world champion Grand prix driver. K. Rudeen. il Sports Illus 19:28-30+ O 7 '63
Off we go! IKF 99-mile enduro at Edwards air force base, Calif. il Hot Rod 16:100-1 Ap '63
Oil the way; Parnelli Jones wins 500-mile race. Newsweek 61:92 Je 10 '63
Old guard has to call it a day; 200-mile race, Milwaukee. K. Rudeen. il Sports Illus 19:18-19+ Ag 26 '63
One from the North; Yankee 300. G. Moore. il Motor T 16:70-3 Ag '64
Pikes Peak. R. Brock. il Hot Rod 17:36-41+ S '64
Pink lady; Donna Mae Mims. Newsweek 62:78 S 16 '63
Pit stops; seconds saved win races. il Motor T 15:52-3 Mr '63
Plymouth's clean sweep; Daytona Beach stock-car race. il Newsweek 63:71-2 Mr 9 '64
Profiles in racing; ed. by M. Muhleman. C. Economaki. il Motor T 15:66-71 Mr '63
Race behind the race at Indianapolis 500. il Bsns W p 118+ Je 6 '64
Race to the top; Pikes Peak hill climb. il Hot Rod 16:108 Je '63
Rallying fast, Paddy's wagon beat them all; Monte Carlo rally. P. E. Ress. il Sports Illus 20:48-50 F 3 '64
Rebirth of sedan racing. L. Nehamkin. il Motor T 15:84-5 S '63
Rhubarb at Indy. il Time 81:82-3 Je 7 '63
Riding it out; U.S. auto club's championship at Trenton, N.J. il Newsweek 64:53 Ag 3 '64
Riverside 400. B. Russo. il Hot Rod 16:104 O '63
Roar of triumph for U.S. engines; Cooper-Cobra wins Riverside Grand prix. K. Rudeen. il Sports Illus 19:20-1 O 21 '63
Rod alert! Bonneville. D. Francisco. il Hot Rod 17:46-51+ D '64

AUTOMOBILE racing—*Continued*
Scourge of Hangover Alley; speed festival at Nassau. B. Ottum. il Sports Illus 21:68-9 D 14 '64
Sebring: Cobra vs. Ferrari. P. Biro. il Motor T 16:58-61 Jl '64
Sebring results. il Motor T 15:81 Je '63
Second annual Riverside 500. il Hot Rod 17:98 Ap '64
Sedans, rails and gassers; Winter nationals, Pomona, Calif; photographs. L. Schiller. Sat Eve Post 237:58-61 Ja 4 '64
Shades o' Muroc; SCTA opener, El Mirage, Calif. L. Smith. il Hot Rod 16:42-5 Ag '63
Shell 4000-mile rally; Cross-Canada automobile rally. B. Cummins. il Motor T 15:80-1 Jl '63
Shell 4000 rally. B. Cummins. il Motor T 16:70-3 Jl '64
Showdown at Watkins Glen; U.S. Grand prix. B. Ottum. Sports Illus 21:91+ O 5 '64
'63 Winternationals. L. Smith. il Hot Rod 16:60-75+ My '63
'64 drag rules. J. Hart. il Hot Rod 17:84-5+ F '64
Smokey Yunick speaks; ed. by M. Muhleman. S. Yunick. il Motor T 15:82 O '63
Speed and women; excerpts from All but my life. S. Moss and K. W. Purdy. il Atlan 212:110-20+ O '63
Speed in bright repose; Indianapolis 500-mile race; with photographs by Martin Nathan. Sports Illus 20:34-9 Je 1 '64
Sport of the speed demons; Trotters hot rod club. il Ebony 19:113-14+ N '63
Stock car foresight and hindsight. M. Muhleman. il Motor T 16:70-3 Mr '64
Stock hop. J. Hart. il Hot Rod 17:84-7 O '64
Stockers storm at the Nationals; Indianapolis. J. Wright. il Motor T 16:54-5 D '64
Stocks boom at the Winternationals. B. McVay. il Motor T 16:62-5 My '64
Stocks zig-zag at Riverside. R. Brock. il Hot Rod 16:26-9+ Ap '63
Swoop of a secret weapon; stock-car races, Daytona 500. H. Horn. il Sports Illus 20:26-8+ Mr 2 '64
Tempest fugit; American challenge cup. il Time 81:62 Mr 1 '63
This car's dying on us. F. Graham, jr. il Sat Eve Post 236:22-4 Je 1 '63
Top ten. L. Smith. il Hot Rod 16:84-5 Mr '63; 17:42-3 Ja '64
Turbine on the hell circuit; Le Mans. il Time 81:69 Je 28 '63
Twenty-four hours at Le Mans. il Motor T 16:66-9 O '64
22° Grand prix automobile; with reproductions of paintings by A. Parker. Sports Illus 20:44-53 My 11 '64
Two against the clock at Indy. K. Rudeen. il Sports Illus 18:26-8+ Je 10 '63
Two from the South; Rebel 300, World 600. M. Muhleman. il Motor T 16:74-9 Ag '64
Two old shoestringers jolt the jet set; Wingfoot Express on the Bonneville Salt Flats. H. Gorey. il Sports Illus 21:66-7 O 12 '64
Two stroke stuff. T. Medley. il Hot Rod 17:102 Mr '64
Ugliest, cheapest and best in the world; jet car at Bonneville Salt Flats. H. Gorey. il Sports Illus 21:24-5 N 9 '64
USAC championship opener; from Phoenix to Indy by way of Trenton. il Motor T 16:82-3+ Je '64
U.S. fuel and gas championship; Bakersfield, Calif; photographs. Hot Rod 16:48-51 Je '63
Unser's hill! Pikes Peak. il Motor T 16:70-3 O '64
What makes Roger race. G. Rogin. il Sports Illus 18:58-62+ Mr 25 '63
Who really wins the Indianapolis. A. F. Gonzalez, jr. il Sci Digest 55:8-13 My '64
Will mechanics make the difference at Daytona? il Pop Sci 184:76-9+ F '64
Willow Springs kart enduro. L. Smith. il Hot Rod 16:80-1 Je '63
Winah! Jack Williams. B. Greene. il Hot Rod 17:34-5 S '64
Winternationals. J. Wright. il Motor T 15:68-73 My '63
With a nudge for luck; Surtees becomes the 1964 Grand prix champion. il Time 84:42 N 6 '64
With girdle & glue; Clark wins South Africa Grand prix. il Time 85:72 Ja 15 '65
World titles at stake; drag racing's 1964 World points championships. Hot Rod 17:88-90 My '64
World's fastest farmer: J. Clark. il Life 55:91-2 N 1 '63
Yankee 300. R. Brock. il Hot Rod 17:84-5 Jl '64
Yankee 300; stock car race, Indianapolis. G. Moore. il Motor T 15:74-7 Jl '63
Zinging in the rain; Solitude grand prix. il Time 84:42 Jl 31 '64
See also
Automobile speed records
Automobiles, Racing
Karting
Speedways

Accidents and injuries

See Sports—Accidents and injuries

History

Automotive milestones; Mulford's leisurely Knox-Indy, 1912. il Motor T 15:60-1+ Jl '63

AUTOMOBILE radios. See Automobiles—Radio equipment
AUTOMOBILE renting. See Automobiles—Renting
AUTOMOBILE replacement parts. See Automobile parts
AUTOMOBILE service stations
Here come the car clinics; Mobil repair center. D. Francis. il Pop Sci 182:53-6+ Mr '63
New kind of gusher; oil company diversification. il Time 82:59-60 Ag 2 '63
One stop for gas, food, lodging. il Bsns W p 118+ Je 29 '63
Running without gas in Mexico. il Bsns W p96+ S 19 '64
Truck stop goes fancy; Toledo 5. il Bsns W p 108-9+ Mr 16 '63

Employees

Retraining fills a gap; Toledo branch, Ohio state employment service. il Bsns W p 164 Ap 20 '63

AUTOMOBILE shows. See Automobiles—Exhibitions
AUTOMOBILE speed records
Bonneville '64; rough, windy and wet. E. Dahlquist. il Hot Rod 17:36-45 N '64
Bonneville speed week. C. Nerpel. il Motor T 15:62-7 D '63
Continental Divide raceways grand opener. il Hot Rod 17:48-9 S '64
Cool run for an old hot rodder; C. Breedlove in the Spirit of America. H. Gorey. Sports Illus 19:46-8+ Ag 19 '63
Craig Breedlove streaks! J. Wright. il Motor T 15:80 O '63
Don Garlits' speed secrets. R. Brock. il Hot Rod 17:28-35+ N '64
Dream of speed; C. Breedlove's Spirit of America. il Time 82:51 Ag 16 '63
Driving a world's record; 407 miles per hour. C. Breedlove. il Pop Mech 120:87-92+ N '63
Dry lakes; Southern California timing association. L. Smith. il Hot Rod 17:72-5 Ja '64
Envoys of speed. il Hot Rod 17:94-5 Ja '64
Jet ace; three-wheeled Spirit of America. il Newsweek 62:74-5 Ag 19 '63
National drag racing records. See issues of Hot rod to May 1963
Official Winternationals champions. Hot Rod 17:24 Ap '64
'63 Bonneville speed trials. B. Greene. il Hot Rod 16:60-73+ N '63
Spirit of America. D. Francisco. il Hot Rod 16:26-33 O '63
World land speed records. il Motor T 17:74-7 Ja '65
AUTOMOBILE speedways. See Speedways
AUTOMOBILE styling. See Automobiles—Design
AUTOMOBILE thefts. See Automobiles, Theft of
AUTOMOBILE tires. See Tires, Automobile
AUTOMOBILE tools. See Tools
AUTOMOBILE touring
It starts straight and gentle but just you wait; northwestern California. il Sunset 132:26+ My '64
Redwood country. H. Papashvily. il Holiday 35:20+ Mr '64
Tips on touring. C. Lane. See issues of Travel to September 1963
Vacationing on wheels; symposium. il Pop Sci 184:106-26+ My '64
We took the back way home. J. Stuart. il Am For 69:40-1+ N '63
See also
Automobile trailers

Accommodations

See Automobile trailer camps; Motels

Central America

First pleasure drive to Panama. T. Stimson. il Pop Mech 119:86-91 My '63

Europe, Western

Personal business; seeing Europe by car. Bsns W p 125-6 Ag 22 '64

AUTOMOBILE touring—*Continued*

Latin America

How's the driving south of Mexico? Sunset 134:26-7 Ja '65

Mexico

Mexican weekends. T. B. Lesure. il Travel 123:44-7 Ja '65

United States

Back roads lead to discovery. B. D. Laschever. il Pop Phot 52:140-1 Ap '63
Cross country camping. P. Geraci. il Travel 119:31-3+ My '63
Cross-country editor; reports on national boom in auto camping. H. Grey. il Field & S 67:36-7+ F '63
Delightful Dixieland trail. il Bet Hom & Gard 42:119-22 Mr '64
From sun-clad sea to shining mountains. R. Gray. il Nat Geog Mag 125:542-89 Ap '64
How to read a road map. G. M. Schultz. il Todays Health 41:14-17+ Mr '63
Open road for women. K. D. Fishman. Mlle 59:110-11+ Je '64
Travel USA. il Look 28:68-85+ My 5 '64
Traveling by car; excerpt from Seventeen book of etiquette and entertaining. E. A. Haupt. Seventeen 23:32 Je '64
Will you drive to the fair? il Sunset 132:45-6+ Je '64
See also
Roads—United States

History

Automotive milestones; first car across the U.S.-Winton, 1903. il Motor T 15:60-1+ My '63
Surrounding hills; driving a Model T from Chicago-West coast in 1924. E. Hahn. New Yorker 40:184+ D 5 '64

AUTOMOBILE towing. See Towing

AUTOMOBILE traffic. See Road traffic

AUTOMOBILE trailer camps
Booked for travel; the mysterious West. H. Sutton. il Sat R 47:36-9 F 15 '64
Cross-country editor; reports on national boom in auto camping. H. Grey. il Field & S 67:36-7+ F '63
Trailer your boat and tent to Florida; ten top trailer-boat camps. K. Ferguson. il Motor B 112:36-9 D '63

AUTOMOBILE trailers
Booked for travel; the mysterious West. H. Sutton. il Sat R 47:36-9 F 15 '64
Choosing a travel trailer. il Consumer Bul 46:2+ Jl '63
Fit your car for your trailer. R. Huntington. il Consumer Bul 48:2+ F '65
Happy ways of trailering. H. Peterson. il Sports Illus 18:68-74 My 13 '63
Hitch & go. C. Isica. See issues of Motor trend
Hitch-um and pitch-um camping. F. M. Krysiak. il Recreation 57:130-1 Mr '64
How to handle any trailer. K. Mason. il Outdoor Life 133:66-8+ Je '64
How to put a wall tent on wheels. P. Geraci. il Pop Sci 185:126-8 Jl '64
Inside look at mobile homes. il Good H 158: 124 Ja '64
Mobile home living. E. T. Kienz. il Consumer Bul 46:2+ S '63
Mobile homes. il Consumer Bul 47:6-12 Je '64
New way to find our lost frontier. R. Cantwell. il Sports Illus 18:32-5+ My 20 '63
Their dream house is on wheels. S. Gordon. il Look 28:49-51 Ja 14 '64
Track-testing trailers. C. Isica. il Motor T 16:86-7+ F '64
Trailer traveling in the U.S. il Consumer Bul 47:13-16 Ag '64
Trailer treks. F. M. Simison. il Travel 119: 40-4 Mr '63
Transcontinental trailer test. R. Barlow. il Field & S 68:51-3 F '64
Vacations on wheels. il Pop Sci 182:118-32+ My '63
What's new in trailers & trailer living. Changing T 17:30 Ag '63
You can save money tenting on two wheels. B. Smallman. il Pop Sci 184:124-5 My '64
See also
Automobile boat trailers
Campers and coaches, Truck

Parking

Hitch & go; driving to the World's fair; parking problems. C. Isica. il Motor T 16: 94-7 Ag '64

AUTOMOBILE trips. See Automobile touring

AUTOMOBILE warranty. See Warranty

AUTOMOBILE washing. See Automobiles—Cleaning

AUTOMOBILE wheels. See Automobiles—Wheels

AUTOMOBILE wiring. See Automobiles—Electric wiring

AUTOMOBILE workers. See Automobile factories—Employees; Automobile mechanics (persons)

AUTOMOBILES
Automakers and their mighty works. R. Armstrong. il Sat Eve Post 237:15-27 S 19 '64
Automobiles. il Consumer Rep 29:386-426 D '64
Automobiles (cont) Sports Illus 18:51-3 Ap 22 '63
Automobiles; 1964 model review. R. Huntington. il Consumer Bul 46:14-20 N '63
Autos 1963-1964. il Consumer Rep 28:152-85; 29:160-93 Ap '63, Ap '64
Avanti, a step forward by Studebaker. R. Brock. il Hot Rod 16:26-31+ Je '63
Barracuda! B. McVay. il Motor T 16:26-7 My '64
Barracuda. R. Brock. il Hot Rod 17:26-9 Jl '64
Box score on 1964 cars. il Pop Sci 184:64-7 Ja '64
Cadillac, Imperial, and Lincoln. Consumer Rep 29:300 Je '64
Cadillac owners praise handling comfort, find ash trays distressing. il Pop Mech 119:78-81+ Je '63
Car as hero; eight unforgettable cars from books. il Vogue 142:124-7+ N 1 '63
Car of the year; Rambler. il Motor T 15:20-45+ F '63
Car of the year; the 1964 Fords. C. Nerpel. il Motor T 16:32-62 F '64
Cars in your family. il Bet Hom & Gard 42: 14+ Je; 14+ Jl; 20-1+ Ag; 29-30+ S; 38+ O; 38+ N '64; 43:6+ Ja '65
Chrysler Newport; Oldsmobile Dynamic 88; Pontiac Catalina. il Consumer Bul 46:24-7 Mr '63
Crash! are small cars death traps? E. D. Fales, jr. il Pop Sci 185:50-3+ Ag '64
Dangerously attractive; new Chevrolet: Chevelle. Time 82:56-7 Ag 30 '63
Dodge: lots of go with plenty of whoa. A. Markovich. il Pop Sci 183:64-6 D '63
Dodge owners crow over quality, grouse about headroom. il Pop Mech 119:102-5+ Ap '63
Emotion key to turbine Chrysler's gas turbine car. E. Hall. Sci N L 85:228 Ap 11 '64
Falcon Challenger. J. Wright. il Motor T 15: 50-1 Mr '63
Family car gets back its frills. il Bsns W p 100-2 Ja 9 '65
Ford Constellation. il Hot Rod 17:86-7 Ag '64
Ford's wildest Mustang. P. O'Shea. il Hot Rod 17:26-9 Je '64
Four full-size cars; Cadillac, Ford, Chevy and Dodge V8. il Consumer Rep 28:238-42 My '63
Four 1965 automobiles; Dodge Coronet V-8; Dodge Dart 6; Falcon 6 and Falcon Futura V-8. il Consumer Bul 48:12-15 Ja '65
Handy hideaways for campgear. M. Lindberg. il Field & S 68:120-1 My '63
Hot rod X-rays the 65's; American motors, Chrysler corp, Ford motor co, and General motors corp. R. Brock. il Hot Rod 17:26-37+ O '64
How a car works: a primer for your wife. H. Wolf. il Esquire 62:200-3 D '64
How owners rate their new Chevelles. il Pop Mech 121:87-91+ F '64
How they get a stock car ready for Daytona. W. S. Griswold. il Pop Sci 182:76-7+ F '63
Lark Custom V-8; Rambler Ambassador V-8; Rambler American 220; Valiant V-100. il Consumer Bul 46:15-19 Je '63
Less weight means more Ford. R. Brock. il Hot Rod 16:40-3+ Jl '63
Little Chevy makes a lot o' jeep. D. Francisco. il Hot Rod 16:76-81 My '63
Mauna Kea hillclimb; first vehicle to reach the top. R. Brock. il Hot Rod 16:48-51+ Ap '63
New ones, 1965. il Motor T 16:24-47 O '64
New wheels in town; the '65 cars. il Vogue 144:120-1 N 15 '64
Nimble handling delights, scant headroom depresses Valiant owners. il Pop Mech 119: 90-3+ Je '63
1965 cars. il Changing T 18:7-12 D '64
1964 cars and station wagons. il Changing T 17:6-12 D '63
1963-1964 cars; full-size models. Consumer Bul 46:16-19 Mr '63; 47-18-26 Ap '64

AUTOMOBILES—*Continued*

Owners praise Pontiac's plush handling, chrome-free style; Falcon owners love its' new style, old thrift. il Pop Mech 121:90-4+ Mr '64

Owners report; Chrysler; Buick. il Pop Mech 119:80-3+ My '63

Owners report; troubles are little for owners of big Chevrolets. il Pop Mech 119:85-9+ F '63

PM drives Chrysler's new gas turbine. il Pop Mech 120:26-9 Jl '63

PM owners report; nimble Olds F-85 pleases owners; mileage, transmission draw fire. il Pop Mech 120:76-9+ Jl '63

PM owners report; Plymouth owners: handling tops headroom; Chevy's ride pleases more than mileage. il Pop Mech 121:90-9+ Ap '64

Report from the driver's seat; Ambassador: Rambler's hot one. A. Markovich. il Pop Sci 183:92-3 Jl '63

Six with four wheel drive; Jeep CJ series. C. Isica. il Motor T 16:38-41 Mr '64

'64 look. D. Francis and A. Markovich. il Pop Sci 183:65-89+ O '63

Skylark: Buick's sporty special. A. Markovich. il Pop Sci 182:80-1 Je '63

Some hazards in early 1965 cars. Consumer Rep 30:4 Ja '65

Spotlight on the Falcon Sprint. J. Whipple. il Pop Mech 119:28+ Je '63

Spotlight on the Jeep Wagoneer. E. Nelson. il Pop Mech 119:44+ My '63

Spotlight on Valiant's new V8. J. Whipple. il Pop Mech 121:42+ F '64

Tempest's style and power please, but the transmission noise annoys. il Pop Mech 119:92-5+ Ap '63

Test driving Ford's new Mustang. J. Wright. il Motor T 16:28-31 My '64

Three full-size cars: Chevrolet Impala; Plymouth Fury; Ford Galaxie 500. il Consumer Rep 29:37-9 Ja '64

Three low-priced full-sized V-8s; Plymouth Fury III V-8, Chevrolet Impala, Ford Custom 500 V-8. il Consumer Rep 30:38-41 Ja '65

Three 1965 automobiles: Chevelle 6 and V-8; Mercury Monterey. il Consumer Bul 48:17-20 F '65

Three 1963 automobiles: Cadillac 62; Dodge 330-6; Lincoln Continental. il Consumer Bul 46:11-16 Ap '63

Tried & true; Chrysler's 1964 models. Time 82:63 Ag 23 '63

Twenty-five years with Mercury. il Motor T 15:40-3 O '63

Two high-powered intermediates: Oldsmobile F-85 and Ford Fairlane 500. il Consumer Rep 29:251-3 My '64

Two 1965 automobiles: Ford Fairlane 500 6, Ford custom V-8. il Consumer Bul 47:19-22 D '64

What's new on the '65 cars? R. Huntington. il Consumer Bul 47:6-12 N '64

Where, oh where, has my little car gone? D. Francis. il Pop Sci 183:53-4 N '63

Whizz-quiz on cars. O. Gendebien and J. Jerome. il Vogue 142:114-19+ N 1 '63

Wh-o-o-o-sh, here come the turbines! B. Greene. il Hot Rod 16:74-7 Jl '63

See also

Automobile graveyards
Sports cars
Station wagons
Taxicabs

Accessories

See Automobiles—Equipment

Accidents

See Traffic accidents

Advertising

See Automobile industry and trade—Advertising

Air conditioning

Automobile air conditioners. il Consumer Bul 47:16 Jl '64

Car air conditioning: is this your year? D. Francis. il Pop Sci 183:82-5 Jl '63

Cool cars. Time 81:55 Mr 22 '63

Keep cool. il Motor T 15:26-9 Je '63

Keeping cool at the wheel. Bsns W p32 Jl 13 '63

Anecdotes, facetiae, satire, etc.

Judgment day traffic jam. P. D. Lagomarcino. New Repub 150:5 F 15 '64

Axles

Build yourself an axle. L. Smith. il Hot Rod 16:82-3+ F '63

Ford axle for Chevys. E. Dahlquist. il Hot Rod 17:92-3 F '64

Batteries

See Storage batteries

Bodies

Basic body dimensions. il Consumer Rep 28:164-71 Ap '63

Bodies and dimensions. il Consumer Rep 29:176-7 Ap '64

Bodies: styling and a wagon innovation. Consumer Rep 28:154 Ap '63

Fastback comeback. M. Lamm. il Motor T 16:32-3 S '64

Fiberglass futures. B. Fendell. il Motor T 16:96-101+ N '64

How to get a good body-repair job. E. D. Fales, jr. il Pop Sci 183:45-9+ S '63

Know your car; differentials, suspension systems, steering controls, brakes, and body construction. R. Temple. il Motor T 15:66-71 F '63

Royalite on a regal line; laminated plastic body of new Cord. W. P. Bowlin. il Motor T 16:70-1 D '64

Brakes

See Brakes, Automobile

Camping equipment

Build this car-top chuck box. N. R. DeYoung. il Pop Sci 184:111 My '64

Eleven ways to get more fun out of camping. il Pop Sci 184:120-1 My '64

Family and fishing? roll 'em together. T. McNally. il Outdoor Life 131:49-51+ My '63

Family camper comes of age. il House B 106:70-1 Ap '64

Rough-country camper. R. McCluskey. il Field & S 67:76 F '63

Traveling companions. il Good H 158:188+ My '64

Vacations on wheels. il Pop Sci 182:118-32+ My '63

What's new for the road. il Pop Sci 184:126 My '64

Your family camping outfit; Cost low, fun unlimited. R. McCluskey. il Field & S 67:38-41 F '63

See also

Automobile trailers
Campers and coaches, Truck

Cams

Cam timing for street and strip. J. Hart. il Hot Rod 17:74-7 D '64

Free 'n' easy cam. il Hot Rod 17:78-9 S '64

New variables: camshaft & compression. R. Huntington. il Motor T 16:50-1+ My '64

Will camshafts be kicked upstairs? R. Huntington. il Motor T 16:56-7+ Jl '64

Carburetors

See Carburetors

Care

Car noises, smells & drips. il Changing T 18:41-2 Ap '64

Fixing your car for overloads. Sunset 133:154+ N '64

How to keep the value of your car high! F. Olmsted. il Bet Hom & Gard 41:58-9 S '63

Now is the time to get your car ready for winter. il Bet Hom & Gard 42:38+ N '64

Rough it right. V. L. Oertle. il Motor T 15:52-7 My '63

Spring car care. H. R. Pfister. il Pop Sci 182:158-62 Ap '63

Summer driving. C. Isica. il Motor T 16:32-5 Je '64

Those service-free cars. il Changing T 17:19-20 My '63

See also

Anti-freeze solutions
Automobiles—Repairing

Chassis

Boxing the rails. L. Smith. il Hot Rod 16:38-9 Mr '63

XR-6; chassis conclusion. L. Smith. il Hot Rod 16:70-3 Ap '63

Cleaning

Aids you need for car cleaning. il Good H 157:155 S '63

Attracting the unwashed. il Time 84:78 Ag 28 '64

Automobile polishes and waxes. il Consumer Bul 46:8-10 S '63

Clutches

When a clutch lets go! photographs. B. Hegge. Hot Rod 16:105 O '63

AUTOMOBILES—*Continued*

Collectors and collecting

Automotive milestones; the passing of Clinton Reynolds' strange car collection. L. Payne. il Motor T 16:80-3 Ja '64
Bugattis on the move. M. Lamm. il Motor T 16:80-1 S '64
Franklin Pursuit Phaeton. E. J. Antrobus. il Motor T 15:56-9 Jl '63
London to Brighton, or bust. J. Stewart-Gordon. il Read Digest 83:217-20 N '63
Model-A-ing we will go. E. Bain. il Hot Rod 16:95 Je '63
Motor trend's rare car collection (cont) R. Temple. il Motor T 15:76-7 F; 76-7 Mr; 76-7 Ap '63
Newfangled invention. il Esquire 59:84-5 My '63
Old-car craze shifts into high. J. Keats. il N Y Times Mag p50+ S 29 '63
Personal business; antique autos. Bsns W p 105-6 Ag 17 '63
Sixty-six years, and still steaming. S. Jackson. il Motor T 15:72-3 Je '63
They don't build 'em like that any more. il Sunset 130:24+ Ap '63
Vintage cars return, brand-new. il Bsns W p 158-60+ D 5 '64
Wonderful world of antique cars. H. E. Dark. il Pop Sci 184:82-7+ Ja '64

Corrosion

See Corrosion and anticorrosives

Cost of operation

Good ways to save on gasoline costs. il Good H 158:159 Mr '64
Your best used car buy. il Motor T 15:52-5 D '63

Dashboards

Build a dash. L. Smith. il Hot Rod 17:42-5 Je '64

Depreciation

See Depreciation

Design

Airy tricks on Cougar II. il Pop Mech 121:112 Ja '64
Automobiles of 1964. il Consumer Bul 47:13-23+ F '64
Autos get longer for 1964. Bsns W p32-3 Je 22 '63
Autos of the future; the changes to look for. il U S News 55:50-1 S 2 '63
Beetle does float; Volkswagen. H. Horn. il Sports Illus 19:58-62+ Ag 19 '63; Same abr. with title Beetle that runs like a car. Read Digest 85:210-14 Jl '64
Birth of a new breed of car. A. Rothenberg. il Look 28:112-13 My 5 '64
Buyers want cars bigger, fancier. il Bsns W p33 My 4 '63
Cadillac kicks up its heels; adds sportier models. il Bsns W p98+ Ag 17 '63
El Camino: Chevelle's truck with class. R. Brock. il Hot Rod 17:34-7 Ap '64
Car design and accident proneness. Consumer Rep 28:185 Ap '63
Car design and public safety; Corvair criticized for design flaws. J. Ridgeway. il New Repub 151:9-11 S 19 '64; Reply. H. E. Campbell. 151:38 O 3 '64
Car of the future. il Changing T 17:19-22 N '63
Cars of tomorrow as Detroit dreams. il Newsweek 61:86-7 Je 10 '63
Change is gradual: slabs, cubes & some curves. il Time 84:88-9 S 25 '64
Chevy's Corsa: a European flair with a U.S. feeling. B. Ottum. il Sports Illus 21:96-7 S 21 '64
Chrysler counts on '64s to keep sales climbing. Bsns W p25 Ag 17 '63
Comfort-convenience index to the 1964 cars. il Pop Mech 121:110-11 Ja '64
Compact sixes and a four. il Consumer Rep 29:182-93 Ap '64
Confusion, inc. a few observations on the '64 models. Pop Sci 183:54-5+ N '63
Corvair engineering for 1965; Corvette engineering for 1965. J. Wright. il Motor T 16:48-53 O '64
Corvair Monza 900; Falcon Futura; Tempest V-8; Oldsmobile F-85 Jetfire. il Consumer Bul 46:24-9 My '63
Crystal-balling the '64s. il Motor T 15:32-5 Ag '63
Customizers. il Time 83:54 Ap 10 '64
Designer who laughts at the conventional. il Bsns W p 126 Mr 9 '63
Detroit plays for four-of-a-kind. il Bsns W p62-4+ S 19 '64
Detroit's strategy: a new look for the '65s. il Bsns W p23-4 My 16 '64
Duesenberg lives! il Newsweek 65:64 Ja 11 '65
Editor's auto-graphs. C. Nerpel. Motor T 15:6 Ap '63
Exploring the mystery of design. W. D. Teague. il Sat R 47:48+ O 24 '64
Factory show cars. il Motor T 15:20-5 Ag '63
Fastback forecast. M. Lamm. il Motor T 17:24-5 Ja '65
Flexible world of GM's planning. il Bsns W p 136-8+ O 5 '63
Four special-appeal cars; Ford Mustang, Corvair Monza, Volkswagen, and Opel Kadett. il Consumer Rep 29:396-9 Ag '64
Good times in auto business: no letdown in sight. il U S News 55:66-8 S 30 '63
Henry's wonderful Tin Lizzie. il Newsweek 62:67 Ag 12 '63
How '64 cars will be changed. il U S News 54:51-4 Je 17 '63
How the new cars are selling. il U S News 55:46-8 O 21 '63
If wishes were autos... improvements CU's testing staff would welcome. il Consumer Rep 29:440-1 S '64
Introducing the 1964 Duesenberg, Packard, Stutz and Mercer! D. Bartley. il Esquire 60:200-3 D '63
Introduction to the '65 cars. il Motor T 16:34-64 N '64
Latest of the new models. il U S News 55:14-15 O 7 '63
Midyear models. il Time 83:86 F 14 '64
Mr Moss builds his dream car. D. Bartley. il Esquire 61:80-1+ Mr '64
More for '64, except in price. il Newsweek 62:79 S 30 '63
More on the '65s! M. Lamm. il Motor T 16:22-7 S '64
Motor trend design competition winners. il Motor T 16:50-5 Jl '64
Motor trend design contest. il Motor T 16:68-9 My '64
Motor trend's search for stylists. il Motor T 16:34-6 Ja '64
My days with LeBaron. H. Pfau. il Motor T 16:80-3 Ag '64
New dawn for Duesenberg? G. Moore. il Motor T 16:76-9 S '64
New drive at G.M: front wheel drive on the Holiday. il Time 84:76 D 18 '64
New-model cars keep coming: a record year in sight. il U S News 57:88-90 S 28 '64
New shape at Ford. il Time 82:95-6 S 13 '63
$950 million for plastic surgery in Detroit. il Newsweek 62:88-9 S 23 '63
Ninth annual Look preview: '65 cars. A. Rothenberg. il Look 28:44-58 O 6 '64
1964 cars: service-free or service-prone? il Pop Mech 121:91-5+ Ja '64
1964 cars, what will they be like? D. Francis. il Pop Sci 183:41-4 Jl '63
1964 models: cars & dolls. A. Rothenberg. il Look 27:85-98 O 22 '63
1963 compact cars. il Consumer Bul 46:20-6 Ap '63
Owners like Rambler's handling, thrift, complain of wind whistle. il Pop Mech 119:96-9+ Mr '63
Preview of the '64s. il Newsweek 61:82-4 Ap 15 '63
Previewing the '65s. il Motor T 16:22-7 Ag '64
Projexions. S. MacMinn. il Motor T 15:76-9 O '63
Pure joy of sports cars; with portfolio of paintings by Lemuel B. Line. Fortune 70:167-71 Jl '64
Rambler engineering. R. H. Isbrandt. il Motor T 15:40-5+ F '63
Ride and pep please Ford Galaxie owners more than fuel milage. il Pop Mech 119:108-11+ Mr '63
Showing what makes Chevy run: dealer preview show, Detroit. il Bsns W p96-8 Ag 24 '63
Six compact sedans. il Consumer Rep 29:74-7 F '64
'65 cars. J. Whipple. il Pop Sci 185:65-96 O '64
'65s: classic but jazzy. il Life 57:115-20+ O 16 '64
'64 cars. il Motor T 15:18-33 O; 50-97 N '63
'64 cars, how they compare. il Pop Mech 120:85-9 O '63
'64 look. D. Francis and A. Markovich. il Pop Sci 183:65-89+ O '63
'64s. J. Whipple. il Pop Mech 120:90-103+ O '63
'64½s. Newsweek 62:79 O 28 '63
'63 cars: how they're better in thirty-six little ways. D. Francis. il Pop Sci 182:90-2 Ap '63
'63 Rambler Ambassador, hot and lukewarm. L. Smith. il Hot Rod 16:30-3 Ap '63

AUTOMOBILES—Design—*Continued*
Sleek '65s: styled for the mainstream. il Newsweek 64:88-9 S 21 '64
Small compacts and not-so-small compact cars. il Consumer Bul 47:18-28 My '64
Spotlight on Detroit; forecasts, facts and rumors. See issues of Motor trend
Still preaching compact gospel; American motors. il Bsns W p 86-8+ Ap 11 '64
Styling preview; how the '64s will look. il Motor T 15:22-7 S '63
Sunbeam Imp; Scottish-built automobile. B. McVay. il Motor T 16:58-61 S '64
Taking the '65s out of the box. il Newsweek 63:75 Je 8 '64
There goes (varoom! varoom!) that kandy kolored tangerine-flake baby; custom cars. T. K. Wolfe. il Esquire 60:114-18+ N '63
This is the automobile you will drive in 1985. U S News 57:57 Ag 17 '64
Transverse T-Bird FWD concept in the works for '65; first front-wheel-drive. G. Moore. il Motor T 15:58-9+ My '63
Trend in '64 cars: small models are longer. il U S News 55:14-15 S 23 '63
Turbine-powered auto makes its bow. il U S News 54:16 My 27 '63
Vintage cars return, brand-new. il Bsns W p 158-60+ D 5 '64
What '65 cars will be like. il U S News 56:66-9 Je 8 '64
What you'll find in the '64 cars. il Pop Mech 120:77-81+ Ag '63
What's coming in the '65 cars. D. Francis. il Pop Sci 185:40-3+ Jl '64
What's different about the 1965 cars. il U S News 57:48-51 S 21 '64
What's Ford up to for '63½? R. Brock. il Hot Rod 16:48-51 F '63
What's new in 1963½ cars. D. Francis. il Pop Sci 182:65-9 F '63
What's up for '64? R. Brock. il Hot Rod 16: 40-7+ O '63
Wheels of fortune; seventh annual International automobile show. il Time 81:89 Ap 19 '63
When air began to flow. M. Lamm. il Motor T 16:40-3 My '64
World's autos wear the Italian look; Turin school of auto design. il Bsns W p56-8 N 16 '63
Year for sports cars. il Time 81:90 Je 14 '63
See also
Automobiles—Bodies
Automobiles—Safety devices and measures

Driveshafts

See Automobiles—Propeller shafts

Driving

See Automobile driving

Electric equipment

Amps for camps. P. Geraci. il Pop Sci 184: 112-15 My '64
How to build a three-in-one test meter for your car. L. Buckwalter. il Pop Sci 183:124-7+ Jl '63
How to build your own portable auto analyzer. R. M. Benrey. il Pop Sci 184:94-9+ Je '64
Warning flasher for your car. M. Lincoln. il Pop Sci 184:114-15 Ja '64

Electric wiring

Wiring made easy. T. McMullen. il Hot Rod 16:38-41+ Je '63

Electronic equipment

Fasten your seat belt; how to make an alarm for your car that reminds you. R. M. Benrey. il Pop Sci 183:83-9 Ag '63

Equipment

Automate your rear view mirror; dimming mirrors. C. Caringella. il Pop Electr 18: 61-7+ F '63
Car-top boat carrier. il Sunset 130:60 F '63
Come away with me, Lucille, in my furnished automobile. L. R. Forester. il Am Home 66: 22+ Jl '63
Family car gifts. il Bet Hom & Gard 42:28+ D '64
Happy ways of trailering. H. Peterson. il Sports Illus 18:68-74 My 13 '63
Homemade travel console. il Pop Sci 182: 101 Je '63
Monopoly is embarrassing; Joseph Lucas industries, ltd. il Fortune 68:80+ S '63
New products. See issues of Motor trend
1964 towing options; towing equipment. Motor T 15:30+ N '63
Now: cars made to order for trailer towing. V. L. Oertle. il Pop Sci 182:98-100+ Je '63
What Detroit didn't do for 1965. J. Whipple. il Pop Sci 185:92-6 O '64
What to keep in the car. il Changing T 17: 46 Mr '63
What's new. See issues of Hot rod
See also
Automobile horns
Automobiles—Safety devices and measures
Electric auto-lite company
Thermostats

Exhibitions

Big show by the sea; National custom auto fairs. D. Wells. il Hot Rod 16:72-3 Jl '63
Big show; Winternationals custom auto fair. il Hot Rod 17:38-9 Ap '64
Every one was a dazzler; seventh annual International automobile show. il Newsweek 61:82-3 Ap 22 '63
Fast and the fancy; at Winternationals custom show. il Hot Rod 16:34-9 Ap '63
National custom auto fair. il Hot Rod 16:40-3 D '63
1900 auto show. I. Ross. il Motor T 16:110-16 N '64
1963 showcase; 44th National automobile show, Detroit. il Motor T 15:52-3 F '63
Show biz. il Hot Rod 17:82-3 O; 92-3 N; 96-7 D '64; 18:94-5 Ja '65
Showing what makes Chevy run; dealer preview show. Detroit. il Bsns W p96-8 Ag 24 '63
Slicked up to chase the booming beetle. K. Rudeen. il Sports Illus 18:51-3 Ap 22 '63
Tri-state auto show; photographs. Hot Rod 16:80-1 Jl '63
Turning wheel; General motors permanent automotive transportation exhibit. il Motor T 15:62-7 Jl '63
Wheels of fortune; seventh annual International automobile show. il Time 81:89 Ap 19 '63

Fires and fire protection

Backdrop for a mill; firewall. L. Smith. il Hot Rod 17:82-3 Ag '64
See also
Automobiles, Racing—Fires and fire protection

Frames

Tubing and beams. R. Huntington. il Hot Rod 16:44-7+ Jl '63

Fuel tanks

Editor's auto-graphs. C. Nerpel. il Motor T 16:8-9 S '64

Gearing

Efficient torque flow. R. Brock. il Hot Rod 16:80-3 S '63
4x4 field test; four-wheel-drive camper. R. Barlow. il Field & S 68:68-9+ My '63
Know your car; differentials, suspension systems, steering controls, brakes, and body construction. R. Temple. il Motor T 15:66-71 F '63
MT road test; Toyota Land Cruiser; four-wheel-drive. J. Wright. il Motor T 15:44-9 Jl '63
Other end. E. Dahlquist. il Hot Rod 17:42-5 O '64
Six with four wheel drive. C. Isica. il Motor T 16:38-41 Mr '64
See also
Automobiles—Transmission

Heating and ventilation

'64 Cadillac makes its own weather. D. Francis. il Pop Sci 183:66-8 N '63

History

Album of seven classic automotive pacesetters. C. Borth. il Pop Mech 121:96-102 Ja '64
Antique autos; new collection of prints: Gallery of the American automobile. il Library J 88:2630-3 Jl '63
Automotive milestones; Chadwick, first supercharged car in America. J. L. Beardsley. il Motor T 15:72-5 D '63
Automotive milestones; Elwood Haynes and the Apperson's first ride. il Motor T 15: 60-1 Je '63
Automotive milestones; history of the Cadillac V-16, 1930-1940. N. F. Uhlir. il Motor T 17:78-83 Ja '65
Automotive milestones; Paige 6-66, up and over. J. L. Beardsley. il Motor T 15:62-3+ S '63
Automotive milestones; rebirth of the second Silver Ghost. M. W. Newman. il Motor T 16:84-7 Je '64
Automotive milestones; the car World war I started in. A. Leich and R. Leich. il Motor T 16:78-81 Jl '64
Automotive milestones; the Corvair's granddaddy. M. King. il Motor T 16:84-5 Ag '64

AUTOMOBILES—History—*Continued*
Automotive milestones; the Peugeot that outran time, Indianapolis, 1913. J. L. Beardsley. il Motor T 15:68-71+ O '63
Cadillac V-16; a restoration. P. Schinnerer. il Motor T 15:64-7 S '63
Classic comments. R. J. Gottlieb. See issues of Motor trend
Getaway cars. il Esquire 59:92-3 Mr '63
Last of the great Packards. H. Broda. il Motor T 16:74-5 Mr '64
Locomobile. D. E. Earnshaw. il Motor T 16:78-81 D '64
Mercedes—Knight. B. S. Lane. il Motor T 15:78-81+ Mr '63
New dawn for Duesenberg? G. Moore. il Motor T 16:76-9 S '64
1917 Mercury. il Motor T 15:93 Je '63
Ninety firsts in American automotive history. H. Lozier. il Pop Sci 184:80-3 Mr '64
Rambler history. il Motor T 15:34-9 F '63
Remember? cars that ran on oatmeal and molasses. T. M. Prudden. il Sci Digest 55:80-5 Mr '64
Revolution of the Tin Lizzie. B. Lefferts. il N Y Times Mag p 18-19 Jl 28 '63
Ten best American classics. R. J. Gottlieb. il Motor T 15:112-15 N '63
Ten special-interest cars; symposium. il Motor T 16:73-83 N '64
Untold story of the Model T. A. Nevins. il Pop Sci 183:68-72+ Jl '63
Used cars in Uruguay. L. D. Lee. il Motor T 16:52-4 Mr '64
When air began to flow. M. Lamm. il Motor T 16:40-3 My '64
Why Studebaker? M. Lamm. il Motor T 16:42-5+ Mr '64

Hub caps

Image makers; wheel covers. il Motor T 16:77-9 O '64

Ignition

See Automobile engines—Ignition

Inspection

How to drive and stay alive. A. Rothenberg. il Look 27:64 My 21 '63
Pros and cons of vehicle safety inspection. il Am City 78:110-11 O '63

Insurance

See Insurance, Automobile

Leasing

Rival ways to ride boom in car leasing; finance leasing. il Bsns W p 187-8 My 18 '63

License plates

Ad-versions; New York world's fair advertising on license plates. il Newsweek 62:53 D 30 '63
Froslid's protest; concerning NY world's fair 64 on license plates. New Yorker 39:28 F 8 '64
Hang'em handy. L. Smith. il Hot Rod 16:82-3 N '63
Liberty with license. Time 83:38 Ja 31 '64

Lighting

Amber-colored front parking lights, a backward step in safety. il Consumer Bul 47:39 Ag '64
Brighter headlamps for European cars. Sci N L 86:180 S 19 '64
Got a light? latest taillight innovation; photographs. B. Hegge. Hot Rod 17:52-3 Ag '64
Keep your headlights on the beam. M. J. Schultz. il Pop Mech 120:157-61 Jl '63
Novel electrometer tube; for automatic headlight control; headlight dimmer. C. E. Atkins. il Electr World 70:44-5 O '63

Lubrication

Be leery of those additives & gimmicks for cars. il Changing T 17:15-18 F '63; Same abr. with title Beware of quack tonics for automobiles. Read Digest 82:272-4 Je '63
Check the oil, mister? il Changing T 18:33-6 O '64
Exploding myths about oil changes. H. E. Dark. il Pop Mech 120:93-7+ N '63
Oil is oil is oil is oil but... il Motor T 15:74-7 Je '63
Servicing; follow the manual, not your local mechanic. il Consumer Rep 29:169-70 Ap '64
Servicing the '63s. il Consumer Rep 28:156-8 Ap '63

Maneuverability

Road behavior. Consumer Rep 28:172; 29:170-1 Ap '63, Ap '64

Manufacture

Are cars as good as they used to be? J. N. Miller. Read Digest 84:53-8 F '64
How about it, Detroit? quality of automobiles. R. F. Meyerowitz. New Repub 150:10-13 Ap 4 '64
How I built my wonderful three-hoss shay. G. De Angelis. il Pop Sci 182:37-41 Je '63
Rambler engineering. R. H. Isbrandt. il Motor T 15:40-5+ F '63
See also
Automobile industry and trade

Materials

Aluminum; light, white, versatile. G. E. Herrman. il Motor T 15:108-11 N '63
Fiberglass futures. B. Fendell. il Motor T 16:96-101+ N '64
More plastics per car. il Fortune 70:201 O '64
Royalite on a regal line; laminated plastic of new Cord. W. P. Bowlin. il Motor T 16:70-1 D '64
Tubing and beams. R. Huntington. il Hot Rod 16:44-7+ Jl '63

Names

Car by any other name. P. D. Lagomarcino. New Repub 150:12 Ap 4 '64
F.O.B. nameville; car names. Time 82:80+ S 13 '63

Noise

Noisemakers. C. W. Morton. il Atlan 212:113 Jl '63

Number plates

See Automobiles—License plates

Painting

High temperature paint. L. Smith. il Hot Rod 17:86 F '64

Parking

See Automobile parking

Periodicals

Driving down a new road. il Bsns W p 143-4+ O 10 '64

Prices

New-car prices, all '64 models. Pop Sci 184:117-19 F '64
1964 vs 1963: the price picture. il Consumer Rep 29:178 Ap '64
1963 compact cars. il Consumer Bul 46:24-6 Ap '63
1963 full-size cars, CR's recommendations in five price groups. il Consumer Bul 46:19-23 Mr '63
Price must be right. Newsweek 62:67 S 9 '63
Prices: a starting point for bargaining. Consumer Rep 28:162-3 Ap '63
Will Detroit hold the price line? '64 models. Bsns W p32+ Ag 10 '63

Propeller shafts

Shorten a shaft. L. Smith. il Hot Rod 17:30-1 Jl '64

Purchasing

Are your car costs in line? Bet Hom & Gard 42:89 Ja '64
How to finance that car. il Changing T 18:25-8 Mr '64
If you're buying a new car. R. Huntington. il Consumer Bul 47:10-12 F '64
Special car market. Consumer Rep 29:255 My '64
When they buy a rolling status symbol. J. Keating. il N Y Times Mag p28+ S 27 '64

Radar control

See Road traffic—Radar control

Radio equipment

AM-FM car radio. T. A. Prewitt. il Electr World 69:44-5 Mr '63
Hum interference in car radios. D. T. Geiser. il Electr World 70:80 D '63
New sounds for your car. il Motor T 15:44-7 Ap '63
Rear-deck auto speakers. il Consumer Rep 29:16-17 Ja '64
Which channel is it? L. G. Sands. il Electr World 71:40+ F '64
See also
Police radio
Radio telephone on automobiles
Taxicabs—Radio equipment

Rating

1963 automobile ratings. Consumer Rep 28:173-82+ Ap '63
Ratings of 1964 cars. il Consumer Rep 29:180-2 Ap '64

AUTOMOBILES—*Continued*

Renting

American credit plan includes car rentals. Aviation W 81:36 D 21 '64
Car-rental race: even the losers win. il Newsweek 63:70-2 Ap 6 '64
Discounters stir up auto rental rate fuss. il Bsns W p 108-9 Jl 20 '63
Ford rent-a-car. Time 84:94 N 6 '64
Great odometer mystery. J. Ridgeway. New Repub 152:10-11 Ja 23 '65
Pay-as-you-go-driving. Time 81:75 Mr 1 '63
Personal business; seeing Europe by car. Bsns W p 125-6 Ag 22 '64
Sales & distribution; discount car rentals. L. Morse. Duns R 82:67 O '63
Still in the driver's seat. Time 83:91 Mr 13 '64
When you rent a car. il Changing T 17:45-7 Je '63
See also
Avis rent a car system
Hertz corporation

Repairing

Big idea: a pit shop for car repairs. A. Markovich. il Pop Sci 183:104-5 S '63
Buyer's guide to automobile tools. il Pop Sci 185:72-83 Jl '64
Cadillac V-16; a restoration. P. Schinnerer. il Motor T 15:64-7 S '63
Gasoline alley. E. Rickman. il Hot Rod 17:72-5+ S '64
Gus Wilson's model garage (title varies) M. Bunn. See issues of Popular science monthly
How to get a good body-repair job. E. D. Fales, jr. il Pop Sci 183:45-9+ S '63
℞ for rough idle. M. J. Schultz. il Pop Mech 119:172-5+ F '63
Rising cost of repairs. il Consumer Rep 28:468-9 O '63
Say Smokey; questions and answers. H. Yunick. See issues of Popular science monthly
Shop talk. D. Clark. See issues of Hot rod
Weekend mechanic. R. E. Jennings. il Motor T 17:66-8 Ja '65 (to be cont)
See also
Automobile engines—Repairing
Automobile mechanics (persons)
Automobile service stations

Safety devices and measures

Automobiles can be made much safer. H. E. Campbell. il Consumer Bul 47:35-7 S '64
Bolt-in bars. L. Smith. il Hot Rod 17:80-3 Je '64
Detroit scandal; glamour v. safety in automobile design. Nation 200:42-3 Ja 18 '65
Don't let this happen! Twistlok rated not acceptable. Consumer Rep 28:460-1 O '63
Editor's auto-graphs. C. Nerpel. il Motor T 16:8-9 S '64
Fashion or safety: Detroit makes your choice. R. Nader. il Nation 197:214-16 O 12 '63; Reply. A. Mather. 197:inside cover N 2 '63
Forty-five steps to safer cars. H. E. Campbell. Consumer Bul 47:30-2 O '64
How the experts shop for seat belts. K. N. Anderson. il Todays Health 41:20-5+ Ap '63
Is your car child-safe? H. Dark and P. Dark. il Todays Health 41:14-17 Jl '63
Mowing them down; staged collisions. Nation 198:594 Je 15 '64
1964 car they didn't build. B. H. Frisch. il Sci Digest 55:52-8 Ja '64
Physician's R-x for auto safety. il Todays Health 42:38 N '64
Safer cars: we can do more. A. Rothenberg. il Look 28:M14+ My 19 '64
Safety features in autos. C. J. Potthoff. Todays Health 42:54 Ag '64
Safety features; 1964 contributes little toward the safe car. il Consumer Rep 29:167-8, 179 Ap '64
Safety: missed bets outnumber the improvements. il Consumer Rep 28:160-1 Ap '63
Tiger in your tank. Nation 199:234 O 19 '64
Tires and road safety. J. Ridgeway. New Repub 151:8-10 O 17 '64
Traffic deaths. il Consumer Bul 46:19-21 S '63
Vision of a crashproof car. C. Leedham. il N Y Times Mag p34+ O 25 '64
What to keep in the car. il Changing T 17:46 Mr '63
See also
Brakes, Automobile
Safety belts

Scrapping

See Automobiles—Wrecking

Seats

Back-seat playroom for your VW. H. H. Hauser. il Pop Mech 119:176-7 F '63
Case against bucket seats. R. Baker. il Pop Sci 183:36+ S '63
Glass buckets; photographs. L. Smith. Hot Rod 17:88-9 O '64

Service stations

See Automobile service stations

Signal lights

Blinker minder. F. J. Haines. il Pop Electr 18:61-4 Mr '63
For greater safety, flash those lights! turn-signal lights. L. F. Cortina. il Pop Electr 20:75-6+ Mr '64
Trouble-shoot your turn signals. il Pop Sci 184:125+ Je '64

Skidding

Dawn skid; thrity-four car pile-up on Manhattan's East River drive. il Time 83:63 Mr 20 '64
New facts about skidding. E. D. Fales, jr. il Pop Sci 184:58-61+ Mr '64
Seven deadly skids. E. D. Fales, jr. il Pop Sci 185:59-61+ N '64

Social aspects

Serious epidemic of automania. G. Hechinger and F. M. Hechinger. il N Y Times Mag p 18+ Ag 11 '63

Specifications

Guide to the specifications table. il Consumer Rep 29:172-5 Ap '64
Motor trend's 1964-1965 car specifications (cont) Motor T 15:100-3 N '63; 16:65-8 N '64
1963 full-size cars, CR's recommendations in five price groups. il Consumer Bul 46:19-23 Mr '63

Speed

Case for fast drivers. R. L. Schwartz. Harper 227:65-70 S '63; Same abr. with title What are the real causes of auto crashes? il Read Digest 84:181-2+ Ap '64; Discussion. Harper 227:6 N '63
Riding the washboard; Art Arfons' Green Monster. il Time 84:42-3 N 6 '64
See also
Automobile speed records

Speed governors

Speed minders. R. Huntington. il Motor T 15:40-1+ Je '63

Springs and suspension

Bank that curve! il Motor T 15:54-7 Ap '63
Beating the bounce; suspension systems: from buggy to Sting Ray. R. W. Temple. il Pop Sci 185:102-7+ D '64
Bolt-on road manners; Corvair spring stabilizer. L. Smith. il Hot Rod 16:46-7 Ap '63
Corvair suspension for early Fords. L. Smith. il Hot Rod 17:82-3 F '64
Know your car; differentials, suspension systems, steering controls, brakes, and body construction. R. Temple. il Motor T 15:66-71 F '63

Stability and stabilizers

Bolt-on-road manners; Corvair spring stabilizer. L. Smith. il Hot Rod 16:46-7 Ap '63
$9.95 wheel balancer for automobiles, said to be a fabulous invention: Gyro-Scopic stabilizer. il Consumer Bul 46:24-6 Ag '63
Weight transfer; drag racer. R. Huntington. il Hot Rod 16:76-9 Ap '63

Starting

Don't blame battery when car won't start. Sci N L 85:72 F 1 '64
Hot tips for cold starts. M. J. Schultz and H. E. Dark. il Pop Mech 121:176-82+ Ja '64
What to do if your car is hard to start. F. L. Greenwald. il Pop Sci 185:104-7 N '64

Starting devices

Motor that starts the motor. M. J. Schultz. il Pop Mech 120:158-62+ Ag '63

Steering gear

Keep the power in power steering. M. J. Schultz. il Pop Mech 120:166-70 D '63
Know your car; differentials, suspension systems, steering controls, brakes, and body construction. R. Temple. il Motor T 15:66-71 F '63
Pedal your Model A; and steer it. T. McMullen. il Hot Rod 18:86-7 Ja '65

AUTOMOBILES—Steering gear—*Continued*
Radius rods for under $15. L. Smith. il Hot Rod 16:82-3 My '63
Two hats of science; power steering and brakes. H. Downs. Sci Digest 56:79-82 N '64

Testing

Allstate endurance test. D. Wells. il Hot Rod 17:92-3 D '64
Avanti Allstate cross-country test runs. il Hot Rod 16:104 N '63
Barracuda vs. Mustang. R. Petty. il Pop Sci 185:76-9 N '64
Buick LeSabre road test. J. Wright. il Motor T 16:56-61 My '64
Buick Riviera Gran Sport drive test. B. McVay. il Motor T 16:48-9 D '64
Buick special Skylark. B. McVay. il Motor T 15:56-61 S '63
El Camino; Chevelle's truck with class. R. Brock. il Hot Rod 17:34-7 Ap '64
Chevelle El Camino road test. J. Wright. il Motor T 16:52-7 S '64
Chevy II V-8 road test. B. McVay. il Motor T 16:46-51 Je '64
Chrysler New Yorker Salon road test. B. McVay. il Motor T 16:68-73 Ap '64
Chrysler Newport road test. B. McVay. il Motor T 16:58-63 Je '64
Comet Enduro. il Motor T 16:62-5 Ja '64
Comparing in depth the 1964 Falcon, Tempest, Studebaker, Chevelle, Rambler, Valiant. J. Whipple. il Pop Mech 121:104-9+ Ja '64
Corvair Corsa road test. J. Ethridge. il Motor T 17:26-31 Ja '65
Corvette Sting Ray road test. B. McVay. il Motor T 16:34-9 S '64
Crashmanship. il Newsweek 63:92 Je 15 '64
Dart V-8 road test. J. Wright. il Motor T 16:36-9 Je '64
Daytona trials; 1963 Pure oil performance trials. M. Muhleman. il Motor T 15:70-5 Ap '63
Draggin' Thunderbolt. R. Brock. il Hot Rod 17:26-9+ F '64
Five intermediate sedans; Buick Special V-6, Chevelle Six, Pontiac Tempest Six, Rambler Classic Six, and Studebaker Commander Six. il Consumer Rep 29:130-3 Mr '64
Five medium-priced full-sized V-8s. il Consumer Rep 29:348-51 Jl '64
Four special-appeal cars; Ford Mustang, Corvair Monza, Volkswagen, and Opel Kadett. il Consumer Rep 29:396-9 Ag '64
Hot & cool Pontiac Catalina road test. B. McVay. il Motor T 16:44-9 My '64
How hot is the Mustang? D. Gurney. il Pop Sci 184:55-8+ My '64
How Motor trend road tests new cars. B. McVay. il Motor T 15:38-40+ N '63
Impala road test. B. McVay. il Motor T 16:32-7 My '64
Keep-'em-honest car tests. H. Luckett. il Pop Sci 182:67-72+ Ap '63
Mercedes 220. il Consumer Rep 28:132-3 Mr '63
MT hot Olds F-85 Cutlass road test. B. McVay. il Motor T 16:46-51 S '64
MT 1964 Thunderbird road test. B. McVay. il Motor T 16:54-9 F '64
MT Rambler Classic Typhoon road test. J. Wright. il Motor T 16:54-9 O '64
MT road test: American Rambler. W. Thoms. il Motor T 15:30-3 F '63
MT road test; Avantis, a pair. J. Wright. il Motor T 15:26-31 Ag '63
MT road test; Buick Riviera. J. Wright. il Motor T 15:62-7 Ap '63
MT road test; Buick Skylark road test. J. Wright. il Motor T 15:36-41 D '63
MT road test; Cadillac Sedan de Ville. J. Wright. il Motor T 16:46-51 Mr '64
MT road test; Chevrolet Impala. J. Wright. il Motor T 15:54-9 Mr '63
MT road test; Chrysler 300-J. J. Wright. il Motor T 15:48-53 Ap '63
MT road test; Comet Cyclone. J. Wright. il Motor T 16:34-9 Ag '64
MT road test; Comet S-22 V-8. B. McVay. il Motor T 15:44-9 Ag '63
MT road test; Cortina GT and Estate wagon. J. Wright. il Motor T 16:80-5 Ap '64
MT road test; Corvair Monza Spyder, performance and personality plus! J. Wright. il Motor T 15:42-7 Je '63
MT road test; Dart GT. W. Thoms. il Motor T 15:44-7 S '63
MT road test; Dodge Dart. J. Wright. il Motor T 15:46-51 F '63
MT road test; Dodge 880. J. Wright. il Motor T 15:36-41 My '63; 16:54-9 Ag '64
MT road test; Dodge Polara 500. J. Wright. il Motor T 15:54-9 Ag '63; 16:68-73 F '64
MT road test; Falcon Sprint. J. Wright. il Motor T 16:48-53 F '64
MT road test; Ford Galaxie. J. Wright. il Motor T 15:38-43 Ap '63
MT road test; Ford Galaxie 500-XL. B. McVay. il Motor T 16:38-43 F '64
MT road test; Imperial. B. McVay. il Motor T 15:70-5 Ag '63
MT road test; Imperial Crown coupe. B. McVay. il Motor T 16:80-5 F '64
MT road test; Lincoln Continental. B. McVay. il Motor T 16:28-33 Ap '64
MT road test; Lincoln Continental. J. Wright. il Motor T 15:36-41 Jl '63
MT road test; Mercury. W. Thoms. il Motor T 15:20-5 Mr '63
MT road test; 1964 Mercury road test. J. Wright. il Motor T 15:34-9 O '63
MT road test; 1964 Rambler American road test. B. McVay. il Motor T 15:56-61 D '63
MT road test; 1964 Studebaker Super Lark. J. Wright. il Motor T 15:20-5 D '63
MT road test; Oldsmobile Dynamic 88. B. McVay. il Motor T 15:54-9 Je '63
MT road test; Oldsmobile F-85 Cutlass. B. McVay. il Motor T 15:20-5+ Jl '63
MT road test; Opel Kadett & Caravan 1000. M. Lamm. il Motor T 16:42-6 Ap '64
MT road test; Pontiac 421 H.O. R. Huntington. il Motor T 15:44-9 Mr '63
MT road test; Pontiac Grand Prix. B. McVay. il Motor T 15:46-51 My '63
MT road test; road testing the Oldsmobile Jetstar 88. B. McVay. il Motor T 16:60-5 Ap '64
MT road test; Simca 1000. B. McVay. il Motor T 15:48-51 Je '63
MT road test; Studebaker Super Hawk. J. Wright. il Motor T 15:20-5 Je '63
MT road test; Tempest Le Mans. W. Thoms. il Motor T 15:54-9 F '63
MT road test; the jeep becomes a gentleman. J. Wright. il Motor T 15:34-9 Mr '63
MT road test; two Rambler tests: Classic and Ambassador. J. Wright. il Motor T 15:22-9 F '63
MT road test; Valiant Barracuda. B. McVay. il Motor T 16:40-3 Ag '64
MT road test; Valiant Signet 200. B. McVay. il Motor T 15:20-5 Ap '63
MT road test; Valiant with a V-8. J. Wright. il Motor T 16:32-7 Mr '64
Mustang road test. B. McVay. il Motor T 16:44-9 Ag '64
Mustang 2+2 road test. B. McVay. il Motor T 17:32-7 Ja '65
Oldsmobile Starfire road test. B. McVay. il Motor T 16:40-5 S '64
100,000-mile durability run. il Hot Rod 17:44-5 Mr '64
1,500 miles in a Valiant. A. Markovich. il Pop Sci 182:92-4 Mr '63
Plymouth Savoy road test. il Motor T 16:70-5 Je '64
PS tests the 1896 Ford. D. Francis. il Pop Sci 182:35-6+ Je '63
Popular science tests the hot compacts. D. Francis and A. Markovich. il Pop Sci 182:53-7+ My '63
Racing champ track tests the hot-engined Ford, Chevy, Dodge, Pontiac, Plymouth. T. E. Stimson. il Pop Mech 121:85-90+ Ja '64
Rally packed Barracuda. B. McVay. il Motor T 17:38-43 Ja '65
'65 Corvair: how much better? J. Whipple. il Pop Sci 186:72-5+ Ja '65
'64 Dodge Dart road test. J. Wright. il Motor T 15:30-5 D '63
Stude Lark with R-3 performance. R. Brock. il Hot Rod 17:28-33+ Ja '64
Tempest G.T.O. road test. B. McVay. il Motor T 16:66-71 Ja '64
Testing the new-size Chevrolet: 10,000 miles in a Chevelle. il Pop Sci 184:53-7+ Ja '64
Testing the '65 Ford, Chevrolet, and Plymouth. J. R. Whipple. il Pop Sci 185:48-53+ D '64
Three for the road. J. Wright and others. il Motor T 16:24-35 D '64
Three '63 ½ cars, plus the Chevrolet Impala 6. il Consumer Rep 28:388-91 Ag '63
Two Buick Wildcats road test. B. McVay. il Motor T 16:26-31 Je '64
Valiant V-8 vs. Comet Caliente, which is hotter? A. Markovich. il Pop Sci 184:78-81 Ap '64
See also
Automobile engines—Fuel consumption

Tires

See Tires, Automobile

Towing

See Towing

AUTOMOBILES—*Continued*

Trailers

See Automobile trailers

Transmission

Blower drives. L. Smith. il Hot Rod 17:34-7 Mr '64
Engineering genius of the modern automatic transmission. il Motor T 16:82-5 O '64
Four-speed for sportsmen. B. Greene. il Hot Rod 16:42-5 S '63
GM's new torque converter. R. Huntington. il Motor T 15:71+ D '63
Hydrostatic drive. J. Arthur. il Pop Mech 120:112-15 Ag '63
Torkmaster; a fluid coupling. L. Smith. il Hot Rod 17:38-41 Ja '64
Transmission transplant. R. Huntington. il Hot Rod 17:42-5 Jl '64
Transmissions: a more convenient manual. Consumer Rep 28:155 Ap '63
See also
Automobiles—Gearing

Transportation

Inter-American highway shrinker; Coordinated Caribbean transport, inc. il Sunset 133:73 N '64

Washing

See Automobiles—Cleaning

Wheels

Balance your car's wheels. R. Day. il Pop Sci 185:128-30 D '64
Breakthrough in aluminum wheels. B. McVay. il Motor T 16:66-7 My '64
Image makers; wheel covers. il Motor T 16:77-9 O '64
Mysteries of wheel balancing. E. Rickman. il Hot Rod 17:30-3 F '64
Switch in wheels. L. Smith. il Hot Rod 17:80-2 My '64
Wheels. L. Smith. il Hot Rod 16:26-9+ S; 74-7+ O; 38-43 N '63

Windows

Auto change no one will notice; float glass windows in GM cars. il Bsns W p52+ S 5 '64

Windshield defrosters

Quickee windshield defroster gun. il Consumer Bul 48:35 Ja '65

Windshields

Anti-fog liquids and cloths. il Consumer Bul 46:43+ O '63
Shield chop. L. Smith. il Hot Rod 17:46-7 S '64

Wrecking

Where do old autos go to die? il Newsweek 64:66-9 Jl 20 '64
See also
National auto and truck wreckers association

AUTOMOBILES, Amphibious
Amphibious: demonstration of the Amphicar. New Yorker 39:46-7 N 23 '63
Penguin for a plunge; leak-proof minicar. M. Marshall, jr. il Motor T 17:48 Ja '65

AUTOMOBILES, Care of. See Automobiles—Care

AUTOMOBILES, Experimental
Chrysler Turboflite experimental. il Motor T 15:34-5 My '63
Gas turbine car feasible. Sci N L 85:219 Ap 4 '64
XR-6; chassis conclusion. L. Smith. il Hot Rod 16:70-3 Ap '63

AUTOMOBILES, Flying. See Airplanes, Light—Automobile combinations

AUTOMOBILES, Foreign
Automotive milestone; the Peugeot that outran time, Indianapolis, 1913. J. L. Beardsley. il Motor T 15:68-71+O '63
Automotive milestones: the thundering Blitzen Benz. J. L. Beardsley. il Motor T 16:76-9 Mr '64
Back & forth; Opel Kadett; Ford's new racer. il Time 83:65 Ja 10 '64
Beetle does float; Volkswagen. H. Horn. il Sports Illus 19:58-62+ Ag 19 '63; Same abr. with title Beetle that runs like a car. Read Digest 85:210-14 Jl '64
Bug's big brother; VW 1500. D. Scott. il Pop Sci 183:85-7+ D '63
Car importers face the facts. il Bsns W p 136-8+ Ap 20 '63
Closing in on Volkswagen. Time 82:98 N 29 '63
DM vs. VW; West Germany's product-testing magazine sued by Volkswagen. Newsweek 63:83 Mr 23 '64
Dandy little diesel for $2,660; Japan's popular-prized Isuzu Bellel. F. Clymer. il Pop Sci 185:98-9+ N '64
Driving the latest NSU-Wankel. G. Molter. il Motor T 15:64-5 F '63
European report. See issues of Motor trend
Foreign car market. Consumer Rep 29:254 My '64
Foreign sportsters: fast and fancy. il Pop Sci 183:78-9 S '63
GTO Le Mans. R. Brock. il Hot Rod 16:26-31 D '63
Highlights of the foreign car shows. il Pop Sci 186:84-5 Ja '65
Hip roddy. D. Moon. il Hot Rod 17:100-1 O '64
How owners rate their Volkswagens now! il Pop Mech 120:77-81+ S '63
Kadett vs. VW. Newsweek 62:81-2 D 2 '63
Magnificent dachshund: Grand Mercedes 600. il Time 82:112 N 15 '63
MT road test; Toyota Land Cruiser. J. Wright. il Motor T 15:44-9 Jl '63
New and hot from overseas. il Pop Sci 182:90-1 Mr '63
Opel's new models. B. McVay. il Motor T 16:88-9 Je '64
Princess R; Vanden Plas Princess 4-litre R. il Newsweek 64:61 Ag 31 '64
Remember the Aero Willys? Brazil's luxury car. il Pop Mech 119:56-8 Mr '63
Report from the driver's seat; Saab story. A. Markovich. il Pop Sci 183:90-1+ S '63
Simca's Bertone, a sporty car for the budget-bound. M. Alexander. il Pop Sci 185:72-3 S '64
Slicked up to chase the booming beetle; New York's international automobile show. K. Rudeen. il Sports Illus 18:51-3 Ap 22 '63
Sportiest Alfa. A. Stockton. il Motor T 16:80-1 O '64
Spotlight on Ford's Cortina. E. Nelson. il Pop Mech 119:50+ Ap '63
Spotlight on the Hillman Super Minx. E. Nelson. il Pop Mech 120:34+ Jl '63
Spotlight on the Land Rover. E. Nelson. il Pop Mech 121:32+ Ja '64
Spotlight on the MG 1100. E. Nelson. il Pop Mech 119:38-40 F '63
Spotlight on the Saab 96. E. Nelson. il Pop Mech 121:30+ Mr '64
Sunbeam Imp; Scottish-built automobile. B. McVay. il Motor T 16:58-61 S '64
Super-beetle; 1500 VW. il Newsweek 64:69 S 7 '64
This is a VW? Sportster. V. L. Oertle. il Pop Mech 120:103 N '63
Volvo with v-v-voom! S. Wilder. il Hot Rod 17:80-3+ D '64
Will this Imp bug the beetle? A. Markovich. il Pop Sci 184:80-1 My '64
Wringing out an Imp. M. Priestley. il Pop Mech 120:105 D '63
See also
Station wagons, Foreign

Anecdotes, facetiae, satire, etc.

Greater game, the Mini-Cooper; with drawings by R. Brockbank. Esquire 60:58-61 Ag '63

Design

Novel trio of small foreign cars: Daffodil, MG 1100, and Renault R-8. il Consumer Rep 28:444-7 S '63
Road gets rougher for the Beetle; VW 1200. il Bsns W p47-8+ Ap 18 '64

Prices

Guide to the low-priced foreign cars. il Changing T 18:24-6 Ja '64

Testing

Datsun 410 road test. B. McVay. il Motor T 16:82-5 S '64
Datsun SPL-310 road test. B. McVay. il Motor T 16:60-3 Mr '64
Driving Opel's new Kadette. R. F. Raguse. il Pop Mech 120:107 Jl '63
Mercedes 300 SE road test. B. McVay. il Motor T 16:76-9 Ja '64
MT road test; Fiat 1500. B. McVay. il Motor T 15:50-5 S '63
MT road test; Volvo 122-S and P-1800S. B. McVay. il Motor T 15:50-7 O '63
MT road test; VW 1500, 1200. W. Thoms. il Motor T 15:36-41 Ag '63
Road-test report on the Renault Dauphine with automatic transmission. il Consumer Rep 29:445-7 S '64
Simca Bertone coupe road test. J. Wright. il Motor T 16:52-5 My '64
Studebaker Cruiser road test. B. McVay. il Motor T 16:60-3 Ag '64
Toyota Tiara 1900 road test. B. McVay. il Motor T 16:86-9 O '64

AUTOMOBILES, Foreign—Testing—*Continued*
Triumph's Spitfire 4; road test report. M. Priestley. il Pop Mech 119:122 Ap '63
Volkswagen 1200 road test. W. Thoms. il Motor T 16:50-3 Ag '64

AUTOMOBILES, Government
Afternoon at the track. Nation 196:338 Ap 27 '63
Car in the White House drive. T. Robinson. il Pop Sci 185:80-2 S '64
Now, fewer bureaucrats in limousines. il U S News 57:6 D 28 '64
Now, for JFK: ten copters, four jets, two yachts, big cars. il U S News 55:60-1 Jl 22 '63
Presidential car: it's safer now. il U S News 57:14 O 19 '64
Travel fleets of two presidents. il U S News 55:65 S 16 '63

AUTOMOBILES, Micro midget. See Karts (midget cars)

AUTOMOBILES, Midget. See Karts (midget cars)

AUTOMOBILES, Miniature. See Automobile models

AUTOMOBILES, Old. See Automobiles—Collectors and collecting

AUTOMOBILES, Police
Snowfighting with sirens; Prairie Village, Kan. R. E. Carroll. il Am City 79:92-3 F '64

Electronic equipment

Electronic sirens; mobile p.a. and siren systems on public-safety vehicles. J. Kyle. il Electr World 71:32-3 Ap '64

AUTOMOBILES, Racing
Anatomy of a champion. L. Smith. il Hot Rod 17:39-43+ Mr '64
Another for the monster; Grand prix of endurance, Sebring, Fla. il Time 81:68 Ap 5 '63
Apperson Jack Rabbit; America's first sports car. J. L. Beardsley. il Motor T 16:54-7 Je '64
Best appearing car; at National championship drag races. il Hot Rod 17:38-9 D '64
Beware the blue Cobra; Sebring race. il Time 83:80+ Ap 3 '64
Big itch they call Little John. J. Olsen. il Sports Illus 22:50-4+ Ja 11 '65
Bluebird makes another bid for speed record. il Pop Sci 182:118-19 Ap '63
Bolt-in bars. L. Smith. il Hot Rod 17:80-3 Je '64
Bonneville nationals; wind, water & speed. C. E. Nerpel. il Motor T 16:56-61 D '64
Bonneville's most unusual streamliner. D. Francisco. il Hot Rod 16:48-53+ Mr '63
Can they hit 500 m.p.h? D. Francis. il Pop Sci 185:70-3+ Ag '64
Cars; photographs. See issues of Hot rod
Cars to watch in '63. M. Muhleman. il Motor T 15:28-33 Mr '63
Chevy on a stick. D. Francisco. il Hod Rod 16:80-3+ Ag '63
Class A terror. D. Francisco. il Hot Rod 16:82-4+ D '63
Cobra coupe sequel. P. Biro. il Motor T 16:74-5 My '64
Daytona 500. M. Muhleman. il Motor T 16:70-3 My '64
Detroit back in race; Indianapolis 500. il Bsns W p96-7+ My 25 '63
Dodge chargers. W. Thoms. il Hot Rod 17:48-51 Jl '64
Dragsters on the prowl; Don Garlits and Connie Kalitta. L. Smith. il Hot Rod 17:50-3+ Ja '64
End of an era at Indy; Indianapolis 500-mile race. K. W. Purdy. il Sat Eve Post 237:60-2 My 30 '64
Engines to the rear: with photographs. L. Nehamkin. Motor T 16:64-9 Je '64
Fame and terror at 200 MPH drag racing. M. Kram. il Sports Illus 21:26-8+ Ag 31 '64
Fast cars, fancy targets; reproductions of paintings by T. Rost; text by W. Page. Field & S 68:38-41 Mr '64
Fast Fords and a great Scot; Indianapolis 500-mile race. B. Ottum. il Sports Illus 20:32-5 My 25 '64
Fastest 500. R. Brock. il Hot Rod 17:36-45+ Ag '64
Firecracker 400. M. Muhleman. il Motor T 16:70-5 S '64
500-mph LSR car? E. Dahlquist. il Hot Rod 17:46-7+ Ag '64
500 under attack; race at Indianapolis. K. Rudeen. il Sports Illus 18:18-21 My 27 '63
For Ferrari, some fast company at last; Fords at Le Mans race. P. E. Ress. il Sports Illus 20:51-2 Je 29 '64
Ford GT. R. Brock. il Hot Rod 17:38-41 Jl '64
Ford vs. Chevy at the Indianapolis 500. J. Whipple. il Pop Mech 119:69-73+ My '63
Ford's fast Fairlane 427. J. Wright. il Motor T 16:76-7 Je '64
Ford's up, Jaguar's on deck, Mercedes aims to play. G. Grant. Sports Illus 20:65-6+ My 11 '64
Go get 'em Corvair. D. Francisco. il Hot Rod 16:32-5+ S '63
Hayden Proffitt's stock car secrets. D. Francisco. il Hot Rod 16:32-7 Mr '63
Heating up the Spyder. R. Huntington. il Hot Rod 16:80-3 Mr '63
Heretic with great expectations at the Indianapolis speedway. K. Rudeen. il Sports Illus 18:72-3 Ap 15 '63
How stock is stock? J. Hart. il Hot Rod 17:46-9 Je '64
How stock is stock? NASCAR rules. il Motor T 15:26-7 Mr '63
How to build a brute; East African safari rally. il Pop Sci 184:84-6 My '64
How to build a champion drag stocker; the Ramchargers way. il Hot Rod 16:42-5 Je '63
How to build a Grand national stock car racer; ed. by J. Foster. C. Owens. il Hot Rod 16:36-41+ F '63
If racing sells cars; Ford to enter stock-car races. il Newsweek 61:80 Je 10 '63
If you can't beat them, get them to join you; Ford wins at Milwaukee. B. Ottum. Sports Illus 21:88+ S 7 '64
Impossible tank. L. Smith. il Hot Rod 16:32-5+ D '63
It was snakebite day at Sebring; Ford Cobras vs. Ferraris. H. Whall. il Sports Illus 20:20-3 Mr 30 '64
It'll be a frantic 500. E. Rickman. il Hot Rod 17:32-5 My '64
Japan zeroes in on world racing; first Oriental entrant of Grand prix competition. J. Lovesey. il Sports Illus 21:70-1 Ag 17 '64
Jet age; world land speed record cars, 1964. D. Francisco. il Hot Rod 18:36-43+ Ja '65
Little engine that could; Chrysler vs. Ford. B. Ottum. il Sports Illus 20:106-7 Ap 13 '64
Match race stockers. E. Dahlquist. il Hot Rod 18:80-3 Ja '65 (to be cont)
Merc goes racing. W. Thoms. il Motor T 15:60-3+ Mr '63
Modified circuit. P. Sukalac. il Hot Rod 17:46-51 F '64
Motor sports (cont) il Sports Illus 18:47+ F 25 '63
National champ wins again. L. Smith. il Hot Rod 16:78-9+ Jl '63
National scene. See issues of Hot rod
New breed for Indy; Chevy; Ford. E. Rickman. il Hot Rod 16:32-7 Je '63
1965 stock car predictions. M. Muhleman. il Motor T 17:52-7 Ja '65
Off to the races; Ford's Galaxie. il Time 81:84 Mr 29 '63
Offy answers back. P. Sukalac. il Hot Rod 17:46-51+ Mr '64
Offy strikes back; 200-mile USAC championship at Trenton. Sports Illus 19:7 S 16 '63
Old guard has to call it a day; 200-mile race, Milwaukee. K. Rudeen. il Sports Illus 19:18-19+ Ag 26 '63
Origin of the boat-tail speedster. G. Borgeson. il Motor T 15:72-5+ F '63
Prepping for the salt. E. Rickman. il Hot Rod 16:38-9+ Ag '63
Push vs. pull; front-vs. rear-engine race cars. Sports Illus 20:14 Ap 27 '64
Quarter horse; drag sedan. il Hot Rod 17:78-9 D '64
Quarter-mile hauler. E. Rickman. il Hot Rod 16:48-50+ My '63
Quick Cobra. E. Dahlquist. il Hot Rod 17:34-5 D '64
Race against death; A. Graham's City of Salt Lake. F. Miller. il Read Digest 83:140-6 O '63
Race against time and tide in the outback; four-ton Bluebird. il Sports Illus 18:20-1 My 20 '63
Race behind the race at Indianapolis 500. il Bsns W p 118+ Je 6 '64
Rattlin' good roadster. M. McCarthy. il Hot Rod 17:74-7 Ag '64
Rod alert! Bonneville. D. Francisco. il Hot Rod 17:46-51+ D '64
Scourge of Hangover Alley; speed festival at Nassau. B. Ottum. il Sports Illus 21:68-9 D 14 '64
Sebring: Cobra vs. Ferrari. P. Biro. il Motor T 16:58-61 Jl '64
Sedans, rails and gassers; Winter nationals, Pomona, Calif; photographs. L. Schiller. Sat Eve Post 237:58-61 Ja 4 '63
Shifty Indy car. il Hot Rod 17:88-9 Jl '64
'63 Bonneville speed trials. B. Greene. il Hot Rod 16:60-73+ N '63

AUTOMOBILES, Racing—*Continued*
Some like 'em hot stock; NHRA's modified production class. J. Hart. il Hot Rod 17:48-50 Ap '64
Speed in bright repose; Indianapolis 500-mile race; with photographs by Martin Nathan. Sports Illus 20:34-9 Je 1 '64
Spirit II. il Hot Rod 17:76-7 F '64
Stock car foresight and hindsight. M. Muhleman. il Motor T 16:70-3 Mr '64
Stock hop. J. Hart. il Hot Rod 17:84-7 O '64
Stockers at the Nationals. J. Wright. il Motor T 15:48-51 D '63
Stockers storm at the Nationals; Indianapolis. J. Wright. il Motor T 16:54-5 D '64
Street rod under an Indy ifluence. B. Turney. il Hot Rod 17:84-7 Je '64
Super fuel Xterminator. E. Dahlquist. il Hot Rod 17:26-9 S '64
Swoop of a secret weapon; stock-car races, Daytona 500. H. Horn. il Sports Illus 20:26-8+ Mr 2 '64
Tempest that could have been king. R. Brock. il Hot Rod 16:70-3 Je '63
Thatcher grooms a Plymouth. B. Greene. il Hot Rod 16:82-5 O '63
Things will never be the same at Indy! D. Francis and R. R. Olney. il Pop Sci 184:64-7+ My '64
This one's gone to the races. il Pop Sci 183:55-7+ N '63
Those Stroppe-stock Mercs. il Hot Rod 16:40-5 Ap '63
365 mph with 400 hp? R. Huntington. il Hot Rod 17:30-3 Je '64
Triple-threat 'Vette. L. Smith. il Hod Rod 17:74-7+ O '64
Tune-up for an American assault; twelve-hour race at Sebring. K. Rudeen. il Sports Illus 18:68-9+ Ap 1 '63
Two old shoestringers jolt the jet set; Wingfoot Express on the Bonneville Salt Flats. H. Gorey. il Sports Illus 21:66-7 O 12 '64
Ugliest, cheapest and best in the world; jet car at Bonneville Salt Flats. H. Gorey. il Sports Illus 21:24-5 N 9 '64
Weight transfer; drag racer. R. Huntington. il Hot Rod 16:76-9 Ap '63
Wenderski-Winkel dragster. S. Scott. il Hot Rod 17:52-4 Jl '64
Wild outdoor headers. L. Smith. il Hot Rod 16:78-9 Je '63
Wingfoot express; jet car. T. Bolek. il Hot Rod 16:92-4 Ag '63
See also
Karts (midget cars)

Design

Challenge for the champ. Sports Illus 19:14 N 11 '63
Difference of opinion Indy style. E. Rickman. il Hot Rod 16:44-7+ My '63
Driving a world's record; 407 miles per hour. C. Breedlove. il Pop Mech 120:87-92+ N '63
Race care safety design. G. Moore. il Motor T 15:68-73 Jl '63
Spirit of America. D. Francisco. il Hot Rod 16:26-33 O '63
Wedge. B. Greene. il Hot Rod 17:88-91 Ag '64

Exhibitions

Fifteenth annual Oakland roadster show. L. Smith. il Hot Rod 16:36-9 My '63
Grand national roadster show. D. Wells. il Hot Rod 17:40-3 My '64
National scene. See issues of Hot rod
Seattle custom auto fair; 1963. L. Smith. il Hot Rod 16:70-3 O '63

Fires and fire protection

After the Indianapolis fire: an argument. K. Rudeen. il Sports Illus 20:54-5 Je 22 '64

History

Spry old sport; one-cylinder Sizaire. il Life 56:63-4 Je 19 '64

Insurance

See Insurance, Automobile

Safety devices and measures

Driver's compartment; measures and equipment for drag racers. J. Hart. il Hot Rod 17:98-9 F '64
Race car safety design. G. Moore. il Motor T 15:68-73 Jl '63

AUTOMOBILES, Remodeled
Autocult. il Newsweek 64:92+ D 14 '64
Bad Bascom. D. Francisco. il Hot Rod 16:48-51+ Jl '63
Horsefeathers. E. Dahlquist. il Hot Rod 17:30-3 S '64
Mark 27. L. Smith. il Hot Rod 16:46-51 D '63
MT driver's report; EMPI's impish Sportster. B. McVay. il Motor T 15:30-5 Jl '63
Olds rear gears for early Fords. L. Smith. il Hot Rod 17:70-3 Je '64
Rare, the car, the setting and the atmosphere; photographs. T. Spicola. Hot Rod 17:86-7 Jl '64
Touring for Santa; street rod. il Hot Rod 17:86-7 D '64

AUTOMOBILES, Second-hand. See Automobiles, Used

AUTOMOBILES, Steam
Locomobile. D. E. Earnshaw. il Motor T 16:78-81 D '64

AUTOMOBILES, Theft of
Highway robbery. M. R. Beasley. il Motor T 15:42-5 My '63
What if the car is stolen? il Changing T 18:36-8 F '64

AUTOMOBILES, Three wheel
Cool run for an old hot rodder. H. Gorey. Sports Illus 19:46-8+ Ag 19 '63
Dream of speed; C. Breedlove's Spirit of America. il Time 82:51 Ag 16 '63
How wheeled jet set land-vehicle record; Spirit of America. Pop Sci 183:79 D '63
Jet ace; three-wheeled Spirit of America. il Newsweek 62:74-5 Ag 19 '63
See also
Motor trucks, Three wheel

AUTOMOBILES, Toy
Sidewalk classic. R. Woolson. il Pop Mech 120:146-51+ N; 128-31 D '63
Twelve MPH scoot-car. R. Woolson. il Pop Mech 120:138-44+ Ag '63

AUTOMOBILES, Used
Fine art of used car buying. C. Isica. il Motor T 16:66-9 S '64
Your best used car buy. il Motor T 15:52-5 D '63
Your car (cont) il Consumer Rep 28:385-416 D '63
See also
Automobiles—Wrecking

Prices

Best bets in used cars. il Changing T 17:35-7 Ap '63
How to sell your car. il Changing T 17:15-16 O '63
What's your car worth? Pop Sci 183:69-74 S '63
What's your car worth today? il Pop Sci 183:67-73 Ag '63

AUTOMOBILES in art
Portfolio of antique automobiles. C. Hornung. il Am Artist 27:54-7+ O '63

AUTOMOBILES in government. See Automobiles, Government

AUTOMOBILI turismo sport. See Automobile industry and trade—Italy

AUTOMOTIVE fuel
See also
Automobile engines—Fuel
Tractor engines—Fuel

Storage

Safe fuel storage. D. S. Huber. Suc Farm 62:58-9 Ja '64

AUTOMOTIVE gas turbines. See Gas turbines, Automotive

AUTOMOTIVE industry. See Automobile industry and trade

AUTOMOTIVE magazines. See Automobiles—Periodicals

AUTONETICS division. See North American aviation, incorporated—Autonetics division

AUTONOMIC nervous system. See Nervous system

AUTONOMY
Aid, investment in the future; address, April 23, 1963. U. A. Johnson. Dept State Bul 48:829-34 My 27 '63
Captive nations week, 1963; proclamation, July 5, 1963. J. F. Kennedy. Dept State Bul 49:161 Jl 29 '63
Foreign aid; the essential factors for success; address, May 28, 1963. C. Bowles. Dept State Bul 48:939-45 Je 17 '63
Prelude to independence; address, June 1, 1963. B. Ward. Vital Speeches 29:564-6 Jl 1 '63

AUTOPILOTS. See Automatic pilot (airplanes)

AUTORADIOGRAPHY
Autobiographies of cells. R. Baserga and W. E. Kisieleski. il Sci Am 209:103-8+ Ag '63
Microstructure of polymers by tritium autoradiography. J. D. Moyer and R. J. Ochs. bibliog il Science 142:1316-18 D 6 '63

AUTOTRANSFUSION of blood. See Blood—Transfusion

AUTRY, Ewart A.
How my family cured me of saying: now when I was a boy. Farm J 88:13 Ag '64

AUTRY, Ewart A.—*Continued*
Park your sinuses outside. Read Digest 85: 124-5 D '64
Words with birds. Audubon Mag 67:52-6 Ja '65

AUTRY, Gene
Cowboy tycoon. il por Newsweek 63:57-8 Ja 6 '64

AUTUMN
Analysis of autumn. B. Tufty. il Sci N L 84:183+ S 21 '63
How to make fall your favorite season. L. Mathison. il Farm J 87:76 O '63
Journeys into autumn. B. Tufty. il Sci N L 86:186-7 S 19 '64
Peripatetic reviewer. E. Weeks. Atlan 214: 144+ D '64

Quotations, maxims, etc.
Truth & poetry; ed. by H. V. Wilson. Flower Grower 50:64 S; 64 O '63

AUTUMN crocuses
Colchicum for autumn bloom. B. Brinhart. il Pop Gard 14:22-3+ Jl '63
For flowers in early autumn. il Sunset 133: 148 Ag '64

AUTUMN in the oak woods; story. See Kazakov, Y.

AUTUMN leaves. See Leaves

AUXILIUM Latinum (periodical)
After hours. C. M. Wilson. Harper 226:28-32 My '63

AUXINS
Gibberellin: effect on diffusible auxin in fruit development. K. K. S. Sastry and R. M. Muir. bibliog il Science 140:494-5 My 3 '63

AUYER, Stephen
Low-power stroboscope. Pop Electr 21:61-3+ N '64

AVAKIAN, Alexander
Inventor of the month. S. V. Jones. il por Sci Digest 56:22 Ag '64

AVAKIAN, Emik A.
Scientist seeks cause of own brain injuries. il por Sci N L 83:306 My 18 '63

AVALANCHES
Graceful prelude to death: Buddy Werner and Barbara Henneberger; with report by M. Smith. il Life 56:34-9 Ap 24 '64
I rode with the avalanche patrol; Colorado. E. D. Fales, jr. il Pop Sci 182:112-14+ F '63
Last race: death of skiers, W. Werner and Barbi Henneberger. il Time 83:36 Ap 24 '64
Terror at Twin Lakes. il Pop Sci 182:114-17 F '63

AVANT-garde dancing. See Dancing

AVANT-garde moving pictures. See Moving pictures

AVANT-garde music. See Music

AVANT garde theater. See Theater

AVARELLI, Walter
Judge commits larceny. C. Goren. il Sports Illus 21:90 S 21 '64

AVCO corporation
Avco made its mistakes early; converting from military to civilian work. il Bsns W p 130-1+ Ag 22 '64
C-bank link may aid in re-entry. M. Getler. il Miss & Roc 12:28+ F 11 '63
Shanghaied technicians. Nation 196:435 My 25 '63

AVE Maria (periodical)
Excelsior, Ave Maria! Christian Cent 81:692 My 27 '64

AVEDON, Elliott M.
Park is for people. por Recreation 57:400-1+ O '64

AVENS
Geum. M. P. Kunkel. il(cover) Horticulture 42:42 My '64

AVERILL, Lloyd J.
Is anybody listening? Christian Cent 80:646 My 15 '63
Political fundamentalism in profile. Christian Cent 81:1009-12 Ag 12 '64
Seed pod. Christian Cent 81:863-4 Jl 1 '64
Sexuality in crisis. Christian Cent 80:1196-9 O 2 '63

AVERY, Mary Ellen
Baby specialist explains the fatal illness. U S News 55:8 Ag 19 '63

AVERY, Robert
Biggest bear in the East; ed. by N. Drahos. por Outdoor Life 131:52-5+ My '63

AVIAN sarcoma virus. See Viruses

AVIATION
Hugh Downs column; what happened to flying? H. Downs. il Sci Digest 55:38-41 Je '64
See also
Air travel
Airplanes—Piloting
Balloon ascensions
Private flying

Accident investigation
CAB seeks to confirm clues to F-27 crash. Aviation W 80:41 My 18 '64
Diaries of destruction; flight recorders. F. A. Tinker. il Pop Mech 120:108-12+ Jl '63
Italians protest Indian accident report. Aviation W 79:45 Ag 12 '63
Rome accident probe spotlights investigation conflicts abroad. R. G. O'Lone. Aviation W 81:29 D 14 '64

Accidents
ALPA challenges finding by CAB that crew erred in DC-7 accident. Aviation W 79:52 O 21 '63
Approach decision cited in slick accident. Aviation W 79:45 O 21 '63
Atlanta: aftermath of a tragedy. J. Blank. il Redbook 121:52-3+ Je '63
Attitude indicator blamed in Comet crash; accident at Esenboga airport, Ankara, Turkey, December 21, 1961. Aviation W 78: 118-19+ Ja 21 '63
BAC III crashes on test flight. Aviation W 79: 43 O 28 '63
Cause of DC-7 Alaska crash is undetermined; June 3, 1963. Aviation W 80:45 Ap 27 '64
CAB accident investigation report: board cites 1049H pilot incapacitation; in Flying Tiger line crash, December 14, 1962. Aviation W 80:74-7+ Mr 30 '64
CAB accident investigation report; CAB cites swan impact in Viscount crash. il Aviation W 78:106-7+ Ap 8 '63
CAB accident investigation report: DC-7 crew actions cited in taxi collision; Memphis municipal airport, January 13, 1963. il Aviation W 81:98-9+ N 23 '64
CAB accident investigation report: ditched DC-7C is evacuated successfully. Aviation W 79:83+ D 2 '63
CAB accident investigation report: faulty latch blamed in decompression. Aviation W 79:101+ Ag 12 '63
CAB accident investigation report: ice accretion blamed in Viscount crash; Kansas City, January 29, 1963. Aviation W 81:78-81+ Jl 27 '64
CAB accident investigation report: low approach cited in Adak Island crash. Aviation W 78:191-3+ Je 10 '63
CAB accident investigation report: three-engine go-around cited in crash. Aviation W 79:115+ S 9 '63
CAB accident investigation report: undetected prop reversal blamed in fatal FAA Constellation crash. Aviation W 78:131+ My 20 '63
CAB cites severed wires in 707 crash; New York international airport accident, March 1, 1962. Aviation W 78:43-4 Ja 21 '63
CAB finds shooting caused crash. Aviation W 81:40 N 9 '64
CAB investigates Bonanza crash, sudden plunge of Pan Am's 707. Aviation W 81:39 N 23 '64
CAB teams probe Eastern DC-8 crash. Aviation W 80:42 Mr 2 '64
Crash probe spurs 1958 finding review. Aviation W 80:29 Je 22 '64
Crash spurs ditching recommendations; Flying Tiger flight, September 23, 1962. Aviation W 80:96-105+ Ja 6 '64
Damaged gear may have ruptured fuel, hydraulic lines on Caravelle. Aviation W 79: 46 S 16 '63
Death at 8:58; Pan American clipper 214 crash. il Newsweek 62:48 D 23 '63
Death in the afternoon; Viscount and DC-3 crash over Ankara. Newsweek 61:44 F 11 '63
Death wish; captain and first officer of Pacific air lines flight 773 shot by passenger. il Time 84:22 N 6 '64
Disaster in Wiltshire; British aircraft corp.'s One-Eleven crash. il Newsweek 62:81 N 4 '63
Effort spurred to find C-133 loss cause. C. Brownlow. Aviation W 82:25 Ja 18 '65
Elevator trim suspected in Lodestar crash; CAB accident investigation report. Aviation W 79:86+ Jl 8 '63
Epilogue to disaster; collision over New York city, December 16, 1960. Time 82:50 N 1 '63
Fatality rate rose slightly in 1964; table. Aviation W 82:29 Ja 11 '65
Fifth of a village, gone in an instant; Swissair Caravelle crash at Humlikon. T. Green. il Life 55:42 S 20 '63
Fishermen reel in a U.S. flier; with report by H. Lavallee. il Life 55:49-52 S 13 '63
Girl who refused to die. E. M. Wylie. il Good H 158:92-3+ My '64

AVIATION—Accidents—*Continued*
Go-around technique cited in DC-7 crash; accident at New York international airport, November 30, 1962. Aviation W 79:64-8 D 30 '63
HC-97, HC-54 collide near Bermuda; photographs. Aviation W 81:82-3 Jl 20 '64
Hook-and-ladder helicopters; taking the terror out of air-crash fires. E. Tozer. il Pop Sci 184:114-16 F '64
I was on the ceiling; jet hits air pocket. C. Miller. il Life 55:23 D 6 '63
Instrument tests set in Kennedy accident. Aviation W 80:24 Je 29 '64
Jet procedures in turbulence changed. R. H. Cook. Aviation W 79:43-4 D 16 '63
Liability. T. Bacon. Flying 74:41+ Mr '64
Location of an aircraft impact from gravity waves. D. E. Amstutz and S. Neshyba. il Science 145:921-3 Ag 28 '64
Mohawk 404 crashes in thunderstorm; Rochester-Monroe County airport, July 2, 1963. Aviation W 81:74-9+ Jl 13 '64
Murder in the sky. il Newsweek 63:37-8 My 18 '64
Northwest DC-7C crashes into Pacific, June 3, 1963. Aviation W 81:82-4+ Ag 10 '64
Old man and the glacier. J Liston. il Pop Sci 185:106-9+ O '64
One came back; crashes at Innsbruck, Austria, and Lake Tahoe, Nev. Newsweek 63:66 Mr 16 '64
Pitch-trim unit problem cited in Louisiana DC-8 crash probe. Aviation W 81:30 Jl 20 '64
Plane crashes: are there more than usual? il U S News 56:10 My 25 '64
Rain of death; collision over Ankara. Time 81:31 F 8 '63
Rendezvous. il Newsweek 63:20 Je 29 '64
Rudder malfunction cited in 707 crash; American airlines accident, March 1, 1962 at New York international airport. il Aviation W 78:74-5+ Ja 28 '63
Shooting determined cause in F-27 crash; near San Ramon, Calif, May 7, 1964. Aviation W 82:78-9+ Ja 4 '65
Survivors; crash of plane to Atlanta at Orly, France. H. Gold. il Reporter 28:44-8 F 14 '63
Swissair Caravelle crashes near Zurich. Aviation W 79:51 S 9 '63
Teddy's ordeal; plane crash. il Time 83:20 Je 26 '64
Thriller in a stricken plane; scotch and diapers went, but dolls and Bibles stayed. J. Leveque. Life 54:38B Mr 29 '63
TWA 707 strikes roller, explodes in aborting takeoff at Fiumicino. Aviation W 81:27 N 30 '64
Tubes clue to air crashes. P. Halliday. Electr World 71:83 Ja '64
U.S. seeks to end crash liability limits. R. H. Cook. Aviation W 80:41+ F 10 '64
Unknown factor in jet crashes: clear air turbulence. il Bsns W p65-6+ Ja 18 '64
Village excursion; Swissair crash near Zurich. il Newsweek 62:42 S 16 '63
Village that lost its parents; Swiss hamlet of Humlikon. C. McCarry. il Sat Eve Post 236:96+ D 7 '63
Voice detectives go to work on the mystery crash: Pacific air lines 773. D. Nevin. il Life 56:46-46A My 22 '64
Way out; Pacific air lines turboprop F-27 crash near San Francisco. il Time 83:39 My 15 '64
We have crashed; test of escape procedures. il Newsweek 63:87 Ap 20 '64
Weather cited as major factor in three N.Y. runway overruns. Aviation W 80:41 Ap 13 '64
See also
Airplanes—Ditching
Helicopters—Accidents
Parachuting
Survival (after airplane accidents, shipwrecks, etc)

Anecdotes, facetiae, satire, etc.

Look, but don't touch. B. Glaves. il Flying 75:34-5 Jl '64

Bibliography

Have you read? See issues of Flying

Bird hazards

CAB accident investigation report; CAB cites swan impact in Viscount crash. il Aviation W 78:106-7+ Ap 8 '63
Danger on the runway: how birds cause crashes. E. D. Fales, jr. il Pop Sci 183:90-3+ N '63
Fighting the birds; J. D. F. Hardenberg's recorded distress calls. Time 83:37 Ja 31 '64
Gooney birds of Midway. J. W. Aldrich. il Nat Geog Mag 125:838-51 Je '64

Communication systems

See also
Teletype in aviation

Competitions

Bahamas treasure hunt. P. Shamburger. il Flying 74:45 F '64
Memo from the publisher; Bahamas flying treasure hunt. E. D. Muhlfeld. il Flying 75:6 Ag '64
Status of U.S. aerobatics; preparations for World aerobatic championships. L. N. Parsons. il Flying 74:43-4+ F '64

Crimes

See Crimes aboard aircraft

Exhibitions

Farnborough revisited. W. J. Coughlin. Miss & Roc 15:90 S 14 '64
Flying demonstrations cap Paris air show; with editorial comment. H. J. Coleman. il Aviation W 78:21, 26-31 Je 24 '63
Hanover air show projects reflect increasing trend to joint efforts. C. Brownlow. il Aviation W 80:18-21 My 4 '64
Hardware list for Farnborough display. Aviation W 81:27 S 7 '64
Paris air show. il Miss & Roc 12:14-18 Je 17 '63
Thunderbirds introduce new maneuvers at Paris; Greek air force team displays precision formations; Italian display features double bomb burst. il Aviation W 79:52-7 Jl 15 '63
Transports dominate Farnborough show. H. J. Coleman. il Aviation W 81:26-30 S 14 '64
U.S. military services to increase participation in Paris air show. Aviation W 78:36 My 13 '63

History

See Aeronautics—History

Ice problem

See Airplanes—Ice protection

Instrument flying

Flying the beam when the fog rolls in. C. Leedham. il N Y Times Mag p22+ My 24 '64
No hands landing; all-weather landing system. J. Eberhart. il Sci N L 86:386 D 19 '64
Way which is up. il Esquire 61:88-91 Je '64

International aspects

Aeroflot will fly Tu-114 to U.S.; Il-62 will follow two years later. Aviation W 79:44 D 23 '63
Africa route quest raises issues of diplomacy, race, competition. J. R. Ashlock. Aviation W 82:37 Ja 18 '65
Agencies divided on foreign aviation aid. R. H. Cook. Aviation W 78:38-9 Ap 1 '63
Air transport agreement with Mexico extended; joint statement, August 14, 1963. Dept State Bul 49:371 S 2 '63
Air transport policy approved by President. Dept State Bul 48:784 My 20 '63
Air transport services agreement signed with U.A.R. Dept State Bul 50:845 My 25 '64
Airlines are bystanders in fare dispute. L. L. Doty. Aviation W 78:34-5 My 27 '63
Airlines planning ticket swindle defense. J. W. Carter. Aviation W 80:26-9 Mr 23 '64
Airlines start attack on new U.S. policy. L. L. Doty. Aviation W 78:44 F 18 '63
Anchorage receiving international flights. Aviation W 80:42 Ap 13 '64
Atlantic carriers, foresee higher earnings. il Aviation W 80:174-9 Mr 16 '64
Atlantic fare battle. R. Hotz. Aviation W 78:17 My 27 '63
Aviation dispute with France settled by arbitration. Dept State Bul 50:506 Mr 30 '64
Concorde tests at U.S. facility approved. L. L. Doty. Aviation W 79:38 Jl 15 '63
Confusion clouds international air travel. L. L. Doty. Aviation W 78:40-1 Ap 8 '63
Courtship in the air; Sino-Pakistan air agreement. Time 82:23 S 6 '63
Cutting transatlantic fares. R. Hotz. Aviation W 79:21 Jl 1 '63
Czech carrier stresses route extension. E. Walford. il Aviation W 81:28-30 D 28 '64
DC-8 pool for Europe-South America. Aviation W 78:40 Ap 1 '63
Dublin rights urged for non-Irish airlines. J. W. Carter. Aviation W 81:34-5 N 16 '64
Extension of new supplemental charter rights to Pacific asked. L. L. Doty. Aviation W 80:30 Mr 23 '64

AVIATION—International aspects—*Continued*
Finnair concentrates on route expansion. E. Walford. il Aviation W 81:50-1+ N 9 '64
Foreign carrier concern growing as tourists shift to U.S. airlines. J. R. Ashlock. Aviation W 78:41 Je 10 '63
Greek flag carrier seeking route to U.S. il Aviation W 81:36-7 D 7 '64
Halaby goes to Moscow for Aeroflot talks; SAS move may bar bilateral. Aviation W 79:39 D 9 '63
Hawaii-Tahiti route backed for Pan Am. Aviation W 80:47 Mr 2 '64
IATA fares dispute aids U.S. airlines. L. L. Doty. Aviation W 78:36 Je 3 '63
IATA session delegates face reappraisal. L. L. Doty. Aviation W 79:41 O 14 '63
International air transport; symposium. il Aviation W 79:21+ O 7 '63
International aviation policy of the United States; address, September 10, 1963. G. G. Johnson. Dept State Bul 49:508-13 S 30 '63
Italy hinders TWA all-cargo jet effort. R. H. Cook. Aviation W 80:49-50 Ja 20 '64
Japan renews bid for SF-London route. L. Booda. Aviation W 80:45+ My 18 '64
Japan's rejection of U.S. terms causes route discussion collapse. Aviation W 81:30 Ag 17 '64
Legislators cool to CAB foreign rate plea. J. R. Ashlock. Aviation W 80:28-9 Je 8 '64
Lower cost Trippe. Time 82:84 Jl 5 '63
Lower-fare jet service challenges IATA. W. Wright. il Aviation W 79:40-1 D 2 '63
Mexico and United States sign civil air agreement. Dept State Bul 51:357 S 7 '64
Nations agree to retain IATA fares role. L. L. Doty. Aviation W 79:28-9 Jl 29 '63
New Soviet N.Y.-Moscow route bid seen. L. L. Doty. Aviation W 79:40 Ag 5 '63
New U.S. air policy threatens merger. L. L. Doty. Aviation W 78:38 F 11 '63
New U.S. moves cloud air policy role. L. L. Doty. Aviation W 79:38-9 Ag 12 '63
New U.S. policy backfires in rate fight. L. L. Doty. Aviation W 78:39-40 My 20 '63
New York-Moscow route decision due. L. L. Doty. il Aviation W 80:34+ Ja 6 '64
No lion's share of the skies. Bsns W p34+ Ap 27 '63
North Atlantic carriers bypass IATA, initiate Nassau fare plan. Aviation W 80:36 Ja 13 '64
North Atlantic fares compromise reached. Aviation W 79:45 D 16 '63
OAS studies need for U.S. aviation aid. R. H. Cook. Aviation W 78:43 Ap 15 '63
Pakistan airlines plans to resume transatlantic route after 1966. J. W. Carter. Aviation W 80:27 Je 8 '64
Pakistan, red China sign air service pact. Aviation W 79:31 S 2 '63
Pakistan route could link U.S. Russia. L. L. Doty. Aviation W 79:43 O 21 '63
Pakistan seeks more Russia, China routes. Aviation W 80:50 Ja 20 '64
Pakistani carrier obtains access agreement from Communist China. Aviation W 78:40 Je 24 '63
Pan Am attacks plan to divide transatlantic routes with TWA. J. R. Ashlock. Aviation W 79:41 Ag 5 '63
Pan Am, BOAC reach fare compromise. L. L. Doty. Aviation W 79:38 D 9 '63
Pan American is awarded Tahiti route. L. L. Doty. Aviation W 79:38-9 N 18 '63
Payments deficit stirs international rift. L. L. Doty. Aviation W 79:36-7 N 25 '63
Pilots group maps SST operations policy. H. J. Coleman. Aviation W 79:47+ N 25 '63
Political decisions influence air transport. Aviation W 79:47+ O 7 '63
Power play; international air fares. Newsweek 61:75 My 6 '63
Present El Al jet fleet may be expanded. C. Brownlow. il Aviation W 80:30-2 Je 8 '64
Red China air expansion seen. Aviation W 79:39 S 9 '63
Red China attacks U.S, Japan on routing. Aviation W 79:30 D 30 '63
Regular U.S.-Russia flights now unlikely; with editorial comment. L. L. Doty. Aviation W 80:21, 38-9 F 24 '64
Renewal of NY route offer to Japan due. J. R. Ashlock. Aviation W 80:32-3 Je 29 '64
SAS of the East? Time 84:94 S 25 '64
SAS Prestwick-U.S. services restricted by aviation ministry. Aviation W 80:42 Ap 13 '64
Secrecy on U.S. international air policy stirs fresh controversy. L. L. Doty. Aviation W 78:39 F 4 '63
Secretary assigned leadership in international aviation policy; letter to Secretary Rusk, June 22, 1963. J. F. Kennedy. Dept State Bul 49:160-1 Jl 29 '63
State's international air role increased. Aviation W 78:38 My 6 '63
Storm over the Atlantic. il Time 81:95 My 3 '63
Supplements get Atlantic charter rights. R. H. Cook. Aviation W 80:31 Mr 9 '64
Swissair seeks simplified Atlantic fares. Aviation W 80:41 Je 15 '64
Three carriers indicate general approval of Pan Am Fare proposal. Aviation W 79:30 Jl 8 '63
Transatlantic case delay creates dilemma on foreign competition. Aviation W 79:39 Ag 26 '63
U.K. treasury criticized on Concorde role. H. J. Coleman. Aviation W 80:45+ Ja 27 '64
U.K, U.S. disagree on blind-landing plans. C. Brownlow. Aviation W 78:45+ My 13 '63
United States and Canada hold civil air transport talks; announcement of talks; with joint statement, May 2, 1964. Dept State Bul 50:844-5 My 25 '64
United States and Italy begin civil air transport consultations. Dept State Bul 51:855 D 14 '64
United States and Italy discuss air relations; joint communique, March 23, 1964. Dept State Bul 50:628 Ap 20 '64
U.S. and Japan agree to recess aviation consultations; joint communique; August 5 1964. Dept State Bul 51:313 Ag 31 '64
United States and Mexico conclude civil air transport negotiations. Dept State Bul 51:133 Jl 27 '64
U.S. and Mexico hold air talks. Dept State Bul 48:840 My 27 '63
United States and New Zealand hold civil aviation talks. Dept State Bul 50:549 Ap 6 '64
U.S. and New Zealand sign air transport agreement. Dept State Bul 51:60 Jl 13 '64
U.S, Canada might revise bilateral pact. D. E. Fink. Aviation W 78:34-5 Je 3 '63
U.S.-European air transport rift widens. L. L. Doty. Aviation W 79:28-9 S 2 '63
United States international aviation month, 1964; proclamation, July 28, 1964. L. B. Johnson. Dept State Bul 51:314 Ag 31 '64
U.S.-Mexican traffic dispute unresolved. H. D. Watkins. il Aviation W 81:78-9+ S 14 '64
U.S. participation in Concorde proposed. L. L. Doty. Aviation W 78:40 Je 17 '63
U.S. reveals liberal international policy. R. H. Cook. Aviation W 78:34-5 Ap 29 '63
U.S. seeks to end crash liability limits. R. H. Cook. Aviation W 80:41+ F 10 '64
U.S. views on international air rate policy; statement, July 18, 1963. A. S. Boyd. Dept State Bul 49:247-8 Ag 12 '63
We're losing the supersonic transport race. J. Hannifin and C. J. V. Murphy. il Fortune 69:118-22+ F '64
Who pays the fare? New Repub 149:6 Jl 13 '63
Wide gap separates carriers on fare cut. L. L. Doty. Aviation W 79:38-9 S 30 '63
World airlines face new consolidations. il Aviation W 78:164-5+ Mr 11 '63
See also
International air transport association
International civil aviation organization

Laws and regulations

FAA considers lower small field minimums. Aviation W 78:50 Je 24 '63
FAA plans wide recorder requirements. R. H. Cook. Aviation W 78:43 Mr 25 '63
Overseas flight, or local hop? CAB in jurisdiction dispute. il Bsns W p31-2 D 26 '64
Troubles of private aviation under Russia's closed-sky policy. W. Cloud. Pop Sci 184:23-4+ Mr '64
U.S. seeks to end crash liability limits. R. H. Cook. Aviation W 80:41+ F 10 '64
Washington clipboard. R. Slater. Flying 74:14 Ja '64
Washington clipboard; FAA's proposal to lower area of positive control; with editorial comment. R. Slater. Flying 74:21, 26 Je '64
See also
Air traffic control
United States—Civil aeronautics board

Lightning hazards

I learned about flying from that! ordeal by thunderstorm. J. F. Reynolds. il Flying 74:50+ Ja '64
Spring; flying in thunderstorms. D. Kuhn. Flying 74:60 Ap '64
Would you fly in a storm? J. H. Winchester. Sci Digest 55:85-90 Je '64

AVIATION—*Continued*

Medical aspects

See also
Motion sickness

Meteorological aspects

See Meteorology, Aeronautic

Physiological aspects

I learned about flying from that! killer in the cockpit. R. I. Forrest. il Flying 74:56 Ap '64
Rhythm: transocean and land; affect on athletes. Sports Illus 19:20+ N 25 '63
Time out of joint; fatigue of time adjustment. il Newsweek 63:79 Je 22 '64
What jet travel does to your metabolic clock. S. W. Bryant. il Fortune 68:160-3+ N '63
Why jet travel makes you tired. Sci Digest 56:25 O '64

Safety devices and measures

Buckle up for a safe flight. B. Schapper. il Todays Health 42:46-7+ D '64
Crash tests used to study survival in helicopter impact. D. E. Fink. il Aviation W 78:112-13+ Ap 22 '63
FAA, ATA shown anti-collision system. il Aviation W 78:105+ Ap 15 '63
Operation Skyhook. il Time 84:51 D 4 '64
Pilot talks about air safety; interview. R. Buck. il U S News 54:59 Mr 18 '63
Pursuit of safety. G. R. Wilson. Flying 74: 26 Ap '64
Safety in the airlanes; concerning N.Y. herald tribune series on air safety. J. O'Gara. Commonweal 79:586 F 14 '64
Skyway crash preventers. K. Brown. il Pop Mech 120:106-10+ D '63
What a perfectly lovely smashup. A. F. Gonzalez, jr. il Sci Digest 56:26-31 S '64
See also
Airplanes—Safety devices and measures
Radar in aviation

Statistics

Air traffic by nations, 1962; table. Aviation W 79:70-1 O 7 '63
Fatality rate rose slightly in 1964; table. Aviation W 82:29 Ja 11 '65
U.S. business & utility plane shipments. il Aviation W 78:93 Ap 29 '63

Storm hazards

Boyd sees jet turbulence ban unneeded. J. R. Ashlock. Aviation W 80:37-8 Ja 13 '64
Crewmen fly B-52 damaged in turbulence. il Aviation W 80:27 Mr 9 '64
I learned about flying from that. G. Edwards. il Flying 74:56+ F '64
In the twister's path. G. P. Miga. il Flying 74:44+ Ja '64
Invisible CAT pilots dread. P. C. Geraci. il Pop Mech 121:104-7+ Ap '64
Jet turbulence problems. J. R. Ashlock. il Aviation W 80:38-41 F 17; 45-6 F 24 '64
Near-blizzard snarls airline schedules. J. R. Ashlock. Aviation W 80:38-9 Ja 20 '64
Spring; flying in thunderstorms. D. Kuhn. Flying 74:60 Ap '64
Turbulence: hidden giant in the sky. W. R. Young. il Life 57:86-8+ D 18 '64
Turbulence studies investigate pilot aids. J. R. Ashlock. Aviation W 80:47 Ap 20 '64
Weather cited as major factor in three N.Y. runway overruns. Aviation W 80:41 Ap 13 '64

Stunt flying

Flying flip. G. Infield. Esquire 61:84+ Je '64
International aerobatics. J. Gilbert. il Flying 74:40-2+ F '64
Mad, mad world of the stunt flier. R. Vaughan. il Sat Eve Post 236:26-7 My 18 '63
Status of U.S. aerobatics; preparations for World aerobatic championships. L. N. Parsons. il Flying 74:43-4+ F '64
Tallmantz on-stage. R. Bach. il Flying 74:39+ Ja '64
This one-man flying circus thrilled New York. G. Soule. il Pop Sci 183:210-12 S '63

Transatlantic flights

Airlines oppose new Atlantic area plan. R. G. O'Lone. Aviation W 81:31 S 28 '64
Atlantic shows heavy April-June increase. Aviation W 81:40 Ag 10 '64
Atlantic traffic surging toward record. J. W. Carter. Aviation W 81:26-7 Jl 20 '64
Canadian transatlantic traffic increases. D. A. Brown. Aviation W 81:32 D 21 '64
Eight years before Lindbergh: they flew the Atlantic in 19 days. G. Soule. il Pop Sci 184:77-9 My '64
Flight into the unknown. J. Stewart-Gordon. il Read Digest 82:120-5 Mr '63
Mayday from Charlie Foxtrot. M. Conrad. il Flying 74:52-3+ Je '64
No lion's share of the skies. Bsns W p34+ Ap 27 '63
Nonstop to Moscow; report of flight from Havana. E. Stevens. il Time 81:23 Mr 22 '63
Record smashing Sabreliner; ed. by W. B. Wentz. E. J. Brandreth, jr. il Flying 74: 48+ My '64
Record transatlantic business expected. J. W. Carter. Aviation W 80:40-1 Ap 20 '64
Supplementals get Atlantic charter rights. R. H. Cook. Aviation W 80:31 Mr 9 '64
Transatlantic jubilee. R. Hotz. Aviation W 81: 21 S 14 '64
Transatlantic market competition grows. J. R. Ashlock. il Aviation W 79:38-9 O 7 '63

Transcontinental flights

Competition stirs transcontinental traffic. J. W. Carter. Aviation W 80:26-7 Je 29 '64
Cross country couple. S. Buegeleisen. il Flying 75:48-9+ Jl '64
First nonstop coast-to-coast flight. G. Soule. il Pop Sci 182:82-4 My '63
Last gasp of the tin goose; 1929 Ford trimotor. A Chamberlin. il Sat Eve Post 236: 26-7 Ag 10 '63; Same abr. Read Digest 83: 151-5 D '63
Westward the, what kind of airplane is that, anyway? R. Bach. il Flying 75:50-1+ Jl '64

Transpacific flights

Extension of new supplemental charter rights to Pacific asked. L. L. Doty. Aviation W 80:30 Mr 23 '64
Impact of reduced fares felt in Pacific. H. D. Watkins. il Aviation W 79:156-7+ O 7 '63

Transpolar flights

Australian odyssey. N. Armstrong. il Flying 74:42-4+ Je '64
First flight across the bottom of the world: Cape Town to Christchurch. J. R. Reedy. il Nat Geog Mag 125:454-64 Mr '64

World flights

First round-the-world flight. W. S. Griswold. il Pop Sci 185:60-3 S '64
I flew around the world alone. J. Merriam. il Sat Eve Post 237:77-83 Jl 25 '64
Jerrie Mock: winner take all. B. Vail and D. Edwards. il Flying 75:32-3+ Jl '64
Let's travel around the world. il Mlle 56:66+ F '63

Africa

Africa sees air transport key to growth. R. H. Cook. Aviation W 79:152+ O 7 '63

Alaska

Alaska subsidy shift to post office urged. L. L. Doty. Aviation W 80:52 F 17 '64
Alaskan carriers' future depends on federal aid in reconstruction. R. H. Cook. Aviation W 80:40-1 Ap 13 '64
Bush pilot's deadly, daily game. D. Moser. il Life 57:112-14+ N 27 '64

Canada

Air policy statement urged in Canada. D. E. Fink. il Aviation W 79:149-51 O 7 '63

China (People's Republic)

Red China air expansion seen. Aviation W 79:39 S 9 '63

Ecuador

Military controls Ecuador's civil aviation. R. G. O'Lone. Aviation W 81:91+ S 14 '64

Florida

Winter flying weather in Florida. W. E. Hillig. il Flying 74:52+ F '64

Germany (Federal Republic)

Right of unrestricted air access to Berlin reasserted by U.S; Department statement. Dept State Bul 51:44 Jl 13 '64
U.S, and U.K, France reaffirm right of free air access to Berlin; U.S. statement, August 24, 1964. Dept State Bul 51:368 S 14 '64

Great Britain

Landing a jet without looking; Great Britain's blind landing experimental unit. L. Lader. il Sat Eve Post 237:64-5 F 15 '64
U.K. treasury rejects criticism on control of Concorde financing. H. J. Coleman. Aviation W 80:34 Je 22 '64

AVIATION—*Continued*

Latin America

Lifeline in the air. il Time 84:33 Jl 31 '64

Mexico

Mexican school for pilots. M. Smith. il Américas 16:29-31 Mr '64

Russia

Red flag over the seven seas. H. W. Baldwin. Atlan 214:37-43 S '64

Russians seek boost for private aviation. Aviation W 79:72+ D 2 '63

Underdeveloped areas

Emerging nations' short-haul needs cited. C. Brownlow. il Aviation W 78:39+ Mr 4 '63

United States

International aviation policy of the United States; address, September 10, 1963. G. G. Johnson. Dept State Bul 49:508-13 S 30 '63

Muffled voice. R. B. Parke. Flying 74:18 My '64; Reply. W. K. Lawton. 75:80+ Jl '64

See also

Airlines—United States

United States—Civil air patrol

AVIATION, Commercial. See Aeronautics, Commercial

AVIATION associations

Aerospace calendar. See issues of Aviation week & space technology

Flying calendar. See issues of Flying

Flying in. il Time 81:66 Je 14 '63

See also names of aviation associations, e.g. National business aircraft association

AVIATION clubs

Confederate air force flies at last; World war II fighter planes. D. Jenkins. il Sports Illus 19:58-63 Ag 12 '63

Congressional flying club. C. Newlon. il Flying 74:22+ Mr '64

Flying clubs. il Flying 74:54+ Je; 75:77 Ag '64

AVIATION conferences

Aerospace calendar. See issues of Aviation week & space technology

AVIATION education

Learn to fly, $65 down; I have a story to tell. J. Butterfield. Flying 75:28-30 S '64

See also

Air pilots—Training

Aviation schools

AVIATION fuel. See Airplane engines—Fuel

AVIATION instructors. See Air pilots—Training

AVIATION insurance. See Insurance, Aviation

AVIATION records

U.S. army helicopters set ten flight records. Aviation W 81:25 N 9 '64

World record flight; amphibious rescue plane. il Ebony 18:85-6 Ag '63

AVIATION research. See Aeronautic research

AVIATION schools

Bug buzzers' prep school; Agricultural aviation academy, Minden, Nev. R. Bach. il Flying 74:34-5+ My '64

Learn to fly, $65 down; I have a story to tell. J. Butterfield. Flying 75:28-30 S '64

Mexican school for pilots; International center for training in civil aviation, Mexico city. M. Smith. il Américas 16:29-31 Mr '64

AVIATION workers

See also

Airlines—Employees

AVIATORS. See Air pilots

AVIATORS, Military. See Air pilots

AVINERI, Shlomo

Israel: image and reality. New Repub 151:7-9 S 26 '64

AVINS, Alfred

Maybe it's time to look at the antislavery amendment. U S News 56:82-4 My 11 '64

AVIONIC devices. See Electronic apparatus and appliances

AVIONICS. See Airplanes—Electronic equipment

AVIONICS industry. See Electronic apparatus industry and trade

AVIS rent a car system

This executive has no secretary. T. J. Murray. il Duns R 84:49-50+ O '64

Trying harder. il Time 84:77-8 Jl 24 '64

AVNET electronics corporation

Avnet: ready around the clock. Duns R 81:38 Ja '63

AVOCADOS

See also

Cookery—Fruit

AVON products, incorporated

Avon: the sweet smell of success. S. Freedgood. il Fortune 70:108-13+ D '64

AVON publications, incorporated

Avon launches rounded corner paperbacks. il(p 19-22) Pub W 185:42 Mr 9 '64

AVONDALE shipyards, New Orleans. See Shipyards

AWARDS. See Rewards, prizes, etc.

AWARE, incorporated

Ordeal of John Henry Faulk. J. P. Blank. il Look 27:80-2+ My 7 '63

AWOLOWO, Obafemi

Verdict in Lagos. por Time 82:39 S 20 '63

AXE, Phil

How to be a loser with four aces. M. Cope. il pors Sat Eve Post 237:28-30 Je 6 '64

AXE quadruplets. See Quadruplets

AXELBANK, Albert

Chiang Kai-shek's silent enemies. Harper 227:46-50+ S '63

Going along with the US. New Repub 152:7-8 Ja 9 '65

Japanese cash register. New Repub 151:13-14 S 5 '64

AXELROD, David, and others

Polyoma virus genetic material in a virus-free polyoma-induced tumor. bibliog Science 146:1466-9 D 11 '64

AXELROD, George

George Axelrod. pors Esquire 60:32-5 Jl '63

AXELROD, Julius

Enzymatic formation of adrenaline and other catechols from monophenols. bibliog Science 140:499-500 My 3 '63

AXENROTH, Joseph B.

Forecast; poem. Christian Cent 81:80 Ja 15 '64

AXLES

See also

Automobiles—Axles

AXON, Gordon V.

Jewelry and gemstones. Consumer Bul 47:12-15 My '64

AXUM, Donna

Salesgirl, but does she sell? Miss America. il pors Bsns W p 146-8+ S 14 '63

AYACUCHO exercise. See Military maneuvers

AYALA, Walmir

Seven new Brazilian poets. Américas 16:27-34 F '64

AYARS, Albert L.

How business and industry are helping the schools. Sat R 47:57-8+ O 17 '64

AYDEMIR, Talat

Insurrection II. il Time 81:26 My 31 '63

AYER, N. W, and son

Trends in typography; newspapers compete in Ayer cup typographical competition. R. L. Tobin. il Sat R 47:51-2 Je 13 '64

AYNES, Edith A.

Coming scandal in nursing; ed. by N. G. Stuart. McCalls 91:100-1+ Mr '64

AYNESWORTH, Hugh

(ed) See Oswald, L. H. Oswald's own story as revealed by his diary

AYOTTE, A. E.

Last stand of the alligators? Audubon Mag 66:237-41 Jl '64

AYRE, Michael B.

Office building at new peak. Arch Rec 133:18 Ap '63

AYRES, C. E.

Economic thinking. Commentary 35:356-60 Ap '63

AYRES, Donald L.

Censorship of textbooks; what can the teacher do? NEA J 52:24 My '63

AYRES, Douglas W.

Forms and machine combine to streamline city operations. Am City 79:108-9 Je '64

AYRES, Samuel, 1893-

Fine art of scratching; interview, ed. by H. G. Earl. Todays Health 43:38-41+ Ja '65

AYRTON, Michael

Unwearying bronze. Horizon 7:16-37 Wint '65

AYUB KHAN, Mohammad

Pakistan-American alliance. For Affairs 42:195-203 Ja '64

We have legitimate cause for complaint against U.S.; interview, ed. by S. W. Sanders. por U S News 54:82-3 My 13 '63

about

Disappointments of Ayub Khan. J. H. Huizinga. il Reporter 28:30-1 Je 6 '63

AZALEAS

Azalea color wave. il Sunset 130:92-7 Ap '63

Azaleas bring new life to retirement years. G. Watters. il Pop Gard 15:22-3 Mr '64

Good soil mates. il Flower Grower 51:46-7 Ja '64

Great past, greater future. M. C. Ohlander. il Flower Grower 51:46-9+ Ap '64

Grow azaleas. J. W. Oliver. Pop Gard 15:50 Mr '64

AZALEAS—*Continued*
Hobbyist writes on Ghent azaleas. J. B. Wills. il Horticulture 41:190 Ap '63
How to increase azaleas & other shrubs. M. J. Dietz. il Flower Grower 51:28 Jl '64
How to pick the right azaleas for your climate. House B 105:220-1 My '63
Sunshine for every garden. M. C. Ohlander. il Flower Grower 50:39 Ag '63
These 194 evergreen azaleas will be on sale in California this spring. Sunset 130:256+ Ap '63
Twofold bounty of azaleas. O. K. Moore. il House B 105:164-5+ My '63
AZAÑA, Manuel
Tragedy of Manuel Azaña and the fate of the Spanish Republic, by F. Sedgwick. Review
Christian Cent 81:1563 D 16 '64. L. Fernsworth
AZEOTROPES
Azeotrope of isopropyl alcohol and isopropyl borate. W. D. English and R. L. Kidwell. bibliog il Science 139:341-2 Ja 25 '63
AZHAR university, Cairo. See Colleges and universities—Egypt
AZIMUTH
System transfers azimuth from tower top to ground monitor. M. M. Merlen. il Miss & Roc 13:32-3 Jl 15 '63
AZNAVOUR, Charles
Face of anybody. New Yorker 39:33-5 Ap 6 '63
He even makes married love sound exciting. L. Bell. por Life 56:18 My 22 '64
Sad star. por Newsweek 61:92 Ap 15 '63
Tu parles, Charles. por Time 81:62+ Ap 12 '63
AZORES
See also
Earthquakes—Azores
AZOTUS. See Ashdod
AZRAEL, Jeremy
Soviet freedom: a balance sheet. New Repub 148:18-20 Mr 2 '63
AZTECS
City of the living god; excerpts from Cortés: the life of the conqueror by his secretary. tr. by L. B. Simpson. F. L. de Gómara. il Am Heritage 15:67-79 Ap '64
AZURDIA, Enrique Peralta. See Peralta Azurdia, E.

B

B-9 (dimethylamino succinamic acid) See Growth inhibiting substances (plants)
B-70. See Airplanes, Military—United States
BBC. See British broadcasting corporation
BCG (Bacillus Calmette and Guérin) See Tuberculosis—Vaccines
BCIU. See Business council for international understanding
BCOA. See Bituminous coal operators association
B. F. Goodrich company. See Goodrich, B. F, company
BIA. See United States—Indian affairs, Bureau of
BIE. See Bureau of international expositions
BLM. See United States—Land management, Bureau of
BMC. See British motor corporation
BMEWS. See Ballistic missile early warning system
BMI. See Book manufacturers' institute
BML. See Boston medical library
BNB. See British national bibliography
BOAC. See British overseas airways corporation
BOR. See United States—Outdoor recreation, Bureau of
B.S.F. company
What's in it for Eddie, Bob, and Vic? S. H. Brown. il Fortune 70:139-43+ S '64
BAAL: drama. See Brecht, B.
BAALBEK international festival. See Music festivals—Lebanon
Al BAATH (political party) See Political parties—Arab states
BABB, James T.
New White House library to include 1,780 titles. Library J 88:3180-1 S 15 '63
BABBAGE, Charles
Cranky grandfather of the computer. il por Fortune 69:112-13 Mr '64
Profiles; computer: analytical engine. J. Bernstein. il New Yorker 39:78+ O 19 '63
BABBITT, Milton
New music and the American mainstream. B. Boretz. Nation 198:466-8 My 4 '64
BABCOCK, Havilah
Doing what comes naturally. Field & S 67:32-3+ F '63
Fallen Lady. Field & S 69:68-70+ My '64
Monofilament hates people. Field & S 68:40-2+ My '63
My dog Sam. Field & S 69:46-8+ S '64
Reformation of Bo. Field & S 68:60-2+ Ap '64
What's happening to bob white? Field & S 68:34-6+ D '63
When a man's thoughts are pure. Field & S 69:24-6+ D '64
BABCOCK, Howard
Roadless roamers. Travel 119:60-1 F '63
BABCOCK, Rilyn
Freud frappé. Atlan 212:134-5 O '63
BABCOCK, Tim M.
Montana's top Bonanza. K. W. Anderson. il por Flying 75:37+ Jl '64
BABCOCK and Wilcox company
Bigger equipment for bigger reactors; fabricators of nuclear reactor vessels. Bsns W p 118 Ag 17 '63
BABEL, Isaac
Two stories: Froim Grach and Kolyvushka; tr. by M. Hayward. Commentary 37:36-40 F '64
about
He died for art. il por Newsweek 64:79 Jl 27 '64
His letters hid a secret life. D. Stern. Sat R 47:43-4 S 12 '64
BABES in the wood; musical comedy. See Musical comedies, revues, etc.—Criticisms, plots, etc.
BABIES hospital, New York. See New York (city)—Columbia-Presbyterian medical center
BABIN, Victor
Power of music; address, November 11, 1963. Mus Am 83:159 D '63
BABIN, Vitya
Power of music; address, November 11, 1963. Mus Am 83:158-9 D '63
BABINKA. See Mollusks
BABOONS
Apish origins of human tension. J. E. Pfeiffer. Harper 227:55-60 Jl '63
Baby baboon. il Look 29:69-70+ Ja 26 '65
Better than guinea pigs; experiments on baboons. il Bsns W p68-70+ N 16 '63
Blood groups in anthropoid apes and baboons. A. S. Wiener and J. Moor-Jankowski. bibliog il Science 142:67-9 O 4 '63; Reply. G. B. Rabb. 142:1261 D 6 '63
BABSON, David L.
Real demand is in top-grade stocks; interview. por U S News 55:47-8 S 16 '63
BABSON, Janis
Triumph of Janis Babson; excerpts from Little girl's gift. L. Elliott. pors Read Digest 82:275-86+ Je '63
BABY animals. See Animals, Infancy of
BABY blankets. See Blankets
BABY bottles
Feeding baby through the ages. il Todays Health 42:38-41 Ap '64
BABY care. See Infants—Care and hygiene
BABY carriages
Report on Parents' magazine's consumer service bureau activities. E. M. McCabe. il Parents Mag 39:24+ Ja '64
BABY coverlets. See Coverlets
BABY cribs. See Cribs (beds)
BABY food. See Infants—Nutrition
BABY sitters
Code for baby sitters. D. R. Campbell. Parents Mag 39:54+ Ag '64
No trapped housewives here; a neighborhood baby-sitting exchange. J. Rossio. il Redbook 123:6+ Ag '64
When mothers work. B. Spock. il Ladies Home J 80:140+ Mr '63
BABY want a kiss; drama. See Costigan, J.
BABYLONIAN astronomy. See Astronomy, Assyro-Babylonian
BABYS tears
Ground covers for house plants. E. S. Parcher. il Horticulture 42:38 F '64
BACARDI international, limited. See Distilling industries
BACCALAUREATE addresses
About those "dull" commencement speeches. il Sr Schol 84:7-8 My 15 '64
Food for thought; commencement-week orators. il Newsweek 61:84 Je 17 '63

BACCALAUREATE addresses—*Continued*
That's good advice. il Time 83:76 Je 19 '64
Zest and sanity from Lady Bird; concerning address at Radcliffe. Life 57:4 Jl 10 '64

Anecdotes, facetiae, satire, etc.

Light touch; bona fide commencement speaker. P. Schrag. NEA J 52:13 My '63
BACCALONI, Salvatore
Ergo sum Baccaloni; interview. ed. by C. A. Matz. por Opera N 28:30-1 Mr 28 '64
BACCARAT glass. See Glassware
BACH, Fritz, and Hirschhorn, Kurt
Lymphocyte interaction: a potential histocompatibility test in vitro. bibliog Science 143:813-14 F 21 '64
BACH, G. L.
Inflation, danger ahead? Harvard Bsns R 42:49-61 Jl '64
BACH, George R.
Fight promoter for the battle of the sexes. S. Alexander. il pors Life 54:102-4+ My 17 '63
BACH, Johann Sebastian
Bach by Gould: incomparably the most fascinating. R. Sabin. Am Rec G 31:211-12 N '64
Bach in jazz? two views of the Jacques Loussier trio. R. Sabin; D. Heckman. Am Rec G 30:1065 Jl '64
Bach's greatest hits revisited. Am Rec G 30:506-7+ F '64
Boettcher's Bach, unqualifiedly recommended. H. Glass. Am Rec G 30:944 Je '64
Finally, all twelve of Bach's keyboard concerti. J. W. Barker. Am Rec G 29:534 Mr '63
For Bach, a bacchanal in swing. J. S. Wilson. Hi Fi 14:67-8 Ja '64
For the first time, Bach's St Luke Passion. P. L. Miller. Am Rec G 29:438 F '63
Fresh Bachian delights: Cantate's continuing cantatas. H. Glass. il Am Rec G 30:400-1+ Ja '64
Glenn Gould: a poet and a seeker. R. Sabin. il Am Rec G 30:292-3 D '63
Interpretation of Bach's keyboard works, by E. Bodky. Review
Am Rec G 29:477-80 F '63. I. Kipnis
Living concert, a new Cantate series. J. W. Barker. il Am Rec G 30:215 N '63
Lovely bits, but not by Bach; St Luke Passion. N. Broder. il Hi Fi 13:72 F '63
[Nine cantatas] Am Rec G 30:933-4+ Je '64
On records; Magnificat in D. Opera N 27:32 My 4 '63
On records; St John Passion. Opera N 29:27 O 17 '64
On records; St Matthew passion. Opera N 28:30 My 2 '64
Passion of Our Lord according to St Matthew. J. W. Barker. il Am Rec G 30:280-3 D '63
Performing the Brandenburgs. T. Dunn. Mus Am 83:52-3 My '63
St John Passion. H. Glass. il Am Rec G 31:418-19 Ja '65
Secure in the universe; Bach's modern interpreters. il Time 83:67 Ja 3 '64
Three by Kurt Redel, unabashed admiration. H. Glass. il Am Rec G 30:576-7 Mr '64
Two new recordings of the St John Passion. P. L. Miller. il Am Rec G 30:930-3 Je '64
Well-tempered clavichord. R. Sabin. Am Rec G 30:574-5 Mr '64
What the boys in the Bach room will have. F. V. Grunfeld. Reporter 31:47-8+ N 19 '64
BACH, Richard
Fighter pilot. Harper 227:39-45 Jl '63
Tallmantz on-stage. Flying 74:39+ Ja '64
There's something knocking at the door. Writer 77:13-15+ My '64
What is an antiquer? To keep the antiques flying. Flying 74:24-31+ Ja '64
BACH festivals
Hercules and St John; Carmel Bach festival. A. Bloomfield. Mus Am 83:37+ S '63
BACHAUER, Gina
Gina Bachauer; interview. ed. by S. Fleming. por Hi Fi 13:46 N '63

about

Two great women pianists. Discus. Harper 228:109-10 Ja '64
BACHELOR days; story. See Vivante, A.
BACHELOR; story. See Broyard, A.
BACHELORS
Bachelors for 1963-1964. il Ebony 18:156-8+ Je '63; 19:210-12+ Je '64
Trials of being a bachelor. J. Mann. il Ebony 18:154-7+ Ap '63
See also
Men

Anecdotes, facetiae, satire, etc.

Buchwald anti-bachelor act. A. Buchwald. McCalls 91:68 My '64
BACHMAN, J. Cary
(ed) See Wade, M. Year-round tennis
BACHMANN, Barbara J.
Neurospora. Science 145:301-2 Jl 17 '64
BACHMANN, E. Theodore
Second thoughts on Helsinki. Christian Cent 80:1102-4 S 11 '63
BACHMANN, Gideon
Ermanno Olmi: the new Italian films. Nation 198:540-3 My 25 '64
(ed) See Fellini, F. Disturber of the peace
BACHRACH, Louis Fabian
Louis Fabian Bachrach dies in Boston at age of eighty-two. B. C. Brown. il por Pop Phot 53:36+ N '63
BACHRACH family
Capturing the executive look. il Bsns W p 108+ Ja 18 '64
Every president since Lincoln sat for the Bachrachs. il Life 55:30B-30C Ag 9 '63
BACHVAROFF, Radoslav, and McMaster, P. R. B.
Separation of microsomal RNA into five bands during agar electrophoresis. bibliog Science 143:1177-9 Mr 13 '64
BACILLUS Calmette and Guérin. See Tuberculosis—Vaccines
BACILLUS coli. See Escherichia coli
BACILLUS macerans
Formation and degradation of cyclic dextrins by intracellular enzymes of bacillus macerans. J. A. DePinto and L. L. Campbell. bibliog il Science 146:1064-6 N 20 '64
BACILLUS megaterium
Flickering in protoplasts of bacillus metaterium. D. M. Miller. Science 139:1060 Mr 15 '63
BACILLUS subtilis
Actinomycin resistance in bacillus subtilis. I. J. Slotnick and B. H. Sells. bibliog il Science 146:407-8 O 16 '64
Polyoma virus: production in bacillus subtilis. K. E. Bayreuther and W. R. Romig. bibliog il Science 146:778-9 N 6 '64
BACK, Martha
Sailing is action, thrills, magic. Seventeen 23:74-5+ Jl '64
BACK doors. See Doorways
BACK East; story. See Whedon, J.
BACK packs. See Packs
BACK RIVER
Down the back to the Arctic. A. Hoyt. il Sports Illus 19:34-6+ Ag 26 '63
BACK yard shelters. See Garden houses, shelters, etc.
BACK yards
How to perform a miracle in the back yard. D. X. Manners. il House B 105:164-5+ Mr '63
Magic change for a small narrow lot. P. Palmer. il Pop Gard 15:20-1 Mr '64
Plan your back-yard garden with your family's needs in mind. T. A. Weston. il Am Home 66:38-43+ Ap '63
Winter sports in your own back yard. il Pop Gard 15:47 Ja '64
Yard becomes a garden. il Sunset 133:94 S '64
See also
Outdoor rooms
BACKACHE
What ever happened to lumbago? J. D. Wassersug. il Sci Digest 54:64-8 N '63
What you can do about your aching back. D. Fisher. McCalls 90:45 Ap '63
BACKDROPS. See Photography—Apparatus and supplies
BACKE, Bruce
Low fees may undermine incentive goal. por Aviation W 82:69+ Ja 11 '65
BACKGAMMON
Everyone for backgammon; first annual International backgammon tournament. E. Shrake. il Sports Illus 20:42-4+ My 4 '64
BACKGROUND. See Composition (photography)
BACKGROUND in fiction. See Fiction—Technique
BACKHAUS, Wilhelm
Happy birthday, Herr Backhaus. R. Kammerer. por Am Rec G 30:596 Mr '64
BACKLIN, Hedy
Education for design. Craft Horiz 24:59-60 Mr '64
Laissez-fair. Craft Horiz 23:40-1 S '63
BACKMAN, Jules
Economic forecast: sounder growth. Nations Bsns 51:74-7 Ag '63
Profits will recover more lost ground. Nations Bsns 51:36-7+ D '63
Seven forces will block inflation. Nations Bsns 52:38-9+ Ap '64

BACKMAN, Jules—*Continued*

about

Of dollars and sense. il Ebony 19:64-5 Jl '64

BACKREST. See Boats—Equipment

BACKWARD areas. See Underdeveloped areas

BACKWARD children. See Children, Backward

BACMEISTER, Rhoda W.
Games that teach fair play. Recreation 56: 196-7 Ap '63
How to handle a creative child. Parents Mag 39:38-9+ Ja '64
Saying I'am sorry is not enough. Parents Mag 38:60-1+ Mr '63

BACON, Edmund Norwood
Under the knife, or all for their own good. por Time 84:69-70 N 6 '64

BACON, Francis, viscount St Albans
Francis Bacon. L. Eiseley. bibliog il pors Horizon 6:32-47 Wint '64
Francis Bacon: the temper of a man, by C. D. Bowen. Review
Reporter 29:64-5 Ag 15 '63. S. Eimerl

BACON, Francis, 1910-
Art. M. Kozloff. Nation 197:354+ N 23 '63
Art; exhibition at the Guggenheim museum. M. Kozloff. Nation 197:335-6 N 16 '63
Bacon: the paint of screams. A. Forge. il por Art N 62:38-41+ O '63
Enter Bacon, with the Bacon scream. D. Sylvester. il por N Y Times Mag p24-5+ O 20 '63
Francis Bacon. L. Alloway. il pors Vogue 142:136-9 N 1 '63
Francis Bacon: man under stress. B. Kaufman. Commonweal 79:294-5 N 29 '63
In the new grand manner. il por Time 82:82-3 N 1 '63
Letter from London; exhibition of H. Moore and F. Bacon at Marlborough gallery. M. Panter-Downes. New Yorker 39:100+ S 7 '63
Man, the accident. il por Newsweek 62:110 O 21 '63

BACON, Margaret H.
Bringing home the world. Parents Mag 38: 52+ N '63
Run-down area gets a new look. Parents Mag 38:42-3+ Jl '63

BACON, Martha
Dotty Dimple and the fiction award. Atlan 211:130-3 Mr '63

BACON, Myron L. jr
State computer analyzes city traffic. Am City 79:84-5 D '64

BACON, Richard G.
Why I can't join the John Birch society; letter. pors Look 28:76+ N 3 '64

BACON, Thorn
Liability. Flying 74:41+ Mr '64
Oregon. Flying 75:43-4+ Jl '64

BACON, W. Steve
Who really started World war 1? Pop Electr 20:40-2+ Ap '64; Same abr. with title Computer tells who started World war 1. Sci Digest 56:44-7 Jl '64
—and Nanas, Edward
How we're using rock-bottom radio. Pop Electr 19:51-4+ D '63

BACON
Best ways with bacon; with recipes. il Bet Hom & Gard 42:87-8 O '64
Quick-cook bacon; Brown 'n serve. Consumer Rep 28:215 My '63
What price bacon? il Consumer Rep 29:18-21 Ja '64

BACON-Shakespeare controversy. See Shakespeare, W.—Authorship

BACQUIER, Gabriel
Son of Provence; interview, ed. by A. M. Lingg. por Opera N 29:16 D 26 '64

BACTERIA
Bacteria produce viruses. Sci N L 86:6 Jl 4 '64
Bacterial structure and replication; report on bipartite symposium during the 64th annual meeting of the American society for microbiology. R. M. Cole. Science 146:554+ O 23 '64
Original sex; a kind of sexual mating between caulobacter bacteria. Time 84:85 N 13 '64
See also
Bacillus macerans
Bacillus subtilis
Brucella
Electric power production from bacteriological action
Escherichia coli
Microorganisms
Pseudomonas
Rhodospirillum rubrum

Mutation

See Mutation (bacteria)

Resistance

6-aminopenicillanic acid: inhibition of destruction of cephalosporin C by bacteria. R. B. Walton. bibliog il Science 143:1438-9 Mr 27 '64

BACTERIA, Aerobic
Evolution of a catabolic pathway in bacteria. S. A. Lerner and others. bibliog il Science 146:1313-15 D 4 '64

BACTERIA, Anaerobic
Anaerobic microorganisms in the soil; report on 64th annual meeting of the American society for microbiology. L. E. Casida, jr. Science 145:300-1 Jl 17 '64
Vitamin K compounds in bacteria that are obligate anaerobes. R. J. Gibbons and L. P. Engle. bibliog il Science 146:1307-9 D 4 '64

BACTERIA, Marine
Knots in leucothrix mucor. T. D. Brock. bibliog il Science 144:870-2 My 15 '64
Microbe ties knots in self when crowded; leucothrix mucor. Sci N L 85:393 Je 20 '64

BACTERIA, Pathogenic
Caution on cracked eggs; salmonella derby bacteria. Consumer Rep 28:509 N '63
Cell wall replication in salmonella typhosa. R. M. Cole. bibliog il Science 143:820-2 F 21 '64
Cracked eggs start derby; salmonella derby infection. F. Marley. Sci N L 84:67 Ag 3 '63
Death lurks in the kitchen; salmonella bacillus. Time 84:62 S 18 '64
Eggs salmonella. Newsweek 62:59 Jl 22 '63
Genetic alteration of adenylic pyrophosphorylase in salmonella. G. P. Kalle and J. S. Gots. bibliog il Science 142:680-1 N 8 '63
Helpful humidity; germs in the operating room's air. Time 82:44+ Ag 23 '63
Persistence of bacteria in protoplast form after apparent cure of pyelonephritis in rats. L. B. Guze and G. M. Kalmanson. bibliog il Science 143:1340-1 Mr 20 '64
Salmonella increasing as a cause of food poisoning. Consumer Bul 46:36-7 Je '63
TB-like germ from fowl. Sci N L 83:171 Mr 16 '63
See also
Microorganisms, Pathogenic
Rickettsia
Staphylococci
Streptococci

BACTERIA in electric power production. See Electric power production from bacteriological action

BACTERIAL diseases of plants. See Plants—Diseases and pests

BACTERIAL spores
Heat adaptation and ion exchange in bacillus megaterium spores. G. Alderton and others. il Science 143:141-3 Ja 10 '64

BACTERIOLOGICAL apparatus
Automatic sampling device for study of synchronized cultures of microorganisms. S. F. Petropulos. bibliog il Science 145:268-70 Jl 17 '64

BACTERIOLOGICAL research
Recombination events in the bacterial genus nocardia. J. N. Adams and S. G. Bradley. bibliog il Science 140:1392-4 Je 28 '63

BACTERIOLOGY
Russian bacteriology old. F. Marley. Sci N L 83:307 My 18 '63
See also
Cheese—Bacteriology
Immunity
Viruses

BACTERIOPHAGE
Bacteriophage: an unusual hybrid of serologically unrelated phages P22 and P221. N. Yamamoto. bibliog il Science 143:144-5 Ja 10 '64
DNA from bacteriophage lambda: molecular length and conformation. L. A. MacHattie and C. A. Thomas, jr. bibliog il Science 144:1142-4 My 29 '64
Electron microscopy of single-stranded DNA: circularity of DNA of bacteriophage ϕX174. D. Freifelder and others. bibliog il Science 146:254-5 O 9 '64
Electron microscopy of the replicative form of the DNA of the bacteriophage ϕX174. A. K. Kleinschmidt and others. bibliog il Science 142:961 N 15 '63
Fragment sizes produced from T5 bacteriophage DNA molecules by acid deoxyribonuclease. L. A. MacHattie and others. bibliog il Science 141:59-60 Jl 5 '63
Process of infection with ϕX174; effect of exonucleases on the replicative form. A. Burton and R. L. Sinsheimer. bibliog il Science 142·962-3 N 15 '63
Replication of the RNA of bacteriophage R17. M. L. Fenwick and others. bibliog il Science 146:527-30 O 23 '64

BACTERIOPHAGE—*Continued*
Sequential gene action in the establishment of lysogeny. M. Levine and H. O. Smith. bibliog il Science 146:1581-2 D 18 '64
Transcription in vivo of DNA from bacteriophage SP8. J. Marmur and C. M. Greenspan. bibliog il Science 142:387-9 O 18 '63
BAD GASTEIN, Austria
Travel well. C. Rule. il Travel 120:61-3 S '63
BADEAU, John S.
U.S.A. and U.A.R: crisis in confidence. For Affairs 43:281-96 Ja '65
BADEN-BADEN
Travel well. C. Rule. il Travel 121:47-8 Ja '64
BADEN-POWELL, Sir Robert
Philately of Baden-Powell. H. D. Thorsen, jr. il pors Hobbies 69:99+ N '64
BADER, Jesse M.
Obituary
Christian Cent 80:1070 S 4 '63
BADER, Richard G. and Koczy, F. F.
Biogeochemistry. Science 142:74+ O 4 '63
BADGE of military merit. See Decorations of honor
BADGERS
Nature note. Sci N L 86:379 D 12 '64
BADO, Walter
Man named John; poem. America 109:160 Ag 17 '63
BADRINATH
Himalayan pilgrimage. R. Kulwant. il Travel 121:51-3 Ap '64
BAECK, Leo
He had a covenant to keep. C. Roth. il Sat R 48:31+ Ja 30 '65
BAEKELAND, G. Brooks
By parachute into Peru's lost world. il pors Nat Geog Mag 126:268-96 Ag '64
BAER, Harold and Bowser, R. T.
Antibody production and development of contact skin sensitivity in guinea pigs of various ages. bibliog Science 140:1211-12 Je 14 '63
—and Chaparas, S. D.
Tuberculin reactivity of a carbohydrate component of unheated BCG culture filtrate. bibliog Science 146:245-7 O 9 '64
BAER, Morley
Composition: a discussion with Morley Baer; ed. by L. Jacobs, jr. U S Camera 27:74-7 Jl '64
BAER, Werner, and Simonsen, M. H.
American capital and Brazilian nationalism. Yale R 53:192-8 D '63
BAERWALD, Hans H.
Factional politics in Japan. Cur Hist 46:223-9+ Ap '64
BAEUMLER, Hans Juergen
Girl of ice. por Newsweek 65:56 Ja 18 '65
BAEZ, Joan
Baez & Dylan: a generation singing out. R. Fariña. por Mlle 59:242+ Ag '64
Boy meets girl. G. Waldman. il por Seventeen 23:78+ Ja '64
To prison with love; student sit-in at University of California, Berkeley. il Time 84:60 D 11 '64
BAEZA, Braulio
Conquistadores. por Time 81:33 My 17 '63
Derby victory prance; Chateaugay. W. Tower. il por Sports Illus 18:24-9 My 13 '63
Silent success. Newsweek 61:76 Je 3 '63
BAGASSE
Putting waste to work. il Bsns W p 137-8 Mr 23 '63
BAGDAD copper corporation
Copper is big. il Fortune 69:117-21 Je '64
BAGDIKIAN, Ben H.
Assassin. Sat Eve Post 236:22-7 D 14 '63
Atomic bombs for everyone. Sat Eve Post 236:66-9 Mr 2 '63
Behold the grass-roots press, alas! Harper 229:102-5+ D '64
Big, bold plans of Lyndon the Lucky. Sat Eve Post 237:17-19 D 12 '64
Big brother is listening. Sat Eve Post 237:68-70 Je 6 '64
Bleed, but bleed inwardly. N Y Times Mag p 10+ Ag 9 '64
How strong is the hate vote? Sat Eve Post 237:19-21 O 17 '64
Invisible Americans. Sat Eve Post 236:28-33+ D 21 '63
Juggling that hot potato, the political gift. N Y Times Mag p 14-15+ Mr 22 '64
New light on Sacco and Vanzetti. New Repub 149:13-17 Jl 13 '63
News managers. Sat Eve Post 236:17-19 Ap 20 '63
Rumors: their birth, growth and death. N Y Times Mag p 14+ Je 14; 2 Jl 5 '64
Safari into Washington's netherworld. N Y Times Mag p 12+ Ja 19 '64
Showdown in Arkansas: Win Rockefeller vs. Orval Faubus. Sat Eve Post 237:75-7 S 19 '64
They want to be second. N Y Times Mag p30-3+ O 11 '64
Two party press? New Repub 151:11-12 O 10; 30 O 31 '64; Correction. 151:37 O 17 '64
Unsecretive report on the C.I.A. por N Y Times Mag p 18+ O 27 '63
—and Oberdorfer, Don
Bobby was the boy to see. Sat Eve Post 236:26-9 D 7 '63
about
Raising their voices. por Newsweek 64:48 D 21 '64
BAGELS. See Bread
BAGG, Elma W.
Without a grain of salt; excerpts. Todays Health 42:32-5+ My '64
BAGGAGE. See Luggage
BAGLEY, Wayne
North from the San Juans. il Yachting 115:69-71 Je '64
Northwest Passage. il Yachting 113:52-3 Je '63
BAGLEY, William Chandler
Bagley, Kandel, and the SAE. W. W. Brickman. Sch & Soc 92:258 O 3 '64
Essentialism and American education. W. W. Brickman. Sch & Soc 91:185 Ap 20 '63
BAGNARA, Joseph T. See Obika, M. jt. auth.
BAGNOLD, Enid
Lesson from a tigress; excerpts from The Chinese prime minister. Vogue 143:150-1+ Mr 1 '64
about
Chinese prime minister. Criticism
America 110:148 Ja 25 '64
Nation 198:80 Ja 20 '64
New Repub 150:28 F 1 '64
New Yorker 39:69 Ja 11 '64
Newsweek 63:70 Ja 13 '64
Sat R 47:22 Ja 18 '64
Time il 83:52 Ja 10 '64
Enid Bagnold, the articulate sprite. P. Gardner. Theatre Arts 48:17+ Ja '64
BAGPIPES
Bonny pipes of Scotland. D. MacDonald. il Read Digest 85:112-14 S '64
BAGRIT, Sir Leon
In automation, a British empire. il por Bsns W p82+ Jl 25 '64
BAGROVA, I. IU. See Gavrilov, N. F. jt. auth.
BAGS
Toteable notes. il Seventeen 23:135 D '64
What's the news around school? new look in school bags and loose-leaf binders. il Seventeen 22:150-1 S '63
See also
Handbags
Shopping bags
BAHAISM
Moroccan monarch meets the press; N.B.C.-TV. Christian Cent 80:484 Ap 17 '63
Nonagon; Baha'i charged with heresy. Nation 196:130 F 16 '63
We love all religions. il Time 81:69 Ap 26 '63
BAHAMA ISLANDS
Bahamas for fun and profit. R. Joseph. il Esquire 62:121+ O '64
Bonanza in the Bahamas. il Newsweek 64:88-9+ O 26 '64
Charter in the islands. il Motor B 112:41-4 S '63
Charting the Bahamas. H. Kline. il Yachting 114:58-60+ N '63
Little bit independent. il Time 83:19 Ja 24 '64
Navigation in the islands. E. A. Smith. il Motor B 112:32-3+ D '63
Small boat in the Bahamas. B. Robinson. il Yachting 114:41-4+ N '63
Trade wind world. D. DeFontaine. il Yachting 116:34-6+ N '64
See also
Andros Island
Architecture, Domestic—Bahama Islands
Birds—Bahama Islands
Fishing—Bahama Islands
Grand Bahama
Inagua
San Salvador Island

Climate

Winter weather in the palm belt. W. S. Kals. il Yachting 116:42-3+ N '64

Description and travel

Bahamas. H. Sutton. il McCalls 90:34+ My '63
Bahamas, golden Archipelago. B. Thielen. il Holiday 36:60-73+ D '64
Camera guide. L. Barry. il Pop Phot 52:76-7+ Mr '63
East to Abaco. L. A. Solomon. il Motor B 114:36-9+ S '64
Editor's report: lucky Lucayan; Beach hotel. M. M. Davis. il Travel 121:60 Ap '64

BAHAMA ISLANDS—Description and travel —*Continued*
Florida-Bahamas yachting; symposium. il Yachting 114:45-62+ N '63
Flying bridge view of the out islands. J. Hart. il Yachting 116:46-8+ N '64
Going places, finding things in the Bahamas and Jamaica. D. Beal. il House & Gard 127:38+ Ja '65
Out islands are in. B. Field. Vogue 141:132-4+ F 15 '63
Very private paradise; Lyford Cay. il Holiday 33:88-93 Mr '63
BAHAMA sloops. See Sloops
BAHAMAS flying treasure hunt. See Aviation—Competitions
BAHAMIAN cookery. See Cookery, Bahamian
BAHCALL, John N.
Observational neutrino astronomy. bibliog Science 147:115-20 Ja 8 '65
BAHIA (city) See Salvador, Brazil
BAHR, Leonard
Portraits of Leonard Bahr. L. L. Winslow. il por Am Artist 28:26-31+ D '64
BAHRENBURG, Bruce
New Jersey's search for identity. Harper 228: 87-90+ Ap '64
BAHUTU. See Rwanda—Native races
BAIL, Jay
Game hour; story. Esquire 61:94 Mr '64
BAIL
Bail-bond scandal. D. Oberdorfer. il Sat Eve Post 237:66-7 Je 20 '64
Best bet for bail: a good crook. J. Breslin. il Life 54:15+ Mr 29 '63
Fair bail for all; Manhattan bail project. W. M. Kunstler. Nation 197:52-3 Jl 27 '63
Great bail scandal. R. Goldfarb. New Repub 150:14-17 Je 6 '64; Discussion. 151:30 Jl 4; 30 Jl 11 '64
Must it be bail or jail? M. T. Bloom. Read Digest 84:189-92+ My '64
Race, creed, color or bankroll. Nation 198: 547 Je 1 '64
Something mother would like; first National conference on bail and criminal justice. il Time 83:67-8 Je 12 '64
BAILEY, Anthony
Effect of Barney Fuller; story. Sat Eve Post 237:66-7 My 9 '64
Our footloose correspondents. New Yorker 40:141-2+ O 31 '64
Would little Joan Littlewood were here! Esquire 61:113-15 Ja '64
BAILEY, Charles
When it's right to be wrong. Nations Bsns 52:98-9+ Je '64
BAILEY, Charles W.
LBJ: man in charge. Look 28:24-5 Mr 10 '64
—See Knebel, F. jt. auth.
BAILEY, Donald W.
Mosaic histocompatibility of skin grafts from female mice. bibliog Science 141:631-3 Ag 16 '63
BAILEY, Fred, Jr
Here's what new wheat grades mean. Suc Farm 62:35 My '64
How income averaging can cut your tax bill. Suc Farm 62:36 N '64
What IRS will look for if they audit your tax return. Suc Farm 62:39 Ja '64
BAILEY, Frederick Augustus Washington. See Douglass, F.
BAILEY, George
Again the autobahn. Reporter 29:16+ N 7 '63
Allied disunity and German politics. Reporter 31:14-16 D 31 '64
As they see it. Reporter 29:10+ D 19 '63
From Birmingham. Reporter 28:12+ My 23 '63
Gambit with pawns. Reporter 30:19-20 Ja 2 '64
Is Austria here to stay? Reporter 29:45-8 O 24 '63
Kafka's nightmare comes true. Reporter 30: 15-20 My 7 '64
My Oxford tutor, C. S. Lewis. Reporter 30: 37-8+ Ap 23 '64
Place to sleep in Romania. Reporter 31:33-4 N 5 '64
Religion in the Soviet Union. Reporter 31:25-9 Jl 16 '64
Trouble over Transylvania. Reporter 31:25-30 N 19 '64
Willy Brandt's third Germany. Reporter 30: 33-6 F 13 '64
BAILEY, Herbert S. Jr
Foundations and subsidies; address. Pub W 184:43-7 Jl 15 '63
BAILEY, Howald T.
Herbert's day. Opera N 28:6-7 Ja 25 '64
BAILEY, J. W.
How to beat the summer milk slump. Suc Farm 62:63 Jl '64
How to disinfect your buildings and truck. Suc Farm 61:141 Mr '63
How to help yourself to a bigger lamb crop. Suc Farm 62:74D Ap '64
How to protect lambs against overeating disease. Suc Farm 61:102 N '63
Newborn calves weak? here's what you can do. Suc Farm 61:68 Je '63
Now, get ready for cold weather. Suc Farm 61:85 Ag '63
Prevent feed-lot killers. Suc Farm 61:91 S '63
Tips for culling your dairy herd. Suc Farm 61:83 My '63
Veterinary helps (title varies) See issues of Successful farming
What you can do about cattle warts. Suc Farm 62:113 F '64
BAILEY, James A.
Doctor on wheels. il pors Ebony 19:83-4+ O '64
James Bailey, M.D. B. Dietz. il pors Look 28:29-35 D 15 '64
BAILEY, John A.
Non-profit mass transportation. Am City 78: 148+ S '63
BAILEY, John Moran
Bit of a split. por Time 81:23 My 3 '63
Cutting the cake. por Time 81:29 My 17 '63
Spoils and spoilers; investigation of John P. Kelly agency, Hartford, Conn. Newsweek 61:37 My 13 '63
BAILEY, Kenneth K.
Southern white Protestantism at the turn of the century. bibliog f Am Hist R 68:618-35 Ap '63
BAILEY, Lucille F.
Teaching through trial and error. Sr Schol 84:10T-11T Ap 17 '64
BAILEY, Mildred
Jazz records. W. Balliett. New Yorker 39:86-9 Ag 24 '63
Sad story of Mildred Bailey. R. De Toledano. Nat R 14:204-6 Mr 12 '63
BAILEY, Ralph
Fresh sense of the lovely past. House & Gard 126:176-81+ S '64
BAILEY, Richard W.
Making etched circuit boards. bibliog Electr World 69:38-9 Je '63
Silk-screen printing for panels. Electr World 70:73 Jl '63
BAILEY, Robeson
Lord love a duck. Outdoor Life 135:12+ Ja '65
Old-fashioned trout trip. pors Outdoor Life 133:36-9+ Je '64
BAILEY, Ronald
Flying Coopers are full of dad's spirit. Life 54:92+ My 17 '63
Moon race blots out a town. Life 57:21 S 25 '64
Mysteries Mariner might fathom. Life 58:44 Ja 29 '65
BAILEY, Roy
Paintings of Roy Bailey. W. Caxton, jr. il Am Artist 27:46-51+ F '63
BAILEY, Stephen K.
Education is a political enterprise. por NEA J 53:13 N '64
BAILEY, Zena
Big four speak. por Library J 88:2070-1+ My 15 '63
BAILY, Francis, 1774-1844
Not observed or existing. J. Ashbrook. il por Sky & Tel 26:80-1 Ag '63
BAIN, Barbara, and Lowenstein, Louis
Genetic studies on the mixed leukocyte reaction. bibliog Science 145:1315-16 S 18 '64
BAIN, Ellyne
Model-A-ing we will go. Hot Rod 16:95 Je '63
BAIN, Myrna
Organized labor and the Negro worker. Nat R 14:455 Je 4 '63
Wind at their backs. Nat R 15:243 S 24 '63
BAIN, Wilfred C.
Singing at Indiana. il por Time 83:56+ Mr 27 '64
Wilfred Bain. D. Thorpe. por Mus Am 84:18-19 Ap '64
BAINBRIDGE, John
Letter from Finland. New Yorker 40:141-2+ O 3 '64
Our footloose correspondents. New Yorker 39: 105-6+ N 9 '63
BAINS, Martha
Art & blind children. il Sch Arts 63:3-9 Ja '64
BAIR, William J.
Inhaled radioactive particles and gases. Science 146:440+ O 16 '64
BAIRD, A. K. and others
Chemical variations in a granitic pluton and its surrounding rocks. bibliog Science 146: 258-9 O 9 '64

BAIRD, R. E.
Single sideband simplified. Electr World 69: 52-4+ F '63
Technical institute. Electr World 71:79-81 Mr '64
BAIRD, Spencer Fullerton
For the increase and diffusion of knowledge among men. Hobbies 68:123 N '63
BAIT
Choosing bait and spinning lines. W. Davis. il Outdoor Life 133:84+ Ap '64
Live baits or artificials? W. Davis. il Outdoor Life 134:120-2 O '64
Pretty kettle of dyed baitfish; largemouth bass see red better than other colors. R. H. Boyle. Sports Illus 21:81+ O 5 '64
Tying salmon-roe baits. R. L. Curtis. il Outdoor Life 133:124 My '64
See also
Earthworms
Fishing lures, flies, etc.
Minnows
BAIZERMAN, Saul
Art; exhibition of sculpture by the late S. Baizerman. H. Kramer. Nation 196:127-8 F 9 '63
BAJ, Enrico
Brass in brocade; exhibition at Cordier & Ekstrom gallery. il Time 81:66 F 22 '63
BAJA CALIFORNIA. See California, Lower
BAJOUR; musical comedy. See Musical comedies, revues, etc.—Criticisms, plots, etc.
BAJUSZ, Eörs
Red skeletal muscle fibers: relative independence of neural control. bibliog Science 145: 938-9 Ag 28 '64
BAKAL, Carl
Mathematics of hunger. Sat R 46:16-19 Ap 27 '63
Traffic in guns: a forgotten lesson of the assassination. Harper 229:62-8 D '64
(ed) What can we do to keep peace on earth? Redbook 124:46-7+ Ja '65
BAKALAR, David
One for the books; Transitron stockholders' suit. il por Fortune 67:191-2+ Mr '63
BAKALAR, Leo
One for the books; Transitron stockholders' suit. il por Fortune 67:191-2+ Mr '63
BAKED beans. See Cookery—Vegetables
BAKER, Augusta
Pioneer in the war on poverty: NYPL. pors Library J 89:3376-9 S 15 '64
BAKER, Burton L. See Clark, R. H. jt. auth.
BAKER, C. H.
Signal duration as a factor in vigilance tasks. Science 141:1196-7 S 20 '63
BAKER, Carroll
Baby doll grows up. R. W. Lewis. il pors Sat Eve Post 236:62-5 N 2 '63
Carroll cavorts in Kenya. il pors Life 57:76-8 Jl 17 '64
Housewife in houriland. pors Time 84:74 S 18 '64
BAKER, Chet
Back from the dark side. por Time 83:110+ Ap 17 '64
BAKER, Donald W.
Formal application; poem. Sat R 46:23 My 11 '63
Room within; Mourner; poems. Poetry 104: 26-7 Ap '64
Walkers; poem. Nation 197:328 N 16 '63
BAKER, Dorothy
No visitors till noon; story. Sat Eve Post 236:46-53 Mr 9 '63
BAKER, Edward G.
Now: a court ruling in defense of the neighborhood school. por U S News 55:43 S 23 '63
BAKER, Elizabeth G.
Late Lachaise, uncensored at last. Art N 63:44-5+ Mr '64
BAKER, Elliott
What we were fighting for; story. Sat Eve Post 237:58-60 S 19 '64
BAKER, George Pierce
Tailoring the B-school to new business world. il pors Bsns W p72-4+ Ja 19 '63
BAKER, Gretta
Health quiz. Farm J 88:60J Mr '64
Your health (cont) Redbook 121:28 Ag '63; 122:26 Ja '64
BAKER, H. G.
Evolutionary mechanisms in pollination biology. bibliog Science 139:877-83 Mr 8 '63
BAKER, John C.
Stock options at the crossroads. Harvard Bsns R 41:22-4+ Ja '63
BAKER, Josephine
La Bakhair returns. por Newsweek 63:90 F 17 '64
Jo Baker's fabulous wardrobe. il pors Ebony 19:104-6+ Jl '64
Joséphine Baker chez elle. J. Egan. il por Atlan 214:130+ D '64

BAKER, Kenneth F. See Weinhold, A. R. jt. auth.
BAKER, Kenneth W.
Faith and science; address, February 5, 1963. Vital Speeches 29:437-9 My 1 '63
BAKER, Leonard
Right to work: a hard one for LBJ. Reporter 32:23-5 Ja 14 '65
BAKER, Lucinda
Rivals; story. Redbook 122:56-7 N '63
BAKER, Ora Phelps
Artist of the month. Sch Arts 63:37-8 Ja '64
BAKER, Paul
Baker v. Baylor. Time 81:42 Mr 22 '63
—and Mazess, R. B.
Calcium: unusual sources in the highland Peruvian diet. bibliog Science 142:1466-7 D 13 '63
BAKER, Peter B.
Mismanaged job in packaging. Duns R 82: pt2 169-70 N '63
BAKER, R. S.
From ed. to education. Commentary 37:85-7 Mr; 38:15 Jl '64
People get hooked. Commentary 35:243-6; 36: 171 Mr, Ag '63
BAKER, Robert Gene
L'affaire Baker. K. Crawford. Newsweek 62: 35 N 4 '63
Baker affair. por Newsweek 62:30 O 14 '63
Baker case: news that will not stay managed? il por U S News 56:43-5 F 24 '64
Bobby Baker again. il Newsweek 64:22 S 14 '64
Bobby Baker blossoms. M. Kempton. New Repub 151:7-8 Jl 4 '64
Bobby Baker case. W. V. Shannon. Commonweal 79:561-2 F 7 '64
Bobby Baker revisited; role of Senate rules committee. M. Kempton. New Repub 149: 6-7 N 16 '63
Bobby was the boy to see. B. H. Bagdikian and D. Oberdorfer. il pors Sat Eve Post 236:26-9 D 7 '63
Bobby's long green carpet; breakdown of Bobby's loans. Time 83:26-7 Mr 13 '64
Candidate Baker? il por Newsweek 63:37 Mr 16 '64
Conflict-of-interest ghost walks again. Bsns W p29 O 26 '63
Congress is not on trial, Baker is. J. N. Eller. America 109:697 N 30 '63
Deal. B. Bradlee. il por Newsweek 64:36+ N 16 '64
End of Bobby Baker? Commonweal 80:497 Jl 24 '64
Fast rise of Bobby Baker; with excerpts from testimony before Senate rules committee by D. B. Reynolds, and statement by L. B. Johnson. il por U S News 56:55-9 F 3 '64
Fast talker from Pickens. por Time 82:29-30 O 18 '63
From Washington straight. Cato. Nat R 15: 342, 432 O 22, N 19 '63
He thought big. Nation 197:338 N 23 '63
Heart of the matter. Nation 198:131 F 10 '64
How Baker turned access into an asset. Bsns W p30-1 F 8 '64
How Bobby Baker made some more money; summary of testimony. T. D. Webb, jr; F. E. Law. U S News 56:8 F 17 '64
Influence and loans: latest on Bobby Baker; when LBJ stepped in. U S News 56:8 Mr 16 '64
It's magic; Bobby Baker's financial affairs. il Newsweek 62:31 N 25 '63
Mess in Washington? with interview with J. J. Williams. il por U S News 55:36-8+ N 25 '63
New light on Bobby Baker's activities. il por U S News 56:6 Mr 2 '64
New twists in Baker's trail. Bsns W p25 N 16 '63
One, four, five, six and out. il por Newsweek 63:18 Mr 2 '64
People of the week. U S News 55:18 N 25 '63
Scandal grows and grows in Washington. K. Wheeler and others. il pors Life 55:40-40B+ N 22 '63
Secretary for the Senate majority: the job, and its power. il por U S News 56:43 F 10 '64
Senate looks at its own housekeeping. il por U S News 55:71 N 4 '63
Serv-U man. por Newsweek 62:39 O 7 '63
Still unanswered in the Baker case. por U S News 56:40 Mr 30 '64
That high-living Baker boy scandalizes the capital. il pors Life 55:32-7 N 8 '63
Unanswered questions of the Bobby Baker case. il por U S News 56:42-3 Mr 9 '64
Vender. M. Kempton. New Repub 149:17-20 O 19 '63
See also
Government investigations—Baker case

BAKER, Russell
Capsule history of the vice presidency. Holiday 36:48-9 S '64
Cultural explosion in Washington. Theatre Arts 47:14-15+ Ap '63
Fourteen clues to Washington news. N Y Times Mag p31+ Ap 7 '63
Is this crisis really worthwhile? Read Digest 84:134-5 My '64
Master of the art of the possible. N Y Times Mag p26+ D 1 '63
Now they dance the nomination minuet. N Y Times Mag p 10-11+ Jl 21 '63
Opinion, please, from Washington. Mlle 58: 38+ Mr '64
Speaking out. por Sat Eve Post 237:10+ O 31 '64
BAKER, Samm Sinclair
Good ideas all over the lot. Pop Sci 182:105 Je '63
Inside story for winter gardeners. Pop Sci 184:107 Ja '64
Panel of American women. Ladies Home J 82:33-5+ Ja '65
Stretch your mental muscles; excerpt from Your key to creative thinking. Read Digest 84:35-6+ My '64
BAKER, William A.
Aviza, a 1725 shallop. il Yachting 113:190-2 My '63
BAKER, William O.
Improvements in control systems cited. M. L. Yaffee. Aviation W 81:69+ D 14 '64
BAKERS and bakeries
See also
Kitchens of Sara Lee, incorporated
National biscuit company
Pepperidge farm, incorporated

Wages and hours

Four days on, four off; Bridgford packing co. Bsns W p 120 F 23 '63
BAKER'S dozen; musical comedy. See Musical comedies, revues, etc.—Criticisms, plots, etc.
BAKHLE, Y. S. and others
Precaution in the use of iodine-125 as a radioactive tracer. Science 143:799-800 F 21 '64
BAKING
Bake-sale best sellers. J. Figg. il Suc Farm 61:72-3+ O '63
Baking equipment and procedures. il House & Gard 126:184-6 D '64
Baking techniques and tips. il House & Gard 127:146-7 Ja '65
For some new baking flavors. il Sunset 130: 226+ Ap '63
Out of the oven. il Redbook 120:74-5+ F '63
Relax, dinner's in the oven! P. McBride. il Bet Hom & Gard 41:80 F '63
Some Christmas baking secrets from Scandinavia. il Sunset 133:132+ D '64
See also
Bread
Cake
Food mixes
Pastry
Pie
BAKING contests. See Cookery—Competitions
BAKING utensils. See Kitchen utensils
BAKKE, Jacque, and others
Hidden faces. Design 65:164-5+ Mr '64
BAKKER, Joop
Ecumenism in Morocco. W. Dunphy. America 111:694 N 28 '64
BAL, Arya K. and Gross, P. R.
Asynchronous synthesis of RNA in nucleoli of root meristem. bibliog Science 143:808-10 F 21 '64
Mitosis and differentiation in roots treated with actinomycin. bibliog Science 139:584-6 F 15 '63
BALABAN, Victor, and French, H. F.
Preventing college crack-ups. Parents Mag 38:64+ F '63
BALAIR. See Airlines—Switzerland
BALANCE of nature
Grow little blowfly. Newsweek 62:80 S 9 '63
BALANCE of payments
Administration moves on the payments gap. Bsns W p25 Jl 20 '63
After the dollar wins. Bsns W p 116+ N 23 '63
Ambassadors asked to report on activities in promoting exports; letter, August 2, 1963. D. Rusk. Dept State Bul 49:290 Ag 19 '63
Another way to stop capital flows. Bsns W p 100 Ag 31 '63
Argument heats up on the payments gap; financial men criticize administration policy. il Bsns W p67-8 Je 8 '63
Balance of payments. New Repub 149:4-5 Ag 3; 4-6 Ag 17; 4-6 Ag 31 '63
Balance-of-payments bind. G. Burck. il Fortune 67:112-17 Je '63
Balance of payments. H. Hazlitt. Newsweek 62:90 S 23 '63
Balance of payments; special message to Congress, July 18, 1963. J. F. Kennedy. Dept State Bul 49:250-9 Ag 12 '63
Balance of payments: the real trouble. Newsweek 62:63 S 2 '63
Balance of payments: the worry of the West. il Newsweek 62:71+ Jl 22 '63
Balance of payments, trade expansion, development assistance; excerpts from economic report. L. B. Johnson. Dept State Bul 50: 222-3 F 10 '64
Balancing act. il Fortune 68:54+ D '63
Big comeback for the dollar; with editorial comment. Bsns W p98+, 148 Ap 25 '64
Bigger role for IMF. Bsns W p30 S 21 '63
Boom raises three challenges. M. Nadler. il Nations Bsns 52:31-3 My '64
Continued gold drain. Time 82:24-5 S 13 '63
Critical look at U.S. from Europe. il U S News 55:43 Ag 19 '63
Cure for our payments pain. Bsns W p 168 My 25 '63
Cutting the losses. il Time 83:89 Ap 3 '64
Dollar and the international monetary system. J. W. Angell; reply with rejoinder. E. N. Adams. Science 140:1141-2+ Je 7 '63
Dollar problem. A. O. Stanley. Duns R 81:68+ Ap '63
Easier world credit; concerning Brookings institution report. il Bsns W p 17-18 Ag 3 '63
East-West trade; statement, March 13, 1964. D. Rusk. il Dept State Bul 50:474-84 Mr 30 '64
Economic report of the President; excerpts. J. F. Kennedy. Dept State Bul 48:228-9 F 11 '63
Europe warily eyes the dollar. Bsns W p32+ Ag 17 '63
European interest rates; address, May 21, 1964. C. D. Dillon. Vital Speeches 30:585-8 Jl 15 '64
Europe's competitive threat will ease; U.S. businessmen will get break from shift in balance of payments. C. A. Cerami. il Nations Bsns 51:34-5+ Mr '63
Export economies between East and West. J. Levin. Yale R 52:373-84 Mr '63
Export expansion and balance of payments; remarks, April 7, 1964. L. B. Johnson. Dept State Bul 50:663-4 Ap 27 '64
Exporting inflation. H. Hazlitt. Newsweek 62:78 S 9 '63
Fiscal responsibility; address, September 30, 1963. J. F. Kennedy. Vital Speeches 30:13-14 O 15 '63
For world bankers caution is the word; plan to strengthen payment system. il Bsns W p24-5 Ag 15 '64
Foreign scapegoats; report by congressional Joint economic committee. H. Hazlitt. Newsweek 63:80 Ap 13 '64
Four for our side; four for your side. il Newsweek 61:77 Mr 25 '63
Good as gold. Newsweek 62:59-60 Jl 29 '63
How real is the drain on dollars? il Bsns W p43-4+ S 5 '64
How to solve the payments imbalance. il Newsweek 62:51 Ag 5 '63
Impact of international travel on U.S. balance of payments; statement, November 30, 1964. C. H. Mace. il Dept State Bul 51: 888-90 D 21 '64
Increasing US exports. New Repub 148:5 Mr 9 '63
Inflation is the cause. H. Hazlitt. Newsweek 62:71 Ag 12 '63
International markets; export picture still dismal. A. O. Stanley. Duns R 81:95 My '63
Investment no, aid yes? concerning views of Secretary Dillon. H. Hazlitt. Newsweek 63:84 F 17 '64
Is the gap closing fast enough? il Bsns W p32-3 Ja 2 '65
Japan: search for a better balance. il Bsns W p69 F 22 '64
Japan tries for a second miracle. P. F. Drucker. Harper 226:72-8 Mr '63
Joint Canadian-United States statement on proposed interest equalization tax, July 21, 1963. Dept State Bul 49:256 Ag 12 '63
Keeping U.S. dollars at home; President's proposed interest equalization tax. il Bsns W p 19-22 Jl 27 '63
Labor faces its first major money crisis. il Bsns W p29-30 N 28 '64
Let the dollar drift? concerning the Brookings institution report. H. Hazlitt. Newsweek 62:64 Ag 26 '63
Looking for scapegoats. H. Hazlitt. Newsweek 63:69 Ja 13 '64

BALANCE of payments—*Continued*
Misery with the dollar or happiness? Life 55:4 Ag 2 '63
Monetary fund has its own ideas; increasing world credit. Bsns W p28 S 14 '63
Money: balancing international payments. H. Malmgren. New Repub 150:13-14 Je 20 '64
Money flows and balance-of-payments adjustment; address, October 8, 1964. R. V. Roosa. Dept State Bul 51:669-73 N 9 '64
More credit for world trade; study of international monetary machinery. il Bsns W p25-7 O 5 '63
New monetary boss will pioneer, cautiously; Under Secy. of the Treasury for monetary affairs. Bsns W p25 Ja 9 '65
New strength for dollar. Bsns W p36 Ap 11 '64
Next threat: world money squeeze. il Bsns W p64+ Jl 27 '63
No help to the dollar. H. Hazlitt. Newsweek 62:62 Ag 5 '63
No. 1 dollar defender; Treasury's interest equalization tax. Bsns W p90+ Ag 3 '63
Our international financial position; address, January 21, 1963. M. M. Kimbrel. Vital Speeches 29:303-5 Mr 1 '63
Payments deficit stirs international rift. L. L. Doty. Aviation W 79:36-7 N 25 '63
Payments stalemate. il Fortune 70:32+ N '64
President moves to facilitate use of foreign currencies. Dept State Bul 49:204 Ag 5 '63
President outlines position on balance of payments and trade; statements, October 24 and October 28, 1964. L. B. Johnson. Dept State Bul 51:751-2 N 23 '64
Protecting the dollar with francs and marks; Treasury taps IMF. Bsns W p26 F 22 '64
Push overseas keeps going strong; McGraw-Hill survey. il Bsns W p27-8 S 7 '63
Rebalancing our balance of payments. Sr Schol 85:21 S 30 '64
Saving gold, easier said than done. Nations Bsns 52:34-5+ Mr '64
Sproul urges deficit attack. Bsns W p74 Je 29 '63
Strategy for defending the dollar. Bsns W p 164 Ap 13 '63
Strengthening the international monetary system; remarks and statements, September 30-October 4, 1963. J. F. Kennedy; C. D. Dillon; G. W. Ball. Dept State Bul 49:610-23 O 21 '63
Tax device to stem the outflow of gold; letter. G. A. Freeman, jr. Fortune 68:94 S '63
Timid tinkering; criticism of the President. N. A. Rockefeller. Newsweek 62:24 S 9 '63
To defend the dollar. H. Hazlitt. Newsweek 61:84 My 20 '63
Trade surplus. il Fortune 69:28+ My '64
Two more plans for aid to dollar; Brookings institution and American bankers association. U S News 55:103 Ag 5 '63
United States as a world trader and banker, by H. B. Lary. Review
 Bsns W p 156+ Mr 9 '63
U.S. balance of payments; address, December 30, 1963. R. M. McKinney. Vital Speeches 30:216-20 Ja 15 '64
U.S. balance of payments problem; address, July 8, 1963. T. B. Curtis. Vital Speeches 29:657-62 Ag 15 '63
U.S. improves balance-of-payments position; increases gold holdings; statement; with report by Secretary Dillon. L. B. Johnson. Dept State Bul 51:752-3 N 23 '64
U.S. payments policy: opinions of European central bankers. M. A. Heilperin. Fortune 68:81-2 O '63
Western Europe and the American balance of payments; address, April 6, 1963. G. G. Johnson. Ann Am Acad 348:110-20 Jl '63
What drags the balance down. il Bsns W p55-8+ Jl 27 '63
What's behind the balance-of-payments problem. E. G. Collado. il Sat R 47:34+ Ja 11 '64
When dollars begin to stay home. Bsns W p24 Ag 8 '64
White House holds conference on export expansion; address, September 17, 1963. D. Rusk. Dept State Bul 49:599-601 O 14 '63
Why we are losing gold. B. L. Masse. America 109:340 S 28 '63
Wrong way to protect the dollar. Bsns W p 104 Jl 27 '63
Yankee dollar. M. Mayer. Sat Eve Post 237:28-30 Ja 18 '64

BALANCE of power
After twenty-five years; can the two superpowers keep control? il Newsweek 64:31 S 14 '64
Balance of world power at the start of a new year. il U S News 58:32-3 Ja 4 '65
India and the Soviet Union. S. Gupta. bibliog f Cur Hist 44:141-6 Mr '63
Little England. J. Mander. Commentary 35:139-45 F '63
Marriage of inconvenience. L. Gelber. For Affairs 41:310-22 Ja '63
Scientific revolution: the end of history; adaptation of address, 1963. E. Rabinowitch. Bul Atomic Sci 19:9-12 N '63
Shifts in Soviet strategic thought. T. W. Wolfe. bibliog f For Affairs 42:475-86 Ap '64
Two worlds. S. Chase. Bul Atomic Sci 19:18-20 Je '63
 See also
World politics

BALANCE of trade. See Balance of payments

BALANCE sheets. See Financial statements

BALANCED diet. See Diet

BALANCHINE, George
Balanchine a biography; excerpts. B. Taper. il pors Dance Mag 38:18-21+ F; 14-16+ Mr; 20-1+ Ap; 14-17+ My; 18-19+ Je '64
Balanchine, by B. Taper. Review
 Commonweal 79:552-5 Ja 31 '64. D. McDonagh
 Reporter 30:42-4 Ja 2 '64. M. Schorer
Balanchine: demigod of the dance. il pors Newsweek 63:51-2+ My 4 '64
Balanchine's return to Russia; excerpts from Balanchine. B. Taper. por Harper 227:47-50+ N '63
Ballet in America: one-man show? R. Krokover and H. C. Schonberg. il Harper 229:92-6 S '64; Discussion. 229:13 N '64
Dance. C. Barnes. Nation 196:427-8 My 18 '63
Dance; New York city ballet. R. Krokover. Mus Am 84:54-5 Ja '64
Ford in its future; grants to New York city ballet and the School of American ballet. Time 82:37 D 27 '63
Ford's miracle; grant to strengthen professional ballet in the U.S. Newsweek 62:51 D 23 '63
GB and BG. Newsweek 63:65 My 11 '64
Genius of Balanchine; excerpts from Balanchine. B. Taper. il pors Theatre Arts 47:10-13+ N '63
Great choreographer is sixty. A. Hughes. il por N Y Times Mag p44 Ja 12 '64
Jewel in its proper setting. il pors Time 83:58-63 My 1 '64
Never mind the ginza; Bugaku. il Time 81:38 Mr 29 '63

BALANDIS, Leo S.
Sceptron; a sound-operated fiber-optic brain cell. por Electr World 69:36-7+ Mr '63

BALASSA, Joseph J. See Schroeder, H. A. jt. auth.

BALASURIYA, S. Tissa
Communism in Asia. Commonweal 81:535-8 Ja 22 '65
Ecumenical approach to religions of Asia. Cath World 200:239-45 Ja '65

BALBOA, Vasco Núñez de
From a peak in Darién; Balboa's discovery 450 years ago. E. B. Roberts. il pors Américas 15:40-3 S '63

BALCOMB, Elaine
Judgment of Solomon. Christian Cent 82:106-10 Ja 27 '65

BALCONIES
Balconies organized as facade pattern; Sunset Heights apartments, Los Angeles. il Arch Rec 136:114-15 Ag '64
Balcony buncombe. E. Goble. Arch Rec 133:9 Mr '63
Catwalks for windows high above ground. il Sunset 130:136 Mr '63
Ode to the great 5'x9' outdoors; terrace in New York. S. Blum. il N Y Times Mag p21+ Ap 26 '64

BALD eagles. See Eagles

BALD soprano; drama. See Ionesco, E.

BALDERSTON, Frederick Emery
Policeman who pounds California's S&L beat. il por Bsns W p40-1 Jl 4 '64

BALDET, Fernand
First lady of French astronomy. Sky & Tel 25:77 F '63

BALDEV, B. and others
Gibberellin production in pea seeds developing in excised pods: effect of growth retardant AMO-1618. bibliog Science 147:155-7 Ja 8 '65

BALDNESS
Baldness, now women, too. il Changing T 17:31-2 Ag '63
Man's oldest fallout problem: baldness. W. R. Vath. il Todays Health 41:46-50 Ag '63; Same abr. with title What men and women should know about baldness. Sci Digest 55:20-5 Mr '64
Worry brought me to the edge of breakdown. il Good H 156:10+ My '63

BALDONI, Evelyn D.
Providence takes a hand. Recreation 56:364-5 O '63

BALDWIN, A. B.
Make data processing work for you. por Am City 79:105-6 F '64

BALDWIN, Faith
Lonely man; story. Redbook 123:127 Je '64
Sleight of hand; story. Good H 157:92-3 O '63

BALDWIN, Hanson Weightman
Battle that turned the Nazi tide. N Y Times Mag p23-5+ Ap 14 '63
Fighting ship still sails the sea. N Y Times Mag p 14-15+ Ja 26 '64
Growing risks of bureaucratic intelligence. Reporter 29:48-50+ Ag 15 '63
Managed news; our peacetime censorship. Atlan 211:53-9 Ap '63; Same abr. Read Digest 82:109-14 Je '63
Navy at ebb tide. Reporter 30:35-8 Ja 30 '64
New navy; condensation. Pop Sci 185:65-7+ S '64
Red flag over the seven seas. Atlan 214:37-43 S '64
Should we end the draft? N Y Times Mag p20-1+ S 27 '64
Slow-down in the Pentagon. For Affairs 43: 262-80 Ja '65
Soviet submarine threat. Reporter 31:39-42 S 24 '64
Speaking out. por Sat Eve Post 236:8+ Mr 9 '63
Taking stock of Europe's nuclear defenses. Reporter 28:29-34 Ap 25 '63
Their world ending, but few knew it. N Y Times Mag p7-9+ Jl 26 '64
Twenty-five years ago: Hitler strikes. N Y Times Mag p 11-13+ Ag 30 '64
What three newsmen report about Kennedy news tactics; reprint. U S News 54:42 Ap 15 '63

BALDWIN, James
At the root of the Negro problem... por Time 81:26-7 My 17 '63
Creative dilemma. Sat R 47:14-15+ F 8 '64
Disturber of the peace; interview. ed. by E. Auchincloss and N. Lynch. por Mlle 57: 174-5+ My '63
Letters from a journey; excerpts from Soon one morning; ed. by H. Hill. Harper 226:48-50+ My '63
Liberalism and the Negro. Commentary 37: 25-42 Mr '64
Talk to teachers; address. Sat R 46:42-4+ D 21 '63
There's a bill due that has to be paid. pors Life 54:81-4+ My 24 '63

about

Baldwin: gray flannel Muslim? Christian Cent 80:791 Je 12 '63; Discussion. 80:1057 Ag 28 '63
Black man in America. J. Ciardi. Sat R 46: 13 Jl 6 '63
Blues for Mister Charlie. Criticism
America 110:776-7 My 30 '64
Cath World 199:263-4 Jl '64
Commonweal 80:299-300 My 29 '64
Ebony il por 19:188+ Je '64
Nat R 16:780-1 S 8 '64
Nation 198:495-6 My 11 '64
New Repub 150:35-7 My 16 '64
New Yorker 40:143 My 9 '64
Newsweek il por 63:46 My 4 '64
Sat R 47:27-8 My 2 '64
Sat R 47:36 My 9 '64
Time 83:50 My 1 '64
Time il por 83:96 Je 5 '64
Vogue 144:32 Jl '64
Call to color blindness. W. F. Buckley, jr. Nat R 14:488 Je 18 '63; Reply. M. Whalen. 15:120 Ag 13 '63
Choose something like a star. J. Ciardi. Sat R 47:16 Ja 11 '64
Doom and glory of knowing who you are. J. Howard. il pors Life 54:86B+ My 24 '63
Everybody knows his name. M. Elkoff. il pors Esquire 62:59-64+ Ag '64
I know about the Negroes and the poor. R. J. Dwyer. por Nat R 15:517-18+ D 17 '63
James Baldwin, an original. G. Steinem. il por Vogue 144:78-9+ Jl '64
James Baldwin's search. R. A. Schroth. por Cath World 198:288-94 F '64
James Baldwin's vision. J. Finn. Commonweal 78:447-9 Jl 26 '63; Reply with rejoinder. J. McCudden. 79:75-7 O 11 '63
Kennedy and Baldwin: the gulf. por Newsweek 61:19 Je 3 '63
What color is God? G. Wills. il por Nat R 14:408-14+ My 21 '63; Discussion. 14:507; 15:31+ Je 18, Jl 16 '63

BALDWIN, Marcia
Siebel's flowers; interview. ed. by R. D. Daniels. por Opera N 28:31 Ja 4 '64

BALDWIN, P. C.
Old mill stream; address. January 30, 1963. por Am For 69:28-30+ Ap '63

BALDWIN, Ralph
Plotting revenge for Hoot Mon; to win the Hambletonian. K. Rudeen. il por Sports Illus 18:80 My 20 '63

BALDWIN, Richard D.
Impediments to the acquisition and use of medical knowledge; letter. Science 141: 1237-8 S 27 '63

BALDWIN, Robert H.
Advances in financial management. bibliog f Harvard Bsns R 42:34-5+ Ja '64

BALDWIN, Roger
Common ground for diversity. Sat R 47:43-4 My 16 '64
General Douglas MacArthur. Nation 198:385 Ap 20 '64

about

Roger Baldwin. W. Morris. New Repub 150: 8-10 Ja 25 '64

BALDWIN, William
Who's afraid of Elsie De Wolfe? C. Amory. il por Vogue 141:116-23+ Je '63

BALDWIN HILLS DAM. See Dams—Failures

BÂLE, Switzerland. See Basel, Switzerland

BALEWA, Sir Abubakar Tafawa
African conference; African unity; address, May 24, 1963. Vital Speeches 29:620-2 Ag 1 '63

BALGOOYEN, Henry W.
Alliance for progress; address, December 12, 1962. Vital Speeches 29:325-32 Mr 15 '63

BALI
Bali: Eden's last stand. D. Dodge. il Holiday 34:24+ D '63
Disaster in paradise. W. P. Booth and S. N. Matthews. il Nat Geog Mag 124:436-58 S '63

See also

Tourist trade—Bali

BALIN, Robert P.
Amplifier quiz. Pop Electr 20:63+ F; 64+ Mr '64
Co-inventors quiz. Electr World 73:90 Ja '65
Electromagnetic function quiz. Pop Electr 20:65+ Je '64
Electronic inventors quiz. Pop Electr 19:67+ N '63
Greek alphabet quiz. Pop Electr 19:73+ D '63
Transformer winding quiz. Pop Electr 21:65+ D '64

BALISH, Jacquelyn
Case of the elegant eye. Mod Phot 27:66-71+ Mr '63
Well traveled camera. Mod Phot 27:52+ My '63

BALK, Alfred
How your right to vote was won. Todays Health 42:52-4 F '64
Last dinosaur wins again. Sat Eve Post 236: 72-3 My 11 '63
Malady that motion can cause. Todays Health 41:28-30 Jl '63
Neglected people in today's nursing home. McCalls 91:84-7 S '64; Same abr. with title Shame of our nursing homes. Read Digest 86:161-2+ Ja '65
Voting: how you can get people to the polls. Todays Health 42:52-5 Mr '64
What happens to your ballot on Election day? Todays Health 42:32-5+ N '64
What newlyweds should know about in-laws. bibliog Todays Health 42:56-7+ Ap '64
When the wind blew black blizzards. N Y Times Mag p98-101 N 10 '63
Why don't more Americans vote? Todays Health 42:28-30+ Ja '64
(ed) See Simon, P. Illinois legislature: study in corruption

BALKAN STATES

Description and travel

Balkans in brief. H. Sutton. il Sat R 46:42-5 Je 8; 48-50 Je 15; 18-20 Jl 6; 18-19+ Jl 13; 35-6 Jl 20; 31-3 Ag 3; 36+ Ag 10; 24-6 Ag 17 '63

BALKE, Betty T.
Envy; poem. Christian Cent 81:480 Ap 15 '64

BALL, Charles E.
Here's the story of the best round-up in Texas. il por Farm J 87:36J Ag '63

BALL, Edward
Back of the dynamite. Nation 198:254 Mr 16 '64
Blowup. il por Newsweek 63:67-8 F 24 '64
Florida's railroad war; a few sticks of dynamite. R. G. Sherrill. il Nation 198:227-30 Mr 9 '64
One way to run a railroad and meet work-rule problems. il por U S News 55:67-9 S 2 '63

BALL, F. Carlton
F. Carlton Ball, a California potter. J. Lovoos. il por Am Artist 28:50-5+ Je '64
BALL, George Wildman
Appeal to discontent; address, October 15, 1964. Dept State Bul 51:622-8 N 2 '64
Common problems of industrial and developing countries; statement, March 25, 1964. Dept State Bul 50:634-40 Ap 20 '64
Department opposes restriction of credit to Communist nations; statement, November 21, 1963. Dept State Bul 49:935-6 D 16 '63
Department supports bill to establish National academy of foreign affairs; statement, April 4, 1963. Dept State Bul 48:619-23 Ap 22 '63
Germany and the Atlantic partnership; address, November 15, 1964. Dept State Bul 51:773-4 N 30 '64
Implications for U.S. of breakdown in U.K.-EEC negotiations; text of letter to Senator Paul H. Douglas, February 15, 1963. Dept State Bul 48:412-15 Mr 18 '63
Interdependence, the basis of U.S.-Canada relations; address, April 25, 1964. bibliog f Dept State Bul 50:770-4 My 18 '64
Jean Monnet honored as Mr Europe. Dept State Bul 48:195-7 F 11 '63
NATO and world responsibilities; address, May 7, 1964. Dept State Bul 50:823-8 My 25 '64
Nuclear deterrent and the Atlantic alliance; address, April 26, 1963. Dept State Bul 48: 736-9 My 13 '63
Open system in North-South relations, April 9, 1964. Dept State Bul 50:657-62 Ap 27 '64
Principles of our policy toward Cuba; address, April 23, 1964. Dept State Bul 50:738-44 My 11 '64
Profitable growth and our world position; address, January 9, 1964. Dept State Bul 50:123-8 Ja 27 '64
Reallocation of world responsibilities; address, January 31, 1964. Dept State Bul 50:287-93 F 24 '64; Same. Vital Speeches 30:293-6 Mr 1 '64
Responsibilities of a global power; address, September 18, 1964. Dept State Bul 51:473-8 O 5 '64
Some current issues in U.S. foreign policy; remarks, April 19, 1963; with questions and answers. Dept State Bul 48:688-92 My 6 '63
Strengthening the international monetary system; statement, October 2, 1963. Dept State Bul 49:619-23 O 21 '63
Under Secretary Ball comments on Cyprus situation; television interview, August 9, 1964. Dept State Bul 51:301-2 Ag 31 '64
Under Secretary Ball departs for meetings at London and Paris; statement, November 27, 1964. Dept State Bul 51:847-8 D 14 '64
Under Secretary Ball interviewed on Issues and answers; transcript of interview, February 10, 1963. Dept State Bul 48:369-75 Mr 11 '63
United Nations today; address, October 24, 1964. Dept State Bul 51:694-700 N 16 '64
U.S. regrets misinterpretation of statement on Brazil; statement, March 19, 1963. Dept State Bul 48:521 Ap 8 '63
about
Mr Ball leaves for London talks on Cyprus; U.S. restates position; statement, February 8, 1964. R. J. McCloskey. Dept State Bul 50:284 F 24 '64
Shut up! Nat R 14:145-6 F 26 '63
Slap at de Gaulle. por U S News 54:19 F 4 '63
BALL, Ian Travers-. See Travers-Ball, I.
BALL, John
Wing that breathes. Flying 74:39-41+ Ap '64
BALL, Lucille
Don't laugh when you call me president. pors McCalls 90:51-2 Mr '63
That same wax of Ball again. G. Ace. Sat R 47:14 My 16 '64
BALL, Robert
Britain: if labor wins. il Fortune 69:51-2+ Je '64
Tennis. Sports Illus 19:56-8 O 7 '63
BALL, Robert M.
How safe is your social security pension? interview. por U S News 57:55-8+ D 7 '64
BALL, William B.
Implications of Supreme court decisions for contemporary church-state problems. Cath World 197:296-305 Ag '63
Legal religion in the schools. Cath World 197: 366-71 S '63
Prayer amendments: a Catholic lawyer's view. por Cath World 199:345-51 S '64
Protestants on church-state. Commonweal 79:689-91 Mr 6 '64
Religion in education. America 108:528-30+; 109:15 Ap 20, Jl 6 '63
BALL
Confessions of a stoop ball champion. G. Rogin. Sports Illus 20:75-6+ Ap 20 '64
See also
Softball
BALL bearings. See Bearings (machinery)
BALL lightning. See Lightning
BALL parks. See Baseball fields; Football fields
BALLAD for Bimshire; musical comedy. See Musical comedies, revues, etc.—Criticisms, plots, etc.
BALLAD of Baby Doe; opera. See Moore, D. S.
BALLAD of Jesse Neighbours; story. See Humphrey, W.
BALLAD of John Henry. See Ballads, American
BALLAD of the sad café; drama. See Albee, E.
BALLADS
Richard Dyer-Bennet; interview, ed. by S. Fleming. R. Dyer-Bennet. il Hi Fi 13:16+ Mr '63
See also
Phonograph records—Folk music
BALLADS, American
A man ain't nothin' but a man; Ballad of John Henry. B. Asbell. il Am Heritage 14: 34-7+ O '63
Seventy-five years ago: Casey at the bat. A. Austin. il N Y Times Mag p51+ Je 9 '63
BALLANTINE, William
Death on the high wire. Read Digest 83:53-8 Jl '63
Master of the bulls. Sat Eve Post 237:60-3 S 5 '64
New York's great river. Holiday 36:21-8 Jl '64
Pikes Peak and all that. Holiday 34:18+ Ag '63
Snow-shunning in Arizona. Holiday 36:36+ D '64
Soviet circus wows the U.S.A. Sat Eve Post 236:82-5 O 26 '63
Summer weekend in Idaho. Holiday 36:16+ Ag '64
Sunniest end of California. Holiday 33:22+ F '63
War of nerves on the high wire. Sat Eve Post 237:73-7 F 15 '64
Yellowstone country. Holiday 35:26+ Je '64
BALLARD, Allen B. Jr
Barnyard view of Soviet agriculture. Reporter 28:38-40 My 23 '63
BALLARD, Ernesta Drinker
Citrus. Horticulture 42:17+ Ag '64
Face the facts about gardening indoors. Horticulture 42:22-5 Mr '64
BALLARD, James
Man overboard; story. Atlan 214:74-8 D '64
BALLERINAS. See Dancers
BALLET
Ballet boy at the Met. A. C. Hirzel. il Dance Mag 37:36-7+ S '63
Ballet in America: one-man show? R. Krokover and H. C. Schonberg. il Harper 229: 92-6 S '64; Discussion. 229:13 N '64
Cinderella of the opera. W. Terry. il Opera N 27:8-13 Ap 13 '63
Ford's miracle; grant to strengthen professional ballet in the U.S. Newsweek 62:51 D 23 '63
Fun for the Philistines; theatrical orgies in the opera. F. Stevenson. Opera N 29:14-15 D 26 '64
Historic bonanza for ballet in America: grants from Ford foundation. Dance Mag 38:3-4 Ja '64; Discussion. il 38:34-7+ F '64
I believe. T. Psjovich. il Seventeen 22:215 N '63
José Limon reports on Asia tour. D. Duncan. il Dance Mag 38:31-2 F '64
Met opera ballet thinks big. D. Hering. il Dance Mag 37:35-9+ Jl '63
My life in opera. D. A. Markova. il Opera N 28:8-11 D 21 '63
Presstime news. See issues of Dance magazine
Regional ballet, USA. See issues of Dance magazine
Reviews. S. J. Cohen; D. Hering; M. Marks. See issues of Dance magazine
See also
Choreography
Dancing
Moving pictures—Dance films

BALLET—*Continued*

History

Ballet girls in New York a century ago; excerpts from Women of New York. G. Ellington. il Dance Mag 38:31-3+ Ja '64

Study and teaching

Anatomy for the ballet teacher; ed. by W. Como. R. Gelabert. See issues of Dance magazine
Ballet for bowlers! il Sr Schol 82:20 F 27 '63
Can we improve our Olympic chances? G. Kaywell. il Dance Mag 37:52-7 N '63
Meet Ricki Starr; wrestler with a gimmick. E. Palatsky. il Dance Mag 37:27 My '63
Professor in ballet slippers. N. S. Hey. il Dance Mag 37:48-52 My '63
Special kind of clatter; boys' ballet classes. D. Hering. il Dance Mag 38:58-60 Ja '64
With passionate clarity. J. Battey. il Dance Mag 37:44-8 Jl '63
See also
School of American ballet, incorporated

Austria

On their toes; Aurel von Milloss appointed to newly created position of ballet director F. Willnauer. Mus Am 83:19 F '63

Canada

See also
National ballet of Canada
Royal Winnipeg ballet

Chile

Chilean national ballet. New York state theater. D. Hering. il Dance Mag 39:28-9 Ja '65
Dance; Chilean national ballet. R. Krokover. Mus Am 84:258+ D '64
Dance in Chile. M. Vicuña. il Américas 15:12-17 D '63
Jooss, Conquistadores, and the wheel of fortune. H. Ehrmann. il Dance Mag 38:32-4 N '64
Musical events; performance of Chilean national ballet at New York state theatre. W. Sargeant. New Yorker 40:235 N 21 '64

Cuba

Alicia Alonso and the National ballet of Cuba. T. De Gámez. il Dance Mag 38:30-5 Jl '64

Denmark

See also
Royal Danish ballet

Europe, Western

Trio of spring premieres. il Dance Mag 37:38-9 S '63

France

Stars and soloists of the opera in Paris; Jacob's Pillow. D. Hering. Dance Mag 37:28 O '63

Germany (Federal Republic)

Style in Stuttgart; Württemberg state opera ballet. il Time 83:56 Je 12 '64
Trials and triumphs in Stuttgart; State opera ballet. H. Koegler. il Dance Mag 39:37-9+ Ja '65

Great Britain

Marie Rambert; midwife to the muses. C. Barnes. Dance Mag 37:42-3 Mr '63
See also
Royal ballet, Great Britain

Hungary

Ballet, violins and shish kebab! Bihari. E. Caroll. il Dance Mag 37:27-8 D '63
Hungarian ballets Bihari at Carnegie Hall. J. Maskey. Dance Mag 38:22-3 Ja '64

Mexico

See also
Ballet folklórico of Mexico

Netherlands

Big company in a small country; National ballet of Holland. J. Anderson. il Dance Mag 38:18-19 Jl '64
In the news; Scapino ballet. il Dance Mag 37:47 D '63

Poland

Mazowsze. New York city center. J. Maskey. Dance Mag 38:29 Ap '64

Russia

How large is Soviet ballet? N. Roslavleva. il Dance Mag 37:35-7+ N '63
Nureyev; an autobiography; excerpts. R. Nureyev. il Dance Mag 37:39-43+ My: 38-41+ Je; 17+ Jl '63
Particular treasure; excerpts from Days with Ulanova, with editorial comment by D. Hering. A. E. Kahn. il pors Dance Mag 37:40-8 S '63
See also
Bolshoi ballet
Kirov ballet

Spain

Ballet Granada of Estrellita and Raul W. Como. il Dance Mag 38:50-1+ My '64

BALLET arts associates
Ballet arts associates at Arts and design auditorium. J. Maskey. Dance Mag 37:65+ My '63

BALLET companies
Annual directory of dance attractions, choreographers, and lecturers. il Dance Mag 37:65+ D '63; 38:67-70+ D '64
As of today; problems and procedures in regional ballet; interview, ed. by D. Hering. D. Alexander. Dance Mag 38:48-9+ O '64
Ballet '64: fresh and fun. J. Anderson. il Dance Mag 38:30 S '64
Boston ballet; Boston arts festival. D. Hering. Dance Mag 38:54-5 Ag '64
Can it be true? newly formed Harkness ballet; interview, ed. by L. Joel. G. Skibine. il Dance Mag 38:40-1 Ag '64
Culture in Kabul; Robert Joffrey co. abroad. R. Heitzig. il Dance Mag 37:28+ Ap '63
First chamber dance quartet, Ballet espanol: Ximenez-Vargas, Delacorte theatre. D. Hering. Dance Mag 38:71-2 O '64
First chamber dance quartet, 92nd street Y. M. Marks. Dance Mag 38:30-1 Ap '64
Frolic in motion; Paul Taylor dance company. il Time 82:41 Ag 16 '63
From migrant city to Charley's Lake; sampling of regional ballet companies in the Southwest. D. Hering. il Dance Mag 38:54-7 Ap; 52-5 My '64
In the news; controversy: new Los Angeles co. il Dance Mag 38:38 N '64
Manhattan festival ballet company at Masque theatre. J. Maskey. Dance Mag 38:64 Mr '64
Paul Taylor dance company, Brooklyn academy of music. M. Marks. Dance Mag 38:18 D '64
Preview and a premiere. Juilliard concert hall. M. Marks. Dance Mag 38:73-4 Ap '64
Raduga dancers. H. Yurchenco. Mus Am 84:42 N '64
Raduga dancers; Philharmonic Hall, N.Y. M. Marks. Dance Mag 38:64 N '64
Regional ballet, USA. See issues of Dance magazine
Robert Joffrey ballet in Leningrad. A. Ewing. il Dance Mag 37:40-2 D '63
Style in Stuttgart; Württemberg state opera ballet. il Time 83:56 Je 12 '64
They proudly call it home; San Diego civic theatre. W. Como. il Dance Mag 38:60-1 D '64
Watch that rhapsody to a fig leaf! copyrighted music. G. E. Deakin. il Dance Mag 37:48-9 N '63
See also
American ballet theater
Australian ballet company
Metropolitan opera ballet
National ballet
National ballet of Canada
New York city ballet
Pennsylvania ballet company
Royal ballet, Great Britain
San Francisco ballet (organization)
Western theatre ballet

Gifts, legacies, etc.

Conscience of educational foundations. W. W. Brickman. Sch & Soc 92:199 My 2 '64
Ford foundation's ballet grants. J. Martin. il Sat R 47:47-8+ Mr 28 '64; Discussion. 47:68-9 Ap 25 '64
Historic bonanza for ballet in America: grants from Ford foundation. Dance Mag 38:3-4 Ja '64; Discussion. il 38:34-7+ F '64
Passing out money among artists; Ford foundation grant. R. Evett. New Repub 150:9-10 Ja 18 '64

BALLET dancers. See Dancers

BALLET fans. See Balletomanes

BALLET festivals. See Dance festivals

BALLET folklórico of Mexico
Ballet folklorico. J. Martin. il Sat R 46:55 N 30 '63
Ballet folklorico of Mexico at New York city center. J. Maskey. Dance Mag 38:22 Ja '64
Because Amalia wanted to dance. A. Rankin. il Theatre Arts 47:60-3 O '63; Same abr. with title Born to dance. Read Digest 83:234-40 O '63

BALLET folklórico of Mexico—*Continued*
Doña Amalia's Ballet folklórico de Mexico. D. Duncan. il Dance Mag 37:42 N '63
Mother of them all. il Newsweek 62:75 N 25 '63
Three masks of the deer dancer. O. Maynard. il Dance Mag 38:34-6+ Ja '64
BALLET Granada. See Ballet—Spain
BALLET in moving pictures. See Moving pictures—Dancing
BALLET notation. See Dance notation
BALLET of Central park; story. See Boyle, K.
BALLET phonograph records. See Phonograph records—Dance music
BALLET programs. See Theater programs
BALLET slippers
Positive force: Jimmy Selva. W. Como. il Dance Mag 37:48-50+ F '63
BALLET theatre. See American ballet theater
BALLETOMANES
Stage door brigade. D. Sanders. il Dance Mag 37:22+ S '63
BALLETS
American premiere of Piège de lumière. D. Hering. il Dance Mag 38:28-9 N '64
Balanchine's gift; Nutcracker by New York city ballet. il Newsweek 64:76 D 21 '64
Balletic view of Distant planet. E. Palatsky. il Sat R 47:60-1 S 26 '64
Basketball ballet: But (Goal) il Newsweek 61:57 Je 17 '63
Devil at the keyhole; Mephistophela. R. Page. il Dance Mag 38:33 O '64
Genius of Balanchine; excerpt from Balanchine. B. Taper. il Theatre Arts 47:10-13+ N '63
GB and BG; first performance of Clarinade at the New York state theater. Newsweek 63:65 My 11 '64
Happy ending in Spoleto; world première of Nureyev's Raymonda. Newsweek 64:75 Jl 20 '64
Letter from London; première of Mods and rockers by Western theatre ballet. M. Panter-Downes. New Yorker 39:67+ Ja 25 '64
Letter from Paris; Miraculous mandarin danced by Opéra national hongrois. Genêt. New Yorker 39:157-8 D 14 '63
Letter from Paris; performance of Swan lake by Royal ballet. Genêt. New Yorker 39:191 N 30 '63
Marguerite and Armand; production of Royal ballet. il Theatre Arts 47:22-4 My '63
More interested in new than in old. J. Anderson. il Dance Mag 37:44-7 Je '63
Music to my ears; Arcade. I. Kolodin. Sat R 46:31 Ap 13 '63
Music to my ears; Balanchine's Bugaku. I. Kolodin. Sat R 46:44 Ap 6 '63
Music to my ears; Elektra, with and without. I. Kolodin. Sat R 46:33-4 Je 1 '63
Music to my ears; MacMillan week at the Royal ballet; Invitation. I. Kolodin. Sat R 46:42 My 25 '63
Music to my ears; "on" night at the Met; Les sylphides staged by A. Markova. I. Kolodin. Sat R 47:34+ N 28 '64
Music to my ears; Royal ballet's Symphony and Marguerite and Armand at Metropolitan opera house. I. Kolodin. Sat R 46:22 My 18 '63
Music to my ears; Tudor's Dim lustre. I. Kolodin. Sat R 47:36+ My 23 '64
Musical events; George Balanchine's Bugaku. W. Sargeant. New Yorker 39:148 Mr 30 '63
Musical events; George Balanchine's La valse. W. Sargeant. New Yorker 39:155 S 21 '63
Musical events; performance of Giselle by Royal ballet. W. Sargeant. New Yorker 39:100-1 My 4 '63
Musical events; performance of Rite of spring by Royal ballet. W. Sargeant. New Yorker 39:93-4+ My 18 '63
Musical events; performance of Sleeping Beauty by Royal ballet. W. Sargeant. New Yorker 39:96+ Ap 27 '63
Musical events; performances of Elektra and The invitation, by Royal ballet. W. Sargeant. New Yorker 39:157 My 25 '63
Musical events; Tudor ballets. W. Sargeant. New Yorker 40:167-8 My 16 '64
Never mind the ginza. il Time 81:38 Mr 29 '63
On from iconoclasm; Béjart's ballet to the music of Beethoven's Ninth symphony. il Time 84:83 N 6 '64
Post-script on a "sleeper": Ballet school. D. Hering. il Dance Mag 37:51+ F '63
Recreating Les sylphides; Poetry in movement; presentation by Metropolitan opera ballet. A. Markova. il Opera N 29:13-17 Ja 9 '65
Reviews; presentations of children's ballets at Christmas time. M. Marks. Dance Mag 38:65-6+ F '64
Les sylphides, Metropolitan opera. D. Hering. Dance Mag 39:70-1 Ja '65
Vienna swoons over Nureyev and swans. L. Zamponi. Dance Mag 38:28+ D '64
Why Swan lake dances on; photographs. A. Hughes. N Y Times Mag p48-9 My 12 '63

Choreographies

See Choreography

BALLETS de Madrid. See Dancing, Spanish
BALLIETT, Whitney
Books (cont) New Yorker 39:78+ Je 29 '63
Check list. New Yorker 40:148-50+ N 7 '64
Current cinema (cont) New Yorker 39:96 Jl 27; 50 Ag 3 '63; 40:74+ Jl 11; 93 Jl 18; 56 Jl 25 '64
Jazz. New Yorker 39:89 Jl 20; 123-4 S 14; 157-61 S 21; 138-9 O 5; 130+ N 16 '63; 75-7 Ja 18; 40:133-5 Je 13; 154+ S 12; 145-8 N 7 '64; 117-18+ Ja 16 '65
Jazz concerts. See issues of New Yorker
Jazz records. See occasional issues of New Yorker
Profiles (cont) New Yorker 40:52-4+ My 2 '64; 39:42+ Ja 2 '65
BALLIEUX, Rudy E. and others
Gamma globulin antigenic types defined by heavy chain determinants. bibliog Science 145:168-70 Jl 10 '64
BALLINGER, Ronald B.
Territory of South West Africa. bibliog f Cur Hist 45:361-5 D '63
BALLIOL college, Oxford. See Oxford university
BALLISTIC missile early warning system
Early warning system in full operation. Sci N L 84:361 D 7 '63
Now the guard is up against surprise attack; concerning BMEWS. il U S News 55:71 S 30 '63
Russians believed to have radar with over-the-horizon capabilities; U.S. installing radar to double BMEWS warning time. P. J. Klass. Aviation W 81:19 S 28 '64
Spadats network relies on varied sensors. P. J. Klass. il Aviation W 78:89+ F 18 '63
BALLISTIC missile testing. See Guided missiles—Testing
BALLOON ascensions
Death on the wind. il Newsweek 63:20+ F 3 '64
When flight was silent. D. Gunston. il UNESCO Courier 16:28-32 S '63
BALLOON astronomy. See Balloons—Use in research
BALLOON flies. See Flies
BALLOONFLOWERS
Your garden needs balloon flowers too! M. P. Kunkel. il Pop Gard 15:56-7 Mr '64
BALLOONS
Here comes skyhook logging! R. H. Forbes. il Am For 71:10-13+ Ja '65
Jambo gasbag safari in Africa. A. Smith. il Sat Eve Post 236:40-7 N 9 '63
Ride silent, ride high in a new hot-air sports balloon; Vulcoon. K. Brown. il Pop Mech 119:85-9+ Ap '63
Venerable heated-air balloon studied as space recovery system; Paravulcoon. il Miss & Roc 13:37 S 9 '63
See also
Balloon ascensions
Parachutes

History

When flight was silent. D. Gunston. il UNESCO Courier 16:28-32 S '63

Use in research

Balloon observations during the July eclipse. E. P. Ney. il Sky & Tel 26:251-4 N '63
Balloon's eye view of Mars; Project Stratoscope II. il Bsns W p92-3+ Mr 9 '63
Clear view of Mars; balloon-borne Stratoscope II. il Time 81:74 Mr 15 '63
First flight of Coronascope II. G. Newkirk, jr. and J. D. Bohlin. il Sky & Tel 28:16-19 Jl '64
Infrared astronomy by balloon. J. Strong. il Sci Am 212:28-37 bibliog(p 134) Ja '65
Manned balloon flights. Sci N L 83:101 F 16 '63
Mars observed; Stratoscope. il Newsweek 61:60 Mr 18 '63
Spot positrons from space. Sci N L 85:39 Ja 18 '64
Stratoscope 2 aims for spectral analyses of planets' atmospheres. il Aviation W 78:74-5+ Ap 1 '63
Stratoscope II observes Jupiter and red giants. Sky & Tel 27:16 Ja '64

BALLOONS—Use in research—*Continued*
Stratoscope II: sky-high and starry-eyed. R. Gannon. il Pop Sci 182:86-90+ F '63
See also
Balloons, Meteorological
BALLOONS, Meteorological
Wind shear probe may have varied uses. il Aviation W 82:49+ Ja 11 '65
BALLOT
See also
Suffrage
Voting machines
BALLOT thievery. See Elections—Corrupt practices
BALLOTTINES. See Cookery—Poultry
BALLPARKS. See Football fields; Stadiums
BALLS, Michael. See Ruben, L. N. jt. auth.
BALLS
See also
Baseballs
BALLS (parties)
Little white beds; Bal des petits lits blancs held in Lebanon. il Newsweek 64:45 Jl 20 '64
New Year's dance at the depot; Grand Central station becomes a ballroom. il Life 56: 84-5 Ja 10 '64
Ringer; New Year's eve; First annual bell ringer ball for mental health in Grand Central station. New Yorker 39:24-5 Ja 11 '64
Telstar cotillion; Negro debutantes. il Ebony 18:40+ Jl '63
Wanamaker debut begins and ends up in a rampage; with report by D. Abrahamsen. il Life 55:30-7 S 20 '63
BALLUTE. See Parachutes
BALOGH, Erno
Distant sound. Opera N 29:6-7 D 19 '64
Great opera houses: Budapest. Opera N 27: 28-31 Ap 6 '63
BALOGH, Janos
Safari armed with microscopes. UNESCO Courier 17:24-7 O '64
BALSA, Cesar
Cesar Balsa: A thousand keys to his kingdom. R. Joseph. il por Esquire 59:118-20 Mr '63
BALSAM GROVE, N.C.
Blue Ridge Samaritan. S. Castan. il Look 27:82-4+ Ag 27 '63
BALSAN, Consuelo (Vanderbilt)
Voices of two venerable Vanderbilts; ed. by G. Plimpton. por Life 57:64A-64B+ Ag 14 '64
about
Consuelo Vanderbilt Balsan: portrait of a unique American. V. Lawford. il pors Vogue 141:124-33+ F 1 '63
Duchess who lived and died a Vanderbilt. il pors Life 57:40B D 18 '64
BALTHUS
Draftsmanship as dissection. T. B. Hess. il Art N 62:34-5+ D '63
BALTIMORE, D. and others
Virus-specific double-stranded RNA in poliovirus-infected cells. bibliog Science 143: 1034-6 Mr 6 '64
BALTIMORE
Architecture
New work of Mies van der Rohe. il Arch Forum 119:82-3 S '63
Offices and showrooms for interiors firm; H. Chambers company. il Arch Rec 136: 164-5 D '64
Old Baltimore yields to change; Charles center. il Bsns W p52-4 Mr 30 '63
City planning
Is this the big industry that can keep U.S. going? il U S News 54:72-3 F 25 '63
Old Baltimore yields to change; Charles center. il Bsns W p52-4 Mr 30 '63
Education
Operation understanding; Columbus school. J. Epstein. il NEA J 53:22-4 Mr '64
To be continued: story of Baltimore early school admissions project. A. C. Harding. il NEA J 53:30-2 S '64
Fire department
Backbone fire training has a few new wrinkles. J. J. Killen. il Am City 78:89-91 Jl '63
Galleries and museums
See also
Walters art gallery, Baltimore
Hospitals
High-rise for research in pediatrics. il Arch Rec 136:194-6 O '64
New kind of hospital; Hopkins children's center. il Time 83:81 My 22 '64
Libraries
See also
Enoch Pratt free library, Baltimore
Music
Baltimore and Philadelphia. M. de Schauensee. Opera N 27:26-7 My 4 '63
Baltimore Idomeneo. G. M. Eby. Opera N 28: 33 Ja 4 '64
Baltimore renaissance. L. Cheslock. il Mus Am 83:10-13 Ap '63
Baltimore's balance. Opera N 29:25 S 26 '64
[Musical events] (cont) Mus Am 83:75 Ja: 15 F '63
See also
Baltimore civic opera
Peabody institute, Baltimore
Negroes
Foot in the door. L. B. Dennis. New Repub 150:5 Mr 14 '64
March on Gwynn Oak park. il Time 82:17-18 Jl 12 '63
Stores
New branch for Baltimore department store; Hecht company. il Arch Rec 133:160-3 Je '63
Theater
City theater designed to pay its way; theater block, Charles center. il Arch Rec 136:132-3 D '64
BALTIMORE and Ohio railroad
Broader view. Newsweek 61:67-8 Ap 8 '63
BALTIMORE CHANNEL tunnel. See Tunnels and tunneling, Underwater
BALTIMORE city fire school. See Baltimore—Fire department
BALTIMORE civic opera company
Baltimore's blessing. G. Fitzgerald. il Opera N 29:31 D 26 '64
Opening night: 1964-1965 season. J. Ardoin. Mus Am 84:50 D '64
BALTIMORE Colts (football club) See Football clubs
BALTIMORE COUNTY, Md.
Computer puts a plus in inventory control. W. E. Fornoff. il Am City 79:90-1 N '64
BALTIMORE COUNTY, Md. public library
Aid through aides. J. W. Daniels. il Library J 88:2194-7 Je 1 '63
BALTIMORE museum of art
1914; fiftieth-anniversary show. H. Rosenberg. il Art N 63:38-41 O '64
BALTIMORE orioles. See Orioles
BALTIMORE Orioles (baseball) See Baseball clubs
BALTIMORE; story. See Mazor, J.
BALTIMORE sun
Sun shine. il Newsweek 61:88+ My 6 '63
BALTZER, Fritz
Theodor Boveri; tr. by C. Stern and E. Stern. bibliog Science 144:809-15 My 15 '64
BAMBOO
Giant grasses. il Sunset 132:128-34+ My '64
How to create faux bamboo. il House & Gard 125:112-13 Ja '64
Many uses of bamboo. il Flower Grower 50:34-6 Je '63
BAMBOO fences. See Fences
BAMMEL, Stanley E.
Electronic switch for your oscilloscope. Electr World 71:38-9+ F '64
9-watt transistorized hi-fi amplifier. Electr World 69:46-7+ Mr '63
TD/RFG: Tunnel diode, radio frequency generator. Pop Electr 18:44-7+ F '63
BANANA shrubs
Fragrance of bananas. il Sunset 133:262 N '64
BANANAS, Joe. See Bonanno, J.
BANANAS
All about bananas. M. E. Shepherd. il Horticulture 42:36 F '64
Bananas for southern gardens. N. C. Bezona. il Horticulture 41:374 Jl '63
See also
Cookery—Fruit
BANCROFT, Anne
Redbook dialogue. por Redbook 121:56-7+ Jl '63
What did you want most at seventeen? ed. by A. Ebert. por Seventeen 22:131 S '63
about
Battling Bancroft. il pors Life 57:133-4+ N 20 '64
BANCROFT, George
Ms. that would not scour; centennial of Gettysburg address. Wilson Lib Bul 38: 378-9 Ja '64
BANCROFT, George H. and others
Vacuum: measurement techniques and equipment. Science 146:1694-5 D 25 '64

BAND music
Why bands play on in Philly; cooperative organization of seventeen bands. il Bsns W p52-4 D 28 '63
See also
Phonograph records—Band music
BAND stands. See Bandstands
BANDA, Hastings Kamuzu
Banda: beware of Communists. A. C. McAdam. Christian Cent 81:809-10 Je 17 '64
Challenge for father. por Time 84:63-4 O 2 '64
God's man. Time 84:35 O 9 '64
Gods of Africa smile on Brandeis. Nat R 16: 54-5 Ja 28 '64
Lion of Malawi. P. Schmid. il Reporter 32: 20-2 Ja 14 '65
One-man Banda. il por Newsweek 64:39 Jl 20 '64
Shaky podium. por Newsweek 64:55 O 12 '64
Short-lived elation. A. C. McAdam. Christian Cent 81:1283-5 O 14 '64
Uneasy calm. A. C. McAdam. Christian Cent 81:1408-10 N 11 '64
BANDAGES and bandaging
See also
Splints (surgery)
Tourniquets
BANDARANAIKE, Sirimavo
Music to vote by. por Time 85:26 Ja 29 '65
Quid pro quo. il por Time 83:30 Mr 6 '64
BANDAS, Rudolph G.
Misunderstanding still. America 109:128 Ag 10 '63
BANDER, Edward J.
Convention diary. Library J 89:2962-5 Ag '64
Mr Dooley on law librarians; excerpts from address, 1963. por Library J 89:575-7 F 1 '64
BANDITS. See Brigands and robbers
BANDS (music)
Band concerts in the park. R. W. Stevens. Recreation 56:332 S '63
Bel canto in brass. J. Johnson. il Opera N 29:6-7 D 12 '64
Best band in the land. il Ebony 19:172-8 N '63
Blues becomes big business; Ray Charles enterprises. L. Robinson. il Ebony 18:34-6+ Ap '63
Burning desire; original banjoist with New Orleans rhythm kings. New Yorker 39:37-9 N 2 '63
But only use a 10¢ comb; J. Kweskin's Jug band. il Time 82:37 D 27 '63
Community in complete harmony; Village band of Ridgewood, N.J. B. F. Reinauer, 2d. Am City 78:48 My '63
If you love a parade. C. Brown. il Redbook 120:42 F '63
Jazz; big-band renaissance. il Time 83:41 Mr 27 '64
Jazz; concert performed by C. Basie band at Philharmonic Hall. W. Balliett. New Yorker 40:145-7 N 7 '64
Jazz concerts; D. Ellington band at Carnegie Hall. W. Balliett. New Yorker 40:100-2 Ap 11 '64
Jazz concerts; J. Coltrane, C. Taylor, and A. Blakey at Philharmonic Hall. W. Balliett. New Yorker 39:93-4 Ja 11 '64
Jazz concerts; Modern jazz quartet at Carnegie Hall. W. Balliett. New Yorker 40:88 Ja 9 '65
Jazz concerts; performance by Orchestra U.S.A. at Hunter college. W. Balliett. New Yorker 39:201-3 D 7 '63
Jazz concerts; T. Monk at Philharmonic Hall. W. Balliett. New Yorker 39:92-3 Ja 11 '64
Jazz records; C. Basie band. W. Balliett. New Yorker 40:194-8 O 3 '64
Jazz records; D. Ellington's music. W. Balliett. New Yorker 39:179-83 O 26 '63; 97-101 Ja 25 '64
Jazz records; first and second W. Herman bands, or Herds. W. Balliett. New Yorker 39:124-8 O 12 '63
Jazz records, Original dixieland jazz band. W. Balliett. New Yorker 40:106+ Je 27 '64
Musical events; jazz: T. Monk, at Five spot. W. Balliett. New Yorker 39:89 Jl 20 '63
Our man in London; Salvation army bands. New Yorker 40:47-9 O 24 '64
Playing their way through college; Howard university steel band. il Ebony 19:113-17 D '63
Police band. D. Barthelme. New Yorker 40: 28 Ag 22 '64
Profiles: jazz pianist, E. Hines. W. Balliett. New Yorker 40:39-42+ Ja 2 '65
Profiles; M. L. Williams. W. Balliett. New Yorker 40:52-4+ My 2 '64
Swing band era; ed. by V. E. Hughes, M. Kaminsky. il Harper 226:57-64 Ap '63
Syncopated dirges, ragtime parades. K. Chase. il Américas 16:16-20 Mr '64
Tom-tomcats; Africa's favorite jazz band. il Time 82:32 Ag 2 '63
Tonight hear the Cavaliers; teen dance band. il Seventeen 22:78-9 Jl '63
Wa-wa-wa; jazz bands. New Yorker 39:25-7 Je 1 '63
See also
Band music
Orchestras
BANDS, College
Excellence in junior college; Santa Monica marching band and dance drill team. W. W. Brickman. Sch & Soc 91:297 O 19 '63
Show biz U; football bands. il Newsweek 64: 68-9 N 9 '64
BANDSAWS. See Saws
BANDSTANDS
Multi-purpose pavilion-bandstand; Asbury Park, N.J. K. H. Lee. il Am City 78:157-8 Mr '63
BANDURA, Albert
What TV violence can do to your child. Look 27:46-8+ O 22 '63
BANDY, Orville L.
Aquitanian planktonic foraminifera from Erben Guyot. bibliog Science 140:1402-3 Je 28 '63
Miocene-pliocene boundary in the Philippines as related to late tertiary stratigraphy of deep-sea sediments. bibliog Science 142:1290-2 D 6 '63
BANE, Bill
How to keep racehorses in the running; patching cracked hoofs. S. V. Jones. il por Sci Digest 55:50-1 Ap '64
BANFIELD, A. W. F.
Grizzly territory. Natur Hist 73:22-7 Mr '64
BANGKOK
Description
Letter from Bangkok. E. J. Kahn, jr. il New Yorker 40:165-6+ D 5 '64
Well traveled camera. H. Keppler. il Mod Phot 29:36+ Ja '65
BANGS, Carl
Facing extremism. Christian Cent 81:1623 D 30 '64
BANGS, Lucille S.
Local-state-national. NEA J 52:26 F '63
BANHAM, Reyner
Word in Britain: character. Arch Forum 121: 118-25 Ag '64
BANISTER, Judith
Design in regency silver. Antiques 86:299-303 S '64
Home-bred or Huguenot? Antiques 84:288-93 S '63
BANISTER, Manly
Barrel full of birds. Pop Mech 119:154-7 Mr '63
Bicycle built for two. Pop Mech 119:176-9+ Ap '63
Easel tracing-projector. Pop Mech 120:130-4 Jl '63
Fancy hardboard. Pop Mech 120:173-8 N '63
Make your own sandblaster. Pop Mech 120: 191-5+ O '63
Mobile leaf burner. Pop Mech 120:184-7+ S '63
Sand casting at home. Pop Mech 120:166-72 Jl '63
Scooter that hitches a ride. Pop Mech 121: 182-9 Ap '64
Steam engine (cont) Pop Mech 119:196-9 F '63
Tricks of brazing and hard soldering. Pop Mech 119:170-4 Je '63
BANK, Dick
Track & field. Sports Illus 21:46-7 Jl 27 '64
BANK-ANTHONY, Sir Mobolaji
Who's who in foreign business. por Fortune 69:70 Ap '64
BANK advertising
All this for an ad; nest egg ad for Chase Manhattan. il Bsns W p48-9 F 16 '63
Taking the cages down; bank letters. L. L. L. Golden. Sat R 47:55 F 8 '64
BANK buildings
Bank capitalizes on unique design. il Arch Rec 135:260 F '64
Different kind of skyscraper; First Pasadena state bank. il Arch Forum 120:122-5 Mr '64
Economical office tower; Detroit bank & trust company. il Arch Rec 135:153-6 My '64
Elegant drive-in bank in a park-like setting; Central motor bank, Jefferson City, Mo. il Arch Rec 134:157-62 S '63
New art of banking; Manhattan's Bankers trust co. il Arch Forum 118:106-9 Ap '63
Small banks. il Arch Rec 135:117-32 Ja '64
Such nice places to keep money. il Time 82: 53 D 20 '63
Symbol for savings: massive piers and a mighty concrete grid. il Arch Forum 119: 108-13 O '63
BANK capital. See Banks and banking—Finance
BANK checks. See Checks

BANK consolidations and mergers
Bigger stick; Supreme court decision regarding antitrust laws and banks. Newsweek 62:54 Jl 1 '63
Blocking bank mergers. Time 81:77 Je 28 '63
Chase goes new road for growth; will form holding company. Bsns W p34 Jl 18 '64
Justice gets some sharper teeth; Supreme court decisions reversing mergers approved by regulatory agencies. Bsns W p29-30 Ap 11 '64
Mergers and monopolies; Lexington bank case. R. J. Barber. New Repub 150:9 Je 13 '64
Thunderbolt for bank mergers; ruling in Philadelphia case by Supreme court. Bsns W p80+ Je 22 '63

BANK credit. See Credit

BANK crisis, 1933. See Banks and banking—United States—Crisis, 1933

BANK deposits
See also
Certificates of deposit

BANK deposits, Unclaimed
Billions of dollars unclaimed! A. Rankin. Read Digest 84:77-81 My '64

BANK failures
Bank failures spur Congress. U S News 57:78 Ag 31 '64
Why banks are failing: a top official's warning. U S News 57:11 N 2 '64

BANK for reconstruction and development, International. See International bank for reconstruction and development

BANK holding companies
Shortcut to statewide banking; holding company status. il Bsns W p54+ F 9 '63

BANK loans. See Loans, Bank

BANK notes
See also
American bank note company

BANK of America national trust and savings association
Bank of America eyes a foreign shore. il Bsns W p 123-4+ N 16 '63
BOA's Peterson: no. one man at no. one bank. il Newsweek 62:83-6+ N 4 '63
From a family of bound feet; Dolly Gee. il Time 83:26 Ja 10 '64
New chief takes over nation's biggest bank. U S News 55:26 N 11 '63
Who's to decide if a banker is biased? Bank of America picketed by CORE. Bsns W p29-30 Je 13 '64

BANK of England
Four against the Bank of England; condensation. A. H. Kings. il Read Digest 85: 195-200+ Ag '64

BANK of London and Mexico
How to survive revolutions. il Time 84:64+ Ag 14 '64

BANK of Nova Scotia. See Banks and banking—Canada

BANK of socialist countries. See Banks and banking—Europe, Eastern

BANK of the Commonwealth. See Detroit—Banks

BANK rates. See Interest

BANK robberies. See Robberies and assaults

BANK statements. See Banks and banking—Accounting

BANK stocks. See Bank and banking—Securities

BANK vaults. See Vaults

BANKEI. See Landscape models

BANKER, Harry J.
Arbor day. Am For 69:31+ Ap '63

BANKERS
See also
American bankers association

BANKING. See Banks and banking

BANKING law
New look in bank capital; selling senior securities. il Bsns W p 122+ O 12 '63
Rift on control of banking: nationally chartered banks vs state-chartered banks. il Bsns W p47-8+ F 23 '63
Senior securities, boon for banks? C. M. Williams. il Harvard Bsns R 41:82-94 Jl '63
Why small bankers are unhappy with Washington. U S News 54:112+ My 13 '63
See also
Banks and banking—Regulation

BANKO, Winston E.
Long fight to save the trumpeter swan; excerpt from Trumpeter swan. il Audubon Mag 65:373 N '63

BANKRUPTCY
Bankruptcy caper; case of Joseph Pagano. Newsweek 61:31 Je 10 '63
Bet that failed; Olavarria and Galban Lobo file under Bankruptcy act. Bsns W p70+ Ag 1 '64
Can franchises keep their flavor? Tastee Freez failure. Bsns W p62+ N 2 '63
Making bankruptcy pay. il Time 81:44+ F 22 '63
Rolls razor calls it quits. Bsns W p 114+ Jl 25 '64
Scandal in personal bankruptcy. R. A. Phalon. il Duns R 81:35-6+ Mr '63
SEC wins round on bankruptcies; Supreme court ruling clarifies Bankruptcy act. Bsns W p 114 Ja 23 '65
Shipwreck of an epic fleet; collapse of Manuel Kulukundis. il Bsns W p60-1+ Ag 10 '63
Why the stars go broke. il Ebony 18:84-6+ Jl '63

BANKRUPTCY, Fraudulent. See Fraudulent conveyances

BANKS, Gordon T.
Auction market; reprint. Hobbies 69:110-11 D '64

BANKS, Harold Chamberlain
Battle of the Great Lakes. W. J. Eaton. il Reporter 29:38-40 N 21 '63
Bully Banks. por Newsweek 62:61 Jl 29 '63
Canada gets the ships moving, at a price. por Bsns W p51+ N 2 '63
Lakes open up, but for how long? por Bsns W p 125 Mr 28 '64
Last act? por Newsweek 63:59 My 18 '64
Mutiny on the Great Lakes. T. R. Brooks. Commonweal 79:278-80 N 29 '63
Still the boss. por Newsweek 62:38 N 4 '63
Trouble on the waterfront. il por Time 83: 30 Mr 27 '64
When Canada's Liberals crack down on unions. il por U S News 55:88-90 N 4 '63
Why unions are at war on the Great Lakes. il por U S News 55:91-2 S 23 '63

BANKS, Louis
Japan: the open door with a catch. Fortune 68:134-41+ Jl '63

BANKS, Richard
Impressions in paint and words; with biographical sketch. por Dance Mag 37:40-1 Mr '63

BANKS, William M.
Carbohydrate digestion in the cockroach. bibliog Science 141:1191-2 S 20 '63

BANKS, The (islands) See Outer Banks (islands)

BANKS, Coin
Old mechanical banks. F. H. Griffith. See issues of Hobbies

BANKS and banking
Checks and balances; credit check by bank officials. Newsweek 64:75 Jl 27 '64
See also
Calculating machines—Banking applications
Clearing houses
Credit
Development banks
Discount
Investment banking
Loans, Bank
Mortgage banks
Postal savings banks
Safe deposit boxes
Savings and loan associations
Savings banks
Trust companies
Vaults

Accounting

Boo-boo at the bank; mistake in T. Thaggard's account, Union bank and trust company. D. Nevin. il Life 54:14 Je 28 '63
How much should a banker tell his stockholders? Bsns W p56 N 28 '64

Advertising

See Bank advertising

Anecdotes, facetiae, satire, etc.

Higher banking. S. Beach. Atlan 212:104-6 S '63
How I feel about banks is unbalanced. A. King. il McCalls 91:42+ Ja '64
Letter from Stan Delaplane. S. Delaplane. Todays Health 41:71 Jl '63

Branch banking

Prestige branch bank with an atrium. il Arch Rec 135:128-9 Ja '64
Shortcut to statewide banking; holding company status. il Bsns W p54+ F 9 '63
Suburban branch largely of brick. il Arch Rec 135:132 Ja '64

Check credit plans

Retail credit by stamp; Revolving check-purchase plan. il Bsns W p92 D 26 '64

Checking accounts

All for lolly; British workers to be paid by check. Time 81:92+ Mr 22 '63

BANKS and banking—*Continued*

Consolidation

See Bank consolidations and mergers

Country banks

Banker to his own flesh and blood; Canadian banks. C. Aucoin. New Yorker 40:125-6 Ap 18 '64

Credit service

Getting along with your lender. il Suc Farm 62:39+ Ag '64

See also

Banks and banking—Check credit plans

Finance

New look in bank capital; selling senior securities. il Bsns W p 122+ O 12 '63

Foreign subsidiaries

Bank of America eyes a foreign shore. il Bsns W p 123-4+ N 16 '63

Bankers to the Bush; Britain's Barclays bank. il Time 81:92 Mr 8 '63

Banks that build new businesses around the world. O. Schisgall. Read Digest 82:128-31 F '63

Holding companies

See Bank holding companies

Investments

Senior securities, boon for banks? C. M. Williams. il Harvard Bsns R 41:82-94 Jl '63

They're confident of the market's momentum. il Newsweek 61:75 Ap 29 '63

Laws

See Banking law

Regulation

Banking's newcomers face tougher going; over-banking and competition cutting profit potential. il Bsns W p52+ O 31 '64

In works: new bank controls. U S News 54:112-13 My 6 '63

Keeping closer eye on banks; disclosure of changes in bank control; with editorial comment. Bsns W p21 Ag 8 '64

S&Ls at the $1-billion crossroads. R. Nason. il Duns R 82:43-5+ D '63

State bank men tee off on Saxon; state chartered vs nationally chartered banks. Bsns W p54+ My 11 '63

What's rocking those rocks, the banks. R. Sheehan. il Fortune 68:108-13+ O '63

Securities

Money on the banks. il Fortune 70:65-6+ O '64

Surprise dip in bank stocks. Bsns W p88 Jl 27 '63

Trust departments

Fight over bank trust powers. Bsns W p 116 F 16 '63

What the banks hold in trust; comptroller's study report. il Bsns W p 124+ Je 20 '64

Africa

African development bank established. UN Mo Chron 1:45 O '64

Canada

Innovator at the till. il Bsns W p56-8+ Je 6 '64

Pep pills for Canada's banks; Porter commission's report. Bsns W p 120 My 2 '64

See also

Banks and banking—Country banks

Europe, Eastern

Banking with the West. New Repub 149:11 N 16 '63

France

Credit for Lyonnais. Newsweek 62:64-5 Jl 15 '63

Great Britain

Bankers to the Bush. il Time 81:92 Mr 8 '63

See also

Bank of England

Katanga

Bare cupboard; National bank of Katanga. Time 81:31 F 8 '63

Lebanon

Beirut: the Suez of money. il Time 84:105-6 O 23 '64

Mexico

Bank of pity. R. Condon. Holiday 33:58+ Mr '63

See also

Bank of London and Mexico

Middle East

Prosperous peddler. Time 81:86 Ap 26 '63

Morocco

Disappearing act; American & foreign bank, Tangier. il Newsweek 63:68-9 Je 1 '64

Russia

Capitalistic Russian banks. il Duns R 82:48-9+ O '63

Scotland

Bank solves a liquidity problem; floating branch of the National commercial bank of Scotland. il Bsns W p 120-1 Ag 17 '63

No man's land; National commercial bank of Scotland branch catering exclusively to women. il Newsweek 65:48 Ja 4 '65

Sweden

Bankers to the world; Skandinaviska bank. Time 84:78+ D 18 '64

Switzerland

My secret Swiss stake. M. Kitman. il Sat Eve Post 236:62-3 F 16 '63

Secrecy is golden. Time 84:100 N 27 '64

United States

Another group of bankers looks ahead; commercial bankers. il U S News 55:54 D 16 '63

Are banks behind the times? the case for broad changes; interview. J. J. Saxon. U S News 55:90-3 N 25 '63

Bankerly feud. Newsweek 63:60 Mr 30 '64

Banking feud: LBJ takes a hand. U S News 56:97 Mr 30 '64

Banks hold breath over interest rates. il Bsns W p26-7 D 5 '64

Banks window dressing is hit. U S News 55:116 O 14 '63

Beating the Fed's old rule. Bsns W p 169 S 12 '64

Big banks boost earnings. il Bsns W p60 Ja 26 '63

Bold breed. il Time 84:74 Ag 28 '64

Building up for a big year. il Bsns W p45+ F 22 '64

Cashing union convenience; new services. il Time 81:84+ Je 21 '63

Chase Manhattan wins friends and influences people. il Newsweek 61:74-7 Ap 8 '63

Control the comptroller? il Newsweek 62:85 O 21 '63

Friends speaks out on banking; Columbia-McKinsey foundation lectures. il Bsns W p83-4+ Ap 25 '64

How banks have lured more corporate cash. il Bsns W p68+ Jl 18 '64

Let 315 do it; plan to share a computer center. Time 81:89 F 15 '63

Mr Johnson makes some suggestions. il Newsweek 64:67 D 14 '64

Money makes money. il Time 84:74 Jl 17 '64

More choice for the investor; common trust fund. il Bsns W p 162+ Mr 21 '64

Moving in on leasing's middle men; commercial banks in equipment leasing. Bsns W p80-1 Ag 10 '63

National-bank policy attacked. il U S News 55:122-3 O 21 '63

Off their duffs; James J. Saxon starts new controversy over federal regulatory powers. Newsweek 64:83 N 9 '64

Pinstripe war. Newsweek 61:71-2 My 6 '63

Portrait of growth: California's startling Union bank. J. Thackray. il Duns R 84:44-5+ O '64

Rift on control of banking; nationally chartered banks vs state-chartered banks. il Bsns W p47-8+ F 23 '63

Running out on Smith; new national banks and new branches. New Repub 148:7 My 18 '63

Saxon and the Fed cross swords again; concerning corporate savings in national banks. Bsns W p21 Ja 4 '64

Saxon crusade. il Time 82:101 O 18 '63

What bankers see ahead for business. il U S News 57:98-101 D 14 '64

What's rocking those rocks, the banks. R. Sheehan. il Fortune 68:108-13+ O '63

Why small bankers are unhappy with Washington. U S News 54:112+ My 13 '63

Wright Patman's well-heeled windmills. G. Carr. New Repub 150:11-12 F 8 '64

See also

Bank failures

Bank of America national trust and savings association

Export-import bank of Washington

Federal deposit insurance corporation

Federal reserve banks

Investment bankers association of America

Money—United States

BANKS and banking—United States—See also —*Continued*
Morgan guaranty trust company
Transamerica corporation
United States—Federal reserve board
also subhead Banks under names of cities, e.g. New York (city)—Banks

Crisis, 1933

Day the money stopped; March 6, 1933. C. Bird. il Look 27:84+ Mr 12 '63

Foreign banks

Pin-stripe invaders; foreign banks in the U.S. Time 84:106 O 16 '64

History

Spoils of the bank war: political bias in the selection of pet banks. F. O. Gatell. bibliog f Am Hist R 70:35-58 O '64

BANKS and banking, International
Russia's sterling success; Narodny bank; London. Time 82:90-1 Jl 12 '63
See also
International bank for reconstruction and development
International bank of economic cooperation

BANKS and banking, State. See Banks and banking—United States

BANKS and banking, Trade union
Labor bank fetes its 40th year; Amalgamated bank of New York. Bsns W p67-8 My 25 '63
Union banker; Frankfurt-based bank fur Gemeinwirtschaft. Time 84:61 Jl 31 '64

BANKS ISLAND (Arctic Ocean)
Banks Island: Eskimo life on the Polar Sea. W. O. Douglas. il Nat Geog Mag 125:702-35 My '64

BANNEKER, Benjamin
Pioneers in protest. L. Bennett, jr. il pors Ebony 19:48-50+ Mr '64

BANNER, William P.
Little films that make it big. U S Camera 27:60-1 Ja '64
Reach for the shadows. U S Camera 27:50-1+ Ag '64
Television photography today. U S Camera 26:18-19+ Je '63
Try filters for portraits. U S Camera 27:14+ D '64

BANNERS. See Flags

BANNERTAILS. See Kangaroo rats

BANNISTER, E.
Ditch; story. Seventeen 23:114-15 Mr '64

BANNISTER, Roger G.
What makes the athlete run? excerpt from address. por UNESCO Courier 17:10-19 Ja '64

about

Man who broke the four-minute mile. A. Carthew. il pors N Y Times Mag p66+ Ap 19 '64

BANNOCKBURN, Md.
Friends of Danville; white sympathizers who took action to aid Negro desegregation. A. Karro. America 110:633-5 My 9 '64

BANNON, Barbara A.
Forecast of paperbacks. See issues of Publishers' weekly

BANQUETTES (furniture) See Benches

BANTAM car company. See American Bantam car company

BANTING, Sir Frederick
Victory over the sugar sickness; ed. by J. D. Ratcliff. C. H. Best. por Todays Health 42:56-8+ Mr '64. Same abr. with title How we discovered insulin. Read Digest 84:43-7 Mr '64

BANTUS. See South Africa—Native races

BANUS, Mario D. and others
High pressure transitions in $A^{(III)}B^{(VI)}$ compounds: indium telluride. bibliog Science 142:662-3 N 8 '63

BAPTISM
Baptism: for babies or believers? Church of England's canon law. il Time 85:36 Ja 8 '65
Rich significance of baptism; excerpt from Sacraments of initiation. C. Davis. Cath World 199:293-300 Ag '64
Word. V. P. McCorry. America 110:874-5 Je 27 '64

BAPTIST world alliance
Changing world. P. B. Mather. Christian Cent 80:1086 S 4 '63

BAPTIST world youth conference
Changing world. P. B. Mather. Christian Cent 80:1086 S 4 '63

BAPTISTS
Baptism: conscience and clue for the church, by W. Carr. Review
Christian Cent 81:1145 S 16 '64. R. Goetz
Texas to Tokyo; Baptist evangelical rally. il Newsweek 61:61 Ap 29 '63

BAPTISTS in Cuba
Persecutes Cuban Baptists. Christian Cent 81:1230-1 O 7 '64

BAPTISTS in the United States
American Baptists: to break the bonds of captivity. H. Moody. Christian Cent 80:456-8 Ap 10 '63; Discussion. 80:683 My 22 '63
Ballot box blow-up; Southern Baptist convention. Newsweek 64:69-70 Ag 31 '64
Baptist division; annual assembly. Time 81:84 My 17 '63
Baptist students desegregate; voted to integrate Baptist student union. Christian Cent 81:1582 D 23 '64
Baptists explore church union. Christian Cent 80:734 Je 5 '63
Baptists in travail; Southern Baptist convention. K. Haselden. Christian Cent 80:672-4 My 22 '63
Baptists urged to join COCU. Christian Cent 81:1453 N 25 '64; Reply. J. W. Bradbury. 82:61-2 Ja 13 '65
Behind the front; race issue. Time 83:68+ My 29 '64
Changing times? Southern Baptist convention meetings. Newsweek 62:76 N 25 '63
Common principle. S. I. Stuber. Christian Cent 81:778-80 Je 10 '64
Court invades independent church; Traskwood landmark missionary Baptist church, Benton, Ark. Christian Cent 80:356 Mr 20 '63
Evading the issue; racial crisis in the South. Christian Cent 80:1356-7 N 6 '63
Five million Baptists plan progress drive. il Ebony 20:76-80+ D '64
Healing old wounds; Southern and American Baptists. Time 82:84 O 18 '63
How to tell a Baptist from a Methodist in the South. G. Harmon. Harper 226:58-63 F '63
Jackson's way; National Baptist convention's 84th annual meeting. Newsweek 64:76 S 21 '64
Missouri Baptist board attacks liberalism. Christian Cent 80:638 My 15 '63
Probe ballot-stuffing charges; Southern Baptist convention. Christian Cent 81:1101-2 S 9 '64
Separate and unequal; ABC and SBC at Baptist jubilee celebration. Newsweek 63:82 Je 1 '64
S.B.C. tightens voting procedures. Christian Cent 81:1325 O 28 '64
Southern Baptist seminaries. O. T. Binkley. Christian Cent 80:774-5 Je 12 '63
Southern Baptists break silence. Christian Cent 81:925 Jl 22 '64
Southern Baptists face crisis. Christian Cent 80:604 My 8 '63
Southern Baptists: need for reformulation, redirection. S. S. Hill, jr; discussion. Christian Cent 80:276-7 F 27 '63
Southern Baptists tackle race problem; Southern Baptist convention. Christian Cent 81:1164 S 23 '64
Sterilizing the stereotypes; Southern Baptists not all alike. Christian Cent 81:1517 D 9 '64
Votes to admit Negroes; First Baptist church of Atlanta, Ga. Christian Cent 81:229 F 19 '64
We are statesmen. il Time 84:73 S 18 '64

BAQUERO, Gastón
Before Columbus came. Américas 15:35-9 O '63
Spain, Unamuno, and Hispanic America. Américas 16:8-14 Je '64

BAR. See Lawyers

BAR HIYYA, Abraham
Judaism as a philosophy: the philosophy of Abraham Bar Hiyya, by L. D. Stitskin. Review
Commentary 34:174-6 Ag '62. J. Eckstein; Reply with rejoinder. L. D. Stitskin. 35:76-7 Ja '63

BAR-ILLAN, Willetta
Dinner in ninety seconds. Sci Digest 56:73-80 Ag '64
How to choose the right diet. bibliog Sci Digest 54:32-8 Ag '63

BAR associations
Face on the courtroom floor; feud between Alaska's bar and bench. Time 84:86+ N 13 '64
Open shop for lawyers; case of Lathrop v. Donohue and state bar associations. G. Kaplan. Nat R 16:603-4 Jl 14 '64

BAR mitzvah. See Jews—Rites and ceremonies

BAR-none trading post; drama. See Miller, H. L.

BARALDI, Sonia
Primitive painters of the United States. Américas 15:21-7 N '63

BARAN, Paul A.
Viewing U.S. economy with a Marxist glass. por Bsns W p67-8+ Ap 13 '63

BARATI, George
Quote-unquote; interview, ed. by R. Eyer. por Mus Am 84:33 S '64
BARBADOS
Flying fish and sugar cane. W. Mankowitz. il Holiday 35:72-8+ F '64
See also
Architecture, Domestic—Barbados
Hotels, taverns, etc.—Barbados
Description and travel
Barbados without tours. J. McCarthy. il Holiday 33:96+ F '63
BARBARY sheep. See Mountain sheep
BARBECUE carts. See Serving carts
BARBECUE cookery
Back to basic barbecue. C. Claiborne. il N Y Times Mag p52 Ag 25 '63
Barbecue spectaculars! M. Johnston and others. il Bet Hom & Gard 42:70-5+ Je '64
Barbecue supreme. M. Reynolds and H. R. Silver. il Esquire 62:54-7 Jl '64
Broiling, grilling and barbecuing. il House & Gard 125:204-8 My '64
Budget barbecue. il Ebony 19:110+ Jl '64
Cook it on the grill. Am Home 67:100 Jl '64
Easy summer barbecues. il Redbook 121:74-5+ Jl '63
For barbecue fun; let's have a cookout; with recipes. K. Smith. il Pop Gard 14:55-7 Jl '63
For the barbecue chef. M. Davidson. il Ladies Home J 80:84 Je '63
For the best barbecue ever, feature ribs. J. Figg. il Suc Farm 62:84-5 S '64
Greatest barbecued ribs ever! M. Johnston. il Bet Hom & Gard 41:78-9+ Je '63
Greatest barbecues! il Bet Hom & Gard 41:74-9+ My '63
Home cooking on the range. N. C. Wood. il Ladies Home J 80:74-7+ Je '63
It's barbecue time. il McCalls 91:104-5+ Je '64
Juicy barbecued meats. R. Behnke. il Farm J 87:52-4 Ag '63
More about barbecuing. Ladies Home J 80:90 Je '63
Vegetables on the grill. H. S. Witty. il Flower Grower 50:46+ Ag '63
We smoke four roasts. il Sunset 132:154-7 Mr '64
When it comes to delectable accompaniments for barbecue dining think big! il Am Home 67:60-1+ My '64
BARBECUE grills
Cookout bar and planter. W. C. Leckey. il Pop Mech 120:120-5 Jl '63
For barbecue fun; choose the perfect grill. R. M. Peters. il Pop Gard 14:46-8 Jl '63
How to put a barbecue pit under your picnic table. il Pop Sci 185:116-18 Jl '64
New outdoor grill cooks with sunshine. il House B 105:83 Je '63
Pick a grill for the outdoor chef. il Pop Gard 15:38-9 My '64
Safari grill (uses throw-away fuel) il Consumer Rep 28:366-7 Ag '63
What's new for barbecues? il Bet Hom & Gard 42:76 Je '64
Care
Cleaning your charcoal grill. H. Bartron. House B 105:42 Je '63
Equipment
For barbecue fun; get a good fire going. R. M. Peters. il Pop Gard 14:49 Jl '63
How to build a kabob rack for your barbecue. il Pop Sci 182:99 My '63
BARBECUE sauces. See Sauces
BARBEE, Bobbie
Baseball's untouchables. Ebony 19:153-4 Je '64
BARBER, Jerry, and Brown, G. S.
Secrets of the short game. Sports Illus 18:32-40 F 18; 50-3 F 25 '63
BARBER, Lawrence
Boating on the great river of the West. Motor B 111:34-5+ My '63
Trimaran for Nuka Hiva. il Yachting 114:130+ Ag '63
BARBER, Noel
Rare white truffle. Holiday 35:142+ Je '64
BARBER, Richard J.
Identical bids; billion-dollar coincidence. Nation 196:154-7 F 23; inside cover Mr 30 '63
Mergers and monopolies. New Repub 150:9 Je 13 '64
Windfall for conspiracy. Nation 199:332-3 N 9 '64
BARBER, Rowland
Hail Caesar! Sat Eve Post 236:28+ F 16 '63
BARBER, Samuel
Music to my ears; Barber concerto performed by the New York philharmonic orchestra. I. Kolodin. Sat R 46:33 N 23 '63
Music to my ears; performance of The Trojan women by the New York philharmonic. I. Kolodin. Sat R 46:28 Ap 20 '63
Musical events. W. Sargeant. New Yorker 39:127-8 N 16 '63
Musical events; Barber's Andromache's farewell performed by New York Philharmonic. W. Sargeant. New Yorker 39:153-4 Ap 13 '63
Vanessa. Criticism
Opera N il 28:34 D 28 '63
BARBER, Willard F.
Can the Alliance for progress succeed? bibliog f Ann Am Acad 351:81-91 Ja '64
BARBER of Seville; opera. See Rossini, G.
BARBERINI vase. See Portland vase
BARBERS and barber shops
Clipping the heads of U.S. industry; Terminal barber shop in New York's Waldorf Astoria hotel. il Bsns W p 164-5 Je 15 '63
Anecdotes, facetiae, satire, etc.
Perfect haircut. A. Friendly, jr. il Esquire 59:76-7+ Ap '63
BARBIE dolls. See Dolls
Il BARBIERE di Siviglia; opera. See Rossini, G.
BARBIROLLI, Sir John
Quote-unquote; interview, ed. by M. Brozen. por Mus Am 84:30 Jl '64
about
Little John in big Texas. il por Time 82:63 N 1 '63
Sir John and the jubilee; new three-year contract with the Houston symphony society. H. Roussel il por Mus Am 84:22-3 Ap '64
BARBITURATES
Alcohol & barbiturates: deadly combination. il Time 83:48 Ja 3 '64
Are sleeping pills safe? Sominex. Consumer Rep 30:4 Ja '65
Eserine and amphetamine: interactive effects on sleeping time in mice. C. D. Barnes and F. H. Meyers. bibliog il Science 144:1221-2 Je 5 '64
Growing menace of nice drugs. J. Phipps and R. Robinson. il Good H 157:70-1+ S '63; Same abr. with title Sleeping pills and pep pills; handle with extreme caution! Read Digest 83:103-7 N '63
BARBIZON hotel. See New York (city)—Hotels, restaurants, etc.
BARBIZON school
Daubigny's gentle naturalism; first US exhibition, at the Paint art center and arboreum, Oshkosh, Wis. il Time 83:867+ My 15 '64
BARBOR, Grace
I married an airplane. Read Digest 86:113-17 Ja '65
BARBOT, Clément
Living dead. il pors Time 82:20-1 Jl 26 '63
BARBOUR, Frederick K.
Some Connecticut case furniture. Antiques 83:434-7 Ap '63
BARBOUR, Roger W.
Microtus: a simple method of recording time spent in the nest. Science 141:41 Jl 5 '63
BARCELLA, Ernest L.
All aboard for happy land. Todays Health 41:62-3+ N '63
BARCELONA
Barcelona. M. Lawrence. il Atlan 212:108+ Ag '63
Letter from Barcelona. A. Reid. New Yorker 39:105-6+ My 4 '63
Galleries and museums
Palace for Picasso. E. V. Ronan. il Américas 16:32-7 Jl '64
Picasso comes home; Picasso museum. B. O'Brian. Reporter 30:52-3 My 21 '64
Picasso vs. Franco; Picasso museum. Newsweek 61:57 Ap 8 '63
Music
Barcelona begins. J. Caballol. Opera N 29:32 Ja 30 '65
Barcelona bravos. J. Caballol. il Opera N 27:31 F 2 '63
BARCLAY, C. N.
Very real risk, war by accident. N Y Times Mag p 17+ My 5 '63
BARCLAY, Robert
Composite girl. il U S Camera 27:60-1 Je '64
BARD, Sandra G. See Nemer, M. jt. auth.
BARDEN, John
Educational park: community vs. neighborhood. Nation 198:388-91+ Ap 20 '64

BARDEN, John—*Continued*
That Cleveland newspaper strike. Nation 196: 159-61+ F 23 '63
Unhappy arbiters of values, standards, and tastes. Bul Atomic Sci 19:34-6 D '63; 20:31-2 O '64

BARDOT, Brigitte
Positivement, Mlle Sagan! interview, ed. by R. Grenier. por Ladies Home J 82:42-3+ Ja '65

BAREFOOT in the park; drama. See Simon, N.

BARENBLAT, Hirsch
Jew against Jew. por Time 81:31 Mr 22 '63

BARFORD, George
Father of letter forms. Sch Arts 64:29-32 D '64

BARGAIN sales
Everybody's far-out bargain store; John's bargain stores. il Bsns W p 110+ My 25 '63
Shopper's guide to bargain sales. il Changing T 17:7-11 F '63

BARGAIN with Cashel; story. See Kersh, G.

BARGAINING power. See Collective bargaining

BARGE lines
Lassoing cattle from rails. il Bsns W p 130+ O 19 '63

BARGHOORN, Frederick Charles
Dead hand that still rules Russia. Life 56 10+ Je 19 '64
Strength of the projected union vis-à-vis Russia; address, April 5, 1963. Ann Am Acad 348:54-64 Jl '63
To meet the propaganda challenge. N Y Times Mag p 13+ Ja 19 '64

about

Barghoorn affair and educational exchange. W. W. Brickman. Sch & Soc 92:63 F 22 '64
Barghoorn has a new book due from Princeton in March. Pub W 184:32-3 N 25 '63
Barghoorn mystery. New Repub 149:4-5 N 30 '63
Big brother is still watching. E. Crankshaw. il N Y Times Mag p8+ D 29 '63
Good-by Mr Barghoorn, pleasant journey. il por Newsweek 62:37-8 N 25 '63
Hot line release? Sr Schol 83:20 D 13 '63
People of the week. por U S News 55:18 N 25 '63
Return of the professor. Nat R 15:469 D 3 '63
Scholar as pawn. il por Time 82:27 N 22 '63
Soviet Union rebuked on climate of fear. Christian Cent 80:1490-1 D 4 '63
Tit-for-tat Russians call Yale prof a spy. il pors Life 55:48-9 N 22 '63
Why? Barghoorn case. Nation 197:377 D 7 '63
Will the swaps keep on? il Bsns W p28-9 N 23 '63

BARHAM, Eric G.
Siphonophores and the deep scattering layer. bibliog Science 140:826-8 My 17 '63

BARIL, Earl F. and others
Chromatography of ribonuclease-treated myosin extracts from early embryonic chick muscle. bibliog Science 146:413-14 O 16 '64

BARILKO, Bill
They hurt when he hit them; Toronto Maple Leafs vs Montreal Canadiens. D. Anderson. Sports Illus 18:E5-6+ Mr 4 '63

BARING-GOULD, William S.
Sherlock Holmes, sportsman. Sports Illus 18: 34-46 My 27 '63

BARITZ, Loren
John Adams and his wife, Abigail. Nation 197: 54-5 Jl 27 '63

BARIUM
High pressure X-ray diffraction studies on barium. J. D. Barnett and others. bibliog il Science 141:534-5 Ag 9 '63

BARIUM hydroxide
Acid of krypton and its barium salt. A. G. Streng and A. V. Grosse. bibliog Science 143:242-3 Ja 17 '64
Barium xenate. A. D. Kirschenbaum and A. V. Grosse. bibliog Science 142:580 N 1 '63

BARK
See also
Cinnamon

BARK cloth. See Tapa cloth

BARK paintings. See Art, Australian (aboriginal)

BARKAN, Al
Unions push biggest political campaign; interview. por Nations Bsns 52:38-9+ Ag '64

BARKE, Harvey E.
Late vegetables. Horticulture 42:14-15+ S '64

BARKENTIN, George, family
Family affair: the story of two little models and how they grew. il Mlle 58:76-9 D '63

BARKENTINES. See Sailing vessels

BARKER, B. Devereux, 3d
Island gunkholing paradise. Yachting 114: 38-40+ D '63
Larchmont's 65th. Yachting 114:51+ S '63
Lipton cup. Yachting 113:210+ Ap '63
Minimum cruising auxiliaries. Yachting 115: 71-3+ Ja '64
Twelve-meter spinnmaker jibe. Yachting 115: 57-9+ Je '64
Yachting interviews: Ray Hunt. Yachting 116:47-9+ Jl '64
(ed) See Hood, F. E. Yachting interviews

BARKER, B. Devereux, 3d, and Fowle, L. M.
Marblehead celebrates the 75th anniversary of its race week. Yachting 116:38-9+ Ag '64

BARKER, Bradley S.
200 per cent more space with microfilm. Am City 78:95-6 O '63

BARKER, David
Glass-ware patents of David Barker. A. G. Peterson. il Hobbies 69:66-7 Ag '64

BARKER, Edna L. S.
Covered bridge; poem. Farm J 88:69 Je '64

BARKER, Eric
Death of a poet; poem. Sat R 46:27 Mr 2 '63
Philosopher; poem. Nation 198:102 Ja 27 '64

BARKER, George
Memorial stanzas for Louis MacNeice; poem. Poetry 104:1-3 Ap '64
Sparrow's feather; poem. New Yorker 39:42 Je 8 '63

about

Three from overseas. E. G. Burrows. Poetry 105:209-10 D '64

BARKER, J. M.
Double take on elephant. por Outdoor Life 132:32-5+ N '63

BARKER, John W.
Béatrice & Bénédict. Am Rec G 29:696-8 My '63
Book reviews. Am Rec G 29:887-90 Jl '63
Choral music of George Frideric Handel. Am Rec G 31:24-5+ S '64
From Capitol, the notable EMI series: Musik in alten städten und residenzen. Am Rec G 30:202-6+ N '63
From Command, Sheridan's The school for scandal. Am Rec G 29:422-3+ F '63
From Decca, the Play of Herod. Am Rec G 31:18-19+ S '64
Heinrich Biber. Am Rec G 29:782-3 Je '63
Julian Bream consort in an evening of Elizabethan music. Am Rec G 30:26-9 S '63
Maurice Abravanel conducts the first recording of Handel's oratorio: Samson. Am Rec G 30:396-9 Ja '64
Passion of Our Lord according to St Matthew. Am Rec G 30:280-3 D '63
Saul. Am Rec G 29:844-6+ Jl '63
Treasury of early music. Am Rec G 30:96-100 O '63
Vox is doing us all a vast service. Am Rec G 29:543-5 Mr '63

BARKER, Ronald
Book distribution in the United Kingdom. ALA Bul 57:523-7 Je '63

BARKER, Roy J. and others
Photoflashes: a potential new tool for control of insect populations. bibliog Science 145: 1195-7 S 11 '64

BARKER chipper. See Wood chipping machines

BARKIN, Solomon
Road to the future: a trade-union commission for self-analysis. Ann Am Acad 350:138-47 N '63
—and Blum, A. A.
(eds) Crisis in the American trade-union movement. bibliog Ann Am Acad 350:1-156 N '63
Is there a crisis in the American trade-union movement? the trade unionists' views. Ann Am Acad 350:16-24 N '63

BARKLEY, Bill
U.S. travel shows. Travel 121:49-51 Ja '64

BARLEY
Culture of small barley embryos on defined media. K. Norstog and J. E. Smith. bibliog il Science 142:1655-6 D 27 '63
Take off barley, hustle in soybeans. B. Hardy. il Farm J 87:36-7 Ap '63

BARLOW, Gary
Creative education & the special student. Sch Arts 63:29-34 Ja '64
Student teacher (title varies) See issues of School arts

BARLOW, George W.
Evolution of behavior; report of a symposium at Philadelphia meeting of the AAAS. Science 139:851-2 Mr 1 '63

BARLOW, Horace B. and Hill, R. M.
Selective sensitivity to direction of movement in ganglion cells of the rabbit retina. bibliog Science 139:412-14 F 1 '63
—and Sparrock, J. M. B.
Role of afterimages in dark adaptation. bibliog Science 144:1309-14 Je 12 '64
BARLOW, Roger
4x4 field test. Field & S 68:68-9+ My '63
Transcontinental trailer test. por Field & S 68:51-3 F '64
BARMBRACK. See Bread
BARMORE, Thomas J.
Home-made printed circuits. Electr World 69: 64 My '63
Solid-state 3-watt CB-ham transmitter. Electr World 70:46-7+ O '63
BARNA, Anne O'Neill-. See O'Neill-Barna, A.
BARNACLES
Contraction-band formation in barnacle myofibrils. R. J. Baskin and G. M. Wiese. bibliog il Science 143:134-6 Ja 10 '64
Membrane properties of barnacle muscle fiber. S. Hagiwara and others. bibliog il Science 143:1446-8 Mr 27 '64
Nature note. Sci N L 85:92 F 8 '64
BARNARD, Charles N.
Drive with devils behind you. Sat Eve Post 237:64-5 Mr 7 '64
Smog battle gets hot. Sat Eve Post 237:78+ Ap 25 '64
Sput . . . pop . . . clank . . . varoom! Sat Eve Post 237:66-8 N 14 '64
BARNARD, John
Bare beeches; Trees reflex in forest pool; poems. Yale R 54:234-5 D '64
BARNARD college, New York
Knitted brows on the subway. M. A. Guitar. il Mlle 58:169-71+ Ap '64
Rosemary Park: new president of Barnard. T. Ferrer. il Sat R 46:66-8 Ap 20 '63
There's nothing like a dame. Time 81:48 Ap 26 '63
BARNES, Allan C.
Reducing the hazards of birth. Harper 228: 31-7 Ja '64
BARNES, Benjamin A. and others
Irradiation of the blood: method for reducing lymphocytes in blood and spleen. bibliog Science 145:1188-9 S 11 '64
BARNES, Charles A.
Rig a jig. Outdoor Life 134:62-3 O '64
BARNES, Charles D. and Katzung, B. G.
Stimulus polarity and conditioning in planaria. bibliog Science 141:728-30 Ag 23 '63
—and Meyers, F. H.
Eserine and amphetamine: interactive effects on sleeping time in mice. bibliog Science 144:1221-2 Je 5 '64
BARNES, Clare, jr, and Bowen, Croswell
Scrimshaw collector. Am Heritage 15:8-13 O '64
BARNES, Clive
Britain's new actors; rougher, tougher, angrier. N Y Times Mag p44-5+ O 6 '63
Company that refused to be neglected. Dance Mag 37:30-4 Jl '63
Dance. Nation 196:427-8 My 18 '63
England's national theatre. Nation 197:399-400 D 7 '63
Hochhuth's Representative. Nation 197:287-8 N 2 '63
Marie Rambert; midwife to the muses. Dance Mag 37:42-3 Mr '63
Ninette de Valois retires as director. Dance Mag 38:42-6 Mr '64
Something for everybody, everything for somebody. Dance Mag 38:36-8+ S '64
BARNES, Duncan
Aches, pains and prizes. Sports Illus 21:52-4 O 12 '64
Border pigeon shoot. Sports Illus 18:18-21 Mr 18 '63
Dogs. Sports Illus 19:68-70 N 18 '63
Fishing. Sports Illus 21:46-7 Jl 20 '64
Herring with derring-do. Sports Illus 20:49-51 Mr 16 '64
Hunting (cont) Sports Illus 21:74-6+ N 30 '64
Scuba diving. Sports Illus 19:51 Jl 29 '63
Shooting. Sports Illus 19:89+ S 9 '63
BARNES, Edward Larrabee
Architect Ed Barnes: toward simpler details, simpler forms, and greater unity. il por Arch Forum 119:74-9 Ag '63
New houses by Edward Larrabee Barnes. il Arch Rec 136:139-52 N '64
BARNES, Helen
Sardinia, how to share the renaissance of a lovely island. House B 105:54+ Ag '63
BARNES, Henry A.
Barnes stops, looks, and tells. por N Y Times Mag p21+ Ag 18 '63
Facts and fallacies of traffic engineering; interview. pors Am City 78:114-17 Je '63
Keep 'em rolling to the final jam. P. O'Neil. il pors Life 57:98-100+ N 13 '64
BARNES, John W.
Obituary
Pub W por 186:52 D 28 '64
BARNES, Louis B. and Greiner, L. E.
Breakthrough in organization development; part II: how the grid program did work. Harvard Bsns R 42:139-55 N '64
BARNES, Marion J.
Will they outgrow it? PTA Mag 58:8-10 bibliog(p35) O '63
BARNES, R. Bowling
Thermography of the human body. bibliog Science 140:870-7 My 24 '63
BARNES, Robert E.
School floors warmed by electric heating. Arch Rec 134:165-6 Jl '63
BARNES, Ronald
Glorious carillon. il por Time 82:72+ O 4 '63
BARNES, Roswell Parkhurst
Architect's warning. por Time 83:64 My 1 '64
Roswell P. Barnes retires. Christian Cent 81: 631 My 13 '64
To Roswell P. Barnes on his retirement. E. C. Parker and B. Thompson. Christian Cent 81:1551 D 16 '64
BARNES, Virgil E.
Detrital mineral grains in tektites. Science 142:1651-2 D 27 '63
BARNES and Noble, Incorporated
Barnes & Noble attains four score years and ten. il Pub W 184:106-8 Ag 19 '63
BARNES engineering company
Fever camera; thermograph stock. Newsweek 62:96+ O 14 '63
BARNES foundation, Merion, Pa.
No place for the rabble. L. G. Forer. il Horizon 6:4-7+ Spr '64
BARNESS, Lewis A. and others
Methylmalonate excretion in vitamin B_{12} deficiency. bibliog Science 140:76-7 Ap 5 '63
BARNETT, J. Dean, and others
High pressure X-ray diffraction studies on barium. bibliog Science 141:534-5 Ag 9 '63
X-ray diffraction studies on tin at high pressure and high temperature. bibliog Science 141:1041-2 S 13 '63
BARNETT, Jonathan
Modern history for modern architects. Arch Rec 135:165-8 Mr '64
Will the computer change the practice of architecture? Arch Rec 137:143-50 Ja '65
BARNETT, Lincoln
Who is behind the assault on English? Horizon 5:33-48 Jl '63
BARNETT, Richard
Sixth man. il Time 81:66+ Mr 8 '63
BARNETT, Robert W.
New role of Japan in world affairs: an American policy view; address, October 6, 1964. Dept State Bul 51:586-91 O 26 '64
BARNETT, Ross Robert
Negro's future in the South; interview. por U S News 54:60-4 Je 3 '63
about
Change of command. il por Newsweek 63:26-7 F 3 '64
Dialogue; telephone calls between Attorney General Kennedy and Governor Barnett prior to arrival of Negro student J. Meredith. Newsweek 62:36 O 14 '63
Mississippi mercy. Reporter 28:19 F 14 '63
BARNETT, William F.
Thought for the interim. America 108:440-2 Mr 30 '63
BARNS and stables
At home in a barn. C. Kellogg. il Ladies Home J 80:68-71 Jl '63
Barn gives you soaring space you can't afford to build today. G. Henle. il House B 105: 142-5+ S '63
Beef-feeding barn that cleans itself. D. Hagen. il Farm J 88:43+ F '64
Built for below-zero comfort. J. R. Borcherding. il Suc Farm 62:42-3 F '64
Dairy cattle housing. J. R. Borcherding. il Suc Farm 62:50-1 O '64
New: loose housing, all under one roof. W. J. Fletcher. il Suc Farm 61:28-9 D '63
Raising the roof of an old barn makes room for parties. il House & Gard 123:172-3 My '63
Cleaning
Barn that cleans the cows and itself. B. Fowler. il Farm J 88:28-9+ S '64
Equipment
Best free-stall ideas from sixty-two dairymen. J. R. Borcherding. il Suc Farm 61: 50-1+ N '63
Free-stall housing made a good dairy setup better. J. R. Borcherding. il Suc Farm 61: 36-7 Jl '63

BARNS and stables—Equipment—*Continued*
New partners; slats and loafing stalls. D. Hagen and J. Bickers. il Farm J 87:30-1+ D '63
Now it's loafing stalls for beef. G. C. Lorang. il Farm J 87:34-5+ N '63
Short on bedding? they're using mats. il Farm J 88:52 Mr '64
Total confinement for beef? D. Malena. il Suc Farm 62:48-9 N '64

Floors

Ideas from Britain on how you can make low-cost beef. D. Seim. il Farm J 88:40-2+ F '64
Keep cows on slats? D. Braun. il Farm J 87:34-5+ Mr '63
New partners; slats and loafing stalls. D. Hagen and J. Bickers. il Farm J 87:30-1+ D '63
Slat-floor barn for all types of stock. L. M. Palmer. il Farm J 87:25+ Ag '63
Slatted floors for beef, too? T. Legge. Farm J 87:78 Mr '63
Total confinement for beef? slotted floors. D. Malena. il Suc Farm 62:48-9 N '64

Heating and ventilation

Barn built for summer comfort. J. R. Borcherding. il Suc Farm 62:34-5 Jl '64
Cold weather ideas for livestock. J. Harvey. il Suc Farm 62:53 N '64
Cool just their heads? air conditioning of dairy barns. il Farm J 87:38 Jl '63
Ventilation and insulation. W. J. Fletcher. il Suc Farm 61:40-1+ Ag '63

Sanitation

Easy-cleaning calf pens. D. Hagen and G. Lorang. il Farm J 87:36E Ag '63

BARNSLEY, Alan Gabriel
My three pubs. Harper 228:24+ Ja '64

about

Gabriel Fielding, new master of the Catholic classic? L. M. Grande. Cath World 197:172-9 Je '63

BARNSTABLE, Mass.
Death of a salt pond; Cotuit, Mass. S. Cobb. Audubon Mag 65:70-2 Mr '63

BARO, Gene
Clamdiggers; poem. New Yorker 39:103 S 7 '63
Dancer resting; poem. New Yorker 40:105 Je 27 '64
In the faculty building; poem. New Yorker 39:64 D 28 '63
Some British poets. Poetry 102:193-8 Je '63
Turkey; poem. New Yorker 39:194 N 30 '63

BAROMETERS
Barometers, weather instruments or wall decorations? il Consumer Bul 48:26-9 F '65
Home barometers: ornamental and useful. il Good H 157:153 S '63

BARON, Claire L.
School libraries. Wilson Lib Bul 39:261+ N '64

BARON, Hermine
One baron who could be queen. C. Goren. il Sports Illus 21:64-5 N 2 '64

BARON, Lynn
Dream dorm or nightmare? Mlle 60:109+ Ja '65

BARON, Ruth
Jesus demythologized; poem. Christian Cent 80:1462 N 27 '63

BARON, Samuel
Baroque flute. Mus Am 83:30 Jl '63

—and Buckler, C. E.
Circulating interferon in mice after intravenous injection of virus. bibliog Science 141:1061-3 S 13 '63

—and others
Host cell species specificity of mouse and chicken interferons. bibliog Science 145:814 Ag 21 '64

BARONDES, Samuel H.
Delayed appearance of labeled protein in isolated nerve endings and axoplasmic flow. bibliog Science 146:779-81 N 6 '64

BARONE, Vincent J.
Paperbacks in the social sciences. Sr Schol 83:30T Ja 17 '64

BAROQUE art. See Art, Baroque

BAROQUE music. See Music, Baroque

BARR, Alfred Hamilton, 1902-
Alfred Barr: New York forecaster of trends in modern art. C. Willard. il pors Look 27:86-8 Mr 26 '63
Thinking of today, and eternal things. il por Newsweek 63:50-2 Je 1 '64

BARR, Browne
On parish renewal. Christian Cent 81:1342+ O 28 '64

BARR, Marjorie
Children's library for adults. Library J 88:832-3 F 15 '63

BARR, Thomas C.
Cave ecology. Science 144:321-2 Ap 17 '64

BARRACUDA fishing
Battling barracuda. G. Heinold. il Outdoor Life 134:26-7+ S '64
Old razormouth. A. J. McClane. il Field & S 68:96-8+ Ap '64
Strike of lightning. J. Brooks. il Outdoor Life 135:20-3+ Ja '65

BARRACUDAS
Nature note. Sci N L 85:111 F 15 '64

BARRAT, Robert
De Gaulle's would-be assassins. Commonweal 77:663-4 Mr 22 '63

BARRAULT, Jean Louis
Letter from Paris; performance of Beckett's Oh les beaux jours. Genêt. New Yorker 40:102+ F 22 '64
Life force. il Newsweek 63:96-7 Mr 16 '64
Off Broadway. E. Oliver. New Yorker 40:112+ Mr 14 '64

BARREIROS RODRIGUEZ, Eduardo
Big on his own. il por Time 83:85 Ja 17 '64
Who's who in foreign business. il por Fortune 68:94 N '63

BARREL lifter; story. See Pecile, J.

BARRELS, Tumbling. See Tumbling barrels

BARRENECHEA, Mauro
Fresh start in Santo Domingo. America 108:366-7 Mr 16 '63

BARRESE, Pauline
Winter night; poem. America 112:165 Ja 30 '65

BARRET, Richard Carter
Notes on some types of American art glass. Antiques 85:671-8 Je '64

BARRETT, Alan H. and Lilley, Edward
Mariner-2 microwave observations of Venus. Sky & Tel 25:192-5 Ap '63

BARRETT, Ernestine
Ernestine Barrett ballet company, Carnegie recital hall. J. Maskey. Dance Mag 38:72 Ap '64

BARRETT, George
Catholics and birth control. Read Digest 83:77-82 N '63

BARRETT, Lincoln
She still remains; poem. McCalls 90:152 S '63
When a tree falls; poem. McCalls 91:166 Ap '64

BARRETT, P. and Burke, A.
Colorful Christmas plants. Horticulture 41:602-3 D '63

BARRETT, Patricia
Book review. America 110:106-7 Ja 18 '64

BARRETT, Richard S.
Guide to using psychological tests. Harvard Bsns R 41:138-46 S '63

BARRETT, William C.
Reader's choice. See issues of Atlantic

BARRIENTOS, Maria
Three neglected sopranos. J. M. Alfonte. por Opera N 28:38-9 N 16 '63

BARRIENTOS ORTUÑO, René
In Bolivia: new leader, old problems; in U.S: questions. por U S News 57:8 N 16 '64
Up from veep. por Newsweek 64:58 N 16 '64

BARRIER; story. See Delman, D.

BARRINGER, D. Moreau
Travel far and near; the meteorite search. Natur Hist 73:56-9 My '64

BARRISTERS. See Lawyers

BARRON, Frank, and others
Hallucinogenic drugs; with biographical sketches. Sci Am 210:24, 29-37 bibliog(p 156) Ap '64

BARRON, James
Bloodshed at dawn. C. S. Forester. il por Am Heritage 15:40-5+ O '64

BARRON, Jennie Loitman
Too much sex on campus. Ladies Home J 81:48+ Ja '64; Same abr. Read Digest 84:59-62 My '64

BARRON, Neil
Peace corps in perspective. bibliog Library J 90:196-200 Ja 15 '65

BARRY, Camilla
WLB biography. Wilson Lib Bul 39:503+ F '65

BARRY, Donna
Now the storm is over; poem. America 111:110 Ag 1 '64

BARRY, Joseph A.
Miss Toklas on her own. New Repub 148:21-3 Mr 30 '63
Portrait of Chanel no. 1. N Y Times Mag p30-1+ Ag 23 '64; Same abr. Read Digest 85:261-3+ N '64
Sarajevo revisited, fifty years after. N Y Times Mag p 12-13+ Je 28 '64

BARRY, Les
Camera guide. il Pop Phot 51:80-1+ D '62; 52:76-7+ Mr; 94-5+ Je; 53:84-5+ O; 54+ N '63
On the go. See issues of Popular photography
BARRY, Naomi
Going places, finding things in the Relais de Campagne; excerpts from France personal. House & Gard 125:52+ My '64
John Huston's best of all worlds. House & Gard 126:140-7 D '64
Shops of Europe. Holiday 37:117-22 Ja '65
Walk, walk, talk, talk; People, places and things in the Paris edition of the New York herald tribune. il por Newsweek 61: 52-3 Ap 1 '63
BARRY, Robert M.
For C. Wright Mills. Commonweal 80:643-5 S 18 '64
Sociology today. Commonweal 80:182-3 My 1 '64
BARRY, Ruth E. and Wolf, Beverly
Should vocational guidance be junked? NEA J 52:30-2 D '63
BARRY, Sheila
Let's travel to Portugal. Mlle 59:335-7 Ag '64
BARRY, T. I. and Moore, W. J.
Amethyst: optical properties and paramagnetic resonance. Science 144:289-90 Ap 17 '64
BARRYMORE, Elaine
Life with the great profile. H. Frankel. Sat R 47:28-9 My 2 '64
BARRYMORE family
Barrymores, by H. Alpert. Review
Sat R il 47:39 D 5 '64. J. K. Hutchens
Over the falls. il Newsweek 64:96 D 14 '64
BARS and barrooms
Corruption uncorked in New York. P. Welch and others. il Life 54:22-31+ Ap 5 '63
Desk, hobby bench, and legs and it's also a bar. H. M. Burke, jr. il Pop Sci 184:146-8 Ap '64
English drinking habits. R. Postgate. il Holiday 33:87-8+ F '63
Irish pub. W. Bittner. il Atlan 211:112+ F '63
My three pubs. G. Fielding. il Harper 228: 24+ Ja '64
New case for the old saloon. Life 54:4 My 31 '63
Saloon. G. Carson. il Am Heritage 14:24-31+ Ap '63
Throwaway New Year's eve bar. il Pop Mech 120:136-7 D '63
To get the bars back on their feet. S. Blum. il N Y Times Mag p68+ S 27 '64
Yippee! Scopitone, a cinematic jukebox in Spark's pub south, New York. New Yorker 40:21-2 Jl 11 '64
BARSHAI, Rudolf
Well-tempered muzykanty; Moscow chamber orchestra. il por Time 82:69 N 22 '63
BART, Peter B.
How to read the financial pages without going broke. Harper 227:31-5 Ag '63
Madison avenue (cont) Sat R 46:54 F 9; 58 Mr 9; 64-5 My 11; 54 Je 8; 47 Jl 13; 45+ Ag 10; 78 S 14; 78 N 9; 60+ D 14 '63; 47: 78 Ja 11; 52+ F 8; 126-7 Mr 14; 81 Ap 11 57 Je 13 '64
Money managers. Esquire 60:204 D '63
BARTA, H. E. P.
Economical plating-waste treatment. Am City 79:75-6 Ja '64
BARTELL, H. Robert, jr. See Robinson, R. I. jt. auth.
BARTER-CROISSANT, Rene
Shoot first! excerpts. il Sat R 46:42-3 Mr 16 '63
BARTH, Alan
Civil liberty and individual responsibility; address. Vital Speeches 31:135-9 D 15 '64
Dr Barth (Alan) on America's heart condition. Nat R 16:437 Je 2 '64
BARTH, John
Ambrose his mark; story. Esquire 59:97 F '63
BARTH, Karl
Barth in retirement. por Time 81:58+ My 31 '63
Barth's wisdom on Rome. Christian Cent 80:1019 Ag 21 '63
First & the last. Time 82:44 Ag 30 '63
Karl Barth's theological quest. D. J. O'Hanlon. Commonweal 77:520-1 F 8 '63
BARTH, Merlyn W.
Triggered sweep for improving scopes. Electr World 73:71-4 Ja '65
BARTH-WEHRENALP, G. and Block, B. P.
Inorganic polymers; adapted from two lectures presented in a panel discussion on the Properties of materials. bibliog Science 142: 627-32 N 8 '63
BARTHELME, Donald
Down the line with the annual. New Yorker 40:34-5 Mr 21 '64
L'lapse. New Yorker 39:29-31 Mr 2 '63
Man's face. New Yorker 40:29 My 30 '64
Margins; story. New Yorker 40:33-4 F 22 '64
Marie, Marie, hold on tight; story. New Yorker 39:49-51 O 12 '63
Piano player; story. New Yorker 39:24 Ag 31 '63
Picture history of the war; story. New Yorker 40:28-31 Je 20 '64
Police band. New Yorker 40:28 Ag 22 '64
President; story. New Yorker 40:26-7 S 5 '64
Shower of gold; story. New Yorker 39:33-7 D 28 '63
BARTHOLD, L. O. and Pfeiffer, H. G.
High-voltage power transmission. Sci Am 210:38-47 bibliog(p 150) My '64
BARTILUCCI, Nicholas
Poured-concrete pool wallops gunite alternate by 50 per cent. Am City 79:96-8 Je '64
BARTLESVILLE, Okla.
Bartlesville, Oklahoma. A. Pryce-Jones. Vogue 144:54 D '64
BARTLETT, Bertrice
Stephens college library instruction program. ALA Bul 58:311-14 Ap '64
BARTLETT, Charles
How not to stop Barry. Cato. Nat R 14:489 Je 18 '63
BARTLETT, Elizabeth
Earth age; poem. Cath World 199:181 Je '64
BARTLETT, F. Lewis
Institutional peonage; our exploitation of mental patients. Atlan 214:116-19 Jl '64
BARTLETT, John
On the fringe. H. Frankel. Sat R 47:39 Mr 21 '64
BARTLETT, Mary
Cooking to windward. por Yachting 113:43-5+ F '63
BARTLETT, Paul R.
High seas radiotelephone. Yachting 113:212+ My '63
BARTLETT, Stephen W.
Dialogue between cultures. Sat R 47:44-7+ Jl 18 '64
BARTLEY, Diana
Introducing the 1964 Duesenberg, Packard, Stutz and Mercer! Esquire 60:200-3 D '63
Mr Moss builds his dream car. Esquire 61: 80-1+ Mr '64
Mustang, for those who think young. Esquire 61:86-8 My '64
Whatever happened to sports cars? Esquire 60:82-7+ S '63
BARTÓK, Béla
Bartók on stage. E. Helm. il Hi Fi 14:74-7+ N '64
Exciting and impressive on Everest, Gunter Wand. H. Glass. Am Rec G 30:510-11 F '64
From DGG, the first complete recording of The miraculous mandarin. J. Diether. Am Rec G 30:826-7 My '64
Letter from Budapest. J. Wechsberg. il New Yorker 40:143-54 Mr 14 '64
Letter from Paris; Miraculous mandarin. Genêt. New Yorker 39:157-8 D 14 '63
New wheel for the old hub. J. Lyons. il Am Rec G 29:516-17 Mr '63
On records; Bluebeard's castle. Opera N 28: 30 My 2 '64
Opera comes into its own Bluebeard's castle twice more on discs. E. Salzman. por Hi Fi 13:60-1 Je '63
Simultaneously, from Mercury and Columbia, Bluebeard's castle. C. J. Luten. il Am Rec G 29:690-1 My '63
Vintage Scherzo. Time 81:46 Mr 8 '63
BARTOLINI, Julian
Ambassador by letter. Recreation 57:64-5 F '64
BARTOLINI, R. Paul
Double header in Milwaukee. Library J 89:4737-9 D 1 '64
BARTON, George Wendell, 1925-
Talking in circles. il Newsweek 62:43 D 30 '63
—and Barton, S. H.
Forms of sounds as shown on an oscilloscope by roulette figures. Science 142:1455-6 D 13 '63
BARTON, James L.
Sheik justice. Read Digest 82:132E-132F+ My '63
BARTON, John
Play that never was. il Time 82:37 Ag 2 '63
BARTON, Stephen H. See Barton, G. W. 1925-, jt. auth.
BARTOSHUK, Linda M. and others
Taste of sodium chloride solutions after adaptation to sodium chloride: implications for the water taste. bibliog Science 143: 967-8 F 28 '64
BARTRAM, John
Bartram's garden. C. B. Lees. il Horticulture 42:46-9+ Mr '64

BARTRON, Harold
Cleaning your charcoal grill. House B 105:42 Je '63
BARTSCH, Karl-Heinz
Harder they fall. Time 81:31 F 22 '63
BARTZ, Alice
Book truck service for curriculum enrichment. ALA Bul 57:165 F '63
BARUCH, Bernard
Baruch and his legend. A. A. Blum. por Nation 199:72-3 Ag 24 '64
End of a friendship; with memorandum by E. M. House. C. Seymour. il por Am Heritage 14:8-9+ Ag '63
BARUKSHTIS, Igor
At Red square, no cool sounds allowed; excerpts from interview, ed. by R. Hemming and G. Nikolaieff. por Sr Schol 85:23 D 2 '64
BARWOOD, Aileen Vincent
Life under 150 inches of rain. Sci Digest 54:18-21 O '63
BARY, Shura
Feasting aboard freighters. Travel 122:39-42 N '64
BARYE, Antoine Louis
Bronze menagerie; exhibition at Manhattan's Bernard Black gallery. il Time 83:72 Mr 6 '64
BARYON. See Particles (nuclear physics)
BARZANI, Mustapha
Ultimatum and war; Kurdish tribesmen and Iraqi troops. por Newsweek 61:56 Je 24 '63
BARZEL, Ann
Little Egypt never got to the Chicago fair! Dance Mag 38:62-5 D '64
Looking at television. See issues of Dance magazine
BARZINI, Benedetta
Benedetta Barzini, magnificent Milanese. pors Vogue 143:56-7 Ja 15 '64
BARZINI, Luigi
Automobile classic: the 1907 race from Peking to Paris by car; excerpts. Vogue 144:123-9 N 15 '64
Charmers. Vogue 143:57-8+ Ja 15 '64
Italian character; excerpts from Italians. Harper 229:33-40 Ag '64
BARZUN, Jacques
Bedside reading; a reference book; excerpts from address. Wilson Lib Bul 39:246-7 N '64
Diller, a dollar, a very expensive scholar. Horizon 5:60-3 S '63
BAS-relief printing. See Photography—Printing processes
BASALT
Basalts dredged from the northeastern Pacific Ocean. C. G. Engel and A. E. J. Engel. bibliog il Science 140:1321-4 Je 21 '63
BASCH, Peter
Prop it with a window. P. Caulfield. il Mod Phot 27:74-5 My '63
BASEBALL
Analysis by an expert; world series, ed. by R. Creamer. F. Hutchinson. Sports Illus 19:25 O 14 '63
Baseball: another business facing change; interview. B. Veeck. il U S News 55:56-61 Ag 12 '63
Baseball establishment. B. Veeck. Esquire 62:45-7+ Ag '64
Baseball 1964; can the pitchers stay on top? W. Leggett. il Sports Illus 20:38-41 Ap 13 '64
Baseball tries to keep its bounce. il Bsns W p 144+ Ap 20 '63
Beanball my men? we'll beanball you, Alvin vows darkly. D. Moser. il Life 55:28-28A Jl 26 '63
Beanballs and other headaches. R. Creamer. Sports Illus 19:52 Jl 29 '63
Bets are off. il Newsweek 62:69 Ag 5 '63
Bible in the bullpen. J. Devaney. il Sat Eve Post 237:28-9 My 2 '64
Candid memoirs of Leo Durocher. L. Durocher and E. Linn. il Sat Eve Post 236:26-8+ My 11 '63
Desperate chase; St Louis Cardinals pennant drive. W. Leggett. il Sports Illus 19:20-5 S 23 '63
Dodgers in four. Newsweek 62:82 O 14 '63
Down the drain. il Newsweek 62:63 S 30 '63
Even series; with some fresh faces; day-by-day account of the first five games. W. Leggett. il Sports Illus 21:22-9 O 19 '64
Ex-national sport looks to its image. L. Koppett. il N Y Times Mag p 18-19+ D 20 '64
Five pitch baseball. R. Copeland. Recreation 57:517 D '64
Get any hits Stan? F. Bisher. il Sat Eve Post 236:30+ My 25 '63
Getting close to the sun and the stars; Florida's annual spring training; reproductions of paintings. B. Charmatz. Sports Illus 18:26-34 Mr 4 '63
Home run heaven; Minnesota's Metropolitan stadium. F. Deford. il Sports Illus 20:22-5 My 18 '64
Honest Warren Giles: he always strives to please. G. Holland. Sports Illus 18:32-4+ Je 10 '63
How to succeed; All-star game. Newsweek 64:77 Jl 20 '64
I managed good, but boy did they play bad; manager of San Jose Bees. G. Rogin. il Sports Illus 21:22-6 Ag 17 '64
It ain't what they do it's the way that they do it; New York Mets defeat of Milwaukee Braves. Time 81:44+ Ap 26 '63
It's news only when he loses. J. Murphy. il N Y Times Mag p 133-4+ S 8 '63
Just one more; pitcher. E. Wynn. il Newsweek 62:62-3 Jl 1 '63
K is for Koufax; first game of the world series. il Time 82:49 O 11 '63
Knuckling under; opening game of the world series. il Newsweek 64:68 O 19 '64
Koo-foo the Killer; world series. W. Leggett. il Sports Illus 19:18-25 O 14 '63
Last time around with Stan. T. M. O'Leary. il Sports Illus 19:20-5 O 7 '63
Leo: under the sunset gun. R. Cantwell. il Sports Illus 18:20-4 F 18 '63
Losing twenty games isn't easy; Houston's pitcher D. Farrell. L. Merchant. il Sat Eve Post 236:58-61 Je 8 '63
Man behind The Man; excerpt from Stan Musial: The Man's own story; ed. by R. Broeg. S. Musial. il Look 28:109-10+ Ap 21 '64
Man in the pin-striped suit: Ralph Houk. E. Linn. il Sat Eve Post 236:89-93 S 28 '63
Needed, an Abe Lincoln of baseball. il Ebony 19:110-11 Ap '64
Notes and comment; box scores. New Yorker 39:35-6 Ap 20 '63
Old potato face. il Time 84:36-90+ S 11 '64
On the trail of a hero. E. Graham. il Sports Illus 19:50-5 Ag 26 '63
One ran away. il Time 82:43 Ag 30 '63
Pennant nobody wanted; National league pennant race. Time 84:86 O 9 '64
Pitch like a pro. il Pop Sci 183:100-1 O '63
Pitchers make snails look fast so throw the ball! E. Havemann. il Life 55:17 S 6 '63; Same abr. with title So throw the ball! Read Digest 84:116-18 Ap '64
Pitchers' poverty; Stars shine. il Newsweek 62:56-7 Ag 12 '63
Rap on the knuckles; Yankees v. Cards. Time 84:94-5 O 16 '64
Rational rebel in pinstripes. L. Shecter. il Sports Illus 18:76-8+ My 13 '63
Return of the mahatma. F. Graham, jr. Sat Eve Post 236:66-8 Mr 9 '63
Speed won the world series; Cardinals vs. Yankees. W. Leggett. il Sports Illus 21:36-7 O 26 '64
Sporting scene; world series. R. Angell. il New Yorker 40:224-8+ O 24 '64
Sporting scene: world series over television in New York bars. R. Angell. New Yorker 39:184+ O 26 '63
Stengel ponders. The year of the Berra. L. Koppett. il N Y Times Mag p21+ Ap 12 '64
Tale of two cities: Philadelphia and Baltimore. il Time 84:80 O 2 '64
Tell you what you ought to do, Commissioner Frick; All-star game in Cleveland. R. Creamer. Sports Illus 19:37-8 Jl 22 '63
That magical day; New York Mets score nineteen runs. Time 83:71 Je 5 '64
There's only one way to beat the Yankees. J. Robinson. il Life 55:106A-12 O 4 '63
Truth strikes out. C. Cilo. Nation 199:281-2 O 26 '64
Urgent matter of one index finger; case of S. Koufax. R. Creamer. il Sports Illus 18:20-2+ Mr 4 '63
View from the mound; pitching. il Newsweek 62:57 Jl 15 '63
Warren Spahn: king of the hill. T. Cohane. il Look 27:67-70 Ap 23 '63
Whiz Kids are still going strong; R. Roberts and C. Simmons former Philadelphia Whiz Kids. W. Leggett. il Sports Illus 20:60+ Je 8 '64
Who will win the war of the lefties? Dodgers vs Yankees. R. Creamer. il Sports Illus 19:28-9 S 30 '63
World series continued; spring training games. Sports Illus 20:16 Ap 6 '64
Year of the pitcher. il Time 82:56 S 13 '63
Year that is. il Newsweek 63:73-4 Mr 16 '64
See also
Little leagues
National baseball hall of fame and museum
Radio broadcasting—Sports
Softball

BASEBALL—*Continued*

Anecdotes, facetiae, satire, etc.

They led the league in gags; ed. by D. Anderson. J. Garagiola. il Sat Eve Post 236: 62-3 S 14 '63
World series with Marianne Moore; letter from an October afternoon. G. Plimpton. il Harper 229:50-8 O '64; Reply. M. Moore. 229-91-2+ N '64

Economic aspects

How I didn't buy a ball club; ed. by E. Linn. B. Veeck. il Sat Eve Post 236:78-80 S 7 '63
Money players. Newsweek 64:61 D 14 '64
Speaking out; businessmen are wrecking baseball. J. P. Brosnan. Sat Eve Post 237: 8+ My 30 '64
Success is killing the American league. W. Leggett. il Sports Illus 19:18-21 S 9 '63

History

Antique sports; chips and sawdust from early baseball days (cont) W. P. Ware. il Hobbies 68:116-17 Ap '63
World serious, then and now. A. Daley. il N Y Times Mag p34 S 29 '63

Quotations, maxims, etc.

Take me out to the—; comp. by E. F. Murphy. il N Y Times Mag p94-5 Ap 19 '64

Rules

Balkball. Newsweek 61:84 My 6 '63
Just a second; National league umpires enforce the balk rule. W. Leggett. il Sports Illus 18:14-15+ Ap 22 '63
Monsters on top; batters up against new pitchers. T. C. Brody. il Sports Illus 19: 10-15 Ag 12 '63
Never on Sunday? concerning world series. Sports Illus 21:11 S 21 '64
New stage in baseball's cold war. W. B. Furlong. il N Y Times Mag p36+ My 12 '63
Percentage baseball, by E. Cook. Review Sports Illus il 20:14-17 Mr 23 '64 F. Deford
Spitter is back; outlawed 1920. W. Leggett. il Sports Illus 18:18-21 Je 3 '63

Statistics

Percentage baseball, by E. Cook. Review Sports Illus il 20:14-17 Mr 23 '64. F. Deford

Study and teaching

With mirrors, flat gloves and sawed-up bats. R. Creamer. il Sports Illus 18:56-8 Je 3 '63

Dominican Republic

Invasion from Santo Domingo; Dominican big leaguers. R. Cantwell. il Sports Illus 18: 54-61 F 25 '63

BASEBALL accidents. See Sports—Accidents and injuries

BASEBALL cards. See Picture cards

BASEBALL clubs

After the Yankees what? a TV drama. L. W. Robinson. il N Y Times Mag p44-5+ N 15 '64
Albie Pearson: the littlest Angel. G. Rogin. il Sports Illus 18:62-4+ My 27 '63
Baltimore's two flags; Baltimore Orioles. F. Deford. il Sports Illus 21:12-15 Jl 13 '64
Baseball (cont) il Sports Illus 18:59-61 Mr 11: 65-6 Ap 15; 61-3 My 6; 63-4+ My 20; 48-9 My 27 '63
Baseball hunts greener pastures. il Bsns W p42+ N 7 '64
Baseball's week. See issues of Sports illustrated published during baseball season
Battle for nineteenth; Mets play Washington Senators. il Newsweek 64:66-7 Ag 10 '64
Bauer's birds; Baltimore Orioles. il Newsweek 64:69-70 Jl 27 '64
Big deal; CBS buys Yankees. il Newsweek 64:54-5 Ag 24 '64
Big eye league; Yankees sold to Columbia broadcasting system. il Time 84:74 Ag 21 '64
Big Red surge; bloodiest pennant feud in twenty-four years. W. Leggett. il Sports Illus 21:26-9 O 5 '64
Big sellout; CBS buys New York Yankees; with editorial comment. il Sports Illus 21:8, 12-17 Ag 24 '64
Big Willie's private war with Cousin Don; Giants vs. Dodgers. R. Creamer. il Sports Illus 19:38-9 Jl 1 '63
Bill Dailey, won't you please come in? Minnesota twins. W. Leggett. il Sports Illus 19:26-7+ Jl 1 '63
Blast-off; record home-run pace. il Newsweek 63:54-5 Je 1 '64
Bravura battle for the Braves; Milwaukee Braves fast becoming Atlanta Braves. H. Horn. il Sports Illus 21:32-3+ N 2 '64
Bring on The Monster: D. Radatz of the Boston Red Sox. Time 82:68 Jl 5 '63
Bronx bombs; New York Yankees. il Newsweek 64:50-1 Ag 31 '64
Business of baseball. T. O'Hanlon. il Duns R 83:44-5+ My '64
Call them Mickey's mice or Pluto's pups; Los Angeles Angels. M. Durslag. il Sports Illus 21:44-5 Jl 20 '64
Can't anybody here play this game? excerpt. J. Breslin. il Read Digest 83:193+ Ag '63
Chaplins in pinstripes. Newsweek 61:85 Ap 22 '63
Checkmate for Charlie; Kansas City Athletics. Sports Illus 20:10 Ja 27 '64
Cliffhanger for Yogi and crucial for July; three-game series between Yankees and Orioles. F. Deford. il Sports Illus 21:16-19 Jl 27 '64
Debacle in Cincinnati; Reds go down in defeat. F. Deford. il Sports Illus 21:22-7 O 12 '64
Desperate chase; St Louis Cardinals pennant drive. W. Leggett. il Sports Illus 19:20-5 S 23 '63
Dick Groat and his hitting machine; St Louis Cardinal infield. W. Bingham. il Sports Illus 19:32-4 Jl 22 '63
Dodgers in a dogfight; Speed and a strong leader. W. Leggett. il Sports Illus 19:8-13 S 2 '63
Early birds; Baltimore Orioles. Time 81:51 Je 14 '63
Entertaining team; Dodgers. il Newsweek 64: 81 Jl 13 '64
Everybody up! spring training. il Time 81: 68+ Ap 5 '63
Everything's green & gold in Kansas City. W. Bingham. il Sports Illus 18:24-6+ My 20 '63
Fire the handicapped; the Tigers. Sports Illus 19:15 Jl 1 '63
Fred Hutchinson: angry boss of the Reds. T. Cohane. il Look 27:66-9 Ag 27 '63
Free-swinging Angel who never fears to tread. R. Creamer. il Sports Illus 19:46+ Ag 12 '63
Futile surge amid the shuffle; Cardinals in pennant race. W. Leggett. il Sports Illus 21:98-101 S 21 '64
Gashouse revisited; St Louis Cardinals. il Time 82:66 S 20 '63
Giant issue; manager of the San Francisco Giants denies racial statements. il Newsweek 64:54 Ag 17 '64
Gil Hodges: most nice guy in baseball; manager of Washington Senators. G. Astor. il Look 28:98A-100+ Jl 14 '64
Go Phillies go! il Newsweek 64:46-7 Jl 6 '64
Hands across the infield; New York Yankees. I. R. McVay. il Look 27:79-82+ Jl 16 '63
Happiness is being somewhere else; K.C. A's. F. Graham, jr. il Sat Eve Post 237: 73-7 Ap 4 '64
Happy start for a happy new Willie; W. Mays of San Francisco Giants. F. Deford. il Sports Illus 20:22-7 Ap 27 '64
He sends in the smoke for the green goose; J. Wyatt of Kansas City Athletics. M. Kram. Sports Illus 20:56-8 Je 22 '64
Hot team in the old town; Philadelphia Phillies. W. Leggett. il Sports Illus 18:18-21 Ap 29 '63
How the West was won. il Newsweek 63: 63 Ap 13 '64
How to win friends. il Time 84:70 Jl 3 '64
If it isn't one M it's another; M. Mantle and R. Maris of the Yankees. il Sports Illus 19: 10-15 Jl 8 '63
I'm the worst that's ever been; Baltimore's M. Pappas. G. Rogin. il Sports Illus 20:54-6+ Ap 27 '64
In first place, the Met fans. L. Koppett. il N Y Times Mag p26+ Je 14 '64
It's Metsomania; New York Mets fans. J. Breslin. il Sat Eve Post 237:20-5 Je 13 '64
Lapse of the gods; AL pennant race. Newsweek 64:72 S 21 '64
Laugh off $11 million? Columbia broadcasting system buys New York Yankee baseball club. J. R. Tunis. New Repub 152:11-12 Ja 2 '65
Let's go, Phillies! J. Olsen. il Sports Illus 21: 10-15 Ag 10 '64
Like a big infection; Phillies leading the league. il Time 83:70-1 Je 5 '64
Lively market in lame ducks; trading baseball's stock. B. Surface. il Sat Eve Post 237:66-7 Je 6 '64

BASEBALL clubs—*Continued*
Managing to lose; 1964 world series. il Newsweek 64:72 O 26 '64
Matter of psychology; Baltimore Orioles. Time 84:81 Jl 10 '64
Miracle in St Louis; Cardinals win the pennant. W. Leggett. il Sports Illus 21:22-7 O 12 '64
Mrs Payson's ball park; New York Mets. C. Amory. il Vogue 144:144-5+ S 15 '64
Newcomers. il Time 84:54 Ag 28 '64
Night I met the Mets. P. Mesta. il McCalls 91:23+ O '63
Night the Dodgers got the monkey off their back; Dodger-Giant rivalry. R. Creamer. Sports Illus 19:70+ S 9 '63
1964 looks like year of the Giants in National league. il Ebony 19:157-8+ Je '64
1963 scouting reports. R. Creamer and others. il Sports Illus 18:45-66+ Ap 8 '63
Not enough talkative bats in Cincy; strong pitching, but no hitters. M. Kram. il Sports Illus 21:54-7 Ag 24 '64
Not much to do but eat, sleep and play baseball; Boston Red Sox rookie. F. Deford. il Sports Illus 21:49-50 Ag 3 '64
Nothing stopped the Dodgers. R. Creamer. il Sports Illus 19:26-7 S 30 '63
Oh, give me a home; Kansas City Athletics. Sports Illus 20:8 Ja 6 '64
On top with old Smokey. il Time 82:68 S 27 '63
One small difference; Los Angeles Dodgers, best seventh-place team. Time 84:43 Jl 31 '64
Orlando Cepeda; San Francisco Giants. T. Cohane. il Look 27:84+ My 21 '63
Out in front with a new look; Yankees lead the league. W. Leggett. il Sports Illus 21: 26-9 S 28 '64
Out of the park on a half swing. B. Hellman. Sports Illus 18:85+ Ap 8 '63
Phils take off. G. Astor. il Look 28:87-92 Ag 25 '64
Photo finish; National and American league pennant races. il Newsweek 64:70 O 12 '64
Pitching explosion in paradise; Pittsburgh Pirates. M. Cope. il Sports Illus 18:22-4+ Je 24 '63
Positively Sain; coach for Yankees. H. L. Masin. il Sr Schol 83:48-9 O 4 '63
Richest bonus baby ever; R. Reichardt of the Angels. E. Shrake. il Sports Illus 21:16-21 Jl 6 '64
Rookie from Wampum, Pa; R. Allen of Phillies. W. Leggett. il Sports Illus 20:28-9 Ap 20 '64
Running game comes back. W. Leggett. il Sports Illus 20:40-1 My 4 '64
Sad day for baseball; selling of Yankees to CBS. W. B. Furlong. il Sports Illus 21: 26-7+ S 21 '64
Scouting reports (cont) il Sports Illus 20:49-54+ Ap 13 '64
Scrappy scramblers; Phillies. H. L. Masin. il Sr Schol 85:40 S 30 '64
Secret weapons save the Yanks. R. Creamer. il Sports Illus 19:12-15 Ag 5 '63
So what else is new? il Newsweek 63:76-7 Ap 20 '64
Spahn and who? is the Braves' battle cry. F. Deford. il Sports Illus 20:84-5 Ap 6 '64
Speaking out; businessmen are wrecking baseball. J. P. Brosnan. Sat Eve Post 237: 8+ My 30 '64
Speaking out; they've wrecked the American league; ed. by E. Linn. B. Veeck. Sat Eve Post 237:10+ Jl 11 '64
Sporting scene; Mets at William A. Shea stadium. R. Angell. il New Yorker 40:96+ My 30 '64
Sporting scene; old teams moving, new teams forming. R. Angell. il New Yorker 40:224-8+ O 24 '64
Sporting scene; the Mets at the Polo Grounds. R. Angell. il New Yorker 39:132+ My 25 '63
Star on the wrong team; J. Fregosi of the Angels. F. Deford. il Sports Illus 20:69-70+ Je 1 '64
Strikeout? Newsweek 63:76 Ja 27 '64
Success is killing the American league. W. Leggett. il Sports Illus 19:18-21 S 9 '63
Sweet taste of revenge; Cardinals and Yankees in world series. il Time 84:62 O 23 '64
Tale of two cities; Boston Red Sox and the Kansas City Athletics. Newsweek 61:59 My 27 '63
Television tilts the old ball game; sale of Yankees to CBS; with report by T. Flaherty. il Life 57:87-8 Ag 28 '64
That Johnny Keane is a fine manager is what he sure is; Cardinals' manager. J. Olsen. il Sports Illus 20:110-14+ Ap 13 '64
They went and got 'em; Orioles and White Sox push New York into third place. W. Leggett. il Sports Illus 21:14-19 Ag 31 '64
This pitcher may need relief. J. Brosnan. il Sports Illus 20:24-6+ Mr 16 '64
Those mighty Minnesota muscle sprouts: the Twins. T. Cohane. il Look 27:84-5+ Je 4 '63
Time of trial for Alvin Dark; San Francisco Giants' manager. R. H. Boyle. il Sports Illus 21:26-31 Jl 6 '64
Torments of excellence; Detroit's A. Kaline. J. Olsen. il Sports Illus 20:32+ My 11 '64
Tragic rebirth of the Chicago Cubs. T. Cohane. il Look 28:60+ Je 16 '64
Travelogue; Milwaukee Braves decision to move to Atlanta. il Newsweek 64:72 N 2 '64
Trouble sprouts for the Yankees; attendance war between Yankees and Mets. W. Leggett. il Sports Illus 20:12-15 Mr 2 '64
Two flags for the Cardinals? baseball Cardinals and the football Cardinals pennant winners. E. Shrake. il Sports Illus 21:20-3 N 9 '64
Walt Alston: manager with a hair shirt; Dodger leader. M. Durslag. il Look 27:64+ Jl 30 '63
Weeks that were; first two weeks of the season. Time 83:47 My 1 '64
What every team needs; purchase of Kansas City Athletics by C. O. Finley. il Time 83:30 Ja 24 '64
Whip who put snap in the Phillies; G. Mauch. M. Cope. il Sat Eve Post 237:74-5+ Ag 8 '64
White Sox hex that failed. W. Leggett. il Sports Illus 20:20-1+ Je 29 '64
Why the Yankees fired Berra. J. Ogle. il Look 28:30+ D 29 '64
Wild scramble in the National league; pennant race. il Sports Illus 20:22-7 Je 15 '64
Word for New York is bush. C. McCabe. il Sports Illus 21:56-8+ Ag 3 '64
Yankees: descent from Olympus; once the mightiest team in baseball, now, like Beverly hillbillies, it belongs to CBS. Why? R. Kahn. il Sat Eve Post 237:80-3 S 12 '64
Yankees vs? il Newsweek 62:66 S 23 '63
Youngest Met. G. Zimmermann. il Look 27: 83-7 Jl 2 '63

BASEBALL coaches. See Physical directors

BASEBALL fans
Blank spots in the bleachers. Time 82:62 Jl 26 '63
Dodgers in a dogfight; Speed and a strong leader. W. Leggett. il Sports Illus 19:8-13 S 2 '63
Fantasy world of baseball. J. Brosnan. il Atlan 213:69-72 Ap '64
Gift for making a bad situation much worse; R. Maris. R. Creamer. Sports Illus 18:48-9 My 27 '63
In first place, the Met fans. L. Koppett. il N Y Times Mag p26+ Je 14 '64
It's Metsomania; New York Mets fans. J. Breslin. il Sat Eve Post 237:20-5 Je 13 '64
Old stonefingers, best show around Boston in years. R. Creamer. il Sports Illus 19: 42+ S 2 '63
On the trail of a hero. E. Graham. il Sports Illus 19:50-5 Ag 26 '63
Quaint cult of the Mets; baseball in the Polo Grounds. R. Creamer. Sports Illus 18:61-3 My 6 '63
Success is killing the American league. W. Leggett. il Sports Illus 19:18-21 S 9 '63
Trouble sprouts for the Yankees; attendance war between Yankees and Mets. W. Leggett. il Sports Illus 20:12-15 Mr 2 '64

Caricatures and cartoons

Back at the Rococo ranch. Los Angeles nervous citizens. Sports Illus 19:26-7 S 23 '63

BASEBALL fields
Land of the nonbreaking curve ball; spring training at Geronimo park, Apache Junction, Ariz. M. Herskowitz. il Sports Illus 18:59-61 Mr 11 '63
Longest ninety feet in baseball; with photographs by N. Leifer. Sports Illus 20:32-6 Je 22 '64

BASEBALL gambling. See Gambling

BASEBALL hall of fame. See National baseball hall of fame and museum

BASEBALL in literature
New baseball books. il Library J 88:1727-8 Ap 15 '63

BASEBALL managers
Annual rite of fall; firing the manager. R. Creamer. il Sports Illus 19:49-51 S 16 '63
Gil Hodges: most nice guy in baseball; manager of Washington Senators. G. Astor. il Look 28:98A-100+ Jl 14 '64
1963 scouting reports. R. Creamer and others. il Sports Illus 18:45-66+ Ap 8 '63

BASEBALL managers—*Continued*
Tale of two cities; Boston Red Sox and the Kansas City Athletics. Newsweek 61:59 My 27 '63
That Johnny Keane is a fine manager is what he sure is; Cardinals' manager. J. Olsen. Sports Illus 20:110-14+ Ap 13 '64
Tragic rebirth of the Chicago Cubs. T. Cohane. il Look 28:60+ Je 16 '64
Why the Yankees fired Berra. J. Ogle. il Look 28:30+ D 29 '64
See also
Alston, W.
Berra, L. P.

BASEBALL players
Aftermath. G. Talese. Esquire 59:61-2+ Je '63
Bad boys who gave the game a good name. J. Orr. Esquire 59:56+ My '63
Baseball All America. I. R. McVay. il Look 28:59+ O 20 '64
Baseball All America (cont) T. Cohane and I. R. McVay. il pors Look 27:100+ O 8 '63
Baseball has done it, by J. Robinson. Review New Repub 151:25-6 Jl 11 '64. M. Polner
Baseball 1964: can the pitchers stay on top? W. Leggett. il Sports Illus 20:38-41 Ap 13 '64
Baseball 1963: slim pickings for the rookies. il Ebony 18:61+ Je '63
Baseball's power elite. R. Riger. il Esquire 59:76-7+ Je '63
Baseball's richest rookie; R. Reichardt Los Angeles Angels bonus baby. M. Cope. il Sat Eve Post 237:68-9 S 19 '64
Baseball's untouchables. B. Barbee. il Ebony 19:153-4 Je '64
Big leaguers in Japan. il Newsweek 63:54 Mr 30 '64
Day when all the sentiment stands still; Cooperstown on Hall of fame day. Sports Illus 19:56-7 Ag 19 '63
Debacle in Cincinnati; Reds go down in defeat. F. Deford. il Sports Illus 21:22-7 O 12 '64
Dodgers' troubled giant; slugger F. Howard. W. Leggett. il Sports Illus 20:66+ My 25 '64
Elmer the Great. Newsweek 61:84 F 11 '63
Even series; with some fresh faces; day-by-day account of the first five games. W. Leggett. il Sports Illus 21:22-9 O 19 '64
Fact chart on Negro major league players. Ebony 19:156 Je '64
Gone are rowdy roughing it days; today it's posh plus. M. Smith. il Life 54:70-4+ Mr 29 '63
Greatest pitcher of them all; W. Johnson. L. Koppett. il N Y Times Mag p26+ O 4 '64
Halo, there! possibilities for the Hall of fame. H. L. Masin. il Sr Schol 83:32 S 13 '63
How I know what pitchers will throw. B. Turley. il Sports Illus 21:30-3 Jl 20 '64
How the West was won. il Newsweek 63:63 Ap 13 '64
Innocent abroad on the baseball diamonds. E. Graham. il Sports Illus 18:64-70 Mr 18 '63
Instant homer king! homer totals and homer rates. H. L. Masin. il Sr Schol 84:30 My 15 '64
Invasion from Santo Domingo; Dominican big leaguers. R. Cantwell. il Sports Illus 18:54-61 F 25 '63
Just how dumb can they be? catcher in baseball; photographs. Sports Illus 19:28-32 Ag 19 '63
Let's go, Phillies! J. Olsen. il Sports Illus 21:10-15 Ag 10 '64
Lively market in lame ducks; trading baseball's stock. B. Surface. il Sat Eve Post 237:66-7 Je 6 '64
Longest season. J. Brosnan. il Esquire 59: 94-7 Mr '63
Man behind The Man: excerpt from Stan Musial: The Man's own story; ed. by R. Broeg. S. Musial. il Look 28:109-10+ Ap 21 '64
Man nobody wanted; T. Oliva. Time 83:80 Je 12 '64
Miracle in St Louis; Cardinals win the pennant. W. Leggett. il Sports Illus 21:22-7 O 12 '64
Monsters on top; batters up against new pitchers. T. C. Brody. il Sports Illus 19: 10-15 Ag 12 '63
1963 scouting reports. R. Creamer and others. il Sports Illus 18:45-66+ Ap 8 '63
No more boom; Tom Cheney. Newsweek 61: 93 My 13 '63
Not enough talkative bats in Cincy; strong pitching, but no hitters. M. Kram. il Sports Illus 21:54-7 Ag 24 '64
Not sporting; contract of employment. New Repub 150:7-8 Ja 18 '64
Nothing stopped the Dodgers. R. Creamer. il Sports Illus 19:26-7 S 30 '63
Out in front with a new look; Yankees lead the league. W. Leggett. il Sports Illus 21: 26-9 S 28 '64
Out in the sun again; drawings of spring training. R. Searle. Sports Illus 20:16-23 Mr 2 '64
Phils take off. G. Astor. il Look 28:87-92 Ag 25 '64
Richest bonus baby ever; R. Reichardt of the Angels. E. Shrake. il Sports Illus 21:16-21 Jl 6 '64
Rookie cookies, 1964. H. L. Masin. il Sr Schol 84:36 Ap 3 '64
Rookie cookies, 1963. H. L. Masin. Sr Schol 82:28-9 Mr 27 '63
Rookies, rookies everywhere, and even JFK is talking. T. C. Brody. Sports Illus 18:65-6 Ap 15 '63
Running game comes back. W. Leggett. il Sports Illus 20:40-1 My 4 '64
Scouting reports (cont) il Sports Illus 20: 49-54+ Ap 13 '64
Scrappy scramblers; Phillies. H. L. Masin. il Sr Schol 85:40 S 30 '64
Secret weapons save the Yanks. R. Creamer. il Sports Illus 19:12-15 Ag 5 '63
Slambang of baseball. il Sports Illus 18:38-44 Ap 8 '63
Spahn and who? is the Braves' battle cry. F. Deford. il Sports Illus 20:84-5 Ap 6 '64
Speaking out; they've wrecked the American league; ed. by E. Linn. B. Veech. Sat Eve Post 237:10+ Jl 11 '64
Speaking out; what's left for the left-hander? B. Veeck. Sat Eve Post 236:10+ Mr 16 '63
Spitter is back; outlawed 1920. W. Leggett. il Sports Illus 18:18-21 Je 3 '63
Sporting scene; Mets at William A. Shea stadium. R. Angell. il New Yorker 40:96+ My 30 '64
Sporting scene; the Mets at the Polo Grounds. R. Angell. il New Yorker 39:132+ My 25 '63
Sporting scene; world series. R. Angell. il New Yorker 40:224-8+ O 24 '64
Sporting scene; world series over television in New York bars. R. Angell. New Yorker 39:184+ O 26 '63
Terrific Tony; Minnesota Twins rookie. il Ebony 19:36-8+ Ag '64
They went and got 'em; Orioles and White Sox push New York into third place. W. Leggett. il Sports Illus 21:14-19 Ag 31 '64
This pitcher may need relief. J. Brosnan. il Sports Illus 20:24-6+ Mr 16 '64
When it's three and two; baseball's most dramatic moment, reproductions of paintings. B. Fuchs. Sports Illus 20:42-8 Ap 13 '64
Who will win the war of the lefties? Dodgers vs Yankees. R. Creamer. il Sports Illus 19: 28-9 S 30 '63
Winners and Wynn. il Newsweek 61:95-6 Ap 15 '63
World serious, then and now. A. Daley. il N Y Times Mag p34+ S 29 '63
World's greatest diamond thief. L. Robinson. il Ebony 18:35-6+ My '63
See also names of baseball players, e.g. P. Ward

Recruiting
Slimmer pickings. Sports Illus 18:8 F 25 '63
Squeeze play: high school and college players chosen from general pool. Nation 200:70 Ja 25 '65

Salaries
See Athletes—Salaries

BASEBALL scoreboards. See Scoreboards
BASEBALL stadiums. See Stadiums
BASEBALL umpires. See Umpires (sports)
BASEBALLS
Pitch like a pro; Yankee coach's ball-on-a-stick. il Pop Sci 183:100-1 O '63
BASEL, Switzerland

Architecture
Collaboration in Switzerland. G. Nelson. il Arch Forum 118:118-21 Je '63

BASEMENT recreation rooms. See Recreation rooms
BASEMENTS and cellars
Basic basement ideas. A. C. Borg. il Am Home 67:46-7+ Ja '64
How to redeem a useless basement; How to crown a windowless basement with light. il House & Gard 125:188-9 My '64
Need an idea for your basement? N. Seney. il Bet Hom & Gard 41:60-1 Mr '63

BASEMENTS and cellars—*Continued*
Party basement. il Bet Hom & Gard 41:52+ O '63
Raised basement adds space to neat development house. il Arch Rec 135:124-6 mid-My '64
See also
Dampness in buildings
BASERGA, Renato, and Kisieleski, W. E.
Autobiographies of cells. Sci Am 209:103-8+ Ag '63
BASES, Air. See Air bases
BASES, Guided missile. See Guided missile bases
BASES, Military. See Military bases
BASHFULNESS
But I'm so shy! J. A. Nimrod. il Farm J 87:97 Mr '63
BASIC books publishing company, incorporated
Basic books' first ten years of publishing. Pub W 184:39 D 30 '63
BASIC research. See Research
BASIDIOMYCETES
Spore discharge in basidiomycetes: a unified theory. D. B. O. Savile. bibliog il Science 147:165-6 Ja 8 '65
BASIE, Count
Homage to the Count. il por Time 83:55 Ja 10 '64
Jazz. W. Balliett. New Yorker 40:145-7 N 7 '64
Jazz records. W. Balliett. New Yorker 40: 194-8 O 3 '64
BASIL Seal rides again; story. See Waugh, E.
BASILIO, Carmen
Gentleman's guide to barroom brawling. por Esquire 62:129 O '64
BASKERVILLE family
At the sign of the crest. H. K. Eilers. il Hobbies 68:120-1 N '63
BASKET gardens. See Plants, Potted
BASKETBALL
Abe Lemons and his poor ol' hongry farm boys; basketball coach at Oklahoma City U. F. Deford. il Sports Illus 22:46-7 Ja 4 '65
Ambush of a Don patrol; best USF squad. F. Deford. Sports Illus 19:100 D 23 '63
Basketball for the physically handicapped; excerpts from Book of basketball. I. A. Leitner. il Todays Health 42:50-1+ Ja '64
Basketball week. M. Hyman. See issues of Sports illustrated published during basketball season
Best one-two punch in basketball; photographs. Sports Illus 20:36-41 Mr 9 '64
Better to die than lose; Boston Celtics vs. Los Angeles Lakers. il Time 81:85-6 My 3 '63
Boom went the anvil chorus; Michigan defeats Duke. F. Deford. il Sports Illus 21: 20-1 D 14 '64
Bruin breed. il Time 83:46 Mr 27 '64
Cazzie; Wolverines. il Newsweek 65:40 Ja 4 '65
Cincy goes for a third; NCAA championship. J. Underwood. il Sports Illus 18:24-6+ Mr 11 '63
College basketball. il Time 84:50 D 25 '64
College basketball 1965. F. Deford. il Sports Illus 21:36-8+ D 7 '64
College basketball (title varies) (cont) Sports Illus 18:50-2 F 18; 60-2 Mr 18 '63
Courtship of Lew Alcindor. il Time 85:50 Ja 22 '65
Discovering basketball. A. Menen. Holiday 33:62-3+ F '63
Down Bloody Nose Lane; Michigan vs Ohio state. J. Underwood. il Sports Illus 20:26-8 Ja 27 '64
Final whistle. D. Anderson. il Sat Eve Post 236:34-5 Mr 16 '63
Five tall strangers shoot 'em up; Davidson's basketball team. B. Ottum. il Sports Illus 20:12-13 Ja 13 '64
Fix was on; basketball mess; with editorial comment. J. Breslin. il Sat Eve Post 236: 15-19, 92 F 23 '63
Games that are a ball for all; NCAA championship playoff, with photographs by J. G. Zimmerman. Sports Illus 18:30-6 Mr 18 '63
Greatest high school game ever played! H. L. Masin. il Sr Schol 84:30 Mr 20 '64
Gunners are after Cincy; Duke and Loyola basketball teams. J. Underwood. il Sports Illus 18:22-5 Mr 25 '63
High scoring has become ho-hum; ed. by T. Cohane. B. Cousy. il Look 27:53-4+ F 12 '63
Hoop to-do! H. L. Masin. il Sr Schol 85:27 D 2 '64
How to make contact; Boston Celtics, winners of National basketball association championship. il Time 83:56 My 8 '64
Howland success! sixth grade team at Bolindale elementary school, Howland, Ohio. H. L. Masin. il Sr Schol 84:22 F 28 '64
I owe the public nothing. E. Linn. il Sat Eve Post 237:60-3 Ja 18 '64
King of the hill is no patsy; G. Ireland, coach of Loyola Ramblers. J. Underwood. il Sports Illus 20:50-2 Mr 9 '64
Large field of unfavorites; NCAA championship pairings. J. Underwood. il Sports Illus 20:20-3 Mr 16 '64
Last fling for a wizard; B. Cousy. il Sports Illus 18:16-17+ Ap 22 '63
Meet the new Wilt Chamberlain; San Francisco Warriors. T. C. Brody. il Sports Illus 20:24-5 Mr 2 '64
Miami's picks: Slick and Rick. J. Underwood. il Sports Illus 20:18-19 Ja 20 '64
New deal at Notre Dame; coach J. Dee's change in style of basketball. F. Deford. il Sports Illus 21:28-9 D 21 '64
1964 college basketball. il Sports Illus 19:34-41 D 9 '63
Only game in Panguitch, Utah. J. Underwood. il Sports Illus 18:56-60+ Mr 4 '63
Open the bomb bays! H. L. Masin. il Sr Schol 83:30 D 6 '63
Pro basketball. W. Leggett. il Sports Illus 19:30-2+ O 28 '63
Profiles: W. W. Bradley of Princeton team. J. McPhee. New Yorker 40:40-2+ Ja 23 '65
Purple gang; Evansville's Purple Aces. il Time 85:34-5 Ja 8 '65
Ramblers wreck Cincy; NCAA championship playoff. J. Underwood. il Sports Illus 18:22-5+ Ap 1 '63
Slo break basketball. M. E. Nunes and K. N. Stange. Recreation 57:358-9 S '64
Small men arise; UCLA wins, Kentucky undefeated. F. Deford. il Sports Illus 20:48-9 Ja 6 '64
Smart moves by a master of deception; ed. by F. Deford. F. Ramsey. il Sports Illus 19: 57-63 D 9 '63
Touch and a tooth of gold; G. Johnson of Baltimore Bullets. M. Kram. il Sports Illus 21:60-3 D 21 '64
Two-minute explosion; UCLA startled Kansas state and Duke won national basketball title. J. Underwood. il Sports Illus 20: 16-19 Mr 30 '64
Two once and future champs; Princeton's Bill Bradley and UCLA. F. Deford. il Sports Illus 22:18-21 Ja 11 '65
Two ways to be ranked 1-2; Cincinnati vs Loyola. W. Bingham. il Sports Illus 18: 16-17+ F 4 '63
UCLA's John Wooden. I. R. McVay. il Look 27:93-7 Mr 12 '63
Up to their old tricks. W. Leggett. il Sports Illus 18:53-6 My 6 '63
Urbane Baron concocts another surprise; A. Rupp, Kentucky's basketball coach. J. Underwood. Sports Illus 20:24-5+ F 17 '64
Zone defenses set the style. M. Hyman. il Sports Illus 21:74-80 D 7 '64

Rules

Smart moves by a master of deception; ed. by F. Deford. F. Ramsey. il Sport Illus 19: 57-63 D 9 '63
Zone defenses set the style. M. Hyman. il Sports Illus 21:74-80 D 7 '64
BASKETBALL coaches. See Physical directors
BASKETBALL fans
Almost perfect pilgrimage of Boop and his group; Cincinnati's basketball fans. W. Bingham. il Sports Illus 18:24-5 Ap 1 '63
Only game in Panguitch, Utah. J. Underwood. il Sports Illus 18:56-60+ Mr 4 '63
Uproar in Philadelphia; Penn-Brown game played against Villanova-La Salle cheering. J. Olsen. il Sports Illus 22:18-23 Ja 18 '65
BASKETBALL players
Another big bluff by big Wilt. F. Deford. il Sports Illus 22:18-19+ Ja 25 '65
Basketball All America. T. Cohane and I. R. McVay. il Look 27:109-12+ Mr 26 '63; 28: 80-2+ Mr 24 '64
Basketball and beefeaters. J. McPhee. New Yorker 39:186-90+ Mr 16 '63
Big men on the move; Cincinnati Royals; reproduction of paintings. C. Condak. il Sports Illus 19:40-5 O 28 '63
BYU: land of cuties and twelve tall Cougars. B. Ottum. il Sports Illus 22:26-9 Ja 4 '65
Carbon copies on the court; Tom and Dick VanArsdale. il Life 56:83-5 Ja 17 '64
Cazzie Russell; sophomore cage phenom. il Ebony 19:101-2+ Ap '64
College basketball 1965. F. Deford. il Sports Illus 21:36-8+ D 7 '64
Hoop to-do! H. L. Masin. il Sr Schol 85:27 D 2 '64

BASKETBALL players—*Continued*
How K.C. won an Oscar in the NBA. F. Deford. Sports Illus 20:58+ Ap 20 '64
Key facts about ten of the best. pors Sports Illus 20:22-3 Mr 16 '64
NBA gets a new image. W. Leggett. il Sports Illus 19:30-2+ O 28 '63
1964 All-American H.S. basketball squad. H. L. Masin. il Sr Schol 84:28 My 8 '64
1964 college basketball. il Sport Illus 19:34-41 D 9 '63
1963 All-American h.s. basketball squad. H. L. Masin. il Sr Schol 82:28 My 8 '63
Of charley horses and little old ladies; star forward of Boston Celtics. T. Heinsohn and B. Ottum. il Sports Illus 21:38-40+ O 26 '64
Once again to nowhere; US basketball team. Sports Illus 18:8 Ap 22 '63
Open the bomb bays! H. L. Masin. il Sr Schol 83:30 D 6 '63
Pro basketball roundup. il Ebony 19:71-2+ Ja '64
Scouting reports; top twenty teams (cont) il Sports Illus 19:43-54 D 9 '63; 21:53-8+ D 7 '64
Two once and future champs; Princeton's Bill Bradley and UCLA. F. Deford. il Sports Illus 22:18-21 Ja 11 '65
We are grown men playing a child's game; Celtics B. Russell. G. Rogin. il Sports Illus 19:74-8+ N 18 '63
Who says you can't win 'em all? U.S. basketball players at Olympics. T. C. Brody. il Sports Illus 20:104-5 Ap 13 '64
Year of the knees in the NBA. W. Leggett. Sports Illus 19:84-5 N 25 '63
See also names of basketball players, e.g. B. Cousy

Recruiting

Five athletes, 500 scholarships. il Ebony 19:57-61 O '64
Go get 'em, coaches! J. Underwood. il Sports Illus 19:82-4+ D 9 '63
Scholarship for Barry; recruiters at work. M. Gross. il Sat Eve Post 236:20-3 F 23 '63
Wooing of a seven-foot wonder. G. Walsh. il Sat Eve Post 237:70-1 Mr 14 '64

Training

Court dictator; coach George Ireland. il Newsweek 61:63 F 18 '63

BASKETBALL scouting
Scouting reports. W. Leggett. il Sports Illus 19:32+ O 28 '63
Scouting reports; top twenty teams. il Sports Illus 19:43-54 D 9 '63; 21:53-8+ D 7 '64

BASKETBALL teams
And still champions; Boston Celtics. il Time 82:92+ D 6 '63
Basketball at its toughest; feud between Boston Celtics and Los Angeles Lakers. W. Leggett. il Sports Illus 18:12-17 F 25 '63
Big men on the move; Cincinnati Royals; reproductions of paintings. C. Condak. il Sports Illus 19:40-5 O 28 '63
Can't anybody here beat these guys? Boston Celtics. il Time 85:60 Ja 29 '65
Five midgets and a wink at Nell; unbeaten UCLA team. J. Underwood. il Sports Illus 20:42+ F 24 '64
Follow the bouncing ball from Honolulu to Boston; Boston Celtics win their sixth NBA championship. F. Deford. Sports Illus 20:81-2+ My 4 '64
His hopes hang by an ankle. J. Underwood. il Sports Illus 20:18-21 Mr 23 '64
How K.C. won an Oscar in the NBA. F. Deford. Sports Illus 20:58+ Ap 20 '64
Meet the new Wilt Chamberlain; San Francisco Warriors. T. C. Brody. il Sports Illus 20:24-5 Mr 2 '64
Of charley horses and little old ladies; star forward of Boston Celtics. T. Heinsohn and B. Ottum. il Sports Illus 21:38-40+ O 26 '64
Pack closes on Boston; with drawings by F. Mullins. Sports Illus 21:50-6 O 26 '64
Panic is on again; the Boston Celtics and Russellphobia. B. Ottum. il Sports Illus 21:18-19+ N 9 '64
Pressure, that's our game: U.C.L.A. il Time 83:74-5 Ja 17 '64
Pro basketball roundup. il Ebony 19:71-2+ Ja '64
Red: Boston Celtics. il Newsweek 64:86 N 30 '64
Scouting reports. W. Leggett. il Sports Illus 19:32+ O 28 '63
Scouting reports; top twenty teams (cont) il Sports Illus 19:43-54 D 9 '63; 21:53-8+ D 7 '64
Sixth man: R. Barnett of Los Angeles Lakers. il Time 81:66+ Mr 8 '63
Sporting scene; farewell to Cousy of Boston Celtics. H. W. Wind. New Yorker 39:146+ Mr 23 '63
Unloved five; UCLA Bruins. il Newsweek 63:50 Mr 2 '64
Up to their old tricks; Boston Celtics win National basketball association championship. W. Leggett. il Sports Illus 18:53-6 My 6 '63
Wally's cue: Sidney! Sidney! J. Underwood. il Sports Illus 20:26-8 F 10 '64
We are grown men playing a child's game; Celtics B. Russel. G. Rogin. il Sports Illus 19:74-8+ N 18 '63

BASKETBALL tournaments
Cincy goes for a third; NCAA championship. J. Underwood. il Sports Illus 18:24-6+ Mr 11 '63
His hopes hang by an ankle. J. Underwood. il Sports Illus 20:18-21 Mr 23 '64
Large field of unfavorites; NCAA championship pairings. J. Underwood. il Sports Illus 20:20-3 Mr 16 '64
Two-minute explosion; UCLA startled Kansas state and Duke won national basketball title. J. Underwood. il Sports Illus 20:16-19 Mr 30 '64

BASKETS
Grandma's Indian baskets. C. Miles. il Hobbies 69:112-13+ My '64
Made with popsicle sticks; novel baskets. T. Lau. il Design 65:100-1 Ja '64
See also
May baskets

BASKETS, Waste. See Waste baskets

BASKETT, John
Some aspects of English landscape painting. Antiques 84:581-5 N '63

BASKETTE, Kirtley
Bette Davis' biggest victory. Good H 157:30+ Ag '63
Is he the next Cary Grant? Good H 156:80-1+ Ap '63

BASKIN, Leonard
Of roots and veins: a testament. por Atlan 214:65-8 S '64
On pop art, Blake and Bohemianism; ed. by J. Howard. pors Life 56:41-2 Ja 24 '64

about

Leonard Baskin: art for life's sake. A. Werner. il por Am Artist 28:40-5+ N '64
Pleasant pariah. il pors Life 56:37+ Ja 24 '64

BASKIN, R. J. and Wiese G. M.
Contraction-band formation in barnacle myofibrils. bibliog Science 143:134-6 Ja 10 '64

BASKIN, Samuel
(ed) What's new in higher education? excerpt from Higher education: some newer developments. NEA J 53:54-6 S '64

BASLE, Switzerland. See Basel, Switzerland

BASMAJIAN, J. V.
Control and training of individual motor units. bibliog Science 141:440-1 Ag 2 '63

BASOLO, Domenith Clarence, jr
Buffalo Bill was a piker. H. Peterson. il Sports Illus 21:76+ O 19 '64

BASOV, Nikolai Gennadevich
Nobel prize winners. por Sci N L 86:295 N 7 '64
Research on maser-laser principle wins Nobel prize in physics. J. P. Gordon. por Science 146:897-9 N 13 '64

BASQUE ballads and songs
Basque troubadour. R. Laxalt. il Atlan 212:136+ O '63

BASQUE cookery. See Cookery, Basque

BASQUES
Christmas in Euzkaldunak. D. Taylor. il Todays Health 42:18-19+ D '64
Gourmets of San Sebastian. B. Wason. il Atlan 213:117+ Je '64

BASS, George F.
Underwater archeology: key to history's warehouse. Nat Geog Mag 124:138-56 Jl '63

BASS, Isaac Houston
Heresy of Isaac Houston Bass. H. H. Leard. il por Am For 69:20-1+ S '63

BASS, Richardson
In August: a realization. Seventeen 22:274-5 Ag '63

BASS, Ross
Racism wasn't the issue in Tennessee. B. Kovach. Reporter 31:37-8 S 24 '64

BASS, Saul
Saul Bass on visual excitement; interview. Pop Phot 55:108-9+ Jl '64

BASS, W. A.
In Nashville schools. NEA J 52:48-50 D '63

BASS
America's greatest gamefish. W. Davis. il Outdoor Life 134:34-7+ Jl '64
This is the fish you can't catch too many of: largemouth bass. R. H. Boyle. il Sports Illus 19:34-9 Ag 19 '63

BASS fishing
Backwater bass. W. Blassingame. il Field & S 68:38-40+ Ap '64
Bass for the asking. S. R. Slaymaker, 2d. il Outdoor Life 132:24-7+ N '63
Best bet for bass. R. Tinsley. il Field & S 67:60-1+ Ap '63
Big red drum. G. Heinold. il Outdoor Life 132:64-5+ S '63
Blizzard bass. B. Cary. il Outdoor Life 133:60-1+ Ap '64
Bomb range bass. K. Osborne. il Field & S 69:43-5+ S '64
Bull bass are my hobby. S. Welch. il Outdoor Life 132:36-9+ Jl '63
Bungalow barges, fish bats, and bass. D. Shaw. il Field & S 69:48-51+ My '64
Bussey is best; it's bassy. G. Gresham. il Outdoor Life 133:76-7+ Ap '64
Fish the midnight eel. R. E. Price. il Outdoor Life 132:36-7+ Ag '63
Fishing on the fly. E. A. Bauer. il Outdoor Life 132:17-19+ Jl '63
Float into the past. R. Tinsley. il Outdoor Life 132:17-19+ Ag '63
Fly fishing for smallmouths. A. J. McClane. il Field & S 68:88-90+ Je '63
Fly rod in the surf. P. McLain. il Field & S 69:58-61 O '64
Found: bass bonanza. E. A. Bauer. il Outdoor Life 131:24-7+ F '63
Grand awakening. R. Tinsley. il Outdoor Life 131:50-3+ Mr '63
How to catch big stripers. F. T. Moss. il Field & S 68:54-7+ My '63
How to fish the weeds. E. A. Bauer. il Outdoor Life 134:28-31+ Ag '64
How to outsmart that six-pound bass. D. E. DeKock. il Farm J 87:24 S '63
I am a bit of a fanatic. R. H. Boyle. il Sports Illus 19:64-5 O 21 '63
Loaded with bass. C. Dickey. il Outdoor Life 133:64-5+ Je '64
My favorite striper hotspots. G. Heinold. il Outdoor Life 133:16+ Je '64
New winter favorite. G. E. Gurley. il Outdoor Life 135:72-4 F '65
October bass explosion. R. E. Price. il Outdoor Life 132:56-9+ O '63
Potluck on the Red Cedar. G. Laycock. il Field & S 68:112-14+ S '63
Potomac bass float trip. D. Carpenter. il Am For 69:24-6 Ag '63
Pretty kettle of dyed baitfish; largemouth bass see red better than other colors. R. H. Boyle. Sports Illus 21:81+ O 5 '64
Promised land of bass. T. Janes. il Outdoor Life 131:76-7+ Je '63
Rocks of the Roanoke River. J. Rutherfoord. il Field & S 69:52-5+ My '64
Striped fever. L. Green. il Outdoor Life 133:44-5+ My '64
Stripers in the Hudson. A. Glowka. il Outdoor Life 134:20-3+ Ag '64
Stripers in the river. L. Dietz. il Field & S 68:44-5+ Ag '63
Surfing for channel bass. G. Heinold. il Outdoor Life 133:10 My '64
Tall tule bass. F. H. Ames. il Outdoor Life 133:40-1+ Ja '64
They're all having luck; Bidwell Lake. il Sunset 132:83-4 My '64
Those bizarre bass. C. Elliott. il Outdoor Life 131:62-3+ My '63
Tips for better bass fishing. H. Bradshaw. il Suc Farm 61:92-3 S '63
Tule dippers. H. Hayden. il Field & S 68:54-5+ F '64
Weatherproof fishing. H. F. Blaisdell. il Outdoor Life 133:44-5+ Je '64
West Coast stampede. L. R. Green. il Outdoor Life 131:30-1+ Mr '63
Where the bass never quit. C. Elliott. il Outdoor Life 133:42-3+ F '64
Where the fish are. W. Davis. il Outdoor Life 132:54-6 Ag '63

BASS ROCK, Scotland
Bass Rock gannets. B. Nelson. il Natur Hist 73:32-41 Ap '64

BASSET hounds
How to run a house; by an old basset. C. Morrison. il Look 28:72-3 Ja 14 '64

BASSETT, Charles K.
Hooked feather pattern; blown iridescent glass shades. Hobbies 69:78-9 Je '64

BASSETT, Grace
Ordeal in Okanogan. Nation 197:454-6 D 28 '63

BASSETT, William A. See Takahashi, T. jt. auth.

BASSETTI, Piero
Politics is his business. por Time 82:66-7 Ag 23 '63

BASSEY, Shirley
Shirley Bassey. il pors Ebony 18:108-10+ Mr '63

BASSING, Eileen
Where's Annie: story; excerpt from novel. por Sat Eve Post 236:39-41 F 23 '63

el-BASSIOUNY, M. Y.
(ed) See Read, H. Conversation with Sir Herbert Read

BASSO, Hamilton
Obituary
Pub W 185:52 My 25 '64
Writer as craftsman. M. Cowley. por Sat R 47:17-18 Je 27 '64

BASTIDE, Francois Régis
Phenomenon of Les parapluies de Cherbourg. Vogue 144:184-5+ N 1 '64

BASTIEN, Barbara (Nesbitt)
Study in courage. C. Morrison. il pors Look 27:25-9 My 21 '63

BASTIEN, Robert Eugene
Study in courage. C. Morrison. il Look 27:25-9 My 21 '63

BASTILLE day
Letter from Paris. Genêt. New Yorker 39:84 Jl 27 '63

BASTOGNE, Battle of, 1944-1945. See Ardennes, Battle of the, 1944-1945

BASUTOLAND
Atlantic report. Atlan 213:34+ Ap '64
Different Africa. G. Vincent. il N Y Times Mag p90+ S 13 '64
High commission territories of southern Africa. B. S. Young. bibliog il Focus 14:1-6 D '63
Protectorates under the gun. S. Uys. New Repub 149:9-10 S 28 '63
South Africa: enclaves of trouble. J. Halpern. il Nation 197:49-52 Jl 27 '63
See also
United Nations—Basutoland

BAT boys (baseball) See Baseball

BAT lady; story. See Dursin, M.

BATA shoe company
Shoemaker to the world. il Time 84:120 N 13 '64

BATAAN, Battle of, 1942. See World war, 1939-1945—Campaigns and battles—Pacific

BATCHELOR, Lillian L.
Planning begins in faculty meetings. ALA Bul 57:159-61 F '63
—See Fenwick, S. I. jt. auth.

BATEMAN, Mildred Mitchell
West Virginia's director of mental health. il pors Ebony 19:63-8 Ja '64

BATES, Alan
Two ways to skin a cat. E. Miller. il pors Seventeen 22:137+ My '63

BATES, Billy Prior
Inconsistent progress; poem. Liv Wild 83:4 Spring '63

BATES, Darrell
Quiet island; story. Sat Eve Post 237:38-40 O 24 '64

BATES, Franklin
Rapid watercolors. il por Design 65:158-61 Mr '64

BATES, Guy
County recording in three easy steps. Am City 80:100-1 Ja '65

BATES, Kenneth
Going places, finding things in Venice. House & Gard 125:40+ Mr '64

BATES, M. U.
Black bear turns man-eater. Outdoor Life 131:68-9+ Je '63

BATES, Marston
Can animals survive in a fast-changing world? excerpt from Animal worlds. Audubon Mag 65:276-9, 370-2 S-N '63
Thirstless camel; excerpts from Animal worlds. UNESCO Courier 17:20-1 Jl '64
When a monkey says kwaa he means let's go. N Y Times Mag p 14-15+ Mr 29 '64

BATES, Paul
I fight giant foxtail with fire. Suc Farm 62:105 My '64

BATES, Richard C.
How to have a heart attack; address. Todays Health 41:54 Ag '63

BATES, Ted, and company
Does brainpower require capital? il Bsns W p83-4 D 12 '64

BATES, William K. and Woodward, D. O.
Neurospora β-galactosidase: evidence for a second enzyme. bibliog Science 146:777-8 N 6 '64

BATESON, Frank M.
Next May's eclipse in the Pacific. Sky & Tel 28:210-12 O '64

BATESON, Mary Catherine
Kinesics and paralanguage. Science 139:200 Ja 18 '63

BATH, Phil
Sandy trap for a million golfers. il Sports Illus 20:26-34 Ja 13 '64

BATH, England
Our far-flung correspondents. M. Panter-Downes. New Yorker 39:66+ Ag 24 '63
Pleasures of Bath in the eighteenth century. I. Origo. il Horizon 7:4-15 Wint '65

Historic houses, etc.

Linley House in Bath. H. D. Roberts. il Antiques 83:570-3 My '63

BATH rooms. See Bathrooms

BATHHOUSES
Concrete trees for the beach; Toms River, N.J. P. F. Losi and J. G. Woods. il Am City 78:92-4 O '63

BATHING. See Baths

BATHING suits
All tanked up. il Time 83:50 My 29 '64
Audacious new swimsuits; Las Vegas show girls turn out in fashions for the beach. il Life 58:46-55+ Ja 8 '65
Barely a bore; topless bathing suits. il Time 83:75 Je 26 '64
Big boom in bathing suits. W. Trombley. Sat Eve Post 236:30 Jl 13 '63
Bikinis in the backyard; with photographs by L. J. Schiller. Sat Eve Post 237:18-25 Je 20 '64
Can you top this? women's topless bathing suits. il Newsweek 64:72-3 Jl 6 '64
Decorating the world's beaches. il Bsns W p84-5 F 2 '63
Girls have all the lines. il Sports Illus 19:68-9 S 30 '63
High surfdom. J. Maisel. il Sports Illus 20:60-5 My 18 '64
How did photographers, TV, and the press meet the challenge of the topless swimsuit? L. Barry. il Pop Phot 55:135-9+ N '64
How to buy a swimsuit. il Seventeen 22:204-5 My '63
Keeping bathing suits in top shape. il Good H 156:153 Je '63
Me? in that! topless suits, with report by S. Alexander. il Life 57:54B-57 Jl 10 '64
New swim suits free the sylphs. il Life 56:46-53 Ja 24 '64
Nudity cult. L. Smith. il Sports Illus 22:34-9 Ja 18 '65
Primer for swimmers. il Esquire 59:90-1 My '63
Suited for swimming. Good H 156:208h Ap '63
Suiting up. il Time 81:75 My 3 '63
Sun, sand, and stares. il Newsweek 62:82-3 Jl 22 '63
Swimsuits for summer maneuvers. il Sat Eve Post 236:24-9 Jl 13 '63

BATHROOM fixtures
Colorful new products for bathrooms. Good H 156:170 Ap '63
Elegant décor in bathrooms. il Life 56:68-74+ My 15 '64
How to buy the right bathroom fixtures. Bet Hom & Gard 41:123 N '63
Newest ideas for bathrooms: fixtures, fittings and lights. il House & Gard 125:138-9 Ap '64
See also
Bidets
Plumbing
Water closets

BATHROOM scales. See Scales (weighing instruments)

BATHROOMS
Add a bathroom? il Changing T 17:13-14 Mr '63
Bathing room. il Vogue 143:144-6+ Ap 1 '64
Bathroom for two children: what remodeling can do. il House & Gard 125:134-7 Ap '64
Bathrooms remembered. S. T. Warner. New Yorker 39:33-6 Ja 11 '64
Bathrooms then & now. il Good H 158:46+ Je '64
Big idea bathrooms. N. Seney and F. R. Glass. il Bet Hom & Gard 41:58-61 N '63
Breaking out of the bathroom box. il House B 106:154-7 Ap '64
Bright bathroom? why not! R. Martens. il Farm J 88:68 Je '64
Elegant décor in bathrooms. il Life 56:68-74+ My 15 '64
Family bathrooms need special planning. R. Charles. il Parents Mag 38:75-8+ F '63
Fifty million-dollar bathroom ideas. il McCalls 91:76-83 S '64
Fully engineered bathrooms; well-planned wardrobes. il House & Gard 124:62-7 Jl '63
Gay, gaudy history of the American bedroom and bath. R. Lynes. il McCalls 91:116-17+ O '63
Get rid of those bathroom booby traps! J. Lentz. il Todays Health 42:71 N '64
Hedonism for the destitute: bath time in Japan; excerpt from Kimono mind. B. Rudofsky. il Horizon 7:106-9 Wint '65
Here's one way to add a new bathroom. il Sunset 133:134 O '64
How a low-level budget can produce a high-level bathroom. il House B 105:170-1 S '63
How to make one and a half equal two. il Bet Hom & Gard 42:125 Ap '64
How to plan a bathroom. il Sunset 130:104-8+ Je '63
Luxurious Edwardian bath. il Ladies Home J 81:142 Ja '64
Modern laving. il Time 82:56 D 27 '63
New order of the bath: pretty, practical and full of color. R. W. Houseman. il Am Home 66:32-9 Ja '63
Pampered bath. M. White. il Ladies Home J 81:159-63 O '64
Plan a beautiful bathroom. il Good H 156:114-19+ Ap '63
Save money with a quality bathroom. Am Home 66:78 Ja '63
Two-in-one bath. il Sunset 132:110 F '64
Updating a bathroom without remodeling. il House B 106:184-5 Ap '64
What makes a bathroom up-to-date? il House & Gard 125:128-33 Ap '64

BATHS
Bath can be such fun! L. D. Kirk. il Parents Mag 38:51 S '63
Bath perfect. il Mlle 59:88-9 Je '64
Bathing aids: la différence. il Mlle 57:31 Jl '63
Bathing room. il Vogue 143:144-6+ Ap 1 '64
Baths are more than soap and water. J. Lentz. il Todays Health 42:16+ N '64
Fragrance for your bath. il McCalls 91:136-7 My '64
Hedonism for the destitute: bath time in Japan; excerpt from Kimono mind. B. Rudofsky. il Horizon 7:106-9 Wint '65
Lazy bath; new you. il Seventeen 22:114-15 N '63
Sleeping while weightless; sleep bath. W. Cloud. il Pop Sci 183:21 S '63

BATHS, Infants. See Infants—Care and hygiene

BATHS, Moor and mud
Spas: goo, golf and games; with list of western Europe's historic health resorts. A. Waugh. il Sports Illus 20:88-92+ My 25 '64

BATHS, Mud. See Baths, Moor and mud

BATHS, Vapor
Oak-leaf lunch; Luxor baths in midtown Manhattan. Newsweek 61:91 My 6 '63
Sauna. il Sunset 131:82-6+ S '63

BATHYSCAPHE
Busy depths. Sci Am 210:64 My '64
Down to Thresher by bathyscaph. D. L. Keach. il Nat Geog Mag 125:764-77 Je '64
From research to search; the Trieste. il Newsweek 61:27 Ap 22 '63
Jeeps in the deep: exploring inner space at 4,500 fathoms. W. Cloud. il Pop Sci 185:42-6+ Ag '64
New inner space ships. il Sci Digest 56:14-15 Ag '64
Nuclear sub loss stirs investigation to locate Thresher. il Sr Schol 82:18-19 My 1 '63
Seanauts launched; Diving saucer. B. Tufty. il Sci N L 85:118 F 22 '64
Search for the Thresher; Trieste operations. F. N. Spiess and A. E. Maxwell. bibliog il Science 145:349-55 Jl 24 '64
Search for Thresher; bathyscaphe Trieste. il Time 81:36 Je 28 '63
Sub rescues, four miles deep. S. D. Pursglove. il Pop Mech 120:69-73+ Ag '63
To sea in a saucer; Cousteau diving saucer. il Bsns W p88-9+ F 15 '64
Trieste stalks a trail 1½ miles below the sea in its hunt for the Thresher. il Newsweek 62:27 Jl 8 '63

BATIK
Fabric batik; Javanese; excerpts from Fabric printing. L. Lauterburg. il Sch Arts 63:33-7 N '63
Printed cottons of Java; excerpts from Printed cottons of Asia. T. Osumi. il Craft Horiz 23:28-32 N '63

BATISSE, Michel
International hydrological decade: world-wide programme of scientific research. UNESCO Courier 17:4-9 Jl '64

BATMAN, Tom
Case for registering guns. Sat R 47:18 Ag 1 '64

BATON ROUGE, La.

Governors mansion
See Governors mansions

Sanitary affairs

Sewage problems respect no political boundaries. G. S. Covert. il Am City 78:71-3 F '63

BATON twirling
Twirling at Ole Miss; Dixie national baton twirling institute. T. Southern. il Esquire 59:100+ F '63
BATS
Bats. M. Freedman. il Atlan 212:138-9 D '63
Bats most sensitive of mammals to DDT. Sci N L 86:376 D 12 '64
Bats: sensitivity to DDT. M. M. Luckens and W. H. Davis. bibliog il Science 146:948 N 13 '64
Brown fat: thermogenic effect during arousal from hibernation in the bat. R. L. Smalley and R. L. Dryer. bibliog il Science 140:1333-4 Je 21 '63
Creature of air and darkness. J. Poling. il Read Digest 82:39-40+ Mr '63
Flight of the bats. D. Holland. il Nat Parks Mag 38:8-10+ Ja '64
Fructivorous fliers; Australian fruit bats. K. Breeden. il Natur Hist 73:26-33 My '64
Moth sounds and the insect-catching behavior of bats. D. C. Dunning and K. D. Roeder. bibliog il Science 147:173-4 Ja 8 '65
Nature note. Sci N L 86:13 Jl 4 '64
Night fighters in a sonic duel; moth's use of hearing to evade bats. K. D. Roeder. il Natur Hist 73:32-9 Ja '64
BATSBY, Fred
Big daddies of the Little league. N Y Times Mag p22+ My 31 '64
BATTAGLIA, Lee E.
Wedding of two worlds. il Nat Geog Mag 124:708-27 N '63
BATTELLE, Kenneth
Kenneth club. il Vogue 142:52-5 Jl '63
BATTELLE memorial institute, Columbus, Ohio
Battelle: new contractor's role at AEC lab means diversification for Hanford, growth for institute. J. Walsh. Science 145:905-7 Ag 28 '64
Development and testing of a new book marking system; Se-Lin. N. H. Gaber. il Library J 89:1911-13 My 1 '64
LTP book labeling system goes to market; Se-Lin. G. T. Piez. il ALA Bul 58:554-6 Je '64
BATTEN, Loring W. 3d
Guadalcanal twenty years after. Yale R 52:418-26 Mr '63
BATTEN, Peter
Have zoo, will travel. W. Trombley. il pors Sat Eve Post 237:72-3 Ag 8 '64
BATTERIES, Solar. See Solar batteries
BATTERIES, Storage. See Storage batteries
BATTERS, Baseball. See Baseball players
BATTERSBY, William S. and Wagman, I. H.
Light adaptation kinetics: the influence of spatial factors. bibliog Science 143:1029-31 Mr 6 '64
BATTERY chargers. See Storage battery chargers
BATTERY charging. See Storage batteries—Charging
BATTERY-operated toys. See Electric toys
BATTERY-powered tape recorders. See Magnetic recorders and recording
BATTEY, Jean
With passionate clarity. Dance Mag 37:44-8 Jl '63
BATTING. See Baseball
BATTISTA, O. A.
What ails that, hic, phrenic nerve? Sci Digest 55:27-9 Ja '64
What happens when you die. Sci Digest 55:80-4 My '64
You can invent by accident. Sci Digest 54:87-90 Ag '63
BATTLE, Jean Allen
I don't have time to read. por NEA J 53:13 F '64
BATTLE, Lucius D.
Education: passkey to the future; statement, August 4, 1963. Dept State Bul 49:411-17 S 9 '63
Foreign students in America; problems, progress, and prospects; address, April 24, 1963. Dept State Bul 48:752-8 My 13 '63
Government book programs; summary of address. por Pub W 185:43-5 Je 22 '64
International cooperation in education, science, and culture. Dept State Bul 48:954-7 Je 17 '63
Need to explore inner space: address, July 2, 1964. Dept State Bul 51:110-19 Jl 27 '64
New dimensions in cultural communication; address, December 29, 1962. Dept State Bul 48:92-7 Ja 21 '63
Open society: key to an advancing America; address, October 26, 1963. Dept State Bul 49:864-9 D 2 '63
Role of music in cultural exchange; address, May 22, 1963. Dept State Bul 48:915-17 Je 10 '63
BATTLE of Chesapeake Bay. See United States—History—Revolution—Naval operations
BATTLE of Gettysburg. See Gettysburg, Battle of, 1863
BATTLE of Mussolini; story. See Household, G.
BATTLE of the sexes. See Women and men
BATTLE of the Villa Fiorita; novel. See Godden, R.
BATTLE of the Virginia Capes. See United States—History—Revolution—Naval operations
BATTLEFIELDS
After twenty years: the GI's war fades away. W. C. Heinz. il Sat Eve Post 237:22-30+ D 12 '64
BATTLES
See also
Military history
BATTS, H. Lewis, Jr, and Shomon, J. J.
Super nature center opens. il por Audubon Mag 67:13-15 Ja '65
BATUTSI. See Rwanda—Native races
BATZER, M. M.
Shock cure for fires. il pors Bsns W p30-1 Mr 14 '64
BAUER, Erwin A.
Assiniboine pack trip. Field & S 68:29-31 F '64
Bargain goat hunt. Field & S 69:31-3+ Ag '64
Beartooth adventure. por Outdoor Life 133:48-51+ Je '64
Bugle call for a bull elk. Field & S 68:21-3+ Ag '63
Bulls of Oyster Creek. Outdoor Life 134:48-51+ S '64
Christmas hasenpfeffer. Outdoor Life 132:28-31+ D '63
Earthquake deer. Outdoor Life 131:56-9+ Je '63
Fishing on the fly. Outdoor Life 132:17-19+ Jl '63
Five days for muskies. por Outdoor Life 131:76-9+ Ap '63
Found: bass bonanza. pors Outdoor Life 131:24-7+ F '63
Glacier: the park with everything. Field & S 69:39-41 Je '64
How to fish the weeds. Outdoor Life 134:28-31+ Ag '64
How to hunt foxes. Outdoor Life 133:24-7+ F '64
Jaguar for a gypsy. Outdoor Life 134:24-7+ Jl '64
Midwinter bird hunt. Outdoor Life 131:32-5+ F '63
New land of strange trout. Field & S 68:35-7+ Ap '64
New road to Rocky Mountain trout. por Outdoor Life 131:68-71+ My '63
Robins get around. Field & S 67:59+ Ap '63
Salmon for everyone. pors Outdoor Life 135:40-3+ F '65
Trout find of the year. Outdoor Life 131:36-9+ Mr '63
Ways and ways for ducks. Outdoor Life 134:32-5+ N '64
We fish the ice at night. Outdoor Life 131:16-19 +Ja '63
What every goose hunter should know. Field & S 68:23-5+ D '63
Whitetails for all. Outdoor Life 132:36-9+ O '63
BAUER, F. J. Jr
Compact BCB DX antennas. Pop Electr 22:75-6 Ja '65
Soup up that AM broadcast receiver. Pop Electr 20:56-7 Je '64
BAUER, Francis
Parent and child (cont) N Y Times Mag p 152 Ap 7; 44 Jl 28 '63
BAUER, Hank
Old potato face. il pors Time 84:86-90+ S 11 '64
BAUER, Harry C.
Minority pace. por Library J 89:3923-5 O 15 '64
Rethinking decisions. por Library J 90:206-8 Ja 15 '65
BAUER, Raymond A.
Exploring the exploratory sample. Harvard Bsns R 41:128-31 Mr '63
—and Buzzell, R. D.
Mating behavioral science and simulation. Harvard Bsns R 42:116-24 S '64
BAUER, S. H.
Chemical kinetics in shock tubes. bibliog Science 141:867-79 S 6 '63
—and Resler, E. L. Jr
Vibrational excitation in some four-center transition states. bibliog Science 146:1045-8 N 20 '64
BAUER, W. W.
Boys and girls together; excerpt from Moving into manhood. Todays Health 41:54-5+ S '63

BAUER, W. W.—*Continued*
Problems on the path to manhood; excerpts from Moving into manhood. Todays Health 41:60-1+ O '63
Seven paths to fitness. por Todays Health 41:13+ Ap '63
To keep children fit and hardy. PTA Mag 58:14-16 bibliog(p36) O '63
Where can a boy go for help; excerpts from Moving into manhood. Todays Health 41: 58-9+ N '63

BAUER, Walter C. and Meyer, J. S.
Iodine-125 distribution between follicular colloid and colloid droplets in mouse thyroid gland. bibliog Science 145:1431-2 S 25 '64

BAUGH, Edward J.
Four-way program of sewer rehabilitation. Am City 79:117 Mr '64

BAUGHMAN, U. E.
Can you really protect the president? interview. por U S News 55:38-40 D 23 '63

BAUM, Bernard
Problems are enormous. Sat R 47:57-8+ Ap 18 '64

BAUM, Betty
Integrated club. Parents Mag 38:62-3+ N '63

BAUM, Gilbert, and others
Observation of internal structures of teeth by ultrasonography. Science 139:495-6 F 8 '63

BAUM, Gregory
Birth control and the council. Commonweal 81:280+, 516-17 N 20 '64, Ja 15 '65
Blossoming of Vatican II. Commonweal 81: 130-2 O 23 '64
Confrontation in the council. Commonweal 79:311-13 D 6 '63
End of the deadlock. Commonweal 79:251-3 N 22 '63
End of the session. Commonweal 79:393-6 D 27 '63
Good beginning. Commonweal 81:66-8 O 9 '64
How anti-Semitism found a home in Christian teaching. Commonweal 80:372-3 Je 12 '64
Mid point in the session. Commonweal 81: 191-4 N 6 '64
Montreal: faith and order. Commonweal 78: 505-6+ Ag 23 '63
New spirit at the council. Commonweal 79: 125-9 O 25 '63
Pope and bishops. Commonweal 79:188-91 N 8 '63
Role of bishops in relation to the papacy. por Cath World 198:94-9 N '63
Triumphs and failures. Commonweal 81:377-81 D 11 '64

BAUM, Joseph H.
Profiles; Restaurant associates, inc. G. T. Hallman. il New Yorker 40:62+ O 17 '64

BAUM, Lyman Frank
Father of the Wizard of Oz. D. P. Mannix. il por Am Heritage 16:36-47+ D '64
Wizard of Oz; dramatization. See Schwartz, L. S.

about

Why librarians dislike Oz; reprint. M. Gardner. Library J 88:834-6, 1708+ F 15, Ap 15 '63

BAUM, Vicki
Fool's gold. por Newsweek 63:120 Ap 20 '64

BAUM, Werner A.
University organization for geophysics education; excerpts from address, April 1964. Science 146:619-21 O 30 '64

BAUM, Werner C.
Amateur scientist. Sci Am 211:128-32 O '64

BAUMAN, L. F. and others
Heritability of variations in oil content of individual corn kernels. Science 139:498-9 F 8 '63

BAUMAN, Robert E.
Excerpt from statement to special subcommittee on labor, June 19, 1963. Cong Digest 43:29+ Ja '64

BAUMGARNER, Alice
Questions you ask. See issues of School arts

BAUMGARTNER, Günter, and others
Visual motion detection in the cat. bibliog Science 146:1070-1 N 20 '64

BAUMGARTNER, Wilfrid S.
Boss is a money man. il por Bsns W p80+ Jl 18 '64

BAUMHART, Raymond, and Fitzpatrick, G. D.
Inertia in business ethics. America 108:798-800 Je 1 '63

BAUMILLER, Robert C.
Will the child be normal? America 110:220-1 F 15 '64

BÄUMLER, Hans Jürgen
Flash of fire on the ice. J. Bell. il por Sports Illus 20:52-3 Ja 27 '64

BAUMRUK, Robert
Summer in Chicagoland. ALA Bul 57:575-80 Je '63

BAUN, William L.
Phase transformation at high temperatures in hafnia and zirconia. bibliog Science 140: 1330-1 Je 21 '63

BAUR, Ernst W.
Catalase abnormality in a Caucasian family in the United States. bibliog Science 140:816-17 My 17 '63

BAUSCH & Lomb, incorporated
Getting one-up on the Japanese; B and L's inexpensive microscopes. il Bsns W p84+ O 19 '63
Moves by Bausch & Lomb. Field & S 69:130 My '64
New B.&L. scopes. J. O'Connor. Outdoor Life 132:111 S '63

BAVAGNOLI, Carlo
Winter in Venice: photographs. Life 56:56-64 F 21 '64

BAVARIA
Epicenter. K. Ames. il Newsweek 65:40+ Ja 11 '65

Description and travel

Going places, finding things in southern Germany. D. Beal. il House & Gard 123:12+ F '63
USC focuses on Bavaria. E. Scully. il U S Camera 27:24-5 D '64

BAVARIAN cookery. See Cookery, Bavarian

BAVIER, Robert N. Jr
Analysis of the one-of-a-kind. Yachting 113: 58-60+ My '63
Bob Bavier on spinnaker handling; interview, ed. by B. Robinson. por Yachting 116: 29+ S '64
International YRU meetings. Yachting 114: 140-1 D '63
Sailor takes to outboards. Yachting 114:60-1+ Jl '63
Selecting the Olympic classes. Yachting 115: 62-3+ Ap '64

BAXTER, James H. and Small, P. A. Jr
Antibody to rat kidney: in vivo effects of univalent and divalent fragments. bibliog Science 140:1406-7 Je 28 '63

BAXTER, Richard
Boy meets girl. por Seventeen 23:76+ Ja '64

BAXTER, Tom
For love and money. Flying 75:14 S '64

BAXTER STATE PARK. See Maine—Parks and reserves

BAY, Ellen
Penny. New Yorker 39:99-100+ Je 22 '63

BAY, Ovid
Who's making the money on your beef? il pors Farm J 88:23-5+ Je '64; Same. U S News 56:53-5 Je 29 '64

BAY OF PIGS invasion. See Cuba—History—Invasion, 1961

BAYANIHAN dance company. See Dancing, Philippine

BAYAR, Celâl
How to stay in trouble. il por Time 81:38 Ap 5 '63

BAYER, Edith
Letter to the Ghanaian times. Parents Mag 39:37+ My '64

BAYER company, incorporated
Advertisers and the government missed the boat on the validity of aspirin advertising. Consumer Bul 46:36 My '63
Rx: aspirin for Johnny; Bayer's aspirin for children. M. B. Keiser. il Parents Mag 39:12+ D '64

BAYH, Birch
Excerpt from statement, January 22, 1964. Cong Digest 43:148+ My '64
Imagine me here in D.C; ed. by J. Howard. M. Bayh. il por Life 55:37-8+ Jl 26 '63
Our greatest national danger. Look 28:74+ Ap 7 '64

BAYH, Marvella (Hern)
Imagine me here in D.C! ed. by J. Howard. il pors Life 55:37-8+ Jl 26 '63

BAYLES, Vera T.
Let's arrange chrysanthemums. Pop Gard 15: 42-3 S '64

BAYLEY, Monica
Renewed effort to solve the problem of drop-out. Sch Life 46:11-16 D '63

BAYLISS, Ernie
Old tools learn new tasks. Am City 79:91-3 Ap '64

BAYLOR, Elgin
Best one-two punch in basketball; photographs. Sports Illus 20:36-41 Mr 9 '64

BAYLOR university, Waco, Tex.
Baker v. Baylor. Time 81:42 Mr 22 '63

BAYNE, Stephen Fielding, bp, 1908-
Bishop Bayne to return to U.S. Christian Cent 80:1294 O 23 '63
New Anglican horizons. C. Northcott. Christian Cent 81:134-5 Ja 29 '64

BAYNHAM, Dorsey
Great cities projects. NEA J 52:17-20 Ap '63

BAYREUTH festival
Mists of ecstasy; 150th anniversary of Wagner's birth. il Time 82:56 Ag 23 '63
Notes from abroad. K. Blaukopf. Hi Fi 13: 28+ N '63
Wagner worship in Bavaria. G. M. Loney. Reporter 29:32+ Jl 4 '63

BAYREUTH festspielhaus
House that Wagner built. E. Downes. il Hi Fi 14:49-52+ F '64

BAYREUTHER, K. E. and Romig, W. R.
Polyoma virus: production in bacillus subtilis. bibliog Science 146:778-9 N 6 '64

BAYTOWN, Tex.
See also
Sterling municipal library

BAYVIEW yacht club. See Yacht clubs

BAZAARS, Charitable
Color enhances your bazaar. il Recreation 58: 30 Ja '65
Planning a successful bazaar. J. G. Staley. Bet Hom & Gard 41:98-9 S '63

BAZÁN, José
Who' who in foreign business. por Fortune 67:70 Je '63

BAZELON, David T.
Financial parochialism. Commentary 35:268-72 Mr '63
History, moralism, distortion. Commentary 35:79-81 Ja '63
Non-legislative arts. Commentary 38:82-5 D '64
Non rule in America. bibliog f Commentary 36:438-45 D '63
Some deductions. Commentary 38:67-8 Ag '64

about

Bazelon, pro and con. Commentary 35:250-3 Mr '63

BAZIL, Duane W.
Conversation with Francisco. Christian Cent 80:366-7 Mr 20 '63

BÉ, Allan W. H. and Lott, Leroy
Shell growth and structure of planktonic foraminifera. bibliog Science 145:823-4 Ag 21 '64
—See Saito, T. jt. auth.

BE my guest, incorporated
Unusual business gifts. J. B. Weiner. Duns R 82:61 N '63

BEA, Augustin, cardinal
How the university can further Christian unity; excerpt from Unity of Christians. Cath World 197:8-14 Ap '63
Prejudice and church unity; excerpts from address. America 109:444 O 19 '63

about

Cardinal Bea: an appreciation. G. P. O'Hara. America 108:442-4+ Mr 30 '63
Cardinal mission. por Newsweek 61:70 Ap 15 '63
Cardinal of unity; Cardinal Bea at Harvard university's four-day Catholic-Protestant colloquim. W. M. Abbott. America 108:484 Ap 13 '63
Catholic university reversal. C. D. Kean. Christian Cent 80:565 Ap 24 '63
Ecumenical voices. il por Time 81:52 Ap 5 '63
Letter from Vatican City. X. Rynne. il New Yorker 39:120+ My 11 '63
Vatican II & the Jews. F. E. Cartus. Commentary 39:19-29 Ja '65

BEACH, Fred F. and Ratliff, L. S.
School administrator's need for inservice education. Sch Life 45:16-17 Mr '63

BEACH, Stewart
Higher banking. Atlan 212:104-6 S '63
Pedestrian drift. Atlan 211:114-16 My '63
Penalty short. Harper 226:26+ Mr '63

BEACH, Sylvia
Paris: a little incident in the rue de l'Odéon. K. A. Porter. Ladies Home J 81:54-5 Ag '64

BEACH architecture
All-weather beach house. il House & Gard 123:124-7 Je '63
Beach house with vast expanse of glass. A. C. Borg. il Am Home 66:32-3 Je '63
Beach pavilion on Florida coast. il Arch Rec 134:148-9 Ag '63
Budget beach house: Springs, L.I. G. O'Brien. il N Y Times Mag p76-7 My 3 '64
Dining pavilion over water. il Arch Rec 136: 208-9 S '64
Every room can be a breezeway. il House B 106:82-7 Ja '64
Expandable sand-dune pavilion. il Am Home 67:42-3 Ap '64
House built for the sunset. il House B 105: 142-51+ My '63
Houses from pickle vats; pillbox-shaped beach houses. il Pop Mech 121:121 Ap '64
Open and shut case for privacy. il Am Home 67:44-5 Ap '64
Pavilion-style house overlooks surf. A. C. Borg. il Am Home 66:28-9 Je '63
Raise the house and get all the breezes. il House B 106:88-91+ Ja '64
Restaurant on the beach at Waikiki. il Arch Rec 136:214-15 S '64
Sand castle. il Holiday 35:104-5 My '64
Seaside home in the classical tradition. il Arch Rec 133:50-3 mid-My '63
Simplicity cuts costs for a seaside house. il Arch Rec 136:147-50 Ag '64
Sometimes there's sense in living up in the air. il House B 106:148-53+ Ap '64
Three vacation houses by Wurster. il Arch Rec 136:221-4 S '64
Two faced house. il Am Home 67:36-7 Ap '64
Two for the beach; Fire Island pines. G. O'Brien. il N Y Times Mag p70-1 My 12 '63
See also
Bathhouses

BEACH carriers. See Carriers (equipment)

BEACH clothes. See Clothing and dress

BEACH erosion
Study surf sand by color; Fernandina Beach, Fla. Sci N L 83:221 Ap 6 '63
See also
Shore protection

BEACH HAVEN, N.J.
Elevated tank for sailors. E. R. Dunphey. il Am City 79:16 D '64

BEACH plants. See Seashore vegetation

BEACH sand. See Sand

BEACH shelters. See Shelters

BEACHES
Afternoon at the beach. B. Bidner. Horn Bk 39:416 Ag '63
At bay on the beach. P. K. Brooks. il Sat R 47:70+ O 10 '64
How to feed a beach; saving Greater Los Angeles beaches. il Time 81:51 F 22 '63
See also
Sand dunes
Seashore
Water pollution

Caricatures and cartoons

Conjugal beach. T. Ungerer. Holiday 36:58-61 Ag '64

BEACON Explorer (artificial satellite) See Artificial satellites—Use in research

BEACONS
FAA endorses crash locator beacon use. Aviation W 80:47 Ja 27 '64

BEADED curtains. See Curtains and draperies

BEADLE, George Wells
New biology and the nature of man: adaptation of address, 1963. Bul Atomic Sci 20: 13-17 Mr '64
What Johnny should learn before school; adaptation of address. por Sci Digest 56: 28-33 N '64

BEADS
Beads, beads, beads, beads, beads; paper beads and salt beads. il Design 66:13 N '64

BEADS, Indian. See Indians of North America —Costume and adornment

BEAGLE, Peter S.
Come lady Death; story. Atlan 212:46-53 S '63
Good-by to the Bronx. Holiday 36:96-7+ D '64

BEAGLEHOLE, J. C.
Noble warm-hearted rock; excerpts from address, December 24, 1961. por Library J 88: 2185-8 Je 1 '63

BEAGLES (dogs)
Best rabbit insurance. P. Czura. il Field & S 69:94-5+ Ja '65
First dogs of the land. C. Leedham. il N Y Times Mag p 11 Je 21 '64
Getting beagles started. D. M. Duffey. il Outdoor Life 133:96-8+ Ja '64
Life visits those White House beagles, Him and Her. il Life 56:68A-68B+ Je 19 '64
Soho! the beagles. J. MacVane. il Field & S 68:35-7+ Ja '64
Square pegs and round holes and getting rid of fleas. D. M. Duffey. il Outdoor Life 131: 142-5 Ap '63

BEAL, Doone
Going places, finding things in Bermuda. House & Gard 124:28+ D '63
Going places, finding things in Brazil, Chile and Peru. House & Gard 124:270+ N '63
Going places, finding things in southern Germany. House & Gard 123:12+ F '63
Going places, finding things in Switzerland. House & Gard 124:16-17+ Jl '63

BEAL, Doone—*Continued*
Going places, finding things in the Bahamas and Jamaica. House & Gard 127:38+ Ja '65
Going places, finding things in the two Berlins. House & Gard 126:43-4+ S '64
Grenada. Mlle 59:188+ My '64
BEAL, J. A. and others
Beetle explosion in Honduras. Am For 70: 31-3 N '64
BEALE, Alice. See McCulloch, R. jt. auth.
BEALE, Betty
From the first Mrs MacArthur: an account of rivalry between two famous generals; reprint. U S News 56:20 My 4 '64
Nixon at the Gridiron; reprint. U S News 56: 48 My 11 '64
BEALE, Sir Howard
Medicare, labor, race: how Australia handles them; interview. por U S News 54:92-7 Mr 25 '63
BEALER, Alex W. 3d
Do you really know how to build a fire? House B 106:28+ F '64
BEALS, Margaret
Elizabeth Keen and Margaret Beals at Judson Hall. J. Maskey. Dance Mag 37:68 Je '63
BEAM, Jacob D.
Nuclear test ban and arms control; address, February 28, 1963. Dept State Bul 48:489-93 Ap 1 '63
BEAM-splitting reflex camera. See Cameras
BEAMS
Formwork: time-saver standards. S. Howard. il Arch Rec 136:254 S '64
BEAN, Charles P. and Schmitt, R. W.
Physics of high-field superconductors. bibliog Science 140:26-35 Ap 5 '63
BEAN, John E.
Data-processing center in the State department of education. Sch Life 46:10-11 Jl '64
Research in the State department of education. por Sch Life 45:17-18 My '63
BEAN, Louis H.
Expert sizes up the primary; statement. U S News 56:41 Mr 23 '64
Is the South to be solid again? U S News 56:34 Ja 20 '64
BEAN yellow mosaic virus. See Viruses, Plant
BEANS
Bean with a difference. H. S. Witty. il Flower Grower 51:20 My '64
Beans and beets in the same field. J. Russell. Farm J 88:49 Ja '64
See also
Cookery—Vegetables
Soybeans
BEAR, Firman E.
Soil. Horticulture 42:30-1+ Jl '64
BEAR, Fred
My greatest trophy; tiger with an arrow; ed. by B. East. Outdoor Life 134:40-3+ O '64
BEAR, Marjorie Warvelle
Herbs are for flavor and fragrance. Horticulture 42:18-19+ Ag '64
BEAR, W. Forrest
Don't abandon that leaky silo. Suc Farm 62: 100 My '64
BEAR hunting
Ambush by four bears. E. I. Neighbor. il Outdoor Life 134:32-3+ Jl '64
Archer stalks the mighty grizzly. D. Moser. il Life 55:104-6+ N 8 '63
Bears were bad enough. D. C. Lawrence. il Outdoor Life 132:28-9+ Ag '63
Bears with a handgun. A. J. Georg. il Outdoor Life 135:28-31+ Ja '65
Biggest bear in the East; ed. by N. Drahos. R. Avery. il Outdoor Life 131:52-5+ My '63
Biggest black ever killed; ed. by B. East. D. Streubel. il Outdoor Life 133:46-8+ My '64
Black bear posse. D. Walker. il Outdoor Life 132:40-3+ D '63
Case of the killer grizzly. D. Robertson. il Outdoor Life 134:29-31+ S '64
Dam' bear ain't there! S. R. Harris. il Outdoor Life 134:20-3+ N '64
Dark tragedy; ed. by B. East. D. Mosher. il Outdoor Life 131:20-3+ F '63
Headlong bears. D. Knight. il Outdoor Life 133:36-9+ Mr '64
Here a bear walked. R. Vincent, jr. il Outdoor Life 132:60-1+ O '63
Hunt against odds. B. Munger. il Outdoor Life 131:20-3+ Ja '63
Ice tiger. M. J. Kempner. il Harper 227:36-41 Ag '63
New world record polar bear; ed. by W. E. Anderson. S. Longoria. il Field & S 69: 56-7 O '64
Old Mose of Paddy Mill Creek. L. Dietz. il Field & S 68:58-60+ My '63
One for the bears. J. O'Connor. il Outdoor Life 133:17-19+ Ja '64
Suddenly there was a bear. H. J. Samuels. il Outdoor Life 133:58-9+ Je '64
Terror in the Cassiars. J. Ashlock. il Outdoor Life 131:52-5+ Ap '63
Too much bear. A. LaHa. il Outdoor Life 135:17-19+ Ja '65
BEAR population
Control
See Animal populations—Control
BEARD, Abner H. Jr
River port that became a seaport Américas 15:17-19 My '63
BEARD, James A.
Corkscrew. See occasional issues of House & garden
Dried fruit and nut cook book. House & Gard 126:271+ N '64
Provencal cook book. House & Gard 125:193+ My '64
Pudding and pie cook book. House & Gard 124:169+ D '63
Sausage cook book. House & Gard 123:175+ Ap '63
Sportsman's cook book. House & Gard 126: 219+ O '64
Wine guide for the triumphant huntsman. House & Gard 126:218+ O '64
about
Five girls and a gourmet. il por Seventeen 22:160+ N '63
BEARD, Robert C.
Adjust your compass. Motor B 111:44+ Ap '63
Antenna advice. Motor B 113:64 Ap '64
Don't neglect the electronics department. por Motor B 111:36+ Mr '63
Five steps to silence aboard. Motor B 112:37 N '63
How to put your depth sounder in shape. Motor B 111:52+ My '63
Radiotelephone tips. Motor B 111:88+ Je '63
Self-servicing the automatic pilot. Motor B 113:374-5 Ja '64
BEARDEN, Romare
Bearden: identification and identity. C. Childs. il por Art N 63:24-5+ O '64
Tormented faces. il Newsweek 64:105 O 19 '64
BEARDS
Capsule history of beards. A. Karlen. Holiday 35:50-1 F '64
Rise and fall of the beard. Sci Digest 54:26 O '63
Tea and goatee. Newsweek 63:80 Mr 9 '64
See also
Shaving
BEARDSLEY, J. L.
Apperson Jack Rabbit. Motor T 16:54-7 Je '64
Automotive milestones. Motor T 15:62-3+ S; 68-71+ O; 72-5 D '63; 16:76-9 Mr '64
BEARDTONGUES. See Penstemons
BEARINGS (machinery)
How to make your own plastic bearings. P. McCafferty. il Pop Sci 183:155-7+ O '63
Inside industry; air bearings. H. E. Klein. Christian Cent 80:565 Ap 24 '63
See also
Automobile engines—Bearings
BEARS
Alaska grizzlies regain record book status. B. East. il Outdoor Life 132:10-11+ O '63
Bear facts. J. W. Giles. il Am For 69:26 Jl '63
Bear that almost made me infamous; Smokey Bear's living symbol. K. D. Flock. il Am For 70:20-1+ D '64
Bear that came for supper. R. F. Leslie. il Read Digest 85:75-9 D '64
Bears in my bed. I. L. Marx. il Outdoor Life 134:48-9+ D '64
Beware of Smokey the bear. H. Bloomfield. il Sat Eve Post 237:68-9 S 12 '64
Biggest black bear ever caught. D. Mech. il Sci Digest 54:5-9 N '63
Black bear turns man-eater; fourth case on record. M. U. Bates. il Outdoor Life 131:68-9+ Je '63
Black bears are not always timid. J. McPhee. il Outdoor Life 133:62-5+ Ap '64
Boy and the bear. F. Dufresne. il Field & S 68:24-6+ Ja '64
Don't feed the bears. M. Zook. il Nat Parks Mag 37:7-9 Je '63
Fishing bears; Alaskan brown bears or grizzlies. il Look 27:114-15 N 5 '63
Grizzly territory. A. W. F. Banfield. il Natur Hist 73:22-7 Mr '64
Groucho of the wilds. F. Dufresne. il Read Digest 83:121-5 D '63
Ice tiger. M. J. Kempner. il Harper 227:36-41 Ag '63

BEARS—*Continued*
Left for dead; ed. by D. French. M. Jack. il Outdoor Life 134:36-7+ O '64
Luzi's first swim; baby polar bear. il Look 28:82-4 D 29 '64
Playing with park bears dangerous. Sci N L 83:360 Je 8 '63
Polar babies. il Look 27:78-9 Jl 2 '63
Polar bear on way to sea. Sci N L 84:146 S 7 '63
That Kodiak bear is at the back door. P. Innis. il Audubon Mag 67:16-17 Ja '65

Photographs

See Animals—Photographs

Stories

Loners: story. J. D. Osier. il Liv Wildn 85: 10-15 Wint '64

BEARS (football club) See Football clubs

BEARS, Photography of. See Photography of animals

BEASLEY, Kenneth E.
Changing library scene. por Library J 88: 3155-60 S 15 '63
Question is still open. por Library J 88:4690-3 D 15 '63

BEASLEY, M. R.
Hostess party cues. Am Home 66:25 Ja '63

BEASLEY, M. Robert
Call on your utility company for help. Am Home 66:72-3 O '63
Highway robbery. Motor T 15:42-5 My '63
Time to water. Pop Gard 14:66-7+ Jl '63

BEAST (automaton) See Automatons

BEAST in me; revue. See Musical comedies, revues, etc.—Criticisms, plots, etc.

BEAT generation. See Beatniks

BEAT that bongo; drama. See Huff, B. T.

BEATIE, David
Visit to a national grasslands. il Nat Parks Mag 38:10-13 O '64

BEATIE, Russel H.
Get your pools out of the red. Am City 78: 84-5 Jl '63

BEATIFICATION
Making of a saint. T. Congdon. il Sat Eve Post 236:74-8 Mr 23 '63
Pilgrims at a coffin; beatification of Bishop Neumann. il Newsweek 62:92-3 O 28 '63

BEATING of the girl; story. See Segal, L.

BEATLES
About the awful; the writing Beatle. P. Schickele. Nation 198:588-9 Je 8 '64
Afterthoughts on the Beatles. A. Brien. Mlle 59:239+ Ag '64
Beatle business; record sales. il Time 84:112 O 2 '64
Beatle man; manager for Beatles. New Yorker 39:23-4 D 28 '63
Beatlemania. il Newsweek 62:104 N 18 '63
Beatlemania hits the U.S. Sr Schol 84:21 F 21 '64
Beatles is coming. Newsweek 63:77 F 3 '64
Beatles reaction puzzles even psychologists. Sci N L 85:141 F 29 '64
Beatles' secret. Reporter 30:16+ F 27 '64
Bit by the Beatles! E. Miller. il Seventeen 23:82-3 Mr '64
Brace yourself, they're back; Beatles. il Bsns W p28-9 Ag 22 '64
British exports booming; Beatles. Nat R 16: 142 F 25 '64
Britons succumb to Beatlemania. F. Lewis. il N Y Times Mag p 124-6 D 1 '63
Building the Beatle image. V. Packard. il Sat Eve Post 237:36 Mr 21 '64
Disaster? well, not exactly: there stood the Beatles; with report by G. Cameron. il Life 57:58A-60+ Ag 28 '64
Feeling of youth; Beatles. J. Ridgeway. New Repub 150:6 F 22 '64
George, Paul, Ringo, and John; the Beatles in the United States. il Newsweek 63:54-7 F 24 '64
Here come those Beatles; with report by T. Green. il Life 56:24-31 Ja 31 '64
Hiram and the Animals; comparison with the Beatles. New Yorker 40:40-3 S 12 '64
Hiram's report; the Beatles in New York. New Yorker 40:21-3 F 22 '64
New madness; rhythm-and-blues quartet called the Beatles. il Time 82:64 N 15 '63
No soul in Beatlesville. A. Rinzler. Nation 198:221-2 Mr 2 '64
Our American scrapbook. il pors Life 57: 105-7 O 23 '64
People are talking about the Beatles, four parody singers, now the passion of British young. il Vogue 143:100-1 Ja 1 '64
Report from Hiram; première of Beatles' first picture Hard day's night. New Yorker 40: 25-7 Ag 22 '64
Return of the Beatles. A. G. Aronowitz. il Sat Eve Post 237:22-9 Ag 8 '64
Science looks at Beatlemania. J. A. Osmundsen. il Sci Digest 55:24-6 My '64
Shaggy Englishman story; British long-hairs Rolling Stones and the Beatles. A. Carthew. il N Y Times Mag p 18+ S 6 '64
Unbarbershopped quartet; the Beatles. il Time 83:46+ F 21 '64
What are the Beatles really like? symposium, ed. by E. Miller. il Seventeen 23:236-7+ Ag '64
What the Beatles have done to hair; teen-aged British boys. il Look 28:58-9 D 29 '64
What the Beatles prove about teenagers; interview. D. Riesman. il U S News 56: 88 F 24 '64
Why the girls scream, weep, flip. D. Dempsey. il N Y Times Mag p 15+ F 23 '64
Yeah-yeah-yeah! Beatlemania becomes a part of US history; with report by G. Cameron. il Life 56:34-34B F 21 '64
Yeah, yeah, yeah; Beatles in New York. il Newsweek 63:88 F 17 '64
Yeah! yeah! yeah! music's gold bugs: the Beatles. A. G. Aronowitz. il Sat Eve Post 237:30-5 Mr 21 '64

BEATNIKS
Bye, bye, Beatnik; marriage of G. Corso. il Newsweek 62:65 Jl 1 '63
Poets of retreat. S. Hazo. Cath World 198: 33-9 O '63
There are also Zen Beatniks, western style, in Japan. il Look 27:28 S 10 '63

BEATON, Cecil
Amazing Bruces; the life in London of the American Ambassador and family; photographs. Vogue 144:122-9 S 15 '64
Audrey Hepburn in Givenchy hats: My fair lady to the life. il Vogue 144:118-21 Ag 15 '64
Cléo de Mérode today. il Vogue 143:92-3+ F 15 '64
His Majesty Hassan II, king of Morocco. Vogue 144:224-31 S 1 '64
I don't want to be 'Liza. il Vogue 142:126-33 D '63
Living legends. il Vogue 145:126-7+ Ja 1 '65
My fair lady; excerpts from Beaton's diary. il por Ladies Home J 81:56-65 Ja '64
My two houses. por Vogue 141:130-7+ Mr 15 '63
Plisetskaya; a photographic essay. Vogue 143: 164-71 Ap 1 '64

about

On the street where you live; Miss Doolittle's bedroom. il por Ladies Home J 81:134-6+ Ja '64

BEATON, Leonard
To slow down the nuclear race. N Y Times Mag p 15+ Mr 8 '64

BEATTIE, Bob
Bob Beattie U.S. Olympic ski coach. C. S. Wren. il pors Look 28:80-1+ Ja 28 '64
For his winning ways; coach of the U.S. Alpine program. Sports Illus 21:8 Ag 10 '64
In and out of a jam. D. Jenkins. il por Sports Illus 20:14-19 F 17 '64
Our ski team flies high; with report by M. Smith. il pors Life 56:66-70+ Ja 10 '64
Young team with a mission; Alpine team. il pors Sports Illus 19:22-7 D 2 '63

BEATTIE, James J.
Pride of Kid Galahad, inc. J. Olsen. il pors Sports Illus 21:64-8+ Ag 31 '64

BEATTY, Clyde
Cat man. il Newsweek 61:92 F 18 '63

BEATTY, Jerome, Jr
How J. Gallagher O'Shay got the U.S. space program off the ground. Esquire 62:96-8+ O '64
Orphan Annie under analysis. Sat R 46:35+ O 19 '63
Trade winds. See issues of Saturday review
What's happening to humor? Sat R 47:49 Ag 29 '64

BEATTY, Jim
Every day hard training must make. por Life 54:56-7 Mr 1 '63
I'll run a record mile; ed. by J. N. Bell. pors Pop Mech 119:112-15 Ap '63

about

According to plan; indoor two-mile record. Time 81:78 Mr 15 '63
And now there are two. W. Bingham. il por Sports Illus 18:14-17 Mr 18 '63
It hurts to run. B. Libby. por Sat Eve Post 236:54-5 F 2 '63
Jim Beatty: America's fastest miler. il por Look 27:81 Ap 9 '63
Look! another record. il por Time 81:50 F 22 '63

BEATTY, John, and Beatty, Patricia
I would not coddle the child. Horn Bk 40:149-52 Ap '64
BEATTY, Patricia. See Beatty, J. jt. auth.
BEATTY, Robert
Half price DME. Flying 74:45-6+ Je '64
(ed) See Link, M. Lady's day in the Comanche 400
BEATTY, Talley
Talley Beatty dance company, 92nd street Y. D. Hering. Dance Mag 38:30 My '64
BEAUBIEN, Irénée
Ecumenism in Montreal. America 109:16-17 Jl 6 '63
BEAUBIEN, Nivelle
Negro political progress in New England. A. Morrison. il pors Ebony 18:35-6 O '63
BEAUCARNEA
Pony-tail plant. A. D. Hawkes. il Horticulture 41:143 Mr '63
BEAUCHAMP, Keith, and Zeman, L. E.
Planning a farm pond. Suc Farm 61:36-7 Je '63
BEAUCHAMP, Robert
(ed) Special issue on paperbacks. Sr Schol 83:21T-35T Ja 17 '64
Variations on a theme. Sr Schol 83:26T Ja 17 '64
What's new in paperbacks? Sr Schol 83:22T Ja 17 '64
BEAUMARCHAIS, Pierre Augustin Caron de
Le mariage de Figaro (Marriage of Figaro)
Criticism
New Yorker 40:120+ Mr 7 '64
BEAUMONT, William
Medical museum at a crossroads of history; Prairie du Chien, Wis. K. N. Anderson. il Todays Health 41:60-6 D '63
Window to the human stomach. il Todays Health 43:88 Ja '65
BEAUMONT, Tex.
Sanitary affairs
Operation bootstrap. D. H. Smith. il Am City 78:78-80 Jl '63
BEAUREGARD, Pierre Gustave Toutant
Du Pont storms Charleston; excerpt from Civil war. S. Foote. il Am Heritage 14:28-34+ Je '63
BEAUTIFUL sloops; story. See Jordon, E. H.
BEAUTIFUL travelers; story. See Bongartz, R.
BEAUTIFYING of cities. See Municipal improvement
BEAUTY. See Aesthetics
BEAUTY, Personal
Are you as pretty as you could be? il Seventeen 23:104-5 O '64
Are you the beauty you were meant to be? quiz and answers. il Mlle 57:136-7+ O '63
Be a golden girl. il Seventeen 22:58-9 Je '63
Be the girl with the three good looks. il McCalls 92:118-19+ N '64
Beauty: an eye to spring. D. A. Robinson. il Ladies Home J 81:66-7 Mr '64
Beauty biographies of four young naturals. il Seventeen 23:100-3 O '64
Beauty bulletin. See issues of Vogue
Beauty checkout. See issues of Vogue
Beauty clinic. See issues of Good housekeeping
Beauty, going on fifteen. McCalls 91:108-9 D '63
Beauty is just a b-zzz-zzz away! il Am Home 67:18+ Jl '64
Beauty memo. Mlle 59:96 S '64
Beauty register; private eye on the beauty lives of nine unusual women. il Vogue 145:38-43 Ja 15 '65
Beauty register; ten beauty biographies. il Vogue 144:102-7 Jl '64
Beauty roundup. il Seventeen 23:106-7 Je '64
Beauty spot. il Mlle 59:136-9 S '64
Beauty you don't know you have. il Mlle 57:89-93 O '63
Dear beauty editor. See issues of Seventeen
Drastic beauty treatment. Vogue 144:112-13+ Ag 15 '64
Dressing table talk. See issues of Seventeen
Engagement with beauty; notes from a bride. il Mlle 58:52-3 Ja '64
Every day in every way you're getting prettier and prettier. il McCalls 90:92-5+ F '63
Five times a day, take a beauty break. il McCalls 91:128-9+ Ap '64
Four guest editors hitch a ride on the beauty-go-round. il Mlle 59:316-17 Ag '64
Frankly speaking; who is the most beautiful woman in the world? comp. by G. Wagner. il McCalls 90:34 Je '63
Get ready for fall. il Seventeen 23:138-9 S '64
GH's can't-be-bothered beauty book. il Good H 158:97-100 Ja '64
Good looks. L. D. Kirk. See issues of Parents' magazine & better homemaking
Growing up beautiful. il Redbook 120:76-7 Ap '63
How beautiful can you get? Mlle 57:124-5 Je '63
How do you compete with the girls he meets? il Good H 158:102-5 Mr '64
How I look my best; women in the world of entertainment. R. Drake. il Redbook 122:72-5+ N '63
How much do you want to be pretty? Seventeen 23:72-3 Jl '64
How the bride stayed beautiful all through the honeymoon. il McCalls 90:98-9+ My '63
How to survive the holiday rush. il Redbook 124:70-1+ D '64
How women spoil their looks. R. Drake. il Redbook 123:56-7+ Je '64
Invest in beauty: the backward glance. il Mlle 58:152 N '63
Look-again look; slightly brazen book of beauty. il McCalls 91:80-95 Jl '64
The look you like; questions and answers; ed. by L. Allen. See issues of Today's health
McCall's discovers you; beauty experiment. il McCalls 90:94-7+ Ag '63
Make me over just a little; M. Smaby, a Seventeen fashion council winner. il Seventeen 22:122-3+ S '63
Meet Bonnie, GH's beautiful covergirl wife. il pors Good H 158:120-3 Je '64
Memo to a winter-weary wife or how to get rid of the January look. Am Home 68:36 Ja '65
Memo: to the hostess. Am Home 67:36 N '64
Memo: to you. Am Home 67:34 O '64
Mlle's own beauty adviser. il Mlle 58:117-21 F '64
My teacher is pretty. Am Home 67:12+ S '64
New year; a new you. il Seventeen 23:88-91+ Ja '64; 24:58-63+ Ja '65
Outdoor glow. il Seventeen 22:112-13 N '63
Plan to look your best on vacation. il Redbook 123:72-3 My '64
Pretty confidential. J. Wescott. il Seventeen 22:16 S '63
Project: you; figure. B. Clerke. il Ladies Home J 80:73-6 Mr '63
℞; for beauty in a day. il McCalls 90:158+ My '63
School-day beauty on the go. il Seventeen 22:112-13 F '63
That certain look: partly grooming, partly make-up. il Seventeen 23:112-13 Mr '64
Through the summer looking glass. B. Clerke. Ladies Home J 80:30+ Jl '63
Twenty-five questions and answers. R. Drake. Redbook 123:66-7+ Jl '64
Two faces of summer. il Seventeen 23:102-3 Je '64
Von Sternberg principle; true nature of glamor. J. Von Sternberg. il Esquire 60:90-7+ O '63
We have our own home beauty shop. A. Eby. il Parents Mag 39:84 Jl '64
What comes naturally. D. A. Robinson. il Ladies Home J 81:76-7 Je '64
Who's the beauty on the beach? il Good H 156:88-9+ Je '63
Yesterday and today. D. A. Robinson. il Ladies Home J 81:56-7 Ag '64
See also
Baths
Beauty shops
Cosmetics
Exercise
Hair
Hairdressing
Make-up
Shaving
Skin
Toilet
BEAUTY boxes. See Boxes, cases, etc.
BEAUTY contests
Beauty part; the International beauty congress. il Newsweek 62:84-5 S 9 '63
Beauty's comeback; Miss Thailand of 1964. il Time 84:32 D 18 '64
Big show at Santa Cruz. il Sunset 130:60 Je '63
Miss Universe: beauty from around world. il Ebony 19:102-4+ O '64
Neatest teener: Miss Teen age America pageant at Dallas. D. Wakefield. il Esquire 59:88-9+ Je '63
Salesgirl, but does she sell? Miss America. il Bsns W p 146-8+ S 14 '63
Will the real Miss Rheingold stand out? D. L. Goodrich. il Sat Eve Post 236:48+ N 16 '63
BEAUTY of nature. See Nature
BEAUTY of scenery. See Landscape
BEAUTY part; drama. See Perelman, S. J.

BEAUTY preparations. See Cosmetics
BEAUTY resorts. See Health resorts, watering places, etc.
BEAUTY shops
Beauty the New York way: where to go to get it. Mlle 58:190 Ap '64
Beauty unlimited. il Mlle 56:168-9 Mr '63
First: Kenneth's new beauty salon. New Yorker 39:43-4 Mr 16 '63
How to buy a hairdresser. il Seventeen 22: 34-5 N '63
Invest in beauty: the $20 bonanza; day at Elizabeth Arden's New York salon. il Mlle 59:69-71 Je '64
Kenneth club. il Vogue 142:52-5 Jl '63
Overteased hair: beginning of the end. E. Harris. il Look 27:26-8+ Jl 30 '63
BEAUTY; story. See Greene, G; Heimer, M.
BEAUVOIR, Simone de
Question of fidelity; excerpts from Force of circumstance, tr. by R. Howard. Harper 229:57-64 N; 111-14+ D '64
about
I ain't Abelard. por Newsweek 64:58-9 D 28 '64
Inscrutable priestess; letters to the editor. A. Montagu; J. M. Demos. Harper 230:6 Ja '65
Letter from Paris. Genêt. New Yorker 39:88-91 Ja 11 '64
Letter from Paris; concerning a lecture on literature. Genêt. New Yorker 40:68-70 D 26 '64
BEAVAN, John
Missionary in the theater. N Y Times Mag p28+ O 13 '63
BEAVER, Edmund
How to keep the kids happy on a trip. Bet Hom & Gard 42:93-4 Jl '64
BEAVER, William T.
Isolated mammalian eye: a method for quantitative evaluation of autonomic drugs. bibliog Science 141:1274-5 S 27 '63
BEAVERBROOK, William Maxwell Aitken, 1st baron
Beaver at eighty five. il por Newsweek 63: 94 Je 8 '64
Beaver at eighty-four. il por Time 82:45-6 S 6 '63
Beaverbrook: Britain's rambunctious press lord. I. Ross. por Read Digest 84:155-6+ Mr '64
Eternal apprentice. il por Time 83:58 Je 5 '64
Larger than death. por Time 83:38 Je 19 '64
Lord Beaverbrook, R.I.P. C. Brogan. Nat R 16:722-4 Ag 25 '64
Max the Giant Killer. por Time 81:82+ My 31 '63
BEAVERS, Stacie Virginia
Hospital music clinic. por Recreation 56:479 D '63
BEAVERS
Return of the beaver. S. Anderson. il Natur Hist 73:38-43 O '64
Smarter than a beaver. C. Ford. il Field & S 69:6+ Je '64
BEBOP. See Jazz music
BÉCAUD, Gilbert
On records: Opéra d'Aran. Opera N 28:35 Mr 28 '64
BECHHOEFER, Bernhard G.
Soviet attitude toward disarmament. bibliog f Cur Hist 45:193-9 O '63
Test-ban treaty: some further considerations. Bul Atomic Sci 20:25-7 My '64
BECHTEL, Jenny Bell
Inventive Africans; *kikois* dashing as dresses. pors Time 84:60 S 18 '64
BECHTEL, Louise Seaman
Chapters from Horn book history. Horn Bk 39:412-15 Ag '63
BECHUANALAND
Atlantic report. Atlan 213:34+ Ap '64
High commission territories of southern Africa. B. S. Young. bibliog il Focus 14:1-6 D '63
Protectorates under the gun. S. Uys. New Repub 149:9-10 S 28 '63
South Africa: enclaves of trouble. J. Halpern. il Nation 197:49-52 Jl 27 '63
See also
Hunting—Bechuanaland
United Nations—Bechuanaland
BECK, Alfred H.
St Louis' slurry-seal experiment. Am City 78:78-80 F '63
BECK, Charles B.
Ginkgophyton (psygmophyllum) with a stem of gymnospermic structure. bibliog Science 141:431-2 Ag 2 '63
BECK, Charles E.
Ford in its future. il por Time 81:74 Mr 1 '63
Philco gets the T-Bird look; success of the Ford-Philco merger. il pors Bsns W p45-6+ Ag 17 '63
BECK, Edward C. See Dustman, R. E. jt. auth.
BECK, Ernest Adam
Noncelibate priest. il por Newsweek 64:52 Jl 13 '64
BECK, James H.
Trecento topography. Art N 63:52+ O '64
BECK, James T.
Warehousing and shipping: costs and solutions. por Pub W 184:65+ N 4 '63
BECK, Joan
Senior citizens spark youth to develop talents. Todays Health 42:60-1+ F '64
BECK, Ray
Wonderful white weasel. Outdoor Life 135:48-9+ Ja '65
BECK, Stanley D. and Alexander, Nancy
Hormonal activation of the insect brain. bibliog Science 143:478-9 Ja 31 '64
BECK, Vivian
In defense of educationists. por NEA J 53:16 Mr '64
BECK, Washington
Glass-ware patents of Washington Beck. A. G. Peterson. il Hobbies 69:82-3 O '64
BECKER, Bernard, and Morton W. R.
Taste sensitivity to phenylthiourea in glaucoma. bibliog Science 144:1347-8 Je 12 '64
BECKER, Elmer L. See Schur, P. H. jt. auth.
BECKER, Frank J.
Excerpt from testimony, April 22, 1964. Cong Digest 43:276+ N '64
Prayer hearings; excerpts from statement before House judiciary committee. Sr Schol 84:13T My 15 '64
about
Never say die! says Becker. Christian Cent 81:852 Jl 1 '64
BECKER, Frederick P.
AMA: vested reaction. New Repub 152:12 Ja 23 '65
BECKER, Harry J.
Voluntary health insurance. Cur Hist 45: 92-7+ Ag '63
BECKER, Herman F.
Flowers, insects, and evolution. Natur Hist 74:38-45 bibliog(p70) F '65
BECKER, Joseph
Data processing equipment in libraries. por ALA Bul 58:227-30, 557-60, 714-18, 822-4, 1007-10 Mr, Je, S-O, D '64
—See Tucker, H. W. jt. auth.
BECKER, Ursula Kocher-. See Kocher-Becker, U.
BECKETT, Samuel
Beckett. New Yorker 40:22-3 Ag 8 '64
Beckett & the theater of the concrete. il Time 81:48+ Je 28 '63
Beckett's testament. R. M. Elman. Commonweal 80:416-18 Je 26 '64
Oh les beaux jours. Criticism
New Yorker 40:102+ F 22 '64
Play. Criticism
Commonweal 79:484-5 Ja 24 '64
Nation 198:106 Ja 27 '64
New Repub 150:30 F 1 '64
Sat R 47:25 Ja 25 '64
Time 83:64 Ja 17 '64
Vogue 143:22 F 15 '64
BECKHAM, Charles H. See Soltis, J. D. jt. auth.
BECKHARD, Robert L.
For Warlock, or Heseltine; letter. Sat R 47: 55 D 26 '64
BECKLEY, Addison S.
How to sell more abroad. Nations Bsns 51: 106-10+ Mr '63
BECKLEY, Paul V.
Divas in movieland. Opera N 29:8-13 D 19 '64
Two on the aisle. Sat R 47:36-7 F 8 '64
BECKLEY, W.Va.
Take a ride through a coal mine. J. B. Kessinger. il Am City 78:31 Ap '63
BECKMAN, Lars, and others
Catalase hybrid enzymes in maize. bibliog Science 146:1174-5 N 27 '64
BECKMAN, Margaret
Why not the Bobbsey twins? reprint. Library J 89:4612-13+ N 15 '64
BECKMANN, Dave
Awkward age. PTA Mag 58:23 S '63
BECKMANN, George M.
Role of the foundations. Ann Am Acad 356: 12-22 N '64
BECKMANN, Max
Art; exhiibtion at Museum of modern art. M. Kozloff. Nation 200:66-7 Ja 18 '65
Art galleries; memorial exhibition at the Museum of modern art. R. M. Coates. New Yorker 40:101-3 Ja 23 '65
Courage to die. por Newsweek 64:103+ O 19 '64

BECKMANN, Max—*Continued*
Roar of lions; first retrospective at Manhattan's Museum of modern art. il Time 85:58 Ja 1 '65
Split worlds of Max Beckmann. M. Roskill. il por Art N 63:46-8+ D '64
BECKNER, Jacquie. See Beckner, N. jt. auth.
BECKNER, Neal
Sportfisherman plus! Yachting 116:57+ Ag '64
—and Beckner, Jacquie
International team racing. il Yachting 114: 56-7+ S '63
BECKWITH, Byron DeLa. See DeLa Beckwith, B.
BED linens. See Linen, Household
BED sitting room; drama. See Antrobus, J. and Milligan, S.
BED wetting. See Urine—Incontinence
BEDAN, Richard
March on Frankfort, Ky. America 110:398 Mr 28 '64
BEDAS, Yusuf
Who's who in foreign business. por Fortune 67:66 Ap '63
BEDAU, Hugo
Law and justice. bibliog Nation 196:357-61 Ap 27 '63
BEDDING
Bedding. Consumer Rep 29:43-50 D '64
Bedding isn't what it used to be. il House B 106:81-109 F '64
Choose bedding for comfort and for eye-appeal. J. Holmstrand. il Suc Farm 62:74-5 Ag '64
Mattresses and bedding '64. il Good H 158: 188-90+ F '64
See also
Coverlets
Sheets
BEDDING for animals. See Litter (bedding)
BEDELL, Eugenia
Pick a pair of perfect islands. Sat R 47:74-5+ O 10 '64
BEDFORD, Harry
Sand casting. Design 65:113+ Ja '64
BEDFORD, Sybille
Generations on the gallows. Nation 197:394-5 D 7 '63
Lost art of civilized touring. Esquire 62: 126-31+ N '64
Ruby trial: a chance to redeem a tragedy. por Life 56:36-36B F 28 '64
Violence, froth, sob stuff: was justice done? Life 56:32-34B+ Mr 27 '64
BEDROOM furnishings. See Household furnishings
BEDROOMS
Bedrooms bright with color. il Good H 158: 90-6 Ja '64
Bedrooms designed by teens for teens. il Seventeen 23:130-1 My '64
Bedrooms with comfort complete. il Bet Hom & Gard 42:56-67 My '64
Candid thoughts on the care and feeding of overnight guests; excerpts from Profession: housewife. P. McGinley. Ladies Home J 80: 43+ Jl '63
Charm of over-bed decorating. il Am Home 66:86 Jl '63
Dream room. il Seventeen 23:120-1 O '64
Gay, gaudy history of the American bedroom and bath. R. Lynes. il McCalls 91:116-17+ O '63
George Washington slept here; but you sleep here. il McCalls 91:130-7+ Ap '64
Get more space from your room. il Seventeen 23:200+ S '64
Give your room a trimming. il Seventeen 23:173 F '64
Handy built-ins for the bedroom area. R. Martens. il Farm J 87:58-60 S '63
How to revamp your room. il Seventeen 23: 134-7 S '64
How to squeeze a lot of beautiful new room into very, very little space. il Seventeen 22:214-15 Ag '63
Model rooms. il Seventeen 23:130-3 Mr '64
My sister and I: want a new room; want two rooms! il Seventeen 22:110-11 O '63
On the street where you live; Miss Doolittle's bedroom. il Ladies Home J 81:134-6+ Ja '64
Paper your room: paper-made accessories. il Seventeen 23:190 Ap '64
Rosy retreat for a teen-ager. il House & Gard 126:188-9 S '64
This bedroom has ideas worth study. il Sunset 134:68+ Ja '65
We're upstairs in the attic! Come down and see my new room! il Seventeen 23:134-5 Je '64
See also
Childrens rooms
BEDS
Bedtime story; king-size bed boom. il Newsweek 64:88-9 N 30 '64
Color hits the jackpot. il House & Gard 123: 110-11 Mr '63
Decorating clinic; how to get a big bed in a small room. M. Casserly. il Bet Hom & Gard 41:28, 52-3 Mr '63
Dress up a bed with a headboard that matches the bedspread. il Bet Hom & Gard 41:49 S '63
Extra sleeping space and extra storage space. il Sunset 131:118 O '63
Fold-away bedroom. il Pop Mech 121:166-70 Mr '64
How beds began to grow. il House & Gard 124:192-3 O '63
How to stretch a double bed. il House & Gard 124:253 O '63
Is there a guest in the house? always room for one more. il Seventeen 22:218-19 N '63
Make room for an extra bed. il Good H 156: 108-15 Mr '63
Murphy bed. J. Peter. il Look 28:62 Je 30 '64
Sleep big; larger beds. Time 83:54 Mr 27 '64
Three dreamy ways to sleep without stirring. il House & Gard 124:178-9 O '63
Where can you sleep an extra guest? J. Holmstrand. il Suc Farm 63:86-7 Ja '65
See also
Bedding
Cribs (beds)
Day beds
BEDS, Automobile. See Automobiles—Camping equipment
BEDS, Built in
Spare bunks. il Pop Mech 121:143 Ap '64
BEDS, Sofa. See Sofas
BEDSOLE, Hal
HAL-lelujah! H. L. Masin. il por Sr Schol 83:25 O 18 '63
Very big head getting smaller; USC end. J. Underwood. il pors Sports Illus 19:42-4+ O 21 '63
BEDSPREADS. See Coverlets
BEE culture. See Bees
BEE stings. See Insect bites and stings
BEE venom. See Venom
BEEBE, Bill
Yellow streak. Outdoor Life 132:48-9+ Jl '63
BEEBE, Lucius
Overland limited; excerpts from Central Pacific and the Southern Pacific railroads. Am Heritage 15:54-7+ D '63
Savoy of London. Holiday 33:106-7+ Mr '63
BEEBE, Robert
Passagemaker. Yachting 116:58-60+ O '64
BEECH, Keyes
Happiness is not a princess. McCalls 91:104-5+ Mr '64
BEECH aircraft corporation
Beech parts, supplies distribution grows. E. J. Bulban. il Aviation W 78:96 Ap 1 '63
Beech planning $95-million sales in 1965. il Aviation W 82:28 Ja 18 '65
BEECHAM, Sir Thomas
Notes from our correspondents. F. Aprahamian. il por Hi Fi 14:29+ N '64
BEECHER, John
All you have to do is lie. New Repub 151:9-10 O 24 '64
Little night music. Nation 199:272-5 O 26 '64
On acquiring a Cistercian breviary; poem. Commonweal 77:520 F 8 '63
BEECHING, Richard
Clearing the track; Beeching's plan. Time 81: 98 Ap 5 '63
New blow to the chin; resignation. Time 85:66 Ja 1 '65
Victorian England. A. Burnet. New Repub 148:9-10 Ap 13 '63
BEEF
Any hope of slowing beef imports? Farm J 88:48 Mr '64
Man's best friend, the beefsteak. J. D. Ratcliff. il Todays Health 41:30-4 Je '63
See also
Cookery—Meat
Marketing
See Meat—Marketing
Prices
See Meat—Prices
Terminology
Your primer of beef carcass terms. R. A. Merkel. Suc Farm 62:47 Je '64
BEEF, Frozen. See Meat, Frozen
BEEF cattle. See Cattle, Beef
BEEF grading. See Meat—Grading and standardization

BEEF industry. See Meat industry and trade
BEEF loaf. See Cookery—Meat
BEEF Stroganoff. See Cookery—Meat
BEEGHLY, Charles Milton
Businessmen in the news. por Fortune 67:54 Je '63
BEEKMAN place; drama. See Taylor, S.
BEELKE, Ralph G.
Is art education threatened? Sch Arts 62:15-16 F '63
about
Art educator of the year. por Sch Arts 62:3 Ap '63
BEEMAN, Gary
Trapped in the desert. Read Digest 85:100-5 Ag '64
BEER, Michael
Electron microscopy. Science 144:431 Ap 24 '64
BEER
Ancient beverage center of cultural focus. Sci Digest 53:54-5 F '63
Beer break. M. Kaytor. il Look 27:46 Jl 16 '63
Snob suds; foreign beer imports. il Newsweek 63:80-1 F 17 '64
See also
Brewing industries
Advertising
Sales & distribution; snob appeal sells premium beer. J. F. Olesky. Duns R 84:65-6 N '64
BEER containers
Build a better beer can and the world will... il Newsweek 62:61 Ag 5 '63
BEERBOHM, Sir Max
Unpublished parodies. Atlan 212:76-7 Ag '63
about
Beerbohm revival. J. Epstein. New Repub 150:32-3 Je 27 '64
Books. J. Updike. New Yorker 40:176+ Mr 7 '64
BEERMANN, Wolfgang, and Clever, Ulrich
Chromosome puffs. Sci Am 210:50-8 bibliog(p 156) Ap '64
BEERY, Althea
Preparing children for reading; reprint. Todays Health 41:16+ D '63
BEES
Bee beep. il Time 81:54 My 31 '63
Bee hive in your living room. il Sunset 130: 142+ Ap '63
Bee keeping. il Sunset 130:264+ Ap '63
Bee portrait. R. Kinne. il Pop Phot 52:54-5+ F '63
Bees tend to lose pep on hearing sound waves. Sci N L 84:377 D 14 '63
Division of labor among primitively social bees. C. D. Michener. bibliog il Science 141: 434-5 Ag 2 '63
How science aids our overworked bees. J. W. Poling. il Audubon Mag 65:280-3 S '63
How to milk a bee. il Time 81:66 F 15 '63
Queen bee's perfume. E. Mirel. Sci N L 84: 38 Jl 20 '63
Royal perfume: queen bee. Time 82:52 Jl 19 '63
Smoke that calms bees shortens their lives. Sci N L 85:137 F 29 '64
Sound communication in honeybees. A. M. Wenner. il Sci Am 210:116-22+ bibliog(p 156) Ap '64
Swarm orientation in honeybees. R. A. Morse. bibliog il Science 141:357-8 Jl 26 '63
Venom collection from honey bees. A. W. Benton and others. bibliog il Science 142: 228-9 O 11 '63
See also
Carpenter bees
BEETHOVEN, Ludwig van
Artur Schnabel, a legend reëmergent. P. Hart. Hi Fi 13:65-8+ N '63
Artur Schnabel: the complete Beethoven piano sonatas. R. Kammerer. il Am Rec G 30: 378-80+ Ja '64
Beethoven and Brahms with a master's stamp. H. Goldsmith. Hi Fi 14:124-6 O '64
Beethoven by Elly Ney. R. Kammerer. Am Rec G 30:680 Ap '64
Beethoven is better than ever. F. V. Grunfeld. Reporter 30:42-4 Mr 12 '64
Beethoven's cello sonatas in a partnership of peers. R. C. Marsh. il Hi Fi 14:65 S '64
Beethoven's Christus am Oelberg. H. Glass. Am Rec G 29:860-2 Jl '63
Fidelio. Criticism
New Yorker 39:149 Mr 9 '63
Sat R 46:41 F 9 '63
Fidelio. G. L. Mayer. Am Rec G 31:192-3 N '64
Fidelio pitched for excitement. C. L. Osborne. il Hi Fi 14:123-4 O '64
From Vox, volume II of Brendel's Beethoven; eight sonatas. R. Jones. Am Rec G 30:41 S '63
Furtwängler radio performances on DGG. AM Rec G 30:570-1+ Mr '64
Happy birthday, Herr Backhaus. R. Kammerer. Am Rec G 30:596 Mr '64
Kempff on Beethoven, magnificently refurbished. J. Lyons. Am Rec G 31:130 O '64
Ludwig van Beethoven nine symphonies; Berlin philharmonic orchestra conductor Herbert von Karajan. C. J. Luten. il Am Rec G 30:10-12 S '63
Monteux's Ninth: an exalted kind of humanity. P. L. Miller. Am Rec G 29:622 Ap '63
Music to my ears; Cantata on the death of Emperor Joseph II, played by New York philharmonic orchestra. I. Kolodin. Sat R 48:22 Ja 30 '65
New integral set of the nine; to add to the best. H. C. R. Landon. Hi Fi 13:79-80 S '63
New revelations of the Choral Fantasia. H. Goldsmith. il Hi Fi 14:67-8 S '64
On records; Christus am Oelberg. Opera N 28:35 F 15 '64
On records; Fidelio. Opera N 29:34 D 12 '64
RCA Victor's million-dollar trio; Archduke trio. R. Jones. il Am Rec G 30:389+ Ja '64
Recordings of Beethoven. M. Mayer. Esquire 59:52-3 Ap '63
Sheer power: late Beethovens by the Amadeus. H. Glass. Am Rec G 30:512+ F '64
BEETLEBUNG trees. See Tupelos
BEETLES
Alien beetle on rampage; cereal leaf beetles. il Sci N L 84:83 Ag 10 '63
Antlered grotesque; stag beetle. L. Holmberg. il Natur Hist 73:56-9 F '64
Beetle with go power; stenodus beetle's defense mechanism. il Time 84:49 S 25 '64
Blighted summer; cereal leaf beetles. il Newsweek 62:72 Ag 26 '63
Engravings beneath the bark; Douglas-fir beetles. M. M. Fisher. il Natur Hist 72: 54-6 Ag '63
Jewels that crawl; megazopherus chiliensis. W. I. Fischman. il Sat Eve Post 236:68 My 11 '63
New beetle has toe hold in Corn Belt; cereal leaf beetle. J. Russell. il Farm J 87:25 Jl '63
See also
Elm bark beetles
Fireflies
BEETLES, Southern pine. See Pine—Diseases and pests
BEETS
See also
Sugar beets
BEEVER, Jack
UHF reception. Electr World 70:37-9+ N '63; 71-81 Ap '64
BEFORE the Trojan war; story. See Garro, E.
BEFORE we part; story. See Teall, K. M.
BEGINNING; story. See Young, T.
BEGONIAS
Begonias as house plants most beauty for least care! J. Kramer. Am Home 67:94 N '64
Begonias for beauty. A. B. Turner. il Horticulture 41:346-7 Je '63
Begonias for winter color. J. L. Martin. il Horticulture 41:280-1 My '63
Begonias; new hybrid kallaking. C. Nave and L. Nave. il Horticulture 42:32 Ja '64
Color choices in fibrous begonias. il Sunset 130:313 My '63
Grow this beauty from a bulb; tuberous begonias. il Pop Gard 15:14-15 F '64
How I grow tuberous begonias. A. J. De Blasi. il Flower Grower 51:46+ Mr '64
How to grow & propagate Christmas begonia. E. Javorsky. il Flower Grower 52: 36-7 Ja '65
How to grow happy begonias. il Sunset 131: 154-5 Jl '63
Lettuce begonia. il Pop Gard 15:19 F '64
Mildew on your begonias. Sunset 133:169+ Jl '64
Rex begonias. R. E. Atkinson. il Horticulture 41:623 D '63
Sparkling hues of tuberous begonias. M. H. Reynolds. il Horticulture 41:146 Mr '63
Tuberous begonias. il Bet Hom & Gard 42: 114 Mr '64
BEHAN, Brendan
Beating the gargle. Theatre Arts 47:9 F '63
Dublin in the doldrums. F. Russell. il Nat R 16:612+ Jl 14 '64
End to confusion. por Newsweek 63:72 Mr 30 '64
Gift of gab on the lam. E. Capouya. il por Sat R 47:36-7 Je 20 '64
Obituary
Pub W 185:37 Mr 30 '64

BEHAN, Dominic
Hail to the O'Chief. Life 54:12 Je 21 '63
BEHAVIOR. See Etiquette
BEHAVIOR (psychology)
Behavior: disturbed or disturbing? R. R. Kyllonen. NEA J 53:50-2 S '64
Behavioral pharmacology; report on annual meeting of the Behavioral pharmacology society. B. Weiss. Science 144:730-1 My 8 '64
Critical periods in behavioral development. J. P. Scott; discussion. Science 139:673-4, 1110+ F 15, Mr 15 '63
Do ministers really understand people? L. David and I. David. Good H 156:65+ Mr '63
Do you understand the language of behavior? M. R. Weisbord. il Parents Mag 39:68-9+ F '64
Human behavior, by G. Steiner and B. Berelson. Review
Newsweek il 63:90 F 24 '64
Time il 83:43 F 14 '64
Human behavior unique. Sci N L 86:151 S 5 '64
Inheritance of behavior in infants. D. G. Freedman and B. Keller. bibliog il Science 140:196-8 Ap 12 '63
Injuries and emotions. il Todays Health 42:88-9 F '64
Limits to deviant behavior in the gifted. R. Kelley. il Sch Life 47:4-6 O '64
Need to popularize basic principles; address, November 23, 1963. O. C. Stewart. Vital Speeches 30:255-6 F 1 '64
Outsiders: studies in the sociology of deviance, by H. S. Becker. Review
New Repub 149:23-5 Jl 20 '63. H. J. Gans
Psychiatrist looks at the behavior of nations. Sci Digest 54:21 D '63
Science and television. E. G. Sherburne, jr. Science 143:792-3 F 21 '64; Reply. M. B. Mitchell. 144:246 Ap 17 '64
Vanishing Americans; missing persons. il Newsweek 63:88 F 24 '64
What are people really like? il Changing T 18:31-3 Jl '64
You are not the target, by L. A. Huxley. Review
Time il 81:44 Je 7 '63
See also
Motivation (psychology)
Nostalgia
BEHAVIOR, Criminal. See Criminal psychology
BEHAVIOR, Group. See Group behavior
BEHAVIOR of animals. See Animals—Habits and behavior
BEHAVIORAL sciences
Behavioral genetics and individuality understood; excerpts from discussions at symposiums. J. Hirsch. bibliog il Science 142:1436-42 D 13 '63
Behavioral science and criminal law. E. J. Sachar. il Sci Am 209:39-45 bibliog(p 186) N '63; Reply with rejoinder. J. V. McConnell. 210:8-9 Ja '64
Behavioral sciences: meeting reflects increased interest in issues of public policy; report of discussion at American orthopsychiatric association meeting. E. Langer. Science 139:1038 Mr 15 '63
Empiricism in latter-day behavioral science. V. E. Bixenstine. bibliog Science 145:464-7 Jl 31 '64; Reply. B. F. Skinner. 145:1385+ S 25 '64
Ethology; report on eighth International ethological conference. P. Marler. Science 144:1046-7 My 22 '64
Human behavior, by B. Berelson and G. A. Steiner. Review
Sci Am 211:129-30+ Jl '64. J. Henry
Sci Digest il 55:90-1 My '64. D. Cohen
Science 144:683-4 My 8 '64. J. L. Kennedy
Managing your manpower; industry application of some behavioral science techniques. T. R. Brooks. Duns R 85:65-6+ Ja '65
Mating behavioral science and simulation. R. A. Bauer and R. D. Buzzell. il Harvard Bsns R 42:116-24 S '64
1963-1964 science review. Sci N L 84:389; 86:390 D 21 '63, D 19 '64
Problems of collaborations between social scientists and the practicing professions. L. S. Cottrell, jr. and E. B. Sheldon. Ann Am Acad 346:126-37 Mr '63
See also
Center for advanced study in the behavioral sciences

Bibliography

Race between destruction and adaptability. R. C. North. Bul Atomic Sci 20:26-8 Mr '64

BEHAVIORISM
Behaviorism at fifty. B. F. Skinner. bibliog Science 140:951-8 My 31 '63
See also
Mechanism (philosophy)
BEHENIC acid. See Docasanoic acid
BEHERMAN, Joseph
Volga car man. il por Newsweek 62:76-7 S 9 '63
BEHM, Donald. See Richards, G. C. jt. auth.
BEHME, Bob
Fishing Utah by camper. por Field & S 68:36-9+ F '64
Oregon's September madness. Field & S 68:41-3 S '63
Secret side of Manti-La Sal. Field & S 69:21-3+ D '64
BEHN, Harry
On haiku. Horn Bk 40:166-7 Ap '64
Worlds of innocence. Horn Bk 39:21-9 F '63
BEHR, Edward
Chaos in Castro's Cuba. Sat Eve Post 236:20-2+ Je 8 '63
Crisis over Christine. Sat Eve Post 236:77-85 Jl 13 '63
Day of joy and sadness. Sat Eve Post 237:36-7 Jl 11 '64
I am the strangler! you must believe me! Sat Eve Post 237:74-5 O 10 '64
Red China face to face. Sat Eve Post 237:21-9 N 14 '64
Royal co-ed Christina prepares to enter Radcliffe. Sat Eve Post 236:78-9 S 28 '63
Silent first lady of France. Sat Eve Post 237:64-5 Ja 18 '64
Suicide of an ex-Nazi. Sat Eve Post 237:76-9 Je 13 '64
BEHRENDT, John C.
Distribution of narrow-width magnetic anomalies in Antarctica. bibliog Science 144:993-4+ My 22 '64
—See Bentley, C. R. jt. auth.
—and Laudon, T. S.
Cretaceous fossils collected at Johnson Nunatak, Antarctica. bibliog Science 143:353-4 Ja 24 '64
BEHRMAN, Richard E. and Hibbard, Emerson
Bilirubin: acute effects in newborn rhesus monkeys. bibliog Science 144:545-6 My 1 '64
—See Lucey, J. F. jt. auth.
BEHRMAN, S. N.
But for whom Charlie. Criticism
America 110:657 My 9 '64
Commonweal 80:90 Ap 10 '64
Nation 198:335-6 Mr 30 '64
New Yorker 40:64 Mr 21 '64
Newsweek il 63:70 Mr 23 '64
Sat R 47:21 Mr 28 '64
Time il 83:55 Mr 20 '64
Vogue 143:62 My '64
Lord Pengo. Criticism
Life il 54:51-2 F 22 '63
Nation 196:214 Mr 9 '63
BEICHMAN, Arnold
First electrocution. Commentary 35:410-19 My '63
BEINECKE family
Sperry & Hutchinson's very successful stagnation. S. H. Brown. il Fortune 70:156-9+ N '64
BEINECKE foundation
High cost of writing; Stern and Beinecke funds. J. F. Fixx. Sat R 47:53+ Je 13 '64
BEINECKE rare book and manuscript library. See Yale university—Libraries
BEIRNE, Joseph A.
Dynamic nature of workers' goals. Mo Labor R 86:618-19 Je '63
Excerpt from statement, March 3, 1964. Cong Digest 43:252+ O '64
about
Union that automation built. L. Velie. Read Digest 84:181-2+ Je '64
BEIRUT
Beirut: city of money and mystery. G. Kent. il Read Digest 85:25-6+ N '64
Monopoly game. il Fortune 67:76 Je '63

Banks

See Banks and banking—Lebanon
BEIRUT university. See American university of Beirut
BEISTEGUI, Don Carlos de
Party's over. il Time 83:114 Ap 17 '64
BEISWANGER, George
She danced to feeling. Sat R 47:38 F 8 '64
BEITTEL, Kenneth R.
David's stonewares. por Sch Arts 63:23-7 S '63
—and Burkhart, R. C.
Crafts in education. Craft Horiz 23:8-9 S '63

BEITZ, Berthold
Ambassador from Krupp. il por Time 82:82 Jl 5 '63

BÉJART, Maurice
Coup de disgrâce. Newsweek 63:51 Mr 30 '64
Faustian scandal in Paris. il Time 83:41 Mr 27 '64
On from iconoclasm. il Time 84:83 N 6 '64

BEKIERKUNST, A. and others
Nicotinamide adenine dinucleotidase activity in cells of tuberculous animals. bibliog Science 145:280-1 Jl 17 '64

BEKKERS, William M.
Catholic parenthood; excerpt from address. Commonweal 78:143-4 Ap 26 '63

BEL canto. See Singing

BELAFONTE, Harry
Redbook dialogue. pors Redbook 120:54-5+ Mr '63

BELANGER, Kay
You should disregard the experts. Redbook 121:45+ Jl '63 Same abr with title When parents should disregard the experts. Read Digest 84:87-90 Ja '64

BELAÚNDE TERRY, Fernando
Big winner. il por Newsweek 62:30 D 30 '63
Forcing the issue. Newsweek 63:36-7 Ja 13 '64
Peru's new politics: the hit-or-miss approach. G. Delmas. il Reporter 29:35-8 O 24 '63
President at last. il por Time 81:22 Je 21 '63
President in office. por Time 82:31 Ag 9 '63
Revolution within the law. il por Time 84:71 O 2 '64
Society of colonial dames. New Repub 148:11 Je 22 '63

BELDEN, Louise C.
Billiards in America before 1830. Antiques 87:99-101 Ja '65

BELDOTTI, Lorraine. See Schwartz, R. S. jt. auth.

BELFAST
People of Belfast. B. Moore. il Holiday 35:58-63 F '64

BELFRAGE, Sally
Danville on trial. New Repub 149:11-12 N 2 '63
Haunted house of Ernest Hemingway. Esquire 59:66-7 F '63

BELGIUM
Benelux countries. F. G. Eyck. Cur Hist 47:355-61 D '64
See also
Airlines—Belgium
Automobile industry and trade—Belgium
Festivals—Belgium
Flemings
Insurance, Health—Belgium
Opera—Belgium
Space research—Belgium
Strikes—Belgium
Tariff—Belgium
Trade unions—Belgium
Trials—Belgium

Commercial treaties and agreements
Ratifications of FEN treaty exchanged with Belgium. Dept State Bul 49:484 S 23 '63

Description and travel
Belgium. P. H. Johnson. il Mlle 58:111-12 Ja '64

Foreign relations
Congo (capital Leopoldville)
Congo: an attempt to go back. il Time 83:27 Mr 27 '64
Lesson of the Congo. Nat R 16:1092+ D 15 '64

History
Bibliography
Articles and other books received; Low Countries, comp. by H. H. Rowen. See issues of American historical review

Politics and government
Atlantic report. Atlan 211:18+ My '63

BELGRADE
Balkans in brief. H. Sutton. il Sat R 46:42-5 Je 8 '63
Letter from Belgrade. J. Wechsberg. New Yorker 39:125-6+ S 21 '63

BELGRADE international book fair. See Book fairs

BELHOMME, Albert Constant
GI who chose communism. S. Karnow. il pors Sat Eve Post 236:104-7 N 16 '63

BELIEF and doubt
Man the believer. S. H. Miller. Christian Cent 81:1167-8 S 23 '64
What do you really believe? il Sci Digest 54:73 Ag '63

BELIEF in God. See Faith

BELITT, Ben
Orphaning; Gorge; Poem: Salamander; Second Adam; poems. Poetry 103:219-23 Ja '64
(tr) See Machado, A. From the apocryphal songbook: Abel Martin
(tr) See Neruda, P. Boy with a hare

BELKIN, Daniel A.
Anoxia: tolerance in reptiles. bibliog Science 139:492-3 F 8 '63

BELKIN, Mike
Big word for a small boy. F. Deford. por Sports Illus 18:57-9 Mr 18 '63

BELKNAP, Margaret G.
Sixty-five years afloat! Yachting 115:190 Je '64

BELL, Alex G.
Diploid and endoreduplicated cells: measurements of DNA. Science 143:139 Ja 10 '64

BELL, Alexander Graham
Listen, my heart; condensation of Make a joyful sound. H. E. Waite. il pors Read Digest 82:297-308+ Ap '63
Romance of the Geographic. G. H. Grosvenor. il pors Nat Geog Mag 124:516-85 O '63
Thanks to one Bell, the whole world rings. il Sr Schol 84:5 Mr 13 '64

BELL, Bernice Lloyd
Public library integration in thirteen southern states; excerpts from Integration in public library service in thirteen southern states, 1954-1962. Library J 88:4713-15 D 15 '63

BELL, Charles G.
Battle hymn in Birmingham. Nation 196:370-3 My 4 '63
Queen of night; poem. Ladies Home J 80:43 My '63

BELL, Daniel
Ethnic group. Commentary 37:74-6 Ja '64
Plea for a new phase in Negro leadership. N Y Times Mag p 11+ My 31 '64
Workers' search for security. Mo Labor R 86:614-17 Je '63

BELL, David Elliott
AID summarizes position on 1964 budget figures; memorandum to Secretary Rusk, May 7, 1963. Dept State Bul 48:881-3 Je 3 '63
David E. Bell becomes administrator of AID; statement, December 21, 1962. Dept State Bul 48:66-7 Ja 14 '63
Foreign aid today; address, May 1, 1964. Dept State Bul 50:831-5 My 25 '64
Impact of foreign aid on the American economy; address, October 23, 1963. Dept State Bul 49:830-3 N 25 '63
Improving the effectiveness of US. assistance to international rural development; address, July 27, 1964. Dept State Bul 51:376-83 S 14 '64
Investment opportunities in Asia: address, September 29, 1964. Vital Speeches 31:61-4 N 1 '64
Letter of reply of March 25, 1963, from Administrator Bell to Finance minister Dantas. Dept State Bul 48:560-1 Ap 15 '63
Major objectives of the foreign aid program; address, November 21, 1964. Dept State Bul 51:821-5 D 7 '64
New implications of industrial competition; address, June 10, 1964. Dept State Bul 51:205-9 Ag 10 '64
Reply to opponents of foreign aid. N Y Times Mag p9+ S 1 '63
U.S. national security; address, December 10, 1963. Vital Speeches 30:167-9 Ja 1 '64
about
Anchor man for foreign aid. por Bsns W p50-1+ My 11 '63
David Bell and foreign aid. Atlan 211:8 Je '63
David E. Bell becomes administrator of AID; statement, December 21, 1962. D. Rusk. Dept State Bul 48:65-6 Ja 14 '63
Foreign aid: saved by the Bell? J. Kraft. Harper 226:73-6+ F '63
Foreign aid: the hard line. il por Newsweek 61:27-9 Je 3 '63

BELL, DeWitt
Euripides; poem. Atlan 212:45 S '63
Motorcyclist's song. Atlan 211:71 F '63
Window; poem. Atlan 211:72 F '63
Young man's lament; poem. Atlan 211:78 Je '63

BELL, Dolores
Art and the student teacher. L. B. Kennon and T. Markle. il pors Sch Arts 63:5-10 Ap '64

BELL, Donald
Look at the future. por Mus Am 83:11 Jl '63

BELL, Eugene. See Scott, R. B. jt. auth.

BELL, Gilbert E.
Seabell; owner's comments. Yachting 115:73+ Je '64

BELL, Harriet
Ladies and stocks. New Yorker 39:24-6 D 28 '63
BELL, Harry
How to give the prettiest parties in town. House B 105:182-4 D '63
BELL, J. A. M.
Peripatetic reviewer. E. Weeks. Atlan 211: 128+ My '63
BELL, James
Flash of fire on the ice. Sports Illus 20:52-3 Ja 27 '64
J.F.K. needs Adenauer's problem: *überbeschäftigung*. Life 54:8 Je 7 '63
Old wolf Adenauer sits at bay. Life 54:36-7 Ap 26 '63
BELL, James P.
Five utilities on one bill. Am City 78:91-2 D '63
BELL, Joseph N.
Hell's angels fly again. Sat Eve Post 237: 28-31 N 7 '64
Life without her. Read Digest 85:49-52 S '64
Monorail: a one-track controversy. Sat Eve Post 237:81-2 My 9 '64
Monorails; will they ever get off the ground? Pop Mech 120:69-74+ D '63
U.S. doctor's five years in a red prison. Todays Health 41:26-31 N '63
(ed) See Beatty, J. I'll run a record mile
BELL, Laura
Life music review. Life 56:18 My 22 '64
BELL, Leland
Hélion paints the impossible. Art N 63:36-7+ N '64
BELL, Léonie. See Wilson, H. V. jt. auth.
BELL, Louise Price
For bare spaces, inch plant. Horticulture 41: 284 My '63
BELL, Marie
New York openings; presentation of Racine's Phedre and Berenice. Theatre Arts 48:67 Ja '64
BELL, Marvin
Changes; poem. Nation 198:636 Je 22 '64
Condition; poem. Poetry 105:169 D '64
Wisdom; Admission; poems. Poetry 103:166-7 D '63
BELL, Peter
Aluminum silicate system: experimental determination of the triple point. bibliog Science 139:1055-6 Mr 15 '63
—See Simmons, G. jt. auth
BELL, R. A. and Adkisson, P. L.
Photoperiodic reversibility of diapause induction in an insect. bibliog Science 144:1149-51 My 29 '64
BELL, Winifred
Creative project. Sch Arts 63:24-5 Ap '64
BELL aerosystems company
Bell aerosystems alters LLRV design to better performance. M. Getler. il Miss & Roc 13:16-17 Ag 12 '63
Bell seeks profit gains by reorganization. il Aviation W 81:98-9+ O 26 '64
New yardstick for defense contracts; award of X-22 contract to Bell. Bsns W p30 Je 22 '63
Ride on a cushion of air; Carabao hovercraft. E. Hall. il Sci N L 85:91 F 8 '64
Test of positive expulsion device planned. M. L. Yaffee. il Aviation W 81:59+ O 5 '64
BELL and Howell company
Dear Chris; simplified annual report. Newsweek 63:88 Mr 23 '64
BELL helicopter company
Bell LOH uses fewer, larger components. E. J. Bulban. il Aviation W 80:104-5+ F 17 '64
BELL telephone laboratories
Crystal formation from vapor probed. il Miss & Roc 14:23 Mr 16 '64
Great immortal machine; direct-dialing exchange. il Pop Electr 22:69-70 Ja '65
Profiles; John R. Pierce and project Echo. C. Tompkins. New Yorker 39:49-50+ S 21 '63
BELL telephone system
Bell grows two billion dollars bigger; A.T.&T. and its affiliates. H. B. Jacobs. il N Y Times Mag p29+ Mr 1 '64
Bootleg bonanza; fad for reconditioned antique telephones. il Newsweek 65:64 F 1 '65
Union that automation built; Communications workers of America. L. Velie. Read Digest 84:181-2+ Je '64
See also
Southern Bell telephone and telegraph company
BELLA, Ahmed Ben. See Ben Bella, A.
BELLA VISTA golf club. See Country clubs
BELLADONNA. See Atropine
BELLAH, James Warner
Luncheon at the Plaza; story. McCalls 90: 86-7 Ap '63

BELLAMY, Albert W.
Stockpiling to survive a nuclear attack. Science 138:958-60; 139:675 N 30 '62, F. 15 '63
BELLEAU WOOD, Battle of, 1918
Belleau Wood. il Life 56:74-7 My 22 '64
Bloody Belleau Wood; excerpts from Doughboys. L. Stallings. il Am Heritage 14:65-77 Je '63
BELLER, Victoria
One way to break into photography. H. Smith. il pors U S Camera 27:58-9+ Ap '64
BELLEW, Vincent D.
Experiment in fitness. por Recreation 57:281-2 Je '64
BELLI, Giuseppe Gioacchino
Letter from Rome; exhibit commemorating centenary of death. W. Murray. New Yorker 40:99-100+ Je 27 '64
BELLI, Melvin Mouron
And so to court. Time 84:62 Jl 31 '64
Battle lost, war won. Time 83:57 F 7 '64
Belli for the defense: a flamboyant advocate. il pors Time 82:48 D 20 '63
Casus Belli. il por Time 83:34+ Mr 27 '64
Death for Ruby. il por Time 83:27-8 Mr 20 '64
Flashy lawyer for Oswald's killer. R. W. Lewis. il pors Sat Eve Post 237:28-30 F 8 '64
Good-by, Belli. il por Newsweek 63:19 Mr 30 '64
War of nerves. Newsweek 63:19 Mr 2 '64
BELLINI, Vincenzo
I Puritani. Criticism
Time il 83:58 F 21 '64
Joan Sutherland in La sonnambula. P. L. Miler. il Am Rec G 29:596-8 Ap '63
Master of melos. V. Gui. por Hi Fi 13:35-6+ Je '63
Norma. Criticism
New Yorker 40:120-1 Je 13 '64
On records; I Puritani. Opera N 28:35 Ap 4 '64
On records; La sonnambula. C. J. Luten. Opera N 27:35 Mr 30 '63
La sonnambula. Criticism
New Yorker 39:96-7 Mr 2 '63
New Yorker 39:228 D 14 '63
Opera N 27:33 Mr 23 '63
Opera N 27:2 Mr 30 '63
Opera N 27:17-20 Mr 30 '63
Opera N 27:24-5 Mr 30 '63
Sat R 46:29 Mr 9 '63
Sutherland in I Puritani. P. L. Miller. il Am Rec G 30:656-7+ Ap '64
BELLMAN, Richard
Control theory; with biographical sketch. Sci Am 211:32, 186-90+ S '64
Where is science taking us? por Sat R 47:56 Ap 4 '64
about
Proper study of mankind. Nation 199:263 O 26 '64
BELLO, Andrés
Andrés Bello. G. de Zéndegui. Américas 16: inside cover N '64
Andrés Bello, cultural liberator. P. Grases. il pors Américas 16:1-4 N '64
BELLOISE, Michael
Are you missing out on social security payments? Read Digest 82:73-6 Je '63
BELLONI, Manuel
Look to the heartland. Américas 16:36-9 Ja '64
BELLOW, Saul
Beatrice Webb's America. Nation 197:116 S 7 '63
Herzog visits Chicago; story. Sat Eve Post 237:44-5 Ag 8 '64
Letter to Doctor Edvig; story; excerpt from Herzog. por Esquire 60:61-2 Jl '63
Movies (cont) Horizon 5:109-11 Mr '63
Napoleon street; story; excerpt from Herzog. Commentary 38:30-8 Jl '64
Seize the day; dramatization. See Otis, M.
Wen; drama; text. Esquire 63:72-4+ Ja '65
Writer as moralist. por Atlan 211:58-62 Mr '63
about
Author. D. Boroff. por Sat R 47:38-9+ S 19 '64
Hurtsog, Hairtsog, heart's hog? G. P. Elliott. Nation 199:252-4 O 19 '64
Last analysis. Criticism
Life 57:17 O 30 '64
Nation 199:256-7 O 19 '64
New Repub 151:25-6 O 24 '64
Newsweek 64:105 O 12 '64
Sat R 47:29 O 17 '64
Time 84:92 O 9 '64
Vogue 144:64 N 15 '64

BELLOW, Saul—about—*Continued*
My friend Saul Bellow. A. Kazin. por Atlan 215:51-4 Ja '65
Napoleon St and after. T. Solotaroff. Commentary 38:63-6 D '64
People are talking about. . . por Vogue 144:110-11 N 15 '64
Rights and permissions. P. Nathan. Pub W 186:70 O 5 '64

BELLS
Buddhist bell. L. Springer. il Hobbies 69:54 Je '64
Flower pot patio bells. il Design 64:217 Je '63
Mortars as bells. L. E. Springer. il Hobbies 68:53 N '63
Portrait or figurine bells. L. E. Springer. il Hobbies 67:50-1 F '63
Rare bells in Traphagen museum collection. L. E. Springer. il Hobbies 68:50 Mr '63
Sound of bells. E. Sloane. il Am Heritage 15:100-1 Je '64
Swinging ceramics; bells by Charlee. il Design 65:82-3 N '63
This bear is a wind bell. il Sunset 130:147 Ap '63
See also
Carillons
Doorbells

BELLS, Diving. See Diving bells

BELLSON, Louis
Jazz. W. Balliett. New Yorker 39:76-7 Ja 18 '64

BELLUSCHI, Pietro
Church architecture: the perils of success. M. E. Marty. Christian Cent 80:390-1 Mr 27 '63; Reply. G. Apel. 80:510 Ap 17 '63
Eloquent simplicity in architecture; address, March 1963. Arch Rec 134:131-5 Jl '63
Episcopal church by Belluschi. il Arch Rec 135:145-8 Mr '64
Major synagogue by Belluschi: Temple B'rith Kodesh in Rochester, N.Y. il Arch Rec 134:143-8 N '63

BELMARCH; story. See Davis, C.

BELMONDO, Jean Paul
Breathless man. por Time 84:76+ Jl 10 '64

BELMONT park. See Race tracks

BELMONT stakes. See Horse racing

BELOFF, Max
Appetite for American taste? Sat R 46:21-2 S 7 '63

BELOIT college, Beloit, Wis.
Curriculum changes at Beloit. Sch & Soc 92:210 My 2 '64

Libraries

Campus vs. community. H. V. Deale. bibliog il Library J 89:1696-7 Ap 15 '64

BELOUSSOV, Vladimir V.
Upper Mantle project. UNESCO Courier 16:12-17 O '63

BELT sanders. See Sanding machines

BELTING
High-speed ribbon that sands and grinds; abrasive belts. H. Walton. il Pop Sci 185:136-8 S '64

BELTS, Machine. See Belting

BELTS, Safety. See Safety belts

BELTS of radiation. See Van Allen radiation belts

BELVIDERE, Ill.
Day Chrysler came to town. Duns R 83:pt2 105 Mr '64

BEMAN, Deane
Deane of the amateurs wins again; National amateur public links championship at Detroit. G. S. Brown. il por Sports Illus 19:90+ S 23 '63

BEMELMANS, Ludwig
Franz Josef: a Habsburg marriage. Holiday 35:68-9+ Ja '64
Marvelous mission to Moscow. Holiday 35:108+ F '64
Visit to an Irish castle. il Holiday 33:33-6+ Ap '63

BEMIS, F. Gregg
Some of the principles behind the racing rules. Yachting 113:48+ F '63

BEMIS, Samuel Flagg
International trouble-shooter. Sat R 47:52-3 F 22 '64

BEN, Philip
How worried are the Israelis? New Repub 148:13-14 Ap 20 '63
New Hungary. New Repub 150:7 F 15 '64
New Russia. New Repub 151:7-8 S 19 '64
Pressure on Khrushchev. New Repub 148:7-8 Mr 9 '63
Religion in Russia. New Repub 151:15-16 D 26 '64
Report from Russia. New Repub 150:16-18 Je 13; 15-17 Je 27 '64
Rumania: another split in Communist ranks. New Repub 149:10-13 O 19 '63

BEN BELLA, Ahmed
After a year, it's Ben Bella's Algeria. P. Braestrup. il pors N Y Times Mag p31+ S 29 '63
Algeria going the way of Cuba? il por U S News 55:62 O 14 '63
Algerian strong man; Ben Bella gets more power; also FLN. por U S News 55:26 S 23 '63
Algerians on their own. J. K. Cooley. Reporter 28:37-40 F 28 '63
At least not chaos. il por Time 82:22-3 Ag 16 '63
Atlantic report. Atlan 213:14+ Ap '64
Ben Bella balked. il por Newsweek 62:42 O 14 '63
Ben Bella's approach misfires in Algeria. por Bsns W p65+ O 19 '63
Ben Bella's triumph. J. Daniel. New Repub 149:18-20 Jl 6 '63
Ben Bellism. Time 82:27 Ag 23 '63
Ben Castro? il Newsweek 62:51 S 23 '63
Clash in the Sahara. il por Sr Schol 83:7-9+ N 22 '63
Clean sweep. Newsweek 64:40 Jl 20 '64
Communist take-over of Algeria. R. Colby. il por U S News 57:52-3 Ag 31 '64
Cuba of Africa. il Time 82:37-8 O 18 '63
Evian treaty; Ben Bella laughing at de Gaulle? G. Laffly. Nat R 15:392-5 N 5 '63
Hex? il por Time 81:39 My 17 '63
Man who came to dinner. il por Time 81:27-8 Mr 22 '63
Mystique without typists. il por Newsweek 63:39 My 4 '64
One-man rule in Algeria. C. Sterling. il Reporter 29:32+ O 10 '63
Reflections on the Barbary Coast. R. Kirk. Nat R 15:442 N 19 '63
Road to Cuba. E. Weintal. il por Newsweek 62:38+ S 30 '63
Supreme guide. Time 82:36 S 20 '63
Unrest in the Kabylia; conference with de Gaulle. il por Time 83:36 Mr 20 '64
Year of independence and rising troubles. F. C. Painton. il por U S News 55:92-4 Ag 5 '63

BEN-EFRAIM, Shlomo, and others
Hypersensitivity to a synthetic polypeptide: induction of a delayed reaction. bibliog Science 139:1222-3 Mr 22 '63

BEN Franklin in Paris; musical comedy. See Musical comedies, revues, etc.—Criticisms, plots, etc.

BEN GURION, David
Why Israel wants peace. pors Look 27:62-5 Ag 27 '63

about

Blowup in Mideast? Nasser puts squeeze on Israel. por U S News 54:22 My 20 '63
King David departs. il Newsweek 62:30+ Jl 1 '63
Vale atque ave. il por Time 81:30 Je 28 '63
Visit with Ben Gurion in the desert; Sde Boker. W. G. Blair. il pors N Y Times Mag p 16+ Ja 12 '64
Visitor's welcome. por Time 81:30 Je 7 '63
Why did Ben-Gurion resign? New Repub 148:9 Je 29 '63

BENARDE, Melvin A.
Where is science taking us? Sat R 46:53 Ap 6 '63

BENARY-ISBERT, Margot
On words, singleness of mind, and the genius loci. Horn Bk 40:202-9 Ap '64

BENASUTTI, Marion
Some legends of Christmas; story. Horn Bk 39:573-5 D '63

BENCE-JONES, Mark
Irish eccentrics. Vogue 144:124+ O 1 '64
Notes on Irish life. Holiday 33:136+ Ap '63

BENCH vises. See Vises

BENCHES
Antique cobbler's bench. J. Hand. il Pop Mech 120:162-4 Jl '63
Backs to the wall; benchlike upholstered seats. G. O'Brien. il N Y Times Mag p36-7 Ja 3 '65
Bench for a terrace. L. Burgess. il Flower Grower 52:12 Ja '65
Build a bench around a tree. il Pop Gard 15:43 Ap '64
Build a bench for your garden. il Am Home 66:6 My '63
For barbecue fun; custom-made for comfort. K. Smith. il Pop Gard 14:59 Jl '63
How to make a bench. J. B. Brimer. Flower Grower 51:29 My '64
Log-box bench. F. Stephany and R. Buenger. il Pop Mech 119:148-9 F '63
Put a bench in your garden. B. Miles. il Flower Grower 51:36-7+ My '64
See also
Work benches

BENCHLEY, Nathaniel
Man-about-town; story. New Yorker 38:96 F 9 '63
BENCOMO, Luis
Cuban doctor's decision. B. Asbell. il por Redbook 120:46-7+ Mr '63
BENDER, Eric
Other kind of teaching. Harper 230:48-55 Ja 65
BENDER, Marylin
Finishes that stop soil before it starts. House B 106:134-5+ Mr '64
BENDETSEN, Karl R.
Victory in the cold war; address, February 22, 1963. Vital Speeches 29:372-6 Ap 1 '63
about
Pollution report: Bendetsen of Champion. J. B. Craig. por Am For 70:10-11+ O '64
BENDINER, Alfred
Problem in architecture. Atlan 213:161-3 Mr '64
BENDINER, Robert
Can American teachers teach? Redbook 123: 60-1+ O '64
Illinois: bellwether state? Reporter 31:23-5+ O 22 '64
Quickie results could sway the election. Life 57:125-6+ S 18 '64
Second spot: how to run from it and win. Life 56:98+ My 8 '64
BENDING of wood. See Wood bending
BENDITT, Earl P. and Wedgwood, R. I.
Sudden-death syndrome. Science 143:156-8 Ja 10 '64
—See Smuckler, E. A. jt. auth.
BENDIX, Hans
Elsinore. Mlle 58:127 F '64
BENDIX corporation
Bendix gives up on computers; sale of Computer div. to CDC. Bsns W p36 Mr 9 '63
Bendix seeks LEM landing contract. J. F. Judge. il Miss & Roc 12:26-7+ Mr 11 '63
Bendix simulating lunar magma in laboratory tests. J. F. Judge. il Miss & Roc 14: 36-7 Mr 23 '64
BENEDEK, George B.
Magnetic resonance at high pressure; with biographical sketch. Sci Am 212:17, 102-8 bibliog(p 136) Ja '65
BENEDICT, Albert A. and others
Synthesis of chicken antibodies of high and low molecular weight. bibliog Science 139: 1302-3 Mr 29 '63
BENEDICT, Crawford
American chestnut has a fighting chance. il Audubon Mag 65:108-12 Mr '63
Bird chasing, a progressive art. Harper 228: 30+ Mr '64
BENEDICT, Donald L.
For a reconciled society. Christian Cent 80: 1007 Ag 14 '63
about
Commandos in the city. il por Time 83:56 F 21 '64
BENEDICT, H. M. and others
Chlorophyll content and growth of soybean plants: possible interaction of iron availability and day length. Science 144:1134-5 My 29 '64
BENEDICT, Michaele
Exploring Grecian villages. Travel 119:41-4 Je '63
BENEDICT, Nelson
Sportfishing. See issues of Yachting
BENEDICTINE monasteries. See Monasteries
BENEDICTINES
Ecumenism in Morocco; Benedictine monks at Toumliline. W. Dunphy. America 111: 694 N 28 '64
BENEDICTUS, David
E-type Charlie; story. Seventeen 23:172-3 S '64
Mother love; story. Seventeen 22:148-9 S '63
BENEDIKT, Michael
Continuity of Pierre Bonnard. Art N 63:20-3+ O '64
Country of the hat; Tulips; Time; Pink buds; poems. Poetry 104:164-6 Je '64
Fairfield Porter: minimum of melodrama. Art N 63:36-7+ Mr '64
Motions; poem. Poetry 102:96 My '63
BENEFIT plans, Employees. See Employees benefit plans
BENEFIT societies
Insurance among Negroes prior to the Civil war. J. E. Gloster. bibliog Negro Hist Bul 27:42-3 N '63
BENENSON, Lawrence A.
Governing Buckley by the numbers. Harper 227:76-7 O '63
BENESCH, Reinhold, and others
Spectra of deoxygenated hemoglobin in the Soret Region. bibliog Science 144:68-9 Ap 3 '64
BENEVOLENT societies. See Benefit societies
BENEZET, Louis T.
Half-way to where? NEA J 53:57-8 Ap '64
How good is a college? address, April 21, 1964. Vital Speeches 30:508-10 Je 1 '64
BENGALI poetry
Translations into English
Hölderlin, B. Bose. Poetry 102:380 S '63
BENGE, Joseph B. jr
When the airplane became a lethal weapon. Esquire 62:33-40 Ag '64
BENGSTON, Bennie
Minnesota, your lady's-slipper is showing. il Audubon Mag 66:227 Jl '64
BENHAM, David B.
Simple control for a complex system. por Am City 78:81-3 Ap '63
BENHIMA, Ahmed Taibi
Young power in diplomacy. por Vogue 143:88 Ap 15 '64
BENIETZ, Manuel
Artistry in a bullring is not enough. P. E. Ress. il por Sports Illus 21:44-7 Ag 10 '64
BENIGNUS, Pierre Emil
Benignus killed in crash. Christian Cent 30: 734 Je 5 '63
BENIN sculpture. See Sculpture, Bini
BENIOFF, Hugo
Earthquake source mechanisms. bibliog Science 143:1399-406 Mr 27 '64
BENITEZ, Jaime
Caribbean: our sea of troubles. Sat R 46:11-13+ Jl 13 '63
To salvage or to save; reflections on America's most pressing revolutions; address, May 9, 1963. Vital Speeches 29:535-7 Je 15 '63
BENITÉZ, Manuel
Man from Córdoba. il por Time 83:42+ F 28 '64
BENITO Cereno; drama. See Lowell, R.
BENJAMIN, Curtis G.
Book publishers' interests in reprographic copyright; excerpts from address, May 1963. por Library J 88:2837-41 Ag '63
Books with an international accent; adaptation of address. Sat R 47:39-41 Ag 8 '64
Chinese reprinters and world copyright practice. por Pub W 185:23+ Mr 30 '64
High price of technical books. por ALA Bul 59:61-4 Ja '65
Power of books; address, November 18, 1964. Vital Speeches 31:155-60 D 15 '64
BENJAMIN, Lois
(ed) Sight & sound. McCalls 91:6+ Ja: 6+ Ag; 8+ S; 92:12+ O '64
—and Sheridan, Bart
(eds) Sight & sound. McCalls 91:8 F; 6+ Mr; 8+ Ap; 8+ My; 8+ Je; 8+ Jl '64
BENJAMIN, Mary A.
Current market values of presidential papers (cont) Hobbies 68:110-12 Ap '63
BENJAMIN, Philip
Uncoil like a snake, think serpent. N Y Times Mag p35+ Ag 30 '64
BENJAMIN, William. See Gellhorn, A. jt. auth.
BENJAMIN company
Hard sell in soft cover. il Bsns W p30+ Jl 4 '64
BENN, Anthony Neil Wedgwood
Call me mister! the peers request. C. Hussey. il por N Y Times Mag p 18+ Ag 25 '63
BENNÉ, Ben
Taping session; Benné method of weight reducing. Newsweek 63:78 Ja 27 '64
BENNET, Richard Dyer-. See Dyer-Bennet, R.
BENNETT, Alan
Please feed the lions. il por Mlle 57:96-7+ Je '63
BENNETT, Clifford A.
When the choirs go marching out? America 111:738-9 D 5 '64
BENNETT, Daniel
Glassware patents of Daniel Bennett. A. G. Paterson. il Hobbies 68:82-3 Je '63
BENNETT, David H.
Year of the old folks revolt. Am Heritage 16:48-51+ D '64
BENNETT, Dorothea
Embryological effects of lethal alleles in the t-region. bibliog Science 144:263-7 Ap 17 '64
BENNETT, Edna
Beauty lurks in little things. U S Camera 27:36-7+ S '64
From out of the past. U S Camera 27:60-5+ N '64
Problems automatic cameras can't solve. U S Camera 27:56-9+ Je '64

BENNETT, Edward L. and others
Chemical and anatomical plasticity of brain. bibliog Science 146:610-19 O 30 '64
BENNETT, Fay
Still the harvest of shame. Commonweal 80: 83-6 Ap 10 '64
BENNETT, George W.
This is the fish you can't catch too many of; largemouth bass. R. H. Boyle. il por Sports Illus 19:34-9 Ag 19 '63
BENNETT, Hank
Monthly short-wave report. See issues of Popular electronics
BENNETT, Helen H.
Demonstrating library use to teachers and administrators. ALA Bul 57:161-2 F '63
BENNETT, Isadora
Isadora Bennett. por Dance Mag 37:33 Ap '63
BENNETT, James V.
Cool look at the crime crisis. Harper 228:123-7 Ap '64
James V. Bennett's prisons. R. Goldfarb. New Repub 151:5 S 12 '64
Paroling the warden. il por Time 84:64+ S 4 '64
BENNETT, John Coleman
Concern for theology. Commonweal 78:418-20 Jl 12 '63
about
Bennett elected Union president. Christian Cent 81:7 Ja 1 '64
Bennett: union's eleventh. E. C. Parker. Christian Cent 81:650 My 13 '64
Committed openness. America 110:560 Ap 25 '64
Right on the premises. il por Time 82:53 D 27 '63
Union man. Newsweek 63:63 Ja 6 '64
BENNETT, John Z.
Astronaut; poem. America 110:90 Ja 18 '64
BENNETT, Karen
Misbehaving clouds; poem. Horn Bk 39:642 D '63
BENNETT, Lerone, jr
Adam Clayton Powell. Ebony 18:25-8+ Je '63
Frederick Douglass: father of the protest movement. Ebony 18:50-2+ S '63
Georgia's Negro senator. Ebony 18:25-8+ Mr '63
Masses were march heroes. Ebony 19:35-40+ N '63
Mood of the Negro. Ebony 18:27-30+ Jl '63
Negro who founded Chicago. Ebony 19:170-2+ D '63
Negro woman. Ebony 18:86-90+ S '63
Pioneers in protest. See isues of Ebony beginning March 1964
Uhuru comes to Kenya. Ebony 19:127-8+ F '64
What Negroes can expect from President Lyndon Johnson. Ebony 19:81-4+ Ja '64
BENNETT, Lynn W.
Subjects unlimited! U S Camera 27:74-5+ My '64
BENNETT, M. V. L. and others
Electrotonic junctions between teleost spinal neurons: electrophysiology and ultrastructure. bibliog Science 141:262-4 Jl 19 '63
BENNETT, Margaret, pseud.
Adrift in Jamais-Jamais land. Sat R 46:67 Mr 16 '63
Pursuit of non-excellence. Sat R 47:53 Je 20 '64
Teaching is better with! Sat R 46:82-3 F 16 '63
Telltale art. Atlan 211:116 F '63
Unauthorized report from the committee on the stereotyped librarian. Library J 89: 2285-6 Je 1 '64
When things are looking up. Sat R 46:28 Ag 24 '63
Why not try Ugh! Redbook 121:43 Jl '63
BENNETT, Michael J.
Incident at Boston college. Commonweal 80: 284-5, 422-3 My 29, Je 26 '64
BENNETT, O. B.
Where Negroes have the whites on the run; interview. por U S News 55:68-75 S 9 '63
BENNETT, Paul A.
Adrian Wilson: designer-printer at Tuscany Alley. Pub W 185:66-9+ Ap 6 '64
Betty Binns: designer of textbooks. Pub W 184:96+ S 9 '63
Frasconi work is exhibited; he designs new U.S. stamp. Pub W 184:86+ Jl 1 '63
Hermann Zapf: calligrapher, type designer, master of the book arts. por Pub W 187:72-4+ Ja 4 '65
John Alcorn: artist-designer with a sense of humor. Pub W 185:76-8 Je 1 '64
Morris's Kelmscott adventure revealed in Grolier club exhibit. Pub W 186:108-12 N 9 '64
Oxford university press keepsakes designed by John Begg. Pub W 185:92-5 Ja 6 '64
Robert Frost: best-printed U.S. author, and his printer, Spiral press. Pub W 185:82-6+ Mr 2 '64
Rudolph Ruzicka at eighty: an appreciation. Pub W 184:92-5 Ag 5 '63
Saul and Lillian Marks and their Plantin press in Los Angeles. Pub W 186:114-18 Jl 6 '64
Visit with George Salter; designer, calligrapher, illustrator and teacher. il Pub W 186:82-7 S 7 '64
Ward Ritchie: designer, printer, publisher, man of books. Pub W 186:84-8+ O 5 '64
BENNETT, Rachel
Who's afraid of the big, bad teen-agers? Parents Mag 38:62-3+ Mr '63
BENNETT, Robert
Old hands at it. Hobbies 69:110 Mr '64
BENNETT, Rowena
Santa Claus and the three polar bears; drama. Plays 23:81-5 D '63
Snow-White and Rose-Red; adaptation; drama. Plays 24:53-64 O '64
BENNETT, Tony
Tony's second time around. por Time 83:63 Mr 6 '64
BENNETT, Wallace F.
Excerpt from debate, August 15, 1964. Cong Digest 44:14+ Ja '65
BENNETT, William Andrew Cecil
Wacky like a fox. il por Newsweek 64:68-9 O 12 '64
BENNETT college, Greensboro, N.C.
Whetting the reading appetite. C. H. Marteena. il Wilson Lib Bul 37:579 Mr '63
BENNING, Don
Coach cracks color barrier. il pors Ebony 19:77+ Mr '64
BENNINGTON, Vt.
Brickwork and carpentry on a low budget: Second Congregational church. il Arch Rec 134:142-5 Jl '63
BENNINGTON college, Bennington, Vt.
Bennington college dance group at 92d street Y. J. Maskey. Dance Mag 38:25 Ja '64
Bennington college, 92nd street Y; dance group program. M. Marks. Dance Mag 39:64 Ja '65
Cauldron of creativity. D. Boroff. il Sat R 46:45-7+ D 21 '63
College or career for dancers? Bennington's answer. E. Stodelle. il Dance Mag 38:40-5 S '64
BENNINGTON ware. See Pottery, American
BENNIS, Warren G. See Slater, P. E. jt. auth.
BENNY, Jack
Benny on Broadway. il por Newsweek 61:86 Mr 11 '63
Buck$ Benny rides again. B. Davidson. il pors Sat Eve Post 236:26-8+ Mr 2 '63
Comics, comics; show at the Ziegfeld. R. Gilman. Commonweal 78:47 Ap 5 '63
My dad, Jack Benny; ed. by A. Hano. J. Benny. il pors Good H 157:96-7+ N '63
Thirty-nine. G. Frank. il por McCalls 90:90-1+ Ap '63
Uncle Jack. il por Time 81:60+ Mr 8 '63
BENNY, Joan
My dad, Jack Benny; ed. by A. Hano. pors Good H 157:96-7+ N '63
BENNY; story. See Maloney, R.
BENOIT, Emile
Would disarmament mean a depression? N Y Times Mag p 16+ Ap 28 '63
BENREY, Ronald M.
Brilliant flash times your engine. Pop Sci 183:164-7 O '63
Electronic flash: is it the perfect portable light source? Pop Phot 55:154-5+ N '64
Fasten your seat belt. Pop Sci 183:87-9 Ag '63
Freeze alarm to save your car and pipes. Pop Sci 184:96+ F '64
Heat or humidity? Pop Sci 183:96-7 Ag '63
How to build your own portable auto analyzer. Pop Sci 184:94-9+ Je '64
Inside those tiny new speedlights. Pop Sci 184:130-2+ Je '64
This homemade, battery-powered loud hailer talks big. Pop Sci 184:134-8 Ap '64
BENSCH, K. and others
Granular pneumocytes: electron microscopic evidence of their exocrinic function. bibliog Science 145:1318-19 S 18 '64
BENSEN, Robert
Great debate. Pop Electr 21:76-7+ O '64
BENSER, Walther
Rainy night in old London town. U S Camera 26:80-1 O '63
RFDR cameras: real sharpness. il Mod Phot 27:58-61+ My '63
Slow/fast how sharp? Mod Phot 28:88-9 S '64
When & how to expose for perfect color. il Mod Phot 27:56-9+ Jl '63

BENSLEY, Jackson H. and Gardner, P. M.
Build your own deer camp. Field & S 68:41-3 Ag '63
BENSON, John J. See O'Connell, D. J. jt. auth.
BENSON, Marilyn
Doctors' wives tackle the suicide problem. Todays Health 42:60-3 My '64
BENSON, Mary
South Africa and world opinion. bibliog f Cur Hist 46:129-35+ Mr '64
BENSON, Milo D.
Neglected fruits. Horticulture 42:15 N '64
BENSON-Lehner company
Speeding up computer output. Bsns W p 103 Ap 13 '63
BENSTED-SMITH, Richard
Le Mans: twenty-four hours of what? Atlan 211:110-12 Je '63
BENTLEY, Beth
Ondine; In the rain forest; poems. Poetry 102:25-6 Ap '63
BENTLEY, Charles R. and Behrendt, J. C.
Glaciology. Science 142:415-16 O 18 '63
BENTLEY, Eric
(tr) See Brecht, B. Mother Courage and her children
BENTLEY, Howard B.
City planning and urban renewal. por Library J 88:1621-4 Ap 15 '63
BENTLEY, Martha C.
Children's paperbacks: a long hard look; excerpts from address, October 1964. por Library J 90:309-11 Ja 15 '65
Operation head start materials collection. Library J 89:4606-7+ N 15 '64
BENTLEY, Wilson A.
Snowflake Bentley's magnificent obsession. D. Epstein and R. Epstein. il Read Digest 83:182-6 D '63
BENTON, Allen W. and others
Bee venom tolerance in white mice in relation to diet. bibliog Science 145:1448-9 S 25 '64
Venom collection from honey bees. Science 142:228-9 O 11 '63
BENTON, Brook
Brook Benton. il pors Ebony 18:44-6+ My '63
BENTON, Elizabeth G.
Apple River Canyon State Park. il Nat Parks Mag 37:19 Je '63
BENTON, Robert. See Newman, D. jt. auth.
BENTON, Ruth
Ode to a beer can. Am For 69:34 Ag '63
Unwelcome guests; poem. Am For 70:37 Ap '64
BENTON, William
Big brother's TV set. Esquire 61:98-9+ Mr '64
Progress report on UNESCO. Sat R 47:16-18+ Mr 7 '64
BENTONITE
Petroleum hydrocarbons: generation from fatty acid. J. W. Jurg and E. Eisma. bibliog il Science 144:1451 Je 19 '64
Volume changes of a thixotropic, sodium bentonite suspension during sol-gel-sol transition. D. M. Anderson and others. bibliog il Science 141:1040-1 S 13 '63
BENVENUTO Cellini; opera. See Berlioz, H.
BENYESH-MELNICK, Matilda. See Rapp, F. jt. auth.
BENZEDRINE. See Amphetamines
BENZENE
Benzene synthesized by California chemist. Sci N L 84:328 N 23 '63
BENZENESULFONATES
Detergent foam nuisance. A. Clarke. Sci N L 83:109 F 16 '63
BENZOQUINONE. See Quinones
BENZYL alcohol
1-Octopamine in citrus: isolation and identification. I. Stewart and T. A. Wheaton. bibliog il Science 145:60-1 Jl 3 '64
BENZYL compounds
N^6-benzyladenine: inhibitor of respiratory kinases. V. Tuli and others. bibliog il Science 146:1477-9 D 11 '64
BENZYLADENINE. See Benzyl compounds
BEPPU, Japan
Little "hells" around Beppu on Japan's Inland Sea. il Sunset 131:110-11 O '63
BEQUESTS. See Wills
BERAN, Josef, abp
Freedom for a fighter. por Time 82:86 O 11 '63
News from Czechoslovakia? America 109:443 O 19 '63
What to do with Beran. America 110:783 Je 6 '64
BERBERIAN, Cathy
Frightening the fish. il por Time 82:72 O 4 '63
BERBERS
Ben Bella balked. il Newsweek 62:42 O 14 '63
Clash in the Sahara. il Sr Schol 83:9+ N 22 '63
Double trouble in Algeria. Sr Schol 83:16 N 1 '63
Far and near; Moroccan Berbers cling to feudal ways. C. Wyatt. il Natur Hist 72: 60-2 N '63
BERBOS, James Nickolas
Be home soon, doctor. S. M. Spencer. il por Ladies Home J 80:72-3 D '63
Five came to Aberdeen. A. Lake. il por McCalls 91:106-7+ D '63
Imperturbable man. S. M. Spencer. por Sat Eve Post 236:36 N 16 '63
BERCHER, Harry O.
Harvester tries for richer crop. il pors Bsns W p66-7+ O 3 '64
BERCZELLER, Richard
Our Maximilian. New Yorker 39:45-6+ Ja 25 '64
Red bicycle. New Yorker 40:151-2+ Mr 7 '64
Trip into the blue. New Yorker 39:20-1 Ag 24 '63
BEREAVEMENT
Day the President died; its meaning and impact. G. R. Krupp. il Redbook 122:49+ Mr '64
BERELSON, Bernard, and Freedman, Ronald
Study in fertility control; with biographical sketches. Sci Am 210:22, 29-37 bibliog(p 150) My '64
BERENDT, John
Memoirs of a six-months trainee. Esquire 61:62-5+ Je '64
Patterns of decay. Esquire 59:96-9 Je '63
BERENSON, Bernard
Bernard Berenson: a summing up. I. Origo. Atlan 212:51-8 N '63
Bernard Berenson of Butremanz. M. Fixler. Commentary 36:135-43 Ag '63
Half of B.B. il por Newsweek 63:92 F 24 '64
Last aesthete? S. Alexander. Reporter 29:55-6 Jl 18 '63
Monologue of an old man. V. Lange. New Repub 150:17-19 F 1 '64
Reflections of a self-curious savant. D. C. Rich. il por Sat R 47:30-1 F 29 '64
BERENSTAIN, Janice. See Berenstain, S. jt. auth.
BERENSTAIN, Stanley, and Berenstain, Janice
It's all in the family. See issues of McCall's
BERESHNY, Alex
Alex Bereshny and his international dance company at Carnegie Hall. J. Maskey. Dance Mag 38:66 Ja '64
BERG, Alban
Alban Berg; an upbeat. M. Bernheimer. pors Sat R 47:46-7 S 12 '64
Berg: Wozzeck; excerpts. J. Diether. Am Rec G 31:120-2+ O '64
Lulu. Criticism
Mus Am il 84:10 F '64
Newsweek 62:53-4 Ag 19 '63
Opera N il 28:8-12 S 28 '63
Time il 82:41 Ag 16 '63
Lulu arrives; American stage premiere. A. Young. Mus Am 83:30-1 S '63
Wozzeck. Criticism
New Yorker 39:156-7 D 14 '63
BERG, Fritz
Germany's economic future; address, April 29, 1963. Vital Speeches 29:506-8 Je 1 '63
BERG, Gene
Oscar-bound pace-setter. Sr Schol 84:20 Mr 20 '64
BERG, Gertrude
Dear me, the sky is falling; dramatization. See Spigelgass, L.
BERG, Irving
My son, the safety patrol. Sch Arts 63:39-40 D '63
BERG, Lise Hartmann
Baby-sitter at the fair. G. Zimmermann. il pors Look 28:78-82+ Jl 28 '64
BERG, Stephen
To my friends; poem. New Yorker 40:32 Ja 23 '65
Uncle Will, the gardener; poem. New Yorker 40:44 D 19 '64
Wrists; poem. Poetry 104:160 Je '64

about

Poetry chronicle. J. B. Hall. Poetry 104:52 Ap '64
BERG, W. F.
Processing; the inside story! (cont) Mod Phot 27:86-7 F '63
BERGAMINI, David. See Margenau, H. jt. auth.

BERGANZA, Teresa
On records; Teresa Berganza: Mozart arias; Spanish & Italian songs. por Opera N 28:34 Ja 11 '64
BERGDORF Goodman company. See New York (city)—Stores
BERGÉ, Carol
Unfinished poem. Poetry 104:86-7 My '64
BERGE, Stanley
Trouble with the railroad is... Changing T 18:6 Ap '64
BERGEN, Candice
Two models on modeling. pors Mlle 60:144-7 N '64
BERGEN, Chan
Like artillery coming in. por Outdoor Life 132:44-5+ N '63
BERGEN, Claus
Most adventurous sea painter of his day. G. P. Hunt. por Life 56:3 Ap 17 '64
BERGEN-Belsen camp. See Concentration camps—Germany
BERGEN COUNTY, N.J.
Censorship on teenage reading slated by New Jersey group; Ethical culture society. Library J 88:2218 Je 1 '63
Small library; thinking big; Mid-Bergen federation of free public libraries. E. Locke. Wilson Lib Bul 37:780-1 My '63
BERGER, Elmer
What Pope Paul's visit was not. Christian Cent 81:524 Ap 22 '64
BERGER, Ivan
Audio bookshelf. Sat R 47:60 Ja 25 '64
Audio in the '60s. Sat R 47:55-7+ S 26 '64
Christmas ribbon and magnetic tape. Sat R 47:58 D 12 '64
Fidelity begins in the groove. Sat R 46:57 N 30 '63
Haydn in the park. Sat R 46:53+ My 25 '63
High fidelity reaches its majority. Sat R 48:55 Ja 30 '65
Microphones make the difference. Hi Fi 14:47-50 Ag '64
New trends in stereo kits. Hi Fi 15:57-9+ F '65
Points on portables. Sat R 46:42-3 Je 29 '63
Reels, wheels, and economics. Sat R 47:73 My 30 '64
Ribbons of rust. Sat R 47:57 Mr 28 '64
See now, hear later. Sat R 46:122 O 12 '63
Shown at the show. Sat R 47:73 O 31 '64
'63 hi-fi show. Sat R 46:56-61 S 14 '63
Some matters of degree. Sat R 47:51 F 29 '64
Tape as you go. Sat R 47:65-5 Ap 25 '64
Tape it slow. Sat R 47:67 Je 27 '64
TV: U and non-U. Sat R 46:53 F 23 '63
Uses of diversity. Sat R 47:47+ N 28 '64
BERGER, M. I.
Existential criticism in educational theory; adaptation from address, April, 1963. M. I. Berger. Sch & Soc 92:334-5 N 14 '64
BERGER, Morroe
Black Muslims. Horizon 6:48-65 Wint '64
BERGER, Oscar
Famous faces by Oscar Berger; with footnotes on his celebrated sitters by the artist. il por Am Artist 27:44-9+ O '63
BERGER, Peter L.
Letter on the parish ministry. Christian Cent 81:547-50 Ap 29 '64
Toward a more scholarly ministry. Christian Cent 80:524-7 Ap 24 '63

about

Peter Berger's attack upon Christendom. Christian Cent 80:415 Mr 27 '63; Reply. P. L. Berger. 80:649 My 15 '63
BERGER, Rainer, and others
Radiocarbon dating of bone and shell from their organic components. bibliog Science 144:999-1001 My 22 '64
BERGER, Roland
China today: walking on two legs. Nation 199:352-5 N 16 '64
BERGER, Samuel David
Silent Sam, the pressure man. Time 81:44+ Ap 19 '63
BERGER, Senta
Senta of Vienna. J. Hamilton. il pors Look 28:87-90 O 6 '64
BERGER, Susan
Orientation. NEA J 53:46-8 O '64
BERGER, Thomas
How the West was lost; story. Esquire 61: 76-9 Mr '64
BERGER, Yves
Tips. Pub W 184:94 S 16 '63
BERGERON, Victor Jules
Sf, it's Trader Vic. il por Newsweek 64:83 N 30 '64
BERGES, Ruth
Man Meyerbeer. Opera N 29:6-7 O 17 '64
BERGETHON, K. Roald
Tolerance and the law. Sch & Soc 91:60-1 F 9 '63
BERGGRAV, Kari
Anthuriums. il Horticulture 42:22-3 S '64
BERGH, Arndt, and others
Clip-on D.C. current probe. Electr World 72:41-3+ S '64
BERGH, Helen
Welcome aboard or are you? Sports Illus 18: 34-41 My 13 '63
BERGH, Phil
Slide hobby that grew and grew and grew. R. Miller. por U S Camera 27:26-7 S '64
BERGMAN, G. M.
Negro who rode with Fremont in 1847. por Negro Hist Bul 28:31-2 N '64
BERGMAN, Helene M.
Dwarf evergreens. Horticulture 42:28-30 Ja '64
BERGMAN, Ingmar
Alienation in Ingmar Bergman. H. H. L. Abraham. Commonweal 80:290-2 My 29 '64

about

How Sweden's film god brings in the kronor. il por Bsns W p 128-30 F 29 '64
Ingmar Bergman, the listener. O. Hedlund. il por Sat R 47:47-9+ F 29 '64
BERGMAN, Ingrid
Interview with Ingrid Bergman; ed. by R. Deardorff. pors Redbook 122:52-3+ F '64
Hardly anybody knows him. D. J. Hamblin. il pors Life 57:133-4+ O 16 '64
Visit. J. Hamilton. il pors Look 28:52-9 Je 16 '64
BERGMAN, Jules
Flier's spending companion. Esquire 61:85+ Je '64
Our watchdog at the edge of space. Read Digest 85:56-60 D '64
BERGMANN, Georg
Discovery. P. Caulfield. il Mod Phot 28:64-5+ F '64
BERGMANN, William
Let there be music. por Recreation 56:68-9 F '63
BERGQUIST, Kenneth P.
Military career; address, May 13, 1964. Vital Speeches 30:562-5 Jl 1 '64
BERGS, Victor V. and Groupe, Vincent
Low malignancy of Rous sarcoma cells as evidenced by poor transplantability in turkeys. bibliog Science 139:922-3 Mr 8 '63
BERGSON, Henri
Henri Bergson's message; a philosophy for today. J. C. Fernández. por Américas 15: 10-12 Ag '63
BERGSON, Maria
Designer Bergson. il por Arch Forum 120: 108-11 F '64
BERGSTROM, Per
He stuck in his thumb and pulled out—DNA! Sat R 46:57-8 Mr 2 '63
BERGSTROM, Robert
Bat-off-the-tee. por Recreation 57:231-2 My '64
BERGWIN, Clyde R. and Coleman, W. T.
Egghead of the animal astronauts; excerpts from Animal astronauts: they opened the way to the stars. Todays Health 42:32-5+ Ja '64
BERINGER, Doris
Crayon-cement prints. Sch Arts 63:39-40 My '64
BERINGER, Johann Bartholomew Adam
Lying stones of Dr Johann Bartholomew Adam Beringer, by M. E. Jahn and D. J. Woolfe. Review
Sci Digest il 54:64 D '63. D. Cohen
BERK, J. E. and others
Chromatographic heterogeneity of rabbit serum amylase. bibliog Science 141:1182-3 S 20 '63
BERKA, Roman, and Laska, Vaclav
Declaration for November 17th: the International students' day. Sch & Soc 92:110 Mr 7 '64
BERKELEY, Calif.

Churches

Recent work of William Wilson Wurster; First Unitarian church. il Arch Rec 133:112-15 Ja '63

Education

Nursery for teaching, research, testing. il Arch Rec 133:174-6 My '63

Negroes

Berkeley discriminates. R. S. Wheeler. Nat R 14:497 Je 18 '63
Enlightened ones. Time 81:25 Ap 12 '63
Housing controversy. E. Culver. Christian Cent 80:590 My 1 '63
BERKELEY, Mo.

Education

Junior high addition for a core curriculum. il Arch Rec 134:203-5 O '63

BERKES, Ross N.
Anglo-American alliance. bibliog f Cur Hist 46:275-81+ My '64
India's ties to the Commonwealth. Cur Hist 44:155-9+ Mr '63
Weapons development in the United States. bibliog f Cur Hist 47:65-70+ Ag '64

BERKNER, L. V.
Berkner outlines U.S. space goals, argues against program's critics; summary of address. Aviation W 78:23 My 6 '63
Compelling horizon. Bul Atomic Sci 19:8-10 My '63

BERKOWITZ, Diane
Knowledge; story. Sr Schol 84:22+ My 15 '64

BERKOWITZ, Leonard
Effects of observing violence: with biographical sketch. Sci Am 210:28, 35-41 bibliog (p 152) F; 8 Je '64

BERKS, Robert
Image distilled from 800 pictures; bronze head by R. Berks. il por Life 56:28-31 Ja 3 '64

BERKSHIRE DOWNS raceway. See Race tracks

BERKSHIRE Hathaway, incorporated
Wage chronology; Berkshire Hathaway inc, 1953-64. il Mo Labor R 87:423-8 Ap '64

BERKSHIRE music center
Big brother watches over Tanglewood. E. Coleman. il N Y Times Mag p20+ Je 28 '64

BERKSHIRE symphonic festival
Britten in the Berkshires; American premiere of B. Britten's War requiem. L. Chapin. il Mus Am 83:30 S '63
Choice & an echo; Mozart's Serenade for four orchestras conducted by Erich Leinsdorf. il Time 84:74 Ag 7 '64
Tree grows at Tanglewood; Erich Leinsdorf at Tanglewood. il Time 82:34 Ag 30 '63

BERKSON, Gershon, and Fitz-Gerald, F. L.
Eye fixation aspect of attention to visual stimuli in infant chimpanzees. bibliog Science 139:586-7 F 15 '63

BERKSON, William
Bluhm paints a picture. Art N 62:38-41+ My '63
Michael Goldberg paints a picture. Art N 62:42-5+ Ja '64
Trouble in paradise; Moments; poems. Poetry 102:87 My '63

BERLAND, Theodore
Appendicitis, the forgotten killer. Todays Health 42:22-3+ My '64
Botulism: the killer who came to dinner. Sat Eve Post 237:71-3 Mr 7 '64
Here's why those do-everything lasers don't, yet. Pop Mech 121:102-6+ Mr '64
Hidden dangers of pile remedies. Todays Health 42:50-1+ F '64
Muscular dystrophy. Sat Eve Post 236:40+ D 14 '63
Sore throat can be serious. Todays Health 43:26-7+ Ja '65
Your health. Redbook 121:44+ My; 20+ O '63

BERLE, Adolf Augustus, 1895-
Are we ignoring Latin America? N Y Times Mag p26+ N 24 '63
As the dust settles in Brazil. Reporter 30: 27-8 Ap 23; 8 My 21 '64
Coin of governance. Reporter 30:48+ Je 18 '64
Dialogue? yes; concessions? beware! N Y Times Mag p9+ O 20 '63; 20 Ja 19 '64
How free shall the free market be? N Y Times Mag p 10+ Je 23 '63
Intellectuals and new deals. New Repub 150: 21-4 Mr 7 '64
Is Haiti next? Reporter 28:16 My 23 '63
Latin America's true voice. Sat R 46:14+ Jl 13 '63
Polity in a castle by the sea. Sat R 47:40-1 O 17 '64
Venezuela: the achievement of Don Romulo. Reporter 29:33-4 N 7 '63
When they shout, Yanqui, no! N Y Times Mag p9+ Ja 26 '64

BERLE, Milton
Milton Berle. G. Frank. pors McCalls 91:94-7+ Mr '64

BERLET, H. H. and others
Endogenous metabolic factor in schizophrenic behavior. bibliog Science 144:311-13 Ap 17 '64

BERLIN, I. N.
Desegregation creates problems, too. Sat R 46:66-7 Je 15 '63
Unrealities in teacher education. Sat R 47:56-8+ D 19 '64

BERLIN, Irving
Best things in life are free. il Time 83:68+ Ap 3 '64
Blue skies to you, Irving Berlin. T. Prideaux. il por Life 54:12+ My 3 '63

BERLIN
Back to abnormal. Time 83:24 Ja 17 '64
Berlin: the broken city; symposium. il Atlan 212:86-123+ D '63
Both sides of the wall. L. Van Der Post. il Holiday 36:74-7+ O '64
Celebrations for some. il Time 83:36 Ja 3 '64
Hole in the wall; cross-over permits for Christmas visits. il Time 82:20 D 27 '63
Letter from Berlin (cont) J. Wechsberg. New Yorker 39:41-2+ Ja 18 '64
Lower barrier? negotiations for pass agreement between West Berlin and East Berlin. il Newsweek 64:50 S 28 '64
When the Berlin wall opened up. .. il U S News 55:4 D 30 '63
Willy Brandt's third Germany. G. Bailey. il Reporter 30:33-6 F 13 '64

Art

Art in a divided city. A. Werner. il Am Artist 27:36-41+ Ap '63

Description

Building and rebuilding of Berlin. W. J. Siedler. il Atlan 212:103-9 D '63
Editor's report: Deutschland duo. M. M. Davis. il Travel 122:55-61 S '64

Economic conditions

Berlin's economic future. H. C. Wallich. Atlan 212:130-4 D '63

Galleries and museums

Art in a divided city. A. Werner. il Am Artist 27:36-41+ Ap '63

History

Allied occupation, 1945-

Again the autobahn. G. Bailey. Reporter 29:16+ N 7 '63
Berlin: the erosion of a principle. J. E. Smith. Reporter 29:32-3+ N 21 '63
Conflict over convoys; halt of U.S. army convoy to Berlin by Soviets. Sr Schol 83:19 N 22 '63
Dance of the gooney birds: Russians hold up American convoy en route to Berlin. il Time 82:31-2 N 15 '63
Just when Nikita seemed all smiles; halt of U.S. military convoy en route to Berlin by Soviet troops. il U S News 55:62-3 N 18 '63
Notes and comment; another attempt to dictate the terms of allied access to West Berlin. New Yorker 39:41 N 16 '63
On the autobahn; U.S. army convoy blocked at Marienborn checkpoint. il Newsweek 62: 44+ N 18 '63
Road to Berlin: flare-up in an old trouble spot. il U S News 55:4 O 21 '63
Sparring on the autobahn. New Repub 149:6 N 16 '63

Music

Notes from our correspondents. P. Moor. Hi Fi 14:26+ S '64

Reconstruction

Building and rebuilding of Berlin. W. J. Siedler. il Atlan 212:103-9 D '63

BERLIN, (East Berlin)
Brave buddelers of Berlin. J. O'Donnell. il N Y Times Mag p32-3+ Ap 7 '63
Breaching the wall: the odds grow. A. J. Olsen. il N Y Times Mag p 11+ Ag 9 '64
Day behind the wall. il Sunset 132:43-4 F '64
East Berlin, a red showcase. A. J. Olsen. il N Y Times Mag p22-3 S 8 '63
Going places, finding things in the two Berlins. D. Beal. il House & Gard 126:43-4+ S '64
It is still there; Berlin wall. il Time 82:22-3 Ag 23 '63
Living with the wall. il Bsns W p22-3 Ag 8 '64
People of East Berlin. O. Frei. il Atlan 212: 118-21 D '63
Sunday in East Berlin. K. Strong. Christian Cent 81:1500+ D 2 '64
There's another side to the wall. L. Barry. il Pop Phot 52:20+ F '63
Uneventful day at the Berlin wall. A. J. Olsen. il N Y Times Mag p 14-15+ O 20 '63
U.S. protests Soviet restrictions in East Berlin; U.S. note, July 5, 1963. Dept State Bul 49:138 Jl 22 '63
Violent night. il Newsweek 63:32 Ja 6 '64
Wedding guest crosses the wall. D. Hildebrandt. il N Y Times Mag p36-7+ N 22 '64

Art

Brief return trip to the land of Marx. A. Frankfurter. Art N 61:25 F '63

BERLIN (East Berlin)—*Continued*

Music

Berlin and Munich; visit by Moscow's second opera company. J. H. Sutcliffe; E. D. Echols. il Opera N 29:30-1 Ja 2 '65
Last week, East Berlin. il Time 81:54 My 17 '63
[Musical events] (cont) Mus Am 84:78+ D '64

BERLIN (West Berlin)
Berlin devours you as you arrive. E. Vreeland. Vogue 141:74+ Mr 1 '63
Berlin/1964; with paintings by Gerald Scarfe. H. K. Smith. Esquire 62:35-9 Jl '64
Brave buddelers of Berlin. J. O'Donnell. il N Y Times Mag p32-3+ Ap 7 '63
Going places, finding things in the two Berlins. D. Beal. il House & Gard 126:43-4+ S '64
It is still there; Berlin wall. il Time 82:22-3 Ag 23 '63
Living with the wall. il Bsns W p22-3 Ag 8 '64
President in Germany. Reporter 29:16+ Jl 18 '63
Uneventful day at the Berlin wall. A. J. Olsen. il N Y Times Mag p 14-15+ O 20 '63
Wall has cut my city in half. J. R. Moskin. il Look 27:36+ Je 18 '63
Wedding guest crosses the wall. D. Hildebrandt. il N Y Times Mag p36-7+ N 22 '64
Willy wins. il Time 81:25 Mr 1 '63
Willy wins; West Berlin parliamentary elections. il Newsweek 61:34 Mr 4 '63

Architecture

Acoustics in-the-round at the Berlin philharmonic. R. S. Lanier. il Arch Forum 120:98-105 My '64

Economic conditions

Rising beside the wall. Time 82:91 N 8 '63

Galleries and museums

New work of Mies van der Rohe; Museum of 20th century art. il Arch Forum 119:86-7 S '63

Intellectual life

Dollars to Deutschland; $2,000,000 project to expand the artistic, educational and cultural resources of Berlin. Mus Am 83:19 F '63

Music

[Musical events] (cont) il Mus Am 84:27 Ap; 20 My '64

Politics and government

Brandt's victory. New Repub 148:8 Mr 9 '63

Streets

Kurfurstendamm. Travel 119:22 Ap '63

BERLIN air corridors. See Aviation—Germany (Federal Republic)

BERLIN festival. See Music festivals—Germany (Federal Republic)

BERLIN film festival. See Moving picture festivals

BERLIN philharmonic hall. See Concert halls

BERLIN question, 1945-
American looks at Berlin; address, October 9, 1963. G. C. McGhee. bibliog f Dept State Bul 49:819-24 N 25 '63
Berlin: a new approach. C. Pell. il Nation 196:520-2 Je 22 '63
Berlin wall; what Ike would have done; excerpts from address. D. D. Eisenhower. U S News 56:14 Ap 13 '64
Berlin's new outlook. L. R. Colitt. Nation 197:236-8 O 19 '63
Cold war collision points; Germany. il(p 15) Sr Schol 85:16-17 O 7 '64
Dynamics of progress in central Europe; address, November 11, 1964. G. C. McGhee. Dept State Bul 51:870-6 D 21 '64
Explosive clause; Franco-German treaty of cooperation. Nation 196:150 F 23 '63
Gambit with pawns. G. Bailey. Reporter 30:19-20 Ja 2 '64
Germans and Berlin: one wall, many views. A. Schalk. Commonweal 78:63-5 Ap 12 '63
How big a price for a break in the wall? il U S News 57:16 N 16 '64
No deal on Berlin; hard look at the Berlin situation in the light of the Cuban crisis. D. Brandon. il America 108:192-6 F 9 '63
Ordeal of coexistence, by W. Brandt. Review Sat R 46:26-7 My 18 '63. W. H. Chamberlin
Secretary discusses Berlin in filmed interview; ed. by J. Steele. D. Rusk. Dept State Bul 48:135-7 Ja 28 '63
Senator Pell's intervention. Nation 196:338 Ap 27 '63
Speaking out; Berlin: let's stop courting disaster. C. Pell. Sat Eve Post 237:8-9 F 8 '64
Three's a crowd; three-Germanys theory. Newsweek 63:31 Ja 13 '64
U.S. reiterates allied right of free access to Berlin; exchange of notes between the United States and the Soviet Union, November 21 and December 18, 1963. Dept State Bul 50:8 Ja 6 '64
U.S. rejects Soviet accusations regarding Berlin judges law. Dept State Bul 48:751 My 13 '63

BERLIND, Bruce
Borborygmus; Metric; Érotique; poems. Poetry 101:256-8 Ja '63

BERLINER, Martha D. See Neurath, P. W. jt. auth.

BERLINERS
Berlin: love scales the wall; photographs. Life 56:28-9 Ja 10 '64
Breaks in the wall. Sr Schol 85:17-18 O 21 '64
Celebrations for some. il Time 83:36 Ja 3 '64
Charging admission; fee for visiting relatives in the eastern zone. Time 85:36 Ja 1 '65
Grumbles from the East; visitors from West Berlin. il Time 83:30 Ja 10 '64
Hole in the wall; cross-over permits for Christmas visits. il Time 82:20 D 27 '63
Letter from Berlin (cont) J. Wechsberg. New Yorker 39:41-2 +Ja 18 '64
Little boy at the wall. il Look 27:30-5 Je 18 '63
People of East Berlin. O. Frei. il Atlan 212:118-21 D '63
Tragedy at the wall. il U S News 56:8 Ja 6 '64
Twain shall meet; East and West Berlin reunions. il Time 83:29 Ja 31 '64
When the Berlin wall opened up... il U S News 55:4 D 30 '63

BERLIOZ, Hector
Béatrice & Bénédict. J. Barker. il Am Rec G 29:696-8 My '63
Benvenuto Cellini. Criticism
Opera N il 29:32 Ja 30 '65
Berlioz first Cléopâtre. P. L. Miller. Am Rec G 29:792 Je '63
Berlioz's Béatrice et Bénédict, now the music is recorded in full. C. L. Osborne. il Hi Fi 13:59-60 Je '63
Colossal nightingale. F. Grunfeld. Reporter 29:52-5 D 5 '63
Damnation of Faust. Criticism
New Yorker 40:182 Ap 4 '64
Music to my ears; Ormandy reveals Berlioz: Grande messe des morts. I. Kolodin. Sat R 47:34 Ap 18 '64
Musical events; Berlioz's Requiem, performed by Philadelphia orchestra with Temple university choirs. W. Sargeant. New Yorker 40:98-100 Ap 11 '64
Nuits d'été. J. Maclain. Am Rec G 30:672-4 Ap '64

BERLITZ schools of languages
Language merchants. il Time 81:84 Je 21 '63

BERLOWITZ, Laurence
It is my firm conviction that sole should never be touched by water. Sunset 130:204 My '63

BERMAN, Arthur I.
Observatories in space; with biographical sketch. Sci Am 209:14, 28-37 bibliog(p 140) Ag '63

BERMAN, Eugene
Prodigal return; interview, ed. by F. Merkling. por Opera N 27:12-13 Mr 23 '63
Yeasty surroundings of a fertile imagination. il House B 105:148-9+ Ap '63

BERMAN, Harold J.
Drop those galoshes, comrade. Nation 198:605-6 Je 15 '64
Reappraisal of U.S.-U.S.S.R. trade policy; excerpts from address, March 12, 1964. Harvard Bsns R 42:139-44+ Jl '64

BERMEL, Albert
Four new ways to make a movie. Harper 229:76-81 O '64
How to treat the Broadway malady of 1963. bibliog f Harper 227:56-62 D '63
Miscegenation. New Repub 148:11-12 Mr 23 '63

BERMUDA
Bermuda gone north, satellites discover. Sci N L 86:249 O 17 '64
See also
Fishing—Bermuda
Hotels, taverns, etc.—Bermuda
Sports—Bermuda
Tourist trade—Bermuda

Description and travel

Going places, finding things in Bermuda. D. Beal. il House & Gard 124:28+ D '63
New routes for photo-travelers. L. Barry. il Pop Phot 55:72-3 Ag '64

BERMUDA grass. See Grasses

BERMUDIAN furniture. See Furniture, Bermudian
BERN, Howard A. See Yagi, K. jt. auth.
BERN (city)
Between trains, a walk through Bern. il Sunset 133:38+ N '64
BERNAC, Pierre
Pierre Bernac: Frenchman in New York. por Mus Am 83:19 My '63
BERNAL, Ignacio
Treasure of Teotihuacán; tr. by D. Heyden. Atlan 213:106-11 Mr '64
BERNAM, Mel
Films your store may not carry. Pop Phot 52: 66-7+ Je '63
How to stretch a lens. Pop Phot 53:78-9+ S '63
Today's monobaths: multi-versatile. Pop Phot 52:78-80 F '63
What film, what paper, what developer for portraits? il Pop Phot 53:140-1+ N '63
BERNARD, Richard F. See Wallace, G. J. jt. auth.
BERNARDI, Santiago
Tango. Américas 16:20-6 D '64
BERNARDINE of Siena, Saint
World of San Bernardino. by I. Origo. Review
Commonweal 77:649-51 Mr 15 '63. A. Fremantle
BERNATH, Maja
Childhood's baffling middle years. Parents Mag 38:52-3+ Ap '63
No more bedtime battles. Parents Mag 39: 54-5+ Je '64
Your baby is a high achiever. Parents Mag 39:64-5+ F '64
BERNBACH, William
Meet Doyle Dane's Bernbach. il por Newsweek 63:76 Je 8 '64
BERND, Daniel
Did Goldwater lose? New Repub 151:8-10 D 5 '64
BERND, John M.
Not if, but how. Sr Schol 83:11T O 18 '63
(comp) Resources for teaching about communism and democracy. Sr Schol 83:16T-18T O 18 '63
(ed) Teaching about communism and democracy. Sr Schol 83:11T-19T O 18 '63
BERNE, Robert
Civil defense official describes architect's role. Arch Rec 135:50+ Mr '64
BERNEIS, Regina F.
Culturally disadvantaged child. ALA Bul 59: 53-7 Ja '65
BERNER, Richard C.
Management of manuscript collections. por Library J 88:1615-16 Ap 15 '63
BERNFELD, Peter, and Wan, J.
Antigens and enzymes made insoluble by entrapping them into lattices of synthetic polymers. bibliog Science 142:678-9 N 8 '63
BERNHARD, consort of Juliana, queen of the Netherlands
Developing nations of the world; necessity of working together; address, December 6, 1963. Vital Speeches 30:229-33 F 1 '64
BERNHARD, Berl I.
Equality and 1984; address, June 2, 1963. Vital Speeches 29:594-7 Jl 15 '63
BERNHARDT, Karl S.
Parent and child. N Y Times Mag p50 Ag 25 '63
BERNHARDT, Sarah
Mucha's divine Sarah. il N Y Times Mag p 17 Je 2 '63
She was Tosca. F. Stevenson. por Opera N 28:24-5 Ap 18 '64
BERNHEIM, Evelyne
—See Bernheim, M. jt. auth.
about
Just a click apart. J. Morris. il U S Camera 26:62-5 D '63
BERNHEIM, Marc, and Bernheim, Evelyne
New art of the new Africa. il N Y Times Mag p22-3 O 4 '64
New kind of African woman. il N Y Times Mag p 14-15 Jl 7 '63
On the Peruvian Amazon. Travel 119:41-3 F '63
about
Just a click apart. J. Morris. il U S Camera 26:62-5 D '63
BERNHEIMER, Martin
Alban Berg: an upbeat. Sat R 47:46-7 S 12 '64
Art and the Offering. Sat R 47:58 F 29 '64
Bach and son. Sat R 46:59+ Mr 30 '63
Between Rossini and Verdi. Sat R 46:70 O 26 '63
Casals conducts St Matthew Passion. Sat R 46:54 Je 29 '63
Changing of the guard. Sat R 47:51 D 26 '64
Cultured Cosi from Ringstrasse. Sat R 46: 45 Je 29 '63
Die frau from Munich. Sat R 47:65 S 26 '64
Don Giovanni from Aix. Sat R 47:62 Ja 25 '64
Enter Eurodisc. Sat R 47:58+ Je 27 '64
Four Messiahs. Sat R 47:71 Ja 11 '64
Guglielmo restored. Sat R 47:67 My 30 '64
Handel down to size. Sat R 47:57 Ap 25 '64
Herod of Fleury. Sat R 47:59 D 12 '64
Hindemith at the Philharmonic. Sat R 46:73 My 11 '63
Janacek. Sat R 47:35 My 16 '64
Kempff's debut. Sat R 47:76 O 31 '64
Kuchta's Bruennhilde. Sat R 46:31 D 14 '63
Last recordings of Bruno Walter. Sat R 46: 58-9 D 28 '63
Lehmann's Müllerin. Sat R 47:51 Jl 25 '64
More Scherchen. Sat R 47:65-6 N 28 '64
More taste than torment. Sat R 46:57 My 25 '63
Poppea semi-vitalized. Sat R 46:61-2 F 23 '63
Prey on Schubert. Sat R 47:61 Mr 28 '64
Real Ariadne? Sat R 46:37 Ag 31 '63
Recordings in review. Sat R 46:40-1 Jl 27 '63
Recordings reports. Sat R 46:42, 44 Jl 27 '63
Rehearsed but not revealed. Sat R 46:35 Ag 31 '63
Resnik, more Janacek. Sat R 47:51 My 23 '64
Rigolettos nos. 14 and 15. Sat R 47:67 O 31 '64
St John according to Richter. Sat R 48:51 Ja 30 '65
Schubert's last songs. Sat R 46:75 S 28 '63
Stockhausen's non-lecture. Sat R 47:44+ Ja 25 '64
(comp) Strauss bookshelf. Sat R 47:65 My 30 '64
Strauss then and now. Sat R 47:65 Je 27 '64
Tebaldi's new Desdemona. Sat R 47:34 Ap 18 '64
Television Tiefland. Sat R 47:41 Ag 22 '64
Trial and Utopia. Sat R 47:41 Jl 25 '64
Vintage Handel from Woldike. Sat R 46:49 Je 29 '63
(tr) See Scherchen, H. Musical past and the electronic future
—and Sunde, Peggy
(comps) Bing repertory 1950-63. Sat R 47: 46-7 Ja 25 '64
BERNIER, George M. and Cebra, J. J.
Polypeptide chains of human gamma-globulin: cellular localization by fluorescent antibody. bibliog Science 144:1590-1 Je 26 '64
BERNS, Donald S. and others
C-Phycocyanin: minimum molecular weight. bibliog Science 145:1054-6 S 4 '64
BERNS, Stanley
Dexter rhododendrons. Horticulture 41:320 Je '63
BERNS, Walter
School prayers and religious warfare. Nat R 14:315-18 Ap 23 '63
Sources of law. Nat R 16:690-1 Ag 11 '64
BERNSTEIN, Bart. See Hagan, R. jt. auth.
BERNSTEIN, Burton
Huntley-Brinkley effect; story. New Yorker 40:155-6 N 14 '64
Uttar pradesh; poem. New Yorker 40:121 F 29 '64
BERNSTEIN, Charles
Ordeal of an innocent man. H. M. Greenwald. il pors Sat Eve Post 236:82+ O 5 '63
BERNSTEIN, Edward M.
After the dollar wins. Bsns W p 116+ N 23 '63
BERNSTEIN, Harry
Labor tries a comeback. Nation 197:107-9 S 7 '63
BERNSTEIN, Henry T.
East works with West. Bul Atomic Sci 21: 37-9 Ja '65
BERNSTEIN, Jeremy
Books (cont) New Yorker 39:158+ My 25; 66+ Ag 31; 241-4 N 23 '63; 40:136-41 Je 13; 236+ N 21 '64
Our far-flung correspondents (cont) New Yorker 40:164+ D 12 '64
Profiles (cont) New Yorker 39:58-60+ O 19; 54-6+ O 26 '63
BERNSTEIN, Leonard
Bernstein twice. Discus. Harper 230:99-100 Ja '65
Best of Bernstein; Boston symphony gives United States premiere of Third symphony, Kaddish. H. Rogers. il por Mus Am 84: 14-15 Mr '64
Boy with cheek. il por Time 83:68 F 7 '64
Composer and conductor. B. H. Haggin. New Repub 151:34-6 Ag 8 '64
Dear Mr Bernstein. il por Sr Schol 85:6+ D 2 '64

BERNSTEIN, Leonard—*Continued*
Demonstrator. L. Marcus. il pors Hi Fi 13: 30-3+ My '63
For God and for country; premiere of Kaddish symphony. S. Matalon. Mus Am 84:58 F '64
Giant & a prince. por Time 81:60 F 8 '63
High order of talent. M. Mayer. il pors Opera N 28:6-15 Mr 21 '64
Music to my ears; avant-garde, rear echelon: Philharmonic concert. I. Kolodin. Sat R 47:28 Ja 18 '64
Music to my ears; L. Bernstein's Kaddish symphony. I. Kolodin. Sat R 47:28 Ap 25 '64
Musical events; concert performed by New York philharmonic in Lincoln Center. W. Sargeant. New Yorker 38:112-13 F 2; 39: 156 My 25 '63
Musical events; concert performed by New York philharmonic. W. Sargeant. New Yorker 40:139 My 23 '64
Musical events; Mahler's Second symphony, performed by New York philharmonic. W. Sargeant. New Yorker 39:135-6 O 5 '63
Musical events; performance of Bernstein's Symphony no. 3, by N.Y. philharmonic. W. Sargeant. New Yorker 40:185 Ap 18 '64
One for the road. I. Kolodin. il por Sat R 47:51-2 Ap 25 '64
Prodigal returns; American première of Kaddish symphony. Newsweek 63:77 F 10 '64
Symphony no. 3 Kaddish; to the beloved memory of John F. Kennedy. A. Cohn. por Am Rec G 30:1014-15 Jl '64

BERNSTEIN, Lou
Fulton fish market; photographs. Natur Hist 73:26-9 D '64

BERNSTEIN, Merton C.
Pension mirage. Nation 198:597-9+ Je 15 '64
Push for early retirement. New Repub 151: 23-4 Ag 22 '64
What future for social security? New Repub 152:9-11 Ja 9 '65

BERNSTEIN, Peter L.
Can business grasp the future? Nation 198: 49-51 Ja 13 '64
Does the profit squeeze hurt? Nation 196:94-7 F 2; inside cover Mr 23 '63
Myrdal's long look at us. New Repub 149: 23-4 N 2 '63

BERNSTEIN, Richard B.
Molecular beam scattering at thermal energies. bibliog Science 144:141-50 Ap 10 '64

BERNSTEIN, Richard J.
Educator. Nation 199:512-15 D 28 '64

BERNSTEIN, Saul
No more rumbles; summary of Youth on the streets. Sr Schol 83:2T+ O 11 '63

BERNSTEIN, Theodore M.
Watch your language! excerpts. Read Digest 82:253-5 Je '63
Watch your language! excerpts from More language that needs watching. Read Digest 83:39+ N '63

BEROZA, Morton. See Jacobson, M. jt. auth.

BERRA, Lawrence Peter. See Berra, Y.

BERRA, Yogi
If I don't make it I'll step down; ed. by B. Costello. por Life 56:42 Ja 10 '64

about

Cliffhanger for Yogi and crucial for July. F. Deford. il pors Sports Illus 21:16-19 Jl 27 '64
I got a touch like a blacksmith. G. Holland. pors Sports Illus 19:28-30+ N 11 '63
Mr Berra of the Yankees. il pors Life 56: 37-8+ Ja 10 '64
Myth becomes a manager. il pors Time 82:90 N 1 '63
Out at home. Sports Illus 21:18 N 30 '64
Speed won the world series. W. Leggett. il Sports Illus 21:36-7 O 26 '64
Stengel ponders, The year of the Berra. L. Koppett. il pors N Y Times Mag p21+ Ap 12 '64
Who's laughing now? il por Newsweek 62:93 N 4 '63
Why the Yankees fired Berra. J. Ogle. il pors Look 28:30+ D 29 '64
Yogi of the Yankees; ed. by D. Anderson. J. Garagiola. por Read Digest 85:110-13 Jl '64
Yogi takes over. G. Zimmermann. il pors Look 28:38+ Je 2 '64
Yogi, the commissar. por Time 83:46 Mr 27 '64

BERREMAN, Gerald D.
Fear itself: an anthropologist's view. Bul Atomic Sci 20:8-11 N '64

BERRETTINI, Pietro. See Cortona, P. da

BERRIAULT, Gina
Birth; story. Redbook 122:48-9 F '64
Birthday party; story. Sat Eve Post 237:52-5 D 19 '64
Mistress; story. Esquire 62:120-1 S '64

BERRIES
Fruit makes even lemons taste sweet; miracle fruit. Sci N L 86:168 S 12 '64
Variety in the bramble patch. G. L. Slate. il Horticulture 41:268-9 My '63

See also
Cookery—Fruit

BERRIGAN, Daniel
Come feed the world; poem. Commonweal 79:187 N 8 '63
Henry Moore in the garden; We are in love, the celibates gravely say; Dark word; poems. Poetry 104:12-13 Ap '64
How strange the world; poem. Commonweal 81:155 O 30 '64

BERRIGAN, Philip F.
Christianity in Harlem. Commonweal 81:323-5 N 27 '64

BERRILL, N. J.
Living clocks. Atlan 212:65-9 D '63
Search for life. Atlan 212:35-40 Ag '63

BERRY, Donald J. O. See James, L. K. jr. jt. auth.

BERRY, Edward Cornelius
Famous hotel now college dorm. W. V. Rakestraw. il por Negro Hist Bul 27:140-1 Mr '64

BERRY, Helen K. and others
Deoxycytidine in urine of humans after whole-body irradiation. bibliog Science 142: 396-8 O 18 '63

BERRY, James
Industry and music. Mus Am 84:6-7+ O '64

BERRY, James O.
Not mad at anybody. il Time 84:35-6 N 6 '64

BERRY, James R.
Does your handwriting give you away? Pop Sci 182:104-7+ Ap '63
How document detectives catch crooks. Pop Sci 184:120-2+ Ap '64
Stupid questions about what you eat. Pop Sci 185:74-5+ N '64

BERRY, John N. 3d
John Berry joins Lj staff. por Library J 89:1704 Ap 15 '64
Questioning a question; and some of the answers. E. Moon. Library J 88:2644-7 Jl '63

BERRY, June
IMC in the continuous progress school. por Library J 89:4599-602 N 15 '64

BERRY, K.
Audio output power meter. Electr World 70: 48-9 O '63

BERRY, Paul L.
Development of library resources. bibliog f Ann Am Acad 356:126-32 N '64

BERRY, Robert B.
He hunts with the wild falcon. Sat Eve Post 237:62-5 Je 20 '64

BERRY, S. J. and others
Control of synthesis of RNA and protein in diapausing and injured cercropia pupae. bibliog Science 146:938-40 N 13 '64

BERRY, Wendell
Antennae to knowledge. Nation 198:304-6 Mr 23 '64
Fear of darkness; poem. Nation 198:102 Ja 27 '64
Guest; poem. Nation 198:156 F 10 '64
James Dickey's new book. Poetry 105:130-1 N '64
November 26, 1963; poem. Nation 197:437 D 21 '63
On the front porch; poem. Nation 197:396 D 7 '63
Sparrow; poem. Nation 196:383 My 4 '63
Thief; poem. Nation 198:468 My 4 '64

BERRY-HILL, Henry, and Berry-Hill, Sidney
George Chinnery in India; excerpts from George Chinnery, 1774-1852. Antiques 83: 449-51 Ap '63

BERRY-HILL, Sidney. See Berry-Hill, H. jt. auth.

BERRY syrups. See Syrups

BERRYMAN, Jack H.
Logan Canyon road controversy; anatomy of a principle. il Nat Parks Mag 37:12-15 Jl '63

BERRYMAN, John
Dream song. Harper 226:36 Mr '63
Dream song. Nation 200:87 Ja 25 '65
Nine dream songs. Poetry 103:1-9 O '63
Spender: the poet as critic. New Repub 148: 19-20 Je 29 '63
Three dream songs. Nation 198:539 My 25 '64
Two dream songs. Yale R 52:558-9 Je '63

BERRYMAN, John—*Continued*

about

Mr Bones, he lives. A. Rich. Nation 198:538+ My 25 '64
Verse. L. Bogan. New Yorker 40:242 N 7 '64

BERSON, Arnold, and Keller, Joseph
Shame and glory in the movies. Nat R 16:17-21 Ja 14 '64

BERSON, Solomon A. and Yalow, R. S.
Antigens in insulin determinants of specificity of porcine insulin in man. bibliog Science 139:844-5 Mr 1 '63

BERTELSMANN publishing house. See Phonograph record industry—Germany (Federal Republic)

BERTHEL, John H.
Johns Hopkins digs down. Library J 89:4752-4 D 1 '64

BERTHOLET, René
Lesson learned. il Newsweek 63:37 Ja 13 '64

BERTIL, Guy
What's dimming the city of lights? tr. by B. Kerr. Mlle 59:105+ O '64

BERTOCCI, Peter A.
Extramarital sex and the pill. Christian Cent 81:267-70 F 26 '64

BERTOLAET, Frederick
Culturally deprived in the great cities. Sr Schol 84:5T-6T Ap 24 '64

BERTSCH, Howard
FHA plans expanded lending to farmers; interview. por Suc Farm 61:10+ Mr '63

BERWYN, Ill.
Hospital opens doors to future medical students; MacNeal memorial hospital, Physician development program. il Todays Health 42:57 Ja '64

BERYLLIUM
ARC hard at work on development of beryllium powder. il Miss & Roc 12:27 My 27 '63
Beryllium: effect of ultra-high pressure on resistance. A. R. Marder. bibliog il Science 142:664 N 8 '63
Beryllium picked for structural job. J. F. Judge. il Miss & Roc 14:34+ Ap 6 '64
Recent representative programs involving beryllium technology; table. Aviation W 81:70-1 N 9 '64
Structural applications of beryllium grow. M. L. Yaffee. il Aviation W 81:64-5+ N 9 '64

BESANT, Annie (Wood)
Last four lives of Annie Besant, by A. H. Nethercot. Review
Sat R il 47:35-6 My 30 '64. T. Ali Baig

BESNARD, Marie (Davaillaud)
Trial of Marie Besnard, by M. Besnard. Review
Newsweek il por 61:107 Ap 15 '63

BESS, Donovan
Cosmetics of war. Nation 197:296-8 N 9 '63
Man who taught too well. Nation 196:507-8+ Je 15 '63
Putsch in the GOP. Nation 198:474-7 My 11 '64
Racist proposition: California on trial. Nation 199:179-82 O 5 '64
Sculptor who embarrasses San Francisco. Harper 226:53-7 F '63
Sorcery and society. Nation 199:358-60 N 16 '64
Speaking in tongues: the high church heresy. Nation 197:173-7 S 28 '63

BESSER, Marianne
Problems are part of growing. Parents Mag 39:54-5+ D '64

BESSIE, Michael
Book publishing today; interview. ed. by R. W. Apple, jr. Writer 76:10-11+ F '63

BESSMAN, Samuel P. and Skolnik, S. J.
Gamma hydroxybutyrate and gamma butyrolactone: concentration in rat tissues during anesthesia. bibliog Science 143:1045-7 Mr 6 '64

BESSMERTNOVA, Natalia
Decidedly Bessmertnova. il por Time 83:33 Ja 31 '64

BESSON, Adèle
Letter from Paris. Genêt. New Yorker 40:106+ Ja 9 '65

BESSON, George
Letter from Paris. Genêt. New Yorker 40:106+ Ja 9 '65

BEST, Charles H.
Victory over the sugar sickness; ed. by J. D. Ratcliff. por Todays Health 42:56-8+ Mr '64; Same abr. with title How we discovered insulin. Read Digest 84:43-7 Mr '64

BEST, Ernest E.
Beyond illusion. Christian Cent 81:40-2 Ja 8 '64

BEST, Herman E.
This landfill has real togetherness. Am City 78:27 F '63

BEST, Jay Boyd
Protopsychology; with biographical sketch. Sci Am 208:32, 54-62 bibliog (p 184) F '63

BEST, Winfield
Are smaller families coming back in style? Parents Mag 39:64-5+ N '64

BEST books. See Books and reading—Best books

BEST foot forward; musical comedy. See Musical comedies, revues, etc.—Criticisms, plots, etc.

BEST sellers
Act of folly. A. B. Anderson Pub W 184:20-1 Jl 22 '63
Best seller lists deplored by NYABA. Pub W 183:26-7 My 6 '63
Best sellers. See issues of Publishers' weekly
Best sellers of 1963 as sold to the U.S. trade. A. P. Hackett. il Pub W 185:78-81 Ja 20 '64
Do you remember. .; popular books 1924-1964. A. P. Hackett. il Sat R 47:109-25 Ag 29 '64
Eliminate best seller list, bookseller urges the Times. Pub W 183:124-5 F 11 '63
Forty years of best-sellers; comp. by A. P. Hackett from Publishers' weekly. Sat R 47:92+ Ag 29 '64
Hardcover best sellers of 1964 in the U.S. book trade. A. P. Hackett. il Pub W 187:68-71 Ja 18 '65
1963-64 paperback best sellers in the bookstores. il Pub W 185:70-7 Ja 20 '64; 187:72-8 Ja 18 '65
So you want to write a book; excerpt from The writing and selling of nonfiction. P. R. Reynolds. Sat R 46:48-50 Jl 13 '63; Reply. D. B. Sanborn. 46:43 Ag 10 '63

BESTER, Alfred
Holiday handbook of think machines. Holiday 35:123-8 Mr '64
New age of radio. Holiday 33:56-65+ Je '63
Zany genius of Glenn Gould. Holiday 35:149-54+ Ap '64

BESTER, John
(tr) See Sawako, A. Prayer

BESTOR, Arthur
American Civil war as a constitutional crisis. bibliog f Am Hist R 69:327-52 Ja '64

BETA Persei. See Stars, Variable

BETA rays
Nuclear theory verified; conservation of vector current in nuclear beta decay. C. S. Wu. Sci N L 83:85 F 9 '63

BETANCOURT, Ernesto F.
How to liberate Cuba. New Repub 149:17-18 Jl 13 '63

BETANCOURT, Rómulo
U.S. and Venezuela take firm stand against Communist threats. Dept State Bul 48:445-6 Mr 25 '63
Venezuelan miracle. Reporter 31:37-41 Ag 13 '64

about

Asylum, too, is a human right. Nat R 15:93 Ag 13 '63
Battle the reds are losing. C. Migdail. il por U S News 54:62-3 Mr 4 '63
Betancourt goes double or nothing. por Bsns W p 114+ N 30 '63
Care & feeding of generals. il por Time 82:30 D 27 '63
Democratic precedent. por Newsweek 63:53 Mr 23 '64
Man with a formula to stop Castroism. il por Bsns W p64-5 Mr 2 '63
Most critical area in the world. Life 54:4B F 22 '63
Quest of Romulo Betancourt. il por Sr Schol 82:5 Mr 6 '63
Si, amigo, ballots beat bullets in Venezuela. il por Sr Schol 84:13-15 F 7 '64
Thwarting subversion. Commonweal 77:608 Mr 8 '63
Venezuela builds on oil. T. J. Abercrombie. il por Nat Geog Mag 123:344-87 Mr '63
Venezuela: no. 1 on the Communists most wanted in Latin America list. il por Sr Schol 82:6-9 Ap 3 '63
Venezuela: piracy and violence. il por Newsweek 61:48+ F 25 '63
Venezuela: the achievement of Don Romulo. A. A. Berle. Reporter 29:33-4 N 7 '63
Washington welcome to a friend. il por Time 81:22 Mr 1 '63
Where U.S. won and Castro lost in Latin America. D. B. Richardson. il por U S News 55:92-4 D 16 '63
Will the terrorists get Betancourt? R. Peter. Nat R 15:482 D 3 '63
With impunity & immunity. Time 82:37 Jl 5 '63
Yanquis say si, si for Latin in D.C. il pors Life 54:30-1 Mr 1 '63

BETANCUR-MEJÍA, Gabriel
Education: backbone of the Alliance for progress. Américas 15:2-7 S '63
BETHANY, David G.
A. C. voltage calibrator. il Electr World 69: 56+ Je '63
BETHANY, Ill.
Bethanyites get a bargain. il Am City 78:77 Ag '63
BETHE, Hans
Fermi prize: J. Robert Oppenheimer named to receive annual AEC award. Science 140: 161-3 Ap 12 '63
Nobel award winners announced; physics. Science 142:937-8 N 15 '63
BETHEL, Millard B.
Filth we breathe. Sci Digest 53:6 My '63
BETHESDA, Md.
Churches
Challenge of church libraries. R. S. Smith. bibliog il Library J 88:3000-3 S 1 '63
BETHESDA, Md. Congregational church choir. See Choirs
BETHLEHEM, Jordan
I saw Bethlehem shining. R. C. Davids. Farm J 87:32+ D '63
BETHLEHEM, Pa.
Oldest U.S. drug store; Simon Rau & co. il Travel 121:33-5 Je '64
BETHLEHEM steel corporation
Bessie gets a new boss. il Bsns W p82 F 8 '64
Bethlehem's shifting stars. il Time 82:86+ N 8 '63
Delayed reaction; attack on business negativism in Harper's. Newsweek 62:91 N 18 '63
Out for a bigger steel bite. il Bsns W p82-3+ F 16 '63
Suburbia in the jungle; Indústria e comércio de minérios. Time 85:78+ Ja 29 '65
BETHPAGE, N.Y.
Plainview welcomes paperbacks: high school library's experience. D. Cohen. bibliog il Library J 90:306-8 Ja 15 '65
BETHUNE, Mary McLeod
My last will and testament; reprint of 1955 article. pors Ebony 18:150-6 S '63
BETJEMAN, John
Australia: everything is different. Vogue 142: 182-3 D '63
Lines written to Martyn Skinner. Harper 229: 72 S '64
BETOCCHI, Carlo
Little diary on growing old (XVIII) poem; tr. by I. L. Salomon. Commonweal 77:664 Mr 22 '63
Summer song; tr. by I. L. Salomon. Commonweal 79:250 N 22 '63
BETROTHALS. See Engagements, Marriage
BETTELHEIM, Bruno
Class, color and prejudice. Nation 197:231-4 O 19 '63
Eichmann; the system; the victims. New Repub 148:23-33 Je 15; 30 Je 29 '63
How to ask the right questions about your child. Parents Mag 38:58-9+ F '63
Parents vs. television. Redbook 122:54-5+ N '63
Roadblocks to learning. NEA J 52:23-5 Mr '63
Sex and violence in books, magazines and television. Redbook 123:60-1+ My '64
Speaking out. por Sat Eve Post 237:8+ Ap 11 '64; New Repub 150:20-30 My 9 '64
What children learn from play. Parents Mag 39:48-9+ Jl '64
Why does a man become a hater? Life 56: 78+ F 7 '64
Women: emancipation is still to come. New Repub 151:48-54+ N 7 '64
BETTER business bureaus
When is a bargain not a bargain? Consumer Bul 46:23-4 O '63
BETTER homes and gardens (periodical)
Winners in our 1962 home improvement contest. il Bet Hom & Gard 41:41-2 O '63
BETTI, Laura
People are talking about. . . por Vogue 141: 98-9 Ap 1 '63
BETTI, Ugo
Corruption in the palace of justice; tr. by H. Reed. Criticism
Cath World 198:199-200 D '63
Nation 197:306 N 9 '63
New Repub 149:26+ D 21 '63
New Yorker 39:100+ O 19 '63
Newsweek 62:72 N 18 '63
Theatre Arts 48:68 Ja '64
Time il 82:75 O 25 '63
BETTINA. See Bodin, S.
BETTING. See Book making (betting); Gambling
BETTINSON, Brenda
Patron of the living arts. America 109:93-5 Jl 27 '63
BETTS, Anne
I believe. J. Fritsche. por Seventeen 22:67 Mr '63
BETTS, Edward
Painting in polymer & mixed media. il Am Artist 28:34-9 O '64
BETULIA (asteroid) See Asteroids
BETWEEN two wars; story. See Warner, S. T.
BEUM, Robert
January night; poem. Commonweal 81:449 D 25 '64
BEVAN, Aneuran
Aneuran Bevan, by M. Foot. Review
America 109:243-4 S 7 '63. M. M. McMahon
Newsweek por 62:73-4 Jl 29 '63
Time il por 82:74+ Ag 9 '63
BEVARD, George
Ideas from a small western feeder. il Suc Farm 61:54 O '63
Tips for beef grade-and-yield-selling. Suc Farm 62:116 F '64
BEVATRON
Atom smasher revived. il Sci N L 83:181 Mr 23 '63
BEVER, Wendell
Gobbler goes west. Outdoor Life 131:60-1+ My '63
Pack dog hunt. por Outdoor Life 133:28-31+ Ja '64
BEVERAGES
Beverages. B. M. Stover. il Parents Mag 39:67 Jl '64
Bubbling along; U.S. soft-drink industry. il Time 84:80 Ag 7 '64
Cold-drink war: Kvass vs. Coke. A. Carthew. il N Y Times Mag p21-3 Jl 12 '64
Converting to summer fuel. il Esquire 60: 64-5 Ag '63
Coolers for hot days; with recipes. R. Behnke. il Farm J 88:45 Ag '64
Coolers from Curaçao and Mexico; horchatas. il Sunset 133:124 S '64
Cooling Latin drinks; with recipes. M. Kaytor. il Look 28:76-7 Jl 14 '64
Cups that cheer. il Redbook 122:80-1+ N '63
Delightful drinks for breakfast and brunch parties. J. A. Beard. il House & Gard 123: 184-6 Ap '63
Frosty summer drinks. il Bet Hom & Gard 41:71-2 Jl '63
Great milk shakes. L. S. Bernbach. il Parents Mag 38:76-7 Je '63
He's making a fruit float. il Sunset 133:112 Ag '64
How to keep food and drink cold. N. Craig. il House B 106:102-6 Jl '64
Kvass vs. Coke. New Yorker 40:33-4 Je 6 '64
Low-calorie leap. Newsweek 62:76 Jl 8 '63
Matter of labeling. il Consumer Bul 46:11 S '63
Memorandum; breakfasts. Mile 56:180 Mr '63
Nice cool drink; recipes. il Vogue 143:142-3 Je '64
Open house beverages. il Bet Hom & Gard 42:89-90 D '64
Project alpha; promotion of dietetic soda pop. Tab; by Coca-Cola company. New Yorker 40:33-4 Mr 14 '64
Revive the icy shrub. E. Kinard. il House B 106:20+ Ag '64
Sales bubble for diet drinks. il Bsns W p88+ Je 27 '64
Serve up a quick thirst quencher. il Am Home 67:72+ Jl '64
Summer coolers. il Suc Farm 61:56+ Jl '63
Summer drink and dessert staple: lemons; with recipes. M. Kaytor. il Look 27:48-51 Jl 30 '63
Sweet talk; low-calorie soft drinks. Newsweek 64:59-60 Ag 10 '64
Tempting uses of soup and juices. Good H 156:221 Ap '63
What's your pleasure, Mr President? favorite drinks of the Presidents. il Esquire 63:52-3 Ja '65
See also
Coca-Cola company
Coffee
Liquors
Punch (beverage)
Soups
Tea
BEVERIDGE, William Henry Beveridge, 1st baron
Lord Beveridge, RIP. Nat R 14:270 Ap 9 '63
BEVERLY HILLS, Calif.
Fire prevention, the key to low fire losses. C. C. Benford. il Am City 78:35 N '63

BEVERLY Hills, Calif.—*Continued*
Happy birthday, dear Beverly. R. Lemon. il Sat Eve Post 237:76-81 D 5 '64
Middle-aged myth. il Time 83:48 F 21 '64

Education

As private as public can be; Beverly Hills high school. il Time 82:36 Jl 19 '63

Lighting

Pay-as-you-go brings code-level lighting. E. E. Tufte. il Am City 78:114 D '63

BEVILACQUA, E. M. and Norling, P. M.
Hexanedione from hydrocarbon polymer oxidation. bibliog Science 147:289-90 Ja 15 '65

BEWLEY, Lois
Brief biography. S. Goodman. pors Dance Mag 38:44-5 O '64

BEYER, Evelyn
Montessori in the space age? NEA J 52:35-6 D '63

BEYOND all wonder; story. See Combs, P.

BEYOND the fringe; revue. See Musical comedies, revues, etc.—Criticisms, plots, etc.

BEYOND the fringe (1964) revue. See Musical comedies, revues, etc.—Criticisms, plots, etc.

BEYOND this moment; story. See Robinson, B.

BEZONA, Norman C.
Bananas for southern gardens. Horticulture 41:374 Jl '63
Date palm. Horticulture 41:390-1 Jl '63
Oleander. Horticulture 41:485 S '63

BEZUSZKA, Stanley J.
Mathematics. NEA J 53:48-50 My '64

BHABHA, Homi Jehangir
Promise of nuclear energy. UNESCO Courier 16:14-17 Jl '63

BHARGAVA, S. C.
Inhibition of flowering by light in the short-day plant salvia occidentalis. bibliog Science 147:60-1 Ja 1 '65

BHATIA, Prem
India cracks down on its Communists. Reporter 32:41-3 Ja 28 '65

BHATTACHARJI, Somdev, and Smith, C. H.
Flowage differentiation. bibliog Science 145:150-3 Jl 10 '64

BHUTAN
Murder in Shangri-La. Newsweek 63:58 Ap 20 '64

BIALE, Jacob B.
Growth, maturation, and senescence in fruits. bibliog Science 146:880-8 N 13 '64

BIALER, Severyn
New B. & K. Reporter 31:25-6 N 5 '64
Twenty-four men who rule Russia. N Y Times Mag p26-7+ N 1 '64

BIANCHI, Daniela
Secret agent James Bond's second girl friend. J. Hamilton. il pors Look 27:71-4 D 31 '63

BIANCHI, Eugene C.
California housing and civil rights. America 111:174 Ag 22 '64
Catholic-Orthodox dialogue. America 111:688-91 N 28 '64
Decree on ecumenism. America 111:776 D 12 '64
Lay theologians in parishes. America 109:772-3 D 14 '63
Protestant sanctity. America 111:106-8 Ag 1 '64
Raiment in the space age. America 111:402 O 10 '64
This new generation. America 109:383 O 5 '63
(ed) See Visser't Hooft, W. A. Key figure of the World council of churches discusses Christian unity

BIBB, Leon
Big smacky experience. por Newsweek 64:50-1 Ag 24 '64

BIBBY, Cyril
Science: a tool of culture; address, reprint from Nature. Sat R 47:51-3 Je 6 '64

BIBER, Heinrich Ignaz Franz von
Again Biber from Cambridge, and now Vox too. J. W. Barker. Am Rec G 31:320+ D '64
Heinrich Biber; fifteen Mystery sonatas for violin and continuo. J. W. Barker. Am Rec G 29:782-3 Je '63
Scordatura; and the Mysteries of the rosary. E. Salzman. Hi Fi 13:73-4 Ap '63

BIBERMAN, Lucien Morton
L'affaire Biberman; weapons research facility in Laboratory of applied sciences to close. New Repub 148:7-8 Je 22 '63

BIBLE
Bible; symposium. il Life 57:5-9+ D 25 '64
Bibles once owned by King James I. P. W. Schmidtchen. il Hobbies 69:106-7 Ap '64
Man's eternal dialogue with God. Life 57:6-7 D 25 '64
Roger Williams Bible. P. W. Schmidtchen. il Hobbies 69:106-7 Ja '65
Scripture and tradition, by G. Moran. Review
Cath World 198:185-6 D '63. N. J. McEleny
See also
Creation
Theology

Antiquities

Diggers verify the Bible past. il Life 57:132-8+ D 25 '64
Digging in Jordan substantiates Old Testament. il Sci Digest 53:42-4 Ap '63
They're digging up Bible stories. S. James. il Pop Mech 121:110-14+ Ap '64
See also
Israel—Antiquities

Bibliography

Bibles and related books for the spring holiday season. il Pub W 185:70-3 F 10 '64
Bibles, related books to be heavily promoted as spring holiday gifts. il Pub W 183:76-81 F 11 '63
New gift Bibles, related books for the Christmas season; with editorial comment. il Pub W 184:28-33, 48 S 9 '63
Strong Christmas campaigns for Bibles, related books. il Pub W 186:81-7 S 28 '64

Criticism, interpretation, etc.

Catholic scholars. il Time 81:80-2 My 3 '63
Catholics and the Bible. Commonweal 77:553-4 F 22 '63
Exegete at the manger. J. L. McKenzie. Commonweal 81:439-42 D 25 '64
Fresh orientation in the church. R. Rouquette. Cath World 196:343-50 Mr '63
Historical tradition in the Fourth Gospel, by C. H. Dodd. Review
Christian Cent 81:1598-9 D 23 '64. J. F. Jansen
Interpreting the resurrection. D. T. Rowlingson. bibliog f Christian Cent 80:459-61 Ap 10 '63
Sins of Sodom. Time 82:54 S 6 '63
See also
Bible—Hermeneutics

Bibliography

Biblical potpourri. R. A. Harrisville. Christian Cent 81:1464-6+ N 25 '64
Books about the Bible. Pub W 185:74-5 F 10 '64
Comment on the Bible, 1964; reviews of books. Christian Cent 81:1430-2+ N 18 '64
New gift Bibles, related books for the Christmas season; with editorial comment. il Pub W 184:34-7, 48 S 9 '63
Strong Christmas campaigns for Bibles, related books. il Pub W 186:81-7 S 28 '64

Theory, methods, etc.

See Bible—Hermeneutics

Editions

See Bible—Versions

Evidences, authority, etc.

Computers and Scripture. W. M. Abbott. America 109:696 N 30 '63

Geography

Biblical world. il Life 57:8-9 D 25 '64

Hermeneutics

Existential way of reading the Bible. il Time 83:62 My 22 '64
Logic and the logos; second consultation on hermeneutics at Drew university. R. W. Funk. Christian Cent 81:1175-7 S 23 '64
New hermeneutic: new frontiers in theology, ed. by J. M. Robinson and J. B. Cobb, jr. Review
Christian Cent 81:639-41 My 13 '64. E. C. Hobbs

Illustrations

See Bible—Pictorial illustrations

Interpretation

See Bible—Criticism, interpretation, etc.

Law

See Jewish law

Pictorial illustrations

Rembrandt's Bible drawings. A. Werner. Am Artist 28:52-8+ D '64

Publication and distribution

See also
American Bible society
Bible societies

BIBLE—*Continued*

Reading

Knowledge of Bible ebbs in Europe. Christian Cent 81:878 Jl 8 '64

Study

See Bible study

Theology

Experience in Biblical theology; symposium at Notre Dame university. V. A. McInnes. America 111:804 D 19 '64

Translations

See Bible—Versions

Versions

Anchor Bible: first of thirty-eight hard-cover volumes. il Pub W 186:98-9 O 5 '64
Book for all creeds; Doubleday's Anchor Bible. Time 84:87 O 23 '64
British common Bible? America 109:785-6 D 21 '63; Reply. R. E. Murphy. 110:29 Ja 11 '64
Common-Bible backing. America 109:183 Ag 24 '63
Debut of the Anchor Bible. B. Vawter. Commonweal 81:396-7 D 11 '64
New Testament bookshelf. R. H. Fuller. Christian Cent 80:271-3 F 27 '63
One for all. il Time 82:48+ S 27 '63
Our new translation of the Bible. R. E. Brown. America 111:601-4 N 14 '64; Discussion. 112:168-9 Ja 30 '65
Share common Bible: Catholic edition of the Revised standard version. Christian Cent 81:163 F 5 '64; Reply. B. Vawter. 81:433 Ap 1 '64
That old family Bible. P. W. Schmidtchen. il Hobbies 69:106-7 Jl '64
Translating the Bible. T. H. Gaster. Commentary 36:305-11 O '63
See also
Bible—New Testament—Versions
Bible—Old Testament—Versions

Old Testament

See also
David, king of Israel
Prophets

Manuscripts

Shapira affair, by J. M. Allegro. Review
Sat R 48:30-1 Ja 30 '65. T. H. Gaster

Pictorial illustrations

23rd psalm; in inspiring pictures for your home. R. Martens. Farm J 87:76-7 My '63

Versions

Prophets paraphrased; translation of J. B. Phillips. Time 82:86 N 1 '63

Pentateuch

Jews of Britain; theological schism. Time 83:63 My 22 '64
Law that bound Israel. W. F. Albright. il Life 57:55-6 D 25 '64
Torah for today; new translation. Newsweek 61:87 F 11 '63

Genesis

Creation. il Life 57:16-23 D 25 '64
God chooses a family. il Life 57:24-35 D 25 '64

Exodus

Moses leads his people. il Life 57:42-7 D 25 '64

Joshua

Invasion of the promised land. il Life 57:48-52 D 25 '64

Kings

Conquerors sweep in. il Life 57:66-70 D 25 '64

Psalms

In praise of the Lord. il Life 57:142-6 D 25 '64

New Testament

Additions to the debate. R. G. Gruenler. Christian Cent 80:1240 O 9 '63
Mixed bag. R. H. Fuller. Christian Cent 80:1241-2 O 9 '63
This good news, by Q. Quesnell. Review
America 110:741 My 23 '64. T. A. Johnson
See also
Jesus Christ

Versions

Four publishers simultaneously issue American standard Bible-New Testament. Pub W 185:75 F 10 '64

Gospels

Biblical Instruction; concerning the historical truth of the Gospels. R. E. Murphy. Commonweal 80:418-20 Je 26 '64
Exegete at the manger. J. L. McKenzie. Commonweal 81:439-42 D 25 '64
See also
Jesus Christ—Teaching

Epistles

Kairopractice; concerning authorship of Romans, Corinthians, and Galatians. Time 81:56 Mr 15 '63
Saint and science; computer analysis of Pauline Epistles. Newsweek 62:82 N 18 '63
St Paul and the computer. Sci Am 210:56 Ja '64

Luke

Parables of conflict in Luke, by J. S. Glen. Review
Christian Cent 80:1274-5 O 16 '63. J. P. Love

John

Historical tradition in the Fourth Gospel, by C. H. Dodd. Review
Christian Cent 81:1598-9 D 23 '64. J. F. Jansen
Well, that's one way; Gospel according to John in twentieth-century disguise. il Newsweek 62:93 S 23 '63

Revelation

Revelation. il Life 57:126-9 D 25 '64

BIBLE in the schools. See Public schools and religion

BIBLE societies
United Bible societies. C. Northcott. Christian Cent 81:940 Jl 22 '64
See also
American Bible society

BIBLE society, American. See American Bible society

BIBLE study
Apostolic few. il Time 81:69 My 24 '63
Biblical Instruction; concerning the historical truth of the Gospels. R. E. Murphy. Commonweal 80:418-20 Je 26 '64
Does Sodom love Gomorrah? reading course based on Bible at Newton high. Time 83:44 Mr 20 '64
Fresh orientation in the church. R. Rouquette. Cath World 196:343-50 Mr '63
Go-ahead for Bible scholars; and wayward press. America 110:754 My 30 '64
Gospel truth; what the recent Vatican statement means to modern Catholic biblical scholars. J. A. Fitzmyer. America 110:844-6 Je 20 '64; Reply with repoinder. J. T. Meehan. 111:118-19 Ag 8 '64
Intellectual freedom; Abbot Butler on relation between scholarship and divine teaching. America 111:509-10 O 31 '64
Jerusalem Olympics; third International Bible quiz. Time 84:90+ O 2 '64
Taking the Bible seriously, by L. E. Keck. Review
Christian Cent 80:494 Ap 17 '63. J. P. Love

Bibliography

Books about the Bible. il Pub W 183:81-3 F 11 '63
Christian message and method. America 109:52-5 Jl 13 '63
Liturgy and scripture: 1964; Biblical works. il America 111:745-6+ D 5 '64
New Testament bookshelf. R. H. Fuller. Christian Cent 80:271-3 F 27 '63
Season of renewal; Lenten reading. D. J. O'Hanlon. Commonweal 77:643-5 Mr 15 '63
Systematic theology bookshelf. R. M. Brown. Christian Cent 80:400-2 Mr 27 '63
Updating Bible lore. America 108:615-16+ Ap 27 '63

BIBLICAL drama. See Religious drama

BIBLICAL maps. See Bible—Geography

BIBLICAL seminary in New York
Biblical seminary controversy. E. C. Parker. Christian Cent 80:380 Mr 20 '63; Reply. A. A. Leininger. 80:716 My 29 '63

BIBLIOGRAPHIC services
See also
School libraries—Bibliographic services

BIBLIOGRAPHY
Eccentric bibliography. E. Moon. Library J 88:4167 N 1 '63
See also subhead Bibliography under various subjects, e.g. Childrens literature—Bibliography

Bibliography

Childrens literature

Selecting materials for children and young adults; comp. by E. D. Hodges and F. Fleming. NEA J 54:69-70+ Ja '65

BIBLIOGRAPHY, National
Goals in national bibliography. D. Melcher. Library J 89:2556-9 Je 15 '64

BIBLIOGRAPHY, National—*Continued*

Brazil

Focus on Brazil; seminar on the acquisition of Latin American library materials. I. Zimmerman. Library J 88:3030-1 S 1 '63

BIBLIOTEKSTJÄNST, Lund, Sweden
Bibliotekstjänst (Library service inc) G. Ostling. il Library J 88:4323-5 N 15 '63

BIBLIOTHERAPY
Bibliotherapy for mental health: subject of AHIL conference workshop. Library J 89:214 Ja 15 '64
Books that help children. R. E. Hutcherson. bibliog Library J 88:2083-6 My 15 '63
Reader who needs remotivation. M. T. Moody. il ALA Bul 58:795-7 O '64
Reader with mental and emotional problems. M. C. Hannigan. bibliog il ALA Bul 58:798-803 O '64
See also
Libraries, Hospital

BICARBONATE formate. See Formates

BICKEL, Alexander M.
After a civil rights act. New Repub 150:11-15 My 9 '64
Barry fights the Court. New Repub 151:9-11 O 10 '64
Battle over Brandeis. New Repub 151:25-6 Ag 8 '64
Beyond tokenism. New Repub 150:11-14 Ja 4 '64
Bobby Baker's silence; back to the Fifth. New Repub 150:9-10 Mr 21 '64
Case of New York. New Repub 151:11 D 26 '64
Civil rights act of 1964. Commentary 38:33-9 Ag '64
Civil rights act of 1963. New Repub 149:9-12 Jl 6 '63
Civil rights and the Congress. New Repub 149:14-16 Ag 3 '63
Civil rights, as amended. New Repub 149:7-8 N 16 '63
Civil rights boil-up. New Repub 148:10-14 Je 8 '63
Court intervenes. New Repub 150:5-6 F 29; 28+ Mr 14 '64
Crime and reapportionment. New Repub 148:5 Ap 6 '63
Homosexuality as crime in North Carolina. New Repub 151:5-6 D 12 '64
Integrated cohabitation. New Repub 150:4-5 My 30 '64
Is the federal government helpless? New Repub 151:14 D 26 '64
Justice and the franchise. New Repub 151:17-18 O 31 '64
Liberals and civil rights. New Repub 149:9-10 D 28 '63
Much more than law is needed. N Y Times Mag p7+ Ag 9 '64
New Court. New Repub 148:15-17 Mr 16 '63
Reapportionment & liberal myths. Commentary 35:483-91; 36:344+ Je, N '63
Reapportionment and the courts. New Repub 150:7 Je 27 '64
Sleepers in the civil rights bill. New Repub 150:14-17 F 29 '64
Supreme court fissures. New Repub 151:15-16 Jl 11 '64
What has been done is prologue. New Repub 152:16-18 Ja 9 '65

BICKERS, Jack
How to keep good hired help. Farm J 87:34-5+ D '63
—See Hagen, D. jt. auth.

BICKFORD, Joseph C.
Excesses could cause readjustment. Nations Bsns 52:110 Je '64

BICKMORE, Lee S.
Involvement and leadership; address, October 2, 1964. Vital Speeches 31:55-7 N 1 '64

BICYCLE racing
Another for the accountant; world's best bicycle racer. il Time 82:62 Jl 26 '63
Et tu, Benoni? world-championship race. il Newsweek 62:66 Ag 26 '63
Lure of the wild white noise; J. Simes America's first Olympic cyclist. B. Ottum. il Sports Illus 21:22-5 S 14 '64
Six days; Berlin's bicycle race. il Time 84:41-2 O 16 '64

BICYCLES
Bicycle built for two; tandem bicycle. M. Banister. il Pop Mech 119:176-9+ Ap '63
Hi-cycle. M. G. Hults. il Pop Mech 121:169 Ap '64
Princess R; British peers ride Moulton's low-wheeler. il Newsweek 64:61 Ag 31 '64
Two million bicyclists expected to apply for free reflective tape. il Todays Health 41:67 Ap '63
See also
Cycling

BICYCLING. See Cycling

BIDAULT, Georges
Demned elusive. . . BBC-TV interview. por Newsweek 61:48+ Mr 18 '63
Determined ones. il por Time 81:40 Mr 15 '63
Give us some sous. il Time 81:24-5 Mr 22 '63
No blindfold. il por Newsweek 61:47 Mr 25 '63
One more wedge between Britain and France. por U S News 54:10 Mr 18 '63

BIDDING, Competitive. See Contracts, Government

BIDDLE, Dorothy
Garden club world. See issues of Popular gardening & living outdoors to May 1964

BIDDLE, Edith C.
Cataloging by the bootstrap method. por ALA Bul 58:49-52 Ja '64

BIDDLE, Francis
Aging of Justice Holmes. New Repub 151:19-22 D 19 '64
Holmes and the life of the law. New Repub 149:24-6 Ag 17 '63
How can the lawyer help? New Repub 149:12 Jl 6 '63
Ordeal of William Penn. Am Heritage 15:30-3+ Ap '64

BIDDLE, George
Considered statements; exhibition at Manhattan's Cober gallery. il por Time 81:68 My 3 '63

BIDDLE, James
American art from American collections. Antiques 83:309-16 Mr '63
Nicholas Biddle's Andalusia, a nineteenth-century country seat today. Antiques 86:286-90 S '64

BIDDLE, Nicholas
Nicholas Biddle's Andalusia, a nineteenth-century country seat today. J. Biddle. il por Antiques 86:286-90 S '64

BIDDLE, William W.
Church and community development. Christian Cent 81:106-8 Ja 22 '64

BIDETS
Yikes! il Newsweek 61:84 Ap 22 '63

BIDNER, Bill
Afternoon at the beach. Horn Bk 39:416 Ag '63

BIDRIN. See Insecticides

BIDWELL, R. G. S.
Plant physiology. Science 146:91-2 O 2 '64

BIEBER, Irving
Parent and child. N Y Times Mag p75+ Ag 23 '64

BIEDERMAN, Charles Joseph
Biederman and the new art. F. Getlein. New Repub 148:26-8 F 16 '63

BIEDERMEIER style
Herr Biedermeier in Vienna. R. M. Vetter. il Antiques 84:698-705 D '63

BIELEFELD, Ted
Sculptured door pulls of Ted Bielefeld. J. Pugliese. il Craft Horiz 23:18-19 My '63

BIELEN, Casimir
Teacher's role in politics. NEA J 53:30 O '64

BIELERT, Karl. See Weidaw, R. jt. auth.

BIENNALE, Venice. See Music festivals—Italy

BIENNIALS (plants)
Biennials. B. Black. il Pop Gard 14:39+ Jl '63

BIERBAUM, Milton W. and Sperreng, Robert
Inter-district cooperation. NEA J 52:56 Mr '63

BIERI, Rudolph, and others
Noble gases in sea water. bibliog Science 146:1035-7 N 20 '64

BIERMAN, Jacquin D.
New tax bill and you. Parents Mag 39:14+ Ap '64

BIERMANN, June, and Toohey, Barbara
MARY: teacher's pet. Wilson Lib Bul 39:402 Ja '65
—See Toohey, B. jt. auth.

BIERRING, Franz. See Andersen, S. B. jt. auth.

BIERSTADT, Albert
Uniqueness of Albert Bierstadt. F. Lewison. il por Am Artist 28:28-33+ S '64

BIG business. See Capitalism; Corporations—Size

BIG HOLE BATTLEFIELD NATIONAL MONUMENT
Memorial to an Indian Moses. P. R. Smith, jr. il Nat Parks Mag 37:13-15 F '63; Reply. J. R. Williams. 37:23 S '63

BIG lift (maneuver) See Military maneuvers

BIG man on Beech street; story. See Preston, B. B.

BIG OAK TREE STATE PARK. See Missouri —Parks and reserves
BIG shoo; drama. See Boiko, C.
BIG SUR, Calif.
What are they doing to Big Sur? W. Trombley. il Sat Eve Post 237:24-9 F 15 '64
BIG trees. See Trees
BIGAMY
Lady-killer; Hoch murder case. A. I. Schutzer. il Am Heritage 15:36-9+ O '64
BIGART, Homer
Canada goes to the polls. Reporter 28:29-32 Ap 11 '63
Will the law ever get Hoffa? Sat Eve Post 236:68-71 Mr 30 '63
BIGELOW, Donald N. and Legters, L. H.
(eds) Non-western world in higher education. Ann Am Acad 356:1-167 N '64
BIGELOW, J. S.
Bat and the scientist; poem. Atlan 211:112 Je '63
BIGGINS, John. See Park, R. B. jt. auth.
BIGGS, E. Power
Biggs: on and off the record. E. Helm. por Mus Am 83:49 Ap '63
Vox humana fortissimo. J. M. Conly. Reporter 31:54-5 S 24 '64
BIGHORN hunting. See Mountain sheep hunting
BIGNELL, Edward E.
Pooled facilities and services pay off. por Recreation 57:346-7 S '64
BIGOTRY. See Toleration
BIHARI ballet. See Ballet—Hungary
BIJOU, Calif.
Most complete waste-water treatment plant in the world. W. Priday and others. il Am City 79:123+ S '64
BIKEL, Theodore
So they say; interview. por Mlle 57:234-5 Ag '63
BIKINIS. See Bathing suits
BILDERBACK, Linda G. and others
Distance perception in darkness. Science 145:294-5 Jl 17 '64
BILE
Ornithocholanic acids and cholelithiasis in man. L. Peric-Golia and R. S. Jones. bibliog il Science 142:245-6 O 11 '63
BILHARZIASIS. See Schistosomiasis
BILIARY calculi. See Calculi, Biliary
BILINGUALISM
New look at the bilingual student. L. V. Kosinski. bibliog il Sr Schol 83:14T O 4 '63
BILIRUBIN
Bilirubin: acute effects in newborn rhesus monkeys. R. E. Behrman and E. Hibbard. bibliog il Science 144:545-6 My 1 '64
Shunt bilirubin: evidence for two components. L. G. Israels and others. bibliog il Science 139:1054-5 Mr 15 '63
BILL, Tony
Which way the wind? E. Miller. pors Seventeen 22:84-5+ Je '63
BILL of rights. See United States—Constitution—Bill of rights
BILL of rights day
Bill of rights day, Human rights day; proclamation. L. B. Johnson. Dept State Bul 51:887 D 21 '64
Bill of rights day, Human rights day; proclamation, December 2, 1963. L. B. Johnson. Dept State Bul 50:21 Ja 6 '64
BILLBOARDS
America down the drain; with statement by Secretary Udall. R. H. Boyle. il Sports Illus 21:78-80+ N 16 '64
America the beautiful: let's not lose it. il Changing T 17:25-9 S '63
Billboards, slobs and cemeteries. R. Starnes. Field & S 68:10+ Jl '63
Blue boy in Secaucus; Gainsborough billboard. il Newsweek 65:48 F 1 '65
Let's rescue our roadsides now! M. Frome. Am For 69:10-11+ N '63
Signs of the times. il Recreation 57:380-1 O '64
Three states fight billboard blight. il Arch Forum 118:13 My '63
We're losing the war against slobs. R. Starnes. Field & S 69:12-15 Jl '64
BILLETDOUX, François
Il faut passer par les nuages (Passage through the clouds) Criticism
New Yorker 40:108 Ja 23 '65
BILLIAR, R. D. and others
D-malate: effects on activity of L-malate dehydrogenase in developing sea urchin embryos. bibliog Science 146:1464-5 D 11 '64
BILLIARDS
Battle of the hottest sticks; World's pocket billiards tournament; with drawings by D. Gorsline. Sports Illus 18:32-7 F 25 '63
Billiards in America before 1830. L. C. Belden. il Antiques 87:99-101 Ja '65
Billiards with a beauty treatment. E. Pomerantz. il Holiday 36:110+ S '64
Games worth the candle. Sports Illus 20:8+ Ja 20 '64
Girls take the cue. D. L. Goodrich. il Sat Eve Post 237:24-7 Ap 18 '64
You don't beat Wimpy at the game he loves; World's pocket billiard tournament. T. Fox. Sports Illus 20:58-61 Mr 23 '64
BILLICK, Bill
CQ fish. Pop Electr 20:45-7 Je '64
BILLING
After paying, who gets? Mrs Helen Clark's bills from Manhattan's Flower and Fifth avenue hospital. Time 83:58 Ja 17 '64
Computer that earns a profit; Albuquerque, N.Mex. J. L. Guggino. il Am City 79:102-3 Mr '64
Consolidate your utility bills; Kirkwood, Mo. W. H. Pfitzinger. il Am City 78:80-1 Ag '63
Customers select method of payment; Middletown, Ohio. R. Chesney. Am City 79:22 N '64
Electronic automation fills the bill; Dearborn, Mich. W. B. Godette. il Am City 78:99 N '63
Five utilities on one bill; Anchorage, Alaska. J. P. Bell. il Am City 78:91-2 D '63
Not late once in seven years; DuPage County Wheaton, Ill. J. J. Kelly. il Am City 78: 84-5 F '63
1.2 seconds per bill; Los Angeles County's electronic data-processing system. J. R. Quinn. il Am City 78:105 My '63
We do our own utility billing; Greeneville, Tenn. M. C. Butler. il Am City 78:101-2 S '63
BILLINGS, John Shaw
John Shaw Billings: 1838-1913. F. B. Rogers. bibliog por Library J 88:2622-4 Jl '63; Reply. J. Neufeld. 88:3388 O 1 '63
BILLINGS, Richard
Ape who drives like sixty. Life 56:11 Ja 17 '64
BILLINGS, Mont.
Sequel to a spending dispute. il U S News 54: 10 Ap 15 '63
BILLINGS, Mont, memorial library. See Parmly Billings memorial library
BILLINGSGATE market. See London—Markets
BILLINGSLEY, Bob D.
Learning without eyes. Parents Mag 39:72-3+ S '64
BILLINGTON, David P. and others
Merits of two model testing techniques. Arch Rec 134:225-8 S '63
BILLS, Robert E.
Grouping; learners or learning? Sch Life 45: 10-12+ Je '63
BILLS (legislation) See Legislation
BIMAT film. See Photography—Films
BIMONTE, Richard
Analysis—or autopsy?—on the Italian character. Commonweal 81:425-6 D 18 '64
Art of anti-acting. Reporter 31:49-50+ O 22 '64
Rain check on Utopia. Reporter 30:46-8 Je 4 '64
BIMS, Hamilton J.
Detroit high school challenges nation. Ebony 19:25-8+ Ag '64
Who will get policy baron's fortune? Ebony 19:116-18+ O '64
BINARY number system. See Numeration
BINARY stars. See Stars, Double
BINDER, David
Active coexister visits us. N Y Times Mag p24+ O 13 '63
10,000,000 Hungarians can't be wrong. N Y Times Mag p6-7+ D 27 '64
BINDING (books) See Bookbinding
BINFORD, L. C.
Lands we share; address, May 3, 1963. por Am For 69:16-19+ Jl '63
BING, Rudolf
New mood for critics. por Sat R 47:50-1 F 15 '64

about

Guest editorial: fifteen years with Mr Bing. R. Sabin. Mus Am 84:4+ N '64
He gets his way. il por Newsweek 62:67-8 O 28 '63
Honors for Mr Bing; with photographs. Opera N 27:12-13 Ap 6 '63
Mr Bing makes the Met go. M. Mayer. il pors N Y Times Mag p44-5+ O 11 '64
Mr Bing's day; photographs. Opera N 28: 13-16 F 15 '64
New mood for the new Met. I. Kolodin. il Sat R 47:45-7+ Ja 25 '64; Discussion. 47: 50-1 F 15; 62-4 F 29 '64

BING Crosby tournament. See Golf—Tournaments
BINGER, Carl
Psychiatrist in the looking glass. Harper 228: 62-7 Je '64
BINGHAM, Charlotte
Opening night in Stratford; the insider's game. Vogue 143:199+ Ap 1 '64
Weedy words on chins, love and puppy fat; excerpts from Coronet among the weeds. pors Life 54:98 Ap 26 '63
BINGHAM, George Caleb
Art; exhibition of drawings by G. C. Bingham at Knoedler's. H. Kramer. Nation 196: 212-13 Mr 9 '63
Missouri show; exhibition at M. Knoedler & co. New Yorker 39:26 F 23 '63
Sovereigns; exhibition at Manhattan's M. Knoedler & co. il Time 81:59 Mr 1 '63
BINGHAM, Jonathan B.
Colonialism and the decade of development; address, February 21, 1963. Dept State Bul 48:459-61 Mr 25 '63
Intensification of demographic studies, research, and training; statement, April 3, 1963. bibliog f Dept State Bul 49:28-31 Jl 1 '63
Problems of economic development; statement, October 3, 1963. Dept State Bul 49: 712-21 N 4 '63
Role of the special fund in the U.N. development decade; statement, January 14, 1963. Dept State Bul 48:258-63 F 18 '63
U.S. calls claims of Portuguese arms diversion unfounded; statement, November 29, 1962. Dept State Bul 48:104-5 Ja 21 '63
U.S. comments on activities of U.N. special fund; statement, June 3, 1963. Dept State Bul 49:68-71 Jl 8 '63
U.S. continues to oppose capital development fund; statement, September 9, 1963. Dept State Bul 49:561-3 O 7 '63
U.S. withdraws proposal on Angola opposed by Afro-Asian group; statement, December 20, 1962. Dept State Bul 48:106-7 Ja 21 '63
BINGHAM, June
Sexual morality and the young. Mlle 57:126+ S '63
U.N. parties are hard to digest. N Y Times Mag p 16+ Je 2 '63
BINGHAM, Ralph
Ralph Bingham. J. Walsh. il pors Hobbies 69: 32-5+ Ap '64
BINGHAM, Robert
Gentle ticking noise. Reporter 29:54+ N 7 '63
How to make lawyers wish you'd go away. Reporter 29:42 S 26 '63
Rule of O. Reporter 30:40+ Mr 26 '64
BINGHAM, Sallie
Going away; story. Ladies Home J 80:86-7 N '63
Ice party; story. Atlan 212:54-60 D '63
Neighbors; story. Atlan 213:66-70 Mr '64
BINGHAM, Walter
Bridge (cont) Sports Illus 18:74-5 Ap 15 '63
BINI sculpture. See Sculpture, Bini
BINKLEY, Olin T.
Southern Baptist seminaries. Christian Cent 80:774-5 Je 12 '63
BINKS, Carolyn. See James, H. jt. auth.
BINNEY & Smith, incorporated
It's easy to be creative with crayons. E. M. McCabe. il Parents Mag 38:18+ F '63
BINNS, Betty
Betty Binns: designer of textbooks. P. A. Bennett. il por Pub W 184:96+ S 9 '63
BINNS, Joseph Patterson
Hilton opening. New Yorker 39:20-2 Jl 6 '63
BINOCULAR vision. See Sight
BINOCULARS. See Field glasses
BINOCULARS; story. See Vivante, A.
BINSFELD, Edmund
Communion; poem. America 111:800 D 19 '64
BINSWANGER, Frank G.
Encourage private capital to aid American industry; address, June 6, 1963. Vital Speeches 29:689-90 S 1 '63
BINZEN, Peter H.
Bringing the world to the classroom. Sat R 47:60-2+ Ap 18 '64
BIOASTRONAUTICS. See Space flight—Physiological aspects
BIOCELLS. See Fuel cells
BIOCHEMICAL fuel cells. See Fuel cells
BIOCHEMICAL laboratories. See Biological laboratories
BIOCHEMISTRY
Acid-alkaline balance important to health. Sci N L 86:378 D 12 '64
Activity rhythm in peromyscus: its influence on rates of recovery from nembutal. S. T. Emlen and W. Kem. bibliog il Science 142: 1682-3 D 27 '63
Behavior disruption in cebus monkeys as a function of injected substances. D. C. Ferguson and A. E. Fisher. bibliog il Science 139:1281-2 Mr 29 '63
Biochemical laboratory at Uppsala. V. K. McElheny. il Science 144:1323-5 Je 12 '64
Biochemistry and soil science. A. D. McLaren. bibliog il Science 141:1141-7 S 20 '63
Body's internal balances: what can go wrong. M. Grant. il Life 55:85-6+ N 8 '63
How food finally produces power; the energy factor. il Life 54:48-59+ Mr 29 '63
Key to health: your heredity; interview, ed. by F. R. Schreiber. R. J. Williams. Sci Digest 53:30-9 Ap '63
Life-giving balancing act. R. Campbell. il Life 55:68-81 N 8 '63
Man, a bundle of enzymes. R. Yoshioka. il Sci N L 84:234-5+ O 12 '63
On biochemical variability and innovation; text of paper presented at a symposium on the general physiology of specialized cells. S. S. Cohen. bibliog il Science 139: 1017-26 Mr 15 '63
On the genetic code; address, December 11, 1962. F. H. C. Crick. bibliog Science 139:461-4 F 8 '63
Phenolics of higher plants; report of symposium sponsored by the Plant phenolics group of North America. S. A. Brown. Science 142:1197-8+ N 29 '63
Rapid mixing and sampling techniques; report on colloquium. B. Chance and others. Science 146:1697-9 D 25 '64
Re-creating the pre-life earth. il Time 81:59 Je 7 '63
Thermodynamic equilibria in prebiological atmospheres. M. O. Dayhoff and others. bibliog il Science 146:1461-4 D 11 '64
Underwater guinea pigs help scientists study life. H. M. Schwalb. il Sci Digest 53:6-11 F '63
Upper temperature limit of life. E. S. Kempner. bibliog il Science 142:1318-19 D 6 '63
See also
Bioenergetics
Biosynthesis
Enzymes
Homeostasis
Metabolism
Paleobiochemistry
BIOELECTRONICS. See Medical electronics
BIOENERGETICS
Bioenergetics; report of symposium in London, Ontario. W. C. McMurray. Science 147:413-14 Ja 22 '65
BIOGEOCHEMICAL prospecting. See Prospecting
BIOGEOCHEMISTRY. See Geochemistry
BIOGRAPHICAL dictionaries
See also
Who's who in America
BIOGRAPHIES
Publication explosion; American authors. K. Vanderbilt. Nation 198:219-20 Mr 2 '64
BIOGRAPHY
How much should a biographer tell? S. Spender. Sat R 47:16-19 Ja 25 '64; Discussion. 47:19 Mr 28; 28 Ap 18 '64
Letter from Stan Delaplane. S. Delaplane. Todays Health 41:70 Ag '63
Neglect of the greats; some observations on the problems of writing the biographies of American librarians. E. G. Holley. bibliog il Library J 88:3547-51 O 1 '63
Scientist in biography. H. I. Sharlin. Bul Atomic Sci 19:27-8 N '63
See also
Autobiography
Obituaries
Bibliography
Authors and academicians. G. Hicks; reply with rejoinder. J. F. Mahoney. Sat R 46:19 F 9 '63
Batch of biographies. F. E. Luchs. Christian Cent 80:1549-50 D 11 '63
Biography (cont) F. J. Gallagher. America 108:684-6; 109:673-4; 110:640-2; 111:708-10+ My 11, N 23 '63, My 9, N 28 '64
Book reviews. NEA J 52:56 D '63
BIOLOGICAL and agricultural index
New successor; formerly Agricultural index. Wilson Lib Bul 39:274+ N '64
BIOLOGICAL apparatus and supplies
Continuous recording of cell number in logarithmic and synchronized cultures. T. W. James and N. G. Anderson. bibliog il Science 142:1183-5 N 29 '63
BIOLOGICAL balance. See Balance of nature
BIOLOGICAL batteries. See Electric power production from bacteriological action
BIOLOGICAL chemistry. See Biochemistry

BIOLOGICAL conferences
Microbiology: global aspects; report of conference on Global impacts of applied microbiology. J. M. Birkeland. Science 142:600 N 1 '63
BIOLOGICAL control of insects. See Insects, Injurious and beneficial—Control
BIOLOGICAL cycles. See Periodicity
BIOLOGICAL effects of nuclear particles. See Particles (nuclear physics)—Physiological effects
BIOLOGICAL experiments. See Biology—Experiments
BIOLOGICAL laboratories
Biochemical laboratory at Uppsala. V. K. McElheny. il Science 144:1323-5 Je 12 '64

Safety devices and measures

Caution, byword in biology. J. Viorst. il Sci N L 83:282-3 My 4 '63
BIOLOGICAL photographs. See Photography—Scientific applications
BIOLOGICAL physics
Biophysics; report on international meeting of the Commission on cell and membrane biophysics and the Commission of communication and control processes in biophysics of the International organization for pure and applied biophysics. L. D. Harmon and F. M. Snell. Science 146:276+ O 9 '64
Biophysics; report on International organization for pure and applied biophysics, Paris, 23 June 1964. T. F. Anderson. Science 147:186+ Ja 8 '65
Symposium points to more AF emphasis on hardware; engineering bionics. H. M. David. il Miss & Roc 12:34-5 Ap 1 '63
Upper temperature limit of life. E. S. Kempner. bibliog il Science 142:1318-19 D 6 '63
See also
Biomedical engineering
BIOLOGICAL power. See Electric power production from bacteriological action
BIOLOGICAL research
Biological implications of gas chromatography; with editorial comment. A. Karmen. bibliog il Science 142:161, 163-72 O 11 '63
Biological research in Czechoslovakia. V. K. McElheny. il Science 145:799-802 Ag 21 '64
Biomedical science in Europe. R. P. Grant and others. bibliog Science 146:493-501 O 23 '64
Biopolitics; science, ethics, and public policy. L. K. Caldwell. Yale R 54:1-16 O '64
Cooperative research: biologists plan international study program. E. Langer. Science 143:455 Ja 31 '64
Digital computers in the biological laboratory. R. L. Schoenfeld and N. Milkman. bibliog il Science 146:190-8 O 9 '64
Germfree animals and biological research. M. Pollard. bibliog il Science 145:247-51 Jl 17 '64
Instrumentation for biomedical sciences; report of National biomedical sciences instrumentation symposium. F. Alt. Science 142: 249-52 O 11 '63
Interventions of man in nature. O. W. Garrigan. Cath World 196:292-8 F '63; Reply. W. J. Gibbons. 197:2-3 Ap '63
Laboratory of molecular biology, Cambridge, England. V. K. McElheny. bibliog il Science 144:398-400; 145:36-8 Ap 24, Jl 3 '64
Magnetic resonance in biological systems; report on first International conference on magnetic resonance in biological systems. O. Jardetzky. Science 146:552-3 O 23 '64
Mecca for the world's biologists. il Bsns W p 140-1+ Ag 15 '64
More keys to secrets of life: findings presented at meeting of the Federation of American societies for experimental biology. il Bsns W p82-3 Ap 27 '63
1963-1964 science review. Sci N L 84:389-90; 86:390-1 D 21 '63, D 19 '64
Research in biology: new pattern of support is developing. V. K. McElheny. Science 145:908-12 Ag 28 '64
Semipermeable microcapsules. T. M. S. Chang. il Science 146:524-5 O 23 '64
See also
Biological laboratories
Fishery research
Germ free animals
Salk institute for biological studies, San Diego, Calif.
Zoological research
BIOLOGICAL specimens
Hampered vinyl polymerization by embedding biological objects. A. A. Hofer and E. Lautenschlager. Science 146:69 O 2 '64
L.A.'s fabulous science center. il Sr Schol 84:14T-15T F 7 '64

Collection and preservation

Science in action; the biological collector. J. J. Rudloe. Natur Hist 73:59-62 N '64
BIOLOGICAL transport
See also
Diffusion
BIOLOGICAL warfare
Biological and chemical weapons. R. L. Pfaltzgraff, jr. bibliog f Cur Hist 47:18-24+ Jl '64
DOD weighs new war concept; incapacitating agents. J. Trainor. Miss & Roc 15:14 O 5 '64
Destroyers that leave no wounds; army work on chemical and biological weapons. il Bsns W p 106+ D 5 '64
FAS statement on biological and chemical warfare. Bul Atomic Sci 20:46-7 O '64
Is Russia outstripping us in weapons of mass destruction? address, December 7, 1962. C. H. Coggins. Vital Speeches 29:263-6 F 15 '63
Speaking out; what's so terrible about germ warfare? C. F. Rassweiler. Sat Eve Post 238:12+ Ja 30 '65
Tomorrow's weapons, chemical and biological, by J. H. Rothschild. Review
Bul Atomic Sci 20:35-6 O '64. M. Meselson
Ultimate weapon? Newsweek 61:56 Mr 4 '63

Safety devices and measures

Monitors to detect germs. Sci N L 83:162 Mr 16 '63
BIOLOGY
Biology and the nature of science. G. G. Simpson; discussion. Science 140:762+ My 17 '63
Biology future predicted; ed. by F. Marley. C. D. Leake. Sci N L 83:259 Ap 27 '63
Biology is not a totem pole; letter. C. C. Davis. Science 141:308+ Jl 26 '63
Biology today. B. Commoner. bibliog il NEA J 53:17-20 Mr '64
Books in review; perspectives in biology. J. Oppenheimer. Natur Hist 74:6+ F '65
New perspectives in biology; report of symposium. J. T. Edsall. Science 143:267-8 Ja 17 '64
See also
Adaptation (biology)
Biological research
Biomathematics
Cells
Death (biology)
Enzymes
Evolution
Genetics
Life (biology)
Marine biology
Mutation (biology)
Regeneration (biology)

Classification

Onward and upward with the sciences; ecology and taxonomy expeditions of the New York botanical garden. G. T. Hellman. il New Yorker 40:41-2+ My 30 '64

Experiments

Purpose of experiments. P. Weiss. il Sat R 47:92-4 Ja 4 '64

Nomenclature

New biology and the nature of man; adaptation of address, 1963. G. W. Beadle. Bul Atomic Sci 20:13-17 Mr '64

Study and teaching

Biology departments should buy natural preserves; letter. L. F. Yntema. Science 144: 12 Ap 3 '64; Reply. F. H. Bormann. 144:953 My 22 '64
Biology is changing, too; curriculum changes at every level from elementary school through college. A. Grobman. il Sat R 46: 67-9+ S 21 '63
L.A.'s fabulous science center. il Sr Schol 84:14T-15T F 7 '64
Student performane in new high school biology programs. H. Grobman. bibliog il Science 143:265-6 Ja 17 '64

Textbooks

Embattled textbooks. Sci Am 211:56-7 O '64
BIOLUMINESCENCE. See Luminescence, Biological
BIOMATHEMATICS
Math killing to animals. Sci N L 84:166 S 14 '63
Mathematics in the biological sciences. E. F. Moore. il Sci Am 211:148-54+ bibliog(p270) S '64
BIOMEDICAL engineering
Emphasis urged for biomedical research. il Aviation W 81:54+ N 23 '64
BIONICS. See Cybernetics

BIONOMICS. See Ecology
BIOPHYSICS. See Biological physics
BIOSATELLITE. See Artificial satellites—Use in research
BIO-SCIENCES information exchange. See Smithsonian institution—Science information exchange
BIOSYNTHESIS
Aromatic biosynthesis and metabolism; report of symposium. A. J. Finlayson. Science 142:981-2 N 15 '63
Biosynthesis of unsaturated fatty acids in microorganisms. J. Erwin and K. Bloch. bibliog il Science 143:1006-12 Mr 6 '64
Carbamyl phosphate synthesis in the earthworm lumbricus terrestris. S. H. Bishop and J. W. Campbell. bibliog il Science 142:1583-5 D 20 '63
Erythromycin: mode of action. A. D. Wolfe and F. E. Hahn. bibliog il Science 143:1445-6 Mr 27 '64
Estrone inhibition of cholesterol biosynthesis at the mevalonic acid stage. A. J. Merola and A. Arnold. bibliog il Science 144:301-2 Ap 17 '64
Fatty acid synthesis by subcellular fractions of lung tissue. E. G. Tombropoulos. bibliog il Science 146:1180-1 N 27 '64
Fungi of lichens. V. Ahmadjian. il Sci Am 208:122-30+ F '63
Gene-enzyme relations with histidine biosynthesis in yeast. G. R. Fink. bibliog il Science 146:525-7 O 23 '64
Inhibition of adhesiveness and aggregation of dissociated cells by inhibitors of protein and RNA synthesis. M. H. Moscona and A. A. Moscona. bibliog Science 142:1070-1 N 22 '63
Lipopolysaccharide of the gram-negative cell wall. M. J. Osborn and others. bibliog il Science 145:783-9 Ag 21 '64
Nicotinic acid biosynthesis: control by an enzyme that competes with a spontaneous reaction. A. H. Mehler and others. bibliog il Science 145:817-19 Ag 21 '64
Protein biosynthesis: some alternative considerations on the current hypothesis. R. W. Hendler. bibliog Science 142:402-5 O 18 '63
Reversible sonic inhibition of protein, purine, and pyrimidine biosynthesis in the living cell. V. W. Burns. bibliog il Science 146:1056-8 N 20 '64
Succinic ester and amide of homoserine: some spontaneous and enzymatic reactions. M. Flavin and others. bibliog il Science 143:50-2 Ja 3 '64
BIOTIC communities. See Ecology
BIOTRONES. See Greenhouses
BIPARTISANSHIP. See Partisanship
BIPES biporus. See Lizards
BIPLANES. See Airplanes
BIRCH, Jack W. and others
Early admission of able children to school. bibliog Sch Life 46:7-9 Je '64
BIRCH, John
Life of John Birch, by R. H. W. Welch, jr. Review
New Repub 151:28+ O 17 '64. C. B. Marshall
BIRCH, John, society. See John Birch society
BIRCH, William G.
What you should know about cesareans. Parents Mag 40:38-9+ Ja '65
BIRCH
Nature note: white birch. Sci N L 87:11 Ja 2 '65
BIRCHFIELD, Marilyn
How to succeed as a nursing mother. Parents Mag 39:40-1+ My '64
BIRD, Caroline
Day the money stopped. Look 27:34+ Mr 12 '63
Portrait of you as a guinea pig. Esquire 60:64-70 O '63
Real diamonds vs. real blue chips. N Y Times Mag p69+ Ap 14 '63
Speaking out; more people should be servants. por Sat Eve Post 237:6+ Je 20 '64; Same abr. with title Help wanted. Read Digest 85:235-7+ N '64
BIRD, Charles F.
Little city gets sewage treatment. Am City 79:85-7 F '64
BIRD, Henry L.
Island joins the march. P. S. McGhee. il Nation 198:51-2 Ja 13 '64
BIRD, John
Bill Scranton, a reluctant candidate. Sat Eve Post 237:73-7 Ja 18 '64
Farmers face their toughest choice. Sat Eve Post 236:74-6 My 18 '63
Mill grinds fine by the Brandywine. Sat Eve Post 236:34+ Jl 27 '63
When farmers go on strike. Sat Eve Post 237:30+ N 21 '64
Will he or won't he? Sat Eve Post 237:21-3 Mr 7 '64
Wonderful, wide, backslapping world of Rotary. Sat Eve Post 236:58-62 F 9 '63
Worm learns. Sat Eve Post 237:66-7 Mr 28 '64
(ed) See Fischer, A. J. Father of ten looks to the future
(ed) See Fischer, A. J. Our life will never be the same
(ed) See Fischer, M. A. Fischer quints at home
(ed) See Fischer, M. A. What a year it has been
BIRD, Marjorie Winifred
This prince led Cinderella to death. C. McCarry. il por Sat Eve Post 237:20-1 My 16 '64
BIRD, Thomas E.
Ecumenics and the East. Commonweal 79:220-2 N 15 '63
Pilgrim in the Holy Land. Commonweal 79:479-81 Ja 24 '64
BIRD banding
On the trail of our wandering birds. J. K. Terres. il Audubon Mag 66:100-3 Mr '64
Owl that stays at home. G. Laycock. il Field & S 69:41+ Jl '64
BIRD baths, etc.
Bird baths. I. B. Wasson. Audubon Mag 65:179-80 My '63
Small pools will bring songbirds to your garden. il Pop Gard 16:34-6 Ja '65
These are all for the birds. il Sunset 130:110+ F '63
You can make this birdbath for a song. H. Sibley. il Pop Mech 120:74 S '63
BIRD calling
How to call ducks. R. M. Russell. il Outdoor Life 133:44-7+ Ja '64
Turkey talk. C. Conley. il Field & S 68:36-7+ N '63
You can talk to quail. D. H. Chapman. il Field & S 69:8-9+ Ja '65
BIRD census
600 club: America's top-ranking birders. S. Keith. il Audubon Mag 65:376-7 N '63
BIRD charcoal. See Charcoal
BIRD dogs
What's a good dog? D. M. Duffey. il Outdoor Life 133:114-17 F '64
See also
Beagles (dogs)
Pointers (dogs)
Retrievers
Training
See Dogs—Training
BIRD feeders. See Feeders (birds)
BIRD flight. See Birds—Flight
BIRD gardens
Bush in the hand. B. Hendricks. Audubon Mag 65:116-19 Mr '63
BIRD houses
Barrel full of birds. M. Banister. il Pop Mech 119:154-7 Mr '63
Birdhouse in an A-frame. il Sunset 132:126 Ap '64
Bluebird of Humbleness. il Sports Illus 18:10+ My 6 '63
Helping hand to the bluebird. J. K. Terres. il Flower Grower 51:24-5+ Je '64
House for Jenny-wren. M. Adams. il Flower Grower 50:49 Je '63
It's a bamboo birdhouse. il Sunset 132:108+ F '64
Perk up that plain wall; dummy birdhouse cupola. H. Sibley. il Pop Mech 120:128-9 Ag '63
These are all for the birds. il Sunset 130:110+ F '63
See also
Dove-cotes
BIRD in the house; story. See Laurence, M.
BIRD phonograph records. See Phonograph records—Animal records
BIRD photography. See Photography of birds
BIRD populations
Bird population levels. C. W. Buchheister. Audubon Mag 66:360 N '64
BIRD repellents
Bird chasing, a progressive art. C. Benedict. il Harper 228:30+ Mr '64
BIRD sanctuaries
England's famous waterfowl park; Severn wildfowl trust. il Sunset 133:41+ Ag '64
Fifty years as an outdoor laboratory; White memorial foundation, Litchfield, Conn. il Audubon Mag 65:206-7 S '63
Pelican; Jamaica Bay wildlife refuge. New Yorker 40:48-9 N 14 '64

BIRD sanctuaries—*Continued*
Prairie chicken and his friends; Buena Vista marsh, Wis. G. Laycock. il Field & S 68:52-3+ S '63
Slaughter at Swan Lake. D. McKinley. Audubon Mag 66:144-5 My '64; Discussion. 66:270; 67:5-7 S '64, Ja '65
Two new wildlife refuges are authorized; Ravalli refuge, Mont. and Hatchie refuge, Tenn. Nat Parks Mag 38:16 Mr '64
See also
Wildlife sanctuaries

BIRD shooting. See Shooting

BIRD songs. See Birds—Song

BIRD study
Bird finding. O. S. Pettingill, jr. See issues of Audubon magazine
Bird watching; a hobby you may enjoy. il Good H 158:170 Ap '64
Death road for the condor. R. Macdonald. il Sports Illus 20:86-9 Ap 6 '64
Earning your life list; reprint. D. S. Rowe. il Audubon Mag 66:70-3 Mr '64
Electric eye counts 300 flights a day by parent birds. T. Shoemaker. il Audubon Mag 66:90 Mr '64
How not to go looking for owlets. M. Byers. il Life 56:33 My 15 '64
How to enjoy more nature activity. H. Saltford. Audubon Mag 65:47-50 Ja '63
How's your gamebird savvy? quiz. D. Du Bois. Outdoor Life 134:38-9 Jl '64
In defense of bird watching. J. P. Jackson. il Am For 70:37+ My '64
Magic number. Sports Illus 18:13 My 6 '63
Memorable days with Ludlow Griscom. C. Wellman. il Audubon Mag 66:247-9 Jl '64
Miss Wiley reaccompanied; ambulatory nature-study session on shorelands of Rye. New Yorker 39:41-3 N 9 '63
Words with birds. E. A. Autry. Audubon Mag 67:52-6 Ja '65
See also
Audubon nature camps
Photography of birds

BIRD watching. See Bird study

BIRDBATHS. See Bird baths, etc.

BIRDHOUSES. See Bird houses

BIRDS
Bird finding. O. S. Pettingill, jr. See issues of Audubon magazine
Birds in your garden. J. K. Terres. il Pop Gard 15:12 S; 4 N '64; 16:8 Ja; 12 F '65
Pet birds: how to tell singers from swingers. il Good H 157:172-3 D '63
Seven big how's for attracting songbirds. H. E. Saintsaver. Audubon Mag 65:311-13 S '63
See also
Game birds
Ornithology
Shore birds
Water birds
also names of birds, e.g. Chickadees

Accidents and hazards

Freeing flamingos from anklets of death. J. G. Williams. il Nat Geog Mag 124:934-44 D '63
Operation duck rescue; oil flooding of the Mississippi. E. Peller. il Audubon Mag 65:364-7 N '63
Tests show forty species of birds poisoned by DDT. G. J. Wallace and R. F. Bernard. Audubon Mag 65:198-202 Jl '63
Tower for tv; 30,000 dead birds. C. A. Kemper. il Audubon Mag 66:86-90 Mr '64
See also
Aviation—Bird hazards

Banding

See Bird banding

Collisions with airplanes

See Aviation—Bird hazards

Eggs

See Birds eggs

Flight

How fast was it going? H. G. Tapply. il Field & S 68:64 O '63
Radio-toting pigeon; project to elucidate mysteries of bird flight. Sci Digest 57: inside cover Ja '65
Watching bird flights by radar. P. E. Hughes. il Audubon Mag 66:182-4 My '64

Food and feeding

Birds will come if there's water. A. F. W. Vick, jr. il Horticulture 42:22-3 Je '64
Food for winter birds. B. McKrill. Audubon Mag 66:394 N '64
Fruits bring eleven species to feeders. V. E. Davison. il Audubon Mag 66:322-5 S '64
How to cultivate birds in your garden. J. Hersey. il House & Gard 124:250-1+ O '63
101 foods for cardinals. V. E. Davison. il Audubon Mag 65:180-3 My '63
Prince for your garden. J. D. Walters. il Flower Grower 50:20-1+ N '63
Something for the birds. H. Gantner. il Flower Grower 51:21 O '64
Songbird secrets. A. M. Rockefeller. il Audubon Mag 66:119-23, 186-90 Mr-My '64
They eat out of her hand. Mrs W. Campbell. Audubon Mag 65:308+ S '63
Warm greetings on cold days. R. C. Williams. Audubon Mag 65:378-80 N '63
See also
Bird gardens
Feeders (birds)

Habits and behavior

Bird chasing, a progressive art. C. Benedict. il Harper 228:30+ Mr '64
Birds are picky about taking baths. Sci N L 86:249 O 17 '64
Components of recognition in ducklings. G. Gottlieb. il Natur Hist 74:12-19 bibliog(p70) F '65
Early arousal and imprinting in chicks. W. R. Thompson and R. A. Dubanoski. bibliog il Science 143:1187-8 Mr 13 '64
First impressions. il Newsweek 61:87 F 25 '63
Following and imprinting: effects of light and social experience. J. M. Polt and E. H. Hess. bibliog il Science 143:1185-7 Mr 13 '64
How to protect your plants from bird marauders. il Sunset 130:210+ Je '63
Imprinting: a reassessment. P. H. Klopfer. bibliog il Science 147:302-3 Ja 15 '65
Imprinting in birds. E. H. Hess. bibliog il Science 146:1128-39 N 27 '64
Imprinting in nature. G. Gottlieb. bibliog Science 139:497-8 F 8 '63
Shell menace; egg shell removal by black-headed gulls. N. Tinbergen. il Natur Hist 72:28-35 Ag '63
See also
Birds—Food and feeding
Courtship of birds
Periodicity

Hazards

See Birds—Accidents and hazards

Migration

Birds on the cruise deck. R. Howard. Audubon Mag 67:8-9 Ja '65
California sparrows return from displacement to Maryland. L. R. Mewaldt. bibliog il Science 146:941-2 N 13 '64
Homeostasis of the nonfat components of migrating birds. E. P. Odum and others. bibliog il Science 143:1037-9 Mr 6 '64
More ducks to migrate down four U.S. flyways. Sci N L 84:168 S 14 '63
On the trail of our wandering birds. J. K. Terres. il Audubon Mag 66:100-3 Mr '64
Satellites track animals. B. Tufty. Sci N L 83:130 Mr 2 '63
Secrets of migration; excerpt from The migrations of birds. tr. by C. Sherman. J. Dorst. il Audubon Mag 65:12-15, 102-6, 240-3+ Ja-Mr, Jl '63
Seventeen flyways over the Great Lakes. J. P. Perkins. il Audubon Mag 66:294-9; 67:42-5 S '64, Ja '65
Space tracks: bioelectronics extends its frontiers. D. W. Warner. il Natur Hist 72:8-15 F '63
Spring migration at Point Pelee. O. S. Pettingill, jr. il Audubon Mag 66:78-80 Mr '64
Watching bird flights by radar. P. E. Hughes. il Audubon Mag 66:182-4 My '64
Wild birds migrate from British winter. Sci N L 83:169 Mr 16 '63
See also
Orientation

Nests

See Nests

Orientation

See Orientation

Photographs

Caught in midair; excerpts from I went to the woods. R. Austing. N Y Times Mag p 106-7 Ap 12 '64

Physiology

Homeostasis of the nonfat components of migrating birds. E. P. Odum and others. bibliog il Science 143:1037-9 Mr 6 '64
Nasal salt gland: independence of salt and water transport. T. Inoue. bibliog il Science 142:1299 D 6 '63

BIRDS—*Continued*

Protection

Bill Huey's birds; New Mexican duck. W. B. Morse. il Am For 69:26-7+ D '63
Garden is a place for birds. E. A. Mason. il Horticulture 42:18-19+ My '64
Is mourning dove management really management? H. M. Weber. il Am For 69:32-3+ S '63
Right hand and left. P. M. Tilden. Natur Hist 72:65-6 D '63
See also
Bird sanctuaries
Ducks unlimited, incorporated

Quotations, maxims, etc.

On the fly; nature of birds; comp. by E. F. Murphy. il N Y Times Mag p77 Ap 26 '64

Sanctuaries

See Bird sanctuaries

Song

Bird songs. J. Vosburgh. il Pop Gard 14:26-7+ Mr '63
Contrapuntal bird songs; courtship duet by African shrike. Sci Am 208:80+ My '63
Culturally transmitted patterns of vocal behavior in sparrows. P. Marler and M. Tamura. bibliog il Science 146:1483-6 D 11 '64
Record boom in bird songs. J. Boswall. il Audubon Mag 66:48-50 Ja '64
Songbirds sensitive. Sci N L 84:134 Ag 31 '63
Words with birds. E. A. Autry. Audubon Mag 67:52-6 Ja '65

Study

See Bird study

Australia

See also
Bowerbirds
Diamondbirds

Bahama Islands

Nearby Bahamas are rich in bird life. R. D. Ross. il Audubon Mag 65:204-5 Jl '63
See also
Flamingos

Connecticut

Senators hear Peterson on osprey decline; summary of address, April 22, 1964. R. T. Peterson. Audubon Mag 66:276-7 S '64

Florida

Bird finding; Florida is rich in birdlife. O. S. Pettingill, jr. il Audubon Mag 65:270-3 S '63

Ireland

Grand sportin' bird. W. Page. il Field & S 68:64-7 My '63

Israel

Spring of winter arrives in Israel. P. Arnold. il Audubon Mag 65:386-7 N '63

Japan

Familiar shore birds in Japan. D. Amadon. il Natur Hist 72:48-51 Ap '63

Manitoba

Bird finding; Churchill, on Hudson Bay. S. Pettingill. il Audubon Mag 65:41-3 Ja '63

Michigan

When a state spray kills the state bird; Michigan's robin redbreast. A. G. Etter. il Audubon Mag 65:134-7 My '63

New Guinea

See also
Bowerbirds

New York (state)

Bird finding in the Adirondacks. O. S. Pettingill. il Audubon Mag 65:138-41 My '63

North America

Song and garden birds of North America, by A. Wetmore and others. Review
Nat Geog Mag 126:552-7 O '64. M. B. Grosvenor
See also
Bird census

North Dakota

Dispossessed sandhill cranes of the Missouri River. J. W. Johnson. il Audubon Mag 65: 212-17 Jl '63

Peru

Rarely seen songbirds of Peru's high Andes. W. G. George. il Natur Hist 73:26-9 O '64

Rhode Island

Block Island converts a skeptic. O. S. Pettingill, jr. il Audubon Mag 66:346-50 N '64

South Dakota

Dispossessed sandhill cranes of the Missouri River. J. W. Johnson. il Audubon Mag 65: 212-17 Jl '63

Tennessee

Winter feeders in Nashville. J. E. Wills. Audubon Mag 65:46-7 Ja '63

Texas

Why Texas is proud of the Edwards Plateau. O. S. Pettingill, jr. il Audubon Mag 66:11-13 Ja '64

Trinidad (island)

Bird painting in a tropical valley. D. Eckelberry. il Audubon Mag 66:284-9 S '64

United States

Magic number. Sports Illus 18:13 My 6 '63
Some fine feathered friends; photographs. D. Bleitz. Read Digest 84:136-43 My '64

BIRDS, Effect of light on. See Light—Physiological effects

BIRDS, Extinct
Flightless birds face extinction. A. Scholes. il Sci N L 85:26 Ja 11 '64
Genus of extinct goose found in desert; Brantadorna downsi. Sci N L 85:104 F 15 '64

BIRDS, Fossil
Genus of extinct goose found in desert; Brantadorna downsi. Sci N L 85:104 F 15 '64

BIRDS as carriers of infection
Bird trap; measures against bird-borne disease-bearing ticks. il Sci Digest 56:64-8 N '64
Fatal infections traced to bird sanctuary area. Sci N L 84:38 Jl 20 '63
Pigeons and cryptococcosis, letter; J. D. Schneidau, jr. Science 143:525 F 7 '64
See also
Pigeons as carriers of infection

BIRDS eggs
Our man in Spaxton; repairing birds' eggs. New Yorker 40:37-9 My 23 '64

BIRDS in art
Audubon, the artist. E. H. Dwight. il Audubon Mag 65:20-3 Ja '63
Audubon treasury. il N Y Times Mag p80 O 6 '63
Audubons; exhibition of original drawings of Birds of America, at John James Audubon gallery of New York historical society. New Yorker 40:21-2 Ag 8 '64
Bird painting in a tropical valley; Trinidad. D. Eckelberry. il Audubon Mag 66:284-9 S '64
See also
Design, Decorative—Animal forms

BIRDS in cities
Kill those pigeons? il Time 82:62 O 18 '63
Perils of pigeons. il Newsweek 62:80 O 14 '63
Please don't feed the pigeons! pigeon control programs. J. C. Devlin. Read Digest 85: 12E-12F+ Ag '64
Shooters solve the pigeon problem! Indianapolis pigeon rid project. C. Conley. il Field & S 68:10-11+ D '63

BIRD'S-nest ferns
Try a bird's nest fern. A. D. Hawkes. il Horticulture 42:10-11 Ja '64

BIRDS of prey
Last call for the birds of prey; condensed from address. R. C. Clement. Audubon Mag 67:37 Ja '65
See also
Condors
Falcons

BIREFRINGENCE. See Refraction, Double

BIRGE, Vincent
Long trail. Recreation 56:228-9 My '63

BIRKELAND, Jorgen M.
Microbiology: global aspects. Science 142:600 N 1 '63

BIRLEY, Robert
Switch at Eton. Time 81:61 Mr 15 '63

BIRMINGHAM, Stephen
Beautiful, bedeviled Adirondacks. Holiday 36:42-7+ Ag; 6+ N '64
Boy behind the door; story. Sat Eve Post 236:42-3 Ap 27 '63
Florida dream. Holiday 34:62-81 D '63
Greatest one-man show on earth; Walt Disney. McCalls 91:98-101+ Jl '64; Same abr. with title Walt Disney: imagination unlimited. Read Digest 85:272-3+ N '64
Main line. Holiday 36:86-95+ D '64
New England prep school. Holiday 35:38-49+ F '64

BIRMINGHAM, Stephen—*Continued*
Rich, rich Grosse Pointe. Holiday 35:60-5+ My '64
What have they done to Irene Dunne. McCalls 91:100-1+ Ag '64
Why men think women talk too much. Redbook 121:43+ Je '63

BIRMINGHAM, Ala.
Birmingham: we can say things in the open. il Newsweek 64:23 D 14 '64
Case history of a sick city. il Newsweek 62:23-4+ S 30 '63
Coming home from Birmingham: reflections on tragic southern city. W. Hamilton. Christian Cent 80:1302-3 O 23 '63
In defense of two cities. R. Moley. Newsweek 63:110 Ap 27 '64
Root of the trouble in Birmingham. M. McGrory. America 109:411 O 12 '63

Crime

Birmingham church bomber. G. McMillan. il Sat Eve Post 237:15-19 Je 6 '64
Farce in Birmingham. il Time 82:27-8 O 18 '63
Half-cocked. il Newsweek 62:35 O 14 '63
New bombing terrorists of the South call themselves Nacirema: American spelled backward. G. McMillan. Life 55:39-40 O 11 '63

Hotels, restaurants, etc.

Barbecue and the bar; Ollie's in Birmingham resists public-accommodations section of Civil rights act. il Newsweek 64:32 S 28 '64
Beyond a doubt; Negroes served at Ollie's barbecue. il Time 84:13-14 D 25 '64
Ollie McClung's big decision. M. Durham. Life 57:31 O 9 '64

Negroes

After Birmingham riots, troubles linger on. il U S News 54:40-2 My 27 '63
After Birmingham riots: who has gained? il U S News 54:46-7 Je 17 '63
Alabama bombers kill four Negro girls. Christian Cent 80:1160 S 25 '63
As racial troubles broke loose in Alabama. il U S News 54:8 My 13 '63
Battle hymn in Birmingham. C. G. Bell. Nation 196:370-3 My 4 '63
Beginning in Birmingham. V. Harding. il Reporter 28:13-19 Je 6 '63; Discussion. 29:5 Jl 4 '63
Birmingham, a city. Commonweal 78:212-13 My 17 '63
Birmingham after the bombing. il U S News 55:38-40 S 30 '63
Birmingham, Alabama: a city in fear. J. D. Brown. il Sat Eve Post 236:11-19 Mr 2 '63
Birmingham: an Alabaman's great speech lays the blame. C. Morgan, jr. il Life 55: 44B-44C S 27 '63
Birmingham and after. W. F. Buckley, jr. Nat R 14:397 My 21 '63; Reply. B. Hamby. 14:507+ Je 18 '63
Birmingham and the law. New Repub 148:3-4 My 25 '63
Birmingham church bomber. G. McMillan. il Sat Eve Post 237:15-19 Je 6 '64
Birmingham: I saw a city die; ed. by T. B. Morgan. C. Morgan, jr. il Look 27:23-5 D 3 '63
Birmingham: keeping our fingers crossed. R. Evans and R. Novak. New Repub 151:17-18 Ag 8 '64
Birmingham lull: illusion of racial peace. K. Haselden. Christian Cent 80:1294-5 O 23 '63
Birmingham: my God, you're not even safe in church. il Newsweek 62:20-3 S 30 '63
Birmingham: the fuse gets shorter. il Bsns W p32-3 S 28 '63
Birmingham, U.S.A.: look at them run. il Newsweek 61:27-8 My 13 '63
Birmingham's choice. il Newsweek 61:26-7 My 27 '63
Birmingham's ordeal. Am City 78:7 Je '63
Birth of a nation. M. Ascoli. Reporter 28:12 Je 6 '63
Bombs and duds; Kenneth C. Royall and Earl H. Blaik, the President's Birmingham peace team. Newsweek 62:40 O 7 '63
Boomerang in Birmingham. America 108: 705-6 My 18 '63
Bull at bay; E. Connor retires as commissioner of public safety. il Newsweek 61:29-30 Ap 15 '63
Connor and King. il Newsweek 61:28+ Ap 22 '63
Crisis in Birmingham; federal government's part. W. V. Shannon. Commonweal 78:238-9 My 24 '63
Death of an innocent: bomb that killed four children in Birmingham. W. B. Huie. il Look 28:23-5 Mr 24 '64
Dogs, kids & clubs. il Time 81:19 My 10 '63
Explosion in Alabama. il Newsweek 61:25-7 My 20 '63
Freedom, now. il Time 81:23-5 My 17 '63
From a European's perspective. H. M. Rubin. Reporter 28:19 Je 6 '63
From Birmingham. G. Bailey. Reporter 28: 12+ My 23 '63
Grounds for hope in Birmingham. R. B. Fulton. Christian Cent 81:1012-13 Ag 12 '64
In the Birmingham jail. B. Deming. Nation 196:436-7 My 25 '63
Last chance for white Alabama? Birmingham's mayor cracks the door. Christian Cent 80:574 My 1 '63
Letter from Birmingham jail; reply to criticism of eight clergymen. M. L. King, jr. Christian Cent 80:767-73 Je 12 '63; Discussion. 80:986 Ag 7 '63; Same with editorial comment. il Ebony 18:23-6+, 98-9 Ag '63
Massacre of the innocents. America 109:338 S 28 '63
Negroes press for showdown in South. il Bsns W p24-6 My 11 '63
Off the streets; race conflict. il Time 81:16 My 31 '63
Peace with justice. Commonweal 78:268 My 31 '63
Poorly timed protest; Birmingham Negroes. il Time 81:30-1 Ap 19 '63
Postscript on Birmingham. Reporter 29:16 Ag 15 '63
Prize and the risk. J. E. Evans. U S News 54:120 My 20 '63
Racial crisis moves toward showdown. Christian Cent 80:667 My 22 '63
Racial crisis summons President's leadership. Christian Cent 80:766 Je 12 '63
Resounding cry. il Time 81:22 My 24 '63
Six days in Alabama: a journal. R. Gutwillig. Mlle 57:116-17+ S '63; Reply. T. C. Turner. 58:38+ D '63
Sunday school bombing. il Time 82:17 S 27 '63
Tension growing over race issue. il U S News 54:37-9 My 20 '63
Test for nonviolence. S. C. Rose. Christian Cent 80:714-16 My 29 '63
They fight a fire that won't go out. il Life 54:26-36 My 17 '63
Time to speak, by C. Morgan, jr. Review
New Repub 150:20+ My 23 '64. J. E. Patterson
Toward peace with justice in Birmingham. Christian Cent 80:515 Ap 24 '63
Truce team in Alabama. il U S News 55:28 O 7 '63
U.S. image not damaged by Birmingham riots; Charge outside agitation to deny own guilt. Sci N L 83:361 Je 8 '63
U.S. troops in Alabama; Governor, President, and the law; telegrams, text of law. G. Wallace; J. F. Kennedy. U S News 54: 40-1 My 27 '63
Violence obscures issue in Birmingham. Christian Cent 80:636 My 15 '63
Voices of Birmingham. D. Cort. il Nation 197:46-8 Jl 27 '63
Who is guilty in Birmingham? C. Morgan jr. Christian Cent 80:1195-6 O 2 '63
Why not enforce the law? Nation 196:413 My 18 '63

Politics and government

Beginning in Birmingham. V. Harding. il Reporter 28:13-19 Je 6 '63; Discussion. 29:5 Jl 4 '63
Birmingham: the fuse gets shorter. il Bsns W p32-3 S 28 '63
Bustling Birmingham; mayoralty election. R. Cleghorn. New Repub 148:9 Ap 20 '63
White sit-ins; segregationist vs. moderate mayor-council government. Newsweek 61: 26+ Ap 29 '63
Who is guilty in Birmingham? C. Morgan jr. Christian Cent 80:1195-6 O 2 '63

BIRMINGHAM, England
Race trouble in Birmingham, England, too. il U S News 56:102-4 Mr 23 '64

BIRMINGHAM-Southern college, Birmingham, Ala.
Genesee and Birmingham. M. Turnipseed. Christian Cent 80:1239 O 9 '63

BIRNBAUM, M. R.
From farmers' market to parking ramp. Am City 78:128+ Mr '63

BIRNBAUM, Max
Whose values should be taught? Sat R 47:60-2+ Je 20 '64

BIRNBAUM, Norman
Politics of the possible: the British scene. Nation 196:244-7 Mr 23 '63
Sir Alec takes over. Nation 197:316-18 N 16 '63
Stirrings in West Germany. Commentary 37:53-8 Ap '64

BIRNEY, Alice McLellan
Being wise in membership; affirming a new concept of parenthood. B. W. Overstreet. il PTA Mag 58:7-9 D '63

BIRNEY, Arthur A.
People you meet. Yachting 114:32-3+ D '63

BIRNEY, Earle
Looking from Oregon; poem. Atlan 214:146 N '64

About

Canadian chronicle. K. McRobbie. Poetry 103:268-9 Ja '64

BIRNIE, Whitt
My most exciting summer ever: in Europe! pors Seventeen 23:116-17+ Je '64

BIRNN, Roland
U.S. Coast guard auxiliary. See issues of Yachting

BIRNS, Harold
Good gracious! living in the Decibel arms. M. A. Guitar. il N Y Times Mag p55-6+ D 1 '63

BIRNSTIEL, Max L. and Flamm, W. G.
Intranuclear site of histone synthesis. bibliog Science 145:1435-7 S 25 '64
—and others
Nucleolus: a center of RNA methylation. bibliog Science 142:1577-80 D 20 '63

BIRO, Pete
Cobra coupe sequel. il Motor T 16:74-5 My '64
Sebring: Cobra vs. Ferrari. Motor T 16:58-61 Jl '64
Snake in the water! Hydrocobra. Motor T 16: 74-6 O '64
Touring car called Apollo. il Hot Rod 17:74-7 Jl '64

BIRRELL, Lowell M.
Back home in handcuffs. il por Newsweek 63:78 My 4 '64
Companies Birrell left behind. il por Bsns W p96+ My 2 '64

BIRREN, James E. and others
Reaction time as a function of the cardiac cycle in young adults. bibliog Science 140:195-6 Ap 12 '63

BIRTH. See Childbirth

BIRTH, Multiple
Multiple births foretold; detecting heart-beats of unborn babies. Sci N L 84:338 N 30 '63
Why are twins so special? C. B. Hicks. il Todays Health 41:18-21+ D '63
See also
Quintuplets

BIRTH certificates. See Registers of births, etc.

BIRTH control
Accenting the positive. America 108:389 Mr 23 '63
Advocate birth control. Sci N L 83:258 Ap 27 '63
Again, the pill; church's teaching on contraception. America 110:306-7 Mr 7 '64
Big breakthrough seen in birth control action. Sci N L 85:350 My 30 '64
Birth control: a new attitude by Catholics? U S News 55:11 S 9 '63
Birth control and policy. America 108:662 My 11 '63
Birth control and public aid: eastern Pennsylvania. H. W. Fry. Christian Cent 81: 438+ Ap 1 '64
Birth control and public policy. J. O'Gara. Commonweal 78:504 Ag 23 '63; Reply. E. J. Pawlak. 80:52+ Ap 3 '64
Birth control and the Council. G. Baum. Commonweal 81:280+ N 20 '64; Reply with rejoinder. R. W. Crooker. 81:515-17 Ja 15 '65
Birth control and the poor: a solution; Mecklenburg County, N.C. J. Shepherd. il Look 28:63-7 Ap 7 '64; Same abr. Read Digest 85:111-14 Ag '64
Birth control and welfare; concerning policy statement of New York state board of social welfare. Commonweal 79:560-1 F 7 '64
Birth control by surgery. J. Ridgeway. New Repub 151:9-11 N 14 '64
Birth control; Catholic attitude. America 111:476-7 O 24 '64
Birth control: Catholic opinion varies widely on Rock's new book. D. S. Greenberg. Science 140:791-2 My 17 '63
Birth control: Catholic problems. Commonweal 81:216 N 13 '64
Birth control: Catholics take a new look; excerpts from address, June 23, 1964. Paul VI. U S News 57:14 Jl 6 '64
Birth control devices and debates engross the U.S. il Life 54:37-40B My 10 '63
Birth control: end of a taboo. D. Burnham. Nation 200:85-6 Ja 25 '65
Birth control hot issue. E. Mirel. Sci N L 83: 309 My 18 '63
Birth control: how much federal help? U S News 54:11 Ap 29 '63
Birth control laws; changing Catholic attitude. America 111:544-5 N 7 '64
Birth control: National academy issues report calling for major effort in population planning. D. S. Greenberg. Science 140:281-2 Ap 19 '63; Reply. H. Frederiksen. 143: 197 Ja 17 '64
Birth control; our disgraceful ignorance. J. T. Edsall. il Nation 196:499-503 Je 15 '63
Birth control series. America 109:146 Ag 17 '63
Birth control: the pill and the church. il Newsweek 64:51-5 Jl 6 '64
Birth control, welfare funds, and the politics of Illinois. H. Bruno. il Reporter 28:32-5 Je 20 '63
Birth regulation; concerning an article by the Rev J. A. O'Brien. il Newsweek 62:82 S 9 '63; Reply. America 109:345-6 S 28 '63
Blackout on birth control; NBC-TV cancels program after Catholic bishops object. Newsweek 65:52 Ja 18 '65
Case for birth control. C. Senior. il Parents Mag 38:84-5+ O '63
Catholic parenthood; excerpt from address. W. M. Bekkers. Commonweal 78:143-4 Ap 26 '63
Catholics and birth control. J. O'Gara. Commonweal 78:320 Je 14 '63
Catholics and birth control; a bold re-examination. G. Barrett. Read Digest 83:77-82 N '63
Catholics support planned parenthood. Christian Cent 80:1021 Ag 21 '63
Catholics take a new look at the pill. J. Star. il Look 28:71-2+ S 8 '64
Child spacing. America 110:360 Mr 21 '64
Child spacing: the mathematical probabilities. A. J. De Bethune. bibliog il Science 142: 1629-34 D 27 '63; Discussion. 143:995, 1394; 144:365-6, 795, 1531 Mr 6, 27, Ap 24, My 15, Je 26 '64
Church and the pill. R. E. Hall. il Nation 199: 191-3 O 5 '64
Coming: new birth control measures. H. G. Lawson. Sci Digest 55:86-90 Mr '64
Conjugal love and conjugal morality. R. A. McCormick. America 110:38-42 Ja 11 '64
Contraception and Catholics: a new appraisal, by L. Dupré. Review
Commonweal 81:104 O 16 '64. R. T. Francoeur
Contraception and holiness. Review
Commonweal 81:360-2 D 4 '64. C. E. Curran
Debate on birth control; Catholic theologians. M. J. O'Neill. New Repub 151:9 Jl 4 '64
Doctor Rock's book; Catholic response. Commonweal 78:213-14 My 17 '63
Don't knock Dr Rock. M. Novak. America 108:728 My 25 '63; Reply. R. B. Moynihan. 109:1 Jl 6 '63
Dutch bishops on the pill. America 110:531 Ap 18 '64; Reply. 110:696 My 23 '64
Encore: no birth control. H. G. Lewis. Christian Cent 81:940 Jl 22 '64; Reply. C. Chotkowski. 81:1177 S 23 '64
Facts behind the momentous controversy about the church and the pill. J. C. G. Conniff. McCalls 92:52+ O '64
Family planning in an exploding population; Roman Catholic opinion. J. A. O'Brien. Christian Cent 80:1050-2 Ag 28 '63
Family planning in Ireland. America 109:724 D 7 '63
Family planning tricky with calendar method. Sci N L 85:21 Ja 11 '64
Family size. R. A. McCormick. America 110:1-2 Ja 4 '64
Father O'Brien's article. J. C. Knott. America 109:225 S 7 '63; Discussion. 109:333-4, 345-6 S 28 '63
Fertility and control. America 110:8-9 Ja 4 '64
For women only, by B. L. Cinberg. Review
America 110:620-1 My 9 '64
Has the time come? sign of a Catholic birth-control thaw. Newsweek 63:90 Je 8 '64
Husband and wife report. America 109:660-2 N 23 '63; Discussion. 110:1, 270 Ja 4, F 29 '64
Illinois birth control policy in peril. Christian Cent 80:389-90 Mr 27 '63
Illinois Senate ousts a birth control champion. Christian Cent 80:637-8 My 15 '63
Judgment on the pill; conference of priests and doctors at St Joseph's seminary, Edmonton, Alberta. America 110:782 Je 6 '64
Land of the free; state-sponsored family planning in Illinois. America 109:68 Jl 20 '63
Let's end the war over birth control. J. A. O'Brien. Christian Cent 80:1361-4 N 6 '63

BIRTH control—*Continued*
Love, O love, O careful love. J. H. Adams. il America 109:481-4 O 26 '63; Discussion. 109:658-9; 110:1, 149 N 23 '63, Ja 4, F 1 '64
Most vexing problem. Newsweek 64:71 O 19 '64
Need for birth control. Sci N L 85:221 Ap 4 '64
Neo-Puritans; birth-control clinics of Maryland. America 110:501 Ap 11 '64
New approach; debate at the second Vatican council. il Newsweek 64:86 N 9 '64
New battle over birth control. A. Q. Maisel. Read Digest 82:54-9 F '63
New boom in birth control. R. Hermann. il Sci Digest 54:5-9 Jl '63
No more Galileos; bishops plea for modification of Roman Catholic objections. Time 84:51 N 6 '64
Old birth-control methods studied. Sci Digest 54:78 D '63
Outlook for world population. J. M. Stycos. Science 146:1435-40 D 11 '64
Pill for Catholics? Newsweek 63:73 My 25 '64
Pope's words; with statement. America 111: 33 Jl 11 '64
Population and the Council. America 109:477 O 26 '63
Population and the pill. W. E. Boggs. New Repub 148:13-14 Ap 13 '63
Population control; concerning report by the National academy of sciences. New Repub 148:7 Ap 27 '63; Reply. L. H. Day. 149:31 Jl 6 '63
Population myths. D. H. Wrong. Commentary 38:61-4 N '64
Population: new U.S. interest in offering assistance reveals lags in underdeveloped nations. D. S. Greenberg. Science 143: 1016-17 Mr 6 '64
Population: planning group hears encouraging reports on efforts to start Latin American programs. D. S. Greenberg. Science 144:513-15 My 1 '64; Reply with rejoinder. W. D. Bellamy. 144:1409-10 Je 19 '64
Population planning: missions told that U.S. is now receptive to requests for some assistance. D. S. Greenberg. Science 140:1291 Je 21 '63
Population planning: 1963 marked by reduction of controversy and shift in government attitude. D. S. Greenberg. Science 142:1554-6 D 20 '63
President approves population studies. Christian Cent 80:605 My 8 '63
Public policy on birth control; possible attitudes of the Catholic community on state involvement. J. E. Dunsford. America 111: 132-4 Ag 8 '64
Question of morality. Christian Cent 80:571-2 My 1 '63; Discussion. 80:833 Je 26 '63
Regulate birth rate. Sci N L 83:372 Je 15 '63
Report on fertility research. W. J. Gibbons. Cath World 197:44-50 Ap '63
Responsible parenthood; symposium. Commonweal 80:311-38+ Je 5 '64; Discussion. 80:486 Jl 10; 548 Ag 7 '64
Rethinking birth control; Roman Catholic views. Christian Cent 81:1133-4 S 16 '64
Rhythm method doomed. Sci N L 85:182 Mr 21 '64
Rhythm method failure. Sci N L 85:109 F 15 '64
Rhythm symposium; CAIP conference. America 111:540-1 N 7 '64
Roman Catholics: a new view on birth control; Rev. L. Janssens endorses oral contraceptive pills. il Time 83:59-60 Ap 10 '64; Discussion. America 110:563, 751 Ap 25, My 30 '64
Roman Catholics; answer on the way. Time 84:74 Jl 3 '64
Say little, do a lot; official U.S. government policy. Time 85:55 Ja 29 '65
Sex behavior neglected. Sci N L 83:322 My 25 '63
Speaking out; Catholic mother tells, why I believe in birth control. R. Ruether. Sat Eve Post 237:12+ Ap 4 '64
Speaking out: it is time to end the birth-control fight. J. Rock. Sat Eve Post 236: 10+ Ap 20 '63
Steps toward legalized birth control. Christian Cent 81:1581 D 23 '64
Tell me, doctor. G. Pincus. Ladies Home J 80:50+ Je '63
Temperature method. A. W. Kane. il America 110:596+ My 2 '64; Discussion. 110:768-70 My 30 '64
Time has come: a Catholic doctor's proposals to end the battle over birth control, by J. Rock. Review
America 108:608-11 Ap 27 '63. J. S. Duhamel
Christian Cent 80:699-700 My 29 '63
Commonweal 78:392-7 Jl 5 '63. H. Ratner and R. M. Brown; Discussion. 78:480-3 Ag 9 '63
Nat R 15:70 Jl 30 '63. R. J. Needles
Parents Mag 38:38 S '63. R. E. Hall
To control births; support for worldwide program. il Newsweek 61:62 Ap 29 '63
Unmanaged news; contraceptives at state expense to women on relief. America 108:701 My 18 '63
Urge expanded birth control study. Christian Cent 80:1068 S 4 '63
Use of population as weapon. W. Davis. il Sci N L 83:115 F 23 '63
Welfare birth control. America 110:157 F 1 '64
What modern Catholics think about birth control, ed. by W. Birmingham. Review
Commonweal 81:523-5 Ja 15 '65. G. Wills
Where is the consensus? concerning Father L. Janssens article on the progesterone pill. Commonweal 79:737 Mr 20 '64; Reply. M. Novak. 80:149 Ap 24 '64
Whither the pill? R. A. McCormick. Cath World 199:207-14 Jl '64
Will the church's teaching on birth control change? excerpt from Contemporary moral theology. J. C. Ford and G. Kelly. Cath World 198:87-93 N '63
Women and rhythm. Commonweal 77:607-8 Mr 8 '63; Discussion. 78:137-9, 306-7, 399-401 Ap 26, Je 7, Jl 5 '63
See also
Church and social problems
Contraceptives

Canada

Spacing births; families in Montreal test the control of fertility by means of the thermometer. R. B. Ganley. America 110:366-7 Mr 21 '64

China (People's Republic)

China's second experiment. F. Nossal. Nation 196:503-5 Je 15 '63

India

How to save a few million lives, and save money at the same time. J. Fischer. Harper 229:14+ O '64; Discussion. 229:4+ D '64

Japan

Birth control in Japan. W. Clifford. il Look 27:60-1 F 26 '63

Latin America

Brake on the Alianza. H. Rosenhouse. New Repub 150:19-21 Mr 28 '64
Latin America turns to family planning. A. Q. Maisel. Read Digest 84:189-90+ Ap '64
Latin-American Catholics and birth control. L. Gross. il Look 28:93-4+ Jl 14 '64

Mexico

Mexico resists the pill. A. F. Corwin. Nation 198:477-80 My 11 '64

Taiwan

Study in fertility control. B. Berelson and R. Freedman. il Sci Am 210:29-37 bibliog(p 150) My '64

United States

See Birth control

BIRTH defects. See Deformities

BIRTH rate
See also
Birth control
Population, Increase of

Europe

Baby boom moves from U.S. to Europe. il U S News 56:67 Mr 30 '64

France

L'amour for la patrie. Time 82:31 Jl 26 '63

Japan

Japan's birth rate, the trend turns. E. Chapin. il N Y Times Mag p44+ O 25 '64

United States

Baby boom moves from U.S. to Europe. il U S News 56:67 Mr 30 '64
Boom in babies: is it slowing down? il U S News 57:12 S 28 '64
End of the baby boom? Newsweek 63:94 Je 15 '64

BIRTH rate—United States—*Continued*
End to the baby boom. il U S News 56:83-4 Mr 2 '64
Have stork's wings been clipped a bit? il Bsns W p28 Jl 25 '64
Not so explosive. Time 83:74 Je 12 '64
BIRTH; story. See Berriault, G.
BIRTHDAY cake. See Cake
BIRTHDAY parties. See Childrens parties
BIRTHDAY party; story. See Berriault, G.
BIRTHDAY party; story. See Mrozek, S.
BIRTHDAY pie; drama. See McGowan, J.
BIRTHDAY present; story. See Wendland, A.
BISCAYNE BAY
Small rebellion in Miami. P. Redford. Harper 228:96-8+ F '64
BISCH, Jørgen
This is the China I saw. il por Nat Geog Mag 126:591-640 N '64
BISCH, Louis E.
Turn your sickness into an asset. Read Digest 83:90-3 D '63
BISCHOFF, Henry
Helping foreign students. America 109:566-8 N 9 '63
BISCUIT and cracker industry
See also
National biscuit company
BISCUITS
Cloud biscuits for heavenly eating. il Bet Hom & Gard 42:88 S '64
Here are two new biscuits. Sunset 132:128 F '64
Ingenuity with refrigerator biscuits. Sunset 130:235 Ap '63
BISE, Margaret
Parents help with audio-visual aids. Wilson Lib Bul 37:787-8+ My '63
BISHER, Furman
Get any hits Stan? Sat Eve Post 236:30+ My 25 '63
BISHKO, C. J.
(comp) Articles and other books received; Spain and Portugal. See issues of American historical review
BISHOP, Amelia. See Bottorff, O. jt. auth.
BISHOP, Barry C.
How we climbed Everest. il pors Nat Geog Mag 124:474-507 O '63
Mount Rainier; testing ground for Everest. il por Nat Geog Mag 123:688-711 My '63
BISHOP, Claire Huchet
Information trap. Commonweal 79:228-9 N 15 '63
Learning about poverty. Commonweal 81:201-2 N 6 '64
Learning bigotry. Commonweal 80:264-6 My 22 '64
Selected list of children's books. Commonweal 79:229-39 N 15 '63
—and Graves, E. M.
Selected list of children's books. Commonweal 80:266-75 My 22 '64
BISHOP, Elizabeth
Burglar of Babylon; poem. New Yorker 40: 56-7 N 21 '64
(tr) See De Melo Neto, J. C. From The death and life of a Severino
BISHOP, Gloria Wade
Four and a half days in Atlanta's jails. Atlan 214:68-70 Jl '64
BISHOP, Jerry E.
How we're fighting illness from animals. Sci Digest 53:54-7 My '63
BISHOP, Jim
Last loving remembrance of John F. Kennedy; excerpts from Day in the life of President Kennedy. por Good H 158:71-4+ Mr '64
Off the cuff. A. Marple. Writer 77:7-8 O '64
BISHOP, Julia Ann
Helping neglectful parents. bibliog f Ann Am Acad 355:82-9 S '64
BISHOP, Leo K.
Pulpit-pew problem. Christian Cent 81:968 Jl 29 '64
BISHOP, M. P. and others
Intracranial self-stimulation in man. bibliog Science 140:394-6 Ap 26 '63
BISHOP, Norman I. See Weaver, E. C. jt. auth.
BISHOP, Stephen H. and Campbell, J. W.
Carbamyl phosphate synthesis in the earthworm lumbricus terrestris. bibliog Science 142:1583-5 D 20 '63
BISHOPS
Baiting the layman. J. O'Gara. Commonweal 81:32 O 2 '64; Reply. W. J. Smith. 81:240-1 N 13 '64
Bishops and responsibility; meaning of collegiality. America 110:249 F 22 '64
Bishops differ on conference powers. Christian Cent 80:1457 N 27 '63
Bishops vote rule by divine right. Christian Cent 80:1394 N 13 '63
Cardinal Spellman reminisces. Christian Cent 80:1531 D 4 '63
Church's Catholicity; council of bishops. America 111:372 O 3 '64
Collegiality: Catholic episcopate; with editorial comment. L. M. Orsy. America 110:754, 760-3 My 30 '64
First council of the Vatican: the American experience. by J. Hennesey. Review Commonweal 79:574-6 F 7 '64. J. Ratté
Future role of bishops. W. M. Abbott. America 110:6 Ja 4 '64
Grass-roots collegiality. America 110:664 My 16 '64
How is the Council going? G. Weigel. America 109:730-2 D 7 '63
Papal primacy at Vatican II. America 111: 343 S 26 '64
Paul VI and the bishops. O. Hastings. il Reporter 29:23-5 D 19 '63
Pope and bishops. G. Baum. Commonweal 79: 188-91 N 8 '63
Roberts ruling; episode in Los Angeles. America 111:100 Ag 1 '64
Role of bishops in relation to the papacy. G. Baum. Cath World 198:94-9 N '63
U.S. bishops want new look at church-state issue. Christian Cent 80:1357-8 N 6 '63
Unprecedented changes. America 108:323 Mr 9 '63
Vatican II: a look ahead. D. J. O'Hanlon. America 109:347-9+ S 28 '63
Vatican II re-educates the American bishops. J. Cogley. il N Y Times Mag p35+ N 22 '64
See also
Vatican council, 2d
BISHOP'S company. See Theater, Traveling
BISLETI, Sieuwke, marchesa
Marchesa Sieuwke Bisleti in Kenya. S. G. Wood. il pors Vogue 142:64-7 Jl '63
BISMARCK, Elisabeth von, countess
Countess Ferdinand von Bismarck. F. Nourissier. il pors Vogue 142:180-5+ S 15 '63
BISMUTH
Isotopes
Negative temperature coefficient of resistance in bismuth I. P. C. Souers and G. Jura. bibliog il Science 143:467-9 Ja 31 '64
BISON
Rare European bison born at Philadelphia zoo. il Sci N L 85:387 Je 20 '64
BISPLINGHOFF, R. L.
Supersonic transport; with biographical sketch. Sci Am 210:18, 25-35 Je '64
BISS, Gerald
London doctor tells his story; interview, ed. by J. Fromm. por U S News 55:65-6 N 4 '63
BISSELL, Richard
Lima I love you, oddly enough. Holiday 35: 46-55+ Je '64
BISSELL, Richard Mervin, jr
Game to the end. il por Newsweek 62:20+ Ag 12 '63
BISSIER, Julius
Incantations in color. il por Time 82:70-1 N 8 '63
BISSIÈRE, Roger
Venice: the biennale. J. Guth and F. Guth. il Craft Horiz 24:48 S '64
BIT of gravy; story. See Donohue, H. E. F.
BITES, Venomous. See Venom
BITKER, Marjorie M.
Blessings of life before breakfast. Read Digest 84:56-8 Ja '64
BITS, Lathe. See Lathes
BITSIOS, Dimitri S.
Efforts of Force commended. UN Mo Chron 1:12 O '64
BITTERBRUSH
Needed, a who's who for shrubs. W. B. Morse. il Am For 70:30-1+ My '64
BITTERMAN, M. E.
Evolution of intelligence; with biographical sketch. Sci Am 212:17, 92-100 Ja '65
BITTERSWEET
Bittersweet. D. L. Roberson. il Horticulture 41:500 O '63
BITTLE, Camilla R.
Happily ever after; story. Redbook 123:144-58 Ag '64
Sugar-bowl dream; story. McCalls 90:70-1 Jl '63
Whole wide world; story. Ladies Home J 80: 68-9 Ja '63
Why do you want to write? Writer 77:18-19 Ag '64
BITTLE, William E. See Geis, G. jt. auth.
BITTNER, William
Irish pub. Atlan 211:112+ F '63
Oases outside Dublin. Atlan 213:168+ Mr '64

BITUMINOUS coal industry. See Coal industry
BITUMINOUS coal mines. See Coal mines and mining
BITUMINOUS coal operators association
Coal miners and the new coal contract. Mo Labor R 87:III-IV My '64
BITUMINOUS sand
Boiling the oil out of stubborn sands; Athabasca oil sands. il Bsns W p66 F 9 '63
BIVALVES. See Mollusks
BIXENSTINE, V. Edwin
Empiricism in latter-day behavioral science. bibliog Science 145:464-7 Jl 31 '64
BIZET, Georges
Best grand-opera Carmen on records. C. L. Osborne. il Hi Fi 14:63-4 S '64
Callas Carmen. P. L. Miller. il Am Rec G 31:403 Ja '65
Carmen. Criticism
New Yorker 40:182 O 10 '64
Opera N 28:32 D 14 '63
Leontyne Price as Carmen. P. L. Miller. il Am Rec G 31:10-12 S '64
On records; R. Resnik's Carmen. Opera N 28:37 Mr 14 '64
On records; L. Price's Carmen. Opera N 29: 35 N 14 '64
Regina Resnik's Carmen. G. L. Mayer. il Am Rec G 30:382-3+ Ja '64
BIZZI, Emilio, and Brooks, D. C.
Pontine reticular formation: relation to lateral geniculate nucleus during deep sleep. bibliog Science 141:270-2 Jl 19 '63
—and others
Vestibular nuclei: activity of single neurons during natural sleep and wakefulness. bibliog il Science 145:414-15 Jl 24 '64
BJERKOE, Ethel Hall
George Hepplewhite, English cabinet-maker. Hobbies 69:90-2 Jl '64
Thomas Sheraton. Hobbies 69:90-1 Ag '64
BJOERKO, Treaty of. See Russo-German treaty, 1905
BJOERLING, Rolf
Rolf. Newsweek 63:51 Mr 30 '64
BJONER, Ingrid
Countess from the North; interview, ed. by R. D. Daniels. por Opera N 29:27 Ja 2 '64
BJÖRLING, Jussi
Historical records. A. Favia-Artsay. por Hobbies 67:30-1 F '63
BLACIC, J. D. See Griggs, D. T. jt. auth.
BLACK, A. L. and others
Water turnover in cattle. bibliog Science 144: 876-8 My 15 '64
BLACK, Alice, pseud.
No cure as yet. America 110:712-14 My 23 '64
BLACK, Ann
Dream of spring. Recreation 56:62-3 F '63
BLACK, B. Coursin
Proof paper; darkroom in the sun. Sch Arts 63:11-13 My '64
BLACK, Barbara
Before winter comes. Pop Gard 14:18-21+ N '63
Best time of year: spring planting. Pop Gard 14:28-32 Mr '63
Beware of garden gyps (cont) Pop Gard 14: 52+ Ap '63
Biennials. Pop Gard 14:39+ Jl '63
Daylilies, midsummer delight. Pop Gard 15: 71+ Jl '64
Gardener's guide to the New York world's fair. Horticulture 42:12+ My '64
Have fun, competing in a flower show. Pop Gard 14:18-19+ My '63
More light on African-violets. Flower Grower 50:28-9+ S '63
Peonies. Pop Gard 14:30-2+ S '63
Roses. Pop Gard 15:24-6 S '64
Two months of glorious bloom from tulips. Pop Gard 15:8-10 N '64
What a team, what a garden. Flower Grower 51:28-9+ Je '64
BLACK, Eugene R.
Brighter than 400 candles. Sr Schol 84:13T+ F 21 '64
BLACK, Fred B. Jr
Long short cut. por Bsns W p28+ My 30 '64
BLACK, Harold
Reporter at large. C. Trillin. New Yorker 39:50+ Jl 27 '63
BLACK, Hillel
Scandal of educational testing; excerpt from They shall not pass. Sat Eve Post 236:72+ N 9 '63
This is war. Sat Eve Post 237:60-3 Ja 25 '64
BLACK, Hugo La Fayette
Civil-rights rulings: what they mean: excerpts from statements. por U S News 57:41 D 28 '64
What the Court said about congressional districts; excerpts from statement. por U S News 56:32 Mr 2 '64
About
Douglas vs. Black: old friends fall out. por U S News 54:20 Je 17 '63
Justice Black and the absolute. J. Grossman. Commentary 36:244-8 S '63
Limits that create liberty & the liberty that creates limits. il pors Time 84:48-50+ O 9 '64
BLACK, Irma Simonton, and Blos, J. W.
Should preschool children be taught the three R's? PTA Mag 59:24-6 bibliog(p36)
BLACK, James F.
Weather control: use of asphalt coatings to tap solar energy. Science 139:226-7 Ja 18 '63
BLACK, John D.
Sheepskin squeeze. Time 81:64 Mr 1 '63
BLACK, Kitty
(tr) See Anouilh, J. Rehearsal
BLACK, Lou
Burning desire; original banjoist with New Orleans rhythm kings. New Yorker 39:37-9 N 2 '63
BLACK, Mary C.
Erastus Salisbury Field and the sources of his inspiration. Antiques 83:201-6 F '63
BLACK, Maurice M. and Ansley, H. R.
Histone staining with ammoniacal silver. bibliog Science 143:693-5 F 14 '64
BLACK, Max
Books. Sci Am 210:141-2+ Mr '64
BLACK, Perry, and Myers, R. E.
Visual function of the forebrain commissures in the chimpanzee. bibliog Science 146:799-800 N 6 '64
BLACK, Robert F. and Laughlin, W. S.
Anangula: a geologic interpretation of the oldest archeologic site in the Aleutians. bibliog Science 143:1321-2 Mr 20 '64
BLACK, Sam
Australian visit. il Sch Arts 64:31-4 O '64
Critics criticized. Sch Arts 63:2 My '64
BLACK, Shirley Temple
Tomorrow I'll be thirty-five. por McCalls 90: 83+ My '63
BLACK, Susan M.
Grave collector. Harper 228:26+ Je '64
New York for next to nothing. Holiday 34: 108+ Jl '63
Ramses to Rembrandt to Wright; story. Atlan 212:71-3 S '63
Reporter at large. New Yorker 39:63-4+ D 7; 89-91+ D 14 '63
BLACK, Virginia M.
Cruisemanship. Travel 120:35-7 N '63
BLACK and Decker manufacturing company
At the top and busy climbing. il Bsns W p91+ N 21 '64
BLACK angels; story. See Friedman, B. J.
BLACK bear hunting. See Bear hunting
BLACK bears. See Bears
BLACK blizzards. See Dust storms
BLACK brant. See Geese, Wild
BLACK death
Black death. W. L. Langer. il Sci Am 210: 114-18+ bibliog(p 152) F '64
See also
Plague
BLACK-drum fishing. See Drumfish fishing
BLACK-footed ferret. See Ferrets
BLACK-footed gooneys. See Albatrosses
BLACK Hawks (hockey team) See Hockey teams
BLACK-headed gulls. See Gulls
BLACK HILLS, S.D.
Magic mountains of the West. H. Bradshaw and V. Bradshaw. il Todays Health 42:34-7+ Ag '64
BLACK HILLS passion play. See Passion plays
BLACK is my favorite color; story. See Malamud, B.
BLACK Jews of Harlem (sect) See Sects
BLACK light. See Infrared rays
BLACK magic. See Witchcraft
BLACK marlin fishing. See Fishing; Salt water fishing
BLACK Muslim movement
Black Muslims. M. Berger. il Horizon 6:48-65 Wint '64
Black Muslim hope: C. Clay. Sports Illus 20: 8 Mr 16 '64
Enter Muhammed? Nat R 14:519-21 Jl 2 '63
Feud within the Black Muslims. G. Samuels. il N Y Times Mag p 17+ Mr 22 '64
I like the word black; increasingly militant mood. il Newsweek 61:27-8 My 6 '63
Integration: as Negro champ views it; excerpts from news conference. C. Clay. il U S News 56:20 Mr 16 '64
Malcolm X; charismatic demagogue: interview, ed. by A. B. Southwick. Malcolm X. Christian Cent 80:740-1 Je 5 '63

BLACK Muslim movement—*Continued*
Miami notebook: Cassius Clay and Malcolm X. G. Plimpton. il Harper 228:54-61 Je '64
Muhammad speaks. J. O'Gara. Commonweal 78:130 Ap 26 '63
My face is black, by C. E. Lincoln. Review
Christian Cent 82:82 Ja 20 '65. G. S. Wilmore, jr
Negro racists. Nation 196:278 Ap 6 '63; Reply. J. Mahrer. 196:inside cover Ap 20 '63
New move by the Black Muslims. il U S News 54:14 Mr 11 '63
Now hear the message to the Black Muslims from their leader; with photographs by E. Arnold. E. Muhammad. Esquire 59:97-101 Ap '63
Ominous Malcolm X exits from the Muslims. M. Crawford. il Life 56:40-40A Mr 20 '64
Two ways: Black Muslim and N.A.A.C.P. G. Samuels. il N Y Times Mag p26-7+ My 12 '63
When the word is given, by L. E. Lomax. Review
Nation 198:56-8 Ja 13 '64. W. Morris
Newsweek 62:107 N 4 '63
White devil's day is almost over; with report by G. Parks. il Life 54:22-33+ My 31 '63
Why Black Muslims are focusing on the Nation's capital now. il U S News 54:24 My 27 '63
Why 400,000,000 follow Mohammed. R. Payne. il N Y Times Mag p 18+ Ag 4 '63; Discussion. p2+ Ag 25 '63

BLACK raspberries. See Raspberries

BLACK snakeroot
Big, bold exuberant perennials. C. Holway. il Horticulture 41:164 Mr '63

BLACK snakes. See Snakes

BLACK snowflakes; story. See Horgan, P.

BLACK walnut trees. See Walnut trees

BLACKBURN, Albert W.
Blackburn memo criticizes TFX decision. Aviation W 78:79-83 Je 3 '63

BLACKBURN, Fred A.
In riverbottom wilds. il Liv Wildn 83:5-10 Spring '63
Marten and I. Nat Parks Mag 38:11-14 Ap '64

BLACKETT, Patrick M. S.
Sensible shopping in the supermarket of science. UNESCO Courier 16:30-1 Jl '63

BLACKJACK (game)
Hit me easy. il Newsweek 63:64 Ap 13 '64
It's bye! bye! blackjack. D. E. Scherman. il Sports Illus 20:18-20+ Ja 13 '64; Same abr. Read Digest 84:223-6 Je '64
Professor who breaks the bank. P. O'Neil. il Life 56:80-2+ Mr 27 '64

BLACKLISTING
Fear on trial, by J. H. Faulk. Review
New Repub 151:17-18+ D 5 '64. R. M. Elman
Newsweek 64:105-6 N 16 '64
Sat R 47:34-5 N 14 '64. G. Seldes
Jaime García Terrés and the *lista negra*. F. H. Wardlaw. Harper 230:16+ Ja '65
Ordeal of John Henry Faulk. J. P. Blank. il Look 27:80-2+ My 7 '63
Still with us; The defenders. Commonweal 79:495-6 Ja 31 '64
Under two flags; P. Seeger blacklisted by NBC, CBS and ABC. Nation 196:279 Ap 6 '63
See also
Communism—United States—Anti-Communist measures

BLACKMAIL. See Extortion

BLACKMAN, Honor
All honor Honor. A. Carthew. il pors N Y Times Mag p73-5 Mr 1 '64

BLACKMAN, Leonard S.
Teaching machines and the mentally retarded. Sch Life 46:10-12 N '63

BLACKMAN, Robert L.
Bob Blackman and his Big Green. C. S. Wren. il pors Look 28:89-92+ N 3 '64

BLACKMAN, Samuel G.
Quarterbacking a nation's news. J. F. Fixx. por Sat R 46:48-9 Ag 10 '63

BLACKMON, Rosemary
New Japan. Vogue 144:84-5+ Ag 15 '64

BLACKOUTS. See Loss of consciousness

BLACKPOOL, England
Blackpool: the English fun-and-chips holiday town. S. Delaney. il Vogue 141:100-1+ Je '63

BLACKSMITHING
See also
Forging
Horseshoeing

BLACKSMITHS
Shoein' horses; a mighty man is he; training of farriers. W. B. Norse. il Am For 70:32-4 O '64

BLACKSTONE, Bruce I.
More teachers for business education. Sch Life 45:23 My '63
Shorthand: 60 B.C. to 1884. Sch Life 47:12 N '64

BLACKWELL, Sir Basil
Profiles; B. H. Blackwell, ltd, Oxford. V. Mehta. il New Yorker 40:66+ O 31 '64

BLACKWELL, Elizabeth
America's first woman physician. J. Lentz. por Todays Health 42:36-7+ Ja '64

BLACKWELL, R. Quentin, and Huang, J. T. H.
Abnormal hemoglobin studies in Taiwan aborigines. bibliog Science 139:771 F 22 '63

BLACKWOOD, Paul E.
Science in the elementary school. Sch Life 47:13-15+ N '64

BLADDER
Surgery
Severe bladder defect repaired by surgery. Sci N L 83:198 Mr 30 '63

BLADES, Saw. See Saws

BLAGONRAVOV, A. A.
Academician Blagonravov to Dr Dryden; letter, August 1, 1963. Dept State Bul 49:405 S 9 '63

BLAIK, Earl H.
Red Blaik predicts: two-platoon football is coming back; ed. by T. Cohane. por Look 27:94+ N 5 '63
Truce team in Alabama. il por U S News 55:28 O 7 '63

BLAINE, Graham B.
Children of divorce. Atlan 211:98-101 Mr '63

BLAINE, Nell
Jane streeters; Jane street group at Knoedler's, New York. il por Newsweek 62:100 S 23 '63

BLAIR, Abbie
Family for Freddie. Read Digest 85:49-52 D '64
If you're thinking of adoption. Parents Mag 39:52-3+ Ag '64

BLAIR, Gordon
Plumbing for horsepower. Hot Rod 17:78-80 Ag '64
Truth about ram tuning. Hot Rod 17:78-81 Jl '64

BLAIR, James P.
Home to lonely Tristan da Cunha. il Nat Geog Mag 125:60-81 Ja '64

BLAIR, John M.
Annals of legislation. R. Harris. New Yorker 40:48-50+ Mr 14; 80+ Mr 21 '64

BLAIR, Lewis Harvie
Southerner's answer to the Negro question. C. V. Woodward. il Reporter 30:39-44 F 27 '64

BLAIR, Lynn
Bright gifts; interview, ed. by R. D. Daniels. por Opera N 27:32 Mr 16 '63

BLAIR, W. Granger
Visit with Ben Gurion in the desert. N Y Times Mag p 16+ Ja 12 '64

BLAIR, William L.
Construct a milliwatt meter. Electr World 71:82-3 Mr '64

BLAIR House. See Washington, D.C.—Historic houses, etc.

BLAIS, Marie Claire
Reporter at large. E. Wilson. New Yorker 40:104+ N 21 '64

BLAISDELL, Harold F.
Americana of angling. Field & S 69:46-7+ My '64
April trout look down. por Outdoor Life 131: 72+ Ap '63
Big bugs bug big pike. por Outdoor Life 134:42-3+ S '64
Smelt have me hooked. por Outdoor Life 131: 30-1+ F '63
Weatherproof fishing. Outdoor Life 133:44-5+ Je '64

BLAISDELL publishing company
Blaisdell will publish history of physics series. Pub W 184:65 N 11 '63

BLAKE, Elias, Jr
Ghosts of dead stereotypes. Negro Hist Bul 26:212-14 Ap '63

BLAKE, Eugene Carson
Let's put Christ in Christmas. por Ebony 19:64 D '63
Union proposal two years later; excerpt from reply appended to The challenge to reunion, by R. M. Brown and D. H. Scott. Christian Cent 80:394-8 Mr 27 '63
about
Blake's second thoughts. il por Time 85:89 Ja 29 '65
Catholics honor Blake as racial reconciler. Christian Cent 81:133 Ja 29 '64
March on Gwynn Oak park. il por Time 82: 17-18 Jl 12 '63
United Presbyterian general assembly. P. R. Carlson. Christian Cent 81:812+ Je 17 '64

BLAKE, Harlan M. and Jones, W. K.
In defense of antitrust. Fortune 70:135+ Ag '64
BLAKE, Patricia
How the U.S. funeral has grown. Life 55: 107-8 S 20 '63
Long research and the happy payoff. Life 56:88-9 Ap 3 '64
BLAKE, Peter
Better than mere cubage. Arch Forum 119:124 D '63
Can New York be saved? Sat R 48:16-18+ Ja 23 '65
Secret scrapbook of an architectural scavenger. Arch Forum 121:81-114 Ag '64
Speaking out; excerpt from God's own junkyard. por Sat Eve Post 236:14+ O 5 '63
BLAKE, R. L. and others
Solar X-ray spectrum below 25 angstroms. Science 146:1037-8 N 20 '64
BLAKE, Robert R. and Mouton, J. S.
Breakthrough in organization development; part I: how the grid program should work. Harvard Bsns R 42:135-8 N '64
BLAKE, Rosemary
Choicest co-ed. por Esquire 60:74 S '63
BLAKE, William
Key to William Blake; Mellon lectures at the National gallery of art, Washington. M. W. Hess. Christian Cent 80:1027-8 Ag 21 '63
William Blake: poet, printer, prophet, by G. Keynes. Review
Nation 200:91-2 Ja 25 '65. J. E. Grant
BLAKEMORE, Barbara
When Redbook looks for stories. Writer 77:26 D '64
BLAKEMORE, W. B.
If Tom is half as old as Will ... Christian Cent 81:489-92 Ap 15 '64
BLAKESLEE, Alton L.
Can diet prevent heart attacks? Sat Eve Post 237:66-7 Ja 25 '64
Today's health news. See issues of Today's health
—and Stamler, Jeremiah
Your heart and your future; excerpts from Your heart has nine lives. Todays Health 42:23-5+ Jl '64
BLAKEY, G. Robert
Discrimination, unions and Title VII. America 111:210-12 Ag 29 '64
BLANCH, Lesley
God rest ye merry teddy bear; excerpt from Under a lilac-bleeding star. Vogue 142:102+ D '63
Star of Venus. Vogue 144:194-201 N 1 '64
BLANCHARD, Duncan C.
Sea-to-air transport of surface active material. bibliog Science 146:396-7 O 16 '64
BLANCHARD, Felix Anthony
Chip off the old Doc. T. Cohane. il pors Look 28:99-102+ D 1 '64
BLANCHARD, Felix Anthony, 3d
Chip off the old Doc. T. Cohane. il pors Look 28:99-102+ D 1 '64
BLANCHARD, Fessenden S.
Hudson River: cruising gateway. Yachting 113:42-5+ Mr '63
BLANCHARD, Hazel A.
NEA convention, 1963 style. NEA J 52:23 F '63
NEA's new membership requirements. NEA J 52:46-7 Ap '63
Vast, unhurried poise, good will, and honesty. PTA Mag 57:20 F '63
BLANCHARD, J. R.
California's problem building adds wings. Library J 89:4750-2 D 1 '64
BLANCHARD springs caverns. See Caves
BLANCHETTE, Herbert W.
Second hundred years. Negro Hist Bul 27: 180 Ap '64
BLANCO, Antonio, and Zinkham, W. H.
Lactate dehydrogenases in human testes. bibliog Science 139:601-2 F 15 '63
BLAND-CARTER, Lillie
Is this my heritage? mother to son; poem. Negro Hist Bul 27:84 Ja '64
Poem: Who is my neighbor? that would I know. Negro Hist Bul 27:28 N '63
We walk in darkness; poem. Negro Hist Bul 27:86 Ja '64
BLANK, David M.
Man for all seasons at CBS. por Bsns W p 126-8+ Ag 10 '63
BLANK, Joseph P.
Atlanta: aftermath of a tragedy. Redbook 121: 52-3+ Je '63
Boy's trial by fire. Read Digest 83:91-6 N '63
Child is lost. Redbook 120:48-9+ F '63
Incredible escape. Read Digest 84:159-62+ My '64
Ordeal of John Henry Faulk. Look 27:80-2+ My 7 '63
(ed) See Bucky, T. L. Einstein: an intimate memoir
BLANK, Martin, and Feig, Steven
Electric fields across water-nitrobenzene interfaces. bibliog Science 141:1173-4 S 20 '63
BLANKETS
Baby blankets: a minority report. Consumer Rep 29:215-16 My '64
See also
Electric blankets, coverlets, etc.
BLANTON, Smiley
Can we learn not to hate? ed. by A. Gordon. Good H 156:73+ F '63
BLARNEY castle
Blarney stone. il Sunset 131:32 D '63
BLASER, Larry
Stereo indicator light circuit. Electr World 69:72 My '63
BLASICK, Henry J.
Determination in Baytown. Library J 88:4538-40 D 1 '63
BLASINGAME, Ralph, Jr
188 in Pa; summary. Wilson Lib Bul 37:834 Je '63
Pennsylvania LA conference hears first report on Blasingame survey; excerpts from report. Library J 89:4767-8 D 1 '64
Recruitment, a part of library development. ALA Bul 57:450-2 My '63
about
Pa. state librarian honored. Library J 88: 2484 Je 15 '63
Top library posts involved in two major job changes. Library J 88:4341 N 15 '63
BLASIS, Carlo
1844 letter from Italy to Denmark. L. Moore. il por Dance Mag 38:52-3+ F '64
BLASS, Walter P.
Economic planning, European-style. bibliog f Harvard Bsns R 41:109-20 S '63
BLASSINGAME, John W.
Negro chaplains in the Civil war. bibliog Negro Hist Bul 27:24+ O '63
BLASSINGAME, Wyatt
Backwater bass. pors Field & S 68:38-40+ Ap '64
Chaos in heaven. Field & S 68:38-9+ Ja '64
Millions of dam fish. Outdoor Life 133:34-5+ Ja '64
BLAST furnaces
Hot breath of Armco's Amanda. il Fortune 69:133-5 My '64
BLASTING
See also
Atomic blasting
BLASTING, Atomic. See Atomic blasting
BLATNIK, John A.
Excerpt from statement, March 26, 1962. Cong Digest 43:240+ O '64
BLATT, Genevieve
Cleaning it up. por Time 83:24 My 8 '64
BLATTIDAE. See Cockroaches
BLATZ, Hanson
Radiation exposure records. Science 140:770 My 17 '63
BLAU, Amram
Most Orthodox Orthodox; Mea She'arim, Jerusalem. il por Time 82:38 Ag 9 '63
BLAU, Herbert
I don't wanna play. Sat R 47:32+ F 22 '64
BLAU, Sidney
Help your child like himself. Parents Mag 38:62-3+ D '63
How to cope with stage fright. Parents Mag 38:66-7+ My '63
Modesty is back in style. Parents Mag 38:51+ Mr '63
BLAUE reiter, Der. See Art, Abstract
BLAUKOPF, Kurt
Notes from our correspondents (cont of) Notes from abroad. See issues of High fidelity
BLAUSHILD, Babette
Confessions of an unpublished writer. Sat R 46:21 Mr 9 '63
BLAVATSKY, Helene Petrovna (Hahn-Hahn)
Theosophist Helena Blavatsky. W. S. Smith. Christian Cent 80:1002-5 Ag 14 '63; Discussion. 80:1244-6 O 9 '63
BLAXALL, Arthur William
Arthur Blaxall arrested in South Africa. Christian Cent 80:606-7 My 8 '63
A. W. Blaxall sentenced to six-month jail term; Johannesburg. Christian Cent 80: 1324 O 30 '63
Sentence on A. W. Blaxall will not be applied. Christian Cent 80:1358 N 6 '63
BLEACH prints. See Prints
BLEACHERS. See Grandstands
BLEACHING materials
Bewildered by bleaches? Bet Hom & Gard 42: 104-5 O '64

BLEACHING materials—*Continued*
How a bleach helps in your family's laundry. E. M. McCabe. il Parents Mag 38:20+ Ag '63
Newest types of laundry bleaches. il Consumer Rep 29:376-8 Ag '64
BLECHMAN, Burt
How much? dramatization. See Hellman, L. My mother, my father and me
BLECHMAN, Fred
Build a telephone beeper. Pop Electr 19:57-9+ D '63
Buyers' guide for portable tape recorders. Pop Electr 18:67-70+ Ap '63
Electronic stop watch. Pop Electr 19:51-4+ O '63
MPX meter. Pop Electr 19:41-4+ N '63
Pickup pranks. Pop Electr 19:60-1+ Ag '63
Standing waves: do they? Pop Electr 20:61-4+ Je '64
Tape-winding nomogram. Electr World 72:38-9 O '64
That vile interference. Pop Electr 18:77-81+ Mr '63
Transistor-photocell color organ. Electr World 72:41-3 Jl '64
BLEECK, John
Place downstairs. il Time 81:65-6 My 3 '63
BLEEDERS disease. See Hemophilia
BLEEDING. See Hemorrhage
BLEI, Ira. See Carroll, B. jt. auth.
BLEIFELD, Stanley
Sculptor hails the Bible. il por Life 54:105-7 Je 28 '63
BLEITZ, Don
Some fine feathered friends. il Read Digest 84:136-43 My '64
BLENDERS, Electric. See Electric apparatus and appliances, Domestic
BLENNERHASSETT ISLAND
Bewitching Blennerhassett. B. A. Roth. il Travel 119:48-50 Ap '63
BLESS Charlie; story. See Fineman, M.
BLESSED day; story. See Rogin, G.
BLESSED Sacrament. See Lords Supper
BLEWETT, John
World resounds: Tokyo. America 109:767-8 D 14 '63
BLEWETT, Stephen E.
Crash detective. il pors Motor T 15:42-3 D '63
BLIGH, William
Martinet or martyr. W. Goldhurst. il por Horizon 5:42-8 S '63
BLIGHTED areas. See Slums
BLIMPS. See Airships
BLIND
If you had a choice. P. Putnam. Sat R 46:29+ O 26 '63
Just an average lawyer. H. Rezatto. il Read Digest 82:145-8+ My '63
Light in a dark world; how you can help the visually handicapped child. R. W. White. bibliog Library J 88:4817-20+ D 15 '63
NAVH helps the visually handicapped; school children with sight problems. L. Marchi. il Library J 88:4821-2+ D 15 '63
Our teacher sees with her hands. S. Gordon. il Look 27:116a-116e Ap 23 '63
Painted in darkness; ed. by A. Gordon. C. W. E. Jordan. il Read Digest 83:140-4 N '63
Spectacle that astonished Salonica; international trade fair. D. Wharton. Read Digest 83:113-16 S '63
Study in courage. C. Morrison. il Look 27:25-9 My 21 '63
See also
Libraries—Work with blind
Education
Art & blind children. M. Bains. il Sch Arts 63:3-9 Ja '64
Learning without eyes; blind with sighted at Agnes Cotton elementary school, San Antonio, Tex. B. D. Billingsley. il Parents Mag 39:72-3+ S '64
Visually handicapped youngster in art. I. Borodziej. il Sch Arts 63:27-8 Ja '64
Employment
Blind leader of the sighted; VA clinical social worker. il Ebony 19:60-2+ Mr '64
BLIND, Apparatus for the
Device enables blind to operate switchboard. il Todays Health 41:73 Ag '63
New ultrasonic radar for the blind. W. S. Bacon. il Pop Electr 20:49+ Ja '64
BLIND, Books for the
Aid for the visually handicapped, by J. H. Prince. Review
ALA Bul 58:324-5 Ap '64. G. T. Piez
Aids for the reader with changing vision. R. W. Fingeret. il ALA Bul 58:792-4 O '64
It's like this, cat, to appear soon in braille and talking-book editions. il Library J 89:1839-40 Ap 15 '64
That the blind may read. A. R. McGratty. America 108:792-3 Je 1 '63
See also
Talking books
BLIND landing of airplanes. See Airplanes—Landing
BLIND riveting. See Rivets and riveting
BLINDNESS
Blindness: its relation to age of menarche. L. Zacharias and R. J. Wurtman. bibliog il Science 144:1154-5 My 29 '64
What causes blindness. Sci Digest 56:79-80 Jl '64
See also
Blind
Color blindness
Eye banks
BLINDNESS, National society for the prevention of. See National society for the prevention of blindness
BLINDS
Bright, breezy easy windows. il Life 54:108-10 Mr 8 '63
BLINDS, Duck. See Duck blinds
BLINDS in nature photography. See Photography—Apparatus and supplies
BLINKING lights. See Electric lamps, Flashing
BLISS, Anthony A.
Year-round employment. Opera N 29:8-11 O 17 '64
BLISS, Charles M.
Profits will improve further. Nations Bsns 52:108 Je '64
BLISS, Ray Charles
Beyond ideology. il por Time 85:19-20 Ja 22 '65
Ohio's Ray Bliss: the GOP picks a chairman. por Newsweek 65:25 Ja 25 '65
Two indispensable men. R. Moley. Newsweek 61:96 F 11 '63
Why Republicans chose Ray Bliss. il por U S News 58:22 Ja 25 '65
BLISS, Robert Woods, collection of pre-Columbian art. See Art—Private collections
BLITZ, Gérard
Bargain vacations in paradise. J. Stewart-Gordon. il Read Digest 84:217-18+ My '64
Mr Blitz and the total vacation game; Club Méditerranée. G. Rogin. il por Sports Illus 19:48-59 Jl 1 '63
BLITZER, Leon
Dynamical model for demonstrating satellite motions. Sky & Tel 29:16-18 Ja '65
BLITZSTEIN, Marc
Blitzstein's legacy. Newsweek 63:58 My 25 '64
Cradle still rocks. G. Weales. Reporter 30:46+ My 21 '64
Obituary
Newsweek 63:77 F 3 '64
Sacco and Vanzetti. Criticism
Newsweek 63:58 My 25 '64
BLIVEN, Bruce, 1889-
By 1966 half of us will be under twenty-five. N Y Times Mag p47-8+ D 8 '63
Mama, they've begun again! Am Heritage 16:12-16+ D '64
My most unforgettable character. Read Digest 85:129-33 Ag '64
Our legacy from Mr Jefferson. Read Digest 82:160-2+ Mr '63
Unions and automation: truce on the West coast. il Reporter 29:35-8 N 7 '63
Using our leisure is no easy job. N Y Times Mag p 18-19+ Ap 26 '64
Why is the sky dark at night? Read Digest 83:203-4+ Jl '63
BLIVEN, Bruce, 1916-
Annals of business. New Yorker 39:83-4+ Mr 23 '63
BLIVEN, Naomi
Books (cont) New Yorker 39:82+ Ag 10; 151-7 S 7 '63; 40:195-6+ Ap 18; 167-70+ Je 6; 96+ Jl 18; 198+ S 26 '64; 70-2 Ja 2 '65
Number of love is always odd; story. New Yorker 39:133-5 Je 8 '63
BLIXEN, Karen (Dinesen) baronesse
Isak Dinesen: in praise of radiance. C. McCullers. por Sat R 46:29+ Mr 16 '63
BLIZZARDS. See Snowstorms
BLOCH, Alfred
Repairs on the Marxian palace. Sat R 46:38-9 Je 22 '63
BLOCH, Charles
New dissent to a Robert Kennedy speech: excerpts from statement. U S News 55:10 O 28 '63

BLOCH, Herbert A.
Juvenile gang; a cultural reflex. bibliog f Ann Am Acad 347:20-9 My '63

BLOCH, Joseph W.
Strike and discontent. Mo Labor R 86:645-51 Je '63

BLOCH, Konrad Emil
Friends share Nobel prize. por Sci N L 86: 263 O 24 '64
Nobel laureates: Bloch and Lynen win prize in medicine and physiology. E. P. Kennedy and F. H. Westheimer. il por Science 146: 504-6 O 23 '64
Secrets of cholesterol. il por Time 84:94 O 23 '64
—See Erwin, J. jt. auth.

BLOCH, M. R.
Social influence of salt; with biographical sketch. Sci Am 209:28, 88-96+ Jl '63

BLOCH, Richard L.
Art is a growing thing. Sat R 47:62-3 O 17 '64

BLOCHMAN, Lawrence G.
Let's remove the stigma from leprosy. Todays Health 43:30-3 Ja '65

BLOCK, B. P. See Barth-Wehrenalp, G. jt. auth.

BLOCK, Herbert Lawrence
Chips off the new Herblock; excerpts from Straight Herblock. il Sat R 47:80-1 N 14 '64

about

Good loud holler. il por NEA J 52:36-7 Mr '63
Herblock's golden key. J. Star. il pors Look 27:62+ F 26 '63
In Herblock, the world is almost exclusively political. F. Getlein. Commonweal 81:332-4 N 27 '64

BLOCK, Jean (Libman)
Dynamic retirement is their goal. Read Digest 84:195-6+ Ja '64
Hello, I want to speak to the oven. House & Gard 126:208-9+ O '64
Homemade money. Good H 157:30-2+ Jl '63
My most unforgettable character. Read Digest 85:107-12 D '64
What it takes to be wife, mother and heart surgeon. Good H 156:34+ My '63

BLOCK, Joseph L.
Government, labor and management; address, December 3, 1962. Vital Speeches 29: 250-4 F 1 '63

BLOCK, Marvin A.
If there's an alcoholic in the family. Parents Mag 39:52-3+ N '64
Latest on over-drinking; interview. por U S News 56:50-6 Je 15 '64; Same abr. with title When does social drinking become over-drinking? Read Digest 85:107-11 S '64; Correction. U S News 56:16 Je 22 '64

BLOCK, Michel
Music to my ears; pianists Block and Lhevinne. I. Kolodin. Sat R 46:23 F 2 '63

BLOCK, Ruth
(comp) In brief, the law. N Y Times Mag p60 Ag 9 '64
(comp) To sleep, perchance to analyze. N Y Times Mag p 10+ Ja 10 '65

BLOCK, Victor
Homemaker service: substitute for mothers. Todays Health 43:60-3+ Ja '65

BLOCK, Heart. See Heart block

BLOCK ISLAND
Block Island converts a skeptic. O. S. Pettingill, jr. il Audubon Mag 66:346-50 N '64

BLOCK parents
Keep them safe from child molesters; block parents. P. K. McCauley. il Parents Mag 39:50-1+ D '64
Plan to protect schoolchildren. il U S News 58:14 Ja 11 '65

BLOCK printing
Three areas of playing-card printing; early block printing. D. Powills. il Hobbies 69: 118-19+ Ag '64
See also
Linoleum block printing

BLOCK prints, Linoleum. See Linoleum block prints

BLOCK puzzles. See Puzzles

BLOCKADE
Blockade. D. Lawrence. U S News 54:112 Mr 18 '63
Cuba & the peace movement. N. Glazer; discussion. Commentary 35:438-43 My '63
Dramatic flourish, empty gesture; breakdown of U.S. trade embargo on Cuba. il Time 83: 23 F 28 '64
Law and the quarantine of Cuba. A. Chayes. For Affairs 41:550-7 Ap '63
Wayward buses to Cuba. Life 56:4 Ja 24 '64
See also
European war, 1914-1918—Blockades

BLOCKER, Joel
(ed) See Singer, I. B. Interview

BLOCKS. See Pulleys

BLOCKS, Building. See Building blocks

BLOCKS, Toy. See Toys

BLOEMKER, Al
Indy's $150,000 questions. Pop Sci 184:66-7 My '64

BLOESCH, Donald G.
Virgin birth defended. Christian Cent 80:493-4 Ap 17 '63

BLOLAND, Paul A.
Student-faculty council revisited. Sch & Soc 91:216-18 My 4 '63

BLONSKY, Marshall. See Aronowitz, A. jt. auth.

BLOOD. Johnny. See McNally, J. V.

BLOOD
Blood substance kills disease-causing fungus. Sci N L 85:73 F 1 '64
Dialysis of sleep and waking factors in blood of the rabbit. M. Monnier and L. Hösli. bibliog il Science 146:796-8 N 6 '64
Facts about the Rh factor. H. F. Philipsborn. Parents Mag 38:135-7 D '63
Inhibition of specific binding of antibody to the Rh_0(D) factor of red cells in antibody excess. S. P. Masouredis and others. bibliog il Science 145:1197-9 S 11 '64
Patient to patient. Time 82:78 N 15 '63
Red blood cells; change in shape in capillaries. M. M. Guest and others. bibliog il Science 142:1319-21 D 6 '63
Sulfate transport in human red cells: inhibition by some uncouplers of oxidative phosphorylation. A. Omachi. bibliog il Science 145:1449-50 S 25 '64
See also
Erythrocytes
Hemoglobin

Agglutination

N-Ethylmaleimide inhibition of horseshoe crab hemocyte agglutination. F. T. Bryan and others. bibliog il Science 144:1147-8 My 29 '64
Human blood group A_1 specific agglutinin of the butter clam saxidomus giganteus. H. M. Johnson. bibliog il Science 146:548-9 O 23 '64
Reovirus hemagglutination: inhibition by N-acetyl-D-glucosamine. L. D. Gelb and A. M. Lerner. bibliog il Science 147:404-5 Ja 22 '65
See also
Hemagglutinin

Analysis and chemistry

Angiotensinase with a high degree of specificity in plasma and red cells. P. A. Khairallah and others. bibliog il Science 140: 672-4 My 10 '63
See also
Blood—Proteins

Circulation

Aortico-pulmonary glomus tissue distribution and blood supply in the adult cat. M. A. Verity and others. bibliog il Science 145: 172-3 Jl 10 '64
Blood flow through muscle; investigators in the physiological research field. S. S. Sobin. Science 140:702 My 10 '63
Phase separation in suspensions flowing through bifurcations: a simplified hemodynamic model. G. Bugliarello and G. C. C. Hsiao. bibliog il Science 143:469-71 Ja 31 '64
Seal & man without air: a common defense. il Time 82:74 D 6 '63

Circulation, Disorders of

Great brain robbery. il Time 84:68 O 30 '64

Coagulation

Balloon clears arteries. Sci N L 83:402 Je 29 '63
Blood clotting; enzymic activation; report on symposium. J. H. Ferguson. Science 144: 1159 My 29 '64
Heparin bonding on colloidal graphite surfaces. J. L. Gott and others. bibliog il Science 142:1297-8 D 6 '63
Paracrystalline forms of fibrinogen. C. Cohen and others. bibliog il Science 141:436-8 Ag 2 '63
Scanning the lungs for blood clots. il Time 84:64 Jl 17 '64
Shower of little clots. il Time 83:72 F 21 '64
Some clots disappear of their own accord. Sci N L 86:344 N 28 '64
Waterfall sequence for intrinsic blood clotting. E. W. Davie and O. D. Ratnoff. bibliog il Science 145:1310-12 S 18 '64
See also
Anticoagulants (medicine)

BLOOD—*Continued*

Collection and preservation

See also
Blood banks

Corpuscles and platelets

Erythroid homeostasis in normal and genetically anemic mice: reaction to induced polycythemia. R. L. Niece and others. bibliog il Science 142:1468-9 D 13 '63
Polyploidy and endoreduplication in human leukocyte cultures treated with β-mercaptopyruvate. J. F. Jackson and K. Lindahl-Kiessling. bibliog il Science 141:424-6 Ag 2 '63
See also
Lymphocytes

Dialysis

See Kidneys, Artificial

Diseases

See also
Anemia
Galactosemia
Hemophilia
Leukemia
Polycythemia

Freezing

Reversible agglomeration used to remove dimethylsulfoxide from large volumes of frozen blood. C. E. Huggins. bibliog il Science 139:504-5 F 8 '63

Pigments

See also
Hemocyanin

Plasma

Collagen-like protein in human plasma. H. Keiser and others. bibliog il Science 142:1678-9 D 27 '63
See also
Blood donors

Pressure

See Blood pressure

Proteins

Blood brothers; man and ape. il Newsweek 63:52 Mr 2 '64
Cerebrally active small moiety from taraxein-like blood fractions. T. F. Redick and others. bibliog il Science 141:646-7 Ag 16 '63
Hereditary deficiency of serum α_1-antitrypsin. F. Kueppers and others. bibliog il Science 146:1678-9 D 25 '64
Inulin and albumin absorption from the proximal tubule in necturus kidney. W. N. Scott and others. bibliog il Science 146:1588-90 D 18 '64
Lactate dehydrogenase variant from human blood: evidence for molecular subunits. S. H. Boyer and others. bibliog il Science 141:642-3 Ag 16 '63
Mental illness cure in brain chemistry; taraxein. Sci N L 84:357 D 7 '63
Plasma protein synthesis in the liver: method for measurement of albumin formation in vivo. E. B. Reeve and others. bibliog il Science 139:914-16 Mr 8 '63
Serum albumin: polymorphism in man. G. Efremov and M. Braend. bibliog il Science 146:1679-80 D 25 '64
Serum protein synthesis by the fetal rat. P. C. Kelleher and others. bibliog il Science 139:839-40 Mr 1 '63
Sex-associated differences in serum proteins of mice. E. Espinosa and others. bibliog il Science 144:417-18 Ap 24 '64
Spectrophotometric titrations of human serum albumin and reduced carboxymethylated albumin. D. S. Eisenberg and J. T. Edsall. bibliog il Science 142:50-1 O 4 '63
See also
Gamma globulin
Serum globulins

Serum

See Serum

Testing

Fifty cent test may thwart disease; detection of Wilson's disease. Bsns W p98 Mr 9 '63
Human blood typing uses cattle serum. Sci N L 85:168 Mr 14 '64

Transfusion

Antibodies to genetic types of gamma globulin after multiple transfusions. J. C. Allen and H. G. Kunkel. bibliog il Science 139:418 F 1 '63
Blood transfusion helps dog transplant take. Sci N L 86:117 Ag 22 '64
Bowery blood. Time 81:78 Ap 19 '63
Heating up the blood. il Time 84:64 N 13 '64
Lurking risks of transfusion. K. Wheeler. il Life 54:70-2+ F 15 '63; Same abr. with title Transfusion; a mixed blessing. Read Digest 84:101-5 Mr '64
Persistent mitosis of transfused homologous leukocytes in children receiving antileukemic therapy. R. H. Levin and others. bibliog il Science 142:1305-6+ D 6 '63
Saved by her own blood; autotransfusion of rare blood. il Time 82:52 N 29 '63
Transfusions in the womb. il Time 85:43 Ja 15 '65
Warm blood transfusions control massive bleeding. Sci N L 83:350 Je 1 '63
Womb transfusion. Newsweek 62:68 O 7 '63

BLOOD banks
Are blood banks a business? il Bsns W p29 S 5 '64
Banking on blood. Newsweek 62:68 D 23 '63
Blood bank mess. il Changing T 17:25-9 Jl '63
Credit at the blood bank. M. T. Whitis. il Parents Mag 39:58+ D '64
Lurking risks of transfusion. K. Wheeler. il Life 54:70-2+ F 15 '63
6,000,000 pints of blood is not enough. L. Galton. il N Y Times Mag p38+ Mr 29 '64

BLOOD brotherhood
Underworld borrows rites from witchcraft. Sci N L 84:139 Ag 31 '63

BLOOD cells. See Blood

BLOOD clotting. See Blood—Coagulation

BLOOD donors
Lurking risks of transfusion. K. Wheeler. il Life 54:70-2+ F 15 '63; Same abr. with title Transfusion; a mixed blessing. Read Digest 84:101-5 Mr '64
Patient to patient. Time 82:78 N 15 '63
Patients serve as own blood donors. il Sci Digest 53:32-3 My '63
6,000,000 pints of blood is not enough. L. Galton. il N Y Times Mag p38+ Mr 29 '64
See also
Blood—Transfusion
National rare blood bank

BLOOD groups
Blood group studies with turtles. W. Frair. bibliog il Science 140:1412-14 Je 28 '63
Blood groups in anthropoid apes and baboons. A. S. Wiener and J. Moor-Jankowski. bibliog il Science 142:67-9 O 4 '63; Reply. G. B. Rabb. 142:1261 D 6 '63
Blood groups of chimpanzees: demonstrated with isoimmune serums. J. Moor-Jankowski. bibliog il Science 145:1441-3 S 25 '64
First linkage of a species antigen in the genus streptopelia. W. J. Miller. bibliog il Science 143:1179-80 Mr 13 '64
Galactosidase action on human blood group B active escherichia coli and ox red cell substances. G. F. Springer and others. bibliog il Science 146:946-7 N 13 '64
Genetics and the human race. W. C. Boyd. bibliog il Science 140:1057-64 Je 7 '63
Hemoglobin $G_{Coushatta}$: a new variant in an American Indian family. R. G. Schneider and others. bibliog il Science 143:697-8 F 14 '64
Human blood typing uses cattle serum. Sci N L 85:168 Mr 14 '64
Prezygotic selection in ABO blood groups. E. Matsunaga and Y. Hiraizumi; discussion. Science 137:861-2; bibliog 139:406-7 S 14 '62, F 1 '63
Rare type of blood; Shabalala-type. il Time 84:96-7 O 2 '64
See also
Rh factors

BLOOD knot; drama. See Fugard, A.

BLOOD pressure
Autoregulation of blood flow; research workshop. P. C. Johnson and others. Science 140:203-5 Ap 12 '63
Blood pressure changes during human sleep. F. Snyder and others. bibliog il Science 142:1313-14 D 6 '63
Cardiovascular disease; report of conference on Psychophysiologic aspects of cardiovascular disease. G. Saslow. Science 142:601+ N 1 '63
Parson's gift to medicine. Todays Health 41:66 Ag '63
Pill to fight mental depression; Eutonyl. Bsns W p76+ Ap 13 '63
Stop worrying about low blood pressure. A. C. Corcoran and I. H. Page. il Todays Health 41:24-5+ N '63
Tonic influence of rostral brain structures on pressure regulatory mechanisms in the cat. D. J. Reis and M. Cuénod. bibliog il Science 145:64-5 Jl 3 '64; Reply with rejoinder. R. L. Katz and others. 145:1459-60 S 25 '64
See also
Hypertension

BLOOD pump. See Heart. Artificial
BLOOD; story. See Singer, I. B.
BLOOD sugar
Hypoglycemia; a potent stimulus to secretion of growth hormone. J. Roth and others. bibliog il Science 140:987-8 My 31 '63
BLOOD tests. See Blood—Testing
BLOOD transfusion. See Blood—Transfusion
BLOOD types. See Blood groups
BLOOD vessels
Blood vessels of the mammalian renal medulla. R. K. Plakke and E. W. Pfeiffer. bibliog il Science 146:1683-5 D 25 '64
Phase separation in suspensions flowing through bifurcations: a simplified hemodynamic model. G. Bugliarello and G. C. C. Hsiao. bibliog il Science 143:469-71 Ja 31 '64
See also
Aorta
Capillaries

Diseases

See also
Aneurysm

Surgery

Balloon clears arteries. Sci N L 83:402 Je 29 '63
Forerunner in vascular surgery; J. Hunter. Todays Health 42:65 Ap '64
Gilding the veins. America 111:648 N 21 '64
Lifesaving triumphs of arterial surgery. J. D. Ratcliff. Read Digest 84:101-4 My '64
Rare artery surgery saves seventy-two year-old man. Sci N L 84:361 D 7 '63
Repairing the royal aorta. il Time 84:52 D 25 '64
Surgeon; Duke of Windsor's operation. il Newsweek 64:34-5 D 28 '64
Surgeons now repair or replace your damaged arteries. J. D. Ratcliff. il Todays Health 42:58-9+ My '64; Same abr. with title Lifesaving triumphs of arterial surgery. Read Digest 84:101-4 My '64
BLOODROOT
Bloodroot; hepatica. I. D. Jolly. il Horticulture 41:463 S '63
BLOODSUCKING insects
See also
Kissing bugs
BLOOM, Arthur L. and Stuiver, Minze
Submergence of the Connecticut coast. bibliog Science 139:332-4 Ja 25 '63
BLOOM, Claire
Bloom in love. C. R. Jennings. il pors Sat Eve Post 237:70-1 S 12 '64
BLOOM, F. E. See Salmoiraghi, G. C. jt. auth.
BLOOM, John
Britain: how Bloom withered. il por Fortune 70:53-4+ O '64
Rolls razor calls it quits. por Bsns W p 114+ Jl 25 '64
Supa John. il por Newsweek 63:67 Mr 2 '64
Trouble in never-never land. por Time 84:82 Jl 24 '64
Wilting Bloom. Newsweek 64:68 Jl 27 '64
BLOOM, Murray Teigh
California cleans its courts. Read Digest 82:91-3 Mr '63
Closing costs: a booby trap for unwary homebuyers. Read Digest 83:138-42 D '63
Else Staudinger's 100-million-dollar gift to Uncle Sam. Read Digest 85:189-90+ Ag '64
How-to-get-rich-in-the-stock market clubs. N Y Times Mag p72+ Ap 28 '63
Is your pension safe? New Repub 151:13-15 O 31 '64
Must it be bail or jail? Read Digest 84:189-92+ My '64
New way out of debt. Read Digest 85:134-7 Ag '64
One-up-in-the-airmanship. N Y Times Mag p28+ Ja 10 '65
Part money plays in marriage. Read Digest 82:83-6 My '63
Why it costs so much to have a baby. Redbook 121:62-3+ S '63
BLOOM, Samuel W.
Process of becoming a physician. bibliog f Ann Am Acad 346:77-87 Mr '63
BLOOMBERG, Claire M. and Troupe, C. H.
Big brothers to troubled children. NEA J 53:22-5 Ja '64
BLOOMER, H. B.
Iran: remolding a nation nearer to the heart's desire. Reporter 30:32-6 Ja 16 '64
BLOOMER, Robert Oliver
Rock doc; geology professor. C. Kocivar. il pors Look 27:M8+ N 5 '63
BLOOMFIELD, Arthur
Hercules and St John. Mus Am 83:37+ S '63
BLOOMFIELD, Howard
Beware of Smokey the bear. Sat Eve Post 237:68-9 S 12 '64
Yachtsman's dreamboat. Yachting 114:57-9+ O '63
BLOOMFIELD, Lincoln P.
Politics of outer space. Bul Atomic Sci 19:12-14 My '63
BLOOMFIELD, Roger C.
Seagoing squirrel. il Field & S 68:117 My '63
BLOOMFIELD, N.J, public library
Town steps back into history and the library helps pave the way. R. F. Diamond. il Wilson Lib Bul 37:578-9 Mr '63
BLOOMFIELD HILLS, Mich. See Detroit
BLOOMINGDALE, Samuel J.
Bloomingdale's Bloomingdale. New Yorker 40:47-8 N 7 '64
BLOOMINGDALES (store) See New York (city)—Stores
BLOS, Joan W. See Black, I. S. jt. auth.
BLOSS, Meredith
Responding to manifest needs. por(p3242) Library J 89:3252-4 S 15 '64
BLOSSOMING of plants. See Plants, Flowering of
BLOTNER radar ballistic site, Maine. See Proving grounds
BLOTTING paper
Rise and fall of the blotter. il Changing T 18:32 O '64
BLOUGH, Donald S. and Schrier, A. M.
Scotopic spectral sensitivity in the monkey. bibliog Science 139:493-4 F 8 '63
BLOUGH, Roger M.
Art of being secure: address. January 21, 1964. Vital Speeches 30:282-6 F 15 '64
Backing for a tax cut, steel's Blough speaks out; summary of news conference. por U S News 55:10 Ag 12 '63
Roger Blough on the problems of steel pricing. Fortune 71:139 Ja '65
Spokesmen for steel and rails see era of labor peace ahead; excerpts from statement. U S News 57:98 O 19 '64

about

Big Steel's policy: no pressure on race issue. por U S News 55:24 N 11 '63
Speaking out. por Time 83:83 My 8 '64
U.S. steel adopts new corporate look; sales operations centralized. por Bsns W p29 S 21 '63
U.S. steel strips for a fight. il por(cover) Bsns W p 114-16+ S 28 '63
BLOUNT, Charlotte
Pictures help books come alive. Parents Mag 38:48-9+ Ap '63
BLOUNT, Jack D. See Haskett, T. R. jt. auth.
BLOUSES
Blouses. il Consumer Bul 46:11-15 Ag '63
See also
Judy Bond, incorporated
BLOW, Michael
Professor Henry and his philosophical toys. Am Heritage 15:24-6+ D '63
BLOW us something good, sirocco; story. See Smith, S. E.
BLOWER-vacuums. See Garden tools, equipment and supplies
BLOWERS, Snow. See Snow blowers, throwers, etc.
BLOWFLIES
Fine structure of the interpseudotracheal papillae of the blowfly. J. R. Larsen. bibliog il Science 139:347 Ja 25 '63
Phenoloxidase system of the blowfly, calliphora erythrocephalo. C. E. Sekeris and D. Mergenhagen. bibliog il Science 145:68-9 Jl 3 '64
Sclerotization in the blowfly imago. C. E. Sekeris. bibliog il Science 144:419 Ap 24 '64
BLUCK, D. R. Y.
Far East's lively little airline; Cathay Pacific. il por Bsns W p 120+ S 14 '63
BLUE baby. See Tetralogy of Fallot
BLUE boy in black; drama. See White, E.
BLUE elder. See Elder
BLUE geese. See Geese, Wild
BLUE LAKE, Washington (state) See Grand Coulee
BLUE laws. See Sunday legislation
BLUE rider (group) See Art, Abstract
BLUE RIDGE MOUNTAINS
Blue Ridge parkway. J. T. Starr. il Atlan 211:120-1 My '63
See also
Shenandoah National Park
BLUE RIDGE parkway. See Roads—United States
BLUE whales. See Whales

BLUEBERRIES
Two good reasons to hedge with blueberries. I. Brown. il Flower Grower 52:18 Ja '65
See also
Cookery—Fruit
BLUEBIRD houses. See Bird houses
BLUEBIRDS
Bluebird of Humbleness. il Sports Illus 18: 10+ My 6 '63
Bluebirds returning? Mrs C. S. Runk. Audubon Mag 66:56 Ja '64
Welcome home the bluebird. J. D. Walters. il Flower Grower 50:36-7+ Mr '63
BLUEBONNETS (flowers)
Bluebonnet blooms deep in the heart of Texas. R. F. Caldwell. il Audubon Mag 66:97 Mr '64
BLUEFISH fishing
Best ways to bluefish. G. Heinold. il Outdoor Life 134:10-11 Ag '64
Blues around the clock; off New Jersey, party-boat fishing. M. Rosko. il Outdoor Life 134:60-1+ S '64
First day blues. C. Conley. il Field & S 68: 40-1+ Jl '63
Fishing for snapper blues. G. Heinold. il Outdoor Life 132:64+ Jl '63
Fishing tidal rivers. G. Heinold. il Outdoor Life 131:20+ Je '63
IQ of blue. J. Guy. il Outdoor Life 132:52-3+ Ag '63
BLUEGILL fishing. See Sunfish fishing
BLUEGRASS. See Grasses
BLUES (music) See Negro music
BLUES for Mr Charlie; drama. See Baldwin, J.
BLUETS
Two attractive native ground covers. I. D. Jolly. il Horticulture 41:68 F '63
BLUFIN tuna fishing. See Tuna fishing
BLUHM, Norman
Bluhm paints a picture. W. Berkson. il por Art N 62:38-41+ My '63
BLUM, Albert A.
Baruch and his legend. Nation 199:72-3 Ag 24 '64
Labor at the crossroads. Harvard Bsns R 42: 6-8+ Jl '64
Prospects for organization of white-collar workers; excerpt from address. bibliog f Mo Labor R 87:125-9 F '64
—See Barkin, S. jt. auth; jt. ed.
BLUM, B. Alquit-. See Alquit-Blum, B.
BLUM, Barton M.
Combat those bluebird blues. Field & S 69: 32-4+ N '64
Great Bay bonanza. Field & S 68:86-8+ D '63
BLUM, David
Look at the future. por Mus Am 83:10 Jl '63
BLUM, Edwin Harvey
Saving grace. Criticism
New Yorker 39:86+ Ap 27 '63
Newsweek 61:54 Ap 29 '63
BLUM, Etta
Blackbird and the gingko tree; poem. Poetry 101:249 Ja '63
Fog at Brighton; poem. Poetry 103:162 D '63
(tr) See Alquit-Blum, B. Three poems: I drew you out of that particular night; Is there a darkness then which was not once light; Since I scarcely know what to do with you
BLUM, Harold F.
Skin cancer and sunlight. Science 145:1339-40 S 18 '64
BLUM, Murray S. See Moser, J. C. jt. auth.
BLUM, Ralph
Books. Vogue 144:66 N 15 '64; 145-26 Ja 15 '65
Mount Ararat seen from afar; story. Mlle 58:150-1 Mr '64
On the night train to Moscow; story. Sat Eve Post 237:38-40 My 2 '64
Reporter at large. New Yorker 39:55-6+ N 2; 59-60+ N 9; 59-60+ N 16 '63
Rites of passage; story. Sat Eve Post 237: 38-44 S 19 '64
BLUM, Richard H.
Malpractice suits, can the patient recover? Nation 196:139-41 F 16 '63
BLUM, Sam
About: accidents. N Y Times Mag p29-30+ My 17 '64
Child from thirty to forty. Esquire 60:95-7 Ag '63
Child's friends. Redbook 121:49+ My '63
Help for sidewalk superintendents. N Y Times Mag p30-1+ O 4 '64
Honesty and dishonesty. Redbook 124:46-8+ D '64
Incredible story behind a cancer cure. Redbook 123:40-1+ Je '64
Ode to the great 5'x9' outdoors. N Y Times Mag p21+ Ap 26 '64
Safety last. Redbook 121:56-7+ S '63
To get the bars back on their feet. N Y Times Mag p68+ S 27 '64
What goes up must come down. N Y Times Mag p 10-11+ D 27 '64
What makes a good father. Redbook 122:38-9+ Ja '64
Why young couples feel trapped. Redbook 123:62-3+ S '64
BLUM, Virgil C.
Are we really teaching democracy? Cath World 197:21-7 Ap '63
Freedom and equality. Commonweal 79:511-15 Ja 31 '64
Tax credits for education. America 110:669-72; 111:97 My 16, Ag 1 '64
BLUME, Peter
Art galleries; exhibition of two paintings and fifty or more drawings at the Durlacher. R. M. Coates. New Yorker 40:169 N 7 '64
BLUMENFELD, Hans
Urban pattern. Ann Am Acad 352:74-83 Mr '64
BLUMENFELD, Harold
Blumenfeld of UPI. M. R. Weiss. il pors Sat R 47:69-70 My 9 '64
BLUMENFELD, Serge
Rising threat of tetanus. Parents Mag 39:129-30 Je '64
BLUMENSON, Martin
Books. A. J. Liebling. New Yorker 39:216-18+ O 19 '63
BLUMENTHAL, Joseph
Robert Frost: best-printed U.S. author, and his printer, Spiral press. P. A. Bennett. il Pub W 185:82-6+ Mr 2 '64
BLUMENTHAL, Lassor
Are trade shows worth it? Duns R 83:39-40+ Je '64
Big machines think small. Duns R 84:pt2 106-9+ S '64
Brand-new industrial package. Duns R 82:pt2 136-8+ N '63
Containerization: the route to integrated transportation. Duns R 83:pt2 110-13+ Je '64
How to cut purchasing costs. Duns R 83:53-4+ Mr '64
Persuading the consumer to buy more. Duns R 84:101 D '64
Should management take sabbaticals? Duns R 83:45-6+ Ja '64
BLUMENTHAL, W. Michael
Commodity trade and economic development; statement, April 30, 1963. Dept State Bul 48:844-8 My 27 '63
From shill to ambassador. il por Newsweek 63:80 My 11 '64
World coffee agreement and U.S. foreign economic policy; address, January 14, 1963. Dept State Bul 48:218-23 F 11 '63
BLUMER, Max, and others
Pristane in zooplankton. bibliog Science 140: 974 My 31 '63
—See Thomas, D. W. jt. auth.
BLUMROSEN, Alfred W.
Individual and the union. Mo Labor R 86: 659-95 Je '63
BLUNDERBUSSES
Blunderbus. C. S. Worman. il Hobbies. 69: 126-7 Ja '65
BLUNDERS
Do you talk double-take? C. Ford. Read Digest 85:101-2 N '64
French postcards; Jean-Charles collection of boners. il Newsweek 61:88 My 20 '63
See also
Bulls, Colloquial
BLUNT, Caroline
Love & merry Christmas. Parents Mag 39:35+ D '64
BLURBS. See Books—Advertising
BLUSH worts
Lipstick plant. Mrs W. H. Hull, jr. il Horticulture 42:46 Ja '64
BLUSHING
What makes you blush? questions and answers. J. E. Brown. il Read Digest 85:53-4 O '64
BLY, Robert
Come with me; Unanswered letters; Beauty of women; Fall; Driving north from San Francisco; On a cliff; Testament; Poem in praise of solitude; poems. Poetry 104:365-8 S '64
(tr) See Ibsen, H. On the murder of Abraham Lincoln
BLY, Wayne
Adventures in nature. Recreation 57:115 Mr '64

B'NAI b'rith

Anti-defamation league

Anti-defamation league marks 50th year. Christian Cent 80:796 Je 19 '63
Danger on the right, by A. Forster and B. Epstein. Review
Nat R 16:855-6+ O 6 '64. W. F. Buckley, jr
Fight against prejudice. T. B. Morgan. Look 27:66+ Je 4 '63
Golf anyone? ghettoization on the golf links. il Newsweek 61:104-5 Mr 25 '63
View from the ten-yard line; 50th anniversary. il Time 81:21 F 8 '63

BOAR hunting
Boar for the Bronx; ed. by L. Miracle, J. Altieri. il Outdoor Life 131:48-51+ Je '63

BOARD games. See Games

BOARD of governors of the Federal reserve system. See United States—Federal reserve board

BOARD of trade, Chicago. See Chicago board of trade

BOARDING homes for children. See Foster home care

BOARDING houses
Mama and the roomer. K. Forbes. Read Digest 82:228E-228F Ap '63

BOARDMAN, Fon
Cooperative advertising: how to make it cooperative; summary of address. Pub W 186:18-20 O 26 '64

BOARDMAN, Walter S.
What good is an opossum? Nat Parks Mag 38:19 Je '64

BOARDS, Federal. See United States—Executive departments

BOARDS, Fiber. See Fiber board

BOARDS, Ironing. See Ironing boards

BOARDS, Recreation. See Recreation—Administration

BOARDS of directors. See Corporations—Directors

BOARDS of education. See School boards

BOARMAN, Patrick M.
Reform for the union movement? three writers suggest ways. por U S News 54:88-9 Je 24 '63

BOAT adhesives. See Adhesives

BOAT building. See Boatbuilding

BOAT camping. See Camping

BOAT club dance; drama. See Robinson, C.

BOAT clubs
Fastest club in America; Chain-O-Lakes boat club. J. Stoltz. il Motor B 111:43-4+ Je '63
Meet the Antique boat and yacht club. il Motor B 113:142 Je '64
Outboard club of the year; Tacoma outboard club. J. Plumb. il Yachting 117:118-19+ Ja '65
Unique boating club: Great Lakes cruising club. il Motor B 111:24-5 Je '63
See also
Yacht clubs

BOAT docks. See Docks

BOAT harbors. See Marinas

BOAT horns. See Horns (signals)

BOAT houses. See Boathouses

BOAT inspection. See Motor boats—Inspection

BOAT landings. See Docks; Piers

BOAT propellers. See Propellers

BOAT racing
Fifty seven boats started a rugged twelve-day race in Texas; only two finished. il Life 54:107-9+ Je 7 '63
Why not go racing? P. Stanford. Yachting 113:184-6 Mr '63
See also
Motor boat racing
Rowing
Sailboat racing
Yacht racing

BOAT shows. See Boats—Exhibitions

BOAT signals. See Signals and signaling

BOAT stealing. See Boats, Theft of

BOAT surfing. See Surf riding

BOAT surveys. See Motor boats—Inspection

BOAT thefts. See Boats, Theft of

BOAT trailers. See Automobile boat trailers

BOAT trips. See Boats and boating

BOAT yards. See Boatyards

BOATBUILDING
Amateurs build a racing fleet. R. S. Obrig. il Yachting 115:193-4+ My '64
America's cup sloops abuilding. W. H. Taylor. il Yachting 115:30-1+ F '64
Aviza, a 1725 shallop. W. A. Baker. il Yachting 113:190-2 My '63
Bahamian boatbuilding. W. R. Johnson, jr. il Motor B 112:30-1+ D '63
Beware of copycat boats! fiberglass copies of famous hulls. J. Martenhoff. il Pop Sci 184:110-11+ Ja '64
Boating business; news and views of the industry (cont of) News of the industry. See issues of Yachting to February 1965
Boating comes of age. J. E. Choate. il Yachting 117:94-7+ Ja '65
Build your own dinghy. il Motor B 112:109 Ag '63
Building a Bermuda 40. il Yachting 113:60-1+ Je '63
Building a new boat. W. T. Spaith. il Yachting 114:42-5+ Ag; 42-4+ S '63
Building of Laura II. R. L. Carlson. il Motor B 114:60+ D '64
Diamond jubilee at Port Clinton; tribute to one of America's finest boatbuilders: Matthews. il Motor B 115:103-5+ Ja '65
Dinghies U.S.A. where to find them. il Motor B 112:110 Ag '63
Family of racing giants: the Jacobys; interview. E. Jacoby. il Motor B 112:44-5+ Jl '63
How to build a fold-up hinged boat. J. Payne. il Pop Sci 184:116-19 My '64
Hydro dynamic. A. Mikesell. il Pop Mech 119:144-52+ Mr '63
John's other wife; a home-built houseboat. J. Gale. il Motor B 111:45-6+ F '63
Majestic workboats of a Portuguese lagoon; *moliceiros.* N. Flowers. il Natur Hist 74:20-5 F '65
Peggy Grebe carries on a tradition. E. Knudsen. il Motor B 113:98+ Ap '64
Retire and cruise. C. Stoessel. il Motor B 113:38-9+ Ap '64
Sandwich fiberglass construction technique. T. Rogers. il Motor B 112:74+ O '63
Sports sled. A. Mikesell. il Pop Mech 121:144-50+ Mr '64
Staudacher: man with a mission. E. Crimmin. il Motor B 115:109-11+ Ja '65
Stuff of which boats are made; wood, steel, aluminum, fiberglass; symposium. il Motor B 114:21-41 D '64
Two-in-one camper boat. A. Mikesell. il Pop Mech 120:166-70 S '63
Unsinkable Jonboat wears a foam life jacket. K. Vining. il Pop Sci 184:131-3+ F '64
We build a boat. E. Robberson. il Yachting 115:38-40+ F '64
You and your naval architect. E. Monk. il Yachting 114:41+ D '63
Yum Yum; an inboard utility boat. J. Atkin. il Motor B 114:52-3+ O '64
See also
Boats—Launching
Yacht building

BOATBUILDING tools. See Tools

BOATELS. See Motels

BOATHOUSES
Build yourself a boathouse. D. M. Christian. il Motor B 111:54-5+ My '63
Sophisticated boathouse. il House & Gard 123:118-21 Je '63
Take-it-easy rooms. il House & Gard 123:98-9 Je '63

BOATING, Photography of. See Photography of sports

BOATMAN, S. G. See Buttery, B. R. jt. auth.

BOATS

Care

Boating short cuts. il Pop Mech 119:142-3 Mr '63
Care and repair of aluminum craft. F. M. Paulson. il Field & S 68:36-90 N '63
Care for sails and metalwork now! W. Britton. il Motor B 112:28+ O '63
Commissioning hints. W. H. deFontaine. il Yachting 113:69 Ap '63
Common sense about hurricanes. F. T. Moss. il Motor B 114:50-3 Ag '64
Fitting out; symposium. il Yachting 113:60-8+ Ap '63
Maintenance; symposium. il Yachting 115:42-8+ Ap '64

Collectors and collecting

Meet the Antique boat and yacht club. il Motor B 113:142 Je '64

Design

Boating bulletins; new trends, new products. il Pop Mech 119:132-7 Mr '63
Boating trends for 1964. J.A. Emmett. il Outdoor Life 133:56-60+ F '64
Boats look like boats again. H. Whall. il Sports Illus 20:16-17 Ja 20 '64

BOATS—Design—*Continued*
Carnival of new way-out watercraft. il Pop Mech 120:82-5 Jl '63
Designs. See issues of Yachting
Know your hulls. J. A. Emmett. il Outdoor Life 132:74-6 D '63
Latest boating trends. J. A. Emmett. Outdoor Life 131:56+ F '63
New trends in hull design. F. M. Paulson. il Field & S 69:38-40 Ja '65
Two-in-one camper boat. A. Mikesell. il Pop Mech 120:166-70 S '63
What's new for boating in '63. J. Roe. il Pop Sci 182:113-35 Mr '63

Electric equipment

Boats for restricted waters. J. A. Emmett. il Outdoor Life 133:28+ Je '64
Caring for the electrical system. B. Whittier. il Yachting 113:62-3+ Je '63
Electrical and electronic. E. Robberson. il Yachting 115:44-5+ Ap '64
Installing a marine generating plant. C. Kucyn. il Motor B 112:38-9+ N '63
What you should know about alternators. E. Robberson. il Yachting 113:40-2+ F '63

Electronic equipment

Electrical and electronic. E. Robberson. il Yachting 115:44-5+ Ap '64
Electronic boating aids. E. Robberson. il Yachting 114:51-3+ Jl '63
New era in marine electronics. L. Craig. il Motor B 112:31-3+ N '63

Equipment

Boat owners sound off. J. A. Emmett. il Outdoor Life 134:82-4 D '64
Crisis kit for your boat. P. K. Snook and M. Michaelson. il Pop Mech 121:154 Mr '64
Equipment 64-65. il Motor B 113:164-83+ Ja '64; 115:162-80+ Ja '65
Fitting out; symposium. il Yachting 113:60-8+ Ap '63
Gadgets & gilhickies. H. DeFontaine. See issues of Yachting
Keep your galley shipshape. il Pop Sci 184:162 My '64
Maintenance; symposium. il Yachting 115:42-8+ Ap '64
New ideas in boating; nautical gadgets. F. M. Paulson. il Field & S 69:42-3 Ja '65
New year, new gear. F. M. Paulson. il Field & S 68:86-91 F '64
PS outfits seven boats for 1963. il Pop Sci 182:116-19+ Mr '63
Reversible backrest. A. I. Allison. il Outdoor Life 134:120 Ag '64
Rig your boat for hunting. J. A. Emmett. il Outdoor Life 132:126+ O '63
Six bits of luxury for your boat. P. K. Snook. il Pop Mech 121:152-3 Mr '64
Swimming ladder for your boat. G. P. Manning. il Motor B 113:31+ Mr '64
Waterfront news. See issues of Yachting
What's new? See issues of Motor boating
What's new for boating? F. M. Paulson. il Field & S 67:68-73 F '63
What's new in boating. J. Roe. il Pop Sci 184:142-5+ F '64
What's new in boats. il Changing T 18:34-6 Ap '64
What's up below. C. Darlington. il Motor B 113:46-8 Mr '64
Yachting interviews; ed. by M. Wiley. H. Adams. il Yachting 115:66-7+ Je '64
See also
Anchors
Horns (signals)
Motor boats—Equipment
Pumps
Radio telephone on ships, boats, etc.
Rope
Speedometers

Exhibitions

Boat-show calendar. Outdoor Life 135:67 Ja '65
For the good life afloat; National boat show. il Bsns W p28-9 Ja 19 '63
Meet the Seasoned skipper; Marine trades show in Chicago. il Motor B 112:21+ N '63
Sea fever; world's biggest boat show opens in Manhattan. il Time 85:37 Ja 22 '65
Yachting's boat show. il Yachting 115:127-32+ Ja '64; 117:127-32+ Ja '65
See also
Motor boats—Exhibitions

Fastenings

See Fastenings (machinery)

Finance

Boat financing. C. R. Meyer. il Motor B 113:258+ Ja '64
First plans and a budget. Motor B 111:22 Mr '63

Floors

No-slip floor for your boat. V. L. Oertle. il Pop Mech 121:151 Mr '64

Heating and ventilation

Small boat ventilation. H. Rubinkam. il Yachting 115:150 F '64

Launching

Boat is an island; Hawaiian launching ceremony. N. J. Lays. il Motor B 115:94-7+ Ja '65
Bringing that new boat home. B. Clede. il Motor B 113:36-7+ Ap '64
Lifting rings for your boat. il Sunset 132:136+ Je '64

Licensing

See Boats—Registration

Materials

Boat owners sound off. J. A. Emmett. il Outdoor Life 134:82-4 D '64
Boating comes of age. J. E. Choate. il Yachting 117:94-7+ Ja '65
Dynel, newest in overlay materials. M. Penzer. il Motor B 112:44-5 O '63
Like trees, boats should be wooden. H. Whall. il Sports Illus 22:42+ Ja 25 '65
Stuff of which boats are made; wood, steel, aluminum, fiberglass; symposium. il Motor B 114:21-41 D '64
Yachting asks about fiberglass boats; symposium, ed. by E. Robberson. il Yachting 115:45-8+ My '64
Yachting asks about wooden boats; questions and answers. il Yachting 114:60-3+ O '63
Your boat in A.D. 2063. H. A. Calahan. il Motor B 111:26-7+ Mr '63

Mooring

ABCs of anchoring. G. P. Manning. il Pop Mech 119:142-6 My '63
Speaking of moorings. R. P. Davis. il Motor B 113:48-51 My '64

Names

Good name, better than precious ointment. M. H. Farnham. il Motor B 113:20-3 F '64
Mystique of boat names. il Motor B 111:46-7 Mr '63

Painting

Pointers on painting. F. M. Paulson. il Field & S 67:124-9 Ap '63

Propellers

See Propellers

Purchasing

Boats to sail, row or paddle. il Changing T 17:43-6 My '63
Buying a used boat. il Pop Sci 182:128-30+ Mr '63
Holiday handbook of small-boat sailing. W. P. Bradley. il Holiday 36:97-100 Ag '64

Radio equipment

See Radio apparatus on ships, boats, etc.

Registration

Documentation of a yacht. R. Brindze. il Yachting 113:48-9+ My '63

Renting

Renting a boat. J. A. Emmett. il Outdoor Life 131:132-6 My '63
Sail it now, sink it later. H. Whall. il Sports Illus 21:18-19 Ag 24 '64

Repairing

Commissioning hints. W. H. deFontaine. il Yachting 113:69 Ap '63
First-aid for foundering dinghies. N. Meiners. il Motor B 113:32-3+ Mr '64
How to keep your fiberglass boat young and floating. G. Daniels. il Pop Sci 185:98-100+ S '64
How to make laminated sister ribs. il Motor B 113:28-9+ Mr '64
New or old, is she your first boat? Do-it-yourself: suggestions. J. Emmett. il Yachting 115:52+ Ap '64
New way to save an old boat. G. Daniels. il Pop Sci 182:127-30 F '63
New wonder products for boat repairs. G. Daniels. il Pop Sci 182:123-5+ Mr '63
Ten timesaving tips. G. F. Stillwell. il Motor B 111:152+ Ag '63

Sanitation

Boat sanitation. E. Robberson. Yachting 116:52-5+ O '64

BOATS—*Continued*

Seats

Re-upholster your helmsman's seat; vinyl upholstery. N. Meiners. il Motor B 113:30+ Mr '64

Speed

See also
Speedometers

Storage

Boats, boatyards and yachtsmen. W. Britton. il Motor B 112:30-1+ O '63
Pieces and quiet; inquiry into the hibernation of the hydroplane. E. Crimmin. il Motor B 111:137-9 F '63
Putting your boat to bed. F. M. Paulson. il Field & S 69:120-4 O '64
Wintering in the Chesapeake; wet storage. F. Kern. il Yachting 114:28-30+ D '63

Transportation

Car-top boat carrier. il Sunset 130:60 F '63
Piggy-back boats. F. M. Paulson. il Field & S 68:102-5+ O '63
Small boats on the move. J. Coverdale. il Yachting 114:52-3 O '63
See also
Automobile boat trailers

BOATS, Fire. See Fireboats
BOATS, Ice. See Ice boats and ice boating
BOATS, Police. See Police boats
BOATS, Remodeled
Boy and a boat; rejuvenated tug. M. Wiley. il Yachting 115:138 F '64
Day sailer to capsule cruiser. J. A. Livingston. il Yachting 114:66+ Jl '63
Steam returns to the San Juans. W. Howland. il Yachting 113:40-1+ Mr '63
BOATS, Rubber
Craft you can tote. J. A. Emmett. il Outdoor Life 135:112-15 F '65
BOATS, Theft of
Look out for harbor pirates! D. C. Fales. il Yachting 116:52-3+ Jl '64
Pirate's eye view of boating; marine theft. G. A. Alton. il Yachting 116:50-1+ Jl '64
BOATS, Used
Buying a used boat. il Pop Sci 182:128-30+ Mr '63
How to buy a used rig. J. A. Emmett. il Outdoor Life 134:126-8 O '64
BOATS and boating
All kinds of people go to sea in whalers. C. Phinizy. il Sports Illus 19:48-50 Jl 29 '63
Beauty part of rowing. W. G. Wing. il Harper 227:26+ S '63
Best years are boating years. Motor B 111:21 F '63
Boating. J. A. Emmett. See issues of Outdoor life
Boating (cont) il Sports Illus 18:52-4 Mr 18 '63
Boating; ed. by F. M. Paulson. See issues of Field & stream
Boating bulletins; new trends, new products. il Pop Mech 119:132-7 Mr '63
Boating in the Land of Lincoln. C. B. Meurer. il Motor B 111:29+ Je '63
Boating manners. R. J. Sullivan. il Motor B 112:46+ D '63
Boating 1963. G. B. Leonard. il Look 27:33-42 Jl 16 '63
Boating on the great river of the West. L. Barber. il Motor B 111:34-5+ My '63
Boating '64. J. Speirs. il Pop Mech 121:133-40+ Mr '64
Boating west of the great divide. il Motor B 111:24-5 My '63
Boats to sail, row or paddle. il Changing T 17:43-6 My '63
Budget boating vacation: the Columbia Basin. D. Bolding. il Field & S 68:61-3 Je '63
By boat into the Cascade wilderness; Lake Chelan. il Sunset 133:18-20 Ag '64
Calendar of coming events. R. B. Smith. See issues of Motor boating
Canal Zone motorboating. N. Robinson and D. Robinson. il Motor B 111:44-5+ My '63
Cold weather outboarding. B. Whittier. il Yachting 116:48-9+ D '64
Dinghies U.S.A. A. Knapp. jr. il Motor B 112:35 Ag; 103 O '63
Dinghies U.S.A. where to find them. il Motor B 112:110 Ag '63
Dinghy cruise to Turkey; from Cyprus. G. Gaskill. il Yachting 115:48-50+ Mr '64
Down to the sea for fun; with photographs by J. Zimmerman. Sat Eve Post 237:28-37 Ap 25 '64
Family boating on Puget Sound. il Motor B 111:143-4 My '63
Fiberglass boats, construction and maintenance. B. Cobb, jr. See issues of Yachting
Fishing dory. J. A. Emmett. il Outdoor Life 134:122-3+ S '64
Gam. See issues of Yachting to March 1964
High road, low road, Buchans take the blow road. E. Crimmin. Motor B 111:146-7 My '63
It's the season for boats and more boats. il Newsweek 63:80-2+ Je 15 '64
Job for everyone. il Motor B 111:23 Mr '63
Living aboard, a way of life. B. Simpson. il Yachting 115:57+ My '64
Look again, old-timer! M. A. Scott. il Motor B 112:41-3+ Jl '63
Miami's wet, windy stadium. J. Martenhoff. Motor B 113:106+ Je '64
Midwest is dinghy country, too. E. J. Knudsen. il Motor B 112:39 Ag '63
New England, U.S. dinghy cradle. il Motor B 112:36-7+ Ag '63
News from overseas. Yachting 115:224-5 My '64
News from yachting centers. See issues of Yachting
1965 bountiful year for boatmen. F. M. Paulson. il Field & S 69:36-44 Ja '65
1964 lineup of new boats and motors. F. M. Paulson. il Field & S 68:27-34 Ja '64
Northern squall eclipses southern sun. E. Crimmin. Motor B 112:106-7+ S '63
One-day cruise on the Lady Rose. Sunset 134-8 Ja '65
Outdoor life boating, 1964-1965. J. A. Emmett. il Outdoor Life 133:52-60+ F '64; 135:52-67+ Ja '65
People you meet. A. A. Birney. il Yachting 114:32-3+ D '63
Puget Sound; the climate, topography, tempo, life, but in particular, the boating. E. Crimmin. il Motor B 111:30-2+ My '63
Reaching ahead; special selection of upcoming events, April through October. il Motor B 113:22-3 Mr '64
Relics from the rapids. S. F. Olson. il Nat Geog Mag 124:412-35 S '63
Remember '63? il Motor B 113:66-74 Ja '64
Reporter at large; Current River, Mo. B. Roueché. il New Yorker 39:48-50+ Ap 6 '63
Seasoned skipper. See issues of Motor boating
Six common boating problems. J. Martenhoff. il Pop Sci 184:165-6+ Ap '64
'64 boats for unquiet people. W. T. McKeown. il Esquire 61:72-5 Mr '64
Sliding up a damp chute. B. Goldrath. il Field & S 68:46-7 Jl '63
Some terrific Pacific dinks. il Motor B 112:40 Ag '63
Southern style dinghies. il Motor B 112:39 Ag '63
Space-age boating. E. Crimmin. il Motor B 113:26-8+ F '64
Stuff of which boats are made; wood, steel, aluminum, fiberglass; symposium. il Motor B 114:21-41 D '64
Tent-boating: fun for the men of the family. P. Neuhaus. il Todays Health 41:51 Ag '63
Through the glass you see an underwater coral world; Hawaii's offshore waters. il Sunset 132:28+ F '64
Through the mangrove wilderness; southwest Florida. M. Hunn. il Yachting 114:54-5+ N '63
To Alaska by outboard. il Yachting 114:42-3 D '63
Trailer cruising northeast. E. R. Thornton. il Motor B 111:32-4+ Ap '63
Trailer down to New Orleans. K. Ferguson. il Motor B 113:84-5+ Ja '64
Trailer trek to Timagami. F. M. Paulson. il Field & S 68:64+ Ap '64
True or false of boating. J. A. Emmett. il Outdoor Life 131:74-6 Ja '63
Under the lee of the longboat. See issues of Yachting
Water rats. S. Iselin. Mlle 57:140-3+ My '63
West Coast skippers stay afloat. C. West. il Motor B 112:28-9+ D '63
What's new? See issues of Motor boating
What's new for boating in '63. J. Roe. il Pop Sci 182:113-35 Mr '63
What's new in boats. il Changing T 18:34-6 Ap '64
Whittled wooden jury rig prop brings boatman home safely. N. Tashman. il Motor B 113:372 Ja '64
With sails, an outboard, or a paddle. il Sunset 130:72 My '63
Wonderfully wild world of boating; photographs. M. Penzer. Motor B 113:37-41 Mr '64

BOATS and boating—*Continued*
Yachting asks about fiberglass boats; symposium, ed. by E. Robberson. il Yachting 115:45-8+ My '64
Yachting asks about wooden boats; questions and answers. il Yachting 114:60-3+ O '63
Year that was. il Motor B 115:62-75 Ja '65
Yes, we keep our boat in a closet. R. Marx. il Pop Sci 184:163-6 My '64
You can start small in boating. il Pop Sci 184:160 Ap '64
You couldn't be here without a boat; symposium. il Pop Sci 184:124-7+ F '64
See also
Airboats
Canoe trips
Catamarans
Catboats
Circle line-sightseeing yachts, incorporated
Cookery, Marine
Cruising
Decks
Ferries
House boats
Hydrokarts
Junks
Kayaks
Marinas
Navigation
Outboard boating club of America
Rafts
Regattas
River trips
Rowing
Sailboats
Sailing
Sails
Women in boating
Yachts and yachting

Accidents

On the water front; weekend sailors. il Newsweek 64:79 Jl 20 '64
Perils of the surface. il Time 82:56 Jl 5 '63
To aid hospitalized driver. B. Ruskauff. il Motor B 111:134-5 F '63
Water torture; photographs; with report by R. Vaughan. R. Huntzinger. Sat Eve Post 236:30-4 Ag 24 '63
What did they do wrong? il Pop Sci 184:137 F '64
What did they do wrong? J. Liston. il Pop Sci 183:110-11 Jl; 85 Ag '63
See also
Fishing—Accidents and injuries

Anecdotes, facetiae, satire, etc.

Cruising tips. E. Crimmin. il Motor B 111:40-1+ Ap '63
First mate to Bligh. B. B. Carton. Mlle 57:218-19+ My '63
Ladies Thursday afternoon; sailing and sinking society. T. J. King. il Yachting 115:74-5+ Ja '64
Mopey Dink. K. Collins. il Yachting 113:42-4+ Je '63
Never a dull moment. M. Rumsey. il Motor B 112:27+ Ag '63
Oh paradise! il Motor B 113:42-3 Ap '64
Vulgar boatmen. W. J. Gold. il Life 54:8+ My 17 '63

Bibliography

Best in boating books. Motor B 112:28 N '63
Book reviews. See issues of Yachting
Yachtsman's bookshelf; comp. by J. DeGraff (cont) Yachting 114:162+ N; 122+ D '63

Caricatures and cartoons

Are you taking your boat to the races? Yachting 116:73 S '64

History

Ships through the ages: a saga of the sea. A. Villiers. il Nat Geog Mag 123:496-545 Ap '63

Laws and regulations

Are you asking for more laws? W. Robberson. Yachting 113:164-5 Je '63
Boat sanitation. E. Robberson. Yachting 116:52-5+ O '64
Boating laws and regulations. W. T. Stone. il Yachting 115:49-51+ Ap '64
Boatman's rules of the road. il Outdoor Life 133:58-9 F '64
Cruising club measurement rule. G. M. Curtis, jr. il Yachting 115:44-6+ Mr '64
Documentation of a yacht. R. Brindze. il Yachting 113:48-9+ My '63
Florida's new boating laws. J. Martenhoff. Motor B 112:113-14 Ag '63
Help, but at a price. J. P. Dunne. il Motor B 114:40-1+ S '64
How many boating mistakes can you find here? il Outdoor Life 135:58-9 Ja '65
Lake George patrol. M. Crook. il Yachting 115:96-7+ Ja '64
Red tape and blue water. M. B. Petersen. il Motor B 112:26+ Ag '63
Right-of-way. G. B. Leonard. il Look 27:42 Jl 16 '63
Sail it now, sink it later. H. Whall. il Sports Illus 21:18-19 Ag 24 '64
Skipper: just how liable are you? J. W. Giles. Motor B 113:248+ Ja '64
Tricks of match racing; excerpt from Cornelius Shields on sailing. C. Shields. il Sports Illus 20:38-47 Je 29 '64
Washington report. W. T. Stone. See issues of Yachting
Water torture; photographs; with report by R. Vaughan. R. Huntzinger. Sat Eve Post 236:30-4 Ag 24 '63

Anecdotes, facetiae, satire, etc.

There oughta be a lawr. E. Crimmin. Motor B 111:147-8 Je '63

Lightning hazards

Struck by lightning. C. B. Ford. il Yachting 115:63-5+ Je '64

Safety devices and measures

Automatic systems for safety. H. Holcomb. il Motor B 112:34-6 N '63
Boating safety suggestions from the coast guard. Yachting 115:116 My '64
Boats in distress. J. A. Emmett. il Outdoor Life 131:106-9 Je '63
Fifty suggestions for safe trips by canoe or boat. E. J. Slezak. Recreation 57:137 Mr '64
Foam boat flotation. L. Oertle. il Suc Farm 61:101 S '63
Foul weather ahead. J. A. Emmett. il Outdoor Life 132:84-7 Jl '63
How to get invited back. J. A. Emmett. il Outdoor Life 132:86-8 Ag '63
How to have a safe boat trip. A. E. Cullen. il Todays Health 41:38-41 Ag '63
Lesson taught by a shoelace. E. Crimmin. il Motor B 114:54+ Jl '64
Modern boats and motel-T boating. T. Cofield. Motor B 113:46+ Je '64
Picking up a man overboard. W. H. deFontaine. il Yachting 115:95 Ja '64
Plotting tomorrow's course. B. Woodward. Motor B 113:37 Je '64
Post war progress; courtesy boat exams and public instruction. il Motor B 113:34-5+ Je '64
Rooster tales. E. Rickman. il Hot Rod 17:104-5 S '64
Safe boating instruction afloat. il Motor B 112:42-3+ Ag '63
Safe boating is fun. il Motor B 113:156 Je '64
Safety for family sailors. W. T. McKeown. il Am Home 67:42 Jl '64
Safety is positive, it is simply doing things right. il Motor B 111:32-3+ Je '63

Statistics

Facts and the figures (cont) J. E. Choate. Yachting 115:151-2 F '64

Study and teaching

Boating skills taught the painless way. il Motor B 112:114-15 Jl '63
Classroom on the Sound; Commack union free school district, L. I. W. G. Tabel. Motor B 112:82 Ag '63
Post war progress; courtesy boat exams and public instruction. il Motor B 113:34-5+ Je '64
Safe boating instruction afloat. il Motor B 112:42-3+ Ag '63

Terminology

Salt in our talk. J. Martenhoff. il Motor B 113:19+ F '64

BOATYARDS
Boats, boatyards and yachtsmen. W. Britton. il Motor B 112:30-1+ O '63
Do-it-yourself boatyard. W. C. Morrison. il Yachting 115:198+ My '64

BOAZ, Martha
Passage to Pakistan. por Wilson Lib Bul 38:478-9 F '64

BOAZ, Willard D.
Pica; prevalent, peculiar, poisonous. PTA Mag 58:22-4 D '63

BOB, Murray
Paperback utopia. por Library J 88:1941-2 My 15 '63

BOB MARSHALL WILDERNESS AREA. See Wilderness areas

BOB whites. See Quails

BOBBIE Brooks, incorporated
$100 million in rags. S. Freedgood. il Fortune 67:151-4+ My '63

BOBBIES. See Police—Great Britain

BOBCAT hunting
Great little cat. B. East. il Outdoor Life 135:24-7+ Ja '65

BOBCATS
Water-happy wildcats. J. Yoakum. il Audubon Mag 66:166-7 My '64

BOBSLEDDING. See Coasting

BOBWHITE shooting. See Quail shooting

BOBWHITES. See Quails

BOCCA, Geoffrey
Marcello Mastroianni: reluctant lover. McCalls 91:64+ My '64
Spectacular cult of Ian Fleming. Sat Eve Post 236:66-8 Je 22 '63
They kept the old flag flying. Horizon 5:74-81 S '63
Those student tours to Europe: what really goes on. McCalls 90:92-3+ Jl '63
Young grandees on tour. Sat R 46:58-60 Mr 16 '63

BOCCACCIO, Giovanni
BCD trilogy, Boccaccio. P. W. Schmidtchen. il por Hobbies 68:106-7 F '64

BOCHNER, Salomon
Revolutions in physics and crises in mathematics. bibliog Science 141:408-11 Ag 2 '63

BOCK, Fred G. and others
Tumor-promoting activity of extracts of unburned tobacco. bibliog Science 145:831-3 Ag 21 '64

BOCK, Frederick
Banner day; For Richie; Vegetation; October silence; poems. Poetry 102:217-20 Jl '63
Factoryland; poem. Nation 196:290 Ap 6 '63
Falls; poem. Nation 197:36 Jl 13 '63
For George, with vim; poem. Christian Cent 80:233 F 20 '63
Man parked on roadside; Summer despite; Lost image; Recovery; poems. Poetry 103: 284-7 F '64
Three variations on finding's keeping; poem. New Repub 149:27 Ag 31 '63

BOCK, Walter
Book project. Sch Arts 64:17-18 N '64

BOCKELMAN, Wilfred
I'm hoping to meet more Catholics. America 111:67-9 Jl 18 '64

BODARD, Mag
Phenomenon of Les parapluies de Cherbourg. V. Cowles. il Vogue 144:214-15+ N 1 '64

BODE, Vernon C. and others
Daily rhythm of luciferin activity in gonyaulax polyedra. bibliog Science 141:913-15 S 6 '63

BODEGA BAY, Calif.
Bodega: symbol of a national crisis. K. S. Roe. il Am For 69:22-5 D '63
Outrage on Bodega Head. G. Marine. il Nation 196:524-7 Je 22 '63; Discussion. 197:62 Ag 10 '63

BODENHEIM, Maxwell
Squash & stretch. M. Klonsky. il pors Esquire 60:162-3+ D '63

BODET, Jaime Torres
Fifteen years ago; address, December 10, 1948. UNESCO Courier 16:4-5 D '63

BODIAN, David, and Taylor, Naomi
Synapse arising at central node of Ranvier, and note on fixation of the central nervous system. bibliog Science 139:330-2 Ja 25 '63

BODIEN, Gordon, and Pratt, L. C.
Blow snow off the bridges. Am City 79:71-2 Ja '64

BODIN, Simone
Bettina's Nile diary; tr. by A. Foulke. pors Vogue 143:132-7+ Ja 1 '64

about

Bettina: a woman of change. F. Nourissier. il pors Vogue 143:138-45+ Ja 1 '64

BODINGTON, Deryk
Snow eaters of Alberta. Natur Hist 73:60-1 F '64

BODMAN, Tim
New life in a leprosarium. Recreation 57:62 F '64

BODMER, Karl
Carl Bodmer's unspoiled West; with portfolio. M. B. Davidson. il Am Heritage 14:43-65 Ap '63

BODSWORTH, Fred
Greatest of all outdoors. Holiday 35:175-82 Ap '64

BODY, Human. See Physiology

BODY chemistry. See Biochemistry

BODY fat. See Fat

BODY fluids
Sea within us; excerpts from Man and his body. B. F. Miller and R. Goode. Read Digest 82:192C-192D+ Mr '63
See also
Gastric juice

BODY size. See Size

BODY temperature. See Temperature, Animal and human

BODY water. See Water in the body

BOEBEL, Jim. See Osheroff, A. jt. auth.

BOECKH, Jurgen, and others
Olfactory receptor response to the cockroach sexual attractant. bibliog Science 141:716 Ag 23 '63

BOEGLI, Janet Claire
My life as a Peace corps girl; ed. by A. St George. Good H 156:84-5+ Ap '63

BOEHM, George A. W.
Alchemy of ultrahigh pressure. Fortune 70: 144-8+ O '64
Bringing engineers up to date. Fortune 67: 120-1+ My '63
Inexhaustible riches from the sea. Fortune 68:132-7+ D '63; Same abr. Read Digest 84:111-15 Ap '64
Reliability engineering. Fortune 67:124-7+ Ap '63
Science of being almost certain. Fortune 69: 104-7+ F '64
Tapping nature's storehouse of violent energy. Fortune 68:130-4+ Ag '63
That wonderful machine, the brain. Fortune 67:125-9+ F '63
What radiation can do for the production line. Fortune 70:140-3+ D '64

BOEHM, Karl. See Böhm, K.

BOEHRINGER, Carl H.
Meeting with the West. Am Heritage 14:16-31 Ag '63

BOEING company
Aerospace alliance; Seattle's Boeing co. acquires an interest in Bölkow GmbH. Time 85:64 Ja 8 '65
Boeing gets $60-million Lunar orbiter award. Miss & Roc 14:13 Ja 6 '64
Boeing holding out on union shop issue. Bsns W p54+ Ap 13 '63
Boeing seeks settlement in profits cases. K. Johnsen. Aviation W 82:29 Ja 25 '65
Boeing steps up efforts in cryogenics research. R. Twiss. Miss & Roc 16:36-7 Ja 11 '65
Boeing strike delayed pending IAM vote. Aviation W 78:36 My 6 '63
Boeing to build lunar orbiter. Aviation W 79:22 D 30 '63
Boeing weighs plans for 707 successors. H. D. Watkins. Aviation W 82:36-7 Ja 25 '65
Challenge met in Minuteman management. R. Twiss. il Miss & Roc 13:36 Jl 22 '63
Compromise ends tension at Boeing. Bsns W p 166 Ap 20 '63
Filling that defense void. Time 84:95-6 O 9 '64
How the Pentagon is run: what TFX fight shows; with excerpts from statement by R. S. McNamara. il U S News 54:54-7 Ap 22 '63
Impasse at Boeing. America 108:190-1 F 9 '63
IAM prepares for Boeing strike. Aviation W 78:37 Ap 15 '63
NASA, Boeing resuming life-support tests. H. M. David. il Miss & Roc 14:28-9 Ja 27 '64
NASA explains choice of Boeing over Hughes in Lunar orbiter award. Miss & Roc 14:13 Mr 9 '64
Phasing out the air force? contract for TFX. Nat R 14:223-4 Mr 26 '63
Strike by IAM at Boeing averted. Aviation W 78:37 Ap 22 '63
Supreme court refuses to hear appeal in Boeing renegotiation. K. Johnsen. Aviation W 80:30 My 11 '64
TFX plane: what the fight is about. il U S News 54:61-3 Mr 25 '63
Tactical fighters; TFX hearing. Reporter 28: 12 Ap 11 '63
Wage chronology: the Boeing co. Washington plants 1962-65. il Mo Labor R 87:900-3 Ag '64
What Boeing and union agreed on; machinists union. U S News 54:96 Ap 29 '63
Where pressure is rising against the union shop. il U S News 54:105-6 Ap 22 '63
Why Wichita said no; rejection of new contract between the Boeing co. and the International assn. of machinists. il Bsns W p 106 Ap 27 '63
Workers reject new Boeing contract. Aviation W 78:27 Ap 29 '63
Workers vote on final Boeing proposal. Aviation W 78:29 Ap 1 '63

BOEKE, Harley C.
Treating troublesome waters. Am City 79: 100-2 F '64
BOERMA, A. H.
World food programme. UN Mo Chron 1: 72-6 N '64
BOERNER, Alfred L.
Alfred L. Boerner botanical gardens. C. B. Lees. il Horticulture 42:34-7 Ap '64
BOERNER botanical gardens, Wisconsin. See Botanical gardens
BOETH, Richard
New face, old pro. Sat R 46:21-3 D 28 '63
BOETTINGER, Henry M.
Man on the move. por Duns R 81:54-5 Ap '63
BOFORS, ab. See Sweden—Industries
BOGAN, Louise
Verse (cont) New Yorker 39:173-5 Ap 27; 210-12 O 12 '63; 40:178+ Ap 11; 238+ N 7 '64
BOGARDE, Dirk
Unpublic life. por Time 83:66 Ap 3 '64
BOGART, Humphrey
Bogey worship. il por Time 83:80-1 F 7 '64
Bogie in excelsis. P. Bogdanovich. por Esquire 62:108-9+ S '64
BOGART, Max
(ed) Special issue on paperbacks. Sr Schol 85:17T-26T+ D 2 '64
BOGDANOVICH, Peter
Autumn of John Ford. Esquire 61:102-4+ Ap '64
Bogie in excelsis. Esquire 62:108-9+ S '64
BOGEN, L. H.
Enlarge upon your problems. U S Camera 26: 66-7+ S '63
BOGEN, Miriam Belle
Guide to cookbook entertaining. Atlan 214: 107 S '64
BOGERT, Charles M.
Little snakes with hands. Natur Hist 73:16-25 Ag '64
BOGGESS, Rough A.
Oklahoma City, a glorious discontent. Mus Am 84:64+ Ja '64
BOGGS, J. Caleb
Excerpt from debate, September 25, 1964. Cong Digest 43:305+ D '64
BOGGS, James
View from Harlem. A. B. Spellman. Nation 198:656-7 Je 29 '64
BOGGS, Jean Sutherland
Picasso and the nude. Art N 62:29-31+ Ja '64
Toronto treasures, universal and university. Art N 61:32-4+ F '63
BOGGS, William E.
Bullets of light. New Repub 148:5 Mr 16 '63
Man on the moon. New Repub 149:6-7 Ag 3; 30 S 14 '63
Plane in a poke. New Repub 149:7 N 2 '63
Plane nobody wants. New Repub 149:12-14 S 14 '63
Population and the pill. New Repub 148:13-14 Ap 13 '63
Specter of science. New Repub 150:19-20+ Ap 18 '64
That mysterious A-11. New Repub 150:14-15 Mr 14 '64
BOGOTÁ, Colombia

Description

Down and up in Bogota. M. M. Davis. il Travel 122:50-3 Jl '64

Housing

Twin duplexes in Colombia. il Arch Forum 118:95 Ap '63
BOGUS (printing industry) See Featherbedding (industrial relations)
BOHAN, Eleanor
Reader's choice. Travel 121:13 Ja '64
BOHANNAN, Paul
Place for all things. Natur Hist 73:54-61 O '64
BOHANNON, Richard
Doctor with one foot in space. K. N. Anderson. il pors Todays Health 42:32-5+ D '64
BOHANON, Eunice Blake
American specialist abroad. Horn Bk 40:642-5 D '64
La BOHÈME; opera. See Puccini, G.
BOHEMIANISM
See also
Beatniks
BOHLIN, J. Davis. See Newkirk, G. jr, jt. auth.
BÖHM, Karl
Böhm portrait. il pors Mus Am 83:12-13 Mr '63
Music master; photographs. E. Cook. Opera N 27:12-13 F 16 '63
BOHMRICH, J. J.
Prestolite builds a new world. por Bsns W p63-4+ D 14 '63
BOHN, Buddy
One-man peace corps. il por Time 81:42+ F 8 '63
BOHN, William
On call with an audio doctor. L. Marcus il por Hi Fi 13:61-4 N '63
BOHR, David F.
Vascular smooth muscle: dual effect of calcium. bibliog Science 139:597-9 F 15 '63
BOHR, Niels Henrik David
Inside story on the A-bomb; excerpt from article. J. R. Oppenheimer. il U S News 57:8 D 21 '64
Philosophy of Niels Bohr. A. Petersen. por Bul Atomic Sci 19:8-14 S '63
Science milestone. G. Gamow. il pors Sci Digest 53:71-8 My '63
BOIGNY, Félix Houphouet-. See Houphouet-Boigny, F.
BOIKO, Claire
Big shoo; drama. Plays 24:41-6 O '64
Christmas revel; drama. Plays 24:39-50, 86 D '64
Exterior decorator; drama. Plays 23:60-4 Mr '64
Franklin reversal; drama. Plays 24:47-53 N '64
Marmalade overture; drama. Plays 24:79-81 N '64
Penny wise; drama. Plays 24:78-82 Ja '65
Peter, Peter, Peter! drama. Plays 23:45-54 F '64
Punctuation proclamation; drama. Plays 23: 65-8, 96 Ap '64
Sun up! drama. Plays 23:73-6 Ap '64
T party; drama. Plays 23:78-82 N '63
Terrible Terry's surprise; drama. Plays 22: 42, 65-70 Ap '63
Trouble in tree-land; drama. Plays 23:83-6, 108 My '64
BOILED eggs. See Cookery—Eggs
BOILER plates
Critical Apollo test modules produced. il Aviation W 79:124-31+ Jl 22 '63
BOILERS
Hyprox to cut altitude chamber cost; Thiokol steam generator. R. Hawkes. il Miss & Roc 12:27 Ap 22 '63
BOILING water reactors. See Nuclear reactors
BOISE Cascade corporation
Action in Idaho. il Time 82:78+ D 20 '63
Bared by a B-school; Stanford students at Boise Cascade corp. il Bsns W p90+ Mr 14 '64
Idaho woodsman makes the chips fly; lumbering industry. il Bsns W p 144+ O 12 '63
BOISEN, H. L.
Untortured Butler. Library J 88:4571-3 D 1 '63
BOJE, Walter
New look in color. U S Camera 27:52-7+ N '64
BOK, Bart J.
International discussion of Milky way research. por Sky & Tel 26:4-7 Jl '63
Large cloud of Magellan; with biographical sketch. Sci Am 210:18, 32-41 Ja '64
BOKELMAN, W. Robert, and Deering, E. C.
Bonds for educational purposes, sales, interest rates, et cetera; colleges and universities. See issues of School life
BOKER, Alouise
Well traveled camera. D. L. Miller. il Mod Phot 27:38+ Je '63
BOLAND, Charles Michael
Getting under way for Christmas. por Pub W 186:36-40 Ag 24 '64
BOLDEN, Abraham
Mr Q mystery. il por Newsweek 63:20 Je 1 '64
BOLDING, Dick
Budget boating vacation: the Columbia Basin. Field & S 68:61-3 Je '63
BOLDINI, Giovanni
Portrait of a master; reprint, tr. by J. W. Freeman. D. Cecchi. il por Opera N 28:6-9 F 15 '64
BOLEK, Tony
Wingfoot express. Hot Rod 16:92-4 Ag '63
BOLER, John F.
Role of the will. Commonweal 80:374 Je 12 '64
BOLES, Paul Darcy
Daughter of the chief of police; story. Sat Eve Post 237:50-1 S 26 '64
Kindred heart; story. Seventeen 22:126-7 O '63
Lucas and Jake; story. Ladies Home J 80:68 Mr '63
Please get serious! story. Seventeen 23:82-3 D '64

BOLES, Paul Darcy—*Continued*
Summer in a shell; story. Seventeen 23:124-5 Je '64
Summerhouse; story. Seventeen 23:220-1 Ag '64
Talent for delight; story. Seventeen 23:126-7 Mr '64
Treasure; story. Seventeen 22:108-9 F '63

BOLES, Robert
Whats your problem? story. New Yorker 40:55-8 O 17 '64

BOLEY, Okla.
Boley round-up time. il Ebony 20:100+ N '64
Dream that faded; all-Negro town. G. Geis and W. E. Bittle. il N Y Times Mag p47+ D 6 '64

BOLIDES. See Meteors

BOLIVIA
Bolivia; Peace corps volunteers. E. S. Dennison. il Nat Geog Mag 126:314-19 S '64
See also
Americans in Bolivia
Economic assistance in Bolivia
Elections—Bolivia
Strikes—Bolivia
Tin mines and mining—Bolivia

Economic conditions

Back to work: Catavi miners. Newsweek 62:51 S 9 '63
Bolivia: revolt in the mountains; on-scene report. M. J. Kubic. il Newsweek 62:46-7 Ag 26 '63
Bolivians trek eastward. R. E. Crist. il Américas 15:33-8 Ap '63
Can anybody save Bolivia? J. N. Wallace. il U S News 57:64-6 D 21 '64
Friendly U.S. ear. Newsweek 62:38 N 4 '63
High, hard land. il Time 82:41 N 1 '63
Solvency & self-respect; tin mines. Time 82:27 Ag 16 '63
Tin-plated trouble. il Newsweek 62:48 Ag 19 '63

Foreign relations

President Paz of Bolivia visits United States; text of communique between President Kennedy and President Paz, October 23, 1963. J. F. Kennedy and V. Paz Estenssoro. Dept State Bul 49:787-8 N 18 '63

Politics and government

Blowup in Bolivia: why, what to expect. il U S News 57:6 N 9 '64
Coup topples Paz. il Sr Schol 85:20 N 18 '64
Durable master. Newsweek 63:52+ My 25 '64
Free at last; American hostages in Bolivia. il Time 82:29 D 27 '63
General in charge. Time 84:56+ N 13 '64
In Bolivia: new leader, old problems; in U.S: questions. U S News 57:8 N 16 '64
Last musketeer. Newsweek 63:57 Je 15 '64
Military rule in Bolivia. New Repub 151:5-6 N 21 '64
New success story in Latin America. il U S News 56:62-3 Je 15 '64
New voice of moderation. Time 83:30 Mr 27 '64
On the brink. il Newsweek 62:35-6 D 23 '63
Plot or play? il Time 85:35 Ja 15 '65
Preventing trouble before it starts. Time 84:66+ O 2 '64
Progress toward a third term. il Time 83:34 My 29 '64
Ruling rivalries. Newsweek 63:47 F 10 '64
State of anarchy. il Time 84:35 N 20 '64
Tin-plated trouble. il Newsweek 62:48 Ag 19 '63
Up from veep. Newsweek 64:58 N 16 '64

Religious institutions and affairs

News of the Christian world. Christian Cent 81:1382 N 4 '64

Riots

Springtime in the Andes. il Newsweek 64:60 N 9 '64
View from the volcano; rioting students. il Time 84:30 N 6 '64

Social conditions

Bolivians trek eastward. R. E. Crist. il Américas 15:33-8 Ap '63

BOLIVIAN hemorrhagic fever. See Hemorrhagic fever

BOLL weevils
Weevils resist poison more at dawn, less later. Sci N L 85:393 Je 20 '64

BOLLANDISTS
Who's who of saints; Analecta Bollandiana. il Time 81:60 My 31 '63

BOLLES, Blair
Residual nationalism: a rising threat to projected European union. bibliog f Ann Am Acad 348:102-9 Jl '63

BOLLING, Richard
Congressman's view of the problem; excerpts from House out of order. New Repub 151:13-14 N 21 '64

BOLLINGEN prize in poetry
Poems split from granite; enriched Bollingen prize awarded to H. Gregory. Time 85:94 Ja 29 '65

BOLLINGER, Richard A.
Brethren and the church. Christian Cent 81:1062-3 Ag 26 '64

BOLM, Adolph
Perspective on Adolph Bolm (cont) J. Dougherty. il pors Dance Mag 37:44-7+ F; 50-3 Mr '63

BOLOGNA biennial of old masters. See Art—Exhibitions

BOLOGNA book fair for children and youth. See Book fairs

BOLSHEVISM. See Communism—Russia

BOLSHOI ballet
Post-script on a "sleeper": Ballet school. D. Hering. il Dance Mag 37:51+ F '63
Reviews; Stars of the Bolshoi at Madison Square Garden. J. Maskey. il Dance Mag 37:32-3 D '63

BOLSHOI opera company. See Opera—Russia

BOLSHOI theater, Moscow. See Opera houses

BOLT, Bruce A. See Christensen, M. N. jt. auth.

BOLT, Robert
Man for all seasons; text. por Theatre Arts 47:33-66 My '63

BOLTIN, Lee
Reviews. Natur Hist 73:4-8 Ap '64

BOLTON, Charles D.
Anatomy of a new politics. Nation 198:529-33 My 25 '64
Peace movement: a program for the future. Nation 197:278-81 N 2 '63
Resolving vicious circles in international affairs. Bul Atomic Sci 19:17-20 Ap '63

BOLTON, Robert H.
Brazil: land of massive problems. Christian Cent 81:1235-9 O 7 '64

BOLTON, William
(ed) That's a good question. See issues of Today's health

BOLTS and nuts
Fastener for every purpose. il Bsns W p 164-6 My 16 '64
1964 Chrysler corp. engineering. J. Wright. il Motor T 15:28-31 S '63
Tighten the tiny ones too. T. Green. il Hot Rod 16:74-7 S '63

BOMAR, Cora Paul, and Jenkins, Clara
EB school library award: Durham County, North Carolina. pors Wilson Lib Bul 39:397-8 Ja '65
—See Johnson, F. K. jt. auth.

BOMARZO gardens. See Gardens—Italy

BOMB detectors. See Detectors

BOMBAY
Hustler's reward. il Time 83:33-4 Ja 10 '64

BOMBING games. See Games

BOMBING planes. See Airplanes, Military

BOMBS
French Canada's strange revolt; role of FLQ (Quebec liberation front) L. Bergquist. il Look 27:90-4+ D 3 '63
Horror explodes in a Canadian mailbox. il Life 54:40-40A Je 7 '63
Saigon: explosion by a brazen enemy. il Life 58:28-9 Ja 8 '65
Sniffer may detect bombs on aircraft. P. J. Klass. il Aviation W 81:42+ N 16 '64

BÖMMEL, H. E. and others
Indium antimonide: superconductivity of the metallic form. Science 139:1301-2 Mr 29 '63
Superconductivity of metallic indium telluride. Science 141:714 Ag 23 '63

BON AMI company
Roy Cohn. M. Kempton. New Repub 148:15-17 Ap 20 '63

BONAIRE
See also
Geology—Bonaire

BONANNO, Joseph
Slippery Bananas. il Newsweek 65:18-19 Ja 4 '65
Who's got Bananas? il por Newsweek 64:38 N 2 '64

BONAPARTE, Napoléon. See Napoléon I, emperor of the French

BONAPARTE family
Golden bees, by T. Aronson. Review Time il 84:120+ S 18 '64

BOND, Bud
How to win a bond program. Am City 79:120-1 Mr '64

BOND, F. Fraser
This business of style. Writer 77:27-8 Jl '64

BOND, Fred
Color workshop. See issues of Modern photography

BOND, Selah
Automatic wiring checkouts. Electr World 73:46-7 Ja '65

BOND campaigns. See Municipal bonds

BOND street. See London—Streets

BONDE, Per
Subjective rangefinder. P. Caulfield. il Mod Phot 28:64-71+ My '64

BONDER, James B.
Your child's intelligence; reprint. Todays Health 41:45 Ag '63

BONDING. See Insurance, Surety and fidelity

BONDS
As investors weigh the chances today. il U S News 56:92-4 Ja 13 '64
Bond dealers are betwixt and between. il Bsns W p 164 S 26 '64
Bond stickler: how deep the well? il Bsns W p83-4 Ap 4 '64
Bonds that behave like stocks. il Fortune 70: 78 Ag '64
How to handle your money now; as experts see it; symposium. il U S News 58:44-8 Ja 4 '65
New war between the states: tax subsidies for industry; industrial band programs. il U S News 55:117-18 N 25 '63
Reverse option on new bonds; registered vs coupon bonds. Bsns W p60 Je 15 '63
See also
State bonds

Rating

Assessing gilt; nation's three bond-rating services. il Time 84:58 D 25 '64

Taxation

See Taxation of bonds, securities, etc.

BONDS, Chemical. See Chemical bonds

BONDS, Fidelity. See Insurance, Surety and fidelity

BONDS, Government
Big bond issues up to voters. U S News 57: 117-18 S 28 '64
Bond issues: how voters decided. U S News 55:131 N 18 '63
Check up on your savings bonds. il Changing T 18:15-17 S '64
A look at votes on bond issues. U S News 57: 108+ N 16 '64
Merrill Lynch buys up bond house. Bsns W p24-5 My 16 '64
Push to sell bonds in foreign currency. il Bsns W p88-9 Mr 30 '63
U.S. savings bonds; sales go up. U S News 54:112 Ap 15 '63
Why people buy savings bonds. U S News 56: 96 Mr 30 '64
See also
State bonds

BONDS, Municipal. See Municipal bonds

BONDS, School. See School finance

BONDS, State. See State bonds

BONE, Ray
We witches are simple people. por Life 57: 60+ N 13 '64

BONE
Cell system in which rate and amount of protein synthesis are separately controlled. O. Landeros and H. M. Frost. bibliog il Science 145:1323-4 S 18 '64
Heparin enhancement of factors stimulating bone resorption in tissue culture. P. Goldhaber. bibliog il Science 147:407-8 Ja 22 '65

BONE, Artificial
Imitation bone made from clay-like material; cerosium, oxide of aluminum impregnated with epoxy resin. Sci N L 86:396 D 19 '64

BONE, Transplantation of. See Transplantation of organs, tissues, etc.

BONE bank. See Orthopedia

BONE cell. See Cells

BONE marrow. See Marrow

BONE surgery. See Orthopedia

BONEFISH fishing
Bay of Pigs. G. X. Sand. il Field & S 67:54-5 Mr '63
Fox of the flats. il Time 83:50-1 Ja 31 '64
How to bag bonefish. G. Heinold. il Outdoor Life 134:14-15+ N '64

BONERS. See Blunders

BONES
Accuracy of bone mineral measurement. R. B. Mazess and others. bibliog il Science 145:388-9 Jl 24 '64
Bones make the walker. E. Mirel. Sci N L 83: 117 F 23 '63
Collagenolytic activity in mammalian bone. J. F. Woods and G. Nichols, jr. bibliog il Science 142:386-7 O 18 '63
Compact bone deficiency in protein-calorie malnutrition. S. M. Garn and others. bibliog il Science 145:1444 S 25 '64
Compact bone in Chinese and Japanese. S. M. Garn and others. bibliog il Science 143: 1439-40 Mr 27 '64
Fluoride: its effects on two parameters of bone growth in organ culture. W. R. Proffit and J. L. Ackerman. bibliog il Science 145:932-4 Ag 28 '64
Indian bones tell health story. Hobbies 68: 115 Je '63
Vertebrate hard tissues; report on special symposium of the section of vertebrate morphology of the American society of zoologists. C. Gans. Science 144:323-4 Ap 17 '64
See also
Bone
Fractures
Skeleton

BONES, Fossil. See Paleontology

BONEY, Knowles
Identification of Liverpool porcelain of the early period, 1756-1765. Antiques 86:728-31 D '64

BONFANTE, Jordan
African students at iron curtain schools flee a hateful epithet: *cherni maimuni*. Life 54:19 Mr 15 '63
Doctor: I went ahead, the first eye, the second. . . Life 57:38-41 N 20 '64
He walks in his silent sadness. Life 56:48+ Mr 27 '64
In his room the end comes. Life 54:28 Je 14 '63
Mafia in trouble on its home grounds. Life 56:96-103 Mr 6 '64
Spy-master unmasked. Life 56:39-40+ F 28 '64
This boy witnessed the wrath of Allah. Life 54:36-8 Mr 8 '63
With the commandos in an assault on a peak. Life 57:40-1 S 18 '64
(ed) See McCarthy, M. Gingery sample of McCarthy views

BONFIRE; story. See O'Hara, J.

BONGARTZ, Roy
Beautiful travelers; story. Sat Eve Post 236: 56-64 Je 15 '63
Do these Indians really own Florida? Sat Eve Post 237:62-3+ F 1 '64
For Benny, much loved; story. New Yorker 39:38-46 S 14 '63
Gloria; story. New Yorker 39:42-8 Mr 23 '63
Pass go and retire. Sat Eve Post 237:26-7 Ap 11 '64
Steel ball; story. Sat Eve Post 238:60-2 Ja 16 '65
Superswamp; Cypress gardens. Sat Eve Post 236:78-81 N 23 '63

BONHAM, Margaret
Man in a corner; story. Sat Eve Post 236: 48-9 S 7 '63

BONHAM, Ron
Bearcat rifle. H. L. Masin. por Sr Schol 84: 30 Mr 6 '64

BONHEUR, impair et passe; drama. See Sagan, F.

BONIFAZ NUÑO, Rubén
Smoke; poem, tr. by J. F. Nims. Atlan 213: 148 Mr '64

BONIN, James J. See Gans, C. jt. auth.

BONINO, José Miguez
Vatican II and Latin America. Christian Cent 81:1616-17 D 30 '64

BONINSEGNA, Celestina
Three neglected sopranos. J. M. Alfonte. por Opera N 28:38 N 16 '63

BONIS, L. J. and Hausner, H. H.
Surface phenomena. Science 145:955-6+ Ag 28 '64

BONIS, William D.
Road to self-fulfillment. Christian Cent 81: 1365-6+ N 4 '64

BONITO fishing
Far-flung Atlantic bonito. G. Heinold. il Outdoor Life 134:10-11+ D '64

BONK, James
Lamentations of Nicodemus; poem. America 111:384 O 3 '64
Lines to Christopher. America 111:189 Ag 22 '64

BONN, George S.
Science-technology periodicals. Library J 88: 954-8 Mr 1 '63
Scientific information and the government. Library J 88:4164-6 N 1 '63
(comp) Technical books of 1962. por Library J 88:933-9 Mr 1 '63
(comp) Technical books of 1963. por Library J 89:1015-21 Mr 1 '64

BONN
Beethoven hall. G. E. K. Smith. il Arch Rec 134:190-1 O '63
Deadbeat diplomacy. Time 82:42+ O 4 '63

Description

C'est si Bonn. il Time 83:30 My 29 '64

BONN festival. See Music festivals—Germany (Federal Republic)

BONNARD, Pierre
Art galleries; memorial exhibition at Museum of modern art. R. M. Coates. New Yorker 40:166+ O 24 '64
Art; retrospective at the Museum of modern art. F. Getlein. New Repub 151:25-6 D 5 '64
Bonnard; expressionist of pleasure; exhibition at the Museum of modern art. M. Kozloff. Nation 199:286-8 O 26 '64
Continuity of Pierre Bonnard. M. Benedikt. il por Art N 63:20-3+ O '64
Distant witness; retrospective show at Manhattan's Museum of modern art. il pors Time 84:96-8 N 13 '64
Moi, j'observe. il por Newsweek 64:103 O 12 '64
Nephew. New Yorker 40:50-1 N 7 '64
People are talking about Terrace at Vernon. il Vogue 144:174-5 O 1 '64

BONNEL, Ulane
LC expands photocopying program of European manuscripts & archives. Library J 88:1496-8 Ap 1 '63

BONNER, Charles
My son came late. Harper 229:71-3 S '64

BONNER, Herbert C.
United States merchant marine; address, November 15, 1963. Vital Speeches 30:186-9 Ja 1 '64

BONNER, James, and Tso, P. O. P.
Histone biology and chemistry. Science 141:651+ Ag 16 '63

BONNER, John Tyler
How slime molds communicate; with biographical sketch. Sci Am 209:14+, 84-6+ bibliog(p 140) Ag '63

BONNER brothers
Four against the odds. il Ebony 18:55-6+ My '63

BONNET, Honoré
Sweet triumph of Napoleon Bonnet. H. Horn. por Sports Illus 20:17 F 17 '64

BONNY, John
Builders of anything, anywhere. il por Bsns W p58-9+ D 5 '64

BONO, Philip
How to bring a booster back alive. Pop Sci 183:80-1 Jl '63
Large reusable booster designs studied; report presented at American astronautical society meeting; ed. by C. M. Plattner. Aviation W 78:52-3+ F 4 '63

BONSAI. See Trees, Dwarf

BONTECOU, Lee
It's art, but will it fly? three-dimensional structure for Lincoln Center's New York state theater. il pors Life 56:43-4+ Ap 10 '64

BONTEMPS, Arna
Negro awakening: what librarians can do. por Library J 88:2997-9 S 1 '63

BONTING, Sjoerd L.
Scientist-minister begins dual career. il por Todays Health 41:84 D '63

BONUS expeditionary force. See Service men. Discharged

BONUS system
General motors bonus system: an indispensable incentive. A. P. Sloan, jr. Fortune 69:125+ Ja '64
Special bonuses for Belgian unionists. R. A. Senser. Mo Labor R 87:928-9 Ag '64
Success with largesse; year-end bonuses. Time 85:64-5 Ja 1 '65
See also
Incentives in industry

BONUSES, Service mens. See Service mens bonuses

BONWIT Teller. See New York (city)—Stores

BONYNGE, Richard
Question of style. Mus Am 84:44-5 D '64

BOOBIES (birds) See Gannets

BOOHER, Edward E.
Take your blinders off, there's a new day ahead! summary of address. por Pub W 185:33-5 Mr 9 '64

BOOK advertising. See Books—Advertising

BOOK and periodical giving campaigns
For the record: book drives; a statement by the ALA international relations committee. ALA Bul 57:191 F '63

BOOK awards, National. See National book awards

BOOK binding. See Bookbinding

BOOK buying
Book buying; who? what? where? when? why? R. H. Brown. il Pub W 185:16-19 My 11 '64

BOOK buying, Personal. See Libraries, Private

BOOK buying for libraries. See Libraries—Acquisitions

BOOK buying for school libraries. See School libraries—Acquisitions

BOOK cases. See Bookcases

BOOK catalogs. See Catalogs, Library

BOOK censorship. See Censorship

BOOK clubs
Book club selections. See issues of Publishers' weekly to December 30, 1963
Bringing books to children; Weekly reader children's book club. P. Fenner. Library J 88:4823-5 D 15 '63
How our library runs a school-wide book club; Lake View H.S. Chicago. R. Fish. Sr Schol 82:21T Mr 13 '63
New book club launched in England; Bookplan. Pub W 185:101 Je 8 '64
New book club to be promoted through churches; Christian growth children's reading program. Pub W 185:57 Ap 20 '64
New British book club announces first tests; Bookplan. Pub W 185:32 Ap 6 '64
Optimist books for boys; Kettle Moraine school, Wisconsin. W. G. Zahn. Sr Schol 82:23T Mr 13 '63
Take three, they're free. D. Dempsey. Sat R 47:42-3 F 15 '64
Time's int'l book society sells out first selection. Pub W 185:46 My 25 '64
See also
Book-of-the-month club

BOOK collecting
Junior book collectors; book fair with a twist; Louis Pasteur junior high school, Los Angeles, Calif. H. J. Kunkle. il Wilson Lib Bul 38:176-7 O '63
See also
Libraries, Private

BOOK covers
Art tips for bookbinding. P. Johnson. il Design 65:68-74 N '63
Books and book jackets in the Litho show. il Pub W 183:72-4 Ap 8 '63
Cover story: book jackets, 1962. il Pub W 183:90-5 Mr 4 '63
Improved foils, multiple-station presses, widen use of roll leaf. N. Zelman. il Pub W 185:90+ Mr 2 '64
Jackets in the library, please; Allentown public library, Pa. E. K. Sanders. Library J 88:4108 N 1 '63; Discussion. 88:4680 D 15 '63
Pre-printed covers: how to reduce casing-in problems. N. B. Leitner. il Pub W 185:80-2 Ap 6 '64
Production and design aspects of Time's distinctive paperback program. il Pub W 187:86-8 Ja 4 '65
Symbolism in university press jacket design. G. Gore. il Pub W 187:92-4 Ja 4 '65

BOOK design
Adrian Wilson: designer-printer at Tuscany Alley. P. A. Bennett. il Pub W 185:66-9+ Ap 6 '64
AIGA panel: have designers become obsolete because of new technology? summaries of addresses. Pub W 186:70-2 D 7 '64
AIGA's Fifty books: a review of the 1963 show. R. F. Neale. bibliog il Pub W 183:56+ My 6 '63
AIGA's fifty books as seen by a production man. I. B. Simon. il Pub W 185:78-9+ My 4 '64
Bookmaking and changing standards and tastes; address to AIGA, Fifty books dinner; with editorial comment. A. Heckscher. Pub W 183:22-4, 32 My 6 '63
Books in the making: 20th century techniques produce 17th century series, Anchor books. il Pub W 183:86-7 My 6 '63
Design in paperbacks: a report from NAL. il Pub W 183:76-8 Ap 8 '63
Illustrations for books. H. C. Pitz. il Design 65:120-5+ Ja '64
International book design seen at Frankfurt fair. Pub W 184:84+ N 4 '63
Planning, printing and prayer: Columbia encyclopedia, third ed. il Pub W 184:80-1 N 4 '63
RPG panel: design of religious books for contemporary appeal. il Pub W 186;76-7 D 7 '64
Saul and Lillian Marks and their Plantin press in Los Angeles. P. A. Bennett. il Pub W 186:114-18 Jl 6 '64
Singapore to Istanbul: printing design and production from seven countries; with report by M. Glick and E. H. Glick. il Pub W 183:84-6+ Mr 4 '63

BOOK design—*Continued*
Triumph at Yale: Albers' Interaction of color. il Pub W 184:78-9 N 4 '63
Visit with George Salter; designer, calligrapher, illustrator and teacher. P. A. Bennett. il Pub W 186:82-7 S 7 '64

Bibliography

Books about books and graphic arts. C. B. Grannis. Pub W 184:70-4+ D 2 '63

Competitions

Maine jury chooses winners in 1962 midwestern books competition. Pub W 183:78+ Ap 8 '63
New York jury picks thirty-five titles in Midwestern books competition; Nineteen books selected in Southern books competition. Pub W 185:77-8 Ap 6 '64

BOOK digests. See Books, Condensed
BOOK discarding. See Libraries—Book discarding
BOOK drives. See Book and periodical giving campaigns
BOOK editors. See Editors and editing
BOOK exhibits
ABA international exhibit. il Pub W 184:35-7 Jl 1 '63
AIGA's fifty books as seen by a production man. I. B. Simon. il Pub W 185:78-9+ My 4 '64
Design or content? AIGA 1961-1962 show of children's books. A. Dalgliesh. Sat R 46:44 My 11 '63
Fifteenth Chicago book clinic show: a useful exhibition. bibliog il Pub W 186:118-21 Jl 6 '64
Fifty books and the pursuit of excellence. D. A. Way. Pub W 184:92+ S 9 '63
Gulf publishing co. opens oil industry book display. Pub W 185:53 Ap 20 '64
Indian educators view low-cost college texts. il Pub W 183:32-3 Mr 18 '63
Librarians assess experimental publishers' New books preview. Library J 88:4831-2 D 15 '63
Lindsay and L'Engle speak at N.Y. New books preview. il Library J 89:3280 S 15 '64
Martin Mayer, Leland B. Jacobs speak at New books preview. Library J 88:3277-8 S 15 '63
New England book show, 1963: a jury picks twenty-eight books. il Pub W 185:72+ Ap 6 '64
Philadelphia book show jurors single out twenty books. il Pub W 183:95-6 Je 3 '63
Printing and the mind of man; exhibition, London, July 16-27. Pub W 184:67 Jl 1 '63
Rounce & Coffin club's 23rd western books exhibition. il Pub W 185:96-9 My 4 '64
700 library buyers attend 1964 New books preview. il Pub W 186:33-4 S 14 '64
Sixth Salon du livre April 2 to April 7. Pub W 185:30 Mr 16 '64
Western books 1963 on continental tour. Pub W 183:97-8 Je 3 '63
See also
Book fairs
Combined book exhibit (organization)
Library exhibits
BOOK fairs
Antiquarian book fair attracts record crowds in New York City. il Pub W 183:22-3 Ap 22 '63
Antiquarian book fair offers diverse materials. Pub W 185:32-3 My 11 '64
La bataille de Francfort; eye-witness report by a first-timer; Frankfurt book fair. R. E. Bye. il Pub W 186:26-30 O 19 '64
Book fair for boys and girls at Nashville Baptist store. il Pub W 186:44-6 D 7 '64
Book fair will be held at Nashville Baptist store; Macy's book fair in New York, Chaplin movies in suburbia. il Pub W 186:62-3 N 2 '64
Bookshows for seniors only. R. H. Dumas. il Library J 89:1828-9 Ap 15 '64
Bookstore fair alerts public to variety of juveniles; Baptist book store, Atlanta, Ga. il Pub W 185:95 F 10 '64
Buenos Aires holds a book fair. Pub W 186:53 N 16 '64
CBC promotion materials, fairs, book week '64. il Pub W 186:104-8 Jl 13 '64
Conference on book fairs stresses the practical. J. F. Dougherty. il Pub W 185:20-3 My 11 '64
Doing the Frankfurt scene. Pub W 184:28-30 S 16 '63
Editorial; Buchmesse at Frankfort-on-the-Main. A. Frankfurter. Art N 62:21+ D '63
Festival in Hawaii. M. Brown. il Sat R 46:54 N 9 '63
Frankfurt book fair, 1963, attracts 2000 exhibitors. Pub W 184:84 S 16 '63
Frankfurt book fair, 1963; with editorial comment. P. Rosenwald. il Pub W 184:18-25, 35 N 4 '63
Good-looking children's books at book fair in Bologna; Bologna book fair for children and youth. E. Mandel. il Pub W 186:66+ Ag 3 '64
Information retrieval at a book fair; Minneapolis public library. il Library J 88:962-3 Mr 1 '63
Inter-American book fair and seminar in Mexico city. P. S. Jennison. il Pub W 186:38-41 Jl 20 '64
International book design seen at Frankfurt fair. Pub W 184:84+ N 4 '63
Israel int'l book fair in Jerusalem, April 20-28. Pub W 183:34 Mr 11 '63
Junior book collectors; book fair with a twist; Louis Pasteur junior high school, Los Angeles, Calif. H. J. Kunkle. il Wilson Lib Bul 38:176-7 O '63
London's first World book fair: trade show or public fair? E. Moon. il Pub W 186:24-9 Jl 27 '64
Manual for a successful book fair. il Sr Schol 84:11T-17T F 14 '64
New look at the N.Y. times national book fairs, 1936-37. N. Paige. Pub W 184:28-30 D 30 '63
New World book fair set for London, June, 1964. P. J. Rosenwald. il Pub W 184:23-4 Jl 22 '63
Promoting, planning and producing book fairs. Q. Hawkins. Pub W 186:171-5 Jl 13 '64
Selling American literary works behind the iron curtain; Belgrade international book fair. H. Lottman. Pub W 187:30-3 Ja 4 '65
Three cheers for books! CBC show promotion materials, announces major book fairs. il Pub W 184:145-8 Jl 8 '63
Washington post book fair shown in New Delhi, Karachi. il Pub W 183:70-1 Ap 15 '63
Whetting the reading appetite; Bennett college, Greensboro, N.C. C. H. Marteena. il Wilson Lib Bul 37:579 Mr '63
Why a book fair? N. Hoopes. Sr Schol 84:4T+ F 14 '64
World's fair, Schmorld's fair; San Antonio to have teen fair; State-library-sponsored bookmobile. Library J 89:1399+ Mr 15 '64
BOOK illustration. See Illustration of books and periodicals
BOOK illustrators. See Illustrators
BOOK indexes. See Indexes
BOOK industries and trade
Awareness of quality is theme of AAUP production discussions. il Pub W 186:110-12 Jl 6 '64
Banker looks at book manufacturing; with editorial comment. C. F. Bound; C. E. Phillips. Pub W 183:72+, 49 Je 3 '63
BMI convention: management techniques and personnel problems; summaries of addresses at 32d annual meeting. Pub W 186:64+ D 7 '64
BMI convention: new attitudes, new demands, advanced technology; summaries of addresses at 32nd annual meeting; with editorial comment. il Pub W 186:79, 80-2+ N 9 '64
Bookmaking; see first issue of each month of Publishers' weekly
Distribution of books; symposium. il ALA Bul 57:505-34+ Je '63
Fifty books and the pursuit of excellence. D. A. Way. Pub W 184:92+ S 9 '63
New efforts that have to be made. C. B. Grannis. Pub W 185:73 Je 22 '64
Westprint '64; items of book industry interest. L. D. Osborne. il Pub W 186:102-4+ Jl 6 '64
See also
Book jobbers
Book manufacturers' institute
Bookazine company, incorporated
Books—Prices
Booksellers and bookselling—United States
Printing
Publishers and publishing
Royalties

Finance

Storage cost cuts profits; BMI to revise customs. Pub W 184:151-2 Jl 8 '63

International aspects

Are U.S. book sales abroad better than we deserve? D. Melcher. Pub W 186:56 Jl 20 '64; Reply. G. C. Simons. 186:23-4 S 7 '64
AAUP; international cooperation: discussions and decisions. il Pub W 186:30-4 Jl 6 '64

BOOK industries and trade—International aspects—*Continued*
Bowker company plans to issue international publishing yearbook; Publishers' world. Library J 89:4496 N 15 '64
Bowker plans yearbook for international book business. Publishers' world. Pub W 186:46 N 9 '64
Foreign sales, foreign services, reviewed at AIGA clinic. Pub W 183:92-4 F 4 '63
Foreign trade: book bank scheme; Africa developments. il Pub W 185:35-7 My 18 '64
International trade developments; 1963-64 in review; Pub W 185:87-8 Ja 20 '64; 187:84-5 Ja 18 '65
International White House library project completed. Pub W 184:31 O 7 '63
Power of books; address, November 18, 1964. C. G. Benjamin. Vital Speeches 31:155-60 D 15 '64
See also
Inter-American scholarly book center

Law

But can you do that? H. F. Pilpel. See occasional issues of Publishers' weekly
Whole new world may open for use of subsidiary rights; New York law on the right of privacy. H. F. Pilpel. Pub W 185:63-4 F 3 '64

Statistics

Publisher-manufacturer relations: trade books; symposium. il Pub W 184:80+ O 14 '63
U.S. book exports & imports, 1962. il Pub W 184:25-6 D 2 '63

Asia, Southern

Book trade organization progressing in south Asia. P. S. Jennison. il Pub W 183:35-7 Ap 15 '63

Canada

Buying around stifles development of a healthy Canadian book trade; adaptation of address. R. A. Browne. Pub W 185:24-8 Je 1 '64

England

See also
Booksellers and bookselling—England

Europe, Western

Adclub session on European advertising and promotion; summary of address. P. Rosenwald. Pub W 186:49 N 16 '64

France

See also
Publishers and publishing—France

Great Britain

Book distribution in the United Kingdom. R. Barker. ALA Bul 57:523-7 Je '63
U.S. and the U.K. in world book markets. R. H. Smith. Pub W 184:33 O 21 '63
See also
Publishers and publishing—Great Britain

Latin America

Inter-American book fair and seminar in Mexico city. P. S. Jennison. il Pub W 186:38-41 Jl 20 '64

Netherlands

Long-term market planning in Holland, Germany, France. Pub W 186:33-4 O 19 '64

Russia

Book distribution in the USSR. K. Enoch and R. W. Frase. bibliog il ALA Bul 57:518-23 Je '63

United States

American books abroad. P. S. Jennison. il Bul Atomic Sci 19:31-3 D '63
AAUP session scans problems of short-run scholarly books. il Pub W 184:76+ Jl 1 '63
Book export and import; trends and significance. R. H. Smith. Pub W 184:28 D 9 '63
BMI leaders, printers urge no reduction in tariffs. Pub W 185:132 F 3 '64
BMI; report of convention; with editorial comments. il Pub W 184:37, 69, 70-2+ O 14; 61, 64-5+ N 4 '63
Book trade and the current session of Congress. R. H. Smith. Pub W 184:38 N 25 '63
Bookmaking and changing standards and tastes; address to AIGA, Fifty books dinner; with editorial comment. A. Heckscher. Pub W 183:22-4, 32 My 6 '63
Changing requirements of book publishing; address. H. J. McBain. Pub W 184:72-4 N 4 '63
Dialog between manufacturers and publishers. C. B. Grannis. Pub W 186:79 O 5 '64
Goals for 1965: book trade association leaders look at the year ahead; symposium with editorial comment. il Pub W 186:30-4, 55 D 28 '64
Legislative outlook for the book industry, 1964-65. R. H. Smith. Pub W 185:36 Mr 23 '64
1963-64 in review; news, trends and statistics in the American book industry. il Pub W 185:82-6 Ja 20 '64; 187:79-84 Ja 18 '65
Power of books; address, November 18, 1964. C. G. Benjamin. Vital Speeches 31:155-60 D 15 '64
Reducing the confusion between publishers and manufacturers. Pub W 183:68+ Ap 8 '63
Revised import figures show 13 per cent gain in 1963. il Pub W 186:50 D 28 '64
Take your blinders off, there's a new day ahead! summary of address. E. E. Booher. Pub W 185:33-5 Mr 9 '64
There must be a basis for a meeting of minds. C. B. Grannis. Pub W 185:45 Je 1 '64
Trade barriers; publishers ask tariff reduction, manufacturers seek retention. il Pub W 185:27-31 Mr 2 '64
U.S. and U.K. in world book markets. R. H. Smith. Pub W 184:33 O 21 '63
U.S. book exports and imports, 1963; with editorial comment. il Pub W 186:36-8, 50 O 5 '64; Correction. 186:31 O 12 '64
See also
Franklin publications, incorporated
Publishers and publishing—United States

BOOK jackets. See Book covers

BOOK jobbers
How to buy them when you need them; elimination of problems in paperback orders. H. Finch. Sr Schol 83:24T Ja 17 '64
NACS associates oppose NACSCORP paperback service. Pub W 185:26-7 My 11 '64
Need for a network of paperback suppliers; Doubts that commercial wholesalers can succeed; with editorial comment. S. D. Keeper; J. P. Dessauer. Pub W 185:27-8, 61 Je 15 '64
Paperback distribution: booksellers and wholesalers. R. H. Smith. Pub W 186:50 N 9 '64
See also
Bookazine company, incorporated

BOOK lending, Library. See Libraries—Circulation, loans, etc.

BOOK lists. See Books and reading—Best books; Childrens literature—Bibliography; Reading lists

BOOK losses. See Libraries—Book losses

BOOK making (betting)
Betting with Bill; world's biggest bookie. Time 82:109-10 N 15 '63
Dagenham caper; bettors' syndicate coup at Greyhound stadium. Newsweek 64:38+ Jl 13 '64
Operation sandpaper; gambling coup at Greyhound stadium in London. il Time 84:40 Jl 10 '64
Profile of a bookmaker. M. Cope. Sat Eve Post 236:34+ Ap 27 '63
Quack medicine; proposal to license off-track betting. Nation 197:151 S 21 '63
See also
Ladbroke and company

BOOK manufacturers' institute
Book industry profit-ailment diagnosed in new BMI study. Library J 88:3578-9 O 1 '63
BMI convention: management techniques and personnel problems; summaries of addresses at 32d annual meeting. Pub W 186:64+ D 7 '64
BMI convention: new attitudes, new demands, advanced technology; summaries of addresses at 32nd annual meeting; with editorial comment. il Pub W 186:79, 80-2+ N 9 '64
BMI leaders, printers urge no reduction in tariffs. Pub W 185:132 F 3 '64
BMI; report of convention; with editorial comments. il Pub W 184:37, 69, 70-2+ O 14; 61, 64-5+ N 4 '63
1963-64 in review. il Pub W 185:92 Ja 20 '64; 187:92-3 Ja 18 '65
Storage cost cuts profits; BMI to revise customs. Pub W 184:151-2 Jl 8 '63
Technical committees and their work. il Pub W 184:70+ N 4 '63
Tomorrow's planning today is theme of BMI convention; 32nd annual meeting. Pub W 186:90+ O 5 '64

BOOK marking. See Books—Labeling, marking, etc.

BOOK marks. See Bookmarks

BOOK of common prayer. See Church of England—Book of common prayer

BOOK of hours of Catherine of Cleves. See Hours, Books of

BOOK-of-the-month club
Book-of-the-month library awards increased to fifty-two. Pub W 184:38 S 23 '63
See also
Dorothy Canfield Fisher library awards

BOOK orders, School libraries. See School libraries—Acquisitions

BOOK paper. See Paper

BOOK prices. See Books—Prices

BOOK processing in libraries. See Libraries—Technical processes

BOOK rarities
Books. P. W. Schmidtchen. See issues of Hobbies
Hot paper; stolen manuscripts from Saragossa cathedral in new Beinecke library, Yale. Newsweek 64:88 N 16 '64
IPEX: printing and the mind of man. J. M. Wells. il Pub W 184:85-6+ S 9 '63
Prospecting in the West; Western Americana institute sponsored by the ACRL rare books section and RSD history section. G. D. McDonald. Library J 88:3021-2 S 1 '63
Rare book collection purchased by Newberry library for $2.75 million; Louis H. Silver collection. Library J 89:2570 Je 15 '64
Rare book dealer sues Silver estate. Pub W 186:24-5 Ag 17 '64
Stolen from Spanish cathedral, rare manuscripts found at Yale; Beinecke library of rare books and manuscripts. Library J 89: 4771-2 D 1 '64
$2.75 million rare book sale sets record; Louis H. Silver collection, Newberry library, Chicago. Pub W 185:47 My 25 '64
See also
Antiquarian booksellers association of America
Association of college and research libraries—Rare books section
Hours, Books of

Collections

See Libraries—Special collections

BOOK repairing. See Books—Conservation and restoration

BOOK restoration. See Books—Conservation and restoration

BOOK review digest
Book review digest announces changes and additions for 1963. Library J 88:1500 Ap 1 '63

BOOK reviewers. See Critics

BOOK reviews
Band together for quality reviewing. H. F. Silverman. Library J 88:2368+ Je 15 '63; Discussion. 88:2806+, 3136+, 4106+ Ag, S 15, N 1 '63
Big four speak; symposium. il Library J 88: 2069-80 My 15 '63
Children's book council surveys newspaper reviews. Pub W 183:36 My 27 '63
Critically your Century; reviews of books. Christian Cent 80:324 Mr 13 '63
Critics approved! reviews before announcement of 1963 Newbery and Caldecott winners. Library J 88:1294-6 Mr 15 '63
Lack of newspaper book reviews hurts some N.Y. bookstores. Pub W 183:48 Mr 18 '63
Mrs Roosevelt and children's books. H. Ferris. il Library J 89:2149-51+ My 15 '64
New York times changes daily book review policy. Pub W 183:43 Je 3 '63
Newspapers and the culture beat. il Pub W 183:31-6 Mr 25 '63
Reviewing children's books: a cooperative venture; Eastern Massachusetts children's book review committee. P. L. Moulton. Library J 88:1723-4 Ap 15 '63
Reviewing of religious books in general media; Religious publishers group panel. il Pub W 183:24-6 My 27 '63
Reviewing philosophy: adult books for young adults. L. Bulman. Library J 89:1878-9 Ap 15 '64
Rewards and hazards of book reviewing: Los Angeles trade-technical college; Los Angeles herald-examiner. H. Lash. ALA Bul 57:860-1 O '63
Scientist reviewers beware; letter. M. Mead. Science 141:312-13 Jl 26 '63; Discussion. 142:154 O 11 '63
Ship of fools & the critics. T. Solotaroff; discussion. Commentary 35:247-50 Mr '63
Tools for selection. R. Lekachman; D. Lorenz; J. E. Frey. il Wilson Lib Bul 39: 325-34 D '64
Tour of the Times book review. B. Daniels. Nat R 14:202-3, 253-4 Mr 12-26 '63
Two book review magazines appear, by teenagers for teenagers; On the book beat, Scrutinize. Library J 88:1742 Ap 15 '63
Unbent twigs; children's unfavorable book reports. E. Rudin. Library J 88:4408 N 15 '63
See also
Literary criticism
New York review of books
New York times book review

Anecdotes, facetiae, satire, etc.

How not to read a book. D. Dempsey. Sat R 47:32-3 Ag 15 '64
Orchids for Miss Hightower. W. Sheed. Commonweal 78:145-6 Ap 26' 63

BOOK sales
One-day book sale grosses $11,000; M. G. Hurtig booksellers ltd, in Edmonton, Alta. il Pub W 185:50-2 Ap 13 '64
Retailing and overstock: the annual markdown sale; Doubleday book shop organization. Pub W 185:50 My 11 '64

BOOK selection
Blue chip book selection; serious fiction and poetry. E. Moon. Library J 89:2562+ Je 15 '64
Book selection: education or communication? with editorial comment. A. Lake; J. S. Dunn. il Wilson Lib Bul 37:670-6 Ap '63
Book selection for the culturally deprived. T. F. Parker. bibliog il Library J 89:3260-5 S 15 '64; Reply. H. E. A. Hassan. 89: 4674+ D 1 '64
Book selection: publication of Selection and acquisition procedures in medium-sized and large libraries. Wilson Lib Bul 38:233 N '63
Choosing the right book today: children's books; symposium, with editorial comment. bibliog il Library J 89:4963-75 D 15 '64
Complaints and answers; address, May 1962. A. Thomas. Library J 88:510-12 F 1 '63
Courage and cowardice; address, November 15-17, 1962. E. Castagna. il Library J 88: 501-6 F 1 '63
Criteria and the individual. C. W. Field. Horn Bk 40:527-9 O '64
Freedom to browse. B. Poll. il Library J 88: 1734 Ap 15 '63
Friends and True friends in New City. E. T. Moore. ALA Bul 57:387-8 My '63
Game of chicken: some librarians afraid to apply standards, pressured by cries of freedom; reprint. R. D. Franklin. Library J 89: 3918-19 O 15 '64
I may, I might, I must; address, May 1962. D. Broderick. Library J 88:507-10 F 1 '63; Discussion. 88:1090+, 1924+ Mr 15, My 15 '63
Librarian's syndrome; letter to the editor. G. A. Somers. Library J 89:4672+ D 1 '64
Mirror, mirror on the wall; importance of fiction. D. E. Gerard. Library J 90:192-5 Ja 15 '65
New provincialism; for ones local area but anti-other areas in childrens literature. D. Broderick. il Library J 89:4121-2 O 15 '64
1964 new books preview planned by Bowker company and LPRC. il Library J 89:2308 Je 1 '64
Oil for the lamps of knowledge; Franklin publications program for developing countries. J. E. Daily. il Library J 89:4483-7 N 15 '64
Our own poverty; library book collections. J. Berry. Library J 89:3274 S 15 '64
Problem books revisited; excerpts from report on survey of small public library's book selection practices in controversial areas. R. B. Agler. il Library J 89:2019-30 My 15 '64; Reply. R. S. Bravard. 89:2470+ Je 15 '64
Reviewing philosophy: adult books for young adults. L. Bulman. Library J 89:1878-9 Ap 15 '64
School libraries. P. Sullivan. Wilson Lib Bul 38:793 My '64
School library book catalog; preparation by committee of professional librarians. Wilson Lib Bul 38:713-14 My '64
Search for sample books; Franklin book programs. J. E. Daily. il Wilson Lib Bul 39: 59-61+ S '64
Selection, not censorship; letter to the editor. R. M. Pearl. Library J 89:428 F 1 '64
Serving the teenager. G. D. Mitchell, 3d. il Library J 89:1817-19 Ap 15 '64
Tools for selection. R. Lekachman; D. Lorenz; J. E. Frey. il Wilson Lib Bul 39: 325-34 D '64
Youth involvement in book selection. D. R. Watts. Wilson Lib Bul 39:83 S '64
See also
Booksellers and bookselling—Stock
Libraries—Acquisitions
School libraries—Acquisitions

BOOK series. See Series, Book

BOOK shelves. See Bookcases

BOOK storage. See Books—Storage

BOOK thefts
- Federal prosecution of fraudulent dealers; book losses at Scranton public library. ALA Bul 58: 304 Ap '64
- Investigation of alleged frauds; book losses at Scranton, Pa., public library. Wilson Lib Bul 38:604+ Ap '64

BOOK therapy. See Bibliotherapy

BOOK titles. See Titles of books, stories, etc.

BOOK trucks. See Library furniture and equipment

BOOK vendors. See Vending machines

BOOK week
- Book week: are booksellers forgetting an opportunity? J. F. Dougherty. Pub W 184:36 N 4 '63
- Catholic book week. il Wilson Lib Bul 38: 382 Ja '64; Discussion. 38:463, 736 F, My '64
- Children's book week. il Wilson Lib Bul 38: 174-5 O '63
- Children's book week 1964. il Library J 89: 3412 S 15 '64
- CBC promotion materials, fairs, book week '64. il Pub W 186:104-8 Jl 13 '64
- Critics' choices for Catholic book week. Commonweal 77:573; 79:667-75 F 22 '63, F 28 '64
- Emphasis on books; Catholic book week. D. L. Flaherty. America 110:258-9 F 22 '64
- Swing into books. Wilson Lib Bul 39:15 S '64
- Three cheers for books! CBC shows promotion materials, announces major book fairs. il Pub W 184:145-8 Jl 8 '63
- Three cheers for children's book week. P. Fenner. il Horn Bk 39:486-9 O '63

BOOK week (periodical)
- Book week lists writers, schedules special features. Pub W 184:42 S 9 '63
- Herald tribune to publish new literary magazine; Book week, in Washington post and San Francisco examiner. Library J 88:3186 S 15 '63
- N.Y. trib's Book week to Washington, San Francisco. Pub W 184:36 Ag 12 '63

BOOKAZINE company, incorporated
- Bookazine expands plant, stock and service. il Pub W 186:14-17 O 26 '64

BOOKBINDING
- Additional listings of bindings for children's books in libraries. Pub W 183:90+ F 4 '63
- Bookbinding by Florence Walter. Y. Uchida. il Craft Horiz 24:28-30 Jl '64
- Book-making regressing? letter to the editor. R. H. Donahugh. Library J 88:4680+ D 15 '63
- Children's libraries. B. S. Moody. Wilson Lib Bul 37:704 Ap '63
- French bookbinding shown at Crafts museum; New York. il Pub W 185:126+ F 3 '64
- Many basic juveniles are unavailable in bookshops; only available in library bindings. Pub W 185:152-3 F 24 '64
- Modern French book art; exhibition at the Museum of contemporary crafts in New York. P. Lada-Mocarski. il Craft Horiz 24: 36-41 Ja '64
- Paperbacks for college-bound students; project of NYLA's Adult services division; with list of binders. C. E. Hieber. bibliog Library J 89:185-90 Ja 15 '64
- Philadelphia bookseller comments on library bindings. Pub W 185:63 Mr 2 '64
- Publishers' library editions; progress and problems viewed. Pub W 185:108+ F 3 '64
- Varieties of binding shown at Childrens' book council library. il Pub W 183:126-7 F 18 '63

See also

Book covers

BOOKBINDING machinery
- Electronic perfect binders, inc: a new plant for paperbacks. il Pub W 184:64-6 D 2 '63

BOOKCASES
- Built-in bookcase wall. il Bet Hom & Gard 41:44 S '63
- Child's garden of bookshelves. il House & Gard 123:208-9 Ap '63
- Divide a room with books. il Bet Hom & Gard 41:104D F '63
- Floating bookshelves. R. J. DeCristoforo. il Pop Mech 119:158 Mr '63
- How to live with books. il Sunset 130:86-9 F '63
- Shelves for books and. . . G. O'Brien. il N Y Times Mag p44-6 F 23 '64
- Shelves: new high in style. il McCalls 91:98-103 F '64
- This bookcase comes apart. il Sunset 132: 165 Ap '64

BOOKCHARGING machines. See Libraries—Charging systems

BOOKER, Erma Barbour
- Signs of spring. Sch Arts 62:35-6 Ap '63

BOOKER, Henry G.
- Academic organization in physical science. Science 146:35-7 O 2 '64
- Proposal for an international union of solar system physics. Science 141:673-4 Ag 23 '63
- University education and applied science. Science 141:486+ Ag 9 '63

BOOKER, Simeon
- Andrew Hatcher makes good. Ebony 18:69-70+ O '63
- Burke Marshall: quiet fighter for civil rights. Ebony 19:90-2+ My '64
- How JFK surpassed Abraham Lincoln. Ebony 19:25-8+ F '64
- How Republican leaders view the Negro. Ebony 19:25-8+ Mr '64
- New face in Congress. Ebony 20:73-4+ Ja '65
- New, new, new, Negro, Esq; address, September 26, 1964. Vital Speeches 31:53-5 N 1 '64

BOOKING agencies. See Theatrical agencies

BOOKKEEPING
- Simplified bookkeeping procedure for booksellers. il Pub W 186:116-18 S 28 '64

See also

Accounting

BOOKLETS. See Pamphlets

BOOKLIST (periodical)
- Reviewing decline; concerning reviews of subscription books; reprint. M. K. Goggin and L. M. Seaberg. Library J 89:1687 Ap 15 '64

BOOKMAKING (betting) See Book making (betting)

BOOKMAN'S manual. See Reader's adviser

BOOKMARKS
- Make your mark. il Am Home 66:40-1+ N '63

BOOKMOBILES
- Don't undersell good bookmobile service. G. K. Schenk. Wilson Lib Bul 38:201 O '63
- Mission to Malagasy. il Library J 89:4476-7 N 15 '64

BOOKPLAN. See Book clubs

BOOKS

See also

Textbooks

Advertising

- Ad club seminar on book advertising. Pub W 185:49-50 My 25 '64
- Ads help sci-tech retail mailing lists; McGraw-Hill book store in New York. il Pub W 184:84-6 N 11 '63
- Books for young people; book and its blurb. A. Dalgliesh. il Sat R 46:42-3 S 21 '63
- Cooperative advertising: how to make it cooperative; summary of addresses. F. Boardman; W. Davies. Pub W 186:18-20 O 26 '64
- Editor's role in ads cited by Adclub speakers. Pub W 186:39-40 N 2 '64
- Effective use of advertising and publicity; summary of panel discussion at Denver ABA meeting. il Pub W 184:24-7 N 18 '63
- February-May: a calendar of some 200 leading campaigns. il Pub W 185:190-224 Ja 27 '64; 187:214-52 Ja 25 '65
- FTC charges Calories don't count. Pub W 184:34 O 7 '63
- 5.9 per cent rise in newspaper ads indicated by book firms. il Pub W 186:36-7 D 14 '64; Correction. 187:68 Ja 11 '65
- Former ad chiefs' advice: describe the book; summary of addresses. C. Denhard and F. Spier. il Pub W 185:54-5 F 17 '64
- Fort Worth shops' Xmas co-op ads boost business year round. Pub W 187:308-9 Ja 25 '65
- Grosset's promotion plan offers free display aids. il Pub W 185:26-7 Mr 16 '64
- How to tell a novel by its cover. M. J. Arlen. Life 57:11 Ag 21 '64
- Is the puff in danger? S. Richardson. Pub W 184:22 Jl 22 '63
- January books; some leading publishers' promotions. il Pub W 184:18-29 N 25 '63
- January books: some major promotions announced by publishers. il Pub W 186:26-34 N 2 '64
- Librarians view publishers' promotion and advertising; summary of addresses. M. Davis; A. Angoff. Pub W 184:33-5 D 2 '63
- New look in university press advertising. F. Spier. il Pub W 184:22-30 O 7 '63
- Newcomers. P. Bart. Sat R 46:54 F 9 '63
- Newspapers and the culture beat. il Pub W 183:31-6 Mr 25 '63
- Publishers' adclub covers cooperative advertising. Pub W 185:41-2 Mr 2 '64
- Publishers' adclub discusses mail order advertising. Pub W 185:56-7 Ap 20 '64

BOOKS—Advertising—*Continued*
PPA meeting discusses travel tie-ins. Pub W 185:43 Mr 9 '64
Respondents deny FTC's calories charges. Pub W 185:52 Ja 13 '64
Schlesinger protests use of quote in promotion of Buckley title. A. Schlesinger, jr. Pub W 183:12-13 Ap 22 '63; Reply with rejoinder. W. F. Buckley, jr. 183:31 Ap 29 '63
Sellarama on view in two N.Y.C. stores. il Pub W 184:46 O 28 '63
Shop and library team up in book promotion plan. Pub W 184:171 Jl 8 '63
Store windows and in-store display. T. Huntington. Pub W 185:76-8 Ja 6 '64
Sussman talks on newspaper strike & book advertising. Pub W 183:134-5 F 18 '63
Take a bow: Michael Gross. il Pub W 184:22-8 D 30 '63
Uses and abuses of point-of-sale material. R. A. Carter. Pub W 187:53-6 Ja 4 '65
Value of book advertising debated at Adclub. Pub W 183:25-6 Ap 22 '63; Reply. J. B. Agel. 183:15 My 6 '63
Yellow pages advertising effective for bookshops. il Pub W 186:43-4 Ag 3 '64
See also
Book week
Booksellers and bookselling—Publicity

Classification
See Classification

Competitions
Cincinnati bookmen judge Southern books competition. Pub W 184:89-90 Jl 1 '63

Conservation and restoration
New R for old books offered by Vatican institute. Library J 88:2475 Je 15 '63
Parchment patients; Vatican's institute for the scientific restoration of books. il Newsweek 61:90 Ap 8 '63

Exhibitions
See Book exhibits

Labeling, marking, etc.
Adhesives for book labels. G. T. Piez. ALA Bul 57:1051-2 D '63
Book labeling system marketed: Se-Lin. G. T. Piez. ALA Bul 58:410-11 My '64
Book marking analysis. N. H. Gaber. il Library J 89:1503-7 Ap 1 '64; Discussion. 89: 2000+ My 15 '64
Development and testing of a new book marking system; Se-Lin. N. H. Gaber. il Library J 89:1911-13 My 1 '64
LTP book labeling system goes to market; Se-Lin. G. T. Piez. il ALA Bul 58:554-6 Je '64

Microscopic and miniature editions
Little books; use of vending machines. New Yorker 40:40 Ap 18 '64

Mutilation, defacement, etc.
Malicious mischief, British style: Islington public libraries; summary. A. Connell. Wilson Lib Bul 37:750 My '63

Paper covered books
See Paperback books

Pirated editions
See Copyright—Unauthorized reprints

Prices
High cost of reading. D. Dempsey. Sat R 47:54-5 Ja 11 '64; Discussion. 47:21 F 8 '64
High price of technical books. C. G. Benjamin. ALA Bul 59:61-4 Ja '65
Price of cut-price bookselling; summary of panel discussion at Dallas ABA meeting. il Pub W 184:30-5 N 18 '63
Selling below cost should be prohibited. J. D. Kahn. Pub W 183:48 Ap 1 '63
See also
Libraries—Finance
Price cutting

Repair
See Books—Conservation and restoration

Reprints
Authors ask new policy on royalties and reprints. Pub W 186:36-8 Jl 27 '64
Fifty-fifty split; reprint and book club royalties. P. Nathan. Pub W 184:19-21 D 30 '63
Rights and permissions: fifty-fifty split. P. Nathan. Pub W 184:45 S 23 '63
Rights and permissions; reprint and book club royalties. P. Nathan. Pub W 184:42-3 O 21 '63
See also
Paperback books

Reprints, Unauthorized
See Copyright—Unauthorized reprints

Storage
Space problem; concerning report: Yale's selective book retirement program. Wilson Lib Bul 38:444-5 F '64
See also
Warehouses

Translations
See Translations and translating

BOOKS, Abridged. See Books, Condensed
BOOKS, Censorship of. See Censorship
BOOKS, Condensed
Let's pep up those old classics. D. E. Scherman. Life 57:22 O 9 '64
BOOKS, Filmed. See Film adaptations
BOOKS, Illustration of. See Illustration of books and periodicals
BOOKS, Paper covered. See Paperback books
BOOKS, Rare. See Book rarities
BOOKS, Rental of. See Libraries, Rental
BOOKS, Shipment of. See Shipment of books
BOOKS, Theft of. See Book thefts
BOOKS and reading
American adults read more fiction; findings of ALA report. Wilson Lib Bul 38:441 F '64
ALA bulletin views book distribution. C. B. Grannis. Pub W 183:42 My 27 '63
Best-read city in the U.S.A.: Pasadena. S. Grafton. il McCalls 90:48+ Ap '63
Book committee chairman reports survey on housewives' reading; excerpts from address, December 10, 1964. N. H. Strouse; with summary. Library J 90:212-13, 328 Ja 15 '65
Book distribution. D. Lacy. ALA Bul 57: 505-6 Je '63
Book week: are booksellers forgetting an opportunity. J. F. Dougherty. Pub W 184:36 N 4 '63
Books. See issues of Esquire
Books. J. Stafford; E. Wensberg. See issues of Vogue
Books and the crisis in U.S. education. F. Keppel. il Pub W 183:30-2 Je 3 '63
Books: under cover. C. Stinnett. Ladies Home J 81:17-18 Jl; 16 Ag '64
Can your reader identify? N. R. Ainsworth. Writer 77:22-4 My '64
Catcher named favorite book in PAL student essay contest. Library J 88:2090-1 My 15 '63
College graduate as a lifetime reader; excerpts from address. J. S. Diekhoff. ALA Bul 58:995-7+ D '64
Curl up and read. See issues of Seventeen
Curl up and read. H. G. First. See issues of Seventeen to July 1963
Death of the reader. W. Morris. Nation 198:53-4 Ja 13 '64
Eating up the classics. F. E. Wagner. il NEA J 52:24-6 F '63
Franklin book program for the U.S.? F. Jennings. Sat R 47:43 D 19 '64
Gresham's law of literature; simplified books. A. Loftis and R. Marshall. il Sat R 46:64-5 S 21 '63
I don't have time to read. J. A. Battle. NEA J 53:13 F '64
Idea of the book. R. Stokes. Library J 88: 4588 D 1 '63
Learning: a lifelong process; excerpts from address, May 21, 1964. M. Long. Library J 90:188-91, 195 Ja 15 '65
Letter on reading. R. M. Hutchins. ALA Bul 57:1027-33 D '63
Library and the teen age; concerning College preparatory reading list by Nioga library system. D. R. Watts. Wilson Lib Bul 38: 795 My '64
Library honors program: Cherokee jr. high school, Madison, Wis. M. Moss. Wilson Lib Bul 38:298 N '63
Life book review. See issues of Life March 27, 1964-
Medium sized P.L.'s report circulation increase in fiction; ALA report. Library J 89:586+ F 1 '64
Mr Jenkins sees it through. D. Dempsey. il Sat R 47:88+ Ag 29 '64
Mutations in the body politic; influential books of the past forty years; with list. R. Girson. il Sat R 47:74-86+ Ag 29 '64
Nation's reading interests outlined in ALA report. Library J 88:530-1 F 1 '63

BOOKS and reading—*Continued*
New officers, new plans at Nat'l book committee; report on reading habits. il Pub W 186:45-8 D 28 '64
New York newspaper strike has little effect on book reading. Library J 88:531-2 F 1 '63
On the encouragement of reading. J. Shera. Wilson Lib Bul 39:169+ O '64
On the fringe. H. Frankel. Sat R 46:22-3 Jl 6 '63
Outlook tower; books of interest to high school students, comp. by M. C. Scoggin. See issues of Horn book magazine
Paths to the mountain. D. D. Collier. Horn Bk 39:322-6 Je '63
Philip Roth talks to teens. P. Roth. Seventeen 22:170+ Ap '63; Excerpts. Library J 88:1738 Ap 15 '63
Reading is the key. R. H. Viguers. Horn Bk 40:147 Ap '64
Reading I've liked. C. Fadiman. See issues of Holiday
Reading: Negro youths' quest for certainty. E. J. Josey. Negro Hist Bul 27:158-9+ Ap '64
Right to read; religious sisters and brothers run the risk of becoming illiterate. America 109:250 S 14 '63
Sellers' market. il Newsweek 62:104 N 4 '63
Significant adult books for young people, 1963. Wilson Lib Bul 38:597-8 Ap '64
Special book issue; symposium. bibliog il Sr Schol 84:13T-21T Mr 6 '64
Taming the young barbarian; excerpts from address, 1963. M. Edwards. il Library J 89: 1819-21 Ap 15 '64
Three antidotes for current cases of literary poisoning. A. Gingrich. Esquire 62:6 O '64
Twenty bookes, clad in blak or reed. J. Jerome. Harper 228:100+ Je '64
Under cover. A. Hine. Ladies Home J 81: 20+ O '64
Under cover. C. Stinnett. Ladies Home J 81: 17-18 Jl; 16 Ag; 17-18 S; 33-4 N '64
Wayward reader. C. Fadiman. Holiday 36: 26+ N '64; 37:33-4 Ja '65
What are we all here for? serving the young adult. J. V. Frost. Library J 89:4979-80 D 15 '64
What books for the young adult? publisher asks, librarian answers. A. Craig; J. Rowell. Library J 89:4103-6 O 15 '64
Why people read books. bibliog Changing T 18:19-20 S '64
YASD committee chooses Interesting adult books for young people, 1962. Library J 88: 1743-4 Ap 15 '63
YASD picks thirty adult books of 1963 as good reading for US teenagers. Library J 89: 1398 Mr 15 '64
See also
Best sellers
Book buying
Book selection
Childrens literature
Childrens reading
Clergy—Reading
College students—Reading
Junior great books program
Libraries
Libraries and readers
Moving pictures and reading
National book committee
Reading lists
Reference books
Religious literature
Service mens reading
Teachers—Reading
Textbooks

Anecdotes, facetiae, satire, etc.

Ultimate teaching machine. R. J. Heathorn. il Harper 226:52 Ap '63

Best books

ALA includes five fiction titles in notable books of 1963. il Library J 89:1204-6 Mr 15 '64
ALA's lists of notable books for adults and young people. Pub W 183:25-7 Mr 18 '63
ALA's notable books of 1962 include ten fiction titles. Library J 88:1129-30 Mr 15 '63
Books; critics' choices for Christmas. Commonweal 81:357-9 D 4 '64
Books to be noted, 1963-1964. America 108: 675-6+; 109:664-5+; 110:635+; 111:698+ My 11, N 23 '63, My 9, N 28 '64
Critics' choices for Catholic book week. Commonweal 77:573 F 22 '63
Great books in paperback. J. L. Jarrett. il Sat R 46:66-7 Mr 23 '63
Letter from Paris; new books of special interest for Catholics. A. Fremantle. Commonweal 80:210-12 My 8 '64
Literary sampler; excerpts from new and forthcoming books. Sat R 46:28-9+ O 5 '63
Look back at the year's best. G. Hicks. Sat R 46:33-4 D 28 '63
New books appraised; ed. by M. Cooley and others. See issues of Library journal
Notability and permanence; concerning notable books of 1963 of Notable books council. E. Moon. Library J 89:1201+ Mr 15 '64
Notable books council; American library association. Wilson Lib Bul 37:614+ Ap '63
Notable books of 1962: a selected list. ALA Bul 57:257-8 Mr '63; Same. NEA J 52: 51-2+ My '63
Notable books of 1963: a selected list. ALA Bul 58:223-4 Mr '64; Same. Pub W 185:40-1 Mr 2 '64; NEA J 53:74-5 Ap '64; Wilson Lib Bul 38:590+ Ap '64
Notability and permanence; concerning notable books of 1963 of Notable books council. E. Moon. Library J 89:1201+ Mr 15 '64; Discussion. 89:1890+ My 1 '64
Significant adult books for young people, 1963. NEA J 53:34 Mr '64
See also
Adult education—Great books program
Best sellers
Book selection
Reading lists

Bibliography

Autumn highlights. M. E. Marty. Christian Cent 80:1214-16 O 2 '63
Autumn leaves a bounty of books: forthcoming publications. il Sat R 46:26-7+ O 5 '63
Books to come; ed. by I. E. Stokvis and J. Putnam. Library J 88:594-6+, 3658-93+; 89:670-2+, 2378-450, 3788-888 F 1, O 1 '63, F 1, Je 1, O 1 '64
Bookworm's boutique. House & Gard 124:188+ D '63
Bookworm's boutique; eighteen suggestions you might add to your Christmas list. House & Gard 126:36-7+ N '64
Bounty: the year's books. il Newsweek 64: 82+ D 21 '64
Christianity and literature bookshelf. Christian Cent 80:1466-7 N 27 '63; Reply. P. Schlueter. 81:182 F 5 '64
Church library choice. Christian Cent 80: 1172, 1241, 1310, 1339 S 25, O 9, 23-30 '63
Critics' choices for Catholic book week. Commonweal 79:667-75 F 28 '64
Critics' choices for Christmas. Commonweal 79:319-26 D 6 '63
Ex libris: choices of outstanding people. See issues of Christian century to June 10, 1963
Fall kicks off the big book. P. Bunker. il Sat R 47:37-8 O 3 '64
Fall survey of books; promise of the season. M. E. Marty. Christian Cent 81:1205-6 S 30 '64
Fanfare for fall: season's parade of new books. D. L. Flaherty. America 109:428-30 O 12 '63
For Christmas. K. G. Jackson. Harper 227: 126-7 D '63
Forecast: books for spring reading. Sat R 46: 31+ Ap 20 '63
History heads the list: new adult non fiction. H. Finch. Sr Schol 85:22T O 7 '64
In praise of over-the-shoulder reading. D. C. Davis. il Sr Schol 83:10T-12T O 4 '63
Interesting adult books for young people. 1962. NEA J 52:64+ Mr '63
Life guide. See issues of Life
Literary luxuries. J. H. Smylie. Christian Cent 81:1530-2+ D 9 '64
Look at the fall books. D. L. Flaherty. America 111:414-15 O 10 '64
New books by recent contributors. New Repub 149:28 D 21 '63
No lollipop. F. Hascall. Horn Bk 39:86-91 F '63
Potpourri. P. Adams. See issues of Atlantic
Reader's adviser, tenth edition; ed. by H. R. Hoffman. Review
Pub W 186:34-5 S 21 '64. D. M. Glixon
SR's check list of new books; comp. by L. Miller (title varies) See issues of Saturday review to May 25, 1963
SR's check list of scholarly books; comp. by R. Brown. Sat R 47:50-1 My 30 '64
SR's checklist of the week's new books (cont of SR's checklist of current books) comp. by R. Brown. See issues of Saturday review beginning June 1, 1963
Season in history. Christian Cent 81:365 Mr 18 '64
Season of renewal; Lenten reading. D. J. O'Hanlon. Commonweal 77:643-5 Mr 15 '63

BOOKS and reading—Bibliography—*Continued*
September books; some top campaigns of the early fall season. il Pub W 183:64-83 Je 10 '63; 185:58-77 Je 8 '64
Something new under the sun; books for young adults. J. M. Losinski. il Sr Schol 85:23T O 7 '64
Spring is for new-book lovers; comp. by P. Bunker. Sat R 47:37-8 Ap 18 '64
Spring reading roundup; comp. by H. R. Finch. il Sr Schol 82:18T-19T Mr 13 '63
Summer books to come; ed. by I. E. Stokvis and J. Putnam. Library J 88:2284-351+ Je 1 '63
Tabulating Ex libris; choices of outstanding people. M. E. Marty. Christian Cent 80: 982-3 Ag 7 '63
This week. See issues of Christian century
Time listings. See issues of Time
To one and all, a good book; comp. by P. Bunker. il Sat R 46:39-43+ D 7 '63
Wanted: new adult materials; Adult services, New York public library. K. L. O'Brien. Sr Schol 85:24T O 7 '64
Writer as middleman. B. DeMott. Harper 227:88+ Jl '63

International aspects

ABPC-ATPI holds meeting on overseas book programs; symposium. Pub W 185:27-9 Ap 6 '64
American books abroad. P. S. Jennison. il Bul Atomic Sci 19:31-3 D '63
AAUP; international cooperation: discussions and decisions. il Pub W 186:30-4 Jl 6 '64
Experiment in India; value of books in diplomacy. J. K. Galbraith. il Sat R 47:20-3 Ag 15 '64
Government book programs; summary of address. L. Battle. il Pub W 185:43-5 Je 22 '64
Harry Most named to Committee on international book programs. Dept State Bul 49: 933 D 16 '63
International White House library project completed. Pub W 184:31 O 7 '63
Secretary Rusk urges Americans to join Books USA campaign; statement, May 1, 1963. D. Rusk. Dept State Bul 48:806 My 20 '63
U.S. training program set for overseas publishers. Pub W 186:151 Jl 13 '64
See also
Inter-American scholarly book center

Quotations, maxims, etc.

Reading matter; some lines for National library week. comp. by E. F. Murphy. il N Y Times Mag p66 Ap 12 '64

Readability

See Readability (literary style)

Reading aloud

Culture for the savages; a mother's way of introducing her children to Shakespeare. G. Goff. il Redbook 120:6+ Ap '63
For reading out loud! C. Dane. PTA Mag 58:13 N '63
How to read a bedtime story. H. A. Littledale. il Parents Mag 38:69+ N '63
Peace of great books. E. F. Hunter. bibliog il Horn Bk 40:651-9 D '64
Stories to read aloud at Christmas time. L. Wilcox. il House B 105:24 D '63

Study and teaching

See Literature—Study and teaching

France

Letter from Paris. Genêt. New Yorker 39: 133-4+ O 12 '63
Oyster and the book. E. Clark. Yale R 52: 366-72 Mr '63

India

Book project in India; summary of address. J. K. Galbraith. Pub W 185:45-7 Je 22 '64

Poland

Fading freedoms; limited publication of intellectual reviews and new books challenged by intellectuals. Newsweek 63:45 My 11 '64

Russia

Impressive power of Soviet libraries reported by U.S. delegates to Russia. Library J 88: 528-9 F 1 '63
What the Soviets read about America. E. Wasiolek. il Sat R 47:26-7 My 9 '64

United States

See Books and reading

BOOKS and reading, influence of. See Literature, Influence of

BOOKS as gifts
Bookstores find handsome gift books promise a good holiday season. il Pub W 186:63-5 N 9 '64
Children's books for Christmas giving. G. Shalit. il McCalls 92:90+ D '64
Gift books; some of the picture books are readable too. il Time 84:114+ D 4 '64
Gift to give? a book, of course. P. Bunker. Sat R 47:51-5+ D 5 '64
Poor man's guide to Christmas. H. Frankel. Sat R 47:37-9 D 5 '64
Season in a nutshell. H. Frankel. Sat R 46:38+ D 7 '63

Anecdotes, facetiae, satire, etc.

Adeste Brentano's! R. Angell. il New Yorker 40:53 N 28 '64

BOOKS for boys. See Childrens literature
BOOKS for children. See Childrens literature
BOOKS for sailors. See Service mens reading
BOOKS for the blind. See Blind, Books, etc. for the
BOOKS for the sick
See also
Libraries, Hospital
BOOKS have wings; drama. See Indick, B. P.
BOOKS USA, incorporated
Books USA names officers at incorporation meeting; organization formed to send paperbacks abroad. Library J 88:3564 O 1 '63
BOOKSELLERS and bookselling
Act of folly. A. B. Anderson. Pub W 184:20-1 Jl 22 '63
Booksellers can sell to libraries. F. H. Potter. Pub W 185:125-8 Je 8 '64
Booksellers find salable new books promise strong fall season. Pub W 184:44-5 O 28 '63
Bookseller's public relations. W. L. Safire. il Pub W 184:25-7 O 21 '63
Call of books. J. A. Duffy. Pub W 185:46 Mr 30 '64
Censorship: a bookseller's view. T. Huntington. Pub W 185:57 Mr 2 '64
Censorship: strategy for defense. P. S. Jennison. Pub W 185:58-61 Mr 2 '64
Direct mail for retail bookstores. M. A. Levin. Pub W 186:53-5 S 21 '64
Don't sell books; personal approach to bookselling. D. Thompson and M. Johnson. Pub W 185:45+ Mr 16 '64
How can the industry create more bookstores? R. Vanderhoef. il Pub W 185:36-8 Ja 13 '64
How do you handle special orders? Pub W 185:65-7 My 25 '64
How to handle incoming merchandise. Pub W 186:175-6 Jl 13 '64
If you want a book, any book: basic reference tools needed by booksellers. E. A. Geiser. Pub W 186:50-3 D 14 '64
It's a matter of salesmanship. P. Anderson. Pub W 183:48-50 Mr 18 '63
Managing a branch bookstore: problems and responsibilities. L. A. Weber. Pub W 186: 62-3 O 5 '64
More than 2000 attend ABA's 63rd annual meeting; Eisenhower, Allen Dulles speak at exhibit. il Pub W 183:54-5 Je 17 '63
Personal selling, or self-service. G. Jennings. Pub W 187:124-5 Ja 18 '65
Role of the publisher's salesman in today's market. F. Watts. Pub W 187:121-4 Ja 18 '65
Should retailers sell to libraries? F. Watts. Pub W 185:120-2 Ja 20 '64
Simplified bookkeeping procedure for booksellers. il Pub W 186:116-18 S 28 '64
Ten suggestions for increasing sales; art books and magazines. il Pub W 184:104-5 Ag 19 '63
What do you mean, practical experience? E. Young. Pub W 185:63-5 My 25 '64
What to tell the neophyte: bookselling is a good career. J. F. Albright. Pub W 185:47-9 Mr 30 '64
See also
Books—Prices
College bookstores
Libraries and booksellers

Childrens literature

Children's department at Christmas time. B. Campbell. Pub W 184:40 Ag 19 '63
Expanding the market for children's books; summaries of addresses. P. Johnson, jr; J. F. Dougherty; L. Russ. Pub W 185:42-5 Je 29 '64
Getting the right book to the right child at the right time. E. C. Lowry. bibliog Pub W 185:91-3 F 3 '64
Juvenile paperbacks or the curious case of Curious George. L. Russ. Pub W 185:44-5 Mr 16 '64

BOOKSELLERS and bookselling—Childrens literature—*Continued*
Let the children's books shout, or A plea for more window display. L. Russ. Pub W 186: 93-5 Ag 24 '64
Sixty days with a salesbook: a reviewer sells at Christmas. J. F. Dougherty. Pub W 185: 61-2 F 3 '64

Jewish literature

From Jerusalem to the West; from Bamberger and Warhman bookstore to UCLA. Wilson Lib Bul 37:822 Je '63

Medical literature

Medical books in the world market. P. Perles. Pub W 183:41-2 Ap 15 '63

Paperback books

ABA regionals: paperback books in the bookstore; summaries of panel discussions and addresses at Boston and Cleveland meetings, with editorial comment. il Pub W 186: 36-43, 50 N 9 '64
Book is to buy; elementary school paperback bookstore. R. E. Newman. il Sat R 48:58-9 Ja 16 '65
Bowker offers inventory cards for titles in PBIP. Pub W 186:25 Ag 17 '64
Distribution of paperbound books. P. Johnson, jr. ALA Bul 57:534+ Je '63
Inventory control system for paperbacks. Pub W 186:40 S 7 '64
Mad Tom books: a venture in roadside selling of paperbacks; Manchester, Vt. P. Johnson, jr. il Pub W 186:38-40 O 5 '64
NACS: making the college store a force in education; symposium. il Pub W 183:27-33 My 27 '63
New kid in school; Buffalo, N.Y, paperback program makes good. A. M. Fox. Library J 88:3254-7 S 15 '63
New paperback revolution; retail sales upsurge. L. Schwartz. Pub W 184:25-6 S 30 '63
1963-64 paperback best sellers in the bookstores. il Pub W 185:70-7 Ja 20 '64; 187: 72-8 Ja 18 '65
Order out of chaos? paperbacks and the twenty six categories. E. Leonard. Pub W 185:43-4 Mr 16 '64
Paperback books: their promotion by booksellers; summary of panel discussion at the Denver ABA meeting. il Pub W 184:18-21 N 18 '63
Paperback flood: will retailer resistance force a slowdown? Pub W 185:29-30 Ap 13 '64
Paperbacks in Larchmont. C. B. Anderson. Pub W 185:86-7 Ap 27 '64
Paperbacks in the classroom. H. L. Stocker. Library J 89:318-19+ Ja 15 '64
Paperbacks in the general bookstore. G. R. Smith. Pub W 186:43-5 O 19 '64
Selling paperbacks to the educational market; ABPC symposium; with editorial comment. il Pub W 183:24-7, 49 Je 3 '63
Unusual fixtures sell paperbacks in Holland. il Pub W 183:26-7 Ap 8 '63

Publicity

Autographing parties: a community service. A. Udin. il Pub W 185:77-9 F 17 '64
Teen-age girl and the book market. K. Corinth. il Pub W 186:18-21 Ag 17 '64

Religious literature

Bibliophilic bibliopolist; Blessing book stores, Chicago, now Alec R. Allenson, inc, Naperville. Christian Cent 81:1223 S 30 '64
Lutherans open 16th store; move Puerto Rico store. il Pub W 185:96-8 F 10 '64
Some facts and factors in the religious book market. C. B. Grannis. Pub W 183:98-9 F 11 '63

Second hand books

Bibliophilic bibliopolist; Blessing book stores, Chicago, now Alec R. Allenson, inc, Naperville. Christian Cent 81:1223 S 30 '64

Statistics

ABPC statistical survey shows 1961-1963 trends in sales. Pub W 184:13-15 D 16 '63; 186:25-7 S 14 '64
Consumer patterns surveyed in three major cities: New York, Washington and San Francisco. Pub W 184:35-6 N 25 '63
January business affected by strikes and bad weather. Pub W 183:53 F 25 '63

Stock

ABC's of stocking the bookstore. H. J. Houlihan. il Pub W 186:55-60 Jl 27 '64
Ways in which authors and booksellers can cooperate to sell books. P. Smith. Pub W 186:14-17 Ag 17 '64

Technical literature

New technical book store in a million dollar market. il Pub W 183:43-5 Ap 15 '63
Service is the keynote of Boston shop's technical book department; Book clearing house. il Pub W 185:75-6 Ap 20 '64
Technical books and their sale examined at Denver ABA meeting; summary of addresses. M. Simons; J. Feyock. il Pub W 184: 30-1 N 11 '63
What this country needs are fifty more technical bookstores. il Pub W 186:72-4 N 16 '64

Alaska

Letter from Anchorage. J. Stewart. Pub W 185:21 Ap 13 '64

California

Calif. shop offers unique service to good customers; Tiburon books. il Pub W 185: 51-3 Mr 16 '64
Carmel bookshop opens branch in shopping center. il Pub W 185:93 Ap 27 '64
Downtown L.A. store celebrates seventy-five years of bookselling; Fowler brothers. il Pub W 184:58-9 D 30 '63
How to prepare for Christmas; Campbell's book store, Los Angeles. R. B. Campbell. Pub W 184:38-9 Ag 19 '63
Impulse buying, dominant factor at Pickwick's suburban shop; Hollywood. il Pub W 186:28-9 D 7 '64
L.A. paperback store in full operation after fire; Book fair in Westwood Village, Los Angeles. Pub W 185:238 Ja 27 '64
New Sacramento store is open every night in the week; Tower books. il Pub W 184: 49-50 O 14 '63
Obscenity: U.S. style; United States of America vs. West Coast news co, inc; reprint. R. R. Kirsch. ALA Bul 58:269-72 Ap '64
Store moves from downtown to large shopping center; Bookfinders, Chula Vista. il Pub W 184:48 O 14 '63
Unusual wrapping paper used by Berkeley store; illustrated with famous marks of printers of the 16th century. il Pub W 186: 46 D 7 '64

Canada

Canadian booksellers association holds its twelfth annual convention. I. Kropotkin. il Pub W 183:39-42 Je 3 '63
Canadian booksellers meeting dealt constructively with trade problems; thirteenth annual convention of the Canadian booksellers association. I. Kropotkin. il Pub W 185:28-31 Je 1 '64
One-day book sale grosses $11,000; M. G. Hurtig booksellers ltd, in Edmonton, Alta. il Pub W 185:50-2 Ap 13 '64
Paperback store is opened in Toronto public library; Classic's little books, inc. Pub W 184:54 Jl 29 '63

Colorado

Chinook bookshop: five years of growth; Colorado Springs. il Pub W 186:328-31 Ag 31 '64
Village bookstore in Boulder, Colo. adds trade books to technical stock. il Pub W 184:86-8 N 11 '63

Connecticut

Getting under way for Christmas; Boland's in New Canaan. M. C. Boland. il Pub W 186:36-40 Ag 24 '64
New Canaan book shop: progress report; 1958-1964. E. Young. il Pub W 185:87-91 Ap 27 '64

England

Bumpus sold to Robert Drummond; John and Edward Bumpus ltd, London. Pub W 185: 238 Ja 27 '64
Fanny Hill found obscene in London. Pub W 185:135-6 F 24 '64
Profiles; B. H. Blackwell, ltd, Oxford. V. Mehta. il New Yorker 40:63-4+ O 31 '64; 87 Ja 9 '65

Florida

Fairs held in slow months stir up business activity; Bates book shoppe, Daytona Beach. il Pub W 186:65-6 O 5 '64
New technical book store in a million dollar market. il Pub W 183:43-5 Ap 15 '63
What books can do for toy sales; Carousel book and toy shop, Miami Beach, Fla. P. Johnson, jr. il Pub W 183:156-9 F 18 '63

France

Brentano's Paris; a new era. il Pub W 183:90-2 Ap 15 '63

BOOKSELLERS and bookselling—*Continued*

Georgia

Bookstore fair alerts public to variety of juveniles; Baptist book store, Atlanta, Ga. il Pub W 185:95 F 10 '64

4000-square-foot shop to open in Atlanta; Lenox Square bookstore. Pub W 184:43-4 O 28 '63

Great Britain

Maxwell's bookshop: new store in Oxford, England, embodies many new concepts. il Pub W 184:34-7 S 23 '63

U.K. bookstore chain starts mail order bookselling; W. H. Smith & son, ltd. Pub W 186:36-7 S 14 '64

See also
Booksellers association

Illinois

Barbara's bookshop, Chicago: a modern personal store. il Pub W 184:52-4 Ag 12 '63

Chestnut Court, Winnetka, Ill: a personal bookshop with a flair. il Pub W 184:68-70 S 2 '63

Chicago booksellers join to fight censorship; Greater Chicago booksellers association established. Pub W 186:83+ Jl 6 '64

Chicago: new censorship capital. E. J. Gaines. ALA Bul 58:983-4 D '64

Kroch's & Brentano's to open 5700-square-foot store; Chicago. il Pub W 184:66-7 S 2 '63

Israel

From Jerusalem to the West; from Bamberger and Warhman bookstore to UCLA. Wilson Lib Bul 37:822 Je '63

Italy

Giangiacomo Feltrinelli: Italian publisher-bookseller pioneers to new book markets. P. J. Rosenwald. il Pub W 185:56-60 F 3 '64

Rome store specializes in American books; American bookshop. il Pub W 184:34-5 S 16 '63

Japan

Baptists open new bookstore in busy section of Tokyo. Pub W 186:115 S 28 '64

Kansas

Kansas store to mark seventy years of bookselling; Goldsmith's, inc. Wichita. Pub W 184:101-2 S 16 '63

Maryland

Bookstore's first print sale is overwhelming success; Cokesbury book store in Baltimore. il Pub W 185:51 Mr 16 '64

Massachusetts

Andover bookstore: relocated and thriving. R. White. il Pub W 185:36-8 Mr 9 '64

Bookselling; Phillips book store, Cambridge. il Pub W 186:69-73 Jl 20 '64

Cambridge shop fifty years old, moves to larger quarters; Phillips book store. Pub W 185:81 F 17 '64

Harvard square's bookshops listed as guide for students. il Pub W 184:55-6 Jl 29 '63

Lauriat's South Shore store a successful enterprise; Braintree. il Pub W 185:130-2 Je 8 '64

Odyssey book shop opens in South Hadley, Mass. D. S. Patee. il Pub W 185:71-3 My 25 '64

Old Holyoke store gives up most sidelines for books; Daniel F. Waters company. il Pub W 184:38-9 D 16 '63

Service is the keynote of Boston shop's technical book department; Book clearing house. il Pub W 185:75-6 Ap 20 '64

Netherlands

Dutch store builds business on imports; Berkhout's academische boekhandel. il Pub W 184:30-3 S 16 '63

New Hampshire

Hardbound and paperbound books intermingled in New Hampshire shop; Apple tree book shop, Concord. il Pub W 186:66-8 N 9 '64

New Jersey

Shop and library team up in book promotion plan. Pub W 184:171 Jl 8 '63

New Mexico

Four bookstores in the Southwest and the West; Taos book and mission shop, Taos, and Mesilla design center, Mesilla. R. Potter. il Pub W 185:39-42 Ja 13 '64

New York (state)

Bible sales increase at Benziger bros. N.Y. store. il Pub W 186:114-15 S 28 '64

Bookselling in Garden City. il Pub W 184:172-6 Jl 8 '63

Branch shop opened in N.Y. by New Canaan bookseller; Boat locker. Pub W 184:62-3 D 30 '63

Brandell's has largest stock of paperbacks on Long Island. il Pub W 185:44-5 Ap 6 '64

Broadway (N.Y.C.) bookstore has attractive design; the Book mark. il Pub W 183:43-5 My 6 '63

Cokesbury store near U.N. attracts foreign visitors; in Church center for the United Nations, NYC. il Pub W 186:118 S 28 '64

Community role of the bookseller. G. Light. il Pub W 185:47-8 My 11 '64

Eliot books: where a physician can satisfy all of his book needs. il Pub W 183:38-40 Ap 15 '63

Fourth travelers bookshop opened in N.Y. il Pub W 184:46-8 D 2 '63

God rest you merry, bookseller; Canterbury bookshop, New York city. M. L. Thompson. Pub W 185:94-5 F 3 '64

Greenwich Village bookshop to move early in 1965. il Pub W 186:46-7 O 19 '64

Harcourt, Brace & World store: most elegant bookshop in N.Y.C. il Pub W 184:28-31 O 14 '63

Laurel book center: a new Fifth avenue shop. il Pub W 186:68-9 D 28 '64

Macy's book fair in New York, Chaplin movies in suburbia. il Pub W 186:62-3 N 2 '64

Mail order sales help paperback bookseller; Bookcase, inc.; New York city. il Pub W 185:51-2 Mr 30 '64

Materials for learning, inc: children's book specialist. il Pub W 183:44-5 Ap 8 '63

New and old bookstores in Brooklyn Heights. il Pub W 183:44-7 Ap 22 '63

New Rizzoli international bookstore; New York city. il Pub W 186:24-9 N 30 '64

Nostalgic twins; Liveright book shop. New Yorker 39:24-6 Mr 2 '63

Paper book stores, inc. plans chain; Paper-book-card stores, New York city. il Pub W 184:55-7 S 23 '63

Three foreign-language bookstores; New York city. il Pub W 185:77-81 Je 15 '64

Three new paperback stores in N.Y.C. il Pub W 184:49-52 O 7 '63

Well-publicized party sells 300 copies of book; Economy bookstore in Syracuse. il Pub W 186:62-3 Jl 27 '64

Wise men fish here: the Gotham book mart. L. Caine. il Pub W 187:38-42 Ja 11 '65

World affairs book center appoints new manager: David W. Griffin. Pub W 185:64 Je 29 '64

North Carolina

Asheville's modern, personal bookshop. il Pub W 184:46-9 O 21 '63

Ohio

Flemings' Columbus, opens branch in Northland shopping center. il Pub W 186:54-6 S 14 '64

Progress report of Cleveland shopping center store; Fields' book store. il Pub W 185:54-5 Mr 9 '64

Two successful stores in shopping centers; Burrows. Cleveland. il Pub W 184:60-2 D 30 '63

Oklahoma

It was the year of the great don't-care. L. Meyer. Pub W 185:80-1 Ja 6 '64

Oregon

Why one personal bookshop is going out of business; the Book Stall in Portland, Ore. Pub W 183:72-4 F 4 '63

Pakistan

Pakistan's need for professional books spurs growth of Lahore bookshop; Mirza book agency. il Pub W 185:77-9 Ap 20 '64

Pennsylvania

Gross increase of fourteen per cent a year realized by small York shop; Colonial book store, inc. J. T. Consolino. il Pub W 186:50-2 N 23 '64

Leary's book store featured in Business week; Philadelphia. Pub W 186:60 O 5 '64

Old bookworm keeps turning slowly; Leary's book store, Philadelphia. il Bsns W p81-2+ S 12 '64

Pa. store successful with back-to-school promotions; L. B. Herr in Lancaster. Pub W 186:64-5 O 5 '64

York, Pa. wholesaler opens bookstore in shopping center, Bookland, inc. il Pub W 187:83-5 Ja 11 '65

BOOKSELLERS and bookselling—*Continued*

Russia

Book distribution in the USSR. K. Enoch and R. W. Frase. bibliog il ALA Bul 57:518-23 Je '63
Tips. Pub W 183:53 Mr 4 '63

Tennessee

Book fair for boys and girls at Nashville Baptist store. il Pub W 186:44-6 D 7 '64
Book fair will be held at Nashville Baptist store. Pub W 186:62 N 2 '64

Texas

Fort Worth shops' Xmas co-op ads boost business year around. Pub W 187:308-9 Ja 25 '65
Four bookstores in the Southwest and the West; Bassett center book store, El Paso. R. Potter. il Pub W 185:43-4 Ja 13 '64
Midland shop one of few Texas shops opened downtown; Chaucer book store. Pub W 185:79 Ja 6 '64
Personal bookshop in a department store; book department of Mayer & Schmidt in Tyler. il Pub W 186:44-5 Ag 17 '64

United States

After six years: the Doubleday merchandising plan. il Pub W 186:24-7 D 7 '64
ABPC: proposals to expand the prime market; with editorial comment. il Pub W 185:52-8, 73 Je 22 '64
ABA booksellers examine the tools and skills of management; annual convention. il Pub W 184:24-9 Jl 1 '63
ABA expanding sales through effective bookstore promotion; symposium. il Pub W 185:35-45 Je 29 '64
ABA: highlights of the 64th booksellers convention; symposium. il Pub W 185:41-58 Je 22 '64
ABA highlights of the 63rd booksellers' convention; symposium; with editorial comment. il Pub W 183:28-35, 52 Je 24 '63
ABA regional meetings: Denver, Dallas, New Orleans; summaries of panel discussions and addresses. il Pub W 184:18-40 N 18 '63
ABA regionals: book distribution and trade relations; summaries of panel discussions and addresses at Boston and Cleveland meetings. il Pub W 186:30-6 N 9 '64; Reply. L. Epstein. 186:21-2 D 7 '64
American bookselling in the 1960's; excerpts from American reading public. T. Wilentz. Pub W 183:42-50 Je 17 '63
Better focus on bookselling. C. B. Grannis. Pub W 184:90 S 16 '63
Bookseller serves the community, but who serves him? G. Light. ALA Bul 57:528-30 Je '63
Booksellers optimistic about Christmas business. il Pub W 184:16-18 D 9 '63
Bookselling (cont of) Retailing. See issues of Publishers' weekly
Christmas novelties unusual merchandise: more ways to capture impulse sales. il Pub W 184:72-7 Ag 19 '63
Cruise ship bookshop sells best sellers, cookbooks. Pub W 184:42 S 30 '63
Excellent Christmas business; deliveries still troublesome. il Pub W 187:126-7 Ja 18 '65
Fewer shops opened, fewer closed in 1963. Pub W 185:127-8 Ja 20 '64
Free delivery service and telephone ordering are assets. R. H. Smith. Pub W 184:89 Ag 19 '63
Goals for 1964; Book industry association president looks ahead; symposium. Pub W 185:46-9, 63 Ja 6 '64
Juvenile series promotion increases traffic, ups sales; North star books. il Pub W 183:155 F 18 '63
Lasser survey; step toward understanding; new era of bookseller-publisher communication. J. A. Duffy. Pub W 186:61 O 5 '64
More books but faster, faster please. J. A. Duffy. Pub W 185:119 Ja 20 '64
More shops opened in 1964; fewer were closed. Pub W 187:128 Ja 18 '65
New light on order fulfillment. C. B. Grannis. Pub W 186:40 S 7 '64
One out of four comes back! how costly are returns to the bookseller and the publishers? F. Watts. Pub W 186:51-3 S 7 '64; Reply. R. B. Igoe. 186:55 S 21 '64
One out of four comes back! how costly are returns to the bookseller and the publishers? F. Watts. Pub W 186:51-3 S 7 '64; Discussion. 186:55 S 21, 58-61 N 2 '64
Photo books are good sellers: are booksellers in the picture? P. Andrews. il Pub W 183:21-5 Mr 11 '63
Records in a bookstore: a new look. D. Ross. il Pub W 184:41-3 Ag 19 '63
Sellers' market. il Newsweek 62:104 N 4 '63
Short history of the ABA book buyer's handbook. G. Jennings. Pub W 186:57-8 N 2 '64
Supreme court petitioned to review "Tropic" conviction. Library J 88:1496 Ap 1 '63
Trade winds; colorful bookshops, with coffee and books. J. G. Fuller. Sat R 47:8 Ja 25 '64
Tropic of cancer before the Supreme court. Wilson Lib Bul 37:612+ Ap '63
Vanishing bookstore. D. Dempsey. il Sat R 46:18-19 Ag 10 '63
Xmas retail sales best since 1959. il Pub W 185:123-6 Ja 20 '64
See also
American booksellers association
Christian booksellers association
Department stores—Book departments

Utah

Two successful stores in shopping centers; Deseret book company, Salt Lake City. il Pub W 184:60-2 D 30 '63

Vermont

Mad Tom books: a venture in roadside selling of paperbacks; Manchester. J. Johnson, jr. il Pub W 186:38-40 O 5 '64

Washington, D.C.

Hecht added technical dept: to build volume; Hecht's book department. Pub W 184:84 N 11 '63
Kann's book department moved to street floor. Pub W 186:56 S 21 '64
Samuel Yudkin loses National airport concession. Pub W 184:30-1 D 2 '63
Shop's growth attributed to innovations, renovations; Savile bookshop. Pub W 184:38 D 9 '63

Washington (state)

To serve the Pacific Northwest: Stacey's new store in Seattle. il Pub W 184:32-5 N 11 '63

Wisconsin

If discounters threaten, don't panic, fight back. H. W. Schwartz. Pub W 185:30-1 Mr 30 '64

Wyoming

Four bookstores in the Southwest and the West; Shafer's books, Cheyenne. R. Potter. il Pub W 185:42-3 Ja 13 '64

BOOKSELLERS association
Booksellers but no books. P. Rosenwald. Pub W 186:22-3 Ag 3 '64

BOOKSELLERS association of America. Antiquarian. See Antiquarian booksellers association of America

BOOKSHELVES. See Bookcases

BOOKSTORES. See Booksellers and bookselling; College bookstores

BOOLA boola, Babe Ruth, and a jug of whiskey sours; story. See White, M.

BOOLEAN algebra. See Algebra, Boolean

BOOLOOTIAN, Richard A. and Campbell, J. L.
Primitive heart in the echinoid strongylocentrotus purpuratus. bibliog Science 145:173-5 Jl 10 '64

BOOMERANGS
Boomerang; the stick that returns. D. Rudolph. il Pop Mech 121:156-8+ Ap '64

BOOMS, Real estate. See Real estate business

BOONE, A. Gordon
Bear at bay. por Newsweek 61:19-20 Mr 4 '63

BOONE, Daniel
World of Daniel Boone. R. P. Warren. por Holiday 34:162+ D '63

BOONE, Richard W.
National service program; interview. NEA J 52:28+ Ap '63

BOONE COUNTY, Ark.
Decentralization and new equipment boost work output. J. R. Holt. il Am City 79:31 Ag '64

BOORE, J. P.
Old glass paperweights. Hobbies 69:82-5+ Mr; 82-4 Ag '64

BOORMAN, Howard L.
Slogans in bloom. Sat R 46:32-3 Mr 9 '63

BOOSTERS for space vehicles. See Space vehicles—Propulsion systems

BOOTH, Arch N.
Making self-government work; address, May 21, 1963. Vital Speeches 29:606-8 Jl 15 '63

BOOTH, Norman J. See Brieland, D. jt. auth.

BOOTH, Philip
Public systems for distributing risks to security. bibliog f Mo Labor R 86:622-9 Je '63

BOOTH, Philip E.
August 1942; poem. Poetry 101:338 F '63
Heavy poet; Seeing Auden off; Dancer; Rain; poems. Poetry 104:235-7 Jl '64
Offshore; poem. Atlan 213:68 Ja '64
Seaweed; poem. New Repub 150:19 F 15 '64
BOOTH, Windsor P. and Matthews, S. N.
Disaster in paradise. por Nat Geog Mag 124:436-58 S '63
BOOTHBY, Robert John Graham Boothby, baron
Filling in the blanks; Boothby and the Sunday mirror. Time 84:52 Ag 14 '64
Smeared peer revenged. il por Newsweek 64:40 Ag 17 '64
BOOTLEGGING
Night they raided the snake-juice still. V. H. Perera. Vogue 144:58+ D '64
Noble experiment, Indian style. T. F. Brady. il N Y Times Mag p24+ F 16 '64
BOOTS, Rubber, plastic, etc. See Shoes, Rubber, plastic, etc.
BOOTS and shoes. See Shoes
BOPLANT (calf cartilage) See Orthopedia
BOQUIST, W. P.
Astronomical photography with the new XR film. il Sky & Tel 27:12-14 Ja '64
BORA BORA, Society Islands
Islands under the wind. il H. Sutton. Sat R 47:23-4 My 2 '64
BORATES
Azeotrope of isopropyl alcohol and isopropyl borate. W. D. English and R. L. Kidwell. bibliog il Science 139:341-2 Ja 25 '63
See also
Ulexite
BORCH, Fred J.
Our common cause in world competition; address, November 9, 1964. Vital Speeches 31:115-18 D 1 '64
about
Electric's new general. por Time 82:104+ O 18 '63
GE shifts herald harder consumer sell. il por Bsns W p88 O 12 '63
New boss at GE. por Newsweek 62:86 O 21 '63
BORCHARDT, Georges
Report on French publishing. Pub W 184:33-5 Ag 12 '63; 186:29-31 Jl 27 '64
BORDE, Percival
Everyman's African roots. D. Leddick. por Dance Mag 38:20-1 O '64
BORDEAUX wines. See Wine
BORDEN, Lizzie
Faces from the past. R. M. Ketchum. por Am Heritage 15:28-9 Ap '64
BORDEN case. See Murder
BORDEN company
Borden's green pastures. il Time 81:86+ Mr 29 '63
Milk & chips; Borden company to acquire the Wise potato chip co. Time 84:98+ O 9 '64
BORDER war, Indian-Chinese. See India—Boundaries
BORDERS, Flower. See Garden borders
BORDES, Denise de Sonneville-. See Sonneville-Bordes, D. de
BORDIN, Edward S.
True or false? tests tell the story. PTA Mag 59:4-6 Ja '65
BOREDOM
Temptations of boredom. V. S. Pritchett. il Holiday 37:8+ Ja '65
BOREK, Ernest. See Srinivasan, P. R. jt. auth.
BORELLI, Pat D.
Make high contrast negatives. U S Camera 27:68-9 My '64
BORERS (insects)
See also
Shipworms
BORETZ, Benjamin
Music. See occasional issues of Nation
Records (cont) Nation 196:107-8, 535-6; 197:308, 374-6, 441-2; 198:155-6, 514-15, 639-40; 199:127-8, 364, 472-4; 200:94-6 F 2, Je 22, N 9, 30, D 21 '63, F 10, My 18, Je 22, S 14, N 16, D 14 '64, Ja 25 '65
BORG-Warner corporation
Next, please; Norge's new president. il Newsweek 64:71 Ag 17 '64
Spotting the right bases overseas. il Bsns W p 104+ Ag 10 '63
BORGE, Victor
Broadway postscript: Comedy in music. H. Hewes. Sat R 48:32 Ja 2 '65
Comedy in music. Time 84:81 N 20 '64
Stage; V. Borge back in New York. W. Sheed. Commonweal 81:354 D 4 '64
Victor Borge. America 111:758 D 5 '64
BORGES, Jorge Luis
Letter from Buenos Aires. A. Neish. Nation 196:273 Mr 30 '63
BORGESE, Elisabeth Mann
Adventure; story. Vogue 141:75 My '63
Afternoon with Nehru. Nation 198:506-8 My 18 '64
Ecumenical council: empire to commonwealth. Nation 200:51-5 Ja 18 '65
Italy: a new village around an old fountain. Nation 196:327-9 Ap 20 '63
Vision of a modern church. Nation 198:46-9 Ja 13 '64
BORGESON, Griff
Origin of the boat-tail speedster. Motor T 15:72-5+ F '63
BORGHESE, Giovanni, prince
Horrors of Bomarzo; interview, ed. by M. L. B. Ambrosini. Harper 228:66-71 Ap '64
BORGHINI, Federico
Treasury of sacred art. Américas 15:8-12 Ap '63
BORGMANN, Dmitri
Daft fad. il por Newsweek 64:104 N 2 '64
BORGNINE, Ernest
Ernest Borgnine: TV's howling new success. C. Brossard. il pors Look 27:32a-32b+ Jl 16 '63
BORGSTEDT, Harold H. See Distefano, V. jt. auth.
BORIN, V. L.
Who killed Diem and why? Nat R 16:441-6 Je 2 '64
BORING, Edwin G.
Books. Sci Am 209:159-60+ Jl '63; 210:145-6+ Ap '64
Cognitive dissonance: its use in science. bibliog Science 145:680-5 Ag 14 '64
BORIS Godunov; opera. See Musorgskii, M. P.
BORIS Godunov (operatic character) See Characters in opera
BORIS; story. See Levinson, D.
BORK, George Paul
Big man in any league. G. Brown. il Sports Illus 19:54-6 N 11 '63
BORK, Robert H.
Civil rights: a challenge. New Repub 149:21-4 Ag 31; 36 S 21 '63
—and Bowman, W. S. Jr
Crisis in antitrust. Fortune 68:138-40+ D '63
BORKLUND, C. W.
DOD performance system explained. Miss & Roc 13:31-2+ S 16 '63
BORLAND, Hal
August bounty; excerpt from Sundial of the seasons. Read Digest 85:29-30+ Ag '64
Day begins... Read Digest 85:210-12 O '64
False conservationists; reprint. por Audubon Mag 66:367 N '64
February; poem. McCalls 91:156 F '64
about
Bit of the Thoreau. il por Newsweek 63:82 Ap 6 '64
Hal Borland and the voice of nature. J. C. Devlin. il por Audubon Mag 66:175-7 My '64
BORMAN, Frank
Get rid of the pogo bounce. Life 55:84 S 27 '63
BORN, Hedwig
Unwritten code. Bul Atomic Sci 19:30-1 My '63
BORN, Max
What is left to hope for? por Bul Atomic Sci 20:2-5 Ap '64
BORNEO
See also
North Borneo
Sarawak
BORNSTEIN, Paul, and others
Intermolecular cross-linking of collagen and the indentification of a new beta-component. bibliog Science 144:1220-1; 145:837 Je 5, Ag 21 '64
BOROBUDUR, Java
Celestial musicians of Borobudor. il UNESCO Courier 17:24-5 Je '64
BORODIN, Aleksandr Profir'evich
Professor Borodin's indulgence. D. Lloyd-Jones. il por Hi Fi 13:28-30+ Je '63
BORODZIEJ, Irena
Visually handicapped youngster in art. Sch Arts 63:27-8 Ja '64
BOROFF, David
Air force academy: a slight gain in altitude. Harper 226:86-8+ F '63
Author: S. Bellow. Sat R 47:38-9+ S 19 '64
Beach, Bohemia, barracks, Brooklyn. N Y Times Mag p64+ S 29 '63
Cambridge on the range. Sat R 47:48-50+ Je 20 '64
Case for the asphalt campus. N Y Times Mag p 15+ Ap 21 '63
Cauldron of creativity. Sat R 46:45-7+ D 21 '63

BOROFF, David—*Continued*
College intellectual, 1965 model. N Y Times Mag p36-7+ D 6 '64
Drinking in German dreaming in French. Mlle 56:130-1+ F '63
Education comes of age. Parents Mag 38: 74+ F '63
Fort Hood: Sparta goes suburban. Harper 228:46-53 Ja '64
No place left to hide. Sat R 47:47 Mr 21 '64
Plea to save the liberal arts. N Y Times Mag p 18+ My 10 '64
St John's college. Sat R 46:58-61+ Mr 23 '63
Status seeking in academe. Sat R 47:45-7 D 19 '64
That science center called M.I.T. N Y Times Mag p 18-19+ Ag 18 '63
Training talent in the arts. Parents Mag 39: 76-7+ F '64

about

West Point & all that. il por Time 81:49-50 F 8 '63

BOROMÉ, Joseph A.
Bellini and the Sleepwalker. Opera N 27:24-5 Mr 30 '63
Great opera houses: The Bolshoi. Opera N 28:26-31 F 29 '64

BORON
Air force admits big potential for boron filament structures. W. Beller. il Miss & Roc 14:22-3 Je 15 '64
Boron. A. G. Massey. il Sci Am 210:88-94+ Ja '64
Boron: another form. R. H. Wentorf, jr. bibliog il Science 147:49-50 Ja 1 '65

BOROS, Julius
Old pro; U.S. Open champion. il pors Time 82:68+ Jl 5 '63
Sporting scene. H. W. Wind. New Yorker 39: 44+ Jl 6 '63

BOROUGH halls. See City halls

BOROUGH names. See Names, Geographical

BOROWITZ, Eugene B.
Jewish need for theology. Commentary 34: 138-44; 35:166-7 Ag '62, F '63
Tension in reform Judaism. Christian Cent 81:729-32 Je 3 '64

BORRAS Y ALMANZA, Mirtha Margarita
Girl spy against Castro. A. St George. il pors Look 28:60-5 D 29 '64

BORROWING of money. See Credit; Debt

BORROWMAN, Merle
Conant, the man. Sat R 46:58-60 S 21 '63

BORSOS, Tibor. See Rapp, H. J. jt. auth.

BORST, Piet. See Weissmann, C. jt. auth.

BORSUK, Robert
Amateur speaks. il U S Camera 26:70-1 Ap '63

BORTH, Christy
Album of seven classic automotive pacesetters. Pop Mech 121:96-102 Ja '64

BORTON, James W. See Borton, N. jt. auth.

BORTON, Nan, and Borton, J. W.
Turkey. pors Nat Geog Mag 126:330-3 S '64

BOSC, Robert
Algeria: year I of independence. America 108: 362-5 Mr 16 '63

BOSCH, Jose M.
Drum-beating for rum; Bacardi's comeback. il por Bsns W p 102-4+ O 12 '63

BOSCH, Juan
In Haiti, terrible tyranny; interview. ed. by C. Migdail. por U S News 54:40 My 20 '63
Indelible spot; story. tr. by H. W. Shlaudeman. Sat Eve Post 236:78-9 N 16 '63

about

After Bosch. New Repub 149:4 O 5 '63
After Trujillo, a reformer with a mission. T. Szulc. il por N Y Times Mag p30+ S 8 '63
Caribbean failure. Commonweal 79:64-5 O 11 '63
Days of doubt in Dominican Republic. Sr Schol 83:20 O 18 '63
Democracy derailed in the Dominican Republic. il Sr Schol 83:4-7 O 25 '63
Fall of Juan Bosch. N. Gall. il Nation 197: 253-6 O 26 '63
If it's war in Haiti, who'll win? C. Migdail. por U S News 54:44 My 13 '63
Latest revolt in Caribbean: its meaning for U.S. il por U S News 55:66-7 O 7 '63
New man for the Dominicans. New Repub 148: 8 Mr 2 '63
Nonintervention: a shield for Papa Doc. G. Sherman. il Reporter 28:27-9 Je 20 '63
Question mark. il por Time 81:29 Mr 8 '63
Santo Domingo: the empty showcase. D. A. Allan. il Reporter 29:28-31 D 5 '63
Shuffle to the right. il por Newsweek 62:64 O 7 '63
U.S.-backed reform flops as Bosch gets the bounce. S. Halper. il por Life 55:49-50 O 18 '63
Why Bosch fell. V. Alba. New Repub 149:12-14 O 12 '63

BOSCOBEL (historic house) See New York (state)—Historic houses, etc.

BOSE, Buddhadeva
Hölderlin; poem. Poetry 102:380 S '63

BOSENBARK, George V.
Stowaway frog. Yachting 114:124-5 Ag '63

BOSIS, Lauro de
Rendezvous with Pegasus. H. Bowser. Sat R 47:14 Mr 14 '64

BOSMAJIAN, Haig A.
Anti-communism in the grade schools. bibliog f Sch & Soc 91:93-6 F 23 '63

BOSS, Mary F.
Let's eat. Am For 69:2-3+ D '63
Portrait of a predator. Flower Grower 50:53-4 Ag '63

BOSS rule
Barry Goldwater talks about liberals and liberalism; excerpts from address, June 27, 1963. B. Goldwater. il U S News 55:44-5 Jl 8 '63
City bosses and political machines; symposium, ed. by L. S. Greene. bibliog f il Ann Am Acad 353:1-121 My '64
Fraud! fraud! A. B. Callow, jr. il N Y Times Mag p60+ S 27 '64
See also
Politics, Corruption in

BOSSA nova. See Jazz music

BOSSUET, Jacques Bénigne, bp
Splendid bishop. J. Ratté. Commonweal 79: 290-1 N 29 '63

BOSTON, Lucy M.
Message from Green Knowe; excerpt from address. Horn Bk 39:259-64 Je '63

BOSTON

Architecture

Athenian reach. W. Evans. il Fortune 69: 138-42 Je '64
Boston: building a heritage. W. McQuade. il Arch Forum 120:68-9 Je '64
Boston makes a comeback. il U S News 57: 52-4+ S 21 '64
Boston's stage government center approved. il Arch Rec 135:26 Ja '64
Final plan unveiled for Boston's new government center. il Arch Rec 133:14-15 My '63
New center for Boston. il Arch Forum 120: 88-9 F '64
Special issue: Boston. il Arch Forum 120:63-124 Je '64

Art

Reviews: Boston. J. H. Kay. Art N 63:17+ S '64

Banks

Staid Boston trustee tries a new venture; management consultant. il Bsns W p72+ O 17 '64
Strategic withdrawal; no increase of loan interest rates. Time 84:97 D 11 '64

City hall

Great plaza for Boston's government center. il Arch Rec 135:192-4 Mr '64

City planning

Boston makes a comeback. il U S News 57: 52-4+ S 21 '64
Boston: rebuilding a city. D. B. Carlson. il Arch Forum 120:79-87 Je '64
Boston: what can a sick city do? W. McQuade. il Fortune 69:132-7+ Je '64
Bulldozers and bureaucrats. W. Von Eckardt. New Repub 149:15-19 S 14 '63
Conference on Boston renewal; Colloquium on church and synagogue in Boston renewal. J. L. Hofford. Christian Cent 81:346-8 Mr 11 '64
Old Boston spruces up. il Bsns W p 130+ Ap 13 '63
Prudential master plan; Back Bay area. il Arch Rec 135:190-1 Mr '64
Under the knife, or all for their own good. il Time 84:60+ N 6 '64

Crime

Fear walks home with the women; with report by M. Byers. il Life 54:16-21 F 15 '63
Hunt for the strangler. il Newsweek 63:31 F 24 '64
Mad strangler of Boston. E. S. Gardner. il Atlan 213:49-56 My '64
Now a seer helps stalk the Boston strangler. P. Mandel. il Life 56:49-50 Mr 6 '64
Phantom strangler; tenth strangle victim. Time 81:20 Mr 22 '63
Search for the strangler; tactical patrol force of Boston. J. Iams. il Sat Eve Post 236: 28+ My 18 '63

BOSTON—*Continued*

Description

Southie is my home town; why the Irish love South Boston. J. McCarthy. Holiday 35: 60-1+ Mr '64

Economic conditions

Lean times in Boston; depression and the drys. C. W. Morton. Atlan 211:47-54 F '63

Education

Boston's backwardness. il Time 82:116 O 4 '63
Dialogue among pickets. H. Cox. Commonweal 79:245-6 N '63; Reply with rejoinder. J. A. Murray. 79:485-6 Ja 24 '64
Quiet revolution; white college students tutor Negro high school youngsters at After school programs. J. F. Warner. il Sat R 47:80-1+ My 16 '64
Universities: tall new symbols of their significance; sixty odd colleges and universities in the Boston region. D. Canty. il Arch Forum 120:114-23 Je '64

Galleries and museums

See also
Boston museum of fine arts

Harbor

Old seaport: planning a window on the world; Boston. il Arch Forum 120:94-7 Je '64

Historic houses, etc.

Boston's Old corner to be restored. Pub W 184:69 N 11 '63

History

Boston accent: brisk saga of a city. W. McQuade. il Arch Forum 120:70-8 Je '64
Great interlude, by F. Russell. Review
Nat R 16:691-3 Ag 11 '64. Chamberlain

Hospitals

Young and daring; Peter Bent Brigham hospital. il Newsweek 61:55 F 11 '63

Hotels, restaurants, etc.

Ritz changes hands but not its cachet. il Bsns W p30-1 O 10 '64

Housing

Bulldozers and bureaucrats. W. Von Eckardt. New Repub 149:15-19 S 14 '63
New Boston high-rise with small suites; Charlesbank apartments. il Arch Rec 134: 212-13 S '63
Tragedy of a vertical slum. R. Tunley. il Sat Eve Post 236:89-93 Je 29 '63

Industries

R&D: new awareness in Congress of stimulus of federal research stirs envy of areas like Boston. J. Walsh. Science 139:1273-5 Mr 29 '63
Why Boston is puzzled by a federal economy move. il U S News 57:84-6 N 23 '64

Libraries

See also
Boston public library

Music

Boy with cheek: Bernstein's Kaddish symphony. il Time 83:68 F 7 '64
Hub witchery. W. A. Storrer. Opera N 27:33 Ap 13 '63
[Musical events] (cont) il Mus Am 83:76 Ja; 20-1 Ap; 115+ D '63; 84:14-15 Mr; 17 My; 63 D '64
See also
Boston opera group, incorporated
Boston symphony orchestra

Negroes

Quiet revolution; white college students tutor Negro high school youngsters at After school programs. J. F. Warner. il Sat R 47:80-1+ My 16 '64
Rally on the Common; Boston demonstration. America 108:729 My 25 '63

Newspapers

See also
Globe (Boston)

Police

Strike that made a president. F. Russell. il Am Heritage 14:44-7+ O '63

Police department

Boston survey stresses police reorganization. il Am City 78:28 Ag '63
Radio system that thinks. E. L. McNamara. il Am City 79:22 D '64

Public buildings

Coordinated architecture for government center. il Arch Rec 135:195-200 Mr '64

Social conditions

Boston tomorrow: problems, prospects, and ideas. il Arch Forum 120:124 Je '64
Close-up on poverty; O'Haires. M. Harrington. il Look 28:64-72 Ag 25 '64

Social life and customs

Urban villagers, by H. Gans. Review
Commentary 35:544-7 Je '63. M. Parenti

Stores

Bargains beneath Boston; Filene's basement. il Time 82:76 S 27 '63

Taxation

Boston's lower taxes. Newsweek 61:39 Je 24 '63

Transportation

Transportation: if it gets any worse, it may never get better. B. Spring. il Arch Forum 120:108-13 Je '64

BOSTON and Maine railroad
Happy commuters! il Newsweek 61:79 F 25 '63
Help for commuters. il U S News 54:88-9 Mr 18 '63
Where a rail subsidy failed to end red ink. U S News 55:9 D 23 '63

BOSTON ballet. See Ballet companies

BOSTON Celtics (basketball team) See Basketball teams

BOSTON Children's medical center. See Children—Hospitals

BOSTON college
Boston beacon. il Time 81:46+ Ap 26 '63
BC's Catholic campus. il Newsweek 61:56 Ap 29 '63
Graduate now, pay later; class of 1964 to provide scholarships. Newsweek 63:100+ My 25 '64
Incident at Boston college; dismissal of Dr Paul M. Michaud. M. J. Bennett. Commonweal 80:284-5 My 29 '64; Reply with rejoinder. R. F. Drinan. 80:420-3 Je 26 '64

BOSTON cooking school cookbook. See Cookbooks

BOSTON marathon. See Running

BOSTON medical library
Opening the chambered nautilus; evaluation of uncataloged material for Francis A. Countway library. L. Ash. il Library J 89:2040-3 My 15 '64

BOSTON museum of fine arts
Additions to the Karolik collection in Boston. R. Davidson. il Antiques 83:218 F '63
Big dig for the lost earring. J. Howard. il Life 56:75-6+ My 1 '64
Boston museum buys a masterpiece of martyrdom. il Life 55:64-5 O 18 '63
Flemish anonymous; Martyrdom of St Hippolytus, at Boston's museum of fine arts. il Time 82:86-7 O 18 '63
Gilding the lily; exhibit at Boston museum of fine arts. il Time 82:58-61 N 8 '63

BOSTON opera company
Boston opera company; fifth season, 1913-1914. H. M. Palmer. il Hobbies 69:30-1+ Ap '64

BOSTON opera group, incorporated
Berg and Bellini in Boston. W. A. Storrer. il Opera N 28:32-3 Mr 21 '64
No ban on Lulu. H. Rogers. il Mus Am 84:10 F '64
Persistent one; Boston opera group. il Time 83:58 F 21 '64
Renaissance woman. Q. Eaton. il Opera N 28:26-9 Ap 18 '64

BOSTON public library
Newspaper gap. E. J. Montana, jr. il Library J 89:1194-7 Mr 15 '64; Correction. 89: 2260 Je 1 '64
Panel to advise Boston on architect for addition. Library J 88:2659 Jl '63
Supermarket come-on: paperback experiment with young adults. J. Manthorne. il Library J 90:302-5 Ja 15 '65

BOSTON Red Sox (baseball) See Baseball clubs

BOSTON safe deposit and trust company. See Boston—Banks

BOSTON symphony orchestra
Balancing accounts. H. Rogers. Mus Am 83: 20-1 Ap '63
For music, not money; orchestra's deficit. il Bsns W p22-3 Ag 1 '64
Home at last. il Newsweek 63:84 Ap 13 '64
Leinsdorf in Boston. J. M. Conly. il Hi Fi 13:44-7+ D '63
Music to my ears; presentation of Menotti's Death of the Bishop of Brindisi. I. Kolodin. Sat R 47:28 N 7 '64

BOSTON symphony orchestra—*Continued*
Musical events; Britten's War requiem. W. Sargeant. New Yorker 39:173-4 N 2 '63
Musical events; performance of Menotti's cantata Death of the Bishop of Brindisi. W. Sargeant. New Yorker 40:231 O 31 '64
Musical events; two concerts at Philharmonic Hall. W. Sargeant. New Yorker 40:100 Ap 11 '64
New Boston tea party. Sat R 46:73 Mr 30 '63; Discussion. 46:72-3 Ap 27; 62 My 25 '63
Prodigal returns; American première of Bernstein's Kaddish symphony. Newsweek 63:77 F 10 '64

Anecdotes, facetiae, satire, etc.

Impregnable Boston symphony; Mr Cabot meets the chorus crasher. J. Roddy and H. B. Cabot. Harper 227:35-8 Jl '63

BOSTON university
Integrated campus for Boston university's landlocked site. il Arch Rec 135:161-70 My '64

BOSTWICK, George Herbert, jr
How to be an amateur. por Newsweek 63:63 My 18 '64

BOSWALL, Jeffery
Record boom in bird songs. Audubon Mag 66:48-50 Ja '64

BOSWELL, F. W. C. and Pappas, G. D.
Electron microscopy. Science 142:686-8 N 8 '63

BOSWELL, James
Books. W. Balliett. New Yorker 39:78+ Je 29 '63
Master confessor. H. Pearson. il Sat R 46:26 Ap 13 '63

BOSWELL steps out; story. See Elkin, S.

BOTANICAL chemistry
Continuous extraction during treatment with ultrasound. J. A. Lott and A. E. DeMaggio. bibliog il Science 139:825-6 Mr 1 '63
See also
Growth promoting substances (plants)
Photosynthesis

BOTANICAL gardens
Alfred L. Boerner botanical gardens. C. B. Lees. il Horticulture 42:34-7 Ap '64
Garden for every child, Royal botanical gardens, Hamilton. L. Laking. il Flower Grower 51:36+ F '64
Green thumb that paid off; El Pinar, Bogota, Colombia. L. Zalamea. il Américas 15:29-33 F '63
Norfolk botanical garden. F. Heutte. il Horticulture 42:26-7 S '64
Pacific tropical botanical garden. P. B. Sears. Science 147:241 Ja 15 '65
See also
Brooklyn botanic garden
Fairchild tropical garden, Coconut Grove, Fla.
Montreal botanical garden
New York botanical garden

BOTANICAL research
Yes, tall oaks from little acorns grow. C Peet. il Am For 69:24-7 O '63

BOTANICAL taxonomy. See Botany—Classification

BOTANISTS
See also
Bartram, J.
Henry, M. G.

BOTANY
Botany fit to survive? Sci N L 84:198 S 28 '63
Compleat botanist; adaptation of address, December 30, 1963. A. J. Sharp. bibliog Science 146:745-8 N 6 '64
See also
Mutation (botany)

Classification

Perspectives in chemotaxonomy. R. E. Alston and others. bibliog il Science 142:545-52 N 1 '63
See also
Botany—Nomenclature

Ecology

Airborne algae: their abundance and heterogeneity. R. M. Brown, jr, and others. bibliog il Science 143:583-5 F 7 '64
Photoelectric ecosystem. N. E. Armstrong and H. T. Odum. bibliog il Science 143:256-8 Ja 17 '64
Species abundance: natural regulation of insular variation. T. H. Hamilton and others. bibliog il Science 142:1575-7 D 20 '63; Reply with rejoinder. D. R. Dawdy. 146:1074-5 N 20 '64
See also
Forest ecology
Plant communities

Embryology

See also
Germination

Nomenclature

Linneaus. G. H. M. Lawrence. il Horticulture 42:22-3 N '64
Roses are rubra, violets are coerulea. M. H. Arnold. il Horticulture 41:364-5 Jl '63

Paleontology

See Paleobotany

Pathology

See Plants—Diseases and pests

Physiology

See also
Growth (plants)
Plants—Respiration
Plants—Transpiration
Spiral growth and movement
Tropism (botany)

Alaska

Plant hunter goes in search of Alaska's arctic plants. il Flower Grower 51:22-3 Mr '64

Australia

Wonderful wattle tree. M. Buttner. il Am For 70:30-1 Jl '64

California

California's methuselah trees. W. F. Heald. il Am For 70:34-5 Mr '64
Waves of spring color in Antelope Valley. il Sunset 132:82-9 Ap '64

Florida

Florida's unusual trees. M. Hunn. il Am For 70:17-19 Ap '64
Shrubs in Florida. P. Dempsey. il Horticulture 42:18-21 N '64

Hawaii

Archipelagic refuge. B. Stone. il Natur Hist 72:32-9 N '63
Pacific tropical botanical garden. P. B. Sears. Science 147:241 Ja 15 '65

Malaysia

Malaysia's giant flowers and insect-trapping plants. P. A. Zahl. il Nat Geog Mag 125:680-701 My '64

New Hampshire

Mt Washington floras. il Natur Hist 72:40-3 F '63

New Jersey

Botanical field meeting; report on North East section of the Botanical society of America. R. K. Zuck. Science 145:1216 S 11 '64

New Zealand

Wild flowers of New Zealand. C. Wylie. il Horticulture 41:370-1 Jl '63

South Africa

Floral inheritance. E. Scholtz. il Natur Hist 72:26-31 My '63

BOTANY, Medical
Going to seed; hallucinatory drug LSD in morning glory seeds. il Newsweek 62:59 Jl 22 '63
Green medicine, by M. B. Kreig. Review Sci Digest il 56:89-90 S '64. D. Cohen
Medieval codex of Italy; Tacuinum sanitatis. K. Kup. il Natur Hist 72:30-41 D '63
Renaissance in botanical drugs. J. A. Mirt. il Todays Health 41:42-5+ My '63
See also
Ginseng

BOTELHO, Stella Y.
Tears and the lacrimal gland; with biographical sketch. Sci Am 211:18, 78-84+ bibliog (p 142) O '64

BOTFLIES
Human botfly. Time 84:82 Jl 10 '64

BOTH, Ernst E.
Recent visual observations of Mars. il Sky & Tel 26:17-19 Jl '63

BOTH barrels; story. See Stuart, J.

BOTSFORD, Harry
Trout superlative. Field & S 68:48-9+ Mr '64

BOTSFORD, Keith
Listening to Pedro Martinez. Commentary 38:46-50 Jl '64
Mexico follows a solo camino. N Y Times Mag p20+ Ap 26 '64
Modesty in exuberance. Nation 196:184-5 Mr 2 '63
Rising expectations. Commentary 37:85-6 F '64

BOTT, George
Literature and English Lakeland. Sr Schol 85:12T Ja 7 '65
BOTTICELLI, Sandro
Dante's Divine comedy in Esperanto. il UNESCO Courier 16:32-3 Je '63
BOTTLE brushes (shrubs)
Bottlebrush buckeye. G. Taloumis. il Pop Gard 15:11-12 N '64
BOTTLE cap removers. See Cap removers
BOTTLE feeding. See Infants—Nutrition
BOTTLED eggs. See Eggs—Marketing
BOTTLED portraitures. See Portrait painting
BOTTLENOSE dolphin. See Dolphins (mammals)
BOTTLES
Atterbury bottle and jar designs. A. G. Peterson. il Hobbies 69:72-3 Jl '64
Bleach-bottle bonanza. W. Waltner and E Waltner. il Pop Mech 120:146-7 Ag '63
Hippest flask. il Esquire 62:94-5 O '64
Soda bottle, a home hazard. Consumer Bul 46:15 Ag '63
Some notes on commemorative bottles. T. H. Marsh. il Hobbies 67:86-7 F '63
Why and how to decant wines. J. A. Beard. il House & Gard 124:168+ D '63
World's fanciest pill bottles; adaptation of address. G. E. Griffenhagen. il Todays Health 42:42-5+ D '64
See also
Baby bottles
BOTTORFF, Oeita, and Bishop, Amelia
Recreation and your church. Recreation 56:476-7 D '63
BOTTY, Ken
Duck hunters: take to the swamps. pors Outdoor Life 132:48-9+ O '63
BOTULINUM toxin. See Toxins and antitoxins
BOTULISM
Botulinus toxin: effect on the central nervous system of man. H. R. Tyler. bibliog il Science 139:847-8 Mr 1 '63
Botulism: the killer who came to dinner. T. Berland. il Sat Eve Post 237:71-3 Mr 7 '64
Canned chili peppers cause two deaths. Sci N L 85:361 Je 6 '64
Death can come in cans. Time 83:31 Ja 24 '64
Deaths from botulism. Sci N L 84:246 O 19 '63
Facts behind the botulism scare. Good H 158:159-60 My '64
Freezing to be safe; Great Lakes fishing industry. il Bsns W p36 N 9 '63
Hardy germ holds up nuclear food processing; organism that causes botulism. il Todays Health 42:60 Mr '64
Let's talk about food. P. L. White. Todays Health 42:15-16+ F '64
Moving in on a menace. Bsns W p 132+ Ja 25 '64
Mystery of the botulism-poisoned fish; Great Lakes smoked fish. Consumer Rep 29:84 F '64
Sniff before you eat. il Sci Digest 55:61 Ja '64
Tragic breakfast; plastic-wrapped smoked whitefish. il Newsweek 62:80 O 21 '63
Two tuna sandwiches. il Newsweek 61:76 Ap 1 '63
Wanted: botulism E antiserum. Sci Digest 55:84 My '64
BOUCHÉ, Louis
Art galleries; exhibition at the Kraushaar. R. M. Coates. New Yorker 40:166+ N 7 '64
BOUCHÉ, René Robert
Elegant and tony; portraitist of the famous and the fashionable. il por Newsweek 62:61 Jl 22 '63
René Bouché, 1906-1963: an appreciation. W. S. Lieberman. il por Vogue 142:184-9 S 1 '63
BOUCHER, Anthony
San Francisco interim. Opera N 29:26-7 S 26 '64
BOUCHET, Barbara
Ease of Europa. il pors Esquire 61:114-15 Ap '64
BOUDART, Michel. See Kohn, H. W. jt. auth.
BOUDIN, Stéphane
Mrs Guest and Monsieur Boudin. il por Vogue 141:148-9+ Ap 1 '63
BOUGAINVILLEA
How to plant a bougainvillea. il Sunset 132:256 Ap '64
BOUGHTON, H. G.
Wicked kings. Outdoor Life 131:60-1+ Je '63
BOULDER, Colo.
Water supply
We had to try twice. E. R. Turner. il Am City 78:122-4 Je '63
BOULDING, Kenneth E.
Hymn for cold warriors. Christian Cent 80:492 Ap 17 '63
BOULEZ, Pierre
Long-wave composer. por Newsweek 61:90 My 20 '63
Music to my ears; Pierre Boulez, group of one. I. Kolodin. Sat R 46:39 Je 8 '63
Two B's; Boulez first appearance in London as conductor and composer. M. Cooper. Mus Am 84:28+ Ap '64
BOULTING, John Edward
Pitfalls of pratfalls; Boulting brothers comedies. W. Sheed. Commonweal 78:402-4 Jl 5 '63
BOULTING, Roy
Pitfalls of pratfalls; Boulting brothers comedies. W. Sheed. Commonweal 78:402-4 Jl 5 '63
BOULWARE, Lemuel R.
Case for Boulwarism. H. R. Northrup. bibliog f il Harvard Bsns R 41:86-97 S '63
BOULWARE, Marcus H.
J. Finley Wilson, fraternal orator. bibliog Negro Hist Bul 27:67-8 D '63
BOUND, Charles F.
Keys to the future. Pub W 183:82+ Je 3 '63
BOUNDARIES
President Johnson calls upon Soviet Union for concrete actions to promote peace; exchange of letters. L. B. Johnson; N. Khrushchev. Dept State Bul 50:157-63 F 3 '64
See also subhead Boundaries under names of countries, states, etc. e.g. India—Boundaries
BOUNDARY and water commission, International. See International boundary and water commission (United States and Mexico)
BOUNDARY layer
Cavity injection explored for hypersonic cooling use. M. L. Yaffee. il Aviation W 82:36-8 Ja 4 '65
Hunting the wily boundary layer. R. Bach. Flying 74:38 Ap '64
Jet boundary layer flap doubles 707 lift. G. C. Wilson. il Aviation W 80:36-7 My 25 '64
Peruvians study rotating-cylinder flap. D. A. Brown. il Aviation W 81:70-1+ D 7 '64
BOUNTIES for animals. See Animals, Predatory—Bounties
BOUNTY mutiny. See Mutiny
BOUQUETS
Beginners' bouquets and what to do with them. il Bet Hom & Gard 42:120 Je '64
BOUQUETS, Dried. See Flowers, Dried
BOURBON open golf tournament. See Golf—Tournaments
BOURBON whiskey. See Whiskey
BOURDET, Claude
Wrong Europe. Nation 196:191-5 Mr 9 '63
BOURJAILY, Vance
Fitzgerald attends my Fitzgerald seminar. Esquire 62:110-11+ S '64
Memoirs of an ace. Esquire 62:29-32+ Ag '64
One hell of a duck hunt. Esquire 60:98-100+ O '63
Outdoors. Esquire 61:168-70 Ap; 57+ Je; 62:40+ S; 40+ O; 96-8 D '64
Speaking out. por Sat Eve Post 237:6+ F 15 '64
You can tell a hunter by what he hunts. N Y Times Mag p38-9+ N 29 '64
BOURKE, George
From tip to top in Florida. See issues of Travel
BOURKE, Kathleen
Fun-to-make holiday decorations for Thanksgiving. Pop Gard 14:28-9 N '63
BOURKE, Sharon
Cafe; Household poem; poems. Poetry 101:245 Ja '63
BOURKE, William
Copyreaders. Atlan 212:130 O '63
BOURKE-WHITE, Margaret
Great lady with a camera; excerpts from Portrait of myself. pors Life 54:85-8+ Je 28 '63
about
Focussing a wide angle lens on life. W. L. Rivers. il pors Sat R 46:24-5 Je 29 '63
BOURNE, Laurence M.
Tulipomania. Horticulture 41:264 My '63
BOURNONVILLE, August
Blasis to Bournonville. L. Moore. il por Dance Mag 38:52-3+ F '64
BOUTON, Ellen Naylor, and Pettigrew, T. F.
When a priest made a pilgrimage. Christian Cent 80:363-5 Mr 20 '63
BOUTROS-GHALI, Boutros
Addis Ababa charter. bibliog f Int Concil 546:5-62 Ja '64

BOUTWELL, Albert
Birmingham's mayor cracks the door. Christian Cent 80:574 My 1 '63
BOUTWELL, William D.
What's happening in education? See issues of PTA magazine
BOUVIER family
Origins. New Yorker 39:25-7 Je 15 '63
BOUWERS telescope. See Telescope
BOVEE, Bob
Species rhododendrons. Pop Gard 14:74-5 My '63
BOVERI, Theodor
Theodor Boveri; tr. by C. Stern and E. Stern. F. Baltzer. bibliog il por Science 144:809-15 My 15 '64; Reply. S. Peller. 144:1409 Je 19 '64
BOVET, Daniel
Homo sapiens, that strange paradox. UNESCO Courier 16:56-7 Jl '63
BOVINE mastitis. See Mastitis
BOVINE tuberculosis. See Tuberculosis in cattle
BOVINE virus diarrhea. See Cattle—Diseases and pests
BOW, Amelae
Serving the handicapped child. Wilson Lib Bul 38:170-2 O '63
BOW, Frank T.
Excerpt from address, April 1, 1963. Cong Digest 42:209+ Ag '63
Great manpower grab. Read Digest 85:61-7 O '64
BOW and arrow
Changes in bow design. G. H. Gillelan. il Outdoor Life 131:62-3+ Ja '63
Right bow weight. G. H. Gillelan. il Outdoor Life 133:18+ Mr '64
See also
Hunting with bow and arrow
BOW and arrow hunting. See Hunting with bow and arrow
BOW pottery. See Pottery, English
BOW sights
Bowsights for bowmen. G. H. Gillelan. il Outdoor Life 134:74-5+ D '64
BOWDEN, M. G.
Principal and the school librarian. Wilson Lib Bul 37:572-3+ Mr '63
BOWDITCH, Nathaniel
Guide over the pathless oceans. A. B. Moody. por Motor B 111:114+ Mr '63
BOWDOIN college, Brunswick, Me.
Designing with deference; Bowdoin college senior center. il Arch Rec 133:142-4 Mr '63
General education for college seniors. Sch & Soc 91:302 O 19 '63
Place where you can follow the footnote back home; report of symposium. E. Moon. il Library J 88:1412-16 Ap 1 '63
Spike's peak; new sixteen-story Senior center. il Newsweek 64:65 N 2 '64
BOWE, Kay
Tree of Christmas. Am For 69:16-17+ D '63
BOWEN, Carroll G.
When universities become publishers. bibliog Science 140:599-605 My 10 '63
BOWEN, Croswell
Cigarettes and the ad man. New Repub 150:6 My 9 '64
—See Barnes, C. jr, jt. auth.
BOWEN, Elizabeth
Enchanted centenary of the brothers Grimm. N Y Times Mag p28-9+ S 8 '63
Tips. Pub W 185:81 F 3 '64
BOWEN, Howard R.
Individuality at Iowa. il por Time 84:60-1 D 11 '64
BOWEN, I. S.
Explorations with the Hale telescope; adaptation of address, May 15, 1964. Science 145:1391-8 S 25 '64
BOWEN, J. David
Bolivia's revolution comes of age. Reporter 29:34-6 S 26 '63
BOWEN, William
Chicago: they didn't have to burn it down after all. Fortune 71:142-6+ Ja '65
Executive compensation: the new wave. Fortune 70:176-8+ N '64
How they put gusto into Schlitz. Fortune 70:106-9+ O '64
Who owns what's in your head? Fortune 70:175-8+ Jl '64
BOWER, Warren
Brief fiction in the big time. Sat R 47:31 Ag 22 '64
Masters of instant truth. Sat R 46:26 Jl 20 '63
BOWERBIRDS
Evolution of bowerbirds. E. T Gilliard. il Sci Am 209:38-46 bibliog(p 140) Ag '63; Reply with rejoinder. R. K. Selander. 209:10+ D '63
BOWERING, George
Far from the shore; poem. Atlan 214:148 N '64
BOWERS, Blair. See Johnson, B. jt. auth.
BOWERS, Dan
Don't let H.O. spoil your fishing. Field & S 69:38-40 N '64
BOWERS, Edgar
From the seventeenth century. Poetry 104:120-1 My '64
BOWERS, Faubion
Crisis in Japanese translation. New Repub 148:32-3 Mr 23 '63
Dance. Nation 197:116-18 S 7 '63
Feast of astonishments. Nation 199:172-5 S 28 '64
Great discovery of royal Chhau. Dance Mag 38:40-1+ Mr '64
Mystery and the wonder: Shanta Rao. Dance Mag 37:46-9 O '63
Nameless new dance. Harper 229:20+ D '64
Puppet theatre from Moscow. Theatre Arts 47:24-5 O '63
BOWERS, Raymond
Plasmas in solids; with biographical sketch. Sci Am 209:30, 46-53 bibliog(p 186) N '63
BOWERS, W. S. and Thompson, M. J.
Juvenile hormone activity: effects of isoprenoid and straight-chain alcohols on insects. bibliog Science 142:1469-70 D 13 '63
BOWERY. See New York (city)—Streets
BOWES, Anne L.
My most unforgettable character. Read Digest 84:114-18 F '64
BOWFIN fishing
Choupique by the sackful. L. Dietz. il Field & S 68:42-3+ Mr '64
BOWFISHING. See Fishing with bow and arrow
BOWHUNTING regulations. See Game laws
BOWIE, Robert R.
Tensions within the Alliance. For Affairs 42:49-69 O '63
BOWKER, R. R, company
Attempt to censure Bowker company fails at Southwestern LA meeting. Library J 89:4490 N 15 '64
Bowker at Frankfurt: U.S. book information center. il Pub W 184:84-5 S 16 '63
Bowker company plans to issue international publishing yearbook; Publishers' world. Library J 89:4496 N 15 '64
Bowker greatly expands book trade directory. Library J 88:3819 O 15 '63
Frederic Melcher library of books about books; children's collection. A. J. Richter. il Library J 89:4118-20 O 15 '64
Libros en venta: Hispanic bibliography. M. C. Turner. il Library J 89:2559-61 Je 15 '64
See also
Carey-Thomas award
BOWL football games. See Football
BOWLES, Chester
Century later: the new commitment. Sat R 46:14-17 Ap 13 '63
Developing nations' greatest need. N Y Times Mag p 15+ Ap 12 '64
Excerpt from address, April 24, 1963. Cong Digest 42:184+ Je '63
Foreign aid: the essential factors for success; address, May 28, 1963. Dept State Bul 48:939-45 Je 17 '63
Myths about Africa and the reality. N Y Times Mag p8+ Je 16 '63
New perspectives on the United States' world relationships; address, April 29, 1963. Dept State Bul 48:817-23 My 27 '63
Not enough food for too many people. N Y Times Mag p7+ S 6 '64
Return to India: the Ambassador's view. N Y Times Mag p20-1+ N 10 '63
Speaking out. por Sat Eve Post 236:8+ My 18 '63
Untouchable rupees. Harper 229:4+ D '64
Why foreign aid; address, April 24, 1963. Dept State Bul 48:777-84 My 20 '63
about
Back from limbo. il por Time 81:22-3 Ap 12 '63
Chester's odyssey. por Newsweek 61:27-8 Ap 15 '63
BOWLES, K. L.
Measuring plasma density of the magnetosphere. bibliog Science 139:389-91 F 1 '63
BOWLES, Paul
Journey through Morocco. Holiday 33:42-53+ F '63
BOWLIN, William P.
Royalite on a regal line. Motor T 16:70-1 D '64

BOWLING
Ballet for bowlers! il Sr Schol 82:20 F 27 '63
Bowl 'em over. Recreation 57:91 F '64
Don Scott clicks on TV bowling show. il Ebony 20:87-8+ D '64
Guy named Smith is striking it rich. R. Boyle. il Sports Illus 19:36-8 N 25 '63
Timeless sport. A. A. Fisk. Recreation 57: 517+ D '64

BOWLING alleys
Bowling goes bourgeosis. R. Lynes. il Horizon 5:89-95 Mr '63

Equipment and supplies

New job for computers; ScoRite, automatic score keeper. W. R. Wise. il Pop Electr 21:46 O '64

BOWLING pins
Is there a rabbit in your bowling pins? S. James. il Pop Mech 121:85-8+ Ap '64

BOWLS
These are gouge bowls. il Sunset 130:144 Mr '63

BOWMAN, Garda W.
What helps or harms promotability? Harvard Bsns R 42:6-8+ Ja '64

BOWMAN, Hazel C.
I stayed home and went around the world. por Sr Schol 84:10T Mr 20 '64

BOWMAN, M. C. and others
Chlorinated insecticides: fate in aqueous suspensions containing mosquito larvae. bibliog Science 146:1480-1 D 11 '64

BOWMAN, Robert L.
Medical electronics. Science 141:1069-70 S 13 '63
Spectrophotofluorometry: biological techniques. Science 142:267-8+ O 11 '63
—See Prager, D. J. jt. auth.

BOWMAN, Ward S. jr. See Bork, R. H. jt. auth.

BOWRON, A. W.
Consultants' column (cont) Library J 88:2460 Je 15 '63

BOWSER, Hallowell
Amy Loveman award 1963. Sat R 46:22 Je 8 '63
Devourers of genius. Sat R 47:34 F 22 '64
Edith Anisfield Wolf: 1889-1963. Sat R 46:23 Ap 13 '63
Frederic G. Melcher: 1879-1963. Sat R 46:29 Mr 30 '63
Memorial to an American critic. Sat R 47: 24 Mr 28 '64
Rendezvous with Pegasus. Sat R 47:14 Mr 14 '64
Reunion on Channel 13. Sat R 46:18-19+ Ap 6 '63
Revelation on the East River. Sat R 47:24 S 12 '64
Rusty bells of hope. Sat R 46:24 Je 22 '63
Surplus people. Sat R 46:12 Ag 17 '63
Sweet, spontaneous humanity. Sat R 46:24 Ap 27 '63
Twilight of the dove. Sat R 46:20 My 18 '63
Wings of madness. Sat R 47:26 O 24 '64

BOWSER, Robert T. See Baer, H. jt. auth.

BOWYER, S. and others
Cosmic X-ray sources. bibliog Science 147: 394-8 Ja 22 '65
Lunar occultation of X-ray emmission from the crab nebula. bibliog Science 146:912-17 N 13 '64

BOX cameras. See Cameras

BOX car to the West; story. See Keats, J.

BOX cars. See Railroads—Freight cars

BOX dinners. See Dinners

BOX elder
Would you like a glowing tree? silver variegated box elder. il Sunset 131:278 O '63

BOXCARS. See Railroads—Freight cars

BOXERS
Dingy, sprightly home of the good ones: Fifth street gym in Miami Beach. T. Maule. il Sports Illus 20:70-2+ Ap 6 '64
For boxing: a year of decision. R. H. Boyle. il Sports Illus 22:20-1 Ja 4 '65
Four who baffled Liston. M. Sharnik. il Sports Illus 20:60-2+ F 10 '64
See also names of boxers, e.g. J. Giardello

BOXES, cases, etc.
Beautiful case for Christmas. il Am Home 66:6 D '63
Built for fun in your home workshop; multipurpose box. il Am Home 67:23 S '64
Eggshell giftware; mosaic-styled designs for boxes. B. Ruff. il Design 64:157 Mr '63
Tackle boxes. A. J. McClane. Field & S 69: 74 D '64
Where do you put it all? beauty boxes, etc. for storing cosmetics. il Redbook 123:76-7+ O '64
See also
Christmas boxes

BOXES, Display. See Exhibition cases

BOXES, Music. See Music boxes

BOXFISH. See Fishes

BOXING
Accra-phobia; Ghana's first world championship fight. Newsweek 63:96+ My 25 '64
Aftermath. Time 81:70 Ap 5 '63
All week long the word was Griffith: Griffith-Rodriguez fight. R. H. Boyle. il Sports Illus 18:24-5+ Je 17 '63
And I'm already the greatest! Clay-Liston fight. il Newsweek 63:50-1 Mr 9 '64
Anything goes; welterweight fight between Emile Griffith and Luis Rodriguez. il Time 83:51 Je 19 '64
At the fair with fat Buster; winner of Olympic trials. R. H. Boyle. il Sports Illus 20:26-8+ Je 1 '64
Baleful look of a new Liston. L. Shecter. Sports Illus 19:76-82+ O 14 '63
Ban boxing? Newsweek 61:84 Ap 8 '63
Big Bus. il Ebony 19:142-4+ S '64
Big Bus; Buster Mathis. il Life 57:95-6 Jl 3 '64
Black champion, by F. Farr. Review Nation 198:660-1 Je 29 '64. W. Ward
Boxing killed my husband. G. Moore. il Ebony 18:131-2+ Jl '63
Boxing mess, and what to do about it. J. Dempsey. Read Digest 83:85-90 O '63
Boxing mess: why I want to get out. W. D. Fugazy. il Sat Eve Post 236:28-30+ Ap 6 '63
Boxing's feet of Clay. Sat Eve Post 237:86 Ap 18 '64
C. Marcellus Clay esq; with photographs taken in London. Sports Illus 18:18-25 Je 10 '63
Case of the frustrated fighter. M. Morgan. il Sat Eve Post 236:71-2 My 18 '63
Cassius Clay. Cassius X, Muhammad Ali. R. Lipsyte. il N Y Times Mag p29+ O 25 '64
Champ's fist was on the sparrow's eye; Willie Pastrano-Goyo Peraltas fight. T. Maule. il Sports Illus 20:48+ Ap 20 '64
Comeuppance for Joey. Sports Illus 21:15 N 2 '64
Continental comeback; Patterson in Sweden. J. Lovesey. il Sports Illus 20:44-6 Ja 20 '64
Days of wine and bloody noses; excerpt from Million dollar gate. J. Kearns and O. Fraley. il Sports Illus 20:50-4+ Ja 20 '64
Dream: C. M. Clay. il Time 81:78-81 Mr 22 '63
Duel in the sun. S. D. Smith. il N Y Times Mag p72-3 Ag 9 '64
'E said 'e would and 'e did; Clay-Cooper fight. H. Horn. il Sports Illus 19:42-5 Jl 1 '63
Eleven men behind Cassius Clay. H. Horn. il Sports Illus 18:62-8+ Mr 11 '63
End of a long, dirty road. Sports Illus 20:5 Ja 20 '64
End of the street; Moore-Ramos fight. Time 81:54 Mr 29 '63
Familiar refrain; intramural feud: Madison Square Garden vs Garden state sports corporation. Sports Illus 19:19-20 D 23 '63
Fast hands and purple lights; Torres-Olson light-heavyweight fight. E. Shrake. il Sports Illus 21:30-1 D 7 '64
Fight in Sweden between boxing's forgotten men; F. Patterson and E. Machen. T. Maule. il Sports Illus 21:50-2 Jl 6 '64
Fix that wasn't; Clay-Liston fight. Sports Illus 20:17 Ap 13 '64
Floyd's fight to save his pride. P. Hamill. il Sat Eve Post 237:76-8 Je 27 '64
For boxing: a year of decision. R. H. Boyle. il Sports Illus 22:20-1 Ja 4 '65
Four who baffled Liston. M. Sharnik. il Sports Illus 20:60-2+ F 10 '64
Greatest fights of the century. R. Riger. il Esquire 60:188-91 D '63
He didn't know the gloves were loaded; Dempsey-Willard fight; excerpt from Million-dollar gate; with editorial comment. J. Kearns and O. Fraley. il Sports Illus 20:4, 48-56 Ja 13 '64
He fought, talked, then died. il Life 54:41-2 Ap 5 '63
Heavyweight muddle. R. Boyle and M. Sharnik. il Sports Illus 18:12-15 Mr 25 '63
How good is Cassius Clay? H. Nipson. il Ebony 19:77-80+ Ap '64
I killed a man. R. Donoghue. il Sat Eve Post 236:65-6 Mr 23 '63
I live with myself; Patterson-Liston fight. ed. by G. Rogin. F. Patterson. Sports Illus 19:27 Ag 5 '63

BOXING—*Continued*
I want to destroy Clay; ed. by M. Gross. F. Patterson. Sports Illus 21:42-4+ O 19 '64
I'm a little special; with editorial comment. C. Clay. il Sports Illus 20:4, 14-15 F 24 '64
Jeff, it's up to you! excerpts from Black champion; with editorial comment. F. Farr. il Am Heritage 15:64-77 F '64
King David and the Black Bull; Rodriguez-Griffith fight. H. Horn. il Sports Illus 20:18-21 Je 22 '64
Liston turned on the evil eye, Clay didn't notice; with report by J. R. McDermott. il Life 56:34-9 Mr 6 '64
Liston's edge: a lethal left; Liston-Clay fight. T. Maule. il Sports Illus 20:18-21 F 24 '64
Long ago; Robinson-Giardello fight. il Time 82:71 Jl 5 '63
Look at Cassius Clay; biggest mouth in boxing. A. Poinsett. il Ebony 18:35-6+ Mr '63
Loser. G. Talese. Esquire 61:65-8+ Mr '64
Man, the rabbit & the boy. il Time 82:52 Ag 2 '63
Many faces of Mr Mac; promoter of the Liston-Clay fight. G. Rogin. il Sports Illus 20:54-6+ F 17 '64
Match made in the jungle; R. Carter vs J. Giardello. M. Gross. il Sat Eve Post 237:76-8 O 24 '64
Meaning for a middleweight. R. Hoban. il Holiday 36:151-2+ N '64
Measured look at the big fight; Liston vs. Patterson. il Sports Illus 19:12-15 Jl 22 '63
Miami notebook: Cassius Clay and Malcolm X. G. Plimpton. il Harper 228:54-61 Je '64
Mighty desirable fellow; J. Giardello. J. Underwood. il Sports Illus 20:30-2+ My 18 '64
Most expensive sports event in history; Sonny Liston-Cassius Clay fight. il Sports Illus 20:24-5 Ja 27 '64
Murder on the BBC; Clay-Cooper fight. il Time 81:66 Je 28 '63
Muslim champ. M. Cope. il Sat Eve Post 237:32-4+ N 14 '64
Only way to save boxing. Sat Eve Post 236:82 My 4 '63
Plan to save boxing. H. Nipson. il Ebony 19:59-60+ My '64
Playing grownups; C. Clay was training for rematch with S. Liston. il Time 84:104-5 N 13 '64
Poet and the boxer. R. Cantwell; G Peeters. il Sports Illus 20:62-72 Mr 2 '64
Prefight moods of Sonny Liston. M. Kram. il Sports Illus 21:34+ N 2 '64
Pride of Kid Galahad, inc. J. Olsen. il Sports Illus 21:64-8+ Ag 31 '64
Relief to royalty on hope, hash, and Corn. F. Graham, jr. Sports Illus 18:E7-E8+ Ap 15 '63
Rueful dream come true; Clay-Liston championship fight. H. Horn. il Sports Illus 19:26-7 N 18 '63
Run, Cassius, run; Clay-Liston fight on closed-circuit TV, at RKO 86th street. New Yorker 40:43-4 Mr 7 '64
Samuelson's law. Nation 198:359 Ap 13 '64
Smile on the face of the Tiger; Dick Tiger, Gene Fullmer fight in Africa. J. Olsen. il Sports Illus 19:12-19 Ag 19 '63
Sonny Liston: king of the beasts. G. Astor. il Look 28:67-8+ F 25 '64
Sporting scene; Clay vs. Jones fight. A. J. Liebling. New Yorker 39:122+ Mr 30 '63
Sporting scene; Patterson vs. Liston return fight. A. J. Liebling. il New Yorker 39:62+ Ag 10 '63
Still hurt and lost; memories of C. Clay and S. Liston fight. G. Rogin. il Sports Illus 21:22-7 N 16 '64
Sting of the Louisville lip. T. Maule. il Sports Illus 20:50-1 F 17 '64
Sugar daddy with a bongo beat; U. Ramos in Japan. L. Griggs and R. D. Lozano. il Sports Illus 20:66-7 Mr 16 '64
Ten thousand words a minute. N. Mailer. Esquire 59:109-20 F '63
Tenth death; Ernie Knox. il Time 82:84 O 25 '63
This is what Clay says he wants; photographs of Patterson-Liston fight. R. H. Boyle. Sports Illus 19:22-6 Ag 5 '63
Tiger strikes; first world championship fight in Africa. Newsweek 62:47 Ag 19 '63
To fight or not to fight? Clay-Liston rematch. R. H. Boyle. il Sports Illus 21:28-31 S 7 '64
Who can beat him? Liston v. Patterson. il Newsweek 62:68-9 Ag 5 '63
With mouth & magic; Clay-Liston fight. il Time 83:66+ Mr 6 '64
Yes, it was good and honest; Liston-Clay fight. T. Maule. il Sports Illus 20:20-5 Mr 9 64
You can't keep a bad boy down; Giardello vs. Dick Tiger. M. Sharnik. il Sports Illus 19:18-19 D 16 '63
See also
Government investigations—Boxing

Accidents and injuries

See Sports—Accidents and injuries

Moral and religious aspects

Boxing kills three more. Christian Cent 80:515-16 Ap 24 '63
Death of a champion; Moore-Ramos fight. M. Sharnik. il Sports Illus 18:18-21+ Ap 1 '63
Should professional boxing be banned? pro and con discussion. il Sr Schol 82:22-3 Ap 17 '63

Publicity

He beats the drums for champs and bums; H. Conrad. R. H. Boyle. il Sports Illus 19:20-2+ Jl 8 '63

Safety devices and measures

Search for ring safety. Sports Illus 18:16+ Ap 15 '63

BOXING decisions. See Sports—Judging
BOY, Angelo V.
Teaching as counseling. Sr Schol 83:12T N 8 '63
BOY behind the door; story. See Birmingham, S.
BOY in a boater; story. See Gillespie, S.
BOY scouts
God and country; National Protestant committee on scouting award. P. E. Pierce. Christian Cent 81:970 Jl 29 '64
30,000 boys and a merit badge; Boy scout forestry merit badge. R. Sheldon. il Am For 70:21+ My '64
Young army pitches camp at Valley Forge. il Bsns W p26-7 Jl 25 '64

Cubs

Revolt of Pack 26. Newsweek 61:69 Je 10 '63
BOY vs. girl; story. See Heifetz, A.
BOY with the eagle laugh; story. See Combs, P.
BOYCOTT
As a boycott hit U.S.-Russia wheat deal. il U S News 56:6 Mr 2 '64
Boycott road to rights. Time 81:95 Je 7 '63
Death in Bonduel; ethics of farmers' boycott of livestock sales. America 111:344 S 26 '64
Testing labor's ultimate weapon; boycott of unfair goods. il Bsns W p50+ Jl 25 '64
Thorny issues for High court. Bsns W p 116 O 12 '63
See also
Blacklisting
BOYCOTTS, School. See School boycotts
BOYD, Alan S.
Boyd reappointment viewed as certainty. L. L. Doty. Aviation W 79:45 D 23 '63
U.S. views on international air rate policy; statement, July 18, 1963. Dept State Bul 49:247-8 Ag 12 '63

about

CAB feels wind from Northeast; refusal to renew Northeast airlines' Florida certificate. il por Bsns W p45-6+ O 5 '63
BOYD, Aquilino
Anti-U.S. diplomats; two spokesmen for Panama. por U S News 56:16 F 3 '64
U.N. diplomat in action. Time 83:34 My 29 '64
BOYD, Catherine
Orphan for Christmas; story. Redbook 122:66-7 D '63
BOYD, Edmond
Do not disturb. Travel 120:38-40 N '63
BOYD, F. R.
Geological aspects of high-pressure research. bibliog Science 145:13-20 Jl 3 '64
BOYD, Harper W. jr, and Levy, S. J.
New dimension in consumer analysis. bibliog f Harvard Bsns R 41:129-40 N '63
BOYD, John T.
Fall foliage focus: Maine. Travel 122:24-7 O '64
BOYD, Julian P.
Modest proposal to meet an urgent need; address. bibliog f Am Hist R 70:329-49 Ja '65
BOYD, Malcolm
Battle of McComb. Christian Cent 81:1398+ N 11 '64
Clown-artist's chronicle. Christian Cent 81:1310+ O 21 '64

BOYD, Malcolm—*Continued*
Movies. Christian Cent 82:113-14 Ja 27 '65
Quartet on race. Christian Cent 81:1064-5 Ag 26 '64
BOYD, T. Gardner
Elementary school industrial arts in Kansas City. NEA J 53:32-3 Ja '64
BOYD, V. E.
Advertising: a public servant; address, November 19, 1964. Vital Speeches 31:153-5 D 15 '64
BOYD, Waldo T.
Build a modern crystal set. Pop Electr 21:53-5+ Jl '64
How to build a battery-powered lawn mower. Pop Sci 182:110-12+ Je '63
BOYD, William C.
Genetics and the human race. bibliog Science 140:1057-64 Je 7 '63
BOYD-ORR, John Boyd Orr, 1st baron
Where are they now? por Newsweek 61:16 Je 17 '63
BOYDEN, Anthony
How could it have happened again? ed. by J. Gold. por Yachting 116:57+ N '64
Methodical Mr Boyden; ed. by J. Lovesey. por Sports Illus 20:72-3 Mr 16 '64
BOYDEN, John
Look at the future. por Mus Am 83:11 Jl '63
BOYER, Charles
Bedroom pirate. il pors Time 84:66+ S 11 '64
BOYER, David S.
Over and under Chesapeake Bay. il Nat Geog Mag 125:592-612 Ap '64
BOYER, Don R.
Hypoxia: effects on heart rate and respiration in the snapping turtle. bibliog Science 140:813-14 My 17 '63
BOYER, Marie France
Look first at the face. Gowland. por Pop Phot 55:22+ N '64
BOYER, P. D.
Phosphohistidine. bibliog Science 141:1147-53 S 20 '63
BOYER, Raymond F.
Coal mine disasters: frequency by month. bibliog Science 144:1447-9 Je 19 '64
Coal mine disasters. Sci N L 86:15 Jl 4 '64
BOYER, Ruth
Narrow band weaving among the Yoruba of Nigeria. Craft Horiz 24:28-9+ N '64
BOYER, Samuel H. and others
Lactate dehydrogenase variant from human blood: evidence for molecular subunits. bibliog Science 141:642-3 Ag 16 '63
Myoglobin: inherited structural variation in man. bibliog Science 140:1228-31 Je 14 '63
BOYER, William H.
Our mistaught GIs. Nation 197:361-4 N 30 '63
BOYKIN, Edward
(ed) See Jefferson, T. Affectionately yours; excerpt from To the boys and girls
BOYKIN, John E. See Grant, B. jt. auth.
BOYKO, Anatole
Inside a globular star cluster. il Sky & Tel 28:269-71 N '64
BOYLE, Andrew
Home's home run. America 109:563 N 9 '63
Letter from Europe. America 108:668-9 My 11 '63
Strategy for life. America 110:133 Ja 25 '64
World resounds: London. America 109:771 D 14 '63
BOYLE, Sir Edward
Education minister's view of education; address, July 5, 1963. Sch & Soc 92:53-8 F 8 '64
BOYLE, Hal
Education comes to a Boyle. Read Digest 85:240B N '64
BOYLE, Kay
Ballet of Central park; story. Sat Eve Post 237:44-8 N 28 '64
Teaching of writing. NEA J 53:11-12 Mr '64
Voice from the future. Holiday 36:12+ O '64
about
Poetry chronicle. R. Howard. Poetry 102:253-9 Jl '63
BOYLE, Robert
Gases: molecules in motion. il Sci Digest 54:79-81 D '63
BOYLE, Robert H.
America down the drain. Sports Illus 21:78-80+ N 16 '64
College football. Sports Illus 19:46-7 S 2 '63
Fishing. Sports Illus 19:64-5 O 21 '63; 20:50+ Mr 30; 21:81+ O 5 '64
Sonny slams ahead. Sports Illus 19:12-15 Jl 29 '63
BOYLE, Sarah Patton
Inside a segregationist. pors Ebony 18:53-4+ Je '63
Price of brotherhood. pors Ebony 18:79-80+ S '63
BOYLE, W. A.
Miners gear for double trouble. por Bsns W p67 D 5 '64
Miners' new leader works another seam. il por Bsns W p 121-2 Mr 28 '64
New UMW president; protégé of John L. Lewis. por U S News 54:20 F 4 '63
UMW gives the nod to Boyle. por Bsns W p70+ Ja 26 '63
UMW seeks job security, safety. por Bsns W p68 Ja 4 '64
BOYNE, Walt
Wiltshire boulevard to Broadway in sixty minutes. Sci Digest 53:66-8 Je '63
BOYNTON, Robert M. and others
Hue-wavelength relation measured by color-naming method for three retinal locations. bibliog Science 146:666-8 O 30 '64
BOYS
Boy's advice on coping with boys; questions and answers. H. Makow. Seventeen 24:92 Ja '65
Boys and other beasts; excerpts. B. Lang. McCalls 91:68+ F; 74+ Mr; 78+ Ap '64
College boy counsels on boy problems; questions and answers. S. Adams. Seventeen 23:98 Ja '64
From a boy's point of view. J. Wescott. See issues of Seventeen
How to hold a boy without hanging on; questions and answers. A. Wood. il Seventeen 22:216-17+ Ag '63
Letters to boys; excerpt from Seventeen book of etiquette and entertaining. E. A. Haupt. Seventeen 23:16 Jl '64
Perfume to dream on. il Seventeen 23:140-1 F '64
Ross and his rifle; ten-year-old boy on first hunting trip. D. Peck. il Outdoor Life 131:36-9+ F '63
Should boys be taught to fight back? J. A. Moran. il Parents Mag 39:44-5+ Je '64
Should he shoot the Magnum? J. Rychetnik. il Outdoor Life 133:38-41+ F '64
Sock is not a simple thing; two-year-old Michael Edward Frith of Anaheim, Calif. il Look 27:88a-88c F 26 '63
Status seekers, junior grade. M. A. Guitar. il N Y Times Mag p47-8 Ag 16 '64
Strange ways of boys; questions and answers. A. Wood. il Seventeen 22:136-7+ N '63
There's always dames. C. Ford. il Field & S 68:6+ Ag '63
Where can a boy go for help; excerpts from Moving into manhood. W. W. Bauer. il Todays Health 41:58-9+ N '63
Who's teaching whom? D. Llewellyn. il Outdoor Life 133:66-8 Mr '64
See also
Adolescence
Boys' life (periodical)
Caddies (golf)
Farm boys
Gangs
High school students
Juvenile delinquency
Runaway boys and girls
BOYS as cooks. See Cookery by children
BOYS books. See Childrens literature
BOYS clothing. See Clothing and dress—Children
BOYS clubs
They help boys want to be educated; Chicago boys clubs. A. Q. Maisel. Read Digest 83:100-4 D '63
BOYS food preferences. See Food preferences
BOYS from Syracuse; musical comedy. See Musical comedies, revues, etc.—Criticisms, plots, etc.
BOYS' life (periodical)
For all boys. F. C. Smith. Writer 77:22-4 N 64
BOYS nation. See Citizenship, Education for
BOYS ranch, Amarillo, Tex.
Where the boys are at home on the range. B. Hibbs. il Read Digest 82:112-17 Ap '63
BOYS rooms. See Childrens rooms
BOYS schools. See Private schools
BOYS shirts. See Shirts
BOYS states. See Citizenship, Education for
BOZELL, L. Brent
Claims of the Court. Nat R 16:29-31 Ja 14 '64
Court enjoins God. Nat R 16:775-6 S 8 '64
Lesson of Cambridge and Salisbury: was violence necessary? Nat R 15:145-7 Ag 27 '63
National trends (cont) por Nat R 14:313+, 354, 398, 445 Ap 23-Je 4 '63
Notes and asides. il Nat R 16:346+ My 5 '64

BOZELL, L. Brent—*Continued*
Saving our children from God. Nat R 15:19-22+ Jl 16 '63
To mend the tragic flaw. Nat R 14:199-200 Mr 12 '63
about
Minds of Barry Goldwater. R. H. Rovere. Harper 229:39-42 S '64
BRACELAND, Francis J.
Psychiatry today. Commonweal 80:172-4 My 1 '64
—and Stock, Michael
Deep roots of prejudice; excerpt from Modern psychiatry: a handbook for believers. pors Cath World 198:109-14 N '63
BRACELETS, Medic-alert. See Identification tags, bracelets, etc.
BRACEROS. See Mexicans in the United States
BRACKEN, Peg
Etiquette, the social whirl, & all that jazz. Ladies Home J 80:38+ D '63
I try to behave myself: excerpts. Ladies Home J 81:20+ Ja; 26+ Mr '64
Peach called Bracken. H. Frankel. Sat R 47:22-3 S 5 '64
Tips. Pub W 185:58-9 My 25 '64
BRACKER, Milton
Bitter, frustrated, divided: Cuba's refugees. N Y Times Mag p7+ Ap 21 '63
Coelacanth saga. N Y Times Mag p84+ O 6 '63
Misszen and hitszen; donor and blitzen; poems. N Y Times Mag p32-3+ D 8 '63
Never again; story. Redbook 121:66-7 O '63
BRADBURY, John
School libraries. Wilson Lib Bul 39:419 Ja '65
BRADBURY, Malcolm
American women are rude. N Y Times Mag p48+ Mr 29 '64
First nymphet? Mlle 57:182-5+ My '63
Opinion, please from New Haven. Mlle 60:40+ D '64
Rise of the Redbrick. Holiday 34:84-7+ N '63
BRADBURY, Ray
Cold wind and the warm; story. Harper 229:61-9 Jl '64
Kilimanjaro machine; story. Life 58:68-72 Ja 22 '65
about
Allegory of any place. il Time 84:85-6 O 30 '64
Man who drives the Kilimanjaro machine. G. P. Hunt. por Life 58:3 Ja 22 '65
Ray Bradbury and the Irish. B. Cook. Cath World 200:224-30 Ja '65
Taste for pandemonium. A. Knight. Sat R 47:31 D 5 '64
WLB biography. L. Ash. por Wilson Lib Bul 39:268+ N '64
World of Ray Bradbury; dramatization of stories. Criticism
Nation 200:92-4 Ja 25 '65
Sat R 47:31 D 5 '64
BRADBURY, Will
Big Lew's message to scouts shh! I'm busy. Life 58:53-4 Ja 29 '65
BRADBURY family
Bradbury coat-of-arms. H. K. Eilers. il Hobbies 68:126 Mr '63
BRADDOCK, James J.
Relief to royalty on hope, hash and Corn. F. Graham, jr. por Sports Illus 18:E7-E8+ Ap 15 '63
BRADDOCK, Robert L.
Insuring the insurers. il pors Bsns W p 125-6+ My 18 '63
BRADDS, Gary
Bradds-and-butter man. H. L. Masin. il por Sr Schol 84:44 F 14 '64
BRADEN, Thomas W.
I was the target of a hate campaign. por Look 27:54+ O 22 '63
about
Braden's round. Newsweek 61:54 Ap 1 '63
We want teachers who are educated. por Time 81:74 My 10 '63
BRADER, Marion
Chichen Itzá, Mexico's mystic city of death. Sr Schol 84:11T Mr 20 '64
BRADERMAN, Eugene M.
200 million new customers for U.S? interview. por U S News 55:40-3 N 4 '63
BRADFORD, Jean
Ladies, please come to order! Redbook 120:41+ Mr '63
BRADFORD, Mary Rose
My short, happy life in the theater. Atlan 211:136+ Mr '63
BRADLAUGH, Charles
Charles Bradlaugh and the secularists. W. S. Smith. Christian Cent 80:331-4 Mr 13 '63
BRADLEE, Benjamin
He had that special grace. Newsweek 62:38 D 2 '63
BRADLEY, Bill
Ivy leaguer is the best; Princeton's basketball player. F. Deford. il pors Sports Illus 21:36-8+ D 7 '64
Paying to play. il por Time 82:64-5 D 20 '63
Profiles. J. McPhee. por New Yorker 40:40-2+ Ja 23 '65
BRADLEY, C. Paul
Formation of Malaysia. bibliog f Cur Hist 46:89-94+ F '64
BRADLEY, Dan Beach
King and us. A. Robertson. il por Horizon 6:18-25 Wint '64
BRADLEY, Gertrude G.
Let them go free; ed. by M. G. Ward. Read Digest 85:121-4 Ag '64
BRADLEY, James
Discovery of stellar aberration. A. B. Stewart. il Sci Am 210:100-8 bibliog(p 152) Mr '64
BRADLEY, Jane Buel
Listening heart. bibliog Wilson Lib Bul 37:677-9+ Ap '63
BRADLEY, Omar Nelson
Brad vs. Monty: an old feud revived; summary of interview. por U S News 58:55 Ja 18 '65
BRADLEY, S. G. See Adams, J. N. jt. auth.
BRADLEY, Sam
Amid unbelief and darkened fields; poem. Christian Cent 81:1584 D 23 '64
Christmas, conscience, battle-waste; poem. Christian Cent 80:1583 D 18 '63
Out in the no. 7; poem. Nation 196:272 Mr 30 '63
Outreach; poem. Christian Cent 80:359 Mr 20 '63
BRADLEY, W. C., memorial library. See W. C. Bradley memorial library, Columbus, Ga.
BRADLEY, W. H.
Unmineralized fossil bacteria. bibliog Science 141:919-21 S 6 '63
BRADLEY, Wendell P.
Cambridge, Maryland: failure on race street. Reporter 29:20-2 Jl 4 '63
Holiday handbook of small-boat sailing. Holiday 36:97-100 Ag '64
BRADLEY, William Warren. See Bradley, B.
BRADNER, Hugh
Seismic measurements on the ocean bottom. bibliog Science 146:208-16 O 9 '64
BRADSHAW, George
Eating at the fair, N.Y. Vogue 144:114-15 Jl '64
BRADSHAW, Glenn R.
Glenn R. Bradshaw uses casein on rice paper; with biographical sketch. il por Am Artist 29:44-5+ Ja '65
BRADSHAW, Hank
Autumn jackpot. Outdoor Life 132:44-7+ S '63
Calling all fox squirrels. por Field & S 69:65-7+ S '64
Homemade auger speeds ice fishing. Pop Sci 184:154 F '64
How to get started in trap and skeet: the sport for sharpshooters. Pop Sci 185:142-6+ O '64
Ice fishing, it's the greatest. Suc Farm 61:116 F '63
Little old BB gun. Pop Sci 185:86-9+ D '64
Minnesota brush bucks. pors Field & S 69:138-41+ O '64
New reels, they take the fumbling out of fishing. Pop Sci 185:122-5+ Ag '64
Santa Claus brought waterfowl. por Outdoor Life 135:32-3+ Ja '65
Sneaky art of fooling fish. Pop Sci 184:150-5 Mr '64
Snowmobile lakers. Field & S 69:27-9+ Ja '65
Ten on-the-spot fixes for your fishing reels. Pop Sci 184:150-3 Je '64
Tips for better bass fishing. il Suc Farm 61:92-3 S '63
Tips for planning a hunting trip this fall. Suc Farm 61:38+ S '63
Wing dam walleyes. Field & S 68:10-11 My '63
—and Bradshaw, Vera
For great fishing, try Canada. il Suc Farm 61:67 Je '63
Future physician's clubs attract teen-agers to the medical profession. Todays Health 42:54-7 Ja '64
Magic mountains of the West. il Todays Health 42:34-7+ Ag '64
Mississippi River adventure. il Suc Farm 61:50-2 Ag '63
Now you can camp at the Rosebud Indian reservation. il Suc Farm 62:48 Ag '64
Space ball. Pop Sci 182:110-11 F '63

BRADSHAW, Homer Vernon
U.S. doctor's five years in a red prison. J. N. Bell. il por Todays Health 41:26-31 N '63

BRADSHAW, Lillian Moore
Consultants' column (cont) Library J 88:1634, 3806+ Ap 15, O 15 '63

BRADSHAW, Vera. See Bradshaw, H. jt. auth.

BRADY, Charles
Dream of trees; poem. America 111:801 D 19 '64
Incident at Jairus' house; poem. America 110:672 My 16 '64

BRADY, Diamond Jim. See Brady, J. B.

BRADY, Frank B.
All-weather aircraft landing; with biographical sketch. Sci Am 210:20, 25-35 Mr '64

BRADY, James Buchanan
God, Nell, ain't it grand? Diamond Jim's appetite; excerpts from American heritage cookbook. C. Amory. il Horizon 6:14-15 Sum '64

BRADY, John Paul, and Levitt, E. E.
Nystagmus as a criterion of hypnotically induced visual hallucinations. bibliog Science 146:85-6 O 2 '64

BRADY, Mildred Edie
Cigarette advertising; testimony presented before FTC. Consumer Rep 29:246-50 My '64

BRADY, Philip
Beetlebung tree. Am For 69:52 My '63

BRADY, Thomas F.
Noble experiment, Indian style. N Y Times Mag p24+ F 16 '64

BRADY, Todd
High time for all at the Bourbon open. B. Surface. il Sports Illus 18:60-2 Je 10 '63

BRADYKININ. See Kallikrein

BRAEND, Mikael. See Efremov, G. jt. auth.

BRAESTRUP, Peter
After a year, it's Ben Bella's Algeria. N Y Times Mag p31+ S 29 '63
New dilemmas for the *pieds noirs*. N Y Times Mag p28+ My 26 '63

BRAGALINE, Edward A.
Paintings and antiques. R. Davidson. il Antiques 84:556-61 N '63

BRAHE, Tycho
New star of 1572 is still exploding. C. D. Hellman. il Sat R 47:39-43 Jl 4 '64
Phoenix of astronomers. C. A. Ronan. il por Natur Hist 74:52-7 Ja '65

BRAHM, Walter
Challenge of change; excerpts from address, October 19, 1962. por Library J 88:3164-5 S 15 '63
Logic or lip service? address, April 1964. por Library J 89:3093-8 S 1 '64
On the grindstone. Library J 90:78-9 Ja 1 '65

BRAHMS, Johannes
Again, Kempff, with Brahms, the secret is understatement. R. Sabin. Am Rec G 31:134 O '64
Beethoven and Brahms with a master's stamp. H. Goldsmith. Hi Fi 14:124-6 O '64
Brahms by Fleisher and the Juilliard quartet. R. Sabin. Am Rec G 30:219 N '63
Brahms piano concertos in fruitful collaborations. H. Goldsmith. il Hi Fi 13:70-1 Mr '63
Happy news on a tenth anniversary. Hi Fi 14:41 Ap '64
On records; German requiem. Opera N 28:35 Mr 7 '64
On records; German requiem. C. J. Luten. Opera N 27:35 Ap 6 '63
On records; Liebeslieder. Opera N 28:35 F 22 '64
Protestant requiem for a Roman Catholic President. J. W. Barker. il Am Rec G 30:598-9 Mr '64
Szeryng's (and Rubinstein's) Brahms. N. Lang. Am Rec G 29:444-5 F '63

BRAIDWOOD, Robert J.
Out of the stone age. il por Newsweek 64:66 N 2 '64

BRAILLE. See Blind, Books, etc. for the

BRAIN
Alcohol consumption in rats: effects of intracranial injections of ethanol. R. D. Myers. bibliog il Science 142:240-1 O 11 '63
Behavioral-neurochemical correlation in reactive and nonreactive strains of rats. H. S. Sudak and J. W. Mass. bibliog il Science 146:418-20 O 16 '64
Brain aroused by silence; reticular formation. Sci N L 86:198 S 26 '64
Brain, morals, and politics. A. Szent-Györgyi. Bul Atomic Sci 20:2-3 My '64
Brain reflexes; report on international conference. D. P. Purpura and H. Waelsch. Science 143:598+ F 7 '64
Brain reserve may be greater than realized. Sci N L 84:264 O 26 '63
Brain vs. the machine. J. W. Krutch. Sat R 47:17-19+ Ja 18 '64
Callosal section: its effect on performance of a bimanual skill. G. Ettlinger and H. B. Morton. bibliog il Science 139:485-6 F 8 '63
Caudate-induced cortical potentials: comparison between monkey and cat. S. Goldring and others. bibliog il Science 139:772 F 22 '63
Cells that communicate. D. G. Cooley. il Todays Health 41:20-5+ My; 38-41+ Je '63
Cerebral white matter: selective spread of pneumococcal polysaccharides. S. Levine. bibliog il Science 139:605-6 F 15 '63
Cerebrally active small moiety from taraxein-like blood fractions. T. F. Redick and others. bibliog il Science 141:646-7 Ag 16 '63
Chemical and anatomical plasticity of brain. E. L. Bennett and others. bibliog il Science 146:610-19 O 30 '64
Chemical brain control. Sci N L 85:214 Ap 4 '64
Chemistry of behavior; chemical processes in the brain can determine emotional behavior. il Newsweek 63:52 Je 22 '64
Cockroach brain surgery. Sci N L 85:174 Mr 14 '64
Control of the brain. R. Coughlan. il Life 54:90-2+ Mr 8; 81-2+ Mr 15 '63
Disinhibition after prefrontal lesions as a function of duration of intertrial intervals. S. Brutkowski and J. Dabrowska. bibliog il Science 139:505-6 F 8 '63
Do your brain molecules change their shape when you think? Sci Digest 53:26-7 Ap '63
Electrical transmission at an excitatory synapse in a vertebrate brain. E. J. Furshpan. bibliog il Science 144:878-80 My 15 '64
Electroencephalographic changes after prolonged sensory and perceptual deprivation. J. P. Zubek and G. Welch. bibliog il Science 139:1209-10 Mr 22 '63
Electroencephalographic desynchronization during deep sleep after destruction of midbrain-limbic pathways in the cat. G. Carli and others. bibliog il Science 140:677-9 My 10 '63
Ependymal cilia: distribution and activity in the adult human brain. W. C. Worthington, jr. and R. S. Cathcart, 3d. bibliog Science 139:221-2 Ja 18 '63
Exercised brains. Sci Am 212:52 Ja '65
Gap between the ears; new concepts of perception. il Newsweek 63:39 My 11 '64
Great cerebral commissure; split-brain studies. R. W. Sperry. il Sci Am 210:42-52 bibliog(p 152) Ja '64
Heart rate changes after reinforcing brain stimulation in rats. W. J. Meyers and others. bibliog il Science 140:1233-5 Je 14 '63; Reply. R. B. Malmo. 144:1029-30 My 22 '64
Heart rate: differential effects of hypothalamic and septal self-stimulation. J. Perez-Cruet and others. bibliog il Science 140:1235-6 Je 14 '63; Reply. R. B. Malmo. 144:1029-30 My 22 '64
Hormonal activation of the insect brain. S. D. Beck and N. Alexander. bibliog il Science 143:478-9 Ja 31 '64
How a violent encounter is perceived all depends upon the brain. R. Campbell. il Life 54:73-5, 76A Je 28 '63
How the machine called the brain feels and thinks. D. E. Wooldridge. il N Y Times Mag p24+ O 4 '64
Interaction of positive and negative reinforcing neural systems. E. S. Valenstein and T. Valenstein. bibliog il Science 145:1456-8 S 25 '64
Intracranial reward delay and the acquisition rate of a brightness discrimination. R. E. Keesey. bibliog il Science 143:702-3 F 14 '64
Intracranial self-stimulation in man. M. P. Bishop and others. bibliog il Science 140:394-6 Ap 26 '63
Isolation of the monkey brain: in vitro preparation and maintenance. R. J. White and others. bibliog il Science 141:1060-1 S 13 '63
Laboratory monkey business, breakthrough in brain research. Pop Sci 185:19-20 Ag '64
Lateral geniculate nucleus and cerebral cortex: evidence for a crossed pathway. M. Glickstein and others. bibliog il Science 145:159-61 Jl 10 '64
Live brains in the lab; Cleveland metropolitan general hospital researchers keep isolated monkey brains alive. il Time 83:72 Je 19 '64
Loneliness affects brain. Sci N L 87:38 Ja 16 '65
Low dose radiation of the developing brain. S. P. Hicks and C. J. D'Amato. bibliog il Science 141:903-5 S 6 '63

BRAIN—*Continued*
Microscopic brains; adaptation of address. V. G. Dethier. bibliog Science 143:1138-45 Mr 13 '64; Reply. W. N. Tavolga. 144:1533 Je 26 '64
Midbrain reticular influences upon single neurons in lateral geniculate nucleus. T. Ogawa. bibliog il Science 139:343-4 Ja 25 '63
Mirror display in the squirrel monkey, saimiri sciureus P. D. MacLean. bibliog il Science 146:950-2 N 13 '64
Norepinephrine and 3,4-dihydroxyphenethylamine turnover in guinea pig brain in vivo. S. Udenfriend and P. Zaltzman-Nirenberg. bibliog il Science 142:394-6 O 18 '63
Nucleus of the trapezoid body: dual afferent innervation. J. M. Harrison and R. Irving. bibliog il Science 143:473-4 Ja 31 '64
Our brains are getting smaller says evolutionist. Sci Digest 54:58-9 Jl '63
Poisoning by DDT: relation between clinical signs and concentration in rat brain. W. E. Dale and others. bibliog il Science 142:1474-6 D 13 '63
Pontine reticular formation: relation to lateral geniculate nucleus during deep sleep. E. Bizzi and D. C. Brooks. bibliog il Science 141:270-2 Jl 19 '63
Pulmonary edema as a consequence of hypothalamic lesions in rats. R. W. Reynolds. bibliog il Science 141:930-2 S 6 '63
Reversible section of the brain by a wall of cold. R. Byck and P. Dirlik. bibliog il Science 139:1216-18 Mr 22 '63
Stress response controlled by brain. Sci N L 84:4 Jl 6 '63
Study brain isolation. F. Marley. Sci N L 86:263 O 24 '64
Test of Deutsch's drive-decay theory of rewarding self-stimulation of the brain. S. S. Pliskoff and T. D. Hawkins. bibliog il Science 141:823-4 Ag 30 '63; Reply with rejoinder. J. A. Deutsch. 142:1125-6 N 29 '63
That wonderful machine, the brain. G. A. W. Boehm. il Fortune 67:125-9+ F '63
Thin air affects brain. Sci N L 83:286 My 4 '63
Timing behavior after lesions of zona incerta and mammillary body. P. Ellen and E. W. Powell. bibliog il Science 141:828-30 Ag 30 '63
What is your brain power? H. Earle. il Todays Health 41:50-5 O '63
Why we have two brains. K. B. Mishler. il Sci Digest 56:81-4 Ag '64
See also
Cerebellum
Cerebral cortex
Hypothalamus
Intellect
Memory
Nervous system
Pituitary body

Diseases

See also
Amaurotic family idiocy
Aphasia
Cerebral hemorrhage
Mental illness

Localization of functions

Activating and synchronizing centers in cat brain: electroencephalograms after lesions. A. Camacho-Evangelista and F. Reinoso-Suárez. bibliog il Science 146:268-70 O 9 '64
Caudate nucleus lesions: behavioral effects in the rat. S. L. Chorover and C. G. Gross. bibliog il Science 141:826-7 Ag 30 '63
Chemical stimulation of the brain; releasing drives such as hunger and thirst. A. E. Fisher. il Sci Am 210:60-8 Je '64
Control and training of individual motor units. J. V. Basmajian. bibliog il Science 141:440-1 Ag 2 '63
Habituation of responses to novel stimuli in monkeys with selective frontal lesions. C. M. Butter. bibliog il Science 144:313-15 Ap 17 '64
Man's mysterious memory machine. D. E. Wooldridge. il Harper 226:57-63 Je '63
Plasma corticosteroids: changes in concentration after stimulation of hippocampus and amygdala. A. J. Mandell and others. bibliog il Science 139:1212 Mr 22 '63
Speech sound discrimination by cats. J. H. Dewson, 3d. bibliog il Science 144:555-6 My 1 '64
Time factors in interhemispheric transfer of learning. O. S. Ray and G. Emley. bibliog il Science 144:76-8 Ap 3 '64
Tonic influence of rostral brain structures on pressure regulatory mechanisms in the cat. D. J. Reis and M. Cuénod. bibliog il Science 145:64-5 Jl 3 '64; Reply with rejoinder. R. L. Katz and others. 145:1459-60 S 25 '64
Uncommitted cortex; the child's changing brain. W. Penfield. Atlan 214:77-81 Jl '64
Visual function of the forebrain commissures in the chimpanzee. P. Black and R. E. Myers. bibliog il Science 146:799-800 N 6 '64
Visual motion detection in the cat. G. Baumgartner and others. bibliog il Science 146:1070-1 N 20 '64

Surgery

Awake through a brain operation. A. Anselmo. Read Digest 85:53-7 Jl '64
Brain surgery for pain. Sci N L 85:36 Ja 18 '64
Brain tumor fears eased by statistics. Sci Digest 53:46 Mr '63
Creating brain lesions reduces mental illness. Sci N L 86:340 N 28 '64
Deepfreeze surgery fights nervous diseases. Sci N L 86:151 S 5 '64
Electric wires in brain aid epilepsy surgery. Sci N L 83:281 My 4 '63
Freezing can destroy tumorous pituitary. Sci N L 84:366 D 7 '63
Living brain; isolated monkey brain. il Life 57:33-4 Jl 31 '64
Man with two brains. il Newsweek 62:90 O 28 '63
Now, knifeless brain surgery. il Sci Digest 55:71-2 Mr '64
Patching brain blowouts; operation for cranial aneurysm. Sci Digest 56:20-1 D '64
Sad victory for a heavyweight; A. Lavorante paralyzed by blow; with report by R. Stolley. il Life 55:97-8+ S 27 '63

Wounds and injuries

Brain damage detected by radioactive isotopes. Sci N L 86:233 O 10 '64
Brain injuries at birth. Sci N L 86:71 Ag 1 '64
Concussion of the brain; first aid. C. J. Potthoff. Todays Health 42:70 Mr '64
How a knockout hurts the brain. W. Cloud. Pop Sci 183:29 O '63
How a knockout kills. F. B. Byrom. il Sci Digest 54:23-7 S '63
Neuropathology of certain forms of mental retardation; address, February 12, 1963. W. F. Windle. bibliog Science 140:1186-9 Je 14 '63
Ordeal of Linda Harris. T. Irwin. il Good H 158:42+ F '64

BRAIN hemorrhage. See Cerebral hemorrhage
BRAIN surgery. See Brain—Surgery
BRAIN waves
Brain monitor operates inside astronaut helmet. Sci N L 84:133 Ag 31 '63
Talk via brain waves. W. MacLaurin. Sci N L 86:275 O 31 '64
BRAINE, John Gerard
WLB biography. C. Hines. por Wilson Lib Bul 38:297 N '63
BRAINSTORMING. See Ideas
BRAINWASHING
Who can resist brainwashing? il Sci Digest 55:67 My '64
BRAITHWAITE, William Stanley
In memoriam: William Stanley Braithwaite; poem. H. Hill. Negro Hist Bul 26:218 Ap '63
BRAKE, Brian
Kipling's India. il Horizon 6:67-71 Autumn '64
Prodigious output of the East; photographs. Life 55:166-79+ D 20 '63
BRAKE fluids
Make sure your brake fluid won't kill you. S. D. Pursglove. il Pop Mech 120:98-100+ S '63
BRAKES, Airplane
USAF performs tests on XB-70 brakes. il Aviation W 78:67+ Mr 18 '63
BRAKES, Automobile
Brakes in a bad way! M. Lamm. il Motor T 16:62-5 S '64
Chevy tops the trials; Pure oil performance trials. M. Muhleman. il Motor T 16:36-9 Ap '64
Disc brakes. R. Huntington. il Hot Rod 17:28-33 D '64
Don't drill drums; reprint. Hot Rod 17:92-3 Ag '64
Drums along the highway (cont) R. Jennings. il Hot Rod 16:72-5+ F; 70-5+ Mr '63
Good brake job for your car. il Changing T 18:42-4 S '64
Know your car; differentials, suspension systems, steering controls, brakes, and body construction. R. Temple. il Motor T 15:66-71 F '63

BRAKES, Automobile—*Continued*
Let's have cars that will stop! H. Luckett. il Pop Sci 184:59-64 Ap '64
Lifting the lid on power brakes. M. J. Schultz. il Pop Mech 121:178-82+ F; 174-7 Mr '64
Pedal your Model A; and steer it. T. McMullen. il Hot Rod 18:84-5 Ja '65
Safe-stop lever. D. Roulston. il Hot Rod 17:108-9 O '64
Stop stop stop; disc brake. J. Wright. il Motor T 16:60-1 Ja '64
Taking the panic out of braking. il Pop Mech 119:98-9 Je '63
Two hats of science; power steering and brakes. H. Downs. Sci Digest 56:79-82 N '64
What's coming in disc brakes. R. Huntington. il Motor T 16:90-5 N '64
BRAMLETT, Betty Jane
Glass on glass. Sch Arts 62:39 Ap '63
BRANCH, Harllee, jr
Private power in TVA's backyard. il por Bsns W p 176-8+ O 17 '64
BRANCH, Judson
Allstate's catchall companion. il por Bsns W p47-8+ S 7 '63
BRANCH banking. See Banks and banking—Branch banking
BRANCH factories, Foreign
Case of the multiplant manufacturer; excerpts from European problems in general management. R. C. K. Valtz. il Harvard Bsns R 42:12-16+ Mr '64
Management of international production; excerpts from research report. C. W. Skinner. il Harvard Bsns R 42:125-36 S '64
BRANCH libraries. See Libraries—Branches and stations
BRANCHE, Stanley E.
Old Scratchhead wakes up in Chester, Pennsylvania. S. Klaw. il Reporter 30:33-4 Je 18 '64
BRANCO, Humberto Castello. See Castello Branco, H.
BRAND, J. L.
American association for the history of medicine. Science 145:302-3 Jl 17 '64
BRAND, Paul
Paul Brand and his mission. N. Cousins. il pors Sat R 47:21-3+ O 3 '64; Reply. P. W. Brand. 47:25 N 21 '64
BRAND marks. See Trade marks
BRAND names. See Trade names
BRANDBORG, Stewart M.
On the carrying capacity of wilderness; excerpt from address, August 26, 1963. pors Liv Wildn 84:28-33 Sum '63
Sawtooth wilderness supported; remarks, September 4, 1963. Liv Wildn 85:37-9 Wint '64
BRANDEIS, Louis Dembitz
Justice on trial, by A. L. Todd. Review
New Repub 151:25-6 Ag 8 '64. A. M. Bickel; Correction. A. L. Todd. 151:38 Ag 22 '64
Revolutionary then, orthodox now. Bsns W p94 Ap 20 '63
BRANDEIS university, Waltham, Mass.
For freedom; anti-Sachar resolution. Newsweek 61:86 My 6 '63
Gods of Africa smile on Brandeis. Nat R 16:54-5 Ja 28 '64
Lesson in unity. il Arch Rec 133:169-72 Ap '63
Skylights for studios. il Arch Forum 118:84-5 Mr '63
Treasures on campus: pop goes Brandeis! Rose art museum. L. Lerman. il Mlle 58:74-5+ D '63
BRANDEL, Arthur
Negroes tip the scales. New Repub 150:6 My 30 '64
BRANDEL, Max
I shall not look upon his like again. Horizon 6:96-7 Spr '64
Typographical escapades. Horizon 7:38-9 Wint '65
BRANDES, Ely M.
Manpower and the new pariahs. Reporter 30:17-19 Mr 26 '64
BRANDO, Marlon
Ambassador Brando. il pors Life 54:45-7 My 10 '63
Brando fights for civil rights; interview. pors Ebony 18:60-2+ O '63
BRANDON, Donald
De Gaulle's pursuit of grandeur; excerpt from American foreign policy. Cath World 199:224-9 Jl '64
Illusion of victory. Commonweal 78:473-6 Ag 9 '63
No deal on Berlin. America 108:192-6 F 9 '63
BRANDON, Henry
New renaissance man. Sat R 47:18+ Ag 29 '64
1964: who's ahead? Mlle 58:130-1 Mr '64
State of affairs. See issues of Saturday review
Untold story of the Cuban crisis. Sat R 46:56-7 Mr 9 '63
Weighing the advantages. Sat R 46:16+ N 2 '63
Witness in the White House. Sat R 46:85-6 Mr 16 '63
(ed) See Schlesinger, A. jr. Schlesinger at the White House
(ed) See Ustinov, P. Peter Ustinov speaking
BRANDON, William
Wish is for wanting; story. Good H 158:90-1 My '64
BRANDRETH, E. J. jr
Record smashing Sabreliner; ed. by W. B. Wentz. Flying 74:48+ My '64
BRANDRISS, Michael W.
Methotrexate; suppression of experimental allergic encephalomyelitis. Science 140:186-7 Ap 12 '63
BRANDS, National. See National brands
BRANDT, Carl
Simple flash exposures. U S Camera 26:52 F '63
BRANDT, Heidi
Heidi Brandt, illustrator & painter. R. Day. il por Am Artist 27:18-23+ D '63
BRANDT, John C.
Radar observations of the Corona and Mariner II measurements of the flux in the solar wind. bibliog Science 146:1671-2 D 25 '64
BRANDT, John H.
By dunung and bouj. Natur Hist 72:26-9 F '63
BRANDT, K. F. See Rockstein, M. jt. auth.
BRANDT, Karl
Population dilemma; address, June 27, 1963. Vital Speeches 29:629-31 Ag 1 '63
Relationship of sound money to freedom; address, April 8, 1964. Vital Speeches 30:623-8 Ag 1 '64
BRANDT, Nat
New York's great fire that wasn't. N Y Times Mag p 109-10+ N 22 '64
BRANDT, Rex
Brush and watercolor; excerpts from Watercolor landscape. Design 65:114-19+ Ja '64
BRANDT, Thomas O.
Bull market in foreign languages. Sch & Soc 92:225-7 Sum '64
BRANDT, Willy
Exclusive Senior scholastic interview. por Sr Schol 83:16+ N 15 '63

about

Erhard vs. Brandt. Newsweek 63:44 Mr 16 '64
Qualified triumph. il Newsweek 63:40 Mr 2 '64
Wall has cut my city in half. J. R. Moskin. il pors Look 27:36+ Je 18 '63
Willy Brandt's third Germany. G. Bailey. il Reporter 30:33-6 F 13 '64
Willy wins. il por Time 81:25 Mr 1 '63
Willy wins; West Berlin parliamentary elections. il por Newsweek 61:34 Mr 4 '63
BRANDT, Yanna
Off-camera close-up. K. K. Waller. il por Mlle 56:114-15+ F '63
BRANDY
Cognac on the rocks? il Bsns W p 112-13 N 21 '64
In search of cognac. G. Henle. il House B 105:206-7+ O '63
BRANFORD, Conn.
Aerial photos reduce costs, aid planning studies. il Am City 79:96 F '64
BRANFORD electric railway association
Trolley museum; Branford, Conn. il Travel 120:45-7 Ag '63
BRANIFF airways
Golden castles of Troy V. Post. S. H. Brown. il Fortune 71:154-9+ Ja '65
BRANSON, Edwina R.
Impromptu teaching in Norway. Sr Schol 84:12T-13T Mr 20 '64
BRANSTEN, Thomas R.
How to survive the Sorbonne. Mlle 59:100-2+ Je '64
—and Brown, S. H.
Machines Bull's computer crisis. Fortune 70:154-5+ Jl '64
BRANT. See Geese, Wild
BRANTADORNA downsi. See Birds, Extinct
BRANTLEY, Bill, and others
When and where to invest off the farm. Suc Farm 62:52+ N '64
—See Davis, V. W. jt. auth.
BRANTLEY, George D.
Diploma-giving principal; St Louis's Charles Sumner high school. il pors Ebony 18:76+ Je '63

BRANTLEY, Howell
Underground power distribution cuts costs, promotes city growth. Am City 80:93-4 Ja '65

BRANZELL, Karin
Daughter of the gods. F. Robinson. pors Opera N 29:26-8 D 26 '64

BRAQUE, Georges
At the cubist root. por Time 82:66 S 13 '63
Braque festival. New Yorker 40:32 Mr 28 '64
Braque in America. E. F. Fry. Nation 198: 512-14 My 18 '64
Braque: pre-cube to post-Zen. J. Richardson. il Art N 63:29-31+ Ap '64
Braque's birds and billiards. il Sports Illus 19:13 S 9 '63
Death of a master. il por Newsweek 62:45 S 9 '63
Georges Braque: a memoir. A. Frankfurter. Art N 62:21 O '63
Letter from Paris. Genêt. New Yorker 39: 185-6+ S 14 '63

BRASEFIELD, C. J.
Fission product gamma activity with northerly winds and with southerly winds. bibliog Science 142:952-3 N 15 '63

BRASILIA, Brazil
Brasilia. J. E. Searles. il Sch Arts 63:24-8 O '63
Growing pains for a frontier capital. il Bsns W p 116-18 Ap 20 '63
Life on the fly. il Time 82:27 Ag 30 '63
Why move a capital? R. E. Crist. il Américas 15:13-17 Ag '63

BRASILIA. University, Brazil. See Colleges and universities—Brazil

BRASSENS, Georges
Bear of Montparnasse. por Time 84:93 N 13 '64
Immortal bear? por Newsweek 65:72-3 F 1 '65

BRASSIERES
Bra makers get a lift from fashion's plunge. il Bsns W p64+ Ap 4 '64
Support for the needy; deep-cut bras. il Time 83:64 F 14 '64
Take a fashion lesson; do's, don'ts and dressing room decorum. il Seventeen 23:67 O '64

BRAUDE, A. I.
Bacterial endotoxins; with biographical sketch. Sci Am 210:20, 36-45 bibliog(p 152) Mr '64

BRAUN, Dick
(ed) Dairy. See issues of Farm journal
(ed) Poultry. See issues of Farm journal

BRAUN, Ernest
Photographs to live with. il U S Camera 27: 22-3+ S '64

BRAUN, Henry
My crowns; poem. Nation 197:370 N 30 '63

BRAUN, Sigismund von
Future of Germany; address, January 13, 1964. Vital Speeches 30:365-9 Ap 1 '64

BRAUN, Wernher von. See Von Braun, W.

BRAUN-MENENDEZ, Mauricio, family
Lords of Patagonia. il Time 82:103 N 1 '63

BRAUNER, Charles J.
Improving education as a subject of study; excerpt from American educational theory. bibliog Sch & Soc 92:25-9 Ja 25 '64

BRAUNWALD, Nina Starr
Days are busy for only woman open-heart surgeon. J. G. Harmount. il pors Todays Health 41:31 Jl '63
What it takes to be wife, mother and heart surgeon. J. L. Block. il pors Good H 156:34+ My '63

BRAVEMAN, Mal
Face of anybody. New Yorker 39:34-5 Ap 6 '63

BRAVERMAN, Harry
Prophet to the end. Nation 197:350-2 N 23 '63

BRAWLING. See Fighting, Hand-to-hand

BRAY, Barbara
Apostle of affliction. UNESCO Courier 16:4-8 Mr '63

BRAY, Donald W.
Chile enters a new era. Cur Hist 48:21-5+ Ja '65

BRAY, J. Roger
Chronology of a small glacier in eastern British Columbia, Canada. Science 144:287 Ap 17 '64

BRAYBROOKE, Neville
Blimey, it's balmy! Sat R 46:42+ Ap 13 '63
Brush up your Shakespeare. Sat R 47:92+ Mr 14 '64
Poetry of Robert Lowell. Cath World 198: 230-7 Ja '64
Simone Weil and Edith Stein: modern mystic-martyrs. Christian Cent 81:1461-3 N 25 '64

BRAYMAN, Harold
Communication in our modern society; address, October 13, 1964. Vital Speeches 31:50-3 N 1 '64

BRAZELTON, T. Berry
Toilet teaching made easy. Parents Mag 38:46-7+ Je '63
Why some babies cry so much. Parents Mag 39:56-7+ Ap '64

BRAZIER, Mary A. B.
Electrical activity of the nervous system. bibliog Science 146:1423-8 D 11 '64

BRAZIL
Brazil: a study in delusion. L. Gross. il Look 28:78 Je 2 '64
Brazil: complex giant. H. O. Sternberg. For Affairs 43:297-311 Ja '65
Brazil: giant in chains. il Sr Schol 82:10-13+ My 8 '63
Brazil: land of massive problems. R. H. Bolton. Christian Cent 81:1235-9 O 7 '64
Brazil: prelude to crisis. G. Murray. Christian Cent 81:588-9 Ap 29 '64
Ethnic democracy: the Brazilian example. G. Freyre. il Américas 15:1-6 D '63
Goal: economic freedom. C. L. Hulet. Sat R 47:43-4 F 15 '64
Potential in Brazil. J. J. Johnson. Cur Hist 46:1-7 Ja '64

See also
Advertising—Brazil
Agriculture—Brazil
Bibliography, National—Brazil
Brasília
Communication and traffic—Brazil
Communism—Brazil
Economic assistance in Brazil
Electric power—Brazil
Finance—Brazil
Food supply—Brazil
Hunting—Brazil
Iguassú Falls
Investments, Foreign (in Brazil)
Land tenure—Brazil
Marajo (island)
Mato Grosso
Minas Gerais, Brazil
Missions—Brazil
Money—Brazil
Monte Alto
Natural resources—Brazil
Newspapers—Brazil
Paleontology—Brazil
Paraná
Penedo
Pernambuco (state)
Petroleum industry and trade—Brazil
Political campaigns—Brazil
Portuguese language in Brazil
Salvador
São Paulo
Space research—Brazil
Technical assistance in Brazil
Theater—Brazil

Air force
Bello Antonio; dispute over aircraft carrier Minas Gerais. il Newsweek 65:46 Ja 25 '65

Civilization
Bandeirantes and pioneers, by V. Moog; tr. by L. I. Barrett. Review
Nat R 16:736-7 Ag 25 '64. E. M. von Kuehnelt-Leddihn

Commerce
Contrabando: big in Brazil; with report by M. J. Kubic. il Newsweek 62:46-7 Jl 8 '63
Terms of trade and the Brazilian balance of payments; address, January 29, 1963. L. Gordon. il Dept State Bul 48:284-93 F 25 '63

Economic conditions
Atlantic report. Atlan 213:32+ Mr '64
Blame August. Time 82:32 Ag 9 '63
Brazil: anti-inflation plans collapse. il Bsns W p80 Ag 3 '63
Brazil: 2 billion dollars from U.S. and yet—. il U S News 54:44-7 Ap 1 '63
Brazil's big dust bowl. K. W. Seegers. il Read Digest 83:212-16+ Jl '63
Brazil's Goulart: power for the sake of what? il Newsweek 61:48-50+ Mr 11 '63
Country where inflation is the way of life. D. B. Richardson. U S News 55:67-9 Ag 12 '63
Development of Brazil. C. Furtado. il Sci Am 209:208-12+ bibliog(p308+) S '63
Great whirligig; inflation. il Time 84:43 O 23 '64
Help from abroad. Time 84:28 Jl 10 '64
How to do business amid chaos; inflation in Brazil. il Time 83:95-6 Mr 6 '64
Inflation as a way of life. il U S News 57:95 Jl 20 '64
Long, tricky path facing Brazil; with editorial comment. Bsns W p72+, 188 Ap 11 '64

BRAZIL—Economic conditions—*Continued*
Pope Paul to Brazil? America 112:33 Ja 9 '65
Printing-press economy. il Fortune 67:63-4+ Mr '63
Social-minded archbishop. E. K. Culhane. America 109:5 Jl 6 '63
Spinning spiral. il Newsweek 64:79-80 N 16 '64
Texas-size slum; Brazil's Northeast. il Newsweek 61:55 Mr 11 '63

Economic policy

Brazil gums up plans for its own rescue; inflation, strikes, and political crises. il Bsns W p54-6 N 9 '63
Brazil: what kind of revolution? C. Furtado. For Affairs 41:526-35 Ap '63
Campos plan. Time 84:27 Ag 21 '64
Close-up of Brazil three months after revolution. U S News 57:94-5 Jl 20 '64
Development of Brazil. C. Furtado. il Sci Am 209:208-12+ bibliog(p308+) S '63
Economic progress and Brazilian nationalism. D. Goulet. Cath World 198:314-19 F '64
Economic troubles are not being solved. il Time 81:26-7 Je 7 '63
Help on an if basis. il Time 81:30 Ap 5 '63
Printing-press economy. il Fortune 67:63-4+ Mr '63
Rio's fiscal surgeon. il Bsns W p 100+ Je 13 '64
Stirrings of reform. Newsweek 63:50 My 11 '64
Toward a new economics. Time 83:34 Je 5 '64
U.S. and Brazil reach understanding in economic and financial talks; exchange of letters. F. C. S. T. Dantas; D. E. Bell. il Dept State Bul 48:557-61 Ap 15 '63
Very long shot. New Repub 148:10 Mr 30 '63

Economic relations

American capital and Brazilian nationalism. W. Baer and M. H. Simonsen. Yale R 53: 192-8 D '63

Foreign relations

Cool toward Tito. il Newsweek 62:32 S 30 '63
United States and Brazil pledge continued cooperation; exchange of letters, December 13 and December 18, 1963. L. B. Johnson; J. Goulart. Dept State Bul 50:47-9 Ja 13 '64

History

Brazil; excerpt from Brazil on the move. J. Dos Passos. il Sat R 46:80-3+ O 12 '63

Industries

Backland's capitalism; Project Asimow. Time 84:66 Ag 14 '64
Brazil. C. F. Jones. il Focus 15:1-6 N '64
Rothschilds of the south. Time 81:30 Je 28 '63
State of awakening: Mina Gerais. il Time 82:34 Jl 5 '63
Suburbia in the jungle; Indústria e comércio de minérios. Time 85:78+ Ja 29 '65

Intellectual life

Speaking of Brazil. A. Filho. il Américas 15: 34-6 F '63

Native races

See Indians of South America—Brazil

Navy

Bello Antonio; dispute over aircraft carrier Minas Gerais. il Newsweek 65:46 Ja 25 '65

Politics and government

Amazon in flood. Nat R 16:391 My 19 '64
Another coup? il Newsweek 62:74 O 21 '63
April fool's day in Brazil. F. de Alencar Arraes. Commonweal 80:192-3 My 8 '64
Arrested: a big yaw to the left. il Life 56: 38B-38C Ap 17 '64
As the dust settles in Brazil. A. A. Berle. Reporter 30:27-8 Ap 23 '64; Discussion. 30: 6+ My 21 '64
Brazil and Chile. New Repub 150:5-6 Ap 11 '64
Brazil in perspective; the Goulart ouster. A. G. Frank. Nation 198:408-11 Ap 27 '64
Brazil in quandary. J. J. Johnson. Cur Hist 48:9-15+ Ja '65
Brazil: success without cheers. il Newsweek 65:46-7 Ja 11 '65
Brazil: the new government; address, June 23, 1964. C. Lacerda. Vital Speeches 30: 717-19 S 15 '64
Brazil: what kind of revolution? C. Furtoda. For Affairs 41:526-35 Ap '63
Brazilian coup. Commonweal 80:100 Ap 17 '64
Brazil's adroit new leader. M. J. Kubic. il Reporter 31:21-3 D 17 '64
Brazil's Goulart: power for the sake of what? il Newsweek 61:48-50+ Mr 11 '63
Brazil's Goulart skirts the abyss. J. De Onis. il N Y Times Mag p20+ Ag 18 '63
Cabinet maker. il Time 81:21 Je 28 '63
Cauldron of Brazil. Nation 198:357 Ap 13 '64
Chaos compounded. Time 82:33 O 18 '63
Country that saved itself. C. W. Hall. il Read Digest 85:133-58 N '64
Crossing out the ex; Kubitschek ostracized. Time 83:30+ Je 19 '64
Dangers of politics. il Newsweek 62:51 S 9 '63
Disillusion. Nation 198:406 Ap 27 '64
End of the purges. Time 84:54 O 16 '64
Goodbye to Jango. il Time 83:26-7 Ap 10 '64
Goulart audit. il Time 83:36+ My 1 '64
Goulart forced out. il Sr Schol 84:18-19 Ap 17 '64
Goulart goes over brink in Brazil; military rebellion. il Bsns W p27 Ap 4 '64
Goulart's gone, but Brazil's problems stay. il Newsweek 63:37-8 Ap 13 '64
Goulart's legacy. R. Peter. Nat R 16:358 My 5 '64
Half a loaf. Newsweek 64:60-1 N 2 '64
Hammer & the anvil. il Time 82:53-4 N 15 '63
Hard line. il Time 84:40 D 4 '64
Headway at last. il Time 85:30-1 Ja 22 '65
How red is Brazil? L. Gross. il Look 27:111+ My 21 '63
Hungry revolution. Newsweek 63:57-8 Je 15 '64
Imbalance in Brazil. R. E. Poppino. Cur Hist 44:100-5+ F '63
Long, tricky path facing Brazil; with editorial comment. Bsns W p72+, 188 Ap 11 '64
Man from above. il Time 82:29-30 D 27 '63
Marry in haste. . . il Newsweek 63:60+ Ap 20 '64
Milk, motherhood and the American flag. New Repub 150:10-11 Ja 4 '64
More time; election postponed. il Time 84:36 Jl 24 '64
Most dangerous man in Brazil. J. Dos Passos. il Nat R 15:53-7 Jl 30 '63
Mutiny of the mariners. il Newsweek 63:49 Ap 6 '64
Now with Castro turned back; a new start for Brazil. il U S News 56:73-4 Ap 20 '64
Part of what was wrong; political corruption. il Time 84:22-3 Jl 3 '64
Point of disorder. il Time 82:36 D 13 '63
Political what's what. New Repub 150:8 Ap 18 '64
Quest for moderation. Newsweek 63:59 Ap 27 '64
Quickstep to the left. Newsweek 63:54 Mr 23 '64
Revolution in Brazil, by I. L. Horowitz. Review
Nat R 16:949-51 N 3 '64. J. W. F. Dulles
Nation 198:630-2 Je 22 '64. L. Wiznitzer
Right turn in Brazil. Bsns W p31 Je 13 '64
Road back. il Time 83:24 Ap 24 '64
Seeds of injustice? National security council blacklist. il Time 83:50 Je 12 '64
Seven days in April. Nat R 16:308 Ap 21 '64
Shaking down. Newsweek 64:40 Ag 3 '64
Silencing Furtado. New Repub 150:4 My 2 '64
State of chaos. il Time 82:33 O 11 '63
Suppressing the future. R. H. Chilcote. Nation 199:368-70 N 23 '64
Tale of two cities; São Paulo and Recife. M. J. Kubic. il Newsweek 64:47 Ag 24 '64
Three who hold key to Brazil's future. U S News 56:16 Ap 27 '64
Toward profound change. il Time 83:49-50 Ap 17 '64
Under the volcano. Nation 198:614 Je 22 '64
U.S.-Brazilian witch hunt. Nation 199:206-7 O 12 '64
Vote of confidence. il Newsweek 61:48 Ap 8 '63
When executives turned revolutionaries. P. Siekman. il Fortune 70:147-9+ S '64

Race problems

Black and white. il Newsweek 64:46+ S 7 '64

Religious institutions and affairs

News of the Christian world (cont) Christian Cent 80:445-6; 81:278, 1408 Ap 3 '63, F 26, N 11 '64
See also
Catholic church in Brazil

Social conditions

Brazil's big dust bowl. K. W. Seegers. il Read Digest 83:212-16+ Jl '63
Conscience and anti-communism; challenge of sub-human conditions. H. Camara. Commonweal 81:407-8 D 18 '64

BRAZIL—Social conditions—*Continued*
Heads of lettuce; Brazil's bishops appeal for social change now. America 110:663 My 16 '64
On the road in Brazil. M. Miller. il Harper 227:65-70+ O '63
Operation Nordeste; Brazil's bold programme in the hunger campaign. J. de Castro. il UNESCO Courier 16:24-31 My '63
Sister Dulce. S. Seegers and K. Seegers. il Cath World 199:230-7 Jl '64

Social history

Mansions and the shanties, by G. Freyre. Review
Time 81:28 Ap 26 '63

BRAZIL and the United States
Brazil's Goulart: power for the sake of what? il Newsweek 61:48-50+ Mr 11 '63
Economic progress and Brazilian nationalism. D. Goulet. Cath World 198:314-19 F '64
Potential in Brazil. J. J. Johnson. Cur Hist 46:1-7 Ja '64

BRAZILIAN folk drama. See Folk drama, Brazilian

BRAZILIAN literature
See also
Brazilian poetry

BRAZILIAN music. See Music, Brazilian

BRAZILIAN poetry
Modern Brazilian poetry: an anthology, ed. by J. Nist. Review
Nation 196:184-5 Mr 2 '63. K. Botsford
Seven new Brazilian poets. W. Ayala. il Américas 16:27-34 F '64

Translations into English

From The death and life of a Severino; excerpts, tr. by E. Bishop. J. C. De Melo Neto. Poetry 103:10-18 O '63

BRAZILIANS
People of Rio; Cariocas. L. Gross. il Look 27:54-64 Je 4 '63

BRAZING
Exothermic process promises brazing applications in space. J. F. Judge. il Miss & Roc 13:48+ S 30 '63
Gadgets & gilhickies; silver alloy brazing. T. Moore. il Yachting 115:77+ My '64
Tricks of brazing and hard soldering. M. Banister. il Pop Mech 119:170-4 Je '63

BRAZZAVILLE
Violence in Africa; developments in Togo, Brazzaville and Dahomey. T. P. Melady. America 109:734-5 D 7 '63

BREACH; story. See Senesi, M.

BREAD
Bagel and lox; comments. il McCalls 90:128-9+ My '63
Bread. R. Godden. House & Gard 123:136-7+ Ap '63
Bread like grandmother baked; with recipes. J. Figg. il Suc Farm 61:94-5+ Mr '63
Bread takes the cheese. G. Claiborne. il N Y Times Mag p77-8 My 5 '63
Breads to bake for Easter. J. Figg. il Suc Farm 62:110-11+ Mr '64
Breads to serve hot, with coffee. il Sunset 133:192+ N '64
Cheese corn crisps. il Good H 156:176 Ap '63
Christmas breads to serve and to give. il Parents Mag 38:69-72 D '63
Crisp bread good with pasta. il Sunset 133:152 S '64
Crusty Irish soda bread. il Sunset 130:208 Mr '63
Easter breads. il Bet Hom & Gard 41:83-4 Ap '63
Flavors of bread. il Bet Hom & Gard 42:68-9+ Mr '64
For Twelfth night, three kings' bread. il Sunset 132:88 Ja '64
Fragrant cinnamon bread. il Bet Hom & Gard 43:86 Ja '65
Fragrant nut pinwheels. Sunset 132:218 Ap '64
Have a taste of golden Christmas tree bread. il Sunset 133:54-7 D '64
Have some Navajo fry bread. il Sunset 133:122 S '64
Here is a hot surprise bread; wheatless bread called rieska. il Sunset 132:153 Mr '64
Holiday breads. il Good H 157:68-9+ D '63
Holiday quick breads. Parents Mag 38:127+ D '63
Homemade bread doughs into your freezer. il Sunset 132:154+ F '64
Hot rolls. il Bet Hom & Gard 42:93-4 F '64
How to make your husband miss the 8:13. il Am Home 67:62+ Mr '64
How to pop a perfect popover time after time after time. il Sunset 130:114-15 My '63
Irish serve barmbrack on Halloween. il Sunset 133:204 O '64
Joke: bread is made from wheat. Sci Digest 54:54 O '63
Making your own croissants. il Sunset 132:234+ Ap '64
No bread like homemade bread; with recipes. J. Hewitt. il N Y Times Mag p92+ D 6 '64
Nut breads. il Bet Hom & Gard 41:93-4 N '63
Psst! Christmas breads too. il Am Home 66:48+ D '63
Quick bread bests. il Suc Farm 61:89-90 F '63
Sourdough hot breads. B. Pierson. Farm J 88:89 Mr '64
Step by step to homemade bread. il Parents Mag 38:126 D '63
Step by step to rich nut bread. il McCalls 90:130-1+ My '63
Successful recipes; quick bread. il Suc Farm 62:81-2 N '64
Surprise is the bread. il Sunset 131:105 Ag '63
Surprise them with bagels. il Sunset 134:106+ Ja '65
Susan makes a pinwheel sandwich loaf. il Good H 157:136 Jl '63
Susan, our teenage cook, makes fabulous refrigerator rolls. il Good H 157:152 N '63
Sweet perfection with your coffee. il McCalls 91:144-5+ My '64
Tall and fragrant loaf for Easter; Finnish Easter bread. il Sunset 132:98-9 Mr '64
These buns are Arab bread. il Sunset 130:164 Je '63
Three great breads; with recipes. il Bet Hom & Gard 43:70-1+ Ja '65
To bagelville and beyond. H. Sutton. Sat R 47:36+ N 21 '64; Discussion. 47:33 D 12; 21 D 26 '64; 48:43 Ja 9; 21 Ja 16; 37 Ja 23; 21 Ja 30 '65
Two days to make, but it's worth it; salt rising bread. il Sunset 132:168 Ap '64
Whittling away at the staff of life. Consumer Rep 29:366-7 Ag '64
See also
Coffee cake

BREAD and butter shop; drama. See Miller, H. L.

BREAD LOAF writers conference. See Authors conferences

BREAKFAST foods. See Cereal foods

BREAKFASTS
Ambitious young cooks serve breakfast. il Sunset 130:217-18 Ap '63
Bagel and lox; comments. il McCalls 90:128-9+ My '63
Breakfast in the sun. il McCalls 90:110-11+ Je '63
Breakfast recipes to start the day right. G. Maddox. il Todays Health 42:24-9 S '64
Come for breakfast. il House & Gard 123:168-72+ Ap '63
Easter breakfast idea from Portugal. il Sunset 132:182+ Mr '64
French toast; breakfast menus; with recipes. il McCalls 91:108-9+ S '64
Ice cream for breakfast. il Seventeen 23:159 My '64
Memorandum. Mlle 56:180 Mr '63
See also
Brunches

BREAKSTONE, Arthur L.
Summer weekend project. Pop Gard 15:10-11 Jl '64

BREAM, C. C. jr.
Rehabilitative recreation in VA hospitals. por Recreation 57:224-6 My '64

BREAST cancer. See Cancer

BREAST feeding. See Infants—Nutrition

BREATH, Shortness of. See Emphysema

BREATHING. See Respiration

BREATHITT, Edward T.
Reception. New Yorker 40:27-8 F 29 '64

BREAUX BRIDGE, La.
Crawfish capital celebrates. il Bsns W p30-1 Ap 25 '64

BREBNER, Winston
Seafaring New England. Holiday 34:18+ Jl '63

BRECHER, Edward. See Brecher, R. jt. auth.

BRECHER, George. See Robinson, S. H. jt. auth.

BRECHER, Ruth, and Brecher, Edward
Don't take the police for granted. Parents Mag 39:56-7+ Mr '64
Fundamentals for survival. Parents Mag 38:45+ Je '63
Having a baby your own way. Redbook 122:69-80 F '64
How to give up smoking; maybe. N Y Times Mag p 16+ Ja 26 '64
Is our environment poisoning us? Parents Mag 38:72-3+ O '63

BRECHER, Ruth, and Brecher, Edward—*Cont.*
Military's limited war against segregation. Harper 227:79-82+ S '63
Money-saving guide to meat. Redbook 121: 84-92 O '63
Nursing homes. Consumer Rep 29:30-6, 87-92, 139-42, 194-8 Ja-Ap '64
Parks that pay for themselves. Read Digest 83:258-62 N '63
Smoking and lung cancer. Consumer Rep 28:265-80 Je '63
Tragic inefficiency of our hospital emergency wards. Redbook 123:55+ S '64
What will they be when they grow up? Parents Mag 38:62-3+ F '63

BRECHT, Bertolt
Arturo Ui. Criticism
Cath World 198:263-4 Ja '64
Commonweal 79:314+ D 6 '63
Nation 197:403-4 D 7 '63
New Repub 149:26 D 21 '63
Newsweek 62:71 N 25 '63
Sat R 46:24 N 30 '63
Baal. Criticism
Nation 196:381 My 4 '63
Brecht in perspective. A. Pryce-Jones. por Theatre Arts 47:22-4 Je '63
Brecht is global, except here. H. Clurman. il N Y Times Mag p30-1+ N 3 '63
Der hofmeister (Tutor) tr. by G. Nellhaus. Criticism
Theatre Arts il 47:58-9 O '63
Man's a man. Criticism
Theatre Arts 47:67 F '63
Mother Courage and her children; tr. by E. Bentley. Criticism
Cath World 197:143-4 My '63
Commonweal 78:141-2 Ap 26 '63
Nation 196:314-15 Ap 13 '63
New Repub 148:35-6 Ap 13 '63
New Yorker 39:71 Ap 6 '63
Newsweek il 61:85 Ap 8 '63
Reporter 28:39-40 My 9 '63; Discussion. 28:8 Je 6 '63
Sat R 46:20 Ap 13 '63
Theatre Arts il(p 13) 47:14-15 My '63
Time il 81:56 Ap 5 '63
Relentless specter of Brecht; with report by T. Prideaux. il por Life 57:112B-118+ S 18 '64

BRECK, Park
Snap in the deep. L. Barry. il Pop Phot 54: 20+ F '64

BREDA, Jeremie
Life in Haiti: voodoo and the church. Commonweal 78:241-4 My 24 '63

BREDELL, Roscoe G.
Unkempt, unswept label touches off a storm. por Am City 79:114-15 O '64

BREE, Germaine
Between silence and rhetoric. Sat R 47:38+ N 7 '64
Corpuscles of her corpus. Sat R 47:42 My 23 '64
Distrusting the Gaul. Nation 198:377-9 Ap 13 '64
Happiest when he was the sadist. Sat R 46:58+ S 28 '63

BREEDEN, Kay
Fructivorous fliers. Natur Hist 73:26-33 My '64

BREEDER reactors. See Nuclear reactors

BREEDING
See also
Cattle breeding
Eugenics
Inbreeding
Swine breeding

BREEDLOVE, Craig
Driving a world's record; 407 miles per hour. por Pop Mech 120:87-92+ N '63
Fast, wet, and almost dead. H. Gorey. il por Sports Illus 21:72-4 O 26 '64
about
Cool run for an old hot rodder. H. Gorey. por Sports Illus 19:46-8+ Ag 19 '63
Dream of speed. il por Time 82:51 Ag 16 '63
Jet ace: three-wheeled Spirit of America. il Newsweek 62:74-5 Ag 19 '63

BREEN, Whilden P. 1927?-
Long voyage in inner space. T. Flaherty. il pors Life 54:119-20 My 17 '63

BREGENZ festival. See Music festivals—Austria

BREHM, Margaretta
Tour. New Yorker 40:28-30 Je 13 '64

BREIDENBACH, Andrew W. and Lichtenberg, J. J.
DDT and dieldrin in rivers: a report of the National water quality network. bibliog Science 141:899-901; 142:1021 S 6, N 22 '63

BREITFELLER, Carl J.
Swinging prison priest. D. R. Maxey. il pors Look 28:24-9 D 29 '64

BRELIS, Dean
M.I.T. Holiday 33:66-75+ Mr '63

BREMNER, Ruth Ray
That convent wall. America 111:456-7 O 17 '64

BREMSER, L. W.
Two-stage water-plant expansion. Am City 78:78-80 D '63

BRENAN, Gerald
One man's story. por Time 81:118 Ap 19 '63

BRENNA, Virgilio
Our neighbor the moon; excerpts from The moon. il Look 27:68-74+ N 5 '63

BRENNAN, Blythe Morley
Albert. McCalls 90:106-7+ Je '63

BRENNAN, Eileen G. and others
Atmospheric aldehydes related to petunia leaf damage. bibliog Science 143:818-20 F 21 '64

BRENNAN, Maeve
Carpet with the big pink roses on it; story. New Yorker 40:47-50 My 23 '64
Drowned man; story. New Yorker 39:26-33 Jl 27 '63
Free choice; story. New Yorker 40:26-36 Jl 11 '64
In and out of never-never land; story. New Yorker 39:28-36 Jl 6 '63

BRENNAN, William Joseph, 1906-
Inside view of the High court. N Y Times Mag p35+ O 6 '63
Law, liberty and libraries; excerpts from address, May 1, 1963. por Library J 88:2417-20 Je 15 '63
Teaching about civil rights. por NEA J 52: 43 Mr '63

BRENNER, Anita
Critic's view. Atlan 213:131-41 Mr '64

BRENNER, L. J. and Ecker, E. E.
Differences in complement titers of serums from spaced bleedings in guinea pigs. bibliog Science 145:400-1 Jl 24 '64

BRENNINKMEYER, C. and A, company
Suited for expansion. il Time 82:74 Jl 19 '63

BRESCIANI, Francesco
DNA synthesis in alveolar cells of the mammary gland: acceleration by ovarian hormones. bibliog Science 146:653-5 O 30 '64

BRESLIN, James
Best bet for bail: a good crook. Life 54:15+ Mr 29 '63
Can't anybody here play this game? excerpt. Read Digest 83:193+ Ag '63
Death in emergency room no. one. Sat Eve Post 236:30-1 D 14 '63
Fix was on. Sat Eve Post 236:15-19 F 23 '63
It's Metsomania. Sat Eve Post 237:20-5 Je 13 '64
Old Indian's last stand. Life 54:119-20+ Ap 5 '63
Still they come to the hillside. Sat Eve Post 237:22-3 N 21 '64
about
Keep me going. por Newsweek 61:90 My 6 '63

BRESLOW, Paul
Movies. Vogue 143:31 Ja 15; 20 F 15; 64 Mr 15; 52 Ap 15 '64
TV and the public interest. Commentary 35:264-8 Mr '63

BRESSLER, Ray
Ballplayer's moose hunt. pors Outdoor Life 135:66-9+ F '65
Deer hunting with dad. pors Outdoor Life 133:60-3+ My '64

BRESSON, Henri Cartier-. See Cartier-Bresson, H.

BRETH, Fred E.
France's amazing beef machine. Sci Digest 56:37-42 N '64
What you don't know about milking cows. Sci Digest 55:39-44 Ja '64

BRETHREN, Church of the. See Church of the Brethren

BRETHREN in Christ. See Mennonites

BRETZKE, David J.
You must have a garbage-disposal unit. Am City 79:177 Je '64

BREUER, Gustl
Ariadne renascent. Opera N 27:28-9 F 16 '63
Art of Elisabeth Schumann. Am Rec G 29: 780-1 Je '63
Die goettliche Kurz and others. Am Rec G 30:884-5 My '64
Everything in its time. Opera N 29:26-8 D 19 '64

BREUER, Herb
Swing high, swing low. il U S Camera 27:52-3 Ja '64

BREUER, Marcel
Architectural details. il Arch Rec 135:121-36 F '64

BREUER, Robert
Case of hard-earned bread. Hi Fi 14:42-5+ Je '64
Strauss and his contemporaries. Sat R 47:64-5 My 30 '64
Strauss, Krauss, and Capriccio. Sat R 46:60-1 O 26 '63
BREVARD music festival. See Music festivals —North Carolina
BREVERMAN, Harvey
Some notes on drawing. il por Am Artist 28:36-41+ Ja '64
BREVOORT, H. F.
Focusing on nature; ed. by B. Hering. il por Pop Sci 183:132-4+ Ag '63
BREWER, David J.
United States a Christian nation; address, 1905. U S News 55:108+ O 28 '63
BREWER, Ernest J.
Municipal purchasing and public relations. Am City 78:98-9 Ag '63
BREWER, James Fitzgerald
Now what's wrong with the foreign-aid program? America 108:224-7 F 16 '63
BREWER, Leo
New chemical theory. Sci N L 85:403 Je 27 '64
BREWER, William Conant, jr
Home to the sea. Motor B 113:114-15+ Ja; 24-5+ F; 52+ Mr '64
Schizophrenic sailor. Yachting 115:196-9 Mr '64
BREWERIES
See also
Liebmann breweries, incorporated
BREWING
Automatic beer; continuous-flow brewing. il Time 84:98 S 4 '64
BREWING industries
Are the drinkers doing their part? il Bsns W p 106+ Ap 13 '63
Tax ruling may open new markets to beer; beer concentrate. Bsns W p34 S 7 '63
Who drinks? the brewers's dilemma. il Newsweek 64:66-8 Ag 24 '64
See also
Anheuser-Busch, incorporated
Carling brewing company
Schlitz, Joseph, brewing company
BREWSTER, Evelyn
Denver: rapport and Round robin. Wilson Lib Bul 38:275-8 N '63
BREWSTER, Kingman, 1919-
Is the Ivy league still the best? il pors Newsweek 64:65-8+ N 23 '64
New Haven, safe haven. il pors Time 83:73-4 Ap 17 '64
New prexy marches into office at Yale. il por Life 56:45 Ap 24 '64
President Brewster. New Yorker 39:22-4 Ja 11 '64
Student to president. por Newsweek 62:103 O 21 '63
Y of it all. por Time 82:51 O 18 '63
Yale inauguration. New Yorker 40:42-3 Ap 25 '64
BREYERE, Edward J. and Williams, L. B.
Antigens associated with a tumor virus: rejection of isogenic skin grafts from leukemic mice. bibliog Science 146:1055-6 N 20 '64
BREZHNEV, Leonid Il'ich
Peaceful co-existence; address, October 19, 1964. Vital Speeches 31:38-40 N 1 '64
—See Khrushchev, N. S. jt. auth.
about
After Khrushchev what? with report by K. Lachmann. il pors U S News 57:39-45 O 26 '64
B after K! por Newsweek 62:26 D 23 '63
Communists in gray flannel suits. H. Tanner. il pors N Y Times Mag p 11+ Ag 2 '64
Fall of Nikita K; with comment on the world's news fronts. il por Sr Schol 85:17-18+, 24 O 28 '64
Heir apparent in Kremlin. por Bsns W p34 Jl 18 '64
Heir to Khrushchev? Brezhnev steps up. il por U S News 57:16 Jl 27 '64
Kremlin chiefs pledge business as usual. il pors Bsns W p30-3 O 24 '64
New B. & K. S. Bialer. il Reporter 31:25-6 N 5 '64
New men at the top in the Kremlin. por U S News 57:21 O 26 '64
New number one man was a party prodigy. il por Life 57:34-5 O 23 '64
New president for the USSR and the man to watch. America 111:99-100 Ag 1 '64
Revolt in the Kremlin. il pors Time 84:28-31 O 23 '64
Successor confirmed. Time 84:30 Jl 24 '64
Two for one: after K, the gray-flannel men move in. por Newsweek 64:46-7 O 26 '64
Who runs Russia now? il por U S News 57:52-4+ N 9 '64
BRIARCLIFF junior college, Briarcliff Manor, N.Y.
Trim house for girls' campus. il Arch Forum 118:88-9 Mr '63
BRIBERY
Apropos; Wally Butts-Bear Bryant affair. Sports Illus 18:13 My 27 '63
Case history of a favor. Christian Cent 81:415 Mr 25 '64
Empires of toothpicks; Playboy club's liquor license. Nation 196:366 My 4 '63
Fix was on: basketball mess; with editorial comment. J. Breslin. il Sat Eve Post 236:15-19, 92 F 23 '63
Many-armed bandit; bill to ban slot machines in Maryland. Newsweek 61:27 Ap 1 '63
Name of the game; Georgia vs. Alabama. Sat Eve Post 236:82 Ap 27 '63
Our own public scandal; address, August 7, 1963. E. P. Neilan. Vital Speeches 29:730-2 S 15 '63; Same abr. with title Political immorality, a speech that rocked Congress. Read Digest 83:126-9 N '63; Excerpts. U S News 55:102-3 Ag 26 '63
Shadow over pro football. T. Maule. il Sports Illus 18:10-11 Ja 28 '63
Thin gray line. M. Mannes. McCalls 91:53+ Ja '64; Same abr. Read Digest 84:63-3 Ap '64
True crisis; corruption in sports. J. Underwood. il Sports Illus 18:16-19+ My 20 '63
See also
Politics, Corruption in
BRICE, Fanny
Girl named Fanny. B. Rose. il por McCalls 90:52+ S '63
BRICE, Mary Anne
Have job, will travel. Mlle 60:168+ N '64
BRICK. See Bricks
BRICK construction
Bold expression in brick and concrete. il Arch Rec 135:80-3 mid-My '64
Brick bearing walls emerge in a new form. il Arch Rec 134:186-91 N '63
Bricks without straw bosses. J. Lear. il Sat R 47:45-9 F 1 '64
Designer's sketchbook. il Am Home 67:28+ Mr '64
New forms for an age-old material: brick. A. C. Borg. il Am Home 67:54-7 Mr '64
Suburban branch largely of brick. il Arch Rec 135:132 Ja '64
BRICK floors. See Floors, Brick
BRICKER, John W.
Views of a veteran. R. Moley. Newsweek 64:108 D 7 '64
BRICKMAN, William W.
Conant, Koerner, and the history of education. bibliog f Sch & Soc 92:135-9 Mr 21 '64
Education as foreign policy. Sat R 47:61-2 D 19 '64
Foreign books for educators. Sch & Soc 91:149-54, 381-7 Mr 23, N 30 '63
Scholar-educator in an age of automation. Sch & Soc 92:314-15 O 31 '64
U.S. books for educators. Sch & Soc 91:246-57, 310-20, 440-6; 92:242-50, 418-25 Sum, O 19, D 28 '63, Sum, D 26 '64
BRICKS
Bricks to use around the house. il Changing T 18:39-40 Jl '64
See also
Brick construction
BRIDAL showers. See Entertaining
BRIDE, Joseph
Candy-apple paint, nerf bars and monsters. Life 57:98 O 16 '64
BRIDENBAUGH, Carl
Great mutation; address. Am Hist R 68:315-31 Ja '63
BRIDES showers. See Entertaining
BRIDGE (game)
Another lesson from a master. C. Goren. il Sports Illus 21:72-3 O 12 '64
Art of leading misleadingly; 1963 world championship. C. Goren. il Sports Illus 21:53 Ag 24 '64
Avoiding the no point system; risking divorce playing bridge with your spouse. L. W. Robinson. il N Y Times Mag p 19+ Ap 19 '64
Bad role for Omar the actor. C. Goren. il Sports Illus 21:82 O 19 '64
Big hand for Big Lew. C. Goren. il Sports Illus 21:57 Ag 10 '64
Bridge. C. Goren. See issues of Sports Illustrated
Bridge for two players only. C. H. Goren. il McCalls 90:38+ Jl '63

BRIDGE (game)—*Continued*
Chicago bridge. Newsweek 62:68 Ag 26 '63
Chinese took them to the cleaners; World Olympiad. C. Goren. il Sports Illus 20:66 Je 15 '64
Cruise ship with a thousand decks. C. H. Goren. il McCalls 90:28+ Je '63
Don't fool around with fancy gadgets; two-diamond bid to announce three-suiter. C. Goren. il Sports Illus 21:57 D 14 '64
End of a Canada dry spell; Masters knockout team championship. C. Goren. il Sports Illus 21:72 Ag 17 '64
Even experts can fumble. C. H. Goren. il McCalls 90:36+ Ap '63
Fifty-two characters who found authors. C. H. Goren. il McCalls 91:34+ F '64
Goren's new formula; ed. by J. Olsen. C. H. Goren. il Sports Illus 20:32-8+ F 17; 24-8+ F 24; 32-4+ Mr 2; 28-30+ Mr 9; 52-3+ Mr 16 '64
Italy deals itself another winner; World bridge Olympiad. D. Jenkins. il Sports Illus 20:78+ My 25 '64
Judge commits larceny; W. Avarelli of Italian world Olympiad team. C. Goren. il Sports Illus 21:90 S 21 '64
Lost in the Blackwood. C. H. Goren. il McCalls 91:24+ Ja '64
My favorite bridge stories. C. H. Goren. il McCalls 90:38+ S '63
Never trump your partner's ace! C. H. Goren. il McCalls 90:62 Mr '63
Never underestimate an overbidder. C. Goren. il Sports Illus 20:78 My 18 '64
New bridge game; Chicago. N. W. Pearson. Vogue 141:100+ My '63
New bridge laws. C. H. Goren. il McCalls 90:32+ My '63
One baron who could be queen; Pacific Northwest regional championships in Seattle. C. Goren. il Sports Illus 21:64-5 N 2 '64
See the bridge stars shine! C. H. Goren. il McCalls 91:62+ My '64
Seven deadly sins. il McCalls 92:90+ N '64
Slam-bang slams. C. H. Goren. il McCalls 91:72+ Ap '64
Sure cure for hard luck. C. H. Goren. il McCalls 91:28+ Mr '64
Test of skill for the holiday season; ten problems in bidding and two special puzzles. C. Goren. il Sports Illus 21:78-80 D 21 '64
Three pairs for one team; competition for positions on North America 1965 world championship team. C. Goren. il Sports Illus 21:88-9 N 23 '64
Two crucial boards that helped Italy to victory. C. Goren. il Sports Illus 20:80 My 25 '64
U.S. prepares an assault on bridge Italian style; Italians favored to win. C. Goren. il Sports Illus 20:108-9 Ap 13 '64
What shall I lead? C. H. Goren. il McCalls 91:58+ N '63
When you meet a freak hand. C. H. Goren. il McCalls 90:30+ F '63
Who's afraid of no trump? C. H. Goren. il McCalls 91:36+ Je '64
Who's afraid of Santa Claus? C. H. Goren. il McCalls 91:36+ D '63
See also
American contract bridge league
BRIDGE, Flying. See Navigating bridge
BRIDGE building. See Bridges
BRIDGE CANYON DAM (proposed) See Dams
BRIDGE clubs
King of clubs. C. H. Goren. il McCalls 90:18+ Ag '63
BRIDGE diodes. See Diodes
BRIDGE players
End of a Canada dry spell; Masters knockout team championship. C. Goren. il Sports Illus 21:72 Ag 17 '64
Far Eastern bid for supremacy; World Olympiad. C. Goren. il Sports Illus 21:42 Jl 20 '64
Great bridge battle! C. H. Goren. il McCalls 91:36+ O '63
Italy deals itself another winner; World bridge Olympiad. D. Jenkins. il Sports Illus 20:78+ My 25 '64
Judge commits larceny; W. Avarelli of Italian world Olympiad team. C. Goren. il Sports Illus 21:90 S 21 '64
Leading ladies who were not there; women's teams. C. H. Goren. il McCalls 92:40+ O '64
Little major's minor mishap. C. Goren. il Sports Illus 20:76 Je 1 '64
Old hands with new tricks; North American entry in the 1965 world championship. C. Goren. il Sports Illus 21:95-7 D 7 '64
One-man team in a partnership game; Lew Mathe. C. Goren. il Sports Illus 22:55 Ja 18 '65
Other side of point count. C. Goren. il Sports Illus 21:56-7 Jl 27 '64
Some who cannot see, see best; Summer nationals. C. Goren. il Sports Illus 22:48 Ja 4 '65
Trumps for business; World bridge Olympiad. il Bsns W p34 My 9 '64
Two kids and a pair of foxes. C. Goren. il Sports Illus 20:52+ Ap 20 '64
Two women with sharpened fingernails; World bridge team championship. C. Goren. il Sports Illus 21:58-9 N 9 '64
Words will never hurt them; U.S. women's Olympiad. C. Goren. il Sports Illus 20:70-1 My 11 '64
BRIDGE tournaments
Bridge, Italian style; second World bridge team Olympiad. il Newsweek 63:96 My 25 '64
Far Eastern bid for supremacy; World Olympiad. C. Goren. il Sports Illus 21:42 Jl 20 '64
Leading ladies who were not there; women's teams at the bridge Olympics in New York. C. H. Goren. il McCalls 92:40+ O '64
No Jack Dalton to save the day; Masters knockout team championship, Toronto. C. Goren. il Sports Illus 21:59 S 28 '64
Some who cannot see, see best; Summer nationals. C. Goren. il Sports Illus 22:48 Ja 4 '65
Trumps for business; World bridge Olympiad. il Bsns W p34 My 9 '64
Two women with sharpened fingernails; World bridge team championship. C. Goren. il Sports Illus 21:58-9 N 9 '64
Words will never hurt them; U.S. women's Olympiad. C. Goren. il Sports Illus 20:70-1 My 11 '64
Work of fine Italian hands; world championship. W. Bingham. Sports Illus 19:28+ Jl 1 '63
BRIDGEPORT, Conn.

Crime

Clergy patrol; volunteers riding with patrol cars on trouble spots where teen-age tension spills over. America 111:172 Ag 22 '64

Education

State associations work closely with locals; Connecticut education association. W. J. Sheehan. NEA J 53:20-1 F '64
BRIDGER, James
Heroes and heroism in the Yellowstone country. G. Caesar. Holiday 34:50-1+ Ag '63
BRIDGER wilderness area. See Wilderness areas
BRIDGERS, John
Coach even the faculty likes. M. Sharnik. il por Sports Illus 19:52+ N 18 '63
BRIDGES, Harry
Man who made the most of automation. por Time 82:19 D 27 '63
New Harry Bridges. F. Porter. New Repub 149:5-6 O 26 '63
Strange twilight of Harry Bridges. B. H. Wolfe. por Harper 228:78-80+ Mr '64
BRIDGES, Lucas, family
Tierra del Fuego; excerpts from The cloud forest. P. Matthiessen. il Américas 16:36-42 F '64
BRIDGES, Rocky
I managed good, but boy did they play bad. G. Rogin. il pors Sports Illus 21:22-6 Ag 17 '64
BRIDGES
Bridge. G. Talese. il Esquire 62:136-44+ D '64
Graceful park bridge wins award; Chicago. R. A. Black. il Am City 78:22 Je '63
Highway sculpture: the fantastic bridges of Paolo Soleri. il Arch Forum 119:84-7 O '63
To get to the other side; soaring steel & floating concrete; with colored photographs. il Time 84:62-9 Ag 28 '64
See also
Chesapeake Bay bridge-tunnel
also subhead Bridges under names of cities, e.g. New York (city)—Bridges

Floors

Many hands saved this deck; Racine, Wis. W. J. Chadwick. il Am City 78:76-7 Jl '63
℞ for a sick bridge; grid floor, Pulaski bridge, Amsterdam, N.Y. A. Lichtenstein. il Am City 79:104-6 S '64
Roughed-up deck cuts skidding accidents; Lake Washington's floating bridge. il Am City 78:118 S '63
Scale-free bridge deck; intercity viaduct, Kansas City. il Am City 79:80-1 Ja '64

Lighting

High-level lighting for a new lower level; George Washington Bridge. il Am City 78:117-18 F '63

BRIDGES—*Continued*

Maintenance and repair

New plates save an old bridge; Rockford, Ill. S. E. Scholl. il Am City 78:110-11 My '63

℞ for a sick bridge; grid floor, Pulaski bridge, Amsterdam, N.Y. A. Lichtenstein. il Am City 79:104-6 S '64

Scale-free bridge deck; intercity viaduct, Kansas City. il Am City 79:80-1 Ja '64

BRIDGES, Arched

Building a mighty arch bridge; Cold Spring Canyon bridge, Calif. R. R. Olney. il Pop Sci 183:112-13 O '63

BRIDGES, Floating. See Bridges, Pontoon

BRIDGES, Foot

Footbridge to cross a pool. il Sunset 133:138+ N '64

BRIDGES, Natural

Arches and bridges of stone; Utah. W. Luce. il Natur Hist 73:42-7 Ag '64

BRIDGES, Pontoon

Roughed-up deck cuts skidding accidents; Lake Washington's floating bridge. il Am City 78:118 S '63

BRIDGES, Suspension

To get to the other side; soaring steel & floating concrete; with colored photographs. il Time 84:62-9 Ag 28 '64

BRIDGES, Wooden

See also

Covered bridges

BRIDGHAM, William

Parking meters keep downtown alive. por Am City 79:129+ S '64

BRIDGMAN, Charles F. and Eldred, Earl

Hypothesis for a pressure-sensitive mechanism in muscle spindles. Science 143:481-2 Ja 31 '64

BRIDGMAN anvils. See Electric resistance

BRIDSTON, Keith

La dolce vita ecumenica. Christian Cent 80: 679 My 22 '63

Role of the World council. Christian Cent 81: 330-1 Mr 11 '64

BRIELAND, Donald, and Booth, N. J.

Child guidance as a community service. bibliog f Ann Am Acad 355:105-11 S '64

BRIEN, Alan

Afterthoughts on the Beatles. Mlle 59:239+ Ag '64

Joan Littlewood. Vogue 144:160-1+ S 15 '64

Living legends. Vogue 145:124-5+ Ja 1 '65

Openings, London. See issues of Theatre arts

Opinion, please from London. Mlle 58:30+ F '64

BRIER, Herb S.

Across the ham bands. See issues of Popular electronics

BRIERLEY, G. P. and others

Participation of an intermediate of oxidative phosphorylation in ion accumulation by mitochondria. bibliog Science 140:60-2 Ap 5 '63

BRIG; drama. See Brown, K. H.

BRIGADOON; musical comedy. See Musical comedies, revues, etc.—Criticisms, plots, etc.

BRIGANDS and robbers

I am but a simple murderer; death of M. I. Kilit. il Time 84:35 Jl 24 '64

Killers; rural gang warfare in Colombia. Newsweek 62:40 Ag 5 '63

New-style bank robber. F. Sondern, jr. il Read Digest 83:33-4+ D '63

Senseless slaughter; Aranguren massacre, Colombia. il Time 82:21 Ag 23 '63

BRIGGS, Asa

Technology and economic development; with biographical sketch. Sci Am 209:24, 52-61 bibliog(p306) S '63

BRIGGS, Ellis O.

Bureaucracy abroad. por Time 82:22 Jl 5 '63

Case against a West Point for diplomats. N Y Times Mag p20+ My 3 '64

Sad state of the Department of state: the hog-tied ambassador. por Esquire 60:100-1+ S '63

Speaking out. por Sat Eve Post 236:8+ S 14 '63

Speaking out; waste in the world of diplomacy. por Sat Eve Post 236:10+ F 2 '63

BRIGGS, Jon

Curl up and read. Seventeen 23:16 O '64

BRIGGS-Weaver machinery company

Industrial tent show; ShowMart. il Bsns W p 130 O 5 '63

BRIGHAM, Dan

New super-smooth metal substitute. Sci Digest 53:27-30 Mr '63

BRIGHAM, Robert

All the comforts of home up where polar bears play. Life 57:34A-34C Jl 17 '64

China's Chou, the difficult guest. Life 57:45 N 20 '64

Hosts with the most toasts. Life 55:123-6 S 13 '63

New B & K show opens in Red square. Life 57:40-42B O 30 '64

Polaris sub prowls the sea. Life 54:22-31 Mr 22 '63

Prairie schooner rolls into Moscow. Life 57:121-3 N 6 '64

Professor is ready. Life 55:59-60+ S 6 '63; Same abr. with title Erhard, Germany's new chancellor. Read Digest 83:119-22 N '63

Russia: no, no, this cannot be true. Life 55:129-30 D 6 '63

Up they claw in winter's Alpine epic. Life 54:22-5 F 15 '63

about

Gloucesterman in Russia. G. P. Hunt. il por Life 57:3 Jl 17 '64

BRIGHAM Young university, Provo, Utah

BYU: land of cuties and twelve tall Cougars. B. Ottum. il Sports Illus 22:26-9 Ja 4 '65

BRIGHT, James R.

Opportunity & threat in technological change. Harvard Bsns R 41:76-86 N '63

BRIGHT children. See Children, Gifted

BRIGHTBILL, Charles K.

Leisure, its meaning and implications; excerpts from address. por Recreation 57: 10-11 Ja '64

BRIGHTMAN, Anna

Window curtains in colonial Boston and Salem. Antiques 86:184-7 Ag '64

Woolen window curtains. Antiques 86:722-7 D '64

BRIGHTWATERS, N.Y.

Goodbye, lily pads. G. J. Guinta. il Am City 79:14 Mr '64

BRIGS. See Sailing vessels

BRILL, Harry

Educating youth; the cruel solution. Nation 198:296-7 Mr 23 '64

BRILL, Robert H.

Ancient glass. Sci Am 209:120-30 bibliog (p 188) N '63

BRILL, Winston J. and others

Anaerobic formate oxidation: a ferredoxin-dependent reaction. bibliog Science 144:297-8 Ap 17 '64

BRIMER, John Burton

Back up your planting. il Flower Grower 50: 30-1 S '63

Basic garden layout. Flower Grower 52:43-4 Ja '65

Build good design into your garden pool. il Flower Grower 50:22-3 Mr '63

Built-in shade. il Flower Grower 51:22-3 S '64

Five flower boxes for your porch or patio. Pop Sci 185:108-9 Jl '64

Five ways to give your home a lot of parking. Pop Sci 185:108-11 S '64

Flower grower's home garden notebook. See issues of Flower grower beginning June 1964

How to make a bench. Flower Grower 51:29 My '64

How to make a pomander. Flower Grower 50: 56 D '63

Ideas to profit by; woodland garden of bulbs. Flower Grower 51:27 S '64

Italian accent; excerpt from European sketchbook. Flower Grower 50:28-9 Je '63

Lath house will protect shade lovers from hot sun. il Flower Grower 50:22-3 Ag '63

Translation from German gardens. il Flower Grower 50:34-5 Mr '63

Well dressed for winter. Flower Grower 51:34 N '64

BRINDLEY, G. S.

Afterimages. Sci Am 209:84-90+ O '63

BRINDLEY, Larry W.

Parallel-resistor chart. Electr World 70:31 N '63

Phase-shift nomogram. Electr World 72:31 N '64

BRINDLEY, Robert H.

TV sewer inspection. Am City 79:87-9 Ja '64

BRINDZE, Ruth

Documentation of a yacht. Yachting 113:48-9+ My '63

BRINHART, Betty

Colchicum for autumn bloom. Pop Gard 14: 22-3+ Jl '63

Divide crowded day-lilies for more bountiful bloom. Flower Grower 51:45-6 Ag '64

Exotic Hawaiian ti plant. Horticulture 41: 478-9 S '63

BRINHART, Betty—*Continued*
Factor of plant growth: soil temperature. Horticulture 41:172 Mr '63
How to garden like an expert. Pop Gard 14:52-3 Mr '63
Lime your soil. Horticulture 41:554-5 N '63
Most popular salad vegetable. Pop Gard 14:40+ Ap '63
Soil air essential for good plant growth. Horticulture 41:92-3 F '63
Time to heal tree wounds. Flower Grower 50:25-6 Mr '63
Use sawdust and enjoy a weed-free garden. Flower Grower 51:42-3 Jl '64
Window gardens are interesting. Horticulture 42:54 Ja '64

BRINKLEY, David
Elections are no fun anymore. Look 28:35+ Jl 14 '64
Goodman and the TV networks. New Repub 148:39 Mr 23 '63
about
David Brinkley and his golden key. C. S. Wren. il pors Look 28:44+ F 25 '64
On the news beat. il por Newsweek 63:74-5 Je 1 '64

BRINKLEY, William
Great Gonzales. Holiday 34:85-90+ Jl '63

BRINKMAN, Oscar H.
Excerpt from testimony before subcommittee on housing, February 27, 1964. Cong Digest 43:125+ Ap '64

BRINKMEYER, Susan
Backing the meliorist. por Library J 88:1113-14 Mr 15 '63

BRINLEY, Ann
Classrooms as big as all outdoors. NEA J 53:44-5+ Ap '64

BRINNIN, John Malcolm
As I was going to St Ives. Atlan 211:118+ Je '63
Ascension: 1925; poem. New Yorker 39:142 My 25 '63
Giant turtle grants an interview; poem. New Yorker 39:30 Je 29 '63
Letter from an island; poem. New Yorker 40:36 D 19 '64
Not far from Ararat; poem. Atlan 212:98 Ag '63
Skin diving in the Virgins; poem. New Yorker 39:30 Ja 4 '64
about
Long reach, strong speech. B. Cutler. Poetry 103:387 Mr '64

BRINTON, Crane
Many mansions; address, December 29, 1963. Am Hist R 69:309-26 Ja '64

BRIOCHE. See Bread

BRIQUETS (fuel)
Backyard picnickers burn 350,000 tons of charcoal. Sci N L 84:72 Ag 3 '63

BRISCOE, Anne
Is this card necessary? Farm J 88:71 D '64

BRISCOE, Keith G.
Man of many talents. por Recreation 57:89-90 F '64

BRISTLECONE pine. See Pine

BRISTOL aeroplane company
Bristol reports 1963 profit of $9.3 million. Aviation W 80:95+ Je 29 '64

BRITAIN'S lawn tennis association
Forecast for the ILTF. Sports Illus 20:10 Ja 27 '64

BRITISH
For the British it's odd man in. B. Hollowood. il N Y Times Mag p48-9+ Ja 24 '65
Portrait of Britain in the fat years. il N Y Times Mag p 12+ Ap 28 '63
See also
English

BRITISH actors and actresses. See Actors and actresses; Kemble family

BRITISH aircraft corporation
Battling for new jet trade: Douglas DC-9 to counter Britain's BAC-111. il Bsns W p52+ Mr 23 '63
British jet out in front; short-range jet field. il Bsns W p26 Jl 27 '63
New BAC 111 version proposed; production rate increases. il Aviation W 81:38-41 S 7 '64

BRITISH amateur golf tournament. See Golf—Tournaments

BRITISH artificial satellites. See Artificial satellites, British

BRITISH association for the advancement of science
British association for the advancement of science; report of annual meeting. C. D. Leake. Science 142:688-9 N 8 '63

BRITISH automobiles. See Automobiles, Foreign

BRITISH aviators. See Air pilots

BRITISH book centre, New York
British book centre sale grosses $5000. Pub W 186:83 Jl 6 '64
Retail expansion at the British book centre. il Pub W 185:54-5 My 18 '64

BRITISH broadcasting corporation
BBC-2; new network. Newsweek 63:102 Ap 27 '64
Demned elusive. . . BBC-TV interview with G. Bidault. il Newsweek 61:48+ Mr 18 '63
Goldie's gang. Newsweek 61:86 Ap 29 '63
Onward and upward with the arts: Third programme. V. Mehta. New Yorker 39:98+ My 18 '63
Third channel for British telly; Independent television. A. Carthew. il N Y Times Mag p 13+ Mr 29 '64

BRITISH CAMEROONS. See Cameroons, British

BRITISH COLUMBIA
See also
Columbia River
Harrison Lake
Vancouver Island
Victoria

Description and travel

From Oroville to Keremeos. il Sunset 133:21 Jl '64

Industries

Timber rush. il Fortune 70:71-2+ N '64

Parks and reserves

Assiniboine pack trip. E. A. Bauer. il Field & S 68:29-31 F '64

Politics and government

Wacky like a fox. il Newsweek 64:68-9 O 12 '64

BRITISH COMMONWEALTH. See Commonwealth of nations

BRITISH cookery. See Cookery, English

BRITISH council of churches
One flock, no shepherd; Christian case for abstinence from sexual intercourse before marriage. America 110:784 Je 6 '64

BRITISH economic assistance. See Economic assistance, British

BRITISH European airways corporation
BEA shows loss for fiscal year, links deficit to social services. Aviation W 79:30 S 2 '63

BRITISH Ford. See Ford motor company, limited, Dagenham, England

BRITISH GUIANA
Calling for help. Time 81:22 Je 21 '63
Dubious charge. Nation 197:171 S 28 '63
Open season on Indians. Newsweek 62:47 Jl 15 '63
Race war. Time 83:34+ Je 5 '64
See also
Communism—British Guiana
Elections—British Guiana
Strikes—British Guiana
United Nations—British Guiana

Commerce

Gimpex way; Guiana import-export corp. Time 82:55 O 4 '63

Labor policy

British Guiana strike settlement. Mo Labor R 86:1069-70 S '63

Politics and government

Admission of failure; Cheddi Jagan's agricultural workers' union. Time 84:29 Ag 14 '64
Atlantic report. Atlan 214:18+ Jl '64
British Guiana: another Cuba in the making? E. Lyons. il Read Digest 82:118-23 Ap '63
Can Jagan hold on? C. C. Moskos, jr. New Repub 150:10-11 Mr 21 '64
Cheddi against the field. il Time 84:44 N 27 '64
Dentist at work. il Newsweek 62:59 S 23 '63
Husband & wife team. il Time 81:27 My 3 '63
Jagan must resign! Newsweek 61:66 Je 24 '63
Jagan thwarted again. Newsweek 62:64 N 11 '63
Jagan's future. New Repub 149:10 N 16 '63
Janet's challenge. il Newsweek 63:58 Je 15 '64
Making chaos. il Newsweek 63:52 My 11 '64
Nearness to civil war. Time 82:43 Jl 12 '63
New boss: Sir Richard Luyt assumes emergency power. il Time 83:36 Je 26 '64
Picking up the pieces. Newsweek 62:49 Jl 22 '63
Politics of violence. Newsweek 63:60-1 Je 8 '64

BRITISH GUIANA—Politics and government—*Continued*
Prelude to independence. T. E. M. McKitterick. il Nation 197:179-81 S 28 '63
Record straightening? Newsweek 61:46 Ap 29 '63
Seething land; with report by J. Barnes. il Newsweek 62:33-4 Jl 1 '63
Sir Richard's coup. Newsweek 63:50 Je 29 '64
Stoning the prime minister. il Time 81:42 Je 14 '63
Strike goes on. Newsweek 61:52 My 27 '63
Terror in the sugar cane. Time 83:42 Mr 13 '64
Tie that binds; Forbes Burnham sworn in as premier. il Newsweek 64:32 D 28 '64
With love from London. New Repub 149:9 Jl 13 '63
Working to divide. Time 83:48 Je 12 '64

Race problems

Politics of violence. Newsweek 63:60-1 Je 8 '64
Red's own race war in Guiana: signs of another Congo. il U S News 56:60-1 Je 15 '64
Shaky truce in a race war. il U S News 55:52 Jl 22 '63

Riots

Letter from the publisher; experience of Time's correspondent M. Garcia. B. M. Auer. Time 84:25 N 27 '64

BRITISH HONDURAS
British Honduras, delightful. il Sunset 131:22+ D '63
Promise of self-government. il Time 82:32 Ag 9 '63
See also
Fishing—British Honduras
BRITISH humor. See Humor, English
BRITISH international drag festival. See Automobile racing
BRITISH labor party. See Labor party (Great Britain)
BRITISH library association. See Library association
BRITISH military assistance. See Military assistance, British
BRITISH money. See Money—Great Britain
BRITISH motor corporation
Britain's auto giant goes into top gear. il Bsns W p 124+ Mr 9 '63
BRITISH museum
Book thieves operate on national levels. Library J 88:4186 N 1 '63
British museum bill. J. Wakeman. il Wilson Lib Bul 37:782-5+ My '63
BRITISH musicians. See Musicians, English
BRITISH national bibliography
Book in hand: subject specialization, interregional cooperation. E. Moon. Library J 89:3704+ O 1 '64
BRITISH national theatre. See Theater—Great Britain
BRITISH national union of teachers. See Teachers unions
BRITISH NORTH BORNEO. See North Borneo
BRITISH Open. See Golf—Tournaments
BRITISH overseas airways corporation
Amery nearing VC.10 decision. Aviation W 81:34 Jl 13 '64
Amery reshuffles BOAC board; deputy chairman plans to resign. Aviation W 79:41 D 9 '63
British carriers to form Jamaican airline. J. R. Ashlock. Aviation W 78:40 Mr 18 '63
BOAC deficit climbs to $215.6 million. Aviation W 79:43 O 28 '63
BOAC has $253-million deficit. Aviation W 81:48 N 9 '64
BOAC presses for government decisions on routes, cargo jets. Aviation W 81:32 Ag 3 '64
BOAC staff cut scored by Labor party. H. J. Coleman. Aviation W 81:36 O 12 '64
BOAC to drop NY-San Francisco route after review of services. J. W. Carter. Aviation W 81:32 S 28 '64
BOAC to reduce fleet, cut staff by 800-900. Aviation W 78:41 My 13 '63
BOAC VC.10 fight ends in compromise. L. L. Doty. Aviation W 81:26 Jl 27 '64
Financial plight is major obstacle confronting new BOAC chairman. H. J. Coleman. Aviation W 79:39-40 D 2 '63
Flying under pressure. il Time 84:61 Jl 31 '64
Let's travel around the world. il Mlle 56:66+ F '63
Mixture that pains a state-run airline. il Bsns W p78-80 Je 15 '63
Parliamentary unit says BOAC should get VC.10 compensation. H. J. Coleman. Aviation W 80:28 Je 29 '64
Piloting BOAC out of the storm; revising route structure. il Bsns W p 124+ S 19 '64

BRITISH painting. See Painting, British
BRITISH poetry. See English poetry
BRITISH portraits. See Portraits, British
BRITISH posters. See Posters
BRITISH press. See Newspapers—Great Britain
BRITISH press council. See Newspapers—Great Britain
BRITISH racing motors. See Automobile industry and trade—Great Britain
BRITISH railways board
New blow to the chin; resignation of chairman. Time 85:66 Ja 1 '65
BRITISH royal ballet. See Royal ballet, Great Britain
BRITISH royal collection. See Art—Private collections
BRITISH scientists. See Scientists, British
BRITISH secretaries. See Secretaries
BRITISH secularism. See Secularism
BRITISH singers. See Singers
BRITISH SOMALILAND. See Somalia
BRITISH SOUTH AFRICA company
Relic of empire; British South Africa's mineral rights in Northern Rhodesia. il Time 84:103 O 9 '64
BRITISH spies. See Spies
BRITISH standards institution
Transliteration of modern Russian. J. Orne il Library J 88:4157-60 N 1 '63
BRITISH students
Rise of the Redbrick; Leicester university. M. Bradbury. il Holiday 34:84-7+ N '63
BRITISH trades union congress. See Trades union congress
BRITISH travel and holidays association
Sceptered isle in holiday humor; Shakespeare's 400th birthday. il Bsns W p 146-8 Ap 18 '64
BRITISH united airways
BUA pushes VC.10 use in Latin America. H. J. Coleman. Aviation W 81:43 O 26 '64
BRITISH VIRGIN ISLANDS
Amphibious resorts; six acres and a sea full of glories: Marina Cay. C. Phinizy. il Sports Illus 20:22-9 Ja 20 '64
BRITT, George
During the blackout. New Repub 148:6-7 Ap 13 '63
BRITTANY
Brittany: dragon country. E. Clark. il Vogue 144:144-7+ O 15 '64
Oyster and the book. E. Clark. Yale R 52:366-72 Mr '63
See also
Locmariaquer, France
BRITTEN, Benjamin
Benjamin Britten; musician of the year; interview, ed. by J. Warrack. por Mus Am 84:20-1+ D '64
Britten looking back; reprint. por Mus Am 84:4-6 F '64
On winning the first Aspen award; address. pors Sat R 47:37-9+ Ag 22 '64

about

Benjamin Britten's Sechs Hölderlin-fragmente. J. Diether. il Am Rec G 30:386-8 Ja '64
Benjamin Britten's War requiem. B. H. Haggin. New Repub 149:28-9 Ag 17 '63
Benjamin Britten's War requiem. E. Salzman. il Hi Fi 13:51-2 Jl '63
Britten at fifty, a protean composer. C. Reid. il pors N Y Times Mag p38-9+ N 17 '63
Britten in the Berkshires. L. Chapin. il Mus Am 83:30 S '63
Britten-san; Aldeburgh première of Curlew River. Time 83:72 Je 26 '64
Britten's War requiem. I. Kolodin. por Sat R 46:45-6 My 25 '63
Bundle for Britten; Aspen award. A. Young. il por Mus Am 84:18-19 S '64
Fresh life for an old genre. J. Diether. il Am Rec G 31:292-5 D '64
From London, Britten's overpowering War requiem. J. Diether. il por Am Rec G 29:916-19+ Ag '63
High honor for a shy genius. T. Green. il pors Life 57:41-2 Ag 7 '64
In the call of the cuckoo. por Time 82:39 D 20 '63
Midsummer night's dream. Criticism
New Yorker 39:99-100 My 4 '63
Sat R 46:67+ My 11 '63
Music. B. Boretz. Nation 197:334-5 N 16 '63
Music to my ears: Britten's War requiem at Tanglewood. I. Kolodin. Sat R 46:35 Ag 10 '63

BRITTEN Benjamin—about—*Continued*
Musical events; Britten's War requiem, performed by Boston symphony. W. Sargeant. New Yorker 39:173-4 N 2 '63
Notes from abroad; Britten's Requiem. C. Reid. por Hi Fi 13:18+ Ap '63
On records; War requiem. por Opera N 28:34 D 7 '63
Operas of Britten. D. Mitchell. il por Mus Am 84:22-5+ D '64

BRITTEN, E. J.
Chromosome number of rose clover, trifolium hirtum. bibliog Science 142:401-2 O 18 '63

BRITTEN, R. J.
Complementary strand association between nucleic acids and nucleic acid gels. bibliog Science 142:963-5 N 15 '63

BRITTON, Nan
Four mysteries of Warren Harding. F. Russell. il por Am Heritage 14:4-9+ Ap '63

BRITTON, Wright
Anchoring tips. Motor B 112:132 Jl; 111 Ag; 125 S; 115 O '63; 113:256 Ja '64
Anchors and anchoring: basic principles. Motor B 111:48-9+ My '63
Boats, boatyards and yachtsmen. Motor B 112:30-1+ O '63
Care for sails and metalwork now! Motor B 112:28+ O '63
Delight around Denmark. Motor B 111:90-2+ F; 126+ Mr '63

BRIZOLA, Leonel
Brizola under attack. Time 82:23 Jl 19 '63
Revolution in Brazil, by I. L. Horowitz. Review
Nat R 16:949-51 N 3 '64. J. W. F. Dulles
Unmissing man. il por Time 83:48 My 15 '64

BROADBENT, Elizabeth
Advice; poem. Horn Bk 39:331 Je '63
Wind-chaser; poem. Horn Bk 40:33 F '64

BROADCASTING companies. See Radio broadcasting; Television broadcasting

BROADWAY, New York (theater district) See New York (city)—Theater

BROADWAY actors and actresses. See Actors and actresses

BROADWAY spectaculars. See Electric signs

BROCINER, Victor
Loudspeakers for transistor amplifiers. Electr World 71:42-4+ Ja '64

BROCK, Carol
Hostess notebook. See issues of Good housekeeping

BROCK, H. I.
Seven lively limericks. Read Digest 84:242C Je '64

BROCK, Lou
Player of the week; Cubs outfielder. por Sports Illus 21:115 S 21 '64

BROCK, Stanley E.
Make like an Indian. Outdoor Life 133:40-3+ Je '64
Poppy was a real hunting dog. Outdoor Life 133:36-9+ Ja '64

BROCK, Thomas D.
Knots in leucothrix mucor. bibliog Science 144:870-2 My 15 '64
—and Wooley, S. O.
Streptomycin as an antiviral agent: mode of action. bibliog Science 141:1065-7 S 13 '63

BROCKEL, Harry C.
Today's port, a trade and transport hub. Ann Am Acad 345:95-102 Ja '63

BROCKTON, Mass. public library
Birchers denied access to Massachusetts library. Library J 88:2462 Je 15 '63

BROCKWAY, Allan R.
Modern abolitionists. Christian Cent 81:1464 N 25 '64

BRODA, Engelbert
When exchange is not really exchange. Bul Atomic Sci 20:23-5 N '64

BRODA, Hal
Last of the great Packards. Motor T 16:74-5 Mr '64

BRODE, Wallace R.
Approaching ceilings in the supply of scientific manpower; excerpts from address, February 19, 1963. bibliog Science 143:313-24 Ja 24 '64

BRODER, David S.
Able and willing Eugene McCarthy. New Repub 150:8-9 Je 20 '64
Great speeches aren't necessarily good politics. N Y Times Mag p7+ Mr 29 '64
Men behind the men who—. N Y Times Mag p 15+ Ja 5 '64
Triple-H brand on the vice-presidency. N Y Times Mag p30-1+ D 6 '64
What makes a great senator? N Y Times Mag p 15+ Je 14 '64
What's the best road to the White House? N Y Times Mag p28+ S 22 '63
Why the candidates are targets for mudslingers. N Y Times Mag p 19+ S 27 '64

BRODER, George, and Weil, M. H.
Excess lactate: an index of reversibility of shock in human patients. bibliog Science 143:1457-9 Mr 27 '64

BRODER, Nathan
Cosi comes again, with wonderful things. Hi Fi 13:55-6 My '63
Lovely bits, but not by Bach. Hi Fi 13:72 F '63
Mozart; five different views, and all faithful. Hi Fi 14:69-70 Ap '64
Mozart's horn concertos thrice recorded. Hi Fi 14:92 N '64

BRODERICK, Dorothy M.
Children's libraries. Wilson Lib Bul 38:209 O '63
I may, I might, I must; address, May 1962. por Library J 88:507-10 F 1 '63
New provincialism. Library J 89:4121-2 O 15 '64
On misplaced devotion. Library J 90:314-15 Ja 15 '65
Second letter to sports writers. Library J 89:4608-9 N 15 '64
Toward a new formula. por Library J 89:4972-5 D 15 '64

BRODERSON, Morris
That heavy secret; exhibition at Manhattan's Downtown gallery. il Time 81:56 Mr 1 '63

BRODIAEA uniflora. See Spring star flowers

BRODIE, Bernard
What price conventional capabilities in Europe? Reporter 28:25-9+ My 23 '63

BRODIE, David A. and Marshall, R. W.
Gastric content of fasted primates: a survey. bibliog Science 141:174-5 Jl 12 '63

BRODIE, Fawn M.
Hidden, the unknowable, the unthinkable. Horizon 5:110-17 Jl '63

BRODIE, Israel
Heretical rabbi. por Newsweek 63:66 My 18 '64

BRODKEY, Harold
Abundant dreamer; story. New Yorker 39:58-64 N 23 '63
Well-regulated impulse; story. Esquire 62:86-9 O '64
Winter; poem. New Yorker 40:110 F 22 '64

BRODOVITCH, Alexey
Unforgettable. Pop Phot 54:84-5 Je '64

about

Critic's choice. B. Downes. il Pop Phot 55:64-5 Ag '64

BRODSKY, Jack
Cleopatra papers; excerpts. por Esquire 60:33-7+ Ag '63

BRODSKY, Joseph
Case against Brodsky. Time 84:43 Jl 3 '64
Trial of a poet. Newsweek 64:34+ S 14 '64

BRODY, Stuart, and Yanofsky, Charles
Independent action of allele-specific suppressor mutations. bibliog Science 145:399-400 Jl 24 '64

BRODY, Thomas C.
Baseball. Sports Illus 18:50-2 F 18; 65-6 Ap 15 '63
Basketball. Sports Illus 20:104-5 Ap 13 '64
College football. Sports Illus 21:54-5 N 2; 65-6 N 16; 68+ N 23; 58-60 D 14 '64
Hockey. Sports Illus 20:56+ Mr 30; 89-90+ My 4 '64
Pro football scouting reports. Sports Illus 19:64-8 S 9 '63
Rowing. Sports Illus 18:50+ Je 3 '63; 21:53-4 Jl 6 '64
Track. Sports Illus 20:68-9 Mr 16 '64
Track & field (title varies) Sports Illus 20:68-9 Mr 16; 21:68-9 Ag 17 '64

BROECKER, Wallace
Radiocarbon dating: a case against the proposed link between river mollusks and soil humus. bibliog Science 143:596-7 F 7 '64
—See Richards, H. G. jt. auth.

BROEDERBOND (League of brothers)
Blood brothers. Newsweek 62:65 D 9 '63

BROEDLING, W. E.
Fruit of Jove. Horticulture 41:69 F '63

BROEG, Robert
(ed) See Musial, S. Man behind The Man

BROFFLE, Robert W.
New maintenance center brings order out of chaos. Am City 79:93-5 O '64

BROGAN, Colm
At home with Sir Alec. Nat R 15:567-8 D 31 '63
Britain's scandalous spy case. Nat R 14:195-6+ Mr 12 '63
Letter from London. Nat R 16:1015-16+ N 17 '64
Lord Beaverbrook, R.I.P. Nat R 16:722-4 Ag 25 '64
Low life above stairs. Nat R 16:153-5 F 25 '64
Profumo affair. Nat R 14:528-9+ Jl 2 '63

BROGAN, Colm—*Continued*
Ten days that shook the Exchequer. Nat R 17:57-8 Ja 26 '65
View of a Goldwater administration from abroad. Nat R 16:595-7 Jl 14 '64

BROGAN, D. W.
American personality; excerpt from American aspects. Sat R 48:34-5 Ja 2 '65
Blessing in disguise. America 108:262-3+ F 23 '63
Europe nervously watches our election. N Y Times Mag p 15+ O 4 '64
Fat boy of England. Harper 226:80-1 Ap '63
Highest office; excerpt from American aspects. Am Heritage 15:4-9 Ag '64

BROGAN, Denis
He also served. Sat R 47:33-4 Mr 7 '64

BROGAN, Hugh
Britain in the 'sixties: a rejoinder. Yale R 53:149-60 O '63

BROGDON, Wallace M. and Koelsche, C. L.
Science education programs in Georgia high schools. Sch & Soc 91:195-7 Ap 20 '63

BROIDO, A.
Surviving fire effects of nuclear detonations. Bul Atomic Sci 19:20-3 Mr '63
—and Nelson, M. A.
Ash content: its effect on combustion of corn plants. bibliog Science 146:652-3 O 30 '64

BROILERS, Electric. See Electric broilers

BROILING
Bonus benefits of broiler and oven. B. G. Wadsworth. il Parents Mag 39:34 Mr '64
Broiling, grilling and barbecuing. il House & Gard 125:204-8 My '64
These tasty recipes will make you an outdoor grill expert. G. Maddox. il Todays Health 42:24-9 My '64

BROKAW, Arthur T.
Isolating the causes of infiltration. pors Am City 79:80-1 D '64

BROKAW, C. J. and Wright, Leigh
Bending waves of the posterior flagellum of ceratium. bibliog Science 142:1169-70 N 29 '63

BROKEN bones. See Fractures

BROKERS
Breathing spell on SEC action. Bsns W p 170+ Ap 20 '63
Broker's fastest messengers. il Bsns W p83-4+ O 10 '64
Brokers look to cut their own loan costs. il Bsns W p72+ D 26 '64
Brokers seek right to go public. Bsns W p 166 S 26 '64
Housekeepers; practices of brokerage firms. Fortune 69:242+ Ap '64
New controls for brokers? U S News 54:115-16 My 13 '63
No hostility in Securities report. U S News 54:97 Ap 1 '63
Pleasing the ancestors: Tokyo's Nomura securities co. ltd. il Time 81:87-8 Je 21 '63
Sweet deal; Merrill Lynch, Pierce, Fenner & Smith-C. J. Devine & co. merger. il Time 83:93 My 22 '64
What safeguards are there for today's investors? U S News 55:81-2 D 23 '63
Why brokers yearn to merge. Bsns W p78-80 Ag 31 '63
See also
Donaldson, Lufkin and Jenrette, incorporated
Haupt, Ira, and company
Investment banking
Loeb, Carl M. Rhoades and company
Merrill Lynch, Pierce, Fenner and Smith incorporated
Salomon brothers and Hutzler

Advertising

U.S. pitch at British investors stirs the city: Merrill Lynch's advertising. il Bsns W p 134+ Ap 13 '63
Wall street looks at its image. G. Lazarus. Sat R 47:84-6 N 14 '64

Commissions

Brokers brace for a squeeze on commissions. Bsns W p96+ Ja 16 '65
Brokers split on fee hike. Bsns W p20 Ja 2 '65

BROKERS, Marriage. See Marriage brokers

BROKERS, Real estate. See Real estate agents

BROMAGE, P. R. and others
Local anesthetic drugs: penetration from the spinal extradural space into the neuraxis. bibliog Science 140:392-4 Ap 26 '63

BROMBERG, Conrad
Defense of Taipei. Criticism
Commonweal 79:663 F 28 '64

BROMELIADS
Bizarre brilliant bromeliads. J. Kramer. il Flower Grower 50:42-4 O '63
Decorative indoor plants: bromeliads. M. H. Drummond. il Horticulture 41:504-5 O '63

BROMINE
Bromine analysis in 5-bromouracil-labeled DNA by X-ray fluorescence. L. Zeitz and R. Lee. bibliog il Science 142:1670-3 D 27 '63
Effect of bromination on the biological activities of transfer RNA of escherichia coli. C. T. Yu and P. C. Zamecnik. bibliog il Science 144:856-9 My 15 '64

BROMODEOXYURIDINE
5-bromodeoxyuridine: effect on myogenesis in vitro. F. Stockdale and others. bibliog il Science 146:533-5 O 23 '64

BROMOPHENOL blue
New dye test reported for severe burn injuries. Sci N L 85:328 My 23 '64

BRONCHITIS
Bronchitis or emphysema? Sci N L 84:211 O 5 '63

BRONCO busting. See Rodeos

BRONCOS (football club) See Football clubs

BRONIAREK, Zygmunt
Communist at the White House. pors Sat Eve Post 237:62-3 My 2 '64

BRONK, J. Ramsey
Thyroid hormones: control of terminal oxidation. bibliog Science 141:816-18 Ag 30 '63

BRONOWSKI, J.
Abacus and the rose; a dialogue after Galileo. Nation 198:4-17 Ja 4 '64
Biography of an atom and the universe. N Y Times Mag p 19+ O 13 '63; Same abr. with title Amazing biography of an atom. Read Digest 84:133-6 Ja '64
Books. Sci Am 208:169-70+ Je '63; 210:130+ Je '64
Clock paradox; with biographical sketch. Sci Am 208:34, 134-6+ bibliog(p 186) F '63

BRONSON, F. H. See Marsden, H. M. jt. auth.

BRONSTON, Samuel
Brain in Spain. il por Time 82:57 Jl 12 '63

BRONTË, Emily
Wuthering Heights; dramatization. See Olfson, L.

BRONTËS (dramatic reading) See Dramatic readings

BRONX, N.Y.
Good-by to the Bronx. P. S. Beagle. Holiday 36:96-7+ D '64
Outdoors in the city's shadow; Riverdale. H. Williams. il Natur Hist 72:32-41 My '63

BRONX high school of science. See New York (city)—Education

BRONX zoo. See New York zoological park

BRONZE
See also
Bronzes

BRONZE age
Bronze age seen in granite. H. Arbman. il Natur Hist 73:36-43 N '64

BRONZE doors. See Doors

BRONZE founding
Craft of bronze casting. L. Campbell and M. Millikan. il Craft Horiz 23:26-33+ Ja '63
University bronze foundry; University of Wyoming. R. I. Russin. il Am Artist 27:46-51+ D '63
Unwearying bronze. M. Ayrton. il Horizon 7:16-37 Wint '65

BRONZES
Africa: the face behind the mask. B. Davidson. il Horizon 5:48-51 Mr '63
Bronze-age treasures discovered in China. T. W. Ouyang. il Art N 63:40-1 Ja '65
Bronze mounts and a new label. B. Ginsburg. il Antiques 83:459 Ap '63
Bronzes of Luristan. B. Goldman. il Natur Hist 73:12-21 My '64
English bronze wool weights. J. P. Hudson. il Antiques 84:691-3 D '63
Great Luristan mystery; Louvre exhibition. P. Amiet. il Art N 62:24-6+ Ap '63
René Joffroy and the Vix krater. il Horizon 7:2-3 Wint '65
Royal ease along the Niger; Tsoede bronzes. W. Fagg. il Horizon 5:51 Mr '63
Tsin Ning pot. J. Brzostoski. il Craft Horiz 24:34-5 Ja '64
Unwearying bronze. M. Ayrton. il Horizon 7:16-37 Wint '65
See also
Bronze founding

Exhibitions

Introducing the sculpture of George Spaventa. F. O'Hara. il Art N 63:44-7 Ap '64

BROOK-SHEPHERD, Gordon
Pursuit of guilt; Germany's final roundup of war criminals. Atlan 214:76-80 S '64
Right honourable foreign secretary. Reporter 29:31-3 Jl 18 '63
(ed) See Walker, P. G. Labour's shadow diplomacy
BROOK trout. See Trout
BROOKE, Bissell
Mr Washington and laughter. Hobbies 68:28 Mr '63
BROOKE, Charles Frederick Tucker
William to Tucker to Jess. J. Shera. Wilson Lib Bul 38:677 Ap '64
BROOKE, Dinah
Letter; story. New Yorker 40:52-7 N 7 '64
BROOKE, Edward W.
Brooke of Massachusetts; a Negro governor on Beacon Hill? E. R. F. Sheehan. por Harper 228:41-7 Je '64
Negro political progress in New England. A. Morrison. pors Ebony 18:26-8 O '63
BROOKE, John Mercer
Ordeal of the Kanrin Maru; with editorial comment. E. V. Warinner. il Am Heritage 14:95-7 Ag '63
BROOKE, Rupert
Ethereal barrel organ. il Newsweek 64:78 Ag 31 '64
Rupert Brooke, by C. Hassall. Review
Commonweal 80:642-3 S 18 '64. S. Hynes
Nat R 16:776+ S 8 '64. S. Leslie
New Yorker 40:233-8+ O 10 '64. M. Panter-Downes
BROOKES, William Penny
Baron de Coubertin, indeed! Sports Illus 21:16 N 9 '64
BROOKHAVEN, N.Y.
Mixed bag at Suffolk; Suffolk lodge game preserve at Brookhaven, L. I. A. MacBain. il Field & S 68:160+ My '63
BROOKHAVEN national laboratory
Omega minus. New Yorker 40:39-40 Mr 7 '64
Omega-minus experiment. W. B. Fowler and N. P. Samios. il Sci Am 211:36-45 O '64
Our far-flung correspondents; CERN (Conseil européen pour la recherche nucléaire) J. Bernstein. New Yorker 40:164+ D 12 '64
BROOKING, Walter J. and Mahar, M. H.
Libraries for technical education programs. bibliog Sch Life 47:9-13 O '64
BROOKINGS institution
Two more plans for aid to dollar. U S News 55:103 Ag 5 '63
BROOKLINE country club course. See Golf courses
BROOKLYN
Beach, Bohemia, barracks; Brooklyn. D. Boroff. il N Y Times Mag p64+ S 29 '63
Pad in Brooklyn Heights; Brooklyn's Brook farm. O. Evans. Nation 199:15-16 Jl 13 '64

Churches

Rebel in a Brooklyn pulpit. S. Castan. il Look 27:59-60+ Mr 26 '63

City planning

Brooklyn to get a town center. il Am City 79:78 Ja '64

Crime

As violence grows in a big city; radio-car patrols of Hasidic Jews. il U S News 56:6 Je 8 '64
Citizen crimebusters, one answer to city violence; Jewish citizens' patrol force. il U S News 57:62-4 Jl 13 '64
Maccabees and the Mau Mau. Nat R 16:479 Je 16 '64
Maccabees ride again; Hasidic Jews patrol Crown Heights. A. G. Aronowitz. il Sat Eve Post 237:32+ Je 27 '64
Only in Brooklyn; Hasidic Jewish patrols in Crown Heights. il Newsweek 63:52 Je 8 '64
Reporter at large; girls' gang in Brownsville section of east Brooklyn. R. Rice. il New Yorker 39:153-4+ O 19 '63

Description

Marianne Moore's Brooklyn. P. Coffin. il Look 27:54f+ My 7 '63

Education

Report recommends more cooperation among Brooklyn's academic libraries. Library J 88:3810 O 15 '63

Music

Brooklyn bonanza. F. Stevenson. Opera N 29:31 D 26 '64
Brooklyn Heights. F. Stevenson. Opera N 28:25 S 28 '63
Salmaggi's stand. W. A. Storrer. Opera N 28:25 My 2 '64
See also
Brooklyn academy of music
Brooklyn philharmonia

Negroes

Bedford-Stuyvesant. F. C. Shapiro. New Yorker 40:23-6 Ag 1 '64
Through a black man's eyes; ed. by E. Dunbar. G. Starks. il Look 27:31-5 D 17 '63
BROOKLYN academy of music
Great opera houses. Q. Eaton. il Opera N 29:28-33 Ja 9 '65
BROOKLYN botanic garden
Garden? Japanese garden, Ryoanji. New Yorker 39:27-9 S 7 '63
Gardeners under glass. M. A. Guitar. il N Y Times Mag p62+ My 12 '63
Japan is nearer than you think! photographs. M. Perry. Flower Grower 50:26-7 Je '63
BROOKLYN children's museum
Curators a-borning; junior curators. il N Y Times Mag p68 My 26 '63
They dig for history. il Parents Mag 39:46-7 Jl '64
BROOKLYN college

Library

College library recruits with an exhibit and a symposium. R. Z. Sellers. Library J 88:1105-7 Mr 15 '63
BROOKLYN museum
Jan Martense Schenck house in the Brooklyn museum. M. D. Schwartz. il Antiques 85:421-8 Ap '64
BROOKLYN navy yard. See Navy yards and naval stations
BROOKLYN philharmonia
Orchestra grows in Brooklyn. S. Landau. Mus Am 84:56-7 Jl '64
BROOKLYN public library
Brooklyn pl spurs registration with help of NYC board of educ. Library J 89:338 Ja 15 '64
Library service to neighborhood areas; summary of address. F. R. St John. Wilson Lib Bul 37:743 My '63

Branches

Brooklyn public library branches suffer attacks of vandalism. il Library J 89:1573-4 Ap 1 '64
Brownsville children's library. S. G. Walton. Horn Bk 40:236 Je '64
Day in Bedford Stuyvesant: Macon branch. E. Moon. il Library J 89:3689-93 O 1 '64
Joiner and goer service to Bedford Stuyvesant area. K. Molz. il Wilson Lib Bul 38:349-51 D '63
BROOKS, Alan
October; poem. Horn Bk 39:531 O '63
BROOKS, Albert Neal Dow
Carter G. Woodson clubs. Negro Hist Bul 26:180 F '63
John Fitzgerald Kennedy. Negro Hist Bul 27:49 D '63
Martyr on Alabama racial tightrope. Negro Hist Bul 26:230-2 My '63
Public education in Washington. Negro Hist Bul 26:196-7 Mr '63
So you like to travel. Negro Hist Bul 26:204+ Mr '63
Why Negro history association? por Negro Hist Bul 27:189 My '64
Words to teachers. por Negro Hist Bul 27:196 My '64

about

Albert N. D. Brooks, editor: 1951-1964. il pors Negro Hist Bul 27:185-203 My '64
BROOKS, Cleanth
History, tragedy, and the imagination in Absalom, Absalom! Yale R 52:340-51 Mr '63
BROOKS, Dana C. See Bizzi, E. jt. auth.
BROOKS, Deton J. Jr
Helping Cook County's culturally deprived adults. NEA J 52:29-30 Ap '63
BROOKS, Donald
New kind of sweater girl. il por Life 56:103+ Ap 10 '64
BROOKS, Earle. See Brooks, R. jt. auth.
BROOKS, Edward M.
Why was last December's lunar eclipse so dark? il Sky & Tel 27:346-8 Je '64
BROOKS, Garnet
Canada's Caruso. il pors Ebony 20:177-8+ D '64
BROOKS, George W.
Case for teachers' unions; excerpt from address. Mo Labor R 87:292 Mr '64
Security of worker institutions. Mo Labor R 86:652-8 Je '63

BROOKS, Gwendolyn
Sight of the horizon; poem. Ebony 18:27 S '63

about

Long reach, strong speech. B. Cutler. Poetry 103:388-9 Mr '64

BROOKS, Helen Fislar
Papa's disappearing Christmas tree. Todays Health 41:30-3+ D '63
When May day was a gay day. Todays Health 41:38-41+ My '63

BROOKS, James
As paint leaves brush; exhibition at Whitney museum of American art. il por Time 81:52-3+ F 8 '63
James Brooks and the abstract inscape. I. H. Sandler. il por Art N 61:30-1+ F '63

BROOKS, James W.
Menace to American hunting? por Outdoor Life 131:34-5+ My '63

BROOKS, Joe
Best all-round trout fly. por Outdoor Life 132:64-5+ O '63
Fisherman's tour of Scotland. pors Outdoor Life 131:28-31+ Ja '63
Fly rod tarpon. por Field & S 67:34-5 F '63
Mighty trout of the Mighty Mo. pors Outdoor Life 131:56-9+ Ap '63
Mystery fish of the sea. Field & S 69:40-1+ Ag '64
River with a past, and a future. Field & S 69:12-14+ O '64
Skaters' waltz. por Field & S 69:60-1+ My '64
Strike of lightning. por Outdoor Life 135:20-3+ Ja '65
Tailers. pors Outdoor Life 132:36-7+ N '63
Those deadly blondes. por Outdoor Life 132:24-7+ D '63
Virgin Islands discovery. Outdoor Life 135:62-3+ F '65
Wahoo are sudden. por Field & S 68:38-9+ N '63
Whitefish magic. Outdoor Life 132:30-1+ Jl '63

BROOKS, John
Annals of business (cont) New Yorker 39:37-8+ Ja 11; 40-160+ N 14 '64
Annals of finance. New Yorker 39:35-6+ Ag 31 '63
Hard sell and the soft sell. Consumer Rep 28:402-3 Ag '63
Look at the paperbacks. Consumer Rep 28:306-7 Je '63; Excerpts. Library J 89:315-17 Ja 15 '64
Most improveablest land. Am Heritage 15:62-3+ O '64
New York in fair time; evaluation of city guide books. Consumer Rep 29:199-201 Ap '64
Onward and upward with the arts. New Yorker 39:41-2+ Je 1 '63
Profiles (cont) New Yorker 39:49-50+ Ap 27 '63
Ways of death. Consumer Rep 29:40-3 Ja '64
What you can't find in paperback. Consumer Rep 29:258-9 My '64

BROOKS, Marta, and Elledge, Eugene
Eye of the octopus. Library J 89:320-1+ Ja 15 '64

BROOKS, Patricia K.
At bay on the beach. Sat R 47:70+ O 10 '64
Booked for travel. Sat R 47:30-1 O 3 '64
Civil war; what cooked? Am Home 66:64+ My '63
Going places, finding things in Madrid. House & Gard 126:32+ D '64
Remains of Spain are mainly a strain. Sat R 46:93+ O 12 '63
Restaurant English. Sat R 47:35 Ap 11 '64
Take me out to the fairgrounds. Sat R 47:86+ Mr 14 '64

BROOKS, Paul
Canyonlands; new national park? Atlan 211:52-7 Mr '63
Congressman Aspinall vs. the people of the United States. Harper 226:60-3 Mr '63
Golden plains of Tanganyika. Horizon 7:80-9 Wint '65
Mexico's California. il Atlan 214:69-73 S '64

BROOKS, Philips
Philips Brooks: spokesman for freedom. J. R. Phillips. por Negro Hist Bul 27:10 O '63

BROOKS, Rhoda, and Brooks, Earle
Ecuador. pors Nat Geog Mag 126:338-45 S '64

BROOKS, Robert M.
Book reviews. America 110:102 Ja 18 '64

BROOKS, Steve
Psychiatrist. il por Time 81:93 Ap 19 '63

BROOKS, T. E.
Hat my mother bought me; story. Seventeen 22:132-3 My '63

BROOKS, Thomas R.
Are demonstrations self-defeating? Commonweal 79:98-100 O 18 '63
Better day for brother Randolph. Reporter 29:23 D 5 '63
Blood brotherhood in Harlem? Commonweal 80:282-3 My 29 '64
Detroit: new model in city hall. Reporter 30:25-7 Ap 9 '64
Domestic peace corps? Commonweal 78:131-3 Ap 26 '63
End to featherbedding? Commonweal 78:301-3 Je 7 '63
Hoffa wins again. Reporter 28:34-5 My 23 '63
Labor backlash? Commonweal 81:93-5 O 16 '64
Labor: the enigma of the unions. Duns R 81:pt2 S135-6+ Je '63
Long, hot summer. Commonweal 80:189-90 My 8 '64
Look ahead to the auto negotiations. Reporter 30:27-9 My 21 '64
Managing your manpower. See issues of Dun's review and modern industry
March of the robots. Duns R 81:40-1+ Ja '63
Mutiny on the Great Lakes. Commonweal 79:278-80 N 29 '63
New York's boycott: what did it prove? Reporter 30:32-4 F 27 '64
Of cars and steel and tottering guideposts. Reporter 31:23-5 D 17 '64
People, vitality and AT&T. Duns R 81:53-5+ Ap '63
Revolt against Hoffa? Commonweal 79:385-6 D 27 '63
Settlement in steel. Commonweal 78:449-52 Jl 26 '63
3M's formula for new products. Duns R 82:32-4+ Ag '63
(ed) See Snyder, J. I. jr. Does automation require a new economy

BROOKS, Van Wyck
Memorial to an American critic; Van Wyck Brooks library memorial fund. H. Bowser. il Sat R 47:24 Mr 28 '64
Obituary
Pub W 183:36 My 13 '63
Van Wyck Brooks: a bibliography. W. Sullivan. Sat R 46:19 My 25 '63
Van Wyck Brooks: a career in retrospect. M. Cowley. il por Sat R 46:17-18+ My 25 '63

BROOKS, William R.
Harvester of the skies. J. Ashbrook. il por Sky & Tel 25:198-9 Ap '63

BROOKS, Win
Strike the young hawk gently; story. Read Digest 83:247-9 N '63

BROOKS, creeks, etc.
Are you a sap for the ribbon cutters? destruction of fishing streams through highway building. A. Grahame. il Outdoor Life 131:10-12+ Je '63; Reply with rejoinder. R. M. Whitton. 132:4+ S '63

BROOKS comet. See Comets

BROOME, Harvey
Broome addresses educators; August 21, 1963. por Liv Wildn 84:45-7 Sum '63
Plans for outdoor recreation. Liv Wildn 82:21-3 Wint '62

BROOMS, Street cleaning. See Street cleaning apparatus

BROPHY, Brigid
Speaking out. por Sat Eve Post 236:10+ N 2 '63

BROPHY, John A. See Leighton, M. M. jt. auth.

BROPHY, Marjorie
Every day is mother's day. See issues of Good housekeeping

BROSIO, Manlio
Letter to President Johnson, October 6, 1964. Dept State Bul 51:673 N 9 '64
President Johnson meets with NATO Secretary General; exchange of toasts at luncheon and remarks on departing from Offutt air force base, September 29, 1964. Dept State Bul 51:583-5 O 26 '64

about

Man who. . . Newsweek 63:44 My 18 '64

BROSNAN, Dennis William
Hell of a different way to run a railroad. H. B. Meyers. il por Fortune 68:100-9+ S '63

BROSNAN, Jim
Fantasy world of baseball. Atlan 213:69-72 Ap '64
Little leaguers have big problems, their parents. Atlan 211:117-20 Mr '63
Longest season. Esquire 59:94-7 Mr '63
Speaking out. por Sat Eve Post 237:8+ My 30 '64

BROSNAN, Jim—*Continued*
This pitcher may need relief. por Sports Illus 20:24-6+ Mr 16 '64
Truth strikes out. C. Cilo. Nation 199:281-2 O 26 '64
BROTH. See Soups
BROTHELS. See Prostitution
BROTHER-in-the-Lord Ora Gumbs: story. See Meserve, N.
BROTHERHOOD of locomotive firemen and enginemen
Beyond the last mile. il Time 82:13-16 Jl 26 '63
Firemen survive cutbacks. Bsns W p 105-6 My 16 '64
BROTHERHOOD of man
Word. V. P. McCorry. America 111:760 D 5 '64
Bibliography
Books for brotherhood; Commonweal 77:564-5; 79:628-30 F 22 '63, F 21 '64
BROTHERHOOD of railway clerks
Rail union makes bid for 12,700 at United; 3,000 are ex-members. Aviation W 78:41 F 11 '63
BROTHERHOOD week
Negro history and the modern Uncle Tom. Negro Hist Bul 27:134-5 Mr '64
BROTHERHOODS, Railroad. See Trade unions—United States
BROTHERHOODS, Religious
See also
Brothers (Catholic)
BROTHERS, Joyce
On being a woman. por Good H 158:30-3 F; 48-50 Mr; 40+ Ap; 52+ My; 62+ Je '64
BROTHERS
Capital brotherhood; photographs. G. Tames. N Y Times Mag p96 My 5 '63
My two sons. Redbook 122:8+ Ja '64
BROTHERS (Catholic)
Only a brother? C. J. McNaspy. America 108:744-5 My 25 '63
BROTHERS and sisters. See Siblings
BROTHERS; story. See Thompson, J.
BROUDY, Harry S. and others
New look at readiness; excerpt from Democracy and excellence in American secondary education. bibliog Sch & Soc 91:424-30 D 28 '63
BROUGH, James
Auction! excerpt. McCalls 90:112-13+ Ap '63
Dog who lives at the Waldorf; story. McCalls 91:128-9 My '64
(ed) See Dionne, A. and others. Dear quints, with love from the quints
(ed) See Dionne, A. and others. We were five
BROUGHER, Linda
Winter thoughts; poem. Horn Bk 40:662 D '64
BROUGHTON, James
Birds of America; poem. Poetry 104:154-5 Je '64
BROUGHTON, T. Robert S.
(comp) Articles and other books received; ancient. See issues of American historical review
BROUGHTON family
Broughton coat-of-arms. H. K. Eilers. il Hobbies 69:120-1+ Ja '65
BROUSSE, Charles
Blonde bond. Time 82:17 D 20 '63
BROUWER, Dirk
Orbits in the solar and stellar systems. Science 146:1602-3 D 18 '64
BROUWER, Paul J.
Power to see ourselves. Harvard Bsns R 42:156-62+ N '64
BROWALLIA
Bow to browallia. F. W. Patch. il Flower Grower 51:30 Je '64
BROWARD COUNTY, Fla.
Cooperative purchasing. A. C. Dobay. il Am City 78:134+ My '63
BROWER, Brock
Brothers Cassini. Esquire 59:61-4+ F '63
Comeback; story. Sat Eve Post 237:52-4 N 28 '64
Flag and I. Esquire 63:67-9+ Ja '65
Last chance for Junior. Sat Eve Post 236:32-3 Jl 27 '63
Long day's monotony of TV. Sat Eve Post 237:76-8 S 26 '64
Man-machines may talk first to Dr Shannon. Vogue 141:88-9+ Ap 15 '63
1939: now that was a World's fair! Esquire 61:61-5+ Ap '64
A saint is a saint, you know. Sat Eve Post 237:22-3 D 5 '64
Vulgarization of American demonology. Esquire 61:94-9+ Je '64
BROWER, Charles H.
How to be a failure. Read Digest 86:144-5 Ja '65
Let's dare to be square. Read Digest 82: 49-51 Ap '63
Squares America needs; reprint. por U S News 56:70-2 Ap 6 '64
BROWER, Lincoln Pierson, and others
Mimicry: differential advantage of color patterns in the natural environment. bibliog Science 144:183-5 Ap 10 '64
BROWERE, John Henri Isaac
Day Jefferson got plastered. D. B. Webster, jr. il Am Heritage 14:24-7 Je '63
BROWN, Aaron H.
It's bogus; but is it featherbedding? (cont) Nat R 14:127 F 12 '63
BROWN, Alan A.
Holiday quiz. Holiday 34:117 S '63
BROWN, Alphonse Theo
Poet and the boxer. R. Cantwell; G. Peeters. il Sports Illus 20:62-72 Mr 2 '64
BROWN, Andrew H.
Sweden, quiet workshop for the world. Nat Geog Mag 123:451-91 Ap '63
BROWN, Arlo, Jr
Crash program for parkland acquisition. por Recreation 57:397-9 O '64
BROWN, Arthur Whitten
Flight into the unknown. J. Stewart-Gordon. il por Read Digest 82:120-5 Mr '63
BROWN, Aubrey N. Jr
Presbyterians, U.S: enroute to broader concerns. Christian Cent 80:1577-80 D 18 '63
BROWN, B. Frank
Answer to dropouts; the nongraded high school. Atlan 214:86-90 N '64
Charles Keller: impassioned advocate. Sat R 46:72+ N 16 '63
Cape Kennedy's high school for sky-high learning. B. Asbell. il PTA Mag 58:14-16 Ja '64
Melbourne: ungraded high. H. Langer. il por Sr Schol 83:18T-19T O 4 '63
BROWN, Beth
Responsibilities of a dog owner. Bet Hom & Gard 42:117 My '64
When you choose a cat. Bet Hom & Gard 42:144 N '64
BROWN, Betty B.
Success with rhododendrons. Flower Grower 51:37+ F '64
BROWN, Betty C.
Automation will dominate Chicago MPDFA show. Pop Phot 54:74-7+ Ap '64
Democrats and 389 photographers. il Pop Phot 55:140-1+ D '64
Louis Fabian Bachrach dies in Boston at age of eighty-two. Pop Phot 53:36+ N '63
BROWN, Bob W. See Buchanan, H. A. jt. auth.
BROWN, Burke L. and Fuerst, Robert
Ethylene oxide sterilization of tissue culture media. bibliog Science 142:1654-5 D 27 '63
BROWN, Carl
Nation of faith and works. Am For 69:11 Je '63
BROWN, Carlton
What's new in records. See issues of Redbook
BROWN, Carol Fradkin
Eye, ear, um, erica, zing! king; poem. Esquire 61:119 Mr '64
BROWN, Cecil
(ed) See Eisenhower, D. D. As Ike sees the candidates now
BROWN, Charles A.
Lloyd Leftwich, Alabama state senator. bibliog Negro Hist Bul 26:161-2 F '63
Reconstruction legislators in Alabama. bibliog Negro Hist Bul 26:198-200 Mr '63
William Hooper Councill; Alabama legislator, editor and lawyer. bibliog Negro Hist Bul 26:171-2 F '63
BROWN, Charles E.
Schools in Newton; experiment in flexibility. Atlan 214:74-8 O '64
This task is ours; excerpts from address, April 5, 1963. Library J 88:4434-6 N 15 '63
BROWN, Clarence J.
Excerpt from debate, April 7, 1964. Cong Digest 43:177+ Je '64
BROWN, Courtney C.
Last say on the company way. Sat R 47:55 F 22 '64
about
Business school with a rising star. il por Bsns W p56-60+ My 2 '64
BROWN, Dale W.
Baugo and Zagorsk: extremes in encounter. Christian Cent 81:52+ Ja 8 '64
BROWN, Darrell F.
New steelhead thrills. por Outdoor Life 134: 42-3 D '64
BROWN, Dolores
Wild wolf hunt. Outdoor Life 134:17-19+ D '64

BROWN, Dorothy Foster
Button collecting. See issues of Hobbies
BROWN, Earle
Feldman and Brown. Mus Am 83:33-4 N '63
BROWN, Edmund Gerald Pat
How to put the states back in business. Harper 229:98+ S '64

about

Campaign against death. J. Star. il Look 27:29 My 7 '63
Just a term of endearment. Time 81:22 Je 7 '63
Pat Brown: LBJ's '64 running mate? il por U S News 55:9 D 30 '63
BROWN, Elmer
Democracy's way at the ITU. por Bsns W p78+ Je 6 '64
BROWN, Esther Lucile
Meeting patients' psychosocial needs in the general hospital. Ann Am Acad 346:117-25 Mr '63
BROWN, George Alfred
Left vs. right in Britain's Labor party. por U S News 54:20 F 18 '63
Non-U Socialist. Newsweek 62:25+ D 30 '63
Search for an heir. il por Newsweek 61:33+ F 4 '63
BROWN, George M. and Levy, H. A.
Sucrose: precise determination of crystal and molecular structure by neutron diffraction. bibliog Science 141:921-3 S 6 '63
BROWN, Georgia
Sweet Lillian Klot. Newsweek 61:75 Ap 1 '63
BROWN, Gifford
News of the week in review. New Yorker 39:66+ Ja 4 '64
BROWN, Gordon C. and others
Rubella antibodies in human serum: detection by the indirect fluorescent-antibody technique. bibliog Science 145:943-5 Ag 28 '64
BROWN, Gregory N.
Cesium in liriodendron and other woody species: organic bonding sites. bibliog Science 143:368-9 Ja 24 '64
BROWN, Gwilym S.
College football. Sports Illus 19:54-6 N 11; 77-9 N 25 '63
Golf (cont) Sports Illus 19:42-4 Ag 26; 53 D 16 '63; 20:48-50 F 10; 81-2+ My 18; 21: 84-5 N 23; 59-60+ N 30 '64
Track (title varies) (cont) Sports Illus 18: 38-9+ F 25 '63
Track & field (title varies) (cont) Sports Illus 18:38-9+ F 25 '63; 22:52-4 Ja 18 '65
BROWN, H. Douglas
Gems and minerals. See issues of Hobbies
BROWN, Harold
Brown oversees all military RDT&E. il Miss & Roc 12:80-1+ Mr 25 '63
BROWN, Harold O. J.
Death of God in modern theology. Nat R 16:452-4+ Je 2 '64
BROWN, Harriett B. and Sinnette, E. D.
School library progress for children in a depressed area. bibliog pors ALA Bul 58: 643-7 Jl '64
BROWN, Harrison
Planetary systems associated with main-sequence stars. bibliog Science 145:1177-81 S 11 '64
BROWN, Harry
On an autumn day; poem. Sat R 47:31 Mr 14 '64
BROWN, Helen Evans
Hawaiian cook book. House & Gard 126:103-8 Jl '64
Southwest cook book. House & Gard 124: 129+ Ag '63
BROWN, Helen Gurley
Bosses make lousy lovers. J. Didion. il pors Sat Eve Post 238:34+ Ja 30 '65
Meat loaf, anyone? por Newsweek 64:53 Ag 31 '64
Singular girl's success. S. Alexander. il pors Life 54:60+ Mr 1 '63
What price the single girl? il por Esquire 62:108-9 O '64
BROWN, Ileen C.
Black raspberries for an edible hedge. Horticulture 41:62 F '63
Two good reasons to hedge with blueberries. Flower Grower 52:18 Ja '65
BROWN, Ivor
Critics and creators. Sat R 46:11-13+ Ag 10 '63
How Shakespeare spent the day. Sat R 47: 14-17+ Ap 4 '64
BROWN, J. Bush-. See Bush-Brown, J.
BROWN, J. Douglas
Squeeze on the liberal university. Atlan 213: 84-7 My '64

BROWN, J. Scott
There's nothing like a rose. I. McLendon. il por Pop Gard 15:20-2 F '64
BROWN, James F.
Khrushchev's European allies. New Repub 148:18-20 Mr 30 '63
BROWN, James M. 3d
Interim collection. E. Gaines. il Antiques 84: 592-5 N '63
BROWN, James R.
Citizens for educational freedom. America 110:194-6 F 8 '64
BROWN, Jeff
My life in art: story. New Yorker 39:127-8 My 4 '63
Sidney on skis; story. Sat Eve Post 237:44-51 F 8 '64
Someone has to say something; story. Redbook 121:52-3 Ag '63
BROWN, Jessie L.
Road less traveled by. bibliog f Negro Hist Bul 27:144-5 Mr '64
BROWN, Jimmy, and Cope, Myron
Jimmy Brown's own story. . .football bruisers I've bumped into; excerpts from Off my chest. pors Look 28:104-12+ O 20 '64
Jimmy Brown's own story. . . my case against Paul Brown; excerpts from Off my chest. pors Look 28:62-4+ O 6 '64

about

Brown on Brown. Newsweek 64:62-3 N 16 '64
Controversial Jim Brown. A. Poinsett. il pors Ebony 20:65-6+ D '64
From pigskins to redskins. il pors Life 57:67-8+ S 18 '64
He's the greatest since Jim Thorpe. J. Flynn. il pors Life 55:47-9 O 25 '63
Jimmy, the Giant killer. il Time 82:84 O 25 '63
Knack for running. il pors Time 82:66+ O 4 '63
People are talking about Jim Brown of the Cleveland Browns. il por Vogue 142:122-4 D '63
Plan that worked; Cleveland Browns vs New York Giants. T. Maule. il Sports Illus 19:16-19 O 21 '63
Pro football's mightiest player. A. Poinsett. il pors Ebony 19:32-4+ Ja 64
BROWN, Joe
Annals of medicine. B. Roueché. New Yorker 39:176+ O 12 '63
BROWN, Joe David
Birmingham, Alabama: a city in fear. Sat Eve Post 236:11-19 Mr 2 '63
Dreyfus case. por(p4) Sports Illus 20:62-4+ Mr 30 '64
Governor's happy lady. Sat Eve Post 236: 15-19 Je 22 '63
Kind word for drink. Sat Eve Post 236: 64-6 My 25 '63
Rifle called Daisy. Sports Illus 18:58-64+ Ap 29 '63
Star and sportsman riding a wave. Sports Illus 21:84-6+ O 26 '64
Whooping baron of the prairie. Sports Illus 19:60-2+ N 4 '63
BROWN, John
Five brave Negroes with John Brown at Harpers Ferry. por Negro Hist Bul 27:164-9 Ap '64
John Brown: God's angry man. L. Bennett, jr. il pors Ebony 20:96-8+ D '64
BROWN, John Lott. See Sechzer, J. A. jt. auth.
BROWN, John Mason
Heritage of Edith Hamilton: 1867-1963. Sat R 46:16-17 Je 22 '63
More than 1,001 first nights. Sat R 47:46-8 Ag 29 '64
What's right with the theatre; excerpt from Dramatis personae. Sat R 46:19-21 My 11 '63
BROWN, Jonathan M.
Zurbarán's claims to fame. Art N 63:31-3+ Ja '65
BROWN, Joseph G.
Election of 1864. Hobbies 69:28-30 Ag '64
BROWN, Judith Ellen
What makes you blush? questions and answers. Read Digest 85:53-4 O '64
Why people faint. Todays Health 41:18-19+ Ag '63
BROWN, Karl
Carl Hastings Milam, 1884-1963. Library J 88:3586 O 1 '63
BROWN, Kenneth E. and Obourn, E. S.
Mathematics and science teachers in U.S. high schools; excerpt from report. Sch Life 45:24-5 Ja '63
BROWN, Kenneth H.
Author says he had plenty to yell about. J. R. McDermott. il por Life 55:40+ Ag 16 '63

BROWN, Kenneth H.—*Continued*
Brig. Criticism
Commonweal 78:303-4 Je 7 '63
Life il 55:39 Ag 16 '63
Nation 198:58 Ja 13 '64
New Repub 148:28-9 Je 1 '63
New Yorker 39:57-9 My 25 '63
Newsweek 61:93 My 27 '63
Theatre Arts il 47:11 Jl '63
BROWN, L. H.
Expanding your dairy herd? Suc Farm 61: 38 My '63
BROWN, La Vyrne Hanson
December trees; poem. Am For 69:45 D '63
From Brown County, Indiana; poem. Am For 70:54 S '64
BROWN, Lawrence R.
Parkinson's folly. Nat R 16:163-5 F 25 '64
BROWN, Luther J.
World record flight. il pors Ebony 18:85-6 Ag '63
BROWN, Mackey
Living in tune with time. Sat Eve Post 236:26-7 Mr 30 '63
BROWN, Marcia
Festival in Hawaii. Sat R 46:54 N 9 '63
BROWN, Margery Finn
I wisk you a Merry Christmas; story. Redbook 124:44-5 D '64
Mary; story. Redbook 122:48-9 D '63
O the days of the Kerry dancing; story. Redbook 122:54-5 Mr '64
BROWN, Margery W.
Art classes. Sch Arts 63:24-8 Je '64
BROWN, Marjorie L.
Welter of warts. Christian Cent 81:966 Jl 29 '64
BROWN, Marvin L.
(ed) See Riedesel, F. C. L. V. Baroness on the battlefield
BROWN, Melancthon S. and Mosher, H. S.
Tarichatoxin: isolation and purification. bibliog Science 140:295-6 Ap 19 '63
BROWN, Nancy
Individualists; Mlle's annual Merit awards. il por Mlle 58:72-3 Ja '64
BROWN, Nona B.
Inquiry into the feminine mind. N Y Times Mag p 17+ Ap 12 '64
BROWN, Norman O.
How Hieronymus Bosch and Norman Brown would change the world. T. B. Morgan. il Esquire 59:100-2+ Mr '63
BROWN, Pat. See Brown, E. G. P.
BROWN, Paul
Jimmy Brown's own story. . . my case against Paul Brown; excerpts from Off my chest. J. Brown and M. Cope. il pors Look 28:62-4+ O 6 '64
Team on trial; Cleveland Browns. B. August. il por Sat Eve Post 236:86-8 N 23 '63
BROWN, Paul K. and Wald, George
Visual pigments in single rods and cones of the human retina. bibliog Science 144:45-6+ Ap 3 '64
BROWN, Peter
Banning of Peter Brown. K. N. Carstens. Christian Cent 81:1274 O 14 '64
BROWN, Philip S.
Tempting, colorful drinks of Hawaii. House & Gard 126:100+ Jl '64
BROWN, Mrs Porter
Elects woman to high office; general secretary to its Board of missions. Christian Cent 81:1198 S 30 '64
Methodist missions retooled. B. Thompson. Christian Cent 81:1273 O 14 '64
BROWN, R. Hanbury
Stellar interferometer at Narrabri observatory. Sky & Tel 28:64-9 Ag '64
BROWN, R. Malcolm, Jr, and others
Airborne algae: their abundance and heterogeneity. bibliog Science 143:583-5 F 7 '64
BROWN, Rachel
Summer in Cambridge, Maryland. Horn Bk 40:315-19 Je '64
BROWN, Ray E.
Why hospital costs are rising so fast; interview. por U S News 56:73-5 My 25 '64
BROWN, Raymond E.
Our new translation of the Bible. America 111:601-4 N 14 '64
BROWN, Richard H.
Book buying: who? what? where? when? why? Pub W 185:16-19 My 11 '64
BROWN, Robert
Private. New Yorker 40:27-8 Ja 16 '65
BROWN, Robert L.
City slicker. Field & S 67:10-11 F '63
BROWN, Robert McAfee
Ecumenical conversations. America 108:808-10 Je 1 '63
Ecumenism behind bars. Commonweal 80:600-2 S 4 '64
Open letter to the American bishops. Commonweal 80:411-16 Je 26 '64
Open letter to the New Yorker. Christian Cent 80:956-7 Jl 31 '63
Protestant assessment. Commonweal 79:396-8 D 27 '63
Protestant hopes for the Vatican council. por Look 28:21-7 O 6 '64
Protestant viewpoint (cont) Commonweal 77: 491-2, 596-7, 621; 78:133-5, 369-71; 79:73-5, 165-7, 280-3, 626-7+; 81:14-16, 69-71, 330-1, 442-5 F 1, Mr 1-8, Ap 26, Je 28, O 11, N 1, 29 '63, F 21, S 25, O 9, N 27, D 25 '64
Rock book; Protestant viewpoint. Commonweal 78:395-7 Jl 5 '63
Spotlight on California. Christian Cent 81: 1202-4 S 30 '64
Systematic theology bookshelf. Christian Cent 80:400-2 Mr 27 '63
Voice of the good shepherd; Pope John. Commonweal 78:369-71 Je 28 '63
BROWN, Roderick Haig-. See Haig-Brown, R.
BROWN, Roosevelt
Left tackle. W. N. Wallace. il por N Y Times Mag p 137-41+ N 8 '64
BROWN, Rosellen
Cummington cemetery; poem. Mlle 56:44 F '63
BROWN, Ruth
(comp) SR's check list of current books (title varies) See issues of Saturday review beginning June 1, 1963
(comp) SR's check list of 1963's books on Latin America. Sat R 46:16+ O 12 '63
(comp) SR's check list of scholarly books. Sat R 47:50-1 My 30 '64
BROWN, Sanborn C.
Science's exciting new frontier. Sci Digest 56:83-8 O '64
BROWN, Sandford
Color catches fire. Sat Eve Post 236:74-5 Ag 10 '63
World of play. Sat Eve Post 237:17-21 D 19 '64
BROWN, Seyom
Universal nuclear deterrent force. Bul Atomic Sci 19:20-4 Ap '63
BROWN, Spencer W. and Nur, Uzi
Heterochromatic chromosomes in the coccids. bibliog Science 145:130-6 Jl 10 '64
BROWN, Stanley H.
Golden castles of Troy V. Post. Fortune 71: 154-9+ Ja '65
How to manage a conglomerate making. Fortune 69:154-7+ Ap '64
Magnavox goes its own golden way. Fortune 69:112-15+ F '64
Sperry & Hutchinson's very successful stagnation. Fortune 70:156-9+ N '64
Under Marion Harper's big tent. Fortune 69: 128-32 My '64
What's in it for Eddie, Bob, and Vic? Fortune 70:139-43+ S '64
Who's to blame for Riklis? Riklis? Fortune 68:136-7+ O '63
—See Branstcn, T. R. jt. auth.
BROWN, Stewart A.
Phenolics of higher plants. Science 142:1197-8+ N 29 '63
BROWN, Thomas H. and others
Xenon tetrafluoride: fluorine-19 high-resolution magnetic resonance spectrum. bibliog Science 140:178 Ap 12 '63
BROWN, Tom
Rookies, rookies everywhere, and even JFK is talking. T. C. Brody. por Sports Illus 18:65-6 Ap 15 '63
BROWN, W. Norman
South Asia studies: a history. Ann Am Acad 356:54-62 N '64
BROWN, Walter L.
Radiation belt intensity dispute grows; summary of study presented at meeting of the American physical society; ed. by W. C. Wetmore. Aviation W 78:60-1+ F 4 '63
BROWN, Wenzell
Advice can be dangerous. Writer 78:19-21 Ja '65
BROWN, Sir William Brian Pigott-, 3d bart. See Pigott-Brown, W. B.
BROWN, William Fuller, Jr
Magnetism: a decade of conferences. Science 147:73-4 Ja 1 '65
BROWN bears. See Bears
BROWN fat. See Fat
BROWN sugar. See Sugar
BROWN university, Providence, R.I.
Brown grows the ivy. Newsweek 64:79 O 12 '64
Library
Xerox applications. L. G. Vagianos. Library J 88:1792 My 1 '63
BROWNE, Anthony Montague
Old master; personal secretary to W. Churchill. New Yorker 40:50-1 N 21 '64

BROWNE, Dan
Two islands; story. Atlan 213:91-5 Je '64
BROWNE, Henry J.
Changing city, changing parish? por Cath World 198:170-6 D '63
BROWNE, Peter
They take snapshots in sound. Read Digest 82:151-3+ My '63
BROWNE, R. A.
Buying around stifles development of a healthy Canadian book trade; adaptation of address. Pub W 185:24-8 Je 1 '64
BROWNE, Roger J.
Vendor-relations office. Am City 78:153 O '63
BROWNE, Roland A.
Roses, how to select wisely. Flower Grower 51:32+ F '64
BROWNE, Sir Thomas
Works of Sir Thomas Browne, ed. by G. Keynes. Review
Nation 199:282 O 26 '64. K. Rexroth
BROWNE, W. J.
Canadian renewal. America 110:675-6 My 16 '64
BROWNE-MAYERS, Albert N.
Uses of experience. Sat R 47:24 D 12 '64
BROWNELL, Ann
Letter from Connecticut. Nat R 16:231-2+ Mr 24 '64
BROWNELL, Herbert
Speaking out. por Sat Eve Post 237:10+ Ap 18 '64
BROWNIAN movements
Brownian movement in color photomicrography. H. F. Sassoon and M. H. C. Parsons. Science 139:1285-6 Mr 29 '63
BROWNIE cameras. See Cameras
BROWNIES. See Cake
BROWNIES (club) See Girl scouts
BROWNING, Bill
Montana's Territorial centennial. Travel 121:39-41 Je '64
BROWNING, Carolyn
Masks from mesh. Sch Arts 63:22 Mr '64
BROWNING, Elizabeth (Barrett)
Robert Browning's copy of Aristotle. P. W. Schmidtchen. il Hobbies 68:106+ Ag '63
BROWNING, Grace B.
First year. McCalls 91:218 N '63
BROWNING, James
Weinstock's Donizetti. Opera N 28:36 Ja 18 '64
Yankee diva. Opera N 29:34 D 26 '64
BROWNING, Norma Lee
Why women go wig-happy. Sat Eve Post 236:68-70 F 23 '63
BROWNING, Robert
Browning and Kierkegaard as heirs of Luther. M. W. Hess. Christian Cent 80:799-801 Je 19 '63
Robert Browning's copy of Aristotle. P. W. Schmidtchen. il por Hobbies 68:106+ Ag '63
BROWNING, W. E. jr. See Silverman, M. D. jt. auth.
BROWNLEE, J. L.
Councilmen are smart. Am City 78:105-6 Je '63
BROWNLEE, John
New Manhattan project; address, November 11, 1963. Mus Am 83:162 D '63
BROWNLOW, Cecil
Israel aircraft planning major reshuffle. Aviation W 80:104-5+ Je 15 '64
BROWNS (football club) See Football clubs
BROWNSTEIN, Philip N.
Federal housing agencies encouraging good design. Arch Rec 136:108-9 Ag '64
BROWNSTONES (houses) See New York (city)—Architecture
BROWNSVILLE, Tex.

Education

Reaching students through the arts; Latin American students. Mrs D. Morris. il Sr Schol 84:9T Ap 24 '64
BROWNSVILLE children's library. See Brooklyn public library—Branches
BROWNWOOD, Tex.
Lift-dome auditorium. J. Clary. il Am City 78:100-1 O '63
BROYARD, Anatole
Bachelor; story. New Yorker 40:26-9 Jl 25 '64
BROZEN, Michael
Portrait of a music publisher. Mus Am 83:36 O '63
BRUBACHER, R.
Know when to holler for help. Am City 79:92-3 My '64
BRUBAKER, K. K. See Jacobs, M. E. jt. auth.
BRUCE, David K. E.
Amazing Bruces; the life in London of the American Ambassador and family; with photographs by C. Beaton. Vogue 144:122-9+ S 15 '64
BRUCE, Evangeline (Bell)
Amazing Bruces; the life in London of the American Ambassador and family; with photographs by C. Beaton. Vogue 144:122-9+ S 15 '64
Busy life of the ambassador's wife. il pors Look 27:54-6+ Ag 13 '63
Evangeline Bruce: her listening gaiety. P. de Rothschild. il pors Vogue 144:128-9+ S 15 '64
BRUCE, Harry
Great Lakes labor war. Nation 197:298-300 N 9 '63
BRUCE, Jeanette
Without obligation; story. Redbook 122:60-1 Mr '64
BRUCE, John A. See Shoemaker, W. J. jt. auth.
BRUCE, Lenny
Bruce's trial. por Newsweek 64:76 Jl 20 '64
Comedy of Lenny Bruce. A. Goldman. Commentary 36:312-17 O '63; Discussion. 37:20 F '64
Let's nix the sicknicks. R. Ruark. il por Sat Eve Post 236:38-9 Je 29 '63
Profane comedy. por Time 84:88 N 13 '64
Trial of Lenny Bruce. A. Goldman. New Repub 151:13-14 S 12 '64
BRUCE PENINSULA, Ontario
Ontario's Bruce: blue heart of the Great Lakes. K. Ferguson. il Motor B 114:42-3+ Jl '64
BRUCELLA
Brucella-agglutinating antibodies: relation of mercaptoethanol stability to complement fixation. R. K. Anderson and others. bibliog il Science 143:1334-5 Mr 20 '64
Interferon production in chickens injected with brucella abortus. J. S. Younger and W. R. Stinebring. bibliog il Science 144:1022-3 My 22 '64
BRUCELLOSIS in swine
Launch mass attack on swine brucellosis. il Suc Farm 61:104 F '63
BRUCH, Hilde
Psychology of dieting. Ladies Home J 82:66 Ja '65
BRUCH, Max Christian
Ambition lost. E. Gerken. il por Opera N 27:28-9 F 2 '63
BRUCK, Gene
Imports. See issues of High fidelity to April 1964
BRUCKER, Herbert
Two centuries of the Hartford courant. Sat R 47:62-4 My 9 '64
Ultimate weapon; excerpts from address. por Time 81:65 My 3 '63
When the press shapes the news. Sat R 47:75-7+ Ja 11 '64
BRUCKNER, Anton
Baffling case of Anton Bruckner; with discography. H. C. R. Landon. il Hi Fi 13:46-8+ F '63
From among the symphonic treatises of Anton Bruckner. H. Goldsmith. il Hi Fi 13:67-8 D '63
From Angel, DGG, and Amadeo, a feast of Bruckner's church music. J. Diether. il Am Rec G 29:850-2 Jl '63
Furtwängler radio performances on DGG. Am Rec G 30:570-1+ Mr '64
Klemperer's Bruckner: two views. J. Diether; C. J. Luten. Am Rec G 29:446-7 F '63
Music to my ears: Bruckner cycle III, played by New York philharmonic. I. Kolodin. Sat R 48:63 Ja 9 '65
Musical events; comparison of A. Bruckner and G. Mahler. W. Sargeant. New Yorker 39:136-8 O 5 '63
Musical events; first performance of Bruckner cycle by N.Y. philharmonic. W. Sargeant. New Yorker 40:222-3 O 24 '64
Musical events; performance of Bruckner's Ninth symphony by Manhattan school of music. W. Sargeant. New Yorker 40:192-4 Ap 25 '64
Musical events; performance of Bruckner's Sixth symphony by N.Y. philharmonic. W. Sargeant. New Yorker 40:55 D 26 '64
On records; Mass no. 3. C. J. Luten. Opera N 28:34 O 19 '63
Strange case of Bruckner's Eighth: five recorded performances of three different editions. J. Diether. por Am Rec G 30:498-500 F '64
BRUCKSHAW, J. M.
New tools to map our hidden mineral wealth. UNESCO Courier 17:28-32 Ja '64

BRUDERHOF. See Society of brothers
BRUELL, Jan H.
Additive inheritance of serum cholesterol level in mice. Science 142:1664-5 D 27 '63
BRUGES, Belgium
Back-tracking four centuries. L. Barry. il Pop Phot 53:24+ N '63
BRUMBERG, Abraham
Screws are tightened again. Reporter 28:21-4+ My 9 '63
Tempest in a gallery. New Repub 148:17-20 F 16 '63
BRUMEL, Valerii
Track & field. pors Sports Illus 18:38-41 F 4 '63

about

Coaches view Brumel and some U.S. rivals. il por Sports Illus 18:41 F 4 '63
Record prospect. Sports Illus 18:8 Mr 18 '63
BRUMIDI, Constantino
Letter from the publisher. B. M. Auer. Time 85:11 Ja 22 '65
BRUMMELL, O. B.
Artistic ferment of Mexico today. Hi Fi 15:69-70 F '65
Badmen; fable bows to fact. Hi Fi 13:127-8 O '63
Do not go gentle into that good night. Hi Fi 14:65 Je '64
Folk music. Hi Fi 14:103-5 Mr; 89 My; 79-80 Jl; 123 S; 131 N '64; 15:97-8+ Ja '65
Sound of saudade. Hi Fi 14:106-10 O '64
BRUN, Helen L.
Rideau, with four feet apiece. por Motor B 114:28-9+ Jl '64
BRUNAUER, Stephen, and Copeland, L. E.
Chemistry of concrete; with biographical sketches. Sci Am 210:24+, 80-6+ Ap '64
BRUNCHES
Be a carefree weekend hostess at a brunch; with recipes. il Am Home 67:56-7+ Je '64
Come for brunch. il Sunset 131:196-7 O '63
Sunday brunch. il Redbook 120:80-1+ Ap '63
Table for two. Ladies Home J 81:34 D '64
Turkey time; Sunday brunch, with recipes. M. Kaytor. il Look 27:56+ N 19 '63
BRUNEAU CANYON, Idaho. See Canyons
BRUNEI (sultanate)
More panic in southeast Asia. New Repub 148:8 F 9 '63
Oil tanker. il Time 81:90 F 22 '63
Our far-flung correspondents; Federation of Malaysia. R. Shaplen. New Yorker 39:158-63 Ap 6 '63
Troubles of becoming a nation; the story of Malaysia. R. P. Martin. il U S News 54:81-2 Ap 15 '63
BRUNER, Jerome Seymour
Harvard's Bruner and his yeasty ideas. A. T. Weil. por Harper 229:81-6+ D '64
Kids and computers; summary of address. Sr Schol 83:3T N 22 '63
Nongraded high school. Sat R 47:71-2 Ja 18 '64
Structures in learning. NEA J 52:26-7 Mr '63
—and Potter, M. C.
Interference in visual recognition. bibliog Science 144:424-5 Ap 24 '64
BRUNER, Louise
Edgar Miller; a versatile artist & craftsman. Am Artist 27:38-43+ My '63
BRUNER, Margaret E.
Christmas eve meditation; poem. Recreation 57:497 D '64
BRUNFELSIAS
It is yesterday-today-tomorrow. il Sunset 132:248 Je '64
BRUNGARD, Mrs Edward G.
City revitalized. por Recreation 56:267+ Je '63
In the swim in St Louis. por Recreation 56:308-9+ S '63
BRUNI, Thomas G.
Foreign language paperbacks. Sr Schol 83:33T Ja 17 '64
BRUNING, Walter F.
How to keep your yard neat without really trying. Pop Sci 183:102-4 Jl '63
BRUNNER, Emil
Emil Brunner and the wide-open spaces. Christian Cent 80:255 F 20 '63
Theology of Emil Brunner: pro and con. R. H. Bryant. Christian Cent 81:81-4 Ja 15 '64
BRUNO, Hal
Birth control, welfare funds, and the politics of Illinois. Reporter 28:32-5 Je 20 '63
Chicago ain't ready for reform. Reporter 28:41-3 Mr 28 '63
Chicago's hillbilly ghetto. Reporter 30:28-31 Je 4 '64
BRUNO, John
Cold. New Yorker 39:21-2 Je 22 '63
BRUNSCHWIG, Alexander
Most radical operation. il por Time 84:49 Jl 31 '64
BRUNTON, Patricia B.
Make your own Christmas sampler. Todays Health 42:40-1 D '64
BRUSH, Alan H. and Allen, Kenneth
Astaxanthin in the cedar waxwing. bibliog Science 142:47-8 O 4 '63
BRUSH burners. See Refuse incinerators
BRUSH collection. See Refuse and refuse disposal
BRUSH drawing
New technique with a familiar medium. A. Grissett. il Sch Arts 62:15 Je '63
BRUSH fires
Day our block burned down. J. Stang. il Good H 157:72-3+ Ag '63
No end to disaster; suburbs of Los Angeles. il Time 83:19 Mr 27 '64
BRUSHES
Brushes to make cleaning easier. il Good H 156:138-9 Mr '63
BRUSSELS

Music

Belgian melange; Brussels' national opera. L. Mueller. il Opera N 28:34 Mr 21 '64
Brussels bouquet. L. Muller. il Opera N 27:33 F 16 '63
BRUSSELS sprouts
See also
Cookery—Vegetables
BRUSTAT, August W.
Goals of learning; address, February 11, 1963. Vital Speeches 29:554-8 Jl 1 '63
BRUSTEIN, Robert
Art, non-art: the curse of official culture. New Repub 151:85-8+ N 7 '64
Theater. See issues of New republic
BRUSTLEIN, Daniel
Religious art without God. J. Tworkov. il pors Art N 63:32-5+ N '64
BRUTKOWSKI, Stefan, and Dabrowska, Jadwiga
Disinhibition after prefrontal lesions as a function of duration of intertrial intervals. bibliog Science 139:505-6 F 8 '63
BRUXISM. See Teeth
BRY, Michael E.
Whitby abbey. il U S Camera 27:45 Ap '64
BRYAN, C. D. B.
Part of growing up; story. Good H 158:98-9 F '64
What are you thinking about? story. New Yorker 39:46-9 N 16 '63
BRYAN, Diana
Notes for the hostess. See issues of House & garden incorporating Living for young homemakers
BRYAN, F. T. and others
N-Ethylmaleimide inhibition of horseshoe crab hemocyte agglutination. bibliog Science 144:1147-8 My 29 '64
BRYAN, J. 3d
Don Juan of Spain. Holiday 33:96-9+ My '63
Evil eye. Holiday 35:58-9+ My '64
Fine feathers for hire. Holiday 34:44+ D '63
Greatest con man of all. Holiday 36:46+ D '64
Lightning guide to Liechtenstein. Holiday 33:78-83+ Mr '63
Lightning guide to Lisbon. Holiday 37:52-3+ Ja '65
Lightning guide to Luxembourg. Holiday 35:54-9 Mr '64
Small, proud, cream-colored hotel. Holiday 34:62-3+ S '63
BRYAN, James E.
American library association and civil rights: excerpts from report, July 1963. ALA Bul 57:747 S '63
Needs of libraries and what ALA is doing about them. ALA Bul 57:319-21 Ap '63
Students and libraries. ALA Bul 57:213 Mr '63
Students, libraries, and the educational process; excerpt from address, June 22, 1962. Sch & Soc 91:39-41 Ja 26 '63
BRYANT, Sir Arthur
Good King Teddy, a proper sport. Life 56:15+ My 22 '64
BRYANT, Farris
Case for freedom: a governor's view: testimony before the Senate commerce committee. por U S News 55:11 Ag 12 '63
Excerpt from testimony, July 29, 1963. Cong Digest 42:277+ N '63
BRYANT, H. Stafford, Jr. See Reed, H. H. jr, jt. auth.
BRYANT, Jack W.
Administrator's view: library promotion. por Wilson Lib Bul 39:464-7 F '65
Like diamonds from Tiffany's. por Library J 89:199-201 Ja 15 '64
BRYANT, Nelson
Destination, ducks. pors Outdoor Life 134:32-3+ D '64

BRYANT, Nelson—*Continued*
Remote ponds near home. pors Outdoor Life 131:76-7+ My '63
Trout after dark. pors Outdoor Life 132:44-5+ Jl '63
BRYANT, Paul
Balm for a gloomy bear. Time 83:51 F 14 '64
Days of decision. Newsweek 63:65 F 17 '64
Gridiron on the grid. Nation 196:299 Ap 13 '63
Name of the game. Sat Eve Post 236:82 Ap 27 '63
Scandalous notes. D. Jenkins. il Sports Illus 18:24-5+ Ap 8 '63
Story of a college football fix; Georgia versus Alabama. F. Graham, jr. il pors Sat Eve Post 236:80-3 Mr 23 '63; Discussion. Sports Illus 18:18-21 Mr 25 '63; Time 81:51 Mr 29 '63; Newsweek 61:51 Ap 1 '63
Trial that has the South seething; college football fix; Georgia versus Alabama. D. Jenkins. il por Sports Illus 19:18-21 Ag 5 '63
BRYANT, Robert H.
Theology of Emil Brunner: pro and con. Christian Cent 81:81-4 Ja 15 '64
BRYANT, Samuel W.
How's the annual report coming? Fortune 69:104-7+ Ja '64
Keeping executives healthy. Fortune 67:122-3+ Ap '63
What jet travel does to your metabolic clock. Fortune 68:160-3+ N '63
BRYCE, John
Glass-ware patents of John Bryce. A. G. Peterson. il Hobbies 69:74-5 S '64
BRYCE, Mayo
Identifying the role of the arts in education. Sch Arts 62:29 Ap '63
BRYCE CANYON NATIONAL PARK
December visit to Bryce. il Sunset 131:55 D '63
BRYDON, Margaret Wylie, and Ziegler, E. E.
May witch; drama. Plays 22:69-78 My '63
BRYK, Rut
Pair of designing Finns. R. Moss. il por Horizon 5:62-7 Jl '63
BRYNES, Asher
Apostle to the Cabinet. New Repub 148:21-2 F 2 '63
Chickens and votes. New Repub 149:14-15 O 26 '63
$500 million mistake. New Repub 151:11-14 S 26 '64
Golden rule. New Repub 148:20-1 Mr 9 '63
How now, brown cow? New Repub 148:8 Ap 20 '63
LBJ and the farmers. New Repub 150:15-16 F 15 '64
Overproduction in American agriculture. New Repub 149:24-6 Jl 13 '63
Regulating AT&T. New Repub 151:11-14 O 3 '64
To him that hath. New Repub 148:9 Mr 30 '63
Virtue in business. New Repub 148:21-3 My 11 '63
What's public property? New Repub 148:6 Ap 6 '63
BRYSON, David Lyman
Development of mouse eggs in diffusion chambers. bibliog Science 144:1351-3 Je 12 '64
BRYSON, John
Holy Land. il Ladies Home J 81:49-55 Ap '64
Palm Springs. il Sat Eve Post 236:16-21 Mr 30 '63
BRYSON, Reid A. and others
Radiocarbon and soil evidence of former forest in the southern Canadian tundra. bibliog Science 147:46-8 Ja 1 '65
BRYSON, Vernon, and Vogel, H. J.
Evolving genes and proteins. Science 147:68-71 Ja 1 '65
BRZEZINSKI, Zbigniew
After the test ban. New Repub 149:18-21 Ag 31 '63
Calculations and suggestions. Newsweek 62:52 N 25 '63
Moscow and the M.L.F: hostility and ambivalence. For Affairs 43:126-34 O '64
Russia and Europe. For Affairs 42:428-44 Ap '64
Threat and opportunity in the Communist schism. For Affairs 41:513-25 Ap '63
Victory of the clerks. New Repub 151:15-18 N 14 '64
What Communist breakup means to us; interview. por Nations Bsns 52:34-5+ Je '64
With test-ban treaty, has Khrushchev changed his ways? interview. por U S News 55:72-3 S 30 '63
BRZOSTOSKI, John
Iran: light vs. darkness. Art N 63:39-41+ Sum '64
Tsin Ning pot. Craft Horiz 24:34-5 Ja '64

about
How to make a monster. F. De Wys. il Design 65:19-21 S '63
BUBASH, George R. and others
Microsporum nanum: first recorded isolation from animals in the United States. bibliog Science 143:366-7 Ja 24 '64
BUBBLE chambers
Cover; view inside hydrogen bubble chamber at the Lawrence radiation laboratory. il Sci Am 210:4 F '64
BUBBLES, John
Bubbles bounces back. il pors Ebony 20:49-50+ Ja '65
BUBER, Martin
I-thou & I-it. por Time 82:49 Jl 12 '63
Interpreting Hasidism; tr. by M. Friedman. Commentary 36:218-25 S '63
Martin Buber's Hasidism. G. Scholem; discussion. Commentary 33:161-3 F '62; 37:18-20 F '64
Responses & reactions (cont) N. Mailer. Commentary 35:146-8, 335-7, 517-18; 36:164-5 F, Ap, Je, Ag '63
Rootless mysticism. I. B. Singer. Commentary 39:77-8 Ja '65
World to make real. R. B. Gittelsohn. por Sat R 47:26+ Ag 1 '64
BUBLEY, Esther
Portrait of a place. il U S Camera 26:58-61 Mr '63
BUBONIC plague. See Plague
BUCHAN, Alastair
American commonwealth? Harper 226:95-101 Je '63
Atlantic defense; keeping the door open for France. New Repub 152:11-14 Ja 9 '65
Is this NATO crisis necessary? New Repub 151:19-21 Ag 8 '64
Nassau reconsidered: what can America and Britain do now? New Repub 148:21-3 Mr 2 '63
Partners and allies. For Affairs 41:621-37 Jl '63
Systems in collision. New Repub 150:15-16+ My 23 '64
BUCHANAN, Colin
Letter from London. M. Panter-Downes. New Yorker 39:65-6 Ja 25 '64
BUCHANAN, Henry A. and Brown, B. W.
Speaking out. pors Sat Eve Post 237:10+ O 24 '64
BUCHANAN, James
James Buchanan, fifteenth President 1857-1861. F. Freidel. il pors Nat Geog Mag 127: 118-21 Ja '65
BUCHANAN, Patrick J.
Jefferson City: the pen that just grew. Nation 199:355-7 N 16 '64
BUCHANAN, Virginia
Travel enriches our Christmas. Travel 122:47-9 D '64
BUCHAREST
Balkans in brief; Bucur and the big city. H. Sutton. il Sat R 46:18-20 Jl 6 '63
BUCHBAUM, Walter H.
Automatic degausser for color TV. Electr World 72:53 S '64
BUCHENWALD concentration camp. See Concentration camps—Germany
BUCHHEIMER, Naomi
Dropouts. Sr School 84:1T-2T Ap 17 '64
BUCHHEISTER, Carl W.
President reports to you. See issues of Audubon magazine
BUCHMAN, Frank
Music at midnight. Criticism
Nat R 14:465-7 Je 4 '63
BUCHMUELLER, A. D.
Pressures on the American family. Sch & Soc 91:244-5 Sum '63
Teen-age code of conduct for parents. PTA Mag 59:4-7 bibliog(p37) O '64
Two is the age of firsts. McCalls 90:102-3 Ag '63
BUCHSBAUM, Walter H.
Calibrating test equipment. Electr World 70: 43-5+ Ag '63
Digital readouts. Electr World 69:33-5+ F '63
Electronic anesthesia. Electr World 70:27-9 S '63
New TV designs for 1964. Electr World 71: 51-4+ Mr '64
Shielded cables. Electr World 72:36-8+ N '64
U.H.F. tuners for 1964 TV sets. Electr World 71:28-30+ Je '64
Understanding color TV demodulators. Electr World 70:44-7 Jl '63
Understanding telemetry. Electr World 71:25-8 Ap '64
BUCHWALD, Art
All unquiet on the Potomac. Read Digest 83: 185-6+ Jl '63

BUCHWALD, Art—*Continued*
Art Buchwald tax plan; excerpt from I chose capitol punishment. Read Digest 84:12H Mr '64
Buchwald anti-bachelor act. McCalls 91:68 My '64
Business is awful. McCalls 91:52 D '63
City the world loves: Paris. McCalls 91:66 F '64
Cottage for sale. McCalls 91:44 Je '64
Guilty party is Art Buchwald. por McCalls 90:54 My '63
Hooray for commercials! Read Digest 84:27-8 My '64
Household help! McCalls 90:50 Ap '63
Man who promised marriage. por McCalls 90:36 Je '63
Problems of being the perfect husband. por McCalls 90:28 Jl '63; Same abr. Read Digest 83:231-2 O '63
Sing along with Art Buchwald. por McCalls 90:42 S '63
What is your divorce potential? por McCalls 91:86 O '63; Same abr. with title Warning all wives! Read Digest 84:129-30 F '64
What makes a man propose? McCalls 91:62 N '63
What's my desk doing out in the hall? Read Digest 83:75-8 D '63
When Martha goes to Washington. McCalls 91:34 Ap '64
You too can be fat and love it. McCalls 90:16 F '63

about

Buchwald's Washington. il por Time 82:62+ S 20 '63
Life imitates Art. Time 84:73 D 18 '64

BUCHWALD, H. Dieter, and others
Identity of tarichatoxin and tetrodotoxin. bibliog Science 143:474-5 Ja 31 '64

BUCK, Ellsworth
Lifting the lid on Labrador. Am For 70:28-31+ Ag '64

BUCK, Pat
Our Johnny-come-lately baby. Parents Mag 38:52-3+ D '63

BUCK, Paul
Credo reconsidered; excerpts from Libraries and universities. por Library J 89:4295-300 N 1 '64

BUCK, Pearl (Sydenstricker)
Court of love; story; excerpt from Living reed. Good H 157:74-5 S '63
India, India; story. McCalls 91:88-9 S '64
Legend of Tchi-Niu; adaptation. McCalls 91:114-15+ My '64
My world. por Ladies Home J 81:36+ N '64; 82:18+ Ja '65
Nineteen stockings by the chimney piece. Read Digest 83:49-52 D '63
Pursuit of happiness. por Seventeen 22:112+ D '63
Sacred skull; story. Sat Eve Post 236:38-41 Mr 16 '63
Sexual revolution; excerpts from Children for adoption. por Ladies Home J 81:43-5+ S '64

BUCK, Robert
Pilot talks about air safety; interview. por U S News 54:59 Mr 18 '63

BUCK, Susan
Life among the libs (Hunter college division) Nat R 16:275-7+, 329 Ap 7-21 '64

BUCK, William Alvadore
Grow the delectable radish for all it's worth. House B 105:214-16 My '63
Off-duty joys of gardening. House B 105:194-7 Mr '63
Potatoes from the Incas. Horticulture 43:40-3 Ja '65

BUCK hears the call; story. See London, J.

BUCKET seats. See Automobiles—Seats

BUCKEYE, Ariz.
Brackish water becomes fresh. W. G. Hamner. il Am City 78:115-16 Mr '63

BUCKINGHAM, Sue, and others
Pulmonary alveolar cell inclusions: their development in the rat. bibliog Science 145:1192-3 S 11 '64

BUCKINGHAM palace
Time clocks coming? maintenance of royal residences. il Bsns W p56 Jl 20 '63

BUCKLER, Charles E. See Baron, S. jt. auth.

BUCKLER, Ernest
Little flag for mother. Farm J 87:69-70 My '63

BUCKLEY, Charles E.
Fine Federal furniture attributed to Portsmouth. Antiques 83:196-200 F '63
Furniture of New Hampshire. Antiques 86:56-61 Jl '64

BUCKLEY, Charley
Bad night for bosses. il por Newsweek 63:29-30 Je 15 '64

BUCKLEY, Francis J.
Vietnam dilemma. America 109:238-40 S 7 '63

BUCKLEY, Isabelle P.
We respect this approach to child discipline. Bet Hom & Gard 41:25+ Je '63

BUCKLEY, John P.
Unconventional way. Am City 79:96-8 Ja '64

BUCKLEY, Noel
Clubs of business. Duns R 82:28-31+ Ag '63
Fortunes in franchising. Duns R 83:36-7+ Ap '64
How Sears, Roebuck plans for the future. Duns R 82:44-6+ O '63
Idle fifth man in the office. Duns R 82:47-8+ N '63
Maintenance: the wasted dollars. Duns R 83:pt2 123-4+ Mr '64
Offbeat profits on Wall Street. Duns R 82:37+ S '63
Payoff in design. Duns R 84:pt2 115-17+ S '64
Private carriage: the fifth method. Duns R 83:pt2 145-6+ Je '64

BUCKLEY, Priscilla L.
I'm a sad fat boy. Nat R 16:498+ Je 16 '64
Odd sad waif. Nat R 16:199-200 Mr 10 '64
Personal observations from abroad: free and less free. Nat R 16:809-12 S 22 '64
Taiwan, the joyous and proud. Nat R 14:152-3 F 26 '63
Theater (cont) Nat R 14:535-7; 16:546-7 Jl 2 '63, Je 30 '64

BUCKLEY, Thomas
Artful pursuers of artful dodgers. N Y Times Mag p90+ S 8 '63

BUCKLEY, William Frank, 1925-
Answers for conservatives; questions and answers. Nat R 16:145-6+ F 25 '64
Assault on Whittaker Chambers. Nat R 16:1098-102 D 15 '64
Atlantic City without the girls. Nat R 16:763-5 S 8 '64
Ecce Ike. Nat R 15:487-8+ D 3 '63
Hang on to your hats. Nat R 14:822-4 Ap 28 '63
Inviting Communists to speak at colleges; address, 1962. Nat R 15:343-5+ O 22 '63
On the right. See issues of National review
Speaking out. por Sat Eve Post 237:8+ O 17 '64
Vile campaign. Nat R 16:853-6+ O 6 '64

about

How to attack a liberal. S. Allen. Nat R 14:149-52 F 26 '63
Lion of conservatism. por Newsweek 61:94-5 My 13 '63
Won't you come into my parlor? J. Chamberlain. Nat R 14:367-8 My 7 '63

Anecdotes, facetiae, satire, etc.

Governing Buckley by the numbers; fantasy in 2,000 digits. L. A. Benenson. Harper 227:76-7 O '63

BUCKLEY, William W.
Small city enjoys big-sweeper economy. Am City 79:177-8 O '64

BUCKLEY school, New York. See Private schools

BUCKLIN, Ella
(ed) Motion picture previews. See issues of PTA magazine

BUCKMAN, Gertrude
Jobs that could only happen here. Mlle 58:152-3+ Ap '64
Life of a wife. Mlle 58:96-7+ Ja '64
Off-Broadway girls. Mlle 58:132-3+ N '63
Thought behind ACCION. Mlle 60:106-8+ Ja '65

BUCKNER, Jess
Fallout filters. pors Am City 78:107-8 Je '63

BUCKS COUNTY, Pa.
Against almost impossible odds; swampy slum into attractive park. R. W. Pierson and R. E. Nagle. il Am City 79:112-13 S '64
Winter in Bucks County; excerpts from Private line in Bucks County. W. Teller. il Atlan 211:78-81 Mr '63

BUCKS COUNTY playhouse. See New Hope, Pa.—Theater

BUCKTHORN
Speedy Italian buckthorn. il Sunset 132:184+ F '64

BUCKWALTER, Len
Comments on the new CB rules. Electr World 72:42-3 N '64
Eight electronic experiments with a transistor breadboard. Pop Mech 120:200-3 N '63
Guide to stereo shelving. Hi Fi 14:50-2+ Je '64
How to build a three-in-one test meter for your car. Pop Sci 183:124-7+ Jl '63

BUCKWALTER, Len—*Continued*
New citizens band circuits. Electr World 69: 48-9+ Ap; 32-3 Je; 70:41+ S; 36+ N '63; 71:32-3+ Ja; 46-7+ Mr; 46-7+ My; 72:34-5+ Jl; 54-5+ O '64; 73:50-1 Ja '65
Two-mile boat horn. Pop Mech 120:178-9 Ag '63
—and Francois, Bill
Fuel cells: electricity in a promising new package. Pop Mech 119:102-6+ Mr '63
—and Steckler, Larry
Two-way CB radios. Pop Mech 120:92-5 Jl '63
BUCKY, Thomas Lee
Einstein: an intimate memoir; ed. by J. P. Blank. Harper 229:43-8 S '64
BUDAPEST
No end to liberation. Time 83:39 Ap 3 '64

Description

Left bank. H. Sutton. il Sat R 46:24-6 Ag 17 '63
Letter from Budapest. J. Wechsberg. il New Yorker 40:121-2+ Mr 14 '64
To Buda and to Pest. H. Sutton. il Sat R 46: 36+ Ag 10 '63

Music

Berg takes Budapest. K. Kristof. il Opera N 28:26 My 2 '64
Budapest generations. K. Kristof. Opera N 28:34 D 28 '63
Great opera houses. E. Balogh. il Opera N 27:28-31 Ap 6 '63
[Musical events] (cont) Mus Am 83:163 D '63
Notes from abroad. D. Stevens. Hi Fi 13: 40+ S '63
Samson on the Danube. K. Kristof. Opera N 28:32 F 1 '64

Social life and customs

Gay until tomorrow; Farsang ball. il Time 81:30 F 22 '63
BUDAPEST opera house. See Opera houses
BUDD company
Budd pulls a switch; bid on stainless steel subway cars. Bsns W p26 Jl 6 '63
BUDDHISM and Christianity. See Christianity and other religions
BUDDHIST sculpture. See Sculpture, Buddhist
BUDDHISTS
Again, the Buddhists in South Viet Nam. il Time 83:27-8 Je 5 '64
Again Thich Tri Quang. America 110:784 Je 6 '64
Anagarika Dharmapala, Buddhist missionary and educator. W. Rahula. Sch & Soc 92:383-5 D 12 '64
Anarchy & agony. il Time 84:33-4 S 4 '64
Beat them; Buddhist campaign no longer a dispute over religious toleration. il Newsweek 62:46 Ag 19 '63
Behind the Buddhist unrest in southeast Asia. N. F. Busch. Read Digest 83:94-9 D '63
Brutality in Vietnam. Christian Cent 80:950 Jl 31 '63
Buddha on the barricades. il Time 84:38-42+ D 11 '64
Buddhist crisis; South Viet Nam. il Time 82:24-6 Jl 26 '63
Buddhists fight Diem with sit-downs and suicides. il Life 55:24-5 Ag 2 '63
Buddhist way. il N Y Times Mag p 11 S 1 '63
Buddhist way in Vietnam. J. Langguth. il N Y Times Mag p29+ O 11 '64
Death v. the family; second Buddhist priest to burn himself to death. Time 82:23 Ag 16 '63
Dictatorial regime; Khanh promoted to president; Buddhists again threaten trouble. il Time 84:26-7 Ag 28 '64
Diem and the Buddhists. H. G. Fairbanks. Commonweal 78:452-4 Jl 26 '63
Diem, the Mandarin. America 109:111-12 Ag 3 '63
Diem's other crusade: against Vietnamese Buddhists. New Repub 148:5-6 Je 22 '63
Dissatisfied Buddhists; South Vietnam Buddhists. Newsweek 64:34 S 7 '64
Edge of chaos. S. Karnow. il Sat Eve Post 236:27-37 S 28 '63
Exploding power of the Buddhists; instability in Vietnam. il Life 57:34-41 D 11 '64
Faith that lights the fires. il Time 82:29 Ag 23 '63
Fiery protest; self-sacrifice of Thich Quang Duc. il Newsweek 61:63 Je 24 '63
Fighting the reds & the bonzes. Time 84:32 D 18 '64
Flames & music. il Time 82:41 O 11 '63
Heart of Quang Duc. il Time 82:33 Jl 5 '63
Hunger & desperation; South Viet Nam's top three monks begin a forty-eight hour fast in their campaign to bring down Premier Tran Van Huong. Time 84:21 D 25 '64
Job on Diem; Buddhist campaign on the issue of religion. America 110:758 My 30 '64
Letter from Saigon. R. Shaplen. New Yorker 40:179-86+ S 19 '64
Looking east; movement toward Buddhism. il Newsweek 62:92 D 2 '63
Mandarins of Hué. Newsweek 61:49-50 My 27 '63
Meditation of U Thant. G. Samuels. il N Y Times Mag p32-3+ D 13 '64
Out of the frying pan; Buddhist demonstrations in Viet Nam. il Newsweek 65:34+ F 1 '65
Pressure on Diem and on the UN. America 109:544 N 9 '63
Question for the press. America 109:472 O 26 '63
Question in Saigon. America 111:286-7 S 19 '64
Real trouble in Vietnam. il U S News 57: 46 D 14 '64
Reporting from Saigon; possible political motivation behind the Buddhist anti-government campaign. America 109:152 Ag 17 '63
Reprise from the pagodas. il Time 84:38 D 4 '64
Rome and Saigon. Christian Cent 80:1067 S 4 '63
Saigon in perspective. America 109:126 Ag 10 '63
Saigon summary. M. Higgins. America 110: 18-21 Ja 4 '64
Same old Diem; anti-Buddhist measures. Nation 196:538 Je 29 '63
South Viet Nam; new phase. il Time 84:29 S 11 '64
South Vietnam. New Repub 148:9 Je 29 '63
Suicide series; South Viet Nam. il Time 82:28 Ag 23 '63
Tear gas & burning books; anti-American outburst in South Viet Nam. il Time 85:25 Ja 29 '65
Tiger by the tail; charges of anti-Buddhist discrimination. America 109:207-8 Ag 31 '63
Trial by fire; self-sacrifice of monk, Thich Quang Duc in Viet Nam. il Time 81:32 Je 21 '63
Two views of Vietnam. America 109:223 S 7 '63
Ugly Americans of Vietnam; with editorial comment. M. Higgins. il America 111:367, 376-82 O 3 '64
Vietnam dilemma. V. S. Kearney; F. J. Buckley. America 109:237-40 S 7 '63
Vietnam's future: All bets are off. il Newsweek 62:35-6 Ag 26 '63
Vietnam's militant Buddhists. D. Warner. il Reporter 31:29-31 D 3 '64
War in the pagodas: who is the enemy? il Newsweek 62:35-6+ S 2 '63
What's really going on in Vietnam. Ngo-dinh-Thuc. il Nat R 15:388-90 N 5 '63
When a monk became a human torch: What U.S. has at stake. il U S News 54:8 Je 24 '63
BUDDING. See Grafting
BUDER, Leonard
Parent and child. N Y Times Mag p82+ My 26 '63
BUDGE, Hamer H.
Mr Johnson flunks. Nation 198:613 Je 22 '64
BUDGET

Canada

Bungled budget of Canada's Liberals; with editorial comment. Bsns W p34+, 124 Je 29 '63
Canada starts back to business as usual. Bsns W p34 Jl 13 '63
Getting it back from the foreigners. New Repub 149:8 Jl 13 '63
Pearson loses round one. R. E. Spencer. Nation 198:43-6 Ja 13 '64
Where deficits are no concern. il U S News 55:76-8 S 2 '63

Europe, Western

Where deficits are no concern. il U S News 55:76-8 S 2 '63

France

Sincere budget. Time 84:25 S 25 '64

Great Britain

Britain gets a budget; tax cuts and higher spending. Bsns W p27 Ap 6 '63
Britain's budget bets on expansion. Bsns W p27-8 Ap 18 '64
Could have been worse, but is it good enough? Time 84:39-40 N 20 '64
How Britain does it. E. L. Dale, jr. New Repub 148:7-8 Mr 30 '63
Letter from London. M. Panter-Downes. New Yorker 40:197-8 N 21 '64

BUDGET—*Continued*

India

Date with Desai. Time 81:33 Mr 8 '63

Russia

Soviet military budget. T. Sosnovy. bibliog f il For Affairs 42:487-94 Ap '64

United States

Are we looking at the wrong budget? W. W. Howard. il Reporter 28:41-2+ My 23 '63; Discussion. 28:8-9 Je 20 '63
As Johnson swings the economy ax. il U S News 56:4 Ja 6 '64
Basic defense, space efforts to continue. G. C. Wilson. Aviation W 82:16-17 Ja 4 '65
Brighter look for the budget. U S News 55: 120 N 11 '63
Budget authorities speak out on spending; symposium. il Nations Bsns 51:86-8+ My '63
Budget box score. America 111:99 Ag 1 '64
Budget fight heating up. Bsns W p26-7 Ap 6 '63
Budget: $14.9 billion asked for research in fiscal 1964. J. Walsh. Science 139:394-5 F 1 '63
Budget: it's really 125 billion dollars. il U S News 58:76-7 Ja 11 '65
Budget of the United States government for the fiscal year ending June 30, 1964; excerpts from budget message. J. F. Kennedy. il Dept State Bul 48:224-8 F 11 '63
Budget of the United States government for the fiscal year ending June 30, 1965; with excerpts from Budget message of the President. il Dept State Bul 50:218-22 F 10 '64
Budget: requests for R&D funds edge above $15 billion mark for a fiscal year of austerity. J. Walsh. il Science 143:337-8 Ja 24 '64
Budget revisited. il Fortune 67:44+ Mr '63
Budget sets a new style; with editorial comment. il Bsns W p23-4, 136 Ja 25 '64
Built-in boost for spending; Johnson's pressure for cuts. il Bsns W p25 D 14 '63
Business roundup; unstabilizing budget. il Fortune 69:27-8 F '64
Cheering budget promise. Life 56:4 Ja 17 '64
Congress vs. spenders. il Bsns W p25-6 F 23 '63
Deficits as a policy. H. Hazlitt. Newsweek 61: 76 F 4 '63
Demag, Tex. concerning State of the Union message. Nat R 16:54 Ja 28 '64
Democrats volunteer a Republican budget. J. N. Eller. America 108:631 My 4 '63
Do deficits make jobs? H. Hazlitt. Newsweek 61:81 Ap 22 '63
Dread of a surplus. H. Hazlitt. Newsweek 64:69 Jl 20 '64
Economic goals: view from the White House; address, November 19, 1964. L. B. Johnson. Sat R 48:28-30 Ja 9 '65
Estimates vs. reality. H. Hazlitt. Newsweek 63:70 F 10 '64
Excerpt from letter to representative C. A. Halleck, March 26, 1963. D. D. Eisenhower. Cong Digest 42:140 My '63
Federal budget hides big spending. il Nations Bsns 51:100-1+ D '63
15 per cent of budget for R&D; $6.1 billion budget for space research. W. Davis. Sci N L 83:67 F 2 '63
Financing seven years of deficit; with editorial comment. il Bsns W p 126+, 156 F 23 '63
First glimpse of a balanced budget. il Bsns W p 126+ My 16 '64
From Washington straight. Cato. Nat R 14: 228 Mr 26 '63
Giving & taking; preparation of budget for fiscal 1966. Time 85:29 Ja 1 '65
Going along with Johnson on budget. il Bsns W p25 My 2 '64
Government spending, it'll never be cut. il Changing T 17:6-10 Ag '63; Same abr. with title Up, up, up, the relentless rise in government spending. Read Digest 83:231-2+ N '63
GOP budget-cutters face uphill battle. Bsns W p26-7 Mr 16 '63
Great almoner. R. Moley. Newsweek 63:88 Mr 2 '64
Hitting a fiscal target. il Bsns W p23-4 O 31 '64
How a top Democrat would cut budget. U S News 54:22 Mr 18 '63
How good is the Kennedy style? Fortune 67: 91-2 Je '63
How LBJ's budget is making out. il U S News 57:109-10 N 9 '64
How much should government do? K. Gordon. il Sat R 48:25-7+ Ja 9 '65
How to be conservative. Nation 197:210 O 12 '63
How to cut a budget. il Newsweek 63:15 Ja 20 '64
How to spot false budget cuts. V. J. Burke. il Nations Bsns 52:42-3+ F '64
If you want to know how the budget can be cut. il U S News 54:46-7 Mr 25 '63
In sight: budget of 100 billions; summary of testimony. D. Dillon. U S News 55:100 Ag 26 '63
In tune with his goals. Bsns W p 17 Ja 2 '65
Johnson's first budget; to break all records. il U S News 55:30-1 D 23 '63
Johnson's miracle. New Repub 150:3-5 Ja 18 '64
Johnson's program and its prospects; concerning State-of-the-Union message. il U S News 56:29-31 Ja 20 '64
Keeping up the budget squeeze. il Bsns W p 19 My 30 '64
Kermit Gordon; the President's affable no man on the budget. Newsweek 63:66-7 Ja 27 '64
Latest on the budget: about 100 billions. U S News 56:8 Ja 13 '64
Let's spend more. H. Rowen. New Repub 148:13-16 My 25 '63
Letter from Washington; concerning State of the Union message. R. H. Rovere. New Yorker 39:35-6+ Ja 25 '64
LBJ and the budget: the outlook. il U S News 57:107-8 N 16 '64
LBJ looks ahead to more red ink. il U S News 58:73-4 Ja 4 '65
LBJ's brand goes on the economy; with editorial comment. il Bsns W p71-4+, 136 Ja 25 '64
Man on the moon, men on the dole; reprint. J. Reston. Aviation W 78:21 Ap 22 '63
Man with a $100-billion budget. il Bsns W p 100+ Jl 20 '63
Mr Economy; President hopes to keep 1966 budget under $100 billion. Newsweek 65:12+ Ja 4 '65
Neither extravagant nor miserly. il Time 85: 19B Ja 29 '65
New budget: same old magic. il Newsweek 65:19-20 F 1 '65
New patterns for military spending. il Bsns W p24-5 Ag 31 '63
1964 numbers game. il Bsns W p25-6 Ja 18 '64
Now: a revised federal budget and a new criticism of U.S. spending. U S News 56: 88 Je 1 '64
$100 billion line. Newsweek 63:18-19 Ja 13 '64
President committed to war on poverty. J. N. Eller. America 110:182 F 8 '64
Principles of defense management; excerpts from message to Congress, January 18, 1965. L. B. Johnson. Aviation W 82:17 Ja 25; Miss & Roc 16:11 Ja 25 '65
Real truth about the federal budget. C. Stevenson. Read Digest 82:49-54 My '63
'65 budget: more for less? il Sr Schol 84:20 F 7 '64
Sound, not fury. W. J. Coughlin. Miss & Roc 14:46 Ja 6 '64
Spending control and the tax cut. Bsns W p 160 N 2 '63
Spending hold-down shows in budget. il Bsns W p24-5 Jl 25 '64
State of the Union; address, January 8, 1964. L. B. Johnson. Dept State Bul 50:110-11 Ja 27 '64; Same. il U S News 56:66-9 Ja 20 '64; Vital Speeches 30:194-7 Ja 15 '64; Cur Hist 46:176-8+ Mr '64
State of the Union; concerning President Johnson's first State of the Union message. il Time 83:11-12 Ja 17 '64
Tax cut comes first; concerning Kennedy's State of the Union and budget messages. il Bsns W p23-6 Ja 19 '63
Tax cut in wonderland. H. Hazlitt. Newsweek 62:90 N 4 '63
Tax cuts & Puritans. Time 81:16-17 F 8 '63
Tax plan: deficit worries Congress; Kennedy's tax cut proposals. il Bsns W p25-6 F 2 '63
Tax reduction and balanced budget; address, October 8, 1963. D. Dillon. Vital Speeches 30:44-7 N 1 '63
Taxes & spending: where the money goes. il Nations Bsns 51:36-7 Ap '63
Taxes & spending: why the budget must be cut; interview. J. L. McClellan. il Nations Bsns 51:38-9+ Ap '63
Taxes; to cut or not to cut. il Sr Schol 82:5-7 Ja 30 '63
That fiscal revolution. H. Hazlitt. Newsweek 64:60 Ag 10 '64
That man (LBJ) made a lot of friends; business comments on the President's $97.9 billion budget. il Newsweek 63:63-4 Ja 20 '64

BUDGET—United States—*Continued*
Their finest hour. Nation 196:81 F 2 '63
This month's feature: Congress & the proposed federal budget. Cong Digest 42:131-9+ My '63
This month's feature: President's tax revision program. il Cong Digest 42:99-107+ Ap '63
Treasury due to borrow less. Bsns W p90 Jl 20 '63
Trouble ahead. R. Hotz. Aviation W 81:11 D 7 '64
Uncuttable budget. R. D. Novak. Reporter 28:41-2+ Ap 25 '63
Under attack: Johnson budget. U S News 56:95 Ap 6 '64
U.S. will tighten up spending. Bsns W p75-6+ O 5 '63
War on want, at home; State of the Union message; with editorial comment. il Bsns W p 19-21, 112 Ja 11 '64
Watch those lights. il Time 83:13-14 Ja 31 '64
Well, it's not as bad as they said they expected. Time 82:18 Jl 26 '63
When do we get rid of budget deficits? D. Lawrence. U S News 56:96 Ja 20 '64
When the first bills come in for the Great society. il U S News 57:115 D 7 '64
When will it be safe to balance the budget? E. L. Dale, jr. il N Y Times Mag p 14-15+ Ja 24 '65
Where deficits are no concern; Western Europe and Canada. il U S News 55:76-8 S 2 '63
Wilbur Mills grinds exceedingly fine. il Newsweek 62:61 Ag 19 '63
See also
Taxation—United States
United States—Appropriations and expenditures

BUDGET, Business
Business budgets; to each his own; Budget executives institute. il Bsns W p76+ My 30 '64

BUDGET, Household
Do you fight about money? with program for discussion group, by E. G. Neisser. E. M. Stern. il Parents Mag 38:38+, 54-5+ My '63
Enjoy a budget? we do, honest! L. Campbell. il Farm J 89:61-2+ Ja '65
Family financial program. il Changing T 17:39-43 Ag; 41-5 S; 41-5 O; 39-43 N '63
Family money questions answered. See issues of Better homes and gardens
Family spending: see how it changes. il Changing T 18:43-5 Mr '64
Fifteen ways to save money. il Changing T 18:35-8 Jl '64
High cost of scrimping. il Good H 157:12+ Jl '63
How to make your dollars go further. E. Peterson. il Suc Farm 62:79+ S '64
How women feel about money. G. H. Gallup and S. Grafton. il McCalls 91:74-7+ Jl '64
Intercity differences in family food budget costs. J. C. Brackett. il Mo Labor R 86:1189-94 O '63
Low finance; questions and answers. J. Goodsell. il Ladies Home J 80:42 Ap '63
Making your money count (cont of) Family money management. S. Margolius. il Ladies Home J 80:38 Ja; 22 Ap; 31 Je; 16 Jl '63
Money in the American home. Am Home 68:17+ Ja '65
Money talk for newlyweds. il Changing T 17:6-17 Je '63
Newlyweds, a market unto themselves. il Bsns W p98-100 N 2 '63
Part money plays in marriage. M. T. Bloom. Read Digest 82:83-6 My '63
Sylvia Porter's advice to young wives about money; questions and answers. S. Porter. il Redbook 124:62-3+ N '64
Ten biggest mistakes in any woman's budget. G. H. Gallup and S. Grafton. McCalls 91:46+ Ag '64
We can't afford it. E. Hill. Read Digest 86:123-5 Ja '65
Why you feel pinched; more we make, the less we seem to have. il Changing T 18:7-12 N '64

BUDGET, Municipal
Cities feel the squeeze. il Bsns W p26-8 Mr 9 '63

BUDGET, Personal
Can this marriage be saved? D. C. Disney. Ladies Home J 81:34+ O '64
Money managers. P. Bart. Esquire 60:204 D '63
Money manners; excerpt from Seventeen book of etiquette and entertaining. E. A. Haupt. Seventeen 23:26 Ap '64
Much ado about money; with group discussion program, by E. J. LeShan. E. N. Ryan and D. R. McNeil. il Parents Mag 39:20, 44-5+ My '64
That matter of money; questions and answers. A. Wood. il Seventeen 23:162-3+ S '64
We can't afford it. E. Hill. Read Digest 86:123-5 Ja '65
Young people and money. V. Weingarten. Bet Hom & Gard 42:80+ F '64
See also
Childrens allowances
Finance, Personal
Saving and savings

BUDGETS, Library. See Libraries—Finance

BUDNIK, Dan
Get close for girl stoppers. P. Caulfield. il Mod Phot 27:88-9 Je '63
Magic eye of Dan Budnik. il U S Camera 26:64-9 Ap '63

BUDNY, Lorraine
Who said mulching is easy? Pop Gard 14:80-1 Jl '63

BUDOWSKI, P. and others
Provitamin A_2 from lutein. bibliog Science 142:969-71 N 15 '63

BUDS
Index to next spring's growth. V. Argo. il Natur Hist 73:52-6 Ja '64

BUDWORMS, Spruce. See Spruce budworms

BUECHLER, James
John Sobieski runs; story. Sat Eve Post 237:54-8 O 10 '64

BUEGELEISEN, Sally
Cross-country couple. por Flying 75:48-9+ Jl '64

BUELL, John
Reporter at large. E. Wilson. New Yorker 40:115-16+ N 14 '64

BUENA VISTA marsh, Wis. See Bird sanctuaries

BUENOS AIRES

Music

New opera in Buenos Aires. J. Vincent. il Américas 16:35-8 O '64
Tango. S. Bernardi. il Américas 16:20-6 D '64
Verdi at the Colon. G. Knepler. il Opera N 28:32-3 D 21 '63

BUERGER, Johanna B.
Achimenes on the terrace. Horticulture 41:321 Je '63

BUERGER, M. J. and Dollase, W. A.
Shape of the recorded area in precession photographs and its application in orienting crystals. Science 145:264-5 Jl 17 '64
—and Wuensch, B. J.
Distribution of atoms in high chalcocite, Cu_2S. bibliog Science 141:276-7 Jl 19 '63

BUETTNER, Konrad J. K. and Kern, C. D.
Infrared emissivity of the Sahara from Tiros data. bibliog Science 142:671 N 8 '63

BUFANO, Beniamino Benvenuto
Sculptor who embarrasses San Francisco. D. Bess. il por Harper 226:53-7 F '63

BUFFA, Elwood S. and others
Allocating facilities with CRAFT. Harvard Bsns R 42:136-47+ Mr '64

BUFFALO, Mo.
Man in Missouri; D. A. Mallory's donations. Time 81:102-3 My 17 '63

BUFFALO, N.Y.

Galleries and museums

See also
Albright-Knox art gallery

Hospitals

Surgeon for all seasons; Roswell Park memorial institute. il Newsweek 64:92 O 19 '64

Libraries

See also
Buffalo and Erie County, N.Y. public library

Music

[Musical events] (cont) il Mus Am 83:16 F '63; 84:56-7 Ja; 24 Jl '64

BUFFALO; story. See Mostert, N.

BUFFALO and Erie county, N.Y, public library
Scholarship realities; letter to the editor. P. M. Rooney. Library J 89:2904+ Ag '64

BUFFALO Bill. See Cody, W. F.

BUFFALO Bills (football club) See Football clubs

BUFFALO hunting
Buffalo Bill was a piker; D. C. Basolo's one-day record for buffalo kills. H. Peterson. il Sports Illus 21:76+ O 19 '64
Buffalo make me nervous. J. O'Connor. il Outdoor Life 132:20-3+ Ag '63

BUFFALO university. See New York state university—University at Buffalo
BUFFALOES
Cape buffalo. J. O'Connor. il Outdoor Life 134:36-9+ D '64
Last buffalo in Kalamazoo. B. Gilbert. il Sports Illus 18:E5-7 My 6 '63
BUFFET meals
Bountiful buffet for twenty. Ladies Home J 80:84-5 D '63
Curry buffet dinner for twenty. Vogue 141: 184 My '63
Do-it-yourself wedding buffet. il Ebony 19: 194+ Je '64
Isn't this a wonderful idea for a buffet dinner party? il Redbook 122:78-9+ N '63
Lap food. il Life 57:152-3+ O 16 '64
Little kitchen, big party. M. J. Engel. il Ladies Home J 80:102-3+ S '63
Luncheon buffet or a picnic with wines. il Sunset 131:128-30+ S '63
Patio party for teens. il Pop Gard 15:82 Jl '64
Patio tables for easy entertaining. il Pop Gard 15:40-1 My '64
Serve a leisurely buffet when the moon comes up; with recipes. il Am Home 67:58-9+ Je '64
Success with buffets. Bet Hom & Gard 41: 25 N '63
BUFFETS (furniture)
This wall-hung buffet once sat on four legs. il Sunset 133:130+ O '64
BUFFIE, Edward G. and Shane, H. G.
Who does Johnny's homework? PTA Mag 58:30-2 bibliog(p36) Ja '64
BUFORD, Curtis D.
Railroads have quit slumbering. Ann Am Acad 345:58-65 Ja '63
BUFORD, John Lester
Why belong to an NEA department? NEA J 52:47 F '63
BUG repellents. See Insect baits and repellents
BUGAY, John
Cruising the Santa Barbara Channel Islands. Yachting 113:40-2+ My '63
BUGBEE, Emma
Eleanor Roosevelt: my most unforgettable character. Read Digest 83:91-7 O '63
BUGLIARELLO, George, and Hsiao, G. C. C.
Phase separation in suspensions flowing through bifurcations: a simplified hemodynamic model. bibliog Science 143:469-71 Ja 31 '64
BUGS, Artificial. See Fishing lures, flies, etc.
BUHL, Bob
Big league batter with the built-in slump. R. Creamer. il por Sports Illus 18:66-9 Je 10 '63
BUHLER, Kathryn
Nine colonial sugar boxes. Antiques 85:88-91 Ja '64
BUICK motors division. See General motors corporation—Buick motors division
BUIE, T. S.
Rail fences. Am For 70:44-6 O '64
BUILDING
Across the land: men at work. il Newsweek 63:92-3 My 18 '64
Build right and prevent decay and termites. A. B. Parker. il House B 106:112-13+ F '64
Careful house hunter. il Time 81:91 Ap 5 '63
Dazzling new shows for sidewalk superintendents; revolutionary building methods. I. Wolfert. Read Digest 83:134-7 D '63
Going up; jump in construction spending. il Time 83:63 Ja 10 '64
Help for sidewalk superintendents. S. Blum. il N Y Times Mag p30-1+ O 4 '64
How to be a sidewalk superintendent; with drawings by H. B. Comstock. R. Gannon. Pop Sci 185:122-5+ O '64
Labor and material requirements for one-family houses. H. J. Rothberg. il Mo Labor R 87:797-800 Jl '64
Life guide; construction sites. il Life 55: 7 S 6 '63
Science of successful sidewalk super-intendency. il Changing T 17:39-40 O '63
Secret scrapbook of an architectural scavenger. P. Blake. il Arch Forum 121: 81-114 Ag '64
Sidewalk history; sidewalk superintendent. il Newsweek 62:98 O 14 '63
Structure & design; ed. by W. McQuade. il Fortune 70:177-8+ O; 205-6+ N; 176-8+ D '64
What it takes to be a client. D. Canty. il Arch Forum 119:84-7 Jl; 92-5 S; 94-7 D '63; 120:104-7 F; 106-9 Ap '64
See also
Brick construction
Earthquakes and building
Flashing
Foundations
Framing (building)
Roofs
Struts
Windowless construction
Wood construction

Bibliography

New literature for home-planning. Arch Rec 135:155+ mid-My '64
Technical books. Arch Rec 135:254+ My '64

Contracts and specifications

How to go from concept to construction. D. Canty. il Arch Forum 120:104-7 F '64

Cost

Apartment roundtable asks: what price urban living? il Arch Forum 120:84-91 Mr '64
Architecture as total community: the challenge ahead. A. Mayer. Arch Rec 136:157-62 Jl '64
Big, comprehensive high school at low cost. il Arch Rec 135:156-7 F '64
Building construction costs. M. L. Matthews. See issues of Architectural record to November 1964
Building construction costs. W. H. Edgerton. il Arch Rec 136:28 D '64; 137:20 Ja '65
Construction cost indexes. See issues of Architectural record
Cost of Record houses near you. il Arch Rec 135:128 mid-My '64
How one large office uses construction cost estimates; summary of views and procedures at Smith, Hinchman & Grylls associates, inc. W. B. Foxhall. il Arch Rec 135:106+ My '64
Lesson in how much things cost. il House B 105:172-3 S '63
To start your home improvement. il Bet Hom & Gard 41:6+ O '63
Why new houses cost too much. A. M. Watkins. il Sat Eve Post 236:19-25 S 21 '63
See also
School buildings—Cost

Employees

See Building workers

Estimates

How one large office uses construction cost estimates; summary of views and procedures at Smith, Hinchman & Grylls associates, inc. W. B. Foxhall. il Arch Rec 135:106+ My '64

Finance

See also
Mortgages

Regulations

See Building laws and regulations

Specifications

See Building—Contracts and specifications

Statistics

Building heads for a new record year. il Arch Forum 119:5 Ag '63
Building picture. G. A. Christie. Arch Rec 135:143 Ja '64
Current trends in construction. H. C. F. Arnold. See issues of Architectural record to June 1964
F. W. Dodge construction outlook for 1964. il Arch Rec 134:141-8 O '63
1964 forecast: $28.6 billion for new buildings. M. L. Colean. Arch Forum 119:100-1 N '63
Solid housing. Fortune 68:46 O '63
BUILDING, Adobe
Hugo Reid adobe near Los Angeles, California. G. Norman-Wilcox. il Antiques 84:168-71 Ag '63
Readers ask us about adobe. Sunset 132:86-8 F '64
BUILDING, Bombproof
New York plans protection for children. A. E. Sigal. Arch Rec 133:172 F '63
BUILDING, Ice and snow
City under the ice cap; Camp Century, Greenland. L. D. Hamilton. il Am City 78:100-2 Jl '63
BUILDING, Stormproof
High winds make missiles of building parts at Guam. il Arch Rec 133:186 F '63
Nested hurricane screens shield windows. il Arch Rec 135:186 Je '64
BUILDING and earthquakes. See Earthquakes and building
BUILDING appraisal. See Valuation
BUILDING blocks
Building blocks, dirt cheap; Cinva-Ram blocks. D. S. Stroetzel. il Read Digest 84: 234-8 My '64

BUILDING blocks—*Continued*
Earth bricks by the millions; Cinva-Ram blocks. D. S. Stroetzel. il Américas 16:5-9 Ap '64; Same abr. with title Building blocks, dirt cheap. Read Digest 84:234-8 My '64

BUILDING codes. See Building laws and regulations

BUILDING costs. See Building—Cost

BUILDING fittings
Components program for California schools. il Arch Rec 135:167-9 Ja '64
New products for the house. il Arch Rec 135:129+ mid-My '64
Product reports. See issues of Architectural record
Products. See issues of Architectural forum to July 1964
Quality is like money in the bank. Bet Hom & Gard 41:30+ My '63
School component designs, costs revealed; California's program. il Arch Rec 135:166-72 F '64
What's new at the builders' show. il House & Gard 123:210-12 Ap '63

BUILDING industry
America's biggest stagnant industry. il Arch Forum 118:73 F '63
Big cities report on building prospect. il Arch Forum 120:7+ F '64
Boom with a nervous tone. il Bsns W p30-2 Jl 13 '63
Bricks without straw bosses. J. Lear. il Sat R 47:45-9 F 1 '64
Building a base for prosperity; apartment and home building. il Bsns W p20-1 D 21 '63
Building boom feels the brake of caution. il Bsns W p 113-14+ Mr 23 '63
Building takes a pause. il Bsns W p82+ Je 20 '64
Business outlook; signs of real improvement. Bsns W p21-2 Je 1 '63
Construction boss. il Ebony 18:105-8+ Jl '63
Construction: public money fuels growth. il Bsns W p 118+ Mr 23 '63
Contractors bid for progress. il Arch Forum 118:125-7 Je '63
Experts see a continuing building boom. il Arch Forum 119:5+ D '63
Feel of the forest. F. B. Quigg. il Am For 69:28-31+ N '63
Foreign builders get a beachhead; newest look on U.S. skyline. il Bsns W p84-6+ My 11 '63
Housing raises the roof; survey of builders; with chart. Fortune 67:40+ Ap '63
Housing turns a corner; apartment and home building. il Bsns W p 19-20 D 19 '64
Housing's prospects look a little better. il Bsns W p27-8 My 4 '63
Industry scrambles to get plants built; Engineering news-record report. il Bsns W p54-5 D 26 '64
Is the building boom headed for trouble? il U S News 56:99-101 Je 8 '64
Is the building boom tapering off? il U S News 55:62-4 S 30 '63
Large components systems discussed at convention of the Producers' council. Arch Rec 134:70 D '63
Latest on building boom; with charts. U S News 57:96-7 S 21 '64
Manufacturers reject research subsidy; National construction industry research and development conference. il Arch Forum 119:10-11 D '63
New architecture of Castro's Cuba. D. Rowntree. il Arch Forum 120:122-5 Ap '64
New signs of trouble in the building boom. il U S News 56:92-3 Mr 9 '64
New York tops out its building boom. il Bsns W p34+ Ag 29 '64
1964 construction outlook at midyear. G. A. Christie. il Arch Rec 136:18 Jl '64
100 biggest building clients in the U.S. (cont) il Arch Forum 119:91-3 Ag '63; 121:14-16 Jl '64
One hundred biggest building contractors in the U.S. il Arch Forum 118:122-4 Je '63
$120 billion in construction in 1975; forecast by F. W. Dodge corporation. G. A. Christie. il Arch Rec 134:173-80 S '63
Private spending will strengthen prosperity. R. Newcomb. il Nations Bsns 52:40-1+ S '64
Shell home builders try for a comeback. il Bsns W p83-4+ Mr 9 '63
Too much too soon? Time 83:84 Je 26 '64
Where there's life, there's business. il Bsns W p 16 Jl 4 '64
See also
Contractors
Houses, Prefabricated

Employees

Negroes push harder for construction jobs. il Bsns W p66+ Je 15 '63

Labor conditions

Labor and material requirements for public housing. S. F. Miller. il Mo Labor R 87:1029-32 S '64

Great Britain

British system builds from the top down. il Arch Forum 120:92-5 Mr '64

BUILDING laws and regulations
Building boom feels the brake of caution. il Bsns W p 113-14+ Mr 23 '63
Codes cover an experimental house; Rockville, Md. W. A. Scheiber. il Am City 78:83-4 Ag '63
St Louis takes the cure; a case history for ailing cities. A. M. Watkins. il Harper 229:66-70 Ag '64
What you should know about building codes. House & Gard 124:36+ N '63
Who is blocking building code reforms? A. M. Watkins. Am Home 66:31+ Ja '63
Why new houses cost too much. A. M. Watkins. il Sat Eve Post 236:19-25 S 21 '63
See also
Plumbing laws and regulations
Zoning

BUILDING maintenance. See Buildings—Maintenance and repair

BUILDING materials
Basic guide to low maintenance. D. X. Manners. House B 106:150-2 Mr '64
Bricks without straw bosses. J. Lear. il Sat R 47:45-9 F 1 '64
Classic elegance in sturdy materials. il Arch Rec 133:106-9 mid-My '63
Double-duty building materials. il House & Gard 124:246-7 O '63
Exploit the riches of inexpensive materials. il House B 106:110-13+ Je '64
Fight for the home. il Time 83:87 My 1 '64
Houses will be different. Changing T 18:6 S '64
How can you make them people-proof? il Arch Forum 118:100-1 Ap '63
Latest ways to modernize your home. il Pop Mech 120:138-43 S '63
Materials, systems differ in four deployable schools. il Arch Rec 133:182-5 F '63
Natural materials and landscape blend in open-plan house. il Arch Rec 133:110-13 mid-My '63
New products for the house. il Arch Rec 133:132+ mid-My '63; 135:129+ mid-My '64
Plastic planks. J. Joseph. il Pop Mech 120:132-3+ O '63
Product reports. See issues of Architectural record
Products. See issues of Architectural forum to July 1964
Quality is like money in the bank. Bet Hom & Gard 41:30+ My '63
Revoluntary building material; boron fibers from borax. U S News 56:12 Je 29 '64
Secret scrapbook of an architectural scavenger. P. Blake. il Arch Forum 121:81-114 Ag '64
Spring roundup of new building materials. A. J. Maher. il Pop Mech 121:128-33 Ap '64
What you need to know before you build in the tropics. A. B. Parker. il House B 106:102-3+ Ja '64
What's new at the builders' show. il House & Gard 123:210-12 Ap '63
Your second home: design and material selection. il Am Home 67:20+ Ap '64
See also
Aluminum, Structural
Bricks
Concrete
Concrete blocks
Plastics
Plywood industry
Roofing

BUILDING research
Future of research; excerpts from paper. R. Llewelyn-Davies and P. Cowan. Arch Rec 136:105+ S '64
How will labor attack research for building? British construction industry. Arch Rec 136:304+ N '64
Research for building: the big battle rages in Washington. B. P. Spring. il Arch Forum 119:122-3+ S '63
Washington debates building research. il Arch Forum 118:5 Ap '63

BUILDING service employees' international union
House the janitors built; Marina City Chicago. G. Cross. il Read Digest 82:201-4 F '63
Marina City. J. M. Liston. il Pop Sci 182:82-5+ Ap '63
Union support of towers toppling. il Bsns W p 108 My 16 '64

BUILDING sites
Architecture as total community: the challenge ahead. A. Mayer. Arch Rec 136:157-62 Jl '64

BUILDING sites—*Continued*
Before you buy a house, look at the landscape. J. Fanning. il Pop Gard 15:55-7 Jl '64
Better homes for all America! J. D. Bloodgood. il Bet Hom & Gard 42:40-3 Mr '64
Buy a lot and build? il Changing T 17:31-3 Jl '63
Campus planning; California; symposium. il Arch Rec 136:175-204 N '64
Formal house planned for a river view. il Arch Rec 135:64-7 mid-My '64
Foundation planting. il House & Gard 125: 128-31 F '64
House with a built-in landscape. il House & Gard 125:170-3 My '64
Large school shaped by its site; William B. Ward school, New Rochelle, N.Y. il Arch Forum 120:120-1 My '64
Look twice before cutting. D. White. il Flower Grower 50:45+ Mr '63
Machine factory with a woodland setting. il Arch Rec 134:126-7 D '63
Offices built along a highway; Northwestern mutual insurance company of Seattle, Raleigh, N.C. il Arch Rec 136:162-3 D '64
Purposefully regional architecture; country house by Winston Elting in the Pennsylvania countryside. il Arch Rec 137:135-42 Ja '65
Staggered walls exploit site irregularities. il Arch Rec 135:112-15 mid-My '64
Sunny house for a wooded site. il Arch Rec 135:169-72 Mr '64
Two-level site solution. il Arch Rec 133:156-7 Mr '63
Urbanity in the lush Nuanu Valley. il House B 106:104-7 Ja '64
Why, where, & how to build your second home. Am Home 67:16 Ap '64
See also
Hillside architecture
Housing projects—Site planning

BUILDING tools. See Tools

BUILDING trades. See Building industry

BUILDING trades unions
N.Y. unions fight decline in building. Arch Forum 119:11 Jl '63

BUILDING workers
Bridge. G. Talese. il Esquire 62:136-44+ D '64
Not racism, but nepotism. il Time 82:14 Ag 9 '63

BUILDINGS
See also
Public buildings

Cleaning

New look in Paris; five-year cleaning campaign. A. Rothberg. Commonweal 77:514-15 F 8 '63
Paris takes an epic bath. J. Daniel. il Read Digest 83:174-80 Ag '63

Maintenance and repair

How can you make them people-proof? il Arch Forum 118:100-1 Ap '63
See also
Allied maintenance corporation

Models

See Architectural models

Orientation

See Orientation (architecture)

Valuation

See Valuation

BUILDINGS, Bombproof. See Building, Bombproof

BUILDINGS, Photography of. See Photography of buildings and structures

BUILDINGS, Portable
See also
School buildings, Portable

BUILDINGS, Prefabricated
Metal prefabs are coming of age. il Arch Forum 118:124-7 Ap '63
Moscow landscape 1963: it's instant housing! il Life 55:34-41 S 13 '63
Packaged buildings. W. J. Fletcher. il Suc Farm 62:64-5 Ag '64
Swiss prefabrication. il Arch Forum 120:82-3 Mr '64
See also
Hospitals, Prefabricated
Houses, Prefabricated

BUILDINGS, Remodeled
See also
Houses, Remodeled

BUILDINGS, Restoration of. See Architecture—Conservation and restoration

BUILDINGS, Round
Shopping go-round at Macy's; Queens store. il Bsns W p34 F 15 '64

BUILDINGS, Stormproof. See Building, Stormproof

BUILDINGS, Underwater. See Underwater structures

BUILDINGS, Wrecking of. See Wrecking

BUILDINGS in art. See Architecture in art

BUILT in beds. See Beds, Built in

BUILT in furniture. See Furniture, Built in

BUKHARA, Russia
God rest ye merry teddy bear; excerpt from Under a lilac-bleeding star. L. Blanch. Vogue 142:102+ D '63

BUKOWSKI, Charles
Home and the dragon: U.S. poetry before and after the beats. L. Holland. por Américas 16:28-32 Ja '64
Seven poets and a playwright. D. Stuart. Poetry 104:263 Jl '64

BUKSTEIN, Ed
Binary computer codes and ASCII. Electr World 72:28-9 Jl '64
Computer input-output equipment. Electr World 72:52-4+ N '64
Data flow in digital computers. Electr World 72:36-7+ Ag '64
Electric shock on purpose. Electr World 69: 29-32+ F '63

BULANGO affair; story. See Edqvist, D.

BULBS
Annuals, perennials, summer bulbs for 1964. H. Mason. il Bet Hom & Gard 42:58-63 Mr '64
Bulb planting. V. H. Ries. il Horticulture 41:562-3 N '63
Bulb planting guide for fall; comp. by P. F. Frese. Pop Gard 15:62-3 S '64
Bulb planting reminder. il Horticulture 42: 38-9 O '64
Bulbs. M. Costigan. il Horticulture 41:454-5 S '63
Bulbs in the deep South. J. L. Russell, jr. il Flower Grower 50:67-8 Ap '63
Early bird bulbs. B. Miles. il Flower Grower 50:26-7+ S '63
Fall bulbs. M. M. Graff. il Horticulture 42: 14-16 Ag '64
Fall-sown annuals hide ripened bulb foliage in spring. M. Costigan. il Flower Grower 50:18-20 O '63
Flowers of spring are in these bulbs. il Flower Grower 50:24-8 O '63
For gardeners in Utah, these will bloom in March. il Sunset 131:286 O '63
Glorious spring color, yours for the planting. H. Mason. il Bet Hom & Gard 42:62-7+ O '64
Growing bulbs in pots indoors. K. S. Taylor. il Horticulture 42:24-7+ N '64
Holland in bloom. J. H. Winchester. il Travel 119:28-30 F '63
How to buy a better bulb. il Bet Hom & Gard 41:126-7 O '63
Ideas to profit by; woodland garden of bulbs. J. B. Brimer. il Flower Grower 51:27 S '64
It's time to plant bulbs. il Changing T 18:18 S '64
Making bulb arrangements. il Sunset 131:298+ O '63
More ideas for bulb highlights. il Pop Gard 15:38-9 S '64
My golden spring. C. Lisle. il Flower Grower 51:24-5 S '64
Plant a spring bulb show in your garden this fall. Am Home 67:89-90 O '64
Plant bulbs for spring. D. H. Jenkins. il Parents Mag 39:164 N '64
Salute to the Hollanders and their bulbs. T. A. Weston. il Am Home 66:27-9 O '63
Some new bulbs for fall. il Horticulture 41: 483 S '63
Spring bulb make-up kit. M. M. Graff. House & Gard 124:204-5+ S '63
Spring bulb story must begin in the fall. il Flower Grower 51:24-6 O '64
Spring bulbs earlier. J. Unterecker. il Flower Grower 50:37+ N '63
Spring; make the most of it with small bulbs. G. S. Wister. il Horticulture 42:14-18 Mr '64
Summer bulbs; with drawings by V. Howie. Horticulture 42:34-5 Je '64
True bulbs sit for their portrait. il Sunset 133:94-9 O '64
You can put a better face on spring. il House & Gard 124:158-61 S '63
See also
Camasses
Forcing (plants)
Narcissus
Tulips

Storage

Dig gladiolus corms and store over the winter; photographs. Flower Grower 51:48 O '64

BULBS—Storage—*Continued*
How to store summer bulbs. V. Howie. il Horticulture 42:36-7 O '64
BULEN, William A.
Biological nitrogen fixation. Science 147:310-12 Ja 15 '65
BULFINCH, Charles
Bulfinch's houses for Mrs Swan. J. Kirker. il Antiques 86:442-4 O '64
BULFINCH, Thomas
On the fringe. H. Frankel. Sat R 47:39 Mr 21 '64
BULGARIA
See also
Airlines—Bulgaria
Foreign students in Bulgaria
Sofia
Taxation—Bulgaria

Commerce

Department states views on trade relations between U. S. and Bulgaria; Department statement, July 2, 1963. Dept State Bul 49:141 Jl 22 '63

Economic conditions

Bulgaria under Soviet leadership. L. A. D. Dellin. Cur Hist 44:281-7 My '63
Life of a lap dog. il Time 84:26-7 S 25 '64
BULGARIA and the United States
Minister Eugenie Anderson speaks on Bulgarian television and radio; July 3, 1963. E. Anderson. Dept State Bul 49:141 Jl 22 '63
BULGARIAN literature
See also
Childrens literature—Bulgaria
BULGE, Battle of the. See Ardennes, Battle of the, 1944-1945
BULGER, Paul
President views art education. Sch Arts 63:36-8 Mr '64
BULGUR
Cooking with bulgur wheat. Sunset 131:209 O '63
BULK bin field handling. See Fruit handling
BULKELEY, Houghton
Aaron Roberts and the southeastern Connecticut cabinetmaking school. H. Comstock. il Antiques 86:437-41 O '64
BULKLEY, Robert J. jr
PT's ride again; excerpt from At close quarters. Motor B 112:28-31 Jl '63
BULL, Hedley
International order and the dispersion of nuclear weapons. Science 144:677-8+ My 8 '64
BULL, Ronnie
Workhorse Texas Bull; running back of Chicago Bears. J. Olsen. Sports Illus 19:52-4 O 14 '63
BULL, Sandy
This record is important: the innate musicality of Sandy Bull. W. Rhodes. por Am Rec G 29:899 Jl '63
BULL, William E.
Sonny LeMatina? il Newsweek 63:79-80 Mr 9 '64
BULL fights. See Bullfights
BULL-horn acacias. See Acacias
BULLARD, Robert W. See Van Beaumont, W. jt. auth.
BULLDOGGING. See Rodeos
BULLDOZERS
Gentle bulldozers of Peoria. G. Cross. il Fortune 68:166-71+ Jl '63
BULLEN, Beverly A.
How to stay on a diet. Seventeen 23:176-7+ S '64
BULLER, Bonner I.
My trailer does more than haul a boat. Pop Sci 182:134-6+ F '63
BULLETIN, Philadelphia
Do newsmen have special rights in court? R. L. Tobin. Sat R 46:59-60 Ap 13 '63; Reply. J. C. Crumlish, jr. 46:49+ Je 8 '63
Evening bulletin test case. R. L. Tobin. Sat R 46:55 My 11 '63
Newspaper and public library tangle over secret records; Philadelphia evening bulletin vs. Free library of Philadelphia. Library J 88:3042 S 1 '63
BULLETIN of the atomic scientists
Atomic age, ed. by M. Grodzins and E. Rabinowitch. Review
New Yorker 40:136-41 Je 13 '64. J. Bernstein
New Year's thoughts 1964. E. Rabinowitch. Bul Atomic Sci 20:2+ Ja '64
Our common enterprise. Bul Atomic Sci 19:24 S '63
Turning back the clock. Time 83:52-3 Ap 10 '64
BULLETS
Practice bullets for regular guns; Accra-Wax, CCI Red-Jet, and Speer Target-38. Consumer Rep 29:138 Mr '64
See also
Cartridges
BULLFIGHTERS
Artistry in a bullring is not enough. P. E. Ress. il Sports Illus 21:44-7 Ag 10 '64
BULLFIGHTS
Brave matadora explains the bullfight; drawings by R. Riger. P. McCormick. Sports Illus 18:38-44+ Mr 11 '63
Bullfighting. R. D. Lozano. il Sports Illus 18:68+ Ap 15 '63
Fighting Yankee of Seville; matador. R. Daley. il Sat Eve Post 237:62-3 Ap 11 '64
Man from Córdoba. il Time 83:42+ F 28 '64
Spanish spectacle. il Holiday 35:160 Je '64
BULLFROGS. See Frogs
BULLOCK, Adeline
When baby is ill. Parents Mag 39:154-5 S '64
BULLOCK, Helen Duprey
Dining with the presidents; with recipes. Am Home 67:58-9+ N '64
BULLOCK, Milon W. See Burdette, W. J. jt. auth.
BULLOCK, Theodore H.
Neurophysiology: United States-Japan joint symposium. Science 144:1361-4 Je 12 '64
BULLOUGH, Vern L.
Mormon writ and modern ethics. Nation 196:291-2 Ap 6 '63
BULLS
Are you using the right dairy bull? questions and answers. C. E. Meadows. il Suc Farm 61:42-3 O '63
Breeding the bravest of bulls; in Spain. il Bsns W p 116-17+ My 25 '63
Bulls need a physical, too. O. Bay. il Farm J 88:58H N '64
He doubled his bull power. C. Peterson, jr. il Suc Farm 62:120 Ap '64
How much should you pay for a beef bull? G. W. Litton. il Suc Farm 61:72 Je '63
Husbandry? Aberdeen Angus bull $176,400. il Newsweek 62:62 Ag 19 '63
They fed out 100 bulls! D. Malena and B. Rust. il Suc Farm 62:32-3 D '64

Performance records and registration

See Cattle, Beef—Performance records and registration
BULLS, Colloquial
Games; the Irish bull. J. Ciardi. Sat R 47:10 Ag 8 '64
Taurus revisited, or Was that bull Irish? J. Ciardi. Sat R 47:37-8 O 10 '64
BULLS, Irish. See Bulls, Colloquial
BULLS, Papal
Language of Rome; papal documents. America 111:652 N 21 '64
BULMAN, Learned
Reviewing philosophy. Library J 89:1878-9 Ap 15 '64
BULOVA watch company
Swiss seek to turn their watches ahead; challenge to Bulova's Accutron. il Bsns W p42-4+ Ja 9 '65
BÜLOW-HÜBE, Torun
Jewelry by Torun. A. Karlikow. il Craft Horiz 23:20-1+ Jl '63
BULTMAN, Fritz
Achievement of Hans Hofmann. Art N 62:43-5+ S '63
BULTMANN, Rudolf
Bultmann: stone of stumbling. Christian Cent 80:383 Mr 20 '63
New search for the historical Jesus. il Time 81:68+ Je 21 '63
BUMBLEBEES
Smell, sex and survival in animals. K. Von Frisch. il Sci Digest 53:65-72 F '63
BUMBRY, Grace
Grace Bumbry: a singer comes home. V. Kelly. il pors Look 27:66+ F 26 '63
BUMSTEAD, John C.
Cut water-planning guesswork. Am City 78:102-4 My '63
BUNAU-VARILLA, Philippe
Man who invented Panama. E. Sevareid. por Am Heritage 14:106-10 Ag '63
Panama Canal lobby of Philippe Bunau-Varilla and William Nelson Cromwell. C. D. Ameringer. Am Hist R 68:346-63 Ja '63
BUNCH, T. E. and Cohen, A. J.
Coesite and shocked quartz from Holleford Crater, Ontario, Canada. bibliog Science 142:379-81 O 18 '63
BUNDY, Edgar C.
$ucce$$ of Major Bundy. Christian Cent 80:991 Ag 7 '63

BUNDY, F. P.
Diamond synthesis with Bridgman opposed-anvil apparatus. bibliog Science 146:1673 D 25 '64
—and Kasper, J .S.
New dense form of solid germanium. bibliog Science 139:340-1 Ja 25 '63
BUNDY, Horace
Pilgrim's progress: Horace Bundy and his paintings. H. O. Shepard. il por Antiques 86:445-9 O '64
BUNDY, McGeorge
Excerpt from address, October 4, 1962. Cong Digest 42:238+ O '63
Next steps toward peace: some notes on the two-legged process; address September 30, 1963. Dept State Bul 49:625-30 O 21 '63
Presidency and the peace. For Affairs 42: 353-65 Ap '64
Scientist and national policy; address. December 27, 1962. Science 139:805-9 Mr 1 '63

about

JFK's McGeorge Bundy; cool head for any crisis. il pors Newsweek 61:20-4 Mr 4 '63
Mr Whitney Griswold and his successor. Nat R 14:350 My 7 '63
Second most important brothers in Washington. por Time 82:33 N 15 '63
BUNDY, Mary Lee
Behind central processing. por Library J 88: 3539-43 O 1 '63
BUNDY, William Putnam
Assistant Secretary Bundy comments on southeast Asia developments in Voice of America interview; ed. by W. McCrory. Dept State Bul 51:334-9 S 7 '64
Mr Bundy interviewed on red China's nuclear testing, October 16, 1964. Dept State Bul 51:616-17 N 2 '64
Progress and problems in east Asia: an American viewpoint; address, September 29, 1964. Dept State Bul 51:534-42 O 19 '64
United States and Korea reaffirm policy of cooperation: joint statement, October 3, 1964. Dept State Bul 51:542 O 19 '64

about

New top man on Far East. por U S News 56: 19 Mr 16 '64
Second most important brothers in Washington. por Time 82:33 N 15 '63
BUNGALOWS
Ways to grow with a bungalow. R. Martens. il Farm J 87:26-7 Ag '63
BUNGE corporation
Global grain dealer and more besides. il Bsns W p56-8+ O 19 '63
BUNIM, Joseph J.
What doctors are learning about arthritis; questions and answers, ed. by H. G. Earl. por Todays Health 42:38-9+ Ag '64
BUNK beds. See Beds
BUNKER, Don L.
Computer experiments in chemistry. Sci Am 211:100-8 Jl '64
BUNKER, Ellsworth
First special Inter-American conference provides for admission of new members to Organization of American states; statement, December 17, 1964; with text of the Act of Washington. Dept State Bul 52:46-9 Ja 11 '65
OAS council moves to assist in solving U.S.-Panama dispute; statements, January 31 and February 4, 1964. bibliog f Dept State Bul 50:300-4 F 24 '64

about

Another job for the U.N. Time 81:31-2 My 10 '63
New man at OAS. por Newsweek 63:36 Ja 13 '64
President names Ellsworth Bunker ambassador to OAS; statement, January 2, 1964. L. B. Johnson. Dept State Bul 50:143 Ja 27 '64
BUNKER, George Maverick
Millions under Martin Marietta's mattress. C. J. V. Murphy. il por Fortune 68:134-41+ N '63; 69:76+ F '64
BUNKER, Patricia
Fall kicks off the big book. Sat R 47:37-8 O 3 '64
Gift to give? a book, of course. Sat R 47: 51-5+ D 5 '64
(comp) Spring is for new-book lovers. Sat R 47:37-8 Ap 18 '64
(comp) To one and all, a good book. Sat R 46:39-43+ D 7 '63
BUNKER, Wally
Strictly for the birds. H. L. Masin. por Sr Schol 85:38 S 23 '64
BUNKER HILL, Battle of, 1775
Black patriots were heroes at first major battle of Revolution. A. Morrison. il Ebony 19:44-6+ F '64
BUNKER-Ramo corporation
New face in computers; computer control systems. il Bsns W p32 Ja 25 '64
BUNKS. See Beds; Beds, Built in
BUNN, Martin
Gus Wilson's model garage (title varies) See issues of Popular science monthly
BUNNELL, R. H.
Vitamin B_6; report on International symposium on vitamin B_6. Science 146:674-7 O 30 '64
BUNNING, Jim
Player of the week; Philadelphia Phillies perfect game. il por Sports Illus 20:69 Je 29 '64
BUNRATTY castle. See Castles
BUNSHAFT, Gordon
Any form you need; headquarters for the Emhart manufacturing co, Conn. il por Time 82:44-5+ Ag 2 '63
BUNTING, John R.
Disturbing economics of affluence; excerpts from Hidden face of free enterprise. Duns R 83:40-1+ Ap '64
What's ahead for business? Atlan 213:72-5 Je '64
BUNTING, Mary F.
Just what is a landscape architect? Horticulture 41:88-9 F '63
Water adds coolness to the garden. Horticulture 41:318-19 Je '63
BUÑUEL, Luis
Two on the aisle. P. V. Beckley. il Sat R 47:36-7 F 8 '64
BUNZEL, Peter
Does everybody here like Jack? Life 54:103-5+ Mr 22 '63
Edie wins a big one. Life 54:95-6+ Ap 5 '63
There's method in Newman's marriage. Life 55:50-1 Jl 5 '63
When I'm with dancers I am a loner. Life 54:66-7 Je 21 '63
BUOY; story. See Mountzoures, H. L.
BUR oak. See Oak
BURBANK, Muriel D.
Washout technique. Sch Arts 63:16-17 Je '64
BURCA, Richard
Holiday I'll never forget. Read Digest 84:64-8 Je '64
BURCH, Claire
Day Elizabeth was born. McCalls 90:46 Je '63
For John F. Kennedy, November 26, 1963; poem. McCalls 91:186 Mr '64
Hill; poem. Mlle 58:42 Ja '64
I remember Eda Lou. Sat R 46:14-16 Je 29 '63
Lines from inside the Promised Land. New Repub 148:24 Ap 20 '63
Magic moment; poem. McCalls 90:141 Jl '63
Notes on a blast; poem. Sat R 46:16 Ap 13 '63
One-woman show. por Redbook 123:8+ Je '64
Winter bargains; poem. Sat R 47:160 Ag 29 '64
World inside; poem. McCalls 91:180 O '63
BURCH, Dean
Bye, bye Burch? il por Newsweek 64:19-21 D 21 '64
Clearing the underbrush. il por Time 84:24 D 18 '64
Hand at the helm. por Time 84:28A Jl 24 '64
Pen pal for Dean. Time 85:17 Ja 8 '65
BURCH, Thomas K.
Population and parenthood. Commonweal 80: 328-31 Je 5 '64
BURCHARD, Marshall
Yale's School of art and architecture. Arch Forum 120:80-3 F '64
BURCK, Gilbert H.
Assault on fortress I.B.M. Fortune 69:112-16+ Je '64
Balance-of-payments bind. Fortune 67:112-17 Je '63
Boundless age of the computer. Fortune 69: 100-11+ Mr; 140-5+ Ap; 112-16+ Je; 70: 124-6+ Ag; 120-1+ O '64
Chemicals: the reluctant competitors. Fortune 68:148-53+ N '63
In electrical manufacturing, the word is rationalize. Fortune 68:110-15+ S '63
Knowledge: the biggest growth industry of them all. Fortune 70:128-31+ N '64

BURCK, Gilbert H.—*Continued*
No bed of feathers. Life 55:23 S 27 '63
You may think the corporate profit tax is bad, but... Fortune 67:86-9+ Ap '63
—and Parker, S.
Prime mover begins to move. Fortune 67:110-14+ F '63
BURCKHARDT, Rudolph
Rudolph Burckhardt: multiple fugitive. A. Katz. il por Art N 62:38-41 D '63
BURCKHARDT, Sigurd
Of order, abstraction, and language. Yale R 53:533-50 Je '64
BURDEN, Amanda
Young joyous life. V. Lawford. il pors Vogue 145:178-85+ F 1 '65
BURDEN, Jean
Way of knowing; excerpts from address. bibliog Mlle 58:73+ D '63
BURDEN, S. Carter, Jr
Young joyous life. V. Lawford. il pors Vogue 145:178-85+ F 1 '65
BURDEN, Shirley
I wonder why; condensation. il Read Digest 84:97-107 F '64
BURDEN, William
William Burden collection. il por Vogue 143:86-7 Ja 15 '64
BURDETTE, Walter J. and Bullock, M. W.
Ecdysone: five biologically active fractions from Bombyx. bibliog Science 140:1311 Je 21 '63
BURDETTE and company
Boston printing firm enters trade publishing. Pub W 184:32 O 28 '63
BURDICK, Eugene
480; novel. Sat Eve Post 237:44-6 Je 13; 36-7 Je 20; 40-2 Je 27 '64
From gold rush to sun rush. N Y Times Mag p36-7+ Ap 14 '63
They ride the big surf. Read Digest 83:224-30 Jl '63
Trailing a curious political animal. N Y Times Mag p 10+ My 31 '64
—See Lederer, W. J; Wheeler, H. jt. auths.
—and Lederer, W. J.
Ugly American revisited. pors Sat Eve Post 236:78-81 My 4 '63
BUREAU of commercial fisheries. See United States—Fish and wildlife service
BUREAU of customs. See Customs service—United States
BUREAU of educational and cultural affairs. See United States—State, Department of—Educational and cultural affairs, Bureau of
BUREAU of international expositions
Onward and upward with the arts. J. Brooks. New Yorker 39:42+ Je 1 '63
BUREAU of marine inspection and navigation. See United States—Coast guard
BUREAUCRACY
Big shuffle; House census and government statistics subcommittee study problem of paper work. Newsweek 65:28 Ja 11 '65
Case for bureaucracy. H. Cleveland. il N Y Times Mag p 19+ O 27 '63
Conflicting policies decrease public's trust in government. F. Morley. il Nations Bsns 51:27-8 Ap '63
Dilemmas of power; excerpt from Rise of the West. W. H. McNeill. Sat R 46:50-1 N 2 '63
House prober charges federal paperwork wastes your money; interview. A. Olsen. Nations Bsns 52:84-6+ S '64
How to get better government; interview, ed. by P. F. Healy. E. P. Neilan. il Nations Bsns 51:40-1+ My '63
How to save money; an open letter to Congressman John J. Rooney. H. S. Villard. Harper 228:17+ Ja '64
Muddle of megalopolis. A. M. Sullivan. Duns R 84:86 D '64
Paper-work jungle. H. Hazlitt. Newsweek 64:50 D 28 '64
Personal observations from abroad: free and less free; red tape in Warsaw. P. L. Buckley. Nat R 16:809-12 S 22 '64
Political frustration: cause and cure. R. Rienow and L. T. Rienow. Sat R 46:25-8 S 28 '63; Discussion. 46:29 O 19 '63
Red tape: what it costs in taxes, in headaches. il U S News 55:79-81 Ag 19 '63
Sad state of the Department of state: the hog-tied ambassador. E. Briggs. Esquire 60:100-1+ S '63
Washington insight; Kennedy and the intellectuals. J. Kraft. Harper 227:112+ N '63
Working man's Washington. J. D. Weaver. Holiday 36:74-5+ D '64
Yardstick for red tape. Bsns W p38 S 12 '64
BUREAUCRATS. See Public officers
BUREAUS of United States government. See name of bureau, inverted, under United States, e.g. United States—Indian affairs, Bureau of

BURFORD, Byron
Where do we go from here? F. Getlein. New Repub 149:34-5 N 2 '63
BURFORD, William
Spell; poem. Nation 199:409 N 30 '64
about
Five poets. T. Cassity. Poetry 103:195-7 D '63
BURGAN, Robert L.
How to have plenty of parks. por Am City 78:118-19 Je '63
BURGEES. See Flags
BURGER, Chester
Don't let your travel slide show fail. Pop Phot 52:130+ Ap '63
BURGER, Ralph W.
Making change at A.&P. Time 81:86 Mr 22 '63
Pinching 500,000,000,000 pennies. il por Fortune 67:104-9+ Mr '63
BURGERT, Robert
(ed) Special issue on A-V instruction. por Sr Schol 85:8T-10T+ Ja 21 '65
BURGESS, Alan
(ed) See Martin, S. Night the world fell down
BURGESS, Frederick
Profiles; Church of St Matthew and St Timothy. R. Rice. il New Yorker 40:41-2+ Ag 1 '64
BURGESS, Gelett
Have you an educated heart? excerpts from The bromide and other theories. Read Digest 82:180G Mr '63
BURGESS, Guy Francis de Moncy
Kim. il Time 81:39 Mr 15 '63
Love, Kim. Newsweek 61:45 Mr 18 '63
BURGESS, Howard F.
Miniature voltage regulators. Electr World 71:82-3 F '64
BURGESS, Lorraine
Put spring in a bottle. il Flower Grower 50:26-7 N '63
BURGESS, Robert
Rocky road of HR 6386; excerpts from testimony. Nat R 15:429 N 19 '63
BURGESS, Robert F.
Decoys for doves. Outdoor Life 132:44-7+ D '63
Florida's sturgeon spree. por Outdoor Life 131:44-7+ Mr '63
BURGESS, Thornton W.
Thornton W. Burgess recalls a ninety-year romance with nature. D. M. Fox. il pors Audubon Mag 66:312-13 S '64
BURGESS, William C.
Glue sniffing. PTA Mag 58:15-17 Mr '64
BURGLARY and burglars
Aristocrats of crime; jewel thieves. C. Remsberg and B. Remsberg. il N Y Times Mag p9 +D 27 '64
Burglar sizes up your house. il Read Digest 84:84-6 F '64
Celebrity watchers. Newsweek 63:77 Ja 27 '64
Reporter at large. S. Black. il New Yorker 39:63-4+ D 7; 89-91+ D 14 '63
Ten best ways to outwit burglars. D. X. Manners. il House B 106:100-1+ Jl '64
BURGLARY insurance. See Insurance, Burglary
BURGOYNE, John
Baroness on the battlefield; excerpts from Baroness von Riedesel and the American revolution, ed. and tr. by M. L. Brown. F. C. L. V. Riedesel. il pors Am Heritage 16:64-79 D '64
March to Saratoga, by H. Bird. Review
Reporter 28:54-5 My 23 '63. R. P. Knapp, jr
BURGOYNE'S invasion, 1777
March to Saratoga, by H. Bird. Review
Reporter 28:54-5 My 23 '63. R. P. Knapp, jr
BURHANS, R. W.
Sohio Project moonbeam. por Sky & Tel 25:128-31 Mr '63
BURHOE, Ralph W.
AAAS affiliate. Science 139:1226+ Mr 22 '63
BURIAL
See also
Cremation
Undertakers and undertaking
BURIAL, Cost of. See Funerals, Cost of
BURIAL mounds. See Mounds and mound builders
BURIAL rites. See Funeral rites and ceremonies
BURIED treasure. See Treasure trove
BURK, Bruce
Belt sander that works on its side. Pop Sci 185:162-3 N '64
BURK, Dale A.
Big fish lake, a sequel. Field & S 69:44 O '64
BURKA, Edward R. See Marks, P. A. jt. auth.

BURKE, A. See Barrett, P. jt. auth.
BURKE, Arleigh
Where America is weakest; interview. pors U S News 57:66-70 Jl 13 '64
BURKE, Billie
Ziegfelds' girl; excerpts. P. Ziegfeld. il pors Ladies Home J 81:62-4+ Jl; 107-11 Ag '64
BURKE, C. G.
Lost inquiry. Hi Fi 13:54-6+ F '63
BURKE, Edmund
Relevance of Edmund Burke, ed. by P. J. Stanlis. Review
Nat R 16:1111 D 15 '64. R. Kirk
BURKE, George E.
Ol' swimmin' hole goes modern. Am City 79: 100-1 Mr '64
BURKE, Herbert C.
There are matters; poem. Commonweal 79: 721 Mr 13 '64
To my young daughter; poem. Cath World 197:386 S '63
BURKE, Howell M. jr
Desk, hobby bench, add legs and it's also a bar. Pop Sci 184:146-8 Ap '64
BURKE, James
Independent Afghans openly play the U.S. against Russia. il Life 55:20-7 Ag 9 '63
James Burke, 1915-1964. G. P. Hunt. por Life 57:3 O 16 '64
BURKE, Kenneth
Here and now; Assertion to end on; poems. Poetry 105:188-9 D '64
To the memory of E. E. Cummings; poem. Poetry 102:31-7 Ap '63
BURKE, Mary C.
Going places, finding things on a Mississippi paddle wheeler. House & Gard 126:44-6+ N '64
BURKE, Morton H.
Me technician, you engineer; story. Pop Electr 18:55 F '63
BURKE, Roy O.
Fall decorative panels. Sch Arts 63:15-16 N '63
BURKE, Thomas J. M.
Sublimely subliminal; first doctoral thesis on Public relations of religious institutions in a pluralistic society. il por Newsweek 62: 78-9 Jl 15 '63
BURKE, Vincent J.
Congress and Kennedy, what's coming. Nations Bsns 51:38-9+ Jl '63
How to spot false budget cuts. Nations Bsns 52:42-3+ F '64
Mislabeled bills mislead voters. Nations Bsns 51:92-5 F '63
Wandering paths of a transit bill. Reporter 31:31-3 Jl 16 '64
BURKETT, Warren
Apollo add-on is $500 million. Miss & Roc 14:14 Je 29 '64
Coming: big space decision. Sci Digest 56:50-6 O '64
Eight Gemini astronaut suits begun. Miss & Roc 14:31 My 25 '64
First unmanned Gemini flight will be orbital shot. Miss & Roc 13:16-17 Jl 15 '63
Hybrids work geared to lunar survey role. Miss & Roc 14:38 Mr 9 '64
MSC begins testing reliability of water-cooled Apollo space suit. Miss & Roc 14:28 Je 22 '64
NASA planning Mars expedition. Miss & Roc 12:34+ My 13 '63
New astronauts show strong academic backgrounds. Miss & Roc 13:20 O 28 '63
New astronauts to provide manpower for three lunar landings. Miss & Roc 13:32 S 30 '63
Reorganization at MSC to aid project heads. Miss & Roc 13:16 N 11 '63
Soviets leading in fusion research. Miss & Roc 16:14 Ja 25 '65
BURKHARDT, Frederick
National humanities foundation; summary of report, ed. by C. B. Grannis. Pub W 186:35 D 7 '64
BURKHARDT, Robert
Comsat; speculation in the space age. New Repub 150:11-13 Je 27 '64
How to lie successfully to the lie detector. New Repub 150:6-7 My 16 '64
On the Savannah. New Repub 151:13 Jl 11 '64
Sonic boom town. New Repub 151:5-6 Ag 22 '64
BURKHART, David
David's stonewares. K. R. Beittel. il por Sch Arts 63:23-7 S '63
BURKHART, Penny
Stitchery. Sch Arts 62:21-2 F '63
BURKHART, Robert C.
Conditions increasing self-reflective learning in art; research report. Sch Arts 64:23-30 O '64
Depth's four dimensions. Sch Arts 62:30-1 Ap '63
Workshop, four-hand throwing. Craft Horiz 23:54-5 My '63
—See Beittel, K. jt. auth.
BURKHOLDER, J. Lawrence
Peace churches as communities of discernment. Christian Cent 80:1072-5 S 4 '63
BURKLEY, George G.
Johnson's health his doctor's report; questions and answers. U S News 58:11 Ja 11 '65
BURKS, Ardath W.
Japan: the kitchen and the garden. bibliog f Cur Hist 46:230-7 Ap '64
BURKS, Craighill S. and Dowell, R. L.
We have left no art unturned. NEA J 53: 22-4 My '64
BURKS, David
Future of Castroism. Cur Hist 44:78-83+ F '63
BURLAGE, Carl J.
Looking at youth's problems; American view. America 108:230-1 F 16 '63
BURLESON, Dyrol
Very fast crowd at the tape. G. S. Brown. il por Sports Illus 20:28-9 Je 15 '64
BURLESON, Omar
Winning the Weevils. il por Time 82:36 O 4 '63
BURLESQUE. See Vaudeville
BURLINGAME, Robert
Old poet; poem. Sat R 47:23 Ag 8 '64
BURLINGTON industries, incorporated
Avoiding the curse of the company town; Burlington industries development of Cramerton, N.C. il Bsns W p48+ Ag 22 '64
What happened at Burlington when the king dropped dead. S. Freedgood. il Fortune 69:104-11+ Je '64
BURLS
Burlwood, royalty's wood? H. L. Mitchell. il Am For 70:22-5 D '64
BURMA
Letter from Burma. D. Richie. Nation 197: 77-8 Ag 10 '63
See also
Colleges and universities—Burma
Communism—Burma
Forests and forestry—Burma
Pagan
Women—Burma
Description and travel
Burma: gentle neighbor of India and red China. W. R. Moore. il Nat Geog Mag 123:153-99 F '63
Burma village; photo report. U S News 54: 70-1 Ap 1 '63
Foreign relations
Burma: drifting into an uncertain future. il Sr Schol 84:6-8 Ap 17 '64
Gourd amid cactuses. V. S. Kearney. il America 110:345 Mr 14 '64
Where reds may take over a key country. il U S News 54:69 Ap 1 '63
Politics and government
Army socialism. il Time 81:32 F 22 '63
Burma: drifting into an uncertain future. il Sr Schol 84:6-8 Ap 17 '64
From democracy to dictatorship in Burma. J. Silverstein. bibliog f Cur Hist 46:83-8+ F '64
Left full rudder. Newsweek 61:46 Mr 11 '63
Not much left to nationalize. Time 82:33-4 D 13 '63
Way to socialism & havoc. Time 82:20-1 Ag 30 '63
BURMA-Shave signs. See Advertising, Outdoor
BURMEISTER, W. L. and Schwarz, C. W.
Coded signal warns of sewer surcharge. Am City 78:96-7 S '63
BURNERS
Snecma builds design capabilities with fully modulated afterburner. Aviation W 78:67+ Je 10 '63
BURNERS, Oil. See Oil burners
BURNESS, Jean F.
Service, standards, and surveys. Library J 88:2844-6 Ag '63
BURNET, Alastair
Blushing James Bond. New Repub 149:9-10 Ag 17 '63
Britain's North-South problem. New Repub 148:17-18 My 11 '63
Caligula's horse. New Repub 149:10-11 N 2 '63
Labour's first few weeks. New Repub 151:11-12 N 14 '64
State of British morals. New Repub 149:11-12 S 21 '63

BURNET, Alastair—*Continued*
Still the Trojan horse. New Repub 148:8-9 F 2 '63
That cad, Profumo. New Repub 149:6 Jl 6 '63
Victorian England. New Repub 148:9-10 Ap 13 '63
Why Tory hopes are rising. New Repub 151: 8-9 O 10 '64
BURNET
Burnet. M. Reay. Horticulture 41:99 F '63
BURNETT, Allison L. See Haynes, J. jt. auth.
BURNETT, Carey C.
From city dump to industrial park. Am City 78:95-6 Jl '63
Growth follows the water mains. Am City 78: 132-3 Je '63
BURNETT, Carol
My friend Julie Andrews; ed. by H. Markel. por Good H 157:34+ N '63
One battle I had to win; ed. by R. Hochstein. por Good H 156:86-7 My '63
Redbook dialogue: Peter Sellers & Carol Burnett. pors Redbook 122:60-1+ D '63
What did you want most at seventeen? ed. by A. Ebert. por Seventeen 22:130 S '63

about

Adventures of Carol Burnett in her movie bow. il pors Look 27:90-2+ S 24 '63
Life, love and laughter of Carol Burnett. N. G. Stuart. il pors Ladies Home J 80: 72-3+ Ap; 34+ My '63
Only girl who acts with her back and front, too. E. Havemann. il pors Life 54:85-6+ F 22 '63
BURNETT, Ivy Compton-. See Compton-Burnett, I.
BURNETT, Wanda M.
Can you blame it on the weather? Parents Mag 39:50-1+ N '64
BURNETTE, Frances
(comp) Brush up your Shakespeare! recordings. Wilson Lib Bul 38:655+ Ap '64
BURNEYVILLE, Okla.
Nobody loses at the Poor boy open; Waco Turner open. E. Shrake. il Sports Illus 20: 28-31 My 11 '64
BURNFORD, Sheila
Time out of mind; excerpt from Fields of noon. Atlan 214:38-43 Jl '64
Walking; excerpt from Fields of noon. Atlan 214:66-70 Ag '64
William; story. Atlan 212:72-5 Ag '63; Same abr. with title Long day for William. Read Digest 84:125-8 F '64
BURNHAM, David
Air force coins a word. Reporter 28:32-3 Je 6 '63
Birth control: end of a taboo. Nation 200: 85-6 Ja 25 '65
BURNHAM, Donald Clemens
Breaking a pattern of woes. il Bsns W p90-3 Ag 31 '63
Burnham of Westinghouse. por Fortune 68:59 S '63
Mr Automation. por Time 82:73-4 Jl 26 '63
New life in an old giant. il por Time 84:97-8 O 30 '64
New man at the top for Westinghouse. por Bsns W p72 Jl 20 '63
Quiet surprise. por Newsweek 62:60 Jl 29 '63
BURNHAM, Forbes
Reds' own race war in Guiana: signs of another Congo. il por U S News 56:60-1 Je 15 '64
Where a Communist leader was voted out. il por U S News 57:16 D 21 '64
BURNHAM, James
Coming ADA government? Nat R 16:954-9 N 3 '64
Does ADA run the New frontier? Nat R 14: 355-62 My 7 '63
Landside view. Nat R 16:317-18 Ap 21 '64
Political notes from the prairies. Nat R 16: 278-9 Ap 7 '64
Third world war. See issues of National review
BURNHAM, Rufus Bradford
What's new when you get there. Motor B 112:34-7+ S '63
BURNHAM, Walter Dean
After JFK, what? Commonweal 79:340-3 D 13 '63
Democracy and the Court. Commonweal 80: 499-503 Jl 24 '64
Democracy at home and imperial policy abroad. Commonweal 80:639-40+ S 18 '64
Eisenhower as man, Eisenhower as mystique. Commonweal 79:408-9 D 27 '63
Goldwaterite revolution. Commonweal 80:531-5, 613-14 Ag 7, S 4 '64
G.O.P. crisis. Commonweal 80:373-4 Je 12 '64
Has Congress a future? Nation 196:545-8+ Je 29 '63
Hobbling the Constitution. Commonweal 78: 531-3 S 6 '63
Lippmann distilled; an apprehensive view of mass society. Commonweal 78:459-61 Jl 26 '63
One voter, one vote. Commonweal 80:12-15 Mr 27 '64
Reading the returns. Commonweal 79:271-4 N 29 '63
Recovering from Barry. Commonweal 81:319-22 N 27 '64
Republican campaign strategy. Commonweal 80:287-90 My 29 '64
Schizophrenia in the G.O.P. Commonweal 79: 5-10 S 27 '63
BURNING; drama. See Hamilton, W.
BURNING in effigy. See Executions in effigy
BURNING of land
See also
Weeds—Control by fire
BURNLEY, Rose Marie
Redbook's guide to easier housecleaning. Redbook 123:81-8 My '64
Time-saving, money-saving advice from your repairman. Redbook 121:58-9+ Ag '63
BURNS, Allan F. See White, J. L. jt. auth.
BURNS, Arthur Edward
History of planned generosity. Sat R 47:33-4 Ag 1 '64
Material outlook for mankind. Sat R 47:44-6 Je 6 '64
World war on poverty. Sat R 48:53 Ja 9 '65
BURNS, Arthur F.
Excerpt from testimony before Joint economic committee, February 4, 1963. Cong Digest 42:109+ Ap '63
A look at the business future; excerpts from address, 1964. por U S News 57:92-3 Ag 17 '64
Of growth and gain. Reporter 29:52+ S 12 '63
Top authority's plan to get the economy rolling; statement. por U S News 54:98-101 F 18 '63

about

Business outlook: Burns vs. Heller. por U S News 57:63 S 7 '64
Tax cut every year? T. G. Harris. por Look 28:70+ O 20 '64
BURNS, Jack
Aloha a la sinistra. L. V. Cott. il Nat R 15:57-8 Jl 30 '63
BURNS, James MacGregor
Despite the hoopla, it's the best system. N Y Times Mag p 11+ Ap 26 '64
Editor-in-chief of democracy. Sat R 46:19-20 Ag 3 '63
Goldwater challenges the four-party system. N Y Times Mag p7+ Je 28 '64
Legacy of the 1,000 days. N Y Times Mag p27+ D 1 '63
President: a free man first. Sat R 47:27-8 Ap 11 '64
President behind the candidate. por Life 57:95-6+ O 9 '64
President Kennedy's place in history: a new size-up; interview. por U S News 57:64-6 N 23 '64
Speaking out. por Sat Eve Post 237:12+ Ja 25 '64
BURNS, John Anthony
Aloha has many meanings. A. E. P. Wall. America 111:148 Ag 15 '64
BURNS, John H. and others
Xenon tetrafluoride molecule and its thermal motion: a neutron diffraction study. bibliog Science 139:1208-9 Mr 22 '63
BURNS, John L.
RCA's signal: coming in strong. il por Bsns W p 110-12+ Je 29 '63
BURNS, Lillian G.
Housing act and higher education. bibliog f Sch & Soc 91:211-12 My 4 '63
BURNS, Madeleine
Making of a model. il pors Seventeen 22:84-5+ Jl '63
BURNS, Richard
This is the fabric itself. por Library J 88:4701-3 D 15 '63
BURNS, Roger G. and Fyfe, W. S.
Site of preference energy and selective uptake of transition-metal ions from a magma. bibliog Science 144:1001-3 My 22 '64
BURNS, Sheila
Stamps. See issues of Senior scholastic
BURNS, Victor W.
Reversible sonic inhibition of protein, purine, and pyrimidine biosynthesis in the living cell. bibliog Science 146:1056-8 N 20 '64
BURNS, Vincent M.
Ethics in government: a poisonous atmosphere. Cath World 200:78-83 N '64

BURNS, W. Haydon
Astounding results. il por Time 84:41-2 N 13 '64

BURNS and scalds
Beautiful gamble for Johnny; doctors save child with eighty-five per cent of his body burned. A. Lake. il McCalls 91:62+ S '64
Boy's trial by fire. J. P. Blank. il Read Digest 83:91-6 N '63
Burn accidents: an unrecognized menace. il Sci Digest 57:32-3 Ja '65
Burns affect emotions. E. Mirel. Sci N L 83: 179 Mr 23 '63
Early grafting saves lives of severely burned. Sci N L 85:25 Ja 11 '64
New dye test reported for severe burn injuries. Sci N L 85:328 My 23 '64
New healer for the burn victim. Bsns W p 124+ N 21 '64
Patients nobody wanted; Shriners' burns-treatment program. A. Lake. il Sat Eve Post 237:87-91 D 5 '64
Sarge. M. M. Moore. Read Digest 86:49-52 Ja '65
Six-day shower cure. Sci Digest 56:52-3 Ag '64

BURNSHAW, Stanley
Three notable collections. L. Untermeyer. Poetry 103:385-6 Mr '64

BURNSVILLE, Minn.
Speedy electronics map a new city. il Am City 79:30 D '64

BURR, Gray
Sailing, sailing; poem. New Yorker 39:42 S 14 '63

BURR, Harry B.
Why penalize firms hiring handicapped workers? Harvard Bsns R 41:56-8 Jl '63

BURR, Robert N.
Recent developments in Latin-American history. bibliog f Ann Am Acad 353:122-30 My '64

BURRAGE, Albert C.
Vegetables. Horticulture 42:22-5+ Ap '64
Wintering roses. Horticulture 42:40-2 O '64

BURRI, Rene
Red China spruced up for show; photographs. Life 57:97-102 Jl 17 '64

BURRIER, Tom
Operation budworm: Washington. Am For 69:28-9 S '63

BURRO saddles. See Saddles

BURROUGHS, Edgar Rice
Tarzan revisited. G. Vidal. il Esquire 60:192-3+ D '63

BURROUGHS, John
Big idea: an empty room. por Pop Sci 183:118 S '63
Build a movie step-by-step. Pop Phot 52: 88+ Ja '63
Four seasons bowl. Pop Mech 121:152-5 Ja '64
How to custom-build a carrying case. Pop Sci 182:107-10 My '63
How to get started with a metal lathe. Pop Sci 182:106-10+ Mr '63
Pop goes the rivet. Pop Sci 185:156-7 N '64
Portraits like the pros. Pop Mech 121:166-70 F '64
Secret of precision woodwork. Pop Sci 184: 121-3+ F '64
Taking pictures that do a job. Pop Sci 184: 128-9 Je '64
Three power take-offs for a flexible shaft. Pop Mech 121:190-1 Ap '64

BURROUGHS, John, 1837-1921
Our alliance with nature; excerpt from address, delivered on acceptance of John Burroughs medal, April 6, 1964. J. Hay. Audubon Mag 66:395-8 N '64

BURROUGHS, William
Tangier. por Esquire 62:114-19 S '64

about

Notes on Burroughs. M. McLuhan. Nation 199:517-19 D 28 '64

BURROUGHS, Wise, and Ewing, S. A.
Beef additives. Suc Farm 61:100 N '63

BURROUGHS corporation
Space & defense group seeks 10-15 per cent sales hike. Miss & Roc 12:35 My 27 '63

BURROWING, Animal. See Animals—Habits and behavior

BURROWS, Alvina Treut
Language arts and language learners. PTA Mag 59:28-30 bibliog(p36) N '64

BURROWS, E. G.
Day grandmother died; Saratoga; poems. Poetry 104:217-20 Jl '64
Three from overseas. Poetry 105:207-10 D '64

BURSITIS
Bursitis, grin and bear it. il Sci Digest 55:83 F '64

BURSK, Edward C.
'64
Businessman's bookshelf. Sat R 47:44 Ja 11 '64; 48:18+ Ja 9 '65
Goad to economic growth. Sat R 46:21-2 Je 1 '63

BURSTEIN, Herman
How a tape recorder works. Pop Phot 53:64-5+ S '63
Shopping guide to tape recorders for the home. Pop Phot 53:50+ S '63
Tape-recorder equalization curves. Electr World 72:38-40 Jl '64
Which tape to use? Electr World 70:34-5 N '63

BURSTEIN, Pinchas. See Maryan

BURT, Al
Cuban exiles: the mirage of Havana. Nation 200:76-9 Ja 25 '65
Haiti: alternatives to tyranny. Nation 200: 10-12 Ja 4 '65

BURT, David
Detour to sculpture. il Am Artist 28:30-5+ Ja '64

BURT, Nathaniel
Philadelphia plain & fancy. Horizon 5:4-27 Jl '63
Race and renaissance in Philadelphia. Harper 229:64-70 S '64

BURTON, Alice, and Sinsheimer, R. L.
Process of infection with ϕX174: effect of exonucleases on the replicative form. bibliog Science 142:962-3 N 15 '63

BURTON, Benjamin
What's in a meal? Américas 15:1-6 F '63

BURTON, Philip
Other Burton. L. Hershey. il por McCalls 92:86+ Ja '65

BURTON, Richard
Candid look at Becket and myself. por Life 56:85-6 Mr 13 '64
Visit with Richard Burton; interview, ed by J. Roddy. por Look 28:47 Ja 28 '64
—See Muggeridge, M. jt. auth.

about

Beginning writer. il por Time 84:82 O 30 '64
Burton and the girls. il pors Look 28:40-2+ Ja 28 '64
Burton's Hamlet. J. McLaughlin. Cath World 199:308-12 Ag '64
Dickenliz in Toronto. Newsweek 63:78 F 10 '64
Drama the cameras missed; ed. by M. Davidson. T. Victor. il pors Sat Eve Post 237: 24-8+ Jl 11 '64
Elizabeth Taylor talks about Cleopatra; ed. by J. Hamilton. E. Taylor. il pors Look 27:41-7+ My 7 '63
Funny thing happened on the way to decorum. por Time 83:56 Ja 3 '64
Hamlet of brain and passion. G. Rogoff. por Hi Fi 14:51-2 Jl '64
Liz and Dick put iambics in the big time. T. Prideaux. Life 57:12 Jl 24 '64
Man on the billboard. il pors Time 81:70-4 Ap 26 '63; Same abr. with title Anatomy of an actor. Read Digest 83:104-9 Jl '63
Millionairess. il Time 81:50 Je 7 '63
Other Burton. L. Hershey. il por McCalls 92:86+ Ja '65
Perils of Mexican divorce. il por Time 82: 34 D 27 '63
Prince of thought. por Time 83:65 Ap 17 '64
Something to write home about. il por Time 84:62 Jl 3 '64
Theater: New York performance of Hamlet. G. Wills. Nat R 16:458-9 Je 2 '64
We will dance. por Newsweek 64:73 D 21 '64

BURTON, Sir Richard Francis
Burton, by B. Farwell. Review
Time il por 83:110+ F 28 '64
From battlefield to bazaar. H. T. Moore. por Sat R 47:31-2 F 29 '64
Hidden, the unknowable, the unthinkable. F. M. Brodie. il pors Horizon 5:110-17 Jl '63

BURTON, Sybil
Sybil Burton starts over. J. Krantz. por McCalls 91:108+ Ap '64

BURTON, Walter E.
Camera attachment to give shadowless lighting. Pop Sci 185:136-7 N '64
Compound slide rest for your wood lathe. Pop Mech 119:190-4+ F '63
Four special jobs for a saber saw. Pop Sci 182:148-50 F '63
Grind anything anywhere. Pop Mech 121:188-91 Mr '64
Hammer crafting sheet metal. Pop Mech 119: 140-2 Ap '63
Homemade power hacksaw for less than $20. Pop Sci 184:162-6+ F '64
Precision indexer for your jigsaw. Pop Mech 119:194-6+ Mr '63

BURTON, William E.
Cleaner tools for the dentist; dental equipment blamed for cross-contamination. il Bsns W p80-2 O 5 '63
BURUNDI
Chou En-lai and the Watusi. C. Sterling. il Reporter 30:22-4 Mr 12 '64; Reply. G. Nyangoma. 30:8 Ap 9 '64
Down to size; assassination of premier. Time 85:25-6 Ja 29 '65
Peking puts up a Congo command post. R. Rowan. il Life 57:66A-66B D 18 '64
Rwanda and Burundi. R. Y. Gildea, jr. and A. Taylor. bibliog il Focus 13:1-6 F '63
Native races
Africa's dilemma. V. S. Kearney. America 110:274 F 29 '64
Kill thy neighbor; Watusis murdered by Bahutu tribesmen. J. P. Nugent. il Newsweek 63:51 F 24 '64
Rise and fall of the Watusi; slaughter of Tutsi by Bahutu. E. Huxley. il N Y Times Mag p 10+ F 23 '64
Where black slaughters black: death of the Watusi; revolt of Bahutu. A. J. Meyers. il U S News 56:50-1 F 24 '64
BURUSHO
Hunza in the Himalayas. J. Clark. il Natur Hist 72:38-45 O '63
BURWEN, Richard S.
Transistors vs tubes for hi-fi. Electr World 70:85 D '63
BURY, Pol
Art galleries: exhibition at Lefegre. R. M. Coates. New Yorker 40:163-4 N 7 '64
BUS stations. See Motor bus lines—Stations
BUS tokens. See Tokens
BUS travel. See Motor bus travel
BUSBY, Horace
Closing the word gap? il por Newsweek 63:23 Ap 13 '64
People of the week. por U S News 56:16 Ap 13 '64
When Johnson plans a speech—. por U S News 56:33 F 3 '64
BUSCH, August A. Jr
Promotional flair keeps Busch on top. il pors Bsns W p 112-14+ Ap 13 '63
BUSCH, Noel F.
Behind the Buddhist unrest in southeast Asia. Read Digest 83:94-9 D '63
TR, the strenuous life of a great American; excerpts from T.R: the story of Theodore Roosevelt. Read Digest 83:237-43+ Jl '63
Two minutes to noon; condensation. Read Digest 84:221-6+ Mr '64
U Thant; inscrutable shepherd of the U.N. Read Digest 84:63-7 Mr '64
BUSCH, Wilhelm
Rolf Hochhuth: equivocal Deputy. E. Alexander. il America 109:416-18+ O 12 '63; Discussion. 109:518-20, 691 N 2, 30 '63
BUSCH gardens. See Florida—Parks and reserves
BUSCHKE, Herman
Retention in immediate memory estimated without retrieval. bibliog Science 140:56-7 Ap 5 '63
BUSES, Motor. See Motor buses
BUSH, Emily
Winter landscapes. il Horticulture 43:28-9+ Ja '65
BUSH, George
Republican party and the conservative movement. por Nat R 16:1053-4 D 1 '64
about
Bush grows in Texas. Newsweek 62:30 S 30 '63
Cactus-nasty campaign. il por Time 84:39 O 16 '64
BUSH, George S.
Carmel's key to happy retirement: help, not a handout. Todays Health 42:58-9+ Ja '64
BUSH, George Washington
George Washington of Centralia Washington. W. S. Savage. bibliog Negro Hist Bul 27:44-7 N '63
BUSH, Howard. See Henneberger, R. M. jr, jt. auth.
BUSH, Joseph Bevans
Death of Lizzie Miles ends great era of blues shouters. Negro Hist Bul 27:69 D '63
Is America Christian? Negro Hist Bul 27:173+ Ap '64
BUSH, Monroe
New direction from Asilomar. Am For 69:27+ Jl '63
Reading about resources. See issues of American forests

BUSH, Prescott
Rockefeller under fire. Bush urges that he withdraw; summary of address. por U S News 54:20 Je 24 '63
BUSH, Vannevar
Vannevar Bush speaks; excerpts from statement, November 21, 1963. Science 142:162 D 27 '63
We're moving deeper into welfare state; interview. por Nations Bsns 51:36-7+ Mr '63
about
Tomorrow's pioneers. F. L. Phelps. il Américas 15:20-8 F '63
BUSH-BROWN, J.
Guide to wise plant selection. Horticulture 41:514 O '63
BUSH poppies
Striking California natives: the bush poppies. M. G. Schmidt. il Horticulture 41:420 Ag '63
BUSHELL, Edward
Ordeal of William Penn. F. Biddle. il Am Heritage 15:107-10 Ap '64
BUSHMEN. See Africa—Native races
BUSHNELL, Louise
New lamps for old? centralism; address, November 11, 1964. Vital Speeches 31:112-14 D 1 '64
BUSHNELL, Philip R.
Revised conclusion of James Reston. Nat R 14:449-50+ Je 4 '63
BUSINESS
Individualism and big business, by L. R. Sayles. Review
Reporter 30:47+ Ja 16 '64. J. W. Ward
National agenda for 1964: symposium presented with the Committee for economic development. T. O. Yntema. il Sat R 47:19-32+ Ja 11 '64
What's ahead for business? J. R. Bunting. Atlan 213:72-5 Je '64
Who speaks for business? Duns R 83:35 Mr '64
See also
Christmas business
Competition
Free enterprise
Ideas in business
Inventories
Profit
Retail trade
Success
Anecdotes, facetiae, satire, etc.
Still pricking business balloons; S. Mead before businessmen at UCLA. il Bsns W p90+ Mr 21 '64
Bibliography
Business books of 1963; comp. by C. Georgi. il Library J 89:1026-32 Mr 1 '64
Business books of 1962; comp. by M. Stone. il Library J 88:944-8 Mr 1 '63
Business books to come; ed. by I. E. Stokvis and J. Putnam. Library J 88:4242-6; 89:1120-6, 2830-4, 4392-8 N 1 '63; Mr 1, Jl, N 1 '64
Business books to come; ed. by M. Cooley and I. E. Stokvis. Library J 88:1030-9 Mr 1 '63
Businessman's bookshelf. E. C. Bursk. Sat R 47:44 Ja 11 '64; 48:18+ Ja 9 '65
Executive bookshelf. See issues of Dun's review and modern industry
Summer business books; ed. by I. E. Stokvis and J. Putnam. Library J 88:2734-8+ Jl '63
Directories
Guide to management services. Duns R 85: pt 2 119-34+ Ja '65
Exhibitions
See Exhibitions
Foreign expansion
Aerospace alliance; Seattle's Boeing co. acquires an interest in Bölkow GmbH. Time 85:64 Ja 8 '65
American business overseas; address, April 8, 1963. N. Erin. Vital Speeches 29:497-9 Je 1 '63
American plants abroad. F. Kowalski. Nation 197:197-9 O 5 '63; Reply. E. C. Daum. 197: inside cover O 26 '63
Back to glamour; aluminum industry. il Time 82:88 D 13 '63
Box office buzzes overseas; expansion of U.S. movie makers. il Bsns W p64+ N 7 '64
Chrysler soups up foreign sales. il Bsns W p47-8 F 8 '64
European market: will it blast off? il Bsns W p22 Jl 4 '64
Flying trade show. il Bsns W p76+ D 12 '64

BUSINESS—Foreign expansion—*Continued*
French slap at U.S. investment. Bsns W p 149 O 24 '64
German defense minister orders plans to buy TF-104Gs shelved. Aviation W 79:32 N 11 '63
He's building a business bridge; M. Sindona of Italy. il Bsns W p 128-30+ O 10 '64
How to go international; excerpts from Handbook of international marketing. A. O. Stanley. il Nations Bsns 51:90-2+ S '63
How world trade will change. il Nations Bsns 52:38-9+ S '64
It's a spryer Singer. E. K. Faltermayer. il Fortune 68:144-8+ D '63
Little red wagon heads west. il Bsns W p49-50+ S 19 '64
Mining new markets for nickel; Falconbridge. il Bsns W p62-4+ S 5 '64
Now the transnational enterprise. D. F. Kircher. Harvard Bsns R 42:6-8+ Mr '64
Organizing for profit overseas. Bsns W p 112+ My 23 '64
Overseas boom in door-to-door selling. T. J. Murray. il Duns R 84:35-7+ N '64
Overseas: tumult & transformation. il Duns R 81:pt2 S117-20 Mr '63
Paper world of Karl Landegger. E. K. Faltermayer. il Fortune 70:168-71+ N '64
Public projects abroad offer U.S. big market. Nations Bsns 52:76+ My '64
Showcase for U.S. exports. il Fortune 69:67-8 Mr '64
Spotting the right bases overseas; Borg-Warner international. il Bsns W p 104+ Ag 10 '63
Stronger foreign competition coming; symposium of top executives from Europe and Japan. il Nations Bsns 52:55-8+ Ja '64
Those American managers don't impress Europe; excerpts from Americanization of Europe. E. A. McCreary. Fortune 70:138-9+ D '64
Trade, property, and the dollar. il Fortune 68:129-30 Jl '63
U.S. tractors plow some global fields. il Bsns W p 174+ O 24 '64
What not to do when going to Europe. il Time 84:82 Ag 21 '64
Why American companies are going abroad; interview. R. R. Eppert. il U S News 56:64-7 F 10 '64
Worldwide inflation: what it means to U.S. il U S News 55:58-60 O 28 '63
You can shape business climate; symposium. il Nations Bsns 51:61-4 Jl '63
Your foreign showcase. il Bsns W p 104+ Ag 29 '64
See also
Corporations—Foreign subsidiaries

Forms, blanks, etc.

Memo on memos (six copies, please) T. Irwin. il N Y Times Mag p46+ N 17 '63
Paper tiger; unnecessary paperwork. Time 83:94 Ap 24 '64

Anecdotes, facetiae, satire, etc.

How to outwit forms. J. E. Leffler. il Atlan 213:122 F '64

History

Now it's more of a science; reports of study by Harvard graduate school of business. bibliog il Bsns W p44+ D 28 '63
Revolutionary then, orthodox now; scientific management. Bsns W p94 Ap 20 '63

International aspects

Are we gaining or guessing abroad? address, March 27, 1963. F. C. Foy. Vital Speeches 29:421-5 My 1 '63
Business hot line. Bsns W p56+ O 24 '64
International markets. A. O. Stanley. See issues of Dun's review and modern industry to June 1963
Now the transnational enterprise. D. F. Kircher. Harvard Bsns R 42:6-8+ Mr '64
Organizing a worldwide business. G. H. Clee and W. M. Sachtjen. il Harvard Bsns R 42:55-67 N '64
Parallel roles of business and diplomacy in an era of expanding frontiers; address, May 19, 1964. G. C. McGhee. Dept State Bul 51:18-25 Jl 6 '64
Planning in a worldwide business. M. H. Pryor, jr. il Harvard Bsns R 43:130-9 Ja '65
U.S. capital stirs fear in Europe. il Bsns W p 114+ D 5 '64
World business; how it affects you. See issues of Nation's business
Your competitors; address, November 21, 1963. P. Steele. Vital Speeches 30:373-6 Ap 1 '64
See also
United States—State, Department of—Advisory committee on international business problems

Periodicals

There's no business like business. N. L. Cahners. il Sat R 48:72-3 Ja 9 '65

Political aspects

Anti-communism & the corporations. A. F. Westin. Commentary 36:479-87 D '63; Correction. 38:16 Ag '64; Discussion. 37:19-24 Ap; 14 Je; 38:6 N '64
Big business fails America. S. Screven; reply. R. Baumhart. America 108:184 F 9 '63
Business and Johnson savor a love feast. il Bsns W p28-9 Ja 18 '64
Business and politics, 1964; symposium, ed. by S. A. Greyser. il Harvard Bsns R 42:22-4+ S '64
Business, and the party platforms. T. O'Hanlon. il Duns R 84:55-7+ O '64
Business stays hopeful. Bsns W p37 N 7 '64
Businessmen's vote: it's going to be a tough decision. il Bsns W p23-5 S 5 '64
Campaign in the plants. il Time 84:100 O 9 '64
Cocktail hour guide to election economics; effects of election on the economy; or vice versa. Bsns W p34 Ag 22 '64
Coming: biggest role ever for business. il Nations Bsns 51:34-5+ N '63
Corporation, the employee, and politics; presidents' panel report. G. R. Rosen. il Duns R 84:38-40+ Jl '64
Free enterprisers: Kennedy, Johnson, and the business establishment, by H. Rowen. Review
New Repub 151:26-8 S 19 '64. R. L. Strout
Newsweek 64:94-5 S 21 '64
H. L. Hunt: portrait of a super-patriot; Life line. R. G. Sherrill. Nation 198:182-95 F 24 '64
How business failed Dallas. R. A. Smith. il Fortune 70:156-60+ Jl '64
How businessmen can fight big government and win. D. G. Wood. Harper 227:77-81 N '63
How businessmen can serve their country; interview, ed. by B. Hibbs. G. Romney. Read Digest 83:76-80 O '63
How LBJ is wooing businessmen; businessmen who came to dinner. U S News 56:58 My 11 '64
How many businessmen for whom? newly formed group of forty-five, the National independent committee for President Johnson and Senator Humphrey. il Newsweek 64:67-8 S 14 '64
How reapportionment threatens business. il Nations Bsns 52:94-7 D '64
In defense of politics; address, January 25, 1963. J. P. Mitchell. Vital Speeches 29:340-3 Mr 15 '63
In the making: a Romney boom? il U S News 54:19 My 13 '63
Industry's brains help a state; Ohio's Little Hoover commission. il Bsns W p 131 N 23 '63
JFK in a truce with business? il U S News 54:35-6 Je 3 '63
LBJ talked calories and profits at White House business lunch. il Newsweek 64:57-8 Ag 3 '64
L.B.J.'s romance with business. H. B. Meyers. il Fortune 70:130-3+ S '64
Man in grey flannel levis; corporations and Johnson or Goldwater administration. Nat R 16:800-1 S 22 '64
Man is the central element; excerpts from address. D. Rockefeller. Fortune 68:78 N '63
Politics and the business outlook. il U S News 57:60-2 S 7 '64
What business can do for America. J. F. Kennedy. Nations Bsns 51:29-31+ S '63
When executives turned revolutionaries in Brazil. P. Siekman. il Fortune 70:147-9+ S '64
When politics rip apart old loyalties. il Bsns W p38+ O 24 '64
Where businessmen support Kennedy. Nations Bsns 51:34-5+ F '63
Why businessmen make good politicians; interview. H. T. Schneebeli. Nations Bsns 51:94-8+ N '63
Why canny investors are sitting it out. il Bsns W p 164+ S 12 '64
Your competitors; address, November 21, 1963. P. Steele. Vital Speeches 30:373-6 Ap 1 '64

BUSINESS—*Continued*

Public relations

Businessman and his critics; excerpt. D. Finn. Sat R 47:60-2+ S 12 '64
Charting a new pathway; government-business relationships. L. L. L. Golden. Sat R 47:132 Mr 14 '64
Corporate censorship. P. B. Bart. Sat R 47:57 Je 13 '64
Hard look at public relations. L. H. Naum. il Duns R 84:47+ N '64
If I were a company president. P. F. Drucker. Harper 228:16+ Ap '64; Reply. R. S. Taplinger. 228:12+ Je '64
Message to company presidents. W. J. Coughlin. Miss & Roc 13:46 Jl 15 '63
New business spokesman urges positive approach. C. B. Seib. il Nations Bsns 52:42-3+ My '64
Out in the open; Securities and exchange commission's report on corporate publicity and public relations. L. L. L. Golden. Sat R 46:52-3 Jl 13 '63

Small business

See Small business

Social aspects

Are businessmen speaking out? presidents' panel report. il Duns R 82:31-3 N '63
Do corporations have a social duty? A. Hacker. il N Y Times Mag p21+ N 17 '63
Family business. R. G. Donnelley. bibliog f il Harvard Bsns R 42:93-105 Jl '64
How businessmen can fight big government and win. D. G. Wood. Harper 227:77-81 N '63
Ideological debate dividing businessmen. il Bsns W p201-2 S 12 '64
Innocence of U.S. steel; role of the corporation in the community. C. O. Rice. il Commonweal 80:504-6 Jl 24 '64
Is business socially responsible? J. W. Clark. America 110:250-2 F 22 '64
Management of voluntary welfare agencies. E. Lippincott and E. Aanestad. Harvard Bsns R 42:87-98 N '64
Myth of the American way. K. Watson. Christian Cent 80:328-30 Mr 13 '63
Prosperity gap. S. M. Linowitz. Sat R 48:42 Ja 9 '65
Troubled conscience of American business; excerpts from Myths and mythmakers in the modern economy. B. Nossiter. Harper 227:37-43 S '63; Discussion. 227:8+ N '63

BUSINESS, Retirement from. See Retirement from business, etc.

BUSINESS administration. See Business management and organization

BUSINESS airplanes. See Airplanes, Business

BUSINESS and art. See Art and industry

BUSINESS and education
Education: the business stake. Nations Bsns 51:14+ S '63
How business and industry are helping the schools. A. L. Ayars. il Sat R 47:57-8+ O 17 '64
Industry's stake in education; address, January 16, 1963. C. G. Mortimer. Vital Speeches 29:270-3 F 15 '63
What can we learn from industry? S. Solomon. il Sr Schol 85:12T Ja 14 '65
See also
Corporations—Charitable contributions

BUSINESS and professional women
Happily ever after; four San Francisco stories. R. Hoffmann. il Mlle 59:140-3 My '64
New job for Joan. M. Crawford. il Look 27:50-1+ D 17 '63
Where the boys are not; Barbizon hotel, New York. N. Robertson. il Sat Eve Post 236:28-33 O 19 '63
See also
Married women—Employment
Secretaries
Women as executives

BUSINESS and race problems
Smoothing a way for rights law; efforts of business groups. Bsns W p32 Je 20 '64

BUSINESS and state. See Industry and state

BUSINESS and the community. See Business—Social aspects

BUSINESS arbitration. See Arbitration, Commerical

BUSINESS budgets. See Budget, Business

BUSINESS charts
Organization for efficient practice; Nolen-Swinburne and associates. H. H. Swinburne. il Arch Rec 133:155-8 F '63

BUSINESS committee for tax reduction
Mobilizing business; with editorial comment. Bsns W p28-9, 148 My 4 '63

BUSINESS communication. See Communica-tion in management

BUSINESS conditions
Behind the growth of the economy. il Bsns V p25-6 Je 1 '63
Boom raises three challenges. M. Nadler il Nations Bsns 52:31-3 My '64
Business and finance. See issues of News-week
Business outlook. See issues of Business wee
Business roundup. See issues of Fortune
Business tides. H. Hazlitt. See issues o Newsweek
Can business grasp the future? P. L. Bern-stein. il Nation 198:49-51 Ja 13 '64
Cities in the U.S. where business is best with charts. U S News 55:54-7 Jl 1 '63; 57 ,62-5 Ag 10 '64
Economic projection. Duns R 81:29 Je '63
Effect of tax cut on business. il U S New 56:35-7 Mr 9 '64
Effects of change; Wall Street's reaction t death of President. il Time 82:89 N 29 '6
Find the lag. Nations Bsns 51:114 Mr '63
From business, a contented purr. il Bsns V p23-5 Ap 4 '64
Hail to the chiefs. il Time 83:91 Ap 24 '64
How business reacted in past to death of president. U S News 55:50 D 9 '63
How they're spending their tax-cut mone il Time 83:79 Je 26 '64
LBJ: all right, men, hold that line. News-week 63:71 My 11 '64
New & exuberant. il Time 81:73-7 My 3 '63
New gains in business: how strong. il U News 54:36 F 11 '63
Newsweek survey: better business ahead bu no boom. il Newsweek 62:66-8 S 2 '63
Not enough bigness in business? il U News 57:88 Jl 27 '64
Now business spending joins the rise. U News 56:59 Mr 16 '64
Plus & minus; business activity of the week See issues of U.S. news & World repor
Price of prosperity. il Time 82:93 O 11 '63
Renewed faith; reaction after Kennedy as-sassination. il Newsweek 62:77-80 D 9 '6
Spotlight in business. See issues of News-week
Spring fever chart of business: up. il Lif 54:36 My 3 '63
State of business; the long gain. il Time 83 79 Mr 27 '64
Stripped for action. il Bsns W p25-6 Ap 1 '64
Trend of American business. See issues c U.S. news & World report
Trend of business. J. Phillips. See issues c Dun's review and modern industry
U.S. business. See issues of Time
Warmth of spring. Time 83:83 My 8 '64
Washington desk. J. R. Slevin. Duns R 81: My '63
What challenges lie ahead; symposium. Nations Bsns 51:60+ N '63
What happens to business now. il U S New 55:48-50 D 9 '63
What went right. Fortune 67:103-4 My '63
What's needed to give business a boost. U S News 54:37-8 Mr 11 '63
Where people are spending their money. U S News 55:72-3 D 2 '63
Why business sings the February blues. Bsns W p32 F 9 '63
Why Kennedy is worrying about the busines outlook. il U S News 54:35-6 Mr 11 '63
See also
Business cycles
Business depression
Business forecasting
Economic conditions
Industrial statistics
Inflation (finance)
Investments

BUSINESS conferences
Make your meetings more worth while. H. I Zelko. il Nations Bsns 52:92-4+ S '64

BUSINESS consolidations and mergers
American hardware marries for love. il Bsn W p 144+ My 16 '64
Another Transamerica? ITT announced plar to acquire Avis, inc. Bsns W p29 Ja 23 '
Antitrust turns tougher. il Bsns W p98-100- S 12 '64
Attraction of opposites; Radio corporatio of America offers to absorb Prentice-Ha inc. Time 84:58 D 25 '64
Back of worry over mergers; latest figure on profits. il U S News 56:74 Je 1 '64
Bigger the badder? Newsweek 63:74+ Je 1 '64
Blocking a merger in advance. Bsns W p90 My 4 '63
Brothers move on; Smith brothers merge into Warner-Lambert pharmaceutical c il Time 83:86 F 21 '64

BUSINESS consolidations and mergers—*Cont.*
Bulldog in Chrysler's stable? plans to acquire Mack truck; will Justice dept. approve? Bsns W p28-9 My 9 '64
Court narrows road to corporate growth; hits mergers and joint ventures. Bsns W p30-1 Je 27 '64
Destiny of dynasties; Fiat buys one-third of Olivetti. il Time 83:106 Ap 17 '64
Economic courtships; Belgium's Gevaert photo-producten and Germany's Agfa. Time 83:98+ F 28 '64
End of a feud; E.N.I. and Gulf Italia. il Time 83:101 F 28 '64
GE tries for two feet in the door; dickering with Italy's Olivetti for Europe's computer market. Bsns W p 112+ Ag 15 '64
Giant that makes almost anything; FMC corp. to absorb American viscose. il Bsns W p58+ Mr 9 '63
Hard line; Justice department challenges proposed Chrysler merger with Mack trucks, inc. Newsweek 64:60 Ag 31 '64
Heavy-duty, high gear merger; White motor and Cummins engine. Bsns W p94+ O 5 '63
How a radio chain got into pest control; Rollins broadcasting purchases Orkin exterminating. Bsns W p65-6+ Jl 11 '64
If you're big, grow from within; Justice dept. to Chrysler and Mack. Bsns W p26 Ag 8 '64
Is antitrust hurting growth? address. J. J. Scott. il Duns R 83:55-6+ My '64
It's no longer just grind, grind at Norton. il Fortune 68:118-23+ Ag '63
Litton's drive shifts into a quieter key. il Bsns W p27-8 S 5 '64
Lure for pure. il Time 84:79 Jl 3 '64
Mergers and acquisitions. See occasional issues of Aviation week & space technology to April 20, 1964
Mergers keep growing; with a difference. Bsns W p64+ Mr 21 '64
Need for a hot line. Fortune 68:119-20 N '63
New crackdown on business? il U S News 56:39-41 My 25 '64
New powers for trustbusters. il Time 84:77 Jl 3 '64
New suitor bids for Pure oil's favors. Bsns W p20 Jl 4 '64
New thorns strewing the road to mergers; companies resist acquisition. il Bsns W p58+ N 9 '63
Sharpening the law on antitrust. il Bsns W p32-4 O 5 '63
Some benefits of looking backward; address, November 18, 1964. G. H. Love. Vital Speeches 31:183-5 Ja 1 '65
Supreme court vs. corporate mergers. M. Handler and S. D. Robinson. il Fortune 71: 164-5+ Ja '65
Sweet deal; Merrill Lynch, Pierce, Fenner & Smith - C. J. Devine & co. merger. il Time 83:93 My 22 '64
Trade and mark; Smith brothers merged into Warner-Lambert pharmaceutical co. Newsweek 63:68+ F 24 '64
Trustbusters in Tucson; Arizona daily star bought by the Daily citizen. Time 85:67 Ja 15 '65
Trying even harder; merger of International telephone & telegraph co. and Avis rent a car. Time 85:67 Ja 22 '65
Union's arbitration demand upheld in merger situation; Supreme court's ruling. Pub W 185:31-2 Ap 13 '64
U.S. antitrust action: big is bad? il Newsweek 63:72-3+ Je 29 '64
What's an acquisition worth? J. Thackray. il Duns R 83:36-8+ Mr '64
What's next in antitrust? interview, ed. by G. R. Rosen. W. H. Orrick, jr. Duns R 83:35-6+ Je '64
When managerial styles clash. il Bsns W p65-6+ N 30 '63
Why businessmen keep a worried eye on Washington. il U S News 54:55-7 Ap 1 '63
Why mergers go wrong. B. McLagan. il Duns R 84:40-1+ N '64
See also
Bank consolidations and mergers
Railroads—Consolidations and mergers

BUSINESS consultants
Expertland, by R. Sommer. Review
Bsns W il p63+ Ag 24 '63
Experts and the editors. Duns R 81:3 My '63
Famous firsts: high priest of efficiency. Bsns W p 100+ Je 22 '63
Famous firsts: man who asked the right questions. Bsns W p 74-5 Ag 31 '63
Get your money's worth from specialists. N. Stewart. Nations Bsns 52:96+ Ap '64
Mating behavioral science and simulation. R. A. Bauer and R. D. Buzzell. il Harvard Bsns R 42:116-24 S '64
Negroes get a hand. il Bsns W p38 Je 27 '64
Peter Drucker: troubleshooter at the top. P. Korenvaes. Duns R 84:43+ Jl '64
Staid Boston trustee tries a new venture; management consultant. il Bsns W p72+ O 17 '64
Thorough approach to foreign markets; use of consultants in international commerce; address, June 18, 1963. L. V. Kleydorff. Vital Speeches 29:631-3 Ag 1 '63
What management consultants can do; with list of twenty-five top-line consultants. il Bsns W p88-90+ Ja 23 '65
See also
McKinsey and company

BUSINESS correspondence. See Commercial correspondence

BUSINESS council
In gauging the boom, watch June; semiannual meeting. il Newsweek 64:81 O 26 '64
Soup & chips. il Time 84:97-8 D 11 '64

BUSINESS council for international understanding
Are we gaining or guessing abroad? address, March 27, 1963. F. C. Foy. Vital Speeches 29:421-5 My 1 '63

BUSINESS cycles
America's great depression, by M. N. Rothbard. Review
Nat R 16:456-8 Je 2 '64. L. M. Spadaro
Importance of being on time. G. Terborgh. il Fortune 69:136-7 My '64
Is the long cycle why we don't grow? creeping pace of industrial growth. il Bsns W p78+ F 16 '63
Long cycle: hidden force in the economy. B. G. Hickman. il Duns R 82:48-9+ D '63
Strains and restraints. il Fortune 70:27-8 O '64
What ever happened to the business cycle? il Time 83:79 Je 5 '64
Why future recessions will be mild; symposium. il Nations Bsns 51:52+ N '63
See also
Business conditions

BUSINESS depression
Amidst prosperity, recession warnings. il Newsweek 62:75-6 N 4 '63
Entrepreneurship and the depressed area. S. F. Reed. Yale R 54:31-40 O '64
History repeats? excerpts from editorial of February 28, 1958. D. Lawrence. U S News 54:100 Ap 1 '63
In Hazard, Ky. D. Wakefield. Commentary 36:209-17 S '63
Is recession inevitable? interview, ed. by G. R. Rosen. H. C. Wallich. Duns R 84:30-1 Ag '64
Lean times in Boston; depression and the drys. C. W. Morton. Atlan 211:47-54 F '63
Long cycle: hidden force in the economy. B. G. Hickman. il Duns R 82:48-9+ D '63
No more depressions? interview. W. W. Heller. il U S News 56:58-63 Je 29 '64
Ordeal of Herbert Hoover. C. N. Degler. Yale R 52:563-83 Je '63
Recess or recession? D. Lawrence. U S News 54:108 Mr 4 '63
Why U.S. can't afford a slump. il U S News 57:102 D 14 '64

BUSINESS districts
Award winning mall; Knoxville, Tenn. J. J. Duncan. il Am City 79:74-5 N '64
Beauty in the business district; Oakland, Calif. il Am City 79:113 O '64
Downtown area: how to clean it up and make it pay; Boston. D. B. Carlson. il Arch Forum 120:98-101 Je '64
Downtown snarl: a case for sorting, stacking, and storing. il Arch Forum 119:78-83 O '63
First Cullen center units opened; Houston, Tex. il Arch Rec 134:153-6 Ag '63
Here's way to rebuild your city; downtown Rochester, N.Y. il Nations Bsns 52:34-5+ My '64
Long-term benefits of a shoppers' mall; Kalamazoo, Mich. C. H. Elliott. il Am City 79: 91-2 Mr '64
Midtown plaza promotes a Rochester building boom. il Arch Forum 121:8 Jl '64
New nerve centers in Downtown, U.S.A. il Bsns W p 13 Jl 4 '64
Planning the downtown center: symposium, with introd. by M. F. Schmertz. il Arch Rec 135:177-200 Mr '64
Pomona sets a pattern: downtown pedestrian mall. H. A. Faull. il Am City 79:77-8 Ja '64
Rome builds a new forum for business. il Bsns W p 120-1+ D 5 '64
Shopping center moves back to midtown. il Fortune 71:190+ Ja '65
Ten-acre superblock planned for Dallas. il Arch Rec 136:14 Jl '64

BUSINESS districts—*Continued*
Ten steps to a healthier downtown. J. S. Sharp. il Am City 79:97-8 F '64
Transit-way unveiled for Minneapolis. O. D. Gay. il Am City 78:113 Jl '63
BUSINESS economists. See Economists
BUSINESS education
B-school grads: are they aiming too high? Harvard grads. il Bsns W p52 My 25 '63
B-schools for Britain; concerning Lord Franks plan. Bsns W p84+ D 7 '63
B-schools run hard in the race for talent. il Bsns W p 152+ N 16 '63
B-schools seek a wider world; conference on international business programs, Indiana university. il Bsns W p 124+ D 14 '63
Case studies teach high school history; case study method. il Bsns W p94 F 1 '64
College attuned to business; Northwood institute, Midland, Mich. il Bsns W p 143-4+ S 7 '63
Deans' club peps up. il Bsns W p 116-18 My 16 '64
Education for an expanded export trade. Sch Life 46:12 N '63
Famous firsts: how business schools began. il Bsns W p 114+ O 19 '63
Go to the Château; European institute of business administration at Fontainebleau. il Newsweek 61:76 Je 10 '63
More teachers for business education. B. I. Blackstone. il Sch Life 45:23 My '63
New report card on the business schools. R. Sheehan. il Fortune 70:148-50+ D '64
Peru gets B-school; launching of graduate program in business administration in Lima by Stanford university. Bsns W p 174 Je 15 '63
Poor man's B-school; correspondence course in management. il Bsns W p 160+ Je 6 '64
Ringing a bell for B-school support. Bsns W p 172 N 7 '64
Search for talent; new business schools abroad. il Time 82:91 D 13 '63
Teenage look at business. il Bsns W p 152-4 Je 27 '64
Trade education program. A. O. Stanley. Duns R 81:96-8 My '63
Trilingual business education; European institute of business administration, Fontainebleau. il Fortune 69:51-2+ F '64
What one top company wants; excerpts from address. J. J. Scanlon. Nations Bsns 52:68+ Ap '64
What's ahead for business education; symposium. il Nations Bsns 52:40-1+ Ap '64
See also
Columbia university—Graduate school of business
Executives—Training
Industrial management—Study and teaching
Stanford university, Stanford, Calif.—Graduate school of business
BUSINESS enterprises
Diamond-studded coyote; C. Trouyet of Mexico City. il Time 82:115 D 6 '63
Farm boy who's going to town; K. Osano of Japan. Time 83:93-4 Ap 3 '64
How to start a business. A. Poinsett. il Ebony 19:85-6+ Jl '64
BUSINESS enterprises, New. See New business enterprises
BUSINESS entertaining
Biggest thank you party; Chicago postmaster, the host. il Ebony 19:55-6+ F '64
Business practices under the new T&E rules. V. H. Rothschild, 2d. il Duns R 82:40-2+ N '63
Company Santas sober up. il Bsns W p29 D 14 '63
Famous faces of forty years; Time's 40th anniversary celebrations. il Life 54:77-82D+ My 17 '63
Free anything gets put off limits. il Bsns W p28-9 N 21 '64
Making the publishing party rounds. H. Frankel. Sat R 47:36+ O 3 '64
Moline's biggest bash; opening of Deere & co.'s Saarinen-designed headquarters. il Bsns W p62-4 Je 20 '64
Personal business; deducting travel and entertainment expenses. Bsns W p89 Ap 6 '63
See also
Entertaining in sales promotion

Anecdotes, facetiae, satire, etc.

Be my host. L. Anders. il Harper 227:43-6 N '63
BUSINESS ethics
Big business fails America. S. Screven; reply. R. Baumhart. America 108:184 F 9 '63
Business conscience, by L. H. Hodges. Review New Repub 148:21-3 My 11 '63. A. Brynes Sat R 46:31 My 11 '63. K. Schriftgiesser
Business ethics and the individual. Duns R 81:31 Ja '63
Church and the businessman; plea for greater understanding. J. C. Worthy. Christian Cent 80:1232-4 O 9 '63
Corrupt society; with foreword by the editors. F. J. Cook. Nation 196:453-96a Je 1 '63; Discussion. 196:inside cover Je 22; inside cover Je 29 '63
Deceptive business practices; address, February 21, 1963. S. J. Insalata. Vital Speeches 29:473-5 My 15 '63
Ethical aftermath of profit; address, August 8, 1963. E. Maher. Vital Speeches 29:735-6 S 15 '63
Government and business; address, October 30, 1963. L. B. Mason. Vital Speeches 30:134-8 D 15 '63
Inertia in business ethics. R. Baumhart and G. D. Fitzpatrick. America 108:798-800 Je 1 '63
Myth of the American way. K. Watson. Christian Cent 80:328-30 Mr 13 '63
On the job ethics, ed. by C. P. Hall. Review America 110:332 Mr 14 '64. B. L. Masse
Pick the middle road for success. W. Letwin. Nations Bsns 52:76-7 Ag '64
Sins they commit; business and political ethics. America 109:72 Jl 20 '63
TV searches the business soul; lectures by professor of marketing at St Joseph college, Philadelphia. il Bsns W p99-100 Mr 28 '64
See also
Better business bureaus
Competition
Trade practices
Trade secrets
BUSINESS etiquette. See Etiquette
BUSINESS expansion. See Industrial expansion
BUSINESS expenses. See Expense accounts (business)
BUSINESS failures
Business failures. R. Wyant. See issues of Dun's review and modern industry
See also
Bank failures
Bankruptcy
BUSINESS films. See Moving pictures in industry
BUSINESS flying. See Airplanes in business
BUSINESS forecasting
Another group of bankers looks ahead; commercial bankers. il U S News 55:54 D 16 '63
Balance tips to the bulls; mutual fund managers outlook. il Bsns W p 132+ Mr 16 '63
Balanced gains for business; forecast for second-half of '63. Bsns W p25-6 My 18 '63
Banker's formula for good times in '64; excerpts from address. W. F. Butler. U S News 56:66-7 F 3 '64
Big if's. il Fortune 69:27-8 Mr '64
Boom LBJ sees ahead. il U S News 56:29-31 F 3 '64
Bounce is missing. il Bsns W p27 D 14 '63
Business after the election; with charts. U S News 57:96-8 N 9 '64
Business outlay surge brings a few worries; price boosts and boom psychology. il Bsns W p25-6 Mr 14 '64
Business outlook: all signs point up. il U S News 54:38-9 Je 3 '63
Business outlook: Burns vs. Heller. il U S News 57:63 S 7 '64
Business spending: 12 per cent more. il Bsns W p25-6 D 12 '64
Business upturn: how big? how long? il U S News 54:39-41 Mr 25 '63
Businessmen's expectations. il Duns R 81:11 Mr; 15 Je '63
Businessmen's expectations. K. Dieter. il Duns R 83:11 Je; 84:11 S; 11 D '64
Businessmen's expectations. W. A. Duvel. il Duns R 82:11 S; 11 D '63; 83:11-12 Mr '64
Can good times go on and on? here are answers from leading businessmen. U S News 55:70 O 28 '63
Coming: faster business growth; questions and answers. P. J. Lovewell. il Nations Bsns 51:31-3+ My '63
Coming up roses. il Bsns W p23-5 Mr 14 '64
Complacency ltd. il Fortune 69:23-4 My '64
Economy's DEW line. Time 84:79 Ag 21 '64
Experts analyze investment outlook. C. M. Bliss; A. P. Haake, jr; J. C. Bickford. il Nations Bsns 52:106-8+ Je '64
Experts predict stock market outlook; symposium. il Nations Bsns 51:56-8+ Je '63
First finding, up 4 per cent; McGraw-Hill capital spending survey; with editorial comment. il Bsns W p25-7, 152 N 9 '63

BUSINESS forecasting—*Continued*
Focus on '64; symposium. il Nations Bsns 51:33-9+ D '63
Great opportunities ahead; successful businessman of 1975; symposium. Nations Bsns 52:28-9+ Ja '64
How bankers size up the outlook now; poll investment bankers. il U S News 55:50-3 D 16 '63
How to keep the expansion going. Bsns W p 144 My 9 '64
How to rate the forecasters; NBER study. Bsns W p39-40 Ja 9 '65
How top businessmen rate the year ahead. U S News 54:78 My 20 '63
If taxes are cut; the chances of a boom. il U S News 54:32 F 11 '63
Importance of being on time. G. Terborgh. il Fortune 69:136-7 My '64
In spring, the bears still growl. il Bsns W p26-7 My 2 '64
Is a boom ahead for business? il U S News 54:37-9 Ap 29 '63
Is inflation on the way? a look ahead. il U S News 55:25-8 D 23 '63
Is it to be a real boom for U.S? what businessmen say about the outlook. il U S News 56:56-61 Mr 23 '64
Leading economists size up the business outlook; symposium. il U S News 58:54-63 Ja 4 '65
Look ahead. See issues of Nation's business
A look at the business future; excerpts from address, 1964. A. F. Burns. U S News 57:92-3 Ag 17 '64
Management problems in 1963; interviews with executives. il Harvard Bsns R 41:6-8+ Ja '63
Nation's business outlook symposium. il Nations Bsns 51:40-1+ N '63
Nation's business survey; views of key men. il Nations Bsns 52:56-8+ Jl '64
New guides help you plan. H. Wolozin. Nations Bsns 51:64-7 Ag '63
New note; exuberance and worries. il Fortune 70:27-8 N '64
New upturn in business soon? il U S News 55:31-3 Ag 19 '63
Optimists; economy's growth will continue. Newsweek 64:66+ Jl 13 '64
Outlook for business; address, December 5, 1963. J. D. Wilson. Vital Speeches 30:169-72 Ja 1 '64
Profitless prosperity is on the way out. il Bsns W p54-5 Ja 4 '64
Proposal for better business forecasting; adaptation of address. W. W. Leontief. Harvard Bsns R 42:166-7+ N '64
Ready to build again; McGraw-Hill survey. il Bsns W p25-7 Ap 25 '64
Recovery to growth. il Fortune 68:41-2+ Jl '63
Report on the business outlook; forecast by industry economists. il U S News 57:109-11 O 12 '64
Those static statistics. Time 84:88+ Jl 10 '64
Tighter money ahead? il U S News 54:102-3 F 25 '63
To settle an argument, what five economic advisers see ahead; symposium. U. S. News 57:60-2 S 14 '64
Top executives tell Nation's business readers: why next year looks good; symposium. il Nations Bsns 51:31-3+ Jl '63
Trend of American business. See issues of U.S. news & World report
U.S. thirty-seven years from now. il U S News 54:70-1 F 11 '63
Up, if taxes go down; impact of a tax cut on U.S. business in 1964; McGraw-Hill capital spending survey. il Bsns W p28-9 N 9 '63
Visibility now. il Fortune 67:39-40 Ap '63
Vote of confidence in good times; with chart. U S News 57:63 D 28 '64
Wall Street's view: a modest price gain. il Bsns W p70-2 D 28 '63
What bankers see ahead for business. il U S News 55:50-1 O 21 '63; 57:98-101 D 14 '64
What business leaders see ahead. U S News 57:114 O 26 '64
What experts see next for business. il U S News 57:37-8 N 30 '64
What the future holds for business; interview. P. A. Samuelson. il U S News 57:64-8+ D 14 '64
What top economists see ahead for business; symposium. il U S News 56:64-72 Ja 13 '64
What top executives expect in 1965. il Nations Bsns 52:29-31+ D '64
When spending hits 600 billions. il U S News 55:46 Jl 22 '63
Where business is heading; as seen by economists for big companies. il U S News 55:43-5 O 7 '63
Wrong time for pipe dreams. Bsns W p 124 Ja 18 '64
Year for caution, but not for alarm; symposium. il Bsns W p56-8 Ja 2 '65
See also
Forecasts (economics)
BUSINESS forms. See Business—Forms, blanks, etc.
BUSINESS games. See Management games
BUSINESS gifts. See Gifts in business
BUSINESS hours
See also
Libraries—Hours of opening
BUSINESS insurance. See Insurance, Business
BUSINESS journals. See Business—Periodicals; Trade journals
BUSINESS letters. See Commercial correspondence
BUSINESS liquidation. See Liquidation
BUSINESS location. See Location in business and industry
BUSINESS magazines. See Business—Periodicals
BUSINESS management and organization
American vs. European management philosophy. O. H. Nowotny. bibliog f il Harvard Bsns R 42:101-8 Mr '64
Big management shake-up. J. B. Weiner. Duns R 83:30-1+ Je '64
Big power of little ideas; excerpts from Managing for results: economic tasks and risk-taking decisions. P. F. Drucker. Harvard Bsns R 42:6-8+ My '64
Black figures and red faces. Duns R 84:31 Jl '64
Care and feeding of the profitable product; excerpts from Managing for results: economic tasks and risk-taking decisions. P. F. Drucker. Fortune 69:133-5 Mr '64
Case of the unproductive products. S. A. Greyser. il Harvard Bsns R 42:20-2+ Jl '64
Changing American executive; symposium. Duns R 83:38-40+ Ja '64
Coming: new jobs, new titles. S. Schuler. Nations Bsns 51:40-1+ Je '63
Corporation at war with itself. W. E. Moore. il Duns R 81:58-60 Ap '63
Cutting back middle management: new shine to Scovill. J. B. Weiner. il Duns R 84:34-5+ Jl '64
Democracy is inevitable. P. E. Slater and W. G. Bennis. bibliog f Harvard Bsns R 42:51-9 Mr '64
Dilemma of decentralization; symposium, ed. by T. O'Hanlon. il Duns R 84:41-2+ S '64
Dis-organization man. J. B. Weiner. il Duns R 83:32-4+ Ap '64
Disturbing economics of affluence; excerpts from Hidden face of free enterprise. J. R. Bunting. il Duns R 83:40-1+ Ap '64
Double talk cuts egghead's value to business. G. S. Odiorne. il Nations Bsns 51:92-4 Ap '63
Downwardly mobile; demotion instead of dismissal. Newsweek 62:59 D 16 '63
Drawing the rules from history. Bsns W p46+ Ag 3 '63
Ethical aftermath of profit; address, August 8, 1963. E. Maher. Vital Speeches 29:735-6 S 15 '63
Every man for himself; decentralized management. Bsns W p84+ S 19 '64
Executive decision; address, April 24, 1964. J. E. Swearingen. Vital Speeches 30:506-8 Je 1 '64
Famous firsts: bringing brainwork to the fore. Bsns W p54+ F 15 '64
Famous firsts: carrying the gospel to Europe. Bsns W p63-4 N 23 '63
Famous firsts: charting a way to democracy. Bsns W p44+ Ja 11 '64
Famous firsts: discoveries from looking inward. Bsns W p 152+ Je 6 '64
Famous firsts: extending the scientific gospel. Bsns W p 132+ Ap 18 '64
Famous firsts: organizing a profession. Bsns W p87-8 Mr 21 '64
Gentle art of stitch-in-timemanship; trade relations director. il Bsns W p74 My 11 '63
Great GM mystery. H. Wolff. bibliog f Harvard Bsns R 42:164-6+ S '64
Growth companies. J. B. Weiner. il Duns R 84:40-3+ O '64
Here's know-how you'll need; views of key men. Nations Bsns 52:66-7 Jl '64
How companies build on success. C. A. Cerami. il Nations Bsns 52:38-9+ Mr '64
How companies will win success; interview. Nations Bsns 52:26-7+ Ja '64
How General motors did it. R. Sheehan. il Fortune 67:96-111+ Je '63

BUSINESS management and organization—*Continued*
How Sears, Roebuck plans for the future. N. Buckley. il Duns R 82:44-6+ O '63
How to evaluate corporate strategy. S. Tilles. bibliog f Harvard Bsns R 41:111-21 Jl '63
How to go international; excerpts from Handbook of international marketing. A. O. Stanley. il Nations Bsns 51:90-2+ S '63
How to head off trouble. N. Stewart. il Nations Bsns 52:68-70+ Ag '64
How to run a growing company. L. A. Allen. il Nations Bsns 53:68-70+ Ja '65
Japanese giant that wouldn't stay dead; Mitsubishi group. R. Lubar. il Fortune 70:141-9+ N '64
Jersey Standard's corporate longevity. il Duns R 81:28-30+ Mr '63
Job of being president. Duns R 81:26-7+ Mr '63
Keep your business in balance. N. Stewart. il Nations Bsns 52:90-2+ N '64
Make the most of new ideas. C. A. Cerami. Nations Bsns 52:50-2+ Jl '64
Make your time more productive. A. Uris. il Nations Bsns 51:98+ Ap '63
Man in management; address, January 15, 1963. H. C. Alexander. Vital Speeches 29:312-14 Mr 1 '63
Management in the future; symposium. il Nations Bsns 51:55-73 Jl '63
Management ways of General electric. J. Thackray. il Duns R 82:28-30+ N '63
Managing for business effectiveness. P. F. Drucker. il Harvard Bsns R 41:53-60 My '63
Minority owners can avoid squeeze-outs. F. H. O'Neal. Harvard Bsns R 41:150-2+ Mr '63
Mismanaged job in packaging. P. B. Baker. il Duns R 82:pt2 169-70 N '63
Mysterious management committee. S. Nicholson. il Duns R 81:57-9+ My '63
New art of free-form management. J. B. Weiner. il Duns R 84:30-2+ D '64
No easy road to market orientation. R. W. Lear. il Harvard Bsns R 41:53-60 S '63
Now it's more of a science; reports of study by Harvard graduate school of business. bibliog il Bsns W p44+ D 28 '63
Old gun, new ramrod. il Bsns W p 168-70+ Je 15 '63
Organizing a worldwide business. G. H. Clee and W. M. Sachtjen. il Harvard Bsns R 42:55-67 N '64
Organizing for profit overseas. Bsns W p 112+ My 23 '64
Parkinson cautions: there's danger in growth; interview. C. N. Parkinson. Nations Bsns 52:36-7+ My '64
People, vitality and AT&T. T. R. Brooks. il Duns R 81:53-5+ Ap '63
Pink slips and chief executives. L. Wolman. il Duns R 81:47-8+ F '63
Playing guinea pig: Britain's Glacier metals co. ltd. il Bsns W p 166+ N 7 '64
Practical planning for small business. R. A. Golde. bibliog f il Harvard Bsns R 42:147-55+ S '64
President and corporate planning. M. L. Mace. Harvard Bsns R 43:49-62 Ja '65
Principles of effective management; excerpts from New patterns of management. R. Likert. Harvard Bsns R 41:103 N '63
Problem in organization. S. Nicholson. il Duns R 81:43-4+ Je '63
Profit teams of management. J. B. Weiner. il Duns R 84:36-7+ S '64
Russians yearn for the managerial mind. D. W. Ewing. Harper 230:67-72 Ja '65
Sales managers must manage. R. O. Leon. il Harvard Bsns R 42:107-14 My '64
Should management own more stock? J. J. Friedman. il Duns R 81:52-3 My '63
Six challenges for tomorrow's manager. J. H. Healey. il Duns R 84:60-1+ O '64
Six enemies of executive output. J. A. Patton. il Duns R 81:33-4+ Mr '63
Stretching the span of management. G. G. Fisch. bibliog f il Harvard Bsns R 41:74-85 S '63
Ten best-managed companies. il Duns R 81:32-4+ Ja '63
Transferring research results to operations. J. B. Quinn and J. A. Mueller. il Harvard Bsns R 41:49-66 Ja '63
Twelve fables of research management. P. F. Drucker. il Harvard Bsns R 41:103-8 Ja '63
V.P. for the future: corporate planner. il Time 81:89 My 10 '63
What is the manager? H. Sonthoff. bibliog f Harvard Bsns R 42:24-6+ N '64
What makes a best-managed company? J. B. Weiner. il Duns R 82:40-2+ D '63
What makes a growth company? top thirteen. J. B. Weiner. il Duns R 84:30-2+ N '64
What makes GM go. T. R. Brooks. il Duns R 82:30-2+ S '63
What's ahead in management? interviews with executives. ed. by J. B. Weiner. Duns R 85:32-3+ Ja '65
See also
Budget, Business
Business consultants
Calculating machines—Business applications
Conflict of interests (business)
Council for international progress in management
Decision making
Executive ability
Executives
Featherbedding (industrial relations)
Hotel management
Industrial management and organization
Industrial relations
International academy of management
Inventories
Marketing
Systems management

Bibliography

Some trophies from the jungle. il Bsns W p 140 F 16 '63

BUSINESS men
Business and labor meet the President. il Newsweek 62:65 D 16 '63
Businessmen in the news. See issues of Fortune
Businessmen who love the land. il Fortune 67:114-21 Mr '63
Church and the businessman; plea for greater understanding. J. C. Worthy. Christian Cent 80:1232-4 O 9 '63
Corrupt society. F. J. Cook. Nation 196:474-5 Je 1 '63
Government-business team that works; trade missions. A. Fontaine. Read Digest 83:111-14 D '63
Hidden face of free enterprise: the strange economics of the American businessman, by J. R. Bunting. Review
Bsns W il p 164+ Je 6 '64
Individualism and big business, by L. R. Sayles. Review
Bsns W il p 100 O 5 '63
Lonely wife; wife of a traveling man. J. Krantz. il McCalls 91:142-3+ N '63
Lost leaders of business; editorial. Duns R 82:25 Ag '63
Main Street standards. Duns R 84:29 D '64
Mammon's untouchables. Duns R 85:31 Ja '65
Mind of the businessman. B. L. Masse. America 111:296-8 S 19 '64
Personal business; U.S. businessmen in Europe, to mix business with pleasure. Bsns W p 107-8 My 30 '64
World of the renaissance executive. il Newsweek 62:92-4 N 18 '63
See also
Capitalists and financiers
Executives

Anecdotes, facetiae, satire, etc.

Self-made nitwit. W. F. Miksch. Atlan 214:107-8 Ag '64

Health and hygiene

See Men—Health and hygiene

Political activities

See Business—Political aspects

BUSINESS men as public officers. See Public officers
BUSINESS mens clubs. See Clubs; Kiwanis clubs
BUSINESS mens lunches. See Lunches
BUSINESS offices. See Offices
BUSINESS organization. See Business management and organization
BUSINESS recession. See Business depression
BUSINESS records
AAUP production facts and figures needed for wise management. R. Kinney; W. C. Becker; W. Sloane. il Pub W 184:68-9+ Jl 1 '63
Grolier using new record storage plan. il Pub W 184:35 Jl 29 '63
How to get rid of paper; corporate archivist. il Time 83:74 Ja 3 '64
Stemming the paper torrent. il Duns R 84:pt2 110-12+ S '64
This firm threw its files away; retail store chain, Marks and Spencer. il U S News 55:69 Jl 29 '63
See also
Business—Forms, blanks, etc.
BUSINESS research
See also
Market research
Operations research

BUSINESS schools. See Business education
BUSINESS secrets. See Trade secrets
BUSINESS statistics
Figures of the week. See issues of Business week
Fourteen important ratios in twelve retail lines, 1962. il Duns R 82:38-9 N '63
See also
Business forecasting
BUSINESS tax
Constitutional balm for an old sore; occupation taxes in Minnesota's mining industry. Bsns W p 112 S 14 '63
BUSINESS trips. See Travel
BUSONI, Ferruccio
Dr Faust; presentation in New York. F. Merkling. Opera N 29:31 Ja 2 '65
Music to my ears; Busoni's Faust and other novelties. I. Kolodin. Sat R 47:29+ D 19 '64
BUSTAD, L. K.
Radioiodine: its nature and effects. Science 142:510+ O 25 '63
BUSTAMANTE, Sir Alexander
Race with unrest. por Time 84:50 O 30 '64
BUSTANI, Emile
Ninth life. Newsweek 61:48 Mr 25 '63
BUSTELLI, Franz Anton
Rococo retrospective; exhibition of figurines. il Time 82:40-1 Ag 30 '63
BUSWELL, James H.
Add fall color to your outdoor living room with chrysanthemums. Pop Gard 14:48+ My '63
BUT for whom Charlie; drama. See Behrman, S. N.
BUTCHER, Charles
Axles and cones. New Yorker 40:28-9 Ja 16 '65
BUTCHER, Russell D.
Freeways versus redwoods. Nat Parks Mag 38:12-15 Je '64
Redwoods and the fragile web of nature. Audubon Mag 66:172-4 My '64
BUTCHER, Wilfred F.
Separatists in Quebec. Christian Cent 80:742-4 Je 5 '63
BUTENKO, John W.
Include the women. il por Time 84:34 D 11 '64
Quiet man. il Newsweek 62:44+ N 11 '63
BUTKUS, Dick
Killer whale. H. L. Masin. por Sr Schol 85:28 N 4 '64
Special kind of brute with a love of violence. D. Jenkins. il pors Sports Illus 21:30-2+ O 12 '64
BUTLER, Clay P. and Jenkins, R. J.
Temperature of an iron meteoroid in space. Science 142:1567-8; 44:81 D 20 '63, Ap 3 '64
Thermal properties of meteoritic iron from 150° to 300° Celsius. Science 139:486-7 F 8 '63
BUTLER, D. E.
Why American political reporting is better than England's. Harper 226:14+ My '63
BUTLER, Dick
Say it with care, or say it with confidence. Motor B 115:100+ Ja '65
BUTLER, Donald E.
Angry is the morning; story. Cath World 198:251-6 Ja '64
BUTLER, George D.
Hooked! Recreation 56:253 Je '63
Is your playground surfacing safe? Recreation 56:193-4 Ap '63
Supply and demand. Recreation 56:120-2 Mr '63
BUTLER, Henry
Measure of Menotti. Opera N 28:27 F 8 '64
To be a Bernhardt. Harper 227:56-61 Ag '63
BUTLER, Joseph T.
Hudson River Valley portfolio. Antiques 85:432-7 Ap '64
Sunnyside at Tarrytown, New York. Antiques 84:175-8 Ag '63
BUTLER, Minnis C.
We do our own utility billing. Am City 78:101-2 S '63
BUTLER, Richard Austen
Disarmament; address, February 25, 1964. Vital Speeches 30:331-6 Mr 15 '64
Foreign affairs; address, November 26, 1963. Vital Speeches 30:139-41 D 15 '63
Problems of the future; address, June 16, 1964. Vital Speeches 30:578-82 Jl 15 '64
about
Filling a Tory gap; Butler as prime minister. por U S News 55:24 O 21 '63
Three times almost prime minister. por Time 82:35 O 18 '63
BUTLER, Ruth M.
Is disrespect inevitable? PTA Mag 57:24-6 bibliog(p36) Mr '63
BUTLER, William
November 25, 1963; poem. Harper 228:72 F '64
BUTLER, William B.
Right to be free without a fee. Sat R 47:28 Je 27 '64
BUTLER, William Frank
Banker's formula for good times in '64; excerpts from address. por U S News 56:66-7 F 3 '64
Trade and the less developed area. For Affairs 41:372-83 Ja '63
BUTLER university, Indianapolis
Many-faceted stage for the performing arts; Clowes memorial hall. il Arch Forum 119:98-105 D '63
Untortured Butler; new library. H. L. Boisen. il Library J 88:4571-3 D 1 '63
BUTTENHEIM, Edgar J.
Obituary
Am City por 80:4-5 Ja '65
BUTTER, Charles M.
Habituation of responses to novel stimuli in monkeys with selective frontal lesions. bibliog Science 144:313-15 Ap 17 '64
BUTTER
Australians sprinkle powdered butter. Sci Digest 53:62 Mr '63
Butter bird in nest. il Good H 157:220 D '63
Fresh butter, old-fashioned buttermilk, and fresh cottage cheese. il Sunset 131:78-81 S '63
Some very special butters. il McCalls 91:154-5+ N '63
BUTTER molds
Look what shape the butter's in. il Sunset 133:172-3 N '64
BUTTER substitutes
Tariff schedule on importation of butter oil amended; proclamation, October 5, 1963. J. F. Kennedy. Dept State Bul 49:685 O 28 '63
BUTTERCUPS
Keeping an eye on ranunculus; four diseases that sometimes affect ranunculus. il Sunset 132:276-7 Ap '64
Put ranunculus in this month. il Sunset 131:256 N '63
BUTTERFIELD, James
Learn to fly, $65 down. Flying 75:28-30 S '64
BUTTERFIELD, Roger
Camera comes to the White House. Am Heritage 15:33-48 Ag '64
BUTTERFLIES
Butterfly farmer. il Pop Mech 119:120-1 Mr '63
Lowly disguise of the giant swallowtail. M. L. Donahue and R. J. Donahue. il Audubon Mag 66:320-1 S '64
Mid-summer is busy season for butterflies. il(p49) Sci N L 84:53 Jl 27 '63
Monarch: jeweled traveler of the skies. P. Farb. il Read Digest 83:70-4 S '63
Monarch's emergence. A. B. Klots. il Natur Hist 73:50-3 My '64
Mystery of the monarch butterfly. P. A. Zahl. il Nat Geog Mag 123:588-98 Ap '63
On the character of color; with photographs. A. B. Klots. Natur Hist 72:30-9 Je '63
Smell, sex and survival in animals. K. Von Frisch. il Sci Digest 53:65-72 F '63
See also
Imported cabbage worms
Migration
Mystery of the monarch butterfly. P. A. Zahl. il Nat Geog Mag 123:588-98 Ap '63
Ocean hopping monarch. L. H. Newman. il Audubon Mag 66:106-9 Mr '64
BUTTERFLY valves. See Valves
BUTTERMILK
Fresh butter, old-fashioned buttermilk, and fresh cottage cheese. il Sunset 131:78-81 S '63
BUTTERNUT trees
Tenacious butternut. W. M. Harlow. il Am For 69:37 S '63
BUTTERS, Dorothy G.
Escape! story. Good H 158:90-1 Je '64
BUTTERSWORTH, James E.
Marine paintings by two Buttersworths. H. Comstock. il Antiques 85:99-103 Ja '64
BUTTERSWORTH, Thomas
Marine paintings by two Buttersworths. H. Comstock. il Antiques 85:99-103 Ja '64
BUTTERY, B. R. and Boatman, S. G.
Turgor pressures in phloem; measurements on hevea latex. bibliog Science 145:285-6 Jl 17 '64
BUTTNER, Marguerite
Wonderful wattle tree. Am For 70:30-1 Jl '64

BUTTON, Dick
America on ice. Am Heritage 14:38-49 F '63
BUTTONS
Button collecting. D. F. Brown. See issues of Hobbies
BUTTONS, Campaign. See Campaign buttons, etc.
BUTTS, Wally
Balm for a gloomy bear. Time 83:51 F 14 '64
Butts reverses field to try for full $3,060,000. Pub W 185:77 F 10 '64
Curtis publishing hit with $3,060.000 libel verdict. Pub W 184:45 S 2 '63
Dramatic moment. il Sports Illus 19:26-7 Ag 26 '63
Fix or fiction? il por Time 82:38+ Ag 16 '63
Gridiron on the grid. Nation 196:299 Ap 13 '63
High cost of libel. il por Newsweek 62:72-3 S 2 '63
How much can coach Butts keep? 3-million-dollar libel award. por U S News 55:6+ S 2 '63
It's not the money, it's the vindication; with editorial comment. R. H. Boyle. il por Sports Illus 19:5, 46-7 S 2 '63
Libel judgement against Curtis reduced to $460,000. Pub W 185:239 Ja 27 '64
Money for the Post. Time 83:43 Ja 24 '64
Name of the game. Sat Eve Post 236:82 Ap 27 '63
Scandalous notes. D. Jenkins. il Sports Illus 18:24-5+ Ap 8 '63
Sophisticated muckraking. il Time 82:34 Ag 23 '63
Story of a college football fix; Georgia versus Alabama. F. Graham, jr. il pors Sat Eve Post 236:80-3 Mr 23 '63; Discussion. Sports Illus 18:18-21 Mr 25 '63; Time 81:51 Mr 29 '63; Newsweek 61:51 Ap 1 '63
$3,060,000 worth of guilt. por Time 82:37+ Ag 30 '63
Trial that has the South seething; college football fix: Georgia versus Alabama. D. Jenkins. il por Sports Illus 19:18-21 Ag 5 '63
BUTYL bromide
Coupling of butyl bromide on hot magnesium. F. L. Lambert and others. bibliog Science 146:1049 N 20 '64
BUTYRIC acid
Differential estimation of gamma-butyrolactone and gamma-hydroxybutyric acid in rat blood and brain. N. J. Giarman and R. H. Roth. bibliog il Science 145:583-4 Ag 7 '64
Gamma hydroxybutyrate and gamma butyrolactone: concentration in rat tissues during anesthesia. S. P. Bessman and S. J. Skolnik. bibliog il Science 143:1045-7 Mr 6 '64
Irreparable mutations and ethionine resistance in neurospora. R. L. Metzenberg and others. bibliog il Science 145:1434-5 S 25 '64
BUTZ, J. S. jr
Shortcut to engine design; scaled powerplants. Flying 74:49+ My '64
BUXTON, C. Lee
Unborn baby's movements. Redbook 123:32+ Ag '64
BUXTON, Nigel
Lovely lodgings, low-priced. Mile 56:205+ Mr '63
BUYER, Bob
My sap runneth all over. Life 54:10 Ap 19 '63
BUYERS guides. See Consumer education
BUYING. See Purchasing; Purchasing, Household; Shopping and shoppers
BUYING motives. See Market research
BUYING of paintings. See Pictures—Purchasing
BUYUK ISLAND
Peaceful day on Büyük Ada. il Sunset 133:8 S '64
BUYUKMIHCI, Hope Sawyer
Unexpected refuge. il Audubon Mag 65:100-1 Mr '63
BUZZELL, Robert D.
Is marketing a science? bibliog f Harvard Bsns R 41:32-4+ Ja '63
—See Bauer, R. A. jt. auth.
BY-elections. See Elections—Great Britain
BYARS, Joseph C.
Twice 360°! Yachting 116:64-5+ Jl '64

about

Over, under and over again. H. Whall. il Sports Illus 20:32-3 Je 1 '64
BYCK, Robert, and Dirlik, Paul
Reversible section of the brain by a wall of cold. bibliog Science 139:1216-18 Mr 22 '63
BYE, Richard E.
La bataille de Francfort; eye-witness report by a first-timer. Pub W 186:26-30 O 19 '64
BYERS, G. L. and others
Moisture release from cut alfalfa. bibliog Science 143:1183 Mr 13 '64
BYERS, Margery
How not to go looking for owlets. Life 56:33 My 15 '64
When I hear the bell or a knock on the door, I panic. Life 54:18-19 F 15 '63
BYFIELD, L. E.
Four-way oscillator. Pop Electr 20:59 F '64
BYKOVSKII, Valerii Feodorovich
Hawk. il por Newsweek 61:68 Je 24 '63
His and hers. il por Newsweek 62:46 Jl 1 '63
Romanoff & Juliet. il por Time 81:26+ Je 21 '63
Soviets push ahead in the space race. por U S News 54:8 Je 24 '63
See also
Space flight—Manned flights—Bykovskii flight, 1963
BYLINSKY, Gene
Computer monster. New Repub 151:23-5 O 3 '64
—and Howard, W. E.
Hot rocket to nowhere. Sat Eve Post 236:78-81 N 9 '63
BYNUM, Mrs C. W.
Musician collects miniature pianos and organs. S. A. Parvin. il por Hobbies 68:122 Jl '63
BYNUM, Jim
Bulldogger. il por Time 82:33-4 S 6 '63
BYNUM, Ruth
More about textbooks; summary. Wilson Lib Bul 37:805 My '63
BYPASS jet engines. See Jet airplane engines
BYRD, C. W.
How silent the forest; poem. Am For 70:6 Ap '64
BYRD, Harry Flood
As Byrd sees himself: last of the old new dealers; excerpts from address. por U S News 54:20 Ap 15 '63
Big government, big spending; warning from Senator Byrd; excerpt from address, August 31, 1963. por U S News 55:50-1 S 9 '63
Byrd's-eye views; address, August 15, 1964. Vital Speeches 30:713-15 S 15 '64
Excerpt from statement, March 29, 1963. Cong Digest 42:140+ My '63
Massive federal spending; concentration of national power; address, May 3, 1963. Vital Speeches 29:514-20 Je 15 '63
Six deficits in a row? excerpts from address, January 30, 1964. U S News 56:12 F 10 '64

about

Meet the Honorable Harry (the rare) Byrd. W. S. White. por Read Digest 82:205-7+ Ap '63
Tax cuts & Puritans. Time 81:16-17 F 8 '63
BYRD, Robert Carlyle
Skeleton in the closet. C. D. Kean. Christian Cent 80:1148-9 S 18 '63
BYRD, William, 1542?-1623
On DGG and London, the genius of William Byrd. J. W. Barker. Am Rec G 31:228-9 N '64
BYRD, William, 1674-1744
Duchess and William Byrd. T. Thorne. il Antiques 84:562-5 N '63
BYRD family
Byrd coat-of-arms. H. K. Eilers. il Hobbies 69:126-7+ N '64
BYRNE, Brendan
How teenagers can combat adult delinquency; address, April 5, 1963. Vital Speeches 29:540-2 Je 15 '63
BYRNE, Donn. See Golightly, C. jt. auth.
BYRNE, James
Sheltered life. il pors Newsweek 64:75 Jl 27 '64
BYRNE, Katharine
Marvin's mother. Commonweal 80:395-7 Je 19 '64
BYRNE, William D.
Public bids on bonds vs. negotiated sale. Am City 79:135-6+ Ag '64
BYRNES, Asher
Turning gold into sand. New Repub 150:21-3 F 22 '64
BYRNES, James F.
Mr Byrnes' views. R. Moley. Newsweek 64:100 D 14 '64
Quiet South Carolina. R. Moley. Newsweek 63:100 Mr 23 '64
BYRNES, John W.
How Republicans would cut taxes and avert financial disaster; excerpts from address, September 20, 1963. U S News 55:85 S 30 '63
Kennedy tax bill; Republican view; summary of statement. U S News 54:104 F 25 '63

BYRNES, John W.—*Continued*
about
Leave it to Johnny. por Time 83:14 Ja 17 '64
Winning the Weevils. il Time 82:36 O 4 '63
BYRNES, Thomas
Songs for a small gardener. McCalls 91:96-7 Ag '64
BYROM, F. B.
How a knockout kills. Sci Digest 54:23-7 S '63
BYRON, George Gordon Noël Byron, 6th baron
Lord Byron's wife, by M. Elwin. Review Sat R il por 46:29-30 My 11 '63. H. T. Moore
BYRON, Gilbert
Thoreau and fellow mammals. Audubon Mag 65:374-5 N '63
BYRON, William J.
Few jobs for our youth. America 108:801 Je 1 '63
BYZANTINE art. See Art, Byzantine
BYZANTINE empire
Byzantium: the other half of the world. P. Sherrard. il Horizon 5:4-34 N '63
BYZANTINE music. See Music, Byzantine
BYZANTINE rite
Rumanian tragedy; anniversary of the dissolution of the Eastern rite church of Rumania. America 110:471 Ap 4 '64

C

CAB. See United States—Civil aeronautics board
CAIP. See Catholic association for international peace
CAP. See United States—Civil air patrol
CARE. See Cooperative for American relief everywhere, incorporated
CAT (Clear air turbulence) See Atmospheric turbulence
CATV (community antenna television systems) See Television antennas
C. and A. Brenninkmeyer company. See Brenninkmeyer, C. and A. company
CBA. See Christian booksellers association
CBC. See Canadian broadcasting corporation; Childrens' book council
CBE. See Council for basic education
CBS. See Columbia broadcasting system
C. B. Sheridan company. See Sheridan, C. B, company
CCA. See Cruising club of America
CCAR. See Central conference of American rabbis
CCC. See Commodity credit corporation; United States—Civilian conservation corps
CCD. See Confraternity of Christian doctrine
CCMC. See United States—Committee on the costs of medical care
CCSA. See Christian committee for service in Algeria
CCTV. See Television, Closed circuit
CD. See Certificates of deposit
CD (Chamber of deputies) See Italy—Parliament—Chamber of deputies
CDC. See Control data corporation; United States—Communicable disease center, Atlanta, Ga.
CDC pharmaceutical, incorporated. See Cove vitamin and pharmaceutical, incorporated
CDL. See Citizens for decent literature
CEA. See United States—Council of economic advisers
CED. See Committee for economic development
CEF. See Citizens for educational freedom
CEP. See Citizenship education project
CERN (Conseil européen pour la recherche nucléaire) See European organization for nuclear research
CF. See Cystic fibrosis
CFM. See Christian family movement (organization)
C. H. Wills and company. See Wills, C. H, and company
CIA. See United States—Central intelligence agency
CIAP (Inter-American committee on the Alliance for progress) See Alliance for progress
CILA (Centro Interamericano de libros académicos) See Inter-American scholarly book center
CINE. See Council on international nontheatrical events
CIOS international management congress. See International congress for scientific management
CIPM. See Council for international progress in management
CISV. See Childrens international summer villages
CLA. See California library association
CLAM (chemical low-altitude missile) See Guided missiles
CLR. See Council on library resources, incorporated
CMU. See Chlorophenyl dimethylurea
CND. See Campaign for nuclear disarmament (organization)
COC (Combat operations center) See North American air defense command
COFO. See Council of federated organizations
COMAP. See Commerce committee for the Alliance for progress
COMECON. See Council for mutual economic assistance
COPE. See American federation of labor and Congress of industrial organizations—Committee on political education
CORE. See Congress of racial equality
COSGO. See Council of state governments
COSPAR. See International council of scientific unions—Committee on space research
CPA. See Catholic press association
CPIF (cost plus incentive fee) See Incentives in industry
CPM (critical path method) See Critical path analysis
CPSU (Congress of the Communist party of the Soviet Union) See Communist party (Russia)
CRD (chronic respiratory disease) See Poultry —Diseases and pests
CRI. See Composers recordings, incorporated
CROP. See Christian rural overseas program
CSD. See American library association—Children's services division
CSG. See Council of state governments
CU. See Consumers union of United States
CWA. See Communications workers of America
CWS. See Church world service
CAB drivers. See Taxicab drivers
CABANISS, Edward H.
Meet GEVIC, the computer that flies. S. V. Jones. il por Sci Digest 55:76-7 Ja '64
CABARETS. See Music halls (variety theaters, cabarets, etc)
CABBAGE butterflies. See Imported cabbage worms
CABBAGE harvesting machinery. See Harvesting machinery
CABIN cruisers. See Yachts and yachting
CABIN in the sky; musical comedy. See Musical comedies, revues, etc.—Criticisms, plots, etc.
CABINET (United States) See United States—Cabinet
CABINET officers
From Washington straight. Cato. Nat R 16:1095 D 15 '64
Who's to be who in the new Johnson term. il U S News 57:27-9 D 21 '64
Why top-level jobs changed hands at the Pentagon. U S News 55:26 O 28 '63
See also
United States—Cabinet
CABINETMAKERS
Fine Federal furniture attributed to Portsmouth. C. E. Buckley. il Antiques 83:196-200 F '63
Meeks family of cabinetmakers. J. N. Pearce and others. il Antiques 85:414-20 Ap '64
Personal experiences of an old New York cabinetmaker; ed. by E. A. Ingerman. E. Hagen. il Antiques 84:576-80 N '63
See also
Hartshorne, E.
Lannuier, C. H.
Quervelle, A. G.
Roberts, A.
Wahl, J. G.
CABINETS (furniture)
ABCs of building chests and cabinets. R. J. De Cristoforo. il Pop Sci 185:116-21 N; 132-5 D '64; 186:132-6 Ja '65 (to be cont)
Furniture with a built-in bonus. il House B 105:222-3 O '63
Hi-Fi. C. L. Osborne. Opera N 27:35 F 16 '63

CABINETS (furniture)—*Continued*
How to decorate a utility box. il Sunset 130:131-2 Je '63
Rhenish cabinet of the eighteenth century. R. C. Smith. il Antiques 87:68-72 Ja '65
Two built-in storage units to solve two different problems. il House B 105:72+ O '63
Variable curio cabinet. il House & Gard 126: 228-9 S '64
See also
Kitchen cabinets
Phonograph cabinets

CABINETS, Built in. See Furniture, Built in

CABINS
A-frame assumes a more comfortable shape. il Sunset 130:118 Je '63
Build your own deer camp. J. H. Bensley and P. M. Gardner. il Field & S 68:41-3 Ag '63
Four-level igloo for fourteen; ski house, West Dover, Vt. F. R. Smith. il Sports Illus 19:44-7 D 16 '63
How to find your cabin in the pines. C. Schoenfeld. il Field & S 67:43-5+ Mr '63
How to prefab a vacation cabin in a home shop. B. Smallman. il Pop Sci 184:100-6 Ap '64
Life guide; cabins for amateur carpenters. il Life 54:17 My 31 '63
Low-cost cabin you can build for yourself. il Am Home 67:80+ Je '64
Retreat to the wilds but, keep the convenience of plumbing and a modern kitchen. il House B 105:56-9 Jl '63
Snow country retreat; Vermont ski house. B. Plumb. il N Y Times Mag p28-9 D 29 '63
Strictly a dream-boat, but loaded with ideas. il Good H 157:89-91 Jl '63
Sun and ski cabin on a mountain. A. C. Borg. il Am Home 66:30-1 Je '63
$10,000 mountain retreat. il House & Gard 123:122-3 Je '63
Tepee cabin. il Sunset 130:112-13 Mr '63
This cabin is really a vacation village. il Sunset 132:114-15 My '64
This vacation house is just 729 square feet. il Sunset 133:81 Jl '64
Winter-summer vacation house: there's no need to exclude comfort. C. C. Calkins. il House B 105:96-7 F '63
Winter vacation houses. J. Peter. il Look 27: 40-1 F 12 '63

CABLE, Harold
Way-out Cinderella; drama. Plays 23:23-35 My '64

CABLE, Mary
Emperor's monumental folly. Horizon 5:32-9 My '63
Wall: painted clay. Craft Horiz 23:27-31+ My '63

CABLES, Submarine
AMR cable enhances tracking reliability. P. J. Klass. il Aviation W 79:104-6+ Ag 5 '63
Before you get too excited about the new Telstar. il U S News 54:46-7 My 20 '63
Cross talk on what cables should carry; fights between telephone and telegraph companies. Bsns W p 116+ F 22 '64
Cutting in on the line; A.T.&T. refused permission to transmit printed as well as spoken communications through its transatlantic cables. il Time 83:83 Mr 27 '64
Down to the sea with phone lines. il Bsns W p70-1 Jl 4 '64
Extreme reliability vacuum tubes. il Electr World 73:41 Ja '65
San Francisco calling Tokyo under water. il Sr Schol 82:18 Ap 3 '63
Transmission from U.S. to Australia via Commonwealth cable opened; statement, December 2, 1963. D. Rusk. Dept State Bul 49:969 D 23 '63
Transpacific telephone. Sci Am 210:64 Ap '64
See also
Telephone cables

CABLES, Telephone. See Telephone cables

CABLEWAYS
Aerial tram conquers a peak in California; Mt San Jacinto tramway. il Bsns W p32-3 Ap 27 '63
New way to get a ride out of Palm Springs: biggest tramway soars skyward. il Life 55: 51+ N 1 '63
Sonata for a sherpa; aerial tramway at Palm Springs. H. Sutton. il Sat R 47:26-7 F 1 '64
World's longest aerial tramway; Mt San Jacinto, Calif. R. R. Olney. il Pop Sci 183:40-3 Ag '63

CABLING of trees. See Trees, Care of

CABOT, Henry B. See Roddy, J. jt. auth.

CABOT, Richard C. and Dicks, R. L.
Wisdom of the body; excerpts from Art of ministering to the sick. Read Digest 84: 24B Ja '64

CABRAL, Donald Reid
Struggling forward. por Time 83:28 Ap 10 '64

CACHIN, Françoise
Duality of Delacroix. Art N 62:38-41+ Sum '63

CACTUS
Colorful Christmas plants. P. Barrett and A. Burke. il Horticulture 41:602-3 D '63
How to grow cactus from seed. W. B. Carter. il Horticulture 42:44+ Ap '64
Landscaping with cactus. il Sunset 132:228+ Je '64
Saguaro: a population in relation to environment. W. A. Niering and others. bibliog il Science 142:15-23 O 4 '63
See also
Epiphyllums
Peyote

CADAVERS
On giving oneself away. E. T. Harris. Harper 229:99-101 D '64

CADDEN, Vivian
Husbands and love. Redbook 120:62-3+ Ap '63
John F. Kennedy's tribute to his older brother. Redbook 122:46-7+ F '64
Parent and child. N Y Times Mag p89-90 Ap 28 '63
Why babies die. Redbook 122:58-9+ N '63
(ed) See Krohner, L. Husband's diary of his wife's pregnancy

CADDIES (golf)
I'll-carry-my-own-bag dept. Sports Illus 21:9 D 14 '64
Man behind the golfer. W. B. Furlong. il N Y Times Mag p72+ O 11 '64
Vanishing knave of clubs. B. Gilbert. il Sat Eve Post 237:68+ Je 20 '64

CADES COVE. See Great Smoky Mountains National Park

CADILLAC, Mich.

Water supply

Wells replace surface supply P. H. Jones. il Am City 78:74-5 Jl '63

CADILLAC motor car division. See General motors corporation—Cadillac motor car division

CADMIUM
Cadmium: uptake by vegetables from superphosphate in soil. H. A. Schroeder and J. J. Balassa. bibliog il Science 140:819-20 My 17 '63

CADWALADER, Mary H.
Anguish of a couple whose six babies have died one after another. Life 55:8+ Jl 12 '63

CAESAR, Caius Julius
Legacies of Julius Caesar and Rome. Sr Schol 84:5+ Mr 20 '64

CAESAR, Gene
Heroes and heroism in the Yellowstone country. Holiday 34:50-1+ Ag '63

CAESAR, Sid
Hail Caesar! R. Barber. il pors Sat Eve Post 236:28+ F 16 '63
How to pitch a ball game in five hours. T. Cohane. il pors Look 27:99-101 F 26 '63

CAESAREAN section. See Cesarean section

CAESARS. See Roman emperors

CAETANI, Marguerite (Chapin) principessa
Letter from Paris. Genêt. New Yorker 39:86+ Ja 25 '64

CAFE Crown; musical comedy. See Musical comedies, revues, etc.—Criticisms, plots, etc.

CAFÉ de la paix. See Paris—Hotels, restaurants, etc.

CAFÉ filtre; story. See Vivante, A.

CAFETERIAS
Self-help; Tad's steaks, inc; New York. New Yorker 39:34 Mr 9 '63

CAFFEINE
Can't sleep? don't blame coffee. Sci Digest 54:81-2 Jl '63

Physiological effects

Alcohol and caffeine: effect on inferred visual dreaming. S. C. Gresham and others. bibliog il Science 140:1226-7 Je 14 '63

CAFRUNY, Edward J. See Komorn, R. M. jt. auth.

CAGE, John
Far-out at the Philharmonic. il Time 83:79-80 F 14 '64
John Cage: builder of new music. P. B. Yates. Vogue 144:225-9 O 1 '64
Music marathon; Satie's Vexations repeated 840 times. Newsweek 62:95 S 23 '63

CAGE, John—*Continued*
Mycophiles: annual banquet. New Yorker 40:22-4 Ja 9 '65
Profiles. C. Tomkins. por New Yorker 40:64-6+ N 28 '64
Shoot the piano player. Time 82:54 S 20 '63
CAGES
House for your Easter rabbits. il Sunset 130:134 Ap '63
CAGES; drama. See Carlino, J.
CAGGIANO, Richard C.
Amateur scientist; extraction of growth-promoting substances from cantaloupe. Sci Am 211:100-3 Ag '64
CAHAN, Cora
Brief biography. S. Goodman. pors Dance Mag 37:46-7 Mr '63
CAHAN, William G.
Cancer links in chain smoking. Sat R 46:38-9 Ag 24 '63
CAHEN, Alfred
Obituary
Pub W por 184:89 S 16 '63
CAHILL, Edward A.
Undeserving. Nation 196:inside cover Ap 27 '63
CAHILL, James
Multiplicity inside a mystique. Sat R 47:45 D 12 '64
CAHN, Edmond
Store of wisdom. Nation 199:83 S 7 '64
CAHN, Patricia Lovelady
How to prepare your child for the world of the '70s. McCalls 92:53+ Ja '65
(ed) See Diebold, J. When will your husband be obsolete?
CAHN, William
Intellectual freedom committee protests censorship in Nassau. Library J 89:2300-1 Je 1 '64
CAHNERS, Norman L.
There's no business like business. Sat R 48:72-3 Ja 9 '65
CAHOKIA, Ill.
Prehistoric city had Indian woodhenge. il Sci N L 86:86 Ag 8 '64
CAICOS ISLANDS
Li'l orphan islands. T. J. King. il Travel 122:61-2+ N '64
CAILLOIS, Roger
Shore of exile. UNESCO Courier 17:14-15 Je '64
Uncharted lands, neglected masterpieces in the world of translations. UNESCO Courier 16:4-5 F '63
CAIMANS. See Alligators
CAIN, Arthur H.
Alcoholics anonymous: cult or cure? bibliog f Harper 226:48-52 F '63
Speaking out. por Sat Eve Post 237:6+ S 19 '64
CAIN, Emily
Cassius's castle; story. New Yorker 39:50-6 N 23 '63
CAIN, James E.
High-power photocell. Electr World 71:44-5 Mr '64
CAIN, Stanley A. and others
Wildlife management in the national parks. por Liv Wildn 83:11-19 Spring '63
CAINE, Lynn
Wise men fish here: the Gotham book mart. Pub W 187:38-42 Ja 11 '65
CAIRO conference of non-aligned countries. See Conference of heads of state or government of non-aligned countries, Cairo, 1964
CAISSON disease
Ice pack relieves bends. Sci N L 83:66 F 2 '63
CAJORI, Charles
Cajori: the figure in the scene. L. Finkelstein. il Art N 62:38-41+ Mr '63
CAJUN-country tournament. See Golf—Tournaments
CAKE
Bake a batch of bars. il McCalls 90:128-9+ S '63
Bake a Christmas log. il Sunset 131:64-5 D '63
Bake a Christmas tradition, fruitcake; with recipes. J. Figg. il Suc Farm 61:46-7 D '63
Be an angel and bake a foam cake. il Am Home 67:56-7, 64+ Ap '64
Birthday party; with recipes. il McCalls 90:112-13+ F '63
Blue ribbon Hereford cake. B. G. La Roche. il Farm J 87:78-9 My '63
Brave cake for St Valentine's day; build it four layers high. il Sunset 130:128 F '63
Cake by pounds. C. Claiborne. il N Y Times Mag p69 Ag 18 '63
Cake of the month. See issues of Good housekeeping
Cakes for frosting artists. il Bet Hom & Gard 41:112-13 F '63
Coffee-hour recipes that intrigue guests. G. Maddox. il Todays Health 42:50-5 O '64
Cup that cheers. il McCalls 91:122-3+ Mr '64
Desserts with a Viennese accent. C. Claiborne. il N Y Times Mag p39 D 20 '64
Dutch treat: best chocolate cakes. il McCalls 92:92-3+ Ja '65
Farm women really can cook! with recipes. B. Pierson. il Farm J 88:64+ N '64
Flavor is your choice. il Bet Hom & Gard 42:70-1+ Mr '64
Frozen cookie cakes; and not a bit of baking! with recipes. il Seventeen 22:146-7+ N '63
Fruitcakes. il Good H 157:66-7+ D '63
Fruitcakes. il Redbook 122:68-9+ D '63
Germans call it a sandtorte. il Sunset 131:98 Ag '63
Give the party a big blast off! tisket a tasket cake; now hear this, a ship ahoy cake. il Am Home 67:54-6+ S '64
Groom's cake. il Bet Hom & Gard 42:82 Je '64
Happy birthday cakes. il Redbook 123:76-9 My '64
How to make a sweet cherry cake. il Sunset 132:202+ Je '64
How to make your Christmas log. il Sunset 131:160-1 D '63
If you are fond of spice cake. Sunset 130:124 F '63
It's a carousel cake. il Sunset 130:192+ Ap '63
Kids' own cake. il McCalls 92:96-7+ Ja '65
Lady Baltimore. il McCalls 91:96-7+ Ja '64
Made with molasses. il Suc Farm 61:89-90 Ap '63
Most festive, luscious, bowl-licking cakes a creature ever stirred! il Am Home 66:46-7+ D '63
Out-of-the-ordinary pound cakes. il Sunset 131:127 Jl '63
Peach cherry pineapple strawberry lime lemon. . . perfect cakes. il McCalls 92:94-5+ Ja '65
Pound cake that's chocolate. il Sunset 133:110 Jl '64
Prize brownies. il Bet Hom & Gard 42:91-2 S '64
Quilted fruitcake for mother. il Sunset 132:253+ My '64
Rich as royalty and light as air; sponge roll. C. Claiborne. il N Y Times Mag p 100+ S 20 '64
Seven ways to say I love you; with recipes. il Seventeen 22:140-1+ F '63
Spice cake from bread dough. il Sunset 133:148 S '64
Step by step angel-food cake. il McCalls 91:112-14+ S '64
Step by step to an all-star roll. il McCalls 91:154-5+ Ap '64
Strawberry nutmeg ring. V. V. Voboril. il Good H 158:182+ Mr '64
These are signature cakes. il Sunset 132:210+ Ap '64
This cake uses the egg whites. il Sunset 132:233 My '64
This twelve-decker is Hungarian. il Sunset 130:156 F '63
Three tasty, tempting cakes. Good H 156:174 Ap '63
Tortes: the conversation-piece dessert; with recipes. L. W. Gilliam. il Farm J 88:68-9 D '64
When you know guests are coming, bake a cake! J. Figg. il Suc Farm 62:78-9 N '64
You start with ground walnuts: karidopita. il Sunset 132:198+ Ap '64
See also
Cheesecake
Coffee cake
Gingerbread
Shortcake
Wafers
CAKE decorations. See Icings
CAKE frosting mix. See Food mixes
CAKE mixes. See Food mixes
CALAHAN, Edward Augustin
Ticker. New Yorker 40:22-3 Jl 18 '64
CALAHAN, Harold Augustin
Incident I'll never forget. Yachting 115:218-19 My '64
With tools, it's how you use 'em. Motor B 113:24-5+ Mr '64
Your boat in A.D. 2063. Motor B 111:26-7+ Mr '63
about
Ticker. New Yorker 40:22-3 Jl 18 '64
CALANDRA, Alexander
How is science being taught? PTA Mag 59:4-6 bibliog(p35) D '64

CALAS, Jean
Voltaire and the Calas case, by E. Nixon. Review
Commonweal 78:113-16 Ap 19 '63. L. F. X. Mayhew

CALAS, Nicolas
Double-axes to grind. Art N 63:52-3 O '64

CALCIFICATION
Amino acids in the proteins from aragonite and calcite in the shells of mytilus californianus. P. E. Hare. bibliog il Science 139:216-17 Ja 18 '63
Calcification of deciduous teeth in rhesus monkeys. D. R. Swindler and H. A. McCoy. bibliog il Science 144:1243-4 Je 5 '64
Calciphylaxis: passive transfer. H. Selye and others. bibliog il Science 143:365-6 Ja 24 '64
New search for the fountain of youth. J. D. Ratcliff. Read Digest 83:69-74 D '63
Vertebrate hard tissues; report on special symposium of the section of vertebrate morphology of the American society of zoologists. C. Gans. Science 144:323-4 Ap 17 '64

CALCITE
Calcite-aragonite equilibrium. G. Simmons and P. Bell. bibliog il Science 139:1197-8 Mr 22 '63; Reply. W. A. Crawford and W. S. Fyfe. 144:1569-70 Je 26 '64
Oxygen isotope fractionation between coexisting calcite and dolomite. J. N. Weber. bibliog il Science 145:1303-5 S 18 '64
Sea water: saturation with apatites and carbonates. J. R. Kramer. bibliog il Science 146:637-8 O 30 '64

CALCIUM
Microdetermination of calcium by aequorin luminescence. O. Shimomura and others. bibliog il Science 140:1339-40 Je 21 '63
Polar transport of calcium in the primary root of zea mays. E. C. Evans, 3d. bibliog il Science 144:174-7 Ap 10 '64
Strontium and calcium reabsorption in renal tubules of the newt, triturus pyrrhogaster. R. Ichikawa and others. bibliog il Science 144:53-4 Ap 3 '64
Strontium and calcium uptake by the green alga, oocystis eremosphaeria. N. R. Kevern. bibliog il Science 145:1445-6 S 25 '64; Reply with rejoinder. L. G. Williams. 146:1488 D 11 '64
Vascular smooth muscle: duel effect of calcium. D. F. Bohr. bibliog il Science 139: 597-9 F 15 '63

CALCIUM carbonate
Calcium carbonate: factors affecting saturation in ocean waters off Bermuda. R. F. Schmalz and K. E. Chave. bibliog il Science 139:1206-7 Mr 22 '63
Electrolytic conductance of sea water: effect of calcium carbonate dissolution. K. Park. bibliog il Science 146:56-7 O 2 '64
High pressure solubility of calcium carbonate in seawater. R. M. Pytkowicz and D. N. Conners. bibliog il Science 144:840-1 My 15 '64
X-ray diffraction data on two high-pressure phases of calcium carbonate. B. L. Davis. bibliog il Science 145:489-91 Jl 31 '64

CALCIUM hydroxide
Ion-exchange removal of sodium chloride from water with calcium hydroxide as recoverable regenerant. K. Popper and others. bibliog il Science 141:1038-9 S 13 '63

CALCIUM in the body
Calcium absorption in man: based on large volume liquid scintillation counter studies. L. Lutwak and J. R. Shapiro. bibliog il Science 144:1155-7 My 29 '64
Calcium: unusual sources in the highland Peruvian diet. P. T. Baker and R. B. Mazess. bibliog Science 142:1466-7 D 13 '63
Chelation of calcium by lactose: its role in transport mechanisms. P. Charley and P. Saltman. bibliog il Science 139:1205-6 Mr 22 '63
Heart action potential: dependence on external calcium and sodium ions. R. K. Orkand and R. Niedergerke. bibliog il Science 146:1176-7 N 27 '64
See also
Calcification

CALCIUM oxalate
Crystal structure of weddellite. C. Sterling. bibliog il Science 146:518-19 O 23 '64

CALCULATED risk; drama. See Hayes, J.

CALCULATING charts. See Charts, Calculating

CALCULATING machine simulators. See Simulators

CALCULATING machines
Analytical engine, by J. Bernstein. Review
Esquire 62:18+ O '64
New Repub 151:23-5 O 3 '64. G. Bylinsky
Animated movies made by computer. Sci N L 85:287 My 2 '64
Automatic information processing in western Europe. G. Salton. bibliog Science 144:626-32 My 8 '64
Automation of patents. E. Hall. Sci N L 84: 213 O 5 '63
Big whir: computers spin problems and profits. il Newsweek 62:92-4+ O 21 '63
Binary computer codes and ASCII; American standard code for information interchange. E. Bukstein. il Electr World 72:28-9 Jl '64
Boundless age of the computer; with editorial comment. il Fortune 69:97-8, 100-11+ Mr; 140-5+ Ap; 153-6+ My; 112-16+ Je; 70:124-6+ Ag; 120-1+ O '64
Brainy breed: annual conference of Association for computing machinery. il Time 82: 78 S 6 '63
Challenge of automation. il Newsweek 65: 73-8+ Ja 25 '65
Computer age in psychoanalysis. F. R. Schreiber and M. Herman. Sci Digest 57: 18-19 Ja '65
Computer as a botanist; a British experiment in artificial intelligence. W. T. Williams. Sat R 46:44-5 Je 1 '63
Computer can read almost illegible writing. Sci N L 86:278 O 31 '64
Computer composition used in production of novel. Pub W 185:36 Je 1 '64
Computer costs increase. Sci N L 86:246 O 17 '64
Computer own designer; Fixed plus variable structure computer. Sci N L 86:260 O 24 '64
Computer shows how Shelley aped Milton. Sci N L 86:297 N 7 '64
Computer simulates people with problems; Homunculus. Sci N L 85:347 My 30 '64
Computer system mixes science, business tasks; System/360. Sci N L 85:248 Ap 18 '64
Computer talks fast with great accuracy; SECO. Sci N L 83:374 Je 15 '63
Computer teaches writing. Sci N L 83:87 F 9 '63
Computer that reads. Sci N L 83:228 Ap 13 '63
Computerizings. V. Torrey. il Atlan 212:140-3 D '63
Computers. S. M. Ulam. il Sci Am 211:202-8+ bibliog(p272) S '64
Computers in science fiction. M. Ascher. bibliog f Harvard Bsns R 41:40-2+ N '63
Computers leave the high cost era. Bsns W p34 Ag 15 '64
Computers now plan daily hospital menus. il Todays Health 42:86 Ap '64
Computers of tomorrow. M. Greenberger. il Atlan 213:63-7 My '64
Do-all thinkmachine; System/360. il Time 83:117 Ap 17 '64
Electrochemical nerve cells under study. B. Miller. il Aviation W 78:103+ F 18 '63
Firm studying method to grow computers. Miss & Roc 14:22 Mr 16 '64
Going after the leader; IBM's System 360 and RCA's Spectra 70. il Bsns W p 122+ D 12 '64
Harris-Intertype computers made especially for type composition. il Pub W 185:62-5 Ap 6 '64
Harvard computer finds English language fuzzy. Sci N L 84:346 N 30 '63
Imitation of man by machine. U. Neisser. bibliog Science 139:193-7 Ja 18 '63; Discussion. 140:212-14+ Ap 12 '63
Information revolution. G. L. Haller. il Sci Digest 55:69-73 My '64
Information systems: learning, adaptation, and control; report of Computer and information science symposium. J. T. Tou. Science 141:1070+ S 13 '63
IBM unwraps its billion-dollar gamble; System/360 data equipment. il Bsns W p67-8+ Ap 11 '64
IBM v. the others. il Time 81:86+ Mr 8 '63
Is the computer running wild? il U S News 56:80-4 F 24 '64
Look what those knucklehead machines are doing! S. D. Pursglove. Read Digest 82: 278-80 Ap '63
Machine that reads writing. S. V. Jones. Sci Digest 55:52-3 F '64
Machines Bull's computer crisis; France's proud business-machine firm. T. R. Bransten and S. H. Brown. il Fortune 70:154-5+ Jl '64
Machines smarter than men? interview. N. Wiener. il U S News 56:84-6 F 24 '64; Same abr. Read Digest 84:121-4 My '64
Man-computer relationship. D. L. Johnson and A. L. Kobler; discussion. Science 139: 1231-2+ Mr 22 '63
New tool, new world; electronic computers. il Bsns W p70-1+ F 29 '64

CALCULATING machines—*Continued*
Now System 360. il Newsweek 63:91-3 Ap 20 '64
Profiles; computer: analytical engine. J. Bernstein. il New Yorker 39:58-60+ O 19; 54-6+ O 26 '63
Profiles; computers in scientific and industrial research in Cambridge and vicinity. C. Rand. New Yorker 40:57-8+ Ap 18 '64
Quotations by computer; New York's American stock exchange Am-Quote system. Time 83:61 My 22 '64
RCA takes aim on big computer sales. C. D. LaFond. il Miss & Roc 15:32-3 D 14 '64
Science and the poltergeist. Duns R 82:27 N '63
Small memory for large numbers; ceramic memory units. il Time 83:53 Mr 27 '64
Special computer for printers. il Bsns W p 102 Mr 7 '64
Speeding up computer output. Bsns W p 103 Ap 13 '63
Storing sparks tomorrow; necessity for a degree of standardization and compatibility; excerpt from Promise and challenge of the computer. D. Sarnoff. Sat R 48:95 Ja 2 '65
There's even one that says: oh, that tickles. il Time 84:89 N 6 '64
War of the computers: Nov. 3. D. F. Nolan. il Sci N L 86:250-1 O 17 '64
What is a computer? reprint. K. Kizer. il Sci Digest 57:75-8 Ja '65
White-collar automation. T. O'Toole. il Reporter 29:24-7 D 5 '63
Why GE is joining Olivetti; hopes to get European computer market. il Bsns W p 140+ S 12 '64
See also
Control data corporation
Cybernetics
Data processing centers
Electronic data processing
International business machines corporation
Programming (calculating machines)
Programming languages (calculating machines)

Aeronautic applications

Adaptive computer utilizes microcircuits. B. Miller. il Aviation W 80:87-9+ My 11 '64
Airborne-ground computer series shares common logic structure. il Aviation W 80: 91 Ap 20 '64
Army to use computers to simulate radio frequency interference problems. C. D. LaFond. il Miss & Roc 14:26-7 Je 22 '64
Computer is vital tool for logistics. Aviation W 81:57+ mid-D '64
Computer-planned flights cut costs. Sci N L 87:41 Ja 16 '64
Computer simplifies Loran-C navigation. P. J. Klass. il Aviation W 80:93+ Je 15 '64
IBM in used airplanes. P. Korenvaes. Duns R 82:55-6 D '63
Jet takeoff computer undergoes testing. il Aviation W 81:81-2 O 5 '64
Microcircuits add to computer capability. B. Miller. il Aviation W 80:230-3 Mr 16 '64
Modular data system designed for Shrike. il Aviation W 81:71-2 Ag 17 '64
Navy adopts new ASW avionics approach. P. J. Klass. il Aviation W 79:64+ Jl 8 '63
Navy test of thin-film computer planned. R. D. Hibben. il Aviation W 81:74-5+ O 5 '64
Phoenix missile computer data revealed. B. Miller. il Aviation W 80:54-5 F 24 '64
Sophisticated thin-film computer holds aerospace system potential. C. D. LaFond. il Miss & Roc 15:33+ O 19 '64

Agricultural applications

Computers now foretell how fast plant will grow. Sci N L 84:168 S 14 '63
New records turn up surprises. D. Braun. Farm J 87:58A Ap '63
Will the computer change the practice of architecture? J. Barnett. il Arch Rec 137: 143-50 Ja '65

Analog computers

Amateur scientist; simple analogue computer that simulates Pavlov's dogs. H. S. Hoffman. il Sci Am 208:159-60+ Je '63
Analog computation; Institute on analog computation, at Catholic university of America, Washington, D.C. B. P. Shah. Science 141:448 Ag 2 '63
Automated photographer. P. Farber. il U S Camera 27:48-9+ S '64
Automation surge. W. Wingo. il Sci N L 84: 294 N 9 '63
Inventor of the month; the computer that plans ahead; Planalog. il Sci Digest 55: 52-3 Je '64

Anecdotes, facetiae, satire, etc.

Authentic document. Christian Cent 80:1595 D 18 '63
Warning impulse timing and computing haversack. J. Slate. Fortune 69:157-8+ My '64

Architectural applications

Advice from a wise old computer; change in plans for junior college in St Louis. Time 84:43 Jl 17 '64
New computers may provide big-job planning assistance. il Arch Rec 135:86+ Mr '64
Tighter use of room; scheduling space through computer, new junior college, St Louis. Bsns W p79 Jl 18 '64

Astronomical applications

Computer helps compile astronomical tables. Sci N L 85:121 F 22 '64
Computer shows how real stars behave. Sci N L 85:280 My 2 '64
Secret of Stonehenge. G. S. Hawkins. il Harper 228:96-9 Je '64

Banking applications

Banks open a new window; with suggestions by C. A. Agemian. il Bsns W p 156+ O 17 '64
Electronics in banking; MICR and ERMA. K. Gilmore. il Electr World 69:29-32+ Ap '63
Let 315 do it; plan to share a computer center. Time 81:39 F 15 '63
Victory for the Bull; French Machines Bull's Eurocheck. il Time 81:112 My 17 '63

Business applications

Big board takes on assembly line look; New York stock exchange's automation program. il Bsns W p 110-11+ N 14 '64
Big machines think small. L. Blumenthal. il Duns R 84:pt2 106-9+ S '64
Broker's fastest messengers. il Bsns W p83-4+ O 10 '64
Business hot line. Bsns W p56+ O 24 '64
Buy by computer. J. W. Widing, jr. and C. G. Diamond. il Harvard Bsns R 42: 109:20 Mr '64
Buying computers by the dozen; desk-sized Monrobot XI. Bsns W p45-6 Jl 20 '63
Computer gets nearer. il Bsns W p88+ Ja 18 '64
Computer puts a plus in inventory control; Baltimore County, Md. W. E. Fornoff. il Am City 79:90-1 N '64
Computer ships the shoes; Genesco's automatic shipping sorter. il Bsns W p96-7+ Jl 11 '64
Computers take to prophecy. il Bsns W p47-8 Je 1 '63
EDP tells Main St. il Bsns W p66 Ag 8 '64
Electrons that add; Anita, a desk-top electronic computer. il Bsns W p82-3 D 28 '63
Insurance man's best friend. il Bsns W p 100+ N 7 '64
Now retailers put it all on tape. il Bsns W p30-1 Ja 16 '65
Office: the great information revolution; symposium. il Duns R 82:pt2 94-100+ S '63
Precise profit predicting; security analysis. Bsns W p86 Jl 6 '63
Stemming the paper torrent. il Duns R 84: pt2 100-12+ S '64
You can be replaced. il Newsweek 63:62 My 4 '64

Chemical engineering applications

Computer experiments in chemistry. D. L. Bunker. il Sci Am 211:100-8 Jl '64

Circuits

Microcircuits add to computer capability. B. Miller. Aviation W 80:230-3 Mr 16 '64

Communication applications

Chrysler's computer does the talking faster and cheaper. il Bsns W p52-3 Ag 24 '63

Control applications

Control theory. R. Bellman. il Sci Am 211: 186-90+ S '64
New face in computers; computer control systems. il Bsns W p32 Ja 25 '64

Cooperative use

Computer that grows with you; DEC's PDP-6. il Bsns W p56+ Mr 14 '64
Computers feed many mouths; MIT's project MAC. il Bsns W p54-5 F 1 '64
IBM offers new computer plan; time-sharing. Bsns W p28 D 19 '64

CALCULATING machines—*Continued*

Design

Redundancy in computers; extra parts to suppress errors. W. H. Pierce. il Sci Am 210:103-6+ bibliog(p 152) F '64

Digital computers

Automation surge. W. Wingo. il Sci N L 84: 294 N 9 '63
Autonetics expects 20-cu.-in. digital computer to be ready in three to four years. R. Pay. il Miss & Roc 15:27-8 O 26 '64
Computer logic fundamentals. S. Lukens. il Electr World 71:46-8 Je '64
Computer poetry or, Sob suddenly, the bongos are moving. F. P. Tullius. il Harper 227: 24+ D '63
Computer simulation of consumer behavior. W. D. Wells. Harvard Bsns R 41:93-8 My '63
Data flow in digital computers. E. Bukstein. il Electr World 72:36-7+ Ag '64
Digital computer-TV displays gaining favor for operations C&C use. C. D. LaFond and R. Pay. il Miss & Roc 15:38-9+ O 5 '64
Digital computers in the biological laboratory. R. L. Schoenfeld and N. Milkman. bibliog il Science 146:190-8 O 9 '64
Foxboro takes industry's measure. il Bsns W p 146+ O 3 '64
From surplus a bargain computer; Univac. A. Erxleben. il Pop Electr 18:42-4 Je '63
High-speed automatic analysis of biomedical pictures. R. S. Ledley. bibliog il Science 146:216-23 O 9 '64
Holiday handbook of think machines. A. Bester. il Holiday 35:123-8 Mr '64
Intricate Hardy-Cross mazes bow to a computer; water-system design; Waterford Township, Mich. P. M. Hampton. il Am City 79:107-8 S '64
Magnetic core memories. R. B. Rusch. il Electr World 71:37-9 Ap '64
New printer is fast computer mate. il Miss & Roc 13:38 Jl 1 '63
Ninety-nine per cent accurate. Newsweek 62: 84 Jl 22 '63
Personality test interpretation by digital computer. B. Kleinmuntz. il Science 139:416-18 F 1 '63
Precision digital tide gauge. F. E. Snodgrass. bibliog il Science 146:198-200+ O 9 '64
Simultaneous studies of firing patterns in several neurons. G. L. Gerstein and W. A. Clark. bibliog il Science 143:1325-7 Mr 20 '64
System simplifies computer use. R. Pay. Miss & Roc 14:35-6 Je 15 '64
Trainers teach digital computer basics. P. J. Klass. il Aviation W 78:77 Mr 25 '63

Educational applications

Computer to teach college students. Sci N L 86:232 O 10 '64
Dial H for history. il Newsweek 63:76-7 Mr 2 '64
Plug-in schools: next step in educational design? B. P. Spring. il Arch Forum 119:68-73 Ag '63

Engineering applications

Computer helps design mechanical systems; program determines heating and cooling loads. il Arch Rec 137:179-80 Ja '65
Intricate Hardy-Cross mazes bow to a computer; water-system design; Waterford Township, Mich. P. M. Hampton. il Am City 79:107-8 S '64
Role of the computer in engineering practice. M. P. Levy and others. il Arch Rec 134:158-61 Ag '63

Government applications

Big-brother 7074 is watching you. R. Gannon. il Pop Sci 182:86-8+ Mr '63
Committee will study use of ADP. Miss & Roc 15:15 S 28 '64
Computer pool fought. Sci N L 84:77 Ag 3 '63
Computerized slander. Nation 199:84 S 7 '64
Computing ad absurdum. H. Schenck, jr. Nation 196:505-7 Je 15 '63
IBM to build new reading machine for social security. Pub W 186:90 S 7 '64
New tax detective: a gimlet-eyed machine. il Bsns W p96-7 F 8 '64
Redistricting by computer. Sci Am 210:57 Mr '64
What new tax law will mean: interview. M. M. Caplin. Nations Bsns 52:38-9+ F '64

History

Cranky grandfather of the computer. il Fortune 69:112-13 Mr '64
Historic computer paper found after twenty years. Sci N L 86:120 Ag 22 '64

Industrial applications

Allocating facilities with CRAFT. E. S. Buffa and others. il Harvard Bsns R 42:136-47+ Mr '64
Brain for most tools. il Bsns W p 116 F 8 '64
Computers speed the design cycle. il Bsns W p 134+ N 7 '64
How computers did the job at Seadrift; Union carbide's ethylene plant. il Bsns W p 146+ N 9 '63
Machines reproducing. J. Eberhart. Sci N L 85:303 My 9 '64
Next for computers: central control. Bsns W p44-5 Ja 2 '65
Office: management's billion-dollar system; symposium. il Duns R 84:pt2 101-12+ S '64
Only one out of three pays for itself; report by McKinsey & co. il Bsns W p 152+ Ap 13 '63
Programming a cake; computer as head chef. il Bsns W p 154-6+ Mr 14 '64
Resourceful computer application keeps Hercules plant on schedule. J. F. Judge. il Miss & Roc 15:28+ Jl 13 '64
Sales & distribution; scheduling tasks made easy. J. B. Weiner. Duns R 83:69 F '64
Tape can run the machine better. il Bsns W p 100-2+ Mr 30 '63
Tomorrow's plant now; Western electric's Kansas City plant. il Bsns W p52-3+ Ag 1 '64
Top management and computer profits. J. T. Garrity. Harvard Bsns R 41:6-8+ Jl '63
When bottlenecks need to be broken. il Bsns W p47-8 Ag 29 '64

Input-output equipment

Computer input-output equipment. E. Bukstein. il Electr World 72:52-4+ N '64
Eye for computers is quick as a wink; Programmable film reader. il Bsns W p80 S 19 '64

Legal applications

Automating the archives; computer to take over the lawyer's plodding search through archives. Time 82:82 D 13 '63
Computer analysis of the nuclear test ban treaty. R. A. Langevin and M. F. Owens. bibliog il Science 146:1186-9 N 27 '64
Computers may tip the scale of justice. il Bsns W p45-6 Ag 22 '64
Space age electronics; address, June 16, 1964. H. Ellenbogen. Vital Speeches 30:662-5 Ag 15 '64
Univac for the defense; automation can save a lawyer time. Newsweek 62:55 D 16 '63
When computers do the digging; hunt through case and statute books. il Bsns W p54+ Ja 23 '65

Literary applications

Aquinas on IBM tape. America 111:433-4 O 17 '64
Books in the making; Concordance to the poems of Emily Dickinson published with the aid of computer. Pub W 187:100 Ja 4 '65

Manufacture

Battle of the computer marketeers. il Fortune 71:171-2 Ja '65
Machines Bull hits bearish times; La compagnie des machines Bull. il Bsns W p58+ Ja 25 '64

Mapping applications

Computer program for printing undeformed Fourier maps. J. D. H. Donnay and H. Takeda. il Science 143:1162-3 Mr 13 '64

Materials

Material for smaller, faster computers; ceramic. Sci N L 85:232 Ap 11 '64

Medical applications

Bionic computers. K. Gilmore. il Electr World 69:25-8+ Mr '63
Computer analyzes blood constituents. Sci N L 83:343 Je 1 '63
Computer heart pictures. Sci N L 86:52 Jl 25 '64
Computer that helps rebuild lives. A. Hamilton. il Sci Digest 56:19-23 S '64
Computerized eating; arm-aid for the paralyzed. il Newsweek 64:104 S 21 '64
Computers aid doctors; in compiling mental case histories. Sci N L 85:342 My 30 '64
Computers fight disease. W. Wingo. Sci N L 84:69 Ag 3 '63
Computers: new medical research tool. K. N. Anderson. il Todays Health 42:34-9 F '64
Mechanical brains will aid doctors. Sci Digest 53:45 Mr '63

CALCULATING machines—Medical applications —*Continued*
My doctor, the computer. il Newsweek 61:59 F 18 '63
Now Dr Robot enters the scene. L. Lasagna. il N Y Times Mag p 15+ Je 16 '63
Scientist seeks cause of own brain injuries. il Sci N L 83:306 My 18 '63
Sick? let a computer do the diagnosis. S. Gibson. il Pop Electr 21:45-8+ N '64
Transistorized M.D; systems for monitoring patients. L. Lessing. il Fortune 68:130-4+ S '63

Meteorological applications

Carla's computer. il Pop Electr 18:48-9 Ap '63
Computer grows clouds and produces rain. Sci N L 83:72 F 2 '63
Forecasting by computer. A. Ewing. Sci N L 84:87 Ag 10 '63
Foretell future weather. Sci N L 85:404 Je 27 '64
Thunderstorm violence. T. Neville. Sci N L 84:135 Ag 31 '63
Weather computers. R. C. Cowen. il Nation 198:71-3 Ja 20 '64; Same abr with title Needed, umbrella weather forecasting. Sci Digest 55:25-9 Ap '64

Military applications

473L to aid in worldwide USAF control. B. Miller. il Aviation W 81:49+ Ag 3 '64
Machine that learns may be recon aid. P. J. Klass. il Aviation W 79:84-7 Ag 26 '63
Security is too important to be left to computers. F. X. Kane. Fortune 69:146-7+ Ap '64
Vector technique speeds C&C computer capability. il Miss & Roc 13:32-4 D 2 '63

Miniaturization

See Miniature electronic equipment

Municipal applications

Automation anticipates $165,000 saving on alimony checks; Akron, Ohio. F. P. Yacobucci. il Am City 79:106-7 O '64
Computer that earns a profit; Albuquerque, N.Mex. J. L. Guggino. il Am City 79:102-3 Mr '64
Computer that pays its way; Greensboro, N.C. C. M. Conway. il Am City 79:102-3 S '64
Electronic automation fills the bill; Dearborn, Mich. W. B. Godette. il Am City 78:99 N '63
Let the computer tabulate your traffic counts. D. H. Johnson. il Am City 78:135 Mr '63
Not late once in seven years; DuPage County Wheaton, Ill. J. J. Kelly. il Am City 78:84-5 F '63

Musical applications

Digital computer as a musical instrument. M. V. Mathews. bibliog il Science 142:553-7 N 1 '63

Readout systems

Digital readouts. W. H. Buchsbaum. il Electr World 69:33-5+ F '63

Scientific applications

AEC is first customer for Control data 6600. Aviation W 79:85 S 2 '63
Computer probes atom. il(p 161) Sci N L 86:167 S 12 '64
Condensation model producing crystalline or amorphous tetrahedral networks. R. Ordway. bibliog il Science 143:800-1 F 21 '64
Direct readout of sediment analyses by settling tube for comuter processing. J. M. Zeigler and others. il Science 145:51 Jl 3 '64
Information-processing models in psychology. W. R. Reitman. bibliog Science 144:1192-8 Je 5 '64
Two computers solve problems together; GEORGE and FLIP solving scientific problems. Sci N L 85:57 Ja 25 '64

Space flight applications

Autonetics expects 20-cu.-in. digital computer to be ready in three to four years. R. Pay. il Miss & Roc 15:27-8 O 26 '64
Burroughs gets Gemini and Agena guidance job. C. Butler. Miss & Roc 15:70 S 14 '64
Computers, integration top trends. il Miss & Roc 12:25-6+ My 20 '63
Dwarf to guide Apollo; G&N. V. Torrey. il Pop Mech 121:116-19+ F '64
First Gemini computer model completed. R. D. Hibben. il Aviation W 79:58-9+ Jl 15 '63
First of some fifty block II Apollo G&N computers is due by mid-1965. R. Pay. il Miss & Roc 15:36-7 S 7 '64
First Saturn V guidance computer, data adapter prototypes due at Marshall. C. D. LaFond. il Miss & Roc 15:31-2 N 2 '64
Gemini digital command system readied by Radiation, inc. M. Getler. il Miss & Roc 13:32-3 Jl 22 '63
Giant data system developed for Nike-X. Aviation W 81:49 N 30 '64
Math model trouble-shoots Minuteman. Miss & Roc 12:40 F 25 '63
Meet GEVIC, the computer that flies. S. V. Jones. il Sci Digest 55:76-7 Ja '64
Microcircuits add to computer capability. B. Miller. il Aviation W 80:230-3 Mr 16 '64
Saturn computer uses voter redundancy. P. J. Klass. il Aviation W 81:47-8 N 2 '64
Space computer techniques under study. B. Miller. il Aviation W 80:72-3+ Mr 23 '64
Space role seen for new computer. M. Getler. il Miss & Roc 12:31+ My 27 '63
Special report: advanced displays. il Miss & Roc 15:27-8+ O 5 '64
System could improve orbit gauging. Miss & Roc 13:16 N 4 '63
Vector technique speeds C&C computer capability. il Miss & Roc 13:32-4 D 2 '63

Transportation applications

Automated commuting. Sci N L 86:15 Jl 4 '64
Computer out-thinks. S. Cass. il Am City 79:98-9 Ag '64
State computer analyzes city traffic; Green Bay, Wis. M. L. Bacon, jr. il Am City 79:84-5 D '64
Technology: methods and machines to shape the future. B. P. Spring. il Arch Forum 119:88-93 O '63

CALCULI, Biliary
Formation of gallstones triggered by imbalance. Sci N L 83:297 My 11 '63

CALCULI, Dental
Tartar agent detected. Sci N L 86:181 S 19 '64

CALDECOTT medal
Book award jury hails big boy, little boy, Cat and Wild things. Library J 89:1391 Mr 15 '64
Critics approved! reviews before announcement. Library J 88:1294-6 Mr 15 '63
Ezra Jack Keats. A. Duff. il Library J 88:1292-4 Mr 15 '63
Loud silence. E. Rudin. Library J 89:900 F 15 '64; Discussion. 89:1800+ Ap 15 '64
Maurice Sendak. U. Nordstrom. il Library J 89:1374-6 Mr 15 '64
Newbery and Caldecott awards. il ALA Bul 57:335 Ap '63
Newbery and Caldecott runners-up; symposium. il Library J 89:1377-82 Mr 15 '64
Newbery and Caldecott winners: Emily Neville, Maurice Sendak. il Pub W 185:30-2 Mr 9 '64
Newbery-Caldecott awards. il Wilson Lib Bul 38:617 Ap '64
Newbery-Caldecott medals: Madeleine L'Engle, Ezra Jack Keats win 1963 awards. il Pub W 183:18-20 Mr 11 '63

CALDER, Alexander
Alexander Calder. N. Guppy. il por Atlan 214:53-60 D '64
Art galleries; exhibition at the Guggenheim museum. R. M. Coates. New Yorker 40:165-6+ N 21 '64
Arts; retrospective at the Guggenheim museum, New York. C. J. McNaspy. America 111:759 D 5 '64
Calder. B. Chernow. il por Sch Arts 63:24-7 D '63
Calder show: retrospective exhibition at the Guggenheim museum in New York. B. Kaufman. Commonweal 81:398-9 D 11 '64
Connecticut colossi Gargantualand. il por Time 83:72 F 28 '64
Letter home. J. Jones. Esquire 61:28+ Mr '64
Man who made sculpture move. J. Canaday. il N Y Times Mag p32-3 N 1 '64
Mobile eye. il por Newsweek 64:98 N 16 '64
Second fame: good food. N. Lyon. il por Vogue 145:152-4 Ja 1 '65
Toys for all ages. il por Time 84:96-9 N 20 '64

CALDER, Alexander, family
At the Calders. F. Du Plessix. il House & Gard 124:154-9+ D '63

CALDER, Nigel
Control and use of technology. Nation 200:3-5 Ja 4 '65
Technology and the investor. Bul Atomic Sci 20:47-8 Ap '64

CALDER, Ritchie
Foreign aid: how firm a foundation? Reporter 28:34-6 F 28 '63
Gastronomy for the bold. UNESCO Courier 16:21-5+ F '63

CALDER, Ritchie—*Continued*
More food for southeast Asia. Bul Atomic Sci 19:31-2 Mr '63
Peaceful uses for military energy. R. Calder. il UNESCO Courier 17:29-32 N '64
World of opportunity; excerpt. UNESCO Courier 16:4-9 Jl '63

CALDERÓN, Pedro
Music to my ears; assistant conductors of the Philharmonic. I. Kolodin. Sat R 47:34+ F 15 '64
Triumphant trio. por Time 81:62 Ap 12 '63
Word with Pedro Calderón. J. Villaverde. il por Américas 15:38-9 Jl '63

CALDERÓN DE LA BARCA, Pedro
Life is a dream (La vida es sueño) tr. by R. Campbell. Criticism
New Yorker 40:136+ Mr 28 '64

CALDERONE, Mary Steichen
Adolescent sexual behavior: whose responsibility? excerpts from address, May 1964. PTA Mag 59:4-7 S '64
Love and sex. Redbook 122:39+ F '64; Same abr. with title There are no shortcuts to marriage. Read Digest 85:68-70 Ag '64

CALDWELL, Judy H.
Conservation careers in government. Nat Parks Mag 37:17-18 N '63
Stronghold: story of a man and a mountain. Nat Parks Mag 37:16 Ag '63

CALDWELL, Ken
Special-interest cars. Motor T 16:82 N '64

CALDWELL, Lynton K.
Biopolitics: science, ethics, and public policy. Yale R 54:1-16 O '64

CALDWELL, Millard
Judicial usurpation; address, January 31, 1964. Vital Speeches 30:317-20 Mr 1 '64

CALDWELL, Ralph M. See Yirgou, D. jt. auth.

CALDWELL, Roberta F.
Bluebonnet blooms deep in the heart of Texas. Audubon Mag 66:97 Mr '64

CALDWELL, Sarah
Quote-unquote; interview, ed. by H. Rogers. por Mus Am 84:104 D '64

about

Persistent one. il por Time 83:58 F 21 '64
Renaissance woman. Q. Eaton. il pors Opera N 28:26-9 Ap 18 '64

CALDWELL, Taylor
Speaking out. por Sat Eve Post 236:8+ My 25 '63
T.L.C, keep your paws off me! Nat R 15:103-4 Ag 13 '63

CALDWELL, William, family
Mommy, do white puppies like us? Project friendship. G. McMillan. il Good H 157:64+ O '63

CALENDAR
For tidier time; world calendar. G. Vincent. il N Y Times Mag p78-80+ Ja 12 '64
Gregorian calendar was meant to keep seasons in their places. T. D. Nicholson. il Natur Hist 73:42-5 Mr '64
Way out of the calendar mess; thirteen identical months. il Look 28:39+ D 1 '64
Who wants a tidy calendar? J. Skow. il Sat Eve Post 237:38-9 Mr 7 '64

CALENDAR, Chinese
Notes on China's ancient calendar. J. L. Friend. il Sky & Tel 26:329 D '63

CALENDARS
Daze to come; Chases' calendar of annual events. Newsweek 64:98 D 7 '64
Engagement, wall calendars: traffic builders in a bookstore. il Pub W 184:59-60+ Ag 19 '63
Glamor; make her a calendar girl. P. Gowland. il Pop Phot 54:14+ My '64
Make your own Advent calendar. il Sunset 131:110 D '63

CALF pens
Easy-cleaning calf pens. D. Hagen and G. Lorang. il Farm J 87:36E Ag '63
Low-cost calf shelter. L. Elam. il Suc Farm 61:88 O '63

Floors

Healthier calves with slat floors. il Farm J 88:50F My '64

CALF self feeders
Merry-go-round calf feeder. J. W. Aberle. il Farm J 87:58R Ap '63

CALHOUN, John C.
Secretary of our early wars. C. A. Madison. il Sat R 46:32-3 Je 15 '63

CALHOUN, Lillian S.
Woman on the go for God. Ebony 18:78-81+ My '63

CALHOUN, William J.
How to get what you want. por Recreation 57:551-2 D '64

CALIAN, Carnegie Samuel
Armenian church and ecumenism. Christian Cent 81:1007-8 Ag 12 '64
Eastern orthodoxy seen through Protestant eyes. por Cath World 200:300-6 F '65

CALIBRATION
Calibrating test equipment. W. H. Buchsbaum. il Electr World 70:43-5+ Ag '63
Instrument calibration and repair technician; electronics technicians and engineers. G. C. Gedney and F. M. Winterburg. il Electr World 70:28-9 Ag '63

CALIBRATION oscillators. See Oscillators

CALIBRATORS
A.C. voltage calibrator. D. G. Bethany. il Electr World 69:56+ Je '63
Inexpensive scope and VOM calibrator. H. R. Newhoff. il Pop Electr 21:57-9 O '64

CALIBRATORS, Radio. See Radio instruments

CALIFORNIA
California story. Nation 196:130 F 16 '63
California; too much, too soon; symposium. il Esquire 59:65-77+ My '63
Nation that moved West. il Sr Schol 82:6-9+ My 8 '63

See also
Agriculture—California
Airports—California
Architecture, Domestic—California
Art—California
Booksellers and bookselling—California
Botany—California
Cascade Range
Catalina Island
Colleges and universities—California
Courts—California
Education—California
Elsinore, Lake
Festivals—California
Fishing—California
Forests and forestry—California
Gardens—California
Housing—California
Hunting—California
Irrigation—California
Kings Canyon National Park
Klamath Mountains
Klamath River
Law—California
Libraries—California
Mines and mineral resources—California
Mission Bay
Mojave Desert
Music festivals—California
Paleontology—California
Plumas County
Public welfare—California
Roads—California
Russian River
Salton Sea
Sequoia National Park
Sierra Nevada
Tahoe, Lake
Tourist trade—California
Water supply—California
White Mountains, Calif.

Anecdotes, facetiae, satire, etc.

How to face the move to California. H. Sargent. il Esquire 59:70 My '63

Antiquities

See Indians of North America—Antiquities—California

Description and travel

California's golden coast; Better homes & gardens family-planned vacation. il Bet Hom & Gard 42:133-6 My '64
Come cruise California! C. West. il Motor B 111:26-9+ My '63
Cornishman looks at California A. L. Rowse. Mlle 59:124+ My '64
Giant playground. C. Phinizy. il Sports Illus 19:28-39 Ag 12 '63
It starts straight and gentle but just you wait; northwestern California. il Sunset 132:26+ My '64
New picture book portrays the face of California. il Sunset 130:120-5 My '63
Poking around in Owens Valley. il Sunset 130:92-9 My '63
Sunniest end of California. B. Ballantine. il Holiday 33:22+ F '63
Touring the redwood country by rail car. il Sunset 130:24+ Mr '63
Travel & camera. M. Orovan. il U S Camera 27:26-7 Mr '64
Visit California's glamourland. W. R. Wilson. il Suc Farm 62:58-9+ Mr '64
Vogue's shop hound in California. Vogue 141:148-9 Je '63
Whipples are almost untouched. il Sunset 132:34+ F '64

CALIFORNIA—*Continued*

Highways, Division of

Redwood totem. H. Gilliam. il Nation 199:91-3 S 7 '64

Historic houses, etc.

Hugo Reid adobe near Los Angeles, California. G. Norman-Wilcox. il Antiques 84:168-71 Ag '63

History

Era of discovery. P. M. Tilden. il Natur Hist 72:58-64 Ag '63
From gold rush to sun rush. E. Burdick. il N Y Times Mag p36-7+ Ap 14 '63
Negro who rode with Fremont in 1847. G. M. Bergman. Negro Hist Bul 28:31-2 N '64
See also
San Francisco—History

Industries

California firms study contract warnings. H. D. Watkins. il Aviation W 79:74-7 Jl 29 '63
She's a big girl; California wine industry. J. Deever. il Sat Eve Post 236:58-61 D 21 '63

Missions

See also
Santa Barbara mission

Parks and reserves

Finding the Mt Everest of all living things. P. A. Zahl. il Nat Geog Mag 126:10-51 Jl '64
Forest walking and forest camping; Prairie Creek Redwoods State Park. il Sunset 131:19-20 S '63
Freeways versus redwoods. R. D. Butcher. il Nat Parks Mag 38:12-15 Je '64
Hardest working water in the world; Big Creek development with playground, Camp Edison-Shaver Lake. A. S. Green. il Am For 70:28-30 Je '64
New state parks for California. il Sunset 133:30-2+ N '64
Redwoods and the fragile web of nature. R. D. Butcher. il Audubon Mag 66:172-4 My '64
Shady stop-off in the San Joaquin. il Sunset 130:84 My '63

Police

No fair! the student strike at California; with editorial comment. G. Marine. il Nation 199:477, 482-6 D 21 '64

Politics and government

Another upset victory for the Republicans. U S News 54:10 Je 24 '63
Anything can happen in California, and did. New Repub 151:6 N 14 '64
Backlash may do it. M. Ryskind. Nat R 16:968 N 3 '64
Big Daddy's lockup. Newsweek 62:25 Ag 12 '63
California: a wild card in the deck; amendment designed to establish racial discrimination as a property owner's right. J. Lewis. Reporter 31:29+ O 22 '64
California Democrats: battle royal for the Senate. B. Stout. Reporter 30:21-4 My 7 '64
California Republicans: are the Birchers taking over? J. Wood. Reporter 30:24-6 My 7 '64
California's primary explosion. K. Hendrick: D. Bess. il Nation 198:472-7 My 11 '64
Call from California; convention of California Democratic council. il Newsweek 63:22 Mr 9 '64
Clair's health. il Newsweek 63:19 F 3 '64
Democratic battle with big stakes. il U S News 56:19 My 11 '64
Difficulty of selling soap; race for Democratic nomination to the U.S. Senate. Time 83:20 My 29 '64
Engle's decision; withdrawal from primary. Newsweek 63:20 My 11 '64
Half-loaves. Newsweek 62:25 Jl 1 '63
In California, a split among Democrats; Senator Clair Engle and State Controller Alan Cranston. il U S News 56:16 Mr 9 '64
Jesse Unruh. Big Daddy of California. E. Cray. Nation 196:199-207 Mr 9 '63
Just a term of endearment. Time 81:22 Je 7 '63
Just call him senator; Murphy's victory over Pierre Salinger. il Time 84:42 N 13 '64
Like a lone tree; Republican landscape. Time 81:24 Je 7 '63
No kidding; race for the Senate nomination. il Time 83:25-6 My 8 '64
No place to go but up; Democratic senatorial nomination. il Newsweek 63:30 My 25 '64
Nomination by association. il Time 83:36 Je 12 '64
Republicans; one up in California. Newsweek 61:16-17 F 4 '63
Right turn in California? M. Fjeldsted. New Repub 152:18 Ja 16 '65
Round vs square in California. A. D. Kopkind. New Repub 150:9-11 My 30 '64
Salinger swings for Senate. R. Ajemian. il Life 56:43 Ap 3 '64
Senator Salinger: a controversial appointment. il U S News 57:12+ Ag 17 '64
Shooting at Big Daddy. Time 82:18 Ag 23 '63
Slurbia: chaotic system of local government. il Newsweek 62:94 S 23 '63
Son of the Birch; Robert A. Gaston, elected president of California's Young Republicans. il Newsweek 61:27-8 Mr 4 '63
Strange case of Thomas Kuchel. Cato. Nat R 16:716 Ag 25 '64
Temperature normal. New Repub 151:10 Jl 4 '64
Turnabout; California Republican assembly. Newsweek 61:28 Mr 11 '63
Vacuum at the top. Newsweek 61:33-4 Je 10 '63
Winner take all; special election, 23rd congressional district. Time 81:20 Je 21 '63

Population

From gold rush to sun rush. E. Burdick. il N Y Times Mag p36-7+ Ap 14 '63

Public utilities commission

$500 million mistake; regulating AT&T the world's biggest business. A. Brynes. New Repub 151:11-14 S 26 '64
Regulating AT&T. A. Brynes. New Repub 151:11-14 O 3 '64

Race problems

How Los Angeles eases racial tensions; Commission on human rights. P. Deutsch and R. M. Deutsch. Read Digest 85:86-90 O '64
Proposition fourteen, concerning the sale or rental of California real estate properties. il Time 84:23 S 25 '64
Racist proposition: California on trial. D. Bess. Nation 199:179-82 O 5 '64

Recreation

See Recreation—United States

Religious institutions and affairs

News of the Christian world (cont) Christian Cent 80:253-4, 344+, 660-1, 692, 1146+, 1476; 81:93-4, 216+, 248, 532, 1020-2, 1472-4 F 20, Mr 13, My 15-22, S 18, N 27 '63, Ja 15, F 12-19, Ap 22, Ag 12, N 25 '64

Social conditions

Forgetting Pearl Harbor; Japanese cultural influence. il Newsweek 64:97-8 D 7 '64
From gold rush to sun rush. E. Burdick. il N Y Times Mag p36-7 Ap 14 '63

Social life and customs

California: the new society, by R. Nadeau. Review
Sat R 46:41 N 23 '63. M. R. Freedman
Depressed in California. A. McIntyre. Esquire 59:67+ My '63

CALIFORNIA, GULF OF
Cruising the Sea of Cortéz; excerpt. S. Murray. il Motor B 114:37-9 N '64
See also
Fishing—California, Gulf of

CALIFORNIA, LOWER
Baja California. C. West. il Yachting 116:44-7+ O; 58-9+ N '64
Land of the buzzard and the Coromuel; photographs by J. Maisel; with account by J. Olsen. Sports Illus 22:56-68 Ja 18 '65
Last chance at Land's End. R. Joseph. il Esquire 62:88-9+ Jl '64
Mexico's California. P. Brooks. il Atlan 214:69-73 S '64
Surprises of Baja. il Sunset 131:74-87 N '63
See also
Fishing—California, Lower
Hunting—California, Lower

CALIFORNIA big trees. See Sequoia

CALIFORNIA condors. See Condors

CALIFORNIA earthquakes. See Earthquakes—United States

CALIFORNIA institute of technology
See also
Jet propulsion laboratory

CALIFORNIA library association
California LA presents plan for public library improvement. Library J 88:742 F 15 '63
Intellectual freedom theme of the pre-conference. Wilson Lib Bul 39:304 D '64

CALIFORNIA library association—*Continued*
Mr and Mrs Grundy in the library and in court; CLA pre-conference meeting on Intellectual freedom; excerpts from report with editorial comment. H. M. Madden. Library J 89:4857-62 D 15 '64
Writers discuss automated world at CLA. Library J 89:593 F 1 '64

CALIFORNIA medical association
To teen-age smokers. Newsweek 61:86 Ap 8 '63

CALIFORNIA newts. See Newts

CALIFORNIA poppies
California poppies; new unusual colors. R. E. Atkinson. il Horticulture 42:30 F '64
Your state flower; California-poppy, California. L. Krelove. il Flower Grower 50:26 My '63

CALIFORNIA primary. See Primaries

CALIFORNIA state college, San Jose
College-supported faculty research programs. R. H. Woodward. Sch & Soc 91:109+ Mr 9 '63

CALIFORNIA state colleges. See Colleges and universities—California

CALIFORNIA. University
California: as enrollment bulge hits higher education system, state banks on its master plan. J. Walsh. Science 144:34-5 Ap 3 '64; Reply. L. B. Loeb. 144:1178-9 Je 5 '64
California's new campuses. il Arch Rec 136:175-99 N '64
Exploding University of California. W. Trombley. il Sat Eve Post 237:22-9 My 16 '64
Field-free laboratory in a wooded setting; Lawrence radiation laboratory, University of California, Berkeley. il Arch Rec 134:184-7 S '63
Gripes not of wrath. Newsweek 63:80 F 10 '64
New frontier of higher education. D. Canty. il Arch Forum 118:96-103 Mr '63
Planning for a hundred tomorrows; southern California. il Bsns W p74-5+ O 24 '64

Berkeley campus

Battle of Sproul Hall; protest against ban on political activities, with report by J. M. Russin. il Newsweek 64:44+ D 14 '64
Berkeley: does that banner still wave? Free speech movement. G. A. Harrison. New Repub 151:7-8 D 19 '64
Campus agitation vs. education. Life 58:4 Ja 22 '65
Campus uproar that is blamed on reds. il U S News 57:12 D 14 '64
Climate at Berkeley; discipline and the issue of political protests. il Time 84:30 D 25 '64
Détente at Berkeley? M. Meyerson appointed acting chancellor. Newsweek 65:52 Ja 18 '65
Escalation in California. N. Cousins. Sat R 48:20 Ja 30 '65
Extremism in the defense of... R. E. Fitch. Christian Cent 82:11-15 Ja 6 '65
Freedom to learn but not to riot. S. Hook. il N Y Times Mag p8-9+ Ja 3 '65
Lesson of Berkeley; question of student political activities. S. M. Lipset and P. Seabury. il Reporter 32:36-40 Ja 28 '65
Negro writer in the United States. H. W. Fuller. il Ebony 20:126-8+ N '64
New man at Berkeley. Time 85:50+ Ja 15 '65
No fair! the students strike at California. G. Marine. il Nation 199:482-6 D 21 '64; Discussion. 199:477-8 D 21 '64; 200:inside cover Ja 11 '65
Panty raids? no! tough campus revolt. il Life 57:46A-46B D 18 '64
Savio onstage; battle over political activities on campus. il Newsweek 64:71 D 21 '64
To prison with love; student sit-in. il Time 84:60 D 11 '64
What happened at Berkeley. J. Cass. il Sat R 48:47-8+ Ja 16 '65
When students try to run a university. il U S News 57:43 D 21 '64
You don't shoot mice with elephant guns; free speech movement. S. Alexander. Life 58:27 Ja 15 '65

Davis campus

Cow college conversion. il Time 82:79 N 29 '63

Libraries

California's problem building adds wings. J. R. Blanchard. il Library J 89:4750-2 D 1 '64

Irvine campus

Irvine campus; with statement by D. G. Aldrich. il Arch Rec 136:186-91 N '64

Libraries

See also
California. University—Davis campus—Libraries
California. University—Los Angeles campus—Libraries

Los Angeles campus

Bringing engineers up to date; G. A. W. Boehm. il Fortune 67:120-1+ My '63
From Jerusalem to the West; from Bamberger and Warhman bookstore to UCLA. Wilson Lib Bul 37:822 Je '63
Professional theatre on campus. P. Greene. il Theatre Arts 47:62-3+ F '63
UCLA invites you to come and see. il Sunset 133:76-8 S '64
Upgrading courses for lady brass; UCLA management seminars. Bsns W p 156+ N 16 '63

Libraries

UCLA in three stages. P. Miles. il Library J 89:4746-9 D 1 '64

San Diego campus

San Diego campus; with statement by H. York. il Arch Rec 136:192-9 N '64
San Diego: new general campus for University of California plots an unconventional course. J. Walsh. Science 144:658-60 My 8 '64

Santa Cruz campus

Santa Cruz campus; with statement by D. E. McHenry. il Arch Rec 136:176-85 N '64

CALIFORNIA wines. See Wine

CALIFORNIANS
Trailing a curious political animal; California primary. E. Burdick. il N Y Times Mag p 10+ My 31 '64
Who are the losers? California's proposed lottery. R. W. Moon. Christian Cent 81:1104-5 S 9 '64
Why do you like living in California? with answers. il Esquire 59:68-9 My '63

CALIGNUM. See Fungicides

CALISHER, Hortense
Little did I know; story. Sat Eve Post 236:46-50 Je 8 '63
Textures of life; story. Redbook 120:139-70 Mr '63

about

WLB biography. E. Gottesfeld. por Wilson Lib Bul 37:599 Mr '63

CALITRI, Charles J.
Language and the dignity of youth. Sat R 46:46-7+ Jl 20 '63

CALKING
Calking compounds. il Consumer Bul 47:27-9 O '64
Johnny, get your calking gun. S. J. Howard. il Pop Mech 120:156-60 N '63
Seal out frosty winter drafts. Am Home 67:110-11 O '64

CALKINS, Carroll C.
How to live with spring ten months a year. House B 105:157-63+ Mr '63
How to rescue land lost on a slope. House B 105:174-7+ Ap '63

CALKINS, Frank
Compleat alibier. Field & S 69:54-5+ O '64
What to do in a pinch. Field & S 68:44-6+ N '63
Where the ducks are. Field & S 69:41-3+ N '64

CALKINS, John
Mio, Michigan: strictly for the birds. Am For 69:6+ Je '63

CALL, Hughie
Little kingdom; excerpt. Redbook 123:34-42 Jl '64; Same abr. with title Horse for Wezie. Read Digest 85:85-8 S '64

CALL girl; story. See Mehta, V.

CALL it virtue; drama. See Pirandello, L.

CALLA lilies
For a surprise next summer. Sunset 131:293 N '63

CALLAGHAN, Elizabeth P.
Religious gifts. McCalls 91:50+ D '63

CALLAGHAN, James
Ten days that shook the Exchequer. C. Brogan. il Nat R 17:57-8 Ja 26 '65

CALLAGHAN, Morley
Books. E. Wilson. New Yorker 39:139-42+ F 23 '63; Reply. M. Hemingway. 39:160+ Mr 16 '63

CALLAHAN, Daniel
Authority and the theologian. Commonweal 80:319-23, 513-14 Je 5, Jl 24 '64
Catholic freedom and Mr Wills. Commonweal 80:607-9; 81:74 S 4, O 9, '64

CALLAHAN, Daniel—*Continued*
Catholic responsibility for unity. Commonweal 77:646-7 Mr 15 '63
Dilemma of the Catholic layman; excerpt from Mind of the Catholic layman. Cath World 198:80-6 N '63
Freedom of priests. Commonweal 79:95-8 O 18 '63
In praise of Father DuBay. Commonweal 80:408-9 Je 26 '64
Into the briar patch. Commonweal 79:501-3 Ja 31 '64
New pluralism: from nostalgia to reality. Commonweal 78:527-31 S 6 '63
Nobody here but us pluralists. America 109: 733-4 D 7 '63
Quest for honesty. Commonweal 80:137-40, 263 Ap 24, My 22 '64
Schools. Commonweal 81:473-6 Ja 8 '65
Seeds behind the wall. Commonweal 78:275+ My 31 '63

CALLAHAN, Harry
Callahan shows, East & West, mark his book's publication. G. A. Young and H. M. Kinzer. il Pop Phot 54:28+ Je '64
Double exposure. M. R. Weiss. il por Sat R 47:36-8 S 26 '64

CALLAHAN, Maurice
Airport water works requires more systems. Am City 79:93-4 Mr '64

CALLAHAN, William R. See Clifford, R. J. jt. auth.

CALLANISH. See Callernish, Scotland

CALLAO, V. and others
Toxohormone inhibitory effect on the growth of an unstable strain of yeast. bibliog Science 142:1668-9 D 27 '63

CALLAS, Maria
Maria Callas; interview, ed. by E. Gelatt. pors Hi Fi 15:42-7 F '65
My lonely world, a woman looking for her voice; interview, ed. by P. Dragadze, with editorial comment. pors Life 57:61-2, 64+ O 30 '64

about

Art of Maria Callas. E. Greenfield. pors Hi Fi 14:42-6+ Mr '64
Bel canto revival. Discus. Harper 228:124-5 My '64
Callas today. J. Ardoin. il por Mus Am 84:30-1 D '64
Callas Tosca. T. Heinitz. Sat R 47:57+ F 29 '64
Callas's Carmen. il por Newsweek 65:73 F 1 '65
Letter from London. M. Panter-Downes. New Yorker 39:116 F 15 '64
Letter from Paris; performance of Bellini's Norma. Genêt. New Yorker 40:120-1 Je 13 '64
Maria Callas. pors Vogue 143:170-1 My '64
Maria Callas in Paris. J. Maclain. por Am Rec G 30:492-3 F '64
Notes from our correspondents; Tosca rehearsal, Royal opera house, London. H. Wild. por Hi Fi 14:28+ Ap '64
On Angel, the latest from Maria Callas. G. L. Mayer. Am Rec G 31:205 N '64
Question of majesty. W. Cecil. Sat R 47:56-7+ Ap 25 '64

CALLAWAY, Helen Lund
Doers, not do-gooders, the Peace corps in Nigeria. Mlle 57:126-9+ Je '63

CALLE, Paul
I saw Atlas 9 take off! il Am Artist 27:58-9+ O '63

CALLERNISH, Scotland
Callanish, a Scottish Stonehenge. G. S. Hawkins. il Science 147:127-30 Ja 8 '65

CALLERY, Sean
Drama in Britain. Commonweal 81:461-2 D 25 '64

CALLIES, Gonzaga
Looking at youth's problems; French view. America 108:231-2+ F 16 '63

CALLIGRAPHY. See Penmanship

CALLIGRAPHY, Chinese. See Chinese language—Writing

CALLING, Animal. See Animal calling

CALLIPHORA erythrocephala. See Blowflies

CALLISON, Charles
Facts about Wilderness bill. Liv Wildn 82: 11-16 Winter '62
National capital report. See issues of Audubon magazine
Yukon River features. Liv Wildn 83:28-9 Spring '63

CALLOT, Jacques
Callot: the miniature universe. il Art N 62:37+ Mr '63

CALLOW, Alexander B. Jr
Fraud! fraud! N Y Times Mag p60+ S 27 '64

CALLOW, Sister Mary Anastasia
What is it in the mind; poem. Commonweal 81:328 N 27 '64

CALLOWAY, Doris Howes
Minimum ecological systems for man. Science 147:184+ Ja 8 '65

CALLUNA. See Heathers

CALLUS (botany)
Endive plantlets from freely suspended cells and cell groups grown in vitro. I. K. Vasil and others. bibliog il Science 146:76-7 O 2 '64

CALLWOOD, June
Eight days make a miracle. McCalls 91:34+ Ja '64
One sure way to happiness; excerpt from Love, hate, fear, anger and the other lively emotions. Read Digest 85:93-6 N '64

CALMER, Ned
Duce's dream was nightmare. Sat R 47:49 My 16 '64

CALMETTE, Léon Charles Albert
Birth of a new vaccine. il por UNESCO Courier 17:10-11+ Ap '64

CALORIES, Food. See Diet; Food values

CALORIMETRY conference
Calorimetry: report on 18th annual calorimetry conference. G. T. Armstrong. Science 143:158-60+ Ja 10 '64
Calorimetry; report on 19th conference, Washington, D.C, 13-16 October 1964. W. N. Hubbard. Science 147:312-14 Ja 15 '65

CALTHORP family
Calthorp coat-of-arms. H. K. Eilers. il Hobbies 68:120-1 Ja '64

CALVERT, W. and others
Ionosphere Explorer I satellite: first observations from the fixed-frequency topside sounder. bibliog Science 146:391-5 O 16 '64

CALVES
Calf-raising ideas from three experts. il Suc Farm 61:68+ F '63
They guarantee high producers. G. Lorang. Farm J 88:50 Ja '64

Diseases and pests

Newborn calves weak? here's what you can do. J. W. Bailey. Suc Farm 61:68 Je '63

Feeding

Farmers report roughage cuts calf costs. Suc Farm 61:11 Je '63
New way to raise calves. C. E. Ball. Farm J 88:50L Ja '64
Push heifers for early breeding? D. Hagen and J. Russell. il Farm J 88:24-5+ Ag '64
This feed makes calves grow faster. O. Bay. il Farm J 88:42 N '64
See also
Calf self feeders

Marketing

Big new market for your calves. L. Palmer. Farm J 88:46 O '64

Prices

Here's feeder-buying advice from the pros. R. Black. Farm J 88:38 N '64

Transportation

See Cattle—Transportation

CALVIN, John
Calvin after 400 years. J. T. McNeill. Christian Cent 81:702-4 My 27 '64
Calvin and the knowledge of God. T. F. Torrance. por Christian Cent 81:696-9 My 27 '64
Calvin: The origins and development of his religious thought, by F. Wendel. Review
Christian Cent 81:1309-10 O 21 '64. E. A. Dowey, jr
Calvin without myths. K. McDonnell. il Commonweal 81:163-6 O 30 '64
Calvin's influence in Scotland and England. J. K. S. Reid. Christian Cent 81:699-701 My 27 '64

CALVINISM
Calvin after 400 years. J T. McNeill. Christian Cent 81:702-4 My 27 '64
Calvin and the knowledge of God. T. F. Torrance. Christian Cent 81:696-9 My 27 '64
Calvin without myths. K. McDonnell. il Commonweal 81:163-6 O 30 '64
Calvinism and democracy: some political implications of debates on French reformed church government, 1562-1572. R. M. Kingdon. bibliog f Am Hist R 69:393-401 Ja '64
Calvin's influence in Scotland and England. J. K. S. Reid. Christian Cent 81:699-701 My 27 '64
Renegade reformed; graduates of Calvin college. Christian Cent 80:815 Je 19 '63

CAMACHO-EVANGELISTA, A. and Reinoso-Suárez, F.
Activating and synchronizing centers in cat brain: electroencephalograms after lesions. bibliog Science 146:268-70 O 9 '64
CÂMARA, Helder Pessôa, abp
Challenge to Latin America; excerpts from address. America 110:590 My 2 '64
Conscience and anti-communism. Commonweal 81:407-8 D 18 '64
about
New houses for Rio. V. Sanson. il por Américas 16:32-3 D '64
Pope's man in Recife. por Time 83:60 Mr 27 '64
CAMARGO, Alberto Lleras. See Lleras Camargo, A.
CAMARGO, Pedro Pablo
Human rights and democracy. Américas 15:33-6 My '63
CAMASSES
Camassia esculenta. il Horticulture 41:467 S '63
CAMASSIA esculenta. See Camasses
CAMBODIA
Sihanouk, prince under pressure. S. S. King. il N Y Times Mag p42+ S 13 '64
See also
Economic assistance in Cambodia
United Nations—Cambodia
Boundaries
Cambodia; Security council appoints mission. UN Mo Chron 1:25-30 Jl '64
On the borderline; three-nation U.N. committee to investigate Cambodia's complaints. F. Sully. il Newsweek 63:39-40 Je 22 '64
Security council continues debate on Cambodian complaint; two statements, May 26, 1964. A. E. Stevenson. Dept State Bul 50:937-41 Je 15 '64
Security council team to examine Cambodia-Viet-Nam border areas; statement, June 4, 1964; with text of resolution. A. F. Stevenson. Dept State Bul 50:1002-4 Je 29 '64
U.S. calls for frontier patrol to help prevent border incidents between Cambodia and Viet-Nam; statement, May 21, 1964. A. E. Stevenson. bibliog f Dept State Bul 50:907-13 Je 8 '64; Same. Vital Speeches 30:483-7 Je 1 '64
Description and travel
Cambodia: Indochina's neutral corner. T. J. Abercrombie. il Nat Geog Mag 126:514-51 O '64
Foreign relations
Cambodia, China and the U.S. Nation 199:365 N 23 '64; Reply. Norodom Sihanouk. 200:inside cover Ja 25 '65
Cambodia; why the crisis? New Repub 150:8-10 Ja 4 '64
Cambodia's high-wire act. il Sr Schol 84:8-10 My 1 '64
Chantrea incident; South Vietnamese raid Cambodian border village. il Newsweek 63:34 Ap 6 '64
China's new kinsman. T. Okla. New Repub 149:13-15 Jl 20 '63
Country that's neutral in favor of Communists. R. P. Martin. il U S News 56:80-2 Ap 27 '64
End of US aid. New Repub 149:7 N 30 '63
Man of sensitivity; Prince Norodom Sihanouk. Newsweek 62:28 D 23 '63
Off again. Newsweek 63:48+ Mr 23 '64
On the tightwire. il Newsweek 64:53-4 N 23 '64
Oriental touch. Newsweek 63:26 Ja 6 '64
Our far-flung correspondents. R. Shaplen. New Yorker 40:150+ Ap 18 '64
Slumbering prince. il Time 82:24 D 27 '63
There goes Cambodia. D. Warner. il Reporter 30:27-30 Mr 26 '64
When a neutralist turned on the U.S. il U S News 56:14 Mr 23 '64
Whose hour? il Newsweek 62:58 D 2 '63
Will Cambodia go Communist? J. A. Rose. il Sat Eve Post 237:68+ Mr 28 '64
See also
Cambodia—Boundaries
Politics and government
Balance of menaces. Time 82:40+ N 29 '63
Cambodia's high-wire act. il Sr Schol 84:8-10 My 1 '64
Country that's neutral in favor of Communists. R. P. Martin. il U S News 56:80-2 Ap 27 '64
Drift to the left. il Time 83:35 Mr 20 '64
Ghoulish glee. Time 82:18+ D 20 '63
Man who wouldn't be king. il Time 81:28+ F 8 '63
Prince & the dragon. il Time 83:32-6 Ap 3 '64
CAMBON, Glauco
Between Aristotle and Plato. Poetry 102:198-201 Je '63
Two poets of New York. Poetry 102:266-8 Jl '63
CAMBRIDGE, Godfrey MacArthur
Laugh at this Negro, but darkly. M. Gussow. pors Esquire 62:94-5+ N '64
CAMBRIDGE, Md.
Cambridge, Maryland: failure on race street. W. P. Bradley. il Reporter 29:20-2 Jl 4 '63
Cauldron of hate. il Time 82:17-18 Jl 19 '63
Gloria, Gloria. M. Kempton. il New Repub 149:15-17 N 16 '63
Gloria Richardson. il Ebony 19:23-6+ Jl '64
In troubled Cambridge: Negro heads city council. U S News 57:12 Ag 3 '64
Lesson of Cambridge and Salisbury: was violence necessary? L. B. Bozell. Nat R 15:145-7 Ag 27 '63
Negro rights subjected to local white whims. Christian Cent 80:1227 O 9 '63
People in a trap. S. Alsop. il Sat Eve Post 237:12 Je 6 '64
Spark in Cambridge; clash between Negroes and National guard. il Newsweek 63:33-4 My 25 '64
Stillness in Cambridge. il Time 82:10 Ag 2 '63
Summer in Cambridge, Maryland. R. Brown. Horn Bk 40:315-19 Je '64
Thirty miles divide folly and reason; Cambridge and Salisbury, Md; with report by M. Durham. il Life 55:18-25 Jl 26 '63
Where Negroes didn't vote on integration. il U S News 55:6 O 14 '63
Who can we surrender to? R. A. Liston. il Sat Eve Post 236:78-80 O 5 '63; Reply. 236:82 N 2 '63
Why race troubles hit one city, spare another; a case study: Cambridge and Salisbury, Md. il U S News 55:78-80 Ag 5 '63
Zealot's stand. Time 82:30 O 11 '63
CAMBRIDGE, Mass.
Oxford & Cambridge; school board's refusal to rent a high school auditorium. Time 81:20 F 8 '63
Profiles; center of a new world. C. Rand. il New Yorker 40:43-8+ Ap 11; 57-8+ Ap 18; 55-6+ Ap 25 '64
Architecture
Instead of an abandoned factory; Technology square industrial center. il Am City 78:89 O '63
Cemeteries
Trees of Mount Auburn. D. Wyman. il Horticulture 42:38-9+ Je '64
Music
Cambridge feast. W. A. Storrer. Opera N 27:31 F 2 '63
Streets
Little green space; citizens protests over changing Memorial Drive. il Time 83:64 F 14 '64
CAMBRIDGE circus; revue. See Musical comedies, revues, etc.—Criticisms, plots, etc.
CAMBRIDGE university
Cambridge's revenge: dons say Hailsham threatens U.S. support, block honorary degree for him. D. S. Greenberg. Science 140:282-3 Ap 19 '63
Churchill college, a modern university college. J. Cockcroft. Science 146:502-4 O 23 '64
Libraries
New building abroad. il Arch Forum 118:104-5 Je '63
CAMBRIDGE university press
Cambridge moves warehouse and accounting. il Pub W 183:28-9 Mr 18 '63
CAMDEN, Ark.
Paper-bag collection on request. G. G. Fox. il Am City 79:14 O '64
CAMELLIA exhibits. See Flower exhibits
CAMELLIAS
Camellia pattern on a wall. il Sunset 130:178 F '63
Camellias are moving north. J. Threlkeld. il Pop Gard 14:32-3+ F '63
Camellias outdoors in the North. D. Gurin. il Horticulture 42:44-5 N '64
Camellias require winter protection in northern regions. M. J. Dietz. il Flower Grower 51:48 N '64

CAMELLIAS—*Continued*
From Blue Danube to waltz time: saluenensis hybrid camellias. il Sunset 132:68-9 F '64
To start a camellia off right, refill the planting hole like this. il Sunset 134:126-7 Ja '65

CAMELS
Compleat camel. D. Stivens. il Sci Digest 56:25-7 N '64
How the camel conquers thirst. Time 84:55 Jl 17 '64
Thirstless camel; excerpts from Animal worlds. M. Bates. il UNESCO Courier 17:20-1 Jl '64

CAMERA cases
Cases for guys on the go. il U S Camera 27:50-1+ Jl '64
How to custom-build a carrying case. J. Burroughs. il Pop Sci 182:107-10 My '63
Large camera. A. Feininger. Mod Phot 28:30+ Ap '64

CAMERA clubs
Group travel. L. Pett. il Pop Phot 52:134-5 Ap '63
Heliographers; new photographic movement. J. N. Uelsmann. il U S Camera 27:61-5 My '64
Photography is possible. B. Reed. il Sch Arts 62:11-13 Ap '63
See also
Moving picture clubs

CAMERA dealers
Revolutionary technique in camera merchandising. S. Nathan. U S Camera 26:36 Je '63

CAMERA lenses. See Lenses, Photographic

CAMERA shutters
Cork-screw camera. H. Keppler. il Mod Phot 27:74-5 Mr '63
How slow is your slow shutter? G. Gilbert. il U S Camera 26:78-9+ N '63
Identification game. C. Wright. Pop Phot 55:113 S '64
Polaroid color pack camera. E. Hannigan. il U S Camera 26:50-3 O '63
Sensational is word for new Agfa patent. Pop Phot 52:32+ Je '63
Test your shutter's accuracy. J. S. Paul. il U S Camera 27:36+ D '64

CAMERA stores. See Photographic apparatus industry and trade

CAMERA tripods
Fictions, fantasies & truth about tripods. il Mod Phot 28:76-9+ Ag '64
Large camera. A. Feininger. Mod Phot 28:36+ Ja '64
Movie maker. M. A. Matzkin. il Mod Phot 27:94 Mr; 86+ Ap; 92+ My '63
Twin lens. F. Henle. il Pop Phot 52:16 Mr '63

CAMERAS
Accent on transistors. C. Wright. il Pop Phot 54:108-9 Ap '64
Ad libs; pinholes. P. Farber. il U S Camera 26:20+ Je '63
Amateur scientist; on constructing highspeed cameras for photographing fleeting events. W. Gannaway. il Sci Am 211:118-24+ Jl '64
Are German cameras better? il U S Camera 27:42-3 N '64
Aren't RFDR cameras really sharper? E. Meyers and H. Keppler. il Mod Phot 27:68-9+ S '63
Army service testing new recon camera. D. A. Brown. Aviation W 81:26 Ag 17 '64
As I see it: Kodak Instamatic system. E. Hannigan. il U S Camera 26:40 Je '63
Automatic electric-eye 35mm. cameras. il Consumer Bul 46:2+ Je '63
Automatic eyes. W. J. Sumits. Pop Phot 52:87 My '63
Automatics need help in thinking: here's why and how you can do it. H. Keppler. il Mod Phot 27:24+ Jl '63
Automation and how to live with it. D. B. Eisendrath, jr. Pop Phot 53:8+ O '63
Automation will dominate Chicago MPDFA show. B. C. Brown. il Pop Phot 54:74-7+ Ap '64
Bargains in rangefinder cameras. D. L. Miller. il Mod Phot 27:62-3+ My '63
Behind the scenes. See issues of Modern photography
Beseler Topcon Super D; behind-the-lens meter system. D. Gerritt. il U S Camera 26:62-3+ O '63
Bits & pieces. W. J. Sumits. Pop Phot 54:101 Mr '64
Camera sees all sides at once; periphery camera. il Pop Mech 120:131 O '63
Cameras focus on U.S. buffs; Japan and West Germany. il Bsns W p56-8+ Mr 23 '63
Cameras: what's new, what's next. B. H. Frisch. il Sci Digest 53:16-20 Je '63
Challenge of marine photography. il Motor B 112:36-9+ Jl '63
Check your camera. Field & S 68:124 My '63
Committee for a sane policy in automation; interview, ed. by H. Shaman. M. Forscher. Pop Phot 55:39+ O '64
Compact camera for home and abroad; Brownie Flashmite. J. J. Simpkins. Flower Grower 50:71 Ap '63
Compare 'em: 35mm. half frame & ultraminiatures. H. Keppler. il Mod Phot 27:62-3+ Ag '63
Comparing the new quick loaders; Instamatic cameras. K. Brown. il Pop Mech 120:112-15+ O '63
Complete SLR guide. D. L. Miller. il Mod Phot 28:85+ Jl '64
Converter lenses for single-lens reflex cameras. il Consumer Bul 47:23-5 D '64
Cora Wright's guide through the maze of exposure automation; with editorial comment. C. Wright. il Pop Phot 54:46, 49-59+ Mr '64
Crash course in color. A. Francekevich. il Pop Phot 53:45-57+ Jl '63
Creative color; new 35 format. A. Rothstein. U S Camera 26:9-10 Je '63
Creative color; single frame. A. Rothstein. U S Camera 28:8+ Ja '65
Dateline: Chicago. il U S Camera 27:56-60 My '64
Dateline: Germany; photokina. W. Clark. il U S Camera 26:56-61+ Je '63
Do you need a better camera? N. Rothschild. Pop Phot 54:95-6 My '64
Don't be a sucker shopper! W. G. McClanahan. U S Camera 27:41+ D '64
Don't knock the box. D. H. Moore. il U S Camera 27:54-5 Ap '64
Electric-eye 35mm. cameras. il Consumer Bul 46:19-22 Jl '63
Equipment preview '65; Master photo dealers' and finishers' association, Chicago. il Mod Phot 28:82-3 My '64
Experiences with cooled color emulsions; thermoelectric camera. A. A. Hoag. il Sky & Tel 28:332-4 D '64
Filming with the Fairchild 8. D. C. Thomas. il Pop Phot 53:99+ S '63
First camera with CdS cell. C. Wright. il Pop Phot 52:76 F '62
First SLR through-the-lens meter. il Pop Sci 183:133 D '63
For travel picture insurance, pre-check your equipment. C. Wright. il Pop Phot 52:136-7 Ap '63
Full story on half frame. il U S Camera 27:46-9+ Ag '64
Future techniques; camera automation. J. Reidy. il U S Camera 26:12-13 Je '63
Here's what's new! il Pop Phot 52:43-58 Je '63
How do SLR cameras differ? il Mod Phot 28:64-5 S '64
How far have we gone? Ansco Memo 35mm camera. G. Zygmund. il Mod Phot 27:48+ O '63
How far have we gone? Kodak no. 1. E. M. Fusco. il Mod Phot 27:40 Ag '63
How far have we gone? Vidax. J. Wolbarst. il Mod Phot 28:14-15 N '64
How to buy cameras. E. Meyers. il Mod Phot 28:134-5 D '64
How to choose and test cameras, lenses, meters, electronic flash units. Mod Phot 27:14-16+ D '63
How to live with automation. D. B. Eisendrath, jr. Pop Phot 55:12+ N '64
How to use small-camera bellows & extension tubes. N. Rothschild. il Pop Phot 54:42-7+ F '64
How wide can you get? M. Adler. il U S Camera 26:58-9+ S '63
Human bone marrow distribution shown in vivo by iron-52 and the positron scintillation camera. H. O. Anger and D. C. Van Dyke. bibliog il Science 144:1587-9 Je 26 '64
Instamatic v. rapid. il Time 84:98 S 4 '64
Instant 35mm. H. Keppler. il Mod Phot 27:72-3 Je '63
It wasn't here! B. Schwalberg. il U S Camera 26:59+ Je '63
Keppler on the SLR. H. Keppler. See issues of Modern photography
Kodak Instamatic cameras. il Consumer Bul 46:14-17 D '63
Kodak introduces instant loading. il Pop Phot 52:45-6 My '63
Koni/Omega Rapid. S. Nathan. il U S Camera 26:64-5+ O '63
Large camera. A. Feininger. See issues of Modern photography
Limitations and advantages of automation. A. Rothstein. U S Camera 26:8+ Jl '63
Look what's happening to SLRs. P. Wahl. Pop Sci 186:142-5+ Ja '65
MPDFA and photokina previews. il Pop Phot 52:67-9+ Ap '63

CAMERAS—*Continued*
Modern techniques with 2¼. E. Meyers. il Mod Phot 28:82-3 N '64
Modern tests. See issues of Modern photography
More than 300 new still & movie cameras & how they compare; comp. by D. L. Miller and M. A. Matzkin. il Mod Phot 27:99-128 D '63
Mutars: one Rollei becomes three. F. Henle. il Pop Phot 54:32 Ap '64
Mutars; Rollei's answer to interchangeability. N. Rothschild. il Pop Phot 52:102-5 My '63
Nature and the camera. D. Linton. il Natur Hist 72:65-8 Ap '63
New at the show; report on 40th Master photo dealers' and finishers' association national convention and trade show. il Pop Phot 54:87-97 Je '64
New format: 46-mm? W. J. Sumits. il Pop Phot 52:91 Mr '63
New product report. See issues of U.S. camera
New products. See issues of Modern photography to November 1963
New wonder camera for nature close-ups: Startech cameras. J. C. Schmid. il Audubon Mag 65:266-8 S '63
Nikonos: the toughest 35. P. Leonian. il US Camera 27:58-9+ S '64
1965 preview. il Mod Phot 28:90-7 Je '64
1964 preview of photo products. il Mod Phot 27:51-63+ Je; 84-7+ Jl '63
1964-1965 directory & buying guide. il Pop Phot 53:66-130 N; 70-135 D '63; 55:1A-64A N '64
No eye-level SLR for you? why not build your own? H. Keppler. il Mod Phot 28:17 N '64
Non-reflexes are okay, too. N. Rothschild. Pop Phot 53:95-6 S '63
One man's predictions; automation. D. B. Eisendrath, jr. Pop Phot 52:66+ Ap '63
Oscilloscope photography in industry; CRO cameras. R. A. Shiver. il Electr World 69:53-6+ Mr '63
Panoramic camera for under $40; Russian-made spaceview 2. P. Schroeder. il Pop Phot 54:54-5+ F '64
Photo show roundup; Chicago trade show. il U S Camera 27:90-1 Je '64
Photography season starts at the flower show. J. J. Simpkins. il Flower Grower 51:59 Mr '64
Photography's most-asked question. N. Rothschild. Pop Phot 53:189-91 D '63
Photokina postscript. il Pop Phot 53:70-2+ Jl '63
Pinhole camera. P. R. Farber. il U S Camera 26:58-9+ Ap '63
Pocket studio. J. Foldes. il U S Camera 26:56+ N '63
Polaroid back for Hasselblad. S. Nathan. il U S Camera 26:14 Je '63; 27:26+ F '64
Preview of photo show equipment. il U S Camera 27:37-44 Ap '64
Put together a complete SLR outfit for under $100. E. Meyers. il Mod Phot 28:84-5 Mr '64
RF or SLR, which is the real you? M. Edelson and J. Ward. il U S Camera 27:40-5 S '64
RFDR cameras: real sharpness. W. Benser. il Mod Phot 27:58-61+ My '63
Revolution in 35 mm. cameras. il Consumer Bul 47:2+ O '64
Saturn's camera system most elaborate ever. il Sci N L 85:98 F 15 '64
70mm, fad or future? S. Nathan. U S Camera 26:33-5 My '63
Shutter bugging. il Seventeen 22:186-7 My '63
SLR cameras compared! D. L. Miller. il Mod Phot 27:60-7 S '63
SLR's without moving mirrors: the split-beam system. B. Pierce; N. Rothschild; R. W. Vesey. il Pop Phot 54:64-7+ Je '64
Sky cameras: America's cold-war sentinels. C. P. Gilmore. il Pop Sci 183:116-21+ O '63
Some speculations on the Leicaflex. N. Rothschild. il Pop Phot 55:46+ D '64
Special 35-mm issue; symposium, with editorial comment. il Pop Phot 55:30, 33-63+ Ag '64
Stick with a simple camera. il Changing T 18:41-3 N '64
Still cameras designed for lunar mission. W. Wright. il Aviation W 79:55-6+ N 25 '63
Subminiature; symposium. il Pop Phot 53:35-49+ Ag '63
T system. H. Shaman. il Pop Phot 53:64-7 Jl '63
Techniques tomorrow; Artronic shutter & the auto focusing canon. B. Sherman. il Mod Phot 27:60-1 Jl '63
Techniques tomorrow; automation in camera and lens making. B. Sherman. Mod Phot 27:48+ N '63
Techniques tomorrow; camera used by Mercury astronauts. B. Sherman. il Mod Phot 28:12-13 Jl '64
Test report: the amphibious Nikonos. R. Kinne. il Pop Phot 54:70-3+ Mr '64
Test reports. See issues of Popular photography
Tests of three new single-lens reflex cameras. il Consumer Bul 47:6-8 My '64
They said it couldn't be done, and it wasn't: Voigtlander camera designs. H. Keppler. il Mod Phot 28:58-61 F '64
35mm. J. Wolbarst. See issues of Modern photography
35mm cameras. il Consumer Rep 28:529-34 N '63
35mm; Rapid system vs Instamatic. J. Wolbarst. Mod Phot 29:50+ Ja '65
35mm techniques. P. Stackpole. See issues of U.S. camera
Thoughts on the Instamatic. W. J. Sumits. Pop Phot 53:91 S '63
Through the looking glass; SLR. il U S Camera 27:44-7 D '64
Today's 8mm cartridges are versatile, tomorrow's may be instamatic. M. A. Matzkin. il Mod Phot 28:86-7+ F '64
Twenty exposures in only one second. G. P. Hunt. il Life 57:3 Ag 7 '64
TLR, the second most popular camera. il U S Camera 27:44-7 Jl '64
2¼ camera rundown; comp. by D. L. Miller. il Mod Phot 28:74-7 N '64
2¼ SLR color way in. P. Caulfield. il Mod Phot 27:54-6 S '63
2¼ SLR color way out. P. Caulfield. il Mod Phot 27:57-9 S '63
256 new cameras & how they compare; comp. by D. L. Miller. il Mod Phot 28:109-32 D '64
Two new single-frame cameras and a slide projector. il Consumer Bul 47:29-31 Je '64
Two worlds in one picture. C. Phinizy. il U.S. Camera 26:38-9+ Jl '63 Reply. P. Stackpole. 26:12 S '63
U.S. camera compares; Hasselblad; Bronica. il U S Camera 26:60-3+ Ap '63
U.S. camera test reports (cont of) New product report. il U S Camera 27:60-3+ Ag; 60-1+ S; 88+ N '64; 28:80-1+ Ja '65
Un-miniature ultra-miniature; Tessina. J. Foldes. il U S Camera 26:68-9+ N '63
Vagabond camera. W. Lane. il Travel 120:52-3 N '63; 121:58-9 Ap; 122:56-7 Ag '64
Versatile second camera; subminiature. B. Hering. il Pop Sci 183:132-3+ Jl '63
What you'll see in '63. il U S Camera 26:74-7+ My '63
What'll you have in 35? il U S Camera 26:40-1 Jl '63
What's a Panophic? N. Rothschild. il Pop Phot 55:50-1+ O '64
What's new at the camera shows. B. Hering. il Pop Sci 182:126-9 Je '63
What's wrong with equipment design? N. Rothschild. Pop Phot 55:109-11 S '64
Which viewing system for you? J. Foldes il U S Camera 27:66-9 F '64
Your leisure (cont) il Consumer Rep 28:304-32 D '63
See also
Eastman Kodak company
Graflex camera
Moving picture cameras
Photography
Polaroid Land cameras
Television cameras
View finders

Anecdotes, facetiae, satire, etc.

Is automation really necessary? A. Prado. il U S Camera 27:42 Mr '64

Care

Clean-living camera. C. Wright. Pop Phot 54:97-8 My '64
How to care for cameras. T. Karp. il Mod Phot 28:138+ D '64
Keep 'em working. M. Edelson. il U S Camera 28:56-7+ Ja '65
Large camera. A. Feininger. Mod Phot 28:30+ Ap '64

Collectors and collecting

Bring on the oldies. G. Gilbert. il U S Camera 27:16+ Je '64

History

Landmark cameras. B. Newhall. il Pop Phot 55:142-7 D '64

Loading

Bulk load and save. C. Wright. il Pop Phot 55:40-3+ Ag '64

CAMERAS—Loading—*Continued*
Comparing the new quick loaders. K. Brown. il Pop Mech 120:112-15+ O '63
Fastest loading in 35-mm! B. C. Brown. il Pop Phot 55:56-7+ Ag '64
From 1936 to 1964 quick, quicker, quickest loading! L. Drukker. il Pop Phot 55:108+ O '64
Idea that clicked; instant-load cartridge-camera system. R. L. Hering. il Pop Sci 183:134-7+ D '63
Now: cameras you load like a gun; Instamatic camera. B. Hering. il Pop Sci 182:112-13 My '63
Rapid vs Instamatic loading. P. Farber. il U S Camera 27:18+ N '64
35mm; new Rapid system. J. Wolbarst. Mod Phot 28:28+ O '64

Mounting

Sliding camera mount. W. E. Burton. il Pop Mech 120:162-3 S '63

Testing

How to test cameras. E. Meyers. il Mod Phot 28:136-7 D '64

CAMERAS, Used
Buying a good used camera. C. H. Crandall. il Pop Mech 120:118-21 Ag '63
Eight top RFDR camera buys. D. L. Miller. il Mod Phot 28:80-1+ My '64
1964 used camera buying guide; comp. by N. M. Grossman. il Mod Phot 27:66-98 D '63
Pictures in a moment; super bargains. J. Wolbarst. il Mod Phot 28:12 My '64
Should you buy a used camera without flash synchronization? comp. by A. C. Muller. Mod Phot 27:98 D '63
281 used cameras & how they compare; comp. by N. M. Grossman. il Mod Phot 28:77-108 D '64

CAMERMAN, N. and Trotter, J.
5-iodo-2'-deoxyuridine: relation of structure to its antiviral activity. bibliog Science 144:1348-50 Je 12 '64

CAMERON, A. G. W.
Birth of the elements; excerpt from address, December 5, 1962. il Sky & Tel 25:254-7 My '63
Communicating with intelligent life on other worlds; adaptation of address, March 27, 1963. Sky & Tel 26:258-61 N '63
—See Jastrow, R. jt. auth.

CAMERON, Dale C.
Treatment of narcotic addicts. Todays Health 41:12+ O '63

CAMERON, Eleanor
Dearest freshness deep down things; excerpt from address, March 14, 1964. Horn Bk 40:459-72 O '64
Of style and the stylist. Horn Bk 40:25-32 F '64
Unicorn; poem. Horn Bk 39:474-5 O '63

CAMERON, Elizabeth
John F. Kennedy library exhibit. Wilson Lib Bul 39:63-5 S '64
Made in the house. Wilson Lib Bul 38:550-1 Mr '64

CAMERON, Frank
Look what's cooking with natural gas! Read Digest 83:204C+ O '63

CAMERON, Gail
Cool brain behind the bonfire. Life 57:62+ Ag 28 '64
Life TV review. Life 57:17 D 4 '64
We've got 'em, luv, and it's all gear. Life 56:34B F 21 '64

CAMERON, J. M.
Awaiting the second spring. Commonweal 79:65-6 O 11 '63
Closing the door. Commonweal 80:386-8 Je 19 '64
Conservative comeback? Commonweal 79:562-4 F 7 '64
From Britain; reaction to Goldwater. Commonweal 80:563-4 Ag 21 '64
Humane and sane. Commonweal 79:338 D 13 '63
Profumo affair. Commonweal 78:445-6 Jl 26 '63

CAMERON, James
Albania: the last Marxist paradise. Atlan 211:41-50 Je '63
Cuba's fumbling Marxism. Atlan 214:92-6+ S '64

CAMERON, John R. and Sorenson, James
Measurement of bone mineral in vivo: an improved method. bibliog Science 142:230-2 O 11 '63

CAMERON, Nigel
Eternal dance of India. Horizon 5:64-73 S '63

CAMERON, Roderick
Australia, where surf-riding is flying on wings of foam. Vogue 143:119-20+ My '64

CAMERON, W. R.
W. R. Cameron stresses line, light and form; with biographical sketch. il por Am Artist 27:34-5 Mr '63

CAMERON, Zita. See Connor, D. M. jt. auth.

CAMERON, Mo.
Light touch brightens a dismal downtown. J. D. Arnold. il Am City 78:119 D '63

CAMERON iron works, incorporated
Forging shop turns its back on suppliers. il Bsns W p 194-6+ My 18 '63

CAMEROUN
Northern Cameroons; judgment of International court of justice. U N Rev 11:41-2 F '64
See also
Railroads—Cameroun

CAMEROUNS, British
Northern Cameroons; judgment of International court of justice. U N Rev 11:41-2 F '64

CAMINO, Paco
Artistry in a bullring is not enough. P. E. Ress. il por Sports Illus 21:44-7 Ag 10 '64
In Mexico, Paco Camino is hailed as número uno. R. D. Lozano. il por Sports Illus 18:68+ Ap 15 '63

CAMOUFLAGE
See also
Color of animals
Mimicry (biology)

CAMP, Dolph
Guidance worker in the State department of education. Sch Life 46:6-9 Jl '64

CAMP, John R.
Rich wasteland. Américas 15:11-14 Jl '63

CAMP, Ray
Camouflaged bunnies. Field & S 68:28-30+ N '63
Too good to shoot. Field & S 67:56-7+ Mr '63

CAMP cars. See Automobiles—Camping equipment

CAMP Century. See Building, Ice and snow

CAMP cookery
Advice to cooks. T. Trueblood. il Field & S 68:16+ N '63
Cooking afloat and cooking ashore. il Sunset 133:48-53 Jl '64
Gourmet travel kit: seasonings, flavorings, drink additives. M. Kaytor. il Look 28:88-9 My 5 '64
On-the-move cook book. B. Edgar. il House & Gard 123:148 Je '63
What's for chow? C. B. Colby. Outdoor Life 132:88-9+ Jl '63
Your camp kitchen. C. B. Colby. il Outdoor Life 134:124-7 S '64

CAMP-cooking utensils. See Kitchen utensils

CAMP counselors and directors
Counselor, yours is a tough assignment. S. T. Woal. Recreation 57:111 Mr '64

CAMP discipline. See Discipline

CAMP EDISON-SHAVER LAKE. See California—Parks and reserves

CAMP Enterprise. See Business education

CAMP equipment. See Camping outfits

CAMP fire girls
Conservation and the Camp fire girls. il Nat Parks Mag 38:8-10 N '64

CAMP fires
See also
Fire making

CAMP lanterns. See Lanterns

CAMP sites. See Camps

CAMP stools. See Stools

CAMP stoves
Solid-fuel stove; Sportsman's galley stove. C. Conley. il Field & S 68:91 N '63

CAMPAIGN buttons, etc.
Buttons pick the victor. il Bsns W p34 Jl 25 '64

CAMPAIGN for nuclear disarmament (organization)
Aldermaston's amen? sixth Aldermaston march. il Time 81:35 Ap 26 '63
Reporter at large; Aldermaston march. D. Lang. il New Yorker 39:35-6+ Je 22 '63
Ruptured peace movement. J. B. Priestley. Nation 197:251-3 O 26 '63; Discussion. 197: inside cover N 23 '63

CAMPAIGN funds
Barbecue: sponsored by Young citizens for Johnson, at Gracie Mansion. New Yorker 40:22-3 Ag 29 '64
Delegates, not dollars. Commonweal 80:528-9 Ag 7 '64
Disadvantage of being earnest; issue of political financing. Reporter 32:14 Ja 14 '65
F. Scott Fitzjohnson; LBJ campaign barbecues. il Newsweek 64:52 Ag 31 '64

CAMPAIGN funds—*Continued*
Fat cats are hard to find. W. Pincus. Reporter 31:34-6 Ag 13 '64
Goldwater's diggins. Nation 199:61-2 Ag 24 '64
Here's the way politicians sell tickets at $100 a head. il U S News 56:60 Je 8 '64
High cost of being elected. il U S News 58:40 Ja 4 '65
High cost of winning; violation of federal laws on campaign financing. Newsweek 65:16-18 Ja 4 '65
It was a 200-million-dollar political campaign. il U S News 57:41-2 N 9 '64
Knife-and-fork route to campaign dollars. il U S News 56:44-5 My 25 '64
Million-dollar loser looks at campaigning. A. Cranston. Fortune 70:124+ N '64
Money and politics. Nation 200:2 Ja 4 '65
Money comes easily; GOP campaign. il Bsns W p 19-20 Ag 1 '64
New approach to campaign finances; private donations to presidential election campaigns. A. Heard. il N Y Times Mag p50+ O 6 '63
Politicians tap the little guy. Bsns W p32 Mr 9 '63
Politics: the rich man's game. I. Sclanders. Nation 198:215-16 Mr 2 '64
Tax incentives for campaign contributions? pro and con discussion. Sr Schol 83:8-9 N 1 '63
Who pays the campaign bills? il Sr Schol 85:22 S 23 '64

CAMPAIGN furniture. See Furniture

CAMPAIGN literature
Case for bookburning; political pamphlets. Christian Cent 81:1415 N 11 '64
Hall of defamers; paperbacks a major weapon of political warfare. T. Clancy. America 111:520-2 O 31 '64; Reply with rejoinder. M. Burke. 111:762 D 12 '64
Help keep campaign literature fair. Christian Cent 81:1004 Ag 12 '64
None dare call it reason. Christian Cent 81:1351 O 28 '64
Package of political poison; analysis and criticism of None dare call it treason, by J. A. Stormer; reprint. R. W. Smith. Christian Cent 81:1263-4 O 14 '64
Pop literature of the radical right. B. Galphin. New Repub 151:22-5 O 10 '64
See also
Political poetry

CAMPAIGN oratory
Tumult & the shouting; excerpts from presidential campaign speeches. il Am Heritage 15:88-9 Ag '64
Quotations, maxims, etc.
Oratory in season; comp. by E. F. Murphy. il N Y Times Mag p28 O 4 '64

CAMPAIGN slogans. See Slogans

CAMPAIGN songs
November songs. il N Y Times Mag p 150-1 S 13 '64

CAMPAIGNE, Jameson G. Jr
Intellectual underbrush. Nat R 16:779-80 S 8 '64
On target. Nat R 15:444-5 N 19 '63

CAMPAIGNS, Political. See Political campaigns

CAMPAIGNS, Presidential. See Presidential campaigns

CAMPANULAS
Indoor campanulas. M. E. Ross. il Horticulture 41:414 Ag '63

CAMPBELL, Alan K. and Sacks, Seymour
Goldwater seeks a new coalition. N Y Times Mag p22+ Ag 23 '64

CAMPBELL, Alex
Between education and catastrophe. New Repub 151:19-20 O 31 '64
Born to rule. New Repub 150:21+ My 2 '64
Mild Mr Rusk. New Repub 150:13-16 Ap 11 '64
Wealth of West Germany. New Repub 151:24-6 D 26 '64

CAMPBELL, B. H.
We moved to a small town. por Redbook 122:20+ F '64

CAMPBELL, Blanche
Children's department at Christmas time. Pub W 184:40 Ag 19 '63

CAMPBELL, Bryn
World's most unusual camera store: Wallace Heaton ltd. Pop Phot 54:61-3+ Je '64

CAMPBELL, Daniel R.
Code for baby sitters. Parents Mag 39:54+ Ag '64

CAMPBELL, David R.
Crafts for the aging; excerpts from introduction. Craft Horiz 23:8-9 Ja '63
about
David R. Campbell, 1908-1963. Mrs V. Webb. por Craft Horiz 23:8-9 My '63

CAMPBELL, Donald
Bluebird to happiness. il por Time 84:58 Jl 24 '64
Race against time and tide in the outback. il Sports Illus 18:20-1 My 20 '63
Speed king? or, Just son of speed king? K. Rudeen. il pors Sports Illus 19:56-61 Jl 29 '63

CAMPBELL, Douglas Gordon
Dangers in pesticides; excerpt from interview. Consumer Bul 47:33-6 Jl '64

CAMPBELL, Francean
Vancouver festival. Mus Am 83:9 Ag '63

CAMPBELL, Frank
Callery pear. Horticulture 42:24 Je '64

CAMPBELL, Frank L.
Tribute to F. R. Moulton; letter. Science 141:311 Jl 26 '63

CAMPBELL, Henry C.
Comment from Canada; excerpts from report. Library J 88:2468 Je 15 '63
Multi-lingual library. Wilson Lib Bul 38:68-9+ S '63

CAMPBELL, Henry J. Jr. See Cerniglia, V. J. jt. auth.

CAMPBELL, Horace E.
Automobiles can be made much safer. Consumer Bul 47:35-7 S '64
Forty-five steps to safer cars. Consumer Bul 47:30-2 O '64

CAMPBELL, Ian Douglas, 11th duke of Argyll. See Argyll, I. D. C.

CAMPBELL, J. B.
Synthetic elastomers. bibliog Science 141:329-34 Jl 26 '63

CAMPBELL, James L. See Boolootian, R. A. jt. auth.

CAMPBELL, James W. See Bishop, S. H. jt. auth.

CAMPBELL, Lady Jean
Lady is a legman. por Newsweek 63:46-7 Ja 6 '64

CAMPBELL, John C.
Jugoslavia: crisis and choice. For Affairs 41:384-97 Ja '63

CAMPBELL, John Carden
Honeycomb house for all seasons. il Sports Illus 20:40-5 Mr 23 '64

CAMPBELL, John W.
Science fact, science fiction. Writer 77:26-7 Ag '64

CAMPBELL, Jule
Sporting look (cont) Sports Illus 18:32-3 F 4 '63

CAMPBELL, L. Leon. See DePinto, J. A. jt. auth.

CAMPBELL, Lawrence
Animal kingdom of Anne Arnold. Art N 63:32-3+ D '64
Creative casting. Craft Horiz 23:10-17+ N '63
Elaine deKooning: portraits in a New York scene. Art N 62:38-9+ Ap '63
Elias Goldberg paints a picture. Art N 62:42-5+ N '63
Five Americans face reality. Art N 62:25-7+ S '63
Hopper: painter of thou shalt not. Art N 63:42-5+ O '64
Lester Johnson on the Bowery. Art N 62:46-7+ F '64
Lewitin: cabalist fabulist. Art N 63:28-30+ Ja '65
Marisol's magic mixtures. Art N 63:38-41+ Mr '64
Pousette-Dart: circles and cycles. Art N 62:42-5+ My '63
—and Millikan, Moria
Craft of bronze casting. Craft Horiz 23:26-33+ Ja '63

CAMPBELL, Louise
National academy of sciences: 100th anniversary program. Science 142:561-3 N 1 '63
Science in Japan. bibliog Science 143:776-82 F 21 '64

CAMPBELL, Lucille
Enjoy a budget? we do, honest! por Farm J 89:61-2+ Ja '65

CAMPBELL, Marjorie D.
Scuola di Severino; a new home. Sch Arts 62:12-16 My '63

CAMPBELL, Marjorie Wilkins
Canada's dynamic heartland Ontario. Nat Geog Mag 124:58-97 Jl '63

CAMPBELL, Pamela
Student speaks. por Mus Am 83:8 Je '63

CAMPBELL, Reginald John
R. J. Campbell at City temple. W. S. Smith. Christian Cent 80:1132-4 S 18 '63

CAMPBELL, Robert
Circuits of the senses. Life 54:64-76B+ Je 28 '63
Life-giving balancing act. Life 55:68-81 N 8 '63

CAMPBELL, Robert B.
How to prepare for Christmas. Pub W 184:38-9 Ag 19 '63

CAMPBELL, Roy
(tr) See Calderón de la Barca, P. Life is a dream
CAMPBELL, Sandy
Mr Forster of King's. il Mlle 59:80-1+ Je '64
CAMPBELL, Spencer
Vision in the valley. il por Newsweek 63:82-3 Je 29 '64
CAMPBELL, T. L.
ACHEMA, world's largest chemical engineering congress, shows scientific instruments of twenty-three nations. Science 145:1026-35 S 4 '64
What's new in research instruments. bibliog Science 144:892-8 My 15 '64
CAMPBELL, Thomas
If Tom is half as old as Will. . . W. B. Blakemore. Christian Cent 81:489-92 Ap 15 '64
CAMPBELL, Mrs Willard
They eat out of her hand. Audubon Mag 65: 308+ S '63
CAMPBELL soup company
Artistry, science, skill=flavorable food. M. B. Keiser. il Parents Mag 39:12+ O '64
In the soup and happy to be there. il Bsns W p 124-6+ F 15 '64
Soup & chips. il Time 84:97-8 D 11 '64
Three-course dinners; TV-dinners. Consumer Rep 28:412 S '63
CAMPERS and coaches, Truck
At home in a bus. H. Sutton. il Sat R 47:45-7 D 5 '64
Big circle tour. B. W. Dalrymple. il Field & S 69:66-9+ O '64
Big-family camping. B. Conaway. il Field & S 67:46-51 Mr '63
Boats for campers. J. A. Emmett. il Outdoor Life 131:100-2 Mr '63
Campers. V. L. Oertle. il Motor T 15:62-5 Je '63
Car camping bonus section; symposium. il Field & S 68:42-50 F '64
Country home will do 60 m.p.h. J. M. Liston. il Pop Sci 185:146-7 Jl '64
Fold-flat camper. il Pop Mech 120:81 D '63
4x4 field test; four-wheel-drive camper. R. Barlow. il Field & S 68:68-9+ My '63
Hitch & go. C. Isica. See issues of Motor trend
In way to camp out. il Time 84:42 Ag 28 '64
Instant camper on a pickup. F. Harvey. il Pop Sci 184:122-3 My '64
Land yacht, a new breed of rolling home. il House B 106:135-47+ Ap '64
Modern wagon train on a worldwide ramble. il Bsns W p56-8 D 19 '64
1964 truck campers. V. L. Oertle. il Pop Sci 184:106-10+ My '64
Pickup camper paradise. R. Cannon. il Field & S 67:70-3+ Ap '63
Scout camper; compact and convenient. R. McCluskey. il Field & S 67:184-5 Ap '63
Six can eat and sleep in camper. il Pop Mech 120:106 Jl '63
There's a long, long trail; camp equipment. il Bsns W p34-5 N 2 '63
Vacationing on wheels. il Consumer Bul 46: 16-19 Ag '63
Vacations on wheels. il Pop Sci 182:118-32+ My '63
Wheel estate; factory-built mobile homes. il Time 84:98 D 11 '64
Workhorse and playboy; Tow a tent or a little house. il Field & S 67:42-7 F '63
CAMPING
Ahead; summer week ends in the great outdoors. G. Laycock. il Todays Health 41:46-9+ My '63
All-season camping. il Recreation 56:115-18 Mr '63
Big circle tour. B. W. Dalrymple. il Field & S 69:66-9+ O '64
Camp season's coming. F. Fielding-Jones. il Parents Mag 38:68-9+ Mr '63
Camping. C. B. Colby. See issues of Outdoor life
Camping and outdoor recreation; symposium. il Recreation 57:103-20 Mr '64
Camping as related to leisure. A. R. Martin. Recreation 56:112 Mr '63
Car camping bonus section; symposium. il Field & S 68:42-50 F '64
C'mon, try boat-camping. il Motor B 114:25-7 Jl '64
Cross country camping. P. Geraci. il Travel 119:31-3+ My '63
Exodus East: New York world's fair, tips for campers and owners. D. B. Huyck. il Am For 70:34-7 F '64
EV and camping clubs. D. B. Huyck. il Am For 70:10-11+ Je '64
Glacier: the park with everything. E. A. Bauer. il Field & S 69:39-41 Je '64
How to camp out and enjoy it. P. Czura. il Todays Health 42:32-5+ Jl '64
How we discovered America. L. Hillary. il Redbook 121:60-1+ Je '63
Need camping information? Am For 69:17 Mr '63
New way to find our lost frontier. R. Cantwell. il Sports Illus 18:32-5+ My 20 '63
Our loving public. W. W. Huber. il Am For 69:6-7+ Ag '63
Seattle to Seattle in 3,600 miles. B. Kocivar. il Look 28:80-3 My 5 '64
So you want to entertain the public! private outdoor recreation industry. P. E. McDowell. il Am For 70:22-5+ Ja '64
Some human aspects of camping; report of survey. W. T. Moss. il Am For 70:24-5+ Ag '64
Try camping for summer fun. C. Allen. il Ebony 18:127-8+ Je '63
You don't have to be a hero; automobile camping. M. Rubenstein. il Field & S 68: 40-2+ F '64
See also
Camp cookery
Camping outfits
Outdoor life
Sierra club
Activities
Camp for your child; with study-discussion program. E. G. Osborne. bibliog il PTA Mag 58:28-30, 35-6 My '64
Camping: day and night. il Recreation 56: 124-6 Mr '63
Experiment in fitness; Eastchester, N.Y. V. D. Bellew. Recreation 57:281-2 Je '64
Factors affecting the day camp program. V. Musselman. il Recreation 56:131-4 Mr '63
Something new for campers. E. M. Stern. il Parents Mag 39:58-9+ Mr '64
Tepee on the hilltop; St Louis YMCA camps. L. Congdon. Recreation 57:117 Mr '64
What can we do with Peter? K. B. Webb. Recreation 57:103-4 Mr '64
Anecdotes, facetiae, satire, etc.
Tenting tonight—CCCreatively. P. Welch. il Life 55:10 Jl 19 '63
Bibliography
For families who want to camp by themselves. Consumer Rep 28:194-5 Ap '63
Educational aspects
Art experiences in camping. R. E. Dodson. Recreation 56:135+ Mr '63
What can we do with Peter? K. B. Webb. Recreation 57:103-4 Mr '64
What's going on here? R. E. Roth. Recreation 57:118-20 Mr '64
Health aspects
Camp sanitation. C. B. Colby. Outdoor Life 134:90-1+ Ag '64
Safety devices and measures
Factors affecting camping facilities. S. W. Stocker. Recreation 56:142 Mr '63
Fifty suggestions for a safe over-night. E. J. Slezak. Recreation 56:130 Mr '63
Get fit for a trip to the woods. B. J. Plummer. il Parents Mag 38:60-1+ My '63
Stay healthy in camp. C. B. Colby. Outdoor Life 132:126-8 S '63
California
Autumn camping on the Feather. il Sunset 133:69+ O '64
For the boating, the camping, and the unusual trout. il Sunset 130:64+ My '63
Canada
Big-family camping. B. Conaway. il Field & S 67:46-51 Mr '63
Tremblant: big wilderness; ideal camping, fishing, boating. C. B. Colby. il Outdoor Life 133:22-4+ Je '64
Europe
How is camping in Europe? Sunset 132:58+ Ap '64
Europe, Western
Germans take lead in economy travel. il Bsns W p30-1 Jl 20 '63
Great Britain
Camping in Great Britain; Americans! you never had it so good! L. B. Sinden and J. A. Sinden. il Am For 71:34-7+ Ja '65
Maine
Bush-queer canoe trip. E. W. Smith. il Field & S 69:40-2+ My '64

CAMPING—*Continued*

Massachusetts

Camp study for Boston area. Recreation 57: 138 Mr '64

Mexico

Camping south of the border. P. Crabtree. il Am For 69:48-51+ My '63

New York (state)

Camping at thirty below. S. James. il Pop Mech 121:128-32+ Ja '64
Family camping in wilderness. Liv Wildn 83: 28 Spring '63

Oregon

Sports fitness camps; Portland. D. Graham. il Recreation 57:280-1 Je '64

United States

See Camping

Washington (state)

Budget boating vacation: the Columbia Basin. D. Bolding. il Field & S 68:61-3 Je '63

CAMPING outfits
Air mattresses. il Consumer Rep 28:122-6 Mr '63
Better night's sleep. C. B. Colby. il Outdoor Life 132:102-4 N '63
Camper's tool kit. C. B. Colby. Outdoor Life 131:112-14 F '63
Camping and picnicking. il Consumer Bul 29: 318-38 D '64
Camping thirty below. S. James. il Pop Mech 121:128-32+ Ja '64
Camping tips. il Bet Hom & Gard 41:106D Je '63
Containers for everything; for campers. C. B. Colby. Outdoor Life 132:130-1 O '63
Cooking kits. T. Trueblood. il Field & S 68: 16+ F '64
Dry run for '63. C. B. Colby. Outdoor Life 131:38-9 Je '63
Gifts campers want. C. B. Colby. il Outdoor Life 132:78-80 D '63
How to camp out and enjoy it. P. Czura. il Todays Health 42:32-5+ Jl '64
How to save loafing time. il Sunset 131:172 O '63
Instant camp mattress. C. Conley. il Field & S 68:145 Ap '64
Kitchen fly for campers. C. Pelander. il Pop Mech 119:132-3 Je '63
Make your canoe a cruising camper. F. M. Paulson. il Field & S 69:86-8+ Jl '64
New ideas for campers. C. B. Colby. il Outdoor Life 134:88-90 D '64
Newest camp gear. C. B. Colby. il Outdoor Life 131:40+ Ap '63; 133:22-4+ My '64
Pamper your camp gear. B. Knox and W. Knox. il Pop Mech 120:111-13+ S '63
Questions I'm asked. C. B. Colby. il Outdoor Life 134:14+ O '64
There's a long, long trail; camp equipment. il Bsns W p34-5 N 2 '63
Treat gear to shed water. C. B. Colby. Outdoor Life 133:104-5+ F '64
Why rough it? C. B. Colby. Outdoor Life 131:110-12 Mr '63
Your family camping outfit: Cost low, fun unlimited. R. McCluskey. il Field & S 67: 38-41 F '63
Your leisure (cont) il Consumer Rep 28:332-44 D '63
See also
Automobiles—Camping equipment
Camp cookery
Knapsacks
Packs
Refrigerators, Portable
Sleeping bags
Station wagons—Camping equipment
Tents

CAMPION, Donald R.
Books to be noted; home scene. America 108: 687-91; 110:651-3 My 11 '63, My 9 '64
Campus corner. America 108:198, 266, 302, 337, 367, 406, 467, 532, 639, 751; 109:45; 110:437, 569, 825 F 9, 23-Mr 23, Ap 6, 20, My 4, 25, Jl 13 '63, Mr 28, Ap 25, Je 13 '64
Constitution on the church. America 111:777-8 D 12 '64
Council jottings. America 109:90, 110, 130, 150, 186, 206, 229, 254 Jl 27-S 14 '63
Five views of the council. America 110:816-19 Je 13 '64
How Protestants see others. America 108:428 Mr 30 '63
Letter from the council. America 111:374-5, 406-7, 446-7, 478-9, 512-13, 546-7, 592-3, 654-5, 736-7 O 3-N 21, D 5 '64
Loss and gain. America 110:10-14 Ja 4 '64
New world, new church. America 110:709-11 My 23 '64
Third session. America 111:252-4 S 12 '64
World resounds: Rome. America 109:768 D 14 '63
—and O'Hanlon, D. J.
Council jottings. America 109:341-3, 377-8, 409-10, 446-7, 479-80, 508-10, 553-5, 626-7, 654-5, 701-2, 765-6, 791 S 28-N 30, D 14-21 '63

CAMPION, Howard A.
Financing the public junior college. NEA J 53:67-8 O '64

CAMPION award. See Catholic book club

CAMPOBELLO PARK. See Roosevelt Campobello International Park

CAMPOS, Roberto de Oliveira
Rio's fiscal surgeon. il por Bsns W p 100+ Je 13 '64
Self-criticism. Newsweek 63:36 F 24 '64

CAMPS
Camp double dividend; camp grandparents at Madison-Felicia. M. Weston. il N Y Times Mag p62+ Ag 18 '63
Camp for your child; with study-discussion program. E. G. Osborne. bibliog il PTA Mag 58:28-30, 35-6 My '64
Camp isn't just for kids; family camp. H. McKinley. il Parents Mag 38:52-3+ Jl '63
Camp season's coming. F. Fielding-Jones. il Parents Mag 38:68-9+ Mr '63
Camping: day and night. il Recreation 56: 124-6 Mr '63
Camping: French, yoga, and TV; growing collection of expensive, exotic hideaways. il Newsweek 63:82-3 Je 22 '64
Campsite layout. C. B. Colby. il Outdoor Life 132:90+ Ag '63
Day camping, an answer to summer needs; Slim Baker day camp, Bristol, N.H. R. P. Ledger. Recreation 57:116-17 Mr '64
Factors affecting the day camp program. V. Musselman. il Recreation 56:131-4 Mr '63
I can lick every person in this camp! a school social worker at a day camp. M. B. Crock. il NEA J 53:52-3 N '64
My favorite campgrounds. C. B. Colby. il Outdoor Life 134:102-4+ N '64
Planning camps. J. H. Salomon. il Recreation 56:139-41 Mr '63
Rescaling fees and charges. Recreation 57: 243 My '64
Something new for campers. E. M. Stern. il Parents Mag 39:58-9+ Mr '64
Summer camps. il Seventeen 22:138-9+ Ap '63
Summer camps. W. Como. il Dance Mag 37: 60-4 Ap; 61 My '63
Tepee on the hilltop; St Louis YMCA camps. L. Congdon. il Recreation 57:117 Mr '64
When science is fun; with list of science camps. I. L. Slesnick. il Sci Digest 55:73-4 Je '64
Where to go camping. Consumer Rep 28:215 My '63
See also
Audubon nature camps
Camping
Military training camps
Music camps

Activities

See Camping—Activities

Europe, Western

Camps across the sea. L. Hadley. il N Y Times Mag p47-8 F 23 '64
European camps for kids. J. P. Harmon. il Travel 119:48-50 Je '63

Russia

Moffetts go a-moseying; account of a Communist young pioneer camp. H. Moffett. il Life 55:100-2+ S 13 '63

CAMPS, Forestry. See Forestry camps

CAMPS, Military
See also
Military training camps

CAMPS for the handicapped
Day camp for the mentally retarded. R. Stockhamer. Recreation 56:236-7 My '63

CAMPUS government. See Self government in education

CAMPUS life. See Student life

CAMPUS parking. See Automobile parking

CAMRAS system. See Video tape recorders and recording

CAMS
See also
Automobiles—Cams

CAMUS, Albert
Riddle. Atlan 211:83-5 Je '63

CAMUS, Albert—*Continued*

about

Albert Camus: ex post facto convert. Christian Cent 80:191 F 6 '63
Camus as journalist. J. Daniel. New Repub 150:19-21 Je 13 '64
Camus notebooks. A. J. Liebling. New Yorker 39:128+ F 8 '64
Charting a literary log. J. Cruickshank. por Sat R 46:25+ Ag 31 '63
Early Camus. A. E. Mayhew. Commonweal 79:173-4 N 1 '63
Finger exercises. D. Littlejohn. Reporter 29: 62-4 O 24 '63
Individual. por Time 82:86 Jl 26 '63

CAN, Ngo-dinh-. See Ngo-dinh-Can

CAN I stay here? story. See O'Hara, J.

CANADA, A. J.
Early American spice rack. Pop Mech 121: 160-1 Mr '64

CANADA
Canada; symposium. il Atlan 214:100-8+ N '64; Discussion. 215:30+ Ja '65
Canada; symposium. il Holiday 35:1-220 Ap '64
Unknown Canadians. I. Mothner. il Look 27: 56-8+ Ap 9 '63

See also
Aeronautics, Military—Canada
Aerospace industries—Canada
Airlines—Canada
Airplane industry and trade—Canada
Airplanes, Military—Canada
Arbitration, Industrial—Canada
Back River
Banks and banking—Canada
Birth control—Canada
Book industries and trade—Canada
Booksellers and bookselling—Canada
Camping—Canada
Civil service—Canada
Crime and criminals—Canada
Dams—Canada
Education—Canada
Education and state in Canada
Elections—Canada
Fishing—Canada
Flags—Canada
Forests and forestry—Canada
French Canadians
Geology—Canada
Great Bear Lake
Hudson Bay
Hunting—Canada
Insurance, Health—Canada
Insurance, Unemployment—Canada
Investments, Foreign (in Canada)
Lake of the Woods, Minnesota and Canada
Mines and mineral resources—Canada
Music festivals—Canada
Natural resources—Canada
Newspapers—Canada
Northwest, Canadian
Opera—Canada
Periodicals—Canada
Political campaigns—Canada
Public opinion—Canada
Quebec (province)
Research—Canada
Rideau Canal
Science—Canada
Shipping—Canada
Space research—Canada
Taxation—Canada
Trade unions—Canada
Trials—Canada
United Nations—Canada

Armed forces

Canada may merge three armed services. J. W. Carter. il Aviation W 80:303+ Mr 16 '64
Hellyer-McNamara defense talks planned. Aviation W 80:33 Je 15 '64
Unification of Canadian services to have heavy industry impact. Aviation W 80:94+ Ap 27 '64

Army

Here come the Van Doos; Royal 22nd regiment in Cyprus. Time 83:23 Mr 27 '64

Bibliography

Look northward! books by Canadians and about Canada, for American chilldren and young adults. S. A. Egoff and R. A. Hagler. Library J 88:4421-8 N 15 '63

Commerce

And that ain't hay; sale of 300 million bushels of wheat to Soviet Russia. Newsweek 62:59 S 23 '63
Bread for Russia; big wheat export deal. Time 82:42 S 20 '63
Canada looks south; trade fair in Philadelphia. il Bsns W p 178-80 N 16 '63
Canada's prosperity hangs on foreign sales; in finished goods. il Bsns W p34+ Ja 16 '65
Canadian-American relations construct a solid foundation for effective world trade; address, April 22, 1963. R. W. Macaulay. Vital Speeches 29:503-6 Je 1 '63
China isn't buying. Newsweek 62:34 Jl 1 '63
Farm boom that red trade built. il U S News 56:98-100 Je 29 '64
For and against the grain. Reporter 29:14+ O 10 '63
Massive wheat sale to U.S.S.R. Sr Schol 83: 8-9 O 4 '63
Rush to trade with reds; will U.S. join it? il U S News 55:51-2 S 30 '63
Soviet-Canadian deal stirs a wheat tempest. Bsns W p28 S 21 '63
Spreading wealth. il Time 83:35 Ja 3 '64
Trade with the reds: a bonanza for Canada. il U S News 56:64 Mr 2 '64
Tramps reap the harvest; Russian demand for ships to carry Canadian wheat. Bsns W p28 S 28 '63
Wheat-sale dividend: new strength for Pearson. U S News 55:16 S 30 '63

Defenses

Bomarc for Canada. M. Halperin. New Repub 148:6-7 Mr 2 '63
Canada, a weakening ally? il U S News 54:41 F 11 '63
Canada explodes over nuclear warheads. il Bsns W p28-9 F 9 '63
Canada's option. Commonweal 77:505 F 8 '63
Canadian defense policy shift looms after voting. D. E. Fink. il Aviation W 78:288-9+ Mr 11 '63
Defense policy topples Canada's leaders. Aviation W 78:30 F 11 '63
Explosion on Parliament hill. N. McKenty. America 108:267 F 23 '63
Gift from Washington. Time 81:31 Ap 5 '63
Hellyer-McNamara defense talks planned. Aviation W 80:33 Je 15 '64
Here the U.S. fights the coldest war; with report by C. Mydans. il Life 54:18-27 Mr 1 '63
How can Canada make her most effective contribution to collective security? address, January 12, 1963. L. B. Pearson. Vital Speeches 29:290-3 Mr 1 '63
Nuclear blowup. Newsweek 61:52 F 11 '63
Nuclear issue may cause Canadian elections. Aviation W 78:37 F 4 '63
U.S. and Canadian negotiations regarding nuclear weapons; Department statement, January 30, 1963. Dept State Bul 48:243-4 F 18 '63
Washington gives Canada an election and an issue; with statement by U.S. Department of state. W. H. Hessler. Reporter 28:29-31 F 28 '63; Discussion. 28:6+ Mr 28 '63

See also
Canada—Navy
Canada-United States ministerial committee on joint defense
North American air defense command

Description and travel

Across the vast land. V. S. Pritchett. il Holiday 35:52-69+ Ap '64
Along the Trans-Canada highway with boys and station wagon. R. L. Ornauer. il Redbook 122:60-1+ F '64
Autoless adventure West. R. Meyer, jr. il Travel 120:38-42 Jl '63
Crisis in beautiful, bewildered Canada; photographs; with report by I. Mothner. D. Kirkland. Look 27:49-58+ Ap 9 '63
Down east to Nova Scotia. W. Parks. il Nat Geog Mag 125:852-79 Je '64
Enchanting eastern Canada. il Bet Hom & Gard 41:107-10 Je '63
Greatest of all outdoors. F. Bodsworth. il Holiday 35:175-82 Ap '64
On the trail of the voyageurs. M. S. Edsall. il Travel 120:42-4 Ag '63
Personal business. Bsns W p77-8 Ag 1 '64
See Canada and live. H. Sutton. il McCalls 90:166-7+ Mr '63
Teen travel talk. il Seventeen 23:28 Jl '64
Trail-blazing a vacation. J. V. Edsall and M. S. Edsall. il Outdoor Life 131:56-9+ My '63
Travel notes. R. Joseph. Esquire 62:114+ D '64

Economic conditions

Canada's boom lies year away. il Bsns W p22-3 D 28 '63
Doing fine north of the border. il Bsns W p29-30 O 3 '64
Healthier neighbor. il Time 82:84 Jl 5 '63
Pearson's frontier. il Fortune 68:113-14+ Jl '63

CANADA—*Continued*

Economic policy

Canada plans new pinch on outsiders; pressure on U.S. business. il Bsns W p27 F 15 '64
Canada's planners walk a tightrope; new Economic council. il Bsns W p 146+ Mr 14 '64
Canadianism today; address, February 20, 1963. N. R. Crump. Vital Speeches 29:394-7 Ap 15 '63
Pearson's budget bombshell. Bsns W p40-2 Je 22 '63
Pearson's frontier. il Fortune 68:113-14+ Jl '63
Plan or no plan or un-plan? address June 3, 1963. W. E. McLaughlin. Vital Speeches 29:636-9 Ag 1 '63
Thawing icebound jobs; winter homebuilding in Canada. Bsns W p 112 N 23 '63
Will they or won't they sell shares in Canada? il Bsns W p50+ Ja 25 '64
See also
Budget—Canada

Economic relations

United States

Canada plans new pinch on outsiders; pressure on U.S. business. il Bsns W p27 F 15 '64
Changing scene in Canada; address, April 20, 1964. W. L. Gordon. Vital Speeches 30:450-2 My 15 '64
Common market for North America; address, February 20, 1964. L. A. Townsend. Vital Speeches 30:381-4 Ap 1 '64
Impact of American business. R. M. Fowler. il Atlan 214:119-23 N '64
Pearson's progress; Canada after a year of Liberal government. W. H. Hessler. il Reporter 30:24-9 Mr 12 '64
United community of North America; address, September 30, 1964. E. Lamb. Vital Speeches 31:46-8 N 1 '64
U.S.-Canada brawl: a matter of capital. Bsns W p29-30 N 2 '63
When Canada looks to its future. il U S News 55:62-5 Ag 5 '63
See also
Joint United States-Canadian committee on trade and economic affairs

Exploration

Relics from the rapids; divers explore the watery highway of Canada's voyageurs. S. F. Olson. il Nat Geog Mag 124:412-35 S '63

Foreign relations

Canada, Britain, U.S: can Pearson tie them closer? il U S News 54:21 Ap 29 '63
Canada in search of its role. J. W. Holmes. For Affairs 41:659-72 Jl '63
Canadianism today; address, February 20, 1963. N. R. Crump. Vital Speeches 29:394-7 Ap 15 '63
Diplomacy of a middle power. J. W. Holmes. Atlan 214:106-8+ N '64

France

Honest broker. Newsweek 63:47 Ja 27 '64

Latin America

Canada and Latin America; remarks, February 1964. J. M. Dessureault. il Américas 16:36-7 Ap '64
Canada and the O.A.S. D. O'Brien. Commonweal 79:71-2 O 11 '63

United States

After the big two talks: what to expect. U S News 54:8 My 20 '63
Ahead: a friendlier Canada. il U S News 54:46 Ap 22 '63
As Canada heads for showdown at the polls. il U S News 54:48 Ap 8 '63
Atlantic report. Atlan 212:12+ Jl '63
Atmosphere of trust. il Newsweek 61:57 My 20 '63
Canada, a weakening ally? il U S News 54:41 F 11 '63
Canada blasts friendly old US. il Life 54:26-7 F 15 '63
Canada explodes over nuclear warheads. il Bsns W p28-9 F 9 '63
Canada, U.S. drift toward unity; with editorial comment. il Bsns W p24-5, 192 O 17 '64
Canadian Prime Minister visits Washington; U.S. and Canada agree on Columbia River development and establishment of Campobello Park; joint communique; with joint statements and texts of agreements; January 21-23, 1964. L. B. Johnson; L. B. Pearson. Dept State Bul 50:199-206 F 10 '64
Diefenbaker falls: did he jump or was he pushed? il Newsweek 61:33-6 F 18 '63
Good neighborhood. L. B. Pearson. For Affairs 43:251-61 Ja '65
How can Canada make her most effective contribution to collective security? address, January 12, 1963. L. B. Pearson. Vital Speeches 29:290-3 Mr 1 '63
Interdependence, the basis of U.S.-Canada relations; address, April 25, 1964. G. W. Ball. bibliog f Dept State Bul 50:770-4 My 18 '64
Neighbors agree on nuclear arms. Sr Schol 83:7-8 S 20 '63
North America, the open continent; address, June 16, 1963. W. R. Tyler. Dept State Bul 49:93-7 Jl 15 '63
Now U.S. is the issue in Canada. il U S News 54:31-2 F 18 '63
President Kennedy and Prime Minister Pearson of Canada hold talks; joint communique, May 11, 1963. J. F. Kennedy and L. B. Pearson. Dept State Bul 48:815-17 My 27 '63
Washington gives Canada an election and an issue; with statement by U.S. Department of state. W. H. Hessler. Reporter 28:29-31 F 28 '63; Discussion. 28:6+ Mr 28 '63
Weekend at Jack's. il Time 81:32 My 17 '63
What's bothering Canada now about the U.S. il U S News 55:42-3 O 28 '63
Will Canada break up? a story of tensions. il U S News 57:56-7 N 2 '64
Working together: Columbia River project and Roosevelt International Park, Campobello. il Sr Schol 84:20 F 21 '64

History

Nation in the making. B. Hutchinson. il Holiday 35:70-1+ Ap '64
Quebec's quiet revolution. C. de Mestral. Christian Cent 81:1268-70 O 14 '64
Reporter at large; concerning F. Parkman's great history. E. Wilson. New Yorker 40:71-2+ N 14 '64

Indians

See Indians of North America—Canada

Industries

See also
Forests and forestry—Canada
Mines and mineral resources—Canada
Mining industry and finance—Canada
Wood pulp industry

Intellectual life

Arts in Canada: a search for identity. H. MacLennan. il Mus Am 83:12-13+ S '63
Reporter at large; an American's notes on Canadian culture. E. Wilson. il New Yorker 40:63-6+ N 14; 64-6+ N 21; 143-4+ N 28 '64

Languages

Language shows prejudice. E. Mirel. Sci N L 84:149 S 7 '63

Maps

Canada. Holiday 35:50-1 Ap '64
Powerful neighbors join hands across the Great Lakes. Nat Geog Mag 124:98, sup (folded map) Jl '63

National health service

Recommend national health service; Royal commission on health services. Christian Cent 81:876 Jl 8 '64

National library

Office for library resources urged for National library of Canada. Library J 88:4720-1 D 15 '63

Navy

New ASW trainer improves readiness of Canadian fleet. M. Getler. il Miss & Roc 13:26-7 D 16 '63

Politics and government

Ahead: a friendlier Canada. il U S News 54:46 Ap 22 '63
Angry welcome for a Queen; French revolt that threatens Canada. R. Sherrod. il Sat Eve Post 237:19-23 O 10 '64
Atlantic report. Atlan 213:34+ Je '64
Canada in search of its role. J. W. Holmes. For Affairs 41:659-72 Jl '63
Canada, U.S. drift toward unity; with editorial comment. il Bsns W p24-5, 192 O 17 '64
Canada's crisis. M. R. MacGuigan. Commonweal 79:747-9 Mr 20 '64; Reply. R. A. Jones. 80:121-2 Ap 17 '64
Canada's sixty big days. il Bsns W p34 Ap 27 '63
Changing the guard. Time 81:28 Ap 26 '63

CANADA—Politics and government—*Cont.*
Confusion in Canada. New Repub 148:6 F 23 '63
Crisis in Canada. N. McKenty. America 111:135 Ag 8 '64
Diefenbaker falls: did he jump or was he pushed? il Newsweek 61:33-6 F 18 '63
Diefenbaker vision. I. Sclanders. Nation 198:387-8 Ap 20 '64
Diefenbaker's shambles. Time 81:29 F 15 '63
Do they really hate us in Canada? J. Atwater. il Sat Eve Post 236:15-21 Ap 6 '63
Good neighborhood. L. B. Pearson. For Affairs 43:251-61 Ja '65
Government crisis north of the border. il Sr Schol 82:4 F 20 '63
Into the fire. Newsweek 64:43-4 D 14 '64
Mr Pearson's troubles. Time 84:29 Jl 10 '64
New frontier north. Newsweek 61:46 Ap 29 '63
New leader. il Time 81:33-7 Ap 19 '63; Same abr. with title Lester Pearson: Canada's new leader. Read Digest 83:130-4 Ag '63
Nuclear blowup. Newsweek 61:52 F 11 '63
Pearson loses round one. R. E. Spencer. Nation 198:43-6 Ja 13 '64
Pearson's progress; Canada after a year of Liberal government. W. H. Hessler. il Reporter 30:24-9 Mr 12 '64
Quebec guerrillas; Canada faces secession. R. E. Spencer. il Nation 198:283-6 Mr 23 '64
Quebec lieutenant. Newsweek 63:45 F 3 '64
Quebec revolution. A. Harrigan. il Cath World 199:109-15 My '64
Quebec's quiet revolution. C. de Mestral. Christian Cent 81:1268-70 O 14 '64
Search for unity. il Time 84:48 S 18 '64
Sixty day blues. il Time 81:20 Je 28 '63
Time out for a troubled neighbor. L. L. L. Golden. il Sat R 47:28-9 Jl 4 '64
Violence is inevitable; Quebec terrorists. Newsweek 64:46 S 14 '64
When friends fall out. il Time 81:32 F 8 '63
With a confident air. Time 81:39 My 10 '63
Year-end report. Newsweek 63:44 My 4 '64
See also
Elections—Canada
Federal and provincial relations (Canada)
French Canadians
Political parties—Canada

Popular culture

Canadiana: one man's view. M. Richler. Holiday 35:41+ Ap '64

Religious institutions and affairs

Canadian judge bars atheists. Christian Cent 81:1260 O 14 '64
News of the Christian world (cont) Christian Cent 80:284-6, 1448, 1479-80; 81:89, 942-3, 1374-6 F 27, N 20-27 '63, Ja 15, Jl 22, N 4 '64
See also
Catholic church in Canada
Presbyterian church in Canada
United church of Canada

Royal Canadian mounted police

Crime problem in Canada; how the mounties handle it; interview, ed. by K. M. Chrysler. C. W. Harvison. il U S News 55:66-8 Jl 29 '63
Modern mounties. il Time 82:44 N 8 '63
Rescue! E. R. Thornton. il Field & S 67:34-6+ Mr '63

Social life and customs

Scotch in Canada; excerpts from Scotch. J. K. Galbraith. il Harper 228:35-40 Je; 229:79-84 Jl; 77-80 Ag '64

Transport, Department of

Toll booth in the sky. il Bsns W p 138 F 16 '63

Treaties

Exchange of notes on Columbia River treaty and downstream power benefits, January 22, 1964; with Annex and attachment relating to terms of sale. P. Martin; D. Rusk. Dept State Bul 50:201-6 F 10 '64
U.S. and Canada hold Columbia River treaty ceremonies; remarks, with exchange of notes, executive order, and Canadian entitlement purchase agreement. L. B. Johnson; L. B. Pearson. Dept State Bul 51:504-16 O 12 '64
U.S. and Canada to tame a river. il U S News 55:44 D 30 '63

CANADA and the United States
Canada under Old Glory. D. Cort. il Nation 199:51-3 Ag 10 '64
Canadians answer a question; with discussion. C. Emmet. America 108:563-6 Ap 20 '63
Do they really hate in Canada? J. At-
water. il Sat Eve I 236:15-21 Ap 6 '63
United States, Canad and leadership in
international cooperat address, July 25,
1964. W. A. Harriman ept State Bul 51:
237-41 Ag 17 '64
What is Canada? J. Co Atlan 214:100-
5 N '64
CANADA cup matches. See -Tournaments
CANADA geese. See Geese.
CANADA trade fair, Philad See Ex-
hibitions
CANADA trust company. See T mpanies
CANADA-United States ministe mmittee
on joint defense
U.S.-Canada committee reviews nt de-
fense problems. Dept State 1:45-6
Jl 13 '64
CANADAIR, limited
Canadair completes CL-84 VTO rn.
D. E. Fink. il Aviation W 79:70 25
'63
CANADAY, John
Albrecht Dürer. Horizon 6:16-31 Su
Back to the nude. Horizon 5:90-6 S '6
Bizzarre denizens of Lautrec's world. Times Mag p 14-15+ F 2 '64
Critic surveys the party line in art. Times Mag p 18-19+ Ja 5 '64
Familiar truths in clear and beautiful la uage. Horizon 6:88-105 Autumn '64
Manet. Horizon 6:84-105 Wint '64
Mantegna of Mantua. bibliog f Horizon 6:7 89 Spr '64
Parent and child. N Y Times Mag p61+ Ja 17 '65
Picasso. Horizon 7:65-79 Wint '65
Pop art sells on and on, why? N Y Times Mag p7+ My 31 '64
Spanish castle on Fifth avenue. N Y Times Mag p 106-7 N 22 '64

about

Canaday affair. New Yorker 39:20-2 Ja 4 '64
CANADIAN ARCTIC REGIONS. See Arctic Regions
CANADIAN art. See Art, Canadian
CANADIAN artificial satellites. See Artificial satellites, Canadian
CANADIAN authors. See Authors, Canadian
CANADIAN battalions. See Canada—Army
CANADIAN booksellers association
Canadian booksellers association holds its twelfth annual convention. I. Kropotkin. il Pub W 183:39-42 Je 3 '63
Canadian booksellers meeting dealt constructively with trade problems. I. Kropotkin. il Pub W 185:28-31 Je 1 '64
CANADIAN breweries limited
Automatic beer; continuous-flow brewing. il Time 84:98 S 4 '64
CANADIAN broadcasting corporation
Television & Canadian culture; adaptation of address. N. Compton. Commentary 38:75-9 N '64
CANADIAN center for the performing arts. See Ottawa—Canadian center for the performing arts
CANADIAN coins. See Coins
CANADIAN composers. See Composers, Canadian
CANADIAN dancing. See Dancing, Canadian
CANADIAN dental association
Toronto versus Ottawa; statement of the Council on research, concerning antifluoridation article in Saturday review. Sat R 47:48-9 My 2 '64
CANADIAN Eskimos. See Eskimos
CANADIAN guides. See Guides
CANADIAN Indians. See Indians of North America—Canada
CANADIAN labor congress
Canada's labor umpire faces first rhubarb. Bsns W p 100+ O 24 '64
CANADIAN library association
Service, standards, and surveys; Canadian library association meets in Winnipeg. J. F. Burness. Library J 88:2844-6 Ag '63
Shall we have another? nineteenth annual conference. D. W. Halliwell. il Library J 89:2957-60 Ag '64
CANADIAN literature
Northern muse. R. Davies. Holiday 35:10+ Ap '64
Reporter at large; an American's notes on Canadian culture. E. Wilson. il New Yorker 40:63-6+ N 14 '64
See also
Authors, Canadian

Bibliography

Fifty Canadian books. Holiday 35:20-1 Ap '64

PROVINCES. See
CANADIAN MARITIManada
Maritime Provinceice. See Canada—Royal
CANADIAN mounted police
Canadian mountresearch council. See
CANADIAN nationcouncil of Canada
National researWEST. See Northwest,
CANADIAN NOR
mpany
Canadian
CANADIAN oper. Ubriaco. Opera N 29:33
Toronto quintC railway
D 19 '64 a railroad. il Time 84:92+
CANADIAN P
One way t research institute
Jl 10 '64 on war. J. Robbins and J.
CANADIANRedbook 123:54-5+ My '64
One mantry
Robbinnicle. P. Webb. Poetry 104:385-
CANADIA
Canadi large; an American's notes on
92 Sculture. E. Wilson. New Yorker
Repor 14 '64
Careindeer. See Caribou
40
S
CANreally hate us in Canada? J. At-
CAl il Sat Eve Post 236:15-21 Ap 6 '63
Ethnics or New Canadians. il News-
'63:48 Je 22 '64
wn Canadians. I. Mothner. il Look 27:
+ Ap 9 '63
e also
h Canadians
Scotians

Caricatures and cartoons

e people to the north. Holiday 35:76-83
Ap '64

NADIENS (hockey team) See Hockey teams

NAL, Antonio
Antonio Canale. C. B. Johnson. il Sch Arts 64:52 S '64
Canaletto in Canada. B. E. Smith. il Art N 63:26-9+ N '64
From Venice with love. il por Time 84:88-90 O 16 '64
Sun, air, sea. il Newsweek 64:94 N 9 '64

CANAL, Giovanni Antonio. See Canal, A.

CANAL ZONE. See Panama Canal Zone

CANALES, Paul del Rio
Red pimpernel? por Newsweek 62:32-3 S 30 '63

CANALETTO. See Canal, A.

CANALS
Canal route problems; second canal connecting the Atlantic and Pacific Oceans. B. Tufty. Sci N L 85:75 F 1 '64
Good case for a new canal. Life 56:4 Mr 6 '64
Will a new Big ditch be built? alternate sea-level waterway through Central American isthmus. il Bsns W p45-7 F 15 '64
See also
Panama Canal

Canada

See also
Rideau Canal
Welland Ship Canal

Central America

President approves bill for study of sea-level canal site; statement, September 24, 1964. L. B. Johnson. Dept State Bul 51:554 O 19 '64

Netherlands

Cruising Amsterdam's canals. il Sunset 130: 56+ Ap '63

United States

See also
Florida Ship Canal project

Washington (state)

Fact or pipe dream? a Puget Sound to Columbia River Canal. il Motor B 111:33+ My '63

CANAN, James W.
Second chance for ninety men in Norfolk. Reporter 31:34-6 Jl 16 '64

CANAPÉS
Fast and fancy canapés. il Am Home 67:56-7+ D '64

CANAVAN, Francis P.
Books to be noted: world scene. America 108:675-6+ My 11 '63
Cigarettes and brimstone. America 110:154 F 1 '64
Conscience and pluralism. America 110:536-9 Ap 18 '64
Disenchantment of General de Gaulle. America 111:123 Ag 8 '64
Freedom to die. America 110:33 Ja 11 '64
Gentle thoughts on murder. America 110:503 Ap 11 '64
New education bill. America 112:108-9+ Ja 23 '65
New pluralism or old monism. America 109: 556-8+, 734 N 9, D 7 '63
Opening the religious press. America 108: 336-7 Mr 9 '63
Peace on earth. America 108:876 Je 22 '63
Politics of religious equality. America 108: 664-7 My 11 '63
School: whose is it? America 111:153-6, 300-1 Ag 15, S 19 '64
Schools under fire. America 110:444 Mr 28 '64
Washington front. America 108:703 My 18 '63
Whose constitution is it? America 110:867-8 Je 27 '64

CANAVERAL, CAPE. See Kennedy, Cape

CANAVERAL, PORT. See Port Canaveral, Fla.

CANAVERAL press
Canaveral now publisher of Burroughs hardbounds. Pub W 184:26 D 16 '63

CANBERRA (ship) See Ocean liners

CANBY, Edward Tatnall
Taping FM stereo. Hi Fi 13:45-7+ Ag '63

CANBY, Henry Seidel
SRL's first editorial; excerpts. Sat R 47:61-2 Ag 29 '64

about

Dr Canby and his team. M. Cowley. il por Sat R 47:54-5+ Ag 29 '64

CANBY, Minn.
Instant police via citizens-band radio. C. E. Kittelson. il Am City 78:147 D '63

CANCER
Cancer; address, August 31,1964. W. G. Scott. Vital Speeches 30:762-6 O 1 '64
Cancer taught me to be brave. il Good H 158:12+ Mr '64
Cancer that cures itself. Sci Digest 55:85 F '64
Cancer: the outlook is mixed. il Sci Digest 54:51 N '63
Cervical cancer, detectable, curable, yet commonly fatal. Consumer Rep 29:450-1 S '64
Courage vs. cancer; case of N. Wynn. J. Hopkins. Good H 156:36+ Ap '63
Danger of lung cancer in asbestos workers; also of asbestosis. Sci N L 86:276 O 31 '64
Enchanted child. S. G. Goodrich. Ladies Home J 80:58 O '63
Facts about breast cancer. J. D. Ratcliff. Read Digest 82:68-71 Mr '63
How much should a cancer victim know? il Sci Digest 54:49-50 N '63
How not to die of cancer; case of W. Powell. il Time 81:54 My 10 '63
Medicines of tomorrow; excerpts from Science book of modern medicines. D. G. Cooley. il Todays Health 41:38-42 N '63
My life with cancer. O. S. Davis. Ladies Home J 81:68-9+ O '64
Physicians and patients neglect ovarian cancer. Sci N L 85:277 My 2 '64
Prostate cancer: needless killer. J. D. Ratcliff. Read Digest 83:147-50 S '63
Reassuring facts about the breast cancer controversy. S. Frank. Good H 158:96-7+ My '64
Skin tumorigenesis by 7,12-dimethylbenz(a) anthracene: inhibition by actinomycin D. H. V. Gelboin and M. Klein. bibliog il Science 145:1321-2 S 18 '64
Symptoms that can cause false cancer fears. Good H 158:159-60 F '64
Valley of compassion; Valley aid for cancer program in San Fernando Valley. D. Gregory. il Look 27:116-18+ O 22 '63
Waiting for the smoke signal; report from U.S. government. il Bsns W p 150-2+ S 7 '63
William Gargan's finest role: esophageal speech. C. B. Wall. Read Digest 83:49-54 S '63
See also
Cancer research
Sarcoma
United States—President's commission on heart disease, cancer and stroke

Causes

. . . And slow death. Read Digest 82:49-53 F '63
Athletes in smoke switch; series ads by the American cancer society. il Sr Schol 83: 19 N 22 '63
Cancer education. Sr Schol 82:3T+ My 1 '63
Cancer from plastics? Sci N L 87:55 Ja 23 '65
Cell division and cancer; report of international symposium on the control of cell division and the induction of cancer. C. C. Congdon. Science 142:252-3+ O 11 '63

CANCER—Causes—*Continued*
Cigarette controversy: a storm is brewing. L. M. Miller and J. Monahan. il Read Digest 83:91-9 Ag '63
Cigarettes and cancer. C. A. Betts. Sci N L 87:54 Ja 23 '65
Fumes from street tars seen as cancer threat. Sci N L 86:162 S 12 '64
Hormone excretion patterns in breast and prostate cancer are abnormal. E. Stern and others. bibliog il Science 145:716-19 Ag 14 '64
Lung cancer, arsenic linked in British study. Sci N L 84:89 Ag 10 '63
Mines cause lung cancer. Sci N L 84:150 S 7 '63
New hint to cancer cause in moclecular structure. Sci N L 85:82 F 8 '64
Old virus infection may trigger lung cancer. Sci N L 85:211 Ap 4 '64
Reporter at large. T. Whiteside. il New Yorker 39:67-8+ N 30 '63
Skin cancer and sunlight; report on conference. H. F. Blum. Science 145:1339-40 S 18 '64
Smoking and lung cancer. R. Brecher and E. Brecher. il Consumer Rep 28:265-80 Je '63
Smoking causes cancer; excerpts from report. F. Marley. Sci N L 85:51-2 Ja 25 '64
Smoking, health, and a giant industry. il U S News 55:84-6 D 2 '63
To smoke or not to smoke; questions and answers; Tobacco institute replies. Sci N L 83:263+ Ap 27 '63
Tumor-promoting activity of extracts of unburned tobacco. F. G. Bock and others. bibliog il Science 145:831-3 Ag 21 '64
U.S. sums it up: quit smoking; Surgeon General's report. il Bsns W p42-4+ Ja 18 '64

Diagnosis

Cancer detected by X-ray examination. Sci N L 83:232 Ap 13 '63
Color movies find hidden cancers. G. J. Jaffe. il Sat Eve Post 236:72+ Je 29 '63
Lung cancer diagnosed when X-rays are normal. Sci N L 83:312 My 18 '63
Lung cancer diagnosis. Sci N L 86:405 D 26 '64
Making cancer glow. il Time 84:50 Ag 7 '64
New test for early detection of breast cancer. Good H 156:159-61 My '63
New throat cancer test. Sci N L 86:270 O 24 '64
Painless new way to detect breast cancer. R. Lescher. Ladies Home J 80:13+ Ap '63
Pap by mail. il Newsweek 61:59 F 4 '63
Teach cancer detection to family dentists. Todays Health 41:68 O '63
Ultraviolet absorption in epidermoid cancer cells. L. A. Kamentsky and others. bibliog il Science 142:1580-3 D 20 '63

Prevention and control

Breast cancer control. il Sci N L 83:277 My 4 '63
Cancer stalemate. Newsweek 64:66 S 28 '64
Cancer tissue immunity seen for patients. Sci N L 84:8 Jl 6 '63
Tips for your home and family; cancer can be cured. Todays Health 41:69-70 Ap '63
See also
American cancer society

Statistics

Breast cancer survivors. Sci N L 83:370 Je 15 '63
Cancer deaths reported equal to cancer cures. Sci N L 86:296 N 7 '64
Cancer survival higher. Sci N L 86:214 O 3 '64
Latest statistics released by the American cancer society. Time 84:76 N 6 '64
Lung cancer patient survives seven years. Sci N L 84: 344 N 30 '63
1963 cancer prediction. Sci N L 83:286 My 4 '63
Shattering the myth. Time 82:44 Ag 23 '63
Statistics of survival. Time 81:78 Ap 19 '63
Surgery helps survival of aged cancer patients. Sci N L 84:277 N 2 '63

Therapy

After breast cancer; learning to live again. S. Robinson. McCalls 91:32+ Ap '64
Another whisper, another wait. il Time 81: 66+ My 31 '63
Cancer surgery advised soon after X-ray; Lung cancer survival improves with treatment. Sci N L 87:54 Ja 23 '65
Cancer therapy: a possible new approach. A. Szent-Gyorgyi and others. bibliog Science 140:1391-2 Je 28 '63; Reply. M. B. Yatvin. 142:339+ O 18 '63
Cancer treatment helped by oxygen pressure. Sci N L 84:360 D 7 '63
Cancerous spongy bones recalcify with fluoride. Sci N L 87:57 Ja 23 '65
Drug-treated cancer victims bear children. Sci N L 84:345 N 30 '63
Fight fire with fire in treatment of cancer; female hormones. Sci Digest 53:76 Ap '63
Growth-inhibiting agents from mercenaria extracts: chemical and biological properties. M. R. Schmeer. bibliog il Science 144:413-14 Ap 24 '64
Heat destroys cancer. F. Marley. Sci N L 86:18 Jl 11 '64
New hope for conquering childhood cancer. M. Markham. Parents Mag 39:62-3+ N '64
New problems for surgery; excerpts from address, December 30, 1963. F. D. Moore. Science 144:388-92 Ap 24 '64
Outlook for cancer. Sci N L 86:2 Jl 4 '64
Will chemicals cure cancer? excerpt from Savage cell. P. McGrady and M. Morgan. il Sat Eve Post 237:68-70 My 16 '64
See also
Krebiozen
Laetrile

Vaccines

Cancer vaccine in near future foreseen. Sci N L 84:397 D 21 '63
Cancer vaccine possible. Sci N L 86:382 D 12 '64
Closing in on a cancer vaccine. il Bsns W p72+ F 22 '64
Preparation of retine from human urine. A. Hegyeli and others. il Science 142:1571-2 D 20 '63

CANCER in animals
Domestic animal cancer rate highest in cows. Sci N L 83:121 F 23 '63

CANCER in fishes
Polymer similar to polydeoxyadenylate-thymidylate in various tissues of a marine crab. T. Y. Cheng and N. Sueoka. bibliog il Science 143:1442-3 Mr 27 '64

CANCER producing substances
Benzo(a)pyrene and other polynuclear hydrocarbons in charcoal-broiled meat. W. Lijinsky and P. Shubik. bibliog il Science 145:53-5 Jl 3 '64
Effects of polycyclic aromatic carcinogens on viral replication: similarity to actinomycin D. E. De Maeyer and J. De Maeyer-Guignard. bibliog il Science 146:650-1 O 30 '64
Growth inhibition of sarcoma and carcinoma cells of homozygous origin. K. E. Hellström. bibliog Science 143:477-8 Ja 31 '64
Mutagenic and carcinogenic agents; annual symposium; Biology division of the Oak Ridge national laboratory. R. Dulbecco. Science 145:300 Jl 17 '64

CANCER research
Atomic drill may prove aid in cancer research. il Todays Health 42:20 N '64
Battle against cancer; is a breakthrough near? W. Goodman. Ladies Home J 81:37-9+ Ag '64
Bright future foreseen. A. Ewing. Sci N L 85:23 Ja 11 '64
Cancer, a new look at what's happening. S. S. Steinberg. Suc Farm 61:92+ Ap '63
Cancer, heredity linked. Sci N L 86:19 Jl 11 '64
Cancer immunizing is aim. Sci N L 86:215 O 3 '64
Cancer-inducing DNA; excerpt from report. H. Curtis. Sat R 46:52 F 2 '63
Cancer is yielding up its secrets; excerpt from Savage cell. P. McGrady and M. Morgan. il Sat Eve Post 237:19-23 My 9 '64
Cancer; relation of prenatal radiation to development of the disease in childhood. E. J. Sternglass. bibliog il Science 140:1102-4 Je 7 '63; Discussion. 141:1109+; 142:448; 143: 994-5 S 13, O 25 '63, Mr 6 '64
Cancer therapy: a possible new approach. A. Szent-Gyorgyi and others. bibliog Science 140:1391-2 Je 28 '63; Reply. M. B. Yatvin. 142:339+ O 18 '63
Cancer, thyroid link. F. Marley. Sci N L 86: 243 O 17 '64
Cancer vaccine possible. Sci N L 86:382 D 12 '64
Chromosome number and morphology of a human preinvasive neoplasm. R. M. Richart and P. A. Corfman. bibliog il Science 144: 65-7 Ap 3 '64
Cigarette controversy: a storm is brewing. L. M. Miller and J. Monahan. il Read Digest 83:91-9 Ag '63
Closing in on a cancer vaccine. il Bsns W p72+ F 22 '64

CANCER research—*Continued*
Communiqué on cancer. il Newsweek 63:80 Ap 6 '64
Cytology; tenth annual meeting of the American society of cytology. C. A. Hellwig. Science 140:1106+ Je 7 '63
Defective cancer virus; Rous sarcoma virus. H. Rubin. il Sci Am 210:46-52 Je '64
Double life of the Drs Ambrus; with photographs. Sci Digest 54:48-55 D '63
Experimental ethics. il Newsweek 63:48 F 3 '64
From fowl to woman? Time 83:79 Ap 3 '64
Genetic disparity and cancer induction by normal tissue implants in amphibia. L. N. Ruben and M. Balls. bibliog Science 146:1321-2 D 4 '64
Growth-inhibiting agents from mercenaria extracts: chemical and biological properties. M. R. Schmeer. bibliog il Science 144:413-14 Ap 24 '64
Human experimentation: cancer studies at Sloan-Kettering stir public debate on medical ethics. E. Langer. Science 143:551-3 F 7 '64; Discussion. 144:486; bibliog 145:768 My 1, Ag 21 '64
Hydroxyurea: inhibitory effect on DNA metabolism. C. W. Young and S. Hodas. bibliog il Science 146:1172-4 N 27 '64
Nobelist offers hope. Sci N L 86:214 O 3 '64
Nobelist's cancer theory; balance between promine and retine. W. Wingo. Sci N L 84:19 Jl 13 '63
Promote & retard. il Time 82:43 Ag 2 '63
Sabin to do cancer study. Sci N L 83:274 My 4 '63
Smoking as cancer risk. Sci N L 83:91 F 9 '63
Strategy for life; proposed international Cancer research institute. A. Boyle. America 110:133 Ja 25 '64
Temperature-dependent histotypic changes in Walker carcinosarcoma in the chorioallantois. J. Leighton and others. il Science 141:1181-2 S 20 '63
Thalidomide cancer cure? Sci N L 83:71 F 2 '63
Transformation of cells in vitro by viruses. R. Dulbecco. bibliog Science 142:932-6 N 15 '63
Tumor cells return to normal functioning. Sci N L 83:313 My 18 '63
Virus clue to cancer. Sci N L 86:163 S 12 '64
Will chemicals cure cancer? excerpt from Savage cell. P. McGrady and M. Morgan. il Sat Eve Post 237:68-70 My 16 '64
See also
United States—National cancer institute

CANCER tests. See Cancer—Diagnosis

CANCER virus
Adenovirus-like particles from cancers induced by adenovirus-12 but free of infectious virus. K. O. Smith and J. L. Melnick. bibliog il Science 145:1190-2 S 11 '64
Cancer-inducing DNA; excerpt from report. H. Curtis. Sat R 46:52 F 2 '63
Cancer is yielding up its secrets; excerpt from Savage cell. P. McGrady and M. Morgan. il Sat Eve Post 237:19-23 My 9 '64
Closing in on a cancer vaccine. il Bsns W p72+ F 22 '64
Crystallization of SE polyoma virus. W. T. Murakami. bibliog il Science 142:56-8 O 4 '63
Death comes to a cancer virus. L. Engel. il N Y Times Mag p25+ N 8 '64
Defective cancer virus; Rous sarcoma virus. H. Rubin. il Sci Am 210:46-52 Je '64
Defective virus; Rous sarcoma virus. Sci Am 208:74+ Je '63
Epidermal papillomas with virus-like particles in flathead sole, hippoglossoides elassodon. S. R. Wellings and R. G. Chuinard. bibliog il Science 146:932-4 N 13 '64
Near disaster with the Salk vaccine; tumor-producing simian virus content. A. J. Snider. Sci Digest 54:40-1 D '63
New papovavirus contaminating Shope papillomata. J. W. Hartley and W. P. Rowe. bibliog il Science 143:258-60 Ja 17 '64
Niles cluster. il Newsweek 61:88-9 Ap 22 '63
Oncogenic effect of human adenovirus type 12, in mice. Y. Yabe and others. bibliog il Science 143:46-7 Ja 3 '64
Polyoma virus genetic material in a virus-free polyoma-induced tumor. D. Axelrod and others. bibliog il Science 146:1466-9 D 11 '64
Polyoma virus: production in bacillus subtilis. K. E. Bayreuther and W. R. Romig. bibliog il Science 146:778-9 N 6 '64
Reovirus and wound-tumor virus; serological cross reactivity. G. Streissle and K. Maramorosch. bibliog Science 140:996-7 My 31 '63
Simian virus 40: isolation of two plaque types. J. L. Riggs and E. H. Lennette. bibliog il Science 147:408-9 Ja 22 '65
Transformation of cells in vitro by viruses. R. Dulbecco. bibliog Science 142:932-6 N 15 '63
Tumors induced in hamsters by simian virus 40; persistent subviral infection. P. Gerber. bibliog il Science 140:889-90 My 24 '63
Virogenic hamster tumor cells: induction of virus synthesis. P. Gerber. bibliog il Science 145:833 Ag 21 '64
Virus-causing tumor. Sci N L 84:261 O 26 '63
Virus is cancer cause. Sci N L 83:190 Mr 23 '63
Viruses blamed for cancer. il Bsns W p 142+ Ap 25 '64
Viruses, cancer link. Sci N L 83:274 My 4 '63

CANCIO, Marta. See Toro-Goyco, E. jt. auth.

CANDAU, M. G.
World health day 1963; message, April 7, 1963. U N Rev 10:15 Ap '63

CANDELA, Félix
Prisoner of geometry. il Time 81:60 Je 28 '63

CANDELABRA. See Candlesticks

CANDID photography. See Photography

CANDIDA albicans. See Fungi, Pathogenic

CANDIDA by Bernard Shaw; story. See Cozzens, J. G.

CANDIDA; drama. See Shaw, G. B.

CANDIDATES, Political
Astronaut's progress; countdown in Ohio. R. L. Maher. il Nation 198:131-3 F 10 '64
Burdened by Barry; Republican congressional candidates. Time 84:26-7 O 9 '64
California; Arkansas; Texas; Illinois. il Time 84:34-9 O 16 '64
Can a Kennedy beat the Republican in New York? il U S News 57:31-2 Ag 31 '64
Congress race: running hard to stand still. il Bsns W p53-4+ O 10 '64
Everybody's doing it. il Newsweek 64:36+ N 2 '64
Florida red-head. Nation 198:520 My 25 '64
Focus on Nov. 3. Nat R 16:12, 53, 96, 140, 220 Ja 14-F 25, Mr 24 '64
Foretaste; the kind of criminal assault against conservatives. Nat R 15:141 Ag 27 '63
Glenn in orbit. Nation 198:111 F 3 '64
Heebie-jeebies; New York senatorial candidates. il Newsweek 64:30+ Ag 17 '64
Hello, Happy Chandler! J. Sellers. Nat R 14:399 My 21 '63
Into Senate race: astronaut Glenn. il U S News 56:15 Ja 27 '64
Key Republican candidates. Sat Eve Post 237:86 O 24 '64
Major congressional contests. il Sr Schol 85:19 S 23 '64
Newsman v. newsman; candidates for Congress from Westchester. il Time 83:79 Mr 20 '64
On being a candidate. H. S. Hughes. Commentary 35:123-31 F '63
On rewarding friends. Nation 198:177 F 24 '64
One man, one vote, two offices. Nation 197:337-8 N 23 '63
Political parties need more than your money. M. Smith. il Nations Bsns 51:21-2 S '63
Politics: the rich man's game. I. Sclanders. Nation 198:215-16 Mr 2 '64
Races for governor. Time 84:26-7 O 23 '64
Rough ride for a hero; senatorial contest in Ohio. S. Alsop. il Sat Eve Post 237:14 Mr 14 '64
Salinger swings for Senate, there's bedlam in California. R. Ajemian. il Life 56:43 Ap 3 '64
Senate races. Time 84:36-7 O 16 '64
Senate races, 1964 election. W. V. Shannon. Commonweal 81:85-6 O 16 '64
Some familiar names on the '64 ballots. il U S News 56:22 My 25 '64
Speaking out; we want our politicians to be hypocrites. W. F. Buckley, jr. Sat Eve Post 237:8+ O 17 '64
Taft, Homney, Percy; a trio of G.O.P. stars fighting hard not to be buried with Barry. R. Ajemian. il Life 57:32-7 O 30 '64
Tight Senate race; the uncertain length of LBJ's coattails. P. R. Wieck. New Repub 151:7-8 O 24 '64
Tired of being sick and tired. J. DeMuth. Nation 198:548-51 Je 1 '64
Veep, veep; question of running mate for Lyndon Johnson. Time 82:12 D 20 '63
Where Democrats are rocking the boat. pors U S News 56:44 Ap 6 '64
Why I won; why I lost; candidates' own analysis. U S News 57:129-30+ N 16 '64; Correction. 57:16 N 23 '64

CANDIDATES, Political—*Continued*
Will Republicans gain some governors? il U S News 57:10 N 2 '64
See also
Political campaigns
Presidential candidates
Presidential candidates—1964
Vice-Presidential candidates
Vice-Presidents—United States

Anecdotes, facetiae, satire, etc.

Non-partisan, transistorized candidate. I. Shapiro. New Repub 150:11-12 Mr 28 '64
CANDIED fruit. See Confectionery
CANDLE holders. See Candlesticks
CANDLE stands. See Candlesticks
CANDLER, Julie
Traveling safely with children. Redbook 121: 40-1 Jl '63
CANDLES
Candlelight for Christmas. il Redbook 122: 72-3+ D '63
Creativity to burn. il Design 66:25-6 N '64
For real outdoor glamour candles by the score. il House B 105:108-9 Ag '63
Handsome gift candles. W. Waltner and E. Waltner. il Pop Mech 120:145-7 D '63
How to make a bottle candle. il Sunset 130: 182 My '63
How to make scented candles. il Sunset 133: 96 D '64
Painted with melted crayons; lovely candle is wax-on-wax decorated. il Design 65:65 N '63
There is nothing prettier than candlelight. il Am Home 67:52-3+ N '64
What's better at Christmas than red and green and candlelight? R. Martens and R. Miller. il Farm J 88:64-5 D '64
CANDLESTICKS
Benjamin Gerrish, brazier. R. H. Randall, jr. il Antiques 85:320-1 Mr '64
Double-spiral candlestick. E. R. Haan. il Pop Mech 119:140-1+ My '63
Festive flattery for candles. il House & Gard 123:28-9 F '63
Making Christmas candle holders. il Sunset 131:83 D '63
There is nothing prettier than candlelight. il Am Home 67:52-3+ N '64
CANDY
Bright burst of candy making; Christmas candy, with recipes. il Seventeen 23:110-11+ D '64
Candies. il Good H 157:70-1+ D '63
Candy & cookie cookbook. il Parents Mag 38:83+ N '63
Christmas candies. il Bet Hom & Gard 41: 73-4 D '63
Christmas is for giving; sweet-tooth gifts; with recipes. il Suc Farm 62:52+ D '64
Here are ideas for all the candy makers; with recipes. il Sunset 133:118+ D '64
Make our cover Santa lollipop. Good H 157: 8 D '63
Say it with sweets. il McCalls 92:138-9+ D '64
Sugarplum season. C. Claiborne. il N Y Times Mag p 108+ D 1 '63
Sweet challenge of candymaking; with recipes. G. Maddox. il Todays Health 41: 46-51 N '63
What a boot. il Am Home 66:44-5+ D '63
Wrap up Christmas: the easiest Christmas candy. il Seventeen 22:110-11 D '63
See also
Confectionery
CANDY aspirin. See Aspirin
CANDY industry and trade
Dash of poly sorbate-60 & zein; reprint. O. Powers. Consumer Bul 46:14 My '63
Only the box stays the same; Whitman Sampler. il Bsns W p 130-2+ Je 20 '64
This chocolate isle; British candymakers. il Time 81:85 Ap 26 '63
CANE, Melville
Bees, after rain; poem. McCalls 91:229 O '63
CANE furniture. See Furniture
CANEL, Eli B.
El As is the voice of America; broadcasts world series in Spanish. R. H. Boyle. il por Sports Illus 19:33-4+ O 14 '63
CANHAM, Erwin D.
Hard way to the middle course. Sat R 46: 42-3 N 9 '63
CANINO, Leda
World opens. por Dance Mag 38:46-7 O '64
CANNAN, R. Keith
Atomic bomb casualty commission: the first fifteen years. Bul Atomic Sci 19:45-8 O '63
CANNAS
Dwarf cannas. L. K. Powell. il Pop Gard 14:44 Ap '63
Pfitzer's cannas are dwarfs. il Sunset 133: 163 Ag '64
CANNAVO, Anthony J.
Mercury city, U.S.A. Am City 78:121 Mr '63
CANNED food
Adventures in home cooking. S. Spitzer. il Holiday 34:99-104 S '63
Homemakers confident of canned food safety. Sci N L 83:347 Je 1 '63
How long may canned goods be stored? Consumer Bul 46:14 Mr '63
Instant cook. L. Stilwill. il Ladies Home J 80:161-2 O '63
Nationwide search for four million cans. il Life 54:43-4+ Ap 26 '63
Tuna back in favor. Time 82:92+ N 29 '63
Tuna fish; the favorite canned seafood. il Consumer Rep 29:82-4 F '64
Tuna scare. il Time 81:79 Ap 26 '63
Tuning up tuna. Newsweek 62:60-1 Ag 5 '63
See also
Fruit, Canned
Libby-McNeill and Libby
CANNED fruit. See Fruit, Canned
CANNES, France
Well traveled camera. il Mod Phot 28:36+ My '64
CANNES international film festival
Cannes: cinema and semantics. H. Alpert. il Sat R 47:20-1 Je 6 '64
Eyestrain at Cannes. R. Steel. Commonweal 80:361-4 Je 12 '64
CANNIBALISM
Atrocities seen as rites. B. Tufty. Sci N L 86:371 D 12 '64
Plea to the Fijians. N. Cousins. il Sat R 47:14-15 Jl 25 '64
CANNING, Charles John Canning, earl
Our man in London. New Yorker 40:48-51 N 28 '64
CANNING, Victor
Margin of peril; story. Ladies Home J 80: 64-5 My '63
CANNING and preserving
Prepare now, enjoy later. J. Hewitt. il N Y Times Mag p41 Jl 26 '64
Sweet taste of summer. H. S. Witty. il Flower Grower 51:38 O '64
See also
Food preservation and preservatives
Fruit—Preservation
CANNON, Carl
Tour. New Yorker 40:27-30 Je 13 '64
CANNON, Charles E.
Largest sewer photo inspection. Am City 80: 98-9 Ja '65
CANNON, Clarence
Above inhibition. por Time 81:28-9 My 17 '63
Cannon to Mahon. Cato. Nat R 16:439 Je 2 '64
Exit Clarence Cannon. por Newsweek 63: 31-2 My 25 '64
Guardian. por Time 83:22 My 22 '64
CANNON, Gaine
Blue Ridge Samaritan. S. Castan. il pors Look 27:82-4+ Ag 27 '63
CANNON, Grace B.
Culture of insect salivary glands in a chemically defined medium. bibliog Science 146: 1063 N 20 '64
CANNON, Gus
I'm a yard man. por Time 81:46+ Ap 5 '63
CANNON, Helen L.
Geology and trace elements: relation to nutrition. Science 143:704+ F 14 '64
CANNON, Howard W.
Speaking out. por Sat Eve Post 236:10+ Je 15 '63
CANNON, P. and Conlin, E. T.
Magnesium compounds: new dense phases. Science 145:487-9 Jl 31 '64
CANNON, Poppy
Revolution in the kitchen. Sat R 47:54-7 O 24 '64
CANNON, Ralph A.
Pornography, sex and the church. Christian Cent 80:576-9 My 1 '63
CANNON, Ralph S. jr, and others
Lead isotope variation with growth zoning in a galena crystal. bibliog Science 142:574-6 N 1 '63
CANNON, Ray
Pickup camper paradise. pors Field & S 67: 70-3+ Ap '63
CANNON. See Ordnance
CANNON, Toy. See Toys
CANOE racing
Tippy canoe, kayaks, too; West River slalom, Jamaica, Vt. il Newsweek 63:79 Je 1 '64
CANOE trips
Down the back to the Arctic. A. Hoyt. il Sports Illus 19:34-6+ Ag 26 '63

CANOE trips—*Continued*
Make your canoe a cruising camper. F. M. Paulson. il Field & S 69:86-8+ Jl '64
Not so gently down the stream. A. Higgins. il Sports Illus 18:34+ Ap 29 '63
Planning a float trip. J. A. Emmett. il Outdoor Life 131:12+ Ap '63
Waters of the Allagash. H. Clepper. il Am For 70:14-18+ N '64
CANOES and canoeing
Down the Quinault in a cedar dugout. il Sunset 130:22+ Je '63
Exaltation at the smokehole. B. Gilbert. il Sports Illus 20:76-82+ Ap 27 '64
Pole your canoe. B. Riviere. il Field & S 68:50-3+ My '63
Renew your canoe. F. M. Paulson. il Field & S 67:88-92 Mr '63
Selecting a canoe. J. A. Emmett. il Outdoor Life 133:38+ Ap '64
CANON law. See Ecclesiastical law
CANONIZATION
Pope confers sainthood on twenty-two African martyrs. E. B. Thompson. il Ebony 20:23-6+ Ja '65
Saints Mbaga and Mukasa. America 111:505 O 31 '64
See also
Beatification
CANONSBURG, Pa.
Small city enjoys big-sweeper economy. W. W. Buckley. il Am City 79:177-8 O '64
CANS. See Tin cans
CANS, Aluminum. See Aluminum cans
CANT, Gilbert
Nature. Sports Illus 21:53-5 Ag 10 '64
CANTALOUPES. See Muskmelons
CANTATAS
Argentine Atlantis. G. Knepler. Opera N 28:27 S 28 '63
See also
Phonograph records—Cantatas
CANTAVE, Leon
Final encounter; Cantave's defeat. Newsweek 62:65 O 7 '63
There'll be another Haiti revolt soon, but. . . il por U S News 55:10 Ag 19 '63
CANTERBURY, Arthur Michael Ramsey, abp of. See Ramsey, A. M.
CANTERBURY, Conn.
Canterbury tale; school for Negro girls in Connecticut, 1832-34. R. Rushmore. Reporter 28:46-7 Ap 25 '63
CANTERBURY tales; drama. See Olfson, L.
CANTERO CUADRADO, Pietro, bp
Spanish prelate dampens Protestant hopes. Christian Cent 80:734 Je 5 '63
CANTERVILLE ghost; drama. See Wilde, O.
CANTILEVER girders. See Girders
CANTLON, J. E. See Curtis, E. J. C. jt. auth.
CANTON, Ohio
Miniature Rockefeller plaza in a midwest city. il Arch Forum 120:98-101 Ja '64
CANTON, Tex.
Texas dog days. C. A. Nicholson. il Field & S 69:44-6 D '64
CANTOR, Arthur
Plight of the play producer; excerpts from address. por Cath World 200:103-8 N '64
Weep not for Broadway. Theatre Arts 47:19-20 Jl '63
CANTRIL, Hadley
Study of aspirations; with biographical sketch. Sci Am 208:32, 41-5 bibliog(p 184) F '63
CANTWELL, Mary
Paris: a designer's debut. Mlle 58:147-9+ Mr '64
CANTWELL, Robert
Columbia: a gem of a river. Sports Illus 20:56-60+ F 24 '64
Era shaped by war. Sports Illus 21:36-8+ N 30 '64
Food. Sports Illus 19:52-5 O 28 '63
Grey Owl: mysterious genius of nature lore. Sports Illus 18:112-14+ Ap 8 '63
High road to a wild paradise. Sports Illus 19:48-52+ Ag 5 '63
New way to find our lost frontier. Sports Illus 18:32-5+ My 20 '63
Silver anniversary. Sports Illus 19:64-6 N 11 '63
CANTY, Donald
Architecture and the urban emergency. Arch Forum 121:172-9 Ag '64
Fight to tame the urban freeway takes a positive new turn. Arch Forum 119:68-73 O '63
New frontier of higher education. Arch Forum 118:96-103 Mr '63
Strength or banality? Arch Forum 119:68-72 D '62
What it takes to be a client. Arch Forum 119:84-7 Jl; 92-5 S; 94-7 D '63; 120:104-7 F; 106-9 Ap '64
CANVASSING
Avon: the sweet smell of success. S. Freedgood. il Fortune 70:108-13+ D '64
Don't be gypped by mail-order firms. Consumer Bul 47:38-40 Mr '64 (to be cont)
Overseas boom in door-to-door selling. T. J. Murray. il Duns R 84:35-7+ N '64
Sales & distribution; door-to-door selling. K. Schwartz. Duns R 81:97-8 Ap '63
Salesman at the door. il Changing T 17:25-9 Ag '63
Shoes that come to your door; Charles C. Eaton co; Brockton, Mass. il Bsns W p86+ Ag 22 '64
CANYONLANDS NATIONAL PARK
Canyonlands; new national park? P. Brooks. il Atlan 211:52-7 Mr '63
Canyonlands, our newest national park. il Nat Parks Mag 38:17 N '64
Hearings held on Canyonlands National Park. Nat Parks Mag 37:14 Je '63
Let's get going in the Canyonlands. A. W. Smith. il Nat Parks Mag 37:2 F '63
CANYONS
Biological visit to McKittrick Canyon. F. R. Gehlbach. il Nat Parks Mag 37:4-7 Mr '63
Can you toss a rock across this canyon? il Sunset 131:48 S '63
Canyon of the Rogue on foot, by boat, by car; Rogue River Canyon, Ore. il Sunset 131:57+ S '63
Logan Canyon road controversy: anatomy of a principle. J. H. Berryman. il Nat Parks Mag 37:12-15 Jl '63
West Texas wonderland. W. F. Heald. il Travel 119:45-6 Mr '63
See also
Glen Canyon
CANZONERI, Robert
One lion, once; poem. Sat R 46:46 S 21 '63
CAOUETTE, Réal
Angry French Canadians. il por Sat Eve Post 236:20 Ap 6 '63
Demagogue from Quebec. il por Time 81:21 Mr 29 '63
French leave; fifth political party. Time 82:46 S 13 '63
CAP removers
Cap removers. il Consumer Rep 28:386-7 Ag '63
CAPA, Robert
Many faces of war; excerpts from Faces of war. il por N Y Times Mag p30-1 Ap 19 '64
War memorial. M. R. Weiss. il por Sat R 47:34-6 Je 6 '64
CAPACITANCE, Electric. See Electric capacitance
CAPACITORS. See Electric capacitors
CAPACITORS, Radio. See Radio capacitors
CAPACITY bridge. See Radio instruments
CAPANA dello Zio Tom; opera. See Trecate, L. F.
CAPDEVILA, Arturo
Sail away innocent; story. Américas 16:32-8 Mr '64
CAPE BRETON ISLAND
Scottish touch: Cape Breton. H. Maclennan. il Holiday 35:86-7+ Ap '64
CAPE buffalo hunting. See Buffalo hunting
CAPE buffaloes. See Buffaloes
CAPE CANAVERAL lighthouse. See Lighthouses
CAPE COD
New look of old Cape Cod. B. Thielen. il Holiday 34:30-43 S '63
Walk with Thoreau: Cape Cod revisited. W. J. Burke. il Look 27:37-41 Jl 2 '63
See also
Hyannis Port, Mass.
CAPE COD catboat. See Catboats
CAPE CORAL, Fla.
Supplemental water plant came first. R. G. Shanklin jr. and R. A. Cuevas. il Am City 79:153-5+ O '64
CAPE KENNEDY. See Kennedy, Cape
CAPE LOOKOUT NATIONAL SEASHORE (proposed) See National parks and reserves—United States
CAPE MAY, N.J.
Asphalt promenade. J. P. Sweitzer. il Am City 78:95-6 N '63
CAPE MAY CITY, N.J. See Cape May, N.J.
CAPE MAY COUNTY, N.J.
Mosquitoes, beware! foggers go to school. B. M. Lafferty. il Am City 79:100-1 S '64
CAPERS
Flavor caper. il Bet Hom & Gard 42:112-13 Mr '64
CAPET, Hugh
Death for Tahiti. Atlan 212:73-4 Jl '63

CAPILLARIES
Red blood cells: change in shape in capillaries. M. M. Guest and others. bibliog il Science 142:1319-21 D 6 '63

CAPILLARITY
See also
Surface tension

CAPITAL
Venture capital from inside the stock family; Occidental petroleum lines up investors. Bsns W p66+ Mr 23 '63
Venture capital: money in a hurry. R. Nason. il Duns R 82:34-5+ N '63
Why men take risks; excerpts from The enterprising man. Nations Bsns 52:121-2+ O '64
See also
Liquidity (economics)
Profit

CAPITAL development fund. See United Nations—Capital development fund

CAPITAL gains tax. See Income tax—Capital gains tax

CAPITAL investments
Bounce is missing; spending plans of business in 1964. il Bsns W p27 D 14 '63
Business expects big gains. il Nations Bsns 51:33-5+ D '63
Business outlay surge brings a few worries; price boosts and boom psychology. il Bsns W p25-6 Mr 14 '64
Business spending: 12 per cent more. il Bsns W p25-6 D 12 '64
Capital complications; Europeans to rely more on their own capital markets. il Fortune 69:75-6 Ap '64
Capital spending: a freshening breeze. il Newsweek 61:82-5 Mr 18 '63
Capital spending up 9 per cent now; McGraw-Hill survey. il Bsns W p25-7 F 8 '64
Capital upswing. il Fortune 69:28+ Je '64
Caution; appropriations decline. il Newsweek 63:70+ Mr 2 '64
Confirming the trend; McGraw-Hill survey. il Bsns W p28 Je 13 '64
Controlled rise. il Newsweek 63:67 Je 1 '64
Defying gravity. il Newsweek 64:63 S 7 '64
Every man his own banker. il Bsns W p24-5 F 15 '64
First finding, up 4 per cent; McGraw-Hill capital spending survey; with editorial comment. il Bsns W p25-7, 152 N 9 '63
Fresh wave of vigor; U.S. capital spending on the rise. il Bsns W p25-7 S 7 '63
Fuel for the boom. il Newsweek 64:68 D 14 '64
Guaranteed investment. Fortune 69:32+ Mr '64
How to use decision trees in capital investment. J. F. Magee. il Harvard Bsns R 42:79-96 S '64
How world's biggest profit makes jobs; General motors' $2 billion expansion. il Nations Bsns 52:40-1+ Jl '64
Importance of being on time. G. Terborgh. il Fortune 69:136-7 My '64
Industry's plans edge up. il Bsns W p32+ Je 15 '63
Investment marches on. Fortune 67:40+ Je '63
Investment: to the crest. il Fortune 70:28+ D '64
Living higher on the hog; Billions in search of a top return. il Bsns W p 166-8+ O 19 '63
Longest boom still going strong. il Bsns W p 130-2 S 19 '64
Machinery, tools lead the way. il Bsns W p39-40 Ja 11 '64
Money rates face new push. Bsns W p 142 O 26 '63
More push for plant; latest Commerce-SEC report. il Bsns W p27-8 Mr 16 '63
New profits from new plants. il Duns R 81:pt2 S92-4+ Mr '63
Paper leads the expansion parade. il Bsns W p70+ S 5 '64
Pause before the push. il Newsweek 61:77-8 Je 17 '63
Plans for spending rise again; with editorial comment. il Bsns W p72-4, 132 Ap 27 '63
Pressures for capital. il Fortune 68:50+ D '63
Prime mover begins to move. G. Burck and S. Parker. il Fortune 67:110-14+ F '63
Profits follow the boom line. il Bsns W p 134+ S 19 '64
Ready to build again; McGraw-Hill survey. il Bsns W p25-7 Ap 25 '64
Realism in corporate real estate. A. Rabinowitz. bibliog f il Harvard Bsns R 41:62-9 N '63
Risk analysis in capital investment. D. B. Hertz. bibliog f il Harvard Bsns R 42:95-106 Ja '64
Spending goes up, but not so fast. il Bsns W p38-9 N 7 '64
Strains and restraints. il Fortune 70:27-8 O '64
Surge in capital spending. il Time 83:87 Mr 6 '64
Tax credit gets to work at last. Bsns W p60+ Ja 19 '63
Taxes & spending: how investment creates jobs. il Nations Bsns 51:40-1+ Ap '63
Visibility now. il Fortune 67:39-40 Ap '63
What boosts capital spending. Bsns W p89 Jl 6 '63
Why steelmen raise the ante; capital spending boom. il Bsns W p 144+ N 16 '63

CAPITAL punishment
Bitter battle over capital punishment. J. Star. il Look 27:23-8 My 7 '63
California: death double-headers. Newsweek 61:33 Ap 22 '63
Capital punishment; ban proposed. New Repub 148:5 Je 8 '63
Counsel for the doomed. Newsweek 61:36-7 Mr 25 '63
Death penalty and fair trial. W. E. Oberer. Nation 198:342-4 Ap 6 '64
Demise of the gallows; House of commons in London votes to abolish the death penalty for murder. America 112:99 Ja 23 '65
Edging away from capital punishment. S. McBee. New Repub 152:11-12 Ja 30 '65
End to hanging; bill passed in the House of commons. il Time 85:36-7 Ja 1 '65
Entering wedge; death penalty in New York. Newsweek 61:38 My 20 '63
Is the death sentence dying? il Newsweek 61:31+ F 11 '63
Justice and the death penalty. D. R. Gordon. Christian Cent 80:955 Jl 31 '63
Last chance on death row. H. Lavine. il Sat Eve Post 236:76+ Je 29 '63
On the way out. Nation 199:367 N 23 '64
Phone call. C. C. Reid. Harper 228:164-6 Ap '64
Rope's end; Britain abolishes death penalty. il Newsweek 65:27 Ja 4 '65
Someone had a good idea; New York law. Nation 196:298 Ap 13 '63; Reply. N. Redlich. 196:inside cover Ap 27 '63
Trend against hanging. America 108:213 F 16 '63
Waiting for the firing squad. A. Ladas. il Harper 229:87-90 N '64
See also
Electrocution

CAPITAL spending. See Capital investments

CAPITALISM
Beyond imperialism. G. Lichtheim. New Repub 148:17-19 Mr 16 '63
Businessman looks at today's big issues; excerpts from address, November 5, 1964. T. O. Yntema. il U S News 57:100-4 N 30 '64
Can anyone explain capitalism? R. J. Monsen, jr. Sat R 46:13-15+ D 14 '63
Consider the horse; or, A study of U.S. capitalism. G. Schwartz. il N Y Times Mag p20+ O 4 '64
Fences against power. S. W. Rousseas. Nation 196:343-6+ Ap 27 '63
Goldwater view of economics. M. Friedman. il N Y Times Mag p35+ O 11 '64
National capitalism; address, October 15, 1964. C. T. Garland. Vital Speeches 31:109-12 D 1 '64
New trend in Russia: creeping capitalism. il U S News 57:119-20 S 28 '64
Nor capitalism, either. America 107:1266 D 22 '62; Discussion. 108:397 Mr 23 '63
Postwar advance of the five hundred million. M. Ways. il Fortune 70:104-9+ Ag '64
President Frei on U.S. capitalism; reprint. E. Frei. America 111:285 S 19 '64
Slogan for the unwary. America 109:346 S 28 '63
This problem of bigness; excerpt from Justice for all. B. L. Masse. America 111:128-30 Ag 8 '64
Viewing U.S. economy with a Marxist glass; analysis of capitalism's troubles. il Bsns W p67-8+ Ap 13 '63
See also
Business
Free enterprise
Technocracy

CAPITALISM and communism. See Communism and democracy

CAPITALISTS and financiers
Antidisestablishmentarianism. S. Alsop. Sat Eve Post 237:22 S 26 '64
Brothers Zilkha: a new world. il Bsns W p80-2+ My 9 '64
Set of mere money-getters? A. Nevins. Am Heritage 14:50-1+ Je '63
This man Ludwig. Time 82:60+ Ag 2 '63
See also
Millionaires
Rich, The

CAPITALS (cities)
State capitals go radical; photographs. A. L. Huxtable. N Y Times Mag p38-9 My 12 '63

CAPITOL (United States) See United States—Capitol

CAPITOL records, Incorporated
High quality classics at half price; paperback classics. P. Hart. Hi Fi 13:96 S '63

CAPITOLS
State capitals go radical; photographs. A. L. Huxtable. N Y Times Mag p38-9 My 12 '63

CAPLAN, Ralph
Topcoat. New Yorker 39:170-2+ O 5 '63

CAPLIN, Alfred Gerald. See Capp, A.

CAPLIN, Mortimer Maxwell
What new tax law will mean; interview. por Nations Bsns 52:38-9+ F '64
What's wrong with today's income tax; interview. pors U S News 57:66-70 Ag 17 '64; Same abr. Read Digest 85:173-4+ N '64

about

Easing expense accounts. il por Time 82:77 Jl 5 '63
Expense-account meals: what the rules really are. il U S News 54:96+ Mr 4 '63
Is taxpayers' revolt brewing? il por U S News 54:37-9 Ap 8 '63
Latest word on expense accounts. U S News 55:105 S 30 '63
Mortimer Caplin: the man who takes your money. B. Herndon. il por Sat Eve Post 236:70+ Ap 13 '63
Pulling the tax punch. il Bsns W p34 Ap 6 '63
Your friendly tax collector. il pors Life 54:69-72 Mr 1 '63

CAPONE, Alphonse
Chicago; shades of Capone. V. W. Peterson. Ann Am Acad 347:30-9 My '63

CAPONE, Carmine
Reluctant sailor: a self-portrait. por Esquire 61:100-1+ My '64

CAPONIGRO, Paul
Caponigro. J. Deschin. por Pop Phot 55:31 N '64

CAPORALE, Rock
Last council? excerpt from Vatican II. America 111:307-9 S 19 '64

CAPOTE, Truman
Two-headed calf. Vogue 143:168-71 Ap 1 '64

about

Author in search of a character. S. Kauffmann. New Repub 148:21-2+ F 23 '63
Capote collected. D. Littlejohn. Commonweal 78:187-8 My 10 '63
Fabulist. por Newsweek 64:58 D 28 '64

CAPOUYA, Emile
Cornered market on morals. Sat R 46:34 O 19 '63
Critic selects his own society. Sat R 47:25-6 Ap 4 '64
Cry against a decision of silence. Sat R 47:41-2 Mr 21 '64
Days of the dangerous virtues. Sat R 47:30+ F 8 '64
Documents of the struggle for public decency. Sat R 47:13+ Jl 25 '64
Evolution of an instinct. Sat R 47:41-2 Je 6 '64
Gift of gab on the lam. Sat R 47:36-7 Je 20 '64
Market value of a man. Sat R 47:33-4 D 19 '64
Move toward immobility. Sat R 46:36-8+ N 16 '63
On crying for the moon. Sat R 46:20 Ag 31 '63
On unperfect actors. Sat R 46:40-1 D 14 '63
Things seem as bad as they seem. Sat R 47:43 My 16 '64
Varieties of love. Nation 197:457-9 D 28 '63
What we don't know might kill us. Sat R 47:26-7 Mr 28 '64
Woman: woe to man? Sat R 47:47-8 D 12 '64

CAPP, Al
Can TV be saved? por Esquire 60:211+ D '63
Mother and her secret. Read Digest 84:45-6 My '64
What's wrong with men's clothes. Sat Eve Post 236:20-1 Je 1 '63

about

Al Capp, critic. Newsweek 61:78 Ap 1 '63
Shmoo's return; Li'l Abner comic strip. il New Yorker 39:39-40 O 26 '63

CAPPADOCIA
Rock monasteries of Cappadocia; excerpt from A time to keep silence. P. L. Fermor. il Horizon 6:66-73 Wint '64

CAPPELL, Sylvain
Mad for math. por Newsweek 61:94 Mr 18 '63

CAPRALOS, Christos
Sculptor of gods; bronzes at Martha Jackson gallery. il Time 82:90-1 D 6 '63

CAPREOMYCIN. See Antobiotics

CAPRIO, Ralph G. and Crann, Frank
Resourceful street maintenance. Am City 78:96-7 Ap '63

CAPTAIN'S boar hunt; story. See Ely, D.

CAPTAINS of ships. See Shipmasters

CAPTIVE finance companies. See Finance companies

CAPTIVE nations week
Captive nations week, 1964; proclamation. L. B. Johnson. Dept State Bul 51:63 Jl 13 '64

CAPTIVE; story. See Coates, R. M.

CAPTURE of animals. See Animals—Capture

CAPUTO, Vincent F.
Moral deterrent; address, February 1, 1963. Vital Speeches 29:381-3 Ap 1 '63
Year 2000; address, September 23, 1964. Vital Speeches 31:10-15 O 15 '64

CAR clubs. See Automobile clubs

CAR coats. See Coats

CAR shelters. See Shelters

CAR-top carriers. See Automobiles—Equipment

CARACAS, Venezuela

Police

Comic cops. il Time 82:30 S 6 '63

CARADON, Hugh Foot, baron
Ferment in Africa. Christian Cent 81:1491-3 D 2 '64

CARAMOOR festivals. See Music festivals—New York (state)

CARAVAGGIO, Michelangelo Merisi da
Our far-flung correspondents. R. M. Coates. New Yorker 39:182-4+ N 2 '63

CARAVAN, John
Primary report. Nat R 16:448 Je 2 '64

CARAVANS
Isn't this a pleasant way to tour Ireland? U-drive caravan costs $45 a week plus oats. il Sunset 130:34-6 Mr '63

CARAVANS; novel. See Michener, J. A.

CARBAMYL phosphate
Carbamyl phosphate. M. E. Jones. bibliog il Science 140:1373-9 Je 28 '63
Carbamyl phosphate synthesis in the earthworm lumbricus terrestris. S. H. Bishop and J. W. Campbell. bibliog il Science 142:1583-5 D 20 '63
Neurospora mutant lacking an arginine-specific carbamyl phosphokinase. R. H. Davis. bibliog Science 142:1652-4 D 27 '63

CARBARYL. See Insecticides

CARBINES. See Rifles

CARBOHYDRATES
Conglutination: specific inhibition by carbohydrates. M. A. Leon and R. Yokohari. bibliog il Science 143:1327-8 Mr 20 '64
Tuberculin reactivity of a carbohydrate component of unheated BCG culture filtrate. H. Baer and S. D. Chaparas. bibliog Science 146:245-7 O 9 '64

CARBON
Artificial inspiration; our dependency of three principle key elements. il Sci Digest 57:86-9 Ja '65
Biography of an atom and the universe. J. Bronowski. il N Y Times Mag p 19+ O 13 '63; Same abr. with title Amazing biography of an atom. Read Digest 84:133-6 Ja '64
Carbon: a new crystalline phase. R. B. Aust and H. G. Drickamer. bibliog il Science 140:817-19 My 17 '63

Isotopes

Carbon-14 in clinical research; report on conference. G. V. LeRoy. Science 144:731-2 My 8 '64
Carbon isotope abundance in meteoritic carbonates. R. N. Clayton. bibliog il Science 140:192-3 Ap 12 '63
Early history of carbon-14. M. D. Kamen. bibliog il Science 140:584-90 My 10 '63; Reply. E. C. Pollard. 140:1268 Je 21 '63; Rejoinder. 141:861-2 S 6 '63
Fractionation of sulfur and carbon isotopes in a meromictic lake. E. S. Deevey, jr. and others. bibliog il Science 139:407-8 F 1 '63
Isotope ratios in marine mollusk shells after prolonged contact with flowing fresh water. J. N. Weber and A. La Rocque. bibliog il Science 142:1666 D 27 '63
Natural carbon-14 activity of organic substances in streams. A. A. Rosen and M. Rubin. bibliog il Science 143:1163-4 Mr 13 '64

CARBON—Isotopes—*Continued*
Radioautographic evidence for the incorporation of leucine-carbon-14 into the mitotic apparatus. D. W. Stafford and R. M. Iverson. bibliog il Science 143:580-1 F 7 '64
Radiocarbon activity of shells from living clams and snails. M. Rubin and D. W. Taylor. bibliog il Science 141:637 Ag 16 '63
Radiocarbon dating: a case against the proposed link between river mollusks and soil humus. W. Broecker. bibliog il Science 143:596-7 F 7 '64; Reply. M. L. Keith and G. M. Anderson. 144:890 My 15 '64
See also
Radiocarbon dating
CARBON compounds
See also
Hydrocarbons
CARBON dioxide
Stomatal penetration of wheat seedlings by stem and leaf rust; effect of light and carbon dioxide. D. Yirgou and R. M. Caldwell. bibliog il Science 141:272-3 Jl 19 '63
Transpiration and stomatal opening with changes in carbon dioxide content of the air. J. E. Pallas, jr. bibliog il Science 147: 171-3 Ja 8 '65
CARBON 14. See Carbon—Isotopes
CARBON monoxide
Carbon monoxide production by a bathypelagic siphonophore. G. V. Pickwell and others. bibliog il Science 144:860-2 My 15 '64
Carbon monoxide's other peril. Sci Digest 55: 74-5 F '64
Gas asphyxia. C. J. Potthoff. Todays Health 41:56 F '63
I learned about flying from that! killer in the cockpit. R. I. Forrest. il Flying 74:56 Ap '64
Monoxide in small doses. il Time 83:44 Ja 17 '64
New treatment devised for carbon monoxide. Sci N L 85:14 Ja 4 '64
CARBON tetrachloride
Carbon tetrachloride poisoning in rats: alteration in ribosomes of the liver. E. A. Smuckler and E. P. Benditt. bibliog il Science 140:308-10 Ap 19 '63
CARBONARI
Carbonari: their origins, initiation rites, and aims. R. J. Rath. bibliog f Am Hist R 69: 353-70 Ja '64
CARBONATE rocks. See Rocks
CARBONATED beverages. See Beverages
CARBONATES
Calcite-dolomite-magnesite stability relations in solutions at elevated temperatures. P. E. Rosenberg and H. D. Holland. bibliog il Science 145:700-1 Ag 14 '64
Thermal reduction of bicarbonate to formate. I. C. Hisatsune and K. O. Hartman. bibliog il Science 145:1455-6 S 25 '64
CARBONDALE, Pa.
City on fire. C. P. Gilmore. il Sat Eve Post 236:83-7 S 7 '63
Towns built over a furnace. il Bsns W p98-100+ My 4 '63
CARBONE, Paul P. See Fishbein, W. N. jt. auth.
CARBONI, Remo
Plaster & burlap. pors Sch Arts 63:16-17 S '63
CARBURETORS
Make your Corvair go. E. Rickman. il Hot Rod 16:52-3+ F '63
More air for Chevy Sixes. il Hot Rod 17:100-1 Ap '64
Return of the single throat. E. Dahlquist. il Hot Rod 17:50-1+ S '64
Should you lay a hand on your carburetor? M. J. Schultz. il Pop Mech 121:176-80+ Ap '64 (to be cont)
CARCINOGENIC substances. See Cancer producing substances
CARD games. See Cards
CARD tables. See Tables
CARDAMOM
Christmas spice; with recipes. C. Claiborne. il N Y Times Mag p97-8 D 8 '63
CARDBOARD cutouts. See Paper work
CARDBOARD dolls. See Paper dolls
CARDENAL, Ernesto
Indian heavens. Américas 16:23-7 Ja '64
CÁRDENAS, Lázaro
U.S. betting on Mexico; but there's trouble ahead. il por U S News 54:45-7 F 25 '63
CARDER, Frederick
Obituary
Hobbies 68:84 F '64
Rockwell collection of Carder's Steuben. E. E. Ericson. il por Hobbies 68:28-9+ My '63
CARDIAC resuscitation
Chest massage for babies. Sci N L 84:223 O 5 '63
Code 99! calls a hospital to battle against death; St Vincent's hospital team; with editorial comment. il Life 56:3, 52B-61 F 28 '64
New fight against sudden death: mouth-to-mouth breathing, heart massage. A. Cutler. il Look 28:44-6+ D 1 '64
New life-saving method: mouth-to-mouth resuscitation and external heart massage. D. W. Larson. il Outdoor Life 132:48-9+ Ag '63
See also
Heart-lung machines
CARDINAL birds
Cardinal. J. K. Terres. il Pop Gard 16:8 Ja '65
101 foods for cardinals. V. E. Davison. il Audubon Mag 65:180-3 My '63
Prince for your garden. J. D. Walters. il Flower Grower 50:20-1+ N '63
CARDINALE, Claudia
Square world of Claudia Cardinale. P. Hamill. por Sat Eve Post 237:62-3 F 29 '64
CARDINALS
And now the search begins for the new pope. R. B. Kaiser. Life 54:57-8 Je 21 '63
Flying red hats. il Time 83:62-3 My 22 '64
Great princes of the church; with photographs by Y. Karsh and D. Lees. Life 54: 29-35 Je 14 '63
Six cardinals: one a pope? il Newsweek 61: 59 Je 17 '63
See also
Popes—Election
CARDINALS (baseball) See Baseball clubs
CARDINALS (football club) See Football clubs
CARDINALS, College of. See Cardinals
CARDINELL, R. L. See Goodfriend, L. S. jt. auth.
CARDIOLOGY. See Heart
CARDIOVASCULAR diseases. See Heart—Diseases
CARDIOVASCULAR strokes. See Heart—Diseases
CARDIOVERTER. See Medical instruments and apparatus
CARDONA, José Miró. See Miró Cardona, J.
CARDOSO, Juan Carlos
Men who came to dinner. por Time 82:43 Jl 12 '63
CARDOSO, Luis Amadeo
Men who came to dinner. por Time 82:43 Jl 12 '63
CARDS
Aluette cards of Brittany (cont) S. Mann. il Hobbies 67:120-1 F '63
Family fun with card games. J. H. Wood. il Recreation 56:400 N '63
Miscellany of playing cards of England. R. Allen. il Hobbies 68:120-1 My '63
Playing cards. D. Powills. See issues of Hobbies
Traditional playing cards of Italy. S. Mann. il Hobbies 68:116-17 S; 118-19+ O; 118-19 N '63
See also
Blackjack (game)
Bridge (game)
Poker
Rummy (game)
CARDS, Advertising. See Advertising cards
CARDS, Catalog. See Catalog cards
CARDS, Greeting. See Greeting cards
CARDS, Picture. See Picture cards
CARDS, Place. See Place cards
CARDWELL, Guy A.
Among cypresses; poem. Sat R 46:33 Ag 24 '63
CARE. See Cooperative for American relief everywhere, incorporated
CARE of firearms. See Firearms—Care
CAREER clubs. See Clubs
CAREER counseling. See Vocational guidance
CAREER diplomats. See United States—Diplomatic and consular service
CAREER girls. See Business and professional women
CAREER literature. See Vocational literature
CAREERS. See Occupations
CAREERS for women. See Woman—Employment; Woman—Occupations
CARELESS talk; story. See Gallant, M.
CAREY, Ann
Girl who means hope to troubled boys. B. Leavitt. il pors Look 27:97-100 Je 18 '63

CAREY, Donald E. and others
Dengue types 1 and 4 viruses in wild-caught mosquitoes in south India. bibliog Science 143:131-2 Ja 10 '64

CAREY, Hugh L.
Equal rights for every tenth American and every seventh child; address, August 9, 1963. Vital Speeches 29:728-30 S 15 '63

About

Don't confuse the issue! concerning address at convention of Citizens for educational freedom. Christian Cent 80:1093 S 11 '63

CAREY, James A.
What happened when my school banned going steady. McCalls 90:69+ Je '63

CAREY, James B.
Excerpt from testimony, April 30, 1963. Cong Digest 43:84+ Mr '64

About

Different way to deal with unions; GE with IUE. il por U S News 55:120-1 O 7 '63
New fuel for IUE power struggle. Bsns W p 118 O 5 '63
Union leaders face growing revolt. por Bsns W p54+ O 3 '64

CAREY, James W.
Ethnic backlash? Commonweal 81:91-3 O 16 '64

CAREY, John A.
Jewelry making. Sch Arts 63:31-2 F '64

CAREY, Walter F.
Easing up on criticism; new C. of C. president; summary of news conference. por U S News 56:16 Ap 27 '64
New business spokesman urges positive approach. C. B. Seib. il por Nations Bsns 52:42-3+ My '64

CAREY-Thomas award
Carey-Thomas award given to Wesleyan university press. il Pub W 185:57-9 Ap 27 '64
Carey-Thomas awards: Shorewood, Yale, Houghton. il Pub W 183:32-4 F 25 '63
Shorewood wins Carey-Thomas for Great drawings. Pub W 183:130 F 18 '63
Wesleyan university press wins Carey-Thomas award. Library J 89:2055-6 My 15 '64
Wesleyan univ. press wins Carey-Thomas award. Pub W 185:49 Ap 20 '64

CARGILL, Incorporated
Big grain trader needs more than grain. il Bsns W p70-4 Ja 4 '64
With the grain. Time 82:102+ O 18 '63

CARGIN, Harold
Juneau knows that machine accounting pays. por Am City 78:94-5 Ap '63

CARGO airlines. See Air freight service

CARGO passenger ships. See Freight vessels

CARGO planes. See Airplanes, Freight

CARGO planes, Military. See Airplanes, Military transport

CARGO ships. See Freight vessels

CARIBBEAN NATIONAL FOREST. See National forests

CARIBBEAN REGION
Caribbean kaleidoscope. T. Mathews. il Cur Hist 48:32-9 Ja '65
Caribbean: our sea of our troubles. J. Benitez. Sat R 46:11-13+ Jl 13 '63
Chips are down in the islands of the sun. A. F. Gonzalez, jr. il Sat R 47:69+ O 10 '64
Coast to coast cruising, and then some. S. Penington. il Motor B 114:22-3+ N '64
Earning your life list; reprint. D. S. Rowe. il Audubon Mag 66:70-3 Mr '64
Sneakers and snorkels: Fish watcher's guide to the Caribbean. F. R. Smith. il Sports Illus 20:36-8+ Ja 20 '64

See also

Air travel—Caribbean Region
Public health—Caribbean Region
Tourist trade—Caribbean Region
West Indies

Description and travel

Atlantic liners extend the sun run; Caribbean winter-cruise circuit. il Newsweek 65:68-70 Ja 11 '65
Caribbean incidentals. Vogue 143:60 Ja 1 '64
Cooking to windward. M. Bartlett. il Yachting 113:43-5+ F '63
North to Antigua; from Martinique. M. P. Ryan. il Motor B 114:42-5 S '64
Personal business. Bsns W p 133 O 12 '63
Pick a place. il U S Camera 27:32-3 F '64
South Seas close to home; photographs by J. Launois; with account by A. Chamberlin. Sat Eve Post 237:26-34+ Mr 14 '64
South to the Islands. D. Street. il Yachting 116:54-6+ Ag '64
Sun islands notebook. L. Barry. il Pop Phot 55:26+ N '64
Sunny islands; symposium. il Mlle 59:174-5+ My '64
Virgin cruising. D. Phillips. il Motor B 114:24-8 N '64
Winter boating vacation guide. il Motor B 112:22-6+ D '63

Politics

Caribbean: a sea of growing despair. il U S News 56:64-8 Mr 23 '64

Religious institutions and affairs

News of the Christian world. Christian Cent 81:345-6, 776 Mr 11, Je 10 '64

CARIBOU
Nomads of the North. J. Rearden. il Am For 69:8+ F '63
North to the dwindling caribou; excerpts from Runes of the North. S. F. Olson. il Audubon Mag 65:346-51 N '63
Return of the native caribou. il Life 56:41-2 Ja 31 '64
Woodland caribou comes home to Maine. B. Geagan. il Nat Parks Mag 38:8-9 My '64

CARIBOU hunting
Going for broke; ed. by M. K. Sloan. S. R. Sloan, 3d. il Outdoor Life 131:72-5+ My '63
Too many caribou. J. Rearden. il Outdoor Life 132:33-5+ S '63

CARICATURES and cartoons
Chips off the new Herblock; excerpts from Straight Herblock. H. L. Block. Sat R 47:80-1 N 14 '64
David Low album selected by Low. D. Low. N Y Times Mag p24-5 S 29 '63
'E's luv'ly. Time 82:71+ N 1 '63
Epic of man (with apologies to Life magazine) F. Krahn. Horizon 5:108-12 S '63
Facing the candidate; Goldwater on the drawing boards. Time 84:61 Ag 7 '64
Famous faces by Oscar Berger; with footnotes on his celebrated sitters by the artist. il Am Artist 27:44-9+ O '63
Feiffer. J. Feiffer. See issues of New republic
Harry, the rat with women, by J. Feiffer. Review
Time 81:84 Je 28 '63
Little M. C. Castberg. Mlle 58:70-1 Ja; 128 F; 108 Ap '64
Look on the light side; selection of cartoons from Look. Read Digest 82:87-90 Je '63
Mauldin on Barry Goldwater. W. H. Mauldin. New Repub 151:13 Jl 4 '64
Road maps to opinion. Time 82:96 O 4 '63
Shah was not amused; offensive West German cartoon. Time 85:26 Ja 22 '65
Some notes on affectation; excerpt. W. Steig. Vogue 141:114-15 F 15 '63
Three contemporary allegories. J. Glashan. Holiday 34:70-5 N '63
Through history with J. Wesley Smith. B. Shafer. Sat R 47:148 Ag 29 '64
To make them laugh. il Time 83:66 My 1 '64
Upside-downs of Little Lady Lovekins and Old Man Muffaroo; excerpts from Incredible upside-downs of Gustave Verbeek. G. Verbeek. Redbook 121:56-7 Je '63
What is the most wonderful feeling in the world? excerpts from Security is a thumb and a blanket. C. M. Schulz. McCalls 91:66 O '63
Wordless workshop. R. Doty and others. See issues of Popular science monthly
X-ray pen; excerpts from Continuous performance. W. Steig. Sat R 46:20-1 F 16 '63
You are his target. G. Millstein. Sat Eve Post 237:38+ O 3 '64
You too can lay an egg; excerpt. B. Waber. il Life 54:113-14+ Ap 5 '63

See also

Comics (books, strips, etc)
Moving pictures—Animated cartoons

CARIES, Dental. See Teeth—Diseases

CARILLONS
Glorious carillon; Washington cathedral's inaugural recital. il Time 82:72+ O 4 '63

CARINGELLA, Charles
Automate your rear view mirror. Pop Electr 18:61-7+ F '63
Big TC. Pop Electr 21:29-32+ Jl '64
Build a stereo indicator. Pop Electr 19:63-5+ S '63
Crystal test meter. Pop Electr 18:61-3 My '63
Grid dip modulator. Pop Electr 18:57-60 Mr '63
Miniature I.F. module superheterodyne pocket receiver. Pop Electr 21:49-52+ D '64
X-line tachometer. Pop Electr 20:41-4 Ja '64

CARIOCAS. See Brazilians

CARL, Herbert A. See Lorenz, J. G.; Price, P. P. jt. auths.
CARLENE, Sister Alice. See Alice Carlene, Sister
CARLESS, Rosa Maria
Village pottery in Iran. Craft Horiz 23:34-5 Jl '63
CARLETON, Alford
For greater unity in east Asia. Christian Cent 81:612+ My 6 '64
CARLETON, Jetta
Moonflower vine; novel. McCalls 90:82-3 F; 100-1 Mr '63
CARLETON, R. Milton
All that glitters is not gold. Horticulture 41: 326-7 Je '63
Herbs: their ancient influences on mankind. Todays Health 42:32-7 Mr '64
Midwest pointers. See issues of Flower grower
Mystery of spring. Todays Health 41:18-19+ Ap '63
Only in America: such autumn color. Todays Health 41:46-9 O '63
Time now to prevent snow mold on lawns. Flower Grower 50:11 O '63
CARLETON, William G.
Government and health before the New deal. Cur Hist 45:71-6 Ag '63
Hawthorne discovers the English. Yale R 53: 395-414 Mr '64
Politics of the 1920's. Cur Hist 47:210-15+ O '64
CARLETON college, Northfield, Minn.
Credo of a college president; excerpt from address, October 13, 1962. J. W. Nason. Sch & Soc 91:214-16 My 4 '63
CARLI, Giancarlo, and others
Electroencephalographic desynchronization during deep sleep after destruction of midbrain-limbic pathways in the cat. bibliog Science 140:677-9 My 10 '63
CARLI, Guido
What the doctor ordered. M. A. Heilperin. il por Fortune 70:60+ O '64
CARLIN, William J.
Civic celebrations don't just happen. por Am City 78:109+ Ap '63
CARLING brewing company
Brewing a river of beer. Bsns W p26 Mr 14 '64
Winning a barrel of beer money; first $200,000 Carling world golf championship. A. Wright. il Sports Illus 21:32-5 S 7 '64
CARLING world golf championship. See Golf—Tournaments
CARLINI, E. A. and Green, J. P.
Acetylcholine-like activity in sciatic nerve. bibliog Science 141:901-2 S 6 '63
CARLINO, Lewis John
Cages. Criticism
Theatre Arts 47:13 Ag '63
Doubletalk. Criticism
New Yorker 40:165 My 16 '64
Newsweek 63:80 My 18 '64
Telemachus Clay. Criticism
Commonweal 79:543-4 Ja 31 '64
New Repub 149:28 D 21 '63
New Yorker 39:146-7 N 23 '63
Sat R 46:35 D 7 '63
CARLISLE, Duke
Duke's day. il por Time 83:56 Ja 10 '64
CARLISLE, Emmett Augustus, 3d. See Carlisle, D.
CARLISLE, G. R.
These beef specialists answer your twenty-one most asked questions. por Suc Farm 61: 46-7 My '63
CARLISLE, Norman
How to cash in on your invention. Pop Sci 183:122-4+ O '63
Now, inventing is easier than ever! Pop Sci 182:72-4+ My '63
They take all the fun out of getting killed! Pop Sci 183:74-6+ N '63
What to do with a bright idea. Pop Sci 185: 110-11+ O '64
World's greatest prospector. Pop Sci 184: 60-3+ My '64
CARLISLE, Olga (Andreyev)
Biographical sketch of Osip Mandelstam. Atlan 211:63 Je '63
Biographical sketch of Anna Akhmatova. Atlan 214:60-1 O '64
Gardens of today and yesterday. Nation 198: 586-8 Je 8 '64
Tips. Pub W 183:53 Mr 4 '63
CARLISLE, Thomas John
Blizzard; poem. Ladies Home J 80:134 Ja '63
Elevation within limits; poem. McCalls 90: 140 S '63
Midnight and morning; poem. Horn Bk 39: 575 D '63
Today; poem. Christian Cent 81:1033 Ag 19 '64
CARLOS, Don. See Charles, prince of Asturias
CARLOS, prince of Bourbon-Parma. See Hugo Carlos
CARLOS
Death of a poet. A. Kerrigan. Nat R 15:306 O 8 '63
CARLOS, Dorcas
Restoring old furniture. House & Gard 125:50+ Ap '64
CARLOTTA, consort of Maximilian, emperor of Mexico. See Charlotte
CARLSBAD, Czechoslovakia. See Karlsbad, Czechoslovakia
CARLSBAD CAVERNS
Flight of the bats. D. Holland. il Nat Parks Mag 38:8-10+ Ja '64
CARLSBAD CAVERNS NATIONAL PARK
Looping the Guadalupes. W. F. Heald. il Travel 120:34-6 O '63
CARLSBAD film festival. See Moving picture festivals
CARLSON, Adeline
Sweet dreams, Mrs Jones. Redbook 121:34+ O '63
CARLSON, Amy
Reader's choice. Travel 121:13 My '64
CARLSON, David B.
Can transportation systems put our cities back together again? Arch Forum 119:62-7 O '63
Downtown's dramatic comeback. Arch Forum 120:98-103 F '64
New look in public housing, too little and too late? Arch Forum 119:116-19 Jl '63
Sam Lefrak; he builds them cheaper by the dozen. Arch Forum 118:102-5 Ap '63
Town and gown. Arch Forum 118:92-5 Mr '63
Urban renewal: a new face on the American city. Arch Forum 119:80-5 Ag '63
Urban renewal for people. Arch Forum 120: 86-9 Ja '64
Yamasaki's first tower. Arch Forum 118:98-113 My '63
CARLSON, Don
Art in the sun. Sch Arts 63:5-9 F '64
CARLSON, Edna Dellinger
Paper angel. NEA J 53:25 D '64
CARLSON, Edward E.
Running hotels with a loose rein. il por Bsns W p92+ F 23 '63
CARLSON, Elmer C.
Stereo in a suitcase. Pop Mech 119:116-20 Je '63
CARLSON, Frank
Excerpt from address, April 3, 1963. Cong Digest 43:216+ Ag '64
CARLSON, Leland H.
(comp) Articles and other books received; British Commonwealth and Ireland. See issues of American historical review
CARLSON, Paul Earle
His last words to his church and his father. Life 57:42B D 4 '64

about

Agonizing choice. il por Newsweek 64:58 N 30 '64
Congo massacre. il pors Time 84:28-32 D 4 '64
Congo ransom: a good man's life; with account by J. Hicks. il pors Life 57:32-42A D 4 '64
Hostages. il por Time 84:36 N 27 '64
Massacre in the Congo: story of a rescue attempt. il U S News 57:41-3 D 7 '64
Ordeal in the Congo. il Sr Schol 85:17-18 D 9 '64
United States cooperates with Belgium in rescue of hostages from the Congo; text of documents, November 16—28, 1964. Dept State Bul 51:838-9, 842 D 14 '64
CARLSON, Paul Earle, family
Don't let my child know, she said, I'll tell them tonight at bedtime. J. Hicks. il pors Life 57:42-42A D 4 '64
CARLSON, R. L.
Building of Laura II. por Motor B 114:60+ D '64
CARLSON, Reynold E.
Key to nature; address, August 1962. por Recreation 56:64-6+ F '63
Wonder as you wander. por Recreation 56: 272-4 Je '63
—and others
Guiding principles for program planning; excerpt from Recreation in American life. Recreation 58:40-1 Ja '65
CARLSON, William Hugh
Oregon plans for expansion. Library J 89:4755-7 D 1 '64
CARLSTON, Charles W.
Tritium-hydrologic research: some results of the U.S. geological survey research program. bibliog Science 143:804-6 F 21 '64

CARLTON, Helen
Life World's fair review. Life 57:18 Jl 17 '64
CARLTON, Lessie, and Moore, R. H.
Individualized reading. NEA J 53:10-12 N '64
CARLTON, Lilyn E.
Last resort. Atlan 213:102-3 Ja '64; Same abr. with title When things get out of whack. Read Digest 84:183-4+ Mr '64
CARMEL, Calif.
Carmel's key to happy retirement: help, not a handout. G. S. Bush. il Todays Health 42:58-9+ Ja '64
CARMEL Bach festival. See Bach festivals
CARMEN; opera. See Bizet, G.
CARMER, Carl
America's Victorian homes. Am Home 67:86-7 Mr '64
Mormons (cont) Am Heritage 14:26-33+ F '63
Tips. Pub W 186:45-6 S 7 '64
CARMI, Ill.
Taming a troublesome water. J. Keim. il Am City 79:157-8 S '64
CARMICHAEL, Earl
Make your parks people-pleasers. Am City 79:104-6 Ap '64
CARMICHAEL, Joel
Christianity on the Nile. Sat R 46:27 Ap 6 '63
CARMICHAEL, Leonard, and Riopelle, A. J.
Primate biology: planning meeting. Science 146:1078+ N 20 '64
CARMICHAEL, Oliver C. Jr
Where the money is. il pors Bsns W p56+ Ag 8 '64
CARNAHAN, Paul H.
Businessmen in the news. por Fortune 71:47 Ja '65
CARNE-ROSS, D. S.
Contemporary Greek. Poetry 101:283-6 Ja '63
CARNEGIE, Andrew
Carnegie and opera. Q. Eaton. il por Opera N 28:27-31 Mr 14 '64
CARNEGIE corporation of New York
New education grants. Sr Schol 83:2T Ja 10 '64
New publication tells story of Carnegie library program. Library J 88:3040 S 1 '63
$266,900,000: private give-away, done by three men. A. Talmey. Vogue 141:103 Je '63
CARNEGIE Hall. See New York (city)—Carnegie Hall
CARNEGIE institute of technology, Pittsburgh
Man & machine at Carnegie tech; Graduate school of industrial administration. il Time 83:52-3 Ap 3 '64
CARNEGIE institution of Washington
Meeting. New Yorker 39:31-3 Je 8 '63
Stars, moths, and birds. New Yorker 40:31-3 Je 6 '64
CARNEGIE international exhibition of art. See Art—Exhibitions
CARNEGIE medals
Carnegie-Greenaway medals given at London dinner. Pub W 186:53-4 Jl 20 '64
CARNEIRO, Robert L.
Science in action. Natur Hist 73:58-9+ Ag '64
CARNELL, Edward John
Christian social ethics. Christian Cent 80: 979-80 Ag 7 '63
CARNER, Charles R.
Are we rejecting our creative children? Todays Health 42:20-3+ F '64
Publishing revival in the second city. por Library J 88:2435-8 Je 15 '63
They make child's play of speech therapy. Today's Health 41:24-7+ Mr '63
CARNEY, Francis M.
Decentralized politics of Los Angeles. bibliog f Ann Am Acad 353:107-21 My '64
New guard; letter. America 111:781-2 D 12 '64
CARNIVAL
After the ball; carnival time in Rio. il Time 81:31 Mr 8 '63
All-out gamboling. il Bsns W p30-1 Mr 2 '63
Changing times; New Orleans Mardi gras. il Newsweek 61:30 Mr 11 '63
Forget about it; *fasching*. il Newsweek 61:40 Mr 4 '63
Life guide; Mardi gras. il Life 56:7 Ja 31 '64
Night of glory; pre-Lenten carnival for Rio's Salgueiro *favela*. il Time 81:23 Mr 1 '63
Reporter at large; Mardi gras parade by Zulu social aid & pleasure club. C. Trillin. New Yorker 40:41-2+ Je 20 '64
CARNIVAL glass. See Glassware
CARNIVALS
Belgium's carnival craze. P. DeMaerel. il Travel 121:44-6 F '64
It's time to plan for carnival in Mazatlán. il Sunset 133:26+ N '64
Life guide; winter carnivals. il Life 56:14 Ja 17 '64
Travel notes; eleventh annual winter carnival, Quebec. R. Joseph. Esquire 62:114+ D '64
CARNIVOROUS plants. See Insectivorous plants
CARNOVSKY, Morris
Everyman's disasters; Connecticut's triumph. por Time 82:44 Ag 16 '63
CARO, José Eusebio
United States in 1850. M. Torres. il por Américas 16:1-8 F '64
CARO y Cuervo institute. See Colombia—Instituto Caro y Curevo
CAROL, Cindy
Gidget was here; ed. by E. Miller. pors Seventeen 22:94-5+ Jl '63
CAROL singing. See Christmas carols
CAROLINA Israelite (newspaper)
Last of the personal journalists? (cont) H. Golden. Sat R 46:48 F 9 '63
CAROLINA rhododendrons. See Rhododendrons
CAROLL, Evelyn
Ballet, violins and shish kebab! il Dance Mag 37:27-8 D '63
CAROLLO, Betty J.
Ten ways to good discipline without spanking. Parents Mag 38:62+ Ap '63
CAROLS
See also
Christmas carols
CARON, Leslie
Ballet is an adolescent passion; interview, ed. by L. Joel. pors Dance Mag 37:26-7 O '63
about
Waif becomes a woman. C. R. Jennings. il pors Sat Eve Post 236:22-3 S 14 '63
CAROTENE
Beta-carotene: thermal degradation. I. Mader. bibliog il Science 144:533-4 My 1 '64
CAROTENOIDS
Carotenoids of cavernicolous crayfish. D. A. Wolfe and D. G. Cornwell. bibliog il Science 144:1467-9 Je 19 '64
Ionene: a thermal degradation product of β-carotene. W. C. Day and J. G. Erdman. bibliog il Science 141:808 Ag 30 '63
CAROUSSO, Georges
New life for a blind deer. Sat Eve Post 237: 77-8 My 9 '64
CAROZZA, Michael J.
We trade concrete for right-of-way. Am City 78:130-1 Je '63
—and Jefford, N. O.
How Fresno upgraded parking-meter service. Am City 78:117+ N '63
CARP
Fish eat weeds to aid power plant operation. Sci N L 86:139 Ag 29 '64
CARP fishing
Summer's hottest fishing. R. Tinsley. il Field & S 68:48-9+ Jl '63
CARPACCIO, Vittore
Carpaccio at the palace; exhibition at Doge's palace. il Time 81:62-5 Je 21 '63
Carpaccio emerges an adventurous conservative. A. Frankfurter. il Art N 62:20-4+ S '63
CARPENTER, Don
Case money; story. Sat Eve Post 237:62-6 S 12 '64
Potomac bass float trip. Am For 69:24-6 Ag '63
Trouting, where? Am For 69:22-3+ Mr '63
CARPENTER, E. W.
Explosion seismology. bibliog Science 147:363-73 Ja 22 '65
CARPENTER, Joseph, Jr
Joseph Carpenter jr, silversmith and clockmaker. A. R. Chase. il Antiques 85:695-7 Je '64
CARPENTER, Marjorie
Today's tensions; address, November 9, 1963. Vital Speeches 30:184-6 Ja 1 '64
CARPENTER, May
Alpine strawberries. Horticulture 42:16-17 F '64
CARPENTER, Roland L. and Goldstein, R. M.
Radar observations of Mercury. bibliog Science 142:381 O 18 '63
CARPENTER bees
Wood-boring carpenter bee; xylocopa. A. W. Eckert. il Sci Digest 53:13-18 Ap '63
CARPENTER center for the visual arts. See Harvard university—Carpenter center for the visual arts
CARPENTERS squares
How to solve math problems with a square. R. Gordon. il Pop Sci 182:132-5 Ap '63
CARPENTRY
See also
Doors
Joints (carpentry)
Woodworking
Work benches

CARPER, Eugene G.
Who attends church? J. L. Hofford. Christian Cent 81:654 My 13 '64

CARPET sweepers
Carpet sweepers. il Consumer Bul 47:17-19 Je '64

CARPET underlays. See Rug pads

CARPET with the big pink roses on it; story. See Brennan, M.

CARPETS. See Rugs and carpets

CARPORTS. See Garages

CARR, Archie
African underground movement. N Y Times Mag p57-8+ S 20 '64
Green turtle; letter to the editor. Américas 16:48 N '64

CARR, Glenn
Wright Patman's well-heeled windmills. New Repub 150:11-12 F 8 '64

CARR, Grant
Aluminum. Motor B 114:28-33 D '64

CARR, Henry
Souped-up Carr! H. L. Masin. pors Sr Schol 82:32 My 1 '63

CARR, James K.
Californian looks at California: address, February 27, 1963. Am For 69:16-19 Ap '63

CARR, Paul
Build the inductaphons. Pop Electr 18:65-8 My '63

CARR, R. E. See Gouras, P. jt. auth.

CARR, Rachel E.
New dimensions. Flower Grower 50:34-5+ Ag '63
Simplicity with chrysanthemums. Flower Grower 50:48-9 O '63
Some basic techniques for good arrangements. Flower Grower 51:50-1 Jl '64

CARR, Warren
Notes from an irrelevant clergyman. Christian Cent 80:879-81 Jl 10 '63

CARR, William G.
Scholastic teacher interviews: William G. Carr; ed. by H. Langer. por Sr Schol 83: 9T-13T Ja 17 '64
Waging peace in the sixties. PTA Mag 59:8-10 O '64
WCOTP primer. por NEA J 53:38-9 O '64

CARRÉ, John le, pseud. See Cornwell, D.

CARRELS, Study. See School libraries

CARREÑO, Virginia
American federal furniture in Argentina. Antiques 84:283-7 S '63

CARRICK, Robert W.
Outboard wells for the small auxiliary. Yachting 117:77-9+ Ja '65
Yachting interviews: Bill Luders. Yachting 116:61+ Ag '64

CARRIER, Warren
Agonist of the intuition. Poetry 101:349-52 F '63

CARRIER pigeons. See Pigeons

CARRIERS
See also
United States—Interstate commerce commission

CARRIERS (equipment)
How to make a beach travois. il Sunset 131: 90+ Ag '63

CARRIERS, Aircraft. See Aircraft carriers

CARRIERS, Car-top. See Automobiles—Equipment

CARRIERS of infection
Intracellular infection and the carrier state. J. E. Smadel. bibliog il Science 140:153-60 Ap 12 '63
See also
Birds as carriers of infection
Insects as carriers of infection
Pigeons as carriers of infection

CARRIGHAR, Sally
To him, the unknown was home. Sat R 47: 40 Je 20 '64

CARRILLO, Elisa A.
Alcide De Gasperi. America 111:156-8 Ag 15 '64

CARRINGTON, C. E.
Rudyard Kipling: he outlives the empire. Horizon 6:60-6 Autumn '64

CARRIÓN, Arturo Morales-. See Morales-Carrión, A.

CARRISON, L. C. See Sclar, C. B. jt. auth.

CARRO, John
Information; Mayor's information center, mobile unit. New Yorker 39:41-2 N 16 '63

CARROLL, Benjamin, and Blei, Ira
Measurement of optical activity: new approaches. bibliog Science 142:200-8 O 11 '63

CARROLL, Daniel B.
Il Duce's destiny. America 110:730-1 My 23 '64

CARROLL, George D.
Richmond, California's new mayor. il pors Ebony 19:94+ O '64

CARROLL, Gertrude
Tribute to Gertrude. D. Duncan. por Dance Mag 37:72-3 F '63

CARROLL, Hattie
Spinsters' ball. il por Time 81:26 F 22 '63

CARROLL, J. Roy, jr
Industrial architecture, proving ground for comprehensive services; condensation of address. Arch Rec 136:167-8 Jl '64

CARROLL, John T.
Movie of the month. Cath World 199:71-2 Ap '64

CARROLL, Paul
Is Miller really a puritan? Sat R 46:29 F 23 '63

CARROLL, Ralph E.
Snowfighting with sirens. Am City 79:92-3 F '64

CARROLL, Wallace
Campaign trail hootenanny. Reporter 31:26-7 O 22 '64

CARROLL, Warren H.
Counterattack at Colorado. Nat R 14:494-5 Je 18 '63

CARROLL, William
Self-employed fire chief. il pors Ebony 18: 59-60+ Mr '63

CARRUTH, Ella K.
Who brought the stork? Sci Digest 53:87-9 Mr '63

CARRUTH, Hayden
Abstruse considerations. Poetry 104:243-4 Jl '64
Closest permissible approximation. Poetry 101:358-60 F '63
Daylight. Poetry 105:194-5 D '64
Freedom and discipline; poem. Nation 198:441 Ap 27 '64
Heart for the gods. Nation 198:171-2 F 17 '64
Intelligence, rebellion, interest. Poetry 104:44-5 Ap '64
Interim report. Poetry 102:389-90 S '63
Kind of revolt. Nation 197:165-6 S 21 '63
Poetic mythology. Poetry 104:369-74 S '64
Poets without prophecy. Nation 196:354-7 Ap 27 '63
Private words and public art. Nation 197: 418-19 D 14 '63
Requiem for God's gardener. Nation 199:168-9 S 28 '64
Scales of the marvelous. Nation 199:442-4 D 7 '64
Silent voices. Poetry 103:191-2 D '63
Spring notes from robin hill; Smallish son; poems. Poetry 103:19-25 O '63
Uses of typology. Poetry 101:424-6 Mr '63
William Carlos Williams as one of us. New Repub 148:30-2 Ap 13 '63
about
Service of friendliness. W. Stafford. Poetry 102:323-4 Ag '63

CARRY, Peter
Baseball's week. Sports Illus 21:69 Jl 6; 66 Jl 27; 67 Ag 24; 76 Ag 31; 124 S 7; 77 S 14; 115 S 21; 100 S 28; 93 O 12 '64

CARRYING. See Lifting and carrying

CARS. See Railroads—Cars

CARS (automobiles) See Automobiles

CARSON, Gerald
Saloon. Am Heritage 14:24-31+ Ap '63
Tax on whiskey? never! Am Heritage 14:62-4+ Ag '63
(ed) See Ogle, C. Speech that toppled a president

CARSON, Johnny
Celebrity register. C. Amory. por McCalls 90:132 Mr '63
Johnny Carson: nighthood's new prince. il pors Look 27:59-60+ Ap 23 '63

CARSON, Lettie Gay
They can't learn without books. Parents Mag 39:74+ Ap '64

CARSON, Mindy
Celebrity register. C. Amory. por McCalls 90:146 Mr '63

CARSON, Rachel Louise
Miss Carson goes to Congress. pors Am For 69:20-3+ Jl; 2 O '63
Moving tides; excerpt from The sea around us. Motor B 112:20-2+ Jl '63
Rachel Carson answers her critics. Audubon Mag 65:262-5+ S '63
about
Celebrity register. C. Amory. por McCalls 90:188 Mr '63
Constance Lindsay Skinner award won by Rachel Carson. Pub W 183:130 F 18 '63

CARSON, Rachel Louise—about—*Continued*
Editorial. por Am For 70:8 My '64
For many a spring. il por Time 83:73 Ap 24 '64
Legacy of Rachel Carson. S. L. Udall. il por Sat R 47:23+ My 16 '64
Life in nature. por Newsweek 63:95 Ap 27 '64
Notes and comment. New Yorker 40:35 My 2 '64
Obituary
Flower Grower 51:42 Je '64
Nat Parks Mag 38:2 My '64. P. M. Tilden
Pub W 185:63-4 Ap 27 '64
Personality portrait. J. Lear. por Sat R 46:45 Je 1 '63
Pesticides; White House advisory body issues report recommending steps to reduce hazard to public. D. S. Greenberg. Science 140:878-9 My 24 '63
Pests and poisons; R. Carson before Senate investigative subcommittee. Newsweek 61:86 Je 17 '63
Rachel Carson memorial fund for research; with tributes to R. Carson. C. W. Buchheister. Audubon Mag 66:208-10 Jl '64
Rachel Carson receives Audubon medal; with acceptance address. J. Vosburgh. il por Audubon Mag 66:98-9 Mr '64
Rachel Carson receives WNBA Skinner award in absentia. il Pub W 183:35 F 25 '63
Rachel Carson vs. pest control. Am City 78:7 Mr '63
Rachel Carson's war. Sr Schol 84:18-19 My 1 '64
Silent spring on the Pacific slope. C. C. Van Fleet. Atlan 212:81-4 Jl '63
Speaking out; the myth of the pesticide menace; concerning Silent spring. E. Diamond. Sat Eve Post 236:16+ S 28 '63
Was Rachel Carson right? B. H. Frisch. il por Sci Digest 56:39-45 Ag '64

Poetry

For Rachel Carson. M. W. Andrews. il Am For 70:16 S '64

CARSON, Rachel, memorial fund for research. See National Audubon society

CARSON, Robert
French touch: Quebec. Holiday 35:72-3+ Ap '64

CARSON, Ruth
Childbirth facts and fads. Parents Mag 38:58-9+ My '63
How to keep teens out of trouble. Parents Mag 39:48-9+ Je '64
New horizons for retarded children. Parents Mag 39:46-7+ D '64
Two-year community colleges. Parents Mag 39:66-7+ Ap '64

CARSTENS, Kenneth N.
Banning of Peter Brown. Christian Cent 81:1274 O 14 '64

CARSTENSEN, Vernon
Doctoral dissertations; excerpts from address. por(p37) Pub W 184:40-1 Jl 15 '63

CARTAGO, Costa Rica
Volcano doctor; Haroun Tazieff's study of Irazú. il Time 83:68+ Ap 24 '64

CARTE, Bridget D'Oyly
Great opera houses: the Savoy theatre. Opera N 29:26-9 D 12 '64

CARTELS, International. See **Trusts. Industrial—International aspects**

CARTER, Albert Howard
Aurora borealis; poem. New Repub 150:18 F 1 '64
Christmas needles; poem. New Repub 149:21 D 21 '63

CARTER, Barbara
Elephants in Tammanyland. Reporter 29:41-3 N 21 '63
How good is old siwash? Reporter 31:55-6 N 19 '64
Jalopy nomads. Reporter 30:31-3 My 7 '64
Lawyer leaves Mississippi. Reporter 28:33-5 My 9 '63
New York city, can it be governed? Reporter 30:42-5 Ja 30 '64
New York's Jim Crow schools: bleak facts and bright visions. Reporter 31:23-6 Jl 2 '64
Organizing the old folks. Reporter 30:31-2 Mr 12 '64
Role of the civil rights commission. Reporter 29:10-14 Jl 4 '63
Visit to Rochester. Reporter 31:16+ Ag 13 '64
Who was Bill Miller? Reporter 31:21-4 N 5 '64

CARTER, Bruce
Personal challenge of teaching drawing. Sch Arts 62:30-3 Je '63

about

American artist in Norway. il Am Artist 27:12 Ap '63

CARTER, Clifton C.
Cliff Carter: LBJ's political liaison man. por U S News 56:20 Ja 13 '64

CARTER, Dorothy Sharp
Lost empire. Travel 120:37-40 O '63

CARTER, Elliott
Music. B. Boretz. Nation 196:294-6 Ap 6 '63

CARTER, Esther
Is the federal government helpless? dismissal of federal conspiracy charges. A. M. Bickel. New Repub 151:14 D 26 '64

CARTER, G. Emmett, bp
Head and heart: catechisms with a modern accent. America 109:40-3 Jl 13 '63
Xavier Rynne book. America 108:906 Je 29 '63; Discussion. 109:30 Jl 13 '63

CARTER, Hodding, 1907-
Double standard for murder? N Y Times Mag p20+ Ja 24 '65
Little Miss Rachel and D. O. Volenty. Read Digest 83:100-2 S '63
Mississippi now: hate and fear. N Y Times Mag p 11+ Je 23 '63
Song was yours. McCalls 91:165 My '64

CARTER, Howard
Science classic; why they dig. por Sci Digest 53:11-15 Je '63

about

King Tut's golden hoard. J. Stewart-Gordon. il Read Digest 84:198-204 Ap '64

CARTER, Hugh
Eight myths about divorce, and the facts. N Y Times Mag p 17+ My 3 '64

CARTER, John
Framed dollar. Harper 227:22+ Jl '63
Wages of fashion. Nation 199:465-6 D 14 '64

CARTER, John Mack
Vote of confidence. por NEA J 52:15 Ap '63

CARTER, John Stewart
No. 6025; poem. New Repub 149:21 D 14 '63

CARTER, Joseph
Birth of a voter. B. Adelman. il pors Ebony 19:88-90+ F '64

CARTER, Joseph C.
Junior leadership pays off. por Recreation 57:178 Ap '64

CARTER, Launor F.
Psychological testing and public responsibility. Science 146:1695-7 D 25 '64

CARTER, Leon J. 3d
Is this my heritage? son mother; poem. Negro Hist Bul 27:84 Ja '64

CARTER, Lillie Bland-. See Bland-Carter, L.

CARTER, Manfred A.
Art critic; poem. Christian Cent 80:238 F 20 '63
Earthquake window; poem. Christian Cent 81:878 Jl 8 '64
Idiot God; poem. Christian Cent 81:546 Ap 29 '64
Night people; poem. Christian Cent 80:429 Ap 3 '63
November 22, 1963: World stage; Monometal; Assassin; Clay figure; poems. Christian Cent 80:1540 D 11 '63
Red flags in snow; poem. Christian Cent 81:360 Mr 18 '64
Refugees; poem. Christian Cent 81:1138 S 16 '64
Soldier waiting; poem. Christian Cent 80:979 Ag 7 '63
Sun on the roadside; poem. Christian Cent 80:1169 S 25 '63
Twilight Christmas; poem. Christian Cent 80:1610 D 25 '63
Yucca prayer; poem. Christian Cent 80:708 My 29 '63

CARTER, Mary
All things bright and beautiful; story. Redbook 120:54-5 Ap '63

CARTER, Meg
Home sewing (cont) Redbook 120:36 Mr; 50 Ap; 121:47 My; 22 Jl; 10 Ag '63

CARTER, Morgan Doug, Jr
Reason; poem. Negro Hist Bul 27:163 Ap '64

CARTER, Richard
What women really think of the Kennedys. Good H 156:73-5+ Je '63

CARTER, Robert A.
Uses and abuses of point-of-sale material. Pub W 187:53-6 Ja 4 '65

CARTER, Robert S.
Norpac race. Yachting 116:35+ O '64

CARTER, Rubin
Baleful look of a new Liston. L. Shecter. por Sports Illus 19:76-82+ O 14 '63
Match made in the jungle. M. Gross. il pors Sat Eve Post 237:76-8 O 24 '64

CARTER, Samuel, 3d
Showdown on the Allagash. Read Digest 85:178-82+ O '64

CARTER, T. Donald
Reviews. Natur Hist 73:4+ Ja '64

CARTER, William, company
Potent packaging. Duns R 83:68+ My '64
CARTER, William B.
How to grow cactus from seed. Horticulture 42:44+ Ap '64
CARTERETTE, Edward C. and Jones, M. H.
Redundancy in children's texts. bibliog Science 140:1309-11 Je 21 '63
—and others
Lateralization of sounds at the unstimulated ear opposite a noise-adapted ear. bibliog Science 147:63-5 Ja 1 '65
CARTHEW, Anthony
All honor Honor. N Y Times Mag p73-5 Mr 1 '64
Britain edges out of the ice age. N Y Times Mag p60+ D 13 '64
Britain's no. 1 book. N Y Times Mag p85-6+ My 10 '64
Cold-drink war: Kvass vs. Coke. N Y Times Mag p21-3 Jl 12 '64
Diamonds are not necessarily forever. N Y Times Mag p46+ O 4 '64
John Bull goes right on smoking. N Y Times Mag p 17+ Ja 19 '64
Man who broke the four-minute mile. N Y Times Mag p66+ Ap 19 '64
Shaggy Englishman story. N Y Times Mag p 18+ S 6 '64
Snuff is not to be sneezed at. N Y Times Mag p90+ Mr 8 '64
Third channel for British telly. N Y Times Mag p 13+ Mr 29 '64
CARTIER, Jean Jacques. See Auclair, J. L. jt. auth.
CARTIER, John O.
Guarantee your grouse. Field & S 68:62-3+ O '63
Technique for northerns. Field & S 67:62-5+ Ap '63
CARTIER, Raymond
Cost of grandeur. il por Newsweek 63:41+ Mr 23 '64
CARTIER-BRESSON, Henri
Spain. il Vogue 143:122-32+ Je '64
This is Castro's Cuba seen face to face. il Life 54:28-43 Mr 15 '63
CARTILAGE
Elasticity of articular cartilage: effect of ions and viscous solutions. L. Sokoloff. bibliog il Science 141:1055-7 S 13 '63
CARTOGRAPHY
Cartography in Africa; United Nations regional cartographic conference for Africa, Nairobi, Kenya, July 1-13, 1963. G. E. Pearcy. Dept State Bul 49:1014-18 D 30 '63
New twist for maps with old instrument. Sci N L 86:201 S 26 '64
See also
Nautical charts
CARTOMANCY. See Fortune telling
CARTON, Bernice B.
Africa's Ivory Coast. Travel 122:44-6 D '64
First mate to Bligh. Mlle 57:218-19+ My '63
CARTONS, Milk. See Milk containers
CARTOONISTS
Down under to Denver; Australia's P. B. Oliphant at the Denver post. il Time 84: 82-3 S 18 '64
Finding a president. il Time 83:52 Ap 10 '64
Going West. Time 83:40 Ja 31 '64
Map for cartoonists. T. Key. il Design 66:2 N '64
See also
Berry, J. O.
Caricatures and cartoons
Feiffer, J.
Goldberg, R.
Mauldin, B.
O'Neill, H. D. 3d
Ramus, M.
Schulz, C. M.
Siné
Smythe, R.
Tim
CARTOONS. See Caricatures and cartoons; Moving pictures—Animated cartoons
CARTRIDGE, Phonograph. See Phonograph—Pickup
CARTRIDGE projectors. See Projection apparatus
CARTRIDGES
Battle of the plastics; plastic shotshells. W. Page. il Field & S 69:128-30 My '64
Cartridges for elk. W. Page. il Field & S 69: 82-5 S '64
Cartridges for mule deer. J. O'Connor. il Outdoor Life 134:66+ S '64
Changes in the shot shell. J. O'Connor. il Outdoor Life 135:70-4 Ja '65
Extra shotgun free; by carrying both old and new style shells. F. McKinley. il Outdoor Life 135:50-1+ F '65
Here come the Magnums. J. O'Connor. il Outdoor Life 134:62-3+ Ag '64
In varmint circles. W. Page. il Field & S 69:98-101 Je '64
Living cartridges, and the dead. J. O'Connor. il Outdoor Life 131:86-90 Mr '63
Medicine for elk and moose. J. O'Connor. il Outdoor Life 132:60-4 Ag '63
Mighty .22 rimfires. J. O'Connor. il Outdoor Life 131:96+ Je '63
New shotshells turn misses into hits; plastic-wrapped shells. S. Latham. il Pop Sci 183: 154-6 S '63
New 6mm. Rem. Field & S 68:61 Ag '63
Old booming Bertha, the .375. J. O'Connor. il Outdoor Life 132:58+ N '63
Reloading plastics. Field & S 69:85-6 S '64
Remington's latest: new handgun and two new cartridges. J. O'Connor. il Outdoor Life 131:120-2 My '63
Shooting; the .270, .280 and .284. J. O'Connor. il Outdoor Life 133:54-8 Ja '64
Summer styles in cartridges. W. Page. il Field & S 68:78-81 Jl '63
Three 7 mm.'s in Africa. J. O'Connor. il Outdoor Life 131:52-6 Ja '63
Two new Winchester cartridges. J. O'Connor. il Outdoor Life 131:118-21 Ap '63
.270 strong as ever. J. O'Connor. il Outdoor Life 135:102+ F '65
Varmint cartridges for thirty years. J. O'Connor. il Outdoor Life 133:102+ Je '64
Weatherby cartridges. J. O'Connor. Outdoor Life 131:127 My '63
What happened to the .256? W. Page. il Field & S 67:58-60 F '63
CARTS
Lumber caddy that rolls to work. il Pop Sci 185:160 O '64
Rolling cart, the new household work horse. il House B 105:172-3+ Ap '63
Wheels for washers, etc; Kitchen Kaddy. il Consumer Rep 30:8 Ja '65
Yard cart you can push or tow. J. Hand. il Pop Sci 183:94-7+ Jl '63
CARTS, Golf bag. See Golf—Equipment
CARTS, Serving. See Serving carts
CARTS, Tea. See Serving carts
CARTUS, F. E.
Vatican II & the Jews. Commentary 39:19-29 Ja '65
CARTWRIGHT, Marguerite
Africans and Asians; outstanding at World's food congress. por Negro Hist Bul 27:6-10 O '63
Diplomats entertain. por Negro Hist Bul 26: 187-8, 216-18 Mr-Ap '63
United Nations correspondent's circle. pors Negro Hist Bul 27:93-4 Ja '64
Visit from a King. por Negro Hist Bul 26: 245-6 My '63
CARTY, Rico
Player of the week; Milwaukee outfielder. por Sports Illus 21:77 S 14 '64
CARUSO the truck driver; story. See Gold, H.
CARUTHERS, R. and others
Interaction of evoked potentials of neocortical and hypothalamic origin in the amygdala. bibliog Science 144:422-3 Ap 24 '64
CARVALHO, Eleazar de
Eleazar de Carvalho: orchestra builder. R. J. Hutcheson. il por Mus Am 84:58-9 My '64
CARVALHO, Jose Vasconcellos de
Brazil hails its king of credit. il por Bsns W p 134+ N 14 '64
CARVER, Bob, and Crimmin, Eileen
Washtub honkers. Field & S 67:12-13 Ap '63
CARVER, John A. jr
People's river; remarks, May 15, 1964. Am For 70:22-5+ N '64
CARVER, Michael J. See Ryan, W. L. jt. auth.
CARVER, R. K. See Ingram, R. L. jt. auth.
CARVER, Thomas R.
Optical pumping. bibliog Science 141:599-608 Ag 16 '63
CARVING (art industries)
Lore from a gemstone carving genius. D. J. Cipnic. il Pop Mech 121:124-7+ Mr '64
Root-carver from Cali. A. Pardo-Tovar. il Américas 16:35-8 N '64
See also
Scrimshaw
Stone carving
Wood carving
CARVING (meat, etc)
Boning meat and poultry. il House & Gard 124:284-6 N '63
How to carve a turkey. il Am Home 66:70+ N '63
How to carve a turkey. il Suc Farm 62:63 D '64
How to carve duck and goose. il House & Gard 123:188-90 Ap '63
How to carve roast beef. il Good H 157:176 D '63

CARVING (meat, etc)—*Continued*
How to carve suckling pig. il House & Gard 124:112-13 Jl '63
How to carve veal. il House & Gard 123:194-5 My '63
What's newest for Christmas carving? il Good H 157:232 D '63
CARVING knives. See Knives
CARY, Bob
Blizzard bass. pors Outdoor Life 133:60-1+ Ap '64
Deer in your pocket. il por Outdoor Life 132: 54-5+ S '63
Lakers at 30 below. Outdoor Life 135:40-1+ Ja '65
We track pheasants. por Outdoor Life 134: 20-3+ D '64
CARY, William L.
Breeze through the corridors. il por Newsweek 63:79 My 25 '64
Wall Street musters its defenses; SEC's study of floor trading and stock specialist. il por Bsns W p84-6 Jl 27 '63
CARYOPHYLLACEAE. See Wild pinks
CASAL, Julián del
Two trailblazers of modernism. R. M. Martínez. por Américas 16:17-19 D '64
CASALS, Pablo
Casals conducts St Matthew Passion. M. Bernheimer. Sat R 46:54 Je 29 '63
Don Pablo. il por Newsweek 63:85 Je 29 '64
Don Pablo revisited. N. Cousins. por Sat R 47:20-1+ Mr 7 '64
Pablo Casals. R. De Toledano. Nat R 14:417-19 My 21 '63
CASANOVA, Pablo González
Mexico looks to the future; tr. by E. Flint. Atlan 213:149-50+ Mr '64
CASAS, Bartolomé de las
Conquest and the cross; summary of address. L. Hanke. il por Am Heritage 14:4-19+ F '63
CASCADE RANGE
By boat into the Cascade wilderness; Lake Chelan. il Sunset 133:18-20 Ag '64
Goat-watching in the Cascades. il Sunset 130: 54+ F '63
World of white. R. L. Nelson. il Audubon Mag 66:92-6 Mr '64
See also
Saint Helens, Mount
CASCO, Wis.
Church ruled liable for damages; ruling against Holy Trinity Catholic church. Christian Cent 80:733 Je 5 '63
CASE, Clifford Philip
Blueprint for a stronger Congress. Sat R 46:23-4+ N 23 '63
Congress, too, has conflicts of interests. N Y Times Mag p 12+ My 19 '63
Cure for sick cities. Sat R 46:12-14 F 9 '63
Senator Case seeks watchdog unit for military, space contracts. Aviation W 78:34 F 25 '63
about
Bakers: $470 tax on $82,000 income; unanswered questions. U S News 56:10 Ap 13 '64
How much politics in contract awards? U S News 54:10-11 F 18 '63
CASE, Everett
Excerpt from statement, August 18, 1961. Cong Digest 42:60+ F '63
CASE, Harold C.
Dilemma for Americans; address, August 22, 1964. Vital Speeches 30:715-17 S 15 '64
To form great individuals; address August 24, 1963. Vital Speeches 29:708-10 S 15 '63
CASE, L. L.
Inner inside story of the Canadian crisis. New Yorker 39:29-31 F 23 '63
CASE, Robert N.
Brave new school libraries. por Wilson Lib Bul 38:763-5 My '64
CASE, Stewart
Leisure, the heart of living. por Recreation 56:224-5 My '63
CASE money; story. See Carpenter, D.
CASE of libel; drama. See Denker, H.
CASE of mistaken identity; drama. See Murray, J.
CASEI, Nedda
Maddalena & Enrico; interview, ed. by E. R. Rizzo. por Opera N 29:16 D 12 '64
CASEL, Odo
Maria Laach revisited. H. A. Reinhold. Commonweal 78:497-500 Ag 23 '63
CASES. See Boxes, cases, etc.
CASES, Tool. See Tool boxes, racks, etc.
CASEWIT, Curtis W.
Successful query letters. Writer 76:15-17 D '63
CASEY, Bernard
Double life of Bernie Casey. il pors Life 57: 123-4 D 4 '64
CASEY, Gene
Blue water bargain. por Outdoor Life 133: 60-3+ Je '64
CASEY, George W.
Confessors and theologians; the pastoral crisis. Commonweal 80:317-19 Je 5 '64
Same always, please. Commonweal 77:487-9 F 1 '63
CASEY, Gerry, and Nagle, Tonia
Danny Kaye. Flying 74:46+ Mr '64
CASEY, James Leslie Lawrence
Casey and his cougar run over California. V. Kraft. il por Sports Illus 19:67-8 N 25 '63
CASEY, W. F.
Get the streets open first. Am City 78:26 Ap '63
CASEY, William Van Etten
Diary of an American Jesuit. America 109: 113-17 Ag 3 '63
CASEY at the bat (ballad) See Ballads, American
CASH discount. See Discount
CASH registers
ABA question box; what kind of cash register for a small bookstore? Pub W 186:69-71 N 16 '64
CASHIN, Bonnie
Tie for the top and a tribute to Bonnie. J. A. Zill. il Sports Illus 18:48-50 My 6 '63
CASHMERE (country) See Kashmir
CASHMERE bouquet. See Glory bowers
CASIDA, John E.
Esterase inhibitors as pesticides. bibliog Science 146:1011-17 N 20 '64
CASIDA, L. E. jr
Anaerobic microorganisms in the soil. Science 145:300-1 Jl 17 '64
CASIMIROA edulis. See Sapotes
CASINOS
Chips are down in the islands of the sun. A. F. Gonzalez, jr. il Sat R 47:69+ O 10 '64
CASKETS, Burial. See Coffins
CASKEY, George B.
Never called on account of rain. Am City 79: 29 Je '64
CASPARI, Ernst
Phylogeny: principles and methods; meeting sponsored by the American society of naturalists. Science 139:773-4 F 22 '63
CASPER, Alfred G. T.
Animal surgeon. il pors Ebony 19:168-70 N '63
CASPER, Billy
If a Texas portent holds true, watch out for Big Billy. G. S. Brown. il por Sports Illus 210:81-2+ My 18 '64
CASPER, John H.
Mono-print printmaking. Sch Arts 64:14-16 N '64
CASPIAN SEA
Sea that spills into a desert. M. A. Garbell. il Sci Am 209:94-100 bibliog(p 140) Ag '63
CASS, James
What happened at Berkeley. Sat R 48:47-8+ Ja 16 '65
While school keeps. See issues of Saturday review
CASS, Lewis
On report, gentlemen! army officers, 1813; ed. by D. Emrich. Am Heritage 14:112 Ag '63
CASS, Sam
Computer out-thinks. Am City 79:98-9 Ag '64
CASSADAY, E. W.
Upgrading simple FM tuners. Electr World 69:80 My '63
CASSEDY, James H.
Stimulation of health research. bibliog Science 145:897-902 Ag 28 '64
CASSEGRAIN telescope. See Telescope
CASSELL, John
On the fringe. H. Frankel. Sat R 47:39 Mr 21 '64
CASSELS, Alan
Fascism for export: Italy and the United States in the twenties. bibliog f Am Hist R 69:707-12 Ap '64
CASSEROLE cookery
Casserole to serve a hungry dozen. Sunset 130: 237 My '63
Chicken casseroles. il Suc Farm 61:90+ Ap '63
Chicken noodle casserole. D. J. Robinson. il Ebony 18:142+ Je '63
Easy casseroles from your pantry shelf. V. T. Habeeb. il Am Home 66:48-9+ O '63
Easy one-dish patio meals. il Pop Gard 15:42 F '64
Freezing & canning cookbook; excerpts. N. Nichols. il Farm J 87:94-7+ Ap '63

CASSEROLE cookery—*Continued*
Glamorous catchall; with recipes. D. Durham. il Ladies Home J 81:150-2+ N '64
How to crisp a casserole! il Bet Hom & Gard 42:92+ Ap '64
Macaroni or spaghetti. il Bet Hom & Gard 43:115-16 Ja '65
Meal in one. il McCalls 91:94-5+ Ja '64
One-dish meals for your busiest days. il Am Home 67:58+ D '64
Why not a casserole brunch? Sunset 132:240+ My '64
CASSIDY, Brendan. See Tierney, E. J. jt. auth.
CASSIDY, Claudia
Chicago: all's well that... Theatre Arts 47:20-1+ Mr '63
CASSIDY, Daniel, jr
Landward pale; poem. Atlan 212:58 S '63
CASSIDY, William A.
Cosmic dust. Science 144:1475-7 Je 19 '64
CASSINI, Charlene (Wrightsman)
Rich girl. il por Time 81:32 Ap 19 '63
CASSINI, Igor
Personal lives: when the sweet life turns sour; a farewell to scandal. Esquire 61:94-5+ Ap '64
about
Brothers Cassini; Oleg and Igor. B. Brower. por Esquire 59:61-4+ F '63
Social notes. Sat Eve Post 236:76 Mr 9 '63
Who's twisting now? il por Newsweek 61:23 F 18 '63
CASSINI, Oleg
Brothers Cassini; Oleg and Igor. B. Brower. por Esquire 59:61-4+ F '63
CASSITY, Turner
Catechism for Cape Malays; Message from Mother Goddam; Meditation under a pith helmet; Shropshire lad in Limehouse; Junker-lied; In the western province; poems. Poetry 102:74-9 My '63
Down there on a visit: poetry in the Netherlands. Poetry 102:38-42 Ap '63
Five poets. Poetry 103:192-8 D '63
Serenade for the vicereine; Hotel Des Indes; East side, West side; Any year at Bad Irgendwo; Leda of the grosse freiheit; Gardens of Proserpine; poems. Poetry 104:346-51 S '64
CASSIUS'S castle; story. See Cain, E.
CASTAGNA, Edwin
Access survey; from the public library administrator's viewpoint. por Wilson Lib Bul 38:342-4 D '63
Challenge and opportunity; excerpts from address, October 12, 1963. Library J 89:1825-7 Ap 15 '64
Climate of intellectual freedom; why is it always so bad in California? address, November 6, 1964. por ALA Bul 59:27-33 Ja '65
Courage and cowardice; address, November 15-17, 1962. por Library J 88:501-6 F 1 '63
Libraries for an affluent society with frayed edges; address, July 3, 1964. ALA Bul 58:635-8 Jl '64
Memo to members. por ALA Bul 58:670-1 S '64
Up to our ears in students; or, Something's got to give; excerpts from address, May 2, 1963. Library J 88:2421-3 Je 15 '63
Wealthier by the world; foreign librarians in Enoch Pratt free library, Baltimore; address, October 1963. por Wilson Lib Bul 39:48-50 S '64
—and Halverson, Rolf
To overcome the myth. pors(p3242) Library J 89:3249-51 S 15 '64
about
New ALA officer. J. D. Henderson. por ALA Bul 57:660+ Jl '63
CASTBERG, Christian
Little M. il Mlle 58:70-1 Ja; 128 F; 108 Ap '64
CASTE
Outlawing of India's caste system. H. Kabir. il UNESCO Courier 16:12-14 D '63
Return to India: the Ambassador's view. C. Bowles. il N Y Times Mag p20-1+ N 10 '63
See also
Untouchables
CASTELLANI, A. and others
Overlap of photoreactivation and liquid holding recovery in escherichia coli B. bibliog Science 143:1170-1 Mr 13 '64
CASTELLANOS, Rosario
Hecuba's testament; poem, tr. by J. F. Nims. Atlan 213:120 Mr '64
CASTELLO BRANCO, Humberto
U.S. and Brazil reaffirm commitment to peace; letter to President Johnson, August 11, 1964. Dept State Bul 51:435 S 28 '64
about
Brazil in quandary. J. J. Johnson. Cur Hist 48:9-15+ Ja '65
Brazil: success without cheers. il por Newsweek 65:46-7 Ja 11 '65
Brazil's adroit new leader. M. J. Kubic. il Reporter 31:21-3 D 17 '64
Half a loaf. Newsweek 64:60-1 N 2 '64
Long, tricky path facing Brazil; with editorial comment. por Bsns W p72+, 188 Ap 11 '64
New president. Newsweek 63:65 Ap 20 '64
Quest for moderation. Newsweek 63:59 Ap 27 '64
Right turn in Brazil. por Bsns W p31 Je 13 '64
Shaking down. por Newsweek 64:40 Ag 3 '64
Toward profound change. il por Time 83:49-50 Ap 17 '64
CASTER, K. E. See Durham, J. W. jt. auth.
CASTER, W. O. and Ahn, Philip
Electrocardiographic notching in rats deficient in essential fatty acids. bibliog Science 139:1213 Mr 22 '63
CASTERS, glides, etc (hardware)
Casters for home use. il Good H 157:147 Ag '63
CASTIELLA, Fernando Maria
Non-Catholics in Spain. America 109:189-92 Ag 24 '63
United States and Spain renew defense agreement. Dept State Bul 49:686-8 O 28 '63
CASTING (fishing) See Fishing
CASTING (sculpture)
Creative casting. L. Campbell. il Craft Horiz 23:10-17+ N '63
Sand casting. H. Bedford. il Design 65:113+ Ja '64
See also
Plaster casts
CASTING, Continuous. See Continuous casting
CASTING, Plastics. See Plastics—Molding
CASTING, Precision. See Lost wax process
CASTING of bronzes. See Bronze founding
CASTING rods. See Fishing tackle
CASTINGS, Steel. See Steel castings
CASTLE, Joellen
Cornfield chemicals club. Recreation 56:409-10 N '63
CASTLE, Nick
Thirty years of Nick Castle. R. Clark. il pors Dance Mag 38:46-9 F '64
CASTLES
Castle in the casbah; Moorish York castle, Tangier, Morocco. S. Kirtland and others. il Look 28:51-8 Ja 28 '64
Elsinore. H. Bendix. Mlle 58:127 F '64
Fabled Mount of St Michael. A. Villiers. il Nat Geog Mag 125:880-98 Je '64
Fit for a king; castles as inns. il Time 81:54 Je 28 '63
Hamlet's castle; Kronborg castle. J. H. Preston. il Holiday 35:24+ Ja '64
In Germany's castle-hotels. il Sunset 132:41+ Mr '64
Live like a king in a castle. L. Lawrence. il Read Digest 83:158-63 Jl '63
Medieval tour; Bunratty castle. J. Park. il Travel 119:16 F '63
Minister's fatal showplace; Vaux and Vaux-le-Vicomte. W. H. Hale. il Horizon 5:76-83 Jl '63
Moats in their eyes; castle living for tourists. Newsweek 64:56+ Jl 13 '64
Mountbatten's Irish retreat. il Life 55:131-3 S 20 '63
Power of dreams: château of the Baron and Baroness Philippe de Rothschild. V. Lawford. il Vogue 142:86-97 Jl '63
Visit to an Irish castle; Luttrellstown castle, County Dublin. L. Bemelmans. Holiday 33:33-6+ Ap '63
CASTO, Robert Clayton
Orpheus; poem. Commonweal 77:509 F 8 '63
CASTOR beans
Biochemical tests indicative of reaction of castor bean to botrytis. C. A. Thomas and R. G. Orellana. bibliog Science 139:334-5 Ja 25 '63
CASTRATION
Feminine behavior in neonatally castrated and estrogen-treated male rats. H. H. Feder and R. E. Whalen. bibliog il Science 147:306-7 Ja 15 '65
RNA synthesis in rat seminal vesicles: stimulation by testosterone. W. D. Wicks and F. T. Kenney. bibliog il Science 144:1346-7 Je 12 '64
CASTRO, Angel, family
Bitter family. il Time 84:28 Jl 10 '64
CASTRO, Fidel
Oh, to punch Khrushchev; excerpts from interview. Time 81:19-20 Mr 29 '63

CASTRO, Fidel—*Continued*

about

Adopted son in revolt. por Newsweek 62:51 S 16 '63
After all of Cuba's troubles, what's ahead for Castro. il por U S News 55:34-5 N 4 '63
Algeria going the way of Cuba? il U S News 55:62 O 14 '63
As the Cubans see Castro. R. Hudson. por Sat R 47:97-9+ O 10 '64
Beard arrives; visit to Russia. Time 81:32+ My 3 '63
Castro, Khrushchev, and Mao. T. Draper. il Reporter 29:27-31 Ag 15 '63
Castro pulls the eagle's tail; retaliatory seizure of U.S. embassy in Havana. il por U S News 55:23 Ag 5 '63
Castro's challenge to U.S.: the real reasons. il por U S News 56:38-9 F 17 '64
Castro's mysterious trip to Russia. il por U S News 56:16 Ja 27 '64
Chaos in Castro's Cuba; with editorial comment. E. Behr. il por Sat Eve Post 236: 20-2+. 72 Je 8 '63
Choice for Latin America: Castro threat or Leoni promise. Newsweek 63:34-6+ Mr 30 '64
Close-up of Cuba after five years of Castro. il por U S News 56:8 Ja 13 '64
Courting Comrade Castro; first visit to the Soviet Union. il pors Newsweek 61:43-4 My 13 '63
Cuba: how Castro wins and U.S. loses. il por U S News 56:66-8 Ap 6 '64
Cuba in Communist world strategy; address, November 15, 1962. L. V. Manrara. Vital Speeches 29:236-40 F 1 '63
Cuba in 1964. J. Burnham. Nat R 16:16 Ja 14 '64
Cuba lives by Castro's moods. R. Eder. il pors N Y Times Mag p 12-13+ Jl 26 '64
Cuba, the lingering debate. il por Sr Schol 82:8-11 Mr 6 '63
Deal Castro wants with U.S. C. Migdail. U S News 57:47 Ag 10 '64
Eager to coexist? il por Newsweek 64:42 Ag 10 '64
Fidel and Lisa; concerning TV interview with Castro. por Newsweek 61:69 My 13 '63
Fidel in wonderland. il por Time 83:18-19 Ja 24 '64
For Castro, triple trouble now. il U S News 56:66 Ap 27 '64
Fruits of Castro's plotting; with editorial comment. S. Alsop. il por Sat Eve Post 236:75-80 Mr 16 '63
Grief of a foe. por Newsweek 62:53 D 9 '63
Horse-trade in Moscow. por Bsns W p25-6 My 4 '63
How Castro tried to rewrite history. il U S News 55:14 D 23 '63
In the works: deal with Castro? por U S News 54:65 Je 17 '63
Is Castro planning to shoot down U-2s? il por U S News 57:12 N 23 '64
Is Cuba ripe for revolt? E. Tetlow. New Repub 148:8-9 F 23 '63
Kremlin climate; visit to Moscow. il por Newsweek 63:38 Ja 27 '64
Laos, Cuba, and two visitors to Moscow. il por Newsweek 61:39-40 My 6 '63
LBJ and Cuba: what comes next. por U S News 55:41 D 23 '63
My advance view of the Cuban crisis. K. Keating. il Look 28:96+ N 3 '64
My brother is a tyrant and he must go. J. Castro. il pors Life 57:22-33 Ag 28 '64
New trouble in Cuba; Castro's woes keep growing. il por U S News 57:14 D 21 '64
Nonstop day with Castro. il pors Newsweek 63:28-9 Mr 2 '64
On with the show; celebration in Santiago de Cuba. il por Time 84:34 Ag 7 '64
Other beard. il por Time 81:27 My 10 '63
Report from Cuba: passion for seed potatoes. J. Gerassi. il por Newsweek 64:44+ Jl 27 '64
Reporter engagé; concerning report by J. Daniel. Newsweek 62:70 D 23 '63
Rethinking Cuba. Christian Cent 80:1191-2 O 2 '63
Sister's view. Newsweek 64:42+ Jl 13 '64
Total recall. il por Newsweek 63:59 Ap 27 '64
Undiplomatic diplomatic move; seizure of U.S. embassy building. il Sr Schol 83:7 S 20 '63
U.S. Cuba and Guantanamo. il por Sr Schol 84:9-11 Mr 13 '64
United States, Cuba, and Castro. by W. A. Williams. Review
New Repub 148:23-4 Ap 20 '63. S. Shapiro
U.S. warns of Castro declaration of war on hemisphere; text of U.S. note, January 30, 1963. D. S. Morrison. Dept State Bul 48:263-4 F 18 '63
Variation on a theme. il por Newsweek 64: 49-50 Jl 20 '64
What a reporter found: after five and a half years of communism; how Cuba looks today. C. Migdail. il por U S News 57:38-40 Ag 31 '64
What are the odds against Castro now? il U S News 55:90-1 D 9 '63
When Castro heard the news. J. Daniel. New Repub 149:7-9 D 7 '63
When Khrushchev and Castro get together. il pors U S News 54:37-9 My 13 '63
Why Castro wants U.S. to bail him out. por U S News 57:62 Jl 20 '64

CASTRO, Josué de
Operation Nordeste. UNESCO Courier 16:24-31 My '63

CASTRO, Juanita
My brother is a tyrant and he must go. pors Life 57:22-33 Ag 28 '64

about

Bitter family. il por Time 84:28 Jl 10 '64
Embarrassing exile. por U S News 57:19 Jl 13 '64
People of the week. U S News 57:19 Ag 31 '64
Sister's view. por Newsweek 64:42+ Jl 13 '64

CASTRO, Raul
Castro, sí; Yanqui, sí; new ambassador to El Salvador. por Time 84:53 S 18 '64

CASTRO, Raúl Silva. See Silva Castro, R.

CASTRO JIJÓN, Ramón
Morning after; coup d'état. por Newsweek 62:49 Jl 29 '63

CASTRO RIBEIRO, Constantino de
Visions & vengeance. Time 82:37 Jl 5 '63

CASTS, Plaster (sculpture) See Plaster casts

CASUALTIES
See also
War casualties

CAT and the canary; drama. See Willard, J.

CAT food
Catering to the cats and dogs. il Bsns W p64-6+ N 9 '63

CAT shows
Cat show; at New York trade show building. New Yorker 39:19-20 Ja 4 '64

ÇATAL Hüyük excavations. See Turkey—Antiquities

CATALASE
Catalase abnormality in a Caucasian family in the United States. E. W. Baur. bibliog il Science 140:816-17 My 17 '63

CATALDO, John W.
Crafts in a technocracy & education. Sch Arts 63:29-33 Ap '64
Editorial. Sch Arts 62:48 My '63

CATALINA ISLAND. See Santa Catalina Island

CATALINA perfume currant. See Ribes viburnifolium

CATALOG card filing. See Files and filing (documents, etc)

CATALOG cards
Cards-with-books program. J. H. Treyz. il ALA Bul 57:433-4 My '63
Catalog card innovation; Wilson catalog cards: typical comments. Wilson Lib Bul 38:798 My '64
LC studies use of perforated tape for reproduction of catalog cards. Library J 89:2303-4 Je 1 '64
Stacey offers L. C. cards with all scientific books. Pub W 184:46 N 18 '63

Reproduction

Imagement for catalog card reproduction; St Paul public library. E. B. Robbins. il Library J 88:3544-6 O 1 '63

CATALOG houses. See Mail order business

CATALOGERS
Quest for catalogers: today and tomorrow; address, April 18, 1963. S. Lubetzky. bibliog il Library J 88:3535-8 O 1 '63; Reply. H. S. White. 88:4506 D 1 '63

CATALOGING
Age of the mass-produced gargoyle. B. Toohey and J. Biermann. il Library J 89:3698-9 O 1 '64
Association of research libraries concentrates on centralized cataloging. J. Skipper. Library J 89:2953 Ag '64
Catalog code revision, 1964; ALA catalog rules, address, June 2, 1964. S. Lubetsky. bibliog Library J 89:4863-5+ D 15 '64
Cataloging by the bootstrap method; Delphi, Ind, public library. E. C. Biddle. ALA Bul 58:49-52 Ja '64; Discussion. 58:255, 261, 431-2 Ap, Je '64

CATALOGING—*Continued*
Changing catalog rules; reprint. M. Dewey. Library J 89:2296 Je 1 '64
S. Lubetzky. 89:3054+ S 1 '64
Fringe benefit in Egypt; cataloging and classification for Assiut university libraries. M. S. Rinehart. il Wilson Lib Bul 39:52-5 S '64
Librarian vs. scholar-user. H. Draper. il Library J 89:1907-10 My 1 '64; Discussion. 89:2694, 3056+ Jl, S 1 '64
Quest for catalogers: today and tomorrow; address, April 18, 1963. S. Lubetzky. bibliog il Library J 88:3535-8 O 1 '63; Reply. H. S. White. 88:4506 D 1 '63
Rare books and automation: NYU's cataloging experiment; use of IBM punch cards. Library J 88:4723 D 15 '63
Subject cataloging: some considerations of costs. D. Gore. il Library J 89:3699-703 O 1 '64; Reply. R. D. Franklin. 89:4238 N 1 '64
See also
Subject headings

Anecdotes, facetiae, satire, etc.

When things are looking up. M. Bennett. Sat R 46:28 Ag 24 '63

Cost

Another chance for centralized cataloging; reprint. R. E. Ellsworth. il Library J 89:3104-7 S 1 '64; Reply. C. MacQuarrie. 89:4236 N 1 '64

CATALOGING, Cooperative
Commercial cataloging services: a directory; comp. by B. Westby. il Library J 89:1508-13 Ap 1 '64; Correction. 89:2311 Je 1 '64
Program for shared cataloging to be developed by ARL; committee, with Library of Congress. Library J 89:1046 Mr 1 '64
Sharing the cataloging load; planning committee of ARL with LC. Wilson Lib Bul 38:525+ Mr '64

CATALOGS
See also
Phonograph records—Catalogs

CATALOGS, Library
Automatic preparation of book catalogs. J. Becker. ALA Bul 58:714-18 S '64
Book catalog. G. K. Schenk. Wilson Lib Bul 37:884 Je '63
Chain indexing is not mysterious; classified catalogs. T. Wilson; reply. T. C. Hines. Library J 88:702 F 15 '63
Cut across the media: school library catalogs. D. E. Hogan. Library J 89:4981-4 D 15 '64
Subject cataloging: some considerations of costs. D. Gore. il Library J 89:3699-703 O 1 '64; Reply. R. D. Franklin. 89:4238 N 1 '64

CATALOGS, Mail order
Catalog cache; with list of mail-order specialists. il Sports Illus 21:54-60 N 16 '64
Christmas catalogs are here. Consumer Bul 46:26 D '63
How catalogues get their sales appeal. il Bsns W p96+ Jl 25 '64
Penney by post. il Newsweek 62:66 Ag 12 '63
See also
Mail order business

CATALOGS, Seed and plant
Catalogs can make your gardening an adventure. A. Murphy. il Horticulture 41:610-12 D '63
Catalogs coming. R. C. Hands. Horticulture 41:612-15 D '63
Catalogues. Pop Gard 15:45 N '64
Catalogues for fireside browsing. B. Nichols. il Pop Gard 14:51+ N '63
Four-color flora. Time 85:42+ Ja 29 '65
1965 catalogs. R. C. Hands. Horticulture 42:41 D '64
That wonderful world of seed and garden catalogs. Consumer Bul 47:14-15 Mr '64

Bibliography

Library plant and seed sources. B. Higgins. Horticulture 41:586 N '63

CATALOGS, Trade
One 33J3663F and a 7J4202F: the buying-by-catalogue boom. il Newsweek 63:88-90 My 25 '64; Same abr. with title Booming business of buying by catalogue. Read Digest 85:189-90+ O '64

Anecdotes, facetiae, satire, etc.

Tool catalogs, a critical appraisal. W. Stanton. Life 56:12+ My 1 '64

CATALYSIS
Alpha-chymotrypsin and the nature of enzyme catalysis. C. Niemann. bibliog il Science 143:1287-96 Mr 20 '64
Infrared spectroscopy and catalysis research. R. P. Eischens. bibliog il Science 146:486-93 O 23 '64
Mass spectral studies of surface catalysis: the production of free radicals at 40°C. T. W. Martin and R. E. Rummel. bibliog il Science 143:797-9 F 21 '64

CATAMARANS
Big cat island-hops in Bahamas. il Pop Sci 182:70-1 My '63
Catamarans and common sense. R. Choy. il Motor B 111:40-1+ F; 86-8+ Mr '63
Clever idea turns two canoes into a cat. il Pop Sci 185:93 Jl '64
DC-14 Phantom. il Yachting 115:61 My '64
52' catamaran motorsailer. il Motor B 112:56+ S '63
How of those hopped-up sailboats. F. Rohr, jr. il Pop Mech 121:108-12+ F '64
Sailing a catamaran. E. F. Cotter. il Yachting 113:48-50+ Je '63
Two hulls are better than one; one-of-a-kind regatta on Biscayne Bay. A. Zich. il Sports Illus 18:12-17 Mr 4 '63
Wissahickon; catamaran of the gay nineties. W. H. Taylor. il Yachting 115:136-7 F '64

Design

Hiolani, a 36' ocean-going cat. il Motor B 111:52 Je '63

CATARACT
Can you see, my son, can you really see? cataracts removed from five Rotolo brothers; with report by J. Bonfante. il Life 57:32-41 N 20 '64
Your eyes their two worst enemies: cataracts and glaucoma. il Changing T 17:17-18 D '63

CATASTROPHES (geology) See Geology—History
CATASTROPHIES. See Disasters
CATBOATS
Other man's boat; Prudence, Cape Cod catboat. W. H. DeFontaine. il Yachting 116:54-5+ D '64
CATCHERS, Baseball. See Baseball players
CATCHPOOL, J. F. See Cherkin, A. jt. auth.
CATCHWORDS. See Slogans
CATE, Curtis
People on fire: the Congo. Atlan 213:91-2+ My '64
Road to Moscow: de Gaulle and the Kremlin. Atlan 212:65-71 Ag '63
CATE, William B.
Dialogue in Portland. Christian Cent 80:745 Je 5 '63
CATECHETICS
Head and heart: catechisms with a modern accent. G. E. Carter. America 109:40-3 Jl 13 '63
Primitive ecumenical catechism; excerpts from reports and messages of major ecumenical conferences. R. French. Christian Cent 80:1505-8 D 4 '63
See also
Catechisms

Bibliography

Readings in Protestant catechetics. W. H. DuBay. Cath World 199:43-9 Ap '64

CATECHISMS
More than a memorial; Heidelberg catechism. Christian Cent 80:198 F 13 '63
CATECHOL
Enzymatic formation of adrenaline and other catechols from monophenols. J. Axelrod. bibliog il Science 140:499-500 My 3 '63
CATECHOLAMINES
Alteration in learning ability caused by changes in cerebral serotonin and catechol amines. D. W. Woolley and T. van der Hoeven. bibliog il Science 139:610-11 F 15 '63; Reply with rejoinder. D. E. McMillan. 145:952 Ag 28 '64
See also
Dopamine
CATEGORY novel. See Fiction
CATER, Douglass
Beyond tokenism. Reporter 29:23-7 O 10 '63
Clay report. Reporter 28:10+ Ap 11 '63
Eisenhower: what did he want? Reporter 29:59-60 N 21 '63
Hard-won destiny of Lyndon Johnson. Reporter 29:17-19 D 19 '63
Politics of poverty. Reporter 30:16-20 F 13 '64
Secret life of the A-11. Reporter 30:16-17 Ap 23 '64
CATER, Harold Dean
Whatever happened to the arts in education? Sch Arts 63:20 F '64
CATERING
Catering Cokers; G. J. Coker & son. New Yorker 40:46 D 12 '64

CATERPILLAR tractor company
Gentle bulldozers of Peoria. G. Cross. il Fortune 68:166-71+ Jl '63
Useful work for disabled; it pays to hire handicapped workers. il Bsns W p48+ My 9 '64
CATERPILLARS
Animal husbandry in the animal kingdom; how and why carpenter ants protect caterpillars. il Time 82:98 D 6 '63
Beware the woolly worm. Time 84:49 Jl 31 '64
Multicolored world of caterpillars. P. Villiard. il Natur Hist 73:24-31 Ap '64
See also
Butterflies
Gipsy moths
Silkworms
CATFISH fishing
Don't let H.O. spoil your fishing. D. Bowers. il Field & S 69:38-40 N '64
Grabbling for those crazy Mississippi cats. H. Peterson. il Sports Illus 20:58-60+ Je 15 '64
Hats off to the cats. R. Tinsley. il Outdoor Life 134:42-3+ N '64
Pothole catfish. R. Tinsley. il Outdoor Life 131:78-80+ Je '63
CATFISHES
Catfish, super-snooper of the deep. J. George. il Read Digest 85:21-2+ Jl '64
See also
Cookery—Fish
CATHARTICS
Irregulars. il Newsweek 61:62-3 Ap 29 '63
CATHAY Pacific (airline) See Airlines—Far East
CATHCART, Robert S. 3d. See Worthington, W. C. jr. jt. auth.
CATHEDRALS
England
Up from the ashes, a great cathedral rises; Coventry. C. W. Hall. il Read Digest 82: 197-200+ Je '63
See also
London—St Paul's cathedral
France
See also
Notre Dame cathedral, Paris
Italy
See also
Rome (city)—St Peter's cathedral
Spain
Crown of Toledo; with photographs by D. Kessel. Life 55:64-75 D 13 '63
CATHERINE II, empress of Russia
Catherine the Great, by Z. Oldenbourg. Review
Newsweek por 65:79 F 1 '65
Sat R il 48:47 Ja 23 '65. I. Spector
CATHERINE, Sister Mary. See Mary Catherine, Sister
CATHERINE of Cleves, Book of hours of. See Hours, Books of
CATHERINE'S crown; story. See Cavanaugh, A.
CATHODE-ray accelerators. See Accelerators (electrons, etc)
CATHODE-ray oscilloscope cameras. See Cameras
CATHODE ray oscilloscopes. See Oscillographs
CATHODE ray tubes
High-speed electronic printer. A. W. Edwards. il Electr World 72:46-8 D '64
Recording storage tubes and their applications. A. S. Luftman. il Electr World 69: 21-4+ My '63
See also
Television receiving apparatus—Picture tubes
CATHODIC protection. See Corrosion and anticorrosives
CATHOLIC action
Lay elite. L. M. Madigan. America 109:193-5 Ag 24 '63
CATHOLIC art. See Christian art and symbolism
CATHOLIC association for international peace
Catholic peacemakers. America 110:217 F 15 '64
On the peace circuit. J. Leo. Commonweal 79:123-4 O 25 '63
Peace fighter. America 110:810 Je 13 '64
CATHOLIC authors
Catholic as writer. W. Sheed; M. Novak. Commonweal 77:560-3+ F 22 '63
Catholic novels & American culture. T. F. Curley. Commentary 36:34-42 Jl '63
Gabriel Fielding, new master of the Catholic classic? L. M. Grande. Cath World 197:172-9 Je '63
Maria Cross, by C. C. O'Brien. Review
Cath World 198:384+ Mr '64. G. Roy
CATHOLIC book awards, National. See National Catholic book awards
CATHOLIC book club
Barbara Ward; recipient of Campion award. America 111:682 N 28 '64
CATHOLIC book week. See Book week
CATHOLIC church
Aggiornamento. Cath World 199:332; 200:3, 72, 136, 199 S '64-Ja '65
Angry young men; advocates of change. America 111:150-1 Ag 15 '64; Discussion. 111:274-6, 606-7+ S 19, N 14 '64
Baptist intellectual's view of Catholicism. H. Cox; reply. P. Blanshard. Harper 226:14 Mr '63
Between Constantinople and Rome. W. A. Visser 't Hooft. Christian Cent 81:1106-8 S 9 '64
Bravest schema; no. thirteen, The church in the modern world. il Time 84:74+ O 30 '64
Break with the past; Mater et magistra and Pacem in terris. M. Novak. Commonweal 78:372-5 Je 28 '63
Cardinal Suenens on the church; interview, ed. by W. M. Abbott. L. J. Suenens. America 108:360-1 Mr 16 '63
Catching up. America 109:92 Jl 27 '63
Catholic church battles its old guard. J. T. Elson. il Life 55:114-15+ O 18 '63
Catholic church: which way now? il U S News 54:37-9 Je 17 '63
Catholic scholars. il Time 81:80-2 My 3 '63
Catholicism: prospects and problems. Christian Cent 80:881-4, 904-7, 930-3 Jl 10-24 '63
Catholics and birth control; a bold reexamination. G. Barrett. Read Digest 83:77-82 N '63
Challenge of Christian freedom; supernatural reality of Christian liberty. J. V. Gallagher. Cath World 197:223-30 Jl '63
Change without fanfare; new board for the implementation of the Constitution on the liturgy. R. W. Rousseau. America 110:694 My 23 '64
Changes in church and world, the work of Pope John. il U S News 54:50-1 Je 10 '63
Changing roles in the church. J. Cogley. Commonweal 80:5-7 Mr 27 '64; Reply. 80:238 My 15 '64
Church and freedom. H. Kung. il Commonweal 78:343-53 Je 21 '63; Discussion. 78: 339, 536-7; 79:108-9 Je 21, S 6, O 18 '63
Church and mankind's future on earth; excerpt from address. E. Schillebeeckx. Cath World 200:218-23 Ja '65
Church and the council: issues behind the speeches on the nature of the church. J. C. Murray. America 109:451-3 O 19 '63
Church's Catholicity. America 111:372 O 3 '64
Clear it with the Vatican. il Time 82:72 S 20 '63
Closed and/or open. J. Powell. America 109: 484-6 O 26 '63
Constitution on the church. D. R. Campion. America 111:777-8 D 12 '64
Dialogue of salvation; Pope Paul VI's first encyclical. Ecclesiam suam. America 111:176 Ag 22 '64
Ecumenical voices. il Time 81:52 Ap 5 '63
Ecumenics and non-Christians; new secretariat for non-Christians. bibliog America 110:753 My 30 '64
Facing the black facts. Newsweek 63:55 F 10 '64
Family planning in an exploding population; Roman Catholic opinion. J. A. O'Brien. Christian Cent 80:1050-2 Ag 28 '63
Father Delp's prison diary. A. Delp. Cath World 196:364-9 Mr '63
Fresh orientation in the church. R. Rouquette. Cath World 196:343-50 Mr '63
Half-breeds; the ordinary priests reaction to modernization. J. Maher. America 111: 743-4 D 5 '64
His church; Pope Paul VI's first encyclical Ecclesiam suam. Newsweek 64:76 Ag 24 '64
Honesty vs. loyalty oaths. J. Cogley. Commonweal 80:249-51 My 22 '64
Layman's hopes. J. O'Gara. Commonweal 81: 87 O 16 '64
Modernist movement and Catholic renewal today. C. D. Nelson. Christian Cent 81:1139-41 S 16 '64
Monoliths: existent and non-existent. R. M. Brown. Commonweal 77:596-7 Mr 1 '63; Reply with rejoinder. U. J. Proeller. 78:249 My 24 '63
New Catholic image: openness to today's world. J. B. Sheerin. Cath World 198:204-7 Ja '64
On discussing freedom; Fr. H. Küng's lecture tour. America 108:663 My 11 '63

CATHOLIC church—*Continued*
Pentecostal gesture; Pope Paul's announcement of new secretariat for relations with non-Christians. America 110:757 My 30 '64
Pope John: the astonishing Catholic pontiff; and why he stirred the world; Pacem in terris. J. Roddy. il Look 27:18-29 Jl 2 '63
Prior mission of the church. E. Hillman. il Cath World 198:238-44 Ja '64
Protestantism and authority. R. M. Brown. Commonweal 81:69-71 O 9 '64; Reply with rejoinder. P. E. Meehl. 81:329-31 N 27 '64
Public image of the Catholic church today; symposium. Cath World 199:352-5 S '64
Radical Rome. C. Northcott. Christian Cent 81:1423 N 18 '64
Representing the community; analogy with democracy. C. Davis. America 111:353 S 26 '64
Second coming. J. Cogley. Commonweal 77:554-5 F 22 '63
Secretariat for non-Christians. Commonweal 80:280-1 My 29 '64
Signs of change stir the Catholic church. J. Roddy. il Look 27:81 Ap 23 '63
Situation normal. Commonweal 79:88 O 18 '63
Spirit bloweth; concerning Father Hans Kung's address at Georgetown university. A. Dun. New Repub 148:8 My 18 '63
Story of schema seventeen: the church in the present-day world. L. Kaufmann. Cath World 200:8-14 O '64
Suggestion for Mr Waugh. J. Cogley. Commonweal 81:120-2 O 23 '64; Discussion. 81:352-4 D 4 '64
Thrust of "progressive" Catholicism. G. A. Lindbeck. Commonweal 79:105-7 O 18 '63
Time for balance. America 111:127 Ag 8 '64
Trials of the church in 1964. America 110:3 Ja 4 '64
Understanding the conservatives. J. Cogley. Commonweal 80:388-9 Je 19 '64; Reply. E. Waugh. 80:547-8 Ag 7 '64
Unfinished reformation: report of statement on the need for a reform of the Roman Catholic church. Time 83:66 F 7 '64
Variety of Catholic attitudes, by T. Westow. Review
Commonweal 79:724 Mr 13 '64. H. A. Reinhold
Vatican hints review of birth control stand; new pill under test may be acceptable to Catholics. Bsns W p25 My 30 '64
Where Pope Paul is leading his church; first encyclical. il U S News 57:42-3 Ag 24 '64
Winds of change in the Catholic church. il U S News 57:54-5 N 2 '64
Word (cont) V. P. McCorry. America 110:128; 111:221, 643-4, 676 Ja 18, Ag 29, N 14-21 '64
Working together; modern lay outlook. C. Davis. America 111:42 Jl 11 '64
See also
Beatification
Church and state
Councils and synods
Ecumenical movement
Encyclicals
Eucharistic congresses
Martyrs
Mass
Modernism
Opus Dei
Papacy
Penance
Popes
Religious orders
Saints
Sisterhoods
Tithes
Vatican
Vatican City
Vatican council, 2d
Vocation (in religion)
Worker priests

Apologetics

See Apologetics

Art

See Christian art and symbolism

Authority

See Church—Authority

Bibliography

Of Catholic interest. W. A. Johnson. Christian Cent 80:1404-7 N 13 '63

Byzantine rite

Patriarch Maximos IV and Vatican council II; interview, ed. by E. Inglessis and E. Inglessis. Maximos IV. Cath World 198:372-9 Mr '64

Ceremonies and practices

Ecclesiastical baroque. J. O'Gara. Commonweal 79:478 Ja 24 '64; Reply. T. Merton. 79:573-4 F 7 '64
Same again please: a layman's hopes of the Vatican council. E. Waugh; discussion. Nat R 13:521; 14:37 D 31 '62-Ja 15 '63; Commonweal 77:487-9 F 1 '63; Newsweek 61:57 F 25 '63; America 108:440-2 Mr 30 '63

Charities

Franciscans and burlesque. America 109:278 S 21 '63
See also
Little brothers of the poor

Clergy

Anticlericalism, American style. Christian Cent 80:419-20 Ap 3 '63
Clerical freedom. Commonweal 78:86-7 Ap 19 '63
Collegiality. America 108:459 Ap 6 '63
Freedom of priests. D. Callahan. Commonweal 79:95-8 O 18 '63; Discussion. 79:285-8, 373-5 N 29, D 20 '63
Limousines and clerics. America 110:181 F 8 '64
Married priest. il Time 84:66 Jl 10 '64
Not peace, but the sword; the new anguish of American Catholicism. E. R. F. Sheehan. il Sat Eve Post 237:20-32+ N 28 '64
Priestly state, marriage or celibacy? by P. Hermand. Review
Time 84:56+ Ag 28 '64
Princes and eunuchs. America 109:652 N 23 '63
Role of bishops in relation to the papacy. G. Baum. Cath World 198:94-9 N '63
See also
Bishops
Cardinals
Priests
Vatican council, 2d

Congregation of the Holy Office

Cardinal Ottaviani: the bulwark. E.-M. Jung. Cath World 199:80-8 My '64
Civil rights in the church. R. A. Graham. America 109:257-60 S 14 '63

Converts

See Converts, Catholic

Dioceses

Catholicism in Los Angeles. A. V. Krebs, jr; J. Leo. il Commonweal 80:467-82 Jl 10 '64; Discussion. 80:463-4, 549-50, 581 Jl 10, Ag 7-21 '64; Christian Cent 81:926 Jl 22 '64
CURE; Los Angeles movement for racial equality and social justice. Commonweal 80:352 Je 12 '64
Postscript on L.A. J. Leo. Commonweal 80:529 Ag 7 '64
Sinus Viridis packers and the neo-Eboraci giants. N. Perrin. New Yorker 39:213-15+ N 9 '63

Discipline

Politics and Catholic freedom, by G. Wills. Review
Nat R 16:730-2+ Ag 25 '64. W. Herberg. Discussion. 16:829-31+ S 22 '64
See also
Obedience (canon law)

Education

Academic man in the Catholic college, by J. D. Donovan. Review
Commonweal 81:21-2 S 25 '64. J. McDermott
Sat R 47:71 Ap 18 '64. G. N. Shuster
America's directory of Catholic colleges 1963. America 109:574-5 N 9 '63
America's 1964 directory of Catholic colleges. America 111:608-9 N 14 '64
Are parochial schools the answer? by M. P. Ryan. Review
Christian Cent 81:595-6 My 6 '64
Commonweal 80:99-100 Ap 17 '64; Reply. F. C. Arricale. 80:258-9 My 22 '64
Sat R 47:77 Mr 21 '64. J. Scanlon
Are we really teaching democracy? V. C. Blum. Cath World 197:21-7 Ap '63
Campus corner. D. R. Campion. America 108:198, 266, 302, 337, 367, 406, 467, 532, 639, 751; 109:45; 110:437, 569, 825 F 9, 23-Mr 23, Ap 6, 20, My 4, 25, Jl 13 '63, Mr 28, Ap 25, Je 13 '64
Canon law on schools. America 112:105 Ja 23 '65
Catholic asks: Are parochial schools the answer? excerpt from Are parochial schools the answer? with excerpts from foreword by E. J. Primeau. M. P. Ryan. il U S News 56:75-6 Ap 13 '64

CATHOLIC church—Education—*Continued*
Catholic campus, by E. Wakin. Review
Sat R 46:80 My 18 '63. G. N. Shuster
Catholic colleges: a modest proposal. L. Swidler. Commonweal 81:559-62 Ja 29 '65
Catholic scholarship. J. F. Mulligan. America 109:288-90 S 21 '63
Catholic science textbooks? V. E. Smith. America 110:78-80+ Ja 18 '64; Discussion. 110:208, 270 F 15, 29 '64
Catholicism on the campus. J. Cogley. Commonweal 78:88-9 Ap 19 '63; Reply with rejoinder. J. R. Crowley. 78:326-7 Je 14 '63
Catholics in higher education; Catholic student on the secular campus. R. J. Clifford and W. R. Callahan. il America 111:288-91 S 19 '64; Discussion. 111:468, 726-7 O 24, D 5 '64
Censorship on campus; a student's plea for granting responsible freedom to Catholic college editors. M. O'Connell. America 111:611-?13 N 14 '64; Discussion. 112:17-18, 95 Ja 2, Ja 23 '65
Christian schools, secular subjects. Brother Fidelian. Commonweal 81:566-8+ Ja 29 '65
Church related schools; shared-time. New Repub 148:4-6 My 11 '63
Crisis in Catholic schools. T. J. Fleming. il Sat Eve Post 236:19-25 O 26 '63
Crisis of growth. America 109:250 S 14 '63
Do we have Catholic colleges? C. J. O'Toole; R. J. Henle. America 109:296-9 S 21 '63; Reply. R. Hoffman. 109:403 O 12 '63
Federal aid and Catholic schools; symposium. il Commonweal 79:501-42 Ja 31 '64; Discussion. 79:633-4, 664-5; 80:150-1 F 21-28, Ap 24 '64
Flexible African church; first Africa-wide meeting on Catholic education planned by the Catholic international education office. America 110:664 My 16 '64
Forward look in Louisville; first Catholic educational conference. America 110:302 Mr 7 '64
Georgeham: 1984. L. Shaw. America 111:214-16 Ag 29 '64; Discussion. 111:485-6 O 24 '64
How the university can further Christian unity; excerpt from Unity of Christians. A. Bea. Cath World 197:8-14 Ap '63
Is the Catholic college an apostolate? C. L. Salm. Cath World 200:211-17 Ja '65
Jubilation; memoir of a Sacred Heart education, tr. by F. Frenaye. C. de Rivoyre. Vogue 144:238-9+ D '64
Merging the colleges. Commonweal 81:556-7 Ja 29 '65
Modest proposal of Mary Perkins Ryan. J. A. O'Connor. Cath World 199:216-23 Jl '64
NORC, round three: study of the effects of Catholic formal education in America. Commonweal 81:555-6 Ja 29 '65
New debate. A. M. Greeley; J. D. Donovan; J. W. Trent. il Commonweal 81:33-42 O 2 '64
New kind of sisters' school. M. McGrory. America 111:206 Ag 29 '64
Opposing Dallas apartheid. America 112:97 Ja 23 '65
Our segregated Catholic schools. J. B. Sheerin. Cath World 196:331-4 Mr '63
Place to learn; Catholic universities in Latin America. il Time 82:41 N 22 '63
Question of relevance; control by the laity. J. McCudden. Cath World 198:7-13 O '63
Reforming the seminaries. J. O'Donoghue. Commonweal 81:194-6 N 6 '64; Discussion. 81:391-2, 466-7+ D 11 '64, Ja 8 '65
Religion and career, by A. M. Greeley. Review
America 110:102 Ja 18 '64. R. M. Brooks
Scholastic teacher interviews: Msgr. O'Neil C. D'Amour; ed. by H. Langer. O. C. D'Amour. il Sr Schol 84:9T-11T Ap 10 '64
Schools and Vatican II. America 112:97 Ja 23 '65
Schools under strain. il Time 83:74+ Mr 20 '64
Script for a beginning; efforts at Marin Catholic high school, Kentfield, Calif. to help interracial understanding. Sister Mary Leona. America 111:256-9 S 12 '64
Separate & superior; St Augustine high school in New Orleans. il Time 85:56 Ja 1 '65
Sit-in at Georgetown. F. E. Kearns. Commonweal 78:94+ Ap 19 '63; Discussion. 78:250-2 My 24 '63
So it's parochialism. M. E. Endres. America 110:823-5 Je 13 '64
Theology in the Catholic college. G. H. Tavard. il Commonweal 78:273-5 My 31 '63; Discussion. 78:455-7 Jl 26 '63
Toward the open college. Sister Helen James John. Commonweal 79:33-6 O 4 '63; Reply with rejoinder. J. F. Flynn. 79:196-7 N 8 '63
University headaches; administrative decisions. America 108:430-1 Mr 30 '63
Where are you going? reasons for the Catholic high school graduate to attend a Catholic college. G. B. Fugate. America 110:673-5 My 16 '64
Why not a second Cadillac? America 110:301 Mr 7 '64; Reply. M. J. Fortunato. 110:388-9 Mr 28 '64
See also
Boston college
Clarke college, Dubuque, Iowa
De Paul university
National Catholic educational association
Notre Dame, Ind. University
Parochial schools, Catholic
Trinity college, Washington, D.C.
Webster college, Webster Groves, Mo.

Eucharist

Welcome innovation; procedure for distributing communion in the Roman rite. America 110:664 My 16 '64

Government

Apostolic senate. America 110:277 F 29 '64
Bishops, under or with the pope? J. B. Sheerin. Cath World 198:139-43 D '63
Confrontation in the council. G. Baum. Commonweal 79:311-13 D 6 '63
Congregation vs. council? America 110:664 My 16 '64
Crisis in Rome; struggle between the bishops and the Roman curia. Newsweek 62:76 N 25 '63
Future role of bishops. W. M. Abbott. America 110:6 Ja 4 '64
Unprecedented changes. America 108:323 Mr 9 '63
See also
Vatican council, 2d

History

Reappraising the reformation. L. Swidler. Commonweal 81:156-8 O 30 '64

Infallibility

Catholic reform and religious liberty. K. Haselden. Christian Cent 80:1570-2 D 18 '63
Papal infallibility. U. J. Proeller; R. M. Brown. Commonweal 78:249 My 24 '63
Understanding the church's teaching office; excerpt from The council in action. H. Küng. Cath World 198:21-7 O '63
Word. V. P. McCorry. America 111:20 Jl 4 '64

Liturgy and ritual

Amen; Liturgy and irredentism. America 110:839 Je 20 '64
Art and the liturgy. S. Hazo. il Cath World 199:286-92 Ag '64
Canadian renewal; a report on the progress of liturgical changes in French and English Canada. W. J. Browne. America 110:675-6 My 16 '64
Changes in the liturgy. F. R. McManus. Commonweal 79:594-6+ F 14 '64
Changes in your missal. America 110:785 Je 6 '64
Coming reforms in the liturgy. F. R. McManus. Cath World 196:335-42 Mr '63
Council and the liturgy. C. J. McNaspy. America 111:778 D 12 '64
First fruits of the spirit; Vatican II's newly proclaimed constitution on sacred liturgy. W. J. Leonard. il America 109:798-801 D 21 '63
It couldn't be done! lay participation in the public worship of the church. America 109:204 Ag 31 '63
Liturgical bonds; three-year cycle of readings. America 109:183 Ag 24 '63
Liturgical challenge. America 110:135-6 Ja 25 '64
Liturgical changes; concerning the council's constitution on the sacred liturgy. America 110:753 My 30 '64
Liturgy: an achievement. G. Young. America 110:14-15 Ja 4 '64
Liturgy and the second Vatican council; constitution on the sacred liturgy. H. A. Reinhold. Cath World 198:347-56 Mr '64
Liturgy: barrier or bond? C. J. McNaspy. America 110:278-80 F 29 '64
New way of worship. il Time 84:66+ N 27 '64
Pastoral liturgy, by J. A. Jungmann. Review
Cath World 197:330-2 Ag '63. J. V. Gallagher
Pope and liturgy changes. America 112:154 Ja 30 '65
Pope orders liturgy changes. Christian Cent 81:199 F 12 '64

CATHOLIC church—Liturgy and ritual—*Cont.*
Progress report on the liturgy. G. S. Sloyan. America 111:179-83 Ag 22 '64; Reply. P. T. Weller. 111:274 S 19 '64
Reform without reformers; changes cannot be fulfilled by decree alone. R. W. Hovda. il Commonweal 80:571-3 Ag 21 '64
Revolution in worship. il Time 82:44 Ag 30 '63
Rites controversy. J. R. Rosenbloom. America 110:544-5 Ap 18 '64
Spirit of Holy week. America 108:457 Ap 6 '63
To the rear, march; letter from an eastern bishop to the priests of his diocese. Commonweal 81:470 Ja 8 '65
Vatican II on music; Constitution on the sacred liturgy. C. J. McNaspy. America 110:55-6 Ja 11 '64
Welcome innovation; procedure for distributing communion in the Roman rite. America 110:664 My 16 '64
Your private devotions. America 111:686 N 28 '64
See also
Liturgical language
Liturgical movement—Catholic church
Liturgical week
Mass
Missals

Bibliography

New books on liturgy. C. J. McNaspy. America 111:187-8 Ag 22 '64

Missions

Go ye therefore, and teach all nations. P. Streit. il N Y Times Mag p 12+ Mr 22 '64
Prior mission of the church. E. Hillman. il Cath World 198:238-44 Ja '64
Vatican II and missions. America 111:444-5 O 17 '64
See also
Catholic medical mission board
Jesuits—Missions

Music

See Church music

Negroes

See also
Church and race problems
National Catholic conference for interracial justice

Public relations

See Church advertising

Relations

Jews

As we await The deputy; questions and answers. J. M. Oesterreicher. il America 109:570-3+ N 9 '63
Backs council draft on Jews. Christian Cent 81:1078 S 2 '64
Billy Rose's message. America 109:187 Ag 24 '63
Cardinal Spellman condemns anti-Semitism. J. B. Sheerin. Cath World 199:268-71 Ag '64; Reply. D. H. Aldeborgh. 200:71 N '64
Catholic church and Nazi Germany, by G. Lewy. Review
Christian Cent 81:886-8 Jl 8 '64. L. D. Streiker
Catholics & Jews: how close? il Time 82:51 N 29 '63
Catholics and Jews. New Repub 150:5-6 Je 27 '64
Christ's Jewishness. Newsweek 62:92 O 28 '63
Controversy on a text. America 111:287 S 19 '64
Council and anti-Semitism. Commonweal 80:407 Je 26 '64
Council and the Jews. America 110:842-3 Je 20 '64; Discussion. 111:1-2 Jl 4 '64
Council declaration on the Jews. J. L. Lichten. Cath World 199:272-8 Ag '64; Discussion. 200:71 N '64
Council on anti-Semitism. America 109:224 S 7 '63
Council on anti-Semitism; concerning talk by G. Weigel to National community relations advisory council. America 109:70-1 Jl 20 '63
Council's text on Jews in jeopardy. Christian Cent 81:1548-9 D 16 '64
Cry against a decision of silence; The deputy, by R. Hochhuth. E. Capouya. il Sat R 47:41-2 Mr 21 '64; Reply. Mrs B. Hecht. 47:28 Ap 18 '64
Danish rabbi speaks; concerning Hochhuth's play, The deputy. America 110:30 Ja 11 '64
Deicide and doctrine. Newsweek 64:81 S 14 '64
Deputy controversy. Christian Cent 81:507-8 Ap 22 '64; Discussion. 81:861-2 Jl 1 '64
Footnote to The deputy dispute: Jews of Rome, the Nazis and the Vatican. C. Mydans. Life 56:21 My 1 '64
Handles Jewish question clumsily. Christian Cent 81:1452 N 25 '64
Hochhuth's Representative. C. Barnes. Nation 197:287-8 N 2 '63
Israel and the pilgrimage. P. S. Konstam. Christian Cent 81:204-6 F 12 '64; Reply. E. Berger. 81:524 Ap 22 '64
Jewish sentiment. M. Himmelfarb. il Commonweal 79:524-7 Ja 31 '64
Jewish statement. Commonweal 81:27-8 O 2 '64
Jews absolved: responsibility for the death of Christ. Sr Schol 85:18 D 9 '64
Jews and Vatican II. America 109:698 N 30 '63
Jews denounce Catholic document; Vatican council's schema on ecumenism as spiritual fratricide. Christian Cent 81:1165 S 23 '64
No letup for Der stellvertreter. E. E. Turner. Christian Cent 80:1269-70 O 16 '63
Nothing more unjust; Pope Paul's allusion to the attacks upon Pope Pius XII in The deputy. America 110:68 Ja 18 '64
Pius and the Jews. America 109:70 Jl 20 '63
Pius XII & the Jews. il Time 82:85-6 N 1 '63
Pius XII and the Jews. P. Land. America 108:730-1 My 25 '63
Pius XII, the Jews, and the German Catholic church. G. Lewy. bibliog Commentary 37:23-35 F '64; Discussion. 37:6+ Je '64
Play that indicts Pope Pius XII. H. Graef. Cath World 197:380-5 S '63
Pope, council and Jews. America 108:427 Mr 30 '63
Recollections of Pius XII. G. A. Gripenberg. America 110:539+ Ap 18 '64
Rolf Hochhuth's The deputy: symposium. Commonweal 79:647-62 F 28 '64; Discussion. 80:46+, 119-21 Ap 3, 17 '64
See or read it first! concerning The deputy. Christian Cent 81:294 Mr 4 '64
Teaching of contempt, by J. Isaac. Review
Commonweal 80:372-3 Je 12 '64. G. Baum
Test of good will; proposed declaration on anti-Semitism. il Time 84:63+ O 9 '64
Third myth. K. Haselden. Christian Cent 80:1491-3 D 4 '63
Vatican and Auschwitz. America 110:668 My 16 '64
Vatican and Jewry: two ecumenical councils, 1869 and 1962. M. L. Gabriel. Cath World 198:157-62 D '63
Vatican II, act III. M. Novak. New Repub 151:7-8 O 17 '64
Vatican II & the Jews. F. E. Cartus. Commentary 39:19-29 Ja '65
Weakened schema on Jews feared. Christian Cent 81:790-1 Je 17 '64
What Catholics think about Jews. Time 84:58 S 11 '64
See also
Vatican council, 2d

Muslims

Greater dialogue; proposal to set up special bureau for relations with the Muslim world. America 111:207 Ag 29 '64
Muslims, too. P. Koch. America 110:326 Mr 14 '64

Orthodox Eastern church

After 500 years, an embrace for unity. il Life 56:27 Ja 17 '64
Catholic-Orthodox dialogue. E. C. Bianchi. America 111:688-91 N 28 '64
Christian exchange; visit of Russian Orthodox churchmen from the Soviet Union. il Newsweek 61:74 Ap 1 '63
Christian summit? Newsweek 62:47 D 23 '63
Did the world watch in vain? meeting between Pope Paul and Athenagoras I. Christian Cent 81:131-2 Ja 29 '64
Ecumenics and the East. T. E. Bird. Commonweal 79:220-2 N 15 '63
Equal dialogue. America 109:547 N 9 '63
Greek primate balks. America 109:339 S 28 '63
Kiss of peace. il Newsweek 63:76 Ja 20 '64
Orthodox initiative. Commonweal 79:64 O 11 '63
Primacy and ecumenism. Commonweal 80:592 S 4 '64
Rumble over a relic; return of supposed skull of Andrew, Greece's patron saint. Christian Cent 81:1197 S 30 '64
Seed planted. il Time 83:36-41 Ja 17 '64
Still deaf to Rome. Time 82:72 S 20 '63
Table-talk with the Russian observers; failure of the Greek Orthodox to send observers to the first session of the council. E. M. Jung. Cath World 196:273-8 F '63
Toward a dialogue: Orthodox churches and Rome. il Time 82:86 O 11 '63
Toward Catholic-Orthodox dialogue. G. A. Maloney and R. H. Marshall, jr. il Cath World 198:295-301 F '64

CATHOLIC church—Relations—*Continued*

Protestant churches

Barth's wisdom on Rome. Christian Cent 80:1019 Ag 21 '63
Charity the first step. K. Haselden. Christian Cent 80:1539-40 D 11 '63
Completing the reformation; renewal of the whole church. Christian Cent 81:1389 N 11 '64
Dialogue at the top. D. J. O'Hanlon. America 109:231-4 S 7 '63; Reply. D. A. Walsh. 109:441 O 19 '63
Dialogue in Portland. W. B. Cate. Christian Cent 80:745 Je 5 '63
Doctor Schlink warns Vatican council. Christian Cent 80:1425 N 20 '63
Door opens wider. D. J. O'Hanlon. America 109:88 Jl 27 '63
Ecumenical first; Roman Catholic archbishop, member of the New Mexico council of churches. Christian Cent 82:6 Ja 6 '65
Ecumenical frontiers; language of official documents. America 109:277 S 21 '63
Ecumenicity, unlimited. Christian Cent 81:227-8 F 19 '64
Ecumenics and laymen in the pew. E. S. Stanton. America 109:210-12 Ag 31 '63
European reaction to the Vatican council. Y. Chabas; F. Luepsen. Christian Cent 80:207-9 F 13 '63
Heirs of Abbé Couturier; Catholic-Protestant dialogue. I. Chabas. Christian Cent 82:41-3 Ja 13 '65
Home base is everywhere; meeting of Commission on world mission and evangelism, in Mexico city. D. Peerman. Christian Cent 81:70-2 Ja 15 '64
How tense are interreligious tensions? J. J. Kane. Cath World 197:351-8 S '63
I'm hoping to meet more Catholics. W. Bockelman. America 111:67-9 Jl 18 '64
Interview with Dr Heiko Oberman; Protestant observer at the first session of the council. ed. by J. B. Sheerin. H. Oberman. Cath World 197:100-6 My '63
Pope sobers talks of Christian unity. Christian Cent 81:1421 N 18 '64
Protestant hopes for the Vatican council. R. M. Brown. il Look 28:21-7 O 6 '64
Protestants on the council. America 108:288-9 Mr 2 '63
Reformation Sunday. Commonweal 81:149-50 O 30 '64
Temperature of Catholic-Protestant tensions. M. E. Marty. Cath World 197:343-50 S '63
Unfinished reformation: a Catholic view. L. J. Putz. Christian Cent 81:109-12 Ja 22 '64
Unity we seek. ed. by W. S. Morris. Review Christian Cent 80:646 My 15 '63. L. J. Averill
Who will answer the Pope's plea? Christian Cent 80:1357 N 6 '63

United Nations

Vatican UN observer. America 110:560 Ap 25 '64

Relations (diplomatic)

Communist countries

Mission to Moscow? thaw between the Holy See and the Communist nations. il Newsweek 61:89 My 20 '63

Germany

Pius XII and the Nazis. R. A. Graham. America 111:742-3 D 5 '64; Reply with rejoinder. F. W. Wentz. 112:2 Ja 2 '65
Pope Pius XII and Germany: some aspects of German-Vatican relations, 1933-1943. G. O. Kent. bibliog f il Am Hist R 70:59-78 O '64

Hungary

Accommodations. Newsweek 64:86 S 28 '64
Breathing room in Hungary. Time 84:66 S 25 '64
Much ado in Hungary; About nothing? settlement between the Vatican and the Communist regime. America 111:367 O 3 '64

Israel

Recognize Israel? America 110:130 Ja 25 '64

United States

Vatican and U.S: closer ties? il U S News 55:37 Jl 15 '63

Roman curia

Breaking the walls; curia and the council. il Newsweek 62:80 D 16 '63
Changes in Roman curia rumored. Christian Cent 81:355 Mr 18 '64
Council and curia. R. Etteldorf. America 109:234-5 S 7 '63; Reply. R. H. Schmandt. 109:336 S 28 '63; Rejoinder. 109:540+ N 9 '63
Crisis in Rome; struggle between the bishops and the Roman curia. Newsweek 62:76 N 25 '63
How new Pope plans to modernize church. il U S News 55:46-8 O 14 '63
Letter from Vatican City. X. Rynne. New Yorker 39:150+ N 30 '63
Paul and the curia. il Newsweek 62:62 S 30 '63
Pope and curia. America 109:380 O 5 '63
Pope increases powers of Catholic bishops. Christian Cent 80:1193 O 2 '63
Pope Paul sets a goal: modernize church machinery. U S News 55:30 O 7 '63
Pope Paul's address to the curia. M. Novak. Commonweal 79:89-90 O 18 '63
Riddle of Pope Paul VI. A. Leone-Moats. il Nat R 15:347-9+ O 22 '63
What happened to curia reform? Christian Cent 81:1101 S 9 '64
What went wrong? il Time 82:52+ D 6 '63
See also
Vatican council, 2d

Societies

Catholic organizations. Commonweal 79:737-8 Mr 20 '64
For Catholic pulpit renewal. W. D. Thompson. Christian Cent 81:644 My 13 '64
Role of Catholic agencies; work directed toward elimination of poverty throughout the world. J. Norris. Commonweal 81:235-7 N 13 '64
See also
American Catholic sociological society
Catholic association for international peace
Catholic Near East welfare association
Knights of Columbus
Newman clubs
Sodalities

Theology

See Theology

CATHOLIC church and art. See Art and religion

CATHOLIC church and communism

Ask Americans to pray for us; ed. by C. Hotchkiss. S. Wyszynski. il Sat Eve Post 236:58-60 F 2 '63
Back of the changes in Vatican policy. il U S News 54:60-1 Ap 29 '63
Church and communism. Commonweal 79:3 S 27 '63
Coming great confusion. E. von Kuehnelt-Leddihn. Nat R 14:314 Ap 23 '63
Communism and the Pope; encyclical Pacem in terris. Commonweal 78:235-6 My 24 '63
Communists in good faith; Italian bishops joint pastoral. America 109:621 N 16 '63
Conditions of peace; concerning John XXIII's recent encyclical. America 109:38 Jl 13 '63
Council, right and left. G. D. Kumlien. Commonweal 79:362-3 D 20 '63
Dialogue Communist style. America 110:397 Mr 28 '64
Divini redemptoris to Pacem in terris. F. S. Meyer. Nat R 14:406 My 21 '63
Encountering communism. Commonweal 80:131-2 Ap 24 '64
Hominibus bonae voluntatis; encyclical Pacem in terris. J. Burnham. Nat R 14:353 My 7 '63
Hungarian slowdown. America 109:86 Jl 27 '63
Kremlin and Vatican; release of Archbishop Josyf Slipyi. America 108:283 Mr 2 '63
Kremlin courts the Vatican; A. I. Adzhubei received by Pope John XXIII. Christian Cent 80:357 Mr 20 '63
New look in diplomacy? America 108:730-1 My 25 '63
New pope; concerning encyclicals of John XXIII and Paul VI. Nat R 16:711+ Ag 25 '64
New Vatican approach to communism. W. Purdy. Cath World 197:216-22 Jl '63
Pacem in terris, Ecclesiam Suam and communism. C. Wallace. Cath World 200:231-8 Ja '65
Pacem in terris. M. Ascoli. Reporter 28:20-1 My 23 '63; Discussion. 28:8 Je 20 '63
Pacem in terris: an opening to the left? V. C. Ferkiss. Cath World 198:100-8 N '63
Peace on earth; Pope John's encyclical. Newsweek 61:70 Ap 15 '63
Pope and communism. Commonweal 78:412 Jl 12 '63
Pope meets Communist. il Time 81:53 Mr 15 '63
Popes and Communists. H. M. Pachter. New Repub 148:15-17 Je 22 '63
Pope's bombshell; meeting with A. Adzhubei. G. D. Kumlien. Commonweal 78:71-2 Ap 12 '63
Riddle of Pope Paul VI. A. Leone-Moats. il Nat R 15:347-9+ O 22 '63

CATHOLIC church and communism—*Continued*
Supranational neutrality. America 108:518 Ap 20 '63
Things old and new in Pacem in terris. J. C. Murray. America 108:612-14 Ap 27 '63
Vatican-Kremlin puzzle. America 109:255 S 14 '63
CATHOLIC church and economics. See Christianity and economics
CATHOLIC church and international relations. See Church and international relations
CATHOLIC church and politics. See Church and politics
CATHOLIC church and psychiatry. See Psychiatry and religion
CATHOLIC church and race problems. See Church and race problems
CATHOLIC church and social problems. See Church and social problems
CATHOLIC church and science. See Religion and science
CATHOLIC church and the press. See Church and the press
CATHOLIC church and war. See War and religion; World war, 1939-1945—Catholic church
CATHOLIC church in Africa
Africa and the council. D. E. Hurley. Commonweal 79:10-12 S 27 '63
Africa speaks to the American Negro; appeal for monastic recruits. B. Luykx. America 110:365 Mr 21 '64
Cartago amputanda est; agreement between the Vatican and government of Tunisia. il Time 84:62 Jl 24 '64
Flexible African church. America 110:664 My 16 '64
Hope of Africa. America 108:605 Ap 27 '63
Resourceful Africa. America 108:186 F 9 '63
CATHOLIC church in Algeria
Algeria; year I of independence. R. Bosc. America 108:362-5 Mr 16 '63
CATHOLIC church in Argentina
We have no childhood; ed. by R. Llewellyn. S. Lombardi. il Sat Eve Post 236:76-7 S 7 '63
CATHOLIC church in Asia
Ecumenical approach to religions of Asia. S. T. Balasuriya. Cath World 200:239-45 Ja '65
CATHOLIC church in Brazil
Brazil: dearth of priests. B. de Margerie. America 108:220-2 F 16 '63
Brazil: social action. J. P. Cotter. America 108:222-3 F 16 '63
Catholicism in Brazil; with editorial comment. B. Tyson; A. Amoroso Lima. America 110:758, 764-7 My 30 '64
Challenge to Latin America; excerpts from address. D. H. Camara. America 110:590 My 2 '64
Pope's man in Recife. Time 83:60 Mr 27 '64
Reaching souls in a stadium; religious pageant. il Time 82:46 S 13 '63
Social-minded archbishop. E. K. Culhane. America 109:5 Jl 6 '63
CATHOLIC church in Canada
Reporter at large; concerning book of letters on French Canada, by Le Frère Untel. E. Wilson. New Yorker 40:64-6+ N 21 '64
CATHOLIC church in Ceylon
Schools in Ceylon. J. P. Cotter. America 109:212-13 Ag 31 '63
CATHOLIC church in China
Rites controversy. J. R. Rosenbloom. America 110:544-5 Ap 18 '64
Word from Peiping. America 110:3 Ja 4 '64
CATHOLIC church in Communist countries. See Catholic church and communism
CATHOLIC church in Cuba
Church in Cuba. America 111:769 D 12 '64
Church in Cuba; a universal dilemma; excerpts from Christianity and revolution. L. Dewart. Commonweal 79:67-9 O 11 '63; Reply with rejoinder. B. Moran. 79:716-19 Mr 13 '64
CATHOLIC church in Czechoslovakia
Collaborationist priests. America 110:621-2 My 9 '64
What to do with Beran. America 110:783 Je 6 '64
CATHOLIC church in England
After four hundred years; England's ecumenical awakening. I. Evans. Commonweal 78:222-4 My 17 '63
Awaiting the second spring. J. M. Cameron. Commonweal 79:65-6 O 11 '63
CATHOLIC church in France
Encounter in a parish; parish congress pioneered by Church of St Sulpice, Paris. M. O'Connor. il Commonweal 80:568-70 Ag 21 '64
French Catholicism, 1964. E. Malatesta. America 110:253-5 F 22 '64
Heirs of Abbé Couturier; Catholic-Protestant dialogue. I. Chabas. Christian Cent 82:41-3 Ja 13 '65
CATHOLIC church in Germany
Catholic church and Nazi Germany, by G. Lewy. Review
America 111:70-2 Jl 18 '64. R. A. Graham
Cath World 200:51-3 O '64. G. N. Shuster
Christian Cent 81:886-8 Jl 8 '64. L. D. Streiker
Commonweal 80:445-8 Jl 3 '64. G. C. Zahn; Discussion. 80:546-7 Ag 7 '64
CATHOLIC church in Germany (Federal Republic)
In Germany, too; criticism of West German Catholicism. America 110:475-6 Ap 4 '64
CATHOLIC church in Great Britain
Closing the door. J. M. Cameron. Commonweal 80:386-8 Je 19 '64
Roman radical in London. C. Northcott. Christian Cent 81:907-8 Jl 15 '64
Unfinished business, by M. Ward. Review
Commonweal 81:123-5 O 23 '64. G. N. Shuster
CATHOLIC church in Hungary
Can anyone free Cardinal Mindszenty? A. Leone-Moats. Nat R 14:491-3 Je 18 '63
Men of good will? Polish-Hungarian relations with the Vatican. America 108:793 Je 1 '63
Mindszenty tragedy. T. Weyr. Commonweal 79:454-7 Ja 17 '64; Discussion. 79:719-21 Mr 13 '64
Rhapsodies in Hungary; negotiations towards a settlement with the Vatican. America 109:208 Ag 31 '63
Two cardinals meet. America 108:627 My 4 '63
CATHOLIC church in India
Christian India. E. De Souza. America 111:87-90 Jl 25 '64
CATHOLIC church in Ireland
In Dublin's fair city; election of a Catholic chancellor. America 110:3 Ja 4 '64
CATHOLIC church in Italy
Italy: problem for Pope Paul. H. W. Flannery. Cath World 197:372-9 S '63
Why communism in Catholic Italy? D. O'Grady. il Cath World 199:102-8 My '64
See also
Church and state in Italy
CATHOLIC church in Latin America
Alliance for progress; address, January 20, 1964. H. H. Humphrey. Vital Speeches 30:307-11 Mr 1 '64
Catholics and Latin America. Commonweal 79:615-16 F 21 '64
FERES study of Latin America. E. K. Culhane. America 111:345-7 S 26 '64
I failed in Puno; Papal volunteer. R. F. Clark. America 112:7 Ja 2 '65; Reply. F. M. Cameron. 112:152 Ja 30 '65
Latin America: the church meets the challenge of change. R. Hoffman. Cath World 197:164-71 Je '63
Latin-American Catholics and birth control. L. Gross. il Look 28:93-4+ Jl 14 '64
New spirit in the church. il Time 82:20 Ag 23 '63
Religion, revolution and reform; ed. by W. D'Antonio and F. B. Pike. Review
Commonweal 81:547-9 Ja 22 '65. A. Stepan
Revolutionary cardinal. Newsweek 62:69 Ag 26 '63
Upsurge in Latin America. America 111:343-4 S 26 '64
Vatican II and Latin America. J. M. Bonino. Christian Cent 81:1616-17 D 30 '64
CATHOLIC church in Malta
Maltese constitution. America 111:147 Ag 15 '64
CATHOLIC church in Poland
Ask Americans to pray for us; ed. by C. Hotchkiss. S. Wyszyński. il Sat Eve Post 236:58-60 F 2 '63
Guerrilla war in Poland. America 111:224 S 5 '64
Intolerance of atheism. America 111:681 N 28 '64
Letter from Warsaw. J. Wechsberg. New Yorker 38:108+ F 9 '63
Men of good will? Polish-Hungarian relations with the Vatican. America 108:793 Je 1 '63
Poland 1963. E. Dunbar. il Look 27:24-8+ Ag 27 '63
Tolerant Polish reds. America 111:397 O 10 '64
CATHOLIC church in Portugal
Protest in Portugal. America 112:33 Ja 9 '65
CATHOLIC church in Puerto Rico
Machismo and the priestly vocation. A. Weigert. il Cath World 199:152-8 Je '64
CATHOLIC church in Quebec. See Catholic church in Canada
CATHOLIC church in Russia
Diary of an American Jesuit. W. V. Casey. il America 109:113-17 Ag 3 '63

CATHOLIC church in South Africa
Catholic bishops on apartheid. D. M. Norman. Christian Cent 81:647-8 My 13 '64
CATHOLIC church in South America. See Catholic church in Latin America
CATHOLIC church in Spain
Delicate matter; broader rights for Protestants. Newsweek 61:78 Je 3 '63
Evolving church. New Repub 150:7-8 Ja 25 '64
Franco and Pope Paul. Christian Cent 80:995-6 Ag 14 '63; Discussion. 80:1276 O 16 '63
New breed in Spain. T. Valcarcel. Cath World 200:155-61 D '64
Religious liberty in Spain. America 111:471 O 24 '64
Spain and freedom. America 112:68 Ja 16 '65
Spanish cardinal makes small concession. Christian Cent 81:165 F 5 '64
CATHOLIC church in Switzerland
Canton of Zurich recognizes Catholic church. Christian Cent 80:925 Jl 24 '63
CATHOLIC church in the Middle East
See also
Catholic Near East welfare association
CATHOLIC church in the Netherlands
In Dutch with the Vatican; provocative articles in De Nieuwe linie. Time 83:72 Je 5 '64
CATHOLIC church in the United States
Ages of American Catholicism. J. Cogley. Commonweal 79:29-31 O 4 '63
American laymen. J. O'Gara. Commonweal 79:364 D 20 '63
America's Catholic community: increasing involvement. B. Cooke. Christian Cent 80:360-2 Mr 20 '63
Anti-climax dept, Tiara div. Commonweal 81:404 D 18 '64
Bishops' statement; apprehension over nonreligious trends in contemporary life. America 109:693 N 30 '63
Catholic novels & American culture. T. F. Curley. Commentary 36:34-42 Jl '63
Catholicism in America: the renewal. il Newsweek 62:66-9 O 14 '63
Catholicism: molder of manpower. J. H. Smylie. Christian Cent 80:1544-6 D 11 '63
Catholics and American goals. J. H. Smylie. Christian Cent 81:140-3 Ja 29 '64
Catholics as immigrants. J. H. Smylie. Christian Cent 80:1396-9 N 13 '63
Charter for laymen, 1822. G. Traynor. Commonweal 81:418-21 D 18 '64; Reply. M. Novak. 81:555+ Ja 29 '65
Church in America. J. J. Hennesey. America 111:448-9+ O 17 '64
Conservative bishops. America 109:151 Ag 17 '63
Dilemma of the Catholic layman; excerpt from Mind of the Catholic layman. D. Callahan. Cath World 198:80-6 N '63
Eyes on the church. America 109:39 Jl 13 '63
Fortieth anniversary symposium: history and present situation of Catholicism in American life discussed by present and past editors of Commonweal. il Commonweal 81:261-80 N 20 '64; Reply. D. I. Segal. 81:498-9+ Ja 15 '65
Good start: proposed archdiocesan dialogue conference in St Louis. Commonweal 81:468-9 Ja 8 '65
How rules changes affect U.S. Catholics. il U S News 57:16 D 14 '64
Let's end the war over birth control. J. A. O'Brien. Christian Cent 80:1361-4 N 6 '63
Liturgical movement: phase three. A. Kavanagh. America 111:183-5 Ag 22 '64
Mass confusion; Mass in English in the US. il Newsweek 64:38 D 28 '64
Mind of the Catholic layman, by D. Callahan. Review
Commonweal 79:171-2 N 1 '63. J. T. Ellis
Reporter 29:56+ N 21 '63. A. M. Greeley
More to come; great change in American Catholicism. J. O'Gara. Commonweal 80:358 Je 12 '64
New debate: Catholic intellectual life. A. M. Greeley; J. D. Donovan; J. W. Trent. il Commonweal 81:33-42 O 2 '64
No hot line to the Vatican. America 109:106 Ag 3 '63
Not peace, but the sword; the new anguish of American Catholicism. E. R. F. Sheehan. il Sat Eve Post 237:20-32+ N 28 '64
Old soldiers never die. J. Cogley. Commonweal 78:214-16 My 17 '63
Pope Paul to the laity. J. O'Gara. Commonweal 79:70 O 11 '63
Reclaiming the city; Baltimore archdiocesan program to co-ordinate parishes. America 109:33 Jl 13 '63
Restraints on American Catholic freedom. J. Victor. bibliog f Harper 227:33-9 D '63
Structures, not rhetoric. J. O'Gara. Commonweal 81:503 Ja 15 '65
U.S. Catholicism: growth or decline? A. M. Greeley. America 111:480-3 O 24 '64
Unlikely cardinal. il Time 84:35-40 Ag 21 '64; Same abr. with title Boston's contrary cardinal. Read Digest 85:119-23 N '64; Reply. America 111:228-9 S 5 '64
Word of thanks. H. Küng. il America 108:826-9 Je 8 '63
See also
Knights of Columbus
CATHOLIC church in Tunisia
Vatican and Tunisia reach agreement. Christian Cent 81:821 Je 24 '64
Vatican-Tunisia accord. America 111:80 Jl 25 '64
CATHOLIC church in Viet Nam (Republic)
Brutality in Vietnam. Christian Cent 80:950 Jl 31 '63
Facts, please. America 109:38-9 Jl 13 '63
Rome and Saigon. Christian Cent 80:1067 S 4 '63
Voice in Vietnam. Commonweal 78:413 Jl 12 '63
CATHOLIC church in Yugoslavia
Tito-Vatican talks? America 110:621 My 9 '64
CATHOLIC churches. See Church architecture
CATHOLIC college graduates. See College graduates
CATHOLIC colleges. See Catholic church—Education
CATHOLIC converts. See Converts, Catholic
CATHOLIC council on civil liberties
Civil liberties. America 109:474 O 26 '63
CATHOLIC education. See Catholic church—Education
CATHOLIC film newsletter
Catholic film newsletter. America 112:68 Ja 16 '65
CATHOLIC high schools. See Catholic church—Education
CATHOLIC hospitals. See Hospitals
CATHOLIC Indian missions. See Indians of North America—Missions
CATHOLIC intellectuals. See Intellectuals
CATHOLIC interracial councils
Church of silence. A. V. Krebs, jr. il Commonweal 80:467-76 Jl 10 '64
More interracial councils. America 110:530 Ap 18 '64
Youth leads; Junior Catholic interracial council of St Louis. W. J. Hutchison. America 111:213 Ag 29 '64
CATHOLIC laymen. See Laity
CATHOLIC library association
ALA go home! Library J 89:4128+ O 15 '64
Catholic library week. M. C. Frederic. Wilson Lib Bul 38:736 My '64
CATHOLIC literature
Harrowing evangel of Flannery O'Connor. R. Drake. Christian Cent 81:1200-2 S 30 '64
See also
Catholic authors
Publishers and publishing—Catholic literature

Bibliography

Books for Christmas gifts. Cath World 198:168-9 D '63
Religion. E. S. Stanton. America 109:675-6; 110:642-4; 111:712-14 N 23 '63, My 9, N 28 '64
Religion. V. de P. Hayes. America 108:680+ My 11 '63
CATHOLIC medical mission board
Medical giants. America 112:155 Ja 30 '65
CATHOLIC Near East welfare association
Mission in the Near East. America 111:506 O 31 '64
No substitute in India. America 111:731-2 D 5 '64
CATHOLIC newspapers. See Catholic press
CATHOLIC periodicals. See Catholic press
CATHOLIC philosophy. See Philosophy
CATHOLIC press
Catholic press. R. G. Hoyt; J. O'Connor. Commonweal 77:534-41 F 15 '63; Reply with rejoinder. A. de Zutter. 78:135-7 Ap 26 '63
Catholic press thaws; Brooklyn tablet and Our Sunday visitor. Christian Cent 80:484 Ap 17 '63
Catholics and Vietnam. Commonweal 79:244-5 N 22 '63; Reply with rejoinder. P. O'Connor. 79:427-8 Ja 10 '64
Catholics on The deputy. America 110:400 Mr 28 '64
Council, the press and theology; address. G. H. Tavard. il Cath World 199:337-44 S '64
Foreign Catholic press. America 110:248-9 F 22 '64
In Dutch with the Vatican; provocative articles in De Nieuwe linie. Time 83:72 Je 5 '64
Sad surfside soliloquy. T. N. Davis. America 108:702 My 18 '63

CATHOLIC press—*Continued*
Too many? Commonweal 78:155-6 My 3 '63
What is a Catholic paper? America 108:426 Mr 30 '63
See also
Commonweal (periodical)
National Catholic reporter
CATHOLIC press association
Catholic press association sponsors new book awards. Pub W 185:33 Mr 23 '64
Sad surfside soliloquy. T. N. Davis. America 108:702 My 18 '63
CATHOLIC-Protestant colloquium, Harvard. See Religious conferences
CATHOLIC-Protestant marriages. See Marriages, Mixed
CATHOLIC relief services. See National Catholic welfare conference
CATHOLIC schools. See Parochial schools, Catholic
CATHOLIC students
Catholic students protest; removal of progressive theologians from Catholic university. Christian Cent 80:1162 S 25 '63
Catholicism on the campus. J. Cogley. Commonweal 78:88-9 Ap 19 '63; Reply with rejoinder. J. R. Crowley. 78:326-7 Je 14 '63
Catholics in college; secular campuses. M. Novak; discussion. Commonweal 78:16-20 Mr 29 '63
Catholics in higher education; Catholic student on the secular campus. R. J. Clifford and W. R. Callahan. il America 111:288-91 S 19 '64; Discussion. 111:468, 726-7 O 24, D 5 '64
For the doubting student; Pittsburgh oratory. il Time 81:53 Mr 15 '63
Problems at State university. R. E. Kavanaugh. America 108:540-4+ Ap 20 '63
Religion and career, by A. Greeley. Review Commonweal 79:436 Ja 10 '64. G. N. Shuster
What makes them tick? Catholic students volunteer groups. America 108:795-6 Je 1 '63
CATHOLIC teachers. See Teachers
CATHOLIC textbooks. See Textbooks
CATHOLIC theological society of America
Catholics and race. America 109:33 Jl 13 '63
CATHOLIC universities. See Catholic church—Education
CATHOLIC university of America
Aftermath and fallout; Catholic university hassle over the acceptability of four prominent theologians as speakers. America 108:387 Mr 23 '63
Breaking the silence. Commonweal 78:4 Mr 29 '63; Reply. 78:249-5 My 24 '63
Catholic students protest; removal of progressive theologians from Catholic university. Christian Cent 80:1162 S 25 '63
Catholic university reversal. C. D. Kean. Christian Cent 80:565 Ap 24 '63
Clearing the air; resolutions of board of trustees. America 108:658 My 11 '63
Controversy within Catholicism; barring Catholic ecumenists from lecturing. C. D. Kean. Christian Cent 80:358-9 Mr 20 '63
Crisis at Catholic U; ban on speakers. il Time 81:58+ Mr 29 '63
Goldfish bowl; ban on Catholic theologians. America 108:329 Mr 9 '63
Murray and Weigel: dialogizing duo. Christian Cent 80:599 My 1 '63
Not always on the day after Sunday. J. N. Eller. America 108:391 Mr 23 '63
Postscript on Catholic U. Commonweal 78:212 My 17 '63
Restraints on American Catholic freedom. J. Victor. bibliog f Harper 227:33-9 D '63
Uninvited; speakers in a student-sponsored lecture series at Catholic university. Commonweal 77:608-9 Mr 8 '63
University headaches; administrative decisions. America 108:430-1 Mr 30 '63
CATHOLIC women, National council of. See National council of Catholic women
CATHOLIC worker movement
Loaves and fishes, by D. Day. Review Christian Cent 80:1308 O 23 '63. E. L. Haselden
CATHOLIC writers. See Catholic authors
CATHOLICISM. See Catholic church
CATHOLICS
Baptist intellectual's view of Catholicism. H. Cox; reply. P. Blanshard. Harper 226:14 Mr '63
Faith and philosophy. R. O. Johann. America 111:487 O 24 '64; Reply. C. G. Marxer. 111:727+ D 5 '64
Honesty vs. loyalty oaths. J. Cogley. Commonweal 80:249-51 My 22 '64
In search of honesty. J. Cogley. Commonweal 79:705-7 Mr 13 '64
Shall we wrangle or reason about reforms? J. B. Sheerin. Cath World 199:203-6 Jl '64
Word; personality v. community. V. P. McCorry. America 109:28-9 Jl 6 '63
CATHOLICS in Germany
Catholic leadership. America 108:455 Ap 6 '63
CATHOLICS in India
Pope visits a lost tribe. A. Menen. il N Y Times Mag p34-5+ N 29 '64
CATHOLICS in Poland
Polish paradox. T. D. Langan. il Commonweal 80:228-32 My 15 '64
CATHOLICS in Southern Rhodesia
Church in Rhodesia. America 110:622 My 9 '64
CATHOLICS in Spain
Loyal opposition. America 109:621 N 16 '63
CATHOLICS in the United States
America's Catholic community: increasing involvement. B. Cooke. Christian Cent 80:360-2 Mr 20 '63
Catholic vote. America 111:766 D 12 '64
Catholic vote is confused. M. Novak. New Repub 151:14-15 Ag 22 '64
Catholicism in America: the renewal. il Newsweek 62:66-9 O 14 '63
Catholics and American goals. J. H. Smylie. Christian Cent 81:140-3 Ja 29 '64
Catholics and isolationism; Peace on earth. J. O'Gara. Commonweal 78:219 My 17 '63
Church attendance. J. H. Fichter. America 108:832-4 Je 8 '63
Church attendance among college graduates. A. M. Greeley. Cath World 197:95-9 My '63
Crisis in Catholic schools. T. J. Fleming. il Sat Eve Post 236:19-25 O 26 '63
Divergent ethics. America 111:686-7 N 28 '64
Fortieth anniversary symposium: history and present situation of Catholicism in American life discussed by present and past editors of Commonweal. il Commonweal 81:261-80 N 20 '64; Reply. D. I. Segal. 81:498-9+ Ja 15 '65
How tense are interreligious tensions? J. J. Kane. Cath World 197:351-8 S '63
Kennedy the Catholic. T. J. Fleming. Nation 198:571-2 Je 8 '64; Discussion. 199: inside cover Jl 13 '64
More to come; great change in American Catholicism. J. O'Gara. Commonweal 80:358 Je 12 '64
Return from Russia. W. Ciszek. America 110:408-11 Mr 28 '64
Striking changes in the way Protestants & Catholics feel about each other. W. Goodman Redbook 122:62-3+ Mr '64
Through rose-colored glasses, darkly. J. O'Gara. Commonweal 77:530 F 15 '63
To the Roman Catholics in the United States of America; reply to a letter from the American Catholic clergy and laity. G. Washington. America 111:3 Jl 4 '64
Who is joining the Peace corps? disturbing questions about Catholic participation. J. M. Cronin and T. E. Cronin; discussion. America 108:69, 228-30 Ja 19, F 16 '63
See also
Catholic worker movement
History
Catholicism: molder of manpower. J. H. Smylie. Christian Cent 80:1544-6 D 11 '63
Catholics as immigrants. J. H. Smylie. Christian Cent 80:1396-9 N 13 '63
CATHOLICS in Viet Nam (Republic)
Anarchy & agony. il Time 84:33-4 S 4 '64
Catholic exodus. Time 84:21-2 D 25 '64
CATHOLICS united for racial equality
CURE; Los Angeles movement for racial equality and social justice. Commonweal 80:352 Je 12 '64
CATHON, Laura E.
Children's libraries. Wilson Lib Bul 38:879 Je '64
CATIONIC proteins. See Proteins
CATLEDGE, Turner
View from the heights. il por Time 84:55-6 S 11 '64
CATLIN, George
He caught the splendor of the first Americans. L. R. Peattie. il Read Digest 85:257-62 O '64
Letter from Paris; exhibition at the American cultural center. Genêt. New Yorker 39:57-8+ D 28 '63
CATLIN, Yates
By barge, river transportation's confluence. Ann Am Acad 345:89-94 Ja '63

CATLING, Patrick Skene
Return of the Redcoats. Esquire 61:74+ Je '64
Third regiment: the President's own. Holiday 35:33-6 Mr '64

CATNIP
Catnip: its raison d'être. T. Eisner. bibliog il Science 146:1318-20 D 4 '64
Growing your own catnip. il Sunset 130:280-1 Ap '63

CATO, pseud.
From Washington straight. See issues of National review

CATO, Bruce G.
Why won't they renew my radiotelephone license? Motor B 113:158+ My '64

CATROW, George C.
Diary of George C. Catrow: excerpts. ed. by G. Crout. NEA J 54:29-30 Ja '65

CATS
Albert. B. M. Brennan. il McCalls 90:106-7+ Je '63
Cat comes on dancing. il Life 55:147+ D 6 '63
Catalina cat. E. R. Choate. il Atlan 212:93-5 N '63
Cat's ability to discriminate oblique rectangles. N. S. Sutherland. bibliog Science 139:209-10 Ja 18 '63
Cats in our lives. A. Suehsdorf. il Nat Geog Mag 125:508-41 Ap '64
Caudate-induced cortical potentials: comparison between monkey and cat. S. Goldring and others. bibliog il Science 139:772 F 22 '63
Hard times for alley cats. P. Montgomery. il N Y Times Mag p47+ Ap 12 '64
Hypothalamic temperature in the cat during feeding and sleep. T. Adams. bibliog il Science 139:609-10 F 15 '63
Losers by a tail? manx cats. Sci Digest 55:41 My '64
When you choose a cat. B. Brown. il Bet Hom & Gard 42:144 N '64
Worlds of two cats: country cat; city cat. J. Peter. il Look 28:49-52 Je 30 '64

Anecdotes, facetiae, satire, etc.

Cat with a telephone number. F. Sparks. il Read Digest 83:21+ Jl '63

Feeding

Balanced diet your pet requires. il Good H 158:162-3 Je '64

Photographs

See Animals—Photographs

Quotations, maxims, etc.

Feline: thoughts for cat week; comp. by E. F. Murphy. il N Y Times Mag p 110 N 3 '63

Training

Your new kitten. il Bet Hom & Gard 41:103 My '63

CATS, Photography of. See Photography of animals

CATS' vision. See Sight (animals)

CATTAFESTA, Richard J.
Artist's view. por Wilson Lib Bul 39:468-71 F '65

CATTAILS
Nature of cohesion within pollen tetrads of typha latifolia. J. J. Skvarla and D. A. Larson. bibliog il Science 140:173-5 Ap 12 '63

CATTELL, David T.
Soviet policies in Latin America. bibliog f Cur Hist 47:286-91+ N '64

CATTELL, Raymond B.
Nature and measurement of anxiety; with biographical sketch. Sci Am 208:33, 96-104 Mr '63

CATTLE
Water turnover in cattle. A. L. Black and others. bibliog il Science 144:876-8 My 15 '64
See also
Calves

Breeding

See Cattle breeding

Breeds

Cattle nobody wanted; Red Angus. O. Bay. il Farm J 87:38-9+ D '63
France's amazing beef machine; Charolais breed. F. E. Breth. il Sci Digest 56:37-42 N '64

Culling

See Cows—Culling

Diseases and pests

Feed lot health mucosal complex. J. B. Herrick. Suc Farm 61:108 O '63
Feed lot health: report on liver abscess. J. B. Herrick. Suc Farm 61:84 N '63
Isolation of a viral agent from pseudocowpox disease. C. Moscovici and others. bibliog il Science 141:915-16 S 6 '63; Reply. C. F. Pait. 142:1422+ D 13 '63
Plan now for healthy feeders this summer. J. W. Bailey. Suc Farm 62:65 My '64
Prevent feed-lot killers. J. W. Bailey. Suc Farm 61:91 S '63
Virus diarrhea; bovine virus diarrhea. J. Herrick. Suc Farm 62:32 N '64
See also
Coccidiosis
Cows—Diseases and pests

Feeding

Are you forcing your cattle to diet? C. E. Summers. il Suc Farm 62:66 O '64
Beef-feeding barn that cleans itself. D. Hagen. il Farm J 88:43+ F '64
Big western feed lots, what you can learn from them. J. I. Sprague. il Suc Farm 61:64-5+ F '63
Changing beef cattle rations? C. E. Summers. Suc Farm 62:35 Ja '64
Cheaper ways to winter beef cows. D. Seim. Farm J 87:40 D '63
Expanding? which way to mechanize. W. J. Fletcher and C. Peterson, jr. il Suc Farm 61:54-5+ Ap '63
Fall feeder situation. B. Brantley. Suc Farm 61:32 Ag '63
Fattening the calf; automation in cattle-raising. il Bsns W p 102-4+ N 9 '63
Feed barley to cattle. Suc Farm 61:62 Ap '63
Feed for pooled cattle: Liberty feed yards. il Suc Farm 62:56 S '64
Feed lot. C. Peterson, jr. il Suc Farm 62:46 Ap '64
Feed on pasture. C. E. Summer and C. Peterson, jr. il Suc Farm 61:62-3 Jl '63
Feeders pool resources; Liberty feed yards. C. Peterson, jr. il Suc Farm 61:34-5+ S '63
For the feeding season: fourteen ways to boost your profit. C. Peterson, jr. and B. Suter. il Suc Farm 61:48-9+ N '63
Four lbs. a day, almost. J. Rohlf. Farm J 87:63 Ap '63
Hay feeders that cut choretime. il Farm J 89:49 Ja '65
Haylage tops corn silage for steers. il Farm J 88:46 My '64
How to balance a feed ration. C. E. Summers. il Suc Farm 61:12 N '63
How to cut feedlot losses from shrink. O. Bay. Farm J 88:66F O '64
How to get better summer beef gains. Farm J 88:32E Ag '64
How to plan a beef feeding layout. P. B. Jones and R. L. Maddex. il Suc Farm 62:38-41 O '64
Ideas from a small western feeder. G. Bevard. il Suc Farm 61:54 O '63
Low-moisture silage for beef cattle. T. W. Perry. il Suc Farm 61:98 My '63
Makes dairy steers finish like beef. D. Hagen. Farm J 87:56 D '63
Managing beef on grass now. G. A. Montgomery. Suc Farm 62:31 Je '64
Money-making feed-lot ideas. C. Peterson, jr. and W. Woods. il Suc Farm 61:52-3 O '63
New eighty per cent supplement, a cost cutter; beef cattle. D. Seim. il Farm J 88:42 O '64
New feed additive may be future cost cutter. il Farm J 88:36 S '64
Report on high-concentrate rations. J. K. Matsushima and T. W. Perry. il Suc Farm 62:46-7 F '64
Scientists report latest research. J. Russell. Farm J 88:48 Ja '64
$7,500 mistake I won't make again. J. A. Rohlf. il Farm J 88:36+ My '64
Should you feed common cattle? E. Uvacek and C. Peterson, jr. il Suc Farm 62:39 Jl '64
These beef specialists answer your twenty-one most asked questions. P. Q. Guyer; G. R. Carlisle; C. E. Summers. il Suc Farm 61:46-7 My '63
Ways to chop your supplement bill. Farm J 88:46 Ap '64
What's ahead for cattle? B. Brantley. Suc Farm 61:37 Ag '63
Wintering beef cattle. H. L. Self; L. S. Pope. il Suc Farm 61:30-1 D '63
See also
Antibiotic feed supplements
Calves—Feeding
Cattle self feeders
Feeding and feeding stuffs

Hormone fattening

Beef additives. W. Burroughs and S. A. Ewing. il Suc Farm 61:100 N '63

CATTLE—*Continued*

Performance records and registration

Payoff from performance testing. C. Peterson jr. il Suc Farm 61:44-5+ S '63

Prices

Farm problem that closely concerns the new President. il U S News 55:76-7 D 16 '63
Hard times on the ranges: why cattle prices are low. il U S News 56:41-5 Ap 13 '64
How low will feeder prices go? il Farm J 88:21+ Jl '64
When will cattle prices get better? il Farm J 88:33+ Ap '64

Testing

Gain most important. Suc Farm 62:82 F '64
Payoff from performance testing. C. Peterson, jr. il Suc Farm 61:44-5+ S '63

Transportation

I flew with the calves; New Jersey to Italian farms; with editorial comment. L. M. Palmer. il Farm J 88:4, 30-1+ N '64
Lassoing cattle from rails. il Bsns W p 130+ O 19 '63
Now they're barging feeders. il Farm J 87:32 Ag '63

CATTLE, Beef

Beef bonanza; Argentine beef. il Time 82:65 Ag 2 '63
Big western feed lots, what you can learn from them. J. I. Sprague. il Suc Farm 61:64-5+ F '63
Experts counsel: don't panic buying feeders. Farm J 88:42 O '64
How to buy feeder cattle. J. A. Rohlf. il Farm J 87:36-7+ O '63
How to produce more lean, tender beef. Farm J 87:38 S '63
How to sell more lean beef. C. Peterson, jr. il Suc Farm 61:74-5 Mr '63
Ideas from Britain on how you can make low-cost beef. D. Seim. il Farm J 88:40-2+ F '64
Large cattle inventory dims long-term outlook. R. Reiman. il Suc Farm 61:103 Ap '63
News from beef meeting; brief report of Coordinated beef improvement conference. C. Peterson, jr. Suc Farm 61:89 S '63
Should you feed common cattle? E. Uvacek and C. Peterson, jr. il Suc Farm 62:39 Jl '64
Six ways to start or expand your beef cow herd. A. L. Neumann. il Suc Farm 62:40-1+ Ja '64
They fed out 100 bulls! D. Malena and B. Rust. il Suc Farm 62:32-3 D '64
What cattlemen should do now. B. Brantley. Suc Farm 62:33 Je '64
What's ahead for cattle? B. Brantley. Suc Farm 61:37 Ag '63
What's new and outlook for. See issues of Successful farming
See also
Beef

Breeds

See Cattle—Breeds

Cost

For the feeding season: fourteen ways to boost your profit. C. Peterson, jr. and B. Suter. il Suc Farm 61:48-9+ N '63
How much should you pay for feeders? il Suc Farm 62:34 S '64
How to figure your beef cow costs. C. Peterson, jr. and A. G. Mueller. il Suc Farm 61:96 Ap '63
What feeders will cost you this fall. C. W. Gifford. il Farm J 87:35+ O '63

Feeding

See Cattle—Feeding

Grading and standardization

Let's give dual grading a chance. J. A. Rohlf. il Farm J 87:31+ My '63

Marketing

City cowmen lose shirts and cattle. C. E. Ball. Farm J 88:60H Mr '64
Consumer's beef dollar: fair share for feeders? B. W. Marion. Suc Farm 62:38+ Mr '64
Futures on the hoof. il Newsweek 64:81-2 D 7 '64
Here's a new idea for selling beef. O. Bay. il Farm J 87:46 O '63
Major changes here in beef cattle trends. R. Reiman. Suc Farm 61:25 Je '63
On-the-rail selling. Suc Farm 61:13 N '63
Tips for beef grade-and-yield selling. G. Bevard. il Suc Farm 62:116 F '64
Who's making the money on your beef? O. Bay. il Farm J 88:23-5+ Je '64; Same. U S News 56:53-5 Je 29 '64

Performance records and registration

First Hereford makes certified meat sire. B. Fowler. Farm J 87:49 F '63
Performance testing, it's really rolling. il Farm J 87:21+ Je '63

Prices

See Cattle—Prices

Statistics

Beef, what the big build-up means; ed. by C. W. Gifford. il Farm J 87:35+ Ap '63

Testing

See Cattle—Testing

Transportation

See Cattle—Transportation

CATTLE, Weight and measurements of
Cover story. il Suc Farm 61:75 Mr '63

CATTLE auctions. See Auctions

CATTLE barns. See Barns and stables

CATTLE breeding
Cattle nobody wanted: Red Angus. O. Bay. il Farm J 87:38-9+ D '63
Crossbreeding beef cattle. C. Peterson, jr. il Suc Farm 62:48-9 My '64
Crossbreeding research. L. N. Hazel. Suc Farm 62:95 My '64
Get a calf from every beef cow. J. B. Herrick. il Suc Farm 61:8 S '63
Push heifers for early breeding? D. Hagen and J. Russell. il Farm J 88:24-5+ Ag '64
Solve dairy cow breeding difficulties. Suc Farm 61:86 N '63
These tricks make cows breed better. J. Russell. Farm J 88:54J Ap '64
Top breeding efficiency. J. W. Bailey. Suc Farm 62:140 Mr '64
You can make more beef with crossbreds. J. Dyer. il Farm J 88:38-9+ My '64
See also
Artificial insemination
Bulls

CATTLE feed. See Feeding and feeding stuffs

CATTLE handling
Handling facilities. C. Peterson, jr. il Suc Farm 61:38+ Je '63
Tips for selecting cattle handling equipment. B. W. Robinson. il Suc Farm 62:71 Mr '64

CATTLE industry and trade
Change rides the range. P. Friggens. il Read Digest 85:182-4+ Ag '64
Farm problem that closely concerns the new President. il U S News 55:76-7 D 16 '63
Fattening the calf; automation in cattle-raising. il Bsns W p 102-4+ N 9 '63
France's amazing beef machine; Charolais breed. F. E. Breth. il Sci Digest 56:37-42 N '64
Hard times on the ranges: why cattle prices are low. il U S News 56:41-5 Ap 13 '64
JFK's tax planners look to the open range. il U S News 54:64-6 Mr 25 '63
Large cattle inventory dims long-term outlook. R. Reiman. il Suc Farm 61:103 Ap '63
Major changes here in beef cattle trends. R. Reiman. Suc Farm 61:25 Je '63
Market weekend for a farming Rockefeller. il Fortune 70:149-53 Jl '64
Plenty of moo, but not enough moola. il Bsns W p32 My 23 '64
Trouble on the range. il Time 83:93-4 F 28 '64
What cattlemen should do now. B. Brantley. Suc Farm 62:33 Je '64
Why the drive to raise cattle prices failed. R. T. Cooper. New Repub 151:7-8 O 3 '64
Your best answer to low beef prices? B. Fowler. il Farm J 88:26-7+ Jl '64
See also
Meat industry and trade

CATTLE self feeders
Dairy system, convertible to beef. il Farm J 87:38-9 My '63
Fit feed lot layout to your needs. P. B. Jones and R. L. Maddex. il Suc Farm 62:54-5 N '64
Self-feeds according to production: Dari-diner. J. Russell. il Farm J 88:49 N '64
Summer feed lot ideas. il Suc Farm 62:44-5 Ag '64
They feed in minutes, and in any weather. B. Brantley. il Suc Farm 61:48 S '63

CATTLE shows
Production helps win this show. il Farm J 87:42 S '63

CATTON, Bruce
—And then Grant took command; excerpt from Centennial history of the Civil war. N Y Times Mag p26-7+ Ap 26 '64
At last Lincoln found a general; excerpt from Centennial history of the Civil war. N Y Times Mag p34-5+ N 24 '63

CATTON, Bruce—*Continued*
Black pawn on a field of peril. Am Heritage 15:66-71+ D '63
Gettysburg: great turning point. N Y Times Mag p9+ Je 30 '63
Moment of decision. Am Heritage 15:49-53 Ag '64
Old Abe the battle eagle. Am Heritage 14:32-3+ O '63
Reading, writing, and history. See issues of American heritage
Thundering water. Am Heritage 15:32-49+ Je '64
While we were marching through Georgia; excerpt from Centennial history of the Civil war N Y Times Mag p28-9+ N 1 '64
(ed) See Ripple, E. H. Civil, and sometimes uncivil, war
CATTON, William B.
First step toward freedom. Sat R 47:30-1 Ag 1 '64
Right man, wrong cause. Sat R 47:40 N 28 '64
CATTON, William R. jr.
Letting George do it won't do it. Nat Parks Mag 38:4-7 Mr '64
CAUDILL, Harry M.
Appalachia: the path from disaster. Nation 198:239-41 Mr 9 '64
Permanent poor; lesson of eastern Kentucky. Atlan 213:49-53 Je '64
Reflections on poverty in America. PTA Mag 58:20-2 Je '64
Warning from Appalachia: we are on our way to becoming a welfare reservation; interview por U S News 56:68-71 My 11 '64
CAUDILL, Rowlett and Scott (firm)
People involvement, research, planning teams, economy and regionalism dictate the designs of Caudill, Rowlett and Scott. il Arch Rec 137:111-26 Ja '65
CAUDILL, William W.
False economies in schoolhouse construction. Sat R 46:72-4+ My 18 '63
CAUFMAN, Howey
Look ma, no hands. il Motor B 112:93 N '63
CAULFIELD, Patricia
Get the picture. See issues of Modern photography
With an SLR? Mod Phot 27:56-63 Ap '63
CAULFIELD, Robert L.
Evaluation of programmed texts. Sch & Soc 91:116-17+ Mr 9 '63
CAULKING. See Calking
CAUSES of death. See Death—Causes
CAUSES of war. See War, Causes of
CAVAFY, Constantine Peter
Contemporary Greek. D. S. Carne-Ross. Poetry 101:284 Ja '63
CAVAGLIERI, Giorgio
Old Jeff to be NYPL's newest branch. il Library J 88:2658-9 Jl '63
CAVALLERIA rusticana; opera. See Mascagni, P.
CAVALLO, Adolph S.
Fresh look at the empire dress. Antiques 86: 310-13 S '64
CAVANAGH, Jerome Patrick
Detroit: new model in city hall. T. R. Brooks. Reporter 30:25-7 Ap 9 '64
Detroit's surprising mayor. T. Nicholson. Harper 227:76-8+ D '63
CAVANAUGH, Arthur
Catherine's crown; story. McCalls 91:82-3 Mr '64
Hanna for hope; story. McCalls 91:74-5 Ag '64
Nights before Christmas; story. McCalls 92: 100-1 D '64
Roseanne of yesterday; story. McCalls 91:140-1 Ap '64
Second glance; story. Redbook 123:62-3 Jl '64
Something bright like a star; story. McCalls 90:84-5 S '63
What I wish (oh, I wish) I had said; story. McCalls 90:68-9 Ag '63
CAVANAUGH, Robert M. See Quinn, J. B. jt. auth.
CAVE, Hugh
After the wedding; story. Good H 158:62-3 Ja '64; Same abr. Read Digest 84:201-4 Mr '64
Creatures of the night; story. Ladies Home J 80:108b-108d S '63
I'll walk you home; story. Good H 158:94-5 Ap '64
In your own back yard; story. Good H 156:84-5 My '63
Listen, I love you; story. Good H 158:84-5 Mr '64
Love is never forgotten; story. Good H 156:82-3 Je '63
CAVE, Ray
Letter from the publisher. S. L. James. por Sports Illus 20:4 Ap 6 '64
CAVE drawings and paintings
African bushman art treasures. A. Friendly. il Nat Geog Mag 123:848-65 Je '63
Green invader; chlorella vulgaris in Lascaux cave. Time 82:63 Jl 5 '63
Green peril; fungus threatens Lascaux frescoes. il Newsweek 61:89 Ap 29 '63
Paintings from the past; rock paintings. E. Mirel. il Sci N L 84:106-7 Ag 17 '63
Stone age art in Spanish caves. il Sunset 131:43-5 O '63
Underground gallery; treasures below the surface of the Lot Valley, France. il Time 83:70 My 8 '64
CAVE fauna and flora
Cave ecology; symposium. T. C. Barr. Science 144:321-2 Ap 17 '64
CAVE-ins. See Mine subsidences
CAVE OF THE CRYSTAL BALLS. See Caves
CAVE; story. See Ford, J. H.
CAVE temples
Travel far and near; art of Ajanta and Ellora. R. S. McCully. il Natur Hist 73: 53-7 bibliog(p63) N '64
CAVENDISH, Henry
Amateur scientist; Cavendish's experiment for determining the constant of gravity. C. L. Stong. il Sci Am 209:267-8+ S '63
CAVERLY, Richard K.
Former Scranton (Pa) librarian charged with embezzlement. Library J 88:2472 Je 15 '63
CAVES
Are you a cave man? questions and answers. J. Daugherty and M. Daugherty. il Sci Digest 54:5-7 D '63
Cave of the Crystal Balls. W. R. Halliday. il Nat Parks Mag 39:13 Ja '65
Cave trophies; aragonite specimens. H. D. Brown. il Hobbies 69:123 Mr '64
Exploring America underground. C. E. Mohr. il Nat Geog Mag 125:802-37 Je '64
Features and significance of the Mount Saint Helens cave area. W. R. Halliday. il Nat Parks Mag 37:11-14 D '63
Longhorn Cavern State Park. W. H. Matthews, 3d. il Nat Parks Mag 37:10-13 Je '63
Mystery hunters of Lovelock cave. N. Karas. il Field & S 69:42-5+ Je '64
Secret caves of Cuba; loaded with IRBMs and submarine facilities. Sat Eve Post 236: 72 Mr 30 '63
Shasta Caverns new this year; open to visitors for the first time. il Sunset 133:62+ O '64
Stalagmites and stalactites; Diamond cave. E. O'Donnell. il Natur Hist 73:22-5 My '64
Wonders of a cave find; in Ozark national forest; with colored photographs by A. Y. Owen. Life 57:49-50+ D 18 '64
See also
Carlsbad caverns
Timpanogos Cave National Monument
CAVIAR
Anyone for caviar? il Bet Hom & Gard 43: 118 Ja '65
If you are puzzled about caviar. Sunset 130: 174-5 Je '63
CAVIAR remembered; story. See La Farge, O.
CAVILL, G. W. K. and others
Venom and venom apparatus of the bull ant, myrmecia gulosa, fabr. bibliog Science 146: 79-80 O 2 '64
CAVINDER, Fred D.
Start them young. Pop Gard 14:72+ F '63
CAVITATION
Cavity formation in thin films of viscous liquids. D. F. Hays and J. B. Feiten. il Science 141:1174-5 S 20 '63
CAXTON, William, jr
Art of Janet Maas Satz. Am Artist 28:26-31+ My '64
Early printers' marks. Am Artist 27:58-9+ F '63
Khouri memorial collection. Am Artist 28:24-9 F '64
Paintings of Roy Bailey. Am Artist 27:46-51+ F '63
Woodcut portfolio. Am Artist 27:50-5+ My '63
CAYEY, Puerto Rico
From septic tanks to secondary treatment. R. M. Guzman. il Am City 78:103-4 N '63
CAYONU excavations. See Turkey—Antiquities
CEANOTHUS. See Deerbrush
CEBRA, John J. See Bernier, G. M. jt. auth.
CECCHI, Dario
Portrait of a master; reprint, tr. by J. W. Freeman. Opera N 28:6-9 F 15 '64
CECIL, Lamar J. R.
Coal for the fleet that had to die. bibliog f Am Hist R 69:990-1005 Jl '64

CECIL, Russell L.
New facts about arthritis. por Parents Mag 39:103-5 Ja '64
CECIL, Winifred
Art song and song art. Sat R 46:47+ Je 29 '63
Question of majesty. Sat R 47:56-7+ Ap 25 '64
Russian songs and singers. Sat R 46:48-9 D 28 '63
Up to standard. Sat R 46:58-9+ Ap 27 '63
CECILY, Sister Mary. See Mary Cecily, Sister
CEDAR CREST college, Allentown, Pa.
Cedar Crest on a cantilever; new library. D. D. Dennis. il Library J 88:4564-6 D 1 '63
CEDAR Hill. See Washington, D.C.—Historic houses, etc.
CEDAR RAPIDS, Ia.

Sanitary affairs

Flyless refuse collection. C. D. Smith. il Am City 78:81-2 D '63
CEDAR RAPIDS, Ia, public library
Sea horses and Apache tears; 1962 summer reading program; letter. S. McDaniel. il Wilson Lib Bul 37:682 Ap '63
CEDAR RIVER watershed. See Watersheds
CEDAR waxwings. See Waxwings
CEILINGS
Cleaning up the ceiling. il Arch Forum 118: 146-9 My '63
Design of ventilating ceilings. il Arch Rec 133:221-2+ Ap '63
Install sound-deadening ceiling tile. il Bet Hom & Gard 41:28 S '63
Integrated ceilings: versatile coffers. B. P. Spring. il Arch Forum 120:115 F '64
Keeping the product exclusive; Armstrong's Luminaire ceilings. il Bsns W p44+ Ja 25 '64
Luminous ceilings where and how to use them. D. X. Manners. il House B 106:186-7+ My '64
Patterned tiles; the new faces of silence. il House & Gard 123:202-3 Ap '63
Pitch a tent ceiling in a small room to give it large-scale glamour. il Bet Hom & Gard 41:42 S '63
These textured ceilings are reed screen. il Sunset 131:94 Jl '63
Wall-to-wall illumination. J. Hand. il Pop Sci 184:150-2 Ap '64
CELA, Camilo José
Inventory of the dark; poem. tr. by A. Kerrigan. Poetry 101:322-4 F '63
Color of seed. A. Kerrigan. Poetry 101:345-9 F '63
CELASTRUS. See Bittersweet
CELBAR, C. Michael
Monk in wood; poem. America 109:486 O 26 '63
CELEBRATIONS
Civic celebrations don't just happen; Findlay, Ohio. W. J. Carlin. il Am City 78:109+ Ap '63
Sentimental trap; excerpts from Profession: housewife. P. McGinley. Ladies Home J 80:20+ N '63
CELEBREZZE, Anthony J.
Excerpt from testimony before subcommittee on the National service corps, June 4, 1963. Cong Digest 43:14+ Ja '64
Excerpt from testimony, February 4, 1963. Cong Digest 42:234+ O '63
Truly effective force in bringing new strength to our schools. PTA Mag 57:21 F '63

about

Is it everybody's big daddy? il por Bsns W p54-8 Ap 4 '64
Rejects parochial school tax aid. Christian Cent 80:765 Je 12 '63
CELEBRITIES
American genii. il Vogue 144:240-3 D '64
Birthday party; Time magazine. New Yorker 39:32-3 My 18 '63
Far out on Long Island. W. K. Zinsser. il Horizon 5:4-27 My '63
Frankly speaking; candid comments on a variety of subjects; comp. by G. Wagner. See issues of McCall's to February 1964
Les hangouts; an insider's tour of the nouveau celebrity haunts. L. Smith. il Esquire 60:140-1 N '63
Honored by Time magazine; eight eminent Negroes. Negro Hist Bul 27:28 N '63
How I look my best; women in the world of entertainment. R. Drake. il Redbook 122: 72-5+ N '63
Man that I marry. R. Hochstein. il Good H 156:86-9 F '63
Most likely to succeed. L. Lerman. il Mlle 57: 154-7 S '63
My children's heroes; celebrities childhood idols and their children's. G. Walker. il Good H 156:84-5+ Je '63
New girl in town. il Esquire 59:72-5 Je '63
Old age brings honor to those who serve. F. Morley. il Nations Bsns 51:27-8 Je '63
Something to talk about. L. Lerman. il Mlle 57:128-31 O '63
Something to talk about: most likely to succeed. L. Lerman. il Mlle 59:160-3 S '64
Squires at large. il Esquire 59:76 Mr; 78 Ap '63; 61:55 Ja; 75 Je; 62:80 Jl '64
Strategy meeting; attempt by fellow theater people to save L. Hansberry's Sign in Sidney Brustein's window. New Yorker 40: 49-51 D 5 '64
Time's 40th anniversary party. il Time 81: 59-68+ My 17 '63
What did you want most at seventeen? symposium, ed. by A. Ebert. il Seventeen 22:130-3 S '63
Wheels on wheels. il Vogue 142:90-3 Ag 15 '63
Who's news; Cleveland Amory's Celebrity register. Newsweek 62:97 D 2 '63
Why the stars go broke. il Ebony 18:84-6+ Jl '63
See also
Great men
Women, Famous

Anecdotes, facetiae, satire, etc.

And a merry Christmas to all. J. Westcott. il Seventeen 23:22 D '64
CELERIAC
Celeriac. L. K. Lantz. Pop Gard 14:100 My '63
CELERY
See also
Cookery—Vegetables
CELESTIAL globes. See Globes, Astronomical
CELIBACY
Married priests? Commonweal 80:223-4 My 15 '64; Reply. G. M. Dalpiaz. 80:301 My 29 '64
Married Roman Catholic priests. J. Roddy. il Look 28:103+ Mr 24 '64; Reply. America 110:405 Mr 28 '64
Priestly state, marriage or celibacy? by P. Hermand. Review
Time 84:56+ Ag 28 '64
CÉLINE, Louis Ferdinand, pseud. See Destouches, L. F.
CELL division (biology)
Automatic sampling device for study of synchronized cultures of microorganisms. S. F. Petropulos. bibliog il Science 145:268-70 Jl 17 '64
Behavior genetics and individuality understood; excerpts from discussions at symposiums. J. Hirsch. bibliog il Science 142: 1436-42 D 13 '63
Bile duct restoration in rana pipiens after ligation of the hepatoduodenal ligament. J. G. Streett, jr. bibliog il Science 143:592-4 F 7 '64
Cell synchrony; report on conference at the Biology division of the Oak Ridge national laboratory. G. M. Padilla and others. Science 147:175-7 Ja 8 '65
Chromosomal and nucleolar RNA synthesis in root tips during mitosis. N. K. Das. bibliog il Science 140:1231-3 Je 14 '63
Continuous recording of cell number in logarithmic and synchronized cultures. T. W. James and N. G. Anderson. bibliog il Science 142:1183-5 N 29 '63
Dictyotene stage of meiosis in mosses. F. J. Dill. bibliog il Science 144:541-3 My 1 '64
Immune response and mitosis of human peripheral blood lymphocytes in vitro. K. Hirschhorn and others. bibliog il Science 142:1185-7 N 29 '63
Mitoses; distribution in mouse ear epidermis. J. V. Frei and others. bibliog il Science 140:487-8 My 3 '63
Mitosis and differentiation in roots treated with actinomycin. A. K. Bal and P. R. Gross. bibliog il Science 139:584-6 F 15 '63
Mitotically synchronized mammalian cells: a simple method for obtaining large populations. E. Robbins and P. I. Marcus. bibliog il Science 144:1152-3 My 29 '64
Persistent mitosis of transfused homologus leukocytes in children receiving antileukemic therapy. R. H. Levin and others. bibliog il Science 142:1305-6+ D 6 '63
Radioautographic evidence for the incorporation of leucine-carbon-14 into the mitotic apparatus. D. W. Stafford and R. M. Iverson. bibliog il Science 143:580-1 F 7 '64
Replication of DNA and cell division in synchronously dividing cultures of euglena gracilis. L. N. Edmunds, jr. bibliog il Science 145:266-8 Jl 17 '64

CELL division (biology)—*Continued*
Somatic mitoses in cells of picea glauca cultivated in vitro. P. G. Risser. bibliog il Science 143:591-2 F 7 '64

CELL growth. See Cells

CELLARS. See Basements and cellars

CELLER, Emanuel
Excerpt from address, January 31, 1964. Cong Digest 43:78+ Mr '64
Excerpt from debate, August 19, 1964. Cong Digest 44:25+ Ja '65

CELLS
Amphibian cell culture: permanent cell line from the bullfrog (rana catesbeiana) K. Wolf and M. C. Quimby. bibliog il Science 144:1578-80 Je 26 '64
Animal cell strains; report on Cell culture collection committee. bibliog Science 146:241-3 O 9 '64
Antibody plaque formation by normal mouse spleen cell cultures exposed in vitro to RNA from immune mice. H. Friedman. bibliog il Science 146:934-6 N 13 '64
Antibody production by nonimmune spleen cells incubated with RNA from immunized mice. E. P. Cohen and J. J. Parks. bibliog il Science 144:1012-13 My 22 '64
Antibody synthesizing cells: appearance after secondary antigenic stimulation in vitro. M. Richardson and R. W. Dutton. bibliog il Science 146:655-6 O 30 '64
Autobiographies of cells. R. Baserga and W. E. Kisieleski. il Sci Am 209:103-8+ Ag '63
Bone cells: biochemical and biological studies after enzymatic isolation. W. A. Peck and others. bibliog il Science 146:1476-7 D 11 '64
Building blocks of life. Todays Health 41:19 N '63
Cell division and cancer; report of international symposium on the control of cell division and the induction of cancer. C. C. Congdon. Science 142:252-3+ O 11 '63
Cell guidance by alterations in monomolecular films. M. D. Rosenberg. bibliog il Science 139:411-12 F 1 '63
Cell life cycle: macromolecular aspects; report of symposium sponsored by the Biology division of the Oak Ridge national laboratory and the Division of biology and medicine of the Atomic energy commission. D. M. Prescott. Science 141:547-8 Ag 9 '63
Cell system in which rate and amount of protein synthesis are separately controlled. O. Landeros and H. M. Frost. bibliog il Science 145:1323-4 S 18 '64
Cell wall replication in salmonella typhosa. R. M. Cole. bibliog il Science 143:820-2 F 21 '64
Cells, just like people, show discrimination. Sci N L 84:88 Ag 10 '63
Cells that communicate. D. G. Cooley. il Todays Health 41:20-5+ My; 38-41+ Je '63
Cellular mechanisms in experimental epileptic seizures. H. Matsumoto and C. A. Marsan. bibliog il Science 144:193-4 Ap 10 '64
Cigarette smoke: charcoal filters reduce components that inhibit growth of cultured human cells. P. S. Thayer and C. J. Kensler. bibliog il Science 146:642-4 O 30 '64
Coenzyme Q: intracellular distribution in rhodospirillum rubrum. A. F. Greene and J. P. Mascarenhas. bibliog il Science 144:1455-6 Je 19 '64
Cytoplasmic interaction between macrophages and lymphocytic cells in antibody synthesis. M. D. Schoenberg and others. bibliog il Science 143:964-5 F 28 '64
Daily rhythm of luciferin activity in gonyaulax polyedra. V. C. Bode and others. bibliog il Science 141:913-15 S 6 '63
DNA's code: key to all life: with report by A. Hills and A. Rosenfeld. il Life 55:70-8+ O 4 '63
Diploid and endoreduplicated cells: measurements of DNA. A. G. Bell. il Science 143:139 Ja 10 '64
Ethylene oxide sterilization of tissue culture media. B. L. Brown and R. Fuerst. bibliog Science 142:1654-5 D 27 '63
Experimental reversal of germ cells in ovaries of fetal mice. C. D. Turner and H. Asakawa. bibliog Science 143:1344-5 Mr 20 '64
Floral induction and the stimulation of cell division in xanthium. R. G. Thomas. bibliog il Science 140:54-6 Ap 5 '63
Homograft target cells: specific destruction in vitro by contact interaction with immune macrophages. G. A. Granger and R. S. Weiser. bibliog il Science 145:1427-9 S 25 '64
How cells attack antigens. R. S. Speirs. il Sci Am 210:58-64 bibliog(p 152) F '64
How cells make antibodies. G. J. V. Nossal. il Sci Am 211:106-15 D '64
Human diploid cell strains; report on symposium on the characterization and uses of human diploid cell strains. L. Hayflick and others. Science 143:976 F 28 '64
Ideas from cell studies. Sci N L 86:341 N 28 '64
Immunologically determined and competent cells are affected differentially by actinomycin D. E. Weiler. bibliog il Science 144:846-9 My 15 '64; Reply with rejoinder. D. W. Talmage. 145:1073-4 S 4 '64
Intercellular diffusion. Y. Kanno and W. R. Loewenstein. bibliog il Science 143:959 F 28 '64
Intercellular electrical coupling at a forming membrane junction in a dividing cell. R. F. Ashman and others. bibliog il Science 145:604-5 Ag 7 '64
Intracellular regulatory mechanisms. H. E. Umbarger. bibliog il Science 145:674-9 Ag 14 '64
Killing of cultured rabbit fibroblasts with isoimmune serum. D. A. Pious and S. E. Mills. bibliog il Science 142:52-3 O 4 '63
Lens development: fiber elongation and lens orientation. J. L. Coulombre and A. J. Coulombre. bibliog il Science 142:1489-90 D 13 '63
Life activity observed. Sci N L 87:37 Ja 16 '65
Lipopolysaccharide of the gram-negative cell wall. M. J. Osborn and others. bibliog il Science 145:783-9 Ag 21 '64
Loss of radioactivity from labeled DNA of primary human amnion cells. R. S. Chang and H. Vetrovs. bibliog il Science 139:1211 Mr 22 '63
Lysosome. C. de Duve. il Sci Am 208:64-72 My '63
New technique helps analyze single cell. Sci N L 85:281 My 2 '64
Nuclear bodies: their prevalence, location, and ultrastructure in the calf. A. F. Weber and S. P. Frommes. bibliog il Science 141:912-13 S 6 '63
Nucleic acid metabolism in L cells infected with a member of the psittacosis group. E. M. Schechter and others. bibliog il Science 145:819-21 Ag 21 '64
On biochemical variability and innovation; text of paper presented at a symposium on the general physiology of specialized cells. S. S. Cohen. bibliog il Science 139:1017-26 Mr 15 '63
Osteoclasts: organization in chick embryo bone. M. L. Tanzer and R. D. Hunt. bibliog il Science 141:1270-2 S 27 '63
Phospholipid-sugar complexes in relation to cell membrane monosaccharide transport. P. G. LeFevre and others. bibliog il Science 143:955-7 F 28 '64
Photosensitizing substance in human serum: effect on HeLa cells. W. B. Wheeler and A. C. Hollinshead. bibliog il Science 141:1279-80 S 27 '63
Plaque assay for measurement of cells infected with zoster virus. F. Rapp and M. Benyesh-Melnick. bibliog il Science 141:433-4 Ag 2 '63
Polyploidy induced by X-rays in Chinese hamster cells in vitro. C. K. Yu and W. K. Sinclair. bibliog il Science 145:508-10 Jl 31 '64
Polyribosomes. A. Rich. il Sci Am 209:44-53 bibliog(p 178) D '63
Polyribosomes: size in normal and polio-infected HeLa cells. A. Rich and others. bibliog il Science 142:1658-63 D 27 '63
Pulmonary alveolar cell inclusions: their development in the rat. S. Buckingham and others. bibliog il Science 145:1192-3 S 11 '64
Reconstruction of tissues by dissociated cells. M. S. Steinberg. bibliog il Science 141:401-8 Ag 2 '63
Redifferentiation of connective tissue cells in serial culture. R. E. Priest and J. H. Priest. bibliog il Science 145:1053-4 S 4 '64
Relationship between nuclear volumes, chromosome numbers, and relative radiosensitivities. A. H. Sparrow and others. bibliog il Science 141:163-6 Jl 12 '63
Responses of single cells in visual system to shifts in the wavelength of light. R. L. De Valois and others. il Science 146:1184-6 N 27 '64
Reversible sonic inhibition of protein, purine, and pyrimidine biosynthesis in the living cell. V. W. Burns. bibliog il Science 146:1056-8 N 20 '64
Root hairs, cuticle, and pits. F. M. Scott and others. bibliog il Science 140:63 Ap 5 '63
Selection of hybrids from matings of fibroblasts in vitro and their presumed recombinants. J. W. Littlefield. bibliog il Science 145:709 Ag 14 '64

CELLS—*Continued*
Sensitivity of cultured mammalian cells to streptomycin and dihydrostreptomycin. M. Moskowitz and N. E. Kelker. bibliog il Science 141:647-8 Ag 16 '63
Serum factor in renal compensatory hyperplasia. L. M. Lowenstein and A. Stern. bibliog il Science 142:1479-80 D 13 '63
Sex differences in cells. U. Mittwoch. il Sci Am 209:54-62 bibliog (p 170) Jl '63
Single cell has its complex world of workers. il Life 54:52-3 Mr 29 '63
Spleen-colony formation in anemic mice of genotype WW^{v}. E. A. McCulloch and others. bibliog il Science 144:844-6 My 15 '64
Surgery in a cell. Newsweek 63:64 Ja 6 '64
Transformation of cells in vitro by viruses. R. Dulbecco. bibliog Science 142:932-6 N 15 '63
Wondrous inner space of living cells. R. Platt. il Read Digest 84:195+ Je '64
X-ray sensitivity and DNA synthesis in synchronous populations of HeLa cells. T. Terasima and L. J. Tolmach. bibliog il Science 140:490-2 My 3 '63
See also
Chromosomes
Cilia and ciliary motion
Cytoplasm
Differentiation (biology)
Lymphoid cells
Mitochondria
Nerve cells
Nuclei, Cellular
Plant cells and tissues

Inclusions

Uricase: localization in hepatic microbodies. Z. Hruban and H. Swift. bibliog il Science 146:1316-18 D 4 '64

CELLS, Electric. See Electric batteries

CELLULAR metabolism. See Tissue metabolism

CELLULOSE
Ash content: its effect on combustion of corn plants. A. Broido and M. A. Nelson. bibliog il Science 146:652-3 O 30 '64
Cellulose synthesized. il Sci N L 85:53 Ja 25 '64

CELLULOSE acetate membrane. See Membranes (technology)

CELOSIA. See Cockscomb

CELTICS (basketball team) See Basketball teams

CEMENT
Chemistry of concrete; mixing portland cement with water. S. Brunauer and L. E. Copeland. il Sci Am 210:80-6+ Ap '64
Expansive cement; ettringite expanding form of calcium sulfoaluminate. Sci Am 211:60 O '64
See also
Concrete
Mortar

CEMENT industry and trade
Eruption of cement on the Hudson; Atlantic cement co. il Fortune 67:126-7 Je '63
Ready-mixed competition. il Bsns W p61-2+ My 23 '64

History

It doesn't come from Portland, Me. Bsns W p62 My 23 '64

Securities

Carving in cement. il Fortune 69:76+ My '64

CEMENTS, Adhesive
New plastic-mending cements. J. Hand. il Pop Sci 182:169-71 My '63

CEMETERIES
Forest Lawn; photographs. Travel 123:41-3 Ja '65
Grave collector; visiting authors graves. S. Black. il Harper 228:26+ Je '64
See also
Cambridge, Mass.—Cemeteries
National cemeteries, American

CENSORSHIP
ABPC hits Conn. plan for censorship commission. Pub W 183:67 Ap 15 '63
Art in court; Candy comes to Chicago. B. Cook. Nation 199:125-6 S 14 '64
Asserts book-banning rumor unfounded; Rome bookstores. Christian Cent 80:1293 O 23 '63
Banned in Rome? America 109:449 O 19 '63
Book banning and juvenile delinquency. J. Ciardi. Sat R 46:16 Ag 10 '63
Book banning in Rome; Kaiser, Rynne and Küng. Christian Cent 80:1260 O 16 '63
Book editors' meeting debates censorship. Pub W 183:43-4 Je 24 '63
Books and banners; case of censoring Dictionary of American slang in California. J. A. King. Sat R 46:28-9+ N 9 '63
Brooklyn cleric and Fanny keep news media scrambling. Library J 89:1575 Ap 1 '64
Catcher goes to sidelines as Va. parents protest use. Library J 88:2088+ My 15 '63
Catcher in rye reapproved for sale in Pa. HS bookstore. Library J 88:4445+ N 15 '63
Censors and the schools, by J. Nelson and G. Roberts, jr. Review
Pub W 183:38-41 F 4 '63
Reporter 28:42+ Je 6 '63. F. M. Hechinger
Censorship: a bookseller's view. T. Huntington. Pub W 185:57 Mr 2 '64
Censorship and the freedom to read: 1963-64 in review. Pub W 185:88-9 Ja 20 '64: 187: 85-7 Ja 18 '65
Censorship around the world. Library J 88: 1964-5, 3041 My 15, S 1 '63
Censorship, by M. L. Ernst and A. U. Schwartz. Review
Sat R 47:27 Ag 22 '64. P. S. Jennison
Censorship coast to coast. Library J 88:2855-6 Ag '63
Censorship of textbooks; symposium. il NEA J 52:18-28 My '63
Censorship on campus; a student's plea for granting responsible freedom to Catholic college editors. M. O'Connell. America 111: 611-13 N 14 '64; Discussion. 112:17-18, 95 Ja 2, 23 '65
Censorship on teenage reading slated by New Jersey group; Ethical culture society of Bergen County, N.J. Library J 88:2218 Je 1 '63
Censorship roundup: a long, hot summer. Library J 88:3282 S 15 '63
Censorship: strategy for defense; booksellers position. P. S. Jennison. Pub W 185:58-61 Mr 2 '64
Chicago booksellers join to fight censorship; Greater Chicago booksellers association established. Pub W 186:83+ Jl 6 '64
Civil liberties group opposes censorship of pornography; British Columbia civil liberties association. Library J 89:1049 Mr 1 '64
Court bans Tropic of cancer; New York state of law. Christian Cent 80:950 Jl 31 '63
Crossing censorship thresholds; letter to the editor. R. D. Franklin. Library J 88:4288 N 15 '63
Defensive about The defenders. E. Moon. Library J 88:2210 Je 1 '63; Discussion. 88: 2580 Jl '63
Fanny Hill judged too obscene for N.J. Pub W 186:48 D 28 '64
Fanny Hill prosecuted in New Jersey. Pub W 185:68 Je 22 '64
Fanny Hill voted obscene, three to two, in New York appeal; with editorial comment. Pub W 185:39-40, 45 Mr 9 '64
Fanny Hill wins decision in New York; with editorial comment. il Pub W 184:42-4, 49 S 2 '63; Discussion. 184:29 S 23 '63
Flaming censorship. Nation 198:311 Mr 30 '64
Freedom to teach and to learn. E. Gordon. il PTA Mag 58:4-7 O '63
Governor dissolves R.I. censorship commission. Pub W 185:100 Je 8 '64
If ever a library needed a friend; burning of book from public library in New City, Rockland County, N.Y. R. H. Smith. Pub W 183: 55 F 4 '63
Illinois Supreme court reverses ban on Tropic; Fanny Hill o.k.'d for sale in New York. Pub W 186:51-2 Jl 20 '64
Impurities in Yorkville; Father Morton Hill's campaign against pornography. M. Kempton. New Repub 148:13-15 Mr 16 '63
In B—G with Mrs Grundy. P. Fryer. il Horizon 6:66-9 Spr '64
Intellectual freedom committee protests censorship in Nassau. Library J 89:2300-1 Je 1 '64
James Baldwin novel banned in New Orleans. Pub W 184:38 Jl 1 '63
Knock on the door; censorship strikes a librarian at home. W. L. Purcell. Library J 88:526+ F 1 '63; Reply. D. A. Seager. 88:1492 Ap 1 '63
Man who corrupted California; on censoring the Dictionary of American slang. S. Flexner. il Esquire 61:82-3+ Mr '64
Massachusetts judge finds Fanny Hill obscene. Pub W 182:32 S 14 '64
Masters of illusion; Defenders television program Book for burning. America 108:487 Ap 13 '63
Month at random; courts and literary censorship. Wilson Lib Bul 38:21 S '63
Nation of peeping toms; with editorial comment. America 112:34, 38 Ja 9 '65
N.Y.C. court finds two guilty of selling Fanny Hill to minor. Library J 89:83 Ja 1 '64
New York city moves to ban Fanny Hill. Pub W 184:64-5 Jl 15 '63
New York injunction vs. Fanny Hill granted. Pub W 184:44 Ag 5 '63

CENSORSHIP—*Continued*
New York state and London both find Fanny Hill obscene. Library J 89:1204 Mr 15 '64
Relief for booksellers from censorship pressures. H. F. Pilpel. Pub W 183:36-7 F 25 '63
R.I. censors' activities ruled unconstitutional; with editorial comment. Pub W 183:42-3, 49 Mr 4 '63
Rome quietly suppresses some council books. Pub W 184:33 O 14 '63
Sale of smut can be stopped. B. M. Silverman. il Parents Mag 40:48-9+ Ja '65
Sex and the Supreme court; with editorial comment. A. Lewis. Esquire 59:6, 82-3+ Je '63
Sex and violence in books, magazines and television. B. Bettelheim. il Redbook 123:60-1+ My '64
Sex, Tallahassee: handbook on homosexuals banned in Dade County. R. H. Williams. New Repub 150:5 My 23 '64
Show that wasn't there; play dealing with race relations banned from Michigan state university's educational television station. R. L. Shayon. Sat R 47:27 Ag 15 '64
Slang dictionary raises heck of a row in Calif. Pub W 184:65 Jl 15 '63
Student freedom; censorship of articles in the Scholastic. Commonweal 78:269-70 My 31 '63; Reply. O. P. Kretzmann. 78:379 Je 28 '63
Summer of censorship. R. H. Smith. Pub W 184:38 Jl 29 '63
Supreme court asked to review Tropic conviction. Pub W 183:43 Mr 4 '63
Supreme court decision limits censorship. Pub W 186:48-9 Jl 6 '64
Supreme court petitioned to review Tropic conviction. Library J 88:1496 Ap 1 '63
Supreme court reverses Florida ban on Tropic; Tropic found obscene in Illinois Supreme court. Pub W 185:48-50 Je 29 '64
Supreme court sits fence on Tropic of cancer. Library J 89:212 Ja 15 '64
Teenage mazagine asks readers: Is censorship fair to teens? Ingenue magazine. Library J 88:2088 My 15 '63
Tempest in a teapot; Rhode Island commission to encourage morality in youth. America 108:322 Mr 9 '63
Tropic of cancer banned as obscene in N.Y. state. Pub W 184:25 Jl 22 '63
Tropic of cancer before the Supreme court. Wilson Lib Bul 37:612+ Ap '63
Tune in on censorship; Sam Benedict show and Defenders. il Wilson Lib Bul 37:724+ My '63
Two booksellers guilty for selling Fanny Hill. Pub W 184:33-5 N 25 '63
Two dangers: smut and censorship. Christian Cent 81:261 F 26 '64
Two Fanny Hill decisions pending in New York. Pub W 184:26-7 Jl 22 '63
US supreme court overrules Rhode Island censors' group. Library J 88:1736 Ap 15 '63
Unvarnished trash upheld by N. Y. Supreme court judge. Library J 88:3812 O 15 '63
Varieties of love. E. Capouya. Nation 197:457-9 D 28 '63
War against good books in American schools. R. Kirk. Nat R 14:407 My 21 '63
War of words, obscenities in Dictionary of American slang. Newsweek 62:69 Jl 29 '63
When someone complains; threats of book banning, Pontiac, Mich. schools. D. P. Whitmer. Sr Schol 83:27T Ja 17 '64
Ye olde sex; new edition of Memoirs of a woman of pleasure banned. Time 82:41 Ag 2 '63
See also
Freedom of the press
Government and the press
Immoral literature and pictures
Information, Freedom of
Intellectual liberty
Libraries—Censorship
Moving picture censorship
Postal censorship
School libraries—Censorship

Bibliography

Nature of our problem: there have been some changes. E. T. Moore. ALA Bul 57:488-92 Je '63

Australia

Baldwin wins in New Zealand; Australian impasse on The group. Library J 89:2300 Je 1 '64

Canada

Canada considers. E. Moon. Library J 88:523 F 1 '63

France

Book censorship in Paris. P. Lennon. Atlan 212:73-6 N '63
Creeping censorship. Newsweek 63:50+ Ap 20 '64

Great Britain

Fanny Hill seized by British police. Library J 89:212 Ja 15 '64
New York state and London both find Fanny Hill obscene. Library J 89:1204 Mr 15 '64

New Zealand

Baldwin wins in New Zealand; Australian impasse on The group. Library J 89:2300 Je 1 '64

Poland

Censorship by any name: control of Catholic press. America 110:472 Ap 4 '64
Unfreedom of Polish writers. T. V. Atkins. New Repub 151:6-7 O 31 '64

Russia

No censorship court battles in USSR! manuscripts don't get that far; summary of news conference. A. P. Rybin. Library J 88:2218-19 Je 1 '63
Russian art & anti-Semitism; with introd. by M. Decter. E. A. Evtushenko; N. S. Khrushchev; M. Romm. Commentary 36:433-7 D '63

Spain

Franco's new commandments. il Time 83:59 Je 5 '64

United States

See Censorship

Viet Nam (Republic)

No change in Saigon; newspapers ordered out of print. Time 83:59 Je 5 '64

CENSORSHIP, Library. See Libraries—Censorship
CENSORSHIP of mail. See Postal censorship
CENTAUR booster. See Space vehicles—Propulsion systems
CENTAUREA
Centaur flowers. V. M. Quist. il Horticulture 41:338-9 Je '63
CENTENARIANS
How to grow old without aging. A. Parry. il Sci Digest 54:86-90 O '63
Man who spoke to Lincoln. il Ebony 18:79-82+ F '63
CENTENNIALS
Montana's Territorial centennial. B. Browning. il Travel 121:39-41 Je '64
CENTER for advanced study in the behavioral sciences
Leisure of the theory class. M. Mayer. Esquire 59:16+ Mr '63
CENTER for cognitive studies. See Harvard university—Center for cognitive studies
CENTER for cultural and technical interchange between East and West. See Hawaii. University, Honolulu—Cultural center
CENTER for documentation and communication research. See Western Reserve university, Cleveland, Ohio—Center for documentation and communication research
CENTER for the gifted child, incorporated. See Toy industry
CENTER for the study of democratic institutions, Santa Barbara, Calif.
Living encyclical; Pacem in terris to be studied by the Center. America 110:857-8 Je 27 '64
Our footloose correspondents. J. Bainbridge. il New Yorker 39:105-6+ N 9 '63
Pacem in terris; international conference to revive the discussion of the encyclical. J. Cogley. Commonweal 80:639 S 18 '64
Working for peace; study of encyclical Peace on earth. America 112:98 Ja 23 '65
CENTER of gravity; story. See Amster, L. J.
CENTER of population. See United States—Population
CENTERPIECES. See Table decoration
CENTIPEDES
Centipede's spiral is live shelter. F. Schremmer. il Natur Hist 72:42-5 My '63
CENTO. See Central treaty organization
CENTRAL AFRICAN REPUBLIC
Colored rulers. G. C. Turner. Negro Hist Bul 27:153 Mr '64
CENTRAL airlines
Central begins equipment modernization. E. J. Bulban. il Aviation W 81:37+ S 28 '64
CENTRAL AMERICA
See also
Automobile touring—Central America
Canals—Central America
Organization of Central American states

CENTRAL AMERICA—*Continued*

Description and travel

To the Panama Canal by car; a first in tourist travel. J. F. Diggs and T. J. O'Halloran. il U S News 54:70-6 My 13 '63

Economic conditions

How to make good without the Canal; Committee for economic development report on Central America. Time 85:31 Ja 1 '65
J.F.K. co-stars in a new Common market; Latinos have a hit; with report by L. Hall. il Life 54:26-35 Mr 29 '63
Presidents' meeting at San José; statements, addresses and remarks, March 18-21, 1963; with Declaration of Central America. J. F. Kennedy. Dept State Bul 48:511-20 Ap 8 '63
Pulling together. Time 81:42 Je 14 '63

Economic policy

Seven presidents. Newsweek 61:54+ Mr 25 '63
See also
Central American program of economic integration

Foreign relations

Castro's neighbors bitter and disillusioned at U.S. il U S News 54:47 Ap 1 '63
Declaration of Central America. il Newsweek 61:40 Ap 1 '63
J.F.K. co-stars in a new Common market; Latinos have a hit; with report by L. Hall. il Life 54:26-35 Mr 29 '63
Theme at Costa Rica: progress: il Sr Schol 82:16 Ap 3 '63
United in spirit and in arms; Rendezvous with destiny; addresses, March 18 and March 21, 1963. J. F. Kennedy. Vital Speeches 29:386-9 Ap 15 '63
What JFK is promising to Central Americans. U S News 54:55 Mr 25 '63

United States

Presidents' meeting at San José; statements, addresses and remarks, March 18-21, 1963; with Declaration of Central America. J. F. Kennedy. Dept State Bul 48:511-20 Ap 8 '63

History

One kind of patriot. il Time 81:29 Ap 26 '63

Politics

Climate of San José. il Time 81:15-16 Mr 22 '63

CENTRAL AMERICA and the United States. See Latin America and the United States

CENTRAL AMERICAN common market. See Central American program of economic integration

CENTRAL AMERICAN program of economic integration
Central America closes ranks. il Bsns W p47-8+ Mr 16 '63

CENTRAL ARIZONA project (proposed)
CAP and TVA: Barry's fine distinction. D. Oberdorfer. Reporter 31:36-8 S 10 '64

CENTRAL Baptist theological seminary, Kansas City, Kan.
Seminary and the racial crisis: Consultation on the church and the racial crisis. A. C. Porteous. Christian Cent 81:147-8 Ja 29 '64

CENTRAL CITY, Colo.
Town with a romantic past lights for the future. W. C. Russell, jr. il Am City 79:116 N '64

Music

Great opera houses: Central City. A. M. Lingg. il Opera N 28:16-20 My 2 '64

CENTRAL CITY festival. See Music festivals—Colorado

CENTRAL CITY opera association, Colorado
Mr Ward's Lady; premiere of Lady from Colorado, by Robert Ward. A. Young. il Mus Am 84:20-1 S '64

CENTRAL conference of American rabbis
Tension in reform Judaism. E. B. Borowitz. Christian Cent 81:729-32 Je 3 '64

CENTRAL heating. See Heating

CENTRAL intelligence agency. See United States—Central intelligence agency

CENTRAL nervous system. See Nervous system

CENTRAL opera service
C.O.S. conference. Q Eaton. Opera N 29:25 O 17 '64

CENTRAL park. See New York (city)—Parks and playgrounds

CENTRAL POINT, Ore.
Boosters end pressure problems. L. Paul. il Am City 78:133-4 D '63

CENTRAL treaty organization
Central treaty organization holds 11th ministerial meeting; statement, April 30, 1963, with final communique. D. Rusk. Dept State Bul 48:841-4 My 27 '63
Central treaty organization meets at Washington; address, April 28, 1964; with final communique. D. Rusk. Dept State Bul 50:766-9 My 18 '64

CENTRAL WASHINGTON state college, Ellensburg
Central Washington state college. V. B. Archer. il NEA J 53:20-2 My '64

CENTRALIA, Wash.
George Washington of Centralia Washington. W. S. Savage. bibliog Negro Hist Bul 27:44-7 N '63

CENTRALIZATION in government
Why I am a Republican. D. D. Eisenhower. Sat Eve Post 237:17-19 Ap 11 '64; Same abr. with title Policies I believe will strengthen this country. Read Digest 85:102-8 Jl '64

CENTRALIZED cataloging. See Cataloging

CENTRALIZED purchasing. See Purchasing, Municipal

CENTRIFUGES
Scientists to swing out in giant centrifuges. Sci N L 86:132 Ag 29 '64

CENTRO interamericano de libros académicos. See Inter-American scholarly book center

CENTURY, Camp. See Building, Ice and snow

CENTURY 21 exposition. See Seattle—Century 21 exposition, 1962

CEPEDA, Orlando
Orlando Cepeda; San Francisco Giants. T. Cohane. il pors Look 27:84+ My 21 '63

CEPHALOSPORIN C
Inhibition of synthesis of the cell wall of staphylococcus aureus by cephalothin. T. W. Chang and L. Weinstein. bibliog il Science 143:807-8 F 21 '64
6-aminopenicillanic acid: inhibition of destruction of cephalosporin C by bacteria. R. B. Walton. bibliog il Science 143:1438-9 Mr 27 '64

CEPHEIDS
Story of U Cephei. O. Struve. il Sky & Tel 25:199-201 Ap '63

CERAGIOLI, Pete. See Jolly, P.

CERAMI, Charles A.
Europe's competitive threat will ease. Nations Bsns 51:34-5+ Mr '63
How companies build on success. Nations Bsns 52:38-9+ Mr '64
How to get most from growth. Nations Bsns 51:34-5+ Jl '63
Make the most of new ideas. Nations Bsns 52:50-2+ Jl '64
Stale in your job? try this. Nations Bsns 51:88-90 O '63
This test spots leaders. Nations Bsns 52:68-70+ My '64
You can improve your business timing. Nations Bsns 51:94-6+ My '63

CERAMIC materials
Foamed ceramic insulation possible. J. F. Judge. il Miss & Roc 13:39 O 21 '63
Imitation bone made from clay-like material: cerosium, oxide of aluminum impregnated with epoxy resin. Sci N L 86:396 D 19 '64
See also
Magnesia

CERAMIC sculpture
John Voyez, fact and fiction (cont) R. J. Charleston. il Antiques 84:429-33 O '63
Swinging ceramics; bells by Charlee. il Design 65:82-3 N '63

CERAMIC shell process. See Lost wax process

CERAMICS. See Pottery

CERATIUM. See Sea urchins

CERATOCYSTIS infection. See Fungi

CERCEK, B. and others
Pulse radiolysis of potassium bromide solutions. bibliog Science 145:919-20 Ag 28 '64

CEREAL foods
Mineral-treated cereal prevents tooth decay. Sci N L 85:183 Mr 21 '64
Tale of a porridge pot: Cream of wheat. M. Keiser. il Parents Mag 40:18+ Ja '65
Telling the world about breakfast. il Time 83:92 Mr 13 '64
See also
Cookery—Cereals

CEREAL leaf beetles. See Beetles

CEREBELLUM
Cerebellar ataxia in hamsters inoculated with rat virus. L. Kilham and G. Margolis. bibliog il Science 143:1047-8 Mr 6 '64
Chemically induced epileptiform seizures in the cat. S. P. Grossman. bibliog il Science 142:409-11 O 18 '63

CEREBELLUM—*Continued*
Interaction of evoked potentials of neocortical and hypothalamic origin in the amygdala. R. Caruthers and others. bibliog il Science 144:422-3 Ap 24 '64

CEREBRAL cortex
Attention, vigilance, and cortical evoked-potentials in humans. M. Haider and others. bibliog il Science 145:180-2 Jl 10 '64
Auditory discrimination by the cat after neonatal ablation of temporal cortex. D. P. Scharlock and others. bibliog il Science 141:1197-8 S 20 '63
Brain information officer; hippocampus. Sci N L 85:245 Ap 18 '64
Cerebral cortex: a sensorimotor amalgam in the marsupialia. R. A. Lende. il Science 141:730-2 Ag 23 '63
Cerebral heterostimulation in a monkey colony. J. M. R. Delgado. bibliog il Science 141:161-3 Jl 12 '63
Convulsant drug action on neuronally isolated cerebral cortex. B. Grafstein. bibliog il Science 142:973-5 N 15 '63
Cortico-subcortical homeostasis in the cat's brain. W. P. Koella and A. Ferry. bibliog il Science 142:586-9 N 1 '63
Enhancement of evoked cortical potentials in humans related to a task requiring a decision. H. Davis. bibliog il Science 145:182-3 Jl 10 '64
Gravitational stress: changes in cortical excitability. A. N. Nicholson. bibliog il Science 145:1458-9 S 25 '64
Hippocampectomy and behavior sequences. D. P. Kimble and K. H. Pribram. bibliog Science 139:824-5 Mr 1 '63
Interaction of evoked potentials of neocortical and hypothalamic origin in amygdala. R. Caruthers and others. bibliog il Science 144:422-3 Ap 24 '64
Lateral geniculate nucleus and cerebral cortex: evidence for a crossed pathway. M. Glickstein and others. bibliog il Science 145:159-61 Jl 10 '64
Long-term stability of visually evoked potentials in man. R. E. Dustman and E. C. Beck. il Science 142:1480-1 D 13 '63
Midbrain hemisection: effect on cortical acetylcholine in the cat. G. Pepeu and P. Mantegazzini. bibliog il Science 145:1069-70 S 4 '64
Postsynaptic potentials and spike patterns during augmenting responses in cat's motor cortex. M. R. Klee and K. Offenloch. bibliog il Science 143:488-9 Ja 31 '64
Sound-evoked potentials in neocortex of unanesthetized opossum. P. C. Nieder and W. Randall. bibliog il Science 144:429-30 Ap 24 '64
Speech sound discrimination by cats. J. H. Dewson, 3d. bibliog il Science 144:555-6 My 1 '64
Visual cortex of the brain. D. H. Hubel. il Sci Am 209:54-62 bibliog(p 186) N '63

CEREBRAL hemorrhage
Episode, by E. Hodgins. Review
Life 56:13 Mr 27 '64. J. K. Galbraith
I came back from a stroke. J. H. Winchester. Read Digest 83:169-74 O '63
Instant stroke diagnosis; thermographic test. il Sci Digest 57:16-17 Ja '65
Pattern of recovery? rehabilitation therapy at the Institutes for the achievement of human potential, Philadelphia. il Newsweek 63:84-5 My 4 '64
Stroke: the killer than can be curbed. R. M. Deutsch and P. Deutsch. Read Digest 85:70-4 D '64
Strokes: new treatments, new hope. il Changing T 18:37-40 Je '64
When a stroke hits. il Newsweek 65:50 F 1 '65

CEREBRAL palsy. See Paralysis

CEREBROMACULAR degeneration. See Amaurotic family idiocy

CEREBROSPINAL meningitis. See Meningitis

CEREBRUM. See Brain

CERF, Bennett
Have a dream. por Seventeen 22:232+ Ag '63
Trade winds. Sat R 47:10+ Ag 29 '64

about

Long happy life of Bennett Cerf. T. B. Morgan. por Esquire 61:112-13+ Mr '64

CERIMANS
Monsters for your shelf. W. Radcliffe. il Flower Grower 51:23 Ja '64

CERIUM
Nature in rock & mineral. P. M. Tilden. il Natur Hist 72:63-7 F '63
See also
Plants—Cerium content

CERIUM oxides
Nature in rock & mineral. P. M. Tilden. il Natur Hist 72:63-7 F '63

CERN. See European organization for nuclear research

CERNIGLIA, V. J. and Campbell, H. J. jr
We borrowed from the steel industry. Am City 79:89-91 My '64

CEROSIUM. See Ceramic materials

CERRUTI, James
Two Acapulcos. Nat Geog Mag 126:848-78 D '64

CERTIFICATES, Aviators. See Air pilots—Licenses

CERTIFICATES of deposit
How banks have lured more corporate cash. il Bsns W p68+ Jl 18 '64
Mysterious $5.5-million; Manhattan casualty case. Bsns W p76-8 Ag 24 '63
New trend in finance: the negotiable C.D. W. A. Law and M. C. Crum. il Harvard Bsns R 41:115-26 Ja '63

CERTIFICATES of merit. See Rewards, prizes, etc.

CERTIFICATES of stock. See Stocks—Certificates

CERTIFICATION of teachers. See Teachers—Certification

CERTIFIED public accountants. See Accountants

CERULOPLASMIN
Body enzyme harnessed. Sci N L 86:19 Jl 11 '64

CERVENY, Walter J.
Color-pattern generators. Electr World 69:50-2+ Mr '63

CERVICAL cancer. See Cancer

CESAREAN section
Cesarean baby dangers; drugs and anesthetics. F. Marley. Sci N L 84:22 Jl 13 '63
Cesarean births: how many are safe? I. Taves. il Look 27:70-2 Ag 27 '63
How many caesareans? Time 81:52 Je 7 '63
Monkey babies quiet after cesarean birth. Sci N L 85:168 Mr 14 '64
What you should know about cesareans. W. G. Birch. il Parents Mag 40:38-9+ Ja '65
When a cesarean birth is necessary. il Good H 157:171 N '63
When are cesarean sections needed? A. V. Greeley. Redbook 123:42+ O '64
Whys of caesareans; Patrick Bouvier Kennedy's death. il Newsweek 62:50+ Ag 19 '63

CESIUM
High pressure polymorphism in cesium. H. T. Hall and others. bibliog il Science 146:1297-9 D 4 '64
See also
Plants—Cesium content

Isotopes

Cesium in liriodendron and other woody species: organic bonding sites. G. N. Brown. bibliog il Science 143:368-9 Ja 24 '64
Cesium-134 in Alaskan Eskimos and in fallout. H. E. Palmer and R. W. Perkins. bibliog il Science 142:66-7 O 4 '63
Decontamination of potato tubers containing cesium-137. H. J. Perkins and G. Strachan. bibliog il Science 144:59-60 Ap 3 '64
Variation of cesium in the ocean. T. R. Folsom and others. bibliog il Science 144:538-9 My 1 '64

CESIUM beam devices. See Time measurements

CESIUM in diet
Lichen, caribou and high radiation in Eskimos. W. O. Pruitt. il Audubon Mag 65:284-7 S '63

CESIUM in the body
Cesium-134 in Alaskan Eskimos. H. E. Palmer and others. bibliog il Science 142:64-6 O 4 '63
Cesium-134 in Alaskan Eskimos and in fallout. H. E. Palmer and R. W. Perkins. bibliog il Science 142:66-7 O 4 '63

CESSNA aircraft company
Cessna acts to widen twin-engine sales; foresees industry growth; summary of address. D. L. Wallace. Aviation W 78:76+ Mr 18 '63
Cessna anticipates record sales this year, studies business jet. Aviation W 82:29 Ja 18 '65

CESTODA
Cestode echinococcus multilocularis in foxes in North Dakota. P. D. Leiby and O. W. Olsen. bibliog Science 145:1066 S 4 '64

CETACEA
See also
Dolphins (mammals)

CÉVENNES
Travels in the Cévennes. J. Masters. il Holiday 36:88-93+ N '64

CEYLON
See also
Education—Ceylon
Government ownership—Ceylon
Petroleum industry and trade—Ceylon
Women—Ceylon

Commerce
Lowering the boom. Newsweek 61:46 F 18 '63

Economic conditions
Leftward lurch. il Time 83:22 Ja 17 '64

Politics and government
Leftward lurch. il Time 83:22 Ja 17 '64
Music to vote by: general election ahead. Time 85:26 Ja 29 '65
Quid pro quo. il Time 83:30 Mr 6 '64

Religious institutions and affairs
Ceylon cries foul. America 109:413 O 12 '63
Mockery in Ceylon. America 109:695 N 30 '63
Of flags and schools; discrimination against Christians. America 109:146 Ag 17 '63

CÉZANNE, Paul
Art; exhibition of Cézanne water colors at Knoedler's. H. Kramer. Nation 196:381-2 My 4 '63
Cézanne: the logical mystery; loan exhibition of watercolors. T. Reff. il Art N 62:28-31 Ap '63
London captures a great Cézanne: Les grandes baigneuses. il Art N 63:48+ Ja '65
Purest genius; water colors at Knoedler's. Newsweek 61:96-7 Ap 22 '63
Watery depths; watercolors at Manhattan's M. Knoedler & co. il Time 81:86-7 Ap 19 '63

CHAABANI, Mohammed
Man on the mountain. il por Time 84:35 Jl 10 '64
To the wall. Time 84:45 S 11 '64

CHABAS, Yves
European reaction to the Vatican council. Christian Cent 80:207-8 F 13 '63
France prepares for Billy Graham. Christian Cent 80:614-15 My 8 '63
Heirs of Abbé Couturier. Christian Cent 82:41-3 Ja 13 '65

CHACE, Hugh R. See Speagle, R. E. jt. auth.

CHACE, Marian
Dance alone is not enough. por Dance Mag 38:46-7+ Jl '64
Power of movement with others. por Dance Mag 38:42-5+ Je '64

CHACHALACA shooting
Chachalaca. C. E. Gillham. il Field & S 68:54-5+ S '63

CHACO CANYON NATIONAL MONUMENT
Pueblo Bonito: the place of the braced-up cliff. O. F. Oldendorph. il Nat Parks Mag 37:4-7 S '63

CHAD
Colored rulers. G. C. Turner. Negro Hist Bul 27:91 Ja '64

CHADWICK, Lynn
Castle tomorrow; L. Chadwick remodels Lypiatt Park. P. Russell. il pors Vogue 142:126-33 Ag 1 '63

CHADWICK, W. J.
Many hands saved this deck. Am City 78:76-7 Jl '63

CHAFEE, John
Highly employable. por Time 84:41 N 13 '64

CHAFETZ, M. E.
How nations drink: the puzzle of alcoholism. Nation 199:401-4 N 30 '64

CHAFFINCHES. See Finches

CHAFING dish cookery
Mobile, noble chafing dish; ten menus, ten recipes, from ten good cooks. il Vogue 141:124-6+ F 15 '63

CHAGALL, Marc
Artist at work: Marc Chagall. C. Lake. il pors Atlan 212:85-112 Jl '63
Canopy of color; new ceiling for the Paris Opéra. il Time 84:78-9 N 6 '64
Chagall affair; painting of Paris opera ceiling. il por Newsweek 62:112+ O 14 '63
Chagall at the Paris Opéra. F. Merkling. il pors Opera N 29:8-12 D 26 '64
I brought Chagall to America. K. Kellen. Esquire 62:60+ D '64
Line on the illogical. G. H. Hamilton. il Sat R 47:32-3 Ap 25 '64
Marc Chagall, by F. Meyer. Review
Commentary 38:57-60 Jl '64. H. Kramer
Marc Chagall's big year; stained-glass window in the United Nations Secretariat building and ceiling for the Paris Opéra. il Life 57:70-7 D 4 '64

CHAGAS, Carlos, Jr
Village beyond despair. T. Armbrister. il Sat Eve Post 236:66-9 N 9 '63

CHAGAS' disease. See Trypanosomiasis

CHAIKIN, Frieda
Art of the mentally retarded on exhibition. P. Vandervoort. il Sch Arts 63:10-12 Ja '64

CHAIN hotels. See Hotels, taverns, etc.

CHAIN-O-LAKES boat club. See Boat clubs

CHAIN saws. See Saws

CHAIN stores
Can farmers control food chains? Bsns W p25 D 19 '64
Chain squeeze; power of big food; with editorial comment. D. Smith. il Nation 198:642, 646-8 Je 29 '64
Nearly all did better. il Bsns W p47 Je 8 '63
Should farmers own food chains? with editorial comment. E. H. Fallon. Farm J 88:54-5, 94 D '64
Supermarts on the Seine; Prisunic of France. il Time 81:95 Ap 12 '63
See also
Food fair stores, incorporated
Great Atlantic and Pacific tea company
Great universal stores, limited
Penney, J. C. company
Safeway stores, incorporated
Variety stores
Winn-Dixie stores, incorporated
Woolworth, F. W, and company

Securities
Shopping the big stores. D. Seligman and others. il Fortune 68:232+ D '63

CHAIR seats
How to weave a sash cord seat. il Sunset 133:120+ O '64

CHAIRS
American triangular turned chair? S. D. Ripley. il Antiques 85:104-6 Ja '64
Captain's chair and its family tree. E. Gaines. il Antiques 85:110-11 Ja '64
Chair for all seasons and many years. P. Doherty. il House B 106:88-91 Ag '64
Chairs for men only; modern Morris chairs. J. Peter. il Look 28:60+ Mr 10 '64
Check list for chair buying. il Am Home 66:79 O '63
Do we sit? no, we collapse; new designs for sitting. S. Wright. il N Y Times Mag p26+ Ap 19 '64
Folding chairs aren't what they used to be. J. Polshek. il House B 105:180-1+ D '63
Four-hour string chair. J. Parker. il Pop Mech 119:166-7 F '63
Give dad a gift the whole family will enjoy. J. Holmstrand. il Suc Farm 61:42-3 D '63
Happy wanderer; occasional chairs. il House & Gard 125:166-7 Je '64
How does your seat rate? il Sci Digest 54:43-4 Ag '63
How to put your feet up in style; tilt-back chairs. il House B 106:124-7 F '64
How to select a reclining chair. Bet Hom & Gard 43:38 Ja '65
In praise of the rocker. il Sci Digest 55:84 F '64
Most comfortable chair. il House & Gard 124:92-3 Jl '63
New dental office chairs. Sci N L 86:130 Ag 29 '64
New slant on comfort; reclining chairs. il House & Gard 123:26-7 F '63
Portuguese painted chairs. R. C. Smith. il Antiques 83:680-3 Je '63
Pull up a chair. il Seventeen 22:183+ My '63
Rockers for '63; with shopping guide. C. Squire. il Pop Gard 14:54 My '63
Rocking chairs for young & old. il Changing T 17:46 O '63
Thumbnail guide to furniture fashions. il Seventeen 23:178-9 Je '64
Under twenty chairs that fit anywhere. il Am Home 67:52-3 Ap '64
Up-to-date antiques. il Life 54:93-4+ Mr 22 '63

Repairing
Uplift for tired chairs. E. R. Haan. il Pop Mech 121:171-2 F '64

CHAISE longues
Inviting lounge. il House & Gard 126:190-1 D '64
Return of a good thing; the semi-chaise. il House B 105:54+ O '63

CHAKIRIS, George
In search of George Chakiris; ed. by E. Miller. pors Seventeen 23:136-7+ Mr '64

CHAKOVSKII, Aleksandr Borisovich
Art for Marx' sake. G. Feifer. il por N Y Times Mag p 12-13+ D 20 '64

CHAKRAVARTI, P. C.
Indian non-alignment and United States policy. Cur Hist 44:129-34+ Mr '63

CHALAROPSIS. See Fungi

CHALCOCITE
Distribution of atoms in high chalcocite, Cu_2S. M. J. Buerger and B. J. Wuensch. bibliog il Science 141:276-7 Jl 19 '63

CHALET, Pierre
Natch; poem. Am For 70:47 My '64
Pine is a pine is a pine; poem. Am For 70:50 Jl '64

CHALLEEN, William W. sr
Dusk-to-dawn lighting. Am City 79:134 S '64

CHALLMAN, Jean C.
Adults si, children no. por Library J 89:807-9 F 15 '64
Nickel-a-day addiction. por Library J 89: 4866-7 D 15 '64

CHALONER, Gwen
Court of King Arithemtic; drama. Plays 23: 35-40 Mr '64
Magic wishing ring; drama. Plays 23:49-54, 60 O '63
Thankful elf; drama. Plays 23:73-7 N '63

CHAMAECYPARIS. See Faith trees

CHAMBER music
Chamber music festival at Library of Congress. il Américas 16:39 O '64
Chamber music in New York. il Mus Am 83:191+ Ja; 32-4 F; 37-40 Mr; 38-43 Ap; 37-40 My; 30-1 Je '63
Reviews: chamber music; concerts in New York. il Mus Am 83:41 N; 264-6 D '63; 84: 54 Ja; 39-42 F; 44-6 Mr; 57-9 Ap; 47-9 My; 46-8 Jl; 50-2 O; 39-40 N; 258 D '64
See also
Phonograph records—Chamber music

CHAMBER of commerce of the United States
National chamber fears federal research role. Sci N L 87:52 Ja 23 '65

CHAMBER of commerce of the United States. Junior. See United States junior chamber of commerce

CHAMBER of deputies. See Italy—Parliament—Chamber of deputies

CHAMBERLAIN, Georgia S.
Painter of patriotic pictures. Hobbies 69:44-5 S '64

CHAMBERLAIN, John
Conservatism of reflection. Nat R 16:198-9 Mr 10 '64
Conservative Miss McCarthy. Nat R 15:353-5 O 22 '63
Only yesterday. Nat R 16:691-3 Ag 11 '64
Political powerhouse in action. Read Digest 85:189-90 N '64
Verdict of history. Nat R 16:1112-13 D 15 '64 '63
Which way with LBJ? Nat R 15:525-7 D 17
Wonderful world of Hubert. Nat R 16:767-9 S 8 '64
Won't you come into my parlor? Nat R 14: 367-8 My 7 '63

CHAMBERLAIN, Joseph W.
Aeronomy. Science 142:414-15 O 18 '63
Airglow and the physics of upper atmospheres. bibliog Science 142:921-4 N 15 '63

CHAMBERLAIN, Neil W.
Lifetime of education. por NEA J 53:11 Ja '64
Retooling the mind. Atlan 214:48-50 S '64
What's ahead for labor? Atlan 214:34-7 Jl '64

CHAMBERLAIN, Neville
Appeasers, by M. Gilbert and R. Gott. Review
Nat R 15:403-4 N 5 '63. A. Lejeune

CHAMBERLAIN, Richard
Doctor Kildare is a doll. M. Durslag. pors Sat Eve Post 236:14-15 Mr 30 '63

CHAMBERLAIN, Roy W. and others
Venezuelan equine encephalitis virus from south Florida. bibliog Science 145:272-4 Jl 17 '64

CHAMBERLAIN, Samuel
Samuel Chamberlain: artist & photographer. F. Johnson. il por Am Artist 29:28-33+ F '65

CHAMBERLAIN, Wilt
Another big bluff by big Wilt. F. Deford. il por Sports Illus 22:18-19+ Ja 25 '65
Big man, big business. L. Robinson. il pors Ebony 19:57-8+ Ag '64
Meet the new Wilt Chamberlain. T. C. Brody. il Sports Illus 20:24-5 Mr 2 '64

CHAMBERLIN, Anne
Commercialization of J.F.K. Sat Eve Post 237:20-1 N 21 '64
Dam the Nile, full speed astern. Sat Eve Post 237:73-7 Je 6 '64
Fabulous Coco Chanel. Ladies Home J 80: 165-70 O '63
Filet of hippo, anyone? Sat Eve Post 238: 78+ Ja 30 '65
How to spend your excess money in New York. Sat Eve Post 237:88+ My 23 '64
Last gasp of the tin goose. Sat Eve Post 236:26-7 Ag 10 '63; Same abr. Read Digest 83:151-5 D '63
Love in Washington. Esquire 61:69+ Ja '64
Russia's total airline. Sat Eve Post 237:63-4 N 28 '64
She dresses the lady pioneers of the New frontier. Ladies Home J 80:134+ N '63
To get lost, hurry up. Sat Eve Post 237:34+ Mr 14 '64
Two cheers for the National geographic. Esquire 60:206-9+ D '63
What are they doing with Gen. Sheridan's horse? Sat Eve Post 237:70-3 My 9 '64
When the Russians try to invade suburbia. Sat Eve Post 236:28-9 Ag 24 '63

CHAMBERLIN, Ralph
Stop that stereotype! Writer 76:26-7 N '63

CHAMBERLIN, William Henry
Chief of postwar Germany. Sat R 47:64 Ap 11 '64
Decline and fall revisited. Sat R 47:18-19 Ag 8 '64
Message from the Mayor. Sat R 46:26-7 My 18 '63

CHAMBERS, George
Samuel; poem. Christian Cent 81:631 My 13 '64

CHAMBERS, Hansi. See Lewis, V. E. jt. auth.

CHAMBERS, Jack A.
Creative scientists of today. bibliog Science 145:1203-5; 147:67 S 11 '64, Ja 1 '65

CHAMBERS, M. M.
Disciplines' new attitude toward higher education. Sch & Soc 91:190-1 Ap 20 '63
Progress in state tax support of higher education. Sch & Soc 91:144-6 Mr 23 '63

CHAMBERS, Paul
Who's who in foreign business. por Fortune 67:88 My '63

CHAMBERS, Stanley Paul
British giant tries for more size. por Bsns W p66-8+ Je 22 '63
Imperial tiger. por Time 81:106 My 3 '63

CHAMBERS, Whittaker
Cold Friday; excerpts. pors Sat Eve Post 237:26-8+ S 5 '64

About

Assault on Whittaker Chambers. W. F. Buckley, jr. il por Nat R 16:1098-100 D 15 '64; Discussion. 17:4+ Ja 12 '65
Blind man's bluff. D. Cort. Nation 199:306-7 N 2 '64
Comfort of Cold Friday. C. Brogan. il Nat R 16:1153-4 D 29 '64
Final search for meaning. G. Hicks. Sat R 48:25-6 Ja 2 '65
Hegel's road to Walden; posthumous book. il por Time 84:108 N 6 '64
Madness, vision, stupidity. I. Howe. New Repub 151:22-4 N 28 '64; Discussion. 152:38 Ja 23 '65; Nat R 16:1100-2; 17:4+ D 15 '64, Ja 12 '65
Total recoil. il por Newsweek 64:108+ N 2 '64

CHAMBERS, Yolande H.
Three-state store chain's vice-president. il pors Ebony 19:36-40+ F '64

CHAMBERS of commerce
Easing up on criticism; new C. of C. president; summary of news conference. W. F. Carey. U S News 56:16 Ap 27 '64
See also
Chamber of commerce of the United States
International chamber of commerce
United States junior chamber of commerce

CHAMBERSBURGH engineering company
Drop forge goes automatic; Chambersburg impacter. il Bsns W p83-4+ O 17 '64

CHAMBLESS, Bill
Instamatic goes to school. Pop Phot 55:58-9+ O '64

CHAMELEONS
Color change: chameleon camouflage. H. G. Dowling. il Natur Hist 73:40-3 F '64
Enigmatic lizard; pygmy chameleon. O. Von Frisch. il Natur Hist 72:46-51 O '63

CHAMLEE, Mario
Mario Chamlee. A. Favia-Artsay. il pors Hobbies 69:30-1+ Jl '64

CHAMPAGNE
Battle of the Marne. il Newsweek 61:78 F 18 '63
Bubbling with ideas; French champagne industry. il Bsns W p30-2 N 16 '63
Champagne complexes. J. Wilson. il House & Gard 123:130+ F '63
No one takes champagne lightly. Vogue 144: 28-9 N 1 '64

CHAMPION, Gower
Dance magazine's 1963 awards. por Dance Mag 38:33+ Mr '64

CHAMPION paper and fibre company
Profit teams of management. J. B. Weiner. il Duns R 84:36-7+ S '64

CHAMPION spark plug company
Franklin club homecoming trek. il Motor T 16:92-3 D '64

CHAMPLAIN, LAKE
Come to Champlain. il Motor B 113:22-9 Ap '64

CHAMPLAIN, LAKE, Battle of, 1814
Victory on Lake Champlain. C. S. Forester. il Am Heritage 15:4-11+ D '63

CHAMPLIN, C. D.
How beastly are the British? Life 57:15 N 6 '64

CHAMPNEY, Benjamin
Benjamin Champney and the American Barbizon. 1850-1857. W. G. Hennessy and F. A. Sharf. il por Antiques 84:566-9 N '63

CHAMPOEG MEMORIAL STATE PARK. See Oregon—Parks and reserves

CHAMPOLLION, Jean François
Cleopatra & Ptolemy gave Champollion his missing clue. il UNESCO Courier 17:10-11 Mr '64

CHAMPS-Elysées. See Paris—Streets

CHANCAY pottery. See Pottery, Peruvian

CHANCE, Britton, 1913-, and Estabrook, R. W.
Mitochondrial structure and function, a compostium. Science 146:957-8+ N 13 '64

—and Parsons, D. F.
Cytochrome function in relation to inner membrane structure of mitochondria. bibliog Science 142:1176-80 N 29 '63

—and others
Cytochrome content of mitochondria stripped of inner membrane structure. bibliog Science 143:136-9 Ja 10 '64
Rapid mixing and sampling techniques. Science 146:1697-9 D 25 '64

CHANCE, Britton, Jr
Development of the Twelve. il Motor B 114: 36-8+ Ag '64

CHANCE, Dean
Player of the week; pitcher of the Angels. por Sports Illus 20:95 Je 15 '64
Who needs to see? il Time 84:58-9 S 25 '64

CHANCE
Best of luck. W. Golding. il Holiday 35:12+ My '64
See also
Probabilities

Anecdotes, facetiae, satire, etc.

Claude Fetridge's infuriating law. H. A. Smith. il Read Digest 82:229-30+ Je '63

CHANCEL, Annie. See Sheila

CHANCELLOR, John M.
More fruitful use of knowledge. por ALA Bul 57:326-9 Ap '63

CHANCELLOR-MADDISON, Jennifer, and Noll, C. R. Jr
Molecular heterogeneity of enzymes: malate dehydrogenase of euglena. bibliog Science 142:60-1 O 4 '63

CHANDELIERS
Antiques; English silver chandelier in dining room of the Governor's palace, Williamsburg. A. Winchester. il Antiques 85:664-5 Je '64
Light up your foyer with style. il House & Gard 125:66-7 Mr '64

CHANDLER, Albert Benjamin
Happy ending in Kentucky. J. A. Maxwell. Reporter 28:22-4 Je 20 '63
Happy's last hurrah. H. H. Martin. pors Sat Eve Post 236:32+ Ag 10 '63
Hello, Happy Chandler! J. Sellers. Nat R 14:399 My 21 '63
Old Happy. pors Time 81:18 Mr 29 '63
Sad day for Happy. il Time 81:22-3 Je 7 '63

CHANDLER, Barbara, and others
Circularity of the replicating form of a single-stranded DNA virus. bibliog Science 143: 46-9 Ja 3 '64

CHANDLER, Dorothy Buffum
Brightness in the air. il pors Time 84:46-58 D 18 '64
Los Angeles hoists flag of culture. il pors Bsns W p32-3 N 21 '64

CHANDLER, Happy. See Chandler, A. B.

CHANDLER, Margaret Irene
Mighty is the sea; excerpt. Sr Schol 82:9 My 15 '63

CHANDLER, Raymond
Casual notes on the mystery novel. Writer 76:13-16+ Jl '63
Raymond Chandler, private eye. R. Schickel. Commentary 35:158-61 F '63

CHANDLER family
Happy Chandlers. il Newsweek 63:93 Je 8 '64

CHANDOS of Aldershot, Oliver Lyttelton, 1st viscount
To England, with love and candor. J. H. Plumb. por Sat R 46:44 N 9 '63; Reply. W. D. Allister. 46:32 D 21 '63

CHANEL, Gabrielle
Chanel look. H. Obolensky. il Redbook 123: 50-3 Je '64
Fabulous Coco Chanel. A. Chamberlin. il pors Ladies Home J 80:165-70 O '63
Portrait of Chanel no. 1. J. Barry. il pors N Y Times Mag p30-1+ Ag 23 '64; Same abr. Read Digest 85:261-3+ N '64

CHANG, Eileen
Return to the frontier. Reporter 28:38-41 Mr 28 '63

CHANG, Hsien-wu. See King, G. W. jt. auth.

CHANG, R. Shihman, and Vetrovs, Helen
Loss of radioactivity from labeled DNA of primary human amnion cells. bibliog Science 139:1211 Mr 22 '63

CHANG, Sea Bong, and others
Aflatoxin B_2: chemical identity and biological activity. bibliog Science 142:1191-2 N 29 '63

CHANG, Shen Chin, and others
Insect chemosterilants with low toxicity for mammals. bibliog Science 144:57-8 Ap 3 '64

CHANG, Te-wen, and Weinstein, Louis
Inhibition of synthesis of the cell wall of staphylococcus aureus by cephalothin. bibliog Science 143:807-8 F 21 '64

CHANG, Thomas M. S.
Semipermeable microcapsules. Science 146: 524-5 O 23 '64

CHANGE
Confederacy of dunces. R. L. Tobin. Sat R 46:47-8 O 12 '63
Diagnosing the American dream. M. W. Fishwick. il Sat R 46:8-11 D 21 '63
Everything nailed down is coming loose; condensation of address. M. W. Fishwick. Sat R 46:11-14 Je 29 '63
Fear or courage? the question that comes before politics. M. Mannes. Vogue 144:106-7 Ag 15 '64
Permanence and change. R. O. Johann. America 109:359 S 28 '63
Taste for change; address, September 23, 1963. J. S. Dickey. Vital Speeches 30:24-5 O 15 '63
World: a sense of history. L. J. Halle. il New Repub 151:92-5+ N 7 '64
See also
Economic change
Social change

CHANGE of heart: story. See Liben, M.

CHANGE of life in women. See Menopause

CHANGELING; drama. See Middleton, T. and Rowley, W.

CHANNEL. See English Channel

CHANNEL ISLANDS, Calif. See Santa Barbara Islands, Calif.

CHANNEL tunnel. See English Channel tunnel (proposed)

CHANNELS
Building grass waterways now. Suc Farm 62:50 Ag '64

CHANNING, Carol
Pace-setters; interview. por Mlle 59:283 Ag '64

about

Carol's dream. il Esquire 63:58-9 Ja '65
Dolly. New Yorker 40:23-4 F 29 '64
Good-bye, Lorelei. Hello, Dolly! G. Millstein. pors Sat Eve Post 237:78-9 F 22 '64
Love letters of a tough critic. W. Kerr. por Life 56:114 Je 19 '64
New Carol Channing. H. Ehrlich. il pors Look 28:58-62 My 19 '64

CHANOCK, R. M. and others
Mycoplasma pneumoniae; proposed nomenclature for atypical pneumonia organism (Eaton agent) bibliog Science 140:662 My 10 '63
—See Tyrrell, D. A. J. jt. auth.

CHANTILLY race track. See Race tracks

CHANTS (Gregorian, plain, etc)
See also
Phonograph records—Chants (Gregorian, plain, etc)

CHANUKAH. See Hanukkah (Feast of lights)

CHAO, E. C. T.
Spalled, aerodynamically modified moldavite from Slavice, Moravia, Czechoslovakia. bibliog Science 146:790-1 N 6 '64

CHAOS, disorder and the late show; story. See Miller, W.

CHAPARAS, Sotiros D. See Bear, H. jt. auth.

CHAPEL, I. C.
Monitor your code. Pop Electr 18:56-7+ Ap '63
RF power capsule. Pop Electr 18:58-9+ F '63

CHAPEL attendance. See Church attendance

CHAPEL services. See Church services

CHAPELLE, Dickey
Fighting priest of South Vietnam. il Read Digest 83:194-200 Jl '63

CHAPELS
Air academy chapel: a critical appraisal. A. Temko; discussion. il Arch Forum 118:19 F '63

CHAPELS—*Continued*
Art and architecture: a new light on monastic design; buildings for Passionist fathers, North Palm Beach, Fla. P. Damaz. il Craft Horiz 23:24-5+ Ja '63
Geometry in New Mexico; private chapel. il Arch Forum 121:154-5 Ag '64
Rock in the forest: Chapel of Saint Rouin, France. il Arch Forum 119:74-5 D '63
Top drawer: U.S. air force academy's interdenominational chapel. Newsweek 62:62 S 30 '63

CHAPERONS
But where are the chaperons? M. W. Lear. il N Y Times Mag p22+ F 23 '64

CHAPIN, Alice Z.
I took a vacation at home. Suc Farm 62:75+ My '64

CHAPIN, Barbara
Shh, the need for do-nothing quietude. Recreation 57:437-8 N '64

CHAPIN, Emerson
Japanese Prince meets girl, by go-between. N Y Times Mag p42+ Mr 22 '64
Japan's birth rate, the trend turns. N Y Times Mag p44+ O 25 '64

CHAPIN, Katherine Garrison
From Attica; poem. New Repub 148:23 Mr 9 '63
Prose he did not write. New Repub 152: 16-17 Ja 2 '65

CHAPIN, Louis
Britten in the Berkshires. Mus Am 83:30 S '63
Walter Piston at seventy. Mus Am 83:34 D '63

CHAPIN, Schuyler G.
Program director. New Yorker 40:40-3 Mr 7 '64

CHAPIN, Thomas T.
When Negro child meets white. Christian Cent 80:1333-4 O 30 '63

CHAPIN, Victor
Farewell to April; story. Seventeen 22:136-7 Ap '63

CHAPLAINS
Father Schönig: circus priest extraordinary. G. Kent. il Read Digest 84:74-8 Je '64

CHAPLAINS, Congressional. See United States —Congress—Chaplains

CHAPLAINS, Hospital
See also
Association of mental hospital chaplains

CHAPLAINS, Military
A.C.L.U. denies attack on chaplaincy. Christian Cent 81:630 My 13 '64
In dubious battle; future of the chaplaincy. Newsweek 63:82 Je 1 '64
Negro chaplains in the Civil war. J. W. Blassingame. bibliog Negro Hist Bul 27:24+ O '63
Peale pulls out all the stops. Christian Cent 81:692 My 27 '64
Study of chaplaincy is proposed. Christian Cent 80:292 Mr 6 '63; Reply. J. D. Forest. 80:586 My 1 '63
View from the Brick chapel. W. V. Kennedy. America 109:184 Ag 24 '63
See also
General commission on chaplains and armed forces personnel

CHAPLAINS, Prison
Swinging prison priest; chaplain for the five District of Columbia prisons in Washington area. D. R. Maxey. il Look 28:24-9 D 29 '64

CHAPLIN, Charles
Books. B. Gill. New Yorker 40:236-44 D 12 '64
Charles the great. il pors Newsweek 64:78-9 Jl 27 '64
Charlie Chaplin at ease. F. Wyndham. il por Vogue 144:112-13 N 15 '64
Charlie's Chaplin. J. Houseman. Nation 199: 222-5 O 12 '64
Dapper wayfarer. R. Hatch. Harper 229:129-32 O '64
Little tramp as told to himself. il pors Time 84:132 O 2 '64
Man named Chaffin. S. Kauffmann. New Repub 151:19-21 O 3 '64
Only the little tramp matters. F. Russell. Nat R 16:1066+ D 1 '64; Correction. 17:77 Ja 26 '65
Real life of the tramp. H. Junker. Commonweal 81:104-5 O 16 '64
Tantalizing look behind Chaplin's mask; his autobiography. H. Lemay. Life 57:24+ O 2 '64
Tramp. por Newsweek 64:112 O 5 '64
Travels with Charlie and friends. A. Knight. por Sat R 47:45 O 10 '64

CHAPLIN, Charles, Jr
Clown-artist's chronicle. M. Boyd. Christian Cent 81:1310+ O 21 '64

CHAPLIN, Geraldine
Charles Chaplin's daughter. pors Vogue 143: 146-7 F 1 '64
New Chaplin in limelight. il pors Life 56:75-7 Ja 31 '64

CHAPMAN, Daniel H.
You can talk to quail. Field & S 69:8-9+ Ja '65

CHAPMAN, Eddie
Big tickle puts the scream too high; ed. by K. Gouldthorpe. Life 55:21-3 Ag 23 '63

CHAPMAN, Frank
Florence May festival. Mus Am 83:7-8 Ag '63

CHAPMAN, Frank M. memorial hall of North American birds. See American museum of natural history, New York

CHAPMAN, Frederick
Cover. il Am Artist 29:4+ F '65

CHAPMAN, Gilbert W.
When executives retire. Duns R 82:63-4+ O '63

CHAPMAN, Herman Haupt
Chapman of Yale. S. T. Dana. pors Am For 69:10+ S '63
Defender of the forestry profession: editorial. A. G. Hall. Am For 69:13 S '63

CHAPMAN, Jane
House designed to please seventy-five women. House B 105:168-78 My '63

CHAPMAN, John
Johnny Appleseed. E. F. Steffek. il Horticulture 42:21 S '64

CHAPMAN, John L.
Expanding spectrum. Harper 229:70-4+ Jl '64

CHAPMAN, Laura Hill
New stereotype. Sch Arts 62:10-11 Mr '63

CHAPMAN, Seville
Do we want fallout shelters? Bul Atomic Sci 19:24-6 F '63

CHAPMAN, William
Two doubles a world apart. Sports Illus 19: 100-2+ N 25 '63

CHAPMAN, William P.
Automatic controls can cut lighting costs. Arch Rec 133:192-3 My '63

CHAPPAQUA, N.Y.
Four pavilions planned in relation to large play areas. il Arch Rec 136:232-3 S '64

CHAPPELL, Fred
Property of hope; story. Sat Eve Post 237: 62-4 My 9 '64
Trout fishing: ritual, not rapture. Holiday 36: 122+ Jl '64

CHAPPELL, William, Jr
Seventeen states vote to destroy democracy as we know it. T. B. Morgan. il Look 27: 76+ D 3 '63

CHAPRALIS, Jim C.
Muskie on his back. Field & S 69:70-1+ S '64

CHAPSAL, Madeleine
Grieving, going on. Reporter 31:54 O 8 '64
Prison of Jean Giono. Reporter 29:30-1 Jl 4 '63

CHAPUT, Donald
Uncle Tom and predestination. Negro Hist Bul 27:143 Mr '64

CHAPUT, Marcel
Reporter at large. E. Wilson. New Yorker 40:177-8+ N 28 '64

CHAR, René
Chanson des etages; Post-scriptum à lettera amorosa; Sept parcelles de Luberon; Les parages d'Alsace; poems, with English tr. by W. Fowlie. Poetry 104:278-95 Ag '64

CHAR
Arctic mystery fish. A. J. McClane. il Field & S 67:72-7+ Mr '63

CHAR fishing
Fiery fish. G. Laycock. il Outdoor Life 131: 64-7+ Je '63
River of records. B. White. il Field & S 68: 122-4+ Je '63

CHARACTER
Conscience and character; with study-discussion program, by R. Strang. G. Langdon and I. W. Stout. bibliog il PTA Mag 58:4-6, 35 F '64
Good character is made, not born. M. E. Goodman. il Parents Mag 39:54-5+ O '64
He could take it; reprint. A. B. Reincke. Read Digest 82:140-2 F '63
Improvement of the human character; address, November 6, 1964. R. H. Amberg. Vital Speeches 31:121-3 D 1 '64
Squares America needs; reprint. C. H. Brower. il U S News 56:70-2 Ap 6 '64
Time for moral courage. B. Graham. Read Digest 85:49-52 Jl '64
Where does character come from? K. S. Bernhardt. il N Y Times Mag p50 Ag 25 '63
See also
Conduct of life
Ethics
Individuality
Responsibility

CHARACTER analysis
Let me explain... C. O. Skinner. il Read Digest 83:79-81 Ag '63
Traits of eminent American psychologists. L. G. Wispé. bibliog il Science 141:1256-61 S 27 '63

CHARACTER education. See Moral education

CHARACTER reading. See Graphology; Palmistry

CHARACTER sketches
Contrary genius of Fidgets' Retreat. H. A. Smith. il Read Digest 84:27-8+ Ja '64
Day the cows didn't come home. J. B. Mosley. il Read Digest 84:112-16 Ja '64
Great-granddad's last battle. R. Froman. il Read Digest 83:25-6+ D '63
Happiest man. D. Kaye. Read Digest 82:94-8 Mr '63
Little Miss Rachel and D. O. Volenty. H. Carter. Read Digest 83:100-2 S '63
Most unforgettable character I've met. See issues of Reader's digest
My most unforgettable character. See issues of Reader's digest
Three lives of David Starr Jordan. F. J. Taylor. Read Digest 82:113-17 My '63

CHARACTERIZATION
Ashtrays in a vacuum. L. Conger. Writer 76:15-17 My '63
Dialogue with distinction. P. S. Curry. Writer 77:11-13+ Jl '64
Fathers and sons in American fiction. E. Rovit. Yale R 53:248-57 D '63
Getting to know your characters. V. Henry. Writer 77:23-5 Ag '64
Goals. F. A. Rockwell. Writer 77:19-21 S '64
Grain in the silo. E. K. Woolvin. Writer 76: 20-1+ N '63
How to live with a hero. J. D. MacDonald. Writer 77:14-16+ S '64
Is fiction here to stay? address, June 4, 1963. M. Cousins. Writer 77:9-15 Ja '64
Keep moving forward. D. C. DeJong. Writer 76:20-1 Je '63
No mirrors, please! D. Gardiner. Writer 77: 16-19 Ja '64
Ship of fools & the critics. T. Solotaroff; discussion. Commentary 35:247-50 Mr '63
Stop that stereotype! R. Chamberlin. Writer 76:26-7 N '63
Those magic one-liners. E. Jensen. Writer 78:9-11 Ja '65
Trouble with trouble. R. A. Knowlton. Writer 76:15-16+ Je '63
Where do characters come from? C. Edwards. Writer 77:10-12+ Mr '64

CHARACTERS in literature
Children's hero; the genteel conspiracy. J. Epstein. il Wilson Lib Bul 38:154-60 O '63; Discussion. 38:162-4, 253+ O-N '63
Control of character. R. Savage. Writer 76: 7-9 Ag '63
Fat boy of England. D. W. Brogan. il Harper 226:89-1 Ap '63
Father of the Wizard of Oz. D. P. Mannix. il Am Heritage 16:36-47+ D '64
Forebears of Falstaff; Shakespeare's Merry wives of Windsor. G. McElroy. Opera N 29: 24-5 Ja 23 '65
History, tragedy, and the imagination in Absalom, Absalom! C. Brooks. Yale R 52: 340-51 Mr '63
James Bond: culture hero. G. Grella. New Repub 150:17-18+ My 30 '64; Reply. D. Kaufman. 150:29 Je 20 '64
Lives and times of Nancy Drew; with excerpts from some mystery stories. il Mile 59:28-39 Jl '64
Salinger; how to love without love. A. Chester. Commentary 35:467-74 Je '63; Reply. M. E. Parrish. 36:350 N '63
Sherlock Holmes, sportsman. W. S. Baring-Gould. il Sports Illus 18:34-46 My 27 '63
Tarzan of the paperbacks. P. Mandel. il Life 55:11-12 N 29 '63
Tarzan revisited. G. Vidal. il Esquire 60:192-3+ D '63
Trilby. T. H. Marsh. il Hobbies 68:82-3 Ja '64
Two heroes: Dietrich of Berne and Hakon of Rogen's saga. R. H. Viguers. Horn Bk 39: 272 Je '63
Vice of kings. G. McElroy. il Opera N 28: 22-5 Ap 4 '64
Where did she come from? why did she go? Mary Poppins. P. L. Travers. il Sat Eve Post 237:76+ N 7 '64
See also
Characterization
Shakespeare, W.—Characters
Uncle Tom

CHARACTERS in opera
Abbé and the image; Manon's author led the life of Des Grieux. G. McElroy. Opera N 28:12-13 D 21 '63
Best of braggarts; first Falstaff. V. Sheean. il Opera N 28:27-9 Mr 21 '64
Boris boom. il Time 81:46 Ap 5 '63
Death of a seamstress; Mimi of Murger's Scènes de la vie de Bohème. A. W. Zorgniotti. Opera N 28:24-5 Mr 14 '64
Elsa of Brabant. E. Gerken. Opera N 28:12 F 1 '64
Meet Papageno. A. M. Lingg. Opera N 28: 24-5 Ja 25 '64
Sequels. E. Gerken. il Opera N 29:24-5 D 19 '64
Tender irony; Mozart's Figaro. E. Downes. il Opera N 29:24-5 Ja 2 '65
Vice of kings. G. McElroy. il Opera N 28: 22-5 Ap 4 '64

CHARAP, Stanley H. and Elfant, R. F.
Magnetism. Science 143:604+ F 7 '64

CHARBONNEAU, Joseph, abp
Reporter at large. E. Wilson. New Yorker 40:160+ N 28 '64

CHARCOAL
Attention bird owners: a penny saved...! bird charcoal. il Consumer Bul 46:22 Jl '63
Backyard picnickers burn 350,000 tons of charcoal. Sci N L 84:72 Ag 3 '63
Look to the heartland; charcoal production in Argentina. M. Belloni. il Américas 16: 36-9 Ja '64

CHARCOAL cookery. See Cookery

CHARCOAL drawing
Kalman Aron, draughtsman. J. Lovoos. il Am Artist 28:30-5+ Mr '64

CHARD
Swiss chard. J. Hersey. Flower Grower 50: 33+ Mr '63

CHARDIN, Pierre Teilhard de. See Teilhard de Chardin, P.

CHARDON, Roland E.
Guatemala. bibliog Focus 13:1-6 My '63

CHARGE accounts (retail trade)
Charge accounts & instalment plans. il Changing T 17:35-8 Mr '63
Drawing a bead on World's fair market; Macy's credit card for out-of-towners. il Bsns W p43-4 F 29 '64
How to establish a simple charge system; booksellers methods. Pub W 185:128-9 Je 8 '64

CHARGERS (football club) See Football clubs

CHARGERS, Battery. See Storage battery chargers

CHARGING systems(libraries) See Libraries—Charging systems

CHARISMATA. See Gifts, Spiritual

CHARITABLE uses, trusts, foundations
Phoenix trust in England presents first grants. Pub W 183:45 Mr 4 '63

CHARITIES
Bank of pity. R. Condon. Holiday 33:58+ Mr '63
Charity: big business, growing bigger. il Sr Schol 85:8+ D 9 '64
Cup of water. America 111:653 N 21 '64
See also
Catholic worker movement
Fund raising
Gifts
Giving
United fund
also subhead Charities under names of cities, e.g. Detroit—Charities

CHARITY
Mutual understanding and friendship; address, December 3, 1964. Paul VI. Vital Speeches 31:132 D 15 '64
True act of charity. M. B. McCoy. Good H 157:104+ Jl '63
Word. V. P. McCorry. America 109:370-1; 111: 144 S 28 '63, Ag 8 '64

CHARITY (plant) See Jacobs ladder

CHARLATANS. See Impostors and imposture

CHARLES I, king of Great Britain
Coffin for King Charles, by C. V. Wedgwood. Review
Time il 84:104 S 4 '64
Execution of Charles I. C. V. Wedgwood. il Horizon 6:41 Sum '64
Hunt for the regicides. A. Winston. il pors Am Heritage 16:26-9+ D '64
King's trial; excerpt from Coffin for King Charles. C. V. Wedgwood. il por Horizon 6:32-40 Sum '64

CHARLES, prince of Asturias
Dark brilliance. K. McDonald. il Opera N 28:24-5 Mr 7 '64

CHARLES, prince of Wales
Prince Charles: a schoolmate's view of a lonely boy. P. Pelham-Jones. il por Redbook 122:72-3+ Ap '64
Princely pauper. por Time 84:40 N 27 '64
Princely price: sale of essays. Newsweek 64-64 N 30 '64

CHARLES, prince of Wales—*Continued*
Teen-age princes and princesses. G. Fisher and H. Fisher. il por Seventeen 23:122-3+ Je '64
When Prince Charles sipped some brandy. por U S News 55:16 Jl 1 '63

CHARLES, Ed
Everything's green & gold in Kansas City. W. Bingham. il Sports Illus 18:24-6+ My 20 '63

CHARLES, R. F.
Successor to Gaitskell. America 108:248 F 23 '63

CHARLES, Ray, 1932-
Blues becomes big business. L. Robinson. il pors Ebony 18:34-6+ Ap '63
That's all right. por Time 81:43 My 10 '63
What's so great about Ray Charles? A. G. Aronowitz. il pors Sat Eve Post 236:74-6 Ag 24 '63

CHARLES, Robert
Does your house have enough hot water? Parents Mag 39:66-7+ Ja '64
Is a swimming pool a wise investment? Parents Mag 39:67-70+ Mr '64
Portfolio of seven award winning homes. Parents Mag 38:77+ Mr '63
Wise ways with windows. Parents Mag 39:81-4+ F '64

CHARLES, Robert, 1937?-
Golf gets its first southpaw hero. A. Wright. il por Sports Illus 18:28+ My 27 '63
One for the left. il por Time 82:50 Jl 19 '63
Sporting scene. H. W. Wind. il New Yorker 39:52+ Ag 3 '63
Winners at work. il por Newsweek 62:55-6 Jl 22 '63

CHARLES F. Orvis company. See Orvis, Charles F. company

CHARLES Pfizer and company. See Pfizer, Charles, and company

CHARLES-ROUX, Edmonde
Living legends. Vogue 145:130-3+ Ja 1 '65
Vogue's eye view of Madame Grès. Vogue 144:97-9 S 15 '64

CHARLES Stewart Mott foundation
Mr Flint. Time 81:19 Je 28 '63

CHARLESTON, Robert Jesse
Beilby glasses. Antiques 83:320-3 Mr '63
Glass souvenirs of the Grand tour. Antiques 83:665-9 Je '63
John Voyez, fact and fiction (cont) Antiques 84:429-33 O '63

CHARLESTON, S.C.

Description

Harbors of history: the Southeast heritage cruise. il Motor B 114:21-9 S '64
Put on your walking shoes when you visit old Charleston. R. Dunlop. il Todays Health 41:44-7+ Ap '63

CHARLESTON PEAK. See Spring Mountains

CHARLESWORTH, James C.
(ed) Africa in motion. bibliog f Ann Am Acad 354:1-152 Jl '64
(ed) New Europe: implications for the United States. bibliog f Ann Am Acad 348:1-163 Jl '63

CHARLEY, Philip, and Saltman, Paul
Chelation of calcium by lactose: its role in transport mechanisms. bibliog Science 139:1205-6 Mr 22 '63

CHARLOTTE, consort of Maximilian, emperor of Mexico
Operator and the emperors; with portfolio. L. Thomas. il pors Am Heritage 15:8-23+ Ap '64

CHARLOTTE, grand duchess of Luxembourg
Golden rose. por Time 83:27 Mr 27 '64
Grande Duchesse: great lady; memories of the first family of Luxembourg. P. Mesta. por McCalls 91:30+ S '64

CHARLOTTE, N.C.
Ready-marked pavements. H. Hoose. il Am City 78:117 Ag '63

CHARLSON, Robert J.
Liquid film hygrometer. Science 143:1031-2 Mr 6 '64

CHARM. See Personality

CHARMATZ, Bill
Getting close to the sun and the stars. il Sports Illus 18:26-34 Mr 4 '63

CHARMED life; story. See Cousins, M.

CHARMS
Dammit all; Dammit dolls. il Newsweek 63:68 F 3 '64

CHAROLAIS cattle. See Cattle—Breeds

CHARRED cross of Coventry. See Cross and crosses

CHARTER of the United Nations. See United Nations—Charter

CHARTERING of airplanes. See Airplanes—Chartering

CHARTERING of yachts. See Yachts—Chartering

CHARTERS, Thomas H.
Build the AUX-9. Pop Electr 21:65-7+ O '64

CHARTS
See also
Business charts

CHARTS, Aeronautical. See Aeronautic charts

CHARTS, Astronomical. See Astronomy—Charts, diagrams, etc.

CHARTS, Calculating
Ascor guide number nomograph for electronic flash. Pop Phot 53:93 S '63
Capacitance nomogram. F. D. Gross. il Electr World 72:31 D '64
Cathode-follower nomogram. A. L. Teubner. il Electr World 70:33 S '63
CB range nomogram. G. Karlin. il Electr World 71:29 Je '64
Coil-winding nomogram. A. L. Teubner. il Electr World 69:33 Ap '63
Delta-Y transformation nomogram. A. L. Teubner. il Electr World 71:31 F '64
Flash calculator. F. R. Shoemaker. il U S Camera 26:30+ Ag '63
Floor and ceiling tile calculator. il Pop Sci 185:119 S '64
Handy nail calculator. il Pop Sci 184:135 My '64
Meter range-extension nomogram. A. L. Teubner. il Electr World 70:37-8 Ag '63
Meter reading conversion nomograms. R. Jones. il Electr World 72:24-5 Ag '64
Mid-frequency amplifier-gain nomogram. K. W. James. il Electr World 71:31+ Je '64
Negative-feedback nomogram. A. L. Teubner. il Electr World 70:31 D '63
Output-transformer chart. il Electr World 70:57 D '63
Parallel-resistor chart. L. W. Brindley. il Electr World 70:31 N '63
Phase-shift nomogram. L. W. Brindley. il Electr World 72:31 N '64
Power & resistor charts. R. Jones. il Electr World 72:33 S '64
RC filter chart. R. K. Re. il Electr World 70:25 Jl '63
Resistor power calculator. R. K. Re. il Electr World 69:37 Je '63
Resistor power-rating nomogram. J. Kyle. il Electr World 71:29 Ap '64
Ripple-filter design chart. A. L. Teubner. il Electr World 70:31 O '63
Tape-winding nomogram. F. Blechman. il Electr World 72:38-9 O '64
Tolerance calculator. R. K. Re. il Electr World 69:25 My '63
Voltage-divider nomogram. D. W. Moffat. il Electr World 71:29+ Mr '64
Wood screw holding-power calculator. il Pop Sci 185:154 N '64

CHARTS, Nautical. See Nautical charts

CHARTS, Stock. See Stocks—Price indexes and averages

CHARYK, Joseph V.
World communications; address, November 17, 1964. Vital Speeches 31:167-71 Ja 1 '65

about

Men who will run Comsat. por Fortune 67:51 Ap '63
People of the week. por U S News 54:25 Mr 11 '63
Taking a flyer in outer space. il por Newsweek 63:85-8+ Mr 16 '64

CHARYN, Jerome
Faigele the idiotke; story. Commentary 35:220-31 Mr '63
God bless Captain Freddy and Private Ming! story. Mlle 58:142-3 Ap '64
On Second avenue; story. Commentary 36:26-33 Jl '63

CHASE, Ada R.
Joseph Carpenter jr, silversmith and clockmaker. Antiques 85:695-7 Je '64

CHASE, Edward T.
Faces of the racial revolution. New Repub 152:29-30+ Ja 23 '65
Four days shalt thou labor? N Y Times Mag p28+ S 20 '64
How many people, how many jobs? New Repub 151:32-3+ Ag 22 '64
How to recover from disarmament. New Repub 148:25-6 Je 1 '63
Impact of technology. New Repub 150:17-18 F 15 '64
Job-finding machine; how to crank it up. Harper 229:31-6 Jl; 11 O '64
Learning to be unemployable. Harper 226:33-40 Ap '63
Politics and technology. Yale R 52:321-39 Mr '63
Quotas for Negroes? Commonweal 79:451-4 Ja 17 '64

CHASE, Edward T.—*Continued*
Replacing the myth of the free price-market system. Commonweal 79:288-90 N 29 '63
Small drop, large bucket. New Repub 150: 30+ Je 27 '64
Supersonic jet: is it worth it? Commonweal 80:9-12 Mr 27 '64
Technology and urban life: address, October 30, 1963. Vital Speeches 30:346-8 Mr 15 '64

CHASE, Francis S.
Teacher education for the next decade; adaptation of address, October 1, 1963. Sch & Soc 92:140-2 Mr 21 '64

CHASE, Ilka
African holiday. Vogue 141:53+ Ap 1 '63
Impressions of Africa. Travel 121:30-2 Je '64
Travellers' tips, far-flinging. Vogue 142:221-3 O 1 '63

CHASE, Kathleen
Syncopated dirges, ragtime parades. Américas 16:16-20 Mr '64

CHASE, Mary
Magic of poetry. NEA J 53:8-11 D '64

CHASE, Mary C.
Practice of playwriting. Writer 76:17-19 Je '63

CHASE, Mary Ellen
Rewards of teaching. Ladies Home J 81: 48+ N '64
Victoria: a pig in a pram. McCalls 91:114-15+ O '63

CHASE, Oscar
Incident in Hattiesburg. H. Zinn. Nation 198:501-4 My 18 '64

CHASE, Randolph M. Jr. See Rapaport, F. T. jt. auth.

CHASE, Salmon Portland
Salmon Portland Chase: rhetorician of abolition. F. W. Hale. bibliog Negro Hist Bul 26:165-8 F '63

CHASE, Sherret S.
Why conservationists are missing a big bet! por Am For 70:14-16 My '64

CHASE, Stuart
Confessions of a town planner. Read Digest 83:133-7 Jl '63
New ways to make modern money. Sat R 47: 30 Ag 8 '64
Two worlds. Bul Atomic Sci 19:18-20 Je '63

CHASE, W. Howard
Total health: address, November 30, 1964. Vital Speeches 31:177-81 Ja 1 '65

CHASE Manhattan bank. See New York (city) —Banks

CHASES' calendar of annual events. See Calendars

CHASES, Police. See Police chases

CHASINS, Abram
Hidden talent for music in every child. McCalls 91:36+ Jl '64

CHASSIS, Automobile. See Automobiles—Chassis

CHASTITY. See Sexual ethics

CHATEAU of Roche-Courbon. See France—Historic houses, etc.

CHATEAUX. See Castles

CHATELAINES (Jewelry)
Treasures and trinkets; the chatelaine. G. Kaler. il Hobbies 69:42+ Ag; 42 S; 42-3+ O '64

CHATFIELD, Chester
Beast of buckless gulch. Outdoor Life 134: 54-5+ O '64
Fastest gunning in the West. Outdoor Life 134:40-1+ S '64
40th buck. Outdoor Life 132:28-9+ Jl '63
Whoop-and-holler salmon. pors Outdoor Life 134:36-9+ Ag '64

CHATFIELD, Jack
Letter to a northern friend. New Repub 148:13-14 My 18 '63

CHATHAM, Josiah G.
Southern Pentecost; address, with editorial comment. America 109:2, 11-12 Jl 6 '63
Toast to America; address, May 13, 1964. America 110:718-19 My 23 '64

CHATMAN, Dan
Youth heads California future farmers. il pors Ebony 19:49-50+ D '63

CHATSWORTH. See England—Historic houses, etc.

CHATTANOOGA, Tenn.
Chattanooga puts its citizens to work. il Am City 79:159+ Ap '64

CHATTANOOGA times
Carrying on a tradition. Time 85:49 Ja 1 '65

CHAUCER, Geoffrey
Canterbury tales; dramatization. See Olfson, L.

about

BCD triology. P. W. Schmidtchen. il por Hobbies 68:106-7 D '63

CHAUSSON, Ernest
Three violinists, three internal perspectives. R. Sabin. il Am Rec G 31:114-16 O '64

CHAUTAUQUA, LAKE
Tiger of Lake Chautauqua. E. P. Clarkson. il Motor B 112:82+ Jl '63

CHAUTAUQUA, N.Y.

Music

[Musical events] il Mus Am 83:31-2 S '63

CHAUTAUQUA institution
Way of life; Chautauqua music festival. J. Ardoin. il Mus 84:14-15 O '64

CHAUTAUQUA summer music festival. See Music festivals—New York (state)

CHAVE, Keith E. See Schmalz, R. F. jt. auth.

CHÁVEZ, Carlos
Artistic ferment of Mexico today. O. B. Brummell. por Hi Fi 15:69-70 F '65
Music to my ears; Chavez No. 6. il Sat R 47:36+ My 23 '64
Musical events; performance by New York philharmonic. W. Sargeant. New Yorker 40:169 My 16 '64
Way to write music. il por Time 83:56 My 15 '64

CHAVEZ ravine, Los Angeles. See Stadiums

CHAYEFSKY, Paddy
Passion of Josef D. Criticism
Commonweal 79:693 Mr 6 '64
New Yorker 40:92 F 22 '64
Newsweek il 63:61 F 24 '64
Sat R 47:26 F 29 '64
Time il 83:62 F 21 '64

CHAYES, Abram
Communications satellite program and the Department of state; statement, April 8, 1964. bibliog f Dept State Bul 50:632-3 Ap 27 '64
European integration and American foreign policy; address, February 9, 1963. Dept State Bul 48:318-22 Mr 4 '63
International organization and space law; address, May 1, 1963. Dept State Bul 48:835-8 My 27 '63
Law and the quarantine of Cuba. For Affairs 41:550-7 Ap '63
Rule of law, now; address, July 3, 1963. Dept State Bul 49:162-7 Jl 29 '63; Same. Vital Speeches 29:696-9 S 1 '63
U.N. charter, the purse, and the peace; address, May 15, 1964. Dept State Bul 50:900-6 Je 8 '64
United Nations, what it is, what it has done; address, March 21, 1963. Dept State Bul 48:562-6 Ap 15 '63
United States trade policies; address, October 3, 1963. Vital Speeches 30:47-51 N 1 '63

CHAYES, Felix
Stereology congress. Science 140:1247-8 Je 14 '63

CHAYOTES
See also
Cookery—Fruit

CHAZE, Elliott
No tallyho. Life 54:19 Mr 8 '63
Once I was a tiger. Life 54:17-18 F 8 '63

CHEATING
See also
Fraud

CHEATING in schoolwork
Classroom incident: symposium. NEA J 54: 54-5 Ja '65
Code of honor: air force cadets accused of stealing examination papers. Time 85:20 Ja 29 '65
Fall from honor: exam cheating scandal at Air force academy. il Newsweek 65:46 F 1 '65

CHECK credit plans. See Banks and banking—Check credit plans

CHECK pilots. See Air pilots

CHECKER, Chubby
Sweet potato pie: a goblin's delight. D. J. Robinson. il pors Ebony 18:134+ O '63

CHECKER motors corporation
Box that tailoring made. il Time 82:62 Ag 2 '63

CHECKING accounts. See Banks and banking —Checking accounts

CHECKS
What you should know about checks; questions and answers. N. G. P. Krausz. Suc Farm 62:74 O '64
See also
Travelers checks

CHECKS and balances (government) See Separation of powers

CHECKUP, Medical. See Physical examinations

CHEESE
Pasteurized process cheese, its development and nutritive value. il Parents Mag 38:42+ S '63

CHEESE—*Continued*
Play on cheeses. M. R. Henry. House & Gard 125:48+ My '64
President amends regulations on imports of blue-mold cheese; proclamation, November 26, 1963. L. B. Johnson. Dept State Bul 49: 970-1 D 23 '63
See also
Cookery—Cheese
Cottage cheese

Bacteriology

He keeps the bacteria jumping. A. K. Klingender. il Sat R 47:51-2 My 2 '64

CHEESE bread. See Bread

CHEESECAKE
Choice of cheesecakes. C. Claiborne. il N Y Times Mag p99-100 S 8 '63
Happy marriage; glazed lemon-cream-cheese cake. il McCalls 92:38 Ja '65
It's the season for cheesecake. il Sunset 133: 124-5 Jl '64

CHEETAHS
Savage encounter. F. McKinley. il Outdoor Life 133:52-3+ Mr '64

CHEEVER, John
Educated American woman; story. New Yorker 39:46-54 N 2 '63
Habit; story. New Yorker 40:45-7 Mr 7 '64
International wilderness; story. New Yorker 39:43-7 Ap 6 '63
Marito in città; story. New Yorker 40:26-31 Jl 4 '64
Mene, mene, tekel, upharsin; story. New Yorker 39:38-41 Ap 27 '63
Metamorphoses; story. New Yorker 39:32-9 Mr 2 '63
Metamorphoses of John Cheever; excerpts from short stories. Time 83:69 Mr 27 '64
Montraldo; story. New Yorker 40:37-9 Je 6 '64
Ocean; story. New Yorker 40:30-40 Ag 1 '64
Swimmer; story. New Yorker 40:28-34 Jl 18 '64
Wapshot scandal; story; excerpt. por Esquire 60:52-4 Jl '63
about
America aglow. C. Ozick. Commentary 38:66-7 Jl '64
Ovid in Ossining. il pors Time 83:66-70+ Mr 27 '64

CHEFS salad. See Salads

CHEHAB, Fuad
Charles the Sweet. Newsweek 64:44 Ag 31 '64

CHEIT, Earl F.
(ed) See Hofstadter, R. Antitrust in America

CHEKHOV, Anton Pavlovich
Late-blooming flowers; story. Ladies Home J 80:74-7 N '63
about
Chekhov, by E. J. Simmons. Review
New Yorker 39:138+ Mr 2 '63. H. Moss
Three sisters; tr. by R. Jarrell. Criticism
America 111:54 Jl 11 '64
Nation 199:37-9 Jl 27 '64
New Yorker 40:56 Jl 4 '64
Newsweek il 64:45 Jl 6 '64
Sat R 46:34 Ag 24 '63
Sat R 47:25 Jl 18 '64
Theatre Arts il(p 11) 47:13 Ag '63
Time il 84:72 Jl 3 '64
Uncle Vanya. Criticism
Newsweek il 62:45 Ag 5 '63
Wingless sea gull. J. Rosselli. Reporter 30: 34-5 Je 4 '64

CHELAN, LAKE
By boat into the Cascade wilderness. il Sunset 133:18-20 Ag '64
Charm-laden Lake Chelan. W. F. Heald. il Travel 119:51-2 Je '63

CHELATION
Metal chelates in analytical chemistry; report on 16th annual analytical symposium. Q. Fernando and others. Science 143:491-2+ Ja 31 '64
Mining the sea; chemical extraction of gold. il Time 83:90 My 15 '64

CHELMINSKI, Rudolph
Greece mourns, a new king inherits a crisis. Life 56:26-9 Mr 27 '64
Into no man's land they walk and then the guns go silent. Life 56:34 Ap 3 '64
Rich waif's wail: I'm sick of moving. Life 55:70 S 6 '63
Two who lay buried for fifty-six hours. Life 55:68+ Ag 9 '63
—See Hall, L. jt. auth.

CHELONIA mydas. See Turtles, Green

CHELSEA flower show. See Flower exhibits

CHELSEA hotel. See New York (city)—Hotels, restaurants, etc.

CHELSEA porcelain. See Pottery, English

CHEMICAL abstracts (periodical)
Chemical abstracts reaches 3 millionth entry. Library J 89:597 F 1 '64
Foreign literature of chemistry. J. L. Wood and others. il Science 140:610-13 My 10 '63

CHEMICAL additives in cattle feed
See also
Antibiotic feed supplements

CHEMICAL additives in food. See Food additives

CHEMICAL analysis. See Chemistry, Analytic

CHEMICAL bonds
Bent chemical bonds. W. H. Flygare. bibliog il Science 140:1179-85 Je 14 '63
Bonding in xenon fluorides and halogen fluorides. K. S. Pitzer. bibliog il Science 139: 414-15 F 1 '63
Condensation model producing crystalline or amorphous tetrahedral networks. F. Ordway. bibliog il Science 143:800-1 F 21 '64

CHEMICAL compounds
See also
Chelation
Intermetallic compounds

CHEMICAL elements
Birth of the elements; excerpt from address, December 5, 1962. A. G. W. Cameron. il Sky & Tel 25:254-7 My '63
Elementary course in elements. il Sci Digest 54:69-71 S '63
He's got the whole world in his hands. A. P. Armagnac. il Pop Sci 182:82-4 Je '63
New batch of man-made rare elements created. Sci N L 85:56 Ja 25 '64
Synthetic elements. G. T. Seaborg and A. R. Fritsch. il Sci Am 208:68-78 bibliog(p200) Ap '63
See also
Earths, Rare
also names of chemical elements, e.g. Technetium

CHEMICAL engineering
See also
Calculating machines—Chemical engineering applications

CHEMICAL formula typewriter. See Typewriters

CHEMICAL geology. See Geochemistry

CHEMICAL industries
After Wiesner report: feeling little pain; pesticide manufacturers. Bsns W p36 My 25 '63
Better things for better living through chemistry? Time 82:17-18 D 20 '63
Chemicals: the reluctant competitors. G. Burck. il Fortune 68:148-53+ N '63
Island in sun adds industry to beaches; Aruba chemical industries. il Bsns W p36-7+ Ja 4 '64
Over the bridge; Germany's Hoechst farbewerke. il Time 81:90+ F 15 '63
Soviet Union: more chemicals. New Repub 149:12 D 28 '63
See also
Chemistry, Technical
Fertilizer industry and trade
General aniline and film corporation
Imperial chemical industries, limited
Interessengemeinschaft farbenindustrie aktiengesellschaft
Monsanto chemical company
Union carbide and carbon corporation

Exhibitions

ACHEMA, world's largest chemical engineering congress, shows scientific instruments of twenty-three nations. T. L. Campbell. il Science 145:1026-35 S 4 '64
Seen at chemical fair; 29th exposition of Chemical industries, New York. Sci N L 84:382 D 14 '63

Great Britain

Chemical company with a whisky base; Distillers co. ltd. il Bsns W p56+ S 19 '64

Russia

Russians try again to heat up chemicals. il Bsns W p89-90+ Mr 28 '64
Selling a plant to Soviets; Fisons weed-killer to be produced in Russia. il Bsns W p52 My 30 '64

United States

See also
Grace, W. R. and company

CHEMICAL laboratories
See also
Lederle laboratories

CHEMICAL literature
See also
Chemical abstracts (periodical)

CHEMICAL low-altitude missile. See Guided missiles

CHEMICAL reactions
Chemical kinetics in shock tubes. S. H. Bauer. bibliog il Science 141:867-79 S 6 '63
Exothermic process promises brazing applications in space. J. F. Judge. il Miss & Roc 13:48+ S 30 '63
Exothermic system selection explained. il Miss & Roc 13:51+ S 30 '63
See also
Alkylation
Catalysis
Oxidation reduction reaction

CHEMICAL reagents
Osmiophilic reagents: new cytochemical principle for light and electron microscopy. J. S. Hanker and others. bibliog il Science 146:1039-43 N 20 '64

CHEMICAL research
Chemistry in the universities. P. H. Abelson. Science 144:251 Ap 17 '64; Reply. A. V. Grosse. 144:797 My 15 '64
1963-1964 science review. Sci N L 84:390-1; 86:391-2 D 21 '63, D 19 '64
See also
Chemistry, Technical—Research
Gordon research conferences

CHEMICAL societies
See also names of chemical societies, e.g. American chemical society

CHEMICAL warfare
Biological and chemical weapons. R. L. Pfaltzgraff, jr. bibliog f Cur Hist 47:18-24+ Jl '64
Chemical warfare in Vietnam. B. Russell. New Repub 149:30-1 Jl 6 '63
Chemical warfare; U.S. government accused by the South Vietnam liberation Red cross. B. Russell. Nation 197:inside cover Jl 6 '63
DOD weighs new war concept; incapacitating agents. J. Trainor. Miss & Roc 15:14 O 5 '64
Destroyers that leave no wounds; army work on chemical and biological weapons. il Bsns W p 106+ D 5 '64
FAS statement on biological and chemical warfare. Bul Atomic Sci 20:46-7 O '64
Is Russia outstripping us in weapons of mass destruction? address, December 7, 1962. C. H. Coggins. Vital Speeches 2:263-6 F 15 '63
Speaking out; what's so terrible about germ warfare? C. F. Rassweiler. Sat Eve Post 238:12+ Ja 30 '65
Tomorrow's weapons, chemical and biological, by J. H. Rothschild. Review
Bul Atomic Sci 20:35-6 O '64. M. Meselson
U.S. comments on U.N. mission's Cambodia-Viet-Nam report; letter, September 9, 1964. A. E. Stevenson. Dept State Bul 51: 527-9 O 12 '64
U.S. replies to Cambodian charge on chemical operations; letter, August 3, 1964. C. W. Yost. Dept State Bul 51:274 Ag 24 '64
U.S. welcomes inquiry of Cambodian charge of chemical operations; text of letter from Ambassador A. E. Stevenson, August 14, 1964. Dept State Bul 51:319 Ag 31 '64
See also
Gases in warfare

CHEMICAL workers
See also
International chemical workers union
Strikes—United States—Chemical workers

CHEMICALS

Physiological effects

Agricultural chemicals, often misused, menace the life of plants, animals, and people. il Consumer Bul 46:27-30 Ap '63
Chemical mind-changers. R. Coughlan. il Life 54:81-2+ Mr 15 '63
First aid; surface injuries. C. J. Potthoff. il Todays Health 42:78 Ja '64

CHEMICALS, Agricultural. See Agricultural chemicals

CHEMICALS, Sterilizing. See Chemosterilants

CHEMILUMINESCENCE. See Luminescence

CHEMISTRY
Chemistry: pure and applied; report of 19th International congress of pure and applied chemistry. R. C. Elderfield. Science 142:72-3 O 4 '63
See also
Alchemy
Biochemistry
Chemical industries
Molecules
Radicals (chemistry)

Periodicals

See also
Chemical abstracts (periodical)

CHEMISTRY, Analytic
Analytical chemistry in nuclear technology; report on seventh conference on analytical chemistry in nuclear technology. M. T. Kelley and others. Science 144:570-2 My 1 '64
Bromine analysis in 5-bromouracil-labeled DNA by x-ray fluorescence. L. Zeitz and R. Lee. bibliog il Science 142:1670-3 D 27 '63
Chemical variations in a granitic pluton and its surrounding rocks. A. K. Baird and others. bibliog il Science 146:258-9 O 9 '64
Chemistry of noble gas compounds. H. H. Hyman. bibliog il Science 145:773-83 Ag 21 '64
Perspectives in chemotaxonomy. R. E. Alston and others. bibliog il Science 142: 545-52 N 1 '63
Specific inhibition of replication of animal viruses. I. Tamm and H. J. Eggers. bibliog il Science 142:24-33 O 4 '63; Reply with rejoinder. T. D. Brock. 143:195-6 Ja 17 '64
See also
Chromatographic analysis
Radioactivation analysis

CHEMISTRY, Colloidal. See Colloids

CHEMISTRY, Industrial. See Chemistry, Technical

CHEMISTRY, Inorganic
See also
Intermetallic compounds

CHEMISTRY, Physical and theoretical
Absolute spectrofluorometer. G. K. Turner. bibliog il Science 146:183-9 O 9 '64
See also
Catalysis
Diffusion
Surface chemistry

CHEMISTRY, Surface. See Surface chemistry

CHEMISTRY, Technical
See also
Distillation

Research

Change ahead for labs. il Bsns W p92+ Ap 4 '64

CHEMISTRY sets. See Toys

CHEMISTS
Chemists; annual fall meeting of American chemical society. New Yorker 39:33-5 S 28 '63
More chemists die young. S. Soloveichik. Sci N L 84:199 S 28 '63

CHEMOSTERILANTS
Insect chemosterilants with low toxicity for mammals. S. C. Chang and others. bibliog il Science 144:57-8 Ap 3 '64
Insect fecundity and fertility: chemically induced decrease. D. S. Grosch. bibliog il Science 141:732-3 Ag 23 '63
Resistance to the chemical sterilant, apholate, in aedes aegypti. E. I. Hazard and others. il Science 145:500-1 Jl 31 '64

CHEMOTHERAPY
Antimicrobial agents and chemotherapy; report on 3rd interscience conference on antimicrobial agents and chemotherapy. D. Perlman. Science 144:322-3 Ap 17 '64
Congenital malformations in hamster embryos after treatment with vinblastine and vincristine. V. H. Ferm. bibliog il Science 141:426 Ag 2 '63; Reply. J. G. Armstrong and others. 143:703 F 14 '64
High hope for a leukemia cure. Bsns W p52 Je 6 '64
Will chemicals cure cancer? excerpt from Savage cell. P. McGrady and M. Morgan. il Sat Eve Post 237:68-70 My 16 '64

CHEN, Chin
Pteropod ooze from Bermuda pedestal. bibliog Science 144:60-2 Ap 3 '64

CHENAULT, James K.
Time to finish the Communist bridgehead. il por Time 82:49 D 6 '63

CHENAULT, John W.
I sold a house to a Negro. E. Moore. il pors Ebony 18:92-4+ O '63

CHENAULT, Price
Correctional institutions helping the functionally illiterate. bibliog f ALA Bul 58:804-9 O '64

CHENEVIX-TRENCH, Anthony
Switch at Eton. por Time 81:61 Mr 15 '63

CHENEY, Frances Neel
Current reference books. See issues of Wilson library bulletin

CHENG, Chu-yuan
Truth about red China's bomb; interview. por U S News 57:28-32 D 28 '64

CHENG, H. H. and others
Variations of nitrogen-15 abundance in soils. bibliog Science 146:1574-5 D 18 '64

CHENG, Tien-hsi
Insect control in mainland China. bibliog Science 140:269-77; 141:577-9 Ap 19, Ag 9 '63

CHENG, Ts'ai-ying, and Sueoka, Noboru
Heterogeneity of DNA in density and base composition. bibliog Science 141:1194-6 S 20 '63
Polymer similar to polydeoxyadenylate-thymidylate in various tissues of a marine crab. bibliog Science 143:1442-3 Mr 27 '64
CHERISHING kind; story. See Stern, R. M.
CHERKIN, Arthur, and Catchpool, J. F.
Temperature dependence of anesthesia in goldfish. bibliog Science 144:1460-2 Je 19 '64
CHERNE, Leo
Preview of change: from now to 1980; interview. por Nations Bsns 53:50-2+ Ja '65
CHERNETSKI, Kent E.
Exchange of postdoctoral students with Japan; letter. Science 146:597 O 30 '64
CHERNOW, Burt
Calder. Sch Arts 63:24-7 D '63
Proposal concerning art education at the elementary level. Sch Arts 63:30 S '63
CHERRIES
Cherries for fruit and flowers. D. Henry. il Horticulture 41:294-5 My '63
See also
Cookery—Fruit
CHERRIES of Sir Cleges; drama. See Hall, M.
CHERRY, Joe H.
Association of rapidly metabolized DNA and RNA. bibliog Science 146:1066-9 N 20 '64
CHERRY trees
See also
Oriental flowering cherry
CHESAPEAKE AND OHIO CANAL NATIONAL HISTORICAL PARK. See Potomac River
CHESAPEAKE and Ohio railway
Big deal in Toledo; purchase of C&O bulk-loading complex. il Bsns W p92+ N 16 '63
Broader view. Newsweek 61:67-8 Ap 8 '63
C&O's happy holders; Greenbrier house parties promote loyalty. il Bsns W p96-8 D 7 '63
CHESAPEAKE BAY
Chesapeake country. N. T. Kenney. il Nat Geog Mag 126:370-411 S '64
Crossing that defies the Atlantic; bridge-tunnel system. il Fortune 67:112-21 Ap '63
Cruising the Chesapeake country. il Motor B 112:22-7 S '63
Delightsome land. R. Deardorff. il Redbook 121:66-7+ My '63
Ferryboat farewell. D. W. Ross. il Travel 119:41-3 Ap '63
New shortcut for North-South travel. il U S News 55:72-3 Ag 5 '63
Over and under seventeen mi. of open sea. il Bsns W p46-8+ Mr 23 '63
River drowned under bay. E. Hall. Sci N L 84:86 Ag 10 '63
Wintering in the Chesapeake. F. Kern. il Yachting 114:28-30+ D '63
Yankee cruises the Chesapeake. M. MacDuffie. il Yachting 116:40-2+ D '64
See also
Smith Island
CHESAPEAKE BAY, Battle of. See United States—History—Revolution—Naval operations
CHESAPEAKE BAY bridge-tunnel
Air key to ocean tunnel. E. Hall. il Sci N L 85:218 Ap 4 '64
Bridge of size. il Time 83:74-5 Ap 24 '64
Coming next spring: a sea voyage by auto. il Newsweek 62:86-7 O 28 '63
Crossing that defies the Atlantic; bridge-tunnel system across Chesapeake Bay. il Fortune 67:112-21 Ap '63
Driving across Chesapeake Bay. il Sci Digest 53:64-9 Mr '63
New route to South leaps bays. il Bsns W p34+ Ap 11 '64
New shortcut for North-South travel; Chesapeake Bay bridge-tunnel. il U S News 55:72-3 Ag 5 '63
Over and under Chesapeake Bay. D. S. Boyer. il Nat Geog Mag 125:592-612 Ap '64
Over and under seventeen mi. of open sea; link Delmarva Peninsula and the Norfolk-Virginia Beach area. il Bsns W p46-8+ Mr 23 '63
Porpoising highway; Chesapeake Bay tunnel-bridge. il Pop Mech 119:94-5 Je '63
CHESAPEAKE BAY retrievers. See Retrievers
CHESAREK, R. F.
How to select an incinerator bucket. Am City 79:80-2 Ag '64
CHESHIRE, Maxine
Dishrags to riches: the saga of Heloise. Sat Eve Post 236:58-61 Mr 2 '63
What is Maggie Smith up to? Sat Eve Post 237:30-2 Ap 18 '64
CHESHIRE, Conn, public library
If your library needs to improve. il Good H 156:169 My '63
CHESLOCK, Louis
Baltimore renaissance. Mus Am 83:10-13 Ap '63
CHESS, Stella, and Thomas, Alexander
Are parents responsible for everything? Parents Mag 39:48-9+ N '64
CHESS
Amazing victory streak of Bobby Fischer. il Sports Illus 20:14-15 Ja 13 '64
Bobby Fischer; best in chess? R. O'Brien. il Sat R 46:22-3 Ap 27 '63; Same abr. with title America's wizard of chess. Read Digest 82:221-2+ My '63
Case of the missing bishop; Kensington high school library, Buffalo, N.Y. D. Pierman. il Wilson Lib Bul 37:580 Mr '63
Chess candidate; owner of Queen's pawn chess emporium. New Yorker 40:43-4 S 19 '64
Chess corner. A. Horowitz. See issues of Saturday review
Master goof in Amsterdam; Interzonal chess tournament. L. Evans. il Sports Illus 21:48 Jl 20 '64
Newest idol; world champion. il Time 81:65 My 31 '63
Poker, pawns, and power; adaptation of address. E. L. Katzenbach, jr. Sat R 46:25 Mr 23 '63
Why not chess in the garden? il Sunset 131:74-6 Jl '63
CHESS players
Amazing Bobby Fischer. P. Lyon. il Holiday 33:125-9+ My '63
Chess nut is a helpless pawn. H. C. Schonberg. il N Y Times Mag p67+ N 29 '64
Squeeze player; Tigran Petrosian. il Newsweek 61:76 Je 3 '63
CHESTER, Alfred
Edward Albee: red herrings & white whales. Commentary 35:296-301 Ap '63
Looking for Genet. Commentary 37:63-7 Ap '64
Salinger; how to love without love. Commentary 35:467-74 Je '63
CHESTER, Marjorie Fatt, and Marek, Richard
Especially for Christmas: fund-raising ideas for churches & clubs; excerpts from McCall's book of fund-raising ideas. McCalls 92:88 N '64
CHESTER, Pa.
Militants; Chester committee for freedom now. O. Moritz. New Repub 150:5-6 My 9 '64
Old Scratchhead wakes up in Chester, Pennsylvania; segregation in the city's schools. S. Klaw. il Reporter 30:31-4 Je 18 '64
CHESTER COUNTY, Pa.
Chester County day. Hobbies 69:90 S '64
CHESTER family
Chester coat-of-arms. H. K. Eilers. il Hobbies 69:124-5 My '64
CHESTERTON, Gilbert Keith
In praise of Chesterton. J. Hart. Yale R 53:49-60 O '63
CHESTERTOWN, N.Y.
Big grader is best for this small town. R. Van Guilder. il Am City 79:97-8 Jl '64
CHESTNUT blight
American chestnut has a fighting chance. C. Benedict. il Audubon Mag 65:108-12 Mr '63
They are bringing back the chestnut tree. J. C. Furnas. il Read Digest 82:129-32 Ap '63
CHESTNUT trees
American chestnut has a fighting chance. C. Benedict. il Audubon Mag 65:108-12 Mr '63
Chestnuts. R. A. Jaynes. il Horticulture 42:16-17+ S '64
Ozark chinkapin. R. R. Thomasson. Pop Gard 14:85+ F '63
They are bringing back the chestnut tree. J. C. Furnas. il Read Digest 82:129-32 Ap '63

Diseases and pests

See also
Chestnut blight
CHESTNUTS
See also
Cookery—Nuts
CHESTS
ABCs of building chests and cabinets. R. J. De Cristoforo. il Pop Sci 185:116-21 N; 132-5 D '64; 186:132-6 Ja '65 (to be cont)
Collectors' notes. E. Gaines. il Antiques 84:82-3 Jl '63
Dead men's chests. K. Lucas. il Travel 121:54-5 F '64
Diversity in Connecticut blockfront. H. Comstock. il Antiques 84:63-7 Jl '63
Small stowaways. G. O'Brien. il N Y Times Mag p70-1 My 10 '64
What to look for when choosing tables and chests. il Bet Hom & Gard 41:124-5 Ap '63

CHET Ager bird and wildlife study center, Lincoln, Neb. See Audubon nature centers

CHETHAM-STRODE, A. and Ferguson, D. E.
Protactinium chemistry. Science 141:444 Ag 2 '63

CHETKOW, B. Harold
Discipline problems in camp. Recreation 57: 136-7 Mr '64

CHEVALIER, Lois R.
Miraculous world of pills that cure. McCalls 90:80-1+ F '63
Welfare mess. Sat Eve Post 236:15-19 My 11 '63

CHEVALIER, Maurice
Seventy-five, and still a one-man show. P. E. Schneider. il pors N Y Times Mag p34-5+ S 8 '63
Solo. New Yorker 38:25-7 F 16 '63

CHEVETOGNE monastery. See Monasteries

CHEVILLE, Roy A.
Mormonism on the move. Christian Cent 80: 1328-30 O 30 '63

CHEW, Geoffrey
All atomic particles equal; summary of address. Sci N L 84:275 N 2 '63
—and others
Strongly interacting particles; with biographical sketches. Sci Am 210:28+, 74-93 bibliog(p 152) F '64

CHEWING gum
See also
Topps chewing gum, incorporated

CHEYENNE frontier days (festival) See Festivals—Wyoming

CHEYENNE MOUNTAIN
Command post for a continent: a hollowed-out mountain; NORAD combat operations center. il U S News 55:49-52 S 23 '63
Mountain fortress for air defense; NORAD's Combat operations center, Colo. il Bsns W p 130-1 Ap 18 '64

CHEZ Vito. See New York (city)—Hotels, restaurants, etc.

CHIANG, Ching-kuo
Next: large-scale uprisings; interview. por U S News 54:41-4 Mr 4 '63

about

Free China's next chief? Chiang Ching-kuo tours U.S. il por U S News 55:26 S 23 '63
Heir apparent. Time 85:23 Ja 22 '65
Little Chiang. il por Time 82:35 S 20 '63
Son of Chiang. il por Newsweek 62:47 S 23 '63

CHIANG, Kai-shek
China 1965: address, December 31, 1964. Vital Speeches 31:198-200 Ja 15 '65

about

Chiang Kai-shek: the crumbling facade. S. Karnow. il por Sat Eve Post 236:101-5 D 7 '63
Chiang Kai-shek's silent enemies. A. Axelbank. Harper 227:46-50+ S '63; Discussion. 227:10+ D '63
Chiang still dreams his dream. T. Durdin. il pors N Y Times Mag p 18-19+ Mr 22 '64
U-2 & a birthday. Time 82:38 N 8 '63
Wanted: a Taiwan policy. New Repub 149: 5-6 S 14 '63

CHIANG, Warren
Miracle for Amanda. T. Wilson. McCalls 91: 52+ Je '64

CHIARI, Roberto Francisco
—See Kennedy, J. F. jt. auth.

about

Inside story of Panama riots. il por U S News 56:48-52 Mr 30 '64
Panama: bluffs, pressures, impasse. il Newsweek 63:45 Ja 27 '64
Panama's milk and sugar President: how a family fortune keeps growing. il por U S News 56:64-5 Ap 6 '64
Rule of the whitetails. il por Time 83:32 F 14 '64

CHICAGO
Chicago: they didn't have to burn it down after all. W. Bowen. il Fortune 71:142-6+ Ja '65
Records go on a diet. S. R. Olsen. il Am City 79:79 Ja '64
Suburban good neighbors identify themselves; South suburban human relations council. Christian Cent 81:901 Jl 15 '64

Airports

Airport water works requires more systems; O'Hare international airport, Chicago. M. Callahan. il Am City 79:93-4 Mr '64
Handy little strip; Chicago's Meigs field. il Bsns W p33 N 9 '63
O'Hare walking distance stirs criticism. R. H. Cook. il Aviation W 79:45+ Jl 15 '63

Architecture

Buildings that inflamed the pride of the citizenry; drawings. N. Solovioff. Fortune 71:147-51 Ja '65
Chicago school of architecture. by C. W. Condit. Review
Nation 200:90 Ja 25 '65. J. Jacobus
House the janitors built; Marina City. G. Cross. il Read Digest 82:201-4 F '63
Innovation in Chicago; United States Gypsum's headquarters. il Arch Rec 135:133-8 Ja '64
Large spans in Chicago. il Arch Forum 118: 120-5 My '63
Living on the top; Marina City. J. Star. il Look 28:53-5+ Ja 14 '64
Marina City. J. M. Liston. il Pop Sci 182: 82-5+ Ap '63
New office building by SOM has unusual site plan, and a well integrated structural and mechanical system; American college of surgeons. il Arch Rec 136:139-43 Ag '64
New work of Mies van der Rohe. il Arch Forum 119:90-1 S '63
View from the 14th floor. Christian Cent 81:1127 S 9 '64

Art

Art news from Chicago (cont) il Art N 62: 19+ Mr; 48 My; 48 Sum; 20 N '63; 53-4 Ja; 63:48 Sum; 52 S '64
Chicago scene. M. Kozloff. Nation 198:352-4, 379-80 Ap 6-13 '64
Review: Chicago. J. Kind. il Art N 63:21-2 My '64

Auditorium theater

Notes from our correspondents. R. C. Marsh. il Hi Fi 14:20+ Ag '64

Banks

Where tax complexities pay off in profits; Chicago's commerce clearing house. il Bsns W p50+ F 22 '64

Board of trade

See Chicago board of trade

Bookstores

See Booksellers and bookselling—Illinois

City planning

Is this the big industry that can keep U.S. going? il U S News 54:74 F 25 '63
Politics of urban renewal: the Chicago findings. by P. H. Rossi and R. A. Dentler. Review
Commentary 35:176-9 F '63. H. J. Gans
Time refuses to back down; Catholic opposition to urban renewal in Chicago. Christian Cent 80:420 Ap 3 '63

Courts

People in trouble. A. Schiller. il Harper 228: 145-9 Ap '64

Crime

Chicago: shades of Capone. V. W. Peterson. Ann Am Acad 347:30-9 My '63
Death in the 24th ward; murder of Alderman Lewis. il Newsweek 61:29 Mr 11 '63
Gang's all here. il Newsweek 63:34+ Je 22 '64
How the mob controls Chicago. B. Davidson. il Sat Eve Post 236:17-27 N 9 '63
Return of the rub-out; murder of Chicago's Alderman Lewis. il Time 81:28 Mr 8 '63
Thirty-five years ago: Chicago's gang wars. S. D. Smith. il N Y Times Mag p45+ F 9 '64
Two views of Chicago. O. W. Wilson; A. Schiller. Harper 228:140-9 Ap '64
Untouchables. Newsweek 61:25-6 Ap 22 '63

Description

Chicago. P. Deutsch and R. Deutsch. il Redbook 122:68-9+ N '63
Mayor Daley's Chicago. J. Dugan. il Holiday 34:84-93+ D '63
Summer in Chicagoland. R. Baumruk. il ALA Bul 57:575-80 Je '63
U.S. city weekends. T. B. Lesure. il Travel 120:28-32+ Jl '63

Education

Chicago school chief center of race controversy. U S News 55:26 O 21 '63
Decentralized urban elementary school for team teaching; James W Johnson elementary school. il Arch Rec 136:234-5 S '64
Doomed ones: school themes by sixth-graders in Chicago. S. Alsop. il Sat Eve Post 237:16 Ap 4 '64

CHICAGO—Education—*Continued*
Education of Big Ben; Negro demands for a loosening neighborhood-school pattern in Chicago. il Time 82:48 Ag 30 '63
Education the year round: the Dunbar school of Chicago. B. C. Willis. Atlan 215:83-6 Ja '65
Embattled boss of Chicago's schools. W. R. Shelton. il Sat Eve Post 236:26-7 O 19 '63
Illiteracy; the key to poverty! B. Asbell. McCalls 91:96-7+ F '64
Montessori in the slums. il Time 84:53-4 Jl 10 '64
This is the city; Hauser report. il Newsweek 63:53 Ap 13 '64
Urban school for progressive education. il Arch Rec 134:214-15 O '63
Working with disadvantaged parents; Special project; District eleven, Chicago. L. G. Daughtery. NEA J 52:18-20 D '63

Education, Board of

Boycotting Ben. Newsweek 62:60 N 4 '63
Chicago answer for dropouts; Education-employment program. il Ebony 18:81-2+ O '63
Chicago close-up; political side of the race issue. il U S News 55:72-3 N 4 '63
De facto superintendent; B. C. Willis. il Time 82:56 N 1 '63
Man who said boo. Newsweek 62:94 O 28 '63
Massive attack on illiteracy: Cook County experience; excerpts from address, July 13, 1963. R. M. Hilliard. il ALA Bul 57:1034-8 D '63
Willis resigns in Chicago. Sr Schol 83:1T O 25 '63

Fire department

Chicago fire department jets around. R. J. Quinn. il Am City 79:89 Jl '64
Snorkel Bob: Chicago's champion fire fighter. K. Detzer. il Read Digest 85:117-20 Ag '64

Galleries and museums

See also
Museum of science and industry, Chicago

Historic houses, etc.

Committee plans restoration of Robie House. il Arch Rec 133:29 Ap '63

History

From a silk handkerchief; libraries. J. W. R. Scurr. il Library J 88:2439-45 Je 15 '63
Negro who founded Chicago. L. Bennett, jr. il Ebony 19:170-2+ D '63

Hotels, restaurants, etc.

Chicago restaurants and night life. E. Mistaras. il ALA Bul 57:565-70 Je '63
Dining out in Chicago. S. Spitzer. Holiday 35:121-4 F '64
Executive on the door; doormen at the Ambassador hotels. il Bsns W p30 My 11 '63
Maxim's gets a twin; Maxim's de Chicago. il Bsns W p30-1 D 14 '63
See also
Night clubs

Housing

Architect Goldberg's Marina City concept. il Arch Rec 134:214-16 S '63
Keeping the outsiders out. E. Richey. il Sat R 46:22-4 O 19 '63; Discussion. 46:20-1, 23 N 30 '63
Kenwood foils the block-busters. E. Richey. Harper 227:42-7 Ag '63
Life in the round; Marina City. il Ebony 20:106-8+ N '64
Living on the top; Marina City. J. Star. il Look 28:53-5+ Ja 14 '64
Refinement in Chicago. il Arch Forum 120:76-7 Mr '64

Intellectual life

Cultural desert for writers? B. Katz. il Library J 88:2430-4 Je 15 '63

Libraries

From a silk handkerchief. J. W. R. Scurr. il Library J 88:2439-45 Je 15 '63
That toddlin' town also reads. W. M. Hartwell. il Library J 88:2426-9 Je 15 '63
See also
Newberry library, Chicago

Moral conditions

Chicago ain't ready for reform. H. Bruno. il Reporter 28:41-3 Mr 28 '63

Music

Jazz records. W. Balliett. New Yorker 40:201-4 D 5 '64
[Musical events] (cont) il Mus Am 83:75 Ja; 33-4 S '63; 84:10-11 F; 26 Ap; 19-20 S; 64+ D '64
Notes from our correspondents. R. C. Marsh. il Hi Fi 14:20+ Ag '64
See also
Chicago opera company
Chicago symphony orchestra
Lyric opera of Chicago

Negroes

Angry at everybody. il Time 82:18-19 Jl 12 '63
Back of Chicago's worry over race violence. il U S News 57:36 Ag 31 '64
Boycott in Chicago. Newsweek 63:30-1 Mr 9 '64
Boycotts, demonstrations. A. P. Klausler. Christian Cent 80:1416+ N 13 '63
Chicago starts moving on equal job question. il Bsns W p22-3 My 30 '64
Chicago story: after Negroes moved in, the trials of a community; excerpts from I went to see the elephant. D. J. Ingle. il U S News 55:96-7 S 16 '63
Gitlow will show you how to shuffle. A. Friendly, jr. New Repub 150:9 My 23 '64
Growing racial unrest in Chicago. il U S News 55:14 Ag 26 '63
Kenwood foils the block-busters. E. Richey. Harper 227:42-7 Ag '63
Mayor and minister booed in Chicago; convention of NAACP. Christian Cent 80:902 Jl 17 '63
Rise of the Negro militant. H. W. Fuller. Nation 197:138-40 S 14 '63
Splitsville, U.S.A; urban renewal and racial segregation. E. Rickey. il Reporter 28:35-8 My 23 '63; Discussion. 29:5 Jl 4 '63
They got too mad. il Time 84:25 Ag 28 '64
War in the North. il Time 81:16-17 My 31 '63
When marchers turned on Chicago's mayor. il U S News 55:10 Jl 15 '63
Where whites staged a protest march. il U S News 55:6 S 23 '63

Newspapers

Burying the story. Time 82:40 Ag 16 '63
See also
Chicago sun-times

Police

How the mob controls Chicago. B. Davidson. il Sat Eve Post 236:17-27 N 9 '63
How the police chief sees it. O. W. Wilson. Harper 228:140-5 Ap '64

Politics and government

Chicago ain't ready for reform. H. Bruno. il Reporter 28:41-3 Mr 28 '63
Clouter with conscience. il Time 81:24-35 Mr 15 '63
Death in the 24th ward; city council election. il Newsweek 61:29 Mr 11 '63
How to beat a voting machine and a drive to make it honest. il U S News 54:63 Ap 8 '63
Last dinosaur wins again. A. Balk. il Sat Eve Post 236:72-3 My 11 '63
More of everything; election results. il Newsweek 61:32 Ap 15 '63
Overwhelming, he said. il Time 81:23-4 Ap 12 '63
Return of the rub-out; murder of Chicago's Alderman Lewis. il Time 81:28 Mr 8 '63

Public buildings

Rehabilitating a police headquarters. P. Gerhardt, jr. il Am City 79:37 Ja '64

Rapid transit

Chicago transit goes air-conditioned. il Am City 79:127 Mr '64

Religious institutions and affairs

Commandos in the city; Chicago city missionary society. il Time 83:56 F 21 '64
High-rise hermits; Edgewater association of clergy and rabbis. il Newsweek 64:56 S 7 '64
News of the Christian world (cont) Christian Cent 80:754-6, 914; 81:124-6, 221-2, 532-3 Je 5, Jl 17 '63, Ja 22, F 12, Ap 22 '64
Time refuses to back down; Catholic opposition to urban renewal in Chicago. Christian Cent 80:420 Ap 3 '63

Riots

Back of Chicago's worry over race violence. il U S News 57:36 Ag 31 '64

Social conditions

Chicago's hillbilly ghetto. H. Bruno. il Reporter 30:28-31 Je 4 '64
Up from apathy, the Woodlawn experiment; excerpts from Crisis in black and white. C. E. Silberman. Commentary 37:51-8 My '64; Discussion. 38:14+ O '64

CHICAGO—Social conditions—*Continued*
When whites migrate from the South. il U S News 55:70-3 O 14 '63

Social life and customs

See also
Night clubs

Stockyards

Chicago gets back a barnyard. il Bsns W p 126-8 Mr 16 '63

Street traffic

Electronic recorder speeds bus travel. il Am City 78:109 F '63

Water supply

Chicago's struggle for clean water. il Bsns W p 127-8 O 24 '64

Worlds Columbian exposition, 1893

Coins and medals of the Columbian exposition. C. French. Hobbies 69:102 O '64
Little Egypt never got to the Chicago fair! A. Barzel. il Dance Mag 38:62-5 D '64

CHICAGO (game) See Bridge (game)

CHICAGO and north western railway
Heavenly way to run a railroad. A. Steinberg. il Read Digest 82:175-80 My '63
Man who likes commuters. il Life 57:61-2 D 4 '64

CHICAGO Bears (football club) See Football clubs

CHICAGO Black Hawks (hockey team) See Hockey teams

CHICAGO board of trade
Boom time hits the Chicago pit. il Bsns W p 106+ O 5 '63

CHICAGO boys clubs. See Boys clubs

CHICAGO city missionary society. See Missionary societies

CHICAGO city news bureau. See News agencies

CHICAGO Cubs (baseball) See Baseball clubs

CHICAGO daily news
Rewriting the Gospels; during Lent. Christian Cent 80:486 Ap 17 '63

CHICAGO fire, 1871. See Fires

CHICAGO in literature
Cultural desert for writers? B. Katz. il Library J 88:2430-4 Je 15 '63

CHICAGO institute of design. See Illinois institute of technology—Institute of design

CHICAGO lyric opera. See Lyric opera of Chicago

CHICAGO museum of science and industry. See Museum of science and industry, Chicago

CHICAGO opera company
Old grandeur. il Newsweek 62:100 O 21 '63

CHICAGO, Rock Island and Pacific railway
Battle for a mighty good road; Union Pacific and North Western covet Rock Island line. il Bsns W p 119-20+ N 2 '63
Much-wanted talent; Jervis Langdon, jr. appointed as chairman. Time 84:106 O 16 '64

CHICAGO sun-times
First in the second city; Chicago sun-times. il Newsweek 64:36 D 28 '64

CHICAGO symphony orchestra
Backstage battle. R. Dettmer. Mus Am 84:10-11 F '64; Discussion. 84:4-5 My '64
Musical events; two concerts. W. Sargeant. New Yorker 40:191-2 Ap 25 '64
Reiner retires. R. Dettmer. Mus Am 83:12-13 Jl '63

CHICAGO tribune
Candy a best seller, but not in Chicago; Chicago trib. presentation for Books today. il Pub W 186:38-9 S 21 '64
View from the Tower. Christian Cent 81:1262-3 O 14 '64

CHICAGO. University
L'affaire Biberman; weapons research facility in Laboratory of applied sciences to close. New Repub 148:7-8 Je 22 '63
Chicago to shut weapons lab. Bsns W p 108 Je 15 '63
Generalist's elysium; Committee on social thought. il Time 83:68 Ja 3 '64
Great art in the elementary library; University of Chicago laboratory schools. M. Seckel. il Library J 88:4813-16 D 15 '63
Return of a giant. il Time 81:38+ My 31 '63

Graduate library school

D.R.S. to G.L.S. J. Shera. Wilson Lib Bul 37:687+ Ap '63

Libraries

Public relations awry on UC public relations library. Library J 88:747 F 15 '63

CHICAGO university laboratory schools. See Schools, Experimental

CHICAGO White Sox (baseball) See Baseball clubs

CHICHEN ITZÁ
Chichen Itzá, Mexico's mystic city of death. M. Brader. il Sr Schol 84:11T Mr 20 '64

CHICHESTER, Francis
Single-handed passages. Yachting 113:43-5+ My '63

about

French sailor first in ocean race. il Motor B 114:88-9 Ag '64

CHICHESTER festival. See Drama festivals

CHICHESTER festival theatre. See Theater buildings

CHICK embryos. See Embryology—Birds

CHICKADEES
Chickadee helps check insect invasion. A. D. Telford and S. G. Herman. il Audubon Mag 65:78-81 Mr '63

CHICKASHA, Okla.
Soil cement streets for six cents a day. B. Sullivan. il Am City 78:88-9 D '63

CHICKEN as food. See Cookery—Poultry

CHICKEN houses. See Poultry houses

CHICKEN pox
Chicken pox: least serious of contagious childhood diseases. F. H. Richardson. il Todays Health 42:27 Ja '64

CHICKENS. See Poultry

CHICKERING, Lisa
Travel-film career girls. il por Pop Phot 54:127+ My '64

CHICKERING, Sherman B.
Beyond make-believe. Sat R 47:28-9 O 10 '64
Change of chemistry. Sat R 46:20-1 Ap 27 '63
Student magazine awards for 1963. Sat R 46:26-7+ S 21 '63

CHICO, Calif.
One year later, still no bomb. G. Talese. Esquire 59:76-7 My '63

CHICO King: popular singer; story. See Rogin, G.

CHICOREL, Marietta
Some leading questions. bibliog por Library J 88:1424-8 Ap 1 '63

CHIDESTER, Ann
Enemy; story. Redbook 123:62-3 O '64

CHIDSEY, Charles A. and others
Biosynthesis of norepinephrine in isolated canine heart. bibliog Science 139:828-9 Mr 1 '63

CHIEF justices. See Judges

CHIEF thing; drama. See Evreinov, N. N.

CHIEFS (football club) See Football clubs

CHIEFS of staffs. See United States—Joint chiefs of staff

CHIFALA, J. A.
Clean sewers on schedule. Am City 78:110-11 Je '63

CHILCOTE, Ronald H.
Suppressing the future. Nation 199:368-70 N 23 '64

CHILD, Julia
Dinner in the great tradition, but with the work shared by four. House B 105:136-43+ D '63
Everyone's in the kitchen with Julia. L. H. Lapham. il por Sat Eve Post 237:20-1 Ag 8 '64
How to sell broccoli. il por Time 83:56 Mr 20 '64
Plain and fancy; the French chef on WGBH-TV. por Newsweek 62:77-8 Jl 15 '63

CHILD accidents. See Accidents

CHILD-adult relationship
Side of your child you never see. M. Westover. il Parents Mag 38:36-7+ Jl '63
Teen-age manners and make-up; with study-discussion program, by E. M. Duvall. R. H. Loeb, jr. bibliog il PTA Mag 58:30-2, 36 D '63
Where can a boy go for help; excerpts from Moving into manhood. W. W. Bauer. il Todays Health 41:58-9+ N '63

See also
Parent-child relationship

CHILD beating. See Cruelty to children

CHILD buyer; drama. See Shyre, P.

CHILD guidance. See Child study

CHILD health. See Children—Care and hygiene

CHILD labor laws and legislation

United States

Should child labor laws be relaxed? pro and con discussion. il Sr Schol 82:8-9 F 27 '63

CHILD molesters. See Children and strangers

CHILD obesity. See Corpulence

CHILD of the hurricane; story. See Harvey, F.
CHILD photography. See Photography of children
CHILD placing. See Adoption; Foster home care
CHILD psychiatry
Are parents responsible for everything? with program for discussion group, by M. R. Sherwin. S. Chess and A. Thomas. il Parents Mag 39:48-9+, 124+ N '64
Child guidance as a community service. D. Brieland and N. J. Booth. bibliog f Ann Am Acad 355:105-11 S '64
What triggers violence? il Newsweek 64:94+ N 16 '64
See also
Mentally handicapped children
CHILD psychology. See Child study
CHILD study
Adults often mistaken in children's abilities. Sci N L 84:139 Ag 31 '63
Are parents responsible for everything? with program for discussion group, by M. R. Sherwin. S. Chess and A. Thomas. il Parents Mag 39:48-9+, 124+ N '64
Are school psychologists helping or hurting your child? il Redbook 122:76-7+ Ap '64
Art of the mentally retarded child. I. Rapaport. il Sch Arts 63:13-17 Ja '64
Big, bad fears of childhood. J. E. Allen and F. H. Allen. il Parents Mag 39:62-3+ Mr '64
Bottle, blanket and thumb; comfort or bad habit? B. Spock. il Redbook 122:26+ F '64
Child guidance as a community service. D. Brieland and N. J. Booth. bibliog f Ann Am Acad 355:105-11 S '64
Children's fears and phobias; with study discussion program, by R. Strang. H. H. F. H. Allen. il Parents Mag 39:62-3+ Mr '64
Children's language: word-phrase relationship. J. Huttenlocher. il Science 143:264-5 Ja 17 '64
Children's stresses and distresses; with study discussion program, ed. by R. Strang. L. B. Murphy. il PTA Mag 59:14-16, 35 O '64
Child's friends. S. Blum. il Redbook 121:49+ My '63
Do you understand the language of behavior? M. R. Weisbord. il Parents Mag 39:68-9+ F '64
Doctor Spock talks with mothers. B. Spock. See issues of Ladies' home journal to September 1963
Everybody's lonesome. D. G. Francisco. il Parents Mag 38:136 Ap '63
Fundamentals for survival; with program for discussion group, by E. G. Neisser. R. Brecher and E. Brecher. Parents Mag 38:35-6+, 45+ Je '63
Guide for parents: your child's mental health. W. W. Wattenberg. bibliog il NEA J 53:35-50 F '64
Help your child like himself; with study-discussion program, by C. W. Mattuck. S. Blau. il Parents Mag 38:37-8, 62-3+ D '63
Helping children cope with stress; with study-discussion program, by R. Strang. E. J. LeShan. bibliog il PTA Mag 58:7-9, 35 Ja '64
How to head off tantrums. I. T. Comfort. il Parents Mag 38:60-1+ D '63
Illness in the family. L. Strong. il N Y Times Mag p67 Ag 18 '63
Let's stop scaring our children. M. J. E. Senn. McCalls 92:74+ O '64
Life and times with a two-year-old. S. H. Fraiberg. il Parents Mag 38:54-5+ D '63
Like mother, like child, or vice versa? Sci Digest 55:44 Ap '64
Living with a genius. L. Strong. il N Y Times Mag p53-4 F 16 '64
Never underestimate the mind of a child. Sci N L 85:125 F 22 '64
Organization child; with study-discussion program. D. Harris and E. Harris. bibliog il PTA Mag 57:22-4, 35 Ap '63
Playing with toy guns; effect of warlike toys and games on children. B. Spock. Redbook 124:24+ N '64
Psychologist's view: children and toys. J. Star. il Look 27:107-14 D 17 '63
Redbook dialogue; Mario Montessori and A. S. Neill discuss their famous schools and their radical approaches to child rearing. M. Montessori and A. S. Neill. Redbook 124:42-3+ D '64
Talk yourself into it; changing a child's actions or attitudes. il Sci Digest 55:66 My '64
Ticking away; childhood tensions and traumas. il Newsweek 63:68-9 Mr 23 '64
What children learn from play. B. Bettelheim. il Parents Mag 39:48-9+ Jl '64
What it's like to be little. W. Keisler. il Parents Mag 39:48-9+ Mr '64
What makes kids run wild? with study-discussion program, by C. W. Mattuck. C. Chilman. il Parents Mag 39:35+, 72 Ja '64
When children get on your nerves; clearing the atmosphere. M. Piers. il PTA Mag 58:21-2 Ap '64
When parents convict themselves. E. J. LeShan. il N Y Times Mag p32 Jl 12 '64
Who says kids want to be understood? D. Van Ark. il Parents Mag 39:40-1+ Jl '64; Same abr. Read Digest 86:39-40+ Ja '65
Will they outgrow it? with study-discussion program, by R. Strang. M. J. Barnes. bibliog il PTA Mag 58:8-10, 35 O '63
See also
Children and death
Childrens questions
Psychology, Educational
CHILD study association of America
Meeting, 1963. A. D. Buchmueller. Sch & Soc 91:244-5 Sum '63
CHILD suicide. See Suicide
CHILD welfare
Child welfare research: a review and critique. E. V. Mech. bibliog f Ann Am Acad 355:20-30 S '64
Custody by committee? Time 84:67-8 S 18 '64
See also
Cruelty to children
Foster home care
Foster parents' plan, incorporated
United Nations children's fund

Canada

Bonus for babies. I. Sclanders. Nation 198:167-8 F 17 '64

Korea (Republic)

Korean waifs and Yankee volunteers. il Todays Health 42:38-9 S '64

Thailand

Bangkok's wonderful Dr Pierra. J. D. Ratcliff. il Read Digest 85:206-8+ S '64

United States

Bill introduced to expand impacted aid. il NEA J 53:4 Ap '64
Birth control, welfare funds, and the politics of Illinois. H. Bruno. il Reporter 28:33-5 Je 20 '63
Don't knock on this door; welfare visits. Nation 196:298 Ap 13 '63; Reply. E. S. Zaretsky. 196:inside cover My 11 '63
Needed: parents pro tem. M. Weston. il N Y Times Mag p96 Ap 21 '63
Programs and problems in child welfare; symposium, ed. by A. Keith-Lucas. bibliog f il Ann Am Acad 355:1-139 S '64
Twenty-fifth child. R. Haitch. il Nation 197:238-41 O 19 '63
See also
Day nurseries
Save the children federation
School social work
United States—Children's bureau
CHILDBIRTH
American way of birth. S. Wilson. Harper 229:48-54 Jl '64; Same abr. Read Digest 85:68-72 O '64
Behavior of infant monkeys: differences attributable to mode of birth. G. W. Meier. bibliog il Science 143:968-70 F 28 '64
Best way to have a baby. H. Thoms and M. J. Hungerford. il Parents Mag 39:56-9+ N '64
Case for and against induced labor. B. Davidson. il Good H 158:58-9+ Ja '64
Child is born. S. Szasz. il Parents Mag 39:50-1 Mr '64
Childbirth facts and fads. R. Carson. il Parents Mag 38:58-9+ My '63
Could you deliver a baby? reprint. R. B. Scott. Sci Digest 56:63-6 D '64
Fewer drugs for happier mothers; natural childbirth. il Time 84:81 S 25 '64
How to tell when labor begins. B. Pisani. Redbook 123:28+ Je '64
Initiation of labor; report on interdisciplinary conference. C. A. Villee. Science 144:82-4 Ap 3 '64
Long hour of birth; ed. by D. C. Disney. M. A. Fischer. il Sat Eve Post 236:31 N 16 '63
My life, my children; ed. by D. C. Disney. M. A. Fischer. il Ladies Home J 80:56-8+ D '63
Notes from a maternity ward. S. H. Rudolph. il Atlan 211:122-5 Mr '63
Reducing the hazards of birth. A. C. Barnes. Harper 228:31-7 Ja '64; Discussion. 228:8+ Mr '64

CHILDBIRTH—*Continued*
Revolution in childbirth? birthsuit. O. Mendels. Ladies Home J 80:40 Ja '63
Should fathers be in the delivery room? Good H 158:171 Je '64
Slow labor speeded. F. Marley. Sci N L 86: 82 Ag 8 '64
Storm over childbirth. M. J. E. Senn. McCalls 90:40+ F '63
Suction found safer than forceps in births. Sci N L 86:121 Ag 22 '64
What to do in emergency childbirth. Good H 158:163 Mr '64
When is it safe to induce labor? J. F. Jewett. Redbook 122:44+ Ap '64
Who made the lamb; excerpts. C. Painter. il Ladies Home J 81:49+ D '64
Why it costs so much to have a baby. M. T. Bloom. il Redbook 121:62-3+ S '63
See also
Cesarean section
Midwives
Obstetrics
Stillbirth

CHILDHOOD. See Children
CHILDHOOD memories. See Reminiscence
CHILDHOOD schizophrenia. See Schizophrenia
CHILDHOOD tuberculosis. See Tuberculosis
CHILDLESSNESS. See Sterility
CHILDREN
Centuries of childhood: a social history of family life, by P. Ariès. Review
Sat R 46:73-4 Mr 23 '63. P. Gay
Sci Am 208:181-2+ Ap '63. D. H. Wrong
Children; symposium. il Atlan 211:86-133 Mr '63
Christmas is for children. J. R. Moskin. il Look 28:48-53 D 29 '64
First time she saw Paris. P. Coffin. il Look 27:88-92 Jl 2 '63
Five-year-old at the fair; Caroline Hadley. H. Ehrlich. il Look 28:64-8 S 8 '64
How four farm boys discovered Christmas; Hovde family. il Farm J 88:32-3+ D '64
I remember, I remember. A. P. Eliasberg. il N Y Times Mag p 38 D 20 '64
Ice cream taster; seven-year-old Lloyd Jose; photographs. Look 27:81+ Mr 12 '63
Kids and cops. B. W. Wyden. il N Y Times Mag p56-7+ F 23 '64
Many realms of childhood: excerpts from Reader for parents. il N Y Times Mag p88+ N 10 '63
Owl in the playpen. B. Gilbert. il Sat Eve Post 237:72+ Jl 11 '64
Strangers in our midst. il Sat Eve Post 237: 74 D 19 '64
They don't make them that way any more. R. P. Smith. il McCalls 90:86-7+ My '63
See also
Cookery by children
Declaration of the rights of the child
Education of children
Eugenics
Family life
Family, Size of
Gifts from children
Girls
Moving pictures for children
Negro children
Parents
Prenatal influences
Preschool children
Siblings
Stepparents
Travel with children

Accidents
See Accidents

Adjustment
See Adjustment, Social

Amusements
See Childrens amusements

Anecdotes, facetiae, satire, etc.
Are children people? excerpts from Profession: housewife. P. McGinley. il Ladies Home J 80:78-9+ Je '63
How to freeze baseball caps and other helpful household hints. J. Mills. il Redbook 121: 64-5+ Jl '63
Lesson in logic. J. P. McEvoy. Read Digest 82:200C F '63
My son Nobody. C. Farley. Redbook 121:38 My '63
My 365 most embarrassing moments. R. Ashley. il Redbook 121:28 My '63

Cancer
See Cancer

Care and hygiene
Beware: hidden threat to young eyes. G. G. Greer. Bet Hom & Gard 42:36 S '64
Child care in Russia: better than ours? M. J. E. Senn. il McCalls 90:40+ Mr '63
Day in the life of a pediatrician; Laurence Gesner Pray of Fargo, N. D. P. Hamill. il Sat Eve Post 237:69-73 D 19 '64
Disease and delinquency. R. I. Jaslow and G. Ebling, jr. il PTA Mag 57:18-20 Je '63
Growing pains. See issues of Today's health
Health plan for young teens. E. F. Kraft. il Parents Mag 39:60-1+ N '64
Healthy children need doctors, too. M. A. Wessel. il Parents Mag 38:70-1+ O '63
Maternal and child health problems. A. Yankauer. bibliog f il Ann Am Acad 355: 112-20 S '64
Messiness from infancy to adolescence. B. Spock. il Ladies Home J 80:48+ Ap '63
Off to school, and ready for it. L. D. Kirk. il Parents Mag 38:30 Ag '63
Revolution in the nursery. A. P. Eliasberg. il N Y Times Mag p61-3 Je 9 '63
School days should be healthy days. F. V. Hein. il Todays Health 42:90 S '64
Schoolchildren can improve their physical condition. Sch Life 46:20 O '63
Toilet teaching made easy. T. B. Brazelton. il Parents Mag 38:46-7+ Je '63
What parents ask about growing pains. M. J. E. Senn. il McCalls 90:70+ My '63
What the schools do (and don't do) to protect children's health. G. G. Greer. Bet Hom & Gard 43:14 Ja '65
Your child's health. L. W. Sauer. See issues of PTA magazine
See also
Child welfare
Children—Growth and development
Children—Nutrition
Children—Preparation for medical and dental care
Infants—Care and hygiene
Posture

Caricatures and cartoons
Golden years. O'Brian. New Yorker 40:32-3 F 29 '64
Small wonders. R. Marcus. See issues of Good housekeeping

Charities, protection, etc.
See Child welfare

Clothing and dress
See Clothing and dress—Children

Day care
See Day nurseries

Diseases
Childhood diseases, not licked yet. Changing T 17:13-15 S '63
Children's problems that go away. P. W. Goldman. il N Y Times Mag p58 Ja 10 '65
Peripatetic reviewer. E. Weeks. Atlan 211: 151 Mr '63
Vaginal disorders in babies and young children. M. J. E. Senn. McCalls 91:32+ Ja '64
Your child's health. L. W. Sauer. See issues of PTA magazine
See also
Amaurotic family idiocy
Chicken pox
Children—Care and hygiene
Communicable diseases
Diphtheria
Galactosemia
Infants—Care and hygiene
Measles
Mumps
Paralysis
Whooping cough

Education
See Education, Elementary; Education of children

Food
See Children—Nutrition

Growth and development
Anger and rivalry in children: Dr Spock talks to a group of Redbook mothers. B. Spock. il Redbook 124:34-5+ Ja '65
Can you predict how tall a child will grow? il Good H 156:156-7 Je '63
Case for intelligent neglect. L. Strong. il N Y Times Mag p97-8 Je 7 '64
Childhood's baffling middle years. M. Bernath. il Parents Mag 38:52-3+ Ap '63
Don't rush them out of childhood; with group discussion program, by E. J. LeShan. M. A. Wessel. bibliog il Parents Mag 39:18+, 48-9+ O '64

CHILDREN—Growth and development—*Cont.*
Elusive child. L. Jacobs, jr. il U S Camera 26:50-1 Je '63
Encourage them to grow. T. Vahanian. Parents Mag 38:122 O '63
Family business in brief. A. P. Eliasberg. il N Y Times Mag p34 Jl 14 '63; p42 Je 21; p87-8 D 13 '64
Hard day's night of today's students. E. J. LeShan. il N Y Times Mag p 104+ S 27 '64
Homes that nurture intellect; with study-discussion program, by D. B. Harris and E. S. Harris. W. G. Hollister. bibliog il PTA Mag 57:8-10, 36 My '63
How to test a baby's intelligence. il Sci Digest 55:8-11 Ja '64
Is it a problem or just a stage? C. Chilman. il Parents Mag 38:66-8 N '63
Kids should be bored sometimes. R. W. Wells. il Parents Mag 38:64-5+ N '63; Same abr. Read Digest 83:19+ N '63
Male and female; excerpts from Children tell stories: an analysis of fantasy. E. G. Pitcher. il Atlan 211:87-91 Mr '63
Moving toward maturity: the mind at 3+; with study-discussion program, by R. Strang. J. W. Kessler. bibliog il PTA Mag 57:22-4, 35 F '63
Play is child's work. A. Schwartz. il Parents Mag 38:74-5+ N '63
Problems are part of growing; with program for discussion group by M. R. Sherwin. M. Besser. il Parents Mag 39:14, 54-5+ D '64
Sentences, a clue to your child's development. F. R. Schreiber. il Todays Health 41:26-9+ Ap '63
They all fall down. M. R. Weisbord. il Parents Mag 38:54-5+ Mr '63
Three is a threshold. R. Kramer. il N Y Times Mag p 122+ O 18 '64
Up-and-coming threes. J. L. Hymes, jr. and T. Taylor. il Parents Mag 39:56-7 Je '64
What will they be when they grow up? with program for discussion group, by M. R. Sherwin. R. Brecher and E. Brecher. il Parents Mag 38:38, 62-3+ F '63
Why African babies are more intelligent. R. Dean and M. Geber. il Sci Digest 56:35-40 S '64
Why they never stick to anything; with program for discussion group by M. R. Sherwin. H. S. Arnstein. il Parents Mag 39:16, 52-3+ D '64
Will they outgrow it? with study-discussion program, by R. Strang. M. J. Barnes. bibliog il PTA Mag 58:8-10, 35 O '63
Wonderful world of two. J. L. Hymes, jr and T. Taylor. il Parents Mag 39:52-3 My '64
Worlds of innocence. H. Behn. il Horn Bk 39:21-9 F '63
You have to let your kids go! with study discussion program, by M. Smart. H. H. Work. il Parents Mag 39:16+, 60-1+ Mr '64
See also
Child study
United States—National institute of child health and human development

Hairdressing

See Hairdressing

Health

See Children—Care and hygiene; Health

Hospital care

See Hospital care

Hospitals

Giving hope. il Time 84:54 S 4 '64
Under pressure; Boston's Children's hospital medical center. il Newsweek 61:58-9 F 18 '63

Humor

See Humor

Jealousy

See Jealousy

Language

Children's language: word-phrase relationship. J. Huttenlocher. il Science 143:264-5 Ja 17 '64
From two to five, by K. Chukovsky, tr. and ed. by M. Morton. Review
Sat R 46:55-6 D 21 '63. K. Taylor
How babies learn to talk. E. H. Lenneberg. il Parents Mag 39:66-7+ S '64
How speech grows; with study-discussion program, by R. Strang. M. M. Lewis. bibliog il PTA Mag 59:8-10, 35 N '64
How your youngster learns to talk. R. Rogers. il Parents Mag 38:50-1+ Ap '63
Ka-platz; delight in the unexpected. W. Kelly. il Atlan 211:92-6 Mr '63
Sentences, a clue to your child's development. F. R. Schreiber. il Todays Health 41:26-9+ Ap '63

Law

Do children have rights? M. G. Paulsen. il PTA Mag 58:7-9 F '64
Guardianship: every child's right. I. Weissman. bibliog f Ann Am Acad 355:134-9 S '64
Helping the child who comes into conflict with the law. R. G. Farrow. Ann Am Acad 355:90-7 S '64
Judgment of Solomon; child custody proceedings. E. Balcomb. Christian Cent 82:106-10 Ja 27 '65
Licensing of child-care facilities. C. B. Corry. Ann Am Acad 355:128-33 S '64
See also
Juvenile courts
Parent and child (law)

Management and training

Affluent child; with study discussion program by the authors. D. Harris and E. Harris. bibliog PTA Mag 58:27-9, 35-6 Mr '64
Anger and rivalry in children: Dr Spock talks to a group of Redbook mothers. B. Spock. il Redbook 124:34-5+ Ja '65
Are you cheating your child out of a living? M. C. Kohler and A. Fontaine. il Good H 157:76-7+ S '63
Bringing up children: the American vs. the British way. E. Wintour. Harper 229:58-63 Ag '64; Discussion. 229:11-12 O '64
Captain Really and the fabulous stair-mounter. N. Hartshorne. il Harper 228:46-9 F '64
Casual touch; excerpt from Sixpence in her shoe. P. McGinley. Ladies Home J 81:22+ Jl '64
Child and the society; excerpt from Development in early childhood: the preschool years. D. B. Gardner. Sch & Soc 92:157-61 Ap 4 '64
Child care created by mother. A. Eisenberg and H. Eisenberg. il Ladies Home J 81:56-7+ Je '64
Children are people too! W. Abraham. il Todays Health 43:28-9+ Ja '65
Chores that children like. S. H. Fraiberg. il Parents Mag 39:58-9+ Ap '64
Chores, they still breed character. G. Hechinger. il N Y Times Mag p50 Ag 9 '64
Conscience and character; with study-discussion program, by R. Strang. G. Langdon and I. W. Stout. bibliog il PTA Mag 58:4-6, 35 F '64
Discipline: where fathers fail. B. Spock. il Redbook 123:48-9+ Jl '64
Don't be afraid to act like a parent. M. B. Hoover. il Parents Mag 40:52-4+ Ja '65
Don't make tragedies out of trifles. A. McColl. Farm J 88:93 My '64
Don't rush them out of childhood; with group discussion program, by E. J. LeShan. M. A. Wessel. bibliog il Parents Mag 39:18+, 48-9+ O '64
Don't underestimate your children. il Farm J 88:56+ Je '64
Expectations not great enough. L. Wainwright. Life 58:19 Ja 8 '65
Family business. J. W. Levin. il N Y Times Mag p 100 D 8 '63
Family business in brief. A. P. Eliasberg. il N Y Times Mag p79-80 My 17 '64
Family business in brief. R. Kramer. il N Y Times Mag p39 Ja 3 '65
Family clinic. See issues of Parents' magazine & better homemaking
Forgive the little children. J. Wellington. il PTA Mag 58:12-14 Je '64
Good character is made, not born. M. E. Goodman. il Parents Mag 39:54-5+ O '64
Growing pains. See issues of Today's health
Helping the unhappy child. T. D. Engel. il Redbook 121:36 My '63
How my ideas have changed. B. Spock. il Redbook 121:51-5+ O '63
How strict should parents be? J. E. Laird and D. B. Harris. il Parents Mag 39:35+ Ag '64
How to ask the right questions about your child. B. Bettelheim. il Parents Mag 38:58-9+ F '63
How to head off tantrums. I. T. Comfort. il Parents Mag 38:60-1+ D '63
How we manage with eight. R. Weber. il Farm J 88:94 My '64
Janie found a big idea in the attic. L. Wetzel. Farm J 87:62 Mr '63
Little frustration won't hurt. J. W. Levin. il N Y Times Mag p 106+ N 17 '63
Mother, I'd rather do it myself! il Am Home 67:21 S '64
Mud and children. il Farm J 88:90 My '64

CHILDREN—Management and training—*Continued*
Needed: more good parents. J. F. Molloy. il NEA J 52:42-6 S '63
New upper class, the kids. M. Mannes. Vogue 142:46-7+ Jl '63
Nicest thing that happened today; ending the day with pleasant thoughts; reprint. Farm J 88:85 O '64
Organization child; with study-discussion program. D. Harris and E. Harris. bibliog il PTA Mag 57:22-4, 35 Ap '63
Our children in these times. J. L. Hymes, jr. Farm J 87:91-2 F '63
Parents who care, more or less. K. Erickson. il PTA Mag 58:25-7 Je '64
Puppy and biscuit; American versus British system. il Newsweek 63:52 Ja 27 '64
Recipe for raising a good cook. H. Hermann. il Parents Mag 39:55+ Ja '64
Relearning what permissive means. J. L. Hymes, jr. il N Y Times Mag p91 O 27 '63
Revolution in the nursery. A. P. Eliasberg. il N Y Times Mag p61-3 Je 9 '63
Rules for teen-agers: a new social code; Parents council of Washington. il U S News 57:4 D 21 '64
Saying I'm sorry is not enough. R. W. Bacmeister. il Parents Mag 38:60-1+ Mr '63
Self feeding's so easy a baby can do it. A. Swinfen. il Parents Mag 38:60-1+ N '63
Shop along with baby. M. Bernath. il Parents Mag 39:48-50+ Ja '64
Should boys be taught to fight back? J. A. Moran. il Parents Mag 39:44-5+ Je '64
Slowing down the social pace. G. Hechinger. il N Y Times Mag p99 Ap 14 '63
Talking time. R. R. Wilson. Parents Mag 39:79 Jl '64
Ten ways to good discipline without spanking. B. J. Carollo. Parents Mag 38:62+ Ap '63
Toddlers can be taught more than you think. M. K. Frey. il Parents Mag 38:56-7+ My '63; Same abr. with title Children can be taught life, early. Read Digest 83:95-6 Jl '63
Toilet teaching made easy. T. B. Brazelton. il Parents Mag 38:46-7+ Je '63
We have our own home beauty shop. A. Eby. il Parents Mag 39:84 Jl '64
We're bigger than they are! J. B. Kelley. America 109:628-30 N 16 '63
What parents ask most about children. J. H. Pollack. il Todays Health 41:24-7+ F '63
Whatever happened to please? E. S. Ringold. il N Y Times Mag p49-51 D 15 '63
Why did my mother give me away? P. Streit. il N Y Times Mag p53+ Ja 24 '65
You have to say no! E. J. LeShan. il Parents Mag 38:38-9+ Ag '63
Your baby is a high achiever. M. Bernath. il Parents Mag 39:64-5+ F '64
Your child. See issues of Redbook to September. 1963
See also
Childrens allowances
Corporal punishment
Discipline
Honesty
Moral education
Occupations for children
Parent-child relationship

Ancedotes, facetiae, satire, etc.

In one era and out the other: excerpts from Profession housewife. P. McGinley. il Ladies Home J 81:42+ Ap '64

Bibliography

Books for parents; comp. by P. Pinson. See issues of Parents' magazine & better homemaking

Memories

See Reminiscence

Mortality

See also
Infant mortality

Nutrition

Are we drinking too much milk? with special diet for infants. W. W. Sackett, jr. Sci Digest 53:19-25 Ap '63
Everyday nutrition (cont) Parents Mag 38:50 F; 135 Mr; 116 My; 97 Je '63
Feeding the allergic child; with recipes. A. Yenne. il Parents Mag 39:57-8+ My '64
Feeding the younger traveler. B. M. Stover. il Parents Mag 38:72+ My '63
In these schools the popular drink is milk. J. Bickers. il Farm J 87:46 Jl '63
Meal planning for children allergic to wheat, milk and eggs; with recipes. R. Noonan. il Parents Mag 39:59+ My '64
No feeding problems at our house. K. Kuperstock. il Parents Mag 38:69-71+ My '63
Our underweight children. L. W. Sauer. il PTA Mag 58:21-2 Mr '64
Should baby diet, too? P. W. Goldman. il N Y Times Mag p79-80 Ap 12 '64
Teen-agers need to eat more fruit, vegetables. Sci N L 87:25 Ja 9 '65
Three fabulous eaters and how they grew. P. T. Overbeck. il Parents Mag 39:80+ S '64
Today's research for babies' future. M. B. Keiser. il Parents Mag 39:20+ N '64
Twenty questions about children's eating. L. B. Ames and F. L. Ilg. il Am Home 67:32+ S '64
Water intake of normal children. J. S. Walker and others. bibliog il Science 140:890-1 My 24 '63
Why some children hate meals. Sci Digest 56:54-5 Ag '64

Occupations

See Occupations for children

Only child problem

What parents ask about the only child. M. J. E. Senn. McCalls 91:46+ Je '64

Photographs

Children's pictures, for a cause. S. Szasz. il Pop Phot 52:72-5+ Mr '63
Horse-happy Hansen. I. Hansen. Look 28:99-101 Mr 24 '64
Opera's children; a Metropolitan family album. Opera N 28:13-16+ F 1 '64
Pet parade; Princeton, N.J. U S Camera 26:51-3 Jl '63
Pictures to read by; photographs from Joy of children. M. R. Weiss. Sat R 47:40-2 N 21 '64

Preparation for medical and dental care

No fears, no tears at the dentist's. A. Schwartz. il Parents Mag 39:54-5+ N '64

Psychiatry

See Child psychiatry

Psychology

See Child study

Religion

Crisis of faith, by P. Babin. Review
Commonweal 79:409-10 D 27 '63. W. J. Wood
Fountain filled with blood. R. Drake. Christian Cent 80:432-6 Ap 3 '63
See also
First communion

Sayings

And how are your little red constables? R. N. Rood. PTA Mag 59:31 O '64
Children and love. L. Miller. il Redbook 123:58-9+ S '64
Child's garden of misinformation; excerpts. A. Linkletter. il McCalls 90:58 F; 70 Mr '63; 91:70-1 Ja; 58 F; 48+ Mr; 74+ Ap; 70 My; 66 Je; 127 Ag; 59 S '64
Congress, it's my daddy. L. Miller. il Redbook 121:50-1+ Ag '63
Editor's notebook. M. S. Fenner. NEA J 53:78 Ap '64
From the world of Ivan jr; excerpts from From two to five, ed. by J. W. Levin. K. Chukovsky. il N Y Times Mag p22 D 29 '63
Out of the mouths of babes. Parents Mag 39:32 O; 36 N; 30 D '64
What are Americans like? European school childrens observations. J. Robbins. il Redbook 122:56-7+ D '63
What are little boys made of? W. McCaslin. il Read Digest 84:131-3 Je '64
See also
Children's opinions

Sex instruction

See Sex instruction

Social and economic status

Attack on poverty. C. G. Norris. bibliog Horn Bk 40:364-9 Ag '64
Elementary school in the city: a conference report. Sch Life 45:26-34 Je '63
Homes affect mentality. Sci N L 84:210 O 5 '63
See also
Socially handicapped children

Speech

See Children—Language

Suicide

See Suicide

CHILDREN—*Continued*

Surgery

Plastic and reconstructive surgery for children. L. W. Sauer. PTA Mag 58:33-4 Ap '64
See also
Orthopedia

Training

See Children—Management and training

Africa

African babies alert. Sci N L 85:125 F 22 '64
Why African babies are more intelligent. R. Dean and M. Geber. il Sci Digest 56:35-40 S '64

Hong Kong

Hong Kong heartbeat. R. Emerson. il Travel 122:43-4 O '64

Japan

Thousand cranes. B. J. Lifton. il Horn Bk 39:211-16 Ap '63
Tokyo afternoon: to Ueno park to see the children. il Sunset 133:53 O '64

Russia

Child care in Russia: better than ours? M. J. E. Senn. il McCalls 90:40+ Mr '63
What are Americans like? what are Russians like? answers of children in the Soviet Union and United States. B. Asbell. il Redbook 123:52-3+ O '64

United States

Children's crusades in Alabama and Missouri. Christian Cent 80:667 My 22 '63
What are Americans like? what are Russians like? answers of children in the Soviet Union and United States. B. Asbell. il Redbook 123:52-3+ O '64

CHILDREN, Abandoned. See Foundlings

CHILDREN, Adoption of. See Adoption

CHILDREN, Backward
Help for retarded children. il Changing T 18:37-40 Mr '64
Help is a warm puppy; Chicago pet shop of Bob Terese and Corinne Owen. J. Graham and J. Poling. il Ladies Home J 80:28+ N '63
Image of the student in basic education. E. Armstead, jr. Negro Hist Bul 26:174-5 F '63
Marley's ghost. A. R. Doolittle. il NEA J 52:44-5 D '63
Opening doors for the retarded child. K. B. Oettinger. il N Y Times Mag p68-9 My 12 '63
Struggle to mend children's minds. il Ebony 19:58-62+ S '64
These least of the flock. America 111:796 D 19 '64
Where mentally retarded children start new lives; Warren G. Murray children's center, Centralia, Ill. H. G. Earl. il Todays Health 42:26-31 N '64
See also
Mentally handicapped children

Education

Expression through observation. A. Fredette. il Sch Arts 64:22 O '64
Extreme situation: dropouts return to school. P. Goodman. New Repub 149:7 O 19 '63
New horizons for retarded children. R. Carson. il Parents Mag 39:46-7+ D '64
Planning for the educable mentally retarded. H. Goldstein. NEA J 53:34-5 My '64
Teaching machines and the mentally retarded. L. S. Blackman. il Sch Life 46:10-12 N '63
Who makes a menace out of Johnny? R. E. Loewe. il Sat R 46:64-5+ Je 15 '63; Discussion. 46:40-1 Jl 20 '63
See also
Special classes and special schools

CHILDREN, Blind. See Blind

CHILDREN, Crippled. See Cripples

CHILDREN, Cruelty to. See Cruelty to children

CHILDREN, Deformed. See Deformities

CHILDREN, Delinquent. See Juvenile delinquency

CHILDREN, Education of. See Education of children

CHILDREN, Exceptional
College and university programs for the preparation of teachers of exceptional children; with list of institutions. R. P. Mackie and others. Sch Life 45:29-35 Mr '63

CHILDREN, Feral. See Children, Wild

CHILDREN, Gifted
Are we rejecting our creative children? C. Carner. il Todays Health 42:20-3+ F '64
Artist of the month. O. P. Baker. Sch Arts 63:37-8 Ja '64
Artist; paint prodigy J. E. Love. il Ebony 18:115-16+ Mr '63
Be glad your child is different. M. Mead. il Parents Mag 39:70-1+ S '64
Challenge of the gifted. K. Levin. il N Y Times Mag p41-2 Ag 2 '64
Gifted and the creative student. P. A. Witty. bibliog f Sch & Soc 92:183-5 Ap 18 '64
Guarding the gifts of the gifted. J. Whitbread. il N Y Times Mag p92+ My 19 '63
How we discourage creative children. J. K. Lagemann. il Redbook 120:44-5+ Mr '63; Same abr. with title Your child may be more gifted than you think. Read Digest 82:245-6+ My '63
Limits to deviant behavior in the gifted. R. Kelley. il Sch Life 47:4-6 O '64
Living with a genius. L. Strong. il N Y Times Mag p53-4 F 16 '64
Prodigy; eleven year old M. Grost at Michigan state university. il Newsweek 64:79 O 12 '64
Project talent. J. C. Flanagan. il NEA J 53:8-10 Ja '64
Put away your blocks; ten year old Michael Grost enrolls as a regular M.S.U. student. il Time 84:80 O 9 '64
Remarkable life of a little genius; six-year-old Peter Winston. G. Millstein. il Sat Eve Post 237:32+ D 19 '64
Rise of his rage to learn; Barry Wichmann. J. Estes. il por Life 57:80+ D 4 '64
Speaking out; stop pampering gifted children. B. Bettelheim. Sat Eve Post 237:8+ Ap 11 '64; Reply. C. Jencks. New Repub 150:26-8 Ap 25 '64; Rejoinder. 150:29-30 My 9 '64
Virtuoso on the rise. il Ebony 18:124-6 Ap '63
What is a creative child? D. B. Thompson. il Am Home 67:28+ S '64
What you can do about an underachiever. M. Grant. il Parents Mag 38:56-7+ Mr '63
What's happening in education? creative child. W. D. Boutwell. PTA Mag 57:26 Je '63
See also
Children as musicians
High school students, Mentally superior
Special classes and special schools

Education

Why not give your kids a better chance? schools challenging able and ambitious. G. W. Wormley. il Farm J 88:32-3+ S '64

CHILDREN, Handicapped
Disease and delinquency. R. I. Jaslow and G. Ebling, jr. il PTA Mag 57:18-20 Je '63
Handicapped child. C. R. Gardipee. bibliog f Ann Am Acad 355:121-7 S '64
Helping hand for Carol. C. Mallison. il Parents Mag 39:66+ Mr '64

Education

Angels. S. Plapinger. il Ladies Home J 81:47-51 My '64
Education combined with rehabilitation; Institute for the crippled and disabled, New York city. il Arch Rec 133:180-1 My '63
Education of handicapped children. il Sch Life 46:10-13 My '64
Exceptional children's art: symposium, ed. by G. Barlow. il Sch Arts 63:2-38 Ja '64
Physically handicapped in the regular classroom. D. Waleski. il NEA J 53:12-16 D '64
Provisions for handicapped children: P.L. 88-164. Sch Life 46:5 D '63
See also
Institutes for the achievement of human potential, Philadelphia

CHILDREN, Illegitimate. See Illegitimacy

CHILDREN, Mentally handicapped. See Mental handicapped children

CHILDREN, Mentally ill. See Mentally ill

CHILDREN, Mentally superior. See Children, Gifted

CHILDREN, Missing. See Missing persons

CHILDREN, Painting of. See Portrait painting

CHILDREN, Photography of. See Photography of children

CHILDREN, Precocious. See Children, Gifted

CHILDREN, Preschool. See Preschool children

CHILDREN, Problem. See Problem children

CHILDREN, Refugee. See Refugee children

CHILDREN, Runaway. See Runaway boys and girls

CHILDREN, Sick. See Sick, The

CHILDREN, Timid. See Timidity
CHILDREN, Underprivileged. See Children—Social and economic status
CHILDREN, Unwanted
Tragedy of the unwanted child. A. F. Guttmacher. Parents Mag 39:43+ Je '64
CHILDREN, Wild
Dispute tales of children raised by wild animals; feral children. il Sci Digest 53: 32-4 Mr '63
CHILDREN and adults. See Child-adult relationship
CHILDREN and art
We found more than mummies. D. Wilson. il House B 105:204-5 My '63
CHILDREN and death
Children and death. B. Spock. Redbook 122: 36+ Ap '64
Child's-eye view of life and death. M. J. E. Seen. il McCalls 91:64+ Ap '64
Legacy. F. Woodward. Redbook 120:142 Ap '63
CHILDREN and music. See Music and children
CHILDREN and parents. See Parent-child relationship
CHILDREN and race relations. See Interracial cooperation
CHILDREN and religion. See Children—Religion
CHILDREN and strangers
Keep them safe from child molesters; block parents. P. K. McCauley. il Parents Mag 39:50-1+ D '64
Teachers' trading post; protection of children from the dangerous stranger. NEA J 54:56 Ja '65
When the police welcome false alarms; child molesters. G. Marten. PTA Mag 57:30-1 My '63
CHILDREN and television. See Television broadcasting and children
CHILDREN and war. See War and children
CHILDREN as actors
Children caught in adult dramas. il Life 54: 97-100+ F 8 '63
Scholastic teacher interviews: James Allen Jones; ed. by H. Langer. J. A. Jones. il Sr Schol 84:10T-11T F 28 '64
CHILDREN as artists. See Childrens art
CHILDREN as authors
Humphrey the Humpher; gift to central children's room of the Tucson public library. E. Schunk. il Wilson Lib Bul 39:164 O '64
CHILDREN as guests. See Guests
CHILDREN as models
Artists' model children. il N Y Times Mag p 104+ Je 7 '64
Children for rent by the hour. M. Hall. il McCalls 90:90-1+ Ag '63
Family affair: the story of two little models and how they grew. il Mlle 58:76-9 D '63
CHILDREN as musicians
Fiddling legions: Suzuki's child violinists. il Newsweek 63:73 Mr 23 '64
Prodigies. M. Mayer. il Esquire 61:106-7+ My '64
Small-fry violinists. il Look 28:78-80 Jl 14 '64
Wonderful world of Stevie Wonder. il Ebony 18:99-100+ Jl '63
CHILDREN as photographers
Angry young man with a camera; interview. S. Shore. il U S Camera 26:52-3 Je '63
Camera hobby for your child. Bet Hom & Gard 43:20 Ja '65
Innocent camera. E. Leos. il Sch Arts 63:8-15 Mr '64
Instamatic goes to school. B. Chambless. il Pop Phot 55:58-9+ O '64
Kids and cameras go together. P. Korn. il U S Camera 26:28-9+ Je '63
CHILDREN from their games; drama. See Shaw, I.
CHILDREN in art
Children in clay. A. Entis. il Design 64:200-1 Je '63
CHILDREN of migrant laborers

Education

Disadvantaged newcomers to the city. J. M. O'Hara. NEA J 52:25-7 Ap '63
Education for our rural slums. C. H. Karraker. Sch & Soc 91:276-7 O 5 '63
Problems and trends in migrant education. G. E. Haney. Sch Life 45:5-9 Jl '63
CHILDRENS allowances
How do you teach a child the value of money? Bet Hom & Gard 41:8+ F '63
Much ado about money; with group discussion program, by E. J. LeShan. E. N. Ryan and D. R. McNeil. il Parents Mag 39:20, 44-5+ My '64
What parents ask about children's allowances. M. J. E. Senn. il McCalls 90:46+ Ag '63
When children discover money. A. M. Daniels. N Y Times Mag p 109-10 S 13 '64

Anecdotes, facetiae, satire, etc.

Junior capitalists, arise! excerpt from While the humour is on me. J. D. Sheridan. Read Digest 84:36C Ap '64
CHILDRENS amusements
Again it's the tops. E. Merriam. il N Y Times Mag p 14-15 D 22 '63
How to amuse a shut-in child. il Todays Health 42:26-9 D '64
Parent's guide to childhood pleasures; excerpt from Fun for children and parents. A. Schwartz. il Redbook 123:75-82 Ag '64
What will they be when they grow up? with program for discussion group, by M. R. Sherwin. R. Brecher and E. Brecher. il Parents Mag 38:38, 62-3+ F '63
See also
Camping—Activities
Christmas projects
Games
Pinatas
Play
Playgrounds, Home—Equipment
Recreation—Activities
Skateboarding
Story telling
Toys
Vacation projects

Photographs

Child's guide to sport in New York; photographs by B. Davidson; with account by G. Rogin. Sports Illus 20:66-76+ Ap 20 '64
CHILDRENS art
Artist; paint prodigy. J. E. Love. il Ebony 18:115-16+ Mr '63
Buttons, birds and beasts. il Design 64:195 Je '63
By children abroad for children here; display to mark the opening of the new headquarters of the U.S. committee for UNICEF. il N Y Times Mag p22-3 Je 23 '63
Cheerful pillows display children's art. il Sunset 134:88+ Ja '65
Child sets a joyous pattern; grown-ups wear schoolgirl art. il Life 54:47-8 Mr 22 '63
Children of all ages create in a variety of media. E. Madsen. il Sch Arts 62:8-11 My '63
Christmas is craft time; excerpts from Fun crafts for children. il Recreation 57:508-9 D '64
David's stonewares. K. R. Beittel. il Sch Arts 63:23-7 S '63
Drawing approaches for the intermediate grades. M. Kutila. il Sch Arts 62:3-6 Je '63
Evaluating children's art. E. W. Eisner. il Sch Arts 63:20-2 S '63
Exceptional children's art; symposium, ed. by G. Barlow. il Sch Arts 63:2-38 Ja '64
Film-maker; D. Wise, nine-year-old cartoonist. New Yorker 39:25-7 F 15 '64
Floating designs; fifth grade projects. G. Turner and F. Major. il Design 65:104-7 Ja '64
Graduation from kindergarten. J. Hendry. il Sch Arts 63:3 Je '64
Happiness goes on and on; children to draw their own ideas of happiness. il Life 55: 67-8+ O 25 '63
Hurricane in paper collage. E. M. Colbert. il Sch Arts 63:40 O '63
Key to action. M. McMullan. il Sch Arts 63: 5-7 Mr '64
Let's carve a log; fourth grade project in wood sculpture. H. J. McWhinnie. il Sch Arts 63:16-17 F '64
Look, the parade is coming. M. Allen. il Sch Arts 63:13 D '63
Making faces. O. Kitt. il Sch Arts 63:33 O '63
Mark's mob; exhibitors of crayon drawings at open-air art show in Greenwich Village. New Yorker 40:53-4 O 10 '64
Our new school. J. O. Mitchell. il Sch Arts 63:10-11 N '63
Painting, a fundamental art experience for children. W. Stewart. il Sch Arts 63:21-3 N '63
Plan a children's art show. S. James. il Am Home 67:26 N '64
Skyscraper impressions. A. K. MacDonald. il Sch Arts 62:37-8 Ap '63
Summer to remember. F. Green. il Sch Arts 64:14-16 S '64
That lady with a smile; youngsters speak out about the Mona Lisa. il N Y Times Mag p34 S 1 '63
Try totem poles; cardboard mailing tube. F. M. Major. il Design 64:173 Mr '63
We went out to see. M. J. Reinhard. il Sch Arts 64:5-9 Ja '65
Young artists exhibit; third annual Young artists exhibition at Gimbels, Philadelphia. B. Segal. il Sch Arts 64:38-9 Ja '65

CHILDRENS art—*Continued*

Competition

Artist of the month. O. P. Baker. il Sch Arts 63:37-8 Ja '64

Exhibitions

Art of the mentally retarded on exhibition. P. Vandervoort. il Sch Arts 63:10-12 Ja '64
Beauty around our town; art show at Moorpark elementary school, Calif. J. Stillion. il Sch Arts 63:22-4 F '64
Cave for a child. Des Moines art center. Junior art museum exhibit. D. Parker. il Sch Arts 63:14-18 My '64
Children's dream of Christmas. il N Y Times Mag p 10-11 D 22 '63
Junior gallery; Laguna Beach art festival. M. J. Haden. il Sch Arts 63:4-7 Je '64
Magic world of art; a children's center for art appreciation; Tucson public schools spring festival. N. Krevitsky. il Sch Arts 63:11-16 Ap '64
Signs of spring. E. B. Booker. il Sch Arts 62: 35-6 Ap '63
Student art; International school art program. il NEA J 53:31-3 Mr '64
View of two cities; student exchange exhibition Oakland, Calif. and Lisbon, Portugal. D. E. Morrison. il Sch Arts 63:28-30 F '64

CHILDRENS ballets. See Ballets
CHILDRENS beds. See Beds; Cribs (beds)
CHILDRENS book clubs. See Book clubs
CHILDREN'S book council
CBC introduces materials for vacation reading; with editorial comment. il Pub W 185:131, 137 F 24 '64
Children's book council surveys newspaper reviews. Pub W 183:36 My 27 '63
Children's library for adults. M. Barr. il Library J 88:832-3 F 15 '63
Varieties of binding shown at Childrens' book council library. il Pub W 183:126-7 F 18 '63
CHILDRENS book departments. See Booksellers and bookselling—Childrens literature
CHILDRENS book editors. See Editors and editing
CHILDRENS book exhibits. See Book exhibits
CHILDRENS book fairs. See Book fairs
CHILDRENS book talks. See Book reviews
CHILDRENS book week. See Book week
CHILDRENS books. See Childrens literature
CHILDRENS bookshops. See Booksellers and bookselling—Childrens literature
CHILDREN'S bureau. See United States—Children's bureau
CHILDRENS camps. See Camps
CHILDRENS candy aspirin. See Aspirin
CHILDRENS choirs. See Choirs
CHILDRENS clothes. See Clothing and dress—Children
CHILDRENS costume. See Costume
CHILDRENS courts. See Juvenile courts
CHILDRENS dictionaries. See Dictionaries, Childrens
CHILDRENS diseases. See Children—Diseases
CHILDRENS emotions. See Emotions
CHILDRENS encyclopedias. See Encyclopedias
CHILDRENS fears. See Fear
CHILDRENS football. See Football, Childrens
CHILDRENS friends. See Playmates
CHILDRENS furniture. See Furniture, Childrens
CHILDRENS games. See Games
CHILDRENS gardens
Adventures in the vegetable kingdom. E. Finnegan. il Parents Mag 39:50-1+ My '64
Children grow in gardens. I. Zucker. il Pop Gard 15:34-5 Jl '64
Garden for every child, Royal botanical gardens, Hamilton. L. Laking. il Flower Grower 51:36+ F '64
How does your garden grow? il Bet Hom & Gard 42:96 Mr '64
Let's bring children into gardens. H. G. Wendler. il Horticulture 42:36-7+ My '64
CHILDRENS gifts. See Gifts for children
CHILDRENS haircuts. See Haircutting
CHILDRENS historical literature. See Historical literature
CHILDRENS homesickness. See Nostalgia
CHILDREN'S hospital, Boston. See Children—Hospitals
CHILDRENS hotels. See Hotels, taverns, etc.
CHILDRENS humor. See Humor

CHILDRENS international summer villages
I stayed home and went around the world. H. C. Bowman. il Sr Schol 84:10T Mr 20 '64
CHILDRENS letters (by children) See Letters by children
CHILDRENS librarians
It's this way, kid! D. C. Davis. Horn Bk 40:523-7 O '64
Reading is the key. R. H. Viguers. Horn Bk 40:147 Ap '64
Warm puppy is not happiness. J. Shera. Wilson Lib Bul 38:409 Ja '64
CHILDRENS libraries. See Libraries, Childrens; Libraries, Private
CHILDRENS literature
Adult children's books. E. M. Graves. il Commonweal 78:253-4 My 24 '63
Album and the artist. N. Streatfeild. il Horn Bk 40:159-61 Ap '64
Behind the boom in books. M. P. Archer. Sr Schol 85:17T O 7 '64
Bobbsey twins at an orgy. W. J. Smith. Nation 198:633-5 Je 22 '64
Carroll B. Colby and his factual books for youngsters. il Pub W 183:128-9 F 18 '63
Children's book issue; symposium. il Wilson Lib Bul 38:154-72+ O '63
Children's reading; symposium. il Wilson Lib Bul 39:140-67 O '64
Choosing the right book today: children's books; symposium, with editorial comment. bibliog il Library J 89:4963-75 D 15 '64
Creating books; condensation of address, May, 1963. L. Lenski. il Library J 88:3987-90+ O 15 '63
Cry and the creation. M. DeJong. il Horn Bk 39:197-206 Ap '63
Dark corners of the mind: Dickens' childhood reading. H. Stone. il Horn Bk 39:306-21 Je '63
Dearest freshness deep down things; excerpt from address, March 14, 1964. E. Cameron. il Horn Bk 40:459-72 O '64
Dotty Dimple and the fiction award. M. Bacon. il Atlan 211:130-3 Mr '63
Expansion plans for Dell's Harlin Quist books; paperback juveniles. Pub W 185:40-1 Je 1 '64
Faraway lurs and the moon by night. R. H. Viguers. Horn Bk 39:165-6 Ap '63
Father of the Wizard of Oz. D. P. Mannix. il Am Heritage 16:36-47+ D '64
For all boys. F. C. Smith. Writer 77:22-4 N '64
Good bunnies always obey; books for American children. J. Epstein. Commentary 35: 112-22 F '63; Discussion. 36:169-71 Ag '63
Gresham's law of literature; simplified books. A. Loftis and R. Marshall. il Sat R 46:64-5 S 21 '63
Happy days are here again; Happy lion series. H. Frankel. Sat R 47:24-5 Ag 22 '64
He makes c-a-t spell big money. il Bsns W p72-3 Jl 18 '64
Imaginary correspondence; B. Potter and a present day children's book editor. R. Godden. Horn Bk 39:369-75 Ag '63
Information trap. C. H. Bishop. Commonweal 79:228-9 N 15 '63
It's this way, kid! D. C. Davis. Horn Bk 40:523-7 O '64
Key, the door, the road; address, March 20, 1964. M. L'Engle. Horn Bk 40:260-8 Je '64
Kids' books: a happy few amid the junk. R. Wallace. il Life 57:112-14+ D 11 '64
Learning bigotry: anti-Semitism in books for children. C. H. Bishop. Commonweal 80: 264-6 My 22 '64
Let's stop shortchanging young readers; excerpt from Hearth has its reasons. P. McGinley. il Read Digest 84:142-4 Ap '64
Little Toot's twenty-fifth birthday. H. Gramatky. il Horn Bk 40:518-19 O '64
Margin for surprise, by R. H. Viguers. Review
Horn Bk 40:640-1 D '64. F. C. Sayers
Message from Green Knowe; excerpt from address. L. M. Boston. il Horn Bk 39:259-64 Je '63
My father was Uncle Wiggily. R. Garis. il Sat Eve Post 237:64-6 D 19 '64
New books for the slum child. P. J. Groff. Wilson Lib Bul 38:345-8 D '63
New children's books. R. H. Viguers. Harper 227:118+ D '63
News from Narnia. L. H. Smith. Horn Bk 39:470-3 O '63
Nonsensical world of Dr Seuss. D. Freeman. il McCalls 92:115+ N '64
Not recommended. R. H. Viguers. Horn Bk 39:76-8 F '63
Nuts to excelsior. C. M. Craig. Library J 89:4989 D 15 '64
On causes and clouds. R. H. Viguers. Horn Bk 40:249 Je '64

CHILDRENS literature—*Continued*
Paperbacks in the classroom. H. L. Stocker. Library J 89:318-19+ Ja 15 '64
Password is book. F. Sullivan. il PTA Mag 58:28-30 Je '64
Paths to the mountain. D. D. Collier. Horn Bk 39:322-6 Je '63
Power of a child's book; Little red lighthouse. H. H. Swift. il Sat R 46:43 My 11 '63
Rudolph was almost Rollo; Rudolph the red-nosed reindeer. il Newsweek 64:80 D 7 '64
Spreading chestnut tree. A. Dalgliesh. Sat R 46:53 Ag 17 '63
Story of the three bears and the man who didn't write it. J. M. Lexau. il Horn Bk 40:68-94 F '64
Teacher's image in children's literature. F. H. Hektoen. Sr Schol 83:13T O 4 '63
Time of trial, by H. Burton. Review
  Horn Bk 40:302 Je '64. R. H. Viguers
What is a children's classic? A. Dalgliesh. Sat R 46:46 Je 22 '63
What should children read? Pub W 184:156 Jl 8 '63
Where did she come from? why did she go? Mary Poppins. P. L. Travers. il Sat Eve Post 237:76+ N 7 '64
Who'll kill the mockingbirds? D. C. Davis. Horn Bk 39:265-71 Je '63
Why I write for children. E. Unnerstad. Horn Bk 39:110 F '63
Why librarians dislike Oz; reprint. M. Gardner. Library J 88:834-6 F 15 '63; Discussion. 88:1196, 1708+, 3240 Mr 15, Ap 15, S 15 '63
Wild rose, briar rose. M. A. McMillan. il Horn Bk 39:622-8 D '63
Words make the book. R. Godden. il Ladies Home J 81:32+ Ja '64; Same. Writer 77:14-17 Jl '64
Writing the juvenile mystery. P. A. Whitney. Writer 76:14-18 Ap '63
See also
Book selection
Book week
Booksellers and bookselling—Childrens literature
Childrens periodicals
Childrens poetry
Childrens reading
Childrens stories
Fairy tales
Horn book magazine
Libraries, Childrens
Newbery medal
Paperback books
Picture books for children
Scientific literature for children

Anecdotes, facetiae, satire, etc.

In the act; excerpt from Exhibits round table, spoof on Image of the new librarian at ALA meeting. il Library J 89:4112-14 O 15 '64

Bibliography

America balances books for the children. E. Sheehan. America 109:634-8+ N 16 '63
ALA issues its annual list, Notable children's books. Pub W 183:29-30 Ap 1 '63; Same. A L A Bul 57:331-4 Ap '63; Library J 88:1740+ Ap 15 '63; PTA Mag 57:31-2 Je '63; Wilson Lib Bul 37:726+ My '63
Blithe spirits: some children's books for adults to give adults. L. Russ. il Pub W 186:28-31 S 14 '64
Booklist (title varies) comp. by R. H. Viguers and others. See issues of Horn book magazine
Books (cont) E. Maxwell. New Yorker 39:210-12+ N 30 '63; 40:207-10+ D 5 '64
Books for boys & girls; comp. by D. E. Leland. See issues of Parents' magazine & better homemaking
Books for boys and girls; titles published in the past six months. E. Sheehan. il America 110:848-51 Je 20 '64
Books for children: a Christmas list. C. Jackson. Atlan 214:160-4 D '64
Books for children and playful adults. G. Shalit. McCalls 91:48+ D '63
Books for young people. A. Dalgliesh. See issues of Saturday review
Books for younger readers. H. Finch. Sr Schol 82:11T Ap 17 '63
CSD picks fifty-plus children's books as notable reading for boys and girls. il Library J 89:1840-1 Ap 15 '64
Children's book show; 1961-2 choices of AIGA. S. M. Agnew. il Pub W 183:64 Ap 8 '63
Children's books. G. Shalit. il McCalls 91:92+ My '64
Children's books for Christmas giving. E. Sheehan. il America 111:664-73 N 21 '64
Children's books for Christmas giving. G. Shalit. il McCalls 92:90+ D '64
Children's books of 1962-64. NEA J 52:59+ N '63; 53:56-7+ N '64
Children's books; some leading titles to be published this spring. il Pub W 185:90-130 F 24 '64
Children's Christmas book bag. Christian Cent 80:1584-7 D 18 '63
Chosen for children. Christian Cent 81:1497-9 D 2 '64
Fifty nonfiction books children may enjoy. il Good H 157:177 D '63
For a child's library: a paperback book list. Library J 90:312-13 Ja 15 '65
French books for children. S. B. Vogel. Library J 88:4428-33 N 15 '63
Here's help in choosing books to give to children. R. B. Prowitt. il Am Home 67:28 D '64
Junior books appraised; ed. by E. L. Davis and others. See issues of Library journal
Leading children's books for fall. il Pub W 186:113-49 Jl 13 '64
Learning about poverty. C. H. Bishop. Commonweal 81:201-2 N 6 '64
Life guide (cont) il Life 55:15+ N 15 '63
Look northward! books by Canadians and about Canada, for American children and young adults. S. A. Egoff and R. A. Hagler. Library J 88:4421-8 N 15 '63
New books for the young. R. B. Prowitt. Am Home 66:20+ D '63
New fall children's books; comp. by E. L. Davis and P. H. Allen. Library J 89:4152-87 O 15 '64
New fall children's books; comp. by E. L. Davis and others. Library J 88:4028-66 O 15 '63
New spring children's books; comp. by K. Montgomery. Library J 89:1409-38 Mr 15 '64
New spring juvenile books; comp. by E. L. Davis and others. Library J 88:1320-55 Mr 15 '63
1964 Christmas books: advance reviews. P. H. Allen. il Library J 89:4115-17 O 15 '64
1963 Christmas books. il Library J 88:3996-8 O 15 '63
Notable children's books of 1963. il ALA Bul 58:307-10 Ap '64; Same. Pub W 185:61-2 Ap 27 '64; Wilson Lib Bul 38:710+ My '64
On beyond Notable; seventy-five additional 1962 juvenile books. P. H. Allen. Library J 88:2063-5 My 15 '63
Operation head start materials collection: preschool reading readiness program geared to the needs of the disadvantaged child. M. C. Bentley. il Library J 89:4606-7+ N 15 '64
Password is book. F. Sullivan. il PTA Mag 58:28-30 Je '64
Replacements for blacklisted series offered by small libraries project. Library J 89:4996 D 15 '64
Selected list of children's books. C. H. Bishop and E. M. Graves. il Commonweal 80:266-75 My 22 '64
Selected list of children's books. C. H. Bishop. il Commonweal 79:229-39 N 15 '63
Selected list of children's books. E. M. Graves. il Commonweal 78:254-63; 81:203-11 My 24 '63, N 6 '64
Selection of modern classics; comp. by the Office of children's services of the New York public library. Life 57:130 D 11 '64
Some leading children's books to be published this fall. il Pub W 184:107-44 Jl 8 '63
Some spring books for boys and girls. E. Sheehan. il America 108:804-7 Je 1 '63
Spring children's books. Christian Cent 80:746-9 Je 5 '63
Spring children's books. il Pub W 183:90-120 F 18 '63
Take these to your reader; SLJ names forty-three readable, notable, awardable children's books of 1963. il Library J 89:918-20 F 15 '64
Under cover. C. Stinnett. Ladies Home J 81:26+ D '64
See also
Bibliography—Bibliography—Childrens literature

Book reviews

See Book reviews

Censorship

See Censorship

Collectors and collecting

Toronto's historic collections; opening of new Boys and girls house. J. Thomson. Wilson Lib Bul 39:499 F '65

Exhibitions

See Book exhibits

CHILDRENS literature—*Continued*

Illustrations

See Illustration of books and periodicals

Technique

And then what happened? M. G. Clark. Writer 77:23-5 D '64
My heroine helped me. C. Harris. il Horn Bk 40:361-3 Ag '64
New kind of fiction; writing for the reluctant reader. N. R. Ainsworth. Writer 78:26-9 Ja '65
On three ways of writing for children; reprint. C. S. Lewis. Horn Bk 39:459-69 O '63

Bulgaria

Children's libraries; the Bulgarian way; Communist philosophy of juvenile literature. V. Haviland. Wilson Lib Bul 38:487 F '64

Russia

Children's literature in the Soviet Union. M. Rudolph. Horn Bk 40:646-50 D '64
From two to five; concerning book by K. Chukovsky. R. H. Viguers. Horn Bk 40:84-5 F '64

Underdeveloped areas

Children's books in developing countries; address. D. C. Smith, jr. il Horn Bk 39:36-49 F '63

CHILDRENS manners. See Courtesy; Etiquette

CHILDRENS market
Moppets and money. P. Korenvaes. Duns R 82:55 D '63
Small-fry boom. R. Lemon. il Sat Eve Post 237:58-63 D 19 '64

CHILDRENS museums
Museum of childhood. P. Murray. il Horn Bk 40:255-9 Je '64
See also
Brooklyn children's museum

CHILDRENS national book week. See Book week

CHILDRENS opinions
Skyscrapers, cowboys and skinny blondes; child's-eye view of life in America. P. W. Goldman. il N Y Times Mag p94+ N 29 '64
What are Americans like? what are Russians like? answers of children in the Soviet Union and United States. B. Asbell. il Redbook 123:52-3+ O '64
What kids say about rockets. H. Dunn. il Sci Digest 54:65-8 O '63
What kids say about science. H. Dunn. il Sci Digest 56:67-70 O '64

CHILDRENS parties
And one to groan on. J. L. O'Neill. il Am Home 67:17 S '64
Birthday party; with recipes. il McCalls 90:112-13+ F '63
Come to a candy mixer, a party for pint-size people. V. Stanton. il House B 105:152-3+ D '63
Fun and games for parties. E. Julius. il Parents Mag 39:40-1+ Ja '64
Fun with food parties. B. M. Stover. il Parents Mag 39:73+ Mr '64
How to give a birthday party. D. Molyneaux. il House B 105:235+ N '63
How to give three parties children will love. il Am Home 67:62 S '64
Kid catering; Parties unlimited. il Time 81:37 F 8 '63
Perle Mesta's party notebook. P. Mesta. il McCalls 91:26+ D '63
Return to paradise; club dance at YMCA, Seattle, Wash. B. Parks. il Recreation 57:363-4 S '64
Tempting backdrop for a children's party. il House & Gard 124:128-9 D '63
Tree trimming party for the young person and the young in heart. il House B 105:144-5 D '63
Wishing well Christmas party for children. P. Mesta. il McCalls 92:28 D '64
See also
Party favors

CHILDRENS periodicals
Can your reader identify? N. R. Ainsworth. Writer 77:22-4 My '64
New kind of fiction; writing for the reluctant reader. N. R. Ainsworth. Writer 78:26-9 Ja '65
See also
Highlights for children (periodical)

CHILDRENS pets. See Pets

CHILDRENS phonograph records. See Phonograph records—Childrens records

CHILDRENS plays
Persephone, Metropolitan museum of art. M. Marks. il Dance Mag 38:32-3 Je '64

Texts

Middle grades; lower grades. See issues of Plays

CHILDRENS poems (by children)
Horn book league. See issues of Horn book magazine
I never saw another butterfly. ed. by H. Volavkova. Review
Nation 199:411-12 N 30 '64. J. Richard
Magic of poetry. M. Chase. il NEA J 53:8-11 D '64

CHILDRENS poems (for children)
Sweet as a pickle and clean as a pig; a collection of verses for children. C. McCullers. il Redbook 124:49-56 D '64

CHILDRENS poetry
Poet in the playpen. X. J. Kennedy. Poetry 105:190-3 D '64
Transformation of a poet; John Ciardi. P. J. Groff. Horn Bk 40:153-8 Ap '64
Writing children's verse. A. Fisher. Writer 76:21-4 Ap '63
See also
Childrens poems (for children)

CHILDRENS press, incorporated
Field enterprises sues Childrens press. Pub W 184:247 Ag 26 '63

CHILDRENS private libraries. See Libraries, Private

CHILDRENS questions
Answer lady of space; M. S. Niehaus. M. Clapp. il Todays Health 41:20-1+ O '63
Big questions little ones ask. E. Elias. il Parents Mag 39:38-9+ Jl '64
What time is it in Brooklyn? J. Cook. il N Y Times Mag p93-4, O 4 '64

CHILDRENS reading
About books. E. Rudin. Library J 88:3880 O 15 '63
Another kind of camera. A. M. Tredup. il Horn Bk 39:30-5 F '63
Bringing books to children. P. Fenner. Library J 88:4823-5 D 15 '63
CBS introduces materials for vacation reading; with editorial comment. il Pub W 185:131, 137 F 24 '64
Children's reading; symposium. il Wilson Lib Bul 39:140-67 O '64
Former child objects. V. Schultheis. Wilson Lib Bul 37:552 Mr '63
Freedom to browse. B. Poll. il Library J 88:1734 Ap 15 '63
Get more books into the hands of more children. W. D. Boutwell. PTA Mag 59:18 D '64
Letter to parents. N. Larrick. il Sr Schol 84:8T F 14 '64
Massachusetts lns. want, will get more courses in children's reading; role of state Division of library extension. Library J 88:4830 D 15 '63
New books for the slum child. P. J. Groff. Wilson Lib Bul 38:345-8 D '63
New channels for book distribution through the schools. N. Larrick. ALA Bul 57:544-8 Je '63
New children's books. R. H. Viguers. Harper 227:118+ D '63
No eleventh book. M. A. McMillan. Horn Bk 40:251-4 Je '64
Remarkable success. D. Melcher. Library J 89:1836 Ap 15 '64
Sex and violence in books, magazines and television. B. Bettelheim. il Redbook 123:60-1+ My '64
Skip it; open letter to children on reading books. H. Sandburg. Horn Bk 40:86-7 F '64
What did I say, dear? new children's book author talks to herself. M. W. Rodman. il Library J 89:1385-6+ Mr 15 '64
Why not the Bobbsey twins? reprint. M. Beckman. il Library J 89:4612-13+ N 15 '64
Words make the book. R. Godden. il Ladies Home J 81:32+ Ja '64; Same. Writer 77:14-17 Jl '64
Your child and reading; reprint. D. H. Russell. il Todays Health 41:16 N '63
See also
Bibliotherapy
Books and reading
Childrens literature
Childrens periodicals
Comics (books, strips, etc)
Libraries, Childrens
Libraries, Childrens—Projects

CHILDREN'S repertory group. See Childrens plays

CHILDRENS rooms
Bright young bedrooms. D. Sevick. il Bet Hom & Gard 42:46-7 Ja '64
Case for apartness. il House & Gard 124:254-9+ N '63
Children's rooms designed for growing and dreaming. il House & Gard 126:184-7 S '64
Have a creative corner in your room. R. C. Jennette. il Sch Arts 62:33-5 Mr '63

CHILDRENS rooms—*Continued*
Rooms to grow in. E. T. Lawyer and D. Sevick. il Bet Hom & Gard 42:36-9 Ag '64
Study play sleep dens for school agers. il Pop Mech 119:124-31 My '63
Teen-ager's domain. G. O'Brien. il N Y Times Mag p82-3 N 10 '63
These kids love their rooms. J. Holmstrand. il Suc Farm 61:56-9 S '63
What are children's bedrooms made of? il Am Home 67:40-3 S '64
Young rooms: toddlers to teens. il Good H 157:108-16 Ag '63
See also
Nurseries

CHILDRENS sayings. See Children—Sayings

CHILDREN'S services division, American library association. See American library association—Children's services division

CHILDRENS shoes. See Shoes

CHILDRENS speech defects. See Speech defects

CHILDRENS sports. See Sports for children

CHILDREN'S spring book festival awards. See Rewards, prizes, etc.

CHILDRENS stories
Birthday party. G. Berriault. il Sat Eve Post 237:52-5 D 19 '64
When you write for tots. M. Grenier. Writer 77:24 Ap '64

Technique
See Childrens literature—Technique

CHILDREN'S story. See Clavell, J.

CHILDRENS success. See Success

CHILDRENS theater. See Theater, Childrens

CHILDRENS thefts. See Shoplifting

CHILDRENS wards. See Hospitals—Childrens wards

CHILDRENS workshops. See Workshops

CHILDRENS zoos. See Zoological gardens

CHILDRES, Robert
Victims. Harper 228:159-62 Ap '64

CHILDRESS, William
Floral tribute; poem. Mlle 56:219 Mr '63

CHILDS, Charles
Bearden: identification and identity. Art N 63:24-5+ O '64

CHILDS, Marquis William
How would you like to be secretary of state? NEA J 53:57 S '64
What should we tell our children about communism. por Parents Mag 38:66-7+ S '63
Without the consent of the governed. New Repub 150:23-4 Ap 11 '64

CHILE
See also
Atacama Desert
Ballet—Chile
Copper industry and trade—Chile
Elections—Chile
Fishing—Chile
Forests and forestry—Chile
Investments, Foreign (in Chile)
Political parties—Chile
Science—Chile
Tierra del Fuego
United Nations—Chile

Cultural relations
Clarifying an image. il Time 82:56 O 4 '63

Description and travel
Going places, finding things in Brazil, Chile and Peru. D. Beal. il House & Gard 124:270+ N '63

Economic conditions
Chile: an example of U.S. troubles in Latin America. il U S News 57:77-80 N 9 '64
Chile's goal: a doubled income. il U S News 57:76 S 21 '64
New hope for Chile? il Sr Schol 85:12-15 O 21 '64
Science and development in Chile; address, October 9, 1964. D. Rusk. Dept State Bul 51:634-7 N 2 '64

Foreign relations
Then there were three; breaking with Cuba. Newsweek 64:47 Ag 24 '64
To Russia with trade. Time 84:40 D 4 '64

Politics and government
And now to toil. il Time 84:35 N 20 '64
Bid by Marx. il Time 84:27 Ag 21 '64
Brief breathing spell: Frei program. Commonweal 81:4-5 S 25 '64
Chile: an example of U.S. troubles in Latin America. il U S News 57:77-80 N 9 '64
Chile enters a new era. D. W. Bray. Cur Hist 48:21-5+ Ja '65
Chile: revolution of good intentions. M. Wyman. Nation 199:320-1+ N 9 '64
Chile: the last, best hope. L. Gross. il Look 28:80+ Je 2 '64
Chile turns left. D. D. Ranstead. Commonweal 80:594-6 S 4 '64
Chile's leader: pro-American leftist. por U S News 57:21 S 21 '64
Choice for Chile: which way to go left? democratic left or Marxist. il Bsns W p48+ Ag 8 '64
Choice in Chile: left or far left? S. Rothman. il Reporter 31:26-9 Jl 2 '64; Reply. R. E. Zalles. 31:10 S 24 '64
Crucial choice; coming presidential election. il Time 83:50 Ap 17 '64
Elections in Chile. J. P. O'Neill. America 111:226 S 5 '64
First hurdle; Frei negotiates deal with U.S. copper companies. Newsweek 65:29-30 Ja 4 '65
Good news from South America; E. Frei elected president. Life 57:4 S 18 '64
In Chile, a swing to the left; top candidates: E. Frei and S. Allende. il U S News 57:20 S 14 '64
Moderate wins. il Sr Schol 85:30 S 23 '64
New frontiersmen; Frei and his aides. Newsweek 64:65 S 21 '64
New hope for Chile? il Sr Schol 85:12-15 O 21 '64
On the threshold. Newsweek 64:60-1 N 9 '64
Sure winner; three presidential candidates. Newsweek 64:44 Jl 13 '64
Will Chile go Communist? T. Armbrister. il Sat Eve Post 237:69-73 S 5'64
See also
Elections—Chile
Political parties—Chile

Religious institutions and affairs
News of the Christian world (cont) Christian Cent 80:184-6; 81:1472 F 6 '63; N 25 '64

Social conditions
My life as a Peace corps girl; ed. by A. St George. J. C. Boegli. il Good H 156:84-5+ Ap '63

CHILEAN national ballet. See Ballet—Chile

CHILEAN poetry
Five Chilean poets; with poems. J. Donoso. il Américas 16:15-20 My '64

Translations into English
Boy with a hare; tr. by B. Belitt. P. Neruda. Commonweal 81:449 D 25 '64
Four love poems; tr. by S. H. Hastie. P. Neruda. il Mlle 56:90-1 F '63

CHILI con carne. See Cookery—Meat

CHILKOVSKY, Nadia
20th century school of dance. B. Kevles. il por Dance Mag 38:20-2 My '64

CHILMAN, Catherine
Baby puts a strain on marriage. Parents Mag 38:48-9+ Je '63
Ease them into the teens. Parents Mag 39:38-9+ Ag '64
Honesty doesn't come naturally. Parents Mag 38:44-6+ Ag '63
Is it a problem or just a stage? Parents Mag 38:66-8 N '63
It's no fun to be fat. Parents Mag 38:54-5+ Ap '63
What makes kids run wild? Parents Mag 39:35+ Ja '64

CHIMES
See also
Carillons

CHIMNEY pieces. See Fireplaces

CHIMPANZEES
Ape who drives like sixty. R. Billings. il Life 56:11 Ja 17 '64
Apish origins of human tension. J. E. Pfeiffer. Harper 227:55-60 Jl '63
Arithmetic behavior in chimpanzees. C. B. Ferster. il Sci Am 210:98-104+ My '64
Chimp girl. il Sci Digest 55:74-7 My '64
Egghead of the animal astronauts; excerpts from Animal astronauts: they opened the way to the stars. C. R Bergwin and W. T. Coleman. il Todays Health 42:32-5+ Ja '64
Eye fixation aspect of attention to visual stimuli in infant chimpanzees. G. Berkson and F. L. Fitz-Gerald. bibliog il Science 139:586-7 F 15 '63
Man not only toolmaker. N. Lawson. il Sci N L 85:191 Mr 21 '64
Man of the woods. V. Reynolds. il Natur Hist 73:44-51 Ja '64
My life among wild chimpanzees. J. Goodall. il Nat Geog Mag 124:272-308 Ag '63

CHIMPANZEES—*Continued*
Tooling up; chimpanzees who are toolmakers. Newsweek 61:98-9 My 27 '63
Toolmaking chimpanzees. Sci Am 211:48 Jl '64
Zoo story; chimpanzee's paintings hung. Time 83:71 F 21 '64

CHINA
See also
Guerrillas—China
Medicine—China
Taiwan
United States—Foreign relations—China

Antiquities
Ancient dynasty capital excavated in China; underneath the city of Sian. Sci N L 83:155 Mr 9 '63
Cache at Stone-fortress-hill. J. F. Haskins. il Natur Hist 72:30-9 F '63
Tsin Ning pot. J. Brzostoski. il Craft Horiz 23:34-5 Ja '64

Bibliography
Open door, closed heart. R. Payne. Sat R 46:37 Je 15 '63

Boundaries
Mountaintop war in remote Ladakh. W. E. Garrett. il Nat Geog Mag 123:664-87 My '63

Foreign relations
Persistence of tradition in Chinese foreign policy. M. Mancall. bibliog f Ann Am Acad 349:14-26 S '63

Africa
Two Chinas in Africa. L. M. S. Slawecki. For Affairs 41:398-409 Ja '63

United States
Next: large-scale uprisings; interview. C. K. Chiang. il U S News 54:41-4 Mr 4 '63

History
Borders of China. J. Jacquet-Francillon. il New Repub 148:18-22 Ap 20 '63; Reply. W. M. Sacks. 148:38-9 My 4 '63
Chinese and the Russians; excerpt from Peking and Moscow. K. Mehnert. bibliog f Ann Am Acad 349:1-13 S '63
Chinese tradition and modern currents: address, October 31, 1964. T. F. Tsiang. Vital Speeches 31:105-9 D 1 '64
Stake: freedom for half of mankind. B. Ward. il N Y Times Mag p 19+ Ap 14 '63

Religious institutions and affairs
See also
Catholic church in China

Social life and customs
Gentle art of tiny teapot tea. P. Mooho. Esquire 62:180+ D '64
Golden casket: Chinese novellas of two millennia. tr. by C. Levenson from W. Bauer's and H. Franke's German versions of the original Chinese. Review
Sat R 47:63 D 5 '64. C. T. Hsia
Growing up with Confucius. L. Yen. il Holiday 34:108+ N '63

CHINA (People's Republic)
Birthday party. Newsweek 62:45 O 14 '63
Boasts & Daniel Boone: the U.S. nuclear-fueled submarine. Time 85:21 Ja 8 '65
China in the world today; symposium. bibliog f il Cur Hist 47:129-72+ S '64
China: the sun in our hearts. il Newsweek 65:20 Ja 4 '65
China today. J. Jacquet-Francillon. New Repub 148:19-21 Mr 16; 17-21 Mr 23 '63
China's challenge. Commonweal 80:279-80 My 29 '64
Chinese checkers. Christian Cent 82:35-6 Ja 13 '65
Communist China, 1963; symposium. bibliog f il Cur Hist 45:129-77+ S '63
Communist China: what science wants to know about it. J. Lear. Sat R 47:43-6 Mr 7 '64; Discussion. 47:44-6 Ag 1 '64
Future of half the world. Time 83:34 Je 26 '64
How they reacted; when Nikita Khrushchev fell and Peking exploded its nuclear bomb. Newsweek 64:57 N 9 '64
Learning to live with China; symposium. New Repub 151:13-16 S 5 '64
Photographer looks at China. O. Van Noppen. il N Y Times Mag p22-3 N 17 '63
Recognizing China. New Repub 150:5 F 1 '64
Scary pageant in Peking; anti-U.S. demonstration; with photographs by P. Boulat. N. Liber. il Life 57:54-61 S 4 '64
Three weeks in the Middle kingdom. M. Jones. il Horizon 6:58-63 Sum '64
Trip to China. R. Terrill. New Repub 152:9-11 Ja 2; 13-15 Ja 16; 15-16 Ja 23 '65
Waiting for evolution. il Time 84:46-9 N 13 '64
See also
Aeronautics, Military—China (People's Republic)
Agricultural administration—China (People's Republic)
Airlines—China (People's Republic)
Atomic power—China (People's Republic)
Aviation—China (People's Republic)
Colleges and universities—China (People's Republic)
Communism—China (People's Republic)
Education—China (People's Republic)
Food supply—China (People's Republic)
Foreign visitors in China
Moving pictures—China (People's Republic)
Prisons—China (People's Republic)
Public health—China (People's Republic)
Roads—China (People's Republic)
Science—China (People's Republic)
United Nations—China (People's Republic)
Youth—China (People's Republic)

Armed forces
China's military strategy. J. Gittings. Nation 200:43-6 Ja 18 '65
Communist China's capacity to make war. S. B. Griffith, 2d. For Affairs 43:217-36 Ja '65
Communist China's military potential. R. L. Powell. bibliog f il Cur Hist 47:136-42 S '64
Is red China a paper tiger? il U S News 57:76-7 O 19 '64
Ready for action: red China's armies. il Newsweek 64:41 Jl 27 '64
Sino-Soviet military relations. R. L. Garthoff. bibliog f Ann Am Acad 349:81-93 S '63

Boundaries
China's new roads: where do they lead? D. Warner. il Reporter 29:31-3 S 26 '63
Intelligence report: secret Chinese road-building. il Newsweek 61:34 Ap 29 '63
Search for lebensraum? struggle between Russia and red China. il Time 84:40-1 S 18 '64
Sinkiang: Soviet rustlers in China's Wild West. S. Karnow. il Reporter 30:36-9 Je 18 '64
Sino-Indian border war. W. Levi. Cur Hist 45:136-43 S '63
Where troops of red China and Soviet stand toe to toe. il U S News 56:53-4 Ja 6 '64

Commerce
East Africa: enter the Chinese. New Repub 149:10 Ag 31 '63
Seeking bargains for Peking. il Newsweek 61:72-5 My 6 '63
Ties that bind in the Orient; Japan and red China. il Bsns W p60+ Ap 25 '64

Cultural relations
Circus brings message; State Peking acrobatic troupe in Tokyo. il Bsns W p72-3 Mr 2 '63

Defenses
China's military strategy. J. Gittings. Nation 200:43-6 Ja 18 '65
Optimists and the pessimists; shift in power in Russia and explosion of the Chinese nuclear bomb. W. V. Shannon. Commonweal 81:217-18 N 13 '64
Red China gets ready to fire its A-bomb. il Bsns W p32+ Ag 1 '64

Description and travel
Doctor in red China. W. Penfield. il Atlan 214:67-71 D '64
Red China spruced up for show; with photographs by R. Burri. Life 57:97-102 Jl 17 '64
This is the China I saw. J. Bisch. il Nat Geog Mag 126:591-640 N '64

Economic conditions
China: a monster devours itself; excerpts from Ta ta, tan tan (Fight fight, talk talk) V. Chu. il Life 54:86-8+ My 3 '63
China today: walking on two legs. R. Berger. il Nation 199:352-5 N 16 '64
China's economy and its prospects. Y. L. Wu. bibliog f il Cur Hist 47:166-72 S '64
Communist China is a paper dragon. D. S. Zagoria. il N Y Times Mag p40-1+ O 18 '64
How Communist economics failed in China. S. Karnow. il Fortune 68:154-7+ Jl '63
In red China, a new great leap to where? il U S News 54:93-4 Je 24 '63
Inside red China. F. H. Maclean. il Sat Eve Post 236:96+ N 16 '63

CHINA (People's Republic)—Economic conditions—*Continued*
Is red China a paper tiger? il U S News 57:76-7 O 19 '64
Number five; Chinese nuclear explosion. Nation 199:289 N 2 '64
On the economic crisis in Communist China. A. Eckstein. il For Affairs 42:655-68 Jl '64
Red China face to face; with editorial comment. E. Behr. il Sat Eve Post 237:21-9, 86 N 14 '64
Refugee reports on red China. S. Karnow. il Reporter 29:39-42 Jl 18 '63
Running down; effects of the Soviet withdrawal on the Chinese economy. Newsweek 61:36 Ap 1 '63
Truth about red China's bomb; interview. C. Y. Cheng. il U S News 57:28-32 D 28 '64
What Chinese threat means to you. Nations Bsns 51:38-9 Mr '63
Why red China can defy Russia now. il Bsns W p28-9 Jl 20 '63

Economic policy

Centralization versus decentralization in mainland China and the Soviet Union. D. H. Perkins. bibliog f Ann Am Acad 349:70-80 S '63
Economic policy and political power in Communist China. F. Schurmann. bibliog f il Ann Am Acad 349:49-69 S '63
Industrial development in China. Y. L. Wu. bibliog f Cur Hist 45:173-7+ S '63

Economic relations

Communist China's opening to the West. C. F. Nothomb. Reporter 30:36-7 F 13 '64
Sino-Soviet economic relations, 1959-1962. O. Hoeffding. bibliog f il Ann Am Acad 349:94-105 S '63
What Chinese threat means to you. Nations Bsns 51:38-9+ Mr '63
Why China ends its isolation. il Bsns W p26-7 F 1 '64

Foreign relations

Another finger on the button. Christian Cent 81:1259 O 14 '64
Arrogant dragon becomes atomic. D. Chu. il Sr Schol 85:13-16+ N 18 '64
Asia: no rest for U.S. from red pressures. U S News 58:26 Ja 4 '65
Asia's atomic cloud. Sr Schol 85:23 O 28 '64
China: the East wind gains force. il Newsweek 63:43-4 F 17 '64
Chinese bomb. J. Burnham. Nat R 16:910 O 20 '64
Chinese bomb menace. T. G. Harris. il Look 28:28-9 D 1 '64
Communist China's retreat from fantasy. il Newsweek 62:44-6+ N 25 '63
Flexing its muscles? il Newsweek 62:30+ Ag 12 '63
From Washington: the bomb in China. H. Margolis. Bul Atomic Sci 20:36-9 D '64
Getting the war over with. New Repub 150:5 Je 13 '64
Is a race war shaping up? A. J. Toynbee. il N Y Times Mag p26+ S 29 '63
Living with China as a great power. O. E. Clubb. bibliog f Ann Am Acad 351:140-7 Ja '64
Mao: Nationalist first, Communist second. R. Hughes. il N Y Times Mag p 17+ Je 7 '64
Mao now; successful status seeker. il Newsweek 64:49-50 O 12 '64
Now red China makes the bomb; what it means; U.S. view: no need to panic. il U S News 55:38-40 Jl 15 '63
Peking joins the club. Nat R 16:942 N 3 '64
Peking's indispensable front man; Premier Chou En-lai. R. Hughes. il N Y Times Mag p 16+ O 4 '64
Positive proposal; prevention against nuclear threat. Nat R 16:1045 D 1 '64
Real meaning of the test ban. S. Alsop. il Sat Eve Post 236:20 S 28 '63
Red China's bomb: how it alters things in the world. il U S News 57:48-50 O 26 '64
Red China's Chou: edging closer to Moscow? summary of interview. E. L. Chou. U S News 57:21 N 9 '64
Red Chinese test expected. Sr Schol 85:15 O 14 '64
Rethinking China. Christian Cent 80:1091 S 11 '63; Discussion. 80:1305-6 O 23 '63
Russia, China, and the underdeveloped areas. H. Gelman. bibliog f Ann Am Acad 349:130-42 S '63
Should we bomb red China's bomb? Nat R 17:3-10 Ja 12 '65
Sino-Soviet balance sheet in the underdeveloped areas. C. P. FitzGerald. bibliog f Ann Am Acad 351:40-9 Ja '64
Small hello. Newsweek 62:30+ D 23 '63
Truth about red China's bomb; interview. C. Y. Cheng. il U S News 57:28-32 D 28 '64
Two Chinas. P. M. A. Linebarger. Cur Hist 47:162-5 S '64
With red China getting the bomb. il U S News 57:38-9 O 12 '64
See also
China (People's Republic)—Boundaries

Africa

China fans the fires. D. Warner. il Reporter 32:16-20 Ja 14 '65
Chou En-lai and the Watusi. C. Sterling. il Reporter 30:22-4 Mr 12 '64; Reply. G. Nyangoma. 30:8 Ap 9 '64
Chou in Africa. Nation 198:21 Ja 6 '64
Chou's trip: a few crises but not much headway. il Time 83:24-5 F 14 '64
Long spoon of Peking. E. Huxley. Nat R 16:868-9 O 6 '64
Peking puts up a Congo command post. R. Rowan. il Life 57:66A-66B D 18 '64
Red China; ed. by Q. Reynolds. C. P. Tung. il Look 28:21-7 D 1 '64
Sino-Soviet competition in Africa. R. A. Scalapino. For Affairs 42:640-54 Jl '64
Two Chinas in Africa. L. M. S. Slawecki. For Affairs 41:398-409 Ja '63
Us blacks. New Repub 149:10-11 D 28 '63

Asia

China fans the fires. D. Warner. il Reporter 32:16-20 Ja 14 '65
China's relations with her Asian neighbors. D. P. Mozingo. bibliog f Cur Hist 47:156-61+ S '64

Asia, Southeastern

If it comes to war with Communist China. . . il U S News 57:42-3 Jl 13 '64
Peking strikes South. B. B. Fall. bibliog f il Cur Hist 45:151-7 S '63
Who is the real enemy in Vietnam? il U S News 56:33-5 Je 1 '64

Cuba

Castro, Khrushchev, and Mao. T. Draper. il Reporter 29:27-31 Ag 15 '63

France

Chiang lets de Gaulle get off the hook. U S News 56:8 F 24 '64
Embassy row. il Newsweek 63:36-7 Mr 9 '64
France takes the plunge; recognition of red China. Bsns W p26 F 1 '64
France's bow to China; recognition of Communist China. il Bsns W p27-8 Ja 25 '64
In defense of Charles de Gaulle. J. Grigg. il N Y Times Mag p 14+ F 23 '64

India

Alarm rings in India. A. M. Rosenthal. Read Digest 82:84-8 F '63
China: a dragon rampant. H. C. Hinton. Commonweal 77:531-4 F 15 '63
China: jealous neighbor. V. P. Dutt. bibliog f Cur Hist 44:135-40+ Mr '63
See also
India—Boundaries

Indonesia

Awkward visitor; Liu Shao-chi in Indonesia. il Newsweek 61:44 Ap 29 '63

Japan

China and Japan. P. F. Langer. bibliog f Cur Hist 45:144-50+ S '63
Japan's relations with China. P. F. Langer. bibliog f il Cur Hist 46:193-9+ Ap '64

Laos

Peking strikes South. B. B. Fall. bibliog f il Cur Hist 45:151-7 S '63

Russia

As Russia-China talks got under way. U S News 55:20 Jl 15 '63
Battle of the giants. J. O'Gara. Commonweal 77:654 Mr 22 '63
Bear-baiting. J. Burnham. Nat R 16:718 Ag 25 '64
Behind the big red rift. il Sr Schol 83:20-2+ S 13 '63
Behind the Russian-Chinese split; interveiw, ed. by M. Gordey. N. S. Khrushchev. il Look 27:32-3+ F 12 '63
Borders of China. J. Jacquet-Francillon. il New Repub 148:18-22 Ap 20 '63; Reply. W. M. Sacks. 148:38-9 My 4 '63
Can we deal with Moscow? with editorial comment. G. F. Kennan. Sat Eve Post 236:38+, 96 O 5 '63
China: a dragon rampant. H. C. Hinton. Commonweal 77:531-4 F 15 '63

CHINA (People's Republic)—*Continued*

Social conditions

Behind the curtains, bamboo and iron. J. Massey-Stewart. il N Y Times Mag p 12+ Je 16 '63
Tourism for ugly imperialists. il Time 84:30-1 Jl 31 '64
See also
Communism—China (People's Republic)

Territorial expansion

Sino-Indian border war. W. Levi. Cur Hist 45:136-43 S '63

CHINA (People's Republic) and the United States
On teaching Chinese. J. Lear. Sat R 47:61 N 7 '64; Discussion. 47:86-7 D 5 '64

CHINA (porcelain) See Pottery

CHINA and Africa
China's push in Africa. J. K. Cooley. Commonweal 79:424-6 Ja 10 '64

CHINA asters. See Asters

CHINAMPAS
Chinampas of Mexico. M. D. Coe. il Sci Am 211:90-8 Jl '64

CHINESE
Chinese and the Russians; excerpt from Peking and Moscow. K. Mehnert. bibliog f Ann Am Acad 349:1-13 S '63
See also
China—Social life and customs

CHINESE almanacs. See Almanacs, Chinese

CHINESE AMERICANS
I believe; ed. by D. Taylor. K. Fong. Seventeen 23:78 Ag '64

CHINESE artists. See Artists, Chinese

CHINESE astronomy. See Astronomy, Chinese

CHINESE athletes. See Athletes

CHINESE atomic bomb test. See Atomic bombs—Testing

CHINESE calendar. See Calendar, Chinese

CHINESE cookery. See Cookery, Chinese

CHINESE dancing. See Dancing, Chinese

CHINESE date trees. See Jujubes

CHINESE folk drama. See Folk drama, Chinese

CHINESE in Indonesia
Present & future. il Time 81:30 My 31 '63

CHINESE in Southeastern Asia
I am Chinese! I live in the southern ocean! R. Hughes. il N Y Times Mag p9+ Ag 4 '63

CHINESE in the United States
Goodbye and hello; celebration of Chinese New Year at Lichee tree, in Greenwich Village. New Yorker 40:24 F 29 '64
Miracle for Amanda; case of Amanda Chiang Dao. T. Wilson. McCalls 91:52+ Je '64
See also
Chinese Americans

CHINESE junks. See Junks

CHINESE language
Computer for translating. A. Gode. il Sci N L 83:374 Je 15 '63
Machine translation of Chinese. G. W. King and H. W. Chang. il Sci Am 208:124-35 Je '63; Reply with rejoinder. A. G. Oettinger. 209:8+ O '63

Alphabet

Ideograms from ancient China. il UNESCO Courier 17:30-3 Mr '64

Study and teaching

Chinese and Japanese in high school. Sch & Soc 91:288+ O 5 '63
Dawn-to-yawn Chinese; Seton Hall university's summer Chinese language institute. il Newsweek 64:49-50 Ag 3 '64
Instruction in Chinese and Japanese in secondary schools. F. H. Jackson. Ann Am Acad 356:113-18 N '64
On teaching Chinese. J. Lear. Sat R 47:61 N 7 '64; Discussion. 47:86-7 D 5 '64

Writing

Ideograms from ancient China. il UNESCO Courier 17:30-3 Mr '64

CHINESE legends. See Legends, Chinese

CHINESE literature
Golden casket: Chinese novellas of two millennia, tr. by C. Levenson from W. Bauer's and H. Franke's German versions of the original Chinese. Review
Sat R 47:63 D 5 '64. C. T. Hsia
Yung Lo encyclopedia presented to Library of Congress. R. Hilsman; R. D. Rogers. Dept State Bul 49:740 N 11 '63

CHINESE medicine. See Medicine—China

CHINESE New Year. See New Year

CHINESE opera. See Opera, Chinese

CHINESE painting. See Painting, Chinese

CHINESE pear
Callery pear. F. Campbell. Horticulture 42:24 Je '64

CHINESE poetry
Lines by China's poet laureate; Mao Tse-tung's poetry. I. Stewart. il N Y Times Mag p 12+ Mr 29 '64
Twentieth century Chinese poetry: an anthology, tr. and ed. by K. Y. Hsu. Review
Sat R 46:33 S 7 '63. R. Payne

CHINESE prime minister; drama. See Bagnold, E.

CHINESE prints. See Prints

CHINESE propaganda. See Propaganda, Chinese

CHINESE refugees. See Refugees, Chinese

CHINESE students
Talented Chinese youth. Sci N L 83:100 F 16 '63

CHINESE trade fair, Tokyo. See Exhibitions

CHINESE wall; drama. See Frisch, M.

CHINESE wall paintings. See Mural painting and decoration

CHINESE writing. See Chinese language—Writing

CHINGIS Khan. See Jenghis Khan

CHINKS, pseud.
Mr Hardy Lee, his yacht; excerpts, with introd. by Alexander C. Brown. pors Am Heritage 15:24-31 Je '64

CHINNERY, George
George Chinnery in India; excerpts from George Chinnery, 1774-1852. H. Berry-Hill and S. Berry-Hill. il por Antiques 83:449-51 Ap '63

CHINO, Haruo, and Gilbert, L. I.
Diglyceride release from insect fat body; a possible means of lipid transport. bibliog Science 143:359-61 Ja 24 '64

CHINO, Calif.
New strength for old asphalt. E. T. Lynch. il Am City 79:90-1 F '64

CHINOOK salmon fishing. See Salmon fishing

CHINOOK winds. See Winds

CHINOPTILOLITE. See Zeolites

CHINQUAPIN. See Chestnut trees

CHIPLEY, Fla.
Rattling for tourists in northern Florida. J. O'Reilly. il Sports Illus 20:95-6+ Ap 13 '64

CHIPMAN, Abram
LP overview of Debussy's seascape. Am Rec G 30:390-3 Ja '64

CHIPPENDALE, Thomas
In the museums; two letters from Chippendale. R. Davidson. il Antiques 85:220 F '64

CHIPPEWA RIVER
Tale of two rivers. E. Swift. il Am For 70:32-5+ Je '64

CHIPPING machines. See Wood chipping machines

CHIPS with everything; drama. See Wesker, A.

CHIRICAHUA NATIONAL MONUMENT
Behind the scene at Chiricahua. N. N. Dodge. il Nat Parks Mag 37:10-14 Mr '63

CHIRICO, Giorgio de
About the cover: Nostalgia of the infinite; excerpt from Masters of modern art. J. T. Soby. Sat R 47:63 N 14 '64

CHIROPRACTORS
Foot in the door. Newsweek 61:86 Ap 8 '63

CHISELS
Passing of the ice chisel. il Field & S 68:127 Mr '64

CHISHOLM, Brock
Take a lesson from the dinosaur. Parents Mag 39:55+ Ap '64

CHITONS
Chitons. A. G. Melvin. il Hobbies 69:130+ Je '64

CHIVES
How to grow, freeze and dry your own chives. L. Illig. il House B 106:45-6+ Je '64

CHIZCOTT, Paula
Uneasy days before college. Parents Mag 38:40-1+ Jl '63

CHLAMYDOMONAS snowiae. See Algae

CHLORAMPHENICOL
Chloramphenicol in blood: simple chemical estimations in patients receiving multiple antibiotics. D. W. O. Hughes and L. K. Diamond. bibliog il Science 144:296-7 Ap 17 '64

CHLORELLA. See Algae

CHLORIDES
Chlorinated insecticides in the body fat of people in the United States. W. E. Dale and G. E. Quinby. bibliog il Science 142:593-5 N 1 '63

CHLORINATED insecticides. See Insecticides
CHLORINATION of water. See Water purification
CHLORINE
Chlorine pentafluoride. D. F. Smith. Science 141:1039 S 13 '63
Odor of chlorine. Am City 78:7 My '63
Reductive dechlorination of DDT to DDD by yeast. B. J. Kallman and A. K. Andrews. il Science 141:1050-1 S 13 '63
CHLORINE, Liquid
Time bombs in the Mississippi. E. D. Fales, jr. il Pop Sci 182:124-30+ Ap '63
CHLOROFORM
Surgeons used chloroform; study of Battle of Gettysburg. Sci N L 84:30 Jl 13 '63
CHLOROPHENYL dimethylurea
Flavin sensitized photoreactions: effects of 3-(p-chlorophenyl)-1,1-dimethylurea. P. Homann and H. Gaffron. bibliog il Science 141:905-7 S 6 '63
CHLOROPHENYL ethane. See Ethane
CHLOROPHYLL
Chlorophyll *a* appearance in the dark in higher plants; analytical notes. D. W. Kupke and J. L. Huntington. bibliog il Science 140:49-51 Ap 5 '63
Chlorophyll content and growth of soybean plants: possible interaction of iron availability and day length. H. M. Benedict and others. il Science 144:1134-5 My 29 '64
Preservation of chlorophyll in leaf sections by substances obtained from root exudate. H. Kende. bibliog il Science 145:1066-7 S 4 '64
CHLOROPLASTS
Quantasome: size and composition. R. B. Park and J. Biggins. bibliog il Science 144:1009-11 My 22 '64
Ultraviolet inactivation of chloroplast formation in synchronously dividing euglena gracilis. S. F. Petropulos. Science 145:392-3 Jl 24 '64
CHLOROQUINE
Antimalarial drugs cause eye trouble. Sci N L 84:153 S 7 '63
Danger to eyes found in drugs for arthritis. Sci N L 83:370 Je 15 '63
CHLOROSIS (plants)
How to control sorghum chlorosis. Suc Farm 61:63 Je '63
CHLORPROMAZINE
Dissociation and recovery of a response learned under the influence of chlorpromazine or saline. L. S. Otis. bibliog il Science 143:1347-8 Mr 20 '64
Errorless discrimination learning in the pigeon: effects of chlorpromazine and imipramine. H. S. Terrace. bibliog il Science 140:318-19 Ap 19 '63
Fetal death from nicotinamide-deficient diet and its prevention by chlorpromazine and imipramine. I. Fratta and others. bibliog il Science 145:1429-30 S 25 '64
7-Hydroxychlorpromazine: potential toxic drug metabolite in psychiatric patients. T. L. Perry and others. bibliog il Science 146:81-3 O 2 '64
CHOATE, Elizabeth R.
Catalina cat. Atlan 212:93-5 N '63
Gentle art of catching smelts. Atlan 214:93-4 N '64
Give your heart to a dog. Atlan 214:81-4 D '64
Pig tale. Atlan 214:81-4 S '64
CHOATE, Joseph E.
Boating comes of age. Yachting 117:94-7+ Ja '65
Facts and the figures (cont) Yachting 115:151-2 F '64
What made boating grow? por Motor B 112:36+ O '63
CHOATE, Rufus
Gathering storm: a campus view; letters. Am Heritage 14:15 Ag '63
CHOATE, Thomas S.
Border wilderness. il Nat Parks Mag 38:4-7 O '64
CHOATE school, Wallingford, Conn. See Private schools
CHOCOLATE
See also
Cookery—Chocolate

Manufacture

Pass the chocolates; Japanese manufacturers turning out some 400 chocolate products. il Newsweek 63:82 My 11 '64
CHOCOLATE cake; story. See Deal, B. H.
CHODIRKER, W. B. and Tomasi, T. B. jr
Gamma-globulins: quantitative relationships in human serum and nonvascular fluids. bibliog Science 142:1080-1 N 22 '63
CHODOSH, Richard B.
Cowardish and Rodgersy. Newsweek 62:58 D 30 '63
CHOICE (psychology)
Who says you have to choose? V. Hyde. il Redbook 123:33+ Je '64
CHOICE of college. See College, Choice of
CHOICE of occupation. See Occupations
CHOICE of profession; story. See Malamud, B.
CHOIRS
Capital music maker; Bethesda, Md, Congregational church choir. il Ebony 18:91-2+ Jl '63
Littlest scene stealer; United Nations children's choir of Los Angeles. il Ebony 18:63-4+ Jl '63
Musical events; a-cappella concert by choir of St Olaf college, Northfield, Minn, in Philharmonic Hall. W. Sargeant. New Yorker 40:119-21 F 22 '64
Singing saints; Mormon tabernacle choir. il Time 82:66 Jl 26 '63
When the choirs go marching out? C. A. Bennett. il America 111:738-9 D 5 '64
CHOLERA
Cholera years, by C. E Rosenberg. Review
Am Heritage 14:106-7 F '63. B. Catton
These Americans must be gods; U.S. navy doctor in Saigon. S. Karnow. il Sat Eve Post 237:72-3 Ap 25 '64
U.S. navy helps fight Saigon cholera epidemic. Sci N L 85:72 F 1 '64
CHOLESTEROL
Additive inheritance of serum cholesterol level in mice. J. H. Bruell. il Science 142:1664-5 D 27 '63
Can diet prevent heart attacks? A. L. Blakeslee. il Sat Eve Post 237:66-7 Ja 25 '64
Cholesterol: guilt or innocent? L. Engel. il N Y Times Mag p29+ My 12 '63
Cholesterol: guilty or not guilty? J. D. Ratcliff. Read Digest 85:81-4 N '64
Cholesterol in higher plants. D. F. Johnson and others. bibliog Science 140:198-9 Ap 12 '63
Cholesterol lowered. Sci N L 86:243 O 17 '64
Cholesterol similarities shown in study of twins. Sci N L 86:248 O 17 '64
Estrone inhibition of cholesterol biosynthesis at the mevalonic acid stage. A. J. Merola and A. Arnold. bibliog il Science 144:301-2 Ap 17 '64
Food for the heart. il Newsweek 62:70-1 Ag 5 '63
Four fats in the blood: which cause heart attacks? il Time 83:66-7 Je 19 '64
Low-calorie protein diet; cholesterol levels of monks. Sci N L 84:197 S 28 '63
Low cholesterol eggs hit the market. il Farm J 87:52 N '63
Prudent diet; Anti-Coronary club of New York city. Newsweek 64:92 O 19 '64
Secrets of cholesterol; two biochemists share 1964 Nobel prize in physiology and medicine. il Time 84:94 O 23 '64
Surgery lowers cholesterol level. Sci Digest 57:31 Ja '65
CHOLINACETYLASE
Acetylcholine and cholinacetylase content of synaptic vesicles. E. De Robertis and others. bibliog il Science 140:300-1 Ap 19 '63
CHOLINE
Cholinergic action of homogenates of sea urchin pedicellariae. E. G. Mendes and others. bibliog Science 139:408-9 F 1 '63
CHOLINESTERASE
Cholinesterase inhibition in spider mites susceptible and resistant to organophosphate. H. R. Smissaert. bibliog il Science 143:129-31 Ja 10 '64
CHOMICKY, Yar
Plowshares into sculpture. Sch Arts 62:22-4 Mr '63
CHONDRITES. See Meteorites
CHONDRULES
Chondrites and chondrules. J. A. Wood. il Sci Am 209:64-8+ O '63
Oldest solids. Sci Am 208:72-4 Mr '63
CHOPIN, Frédéric François
Honeymoon in a monastery. F. Grunfeld. por Reporter 28:33-6 Je 6 '63
Rubinstein's Chopin waltzes: peerless. C. J. Luten. Am Rec G 31:328 D '64
CHOPS. See Cookery—Meat
CHORAL groups and societies
Fourth man makes the trio tick; Kingston trio. il Bsns W p56-8 F 23 '63
Street singers; Yale Russian chorus. Newsweek 61:57 Je 17 '63
Swinging nuns. S. G. Aronowitz. il Sat Eve Post 237:66-7 Ja 4 '64
Texas boys choir. il Mus Am 83:10-11 Ag '63

CHORAL groups and societies—*Continued*
They sing like temple bells; Korean orphans. il Life 54:41-2+ Ap 12 '63
Whiffenpoofs are expensive. R. G. Kaiser. il Esquire 62:134-7+ N '64
CHORAL music
See also
Handel and Haydn society
Phonograph records—Choral music
CHORAL singing
See also
Choirs
CHOREOGRAPHY
American choreographers' workshop at Fashion institute of technology. M. Marks. Dance Mag 37:149-51 D '63
Appreciation of Jean Cocteau. W. Sorell. il Dance Mag 38:38-41 F '64
Balanchine's return to Russia; excerpts from Balanchine. B. Taper. Harper 227:47-50+ N '63
Ballet '64: fresh and fun. J. Anderson. il Dance Mag 38:30 S '64
Bill Frank, Phyllis Lamhut, Murray, Louis, Henry street playhouse. J. Maskey. Dance Mag 38:32-3 Je '64
Blasis to Bournonville. L. Moore. il Dance Mag 38:52-3+ F '64
Bob Fosse. Dance Mag 37:32 Ap '63
Contemporary dance, inc. presents: The coach with the six insides, 92nd street Y. D. Hering. Dance Mag 38:72 My '64
Dancing along with Mitch. S. Goodman. il Dance Mag 37:30-3+ S '63
Ernie Flatt in action. E. Palatsky. il Dance Mag 38:42-5 D '64
Fabulous career of Bronislava Nijinska. J. Anderson. il Dance Mag 37:40-6 Ag '63
Genius of Balanchine; excerpt from Balanchine. B. Taper. il Theatre Arts 47:10-13+ N '63
In the news. il Dance Mag 37:46 D '63
Manifold implications; A. Halprin. J. Anderson. il Dance Mag 37:44-7 Ap '63
Merri-Mimes in The firebird, Cricket theatre. M. Marks. Dance Mag 38:71 My '64
New choreographers, Clark center for the performing arts. J. Maskey. Dance Mag 39:62+ Ja '65
New choreographers concert at Clark center. M. Marks. Dance Mag 38:29 F '64
New choreographers concert, Clark Center for the performing arts. J. Maskey. Dance Mag 38:65-6 Je '64
New spirit in an ancient dance; World's fair Indonesian dancers. M. Dehn. il Dance Mag 38:16+ S '64
Olga Zampos, Mimi Garrard, Albert Reid, Henry street playhouse. M. Marks. Dance Mag 38:34-5 Je '64
Seconding the motion: interview, ed. by G. Fitzgerald. K. Dunham. Opera N 28:15 D 7 '63
Shakespeare and the choreographer. W. Sorell. il Dance Mag 38:43-5+ My '64
Solitary athlete; Martha Graham and her company; Lunt-Fontanne theatre. D. Hering. il Dance Mag 37:54-9 D '63
Vaganova; excerpts, tr. by V. Litvinoff. Dance Mag 38:40-3 Jl; 42-4+ Ag '64
Who knows how I appear? Murray Louis' Journal. D. Hering. il Dance Mag 37:46-7 N '63
Young choreographers' concert, 92nd street Y. M. Marks. Dance Mag 38:28-9 Jl '64
See also
Dance notation
CHORES, Childrens. See Occupations for children
CHORES, Farm. See Farm chores
CHORIOMENINGITIS. See Meningitis
CHORLEY, Jean Travers
Rewards of collecting. Antiques 86:432-6 O '64
CHOROVER, Stephan L. and Gross, C. G.
Caudate nucleus lesions: behavioral effects in the rat. bibliog Science 141:826-7 Ag 30 '63
CHORUS girls. See Actors and actresses
CHOTZINOFF, Samuel
Conversation with Jascha Heifetz. Holiday 34:89-94+ S '63
Conversation with Leontyne Price. Holiday 35:103-4+ Mr '64
Guilt of Gian Carlo Menotti. Holiday 33:101-2+ Je '63
Musical Russians. Holiday 34:121-6 O '63
(ed) See Rodgers, R. Conversation with Richard Rodgers
(ed) See Rubinstein, A. Conversation with Artur Rubinstein
CHOU, En-lai
Red China's Chou: edging closer to Moscow? summary of interview. por U S News 57:21 N 9 '64
about
Chou in Africa. Nation 198:21 Ja 6 '64
Chou's trip: a few crises but not much headway. il por Time 83:24-5 F 14 '64
How to be friendly without getting seduced; visit to Pakistan. il por Time 83:28 F 28 '64
Looking for Chou. Time 84:40 S 11 '64
Man to watch. il por Newsweek 62:27-8 D 30 '63
Old times or new realities? il por Newsweek 64:45 N 16 '64
On safari. Time 83:39 Ja 3 '64
Peking's indispensable front man. R. Hughes. il pors N Y Times Mag p 16+ O 4 '64
People of the week. U S News 56:19 F 17 '64
Small hello. por Newsweek 62:30+ D 23 '63
Sphinx, anyone? visit to Egypt. il por Time 82:21 D 27 '63
Worry for Johnson: Chou woos U.S. friends. U S News 56:12 Mr 2 '64
Yellow man's burden; visit to Africa. Time 82:22 D 20 '63
CHOU, Kyong Chol
Algol, still a demon star! il Sky & Tel 27: 24-6 Ja '64
CHOU, Wayne W.
Transistors vs tubes for hi-fi. Electr World 71:36+ F '64
CHOU paste. See Pastry
CHOWDER
Party-best tuna chowder. il Seventeen 22:150 Mr '63
CHOY, Rudy
Catamarans and common sense. Motor B 111:40-1+ F; 86-8+ Mr '63
(ed) See Murphy, K. Catamaran to Tahiti
(ed) See Reid, A. Catamaran to Tahiti
CHRIST. See Jesus Christ
CHRIST child's lullaby; story. See Moray, A.
CHRIST-JANER, Albert
Building on the Wright foundation. Sat R 46:36-7 F 2 '63
What part art? por Sch Arts 62:28-31 F '63
CHRISTENING. See Baptism
CHRISTENSEN, Carl J.
Henry Eyring, president-elect. Science 143: 826-8 F 21 '64
CHRISTENSEN, Halvor N. See Harvey, A. M. jt. auth.
CHRISTENSEN, Mark N. and Bolt, B. A.
Earth movements: Alaskan earthquake, 1964. Science 145:1207-8+ S 11 '64
—and Gilbert, C. M.
Basaltic cone suggests constructional origin of some guyots. bibliog Science 143:240-2 Ja 17 '64
CHRISTENSEN, Sigrid Müller-. See Müller-Christensen, S.
CHRISTENSEN, Willam Farr
Professor in ballet slippers. N. S. Hey. il pors Dance Mag 37:48-52 My '63
CHRISTENSON, John E.
Improving educational practices. NEA J 53: 17-18 Ja '64
CHRISTIAN, Dorothy M.
Build yourself a boathouse. il por Motor B 111:54-5+ My '63
CHRISTIAN, Fletcher
Martinet or martyr. W. Goldhurst. il Horizon 5:42-8 S '63
CHRISTIAN, Jack G.
Nitrous oxide produced by the catalytic oxidation of organic nitrogen compounds. bibliog Science 143:573-4 F 7 '64
CHRISTIAN, John E. and others
Body composition: relative in vivo determinations from potassium-40 measurements. bibliog Science 140:489-90 My 3 '63
CHRISTIAN, John J. and Davis, D. E.
Endocrines, behavior, and population. bibliog Science 146:1550-60 D 18 '64
CHRISTIAN, Minas
Minas Christian, conductor Evansville philharmonic, Indiana. R. Eyer. por Mus Am 83:11 My '63
CHRISTIAN, Vance
Food expert teaches at Cornell. il pors Ebony 18:73-4+ Ag '63
CHRISTIAN anti-communism crusade
Be careful; anti-Communist ballads sung at meetings. New Repub 152:8 Ja 23 '65
CHRISTIAN art and symbolism
Arts of Byzantium. D. Smith. il Craft Horiz 23:34-7+ My '63
Church of the Florentine businessmen. il Fortune 67:133-7 Je '63
Church's challenge. C. J. McNaspy. America 110:203-4 F 8 '64
Colonial art and architecture. P. Damaz. il Craft Horiz 23:30-2 S '63

CHRISTIAN art and symbolism—*Continued*
German and Italian embroidery of the middle ages; excerpts from Pictorial history of embroidery. M. Schuette and S. Müller-Christensen. il Craft Horiz 24:23-7+ N '64
Inspired wood carvers of the Gothic age. A. Werner il Am Artist 27:40-5+ D '63
Island of faith in the Sinai wilderness. G. H. Forsyth. il Nat Geog Mag 125:82-106 Ja '64
Lost treasures are seen again; wall paintings in remote churches, Yugoslavia. il Life 54: 52-61 Ap 12 '63
Many mansions; today's art. C. J. McNaspy. America 111:19-20 Jl 4 '64
Mount Sinai's holy treasures. K. Weitzmann. il Nat Geog Mag 125:107-27 Ja '64
Old and new; exhibition of contemporary liturgical art, Philadelphia. C. J. McNaspy. America 109:246+ S 7 '63
Opus anglicanum; English embroiderers loan exhibition at the Victoria & Albert museum, London. A. Frankfurter. il Art N 62:22-5+ D '63
Sculptor hails the Bible. il Life 54:105-7 Je 28 '63
Treasury of sacred art; new museum in Bahian monastery. F. Borghini. il Américas 15:8-12 Ap '63
Treasury treasures; cathedral museums of sacred art masterpieces. M. Zook. il Travel 121:46-7 Je '64
Vestige of colonial splendor; church in Tópaga, Colombia. E. M. Varela. il Américas 15:22-6 Ag '63
See also
Altarpieces
Art, Coptic
Art and religion
Church architecture
Cross and crosses
Glass painting and staining
Icons
Illumination of books and manuscripts
Jesus Christ—Art
Mary, Virgin—Art
Triptychs

Exhibitions

Detroit's fourth biennial. C. J. McNaspy. America 111:362-3 S 26 '64

CHRISTIAN booksellers association
Largest meeting of CBA ever held outside of Chicago. A. Hustwitt. il Pub W 184:38-41 S 9 '63

CHRISTIAN century (periodical)
Announcement; concerning H. E. Fey's retirement. F. Hoskins. Christian Cent 81: 134 Ja 29 '64
Announcement; concerning K. Haselden's appointment as editor. F. Hoskins. Christian Cent 81:358 Mr 18 '64
Announcement; editor H. E. Fey retires. K. Haselden. Christian Cent 81:1078 S 2 '64
Announcement; new corps of interfaith, interracial editors at large. Christian Cent 81:1422 N 18 '64
Announcements; concerning staff members. K. Haselden. Christian Cent 81:1135 S 16 '64
Captive of no party. Christian Cent 81:1255 O 7 '64
Charles Clayton Morrison at ninety; tribute by his friends. Christian Cent 81:1486-8 D 2 '64; Reply. H. S. Leiper. 82:17 Ja 6 '65
Critically your Century; reviews of books. Christian Cent 80:324 Mr 13 '63
Please uncancel your subscription! Christian Cent 81:871 Jl 1 '64
Switch at Century. Time 83:77 Mr 20 '64
Taking political stands; supporting President Johnson. Christian Cent 81:1388 N 11 '64; Discussion. 81:1528, 1622 D 9, 30 '64

CHRISTIAN church (sect) See Disciples of Christ

CHRISTIAN committee for service in Algeria
Relief in Algeria. C. Murray. Christian Cent 81:120-2 Ja 22 '64

CHRISTIAN crusade (organization)
Gospel according to Billy; convention in Dallas. il Newsweek 64:77 Ag 24 '64
Midnight ride of Hargis and Walker; Operation midnight ride. Christian Cent 80:262 F 27 '63
Nameless one. Christian Cent 80:1039 Ag 21 '63

CHRISTIAN democrats (Italy) See Political parties—Italy

CHRISTIAN democrats (Latin America) See Political parties—Latin America

CHRISTIAN doctrine. See Theology

CHRISTIAN doctrine, Confraternity. See Confraternity of Christian doctrine

CHRISTIAN education. See Religious education

CHRISTIAN ethics
Honest to marriage; Christian morals. Christian Cent 81:477 Ap 15 '64; Reply with rejoinder. J. A. T. Robinson. 81:738-9 Je 3 '64
Inertia in business ethics. R. Baumhart and G. D. Fitzpatrick. America 108:798-800 Je 1 '63
Justice and love in the racial crisis. L. D. Kliever. Christian Cent 81:1055-7 Ag 26 '64
Man as nature's man. P. Hefner. Christian Cent 81:1556-9 D 16 '64
Moral response. R. O. Johann. America 108: 761-2 My 25 '63
Morality and beyond, by P. Tillich. Review
Sat R 47:80 Ja 4 '64. J. E. Smith
Morals, new and old. America 110:216 F 15 '64
On keeping human life human. P. Lehmann. Christian Cent 81:1297-9 O 21 '64; Reply. P. Ramsey. 81:1529 D 9 '64
Sir, the word is moral! D. R. Kline. Christian Cent 81:455-8 Ap 8 '64; Discussion. 81:803-4 Je 17 '64
South and Christian ethics, by J. Sellers. Review
Christian Cent 80:302-4 Mr 6 '63. E. Tilson
Where is the consensus? concerning Father L. Janssens article on the progesterone pill. Commonweal 79:737 Mr 20 '64; Reply. M. Novak 80:149 Ag 24 '64
See also
Christianity and economics
Church and social problems
Conscience
Guilt
Social ethics
War and religion

Bibliography

Christian social ethics bookshelf. W. G. Muelder. Christian Cent 80:1336-7 O 30 '63

CHRISTIAN family movement (organization)
Questions meant to stimulate. America 112:5 Ja 2 '65

CHRISTIAN foundation. See Foundations, Charitable and educational

CHRISTIAN giving
See also
Tithes

CHRISTIAN herald
Conducts loaded poll. Christian Cent 81:1549 D 16 '64; Reply with rejoinder. D. Poling. 82:118 Ja 27 '65

CHRISTIAN life
Christian's vocation: a call to status and mission. N. J. McEleney. Cath World 197: 152-8 Je '63
Christ's message to the disinherited; excerpts from Jesus and the disinherited. H. Thurman. Ebony 18:58+ S '63
Committed Christian in the modern world; excerpt from The Christian commitment. K. Rahner. Cath World 198:144-50 D '63
False claim. C. Davis. America 110:514 Ap 11 '64
Inner peace and how to find it; reprint. H. E. Fosdick. Read Digest 83:110-13 Jl '63
Love, O love, O careful love. J. H. Adams. il America 109:481-4 O 26 '63; Discussion. 109:658-9; 110:1, 149 N 23 '63, Ja 4, F 1 '64
Man as servant. J. I. Miller. Christian Cent 81:233-6 F 19 '64
Mightiest force in the universe. N. V. Peale. Read Digest 83:66-9 S '63
My last will and testament; reprint of 1955 article. M. M. Bethune. il Ebony 18:150-6 S '63
No magic key. I. Travers-Ball. America 108: 673-4 My 11 '63
On parish renewal. B. Barr. Christian Cent 81:1342+ O 28 '64
Peace churches as communities of discernment. J. L. Burkholder. Christian Cent 80: 1072-5 S 4 '63
Persons, not things. C. Davis. America 108: 861 Je 15 '63
Quo vadis? A. J. Cronin. il Read Digest 82: 118-20+ My '63
Sense of crisis. R. O. Johann. America 109:795 D 21 '63
Word (cont) V. P. McCorry. America 108:384, 478, 787-8, 872-3, 914-15; 109:248, 268-9, 330-1; 110:658-9, 854-5; 111:199-200, 427-8, 465-6 Mr 16, Ap 6, My 25, Je 15, 29, S 7-21 '63, My 9, Je 20, Ag 22, O 10-17 '64
See also
Conduct of life
Conversion
Holiness
Prayer

CHRISTIAN martyrs. See Martyrs

CHRISTIAN Methodist Episcopal church
Negro Methodists consider union. V. E. Lowder. Christian Cent 81:250+ F 19 '64
CHRISTIAN missions. See Missions
CHRISTIAN names. See Names, Personal
CHRISTIAN pacifism. See Pacifism
CHRISTIAN peace conference, Prague. See Peace conferences
CHRISTIAN roommates; story. See Updike, J.
CHRISTIAN rural overseas program
CROP feeds hungry in Pakistan. Christian Cent 81:957 Jl 29 '64
Multiplying your dollars; Thanksgiving offerings help finance the feeding of needy persons overseas. Christian Cent 81:1453 N 25 '64
CHRISTIAN Science
Her growing daughters; annual meeting of Church of Christ, Scientist. Time 83:60 Je 19 '64
CHRISTIAN Science monitor (newspaper)
Change at the Monitor. il Time 85:37 Ja 8 '65
CHRISTIAN socialism. See Socialism, Christian
CHRISTIAN sociology. See Sociology, Christian
CHRISTIAN theological seminary, Indianapolis
Theological seminary receives large gift. Christian Cent 80:1569 D 18 '63
CHRISTIAN unity. See Church unity
CHRISTIAN year
See also
Advent
CHRISTIANITY
Are we post-Christian? America 108:394, 526 Mr 23, Ap 20 '63; Reply. R. F. Charles. 108:625-6 My 4 '63
Bishop and the debate. M. E. Marty. Christian Cent 81:830-2 Je 24 '64
Challenge of Christian freedom; supernatural reality of Christian liberty. J. V. Gallagher. Cath World 197:223-30 Jl '63
Christian opportunity, by D. de Rougemont; tr. by D. Lehmkuhl. Review
Christian Cent 80:1207 O 2 '63. W. A. Sadler, jr
Christian primer, by L. Cassels. Review
Christian Cent 81:966-8 Jl 29 '64. D. Meade
Christian's dilemma; views of F. Dostoevsky, B. F. Skinner, and Teilhard de Chardin. J. Collignon. il Sat R 47:14-16 Je 27 '64
Christmas and the world. J. V. Schall. Commonweal 79:389-92 D 27 '63
Dilemma of modern belief, by S. H. Miller. Review
Christian Cent 80:1206 O 2 '63. A. P. Klausler
Faith in a secular age. P. Schlueter. Christian Cent 80:805 Je 19 '63
Father Delp's prison diary. A. Delp. Cath World 196:364-9 Mr '63
Fourth American faith, by D. Howlett. Review
Christian Cent 81:1064 Ag 26 '64. T. B. Clark
Greek myths and Christian mystery, by H. Rahner. Review
Commonweal 79:605-6 F 14 '64. A. A. Cohen
Hemlock and the cross: humanism, Socrates and Christ, by G. MacGregor. Review
Christian Cent 80:1107 S 11 '63. L. C. Rudolph
Honest to God, by J. A. T. Robinson. Review
Commonweal il 80:573-4+ Ag 21 '64. T. Merton
Inward law of Christian liberty; excerpt from In the redeeming Christ; toward a theology of spirituality. F. X. Durrwell. Cath World 197:187-92 Je '63
Irrelevance of religion. America 110:861-2 Je 27 '64
Liturgy and mystery. B. Leeming. America 109:153-5 Ag 17 '63
Mightiest force in the universe. N. V. Peale. Read Digest 83:66-9 S '63
Militant ministry, by H. R. Weber. Review
Christian Cent 81:1173 S 23 '64. H. A. Schulz
Moralism vs. Christianity. F. E. Stoeffler. Christian Cent 80:1299-302 O 23 '63; Discussion. 80:1520-1 D 4 '63
Needs of the world; address, December 23, 1963. Paul VI. Vital Speeches 30:198-200 Ja 15 '64
One Protestant voice? Christian Cent 80:1291-2 O 23 '63
Prior mission of the church. E Hillman. il Cath World 198:238-44 Ja '64
Religionless Christianity. Time 81:49-50+ Ap 12 '63
Religionless religion. G. Foley. Christian Cent 80:1096-9 S 11 '63; Discussion. 80:1277-8, 1341-2, 1472 O 16, 30, N 27 '63
Secular meaning of the gospel, by P. M. Van Buren. Review
Christian Cent 80:1208 O 2 '63. W. Hamilton
Servant church. il Time 84:45-9 D 25 '64
Time for Christian candor, by J. A. Pike. Review
Christian Cent 81:1405-6 N 11 '64. W. A. Clebsch
Toynbee dilemma. M. W. Hess. Christian Cent 81:8-9 Ja 1 '64
Turn to religion; address, March 29, 1964. Paul VI. Vital Speeches 30:386-7 Ap 15 '64
Varieties of unbelief, by M. E. Marty. Review
Commonweal 81:490-1 Ja 8 '65. T. Merton
Newsweek 64:90-1 D 7 '64
Wait without idols, by G. Vahanian. Review
Christian Cent 81:769-70 Je 10 '64. R. H. Glauber
Way and its ways, by G. W. Cornell. Review
Christian Cent 80:1373 N 6 '63. D. Meade
See also
Catholic church
Christian ethics
Christian life
Fundamentalism
God
Grace (theology)
Jesus Christ—Teaching
Paul, Saint—Teaching
Protestantism
Religion
Sects
Theology
War and religion

Bibliography

Christianity's search for a new role. J. Pelikan. Harper 229:144-6 D '64

Evidences

See Apologetics

History

Africa's golden past; historical facts challenge notion that Christianity is religion of West. W. L. Hansberry and E. H. Johnson. il Ebony 20:86-92 Ja '65
CHRISTIANITY, Primitive. See Church history—Primitive and early church
CHRISTIANITY and communism. See Catholic church and communism; Communism and religion
CHRISTIANITY and crisis (periodical)
Four-letter sermon. il Newsweek 65:70-1 F 1 '65
CHRISTIANITY and democracy. See Religion and democracy
CHRISTIANITY and economics
Catholicism: molder of manpower. J. H. Smylie. Christian Cent 80:1544-6 D 11 '63
Christian responsibility and world poverty, ed. by A. McCormack. Review
Cath World 199:50-2 Ap '64. W. J. Gibbons
Claim against the West. B. Ward. il Commonweal 81:219-22 N 13 '64
Concerning the education of clergymen. R. Kirk. Nat R 14:238 Mr 26 '63; Reply. A. B. Muller. 14:425 My 21 '63
Jobless challenge the churches: Church and economic life week. Christian Cent 81:69 Ja 15 '64
On the job ethics, ed. by C. P. Hall. Review
America 110:332 Mr 14 '64. B. L. Masse
Religion of life insurance. A. Welsh. Christian Cent 80:1541-3, 1574-6 D 11-18 '63; Discussion. 81:118-19, 239-40 Ja 22, F 19 '64
This problem of bigness; excerpt from Justice for all. B. L. Masse. America 111:128-30 Ag 8 '64
CHRISTIANITY and international affairs. See Church and international relations
CHRISTIANITY and other religions
As Christians face rival religions: an inter-religious strategy for community without compromise, by G. Cook. Review
Christian Cent 80:713 My 29 '63. D. Yu
Buddhism and Christianity, by W. L. King. Review
Christian Cent 80:582 My 1 '63. G. B. Cooke
Catacombs and Khazars. M. Himmelfarb. Commentary 37:72-4 My '64; Discussion. 38:22+ O '64
Catholics & Jews: how close? il Time 82:51 N 29 '63
Christian schools & Israeli children. H. Weiner. Commentary 38:39-45 Jl '64; Discussion. 39:14+ Ja '65

CHRISTIANITY and other religions—*Cont.*
Christian war on anti-Semitism. A. Eisenberg and H. Eisenberg. il Look 28:48+ Je 2 '64
Christianity and Islam in West Africa. K. Hughes. Christian Cent 81:264-7, 298-302 F 26-Mr 4 '64
Christianity and the encounter of the world religions, by P. Tillich. Review
Christian Cent 80:273 F 27 '63. M. C. Ebersole
Christians and Jews: a new rapprochement; excerpt from America is different. S. E. Rosenberg. Christian Cent 81:295-8 Mr 4 '64 '64; Reply. A. T. K. Zadig. 81:801-3 Je 17 '64
Christians & Jews; combatting contempt. il Time 83:66+ My 29 '64
Council reform and reunion, by H. Küng. Review
Christian Cent 80:709-10 My 29 '63. A. J. Wolf; Discussion. 80:829, 864-5 Je 26-Jl 3 '63
Egypt's Christian minority. E. Wakin. Christian Cent 81:332-4 Mr 11 '64
Faith and prejudice: intergroup problems in Protestant curricula, by B. E. Olson. Review
Christian Cent 80:617-19 My 8 '63. F. H. Littell; Reply. B. E. Olson. 80:887 Jl 10 '63
Festivals and judges; twelve weeks of Christmas. M. Himmelfarb. Commentary 35:66-7 Ja '63
Jewish-Christian argument: a history of theologies in conflict, by H. J. Schoeps. Review
Christian Cent 80:1375-6 N 6 '63. L. D. Streiker
Jews and Jesus. Newsweek 62:92-3 D 2 '63
Protestant renewal: a Jewish view. A. J. Heschel. Christian Cent 80:1501-4 D 4 '63
Recurrent pattern: studies in anti-Judaism in modern thought, by N. Rotenstreich. Review
Commentary 38:92-5 N '64. W. J. Dannhauser
Rome & Jerusalem. M. Himmelfarb. Commentary 38:69-73 S '64
Teaching of Contempt, by J. Isaac. Review
Christian Cent 81:805 Je 17 '64. L. D. Streiker
Two worlds or none: Christian missions in secular as well as spiritual milieu. W. J. Danker. Christian Cent 80:737-9 Je 5 '63

CHRISTIANITY and politics. See Church and politics

CHRISTIANITY and psychiatry. See Psychiatry and religion

CHRISTIANITY and science. See Religion and science

CHRISTIANITY and social problems. See Church and social problems

CHRISTIANITY and war. See War and religion

CHRISTIANS
Outside the camp; excerpt from Passion. K. A. Olsson. Christian Cent 80:264-7 F 27 '63

CHRISTIANS and Jews, National conference of. See National conference of Christians and Jews

CHRISTIANS in Africa
All-Africa Christianity; All-Africa conference of churches. E. C. Parker. Christian Cent 80:670-2 My 22 '63
Third thoughts on Africa. H. P. Van Dusen. Christian Cent 81:855-8 Jl 1 '64

CHRISTIANS in Asia
See also
East Asia Christian conference

CHRISTIANS in China
Church in Communist China: a Protestant appraisal, by F. P. Jones. Review
Christian Cent 80:713 My 29 '63. W. J. Danker
What about mainland China? D. M. Stowe. Christian Cent 82:44-6 Ja 13 '65
See also
Catholic church in China

CHRISTIANS in Egypt
Egypt's Christian minority. E. Wakin. Christian Cent 81:332-4 Mr 11 '64

CHRISTIANS in Germany
Sunday in East Berlin. K. Strong. Christian Cent 81:1500+ D 2 '64

CHRISTIANS in India
News of the Christian world. Christian Cent 80:867-8 Jl 3 '63
Pope visits a lost tribe. A. Menen. il N Y Times Mag p34-5+ N 29 '64

CHRISTIANS in Japan
Japanese Christians welcome U.S. servicemen; Japan Christian hospitality center. Christian Cent 80:1537 D 11 '63
Japan's new religions and the Christian community. R. H. Drummond. Christian Cent 81:1521-3 D 9 '64

CHRISTIANS in Malaysia
Christians in newborn Malaysia. A. R. Crouch. Christian Cent 80:1437 N 20 '63; Reply. H. B. Amstutz. 81:244-5 F 19 '64; Rejoinder. 81:465-6 Ap 8 '64

CHRISTIANS in Russia
Children's crusade in reverse: Communist indoctrination of children. D. A. Lowrie. Christian Cent 81:1141-3 S 16 '64
Every child an atheist; Communist indoctrination of children. D. A. Lowrie. Christian Cent 80:776-7 Je 12 '63

CHRISTIANS in South Africa
God, Allah and Ju Ju, by J. Mendelsohn. Review
Christian Cent 80:648-9 My 15 '63. F. D. Lueking
Missionaries' return. Newsweek 63:66 Mr 23 '64
White South African's dilemma. B. Marais. Christian Cent 80:580-1 My 1 '63

CHRISTIANS in Sudan
Genocide in Sudan; Arab repression of Negroes. G. MacEoin. Commonweal 80:539-42 Ag 7 '64
Missionaries' return. Newsweek 63:66 Mr 23 '64
Restive Sudan; missionaries expelled. America 110:355 Mr 21 '64
Sudan continues expulsion of missionaries. Christian Cent 81:1053 Ag 26 '64
Sudan tightens control of Christians. Christian Cent 80:378 Mr 27 '63
Sundown on Christianity in the Sudan. V. J. Dunigan. il Cath World 199:245-52 Jl '64
Trial in the Sudan. America 110:502 Ap 11 '64

CHRISTIANS in Turkey
Turkey restricts clergy moves. Christian Cent 80:387 Mr 27 '63

CHRISTIANSEN, Charles M.
Look ahead at Miami Beach. Recreation 57:55 F '64

CHRISTIANSEN, F. W.
Polygonal fracture and fold systems in the salt crust, Great Salt Lake Desert, Utah. Science 139:607-9 F 15 '63

CHRISTIE, George A.
Building picture. Arch Rec 135:143 Ja '64
Current trends in construction. Arch Rec 133:18 Mr '63
$120 billion in construction in 1975. Arch Rec 134:173-80 S '63
Surveys show mixed market for apartments. Arch Rec 136:18 Ag '64

CHRISTIE, Julie
Julie Christie: a star in eleven minutes. J. Hamilton. il pors Look 28:40-2+ Ag 25 '64
Star is weaned. il por Time 82:57 S 6 '63

CHRISTIE, Robert
Do lie detectors lie? Pop Sci 183:64-7+ S '63

CHRISTIE, Trevor L.
Abu Simbel: legacy of a pharaoh. Sat R 47:80-1+ O 10 '64
Booked for travel. Sat R 47:28-9 S 12 '64
Boomlet in the Johnson country. Sat R 47:37-8 My 23 '64
Fair game. Sat R 47:48+ Mr 14 '64
Kaiser in the Holy Land. Sat R 47:42+ Ja 4 '64

CHRISTINA, princess of Sweden
Royal co-ed Christina prepares to enter Radcliffe. E. Behr. pors Sat Eve Post 236:78-9 S 28 '63

CHRISTMAS
Across the editor's desk. D. Hanson. Suc Farm 61:8 D '63
Christmas is a journey. R. H. Viguers. Horn Bk 40:585 D '64
Christmas is together-time; excerpt. C. M. Schulz. il McCalls 92:118-19 D '64
Christmas message. J. Kennedy. il Look 27:14-15 D 31 '63
Christmas 1963. R. V. Viguers. Horn Bk 39:571 D '63
Christmas 1964: peace on earth? il U S News 57:19 D 28 '64
Christmas on twenty-five cents a week; excerpt from Open heart. E. Weeks. il Read Digest 85:95-6 D '64
Christmas syndrome. F. Leiber. il Sci Digest 54:16-21 D '63
Christmas time! C. Dickens. il Good H 157:60-1 D '63
Do you take time to enjoy the season? L. Strong. Am Home 67:4 D '64
Facts and fancies of Christmas; questions and answers. G. Dugas. House & Gard 124:48+ N '63
First-born among many brethren. Christian Cent 80:1599 D 25 '63
Folly forgiven, or, Christmas is for beginners. R. Lynes. Mlle 58:58-9 D '63

CHRISTMAS—*Continued*
Gift of memory at Christmas. V. Duncan. Hobbies 69:28 D '64
Home for Christmas; excerpt from An old-fashioned Christmas. P. Engle. Redbook 124:35+ D '64
Hopefulness of these times; remarks, December 18, 1964. L. B. Johnson. Dept State Bul 52:41 Ja 11 '65
How to keep Christmas well. M. E. Jenkins. PTA Mag 58:2-3 D '63
If Christmas were only Christmas; reprint. D. Lawrence. U S News 57:76 D 28 '64
Is Christmas just for children? D. B. Thompson. il Am Home 67:18+ D '64
Like a dawning. America 109:788 D 21 '63
Merry Christmas! Christian Cent 81:1607 D 23 '64
Mr Dunkenheimer; my fifth Christmas. A. Morrissett. il Redbook 122:12+ D '63
Nothing can erase Christmas. A. Pryce-Jones. House & Gard 126:136-7 D '64
Our family Christmas. L. Frost. Redbook 122:45+ D '63
Restore Christmas to Christ! Christian Cent 81:1579 D 23 '64
Sailor's Christmas gift. W. Lederer. Sat Eve Post 236:40 D 21 '63
Santa's safety list. Recreation 56:412 N '63
Someday: a real Christmas. D. Lawrence. U S News 55:80 D 30 '63
Travel enriches our Christmas. V. Buchanan. il Travel 122:47-9 D '64
Twenty ways to make Christmas merrier. Am Home 67:30+ D '64
What shall we give the children? il McCalls 92:93 D '64
Without portfolio. C. B. Luce. il McCalls 91: 23+ D '63; 92:24+ D '64
Word (cont) V. P. McCorry. America 109: 810-11; 111:811-12 D 21 '63, D 19 '64
Year we rediscovered Christmas. C. L. Yellin. Redbook 124:10+ D '64
Yuletide: the world wide. P. P. Coleman. il Sr Schol 85:13T D 9 '64
See also
Advent
Jesus Christ—Nativity
Santa Claus

Anecdotes, facetiae, satire, etc.

Deck the halls with boughs of whatchamacallit; old-fashioned family Christmas. W. Stanton. McCalls 92:122-3+ D '64
Legend of Jones City. M. Kantor. McCalls 91:63 D '63

Caricatures and cartoons

Charlie Brown's Christmas stocking. C. M. Schulz. Good H 157:129-44 D '63

Germany

Non-profit style for Christmas; Nuremberg's Christkindlmarkt. il Bsns W p 22-3 D 21 '63

Japan

Ho-ho-ho. il Newsweek 62:33 D 23 '63
Oriental Christmastide. W. P. Woodward. Christian Cent 81:345 Mr 11 '64

Jordan

I saw Bethlehem shining. R. C. Davids. Farm J 87:32+ D '63

Latin America

Christmas in Latin America. K. V. Lyford. il Horn Bk 40:587-95 D '64

Mexico

See also
Pinatas

Russia

Christmas in Moscow. A. Hurlburt. il Look 28:76-9 D 29 '64

Sweden

Lucia day comes early in December. Sunset 133:30 D '64

United States

Christmas I'll never forget; ed. by G. Walker. il Good H 157:17-18+ D '63
Christmas is for children. J. R. Moskin. il Look 28:48-53 D 29 '64
Christmas is for giving; camera's eye view of the Skip Johnson family, Agency, Ia. il Suc Farm 62:47 D '64
Christmas on Nantucket. J. Peter and M. Kaytor. il Look 28:71-7 D 15 '64
Colonial Christmas; Williamsburg, Va. H. W. Dengler. il Am For 70:6-7+ D '64
Everyone is a child at Christmas. M. A. Daily. il Redbook 122:6+ D '63
Festivals and judges; twelve weeks of Christmas. M. Himmelfarb. Commentary 35:66-7 Ja '63
Has Christmas become too commercial? R. Moore. Farm J 87:63 D '63
How four farm boys discovered Christmas; Hovde family. il Farm J 88:32-3+ D '64
I remember, I remember. A. P. Eliasberg. il N Y Times Mag p38 D 20 '64
It could happen this Christmas. V. B. Rose. Farm J 88:59+ D '64
Let's put Christ in Christmas. E. C. Blake. Ebony 19:64 D '63
Life guide; the splendor of Christmas all over. il Life 55:15 N 29 '63
Lighting of the national Christmas tree; remarks, December 22, 1963. L. B. Johnson. Dept State Bul 50:38-9 Ja 13 '64
Notes and comment; in search of the invisible difference in New York city. New Yorker 39:21 D 21 '63
Papa's disappearing Christmas tree. H. F. Brooks. il Todays Health 41:30-3+ D '63
Start your own Christmas custom. J. L O'Neil. Am Home 66:12 D '63
Time of hope, Christmas, 1963. il Newsweek 62:11-12 D 30 '63

Wales

Christmas in Wales; excerpts from Child's Christmas in Wales. D. Thomas. il Look 27:42-6 D 31 '63

CHRISTMAS bear; drama. See McBueen, M. H.
CHRISTMAS begonias. See Begonias
CHRISTMAS boxes
Gift wraps: for use after Christmas. il Seventeen 23:112-13+ D '64
CHRISTMAS breads. See Bread
CHRISTMAS business
America's titanic Christmas package. D. Wharton. il Read Digest 85:200-2+ D '64
Bell ringer. Time 83:73 Ja 3 '64
Booksellers optimistic about Christmas business. il Pub W 184:16-18 D 9 '63
Christmas '63 best sales ever. il Bsns W p 15-16 D 21 '63
Don't wait for Thanksgiving. il Time 82:85 N 22 '63
Excellent Christmas business; deliveries still troublesome; nation's bookstores and department store book departments. il Pub W 187:126-7 Ja 18 '65
Getting under way for Christmas. M. C. Boland. il Pub W 186:36-40 Ag 24 '64
It was the biggest spending binge ever. il Bsns W p 18 D 28 '63
It was the year of the great don't-care. L. Meyer. Pub W 185:80-1 Ja 6 '64
It's a real boom in Christmas shopping. il U S News 55:23-4 D 23 '63
It's a record boom in Christmas shopping. il U S News 57:94-5 D 21 '64
No mink, just a new living room set. il Bsns W p 139+ N 21 '64
Plenty to spend, and ready to buy. il Bsns W p25-7 N 21 '64
Retailers set their sights still higher; 1964 Christmas sales biggest in history. il Bsns W p 14-15 Ja 2 '65
Shoppers flock back to resume buying. il Bsns W p89-90 N 30 '63
Xmas retail sales best since 1959; bookstores. il Pub W 185:123-6 Ja 20 '64
CHRISTMAS cactus. See Cactus
CHRISTMAS candles. See Candles
CHRISTMAS candy. See Candy
CHRISTMAS cards
Artists' Christmas cards. il Am Artist 27:44-8+ N '63
Christmas cards; offered by museums, galleries and UNICEF (cont) il Consumer Rep 28:476-7 O '63
Color clinic; photographic Christmas cards. D. B. Eisendrath, jr. Pop Phot 55:12+ D '64
In the cards; nation's famous choices. il Time 84:34 D 25 '64
Is this card necessary? A. Briscoe. Farm J 88: 71 D '64
It's not too early to plan your color holiday cards. R. Russell. il Pop Phot 53:66-7+ O '63
Psychiatrists psychoanalyze Christmas cards. F. R. Schreiber and M. Herman. il Sci Digest 56:26-8 D '64
Special greeting cards. Pub W 184:77 Ag 19 '63
UNICEF greeting cards (cont) il UNESCO Courier 16:28-9 N '63

Anecdotes, facetiae, satire, etc.

Atrocious Christmas card. M. Dean. il Atlan 212:132-4 O '63
Letter from Stan Delaplane. S. Delaplane. il Todays Health 41:69 D '63; 42:76 D '64

CHRISTMAS carols
Good King Wenslus-slus. F. Russell. Nat R 15:574-5 D 31 '63
Sing, boys, in joyful chorus. il House & Gard 124:150-1 D '63
See also
Phonograph records—Christmas music
CHRISTMAS carols (with music)
Three songs of Mary: O simplicitas; O oriens; O sapientia. M. L'Engle. Horn Bk 39:615-21 D '63
CHRISTMAS cookery. See Christmas dinners; Christmas meals; Cookery; Cookery, Ornamental
CHRISTMAS cookies. See Cookies
CHRISTMAS cribs
Away in a manger. America 109:724 D 7 '63
Christmas crèche figures: sculpture in miniature. B. Snow. il Antiques 86:698-701 D '64
Christmas crib figures. C. H. Fawcett. il Hobbies 69:36+ D '64
How to stage an inspiring crèche. il House & Gard 124:138-43 D '63
Lovely crèches. il Am Home 66:40-1 D '63
CHRISTMAS decorations
Add radiance with holiday magic. J. E. Dwyer. il Pop Gard 15:36-41 N '64
Best-sellers from ten years of House beautiful decorations. il House B 105:28+ D '63
Bright spots you can make. il Am Home 67: 52-3+ D '64
Candy evergreen tree. Good H 157:188 D '63
Children made these ornaments. il Sunset 133: 82 D '64
Christmas claybake. M. White. il Ladies Home J 81:56-9+ D '64
Christmas corners, small & stylish. il McCalls 92:104-5 D '64
Christmas decorating with fruit. il Sunset 133:70 D '64
Christmas ideas. B. G. Wadsworth. il Parents Mag 38:88 D '63
Christmas ideas. il Bet Hom & Gard 41:14+ D '63
Christmas if you're a millionaire. il McCalls 92:114-15+ D '64
Christmas in October? M. L. Ham. il Horticulture 42:18-19 O '64
Christmas is craft time; excerpts from Fun crafts for children. il Recreation 57:508-9 D '64
Christmas is where the hearth is. il Am Home 66:25-31 D '63
Christmas lights twinkle to music. L. A. Wortman. il Pop Electr 21:45-8 D '64
Christmas magic; excerpts. M. Perry. il Flower Grower 51:18-19 D '64
Christmas tree cones; kindergarten projects. E. Sanders. il Design 65:62-3 N '63
Cones for Christmas. H. W. Dengler. il Am For 69:8-11+ D '63
Create these for Christmas. il Pop Gard 14:30-2 N '63
Crowning touches for your holiday decor. il Am Home 66:32-5 D '63
Deck the halls in keeping with your home. il Am Home 67:36-9 D '64
Deck the house for the holidays. L. Marett. il Parents Mag 38:50-1+ D '63
Deck the party scene with paper. il Good H 157:112-14+ D '63
Designs in day-glo; project of sixth graders at Osborne school, Sandusky, Ohio. J. Vanover. il Design 65:48 N '63
Dime store trims make heirloom ornaments. il Bet Hom & Gard 42:10 D '64
Drama in the round. il McCalls 91:84-5 D '63
Embossing, the new easy way to make holiday decorations. P. Hyde. il House B 105: 244-7+ N '63
Festive frosting of paper. il House & Gard 126:124-31 D '64
Focus on folk art. M. C. Cole. il Flower Grower 50:16-19 D '63
Glowing prelude to Christmas. il Good H 157:224 D '63
Holiday decorations. C. MacArthur. il Horticulture 41:598 D '63
House beautiful's tenth annual Christmas collection. il House B 105:174-9 D '63
How to hang Christmas decorations. D. X. Manners. il House B 105:114+ D '63
In the spirit of the season. G. O'Brien. il N Y Times Mag p32-3 D 22 '63
Make a pair of elves. D. L. Brightbill. il Am Home 66:6 N '63
Most inviting door; winning designs from Christmas contest of 1963. il House & Gard 126:132-5 D '64
Ornaments that go from package to tree. il House & Gard 124:144-5 D '63
Plastic decorations you can make in your oven. M. Garrity. il Bet Hom & Gard 42:80-1+ N '64
Put the house in holiday trim. il Good H 157:122-3 D '63
Ready-made wreaths to decorate any door. il Good H 157:159 D '63
Red and green Christmas. il House & Gard 124:124-31 D '63
Shoe box decorations. il Design 66:40-1 N '64
Spherical fantasies you can make yourself. il House & Gard 124:148-9 D '63
These Xmas lights dance to music. L. Wortman. il Pop Sci 183:129-31 D '63
They're fun and they're unpretentious; Christmas ornaments made with straw. il Sunset 133:68-9 D '64
This December issue presents the true Christmas with all the very good things that Better homes & gardens families make and share and love. il Bet Hom & Gard 42:38-65+ D '64
This wreath is frosted carboard; Working with papers and plastics. il Sunset 131:105-6+ D '63
This year, create one new decoration. R. Martens. il Farm J 87:80-1 D '63
Tree lights. il Consumer Rep 28:552-3 N '63
Tree trimming party for the young person and the young in heart. il House B 105: 144-5 D '63
Trees: stars of Christmas. M. Davidson. il Ladies Home J 81:50-3 D '64
Trim up for holiday fun. il Parents Mag 38: 124 D '63
Wire, foil and tissue. il Sunset 131:74-7 D '63
With scissors and stapler little hands can create magnificent baubles of paper. il House & Gard 126:150-4 D '64
Wrappings and trimmings (title varies) (cont) New Yorker 39:185-94 D 14 '63
Wreaths: your most versatile ornaments. il Am Home 66:36-7 D '63
Yarns with a Yuletide twist. il Good H 157: 202 D '63
Your household. Consumer Rep 28:245 D '63
See also
Christmas greens
Christmas projects
Christmas trees
CHRISTMAS decorations, Outdoor
Christmas doorways, bold & beautiful. il McCalls 92:102-3 D '64
Dressing up for Christmas; reprint. J. Q. Copeland. il Recreation 56:452 D '63
Kindle the glow of Christmas. il Pop Gard 14:33-7 N '63
Magi with gifts in your entry window. il Sunset 133:64-5 D '64
Make your yard a Christmas card; Project-a-plan transparencies. D. Swartwout. il Pop Mech 120:138-43 D '63
One gardener's Christmas; Helen Snow Wilson. C. B. Lees. il Horticulture 42:24-7 D '64
Safe outdoor Christmas lighting. Sunset 131: 94+ D '63
Sparkling ideas for outside your house. J. E. Dwyer. il Pop Gard 15:40-1 N '64
Tribute to Christmas. il Am City 78:82 D '63
CHRISTMAS desserts. See Desserts
CHRISTMAS dinner; story. See Mostert, N.
CHRISTMAS dinners
Christmas at grandma's; with recipes. il McCalls 92:132-3+ D '64
Christmas dinner. il Good H 157:94-5 D '63
Christmas dinner: a festive roast. il Sunset 131:78-80 D '63
Christmas dinner with Tommy Davis. il Ebony 19:162+ D '63
Christmas dinners/U.S.A. W. Bar-Illan. il Ladies Home J 81:60-3+ D '64
Christmas is for giving; turkey and the trimmings; with recipes. il Suc Farm 62:54-5+ D '64
Classic Christmas dinners; menus and recipes. il Redbook 124:57-63+ D '64
CHRISTMAS entertainments
Magic of Christmas. G. J. Guetzlaff. il Recreation 56:411-12 N '63
Wassail bowl and the grete boar's hede; Christmas in the manner of old England at three resort hotels. il Sunset 131:44+ D '63
See also
College and school drama
CHRISTMAS eve
Enchanted cottage. M. Cousins. il Good H 157:104-9 D '63
When the Wise man appeared. W. A. Anderson. il Read Digest 86:99-101 Ja '65
CHRISTMAS every day; drama. See McGowan, J.
CHRISTMAS favors. See Party favors
CHRISTMAS gifts
Appropriate gift. il Esquire 60:173-84 D '63
Basic rules of holiday etiquette. il Good H 157:179 D '63

CHRISTMAS gifts—*Continued*
Best buy gifts; 1963-1964. il Consumer Rep 28: 512-16 N '63; 29:520-2 N '64
Boating's best in Christmas gifts. il Motor B 112:22-9 N '63
Christmas beauties: $4 and under; $5 and up. il Seventeen 22:82-5 D '63
Christmas classified. L. Lerman. Mlle 60:138-41 N '64
Christmas gift! L. Lerman. Mlle 58:64-5+ D '63
Christmas gift portfolio. il Esquire 62:181-91 D '64
Christmas gifts for archers. G. H. Gillelan. il Outdoor Life 132:90-1+ N '63
Christmas gifts for travelers. il Sunset 131: 16 D '63
Christmas gifts $25 and under. P. Peterson. il N Y Times Mag p 104-5+ D 8 '63
Christmas is for giving. il Suc Farm 62:48-50+ D '64
Christmas novelties, unusual merchandise: more ways to capture impulse sales. il Pub W 184:72-7 Ag 19 '63
Christmas presents for cooks and their kitchens and their entertaining tables. il Vogue 142:172-3 N 15 '63
Christmas shopper. il Craft Horiz 23:22-3 N '63; 24:20-1+ N '64
Christmas shoppers' science list; for the entire family. F. Snakenberg. il Sci N L 84:298-9 N 9 '63
Christmas: the present idea. Vogue 144:20+ N 15 '64
Christmas tree, 1964; sporting arms and accessories. W. Page. il Field & S 69:54-60 D '64
Especially for Christmas; spoken records. S. Potter. Am Rec G 30:339-40+ D '63
Esquire's Christmas gift guide. il Esquire 60: 97+ D '63; 62:220+ D '64
Fifty thoughtful Christmas presents that don't cost a cent. il Redbook 122:50-1+ D '63
For Christmas. il Farm J 87:68 D '63
Forty stocking stuffers. N. Rothschild. il Pop Phot 51:68-71 D '62
Gifts from museums (cont) il Consumer Rep 28:526-8; 29:544-6 N '63, N '64
Gifts galore to make ahead for Christmas. il Good H 157:118-21+ N '63
Gifts to make. il Seventeen 23:228-9 N '64
Gifts to make and sell at bazaars. R. Martens. il Farm J 87:80-2 O '63
Gifts to make for less than three dollars. il Redbook 122:62-5+ D '63
Gifts to make hobbyists happier than ever. il House & Gard 126:236-7 N '64
Gifts to make this Christmas the best Christmas yet. il House & Gard 124:236-45+ N '63
Gifts to please your favorite people. il Seventeen 23:30 N '64
Gifts $2 and under; $5 and under. il Seventeen 23:160-3 N '64
Giving, getting. N. H. Packer. Reporter 31: 28-30+ D 31 '64
Good housekeeping's famous gift list. il Good H 157:32+ D '63
Grand gifts. Am Home 67:78-9 D '64
How to play Santa Claus. Hi Fi 14:47 D '64
How to warm up a money gift. L. Anderson. il Farm J 87:66 D '63
It's the thought that counts. G. Glueck. il N Y Times Mag p98+ D 1 '63
Keppler on the SLR: valuable picture making trifles. H. Keppler. il Mod Phot 27:20+ D '63
Last call for Christmas. il Esquire 63:70-1 Ja '65
Last minute gifts. Am Home 67:91 D '64
Life guide; records for giving, books for giving. Life 55:27+ D 6 '63
Little beauties: from $1; from $5. il Seventeen 23:86-9 D '64
Little beauty gifts wrapped in beauty. il Good H 157:102-3+ D '63
Nineteen stockings by the chimney piece. P. S. Buck. il Read Digest 83:49-52 D '63
Packable presents: photographic equipment. L. Barry. il Pop Phot 53:162-5+ D '63
Pets: their Christmas pampering. il House & Gard 124:57 N '63
Presents with presence: black and white. il Mlle 58:138-41 N '63
Presents you can't buy. il McCalls 91:68 D '63
Quick gifts-to-make. il Seventeen 22:200-1 N '63
Religious gifts. E. P. Callaghan. McCalls 91:50+ D '63
Santa's odd lots. il Bsns W p36 D 5 '64
Say it with fragrance. il Redbook 122:22 D '63
Science for Santa's sack. F. Snakenberg. il Sci N L 86:314-15 N 14 '64
Send them home with a rare trifle. il House B 105:168-9+ D '63
Short-order Christmas gifts. il Ladies Home J 80:32 D '63
Smart, personal, and rewarding gifts from the darkroom. J. Von Miklos. il Pop Phot 51:72-5+ D '62
Snifter full of nylons. il Newsweek 64:66 D 21 '64
Start making these gifts for Christmas. il Am Home 67:16+ N '64
That's what I want for Christmas! il Changing T 18:42-3 D '64
Thirty gift suggestions for the compleat traveler. il House & Gard 124:58+ N '63
This December issue presents the true Christmas with all the very good things that Better homes & gardens families make and share and love. il Bet Hom & Gard 42:38-65+ D '64
Tiny surprises for a Christmas stocking. il House & Gard 124:62+ N '63
Tip top gifts. il Seventeen 23:208 N '64
'Tis better to give. C. Ford. il Field & S 68: 6+ Ja '64
Touch of the venerable. il Esquire 62:214-15 D '64
Very special gifts for the most important people in the world: your family. il House & Gard 124:52+ N '63
What is a family? A. P. Eliasberg. il N Y Times Mag p28 D 22 '63
Wishing you health, happiness, and the beauty of the season; electric appliances. McCalls 92:42 D '64
Worldwide bazaar. il Ladies Home J 80:139-40+ N '63
See also
Books as gifts
Food as gifts
Gifts in business
Plants as gifts
Wrapping of packages

Anecdotes, facetiae, satire, etc.

Thoughts that count. G. Glueck. N Y Times Mag p 121-2 D 13 '64
To: the finest little old sanitation men in the whole world. A. King. il McCalls 91:44 D '63

CHRISTMAS gifts for children
Cassie and Beth discover the joy of sharing. il Good H 157:48+ D '63
Children's Christmas book bag. Christian Cent 80:1584-7 D 18 '63
For the children. il Good H 157:209 D '63
Life guide; brain-stretching presents to give youngsters. il Life 55:11 N 22 '63
Miniature McCoy; sporting gear in girl-and-boy size. il Sports Illus 19:46-51 D 2 '63
On and off the avenue (cont) New Yorker 39:158+ D 7 '63; 40:204+ D 12 '64
Pockets full of Christmas. il House & Gard 124:268-9+ N '63
Stevie's small allowance gifts, $1 each. il Parents Mag 38:100 D '63
Toy guide for late shoppers. Parents Mag 38:68 D '63
Treats from toyland. il House & Gard 124: 246-7 N '63
See also
Books as gifts
Toys

Anecdotes, facetiae, satire, etc.

Manner of speaking; I'm dreaming of an endowed Christmas. J. Ciardi. Sat R 47: 14+ F 15 '64

CHRISTMAS gifts for men
From a boy's point of view. J. Wescott. il Seventeen 22:38 N; 24 D '63
Gifts for men. New Yorker 39:186-8+ D 7 '63
Gifts for men who like to hang around the house. il House & Gard 126:234-5 N '64
How to buy gifts for the men in your life. il Seventeen 23:150-1 D '64
V.I.P. for a V.I.P. il Mlle 58:112-15 D '63

CHRISTMAS gifts for pets
If you want a special gift for a pet. Good H 157:172 D '63

CHRISTMAS gifts for the home
For the home; $10 and less. il N Y Times Mag p 104-5+ N 24 '63
Gifts for the home, $10 and under. E. Sverbeyeff. il N Y Times Mag p84-5 D 13 '64
Gifts you couldn't give before. il House B 105:170-3+ D '63
Give something for the home from our mountain of down to earth gifts; And give something out of this world. il Am Home 67:40-3 D '64
Kitchen gifts: twice as useful in terry-towel wraps. il Good H 157:158 D '63
Last minute gifts that last for years. il Am Home 66:8 D '63

CHRISTMAS gifts for the home—*Continued*
Later the greater. il Esquire 61:116-17 Ja '64
Old-fashioned Christmas with new ideas. il Parents Mag 38:75+ D '63
On and off the avenue (cont) New Yorker 39:164+ N 30 '63
Promising presents. il Good H 157:182+ D '63
CHRISTMAS gifts for women
Last minute! last minute! last minute! L. Lerman. Mlle 58:106-7+ D '63
On and off the avenue (cont) New Yorker 39:153-6+ N 23 '63; 40:207-8+ N 28 '64
What one beauty editor would give another. Vogue 142:50+ D '63
CHRISTMAS greens
Easy-to-make golden wreath. W. E. Duggan. il Flower Grower 51:15 D '64
Flowers of Christmas. il Recreation 56:451 D '63
What's better at Christmas than red and green and candlelight. R. Martens and R. Miller. il Farm J 88:64-5 D '64
CHRISTMAS in art
Children's dream of Christmas. il N Y Times Mag p 10-11 D 22 '63
CHRISTMAS in old New England; drama. See Clapp, P.
CHRISTMAS in town; story. See Cousins, M.
CHRISTMAS legends
Christ child's lullaby and how it was first heard in the Isles; a Christmas legend from the Outer Hebrides, retold. A. Moray. Mlle 60:110-11+ D '64
CHRISTMAS lighting. See Christmas decorations
CHRISTMAS meals
Christmas at the inns. il McCalls 91:120-7+ D '63
Christmas breads to serve and give. il Parents Mag 38:69-72 D '63
Christmas in Euzkaldunak. D. Taylor. il Todays Health 42:18-19+ D '64
Christmas time savers! il Bet Hom & Gard 42:66-7 D '64
Citrus fruits: updating a Christmas favorite. G. Maddox. il Todays Health 41:38-43 D '63
Good eating through the holidays! V. T. Habeeb. il Am Home 66:42-3+ D '63
Good housekeeping's complete Christmas cookbook. il Good H 157:64-99 D '63
Special holiday food supplement; menus with recipes. il Ladies Home J 80:83-5+ D '63
This December issue presents the true Christmas with all the very good things that Better homes & gardens families make and share and love. il Bet Hom & Gard 42:38-65+ D '64
See also
Christmas dinners
CHRISTMAS music
Music can help make Christmas magic for children. L. Wilcox. il House B 105:166-7+ D '63
See also
Christmas carols
Phonograph records—Christmas music
CHRISTMAS pantomime. See Pantomime
CHRISTMAS parties. See Childrens parties; Entertaining
CHRISTMAS peppermints; drama. See Miller, H. L.
CHRISTMAS plants. See House plants
CHRISTMAS plates. See Pottery, Danish
CHRISTMAS plays
No no Novillis. S. J. Rowland, jr; discussion. Christian Cent 80:214+ F 13 '63
This Christmas let them put on their own play. E. Kinard. House B 105:146 D '63
See also
Pageants
Texts
Christmas bear. M. H. McQueen. Plays 23:69-74, 96 D '63
Christmas every day; dramatization of story by W. D. Howells. J. McGowan. Plays 23:87-95 D '63
Christmas in old New England. P. Clapp. Plays 23:37-44, 58 D '63
Christmas peppermints. H. L. Miller. Plays 23:49-57 D '63
Christmas revel. C. Boiko. Plays 24:39-50, 86 D '64
Christmas starlet. E. J. Dias. Plays 23:15-26 D '63
Christmas tablecloth. A. Fisher. Plays 23:45-8, 58 D '63
Christmas tree surprise. D. Newman. Plays 24:38, 77-80 D '64
Christmas umbrella. J. McGowan. Plays 24:51-60 D '64
Hotel Santa Claus. H. L. Miller. Plays 23:1-13 D '63
Jill-in-the-Box. F. B. Watts. Plays 23:75-80 D '63
Quiet Christmas. M. Hark and N. McQueen. Plays 24:15-28 D '64
Road to Bethlehem. G. DuBois. Plays 23:27-35 D '63
Santa Claus and the three polar bears. R. Bennett. Plays 23:81-5 D '63
Star of Bethlehem. A. C. Martens. Plays 24:1-14 D '64
Toinette and the elves; dramatization of story by S. Coolidge. A. Thane. Plays 23:59-68 D '63
Tree angel; dramatization of story by Judith Martin and Remy Charlip. il House B 105:147-9 D '63
CHRISTMAS poem; story. See O'Hara, J.
CHRISTMAS poetry
All spaces and times are suns. S. Crites. Christian Cent 81:1584 D 23 '64
American Christmas tree. W. Metcalf. il Am For 70:10 D '64
Amid unbelief and darkened fields. S. Bradley. Christian Cent 81:1584 D 23 '64
At Christmas. R. McGovern. Christian Cent 81:1583 D 23 '64
Christmas gift. K. Reeves. Ladies Home J 81:83 D '64
Christmas parable. V. W. Sykes. Farm J 87:83 D '63
Christmas prayer for a year of grace. il McCalls 91:74-7 D '63
First came Christmas. J. Ingalls. Christian Cent 81:1584 D 23 '64
Five Christmas poems. il America 111:800-1 D 19 '64
Gold and frankincense and myrrh. D. Chuk. Christian Cent 81:1588 D 23 '64
Midnight and morning. T. J. Carlisle. Horn Bk 39:575 D '63
Misszen and hitszen; donor and blitzen. M. Bracker. il N Y Times Mag p32-3+ D 8 '63
Poems for Christmas time. America 109:796-7 D 21 '63
Same glad tidings. N. Farber. Horn Bk 40:636-9 D '64
Shepherd's thoughts. R. Spargur. Christian Cent 81:1584 D 23 '64
Sonnet for Christmas. D. L. Metz. Christian Cent 81:1584 D 23 '64
Star to guide us. J. Merchant. il Farm J 88:57 D '64
Those last, late hours of Christmas eve. L. A. Welte. Horn Bk 40:595 D '64
'Tis the season to be frantic. J. Goodsell. McCalls 91:134 D '63
Tree in the plaza. F. B. Jacobs. McCalls 92:162 D '64
CHRISTMAS presents. See Christmas gifts
CHRISTMAS projects
Deck the house for the holdays. L. Marett. il Parents Mag 38:50-1+ D '63
Getting ready for Christmas? J. Gillies. Farm J 88:72+ D '64
CHRISTMAS revel; drama. See Boiko, C.
CHRISTMAS shopping
Don't be a sucker shopper! W. G. McClanahan. U S Camera 27:41+ D '64
How not to get Santa claustrophobia. J. L. O'Neill. Am Home 66:21+ N '63
This can make Christmas shopping easier. il Good H 157:163 N '63
Twenty ways to make Christmas merrier. Am Home 67:30+ D '64
CHRISTMAS snow; story. See Hall, D.
CHRISTMAS stamps. See Postage stamps
CHRISTMAS starlet; drama. See Dias, E. J.
CHRISTMAS stories
Big man on Beech street. B. B. Preston. il Seventeen 22:102-3 D '63
Cherishing kind. R. M. Stern. il Good H 157:58-9 D '63
Christmas carol; excerpts. C. Dickens. il Sat Eve Post 237:24-31 D 19 '64
Christmas dinner. N. Mostert. il Harper 229:69-74 D '64
Christmas fable. B. Montresor. il Opera N 28:6-7 D 28 '63
Christmas in town. M. Cousins. McCalls 92:130-1 D '64
Enchanted cottage. M. Cousins. il Good H 157:104-9 D '63
First gift, first love. R. A. Knowlton. il Good H 157:62-3 D '63
Going ahead. J. Williams. il Sat Eve Post 237:58-60 D 12 '64
How Joey caught the Christmas spirit; ed. by M. Longwell. G. Parker. il Farm J 87:64-5 D '63; 88:89 F '64
I wisk you a Merry Christmas. M. F. Brown. il Redbook 124:44-5 D '64
Last and most blessed Christmas gift. T. Taylor. il McCalls 91:78-9 D '63
Letter home. R. P. Davis. il Motor B 112:27 D '63

CHRISTMAS stories—*Continued*
May your days be merry and bright. W. Shore. il Sat Eve Post 236:44-5 D 21 '63
Merry Christmas, Mr Longfellow. J. Fritz. il Seventeen 22:78-9 D '63
Nice girl for Christmas. J. Fritz. il Seventeen 23:76-7 D '64
Nights before Christmas. A. Cavanaugh. Mc Calls 92:100-1 D '64
1964 Christmas books: advance reviews. P. H. Allen. il Library J 89:4115-17 O 15 '64
No room. S. Q. McCann. il Redbook 124:40-1 D '64
No time like Christmas. C. Ford. Field & S 69:6+ D '64
Orphan for Christmas. C. Boyd. il Redbook 122:66-7 D '63
Please get serious! P. D. Boles. il Seventeen 23:82-3 D '64
Precious herbs of Christmas. R. Sawyer. Horn Bk 39:635-41 D '63
Runaway Christmas stockings. A. Rabin. il Ladies Home J 80:138a D '63
Shepherd. N. Lofts. il Ladies Home J 81:54-5 D '64
Some legends of Christmas. M. Benasutti. il Horn Bk 39:573-5 D '63
Stop here, my friend. M. J. Gerber. il Redbook 124:64-5 D '64
Stories to read aloud at Christmas time. L. Wilcox. il House B 105:24 D '63
This is the Christmas; Serbian folk tale. R. Sawyer. Horn Bk 40:666-73 D '64
'Tis always the same. C. O'Flynn. il Cath World 200:178-84 D '64
Trouble with Christmas. R. Gordon. il McCalls 91:82-3 D '63
You can't run away from Christmas. E. Streeter. McCalls 92:112-13 D '64
CHRISTMAS suppers
Supper dishes. il Good H 157:90-1 D '63
CHRISTMAS tablecloth; drama. See Fisher, A.
CHRISTMAS toys. See Toys
CHRISTMAS tree lights. See Christmas decorations
CHRISTMAS tree nurseries. See Nurseries (horticulture)
CHRISTMAS tree ornaments. See Christmas decorations
CHRISTMAS tree stands
How to make an imaginative Christmas tree base. il House & Gard 176:148-9+ D '64
Points to check about tree holders. il Good H 157:178 D '63
CHRISTMAS tree surprise; drama. See Newman, D.
CHRISTMAS trees
Accent in quality. A. Dickson. il Am For 70:8-9 D '64
All around the place. J. Milton. Pop Gard 15:51 N '64
And a profit in a polyvinyl tree. il Time 84:108+ D 11 '64
Christmas at the Kern's. il Am For 70:2-4 D '64
Christmas tree fit for royal children. il Ladies Home J 80:150-1 D '63
Christmas trees live on. L. D. Martin. il Pop Gard 14:3+ N '63
For a safer Christmas. Consumer Bul 46:25 D '63
46 million Christmas trees. Am For 70:13 D '64
Good-by, Christmas tree. M. Holmes. il McCalls 92:180 D '64
Good uses for old Christmas trees. Good H 157:179 D '63
How to choose and trim a Christmas tree. J. W. Pockriss. il McCalls 92:34 D '64
Importance of water to Christmas trees. Horticulture 42:12 D '64
Introducing the character tree. il Sunset 133:58-61 D '64
Live Christmas tree in a pot. il Sunset 133:160-1 D '64
Make a nut tree. il Suc Farm 62:87 N '64
Most splendid tree; winning ideas from Christmas tree contest of 1962. il House & Gard 124:132-7 D '63
O Christmas tree, O Christmas tree. il Sunset 131:56-63 D '63
Papa's disappearing Christmas tree. H. F. Brooks. il Todays Health 41:30-3+ D '63
They grow high-quality Christmas trees; H. Reiley, Bellaire, Mich. il Suc Farm 61:66-7 D '63
Things you ought to know about Christmas trees. A. M. Sowder. il Am For 69:12-15+ D '63
Tree of Christmas; fir tree. K. Bowe. il Am For 69:16-17+ D '63
Tree trimming party for the young person and the young in heart. il House B 105:144-5 D '63
Tree-trimming tips. K. Murray. il Pop Sci 185:123 D '64
Trees by the million, ready for Christmas. il Bsns W p92-4 D 12 '64
Up in flames on twelfth night. il Sunset 134:75 Ja '65
Variations on Christmas trees. il Design 66:19-20 N '64
Ways to fireproof your Christmas. Suc Farm 62:41 D '64
You can have your tree and keep it too. il Sunset 131:178-9 D '63
CHRISTMAS umbrella; drama. See McGowan, J.
CHRISTMAS wrappings. See Wrapping of packages
CHRISTMAS wreaths. See Christmas greens
CHRISTMAS wreaths, Artificial. See Christmas decorations
CHRISTOPHER, Joe
Player of the week; Met outfielder. por Sports Illus 21:76 Ag 31 '64
CHRISTY, George
Frankie's kids. Good H 158:80-1+ Je '64
(ed) See Cooper, V. B. How I faced tomorrow
(ed) See Melcher, T. Doris Day I know
CHROMAFFIN
Chromaffin cell: electron microscopic identification in the human dermis. M. H. McGavran. bibliog il Science 145:275-6 Jl 17 '64
CHROMATIN
Heterochromatic chromosomes in the coccids. S. W. Brown and U. Nur. bibliog il Science 145:130-6 Jl 10 '64
CHROMATOGRAPHIC analysis
Accurate chromatographic method for sorption isotherms and phase equilibria. F. Helfferich and D. L. Peterson. bibliog il Science 142:661-2 N 8 '63
Biological implications of gas chromatography; with editorial comment. A. Karmen. bibliog il Science 142:161, 163-72 O 11 '63
Chromatographic heterogeneity of rabbit serum amylase. J. E. Berk and others. bibliog il Science 141:1182-3 S 20 '63
Differential estimation of gamma-butyrolactone and gamma-dydroxybutyric acid in rat blood and brain. N. J. Giarman and R. H. Roth. bibliog il Science 145:583-4 Ag 7 '64
Gas chromatography; report on international symposium. A. B. Littlewood. Science 144:1597+ Je 26 '64
Indophenol blue as a chromogenic agent for identification of halogenated aromatic hydrocarbons. S. O. Graham. bibliog il Science 139:835-6 Mr 1 '63
Isotopic molecules: separation by recycle gas chromatography. J. W. Root and others. bibliog il Science 143:676-8 F 14 '64
Toxic residues in soil nine years after treatment with aldrin and heptachlor. A. T. S. Wilkinson and others. il Science 143:681-2 F 14 '64
Bibliography
Gas chromatography, the art and the science. H. W. Habgood. Science 139:579-80 F 15 '63
CHROMITE
Nature in rock & mineral. P. M. Tilden. il Natur Hist 73:59-63 Ja '64
CHROMOSOMES
Abnormalities associated with a chromosome region in the mouse. L. C. Dunn; D. Bennett. bibliog il Science 144:260-7 Ap 17 '64
Acquired chromosomal anomalies induced in mice by injection of a teratogen in pregnancy. T. H. Ingalls and others. bibliog il Science 141:810-12 Ag 30 '63
Case of the two X's. Newsweek 62:68 Jl 29 '63
Christmas factor: dosage compensation and the production of blood coagulation factor IX. O. Frota-Pessoa and others. bibliog il Science 139:348-9 Ja 25 '63
Chromosome aberrations: their role in the etiology of murine leukemia. M. A. Rich and others. bibliog il Science 146:252-3 O 9 '64
Chromosome abnormalities in vitro in human leukocytes associated with Schmidt-Ruppin Rous sarcoma virus. W. W. Nichols and others. bibliog il Science 146:248-50 O 9 '64
Chromosome complements of two species of primates: cynopithecus niger and presbytis entellus. R. N. Ushijima and others. bibliog il Science 146:78-9 O 2 '64
Chromosome number and morphology of a human preinvasive neoplasm. R. M. Richart and P. A. Corfman. bibliog il Science 144:65-7 Ap 3 '64
Chromosome puffs. W. Beermann and U. Clever. il Sci Am 210:50-8 bibliog(p 156) Ap '64

CHROMOSOMES—*Continued*
Chromosome variations. Sci N L 84:51 Jl 27 '63
Chromosomes and miscarriage. Sci Am 210:59 Je '64
Cytoplasmic sterility in drosophila paulistorum which is ultimately dependent on nuclear genes. L. Ehrman. bibliog Science 145:159 Jl 10 '64; Reply with rejoinder. V. G. Meyer. 145:1460 S 25 '64
DNA contents and chromosome Ph[1] and chromosome 21 in human chronic granulocytic leukemia. G. T. Rudkin and others. bibliog il Science 144:1229-32 Je 5 '64
Distributive pairing and aneuploidy in man. R. F. Grell and J. I. Valencia. bibliog Science 145:66-7 Jl 3 '64
Giant polytene chromosomes in hypodermal cells of developing footpads of dipteran pupae. J. M. Whitten. bibliog il Science 143:1437-8 Mr 27 '64
Gynogenesis in salamanders related to amybstoma jeffersonianum. H. C. MacGregor and T. M. Uzzell, jr. bibliog il Science 143:1043-5 Mr 6 '64
Hereditary quiz. J. Daugherty and M. Daugherty. il Sci Digest 56:89-91 N '64
Heterochromatic chromosomes in the coccids. S. W. Brown and U. Nur. bibliog il Science 145:130-6 Jl 10 '64
Lyon & the Mouse. Time 82:64 Jl 26 '63
Mammalian X-chromosome action; inactivation limited in spread and in region of origin. L. B. Russell. bibliog il Science 140:976-8 My 31 '63
Mosaic females. Sci Am 209:70+ N '63
Mosaic histocompatibility of skin grafts from female mice. D. W. Bailey. bibliog il Science 141:631-3 Ag 16 '63
Plastids and mitochondria: inheritable systems. A. Gibor and S. Granick. bibliog il Science 145:890-7 Ag 28 '64
Preferential segregation of chromosomes from a trivalent in haplopappus gracilis. R. C. Jackson. bibliog il Science 145:511-13 Jl 31 '64
Puffs heredity clue. W. Wingo. Sci N L 86:83 Ag 8 '64
Radiation-induced mouse leukemia: consistent occurrence of an extra and a marker chromosome. N. Wald and others. bibliog il Science 143:810-13 F 21 '64
Reduced incidence of persistent chromosome aberrations in mice irradiated at low dose rates. P. C. Nowell and L. J. Cole. bibliog il Science 141:524-6 Ag 9 '63
Rous sarcoma in Chinese hamsters. C. G. Ahlström and others. bibliog il Science 144:1232-3 Je 5 '64
Sex chromatin patterns and the Lyon hypothesis. R. DeMars. bibliog il Science 141:649-50 Ag 16 '63
Sex differences in cells. U. Mittwoch. il Sci Am 209:54-62 bibliog(p 170) Jl '63
See also
Crossing over (genetics)
Genetics

CHROMOSOMES (botany)
Chromosome number of rose clover, trifolium hirtum. E. J. Britten. bibliog il Science 142:401-2 O 18 '63
Development of complete homozygotes of tobacco. G. W. Stokes. bibliog il Science 141:1185 S 20 '63
Genetic activity in a heterochromatic chromosome segment of the tomato. G. S. Khush and others. bibliog il Science 145:1432-4 S 25 '64
Haploids: high-frequency production from single-embryo seeds in a line of Pima cotton. E. L. Turcotte and C. V. Feaster. bibliog il Science 140:1407-8 Je 28 '63
Relationship between nuclear volumes, chromosome numbers, and relative radiosensitivities. A. H. Sparrow and others. bibliog il Science 141:163-6 Jl 12 '63
Somatic mitoses in cells of picea glauca cultivated in vitro. P. G. Risser. bibliog il Science 143:591-2 F 7 '64
Synergistic effect of 5-bromodeoxyuridine and gamma rays on chromosomes. F. K. S. Koo. bibliog il Science 141:261-2 Jl 19 '63
Wheat: reconstitution of the tetraploid component (AABB) of hexaploids. E. R. Kerber. bibliog il Science 143:253-5 Ja 17 '64

CHROMOSPHERE. See Sun—Atmosphere

CHRONIC bronchitis. See Bronchitis

CHRONIC respiratory disease. See Poultry—Diseases and pests

CHRONICLE (San Francisco) See San Francisco chronicle

CHRONICLE-star, Pascagoula. See Pascagoula chronicle-star and advertiser

CHRONOLOGY
See also
Geological time

CHRONOLOGY, Historical
Year one. M. I. Finley. il Horizon 6:4-17 Wint '64

CHRONOMETERS
John Harrison's million-dollar clock. H. Helfer. il Sci Digest 55:62-4 Mr '64

CHRONOMETRY, Mental. See Time perception

CHRYSANTHEMUMS
Add fall color to your outdoor living room with chrysanthemums. J. H. Buswell. il Pop Gard 14:48+ My '63
Best in show. J. Simpkins. il Flower Grower 50:38-42 Je '63
Big ones are as easy to grow as one, two, three. il Flower Grower 51:27 My '64
Bulb for summer color. M. B. Shaffer. Flower Grower 50:41-2 D '63
Chrysanthemums. E. Gantner. il Pop Gard 15:30-1+ My '64
Decorating with fresh chrysanthemums. il Sunset 131:288 O '63
For rivers of color come autumn. il Sunset 130:280 My '63
Garden in a basket. M. W. Stephens. il Flower Grower 50:15-16 Je '63
Getting a fresh start with new mums. P. F. Frese. Pop Gard 15:74 My '64
Grow a mum tree. J. W. Clausen. il Pop Gard 15:21 S '64
How hardy are hardy chrysanthemums? D. Henry. il Horticulture 41:444-5 S '63
Ideas from a chryanthemum master. il Sunset 133:276+ O '64
Shade chrysanthemums for early bloom. K. Clapp. il Horticulture 41:508-9 O '63
Winter protection for chrysanthemums. C. G. Dubois. il Flower Grower 50:62-3 O '63
You can fool them into early blooming. C. A. Lewis. il Flower Grower 51:39-40 Je '64

CHRYSANTHEMUMS, Arrangements of. See Flowers, Arrangement of

CHRYSLER corporation
At the Daytona speedway derby: stock-car racing. il Newsweek 63:75-8 F 24 '64
Bending the guidelines; U.A.W.-Chrysler settlement. il Time 84:29-30 S 18 '64
Big test; gas-turbine engine. il Time 81:90 My 10 '63
Bulldog in Chrysler's stable? plans to acquire Mack truck; will Justice dept. approve? Bsns W p28-9 My 9 '64
Chassis for the masses; the Farmobil. il Newsweek 61:76 My 6 '63
Chrysler counts on '64s to keep sales climbing. Bsns W p25 Ag 17 '63
Chrysler gets aboard British auto boom. Bsns W p54 Je 13 '64
Chrysler makes its turn on to the road back. il Bsns W p 116-18+ O 31 '64
Chrysler move rouses France. Bsns W p 100 Ja 26 '63
Chrysler restyles top ranks. Bsns W p32+ Ja 19 '63
Chrysler settles: what price peace? il Newsweek 64:87-90 S 21 '64
Chrysler soups up foreign sales. il Bsns W p47-8 F 8 '64
Chrysler's computer does the talking faster and cheaper. il Bsns W p52-3 Ag 24 '63
Chrysler's Spanish accent. Time 82:96 O 11 '63
Comeback in Detroit. J. C. Jones. il Sat Eve Post 236:74-6 My 25 '63
Day Chrysler came to town. Duns R 83:pt2 105 Mr '64
Great divide; two-for-one stock split. Newsweek 61:70 F 18 '63
Hard line; challenge by the Justice department to merger with Mack trucks, inc. Newsweek 64:60 Ag 31 '64
Hatching our giant space birds: Saturn boosters of Michoud plant. il Bsns W p57-61 Ja 4 '64
If you're big, grow from within; Justice dept. to Chrysler and Mack. Bsns W p26 Ag 8 '64
Introduction to the '65 cars. il Motor T 16:42-7 N '64
New ones, 1965. il Motor T 16:42-7 O '64
1964 Chrysler corp. engineering. J. Wright. il Motor T 15:28-31 S '63
Peace at a price; Chrysler pact with UAW; with editorial comment. il Bsns W p27-9, 204 S 12 '64
Price of labor peace in the auto industry. il U S News 57:82-5 S 21 '64
Pulling the rug from stock options. Bsns W p 104+ Ja 11 '64
SR's businessman of the year: G. H. Love. W. D. Patterson. Sat R 47:45-6+ Ja 11 '64
'64 cars. il Motor T 15:56-63 N '63

CHRYSLER corporation—*Continued*
Special-interest cars; thirty years of Airflow design. B. Selbrede. il Motor T 16:74 N '64
Sput . . . pop . . . clank . . . varoom! Chrysler-Plymouth national troubleshooting contest. C. N. Barnard. il Sat Eve Post 237:66-8 N 14 '64
Target; Chrysler picked for strike action. Newsweek 64:64 S 7 '64
Target: Chrysler; possibility of an auto strike. Time 84:91 S 4 '64
Test-driving a jet; Chrysler's new turbine engine. il Bsns W p74-6+ Mr 28 '64
That's the jet. il Newsweek 62:94+ N 11 '63
Trail-blazing pact? Sr Schol 85:24 S 30 '64
Trouble shooters; Plymouth's interscholastic automotive program. B. Greene. il Hot Rod 16:36-9 S '63
Turbine drive. Newsweek 61:84-6 My 13 '63
UAW changes target. il Bsns W p82+ S 5 '64
Wage chronology: Chrysler corp; 1961-64. il Mo Labor R 87:904-15 Ag '64
What's new at the Chrysler corporation. J. Whipple. il Pop Sci 185:86-9 O '64
Why union chose Chrysler as target for strike. il U S News 57:73-4 S 7 '64
Will there be a rush for early retirement? il U S News 57:106-8 S 28 '64

Dodge division

Dodge's golden anniversary. il Motor T 15:44-9 O '63

CHRYSOSTOMOS, abp
Russian calls on Pope but Greek snubs him. Christian Cent 80:1193 O 2 '63

CHRYSTIE, Frances N.
Maurice Sendak: an artist best understood by children. Pub W 185:87-9 F 24 '64

CHU, Chang-chao
China unearths its greatest wall-paintings. Art N 62:31-3+ S '63

CHU, Don-chean
(tr) See Wang, L. Y. Housewife becomes literate in Communist China

CHU, Valentin
China: a monster devours itself; excerpts from Ta ta, tan tan (Fight fight, talk talk) Life 54:86-8+ My 3 '63

CHUBBUCK, John
Machine that plugs itslef in. il Sci Digest 56:61-2 Ag '64

CHUCK boxes. See Automobiles—Camping equipment

CHUCK hunting. See Woodchuck hunting

CHUINARD, R. G. See Wellings, S. R. jt. auth.

CHUK, David
Gold and frankincense and myrrh; poem. Christian Cent 81:1588 D 23 '64

CHUKAR shooting. See Partridge shooting

CHUKARS. See Partridges

CHUKOVSKY, Kornei
From the world of Ivan jr; excerpts from From two to five, ed. by J. W. Levin. N Y Times Mag p22 D 29 '63
From two to five. R. H. Viguers. Horn Bk 40:84-5 F '64

CHUONG, Tran-van-. See Tran-van-Chuong

CHUONG, Tran-van-, Mme. See Tran-van-Chuong, Mme

CHURCH, Frank
Atlantic future: Europe's choice. Harper 227:18+ N '63
Conspiracy USA. por Look 29:21-3 Ja 26 '65
Excerpt from address, January 22, 1964. Cong Digest 43:148+ My '64
Korean paralysis. Nation 198:347-8+ Ap 6 '64
What is a liberal? a liberal senator answers. por U S News 54:117-19 My 6 '63

CHURCH, R. J. Harrison
Senegal. bibliog Focus 15:1-6 S '64

CHURCH, Ruth Ellen
Gourmet diet cook book. House & Gard 125:143-5+ Je '64

CHURCH
Also on Sunday; New York city's Judson memorial church. B. Moore and P. Moore. il Mlle 58:66-9 D '63
I am for the churches. R. W. Riis. il Read Digest 84:135-8 Je '64
Interconfessional research; address, February 3, 1964. P. S. Minear. Vital Speeches 30:343-6 Mr 15 '64
Structures of the church, by H. Küng. Review
Commonweal 80:554-5 Ag 7 '64. D. J. O'Hanlon
See also
Catholic church
Christianity
Women and the church

Authority

Authority and the theologian. D. Callahan. Commonweal 80:319-23 Je 5 '64; Discussion. 80:511-14 Jl 24 '64
Authority in the church. A. M. Greeley. Commonweal 80:515-16 Jl 24 '64
Collegiality: Catholic episcopate with editorial comment. L. M. Orsy. America 110:754, 760-3 My 30 '64
From Döllinger to Vatican II; a century too soon? J. Coulson. Commonweal 79:400-3 D 27 '63
New theology. J. Chapin. America 110:469 Ap 4 '64
Politics and Catholic freedom, by G. Wills. Review
Commonweal 80:607-9 S 4 '64. D. Callahan
Primacy and collegiality. America 110:476 Ap 4 '64
Public opinion in the church; excerpts from pastoral letter. R. J. Cushing. Commonweal 78:426-7 Jl 12 '63
Quest for honesty. D. Callahan. Commonweal 80:137-40 Ap 24 '64; Reply with rejoinder. D. P. Gray. 80:262-3 My 22 '64

Bibliography

Nature of the church. D. B. Watermulder. Christian Cent 81:47-9 Ja 8 '64

CHURCH, Negro. See Negroes in the United States—Religion

CHURCH administration. See Church government

CHURCH advertising
Presbyterians jingle; gospel jingles on radio. Christian Cent 80:973 Ag 7 '63; Discussion. 80:1219 O 2 '63
Sublimely subliminal; first doctoral thesis on Public relations of religious institutions in a pluralistic society. il Newsweek 62:78-9 Jl 15 '63

CHURCH and art. See Art and religion

CHURCH and economic problems. See Christianity and economics

CHURCH and education
Religion and the Court. J. O'Gara. Commonweal 78:391 Jl 5 '63
Secular tendency in church-related colleges in Pennsylvania; excerpt from History of higher education in Pennsylvania. S. Sack. bibliog f Sch & Soc 91:430+ D 28 '63
See also
Public schools and religion

CHURCH and international relations
Back of the changes in Vatican policy; Pacem in terris. il U S News 54:60-1 Ap 29 '63
Love and power in today's setting. A. J. Muste. Christian Cent 80:639-42 My 15 '63
Paul VI to U Thant. America 109:91-2 Jl 27 '63
Peacemaking a church calling; colloquy called by Church peace mission, Oberlin, Ohio. P. Peachey. Christian Cent 80:952-4 Jl 31 '63
Political policies. America 109:7-8 Jl 6 '63
They're mad at the Pope. America 111:542 N 7 '64
Thinking the unthinkable; concerning, F. Nolde's address at W.C.C. conference, Buck Hill Falls. Christian Cent 81:627-8 My 13 '64

CHURCH and labor
Dialogue with workers. America 109:106 Ag 3 '63
Joblessness: the coming challenge. L. E. Schaller. Christian Cent 80:171-3 F 6 '63
Pulpit-pew problem. L. K. Bishop Christian Cent 81:968 Jl 29 '64
See also
Worker priests

CHURCH and politics
Anti-Goldwater Protestants. America 111:280 S 19 '64
Backlash and the Catholic vote; Miller's Catholicism. R. W. Gibbons. Christian Cent 81:1303-5 O 21 '64
Catholic on the ticket? America 110:72-3 Ja 18 '64
Catholics for vice president. America 111:98 Ag 1 '64
Changing times and Catholics on the ticket. M. McGrory. America 111:124 Ag 8 '64
Churches' mandate. Christian Cent 81:1419-20 N 18 '64; Discussion. 81:1621 D 30 '64
Concerning the education of clergymen. R. Kirk. Nat R 14:238 Mr 26 '63; Reply. A. B. Muller. 14:425 My 21 '63
How big is the bloc vote? S. M. Lipset. il N Y Times Mag p32-3+ O 25 '64
How religion influences your politics. il Sci Digest 54:39 S '63
Love, hatred and politics. Christian Cent 80:1423-4 N 20 '63

CHURCH and politics—*Continued*
Loyalties in the emerging nations. G. W. Shepherd, jr. Christian Cent 80:206-7 F 13 '63
1964 religious issue. Christian Cent 81:1227-8 O 7 '64
On presenting both sides. Christian Cent 81: 1163-4 S 23 '64
Paul VI on Vietnam. America 109:337 S 28 '63
Politics and pulpit. America 111:404 O 10 '64
Politics in the pulpit; presidential campaign. il Time 84:63 O 9 '64
Puerto Rican Evangelicals oppose religious parties. Christian Cent 80:1490 D 4 '63
Pulpits and politics; presidential campaign and U.S. churchmen. il Newsweek 64:90 N 2 '64
Religion and freedom in the modern world, by H. J. Muller. Review
Christian Cent 81:1014-16 Ag 12 '64. M. E. Marty
Religion is not a political issue. Christian Cent 81:6 Ja 1 '64
Religion not a 1964 issue. Christian Cent 81:1004 Ag 12 '64
Religious vote: when, why and how much? L. H. Fuchs. Cath World 200:285-93 F '65
Sermon that caused a political furor; excerpts; with comments by W. F. Creighton and A. P. Shirkey. F. B. Sayre. il U S News 57:23-4 S 28 '64
See also
Church and state

CHURCH and race problems
Actions speak louder. America 110:32 Ja 11 '64
Aftermath of violence; New York state. T. L. Conklin. Christian Cent 81:1045-6 Ag 19 '64
Another pilgrimage to Jackson; seven ministers barred from Capitol street Methodist church. T. Thompson. Christian Cent 81: 511-12 Ap 22 '64
Appeal to conscience; statement. Commonweal 77:518 F 8 '63
Are southern churches silent? S. Southard. Christian Cent 80:1429-32 N 20 '63
Backlash and Christian faith. R. R. Parsonage. Christian Cent 81:1300-2 O 21 '64
Backlash and the Catholic vote; Miller's Catholicism. R. W. Gibbons. Christian Cent 81:1303-5 O 21 '64
Backlash hits the churches. Christian Cent 81:1004-5 Ag 12 '64
Baltimore story. America 109:256 S 14 '63
Beyond lip service; Methodist church's General conference. Time 83:53 My 15 '64
Bishop Sheen distorts the truth. Christian Cent 80:996 Ag 14 '63
Bishops on racism. America 109:127 Ag 10 '63
Cable to Rome. Nation 198:643 Je 29 '64
Cardinal in Harlem. America 109:86 Jl 27 '63
Catholics and race. America 109:33; 110:276-7 Jl 13 '63, F 29 '64
Catholics and racial bias. America 108:351 Mr 16 '63
CURE; Los Angeles movement for racial equality and social justice. Commonweal 80:352 Je 12 '64
Christian morality and race issues. Life 56:4 Mr 27 '64
Christian obedience in a world we don't control. P. Peachey. Christian Cent 81:458-60 Ap 8 '64
Christian social ethics. E. J. Carnell. Christian Cent 80:979-80 Ag 7 '63; Reply. M. L. Stackhouse. 80:1219 O 2 '63
Christianity in Harlem. P. F. Berrigan. il Commonweal 81:323-5 N 27 '64
Church and civil rights. America 111:122 Ag 8 '64
Church and race: letters to the editor. Christian Cent 80:1032 Ag 21 '63
Churches challenged; National council of churches and southern Presbyterians. America 112:4 Ja 2 '65
Churches meet racial crisis; with text of statement to churches. H. E. Fey. Christian Cent 80:1572-3 D 18 '63
Churches mobilize. America 110:328 Mr 14 '64
Churches will follow. B. E. Mays. Christian Cent 81:513-14 Ap 22 '64
Churchmen admonish West coast realtors. Christian Cent 81:70 Ja 15 '64
Churchmen defend sit-in student. Christian Cent 80:821 Je 26 '63; Discussion. 80:1106, 1239 S 11, O 9 '63
Civil rights and religion. America 111:79 Jl 25 '64
Congress' fateful decision. Christian Cent 80: 1323 O 30 '63; Reply. S. L. Yale. 80:1519-20 D 4 '63
Convenient Catholicism. America 110:815 Je 13 '64
Crisis in American Protestantism. R. Niebuhr. Christian Cent 80:1498-501 D 4 '63
Demonstration defused by Methodist bishops. Christian Cent 80:1489-90 D 4 '63
Denies right to go to church; Capitol street Methodist church in Jackson, Miss. Christian Cent 80:1324 O 30 '63
Dialogue among pickets; segregation in Boston schools. H. Cox. Commonweal 79:245-6 N 22 '63; Reply with rejoinder. J. A. Murray. 79:485-6 Ja 24 '64
Disappointing statement; Bonds of union, written in Rome. Commonweal 79:267-8 N 29 '63; Reply with rejoinder. J. F. Cronin. 79:373 D 20 '63
Disciples on civil rights; International convention of Christian churches. H. E. Fey. Christian Cent 80:1326-7 O 30 '63
Divided flocks in Jackson. G. Forshey. Christian Cent 80:1469-71 N 27 '63
Doing is the difference; Student interracial ministry. America 112:33 Ja 9 '65
Down to brass tacks; recent episcopal directives. America 109:107 Ag 3 '63
Easter in Jackson; Methodist bishops barred from Galloway memorial Methodist church. J. K. Mathews. Christian Cent 81:478-80 Ap 15 '64
11 a.m. Sunday is our most segregated hour. K. Haselden. il N Y Times Mag p9+ Ag 2 '64
Episcopal leadership; Cardinal Cushing on religious and moral responsibility of Catholics. America 111:249 S 12 '64
Evading the issue; racial crisis in the South. Christian Cent 80:1356-7 N 6 '63
Exile from Los Angeles; Rev J. V. Coffield leaves Los Angeles for Chicago. Newsweek 65:57 Ja 11 '65
Faith & prejudice in Georgia; Lovett school's whites-only admission policy. il Time 82: 94 N 15 '63
Faith and prejudice: intergroup problems in Protestant curricula, by B. E. Olson. Review
Commentary 35:455-60 My '63. M. E. Marty; Reply. B. E. Olson. 36:197-9 S '63
Far West bishops on race. America 111:244 S 12 '64
Focus on the central jurisdiction; Methodist general conference. P. Wogaman. Christian Cent 80:1296-8 O 23 '63
For integrated churches; faculty of Vanderbilt divinity school. Christian Cent 80:1194 O 2 '63
Force of conscience; March on Gwynn Oak park. il Time 82:17-18 Jl 12 '63
Getting nowhere fast? J. O'Gara. Commonweal 80:194 My 8 '64
Glorious opportunity; establishment of Emergency commission on religion and race. Newsweek 62:55 Jl 8 '63
Gwynn Oak; nine Catholic priests startled Baltimore by joining with the pickets to protest segregation at an amusement park. T. Mattingly. America 109:136-7 Ag 10 '63; Reply. F. X. Gallagher. 109:249 S 14 '63
Hattiesburg and central Illinois. J. Moore. Christian Cent 81:340-1 Mr 11 '64
Hattiesburg: toward reconciliation; Hattiesburg ministers project. L. Minear. Christian Cent 81:1115-16 S 9 '64
Heart of the matter; pastoral letter officially banning racial discrimination. Nation 196: 218 Mr 16 '63
How do churches get involved? Christian Cent 80:420 Ap 3 '63
In the struggle. Newsweek 62:80 Jl 22 '63
India and the Negro question; here's how Birmingham and Montgomery look to people around the world. I. Travers-Ball. America 109:44-5 Jl 13 '63
Insider stays to fight. C. S. Wren. il Look 28:26-8 S 8 '64
Interracial council; request for amendment specifying that it is un-Christian to discriminate on grounds of race. America 109: 544 N 9 '63
Is America Christian? J. B. Bush. Negro Hist Bul 27:173+ Ap '64
Justice, southern style; Ashton Jones vs Atlanta's First Baptist church. J. Gillies. Christian Cent 81:112-14 Ja 22 '64; Reply. R. O. McClain. 81:270-2 F 26 '64
Last resort. America 109:188 Ag 24 '63
Letter from Williamston. H. Cox. Christian Cent 80:1516-18 D 4 '63
Lincoln memorial seminary; Protestant, Jewish and Catholic seminarians continuous vigil at the Lincoln memorial. America 110:620 My 9 '64
Los Angeles, 1964. il Newsweek 63:82 Je 29 '64
Methodists: crisis of conscience. R. L. Roy. il Nation 198:262-5 Mr 16 '64

CHURCH and race problems—*Continued*
Methodists vote four-year integration. Christian Cent 81:630 My 13 '64
Minister; experiences in Mississippi. B. A. Asbury. il Nation 199:509-12 D 28 '64
Mississippians repudiate religious freedom; Capitol Street Methodist church in Jackson, Miss. Christian Cent 80:1425-6 N 20 '63
Moral miracle; Cardinal Cushing's plea for change of attitude towards Negroes. America 110:785 Je 6 '64
N.C.C. acts on racial crisis. H. E. Fey. Christian Cent 80:797-8 Je 19 '63
N.C.C. visits Clarksdale. S. C. Rose. Christian Cent 80:1104-6 S 11 '63
News of the Christian world. W. M. Wells, jr. Christian Cent 80:837-8 Je 26 '63
No postponement; concerning Jesuit letter on the race question. America 109:762-3 D 14 '63
No private domain; racism at home viewed from the church's mission posts abroad; statements of the Presbyterian board of world missions. Christian Cent 81:184 F 5 '64
Not words but acts. Commonweal 78:444 Jl 26 '63
Notes from an irrelevant clergyman. W. Carr. Christian Cent 80:879-81 Jl 10 '63
On race relations. H. W. Fry. Christian Cent 81:1121-2 S 9 '64
On the road to Washington; opinions of Freedom bus riders. E. A. Spreitzer. America 109:426-7 O 12 '63
Philadelphia, still closed; Catholic attitudes toward racial changes. D. Clark. Commonweal 80:167-70 My 1 '64; Discussion. 80:259-60, 366-9, 451 My 22, Je 12, Jl 3 '64
Pickets, marches or dialogues. J. B. Sheerin. Cath World 198:3-6 O '63
Prayer for these times. T. W. Halloran. America 109:161 Ag 17 '63
Preaching on civil rights. America 111:506 O 31 '64
Presbyterians hold line on school prayers; racial justice. Christian Cent 80:1538 D 11 '63
Priestly witness; protest against failure of the archdiocese to take leadership on civil rights issues. America 112:66 Ja 16 '65
Priests in protest. America 109:91 Jl 27 '63
Priests' pledge on race. America 109:376 O 5 '63
Priest's protest. Time 85:36 Ja 8 '65
Principle and practice. Commonweal 78:492-3 Ag 23 '63
Progress in Little Rock. Christian Cent 80:606 My 8 '63
Proposition fourteen and the liturgy. N. J. Andersen. America 111:658+ N 21 '64; Discussion. 112:49-50 Ja 9 '65
Race and religion. Nation 197:378 D 7 '63
Race race. R. M. Brown. Commonweal 79:73-5 O 11 '63
Racial polls; attitude of Catholics. America 111:541 N 7 '64
Racism and the council. America 109:507 N 2 '63
Racism: the Nation's false religion. Christian Cent 80:166 F 6 '63
Racists challenge Methodists; Methodist bishops barred from Galloway Methodist church, Jackson, Miss. Christian Cent 81:454 Ap 8 '64
Rector resigns under pressure; Scarsdale, N.Y. Christian Cent 80:165 F 6 '63; Discussion. 80:406 Mr 27 '63
Reflections of a Negro priest. B. J. Patterson. Cath World 200:269-76 F '65
Reformed churches take strong stand on race. Christian Cent 81:1077 S 2 '64
Rejecting respectability. Commonweal 78:547-8 S 20 '63
Religion and race. America 110:662 My 16 '64
Religion and race: local efforts. P. B. Mather. Christian Cent 80:412-14 Mr 27 '63
Religion and race; moves of Protestant communions to foster racial unity. America 110:785 Je 6 '64
Religious leaders demand civil rights bill. Christian Cent 81:631 My 13 '64
Ruleville: reminiscence, reflection. R. C. Marius. Christian Cent 81:1169-71 S 23 '64; Discussion. 81:1468 N 25 '64
Sad chapter. Commonweal 80:163-4 My 1 '64
Script for a beginning; efforts at Marin Catholic high school, Kentfield, Calif. to help interracial understanding. Sister Mary Leona. America 111:256-9 S 12 '64
Search for sufficiency; human relations conference. P. B. Mather. Christian Cent 80:1139-40 S 18 '63
Seeing the unseen. Christian Cent 81:387-8 Mr 25 '64
Segregation and suburbia. C. D. Kean. Christian Cent 80:654+ My 15 '63
Seminary and the racial crisis; Consultation on the church and the racial crisis. A. C. Porteous. Christian Cent 81:147-8 Ja 29 '64
Silent minister speaks up. R. Collie. il N Y Times Mag p 12+ My 24 '64; Same. U S News 56:76-9 Je 15 '64
Silent white ministers of the South. G. McMillan. il N Y Times Mag p22+ Ap 5 '64
Southern Baptists break silence. Christian Cent 81:925 Jl 22 '64
Southern Baptists tackle race problem; Southern Baptist convention. Christian Cent 81:1164 S 23 '64
Southern desegregation; Protestant churches. Time 84:92+ D 4 '64
Southern establishment. S. Southard. Christian Cent 81:1618-21 D 30 '64
Southern Pentecost; address, with editorial comment. J. G. Chatham. America 109:2, 11-12 Jl 6 '63
Stand and be counted; Roman Catholics, Jews and Protestants support civil rights bill. il Newsweek 63:90 My 11 '64
Straw in the racial wind; March on Washington. Christian Cent 80:1123 S 18 '63
Students behind the civil rights vigil. M. McGrory. America 110:666 My 16 '64
Toward open hiring; anti-discrimination pledges in church contracts. Commonweal 81:500 Ja 15 '65
Two views on race; Archbishop W. P. Whelan and South African Bishops' conference. America 110:328 Mr 14 '64
Union seminary offers help to its alumni. Christian Cent 80:1022 Ag 21 '63
Voice of the churches. W. V. Shannon. Commonweal 80:226-8 My 15 '64
Waking up to race. il Time 82:79-80 O 4 '63
What can we tell our children? views of a white southern mother and a Negro mother. il Redbook 123:6+ My '64
When a priest made a pilgrimage. E. N. Bouton and T. F. Pettigrew. il Christian Cent 80:363-5 Mr 20 '63
See also
Catholic interracial councils
National Catholic conference for interracial justice
National conference on religion and race
CHURCH and race problems in South Africa
Archbishop approves apartheid. Christian Cent 81:325 Mr 11 '64
Catholic bishops on apartheid. D. M. Norman. Christian Cent 81:647-8 My 13 '64
Joost de Blank comes home. C. Northcott. Christian Cent 81:328 Mr 11 '64
South African bishops. Commonweal 79:704-5 Mr 13 '64
Taylor for de Blank. D. M. Norman. Christian Cent 81:378-80 Mr 18 '64
CHURCH and recreation. See Church work with youth
CHURCH and social problems
Birth control: the pill and the church. il Newsweek 64:51-5 Jl 6 '64
Brazil: social action. J. P. Cotter. America 108:222-3 F 16 '63
Burden of guilt. Christian Cent 81:37-8 Ja 8 '64; Discussion. 81:243 F 19 '64
Campaign opens on poverty in South. Christian Cent 81:325-6 Mr 11 '64
Candle in a dark world; West German Protestant consultation centers to check abortions. America 109:445 O 19 '63
Catholic position on birth control hardens. E. C. Parker. Christian Cent 82:71-2 Ja 20 '65
Catholics and population. J. O'Gara. Commonweal 78:534 S 6 '63
Catholics take a new look at the pill. J. Star. il Look 28:71-2+ S 8 '64
Challenge of Mater et magistra, ed. by J. N. Moody and J. G. Lawler. Review
America 108:407-8 Mr 23 '63. P. Land
Child spacing: the mathematical probabilities. A. J. De Bethune. bibliog il Science 142:1629-34 D 27 '63; Discussion. 143:995, 1394; 144:365-6, 795, 1531 Mr 6, 27, Ap 24, My 15, Je 26 '64
Choosing sides; conference to develop coordinated policies on role of the churches in an urbanized society. Newsweek 64:45 D 21 '64
Christians and the gambling mania. L. M. Starkey, jr. Christian Cent 80:267-70 F 27 '63
Church and community development. W. W. Biddle. Christian Cent 81:106-8 Ja 22 '64
Church and the pill. R. E. Hall. il Nation 199:191-3 O 5 '64
Clergy-laity schism. L. Davis. Christian Cent 81:1455-6 N 25 '64; Discussion. 82:58-61 Ja 13 '65

CHURCH and social problems—*Continued*
Clergy shatter another taboo; Council on religion and the homosexual. Christian Cent 81:1581 D 23 '64
Clerical lobbyists. America 110:624 My 9 '64
Come out the wilderness, by B. Kenrick. Review
Christian Cent 80:431-2 Ap 3 '63. W. Stringfellow
Contraception and holiness, by T. D. Roberts and others. Review
Christian Cent 81:1624 D 30 '64. E. M. Penonzek
Crisis in American Protestantism. R. Niebuhr. Christian Cent 80:1498-501 D 4 '63
Episcopalians consider Megabagdad. J. M. Dabbs. Christian Cent 81:302-3 Mr 4 '64
Furor over funerals; why the cry of scandal? bibliog il Changing T 17:7-12 N '63
Healing community. Christian Cent 80:1043-4 Ag 28 '63
Hong Kong, and interchurch aid. G. Murray. Christian Cent 80:1471-2 N 27 '63
Housing the aged. America 110:621 My 9 '64
ILO and the bishops. B. L. Masse. America 111:797-9 D 19 '64
Italian criminals. America 109:474 O 26 '63
Judgment day along the Potomac; National interreligious convocation on civil rights. G. Richards. America 110:623 My 9 '64
Let's end the war over birth control. J. A. O'Brien. Christian Cent 80:1361-4 N 6 '63
Letter on the parish ministry; reply to an earnest inquirer. P. L. Berger. Christian Cent 81:547-50 Ap 29 '64; Discussion. 81:936 Jl 22 '64
Liberty of love; premarital sex. G. Foley. Christian Cent 81:826-9 Je 24 '64
Limits of charity; suggested establishment of a co-ordinating agency in Rome for social reform. America 109:476 O 26 '63
Liturgy and action. P. J. Riga. Commonweal 81:445-8 D 25 '64
Man as servant. J. I. Miller. Christian Cent 81:233-6 F 19 '64
New guard; letter. F. W. Carney. America 111:781-2 D 12 '64
News of the Christian world. See issues of Christian century
Nonsense on the right. America 111:444 O 17 '64
On fighting poverty. America 111:405 O 10 '64
On the battle line; Episcopal church of the Inner city. il Time 81:52-3 Ap 5 '63
Peace churches as communities of discernment. J. L. Burkholder. Christian Cent 80:1072-5 S 4 '63
Peaceful battle of 1965; concerning Popes message from India. America 112:9 Ja 2 '65
Poor Pope. America 111:685 N 28 '64
Pope John's essay on inequality; Mater et magistra. B. L. Masse. America 108:368-71 Mr 16 '63
Powerhouse break? New York city's freer birth-control policy. Newsweek 63:57 Ja 27 '64
Profiles; Church of St Matthew and St Timothy. R. Rice. il New Yorker 40:41-2+ Ag 1; 37-8+ Ag 8 '64
Proposition fourteen and the liturgy. N. J. Andersen. America 111:658+ N 21 '64; Discussion. 112:49-50 Ja 9 '65
Pulpit-pew problem. L. K. Bishop. Christian Cent 81:968 Jl 29 '64
Religious leaders allied for civic goals. R. G. Howes. Cath World 197:114-19 My '63
Rethinking birth control; Roman Catholic views. Christian Cent 81:1133-4 S 16 '64
Roman Catholics: a new view on birth control; Rev. L. Janssens endorses oral contraceptive pills. il Time 83:59-60 Ap 10 '64; Discussion. America 110:563, 751 Ap 25, My 30 '64
Roots for the rootless. Christian Cent 80:635-6 My 15 '63; Discussion. 80:887 Jl 10 '63
San Francisco plans ahead. America 111:339 S 26 '64
Sociology and the church. America 112:107 Ja 23 '65
Speaking out; Catholic mother tells, why I believe in birth control. R. Ruether. Sat Eve Post 237:12+ Ap 4 '64; Same abr. Read Digest 84:148-50+ Je '64
Speaking out: it is time to end the birth-control fight. J. Rock. Sat Eve Post 236:10+ Ap 20 '63
Time has come. D. W. Ferm. bibliog f Christian Cent 81:903-6 Jl 15 '64; Discussion. 81:1178-9 S 23 '64
Training clergy and laity for the inner city. Christian Cent 80:356 Mr 20 '63
Two revolutions and a war; Economic opportunity act of 1964. T. F. Lord. Christian Cent 81:1334-6 O 28 '64; Reply. E. Walsh. 81:1595 D 23 '64
Unfinished business, by M. Ward. Review
Commonweal 81:123-5 O 23 '64. G. N. Shuster
World poverty and the Christian; symposium. il Commonweal 81:219-37 N 13 '64
See also
Birth control
Christian ethics
Church and politics
Church and race problems
Church work with migrants
Socialism, Christian
Sociology, Christian

CHURCH and state
Baltimore prayer case; . . . to the Supreme court. America 108:245 F 23 '63
Beast from the sea. B. Vawter. il Commonweal 80:253-6 My 22 '64
Catacombs and Khazars. M. Himmelfarb. Commentary 37:72-4 My '64; Discussion. 38:22+ O '64
Changing times; religious issue in American political life; Dr E. S. James and Baptist views. Newsweek 61:77 Mr 4 '63
Church and state under God, ed. by A. G. Huegli. Review
Christian Cent 82:19-20+ Ja 6 '65. D. M. Kelley
Church control of the state? D. Lawrence. U S News 55:116+ S 23 '63
Church, state, and the Jews. A. Hertzberg. Commentary 35:277-88 Ap '63; Discussion. 36:192+ S '63
Church, state and the wall. J. F. Malloy. Cath World 197:231-7 Jl '63
Church-state conference; study conference sponsored by National council of churches. America 110:245 F 22 '64
Clear light on church-state relations. H. E. Fey. Christian Cent 80:735-6 Je 5 '63
Council's religious liberty document. J. B. Sheerin. Cath World 199:140-3 Je '64
Court invades independent church; Traskwood landmark missionary Baptist church, Benton, Ark. Christian Cent 80:356 Mr 20 '63
Do we need public Protestantism? T. G. Sanders. Christian Cent 81:1424-6 N 18 '64
End to ideology. America 108:519 Ap 20 '63
Federal aid for higher education; church-related institutions. E. H. Rutkowski. Commonweal 79:40-3 O 4 '63
Free church, free state. America 111:122 Ag 8 '64
Future of the wall; address. R. M. Hutchins; **reply. M. P. Mullen. America 108:423 Mr 30 '63**
Goldwater on church and state. G. D. Everett. Christian Cent 81:987-9 Ag 5 '64
Griswold on church-state; excerpts from address. E. N. Griswold. America 108:374-5 Mr 16 '63
How separate should government and God be? address, January 22, 1963. H. C. Wilkinson. Vital Speeches 29:337-40 Mr 15 '63
In God we trust. Christian Cent 81:719 My 27 '64
Interfaith dialogue and church-state issues. R. J. Coughlin. America 108:900-3 Je 29 '63
Jefferson's wall and the schools. H. L. Hurwitz. Sr Schol 84:9T F 7 '64
N.A.E. on church-state. D. M. Kelley. Christian Cent 80:454-5 Ap 10 '63
Nature's God and the founding fathers. E. M. Halliday. il Am Heritage 14:4-7+ O '63
New pluralism: from nostalgia to reality. D. Callahan. Commonweal 78:527-31 S 6 '63; Discussion. 79:258-9 N 22 '63; America 109:556-8+, 733-4; 110:308-12 N 9, D 7 '63, Mr 7 '64
New pluralism or old monism. F. Canavan. America 109:556-8+ N 9 '63
Of note: religious liberty; excerpts from address. F. H. Littell. Commonweal 81:486-8 Ja 8 '65
One nation under God? America 111:647 N 21 '64
Our national relationship to God; address, January 25, 1964. S. Thurmond. Vital Speeches 30:357-61 Ap 1 '64
Peacemaking a church calling; colloquy called by Church peace mission, Oberlin, Ohio. P. Peachey. Christian Cent 80:952-4 Jl 31 '63
Politics of religious equality. F. Canavan. America 108:664-7 My 11 '63
Presbyterians on church and state. J. H. Smylie. Christian Cent 80:610-14 My 8 '63
Protestant concepts of church and state, by T. G. Sanders. Review
Commonweal 81:169-70 O 30 '64. P. T. Heffron
Protestants on church-state; National study conference on church and state. W. B. Ball. Commonweal 79:689-91 Mr 6 '64

CHURCH and state—*Continued*
Pure religion and the secularized society. W. Herberg. Nat R 15:188-9 S 10 '63
Religion and public life. W. Herberg. Nat R 15:104-5 Ag 13 '63
Religious freedom; the Court expands a concept. T. G. Sanders. Nation 197:25-8 Jl 13 '63
Religious liberty and atheism. J. B. Sheerin. Cath World 200:264-8 F '65
Religious liberty: Buddhist protests and Catholic principles. J. B. Sheerin. Cath World 197:339-42 S '63
Religious neutrality. J. J. Regan. America 110:74-6 Ja 18 '64
Separate but interacting. H. E. Fey. Christian Cent 81:231-2 F 19 '64; Reply. 81:293-4 Mr 4 '64
Shall we pray? il New Repub 148:4-6 Je 29 '63
Speaking out; a liberal calls for aid to church schools. R. M. Hutchins. Sat Eve Post 236:6+ Je 8 '63; Discussion. Christian Cent 80:819-20, 1141 Je 26, S 18 '63
Tampering lightly by amendment; famous First's provision. Christian Cent 80:923-4 Jl 24 '63
Theological frame of religious liberty. J. D. Hughey. Christian Cent 80:1365-8 N 6 '63; Reply. J. H. Sherman. 81:14-15 Ja 1 '64
Unconstitutional prayers; letters to the editor. Nat R 15:163+ Ag 27 '63
United States a Christian nation; address, 1905; with editorial comment. D. J. Brewer. U S News 55:108+ O 28 '63
U.S. bishops want new look at church-state issue. Christian Cent 80:1357-8 N 6 '63
Wall between church and state, ed. by D. H. Oaks. Review
America 110:106-7 Ja 18 '64. P. Barrett
Wall, not a sieve; separation of church and state. Christian Cent 81:67-8 Ja 15 '64
See also
Liberty of conscience
Parochial schools, Catholic
Protestants and other Americans united for separation of church and state
Public schools and religion
Religious liberty
Secularization

Bibliography

Church and state. D. M. Kelley. Christian Cent 80:1509-12 D 4 '63
CHURCH and state in Africa
Changing church. America 108:432 Mr 30 '63
CHURCH and state in Europe
Crisis of church and state, 1050-1300, ed. by B. Tierney. Review
Commonweal 81:395-6 D 11 '64. R. W. Hanning
CHURCH and state in Great Britain
End to establishment? il Newsweek 65:51-2 Ja 18 '65
For freedom under establishment; interview. A. M. Ramsey. Christian Cent 81:853 Jl 1 '64
CHURCH and state in Hungary
See also
Catholic church in Hungary
CHURCH and state in Israel
Religious freedom in Israel. R. F. Drinan. America 108:456-7 Ap 6 '63
CHURCH and state in Italy
Pope John: new look. P. S. Land. America 108:395-6 Mr 23 '63
CHURCH and state in Poland
See also
Catholic church in Poland
CHURCH and state in Spain
Abbot of Montserrat. America 110:330-1 Mr 14 '64; Reply. V. de la Serna. 110:498 Ap 11 '64
Church and state in Spain. Commonweal 79:560 F 7 '64
Of many things; abbot of Montserrat condemns lack of freedom in Spain. T. N. Davis. America 110:28 Ja 11 '64
Who will liberate Spanish Catholics? Christian Cent 80:1259-60 O 16 '63
See also
Catholic church in Spain
CHURCH and the press
Anatomy of a headline; how the diocesan press reported the announcement of the reform of the curia. A. V. Krebs, jr. America 109:662-4 N 23 '63; Discussion. 110:83-4 Ja 18 '64
Better council coverage; reporting of Vatican II. America 109:473 O 26 '63
Can the press serve the council? E. Tennant. Cath World 197:107-13 My '63
Communications decree: why the dissent? J. B. Sheerin. Cath World 198:267-71 F '64
Council, the press and theology; address. G. H. Tavard. il Cath World 199:337-44 S '64
Deplorable shambles; arrangements for the press. America 109:757 D 14 '63
Excess of zeal. America 108:251 F 23 '63; Discussion. 108:400-1 Mr 23 '63
Interpreting the council; secular press. Commonweal 77:584 Mr 1 '63
Letters from Vatican City, by X. Rynne, Review
Commonweal 78:461-2 Jl 26 '63. J. Leo
Managing the news; American press panel at the Vatican council. J. Leo. Commonweal 81:5 S 25 '64; Reply with rejoinder. E. Von Feldt. 81:102 O 16 '64
Mr NC; retirement of Frank A. Hall. America 110:273 F 29 '64
Monsignor nods. America 110:357 Mr 21 '64
Newsman's tribute; John XXIII. B. McGurn. America 108:857-8 Je 15 '63
Not always on the day after Sunday. J. N. Eller. America 108:391 Mr 23 '63
Press and the council. America 108:252 F 23 '63
Secrecy at the council. F. X. Murphy. America 109:96-7 Jl 27 '63
Vatican beat. il Newsweek 64:102+ O 26 '64
Vietnam controversy. Commonweal 78:444-5 Jl 26 '63
CHURCH architecture
And here are the people! Christian Cent 81:419-20 Ap 1 '64
Architectural *aggiornamento*; newly adopted Constitution on the sacred liturgy. J. L. Amestoy. il Cath World 199:279-85 Ag '64
Award for best sanctuary. America 110:753-4 My 30 '64
Building types study. il Arch Rec 134:131-50 Jl '63
California: mighty piers; Greek Orthodox church of the Holy Trinity in San Francisco. il Arch Forum 121:152-3 Ag '64
Church buildings alive. C. J. McNaspy. America 109:613-15 N 9 '63
Church of the Autostrada. J. M. Fitch. il Arch Forum 121:100-9 Jl '64
Connecticut prayer tent; First Unitarian Congregational society of Hartford. il Arch Forum 121:126-9 Ag '64
Episcopal church by Belluschi; Concord, Mass. il Arch Rec 135:145-8 Mr '64
First Baptist church, Columbus, Ind. H. Weese. il Arch Rec 133:128-31 My '63
Let's stop building cathedrals! C. H. Reid. Christian Cent 81:797-9 Je 17 '64; Discussion. 81:1037-9 Ag 19 '64
Monumental cathedral for the modern age; San Francisco's new Roman Catholic cathedral. il Arch Forum 120:11 Mr '64
National program honors ten churches with design awards. il Arch Rec 135:12-13 Je '64
New directions in church design. P. Gardner. il Christian Cent 81:424-8 Ap 1 '64
Recent work of William Wilson Wurster; First Unitarian church, Berkeley, Calif. il Arch Rec 133:112-15 Ja '63
Reformation, in church design; photographs. N Y Times Mag p8-9 D 20 '64
Religious buildings: stability after the boom. H. C. F. Arnold. il Arch Rec 134:18 Jl '63
Saarinen's church: the North Christian church in Columbus, Ind. il Arch Rec 136:185-90 S '64
Sky-hooks available; seminar at American institute of architects. C. J. McNaspy. America 110:378-9 Mr 21 '64
Strength or banality? D. Canty. il Arch Forum 119:68-72 D '63
Structure of St Sophia; with editorial comment. R. L. Van Nice. il Arch Forum 118:131-8+, 154 My '63; 121:45-9 Ag '64
Superhighway church; Michelucci's St John the Baptist near Florence, Italy. il Time 84:36 Jl 31 '64
Visible expressions of man's faith. il Fortune 70:124-9 D '64
Well balanced Sunday school; Temple Sharey Tefilo, East Orange, N.J. il Arch Forum 119:114-17 D '63
See also
Chapels
Mosques
National conference on church architecture
Synagogues

Bibliography

Architecture roundup. P. Gardner. Christian Cent 81:434-5 Ap 1 '64
CHURCH art. See Christian art and symbolism
CHURCH attendance
And here are the people! Christian Cent 81:419-20 Ap 1 '64
Church attendance. J. H. Fichter. America 108:832-4 Je 8 '63
Church attendance among college graduates. A. M. Greeley. Cath World 197:95-9 My '63

CHURCH attendance—*Continued*
Church on Sunday. America 108:325 Mr 9 '63
Condemn compulsory chapel; for cadets and midshipmen. Christian Cent 81:1388 N 11 '64
Duty to pray? compulsory religious service. il Newsweek 63:62-3 F 24 '64
Protest mandatory chapel; Air force academy. Christian Cent 81:421 Ap 1 '64; Discussion. 81:774, 1178 Je 10, S 23 '64
Service academies require chapel attendance. Christian Cent 81:292 Mr 4 '64
Technology's impact on religion; correlation between family income and church membership. C. M. Cook. Christian Cent 81:1083-5 S 2 '64
Who attends church? Carper's report of Protestants in Massachusetts. J. L. Hofford. Christian Cent 81:654 My 13 '64

CHURCH center, United Nations. See United Nations center, New York

CHURCH choirs. See Choirs

CHURCH colleges. See Denominational colleges

CHURCH conferences. See Religious conferences

CHURCH cooperation. See Religious cooperation

CHURCH councils. See Councils and synods

CHURCH decoration and ornament
Let's stop building cathedrals! C. H. Reid. Christian Cent 81:797-9 Je 17 '64; Discussion. 81:1037-9 Ag 19 '64

CHURCH finance
Backlash hits the churches. Christian Cent 81:1004-5 Ag 12 '64
Givers: big & small; averages of Protestant bodies. Time 84:102 N 13 '64
Money raisers. Time 84:74 S 4 '64
See also
Tithes

CHURCH gardens
Church gardens. H. V. P. Wilson. il Flower Grower 50:36-9+ Ap '63
Gardener; St Bartholomew's Episcopal church. New Yorker 39:34-6 S 21 '63

CHURCH going. See Church attendance

CHURCH government
Calvinism and democracy: some political implications of debates on French reformed church government, 1562-1572. R. M. Kingdon. bibliog f Am Hist R 69:393-401 Ja '64
Connectionalism: the new polity? L. E. Schaller. Christian Cent 81:858-61 Jl 1 '64; Discussion. 81:1039 Ag 19 '64
Episcopacy for our time; search for relevant polity. P. H. Pfatteicher. Christian Cent 81:1361-4 N 4 '64; Discussion. 81:1559-60 D 16 '64
Plan training program for churchmen; church administrators. Christian Cent 81:1166 S 23 '64
Southern Baptists: need for reformulation, redirection. S. S. Hill, jr; discussion. Christian Cent 80:276-7 F 27 '63

CHURCH history
Achievement of Kenneth Scott Latourette. M. E. Marty. Christian Cent 80:336-7 Mr 13 '63
See also
Catholic church—History
Protestantism
United States—Church history

Bibliography

Building a basic theological library. E. S. Gaustad. Christian Cent 80:560-2 Ap 24 '63

Middle ages

See also
Crusades

Primitive and early church

Greek myths and Christian mystery, by H. Rahner. Review
Commonweal 79:605-6 F 14 '64. A. A. Cohen

CHURCH law. See Ecclesiastical law

CHURCH libraries. See Libraries, Church

CHURCH maintenance and repair
Sticky church pew; Port George, Nova Scotia. J. E. Neily. Christian Cent 81:207-8 F 12 '64

CHURCH music
Music; a dismal centennial. C. J. McNaspy. America 109:328-30 S 21 '63
Music; popular and professional. C. J. McNaspy. America 108:383 Mr 16 '63
Musical-liturgical dialogue. C. J. McNaspy. America 110:266 F 22 '64
Musical manifesto; foundation of Church music association of America. C. J. McNaspy. America 111:331-3 S 19 '64
Vatican II on music; Constitution on the sacred liturgy. C. J. McNaspy. America 110:55-6 Ja 11 '64
When the choirs go marching out? C. A. Bennett. il America 111:738-9 D 5 '64
See also
Choirs
Hymns
Mass (music)
Organ music
Phonograph records—Choral music
Phonograph records—Church music

Anecdotes, facetiae, satire, etc.

Grace notes. Christian Cent 81:471 Ap 8 '64

CHURCH music association of America
Musical manifesto; foundation of Church music association. C. J. McNaspy. America 111:331-3 S 19 '64

CHURCH of England
Anglican-Methodist merger. America 108:354 Mr 16 '63
Anglican-Methodist report. C. Northcott. Christian Cent 80:408-9 Mr 27 '63
Anglican-Methodist union proposed in England. Christian Cent 80:325 Mr 13 '63
Anglicans in crises. il Newsweek 63:57 Ja 27 '64
Archbishop is a Protestant. Time 84:54 Jl 31 '64
Baptism: for babies or believers? il Time 85:36 Ja 8 '65
Church in England. il Time 81:57 Mr 8 '63
Empty pews, full spirit. il Time 82:58-61+ Ag 16 '63
End to establishment? il Newsweek 65:51-2 Ja 18 '65
Evangelization of a nation. Christian Cent 80:971-2 Ag 7 '63
Is Anglicanism Protestant? excerpt from World Protestantism. W. H. Van De Pol. Cath World 200:95-9+ N '64
News item: church condemns sin; condemnation of premarital and extra marital sexual relations. Christian Cent 80:1395 N 13 '63
South bank religion; Southwark parish. il Time 82:66-7 Jl 26 '63
Urge to merge; Anglican and Methodist churches. Newsweek 61:46 F 4 '63
See also
Anglo-Catholicism
Protestant Episcopal church

Book of common prayer

Savings and quality in Seabury's web-offset Prayer book. Hymnal. il Pub W 186:74-6 D 7 '64

Clergy

Battle over benefices. Time 83:48 Ja 31 '64
Prescription for survival. C. Northcott. Christian Cent 81:168 F 5 '64
Those mad, merry vicars of England. D. J. Hamblin. il Life 58:76-8+ Ja 29 '65
Women in Anglican pulpits? C. Northcott. Christian Cent 80:1360 N 6 '63

Missions

Merge mission societies. Christian Cent 82:70 Ja 20 '65

CHURCH of England in Africa
Empty pews, full spirit. il Time 82:61+ Ag 16 '63

CHURCH of England in Asia
Empty pews, full spirit. Time 82:63 Ag 16 '63

CHURCH of England in Australia
Empty pews, full spirit. Time 82:63 Ag 16 '63

CHURCH of England in Latin America
Empty pews, full spirit. il Time 82:58-61+ Ag 16 '63

CHURCH of God
Woman on the go for God. L. S. Calhoun. il Ebony 18:78-81+ My '63

CHURCH of Jesus Christ of Latter-day saints. See Mormons and Mormonism

CHURCH of St Matthew and St Timothy. See New York (city)—Churches

CHURCH of Scotland
Church of Scotland assembly; seen from Edinburgh. I. Logan. Christian Cent 81:836-8 Je 24 '64
Church of Scotland assembly; seen from London. C. Northcott. Christian Cent 81:838 Je 24 '64

CHURCH of sounds; story. See Merwin, W. S.

CHURCH of the Brethren
Brethren and the church; second Theological study conference, July 20-24. R. A. Bollinger. Christian Cent 81:1062-3 Ag 26 '64
Church of the Brethren annual conference. R. A. Bollinger. Christian Cent 80:941-2 Jl 24 '63

CHURCH of the Brethren—*Continued*
Church of the Brethren annual conference. R. M. Miller. Christian Cent 81:941-2 Jl 22 '64
Russian Christians visit Church of the Brethren. Christian Cent 80:1125 S 18 '63
CHURCH of the Holy Sepulcher. See Jerusalem —Church of the Holy Sepulcher
CHURCH of the Nazarene
Church of the Nazarene general assembly. M. A. Talnay. Christian Cent 81:948-9 Jl 22 '64
Preach, teach, live, win. Time 84:74 Jl 3 '64
CHURCH organists. See Organists
CHURCH peace mission (organization)
Christian obedience in a world we don't control. P. Peachey. Christian Cent 81:458-60 Ap 8 '64
Peacemaking a church calling; colloquy called by Church peace mission, Oberlin, Ohio. P. Peachey. Christian Cent 80:952-4 Jl 31 '63
CHURCH polity. See Church government
CHURCH property
See also
Secularization
Taxation
Church makes gift in lieu of taxes; Central Presbyterian church, Des Moines. Christian Cent 80:1458 N 27 '63
Church tax exemption; Mrs Madalyn Murray loses suit against Maryland tax officials. America 112:154 Ja 30 '65
Churches feel tax squeeze. B. D. Kolasa. America 111:185-7 Ag 22 '64
Local church pays county; First Presbyterian church, Morrison, Ill. Christian Cent 81: 229 F 19 '64
Mrs Murray's war on God. R. Liston. il Sat Eve Post 237:83-7 Jl 11 '64
Rendering unto Caesar. Time 81:69 Ap 26 '63
Woman who hates churches; Mrs Murray's tax-exemption suit. il Time 83:53-4 My 15 '64
CHURCH related colleges. See Denominational colleges
CHURCH-related housing projects. See Housing projects
CHURCH-related schools. See Church schools
CHURCH schools
Armageddon in Maryland; question of state aid to church-supported colleges and schools. Newsweek 64:72 D 21 '64
Lutherans and school aid. E. C. Parker. Christian Cent 80:263 F 27 '63
Statistics of nonpublic schools. D. B. Gertler. il Sch Life 46:31-6 O '63
See also
Catholic church—Education
CHURCH services
Way Protestants worship; excerpt from Ecumenical dialogue at Harvard. C. C. Richardson. Cath World 199:175-81 Je '64
See also
Church music
Worship
CHURCH statistics
Church thermometer; information from Yearbook of American churches. Christian Cent 82:100-1 Ja 27 '65
CHURCH unity
Anglican-Methodist report. C. Northcott. Christian Cent 80:408-9 Mr 27 '63
Another Oberlin conference. D. L. Day. Christian Cent 80:1334-5 O 30 '63
Baptists urged to join COCU. Christian Cent 81:1453 N 25 '64; Reply. J. W. Bradbury. 82:61-2 Ja 13 '65
Blake's second thoughts; possibility of union. il Time 85:89 Ja 29 '65
Breakthrough in Puerto Rico. V. Clear. Christian Cent 80:1216-18 O 2 '63
Canadian church union plan in process; Anglican church of Canada to the United Presbyterian churches. Christian Cent 80: 1394 N 13 '63
Cardinal of unity; Cardinal Bea at Harvard university's four-day Catholic-Protestant colloquium. W. M. Abbott. America 108:484 Ap 13 '63
Church aid, church unity. America 109:700 N 30 '63
Church unity is a growing thing. F. G. Ensley. Christian Cent 81:10-12 Ja 1 '64
Churches mobilize. America 110:328 Mr 14 '64
Colloquium at Harvard. Commonweal 78:60 Ap 12 '63; Reply. R. E. Murphy. Commonweal 78:356 Je 21 '63
Common burden. Commonweal 79:471-2 Ja 24 '64
Council, reform and reunion, by H. Küng. Review
Christian Cent 80:709-10 My 29 '63. A. J. Wolf; Discussion. 80:829, 864-5 Je 26-Jl 3 '63
Dialoguing churches; Churchmen praying. America 110:179 F 8 '64
Distorts prayer for Christian unity. Christian Cent 81:228 F 19 '64
Do we really mean this unity talk? Christian Cent 81:38 Ja 8 '64; Reply. H. N. Richardson. 81:206-7 F 12 '64
Ecumenical next steps; World interchurch service (proposed) Christian Cent 80:483 Ap 17 '63
Empty pews, full spirit; Anglican communion. il Time 82:58-61+ Ag 16 '63
Episcopacy for our time; search for relevant polity. P. H. Pfatteicher. Christian Cent 81:1361-4 N 4 '64
Family life weakens; statistics. Christian Cent 80:821 Je 26 '63
Frankfurt: the ghost of unity; meeting of World Presbyterian and Reformed alliance. W. D. Wagoner. Christian Cent 81:1089-90 S 2 '64
From dialogue to deeds. Christian Cent 80: 355-6 Mr 20 '63
Fusion at Oberlin; Consultation on church union. K. Haselden. Christian Cent 80:422-3 Ap 3 '63
Glimmering dream; proposed union of United Presbyterian church in the U.S.A. with other denominations. Time 83:82 Ap 24 '64
Grass-roots ecumenism. D. J. O'Hanlon. Cath World 199:8-15 Ap '64
How the university can further Christian unity; excerpt from Unity of Christians. A. Bea. Cath World 197:8-14 Ap '63
Images of unity. Newsweek 62:71 Ag 5 '63
Latin America: testing ground of ecumenism; excerpt from Unity: man's tomorrow. R. Schutz. il Cath World 197:28-35 Ap '63
Luther up to date; fourth assembly of the Lutheran world federation. il Newsweek 62:71 Ag 19 '63
Marching toward merger; Protestant churches of the U.S. Time 83:56 F 21 '64
New beginnings and common worship. America 112:6 Ja 2 '65; Correction. 112:99 Ja 23 '65
One big family; second Anglican congress in Toronto. il Time 82:49 Ag 23 '63
Orthodox: arrival and dialogue. J. S. Romanides. Christian Cent 80:1399-403 N 13 '63
Our local dialogue. J. A. Fichtner. Cath World 196:285-91 F '63
Polity in the churches. America 108:483 Ap 13 '63
Pope Paul's ecumenical perspective; address. A. Dulles. Cath World 200:15-21 O '64
Pray for unity. Christian Cent 81:35 Ja 8 '64
Prayer and unity; with editorial comment. R. M. Brown. Commonweal 77:480, 491-2 F 1 '63
Prejudice and church unity; excerpts from address. A. Bea. America 109:444 O 19 '63
Princeton Consultation; representatives of six Protestant communions at Princeton theological seminary. America 110:592-3 My 2 '64
Progress and perspectives, by G. Baum. Review
Commonweal 77:646-7 Mr 15 '63. D. Callahan
Protestant ecumenical dilemma. W. D. Wagoner; K. Bridston; W. Nicholls. Christian Cent 81:329-32 Mr 11 '64; Discussion. 81:642 My 13 '64
Servant church. il Time 84:45-9 D 25 '64
Seven devilish ways to block church union. J. R. Nelson. Time 81:77-8 My 10 '63
Slavic heritage; encyclical Magnifici eventus. America 108:797 Je 1 '63
Time has come. D. W. Ferm. bibliog f Christian Cent 81:903-6 Jl 15 '64; Discussion. 81: 1178-9 S 23 '64
Together at Harvard; Roman Catholic-Protestant colloquium. J. O'Gara. Commonweal 78:90 Ap 19 '63
Toward Christian unity. America 108:214 F 16 '63
Turning four churches into one; United church of Schellsburg. il Time 84:75 N 20 '64
Two on unity. J. R. Nelson. Christian Cent 82:111-12 Ja 27 '65
Unfinished reformation: a Catholic view. L. J. Putz. Christian Cent 81:109-12 Ja 22 '64
Union, not mere unity. Christian Cent 81: 323-5 Mr 11 '64; Discussion. 81:643-4 My 13 '64

CHURCH unity—*Continued*
Union proposal two years later; excerpt from reply appended to The challenge to reunion, by R. M. Brown and D. H. Scott. E. C. Blake. Christian Cent 80:394-8 Mr 27 '63; Reply. H. F. Reissig. 80:807 Je 19 '63
Unity, by M. Villain. Review
Cath World 199:188-9 Je '64. C. L. Palms
Unity in good works. America 110:68-9 Ja 18 '64
Unity in Oklahoma; Roman Catholic church in Tulsa joins the Tulsa council of churches. Newsweek 63:82 My 4 '64
Unity initiatives. America 110:406 Mr 28 '64
Voices from Odessa; Christian churches spoke to the world about church unity. America 110:330 Mr 14 '64
Whither church unity? America 110:72 Ja 18 '64
Within Protestantism, diversity. M. M. Shideler. Christian Cent 80:295-8 Mr 6 '63; Discussion. 80:498+ Ap 17 '63
See also
Community churches
Ecumenical movement
European conference of churches
Religious cooperation
United church of Christ
World conference on faith and order

Australia

Commission on union reports. R. Mathias. Christian Cent 80:476-7 Ap 10 '63

Great Britain

Anglican-Methodist merger. America 108:354 Mr 16 '63
Evangelization of a nation. Christian Cent 80:971-2 Ag 7 '63
Urge to merge; Anglican and Methodist churches. Newsweek 61:46 F 4 '63

India

Methodists and North India union; plan rejected. R. V. Marble. Christian Cent 80: 1173-4 S 25 '63; Reply. D. B. Bauman. 80: 1473 N 27 '63

CHURCH work
See also
Church and social problems
Evangelistic work

CHURCH work with migrants
Minister who follows the migrants; Migrant ministry program of N.C.C M. Cope. il Sat Eve Post 237:34-6 Ja 4 '64
Out of work in ten years; N.C.C.-sponsored migrant ministry program. H. E. Fey. Christian Cent 80:1230-1 O 9 '63

CHURCH work with the aged
Building for church recreation. L. Mitchell. il Recreation 57:222-3+ My '64

CHURCH work with youth
Building for church recreation. L. Mitchell. il Recreation 57:222-3+ My '64
Recreation and your church; First Baptist church, Plainview, Tex. O. Bottorff and A. Bishop. il Recreation 56:476-7 D '63

CHURCH world service
CWS offers charity bargain; Share our substance. Christian Cent 80:1395 N 13 '63
Dedicate fresh-water distillery; conversion plant on island of Symi. Christian Cent 81: 1358 N 4 '64
How can I help? one great hour of sharing. Christian Cent 81:293 Mr 4 '64
Lauds church aid to the hungry. Christian Cent 80:262 F 27 '63

CHURCHES
See also
Chapels

Air conditioning

Summer cooling for church sanctuaries. R. A. Hanle. il Arch Rec 134:157-9 Jl '63

Maintenance and repair

See Church maintenance and repair

Canada

Sticky church pew; Port George, Nova Scotia. J. E. Neily. Christian Cent 81:207-8 F 12 '64

Colombia

Vestige of colonial splendor; church in Tópaga, Colombia. E. M. Varela. il Américas 15:22-6 Ag '63

Italy

Church of the Autostrada. J. M. Fitch. il Arch Forum 121:100-9 Jl '64

Spain

Light on the altar; Church of the Coronation of Our Lady, Vitoria, Spain. il Arch Forum 119:82-3 D '63

Sweden

Anchor in a parish; Lutheran-Evangelical church, Hökarängen, Sweden. il Arch Forum 119:78-9 D '63

United States

Store-front churches. America 109:693 N 30 '63
See also
Synagogues
also subhead Churches under names of cities, e.g. New York (city)—Churches

Yugoslavia

Lost treasures are seen again; wall paintings in remote churches, Yugoslavia. il Life 54:52-61 Ap 12 '63

CHURCHES and commercialism. See Commercialism

CHURCHES of Christ
Campbellites are coming. il Time 81:97 F 15 '63

CHURCHGOING. See Church attendance

CHURCHILL, Clementine Ogilvy (Hozier) Spencer, lady
Loyalty that has never wavered; excerpt from My darling Clementine. J. Fishman. il pors Life 54:84-6+ Je 14 '63
My darling Clementine; condensation. J. Fishman. il pors Read Digest 84:201-4+ Ja '64
Woman behind the man of the century; excerpt from My darling Clementine. J. Fishman. il pors Life 54:88-90+ Je 7 '63

CHURCHILL, Creighton
California wines; excerpts from Discovering the world of wines. Harper 227:50-5 D '63

CHURCHILL, Mary, duchess of Montagu
Duchess and William Byrd. T. Thorne. il pors Antiques 84:562-5 N '63

CHURCHILL, Randolph Frederick Edward Spencer
Invitation, mystery, surprise; the gardens at Stour. por Vogue 143:152-3+ Mr 1 '64
Low life above stairs. C. Brogan. por Nat R 16:153-5 F 25 '64
Randolph's resignation. por Time 82:92 N 8 '63

CHURCHILL, Sam
Death of a cathedral. Am For 70:28-30 O '64
Mountain goat trailer defies hillsides. il Farm J 88:32C Ag '64
Old shay's last haul, people. Am For 70:61 My '64
What is spring? Read Digest 84:182C My '64

CHURCHILL, Sir Winston Leonard Spencer
Citizen Churchill's view of us; quotations. por N Y Times Mag p29 Ap 14 '63
His words: they still live; quotations. por Newsweek 65:42C F 1 '65
Sir Winston Churchill becomes honorary citizen of United States; acceptance. Dept State Bul 68:715-16 My 6 '63

about

Anniversary of an antediluvian. il pors Time 84:33-4 D 4 '64
Child of the House; final farewell to House of commons. il por Time 84:33 Ag 7 '64
Churchill. C. P. Snow. il pors Look 27:26-33 F 26 '63; Same abr. with title We must never deny our gratitude. Read Digest 82: 66-71 My '63
Churchill. il pors Time 85:31-3 Ja 29 '65
Churchill at ninety: twilight of a hero. Q. Reynolds. il pors Sat Eve Post 237:15-17 N 28 '64
Churchill: last of the big three. il pors U S News 58:20 Ja 25 '65
Churchill, progress of a slow grower. A. J. Toynbee. il pors N Y Times Mag p40-2+ N 1 '64
Churchill: the world's vigil. il por Newsweek 65:35-6 Ja 25 '65
Coat upon a stick. M. Kempton. New Repub 148:12-13 Ap 27 '63
Epic of Sir Winston. il pors Life 58:56-70 Ja 29 '65
Family man. il por Newsweek 64:47+ N 30 '64
Genius hero of the new movie The finest hours. por Vogue 144:186-7 N 1 '64
Great old man's last trip to Commons. A. Moorehead. il pors Life 57:30-1 Ag 7 '64
Last of the giants. L. A. Foley. il por America 112:160-2 Ja 30 '65
London: death of a titan; Churchill's splendid life. il pors Newsweek 65:38A-38D+ F 1 '65

CHURCHILL, Sir Winston Leonard Spencer—about—*Continued*
Loyalty that has never wavered; excerpt from My darling Clementine. J. Fishman. il pors Life 54:84-6+ Je 14 '63
Man of the century. il pors Read Digest 85: 205-8+ D '64; 86:205-7+ Ja '65
Man of the century. il por Sr Schol 85:7+ N 18 '64
Marquis de Lafayette is no precedent; honorary American citizenship. E. T. Folliard. America 108:217 F 16 '63
My darling Clementine; condensation. J. Fishman. il pors Read Digest 84:201-4+ Ja '64
Old master. New Yorker 40:50-1 N 21 '64
Pedestrian approach. Reporter 28:18+ Mr 14 '63
People of the week. il por U S News 54:26 Ap 22 '63
Sir Citizen. por Newsweek 61:25 Ap 22 '63
Sir Winston Churchill observes his 90th birthday; message with proclamation. L. B. Johnson. Dept State Bul 51:856 D 14 '64
To Winston at ninety: happy returns! il pors Life 57:131-2 D 4 '64
Whilst he still lives amongst us. Q. Hogg. il por Life 57:49-50+ D 11 '64
Winston Churchill. New Repub 152:8-9 Ja 30 '65
Winston Churchill, the Yankee Marlborough. R. W. Thompson. pors Vogue 142:134-7+ S 15 '63
Woman behind the man of the century; excerpt from My darling Clementine. J. Fishman. il pors Life 54:88-90+ Je 7 '63

CHURCHILL, Manitoba
Bird finding; Churchill, on Hudson Bay. S. Pettingill. il Audubon Mag 65:41-3 Ja '63

CHURCHILL college. See Cambridge university

CHURCHILL Downs. See Race tracks

CHUTE, B. J.
January thaw; story. Redbook 124:42-3 Ja '65
Thief in the night; story. McCalls 91:112-13 F '64
When the writer comes of age. Writer 76:10-14 My '63

CHUTE, Marchette
London that was Shakespeare's; excerpts from Shakespeare of London. UNESCO Courier 17:14-17+ My '64

CHUTNEYS. See Pickles and relishes

CHYMOTRYPSIN
Alpha-chymotrypsin and the nature of enzyme catalysis. C. Niemann. bibliog il Science 143:1287-96 Mr 20 '64

CIAMPI, Elgin
Status pet. il por Sat Eve Post 237:22-4+ Ja 4 '64

CIARDI, John
Adam and Eve and the third son. Sat R 47:140-3+ Ag 29 '64
At first flower of the easy day; poem. Atlan 211:68 Mr '63
Authors, reading. Sat R 46:123 O 12 '63
Benn; Small Benn; While I was shaving; poems. Sat R 46:20 D 14 '63
Children's hour: about Eskimos; poem. Sat R 47:26 N 21 '64
Christmas wish; poem. Sat R 46:16 D 21 '63
Citation; poem. Sat R 47:18 Ap 25 '64
Cornelia and the Loves of Charles. Sat R 46:35 Ap 13 '63
Dialogue with an audience: the first seven years. Sat R 46:27-9+ S 14 '63
English literature on record. Sat R 46:39 Jl 13 '63
Evensong. Nation 197:115 S 7 '63
Garland of birds; poems. Sat R 47:10 My 2 '64
Gift; poem. Sat R 46:51 S 7 '63
Hamlet by Burton and Scofield. Sat R 47:56-7 Je 27 '64
How free is free verse? Sat R 47:14-15 Mr 21 '64; Same. Writer 77:15-16 Je '64
King who saved himself from being saved; poem. Sat R 47:24 N 14 '64
L'inglese; Envoi; poems. New Yorker 39:78 Ja 18 '64
Manner of speaking. See issues of Saturday review
Miss Priss; Of hurricanes, summer days, and Miss Myra; Fiddle practice; poems. Sat R 47:9 Jl 4 '64
Monster den; poem. Sat R 47:16+ F 22 '64
Monument and magic. Sat R 46:72 My 11 '63
New fable of the grasshopper and the ant; poem. McCalls 90:100-1 My '63
Othello: Olivier triumphant. Sat R 47:54 D 12 '64
Poetry in three dimensions. Sat R 46:22-5 Ap 20 '63
Robert Frost: To earthward. Sat R 46:24 F 23 '63
Shakespeare on record. Sat R 46:53+ S 14 '63
Tales and tellers. Sat R 46:61 N 16 '63
Text two: From Emmanuel Kant: The starry heavens, the moral law; poem. Sat R 47:12 Ap 25 '64
Thomas Stearns Eliot: 1888-1965. Sat R 48: 34-6 Ja 23 '65
Time leaves no time when you're a boy; Speed adjustments; poems. Sat R 47:22 Je 27 '64
WLB autobiography. por Wilson Lib Bul 38: 480-2 F '64
With malice for all. Sat R 46:52 F 23 '63

about

Poetry chronicle. R. Howard. Poetry 102: 252-3 Jl '63
Transformation of a poet: John Ciardi. P. J. Groff. Horn Bk 40:153-8 Ap '64

CICERO, Ill.
Keeps 5,000 bathers in hot water. R. W. Holec. Am City 79:29 Ja '64

CIDER
Ah! apple cider! il McCalls 90:134-5+ S '63
See also
Cookery—Cider

CIEPLAK, John Baptist, abp
Cieplak, protomartyr. America 110:152 F 1 '64

CIGAR industry
Female puffer. il Newsweek 63:80-1+ Mr 23 '64
No cigar smoke dream. Bsns W p 110+ Je 15 '63
What the cigar needs is a good five-cent machine. Time 83:88 My 1 '64

CIGARETTE filters
Answers on filters; correspondence between L. L. Terry and J. S. Cooper. U S News 56:38 Ja 27 '64
Spider web cigarette filter shown at NSF-I. Sci N L 85:297 My 9 '64

CIGARETTE labels. See Labels

CIGARETTES
Alloocimene: absence in cigarette smoke. J. D. Mold and others. bibliog il Science 144: 1572-3 Je 26 '64
Anti-smoking bill planned; Lose eight years of life. il (p33) Sci N L 85:37 Ja 18 '64
Are cigarettes necessary? G. A. Silver. Nation 196:379-80 My 4 '63
Athletes against smoking. Sci N L 85:197 Mr 28 '64
Back to high levels. il Time 84:89-90 N 6 '64
Before your next vacation learn how to savor smoking; and quit! C. Rule. Travel 119: 61-2 Mr '63
Being nonchalant about smoking. Time 83: 42 Ja 24 '64
British stop smoking program offered. Sci N L 85:116 F 22 '63
Burning question: tobacco and politics. D. S. Greenberg. il Reporter 30:34-5 Ja 30 '64
By their own free choice; tobacco and cancer; address, April 6, 1964. T. Sanford. Vital Speeches 30:463-7 My 15 '64
Can the cancer society combat the hidden persuaders? L. Sneed. New Repub 150:12-13 F 8 '64
Can your child break the habit? R. Goldman and P. Goldman. il N Y Times Mag p87-8 Mr 15 '64
Cigarette controversy: a storm is brewing. L. M. Miller and J. Monahan. il Read Digest 83:91-9 Ag '63
Cigarette, emphysema link; Cigarette aversion from electric shock treatment. Sci N L 85:70 F 1 '64
Cigarette radioactivity linked to cancer: effect of polonium. Sci N L 86:105 Ag 15 '64
Cigarette sales: a sharp drop, then signs of an upturn. U S News 56:12 Mr 20 '64
Cigarette smoke: charcoal filters reduce components that inhibit growth of cultured human cells. P. S. Thayer and C. J. Kensler. bibliog il Science 146:642-4 O 30 '64
Cigarette smokers still puffing away. il Bsns W p 148-50 D 14 '63
Cigarette smoking and arteriosclerosis. S. L. Wilens and C. M. Plair; discussion. il Science 139:1096+ Mr 15 '63
Cigarette smoking is a health hazard. il Newsweek 63:48-50 Ja 20 '64
Cigarette warning, the aftermath; reaction of smokers, congressmen, stock market. U S News 56:38-9 Ja 27 '64
Cigarettes and brimstone. F. Canavan. America 110:154 F 1 '64
Cigarettes and cancer. C. A. Betts. Sci N L 87:54 Ja 23 '65
Cigarettes, cancer, death. Christian Cent 80: 1569 D 18 '63
Cigarettes find a defender. Sci Digest 54:66 D '63
Cigarettes; tried and found guilty. L. M. Miller and J. Monahan. Read Digest 84:71-6 Ap '64

CIGARETTES—*Continued*
Cigarettes v. lollipops; case of Edwin M. Green suing the American tobacco co. Time 84:59 D 11 '64
College smoking; how come nobody's stopped? M. A. Guitar. Mlle 59:268-9+ Ag '64
Crash effort for a safer cigarette; concerning the report of Surgeon General's advisory committee on smoking and health. B. Davidson. il Sat Eve Post 237:19-23 Ap 18 '64
Evidence piles up; Cancer society's indictment of cigarettes. il Bsns W p26-7 D 7 '63
Giving up the habit. il Newsweek 65:52 Ja 25 '65
Government report. il Time 83:42 Ja 17 '64
Hazards of teen-age smoking; excerpts from Smoke screen: tobacco and the public welfare. M. B. Neuberger. il Parents Mag 39:51+ Ja '64
Here's the latest on tobacco and health. il U S News 56:44-5 Ja 20 '64
Hot cigarettes; radioactive isotope, polonium-210 in cigarette smoke. il Newsweek 63:54 Ja 27 '64
How to give up smoking; maybe. R. Brecher and E. Brecher. il N Y Times Mag p 16+ Ja 26 '64
How to keep on smoking. Christian Cent 81:159 Ja 29 '64
Huffing and puffing. Newsweek 63:65-6 F 10 '64
I quit smoking, or Cooper's last stand. C. R. Cooper. Read Digest 84:77-80 Ap '64
Irrational state. Nat R 16:97+ F 11 '64
It is less hazardous. il Time 83:60 Ap 17 '64
It won't happen here; effects of Surgeon General's report on tobacco industry. Bsns W p29 F 15 '64
John Bull goes right on smoking. A. Carthew. il N Y Times Mag p 17+ Ja 19 '64
One year later; effect of Surgeon General's report. Time 85:58 Ja 22 '65
Personal business; smoking habit. Bsns W p97 Ja 11 '64
Place your bets: health odds for cigarette smokers. W. Cloud. il Pop Sci 184:23 Mr '64
Polonium-210; a volatile radioelement in cigarettes. E. P. Radford, jr. and V. R. Hunt. bibliog il Science 143:247-9 Ja 17 '64; Discussion. 143:917; 144:366-7, 952-3; 146:86-7 F 28, Ap 24, My 22, O 2 '64
Puffs of peril? Sr Schol 84:17 Ja 31 '64
Radioactivity in tobacco; polonium. Sci N L 85:70 F 1 '64
Reasonably safe smoking; lawsuit against American tobacco co. Newsweek 64:50 D 14 '64
Reporter at large. T. Whiteside. il New Yorker 39:67-8+ N 30 '63
Rugged smoker. Nation 198:83 Ja 27 '64
Safe cigarette. B. H. Frisch. il Sci Digest 55:15-18 My '64
Safe smoking sought. F. Marley. Sci N L 85:5 Ja 4 '64
Semi-final word; delay in publication of government's report on cigarettes and lung cancer. Newsweek 62:81 O 14 '63
Smoke-filled trap. B. Fielding. il NEA J 53:18-20 O '64
Smokers light up less, but habit bounces back. il Bsns W p88-9+ D 12 '64
Smokers' slowdown: how long will it last? U S News 56:6 F 24 '64
Smoking. C. W. Thompson. NEA J 53:66-9 Mr '64
Smoking and cancer: a reverse relationship. il Sci Digest 57:29-30 Ja '65
Smoking and cancer: a verdict; concerning Surgeon General's report. il Sr Schol 84:4-7 F 21 '64
Smoking and diseases. Sci N L 84:325 N 23 '63
Smoking and health. Sr Schol 84:1T Ja 31 '64
Smoking and health: the U.S. decision. il Newsweek 62:61-6 N 18 '63
Smoking and lung cancer. R. Brecher and E. Brecher. il Consumer Rep 28:265-80 Je '63
Smoking causes cancer; excerpts from report. F. Marley. Sci N L 85:51-2 Ja 25 '64
Smoking effects on heart. Sci N L 85:85 F 8 '64
Smoking fire burns hotter; health vs. industry. il Bsns W p32+ Ja 18 '64
Smoking habits: what Surgeon General says; remarks, January 11, 1965. L. L. Terry. U S News 58:14 Ja 25 '65
Smoking hazard. Consumer Bul 47:14-15 Ap '64
Smoking; is polonium the villain? Time 83:31 Ja 24 '64
Smoking report. Sci Am 210:66-7 F '64
Smoking report; concerning Smoking to death? America 110:131 Ja 25 '64
Smoking scare? what's happened to it. il U S News 58:38-41 Ja 11 '65
Smoking; Surgeon General's report. il Consumer Rep 29:112-15 Mr '64
Stop smoking for your own sake and your children's. G. J. Hecht. Parents Mag 39:38 Ap '64
To control smoking habit. Sci N L 87:35-6 Ja 16 '65
To smoke, or not to smoke? il Newsweek 63:70-3 Ja 27 '64
Tobacco: activity masks unrest in industry as government smoking study is prepared for release. E. Langer. Science 142:941-2 N 15 '63
Tobacco: after publicity surge, Surgeon general's report seems to have little enduring effect. D. S. Greenberg. Science 145:1021-2 S 4 '64
Tobacco and the public welfare. M. B. Neuberger. il PTA Mag 58:10-11 My '64
Tobacco-health issue. F. Marley. il Sci N L 84:373 D 14 '63
Tobacco report: PHS study group, after fourteen month survey, agrees that smoking is indeed harmful. D. S. Greenberg. Science 143:227 Ja 17 '64
Trouble is the word; question of tobacco industry's future. il Time 81:73 Je 28 '63
U.S. sums it up: quit smoking; Surgeon General's report. il Bsns W p42-4+ Ja 18 '64
Verdict on cigarets: guilty as charged; concerning Surgeon General's advisory committee report. il Life 56:56A-62+ Ja 24 '64
Villain in smoke: a new view; excerpt from statement, January 29, 1964. L. Terry. U S News 56:61 F 10 '64
Wait and see; Surgeon General's one-year-later report on lethal effects of cigarette smoking. Nation 200:69-70 Ja 25 '65
What a doctor tells his own kids about smoking. R. R. Montgomery. Changing T 18:13-14 S '64
What part will the school play? E. Schneider. Sch Life 46:18 Ag '64
Where there's smoke. Newsweek 62:84 D 16 '63
Where there's smoke. W. Stanton. il McCalls 91:28+ Ag '64
Where there's smoke; smoking since the Surgeon General's report. il Newsweek 65:50-1 Ja 18 '65
Why smoking called habit; Cigarette actions asked; Withdrawal clinics for smokers thrive. Sci N L 85:50 Ja 25 '64
Why stop smoking? New Repub 150:6-7 Ja 25 '64
Will science find a safer cigarette? C. P. Gilmore. il Pop Sci 185:60-1+ Jl '64
Year I won the war against cigarettes. D. Wharton. Read Digest 86:75-8 Ja '65
See also
Smoking

Advertising

Ads in reverse. il Time 82:69 N 15 '63
Ads subtracted. Newsweek 62:62 Jl 1 '63
. . . And slow death. Read Digest 82:49-53 F '63
Ads switch rather than fight; new voluntary code. il Bsns W p 14 D 26 '64
Calling a smoke a smoke. Time 83:84+ My 8 '64
Can $8 billion be disciplined? Christian Cent 81:876 Jl 8 '64; Discussion. 81:1114 S 9 '64
Carlton's tar and nicotine. il Consumer Rep 29:114-15 Mr '64
Case of the smoked mink. V. Hill. New Repub 150:8 Ap 11 '64
Cigarette advertising; testimony presented before FTC. M. E. Brady. il Consumer Rep 29:246-50 My '64
Cigarette code czar; appointment of Robert B. Meyner as administrator of new code for cigarette advertising. America 110:843 Je 20 '64
Cigarette czar; R. B. Meyner picked to administer new Cigarette advertising code. Newsweek 63:64 Je 22 '64
Cigarette manufacturers adopt new code. Christian Cent 81:629 My 13 '64
Cigarette tar derby may be on again; tar, nicotine content on pack. il Bsns W p24-5 Ja 11 '64
Cigarettes and the ad man. C. Bowen. New Repub 150:6 My 9 '64
Drive for the teen-age market; excerpts from The Consumers union report on smoking and the public interest. PTA Mag 58:23-4 O '63
England warns its youth: Britain's anti-smoking ads. R. L. Dean. il America 108:253-5 F 23 '63; Discussion. 108:245, 451 F 23, Ap 6 '63
Ex-chain-smoker's exit. Time 84:87 S 25 '64

CIGARETTES—Advertising—*Continued*
FTC tries to kick the habit; cigarette ads. il Bsns W p28-9 Ja 25 '64
Good advertising. Nation 199:207-8 O 12 '64
No more free smokes. Nation 197:22 Jl 13 '63
Reporter at large. T. Whiteside. il New Yorker 39:68+ N 30 '63
Saga of cigarette ads. S. C. Whitehead and D. A. Goodman. il America 109:387-9 O 5 '63
Should cigarette advertising be curbed as a health menace? pro and con discussion. il Sr Schol 84:8-9 F 21 '64
Smoke-filled code. il Newsweek 63:72 My 11 '64
Smokescreen; cigarette advertising code. J. Ridgeway. New Repub 152:5-6 Ja 9 '65
Tar Czar; Cigarette advertising code. Newsweek 64:46 D 28 '64
Tar czar; Robert R. Meyner appointed to administer the Cigarette advertising code, inc. Time 83:86 Je 19 '64
Tarred on all sides. Time 83:90 F 7 '64
Thinking man's reaction. America 108:191 F 9 '63
Tobacco troubles. P. B. Bart. Sat R 46:45+ Ag 10 '63; Discussion. 46:66 S 14 '63
Too little, too late and inept. Nation 198:470-1 My 11 '64
Washington hearings on cigarette labeling. il Time 83:79-80 Mr 27 '64
Who's in charge here? C. W. Morton. Atlan 214:103 S '64
Words and meaning. il Newsweek 62:62 Ag 26 '63

Anecdotes, facetiae, satire, etc.

Notes and comment. New Yorker 40:39-40 My 16 '64
Smoking without commercials. C. W. Morton. Atlan 213:160 Mr '64

CIGARS
Female puffer. il Newsweek 63:80-1+ Mr 23 '64
New cigar imports. L. Morse. Duns R 82:67-8 O '63
Pipe this; pipe and cigar smoking women. W. K. Zinsser. il Sat Eve Post 237:58-9 My 30 '64
Switch to small cigars, perhaps? Consumer Rep 29:365 Ag '64
Upmannship. S. White. il Horizon 6:104-5 Sum '64
Women and cigars. il Vogue 143:92 My '64

Advertising

Smoke gets in your ears. G. Ace. Sat R 47:18 D 12 '64

CIGNA, Arrigo A. and Giorcelli, F. G.
Iodine-131 thyroid dose from milk in Italy during the period September 1962 to February 1963. bibliog Science 143:379-80 Ja 24 '64

CIGNA, Gina
Rose for Cigna; interview, ed. by B. Fischer-Williams. il por Opera N 29:26-7 Ja 16 '65

CILEA, Francesco
Adriana Lecouvreur. Criticism
New Yorker 38:111-12 F 2 '63
Newsweek il 61:79 F 4 '63
Opera N 27:18-20 F 9 '63
Opera N 27:28-9 F 9 '63
Opera N 27:35 Mr 9 '63
Sat R 46:41+ F 9 '63
On records; Adriana Lecouvreur. J. W. Freeman. Opera N 27:35 F 9 '63
Perfect gentleman. M. J. Matz. il pors Opera N 27:25-7 F 9 '63

CILIA and ciliary motion
Ependymal cilia: distribution and activity in the adult human brain. W. C. Worthington, jr. and R. S. Cathcart, 3d. bibliog Science 139:221-2 Ja 18 '63
Induction of conjugation by cell-free preparations in paramecium multimicronucleatum. A. Miyake. bibliog Science 146:1583-5 D 18 '64
Nervous control of ciliary activity. E. Aiello and G. Guideri. bibliog il Science 146:1692-3 D 25 '64

CILO, Charles
Truth strikes out. Nation 199:281-2 O 26 '64

CIMBALOM
Goulash wagon; cimbalom player Janos Hosszu. il Newsweek 61:75 Ap 1 '63

CIMICIFUGA racemosa. See Black snakeroot

CINCINNATI

City planning

Cincinnati riverfront redevelopment. H. Weese. il Arch Rec 133:138-9 My '63

Finance

Purchasing for pennies a serving. J. G. Krieg. Am City 79:80 Jl '64

Libraries

See also
Public library of Cincinnati and Hamilton County

Music

[Musical events] (cont) Mus Am 83:12 Jl '63; 84:16+ Mr '64

Newspapers

See also
Cincinnatti enquirer

Parks and playgrounds

Reservoir roof supports a lake. C. M. Bolton. il Am City 79:22 O '64

Politics and government

Cincinnati's legal head. il Ebony 18:87-8+ Je '63

Streets

Testing traffic paint. J. G. Krieg. il Am City 79:92-3 N '64

CINCINNATI enquirer
Efficiency in Cincinnati; time and motion study. Time 84:74+ D 4 '64

CINCINNATI milling machine company
Beating the up-and-down cycle. il Bsns W p90-2+ O 19 '63

CINCINNATI public library. See Public library of Cincinnati and Hamilton County

CINCINNATI Reds (baseball) See Baseball clubs

CINCINNATI Royals (basketball team) See Basketball teams

CINCINNATI summer opera association
Cincinnati fauna. M. De Schauensee. Opera N 28:31 O 19 '63
Zoo story. H. S. Humphreys. il Opera N 29:23 O 17 '64
Zoo story; opera company's 44th season. E. Bell. Mus Am 84:22-3 S '64

CINCOTTI, Fausto
Our man on the Settebello. New Yorker 40:41-4 Ap 18 '64

CINDERELLA girl; story. See Ellingson, M.

CINDERELLA summer; story. See Fritz, J.

CINDY; musical comedy. See Musical comedies, revues, etc.—Criticisms, plots, etc.

CINEMA. See Moving pictures

CINEMA rooms. See Recreation rooms

CINEPHONIC cameras. See Cameras

CINNAMON
Spice is the variety of life. V. M. Quist. il Horticulture 42:14-15 Ja '64

CINVA-Ram blocks. See Building blocks

CIOFFERO, Vito
Dangerous necessity to dramatize. R. Steiner. il Pop Phot 54:48-9+ F '64

CIPHERS
Beatrix Potter's code writing. L. Linder. il Horn Bk 39:140-55 Ap '63

CIPNIC, Dennis J.
Lore from a gemstone carving genius. Pop Mech 121:124-7+ Mr '64
Straight-shooting teens. Parents Mag 39:44-5+ Ja '64

CIRCADIAN rhythm. See Periodicity

CIRCLE cutter. See Cutting tools

CIRCLE line-sightseeing yachts. incorporated
Around the Island; boat ride around Manhattan. il U S Camera 27:62-3 Jl '64

CIRCUIT breakers. See Electric circuit breakers

CIRCUIT testers. See Electric circuit testers

CIRCULAR saws. See Saws

CIRCULAR stairs. See Stairways

CIRCULATING libraries. See Libraries

CIRCULATION of the blood. See Blood—Circulation

CIRCULATIONS, Audit bureau of. See Audit bureau of circulations

CIRCULATORY system. See Vascular system

CIRCULATORY system, Plant. See Plants—Translocation

CIRCUMCISION
Circumcision urged to prevent cancer. Sci N L 86:281 O 31 '64

CIRCUMSTANTIAL evidence. See Evidence (law)

CIRCUS
And now, in the center ring, profits. il Bsns W p28-9 Mr 28 '64
Big top goes abroad; Ringling bros, Barnum & Bailey circus, in Europe. il Bsns W p32-3 O 12 '63

CIRCUS—*Continued*
Big top, Moscow; Moscow circus at Madison Square Garden. il N Y Times Mag p69-70 S 15 '63
Brawn lake; Moscow circus in Manhattan. il Time 82:101 O 4 '63
Circusiana. D. Stevens. See issues of Hobbies
Father Schönig: circus priest extraordinary. G. Kent. il Read Digest 84:74-8 Je '64
Giant swing. New Yorker 39:38-9 Ap 20 '63
Milwaukee rolls out the wagons. il Life 57: 90-2 Jl 3 '64
One-ring barrel of fun from Moscow. il Life 55:69-70+ O 18 '63
Popov and co. the Moscow circus. il Newsweek 62:59 S 30 '63
Soviet circus wows the U.S.A. B. Ballantine. il Sat Eve Post 236:82-5 O 26 '63
Summer action, circus. il U S Camera 26:52-3+ Ag '63
Up, up, by the hair she goes. il Life 56:89-90 Ap 17 '64

Equipment

Gaudery on wheels; circus wagons. E. Bedno and J. Bedno. il Am Heritage 16:113-120 D '64

CIRCUS, Amateur
Let's have a circus. G. Haskin. il Recreation 56:186-8 Ap '63

CIRCUS animals

Training

See Animals—Training

CIRCUS in art
Gaudery on wheels; circus wagons. E. Bedno and J. Bedno. il Am Heritage 16:113-20 D '64

CIRCUS performers
Death on the high wire. B. Ballantine. il Read Digest 83:53-9 Jl '63
Tops under the big tops. il N Y Times Mag p22-3 Je 30 '63
See also
Acrobats and acrobatism

CIRCUS; story. See Gallant, M.

CIRKER, Hayward
Scientific paperback revolution. Science 140: 591-4; 141:483-4+ My 10, Ag 9 '63

CISCO fishing
Nothing like it. J. Zumbo. il Outdoor Life 134: 28-31+ D '64

CISMARU, Alfred
American Negro in post-war French drama. Negro Hist Bul 27:79-80 Ja '64

CISSELL, Helen. See Cissell, R. jt. auth.

CISSELL, Robert, and Cissell, Helen
Consumer credit. America 111:552-4 N 7 '64
Is economic growth enough? America 111:65-7 Jl 18 '64

CISZEK, Walter
Father Ciszek's first public statement. America 109:475 O 26 '63
Loneliness of a long-distance Jesuit. America 111:514-17 O 31 '64
Return from Russia. America 110:408-11 Mr 28 '64
Silent years in Siberia. J. B. Donovan. America 111:807 D 19 '64

CITIES and towns
Are cities obsolete? B. Weissbourd. il Sat R 47:12-15+ D 19 '64; Reply. R. E. Singer. 48:37 Ja 23 '65
Cities, by J. Morris. Review
Nat R 16:979-80 N 3 '64. W. A. Rusher
Future of the city (cont) L. Mumford. il Arch Rec 133:119-26 Ja '63
Twilight of cities, by E. A. Gutkind. Review
Arch Forum 118:145+ Mr '63. D. B. Carlson
See also
Capitals (cities)
City and country
City and town life
Company towns
Education, Urban
Housing
Neighborhoods
Playgrounds
Slums
Sociology, Urban
Street lighting

Defenses

See also
Civil defense

Federal aid

See Federal and municipal relations

Gifts, legacies, etc.

Public gifts. J. E. Curtis. Recreation 56: 61 F '63

Growth

Are we committing urban suicide? L. Hazard. Harvard Bsns R 42:152-4+ Jl '64
Central-city upsurge. Am City 79:7 N '64
City in the '60's. il Sr Schol 83:6-9+ O 11; 12-15 O 18 '63
City may be as lethal as the bomb. B. Ward. il N Y Times Mag p22-3+ Ap 19 '64
Delos symposium explores future of urban growth. Arch Rec 136:86 D '64
Demand and trends in prices for urban transit. G. Faux. bibliog f il Mo Labor R 87:277-84 Mr '64
First Asian metro plan conference. R. H. Hamilton. Am City 79:118 N '64
Five challenges to our cities. P. M. Klutznick. Arch Forum 120:106-8 My '64
Land-use facts vs. fables. Am City 78:7 N '63
Place of nature in the city of man. I. L. McHarg. bibliog f Ann Am Acad 352:1-12 Mr '64
Surge to the towns; Asia. B. Ward. il UNESCO Courier 17:5-6 S '64
Those muddy-boots urban problems. Am City 79:7 D '64
Urban explosion in developing nations. P. Mercier. il UNESCO Courier 16:50-5 Jl '63
Urban pattern. H. Blumenfeld. Ann Am Acad 352:74-83 Mr '64
See also
Metropolitan areas

Industries

Big plant-site scramble. il Duns R 83:pt2 104-5+ Mr '64
How to keep industry; Royersford, Pa. H. J. Grossman. il Am City 78:122 S '63
Meat and potatoes. il Newsweek 61:27-8 F 25 '63
Rough-and-tumble of site location. il Duns R 81:pt2 S97-100+ Mr '63
Urban economic development. J. H. Nixon and P. H. Gerhardt. bibliog f Ann Am Acad 352:39-47 Mr '64

Names

See Names, Geographical

Planning

See City planning

Religious life

See City churches

Transportation

See Rapid transit

Water supply

See Water supply

Zone system

See Zoning

Asia

Surge to the towns. B. Ward. il UNESCO Courier 17:5-6 S '64

Colombia

Farmer, city founder, and poet; founding and construction of San Martín de Porres. L. Zalamea. il Américas 15:35-9 N '63

Great Britain

To avert traffic jams: three-level cities? U S News 55:8 D 9 '63

Israel

Israel's three cities. D. Pryce-Jones. Commentary 35:52-5 Ja '63

Italy

Italian province. S. Levarie. il Opera N 28:6-11 Ap 18 '64

Latin America

Latin America's troubled cities. C. M. Haar. For Affairs 41:536-49 Ap '63

Mexico

Mexico's border towns. M. Ross. il Travel 120:32-4 N '63

United States

All around the town; news & notes on our lively, changing cities & suburbs. il Changing T 17:29-30 My '63
Are most cities too ugly to save? interview. E. D. Stone. il U S News 57:82-8 N 30 '64
Big cities try for a comeback. il U S News 57:34-8 D 28 '64
Cities in the U.S. where business is best; with charts. U S News 55:54-7 Jl 1 '63; 57:62-5 Ag 10 '64

CITIES and towns—United States—*Continued*
City in the '60's. il Sr Schol 83:6-9+ O 11; 12-15 O 18 '63
Culturally deprived in the great cities. F. Bertolaet. il Sr Schol 84:5T-6T Ap 24 '64
Cure for sick cities. C. Case. Sat R 46:12-14 F 9 '63
Notes for a gazetteer. P. Hamburger. See occasional issues of New Yorker
Patient will live. J. H. McCrocklin. Am City 78:7 O '63
Right way to save our cities: condensation. J. Jacobs. il Read Digest 84:229-34+ Ap '64
Sick cities, by M. Gordon. Review
Am Heritage 14:109-11 O '63. B. Catton
Smalltown, U.S.A. L. Hanscom. il Newsweek 62:17-20 Jl 8 '63
Specialists diagnose the stricken American city. C. W. Griffin, jr. Sat R 46:22-4 Ag 3 '63
Those muddy-boots urban problems. Am City 79:7 D '64
Train doesn't stop here anymore. il Time 81:28 F 15 '63
Transportation and the city; symposium. il Arch Forum 119:61-95 O '63
Ugly city. J. O'Gara. Commonweal 80:390 Je 19 '64
Urban villagers, by H. Gans. Review
Commentary 35:544-7 Je '63. M. Parenti
Way the U.S. is growing, what it means. il U S News 56:82-5 Ja 13 '64
Woods move into cities; northeastern seaboard. B. Tufty. Sci N L 85:373 Je 13 '64
Wrecking the cities. Nation 199:207 O 12 '64
See also
All-America cities
Metropolitan areas
Municipal government

CITIES and towns, Movement to. See Cities and towns—Growth

CITIES and towns, Ruined, extinct, etc.
Vanished cities of West Africa. H. G. Lawrence. il Negro Hist Bul 27:117-19 F '64
See also
Fatehpur Sikri, India
Petra, Jordan
Troy

CITIZENS arrest. See Arrest

CITIZENS associations
Chattanooga puts its citizens to work. il Am City 79:159+ Ap '64
Citizens and their schools. J. Cass. Sat R 47:55-6 N 21 '64; Reply. R. I. Coun. 47:44 D 19 '64
Little green space; protest of groups in Cambridge, Mass. over changing Memorial Drive. il Time 83:64 F 14 '64
Small rebellion in Miami; Safe progress association. P. Redford. Harper 228:96-8+ F '64
What do they want? biracial human-relations committees. America 109:71-2 Jl 20 '63
See also
White citizens councils

CITIZENS committees. See Citizens associations

CITIZENS councils. See Citizens associations

CITIZENS for decent literature
CDL on the local scene. E. J. Gaines. ALA Bul 59:17-18 Ja '65
Poison in print and how to get rid of it. C. W. Hall. Read Digest 84:94-8 My '64

CITIZENS for educational freedom
Citizens for educational freedom. J. R. Brown. America 110:194-6 F 8 '64; Reply. E. M. O'Keefe. 110:299 Mr 7 '64
CEF on the march. America 108:322 Mr 9 '63; Reply. W. B. O'Connor. 108:423 Mr 30 '63
Equal opportunity in education. M. H. Wagner. America 111:209 Ag 29 '64
Prince Edward's injustice. America 110:328 Mr 14 '64

CITIZENS obligations. See Citizenship

CITIZENS radio service
Antennas for business radio. H. H. Rice. il Electr World 69:33-5+ Mr '63
CB dilemma; a solution. O. P. Ferrell. Pop Electr 21:78-9 N '64
CB dilemma revisited. Pop Electr 22:64 Ja '65
Citizens band radio. il Travel 120:48-9 Ag '63
Citizens radio rules tightened; for hobby-type operation of class D stations. Electr World 72:78 O '64
CB radio-wave propagation. R. L. Conhaim. il Electr World 70:46-8+ D '63
CBers note! the rules have changed. E. S. Maloney. il Motor B 114:82+ N '64
Comments on the new CB rules. L. Buckwalter. Electr World 72:42-3 N '64
Double-duty EICO 772. R. Clark-Duff. il Pop Electr 19:49-51+ Jl '63
FCC and 11 meters: a CBer's view. D. T. Geiser. il Pop Electr 20:59-60 Je '64
FCC report. R. E. Tall. See issues of Popular electronics to December 1963
How tough are the proposed CB regulations? R. L. Conhaim. Electr World 69:26-8+ My '63
New citizens band circuits. L. Buckwalter. il Electr World 69:48-9+ Ap; 32-3 Je; 70: 41+ S; 36+ N '63; 71:32-3+ Ja; 46-7+ Mr; 46-7+ My; 72:34-5+ Jl; 54-5+ O '64; 73: 50-1 Ja '65
New CB regulations. W. A. Stocklin. Electr World 69:8 F '63
New rules to govern CB. Pop Electr 21:55 O '64
New teeth for the FCC. E. S. Maloney. Motor B 111:165 My '63
On the citizens band. M. P. Spinello. See issues of Popular electronics
Proposal to the FCC; a citizens radio technician license. R. L. Conhaim. Electr World 69:48-9 Mr '63
Revamp your CB for better noise limiting. R. L. Winklepleck. il Pop Electr 20:53-4 Ap '64
12-foot transformer for CB. D. T. Geiser. il Pop Electr 18:90 Mr '63
Two-way radio for everyman. C. Dreher. Atlan 214:168+ N '64
Upgrade from CB to business radio. L. G. Sands. il Electr World 70:33 Jl '63

CITIZENS' scholarship foundation. See Foundations, Charitable and educational

CITIZENSHIP
Canadian judge bars atheists. Christian Cent 81:1260 O 14 '64
Citizen and foreign policy; address, September 30, 1963. K. Louchheim. Dept State Bul 49:681-4 O 28 '63
Citizen and his public responsibilities; address, September 12, 1963. J. Randolph. Vital Speeches 30:9-111 O 15 '63
Documents of the struggle for public decency. E. Capouya. Sat R 47:13+ Jl 25 '64
How to fight city hall. A. Levy. Redbook 122: 61+ Ap '64
Marquis de Lafayette is no precedent; honorary American citizenship. E. T. Folliard. America 108:217 F 16 '63
Memorials, yes: this one no: President Kennedy's inaugural summons. J. Ciardi. Sat R 47:20 S 5 '64
New Court. A. M. Bickel. New Repub 148: 15-17 Mr 16 '63
Now 40,000 ex-Americans can be citizens again; Supreme court decision. U S News 56:13 Je 1 '64
Real meaning of dual citizenship. il Good H 158:129 Ja '64
Total living: total citizenship; address, July 11, 1963. E. J. Meeman. Vital Speeches 29: 662-5 Ag 15 '63
Welcome home; Section 352 of the 1952 Immigration and nationality act repealed. il Time 83:57 My 29 '64
See also
Naturalization
Patriotism

CITIZENSHIP, Education for
Boys nation: leadership for young Americans; Boys state on local level. E. Kolowrat. il Sr Schol 83:29+ S 27 '63
Children can learn from politics. E. Simonds. Parents Mag 39:45+ O '64
Citizens now, voters soon; with study-discussion program. F. Patterson and G. Donovan. bibliog il PTA Mag 59:28-30, 37 S '64
Citizenship courses. Sr Schol 84:1T-2T Ja 31 '64
Citizenship education in New York state. Sch & Soc 91:136-7 Mr 23 '63
Concern for civics. Sr Schol 85:1T O 28 '64
Role of the school in developing social responsibility in a free society; excerpt from Social responsibility in a free society. NEA J 52:33-8 N '63
Schools and character development. H. Howe, 2d. Sat R 46:66-7 S 21 '63
See also
Citizenship education project
Encampment for citizenship

CITIZENSHIP education project
It happened in Oklahoma City. B. V. Watkins. NEA J 52:39-40 N '63

CITRATE cleavage enzymes. See Enzymes

CITROËN. See Automobile industry and trade—France

CITRUS flavonoids. See Flavonoids

CITRUS fruit industry
Orange squeeze; damage caused by cold. il Time 81:73 Mr 1 '63
Squeeze is on oranges; last winter's freeze. Bsns W p 158+ S 14 '63
Squeeze play; Hale Indian River orange groves. H. Sutton. Sat R 47:25-6 F 8 '64

CITRUS fruit trees. See Fruit trees

CITRUS fruit trees, Dwarf. See Fruit trees, Dwarf

CITRUS fruits
Adding a touch of tartness; with recipes. J. Hewitt. il N Y Times Mag p77 Ja 12 '64
Citrus. E. D. Ballard. il Horticulture 42:17+ Ag '64
Citrus for winter and spring color. il Sunset 133:170 D '64
Squeeze play; Hale Indian River orange groves. H. Sutton. Sat R 47:25-6 F 8 '64
See also
Cookery—Fruit

CITRUS products. See Citrus fruit industry

CITY and country
Can cities compete with suburbia for family living? C. B. Wurster. il Arch Rec 136:149-56 D '64
Dusty, smeared, musty, moldy, tattered life of P. T. Barnum. W. Saroyan. il Sat Eve Post 237:70-1 Je 13 '64
Environment: land, air, water. R. Revelle. il New Repub 151:25-8+ N 7 '64
Less rural, more wistful America. R. Kluger. Harper 230:94-7 Ja '65
Notes and comment; escaping from the city to Long Island. New Yorker 39:15 Jl 13 '63
Party of one; back to the city which I never should have left. J. Weidman. Holiday 33:17-21+ My '63
Surge to the towns; Asia. B. Ward. il UNESCO Courier 17:5-6 S '64
See also
Country life
Suburban life

CITY and town life
Architecture and the urban emergency. D. Canty. il Arch Forum 121:172-9 Ag '64
Architecture as total community: the challenge ahead. A. Mayer. Arch Rec 135:141-6 Je '64
Background: the urban crisis. R. C. Weaver. il PTA Mag 59:18-20 O '64
Challenge of urbanization. J. Friedmann. bibliog il NEA J 53:42-5 N '64
Changing pattern of urban party politics. F. I. Greenstein. bibliog f il Ann Am Acad 353:1-13 My '64
City destroying itself. R. J. Whalen. il Fortune 70:114-23+ S '64
City life is best, says Hartford firm. E. C. Freedman. il Am City 79:106 Ag '64
How to bring suburban joys to town. House & Gard 125:168-9 My '64
New towns: and fresh in-city communities. A. Mayer. bibliog f il Arch Rec 136:129-38 Ag '64
Ruminations on small towns. R. Kirk. Nat R 15:485 D 3 '63
Something special in vacations. J. K. Lagemann. il Read Digest 82:222-3+ Je '63
Urban social differentiation and the allocation of resources. R. W. Mack and D. C. McElrath. Ann Am Acad 352:25-32 Mr '64
See also
City and country

CITY bonds. See Municipal bonds

CITY budget. See Budget, Municipal

CITY center of music and drama. See New York city center of music and drama

CITY churches
New creation as metropolis, by G. Winter. Review
Christian Cent 80:1007 Ag 14 '63. D. L. Benedict

CITY colleges. See Colleges and universities. Municipal

CITY councils. See Municipal government

CITY dumps. See Municipal dumps

CITY gardens
Annuals blossom in city housing projects. M. Perry. il Flower Grower 51:77-8 Ja '64
City lot dressed up. il Bet Hom & Gard 41:78 O '63
Under city skies. G. O'Brien. il N Y Times Mag p50-1 Je 16 '63
See also
Church gardens
Roof gardens

CITY government. See Municipal government

CITY growth. See Cities and towns—Growth

CITY halls
City hall sets the pace for downtown growth; Ann Arbor, Mich. G. C. Larcom, jr. il Am City 79:93-4 Ja '64
$4,000 borough hall; Philipsburg, Pa. Mrs. R. B Rickard. il Am City 78:127-8 N '63
Hong Kong: new city hall. il Arch Forum 118:114-15 Je '63
Pomona's city hall will use precast concrete, glass. il Am City 79:114 Mr '64
What's been happening to city hall? il Arch Forum 120:98-105 Ap '64
See also
Boston—City hall

CITY improvement. See Municipal improvement

CITY life. See City and town life

CITY manager plan
Leadership in a large manager city: the case of Kansas City. S. T. Gabis. bibliog f Ann Am Acad 353:52-63 My '64

CITY managers
Feminine city managers. A. Stewart. il Am City 79:154+ My '64
Recent city manager appointments. See issues of American city

CITY news bureau of Chicago. See News agencies

CITY noise. See Noise

CITY of Commerce public library, Los Angeles
Commerce converts a warehouse. P. A. Gray. il Library J 89:4730-2 D 1 '64

CITY of London. See London

CITY OF REFUGE NATIONAL PARK. See Hawaii—Parks and reserves

CITY ordinances. See Municipal ordinances

CITY parks. See Parks

CITY planners
Careers in planning; problems of city growth, traffic, land use. il Changing T 17:31-3 F '63

CITY planning
America down the drain; with statement by Secretary Udall. R. H. Boyle. il Sports Illus 21:78-80+ N 16 '64
Beauty and the planners. W. Von Eckhardt. il New Repub 149:21-4 O 5 '63
California: highest living, and a mess. il Arch Forum 119:7-8 O '63
Can cities compete with suburbia for family living? C. B. Wurster. il Arch Rec 136:149-56 D '64
Can transportation systems put our cities back together again? D. B. Carlson. il Arch Forum 119:62-7 O '63
Cities and space: the future use of urban space, ed. by L. Wingo. Review
Bul Atomic Sci 20:30-2 My '64. J. Friedmann
Cities, the new scale; symposium. il Arch Forum 121:171-209 Ag '64
Citizen planner; municipal planning commission in Shelbyville and Ridgely, Tenn. il Am City 79:148+ O '64
Confessions of a town planner. S. Chase. il Read Digest 83:133-7 Jl '63
Culture change and the planner. A. N. B. Garvan. Ann Am Acad 352:33-8 Mr '64
Downtown snarl: a case for sorting, stacking, and storing. il Arch Forum 119:78-83 O '63
Downtown's dramatic comeback. D. B. Carlson. il Arch Forum 120:98-103 F '64
Federal bulldozer: a critical analysis of urban renewal; 1949-1962, by M. Anderson. Review
Nation 200:87-8 Ja 25 '65. S. Greer
Five challenges to our cities. P. M. Klutznick. Arch Forum 120:106-8 My '64
Future of the city (cont) L. Mumford. il Arch Rec 133:119-26 Ja; 119-26 F '63
Hail Megalopolis. Newsweek 63:68 Je 15 '64
Heart of our cities, by V. Gruen. Review
New Repub 152:18-19 Ja 2 '65. W. Von Eckardt
Man's struggle for shelter in an urbanizing world, by C. Abrams. Review
Nation 199:199-201 O 5 '64. D. Gurin
New towns: and fresh in-city communities. A. Mayer. bibliog f il Arch Rec 136:129-38 Ag '64
New towns in America. W. Von Eckardt. New Repub 149:16-18 O 26 '63; Reply. M. Lippman. 149:39 N 2 '63
Place of nature in the city of man. I. L. McHarg. bibliog f Ann Am Acad 352:1-12 Mr '64
Planning the downtown center; symposium, with introd. by M. F. Schmertz. il Arch Rec 135:177-200 Mr '64
Political side of urban development and redevelopment. S. Greer and D. W. Minar. Ann Am Acad 352:62-73 Mr '64
Profiles; C. Doxiadis. C. Rand. New Yorker 39:49-50+ My 11 '63
Public art of city building. D. A. Crane. bibliog f Ann Am Acad 352:84-94 Mr '64

CITY planning—*Continued*
Recreation and urban development: a policy perspective; excerpts from Trends in American living and outdoor recreation. L. Wingo, jr. bibliog f Ann Am Acad 352:129-40 Mr '64
Responsible building. America 111:510 O 31 '64
Right way to save our cities; condensation. J. Jacobs. il Read Digest 84:229-34+ Ap '64
Rudolph calls students to task of urban design. il Arch Rec 135:23+ My '64
Suburbanites cast their votes for city planning; survey by New York's regional plan assn. Arch Forum 119:84-5 D '63
Survival by design. R. Squeri. il Sch Arts 63:12-15 S '63
Technology and urban life: address, October 30, 1963. E. T. Chase. Vital Speeches 30:346-8 Mr 15 '64
Twilight of cities, by E. A. Gutkind. Review
New Repub 148:22-4 F 2 '63. R. Wilkinson
Ugly American. C. W. Griffin, jr. Reporter 30:53-4+ Ja 30 '64
Who is to save our cities? V. Gruen. il Harvard Bsns R 41:107-15 My '63
Within five years; Rockville, Md. il Am City 78:95 Mr '63
See also
Business districts
Cities and towns
Company towns
Housing
Municipal improvement
Regional planning
Streets
Suburbs
Urban renewal
also subhead City planning under names of cities, e.g. New York (city)—City planning

Bibliography

City planning and urban renewal; guide to available reference tools. H. B. Bentley. il Library J 88:1621-4 Ap 15 '63
Designing the environment: a survey of a dozen new books on planning. Arch Rec 136: 78+ Ag '64

Zone system

See Zoning
CITY planning consultants. See Consultants
CITY school systems. See Public schools
CITY streets. See Streets
CITY temple, London. See London—Churches
CITY traffic. See Street traffic
CITY transit. See Rapid transit
CITY trees. See Trees in cities
CIULLA, Sam F.
View from the upstairs porch. Writer 76:9-11 N '63
Winner; story. Redbook 122:66-7 Ap '64
CIVIC centers. See Municipal centers
CIVIC education. See Citizenship, Education for
CIVIC improvement. See Municipal improvement
CIVICS. See Citizenship, Education for
CIVIL aeronautics board. See United States—Civil aeronautics board
CIVIL air patrol. See United States—Civil air patrol
CIVIL aviation. See Aeronautics, Commercial
CIVIL defense
Cases of conscience. J. Ciardi. Sat R 46:10-11 F 2 '63
Civil defense: Congress refuses funds to complete shelter survey and stocking program this year. J. Walsh. Science 140:283-4 Ap 19 '63
Civil defense: debate flares again as two partisans share platform on behavioral science role. D. S. Greenberg. Science 139: 1034-5 Mr 15 '63
Civil defense in a balanced national security. S. L. Pittman. Bul Atomic Sci 20:24-6 Je '64
Civil defense; new program in race with growing apathy and apathy is pulling ahead. E. Langer. Science 140:1078-80 Je 7 '63
Death of Nike-Zeus. E. Ubell and S. H. Loory. il Sat Eve Post 236:15-19 Je 1 '63
Decline of the ostrich; effect of Baltimore television program on civil defense. Nation 197:338 N 23 '63
In a national emergency: what you should know about farm machinery. F. Bailey, jr. Suc Farm 61:44 Mr '63
New A-ICBM city defense studied. M. Getler. Miss & Roc 16:13 Ja 18 '65
Oregon points the way. Nation 196:517 Je 22 '63
Planning for civil defense: five requirements. H. A. Knapp, jr. Bul Atomic Sci 19:39-41+ Ap '63
Scientists and public affairs: though world has changed, they remain preoccupied with the bomb. D. S. Greenberg. Science 142: 1635 D 27 '63; Discussion. 143:430+; 144: 366, 954; 145:7 Ja 31, Ap 24, My 22, Jl 3 '64
Some reflections on civil defense. M. E. Rozen. Bul Atomic Sci 20:21-4 Je '64
Step to disarming; effective civil defense. Sci N L 85:386 Je 20 '64
Stockpiling to survive a nuclear attack. A. W. Bellamy; reply with rejoinder. T. E. Phipps, jr. Science 139:674-5 F 15 '63
Strategy for survival, by T. L. Martin, jr. and D. C. Latham. Review
Bul Atomic Sci 20:35-6 Ap '64. G. S. Stanford
Survival of the fewest; with editorial comment. D. Oberdorfer. il Sat Eve Post 236: 17-21, 84 Mr 23 '63
You & civil defense; guide for teachers, administrators, and school board members. il NEA J 53:39-54 Mr '64
See also
Atomic bomb shelters
Building, Bombproof
Corporations—Defense measures

Communications systems

Maximum-minimum approach to civil-defense communications; St Marys, Ohio. G. A. Gerstner. il Am City 78:131-2 N '63

Germany (Federal Republic)

Civil defense: a German view; reprint. Bul Atomic Sci 19:46-8 F '63
CIVIL defense centers
Just for dancing; civil-defense headquarters, Weaverville, Calif. Nation 196:415 My 18 '63
CIVIL disobedience. See Passive resistance to government
CIVIL engineering
See also
Bridges
CIVIL liberties. See Civil rights
CIVIL liberties union, American. See American civil liberties union
CIVIL liberty. See Liberty
CIVIL marriage ceremonies. See Marriage customs and rites
CIVIL procedure
See also
Appellate procedure
Jury
Process
CIVIL rights
Age of the rights of man; address, October 12, 1963. D. Rusk. Dept State Bul 49:654-8 O 28 '63
Anarchy. D. Lawrence. U S News 54:96 F 4 '63
Can laws make men equal? a minister's answer; sermon, September 13, 1963. W. R. Courtenay. il U S News 55:113-16 N 18 '63
Civil rights message. New Repub 148:4-5 Mr 16 '63
Criminals, cops and the Constitution. Y. Kamisar. il Nation 199:322-6 N 9 '64
Curbing of the militant majority. J. P. Roche. il Reporter 29:34-8 Jl 18 '63; Discussion. 29:8+ Ag 15 '63
Embarrassed American; failure to ratify international human rights conventions. W. Korey. Sat R 47:24-5 O 31 '64; Reply. E. Schwelb. 47:19-20 N 28 '64
Emerging consensus on economic and social development; statement, July 10, 1963. A. E. Stevenson. Dept State Bul 49:265-72 Ag 12 '63
Expanding and protecting human rights throughout the world; statement, July 30, 1964. F. H. Williams. Dept State Bul 51: 418-22 S 21 '64
Fifteenth anniversary of Universal declaration of human rights; statement, December 9, and address, December 8, 1963. A. E. Stevenson; R. N. Gardner. bibliog f Dept State Bul 50:19-24 Ja 6 '64
Fluoride and civil liberty. J. Lear. Sat R 48:91 Ja 2 '65
Food, jobs and human rights; address, September 21, 1963. R. Theobald. Vital Speeches 30:61-4 N 1 '63
Freedoms in tension. J. I. Miller. Christian Cent 81:1332-3 O 28 '64
Human rights: address, January 28, 1964. A. E. Stevenson. Vital Speeches 30:323-6 Mr 15 '64

CIVIL rights—*Continued*
Human rights and foreign policy; excerpts from In pursuit of world order. R. N. Gardner. Sat R 47:23-5+ S 19 '64
Human rights: some next steps; conventions on slavery, forced labor, and political rights of women; address, August 5; President's letter to Senate, July 22, 1963; and texts of conventions. R. N. Gardner; J. F. Kennedy. Dept State Bul 49:320-8 Ag 26 '63
International promotion of human rights; address, December 8, 1963. R. N. Gardner. Vital Speeches 30:207-9 Ja 15 '64
Lie detectors: trial by gadget. S. Meisler. il Nation 199:159-62+ S 28 '64
Pacem in terris a year later. J. Cogley. Commonweal 80:356-7 Je 12 '64
Peace and human rights; address, June 15, 1963. H. Cleveland. Dept State Bul 49:38-43 Jl 8 '63
Psychiatry's threat to civil liberties. T. S. Szasz. il Nat R 14:191-3 Mr 12 '63; Discussion. 14:295 Ap 9 '63
Selassie's message to the Negro. A. Morrison. il Ebony 19:29-32+ D '63
What you should know about democracy and why. Sr Schol 82:21-2 My 1 '63
Winds of change; amendment to deny federal funds to any state in which the program discriminates against American citizens on the basis of race, creed or color. Nation 196:414 My 18 '63

See also
American civil liberties union
Assembly, Right of
Catholic council on civil liberties
Citizenship
Due process of law
Inter-American commission on human rights
International human rights year (proposed)
Natural law
Negroes in the United States—Civil rights
Privacy
Right to counsel
Searches and seizures
United Nations—Commission on human rights
United States—Commission on civil rights
United States—Constitution—Bill of rights
Universal declaration of human rights

Quotations, maxims, etc.

On human rights; comp. by E. F. Murphy. il N Y Times Mag p 118-19 D 8 '63

Study and teaching

Methods of teaching about human rights; excerpt from Teaching human rights. NEA J 52:53 N '63
Teaching about civil rights. W. J. Brennan, jr. NEA J 52:43 Mr '63

South Africa

South Africa, the time bomb ticks; policy of apartheid. A. Sampson. il N Y Times Mag p 11+ Ap 12 '64

United States

American library association and civil rights; excerpts from report, July 1963. J. E. Bryan. ALA Bul 57:747 S '63
Answer to the rise in crime and violence; excerpts from address, September 8, 1964. G. B. McClellan. il U S News 57:89-90 N 9 '64
Can integration be forced by federal law? address. C. E. Whittaker. U S News 56:99-101 Mr 23 '64; Reply. D. Lawrence. 56:108 Mr 30 '64
Civil liberty and individual responsibility; address. A. Barth. Vital Speeches 31:135-9 D 15 '64
Civil rights. il Sr Schol 85:4 O 14 '64
Civil rights and civil wrongs. D. Lawrence. Read Digest 84:127-8 Je '64
Civil rights: federal responsibility; address, November 14, 1964. W. L. Taylor. Vital Speeches 31:143-6 D 15 '64
Civil rights; integration issue; address. July 19, 1963. J. B. Connally. Vital Speeches 29:679-82 S 1 '63
Civil rights: the White House meeting. Newsweek 64:15 Ag 3 '64
Eastland's charge: Communists are moving into civil rights; excerpts from address, July 22, 1964. J. O. Eastland. U S News 57:4 Ag 3 '64
Equality is a two-way street. Nat R 16:710 Ag 25 '64
For civil rights now; text of statement by faculty of Union theological seminary. E. C. Parker. Christian Cent 80:1594 D 18 '63
In polling places of the Nation: the white backlash on race issues. il U S News 56:32 Ap 20 '64
Judgment day along the Potomac; National interreligious convocation on civil rights. G. Richards. America 110:623 My 9 '64
Justice with a southern accent; do our federal courts need emancipating? L. Lusky. Harper 228:69-70+ Mr '64; Discussion. 228:9 My '64
Lawyer's duty in civil rights; pro and con. R. F. Kennedy; J. C. Satterfield. U S News 55:120-3 O 14 '63
Let's be honest with ourselves. D. D. Eisenhower. Sat Eve Post 236:23-5 O 19 '63; Same abr. Read Digest 83:61-8 D '63
McNamara comes under new fire. R. S. McNamara. U S News 55:10 Ag 12 '63
NEA strengthens its stand on question of civil rights. Library J 88:3276-7 S 15 '63
Ombudsman for America; Scandinavian-style grievance man to investigate complaints about the work of bureaucrats. H. S. Reuss. N Y Times Mag p30+ S 13 '64
Open society: key to an advancing America; address, October 26, 1963. L. D. Battle. Dept State Bul 49:864-9 D 2 '63
Outcast of Lebanon; case of J. N. Snavely. R. G. Hummerstone. il Nation 199:303-5 N 2 '64; Reply with rejoinder. E. U. Sowers, 2d. 200:inside cover Ja 11 '65
Protects military civil rights; during security investigations. Christian Cent 80:1537 D 11 '63
Quest for the dream: the development of civil rights and human relations in modern America, by J. P. Roche. Review
Reporter 30:48-50 F 13 '64. K. S. Lynn
Special duty for Republicans. J. V. Lindsay. Harper 227:94-5+ S '63; Reply. J. Goodspeed. 227:12+ N '63
Three wars; poverty, civil rights & the cold war; address, September 24, 1964. C. F. Phillips. Vital Speeches 30:757-9 O 1 '64
What LBJ, as a senator, said about civil rights; excerpts from debate, ed. by J. L. McClellan. U S News 56:14 Ap 27 '64
Wisconsin primary; resistance to integration in the North. Commonweal 80:133 Ap 24 '64
Word and substance; findings of Civil rights commission report. Newsweek 62:42 O 7 '63

See also
Negroes in the United States—Civil rights

Civil rights bill, 1963-1964

After the march: outlook for a new law on civil rights. il U S News 55:37 S 9 '63
After you, Alphonse; compromise bill. R. Horchler. Commonweal 79:214 N 15 '63
As civil rights moves ahead: how business may be policed. il U S News 55:55 N 11 '63
At last, a vote. il Time 83:32 My 15 '64
Backdoor battle. il Newsweek 63:17 Mr 30 '64
Battle begins on civil rights. il U S News 56:31-2 F 10 '64
Better at moralizing than legalizing; Power & the precedent; concerning Title II of civil rights legislative package. Time 82:19-20 Jl 12 '63
Bill as amended. New Repub 150:5 Je 20 '64
Bill passed by House; uncertain future in the Senate. Sr Schol 84:15-16 F 28 '64
Bog-down on civil rights bill. Commonweal 79:88-9 O 18 '63
Case for freedom: a governor's view; testimony before the Senate commerce committee. F. Byrant. U S News 55:11 Ag 12 '63
Caught in crossfire; Halleck on civil rights. U S News 55:24 N 11 '63
Changes in the civil-rights bill. il U S News 56:46-7 Je 1 '64
Choice: taxes or civil rights. Bsns W p30 S 28 '63
Civil rights; a challenge. R. H. Bork. New Repub 149:21-4 Ag 31 '63; Reply. 149:24 Ag 31 '63; Rejoinder. 149:36 S 21 '63
Civil rights act of 1963. A. M. Bickel. New Repub 149:9-12 Jl 6 '63
Civil rights and civil wrongs; reprint. E. F. Cummerford. U S News 56:84-6 F 17 '64
Civil rights and legal wrongs. J. J. Kilpatrick. il Nat R 15:231-6 S 24 '63; Discussion. 15:497+ D 3 '63
Civil rights and the Congress. A. M. Bickel. New Repub 149:14-16 Ag 3 '63
Civil rights, as amended. A. M. Bickel. New Repub 149:7-9 N 16 '63; Discussion. 149:30-1 D 14 '63; 150:31 Ja 11 '64
Civil-rights bill. Reporter 29:12+ Jl 18 '63
Civil rights bill: it will not be denied. il Newsweek 63:17-18 Je 29 '64
Civil rights bill: no limits on the customers. Bsns W p95 Je 29 '63
Civil rights: condition poor. Nation 197:309 N 16 '63

CIVIL rights—United States—Civil rights bill, 1963-1964—*Continued*
Civil rights: it's time to act. Life 56:4 My 29 '64
Civil rights now! Christian Cent 80:1391-2 N 13 '63
Civil-rights plan and your business. il U S News 55:62-4 Jl 29 '63
Civil rights revolt. New Repub 149:3-4 N 2 '63
Civil rights: Senate buckles down as protests build up; Negro leaders push demonstrations. il Bsns W p26-7 My 9 '64
Civil rights strategy. America 110:500 Ap 11 '64
Civil rights tangle: where it is heading. il U S News 56:37-8 My 25 '64
Civil rights, will this summer tell? il Sr Schol 84:8-11 My 15 '64
Civil rites. K. Crawford. Newsweek 63:29 My 4 '64
Clearing path for rights bill. Bsns W p28 My 23 '64
Clerical lobbyists; pressure by the Nation's churches for an acceptable civil rights bill. America 110:624 My 9 '64
Cloture roll call. il Time 83:22 Je 5 '64
Congress' fateful decision. Christian Cent 80: 1323 O 30 '63; Reply. S. L. Yale. 80: 1519-20 D 4 '63
Congress moves, but stays in low gear. il Bsns W p21-2 D 7 '63
Congress: session of reckoning on civil rights affects prospects of new vocational education bill. J. Walsh. Science 140:1196-9 Je 14 '63
Counterrevolt? W. F. Buckley, jr. Nat R 16: 348 My 5 '64
Covenant; with vote on cloture. il Time 83: 15-18 Je 19 '64
Cracking the whip for civil rights. il Newsweek 63:26-8+ Ap 13 '64
Crushed by the coalition. Time 83:14 F 14 '64
Debate in the Senate; a meeting in Birmingham. il Time 83:21-2 Ap 10 '64
Debate on civil rights: March 18, 1964. H. Humphrey; S. Thurmond. U S News 56: 102-4 Mr 30 '64
Did a justice advise on how to write a bill? U S News 55:9 O 14 '63
Dirksen amendments. America 110:558 Ap 25 '64
Dirksen amendments. New Repub 150:3-4 Je 6 '64
Dirksen delivers the souls. M. Kempton. New Repub 150:9-11 My 2 '64
Eenie, meenie; filibuster, cloture. Cato. Nat R 16:439 Je 2 '64
Ev's law. Time 83:23 My 22 '64
Extra innings. il Newsweek 63:26 Ap 27 '64
Facing the civil rights isue. Bsns W p 152 O 12 '63
Falling-off among friends. Time 83:35-6 Ap 17 '64
Filibuster ahead; President's new civil-rights bill. Newsweek 61:34+ Je 24 '63
Filibuster begins. il Newsweek 63:27 Mr 23 '64
Filibuster buster. K. Crawford. Newsweek 63: 38 Mr 16 '64
Final vote. il Time 83:17 Je 26 '64
Five angry men speak their minds; symposium, ed. by G. Samuels. il N Y Times Mag p 14+ My 17 '64
Forced hiring of Negroes; how it would work. U S News 55:83-4 Jl 29 '63
Fresh slant. Newsweek 62:19 S 30 '63
From resistance to resignation. M. Kempton. New Repub 150:6 F 15 '64
From the House with love. Cato. Nat R 16: 144 F 25 '64
From Washington straight. Cato. Nat R 15:96 Ag 13 '63
Gauntlet: drafting of bill. il Time 82:29 O 25 '63
Giving up the battle to win the war. J. N. Eller. America 110:358 Mr 21 '64
Grapes of wrath. K. Crawford. Newsweek 63: 32 F 24 '64
Great game of civil rights. B. J. Esterday. America 109:505 N 2 '63
Great question before the Senate; civil-rights debate. Sat Eve Post 237:86 Ap 18 '64
Halleck and McCulloch; Administration battle. il Newsweek 62:34+ N 11 '63
Hammer of civil rights. M. L. King, jr. il Nation 198:230-4 Mr 9 '64
Heroes on the right; compromise bill of House judiciary committee. M. Kempton. New Repub 149:4 N 9 '63
Historic vote: seventy-one to twenty-nine; cloture vote. il Newsweek 63:25-6 Je 22 '64
How a real Mrs Murphy views the rights plan; reprint. il U S News 55:23 Jl 29 '63
How the civil-rights bill reads now. U S News 56:35 Je 22 '64
How the rights vote was engineered. New Repub 150:17-19 F 29 '64
How Wallace explains his big vote in Wisconsin; interview. G. C. Wallace. U S News 56:34 Ap 20 '64
If rights bill passes: how to hire, fire, promote. il U S News 56:113-15 F 24 '64
If the Kennedys get the power they ask; role of Attorney General. U S News 55:49-50 Jl 8 '63
If you were darker; hearings on President Kennedy's civil-rights legislation. il Newsweek 62:28 Ag 5 '63
It's over. Reporter 31:7 Jl 2 '64
Jam in Congress; taxes and civil rights: dead for '63. U S News 55:74 N 18 '63
Justice for all; the legal package: President's five-point program. America 109:3 Jl 6 '63
Knuckle down, LBJ. Cato. Nat R 16:189 Mr 10 '64
Law. Cato. Nat R 16:528 Je 30 '64
Liberals and civil rights. New Repub 149:5 N 23 '63
Long day. il Newsweek 63:20-2 Ap 6 '64
Looking great. Newsweek 63:19-20 My 4 '64
Making haste slowly. Time 82:22 N 8 '63
Man pressing for a civil-rights law. il U S News 55:19 Jl 15 '63
Maybe it's time to look at the antislavery amendment; Thirteenth amendment. A. Avins. il U S News 56:82-4 My 11 '64
Minuet; cloture vote. Newsweek 63:30+ Je 15 '64
More heat. il Newsweek 62:35-6 Jl 29 '63
Negro leaders meet LBJ; here are the results they see. il U S News 55:48-9 D 16 '63
New civil rights bill. America 108:847 Je 15 '63
Nine young men in charge of integrating America; Attorney General and "general staff." il U S News 55:58-61 Jl 29 '63
Non-whiz kid with the quiet gun. R. Wallace. il Life 55:75-6+ Ag 9 '63
Now, real showdown begins on rights bill. U S News 56:6 Ap 6 '64
Now the voting starts on civil-rights bill. U S News 56:4 My 18 '64
Now you see it, now... Nat R 16:141-2 F 25 '64
On its way into law. il Bsns W p25-8 Je 13 '64
Open letter to the Attorney General; satire. C. Cameron. Nat R 15:78 Jl 30 '63
Play against Goldwater; private property, and civil rights bill. W. F. Buckley, jr. Nat R 15:13 Jl 16 '63
Plea to the South; southern senators cease to obstruct passage of the civil rights bill. America 110:592 My 2 '64
Politics of cloture. E. B. Drew. il Reporter 31:19-23 Jl 16 '64
President supports civil rights legislation. Christian Cent 81:103 Ja 22 '64
President's package; major proposals. Time 81:14-15 Je 28 '63
Pulling lightning; revisions. Newsweek 63:33 My 25 '64
Racial diplomacy. Commonweal 79:155-6 N 1 '63
Racial extremists fill vacuum. Christian Cent 81:539 Ap 29 '64
Religious leaders demand civil rights bill. Christian Cent 81:631 My 13 '64
Reveille in Washington; President's proposals. il Newsweek 62:17-19 Jl 1 '63
Right basis for rights bill. Life 55:4 Jl 19 '63
Rights riddle. K. Crawford. Newsweek 63:30 Ja 27 '64
Russell sounds call for civil-rights fight. U S News 56:8 F 3 '64
Sandman; W. McCulloch. Cato. Nat R 16:482 Je 16 '64
Second emancipation; address, June 16, 1963. J. H. Robinson. Vital Speeches 29:610-13 Ag 1 '63
Selection or discrimination? D. Lawrence. U S News 55:100 N 4 '63
Senate fantasy. Reporter 30:12+ Mr 26 '64
Senate generals in the rights battle. il U S News 56:12 Mr 2 '64
Senate: Mr Humphrey's conquering hosts. M. Kempton. New Repub 150:6-8 Ap 4 '64
Senate to shelve rights bill for weeks; waiting action on tax cut. Bsns W p28-9 F 15 '64
Senator Russell in the last ditch; civil-rights opposition. F. W. Collins. il N Y Times Mag p16+ O 20 '63
Senator Russell of Georgia: does he speak for the South? il Newsweek 62:20-4 Ag 19 '63
Showdown in the Senate. America 110:247 F 22 '64
Showdown in the Senate. Commonweal 79: 616-17 F 21 '64

CIVIL rights—United States—*Continued*
Showdown on civil rights. W. V. Shannon. Commonweal 78:389-90 Jl 5 '63
Sleepers in the civil rights bill. A. M. Bickel. New Repub 150:14-17 F 29 '64; Discussion. 150:36 Mr 7; 28+ Mr 14 '64
Slicing the bread. il Time 83:18 Ap 24 '64
Smoothing a way for rights law; efforts of business groups. Bsns W p32 Je 20 '64
Soft sell. Newsweek 62:21-2 O 28 '63
Sticky questions; racial discrimination by businesses serving the public. Newsweek 62:20-1 Jl 15 '63
Terribly dangerous; President's legislative proposals. il Newsweek 61:27-8 Je 10 '63
That long, hot summer. Nation 198:567 Je 8 '64
That new feeling. Newsweek 63:19 Je 1 '64
They finally did it: they busted the big filibuster; with report by R. B. Stolley. il Life 56:32-7 Je 19 '64
This month's feature: Congress and public accommodations. Cong Digest 42:259-88 N '63
This month's feature: FEPC features of the civil rights bill. Cong Digest 43:67-96 Mr '64
Tipping the balance on civil rights bill; Senator Dirksen bails out the Democrats. Bsns W p20-1 My 30 '64
To fulfill a historic role; Senate commerce committee hearings. il Time 82:18-19 Jl 19 '63
Two concepts of law. Fortune 68:91-2 Ag '63
Up the hill. Newsweek 62:20 Jl 22 '63
Veteran spokesman for the Old South. Bsns W p28-9 Ap 18 '64
Victory and a half. Newsweek 63:15 F 17 '64
View from Everest. Newsweek 63:24+ F 24 '64
View from the Senate gallery. J. N. Eller. America 110:702 My 23 '64
Washington outlook; rising problems. Bsns W p39 Jl 13 '63
We might be lucky; congressional wrangle. Newsweek 62:27-8 N 4 '63
What all the talk is about; major provisions of civil-rights bill. il Newsweek 63:28 Ap 13 '64
What happens when government polices your hiring; Motorola case. il U S News 56:87 Mr 30 '64
What the civil rights bill would do. Time 83:22-3 My 29 '64
What to expect now in a civil-rights law. il U S News 55:74-5 O 21 '63
What white voters tell senators: a survey. U S News 56:36 Ap 6 '64
When is a majority a majority? Senate's civil rights debate. il Time 83:22-6 Mr 20 '64
Where are we at here? bill of House judiciary subcommittee. il Time 82:23-4 N 1 '63
Why a northerner opposed rights bill; excerpts from statement. L. C. Wyman. U S News 56:16 F 24 '64
Why the Negroes continue to revolt. L. E. Lomax. il Look 27:52-4 S 10 '63
Willing to deal. il Time 82:16 Jl 5 '63
With new civil-rights law; how Negroes see the future. il U S News 56:38-9 Je 29 '64
Wooed & the wooing. il Time 83:22 F 28 '64
Wrong priority; cotton-wheat bill, ahead. Nation 198:253 Mr 16 '64
X factor is race. S. Alsop. il Sat Eve Post 237:10 F 8 '64
Zero hour for civil rights. America 110:301 Mr 7 '64
See also
Civil rights act of 1964
Negroes in the United States—Civil rights

CIVIL rights act of 1964
And now enforcement. M. Ascoli. Reporter 31:18 Jl 16 '64
Aptitude tests: under a cloud; Motorola, inc. U S News 57:83-4 D 14 '64
As the U.S. moves on civil rights law. U S News 57:12-13 Jl 27 '64
Atlantic report. Atlan 214:6+ Ag '64
Barbecue and the bar; Ollie's in Birmingham resists public-accommodations section. il Newsweek 64:32 S 28 '64
Big step in right direction. il Ebony 19:90-1 Ag '64
Bill passed, seventy-three to twenty-seven. il Sr Schol 85:21 S 16 '64
Birmingham: keeping our fingers crossed. R. Evans and R. Novak. New Repub 151:17-18 Ag 8 '64
Civil disobedience: an imprimatur. Nat R 16:1134-5 D 29 '64
Civil rights act of 1964. Sch Life 47:13 O '64
Civil rights act of 1964. A. M. Bickel. Commentary 38:33-9 Ag '64
Civil rights act of 1964; respect for law; address, September 18, 1964. N. deB. Katzenbach. Vital Speeches 31:27-9 O 15 '64
Civil rights act; six principal objectives. B. L. Masse. America 111:6 Jl 4 '64
Civil rights and the Constitution. W. J. Davis. America 111:105 Ag 1 '64
Civil rights: the law and the unions. A. H. Raskin. il Reporter 31:23-8 S 10 '64
Continuing debate over public accommodations; pro and con discussion. Sr Schol 85:12-13 S 16 '64
Crisis in race relations: how will it be met? interviews with congressmen around the Nation. U S News 57:26-32 Ag 10 '64
Crucial moment for civil rights. Bsns W p 148 Jl 11 '64
Discrimination, unions and Title VII. G. R. Blakey. America 111:210-12 Ag 29 '64
Following the returns; interstate-commerce clause. R. Moley. Newsweek 64:60 D 28 '64
Government's big stick for enforcing civil rights; with excerpts from statements by T. C. Clark and H. L. Black. il U S News 57:40-2 D 28 '64
Help on civil rights starting at the top. il Bsns W p27 Ag 22 '64
Hoss unhorsed; desegregation of motels and restaurants in St Augustine, Fla. Time 84:51 Ag 14 '64
How new law will police hiring, firing, promoting. il U S News 56:79-80 Je 29 '64
Is it constitutional? application of act to neighborhood restaurants. New Repub 151:6 O 3 '64
Landmark II: equal rights. Life 56:4 Je 26 '64
Law with a conscience. Christian Cent 81 900 Jl 15 '64
Managing your manpower; how employers are preparing for the civil rights act. T. R. Brooks. Duns R 84:57+ N '64
Moment of history; address. L. B. Johnson. il America 111:62-3 Jl 18 '64
Much more than law is needed. A. M. Bickel. il N Y Times Mag p7+ Ag 9 '64
New civil rights law; now to get it enforced. il U S News 57:33-4 Jl 13 '64
Now that the bill has passed. Sat Eve Post 237:88 Jl 11 '64
Ollie McClung's big decision. M. Durham. Life 57:31 O 9 '64
Pickrick capers; test of public accommodations title. il Time 84:62 Jl 31 '64
Quick test coming for civil rights law. il Bsns W p27-8 O 10 '64
Religion-state conference on civil rights legislation. H. A. Jack. Christian Cent 81:1566-7+ D 16 '64
Rights bill upheld; decision on public accommodations section. Sr Sch 85:17-18 Ja 7 '65
Setback in court for the rights act; Birmingham, Ala. U S News 57:8 S 28 '64
Shall now also be equal. il Newsweek 64:17 Jl 13 '64
South learns to live with the civil-rights law. P. Watters. il Reporter 31:44-6 Ag 13 '64
Speaking out; Goldwater is wrong on civil rights. A. Lewis. Sat Eve Post 237:12+ S 26 '64
Stare and bear it. il Newsweek 64:32+ Jl 20 '64
States get a warning on the price of bias; administration's civil rights programs. Bsns W p23-4 Ja 9 '65
Testing the new law: legalists, publicists, activists. P. De Lissovoy. il Nation 199:7-10 Jl 13 '64
Time of testing. il Time 84:26 Jl 10 '64
Upholding Title II; U.S. Supreme court decision. il Newsweek 64:16+ D 28 '64
What editors in the South say now; symposium. U S News 56:40-6 Je 29 '64
What has been done is prologue; carrying out the civil rights act. A. M. Bickel. New Repub 152:16-18 Ja 9 '65
Whose rights? public accommodations section. Nat R 16:1046-7 D 1 '64
Why Goldwater said no to civil-rights bill: address, June 18, 1964. B. M. Goldwater. U S News 56:67-8 Je 29 '64
Why the South took rights law quietly. il Bsns W p28 Jl 11 '64

CIVIL rights commission. See United States—Commission on civil rights

CIVIL rights demonstrations
Acid test; swim-integrators in St Augustine. il Newsweek 63:26-7 Je 29 '64
After the march. Reporter 29:14 S 12 '63
Albany cases. Nation 198:387 Ap 20 '64
Are demonstrations self-defeating? T. R. Brooks. il Commonweal 79:98-100 O 18 '63

CIVIL rights demonstrations—*Continued*

Are you planning a trip to Washington? March on August 28, 1963. S. Lansdowne. America 109:185 Ag 24 '63

As 200,000 marched in Washington. il U S News 55:38-44 S 9 '63

Atlanta: fruits of tokenism. P. Watters. il Nation 198:162-5 F 17 '64

Backlash; excesses in the Negro revolution. il Time 83:17-18 Ap 24 '64

Backlash; M. Galamison at Hofstra university, Hempstead, N.Y. New Yorker 40:25-8 My 30 '64

Battle plan for integration; role of CORE. D. Wakefield. il Esquire 60:101-4+ O '63

Big bite; March on Washington. N. Mailer. Esquire 60:22+ D '63

Big day: end and a beginning. il Newsweek 62:19-22 S 9 '63

Biggest protest march; with account by L. Bennett, jr. il Ebony 19:29-31+ N '63

Black madness; antisegregation demonstrations. Nat R 16:263 Ap 7 '64

Carl Rowan's advice: oust civil-rights quacks; excerpts from address, 1964. C. T. Rowan. U S News 57:14 Ag 17 '64

Children of Birmingham; non-violent action. P. Goodman. Commentary 36:242-4 S '63

Civil rights: Senate buckles down as protests build up; Negro leaders push demonstrations. il Bsns W p26-7 My 9 '64

Civil rights, will this summer tell? il Sr Schol 84:8-11 My 15 '64

Civil writings; letters to the editor. Nat R 15:251-3 S 24 '63

Communique from the Mississippi front; war is the word for the civil-rights struggle. J. Herbers. il N Y Times Mag p34-5+ N 8 '64

CORE: the shock troops of the Negro revolt. M. Mayer. il Sat Eve Post 237:79-83 N 21 '64

Crisis in black and white, by C. E. Silberman. Review
Nation 198:654-6 Je 29 '64. M. Mayer

Cry of foul at the fair. il Newsweek 63:20-1 My 4 '64

Debate in the Senate; a meeting in Birmingham. il Time 83:21-2 Ap 10 '64

Direction of the March. R. L. Zangrando. bibliog il Negro Hist Bul 27:60-4 D '63

Dogs in Maryland; Princess Anne, Md. Newsweek 63:30 Mr 9 '64

Don't tread on Grandmother Peabody; with editorial comment. R. K. Massie. il Sat Eve Post 237:74+, 84 My 16 '64

Editor's easy chair: a small band of practical heroes. J. Fischer. Harper 227:16+ O '63; Discussion. 227:4 D '63

Extremism and the Negro revolution. Sat Eve Post 237:78 Je 20 '64

Fair and foul; opening day of the World's fair. Reporter 30:8 My 7 '64

Fair; opening day. New Yorker 40:39 My 2 '64

Flop; demonstrators on opening day of the New York World's fair. il Time 83:22-3 My 1 '64

For some, the light burned darkly. J. N. Eller. America 109:226 S 7 '63

Four eyes on the Washington march. J. T. Drukin; J. LaFarge. America 109:252 S 14 '63

From demonstration to politics. Nation 198: 158 F 17 '64

Gloria Richardson. il Ebony 19:23-6+ Jl '64

Hammer of civil rights. M. L. King, jr. il Nation 198:230-4 Mr 9 '64

Hattiesburg and central Illinois. J. Moore. Christian Cent 81:340-1 Mr 11 '64

Incident in Hattiesburg. H. Zinn. Nation 198: 501-4 My 18 '64; Discussion. 198:564 Je 8 '64

Is it ever right to break the law? C. Frankel. il N Y Times Mag p 17+ Ja 12 '64

Is the public getting the truth about the race issue? size-up by a panel of editors from North and South. il U S News 55:82-7 N 11 '63

Keeping cool in a hot summer. Christian Cent 81:597 My 6 '64

King wants white demonstrators. Christian Cent 81:724-5 Je 3 '64

King's targets. il Newsweek 63:26+ Je 22 '64

Last resort. America 109:188 Ag 24 '63

Law and order. Commonweal 80:623 S 18 '64

Leftward march. Nat R 16:11-13 Ja 14 '64

Lesson of Cambridge and Salisbury: was violence necessary? L. B. Bozell. Nat R 15:145-7 Ag 27 '63

Letter from Paris; local preliminary Freedom march, August 21, 1963. Genêt. New Yorker 39:182-4 S 14 '63

Letter from Washington; day of the March, August 28, 1963. R. H. Rovere. New Yorker 39:159-66 S 14 '63

Letter from Williamston. H. Cox. Christian Cent 80:1516-18 D 4 '63

Lone wolf of civil rights; B. Rustin. M. Meyer. il Sat Eve Post 237:76-8 Jl 11 '64

Long, hot summer; demonstrators at opening of the World's fair. T. R. Brooks. Commonweal 80:189-90 My 8 '64

Managing your manpower; Negro push for employment opportunities. T. R. Brooks. Duns R 83:59-60 Je '64

March. Nation 197:121 S 14 '63

March gains and losses. il U S News 55:33-5 S 9 '63

March in Washington. il Time 82:11 Ag 30 '63

March; March on Washington. New Yorker 39:30-1 S 7 '63

March on Frankfort, Ky. R. Bedan. America 110:398 Mr 28 '64

March on Washington. M. Kempton. New Repub 149:19-20 S 14 '63

March on Washington: plans and problems grow. il U S News 55:36-7 Ag 26 '63

March: what Negroes expected, what they want next; address, August 26, 1963. A. P. Randolph. U S News 55:82-5 S 9 '63

Marchers' master plan; with editorial comment. W. R. Young and W. Lambert. il Life 55:4, 63-4+ Ag 23 '63

Marching for justice. F. E. Kearns. il Commonweal 78:551-4 S 20 '63; Reply with rejoinder. G. H. Dunne. 79:169-70 N 1 '63

Marching on Washington: an old story to the capital. il U S News 55:29-31 S 2 '63

Marching orders; March on Washington for jobs and freedom. Christian Cent 80:1021 Ag 21 '63

March's meaning; March on Washington. il Time 82:13-15 S 6 '63

Meaning of Negro strategy. D. Danzig. Commentary 37:41-6 F '64; Discussion. 38:6+ Jl '64

Meaning of the March; March on Washington for jobs and freedom. Christian Cent 80: 1043 Ag 28 '63

Mississippi prepares for war. Christian Cent 81:509 Ap 22 '64

More racial violence, North and South. il U S News 57:6 Jl 27 '64

Mother goes to jail; demonstrations in St Augustine, Fla. il Newsweek 63:25 Ap 13 '64

My husband died for democracy; minister killed in Cleveland rights protest. Mrs B. W. Klunder. il Ebony 19:27-30+ Je '64

Negro leaders ban demonstrations. Christian Cent 81:1005 Ag 12 '64

Negro leaders warn: more race troubles. il U S News 56:38 My 25 '64

Negro riots will go on, unless... S. McBee. New Repub 151:22 S 5 '64

New Negro radicalism. S. Lynd. Commentary 36:252-6 S '63

New rights marches on the way. il Bsns W p20 Ag 31 '63

New shape of nonviolence. il U S News 56: 50 Ap 27 '64

No man's land; St. Augustine, Fla. il Newsweek 64:16-17 Jl 6 '64

On the march; biggest single march on the capital in U.S. history. il Newsweek 62: 17-18+ S 2 '63

Organizing a march. il Bsns W p28-9 Ag 24 '63

Outwitting the law's delay. Christian Cent 81:853 Jl 1 '64

Pickets; Downstate medical center hospital in Brooklyn. New Yorker 39:18-19 Ag 10 '63

Placing our bodies . . . Rev. B. Klunder crushed to death. il Newsweek 63:34 Ap 20 '64

Police are for protection. il Ebony 19:56-7 My '64

Pomp, and protest; New York world's fair. il Sr Schol 84:22 My 8 '64

Race race. R. M. Brown. Commonweal 79:73-5 O 11 '63

Race trouble in a model city; Atlanta. il U S News 56:78 F 10 '64

Race violence in the oldest city; St Augustine, Fla. il U S News 56:8 Je 22 '64

Racial extremists fill vacuum. Christian Cent 81:539 Ap 29 '64

Racial strife: a bloody summer ahead? U S News 56:10 Ap 27 '64

Relevant celebration of the emancipation centennial. K. B. Clark. Ebony 18:23-5 S '63

Responsible tactics will win rights sooner. Life 56:4 My 1 '64

Revolution on the march. H. Swados. Nation 197:104-7 S 7 '63

Revolution without hatred; March on Washington. H. E. Fey. Christian Cent 80:1094-5 S 11 '63

CIVIL rights demonstrations—*Continued*
Rights and differences: some notes for liberals; sociological and cultural differences between whites and Negroes. C. L. Crowe. Christian Cent 81:1359-60 N 4 '64
Show goes on, the spoilers lose the day; failure of Brooklyn CORE plans to disrupt opening of Worlds fair. D. Nevin. il Life 56:35 My 1 '64
Since the Supreme court spoke; photographs. N Y Times Mag p 10-11 My 10 '64
Six days in Alabama: a journal. R. Gutwillig. Mlle 57:116-17+ S '63; Reply. T. C. Turner. 58:38+ D '63
Some mob; March on Washington. K. Crawford. Newsweek 62:31 S 9 '63
Some new tactics in civil-rights push; shop-ins; cross-filing; rent strikes. il U S News 56:52 Mr 16 '64
Sophronia's grandson goes to Washington. L. Hellman. il Ladies Home J 80:78-80+ D '63; Reply with rejoinder. R. D. McCord. 81:82 Mr '64
Southerners turn. Nation 198:358 Ap 13 '64
Sponsors of the March on Washington. Negro Hist Bul 27:3-4 O '63
Spring offensive; Negroes plan the future. P. Watters. il Nation 198:117-20 F 3 '64
Stall-in code. Christian Cent 81:623 My 6 '64
Straw in the racial wind; March on Washington. Christian Cent 80:1123 S 18 '63
They come marching up conscience road; Negroes stir up nation in mighty Washington march. il Life 55:20-9 S 6 '63
Throttle the fair, the public be damned. M. Crawford. il Life 56:40-1 Ap 24 '64
Time of demonstrations. Nation 197:291 N 9 '63
To the sound of a different drum. il Newsweek 63:25-6 Ap 27 '64
Toward the other shore; freedom movement as seen by a church leader. V. Harding. il Reporter 29:27-31 O 10 '63
Unsaintly St Augustine; hotbed of racial injustice and strife. il Ebony 19:92-4+ Ag '64
View from Harlem. A. B. Spellman. Nation 198:656-7 Je 29 '64
Vigil: Theological students' vigil for civil rights in front of Lincoln memorial. New Yorker 40:33-4 My 9 '64
We are dedicated: minister killed during school integration demonstrations in Cleveland, Ohio. il Time 83:36 Ap 17 '64
What the Negroes lost in New York. il U S News 56:31-3 My 4 '64
When the plaints go marching in; march on Washington, August 28, 1963. Nat R 15:140 Ag 27 '63
Where racial trouble keeps erupting; St Augustine, Fla. il U S News 57:6 Jl 6 '64
Why Negroes use pressure. America 109:699 N 30 '63
Why the Negroes continue to revolt. L. E. Lomax. il Look 27:52-4 S 10 '63
Why we went; symposium. Christian Cent 81:1061-2 Ag 26 '64
Will a racial protest tie up the World's fair? il U S News 56:6 Ap 20 '64
World's fair stall-in. America 110:587 My 2 '64

CIVIL rights division. See United States—Justice, Department of—Civil rights division

CIVIL rights emblems. See Emblems

CIVIL rights workers
And three letters home from Mississippi. P. Cowan; G. Cowan. Esquire 62:105-6+ S '64
Churches and Mississippi; Mississippi summer project. S. C. Rose. Christian Cent 81:909-10 Jl 15 '64
Civil rights: fantasy's end; bodies of three civil rights workers found. il Newsweek 64:28-9 Ag 17 '64
Crime called conspiracy; Neshoba County's law officers charged with complicity in the murder of three civil rights workers. il Time 84:29-30 D 11 '64
Crusade in Mississippi. A. Poinsett. il Ebony 19:25-8+ S '64
Day of accusation in Mississippi; Mississippians implicated in murder of civil rights workers: with report by D. Nevin. il Life 57:34-9 D 18 '64
Disgrace of Mississippi. America 111:8-9 Jl 4 '64
Ecumenism behind bars. R. M. Brown. Commonweal 80:600-2 S 4 '64 Discussion. 81:44-6 O 2 '64
End terrorist rule! Christian Cent 81:875 Jl 8 '64
Evangelists; Council of federated organizations campaign in Mississippi. il Newsweek 64:30-2 Ag 24 '64
FBI suspects freed; Philadelphia, Miss. Sr Schol 85:19 Ja 7 '65
Grim discovery in Mississippi; bodies of missing civil rights workers. il Time 84:17 Ag 14 '64
Grim roster; disappearance of three civil rights workers. il Time 84:19-20 Jl 3 '64
If we can crack Mississippi. . . J. Atwater. il Sat Eve Post 237:15-19 Jl 25 '64
Indictments this time; case of murdered civil rights workers near Philadelphia, Miss. Time 85:21 Ja 22 '65
Invaders; volunteers for voter-registration drives and cultural programs in Mississippi. il Newsweek 63:25-6 Je 29 '64
It will be a hot summer in Mississippi. R. Woodley. Reporter 30:21-4 My 21 '64
Jesus, no! preliminary hearing of civil-rights murder case in Meridian, Miss. il Newsweek 64:21-2 D 21 '64
Journey to understanding: four witnesses to a Mississippi summer; symposium. il Nation 199:507-16 D 28 '64
Judgment in Mississippi; arraignment and release of twenty-one persons in connection with murder of civil rights workers. G. W. Johnson. New Repub 151:13-14 D 26 '64
Land within a land; deaths of three civil rights workers. Commonweal 80:561-2 Ag 21 '64
Last summer in Mississippi. A. Lake. Redbook 124:64-5+ N '64
Letter from Jackson. C. Trillin. New Yorker 40:80+ Ag 29 '64
Limpid shambles of violence; search for three missing civil rights workers. il Life 57:32-34B Jl 3 '64
Mass arrests in civil-rights killings. il U S News 57:11 D 14 '64
Mississippi. Nat R 16:573-5 Jl 14 '64
Mississippi Democrats; the Freedom Democrats. New Repub 151:4 S 5 '64
Mississippi dilemma. Nat R 16:1136-7 D 29 '64
Mississippi, everybody's scared. il Newsweek 64:15-16 Jl 6 '64
Mississippi; gang law. New Repub 151:5-6 Jl 4 '64
Mississippi murders. America 112:153 Ja 30 '65
Mississippi murders: twenty-one arrests. il Newsweek 64:21-2 D 14 '64
Mississippi: storm signals. il U S News 57:27 Jl 6 '64
Mississippi, summer of 1964: troubled state, troubled time. il Newsweek 64:18-20 Jl 13 '64
Mississippi: the attack on bigotry. C. S. Wren. il Look 28:20-8 S 8 '64
Mystery of Malcolm X. H. J. Massaquoi. il Ebony 19:38-40+ S '64
Naught for your comfort: a case history. Christian Cent 81:895 Jl 8 '64
Next step in Mississippi; boycott of Mississippi goods. Christian Cent 81:1583 D 23 '64
Night and day in Mississippi; arrest of twenty-one Mississippians by the F.B.I. Christian Cent 81:1550 D 16 '64
Our faces, our words, by L. Smith. Review
Sat R 48:51 Ja 9 '65. B. M. Galphin
Philadelphia indictments; case of Mississippi murders. Time 84:29 O 9 '64
Race troubles in South: bodies found, arrests made in summer of discontent. il U S News 57:6 Ag 17 '64
Railroaded to freedom. Nation 199:62-3 Ag 24 '64
Recollection of Michael Schwerner. R. Woodley. Reporter 31:23-4 Jl 16 '64
Search; Mississippi swampland sludged for missing civil rights workers. il Time 84:27 Jl 10 '64
Stranger in Philadelphia, Mississippi. J. Lelyveld. il N Y Times Mag p5+ D 27 '64
Strategic retreat; charges dropped against twenty-one men. il Time 84:23 D 18 '64
Student's dividend in Georgia. New Repub 151:6-7 S 12 '64
Summer in Mississippi; freedom moves in to stay. J. DeMuth. il Nation 199:104-5+ S 14 '64
Their dream is not to be nervous; a volunteer with the Mississippi summer project reports on teaching in a freedom school; interview, ed. by C. Illig. L. Guest. il Mlle 60:164-5+ N '64
Two worlds of Dick Gregory. T. B. Morgan. Holiday 36:125-30+ D '64
Untold story of the Mississippi murders. W. B. Huie. il Sat Eve Post 237:11-15 S 5 '64
Very good folks; eighteen indicted in murder of three civil-rights workers. il Newsweek 65:26+ Ja 25 '65

CIVIL rights workers—*Continued*
We will overcome. R. Coles. New Repub 151: 13 Jl 11 '64
Whose backyard? northern students assist Negro voter registration in Mississippi. America 111:178 Ag 22 '64
Young rebels with a cause. H. Page. il Parents Mag 39:42-5+ D '64
Your representative in Mississippi. Christian Cent 81:925 Jl 22 '64
Youth corps in Mississippi. B. Keating. il N Y Times Mag p6-7 Jl 5 '64
See also
Council of federated organizations
CIVIL service
So you want to work for the government. F. C. Porter. Sat R 47:21-3+ Ap 11 '64
See also
Bureaucracy

Canada

Streamlining Canada's bureaucracy; reorganizing civil servants. Bsns W p 100+ Mr 28 '64

United States

Government service; challenges and rewards. J. W. Macy, jr. Vital Speeches 30:446-8 My 1 '64
Oh, Mister President! excerpt from The image of the federal service. F. P. Kilpatrick and others. Sat R 47:50-1 Mr 7 '64
To restore adventure to American democracy. J. Lear. il Sat R 46:39-42 S 7 '63; Discussion. 47:96 Ja 4 '64
See also
Government employees
CIVIL service commission. See United States—Civil service commission
CIVIL service pensions
New trend in pensions. Bsns W p31 Je 1 '63
CIVIL service training program. See Government employees—Training
CIVIL uniforms. See Uniforms, Civil
CIVIL war (United States) See United States—History—Civil war
CIVILIAN conservation corps. See United States—Civilian conservation corps
CIVILIAN defense. See Civil defense
CIVILIAN-military relations. See United States—Armed forces—Relations with civilians
CIVILIAN relief. See Relief work
CIVILIZATION
Ambiguity of perfection; excerpts from address at Time's anniversary dinner. P. Tillich. Time 81:69 My 17 '63
Battlements of terror; fear as a deterrent? S. A. Coblentz. Christian Cent 81:1329-31 O 28 '64
Descending spiral of ugliness. A. Heckscher. il Recreation 56:315-16+ S '63
Dilemma for Americans; address, August 22, 1964. H. C. Case. Vital Speeches 30:715-17 S 15 '64
Dissent from despair. A. B. Hoag. il N Y Times Mag p21+ Ap 5 '64
Ford, Ward, and Graham; civilization vs self-love. W. F. Buckley, jr. Nat R 15:143 Ag 27 '63
Good non-life. Newsweek 63:68 Mr 30 '64
Hoffa, Hegel, and Hoffer. N. Cousins. Sat R 46:26 Ap 20 '63
Ideals for export; excerpts from address, September 19, 1963. C. H. Malik. Harvard Bsns R 42:51-9 Ja '64
Is civilization progress? C. A. Lindbergh. Read Digest 85:67-74 Jl '64
July 1914—July 1964. W. H. McNeill. For Affairs 42:559-68 Jl '64
Life inside the centrifuge. N. Cousins. Sat R 47:60-1 Ag 29 '64
Meaning of the twentieth century, by K. Boulding. Review
New Repub 151:17-18 D 12 '64. A. Toffler
Men, apes, and termites. J. W. Krutch. Sat R 46:22-5 S 21 '63; Discussion. 46:29 O 12 '63
Might of the West, by L. R. Brown. Review
Nat R 16:975-6+ N 3 '64. F. S. Meyer
Needs of the world; address, December 23, 1963. Paul VI. Vital Speeches 30:198-200 Ja 15 '64
Occasions and protests, by J. Dos Passos. Review
Nat R 16:1072 D 1 '64. D. J. Stewart
One-dimensional man, by H. Marcuse. Review
Newsweek 63:80 Ja 27 '64
Problems 1963: malaise in wonderland; address. J. Heller Sch Arts 62:25-7 Mr '63
Religion and freedom in the modern world, by H. J. Muller. Review
Christian Cent 81:1014-16 Ag 12 '64. M. E. Marty
Second chance. il Ebony 18:88-9 F '63
Self-renewal: the individual and the innovative society, by J. W. Gardner. Review
Science 144:164-5 Ap 10 '64. C. Kerr
Visions of order, by R. M. Weaver. Review
Nat R 16:540-1 Je 30 '64. J. Hart
What we don't know might kill us. E. Capouya. Sat R 47:26-7 Mr 28 '64
Why I dislike western civilization. A. J. Toynbee. il N Y Times Mag p 15+ My 10 '64
Wilderness as a tonic. J. W. Krutch. Sat R 46:15-17 Je 8 '63
Youth; address, August 24, 1964. C. T. Rowan. Vital Speeches 30:721-5 S 15 '64
See also
Acculturation
Anthropology
Atomic age
Culture
Ethics
Intellectual life
Social change
Social progress
Society, Primitive
Technology and civilization
Twentieth century
also subhead Civilization under names of countries, e.g. United States—Civilization

History

Ancient Mesoamerican civilization. R. S. MacNeish. bibliog il Science 143:531-7 F 7 '64
East and West, by C. N. Parkinson. Review
Nat R il 16:163-5 F 25 '64. L. R. Brown
Origins of New World civilization. R. S. MacNeish. il Sci Am 211:29-37 bibliog(p 154) N '64

Philosophy

Freedom to hope. W. E. Hocking. Sat R 46: 12-15+ Je 22 '63

Preservation of records

Ceremonies; contents of the 1964-65 Westinghouse time capsule revealed at New York worlds fair. New Yorker 40:38-9 S 26 '64
Includes Century editorial in Time capsule II; New York world's fair. Christian Cent 81: 1549 D 16 '64
Postscript; time capsules for New York World's fairs of 1939 and 1964. New Yorker 39:18 Je 29 '63
Remains to be seen; New York worlds fair time capsule, 1964. il Newsweek 64:92 S 28 '64
Thirty leading drugs buried in medical time capsule. Sci N L 84:231 O 12 '63
CIVILIZATION, Ancient
Hydraulic civilizations. P. Armillas. il UNESCO Courier 17:60-3 Jl '64
Lima bean people of 6,000 years ago; Chilcas of Peru. il Time 82:49 Ag 2 '63

Bibliography

Greeks, Romans and others. W. M. Abbott. America 110:108-10 Ja 18 '64
CIVILIZATION, Greek
Greece (cont) il Life 54:60-9+ F 8; 60-73 Mr 8; 62-77 My 3; 54-71+ Je 14; 55:52-67 Jl 19 '63
Sirens, Spartans, and Socrates. P. Dixon. il Sat R 47:32-3 Mr 28 '64

Bibliography

Greeks, Romans and others. W. M. Abbott. America 110:108-10 Ja 18 '64
CIVILIZATION, Jewish. See Jews—Civilization
CIVILIZATION, Modern. See Civilization
CIVILIZATION and science. See Science and civilization
CIVILIZATION and technology. See Technology and civilization
CLAAR, James W.
Memo from the publisher (cont) Miss & Roc 12:6 Mr 25; 13:50 S 23 '63; 14:3 Ja 6; 7 Mr 30 '64; 16:6 Ja 4 '65
CLAFLIN, Elizabeth F. See White, L. P. jt. auth.
CLAGUE, Ewan
Buying power, more gains coming; interview. por Nations Bsns 52:31-3+ Ap '64
From the capital to the Catskills; interview. por Sr Schol 84:8T-10T Ja 31 '64
Response to change. Mo Labor R 86:620-1 Je '63
CLAIBORNE, Craig
Food. See issues of New York times magazine
Shellfish cook book. House & Gard 125:173+ Mr '64
CLAIMS
United States and Yugoslavia conclude claims agreement; Department announcement with text of agreement. Dept State Bul 51:830-1 D 7 '64
See also
Insurance—Adjustment of claims
Restitution claims
World war, 1939-1945—Claims

CLAIMS (land) See Homesteads
CLAIN-STEFANELLI, Vladimir
Expert tells why silver coins must go; excerpts from address, 1964. por U S News 57:100-3 D 7 '64
Future of U.S. coinage; address, October 20, 1964. Vital Speeches 31:85-8 N 15 '64
CLAIRE, Nancy
Glamorous paradox. E. Palatsky. il pors Dance Mag 37:30-3 Ag '63
CLAIRMONTE, Frederick F.
Angola: unfinished duel. Yale R 53:1-10 O '63
CLAIROL, Incorporated
Color me anything. Newsweek 62:55 Ag 19 '63
CLAMAN, Henry N. and Talmage, D. W.
Thymectomy; prolongation of immunological tolerance in the adult mouse. bibliog Science 141:1193-4 S 20 '63
CLAMBAKES
Vogue's own menu; a clambake for ten. Vogue 142:134 Ag 1 '63
CLAMPITT, Amy
Books (cont) Audubon Mag 65:56-8, 122+, 186-7, 249-50+, 316+, 388+; 66:58-61, 126+, 192-3, 258+, 329+, 399-400+; 67:58+ Ja-N '63, Ja-N '64, Ja '65
CLAMPS
All-purpose strap clamp. C. Conley. il Field & S 69:77 D '64
CLAMS
Clams are for the digging. A. G. Melvin. il Hobbies 68:130+ Ag '63
Debut of the giant clam. A. G. Melvin. il Hobbies 68:130+ O '63
High time on a low tide; geoduc hunters at Pacific Northwest. V. Kraft. il Sports Illus 21:50-3 D 14 '64
Human blood group A_1 specific agglutinin of the butter clam saxidomus giganteus. H. M. Johnson. bibliog il Science 146:548-9 O 23 '64
Midnight clam chase; shellfishing in polluted waters. J. Ridgeway. New Repub 151:18 S 5 '64
Temperature dependence of the activity of the antitumor factor in the common clam. A. Hegyeli. bibliog il Science 146:77-8 O 2 '64
See also
Cookery—Fish
CLANCY, Jean
Roads make history. B. Zimo. il Sch Arts 63:18-20 Mr '64
CLANCY, Joseph P.
T.S.E. 1888-1965; poem. Commonweal 81:576 Ja 29 '65
CLANCY, Roger M.
How come the spinnaker. Motor B 114:46-7+ Ag '64
Why of nautical language. Motor B 113:368-9 Ja '64
CLANCY, Thomas H.
Books to be noted; home scene. America 109: 668-70; 111:704-5+ N 23 '63, N 28 '64
Hall of defamers. America 111:520-2; 762 O 31, D 12 '64
Human geography of Harlem. America 109: 156-8 Ag 17 '63
CLANTON, Donald C.
Replacements. Suc Farm 62:47+ Ap '64
CLAPP, Gordon
Nation of faith and works. Am For 69:11 Je '63
CLAPP, Kate
Shade chrysanthemums for early bloom. Horticulture 41:508-9 O '63
CLAPP, Marjorie
Answer lady of space. Todays Health 41: 20-1+ O '63
CLAPP, Patricia
Christmas in old New England; drama. Plays 23:37-44, 58 D '63
Friendship bracelet; drama; reprint. Plays 23:43-50, 66 N '63
Signpost; drama. Plays 22:53-9 My '63
CLAPP, Verner Warren
CLR annual report notes computer's cultivated language; excerpts from introduction. Library J 89:82 Ja 1 '64
Permanent/durable book papers. bibliog f ALA Bul 57:847-52 O '63
Role of LC. ALA Bul 58:536 Je '64
Search for push-button library outlined in sixth CLR annual report; excerpts. Library J 88:746 F 15 '63
Unprovocative exactitude; excerpt from Future of the research library. Library J 89:1502 Ap 1 '64
CLAPPER rails. See Rails (birds)
CLAQUE. See Applause
CLARIDGE'S (hotel) See London—Hotels, restaurants, etc.

CLARINET
Garden hose clarinet blows just as sweet. Sci N L 87:9 Ja 2 '65
CLARK, Blake
Good-by to Bobby One-Eye Wilcoxson. Read Digest 82:63-8 F '63
Job for the next Congress: stop the race to the moon. Read Digest 84:75-9 Ja '64
Lyndon Johnson's Lady Bird. Read Digest 83:108-13 N '63
School where fitness counts. Read Digest 85:94-8 S '64
CLARK, Colin
Economics of development. Nat R 14:373-5 My 7 '63
How many starving millions? Nat R 16:522 Je 30 '64
CLARK, David L.
High church tradition of Anglicanism. Commonweal 80:487-8 Jl 10 '64
CLARK, Dennis
Philadelphia, still closed. Commonweal 80: 167-70 My 1 '64
Toward equality. Commonweal 80:518-19 Jl 24 '64
Utopia in the sixties. Cath World 196:357-63 Mr '63
CLARK, Don
Shop talk. See issues of Hot rod
CLARK, Donald E.
Somali foresters, jacks-of-all-trades. por Am For 69:21+ D '63
CLARK, Duncan C.
Some say in ice; poem. New Repub 148:26 Mr 2 '63
CLARK, E. M.
Of leaders and followers; address, May 28, 1963. Vital Speeches 29:602-6 Jl 15 '63
Strength to be free; address, June 18, 1964. Vital Speeches 30:727-30 S 15 '64
CLARK, Eleanor
Brittany: dragon country. Vogue 144:144-7+ O 15 '64
Mass of oyster-workers; story. Yale R 53: 497-521 Je '64
Oyster and the book. Yale R 52:366-72 Mr '63
CLARK, Eugenie. See Moore, J. C. jt. auth.
CLARK, F. Bryan
Endotrophic mycorrhizae influence yellow poplar seedling growth. bibliog Science 140: 1220-1 Je 14 '63
CLARK, F. C. Jr
Rollaway darkroom. Pop Mech 119:148-9 Je '63
CLARK, F. V.
Who asks pale flowers? poem. Ladies Home J 80:124 Je '63
CLARK, Grenville
Need for total disarmament under enforceable world law. Cur Hist 47:93-6+ Ag '64
Solving the inhuman equation. Sat R 46:15-16+ F 16 '63
about
Grenville Clark at eighty. M. K. Harvey. Sat R 46:17 F 16 '63
CLARK, Harry
Yugoslavian library faces 20th century problems. por Library J 88:718-20 F 15 '63
CLARK, Howard R.
Belt-disk sander. Pop Mech 121:193-5 Ja '64
Pistol-grip hold-down. Pop Mech 119:187-8 F '63
CLARK, Jim, 1937?-
Clark on cows and cornering. pors Life 55: 95+ N 1 '63
about
Big day for Clarkhunters at the Glen; Watkins Glen, N.Y. K. Rudeen. il Sports Illus 19:26-8 O 14 '63
Jim Clark, a whizz in a car. P. Laurie. por Vogue 144:289-91 D '64
Jimmy's year. il por Time 82:60+ Jl 12 '63
None so swift as wee Jimmy. K. Rudeen. il pors Sports Illus 19:28-30+ O 7 '63
Old guard has to call it a day. K. Rudeen. il Sports Illus 19:18-19+ Ag 26 '63
With girdle & glue. il por Time 85:72 Ja 15 '65
World's fastest farmer. il pors Life 55:91-2 N 1 '63
CLARK, Jim, 1941?-
Gallatin glissade. Field & S 68:21-3+ Jl '63
Kayak merry-go-round. pors Field & S 69: 32-5 Ja '65
Mail-run adventure. Outdoor Life 134:44-5+ Jl '64
CLARK, Joan R.
Boron-oxygen polyanion in the crystal structure of tunellite. bibliog Science 141:1178-9 S 20 '63
—and Appleman, D. E.
Pentaborate polyanion in the crystal structure of ulexite, $NaCaB_5O_6(OH)_6 \cdot 5H_2O$. bibliog Science 145:1295-6 S 18 '64

CLARK, John
Hunza in the Himalayas. Natur Hist 72:38-45 O '63
CLARK, John F.
Wildlife whittling. Recreation 57:320+ Je '64
CLARK, John W.
Is business socially responsible? America 110: 250-2 F 22 '64
CLARK, John William, 1916-
Poetry chronicle. P. Petrie. Poetry 102:51 Ap '63
CLARK, Joseph S.
Case for democratic liberalism. por Sat R 47:14-17+ Jl 11 '64
Congress and disarmament. Bul Atomic Sci 19:3-8 S '63
Excerpt from address, September 16, 1963. Cong Digest 53:218+ Ag '64
New kind of national election; excerpts from Congress; the sapless branch. Harper 228:72-4+ My '64
With all deliberate delay. New Repub 150: 13-15 Ap 18 '64
World disarmament; address, June 12, 1964. Vital Speeches 30:688-92 S 1 '64
about
Clark's bark; committee rigging in the Senate. K. Crawford. Newsweek 61:30 Mr 4 '63
Non-legislative arts. D. T. Bazelon. Commentary 38:82-5 D '64
Senate establishment; concerning Senator Clark's remarkable speech. J. McCartney. Nation 196:219-21 Mr 16 '63
Teacher's view inside Congress. D. B. Fleming, jr. il NEA J 53:69-72 Ja '64
CLARK, Kenneth B.
More effective techniques. N Y Times Mag p27 S 29 '63
Negro is tired of waiting; interview. por U S News 54:38-40 Je 10 '63
Relevant celebration of the emancipation centennial. por Ebony 18:23-5 S '63
CLARK, Leonard H. and others
Recent developments affecting the secondary school curriculum; excerpt from the American secondary school curriculum. bibliog f Sch & Soc 92:402-13 D 26 '64
CLARK, Margaret Goff
And then what happened? Writer 77:23-5 D '64
CLARK, Marguerite
Suicide in childhood and adolescence. NEA J 53:32-3+ N '64
CLARK, Neil M.
When the turkeys walked. Am Heritage 15: 92-3 D '63
CLARK, Paul
Insider's magazine: The Atlantian. il por Newsweek 62:78 Ag 12 '63
CLARK, Peter
London collector goes for world celebrities. K. V. Hostick. il por Hobbies 69:110 Je '64
CLARK, Phil
Thailand royalty visits the New York botanical garden. por Horticulture 42:32+ Jl '64
Yum yum. New Yorker 39:36-7 Ap 20 '63
CLARK, Ray H. and Baker, B. L.
Circadian periodicity in the concentration of prolactin in the rat hypophysis. bibliog Science 143:375-6 Ja 24 '64
CLARK, Robert B.
Holly identification. Horticulture 42:22-3+ D '64
CLARK, Robert F.
I failed in Puno. America 112:7 Ja 2 '65
CLARK, Rogie
Road through Dixie; poem. Negro Hist Bul 27:128 F '64
What is Negro folklore? Negro Hist Bul 27: 40-1 N '63
CLARK, Ross L.
Ten years of Metro water supply. Am City 79:118-19+ Je '64
CLARK, Roy
Never too busy. Dance Mag 37:16-17 Ap '63
Thirty years of Nick Castle. Dance Mag 38: 46-9 F '64
CLARK, Sandra
My day at the White House. Seventeen 23: 30+ S '64
CLARK, Stanley
Five ways to increase traction. Suc Farm 63: 64 Ja '65
CLARK, Thaddeus B.
Whiteheadian. Christian Cent 81:1064 Ag 26 '64
CLARK, Thomas
Birthday; Winter day; Pass by blue stone; Trouble: poems. Poetry 105:102-5 N '64
By comparison; poem. Nation 200:59 Ja 18 '65
CLARK, Tom C.
Civil-rights rulings: what they mean; excerpts from statements. por U S News 57: 40-1 D 28 '64
CLARK, Veda
Crisis; story. Redbook 122:70-1 N '63
CLARK, W. A. See Gerstein, G. L. jt. auth.
CLARK, W. E.
Prediction of ultrafiltration membrane performance. Science 138:148-9; 139:1125-6 O 12 '62, Mr 15 '63
CLARK, W. Mansfield
Critique of certain parts of the 1961 report of the Commission on enzymes. Science 141:995-6+ S 13 '63
CLARK, Wallace
Famous firsts: carrying the gospel to Europe. por Bsns W p63-4 N 23 '63
CLARK, Walter
Best of the editions of Neblette. Pop Phot 54:69 My '64
Uncle Death; poem. Commonweal 80:638 S 18 '64
CLARK, Willard
Dateline: Germany. U S Camera 26:56-61+ Je '63
CLARK, William
Ten nights in a bar room. Am Heritage 15: 14-17 Je '64
I gave him barks and saltpeter. P. R. Cutright. bibliog il por Am Heritage 15:58-61+ D '63
CLARK, Yvonne
Tenn. state's lady engineer. il pors Ebony 19:75-6+ Jl '64
CLARK-DUFF, Robert
Double-duty EICO 772. Pop Electr 19:49-51+ Jl '63
CLARK FORK. See Columbia River
CLARK institute. See Sterling and Francine Clark art institute, Williamstown, Mass.
CLARKE, Ann
Spring brings science to garden. Sci N L 83:170-1 Mr 16 '63
CLARKE, Arthur Charles
Armchair astronauts. Holiday 33:94-5+ My '63
Everybody in instant touch. Life 57:118-20+ S 25 '64
Fascinating shark. Holiday 36:116 S '64
In the light of the sun. Horizon 5:48-55 N '63
So you're going to Mars? Read Digest 86: 131-5 Ja '65
about
WLB biography. L. Ash. por Wilson Lib Bul 37:598 Mr '63
CLARKE, Austin
Irish chronicle. Poetry 103:185-7 D '63
Three from overseas. E. G. Burrows. Poetry 105:208-9 D '64
Veterans and recruits. S. F. Morse. Poetry 102:334 Ag '63
CLARKE, Beverly L.
Multiple authorship trends in scientific papers. bibliog Science 143:822-4 F 21 '64
CLARKE, Eugene C. Jr
Drop forge goes automatic. il por Bsns W p83-4+ O 17 '64
CLARKE, Gary K.
Birthday parties at the zoo. Am City 78:101-2 Mr '63
CLARKE, Gilmore
Message; meeting on remodelling Washington Square park. New Yorker 40:34-5 Je 6 '64
CLARKE, Ida Winter
Experiment in learning. Dance Mag 38:54-5 N '64
CLARKE, J. Harold
Good culture increases rhododendron hardiness. Horticulture 41:150-1 Mr '63
Plant hardiness. Horticulture 42:28-9 D '64
CLARKE, Mary Anne, 1776-1852
Notes and comment. New Yorker 39:19 Jl 6 '63
CLARKE, Richard
White-collar Negroes. il por Newsweek 63: 86+ Mr 23 '64
CLARKE, Robert F.
Impact of photocopying on scholarly publishing; summary of thesis, March 1963. Library J 88:2625-9 Jl '63
Recruiting new graduates at library schools. por Wilson Lib Bul 38:483-4 F '64
CLARKE, Robert G.
Tailwheel techniques. Flying 74:46-7+ Ap '64
CLARKE, Thatcher
Brief biographies. S. Goodman. il por Dance Mag 38:50-1 F '64
CLARKE family
Clarke coat-of-arms. H. K. Eilers. il Hobbies 69:124 Je '64

CLARKE college, Dubuque, Iowa
Learning for leisure. il Time 84:62 S 4 '64
CLARKSDALE, Miss.
N.C.C. visits Clarksdale. S. C. Rose. Christian Cent 80:1104-6 S 11 '63
CLARKSON, Eleanor Preston
Tiger of Lake Chautauqua. Motor B 112:82+ Jl '63
CLARKSON, Wash.
If your town smells, stop breathing. P. Hirsch. New Repub 150:7-8 Mr 14 '64
CLARY, John
Lift-dome auditorium. Am City 78:100-1 O '63
CLASS attendance. See Colleges and universities—Class attendance
CLASS distinction
Invisible (white) man. W. Sheed. Commonweal 79:570-1 F 7 '64
Urban social differentiation and the allocation of resources. R. W. Mack and D. C. McElrath. Ann Am Acad 352:25-32 Mr '64
See also
Social classes
Untouchables
CLASS reunions. See College graduates
CLASS rooms. See Classrooms
CLASS size
Millions of children and their teachers are being handicapped by overcrowded classes. F. W. Hubbard. il NEA J 52:52-4 Mr '63
CLASS struggle. See Social conflict
CLASS trips. See School excursions
CLASSES, Social. See Social classes
CLASSES, Special. See Special classes and special schools
CLASSICAL education
See also
Humanities
CLASSICAL literature
Classics still top required high school reading lists. Library J 89:4138 O 15 '64
Pocketful of classics. W. Richards. Sr Schol 85:17T D 2 '64
CLASSICAL music. See Music
CLASSICISM
Classicism of Robert Frost. J. F. Nims. il Sat R 46:22-3+ F 23 '63
CLASSICS, The. See Classical literature
CLASSIEBAWN castle. See Castles
CLASSIFICATION
ABC classification for children using school and public libraries, East Orange, N.J. public library. L. K. M. Gorski. Library J 88:4437-40 N 15 '63; Discussion. 89:298 Ja 15 '64
Classification chaos; LP recordings. G. Stevenson. il Library J 88:3789-94 O 15 '63
Dewey or LC? which best for library in college with 5000-6000 enrollment? H. R. Downey. Library J 89:2292-3 Je 1 '64
Fringe benefit in Egypt; cataloging and classification for Assiut university libraries. M. S. Rinehart. il Wilson Lib Bul 39:52-5 S '64
Neglected topic: the cost of classification. D. Gore. il Library J 89:2287-91 Je 1 '64; Reply. D. E. Kremen. 89:2696 Jl '64
Rutgers plans series of seminars on systems for organizing information. Library J 88:1642+ Ap 15 '63
S. R. Ranganathan, one American view; Colon classification. J. Shera. Wilson Lib Bul 37:581-2 Mr '63

Botany

See Botany—Classification
CLASSIFICATION, Decimal
Dewey abroad; survey. Wilson Lib Bul 37:524+ Mr '63
Field study of DDC abroad gets under way this spring. Library J 89:1704+ Ap 15 '64
International federation for documentation. D. J. Foskett. Library J 89:4478-80 N 15 '64
Plans for a field survey of the use of the Dewey decimal classification. Wilson Lib Bul 38:527+ Mr '64
Rutgers plans series of seminars on systems for organizing information. Library J 88:1642+ Ap 15 '63
US and Western bias reduced in Dewey decimal classification; annual report of the Decimal classification office at the Library of Congress. Library J 88:4594-5 D 1 '63
UDC dissected and discussed at first of Rutgers' seminars: Systems for the organization of information report. T. C. Hines. Library J 88:4592-4 D 1 '63
Use of DDC abroad to be studied. Library J 88:980-1 Mr 1 '63
CLASSIFIED defense information. See Defense information, Classified
CLASSIFIED documents. See Security classification (government documents)
CLASSIFIED information. See Security classification (government documents)
CLASSIFIED telephone directories. See Telephone directories
CLASSROOM management
Time to teach; new NEA project. M. M. Provus. il NEA J 53:17-18 My '64
CLASSROOM teachers. See Teachers
CLASSROOM teachers, Department of. See National education association—Department of classroom teachers
CLASSROOMS
Carpets & clusters; schools that look like wheels and circus tents at Greeley, Colo. il Time 84:44 S 25 '64
Four in one; nation's largest classroom. il Newsweek 62:100 N 25 '63
Schoolhousing in 1963; USOE survey begins next month. G. J. Collins. il Sch Life 46:8-11 O '63
Sound isolation between teaching spaces. W. R. Farrell. il Arch Rec 134:229-32 O '63
See also
School decoration
CLASTER, Bert
World's largest kindergarten: Romper room. il por Time 82:71-2 S 13 '63
CLATHRATE. See Crystallography
CLAUDE, Inis L. Jr
OAS, the UN, and the United States. bibliog f Int Concil 547:3-63 Mr '64
CLAUDE of Jesus, Sister
Silence within; poem. Commonweal 80:208 My 8 '64
CLAUSEN, Jane Welday
Grow a mum tree. Pop Gard 15:21 S '64
CLAUSEN, John A.
Social factors in disease. bibliog f Ann Am Acad 346:138-48 Mr '63
—and Straus, Robert
(eds) Medicine and society. bibliog f Ann Am Acad 346:1-148 Mr '63
—See Straus, R. jt. auth.
CLAUSEN, Oliver
(ed) See Hammarskjöld, D. Clues to the Hammarskjold riddle
CLAVELL, James
Children's story; story. Ladies Home J 80:88-9 O '63; Same abr. Read Digest 84:103-7 Je '64
CLAVICHORD music
See also
Phonograph records—Clavichord music
CLAWSON, Del
Winner take all. por Time 81:20 Je 21 '63
CLAY, Cassius
I'll chop that big monkey to pieces. . . pors Life 54:62A+ F 15 '63
I'm a little special. Sports Illus 20:14-15 F 24 '64
I'm the greatest; poem. por Life 54:62B-63 F 15 '63
Integration: as Negro champ views it; excerpts from news conference. por U S News 56:20 Mr 16 '64

about

And I'm already the greatest! il por Newsweek 63:50-1 Mr 9 '64
Black Muslim hope. Sports Illus 20:8 Mr 16 '64
Boxing's feet of Clay. Sat Eve Post 237:86 Ap 18 '64
Cassius Clay, Cassius X, Muhammad Ali. R. Lipsyte. il pors N Y Times Mag p29+ O 25 '64
Cassius Clay: weak on tests, strong on finances. por U S News 56:10 Mr 30 '64
C. Marcellus Clay esq. il pors Sports Illus 18:18-25 Je 10 '63
Cassius X. il por Newsweek 63:74 Mr 16 '64
Cassius X. il por Time 83:78 Mr 13 '64
Champ's African love affair. il pors Ebony 19:85-6+ S '64
Comeuppance for the cocksure Cassius; Clay-Jones fight. H. Horn. il pors Sports Illus 18:16-17+ Mr 25 '63
Dream. il pors Time 81:78-81 Mr 22 '63
'E said 'e would and 'e did. H. Horn. por Sports Illus 19:42-5 Jl 1 '63
Eleven men behind Cassius Clay. H. Horn. il Sports Illus 18:62-8+ Mr 11 '63
First days in the new life of the champion of the world. H. Horn. il pors Sports Illus 20:26-7+ Mr 9 '64
Fix that wasn't. Sports Illus 20:17 Ap 13 '64
$400,000 bellyache. H. Horn. il por Sports Illus 21:30-2 N 23 '64
How good is Cassius Clay? H. Nipson. il pors Ebony 19:77-80+ Ap '64

CLAY, Cassius—about—*Continued*
I want to destroy Clay; ed. by M. Gross. F. Patterson. Sports Illus 21:42-4+ O 19 '64
I whipped him and I'm still pretty; Clay-Liston fight. M. Kempton. New Repub 150:9-10 Mr 7 '64
In the ring. L. Jones. Nation 198:661-2 Je 29 '64
Left hooks and tenterhooks; Clay-Liston title fight. Sports Illus 19:5 Ag 12 '63
Liston turned on the evil eye, Clay didn't notice; with report by J. R. McDermott. il pors Life 56:34-9 Mr 6 '64
Liston's edge: a lethal left. T. Maule. il por Sports Illus 20:18-21 F 24 '64
Look at Cassius Clay; biggest mouth in boxing. A. Poinsett. il pors Ebony 18:35-6+ Mr '63
Man, the rabbit & the boy. il por Time 82:52 Ag 2 '63
Marvelous mouth. T. Wolfe. por Esquire 60:146+ O '63
Miami notebook: Cassius Clay and Malcolm X. G. Plimpton. por Harper 228:54-61 Je '64
Most subdued Cassius. il pors Life 57:81-2 N 27 '64
Muhammad Ali in Africa. il pors Sports Illus 20:20-5 Je 1 '64
Murder on the BBC. il por Time 81:66 Je 28 '63
Muslim champ. M. Cope. il pors Sat Eve Post 237:32-4+ N 14 '64
$100 misunderstanding? il por Newsweek 63:58 F 24 '64
Playing grownups. il por Time 84:104-5 N 13 '64
Prophet's margin; Clay. Newsweek 61:96 Mr 25 '63
Punching brag. por Newsweek 61:93 Mr 18 '63
Ride on, you Lip of Louisville. D. Moser. il por Life 54:66 F 15 '63
Rueful dream come true; Clay-Liston championship fight. H. Horn. por Sports Illus 19:26-7 N 18 '63
Run, Cassius, run. New Yorker 40:43-4 Mr 7 '64
Sporting scene; Clay vs. Jones fight. A. J. Liebling. New Yorker 39:122+ Mr 30 '63
Still hurt and lost. G. Rogin. il pors Sports Illus 21:22-7 N 16 '64
Sting of the Louisville lip. T. Maule. il por Sports Illus 20:50-1 F 17 '64
This is what Clay says he wants; photographs of Patterson-Liston fight. R. H. Boyle. por Sports Illus 19:22-6 Ag 5 '63
To fight or not to fight? R. H. Boyle. il Sports Illus 21:28-31 S 7 '64
With mouth & magic. il pors Time 83:66+ Mr 6 '64
Wot larks! il por Time 81:52 Je 14 '63
Yes, it was good and honest. T. Maule. il pors Sports Illus 20:20-5 Mr 9 '64

CLAY, George
In pursuit of the sound. il por Newsweek 64:64 D 7 '64

CLAY, Henry
Henry Clay: forerunner of Pan-Americanism. C. M. Sterling. il pors Américas 16:1-6 My '64

CLAY, Lucius DuBignon
President Kennedy and General Clay urge restoration of aid funds; interview, August 30, 1963. Dept State Bul 49:476-8 S 23 '63
Tightening up, but no end to aid abroad; interview. pors U S News 54:43 Ap 8 '63
What Berlin means. Atlan 212:87-9 D '63

about

Clay report. D. Cater. Reporter 28:10+ Ap 11 '63
Clay's feat. K. Crawford. Newsweek 61:28 Ap 8 '63
Don't fence him in. por Newsweek 61:80 F 11 '63
Feat of Clay. Nat R 14:265+ Ap 9 '63
General. New Yorker 39:34-5 Mr 30 '63
President receives Clay report on AID program; letter, March 22, 1963. J. F. Kennedy. Dept State Bul 48:574 Ap 15 '63
Tighter purse for foreign aid. il Bsns W p27-8 Mr 23 '63

CLAY
Ion exchange at edge and interlayer in montmorillonites differing in size. E. C. Jonas. bibliog il Science 140:75-6 Ap 5 '63
Montmorillonite-vermiculite interstratification in clays from eocene chalk soils. L. E. DeMumbrum. il Science 140:187-8 Ap 12 '63
Quick clay. P. F. Kerr. il Sci Am 209:132-8+ bibliog(p 188) N '63
Wall: painted clay. M. Cable. il Craft Horiz 23:27-31+ My '63

CLAY committee. See United States—President's advisory committee to strengthen the security of the free world
CLAY modeling. See Modeling
CLAY pigeons. See Trap shooting
CLAY sculpture. See Ceramic sculpture
CLAYBORNE Hill car pool; story. See Robinson, B.

CLAYTON, Donald D.
Chronology of the galaxy. bibliog Science 143:1281-6 Mr 20 '64

CLAYTON, J. T.
New ventilation system that thinks. Suc Farm 62:97 F '64

CLAYTON, James E.
Reapportionment riddle. Reporter 30:34-7 F 27 '64

CLAYTON, Robert N.
Carbon isotope abundance in meteoritic carbonates. bibliog Science 140:192-3 Ap 12 '63

CLAYTON, William L.
Will Clayton: groundbreaker in ideas. E. Roper. por Sat R 46:22-3 My 11 '63

CLAYTON, Mo.
How zoning can bring beauty. C. W. O'Key. il Am City 78:100-1 Ap '63

CLEANERS, Electric. See Vacuum cleaners

CLEANING
How to clean garage floors and driveways. D. X. Manners. il House B 105:60+ N '63
Miracle fabrics, yes, but how do you clean 'em? with cleaning guide. il Changing T 18:7-11 S '64
Removing stains of ball-point pen ink. Consumer Bul 48:29 F '65
Tricks in time keep table linens fine. B. G. Wadsworth. il Parents Mag 38:34 F '63
Valet service for your husband. B. G. Wadsworth. il Parents Mag 39:30 O '64
Wallpaper and interior paint care. B. G. Wadsworth. il Parents Mag 39:28 Ja '64

See also

Carpet sweepers
Dry cleaning machines
House cleaning
also subhead Cleaning, or Care under various subject, e.g. Barbecue grills—Care

CLEANING and dyeing industry
Troubles of coin-ops. il Time 81:92 Ap 5 '63

Wages and hours

Earnings in laundries and cleaning services, June 1963. C. M. O'Connor. bibliog f il Mo Labor R 87:419-22 Ap '64

CLEANING compositions
AWWA rejects ban on hard detergents. il Am City 78:123-4+ Jl '63
Annals of business; soaps and synthetic detergents. T. Whiteside. il New Yorker 40:42-6+ D 19 '64
At last, a disappearing detergent. il Time 81:62 Je 14 '63
Biodegradation of alkylbenzene sulfonate in a simulated septic tank and drain field. A. E. Straus. bibliog il Science 142:244-5 O 11 '63
Cleaners and polishes for glass. il Consumer Bul 46:43+ Ap '63
Closer look at that white tornado; Ajax with ammonia. il Consumer Rep 28:204 My '63
Dangers in mixing household chemicals. Consumer Rep 29:158 Ap '64
Defenseless America. Nation 196:415 My 18 '63
Detergent dilemma. B. Strawn. il Bet Hom & Gard 41:94-5 Ap '63
Detergent-foam bubble about to burst. Am City 79:35 F '64
Detergent foam nuisance. A. Clarke. Sci N L 83:109 F 16 '63
Detergent mess. B. H. Frisch. il Sci Digest 54:72-8 S '63
Detergent problems. Am City 78:22 My '63
Detergent war. il Time 83:65 Ja 31 '64
Detergents, deadly hazard to water birds. R. W. Nero. il Audubon Mag 66:26-7 Ja '64
Detergents in water: another view; amount of ABS (alkyl benzene sulfonate) il U S News 55:76 Ag 19 '63
Detergents really new and improved. il Consumer Bul 47:22-4 Jl '64
Don't let oven cleaning burn you up; use Jifoam. il Consumer Bul 47:13-16 D '64
Edible detergent. Newsweek 62:98+ N 25 '63
Farewell to foaming detergents. Nat Parks Mag 38:16 O '64
Get-ahead home cleaning hints. B. G. Wadsworth. Parents Mag 38:126 Mr '63
How to clean garage floors and driveways. D. X. Manners. il House B 105:60+ N '63
Just how safe is your drinking water? danger of ABS (alkyl benzine sulfonate) il U S News 55:74-5 Jl 15 '63

CLEANING compositions—*Continued*
Lather over detergents; anti-pollution campaigners push for laws. Bsns W p 104 F 16 '63
Look what they're doing to detergents. il Changing T 18:36 Je '64
New battle of suds. Bsns W p 126 My 23 '64
New methods to remove foam wastes found; fighting detergents with detergents. Sci N L 83:363 Je 8 '63
New soft detergents for home use on market. Sci N L 85:155 Mr 7 '64
Oven cleaners. il Consumer Rep 28:399-401 Ag '63
Scouring powders. il Consumer Bul 47:13-15 Ja '64
Synthetic detergents in water and sewage systems; report of Society for industrial microbiology; annual meeting. W. J. Payne. Science 139:197-8 Ja 18 '63
Vanishing detergents. Sci Am 211:84+ S '64
War on foam; new soft detergents. il Newsweek 63:73-4 F 24 '64
What's new for your wash water? J. Gillies. il Farm J 88:70 N '64
Where is science taking us? detergent waste problem. M. A. Benarde. il Sat R 46:53 Ap 6 '63
See also
Lestoil products, incorporated
Lever brothers company

Anecdotes, facetiae, satire, etc.
Why not try Ugh! M. Bennett. il Redbook 121:43 Jl '63

CLEANING machinery and appliances
Are you giving houseroom to health hazards? E. M. Wylie. Am Home 66:14+ Ap '63
Cleaning is easier when you use the right tools. N. Craig. il House B 106:146-7 Mr '64
Get-ahead home cleaning hints. B. G. Wadsworth. Parents Mag 38:126 Mr '63
See also
Dry cleaning machines
Vacuum cleaners

CLEANING of paintings. See Paintings—Cleaning

CLEANLINESS
Messiness from infancy to adolescence. B. Spock. il Ladies Home J 80:48+ Ap '63

CLEAR, Val
Breakthrough in Puerto Rico. Christian Cent 80:1216-18 O 2 '63
Paperback pedagogy. Sat R 47:73 F 15 '64

CLEAR air turbulence. See Atmospheric turbulence

CLEAR LAKE CITY, Tex.
On a Texas prairie, space city for 200,000. il U S News 54:66-9 F 18 '63

CLEAR the path; story. See Rooney, A. B.

CLEAR track; story. See O'Hara, J.

CLEARING houses
Where tax complexities pay off in profits; Chicago's commerce clearing house. il Bsns W p50+ F 22 '64

CLEARING of lakes. See Lakes—Clearing

CLEARING of land
Rock removal simplified. il Flower Grower 50:53 Jl '63

CLEARWATER, Robert G.
Forest bird becomes a city dweller. Audubon Mag 66:256-7 Jl '64

CLEARWATER, Fla.
Ram-fed incinerator. il Am City 79:69-72 D '64

CLEARY, John F.
Unijunction c.w. monitor. bibliog Electr World 71:62+ Ap '64
Unijunction metronome. Electr World 69:78-9 F '63

CLEBSCH, William A.
Candid Christian. Christian Cent 81:1405-6 N 11 '64

CLEDE, Bill
Bringing that new boat home. Motor B 113:36-7+ Ap '64
Tips for handling guns. Suc Farm 62:126+ Mr '64

CLEE, Gilbert H. and Sachtjen, W. M.
Organizing a worldwide business. Harvard Bsns R 42:55-67 N '64

CLEFT lip. See Harelip

CLEFT palate. See Palate, Cleft

CLEGHORN, Reese
Aftermath in Alabama. Reporter 31:34-5 D 3 '64
Angels are white. New Repub 149:12-14 Ag 17 '63
Bustling Birmingham. New Repub 148:9 Ap 20 '63
Dean departs from Ole Miss. Reporter 29:42 O 24 '63
Epilogue in Albany. New Repub 149:15-18 Jl 20 '63
Martin Luther King jr. apostle of crisis. Sat Eve Post 236:15-19 Je 15 '63
Perils of Plaquemines. New Repub 149:8-10 S 21 '63
Revolt of the professors. New Repub 148:5-6 F 2 '63
(ed) Segs. Esquire 61:71-6+ Ja '64
Who speaks for Mississippi? Reporter 31:31-4 Ag 13 '64

CLELAND, Thomas Maitland
Obituary
Pub W 186:56 N 16 '64

CLEMATIS
All clematis don't climb. M. M. Leister. il Horticulture 42:42 F '64
Clematis. D. F. Platt. il Horticulture 42:14-15+ Jl '64
Clematis to frame your doorway. il Pop Gard 15:22 S '64
Look into the future of clematis. A. T. Robinson. il Horticulture 41:198 Ap '63
This lavender-flowered vine is a climber from China. il Sunset 132:295 My '64

CLEMENS, Cyril
Mark Twain and Lyndon B. Johnson. Hobbies 69:112+ Ap '64

CLEMENS, Hans
Triple double. il por Time 82:26 Jl 19 '63

CLEMENS, Samuel Langhorne
Tom Sawyer, pirate; dramatization. See Thane, A.

about

Days of the dangerous virtues. E. Capouya. Sat R 47:30+ F 8 '64
Mark Twain and Lyndon B. Johnson. C. Clemens. Hobbies 69:112+ Ap '64
Mark Twain detective story published by NYPL. Library J 89:1210 Mr 15 '64
Mark Twain from under ground. S. Kauffmann. New Repub 148:20-2 Ap 6 '63
Mark Twain, obscenity, folk songs. R. De Toledano. Nat R 15:160-1 Ag 27 '63
Mark Twain science writer. R. Bass. por Sci Digest 54:47 Ag '63
Mark Twain's San Francisco. B. Taper. il Am Heritage 14:50-3+ Ag '63
Mark (ye) (the) Twain. D. J. Hamblin. por Life 57:13 Jl 10 '64
Mr Dooley's friends; excerpts from Mr Dooley remembers. F. P. Dunne. Atlan 212:77-80+ S '63

CLEMENT, Frank G.
Racism wasn't the issue in Tennessee. B. Kovach. Reporter 31:37-8 S 24 '64

CLEMENT, Roland C.
Last call for the birds of prey; condensed from address. por Audubon Mag 67:37 Ja '65
Whooping crane: today and tomorrow. Audubon Mag 66:74-7 Mr '64

CLEMENT, Rufus E.
U.S. presents independence gifts to Malawi; statement, July 1, 1964. Dept State Bul 51:91-2 Jl 20 '64

CLEMENT, Travers
How to make a reputation. Yachting 113:39+ Mr '63

CLEMENTS, Bob, and Clements, Claire
Teaching drawing at the college level. il Sch Arts 63:31-2 N '63

CLEMENTS, Claire. See Clements, B. jt. auth.

CLEMENTS, Edith S.
Flowers that bloom above the clouds. il Audubon Mag 66:180-1 My '64

CLEMENTS, Joy
Count and countess; interview, ed. by R. D. Daniels. por Opera N 28:16 F 22 '64

CLEMENTS, Julia
Flower festival at Bath, England. Horticulture 41:220-1 Ap '63

CLEMENTS, Robert J.
European literary scene. Sat R 47:28-9 Jl 11; 26-7 Ag 8; 38-9 S 12; 34-5 O 3; 30 N 21; 24-5 D 26 '64; 48:24-5 Ja 30 '65
Laurels in lieu of the lady. Sat R 46:59-60 D 7 '63
Merchants of light. Sat R 46:32-3 S 21 '63
Remembrances from Ricci palace. Sat R 47:64-5 O 24 '64

CLEMENTS, Tom
Amateur scientist. Sci Am 210:136-7+ Ap '64

CLEMSON agricultural college, Clemson, S.C.
Integration with dignity; with editorial comment. G. McMillan. il Sat Eve Post 236:15-21, 80 Mr 16 '63
New semester, a new Negro student. il U S News 54:15 F 11 '63
New term, new South. il Newsweek 61:29 F 11 '63

CLEMSON agricultural college, Clemson, S.C. —*Continued*
Regard for a good name; Harvey Bernard Gantt at Clemson college. il Time 81:20 F 8 '63
South Carolina's moment of truth. H. J. Massaquoi. il Ebony 18:96-8+ My '63

CLENCH, William J.
Top shell man. A. G. Melvin. por Hobbies 68:130+ My '63

CLEOPATRA, queen of Egypt
Then Antony met Cleopatra. R. Payne. il por N Y Times Mag p26-7+ Je 2 '63
Who was Cleopatra? D. Wharton. por Read Digest 83:239-42+ N '63

CLEPPER, Henry
Visit to FAO. por Am For 70:12-15 Ja '64
Waters of the Allagash. Am For 70:14-18+ N '64

CLERGUE, Lucien
Play gypsy, dance gypsy. J. Morris. il U S Camera 27:63-7 Ap '64

CLERGY
Church and the businessman; plea for greater understanding. J. C. Worthy. Christian Cent 80:1232-4 O 9 '63
Clergy patrol; volunteers are riding with patrol cars on trouble spots where teen-age tension spills over. America 111:172 Ag 22 '64
Clergymen have second chance for social security. Christian Cent 81:1422 N 18 '64
Do ministers really understand people? L. David and I. David. Good H 156:65+ Mr '63
Final call for clergy; social security coverage. America 111:766-7 D 12 '64
For the world of tomorrow. R. C. Miller. Christian Cent 81:544-6 Ap 29 '64
I have the most dramatic job in the world. J. S. Stewart. Read Digest 82:62-5 My '63
Image breakers. il Newsweek 61:99-101 Mr 18 '63
Letter on the parish ministry; reply to an earnest inquirer. P. L. Berger. Christian Cent 81:547-50 Ap 29 '64; Discussion. 81:936 Jl 22 '64
Ministerial health and unhealth; concerning articles in Saturday evening post and Look. R. N. Johnson. Christian Cent 80:706-8 My 29 '63
Ministry and institutional demands; concerning articles in Saturday evening post and Look; discussion. Christian Cent 80:335 Mr 13 '63
Ministry as servanthood. R. Hazelton. Christian Cent 80:521-4 Ap 24 '63
New models for ministers; concerning E. Werner's article in the American scholar. Christian Cent 82:4-5 Ja 6 '65
Notes from an irrelevant clergyman. W. Carr. Christian Cent 80:879-81 Jl 10 '63
On clinical pastoral training. R. J. Fairbanks. Christian Cent 80:556-9 Ap 24 '63
Relevant ministries. America 111:648 N 21 '64
17,358 clergymen are half right; Ministers' Vietnam committee. Christian Cent 80:1161-2 S 25 '63; Discussion. 80:1445-6 N 20 '63
Silent minister speaks up. R. Collie. il N Y Times Mag p 12+ My 24 '64; Same. U S News 56:76-9 Je 15 '64
What clergymen tell young people about marriage. T. Morris. Redbook 120:50-1+ Mr '63
When a priest made a pilgrimage. E. N. Bouton and T. F. Pettigrew. il Christian Cent 80:363-5 Mr 20 '63
Why I didn't quit the ministry. N. V. Peale. Sat Eve Post 236:52, 55 Mr 2 '63
See also
Catholic church—Clergy
Celibacy
Church of England—Clergy
Laity
Negro clergy
Theologians
Theological education
Theological students
Women as priests

Costume

Raiment in the space age. E. C. Bianchi. America 111:402 O 10 '64

Reading

Splart theology. R. E. Wentz. Christian Cent 80:398-9 Mr 27 '63

Recruiting

Shopping for preachers. Time 82:94+ N 15 '63

Salaries

Poor as . . . Newsweek 64:72 N 23 '64
Worthy of his hire. Christian Cent 82:6 Ja 6 '65

CLERGY conferences
Earl lectures; interdenominational pastoral conference. E. T. Culver. Christian Cent 81:316-18 Mr 4 '64

CLERICAL dress. See Clergy—Costume

CLERICAL workers. See Office workers

CLERKE, Bruce
Hair: a brush-up course. Ladies Home J 80:110-12 S '63
Through the summer looking glass. Ladies Home J 80:30+ Jl '63

CLERKS, Retail. See Department stores—Employees

CLERMONT, Yves. See Heller, C. G. jt. auth.

CLERODENDRUM. See Glory bowers

CLEVELAND, Frances Folsom
Among those present: First congress of mothers. M. K. Lucas. PTA Mag 57:17 F '63

CLEVELAND, Grover
Among those present: First congress of mothers. M. K. Lucas. PTA Mag 57:17 F '63
President and his critics. W. A. Williams. Nation 196:227-8 Mr 16 '63

CLEVELAND, H. G.
More than ten years of metered taxi fares. por Am City 78:115-16 My '63

CLEVELAND, Harlan
Agony of success; address, November 14, 1963. Dept State Bul 49:845-50 D 2 '63
Caricature of foreign aid; address, December 28, 1962. Dept State Bul 48:60-5 Ja 14 '63
Case for bureaucracy. N Y Times Mag p 19+ O 27 '63
Crisis diplomacy. For Affairs 41:638-49 Jl '63
18th General assembly: fair and a little warmer, with scattered thundershowers; address, September 15, 1963. Dept State Bul 49:553-6 O 7 '63
Evolution of rising responsibility; address, December 13, 1964. Dept State Bul 52:7-12 Ja 4 '65
Great power and great diversity: the perceptions and policies of President Kennedy; address, December 1, 1963. Dept State Bul 49:964-9 D 23 '63
Health for peace and vice versa; address, September 27, 1963. Dept State Bul 49:676-81 O 28 '63
Member of the parish; address, June 6, 1964. Dept State Bul 50:971-6 Je 22 '64
Must we be the world's policeman? N Y Times Mag p 14+ My 3 '64
Not pie-in-the-sky but enlightened self-interest. Sr Schol 83:12T-13T S 27 '63
Peace and human rights; address, June 15, 1963. Dept State Bul 49:38-43 Jl 8 '63
Political year of the quiet sun; address, February 27, 1964. Dept State Bul 50:452-7 Mr 23 '64; Same. Vital Speeches 30:457-60 My 15 '64
Reflections on the Pacific community; address, March 28, 1963. Dept State Bul 48:613-16 Ap 22 '63
Requisites of abundance; address, March 9, 1964. Dept State Bul 50:550-5 Ap 6 '64
Roles and critics of the United Nations; excerpts from address, August 11, 1964. Dept State Bul 51:351-4 S 7 '64
Thirteenth alarm; address, March 21, 1964. Dept State Bul 50:622-6 Ap 20 '64
Toasted breadcrumbs of the future; address, June 3, 1963. Dept State Bul 49:13-17 Jl 1 '63
Two kinds of politics; address, May 8, 1963. Dept State Bul 48:871-6 Je 3 '63
United Nations and the Congo: three questions; address, January 17, 1963. Dept State Bul 48:165-70 F 4 '63
U.N. economic and social council meets at Geneva; statement, July 23, 1964. Dept State Bul 51:241-8 Ag 17 '64
Uses of diversity; address, September 9, 1963. Dept State Bul 49:461-4 S 23 '63

CLEVELAND, Ohio
Heat lamps soothe winter bus patrons. T. W. McNally. il Am City 78:113 D '63
More truck-tire mileage; for municipal fleet. F. D. East. il Am City 79:86-8 Jl '64

City planning

Downtown's dramatic comeback. D. B. Carlson. il Arch Forum 120:100 F '64

Education

Tutor corps; Summer '64 tutor corps. il Time 84:56 Jl 24 '64
See also
Western Reserve university

Galleries and museums

See also
Cleveland museum of art

CLEVELAND, Ohio—*Continued*

Libraries

See also
Cleveland public library

Music

[Musical events] (cont) Mus Am 83:74 Ja; 12 Je '63; 84:13-14 F; 25-6 Ap '64
See also
Cleveland orchestra

Negroes

New neighbors; Mason family in Ludlow, next in Shaker Heights. C. Morrison. il Look 28:38-41 Ja 14 '64
Our middle-class ghettos. J. Horwitz. il Look 28:42-3+ Ja 14 '64
Racial crisis in Cleveland. O. M. Walton. Christian Cent 81:616+ My 6 '64

Newspapers

Strike two; Cleveland's newspaper strike. Time 81:59 Ap 12 '63
Too much power for labor? excerpts from address, February 12, 1963; with excerpts from letter by members of American newspaper guild. L. B. Seltzer. U S News 54:97 F 25 '63
See also
Cleveland plain dealer

Police

Bark like dogs. Nation 199:318 N 9 '64

Race problems

Bark like dogs. Nation 199:318 N 9 '64

Religious institutions and affairs

Another Oberlin conference. D. L. Day. Christian Cent 80:1334-5 O 30 '63

Stores

Tudors at Higbee's. il Pub W 184:22-3 D 2 '63

Theater

Theater in Cleveland. H. Hewes. Sat R 47:23 Mr 21 '64

CLEVELAND Browns (football club) See Football clubs
CLEVELAND museum of art
Before romanticism; neoclassicism exhibit. il Newsweek 64:102+ O 19 '64
Museum evaluations. A. Frankfurter. il Art N 63:26-9+ D '64
CLEVELAND orchestra
Don't tell Szell; Cleveland summer orchestra's recorded radio commercial. Newsweek 62: 50 Jl '63
Glorious instrument. il Time 81:58-60+ F 22 '63; Same abr. Read Digest 82:261-3+ My '63
Musical events; concert at Carnegie Hall. W. Sargeant. New Yorker 38:151-2 F 16 '63
Szell, still storming after fifty years. M. Mayer. il N Y Times Mag p 13+ F 2 '64
CLEVELAND plain dealer
Replying in spades. il Time 81:50 My 31 '63
CLEVELAND playhouse. See Cleveland, Ohio—Theater
CLEVELAND press
Replying in spades. il Time 81:50 My 31 '63
CLEVELAND public library
Linda A. Eastman. R. C. Lindquist. il ALA Bul 57:783-5 S '63
Shut-in; waiting for what? Judd Fund service-to-shut-ins. C. E. Lucioli and D. H. Fleak. il ALA Bul 58:781-4 O '64
CLEVENGER, Max R.
Ultramicrotome: a simple, easily constructed instrument. Science 142:241-2 O 11 '63
CLEVENGER, Sarah
Flower pigments. Sci Am 210:84-8+ Je '64
CLEVER, Ulrich
Actinomycin and puromycin: effects on sequential gene activation by ecdysone. bibliog Science 146:794-5 N 6 '64
—See Beermann, W. jt. auth.
CLIBURN, Van
Texan team makes its musical bow; Luci Baines Johnson and Van Cliburn. il pors Life 57:53-4+ Ag 7 '64
CLICHÉS. See English language—Terms and phrases
CLIFF, Edward P.
APW: a profit formula. Am For 69:28-30+ O '63
CLIFF, Norman. See Ekstrom, R. B. jt. auth
CLIFF diving
Over the cliff, whoosh! il Life 55:43-6 S 6 '63
CLIFF dwellers and cliff dwellings
Solving the riddles of Wetherill mesa. D. Osborne. il Nat Geog Mag 125:155-95 F '64
Three Turkey House; Navajo archeological site near Canyon de Chelly National Monument in Arizona. O. F. Oldendorph. il Nat Parks Mag 38:8-9 Ag '64
CLIFF swallow. See Swallows
CLIFFE, Frank B. Jr. See Uyeki, E. S. jt. auth.
CLIFFE, Lionel
Tanganyika's two years of independence. bibliog f Cur Hist 46:136-41+ Mr '64
CLIFFORD, A. F. and Zeilenga, G. R.
Xenon fluorosilicate and related compounds. bibliog Science 143:1431 Mr 27 '64
CLIFFORD, Clark
Clark Clifford named chairman of Intelligence advisory board. Dept State Bul 48:805 My 20 '63
CLIFFORD, Henry
Floreat Philadelphia. Art N 62:30-1+ My '63
CLIFFORD, James L.
Master of the marble image. Sat R 46:32+ Ag 10 '63
CLIFFORD, Nicholas R.
Enigma of Germany. Commonweal 81:363-6 D 4 '64
CLIFFORD, Richard J. and Callahan, W. R.
Catholics in higher education. America 111: 288-91 S 19 '64
CLIFFORD, William
Birth control in Japan. Look 27:60-1 F 26 '63
Indian cook book. House & Gard 126:197+ S '64
Visit with John D. Rockefeller 3rd. Look 28:78-80 S 8 '64
What to drink with Indian food. House & Gard 126:196+ S '64
CLIFT, David H.
Carl Hastings Milam, 1884-1963. por ALA Bul 57:812 O '63
Fleas come with the dog. Library J 88:1423 Ap 1 '63
CLIFT, John Russell
New glow in steel technology; paintings. Fortune 71:128-35 Ja '65
CLIMATE
Gardener's month. il House & Gard 126:114-15 Jl '64
Handicap for new nations: climate. G. H. T. Kimble. il N Y Times Mag p35+ S 29 '63
Sea level and climate of the past century. W. L. Donn and D. M. Shaw. bibliog il Science 142:1166 N 29 '63
See also
Arctic Regions—Climate
Man—Influence of environment
Paleoclimatology
Plants, Effect of climate on
Weather
CLIMATE and architecture. See Architecture and climate
CLIMATE and health. See Weather—Mental and physiological effects
CLIMATIC thermal adaptation. See Adaptation (biology)
CLIMATOLOGY, Agricultural. See Plants, Effect of climate on
CLIMBING plants
Boston ivy or Virginia creeper. il Sunset 133:285 O '64
Introducing some clinging vines. Sunset 131: 303 O '63
Leafy arbors. il Sunset 132:98-103 Ap '64
These vines are fast growers. il Sunset 132: 268 Mr '64
Vines. E. L. Scullthorp. il House B 105:98-101 Ag '63
Vines. F. Curto. il Horticulture 42:34-6 D '64
When vines grow on structures. il Sunset 130:290 Ap '63
See also
Asarina
Bittersweet
Clematis
Glory bowers
Morning glories
Roses
CLIMBING roses. See Roses
CLINCHFIELD coal corporation
Coal's comeback at Moss no. three. il Fortune 68:130-5 O '63
CLINICAL laboratories. See Medical laboratories
CLINICAL radiology. See Radiology, Medical
CLINICAL thermometers. See Thermometers, Clinical
CLINICS. See Health clinics
CLINTON, Farley
Polished and robust. Nat R 16:362+ My 5 '64
CLINTON, Sir Henry
Portrait of a general, by W. B. Willcox. Review
Sat R por 47:37-8+ Jl 11 '64. E. Wright

CLINTON, Henry Fiennes, 9th earl of Lincoln. See Lincoln, H. F. C.

CLIPPERS, Hedge. See Hedge clippers

CLIPPINGS (books, newspapers, etc.)
Clipping and conflict; letter. D. D. Jensen. Science 142:341+ O 18 '63; Discussion. 142: 1621 D 27 '63

CLIQUES. See Groups (sociology)

CLIVE, John
British history, 1870-1914, reconsidered: recent trends in the historiography of the period. bibliog f Am Hist R 68:987-1009 Jl '63
Trevelyan: the muse or the museum? Nation 196:143-5 F 16 '63

CLIVEDEN (estate) See Country estates—England

CLOCK and watch makers
Sales & distribution; revolution in the watch industry. L. Moreau. Duns R 83:51-2 Je '64
See also
Bulova watch company
United States time corporation

CLOCK paradox. See Relativity (physics)

CLOCK radios. See Radio receiving apparatus

CLOCKS
Amateur scientist; tuning fork with electric drive can make an inexpensive and highly accurate clock. T. Clemens. il Sci Am 210: 136-7+ Ap '64
Beautiful clocks. L. W. Slaughter. il Hobbies 69:50-1+ Ap '64
Clock corner. il McCalls 91:92-3+ Ja '64
Clock to stop all clocks; Engle clock. L. W. Slaughter. il Hobbies 69:50-1 My '64
Clocks of southern France. L. W. Slaughter. il Hobbies 69:50-1+ D '64
Grand "Grande Sonnerie." L. W. Slaughter. il Hobbies 68:46-7+ Ag '63
Joseph Carpenter jr. silversmith and clock-maker. A. R. Chase. il Antiques 85:695-7 Je '64
Lost is not yet found; eighth wonder or Engle clock. L. W. Slaughter. Hobbies 69:50-1+ Jl '64
More of striking time-pieces. L. W. Slaughter. il Hobbies 68:46-7+ Mr '63
More on the Vienna regulator story. L. W. Slaughter. il Hobbies 68:46-7+ Jl '63
Perils of a horological writer. L. W. Slaughter. il Hobbies 69:50-1+ Je '64
Rare multiple dial clock. L. W. Slaughter. il Hobbies 69:50-1+ Ja '65
Rare Thomas Reid clock. L. W. Slaughter. il Hobbies 69:50-1+ O '64
Swinging clocks. L. W. Slaughter. il Hobbies 68:46-7+ N '63
Time on Fifth avenue. New Yorker 39:44-5 Mr 16 '63
Timely topics. L. W. Slaughter. il Hobbies 69:50-1+ S '64
Two English clocks, and Dutch baroque clock. R. Davidson. il Antiques 86:476+ O '64
Two Essex County clocks. D. A. Fales, jr. il Antiques 84:80-1 Jl '63
What's new in clocks? il Good H 157:169 N '63
Winding the clock. L. W. Slaughter. il Hobbies 69:50-1+ N '64
See also
Astronomical clocks
Chronometers

Atomic control
Frequency & time standards. G. E. Hudson. il Electr World 72:20-3 Ag '64
We will now test the time machine. S. Spillman. il Sci Digest 54:57-60 O '63

Collectors and collecting
Problems of collecting. L. W. Slaughter. Hobbies 69:50-1 Mr '64

CLOCKS, Electric
Electric clocks. il Consumer Bul 47:36-9 N '64
Wake up to your song; music box alarm clock. T. Thomas. il Pop Mech 120:176-7 Ag '63

CLOCKS, Electronic
Amateur scientist; electronic chronometer utilizing tunnel diodes. R. L. Watters. il Sci Am 208:157-60+ Mr '63
Crystal controlled time standard. J. H. Phillips. il Electr World 69:34-6 Je '63

CLOETE, Stuart
Honey bird; story. Sat Eve Post 236:42-6 Mr 2 '63
How to write a novel. Writer 77:9-10 Jl '64

CLOFIBRATE. See Atromid S

CLOISONNÉ
Cloisonné teapots. il(p 1) Hobbies 69:30 O '64
Cloisonné the easy way. il Design 64:198-9+ Je '63

CLOISTERS (museum) See Metropolitan museum of art, New York—Cloisters

CLOONAN, E. T.
Meters save water. Am City 79:147-8 Mr '64

CLOONAN, Jack
Workshop: the direct photographic silk screen. Craft Horiz 23:54-5 N '63

CLOPTON, Mrs Carter
Action for aging. Recreation 57:300-1 Je '64

CLOROX chemical company
How a bleach helps in your family's laundry. E. M. McCabe. il Parents Mag 38:20+ Ag '63
P&G is told it must sell Clorox. Bsns W p82-3 D 21 '63

CLOS, Max
5,000 Vietnamese students study, in Paris. N Y Times Mag p38-9+ D 6 '64
Strategist behind the Vietcong. N Y Times Mag p7+ Ag 16 '64
Why the Africans hate Tshombe. N Y Times Mag p24-5+ Ja 10 '65

CLOSE by my side; story. See Randall, F. E.

CLOSE corporations. See Corporations

CLOSE-up photography. See Photography, Close-up

CLOSED circuit television. See Television, Closed circuit

CLOSED-end investment trusts. See Investment companies

CLOSED shop. See Open and closed shop

CLOSETS
Closets crammed with style; with report by S. Wright. il Life 56:46-51+ F 28 '64
Fully engineered bathrooms; well-planned wardrobes. il House & Gard 124:62-7 Jl '63
How to stretch an average closet. il Bet Hom & Gard 42:99 F '64
How to stretch space for storing clothes. il House B 105:192-5 S '63
Open up a closet with a new door and better organized storage. il Bet Hom & Gard 41: 34 S '63
They needed a closet and this is the result! il Am Home 66:88 Ap '63

CLOTHES closets. See Closets

CLOTHES dryers
Automatic clothes dryers. il Consumer Rep 28:369-75 Ag '63
Clothes dryers. il Consumer Bul 47:6-12 O '64
Electric clothes dryers: Speed Queen, Sears Kenmore. Consumer Bul 48:33 Ja '65
Gas clothes dryers. il Consumer Bul 47:27-30 N '64
Is your laundry right for you? R. Charles. il Parents Mag 38:103-5+ O '63
Terrific, timesaving new washers and dryers! Bet Hom & Gard 41:97 O '63
Twenty reasons for owning a dryer. V. T. Habeeb. il Am Home 66:40-1 O '63

Control
Thinking washers sensing dryers. N. Craig. il House B 105:152-3+ Mr '63

CLOTHES hangers

Anecdotes, facetiae, satire, etc.
Wily coat hanger; excerpt from Bird thou never wert. B. Vaughan. Read Digest 85:180A+ S '64

CLOTHES lines. See Clotheslines

CLOTHES washing machines. See Washing machines

CLOTHESLINES
If you prefer outdoor drying. il Sunset 131:134 O 13 '63

CLOTHING, Cold weather
Brother, it's cold out there! M. Wiley. il Yachting 114:48-50+ S '63
Clothes for boating. J. A. Emmett. il Outdoor Life 132:122-4 S '63
50° suit. C. Conley. il Field & S 69:75 Ja '65
Foam-laminated work trousers. Consumer Bul 48:14 F '65
How to dress warmly in winter. B. H. Frisch. il Sci Digest 57:34-41 Ja '65

CLOTHING and dress
Back to school; campus fashions. il Time 84: 104 O 2 '64
Basic wardrobe for vacation travel. il Good H 158:161 My '64
Best dressed women of 1963. il Ebony 18:132-4+ My '63
Better dress codes; pro and con discussion. il Sr Schol 82:14-15 Ap 3 '63
Bottoms up; Jax slacks. il Time 83:60 Ap 3 '64
Buying for a boom; buyers on spree in New York's garment center. il Bsns W p30-1 Je 20 '64
Clothes closet. Consumer Rep 29:207-25 D '64
Come as you are? D. Herold. il Read Digest 85:159-60 Ag '64

CLOTHING and dress—*Continued*
Fair-weather clothes. C. D. Legg. il Farm J 88:100-3 F '64
Female or feminine; problem of growing immodesty. America 109:107 Ag 3 '63
Habit of opera. A. Vanderbilt. il Opera N 27:8-11 Mr 16 '63
How to dress what you have. il Ladies Home J 80:77 Mr '63
Ladies: it's the season to be shifty and smocky; maternity wear. il Newsweek 61:92 My 27 '63
Look what's happened to housedresses! C. D. Legg. il Farm J 87:94-5 F '63
On being naked. T. Sterling. il Holiday 36:8+ Ag '64
Pants for the city? il Life 57:49-50 O 23 '64
Shift to shifts. C. D. Legg. il Farm J 87:71 My '63
Something more comfortable; loungewear. il Bsns W p54-5 D 21 '63
Speaking out; in defense of naked ladies. R. Baker. Sat Eve Post 237:10+ O 31 '64
These are the clothes we'll wear to school. C. D. Legg. il Farm J 87:56-7 Ag '63
Treasures from the foreign bazaars. B. F. Krainin. il Holiday 34:94-9 N '63
What the well dressed woman never forgets. il Good H 157:149 S '63
What's new to wear for fall. C. D. Legg. il Farm J 87:56 S '63
What's sexy? D. Newman and R. Benton. il Mlle 59:66+ My '64
Your self (cont) il Consumer Rep 28:31-79 D '63
See also
Bathing suits
Coats
Collars
Costume design
Costume designers
Dressmaking
Fashion
Foundation garments
Hats
Religious orders—Habit
Sweaters
Trousers
Uniforms

Care

Can you launder your car coat? il Consumer Bul 47:26 O '64
Dress tips. Sr Schol 82:22 Ap 3 '63

Children

Boys' jeans. il Consumer Rep 29:122-5 Mr '64
Family business in brief. A. P. Eliasberg. il N Y Times Mag p34 Jl 14 '63
How Princess Grace chooses children's clothes. H. Obolensky. il Redbook 121:60-5 Ag '63
Out of the rocker; handsomest children's clothes in the U.S. il Time 84:58+ N 27 '64
Selecting kiddies' sleepers for warmth and wear. il Good H 157:194 D '63
Shopping for snowsuits to weather the winter. il Good H 157:160 D '63
Stretch clothes. il Look 27:45-6 My 21 '63

Cleaning

See Cleaning

History

Chic-ness crosses the channel. J. Laver. il N Y Times Mag p86-7+ N 24 '63
Fresh look at the empire dress. A. S. Cavallo. il Antiques 86:310-13 S '64
Now his is hers. G. Glueck. il N Y Times Mag p45+ S 20 '64

Laws and regulations

Necklines make you nervous? W. K. Zinsser. il Sat Eve Post 237:26-9 F 22 '64

Maternity clothes

Chic though pregnant. il Bsns W p32 My 4 '63
How to be the best-dressed mother-to-be. C. D. Legg. il Farm J 88:88 My '64
Waiting game; advertising mother-to-be clothes. il Time 81:71 Mr 15 '63

Men

Bright plumage for the businessman. il Bsns W p30-1 Mr 30 '63
Economics of the rented tuxedo. il Changing T 19:47 Ja '65
Fashions. O. E. Schoeffler. Esquire 61:161 My; 62:109 Ag; 55 O '64
Fashions; European report. O. E. Schoeffler. Esquire 59:12+ Mr '63
Fine feathers for hire. J. Bryan, 3d. il Holiday 34:44+ D '63
Masculine mode. il Time 83:83 F 28 '64
Men's slacks; mail-order and private brands. il Consumer Bul 48:11-13 F '65
New stretch for men's clothing; stretch fabrics. il Bsns W p86-7 Ja 25 '64
Sportswear races to a sales lead. il Bsns W p54+ D 5 '64
What's wrong with men's clothes. A. Capp. il Sat Eve Post 236:20-1 Je 1 '63
See also
United States—Army—Clothing

History

Men's fashions, too, reflect the times. E. Kendall. il N Y Times Mag p 18-19 Ag 2 '64

Renting

Economics of the rented tuxedo. il Changing T 19:47 Ja '65
Fine feathers for hire. J. Bryan, 3d. il Holiday 34:44+ D '63

Size

Juno in limbo; the trauma of size sixteen. M. Mannes. il Harper 229:37-40 Jl '64

Sports clothes

Banner year for American ski clothes. J. A. Zill. il Sports Illus 19:48-9 D 16 '63
Boat wear for '65. M. Wiley. il Yachting 117:112-15+ Ja '65
Brother, it's cold out there! M. Wiley. il Yachting 114:48-50+ S '63
Clothing for bowhunters. G. H. Gillelan. il Outdoor Life 133:12-14 Je '64
Easy does it! M. Wiley. il Yachting 115:67-70 My '64
Geared for cup racing. il Sports Illus 20:50-3 Je 22 '64
Harborside in California. M. Wiley. il Yachting 113:62-7 My '63
Inventive skier's worldly wardrobe. il Life 58:49-50 Ja 29 '65
Kitzbühel look; photographs. L. Dean. Sports Illus 19:62-5 N 25 '63
Morning line on stretch pants; Ski industries America trade show. Sports Illus 18:17 My 13 '63
Saks of safaris. il Newsweek 62:91 O 21 '63
Sporting look. See issues of Sports illustrated
Sportswear races to a sales lead. il Bsns W p54+ D 5 '64
Sporty look: Paris designs at Abercrombie & Fitch, N.Y. il Time 82:65 N 1 '63
Take a fashion lesson; your first ski lesson. il Seventeen 23:88 N '64
Vacation clothes. T. Trueblood. il Field & S 68:24+ Je '63
White New Year. il Sports Illus 18:35-8 Ja 28 '63
Year of the campus cowboy. il Sports Illus 21:40-2 Ag 24 '64

CLOTHING industry
See also
International ladies' garment workers' union

International aspects

Apparel makers get global visas; U.S. fashions have spread around the world. il Bsns W p 104-6+ O 17 '64

Wages and hours

Earnings in men's and boys' suit and coat industry. G. L. Stelluto. il Mo Labor R 87:1035-8 S '64
Earnings in the dress manufacturing industry, March-April 1963. F. W. Mohr. il Mo Labor R 86:1436-8 D '63
Earnings: women's and misses' coat and suit industry, August 1962. F. W. Mohr. il Mo Labor R 86:817-19 Jl '63

Hong Kong

Fashions: the Asian rag race. S. Karnow. il Sat Eve Post 237:24-31 Ja 25 '64
Hong Kong's signs gain in translation; Chinese shop signs rendered literally into English. il Bsns W p 138 Je 6 '64

United States

All the fit that's news to print. G. Greene. il Sat Eve Post 237:77-81 Ap 11 '64
He's a fashion purist with the golden touch. il Bsns W p64-6+ S 12 '64
New wrinkle in no-wrinkle garb. il Bsns W p34+ N 21 '64
$100 million in rags. S. Freedgood. il Fortune 67:151-4+ My '63
Rackful of giants. il Time 81:91-2 Je 7 '63
See also
Hart, Schaffner and Marx
New York (city)—Industries

CLOTTING of blood. See Blood—Coagulation
CLOTURE rule. See United States—Congress—Senate—Rules and practice

CLOUD, Christina
Green needles showing; poem. Am For 69:58 Jl '63
CLOUD, Preston E. Jr
Earth science today; excerpts from address. Science 144:1428-31 Je 19 '64
CLOUD, Wallace
Science newsfront. See issues of Popular science monthly
CLOUD physics
Building blocks of the clouds. J. A. Day. il Natur Hist 74:36-43 Ja '65
CLOUD seeding. See Rain making
CLOUDBURSTS
Cloudburst at Petra. il Time 81:44 Ap 19 '63
CLOUDS
Cloud patterns over tropical oceans. J. S. Malkus. bibliog il Science 141:767-78 Ag 30 '63
Cloud watching can be fun. D. A. Whelpley. il Sci Digest 54:33-6 Jl '63
Latitudinal distribution of cloud cover from Tiros III photographs. A. Arking. bibliog il Science 143:569-72 F 7 '64; Reply. R. Wexler and W. K. Widger, jr. 145:1206 S 11 '64
Low-latitude noctilucent cloud of 15 June 1963. A. B. Meinel and others. il Science 141:1176-8 S 20 '63
Low-latitude noctilucent cloud of 2 November 1963. A. B. Meinel and C. P. Meinel. il Science 143:38 Ja 3 '64; Reply. A. Margoshes. 144:1158 My 29 '64
Lowest temperature in atmosphere recorded; study of noctilucent clouds. Sci N L 84:326 N 23 '63
Noctilucent clouds. R. K. Soberman. il Sci Am 208:50-9 bibliog(p 183) Je '63
Noctilucent clouds and low atmospheric temperatures. Sky & Tel 27:18 Ja '64
Origin of noctilucent clouds; letter. R. S. Iyengar. bibliog Science 145:767 Ag 21 '64
Radio observation of the electromagnetic emission from warm clouds. J. D. Sartor. bibliog il Science 143:948-50 F 28 '64
Rainbow of moonbeams and a high cloud ring of mystery. il Life 54:111-12 My 17 '63
Research frontier; where is science taking us? J. E. McDonald. il Sat R 46:40 Ag 3 '63
Storm clouds. il Am For 69:28-9 Ag '63
Stratospheric cloud over northern Arizona. J. E. McDonald. bibliog il Science 140: 292-4 Ap 19 '63; Discussion. 141:1136 S 20 '63
CLOUDS, Magellanic. See Magellanic clouds
CLOUGH, Desmond
Fact & fancy; reporting the Vassall case. Time 81:62 F 8 '63
CLOUGH, Roy L. Jr
Electric cannon fires BBs. Pop Mech 120:162-3 N '63
Fastest way to build a model plane. Pop Sci 182:137-9 Mr '63
Hoopskirt. Pop Mech 119:155-7+ Ap '63
Model rotor-sailing ship. Pop Mech 120:124-7 Ag '63
Mysterious walking box. Pop Mech 119:167-8 Mr '63
Water bug. Pop Mech 119:128-30 Je '63
CLOVE
Most fragrant scent in the world. C. Claiborne. il N Y Times Mag p98 S 29 '63
CLOVE apples, oranges, etc. See Pomanders
CLOVER
Chromosome number of rose clover, trifolium hirtum. E. J. Britten. bibliog il Science 142: 401-2 O 18 '63
We're in clover. E. C. Polatin. House B 105: 156-7 Je '63
CLOWES memorial hall for the performing arts. See Indianapolis—Clowes memorial hall for the performing arts
CLOWNS
Rodeo clown. C. Lofting. il Life 55:37-8+ Jl 19 '63
Le CLUB, New York. See Night clubs
CLUB Méditerranée. See Vacation villages
CLUB women. See Womens clubs and societies
CLUBB, O. Edmund
Living with China as a great power. bibliog f Ann Am Acad 351:140-7 Ja '64
CLUBHOUSES
Ideal yacht club; designed by R. Bidwell. A. Zich. il Sports Illus 18:32-6 Ap 22 '63
CLUBS
Action for aging; Training for leadership in senior citizens clubs, Austin, Tex. Mrs C. Clopton. il Recreation 57:300-1 Je '64
Big hop on Cheops' top; Adventurers' club of Denmark celebrates twenty-fifth anniversary. il Life 56:35-6 Ja 17 '64
Choice of the turtle; Lucullus Circle spring dinner. Newsweek 61:51-2 Mr 4 '63
Clubs, clubs, and more clubs. G. Glueck. il N Y Times Mag p44 Ap 7 '63
Clubs of business. N. Buckley. il Duns R 82:29-31+ Ag '63
Cornfield chemicals club. J. Castle. il Recreation 56:409-10 N '63
Finding a future in future clubs. P. W. Goldman. il N Y Times Mag p83-4 Mr 8 '64
Indictment. P. A. Deimel; reply. J. B. Gillette. Recreation 56:108 Mr '63
Ingham County's 500 pound club. J. R. Borcherding. il Suc Farm 61:46-7+ Ap '63
Life guide; clubs for all sorts of joiners. il Life 54:15 F 8 '63
More trouble ahead for private clubs? il U S News 56:12 Ap 6 '64
New idea: start a diet club; with recipes. il Seventeen 23:146-7+ Mr '64
Tall girl meets tall boy; Elinor Provonsha and Bill Barbour. S. Gordon. il Look 27: 56-8+ My 21 '63
Teen club forum; teenage dependents of U.S. military personnel stationed abroad. H. Rathner. il Recreation 57:518 D '64
Ten nights club. S. Spaeth. il Opera N 28: 6-7 Ap 11 '64
Where there's smoke; U.S. fire-buff clubs. il Newsweek 61:90 Mr 18 '63
See also
Book clubs
Bridge clubs
Garden clubs
Science clubs of America
Yacht clubs
also names of clubs, e.g. 4-H clubs
also subhead Clubs under names of cities, e.g. New York (city)—Clubs
CLUETT, Sanford L.
Mr Shrink and Stretch. D. Wharton. por Read Digest 85:39-40+ O '64
CLUNIS, David
Even Minnesota has racial flare-ups now. il por U S News 55:8 Jl 8 '63
CLURMAN, Harold
Brecht is global, except here. N Y Times Mag p30-1+ N 3 '63
Challenge of the new theatres. Nation 198: 122-4 F 3 '64
Clifford Odets. Sat R 46:10 S 14 '63
Cocteau. Nation 197:282 N 2 '63
Critic's credo. Nation 199:120-2, 147-8 S 14-21 '64
Director prepares. Theatre Arts 47:16-19+ Ap '63
Happy time. Nation 197:224-6 O 12 '63
Letter from Tokyo. Nation 197:118-20. 147-8 S 7-14 '63
Theatre. See issues of Nation
There's a method in British acting. N Y Times Mag p 18-19+ Ja 12 '64
Where are the new playwrights? waiting. N Y Times Mag p26-7+ Je 7 '64
about
No tickets for Clurman. Nation 197:379 D 7 '63
CLUSTER zoning. See Zoning
CLUSTERS of stars. See Stars—Clusters
CLUTCHES (machinery)
Clutch that slips on purpose; modulated clutch. il Bsns W p81 Je 20 '64
CLUTCHES, Automobile. See Automobiles—Clutches
CLUTTERBUCK, Guy
Who's who in foreign business. por Fortune 67:66 F '63
CLYDE, George Dewey
Showdown in Utah. Time 81:62 My 24 '63
CLYDE, Norman
California's old man of the mountains. A. Hamilton. por Read Digest 83:168C+ O '63
CLYMER, Floyd
Dandy little diesel for $2,660. pors Pop Sci 185:98-9+ N '64
CLYNE, John V.
Who's who in foreign business. por Fortune 68:82 D '63
COACH dogs. See Dalmatian dogs
COACH with the six insides; drama. See Erdman, J.
COACHES (athletics) See Physical directors
COACHING (athletics) See Athletes—Training
COAGULATION of blood. See Blood—Coagulation
COAKLEY, Frances
Faith to faith; poem. Christian Cent 80:710 My 29 '63
COAL
Transportation
Comeback of coal. il Time 81:93-4 Ap 12 '63
Railroads give coal big break; lower rates for unitized train shipments. il Bsns W p34+ Mr 9 '63

COAL and steel community. See European coal and steel community

COAL-burning turbines. See Gas turbines

COAL industry

United States

Coal hits a new vein. il Bsns W p90-3 F 1 '64
Coal's comeback at Moss no. three. il Fortune 68:130-5 O '63
Comeback of coal. il Time 81:93-4 Ap 12 '63
Out of the hole; new ways to use coal. il Newsweek 61:95 Ap 22 '63

See also

Consolidation coal company

COAL mine rescue work. See Mine rescue work

COAL miners

Back to work for French coal miners. il Sr Schol 82:20 Ap 17 '63
General and the miners. E. Taylor. il Reporter 28:15-18 Ap 11 '63
How de Gaulle came out in showdown with miners. il U S News 54:105-6 Ap 15 '63
In Hazard, Ky. D. Wakefield. Commentary 36: 209-17 S '63
Labor vs. de Gaulle. il Bsns W p78-80+ Mr 23 '63
This is Ellis Grigsby's story. J. J. Lindsay. il Newsweek 61:60-1 Ap 1 '63
Why they still go into the mines. J. J. Lindsay. il N Y Times Mag p37+ N 24 '63

See also

United mine workers of America

COAL mines and mining

Accidents and explosions

Cave-in! Sheppton, Pa. A. F. Gonzalez, jr. il Pop Sci 183:43-8+ D '63
Coal mine disasters. Sci N L 86:15 Jl 4 '64
Coal mine disasters: frequency by month. R. F. Boyer. bibliog il Science 144:1447-9 Je 19 '64; Discussion. 145:727; 146:14 Ag 14, O 2 64
From the grave; rescue operations at Sheppton, Pa. il Newsweek 62:28+ S 2 '63
How trapped miners were rescued; Sheppton, Pa. il U S News 55:16 S 9 '63
Industry pitches in to save trapped miners; Sheppton, Pa. coal mine disaster. il Bsns W p26-7 Ag 31 '63
Rescue and death; Sheppton, Pa. il Newsweek 62:26 S 9 '63
Start of a legend? il Time 82:17 S 6 '63
Two pins; Kyushu mine explosion. Time 82:34 N 22 '63
Why they still go into the mines. J. J. Lindsay. il N Y Times Mag p37+ N 24 '63

Equipment

See also

Coal mining machinery

Fires and fire protection

City on fire; Carbondale, Pa. C. P. Gilmore. il Sat Eve Post 236:83-7 S 7 '63
Towns built over a furnace; old coal mines. il Bsns W p98-100+ My 4 '63

Stripping operations

Washington newsletter; strip mining. P. M. Tilden. Natur Hist 72:63 D '63

Wages and hours

Earnings in bituminous coal mines, November 1962. F. L. Bauer. il Mo Labor R 86:1153-6 O '63

Europe, Western

See also

European coal and steel community

France

De Gaulle and the French strikes. A. Werth. Nation 196:239-40 Mr 23 '63
How de Gaulle handles his labor problems. il U S News 54:100 Mr 18 '63
Labor young and old flouts Big Charlie. il Life 54:26-7 Ap 12 '63

Germany (Federal Republic)

Burnt-out coal; plans to close down thirty-six mines. il Time 84:119 N 13 '64

United States

Coal's comeback at Moss no. three. il Fortune 68:130-5 O '63
Gray spring in Hazard. S. Gervis. Commonweal 78:220-2 My 17 '63
King Coal comes back. J. N. Miller. il Read Digest 85:88-94 D '64
Permanent poor; lesson of eastern Kentucky. H. M. Caudill. Atlan 213:49-53 Je '64; Discussion. 214:30 Ag '64
This is Ellis Grigsby's story. J. J. Lindsay. il Newsweek 61:60-1 Ap 1 '63
UMW faces a miner's revolt; independent mining is spreading. Bsns W p70+ Ag 15 '64

See also

Coal industry—United States

COAL mining machinery

Coal: when machines took over. il U S News 54:69-73 Ap 29 '63

COAR, Arthur D.

Detroit branch, ASNLH, launches $50,000 African art drive. por Negro Hist Bul 27: 99-102 F '64

COAST changes

Emerged holocene South American shorelines. H. G. Richards and W. Broecker. bibliog il Science 141:1044-5 S 13 '63
Sea level changes in the past 6000 years: possible archeological significance. F. P. Shepard. bibliog il Science 143:574-6 F 7 '64
Submergence of the Connecticut coast. A. L. Bloom and M. Stuiver. bibliog il Science 139:332-4 Ja 25 '63

COAST defense

USCG auxiliary at war. il Motor B 113:32-3+ Je '64

COAST guard. See United States—Coast guard

COAST guard academy, United States. See United States coast guard academy

COAST guard auxiliary. See United States—Coast guard auxiliary

COASTAL waters. See Territorial waters

COASTING

Inflexible flyer; bobsledding. C. Phinizy. il Sports Illus 20:54-7 Ja 27 '64
Peace of mind on a fragment of wood and steel; sport is luging. il Sports Illus 20:56-7 Ja 27 '64
Two proper Britishers in a bob; Antony Nash and T. Robin Dixon. il Sports Illus 20:22-3 F 10 '64
Witches' pot; bobsled run at Igls. il Time 81:55 F 15 '63

COASTS

See also

Seashore

COAT hangers. See Clothes hangers

COATES, Eric

Coates, V. W, and Morton Gould on his mettle. J. Diether. Am Rec G 30:1032 Jl '64

COATES, Robert M.

Art galleries. See issues of New Yorker
Captive; story. New Yorker 39:36-46 My 25 '63
Different time, a different place; story. New Yorker 40:45-52 S 26 '64
Our far-flung correspondents. New Yorker 39: 176+ N 2 '63

COATING materials. See Finishing materials

COATINGS

Paint finds a new base. il Bsns W p 110-12+ F 8 '64

COATINGS, Protective. See Protective coatings

COATS

Buying guide to women's winter coats. Good H 157:204+ O '63
Can you launder your car coat? il Consumer Bul 47:26 O '64
Sheepskin wheels to the front. il Sports Illus 21:72-3 N 30 '64

COATS of arms. See Heraldry

COATSVILLE, Pa.

Summer Sunday; excerpt from Incident in Coatsville; with editorial comment. E. F. Goldman. il Am Heritage 15:50-3+ Je '64

CO-AUTHORSHIP. See Authorship—Collaboration

COAXIAL cables

Shielded cables. W. H. Buchsbaum. il Electr World 72:36-8+ N '64

COBALT

Isotopes

Cobalt dusting would defeat own purpose; no effect on airplanes or troops. Sci N L 85: 265 Ap 25 '64

COBB, Alan W.

Salt incorporation in natural ices. Science 141:733 Ag 23 '63

COBB, Bernard R.

I learned about flying from that! Flying 74: 50+ Mr '64

COBB, Boughton, jr

Building a stock fiberglass cruiser. Yachting 117:70-2+ Ja '65
Fiberglass boats. See issues of Yachting
Hull; fiberglass. Yachting 115:43+ Ap '64
Large hole in a small boat. Yachting 115: 92-4+ Ja; 62-3+ F '64

COBB, Stanley
Death of a salt pond. por Audubon Mag 65: 70-2 Mr '63
COBB, Tyrus Raymond
My most unforgettable character. F. Haney. il por Read Digest 84:98-102 Je '64
COBB, W. Montague
New dawn in medicine. por Ebony 18:166-8+ S '63
COBIA. See Sergeant fish
COBIA fishing. See Sergeant fish fishing
COBLENTZ, Stanton A.
Battlements of terror. Christian Cent 81: 1329-31 O 28 '64
Successor to democracy. Christian Cent 81:78-80 Ja 15 '64
COBRA (group) See Painting, European
COBRA plants. See Pitcher plants
COBURN, J. R.
Use roller blinds as backgrounds. U S Camera 26:36 My '63
COBURN, John B.
Where did it go wrong? Christian Cent 81: 1040+ Ag 19 '64
COBWEB sempervivums. See Houseleeks
COCA-COLA company
Coke tries new ways to refresh. il Bsns W p 100-1+ Ag 24 '63
Kvass vs. Coke. New Yorker 40:33-4 Je 6 '64
Pepsi v. Coke. il Time 82:101-2 O 18 '63
Project alpha; promotion of dietetic soda pop, Tab. New Yorker 40:33-4 Mr 14 '64
COCCIDAE. See Scale insects
COCCIDIOIDOMYCOSIS. See Fungi. Pathogenic
COCCIDIOSIS
Feed lot problem coccidiosis. J. B. Herrick. Suc Farm 61:86 S '63
COCCINELLIDAE. See Ladybirds
COCCOLITHS, Fossil. See Flagellates, Fossil
COCH, Nicholas K. See Oaks, R. Q. jr. jt. auth.
COCHELL, Shirley
From Alice to Animal farm. Sr Schol 85: 10T S 16 '64
Income tax in the classroom. Sr Schol 82:5T Ap 3 '63
Jackrabbit homesteading. Sr Schol 84:12T F 7 '64
Making the most of literature notebooks. Sr Schol 84:12T Ap 10 '64
Martians in the classroom. Sr Schol 82:9T-10T Mr 6 '63
Monologues. Sr Schol 83:10T O 25 '63
Vocational counseling in the classroom. Sr Schol 85:7T O 28 '64
Writing colorful descriptions. Sr Schol 85: 12T N 18 '64
COCHRAN, Fred
Traveling study collections. Sr Schol 85:21T Ja 21 '65
COCHRAN, Gerald L.
Bottoms up. Yachting 115:144-6 F '64
COCHRAN, Jacqueline
Sweet explosion in the air. P. Ress. il por Sports Illus 19:16-17 Jl 8 '63
COCHRAN, Kenneth W. See Maassab, H. F. jt. auth.
COCHRAN, Tom
My most unforgettable character. Read Digest 85:90-4 Jl '64
COCHRANE, Arthur C.
Deepening the dialogue. Christian Cent 81: 1111 S 9 '64
COCHRANE, John D.
Equatorial undercurrent and related currents off Brazil in March and April 1963. bibliog Science 142:669-71 N 8 '63
COCKCROFT, Sir John
Churchill college, a modern university college. Science 146:502-4 O 23 '64
COCKING, Walter
Obituary
Sr Schol 84:4T Ja 31 '64
COCKNEY English. See English language—Dialects
COCKNEY rhyming slang. See Slang
COCKPITS. See Airplane cockpits
COCKROACHES
Carbohydrate digestion in the cockroach. W. M. Banks. bibliog il Science 141:1191-2 S 20 '63
Cockroach brain surgery. Sci N L 85:174 Mr 14 '64
Defense of mate and mating chamber in a wood roach. H. Ritter, jr. Science 143:1459-60 Mr 27 '64
Inquiline roach responds to trail-marking substance of leaf-cutting ants. J. C. Moser. il Science 143:1048-9 Mr 6 '64
Isolation and identification of the sex attraction of the American cockroach. M. Jacobson and others; reply with rejoinder. D. R. A. Wharton and others. bibliog Science 142: 1257-8+ D 6 '63
Long live the cockroach. E. J. Ritter. il Sci Digest 54:41-4 N '63
Olfactory receptor response to the cockroach sexual attractant. J. Boeckh and others. bibliog il Science 141:716 Ag 23 '63
Outer space enroached. W. Wingo. il(p 161) Sci N L 84:165 S 14 '63
Regenerating tissues from the cockroach leg: a system for studying in vitro. E. P. Marks and J. P. Reinecke. bibliog il Science 143: 961-3 F 28 '64
Triumph of Archy the Cockroach. J. D. Ratcliff. il Read Digest 82:37-8+ My '63
Uric acid in the reproductive system of males of the cockroach blatella germanica. L. M. Roth and G. P. Dateo, jr. bibliog il Science 146:782-4 N 6 '64

Extermination

Safe spray banishes pool bugs; Richmond, Calif. T. M. Wilson. il Am City 79:33 O '64
COCKSCOMB
Celosia, an easily grown annual with flowers of unusual form and vivid colors. M. M. Taylor. il Horticulture 41:246 My '63
COCKTAIL party conversation. See Conversation—Anecdotes, facetiae, satire, etc.
COCKTAILS
Barman; head bartender of the St Regis. New Yorker 40:19-20 Jl 18 '64
Changing cocktail. E. Kinard. il House B 105:12+ F '63
Delightful drinks for breakfast and brunch parties. J. A. Beard. il House & Gard 123: 184-6 Ap '63
New drinks for new and dangerous times. il Esquire 59:72-3 Mr '63; Reply. B. Egorov. 61:99 Ja '64
COCOA BEACH, Fla.
Birds of Cocoa Beach. B. Thielen. Holiday 35: 64-5+ Je '64
See also
Proving grounds
COCONUT
Polynesian palmistry; excerpt from Two-thirds of a coconut tree. H. A. Smith. Sat R 46:70 Mr 16 '63
COCOONS
Enzymatic mechanism for the escape of certain moths from their cocoons. F. C. Kafatos and C. M. Williams. bibliog il Science 146:538-40 O 23 '64
COCOS ISLAND
Anyone for buried treasure? J. Iams. il Sat Eve Post 237:64-6 Je 13 '64
COCTEAU, Jean
To the young of 2000 A.D.; a prophecy told to Pierre Laforêt, tr. by A. Foulke. Vogue 143:72-5+ Ja 1 '64

about

Adieu and adieu. por Newsweek 62:81 O 21 '63
Appreciation of Jean Cocteau. W. Sorell. il pors Dance Mag 38:38-41 F '64
Hommage à Monsieur Jean. H. Kenner. Nat R 15:441+ N 19 '63
Letter from Paris. Genêt. New Yorker 39:200-2+ N 2 '63
Obituary
Nation 197:282 N 2 '63. H. Clurman
Pub W 184:32 O 21 '63
Poet and the boxer. R. Cantwell; G. Peeters. il Sports Illus 20:62-72 Mr 2 '64
Sparrow & the dilettante. por Time 82:38+ O 18 '63
COD, CAPE. See Cape Cod
COD fishing
Patient madmen of Sheepshead Bay. A. Zich. il Sports Illus 18:18-23 F 4 '63
CODDINGTON, Dean C. See Mahar, J. F. jt. auth.
CODE practice oscillators. See Oscillators
CODES (ciphers) See Ciphers
CODES, Housing. See Housing laws and legislation
CODES, Number. See Numbering systems
CODES for calculating machines. See Calculating machines
CODES of behavior. See Children—Management and training
CODLING moths
Good-by codling moth? G. Lorang. Farm J 88:54 O Ap '64
CODY, William Frederick
Buffalo Bill's home town. E. Waldron. por Holiday 34:85-91 Ag '63

CODY, Wyo.
Buffalo Bill's home town. E. Waldron. Holiday 34:85-91 Ag '63
COE, Darrell L.
Old Faithful's winter plume. il Nat Parks Mag 37:8-9 Mr '63
COE, Lee
Eclipse travel to Alaska and western Canada. Sky & Tel 25:202-3 Ap '63
COE, Michael D.
Chinampas of Mexico; with biographical sketch. Sci Am 211:15, 90-8 Jl '64
—and Flannery, K. V.
Microenvironments and Mesoamerican prehistory. bibliog Science 143:650-4 F 14 '64
COE, Peter
Vacuum-packed theater. R. Gilman. Commonweal 79:404 D 27 '63
COEDS. See College students. Women
COEDUCATION
Notes and comment. New Yorker 40:25 Ja 23 '65
Sex differences and education. W. B. Kolesnik. America 108:552-5 Ap 20 '63
COELACANTHS
Coelacanth saga; extinct fish found alive. M. Bracker. il N Y Times Mag p84+ O 6 '63
COENZYMES
Coenzyme Q: intracellular distribution in rhodospirillum rubrum. A. F. Greene and J. P. Mascarenhas. bibliog il Science 144: 1455-6 Je 19 '64
Coenzyme Q: reversal of inhibition of succinate cytochrome c reductase by lipophilic compounds. S. Takemori and T. E. King. bibliog il Science 144:852-3 My 15 '64
COESITE
Coesite and shocked quartz from Holleford Crater, Ontario, Canada. T. E. Bunch and A. J. Cohen. bibliog il Science 142:379-81 O 18 '63
COEUR D'ALENE
Idaho's Coeur d'Alene country. E. De Roo. il Travel 121:42-4 My '64
COEXISTENCE. See International relations
CO-EXISTENCE policy. See United States—Foreign relations—Russia
COFFEE
Break with coffee? medical warning against heavy coffee drinking. il Newsweek 63: 68+ F 17 '64
Bring on the coffee. il House & Gard 125:134-5 F '64
Coffee and your heart. Sci Digest 54:55 O '63
Coffeehouse party. il Ladies Home J 80:107-8 N '63
How coffee gets the way you like it. il Good H 157:145 Ag '63
How much coffee in the pot? il Changing T 17:46 S '63
Secret of perfect coffee. House & Gard 125: 136 F '64
Turkish coffee; with recipe. M. Kaytor. il Look 28:88+ Je 16 '64
See also
Caffeine
COFFEE cake
Serve a piece of coffee cake. il Sunset 130: 204+ Ap '63
Successful recipes. il Suc Farm 62:97-8 Ja '64
Sweet breads you bake in fancy molds. il Sunset 130:114-18 Mr '63
Walnut whirl. R. Behnke. il Farm J 87:62 S '63
COFFEE cups. See Cups
COFFEE houses
Getting involved; exchange of religious ideas at coffee houses. il Newsweek 63:76 Ja 20 '64
COFFEE pots, percolators, etc.
Automatic coffee-makers. il Consumer Rep 29:528-32 N '64
Coffee makers. il McCalls 91:130 F '64
Stronger coffee, but not so instant; Insta-Brewer and Melior. il Consumer Rep 30:5 Ja '65
Universal Regency; new coffee maker that does not stain. il Consumer Bul 47:43 F '64
COFFEE tables. See Tables
COFFEE trade
Department supports legislation to implement coffee agreement; statement, February 25, 1964. W. A. Harriman. Dept State Bul 50: 459-62 Mr 23 '64
High cost of coffee. il Time 84:80 Ag 28 '64
International coffee agreement, 1962; statement, March 12, 1963. G. C. McGhee. Dept State Bul 48:493-7 Ap 1 '63
Less coffee in the cup; international coffee agreement. H. Hazlitt. Newsweek 61:72 Ap 1 '63
Role of the international coffee agreement in today's market; address, January 20, 1964. J. Jacobson. Dept State Bul 50:260-3 F 17 '64
Terms of trade and the Brazilian balance of payments; address, January 29, 1963. L. Gordon. il Dept State Bul 48:289-91 F 25 '63
U.S. indicates intention to ratify international coffee agreement. Dept State Bul 49:109 Jl 15 '63
U.S. to propose action to halt rise in coffee prices; Department statement, January 10, 1964. Dept State Bul 50:143 Ja 27 '64
World coffee agreement and U.S. foreign economic policy; address, January 14, 1963. W. M. Blumenthal. Dept State Bul 48:218-23 F 11 '63
See also
Mexico—Industries
COFFEE trees
Wind without pity; ruin of Brazil's crop. Time 82:67 Ag 23 '63
COFFEE vending machines. See Vending machines
COFFEY, Junior
Fullbacks in motion. H. L. Masin. por Sr Schol 85:44 N 11 '64
COFFEY, Lillian Brooks
Woman on the go for God. L. S. Calhoun. il pors Ebony 18:78-81+ My '63
COFFEY, Patricia V.
Booklists: bugaboo or boon? Wilson Lib Bul 37:855-6 Je '63
COFFEY, Tom
My private war with Hoffa. por Sat Eve Post 237:68-70 Ja 4 '64
COFFEY, Warren
Faith and the issues. Commentary 37:82-5 Mr '64
COFFIELD, John V.
Exile from Los Angeles. por Newsweek 65:57 Ja 11 '65
Priestly witness. America 112:66 Ja 16 '65
Priest's protest. por Time 85:36 Ja 8 '65
COFFIN, Frank M.
Aid and the national interest; address, August 1, 1963. Vital Speeches 29:719-21 S 15 '63
Some perspectives on the current debates on aid; address, September 11, 1963. Dept State Bul 49:514-19 S 30 '63
COFFIN, Patricia
Fabulous, feudal Portugal. Look 28:72-85+ My 19 '64
High wind; poem. Harper 228:100 Ap '64
Lullaby; poem. McCalls 92:124 Ja '65
COFFIN, Robert P. Tristram
Reunion at Thanksgiving; story. PTA Mag 59:19-20 N '64
COFFIN, Tristram
Department of justice. Holiday 33:94-5+ Mr '63
Leo Szilard: the conscience of a scientist. Holiday 35:64-7+ F '64
Senator Fulbright. Holiday 36:34-7+ S '64
COFFIN, William Sloane, jr
Moral values and our universities; excerpts from address, 1964. NEA J 54:8-10 Ja '65
Stand up for what you believe in. Parents Mag 38:49+ D '63
COFFINS
Wood for eternity. F. Korotkin. il Am For 70:28-9 D '64
COFFMAN, Tom
We want Wallace. New Repub 151:14 Jl 11 '64
COFFYN, Frank Trenholm
This one-man flying circus thrilled New York. G. Soule. il por Pop Sci 183:210-12 S '63
COFIELD, Tom
Modern boats and model-T boating. Motor B 113:46+ Je '64
COGAN, David H.
Every man for himself. por Bsns W p84+ S 19 '64
COGAN, Henry
(tr) See Mendes Pinto, F. Voyages and adventures of Ferdinand Mendez Pinto
COGEN, Charles
Scholastic teacher interview; ed. by H. Langer. por Sr Schol 85:7T-8T N 4 '64
about
Big little man. Newsweek 64:71 Ag 31 '64
COGGAN, Blanche
Underground railroad in Michigan. Negro Hist Bul 27:122-6 F '64
COGGESHALL, Roger G.
Summer propagation. Horticulture 42:40-1 Je '64
COGGIN, Mary. See Coggin, T. jt. auth.
COGGIN, Ted, and Coggin, Mary
When cruising the West Indies. Yachting 114: 121 D '63
COGGINS, Cecil H.
Is Russia outstripping us in weapons of mass destruction? address, December 7, 1962. Vital Speeches 29:263-6 F 15 '63

COGLEY, John
Another Saint Francis? Pope John. Commonweal 78:367-9 Je 28 '63
Conversational letter. Commonweal 81:12-14 S 25 '64
Grounds for hope. Commonweal 79:398-400 D 27 '63
Here and there. See occasional issues of Commonweal to October 23, 1964
John A. Ryan: pioneer of Catholic social thought. Commonweal 78:24-5 Mr 29 '63
Layman rediscovered. Commonweal 79:253-5 N 22 '63
Layman's tribute; John XXIII. America 108:856 Je 15 '63
Pacem in terris. Commonweal 80:639 S 18 '64
Poems on postcards. See issues of America to February 8, 1964
Prevalence of violence. Commonweal 79:481-3 Ja 24 '64
Roman diary. America 111:348-51 S 26 '64
Vatican II re-educates the American bishops. N Y Times Mag p35+ N 22 '64
COGNAC. See Brandy
COHALAN, F. D.
Facts are in. Nat R 14:499 Je 18 '63
COHANE, John Philip
Monster; story. Mlle 58:90-1 Ja '64
COHEN, Abraham B.
Constant-voltage sound-distribution systems. Electr World 70:29-32 Jl '63
COHEN, Alexander H.
Alexander H. Cohen: bigger than Barnum. R. Gehman. il pors Theatre Arts 47:20-2+ O '63
Cut to the chase. por Newsweek 61:99 Ap 15 '63
COHEN, Alvin J. See Bunch, T. E. jt. auth.
COHEN, Arthur A.
Hugo Rahner's pursuit of Christian archetypes. Commonweal 79:605-6 F 14 '64
COHEN, Bertram D. See Rosenberg, S. jt. auth.
COHEN, C. J. and Hubbard, E. C.
Libration of Pluto-Neptune. bibliog Science 145:1302-3 S 18 '64
COHEN, Carl
Essence and ethics of civil disobedience. Nation 198:257-62 Mr 16 '64
COHEN, Carolyn, and others
Paracrystalline forms of fibrinogen. bibliog Science 141:436-8 Ag 2 '63
COHEN, Daniel
Behind Cleopatra. Sci Digest 53:5-10 Je '63
Science milestone; Heinrich Schliemann archaeologist extraordinary. Sci Digest 53:79-86 Mr '63
COHEN, David
On comforting a child; poem. Nation 196:295 Ap 6 '63
Plainview welcomes paperbacks. bibliog por Library J 90:306-8 Ja 15 '65
COHEN, Edward P. and Parks, J. J.
Antibody production by nonimmune spleen cells incubated with RNA from immunized mice. bibliog Science 144:1012-13 My 22 '64
COHEN, Elaine Pear
Thoughts on teaching art in the elementary school. Sch Arts 62:33-5 F '63
COHEN, Eli, and Fremon, Suzanne
Will there be jobs for our children? Parents Mag 38:58-9+ N '63
COHEN, Ellis N. and others
Impurity in halothane anesthetic. bibliog Science 141:899 S 6 '63
COHEN, Hennig
How green was our valley. Sat R 48:32 Ja 16 '65
COHEN, I. Bernard
Man who looked to the stars. N Y Times Mag p 19-20+ F 9 '64
COHEN, J. John, and others
Diphtheria antitoxin: antigen-combining and toxin-neutralizing properties of papain fragments. bibliog Science 144:1585-6 Je 26 '64
COHEN, J. M.
Tree of images. Nation 198:199-200 F 24 '64
COHEN, Jacob Gershon-. See Gershon-Cohen, J.
COHEN, John
Psychological time; with biographical sketch. Sci Am 211:24, 116-22+ bibliog(p 156) N '64
COHEN, Joseph W.
New college honors programs; excerpt from address. NEA J 52:49-50 F '63
COHEN, Leon W.
Conference board of the mathematical sciences. Science 140:416-17 Ap 26 '63
Manpower problems: training of mathematicians. Science 140:1111-13 Je 7 '63
COHEN, Manuel Frederick
Career cop. por Time 84:74 Jl 17 '64
Chip off the shoulder. Newsweek 64:78 D 14 '64
LBJ stamp on SEC. por Bsns W p26-7 Jl 18 '64
No hostility in Securities report. U S News 54:97 Ap 1 '63
Up from within. Newsweek 64:64 Jl 20 '64
COHEN, Marcel
Art of writing. UNESCO Courier 17:4-7+ Mr '64
COHEN, Martin
Free for all at the fair. Redbook 123:58-9+ Je '64
Skiing, a family affair. Redbook 122:28+ Ja '64
COHEN, Milton H.
Big board is under fire; special study of the securities markets. il Bsns W p23-4 Jl 20 '63
For Wall Street: tighter rules, fewer secrets; special study of securities markets. il por Bsns W p23-5 Ap 6 '63
COHEN, Nathan
Theater. Nat R 16:289-90, 780-1, 982-3 Ap 7, S 8, N 3 '64
COHEN, Octavus Roy
Landfalls ahead! Travel 123:48-51 Ja '65
COHEN, Robert David
Bones of incontention; poem. New Yorker 40:38 Ag 22 '64
Song for my first child; Noah. New Yorker 40:34 Je 27 '64
COHEN, Ruth
What's their line? Sr Schol 85:10T O 28 '64
COHEN, Sanford, and Pyle, W. C.
Indiana program of job training and work experience for students; excerpt. Mo Labor R 86:161-3 F '63
COHEN, Selma Jeanne
Philippine songs. Sat R 47:61 Je 27 '64
Reviews See occasional issues of Dance magazine
COHEN, Seymour S.
On biochemical variability and innovation; text of paper presented at a symposium on the general physiology of specialized cells. bibliog Science 139:1017-26 Mr 15 '63
COHEN, Sheldon S.
Money men in key spots. por Newsweek 65:63 Ja 11 '65
People of the week. por U S News 58:15 Ja 11 '65
Two are tapped for Treasury. por Bsns W p58 Ja 2 '65
COHEN, Stanley E.
What ails the post office? Nation 197:364-7 N 30 '63
COHEN, Theodore J. See Schmidt, R. A. jt. auth.
COHEN, Wilbur J.
Medical care for the aged. bibliog f Cur Hist 45:98-103+ Ag '63
COHEN, William D. See Glick, J. L. jt. auth.
COHN, Arthur
Electronic music. Am Rec G 30:924-5+ Je '64
Feast of fascinations by Henry Cowell. Am Rec G 30:476-7+ F '64
How Swiss is Swiss music? Am Rec G 29:520-1 Mr '63
Music of Arnold Schoenberg. Am Rec G 30:192-4 N '63
Music of Arnold Schoenberg: now, volume II. Am Rec G 30:394-5 Ja '64
Nine Dutch composers. Am Rec G 29:610-12+ Ap '63
On Cambridge, CRI, and Vox, that supremely individual creative genius, Chas. E. Ives. Am Rec G 30:760-2+ My '64
Stockhausen's Kontakte on DGG; a telling experience. Am Rec G 29:952+ Ag '63
Symphony no. 3 Kaddish; to the beloved memory of John F. Kennedy. Am Rec G 30:1014-15 Jl '64
COHN, Charles Erwin
Add a TV D.C. restorer. Electr World 70:78+ O '63
COHN, Lawrence
Blues; three of a kind. Sat R 46:97+ Mr 16 '63
Bookshelf of the blues. Sat R 47:49+ Je 13 '64
New faces in folk music. Sat R 46:56-7 N 16 '63
Recordings reports (cont) Sat R 46:44 F 9; 50 Je 29; 42 Ag 31 '63; 47:58 Mr 28; 81 O 17 '64
Sad day in Texas and other folk matter. Sat R 47:66-7 N 14 '64
Tribute to a Titan. Sat R 46:57 Je 15 '63
COHN, Marcus
Religion and the FCC. Reporter 32:32-4 Ja 14 '65
COHN, Roy Marcus
Cohn on the defense. Newsweek 63:24+ Ap 6 '64
Cohn's costly toy. por Time 81:88 Mr 22 '63
Death in the family. il Time 83:76 My 1 '64
Everybody's laughing; mistrial. por Newsweek 63:24+ My 4 '64

COHN, Roy Marcus—*Continued*
Fear of high places. Time 84:44 Jl 24 '64
Going which way? il por Time 82:27-8 S 13 '63
Here we go again; more investigations. W. F. Buckley, jr. Nat R 15:272 O 8 '63
Low blow. Nation 198:255 Mr 16 '64
Point of order. por Newsweek 63:21 Mr 2 '64
Rendezvous of the federal prosecutors. M. Kempton. New Repub 150:6-7 Ap 18 '64
Roy and reaction. por Newsweek 62:69 S 16 '63
Roy Cohn. M. Kempton. New Repub 148:15-17 Ap 20 '63
Roy Cohn: is he a liar under oath? with report by K. Wheeler and W. Lambert. il pors Life 55:24-31+ O 4 '63
Trouble catches up with Roy Cohn. il pors Bsns W p32+ S 14 '63
Winner. Newsweek 64:31-2 Jl 27 '64

COHOSH. See Black snakeroot

COIFFURE. See Hairdressing

COILS, Electric. See Electric coils

COILS, Radio. See Radio coils

COIN (counter insurgency aircraft) See Airplanes, Military—United States

COIN operated dry cleaning machines. See Dry cleaning machines

COIN-operated machines. See Jukeboxes

COIN-operated washers and dryers. See Laundries, Commercial

COIN-tossing. See Superstitions

COINAGE. See Silver as money

COINER, Charles T.
Love letter to the Miramichi. Esquire 60:116-19+ S '63

COINS
About that coin shortage. U S News 56:84-5 Je 22 '64
Can ya spare a dime? nationwide coin shortage. il Newsweek 63:36+ Je 15 '64
Coin quiz. C. French. See issues of Hobbies
Coin shortage: why it happened; when it will end; interview. R. A. Wallace. il U S News 57:68-70 Jl 27 '64
Gold for numismatic purposes. C. French. Hobbies 69:102+ Mr '64
Great coin shortage; interview. T. O. Waage; R. Pratt. il Read Digest 86:31-2+ Ja '65
Great coin shortage: what is being done. il U S News 57:12 Jl 13 '64
High art of portraiture on Roman coins. M. Grant. il Horizon 5:33-41 S '63
Monies of antiquity; Greek coins. J. Fagerlie. il Natur Hist 73:20-5 Ja '64
Nation that is short on change; U.S. in coin shortage. il Bsns W p34+ Je 13 '64
Nice piece of change; Canadian coins. Time 85:35 Ja 15 '65
Numismatics. C. French. See issues of Hobbies
Stainless steel coins? il Sci Digest 56:12 D '64
To coin a phrase: E pluribus unum; U.S. coins. il Sr Schol 84:7 Ap 10 '64
See also
Silver as money

Collectors and collecting

Boom times for piggy-bankers. W. Laas and T. Du Bay. il Sat Eve Post 237:66+ F 15 '64
Changes in coin collecting. C. French. Hobbies 67:102+ F '63
Coin collecting by major types. C. French. Hobbies 68:102 Je '63
Coin-collecting craze. il Changing T 18:17-19 Ag '64
Coin shortage: bad; and getting worse. il U S News 56:6 Ap 6 '64
It's not just money. il Time 82:53 Ag 23 '63
Life guide; U.S. numismatics. il Life 54:15 F 22 '63
Mr Coin Collector: he has them all. il Look 28:54-5 D 29 '64
Money changers; Treasury releases silver dollars. il Newsweek 63:27 Ap 6 '64
Money menagerie; Chase Manhattan bank's money museum. il N Y Times Mag p 127 S 8 '63
Notes on coin collecting. C. French. Hobbies 68:102 N '63
Silver rush; new John F. Kennedy half dollars; dwindling supply of silver dollars. il Newsweek 63:62 Mr 30 '64
Turning cartwheels. il Time 83:60+ Ap 3 '64
Turning cartwheels; silver-dollar sale stopped. il Bsns W p27-8 Mr 28 '64
$25,000 handful of change; assembled by Stack's coin co of New York. il Look 27:49-50 F 26 '63
When a nickel is worth a small fortune; speculation or investment? il Bsns W p 132+ D 14 '63

Anecdotes, facetiae, satire, etc.

One man's search for free silver. M. Kitman. il Sat Eve Post 236:78+ O 26 '63

COIT, Anna N.
Problem in pruning is people. Pop Gard 14:51+ Mr '63

COIT, Lew G.
Why buy growth stocks? Changing T 18:7-11 F '64

COIT, Margaret L.
Great presidents are lucky accidents. Look 28:43-4+ Jl 14 '64
He ruled and raised the clan. Sat R 47:20-2 D 19 '64
Magic mail of John and Abigail. Sat R 46:24-5 Ag 10 '63
Partisan review of democracy. Sat R 47:34+ Mr 28 '64

COKER, George J.
Catering Cokers. New Yorker 40:46 D 12 '64

COLA-type beverages. See Beverages

COLANGELO, Joseph G. jr
How to fold a newspaper. Reporter 30:45-7 Ja 16 '64
Second battle of Homestead. Reporter 29:29-31 Jl 18 '63

COLAS, René
Can we stop the cancer of river pollution? UNESCO Courier 17:22-7 Jl '64

COLBERT, Claudette
Claudette Colbert's other home in the sun. il House B 106:98-101 Ja '64

COLBERT, Edwin H.
Dinosaurs of the Arctic. Natur Hist 73:20-3 Ap '64

COLBERT, Ella Mae
Hurricane in paper collage. Sch Arts 63:40 O '63

COLBERT, Frances
What fun it is to garden. Pop Gard 14:57+ S '63

COLBURN, Edwin B.
Committee on Wilson indexes: how it works. ALA Bul 59:35-6+ Ja '65

COLBY, Carroll B.
Camping. See issues of Outdoor life
Carroll B. Colby and his factual books for youngsters. il Pub W 183:128-9 F 18 '63

COLBY, Roy
Communist take-over of Algeria. por U S News 57:52-3 Ag 31 '64

COLBY, S. R. and Warren, G. F.
Herbicides: combination enhances selectivity. bibliog Science 141:362 Jl 26 '63

COLCHICINE
Generalized Shwartzman reaction in the pregnant golden hamster. M. Galton. bibliog il Science 139:923-4 Mr 8 '63

COLCHICUMS. See Autumn crocuses

COLD
Hot and cold quiz. J. Daugherty and M. Daugherty. il Sci Digest 57:83-5 Ja '65
See also
Low temperature research
Low temperatures

Physiological effects

Cold no longer problem in frozen Polar Regions. Sci N L 85:105 F 15 '64

Therapeutic applications

Chilling during radiation aids cancer treatment. Sci N L 85:8 Ja 4 '64
First aid; when to use cold. C. J. Potthoff. Todays Health 42:68 S '64
Immortality by freezing. F. Marley. Sci N L 85:389 Je 20 '64
Prospect of immortality, by R. C. W. Ettinger. Review
Sci Digest 56:46 Ag '64. D. Cohen
To freeze or not to freeze? duodenal ulcers. Time 82:48+ N 8 '63

COLD (disease)
Antibiotics: experts question value in treating colds; FDA issues ban on use in compounds. E. Langer. Science 141:791 Ag 30 '63
Battling the common cold; Vick chemical company. E. M. McCabe. il Parents Mag 38:37+ N '63
Best way to cope with a cold. G. G. Greer. Bet Hom & Gard 42:105 F '64
Complex epidemiology of respiratory virus infections. C. H. Andrewes. bibliog Science 146:1274-7 D 4 '64
Gesundheit! cold comfort. Seventeen 22:128-9+ F '63
It's hard to fake a cold at NIH. Sci N L 83:376 Je 15 '63
No quick cure for common cold. Bsns W p43 Ja 26 '63
Prevent common colds: experimental inhalant, viractin. F. Marley. Sci N L 86:355 D 5 '64

COLD (disease)—*Continued*

Vaccines

Foresee cold vaccine. Sci N L 86:355 D 5 '64
Study new cold vaccine. Sci N L 83:370 Je 15 '63
Vaccine for acute colds; adenovirus vaccine. Sci N L 86:404 D 26 '64

COLD-blooded vertebrates. See Vertebrates
COLD cuts. See Meat
COLD drinks. See Beverages
COLD forging. See Forging
COLD frames
Build a cold frame for year-round use. S. W. Plimpton. il Horticulture 41:468 S '63
Cold frame convert. M.M. Leister. il Flower Grower 50:56-7 Mr '63
Coldframes. R. L. Hering. il Pop Gard 16:16-18 Ja '65
Make a lightweight cold frame cover. R. D. Donaldson. il Flower Grower 51:43 Mr '64
Trap the sun in a coldframe. il Pop Gard 15:58-9 Mr '64
See also
Flats, etc (horticulture)
COLD remedies. See Medicines, Patent, proprietary, etc.
COLD soups. See Soups
COLD treatment of steel. See Steel—Cold working
COLD war. See Communism and democracy; Psychological warfare
COLD war (United States and Russia) See United States—Foreign relations—Russia; Russia—Foreign relations—United States
COLD weather
As freak weather hit all around the globe. il U S News 54:10 F 4 '63
Coldest place on earth; Oymyakon in Siberia. B. Vandano. il Life 58:80-3 Ja 22 '65
Endless freeze; effect of high-altitude wind patterns. il Newsweek 61:47 F 4 '63
Europe's wildest winter. G. Kent. il Read Digest 83:198-201+ S '63
Extreme cold engulfs U.S; Breaking some records but not snow. A. Ewing. Sci N L 83:83 F 9 '63
Opinion, please from London. A. Alvarez. il Mile 58:99-100 N '63
Why we freeze. Bsns W p34 F 2 '63
See also
Winter
COLD weather clothing. See Clothing, Cold weather
COLD weather operations (military) See Military art and science
COLD wind and the warm; story. See Bradbury, R.
COLDFRAMES. See Cold frames
COLDS. See Cold (disease)
COLE, Charles L. and Adkisson, P. L.
Daily rhythm in the susceptibility of an insect to a toxic agent. bibliog Science 144:1148-9 My 29 '64
COLE, Clayton
It's gone silly! Dance Mag 37:35 D '63
COLE, Dandridge M.
Asteroids stir growing interest. Miss & Roc 12:43+ F 25 '63
Mercury, deep freeze of the solar system. por Sat R 47:54-5 F 1 '64
Mercury missions seen more useful than Mars, Venus probes. Miss & Roc 12:34+ Je 24 '63
COLE, Darryl Glenn
Italian colonists in Costa Rica. Américas 15:38-41 Je '63
COLE, David L.
Now Cole takes on automation. A. H. Raskin. il pors N Y Times Mag p26+ Ap 5 '64
COLE, Ed
Ed Cole; the man who hits on all cylinders. por Newsweek 61:69 F 25 '63
COLE, George
Who's who in foreign business. il por Fortune 69:60 My '64
COLE, Jack
It's gone silly! C. Cole. Dance Mag 37:35 D '63
COLE, Leonard J. See Davis, W. E. jr; Nowell, P. C; Tyan, M. L. jt. auths.
COLE, Mabel K.
Where a friend counts most. Farm J 88:84 My '64
COLE, Marget Cochrane
Focus on folk art. Flower Grower 50:16-19 D '63
Line: living plant material. Flower Grower 50:51 My '63
Sunshine in November; easy-to-arrange mums. Am Home 67:10 N '64
COLE, Nat King
Nat King Cole twins. il pors Ebony 18:106-12+ Ag '63
COLE, O. J. See Ping, K. E. jt. auth.
COLE, Roger M.
Bacterial structure and replication. Science 146:554+ O 23 '64
Cell wall replication in salmonella typhosa. bibliog Science 143:820-2 F 21 '64
COLE, Thomas
Mark-up. Newsweek 64:80 D 21 '64
COLE, Tom
Local representative; story. Sat Eve Post 237:58-9 N 21 '64
COLEAN, Miles
1964 forecast: $28.6 billion for new buildings. Arch Forum 119:100-1 N '63
Truth about the cost of money for remodeling. House B 105:188-91 S '63
COLEBROOK, Joan
People of the slums. New Repub 148:18-22 Je 15; 15-18 Je 29 '63
COLEMAN, Elliott
Mockingbirds at Fort McHenry; poem. Poetry 102:243-9 Jl '63
Poetry chronicle. J. B. Hall. Poetry 104:48 Ap '64
COLEMAN, Emily
Big brother watches over Tanglewood. N Y Times Mag p20+ Je 28 '64
From red barn to package and tent. N Y Times Mag p 12-13+ Jl 19 '64
Prima donna. Opera N 29:12-13 O 17 '64
Scaling the high C's with Birgit Nilsson. N Y Times Mag p22-3+ O 13 '63
Stokowski conducts a new life. N Y Times Mag p72+ D 6 '64
COLEMAN, Henry S.
Columbia college: report to headmasters, principals, and counselors, 1963. Sch & Soc 92:239-41 Sum '64
Columbia college: report to headmasters, principals, and counselors, 1962. Sch & Soc 91:148-9 Mr 23 '63
COLEMAN, James Plemon
Election issue who's against JFK most? por U S News 55:15 Ag 19 '63
COLEMAN, James S.
Surplus youth; a future without jobs. Nation 196:439-43 My 25 '63
COLEMAN, Ornette
Back from exile. il pors Time 85:43 Ja 22 '65
Jazz. W. Balliett. New Yorker 40:117-18+ Ja 16 '65
Play sincere. pors Newsweek 65:84 Ja 25 '65
COLEMAN, Patricia P.
At fun-filled fair: fire dances, flume rides, fanciful foods. Sr Schol 84:12T-13T Ap 3 '64
Q and A: student tours at the fair. Sr Schol 84:14T Ap 3 '64
Summertime is tourtime. Sr Schol 84:9T Ap 17 '64
Three Stratfords. Sr Schol 84:22T F 21 '64
Travel tips. Sr Schol 83:11T N 15; 18T D 13 '63; 84:4T Ja 31; 22T Mr 6; 5T My 8; 85:5T S 30 '64
COLEMAN, Thomas
Blessed Virgin Mary; poem. Commonweal 78:284 My 31 '63
COLEMAN, William T. See Bergwin, C. R. jt. auth.
COLER, Myron A.
Creative chat; Conference on education for creativity in the sciences. New Yorker 39:24-5 Je 15 '63
COLERIDGE, Samuel Taylor
Coleridge on himself. B. Deutsch. Poetry 102:128-30 My '63
Coleridge's star within the moon. J. Ashbrook. Sky & Tel 28:335 D '64
COLES, Robert
Child's question. New Repub 150:10-12 Ap 11 '64
How do the teachers feel? Sat R 47:72-3+ My 16 '64
In the South these children prophesy. Atlan 211:111-16 Mr '63
Journey into the mind of the lower depths. New Repub 150:11-12 F 15 '64
Mood and revelation in the South. New Repub 150:17-19 Ap 18 '64
Our streets of violence. New Repub 151:19-21 S 5 '64
Psychiatrists and the poor. Atlan 214:102-6 Jl '64
Question of Negro crime. Harper 228:134-6+ Ap '64
Racial identity in school children. Sat R 46:56-7+ O 19 '63
Terror-struck children. New Repub 150:11-13 My 30 '64
We will overcome. New Repub 151:13 Jl 11 '64
Who's blocking desegregation? New Repub 148:17-20 Je 22 '63
Youth: opportunity to be what? New Repub 151:59-64 N 7 '64

COLES, Robert—*Continued*

about

Integration; what happens to the kids? il por Time 82:46+ Ag 16 '63

COLETTE, Sidonie Gabrielle
Regarde. Time 82:126 O 18 '63

COLETTI, Barbara
(comp) Bard in Britain. Sat R 47:95-6 Mr 14 '64
Traveler's tales. Sat R 47:84-5 O 10 '64

COLEUS
Coleus in and out. H. Guzelis. il Flower Grower 50:67-8 Ap '63
Coleus rainbow from a packet of seed. M. C. Ohlander. il Flower Grower 52:29 Ja '65

COLEY, Curtis G.
Delectable foothills of Spanish painting. Art N 62:22-5+ Mr '63

COLGATE, Lee
Coming of age in Glen Oaks; story. Good H 156:70-1 Mr '63

COLGATE Palmolive company
Mr Hard Sell. il Time 84:102+ D 4 '64

COLGATE university, Hamilton, N.Y.
New Colgate plan of education. Sch & Soc 92:115 Mr 21 '64
Rudolph designs for Colgate. il Arch Rec 135:10 My '64

COLGROVE, Melba. See Shelton, C. R.

COLIE, R. L.
Johan Huizinga and the task of cultural history. bibliog f Am Hist R 69:607-30 Ap '64

COLINVAUX, Paul A.
Origin of ice ages: pollen evidence from Arctic Alaska. bibliog Science 145:707-8 Ag 14 '64

COLITIS
Colitis: causes and treatment. Good H 157:142 Ag '63

COLITT, Leslie R.
Berlin's new outlook. Nation 197:236-8 O 19 '63

COLL, Jerome
After four centuries. America 110:567-9 Ap 25 '64

COLLABORATION, Literary. See Authorship—Collaboration

COLLABORATION with the enemy. See Treason

COLLADO, Emilio G.
Economic development through private enterprise. For Affairs 41:708-20 Jl '63
What's behind the balance-of-payments problem? Sat R 47:34+ Ja 11 '64

COLLAGE
Collage. E. J. Keats. il Horn Bk 40:269-72 Je '64
Collage. S. E. Wider. il Sch Arts 63:16-17 D '63
Collage by Kurt Schwitters. K. Kuh. il Sat R 46:37 F 23 '63
Collage characters. il Design 66:21-3 S '64
Profiles: R. Rauschenberg. C. Tomkins. il New Yorker 40:39-40+ F 29 '64

COLLAGEN
Aging of collagen. F. Verzár. il Sci Am 208: 104-8+ bibliog(p200) Ap '63
Calcified ectodermal collagens of shark tooth enamel and teleost scale. M. L. Moss and others. bibliog il Science 145:940-2 Ag 28 '64
Collagen-like protein in human plasma. H. Keiser and others. bibliog il Science 142: 1678-9 D 27 '63
Collagenolytic activity in mammalian bone. J. F. Woods and G. Nichols, jr. bibliog il Science 142:386-7 O 18 '63
Collagenolytic activity of intact and necrotic connective tissue. E. R. Goldstein and others. bibliog il Science 146:942-4 N 13 '64
Collagenous layer covering the crown enamel of unerupted permanent human teeth. P. T. Levine and others. bibliog il Science 146:1676-8 D 25 '64
Cross-linkages in collagen; report on workshop. R. R. Kohn and others. Science 145: 186-8 Jl 10 '64
Intermolecular cross-linking of collagen and the indentification of a new beta-component. P. Bornstein and others. bibliog il Science 144:1220-1 Je 5 '64; Reply with rejoinder. S. Bakerman. 145:837 Ag 21 '64
Thermal denaturation of collagen in the dispersed and solid state. J. Gross. bibliog il Science 143:960-1 F 28 '64

COLLARS
Swell neck; expandable collars. Newsweek 61:92-3 My 27 '63
Throw away the collar; paper collars and dickies. il Bsns W p67-8+ S 7 '63

COLLECTING. See Collectors and collecting

COLLECTING of taxes. See Tax collection

COLLECTIVE bargaining
Auto bargaining takes on a new complexion. il Bsns W p92+ N 7 '64
Brighter future for collective bargaining. E. R. Livernash. Harvard Bsns R 42:66-70 S '64
Buoyant UAW likes the odds. Bsns W p 124 Mr 14 '64
Case for Boulwarism. H. R. Northrup. bibliog f il Harvard Bsns R 41:86-97 S '63
Changed course in bargaining? U S News 54:94-5 Ap 29 '63
Collective bargaining; big steel passes a big test. il Newsweek 62:51-4 Jl 1 '63
Collective bargaining contracts in India. il Mo Labor R 86:300-1 Mr '63
Collective bargaining for public school teachers. Mo Labor R 87:1297-8 N '64
Collective bargaining: shift for the sixties. T. R. Brooks. il Duns R 82:30-2 Jl '63
Collective bargaining today. T. R. Brooks. Duns R 81:51-2 Je '63
Courts in conflict. T. R. Brooks. Duns R 82:74B D '63
Different way to deal with unions; GE with IUE. il U S News 55:120-1 O 7 '63
Economic dilemmas of collective bargaining. M. Rothbaum. bibliog f Ann Am Acad 350: 95-103 N '63
Effects of NLRB action on the duty to bargain; excerpt from address, May 27, 1964. F. W. McCulloch. Mo Labor R 87:895-8 Ag '64
Influences of employer bargaining associations in manufacturing. M. S. Wortman, jr. il Mo Labor R 86:272-3 Mr '63
Informed neutrals score a triumph; special mediators to reinforce collective bargaining. il Bsns W p43-4+ My 9 '64
IUE chief accuses GE; charge of Boulwarism. il Bsns W p71-2+ S 28 '63
Is labor's wage push more bark than bite? E. K. Faltermayer. il Fortune 69:100-3+ Je '64
Labor outlook hinges on government. il Nations Bsns 51:38-9+ D '63
LBJ brand on the bargaining table; success in rail settlement; with editorial comment. Bsns W p89-91, 124 My 2 '64
Managing your manpower; collective bargaining on the way out? T. R. Brooks. Duns R 82:51 S '63
Managing your manpower; potential problems in bargaining. T. R. Brooks. Duns R 83:75-6 Ja '64
Men who speak for UAW. il Bsns W p43-4+ Je 20 '64
Nationwide strike averted. Sr Schol 84:21 My 8 '64
New mood. il Time 81:89 My 24 '63
New problems for collective bargaining. L. Woodcock. Mo Labor R 86:271 Mr '63
New road opens; pre-bargaining study committee. il Newsweek 61:68+ Ap 29 '63
On the track ahead: a new crisis; railroad work rules. il Bsns W p 108-10+ Ap 11 '64
Rail settlement: a coup for LBJ. il Newsweek 63:67-8 My 4 '64
Railway bargaining. New Repub 150:5 Ap 25 '64
Settlement in steel. T. R. Brooks. Commonweal 78:449-52 Jl 26 '63
Steel will set bargaining pace. Bsns W p46 Ja 2 '65
Strike wanes as a weapon. il Bsns W p43-4 O 10 '64
Talk is brisk. il Bsns W p56 S 12 '64
Talking troubles out at the plant level: company-union dialogue idea. Bsns W p74+ O 19 '63
Tough bargaining, and not just in autos. Bsns W p47-8 Jl 11 '64
Union bargaining strength: Goliath or paper tiger? G. Strauss. bibliog f Ann Am Acad 350:86-94 N '63
Unions' new strategy for bigger bites: coordinated bargaining. Bsns W p 112 Je 13 '64
UAW changes target. il Bsns W p82+ S 5 '64
UAW leans hard on retirement. Bsns W p90 My 30 '64
UAW urges joint studies. Bsns W p81 Mr 30 '63
USW sees no strike: credit to Human relations committee. il Bsns W p29 F 23 '63
USW simmers as steel talks near. il Bsns W p47-8 N 21 '64
When teachers organize; appeal from an impasse; professional negotiation and collective bargaining. Mo Labor R 87:1295-6 N '64

COLLECTIVE bargaining—*Continued*
Where are the reformers? New York newspaper strike. W. F. Buckley, jr. Nat R 14: 227 Mr 26 '63
Why bargaining goes wrong. Life 55:4 Jl 19 '63
See also
Industrial relations
National railway labor conference
COLLECTIVE farms
Russia
Ah, poor Anany; excerpts from Round and about. F. Abramov. il Time 81:30-1 Ap 12 '63
COLLECTIVE security. See International security
COLLECTIVE settlements
Pad in Brooklyn Heights; Brooklyn's Brook farm. O. Evans. Nation 199:15-16 Jl 13 '64
Pitfalls of intentional community; individualism. F. D. Hall. Christian Cent 80:1000-2 Ag 14 '63
Israel
Visit with Ben Gurion in the desert; Sde Boker. W. G. Blair. il N Y Times Mag p 16+ Ja 12 '64
COLLECTORS and collecting
Antiques travel guide. See issues of Antiques
Bucks County home of Mr and Mrs Hiram D. Rickert; excerpt from Living with antiques, ed. by A. Winchester and others. il Antiques 84:306-11 S '63
Collectors display their collections. il Sunset 133:82+ S '64
Collectors' notes. E. Gaines. See issues of Antiques
Do you collect anything? any thing! il Seventeen 24:66-7 Ja '65
Grand tour. E. A. Standen. il Antiques 83: 660-4 Je '63
Harlem's antique collector. il Ebony 18:105-6+ Ap '63
He's got the whole world in his hands; collecting chemical elements. A. P. Armagnac. il Pop Sci 182:82-4 Je '63
On view: collections. M. White. il Ladies Home J 82:58-60 Ja '65
Rock-headed and glassy-eyed; rock-hounds at Prineville, Ore. and bottle collectors in Florida or out West. H. Sutton. il Sat R 47:26-7 D 19 '64
Serious collector of playfulness, and how he lives; home of A. Girard. il House B 105: 134-7 Ap '63
Speaker of the house: your personality; excerpts from Profession: housewife. P. McGinley. Ladies Home J 81:30+ My '64
Treasure from the junkyard. C. Kellogg. il Ladies Home J 80:156-8+ O '63
What do you collect? il Seventeen 23:82-3 Ja '64
See also
Antiques
Autographs
Miniature objects
also subhead Collectors and collecting under various subjects, e.g. Coins—Collectors and collecting
COLLEGE, Choice of
Antidotes for anguish; new types of guide to colleges. Time 84:58 N 6 '64
Applying for college, a guide for high school seniors. Changing T 18:6 O '64
Comparative guide to American colleges, for students, parents, and counselors, by J. Cass and M. Birnbaum. Review
Sat R 47:73-4 N 21 '64. A. Lass
Electronic fathers; computers counsel students. Newsweek 64:55 Jl 20 '64
Going to college. E. H. Miner. Sr Schol 85: 17-18 N 11 '64
How to visit a college. J. S. Diekhoff. il PTA Mag 57:20-2 Mr '63
Looking ahead to college and careers. J. Hawkes. See issues of Seventeen
On tour: tips to prospective campus visitors. Newsweek 62:70 Ag 26 '63
Should you pay for advice on college? il Changing T 18:25-8 D '64
What's the right college for your youngster? J. S. Diekhoff. il PTA Mag 57:4-6 F '63
Where is the ivy greenest? D. Klein. il Seventeen 22:142-3+ Ap '63
Who should go to college? M. C. McIntosh. il Sr Schol 83:16-17 N 8 '63
COLLEGE administration. See Colleges and universities—Administration
COLLEGE administrators. See College officials
COLLEGE admission. See Colleges and universities—Entrance requirements
COLLEGE and school drama
Life guide; college drama. Life 54:15-16 Mr 8 '63
Ring up the curtain on Christmas. D. K. Osborn. Parents Mag 38:65 D '63
Thoughts on university theater. R. A. Duprey. Cath World 198:71-2 O '63
Texts
Junior and senior high. See issues of Plays
COLLEGE and school journalism
Beyond make-believe; second annual SR-U.S. national student association magazine contest. S. B. Chickering. Sat R 47:28-9 O 10 '64
Campus conservative journals. R. Kirk. Nat R 16:449 Je 2 '64
Censorship on campus; a student's plea for granting responsible freedom to Catholic college editors. M. O'Connell. America 111: 611-13 N 14 '64; Discussion. 112:17-18, 95 Ja 2, Ja 23 '65
Change of chemistry. S. B. Chickering. Sat R 46:20-1 Ap 27 '63
Counterattack at Colorado; liberals vs. conservatives, college newspapers vs. B. Goldwater. W. H. Carroll. Nat R 14:494-5 Je 18 '63
Excess of youth; Harvard Lampoon's awards for the worst movies. H. Alpert. Sat R 46: 26 Ap 27 '63
Fl*m*ng's Alligator: ten Bond books in one. il Newsweek 61:88 F 18 '63
Instant newspaper; sixth grade group. F. A. Gritzner. Sr Schol 84:13T My 1 '64
Little magazine that could. J. F. Fixx. Sat R 47:48 Ag 8 '64
Student freedom; censorship of articles in the Scholastic. Commonweal 78:269-70 My 31 '63; Reply. O. P. Kretzmann. 78:379 Je 28 '63
Student magazine awards for 1963. S. B. Chickering. Sat R 46:26-7+ S 21 '63
COLLEGE aptitude tests. See Aptitude tests
COLLEGE architecture
Architecture and man at Yale. V. Scully. il Sat R 47:26-9 My 23 '64
Beloit college science building. H. Weese. il Arch Rec 133:140-2 My '63
Big campus for Chicago; new downtown campus for the University of Illinois. il Arch Forum 121:148-51 Ag '64
Big change on the campus. il Arch Forum 118:76-103 Mr '63
Broad stairs, stone walls and courtyard form handsome gateway to rural campus; Goucher college center. il Arch Rec 134: 117-24 Jl '63
Building campuses from the ground up. il Fortune 70:160-5 N '64
Building types study. il Arch Rec 134:109-24 Ag '63; 135:161-70 My '64
Building years of a Yale man. W. McQuade. il Arch Forum 118:88-93 Je '63
Campus planning; California; symposium. il Arch Rec 136:175-204 N '64
Chicago architects win R.P.I. contest. il Arch Forum 118:11 Mr '63
College and university building. H. C. F. Arnold. il Arch Rec 135:18 My '64
College architecture; the economics and aesthetics. W. McQuade. il Fortune 67:148-50 My '63
College campus that is Main Street; Denison college, Denison, Ia. il Arch Rec 137: 124-6 Ja '65
College plan a cluster pattern; Grand Valley state college, Mich. il Arch Rec 137:127-34 Ja '65
Continuity in New Mexico: university's varied plazas. il Arch Forum 119:108-11 S '63
Designing with deference; medical library at Harvard, and dormitories at the University of Massachusetts, Princeton, M.I.T. and Bowdoin. il Arch Rec 133:133-44 Mr '63
Dorms vs. classrooms. G. A. Christie. il Arch Rec 136:18 N '64
Dramatic renewal on campus; Columbia's Manhattan campus. il Arch Forum 121:114-17 Jl '64
Farewell to ivy; campus architecture in original modern designs. il Bsns W p50-2 F 9 '63
First tower at M.I.T. il Arch Rec 136:135-8 O '64
Fraternities at Stanford; simple shapes climb a hill. il Arch Forum 119:110-13 Jl '63
Fresh breezes in the windy city; outdoor sculpture in Chicago law school's central court. K. Kuh. il Sat R 47:20 Jl 25 '64
Good form; college architect M. Yamasaki. il Newsweek 64:98 N 9 '64
High-rise and low-rise grouping for Michigan campus. il Arch Rec 135:165-8 Ap '64

COLLEGE architecture—*Continued*
Mansions or misplaced slums? concerning report by Educational facilities laboratories. il Time 83:64 F 28 '64
On from antiquity; St Catherine's college at Oxford; Churchill college at Cambridge. il Time 84:114-16 O 2 '64
Planning the community college. il Arch Rec 135:123-32 Je '64
Princeton building with colonnaded facade; Woodrow Wilson school of public and international affairs. il Arch Rec 134:108-10 D '63
Reed college arts center. H. Weese. il Arch Rec 133:136-7 My '63
Rudolph designs for Colgate. il Arch Rec 135: 10 My '64
School for the arts at Yale. il Arch Rec 135: 111-20 F '64
Science building for small liberal arts college. il Arch Rec 136:162-4 N '64
Science center emphasizes bold structure; Science building, University of Miami, Coral Gables, Fla. il Arch Rec 137:122-3 Ja '65
Science hall stresses inner flexibility; Olin hall of science, Colorado college, Colorado Springs, Colo. il Arch Rec 137:120-1 Ja '65
Shells soar in Formosa; Luce memorial chapel at Tunghai university. il Arch Forum 121:136-9 Ag '64
SOM, Rudolph, and Johnson at Yale. il Arch Forum 119:30-1 N '63
University of Illinois spectacular. il Arch Rec 134:111-16 Jl '63
Up from Gothic. il Fortune 67:142-7 My '63
Word in Britain: character; Leicester university. R. Banham. il Arch Forum 121: 118-25 Ag '64
Yale's School of art and architecture; symposium. il Arch Forum 120:62-85 F '64
See also
Dormitories

COLLEGE athlete recruiting. See Athletes—Recruiting

COLLEGE athletes. See Athletes

COLLEGE athletics
Allston Wheat's crusade. M. Epernay. Harper 226:53-7 My '63
Open letter to a college president; Vernon Alden of Ohio U. D. Kazmaier. Sports Illus 19:57-8 O 14 '63
Professional brawn in college. R. Kirk. Nat R 14:284 Ap 9 '63
Uproar in Philadelphia; Penn-Brown game played against Villanova-La Salle cheering. J. Olsen. il Sports Illus 22:18-23 Ja 18 '65
See also
Basketball
Football
National collegiate athletic association
Rowing
Stadiums
Wrestling

COLLEGE attendance. See Colleges and universities—Attendance

COLLEGE bands. See Bands, College

COLLEGE bookstores
Attractive university bookstore: University of Utah. il Arch Rec 133:178-9 Je '63
Big retailer on campus: university co-op at the University of Wisconsin. il Bsns W p42-4 F 2 '63
College enrollment boom: is everybody ready? R. H. Smith. Pub W 184:44 D 30 '63
First three prize-winners in NACS merchandising contest. il Pub W 185:68-70 My 25 '64
Milwaukee college store resumes construction plans. Pub W 185:71 F 3 '64
NACS: can college stores cope with the paperback boom? summary of addresses. B. J. Larson; M. J. Goodman. il Pub W 184: 16-21 D 16 '63
NACS: college stores' convention stresses general books, education; symposium, with editorial comment. il Pub W 185:30-45, 53 My 25 '64
NACS: Doubleday-N.Y.U. merchandising seminar; symposium; with editorial comment. il Pub W 183:22-35, 42 My 20 '63
NACS: making the college store a force in education; symposium. il Pub W 183:27-33 My 27 '63
NACS: management seminar studies how to measure, control pilferage. M. Saul. il Pub W 186:30-3 S 21 '64
Pilferage and some methods of controlling it. F. J. Worthington; J. R. Shaw; D. Staggs. Pub W 185:33-5 My 25 '64
Princeton university store expands book department. il Pub W 185:22-5 Mr 16 '64
See also
National association of college stores

COLLEGE buildings. See College architecture

COLLEGE choirs. See Choirs

COLLEGE deans
Administrator in higher education as an educational leader; excerpt from address. J. A. Fishman. Sch & Soc 91:304-6 O 19 '63

COLLEGE debating. See Debates and debating

COLLEGE degrees. See Degrees, Academic

COLLEGE dormitories. See Dormitories

COLLEGE drama. See College and school drama

COLLEGE dropouts. See Student withdrawals

COLLEGE education
Access to higher education, v 1, by F. Bowles. Review
Sat R 47:77-8 Mr 21 '64. E. S. Wilson
Age of the scholar, by N. M. Pusey. Review
Sat R 46:84 N 16 '63. H. Rosenhaupt
Challenges to public higher education. W. E. Hager. Sch & Soc 91:200-1 Ap 20 '63
Changing character of undergraduate education; address, January 11, 1964. D. B. Truman. Sch & Soc 92:380-3 D 12 '64
Changing objectives in American higher education, 1842-1960. D. . McKenna and others. il Sch & Soc 91:120-3 Mr 9 '63
Charter day ceremonies, UCLA; remarks, February 21, 1964. A. López Mateos. Dept State Bul 50:400-1 Mr 16 '64
College for all? Newsweek 63:73 Ja 13 '64
Disciplines' new attitude toward higher education. M. M. Chambers. Sch & Soc 91:190-1 Ap 20 '63
Education in the year 2,000 A.D; a uniworld university, with local campuses; address, April 10, 1964. R. T. Oliver. Vital Speeches 30:399-401 Ap 15 '64
Expectations and responsibilities in higher education. R. G. Lloyd. Sch & Soc 92:85 F 22 '64
Extended schooling versus higher education. J. F. Ohles. Sch & Soc 92:156-7 Ap 4 '64
Far more than grades; college presidents play up the value of values. Time 84:87 O 2 '64
Federal expenditures and the quality of education: excerpts from address, March 21, 1963. H. Orlans. bibliog Science 142:1625-9 D 27 '63
Greatest college chance; for an American child. Sci N L 84:157 S 7 '63
Half-way to where? or the quantity-quality muddle in college education. L. T. Benezet. NEA J 53:57-8 Ap '64
Higher education in America. C. P. Snow. NEA J 53:11 Ap '64
Higher education 1970. Sr Schol 85:4T N 11 '64
How good is a college? address, April 21, 1964. L. T. Benezet. Vital Speeches 30: 508-10 Je 1 '64
Human equation and the college; excerpts from address. G. L. McConagha. Sch & Soc 91:285 O 5 '63
Hutchins of Chicago. R. A. Nisbet. Commentary 38:52-5 Jl '64
Non-western world in higher education; symposium, ed. by D. N. Bigelow and L. H. Legters. bibliog f il Ann Am Acad 356:1-167 N '64
Scientific age: the impact of science on society, by L. V. Berkner. Review
Sat R 47:72-3 N 21 '64. R. Gross
Sheepskin squeeze. J. D. Black. il Time 81: 64 Mr 1 '63
Some plain talk about higher education; address, October 2, 1964. V. F. Spathelf. Vital Speeches 31:40-3 N 1 '64
Student and his studies, by E. Raushenbush. Review
Sat R 47:70-1+ S 19 '64. F. G. Jennings
Toward better higher education. Sch & Soc 91:301-2 O 19 '63
Two-year community colleges. R. Carson. il Parents Mag 39:66-7+ Ap '64
Universal opportunity for education beyond the high school; adapted from statement. il NEA J 53:58-60 Ja '64
What's going on in schools & colleges. See issues of Changing times
What's happening in education? place in college for average student? W. D. Boutwell. PTA Mag 57:13 Mr '63
What's new in higher education? excerpt from Higher education: some newer developments, ed. by S. Baskin. il NEA J 53:54-6 S '64
Why not three-year colleges? W. Fallaw. Christian Cent 81:601-2 My 6 '64
See also
Colleges and universities—Curriculum
Educational acceleration
Junior colleges
Liberal education
Specialization in education
Technical education

COLLEGE education—*Continued*

Anecdotes, facetiae, satire, etc.

Fable for other times. R. H. Reid. Sch & Soc 92:227-8 Sum '64

Economic aspects

Tax credit for education. America 110:180 F 8 '64

COLLEGE education, Cost of
Aid in the shade; financial aid. Newsweek 64:49 Ag 3 '64
College bound? you can study now, pay later. il U S News 57:52-4 Ag 10 '64
College may cost less than you think. A. P. Nilsen. Suc Farm 62:92 My '64
High costs of higher education. il Sr Schol 85:18 N 11 '64
How to help your children get ready for their future. M. Longwell. il Farm J 88:62-3+ S '64
How will you ever pay for college. il Changing T 18:9-13 Ap '64
Is going to college too expensive? R. Kirk. Nat R 14:456 Je 4 '63
More students are studying now, paying later. R. G. Moon, jr. il Sat R 46:74-5+ Je 15 '63
Parents' feelings about college costs. R. B. Ekstrom and N. Cliff. Sch & Soc 91:99-100 F 23 '63
Top science freshmen spend $2,700 for college. Sci N L 86:361 D 5 '64

COLLEGE education, Value of
Free college after H.S? concerning report by Educational policies commission. Sr Schol 84:4T Ja 31 '64
How to help your children get ready for their future. M. Longwell. il Farm J 88: 62-3+ S '64
Moral values and our universities; excerpts from address, 1964. W. S. Coffin, jr. il NEA J 54:8-10 Ja '65
Spiritual values of education; address, November 20, 1964. J. H. McConnell. Vital Speeches 31:181-2 Ja 1 '65
Substance of the university; address, September 6, 1963. G. P. Harnwell. Vital Speeches 29:756-7 O 1 '63
Where will they go after high school? H. A. Littledale. il Parents Mag 38:58-9+ Ap '63
Which one went to college? J. D. Boyd. il Farm J 88:39+ F '64
Wirtz proposal. W. F. Buckley, jr. Nat R 16: 267 Ap 7 '64

COLLEGE enrollment. See Colleges and universities—Attendance; Junior colleges—Attendance

COLLEGE entrance examination board
Advanced placement: completion of some college work while still in high school. E. M. Gerritz; C. R. Haywood. il NEA J 54:22-4 Ja '65

COLLEGE entrance requirements. See Colleges and universities—Entrance requirements

COLLEGE ethics. See Student ethics

COLLEGE football. See Football

COLLEGE football players. See Football players

COLLEGE fraternities
Amherst's support of fraternities. Sch & Soc 91:81 F 23 '63
Bridge; case for fraternities; address, July 4, 1963. W. P. Shofstall. Vital Speeches 29: 724-7 S 15 '63
Clarification at College Parks; low moral standards among fraternity members. V. E. Lowder. Christian Cent 81:500-2 Ap 15 '64
Facts on fraternities; University of Michigan study. Sch & Soc 91:80 F 23 '63
Fraternities at Stanford: simple shapes climb a hill. il Arch Forum 119:110-13 Jl '63
Friction on fraternity row; pro and con discussion. il Sr Schol 85:14-15 Ja 7 '65
Perils of big brotherhood; Dean Swift; with account by J. Poppy. il Look 27:53-6+ Mr 12 '63; Discussion. 27:20+ Ap 23 '63

COLLEGE freshmen. See College students

COLLEGE girls. See College students, Women

COLLEGE graduates
Address from the class of 1944 to the class of 1963. H. A. Grunwald. il Horizon 5:86-9 My '63
After the B.A. il Newsweek 63:88 My 18 '64
B-schools run hard in the race for talent. il Bsns W p 152+ N 16 '63
Best job offers for '64 college grads. U S News 56:11 Ja 13 '64
Big man on campus bigger than ever; Class of 1964. il Newsweek 63:98+ Je 15 '64
Class of '63; war babies with diplomas. il Bsns W p23-5 Je 15 '63
College grads married, working two years later. Sci N L 84:297 N 9 '63
College graduate as a lifetime reader; excerpts from address. J. S. Diekhoff. ALA Bul 58:995-7+ D '64
Education graduates view education and academic courses. R. C. Preston. bibliog f il Sch & Soc 92:233-7 Sum '64
Executive trends; demand for June grads. Nations Bsns 51:14+ My '63
For the class of '63: job outlook now. W. W. Wirtz. il U S News 54:74-5 Ap 29 '63
How to break in the college graduate. E. H. Schein. Harvard Bsns R 42:68-76 N '64
Industry rushes for Negro grads. il Bsns W p78-80+ Ap 25 '64
Job outlook for the class of '64. il U S News 56:88-9 My 11 '64
Mammon's untouchables. Duns R 85:31 Ja '65
Many commencements of Callie Trent. W. P. Pitt. il Read Digest 84:49-53 Je '64
New breed. A. M. Greeley. America 110:706-9 My 23 '64; Discussion. 110:863-5 Je 27 '64
New debate: Catholic intellectual life. A. M. Greeley; J. D. Donovan; J. W. Trent. il Commonweal 81:33-42 O 2 '64
New world, new church. D. R. Campion. il America 110:709-11 My 23 '64
Not that wind; founding of conservative Winds of freedom foundation at Stanford. Nat R 14:440 Je 4 '63
Starting pay for college graduates: still headed up in most fields; chart. U S News 55:10 Jl 15 '63
Whither the college graduate? Sch & Soc 92:64-5 F 22 '64
See also
College education, Value of
Colleges and universities—Graduate work

Anecdotes, facetiae, satire, etc.

Oh to be a college man! Nat R 14:523 Jl 2 '63

Caricatures and cartoons

Reunion. Stevenson. New Yorker 40:32-7 Je 20 '64

COLLEGE graduates, Women
Job opportunities for women college graduates. S. Swerdloff. bibliog f il Mo Labor R 87:396-400 Ap '64

COLLEGE journalism. See College and school journalism

COLLEGE librarians. See Librarians

COLLEGE libraries
Academic and research libraries to be studied in Pennsylvania. Library J 88:4595 D 1 '63
Academic libraries featured at NBC annual meeting. Library J 89:213-14 Ja 15 '64
Big four: university librarianship in Sweden. G. Ottervik. il Library J 88:4300-5 N 15 '63
Bodley's librarian praises great academic libraries of US; excerpts from address, July 1963. J. N. L. Myres. Library J 88:3810 O 15 '63
Bulletin board; ALA St Louis conference programs of direct interest to libraries in academic institutions. ALA Bul 58:336 My '64
Changing role of the university library; address, October 1962. R. E. Ellsworth. il Library J 88:1405-11 Ap 1 '63
College libraries theme of NBC annual meeting. Pub W 184:23-4 D 16 '63
Development of library resources. P. L. Berry. bibliog f Ann Am Acad 356:126-32 N '64
Higher education legislation goes to rules committee. Library J 88:2653 Jl '63
Inter-university library cooperation demonstrated in two separate projects; Syracuse university and the University of Toronto. Library J 88:4596 D 1 '63
Libraries for technical education programs. W. J. Brooking and M. H. Mahar. bibliog il Sch Life 47:9-13 O '64
New library buildings: some strengths and weaknesses. W. H. Jesse. il Library J 89: 4700-4 D 1 '64
Open-door policy; Methodist college, Fayetteville, N.C. A. W. Stewart. il Wilson Lib Bul 37:860-2 Je '63
Place where you can follow the footnote back home; report of symposium at Bowdoin college. E. Moon. il Library J 88:1412-16 Ap 1 '63
President Kennedy on libraries; summary of special education message and bills. J. F. Kennedy. Wilson Lib Bul 37:709 Ap '63
Research library and the liberal arts; report of symposium at Bowdoin. il Wilson Lib Bul 37:628+ Ap '63

COLLEGE libraries—*Continued*
20,000 vital titles listed in jr. college reference work; Basic books for junior college libraries. Library J 88:2654 Jl '63
See also
Research libraries
also subhead Libraries under names of colleges or universities e.g. Columbia university—Libraries

Anecdotes, facetiae, satire, etc.

Library key club; Hefnerian view of the university library of the future. F. J. Anderson. il Library J 89:1918-21 My 1 '64

Architecture

See Library architecture

Automation

Automation in the reserved books room. E. E. Weyhrauch. Library J 89:2294-6 Je 1 '64

Circulation, loans, etc.

Automated circulation procedure at Southern Illinois university. Library J 88:1133 Mr 15 '63

Classification

See Classification

Cooperation

Georgia: the groves of academe; University center. W. R. Pullen. Wilson Lib Bul 38: 278-80 N '63
Report recommends more cooperation among Brooklyn's academic libraries. Library J 88: 3810 O 15 '63

Gifts, legacies, etc.

Frost books donated to N.Y.U. library. Pub W 185:105-6 Ja 20 '64

Instruction in use

See Libraries—Instruction in use

Periodical collections

Eight New York college libraries survey their periodical holdings; College centre of the Finger Lakes, N.Y. Library J 88:1131 Mr 15 '63

Public relations

Campus vs. community; Beloit college, Beloit, Wis. libraries. H. V. Deale. bibliog il Library J 89:1695-7 Ap 15 '64

Reference work

Anachronistic wizard; the college reference librarian. D. Gore. il Library J 89:1688-92 Ap 15 '64; Discussion. 89:2256+, 3056 Je 1, S 1 '64

Reserve systems

Automation in the reserved books room. E. E. Weyhrauch. Library J 89:2294-6 Je 1 '64

Standards

Inadequacy of college libraries. Sch & Soc 91:347 N 16 '63
Library association recommends standards for college libraries. Library J 89:4492 N 15 '64

Statistics

College library statistics issued in Canada and United States. Library J 88:2221 Je 1 '63

COLLEGE libraries and schools. See Libraries and schools

COLLEGE library architecture. See Library architecture

COLLEGE library catalogs. See Catalogs, Library

COLLEGE life. See Student life

COLLEGE of cardinals. See Cardinals

COLLEGE of education at Fredonia. See New York state university—College at Fredonia

COLLEGE of education at Potsdam. See New York state university—College at Potsdam

COLLEGE of Saint Benedict, St Joseph, Minn.
Flexible design for the performing arts; Benedicta arts center. il Arch Rec 136:116-19 D '64

COLLEGE officials
International orientation for college administrators. L. J. Stiles. Sch & Soc 91:356-8 N 16 '63

COLLEGE PARK, Md.
In the bag for keeps. R. A. Edwards. il Am City 78:89-92 Ap '63

COLLEGE periodicals. See College and school journalism

COLLEGE presidents
College presidents: study finds that techniques for hunting them could stand a lot of improvement. D. S. Greenberg. Science 147:380-1 Ja 22 '65
Non-academic as head of a British university. W. W. Brickman. Sch & Soc 91:135 Mr 23 '63
President under the gun. il Life 58:58-68 Ja 15 '65
University presidency: what it takes. E. Ashby. il Sat R 47:58-9+ N 21 '64; Reply. J. Seeley. 48:46+ Ja 16 '65

Inauguration

See Inaugurations

COLLEGE presidents wives
Lady in a glass house; M. Alden. il Newsweek 64:101 O 19 '64

COLLEGE professors and instructors
Academic social compact. J. A. Fishman. Sch & Soc 92:29-31 Ja 25 '64
Closed society; J. W. Silver of Ole Miss. il Newsweek 62:66+ N 18 '63
College-supported faculty research programs; San Jose state college. R. H. Woodward. Sch & Soc 91:109+ Mr 9 '63
Conservation of professorial time. W. W. Brickman. Sch & Soc 91:79 F 23 '63
Crassest opportunism. Time 84:61 D 11 '64
Faculty research policy. Sch & Soc 92:284 O 17 '64
Great art of public relations. W. H. Fisher. Sch & Soc 92:47 F 8 '64
Guide stands first; professor of library education. J. Shera. Wilson Lib Bul 38:285+ N '63
Interdependence of administration and faculty. R. F. Humphreys. Sch & Soc 92: 48-9 F 8 '64
Once the professor was a teacher. J. G. Kemeny. il N Y Times Mag p 14+ Je 2 '63
Personal business; businessmen return to teaching. Bsns W p 149-50 Je 6 '64
Personnel selection in academic institutions; letter. M. B. Shimkin. Science 143: 637 F 14 '64
Professional staff in U.S. colleges. R. M. Walker. il Sch Life 46:42-3 Ja '64
Professors, research, and taxes. W. W. Brickman. Sch & Soc 92:148+ Ap 4 '64
Seminary professors resign; Southeastern seminary, Wake Forest, N.C. Christian Cent 82:101-2 Ja 27 '65
Teacher sweats it out. il Life 58:56-65 Ja 22 '65
Tenn. state's lady engineer. il Ebony 19: 75-6+ Jl '64
Three myths about the college teacher. B. Dearing. il Sat R 47:65-7 Ja 18 '64
See also
Academic freedom
American association of university professors
Colleges and universities—Teaching
Teachers and students
Theologians

Education

Slogans, labels, and clichés. W. W. Brickman. Sch & Soc 91:53 F 9 '63

Placement

See College professors and instructors—Selection and appointment

Political activities

Goldwater's brain trust. il U S News 57:36 Jl 27 '64
National goals and the university. J. C. Warner. Science 142:462-4 O 25 '63

Publications

Must college teachers publish or perish? P. Woodring. Sat R 47:45-6 Je 20 '64
One against Tufts; case of W. W. Sayre. Newsweek 63:58 Ap 13 '64
Publish-or-perish policy. W. V. O'Connor; L. E. Hurt. NEA J 53:30-2+ D '64
Threshold of what? necessity to publish. il Time 83:86+ Ap 24 '64

Qualifications

Teachers as scholars. F. T. Worrell. Science 147:358 Ja 22 '65

Recruiting

Art of raiding. V. Alden. Life 58:70-2 Ja 15 '65
Meeting the need for college teachers; recruiting more women. Sch & Soc 92:40+ F 8 '64

Retirement

Farewell, groves of academe. pors Time 82:80-1 Jl 12 '63

Salaries

Academic poker game. D. B. Johnson. il Sat R 46:70-1 Je 15 '63
Faculty: new federal survey shows distribution by field and differences in salaries. J. Walsh. Science 144:982+ My 22 '64

COLLEGE professors and instructors—Salaries *—Continued*
Faculty pay: salary-charging practices on federal grants is subject of A.C.E. panel's advice. J. Walsh. Science 140:284+ Ap 19 '63
Piecework pay for professors. D. Wolfle. Science 140:355 Ap 26 '63
Professor's pay. Newsweek 63:79 Mr 9 '64
Research grants, are they worth saving? letter on recommendations of the Committee on sponsored research of the American council on education. J. W. Mehl. Science 142:914-16 N 15 '63

Selection and appointment

Interdenominational search for faculty. Sch & Soc 91:417+ D 28 '63

Supply and demand

Changing nature of the teacher shortage. R. C. Maul. il NEA J 52:41-2 N '63
Education and architecture. Arch Forum 120:63 Ja '64
Meeting the need for college teachers; recruiting more women. Sch & Soc 92:40+ F 8 '64

Tenure

It's publish or perish. W. W. Sayre. il Life 58:66 Ja 22 '65
Kearns case. J. Leo. Commonweal 81:562-6 Ja 29 '65
Should tenure go? case of W. W. Sayre. C. M. Curtis. Nat R 16:864 O 6 '64
Why pick on a fine teacher? case of W. Sayre. Life 56:4 My 15 '64

COLLEGE professors and instructors in literature
New look of Mr Chips. B. Fagin. Sat R 46:57 Jl 20 '63
COLLEGE proficiency examination program. See Education—New York (state)
COLLEGE recruiting. See Employment systems
COLLEGE reunions. See College graduates
COLLEGE rodeos. See Rodeos
COLLEGE scholarships. See Scholarships and fellowships
COLLEGE slang. See Slang
COLLEGE songs
Hail to thee, er . . . da di da. il Time 82:76+ D 13 '63
COLLEGE sororities. See College fraternities
COLLEGE sports. See College athletics
COLLEGE stores association. See National association of college stores
COLLEGE student activities. See Student activities
COLLEGE student forums. See Forums (discussion and debate)
COLLEGE student riots. See Riots
COLLEGE students
Address from the class of 1944 to the class of 1963. H. A. Grunwald. il Horizon 5:86-9 My '63
Campus report: mood of the students; symposium. il N Y Times Mag p24-5+ N 17 '63
Changes in today's college students. il U S News 56:66-71 F 17 '64
Class of '68. T. B. Morgan. il Look 28:19-33 S 22 '64
College crowd. V. Voss. Mlle 58:77+ Ja '64
College intellectual, 1965 model. D. Boroff. il N Y Times Mag p36-7+ D 6 '64
College student behavior; riots in May 1963. W. W. Brickman. Sch & Soc 91:343 N 16 '63
College student in residence. M. R. Feinberg. il N Y Times Mag p93 O 13 '63
Conning the professor. il Time 82:56+ N 1 '63
Culture at college. L. W. Norris. Sch & Soc 92:263-4 O 3 '64
Frontier of service; address, June 8, 1964. R. S. Shriver. America 111:14-16 Jl 4 '64
Home recruiting lures the grads; Toledo's Operation native son. il Bsns W p62-3 Ja 9 '65
Hounds of spring; Princeton students and intercollegiate spring riot season. il Time 81:102 My 17 '63
Jesuit at Dartmouth; reflections on the problem of good and evil in education. T. V. Purcell. America 108:534-6+ Ap 20 '63
Mole at Yale: Allan Kornfeld. il Newsweek 63:84 Je 29 '64
Morals on campus; Harvard university. Christian Cent 80:1426 N 20 '63
Morals on the campus. Newsweek 65:74 Ja 11 '65
Morals revolution on the U.S. campus. il Newsweek 63:52-6+ Ap 6 '64
More on campus mores. D. A. Eldridge. il Sat R 47:57-9+ Je 20 '64
Must the colleges police sex? J. T. Rule. il Atlan 213:55-8 Ap '64; Discussion. 213:42+ Je '64
Personalists. il Time 82:44+ N 22 '63
Privatist ethic and self-fulfillment. H. Stroup. Christian Cent 81:1031-3 Ag 19 '64; Reply. W. D. Bonis. 81:1365-6+ N 4 '64
Reasonable adventurer, by R. Heath. Review
Sat R 47:65-6 Ag 15 '64. D. Yount
Scientist by several other names. E. L. Klingelhofer. Science 142:1123 N 29 '63; Reply. F. Costin. 145:8 Jl 3 '64
Sex and the college girl, by G. Greene. Review
New Repub 150:18-21 Ap 4 '64. C. Jencks; Discussion. 150:28-9 Ap 18; 37-8 My 16 '64
Sex on the campus; evaded problem. L. A. Kirkendall. Nation 198:165-7 F 17 '64
Sexual morality and the young. J. Bingham. Mlle 57:126+ S '63
Sheepskin explosion; bumper crop of incoming freshmen. il Bsns W p23-4 Je 20 '64
Sheepskin squeeze. J. D. Black. il Time 81:64 Mr 1 '63
'63; best college class in history. Life 54:4 Je 21 '63
Speaking out; don't send Johnny to college. H. Kenner. Sat Eve Post 237:12+ N 14 '64
State university of Iowa. C. Kentfield. il Holiday 34:88-91+ N '63
Student and sex. Newsweek 62:71 N 18 '63
Swept with confused alarms: psychological climate on campus. R. Hoffmann. Mlle 59:260-1+ Ag '64
Tormented generation; American students. M. M. Hunt and R. Corman. il Sat Eve Post 236:30, 33-4 O 12 '63
Ugly American undergraduate; adaptation of address, December 7, 1963. C. R. Wilson. Sch & Soc 92:351-4 N 28 '64
What one college freshman found: far from home; Stanford university, Calif. J. Dotson. il Seventeen 24:108-9 Ja '65
White-buck herd; damage done in New York hotels. Newsweek 61:79 Ap 1 '63
Who's cutting up on campus? Life 56:4 My 22 '64
Whose backyard? northern students assist Negro voter registration in Mississippi. America 111:178 Ag 22 '64
Why the students revolt. B. Ward. il Nation 200:81-5 Ja 25 '65
See also
American students in foreign countries
College fraternities
College graduates
Northern student movement
Self government in education
Student achievements
Student demonstrations
Student ethics
Student life
Teachers and students
United States national student association
Young Americans for freedom (organization)
also British students; Russian students; etc.

Adjustment

Freshman blues; with report by D. Jackson. il Life 58:63-72+ Ja 8 '65
Scraping the top of the barrel; creative nonconformist in college. S. J. Idzerda. NEA J 52:14-15 My '63
That crucial freshman year; symposium. NEA J 52:51-4 S '63

Aid

Ability to pay and college attendance. Sch & Soc 91:53 F 9 '63
See also
Scholarships and fellowships
Student loans

Anecdotes, facetiae, satire, etc.

Open letter to Joe college, 1963. Esquire 60:69 S '63
Pressure: buckle under, Winsocki. D. Newman and R. Benton. il Esquire 62:97-100 S '64

Dating

See Dating

Discipline

See Discipline

Elimination from college

See Student withdrawals

Employment

Harvardmen vs. big business. R. Nason. il Duns R 83:41-2+ Ja '64
Industry research pays student bills. il Bsns W p82+ S 19 '64

COLLEGE students—Employment—*Continued*
Polaroid camera means business. B. Goldrath. il U S Camera 27:22+ Je '64
Student-faculty work program; Northland college, Ashland, Wis. E. J. Kernan. Sch & Soc 91:59 F 9 '63

Expenditures

See also
College education, Cost of

Failures

See Student withdrawals

Grading

See Grading and marking (students)

Health and hygiene

College students in trouble; emotionally disturbed students. J. A. Paulsen. il Atlan 214: 96-101 Jl '64
Time of the crack-up. il Newsweek 64:92-3 D 7 '64

Housing

What a way to go; students help to run Tudor-styled mansion in Los Angeles area. il Time 84:44 Ag 28 '64
See also
Dormitories

Mental hygiene

See College students—Health and hygiene

Political activities

Amid the rah-rah: reality; U.S. college mock political conventions. il Time 83:38-9 My 15 '64
Berkeley: does that banner still wave? Free speech movement. G. A. Harrison. New Repub 151:7-8 D 19 '64
Bloomington blooper. Nation 198:338 Ap 6 '64
Campus agitation vs. education. Life 58:4 Ja 22 '65
Campus report: mood of the students; symposium. il N Y Times Mag p24-5+ N 17 '63
Extremism in the defense of . . . R. E. Fitch. Christian Cent 82:11-15 Ja 6 '65
Higher learning; Princeton university host to racists: Malcolm X and Ross Barnett. Nat R 15:384 N 5 '63
Hoadley's test case in Indiana. J. Neugeboren. New Repub 149:14 S 21 '63
Hoosier witch hunt. N. R. Hanson. il Nation 196:443-4 My 25 '63; Discussion. 196:inside cover, 529 Je 22 '63
Inviting Communists to speak at colleges; address, 1962. W. F. Buckley, jr. il Nat R 15:343-5+ O 22 '63
Lesson of Berkeley. S. M. Lipset and P. Seabury. il Reporter 32:36-40 Ja 28 '65
Letter from Paris; strike of university students all over France. Genêt. New Yorker 39:158-61 D 14 '63
Mock four; Oberlin's campus convention. il Newsweek 63:82 My 18 '64
No fair! the students strike at California. G. Marine. il Nation 199:482-6 D 21 '64; Discussion. 199:477-8 D 21 '64; 200:inside cover Ja 11 '65
Political profile of a university class; survey. D. Vinyard. il Sch & Soc 92:291-3 O 17 '64
Savio onstage; battle over political activities on campus at Berkeley campus, University of California. il Newsweek 64:71 D 21 '64
Student academic freedom and communist speakers on campus. S. Jacobson. Sch & Soc 92:336-7 N 14 '64
Survey of the political and religious attitudes of American college students. Nat R 15:279-302 O 8 '63
Troublemakers. B. Somoroff. il Esquire 60: 78-9 S '63
U.S. students in Cuba: how far left? W. Schulz. Nat R 15:229 S 24 '63
What happened at Berkeley. J. Cass. il Sat R 48:47-8+ Ja 16 '65
What Johnny doesn't know; week as visiting resident, at University of Texas. W. F. Buckley, jr. Nat R 16:14+ Ja 14 '64
When & where to speak. il Time 84:68-9 D 18 '64
Wild time on Capitol hill; investigation of students by House committee on un-American activities. il U S News 55:4 S 23 '63

Reading

Lord of the flies goes to college; symposium. New Repub 148:27-8 My 4 '63
One-hundred-dollar understanding; personal library of paperback books. R. Harwell and S. W. Hilyard. bibliog Library J 88:1937-40 My 15 '63
Salinger and Golding: conflict on the campus. F. E. Kearns; discussion. America 108: 242+ F 23 '63

Religion

God on the secular campus, by R. Butler. Review
America 109:711-12+ N 30 '63. A. Sigur
Love without fear, by R. C. Buckle. Review
Nat R 16:320 Ap 21 '64. R. Kirk
Science, religion and student values; plea for a genuine encounter between church and university. O. H. Mowrer. Christian Cent 80:1200-2 O 2 '63; Discussion. 80: 1442+ N 20 '63
Student apostasy. Christian Cent 80:1455-7 N 27 '63; Discussion. 81:86-7 Ja 15 '64
Survey of the political and religious attitudes of American college students. Nat R 15:279-302 O 8 '63
See also
Colleges and universities—Religious life

Selection

See Student selection

Volunteer service

See Volunteer service

COLLEGE students, Catholic. See Catholic students

COLLEGE students, Married
Bride in Boystown. B. Gary. il Mlle 57:290-1+ Ag '63
Designing with deference; married students housing at M.I.T. il Arch Rec 133:140-1 Mr '63
Housewives on campus: I feel alive again! B. Asbell. McCalls 91:136-7+ N '63
How successful are college marriages? E. Hill. il Redbook 123:58-9+ My '64
I went back to college; young mother's story. B. O'Neill. il Redbook 122:6+ N '63

COLLEGE students, Mentally superior
Gifted boy finds his way: B. Wichmann's escape from mediocrity; with report by J. Estes. il Life 57:79-80+ D 4 '64
New college honors programs; excerpt from address. J. W. Cohen. NEA J 52:49-50 F '63

COLLEGE students, Negro. See Negro students

COLLEGE students, Women
American coeds afraid of hard physical work. Sci N L 85:361 Je 6 '64
Choicest co-ed; symposium. Esquire 60:74 S '63
Co-ed's double life; Ann Boyer, junior at Washington university. I. Mothner. il Look 27:45-8 F 12 '63
Housewives on campus: I feel alive again! B. Asbell. McCalls 91:136-7+ N '63
How not to waste college on girls; with study-discussion program. by M. Smart, G. Hechinger and F. M. Hechinger. il Parents Mag 39:40, 70-1+ F '64
Jennifer. C. Illig. Mlle 56:61+ F '63
Knitted brows on the subway; a profile of New York's Barnard college. M. A. Guitar. il Mlle 58:169-71+ Ap '64
Never again, coed; special position of the coed. D. Newman and R. Benton. Mlle 59: 24+ Ag '64
Return of the prodigal. R. Hoffmann. Mlle 58:116+ D '63
Sex on the campus: the real issue. M. Mead; discussion. Redbook 120:16 Mr '63
Where the brains are; girls at M.I.T. il Time 82:51 O 18 '63
Where the girls are. G. C. Keller and G. R. Hawes. il Esquire 61:119-23+ Je '64
See also
Education of women

Dress

See Clothing and dress

COLLEGE students fads. See Fads

COLLEGE students in literature
See also
French students in literature

COLLEGE students libraries. See Libraries, Private

COLLEGE surveys. See Educational surveys

COLLEGE teachers. See College professors and instructors

COLLEGE teaching. See Colleges and universities—Teaching

COLLEGE terms. See College year

COLLEGE theatricals. See College and school drama

COLLEGE vacations. See Vacations

COLLEGE year
Our schools should be open all year. A. S. Flemming. Good H 156:46 Ap '63

COLLEGE year—*Continued*
Plea for the year-round college. E. J. McGrath. il N Y Times Mag p52+ Ap 28 '63
Too much, too soon? Newsweek 62:101 D 2 '63
Triumph or trimonster? trimester plan at Florida state university. Time 82:91 S 13 '63
Why not three-year colleges? W. Fallaw. Christian Cent 81:601-2 My 6 '64

COLLEGES and universities
Assuming the worst; replacement of private by public higher education. America 108: 604-5 Ap 27 '63
College pressure. il Life 58:60-1 Ja 8; 58-68+ Ja 15; 56-65 Ja 22 '65
Culture at college. L. W. Norris. Sch & Soc 92:263-4 O 3 '64
Future of the university. J. W. Gardner. Sat R 46:46 N 2 '63
See also
Academic freedom
Agricultural colleges
College education
College students
Law schools
Specialization in education

Accreditation

Absolute importance of regional accreditation. A. E. Meder, jr. Sch & Soc 91:108 Mr 9 '63
Accreditation in teacher education. Sch & Soc 92:40 F 8 '64

Administration

Academic organization in physical science. H. G. Booker. Science 146:35-7 O 2 '64
Community of scholars, by P. Goodman. Review
Commentary 35:450-4 My '63. H. Taylor
How to remain in the laboratory though head of a department. E. C. Pollard. Science 145:1018-21 S 4 '64; Discussion. 146:598 O 30 '64
Interdependence of administration and faculty. R. F. Humphreys. Sch & Soc 92:48-9 F 8 '64
Leadership of the universities. G. E. Taylor. bibliog f Ann Am Acad 356:1-11 N '64
Matter of form(s) C. Darlington. il Atlan 212:134-7 N '63
Multiversity: are its several souls worth saving? excerpts from Uses of the university. C. Kerr. Harper 227:37-42 N '63
See also
College deans
College presidents
College year
Self government in education
Student selection

Admission standards

See Colleges and universities—Entrance requirements

Attendance

Brains v. bluebloods. Time 83:68 Ja 3 '64
College enrollments and dropouts. W. W. Brickman. Sch & Soc 93:3 Ja 9 '65
College students are going west. H. T. Groat. il Sch & Soc 91:352-4 N 16 '63
Enrollments for advanced degrees. R. M. Walker. il Sch Life 46:26-7 D '63
Higher education; students, institutions, fall 1962. R. M. Walker. il Sch Life 46:26-7 O '63
Next year: 20 per cent more kids. il Time 82:76 D 13 '63
Sheepskin explosion; bumper crop of incoming freshmen. il Bsns W p23-4 Je 20 '64
Speaking out; don't send Johnny to college. H. Kenner. Sat Eve Post 237:12+ N 14 '64
Statistics of attendance in American universities and colleges, 1963-65. G. G. Parker. bibliog f il Sch & Soc 92:5-18 Ja 11 '64; 93: 5-18+ Ja 9 '65
Third force in college enrollments; adaptation of address. S. G. Tickton. il Sat R 47: 70-2 Mr 21 '64
What kind of excellence? V. R. Alden. il Sat R 47:52-3 Jl 18 '64
See also
Student selection

Business schools

See Business education

Choice

See College, Choice of

Class attendance

Cutting, permissive or controlled. J. P. Williams. Sch & Soc 91:306-7 O 19 '63

Cooperation

Brown and Tougaloo. Commonweal 80:280 My 29 '64
Colleges pool resources. America 110:213 F 15 '64
Divided, we fall. Sister Mary Anon. America 110:628-30 My 9 '64
Interinstitutional co-operation in graduate education. Sch & Soc 91:188 Ap 20 '63
Joint university effort. Sch & Soc 91:164+ Ap 6 '63
Midwestern interstate co-operation in higher education; address, July 30, 1963. S. J. Wenberg. Sch & Soc 92:50-1 F 8 '64
Outside educators; graduate students from northern universities teaching at Tougaloo. Sci Am 211:84 S '64
Universities adopt-a-school plan; Northern university aid in raising Negro college standards. il Time 83:63 My 29 '64

Curriculum

A is an A is an A. il Time 81:38+ F 22 '63
Academic, social, and spiritual program at Mount Holyoke college. R. G. Gettell. Sch & Soc 92:270-2 O 3 '64
Current college curriculum; address, September 1962. H. W. Stoke. Sch & Soc 91:88+ F 23 '63
Depth vs. breadth; re-evaluation of traditional curriculum. Newsweek 63:64 Je 8 '64
Disciplines' new attitude toward higher education. M. M. Chambers. Sch & Soc 91:190-1 Ap 20 '63
Five years for college? F. H. Horn. NEA J 53:40-1 N '64
New Colgate plan of education. Sch & Soc 92:115 Mr 21 '64
Non-western world in higher education; symposium, ed. by D. N. Bigelow and L. H. Legters. bibliog f il Ann Am Acad 356:1-167 N '64
On improving college teaching. J. W. Gustad. NEA J 53:37-8 Mr '64
Religious studies on campus. R. J. Gerber. America 111:292-5 S 19 '64
St John's college; four years with the great books. D. Boroff. il Sat R 46:58-61+ Mr 23 '63; Discussion. 46:60 Ap 20 '63
Saving liberal arts. Time 81:71 F 15 '63
Strengthening undergraduate education. Sch & Soc 91:186 Ap 20 '63
See also
Colleges and universities—Education departments

Departments

University organization for geophysics education; excerpts from address, April 1964. W. A. Baum. Science 146:619-21 O 30 '64

Desegregation

Alabama U: a story of two among 4,000. G. Samuels. il N Y Times Mag p 12+ Jl 28 '63
Bargain with the devil; Negro applicants at the University of Alabama. il Newsweek 61:30 Je 10 '63
Before the showdown: Wallace's views; excerpts from statement. G. C. Wallace. U S News 54:19 Je 17 '63
Desegregation on southern campuses. il Sr Schol 82:21 F 13 '63
Desegregation: two ways. America 108:186-7 F 9 '63
Dialogue; telephone calls between Attorney General Kennedy and Governor Barnett prior to arrival of Negro student J. Meredith. Newsweek 62:36 O 14 '63
End and a beginning. il Newsweek 61:29-34 Je 24 '63
Genesee and Birmingham. M. Turnipseed. Christian Cent 80:1239 O 9 '63
Long march; Negro students at University of Alabama. il Time 81:13-17 Je 21 '63
Message from the Dartmouth Christian union. T. Mitchell. Negro Hist Bul 26:186 Mr '63
Nation's crisis crowds in on one man; with report by D. Nevin. il Life 54:77-8+ Je 14 '63
New term, new South. il Newsweek 61:29 F 11 '63
No indictment in case against Walker. U S News 54:19 F 4 '63
Notes and comment. New Yorker 39:19 Je 22 '63
Quiet progress in the South. Life 54:4 F 8 '63
Regard for a good name; Harvey Bernard Gantt at Clemson college. il Time 81:20 F 8 '63
Reporter at large; admission of Negro students to University of Georgia. C. Trillin. New Yorker 39:30-4+ Jl 13; 32-6+ Jl 20; 34-6+ Jl 27 '63

COLLEGES and universities—Desegregation—*Continued*
South Carolina's moment of truth. H. J. Massaquoi. il Ebony 18:96-8+ My '63
Two students. il Newsweek 62:30+ Ag 26 '63
What went on at Ole Miss; excerpts from report by Mississippi legislative committee. il U S News 54:77 My 20 '63

Dining halls

New facility provides five dining rooms. il Arch Rec 134:136-7 Ag '63

Directories

Half-million mark; Lovejoy's college guide. il Newsweek 62:82 D 16 '63

Discipline

See Discipline

Discrimination

Tolerance and the law. K. R. Bergethon. Sch & Soc 91:60-1 F 9 '63

Education departments

Academic social compact. J. A. Fishman. Sch & Soc 92:29-31 Ja 25 '64
Education as an academic discipline. J. Walton. Sch & Soc 92:264-5+ O 3 '64
Teacher education and liberal arts colleges. Sch & Soc 92:220 Sum '64

English departments

How to get rid of good professors: Michigan state university. R. Kirk. Nat R 14:321 Ap 23 '63; Reply. M. Molenda. 14:421 My 21 '63

Enrollment

See Colleges and universities—Attendance

Entrance requirements

Applying for college, a guide for high school seniors. Changing T 18:6 O '64
Big crisis for nation's youth getting into college. il U S News 56:43-6 Ap 27 '64
California: junior colleges are the key to state's own version of an open door policy. J. Walsh. Science 144:155-7 Ap 10 '64
Chaos in college admissions. il Changing T 17:17-20 Ag '63
College entrance exams. C. Jencks. New Repub 148:7 Ap 20 '63
Columbia college: report to headmasters, principals, and counselors, 1963. H. S. Coleman. Sch & Soc 92:239-41 Sum '64
Going to college. E. H. Miner. Sr Schol 85: 17-18 N 11 '64
How they got into college. T. B. Morgan. il Look 28:32-3 S 22 '64
It's time . . . who shall go to college? address. March 16, 1963. E. L. Harden. Vital Speeches 29:430-4 My 1 '63
Knock on any door; increase in applications for admission. il Newsweek 63:84-5 F 24 '64
Open door vs. selective admission. W. C. Wescoe. Sch & Soc 91:138-40 Mr 23 '63
Propaganda for mediocrity. R. Kirk. Nat R 15:108 Ag 13 '63
Record rush for college: are entrance tests unfair? il U S News 56:67-9 Mr 9 '64
Some answers about college admission. R. R. Denny. Bet Hom & Gard 42:114-16 Ap '64
Tightening admission to college; Kent state university. Sch & Soc 91:80 F 23 '63
Touch of greatness. Time 83:41 Ja 24 '64
Trends in college admissions. il Changing T 18:35-6 Mr '64
Way to finish earlier; advanced placement students to enter American university. Time 84:41 Jl 31 '64
What's happening in education? place in college for average student? W. D. Boutwell. PTA Mag 57:13 Mr '63
Who should go to college? M. C. McIntosh. il Sr Schol 83:16-17 N 8 '63
See also
Student selection

Anecdotes, facetiae, satire, etc.

College game. P. Yaeger and others. il Seventeen 23:110-11 Ja '64

Faculties

See College professors and instructors

Federal aid

See Federal aid to education

Finance

Bond sales for higher education: 1962: Office of education survey. W. R. Bokelman and E. C. Deering. il Sch Life 45:20-4 Mr '63
Bonds for educational purposes, sales, interest rates, et cetera; colleges and universities. W. R. Bokelman and E. C. Deering. See issues of School life
Cutthroat competition; public spending for education. America 111:504 O 31 '64
Free higher education. America 109:255-6 S 14 '63
Money for education. America 112:9-10 Ja 2 '65
Progress in state tax support of higher education. M. M. Chambers. Sch & Soc 91: 144-6 Mr 23 '63
Rising costs in higher education. Sch & Soc 91:272+ O 5 '63
Seed money; Ford foundation's special program in education. il Time 84:68-9 Jl 3 '64
Tax credits on college tuition fees. Sch & Soc 91:298+ O 19 '63
See also
Education and state
Federal aid to education

Freshman problems

Preventing college crack-ups. V. Balaban and H. F. French. Parents Mag 38:64+ F '63
That crucial freshman year: symposium. NEA J 52:51-4 S '63

Gifts, legacies, etc.

Business grants to colleges. Sch & Soc 92: 299 O 31 '64
Four good places to put some money. A. Gingrich. Esquire 59:8 Mr '63
Personal business; planned donation program. Bsns W p 109 Je 8 '63
Role of the foundations. G. M. Beckmann. Ann Am Acad 356:12-22 N '64
Wealthier & wiser; biggest gifts in their history for Smith college and Cornell. il Time 84:68 O 23 '64

Graduate work

Advanced degrees: discrimination wanes as a barrier to Negro grad students; other hurdles remain. J. Walsh. Science 141: 1019-21 S 13 '63
After the B.A. il Newsweek 63:88 My 18 '64
Future of humanities in graduate school. Sch & Soc 92:119+ Mr 21 '64
NASA and education; fast growth stirs Senate committee to place brakes on new university grants. D. S. Greenberg. Science 142: 1042 N 22 '63; Reply. H. L. Dryden. 143:427 Ja 31 '64
New Ph.D plan to train scholar-teachers in history; Harvard university. Sch & Soc 92: 222 Sum '64
School for alumni; at Dartmouth. il Time 83: 50 F 7 '64
What's ahead for business education; symposium. il Nations Bsns 52:40-1+ Ap '64
Whys & hows of graduate school. il Changing T 18:19-23 O '64
See also
Seminars

Honors courses

New college honors programs; excerpt from address. J. W. Cohen. NEA J 52:49-50 F '63

Public relations

How Harvard does it. L. L. L. Golden. Sat R 46:76 S 14 '63

Publications

Daring them to think. Time 81:84+ Je 7 '63
For the old grads; college alumni magazines. il Newsweek 62:51 Jl 22 '63
See also
University presses

Anecdotes, facetiae, satire, etc.

Mr America; alumni magazines. J. Fritz. il Atlan 214:125-9 D '64

Religious life

Anti-anythingarians; religion at Stanford. il Newsweek 63:67 Mr 23 '64
Churches and the campus, by J. G. Chamberlin. Review
America 110:104-5 Ja 18 '64. J. E. Rea
God on the secular campus, by R. Butler. Review
America 109:711-12+ N 30 '63. A. Sigur
Commonweal 79:438-9 Ja 10 '64. W. E. Arnold
Religion on campus; Columbia college. America 109:546 N 9 '63
See also
College students—Religion
Inter-varsity Christian fellowship

Research

California: aerospace industry has meant a second gold rush; climate and education get credit. J. Walsh. Science 143:1151-3 Mr 13 '64

COLLEGES and universities—Research—*Cont.*
Centers of excellence: new NSF science development program aims at second twenty universities. J. Walsh. Science 146:1563-6 D 18 '64
Chicago to shut weapons lab. Bsns W p 108 Je 15 '63
College-supported faculty research programs; San Jose state college. R. H. Woodward. Sch & Soc 91:109+ Mr 9 '63
Demler warns of tight controls on R&D; with editorial comment. Miss & Roc 14:14, 46 Mr 23 '64
Distribution of federal research funds. P. H. Abelson. Science 144:491 My 1 '64
Education aid: university survey finds that despite difficulties, U.S. programs highly beneficial. D. S. Greenberg. Science 141:136-8 Jl 12 '63
Faculty research policy. Sch & Soc 92:284 O 17 '64
Federal expenditures and the quality of education; excerpts from address, March 21, 1963. H. Orlans. bibliog Science 142:1625-9 D 27 '63
Federal grants and small institutions; letter. H. R. Albrecht. Science 143:306 Ja 24 '64; Reply. P. E. Cloud, jr. 143:1121 Mr 13 '64
Federal handouts may get skimpier. Bsns W p45-6 My 16 '64
Federal support of science: a formula for cooperation; excerpts from Federal support of basic research in institutions of higher learning. Science 143:1300-3 Mr 20 '64
Freshman research at M.I.T. Sch & Soc 91:55+ F 9 '63
Function of research centers. R. F. DeHaan. Science 140:1362 Je 28 '63
Government and university research. J. L. Doob. Bul Atomic Sci 20:33 Ap '64
Grants and university authority; letter. L. Levin. Science 146:998 N 20 '64
Industrial R&D: competition from universities, non-profits, alarms independent laboratories. E. Langer. Science 144:273-4 Ap 17 '64; Discussion. 144:1293 Je 12 '64
M.I.T; prime contractor contends with problems produced by solving government's problems. J. Walsh. Science 140:164-5+ Ap 12 '63
Methodology of educational research and scholarship. C. V. Good. Sch & Soc 91:140-4 Mr 23 '63
NASA allocations to universities questioned by Senate committee. Aviation W 81:25 Jl 13 '64
New estate. A. M. Weinberg. Bul Atomic Sci 20:16-19 F '64
New NASA program would fund university satellite development. Aviation W 81:35 O 19 '64
Once the professor was a teacher. J. G. Kemeny. il N Y Times Mag p 14+ Je 2 '63
Research and college teaching by students. Sch & Soc 91:135-6 Mr 23 '63
Research and the university. Sch & Soc 91:110+ Mr 9 '63
Research grants, are they worth saving? letter on recommendations of the Committee on sponsored research of the American council on education. J. W. Mehl. Science 142:914-16 N 15 '63
Savants, sandwiches, and space suits. J. H. Munster, jr. and J. C. Smith. Science 145:1276-81 S 18 '64; Discussion. 146:865, 1636-7 N 13, D 25 '64
Space science and the universities; address, May 7, 1963. F. Seitz. Science 141:614-18 Ag 16 '63
Uncle Sam: big man on campus; government research and development spending. il Bsns W p90-2+ N 2 '63
University responsibility. D. Wolfle. Science 140:861 My 24 '63
Vannevar Bush speaks; excerpts from statement, November 21, 1963. V. Bush. Science 142:1623 D 27 '63
When pure science meets pure politics. D. S. Greenberg. il Reporter 30:39-41 Mr 12 '64
See also
Institute for defense analyses

Social life

See Student life

Statistics

See also
Colleges and universities—Attendance

Teaching

Appropriate function of a university. P. H. Abelson. Science 143:11 Ja 3 '64
Course on college teaching. E. Walters. Sch & Soc 91:286-7 O 5 '63
Growth of self-reliance; self-directed study. H. E. Gruber and M. Weitman. Sch & Soc 91:222-3 My 4 '63
How to get rid of good professors; Michigan state university. R. Kirk. Nat R 14:321 Ap 23 '63; Reply. M. Molenda. 14:421 My 21 '63
On improving college teaching. J. W. Gustad. NEA J 53:37-8 Mr '64
See also
College professors and instructors
Seminars

Alabama

See also
Birmingham-Southern college, Birmingham, Ala.

Arizona

See also
Arizona. University

Brazil

Brasília builds a university. T. Mase. il Américas 15:9-11 Je '63
Peace corps needs librarians for University of Brasilia. Library J 89:209 Ja 15 '64

Burma

Burmese innovation: university libraries; letter to the editor. P. Bixler. Library J 90:4 Ja 1 '65

California

California builds big for education. B. Hibbs. Read Digest 83:164-6+ Jl '63
California: junior colleges are the key to state's own version of an open door policy. J. Walsh. Science 144:155-7 Ap 10 '64
California's new state colleges; with introduction by C. Luckman. il Arch Rec 136:200-4 N '64
Campus planning; California; symposium. il Arch Rec 136:175-204 N '64
New frontier of higher education. D. Canty. il Arch Forum 118:96-103 Mr '63
Rah! rah! rah! college for everybody. L. Dickert and A. Seidenbaum. McCalls 91:98+ My '64
See also
California state college, San Jose
California. University
Pitzer college, Claremont
San Diego city college
Santa Monica city college, Calif.
Southern California university, Los Angeles
Stanford university, Stanford, Calif.
University of the Pacific, Stockton, Calif.

Canada

See also
Alberta. University, Edmonton
Denominational colleges

China (People's Republic)

African student in red China; excerpts. E. J. Hevi. Harper 228:63-6+ Ja '64; Same abr. Read Digest 84:139-40+ Mr '64

Colorado

See also
Colorado college, Colorado Springs
Colorado. University

Connecticut

See also
Yale university

Egypt

Every morning in Cairo; teaching creative writing at American university. J. Stuart. il Sr Schol 84:9T-10T My 8 '64
Fringe benefit in Egypt; cataloging and classification for Assiut university libraries. M. S. Rinehart. Wilson Lib Bul 39:52-5 S '64
New university is born: Assiut university. S. A. Huzayyin. il UNESCO Courier 16:41-3 Jl '63
Rector for the resplendent; Cairo's Al Azhar university. il Time 84:36-7 Ag 14 '64

England

Design for a campus: University of Sussex. il Arch Forum 118:90-1 Mr '63
Explosion in Britain; new universities. il Time 82:70-1 O 11 '63
Rise of the Redbrick: Leicester university. M. Bradbury. il Holiday 34:84-7+ N '63
Seven in the sixties; new, independent universities in England. H. A. Ree. il Sat R 46:35-6+ Ag 17 '63
Word in Britain: character; Leicester university. R. Banham. il Arch Forum 121:118-25 Ag '64
See also
Cambridge university
Oxford university

COLLEGES and universities—*Continued*

Florida

See also
Florida agricultural and mechanical university, Tallahassee
Florida Atlantic university, Boca Raton
Florida state university, Tallahassee
Miami university, Coral Gables, Fla.
New college, Sarasota, Fla.

France

French higher education. H. H. Purvis. il Sat R 47:60-1+ Ag 15 '64; Reply. M. J. Fabre. 47:53 S 19 '64
French revolution. Sr Schol 84:2T+ Ap 17 '64
How to survive the Sorbonne. T. R. Bransten. il Mlle 59:100-2+ Je '64
Letter from Paris; strike of university students all over France. Genêt. New Yorker 39:158-61 D 14 '63
Slipping Sorbonne. il Time 82:105 D 6 '63
300,000 French students can't be wrong. P. E. Schneider. il N Y Times Mag p 16-17+ F 9 '64

Georgia

Georgia: the groves of academe; University center. W. R. Pullen. Wilson Lib Bul 38:278-80 N '63
See also
Emory university, Atlanta, Ga.
Georgia. University

Germany (Democratic Republic)

Pfiff's in what you can't see; Humboldt university, East Berlin. R. Hoffmann. il Mlle 60:118-21+ D '64

Germany (Federal Republic)

Daring design for a German library; University of Giessen. W. M. Ostrem. il Wilson Lib Bul 38:406-7 Ja '64
Rebirth at Göttingen. il Time 81:83-4 Ap 12 '63

Great Britain

Five MIT's for Britain? Newsweek 62:60 N 4 '63
Letter from London; concerning Robbins report on higher education. M. Panter-Downes. New Yorker 39:58+ Ja 25 '64
Most invaluable freedom of them all; Britain and America from viewpoint of higher education. K. Tynan. Seventeen 23:148+ Mr '64
Non-academic as head of a British university. W. W. Brickman. Sch & Soc 91:135 Mr 23 '63
Politics and higher education; address, June 10, 1964. E. Hutchinson. bibliog Science 146:1139-42 N 27 '64
Universities for all; concerning the Robbins report on higher education. P. Crane. America 110:37 Ja 11 '64

Illinois

See also
Illinois institute of technology, Chicago
Illinois. University, Urbana
Lake Forest college, Lake Forest, Ill.
Northern Illinois university, DeKalb
Rockford college, Rockford
Roosevelt university, Chicago, Ill.
Shimer college, Mount Carroll, Ill.
Southern Illinois university, Carbondale

India

University town built by a country doctor; Academy of general education, Manipal. P. Almasy. il UNESCO Courier 16:37-40 Jl '63

Indiana

See also
Butler university, Indianapolis
Earlham college, Richmond, Ind.
Indiana. University, Bloomington
Notre Dame, Ind. University

Iowa

See also
Denison college, Denison, Ia.
Drake university, Des Moines, Ia.
Iowa. University, Iowa City
Parsons college, Fairfield, Ia.
Simpson college, Indianola, Ia.

Ireland

In Dublin's fair city; election of a Catholic chancellor. America 110:3 Ja 4 '64

Israel

American coed in Israel; J. West at Jerusalem's Hebrew university. il Ebony 18:105-6+ My '63
Survival through brainpower; Hebrew university, Jerusalem. il Time 84:78 N 13 '64

Japan

Dialogue in Tokyo. America 110:698 My 23 '64
Wave people; staggering competition for entrance to top universities. Time 84:77 S 11 '64

Kentucky

See also
Alice Lloyd college, Pippa Passes, Ky.

Latin America

Back to the books. il Time 81:20-1 Mr 29 '63
Place to learn; Catholic universities in Latin America. il Time 82:41 N 22 '63

Lebanon

See also
American university of Beirut

Louisiana

See also
Tulane university, New Orleans

Maine

See also
Bowdoin college, Brunswick, Me.

Maryland

Church-state confrontation in Maryland; suit to determine the constitutionality of tax funds for church-related colleges. I. G. Zepp, jr. Christian Cent 82:84+ Ja 20 '65
See also
Goucher college, Baltimore
St John's college, Annapolis, Md.

Massachusetts

Universities: tall new symbols of their significance; sixty odd colleges and universities in the Boston region. D. Canty. il Arch Forum 120:114-23 Je '64
See also
Amherst college, Amherst, Mass.
Boston university
Brandeis university, Waltham, Mass.
Harvard university
Massachusetts institute of technology, Cambridge
Mount Holyoke college, South Hadley, Mass.
Smith college, Northampton, Mass.
Springfield college, Springfield, Mass.
Tufts university, Medford, Mass.

Mexico

Mexico's M.I.T; Monterrey institute of technology. P. Duffett. il Sat R 46:40-2+ Ag 17 '63
Yankees again; anti-American lectures at Mexico university. F. Mallari. America 108:630 My 4 '63

Michigan

See also
Grand Valley state college
Kalamazoo college, Kalamazoo, Mich.
Michigan state university of agriculture and applied science, East Lansing

Middle western states

Academic common market; Committee on institutional cooperation. Time 81:41 F 22 '63

Minnesota

On the campuses. W. L. Thorkelson. Christian Cent 81:1092-4 S 2 '64
See also
Carleton college, Northfield, Minn.
Macalester college, St Paul, Minn.
Minnesota. University, Minneapolis

Mississippi

See also
Mississippi. University
Tougaloo Southern Christian college, Tougaloo, Miss.

Missouri

See also
Washington university, St Louis
Webster college, Webster Groves, Mo.

Montana

Rocky road. il Time 81:84 Je 7 '63

Nebraska

See also
Nebraska. University, Lincoln

Nevada

See also
Nevada. University, Reno

New Hampshire

See also
Dartmouth college, Hanover, N.H.

COLLEGES and universities—*Continued*

New Jersey

See also
Fairleigh Dickinson university, Rutherford, N.J.
Princeton university
Rutgers university, New Brunswick, N.J.

New Mexico

See also
New Mexico. University

New York (state)

Eight New York college libraries survey their periodical holdings; College center of the Finger Lakes, N.Y. Library J 88:1131 Mr 15 '63
See also
Briarcliff junior college
Colgate university, Hamilton, N.Y.
Columbia university
Cornell university, Ithaca, N.Y.
Corning community college, N.Y.
Hofstra college, Hempstead, N.Y.
Hunter college, New York
New York state university
New York university
Queens college, New York
Rensselaer polytechnic institute, Troy, N.Y.
Rochester N.Y. University
St Lawrence university, Canton, N.Y.
Sarah Lawrence college, Bronxville, N.Y.
Vassar college, Poughkeepsie, N.Y.

North Carolina

See also
Duke university, Durham, N.C.
High Point college, High Point, N.C.
North Carolina. University
St Andrews Presbyterian college, Laurinburg, N.C.
Salem college, Winston-Salem, N.C.
Wake Forest college, Winston Salem, N.C.

Nova Scotia

See also
St Francis Xavier university

Ohio

Ohio: old laissez-faire attitude on linking education, research, and industry undergoing change. J. Walsh. Science 145:468-70 Jl 31 '64
See also
Antioch college, Yellow Springs, Ohio
Ohio state university, Columbus
Ohio. University, Athens
Western Reserve university, Cleveland, Ohio

Oregon

See also
Oregon state university, Corvallis

Pennsylvania

See also
Duquesne university, Pittsburgh, Pa.
Grove City college, Grove City, Pa.
Haverford college, Haverford, Pa.
Lafayette college, Easton, Pa.
Pennsylvania. University
Pittsburgh. University
Swarthmore college, Swarthmore, Pa.

Philippines

Light in Diliman. il Time 84:69 Jl 3 '64
Report on C.P.R. N. Cousins. Sat R 47:32 Ap 11 '64

Poland

Six centuries of the University of Cracow; Jagiellonian university. K. Estreicher. Sch & Soc 92:327-9 N 14 '64

Rhode Island

See also
Rhode Island. University, Kingston

Russia

It's hard to get into Moscow U. G. Feifer. il N Y Times Mag p44-5+ N 22 '64
Love at Moscow U. Newsweek 63:46 My 11 '64
Soviet university. F. E. MacGregor. America 111:779-80 D 12 '64

South Carolina

See also
Clemson agricultural college, Clemson, S.C.

Southern states

Desegregation on southern campuses. il Sr Schol 82:21 F 13 '63
Southern state university systems. Sch & Soc 92:94 Mr 7 '64

Spain

Salamanca and the Americas. G. de Zéndegui. il Américas 16:5-8 Ag '64

Sweden

Big four: university librarianship in Sweden. G. Ottervik. il Library J 88:4300-5 N 15 '63

Texas

Space in Houston; NASA's arrival bringing new skills and interests to Nation's petrochemical center. D. S. Greenberg. Science 140:618-19 My 10 '63
Texas educational microwave project. R. C. Norris. Sch Life 45:11-13 Ja '63
See also
Corpus Christi. University, Corpus Christi, Tex.
Rice university, Houston, Tex.
Texas agricultural and mechanical college system—Agricultural and mechanical college of Texas, College Station
Texas. University, Austin

United States

Academic freedom; how much is there? A. Hacker. il N Y Times Mag p25+ Je 7 '64
America's directory of Catholic colleges 1963. America 109:574-5 N 9 '63
America's 1964 directory of Catholic colleges. America 111:608-9 N 14 '64
Arts in our colleges. W. Schuman. Mus Am 83:5 Je '63
Banning the campus speaker. W. W. Van Alstyne. Nation 196:267-8+ Mr 30 '63
Big change on the campus. il Arch Forum 118:76-103 Mr '63
Case for the asphalt campus. D. Boroff. il N Y Times Mag p 15+ Ap 21 '63
Changes in today's college students. il U S News 56:66-71 F 17 '64
College crowd. V. Voss. Mile 58:77+ Ja '64
College enrollment boom: is everybody ready? R. H. Smith. Pub W 184:44 D 30 '63
Colleges of America's upper class. G. R. Hawes. il Sat R 46:68-71 N 16 '63
Colleges that still have room. il Changing T 18:13-15 My '64
Colleges with room for students (cont) il Changing T 17:37-9 D '63
Comparative guide to American colleges, by J. Cass and M. Birnbaum. Review Reporter 31:55-6 N 19 '64. B. Carter
Crisis in our colleges. J. F. Meyers. America 110:438-9 Mr 28 '64; Reply. J. I. Domínguez. 110:722-3 My 23 '64
Crystal ball for colleges; address, January 2, 1964. D. L. McKenna. Vital Speeches 30:249-52 F 1 '64
Does the small private college have a future? P. Woodring. Sat R 48:45-6+ Ja 16 '65
Federal aid and higher education. G. E. Snavely. Sch & Soc 91:86-8 F 23 '63
Higher education: fourth branch of government? C. K. Arnold. il Sat R 47:60-1+ Ja 18 '64; Reply. L. H. Fountain. 47:62 Mr 21 '64
Higher education in the 21st century. A. C. Eurich. Atlan 211:51-5 Je '63
How's your state doing in education? il Changing T 18:22-3 N '64
Ideopolis for the world; summary of address. C. Kerr. il Time 81:88+ My 3 '63
Is the Ivy league still the best? il Newsweek 64:65-8+ N 23 '64
Look at higher education; teaching methods of the future; address, January 15, 1963. A. C. Eurich. Vital Speeches 30:28-32 O 15 '63
Multiversity: are its several souls worth saving? excerpts from Uses of the university. C. Kerr. Harper 227:37-42 N '63
National goals and the university. J. C. Warner. Science 142:462-4 O 25 '63
New estate. A. M. Weinberg. Bul Atomic Sci 20:16-19 F '64
New hope for weak colleges; the consortium plan. G. H. Hanford. il Sat R 48:52-3+ Ja 16 '65
Non-western world in higher education; symposium, ed. by D. N. Bigelow and L. H. Legters. bibliog f il Ann Am Acad 356:1-167 N '64
Politics and higher education; address, June 10, 1964. E. Hutchinson. bibliog Science 146:1139-42 N 27 '64
Practical and academic orientations of liberal arts colleges. W. G. Land. bibliog f il Sch & Soc 91:113-15 Mr 9 '63
Public and private college. Sch & Soc 91:297-8 O 19 '63
Squeeze on the liberal university. J. D. Brown. il Atlan 213:84-7 My '64
Status seeking in academe. D. Boroff. il Sat R 47:45-7 D 19 '64
Take-off universities. il Time 81:62-3 My 24 '63
260 colleges that want more students! il Bet Hom & Gard 41:36+ Je '63

COLLEGES and universities—United States— *Continued*
University comes of age; adaptation of address, October 4, 1963. N. M. Pusey. Sch & Soc 92:286-9 O 17 '64
Useful, ornamental, and benign; address, January 19, 1963. M. W. Gross. Vital Speeches 29:314-18 Mr 1 '63
Uses of the university, by C. Kerr. Review Commentary 38:68+ D '64. H. Taylor Sat R 46:80+ N 16 '63. W. K. Selden
What's going on in schools & colleges. See issues of Changing times
Where do they go to college? W. K. Selden. il Sat R 46:72-3 Je 15 '63
See also
Colleges and universities, State
Denominational colleges
Junior colleges
Land grant colleges
Medical colleges
also names of colleges and universities, e.g. Johns Hopkins university

Vermont

See also
Bennington college, Bennington, Vt.
Middlebury college, Middlebury, Vt.

Virgin Islands

College in the islands. D. C. Stewart. il Sat R 47:50-1 Ag 15 '64

Virginia

See also
Virginia state college, Petersburg

Washington, D.C.

Colleges pool resources. America 110:213 F 15 '64
See also
American university, Washington, D.C.
Howard university, Washington, D.C.
Trinity college, Washington, D.C.

Washington (state)

See also
Central Washington state college, Ellensburg
Washington (state) University, Seattle
Western Washington state college, Bellingham

Wisconsin

See also
Wisconsin state college, La Crosse
Wisconsin state college, Oshkosh
Wisconsin state college, Whitewater
Wisconsin. University, Madison

Yugoslavia

Yugoslavian library faces 20th century problems; University library of Zagreb. H. Clark. il Library J 88:718-20 F 15 '63

COLLEGES and universities, Municipal
Problems of urban universities. N. P. Auburn. Sch & Soc 91:73 F 9 '63
Town and gown. D. B. Carlson. il Arch Forum 118:92-5 Mr '63
See also
Adelphi college, Garden City, N.Y.
Hunter college, New York

COLLEGES and universities, State
California: as enrollment bulge hits higher education system, state banks on its master plan. J. Walsh. Science 144:34-5 Ap 3 '64; Reply. L. B. Loeb. 144:1178-9 Je 5 '64
California: junior colleges are the key to state's own version of an open door policy. J. Walsh. Science 144:155-7 Ap 10 '64
Can state colleges educate for excellence? P. Woodring; B. Baum. il Sat R 47:55-8+ Ap 18 '64; Discussion. 47:67 My 16 '64
Facts about state and land-grant universities. Sch & Soc 92:285+ O 17 '64
See also names of state colleges and universities, e.g. Michigan state university of agriculture and applied science, East Lansing

COLLEGES and universities, Traveling
U7S: University of the Seven Seas; new school is a converted liner. il Newsweek 62:60 N 4 '63
University that went to sea; University of the Seven Seas. il Sci Digest 55:40-3 F '64

COLLEGES for Negroes. See Negroes in the United States—Education

COLLEGES for women
Employers rush the girls' schools; government agencies and industries combing the women's colleges for recruits. il Bsns W p 116+ My 18 '63
Where the girls are. G. C. Keler and G. R. Hawes. il Esquire 61:119-23+ Je '64
See also names of womens colleges, e.g. Stephens college, Columbia, Mo.

COLLIE, Alberto
Merlin with magnets; spatial-absolutes at Manhattan's Nordness gallery. il por Time 83:66 Je 26 '64

COLLIE, Malcom
Plumber's sculpture; photographs. Design 66:24-5 S '64

COLLIE, Robert
Silent minister speaks up. pors N Y Times Mag p 12+ My 24 '64; Same. U S News 56:76-9 Je 15 '64

COLLIER, Barnard L.
News and Latin America: a balance sheet. Sat R 46:50-1 O 12 '63

COLLIER, Blanton
Team on trial; Cleveland Browns. B. August. il por Sat Eve Post 236:86-8 N 23 '63

COLLIER, De Fonda Dowdle
Paths to the mountain. Horn Bk 39:322-6 Je '63

COLLIER, H. O. J.
Aspirin; with biological sketch. Sci Am 209:30, 96-104+ bibliog(p 187) N '63

COLLIER, J. R.
Ribonucleic acids of the ilyanassa embryo. bibliog Science 147:150-1 Ja 8 '65

COLLIER, John
Slow recovery since Wounded Knee. Sat R 46:31-2 Je 15 '63

COLLIER, Zena
Innocents; story. McCalls 91:72-3 Ag '64

COLLIER trophy
Collier trophy award (cont) B. Kocivar. il Look 27:141-4+ O 22 '63; 28:34+ O 6 '64
Mercury team wins Collier trophy award. Sci N L 84:260 O 26 '63

COLLIGNON, Joseph
Christian's dilemma. Sat R 47:14-16 Je 27 '64
Uses of guilt. Sat R 47:26-7+ O 31 '64

COLLINGE, Patricia
Please, doctor. New Yorker 40:136+ Ap 25 '64
Stranger on the beach; story. New Yorker 39:76 Je 22 '63

COLLINGWOOD, Charles
Walter Lippmann interviewed by Charles Collingwood; excerpts from CBS program. New Repub 148:15-18 My 18 '63
(ed) See Ochoa, S. How we're cracking the code of life

COLLINS, Bessie F.
Gauntlet, flung at a teen-ager; poem. McCalls 90:132 Ag '63
How big is an angel? poem. McCalls 91:112 Ja '64

COLLINS, Choo Choo
Chemistry: the arts of attraction; ed. by D. Newman. pors Esquire 59:84-5 F '63

COLLINS, Chrystal
Arizona: land for sale. J. Roddy. il pors Look 27:32-5 O 8 '63

COLLINS, Dean
This month in the Northwest (cont of) Things to do this month in the Northwest. See issues of Popular gardening

COLLINS, E. D.
Growth of photography. Hobbies 68:58+ Mr '63
Ship models and ship modeling. Hobbies 69:28-9 My '64

COLLINS, Frederic W.
Senator Russell in the last ditch. N Y Times Mag p 16+ O 20 '63
Senator Williams, public eye. N Y Times Mag p 18+ F 9 '64

COLLINS, George J.
Schoolhousing in 1963. Sch Life 46:8-11 O '63

COLLINS, Howard F.
Impressionism. Sch Arts 62:20-1 Ap '63
New realism. Sch Arts 63:25-6 Mr '64
Stained glass. Sch Arts 63:35-8 D '63

COLLINS, James F.
Hard sell for mercy. il por Bsns W p32+ My 16 '64

COLLINS, John F.
Boston: what can a sick city do? W. McQuade. il por Fortune 69:132-7+ Je '64

COLLINS, John J.
Jim Wynne. Motor B 113:27+ Je '64

COLLINS, John R.
Advances in photosensitive devices. Electr World 72:49-51 D '64
Fixed resistors. Electr World 70:44-6+ S '63
Hall effect. Electr World 69:39-42+ Ap '63
Innovations in receiving tubes. Electr World 72:54-5+ S '64
Magnetostrictive delay lines. Electr World 71:48-9 Ja '64
Modern batteries. Electr World 70:34-6+ O '63
Modern capacitors. Electr World 69:42-4+ My '63
New look in transformers. Electr World 71:36-8 Mr '64
Quantum devices, how they work. Electr World 70:39-41+ D '63
Regulated transistorized power supplies. Electr World 69:40-2 Mr '63
Temperature sensitive devices. Electr World 72:50-2 O '64

COLLINS, Judy
Maid of constant sorrow. por Time 84:74+ Ag 7 '64
COLLINS, Kreigh
Mopey Dink. il Yachting 113:42-4+ Je '63
North Channel. il Yachting 115:36-8+ Mr '64
COLLINS, Larry, and Lapierre, Dominique
Day Paris was liberated. N Y Times Mag p23-5+ Ag 23 '64
COLLINS, LeRoy
Political conventions; address, June 29, 1964. Vital Speeches 30:612-17 Ag 1 '64
Rights of the states; address, December 8, 1963. Vital Speeches 30:369-73 Ap 1 '64
about
Civil-rights referee. por U S News 57:19 Jl 13 '64
How silly can you get? il por Time 84:26-7 Jl 17 '64
COLLINS, Orvis F.
Psychoanalyzing the small businessman. il Bsns W p90+ S 19 '64
COLLINS, Pat
Cataleptic set. il por Time 82:37-8 Ag 2 '63
Hilarious hypnotist. il por Life 56:125-6 My 8 '64
You will go deep asleep. por Newsweek 63: 106+ My 25 '64
COLLINS, Patrick S.
Dead, yes! dying, no! America 109:648 N 23 '63
COLLINS, Robert L.
Inheritance of avoidance conditioning in mice: a diallel study. bibliog Science 143:1188-90 Mr 13 '64
COLLINS, Ruth Philpott
Shelf of St Louis writers. por Wilson Lib Bul 38:865-6 Je '64
COLLISION in the city; story. See McNulty, F.
COLLISIONS, Airplane. See Aviation—Accidents
COLLISIONS, Automobile. See Traffic accidents
COLLISIONS at sea
Collision course; Shalom collision with Stolt Dagali. il Newsweek 65:28+ Ja 11 '65
Collision stations! Melbourne-Voyager collision. Time 83:39 F 21 '64
Left to be answered; questions about the collision between the Shalom and the Stolt Dagali. il Time 84:24 D 4 '64
Ship that bit another in two: Shalom-Stolt Dagali collision; with report by N. Greenblatt. il Life 57:94-8+ D 4 '64
COLLISON, Robert
Continuing barrier; translation & East-West communications. UNESCO Courier 16:6-9 F '63
COLLISTER, Larew M.
Better way than merit pay. NEA J 53:37-8 My '64
COLLOIDS
Volume changes of a thixotropic, sodium bentonite suspension during sol-gel-sol transition. D. M. Anderson and others. bibliog il Science 141:1040-1 S 13 '63
COLLOQUIAL bulls. See Bulls, Colloquial
COLM, Gerhard
Economic base and limits of social welfare. Mo Labor R 86:695-700 Je '63
COLMAN, Hila
Before the weekend. Am Home 67:20 Je '64
COLOGNE
Description
Cologne. J. Naar. Vogue 144:74 S 15 '64
COLOGNE. See Perfumery
COLOMBIA
Deadly debut; Castroite activity. Time 85: 30 Ja 22 '65
Stamping out la violencia. il Time 83:40+ Mr 13 '64
Testing ground in Colombia. J. M. Hunter. bibliog il Cur Hist 46:8-14+ Ja '64
See also
Agriculture—Colombia
Churches—Colombia
Community development—Colombia
Crime and criminals—Colombia
Guerrillas—Colombia
Hunting—Colombia
Land tenure—Colombia
Schools—Colombia
Trade unions—Colombia
Economic policy
Atlantic report. Atlan 212:10+ D '63
New look. il Newsweek 64:47 Ag 17 '64
Instituto Caro y Cuervo
Temple of the Spanish language. G. De Zéndegui. il Américas 16:4-9 Ja '64
Politics and government
Atlantic report. Atlan 212:10+ D '63
Cracks in the showcase. Time 84:48+ D 11 '64
Dictator's comeback. Time 84:29 Ag 14 '64
Systematic approach; El sistema. M. J. Kubic. Newsweek 64:50 Jl 20 '64
Religious institutions and affairs
News of the Christian world. Christian Cent 81:57 Ja 8 '64
COLOMBIAN art. See Art, Colombian
COLOMBIAN poetry
Nadaísta poetry of Colombia; with poem by G. Arango. il Américas 15:28-31 N '63
COLOMBIANS in the United States
United States in 1850; from the letters of a Colombian exile. M. Torres. il Américas 16: 1-8 F '64
COLOMBO, Franco, incorporated. See Music publishing
COLOMBO, John Robert
Recipe for a Canadian novel; after Cyprian Norwid; poem. Atlan 214:118 N '64
COLOMBO plan
How goes the Colombo plan? Time 82:33 N 22 '63
New dimensions for the Colombo plan. M. J. Marks. Dept State Bul 48:977-83 Je 24 '63
COLON (anatomy)
Diseases
See also
Colitis
COLONIAL administration. See Colonies—Administration
COLONIAL architecture. See Architecture, Colonial
COLONIAL history (United States) See United States—History—Colonial period
COLONIAL painting. See Painting, American
COLONIAL pipeline company. See Petroleum pipe lines
COLONIAL press. See Printing—Private presses
COLONIAL Williamsburg garden symposium
Williamsburg announces symposium program. il Flower Grower 51:21-2 Ja '64
COLONIALISM. See Colonies
COLONIES
African's warning: colonialism must disappear. U S News 55:22 Jl 29 '63
Colonialism and the decade of development; address, February 21, 1963. J. B. Bingham. Dept State Bul 48:459-61 Mr 25 '63
How to talk about communism; when colonialism and anticolonialism are the subject. H. Overstreet and B. W. Overstreet. PTA Mag 57:8-10 Ap '63
See also
Imperialism
United Nations—Committee on information from non-self-governing territories
United Nations—Special committee on situation with regard to implementation of declaration on granting of independence to colonial countries and peoples
also subhead Colonies under names of countries, e.g. Portugal—Colonies
Administration
Sullenness under the sun. N. T. di Giovanni. Nation 196:287-9 Ap 6 '63
COLONIES in Africa
United Nations and colonialism in Africa. R. Welensky. Ann Am Acad 354:145-52 Jl '64
COLONNA, Milagros, princess
Princess Milagros Colonna with her children. il por Vogue 143:162-3 Mr 1 '64
COLONNELLO, Attilio
Man from Milan; interview, ed. by F. Stevenson. por Opera N 29:14-15 O 17 '64
COLOPHONS
Secker & Warburg adopts a colophon. Pub W 183:27 Ap 22 '63
COLOR
Color portfolio. il Craft Horiz 24:61-8 My '64
Colorful quiz. J. Daugherty and M. Daugherty. il Sci Digest 55:43-5 My '64
Interaction of color; excerpts. J. Albers. il Art N 62:32-5+ Mr '63
Is it true? primary colors. H. N. Todd and R. D. Zakia. Pop Phot 53:40 N '63
Josef Albers on tour; Smithsonian's traveling exhibition service. F. Getlein. New Repub 149:34-6 S 21 '63
Wonderful ways with color; color wheel. E. G. Snellenberger. il Design 66:27-9 N '64
See also
Dyes and dyeing

COLOR—*Continued*

Psychology

Binasal hemianopia as an early stage in binocular color rivalry. H. F. Crovitz and D. B. Lipscomb. bibliog Science 139:596-7 F 15 '63

Color affects performance. Sci N L 85:141 F 29 '64

COLOR adaptation. See Eye—Accommodation and refraction

COLOR and music. See Music and color

COLOR-balance stabilizer. See Television apparatus

COLOR blindness

Boy who thought pancakes were green. S. S. Rosenberg. il Parents Mag 38:70-1+ F '63

More color-blindness in civilized world. Sci N L 83:233 Ap 13 '63

Receptors of human color vision; with appendix by W. S. Stiles. G. Wald. bibliog il Science 145:1007-17 S 4 '64

Why color-blind? Newsweek 64:64 O 19 '64

COLOR cathode ray tubes. See Television receiving apparatus—Picture tubes

COLOR charts

Color workshop; Munsell color wheel. F. Bond. il Mod Phot 27:12-13 N; 10-11 D '63

Wonderful ways with color; color wheel. E. G. Snellenberger. il Design 66:27-9 N '64

COLOR film processing. See Photography—Developing and developers

COLOR films. See Photography—Films

COLOR filters. See Light filters

COLOR in gardens. See Gardens—Color

COLOR in house decoration

Add a splash of color; Color gives character to a tract house; Color does wonders for an older house. il Am Home 67:58-67 Jl '64

And inside, great decorating! N. Seney. il Bet Hom & Gard 42:44-9 Mr '64

Beat the heat in a cool-looking room. il Suc Farm 61:57 Ag '63

Bravura color coolly controlled. il House & Gard 124:160-3 D '63

Color compounded. G. O'Brien. il N Y Times Mag pt2 p20-1 S 27 '64

Color hits the jackpot. il House & Gard 123: 110-11 Mr '63

Color is pepper. il House & Gard 125:150-3 My '64

Color that makes tradition come alive. M. Gough. il House B 105:134-47 Mr '63

Decorated with a spirit of independence. R. W. Houseman. il Am Home 66:36-9 N '63

Give your everyday a lift; work with color. il Farm J 87:66-7+ Je '63

Here is more of today's great decorating. il Bet Hom & Gard 42:50-7 Mr '64

H&G gives a house individuality with color inside and out; H&G colors for 1965. il House & Gard 126:150-73 S '64

How to concentrate color. il House & Gard 123:102-9 Mr '63

How to cool off a color scheme. M. Casserly. Bet Hom & Gard 41:66-7 Je '63

How to make an old house look as fresh as tomorrow. il House & Gard 123:134-41 My '63

Inspiring new colors, lively but livable. D. Popplestone. il Bet Hom & Gard 41:42-7 Ag '63

Introducing H&G colors for 1964; symposium. il House & Gard 124:121-45 S '63

McCall's guide to color. il McCalls 92:124-5 O '64

Many ways a room can change, all of them rich. il House B 106:166-8 Ap '64

Out of the blues; twenty-eight elements for spring decorating. il Vogue 141:146-7+ Ap 1 '63

Putting color to work. il House & Gard 125:123-49 Mr '64

Settle down with our restful color schemes. E. Gordon. il House B 106:158-63+ Ap '64

She worked with color. il Am Home 67:48-9 D '64

Start a new color scheme with a brightly patterned fabric. il Bet Hom & Gard 41:47 S '63

Think blue. M. White. il Ladies Home J 81: 106-8 S '64

This is color! symposium. il Bet Hom & Gard 41:46-69 Ap '63

White plus. M. White. il Ladies Home J 81: 46-9 Jl '64

White plus color! il Bet Hom & Gard 41: 110 Mr '63

COLOR in school decoration. See School decoration

COLOR matching

Electronic color matcher. R. P. Turner. il Pop Electr 18:51-3 My '63

COLOR mixing

Wonderful ways with color; color wheel. E. G. Snellenberger. il Design 66:27-9 N '64

COLOR names

Zany zane gray. Newsweek 62:48 D 30 '63

COLOR of amphibia

Pteridines as pigments in amphibians. M. Obika and J .T. Bagnara. bibliog il Science 143:485-7 Ja 31 '64

COLOR of animals

Color change: chameleon camouflage. H. G. Dowling. il Natur Hist 73:40-3 F '64

Color polymorphism in Pacific tree frogs. L. E. Resnick and D. L. Jameson. bibliog il Science 142:1081-3 N 22 '63

Polymorphism and population density in the African land snail, limicolaria martensiana. D. F. Owen. il Science 140:666-7 My 10 '63

See also

Albinos and albinism

Color of amphibia

COLOR of darkness; drama. See Violett, E.

COLOR of fishes

Carotenoids of cavernicolous crayfish. D. A. Wolfe and D. G. Cornwell. bibliog il Science 144:1467-9 Je 19 '64

COLOR of flowers

Annuals for summer color. il Am Home 67:4+ Je '64

Cool blues for warm summer. Sunset 132:246 Je '64

Flower pigments. S. Clevenger. il Sci Am 210:84-8+ Je '64

If you obey that April impulse here are favorite plants for summer color. il Sunset 132:110-11+ Ap '64

Nitrogen and potassium effect on the color of red roses. R. S. Lindstrom and P. Markakis. bibliog il Science 142:1663-4 D 27 '63

COLOR of insects

Mimicry: differential advantage of color patterns in the natural environment. L. P. Brower and others. bibliog il Science 144: 183-5 Ap 10 '64

On the character of color; with photographs. A. B. Klots. Natur Hist 72:30-9 Je '63

COLOR of leaves

Many colors: why? New Yorker 40:39-40 S 26 '64

Only in America: such autumn color. R. M. Carleton. il Todays Health 41:46-9 O '63

Set your garden ablaze with autumn color. T. A. Weston. il Am Home 66:34-5 S '63

COLOR of man

See also

Negro race

COLOR of minerals

Apatite: origin of blue color. P. D. Johnson and others. bibliog il Science 141:1179-80 S 20 '63

COLOR organ

Simplified solid-state color organ. D. Lancaster. il Electr World 71:50+ Ja '64

Solid-state 3-channel color organ. D. Lancaster. il Electr World 69:55-8+ Ap '63

Transistor-photocell color organ. F. Blechman. il Electr World 72:41-3 Jl '64

COLOR photography

As I see it. E. Hannigan. U S Camera 27:34 Je '64

Battle against blue. G. E. Parker. il Pop Phot 55:68-9 Jl '64

Black light for brilliant color. P. Farber. il U S Camera 27:38-9+ Ag; 28-9 O '64

Bounce flash for color. C. Wright. il Pop Phot 52:46-9+ Ja '63

Bright color under soft light. il U S Camera 27:35-7 My '64

Candid color portraits. il U S Camera 27:50-1 Ap '64

Color action at night. G. Hoffman. il U S Camera 26:48-9+ Ag '63

Color action at noon. il U S Camera 26:44-7+ Ag '63

Color clinic. D. B. Eisendrath, jr. See issues of Popular photography

Color from B&W. P. Gridley. il Mod Phot 27: 58-9 F '63

Color in astrophotography. G. T. Keene. il Sky & Tel 26:74-6 Ag '63

Color negative or transparency. A. Rothstein. U S Camera 26:39+ Ag '63

Color photography in theory and practice. D. Linton. il Natur Hist 72:62-5+ O '63

Color photography ripe for market. Sci N L 84:280 N 2 '63

Color photos in sixty seconds. B. Hering. il Pop Sci 182:61-4+ F '63

Color: the slower the better? N. Rothschild. Pop Phot 52:77 F '63

COLOR photography—*Continued*
Color workshop. F. Bond. See issues of Modern photography
Confined? cut loose with SLR color. P. Caulfield. il Mod Phot 28:60-3 S '64
Controls in color. il Pop Phot 54:70-9 My '64
Cool it! Warm it! il U S Camera 27:54-7 Ag '64
Crash course in color. A. Francekevich. il Pop Phot 53:45-57+ Jl '63
Creative color. A. Rothstein. See issues of U.S. camera
Creative color; impact of Polacolor on newspaper photography. A. Rothstein. U S Camera 26:14+ O '63
Cross-polarized color. P. Farber. il U S Camera 27:38-9+ Jl '64
Design for color. il U S Camera 27:60-5 F '64
Eliot Porter. P. Caulfield. il Mod Phot 28:52-7+ F '64
Farewell to slides? color prints. A. Francekevich. il Pop Phot 55:16+ S '64
Filters for color; control, correct, create. N. Rothschild. il Pop Phot 52:74-87 Je '63
Five photographers talk color & lenses; ed. by G. Pyle. il Pop Phot 54:82-91+ Ap '64
Flash with color. il U S Camera 26:52-3 D '63
Focus on Jay Maisel. J. Durniak. il Pop Phot 54:76-85+ Mr '64
Form & content in color. R. Hattersley. il Pop Phot 55:84-91 Jl '64
From Norman Rothschild's color notebook. N. Rothschild. Pop Phot 55:64-7+ Jl '64
How can you spot the techniques used for these pictures? il Pop Phot 52:64-74 F '63
How to louse up your color lab. N. Rothschild and L. Zoref. il Pop Phot 55:60-1+ S '64
How to save money on color. N. Rothschild. Pop Phot 55:64-5+ Jl '64
How would you make pictures like these? il Pop Phot 54:56-65 F '64
Instant color photography. W. Siegrist. il Sci N L 83:250-1 Ap 20 '63
Instant color photos! K. Brown. il Pop Mech 119:100-5+ F '63
Is it true? question of color processes. H. N. Todd and R. D. Zakia. Pop Phot 54:16 Je '64
It's here! Polacolor; symposium with portfolio by famous pros. Pop Phot 52:49-63+ Mr '63
It's not too early to plan your color holiday cards. R. Russell. il Pop Phot 53:66-7+ O '63
Keppler on the SLR; shooting color. H. Keppler. Mod Phot 28:14-15 O '64
Landscapes. il U S Camera 26:54-5 F '63
Light for color. il U S Camera 28:50-4 Ja '65
Long exposures for night color. il U S Camera 26:70-2 Mr '63
Mexico, a big photo studio. L. Barry. il Pop Phot 52:30+ Mr '63
New look in color; creative color work in Germany. W. Boje. il U S Camera 27:52-7+ N '64
Norman Rothschild's guide to daylight color slide films. N. Rothschild. il Pop Phot 53:166-75 D '63
Polacolor. il U S Camera 26:52-7 Mr '63
Polaroid color. J. Wolbarst. il Mod Phot 27:60-5+ Mr '63
Problems, solutions in color. D. B. Eisendrath, jr. il Pop Phot 55:51-61 Jl '64
Subdued light for color beauty. il U S Camera 26:66-9 Je '63
Super bright, super sharp, super color. P. Caulfield. il Mod Phot 27:64-7 Je '63
35mm daylight Kodachrome-X. H. Keppler. il Mod Phot 27:80-5+ Mr '63
Try these new cross-polarization techniques. P. Farber. U S Camera 27:30+ S '64
Use the light you've got. H. Keppler. il Mod Phot 29:80-3 Ja '65
Use the sun to dramatize landscapes. P. Caulfield. il Mod Phot 28:68-71 O '64
Vagabond camera. W. Lane. il Travel 120:62-3 O '63
Vagabond camera; Polaroid Land color film. W. Lane. Travel 119:70-1 Ap '63
When & how to expose for perfect color. W. Benser. il Mod Phot 27:56-9+ Jl '63
Which film? H. Keppler. il Mod Phot 27:52-7 F '63
COLOR photography exhibitions. See Photography—Exhibitions
COLOR photography printing. See Photography—Printing processes
COLOR photomicrography. See Photomicrography
COLOR prejudice. See Race prejudice
COLOR printing
Lane's California: an example of uncommon printing. il Pub W 183:90-2 Je 3 '63
Ranges and limits of color reproduction. Pub W 184:80+ Jl 1 '63
Triumph at Yale: Albers' Interaction of color. il Pub W 184:78-9 N 4 '63
See also
Newspapers—Color printing
COLOR prints
See also
Linoleum block printing
COLOR sense
Color discrimination in the cat. J. A. Sechzer and J. L. Brown. bibliog il Science 144:427-9 Ap 24 '64; Summary. Sci Am 210:59 Je '64
Color vision carried in electronic code. il Sci N L 84:37 Jl 20 '63
Hue-wavelength relation measured by color-naming method for three retinal locations. R. M. Boynton and others. bibliog il Science 146:666-8 O 30 '64
Köllner effect and suppression of the view of an eye. H. F. Crovitz. bibliog il Science 146:1329-30 D 4 '64
New theory describes why we see colors; physical rather than chemical reactions. il Sci N L 86:117 Ag 22 '64
Receptors of human color vision; with appendix by W. S. Stiles. G. Wald. bibliog il Science 145:1007-17 S 4 '64
Scotopic spectral sensitivity in the monkey. D. S. Blough and A. M. Schrier. bibliog il Science 139:493-4 F 8 '63
Three-pigment color vision. E. F. MacNichol, jr. il Sci Am 211:48-56 bibliog (p 154) D '64
See also
Retina
COLOR-slide projectors. See Projection apparatus
COLOR slides. See Transparencies
COLOR television. See Television, Color
COLOR television receiving apparatus. See Television receiving apparatus—Color receivers
COLOR vision. See Color sense
COLOR wheel. See Color charts
COLORADO
See also
Booksellers and bookselling—Colorado
Central City opera association
Cheyenne Mountain
Festivals—Colorado
Hunting—Colorado
Libraries—Colorado
Mesa Verde National Park
Mines and mineral resources—Colorado
Music festivals—Colorado
Water supply—Colorado

Description and travel

Pikes Peak and all that. B. Ballantine. il Holiday 34:18+ Ag '63

Industries

Shale oil gets a fresh push. Bsns W p 114 S 7 '63

Politics and government

Case study of a state that switched. il U S News 57:56 D 14 '64

Religious institutions and affairs

News of the Christian world (cont) Christian Cent 80:507-8, 1590; 81:710, 1571 Ap 17, D 18 '63, My 27, D 16 '64
COLORADO avalanches. See Avalanches
COLORADO college, Colorado Springs, Colo.
Science hall stresses inner flexibility; Olin hall of science. il Arch Rec 137:120-1 Ja '65
Split hall for science. il Arch Forum 118:82-3 Mr '63
COLORADO photographic art center. See Photography—Galleries and museums
COLORADO RIVER
Battle of the Colorado. il Time 81:31 Je 14 '63
Bridge Canyon Dam is not necessary; with editorial comment. S. Raushenbush. il Nat Parks Mag 38:2, 4-8 Ap '64
Colorado jackpot. J. Olsen. il Sports Illus 19:52-9 S 2 '63
Colorado River cruise. V. L. Oertle. il Yachting 113:52-3 Mr '63
Colorado River of the West; excerpt from Inverted mountains. W. F. Heald. il Nat Parks Mag 37:4-9 O '63
Colorado waters dispute. N. Hundley, jr. For Affairs 42:495-500 Ap '64
Desert boating. F. M. Paulson. il Field & S 69:57-9+ N '64
Exploring the Colorado: Lee's Ferry to Lake Mead. F. E. Masland, jr. il Nat Parks Mag 38:4-7+ My '64

COLORADO RIVER—*Continued*
Great thirst. New Repub 149:13-14 Jl 6 '63
Mighty Colorado; Pacific Southwest water plan and Bridge Canyon Dam. A. W. Smith. Nat Parks Mag 37:2+ O '63
Pulling the plug. il Time 83:23 Ap 24 '64
Stormy water. il Newsweek 61:26+ Je 17 '63
Too many people, not enough water; coming crisis. il U S News 54:62-4 Je 17 '63
U.S. watering down river. Sci N L 85:181 Mr 21 '64
View from Dead Horse Point. il Sunset 132: 10 Ap '64
War clouds over the Colorado; Marble Canyon case. A. W. Smith. Nat Parks Mag 37:2 Ap '63
Water challenge of the Pacific Southwest; with editorial comment. S. Raushenbush. il Nat Parks Mag 38:2, 4-7 Je '64
Water for thirsty Southwest. il Bsns W p20-1 Ag 31 '63
West's water fight is far from over; Supreme court backs Ariz. over Calif. Bsns W p26 Je 8 '63
See also
Central Arizona project (proposed)
Glen Canyon
Havasu Lake

COLORADO tick fever. See Rocky Mountain spotted fever

COLORADO. University, Boulder
Counterattack at Colorado; liberals vs. conservatives, college newspapers vs. B. Goldwater. W. H. Carroll. Nat R 14:494-5 Je 18 '63
Enter Smiley, ninth president. Newsweek 61: 88 My 20 '63

COLORING books
Color books harmful. il Sci N L 85:244 Ap 18 '64
Colored account; coloring book's influence on young. Newsweek 63:98 Ap 27 '64

COLPRIT, Ernest S.
Consider the lowly juniper. Horticulture 41: 516-17 O '63

COLQUHOUN, Archibald
Lampedusa in Sicily; the lair of the leopard. por Atlan 211:91-3+ F '63

COLQUITT, Betsy Feagan
Epiphany; poem. Christian Cent 82:15 Ja 6 '65
Poem for Friday. Christian Cent 80:461 Ap 10 '63

COLT patent firearms manufacturing company
Colt's new rifle; the M-16. il Time 82:86 N 22 '63

COLT revolvers. See Revolvers

COLTS
Act II: same cast, new set; Preakness race at Pimlico track. W. Tower. Sports Illus 18:69-70 My 20 '63
Best colt is still in the barn. W. Tower. Sports Illus 19:48+ S 2 '63
Big three looked mighty small; Carry Back's comeback in Cleveland. W. Tower and W. Leggett. il Sports Illus 19:16-17 Ag 26 '63
Case of the curious colt; Greentree stable's No Robbery. W. Tower. Sports Illus 18: 49 Ap 29 '63
Dancer, the Scoundrel, and Mr Moon. W. Tower and W. Leggett. il Sports Illus 20: 24-7 Ap 13 '64
Do-it-yourself guide to the two-year-olds; experimental rating list. W. Tower. Sports Illus 19:62 O 21 '63
Giving them the raspberry; Speedy Scot wins. P. Ryan. il Sports Illus 19:70-2 O 14 '63
Good colt is hard to find; Candy Spots and Never Bend. W. Tower. Sports Illus 18:44-6 F 18 '63
It was easy for Never Bend at Hialeah. W. Leggett. il Sports Illus 18:20-1 Mr 11 '63
Kin of Carry Back; Lepanto. Sports Illus 18: 18+ Ap 15 '63
They all are aiming at Ayres; Hambletonian, foremost trotting event. R. A. Hackett. il Sports Illus 21:51-2 Ag 24 '64
Two colts go after one derby; Candy Spots and Never Bend. W. Tower. il Sports Illus 18:18-23 Ap 8 '63
Winner was the Ruler with floppy ears. W. Tower. il Sports Illus 19:16-17 S 16 '63

COLTS (football club) See Football clubs

COLUM, Padraic
Before a row of votive candles; poem. Commonweal 78:199 My 10 '63
Credit to old Ireland. Sat R 47:43 Ap 4 '64
Images of departure; poem. Yale R 52:412-14 Mr '63

COLUMBIA, Mo, public library
Public library gains support; cooperation and 400 borrowers; Daniel Boone regional library, Columbia, Mo. S. Alexander. Library J 88:1102-4 Mr 15 '63
Starting library service to hospitals. T. F. McArthur. ALA Bul 57:859-60 O '63

COLUMBIA, S.C.
From city dump to industrial park. C. C. Burnett. il Am City 78:95-6 Jl '63

Water supply
Growth follows the water mains. C. C. Burnett. il Am City 78:132-3 Je '63

COLUMBIA artists management
Reports: North American artists management. il Mus Am 83:230-9 Ja '63

COLUMBIA broadcasting system
After the Yankees what? a TV drama. L. W. Robinson. il N Y Times Mag p44-5+ N 15 '64
Big deal; CBS buys Yankees. il Newsweek 64:54-5 Ag 24 '64
Big eye league; Yankees sold to Columbia broadcasting system. il Time 84:74 Ag 21 '64
Big sellout; CBS buys New York Yankees; with editorial comment. il Sports Illus 21:8, 12-17 Ag 24 '64
Bulldozer; F. B. Friendly of CBS news. Newsweek 63:56 Mr 16 '64
CBS and NBC: Walter vs. Chet and Dave. il Newsweek 62:62-5 S 23 '63
Feathers and fun; D. Schoenbrun leaves CBS. Newsweek 62:65 Jl 8 '63
Gold in the air; company's finances. Time 82:78 N 22 '63
Great adventure. J. T. Aubrey, jr. il NEA J 52:33-48 O '63
Laugh off $11 million? Columbia broadcasting system buys New York Yankee baseball club. J. R. Tunis. New Repub 152:11-12 Ja 2 '65
Man for all seasons at CBS. Bsns W p 126-8+ Ag 10 '63
Memorandum to a network. L. E. Craine and Mrs L. E. Craine. Sat R 46:28 D 28 '63
Mr CBS. il Time 83:56-7 Ja 31 '64
No. 1 supplier of TV viewers; CBS-TV. il Bsns W p90-1+ Ap 25 '64
On the news beat. il Newsweek 63:74-5 Je 1 '64
Razzle-dazzle; CBS football coverage. Newsweek 64:65 S 28 '64
Saarinen's dark tower; the CBS building and how it grew. E. Lattabee. il Harper 229: 55-61 D '64
Sad day for baseball; selling of Yankees to CBS. W. B. Furlong. il Sports Illus 21: 26-7+ S 21 '64
Television tilts the old ball game; sale of Yankees to CBS; with report by T. Flaherty. il Life 57:87-8 Ag 28 '64
Upstairs was unhappy. il Newsweek 64:44-5 Ag 10 '64
Walter Cronkite: why won't he be himself on TV? I. Taves. il Look 28:74+ Ag 25 '64
Yankee: descent from Olympus; once the mightiest team in baseball, now, like Beverly hillbillies, it belongs to CBS. Why? R. Kahn. il Sat Eve Post 237:80-3 S 12 '64
You might call it CBS distorts. R. Starnes. Field & S 69:20+ S '64

COLUMBIA college. See Columbia university—Columbia college

COLUMBIA encyclopedia
Planning, printing and prayer: Columbia encyclopedia, 3rd ed. il Pub W 184:80-1 N 4 '63

COLUMBIA Jays. See Jays

COLUMBIA-Presbyterian medical center. See New York (city)—Columbia-Presbyterian medical center

COLUMBIA records, incorporated
Change of chairs; interviews, ed. by S. Fleming. il Hi Fi 14:28+ Ja '64
Columbia's 1903 grand opera series; first recordings of opera in America. F. M. Kleeberg. il Am Rec G 29:772-5 Je '63

COLUMBIA RIVER
Boating on the great river of the West. L. Barber. il Motor B 111:34-5+ My '63
Canadian Prime Minister visits Washington; U.S. and Canada agree on Columbia River development and establishment of Campobello Park; joint communique; with joint statements and texts of agreements; January 21-23, 1964. L. B. Johnson; L. B. Pearson. Dept State Bul 50:199-206 F 10 '64
Columbia: a gem of a river. R. Cantwell. il Sports Illus 20:56-60+ F 24 '64
Decision in Oregon. T. Trueblood. il Field & S 69:10-12+ N '64

COLUMBIA RIVER—*Continued*
Gamma emitters in marine sediments near the Columbia River. C. Osterberg and others. bibliog il Science 139:916-17 Mr 8 '63
Hydropower dream come true; congressional approval of Pacific Northwest-Southwest intertie. il U S News 57:70 S 7 '64
In the catbird seat. Newsweek 62:31 D 30 '63
President Johnson proclaims Columbia River treaty; proclamation, September 16, 1964. L. B. Johnson. Dept State Bul 51:507 O 12 '64
River with a past, and a future; Clark Fork of the Columbia River. J. Brooks. il Field & S 69:12-14+ O '64
U.S. and Canada hold Columbia River treaty ceremonies; remarks, with exchange of notes, executive order, and Canadian entitlement purchase agreement. L. B. Johnson; L. B. Pearson. Dept State Bul 51:504-16 O 12 '64
You can still ferry across the Columbia. il Sunset 132:39-40 Ap '64

Power utilization

U.S. and Canada to tame a river. il U S News 55:44 D 30 '63
See also
Grand Coulee power and reclamation project

COLUMBIA RIVER VALLEY
Pictographs along the Columbia. il Sunset 132:24+ Mr '64

COLUMBIA university
City slums vs. a university. il U S News 56: 74-7 Ap 6 '64
Columbia explosion. New Yorker 39:31-2 Ap 6 '63
Columbia's unorthodox seminars. P. Goodman. Harper 228:72-5+ Ja '64
Dramatic renewal on campus; Columbia's Manhattan campus. il Arch Forum 121:114-17 Jl '64
Refreshment on the rock; policymakers from business firms at Arden house. il Time 84:67 Ag 7 '64
Science class; nine to eleven year olds at Columbia's School of engineering and applied science. New Yorker 39:22-3 Ja 4 '64
See also
Barnard college, New York
Teachers college

Columbia college

Changing character of undergraduate education; address, January 11, 1964. D. B. Truman. Sch & Soc 92:380-3 D 12 '64
Columbia college: report to headmasters, principals and counselors, 1962-1963. H. S. Coleman. Sch & Soc 91:148-9; 92:239-41 Mr 23 '63; Reply. A. L. Goren. 91:271 O 5 63, Sum '64

Graduate school of business

Business school with a rising star. il Bsns W p56-60+ My 2 '64

Graduate school of journalism

Fat, fifty & still fertile. il Time 81:53 Ap 26 '63
Pulitzer idea: fifty years old. J. Tebbel. il Sat R 46:52-3 Mr 9 '63; Discussion. 46:78 Ap 13 '63
We don't hurt them. il Newsweek 61:55 Ap 29 '63

Libraries

Koo papers to Columbia; East Asian library. Wilson Lib Bul 38:229 N '63
Oral history collection; concerning publication of catalog. Wilson Lib Bul 38:716 My '64

School of business

See Columbia university—Graduate school of business

School of engineering and applied science

Columbia school of engineering marks 100th year. Arch Rec 135:302 Ap '64

School of general studies

For adults only. il Time 83:44 My 8 '64

School of library service

Columbia library school celebrates 80th (?) anniversary. Library J 88:2477 Je 15 '63

COLUMBIA university press
Columbia exhibition marks seventy years of publishing. il Pub W 186:54 Jl 6 '64

COLUMBIAN exposition of 1893. See Chicago—World's Columbian exposition, 1893

COLUMBINES
Adventure in aquilegia. B. Mellen. il Horticulture 41:331 Je '63

COLUMBIUM
Columbium thrust chamber is test-fired. M. L. Yaffee. il Aviation W 80:47-8 Mr 30 '64

COLUMBUS, Christopher
America, the navigator's error. J. Lear. il Sat R 46:86-8 O 12 '63
Entries in a logbook: a miscellany of facts on the voyagings of Columbus. B. Smith. il Sat R 46:89 O 12 '63
Niña II. E. C. Uriburu. il Américas 15:2-7 Ap '63
San Salvador seen first. B. Tufty. Sci N L 86:294 N 7 '64
They made our world. L. Rosten. il Look 27: 126-7 O 22 '63

Drama

Compass for Christopher. D. Newman. Plays 24:73-6, 82 O '64

COLUMBUS, Ind.

Architecture

Athens on the prairie. W. McCaslin. il Sat Eve Post 237:64-5 Mr 21 '64
Indiana bank is automobile oriented. il Arch Rec 135:118-19 Ja '64

COLUMBUS, Ohio

Stores

Retailing love affair in Ohio; F. & R. Lazarus & co. il Bsns W p 138-9+ O 19 '63

COLUMBUS, Ohio, public library
Paperback pilot project. G. Gordon. il Library J 89:191-2 Ja 15 '64

COLUMBUS, Tex.
Just read the emergency instructions. E. Gold. il Am City 79:22 Ag '64

COLUMBUS day.
Columbus day. G. de Zéndegui. Américas 16: inside cover O '64
Columbus day, 1964; proclamation, October 3, 1964. L. B. Johnson. Dept State Bul 51: 597-8 O 26 '64

COLUMNISTS. See Newspapers—Sections, columns, etc.

COLUMNS (architecture)
Formwork: time-saver standards. S. Howard. il Arch Rec 136:255 S '64

COLUMNS (newspapers) See Newspapers—Sections, columns, etc.

COLUSA, Calif.
How we saved our shade. J. Miller. il Am City 78:24 S '63

COLVIN, Barbara
We inspire remodeling of fire-damaged home. Am Home 66:87 Ap '63

COMA
Psychological changes associated with induced hyperammonemia. M. Eichler. bibliog il Science 144:886-8 My 15 '64
Sad victory for a heavyweight; A. Lavorante paralyzed by blow; with report by R. Stolley. il Life 55:97-8+ S 27 '63

COMAP. See Commerce committee for the Alliance for progress

COMAR, C. L.
Radiation and food: is action needed? Bul Atomic Sci 19:37-40 Mr '63

COMBAT, Personal. See Fighting, Hand-to-hand

COMBATIVENESS
See also
Fighting (psychology)

COMBINED book exhibit (organization)
Combined book exhibit: a peaceful expansion. il Pub W 187:26-30 Ja 4 '65
Combined book exhibit program for communication between paperback book publishers and educational market. Wilson Lib Bul 38:31 S '63
Combined book exhibits. Sr Schol 85:30T O 7 '64

COMBINES. See Harvesting machinery

COMBS, Arthur W.
Can we measure good teaching objectively? NEA J 53:34+ Ja 64

COMBS, Mattie
Books for Osage. I. Mothner. il pors Look 28:60+ Ap 21 '64

COMBS, Prentiss
Beyond all wonder; story. Good H 157:86-7 O '63
Boy with the eagle laugh; story. Read Digest 85:173-4 Jl '64
Image of love; story. Good H 158:60-1 Ja '64

COMBS
Comb collecting. F. C. McKiernan. il Hobbies 69:28-9 Ap '64

COMBUSTION
Ash content: its effect on combustion of corn plants. A. Broido and M. A. Nelson. bibliog il Science 146:652-3 O 30 '64

COMBUSTION chambers. See Automobile engines

COMBUSTION engineering, incorporated
Bigger equipment for bigger reactors; fabricators of nuclear reactor vessels. Bsns W p 118 Ag 17 '63
COME home to us now; story. See Knowlton, R. A.
COME lady death; story. See Beagle, P. S.
COMEBACK; story. See Brower, B.
COMECON. See Council for mutual economic assistance
COMEDIANS
Funny girls. N. Cohen. Nat R 16:982-3 N 3 '64
Polite generation. il Time 82:71 S 13 '63
Thirty-nine; J. Benny. G. Frank. il McCalls 90:90-1+ Ap '63
See also
Allen, W.
Bruce, L.
Lahr, B.
Negro comedians
Winters, J.
COMEDY
See also
Comedians
Commedia dell' arte
Humor
Moving pictures—Comedy
Television broadcasting—Humor
COMEDY of errors; drama. See Shakespeare, W.—Plays
COMET probes. See Space probes
COMETS
Anti-matter may explain comet's brightening; comet Schwassmann-Wachmann. Sci N L 83:261 Ap 27 '63
Comet belt predicted near farthest planet; summary of address. F. I. Whipple. il Sci N L 84:275 N 2 '63
Comet birth near earth; comet Ikeya. Sci N L 86:386 D 19 '64
Comet Everhart, 1964H. il Sky & Tel 28:246 O '64
Comet found near sun during solar eclipse. il Sci N L 84:163 S 14 '63
Comet Ikeya prominent in southern sky. il Sky & Tel 25:196-8 Ap '63
Comet Pereyra. il Sky & Tel 26:300-1 N '63
Comet rediscovered unseen for fifty eight years; comet Holmes. Sci N L 86:201 S 26 '64
Comet Tempel-Swift. Sky & Tel 26:261 N '63
Comet Tomita-Gerber-Honda. il Sky & Tel 28:107-8 Ag '64
Comets' wanderings end eventually in dissipation into space. S. D. Gossner. il Natur Hist 72:52-3 O '63
Did a comet collide with the earth in 1908? Tungus meteorite expedition. K. P. Florenskii. il Sky & Tel 26:268-9 N '63
Disintegrating comets; comet Faye; comet Encke. il Sky & Tel 27:148-9 Mr '64
Doctor Wernher von Braun tells about comets and meteors; questions and answers. W. von Braun. il Pop Sci 184:95-7 Ap '64
Dust in comet Arend-Roland. il Sky & Tel 26:21-2 Jl '63
First tail-wagging comet discovered. il Sci N L 84:323 N 23 '63
Getting acquainted with astronomy. il Sky & Tel 27:22-3, 283-5 Ja, My '64
Harvester of the skies. J. Ashbrook. il Sky & Tel 25:198-9 Ap '63
More news about comet Ikeya. il Sky & Tel 25:278-9 My '63
More observations of comet 1964c. il Sky & Tel 28:174-7 S '64
New comet Alcock. Sky & Tel 25:281 My '63
New comet discovered; Ikeya. Sci N L 86:45 Jl 18 '64
New comet Ikeya 1964f. il Sky & Tel 28:178 S '64
New short-period comet; Kearns-Kwee. il Sky & Tel 27:16 Ja '64
News about comet Alcock. il Sky & Tel 26:33-5 Jl '63
Out of the eclipse; photographing comets at Pleasant Pond, Me. Newsweek 62:80 S 16 '63
Periodic comet Pons-Winnecke found. il Sky & Tel 27:267+ My '64
Photographing comet Ikeya. A. McClure. il Sky & Tel 25:263-6 My '63
Planets and comets: role of crystal growth in their formation. B. Donn and G. W. Sears. bibliog il Science 140:1208-11 Je 14 '63
Probe for comet fluff. Time 82:62+ N 8 '63
Recovery of comet Holmes. J. Ashbrook. il Sky & Tel 28:268 N '64
Scientists plan missions to comets. W. Beller. il Miss & Roc 12:22-3 My 6 '63
Solar system has some two million comets. Sci N L 86:134 Ag 29 '64
Strange comet Humason (1961e) Sky & Tel 28:70 Ag '64
Trans-Neptunian comet belt. Sci Am 211:43 Ag '64
Weighing a comet. il Sky & Tel 26:197-8 O '63
COMFORT, Iris Tracy
How to head off tantrums. Parents Mag 38:60-1+ D '63
COMFORT, J. Earl
St Louis is proud of its European sparrow. Audubon Mag 65:381-3 N '63
COMFORT; story. See Hazzard, S.
COMFORTER; drama. See Molloy, E. A.
COMFREY
Make compost out of comfrey. V. L. Heitmann. il Horticulture 41:456 S '63
COMIC literature. See Humor
COMIC opera. See Opera
COMIC strips. See Comics (books, strips, etc)
COMICS (books, strips, etc)
Athelstan's world; no-nonsense science strip. il Newsweek 61:86 F 18 '63
From Dogpatch to Slobbovia. by A. Capp. Review
Sat R 47:29+ F 29 '64 G. Hicks
Funnies: an American idiom. ed. by D. M. White and R. H. Abel. Review
Newsweek 61:92-3 Je 17 '63
Sat R 46:35+ O 19 '63. J. Beatty, jr
Gallic comic; cartoonist Kincaid's Contes français. il Time 81:86 Ap 12 '63
Good grief, Charlie Schulz! C. R. Jennings. il Sat Eve Post 237:26-7 Ap 25 '64
Just a kid in a big white house; Miss Caroline. il Time 82:56 Jl 26 '63
Moe has a moral. il N Y Times Mag p96+ N 17 '63
Peanuts and the Bible. R. Short. il Américas 16:16-20 Ap '64
Psychiatrist at the drawing board; Nick Dallis. M. Wagner. il Todays Health 41:14-17+ Ag '63
Redrawing the color line; integrated comic strip. il Newsweek 65:45 F 1 '65
Shmoo's return; Li'l Abner comic strip. il New Yorker 39:39-40 O 26 '63
Superman goes to college; Wonder Wart Hog, of University of Texas Ranger. il Esquire 62:106-7 S '64
Tougher than hell with a heart of gold; Little Orphan Annie. il Time 84:71-2 S 4 '64
Unfinished comic crusade. America 109:759 D 14 '63
We let our kids read comic books. N. G. Stuart. il Read Digest 85:124-6 Jl '64
COMING about, sorry! story. See Ackermann, B. J.
COMING back; story. See Randal, V.
COMING home; story. See Didion, J.
COMING of age in Glen Oaks; story. See Colgate, L.
COMING out parties. See Debutantes
COMITA, Gabriel W. and Schindler, D. W.
Calorific values of microcrustacea. bibliog Science 140:1394-6 Je 28 '63
COMITÉ international de l'organisation scientifique. See International congress for scientific management
COMLY, Hunter H.
Children's fears and phobias. PTA Mag 58:7-9 bibliog(p35) Mr '64
Child's questions about sex. PTA Mag 59:7-9 Ja '65
COMMAGENE
Lost civilization. il Sci Digest 53:47-9 My '63
COMMAGER, Henry Steele
Ambiguous American. N Y Times Mag p 16+ My 3 '64
Case against the Republicans. N Y Times Mag p9+ Ja 12 '64
How the lost cause was lost. N Y Times Mag p 10-11+ Ag 4 '63
Is freedom an academic question? Sat R 47:54-6 Je 20 '64
Passport barrier: it must come down. N Y Times Mag p 12+ O 20 '63
To form a much less perfect union. N Y Times Mag p5+ Jl 14 '63
COMMANDOS. See United States—Air force—Air commando groups
COMMEDIA dell' arte
Company of masks. A. Nicoll. il Opera N 29:6-10 Ja 16 '65
COMMEMORATIVE glassware. See Glassware
COMMEMORATIVE stamps. See Postage stamps
COMMENCEMENT addresses. See Baccalaureate addresses
COMMENTARY (periodical)
Double role. Newsweek 63:61-2 Mr 16 '64
COMMERCE
Business around the globe. See issues of Fortune

COMMERCE—*Continued*
Climate of world trade and U.S.-Canadian trade relations; address, September 15, 1963. G. G. Johnson. Dept State Bul 49:543-8 O 7 '63
Commodity trade and economic development; statement, April 30, 1963. W. M. Blumenthal. Dept State Bul 48:844-8 My 27 '63
East-West trade winds. il Time 82:102 S 13 '63
Europe, too, can have a farm problem; Kennedy Round of transatlantic tariff cuts. il Sr Schol 85:10-13 Ja 7 '65
First round of the Kennedy round. il Newsweek 63:78-82 My 11 '64
GATT ministers reach agreement on tariff negotiating procedures; statements, May 16 and May 17, 1963; with resolution on trade negotiations, adopted May 21, 1963. C. A. Herter. Dept State Bul 48:990-6 Je 24 '63
Hard sell abroad. L. Morse. il Duns R 81:46-9+ Ap '63
How world trade will change. il Nations Bsns 52:38-9+ S '64
In Geneva: global collective bargaining. il Newsweek 63:31-4 Ap 6 '64
Industry role in trade negotiations; address, November 24, 1964. W. M. Roth. Dept State Bul 51:853-5 D 14 '64
International trade and African trade problems; text of statement. P. de Seynes. U N Rev 10:9-13 Mr '63
International trade and economic development; statement, May 27, 1963. I. Frank. Dept State Bul 49:173-8 Jl 29 '63
Kennedy round, progress and promise; address, July 17, 1963. W. T. Gossett. Dept State Bul 49:291-6 Ag 19 '63
New force for peace; the International business exchange; address, June 10, 1964. J. P. Austin. Vital Speeches 30:605-8 Jl 15 '64
New geography of trade. R. G. Lucks. Sat R 47:42+ Ja 11 '64
Perspective on the United Nations conference on trade and development; address, February 21, 1964. G. G. Johnson. Dept State Bul 50:410-15 Mr 16 '64
Policy problems in international trade of agricultural products; address, February 6, 1964. C. W. Nichols. Dept State Bul 50:416-23 Mr 16 '64
Reappraisal of U.S.-U.S.S.R. trade policy; excerpts from address, March 12, 1964. H. J. Berman. Harvard Bsns R 42:139-44+ Jl '64
Rising sales overseas. Nations Bsns 52:40-1+ F '64
Robin Hood at Geneva. Time 83:93 Ap 3 '64
Toward a new order in international trade. A. R. Kasdan. Bul Atomic Sci 20:40-3 D '64
Trade and development; with text of joint declaration of representatives of developing countries. il U N Rev 10:35-8 D '63
Trade and other economic problems considered by General assembly. B. Lewandowski. il U N Rev 10:43-5+ Ja '63
Trade and the Atlantic partnership; address, November 16, 1964. D. Rusk. Dept State Bul 51:766-71 N 30 '64
Trade is people, too. B. Pilkington. Christian Cent 81:610+ My 6 '64
Tribute to perservervance; serious beginning of the Kennedy Round. Time 84:100 N 27 '64
World trade and world trouble. Fortune 69:107-8 My '64
World trade haggle; Kennedy round of world-trade talks. New Repub 151:6-7 N 28 '64
World trade issues. Sr Schol 84:22+ Ap 10 '64
See also
Balance of payments
Business
Competition, International
Dumping (commercial policy)
International chamber of commerce
Tariff
United Nations conference on trade and development
World trade week
also subhead Commerce under names of countries, e.g. United States—Commerce

Statistics

Facts and figures of the Americas; foreign trade. il Américas 15:42-3 O '63

Study and teaching

See Business education

COMMERCE, Calif, public library. See City of commerce public library, Los Angeles
COMMERCE, Chambers of. See Chambers of commerce
COMMERCE, Interstate. See Interstate commerce
COMMERCE and industry association of New York
Debate: federal participation in urban-renewal projects; discussion at annual lunch of Property owners committee. New Yorker 40:46-7 D 12 '64
COMMERCE committee for the Alliance for progress
Alliance that is making little progress. il U S News 54:40+ F 25 '63
Great challenge of Latin America; address, May 23, 1963. J. P. Grace. Vital Speeches 29:613-16 Ag 1 '63
Turmoil on Latin aid; with editorial comment. Bsns W p27, 156 F 23 '63
COMMERCE department (United States) See United States—Commerce, Department of
COMMERCIAL arbitration. See Arbitration, Commercial
COMMERCIAL associations
See also
International chamber of commerce
COMMERCIAL banks. See Banks and banking
COMMERCIAL buildings
See also
Office buildings
COMMERCIAL correspondence
Company pen pals. L. L. L. Golden. Sat R 46:58+ Je 8 '63; Reply. J. H. Janis. 46:63+ Jl 13 '63
COMMERCIAL credit. See Credit
COMMERICAL education. See Business education
COMMERCIAL ethics. See Business ethics
COMMERCIAL fertilizers. See Fertilizers and manures
COMMERCIAL fisheries, Bureau of. See United States—Fish and wildlife service
COMMERCIAL laundries. See Laundries, Commercial
COMMERCIAL law
See also
Bankruptcy
Trusts, Industrial—Law
Warranty
COMMERCIAL products
Emergent thing; modern American life and its things. S. Wright. il Mlle 60:124+ D '64
Emigrating to America; Irish merchandise at Lord & Taylor. il Time 82:108 O 11 '63
Months ahead; guide for your work and personal living. See issues of Changing times
Opinion, please from New Haven; impressions of an English visitor in the United States. M. Bradbury. Mlle 60:40+ D '64
Swing to service. L. Morse. il Duns R 82:pt2 133-5 N '63
They've got a secret. il Time 81:87-8+ F 22 '63
Why Russia downgrades planners. Bsns W p98-100+ O 31 '64
See also
Marine products
Products, New
Quality of products

Testing

Consumer service bureau report (cont of) Report on the testing of advertised products. See issues of Parents' magazine and better homemaking
See also
Consumers' research, incorporated
COMMERCIAL travelers
Books promote progress; traveling book and drug salesmen. W. Davis. Sci N L 84:36 Jl 20 '63
COMMERCIAL treaties and agreements
See also
General agreement on tariffs and trade
also subhead Commercial treaties and agreements under names of countries, e.g. United States—Commercial treaties and agreements
COMMERCIALISM
Fruitcakes and yo-yos; Christmas bazaars. Christian Cent 80:1451 N 20 '63
Has Christmas become too commercial? R. Moore. Farm J 87:63 D '63
Mammon & monuments; excerpt from Independent historical societies. W. M. Whitehill. il Am Heritage 14:38-41+ Ag '63
COMMERCIALS. See Radio advertising; Television advertising
COMMISSION of the churches on international affairs. See World council of churches
COMMISSION on a national plan for library education. See American library association—Commission on a national plan for library education

COMMISSION on civil rights. See United States—Commission on civil rights
COMMISSION on current curriculum development. See Association for supervision and curriculum development
COMMISSION on faith and order. See World council of churches
COMMISSION on heart disease, cancer and strokes. See United States—President's commission on heart disease, cancer and stroke
COMMISSION on human rights. See United Nations—Commission on human rights
COMMISSION on money and credit
Verdict on money and credit; report evaluated by Heller committee. Bsns W p98+ Ap 27 '63
COMMISSION on narcotic and drug abuse. See United States—President's advisory commission on narcotic and drug abuse
COMMISSION on narcotic drugs. See United Nations—Commission on narcotic drugs
COMMISSION on religion and race. See National council of the churches of Christ in the United States of America
COMMISSION on the humanities
Library support urged by Humanities commission. Library J 89:2972 Ag '64
Scholarly commission urges humanities foundation; report. Pub W 186:52-3 Jl 6 '64
COMMISSION on the status of women. See United States—President's commission on the status of women
COMMISSION on world mission and evangelism. See World council of churches
COMMISSION to encourage morality in youth. See Rhode Island—Commission to encourage morality in youth
COMMISSION to investigate the assassination of President Kennedy. See United States—President's commission to investigate the assassination of President Kennedy
COMMISSIONER of education. See United States—Education, Office of
COMMITTEE for a sane nuclear policy. See National committee for a sane nuclear policy
COMMITTEE for economic development
Bitter medicine for labor; CED study of union powers. Bsns W p34 Ap 4 '64
Business plan for labor peace; summary of report. U S News 56:90 Ap 6 '64
Can anyone explain capitalism? R. J. Monsen, jr. Sat R 46:13-15+ D 14 '63
Challenge of prosperity. T. O. Yntema. il Sat R 48:23-4 Ja 9 '65
CED: tycoon trap? W. F. Rickenbacker. Nat R 14:155-6 F 26 '63
CED's plan to nourish the top bureaucrats; establishment of Office of executive personnel. il Bsns W p70+ Jl 25 '64
How to make good without the Canal; Committee for economic development report on Central America. Time 85:31 Ja 1 '64
Labor policy controversy. T. R. Brooks. Duns R 83:60-1 Je '64
National agenda for 1964. T. O. Yntema. Sat R 47:19-20 Ja 11 '64
Ringing a bell for B-school support. Bsns W p 172 N 7 '64
COMMITTEE for industrial development. See United Nations—Committee for industrial development
COMMITTEE for non-violent action
Marching through Georgia. Nation 198:82-3 Ja 27 '64
COMMITTEE; musical comedy. See Musical comedies, revues, etc.—Criticisms, plots, etc.
COMMITTEE of seventeen. See United Nations—Special committee on situation with regard to implementation of declaration on granting of independence to colonial countries and peoples
COMMITTEE of twenty-four. See United Nations—Special committee on situation with regard to implementation of declaration on granting of independence to colonial countries and people
COMMITTEE on housing, building and planning. See United Nations—Economic and social council
COMMITTEE on information from non-self-governing territories. See United Nations—Committee on information from non-self-governing territories
COMMITTEE on international nontheatrical events. See Council on international nontheatrical events
COMMITTEE on political education. See American federation of labor and Congress of industrial organizations—Committee on political education
COMMITTEE on rules. See United States—Congress—House of representatives—Committees
COMMITTEE on social thought. See Chicago. University
COMMITTEE on space research. See International council of scientific unions—Committee on space research
COMMITTEE on the costs of medical care
New deal and national health. R. Lubove. bibliog f Cur Hist 45:77-86+ Ag '63
COMMITTEE on the peaceful uses of outer space. See United Nations—Committee on the peaceful uses of outer space
COMMITTEE to strengthen the security of the free world. See United States—President's committee to strengthen the security of the free world
COMMITTEES, Congressional. See United States—Congress—Committees
COMMODITIES. See Commercial products
COMMODITY credit corporation
New wheat premiums fade during storage. O. Bay. Farm J 87:45 My '63
Vanishing surplus: what it means to you. F. Bailey, jr. Suc Farm 62.:80+ Mr '64
COMMODITY prices. See Prices
COMMODITY speculation. See Speculation
COMMON law
See also
Law
COMMON market in western Europe. See European economic community
COMMON stocks. See Stocks
COMMON trust fund. See Trusts and trustees
COMMONER, Barry
Biology today. bibliog NEA J 53:17-20 Mr '64
Government research grants; effect of the new procedures on the individual investigator; letter. Science 140:1048+ Je 7 '63
Scientific statesmanship; adaptation of address, December 10, 1963. Bul Atomic Sci 19:6-10 O '63
COMMONS, House of. See Great Britain—Parliament—House of commons
COMMONWEAL (periodical)
Crime of John Dos Passos. Nat R 17:51-2 Ja 26 '65
For Catholic press month: the Commonweal idea. Commonweal 77:527-8 F 15 '63
Fortieth anniversary symposium. il Commonweal 81:261-80 N 20 '64
Notes and asides. Nat R 15:558 D 31 '63
Responsible journalism by Commonweal. Christian Cent 81:926 Jl 22 '64
What's wrong with Commonweal. N. K. Herzfeld. Commonweal 80:293-6 My 29 '64: Discussion. 80:424-9 Je 26 '64
COMMONWEALTH Edison company
Wage chronology: Commonwealth Edison co. of Chicago, 1962-63. il Mo Labor R 86:1184-6 O '63
COMMONWEALTH of nations
Can the Commonwealth survive? il Bsns W p80-3 Ja 18 '64
Commonwealth: evolution or dissolution? A. C. Turner. Cur Hist 46:257-62+ My '64
India's ties to the Commonwealth. R. N. Berkes. Cur Hist 44:155-9+ Mr '63
It's the uncommon Commonwealth; Britain's overseas commitments. P. Worsthorne. il N Y Times Mag p 12+ Mr 8 '64
Speaking out; England's place in the sun. S. Lloyd. Sat Eve Post 236:6+ Mr 2 '63: Excerpts. U S News 54:26 Mr 11 '63
Will Britain break with its Commonwealth? il U S News 57:83-4 Jl 13 '64
See also
Aden
Australia
British Guiana
Fiji
Prime ministers conferences
Tristan da Cunha (island)
COMMONWEALTH prime ministers conferences. See Prime ministers conferences
COMMUNAL settlements. See Collective settlements
COMMUNES (China [People's Republic])
In red China, a new great leap to where? il U S News 54:93-4 Je 24 '63
Turning the screw. il Time 81:29 Je 7 '63
COMMUNICABLE disease center, Atlanta. See United States—Public health service—Communicable disease center
COMMUNICABLE diseases
Common contagious diseases. P. M. Stimson. il Parents Mag 39:139-42 Mr '64
Meet our medical FBI; excerpts from To save your life. N. D. Spingarn. il Parents Mag 38:78-9+ O '63
See also
Carriers of infection
Immunity
Insects as carriers of infection
United States—Public health service—Communicable disease center

COMMUNICABLE diseases—See also—*Cont.*
Venereal diseases
Virus diseases
Viruses
also names of communicable diseases, e.g. Pneumonia

COMMUNICABLE diseases in animals
How we're fighting illness from animals; zoonoses. J. E. Bishop. il Sci Digest 53:54-7 My '63
Zoonoses; report on international symposium on theoretical questions of natural foci of diseases. N. D. Levine. il Science 143:1464-6 Mr 27 '64

COMMUNICATION (speech, writing, etc)
Communication in our modern society; address, October 13, 1964. H. Brayman. Vital Speeches 31:50-3 N 1 '64
Communication of science information. P. H. Tannenbaum. bibliog il Science 140:579-83 My 10 '63
Communication with other planets; excerpt from We are not alone. W. Sullivan. il Sat R 47:78-9 D 5 '64
Communications; ed. by R. L. Tobin. See issues of Saturday review
Communications in unusual media; report on Northeast electronics research meeting in Boston. A. Orange. Science 147:181-2 Ja 8 '65
Identifying speech disorders in the classroom. N. E. Wood. bibliog Sch Life 45:6-8 Mr '63
Interstellar communication, ed. by A. G. W. Cameron. Review
Sci Am 210:141-6 F '64. J. R. Newman
Kinesics and paralanguage; Interdisciplinary work conference on paralanguage and kinesics, in Bloomington, Ind. M. C. Bateson. Science 139:200 Ja 18 '63
Let's arbitrate communications strikes. Sat R 46:47-8 F 9 '63; Discussion. 46:50-1 Mr 9 '63
Majoring in resistance. H. F. Ellis. Atlan 214:104-6 S '64
Man with the pencil of light; newspapers of tomorrow. R. L. Tobin. il Sat R 47:138-9+ Ag 29 '64
Mass communication and the social sciences. C. S. Steinberg. Sch & Soc 92:105-6 Mr 7 '64
New developments in communications; address, August 11, 1964. F. R. Kappel. Vital Speeches 30:759-62 O 1 '64
New rivalry for Nielsen; Politz media studies. Bsns W p 121 Je 29 '63
Responsibility and mass media. J. Tebbel. Sat R 46:58-9 F 9 '63
Some needed reforms. P. H. Abelson. Science 140:577 My 10 '63
Speakers' and listeners' processes in a word-communication task. S. Rosenberg and B. D. Cohen. bibliog il Science 145:1201-3 S 11 '64
Understanding media, by M. McLuhan. Review
Commentary 39:79-81 Ja '65. N. Compton
What's coming tomorrow from today's telephones. il U S News 56:60-4 Mr 9 '64
See also
Language and languages
Language arts
Public relations

Anecdotes, facetiae, satire, etc.
I know whatcha mean. C. Fadiman. Read Digest 82:229-30 My '63
Opinion, please from New York. R. De Rochemont. Mlle 59:62+ S '64

International aspects
Culture and communication; address, August 15, 1963. R. T. Oliver. Vital Speeches 29:721-4 S 15 '63
New dimensions in cultural communication; address, December 29, 1962. L. D. Battle. Dept State Bul 48:92-7 Ja 21 '63
Secretary inaugurates broadcasts to Latin America via Relay; statement, January 17, 1963. D. Rusk. Dept State Bul 48:171 F 4 '63
Six feet, six hours, one world. W. D. Patterson. Sat R 48:22 Ja 2 '65
Today's trends in world communications; summary of report, World communications by Unesco. il UNESCO Courier 17:4-11 F '64

Religious aspects
Gospel and postliterate man. H. Cox. Christian Cent 81:1459-61 N 25 '64; Discussion. 82:62 Ja 13 '65
Theology: dead letter or living teacher? J. B. Sheerin. Cath World 197:4-7 Ap '63

Social aspects
Strange world of our children; excerpts from address, May 1964. M. B. Mitchell. il PTA Mag 59:8-10 S '64
When the press shapes the news. H. Brucker. il Sat R 47:75-7+ Ja 11 '64; Discussion. 47:46-7 F 8; 123+ Mr 14 '64

Statistics
Facts and figures of the Americas. il Américas 15:42-3 N '63

COMMUNICATION, Animal. See Animals—Language

COMMUNICATION and traffic
See also
Railroads
Space flight—Communication problems

International aspects
See also
Hot line (Washington and Moscow)

Brazil
Hot line; demand for telephones. Newsweek 62:79 O 21 '63

COMMUNICATION in education
Principles for a program of comparable information. A. R. Lichtenberger. bibliog f Sch Life 45:8-10 My '63

COMMUNICATION in management
Art of listening. Bsns W p76+ O 17 '64
Crisis in corporate controls. S. Nicholson. il Duns R 82:38-9+ Jl '63
For better business writing. J. S. Fielden. bibliog f Harvard Bsns R 43:164-6+ Ja '65
Talking to employees. T. R. Brooks. Duns R 82:56-7+ Jl '63
What do you mean I can't write? J. Fielden. il Harvard Bsns R 42:144-8+ My '64
When to speak up. il Nations Bsns 51:88-90+ Mr '63

COMMUNICATION in medicine
Electronics: new force in hospital design. J. Falick. il Arch Forum 120:90-1 Ap '64

COMMUNICATION in science
Communication and comprehension of scientific knowledge; address, October 23, 1963. R. Oppenheimer. Science 142:1143-6 N 29 '63
Experiment in communication: the information exchange group; letter. D. E. Green. Science 143:308-9 Ja 24 '64
Science information; discussion of report by the President's science advisory committee. C. D. Leake. Science 139:1088 Mr 15 '63
Science information: local groups to inform public on policy issues establish a national institute; Scientists' institute of public information. J. Walsh. Science 139:741-2 F 22 '63
Scientific explanation; adaptation of address, September 24, 1963. W. Weaver. Science 143:1297-300 Mr 20 '64
Scientific information and the government; concerning the Committee on scientific information, and the Weinberg reports. G. S. Bonn. il Library J 88:4164-6 N 1 '63
Scientific information exchange in psychology. W. D. Garvey and B. C. Griffith. il Science 146:1655-9 D 25 '64
U.S.-Japan cooperative science program. N. P. Neureiter. Bul Atomic Sci 21:39 Ja '65
See also
Science—Information services

COMMUNICATION research. See Communications research

COMMUNICATION theory. See Information theory

COMMUNICATIONS, Military
Getting the fast word from the farthest front; nation's worldwide military communications network. il Bsns W p 192-4+ N 14 '64
Martin gets award for further work on Random access discrete address. C. D. LaFond. il Miss & Roc 15:23 S 14 '64
Seismic communications under study. Miss & Roc 15:26-7 N 16 '64
Super global complex being built. C. D. LaFond. il Miss & Roc 12:32+ Je 17 '63
See also
Communications satellites—Military applications
Radio communication, Military
United States—Air force—Communication systems

COMMUNICATIONS, Police. See Police communication systems

COMMUNICATIONS research
Art of listening. Bsns W p76+ O 17 '64

COMMUNICATIONS satellite corporation
Apprehension rises in Congress over structure of Comsat corp. K. Johnsen. Aviation W 78:28-9 Mr 25 '63
Approval of Comsat incorporators sought. Aviation W 78:31 F 4 '63
Battle brewing on Comsat board control. Aviation W 81:25 Ag 24 '64
Bringing its stock back to earth. il Bsns W p 106+ D 19 '64

COMMUNICATIONS satellite corporation—*Continued*
Charter members in space; new stock on sale. il Time 83:97-8 Je 12 '64
Charyk details Comsat corp. future. W. Beller. il Miss & Roc 12:24-5 My 13 '63
Communications satellite corporation; special report. il Miss & Roc 15:135-8+ N 30 '64
Comsat, almost a full-fledged company. Bsns W p67 S 26 '64
Comsat board awaits Senate nod. S. Montgomery. Miss & Roc 15:34 S 28 '64
Comsat corp. presses for DOD business. K. Johnsen. Aviation W 81:18 Ag 17 '64
Comsat corp. studies planned. Aviation W 78:37 My 6 '63
COMSAT: Europeans wary of U.S. plan for American-dominated commercial satellite enterprise. E. Langer. Science 142:1637-40 D 27 '63
Comsat firm awards contracts for global system design effort. Aviation W 80:38 Je 15 '64
Comsat firm files $200-million fund plan; with editorial comment. P. J. Klass. Aviation W 80:17, 25-6 My 11 '64
Comsat firm may own 60 per cent of world net. K. Johnsen. Aviation W 81:16-17 Jl 13 '64
Comsat firm to announce stock plan, satellite schedule in report. Aviation W 80:35 Ja 20 '64
Comsat in orbit over Wall Street. il Newsweek 63:73 Je 15 '64
COMSAT: private satellite firm working out ties with government; basic decisions are still open. E. Langer. il Science 142:1558-60 D 20 '63
Comsat problem. P. J. Klass. Aviation W 80:11 Ap 6 '64
Comsat readies RFP's. M. Getler. Miss & Roc 13:35+ N 11 '63
Comsat; speculation in the space age. R. Burkhardt. New Repub 150:11-13 Je 27 '64; Reply. M. D. Reagan. 151:37-8 Jl 25 '64
Comsat stirs hectic trading. Bsns W p 142 Je 6 '64
Comsat stock offered in June. U S News 56:97 My 18 '64
Comsat stock sets a record. U S News 56:102 Je 15 '64
Comsat stock to be issued in early 1964. Aviation W 79:34 O 14 '63
Comsat surge. Newsweek 63:68 F 24 '64
Comsat to let prototype work in January. K. Johnsen. Aviation W 81:28 O 12 '64
Comsat II: commercial system to avoid tie with Defense department; company now faces other problems. E. Langer. Science 146:751-3 N 6 '64
Comsat: U.S. satellite company leads new international venture; system to be ready around 1966. E. Langer. Science 146:624-6+ O 30 '64
Comsat's contest. Newsweek 63:55 Ja 6 '64
Comsat's curve; stock rising steadily. Newsweek 64:68 D 21 '64
Comsat's orbit, how high is up? stock price climbs. il Newsweek 64:94 S 21 '64
Decision due on DOD-Comsat corp. pact. P. J. Klass. Aviation W 80:31-2 Ap 20 '64
DOD-Comsat agreement still possible. H. M. David. Miss & Roc 15:13 Ag 17 '64
DOD-Comsat decision sought. J. Trainor. Miss & Roc 14:10 Mr 23 '64
DOD now favors Comsat channel lease. K. Johnsen. Aviation W 80:19 Mr 23 '64
Dial cloud 7 for Paris or Rome; satellite communications system. Bsns W p78 F 22 '64
Dispute among large carriers clouds role of U.S. Comsat corp. Aviation W 79:26 Jl 8 '63
Dr Fubini or: How I learned to stop worrying and love Comsat corp. W. J. Coughlin. Miss & Roc 14:70 Je 1 '64
Early formation of Comsat staff planned: incorporators confirmed. Aviation W 78:35 Mr 18 '63
Europeans shying at possibility of U.S.-dominated Comsat cooperation. F. G. McGuire. il Miss & Roc 14:28-9 My 4 '64
Everybody wants some of Comsat. il Newsweek 63:87 My 18 '64
Experts say rise in Comsat stock due to scarcity, shortsightedness. M. Getler. Miss & Roc 15:18-19 S 14 '64
FCC Comsat contract role questioned. P. J. Klass. Aviation W 79:33 Ag 19 '63
FCC given Comsat payload data; first launch set for spring, 1965. Aviation W 80:28 Mr 9 '64
FCC procurement restrictions on Comsat corp. are protested. Aviation W 79:33 S 16 '63
Fifteen firms asked to take part in Comsat design competition. K. Johnsen. Aviation W 79:25 D 30 '63
Firms oversubscribe Comsat stock issue. K. Johnsen. Aviation W 80:24 Je 1 '64
Global Comsat pact assures U.S. up to 61 per cent of contract money. Miss & Roc 15:14 Ag 3 '64
High cost of indecision. R. L. Shayon. Sat R 47:176 Ag 29 '64
Hot new issue that burned the pros; Comsat stock price. il Bsns W p 112 Ag 22 '64
House group studies NASA role as Comsat corp. technical adviser. K. Johnsen. Aviation W 80:32 Ap 13 '64
Incentive potential of $4.8 million in Hughes-Comsat corp. contract. Aviation W 80:23 Mr 30 '64
International Comsat agency considered. C. Brownlow. Aviation W 80:34 F 17 '64
International Comsat agreement reached. K. Johnsen. Aviation W 81:25 Ag 3 '64
Launching a satellite company. il Bsns W p 104+ S 7 '63
Launching the satellite business. il Time 83:83-4 F 21 '64
Leak that SEC forgave. Bsns W p 108 F 29 '64
Men who will run Comsat. il Fortune 67:51 Ap '63
Mother Bell in orbit; Comsat sells first shares. Time 83:82 Je 5 '64
NASA Comsat aid opposed in Congress. K. Johnsen. Aviation W 78:30 F 25 '63
NASA Comsat research stirs debate. Aviation W 79:28 Ag 19 '63
No filibuster this time. New Repub 148:8 My 11 '63
One world, one sky. Nation 198:519-20 My 25 '64
Profitless wonder: Comsat stock. il Time 84:75-6 D 18 '64
Profits in space: when do they begin? first sale of stock to public in Comsat. il U S News 56:86-7 Mr 23 '64
Public sale completes Comsat financing. K. Johnsen. il Aviation W 80:19-20 Je 8 '64
Race is on for hottest new issue; first Comsat stock issue. il Bsns W p96-8 My 30 '64
Russia delays Comsat team commitment. Aviation W 80:24 Je 22 '64
Satellite squabble. Newsweek 62:62 Ag 19 '63
Satellites you'll hear from; Relay II, Echo II. il Bsns W p76-7 F 1 '64
Senate role in private company questioned in Comsat firm debate. K. Johnsen. Aviation W 78:33 Ap 29 '63
Sharing in space. Sr Schol 85:25 S 30 '64
Sovereign state of Comsat. H. I. Schiller. il Nation 200:71-6 Ja 25 '65
Space project that makes sense. E. R. Eisman. il Sci Digest 55:56-60 Mr '64
Taking a flyer in outer space. il Newsweek 63:85-8+ Mr 16 '64
Telstar and the taxpayer. Nation 196:318-19 Ap 20 '63
To help run Comsat: three big name directors; Meany, Donner, Kerr. il U S News 57:28 O 5 '64
Two Comsat studies due in mid-February. Aviation W 82:24 Ja 18 '65
Two in orbit; chairman and president of the new corporation. il Newsweek 61:78-9 Mr 11 '63

COMMUNICATIONS satellites
Advanced research for communications satellites. R. J. Mackey, jr. Electr World 71:64 Je '64
Advanced technology series, possible Navaid program highlight future R&D. il Miss & Roc 15:94-6 N 30 '64
Airlines planning two-way Syncom tests. P. J. Klass. Aviation W 81:34 D 7 '64
Before you get too excited about the new Telstar; underwater cables. il U S News 54:46-7 My 20 '63
Communications satellite program and the Department of state; statement, April 8, 1964. A. Chayes. bibliog f Dept State Bul 50:682-3 Ap 27 '64
COMSAT: Europeans wary of U.S. plan for American-dominated commercial satellite enterprise. E. Langer. Science 142:1637-40 D 27 '63
COMSAT: private satellite firm working out ties with government; basic decisions are still open. E. Langer. il Science 142:1558-60 D 20 '63
Comsats, weather stressed; NASA plans. Miss & Roc 12:18 F 18 '63
Cooperation in outer space. R. N. Gardner. For Affairs 41:353-7 Ja '63
Defense wants Comsat system with twenty-four to thirty satellites by 1965. A. P. Alibrando. Aviation W 78:27 Ap 15 '63
Dial cloud 7 for Paris or Rome; satellite communications system. Bsns W p78 F 22 '64

COMMUNICATIONS satellites—*Continued*
Echoes over New Mexico. il Sky & Tel 27:279 My '64
European Comsat plan advances. F. G. McGuire. il Miss & Roc 15:12-13 N 9 '64
Europeans shying at possibility of U.S.-dominated Comsat cooperation. F. G. McGuire. il Miss & Roc 14:28-9 My 4 '64
Everybody in instant touch. A. C. Clarke. il Life 57:118-20+ S 25 '64
Farthest-out company starts to set up shop; new private corporation to operate a space communications system. il Bsns W p26-7 Ja 26 '63
FCC given Comsat payload data; first launch set for spring, 1965. Aviation W 80:28 Mr 9 '64
First TAD set to launch NASA's Syncom III satellite in mid-August. C. Butler. Miss & Roc 15:14 Jl 20 '64
Global communications satellite conference held at Washington. Dept State Bul 51:167 Ag 3 '64
Ground station difficulty delays Syncom. G. Alexander. Aviation W 78:64 F 11 '63
High orbit, redesign to improve Telstar 2. P. J. Klass. il Aviation W 78:30 My 6 '63
Home-made Oscar III Comsat awaits piggyback Agena ride; translater satellite. R. Lindsey. il Miss & Roc 15:31 Jl 6 '64
Hovering satellite relocated; Syncom 2. R. N. Watts, jr. Sky & Tel 27:289 My '64
Improvements planned for second Syncom 1. Aviation W 78:115 Je 10 '63
International Comsat agency considered. C. Brownlow. Aviation W 80:34 F 17 '64
International conference concludes agreements establishing interim arrangements for global communications satellite system; communique, July 24, 1964 together with the texts of two interrelated agreements. Dept State Bul 51:281-90 Ag 24 '64
Latest AT&T station in sky; Telstar II. il Bsns W p92 My 11 '63
Long live Telstar II. Newsweek 61:92 My 20 '63
Medium- and synchronous-altitude satellite mix considered by Comsat. il Miss & Roc 15:136-8+ N 30 '64
Military Comsat desires disclosed; concerning study presented at the Western electronics show and conference. Miss & Roc 13:26-8+ Ag 26 '63
Military Comsat tests to start in 1966. P. J. Klass. Aviation W 81:19 Ag 17 '64
M/R first U.S. journal with cover via Comsat. il Miss & Roc 12:26 My 6 '63
Modified Syncom ready for 22,300-mi. orbit. H. Taylor. il Miss & Roc 13:13 Jl 22 '63
NASA Comsat aid opposed in Congress. K. Johnsen. Aviation W 78:30 F 25 '63
NASA laser communications, tracking effort to double in FY '64. M. Getler. il Miss & Roc 13:22-3 N 18 '63
NBC's Olympic hurdle; question of rights to transmission by satellite. il Bsns W p34 O 10 '64
News from Telstar II; CBS new's Town meeting of the world. R. L. Shayon. Sat R 46:53 N 16 '63
Next Syncom launch attempt delayed by modifications. Miss & Roc 12:15 Ap 8 '63
Olympic TV has a chance; via satellite. Bsns W p 116 My 2 '64
Planners eye Comsats for the 1970's. M. Getler. Miss & Roc 14:16+ Je 15 '64
Profiles; John R. Pierce and Project Echo. C. Tomkins. New Yorker 39:49-50+ S 21 '63
Radiation-proof Telstar; Telstar II. il Time 81:46 My 17 '63
Relaying the future; Syncom III. Newsweek 64:48-9 Ag 31 '64
Russia in on Echo II satellite now in orbit. il Sci N L 85:94 F 8 '64
Satellite communications. W. A. Stocklin. Electr World 71:8 F '64
Satellite for radio hams; Oscar III. Sci N L 83:199 Mr 30 '63
Satellite science and technology. J. R. Pierce. bibliog il Science 141:237-44 Jl 19 '63
Satellites you'll hear from; Relay II, Echo II. il Bsns W p76-7 F 1 '64
Scandinavian Comsat interest. Aviation W 81:189 Jl 6 '64
Second Relay satellite in orbit; Second Echo satellite. R. N. Watts, jr. il Sky & Tel 27:163-5 Mr '64
Secretary inaugurates broadcasts to Latin America via Relay; statement, January 17, 1963. D. Rusk. Dept State Bul 48:171 F 4 '63
Shine on, Echo. Newsweek 63:71 F 3 '64
Shut up, already. il Newsweek 63:50 Ja 27 '64
Signing of communications satellite agreements hailed by the President; statement, August 20, 1964. L. B. Johnson. Dept State Bul 51:348 S 7 '64
Space doctors; patient: Syncom. Sci Digest 54:5 O '63
Space meteorology and communications: a challenge to science and diplomacy; address, April 19, 1963. R. N. Gardner. Dept State Bul 48:740-6 My 13 '63
Space project that makes sense. E. R. Eisman. il Sci Digest 55:56-60 Mr '64
Station Syncom. il Newsweek 61:57 F 18 '63
Stay-putnik; our new Syncom. C. P. Gilmore. il Pop Sci 182:68-71 Mr '63
Synchronous satellite. Sci Am 209:84 S '63
Syncom found by new R&RR tracking system. C. D. LaFond. Miss & Roc 12:36+ Mr 18 '63
Syncom launch planned. il Sci N L 83:86 F 9 '63
Syncom satellite aims at high orbit. Bsns W p 114 F 9 '63
Syncom satellite operates. R. N. Watts. il Sky & Tel 26:195 O '63
Syncom II system opens new doors. il Miss & Roc 13:30 Ag 19 '63
Syncom 3. R. N. Watts, jr. Sky & Tel 28:207 O '64
Syncom III may allow first TV experiments from stationary orbit. il Miss & Roc 15:13 Ag 24 '64
Syncom 3 retransmits first video picture. Aviation W 81:30 S 21 '64
Syncom III satellite brings Olympic pics. il Sci N L 86:254 O 17 '64
Syncom will be another U.S. first. il Miss & Roc 12:15 F 4 '63
Taking a flyer in outer space. il Newsweek 63:85-8+ Mr 16 '64
Talk through space. Sci N L 83:118 F 23 '63
Team has inside track on MACS; medium altitude communications satellite. D. C. Breasted. Miss & Roc 13:14 D 23 '63
Telstar spin-axis studies. Sky & Tel 25:143 Mr '63
Telstar II equipped to handle radiation. il Miss & Roc 12:17 My 6 '63
Telstar II launched. Sci N L 83:310 My 18 '63
Telstar 2 orbited. Aviation W 78:36 My 13 '63
Telstar 2 radiation damage slight. Aviation W 78:37 Je 24 '63
Time of next Telstar shot uncertain. il(p 1) Miss & Roc 12:17 My 13 '63
USAF pushes interim Comsat capability. il Aviation W 81:87+ N 23 '64
U.S. and Japan inaugurate television link via Syncom III; statements, October 7, 1964. L. B. Johnson; D. Rusk; E. Shiina. Dept State Bul 51:591-3 O 26 '64
U.S. delegate reports on space radio communication conference; statement, November 8, 1963. J. McConnell. Dept State Bul 49:835-7 N 25 '63
U.S.-Europe Comsat agreement predicted. C. Brownlow. Aviation W 78:74-5 Ap 22 '63
U.S. fires satellite for link with Africa; Syncom II. Sci N L 84:85 Ag 10 '63
Varied achievements for year-old Telstar. Sci N L 84:35 Jl 20 '63
West Europe firms pushing space efforts. C. Brownlow. Aviation W 78:38-9 Ap 8 '63
Where's Syncom? il Newsweek 61:56 F 25 '63
World communications; the role of satellites; address, November 17, 1964. J. V. Charyk. Vital Speeches 31:167-71 Ja 1 '65
See also
Communications satellite corporation

Electronic equipment

Feasibility of digital microcircuits tested. B. Miller. il Aviation W 80:83-6, 89 F 10 '64
Relay 2 designed for enhanced reliability. K. J. Stein. il Aviation W 79:53+ D 9 '63
Syncom 2 to use multiple-access devices. B. Miller. il Aviation W 78:108-9+ Je 10 '63
Syncom 2 transponders exceed objective. B. Miller. il Aviation W 79:75+ N 18 '63
Telecommunications union seeks Comsat frequencies agreements. Aviation W 79:35 O 14 '63
Transistors face new radiation hazard; initial blackout of Telstar 1. P. J. Klass. il Aviation W 78:85-6+ Ja 21 '63
Worldwide Comsat frequencies allocated. C. Brownlow. Aviation W 79:35-6 N 18 '63

Launching

Another Echo. il Time 83:36 Ja 31 '64
Interest grows in new Echo II pyrazole controlled-inflation scheme. M. Getler. il Miss & Roc 13:18 D 23 '63

COMMUNICATIONS satellites—Launching—*Continued*
Perfect launching; and then a near miss; Syncom into orbit. il Bsns W p61 F 23 '63
Photo sequences show testing actual deployment and inflation of Echo 2 sphere. il Aviation W 80:80-1 F 10 '64
Relay II performance is beautiful in initial test transmission. C. Butler. Miss & Roc 14:36 Ja 27 '64

Military applications

Comsat problem. P. J. Klass. Aviation W 80:11 Ap 6 '64
Comsat II; commercial system to avoid tie with Defense department; company now faces other problems. E. Langer. Science 146:751-3 N 6 '64
DOD balks most military space expansion except in reconnaissance. il Aviation W 78:116-17+ Mr 11 '63
DOD-Comsat agreement still possible. H. M. David. Miss & Roc 15:13 Ag 17 '64
DOD-Comsat decision sought. J. Trainor. Miss & Roc 14:10 Mr 23 '64
DOD now favors Comsat channel lease. K. Johnsen. Aviation W 80:19 Mr 23 '64
DOD plans Atlas Agena backup for military Comsat booster. Aviation W 81:29 O 12 '64
DOD to develop own Comsats; Medium-altitude communications satellite. J. Trainor. Miss & Roc 15:10 Jl 20 '64
DDR&E ponders military Comsat future. I. Stone. il Aviation W 79:40-1+ S 2 '63
DOD's Comsat will be very rugged. il Miss & Roc 16:16 Ja 18 '65
Feasibility of digital microcircuits tested. B. Miller. il Avation W 80:83-6, 89 F 10 '64
Medium altitude Comsat system advantages cited. P. J. Klass. Aviation W 80:33 Ap 13 '64
Military ComSat desires disclosed; concerning study presented at the Western electronics show and conference. Miss & Roc 13:26-8+ Ag 26 '63
Team has inside track on MACS; medium altitude communications satellite. D. C. Breasted. Miss & Roc 13:14 D 23 '63
Technical, ethical study slows AF Comsat. Aviation W 79:25 O 28 '63

Orbits

Comsat orbit terminology. Aviation W 78:109 Je 10 '63
Drifting to work; Syncom II. il Time 82:70 Ag 9 '63
Like the Red Queen; Syncom II. Time 82:49 Ag 2 '63
NASA prepares to orbit Syncom C in debut of thrust-augmented Delta. Miss & Roc 15:11 Ag 17 '64
Russia reports Echo 2 sightings. Aviation W 80:35 F 3 '64
Satellite stays put; Syncom II. il Life 55:47-8 S 20 '63
Stationary Syncom launch planned. Miss & Roc 13:21 D 9 '63
Syncom carries first live telephone talks. Aviation W 79:24 S 2 '63
Syncom orbiting near its station but causing Olympic controversy. W. J. Normyle. Aviation W 81:22 Ag 31 '64
Syncom syndrome. R. Lewis. Bul Atomic Sci 19:43-5 O '63
Syncom II: hovering 22,500 miles up. il Bsns W p26 Ag 3 '63
Syncom II in orbit and operative. il Miss & Roc 13:17 Ag 5 '63
Syncom 2 succeeds in early experiments. G. Alexander. Aviation W 79:75 Ag 5 '63
Syncom 3 drifting to date line station. Aviation W 81:29 Ag 24 '64
Tour de Syncom. il Newsweek 62:75 Ag 12 '63

Testing

Echo II filled to bursting to gain data on rf reflectivity. il Miss & Roc 13:26-7 Jl 22 '63

Tracking

FCC to resolve ground-stations fight. Miss & Roc 15:137 N 30 '64
Peace corps volunteers praise P.E. project; Satellite communications society at Kuala Lumpur technical college. P. Hardberger. il Pop Electr 20:54-5+ Ja '64
Project Telstar; Earth station, Andover, Me. il Arch Rec 133:152-4 Ja '63
Syncom lost and found. il Sky & Tel 25:210-12 Ap '63

COMMUNICATIONS workers

Wages and hours

Earnings of communications workers in 1962. J. C. Bush. il Mo Labor R 86:1157-61 O '63
Wage chronology; Western union telegraph co; 1954-63. W. Fridie. il Mo Labor R 86:1307-22 N '63

COMMUNICATIONS workers of America
As Michigan goes. Bsns W p 154 S 19 '64
Cops and robbers. Newsweek 63:60+ F 3 '64
Union that automation built. L. Velie. Read Digest 84:181-2+ Je '64
Union with tomorrow's problems; automation. il Bsns W p98+ F 29 '64

COMMUNION. See Catholic church—Eucharist; Lords Supper

COMMUNION of saints
Word. V. P. McCorry. America 111:534 O 31 '64

COMMUNISM
Battle over the tomb. il Time 83:26-30 Ap 24 '64
Challenge to freedom in Asia; address, June 14, 1963. R. W. Hilsman. Dept State Bul 49:43-50 Jl 8 '63
Coexistence and the class struggle. R. Aron. New Repub 149:10-11 S 28 '63
Cold Friday; excerpts. W. Chambers. il Sat Eve Post 237:26-8+ S 5 '64
Cold war, a look ahead; address, March 28, 1963. W. W. Rostow. Dept State Bul 48:551-7 Ap 15 '63
Communism's great debate; Sino-Soviet quarrel. il Newsweek 61:51-2+ Je 24 '63
Communist international youth and student apparatus, by H. Romerstein. Review
Sr Schol il 84:18-20 My 8 '64. H. Overstreet and B. Overstreet
Fifth international; Communist split. New Repub 149:6 Jl 20 '63
From the academy; concerning C. Luckman's commencement address at San Diego state college. R. Kirk. Nat R 16:650 Jl 28 '64
Handbook on communism, ed. by J. M. Bochenski and G. Niemeyer. Review
Nat R 16:916-18 O 20 '64. J. Epstein
How to slice the cake; concerning Khrushchev's speeches in Hungary. il Time 83:42 Ap 17 '64
How to talk about communism (cont) H. Overstreet and B. W. Overstreet. il PTA Mag 57:12-14 F; 10-12 Mr; 8-10 Ap; 16-18 My; 8-10 Je '63
Inviting Communists to speak at colleges; address, 1962. W. F. Buckley, jr. il Nat R 15:343-5+ O 22 '63
Is it peaceful? is it coexistence? P. E. Mosely. il N Y Times Mag p7+ S 1 '63
Labels, logic, and communism. B. E. Tabarlet. il Sch & Soc 91:224-5 My 4 '63
Making the world safe for diversity; address, June 8, 1964. T. L. Hughes. Dept State Bul 51:6-17 Jl 6 '64
Mao's heresy. America 110:564 Ap 25 '64
New frontiers without freedom; address, March 16, 1964. E. V. Rickenbacker. Vital Speeches 30:490-4 Je 1 '64
New perspectives on the United States' world relationships; address, April 29, 1963. C. Bowles. Dept State Bul 48:817-23 My 27 '63
New realities. N. Cousins. Sat R 46:22-3 O 5 '63
Paradox of the Marxist philosopher. T. Molnar. bibliog f il Nat R 16:1107-10 D 15 '64
Realities of world communism, ed. by W. Petersen. Review
Nat R 16:361 My 5 '64. R. V. Allen
Reason and ideology; Soviet Union and Communist China. Commonweal 77:481 F 1 '63
Red China's wounded pride. il Newsweek 61:41 F 11 '63
Shifting sands; with report by Leon Volkov. Newsweek 61:45-6 My 27 '63
Sino-Soviet conflict in perspective. R. A. Scalapino. bibliog f Ann Am Acad 351:1-14 Ja '64
Sino-Soviet dialogue. M. Kovner. bibliog f Cur Hist 45:129-35 S '63
Sino-Soviet dispute: communism at the crossroads. M. Kovner. bibliog f Cur Hist 47:129-35+ S '64
Sino-Soviet relations, the question of authority. B. Schwartz. bibliog f Ann Am Acad 349:38-48 S '63
Splintered legacy of Karl Marx. il Newsweek 63:47-8+ Ap 27 '64
Split between Russia and China. E. Crankshaw. Atlan 211:60-5 My '63
Ten delusions of youth; address, February 14, 1963. W. P. Shofstall. Vital Speeches 29:400-3 Ap 15 '63
Threat and opportunity in the Communist schism. Z. Brzezinski. For Affairs 41:513-25 Ap '63
Two dogmas shake the Communist world; Mao's challenge to the supremacy of Moscow. E. Crankshaw. il N Y Times Mag p5+ Jl 21 '63

COMMUNISM—*Continued*
Understanding the Communist challenge (cont) il Sr Schol 82:11-16 F 6; 12-14+ F 13 '63
See also
Anti-Communist movements
Communist countries
Communist parties
World peace council

Anecdotes, facetiae, satire, etc.

Jokes that seep through the iron curtain. P. Streit. il N Y Times Mag p28+ Ap 19 '64

Anti-Communist measures

Asian freedom fighters; meeting of Asian peoples' anti-Communist league in Taipei. Nat R 16:1139 D 29 '64
Ban the. . . Nat R 14:225 Mr 26 '63
Campaign against anti-communism. H. Romerstein. Nat R 14:108 F 12 '63
Communist subversion in the western hemisphere; statement, February 18, 1963. E. M. Martin. Dept State Bul 48:404-12 Mr 18 '63
Making the world safe for diversity; address, June 8, 1964. T. L. Hughes. Dept State Bul 51:6-17 Jl 6 '64
Man with a formula to stop Castroism; Venezuela's Betancourt. il Bsns W p64-5 Mr 2 '63
To clear & to hold; American AID men in South Viet Nam. E. Pace. il Time 83:21 Mr 27 '64
U.S. business fights Latin American reds. il Bsns W p54+ Mr 16 '63
See also
Anti-Communist movements
United States—Foreign relations—Anti-Communist measures

History

If Lenin were alive today. H. Schwartz. il N Y Times Mag p 14+ Jl 14 '63

Study and teaching

Anti-communism in the grade schools; San Mateo County, Calif. H. A. Bosmajian. bibliog f Sch & Soc 91:93-6 F 23 '63
Challenging study; challenge of communism. S. Hook. il N Y Times Mag p25+ O 13 '63
Cold war education; understanding of communism is inadequate; address, June 12, 1963. T. J. Dodd. Vital Speeches 29:586-9 Jl 15 '63
How to talk about communism: when it sets dogma above fact. H. Overstreet and B. W. Overstreet. il PTA Mag 57:16-18 My '63
Nuns' story; course in communism at College of St Thomas. il Newsweek 64:68 Ag 10 '64
Problems of understanding communism. R. Kirk. Nat R 15:23 Jl 16 '63
Teaching about communism. R. I. Miller. il Sat R 46:62-4+ Mr 23 '63; Reply. R. J. Burke. 46:63 My 18 '63
Teaching about communism and Russia. Sch & Soc 92:150 Ap 4 '64
Teaching about communism in the schools. W. W. Brickman. Sch & Soc 91:30 Ja 26 '63
Tyranny of professorial rationalism. R. Kirk. Nat R 14:115 F 12 '63
What should we tell our children about communism. M. Childs. il Parents Mag 38:66-7+ S '63

Africa

Communism's impact on African nationalism; address, May 13,1963. G. M. Williams. Dept State Bul 48:877-81 Je 3 '63
Communist bloc interest in Africa; address, November 18, 1963. G. M. Williams. Dept State Bul 49:929-32 D 16 '63
Promising trends in Africa; address, February 15, 1964. G. M. Williams. Dept State Bul 50:370-3 Mr 9 '64
Road to Johannesburg. E. Huxley. il Nat R 16:351-2+ My 5 '64

Africa, East

Now it's East Africa that is exploding. il U S News 56:34-5 F 3 '64
Red threat in black Africa? R. K. Massie. il Sat Eve Post 237:80-5 Ap 18 '64
Why Africa is in chaos; interview, ed. by J. Fromm. E. Huxley. il U S News 56:46-9 F 17 '64
Witches' brew. E. Huxley. il Nat R 16:191-2 Mr 10 '64

Albania

Albanian-Soviet rift. W. S. Vucinich. Cur Hist 44:299-304+ My '63

Algeria

Communist take-over of Algeria. R. Colby. il U S News 57:52-3 Ag 31 '64

Arab states

Into their own pitfalls. il Newsweek 61:46 My 27 '63

Argentina

Terrorists at work. R. Peter. Nat R 16:638 Jl 28 '64

Asia

Communism in Asia. T. Balasuriya. Commonweal 81:535-8 Ja 22 '65
Emergence of an Asian Communist coalition. A. M. Halpern. bibliog f Ann Am Acad 349: 117-29 S '63
Stake: freedom for half of mankind. B. Ward. il N Y Times Mag p 19+ Ap 14 '63
United States policy in southern Asia. W. C. Johnstone. Cur Hist 46:65-70+ F '64

Asia, Southeastern

Circuses without bread. W. T. Thomas. Christian Cent 80:823 Je 26 '63
How the world's hottest spot looks to me. H. C. Lodge. il Life 56:38D-38F Ap 17 '64
Major crisis for Johnson: southeast Asia falling apart. il U S News 55:42-3 D 23 '63
Malaysia: a tempting target. D. Warner. il Reporter 31:35-8 N 5 '64
Showdown in Vietnam; all-out fight ahead? il Bsns W p28-9 F 8 '64
Situation in the western Pacific; address, April 25, 1964. D. Rusk. Dept State Bul 50:732-7 My 11 '64
Southeast Asia, season of unrest? Sr Schol 82:20 My 15 '63
Stakes in southeast Asia; photographs. N Y Times Mag p 10-11 My 24 '64
U.S. calls for frontier patrol to help prevent border incidents between Cambodia and Viet-Nam; statement, May 21, 1964. A. E. Stevenson. bibliog f Dept State Bul 50:907-13 Je 8 '64; Same. Vital Speeches 30:483-7 Je 1 '64
Western Pacific; address, May 17, 1963. W. A. Schoech. Vital Speeches 29:584-6 Jl 15 '63

Brazil

Brazil: 2 billion dollars from U.S. and yet—. il U S News 54:44-7 Ap 1 '63
Brazil's big dust bowl. K. W. Seegers. il Read Digest 83:212-16+ Jl '63
Breath of the dragon; Chinese communism in Brazil. il Time 84:27-8 S 11 '64
Country that saved itself. C. W. Hall. il Read Digest 85:133-58 N '64
How close the reds came to taking over Brazil. il U S News 56:65 Ap 27 '64; Same abr. with title When Brazil cracked down on the reds. Read Digest 85:159-60 Jl '64
How red is Brazil? L. Gross. il Look 27:111+ My 21 '63
Most dangerous man in Brazil. J. Dos Passos. il Nat R 15:53-7 Jl 30 '63
Revolution: real winners in Brazil and what it means to U.S. D. B. Richardson. il U S News 56:31-3 Ap 13 '64
Spirit of '32. il Time 83:30 Ap 3 '64
See also
Communist party (Brazil)

British Guiana

British Guiana: another Cuba in the making? E. Lyons. il Read Digest 82:118-23 Ap '63
Marxists in trouble: Jagans of British Guiana. il U S News 54:19 Je 24 '63
Reds' own race war in Guiana: signs of another Congo. il U S News 56:60-1 Je 15 '64
Shaky truce in a race war. il U S News 55:52 Jl 22 '63

Burma

Where reds may take over a key country. il U S News 54:69 Ap 1 '63

Canada

See also
Communist party (Canada)

China (People's Republic)

Another finger on the button. Christian Cent 81:1259 O 14 '64
Arrogant dragon becomes atomic. D. Chu. il Sr Schol 85:13-16+ N 18 '64
Can we deal with Moscow? with editorial comment. G. F. Kennan. Sat Eve Post 236: 38+, 96 O 5 '63
China: a monster devours itself; excerpts from Ta ta, tan tan (Fight fight, talk talk) V. Chu. il Life 54:86-8+ My 3 '63
China today: walking on two legs. R. Berger. il Nation 199:352-5 N 16 '64
China: what we know and don't know. M. Frankel. il N Y Times Mag p5-7+ Ag 2 '64

COMMUNISM—China (People's Republic)—*Continued*
Communist army is sympathetic. R. P. Martin. il U S News 54:44 Mr 4 '63
Communist China is a paper dragon. D. S. Zagoria. il N Y Times Mag p40-1+ O 18 '64
Communist China's retreat from fantasy. il Newsweek 62:44-6+ N 25 '63
GI who chose communism; A. Belhomme. S. Karnow. il Sat Eve Post 236:104-7 N 16 '63
Happiness says Mao is a hard day's work. I. Stewart. il N Y Times Mag p34+ S 27 '64
How to end the class struggle. il Time 84:58 O 2 '64
Inside red China. F. H. MacLean. il Sat Eve Post 236:96+ N 16 '63
Love affair of Comrade Wang; utter denial of personal freedom. J. Marcuse. il N Y Times Mag p40-1+ N 8 '64
Mao, at seventy, tries a big leap in the world. R. Hughes. il N Y Times Mag p 10+ F 2 '64
Mao's heresy. America 110:564 Ap 25 '64
My daddy can beat your daddy several centuries from now. il Time 84:30 Jl 31 '64
Myth who speaks for Mao; Lei Feng. J. Marcuse. il N Y Times Mag p30-1+ N 1 '64
Nearer my God to thee; deification campaign of Mao Tse-tung. Newsweek 64:34 Ag 31 '64
New Chinese adventuring threatens Asia. R. Hilsman, jr. il Nations Bsns 51:66-8 D '63
New realities. N. Cousins. Sat R 46:22-3 O 5 '63
Next: large-scale uprisings; interview. C. K. Chiang. il U S News 54:41-4 Mr 4 '63
Red China and the U.S.S.R; transcript of television program State department briefing, broadcast February 11, 1963. Dept State Bul 48:271-83 F 25 '63
Red China; ed. by Q. Reynolds. C. P. Tung. il Look 28:21-7 D 1 '64
Red China face to face; with editorial comment. E. Behr. il Sat Eve Post 237:21-9, 86 N 14 '64
Refugee reports on red China. S. Karnow. il Reporter 29:39-42 Jl 18 '63
Report (limited) from Communist China. J. Marcuse. il N Y Times Mag p9+ My 24 '64
Rethinking China. Christian Cent 80:1091 S 11 '63; Discussion. 80:1305-6 O 23 '63
Return to the frontier. E. Chang. il Reporter 28:39-41 Mr 28 '63
Roots of Chinese ideology. S. Y. Dai. bibliog f Cur Hist 45:158-64+ S '63
Self-bound Gulliver. il Time 82:30-6+ S 13 '63; Same abr. with title Red China: giant in chains. Read Digest 84:157+ F '64
United States policy toward Communist China; address, December 13, 1963. R. Hilsman. Dept State Bul 50:11-17 Ja 6 '64; Same. Vital Speeches 30:203-7 Ja 15 '64
Wilting of the hundred flowers: the Chinese intelligentsia under Mao, by M. Fusheng. Review
Sat R il 46:32-3 Mr 9 '63. H. L. Boorman
See also
Communes (China)

Congo (capital Leopoldville)

As an East-West war heats up in the Congo. il U S News 58:28-9 Ja 4 '65
Will the Congo be another Vietnam? il U S News 57:34-5 D 21 '64

Cuba

Becoming destructive. Time 81:20 My 31 '63
Boycotting Cuba: whose interest does it serve? J. Daniel. New Repub 149:19-22 D 28 '63
Castro tells Cubans: get down to work. il Bsns W p28-9 Ag 10 '63
Chaos in Castro's Cuba; with editorial comment. E. Behr. il Sat Eve Post 236:20-2+, 72 Je 8 '63
Cold war collision points; Latin America. Sr Schol 85:15-16 O 7 '64
Communism's failure in Cuba; an on-the-ground report; reprint. R. S. Knowles. il U S News 54:66-8 Je 17 '63
Communist subversion in the western hemisphere; statement, February 18, 1963. E. M. Martin. Dept State Bul 48:347-56, 404-12 Mr 11-18 '63
Cuba: between promise and decay. R. Eder. il N Y Times Mag p5+ Je 21 '64
Cuba in Communist world strategy; address, November 15, 1962. L. V. Manrara. Vital Speeches 29:236-40 F 1 '63
Cuba in 1964. J. Burnham. Nat R 16:16 Ja 14 '64
Cuba once more. W. Lippmann. Newsweek 63:23 Ap 27 '64
Cuba paints its own shade of red. il Bsns W p46-8+ Je 13 '64
Cuba paper. Christian Cent 81:788-9 Je 17 '64
Cuba: the girl and the slogans. A. Hoppe. il Nation 199:216-17 O 12 '64
Cuba's fumbling Marxism. J. Cameron. Atlan 214:92-6+ S '64
Cuba's role. Commonweal 78:492 Ag 23 '63
Five years of Cuban revolution. R. M. Schneider. bibliog f Cur Hist 46:26-33 Ja '64
Focus on Latin America; Cuba and Castroism. il Sr Schol 83:38-9 O 4 '63
Fresh look at Cuba. J. A. Mackay. Christian Cent 81:983-7 Ag 5 '64; Discussion. 81:1308 O 21 '64
Future of Castroism. D. Burks. Cur Hist 44:78-83+ F '63
Hot enemies & cool friends. il Time 84:34 D 18 '64
I was Castro's prisoner; ed. by B. Lindeman. G. Shamma. il Sat Eve Post 236:78-81 My 18 '63
Inside a Castro terror school. J. D. Marin. Read Digest 85:119-23 D '64
Latest facts on Russia's Cuban base; interview. K. B. Keating. il U S News 54:43-5 F 11 '63
Latin America in eruption. N. Weyl. Nat R 15:244-5 S 24 '63
Liberation of Cuba; address. P. M. Heilman. Vital Speeches 29:391-4 Ap 15 '63
My twenty-eight days in Communist Cuba. L. Bergquist. il Look 27:15-27 Ap 9 '63
Principles of our policy toward Cuba; address, April 23, 1964. G. W. Ball. Dept State Bul 50:738-44 My 11 '64
Red drive in Cuba. S. Synnestvedt. bibliog f Cur Hist 45:216-22+ O '63
Soviet policies in Latin America. D. T. Cattell. bibliog f Cur Hist 47:286-91+ N '64
Study in grey. G. Scott. il Time 82:45 S 20 '63
War for U.S. in Asia, pullback in Cuba? il U S News 54:39-42 My 6 '63
We are the victors. Time 81:40+ Je 14 '63
What's become of Cuba? K. Crawford. Newsweek 62:44 Jl 29 '63
What's going on in Cuba now. U S News 55:8 Jl 1 '63

Czechoslovakia

America, mon amour. Newsweek 61:36 Ap 29 '63
Czech Stalinists die hard. V. A. Velen. For Affairs 42:320-8 Ja '64
Czechoslovakia; a dull drama. I. Duchacek. Cur Hist 44:273-80+ My '63
Kafka's nightmare comes true. G. Bailey. Reporter 30:15-20 My 7 '64
Reform yes, revolution no. M. Frankel. New Repub 151:7-8 D 12 '64
See also
Communist party (Czechoslovakia)

Dominican Republic

Bosch under attack. Newsweek 61:38 Je 10 '63
Latest revolt in Caribbean; its meaning for U.S. il U S News 55:66-7 O 7 '63

Europe, Eastern

Communist rule in eastern Europe. J. M. Montias. For Affairs 43:331-48 Ja '65
Conditions in eastern Europe; statement, March 10, 1964. W. A. Harriman. Dept State Bul 50:485-7 Mr 30 '64
Crumbling of ideology. R. S. Elegant. il Newsweek 64:35-6 Ag 10 '64
European communism and the Sino-Soviet schism. W. E. Griffith. bibliog f Ann Am Acad 349:143-9 S '63
European red empire. G. L. Steibel. il Sr Schol 82:11-16 F 6 '63
Is Russia losing East Europe? C. Foltz, jr. il U S News 56:48-54 Ap 20 '64
Khrushchev's hidden weakness; captive nations; with editorial comment. R. M. Nixon. il Sat Eve Post 236:23-9, 88 O 12 '63; Same abr. without editorial comment. Read Digest 84:59-64 Ja '64
Moscow's satellites; in and out of orbit. A. Shub. il N Y Times Mag p22-3+ Mr 15 '64
New breed behind the iron curtain. G. J. Prpic. America 112:18-20 Ja 2 '65
New communism. S. Alsop. Sat Eve Post 237:10 N 28 '64
World in change; a trip through eastern Europe. E. Griffiths. il Newsweek 62:36-8+ O 28 '63; Same abr. Read Digest 84:119-24 Ap '64

Europe, Western

European communism and the Sino-Soviet schism. W. E. Griffith. bibliog f Ann Am Acad 349:149-52 S '63

France

Archduke replies. O. von Habsburg. Nat R 14:424 My 21 '63; Discussion. 14:472, 509-10; 15:33-4 Je 4-18, Jl 16 '63

COMMUNISM—France—*Continued*
Communism and the French intellectuals: 1914-1960, by D. Caute. Review
Nation 199:496-9 D 21 '64. H. Goldberg
See also
Communist party (France)

Germany

See also
Reichstag fire

Germany (Democratic Republic)

Rule by terror; political kidnaping in East Germany. America 111:104 Ag 1 '64
Silencing a Socrates. il Time 83:23-4 Mr 27 '64
See also
Communist party (Germany [Democratic Republic])

Great Britain

When left-wingers went wild in Britain. il U S News 54:16 Ap 29 '63

Guatemala

Another ex-Communist. E. K. Culhane. America 108:196-8 F 9 '63
My war with Communism, by M. Ydigoras Fuentes. Review
Sat R 46:25 Jl 20 '63. D. Kurzman
Wall over the Caribbean. Nat R 14:267 Ap 9 '63
Where reds may take over next in Latin America. il U S News 54:48-50 Mr 18 '63

Guinea

Ugly American in dark Africa. W. D. Patterson. il Sat R 46:18-20+ Je 22 '63

Haiti

Is Haiti next? A. A. Berle. Reporter 28:16 My 23 '63
Now: new danger next door to Cuba. il U S News 54:40-2 My 20 '63

Hawaii

Aloha a la sinistra. L. V. Cott. il Nat R 15:57-8 Jl 30 '63

Hungary

Humanizing communism. il Time 82:40 S 13 '63
Hungary: renaissance after revolt. D. Holden. il Sat Eve Post 237:38+ Ap 25 '64
Hungary seven years later. A. Rothberg. Christian Cent 80:1174-6 S 25 '63
Letter from Budapest. J. Wechsberg. il New Yorker 40:121-2+ Mr 14 '64
A look inside Hungary; seven years after uprising. A. Kucherov. il U S News 55:50-3 D 30 '63; Correction. 56:9 Ja 6 '64
Personal observations from abroad: free and less free. P. L. Buckley. Nat R 16:809-12 S 22 '64
10,000,000 Hungarians can't be wrong. D. Binder. il N Y Times Mag p6-7+ D 27 '64
While we wait. Time 81:40+ Ap 19 '63

India

See also
Communist party (India)

Indonesia

Can another $1 per person save a country from communism? il U S News 55:86-8 Jl 29 '63
Indonesian communism: a history, by A. C. Brackman. Review
Reporter 28:62-4 Mr 28 '63. D. Warner
Sat R il 46:34+ Mr 9 '63. B. Raffel
New sea of trouble in southeast Asia. il U S News 54:46-8 F 11 '63
Notes of a new nation. J. M. Van der Kroef. il Nat R 15:390-2 N 5 '63
See also
Communist party (Indonesia)

Iraq

New turn in Mideast: anti-red. J. Law. il U S News 54:52 F 25 '63

Italy

Conservatives in Europe too. W. F. Buckley, jr. Nat R 15:387 N 5 '63
Food and revolution. J. Burnham. Nat R 14:490 Je 18 '63
Memo to: JFK re: Italy from: Signor X. Nat R 15:8 Jl 16 '63
Palmiro's prophecy; future of communism in Italy. Time 84:42 S 18 '64
Remember Prague. M. Ascoli. Reporter 28:12 Je 20 '63
Why communism in Catholic Italy? D. O'Grady. il Cath World 199:102-8 My '64
Will Italian democracy survive? D. Futch. Nat R 15:152-3 Ag 27 '63
See also
Communist party (Italy)

Korea (People's Democratic Republic)

U.S. comments on Communist inspired incidents in Korea; Department statements, July 29 and July 30, 1963. Dept State Bul 49:283 Ag 19 '63

Laos

And then there were three. il Time 81:29 Mr 1 '63
Boxed in. il Newsweek 61:44-5 Mr 4 '63
Choices get grimmer in southeast Asia; with editorial comment. il Bsns W p26-7, 180 My 23 '64
Cold war collision points; southeast Asia. il Sr Schol 85:14-15 O 7 '64
Doublecross for the U.S. in Laos. il U S News 54:66-7 Ap 22 '63
Importance of Laos in southeast Asia. F. N. Trager. bibliog f Cur Hist 46:107-11+ F '64
Laos. Nat R 14:345 My 7 '63
Laos peace broken by red moves. il Sr Schol 82:16-17 My 8 '63
Laos: the war that never stops; Communist takeover of Laos. J. A. Rose. il Sat Eve Post 236:78+ Ag 24 '63
New civil war? il Time 81:30 Ap 26 '63
War for U.S. in Asia, pullback in Cuba? il U S News 54:39-42 My 6 '63
When new fighting broke out in Laos. R. P. Martin. il U S News 54:40-1 My 6 '63
Why Laos is critically important; address, June 14, 1964. D. Rusk. Dept State Bul 51:3-5 Jl 6 '64

Latin America

Alliance for progress; address, March 10, 1964. W. W. Rostow. Dept State Bul 50:496-500 Mr 30 '64
Biography of a lost poet. Time 81:21 My 31 '63
Communist subversion in the western hemisphere; statement, February 18, 1963. E. M. Martin. Dept State Bul 48:347-56, 404-12 Mr 11-18 '63
Crisis for capitalism. R. Armstrong. il Sat Eve Post 237:17-29 Mr 21 '64
Cuba, Latin America, and communism; address, September 20, 1963. E. M. Martin. Dept State Bul 49:574-82 O 14 '63
Cuba once more. W. Lippmann. Newsweek 63:23 Ap 27 '64
Fruits of Castro's plotting; with editorial comment. S. Alsop. il Sat Eve Post 236:75-80 Mr 16 '63
Great challenge of Latin America; address, May 23, 1963. J. P. Grace. Vital Speeches 29:613-16 Ag 1 '63
How Communists plan to get Latin America. il U S News 56:56-9 Mr 9 '64
How Russia is using its Cuban base. U S News 54:45 Mr 4 '63
How the Communists plan to win Latin America. R. Armstrong. il Sat Eve Post 236:19-34 Je 29 '63; Same abr. with title What the Communists plan for Latin America. Read Digest 83:205-9+ O '63
Latin America: a broad-brush appraisal. P. W. Quigg. For Affairs 42:399-412 Ap '64
Latin America in eruption. N. Weyl. Nat R 15:244-5 S 24 '63; Reply with rejoinder. R. P. Fried. 15:453+ N 19 '63
Ministers of seven governments meet in Nicaragua; text of final act, April 4, 1963. Dept State Bul 48:719-21 My 6 '63
New Communist patterns in Latin America. C. J. V. Murphy. il Fortune 68:102-7+ O '63
Policy for Latin America. T. D. White. Newsweek 61:59 Mr 25 '63
Reds with arms and cash spreading out from Cuba; Intelligence report. U S News 54:69 Mr 11 '63
Restless Latins offer reds more openings. E. M. Martin. Nations Bsns 51:64-6 D '63
Seven myths about Latin America. D. B. Richardson. il U S News 54:77-9 My 6 '63
Subversion airlift. il Time 81:19 Mr 29 '63
U.S. business fights Latin American reds. il Bsns W p54+ Mr 16 '63
Western hemisphere's fight for freedom; address, September 21, 1964. T. C. Mann. Dept State Bul 51:549-52 O 19 '64
What JFK is promising to Central Americans. U S News 54:55 Mr 25 '63
Where did everybody go? Continental congress of solidarity with Cuba. Time 81:30 Ap 5 '63
Why can't we save Latin America? R. Armstrong. il Sat Eve Post 236:34-6 N 30 '63
* Why Soviets are rushing a military build-up in Cuba. U S News 54:42-3 F 11 '63
Why the new upheaval in Latin America. il U S News 55:43-5 O 21 '63

COMMUNISM—*Continued*

Mexico

Communists' corner; Michoacán. il Time 81: 40+ My 24 '63
Latin America in eruption. N. Weyl. Nat R 15:244-5 S 24 '63

New Zealand

See also
Communist party (New Zealand)

Panama

How reds inflamed Panama. il U S News 56: 8 F 10 '64

Peru

Letter from Peru. N. Gall. Commentary 37: 64-9 Je '64

Philippines

See also
Hukbalahaps

Poland

Letter from Warsaw. J. Wechsberg. New Yorker 38:106+ F 9 '63
Personal observations from abroad: free and less free; red tape in Warsaw. P. L. Buckley. Nat R 16:809-12 S 22 '64
Poland 1963. E. Dunbar. il Look 27:24-8+ Ag 27 '63
Polish paradox. T. D. Langan. il Commonweal 80:228-32 My 15 '64
Slumping between two worlds. il Bsns W p 190-2+ N 16 '63

Rumania

New strain on red empire: nationalism vs. communism. A. Kucherov. il U S News 54:100-2 Je 17 '63
Rumania: satellite out of orbit? il Sr Schol 85:14-16+ O 28 '64
Trouble over Transylvania. G. Bailey. il Reporter 31:25-30 N 19 '64

Russia

Big changes inside Russia. C. Foltz, jr. il U S News 56:54-65 Ja 20 '64
Can we deal with Moscow? with editorial comment. G. F. Kennan. Sat Eve Post 236: 38+, 96 O 5 '63
Cold war will not end in our time. J. Grigg. il N Y Times Mag p7+ F 2 '64
European as revolutionary. I. Howe. New Repub 150:30-2 Mr 7 '64
From Russia, without love; new Institute of scientific atheism. Time 83:60 Mr 13 '64
God in Russia. Newsweek 63:98 Mr 16 '64
Has Russia lost the cold war; is communism failing? il U S News 55:50-4 N 18 '63
Lenin the ideologist. R. V. Allen. Nat R 16: 1024-6 N 17 '64
Listening to Ivan Denisovich. N. Cousins. Sat R 46:18+ F 9 '63
Long look at Stalin, ten years after. E. Crankshaw. il N Y Times Mag p30+ Ap 7 '63
Neither communism nor capitalism. E. Crankshaw. il N Y Times Mag p36-7+ O 6 '63
New realities. N. Cousins. Sat R 46:22-3 O 5 '63
On peace and war in the atomic age; address, April 5, 1963. M. S. Pap. Vital Speeches 29:531-5 Je 15 '63
Quality of life behind the Soviet statistics. H. A. Grunwald. il Fortune 69:146-7+ Mr '64
Red China and the U.S.S.R; transcript of television program State department briefing, broadcast February 11, 1963. Dept State Bul 48:271-83 F 25 '63
Russia, thirty years later. E. von Kuehnelt-Leddihn. Nat R 15:479-81+ D 3 '63
Soviet fathers and sons. G. Feifer. New Repub 148:11-13 Je 1 '63
Soviet revolution, 1917-1939, by R. R. Abramovich. Review
Commentary 35:84-6 Ja '63. R. V. Daniels
Two steps forward, one step back. E. Griffiths. il Newsweek 61:37-40 Ap 8 '63
What's really gone wrong in Russia; interview, ed. by J. Fromm. L. Schapiro. il U S News 54:46-8 Je 10 '63
Why we must put holes in the iron curtain. Life 55:4B S 13 '63
See also
Communist party (Russia)

South Africa

Communism's impact on African nationalism; address, May 13, 1963. G. M. Williams. Dept State Bul 48:877-81 Je 3 '63

United States

Friends of Lee Oswald, inc. Nat R 16:183-5 Mr 10 '64
Gus Hall and the Pope; Communist notes on Pacem in terris. America 109:550+ N 9 '63
New look at U.S. reds; interview. E. E. Willis. Nations Bsns 52:58-60+ My '64
Red Chinese American Negro. W. Worthy. Esquire 62:132+ O '64
Reds make new bid for U.S. youth; FBI director Hoover warns of DuBois clubs of America. il Nations Bsns 52:38-9+ D '64
Remembrance of the red romance. M. Cowley. il Esquire 61:124+ Mr; 78-9+ Ap '64
Soft on communism? charge of Senator Goldwater. W. F. Buckley, jr. Nat R 16:905 O 20 '64
See also
Communist party (United States)

Anti-Communist measures

Anti-communism & the corporations. A. F. Westin. Commentary 36:479-87 D '63; Correction. 38:16 Ag '64; Discussion. 37:19-24 Ap; 14 Je; 38:6 N '64
Communist reprieve. Newsweek 62:16 D 30 '63
Crusade and collect; E. A. Walker and B. J. Hargis. il Newsweek 61:21-2 Ap 1 '63
Department of state questions Freedom academy proposal; statement, February 20, 1964. W. A. Harriman. Dept State Bul 50:462-4 Mr 23 '64
Fair verdict; J. Goldmark. Nation 198:110 F 3 '64
Guns of California. Nation 198:570 Je 8 '64
I was the target of a hate campaign. T. Braden. Look 27:54+ O 22 '63
McCarran act. New Repub 149:6 D 28 '63
Maintaining a free society. Christian Cent 81: 1515-16 D 9 '64
More legal tests ahead. Nations Bsns 52:60 My '64
New Hampshire hangover. Nation 198:566 Je 8 '64
Ordeal in Okanogan. G. Bassett. Nation 197:454-6 D 28 '63
Still with us; The defenders. Commonweal 79:495-6 Ja 31 '64
Why the H.U.A.C. should go. H. E. Fey; discussion. Christian Cent 80:304-5 Mr 6 '63
See also
Conservatism
Freedom academy (proposed)
Government investigations
John Birch society
Loyalty, Oaths of

Uruguay

So it goes; Cultural attaché of the Cuban embassy in Uruguay. R. Peter. Nat R 15:566 D 31 '63

Venezuela

Atlantic report. Atlan 211:31-2+ My '63
Battle the reds are losing. C. Migdail. il U S News 54:62-3 Mr 4 '63
Flunking the reds; Central university of Venezuela. Newsweek 63:50 Je 29 '64
Hooligans; armed forces of national liberation (FALN) Newsweek 61:55 Ap 22 '63
Quest of Romulo Betancourt. il Sr Schol 82:5 Mr 6 '63
Red terror vs. an election; on-the-spot report from Venezuela. D. B. Richardson. il U S News 55:78 D 2 '63
Rooster that cannot crow: FALN, the Armed forces of national liberation; with report by M. J. Kubic. il Newsweek 62:40+ Ag 12 '63
Si, amigo, ballots beat bullets in Venezuela. il Sr Schol 84:13-15 F 7 '64
Subversion si, study no; strike for right to flunk. Time 83:36 Je 26 '64
Target: FALN activities. il Newsweek 61: 54 Je 17 '63
Time to finish the Communist bridgehead. il Time 82:49 D 6 '63
Venezeula: no. 1 on the Communists most wanted in Latin America list. il Sr Schol 82:6-9 Ap 3 '63
Venezuela: piracy and violence. il Newsweek 61:48+ F 25 '63
Where reds are spreading terror. il U S News 54:14 Je 24 '63
Where U.S. won and Castro lost in Latin America. D. B. Richardson. il U S News 55:92-4 D 16 '63
With impunity & immunity. Time 82:37 Jl 5 '63

Viet Nam (Democratic Republic)

Challenge to freedom in Asia; address, June 14, 1963. R. W. Hilsman. Dept State Bul 49:43-50 Jl 8 '63

Viet Nam (Republic)

Cold war collision points; southeast Asia. il Sr Schol 85:14-15 O 7 '64
Diem from the grave; interview, ed. by C. W. Wiley. Ngo-dinh-Diem. Nat R 15:426 N 19 '63

COMMUNISM—Viet Nam (Republic)—*Cont.*
How to beat the reds in southeast Asia; interview, ed. S. W. Sanders. Ngo-dinh-Diem. il U S News 54:70-3 F 18 '63
Is Vietnam going the way of Chiang's China? R. P. Martin. il U S News 57:67-9 O 12 '64
Now it's a war against Americans in Vietnam. il U S News 56:35 Mr 2 '64
Red breakthrough in Vietnam. S. W. Sanders. il U S News 57:84 O 26 '64
Revolution on the Mekong. J. Burnham. Nat R 15:436 N 19 '63
Six months after the coup. T. Molnar. Nat R 16:491 Je 16 '64; Reply with rejoinder. S. Labin. 16:783 S 8 '64
Truth about a war Americans aren't winning. S. W. Sanders. il U S News 55:46-9 Ag 5 '63
Truth about the war U.S. is losing; interview. B. B. Fall. il U S News 57:58-62 S 28 '64
Viet Nam: decisive battle of the cold war; address, May 6, 1964. Tran-van-Chuong. Vital Speeches 30:628-30 Ag 1 '64
Vietnam hangs on U.S. determination. C. J. V. Murphy. il Fortune 60:159+ My '64
Viet Nam: in double jeopardy? il Sr Schol 85:13-17 D 2 '64
Vietnam, resistance or withdrawal? O. Gass. bibliog f Commentary 37:37-45 My '64; Reply. B. B. Fall. 38:6+ S '64
Vietnamese schizophrenia. Nat R 16:186 Mr 10 '64
War for U.S. in Asia, pullback in Cuba? il U S News 54:39-42 My 6 '63
When new fighting broke out in Laos. R. P. Martin. il U S News 54:40-1 My 6 '63
See also
Guerrillas—Viet Nam (Republic)

Yugoslavia

Idealism of Milovan Djilas. B. Raditsa. Commentary 35:149-53 F '63
Jugoslavia: crisis and choice. J. C. Campbell. For Affairs 41:384-97 Ja '63
Yugoslavia: after the Partisan generation. A. Rothberg. Yale R 53:221-32 D '63

Zanzibar

Cuba off Africa? Sr Schol 84:22 F 7 '64
Latest recruit for communism. map U S News 56:6+ Ja 27 '64
Zanzibar: Communist toehold in Africa? il Sr Schol 84:10-12 F 21 '64

COMMUNISM and democracy
Ain't it awful. Nation 198:177 F 24 '64
ANZUS council meets in New Zealand; final communique, June 6, 1963; U.S. delegation. Dept State Bul 48:967-9 Je 24 '63
Atlantic agenda; address, March 16, 1964. W. W. Rostow. bibliog f Dept State Bul 50:578-87 Ap 13 '64
Ban the. . . Nat R 14:225 Mr 26 '63
Bridge and the wall; address, February 15, 1963. M. A. Rapp. Vital Speeches 29:665-8 Ag 15 '63
Change and contrast; governments of Soviet Union, Great Britain, United States. D. Lawrence. U S News 57:148 O 26 '64
Changing cold war; symposium, ed. by D. F. Fleming. bibliog f Ann Am Acad 351:1-179 Ja '64
Cold war collision points. il Sr Schol 85:14-17 O 7 '64
Cold war education; understanding of communism is inadequate; address, June 12, 1963. T. J. Dodd. Vital Speeches 29:586-9 Jl 15 '63
Cold war in perspectives. G. Lichtheim. Commentary 37:21-6 Je '64; Reply with rejoinder. E. Stillman and W. Pfaff. 38:6+ N '64
Cold war will not end in our time. J. Grigg. il N Y Times Mag p7+ F 2 '64
Collective insecurity. M. S. Evans. Nat R 15:201-3 S 10 '63
Communist bloc interest in Africa; address, November 18, 1963. G. M. Williams. Dept State Bul 49:929-32 D 16 '63
Communist conference debates ideology. Christian Cent 80:852 Jl 3 '63
Democracia militante, by E. Auvert. Review Américas il 16:39-41 Mr '64. J. Villaverde
East-West relations today; address, February 18, 1964. G. C. McGhee. Dept State Bul 50:488-96 Mr 30 '64
Fifth freedom, economic freedom; address, February 7, 1963. R. R. Gros. Vital Speeches 29:465-8 My 15 '63
Foreign policy and the American citizen; address, December 10, 1963. D. Rusk. bibliog f Dept State Bul 49:990-6 D 30 '63
Free world split will widen. E. Stillman. il Nations Bsns 52:34-5+ Ap '64
Free world vs. communism, as viewed around the world; address, September 25, 1964. N. P. Auburn. Vital Speeches 31:57-61 N 1 '64
Freedom in the postwar world; address, August 29, 1964. D. Rusk. Dept State Bul 51:362-7 S 14 '64
Freedom; its responsibilities; address, March 13, 1964. J. Kalvoda. Vital Speeches 30:439-41 My 1 '64
Happiness? D. Lawrence. U S News 55:104 Jl 8 '63
Is communism a menace? Russell's answer. B. Russell. il N Y Times Mag p35+ Ap 7 '63; Discussion. p4+ Ap 21 '63
Kennedy, Khrushchev and Mao. J. Burnham. Nat R 15:17 Jl 16 '63
Khrushchev, Mao and orthodoxy. F. S. Meyer. Nat R 14:280 Ap 9 '63
Let's be honest with ourselves; with editorial comment. D. D. Eisenhower. Sat Eve Post 236:26-7, 86 O 26 '63; Same abr. Read Digest 83:61-8 D '63
Letter from Washington; American foreign policy; summary of address. J. F. Kennedy. New Yorker 39:96-8 Je 22 '63
Major national security problems confronting the United States; address, November 18, 1963. R. S. McNamara. Dept State Bul 49:914-21 D 16 '63
Moral deterrent; address, February 1, 1963. V. F. Caputo. Vital Speeches 29:381-3 Ap 1 '63
New Europe and the cold war. D. F. Fleming. bibliog f Ann Am Acad 348:141-55 Jl '63
Our defense needs; the long view. R. L. Gilpatric. For Affairs 42:366-78 Ap '64
Peacemonger answers some questions. A. Etzioni. il N Y Times Mag p 14+ Ap 21 '63
Priorities on a small planet. Fortune 69:71 Ja '64
Pursuit of peace; address, August 2, 1964. D. Rusk. Dept State Bul 51:214-18 Ag 17 '64
Role of Germany in the evolution of world politics; address, September 18, 1963. W. W. Rostow. Dept State Bul 49:536-42 O 7 '63
Secretary Rusk discusses the outlook for 1964 over Japanese television; interview, December 24, 1963. D. Rusk. Dept State Bul 50:40-6 Ja 13 '64
Secretary Rusk interviewed on BBC's Encounter program, May 10, 1964. D. Rusk. Dept State Bul 50:816-22 My 25 '64
Secretary Rusk's news conference of August 16, 1963. D. Rusk. Dept State Bul 49:356-64 S 2 '63
Secretary Rusk's news conference of February 7, 1964. D. Rusk. Dept State Bul 50:274-84 F 24 '64
Secretary Rusk's news conference of January 2, 1964. D. Rusk. bibliog f Dept State Bul 50:81-9 Ja 20 '64
Secretary Rusk's news conference of July 31, 1964. D. Rusk. Dept State Bul 51:221-8 Ag 17 '64
Secretary Rusk's news conference of May 29, 1963; with excerpts from remarks on discrimination and U.S. foreign policy, May 27, 1963. D. Rusk. Dept State Bul 48:931-8 Je 17 '63
Seventeen year trend to Castro; address, January 22, 1963. C. B. Luce. Vital Speeches 29:295-9 Mr 1 '63
Shaping the future; address, January 9, 1964. W. W. Rostow. Dept State Bul 50:177-83 F 3 '64
Soviet soft line towards the West. G. F. Hudson. Cur Hist 45:230-4+ O '63
Squeeze play on U.S. in Asia: the Mao-Sukarno axis. il U S News 56:72-4 My 18 '64
Strength for peace and strength for war; address, October 19, 1963. J. F. Kennedy. Dept State Bul 49:694-7 N 4 '63
Success of foreign aid; it must continue; address, March 3, 1964. C. Raupe. Vital Speeches 30:406-9 Ap 15 '64
Talk of peace but plenty of troubles. U S News 55:19-20 Ag 12 '63
Test: are we the tougher? W. W. Rostow. il N Y Times Mag p21+ Je 7 '64
There is no weakening of the cold war spirit. J. Grigg. il N Y Times Mag p22+ S 27 '64
Three wars; poverty, civil rights & the cold war; address, September 24, 1964. C. F. Phillips. Vital Speeches 30:757-9 O 1 '64
Today's challenge to diplomacy. J. P. Warburg. Bul Atomic Sci 19:2-4 N '63
Troubled international waters; address, March 15, 1963. J. A. Farley. Vital Speeches 29:389-91 Ap 15 '63
United States and Japan: common interests in the building of a peaceful world; address, January 28, 1964. D. Rusk. bibliog f Dept State Bul 50:230-5 F 17 '64

COMMUNISM and democracy—*Continued*
United States, Canada, and leadership in international cooperation; address, July 25, 1964. W. A. Harriman. Dept State Bul 51:237-41 Ag 17 '64
Victory in the cold war; address, February 22, 1963. K. R. Bendetsen. Vital Speeches 29:372-6 Ap 1 '63
Warfare state, by F. J. Cook. Review
Commentary 35:79-81 Ja '63. D. T. Bazelon; Discussion. 35:444 My '63
What Communist breakup means to us; interview. Z. Brzezinski. Nations Bsns 52:34-5+ Je '64
What you should know about democracy and why. Sr Schol 82:20+ My 8 '63
What's happening to the cold war? East-West relations. il Sr Schol 85:14-18 S 16 '64
Who inherited what from whom? D. Lawrence. U S News 54:108 Mr 11 '63
Why we treat different Communist countries differently; address, February 25, 1964. D. Rusk. Dept State Bul 50:390-6 Mr 16 '64
World order in the sixties. R. Ducci. For Affairs 42:379-90 Ap '64

Bibliography

Resources for teaching about communism and democracy; comp. by J. M. Bernd. il Sr Schol 83:16T-18T O 18 '63

Study and teaching

Teaching about communism and democracy; symposium, ed. by J. M. Bernd. il Sr Schol 83:11T-19T O 18 '63

COMMUNISM and literature
Screws are tightened again; Russia. A. Brumberg. il Reporter 28:21-4+ My 9 '63
Specter haunts the Kremlin. E. Lyons. Read Digest 83:55-61 S '63

COMMUNISM and religion
Abolition of God, by H. G. Koch. Review
Christian Cent 81:305 Mr 4 '64. G. Vahanian
Am I conservative? M. Eastman. Nat R 16: 57-8 Ja 28 '64; Discussion. 16:167-9+ F 25 '64
Atheism's resort to mendacity; falsehoods in Science and religion. D. A. Lowrie. Christian Cent 80:1513-16 D 4 '63
Bible still worries Chinese Communists. Christian Cent 80:795 Je 19 '63
Campaign against anti-communism. H. Romerstein. Nat R 14:108 F 12 '63
Children's crusade in reverse; Communist indoctrination of children. D. A. Lowrie. Christian Cent 81:1141-3 S 16 '64
Communist heritage; campaign against religion in the Soviet zone of Germany. America 110:31 Ja 11 '64
Council, right and left. G. D. Kumlien. Commonweal 79:362-3 D 20 '63
Every child an atheist; Communist indoctrination of children. D. A. Lowrie. Christian Cent 80:776-7 Je 12 '63
God in Russia. Newsweek 63:98 Mr 16 '64
Kafka East, Kafka West. H. Cox. il Commonweal 80:596-600 S 4 '64
Nudge from Moscow. America 112:156 Ja 30 '65
See also
Catholic church in Poland

COMMUNISM and the Catholic church. See Catholic church and communism

COMMUNISM in literature
Soviet political satire. G. Struve. New Repub 149:19-22 S 28 '63

COMMUNIST bloc. See Communist countries

COMMUNIST countries
America's brightest opportunities. D. Rusk. Nations Bsns 51:76-8+ Je '63
And trouble, too, in Khrushchev's empire. U S News 54:48 Je 10 '63
Any friend of goulash can't be all bad. Life 56:4 Ap 17 '64
Cold war strategists predict new moves; analyses from top State department policymakers. il Nations Bsns 51:60-8+ D '63
Communist strategies in Asia, ed. by A. D. Barnett. Review
Sat R 47:31+ F 1 '64. F. N. Trager
Communists of the world, unite? R. Lowenthal. il N Y Times Mag p24+ O 25 '64
Cracks in Russia's empire. il U S News 57: 79-81 O 5 '64
Disunity day; May day 1964. il Newsweek 63:45 My 11 '64
Dragging heels. Time 84:24 Ag 21 '64
Era of many Romes. il Time 84:44-6 N 13 '64
How to talk about communism; when colonialism and anticolonialism are the subject. H. Overstreet and B. W. Overstreet. PTA Mag 57:8-10 Ap '63
Iron grip falters. il Bsns W p74+ N 28 '64
Kan pei! Time 83:30-1 Ja 10 '64
Khrushchev mends some fences. C. Wassermann. Reporter 29:36-8 S 26 '63
Khrushchev's European allies. J. F. Brown. New Repub 148:18-20 Mr 30 '63
Myth of Communist solidarity. V. C. Ferkiss. il Cath World 199:159-66 Je '64
Never mind about Marco Polo. il Time 84:40 S 4 '64
Polycentrism and western policy. G. F. Kennan. For Affairs 42:171-83 Ja '64
Russia after Khrushchev. New Repub 151:3-4 O 24 '64
Russia: the pangs of affluence. A. Werth. Nation 198:453-6 My 4 '64
Satellite blues. E. M. von Kuehnelt-Leddihn. Nat R 16:111 F 11 '64
Signs of a showdown. Newsweek 63:46 Mr 23 '64
Sino-Soviet tensions; excerpts from Sino-Soviet relations: retrospect and prospect. P. S. H. Tang. bibliog f Cur Hist 45:223-9 O '63
Wanted: an explanation; reactions to ouster of Khrushchev. Commonweal 81:180 N 6 '64
See also
Agriculture—Communist countries
Council for mutual economic assistance
Europe, Eastern
Public opinion—Communist countries

Commerce

Burying communism. New Repub 150:3-4 Ja 25 '64
Business is business. New Repub 150:3-4 Je 20 '64
Dramatic flourish, empty gesture; breakdown of U.S. trade embargo on Cuba. il Time 83:23 F 28 '64
Farm boom that red trade built; Canada's grain sales. il U S News 56:98-100 Je 29 '64
Flag follows trade. Time 83:27 My 29 '64
How much trade with the reds? Time 82:29-30 N 22 '63
More red trade? Newsweek 63:71 My 11 '64
New drive by reds for trade. il U S News 54:76 Je 10 '63
Trade with Communists. America 110:276 F 29 '64
Trading with the Communists. S. Slessinger. Commonweal 79:710-13 Mr 13 '64
Trading with the devil with a shorter spoon. R. Lubar. il Fortune 69:108-12+ Ap '64
Why help the reds win the cold war? K. B. Keating. Read Digest 83:66-71 O '63

Economic conditions

Bleak year behind the curtain. U S News 56:47 Ja 13 '64
Economic mess. il Time 84:60 Jl 31 '64
No boom in the red empire. il U S News 54:45-7 My 6 '63
Onions, frogs & corpses. il Time 83:106 Ap 17 '64
United States policy in the Pacific; address, August 20, 1963. R. Hilsman. Dept State Bul 49:386-93 S 9 '63

Economic policy

New managers: discovering capitalism in the Soviet bloc. Time 84:112 O 2 '64

Economic relations

Shortages put new pressure on Russia. il Nations Bsns 51:72-3+ O '63

COMMUNIST ethics
How to talk about communism; when the subject is the expedient lie. H. Overstreet and B. Overstreet. il PTA Mag 57:8-10 Je '63

COMMUNIST newspapers
Letter from Paris; closing of left-wing daily newspaper Libération. Genêt. New Yorker 40:109-11 Ja 9 '65

COMMUNIST parties
After Khrushchev what? with report by K. Lachmann. il U S News 57:39-45 O 26 '64
Campaigning in Hungary; Khrushchev's attack on red China. Newsweek 63:50 Ap 20 '64
Communists of the world, unite? R. Lowenthal. il N Y Times Mag p24+ O 25 '64
European communism and the Sino-Soviet schism. W. E. Griffith. bibliog f Ann Am Acad 349:143-52 S '63
Moscow, Peking and the Communist parties of Asia. R. A. Scalapino. For Affairs 41: 323-43 Ja '63
Notes on the Khrushchev ouster. J. Burnham. Nat R 16:952 N 3 '64
Patching up the Communist split? il U S News 57:8 N 16 '64
Reasons why; repercussions following removal of N. Khrushchev. Sr Schol 85:9 N 11 '64

COMMUNIST parties—*Continued*
Splintered legacy of Karl Marx. il Newsweek 63:47-8+ Ap 27 '64
Who's running the red store? Life 56:4 My 22 '64
COMMUNIST party (Brazil)
Brazil's migratory congress of Communists. R. Peter. Nat R 16:274 Ap 7 '64
Leftists purged. il Sr Schol 84:16 Ap 24 '64
COMMUNIST party (Bulgaria)
Bulgaria under Soviet leadership. L. A. D. Dellin. Cur Hist 44:281-7 My '63
COMMUNIST party (Canada)
Communist apparatus in Canada today; address, October 28, 1963. M. Lamb. Vital Speeches 30:141-4 D 15 '63
COMMUNIST party (China [People's Republic])
Brinkmanship phase of Russian and Chinese diplomacy. il Newsweek 63:41 Ap 13 '64
China 1965: counter-offensive and national recovery; address, December 31, 1964. K. S. Chiang. Vital Speeches 31:198-200 Ja 15 '65
Chinese tradition and modern currents; address, October 31, 1964. T. F. Tsiang. Vital Speeches 31:105-9 D 1 '64
Demons in paradise: the Chinese images of Russia. T. A. Hsia. bibliog f Ann Am Acad 349:27-37 S '63
Economic policy and political power in Communist China. F. Schurmann. bibliog f il Ann Am Acad 349:49-69 S '63
Goulash, Mr Mao? revolution, Mr K. il Time 83:31-2 Ap 10 '64
How Communist economics failed in China. S. Karnow. il Fortune 68:154-7+ Jl '63
Red China's wounded pride. il Newsweek 61:41 F 11 '63
Self-bound Gulliver. il Time 82:30-6+ S 13 '63; Same abr. with title Red China: giant in chains. Read Digest 84:157+ F '64
Sino-Soviet relations, the question of authority. B. Schwartz. bibliog f Ann Am Acad 349:38-48 S '63
Two dogmas shake the Communist world; Mao's challenge to the supremacy of Moscow. E. Crankshaw. il N Y Times Mag p5+ Jl 21 '63
COMMUNIST party (Czechoslovakia)
Another purge, another premier. il Time 82:47 O 4 '63
Look who's destalinizing. il Time 81:32-3 My 24 '63
Slansky's ghost; de-Stalinization. Newsweek 61:54 Je 10 '63
COMMUNIST party (France)
Decline of Maurice. il Time 83:28 My 29 '64
Letter from Paris; Paris C.P. Genêt. New Yorker 40:191-2 Ap 18 '64
Letter from Paris; XVII congress. Genêt. New Yorker 40:120+ My 30 '64
New popular front? E. Taylor. il Reporter 28:13-19 Je 20 '63; Discussion. 29:6+ Jl 18 '63
Pavlovian reflex. Newsweek 63:48 My 25 '64
Rumblings on the left. E. Taylor. Reporter 30:15-19 Ja 2 '64
COMMUNIST party (Germany [Democratic Republic])
Harder they fall. Time 81:31 F 22 '63
Stalemate in Germany; sixth congress of the Socialist unity party. T. Prittie. New Repub 148:10-11 F 2 '63
Stalinist rule in East Germany. C. G. Anthon. Cur Hist 44:265-72+ My '63
COMMUNIST party (Hungary)
Hungary faces the future. F. A. Váli. Cur Hist 44:288-93 My '63
COMMUNIST party (India)
India cracks down on its Communists. P. Bhatia. Reporter 32:41-3 Ja 28 '65
COMMUNIST party (Indonesia)
We are going to change this damn world! J. A. Rose. il Sat Eve Post 236:77-81 N 2 '63
COMMUNIST party (Italy)
Catholic, yet Communist, why? R. Neville. il N Y Times Mag p 12+ Je 2 '63
Cure for communism. Newsweek 65:28 Ja 4 '65
Dialogue Communist style. America 110:397 Mr 28 '64
Doing what is possible. Time 84:30 Ag 28 '64
Is Italy going neutral? M. Ascoli. Reporter 29:26-7 N 21 '63
Italian elections. B. Renton. Nation 196:414 My 18 '63
Italians to the polls. America 111:648-9 N 21 '64
Italy's innocent Communists. E. O. Hauser. Read Digest 83:193-5+ N '63
Italy's intellectuals steer to the left. J. M. Cook. il N Y Times Mag p32+ My 26 '63
Khrushchev and the Italian Communists. G. D. Kumlien. Commonweal 81:408-9 D 18 '64
Longo tries Togliatti's shoes. R. Neville. il N Y Times Mag p32+ N 8 '64
Lurching left? il Newsweek 61:47 My 13 '63
New boss; L. Longo elected general secretary. Newsweek 64:42 S 7 '64
Opening for the left. J. Burnham. Nat R 14:400 My 21 '63
Pope John and Communist gains. Marcello. America 108:896 Je 29 '63
Probing Little Moscow; TV's Chet Huntley reporting. il Sr Schol 82:39 Ap 17 '63
Reform or revolution? Newsweek 63:46 Mr 23 '64
Trouble with Italian politics. A. Mennen. il N Y Times Mag p28-9+ N 22 '64
We need you; death of P. Togliatti. Newsweek 64:35 Ag 31 '64
Where did all those Communists come from? F. Canavan. America 108:703 My 18 '63
COMMUNIST party (New Zealand)
Big little man; Secretary-General V. G. Wilcox. Newsweek 64:45 Jl 20 '64
COMMUNIST party (Poland)
Gomulka compromise. W. Z. Laqueur. New Repub 148:11-12 Je 29 '63
Profile of Poland. R. Staar. bibliog f il Cur Hist 44:257-64 My '63
COMMUNIST party (Rumania)
Fathers & sons. il Time 83:27 My 8 '64
COMMUNIST party (Russia)
After Khrushchev: what next? H. R. Swearer. bibliog f Cur Hist 47:257-65 N '64
As Moscow slept, a new era began; resignation of Khrushchev. il Newsweek 64:45-6+ O 26 '64
Battle over the tomb. il Time 83:26-30 Ap 24 '64
Brinkmanship phase of Russian and Chinese diplomacy. il Newsweek 63:41 Ap 13 '64
Change in Russia; Khrushchev deposed. Commonweal 81:147-8 O 30 '64
Chinese criticism of the Soviet Union; excerpts from Hung Chi, journal of the Central committee of the Chinese Communist party. Cur Hist 47:173-6 S '64
Communism: the meaning of the change. S. Alsop. il Sat Eve Post 237:12 D 5 '64
Communists in gray flannel suits. H. Tanner. il N Y Times Mag p 11+ Ag 2 '64
Communists in gray flannel suits. M. Frankel. New Repub 151:7-8 O 31 '64
Consumers' budget. il Time 84:31 D 18 '64
Echoes of Stalinism. A. Werth. Nation 196:308-9 Ap 13 '63
Fathers & sons. il Time 83:27 My 8 '64
Fine clothes, not highfalutin words. Newsweek 62:28 Jl 1 '63
Goulash, Mr Mao? revolution, Mr K. il Time 83:31-2 Ap 10 '64
Hard day's night; story of N. Khrushchev's fall. il Time 84:37-8 O 30 '64
How Nikita & Nina came back to No. 3 Granovsky street. il Time 84:26 N 6 '64
How to survive in the Kremlin. H. Tanner. il N Y Times Mag p26+ N 15 '64
Intelligent woman's guide to politics in the Kremlin. M. Frankel. il McCalls 92:56+ N '64
Khrushchev at seventy; who is next? P. E. Mosely. il N Y Times Mag p 14+ Ap 12 '64
Khrushchev era. New Repub 148:7-8 My 11 '63
Kremlin chiefs pledge business as usual. il Bsns W p30-3 O 24 '64
Kremlin plays Russian roulette; fall of Khrushchev. H. E. Salisbury. il N Y Times Mag p25+ O 25 '64
Kremlin shake-up. America 111:509 O 31 '64
Man to watch; Khrushchev's chief lieutenant, F. R. Kozlov. Newsweek 61:40 Ap 22 '63
Morning after; Russia's new bosses. il Time 84:36-7 O 30 '64
Moscow: which way? S. Alsop. il Sat Eve Post 237:13 N 21 '64
New B & K show opens in Red square. R. Brigham. il Life 57:40-42B O 30 '64
Now for the main event: Communist party congress. Time 81:29 Je 28 '63
Optimists and the pessimists; shift in power in Russia and explosion of the Chinese nuclear bomb. W. V. Shannon. Commonweal 81:217-18 N 13 '64
Peaceful co-existence; address, October 19, 1964. L. I. Brezhnev. Vital Speeches 31:38-40 N 1 '64
Policy debate in Moscow. R. C. Tucker. New Repub 150:7-8 My 16 '64
Revolt in the Kremlin. il Time 84:28-31 O 23 '64
Room at the top. Sr Schol 85:19 D 9 '64
Russia: Khrushchev and after. O. Gass. bibliog f Commentary 36:353-63 N '63
Russia: poetry, politics, and the unpredictable. P. Johnson. il Reporter 29:44-8 N 21 '63

COMMUNIST party (Russia)—*Continued*
Second tremor; post-Khrushchev changes. Newsweek 64:52 N 30 '64
Sino-Soviet relations, the question of authority. B. Schwartz. bibliog f Ann Am Acad 349:38-48 S '63
Stalin-Trotsky split: a lesson for Kremlinologists. J. A. Hough. Reporter 29:37-9 D 5 '63
Structure of the party and the government. il Life 55:82-3 S 13 '63
Suddenly Nikita's day was done; with report by J. K. Jessup. il Life 57:30-40B O 23 '64
Treatment for tularemia & a promotion for the cops. il Time 84:38 N 27 '64
Twenty-four men who rule Russia; presidium and secretariat. S. Bialer. il N Y Times Mag p26-7+ N 1 '64
Two dogmas shake the Communist world; Mao's challenge to the supremacy of Moscow. E. Crankshaw. il N Y Times Mag p5+ Jl 21 '63
Victory of the clerks; what Khrushchev's ouster means. Z. Brzezinski. New Repub 151:15-18 N 14 '64
What really happened to Khrushchev? with editorial comment. S. Alsop and E. Stevens. il Sat Eve Post 237:81-6 N 7 '64; Same abr. without editorial comment. Read Digest 86:90-4 Ja '65
Who runs Russia now? il U S News 57:52-4+ N 9 '64
See also
Russia—Politics and government

COMMUNIST party (United States)
Communists and the march on Washington. Nat R 15:93 Ag 13 '63
Eastland's charge: Communists are moving into civil rights; excerpts from address, July 22, 1964. J. O. Eastland. U S News 57:4 Ag 3 '64
Equality is a two-way street. Nat R 16:710 Ag 25 '64
Is it Communist-backed guerrilla warfare in New York? il U S News 57:25 Ag 3 '64
J. Edgar Hoover speaks out on reds in the Negro movement; excerpts from testimony before House subcommittee; with editorial comment. J. E. Hoover. U S News 56:33, 108 My 4 '64
Legal shrug; Supreme court. Newsweek 63:36 Je 22 '64
Nobody here but us reds; legal protection of democracy. Time 82:34 D 27 '63
Race and radicalism: the NAACP and the Communist party in conflict, by W. Record. Review
Nation 198:658 Je 29 '64. J. Weinstein
Report on the CP. T. F. Coon. Nat R 16:726 Ag 25 '64
Say it isn't so, Morris; letters to the editor. Nat R 15:411 N 5 '63
Specter haunts the American Communist party. A. Herzog. il N Y Times Mag p54+ O 25 '64
When a Communist has talked about it (cont) H. Overstreet and B. W. Overstreet. il PTA Mag 57:12-14 F; 10-12 Mr '63
Zip go the reds. Nation 198:159 F 17 '64

COMMUNIST party (Yugoslavia)
Staying in power without turning grey. Time 84:31 D 18 '64
Trouble in Hollywood; eighth congress. Newsweek 64:39-40 D 21 '64

COMMUNIST propaganda. See Propaganda, Communist

COMMUNIST spies. See Spies

COMMUNIST strategy
Communist strategies in Asia, ed. by A. D. Barnett. Review
Sat R 47:31+ F 1 '64. F. N. Trager
Communist subversion in the western hemisphere; statement, February 18, 1963. E. M. Martin. Dept State Bul 48:347-56, 404-12 Mr 11-18 '63
Dialogue? yes; concessions? beware! A. A. Berle, jr. il N Y Times Mag p9+ O 20 '63; Discussion. p26+ N 10 '63; 19-20 Ja 19 '64
Divided world of communism; interview, ed. by E. Abel. D. Rusk. Dept State Bul 48:644-6 Ap 29 '63
Great deflation. il Time 81:19-20 My 3 '63
How strong is the Soviet bloc? R. F. Staar. bibliog f il Cur Hist 45:209-15 O '63
How the reds make a riot. E. H. Methvin. Read Digest 86:63-9 Ja '65
New Communist patterns in Latin America. C. J. V. Murphy. il Fortune 68:102-7+ O '63
Peace in our time? H. J. Morgenthau. Commentary 37:66-9 Mr '64
Red drive in Cuba. S. Synnestvedt. bibliog f Cur Hist 45:216-22+ O '63
Seven safeguards for dealing with reds. A. Dulles. Nations Bsns 51:66-7+ O '63
Sino-Soviet competition in Africa. R. A. Scalapino. For Affairs 42:640-54 Jl '64
Sweet talk from Moscow, again. Bsns W p 116 Jl 20 '63
Test-ban treaty; address, September 2, 1963. G. Meany. Vital Speches 29:710-12 S 15 '63
U.S. businessman faces the Soviet spy. J. E. Hoover. Harvard Bsns R 42:140-6+ Ja '64
U.S. comments on Venezuelan discovery of Cuban arms cache; Department statement, November 29, 1963. Dept State Bul 49:913-14 D 16 '63
United States tasks on the world scene; address, November 20, 1963. W. W. Rostow. Dept State Bul 49:921-9 D 16 '63

COMMUNIST young pioneer camp. See Camps —Russia

COMMUNISTS
Out of tune; folksinger M. Reynolds and her family. Nat R 16:221 Mr 24 '64
Role of Communists in San Francisco civil rights agitation. M. M. Morton. Nat R 16:578 Jl 14 '64; Correction. 16:741 Ag 25 '64

COMMUNITIES (ecology) See Ecology

COMMUNITIES, Local. See Community life

COMMUNITY and the school. See School and the community

COMMUNITY antenna television systems. See Television antennas

COMMUNITY art centers. See Art centers

COMMUNITY centers
Penny-by-penny; Branford, Conn. community house. J. Trepasso. il Recreation 57:500-1 D '64
Unified diversity in a whole-family community center; Hartford Jewish community center. il Arch Rec 133:141-6 Je '63
See also
Art centers
New York (city)—Community centers
Recreation centers

COMMUNITY centers, Rural
Dream in a bean field; community center for Mileston, Miss. A. Osheroff and J. Boebel. Nation 199:514 D 28 '64

COMMUNITY chests
See also
United fund

COMMUNITY chorus. See Music, Community

COMMUNITY churches
Council of community churches. R. H. Taylor. Christian Cent 80:1058 Ag 28 '63

COMMUNITY colleges. See Junior colleges

COMMUNITY concerts. See Music, Community

COMMUNITY concerts, incorporated
Community concerts: annual conference. il Mus Am 83:240-1 Ja '63

COMMUNITY dance groups. See Dance production

COMMUNITY development
Church and community development. W. W. Biddle. Christain Cent 81:106-8 Ja 22 '64

Colombia

Air force as welfare worker. il Time 83:43 F 21 '64

Venezuela

Big, bad businessmen; Venezuelan institute of community action. E. K. Culhane. America 110:331 Mr 14 '64
Philanthropy is not enough. il Time 81:29 Ap 12 '63

COMMUNITY health service. See Medical service

COMMUNITY life
Arms control and behavioral science; excerpts from address, September 2, 1963. W. H. Goodenough. bibliog Science 144:821-4 My 15 '64
Institute on community organization. W. C. Sutherland. il Recreation 57:242 My '64
Kenwood foils the block-busters. E. Richey. Harper 227:42-7 Ag '63
Up from apathy, the Woodlawn experiment; excerpts from Crisis in black and white. C. E. Silberman. Commentary 37:51-8 My '64; Discussion. 38:14+ O '64
See also
Neighborhoods

COMMUNITY music. See Music, Community

COMMUNITY opera, incorporated, New York
Post-season New York. F. Stevenson. Opera N 28:25 S 28 '63

COMMUNITY organization. See Community life

COMMUNITY planning. See City planning; Regional planning

COMMUNITY progress, incorporated, New Haven, Conn.
Responding to manifest needs; neighborhood center of New Haven public library. M. Bloss. il Library J 89:3252-4 S 15 '64

COMMUNITY recreation. See Recreation
COMMUNITY relations service. See United States—Community relations service
COMMUNITY service
Community action in the West; they landscaped a neglected street. il Sunset 131:177+ S '63
Ladies of Hilo hang flowers high. il Sunset 130:154+ My '63
Run-down area gets a new look; Powelton village, Philadelphia. M. H. Bacon. il Parents Mag 38:42-3+ Jl '63
Try a teamwork association; Blue Ridge estates association, Monroe, Conn. E. D. Fales, jr. il Am Home 66:22+ Ap '63
Women in the service of community and nation; address, February 3, 1964. K. Louchheim. Dept State Bul 50:347-9 Mr 2 '64
See also
Industrial areas foundation
Volunteer service
COMMUNITY shopping centers. See Shopping centers
COMMUNITY surveys. See Social surveys
COMMUNITY television antennas. See Television antennas
COMMUNITY theater. See Theater—Community and little theater movement
COMMUNITY welfare work. See Community service
COMMUNITY workshops. See Workshops
COMMUTER service. See Railroads—Passenger traffic
COMMUTERS
Commuter scooter? il Travel 120:37 S '63
Getting there is the big problem. il Newsweek 61:89-91+ Je 24 '63
Heavenly way to run a railroad. A. Steinberg. il Read Digest 82:175-80 My '63
Help for commuters. il U S News 54:88-9 Mr 18 '63
It's a club on wheels. M. Gunther. il N Y Times Mag p68+ N 1 '64
Poker in the smoker. R. H. Boyle. il Sports Illus 18:24+ Ap 22 '63
Wrong way on the 8:10. S. C. Florman. il N Y Times Mag p72+ My 12 '63
See also
Suburban life
COMO, William
Big noise is jazz-tap. Dance Mag 37:20-1 N '63
Broadway beehive. Dance Mag 37:54-5 Mr '63
Jazz pants age! Dance Mag 38:53-4 Mr '64
Magic glitter. Dance Mag 37:56-7 Je '63
Positive force: Jimmy Selva. Dance Mag 37:48-50+ F '63
Summer camps. Dance Mag 37:60-4 Ap; 61 My '63
(ed) See Gelabert, R. Anatomy for the ballet teacher
COMO, LAKE
Five minutes from Lake Como. J. Egan. il Atlan 213:128+ Ap '64
COMPACT cars. See Automobiles—Design
COMPAGNIE des machines Bull. See Electronic apparatus industry and trade—France
COMPAGNIE financiere de Suez. See Suez Canal
COMPANIES. See Corporations
COMPANY names. See Corporations—Names
COMPANY of Jesus. See Jesuits
COMPANY presidents. See Executives
COMPANY towns
Avoiding the curse of the company town; Burlington industries development of Cramerton, N.C. il Bsns W p48+ Ag 22 '64
NASA industrial cities. Sci N L 83:98 F 16 '63
COMPANY treasurers. See Corporations—Treasurers
COMPANY truck fleets. See Trucking—Private operations
COMPAR corporation
Easing the squeeze on the sales rep. Bsns W p 130-1 Jl 13 '63
COMPARATIVE education. See Education, Comparative
COMPARATIVE education society
Comparative education; Eastern regional conference. G. de Zéndegui. Américas 16:inside cover Je '64
COMPARATIVE mythology. See Mythology
COMPARATIVE religion. See Religions
COMPASS
Adjust your compass. R. C. Beard. il Motor B 111:44+ Ap '63
Compass deviation card. H. DeFontaine. il Yachting 116:50 D '64
Deviation. W. H. Coolidge. Yachting 113:153 F '63
Devil with deviation! remote indicating compass. R. C. Roetger. il Motor B 115:80-1 Ja '65
Economic meaning of the invention of the compass. F. C. Lane. bibliog f Am Hist R 68:605-17 Ap '63
Your friend the compass. J. L. Watkins. il Motor B 113:44-6+ My '64
COMPASS for Christopher; drama. See Newman, D.
COMPATIBILITY (marriage) See Marriage
COMPENSATION (law)
After holocaust, who pays? question of government compensation. il Time 83:58 Ja 17 '64
Paying the victim; government's liability for riot-incurred property damage. Time 84:63 S 11 '64
See also
Damages
COMPENSATION, Unemployment. See Insurance, Unemployment
COMPENSATOR (sound) See Sound—Apparatus
COMPETITION
Chemicals: the reluctant competitors. G. Burck. il Fortune 68:148-53+ N '63
Knocking down the pole; Supreme court's ruling on conflict between Sears, Roebuck and Chicago's Stiffel co. over pole lamps. Time 83:86 Mr 20 '64
Maps and charts; pressure from private firm may bring rise in government's prices. E. Langer. Science 140:373+ Ap 26 '63
Plastics industry paradox. Bsns W p24 Ag 3 '63
Short happy life; new products. il Time 81:88 Mr 29 '63
Soap wars: a strategic analysis. S. Klaw. il Fortune 67:122-5+ Je '63
Storm warnings for those who would proceed; the transportation field. J. K. Knudson. Ann Am Acad 345:32-8 Ja '63
Tomorrow's competition; symposium. il Nations Bsns 51:29-37+ Ag '63
Why businessmen wage price wars. il Bsns W p 154+ N 2 '63
Why competition will be tougher; symposium. il Nations Bsns 51:57-60 Jl '63
Why the competition is sticky; paint manufacturing. Bsns W p 112 F 8 '64
See also
Free enterprise
COMPETITION, International
Europe's competitive threat will ease; U.S. businessmen will get break from shift in balance of payments. C. A. Cerami. il Nations Bsns 51:34-5+ Mr '63
Sourcing abroad for domestic profit. D. J. O'Connell and J. J. Benson. il Harvard Bsns R 41:87-94 Mr '63
Stronger foreign competition coming; symposium of top executives from Europe and Japan. il Nations Bsns 52:55-8+ Ja '64
COMPETITIONS
Big risk for pipe smokers; tobacco company's contest to name a two-year-old colt. E. Havemann. il Sports Illus 20:32-4+ Ap 13 '64
Columbus contest. Negro Hist Bul 27:66 D '63
Most splendid tree; winning ideas from Christmas tree contest of 1962. il House & Gard 124:132-7 D '63
Motor trend design contest. il Motor T 16:68-9 My '64
See also
Beauty contests
also subhead Competitions under various subjects, e.g. Navigation—Competitions
COMPETITIVE bidding. See Contracts, Government
COMPLAINTS
Park your sinuses outside. E. A. Autry. Read Digest 85:124-5 D '64
Whom to complain to? Call for action. Time 84:68 S 25 '64
COMPLEMENT fixation
Fixation of complement to fragments of antibody. A. M. Reiss and O. J. Plescia. bibliog il Science 141:812-13 Ag 30 '63
COMPLEXION. See Skin
COMPOSERS
Bouncing kangaroo; R. Harris, hardly the typical songwriter. Newsweek 62:50 Jl 8 '63
Composers. See issues of Musical America
Composers' letters; ed. by C. R. Reis. il Mus Am 83:14-17 Ja '63
Fie upon Freud! psychoanalysis and composers. P. J. Pirie. il Hi Fi 14:31-3+ Jl '64
Musical events; the modern composer. W. Sargeant. New Yorker 40:54 D 26 '64
See also
Ives, C.
COMPOSERS, American
Americans all (North and South) R. Kammerer; A. Cohn. il Am Rec G 31:392-6 Ja '65

COMPOSERS, American—*Continued*
Jazz composer: a study in symbiosis. G. Lees. Hi Fi 13:55-7+ Ag '63
New musicals, new songwriters. il N Y Times Mag p76+ N 15 '64
New World composers. A. De La Vega. il Américas 16:23-8 Jl '64
See also
Barber, S.
Cage, J.
Carter, E.
Ives, C. E.
Menotti, G. C.
Reynolds, M.
Schwartz, A.
Still, W. G.

COMPOSERS, Argentinian
See also
Ginastera, A.

COMPOSERS, Austrian
See also
Bruckner, A.
Haydn, F. J.
Mahler, G.
Mozart, J. C. W. A.
Schönberg, A.
Schreker, F.
Schubert, F.
Strauss, J.
Webern, A.

COMPOSERS, British
See also
Walton, W.

COMPOSERS, Canadian
Canadian composers: differences, contradictions, anomalies. H. Davidson. il Mus Am 83:20-1+ S '63; Discussion. 83:4 N '63

COMPOSERS, Czech
See also
Janáček, L.

COMPOSERS, Dutch
Nine Dutch composers. A. Cohn. il Am Rec G 29:610-12+ Ap '63

COMPOSERS, English
See also
Delius, F.

COMPOSERS, French
See also
Berlioz, H.
Boulez, P.
Delibes, L.
Massenet, J.
Meyerbeer, G.
Poulenc, F.
Rameau, J. P.
Satie, E.

COMPOSERS, German
Weaver of German opera. R. Eyer. il Opera N 27:8-13 F 2 '63
See also
Bruch, M. C.
Henze, H. W.
Hindemith, P.
Strauss, R.

COMPOSERS, Hungarian
See also
Bartók, B.

COMPOSERS, Italian
See also
Bellini, V.
Bizet, G.
Cilea
Mascagni, P.
Vivaldi, A.

COMPOSERS, Japanese
See also
Dan, I.

COMPOSERS, Latin American
New World composers. A. De La Vega. il Américas 16:23-8 Jl '64

COMPOSERS, League. See League of composers

COMPOSERS, Mexican
See also
Chávez, C.

COMPOSERS, Polish
See also
Moniuszko, S.

COMPOSERS, Russian
Soviet music since Stalin. B. Schwarz. Sat R 46:55-6+ Mr 30 '63
Where is Russian opera? V. Seroff. il Opera N 27:8-11 Ap 6 '63
See also
Borodin, A. P.
Glinka, M. I.
Musorgskii, M. P.
Prokofiev, S.
Rachmaninoff, S. V.
Rimsky-Korsakov, N. A.

COMPOSERS recordings, incorporated
CRI: a sonic showcase for the American composer; with discography. D. Hall. il Library J 88:1826-9 My 1 '63

COMPOSITE photography. See Photomontage

COMPOSITION (art)
Master path: a study of composition. C. Waugh. il Am Artist 27:48-53+ Je '63

COMPOSITION (music)
Music. B. Boretz. Nation 196:233-6 Mr 16 '63
Musical events; technique of musical composition over the past half century. W. Sargeant. New Yorker 39:164-6 S 28 '63
Unreluctant composers; conversation with Mozart, Verdi and Wagner. L. F. Loveday. il Opera N 28:8-11 Ja 25 '64

COMPOSITION (photography)
Before and after. il U S Camera 27:70-3 F '64
Case of the elegant eye. J. Balish. il Mod Phot 27:42-4+ F '63
Change perspective and refresh. L. Barry. il Pop Phot 53:24+ Jl '63
Color workshop. F. Bond. il Mod Phot 28: 11+ Ja; 34+ F; 16+ Ap '64
Color work-shop; shoot still lifes to improve your sense of composition. F. Bond. il Mod Phot 27:66-71+ Mr '63
Composition: a discussion with Morley Baer; ed. by L. Jacobs, jr. M. Baer. il U S Camera 27:74-7 Jl '64
Creative color. A. Rothstein. U S Camera 27:12-13 D '64
Creative color; new 35 format. A. Rothstein. U S Camera 26:9-10 Je '63
Creative color; photo backgrounds, a new technique. A. Rothstein. il U S Camera 27: 8+ F '64
Discovery; techniques of G. Bergmann. P. Caulfield. il Mod Phot 28:64-5+ F '64
Do you have compositional horse sense? J. R. Oswald. il U S Camera 27:80-1+ N '64
Edward Steichen way out; photographs from Steichen: a life in photography. H. Keppler. Mod Phot 28:74-7 F '64
Films & photography. G. Manupelli. il Sch Arts 62:28-32 Mr '63
Focus on Jay Miasel. J. Durniak. il Pop Phot 54:76-85+ Mr '64
From frame to frame. R. Miller. il U S Camera 27:62-3+ S '64
Get the picture; beginner's biggest problem. P. Caulfield. Mod Phot 28:32 Ap '64
Glamor; bringing nature indoors. P. Gowland. il Pop Phot 54:22 Je '64
Glamor; prepare first, shoot later. P. Gowland. il Pop Phot 53:16 D '63
Group problem; photographs by Victor Obsatz. L. Barry. Pop Phot 53:144-5+ N '63
How many rectangles in a square? C. B. Nieberding. il U S Camera 27:89 F '64
How to flatter your subject. G. Pyle. il Pop Phot 53:138-9 N '63
How work trousers hung in 1912. J. Szarkowski. il Pop Phot 54:72-3 Ap '64
Impact! M. A. Matzkin. il Mod Phot 27:60-5 N '63
Importance of composition; excerpt from a Famous photographers school lesson. il U S Camera 27:48-53 F '64
Isolate your color! il U S Camera 26:54-5 D '63
K.K. on komposition. A. Kraszna-Krausz. il Mod Phot 28:80-1 Je; 17+ Jl; 16+ N '64
Ken Heyman. il U S Camera 26:60-5 F '63
Landscapes; make your camera see what your eyes see. C. Allen. il U S Camera 27: 46-7+ Ja '64
Make your pictures shape up! A. Asnis. U S Camera 26:16+ N '63
More than meets the eye. il U S Camera 26: 40-1 N '63
One-light setups. A. Francekevich. il Pop Phot 52:43-5+ Ja '63
Positive and negative forms in and around the figure. P. Pollack. il Pop Phot 54:66-7+ My '64
Recipe for seeing. D. Vestal. U S Camera 27:41+ F '64
Seven steps to good composition. A. Goldsmith. il Pop Phot 53:137-53+ D '63
Shift the point of interest. W. A. Perine. il U S Camera 27:62-3 O '64
Sight of privacy. I. C. Lieb. il U S Camera 26:70-3 F '63
Studies in composition. il U S Camera 27:56-9 F '64
Swing high, swing low. il U S Camera 27: 52-3 Ja '64
35MM scenics; work of the National geographic's photographic staff. P. Caulfield. il Mod Phot 27:74-9 F '63
Tic, tac, toe of composition. P. Farber. il U S Camera 27:54-5+ F '64
Vagabond camera. W. Lane. il Travel 122:64-5 O '64
What the experts say about kids; symposium. il U S Camera 26:49 Je '63
What we all see every day, instants of transfiguration. H. M. Kinzer. il Pop Phot 54:60-1 Mr '64

COMPOSITION (photography)—*Continued*
Wrong exposures for the right reasons. M. Edelson. il U S Camera 28:58-9 Ja '65
Year's best glamor book. J. M. Zanutto. il Pop Phot 52:70-5 Ap '63
See also
Photography—Still life
COMPOSITION (printing) See Typesetting
COMPOSITION, English. See English language—Composition
COMPOST piles. See Fertilizers and manures—Preservation and storage
COMPOSTS. See Fertilizers and manures
COMPREHENSION
Being wise in membership; where learners are gathered together. B. W. Overstreet. il PTA Mag 58:14-16 F '64
See also
Learning, Psychology of
COMPREHENSIVE dwelling policies. See Insurance—All risk policies
COMPREHENSIVE liability insurance. See Insurance, Liability
COMPRESSED food. See Food, Compressed
COMPRESSION amplifiers. See Amplifiers
COMPRESSORS, Air. See Air compressors
COMPROMISE
No compromise. G. R. Wilson. Flying 74:24 F '64
COMPTON, Martha
Flowers that bloom in the spring. Horticulture 41:166-7 Mr '63
COMPTON, Neil
Cool revolution. Commentary 39:79-81 Ja '65
Television & Canadian culture; adaptation of address. Commentary 38:75-9 N '64
COMPTON, Walter A.
Two challenges of Miles laboratories. T. O'Hanlon. il pors Duns R 84:44-6+ N '64
COMPTON-BURNETT, Ivy
Books. R. Adler. New Yorker 40:183-5 My 2 '64
COMPTON advertising, incorporated
All this for an ad; nest egg ad for Chase Manhattan. il Bsns W p48-9 F 16 '63
COMPTROLLER general, Office of. See United States—General accounting office
COMPULSORY arbitration. See Arbitration, Industrial
COMPULSORY education
See also
School age
School attendance
COMPULSORY health insurance. See Insurance, Health
COMPULSORY labor. See Labor, Compulsory
COMPULSORY military service. See Military service, Compulsory
COMPUTER circuits. See Calculating machines—Circuits
COMPUTER dynamics, incorporated
Contractor gets steady check on profits with new PERT-type system. W. Beller. il Miss & Roc 14:38-9+ Ja 13 '64
COMPUTER process control. See Calculating machines—Industrial applications
COMPUTER processing. See Electronic data processing
COMPUTER program languages. See Programming languages (calculating machines)
COMPUTERS. See Calculating machines
COMPUTING machines. See Calculating machines
COMSAT. See Communications satellite corporation
COMSTOCK, Helen
Aaron Roberts and the southeastern Connecticut cabinetmaking school. Antiques 86: 437-41 O '64
American looking glass. Antiques 85:314-19, 438-41, 679-85 Mr-Ap, Je '64
Diversity in Connecticut blockfront. Antiques 84:63-7 Jl '63
Living with antiques (cont) Antiques 83: 186-9 F '63
Marine paintings by two Buttersworths. Antiques 85:99-103 Ja '64
Print processes. Antiques 84:294-301 S '63
Sheffield plate. Antiques 85:209-13 F '64
COMSTOCK, Henry B.
All steel and a yard wide. il Pop Sci 183: 130-4+ O '63
Big idea: a separate building. por Pop Sci 183:106-7 S '63
Can Detroit move in on Indy? Pop Sci 182: 75-8+ My '63
Getting there is half the fun. il Pop Sci 183: 50-3 S '63
Inside IBM's World's fair egg. il Pop Sci 185:58-9+ Jl '64
New portable all-jobs tool. Pop Sci 134:130-3 My '64
They built the roof on the ground. Pop Sci 184:98-101 Mr '64
Want to drive 600 m.p.h? il Pop Sci 185:124-6+ D '64
What! polish with a belt sander? Pop Sci 185:166-7 O '64
Which gauge should you choose? il Pop Sci 184:169-71+ F '64
Why can't we run our railroads like the French? il Pop Sci 183:82-6+ N '63
COMSTOCK, Lloyd
Boy who cried books; address, April 10, 1963. Library J 88:2087 My 15 '63
CONAFAY, Katherine R. See Jenkins, G. G. jt. auth.
CONAKRY, Guinea
Our far-flung correspondents; visit of an American Negro to Guinea. H. Fuller. New Yorker 39:35-6+ Ja 4 '64
CONANT, Grace Richards
German textbooks and the Nazi past. Sat R 46:52-3 Jl 20 '63
CONANT, Howard
What's wrong with U.S. art schools? a reply. Art N 62:41-2+ S '63
CONANT, James Bryant
Conant seeks revolution; excerpts from address. por Sr Schol 84:1T-2T Mr 13 '64
Conclusions on educating America's teachers; excerpt from The education of American teachers. Sch & Soc 92:123-6 Mr 21 '64
On taking education seriously. Reporter 31:18-21 D 3 '64
Quarrel among educators; excerpt from The education of American teachers. Sat R 46: 53-5+ S 21 '63

about

Can American teachers teach? R. Bendiner. il Redbook 123:60-1+ O '64
Conant follow-up; effects of publication of Education of American teachers. Sr Schol 83:1T D 6 '63
Conant teacher education reforms tested. por Sr Schol 85:4T+ D 2 '64
Conant, the man. M. Borrowman. il pors Sat R 46:58-60 S 21 '63
Conant v. the establishment. por Time 83:64 F 28 '64
Conant's credentials; excerpt from Dr Conant and his critics. L. J. Stiles. Sat R 47:56 S 19 '64
Dilemma of federal aid. Time 81:84+ Ap 12 '63
Doctor Conant's bombshell. F. M. Hechinger. Reporter 29:44-6 S 26 '63
Education of American teachers; excerpts from symposium on J. B. Conant's book. NEA J 53:49-53 Ap '64
For the record; Eisenhower vs. McCarthy over Conant to Germany. W. F. Buckley, jr. Nat R 16:188 Mr 10 '64
Parents' magazine honors Dr James Bryant Conant. il por Parents Mag 39:56 F '64
Quest for better teachers: a progress report on the Conant plan. A. Q. Maisel. Read Digest 85:241-4+ O '64
Return to West Berlin. il por Bsns W p36 Je 1 '63
Teaching of teachers: a national scandal? por U S News 55:10 S 30 '63
CONAWAY, Bill
Big-family camping. por Field & S 67:46-51 Mr '63
CONCENTRATED food. See Food, Concentrated
CONCENTRATION camp atrocities. See World war, 1939-1945—Atrocities
CONCENTRATION camps

Germany

Has Hitler's ghost been laid? V. Dabney. il Sat R 46:16-18 Mr 9 '63
I never saw another butterfly, ed. by H. Volavkova. Review
Nation 199:411-12 N 30 '64. J. Richard
Letter from Paris; dedication of monument at Père Lachaise cemetery for dead at Buchenwald. Genêt. New Yorker 40:192 Ap 18 '64
Meditation on Bergen Belsen. F. Russell. Nat R 14:326+ Ap 23 '63
Visit to a Munich suburb. E. Wakin. America 111:235-6 S 5 '64

Poland

Auschwitz business. il Time 83:24 Ja 17 '64
Dering case; surgeon at Auschwitz. M. Ellmann. Commentary 38:19-25 Jl '64
Sickening past; Auschwitz. il Newsweek 63: 29+ Ja 20 '64

CONCENTRATION camps—*Continued*

Russia

One day in the life of Ivan Denisovich, by A. Solzhenitsyn. Review
Sat R 46:27-9 F 9 '63. G. Reavey

CONCEPTION
One hundred unanswered questions about the start of human life. C. G. Hartman. McCalls 91:69+ S '64

CONCERT artists. See Pianists

CONCERT artists guild
Honors for Mr Bing; with photographs. Opera N 27:12-13 Ap 6 '63

CONCERT audiences. See Audiences

CONCERT bands. See Bands (music)

CONCERT halls
Acoustics in-the-round at the Berlin philharmonic. R. S. Lanier. il Arch Forum 120:98-105 My '64
Bloom in the cultural desert; inaugural program of Los Angeles's new Pavilion. A. Knight. il Sat R 47:43-5 D 26 '64
Brightness in the air; opening of Los Angeles Pavilion. il Time 84:46-58 D 18 '64
Buff's elegant pavilion opens in Los Angeles. il Life 57:40-40A D 18 '64
Design for good acoustics in a big hall; Civic auditorium, Jacksonville, Fla. il Arch Rec 136:134-5 D '64
Dramatic hall for the performing arts; Jesse H. Jones Hall, Houston, Tex. il Arch Rec 137:113-15 Ja '65
Los Angeles hoists flag of culture; opening of new Music center and art museum. il Bsns W p32-3 N 21 '64
Multi-purpose hall for opera, concerts, musical comedy; La grande salle, Place des arts, Montreal, Canada. il Arch Rec 136:136-9 D '64
Music for the angels; Los Angeles music pavilion opens. il Newsweek 64:82 D 14 '64
New German theaters and concert halls; views from the audience. G. E. K. Smith. il Arch Rec 134:179-94 O '63
Place des arts; the building. L. MacGillivray. il Mus Am 83:14-15 S '63
Pure hall for music; Warner concert hall, Oberlin college, Oberlin, Ohio. il Arch Rec 136:128-9 D '64
State of the unions; opening of La grande salle, Montreal. H. Davidson. il Mus Am 83: 23+ O '63
Symphony in the round; new Berlin philharmonic hall. il Time 82:78 O 25 '63
Tale of two cities; Berlin's and New York's Philharmonic Halls. il Arch Forum 118:94-9 F '63
See also
New York (city)—Carnegie Hall
Opera houses

CONCERT managers
Managers: U.S; foreign; selective list. Mus Am 83:341-5 D '63
Reports: North American artists management. il Mus Am 83:230-9 Ja '63

CONCERT opera association
Mary Stuart; presentation in New York. F. Merkling. Opera N 29:31 Ja 2 '65
Musical events; concert performance, Donizetti's Maria Stuarda in Philharmonic Hall. W. Sargeant. New Yorker 40:234-5 N 28 '64
Musical events; concert performance of R. Strauss's Die frau ohne schatten in Philharmonic Hall. W. Sargeant. New Yorker 40:148+ Mr 28 '64
Musical events; concert performance of Rameau's Castor and Pollux in Philharmonic Hall. W. Sargeant. New Yorker 40: 116-17 Ja 23 '65
Musical events; concert performance of Verdi's I vespri siciliani at Philharmonic Hall. W. Sargeant. New Yorker 39:96 Ja 25 '64
Musical events; concert version of William Tell at Philharmonic Hall. W. Sargeant. New Yorker 39:146+ Mr 30 '63
Musical events; Intermezzo at Philharmonic Hall. W. Sargeant. New Yorker 39:136-7 F 23 '63
Musical events; revival of Wagner's Rienzi at Lincoln Center. W. Sargeant. New Yorker 39:199-200 D 7 '63
Opera for the ears alone; concert performances. A. Rich. Mus Am 84:61 N '64
Rienzi reborn. F. Merkling. Opera N 28:35 Ja 4 '64
Vespers and dialogues; performance of Verdi's I vespri siciliani. F. Meklin. Opera N 28:33 F 15 '64

CONCERTGEBOUW orchestra, Amsterdam. See Amsterdam concertgebouw orchestra

CONCERTOS
Music to my ears; Barber concerto performed by the New York philharmonic orchestra. I. Kolodin. Sat R 46:33 N 23 '63
See also
Phonograph records—Concertos

CONCERTS
All the world's a stage when the arts move outdoors. il Sr Schol 82:10-11 My 1 '63
Doing the noble thing badly; opening of New York philharmonic Promenades series. il Time 83:44 My 29 '64
It takes push to float a concert; American wind symphony orchestra on Ohio River barge. il Bsns W p30-1 Jl 11 '64
Life guide; new faces and sounds in concerts. il Life 55:17 N 1 '63
Musical events; New York philharmonic's promenade concerts at Philharmonic Hall. W. Sargeant. New Yorker 40:131-3 My 30 '64
Musical events; Promenade concert program of English music. W. Sargeant. New Yorker 40:131-2 Je 13 '64
Musical events; Shakespeare Promenade concert at Philharmonic Hall. W. Sargeant. New Yorker 40:132-3 Je 13 '64
Sandburg makes history at the proms; Promenade concerts in Philharmonic Hall, New York. I. Kolodin. Sat R 46:51 Je 15 '63

Anecdotes, facetiae, satire, etc.

Eine kleine nachtnoise. R. Schoenstein. il Sat R 46:41 Je 29 '63

CONCERTS, Community. See Music, Community

CONCESSIONS (food, etc)
Executive on the door; Majestic doormen, inc, Chicago. il Bsns W p30 My 11 '63
Hawking in blazers; Automatic canteen co. of America. il Newsweek 62:88 N 4 '63

CONCHOLOGY. See Shells (conchology)

CONCIERGES. See Doorkeepers

CONCILIATION, Industrial. See Arbitration, Industrial

CONCILIATION, International. See Arbitration, International

CONCILIUM (periodical)
Concilium appears. America 112:154 Ja 30 '65

CONCORD, Mass.
Bridge to the past; visits to historic places. E. F. Hunter. il Parents Mag 38:64-6+ Mr '63
Yankee ingenuity; instant sidewalks; fire training aid. T. M. Nelson. il Am City 78:109 Je '63

CONCORD, Mass, free public library
Small library: close-up on Concord; with profile. D. Nyren. il Wilson Lib Bul 37: 776, 778-80 My '63

CONCORD, N.H.
Do-it-yourself park; reprint. S. E. U. Whitney. Recreation 57:365 S '64
New England events; festival of art at South Congregational church. Christian Cent 81:470 Ap 8 '64

CONCORDIA publishing house
Concordia: big expansion, 95th anniversary. il Pub W 186:32-3 D 14 '64

CONCRETE
Admixtures for architectural concrete. R. W. Yeakel, jr. il Arch Rec 133:191-4 F '63
Chemistry of concrete. S. Brunauer and L. E. Copeland. il Sci Am 210:80-6+ Ap '64
Leaf silhouettes; patterns in concrete to enhance your patio. A. R. Ball. il Pop Gard 15:12-13 Ja '64
Notes on exposed concrete surfaces. S. Howard. il Arch Rec 136:250-3 S '64
Shrinkless concrete! it's crack-free. J. Joseph. il Pop Sci 184:110-11+ Je '64
Solid advice about ready-mixed concrete. B. Gilmore. Pop Sci 185:142-3+ Jl '64

Painting

Concrete floor paints; latex and solvent for indoor use. il Consumer Rep 28:427-30 S '63
How to paint over concrete. Suc Farm 61: 104 Mr '63

Prestressing

Nine buildings honored by P.C.I. il Arch Rec 134:12-13 S '63
Prestressed units form inverted dome. il Arch Rec 136:198-201 O '64

CONCRETE, Precast
British system builds from the top down. il Arch Forum 120:92-5 Mr '64
Concrete slabs made from precast boxes. K. C. Naslund and A. Moreno. il Arch Rec 134:154-6 Jl '63

CONCRETE, Precast—*Continued*
Development house expresses the character of concrete. il Arch Rec 135:72-5 mid-My '64
Marble strips distinguish precast concrete facades. il Arch Rec 135:184 Je '64
Precast concrete wall frames delivered to building preglazed. il Arch Rec 134:152-3 Jl '63
Precast framing grows taller: three examples. il Arch Rec 134:224-8 O '63
Precast load-bearing exterior wall. il Arch Rec 136:122-3 Ag '64
Precasting culvert prevents traffic hold-up; Montclair, Calif. S. E. Scholl. il Am City 79:89 D '64
Two-story precast panels for factory. il Arch Rec 133:167 Ja '63

CONCRETE blocks
Neo-classic builder house in concrete block. il Arch Rec 133:114-17 mid-My '63
Sculptured house of concrete block. il Arch Rec 133:70-3 mid-My '63

CONCRETE construction
Any form you need; headquarters for the Emhart manufacturing co, Connecticut. il Time 82:44-5+ Ag 2 '63
Artist in concrete; P. L. Nervi. il Read Digest 84:208-11+ F '64
Closer control of concrete construction. W. Howe. Arch Rec 136:156 Ag '64
Concrete step manufacturers; Thompson unit step co, Indianapolis. il Ebony 19:146-9 D '63
Emhart: a bold, pragmatic structure of concrete and steel. il Arch Forum 119:88-95 Jl '63
Lab that jacks built; one-story structure jacked up and first floor and basement built under it. il Bsns W p 138-40 My 9 '64
Stack of concrete barrels. il Arch Forum 118:132-7 Je '63
Studied details in concrete for a message hub; Florists' telegraph delivery association international headquarters, Detroit, Mich. il Arch Rec 133:198-9 Ap '63
Swiss school is a lesson in concrete; School for economic and social studies, St Gallen. il Arch Forum 120:78-81 Ja '64
Three fast concrete systems. il Arch Forum 118:138-41 Je '63
Walls become columns, and vice versa. W. C. Wing. il Arch Rec 135:202-4 Mr '64
See also
Concrete houses

Forms

Formwork: time-saver standards. S. Howard. il Arch Rec 136:254-6 S '64
New techniques enhance slipform potential. il Arch Rec 136:157-8 Ag '64
Reinforced plastic forms produce sharply detailed concrete facade. il Arch Rec 135:182-3 Je '64

CONCRETE floors. See Floors, Concrete

CONCRETE framing. See Framing (building)

CONCRETE houses
Add water, mix & pour. il Time 83:46-9 Ja 24 '64

CONCRETE mixers
Happy wedding: cement mixer and barrow. D. Huff. il Pop Sci 185:146-7 Ag '64

CONCRETE pavements. See Pavements, Concrete

CONCRETE slabs
Cast your own patio slabs. W. Radcliffe. il Pop Mech 119:164-5 My '63
Formwork: time-saver standards. S. Howard. il Arch Rec 136:254 S '64
Precast, prestressed slabs for library. il Arch Rec 133:167 Ja '63

CONDAK, Cliff
Big men on the move. il Sports Illus 19:40-5 O 28 '63

CONDEMNATION of property. See Eminent domain

CONDENSATION
See also
Cloud physics

CONDENSED books. See Books, Condensed

CONDENSERS (electricity) See Electric capacitors

CONDIE, Richard M. and Langer, R. B.
Linear polymerization of a gastroped hemocyanin. bibliog Science 144:1138-40 My 29 '64

CONDIMENTS
See also
Capers

CONDITIONED reflexes. See Conditioned response

CONDITIONED response
Amateur scientist; simple analogue computer that simulates Pavlov's dogs. H. S. Hoffman. il Sci Am 208:159-60+ Je '63
Averaged brain activity following saccadic eye movement. K. Gaarder and others. bibliog il Science 146:1481-3 D 11 '64
Cognitive factors in the extinction of the conditioned eyelid response in humans. K. W. Spence. il Science 140:1224-5 Je 14 '63
Complex visual concept in the pigeon. R. J. Herrnstein and D. H. Loveland. il Science 146:549-51 O 23 '64
Conditioned discrimination in the planarian. C. D. Griffard and J. T. Peirce. il Science 144:1472-3 Je 19 '64
Conditioning of a free operant response in planaria. R. M. Lee. il Science 139:1048-9 Mr 15 '63; Reply with rejoinder. E. S. Halas. 141:390+ Ag 2 '63
Disinhibition after prefrontal lesions as a function of duration of intertrial intervals. S. Brutkowski and J. Dabrowska. bibliog il Science 139:505-6 F 8 '63
Enhancement of evoked cortical potentials in humans related to a task requiring a decision. H. Davis. bibliog il Science 145:182-3 Jl 10 '64
Imprinting in an altricial bird: the blond ring dove streptopelia risoria. E. Klinghammer and E. H. Hess. bibliog il Science 146:265-6 O 9 '64
Luminous figures: factors affecting the reporting of disappearances. J. R. Schuck and others. bibliog il Science 146:1598-9 D 18 '64
Method for discriminative avoidance training. H. M. B. Hurwitz. il Science 145:1070-1 S 4 '64; Reply with rejoinder. F. R. Brush. 146:1599-600 D 18 '64
Outlets for troutlets. Time 83:48+ Mr 13 '64
Perceptual preferences and imprinting in chicks. P. H. Klopfer and J. P. Hailman. bibliog il Science 145:1333-4 S 18 '64
Planaria: memory transfer through cannibalism reexamined. A. L. Hartry and others. bibliog il Science 146:274-5 O 9 '64
Potency of conditioned reinforcers based on food and on food and punishment. G. S. Reynolds. il Science 139:838-9 Mr 1 '63
Proprioceptive discrimination of a covert operant without its observation by the subject. R. F. Hefferline and T. B. Perera. bibliog il Science 139:834-5 Mr 1 '63
Separation of the salivary and motor responses in instrumental conditioning. G. D. Ellison and J. Konorski. bibliog il Science 146:1071-2 N 20 '64
Stimulus polarity and conditioning in planaria. C. D. Barnes and B. G. Katzung. bibliog il Science 141:728-30 Ag 23 '63

CONDOLENCES; story. See Araya, E.

CONDOMINIUM plan ownership. See Apartment houses—Condominium plan ownership

CONDON, Eddie
Anything for Eddie. il por Newsweek 64:47 Ag 3 '64
Grand old man. il por Time 84:46 Jl 31 '64

CONDON, Edward U.
Education for world understanding. Bul Atomic Sci 20:18-19 Mr '64

CONDON, Richard
Bank of pity. Holiday 33:58+ Mr '63
Infinity of mirrors; story; excerpt from novel. Sat Eve Post 237:46-8 Ag 22 '64
Lightning guide to Panama. Holiday 34:82-3 N '63
Manchurian candidate in Dallas. Nation 197:449-51 D 28 '63
Quick look at Mexico. Holiday 35:56-7 Je '64
Show of hands. Holiday 36:12+ S '64

about

Book rental unfair to authors, says novelist Richard Condon. Library J 89:4492 N 15 '64
Rights and permissions. P. Nathan. Pub W 186:60 S 21 '64

CONDON, Vesta
Wander through Wales. Travel 120:36-41 Ag '63

CONDORS
Death road for the condor. R. Macdonald. il Sports Illus 20:86-9 Ap 6 '64
Hope for the California condor; excerpts from report. A. H. Miller and others. il Audubon Mag 67:38-41 Ja '65
Last of the shy condors. il Life 57:75-6 N 27 '64

CONDUCT of life
Are you a grievance collector? I. A. R. Wylie. Read Digest 84:175+ F '64
Art of changing yourself; excerpt from Art of living. W. A. Peterson. Read Digest 82:24B F '63
Artur Rubinstein talks to teens. A. Rubinstein. Seventeen 22:160+ My '63

CONDUCT of life—*Continued*
Centering as dialogue; excerpt from Centering: in pottery, poetry, and the person. M. C. Richards. il Craft Horiz 24:31-3+ Jl '64
Don't tell me I've got it made; father writes to his son. Read Digest 84:90-2 Ap '64
Fine art of keeping one's head. W. FitzGibbon. Read Digest 83:62-5 S '63
Frankly speaking; what is your greatest weakness? G. Wagner. il McCalls 90:164 My '63
From a boy's point of view. J. Wescott. il Seventeen 23:8 F '64
Grasp the nettle, now! O. Schisgall. il Read Digest 85:43-4+ N '64
History lesson. M. E. Jenkins. PTA Mag 58:2-3 Ja '64
How to cope with criticisms. N. V. Peale. Read Digest 84:117-20 My '64
Know the right moment. A. Gordon. Read Digest 83:135-7 Ag '63
Know yourself! excerpt from address, January 21, 1963. J. W. Gardner. Read Digest 83:72-4 N '63
Limits of intimacy. M. M. Hunt. Read Digest 85:69-71 S '64
Man's reach must exceed his grasp; address, March 15, 1963. R. L. Whitt. Vital Speeches 29:439-41 My 1 '63
Minister's mail. J. F. Newton. Read Digest 85:119-21 O '64
My last will and testament; reprint of 1955 article. M. M. Bethune. il Ebony 18:150-6 S '63
My struggle to be myself. il Good H 157:10+ S '63
Myths we live by; excerpts from address. L. Rosten. Redbook 122:35+ Ja '64
Never say never. M. Drury. Read Digest 84:99-100 My '64
Nice people: the habits they have; excerpt from Seventeen book of etiquette and entertaining. E. A. Haupt. Seventeen 23:32 My '64
Party of one; confessions of an anachronism. C. Fadiman. il Holiday 33:11+ F '63
Perils of leisure. D. Gabor. il Horizon 5:102-9 N '63
Pete Seeger talks to teens. P. Seeger. Seventeen 22:148+ N '63
Problems on the path to manhood; excerpts from Moving into manhood. W. W. Bauer. il Todays Health 41:60-1+ O '63
Profit is a dead weight. M. Moore. Seventeen 22:142+ Mr '63
Realms of gold; address, May 6, 1964. L. Crocker. Vital Speeches 30:537-9 Je 15 '64
Redbook dialogue. R. Graves; G. Lollobrigida. il Redbook 121:58-9+ S '63
Rewards of caring. A. Gordon. il Read Digest 83:81-4 O '63
Search. A. Gordon. Read Digest 82:137-8 Ap '63
Self-protection; address, June 5, 1964. T. J. Watson, jr. Vital Speeches 30:598-600 Jl 15 '64
Speaking out; if at first you don't succeed, quit! T. S. Geisel. il Sat Eve Post 237:6+ N 28 '64
Stand up for what you believe in. W. S. Coffin, jr. il Parents Mag 38:49+ D '63
Strength to be free; address, June 18, 1964. E. M. Clark. Vital Speeches 30:727-30 S 15 '64
Ten delusions of youth; address, February 14, 1963. W. P. Shofstall. Vital Speeches 29:400-3 Ap 15 '63
To be a god. A. Wheelis. Commentary 36:125-34 Ag '63; Discussion. 37:10+ Ja '64
Totality of outlook; address, January 24, 1963. B. McEntegart. Vital Speeches 29:299-300 Mr 1 '63
We stopped living on a treadmill. S. K. Parks. il Redbook 121:6+ Ag '63
Whatever became of personal ethics? L. Kronenberger. Horizon 5:60-1 Mr '63
Why save the cream? E. Gorsline. il Farm J 88:81 Mr '64
World belongs to God; address, May 19, 1963. D. Lyons. Vital Speeches 29:542-4 Je 15 '63
See also
Altruism
Anger
Character
Cheating in schoolwork
Christian life
Courtesy
Duty
Early rising
Ethics
Faith
Happiness
Honesty
Human relations
Idleness
Individuality
Kindness
Leisure
Life
Love
Mental hygiene
Obedience
Pleasure
Popularity
Procrastination
Respect
Responsibility
Self control
Self reliance
Service
Time, Use of
Worth

CONDUCTING (music)
Antal Dorati; interview, ed. by S. Fleming. A. Dorati. Hi Fi 13:22 Je '63
Cellist's view of conducting; excerpt from Cellist. G. Piatigorsky. il Sat R 48:47-8+ Ja 30 '65
In fine style; interview, ed. by J. W. Freeman. G. Prêtre. il Opera N 29:13 D 26 '64
Intangible and misunderstood; interview. G. Szell. Mus Am 83:6 My '63
Marathon maestro; interview, ed. by J. W. Freeman. S. Varviso. Opera N 27:15 Mr 30 '63
Mixture of instinct and intellect; interview, ed. by P. H. Lang, with editorial comment. G. Szell. il Hi Fi 15:41, 42-5+ Ja '65
Performing the Brandenburgs. T. Dunn. Mus Am 83:52-3 My '63
Right spirit; interview, ed. by A. M. Lingg. J. Krips. il Opera N 29:24-5 N 14 '64
Special sound; interview, ed. by L. F. Loveday. G. Solti. Opera N 27:14 Mr 23 '63
See also
Conductors (music)

Competitions

See Music—Competitions

CONDUCTIVITY, Electric. See Electric conductivity

CONDUCTORS (music)
Bel canto in brass. J. Johnson. il Opera N 29:6-7 D 12 '64
Concert of conductors. H. Klein. il N Y Times Mag p54-5 My 17 '64
Detroit acclaims James Frazier; minister of music at the Peoples community church. C. W. Thomas. Negro Hist Bul 28:28 N '64
Did you stop? Dimitri Mitropoulos competition. il Newsweek 64:57 D 28 '64
Far-out at the Philharmonic; mechanical maestro. il Time 83:79-80 F 14 '64
Four for the podium; American conductors project subsidized by the Ford foundation. il Newsweek 61:94 My 27 '63
Music to my ears; Mitropoulos competition. I. Kolodin. Sat R 46:28 Ap 20 '63
Musical events; performances by London symphony orchestra in Carnegie Hall under four conductors. W. Sargeant. New Yorker 40:229-31 O 31 '64
Revolt of the brasses. F. Grunfeld. il Reporter 29:48+ Jl 18 '63
We take the critics to the conductors. H. Thompson. Mus Am 83:8 My '63
See also
Abbado, C.
Beecham, S. T.
Bernstein, L.
Böhm, K.
Calderón, P. I.
Christian, M.
Craft, R.
De Carvalho, E.
Dixon, D.
Dunn, T.
Feldbrill, V.
Fiedler, A.
Furtwängler, W.
Karajan, H. von
Krips, J.
Leinsdorf, E.
Maazel, L.
Martinon, J.
Mehta, Z.
Monteux, C.
Monteux, P.
Munch, C.
Ondrejka, R.
Ozawa, S.
Perlea, J.
Reiner, F.
Rucht, K.
Scherchen, H.
Schippers, T.
Singer, J.
Skrowaczewski, S.
Solti, G.
Steinberg, W.

CONDUCTORS (music)—*See also—Continued*
Stokowski, L.
Stokowski, S. A.
Szell, G.
Van Oterloo, W.
Waldman, F.
Walter, B.
Wand, G.
CONE, Fairfax M.
Who shall bell the cat? concerning address to Association of national advertisers. Nation 200:23 Ja 11 '65
World of the renaissance executive. il por Newsweek 62:92-4 N 18 '63
CONE, Richard A. and Platt, J. R.
Rat electroretinogram: evidence for separate processes governing b-wave latency and amplitude. bibliog Science 144:1016-19 My 22 '64
CONE shells. See Shells (conchology)
CONELRAD warning system
Sign-off for Conelrad. Time 82:52 Jl 12 '63
Wanted: an electronic Paul Revere; CONELRAD; NEAR. E. Nanas. il Pop Electr 18:41-3+ F '63
CONENOSED bugs. See Kissing bugs
CONERLY, Charlie
All's well, and all that. Sports Illus 19:16 S 30 '63
CONES, Pine. See Pine cones
CONEY ISLAND aquarium. See Aquariums
CONEYS. See Pikas
CONFECTIONERY
Color it festive; candied fruits and citron. C. Claiborne. il N Y Times Mag p92 N 29 '64
Distinctive treats from your own kitchen; with recipes. il Farm J 88:76-8 N '64
Holiday goodies to serve with pride. B. M. Stover. il Parents Mag 39:61-3+ D '64
See also
Candy
CONFEDERATE air force (club) See Aviation clubs
CONFEDERATE memorial of Stone Mountain. See Stone Mountain monument
CONFEDERATE STATES of America
Operator and the emperors; with portfolio. L. Thomas. il Am Heritage 15:4-23+ Ap '64
See also
United States—History—Civil war
CONFERENCE board of the mathematical sciences
Conference board of the mathematical sciences; new affiliate of AAAS. L. W. Cohen. Science 140:416-17 Ap 26 '63
Manpower problems: training of mathematicians; report of conference on Manpower problems in the training of mathematicians. L. W. Cohen. Science 140:1111-13 Je 7 '63
CONFERENCE of Asian economic planners. See United Nations conference of Asian economic planners
CONFERENCE of eastern college librarians
Eastern college librarians confer on need to reinvent the library. Library J 89:76-7 Ja 1 '64
CONFERENCE of European churches. See European conference of churches
CONFERENCE of governors. See Governors conference, 1963
CONFERENCE of heads of state or government of non-aligned countries, Cairo, 1964
Cairo: comedy of neutralism. Life 57:4 O 23 '64
Cairo conference. il Newsweek 64:43 O 19 '64
Conference of the nonaligned; Cairo conference. H. A. Jack. Christian Cent 81:1364-5 N 4 '64
Fragmenting bloc. Commonweal 81:118-19 O 23 '64
From Cairo: the nonaligned confer. H. A. Jack. Bul Atomic Sci 20:34-5 D '64
Man who wasn't there. il Time 84:45 O 16 '64
Next question; second conference. Newsweek 64:62 O 12 '64
President Johnson sends message to nonalined nations conference. L. B. Johnson. Dept State Bul 51:581-2 O 26 '64
CONFERENCE of the Eighteen-nation committee on disarmament, Geneva, 1962-
Arms control and disarmament; transcript of the television program State department briefing: disarmament, first broadcast, January 14, 1963. Dept State Bul 48:115-27 Ja 28 '63
Assembly calls for new disarmament talks. U N Rev 11:20-5 Ja '64
Back to Geneva. Commonweal 79:559-60 F 7 '64
Eighteen-nation disarmament committee recesses 1964 session; statement, September 17, 1964. W. C. Foster. bibliog f Dept State Bul 51:524-7 O 12 '64
Eighteen nation disarmament conference reconvenes at Geneva; statement, June 9, 1964. W. C. Foster. Dept State Bul 50:1004-7 Je 29 '64
Geneva conference resumes. H. A. Jack. Christian Cent 80:1028-9 Ag 21 '63
Geneva: progress and problems. H. A. Jack. Sat R 47:19+ Je 27 '64
In Geneva, another step toward armistice day. Newsweek 63:37 Ja 27 '64
Long pull at Geneva. il Bsns W p30-2 F 22 '64
Mr Foster leaves for disarmament conference at Geneva; White House statement, January 16, 1964. Dept State Bul 50:163 F 3 '64
Nonaligned in disarmament negotiations. A. S. Lall. Bul Atomic Sci 20:17-21 My '64
Nuclear test ban issue; statement, February 12, 1963. W. C. Foster. Dept State Bul 48: 398-402 Mr 18 '63
Old horse, new odds. il Time 83:26+ Ja 31 '64
President greets resumption of Geneva disarmament talks; statement, by President Kennedy. Dept State Bul 48:340 Mr 4 '63
President Johnson urges disarmament conference to take further steps toward peace; remarks and message January 21, 1964. L. B. Johnson. bibliog f Dept State Bul 50:223-5 F 10 '64
Report of conference of Eighteen-nation committee on disarmament; text of the interim report. S. K. Tsarapkin and C. C. Stelle. U N Rev 10:42-3 O '63
Report of conference of Eighteen-nation committee; text of report to the United Nations disarmament commission and the General assembly on the deliberations January 21, 1964 to September 17, 1964. UN Mo Chron 1:40-3 O '64
Rocky road to a test ban. H. A. Jack. Christian Cent 80:615-16 My 8 '63
Seventeen continue. H. A. Jack. Bul Atomic Sci 20:43-5 Je '64
Still talking. Newsweek 63:49 Mr 16 '64
U.S. calls for exploration of freeze concept; statement, January 31, 1964. W. C. Foster. Dept State Bul 50:350-2 Mr 2 '64
U.S. discusses freeze proposal in disarmament committee; statement, April 16, 1964. A. S. Fisher. bibliog f Dept State Bul 50:756-9 My 11 '64
U.S. makes proposals for safeguards for peaceful nuclear activities and for bomber destruction; statements, March 5 and March 19, 1964. A. S. Fisher. bibliog f Dept State Bul 50:641-5 Ap 20 '64
U.S. outlines verification measures to assure compliance with proposed freeze of strategic nuclear vehicles; statement, August 27, 1964. C. R. Timberlake. Dept State Bul 51:413-17 S 21 '64
U.S. proposes curb on spread of nuclear weapons; statement, February 6, 1964. W. C. Foster. Dept State Bul 50:376-9 Mr 9 '64
Welcome back. Newsweek 63:32 F 3 '64
William C. Foster named to head delegation to disarmament talks; White House Statement, January 10, 1964. Dept State Bul 50: 119 Ja 27 '64
CONFERENCE on congenital malformations. See International conference on congenital malformations
CONFERENCE on technology and human values, Pennsylvania state university. See Educational conferences
CONFERENCE on the discontinuance of nuclear weapons tests, Geneva, 1958-1961
Most urgent step toward peace. J. J. Wadsworth. Redbook 121:54-5+ Ag '63
CONFERENCE on the peaceful uses of atomic energy. See International conference on the peaceful uses of atomic energy, 3d, Geneva, 1964
CONFERENCES
Notes on conferencemanship. C. B. Marshall. New Repub 148:15-17 F 16 '63
Panelizing dissent; report on conference on the Negro writer in the United States. K. Rexroth. Nation 199:97-9 S 7 '64
Thinksville; Airlie house, Warrenton, Va. Newsweek 63:109-10 Mr 16 '64
See also Religious conferences; Scientific conferences and similar headings
Anecdotes, facetiae, satire, etc.
Let's hold a conference: herewith an imaginary dialog between the collector and his quarry. D. S. Greenberg. Science 144:1204-5 Je 5 '64
CONFERENCES, Religious. See Religious conferences
CONFERENCES on science and world affairs. See Pugwash conferences on science and world affairs

CONFESSION
Bless me, father. J. E. Corrigan. America 110:342-4 Mr 14 '64; Discussion. 110:498 Ap 11 '64
Wiping the slate. C. Davis. America 110:720 My 23 '64
CONFESSION (law)
New headache for state courts; question of coerced confessions. il Time 85:62 Ja 22 '65
CONFESSION stories. See Short stories
CONFIDENTIAL (periodical)
Public lives: Confidential magazine; reflections in tranquillity by the former owner, Robert Harrison, who managed to get away with it. T. K. Wolfe. il Esquire 61:87-90+ Ap '64
CONFISCATIONS
See also
World war, 1939-1945—Confiscations and contributions
CONFLICT (psychology)
See also
Dominance, Mixed
CONFLICT, Social. See Social conflict
CONFLICT of interests (business)
Conflict of interest. W. J. Coughlin. Miss & Roc 12:50 F 18 '63; Reply. J. K. Taussig, jr. 12:6-7 Ap 15 '63
CONFLICT of interests (public office)
L'affaire Baker. K. Crawford. Newsweek 62:35 N 4 '63
Baker issue. K. Crawford. Newsweek 63:28 Ap 6 '64
Call this a code? Nation 199:2 Jl 13 '64
Codes of ethics; all honorable men. L. W. Koenig. Nation 198:551-4 Je 1 '64
Conflict-of-interest ghost walks again; F. Korth and R. Baker. Bsns W p29 O 26 '63
Conflict of interest; new law eases restrictions on part-time expert consultants to government. E. Langer. Science 140:882-3 My 24 '63
Congress and the country slicker. Fortune 68:101-2 D '63
Congress, too, has conflicts of interests. C. P. Case. il N Y Times Mag p 12+ My 19 '63
Congress: when the private life of a lawmaker becomes a public affair. L. Stern and E. Knoll. il Esquire 61:82-6 Ap '64
Congressmen and their conflicting interests. I. Ross. Read Digest 85:118-23 Jl '64
Contempt of Congress; bill to compel disclosure of income. Nation 198:22 Ja 6 '64
Ethics in New York. Newsweek 62:33 N 11 '63
First of the month; excerpt from letter in the Harvard alumni bulletin on whether President Kennedy should resign from Harvard's Board of overseers. C. Amory. Sat R 46:6 My 4 '63
From Washington straight. Cato. Nat R 15:342 O 22 '63
Gilpatric's records are new TFX issue. G. C. Wilson. Aviation W 79:27-8 N 11 '63
High price of talent. Newsweek 65:23 Ja 18 '65
How Baker turned access into an asset. Bsns W p30-1 F 8 '64
How searching? investigation of R. Baker by Senate rules and administration committee. il Newsweek 62:26 N 4 '63
Interest in Transitron. Fortune 67:80 Mr '63
Investigating Washington; how far will it go? U S News 55:66 D 2 '63
Johnson's holdings put on ice; in trust for the duration. il Bsns W p23 D 7 '63
Juggling that hot potato, the political gift. B. H. Bagdikian. il N Y Times Mag p 14-15+ Mr 22 '64
Making senators lift lid, a little, on wealth. Bsns W p 18 Jl 4 '64
Mess in Washington? K. Crawford. Newsweek 62:39 N 18 '63
Mess in Washington? with interview with J. J. Williams. il U S News 55:36-8+ N 25 '63
Official integrity. R. Moley. Newsweek 63:88 F 10 '64
Oil transaction draws fire; member of Texas railroad commission. Bsns W p37 Ap 20 '63
Pulling the teeth of conflict of interest. Bsns W p29 Ja 16 '65
Safari into Washington's netherworld. B. H. Bagdikian. il N Y Times Mag p12+ Ja 19 '64
Scandal grows and grows in Washington; the Bobby Baker case. K. Wheeler and others. il Life 55:40-40B+ N 22 '63
Sell it. Nation 198:385 Ap 20 '64
Senate inquiry into sugar & spice; B. Baker case. il Newsweek 62:32-3 N 11 '63
Senate probers scrutinize Korth letters; with statement by F. Korth, October 19, 1963. G. C. Wilson. Aviation W 79:22-4 O 28 '63
Senate TFX probers split on Gilpatric. G. C. Wilson. Aviation W 79:27-9 N 25 '63
TFX probers fly a new route. Bsns W p33 N 23 '63
Their men in Washington. F. J. Cook. il Nation 198:311-30 Mr 30 '64
CONFLICT of laws
Selected essay on the conflict of laws, by B. Currie. Review
Time 85:42 Ja 8 '65
CONFORMITY
Average American afraid to oppose klan. Sci N L 86:84 Ag 8 '64
Cost of conformity; with study-discussion program, by E. M. Duvall. R. Squires. bibliog PTA Mag 58:4-6, 36 Mr '64; Reply. D. Strutz. 58:35 Je '64
Decline of the individual. H. G. Rickover. Sat Eve Post 236:11-13 Mr 30 '63
His wife likes it; James Forstner's beard. Nation 197:271 N 2 '63
One father. J. Ciardi. Sat R 47:15 D 12 '64
Outsiders, studies in the sociology of deviance, by H. S. Becker. Review
Commentary 36:410-12 N '63. H. Dienstfrey; Reply with rejoinder. E. M. Schur. 37:16 Mr '64
Queen Bee of the school; with report of sociologists, ed. by B. Villet. il Life 55:68-80+ O 11 '63
Scraping the top of the barrel; creative nonconformist in college. S. J. Idzerda. NEA J 52:14-15 My '63
CONFRATERNITY of Christian doctrine
Catechism comes to life. E. J. Menninger. America 111:36-8 Jl 11 '64
CONFUCIUS and Confucianism
Growing up with Confucius. L. Yen. il Holiday 34:108+ N '63
CONGDON, Charles C.
Cell division and cancer. Science 142:252-3+ O 11 '63
CONGDON, Kirby
Art as axle grease. Américas 16:12-15 O '64
CONGDON, LeRoy
Tepee on the hilltop. Recreation 57:117 Mr '64
CONGDON, Thomas B. jr
Ann Lowe: society's best-kept secret. Sat Eve Post 237:74-6 D 12 '64
Convict volunteers. Sat Eve Post 236:62-4 Mr 2 '63
Making of a saint. Sat Eve Post 236:74-8 Mr 23 '63
Strange case of Lee Lawrence. Sat Eve Post 236:85-9 Ap 20 '63
CONGDON, William
Eucharistic congress. America 111:805-6 D 19 '64
Sacred art and the artist. America 109:356-8, 648 S 28, N 23 '63
CONGENITAL malformations. See Deformities
CONGER, Lesley
Ashtrays in a vacuum. Writer 76:15-17 My '63
One woman's world; excerpts from Adventures of an ordinary mind. Read Digest 83:55-6 O '63
When you give your heart; story. Good H 157:58-9 Jl '63
CONGLUTINATION
Conglutination: specific inhibition by carbohydrates. M. A. Leon and R. Yokohari. bibliog il Science 143:1327-8 Mr 20 '64
CONGO (capital Brazzaville)
Abbé steps down. Newsweek 62:37+ Ag 26 '63
Congo: what was wrong, what is and will be wrong. A. J. Meyers. il U S News 54:59-61 F 4 '63

Politics and government

Failure of a fetish. il Time 82:27 Ag 23 '63
CONGO (capital Leopoldville)
Across the river & into the mess. il Time 84:27 Ag 28 '64
Adoula and peace with Belgium; address, February 27, 1963. C. Adoula. Negro Hist Bul 26:247-8 My '63
Africa's anti-US kick. New Repub 151:3-4 D 12 '64
Again, the savages; terrorized Kwilu. il Time 83:34 Mr 6 '64
Agonizing choice; 1,000 white civilians held by Congo rebels. il Newsweek 64:58 N 30 '64
Breakdown in the Congo. V. C. Ferkiss. il Commonweal 81:325-8 N 27 '64
Congo rescue. M. Ascoli. Reporter 31:8 D 17 '64
Congo: the mouse that roared. il Newsweek 64:33 Ag 31 '64
Congolese chaos continues. il Newsweek 64:31 D 21 '64
Elation for Moise: army retakes Albertville. il Time 84:45 S 11 '64

CONGO (capital Leopoldville)—*Continued*
Everybody's problem child. R. Howe. New Repub 148:10-12 Ap 27 '63
Hoodlum rebels. il Time 84:43 N 20 '64
Hostages. il Time 84:36 N 27 '64
Imports of trouble; arms for Simba units. il Time 85:29 Ja 15 '65
Is anyone in control? il Time 83:31-2 Je 26 '64
Massacre season. il Time 83:35 F 7 '64
Mirror, mirror. . Newsweek 64:30 D 28 '64
Mission to Addis; Tshombe's request for African troops rejected. Time 84:46 S 18 '64
More the Congo changes; photographs. N Y Times Mag p32-3 S 13 '64
My clothes were blood-soaked, but I never moved; American missionary among rebels in Kwilu province, Congo; ed. by B. Lindeman. R. Hege. il Sat Eve Post 237:84-5 O 3 '64
Needed: a divine force. il Time 84:30 D 18 '64
No end in sight. il Newsweek 64:36+ D 14 '64
On the rampage. Time 83:21 Ja 24 '64
People on fire: the Congo. C. Cate. il Atlan 213:91-2+ My '64
Plus ça change: revival of Belgian influence. Newsweek 62:38+ S 16 '63
Prospects for the Congo. E. Van de Straeten. Negro Hist Bul 26:246-7 My '63
Rebellion in the Congo; with 1,000 whites as hostages. il U S News 57:11 N 30 '64
Rebels collapse. il Time 84:50+ N 13 '64
That man, c'est moi; rebel leader Soumialot. il Time 84:21-2 Ag 14 '64
Trouble for the mercenaries; help for the rebels; Wamba massacre. il Time 85:19 Ja 8 '65
Trying to untarnish Tshombe. Time 85:33-4 Ja 1 '65
Tshombe squeeze. Newsweek 65:26 Ja 4 '65
U.S. informs U.N. of withdrawal of Congo rescue mission; text of letter to the president of the Security council, December 1, 1964. A. E. Stevenson. Dept State Bul 51: 891 D 21 '64
Unresolved. il Newsweek 65:38 Ja 11 '65
Where's the money? Newsweek 61:51 F 11 '63
Worse than Laos? New Repub 150:4 Je 13 '64
See also
Communism—Congo (capital Leopoldville)
Education—Congo (capital Leopoldville)
Guerrillas—Congo (capital Leopoldville)
Katanga
Rites and ceremonies—Congo (capital Leopoldville)
United Nations—Armed forces—Forces in the Congo
United Nations—Congo (capital Leopoldville)
United States—Armed forces—Forces in the Congo
Women—Congo (capital Leopoldville)

Army

Another round in Katanga? concerning ANC (Congolese national army) C. Scott. Nat R 15:478 D 3 '63
Caesars of the bush; Armée nationale congolaise. Time 81:38+ Ap 5 '63
Can the Congo go it alone? C. Sterling. il Reporter 30:27-31 Je 18 '64
Cheers & beers; ex-gendarmes from Katanga to join the Congolese army. Time 84:35 O 9 '64
Congo: Col. Dodds observes; interview, ed. by E. Deverill. W. A. Dodds. il Newsweek 64:48+ N 23 '64
Congo: no rhyme, no reason; with report by P. Webb. il Newsweek 64:40-2 Ag 24 '64
Congo: plugging a sieve with pinheads. R. W. Howe. Reporter 29:37-8 O 10 '63
Congo tries to build an army. J. A. Lukas. il N Y Times Mag p7-9+ Jl 21 '63
Congo turns to the white man; meaning for Africa. F. B. Stevens. il U S News 57:55 S 14 '64
Full circle? retraining of Congolese army. Newsweek 61:54 My 6 '63
Geronimo! Congolese paratroopers trained in Israel. il Newsweek 62:39+ S 16 '63
Help wanted; Tshombe's new mercenary army. il Time 84:36 S 4 '64
Lousy civilian; with report by A. de Borchgrave. il Newsweek 64:56-7 O 12 '64
Sign up here; recruiting mercenaries to fight against the rebels. il Newsweek 64: 38+ S 7 '64
True believers. A. De Borchgrave. il Newsweek 63:46+ Je 15 '64
Tshombe's four hundred. P. Schmid. il Reporter 31:25-6 D 17 '64
White mercenaries on a rabbit hunt; 51st commando at Bumba. L. Garrison. il N Y Times Mag p30-1+ N 15 '64

Economic conditions

Congo: the morning after; reprint. W. Stone. U S News 57:68 Ag 24 '64
New look at the Congo three years later. F. C. Painton. il U S News 55:102-4 N 25 '63
Price of friendship. Newsweek 61:46-7 Mr 11 '63
When will the Congo be ready for independence? C. Sterling. il Reporter 28:25-8 Ap 11 '63

Foreign relations

Congo: another job for U.S. il U S News 57:37 Ag 17 '64
Down to his socks. Newsweek 62:64 D 2 '63
Reading the Russians' mail. Time 82:46-7 N 29 '63
Tshombe talks about U.S. role in the Congo; interview, ed. by A. J. Meyers. M. Tshombe. il U S News 57:50-1 Ag 3 '64

Massacre, 1964

See Congo massacre, 1964

Native races

Back in the bush; Lunda tribe. il Time 82:33 S 27 '63
Isolated people awakes to progress. P. Daerly. Negro Hist Bul 27:77-8 Ja '64

Politics and government

Adoula tries to bind up the wounds. L. Garrison. il N Y Times Mag p25+ My 12 '63
Aftermath in the Congo. H. R. Rudin. Cur Hist 45:341-6 D '63
Arrow in the air. il Newsweek 63:54 F 17 '64
Atlantic report. Atlan 212:16+ S '63
Baby steps; Tshombe coalition government. Newsweek 64:42 Jl 13 '64
Back comes Moses the Beloved. il Time 84:24 Jl 3 '64
Balancing act. il Time 84:29 Ag 7 '64
Boys from Binza. Time 82:36+ N 1 '63
Can the Congo go it alone? C. Sterling. il Reporter 30:27-31 Je 18 '64
Clamping down. Newsweek 62:52+ N 4 '63
Congo; an attempt to go back. il Time 83: 27 Mr 27 '64
Congo: another job for U.S. il U S News 57:37 Ag 17 '64
Congo: end of the fight? il Sr Schol 82:15 Ja 30 '63
Congo: hostages, mercenaries and the CIA. J. Hatch. il Nation 199:452-5 D 14 '64
Congo: no rhyme, no reason; with report by P. Webb. il Newsweek 64:40-2 Ag 24 '64
Congo: the morning after; reprint. W. Stone. U S News 57:68 Ag 24 '64
Congo triumvirate. R. W. Howe. New Repub 151:6 O 24 '64
Congo: what was wrong, what is and will be wrong. A. J. Meyers. il U S News 54:59-61 F 4 '63
Congo's Tshombe: alternating current. il Newsweek 64:44+ O 19 '64
Crisis in search of a country. J. A. Lukas. il N Y Times Mag p27+ N 24 '63
Freedom's blessings. il Newsweek 64:28-30+ Jl 6 '64
Is there a historian in the House? Nat R 14: 185 Mr 12 '63
Katanga and the Congo crisis. C. K. Yearley. Commoweal 77:483-6 F 1 '63
Look who's here again. Nat R 16:639 Jl 28 '64
Looking up. Newsweek 64:42 S 14 '64
Moise Tshombe's Congo comeback. U S News 57:21 Jl 20 '64
New look at the Congo three years later. F. C. Painton. il U S News 55:102-4 N 25 '63
One of those weeks. Newsweek 64:54+ S 21 '64
OAU commission on Congo talks with department officers; Department statement, with joint press communique, September 23 and September 30, 1964. Dept State Bul 51: 553 O 19 '64
Premier no. four. il Time 84:28-9 Jl 17 '64
Putting the Congo together again. L. Loebl. New Repub 148:10-11 Mr 9 '63
Reluctant to reconcile. il Time 84:32 Jl 10 '64
Setback for U.S. in Congo. il U S News 57:46 Jl 13 '64
Snake has all the lines. il Time 84:33-4 Jl 24 '64
Still in trouble. New Repub 151:14 Jl 4 '64
Summary of U.S. recommendations for program of aid to the Congo. Dept State Bul 48:481-4 Ap 1 '63
Take-over; Tshombe government. Newsweek 64:39-40 Jl 20 '64
Terror in the Congo. Newsweek 63:37-8 F 10 '64
Tshombe at bay. il Newsweek 64:40+ Ag 17 '64
Tshombe in wonderland. S. de Gramont. il Sat Eve Post 237:83+ O 3 '64
Tshombe returns. Sr Schol 85:30-1 S 23 '64

CONGO (capital Leopoldville)—Politics and government—*Continued*
Tshombe talks about U.S. role in the Congo; interview, ed. by A. J. Meyers. M. Tshombe. il U S News 57:50-1 Ag 3 '64
Tshombe's Spanish hideaway. il Ebony 19: 100-2+ Ag '64
Ugly face in Africa. J. Davenport. Fortune 67:84+ F '63; Discussion. 67:20 Ap '63
U.S. cites illegal interference in support of Congo rebellion; statement, December 14, 1964. A. E. Stevenson. Dept State Bul 52: 15-24 Ja 4 '65
Vanishing friends: Tshombe's erstwhile African allies. il Time 81:38 F 15 '63
What's happening in the Congo? R. Howe. New Repub 149:10 N 31 '63; Reply with rejoinder. R. J. Bunche. 149:30-1 D 21 '63
When will the Congo be ready for independence? C. Sterling. il Reporter 28:25-8 Ap 11 '63
Why the Africans hate Tshombe. M. Clos. il N Y Times Mag p24-5+ Ja 10 '65
With magic juice & lucky grass; provinces on the brink of anarchy. il Time 83:47 Je 12 '64

CONGO, FRENCH. See Congo (capital Brazzaville)

CONGO massacre, 1964
Actors in Congo's tragedy; photographs. N Y Times Mag p32-3 D 6 '64
Carnage in the Congo. Christian Cent 81: 1547 D 16 '64
Congo massacre. il Life 57:35-9 D 4 '64
Congo massacre. il Time 84:28-32 D 4 '64
Congo: savagery has no excuse. Life 57:6 D 11 '64
Crisis in the Congo; its meaning. A. J. Meyers. il U S News 57:39-41 D 14 '64
Death in the Congo. Commonweal 81:371 D 11 '64
Face death for Christ's sake; Christian missionaries in Congo. Christian Cent 81: 1581 D 23 '64
Killing ground. il Newsweek 64:47-8 D 7 '64
Massacre in the Congo; story of a rescue attempt. il U S News 57:41-3 D 7 '64
La nuit infernale. il Time 84:45-6 D 11 '64
Ordeal in the Congo. il Sr Schol 85:17-18 D 9 '64
U.S. cites illegal interference in support of Congo rebellion; statement, December 14, 1964. A. E. Stevenson. Dept State Bul 52: 15-24 Ja 4 '65
United States cooperates with Belgium in rescue of hostages from the Congo; texts of documents, November 16—28, 1964. Dept State Bul 51:838-46 D 14 '64

CONGOLESE
Crisis in search of a country. il N Y Times Mag p28-9 N 24 '63

CONGREGATIONAL Christian churches. See United church of Christ

CONGREGATIONAL singing. See Church music

CONGREGATIONALISM
R. J. Campbell at City temple. W. S. Smith. Christian Cent 80:1132-4 S 18 '63
See also
Calvinism

CONGRESS (United States) See United States —Congress

CONGRESS, Contempt of. See Contempt of legislative bodies

CONGRESS of racial equality
Battle plan for integration. D. Wakefield. il Esquire 60:101-4+ O '63
Civil rights battle; northern style. il Ebony 18:96-8+ Mr '63
CORE: the shock troops of the Negro revolt. M. Mayer. il Sat Eve Post 237:79-83 N 21 '64
Hotter fires; friction between organizations; with report by K. Fleming. il Newsweek 62:19-21 Jl 1 '63
James Farmer of CORE. Negro Hist Bul 27: 160-1 Ap '64
New shape of nonviolence. il U S News 56:50 Ap 27 '64
Pickets marched in rain, but fair opened anyway. il Bsns W p32 Ap 25 '64
To the sound of a different drum. il Newsweek 63:25-6 Ap 27 '64
What the Negroes lost in New York. il U S News 56:31-3 My 4 '64
Who's to decide if a banker is biased? Bank of America picketed by CORE. Bsns W p29-30 Je 13 '64
Why didn't they hit back? J. Robbins and J. Robbins. Redbook 121:52-3+ Jl '63

CONGRESS of scientists on survival, incorporated
Cyberculture and girls; Conference on the cybercultural revolution. New Yorker 40:21-2 Jl 4 '64
Science talks about peace. C. Dreher. Nation 197:31-3 Jl 13 '63
SOS, fourth year. Nation 199:3 Jl 13 '64

CONGRESS of the Soviet Communist party. See Communist party (Russia)

CONGRESS on the information system sciences
Pentagon's new stress on tactical C&C systems highlights ISS meeting. M. Getler. Miss & Roc 15:18+ D 7 '64

CONGRESS party, Indian. See Indian national congress

CONGRESSES, Eucharistic. See Eucharistic congresses

CONGRESSIONAL candidates. See Candidates, Political

CONGRESSIONAL committees. See United States—Congress—Committees

CONGRESSIONAL country club course. See Golf courses

CONGRESSIONAL elections. See Elections—United States

CONGRESSIONAL flying club of Washington D.C. See Aviation clubs

CONGRESSIONAL investigations. See Government investigations

CONGRESSIONAL library. See United States —Library of Congress

CONGRESSIONAL medal of honor. See Medal of honor (United States)

CONGRESSIONAL page boys. See United States—Congress—Pages

CONGRESSIONAL procedure. See United States —Congress—Rules and practice

CONGRESSIONAL record
Congressional record, fatter every year. il Sr Schol 82:37 F 20 '63

CONGRESSMEN
Adequate number of Democrats. il Time 85: 16-20 Ja 15 '65
Adult congressman. M. Kempton. New Repub 148:11-13 Ap 6 '63
Are there too many lawyers in Congress? A. Hacker. il N Y Times Mag p 14+ Ja 5 '64
Changes on Capitol hill. il U S News 54:20 F 4 '63
Congress and LBJ. New Repub 151:3-5 D 26 '64
Congress on the atomic age. interviews. ed. by R. Steel. D. M. Fraser; J. M. McDade. il Sr Schol 82:16-18 F 20 '63
Contempt of Congress; bill to compel disclosure of income. Nation 198:22 Ja 6 '64
Democrat margin of victory; with list of all Republican congressmen: their defections to and votes in agreement with Democrats. Nat R 16:960-4 N 3 '64
Duties and responsibilities of a congressman to the United States. A. C. Powell, jr. Esquire 60:109-12+ S '63
88th Congress: twenty-four key votes; rating the performance of legislators. il New Repub 151:13-20 O 17 '64
From Washington straight; new faces of '65: House Republicans. Cato. Nat R 17:55 Ja 26 '65
How can you rate your congressman? D. G. M. Coxe. Nat R 14:525-8 Jl 2 '63
How congressmen rate the new President. U S News 55:78-83 D 9 '63
Insider rule for congressmen. Bsns W p 144 N 23 '63
Is the U.S. Congress a rich man's club? il U S News 57:39-41 Jl 13 '64
Mystery tour; visit by four U.S. congressmen to Timbuktu. il Newsweek 64:32 D 21 '64
New stew; headwaiter on congressional junket. il Newsweek 62:32 N 25 '63
Nine men who control Congress. C. M. Roberts. il Atlan 213:63-8 Ap '64
Observations of a freshman in Congress. C. D. Long. il N Y Times Mag p34+ D 1 '63
Pentagon payola; reserve commissions. Nation 197:41 Jl 27 '63
Personal business; your representative in Washington. Bsns W p 141 D 14 '63
Playing politics with war. Christian Cent 80: 227 F 20 '63
Question of the week: how did LBJ vote? U S News 55:47 D 9 '63
Ten who lead Congress. il pors N Y Times Mag p 18-19 My 5 '63
Twenty-three of thirty-six congressional chairmen are still southerners. U S News 58:14 Ja 4 '65
Washington's second banana politicians; Administrative assistants to congressmen and senators. L. L. King. il Harper 230:41-7 Ja '65
Whither the Republicans? R. Evans, jr. Reporter 28:32-4 F 28 '63
Who's who in Congress. Atlan 211:8+ Mr '63
Winning the Weevils. il Time 82:36 O 4 '63
See also
Conflict of interests (public office)
Negro congressmen
Senators
United States—Congress

CONGRESSMEN—*Continued*

Salaries, allowances, etc.

Consolation prize for Congress: new offices; Rayburn building. il U S News 56:46-7 Mr 23 '64
Pay raise for Parliament; but nothing like Congress gets. U S News 57:12 N 30 '64
Rising living standard for congressmen, too. il U S News 58:44-6 Ja 25 '65
What congressmen spent on travel abroad. U S News 54:8 Mr 25 '63

Term

Reforming the House, a four-year term? W. V. Shannon. il N Y Times Mag p22-3+ Ja 10 '65

CONGRESSMEN, Letters to. See Lobbying

CONGRESSMENS families
Congress, it's my daddy. L. Miller. il Redbook 121:50-1+ Ag '63

CONGRESSMENS wives
Double life of a senator's wife; excerpts from One foot in Washington. E. Proxmire. il Redbook 122:66-74 Ja '64
Imagine me here in D.C! ed. by J. Howard. M. Bayh. il Life 55:37-8+ Jl 26 '63

CONGRESSWOMEN
First Congresswoman from overseas; Hawaii's Patsy Mink. il Life 58:49-50+ Ja 22 '65

CONHAIM, R. L.
CB radio-wave propagation. Electr World 70: 46-8+ D '63
How tough are the proposed CB regulations? Electr World 69:26-8+ My '63
Jet transport communications. Electr World 70:27-30+ N '63
Microphones for communications. Electr World 71:51-4 Ap '64
Proposal to the FCC. Electr World 69:48-9 Mr '63
R. F. power output measurements. bibliog Electr World 70:53-6+ O '63
Understanding frequency-control crystals. Electr World 71:36-8+ My '64

CONIFERS
Bunya-bunya and the Montezuma cypress, two unusual conifers. il Sunset 133:256 O '64
Root pressure in conifers. J. W. O'Leary and P. J. Kramer. bibliog Science 145:284-5 Jl 17 '64
See also
Araucaria
Pine

CONIGLIARO, Tony
Not much to do but eat, sleep and play baseball. F. Deford. por Sports Illus 21:49-50 Ag 3 '64

CONJUNCTIVITIS
Conjunctiva contains factor inhibiting growth of Candida albicans. P. J. Kozinn and others. bibliog il Science 146:1479-80 D 11 '64
Trachoma and inclusion conjunctivitis agents: adaptation to hela cell cultures. Y. Mitsui and others. bibliog il Science 145:715-16 Ag 14 '64

CONKLIN, Paul
Big chickens of James and Samuel. Reporter 28:30-1 Je 20 '63

CONKLIN, Peter M. See Ader, R. jt. auth.

CONKWRIGHT, P. Jefferson
P. J. Conkwright and University press book design; excerpt. J. Dreyfus. il Pub W 183:78+ Mr 4 '63
Tribute to a typographic artist. il por Pub W 183:76-7 Mr 4 '63

CONLEY, Clare
All-purpose hunting tool. Field & S 69:127 O '64
Automatic horn honker. Field & S 69:107 S '64
Clapper, clapper, clapper. Field & S 68:35-7+ S '63
Delaware shad. Field & S 68:61-3 Mr '64
First day blues. Field & S 68:40-1+ Jl '63
Half ounce of prevention. Field & S 68:83 Jl '63
Handy meat smoker. Field & S 68:77 D '63
Harder the better. Field & S 68:33-5+ O '63
Have you tried alcohol? Field & S 68:113-14 Je '63
How to con a crappie. Field & S 69:55-7+ Je '64
Hypo-arrow archery. Field & S 68:43-5+ Je '63
Instant camp mattress. Field & S 68:145 Ap '64
Kit-built depth finder. Field & S 68:125-6 My '63
Lightweight backpack. Field & S 68:103-4 S '63
Low-cost heat. Field & S 68:103 F '64
Portable purifier. Field & S 69:133-4 My '64
Portable refrigerator. Field & S 67:107-8 Mr '63
Quick riveter. Field & S 69:91 Ag '64
Shooters solve the pigeon problem! Field & S 68:10-11+ D '63
Solid-fuel stove. Field & S 68:91 N '63
Take-apart trout. Field & S 69:97 N '64
Temperatures in depth. Field & S 68:79 Ag '63
Three meals in your pocket. Field & S 68:111 O '63
Turkey talk. por Field & S 68:36-7+ N '63
Valleys of the West. Field & S 69:82-5 O '64

CONLIN, E. T. See Cannon, P. jt. auth.

CONLY, John M.
Going for baroque. Reporter 31:44-5 N 5 '64
Leinsdorf in Boston. Hi Fi 13:44-7+ D '63
Multiplex muse. Reporter 31:42+ D 17 '64; 32:8 Ja 14 '65
Tape recorders: the new models. Atlan 214: 128-9 Jl '64
Vox humana fortissimo. Reporter 31:54-5 S 24 '64
You get a lot to like. Reporter 30:44+ Je 18 '64

CONLY, Robert L.
Northern Ireland: from Derry to Down. Nat Geog Mag 126:232-67 Ag '64

CONN, Jerome W.
Blood-pressure hormone. Time 81:48 Mr 15 '63

CONNABLE, Roma
Politics, a new, wide-open world for women. Mlle 58:164-7+ Mr '64

CONNALLY, G. Gorden
Garnet ratios and provenance in the glacial drift of western New York. bibliog Science 144:1452-3 Je 19 '64

CONNALLY, Idanell Brill
Since that day in Dallas; ed. by M. Drury. McCalls 91:78-9+ Ag '64

CONNALLY, John B.
Civil rights; integration issue; address, July 19, 1963. Vital Speeches 29:679-82 S 1 '63

about

Close to the land. il pors Time 83:16-20 Ja 17 '64
Others; year after the assassination of President Kennedy. Time 84:34 N 27 '64
Scars & a memory. il por Time 82:27A D 6 '63

CONNALLY, Ron
Poets' encounter. Américas 16:28+ Ap '64
(tr) See Marechal, L. Robot
(tr) See Squirru, R. Death has taken away a friend

CONNALLY, Tom
Tawl Tawm. por Time 82:23 N 8 '63
Too grave a risk: the Connally amendment. by D. Kitchel. Review
Nat R 14:463 Je 4 '63. H. Alexander and H. Alexander

CONNALLY amendment. See International court of justice, The Hague

CONNECTICUT
See also
Architecture, Domestic—Connecticut
Birds—Connecticut
Booksellers and bookselling—Connecticut
Gardens—Connecticut
Geology—Connecticut
Law—Connecticut
Libraries—Connecticut

Historic houses, etc.

Wethersfield: historic houses. B. Armstrong. il Antiques 86:457-61 O '64

Legislature

Death and taxes. Nat Parks Mag 38:16 S '64
Spoils and spoilers; investigation of John P. Kelly agency, Hartford, Conn. Newsweek 61:37 My 13 '63

Politics and government

Conservatives strike up the band. A. Brownell. Nat R 16:231-2+ Mr 24 '64

Religious institutions and affairs

News of the Christian world (cont) Christian Cent 80:962 Jl 31 '63

CONNECTICUT college, New London, Conn.
Rosemary Park: new president of Barnard. T. Ferrer. il Sat R 46:66-8 Ap 20 '63

CONNECTICUT opera association
Hartford masquerade. F. Stevenson. il Opera N 28:33 Ja 4 '64
Hartford stars. W. A. Storrer. Opera N 28: 33 Ap 18 '64

CONNECTICUT RIVER
Cruising the Connecticut. B. Hawkins. il Motor B 113:30-1+ Ap '64
CONNECTICUT VALLEY
Connecticut Valley, where American industry began; with drawings by P. Hogarth. Fortune 68:116-23 D '63
Life along the Connecticut. W. Manchester. il Holiday 33:68-73+ Je '63
CONNECTIVE tissues. See Tissues
CONNECTORS, Electric. See Electric connectors
CONNELL, Alexander
Malicious mischief, British style; Islington public libraries; summary. Wilson Lib Bul 37:750 My '63
CONNELL, Edward A.
Value of consultants; memorandum to Thorne Sherwood. Am City 78:99-100 D '63
CONNELL, Evan S. Jr
Corset; story. Esquire 62:122-3 N '64
Leon & Bébert; story. Sat Eve Post 237:54-5 O 3 '64
Mountains of Guatemala; story. Esquire 62:176-8 D '64
Suicide; story. Sat Eve Post 237:44-9 My 2 '64
CONNELL, Lester
Report (favorable) on a teamsters local. A. H. Raskin. il por N Y Times Mag p53-4+ N 1 '64
CONNELL, Marie Joan
Tempt the less learned. por Library J 88:1115-17 Mr 15 '63
CONNELLY, Dolly
Eskimos get the make-up message. Life 56:17+ Ja 31 '64
Go lightly into the wilderness. Sports Illus 18:20-1 Je 24 '63
Help! the queen is coming. Life 54:12 F 15 '63; Same abr. with title Queen is coming! Read Digest 83:192C-192D+ Ag '63
Muley's enchanted summer. Sports Illus 19:52-8 Jl 8 '63
New lightweight, portable outdoor foods. House B 106:114+ Ag '64
CONNELLY, Marc
Booked for travel. Sat R 47:33-5 S 19 '64
Caloric Copenhagen. Sat R 46:47-8+ Ap 13 '63
CONNELLY, Will
Noise figures of V.H.F. amateur converters. Electr World 72:34-5+ S '64
CONNEMARA, Ireland
Dreamscape of Connemara. W. Sansom. il Holiday 33:41-2+ Ap '63
CONNER, Angela
Aspects of Zanzibar. Reporter 28:44-5 Mr 28 '63
CONNERS, Donald N. See Pytkowicz, R. M. jt. auth.
CONNERY, Donald S.
Lonely quest in Lapland. Sports Illus 20:46-7+ Ja 27 '64
CONNERY, Sean
Bottled in bond: Sean Connery. P. Hamill. il pors Sat Eve Post 237:32-3 Je 6 '64
Canny Scot. il por Time 83:78 Ja 10 '64
Devil of a fellow, this Bond; new movie, Dr No. il pors Life 54:100B+ My 24 '63
Mr Kisskiss Bangbang. L. Mosley. il pors N Y Times Mag p38+ N 22 '64
Sean Connery; the reluctant James Bond. S. Gordon. il pors Look 28:83-6 S 8 '64
T-shirted beer-lover as the suave spy. S. Alexander. il pors Life 56:55-6 Ap 3 '64
CONNIFF, Frank R.
Newsman v. newsman. por Time 83:79 Mr 20 '64
CONNIFF, James C. G.
Facts behind the momentous controversy about the church and the pill. McCalls 92:52+ O '64
CONNOLLY, Cyril
English conquest in the Old Dominion. Art N 62:30-3+ Sum '63
Happy times when Edward was king. Ladies Home J 81:78+ Ja '64
On Cyril Connolly. J. Finn. Commonweal 81:125-7 O 23 '64
CONNOLLY, Francis X.
This New generation. America 109:386 O 5 '63
CONNOLLY, Thomas E.
Indian and the poverty war. America 111:260-1 S 12 '64
CONNOR, Desmond M. and Cameron, Zita
Antigonish and the world. America 108:398-9 Mr 23 '63
CONNOR, Eugene
Bull at bay. il por Newsweek 61:29-30 Ap 15 '63
From Birmingham. G. Bailey. Reporter 28:12+ My 23 '63
CONNOR, John T.
Doing business with a revolution; address, April 24, 1963. Vital Speeches 29:537-40 Je 15 '63
about
Commerce post goes to Connor. por Bsns W p30 D 19 '64
Good choice for a top spot; Secretary of commerce. Bsns W p96 D 26 '64
Johnson cabinet: drug executive, former counsel to OSRD and ONR, will be Secretary of commerce. E. Langer. Science 147:32 Ja 1 '65
Liberal businessman for the Cabinet. il por U S News 57:12 D 28 '64
Prescription for commerce. il por Time 84:12 D 25 '64
Pulling the teeth of conflict of interest. por Bsns W p29 Ja 16 '65
CONNOR, Otelia
Oteliaquette at Chapel Hill. il por Time 82:45-6 Jl 19 '63
CONNOR, Vicki
Summer of the woodpeckers. por Audubon Mag 65:247-8 Jl '63
CONOVER, Grandin
Films. Nation 199:79-80 Ag 24 '64
God's spies. Nation 199:283-5 O 26 '64
Sly natural. Nation 197:303-4 N 9 '63
CONRAD, Charles, Jr
I'll have fifteen guys on my neck. Life 55:84+ S 27 '63
CONRAD, Gordon R.
Unexplored assets for diversification. Harvard Bsns R 41:67-73 S '63
CONRAD, Harold
He beats the drums for champs and bums. R. H. Boyle. il por Sports Illus 19:20-2+ Jl 8 '63
CONRAD, Max
Mayday from Charlie Foxtrot. por Flying 74:52-3+ Je '64
Old man and the glacier. J. Liston. il por Pop Sci 185:106-9+ O '64
CONRAD, Paul
Going West. por Time 83:40+ Ja 31 '64
CONRAD, Pete
Ugly, unearthly bug. por Life 57:85-6+ O 2 '64
CONRAD, Richard
Shoot candid kids. D. L. Miller. il Mod Phot 27:68-73 Ag '63
CONRAD, Sherman
Meal; Nights of passage; Like Lazarus; Mother of God: Montserrat; One hand clapping: poems. Poetry 104:36-40 Ap '64
CONRAT, Heinz Fraenkel-. See Fraenkel-Conrat, H.
CONROY, Hilary
(comp) Articles and other books received; east Asia. See issues of American historical review
Philadelphia meeting, 1963. Am Hist R 69:910-14 Ap '64
CONROY, William B.
Case of the Adirondacks. Recreation 58:15-16 Ja '65
CONSCIENCE
Christian morality and race issues. Life 56:4 Mr 27 '64
Conscience and character; with study-discussion program, by R. Strang. G. Langdon and I. W. Stout. bibliog il PTA Mag 58:4-6, 35 F '64
Making of a conscience. L. Strong. il N Y Times Mag p97-8 S 20 '64
Word. V. P. McCorry. America 111:392-3 O 3 '64
See also
Guilt
Liberty of conscience
CONSCIENCE fund. See United States—Revenue
CONSCIENTIOUS objectors
Conscience and religion; case of the United States v. D. A. Seeger. America 111:771 D 12 '64
Conscience and the law; case of Daniel A. Seeger. America 110:181 F 8 '64
Conscientious nonbeliever; case of Daniel Seeger. il Time 83:59 Ja 31 '64
C.O. sentenced to prison; I. Stolberg. Christian Cent 80:1229 O 9 '63
France: brooms instead of guns. Newsweek 62:45 Jl 15 '63
Freedom of conscience. America 110:759 My 30 '64
Religious agnostic. Newsweek 63:27-8 F 3 '64
Supreme being clause held invalid: Daniel Seeger case. Christian Cent 81:197-8 F 12 '64
They also served. Christian Cent 81:790 Je 17 '64
CONSCIOUSNESS
Brain vs. the machine. J. W. Krutch. Sat R 47:17-19+ Ja 18 '64
Future of God. J. Lear. il Sat R 47:173-5+ Ag 29 '64

CONSCIOUSNESS—*Continued*
Variations in alpha voltage of the electroencephalogram and time perception. J. Anliker. bibliog il Science 140:1307-9 Je 21 '63
See also
Self
CONSCRIPTION. See Military service, Compulsory
CONSEAR, Helen S.
Low-IQ page volunteers. Library J 89:1830-1+ Ap 15 '64
CONSEIL européen pour la recherche nucléaire. See European organization for nuclear research
CONSERVATION associations
See also
American forestry association
Sierra club
CONSERVATION awards. See American forestry association; Thomas L. Stokes award; United States—Interior, Department of
CONSERVATION corps, Civilian. See United States—Civilian conservation corps
CONSERVATION education. See Conservation of resources—Study and teaching
CONSERVATION education association
Broome addresses educators; August 21, 1963. H. Broome. il Liv Wildn 84:45-7 Sum '63
CONSERVATION education center. See National parks association
CONSERVATION hall of fame. See North American conservation hall of fame and museum
CONSERVATION of energy. See Force and energy
CONSERVATION of resources
Ah, wilderness. il Newsweek 62:54-5 S 30 '63
America down the drain; with statement by Secretary Udall. R. H. Boyle. il Sports Illus 21:78-80+ N 16 '64
America the beautiful. Nation 20:41 Ja 18 '65
America the beautiful: going once. . . going twice? il Sr Schol 82:6-9 Ap 24 '63
America's vanishing wilderness. W. O. Douglas. il Ladies Home J 81:37-41+ Jl '64; Same abr. with title To preserve America's glories. Read Digest 86:146-54 Ja '65
Awakening in Massachusetts. J. M. O'Hare. il Recreation 56:262-3 Je '63
Beginning of action: Carl Schurz and John Wesley Powell; excerpt from The quiet crisis. S. L. Udall. il Am For 69:20-3+ O '63
Benton MacKaye: the verdant prophet. E. J. Long. il Am For 70:16-19 Jl '64
Biology departments should buy natural preserves; letter. L. F. Yntema. Science 144:12 Ap 3 '64; Reply. F. H. Bormann. 144:953 My 22 '64
Breakthrough. R. Starnes. Field & S 69:16+ N '64
Californian looks at California; address, February 27, 1963. J. K. Carr. il Am For 69:16-19 Ap '63; Reply. C. R. Ross. 69:63 Je '63
Conscience and conservation. A. M. Sullivan. Duns R 83:108 Ja '64
Conservation; ed. by H. Titus. See issues of Field & stream
Conservation and progress: two inseparables. A. B. Adams. il Nat Parks Mag 37:4-8 N '63
Conservation and the Fort Ord complex. G. Schneider. il Am For 70:22-3+ Ag '64
Conservation is everybody's battle. J. N. Miller. il Read Digest 85:161-6+ Ag '64
Conservation: local and national interests conflict on proposals awaiting action in Congress. E. Langer. Science 143:941-3 F 28 '64; Discussion. 144:135, il 1408-9 Ap 10, Je 19 '64
Conservation year. A. W. Smith. Nat Parks Mag 38:2 D '64
Crime of waste. Duns R 82:128 N '63
Early conservation and the golden era of trout fishing; excerpts from This wonderful world of trout. C. K. Fox. il Am For 70:38-41+ Ja '64
88th's challenge to conservation. Am For 70:9 N '64
False conservationists; reprint. H. Borland. Audubon Mag 66:367 N '64
In business! J. B. Craig. il Am For 70:4-5+ S '64
Is there a cure for the common scold? R. Starnes. Field & S 68:12+ N '63
Keeping the wilderness wild; how it will be done. il U S News 57:65-7 Ag 24 '64
Kennedy backs efforts to save natural beauty. Sci N L 84:216 O 5 '63
Kennedy out West. New Repub 149:5-6 S 28 '63
Land and water conservation fund. il Recreation 57:449-50 N '64
LBJ'S plan to beautify America. il U S News 58:28-30+ Ja 11 '65
Man threatens nature with smog and pollution. Sci N L 84:360 D 7 '63
Meeting the challenges of the third wave, condensation of address, November 7, 1964. C. W. Buchheister. Audubon Mag 67:18-19 Ja '65
Minnesota sets a brisk pace. J. Morris. Am For 69:35+ N '63
Mischief in the melon patch. G. Laycock. il Field & S 69:10-12+ Je '64
Must God's junkyard grow? Life 57:4 Jl 31 '64
National capital report. C. H. Callison. See issues of Audubon magazine
Need for clean water. R. A. Merritt. Am For 70:2 Mr '64
New direction from Asilomar. M. Bush. Am For 69:27+ Jl '63
New horizons; address, September 23, 1964. L. S. Rockefeller. Am For 70:10-13 N '64
News and commentary (cont of) News briefs from the conservation world. See issues of National parks magazine
News briefs from the conservation world. See issues of National parks magazine
One key to employment. Commonweal 80:132-3 Ap 24 '64
Overview: special feature on conservation; excerpts from Conservation in the people's hands. il NEA J 53:33-6+ D '64
Pioneers for peace; address, September 26, 1963. J. F. Kennedy. Dept State Bul 49:631-6 O 21 '63
Planning, a prologue to action; address. F. V. Durand. il Am For 70:26-9+ N '64
Platform for conservation and outdoor recreation; adaptation of address. L. S. Rockefeller. il Recreation 57:446-8 N '64
Policy report of president to trustees of National parks association; November 19, 1963. Nat Parks Mag 38:I-IV Ja '64
President Johnson lauds conservation Congress; excerpts from address. L. B. Johnson. Am For 70:13 N '64
President Kennedy's tour. Liv Wildn 84:45 Sum '63
Project 70: Pennsylvania looks ahead. R. R. Widner. il Am For 70:26-9+ Ja '64
Quiet crisis, by S. L. Udall. Review
Am For il 70:20-1+ Ja '64. M. Bush
New Repub 149:19-20 N 30 '63. M. Straight
Sat R 46:39+ N 23 '63. F. Osborn
Quiet crisis; excerpts. S. L. Udall. il Sat R 46:19-22+ N 23 '63
Quiet crisis or lost cause? W. Stegner. Sat R 47:28+ S 19 '64
Quotable Mr President; excerpts from addresses; ed. by J. Prokop. L. B. Johnson. Am For 70:8+ Ja '64
Reviews; man and nature joined in quiet crisis. W. Vogt. Natur Hist 73:4+ Mr '64
Senator Anderson honored; National conservation award. il Liv Wildn 83:25-8 Spring '63
Should we change the name of conservation? E. S. Hurd. Am For 70:22-3+ Mr '64; Discussion. 70:4 My; 2-3 Je '64
Stewart Udall and the quiet crisis. R. Starnes. Field & S 68:18+ Je '63
This we hold dear. C. P. Anderson. il Am For 69:24-5 Jl '63
Thoughts on the quiet crisis. S. L. Udall. il PTA Mag 58:20-2 My '64
Twelve rivers under protection study. C. H. Callison. Audubon Mag 66:178 My '64
Ugly American. C. W. Griffin, jr. Reporter 30:53-4+ Ja 30 '64
Washington newsletter (cont) P. M. Tilden. Natur Hist 72:63-7 D '63; 73:66-9 Je; 61-3+ D '64
We must stop destroying our natural riches. C. L. Wirth. Parents Mag 39:32 Jl '64
We point with pride; 88th Congress conservation legislation. C. W. Buchheister. Audubon Mag 66:282 S '64
What AFA members think! conservation platform for American forestry. K. B. Pomeroy. Am For 70:6+ My '64
Whose woods these are: the story of the national forests, by M. Frome. Review
Liv Wildn 82:20 Wint '62. C. Davis
Why not PROservation? N. B. Livermore, jr. Am For 70:3+ Je '64
Why we need the Land and water conservation fund bill. C. P. Anderson. Am For 70:24-7+ Mr '64
Wilderness in Montana, a report. J. J. Craighead. il Liv Wildn 85:25-9 Wint '64
See also
Fish protection
Forest conservation
Natural resources
Preservation of landmarks, scenery, etc
Resources for the future, incorporated

CONSERVATION of resources—*See also*—*Cont.*
Soil conservation
United States—Interior, Department of
Water conservation
Watersheds
Wilderness areas
Wildlife conservation

Study and teaching

Conservation activities in the elementary school. F. Olson. NEA J 53:37-8 D '64
Conservation activities in the secondary school. R. G. Culter, jr. NEA J 53:38-40 D '64
Conservation and the Camp fire girls. il Nat Parks Mag 38:8-10 N '64
Conservation education center fall session opens. Nat Parks Mag 37:19 N '63
Conservation in a Girl scout camp; Rockwood National Girl scout camp, Potomac, Md. L. Knox. il Nat Parks Mag 37:14-16 N '63
Conservation workshop in Maryland. R. L. Norden. il Nat Parks Mag 37:9-13 N '63
President Kennedy salutes Grey Towers. il Am For 69:22-3+ N '63
What's going on here? R. E. Roth. Recreation 57:118-20 Mr '64

CONSERVATION of wildlife. See Wildlife conservation

CONSERVATION workshop in Maryland. See Conservation of resources—Study and teaching

CONSERVATISM
American conservative union. Nat R 17:13-14 Ja 12 '65
Answering the hatemongers; radical rightist organizations. Christian Cent 81:1388-9 N 11 '64
Answers for conservatives; questions and answers. W. F. Buckley, jr. Nat R 16:145-6+ F 25 '64; Discussion. 16:293 Ap 7 '64
Campus conservative journals. R. Kirk. Nat R 16:449 Je 2 '64
Campus report: mood of the students; symposium il N Y Times Mag p24-5+ N 17 '63
Conservatism and the Goldwater consensus. F. S. Meyer. Nat R 15:386+ N 5 '63
Conservative affirmation, by W. Kendall. Review
Nat R 14:322-4 Ap 23 '63. W. F. Buckley, jr
Conservative future at stake; Goldwaterism. Life 57:4 Jl 17 '64
Conservative papers, ed. by M. Laird. Review
Nat R 16:496-7 Je 16 '64. M. S. Evans.
Conservative strategy now. F. S. Meyer. Nat R 16:1145 D 29 '64
Conservatives in Europe too. W. F. Buckley, jr. Nat R 15:387 N 5 '63
Conspiracy USA; symposium. il Look 29:21-32 Ja 26 '65
Dallas image unveiled; near-riot after A. Stevenson's address. J. C. Evans. Christian Cent 80:1438-40 N 20 '63
Danger on the right, by A. Forster and B. Epstein. Review
Nat R 16:855-6+ O 6 '64. W. F. Buckley, jr
Dark doings; anti-Communist newsletter Tocsin fighting against right-wing. Nat R 14:396 My 21 '63
Foretaste; the kind of criminal assault against conservatives. Nat R 15:141 Ag 27 '63
Freedom or virtue? L. B. Bozell; discussion. Nat R 13:223-5, 283, 327+; 15:191-5, 319 S 25-O 9, 23 '62, S 10, O 8 '63
Giant stirs. Nation 199:177-8 O 5 '64
Goldwater defines conservatism; interview. B. Goldwater. il N Y Times Mag p25+ N 24 '63
H. L. Hunt: portrait of a super-patriot; Life line. R. G. Sherrill. Nation 198:182-95 F 24 '64
Here come the conservatives. R. J. Whalen. il Fortune 68:106-9+ D '63
Ideological heroin. Christian Cent 81:1355-6 N 4 '64
Inquiry into the new conservatism. A. Hacker. il N Y Times Mag p7+ F 16 '64
Intellectual two-party system. W. Sheed. Commonweal 80:506-8 Jl 24 '64
Is Goldwater moving left? Nat R 15:335+ O 22 '63
It's too early to bind wounds. L. Wainwright. Life 57:31 N 13 '64
Love, hatred and politics. Christian Cent 80:1423-4 N 20 '63
Mood of conservatism. R. Kirk. Commonweal 78:297-300 Je 7 '63
Must conservatives be Republicans? J. Burnham. Nat R 16:1052 D 1 '64
New conservative manifesto. T. G. Harris. il Look 28:19-23 D 29 '64
New political map of America. F. S. Meyer. Nat R 16:687 Ag 11 '64
Not that wind; founding of conservative Winds of freedom foundation at Stanford. Nat R 14:440 Je 4 '63
Ordeal in Okanogan. G. Bassett. Nation 197:454-6 D 28 '63
Order of battle, by J. K. Javits. Review
Sat R 47:41-2 My 23 '64. R. Drummond
Paranoid style in American politics; adaptation of address, November 1963. R. Hofstadter. Harper 229:77-82+ N '64; Discussion. 230:6+ Ja '65
Partisan review of democracy. M. L. Coit. Sat R 47:34+ Mr 28 '64
Political fundamentalism in profile; it shuns reality. L. J. Averill. Christian Cent 81:1009-12 Ag 12 '64; Discussion. 81:1147 S 16 '64
Politics in the twentieth century, by H. J. Morgenthau. Review
Commentary 35:506-16 Je '63. G. Lichtheim
Public enemy. M. S. Evans. il Nat R 17:70-1 Ja 26 '65
Radio right: hate clubs of the air. F. J. Cook. il Nation 198:523-7 My 25 '64
Republican party and the conservative movement; symposium. Nat R 16:1053-6+ D 1 '64
Toward a dynamic conservatism. Fortune 69:106 Ap '64
Triumph of conservatism, by G. Kolko. Review
Nation 198:398-400 Ap 20 '64. J. Weinstein
Tussle in Texas. S. Friedman. Nation 198:114-17 F 3 '64
What a southern conservative thinks. J. J. Kilpatrick. Sat R 47:15-18 Ap 25 '64; Discussion. 47:27-8 My 16; 24 Je 6 '64
What consensus? F. S. Meyer. Nat R 16:912 O 20 '64
What hope for maintaining a conservative opposition? J. Dos Passos. Nat R 16:907-9 O 20 '64
What is a liberal? what is a conservative? J. Roddy. Look 28:19-21 Jl 28 '64
What is conservatism? ed. by F. S. Meyer. Review
Nat R 16:235-6 Mr 24 '64. F. Morley
What next for conservatism? F. S. Meyer. Nat R 16:1057 D 1 '64
See also
Liberalism
Right and left (political science)

CONSERVATIVE party (Great Britain)
Battling Tories. Time 82:34+ O 18 '63
Conservative comeback? J. M. Cameron. Commonweal 79:562-4 F 7 '64
Filling a Tory gap; Butler as prime minister. U S News 55:24 O 21 '63
In Britain, a comeback for the conservatives. U S News 56:8 Mr 16 '64
Is Super Mac to be undone by sex? il Newsweek 61:45-6 Je 24 '63
Letter from London. M. Panter-Downes. New Yorker 39:119-20 F 15 '64
Letter from London; backwash of the Profumo affair. M. Panter-Downes. New Yorker 39:65-7 Ag 3 '63
Letter from London; incoming prime minister. M. Panter-Downes. New Yorker 39:221-2+ N 9 '63
Letter from London; opening session of the House of commons. M. Panter-Downes. New Yorker 39:202+ N 30 '63
Letter from London; Profumo case. M. Panter-Downes. New Yorker 39:66-9 Je 29 '63
Letter from London; seat left vacant by Profumo. M. Panter-Downes. New Yorker 39:93-4 S 7 '63
Lord Home got the job; But he won't keep it long. A. Lejeune; A. Waugh. Nat R 15:438-9 N 19 '63
Lost leader; concerning House of commons debate on Profumo case. il Time 81:22-5 Je 28 '63
Low life above stairs. C. Brogan. Nat R 16:153-5 F 25 '64
Loyal opposition. il Time 84:25 N 6 '64
Price of Profumo: Tories smeared. P. Worsthorne. il Life 54:22-3 Je 21 '63
Struggle for power; Tory succession. Newsweek 62:39-40 Jl 22 '63
Struggle for Tory leadership. il Newsweek 62:59-60 O 21 '63
SuperMac on the ropes. New Repub 148:11-12 Je 22 '63
SuperMac rides out the storm. A. Lejeune. Nat R 15:189-90 S 10 '63
That cad, Profumo. A. Burnet. New Repub 149:6 Jl 6 '63
Tide turning for Britain's Tories? il U S News 55:68 O 28 '63
Time of the trollop. il Time 81:24+ Je 21 '63
Tory succession: a London letter. G. Lichtheim. Commentary 36:468-72 D '63

CONSERVATIVE party (Great Britain)—*Cont.*
Tory tragedy. R. Moley. Newsweek 62:84 Jl 8 '63
12,000,000 who vote Tory. S. Gruson. il p 17+ O 4 '64
Wilson seems shoo-in; probable results of Profumo scandal. il Bsns W p28-9 Je 22 '63
Wilson's magic. New Repub 150:10 My 16 '64
CONSERVATORIES. See Greenhouses
CONSERVES. See Jelly, jam, etc.
CONSISTENCY
Cognitive dissonance: its use in science. E. G. Boring. bibliog Science 145:680-5 Ag 14 '64; Discussion. 146:471-2 O 23 '64
CONSOL. See Radio in navigation
CONSOLAN. See Radio in navigation
CONSOLIDATED aeronautics, incorporated
Pilot report; go jump in the lake. A. H. Sanfelici. il Flying 74:40-1+ Je '64
CONSOLIDATED Edison company of New York
A-bomb on New York's doorstep; Ravenswood power plant. B. H. Frisch. il Sci Digest 54:29-35 O '63
Atomic power plants and cities; fission or fusion? pro and con discussion. il Sr Schol 83:16-17 O 18 '63
Atomic question for the city; proposed nuclear power plant in Queens. R. P. Hunt. il N Y Times Mag p46+ O 6 '63
Con Ed switches plan; hydro power from Labrador. Bsns W p43 Ja 11 '64
Con Ed's atom. Newsweek 63:71 Ja 20 '64
Dig they must . . . nuclear plant in New York city. il Bsns W p82-4+ S 14 '63
Dig they must? proposed hydro power plant at Storm King Mountain. il Newsweek 64:67-8 D 21 '64
Great battle for Storm King. J. Ridgeway. New Repub 151:8-9 N 28 '64
Storm King question; hydropower project in Hudson Highlands. Nat Parks Mag 39:21 Ja '65
CONSOLIDATED gas company of New York. See Consolidated Edison company of New York
CONSOLIDATED gold fields of South Africa, limited. See Gold mines and mining—South Africa
CONSOLIDATION, Railroad. See Railroads—Consolidations and mergers
CONSOLIDATION coal company
Coal, cars & Love. Time 82:78+ Jl 5 '63
Coal hits a new vein. il Bsns W p90-3 F 1 '64
How the railroads are recapturing business; closing of coal pipeline. U S News 54:11 My 20 '63
CONSOLIDATIONS, Business. See Business consolidations and mergers
CONSOLINO, Joseph T.
Gross increase of fourteen per cent a year realized by small York shop. Pub W 186:50-2 N 23 '64
CONSPIRACY
Quiet, conspiracy at work. W. F. Buckley, jr. Nat R 14:188 Mr 12 '63
CONSTABLE, Rosalind
He is saying: look at it. Life 57:68 Jl 10 '64
CONSTABLE, Stuart
Parks and recreation showcase at the World's fair. por Recreation 57:267-9 Je '64
CONSTANCE Lindsay Skinner award
Constance Lindsay Skinner award won by Rachel Carson. Pub W 183:130 F 18 '63
Polly Goodwin receives the Constance Lindsay Skinner award. M. B. King. il Pub W 186:108-10 Jl 13 '64
Rachel Carson receives WNBA Skinner award in absentia. il Pub W 183:35 F 25 '63
CONSTANTA, Rumania
With Ovid in Constanza. H. Sutton. il Sat R 46:31-3 Ag 3 '63
CONSTANTINE II, king of the Hellenes
Greece mourns, a new king inherits a crisis. R. Chelminski. il por Life 56:26-9 Mr 27 '64
Long live the King! il por Time 83:29 Mr 13 '64
Lovely gift to the Greeks. H. Moffett. il pors Life 57:48-50 O 9 '64
Royal wedding. il por Newsweek 64:52+ S 28 '64
Sports hero to king. il por Sr Schol 84:24 Ap 10 '64
Storm over a royal love affair. C. Plimmer and D. Plimmer. il por Redbook 121:60-1+ O '63
Vogue's notebook; royal wedding in Athens. il Vogue 144:98-101 N 1 '64
Wedding for all; marriage of King Constantine to Princess Anne-Marie of Denmark. il Time 84:26 S 25 '64
CONSTANTINE I, the Great, emperor of Rome
They made our world. L. Rosten. il Look 28:43 Ap 7 '64
CONSTANTS, Physical. See Physical constants
CONSTANTSA. See Constanta, Rumania
CONSTANZA. See Constanta, Rumania
CONSTELLATIONS
See also
Orion (constellation)
CONSTITUTION

United States

See United States—Constitution
CONSTITUTION (frigate)
By heaven, that ship is ours! Constitution vs. Guerrière. L. McKee. il Am Heritage 16:4-11+ D '64
Road show for a relic? Old Ironsides for World's fair. Time 81:25 Je 14 '63
CONSTITUTIONAL amendments. See United States—Constitution—Amendments
CONSTITUTIONAL conventions
See also
United States—Constitutional convention, 1787
CONSTITUTIONAL law
How to change laws you don't like. il Time 84:63 Jl 17 '64
See also
Due process of law
Judicial review
United States—Constitutional law
CONSTITUTIONS
See also
Trade unions—Constitutions
CONSTRUCTION. See Building
CONSTRUCTION, Concrete. See Concrete construction
CONSTRUCTION industry. See Building industry
CONSTRUCTION materials. See Building materials
CONSTRUCTION specifications institute
C.S.I. welcomes new specifications format at seventh annual meeting in Detroit. R. E. Fischer. Arch Rec 134:23 Jl '63
CONSTRUCTION workers. See Building workers
CONSULATES (buildings) See Embassies (buildings)
CONSULTANTS
Planners thriving on renewal. il Bsns W p 134+ Jl 25 '64
CONSULTANTS, Business. See Business consultants
CONSULTATION on church union. See Religious conferences
CONSULTATIVE committee for economic development in south and southeast Asia. See Colombo plan
CONSULTING engineers. See Engineers
CONSULTING engineers council
Panels discuss insurance, registration at annual consulting engineers meeting. Arch Rec 133:23 Je '63
CONSUMER bulletin

Anecdotes, facetiae, satire, etc.

Down the line with the annual. D. Barthelme. New Yorker 40:34-5 Mr 21 '64
CONSUMER buying surveys. See Consumer surveys
CONSUMER credit. See Credit; Loans, Personal
CONSUMER education
Buying guide issue. il Consumer Rep 29:1-432 D '64
Consumer health education. S. L. Smith. NEA J 53:62-3 Mr '64
Guide to your buying guide (cont) il Consumer Rep 28:5-30 D '63
Rising tide; third biennial conference of the International organization of consumers' unions. Consumer Rep 29:415 S '64
See also
Consumer protection
CONSUMER fraud bureaus
You can get your money back. A. Eisenberg and H. Eisenberg. Read Digest 84:131-2+ F '64
CONSUMER goods. See Commercial products
CONSUMER price index. See Price indexes
CONSUMER protection
Consumers sue for defective products. Consumer Bul 47:43+ N '64
Consumer's voice in Washington; President's special assistant for consumer affairs. Consumer Rep 30:8 Ja '65
Do shoppers need help from the government? pro and con discussion. E. Peterson; R. H. Levi. il Changing T 18:7-12 Ag '64

CONSUMER protection—*Continued*
Docket: notes on government actions taken to enforce consumer protection laws. See issues of Consumer reports
FDA's problem: more work, too few watchdogs. il Bsns W p26-7 My 11 '63
Frauds against the aged. Consumer Rep 28: 131 Mr '63
Lady watchdog; President's new committee on consumer interests. il Newsweek 63:64 Ja 20 '64
Mrs Consumer; Mrs E. Peterson. Newsweek 64:78+ N 2 '64
New battleground, consumer interest. T. M. Hopkinson. bibliog f Harvard Bsns R 42:97-104 S '64
New era in consumer affairs; President's special assistant for consumer affairs. il Consumer Rep 29:143-4 Mr '64
Scepter for king consumer; in California. il Bsns W p 106+ Mr 30 '63
So far, just a sympathetic ear; Special assistant for consumer affairs. Bsns W p32 F 15 '64
Supreme court and the consumer. il Consumer Rep 29:424-7 S '64
You can get your money back. A. Eisenberg and H. Eisenberg. Read Digest 84:131-2+ F '64

CONSUMER surveys
Annual questionnaire returns (cont) il Consumer Rep 29:8-10; 30:9-11 Ja '64, Ja '65
Carefree, and ready to spend. il Bsns W p26 N 14 '64
George Gallup looks at tomorrow's customer; interview. G. Gallup. il Nations Bsns 52: 68-70+ Mr '64
Handbook of consumer motivations, by E. Dichter. Review
Science 145:907+ Ag 28 '64. E. Langer
How customers make decisions. W. T. Tucker. il Nations Bsns 52:34-5+ Ag '64
In a buying mood; findings of University of Michigan survey research center. Newsweek 62:85 O 21 '63
Spending habits are hard to break; with editorial comment. il Bsns W p27-8, 168 Je 6 '64
Where foreign wares test the U.S. market; World sampler. il Bsns W p 118-19 O 24 '64
Why consumers spend and save; excerpts from Mass consumption society. G. Katona. il Nations Bsns 52:60-2+ O '64

CONSUMERS
Buying power, more gains coming; interview. E. Clague. il Nations Bsns 52:31-3+ Ap '64
Consumer stance. il Fortune 67:44+ Je '63
Consumer's pocketbook. il Fortune 67:40+ Mr '63
Customers play it cool. il Bsns W p23-4 My 23 '64
Five shoppers take a test. Consumer Rep 29: 272 Je '64
Free-spending consumer. il Time 82:63 Ag 23 '63
Important court decisions favor consumers. Consumer Bul 46:36-7 Mr '63
Life-enriched consumer. il Time 84:79 Ag 7 '64
New & exuberant. il Time 81:73-7 My 31 '63
Noble consumer. il Time 81:81 F 22 '63
People are still in mood to buy; report from Survey research center, University of Michigan. il Bsns W p27-8 O 12 '63
Scouting the trail for marketers. il Bsns W p90-1+ Ap 18 '64
Speaker for the house. C. Montgomery. See issues of Good housekeeping
Spending jogs along nicely. il Bsns W p26-7 Jl 11 '64
Still piling up debt, but slower. il Bsns W p75 Ag 22 '64
Taxes and consumer spending. Duns R 84:39 O '64
When offspring fly the coop: parents have time and money to spend. il Bsns W p52-4+ Jl 11 '64
When $2.50+$5 equals $800 million; tax cut will result in increased spending. il Newsweek 63:61 Mr 30 '64
Where experts are worlds apart; Stanford conference. il Bsns W p74+ N 7 '64
Where people are spending their money. il U S News 55:72-3 D 2 '63
Why don't they give the customer a break? il Changing T 17:7-12 S '63
See also
Consumer protection

CONSUMERS' advisory council. See United States—Council of economic advisors

CONSUMERS credit. See Credit

CONSUMERS preferences
Clues for action from shopper preferences; survey of women shoppers in New York city and in Cleveland. S. U. Rich and B. Portis. il Harvard Bsns R 41:132-49 Mr '63
How customers make decisions. W. T. Tucker. il Nations Bsns 52:34-5+ Ag '64
Markets in motion. R. Mainer and C. C. Slater. bibliog f il Harvard Bsns R 42:75-82 Mr '64
Meet tomorrow's customer. P. F. Drucker. il Nations Bsns 51:102-4+Je '63
Myth of the national market. J. B. Weiner. il Duns R 83:40-3+ My '64
Why she really goes to market. H. H. Martin. il Sat Eve Post 236:40-3 S 28 '63; Same abr. with title When a woman goes to market. Read Digest 84:115-18 Mr '64

CONSUMERS' research, incorporated
Magic of a name. Consumer Bul 46:2+ Ap '63

CONSUMERS union of United States
Another misuse of CU's test results; not for commercialization. Consumer Rep 29:316-17 Jl '64
Board of directors of Consumers union announces. C. E. Warne. Consumer Rep 28: 415 S '63
Consumer reports vs. Purex: case dismissed. Consumer Rep 28:471 O '63
Financial report and election of directors. Consumer Rep 29:533 N '64
News for teachers & others; documentary on consumer testing. Consumer Rep 29:6-7 Ja '64
See also
International office of consumers' unions

CONSUMPTION (economics)
Consumer spending. il Fortune 68:40+ O '63
Consumer's day dawns in Land of Rising Sun. il Bsns W p 128-30+ Mr 21 '64
Contrasts in spending by urban families; trends since 1950. K. R. Murphy. il Mo Labor R 87:1249-53 N '64
Contrasts in spending by urban families; variations in 1960-61. K. R. Murphy. il Mo Labor R 87:1408-15 D '64
Europe goes shopping; increasing Americanization of taste. il Bsns W p58-60+ My 18 '63
Excise cut can pack big wallop; if companies pass the savings on to customers. il Bsns W p70+ Ja 16 '65
Future challenges marketing. F. F. Mauser. Harvard Bsns R 41:172+ N '63
Great shopping spree. il Time 85:58-62 Ja 8 '65
Growing strength in small retailing. A. F. Doody and W. R. Davidson. bibliog f Harvard Bsns R 42:69-79 Jl '64
Income and expenditures of low-income families; excerpt from address. A. E. Chase. il Mo Labor R 87:889-90 Ag '64
Industry and individuals in a buoyant, buying mood. il Newsweek 63:79 Mr 23 '64
Is the consumer growing wary? il Bsns W p27 Je 29 '63
Markets in motion. R. Mainer and C. C. Slater. bibliog f il Harvard Bsns R 42:75-82 Mr '64
New dimension in consumer analysis. H. W. Boyd, jr. and S. J. Levy. bibliog f il Harvard Bsns R 41:129-40 N '63
Pinch is on supply. il Fortune 70:27-8+ S '64
Preview of your markets in '75. il Nations Bsns 52:66-70+ N '64
Smart money; riding the upswing hard. Bsns W p25-6 Mr 21 '64
Spending more on luxuries. il Bsns W p25 My 23 '64
$32-billion more to spend; with editorial comment. il Bsns W p23-5, 124 Mr 7 '64
To spend or to save. il Fortune 69:28+ Mr '64
See also
Consumer surveys
Consumers
Supply and demand

CONTACOS, Peter G. and others
Quartan-type malaria parasite of New World monkeys transmissible to man. bibliog Science 142:676 N 8 '63

CONTACT (periodical)
Threat in South Africa. H. Head. New Repub 149:54-5 N 9 '63

CONTACT lenses
But they make marriage contracts with girls who wear contacts. P. Hamill. il N Y Times Mag p59-60+ D 6 '64
Contact lens, exaggerated scare, some real problems. il Life 56:46 Ap 3 '64
Contact lenses. P. Dorman. il Consumer Bul 46:10-11+ Mr '63
Eye make-up and contact lenses. P. Dorman. il Consumer Bul 47:2 My '64
Eye on contact lenses. il Newsweek 63:70 Mr 30 '64

CONTACT lenses—*Continued*
How good are contact lenses? what do wearers say? Sci Digest 54:45-6 Ag '63
Lens insana. il Time 95:43 Ja 29 '65
O.K. for contacts. Time 83:60 Ap 17 '64
See better, look better with contact lenses; but are they safe? C. A. Pirolo. il Pop Sci 184:62-4+ Je '64
Should you wear contact lenses? il Suc Farm 62:141 Mr '64
Sight for sore eyes; scleral contact air lenses for Olympic swimmers. Sports Illus 21:13 S 21 '64
Smaller and better eyes for the human fish; diver's contact air lenses. C. Phinizy. il Sports Illus 19:62-4 D '63
Truth about contact lenses. J. C. Neill. Ladies Home J 81:40+ D '64
What color did you say your eyes were? il Mlle 57:242-3 Ag '63
CONTAGION and contagious diseases. See Communicable diseases
CONTAGIOUS diseases. See Communicable diseases
CONTAINER industry
Growth comes in many packages: American can co. il Bsns W p68+ My 9 '64
CONTAINERS
Containers for everything; for campers. C. B. Colby. Outdoor Life 132:130-1 O '63
Containers to keep food hot or cold. Good H 156:166 My '63
Gasoline in plastic containers; are such containers safe? il Consumer Bul 46:39+ Jl '63
How steel may save an old market. Bsns W p33 D 5 '64
In the bag; taking the filet home to Fido. il Time 84:53 S 4 '64
Industrial packaging: the key word is merchandising. K. August. il Duns R 84:92-3+ D '64
New weapon for aluminum? Bsns W p 142 Ja 26 '63
Persuading the consumer to buy more; multipackaging. L. Blumenthal. il Duns R 84:101+ D '64
Uncanny transformation. il Time 84:104+ O 16 '64
See also
Beer containers
Milk containers
Tin cans
CONTAINERS, Pressurized. See Aerosols
CONTAINERS for flowers. See Vases
CONTAINERS for shipping
Containerization: the route to integrated transportation. L. Blumenthal. il Duns R 83:pt2 110-13+ Je '64
Roll and rock of containerization in transport economics. M. Forgash. Ann Am Acad 345: 115-21 Ja '63
CONTAMINATION of food. See Food contamination
CONTAMINATION of Mars (planet) See Mars (planet)—Contamination
CONTAMINATION of milk. See Milk contamination
CONTAMINATION of surfaces. See Surface contamination
CONTEMPORARY dance, incorporated
Contemporary dance, inc. at 92nd street Y. M. M. Marks. Dance Mag 37:62-3 F '63
CONTEMPORARY furniture. See Furniture
CONTEMPORARY music. See Music
CONTEMPORARY music festival, Venice. See Music festivals—Italy
CONTEMPT of court
Cool on contempt; Supreme court decision to uphold summary criminal-contempt power. il Time 83:57 Ap 17 '64
Jailing a whole local; longshoremen's refusal to load Canadian ship at Chicago. Bsns W p 134+ D 7 '63
Jury trial barred; Supreme court decision to uphold summary criminal contempt power. Sr Schol 84:15-16 Ap 24 '64
Trial without jury; case of Ross R. Barnett and Paul B. Johnson, jr. New Repub 150:5-6 Ap 18 '64
CONTEMPT of legislative bodies
Contempt power, by R. L. Goldfarb. Review New Repub 150:32-3 Mr 7 '64. T. Arnold
CONTENT, J. E. and Morse, B. K.
Simple transistor tester. Electr World 71: 50 My '64
CONTENTMENT
Meaning of security. M. Wolf. il Parents Mag 38:64+ D '63
See also
Happiness
Les CONTES d'Hoffmann; opera. See Offenbach, J.
CONTESTS. See Competitions
CONTINENTAL airlines
Airline takes the marginal route. il Bsns W p 111-12+ Ap 20 '63
Bid to extend three-class fare opposed. J. R. Ashlock. Aviation W 78:36 Ja 28 '63
Bob Six's bag of tricks. I. Ross. il Fortune 67:130-2+ F '63
Continental plans 1970 service after order for three Concordes. Aviation W 79:43 Ag 5 '63
Highflying Robert Six. R. L. Whearley. il Sat Eve Post 236:82+ F 23 '63
Other carriers likely to oppose Continental economy fare ruling. Aviation W 81:34 D 21 '64
Trans World, Continental discuss merger. L. L. Doty. Aviation W 79:34-5 O 28 '63
CONTINENTAL Congress. See United States—Continental Congress
CONTINENTAL DIVIDE raceway. See Speedways
CONTINENTAL drift
Are the continents drifting? J. T. Wilson. il UNESCO Courier 16:4-11 O '63
Big split. il Newsweek 62:81 S 9 '63
Continental drift. J. T. Wilson. il Sci Am 208:86-100 bibliog(p200) Ap '63
Continental drift and the origin of mountains. E. Orowan. bibliog il Science 146:1003-10 N 20 '64
Continents are still on the move. G. H. T. Kimble. il N Y Times Mag p 13+ Jl 21 '63
Drifting continent. Sci Am 208:73 Je '63
Drifting continents. Pop Sci 182:16+ F '63
Evidence continents drift. Sci N L 84:23 Jl 13 '63
CONTINENTAL grain company
Continental's coup. Newsweek 63:65 F 3 '64
Wheat jam is broken, at last. Bsns W p27 Ja 11 '64
CONTINENTAL Illinois national bank and trust company of Chicago
Kangaroo jumps. il Newsweek 64:62 Ag 24 '64
CONTINENTAL insurance company
Tom Lovell paints a Continental soldier of 1781. il Am Artist 27:24-7 Mr '63
CONTINENTAL oil company
Conoco's widening world. R. Sheehan. il Fortune 69:113-17+ Ap '64
Putting Conoco up with majors. il Bsns W p52-3+ N 30 '63
CONTINENTAL shelf station. See Underwater structures
CONTINENTAL slopes
Precipitous continental slopes and considerations on the transitional crust. C. Emiliani. bibliog il Science 147:145-8 Ja 8 '65
Sea pressure forms slopes. B. Tufty. Sci N L 85:215 Ap 4 '64
CONTINENTS
Anchoring of continents. Sci N L 85:2 Ja 4 '64
When the land was young. J. J. Parodiz. il Américas 15:22-5 Jl '63
See also
Continental drift
CONTINI, Jeanne
Illiterate poets of Somalia. Reporter 28:36-8 Mr 14 '63
Winds of change in the Garden of Aden. Reporter 29:28-30 Jl 4 '63
CONTINI, Nina
My first elephant hunt. Seventeen 23:86-7+ Ja '64
CONTINUOUS casting
Big change comes to steel; from open hearth furnace to oxygen furnace and computers. il Bsns W p78-81+ Ag 15 '64
Non-stop way to cast steel. il Bsns W p82-4 Je 1 '63
Steel irons out casting method; vacuum degasser. Bsns W p 104 S 21 '63
Steel without ingots. Bsns W p36 Mr 16 '63
Tower of steel. Time 81:87 Mr 29 '63
CONTINUOUS-progress plan in education. See Ungraded classes
CONTOUR sanders. See Sanding machines
CONTRACEPTION. See Birth control
CONTRACEPTIVES
Birth control cheapest with new plastic coils. Sci N L 86:57 Jl 25 '64
Birth control devices and debates engross the U.S. il Life 54:37-40B My 10 '63
Birth control pill increases blood clotting; Enovid. Sci N L 83:89 F 9 '63
Birth control pills affect thyroid test. Sci N L 84:168 S 14 '63
Birth control pills boom; oral contraceptive. Bsns W p62+ F 23 '63
Birth control: the pill and the church. il Newsweek 64:51-5 Jl 6 '64
Catholics take a new look at the pill. J. Star. il Look 28:71-2+ S 8 '64

CONTRACEPTIVES—*Continued*
Coming: new birth control measures. H. G. Lawson. Sci Digest 55:86-90 Mr '64
Debate on the birth control pill: Catholic controversy. J. B. Sheerin. Cath World 199: 76-9 My '64
Do the pills cause cancer? Time 84:46 Jl 3 '64
Doctor Rock's book; Catholic response. Commonweal 78:213-14 My 17 '63
Dutch bishops on the pill. America 110: 531 Ap 18 '64; Reply. 110:696 My 23 '64
Enovid cleared. Newsweek 62:84 S 30 '63
Enovid: contraceptive pill and recent FDA report clearing it stir continued medical dispute. E. Langer. Science 141:892-4 S 6 '63
Enovid: contraceptive pill is cleared by FDA, but not all the questions have been answered. E. Langer. Science 141:621-2 Ag 16 '63
Enovid exonerated. Newsweek 83:81 Je 29 '64
Extramarital sex and the pill. P. A. Bertocci. Christian Cent 81:267-70 F 26 '64
FDA says enovid safe. Sci N L 84:119 Ag 24 '63
For women only, by B. L. Cinberg. Review America 110:620-1 My 9 '64
Has the time come? sign of a Catholic birth-control thaw. Newsweek 63:90 Je 8 '64
How safe are the birth control pills? J. Devaney. Redbook 120:45+ F '63
In the shadows; contraceptive industry. Time 81:84+ F 15 '63
Intra-uterine devices: a new era in birth control? il Time 84:48 Jl 31 '64
Male pill; diamine. Newsweek 61:94 Ap 15 '63
Morality of the pill; excerpt from Morale conjugale et progestogènes, tr. by M. Ilford. L. Janssens. Commonweal 80:332-5 Je 5 '64
More on the pill. America 111:730 D 5 '64
New birth-control devices. Sci Am 210:54-5 Ja '64
New birth control pill cleared for prescription. Sci N L 83:111 F 16 '63
New birth control pill ready after ten years; norinyl. Sci N L 85:231 Ap 11 '64
New drug market race; birth control pills. il Bsns W p32 Mr 28 '64
One pill birth control. Sci N L 83:134 Mr 2 '63
Pills: more effective, and more of them. il Time 83:64+ Mr 20 '64
Preventing menopause. Newsweek 63:70 Mr 30 '64
Progress in family planning. il Consumer Rep 29:400-3 Ag '64
Safety report on oral contraceptives. Good H 158:123 Ja '64
Setback for birth-control pills; possible cause of breast cancer. Bsns W p32 O 26 '63
Tell me, doctor. G. Pincus. Ladies Home J 80:50+ Je '63
Test for an ancient law; banning of contraceptives. Time 84:44 D 18 '64
Thalidomide birth control. F. Marley. Sci N L 83:231 Ap 13 '63
Toward birth control. Newsweek 61:58 F 25 '63
Uses of pills. America 110:31-2 Ja 11 '64
Vatican hints review of birth control stand; new pill under test may be acceptable to Catholics. Bsns W p25 My 30 '64
Verdict on enovid. Newsweek 62:77 Ag 12 '63
Warning signals; oral contraceptives. America 108:188 F 9 '63
What the pill does. America 111:120 Ag 8 '64
Whither the pill? R. A. McCormick. Cath World 199:207-14 Jl '64

CONTRACEPTIVES (animals)
Barren coil; contraceptive device used on India's sacred cows. il Time 84:28-9 N 6 '64
Contraception for sacred cows. Sci Am 212: 51 Ja '65
Intrauterine foreign body: effect on pregnancy in the rat. L. L. Doyle and A. J. Margolis. il Science 139:833 Mr 1 '63; Reply with rejoinder. E. Eichner. 140:1136 Je 7 '63

CONTRACT bridge. See Bridge (game)

CONTRACT packaging. See Packaging

CONTRACTION, Muscular. See Muscles

CONTRACTORS
Curbs on advice peddlers; regulation issued by Defense dept. Bsns W p86 Je 15 '63
Multi-million dollar building boss; Detroit general superintendent. il Ebony 19:102+ Mr '64
One hundred biggest building contractors in the U.S. il Arch Forum 118:122-4 Je '63; 120:18-20 My '64
Yale's School of art and architecture: the builder. M. Burchard. il Arch Forum 120: 80-3 F '64

CONTRACTS
Music contractor. M. Mayer. Esquire 59:157-64 My '63
See also
Estimates
Leases
Subcontracting
Teachers—Contracts

CONTRACTS, Government
Adamant Admiral. il Time 81:19 Je 21 '63
Arms and the big money men. J. Duscha. il Harper 228:39-47 Mr; 59-65 Ap; 56-62 My '64; Discussion of March issue 228:10+ My '64; Miss & Roc 14:46 Mr 16 '64
Atwood calls reputation best incentive. Aviation W 79:36-7 Ag 12 '63
Better distribution of R&D funds sought; with list of top research & development contractors. K. Johnsen. Aviation W 81: 101+ N 16 '64
Big hopes ride on a big, big transport. Bsns W p28 D 19 '64
Casing rockets in glass; cylindrical cases made of glass. il Bsns W p 108-10+ F 9 '63
Congressional questions remain unanswered on GE support award. A. P. Alibrando Aviation W 78:91+ My 27 '63
Contractor evaluation comments asked. Aviation W 78:32 Ap 15 '63
Contractor gets steady check on profits with new PERT-type system. W. Beller. il Miss & Roc 14:38-9+ Ja 13 '64
Contractors find flaws in new regime; Barbs come from Congress, military. il Miss & Roc 12:66-8 Mr 25 '63
Contracts. See issues of Missiles and rockets
Contracts and procurements (title varies) See issues of Missiles and rockets
Defense managing. Cato. Nat R 16:649 Jl 28 '64
Defense profits will be linked to contractors' performance. Aviation W 79:36 Ag 19 '63
DOD considering new profit guidelines. F. G. McGuire. Miss & Roc 12:15-16 F 25 '63
DOD list of FY 1963; 100 top prime contractors. il Miss & Roc 14:26 Ja 6 '64
DOD lists major research contractors. Aviation W 81:60-5 D 28 '64
Department of defense lists top 100 prime contractors for fiscal 1963. il Aviation W 79:60-3 D 30 '63
DOD may toughen patent policies. Miss & Roc 15:11 D 7 '64
DOD official calls for controlled, short program definition effort. Aviation W 78:127 My 20 '63
DOD regulation seeks first-class fare curb. Aviation W 79:96+ S 16 '63
DOD research awards total $6.1 billion. il Aviation W 78:83+ F 11 '63
DDR&E will monitor briefings. Aviation W 79:36 Ag 26 '63
Directory of major procurement contracts. Miss & Roc 13:190-9 Jl 29 '63; 15:149-54 Jl 27 '64
Employment impact of changing defense programs. J. F. Fulton. bibliog f il Mo Labor R 87:508-16 My '64
Employment of Negroes by government contractors. J. A. Brackett. il Mo Labor R 87: 789-93 Jl '64
Fact and fancy on identical bids. P. W. Cook. jr. Harvard Bsns R 41:67-72 Ja '63
Firms balk; data-sharing clause dropped. Aviation W 78:29 Ap 1 '63
Five firms bidding in AF big solid motor program. Miss & Roc 12:15 F 25 '63
GAO charges windfall on helium program. Bsns W p29 Ja 26 '63
Higher incentive rewards, penalties due. K. Johnsen. Aviation W 78:84-5 Je 3 '63
History lesson. W. J. Coughlin. Miss & Roc 15:46 O 26 '64
House urges more small business awards. Aviation W 82:93 Ja 25 '65
Housekeeping jobs that don't go begging; bidding for development of nuclear rockets. il Bsns W p 146+ Mr 9 '63
How much politics in contract awards? U S News 54:10-11 F 18 '63
How taxpayers pick up the check for picnics; boosting defense plant morale. Bsns W p25 Jl 25 '64
Identical bids; billion-dollar coincidence. R. J. Barber. il Nation 196:154-7 F 23 '63; Reply with rejoinder. W. P. Kennedy. 196: inside cover Mr 30 '63
In defense of the Defense secretary. Fortune 67:81-2+ Ap '63
Incentive contracts may multiply controls. Aviation W 79:98-9 Jl 1 '63
Incentives prove useful, but no cure-all. Aviation W 81:64 Jl 13 '64

CONTRACTS, Government—*Continued*
Industry doubts report to bring changes. W. H. Gregory. Aviation W 78:179-84 Je 10 '63
Industry mixed on DOD's profit system. W. H. Gregory. Aviation W 79:60-3+ S 2 '63
Industry protests increased data-sharing. Aviation W 78:33 Mr 25 '63
Industry's growth problems; excerpts from address. R. I. McKenzie. Aviation W 79:13 S 2 '63
Lack of technical data cited in award. Aviation W 78:32 Je 17 '63
Long short cut; need for an intermediary. Bsns W p28+ My 30 '64
Low fees may undermine incentive goal; cost plus incentive fee. B. Backe. il Aviation W 82:69+ Ja 11 '65
McNamara and his critics. New Repub 148: 5-6 Mr 30 '63
McNamara's 97¢. il Time 82:95 O 25 '63
Major DOD research conttractors listed. il Aviation W 80:95+ Ja 20 '64
Management tightens its aerospace reins; stress on cost reduction, quality control, and delivery time. il Bsns W p96+ S 14 '63
M.I.T; prime contractor contends with problems produced by solving government's problems. J. Walsh. Science 140:164-5+ Ap 12 '63
Missile row in Britain; cost of guided missile contracts. il Bsns W p54 Ag 8 '64
NASA fiscal 1962 procurement doubled. il Aviation W 78:34-5 Ja 28 '63
NASA list of FY 1963 100 top prime contractors. il Miss & Roc 14:18 Ja 20 '64
NASA lists top fiscal '63 contractors. il Aviation W 80:58-60 Mr 30 '64
New actions will ease government competition. il Nations Bsns 52:108-9+ S '64
New GE Apollo role may be challenged. A. P. Alibrando. Aviation W 78:28-9 Ap 22 '63
New yardstick for defense contracts; award of X-22 contract to Bell. Bsns W p30 Je 22 '63
No pain for business; bomb research and monitoring devices. Bsns W p21-2 Ag 3 '63
Non-profit policies face GAO scrutiny. K. Johnsen. Aviation W 81:15 D 28 '64
Orbiter is first big NASA incentive job. R. G. O'Lone. Aviation W 79:32-3 O 7 '63
Pentagon to try single control on contracts; Project 60. Bsns W p 130 N 2 '63
Politics in the arms business? with excerpts from Congressional record. il U S News 54:40-3 My 13 '63
P.D. quick. Aviation W 78:106 Mr 4 '63
Putting profit spur back into contracts; noncompetitive procurement. Bsns W p 107 My 25 '63
R&D: new awareness in Congress of stimulus of federal research stirs envy of areas like Boston. J. Walsh. Science 139:1273-5 Mr 29 '63
Reliability engineering. G. A. W. Boehn. il Fortune 67:124-7+ Ap '63
Relief via Defense. Nation 196:191 Mr 9 '63
Report favors prototype development. B. H. Klein and others. il Aviation W 78:135+ Je 10 '63
Rules outlined to prevent study firms from gaining unfair edge. K. Johnsen. Aviation W 78:39 Je 10 '63
Senator Case seeks watchdog unit for military, space contracts. C. P. Case. Aviation W 78:34 F 25 '63
Small business pacts continue decline. H. M. David. Miss & Roc 16:16 Ja 11 '65
Smarter bargainer. Time 81:91-2 Mr 15 '63
Solicitous giant. il Time 81:25-6 Ap 26 '63
Solutions to cost overruns recommended. Aviation W 79:91+ O 28 '63
Space and defense, a big industry with problems. il U S News 54:48-51 Mr 11 '63
Space crescent. W. S. Ellis. il Nation 199: 211-16, 239-43, 275-7+ O 12-26 '64
STL may make $1-million bonus on Vela Hotel incentive contract. Aviation W 79:28 O 28 '63
Studies of defense contracting. S. Marcus. bibliog f Harvard Bsns R 42:20-2+ My '64
Subsidized morale. New Repub 151:5 S 26 '64
Sweeping source selection changes sought. P. J. Klass. Aviation W 81:24 O 5 '64
System will rate contractors. H. Taylor. il Miss & Roc 12:14 F 11 '63
Tighter cost control proposed by Rickover. Aviation W 80:93-4 Ja 6 '64
Too many generals at work on contracts? concerning report by Stanford research institute. il Bsns W p91 Je 15 '63
Top research contractors listed by DOD. Aviation W 81:87+ D 21 '64
Turbine engine parts policy is criticized. Aviation W 79:35 Jl 1 '63
Unclassified defense contracts: awards by county, state, and metropolitan areas of the United States fiscal year 1962, by W. Isard and G. J. Karaska. Review
Bul Atomic Sci il 19:34-5 S '63. T. Reiner
U.S. seeks industry pay formula. Aviation W 78:26 My 6 '63
What will take up the slack? shrinking of defense procurement; with editorial comment. il Bsns W p50+, 128 Jl 18 '64
When the Pentagon saves; that's a gang of nickels. il Newsweek 63:63-4+ Mr 9 '64
Where the cuts hurt. il Bsns W p56+ Jl 18 '64
See also
Government investigations—Government contracts
Government spending policy
United States—National aeronautics and space administration—Procurement

Labor problems

Government and manpower requirements; excerpt from report, March 9, 1964. Mo Labor R 87:407-13 Ap '64

Renegotiation

See also
United States—Renegotiation board

Subcontracting

F-111 subcontracts monitored closely. E. J. Bulban. Aviation W 79:55+ Ag 26 '63
Industry studies NASA procurement list. G. Alexander. Aviation W 79:29-31 O 28 '63
LEM subs to be chosen by summer. H. Taylor. il Miss & Roc 12:14 F 25 '63
Protect your freedom to subcontract. M. L. Joseph. Harvard Bsns R 41:98-102 Ja '63
CONTRACTS, Teachers. See Teachers—Contracts
CONTRAST photography. See Photography
CONTROL data corporation
Bendix gives up on computers; sale of Computer div. to CDC. Bsns W p36 Mr 9 '63
Computers get faster than ever; high-powered 6600. il Bsns W p28+ Ag 31 '63
Computers speed up; control data's 6800 model. Bsns W p86 D 19 '64
Poor man's IBM. il Time 84:62-3 Ag 14 '64
Small, smart, sharp. il Bsns W p 154+ My 25 '63
CONTROL equipment. See Automatic control
CONTROL forests. See Forests and forestry
CONTROL of credit. See Credit
CONTROL of electromagnetic radiation. See Conelrad warning system
CONTROL of insects. See Insects, Injurious and beneficial—Control
CONTROL of production. See Production control
CONTROL panels (space vehicles) See Space vehicles—Instrument boards
CONTROL towers. See Airports—Control towers
CONTROLLED economy. See Economic planning
CONTROLLED fusion. See Nuclear fusion
CONTROLLER general, Office of. See United States—General accounting office
CONTROLLERS, Air traffic. See Air traffic controllers (persons)
CONTROLLERSHIP
Three for a pyramid; Lionel's Krock, Huffines and Muscat. il Time 81:108+ My 17 '63
CONUNDRUMS. See Riddles
CONVAIR division. See General dynamics corporation—Convair division
CONVALESCENCE
Fun for a young convalescent. P. L. Jensen. il Parents Mag 38:82-3+ O '63
CONVECTION of heat. See Heat—Convection
CONVENIENCE foods. See Food—Ready-to-cook food
CONVENTION delegates. See National conventions (political)
CONVENTION halls. See Auditoriums
CONVENTIONAL war. See War
CONVENTIONS
Convention wives: help or hindrance? il Newsweek 61:82-3 My 13 '63
Meetings; annual spring meetings, conventions, Olympiads, and symposiums in New York. New Yorker 40:41-3 My 16 '64
Travel for the business groups. il Esquire 63: 22B-22L Ja '65
What expense-account rules are doing to conventions. il U S News 54:113-16 Ap 8 '63

CONVENTIONS, Political. See National conventions (political); Political conventions
CONVENTS and nunneries
Culprit in the convent; condensation of Life with Mother Superior. J. Trahey. il Read Digest 83:221-3+ Ag '63
North Dakota community for the Benedictine sisters; Priory of the Annunciation, Bismarck. il Arch Rec 134:95-102 D '63
See also
Secularization
CONVERSATION
Aren't we the lucky little bozos? L. R. Peattie. Read Digest 82:72-4 F '63
Art of talking to boys; excerpts from Boys and other beasts. B. Lang. McCalls 91:58+ Ag '64
From a boy's point of view. J. Wescott. il Seventeen 22:28 Ag '63
Talk of Hollywood. W. Fadiman. Sat R 46: 76-7 N 9 '63
What do I say next? D. Klein. il Seventeen 23:124-5+ O '64
Why men think women talk too much. S. Birmingham. il Redbook 121:43+ Je '63

Anecdotes, facetiae, satire, etc.

I remember Lucadello; baseball fan at a cocktail party. R. Creamer. il Sports Illus 21:29-30+ D 14 '64
When conversation wanes: ask a silly question. M. Doran. Library J 88:1735 Ap 15 '63
CONVERSATION pieces (pictures)
English conversation pieces from the Mellon collection. A. Winchester il Antiques 83: 444-8 Ap '63
German and Austrian conversation pieces of the nineteenth century. A. Von Saldern. il Antiques 86:604-9 N '64
CONVERSATION pits. See Living rooms
CONVERSATION radio programs. See Radio broadcasting—Conversation programs
CONVERSATION television programs. See Television broadcasting—Conversation programs
CONVERSATION with a sacred cow; story. See Menen, A.
CONVERSATIONAL ball; story. See De Vries, P.
CONVERSION
Convict who became a minister. J. Robbins and J. Robbins. il Redbook 124:38-9+ D '64
Vanishing Jews. M. Himmelfarb. Commentary 36:249-51 S '63; Discussion. 37:23 Mr '64
See also
Evangelistic work
CONVERSION of energy. See Force and energy
CONVERTER lens. See Lenses, Photographic
CONVERTERS, Radio. See Radio converters
CONVERTERS, Television. See Television apparatus
CONVERTERS, Thermionic. See Thermionic converters
CONVERTIBILITY of currency. See Currency convertibility
CONVERTIBLE furniture. See Furniture, Convertible
CONVERTS, Catholic
Catholics hit Vatican II; conversions decline in Britain. Christian Cent 81:540 Ap 29 '64
Convert decline. J. A. O'Brien. America 109:382 O 5 '63; Reply. D. Howard. 109:470 O 26 '63; Rejoinder. 109:646 N 23 '63
Ecumenical dialogue and conversions. B. Leeming. Cath World 198:223-9 Ja '64
CONVERTS; story. See Singer, I. J.
CONVICT fish fishing. See Sheepshead fishing
CONVICTS. See Prisoners
CONVULSIONS
Convulsant drug action on neuronally isolated cerebral cortex. B. Grafstein. bibliog il Science 142:973-5 N 15 '63
Febrile convulsions in infant rats, and later behavior. J. Werboff and J. Havlena. bibliog il Science 142:684-5 N 8 '63
See also
Epilepsy
CONWAY, C. M.
Computer that pays its way. Am City 79:102-3 S '64
CONWAY, Edward A.
Peace fighter. America 110:810 Je 13 '64
CONWAY, J. D.
Revising canon law. Commonweal 80:143-6 Ap 24 '64
CONWAY, Jack T.
Politics of protest; address, November 30, 1963. Vital Speeches 30:313-17 Mr 1 '64
CONWAY, John
What is Canada? Atlan 214:100-5 N '64

CONWAY, Moncure Daniel
After Moncure Daniel Conway. J. A. Davidson. Christian Cent 80:277 F 27 '63
Moncure Daniel Conway at South place chapel. W. S. Smith; reply. S. D. Wakefield. Christian Cent 80:468 Ap 10 '63
CONWAY COUNTY, Ark.
How to lynch a newspaper. R. Reed. Atlan 214:59-63 N '64
CONYERS, John, jr
New face in Congress. S. Booker. il pors Ebony 20:73-4+ Ja '65
COOGAN, Jeanmarie
Lady who likes kids. Ladies Home J 80:54 Je '63
My running fight with the Easter bunny. Ladies Home J 80:55-6 Ap '63
So you're Kate's girl! Read Digest 83:219-20+ Jl '63
COOGAN, Joseph P.
Placebo. McCalls 92:68+ O '64
COOGAN, Tim Pat
Sure, and it's County Kennedy now. N Y Times Mag p7-9+ Je 23 '63
COOK, Bruce
Art in court; Candy comes to Chicago. Nation 199:125-6 S 14 '64
Mary McCarthy: one of ours? Cath World 199:34-42 Ap '64
Ray Bradbury and the Irish. por Cath World 200:224-30 Ja '65
COOK, Charles W.
Lifelong collecting has helped keep Virginia man young in spirit. J. Walsh. il por Hobbies 68:36+ F '64
COOK, Clair M.
Man of principle. Christian Cent 80:1171 S 25 '63
Technology's impact on religion. Christian Cent 81:1083-5 S 2 '64
COOK, Don
De Gaulle builds a new France. Sat Eve Post 236:24-8+ N 23 '63
COOK, Donald A.
(comp) Survey of programmed materials. Sr Schol 84:11T Mr 13 '64
Three-minute course on programmed instruction. Sr Schol 84:6T+ Mr 13 '64
—and Sohn, David
(eds) Special issue on programmed instruction. bibliog Sr Schol 84:6T+, 9T-15T Mr 13 '64
COOK, Donald C.
Case against capitalizing leases. bibliog f Harvard Bsns R 41:145-50+ Ja '63
LBJ's advisers: ins+outs=middle. il por Newsweek 64:65-6 Jl 13 '64
We're the most enterprising utility in this country. H. Kay. il pors Fortune 69:138-41+ My '64
COOK, Earnshaw
Baseball is played all wrong. F. Deford. il por Sports Illus 20:14-17 Mr 23 '64
COOK, Emory
High fidelity newsfronts. N. Eisenberg. il Hi Fi 13:35 D '63
COOK, Francis J. pseud
Letter from the Caribbean. Nat R 16:312 Ap 21 '64
COOK, Fred J.
About: the water we need. N Y Times Mag p90+ N 24 '63
CIA: the case builds up. Nation 198:616-18 Je 22 '64
Coming politics of disarmament. Nation 196: 131-5 F 16 '63
Corrupt society. Nation 196:454-496a Je 1 '63
Dig they must, find they what? N Y Times Mag p 19+ My 19 '63
Foundations as a tax dodge. Nation 196:321-5 Ap 20 '63
Hoffa trial. Nation 198:415-39 Ap 27 '64
Murk, smog, smoke, needed: fresh air. N Y Times Mag p 10+ D 29 '63
Ordeal of Captain Kauffman. Nation 197:123-38 S 14 '63
Radio right: hate clubs of the air. Nation 198:523-7 My 25 '64
Taxpayers under the microscope. N Y Times Mag p20+ Ap 12 '64
Their men in Washington. Nation 198:311-30 Mr 30 '64
Warfare state. bibliog f Ann Am Acad 351:102-9 Ja '64
What makes a safe driver safe. N Y Times Mag p79+ Ap 7 '63

about

Who runs America? an examination of a theory that says the answer is a military-industrial complex. D. S. Greenberg; discussion. Science 139:247-8+ Ja 18 '63
COOK, G. D. and others
Transpiration: its effects on plant leaf temperature. bibliog Science 144:546-7 My 1 '64

COOK, Gioia
Leopard. C. H. McBride. il Esquire 62:130-1 S '64
COOK, Jim
Hon dah (be my guest) Am For 69:26-7+ Ap '63
COOK, Joan M.
Books on the women's pages of Times and Tribune; summary of address. Pub W 184: 32-3 D 2 '63
Italy's intellectuals steer to the left. N Y Times Mag p32+ My 26 '63
Parent and child. N Y Times Mag p52 Ja 5; 55 Mr 29; 86+ Ap 19; 19 Jl 5; 93-4 O 4 '64
COOK, Leonard, and others
Ribonucleic acid: effect on conditioned behavior in rats. bibliog Science 141:268-9 Jl 19 '63
COOK, Louis
Professional theatre at Ann Arbor. Theatre Arts 47:29-31 Ag '63
COOK, Paul W. jr
Fact and fancy on identical bids. Harvard Bsns R 41:67-72 Ja '63
COOK, Peter
Please feed the lions. il por Mlle 57:96-7+ Je '63
COOK, Robert
Recreation weight training. por Recreation 57:30-1 Ja '64
COOK COUNTY, Ill.
Helping Cook County's culturally deprived adults. D. J. Brooks, jr. NEA J 52:29-30 Ap '63
High-density communities can preserve open spaces. il Am City 79:110 S '64
Massive attack on illiteracy; excerpts from address, July 13, 1963. R. M. Hilliard. il ALA Bul 57:1034-8 D '63
Property index number. A. J. Salomon. il Am City 79:139+ N '64
COOKBOOK of the United Nations. See Cookbooks
COOKBOOKS
BH&G new cook book hits 10-million sales mark. il Pub W 186:45-6 N 9 '64
Bouillabaisse sellers. il Time 82:78-9 Jl 12 '63
Cooking by the book; excerpts from McCall's cookbook. il McCalls 91:150-2+ O '63
Cooking has changed; Boston cooking school cook book. R. B. Scott. il Todays Health 41:48-51+ S '63
How to get him to marry you; excerpt from Seducer's cookbook. M. Sheraton. il Mlle 57:148-9 O '63
One world of many tastes; Cookbook of the United Nations. C. Claiborne. il N Y Times Mag p 102 O 25 '64
Speaking out; burn those worthless cookbooks. J. McPhee. Sat Eve Post 237:8+ O 3 '64
Without a grain of salt; excerpts. E. W. Bagg. il Todays Health 42:32-5+ My '64
Bibliography
Cook and the book. P. McGinley. il Sat R 47:61-3 O 24 '64
Cookbooks for everyone. Parents Mag 38:93 Jl '63
Cookbooks for fall selling. il Pub W 184:26-41 S 2 '63
Holiday handbook of cookbooks. H. Papashvily. il Holiday 33:149-52 My '63
New cookbooks. Parents Mag 39:20 Ap '64
New foreign cookbooks. Parents Mag 38:162 S '63
COOKE, Alistair
Choosing up sides. Vogue 144:148-9+ O 15 '64
(ed) See Hearst, S. Flags are not enough
COOKE, Bernard
America's Catholic community: increasing involvement. Christian Cent 80:360-2 Mr 20 '63
Interplay of symbols. Christian Cent 80:1307 O 23 '63
Personal development through grace; excerpt from Pastoral catechetics. Cath World 199:371-8 S '64
COOKE, Eileen D. See Krettek, G. jt. auth.
COOKE, Gerald B.
Scouting bridgelands. Christian Cent 80:582 My 1 '63
COOKE, Hope. See Hope Namgyal, maharani of Sikkim
COOKE, Jerry
Most beautiful racetrack in the world; photographs. Sports Illus 20:44-51 Je 8 '64
Zoo's who. Sat Eve Post 236:28-31 Ag 10 '63
COOKE, Morris Llewellyn
Famous firsts: extending the scientific gospel. por Bsns W p 132+ Ap 18 '64
COOKE, Robert E.
Improvement of man; excerpts from address. por Time 83:81 My 22 '64
COOKERY
Adding a touch of tartness; with recipes. J. Hewitt. il N Y Times Mag p77 Ja 12 '64
Adventures in food. See issues of Sunset
Better homes & gardens test kitchen; flavor of Christmas. Bet Hom & Gard 41:64+ D '63
Big dash of pepper; with recipes. C. Claiborne. il N Y Times Mag p89-90 My 19 '63
Blend it round the clock. il McCalls 91:76+ N '63
Bountiful foods on a budget; with recipes. il Good H 157:106-14 S '63
Celebrities' choice. il McCalls 91:142-7+ O '63
Change of pace summertime cooking. il Bet Hom & Gard 41:68-73+ Ag '63
Chic country cooking; with recipes. J. Peter and M. Kaytor. il Look 27:106-7+ My 21 '63
Chilled and choice. J. Hewitt. il N Y Times Mag p47 Je 23 '63
Christmas at the inns. il McCalls 91:120-7+ D '63
Class of '63. il McCalls 90:124-5+ My '63
Classic ingredients to make and give. il Sunset 133:206+ N '64
Clip & file. il Parents Mag 39:95 Ja '64
Cook-ahead meals for hot summer days. G. Maddox. il Todays Health 41:42-5+ Jl '63
Cook-along party. M. J. Engel. il Ladies Home J 81:145-6+ Mr '64
Cook in the cool of the day, eat in the cool of the evening; cool-cooking electric skillet. il McCalls 90:94-5+ Jl '63
Cooking by scent. F. D. Gray. Vogue 142: 104-5 S 15 '63
Cooking by the book; excerpts from McCall's cookbook. il McCalls 91:150-2+ O '63
Cooking club. il House & Gard 124:237-9 O; 284-6 N; 182-3 D '63; 125:147-8 F; 186-8 Mr; 204-8 My; 152-4 Je; 126:208-11 S; 152+ O; 184-6 D '64; 127:146-7 Ja '65
Cooking delights of spring. il Sunset 130: 190-1 Ap '63
Cooking minus mama; easy-to-follow recipes for men and children. B. La Roche. il Farm J 87:61+ Je '63
Cooking up a memory. W. C. Jardine. Bet Hom & Gard 42:114+ N '64
Date with a dish. See issues of Ebony
Dining a la cart, or cooking on the spot. V. T. Habeeb. il Am Home 66:48-51+ My '63
Dining with the Cratchits; with recipes. C. Claiborne. il N Y Times Mag p29 D 22 '63
Dishes to serve again and again. Sunset 133:180-1 O '64
Even the bride can shine as a cook! with recipes. il Good H 156:92-105 F '63
Famous foods from famous places; Top of the fair. il Bet Hom & Gard 42:72-3+ My '64
Fare for the Fourth. C. Claiborne. il N Y Times Mag p42 Je 30 '63
Flavor, the secret of good cooking. M. Johnston and P. McBride. il Bet Hom & Gard 42:66-7+ Mr '64
Food your gang will go for. Polly. il Farm J 88:96+ F '64
For cooks who frequently are short of time. Sunset 130:228+ My '63
Four go easy main dishes; low calorie content. Sunset 133:220+ N '64
Frankly fancy. M. Johnston. il Bet Hom & Gard 41:88-93+ O '63
From the new Vogue book of menus. Vogue 144:192+ O 15 '64
GH keep cool cookbook. il Good H 157:86-103 Ag '63
Good housekeeping's complete Christmas cookbook. il Good H 157:64-99 D '63
GH's happy family budget cookbook. il Good H 157:96-105 S '63
Gourmet diet cook book. R. E. Church. il House & Gard 125:143-5+ Je '64
Great dinners. il Life 56:47-50+ Ja 31; 102-3+ F 21; 92-3+ Mr 27; 110-11+ Ap 24; 126-7+ My 22; 92-3+ Je 26; 57:66-7+ Jl 31; 80-4 Ag 21; 148-9+ S 18; 152-3+ O 16; 122-3+ N 13; 102-3+ D 18 '64; 58: 84-5+ Ja 29 '65
Heat's off summer cooking. il Ladies Home J 80:88-90+ Jl '63
Holiday food ideas. Farm J 87:79 D '63
Holiday open house. il Ladies Home J 81:121+ D '64
Holiday roundup for problem diets. Good H 157:205-8 D '63
Home-cooked country food that sells. N. Nichols. il Farm J 88:74-5 Ap '64
Home cooking. il Redbook 122:64-5+ Ja '64
Hot meals can be a breeze in summer. il Am Home 66:46-7+ Jl '63
How to eat alone and like it; with recipes. il Redbook 123:70-1+ Jl '64
How to serve simply but with flair. B. G. La Roche. il Farm J 87:64-5 S '63

COOKERY—*Continued*
I love my mother's; six top favorites with children; with recipes. il Am Home 67:50-1+ S '64
Instant cook. L. Stilwill. il Ladies Home J 80:161-2 O '63; 81:124 Mr '64
It's easier than you think. il Good H 158: 106-21+ Mr '64
Join the stampede to rotisserie cooking. E. Gordon. il House B 105:188-92+ My '63
Last-minute meals off the shelf. il Redbook 122:64-5+ F '64
Let's eat. M. F. Boss. il Am For 69:2-3+ D '63
Little kitchen, big party. M. J. Engel. il Ladies Home J 80:102-3+ S '63
Long and short of classic recipes. il Am Home 67:64-5+ O '64
Lovely leaping flame; how and when to do it. E. Kinard. il House B 105:154-5+ D '63
Make-ahead magic. M. Johnston. il Bet Hom & Gard 41:70-5+ S '63
Make-it-again recipes. R. Behnke. il Farm J 88:57 Je '64
Male call; man-type dishes. il McCalls 91: 142-3+ My '64
Master menu cook book. P. Harvey. il House & Gard 124:273+ N '63
Meals by the clock. il Redbook 121:80-1+ S '63
Mealtime magic for everyone; wonderful things you can do with soup mixes. il Am Home 68:58-9+ Ja '65
[Month] menus; with recipes. See issues of Sunset
Most fragrant scent in the world: the clove. C. Claiborne. il N Y Times Mag p98 S 29 '63
Most likely to succeed at your next teenage bash. Am Home 67:73-4 S '64
New, new, new for spring. il Good H 156:96-112 Ap '63
New skillets are better. il McCalls 91:38+ Mr '64
1964 timesaver cookbook. H. Mills. il Redbook 123:64-72 Je '64
107 ways to be a happy hostess. il Good H 158:102-19 Je '64
127 bright ideas for busy wives; ways to make the most of your time and energy. il Good H 156:103-26 My '63
Peter Ustinov: I like what tempts my eye: with recipes; interview, ed. by N. Lyon. P. Ustinov. il Vogue 144:223-4 O 1 '64
Portable means for summer pleasure; with recipes. G. Maddox. il Todays Health 42: 42-7 Jl '64
Readers' choice; most requested recipes. C. Claiborne. il N Y Times Mag p22 D 27 '64
Readers choose; recipes. C. Claiborne. il N Y Times Mag p24 D 29 '63
Recipes from a good cook's notebook. Mrs R. A. Dougan. il Suc Farm 62:52-3 Je '64
Redbook's sixty all-time favorite recipes. il Redbook 121:87-96+ My '63
Relax, dinner's in the oven! P. McBride. il Bet Hom & Gard 41:80 F '63
Revolution in the kitchen. P. Cannon. il Sat R 47:54-7 O 24 '64
Saucy main dishes. il Bet Hom & Gard 41: 89-90 My '63
Season's-best taste table; with recipes. il Farm J 87:72-5 D '63
Second fame: good food: menus, recipes, kitchen amenities of celebrated people. N. Lyon. il Vogue 144:239-40 S 1 '64; 145:152-4 Ja 1; 116-18 Ja 15; 186-8 F 1 '65
Shortcut cook. E. Ward-Hanna. il Ladies Home J 80:80 My '63
Skewer cooking around the world. il Sunset 130:154-6+ Je '63
Split-second gourmet with a blender. il Good H 158:176-8+ Mr '64
Spring is a good idea. il Bet Hom & Gard 42:50-77+ Ap '64
Summer dining tips from major restaurants; with recipes. G. Maddox. il Todays Health 41:34-7+ Ag '63
Sunset's kitchen cabinet. See issues of Sunset
Super eating from supermarket specials; with recipes. il Am Home 67:62-3+ O '64
Table for two; late-summer special. Ladies Home J 81:33 S '64
That extra something is brown sugar. il McCalls 91:98-9+ Ja '64
Three menus, six non-cliché switches. Vogue 141:52 F 1 '63
Time & money in the kitchen; convenience foods: economy or extravagance? il Changing T 17:34 F '63
Tips for the cook. il Suc Farm 61:53 D '63
Tips on top-of-range cooking. B. G. Wadsworth. il Parents Mag 39:34 Ap '64
Treasury of favorite Christmas recipes. E. Ward-Hanna. il Ladies Home J 80:142-4+ D '63
Twenty-four short cuts to summer meals. C. Pines. il Parents Mag 38:55-8 Ag '63
Two good cooks are better than one: ed. by R. Behnke. S. Scott. il Farm J 88:76-8 My '64
Two meals cooked at once. Sunset 131:232 N '63
Vogue's own menu. See issues of Vogue from March 1, 1963
Want to succeed in the business? il McCalls 91:148-9+ O '63
What's cooking in farm kitchens? R. Behnke and B. G. La Roche. il Farm J 87:80-1 My '63
When it's 90° in the shade. C. Claiborne. il N Y Times Mag p26 Jl 12 '64
World tour of cool, quick cooking; appliance cook book. il Bet Hom & Gard 41:72-7 Je '63
Your guests cook their own right at the table. il Sunset 133:234+ O '64
See also
Appetizers
Baking
Barbecue cookery
Breakfasts
Buffet meals
Casserole cookery
Catering
Chafing dish. Cookery
Christmas dinners
Christmas meals
Confectionery
Cookbooks
Curry
Desserts
Dinners and dining
Eating
Electronic cooking
Entertaining
Flowers as food
Food
Food mixes
Frying
Kitchen utensils
Luncheons
Lunches
Meals
Menus
Salads
Sauces
Seasonings
Suppers
Thanksgiving dinners
also names of foods, e.g. Griddle cakes

Anecdotes, facetiae, satire, etc.

Culinary end. W. F. Miksch. il Atlan 213:103-4 Ja '64
Guide to cookbook entertaining. M. B. Bogen. il Atlan 214:107 S '64
If you can read, you can cook. . . P. C. King. il Am Home 67:108 Jl '64

Bibliography

See Cookbooks—Bibliography

Competitions

Crisp salads to eat outdoors. il Pop Gard 15:49 S '64
Grand prize winner; with recipes. il Seventeen 22:172+ My '63
Never overdone; Pillsbury grand national bake-off. il Bsns W p32-3 S 21 '63
Summer harvest of good cooking; prize-winning recipes from fairs and festivals. G. Maddox. il Todays Health 41:40-3+ S '63

Study and teaching

Recipe for raising a good cook. H. Hermann. il Parents Mag 39:55+ Ja '64

Terminology

How to decode a European menu. J. Wechsberg. il Sat R 46:44+ Mr 16 '63
Sweet and hot; a wandering gourmet's guide to Latin American cookery. F. Rufe. Sat R 46:73 O 12 '63

Cereals

Cereal for dessert. C. Claiborne. il N Y Times Mag p 112 O 11 '64
Couscous, cereal a l'africaine. C. Claiborne. il N Y Times Mag p 100 S 15 '63
Three greats with hot cereal. il Bet Hom & Gard 42:59 Ja '64

Cheese

Cheers for cheese. C. Claiborne. il N Y Times Mag p85 N 10 '63
Cheese for every taste. il Good H 157:180 D '63
Cheese it! il McCalls 90:124-5+ Ap '63

COOKERY—Cheese—*Continued*
Cheese, menu mainstay; with recipes. J. Figg. il Suc Farm 61:84-5 Ap '63
Cooking with cream cheese. il Bet Hom & Gard 42:75-6 Jl '64
Great for supper; cheese grits. R. Behnke. Farm J 87:66 S '63
More cheese, please. B. B. Smith. il Parents Mag 38:95+ O '63
Rabbits without ears. C. Claiborne. il N Y Times Mag p 108 N 1 '64
Say cheese. il Am Home 66:46-7+ Je '63
Say cheese. M. J. Engel and L. Stilwill. il Ladies Home J 81:112-14 S '64
Substantial cheese dishes. il Farm J 88:79 Ap '64
See also
Cheesecake

Chocolate

Chocolate cream dream. R. Behnke. il Farm J 87:91 Ap '63
How to paint with chocolate. il Sunset 132: 58-9 Ja '64
Superb chocolate cheese pie. R. Behnke. il Farm J 87:78-9 N '63

Cider

Ah! apple cider! il McCalls 90:134-5+ S '63
Touch of cider. il Bet Hom & Gard 42:94 N '64

Corn meal

Corn, alien and domestic. C. Claiborne. il N Y Times Mag p82 My 3 '64
Make-it-yourself cornmeal mix. R. Behnke. il Farm J 87:101-2 F '63

Cream

Unusual behavior of heavy cream. Sunset 133:210 O '64

Cream, Sour

Old world secret. il McCalls 90:122-3 My '63
Sour cream specials. il Suc Farm 61:58+ Je '63

Eggs

Bologna & eggs pancake style. il McCalls 90: 120+ Mr '63
Egg cook book. E. Alston. il House & Gard 123:151+ Mr '63
Eggs betwixt and between. C. Claiborne. il N Y Times Mag p93 Ap 21 '63
Eggs for lunch or for supper. il Sunset 133: 184+ O '64
Eggs, something to crow about! H. S. Sharpe. il Parents Mag 38:69+ Ap '63
For good eggs. C. Claiborne. il N Y Times Mag p58 Mr 29 '64
How to take advantage of a good egg! il Bet Hom & Gard 41:87 Ap '63
Look and cook; boiled eggs. il Bet Hom & Gard 42:96 Ap '64
Making dessert magic with eggs. il Sunset 132:194-6+ My '64
Matzo brie for brunch. il McCalls 91:118-19+ Mr '64
Shellfish and eggs, and you cook right at the table. il Sunset 130:116-17+ F '63
Surplus of Easter eggs? il Am Home 66:70 Ap '63
These good supper dishes start with hard-cooked eggs. R. Behnke. il Farm J 88:76-7 Ap '64
What to do with Easter's eggs. il Sunset 130:242+ Ap '63
See also
Omelets
Soufflés

Fish

All about fish. il Redbook 120:70-1+ Mr '63
Are you fully acquainted with the anchovy? il Bet Hom & Gard 42:106-7 S '64
Ask your fish man to get you a whole albacore. il Sunset 132:156-7+ Je '64
Bring home a fish. il Sunset 131:60-5 Jl '63
Deep sea delicacies. E. Ward-Hanna. il Ladies Home J 81:72-4 Mr '64
Fancy fish in brown paper; battle plan for the feast. E. Graves. il Life 57:125-6 N 13 '64
Fish & fish mates. M. W. Goodman. il Parents Mag 38:71-4+ Mr '63
Fish and shellfish. il Bet Hom & Gard 42:79-80 Mr '64
Fish dinners from your supermarket shelves. G. Maddox. il Todays Health 41:30-3+ Mr '63
Fish fare for Lent. C. Claiborne. il N Y Times Mag p57 F 9 '64
Fish-in-a-fish: Russian specialty, pirog. il Sunset 133:92-3 O '64
Fish is better with fish; with recipes. C. Claiborne. il N Y Times Mag p52 D 15 '63
Four tuna ideas for Lent. Sunset 130:218 Mr '63
French fish classic. C. Claiborne. il N Y Times Mag p77 Ag 23 '64
Holiday for game: birds and salmon; with recipes. M. Kaytor. il Look 27:108-12 D 3 '63
How to steam-cook a whole fish. il Sunset 132:228 Ap '64
Ideas to open the crab season. Sunset 131: 163 D '63
Investigate the huge new world of seafood cookery. E. Yuasa. il House B 105:204-5+ O '63
It is my firm conviction that sole should never be touched by water. L. Berlowitz. Sunset 130:204 My '63
It's time to watch for shad roe. il Sunset 132:220 Ap '64
Learn how to exploit sea food from the world's masters. E. Gordon. il House B 105:124-7+ Je '63
Mahalia Jackson's Lenten recipe. F. De Knight. il Ebony 18:120+ Mr '63
Make a good loaf better with fruit! meat or tuna loaf. il Bet Hom & Gard 42:84-5 O '64
Mediterranean fish dishes; with recipes. M. Kaytor. il Look 27:64-5 S 10 '63
Mowbray tuna casserole. R. Joseph. Esquire 61:38 Ap '64
New dishes to replace your regular eating habits. G. Maddox. il Todays Health 42: 40-5 F '64
Party-best recipe: shrimp blush. il Seventeen 23:150 Mr '64
Poached scallops on the half shell. il Sunset 132:182 Ap '64
Pretty kettle of fish. M. E. Hoehener. il Good H 158:189 Mr '64
Savory salmon mousse. il N Y Times Mag p 101 S 15 '63
Seafood classics; quick versions. Sunset 131: 214-15 O '63
Seafood for summer lunching. Sunset 132: 178+ Je '64
Setting forth the salmon. C. Claiborne. il N Y Times Mag p41-2 Jl 28 '63
Shellfish; a complete guide to buying and preparing. il Redbook 122:78-81+ Mr '64
Shellfish and eggs, and you cook right at the table. il Sunset 130:116-17+ F '63
Shellfish cook book. C. Claiborne. il House & Gard 125:173+ Mr '64
Shrimp egg rolls. il Good H 157:210 O '63
Some differrent recipes. L. Heinold. il Outdoor Life 131:16+ Ap '63
Southern spring favorites; from the kitchen of the Conrad Aikens. M. Kaytor. il Look 27:64-6 Mr 12 '63
Stars from the sea. il McCalls 91:120-1+ Mr '64
Steamed clams; with recipes. M. Kaytor. il Look 28:50-1 Ag 25 '64
Successful recipes; sea food. il Suc Farm 62:109-10 Ap '64
Susan makes shrimp creole. il Good H 156: 159 F '63
Three ways to go with abalone, but first you must pound it properly. Sunset 133:138 Ag '64
Tricks with tuna. il Suc Farm 61:63-4 S '63
Trout for dinner. il Sunset 130:166+ Je '63
Trout in an almond pool. il Life 56:126-7+ My 22 '64
Trout superlative. H. Botsford. il Field & S 68:48-9+ Mr '64
Two quick main dishes using tuna. Sunset 132:149 F '64
You poach it whole in court bouillon; poached whole salmon. il Sunset 132:174+ Mr '64
See also
Chowder

Flowers

See Flowers as foods

Frogs

Frogs of spring are springing for their lives. B. Heilman. il Sports Illus 18:46-8+ Ap 1 '63

Fruit

A is for apples. B. Behen. il Bet Hom & Gard 42:83 O '64
Adaptable avocado. C. Claiborne. il N Y Times Mag p35 Jl 14 '63
All about apples. il Redbook 120:76-7+ F '63
All about pears. il Redbook 121:82-4+ S '63
Anjou, bosc, and comice; winter pears; with recipes. il Sunset 133:170+ O '64
Apple desserts. il Bet Hom & Gard 41:105-6 O '63
Apricots, and four desserts. Sunset 131:118 Jl '63
Berrytime desserts. il Farm J 88:60 Je '64
Blueberry bounty. il McCalls 91:110-11+ Jl '64
Cherry mix for many uses. R. Behnke and D. Groves. il Farm J 88:48-9 Jl '64
Chicken with cherries! il Bet Hom & Gard 42:98 S '64

COOKERY—Fruit—*Continued*
Citrus desserts. il Bet Hom & Gard 42:67-8 Ja '64
Citrus desserts; with recipes. J. Figg. il Suc Farm 63:90-1 Ja '65
Citrus fruits: updating a Christmas favorite. G. Maddox. il Todays Health 41:38-43 D '63
Color it festive; candied fruits and citron. C. Claiborne. il N Y Times Mag p92 N 29 '64
Cooking with citrus. il Sunset 130:192+ Mr '63
Cooking with juicy gravensteins. Sunset 133: 135 Jl '64
Cooking with wild elderberries. il Sunset 131: 118 Ag '63
Cook's discovery: the West's wild fruits and berries. il Sunset 131:109 Jl '63
Desserts with a citrus flavor. Sunset 132:172 Mr '64
Dried fruit and nut cook book. J. A. Beard. il House & Gard 126:271+ N '64
Experimenting with avocados. Sunset 131:212-13 N '63
Forgotten quince. il Sunset 131:106-9 O '63
Fresh fruit pie should show its face. il Sunset 131:106-7 Ag '63
Fruit for a fresh start; with recipes. il Bet Hom & Gard 42:64-9+ Jl '64
Fruit juice. il McCalls 90:126-7+ My '63
Fruits of summer; enjoy them while you may! with recipes. il Am Home 67:68-9+ Jl '64
Garden on your shelf. il McCalls 92:140-2+ O '64
Have you ever cooked chayote? il Sunset 133: 206+ O '64
Have you tried the new spring apples? il Sunset 130:197-8+ Mr '63
How American fruits and vegetables can be used in foreign dishes; with recipes. G. Maddox. il Todays Health 42:44-9 Ag '64
How good the lemon can be. il McCalls 90: 100-1+ Jl '63
Indians called it ibimi; cranberries. C. Claiborne. il N Y Times Mag p96 O 13 '63
It's September: these fruit marvels are in your market now. il Sunset 133:66-9 S '64
Lemon's tart potential. il N Y Times Mag p92 Mr 15 '64
Love of two oranges and two lemons. Vogue 142:92 N 1 '63
Magic midwinter fruits! with recipes. M. Johnston. il Bet Hom & Gard 43:66-9+ Ja '65
[Month] menus; with recipes. See issues of Sunset
New fruit treat is papaya. il Sunset 132:58-63 F '64
New prune treats; with recipes. N. Nichols. il Farm J 89:65+ Ja '65
Old-fashioned strawberry shortcake. il McCalls 91:54 Jl '64
Our eye is on the apple! M. E. Hoehener. il Good H 158:118 Ja '64
Our pick of 5,000 apple recipes. R. Behnke and D. Groves. il Farm J 87:86+ O '63
Peach with no fuzz. Sunset 131:120-1 Jl '63
Pear specialties from good country cooks; with recipes. D. Groves. il Farm J 88: 65+ S '64
Pears made perfect. C. Claiborne. il N Y Times Mag p64+ Je 9 '63
Peerless pear. il McCalls 90:132-3+ S '63
Plums: the outsides and insides. il Sunset 133:58-63 Jl '64
Ripe for berries. E. Ward-Hanna. il Ladies Home J 81:104-5+ Je '64
Saucy cranberry. il McCalls 91:128-30+ D '63
Signs of summer: fresh fruits and berries. G. Maddox. il Todays Health 41:42-5+ Je '63
Something green for winter; avocados. N. Ickeringill. il N Y Times Mag p56 Ja 19 '64
Summer berry delights. Sunset 131:122 Ag '63
Summer drink and dessert staple: lemons; with recipes. M. Kaytor. il Look 27:48-51 Jl 30 '63
Strawberry desserts. il Bet Hom & Gard 42: 89-90 Je '64
Strawberry shortcake. B. M. Stover. il Parents Mag 39:66 Je '64
Strawberry spectacular. il Suc Farm 61:52-3 Je '63
Summer is berry nice. B. B. Smith. il Parents Mag 39:63-5+ Je '64
Susan makes a melon boat salad! il Good H 158:137 Je '64
Sweet ways with lemons. Am Home 66:66-7 S '63
Taste of the pomegranate. C. Claiborne. il N Y Times Mag p58 Ag 30 '64
Top apple desserts; with recipes. B. C. Shelton and B. Davenport. il Farm J 88:80-1 O '64
Top banana. il McCalls 91:138-9+ My '64
Touch of the grape. C. Claiborne. il N Y Times Mag p64+ S 22 '63
While we have fresh apricots. Sunset 132:173 Je '64
Winter experiments with bananas. il Sunset 132:206+ Mr '64
With autumn's melon bonanza. Sunset 131: 152 S '63
See also
Fruit, Dried

Game

Big-game smoked sausage. M. Sinclair. il Outdoor Life 134:10-11 N '64
Bringing home the hippo; African wildlife as food. E. Huxley. il N Y Times Mag p 134-7 N 29 '64
Deerstalker's reward. C. Claiborne. il N Y Times Mag p96 O 4 '64
Holiday for game; birds and salmon; with recipes. M. Kaytor. il Look 27:108-12 D 3 '63
How to cook a duck. R. Coykendall. il Field & S 69:44-5+ N '64
Lord love a duck. R. Bailey. il Outdoor Life 135:12+ Ja '65
Seasonal wild game offers many exotic dishes for the holidays. G. Maddox. il Todays Health 42:50-5 D '64
Six ways to give thanks with game. W. Bar-Illan. il Ladies Home J 81:144-6+ N '64
Sportman's cook book. J. A. Beard. il House & Gard 126:219+ O '64
When the hunter comes home with venison. Sunset 131:210-11 O '63
Wild game, its care and cooking. F. Fortenberry. il Suc Farm 61:81 N '63

Honey

Just add a little honey. Sunset 130:214 Ap '63

Leftovers

Good eating with leftover turkey. Am Home 67:78 N '64
Turkey's her meat; with recipes; ed. by N. Nichols. J. Stone. il Farm J 87:80+ N '63

Meat

Battle plan for the feast; a royal pork roast for wintertime. E. Graves. Life 57: 105-6 D 18 '64
Battle plan for the feast; a steaming brew of beef and beer. E. Graves. il Life 58:87-8 Ja 29 '65
Battle plan for the feast; pot-au-feu. E. Graves. il Life 57:151-2 S 18 '64
Beef a-bubble. il Life 56:92-3+ Je 26 '64
Beef balls Stroganoff with oven-steamed rice. il McCalls 91:146 Ag '64
Beef, translated from the Russian. C. Claiborne. il N Y Times Mag p26 S 1 '63
Benzo(a)pyrene and other polynuclear hydrocarbons in charcoal-broiled meat. W. Lijinsky and P. Shubik. bibliog il Science 145:53-5 Jl 3 '64
Best barbecued steak; with recipes. il Pop Gard 16:67 Ja '65
Better homes & gardens prize tested recipes. il Bet Hom & Gard 41:85-6 S '63
Chili con carne pie. R. Behnke. il Farm J 88:88 Mr '64
Cooking with soup. il Bet Hom & Gard 42:87-8 Ap '64
Coquettish croquettes. il McCalls 92:138-9+ O '64
Cordon bleu italien. D. J. Robinson. il Ebony 18:144+ My '63
Eggplant and lamb together. Sunset 131:254 O '63
Follow-ups for leg of lamb. Sunset 130:179 Ap '63
For the best barbecue ever, feature ribs. J. Figg. il Suc Farm 62:84-5 S '64
For the lunch box; meat and vegetable pasties. il Sunset 131:244+ O '63
Giant party burger for eight! with recipes. il Seventeen 22:158-9+ My '63
Greatest barbecued ribs ever! M. Johnston. il Bet Hom & Gard 41:78-9+ Je '63
Ham for Easter. il Ebony 19:136+ Mr '64
Hamburger, above and beyond. C. Claiborne. il N Y Times Mag p44 Ag 2 '64
Hamburger cook book. P. Harvey. il House & Gard 127:137+ Ja '65
Hamburgers plain and fancy. il Pop Gard 15: 46 Mr '64
Happy marriage; ham in crust with port wine sauce. il McCalls 92:86 D '64
He likes to cook. G. Koenigsberger. il Bet Hom & Gard 41:80 Je '63
Herbs and spices: the secret key to flavor; with recipes. V. T. Habeeb. il Am Home 66:42-3+ Mr '63

COOKERY—Meat—*Continued*
Hot corned-beef barbecues. il Good H 158: 184 Ap '64
Hot dog specials. il Bet Hom & Gard 42:89-90 Je '64
How to carve and garnish filet of beef. il House & Gard 123:36-7 Je '63
How to corn your own beef or pork. Sunset 130:158+ F '63
How to make Hawaiian jerky. il Sunset 130:191 Je '63
If dinner guests are coming and your time is short. il Sunset 132:195-7 Mr '64
Imperial crown roast of pork. il Ebony 19:104+ Ja '64
It's an opera sandwich; Scandinavian hamburger. il Sunset 131:235 N '63
Just put beef in vinegar awhile; sauerbraten. Sunset 132:100 Ja '64
Kitchen adventures with pork. il Ebony 19: 162+ O '64
Lamb Moroccan style. il Look 27:64-5 D 17 '63
Lambs of spring. il McCalls 91:152-3 Ap '64
Larding and barding. il House & Gard 126: 152+ O '64
Lionizing lamb. C. Claiborne. il N Y Times Mag p52 Ja 24 '65
Long lazy country weekend; with recipes. S. Kirtland and others. il Look 28:64-5 Ja 14 '64
M-M-M bacon. il McCalls 91:122-3+ F '64
Make a good loaf better with fruit! meat or tuna loaf. il Bet Hom & Gard 42:84-5 O '64
Make meat loaf. J. Figg. il Suc Farm 62:94-5 Ja '64
Meal in one. il McCalls 91:94-5+ Ja '64
Meat-ball pizzas. il Good H 156:160 Je '63
Meat kabobs. il Bet Hom & Gard 42:75-6 Jl '64
Meat loaves. il Bet Hom & Gard 42:87-8 My '64
Meaty main dishes men will like. il Farm J 88:58-9+ Je '64
Mixer-made meat loaf and other ground beef dishes; with recipes. L. W. Gilliam. il Farm J 88:79 N '64
My own cookbook: hamburgers. B. M. Stover. il Parents Mag 39:60 My '64
New roles for hot dogs and hamburgers. il Redbook 121:68-9+ Ag '63
New-style pork loin roasts. N. Nichols. il Farm J 88:90-2 F '64
Not so humble meat loaf. C. Claiborne. il N Y Times Mag p86 O 27 '63
One rib for two; prime rib of beef. il Sunset 132:108-9 Mr '64
Open a can of ham. il McCalls 90:106-7+ Ag '63
Our four best burgers! M. Johnston. il Bet Hom & Gard 42:74-5+ My '64
Peasant dish fit for a king; with recipes. C. Claiborne. il N Y Times Mag p 108 N 17 '63
Picnics with pâté. C. Claiborne. il N Y Times Mag p45 Ag 16 '64
Pork chop treats. il Bet Hom & Gard 41: 105-6 O '63
Pork in a pie. C. Claiborne. il N Y Times Mag p65 Ja 17 '65
Pot roast cook book. J. A. Beard. il House & Gard 125:123+ Ja '64
Rack of lamb it's both easy and elegant. il Sunset 132:234+ My '64
Ready-carved lamb roast. il Farm J 87:83 O '63
Roast leg of lamb; Irish lamb stew. il Bet Hom & Gard 41:78 Ap '63
Roast specialties. il Bet Hom & Gard 41: 91-2 F '63
Roast with dividends. E. Ward-Hanna. il Ladies Home J 81:72+ Ap '64
Roasting. il House & Gard 124:237-9 O '63
Sauce up lamb for spring. il Bet Hom & Gard 42:112-13 Ap '64
Sausage cook book. J. A. Beard. il House & Gard 123:175+ Ap '63
Sausage! some like it hot. M. Johnston. il Bet Hom & Gard 42:76-81 S '64
Savory pork; with recipes. il Redbook 123: 80-1+ O '64
Savory ways with meat. il Bet Hom & Gard 43:79-80 Ja '65
She is about to make meat rolls. il Sunset 133:117 Jl '64
Simmer till tender. il McCalls 90:114-15+ Mr '63
Six flavorful ways to serve pork. B. G. La Roche. il Farm J 89:66-8 Ja '65
Sizzling kabobs. il Pop Gard 16:44-5 F '65
Some favorite ground beef ideas. Sunset 130: 230+ Ap '63
Spring is here and lamb's on the table! B. Wason. il Am Home 66:54-5+ Ap '63
Spring lamb knows no season. C. Claiborne. il N Y Times Mag p 122+ O 6 '63
Straight from the shoulder; with recipes. il Redbook 124:56-8+ Ja '65
Strike a bargain with beef. il Good H 158: 114-30 My '64
Successful recipes. il Suc Farm 62:113-14 Mr '64
Successful recipes; burgers and hot dogs. il Suc Farm 62:57-8 Jl '64
Table-ready meats. il Bet Hom & Gard 41: 71-2 Jl '63
There's meat and spinach inside. il Sunset 130:238 Ap '63
There's more to lamb than a leg or a chop. il Am Home 67:58+ Ap '64
Tops in chops. il McCalls 90:130-1+ S '63
Tunisian breast of veal. F. DeKnight. il Ebony 18:104+ F '63
Two classic meat dishes served cold. il Sunset 131:114+ Ag '63
Variety meats cookbook; with recipes. J. Olsen. il Parents Mag 38:81+ F '63
Veal continental style; with recipes. M. Kaytor. il Look 28:76-7 O 20 '64
Ways to cook smoked pork. il Sunset 133:164+ S '64
We love sausage when it sizzles. il McCalls 91:106-7+ S '64
With ribs you don't need to be subtle. Sunset 133:134+ Ag '64
Worldly meatball. il McCalls 92:134-5+ O '64
Yuletide meats. il Bet Hom & Gard 42:89-90 D '64

See also
Barbecue cookery
Cookery—Game
Hash
Meat
Stew

Mocha

Making the most of mocha. J. Hewitt. il N Y Times Mag p 100 Je 7 '64

Mushrooms

Agaricus campestris. C. Claiborne. il N Y Times Mag p36 F 2 '64
Cooking with mushrooms. il Bet Hom & Gard 42:67-8 Ja '64
In the West mushrooms are mushrooming. il Sunset 133:188-90+ O '64

Nuts

Cookies with macadamias. Sunset 133:128 Jl '64
Cook's discovery: chestnut flour. Sunset 131: 132 D '63
Dried fruit and nut cook book. J. A. Beard. il House & Gard 126:271+ N '64
Harvest of nut treats. C. Claiborne. il N Y Times Mag p 120 O 18 '64
Nut like no other. C. Claiborne. il N Y Times Mag p83 Ap 19 '64

Poultry

As the Chinese pot roast a duck. il Sunset 132:122 F '64
Ballottines and galantines. il House & Gard 124:182-3 D '63
Best-dressed bird. il McCalls 91:152-3+ N '63
Budget dinners. il Ebony 19:166+ Ap '64
Chicken around the world. il Sunset 131:216-19 O '63
Chicken cacciatore. il Ebony 19:162+ N '63
Chicken casseroles. il Suc Farm 61:90+ Ap '63
Chicken choices. il Bet Hom & Gard 42:91-2 S '64
Chicken hot off the grill. il Pop Gard 15:46 Ap '64
Chicken noodle casserole. D. J. Robinson. il Ebony 18:142+ Je '63
Chicken Véronique. il Bet Hom & Gard 41: 66 Jl '63
Chicken with cherries. il Bet Hom & Gard 42:98 S '64
For a big crowd, a galantine is elegant and not expensive. il Sunset 130:200+ My '63
Freeze turkey in quarters. B. G. LaRoche. il Farm J 88:65 Ja '64
Glass conserves heat, flavor, and aroma; with recipes. il Sunset 133:241-2+ O '64
Golden succulent turkey and smooth gravy. Am Home 66:68-9 N '63
Happy marriage; roast cornish hens with walnut stuffing. il McCalls 92:60 N '64
Holiday bird. C. Claiborne. il N Y Times Mag p 110 N 1 '64
If you forget to thaw the chicken. Sunset 130:183 Je '63
Let's talk turkey! il Bet Hom & Gard 42: 84-5 D '64
Little hens on a spit; Rock Cornish game hens. E. Graves. il Life 57:80-4 Ag 21 '64
Long lazy country weekend; with recipes. S. Kirtland and others. il Look 28:64-5 Ja 14 '64

COOKERY—Poultry—*Continued*
Meal in itself. C. Claiborne. il N Y Times Mag p 150 Ap 7 '63
Rare case of the parts being greater than the whole. P. Peck. il House B 106:180-1+ Ap '64
Ready to try a new stuffing? il Sunset 131: 238 N '63
Roasting. il House & Gard 124:237-9 O '63
Stuffings for birds. il Bet Hom & Gard 41:73-4 D '63
Successful recipes. il Suc Farm 62:83-4 My '64
These recipes make chicken a new dish. G. Maddox. il Todays Health 43:50-5 Ja '65
They're delicate, delicious; Rock Cornish game hens. il Sunset 131:204+ O '63
Try some choice chicken recipes. B. Pierson. il Farm J 88:64+ S '64
Turkey any time. J. Figg. il Suc Farm 61:70-1 My '63
Turkey's her meat; with recipes; ed. by N. Nichols. J. Stone. il Farm J 87:80+ N '63
Two classic turkey stuffings; with recipes. M. Kaytor. il Look 28:38-9 D 29 '64
Up-dated directions for perfect roast turkey. il Farm J 87:85 N '63
Winning chicken recipes. Farm J 87:60 Ag '63
Wonderful double-crust chicken pie. N. Nichols. il Farm J 87:82 My '63

Rhubarb

Going all out with rhubarb. il Sunset 132: 132 F '64
Look and cook. il Bet Home & Gard 41:114B Ap '63
Rhubarb desserts. il Suc Farm 61:74+ My '63

Rice

For salad days, rice. J. Hewitt. il N Y Times Mag p45 My 31 '64
Oven-to-table rice dishes. R. Behnke. il Farm J 88:66-7 Ja '64
Pantry food for special diet needs. il Parents Mag 39:40+ Mr '64
Pup, pup, pup. S. Weeks. il Atlan 212:117-18 Jl '63
Rice. il McCalls 90:116-17+ Mr '63
Rice specialties. il Bet Hom & Gard 41:83-4 Ap '63
Right with rice! il Bet Hom & Gard 42:108 N '64
Ways with rice. il Suc Farm 61:99-100 Mr '63

Snails

Conch ain't got no bone. J. Rainat. il Motor B 112:34+ D '63

Vegetables

Add a touch of rubies; peppers. il McCalls 90:108-9+ Ag '63
All about beans. il Redbook 122:66-7+ F '64
Artful artichoke. il McCalls 90:118-19+ Mr '63
Artichokes: the domesticated thistles; with recipes. M. Kaytor. il Look 28:60-1 Ap 7 '64
Artichokes the Portuguese way. il Sunset 132:152 F '64
Ask for the mild summer squashes. Sunset 132:212-14 My '64
Asparagus specials. il Suc Farm 61:73-4 My '63
Beans; all kinds. il Bet Hom & Gard 42: 101-2 N '64
Best asparagus of the year is in your market now. il Sunset 132:126-7 My '64
Brussels sprouts italiano. il Ebony 18:120+ Jl '63
Butter-steaming. il Sunset 131:170+ N '63
Butter-steaming your spring vegetables. il Sunset 132:220+ My '64
Celebration of celery. C. Claiborne. il N Y Times Mag p 149 Ap 7 '63
Cooked lettuce is a surprise. Sunset 132:218 Mr '64
Corn! with recipes. il Bet Hom & Gard 42:86-7 Je '64
Corn with the fresh cob flavor. Sunset 133: 158 S '64
Delectable root. il N Y Times Mag p86 N 10 '63
Eggplant and lamb together. Sunset 131:254 O '63
For a festive fall. il McCalls 92:136-7+ N '64
Forty-four ways to enjoy beans. A. C. Jubb. il Flower Grower 51:22-4 Jl '64
Four ways with puree; with recipes. C. Claiborne. il N Y Times Mag p41 Ja 3 '65
Fresh vegetables bring spring tonic to the table. G. Maddox. il Todays Health 42:22-7 Mr '64
Grand ways with green beans. il Bet Hom & Gard 41:100-1 O '63
Green bells are so good! bell peppers. S. Krivenko. Flower Grower 50:6+ S '63
Happy marriage: asparagus with hollandaise. il McCalls 91:38 Je '64
Heat-and-eat potato dishes from the freezer; with recipes. D. Groves. il Farm J 88:82-4 O '64
Here are some unusual ways to use instant potatoes. Sunset 130:137-8 F '63
How American fruits and vegetables can be used in foreign dishes; with recipes. G. Maddox. il Todays Health 42:44-9 Ag '64
How to slice, dice, boil, broil, stuff, puff, wash, squash, cream, steam, prepare and care for vegetables. il Am Home 67:54-5+ Ap '64
If spinach is your dish. Sunset 132:178 Ap '64
Instead of the red, try the green. Sunset 131: 140 Ag '63
International favorite: eggplant. il McCalls 90:136-7+ S '63
Is sauerkraut your problem? Sunset 131:202 O '63
Jamaican stuffs a pumpkin. il Sunset 133:166 O '64
Just stuff cheese into chiles. il Sunset 132: 212+ Je '64
Make it with packaged potatoes. Am Home 67:78 Ap '64
No humdrum vegetables at her house! ed. by R. Behnke. P. Williams. il Farm J 88:90-1+ Mr '64
Non-cliche greenery. Vogue 142:122 O 1 '63
Not only on Saturday; baked beans. C. Claiborne. il N Y Times Mag p82 Ap 12 '64
Onions; with recipes. M. Kaytor. il Look 27: 64+ O 22 '63
Other ways to use pumpkin. il Sunset 133: 179-80 N '64
Pepper plenty. J. Hewitt. il N Y Times Mag p 112+ S 13 '64
Prime time for tomatoes. C. Claiborne. il N Y Times Mag p52 Ag 9 '64
Pudding in the pumpkin shell. il Sunset 131: 184 O '63
Pumpkin desserts. il Bet Hom & Gard 42:87-8 O '64
Rose among roots; with recipes. C. Claiborne. il N Y Times Mag p44 Je 21 '64
Sauce is in the artichoke. il Sunset 130:186-7 Mr '63
Seeing vegetables in a new light; with recipes. il Redbook 123:80-1+ S '64
September is prime tomato time; with recipes. il Sunset 133:134-6+ S '64
Serve versatile sweet potatoes; with recipes. B. Pierson. il Farm J 88:72+ N '64
Spinach surprises. il McCalls 90:128-9+ Ap '63
Spring ways with vegetables. il Bet Hom & Gard 42:106-7 Ap '64
Squash. W. Bar-Illan. il Ladies Home J 81: 146-7+ O '64
Successful recipes; vegetables. il Suc Farm 62:83-4 Ag '64
Summer vegetable harvest. J. Figg. il Suc Farm 61:50-1 Jl '63
This is turnips? il Bet Hom & Gard 42:100+ O '64
This summer, explore new ways to cook vegetables. P. Peck. il House B 105:118-19+ Je '63
Tomato cook book. B. Wason. House & Gard 126:121+ Ag '64
Tomato specials. il Bet Hom & Gard 41:81-2 Ag '63
Tomatoes are in. il McCalls 91:108-9+ Jl '64
Two potato surprises. il Sunset 131:208 N '63
Vegetable ideas for Christmas dinner. Sunset 131:140 D '63
Vegetable specials. il Bet Hom & Gard 41: 89-90 Je '63; 42:79-80 Mr '64
Vegetables that sing of spring. L. Shattuck. il Parents Mag 39:81+ Ap '64
Vegetables with flair. W. Bar-Illan. il Ladies Home J 82:94-6 Ja '65
Vegetables you bake in the oven. Sunset 132:86 Ja '64
Ways with onions. il Suc Farm 61:75-6 O '63
Who says potatoes have to be dull! with recipes. il Redbook 123:78-9+ O '64
Zucchini: stuffed, layered, scrambled. Sunset 131:134-5 S '63
See also
Stew

Wine

Cooking with wine. il Am Home 66:56+ O '63
Wine tasters' dinner; with recipes. M. Kaytor. il Look 27:52-5 Jl 2 '63

COOKERY, American
Christmas on Nantucket; with recipes. J. Peter and M. Kaytor. il Look 28:74-5 D 15 '64
Civil war; what cooked? P. K. Brooks. il Am Home 66:64+ My '63

COOKERY, American—*Continued*
Cooking offered a glorious way to serve God; Shaker cookery, with recipes. il Look 28:58-9 D 1 '64
Dutch treat! il Am Home 66:54+ Ja '63
Festive foods from an early American kitchen. il Redbook 122:70-1+ D '63
Fill yourself up, clean your plate; Pennsylvania Dutch people; with recipes. A. Robertson. il Am Heritage 15:56-66+ Ap '64
Food from the 49th. il McCalls 90:130-1+ Ap '63
Heritage recipes, then and now. B. M. Stover. il Parents Mag 40:61+ Ja '65
Home cooking on the range. N. C. Wood. il Ladies Home J 80:74-7+ Je '63
Living is way out in Oklahoma; with recipes. J. Peter and M. Kaytor. il Look 27:60-1 O 8 '63
O.K. baby, it's foodsville. il Esquire 59:72-3 My '63
Out of our past; excerpts from American heritage cookbook. N. Ickeringill. il N Y Times Mag p 111-12 S 27 '64
Southwest cook book. H. E. Brown. il House & Gard 124:129+ Ag '63
Touch of Texas. il McCalls 90:102-4 Jl '63
What ever happened to American cooking? E. Perenyi. il Sat Eve Post 236:68-70 Je 15 '63
Yankee gumbo. C. Claiborne. il N Y Times Mag p79 My 26 '63
COOKERY, Arabian
Castle in the casbah; Moorish York castle, Tangier, Morocco; with recipes. S. Kirtland and others. il Look 28:56-8 Ja 28 '64
These buns are Arab bread. il Sunset 130:164 Je '63
COOKERY, Austrian
Desserts with a Viennese accent. C. Claiborne. il N Y Times Mag p39 D 20 '64
Fond food memories of old Vienna. M. E. Hoehener. Good H 156:140 F '63
COOKERY, Bahamian
Conch ain't got no bone. J. Rainat. il Motor B 112:34+ D '63
COOKERY, Basque
Christmas in Euzkaldunak. D. Taylor. il Todays Health 42:18-19+ D '64
COOKERY, Bavarian
Hearty bar lunch: businessman's treats at Zum Zum, Pan American building; with recipes. M. Kaytor. il Look 28:38-9 Ag 11 '64
COOKERY, Belgian
Belgium's best at your beck and call. M. E. Hoehener. il Good H 157:208 O '63
COOKERY, Chinese
Chicken wings and lamb riblets. Sunset 130:130 F '63
Chinese cooking, an easier approach. Sunset 130:246+ My '63
Chinese have a wonderful way with food. N. C. Wood. il Ladies Home J 80:78-9+ My '63
Holiday handbook of Chinese cooking. M. Ouei. il Holiday 33:125-9 F '63
How the Chinese shun calories. Sunset 132:238 My '64
How to give a dinner party in Chinese. H. K. Kingman. il House & Gard 125:108-11+ Ja '64
How you can make Chinese steam buns. il Sunset 132:188+ Mr '64
Put a dragon in your galley; with recipes. E. L. Slepian. il Motor B 115:88-91+ Ja '65
COOKERY, Danish
Caloric Copenhagen. M. Connelly. il Sat R 46:47-8+ Ap 13 '63
When Danes want to eat, who cares for calories? R. W. Wells. il Sat Eve Post 236:52-4 Je 8 '63
COOKERY, Dutch
Dutch Crhistmas wreath. il Sunset 131:159 D '63
There's cabbage in Hunter's pudding. il Sunset 133:196 N '64
COOKERY, English
Good English food; photographs. M. Kaytor. Look 27:58-9+ F 12 '63
Hearty British food. E. Ward-Hanna. il Ladies Home J 81:74-6 Ja '64
Not just fish 'n' chips. D. Gunston. Travel 121:63-5 F '64
COOKERY, European
Men enjoy hearty dishes of foreign origin. G. Maddox. il Todays Health 42:38-43 Ja '64
COOKERY, Finnish
Food for September's hungers at Chavez ravine or Candlestick; Finnish meat pies (lihakukko) il Sunset 133:60-1 S '64
Summery fare from Finland. M. E. Hoehener. Good H 156:180 My '63
COOKERY, Foreign. See Cookery, International
COOKERY, French
Ballottines and galantines. il House & Gard 124:182-3 D '63
Classic food of France; with photographs by Irving Penn, and recipes. M. Kaytor. Look 27:56-64 My 7 '63
Cordon bleu italien. D. J. Robinson. il Ebony 18:144+ My '63
Everyone's in the kitchen with Julia. L. H. Lapham. il Sat Eve Post 237:20-1 Ag 8 '64
French fish classic. C. Claiborne. il N Y Times Mag p77 Ag 23 '64
Gifts from abroad; with recipes. C. Claiborne. il N Y Times Mag p88 Ap 5 '64
Going to Maxim's. S. Robinson. il McCalls 91:116-17+ Mr '64
Hors d'oeuvres idea. P. Peck. il House B 105:86-7+ Jl '63
Peasant dish fit for a king; with recipes. C. Claiborne. il N Y Times Mag p 108 N 17 '63
Profiles; Mme M. L. Point. J. Wechsberg. New Yorker 39:57-8+ O 5 '63
Provençal cook book. J. A. Beard. il House & Gard 125:193+ My '64
Quiche Lorraine: French main-dish pie; with recipes. M. Kaytor. il Look 28:46-7 S 22 '64
COOKERY, German
German cooking; with recipes. R. W. Wells. il Sat Eve Post 236:64-6 My 4 '63
Germans call it a sandtorte. il Sunset 131:98 Ag '63
COOKERY, Greek
Greece: get your ambrosia here. R. Joseph. il Esquire 61:66-7+ Je '64
These are Greek Easter cookies; koulourakia. il Sunset 132:214 Mr '64
You start with ground walnuts; karidopita. il Sunset 132:198+ Ap '64
COOKERY, Haitian
Food heritage from Haiti. M. E. Hoehener. Good H 156:156 Mr '63
COOKERY, Hawaiian
Hawaiian cook book. H. E. Brown. il House & Gard 126:103-8 Jl '64
Hawaiian idea, fresh coconut waffles. il Sunset 130:174 Mr '63
How to make Hawaiian jerky. il Sunset 130:191 Je '63
New pie idea from Hawaii. il Sunset 130:241 Ap '63
COOKERY, Hungarian
Cream-of-the-crop from Hungary. M. E. Hoehener. il Good H 157:150 Ag '63
COOKERY, Indian (East Indian)
Indian cook book. W. Clifford. il House & Gard 126:197+ S '64
COOKERY, Indonesian
Dutch treat: taste acquired by retired Dutch East Indian colonists; with recipes using American substitutes. M. Kaytor. il Look 28:82-3+ N 3 '64
Here's a cooking adventure to try on guests. il Sunset 130:192+ My '63
Taste of romance; foods of Indonesia. il McCalls 91:112-14+ Jl '64
COOKERY, International
American cooking is going international; with recipes. G. Maddox. il Todays Health 41:38-41+ F '63
Come with us on a cookbook tour! il Good H 158:96-112+ Ap '64
Foods with a foreign flavor. M. E. Hoehener. See issues of Good housekeeping
How American fruits and vegetables can be used in foreign dishes; with recipes. G. Maddox. il Todays Health 42:44-9 Ag '64
Hungry teen-ager's guide to the fair; with recipes. il Seventeen 23:114-15+ F '64
One world of many tastes; Cookbook of the United Nations. C. Claiborne. il N Y Times Mag p 102 O 25 '64
Recipe imports. il Bet Hom & Gard 41:89-90 Mr '63
Round-the-world dinners. A. Wartenberg. il Parents Mag 38:81-4+ S '63
Santa opens up with a world full of goodies; with recipes. il Am Home 67:54-5+ D '64
Select circle of prize pies. Good H 157:220 N '63
Taste of the fair; with recipes. M. Kaytor. il Look 28:104-5 F 11 '64
You can cook like international chefs. B. M. Stover. il Parents Mag 39:71+ O '64
COOKERY, Italian
Change-of-pace Italian foods. M. E. Hoehener. Good H 158:176 My '64
Easter in Italy; the reverent festival. G. Maddox. il Todays Health 41:40-3+ Ap '63
For any holiday meal except Christmas dinner; osso buco. il Sunset 133:104-6+ D '64
From acini to ziti. C. Claiborne. il N Y Times Mag p89 Ap 26 '64
From northern Italy to western America; cannelloni and manicotti. il Sunset 130:180-2+ Ap '63

COOKERY, Italian—*Continued*
Here's a Sicilian antipasto; caponata, a Mediterranean eggplant dish. Sunset 133:122 D '64
Italian provincial. il McCalls 91:150-1+ Ap '64
Pizza party for the college crowd. V. Stanton. il House B 105:156-7+ D '63
Rare white truffle. N. Barber. Holiday 35:142+ Je '64
Saltimbocca: you make it in rolls or in layers. il Sunset 133:196 O '64
Show business right at the table. il Sunset 132:118-19 My '64
Under the broiler, tetrazzini. il Sunset 132:150-1 F '64
When in Rome. . . portfolio of pastas. N. C. Wood. il Ladies Home J 80:74-8+ Ja '63

COOKERY, Jamaican
Celebrated cookery of Miss Molly Maloney; seven Jamaican menus, fourteen recipes. il Vogue 141:56-7+ Mr 1 '63
Jamaican stuffs a pumpkin. il Sunset 133:166 O '64

COOKERY, Japanese
Discover tempura: a non-greasy way of frying in deep fat. E. Gordon and E. Yuasa. il House B 105:126-7+ F '63
Entertain with tempura. T. Morimoto. il Am Home 67:60-2 Ja '64
Investigate the huge new world of seafood cookery. E. Yuasa. il House B 105:204-5+ O '63
Japanese way with charcoal. C. Claiborne. il N Y Times Mag p25 Jl 7 '63
Learn how to exploit sea food from the world's masters. E. Gordon. il House B 105:124-7+ Je '63
Real inside story on sukiyaki. E. Yuasa. il House B 105:156-7+ Ap '63
Sushi picnic with three kinds of sushi. il Sunset 133:198+ O '64
Taste for tempura. C. Claiborne. il N Y Times Mag p90 Mr 15 '64
Tempura in the patio. il Sunset 133:60-3 Ag '64
Try your hand with tofu. Sunset 132:257-8 My '64

COOKERY, Jewish
For Hanukkah, the festival of lights: with recipes. il Am Home 67:24 D '64
Jewish cooking; with recipes. S. Schur. il Sat Eve Post 236:64-6 F 16 '63
Matzo brie for brunch. il McCalls 91:118-19+ Mr '64

COOKERY, Latin American
New York's Spanish restaurants. P. S. Feibleman. il Holiday 34:104-5+ D '63
Sweet and hot; a wandering gourmet's guide to Latin American cookery. F. Rufe. Sat R 46:73 O 12 '63

COOKERY, Lenten. See Lenten menus

COOKERY, Marine
Building your galley. F. M. Paulson. il Field & S 68:74-8 Ag '63
Cooking to windward. M. Bartlett. il Yachting 113:43-5+ F '63
Feasting afloat. E. Ward-Hanna. il Ladies Home J 80:74-6 Jl '63
Foods afloat. F. M. Paulson. il Field & S 68:94-6 S '63
Galley guide for the helpless male. B. Robinson. Yachting 113:56+ Je '63
Meals afloat. J. A. Emmett. il Outdoor Life 134:88-9+ Ag '64
On-the-move cook book. B. Edgar. il House & Gard 123:141+ Je '63
Put a dragon in your galley; with recipes. E. L. Slepian. il Motor B 115:88-91+ Ja '65
Yachting interviews; ed. by M. Wiley. H. Adams. il Yachting 115:66-7+ Je '64
Your buying guide for blue-water cruising. R. P. Kingett. il Motor B 114:44-5+ N '64

COOKERY, Mediterranean
Pizza, Riviera style: pissaladiere. C. Claiborne. il N Y Times Mag p42 F 23 '64

COOKERY, Mexican
Cooking of Mexico. il Sunset 132:94-9+ Je '64
Eating is interesting in Baja. il Sunset 131:191+ N '63
For any holiday meal except Christmas dinner; menudo. il Sunset 133:104-6+ D '64
Mexican main dish sandwich. il Sunset 130:176 Ap '63
Never too hot for chili. C. Claiborne. il N Y Times Mag p50 Ag 11 '63
Pile high the tostadas. il Sunset 130:92-3 Je '63
Travel well. E. N. Dye. Travel 123:55-6 Ja '65

COOKERY, Middle Eastern
Middle East cook book. M. Waldo. il House & Gard 123:133-8 F '63

COOKERY, Moroccan
Castle in the casbah; Moorish York castle, Tangier, Morocco; with recipes. S. Kirtland and others. il Look 28:56-8 Ja 28 '64
Here's what goes into cous-cous. il Sunset 130:249 Ap '63

COOKERY, Near Eastern
Introduction to yogurt. Sunset 130:210-12 My '63

COOKERY, Norwegian
Five delicious dishes from Norway. M. E. Hoehener. Good H 157:150 Jl '63
Fromage for dessert; with recipes. il Sunset 130:186+ Ap '63

COOKERY, Oriental
From China, Japan, Indonesia, and the Philippines; appetizer ideas for New Year's. il Sunset 134:92-3 Ja '65
Partying the oriental way. il Good H 156:118-21+ Mr '63
See also
Cookery, Chinese

COOKERY, Ornamental
Butter bird in nest. il Good H 157:220 D '63
Cookie ballet. il Redbook 122:52-5+ D '63
Easter breads. il Bet Hom & Gard 41:83-4 Ap '63
Elf inn. il Good H 157:84-5+ D '63
Feast your eyes. M. Johnston. il Bet Hom & Gard 41:74-7+ Ap '63
February treats: excerpts from Ebony cookbook, by F. DeKnight. il Ebony 19:118+ F '64
Halloween treat for spooks and goblins. il Pop Gard 14:56 S '63
Have a taste of golden Christmas tree bread. il Sunset 133:54-7 D '64
Holiday snowman. il Good H 157:214 D '63
How to keep a party log. il House & Gard 125:112-17 F '64
Kids' own cake. il McCalls 92:96-7+ Ja '65
Let's celebrate! il Good H 158:108-23 F '64
Paper-doll cookies. L. Stilwill. il Ladies Home J 81:131-2+ Ap '64
Ring tree is a stack of cooky circles. il Sunset 131:66-7 D '63
Try these for extra sparkle; holiday look to simplest foods. il McCalls 91:148 D '63
When the ladies come for luncheon; with recipes. V. T. Habeeb. il Am Home 66:56-8+ Ap '63
See also
Icings

COOKERY, Outdoor
Beach bake. B. M. Stover. il Parents Mag 38:71+ Je '63
Casseroles to cook outdoors; with recipes. il Pop Gard 15:92 Jl '64
Come-and-get-it family picnics. B. M. Stover. il Parents Mag 39:61+ Jl '64
Cooking kits. T. Trueblood. il Field & S 68:16+ F '64
Cooking on the outside (crying on the inside) S. Delaplane. Am Home 67:7 My '64
Cookout foods. il Suc Farm 61:55-6 Jl '63
Cookout tips from teen-agers. G. Maddox. il Todays Health 41:34-7+ My '63
Great American cookout. D. Wharton. Read Digest 82:25-6+ Je '63
Handy meat smoker; Abu smoke box. C. Conley. il Field & S 68:77 D '63
Heat's on; recipes and menus of celebrities, with photographs by V. Valaitis and H. Ries. Sat Eve Post 237:20-7 Je 6 '64
Here are grand plans for the grand picnic. Sunset 131:124+ Ag '63
Indian summer cookout. J. Figg. il Suc Farm 61:60-1 S '63
Latest in covered cooking. il Bet Hom & Gard 41:92-3 Je '63
On-the-move cook book. B. Edgar. il House & Gard 123:141+ Je '63
On this kind of picnic you take your chances; bouillabaisse-like stew. il Sunset 132:90-3 Ap '64
Skillet suppers for campers. Am Home 67:98 Jl '64
These tasty recipes will make you an outdoor grill expert. G. Maddox. il Todays Health 42:24-9 My '64
Vacation cooking, ltd. il Redbook 123:68-9+ Jl '64
You all come to a cookout. M. A. Whitfield. il Parents Mag 38:61+ Jl '63
See also
Barbecue cookery
Camp cookery

COOKERY, Pennsylvania German. See Cookery, American

COOKERY, Philippine
Delicious introduction to the Philippines. il Sunset 132:162+ Je '64

COOKERY, Polynesian
Let's go Polynesian. il Pop Gard 15:50 Ja '64

COOKERY, Portuguese
Caldo verde; with recipes. il Look 28:42-3 S 8 '64
COOKERY, Roman
Old-fashioned Roman Christmas; Forum of the twelve Caesars restaurant. il Esquire 60:228-31 D '63
COOKERY, Russian
Fish-in-a-fish; Russian specialty, pirog. il Sunset 133:92-3 O '64
Name is *pirog*; Russian turnovers. J. Hewitt. il N Y Times Mag p 147 N 15 '64
Reminders of Russian Easters. M. E. Hoehener. il Good H 156:226 Ap '63
Savory, spicy specialties. il Life 55:117-20 S 13 '63
COOKERY, Scandinavian
Cooking Danish and Swedish pancakes. Sunset 133:175-6 N '64
Scandinavian cook book. N. S. Hazelton. il House & Gard 125:137+ F '64
COOKERY, Shaker. See Cookery, American
COOKERY, Sikkimese
We started off with nettle soup. Hope Namgyal, maharani of Sikkim. McCalls 90:170 S '63
COOKERY, Spanish
For any holiday meal except Christmas dinner; paella. il Sunset 133:104-6+ D '64
From Spain a textured custard; grachunera. il Sunset 132:170 Ap '64
Juan Serrano: gourmet guitarist; with recipes. M. Kaytor. il Look 28:66-9 Mr 10 '64
New York's Spanish restaurants. P. S. Feibleman. il Holiday 34:104-5+ D '63
Super for summer. C. Claiborne. il N Y Times Mag p52 Jl 21 '63
COOKERY, Swedish
Christmas spice; with recipes. C. Claiborne. il N Y Times Mag p97-8 D 8 '63
What it takes to make a smorgasbord. Good H 158:170 Je '64
COOKERY, Swiss
High points of Swiss cuisine. M. E. Hoehener. il Good H 158:180 F '64
Quiche Lorraine: Swiss-cheese pie. il McCalls 92:72 O '64
Swiss cook book. il House & Gard 124:169+ S '63
COOKERY, Turkish
September's the time to try a Turkish buffet. il Sunset 133:126+ S '64
COOKERY, Viennese. See Cookery, Austrian
COOKERY, Welsh
Christmas foods of Wales. M. Kaytor. il Look 27:48-9 D 31 '63
COOKERY, Yugoslav
Casserole of chops, pork and lamb; juvedge. il Sunset 132:201 Je '64
Setting a Yugoslavian table. B. S. Brown. Good H 158:174 Je '64
COOKERY books. See Cookbooks
COOKERY by children
Ambitious young cooks serve breakfast. il Sunset 130:217-18 Ap '63
Cookout tips from teen-agers. G. Maddox. il Todays Health 41:34-7+ My '63
For the little people; a cooky zoo. il Bet Hom & Gard 41:125 Mr '63
Happy Mother's day, mommy. il McCalls 91:82+ My '64
He likes to cook; Richard Klecka. il Bet Hom & Gard 41:98 O '63
Mix well: Christmas, children and sugar cookie dough; with recipes. B. Pierson. il Farm J 88:60-1 D '64
My own cookbook. B. M. Stover. See issues of Parents' magazine & better homemaking
My very own cook book. il Am Home 67:52-3+ S '64
Our teenage cook. See issues of Good housekeeping
Young cook cooks for her friends. il Sunset 132:231-2 Ap '64
COOKERY by men
Chefs of the West. See issues of Sunset
Galley guide for the helpless male. B. Robinson. Yachting 113:56+ Je '63
Girl on a gravy train. J. L. O'Neill. il Am Home 67:12 N '64
He likes to cook. Bet Hom & Gard 41:78 Mr; 80 Ap; 80 Je '63; 42:76 Mr; 80 My; 97 Je; 106 O '64
He likes to cook. G. Koenigsberger. il Bet Hom & Gard 41:80 Je '63
He likes to cook; Cliff Robertson; the movies' JFK; with recipes. C. Robertson. il Bet Hom & Gard 41:78 Mr '63
He likes to cook; sports cartoonist W. Mullin. il Bet Hom & Gard 42:80 My '64
He really likes to cook; Harvey Beffa. il Bet Hom & Gard 43:72-3+ Ja '65
Man's cook book. il House & Gard 124:105-10 Jl '63
Next time a boy asks you to dinner, ask him if he's going to cook it! with recipes. il Seventeen 23:96-7+ Ja '64
When daddy does the cooking. il Changing T 18:42 Ag '64
COOKERY contests. See Cookery—Competitions
COOKERY for the sick
Pantry food for special diet needs. il Parents Mag 39:40+ Mr '64
COOKERY on yachts. See Cookery, Marine
COOKIE trees. See Christmas trees
COOKIES
Bar cookies are easy, quick. Sunset 132:208-9 My '64
Best cookies we know how to bake. il Bet Hom & Gard 42:48-9+ Ja '64
Candy & cookie cookbook. il Parents Mag 38:83+ N '63
Cereal cookies. il Bet Hom & Gard 41:91-2 F '63
Christmas cookie cook book. E. Ross. House & Gard 126:175-80 D '64
Christmas-tree cookies. il McCalls 92:136-7+ D '64
Coffeehouse party. il Ladies Home J 80:107-8 N '63
Cookies. B. M. Stover. il Parents Mag 39:18 S '64
Cookies. il Good H 157:80-3 D '63
Cookies; tested in the American home kitchens. il Am Home 66:50-1+ S '63
Cookies children like to eat; with recipes. Farm J 88:62 D '64
Cookies with macadamias. Sunset 133:128 Jl '64
Cooky jar treats. il Suc Farm 61:57-8 Je '63
Five kinds of cookies. Farm J 88:68 Ja '64
For the little people; a cooky zoo. il Bet Hom & Gard 41:125 Mr '63
How to mass-produce holiday cookies. il Sunset 131:150+ D '63
Ice-cream cookies. il Bet Hom & Gard 42:92 My '64
Lace cookies. il Sunset 133:62-3 D '64
Let's take liberties with the macaroon. Sunset 132:98-9 Ja '64
Make the cookies big for the cooky tree. il Sunset 131:62-3 D '63
Mix well: Christmas, children and sugar cookie dough; with recipes. B. Pierson. il Farm J 88:60-1 D '64
New recipes for springeries. il Sunset 131:165-6 D '63
Paper-doll cookies. L. Stilwill. il Ladies Home J 81:131-2+ Ap '64
Quickest way to fill your cookie jar. B. Pierson. il Farm J 88:82-3 Ap '64
Successful recipes; bar cookies. il Suc Farm 62:87-8 S '64
Under the lid of the cooky jar. Sunset 131:223+ O '63
What a boot. il Am Home 66:44-5+ D '63
See also
Cake
COOKING terms. See Cookery—Terminology
COOKING thermometers. See Thermometers, Cooking
COOKING utensils. See Kitchen utensils
COOKING utensils, Electric. See Electric apparatus and appliances, Domestic
COOKS
Best cook in the monarchy. J. Wechsberg. il Esquire 62:76-7+ Jl '64
COOLEY, Donald G.
Cells that communicate. Todays Health 41:20-5+ My; 38-41+ Je '63
Drug is born. Todays Health 41:18-21+ S '63
Hot-weather target: your heart. Todays Health 41:21-7 Jl '63
Medicines of tomorrow; excerpts from Science book of modern medicines. Todays Health 41:38-42 N; 34-6 D '63
New Better homes and gardens basic calorie chart. Bet Hom & Gard 42:58-9+ Ag '64
COOLEY, Harold D.
Excerpt from debate, April 7, 1964. Cong Digest 43:178+ Je '64
COOLEY, John K.
Algerians on their own. Reporter 28:37-40 F 28 '63
China's push in Africa. Commonweal 79:424-6 Ja 10 '64
COOLEY, Margaret, and Stokvis, I. E.
(eds) Business books to come. Library J 88:1030-9 Mr 1 '63
(eds) Scientific, technical and medical books to come. Library J 88:1040-78 Mr 1 '63
—and others
(ed) New books appraised. See issues of Library journal

COOLEY'S anemia. See Anemia
COOLIDGE, Calvin
Lamplight inauguration. C. M. Wilson. il por Am Heritage 15:80-6 D '63
Strike that made a president. F. Russell. il por Am Heritage 14:44-7+ O '63
COOLIDGE, John
Lamplight inauguration. C. M. Wilson. il por Am Heritage 15:80-6 D '63
COOLIDGE, Susan
Toinette and the elves; dramatization. See Thane, A.
COOLIDGE, Thomas B.
Research at the Moscow medical stomatological institute. Science 140:856+ My 24 '63
COOLIDGE, William H.
Deviation. Yachting 113:153 F '63
COOLING
See also
Air conditioning
Gas and oil engines—Cooling
Tractor engines—Cooling
COOLING of food. See Food, Cooling of
COOMBS, Philip H.
Education's role in the developing nations. Sat R 46:29-30 Ag 17 '63
COOMBS, S. W.
Bracero's journey. Américas 15:7-11 D '63
COON, Carleton S.
Origin of races: a new theory; excerpt from The origin of races. Sat R 45:68-9 D 1 '62; 46:57-8 F 2 '63
COON, Nelson
Corn. Horticulture 42:22-5 Ag '64
Flowers all year. por Horticulture 41:526-7 O '63
COON, Thomas F.
Report on the CP. Nat R 16:726 Ag 25 '64
COON hunting. See Raccoon hunting
COONEY, Barbara
Scratchboard illustration. il Horn Bk 40:162-5 Ap '64
COONEY, Robert F.
Jewel basin. Liv Wildn 85:7-9 Wint '64
COONS. See Raccoons
COOPER, Alfred R.
Silica. Science 143:395+ Ja 24 '64
COOPER, Arnold C.
R&D is more efficient in small companies. bibliog f Harvard Bsns R 42:75-83 My '64
COOPER, Charles A.
Trading with the Communists. New Repub 149:9-12 O 12 '63
COOPER, Chuck
Follow a star. por Seventeen 24:77+ Ja '65
COOPER, Courtney Ryley
I quit smoking, or Cooper's last stand. Read Digest 84:77-80 Ap '64
COOPER, David Y. and others
Photochemical action spectrum of the terminal oxidase of mixed function oxidase systems. bibliog Science 147:400-2 Ja 22 '65
COOPER, Duane H.
Must stereo discs sound bad? Electr World 70:42-3 Jl '63
COOPER, G. P. and Kimeldorf, D. J.
Electroencephalographic desynchronization in irradiated rats with transected spinal cords. Science 143:1040-1 Mr 6 '64
COOPER, Gary
Gary Cooper. D. B. Hyatt. il pors McCalls 90:96-7+ Mr '63
Gary Cooper and the real West. il por Pop Phot 52:36 Ap '63
How I faced tomorrow; interview, ed. by G. Christy. Mrs G. Cooper. il pors Good H 157:80-3+ S '63
COOPER, Giles, and McNally, Terence
Lady of the camellias; dramatization of novel by A. Dumas. Criticism
Nation 196:333 Ap 20 '63
New Yorker 39:110 Mr 30 '63
Newsweek 61:78 Ap 1 '63
Theatre Arts il(p 15) 47:70-1 My '63
Time 81:46 Mr 29 '63
COOPER, Gordon
Astronaut's family problems; interview, ed. by W. Peters. por Redbook 121:22+ Je '63
Cooper and his camera tell the great story. pors Life 54:26-35 Je 7 '63
Cooper reports on details of MA-9 flight. por Aviation W 79:61-2+ O 14 '63
about
Astronaut Cooper: insured for $100,000 now. por U S News 54:21 My 20 '63
Cooper shows man can take it in space. il Bsns W p78+ My 25 '63
Cooper to de-pressurize MA-9 craft. H. M. David. Miss & Roc 12:30+ F 18 '63
Finest hour for Atlas. il Bsns W p28-9 My 18 '63
Fourth orbital spaceflight. il por Sci N L 83:311 My 18 '63
Gordo gets a great hello from the kids and kin. il pors Life 54:34-34A My 31 '63
Great Gordo. il pors Time 81:17-21 My 24 '63
He brings it in right on the old bazoo. il pors Life 54:28-33 My 24 '63
His mission is the longest U.S. orbit. il pors Life 54:90-1 My 17 '63
MA-9 boosts hopes for tenth mission. il por(p 1) Miss & Roc 12:10+ My 20 '63
MA-9 experiments vital to rendezvous; plans for eighteen to twenty-two orbit flight. G. Alexander. Aviation W 78:55+ Ja 21 '63
Man on the moon: how soon now? il por U S News 54:35-9 My 27 '63
Man the whole world cheered. il por U S News 54:24 My 27 '63
Nerve center; Goddard space flight center. New Yorker 39:30-2 My 25 '63
Notes and comment. New Yorker 39:23 Je 1 '63
On the bazoo. il por Newsweek 61:61-4 My 27 '63
Six days of glory. il por U S News 54:19 Je 3 '63
Trouble at the controls. il Newsweek 61:74 Je 3 '63
Under whose moon? il por Time 81:15-16 My 31 '63
View from the capsule. Newsweek 63:60 F 17 '64
See also
Space flight—Manned flights—Cooper flight, 1963
COOPER, Gordon, family
Flying Coopers are full of dad's spirit. R. Bailey. il Life 54:92+ My 17 '63
COOPER, Henry
'E said 'e would and 'e did. H. Horn. por Sports Illus 19:42-5 Jl 1 '63
Murder on the BBC. il por Time 81:66 Je 28 '63
COOPER, Irving
Have I got a girl for you! Criticism
New Yorker 39:80 D 14 '63
COOPER, John Sherman
Answer on filters. U S News 56:38 Ja 27 '64
Excerpt from debate, September 25, 1964. Cong Digest 43:306+ D '64
Test ban treaty; address, July 12, 1963. Vital Speeches 30:201-3 Ja 15 '64
COOPER, Joseph D.
Subminiature. Pop Phot 53:40-2 Ag '63
COOPER, Leroy Gordon. See Cooper, G.
COOPER, Martin
English festivals. Mus Am 83:8 Ag '63
Highland measures. Mus Am 84:17-18 O '64
[Musical events] Mus Am 83:20 Mr; 41-2 O'63; 84:57+ Ja '64
No for an answer. Mus Am 84:26 Jl '64
Strife and self-government. Mus Am 84:21 My '64
Two B's. Mus Am 84:28+ Ap '64
COOPER, Michael
Election prospects in Britain. America 111:81 Jl 25 '64
COOPER, R. A. and others
Placenta of the Indian elephant, elephas indicus. bibliog Science 146:410-12 O 16 '64
COOPER, Richard T.
Goldwater in Illinois. New Repub 151:10-13 O 31 '64
James R. Hoffa: the prosecution rests. New Repub 151:6-7 Ag 8 '64
On trial in Chicago. New Repub 150:13-14 Je 6 '64
Relief in Illinois. New Repub 148:8 Je 15 '63
Why the drive to raise cattle prices failed. New Repub 151:7-8 O 3 '64
COOPER, Suzanne T.
Summertime revisited. Am Heritage 14:35-49 Je '63
COOPER, Theodore, and others
Reserpine: its effect on silver-stained structures of the heart. bibliog Science 141:526-7 Ag 9 '63
COOPER, Thomas
On the roots of bias. Christian Cent 81:770-1 Je 10 '64
COOPER, Trudy
I felt calm, I guess I was saying, go, go pors Life 54:34B-36 My 31 '63
COOPER, Veronica (Balfe)
How I faced tomorrow; interview, ed. by G. Christy. pors Good H 157:80-3+ S '63
COOPER union for the advancement of science and art, New York
Museum for the arts of decoration
Antiques. A. Winchester. Antiques 84:555 N '63
Case of the vanishing museum. K. Kuh. Sat R 46:49-50 O 26 '63

COOPER union for the advancement of science and art, New York—Museum for the arts of decoration—*Continued*
Cooper union; committee to study proposals concerning museum's future. Nation 197:379 D 7 '63
Debate about a delight. il Time 82:52 Ag 9 '63
Disappearance of a museum. D. Cort. Nation 197:109-11 S 7 '63; Discussion. 197: inside cover O 5 '63
COOPERATION
Gropius addresses convocation at Williams; excerpts from address. W. Gropius. Arch Rec 134:10 N '63
Try a teamwork association; Blue Ridge estates association, Monroe, Conn. E. D. Fales, jr. il Am Home 66:22+ Ap '63
See also
Collective settlements
Intercommunity cooperation
International cooperation
Interracial cooperation
Library cooperation
Medical cooperation
Religious cooperation
COOPERATION in education. See Colleges and universities—Cooperation; Educational cooperation
COOPERATIVE advertising. See Advertising, Cooperative
COOPERATIVE associations
Feed for pooled cattle; Liberty feed yards. il Suc Farm 62:56 S '64
Feeders pool resources; Liberty feed yards. C. Peterson, jr. il Suc Farm 61:34-5+ S '63
Grass-roots war on poverty; Southern consumers' co-operative chartered as a holding company. America 111:280 S 19 '64
How a subsidized business thrives; rural electric cooperatives. il Nations Bsns 52:36-7+ O '64
REA, a case study of bureaucracy run wild. K. O. Gilmore and E. H. Methvin. il Read Digest 83:81-7 D '63
COOPERATIVE cataloging. See Cataloging, Cooperative
COOPERATIVE education. See Education, Cooperative
COOPERATIVE for American relief everywhere, incorporated
CARE has a program for educational survival, too. il Sat R 46:56 Jl 20 '63
COOPERATIVE grange league federation exchange
GFL-ESFX propose marriage. il Farm J 88: 38+ Ja '64
COOPERATIVE living establishments. See Collective settlements
COOPERATIVE publishing. See Publishers and publishing
COOPERATIVE research. See Research, Cooperative
COOPERATIVE research, College. See Colleges and universities—Research
COOPERATIVE research program. See United States—Education, Office of
COOPERATIVE societies. See Cooperative associations
COOPERATIVE test division. See Educational testing service
COOPERIDER, C. W.
C. W. Cooperider: young old-timer. C. Miles. por Hobbies 69:112-13 Je '64
COOPERSTOWN, N.Y.
See also
National baseball hall of fame and museum
COORDINATED bargaining. See Collective bargaining
COPE, Jack
Heart-of-the-daybreak; story. Reporter 32:46 Ja 28 '65
COPE, Myron
Baseball's richest rookie. Sat Eve Post 237: 68-9 S 19 '64
How to be a loser with four aces. Sat Eve Post 237:28-30 Je 6 '64
Just call me football's greatest scout. Sports Illus 19:32-4+ S 30 '63
King Edward of Pitt. Sat Eve Post 236:22-3 Ap 6 '63
Kiss the guy or tackle him? Sat Eve Post 236:76-7 O 26 '63
Minister who follows the migrants. Sat Eve Post 237:34-6 Ja 4 '64
Mossie Murphy's crusade. Sports Illus 18:18-20+ Ja 28 '63
Muslim champ. Sat Eve Post 237:32-4+ N 14 '64
Pitching explosion in paradise. Sports Illus 18:22-4+ Je 24 '63
Profile of a bookmaker. Sat Eve Post 236: 34+ Ap 27 '63
Showdown for a quarterback. Sat Eve Post 237:28-9 O 17 '64
Sunday's human targets. Sat Eve Post 236:70+ D 21 '63
Whip who put snap in the Phillies. Sat Eve Post 237:74-5+ Ag 8 '64
—See Brown, J. jt. auth.
COPELAND, George
Unique George Copeland. R. Kammerer. il por Am Rec G 30:812-13 My '64
COPELAND, Harold W.
Peonies are forever. Flower Grower 50:20-1+ S '63
COPELAND, Helen
Old embarrassment; poem. Sat R 47:36 S 12 '64
COPELAND, John
Shop vacuum for less than $10. Pop Sci 186: 163-5 Ja '65
COPELAND, John A.
Five brave Negroes with John Brown at Harpers Ferry. por Negro Hist Bul 27:164-9 Ap '64
COPELAND, John Q.
Dressing up for Christmas; reprint. Recreation 56:452 D '63
COPELAND, L. E. See Brunauer, S. jt. auth.
COPELAND, Lammot du Pont
Business and government: cold war should end, Du Pont head says; excerpts from address, February 10, 1964. por U S News 56:16 F 24 '64
Putting first things first. Sat R 47:25+ D 12 '64
World trade; national and corporate interests; address, November 19, 1963. Vital Speeches 30:264-7 F 15 '64
about
Master technicians. il Time 84:97-8 N 27 '64
COPELAND, Richard
Five pitch baseball. por Recreation 57:517 D '64
COPENHAGEN
Sweepers whisk the snow away. J. P. Horton. il Am City 79:76-7 D '64
Airports
Copenhagen terminal fulfills growth role. il Aviation W 82:32-3 Ja 4 '65
Description
Well traveled camera. H. Keppler. il Mod Phot 27:26+ Ag '63
Hotel, restaurants, etc.
Caloric Copenhagen. M. Connelly. il Sat R 46:47-8+ Ap 13 '63
Monuments, statues, etc.
Pray tell, little mermaid, who took your pretty head? il Life 56:28-33 My 8 '64
Tears for a mermaid; decapitation of The Little Mermaid. il Time 83:34 My 1 '64
Music
Copenhagen. S. A. K. Roewade. Opera N 29:29 Ja 2 '65
Great opera houses. E. Palatsky. il Opera N 28:28-31 F 1 '64
Northern lights. S. A. K. Roewade. il Opera N 28:33 Mr 7 '64
Sweden and Denmark. E. H. Palatsky. il Opera N 28:28 O 19 '63
Parks and playgrounds
Many delights of Tivoli. il Sunset 132:79-80 My '64
Theater
Danes' musical hit. il Theatre Arts 47:66-7 Ag '63
COPENHAGEN festival. See Music festivals—Denmark
COPEPODS
Infestation of the copepod acartia tonsa with the stalked ciliate zoothamnium. S. S. Herman and J. A. Mihursky. bibliog il Science 146:543-4 O 23 '64
COPERNICUS, Nichlaus
Copernicus: a universe revealed. W. Golding. il Holiday 35:56-61+ Ja '64
They made our world. L. Rosten. il por Look 28:112-13 D 15 '64
COPLAN, Maxwell
Camera safari. il U S Camera 26:34-5 Ag '63
COPLAND, Aaron
American in London. Newsweek 63:88-9 Je 8 '64
Music from Manhattan; Copland's Music for a great city, played by London symphony orchestra at Royal festival hall, London. por Time 83:60 Je 5 '64
1947-48 Copland, and Previn's conducting debut. J. Diether. il por Am Rec G 30:1096-8 Ag '64
Three by Copland from CRI. R. Kammerer. Am Rec G 30:43 S '63

COPLANS, John
Art news from San Francisco. Art N 63:21+ Ja '65
COPLEY, C. M. jr, and Sadowski, J. L.
Mosquito control for 4¼ cents per person. Am City 78:128-9 Je '63
COPLEY, John G.
Let the water manager help to bring new industry. Am City 79:89-90 Je '64
COPPER
Copper supply can meet future needs. Sci N L 86:248 O 17 '64
Primitive metallurgy; use by people of Cayonu, 7000 B.C. Sci Am 211:62+ D '64
Red-hot copper; Texas Gulf sulphur announces discovery of copper lodes near Timmins, Ontario. il Time 83:97 Ap 24 '64

Prices

Metals prices take a whirl. il Bsns W p27 Mr 21 '64
Pressure on copper market lets up a little. il Bsns W p 36+ S 12 '64
COPPER industry and trade

Chile

Chile and its copper. America 112:38-9 Ja 9 '65
Chile's new deal with U.S. firms. il U S News 58:69 Ja 4 '65
Policy of partnership. Time 85:31 Ja 1 '65
COPPER mines and mining
Copper is big; Bagdad copper corporation. il Fortune 69:117-21 Je '64

Canada

Big copper rush, U.S. financed that, too. il U S News 56:74 My 4 '64

Greece, Modern

Classical approach; Chalcidice mining co. il Time 81:92 Mr 22 '63

Sweden

Oldest corporation in the world; Stora Kopparberg Bergslags Aktiebolag. il Time 81: 96+ Mr 15 '63
COPPER sulfantimonites
Confirmation of the crystal structure of tetrahedrite, $Cu_{12}Sb_4S_{13}$. B. J. Wuensch. bibliog il Science 141:804-5 Ag 30 '63
COPPER sulfate
Here's the score on copper sulfate. J. Russell. Farm J 88:75 F '64
See also
Chalcocite
COPPERHEADS (nickname)
Most unpopular man in the North. L. W. Koenig. il Am Heritage 15:12-15+ F '64
COPPOCK, J. T.
Great Britain. bibliog Focus 14:1-6 Je '64
COPTIC art. See Art, Coptic
COPTIC church
See also
Copts
COPTIC manuscripts. See Manuscripts, Coptic (papyri)
COPTS
Lonely minority: the modern story of Egypt's Copts, by E. Wakin. Review
Sat R il 46:27 Ap '63. J. Carmichael
COPYING
Copying good or bad? M. Young. il Sch Arts 62:19-20 Je '63
COPYING processes
Can publishers pull the plug on copiers? Bsns W p 114 N 21 '64
Copy break; new copying machines. Time 84:98 O 30 '64
Easel tracing-projector. M. Banister. il Pop Mech 120:130-4 Jl '63
Shop pantograph copies anything. J. W. Nash. il Pop Mech 119:164-8 Je '63
Toy rotary duplicator. T. Holloway. il Pop Mech 120:140 Jl '63
See also
Catalog cards—Reproduction
Transparencies—Copying
Xerography
COPYRIGHT
Book publishers' interests in reprographic copyright; excerpts from address, May 1963. C. G. Benjamin. Library J 88:2837-41 Ag '63
Copyright implications in the new science of data storage and retrieval; conference sponsored by copyright committee of the American textbook publishers institute. Pub W 186:20-3 N 30 '64
Import policy clarified on sheets with U.C.C. notice. Pub W 183:123 Je 10 '63

Anecdotes, facetiae, satire, etc.

They couldn't resist the title. R. Schoenstein. Sat R 47:53 F 8 '64

Art

Design protection. L. Epstein. Craft Horiz 24:9-10 Mr '64

International aspects

Protests infringement of British Commonwealth rights. P. Owen. Pub W 184:22 O 21 '63

Letters

Law of letters. R. Hauser. Sat R 46:56-7 F 9 '63

Music

Watch that rhapsody to a fig leaf! copyrighted music. G. E. Deakin. il Dance Mag 37:48-9 N '63
See also
American society of composers, authors and publishers

Unauthorized reprints

ATPI annual meeting; foreign trade: Formosan piracy. il Pub W 183:26-8 My 13 '63
Chinese reprinters and world copyright practice; a Chinese view and a U.S. publisher's reply. I. C. Loh; C. G. Benjamin. Pub W 185:22-9 Mr 30 '64
Formosa piracy: new pleas for a solution. R. H. Smith. Pub W 184:29 D 16 '63
Taiwan's best selling pirates. C. Elliott. Life 55:8 N 15 '63

Great Britain

Eyre & Spottiswoode bow in New English Bible case. Pub W 184:36 N 25 '63
New English Bible copyright upheld. Pub W 184:81 Ag 19 '63

Taiwan

Changes reported in Formosa copyright law. Pub W 184:249-50 Ag 26 '63
Chinese reprinters and world copyright practice; a Chinese view and a U.S. publisher's reply. I. C. Loh; C. G. Benjamin. Pub W 185:22-9 Mr 30 '64

United States

ABPC-ATPI position paper on copyright revision. Pub W 187:275 Ja 25 '65
ABPC, ATPI state views on copyright draft provisions. Pub W 185:65-6 Je 22 '64
American book-Stratford state copyright position; on proposed changes in the copyright law. Pub W 186:43-4 D 28 '64
ATPI annual meeting; copyright revision. Pub W 185:33-5 My 18 '64
ATPI annual meeting; copyright revision and educational publishing. il Pub W 183: 23-6 My 13 '63
ATPI resolves: eliminate the manufacturing clause. Pub W 185:27-8 My 11 '64
Bill to revise copyright law sent to Congress on July 20. Library J 89:2968 Ag '64
Books, rights and educational broadcasting. R. J. Walsh, jr. Pub W 184:30-3 S 23 '63
Breaking the permissions barrier; creative use of books on ETV. N. Paige. Library J 89:3404-5+ S 15 '64
But can you do that? H. F. Pilpel. Pub W 186:29-31 N 30 '64
CBC explores book use by educational broadcasters. Pub W 184:150-1 Jl 8 '63
Comprehensive bill for revision of copyright law sent to Congress. E. Hamer and A. McCormick. ALA Bul 58:682-4 S '64
Computer programs can be registered for copyright. Pub W 185:102 Je 8 '64
Contract that can't be enforced: question of royalty payments after expiration. H. F. Pilpel. Pub W 187:272 Ja 25 '65
Copyright case involves new use of material; unauthorized recording of speech by M. L. King. H. F. Pilpel. Pub W 185:26 Ap 6 '64
Copyright; excerpts from addresses. L. Davis; D. Lacy. Pub W 184:49-50 Jl 15 '63
Copyright: how the procedure operates for books. il Pub W 183:29-31 F 25 '63
Copyright revision and book publishing: ABPC symposium. Pub W 185:34-7 Je 15 '64
Copyright revision and the library of the future. R. H. Smith. Pub W 185:36 My 11 '64
Copyright revision bill. Wilson Lib Bul 39:18 S '64
Copyright revision bill predicted for late 1963. Pub W 183:41 F 25 '63
Copyright revision bill submitted to Congress. Pub W 186:24-5 Ag 3 '64; Discussion. 186: 31 Ag 3; 25 Ag 10 '64
Copyright revisions. D. Wolfle. Science 145: 879 Ag 28 '64
Copyright ruling on flash cards upheld. Pub W 184:47 Ag 5 '63

COPYRIGHT—United States—*Continued*
Copyright: the problems of revising the law; ABPC symposium. il Pub W 183:28-30 Je 3 '63
Copyrighting writing on the wall. D. Dempsey. Sat R 47:39-40 S 19 '64
Copyrights: chapter two; computerized and xerographic material. D. Dempsey. Sat R 47:34-5 O 17 '64; Discussion. 47:19 N 28 '64
Court protects voice and style of talking. H. F. Pilpel. Pub W 186:21-2 O 26 '64
Court upholds coyprights in educational flash cards. Pub W 183:133 F 18 '63
Education groups attack copyright revision bill; with editorial comment. Pub W 186:22-3, 29 Ag 17 '64
Educational groups protest proposed copyright revision. Library J 89:3116 S 1 '64
ETV's copyright stand hit at broadcasters' convention. Pub W 186:44 N 9 '64
Everybody blows up! Two hours to doom and Fail-safe. D. E. Scherman. il Life 54:49-50 Mr 8 '63
Field enterprises sues Childrens press. Pub W 184:247 Ag 26 '63
Great copyright debate: hassle over fair use; educator's and publisher's view point. H. E. Wigren; L. Deighton. 85:12T-13T O 7 '64
Important break in copyright discussions. C. B. Grannis. Pub W 187:41 Ja 4 '65
Law of a community represents its conscience; preparing and selling the answers to problems in copyrighted textbooks. H. F. Pilpel. Pub W 185:25 Ap 6 '64
Library photocopying: the stalemate deepens. R. H. Smith. Pub W 184:41 Ag 12 '63
New service to simplify ETV use of book properties. Pub W 186:150 Jl 13 '64
Rights and permissions. P. Nathan. See issues of Publishers' weekly
There must be a basis for a meeting of minds; manufacturing clause in the U.S. copyright law. C. B. Grannis. Pub W 185: 45 Je 1 '64
Troublesome problem of the innocent infringer. H. F. Pilpel. Pub W 184:27-8 S 30 '63
Whose right to copy? Sr Schol 84:1T-2T F 14 '64
Wonderland of subsidiary rights. P. Nathan. Sat R 46:58-9+ D 14 '63

COQUET, James de
Letter from Paris. Genêt. New Yorker 40: 159-60 Mr 21 '64

CORAH, Norman L. See Johnson, L. C. jt. auth.

CORAL bells
Coral bell, bloom long and abundantly. E. S. Parcher. il Horticulture 41:218 Ap '63
Santa Ana Cardinal; new coral bells. il Sunset 132:294 Ap '64

CORAL reefs and islands
Mass expulsion of zooxanthellae from Jamaican reef communities after hurricane Flora. T. F. Goreau. bibliog il Science 145:383-6 Jl 24 '64
Modern tools probe deep water. D. F. Squires. il Natur Hist 72:22-9 Je '63
See also
Florida Keys

CORBEAU, Louis
Lake Powell is being filled. Motor B 112: 44-6 Ag '63

CORBEILL, Sidney
Pappy takes over the house. G. White. il pors Ladies Home J 80:147-51 Jl '63

CORBETT, Scott
Duty free. Atlan 213:124-6 Ap '64

CORBIN, Kay
Fragrant little iris. Flower Grower 50:28+ Ap '63
Plant these more often. Horticulture 41:425 Ag '63

CORBISHLEY, Thomas
Roman radical in London. C. Northcott. Christian Cent 81:907-8 Jl 15 '64

CORBUSIER, Le. See Le Corbusier

CORBY, Colleen
Follow a star. B. Pindyck. il por Seventeen 24:78+ Ja '65

CORCORAN, A. C. and Page, I. H.
Stop worrying about low blood pressure. Todays Health 41:24-5+ N '63

CORCORAN, Barbara
Standard dream; story. Redbook 120:56-7 Mr '63

CORCORAN gallery of art, Washington, D.C.
Hard edge and hard times at the Corcoran; Twenty-eighth biennial exhibition. F. Getlein. New Repub 148:27-8+ F 2 '63
Mme Don Ton. Time 84:82 N 27 '64

CORCOS, Lucille
Kitchens then & now. il Good H 157:48-9 O '63

CORDASCO, Francesco
50th anniversary of Monroe's Cyclopedia of education. bibliog f Sch & Soc 91:123-4 Mr 9 '63

CORDEIRO, Joseph
Age of the layman. America 111:347 S 26 '64

CORDERO J, Carlos
Spectacular Irazú. Américas 16:21-7 Ap '64

CORDIER, Daniel
Letter from Paris. Genêt. New Yorker 40:84+ Je 27 '64

CORDILLERA VILCABAMBA. See Vilcabamba, Cordillera

CORDINER, Ralph
New high command at G.E. il Fortune 68:65 D '63

CORDLESS electric appliances. See Electric apparatus and appliances. Cordless

CORDLESS shavers. See Razors

CORDOBA (city), Argentina
Córdoba's biennial comes to Washington. J. Gómez-Sicre. il Américas 15:16-19 F '63

CORDS, Electric. See Electric cords

CORDYLINE terminalis. See Ti plant

CORE. See Congress of racial equality

CORE curriculum. See Colleges and universities —Curriculum

CORE sampling
Time's traces in sediment. D. B. Ericson and G. Wollin. il Natur Hist 72:52-61 F '63

CORENA, Fernando
Bass in orbit; interview, ed. by F. Stevenson. por Opera N 27:29 Mr 9 '63

COREY, Albert Bickmore
Albert B. Corey, 1898-1963. B. Catton. por Am Heritage 15:111 F '64

COREY, Richard B. and Zeman, L. E.
Liming pays big dividends. Suc Farm 61:72-3+ F '63

CORFAM. See Leather substitutes

CORFMAN, Philip A. See Richart, R. M. jt. auth.

CORFU (island)
By ferry to ancient Corfu. il Sunset 131:8 O '63

CORINTH, Kay
Teen-age girl and the book market. Pub W 186:18-21 Ag 17 '64

CORINTH, Lovis
Corinth retrospective. M. Kozloff. Nation 199: 230-2 O 12 '64
Razor's edge. il por Newsweek 64:108 O 5 '64
Valhalla revamped. il Time 84:76-7 S 25 '64

CORINTHIANS (organization)
Hands and berths. M. H. Farnham. il Motor B 111:47+ F '63

CORK
Natural cork providing ablative protection for minuteman, Polaris, Scout. J. F. Judge. il Miss & Roc 13:32-3+ O 28 '63

CORK industry
Cork business and how it started. Miss & Roc 13:35 O 28 '63

CORKE, Hilary
Aberdovey; poem. Yale R 53:551 Je '64
Dog that didn't bark. New Repub 148:27-30 Ap 13 '63
Father drowning; poem. Harper 228:67 Je '64
November poppies; poem. New Yorker 40:64 N 14 '64
Salmon remembers; poem. New Yorker 40: 50 My 16 '64
Storm of love; poem. New Yorker 39:52 D 14 '63
Waltz; poem. New Yorker 39:40 My 4 '63

CORLETT, Bruce
Big step toward automation. por Am City 78:104-5 O '63

CORLEY, Ed
Make a film that helps your community. Pop Phot 52:122-3+ Ap '63
Try filming TV! Pop Phot 53:183+ N '63

CORMAN, Cid
Memento; At Santo Spirito; Demonstration; poems. Poetry 104:167-9 Je '64

CORMAN, Rena
Close-up of the normal wife. N Y Times Mag p52+ S 8 '63
—See Hunt, M. M. jt. auth.

CORMAN, Roger
Titillater. Newsweek 63:87-8 Je 29 '64

CORMORANTS
Birds of the sea. A. Sprunt, 4th. il Motor B 112:54+ N '63
Most prosperous bird colony; Guano Islands. H. S. Ullmann. il Audubon Mag 65:150-1 My '63
Wild music. H. F. Ellis. New Yorker 39:58-60 Jl 6 '63

CORMS. See Bulbs

CORN, Morton, and De Maio, Laurence
Sulfate particulates: size distribution in Pittsburgh air. bibliog Science 143:803-4 F 21 '64

CORN
Continuous corn silage, why not? D. Seim. il Farm J 87:51-2 Ap '63
Corn. N. Coon. il Horticulture 42:22-5 Ag '64
Feed ground ear corn. Suc Farm 61:90 N '63
Growing corn to music. C. B. Hicks. il Pop Mech 119:118-21+ My '63
Growth response of the d-5 and an-1 mutants of maize to some kaurene derivatives. M. Katsumi and others. bibliog il Science 144: 849-50 My 15 '64
Labeled oxygen: transport through growing corn roots. C. R. Jensen and others. il Science 144:550-2 My 1 '64
Mutant gene that changes protein composition and increases lysine content of maize endosperm. E. T. Mertz and others. bibliog il Science 145:279-80 Jl 17 '64
10½ per cent-moisture corn for 51c per bushel. W. Lovely. il Suc Farm 61:24 D '63
Tetrasporic embryo-sac formation in trisomic sectors of maize. M. G. Neuffer. bibliog il Science 144:874-6 My 15 '64
Thanks given to corn. B. Tufty. Sci N L 86: 326 N 21 '64
They produce no. 1 corn. W. J. Fletcher. il Suc Farm 62:96 N '64
Thick corn in dry weather? Suc Farm 62:83 F '64
Virus as a mutagenic agent in maize. G. F. Sprague and others. bibliog il Science 141: 1052-3 S 13 '63
Your 1963 guide to weed-free cornfields. Suc Farm 61:28+ My '63
See also
Popcorn

Breeding
Heritability of variations in oil content of individual corn kernels. L. F. Bauman and others. il Science 139:498-9 F 8 '63

Cultivation
Calendarizing corn nets 1,500 extra bushels. Suc Farm 62:31 Ap '64
Continuous corn, are we headed for trouble? L. E. Zeman. il Suc Farm 61:36-7+ D '63
Corn growers do it again! R. D. Wennblom. il Farm J 88:34-5+ S '64
For corn, pour on fertilizer! Suc Farm 61:36 N '63
High-profit trio farmers do it again! il Suc Farm 62:62 F '64
How fast will you boost yields? Suc Farm 62:114 F '64
Ideas from a really big corn grower; Bill Curry of Nebraska. B. Brantley. il Suc Farm 62:136-7 Mr '64
Late report on narrow-row crops. L. E. Zeman. il Suc Farm 61:54-5+ My '63
Less tillage; just as much corn. il Farm J 88:37 D '64
Narrow rows; the coming thing? J. Russell. il Farm J 87:36-7+ Mr '63
135-bushel corn with plow-plant. L. Gerard. il Suc Farm 61:56-7 My '63
One man grows 30,000 bushels of corn. L. Gerard. il Suc Farm 62:50-1 Mr '64
Questions and answers about high-profit trio. il Suc Farm 62:62-3 Je '64
Seventy-five bu. more corn with $15 worth of fertilizer. O. Bay. Farm J 87:46 F '63
They accepted Successful farming's corn growing challenge. L. E. Zeman. il Suc Farm 61:58-9+ Ap '63
They grew 200-bushel corn! can you? L. Gerard. il Suc Farm 61:72-3+ Mr '63
Two hundred bushels twice, and he's aiming higher. R. J. Reiman. il Suc Farm 63:32-3+ Ja '65
When and how to irrigate. Suc Farm 61:91 Ag '63
Which minimum tillage system for you? L. Gerard. il Suc Farm 61:56-7 Ap '63

Diseases and pests
Aphids spread that new corn stunt diseases; compact maize disease. Farm J 88:41 N '64
Corn down? find out why now. J. T. Murdock and L. E. Zeman. il Suc Farm 62:42-3+ O '64
Corn stunt: how big a threat? D. Seim. il Farm J 89:39 Ja '65
New corn stunt disease in Iowa. Farm J 88:37 D '64
Your 1963—1964 guide to insect-free cornfields. Suc Farm 61:39 Ap '63; 62:16 Ap '64
See also
Beetles
Corn rootworms
Corn stunt disease virus

Drying
News are old hands at drying. il Suc Farm 61:44 O '63

Harvesting
Corn handling. V. W. Davis and B. Brantley. il Suc Farm 62:41-5 S '64
Corn harvest ideas to try. P. B. Jones. il Suc Farm 61:44-5 O '63
New: center-cut silage. il Farm J 87:33+ F '63
Three corn harvest ideas. il Farm J 88:42B N '64

History
Domestication of corn. P. C. Mangelsdorf and others. bibliog il Science 143:538-45 F 7 '64; Reply with rejoinder. M. D. W Jeffreys. 145:659 Ag 14 '64

Hybrids
Catalase hybrid enzymes in maize. L. Beckman and others. bibliog il Science 146: 1174-5 N 27 '64
How good is single-cross corn? interview. M. Swearingin. Suc Farm 62:44-5 Ja '64

Moisture content
Facts about high-moisture ear corn. Suc Farm 62:59 N '64
Ten keys to success with high-moisture corn. B. Brantley. il Suc Farm 61:44-5 Ag '63

Prices
Should pay to store corn and soybeans. T. A. Hieronymus. Suc Farm 61:33 S '63

Seeding
Calendarizing corn nets 1,500 extra bushels. Suc Farm 62:31 Ap '64
Corn without plowing. il Farm J 87:44-5+ Ap '63
Is there a better way to plant corn? il Farm J 88:30-1 Je '64
No plowing or cultivating; new way to grow corn. il Suc Farm 61:27 Ap '63
Once over does it! il Suc Farm 61:30 Ap '63
Plow early, then plant with one trip. K. Pyle. il Farm J 87:521 My '63
You can plant corn at speeds over five mph. il Suc Farm 61:70 Ap '63

Storage
Why grain by the ton is dumped on city streets; open-air storage in Hannibal, Mo. il U S News 55:22 N 18 '63

CORN, Sweet
See also
Cookery—Vegetables
CORN fritters. See Fritters
CORN harvesting machinery
Corn picker tune-up. M. E. Long. il Suc Farm 61:47 O '63
How to get the corn out, fast. il Farm J 88:40-1 O '64
CORN meal
See also
Cookery—Corn meal
CORN pickers. See Corn harvesting machinery
CORN picking. See Corn—Harvesting
CORN planters
Four ways to plant in narrow rows. il Farm J 87:58N Ap '63
Get the stand you want. il Suc Farm 62:46+ My '64
You can plant corn at speeds over five mph. il Suc Farm 61:70 Ap '63
CORN planting. See Corn—Seeding
CORN poppers
Three handy appliances. Am Home 67:130 Jl '64
CORN products company
Difference in being president. T. R. Brooks. il Duns R 84:33-4 D '64
CORN rootworms
Corn rootworm eggs live over two winters. il Farm J 89:37 Ja '65
How to cope with new corn rootworm problems. L. E. Zeman. il Suc Farm 62:48-9+ Ja '64
Tough rootworms damage Midwest corn. D. Seim. Farm J 87:44 S '63
CORN silage. See Silage
CORN stunt disease virus
Corn disease moves north. il Suc Farm 62:34 Ag '64
CORNBERG, Sol
Educational alcove; audiovisual student carrel. New Yorker 39:29 S 7 '63
CORNEA
Oxygen uptake from a reservoir of limited volume by the human cornea in vivo. R. M. Hill and I. Fatt. bibliog il Science 142:1295-7 D 6 '63
CORNEA, Artificial
Artificial eye that sees. il Sci Digest 56:19-20 D '64

CORNEA, Surgery of. See Eye—Surgery
CORNEAL lenses. See Contact lenses
CORNEAL transplants. See Transplantation of organs, tissues, etc.
CORNEHLS, Ursula Grüsser-. See Grüsser-Cornehls, U.
CORNEILLE, Pierre
Four poets and two dramatists. W. Fowlie. Poetry 104:191-2 Je '64
CORNELIUS, Jack
My favorite guide. Field & S 68:46-7+ My '63
CORNELIUS, John C.
Joy of giving. Read Digest 84:65-7 Ja '64
CORNELIUS, Royce O.
Needed: solutions, not epitaphs! pors Am For 70:24-7 Je '64
CORNELL aeronautical laboratory
Cornell tests aim at base-heating guidelines. M. Getler. il Miss & Roc 13:24-5+ Ag 19 '63
How to succeed in business without a profit. Miss & Roc 13:29 Ag 19 '63
Lab that generates its own ideas. il Bsns W p46-8+ O 3 '64
CORNELL university, Ithaca, N.Y.
Cornell students study abroad; semester program in New York city. Arch Rec 134:33 N '63
Dimensions of the modern university; address, October 4, 1963. J. A. Perkins. Sch & Soc 92:100-4 Mr 7 '64
Food expert teaches at Cornell. il Ebony 18:73-4+ Ag '63
Lafayette papers acquired by Cornell. Wilson Lib Bul 38:510 Mr '64
Ms. that would not scour; centennial of Gettysburg address. Wilson Lib Bul 38:378-9 Ja '64
Mo is Sa'aid's nickname at Cornell; 64,000 foreign students. il Newsweek 61:59-62+ Ap 22 '63
Taming Cayuga's waters. il Time 81:73-4 Ap 5 '63
Well endowed. Newsweek 64:96 O 26 '64

Libraries

Far above Cayuga's waters; dedication of Cornell's Olin and Uris libraries. J. Shera. Wilson Lib Bul 38:73+ S '63
CORNELSEN, Leroy A.
Economics of training the unemployed. Sch Life 47:17-18 O '64
CORNET, Antonio Gaudí y. See Gaudí y Cornet, A.
CORNFELD, Bernard
Fundman of fundmen. il por Newsweek 64:82-3 D 7 '64
CORNHUSK dolls. See Dolls
CORNING, N.Y.
Corning, N.Y. painting is back home. il Hobbies 68:50-1 Ag '63
CORNING community college, N.Y.
Planning the community college. il Arch Rec 135:123-32 Je '64
CORNING glass center, Corning, N.Y.
Ancient beaker added to Corning museum. il Hobbies 67:82 F '63
Corning, N.Y. painting is back home. il Hobbies 68:50-1 Ag '63
Fletcher Ford collection now shown in Corning museum. il Hobbies 69:91 Je '64
CORNING glass works, Corning, N.Y.
Company that never left town. J. McDonald. il Fortune 70:114-17+ Ag '64
CORNING museum of glass. See Corning glass center, Corning, N.Y.
CORNING science prize
$12,500 Corning prize for science book announced. Pub W 185:31 Mr 16 '64
CORNING ware. See Pyroceram
CORNISH, Charles
In troubled Cambridge: Negro heads city council. por U S News 57:12 Ag 3 '64
CORNISH, George Anthony
New encyclopedia. New Yorker 39:41-2 Mr 16 '63
CORNISH, Samuel E.
Founders of the Negro press. L. Bennett, jr. il por Ebony 19:96-8+ Jl '64
CORNS, Ray
Romance of Pewee Valley. Harper 229:32 S '64
CORNSTALKS
Cornstalk bedding, how to get it in. W. J. Fletcher. il Suc Farm 61:46 O '63
CORNUELLE, Richard C.
New conservative manifesto. T. G. Harris. il por Look 28:20-3 D 29 '64
CORNWALL, Barbara
Cyprus: it might be another Cuba. New Repub 151:8 Jl 11 '64
Dilemma on Cyprus. New Repub 151:12 S 5 '64
CORNWALL, England
Wild music. H. F. Ellis. New Yorker 39:58-60 Jl 6 '63
See also
St Michael's Mount (island)
CORNWELL, David
Inside job? Newsweek 63:80 F 3 '64
Man who came in from the cold. R. Stout. por Mlle 59:60-1 Jl '64
More Le Carré capers. por Time 83:90+ My 29 '64
Spy-master unmasked. J. Bonfante. il pors Life 56:39-40+ F 28 '64
CORNWELL, David G. See Wolfe, D. A. jt. auth.
CORNWELL, Elmer E. jr
Bosses, machines, and ethnic groups. bibliog f Ann Am Acad 353:27-39 My '64
President's most powerful tool. Sat R 48:16-19 Ja 2 '65
CORNWELL, George W.
Private outdoor recreation industry: its management. Am For 69:36-9+ O '63
CORONA, Al, and Corona, Ree
San Francisco's PALS starts them young. Pop Electr 19:55-6 D '63
CORONA, Ree. See Corona, A. jt. auth.
CORONA, Solar. See Sun—Corona
CORONADO, Calif.
Career day. G. D. Hunsaker. Recreation 56:234 My '63
Dune crawler switches to beach patrol. G. D. Hunsaker. il Am City 79:32 N '64
What to do with Othello? problem of the retired officer. Nation 196:317-18 Ap 20 '63
Where the admirals go. il Newsweek 61:90-1 Ap 15 '63
CORONAGRAPH
Coronascope II. il Sky & Tel 26:82 Ag '63
First flight of Coronascope II. G. Newkirk, jr. and J. D. Bohlin. il Sky & Tel 28:16-19 Jl '64
New Climax coronagraph. il Sky & Tel 26:20 Jl '63
CORONAL spectrum. See Spectrum, Solar
CORONARY artery disease. See Arteriosclerosis
CORONARY heart disease. See Heart—Diseases
CORONATION of Poppea; opera. See Monteverdi, C.
CORPORAL punishment
Black Annie; lashings at Mississippi's Parchman penitentiary. Newsweek 61:33 Mr 18 '63
Cane mutiny. Newsweek 63:78 F 3 '64
Corporal punishment in D.C. schools? U S News 54:8 Mr 4 '63
Corporal punishment? opinions differ. J. A. R. Wilson; J. M. Spinning. NEA J 52:18-20 S '63
Paddling pupils unwise. Sci N L 83:322 My 25 '63
Rumblings in D.C. Sr Schol 82:2T-4T Mr 20 '63
Should teachers wield the rod? S. S. Rosenberg. il Parents Mag 39:74-5+ F '64
Spanking of students, what education chief thinks; excerpts from interview. F. Keppel. U S News 54:20 Je 24 '63
Speaking out; bring back the whipping post! whippings in Delaware. S. Lynch. Sat Eve Post 236:6+ Mr 30 '63
Where a court upheld a whipping sentence; Delaware Supreme court. il U S News 54:16 Ap 15 '63
Whiting doesn't spare the rod. K. Detzer. il Read Digest 82:167-70+ My '63
CORPORATE acquisitions. See Business consolidations and mergers
CORPORATE giving. See Corporations—Charitable contributions
CORPORATE planning. See Business management and organization
CORPORATION law
Who owns what's in your head? W. Bowen. il Fortune 70:175-8+ Jl '64
CORPORATION lawyers. See Lawyers
CORPORATION management. See Business management and organization
CORPORATIONS
American economic republic, by A. A. Berle. Review
New Repub 148:21-3 Je 22 '63. P. Green
Corporate clams; secrecy of European businesses. il Time 81:95 Ap 12 '63
Corporation: linchpin of the economy. il Sr Schol 85:12 D 2 '64
How to succeed on company time; writing and publishing a company history. D. Dempsey. Sat R 47:28-9 Jl 18 '64
In defense of corporations. G. L. Philippe. Duns R 81:52-3+ F '63

CORPORATIONS—*Continued*
Minority owners can avoid squeeze-outs. F. H. O'Neal. Harvard Bsns R 41:150-2+ Mr '63
Ten best-managed companies. il Duns R 81: 32-4+ Ja '63
Top money; Fortune's 500. Time 84:88 Jl 10 '64
See also
Business consolidations and mergers
Electric utilities
Family corporations
Farms, Incorporated
Investments
Trusts, Industrial

Accounting

Accounting for inflation. J. Thackray. il Duns R 84:39-40+ D '64
Accounting improvement: how fast, how far? L. M. Savoie. bibliog f il Harvard Bsns R 41:144-50+ Jl '63
Civil war among the auditors. J. Thackray. il Duns R 83:42-4+ Ap '64
Fit your fiscal year to your business. L. E. Newman. il Harvard Bsns R 42:106-9 N '64
On the judging of mince pies. D. J. Fennelly. il Harvard Bsns R 42:77-86 N '64
Profit-planning accounting for small firms. J. Dearden. Harvard Bsns R 41:66-76 Mr '63
See also
Financial statements

Advertising

Image builders go back to print; ads in magazines again. il Bsns W p70 O 31 '64

Charitable contributions

Boost from blue chips; millions to Negro colleges. Bsns W p25 Ag 1 '64
Case that cleared the way; A. P. Smith manufacturing company's unrestricted gift of $1,500 to Princeton university. L. L. L. Golden. Sat R 47:59 S 12 '64
Charity on a business basis. Bsns W p70+ Ja 23 '65
Lincoln Center and corporate support. C. Francis. Mus Am 84:10 O '64
See also
Foundations, Charitable and educational

Defense measures

If the nuclear bomb drops. . . Bsns W p92 Ap 20 '63

Directories

Fortune directory: 500 largest U.S. industrial corporations. il Fortune 68:177-96 Jl '63; 70: 179-98 Jl '64
Fortune directory; 200 largest foreign industrial companies, and the fifty largest U.S. commercial banks, life-insurance, merchandising, transportation, and utility companies. il Fortune 68:139-50 Ag '63; 70:151-62 Ag '64

Directors

Case of the earmarked executives; case study of junior boards of directors; excerpt from European problems in general management, by E. P. Learned and others. F. J. Aguilar. il Harvard Bsns R 41:6-8+ N '63
Inside the board room. il Time 83:96-7 F 28 '64
Men behind the wheels. il Fortune 68:98-100 Ag '63

Employees

See Employees

Finance

Another peak, but by a hair. il Bsns W p53-4 F 2 '63
Are stockholder ranks thinning? il Bsns W p72-3 F 1 '64
Autos, steel, oil lead the parade. il Bsns W p27-8 N 2 '63
Back of worry over mergers; latest figures on profits. il U S News 56:74 Je 1 '64
Best of everything. il Time 83:89 F 7 '64
Big shift in stockholders: who owns U.S. industry now? U S News 56:97-8 Mr 16 '64
Bright, dark spots in the profits picture; with chart. U S News 54:38 F 11 '63
Buildup in cash. il Fortune 70:99-100+ Jl '64
Captive finance companies. V. L. Andrews. il Harvard Bsns R 42:80-92 Jl '64
Cash-flow flap. Fortune 67:204+ F '63
Climb continues, less fast; corporate profits. il Bsns W p 104+ Ja 9 '65
Does the profit squeeze hurt? P. L. Bernstein. Nation 196:94-7 F 2 '63; Reply with rejoinder. E. H. Freedheim. 196:inside cover Mr 23 '63
Du Pont's financial acumen. J. Ross-Skinner. il Duns R 81:42-4+ F '63
Earnings bounce to new high. il Bsns W p34-5 O 24 '64
Earnings; the best ever. il Newsweek 64:58 Ag 3 '64
Every man his own banker. il Bsns W p24-5 F 15 '64
Executive investor; sixteen rapidly growing industries. il Duns R 85:103-4+ Ja '65
Financial goals: management vs. stockholders. G. Donaldson. bibliog f il Harvard Bsns R 41:116-29 My '63
Germany's financial coronaries. H. Nickel and R. Sheehan. il Fortune 69:130-1+ Je '64
How firms finance outlays now; concerning SEC report. U S News 56:86 My 4 '64
How high are profits? address, March 5, 1964. H. Ford, 2d. Vital Speeches 30:433-6 My 1 '64; Same abr. with title How high is up? Read Digest 85:227-30+ S '64; Excerpts. U S News 56:55 Mr 23 '64
How high are profits? Bsns W p99 Ag 10 '63
How they raise money without much of a fuss; private placement of debt issues. il Bsns W p 164+ O 17 '64
It's another big quarter for profits; with chart. U S News 57:95 N 2 '64
It's harder to play follow the leader. il Bsns W p87-8 Jl 20 '63
Living higher on the hog; Billions in search of a top return. il Bsns W p 166-8+ O 19 '63
Longest boom gets new fuel; first-quarter earnings; with editorial comment il Bsns W p23-5, 144 My 9 '64
Lusty, new record for 1963. il Bsns W p22 F 1 '64
More fuel for growth in the profit upswing. il Bsns W p27 Ap 25 '64
More ready money for business. il U S News 57:94 Ag 24 '64
More zoom still ahead. il Bsns W p25-6 Ap 27 '63
Need for a hot line. Fortune 68:119-20 N '63
$1,459,000,000 for GM; and other earnings reports. Newsweek 61:68+ F 11 '63
Private route to new capital; direct placements. J. Ross-Skinner. il Duns R 81:35-6+ Ja '63
Profits: a record '63, better '64; with chart. U S News 56:84 F 10 '64
Profits follow the boom line. il Bsns W p 134+ S 19 '64
Profits: holding a high level. il Bsns W p60+ F 16 '63
Profits put on weight: second quarter report. il Bsns W p25-7 O 12 '63
Profits set another record; with chart. U S News 56:101 My 4 '64
Profits up; going higher? il U S News 55: 98-9 Ag 5 '63
Profits, wages, and prices. il Fortune 70:28+ O '64
Profits will recover more lost ground. J. Backman. il Nations Bsns 51:36-7+ D '63
Record profits. il Fortune 68:44+ S '63
Record-smashing record; rise in profits. il Time 84:57 Jl 31 '64
ROI for new-product policy. P. A. Scheuble, jr. il Harvard Bsns R 42:110-20 N '64
Review of funds-flow analysis. W. B. McFarland. bibliog f Harvard Bsns R 41:162-4+ S '63
Score on business profits: many gains reported, but—. il U S News 54:84+ My 6 '63
Second quarter profits: trend still upward; with chart. U S News 57:71 Ag 3 '64
Second thoughts on going public; management research survey. Bsns W p 114 F 16 '63
Sharpening up. Time 82:64 Ag 23 '63
Some big companies the SEC would like to be hearing from; table. Fortune 67:232 My '63
Still another record; second-quarter earnings. il Bsns W p23-4 Jl 25 '64
Street consensus: new highs lie ahead. il Bsns W p 122+ S 21 '63
Tax device to stem the outflow of gold; letter. G. A. Freeman, jr. Fortune 68:94 S '63
Third-quarter profits: a new high? with chart. il U S News 55:68-70 N 4 '63
United aircraft: success with a wry twist. H. B. Meyers. il Fortune 68:110-15+ D '63
Vote of confidence in good times; with chart. U S News 57:63 D 28 '64
Wall Street's view: a modest price gain. il Bsns W p70-2 D 28 '63
What 17 million shareholders share. M. D. Reagan. il N Y Times Mag p 11+ F 23 '64
Who's to blame for Riklis? Riklis? S. H. Brown. il Fortune 68:136-7+ O '63
Will it be big enough? il Bsns W p 15-16 Ag 3 '63

CORPORATIONS—Finance—*Continued*
Wonderland economics of Sheraton corp. J. Thackray. il Duns R 83:32-4+ Je '64
See also
Bankruptcy
Budget, Business
Capital investments
Dividends
Financial statements
Profit
Small business—Finance
Stock purchase options

Bibliography

Advances in financial management. R. H. Baldwin. bibliog f Harvard Bsns R 42:34-5+ Ja '64

Foreign expansion

See Business—Foreign expansion

Foreign subsidiaries

Accounting for inflation; accounts of Latin American subsidiaries. J. Thackray. il Duns R 84:39-40+ D '64
Bull at the altar; deal with Machines Bull. Fortune 70:59-60+ S '64
Businessman talks about doing business abroad; excerpts from address. A. C. Long. il U S News 56:96-7 My 4 '64
Central America closes ranks. il Bsns W p47-8+ Mr 16 '63
Chrysler soups up foreign sales. il Bsns W p47-8 F 8 '64
Conoco's widening world. R. Sheehan. il Fortune 69:113-17+ Ap '64
Executive trouble abroad. F. N. Parks. Duns R 82:35-6+ Ag '63
Financing overseas expansion. J. G. McLean. il Harvard Bsns R 41:53-65 Mr '63
For new opportunities: now the word is go abroad. il U S News 56:93-6 Je 1 '64
Going continental. il Time 85:73A Ja 29 '65
Is it over, over there? interviews, ed. by J. B. Weiner. L. C. Yaseen; L. C. Hoch. il Duns R 83:pt2 108-10+ Mr '64
Let's be realistic; exports and foreign investment; address, November 17, 1964. K. Rush. Vital Speeches 31:171-4 Ja 1 '65
Machines Bull's computer crisis; France's proud business-machine firm. T. R. Bransten and S. H. Brown. il Fortune 70:154-5+ Jl '64
Multinational companies. il Bsns W p62-4+ Ap 20 '63
Oilmen in new battle of Britain. il Bsns W p66-9 Mr 2 '63
Prestolite builds a new world. Bsns W p63-4+ D 14 '63
Push overseas keeps going strong; McGraw-Hill survey. il Bsns W p27-8 S 7 '63
Salad days for foreign sales; with charts. il Bsns W p56-8+ D 28 '63
Sourcing abroad for domestic profit. D. J. O'Connell and J. J. Benson. il Harvard Bsns R 41:87-94 Mr '63
Tax havens lose charm. Bsns W p 124 S 12 '64
Thriving under fetters; Union carbide India, ltd. il Bsns W p58-60 N 7 '64
U.S. business fights Latin American reds. il Bsns W p54+ Mr 16 '63
Westinghouse now goes all the way. il Bsns W p49-50+ Je 29 '63
What U.S. companies are doing abroad. See issues of U.S. news & World report
Why GE is joining Olivetti; hopes to get European computer market. il Bsns W p 140+ S 12 '64
See also
Branch factories, Foreign

Names

Name game. il Time 83:90 Ap 3 '64
Willys name gone from auto world; now Kaiser jeep corp. Bsns W p72 Mr 16 '63

Political activities

See Business—Political aspects

Public relations

See Business—Public relations

Rating

DOD, NASA study common system for rating company performance. W. H. Gregory. Aviation W 78:95+ F 4 '63

Real estate operations

Humble oil lays out a new Texas town; Bayport development. il Bsns W p67-8 F 8 '64

Reports

See Reports

Size

Industry's influentials: the million-dollar companies. il Duns R 83:pt2 125-6 Mr '64
New weapons against bigness. S. Marcus. Harvard Bsns R 43:100-8 Ja '65
Parkinson cautions: there's danger in growth; interview. C. N. Parkinson. Nations Bsns 52:36-7+ My '64
T.R.B. from Washington; big business. New Repub 151:2 O 3 '64
Thinking small. il Time 81:88 Mr 22 '63
Where is the organization man? L. W. Porter. bibliog f il Harvard Bsns R 41:53-61 N '63

Social aspects

See Business—Social aspects

Taxation

Business expects big gains. il Nations Bsns 51:33-5+ D '63
Business gets a tax break. il U S News 56:101-2 Je 15 '64
Cashing in on the new tax rate. Bsns W p86 D 12 '64
Does brainpower require capital? question of penalty taxes from Ted Bates & co. il Bsns W p83-4 D 12 '64
Don't wait to cut the corporate tax. Bsns W p 116 Mr 30 '63
For corporations: a tax increase? il U S News 54:45 F 4 '63
Making sense of state taxes; three-year study of state levies on business. Bsns W p54 Je 20 '64
Mr Gordon drops a shoe; U.S. investment in Canada. Fortune 69:56+ F '64
More, not less. Time 81:81-2 F 22 '63
New life on leasing. il Duns R 81:65-6+ Ap '63
Profits in focus. il Fortune 69:32+ Je '64
Some companies that were affected by 1962 tax changes. il Fortune 68:262 Jl '63
Tax changes replenish the till. il Bsns W p64 F 9 '63
Tax havens lose charm. Bsns W p 124 S 12 '64
Taxpayers: the 100 biggest. U S News 55:88 Jl 1 '63
What a tax cut will do for corporations, and when. il U S News 55:126-7 O 7 '63
What new tax law will mean; interview. M. M. Caplin. Nations Bsns 52:38-9+ F '64
What's needed for greater growth; views of key men. Nations Bsns 52:64-6 Jl '64
You may think the corporate profit tax is bad, but. . . G. Burck. Fortune 67:86-9+ Ap '63

Treasurers

Sharp-pencil men; corporate treasurer. Time 81:85 Mr 8 '63

Valuation

Defensive stocks that offer a hedge against a possible market selloff. il Duns R 83:131-2+ My '64
Executive investor; dollar averaging and some promising growth stocks. il Duns R 83:77-9 Je '64
Executive investor; in a high but nervous market, look for quality and promise in earnings. il Duns R 84:83-4 Jl '64
Executive investor; list of stocks often found in institutional portfolios. il Duns R 82:75-8 Ag '63
Executive investor; nine stocks with promise in a selective market. il Duns R 82:103+ D '63
Growth companies. J. B. Weiner. il Duns R 84:40-3+ O '64
One type of buyer retreats. Bsns W p90 Mr 7 '64
Some individual stocks that offer good value. il Duns R 84:77-8+ D '64
Tax-selling vs. overall planning. il Duns R 84:141-2+ N '64
What makes a growth company? top thirteen. J. B. Weiner. il Duns R 84:30-2+ N '64
What's an acquisition worth? J. Thackray. il Duns R 83:36-8+ Mr '64

CORPORATIONS and education. See Business and education
CORPS of engineers. See United States—Army—Corps of engineers
CORPSES. See Cadavers
CORPULENCE
Add two pounds daily. Sci N L 83:403 Je 29 '63
Adipose society; West Germany. il Time 82:29 Jl 19 '63
Citrate cleavage enzyme in livers of obese and nonobese mice. M. S. Kornacker and J. M. Lowenstein. bibliog il Science 144:1027-8 My 22 '64
Fat adults from chubby children grow. Good H 157:195 O '63

CORPULENCE—*Continued*
Great balancing act: eating vs. activity. M. F. Trulson and F. J. Stare. il Todays Health 41:35-7+ Je '63
How to tell if you're fat. Farm J 87:60F N '63
Inactivity complicates fat child's problem. il Todays Health 41:78+ D '63
It's no fun to be fat. C. Chilman. il Parents Mag 38:54-5+ Ap '63
Obese are inactive. Sci N L 83:260 Ap 27 '63
Our overweight children. L. W. Sauer. PTA Mag 58:29-30 F '64
People who can't lose weight. A. J. Snider. Sci Digest 55:76-7 Je '64
Who gets fat? il Sci Digest 56:21 D '64
Zero calorie diet. S. Alexander. il Life 55: 105-8+ O 11 '63

Anecdotes, facetiae, satire, etc.

Containers don't count. F. E. Decker and others. il Esquire 59:102-3+ Ap '63
You too can be fat and love it. A Buchwald. il McCalls 90:16 F '63

CORPUS callosum. See Brain

CORPUS CHRISTI. University, Corpus Christi, Tex.
Island library in the round. C. Wrotenbery. il Library J 88:4566-8 D 1 '63

CORREAS, Edmundo
Sarmiento, the educator. Américas 16:27-32 Ag '64

CORREAS
Correas don't like pampering. il Sunset 131: 281 O '63

CORREGIDOR (surrender) See World war, 1939-1945—Philippines

CORRELATION (education)
Our own space project; art-science activity, Cleveland school, Newark, N.J. B. I. Forman. il Recreation 56:286 Je '63
We have left no art unturned; McLean, Va, high school. C. S. Burks and R. L. Dowell. il NEA J 53:22-4 My '64

CORRELL, David L.
Sialic acid-containing glycopeptide from chlorella. bibliog Science 145:588-9 Ag 7 '64

CORRELL, James W.
Adipose tissue; ability to respond to nerve stimulation in vitro. bibliog Science 140: 387-8 Ap 26 '63

CORRERA, Pascual Juan Emilio Arrieta y. See Arrieta y Correra, P. J. E.

CORRESPONDENCE. See Commercial correspondence, Letter writing; International correspondence; Letters

CORRESPONDENCE schools and courses
Filling those educational gaps by mail. S. C. Mitchell. Parents Mag 38:70+ Mr '63
How good are the home study schools? D. L. Miller. il Mod Phot 28:78-9 F '64
Masters; Institute for university studies, Bergenfield, N.J. New Yorker 39:35-6 S 14 '63
Music by mail. B. MacMillan. il Parents Mag 38:76-7+ S '63
Poor man's B-school. il Bsns W p 160+ Je 6 '64
Supervised correspondence courses. H. V. Kelly. il NEA J 52:26-7 N '63
See also
Famous artists schools, incorporated
Famous photographers school

CORRESPONDENTS, Newspaper. See Reporters and reporting

CORRESPONDENTS association, United Nations. See United Nations correspondents association

CORRIDOR; story. See Fuller, E.

CORRIGAN, John E.
Bless me, father. America 110:342-4 Mr 14 '64

CORRIGAN Frye and the FBI; story. See Rhodin, E.

CORRINGTON, Julian D.
Nature and the microscope (cont) Natur Hist 72:61-4 Mr; 61-4 My; 64-8 N '63; 73:58-62 Mr; 65-70 O '64

CORROSION and anticorrosives
Do pennies prevent battery corrosion? il Pop Sci 183:28-30 Jl '63
End to corrosion; cathodic protection. W. Doring. il Motor B 111:155-7 Ap '63
German scientists investigate materials resisting supersonic rain-erosion damage. W. C. Wetmore. il Aviation W 80:110-11+ Ap 27 '64
No steel corrosion with nuclear by-product. Sci N L 83:264 Ap 27 '63
Water-works corrosion. W. E. Edwards. il Am City 78:86-8 F '63
See also
Protective coatings

CORRUPTION in politics. See Politics, Corruption in

CORRUPTION in the palace of justice; drama. See Betti, U.

CORRY, Claud B.
Licensing of child-care facilities. Ann Am Acad 355:128-33 S '64

CORSET; story. See Connell, E. S. jr

CORSETS. See Foundation garments

CORSICA
Jesus for a night; Easter week processions. Time 81:44 Ap 19 '63
See also
Ajaccio
Art—Corsica

CORSINI, R. J. and Howard, D. D.
(eds) Classroom incident; excerpts from Critical incidents in teaching. NEA J 53: 33-4 S '64

CORSO, Gregory
Audience swam for their lives; excerpts from YM-YWHA-sponsored symposium on The state of American poetry today, ed. by J. Scully. Nation 198:244-5+ Mr 9 '64
Notes from the other sides of April: with Negro eyes, with white; excerpt. Esquire 62:86-7+ Jl '64

about

Bye, bye, Beatnik. il por Newsweek 62:65 Jl 1 '63

CORSON, Dale R.
(ed) See Debye, P. J. W. Peter J. W. Debye: an interview

CORSON, John J.
On recruiting federal officials. Science 144: 663-4 My 8 '64

CORSON, Martha
Nice family; story. Redbook 121:62-3 O '63
Twists, angles, and gimmicks. Writer 76:18-20+ My '63

CORT, David
Ambush on the Styx. Sat R 46:21-2 Ag 31 '63
Blind man's bluff. Nation 199:306-7 N 2 '64
California plays ostrich: the earthquake taboo. Nation 199:404-6 N 30 '64
Canada under Old Glory. Nation 199:51-3 Ag 10 '64
Cities downstream. Nation 198:95-7 Ja 27 '64
Crafts reborn. Nation 198:628-9 Je 22 '64
Disappearance of a museum. Nation 197:109-11 S 7 '63
Glossy rats. Nation 197:326-7+ N 16 '63
Gold in the ski hills. Nation 198:120-1 F 3 '64
Mountaineers: dilettantes of suicide. Nation 196:423-4+ My 18 '63
Olympics: myth of the amateur. Nation 199: 157-9 S 28 '64
People vs. pigeons. il Nation 197:368-9 N 30 '63
Quakes, winds and great waves. Nation 198: 363-5 Ap 13 '64
Starving for science. Nation 199:329-31 N 9 '64
View from the scaffold. Nation 196:177-9 Mr 2 '63
Voices of Birmingham. Nation 197:46-8 Jl 27 '63
Wolves and congressmen. Nation 197:216-18 O 12 '63

CORT, John C.
Eight hundred Americans. Commonweal 81: 7-10 S 25 '64

CORTÁZAR, Julio
Julio Cortázar; storytelling giant. J. Duran. il pors Américas 15:39-43 Mr '63

CORTAZZO, Arnold D. and Menefee, A. R.
Exploring a need. Recreation 57:304-5 Je '64

CORTE, Arturo E.
Particle sorting by repeated freezing and thawing. bibliog Science 142:499-501 O 25 '63

CORTÉS, Hernándo
City of the living god; excerpts from Cortés: the life of the conqueror by his secretary, tr. by L. B. Simpson. F. L. de Gómara. il Am Heritage 15:67-79 Ap '64
Cortés, by F. López de Gómara, tr. and ed. by L. B. Simpson. Review
Sat R il 47:36 My 30 '64. L. C. de Morelos
Great confrontations V: Cortes and Montezuma. J. H. Elliott. il pors Horizon 5:92-6 N '63

CORTÉS, Ramiro
Pioneer service to two young composers. R. Sabin. Am Rec G 30:971 Je '64

CORTESE, Ross W.
Profits and problems from the golden years; Seal Beach Leisure World, Calif. il por Bsns W p 132-3+ Ap 11 '64

CORTESI, Arnaldo
Dynasty's end. Time 82:93 N 8 '63

CORTEX, Cerebral. See Cerebral cortex

CORTÉZ, SEA OF. See California, Gulf of

CORTICOSTEROIDS
Cortisone linked to cataracts in the eye. Sci Digest 53:23 Mr '63
Plasma corticosteroids: changes in concentration after stimulation of hippocampus and amygdala. A. J. Mandell and others. bibliog il Science 139:1212 Mr 22 '63

CORTINA, Louis F.
For greater safety, flash those lights! Pop Electr 20:75-6+ Mr '64

CORTINA D'AMPEZZO, Italy
Winter whirl at Cortina D'Ampezzo. il Holiday 33:56-61 F '63

CORTISOL. See Hydrocortisone

CORTISONE
Actinomycin: inhibition of cortisone-induced synthesis of hepatic gluconeogenic enzymes. G. Weber and others. bibliog il Science 142:390-2 O 18 '63
Glycogen deposition in the liver induced by cortisone: dependence on enzyme synthesis. O. Greengard and others. bibliog il Science 141:160-1 Jl 12 '63
Immunity and susceptibility toward cheek pouch transplants of a mouse leukemia. R. A. Adams. bibliog il Science 146:944-5 N 13 '64
Yams, cortisone source, now grown in U.S. Sci N L 83:201 Mr 30 '63
See also
Hydrocortisone

CORTLAND state teachers college. See New York state university—Teachers college at Cortland

CORTONA, Pietro da
Regal hangings in a Quaker temple. il Art N 63:26-7 O '64

CORTOT, Alfred
Anthology of pianism from a more poetic age. H. Goldsmith. por Hi Fi 14:66-7 F '64

CORVALLIS, Ore.
New Corvallis arts center. il Sunset 132:54 Je '64

CORWIN, Arthur F.
Mexico resists the pill. Nation 198:477-80 My 11 '64

CORWIN, Emil
Combating teen-age smoking. PTA Mag 58:4-6 Ap '64

CORY, John Mackenzie
Slow cool burning; address, April 26, 1963. Wilson Lib Bul 38:262-4+ N '63
about
Cory to study library needs of mid-city Philadelphia. Library J 90:89 Ja 1 '65

CORYLUS. See Filbert trees

COSA nostra. See Mafia

COSAND, Joseph P.
Junior college: pros and cons. PTA Mag 59:22-4 Ja '65

COSBY, Bill
Raceless Bill Cosby. il pors Ebony 19:131-2+ My '64
Riiight. por Newsweek 61:89 Je 17 '63
Spy. por Newsweek 64:51 D 14 '64

COSER, Lewis A.
America and the world revolution; ed. by N. Podhoretz. Commentary 36:278-96 O '63
Democratic processes. Commentary 35:260-2 Mr '63
Hard look at labor. Commentary 37:86-8 F '64
New frontiers. Commentary 36:76-8 Jl '63
Visions and revisions. Commentary 36:178-80; 37:12+ Ag '63, Ja '64

COSHOCTON, Ohio
Little people; pygmy cemetery. H. C. Wolfe. Sat R 47:71 N 7 '64

COSKREN, Thomas Marcellus
Is Golding Calvinistic? America 109:18-20 Jl 6 '63

COSMETIC surgery. See Surgery, Plastic

COSMETICS
All tanned, cool, fresh as a daisy. il Seventeen 22:60-1 Je '63
Beauty bulletin; skin cream. il Vogue 143:178-81+ F 1 '64
Beauty checkout. See issues of Vogue
Block that sun. il Consumer Bul 47:2+ Jl '64
Boys & girls together; men's cosmetics. il Time 82:69 N 15 '63
Can she really get rid of her wrinkles? anti-wrinkle lotion. il Changing T 18:46-8 Je '64
Cosmetic allergies. L. D. Kirk. il Parents Mag 38:130 Ap '63
Eskimos get the make-up message. D. Connelly. il Life 56:17+ Ja 31 '64
Everyone enjoys a gift of beauty. L. D. Kirk. il Parents Mag 39:138-9 N '64
Eye make-up and contact lenses. P. Dorman. il Consumer Bul 47:2 My '64
Hollow-wall packaging of cosmetics. il Consumer Bul 46:43+ My '63
Hormone cosmetics don't remove skin wrinkling. Sci Digest 53:76 Ap '63
Hypo-allergenic cosmetics. L. Allen. Todays Health 41:14 Ap '63
It's time for tanning aids. il Seventeen 22:114 Je '63
Little beauty gifts wrapped in beauty. il Good H 157:102-3+ D '63
Little drops of water: moisturizers. il Mlle 59:144-5 O '64
Make it a fragrant Christmas with cosmetics. L. D. Kirk. il Parents Mag 38:146-7 N '63
New unwrinkle. il Time 83:83 Mr 27 '64
New wrinkle; Magic secret lotion a drug, not a cosmetic? il Newsweek 63:92 My 11 '64
Seven women with the grace to blush; new cosmetic called a blusher. Vogue 141:144+ F 1 '63
Summer coolers. il Mlle 57:36 My '63
Summer formula; summertime sunning. D. A. Robinson. Ladies Home J 81:86 Jl '64
Suntanning aids. il Seventeen 23:24 Je '64
Through the summer looking glass. B. Clerke. Ladies Home J 80:30+ Jl '63
Wrinkle lotions; drugs or cosmetics? Consumer Rep 29:319 Jl '64
Your self (cont) il Consumer Rep 28:31-79 D '63
See also
Avon products, incorporated
Beauty, Personal
Beauty shops
Lipstick
Make-up
Toilet
Toilet preparations

COSMETICS for men
Sweet smell of. . . il Newsweek 64:88 N 30 '64

COSMIC dust. See Matter, Interstellar

COSMIC physics
See also
Magnetic field (cosmic physics)

COSMIC radio noise. See Radio astronomy

COSMIC rays
And quiet shines the sun. R. Lewis. Bul Atomic Sci 20:30-2 Ja '64
Cosmic electromagnetic radiation. E. M. Hafner. bibliog il Science 145:1263-71 S 18 '64
Deadly sprays on moon. W. Wingo. Sci N L 84:115 Ag 24 '63
Effects of cosmic rays on meteorites. M. Honda and J. R. Arnold. bibliog il Science 143:203-12 Ja 17 '64
Estimate of neutron albedo on the moon's surface resulting from cosmic radiation. M. V. K. Appa Rao. bibliog il Science 141:530-1 Ag 9 '63
Exploding galaxies. A. R. Sandage. il Sci Am 211:38-47 N '64
Exploding stars and evolution; excerpt from Cosmic radio waves. I. S. Shklovsky. il Sat R 47:41 Jl 4 '64
Supernova electrons. Sci Am 210:71 F '64
Where is the fat proton from? Time 81:74+ Mr 15 '63
See also
Van Allen radiation belts

Measurement

Solar neutrons and the earth's radiation belts. R. E. Lingenfelter and E. J. Flamm. bibliog il Science 144:292-4 Ap 17 '64

Physiological effects

Corn seeds affected by heavy cosmic ray particles. H. J. Curtis and H. H. Smith. bibliog il Science 141:158-60 Jl 12 '63

COSMOGONY
Deep structure of continents. G. J. F. MacDonald. bibliog il Science 143:921-9 F 28 '64
Procreation in space; McCrea theory that matter is created in the dense centers of galaxies. il Time 84:85 D 18 '64
Why is the sky dark at night? B. Bliven. Read Digest 83:203-4+ Jl '63
See also
Creation

COSMOLOGY
Earth and moon: past and future. G. J. F. MacDonald. bibliog il Science 145:881-90 Ag 28 '64
Fashion and competition in science: letter. G. C. McVittie. Science 146:341-2 O 16 '64; Discussion. 147:237-8 Ja 15 '65
Life and death of the universe. il Newsweek 63:63-7 My 25 '64
Man who looked to the stars. I. B. Cohen. il N Y Times Mag p 19-20+ F 9 '64

COSMOLOGY—*Continued*
Planets and comets: role of crystal growth in their formation. B. Donn and G. W. Sears. bibliog il Science 140:1208-11 Je 14 '63
COSMOPOLITAN (periodical)
One photographer+one model=all women. J. Morris. il U S Camera 26:64-71 My '63
COSMOS
Majesty of the cosmos: excerpt from Dialogue on the great world systems. G. Galilei. il UNESCO Courier 17:26 My '64
COSMOS club. See Washington, D.C.—Clubs
COSPAR. See International council of scientific unions—Committee on space research
COSSERY, Albert
Voices from the place of snakes. L. Zimpel. Nation 198:537-8 My 25 '64
COSSIO family
Jai alai goes west. il Bsns W p30-1 S 5 '64
COST
Must we push up costs. H. Hazlitt. Newsweek 63:67 F 3 '64
See also
Labor cost
also subhead Cost under various subjects, e.g. Cattle, Beef—Cost
COST (law)
Getting the feds to pay. Time 84:46 Jl 10 '64
Now, about the fee. Time 82:70 N 15 '63
COST accounting
Control system for architects' office costs. G. R. Keane. il Arch Rec 134:125-6 Jl '63
Cost-cutting set as major industry factor. G. C. Wilson. il Aviation W 81:17-18 Jl 13 '64
Cost of cost reduction. W. J. Coughlin. Miss & Roc 14:58 F 24 '64
Improve your profits day by day! F. O. Hoffman. Harvard Bsns R 41:59-67 Jl '63
Making cost control work. R. Likert and S. E. Seashore. bibliog f il Harvard Bsns R 41:96-108 N '63
Profit-planning accounting for small firms. J. Dearden. Harvard Bsns R 41:66-76 Mr '63
See also
Estimates
Value analysis
COST control. See Cost accounting
COST depends on what you reckon it in; story. See Gerber, M. J.
COST of advertising. See Advertising—Cost
COST of college education. See College education, Cost of
COST of food. See Food—Prices
COST of living
Control of inflation, like charity, begins at home. M. Smith. il Nations Bsns 51:23-4 O '63
On the town; cost of a night out. Newsweek 61:80 Ap 22 '63
See also
Budget, Household
Prices
Standard of living

Statistics

International binge. il Time 81:78 Je 28 '63

Latin America

Facts and figures of the Americas (cont) Américas 16:47 Je '64

United States

Americans get more for their money. il Nations Bsns 52:106-7 My '64
Consumer and wholesale prices; tables. See issues of Monthly labor review
How living costs vary by cities. il Changing T 17:21-3 My '63
If creeping inflation begins to run; ways of controlling inflation. H. C. Wallich. il N Y Times Mag p34+ S 13 '64
Intercity differences in family food budget costs. J. C. Brackett. il Mo Labor R 86:1189-94 O '63
See also
Food—Prices
Price indexes
Prices—United States
COST of living adjustments. See Wages—Cost of living adjustments
COST of medical service. See Medical service, Cost of
COST plus incentive fee. See Incentives in industry
COSTA, Mary
Epitome. por Newsweek 63:80 Ja 20 '64
Music to my ears; debut of Mary Costa. I. Kolodin. Sat R 47:44 Ja 25 '64
TV jingle singer makes debut at the Met; with interview. ed. by D. Zeitlin. il pors Life 56:37-41 Mr 13 '64
That's right, honey. il pors Time 83:70-1 Ja 17 '64
COSTA RICA
See also
Cartago
Hunting—Costa Rica
Land tenure—Costa Rica
San José

Economic policy

He helps workers become capitalists. D. S. Stroetzel. Read Digest 84:181-5 F '64

Religious institutions and affairs

News of the Christian world. Christian Cent 80:1034-6; 81:891-2 Ag 21 '63, Jl 8 '64
COSTA RICA and the United States
President Orlich of Costa Rica visits Washington; text of joint communique, July 1, 1964. L. B. Johnson and F. J. Orlich. Dept State Bul 51:81 Jl 20 '64
COSTADERIA selloana. See Pampas grass
COSTANTIN, LeRoy L. and others
Localization of calcium-accumulating structures in straited muscle fibers. bibliog Science 147:158-60 Ja 8 '65
COSTELLO, Donald P.
Salinger and his critics. Commonweal 79:132-5 O 25 '63
COSTELLO, Frank
Compliment from Mr C. Time 83:54 F 28 '64
COSTIGAN, James
Baby want a kiss. Criticism
Nation 198:496 My 11 '64
Newsweek 63:46 My 4 '64
Sat R 47:21 My 2 '64
Time il 83:50 My 1 '64
COSTIGAN, Madeleine
Bulbs. Horticulture 41:454-5 S '63
Fall-sown annuals hide ripened bulb foliage in spring. Flower Grower 50:18-20 O '63
Perennials. Pop Gard 15:30-1+ Ap '64
Shrub aristocrats. Horticulture 42:32-3 F '64
Tips on pruning roses. Horticulture 41:238 Ap '63
Try iris in your garden. Horticulture 41:329 Je '63
COSTUME
Paper bag props for holiday fun; account by The paper bag players. il Parents Mag 39:48-9+ D '64
Trick or treat costumes. il Pop Mech 120:158-62 O '63
See also
Academic costume

Collections

First ladies collection. Hobbies 68:51 Mr '63
Mantles of greatness; photographs of Lincoln Center fashion gala '63. Opera N 27:30-2 Mr 2 '63

Exhibitions

See also
Metropolitan museum of art, New York—Costume institute

Egypt

For the well-dressed fellah. il Time 84:30 Ag 7 '64

Japan

Inro art. W. Grimmich. il(p 1) Hobbies 68:28 N '63
COSTUME, Indian. See Indians of North America—Costume and adornment
COSTUME, Military. See Uniforms, Military
COSTUME, Religious. See Religious orders—Habit
COSTUME, Theatrical
Body by MacLaine, in originals by Edith Head. C. R. Jennings. il Sat Eve Post 236:24-9 N 30 '63
Broadway beehive: Herbet's theatrical dance supplies. W. Como. il Dance Mag 37:54-5 Mr '63
Check came to 'The circle O': Circle fabrics. W. Como. il Dance Mag 39:63 Ja '65
I don't want to be Liza; Audrey Hepburn's costumes for film of My fair lady photographed by C. Beaton. il Vogue 142:126-33 D '63
Jazz pants age! W. Como. il Dance Mag 38:53-4 Mr '64
Jo Baker's fabulous wardrobe. il Ebony 19:104-6+ Jl '64
Living figures. P. Hall. il Opera N 29:6-9 N 14 '64
Mantles of greatness; photographs of Lincoln Center fashion gala '63. il Opera N 27:30-2 Mr 2 '63
Metropolitan season; scene and costume sketches in color for 1963-64, with complete roster. Opera N 28:17-20 O 19 '63
My fair lady; excerpts from Beaton's diary. C. Beaton. il Ladies Home J 81:56-65 Ja '64

COSTUME design
All about Yves. il Time 82:46 Ag 9 '63
And not a stitch on underneath. il Life 57:45-6+ Jl 3 '64
Barefoot tycoon makes lillies bloom all over. il Life 54:105-9 F 8 '63
Brash new breed of British designers. il Life 55:78-85 O 18 '63
Chanel look. H. Obolensky. il Redbook 123:50-3 Je '64
Damsels and donkeys: costume exhibition at Boston's museum of fine arts. Newsweek 62:112 O 21 '63
Dazzling flair from Spain. il Life 57:72-81 O 9 '64
Fresh look at the empire dress. A. S. Cavallo. il Antiques 86:310-13 S '64
Galanos. E. Merriam. il Sat Eve Post 236:54+ O 26 '63
Girl with the Galanos air. il Holiday 33:74-9 Je '63
Inventive Africans; *kikois* dashing as dresses. il Time 84:60 S 18 '64
Me? in that! topless suits, with report by S. Alexander. il Life 57:54B-60+ Jl 10 '64
Meanwhile, at the ranch; fall collection previews. il Time 81:54 Je 21 '63
More's the Pitti. il Time 84:44 Jl 31 '64
Necklines take the plunge. il Life 56:70-1 Ja 3 '64
Pajama game; pants for women. il Time 84:67 Jl 3 '64
Paris: a designer's debut. M. Cantwell. il Mlle 58:147-9+ Mr '64
Paris clothes go pretty; photographs by B. Glinn. Sat Eve Post 236:22-7 Mr 16 '63
Paris: straight talk on the new French clothes. D. Vreeland. il Vogue 141:118-19+ Mr 1 '63
Patriotic heyday for fashions U.S.A. il Life 54:56-60+ F 22 '63
Portrait of Chanel no. 1. J. Barry. il N Y Times Mag p30-1+ Ag 23 '64; Same abr. Read Digest 85:261-3+ N '64
Pucci: sportswear king of the world. E. Sheppard. il Ladies Home J 80:55-61 Jl '63
Specialties of the house. J. T. Stark. il Look 28:122-4+ My 19 '64
Young designer changes things; Soviet fashion industry. il Life 55:113-14 S 13 '63
Yves Saint Laurent. J. T. Stark. il Look 28:84-8 Jl 14 '64
See also
Costume, Theatrical
Fashion
COSTUME designers
Ann Lowe: society's best-kept secret; only Negro American dress designer. T. B. Congdon, jr. il Sat Eve Post 237:74-6 D 12 '64
Brash new breed of British designers. il Life 55:78-85 O 18 '63
Chelsea invasion. il Time 84:52+ N 20 '64
Fashion trendmakers: fall 1964. T. Owett. il Ladies Home J 81:46-51 S '64
Necklines make you nervous? W. K. Zinsser. il Sat Eve Post 237:26-9 F 22 '64
Sacrebleu! Time 81:95 Mr 22 '63
Seven philosophers of fashion. B. W. Wyden. il N Y Times Mag p22-3 Jl 19 '64
See also
Brooks, D.
Cashin, B.
Chanel, G.
Galanos, J.
Head, E.
Khanh, E.
Mainbocher
Norell, N.
Paul, Mme
Pipart, G.
Pucci Di Barsento, E.
St Laurent, Y. M.
Tiffeau, J.
Toudouze, A.
Trigère, P.
Zaitsev, V. M.
COSTUME jewelry. See Jewelry
COSULICH, W. F. and Keevan, Thomas
This sewage plant gains friends. Am City 78:78-80 N '63
COSWA conferences. See Pugwash conferences on science and world affairs
CÔTE D'AZUR. See Riviera
COTHRAN, Tilman C.
Negro civil rights leaders; address, October 2, 1963. Vital Speeches 30:84-7 N 15 '63
COTILLIONS. See Balls (parties)
COTNER, Thomas E.
Would you like to teach overseas? Sr Schol 83:7T O 25 '63
COTT, Lawrence V
Letter from Hawaii. Nat R 15:57-8 Jl 30 '63
COTTAGE cheese
Fresh butter, old-fashioned buttermilk, and fresh cottage cheese. il Sunset 131:78-81 S '63
Hydrochloric acid used to make cottage cheese. Sci N L 85:392 Je 20 '64
COTTAGE industries
Homemade money. J. L. Block. il Good H 157:30-2+ Jl '63
COTTAGES
Expansible woodland cottage. il House & Gard 123:128-9 Je '63
Long lazy country weekend. S. Kirtland and others. il Look 28:61-5 Ja 14 '64
Vacation houses. il Sunset 132:106-13 My '64
Your second home. il Am Home 67:16+ Ap '64
COTTER, Edward F.
Sailing a catamaran. Yachting 113:48-50+ Je '63
COTTER, James P.
Brazil: social action. America 108:222-3 F 16 '63
Schools in Ceylon. America 109:212-13 Ag 31 '63
COTTON, F. A. and others
Mononuclear and polynuclear chemistry of rhenium (III): its pronounced homophilicity. bibliog Science 145:1305-7 S 18 '64
COTTON, Neal
Mexican crafts. Sch Arts 62:14-16 Ap '63
COTTON, Robert A.
For longer incinerator life. Am City 78:92-4 N '63
COTTON
Ancient cotton boll sets American identity. Sci N L 85:136 F 29 '64
Antiquity of American polyploid cotton. C. E. Smith, jr. and R. S. MacNeish. bibliog il Science 143:675-6 F 14 '64
Haploids: high-frequency production from single-embryo seeds in a line of Pima cotton. E. L. Turcotte and C. V. Feaster. bibliog il Science 140:1407-8 Je 28 '63
Hybrids
Antiquity of American polyploid cotton. C. E. Smith, jr. and R. S. MacNeish. bibliog il Science 143:675-6 F 14 '64
Prices
Across the editor's desk. D. Hanson. Suc Farm 61:10 My '63
Congress cuts cloth to fit textile men. Bsns W p34+ Ap 18 '64
Uses
Many uses of cotton swabs. Good H 156:141 Mr '63
COTTON bowl parade. See Dallas—Parades
COTTON exchanges
King Cotton loses big one in New Orleans; victim to federal policies. il Bsns W p28-9 Jl 18 '64
King Cotton's road to ruin. Life 57:4 Jl 24 '64
Last boll; government subsidies close New Orleans cotton exchange. Time 84:76 Jl 17 '64
COTTON fabrics
Printed cottons of Java; excerpts from Printed cottons of Asia. T. Osumi. il Craft Horiz 23:28-32 N '63
U.S. and Philippines conclude cotton textile agreement; announcement of initialing, with U.S. note and square yard equivalent conversion factors. il Dept State Bul 50:383-5 Mr 9 '64
Useful facts to know about cottons. Good H 157:130 Jl '63
Protection
Rot-resistant finish; rotproofing and weatherproofing of cotton fabric. Sci N L 86:181 S 19 '64
COTTON finishing
Rot-resistant finish. Sci N L 86:181 S 19 '64
COTTON goosing
Goosing the cotton. il Time 81:60 Ap 26 '63
COTTON growing
Mechanized plasticulture; polyethylene film mulches. il Time 81:75 Ap 19 '63
COTTON hybrids. See Cotton—Hybrids
COTTON industry and trade
Bumper crop. il Newsweek 62:96+ N 11 '63
Costly chaos in cotton, time to end it! R. S. Strother. Read Digest 82:149-50+ Je '63
Cotton textile agreements concluded with Greece and Turkey; Department announcement; with texts of US. notes, July 17, 1964. G. G. Johnson. il Dept State Bul 51:290-4 Ag 24 '64

COTTON industry and trade—*Continued*
Cotton textile arrangement concluded with Jamaica; Department announcement, October 2, 1963; with text of agreement. il Dept State Bul 49:645-6 O 21 '63
King subsidy; for domestic textile mills. New Repub 149:7-8 D 14 '63
Last boll; government subsidies close New Orleans cotton exchange. Time 84:76 Jl 17 '64
Record of U.S. participation during second year of long-term cotton textile arrangement; statement, December 1, 1964. S. Nehmer. Dept State Bul 52:49-56 Ja 11 '65
Rotton cotton? European complaints about the condition of U.S. cotton. il Time 83:89 Je 19 '64
U.S. and Hong Kong announce cotton textile agreement. il Dept State Bul 51:517-18 O 12 '64
U.S. and Hong Kong conclude cotton textile agreement; joint announcement, November 15, 1963. Dept State Bul 49:933-4 D 16 '63
United States and India conclude cotton textile agreement; Department announcement; with exchange of notes effecting the agreement; exchange of notes concerning category thirty-six exports. il Dept State Bul 50:914-17 Je 8 '64
United States and Japan conclude arrangement for cotton textile trade, 1963-65; joint announcement, exchange of notes and letters between Ambassador Ryuji Takeuchi and Assistant secretary of state for economic affairs G. Griffith Johnson, and attachments Dept State Bul 49:440-9 S 16 '63
U.S. and Republic of China conclude textile arrangement; Department announcement, October 22, 1963, with exchange of notes between Ambassador Jerauld Wright and the Chinese Minister of foreign affairs. il Dept State Bul 49:789-92 N 18 '63
U.S. and Spain conclude cotton textile agreement; Department announcement, with agreement and related letters, October 30, 1964. il Dept State Bul 51:794-7 N 30 '64
U.S. and Yugoslavia conclude cotton textile agreement; Department announcement, October 5, 1964, with agreement and related letters by G. G. Johnson. il Dept State Bul 51:602-5 O 26 '64
U.S. participation in long-term cotton textile arrangement; statement, December 3, 1963. S. Nehmer. Dept State Bul 50:96-101 Ja 20 '64
See also
Anderson, Clayton and company
Cotton exchanges

Wages and hours
Earnings in cotton textile mills, May 1963. C. M. O'Connor. il Mo Labor R 87:673-6 Je '64

COTTON mills

Employees
Earnings in cotton textile mills, May 1963. C. M. O'Connor. il Mo Labor R 87:673-6 Je '64

COTTON prints. See Cotton fabrics

COTTON textile workers. See Cotton mills—Employees

COTTONTAIL hunting. See Rabbit hunting

COTTRELL, Alvin J.
United States military posture today. bibliog f Cur Hist 47:71-6+ Ag '64

COTTRELL, Leonard, 1913-
Transport East to buried kingdoms. Sat R 47:34 Mr 7 '64

COTTRELL, Leonard S. Jr, and Sheldon, E. B.
Problems of collaboration between social scientists and the practicing professions. Ann Am Acad 346:126-37 Mr '63

COTTRELL, W. F. and Young, K. E.
Tote barrels. Am City 78:117-18 My '63
—See Dennin, C. jt. auth.

COTUIT, Mass. See Barnstable, Mass.

COUBERTIN, Pierre de
Sport is education; excerpts from address, October 28, 1963. R. Maheu. il UNESCO Courier 17:4-9 Ja '64

COUCH, Frank
Tests check roofing system for huge plant. Arch Rec 137:175-8 Ja '65

COUCH, Lou
Plan now, retire later. NEA J 52:11-12 My '63

COUELLE, Jacques
Village of foetuses; housing development for millionaires on the slopes of the Maritime Alps. il Time 82:57 N 22 '63

COUGAR hunting. See Puma hunting

COUGHLAN, Robert
Control of the brain. Life 54:90-2+ Mr 8; 81-2+ Mr 15 '63
Directors. Life 55:156-8+ D 20 '63
Tangled drama and private hells of two famous scientists. Life 55:87A-94+ D 13 '63
Two birds bet a million on a club in the bush. Sports Illus 18:84-8+ My 20 '63
Who was the man Jesus? Life 57:86-96+ D 25 '64

COUGHLIN, Bernard J.
Interfaith dialogue and church-state issues. America 108:900-3 Je 29 '63

COUGHLIN, William J.
Editorial. See issues of Missiles and rockets

COUILLARD, J. L. E.
Canada's planners walk a tightrope. il por Bsns W p 146+ Mr 14 '64

COULEE DAM. See Grand Coulee power and reclamation project

COULETTE, Henri
Black angel; poem. New Yorker 39:48 N 16 '63
Sickness of friends; poem. New Yorker 40:63 N 21 '64

COULIBALY, Sori
Progress achieved in the field of decolonization. UN Mo Chron 1:85-91 Je '64

COULOMBRE, Alfred J. See Coulombre, J. L. jt. auth.

COULOMBRE, Jane L. and Coulombre, A. J.
Lens development: fiber elongation and lens orientation. bibliog Science 142:1489-90 D 13 '63

COULSON, John
From Döllinger to Vatican II; a century too soon? Commonweal 79:400-3 D 27 '63

COULTER, Edith M.
Annual Edith M. Coulter lecture. por Library J 89:2528 Je 15 '64

COULTER, Francis C.
Shakespeare and the garden. Pop Gard 15:14+ S '64

COUMARIN
Glucosides of coumarinic and o-coumaric acids in the tonka bean. F. A. Haskins and H. J. Gorz. bibliog il Science 139:496-7 F 8 '63

COUNCIL, James
Cases of conscience. J. Ciardi. Sat R 46:10-11 F 2 '63

COUNCIL for a livable world
Scientists in politics: Council founded by Szilard brings cash and sophistication to lobbying. E. Langer. Science 145:561-3 Ag 7 '64

COUNCIL for basic education
High school English textbooks: a critical examination, by J. J. Lynch and B. Evans. Review
Sat R 46:54 D 21 '63. J. F. Warner
Miseducation of American teachers, by J. Koerner. Review
Newsweek 61:96 My 13 '63
Scholastic teacher interviews: Mortimer Smith; ed. by H. Langer. M. Smith. il Sr Schol 84:9T-12T My '64

COUNCIL for international progress in management
Spreading the business gospel; industrialists and educators for developing countries at U.S. business schools. il Bsns W p99-100 S 7 '63

COUNCIL for mutual economic assistance
COMECON. A. Korbonski. bibliog f il Int Concil 549:3-62 S '64
COMECON's woes. il Time 81:78 My 31 '63
Rotten fruit. Newsweek 62:38-9 S 2 '63
Soviets push on western markets; Comecon pipeline. il Bsns W p94-5+ Mr 2 '63

COUNCIL for united civil rights leadership
Angels are white; who pays the bills for civil rights? R. Cleghorn. New Repub 149:12-14 Ag 17 '63

COUNCIL of economic advisers. See United States—Council of economic advisers

COUNCIL of Europe
For France, the power of isolation. il Newsweek 61:38+ F 18 '63

COUNCIL of Europe exhibition of Byzantine art. See Art—Exhibitions

COUNCIL of federated organizations
And three letters home from Mississippi. P. Cowan; G. Cowan. Esquire 62:105-6+ S '64
Battle of McComb. M. Boyd. Christian Cent 81:1398+ N 11 '64
Cat and mouse game. E. Sutherland. il Nation 199:105-8 S 14 '64
Churches and Mississippi; Mississippi summer project. S. C. Rose. Christian Cent 81:909-10 Jl 15 '64
Educator; Mississippi summer project. R. J. Bernstein. il Nation 199:512-15 D 28 '64
Evangelists; program in Mississippi. il Newsweek 64:30-2 Ag 24 '64
It will be a hot summer in Mississippi. R. Woodley. Reporter 30:21-4 My 21 '64
Lawyer; experience in Mississippi. W. M. Kunstler. il Nation 199:507-9 D 28 '64

COUNCIL of federated organizations—*Cont.*
Letter from Jackson. C. Trillin. New Yorker 40:80+ Ag 29 '64
Life for a vote. J. Hersey. il Sat Eve Post 237:34-8+ S 26 '64
Youth corps in Mississippi. B. Keating. il N Y Times Mag p6-7 Jl 5 '64
COUNCIL of state governments
Confederacy revived. America 108:821 Je 8 '63
Reaction's refuge; proposed constitutional amendments. K. Crawford. Newsweek 61:31 Je 3 '63
COUNCIL on international nontheatrical events
When movies joined the jet set; choice of nontheatrical and short-subject motion pictures for international festivals. J. Tebbel. il Sat R 47:78-9 N 14 '64
COUNCIL on library resources, incorporated
Almost $100,000 in grants and contracts. Wilson Lib Bul 37:833 Je '63
CLR annual report notes computer's cultivated language; excerpts from introduction. V W Clapp. Library J 89:82 Ja 1 '64
CLR awards $265,000 in grants, contract. Pub W 186:35-6 S 14 '64
CLR finances two projects in automation and information storage. Library J 88:2860 Ag '63
CLR grant for subject headings list to aid Latin American librarians. Library J 89:2566 Je 15 '64
CLR grant to aid study of law school libraries. Library J 89:2306 Je 1 '64
CLR leads the field in support of library-oriented research; CLR awards grants and contracts totaling almost $100,000. Library J 88:1966-7 My 15 '63
Council on library resources, inc; summary of annual report. Wilson Lib Bul 39:371 Ja '65
Council on library resources report shows 1964 grants totaled $1,037,948. Library J 89:4875-6 D 15 '64
Council on library resources: several grants. Wilson Lib Bul 39:15-16 S '64
Council on library resources: three grants. Wilson Lib Bul 38:31 S '63
Manuscript catalog, research manual aided by Council on library resources. Library J 89:829 F 15 '64
Search for push-button library outlined in sixth CLR annual report; excerpts. V. W. Clapp. Library J 88:746 F 15 '63
$74,140 in grants made by Library resources council. Pub W 183:132 F 18 '63
COUNCIL secretaries, Association of. See Association of council secretaries
COUNCILL, William Hooper
William Hooper Councill; Alabama legislator, editor and lawyer. C. A. Brown. bibliog Negro Hist Bul 26:171-2 F '63
COUNCILMAN, Emily Sargent
This moment's miracle; poem. Christian Cent 81:294 Mr 4 '64
COUNCILS and synods
Last council? excerpt from Vatican II. R. Caporale. America 111:307-9 S 19 '64
Opening to the laity; diocesan synods. America 109:66 Jl 20 '63
Structures of the church, by H. Küng. Review
Commonweal 80:554-5 Ag 7 '64. D. J. O'Hanlon
See also
Vatican council, 2d
COUNSELING
Counseling for Catholics. R. F. Drinan. America 109:209 Ag 31 '63
Do ministers really understand people? L. David and I. David. Good H 156:65+ Mr '63
Guidance problems: cultural or cosmic? R. Mammarella and J. Crescimbeni. il Sat R 47:67+ N 21 '64; Discussion. 47:44 D 19 '64
Minister as therapist. Newsweek 61:62 My 6 '63
Protestant pastoral counseling, by W. E. Oates. Review
Christian Cent 80:430-1 Ap 3 '63. O. H. Mowrer
Young living; questions and answers. A. Wood. See issues of Seventeen
See also
Marriage counseling
School counselors
Vocational guidance
COUNSELING, Educational. See Educational guidance
COUNSELING service, School. See Personnel service (education); School counselors
COUNSELORS
See also
School counselors

COUNSILMAN, James
All-out agony at Indiana U. il por Life 56:94-6 Ap 10 '64
Doctor who makes agony and fun pay off. R. Lardner. il pors Sports Illus 20:48+ Mr 23 '64
Formula: hurt, pain, agony. il por Time 82:42 Ag 23 '63
COUNTERESPIONAGE. See Spies
COUNTERFEIT castle; story. See Knowlton, R. A.
COUNTERFEIT money. See Counterfeits and counterfeiting
COUNTERFEITS and counterfeiting
Making money. B. Surface. il N Y Times Mag p86+ O 18 '64
Moonlight mint. Newsweek 62:29 Ag 5 '63
COUNTER-insurgency aircraft. See Airplanes, Military—United States
COUNTERS (electrons, ions, etc)
Device records radiation in eighteen different sites. il Sci Digest 53:74-5 Ap '63
Radiation counter helps ascertain human growth. Sci N L 85:9 Ja 4 '64
See also
Geiger-Müller counters
COUNTERS (furniture) See Furniture
COUNTERS, Kitchen. See Kitchen furniture
COUNTESS; story. See Rama Rau, S.
COUNTRIES. See Nations
COUNTRY and city. See City and country
COUNTRY auction; story. See Fremantle, A.
COUNTRY banks. See Banks and banking—Country banks
COUNTRY clubs
Big splash for bath and tennis; Lake Bluff, on Chicago's North shore. F. Deford. il Sports Illus 19:36-41 S 2 '63
Golf anyone? ghettoization on the golf links. il Newsweek 61:104-5 Mr 25 '63
If you see a snake, hit it; Bella Vista and La Hacienda golf clubs, Mexico. il Sports Illus 19:20-2+ Ag 26 '63
Personal business; club officers. Bsns W p 181-2 Ap 20 '63
Where is the golf course of the workers? G. S. Brown. il Sports Illus 19:42-4 Ag 26 '63
COUNTRY doctors. See Physicians
COUNTRY estates
Beyond the green gate; President Kennedy's home on Rattlesnake Mountain. il Time 81:17 Mr 1 '63
Dream house; John F. Kennedy's new hideaway on Rattlesnake Ridge. il Newsweek 61:27 Mr 25 '63
Irving Penn's love letter to a farm. il Vogue 142:120-9 Ag 15 '63
Tenants for the new Kennedy place; on Rattlesnake Mountain. il U S News 54:16 My 6 '63

England

Britain's Cliveden set: back in the headlines. il U S News 55:64-5 Jl 15 '63
One gilded night with the Duke; Woburn abbey. W. Petschek. il Ladies Home J 81:143-4 O '64

Ireland

Young, lyric Irish life of the Desmond Guinesses at Leixlip castle and its folly. V. Lawford. il Vogue 144:144-55+ N 15 '64
COUNTRY houses
Leland Haywards of Haywire house. V. Lawford. il Vogue 143:124-7+ F 15 '64
COUNTRY life
Boyhood on the prairie; adaptation of address. B. Hibbs. il Read Digest 85:111-13 N '64
Boys, bears, and bugs. R. Starnes. Field & S 69:14-15+ Ag '64
Country living in the West. il Sunset 132:140+ Ap; 110+ Je '64
See also
City and country
Farm life
Outdoor life
Recreation, Rural
Vacations
Village life

Anecdotes, facetiae, satire, etc.

Department of amplification; letter. N. Perrin. New Yorker 39:63-5 Jl 6 '63
COUNTRY music. See Folk music, American
COUNTRY music festival. See Music festivals—Tennessee
COUNTRY tweeds, incorporated
How coat maker takes its show on the road. il Bsns W p52-3 Ap 17 '63

COUNTRY wife; drama. See Wycherley, W.
COUNTRY women. See Farm women
COUNTRYMAN, Peter
Ivy-league integrationists. R. W. Apple, jr. il Reporter 28:32-4 F 14 '63
Remarkable story of the dropouts and the college students. A. Fontaine. McCalls 91: 26+ Mr '64
COUNTS, Mel
Counts-down. H. L. Masin. il por Sr Schol 82:24 Mr 20 '63
COUNTY agents
See also
Home economics—Extension work
COUNTY finance. See Local finance
COUNTY libraries. See Libraries, County
COUNTY officers
See also
Sheriffs
COUNTY park systems. See Parks
COUNTY purchasing. See Purchasing, County
COUNTY records
County recording in three easy steps: Shelby County, Tenn. G. Bates. il Am City 80: 100-1 Ja '65
COUNTY recreation. See Recreation, Rural
COUNTY taxation. See Taxation, County
COUPON advertising. See Books—Advertising
COUPONS
Case of the smoked mink. V. Hill. New Repub 150:8 Ap 11 '64
See also
Trading stamps
COUPS d'etat. See Revolutions
COURAGE
Cancer taught me to be brave. il Good H 158:12+ Mr '64
Death on the high wire. B. Ballantine. il Read Digest 83:53-9 Jl '63
I enjoy myself most when I'm scared. I. A. R. Wylie. Read Digest 82:77-80 Je '63
Wonderful legacy of Dr Bob McCarthy. A. Hirshberg. il Good H 156:68-9+ Mr '63
See also
Heroes
COURAGE is a private affair; story. See Fortinberry, B.
COURANT, Richard
Mathematics in the modern world: with biographical sketch. Sci Am 211:28, 40-9 bibliog(p269) S '64
COURANT (newspaper) See Hartford, Conn.—Newspapers
COURNOT, Michel
Maeghts' museum. Vogue 144:190-1+ O 15 '64
COURSES of study
Curriculum changes and the librarian; excerpts from address, October 1964. A. Frazier. il Wilson Lib Bul 39:389-91 Ja '65
Education: PSAC panel draws on experience of curriculum reform to point way to wider innovation. J. Walsh. Science 144:394-5 Ap 24 '64
Elementary school in the city: a conference report; curriculum. Sch Life 45:16-22 Jl '63
Fountains of reform; curriculum change in local school systems. il Time 84:92-3 S 18 '64
How to improve your school's curriculum. M. Mayer. Bet Hom & Gard 42:122+ N '64
Is the curriculum our business? with study-discussion program, by D. B. Harris and E. S. Harris. A. H. Marckwardt. bibliog il PTA Mag 58:7-9, 35-6 Ap '64
Requirements for major curriculum revision; excerpt from New curricula. J. R. Zacharias and S. White. Sch & Soc 92:66-72 F 22 '64
What's happening in education? W. D. Boutwell. PTA Mag 58:13-14 Mr '64
See also
Association for supervision and curriculum development
Colleges and universities—Curriculum
High schools—Curriculum
COURT fools. See Jesters
COURT marshals. See United States marshals
COURT martial. See Courts martial
COURT music, Japanese. See Music, Japanese
COURT of justice, International. See International court of justice. The Hague
COURT of King Arithmetic; drama. See Chaloner, G.
COURT of love; story. See Buck, P. S.
COURT procedure. See Procedure (law)
COURT reporting (by newspapers) See Newspaper court reporting

COURTAULDS, limited
Comeback at Courtaulds. il Time 82:32+ Jl 5 '63
Tougher Courtaulds comes out fighting. il Bsns W p97-8 D 21 '63
COURTENAY, Walter R.
Can laws make men equal? a minister's answer; sermon, September 13, 1963. por U S News 55:113-16 N 18 '63
COURTESY
And now a word from the youngsters. M. A. Guitar. il N Y Times Mag p79-80 My 3 '64
Good character is made, not born. M. E. Goodman. il Parents Mag 39:54-5+ O '64
Have you an educated heart? excerpts from The bromide and other theories. G. Burgess. Read Digest 82:180G Mr '63
Manners are from the heart; with program for discussion group, by E. J. DeShan. S. H. Strait. bibliog il Parents Mag 38:40+, 72-3+ N '63; Same abr. without program. Read Digest 84:193-4 Je '64
Now Moscow debates its manners. G. Feifer. il N Y Times Mag p28+ Ag 23 '64
Of Martians and mores. R. Reppert. Read Digest 83:36B S '63
Parent's thoughts on good manners. A. Gordon. Bet Hom & Gard 42:112-13 N '64
Quality of rudeness. N. Pileggi. Esquire 61: 98 Ja '64
Respecting people and titles. Christian Cent 81:229 F 19 '64
Whatever happened to please? E. S. Ringold. il N Y Times Mag p49-51 D 15 '63
Who killed chivalry? D. Fairbanks, jr. McCalls 92:117+ N '64
Who'll take the hi-road? C. Fadiman. Read Digest 82:78-80 Ap '63
Why do women have to be so rude? R. Lynes. McCalls 91:71+ Ag '64
See also
Etiquette
Sportsmanship
COURTROOMS
Room with a view; new-style courtroom in Tacoma, Wash. il Time 83:54 Je 19 '64
COURTS
See also
Criminal procedure
Judges
Traffic courts

Alaska

Face on the courtroom floor; feud between Alaska's bar and bench. Time 84:86+ N 13 '64

Arkansas

Court invades independent church; Traskwood landmark missionary Baptist church, Benton, Ark. Christian Cent 80:356 Mr 20 '63

California

California cleans its courts. M. T. Bloom. Read Digest 82:91-3 Mr '63

Europe, Western

See also
Justice, Administration of—Europe, Western

Florida

Railroaded to freedom. Nation 199:62-3 Ag 24 '64

Georgia

Student's dividend in Georgia. New Repub 151:6-7 S 12 '64

Great Britain

Outward signs of inward grace; life of legal London. F. Cowper. il Horizon 6:34-5 Spr '64

Louisiana

Unfair integration. Time 84:76 N 20 '64

Russia

Russia's courts of public pressure; Comrades' courts. R. S. Sharlet. Nation 200:55-7+ Ja 18 '65
See also
Justice, Administration of—Russia

Spain

Valencia's tribunal of waters. R. Littell. il Read Digest 83:126-30 D '63

Texas

Untold story of Jack Ruby. E. Linn. il Sat Eve Post 237:24-6+ Jl 25 '64

United States

Cracks in the closed society; criticism of the United States Supreme court and Mississippi's courts. Time 85:62 Ja 22 '65
Fascinating & frenetic Fifth: Deep South's Fifth circuit court of appeals. il Time 84:46+ D 4 '64

COURTS—United States—*Continued*
Federal courts: justice across state boundaries. il Sr Schol 84:31 F 14 '64
Judicial usurpation; address, August 13, 1963. J. M. Harlan. Vital Speeches 29:706-8 S 15 '63; Excerpts. U S News 55:49 Ag 26 '63
Justice with a southern accent; do our federal courts need emancipating? L. Lusky. Harper 228:69-70+ Mr '64; Discussion. 228: 9 My '64
Rage to remove; removal of charges from state to federal courts. il Time 84:88 O 30 '64
Should the U.S. have a labor court? T. R. Brooks. Duns R 83:59-62 Mr '64
When a Negro is on trial in the South. B. M. Galphin. il N Y Times Mag p 17+ D 15 '63
See also
Justice, Administration of—United States
Small claims courts
United States—Supreme court
also subhead Courts under names of cities, e.g. Jacksonville, Fla.—Courts

Wisconsin

Church ruled liable for damages; ruling against Holy Trinity Catholic church, Casco. Christian Cent 80:733 Je 5 '63

COURTS (architecture) See Courtyards

COURTS, Municipal
State & local courts: foundation of the judicial system. il Sr Schol 84:32 F 14 '64
See also
Jacksonville, Fla.—Courts

COURTS, State
Bar's side of Canon 35. J. H. Yauch. Sat R 46:61-2 Mr 9 '63
Rage to remove; removal of charges from state to federal courts. il Time 84:88 O 30 '64
State & local courts: foundation of the judicial system. il Sr Schol 84:32 F 14 '64

COURTS martial
Soldier's work between two wars. D. MacArthur. il Life 57:56+ Jl 3 '64

COURTS of appeal. See Appellate procedure

COURTS of small claims. See Small claims courts

COURTSHIP
Ex-bachelor tells girls how to get your man. Ebony 18:158 Ap '63
Hazards of city courtship. W. K. Zinsser. Read Digest 82:41-2+ Ap '63
Inside psychiatry today; psychiatry looks at courtship. F. R. Schreiber and M. Herman. Sci Digest 56:68-9 Ag '64
Long-distance romance, can it last? questions and answers. A. Wood. il Seventeen 23:134-5+ O '64
Whatever happened to courtship? A. Moss. Mlle 56:151+ Ap '63
See also
Dating

Anecdotes, facetiae, satire, etc.

Man who promised marriage. A. Buchwald. il McCalls 90:36 Je '63

COURTSHIP of birds
Birds strut, soar, sing and dance for a mate; excerpt from Encyclopedia of American birds. J. K. Terres. il Audubon Mag 65: 172-5 My '63
Evolution of bowerbirds. E. T. Gilliard. il Sci Am 209:38-46 bibliog(p 140) Ag '63; Reply with rejoinder. R. K. Selander. 209:10+ D '63
Reproductive behavior of ring doves. D. S. Lehrman. il Sci Am 211:48-54 N '64

COURTSHIP of insects
Clustering wasps, and why they cluster. H. E. Evans. il Audubon Mag 65:236-7 Jl '63
Courtship among the insects. M. Eastman. il Audubon Mag 65:152-4 My '63; Same abr. with title Love among the insects. Read Digest 82:193-6 Je '63
Courtship sound production in two sympatric sibling drosophila species. I. Waldron. bibliog il Science 144:191-3 Ap 10 '64
Love among the insects; malachiidae beetles. il Time 82:66 O 11 '63

COURTYARDS
Atrium brings nature into a home. il Am Home 66:38-41 S '63
Atrium house. il House B 105:57-79 Ag '63
Courtyard all its own. il Bet Hom & Gard 42:40+ Je '64

COUSCOUS
See also
Cookery—Cereals

COUSINS, Frank
Unions get new role in Britain. Bsns W p95-6 O 24 '64

COUSINS, Margaret
Charmed life; story. McCalls 90:66-7 Jl '63
Christmas in town; story. McCalls 92:130-1 D '64
Enchanted cottage. Good H 157:104-9 D '63
Feminine mystique; story. McCalls 91:72-3 Je '64
Friend of a friend; story. McCalls 90:98-9 Mr '63
Is fiction here to stay? address, June 4, 1963. Writer 77:9-15 Ja '64
New girl. Good H 157:74-85 Ag '63
Peace on earth; poem. McCalls 91:173 D '63
Suburban matron's story; story. McCalls 91: 104-5 N '63

COUSINS, Norman
Danger beyond smoking. Sat R 47:22 Ja 25 '64; Same abr. Read Digest 84:41-2 My '64
Douglas MacArthur. Sat R 47:18-19 My 2 '64
Feast of reason. por NEA J 54:11 Ja '65
Jungle doctor go home. Sat R 46:30 Mr 16 '63; Same. Sci Digest 54:44-52 Jl '63
More talks with the Russians. Sat R 47:30 S 26; 30-1 O 10 '64
Nehru: man and symbol. Sat R 47:17-21+ Je 20 '64
Notes on a 1963 visit with Khrushchev. Sat R 47:16-21+ N 7 '64
Paul Brand and his mission. Sat R 47:21-3+ O 3 '64

COUSTEAU, Jacques Yves
At home in the sea. pors Nat Geog Mag 125: 465-507 Ap '64
Ocean-bottom homes for skin divers. Pop Mech 120:98-103+ Jl '63
—and Dugan, James
Fish named Ulysses; excerpt from The living sea. Read Digest 83:188-92+ S '63

about

Fish men. il por Newsweek 62:64-5 Jl 29 '63
Home in the deep. il por Time 82:40 Jl 26 '63
Man's future beneath the sea. W. Johnson. il Sr Schol 85:6-9+ Ja 7 '65
Portrait of homo aquaticus. J. Dugan. il pors N Y Times Mag p38-9+ Ap 21 '63
Seanauts launched. B. Tufty. il Sci N L 85: 118 F 22 '64
To sea in a saucer. il por Bsns W p88-9+ F 15 '64
Underwater pioneer. il por Sr Sch 85:20 Ja 7 '65

COUSTEAU saucer. See Bathyscaphe

COUSY, Bob
High scoring has become ho-hum; ed. by T. Cohane. pors Look 27:53-4+ F 12 '63

about

Better to die than lose; Boston Celtics vs. Los Angeles Lakers. il por Time 81:85-6 My 3 '63
Final whistle. D. Anderson. il pors Sat Eve Post 236:34-5 Mr 16 '63
Last fling for a wizard. J. Underwood. il pors Sports Illus 18:16-17+ Ap 22 '63
No fast break for the Cooz. W. Leggett. il por Sports Illus 19:20-1 D 16 '63
Sporting scene. H. W. Wind. New Yorker 39:146+ Mr 23 '63
We love ya, Cooz. pors Newsweek 61:50 Ap 1 '63

COUTANT, Charles C.
Insecticide Seven: effect of aerial spraying on drift of stream insects. bibliog Science 146:420-1 O 16 '64

COUTTS, Frederick L.
Our man in London. New Yorker 40:47-9 O 24 '64
Steady as before. por Time 82:86+ O 11 '63

COUVE DE MURVILLE, Maurice
French foreign policy; address, October 29, 1963. Vital Speeches 30:72-5 N 15 '63
French foreign policy; address, November 3, 1964. Vital Speeches 31:101-5 D 1 '64
Nationalism; address, April 28, 1964. Vital Speeches 30:487-90 Je 1 '64
Question at issue; address, January 29, 1963. Vital Speeches 29:333-4 Mr 15 '63
Why de Gaulle is challenging U.S; interview. por U S News 56:70-5 Mr 16 '64

about

Deadlock, or deathblow? il por Time 81:34 My 17 '63
Pebbles in the pond. il pors Time 83:26-30 F 7 '64

COVE vitamin and pharmaceutical, incorporated
Federal jury indicts four over Calories don't count. Pub W 185:30 Mr 23 '64

COVENANT of the League of Nations. See League of Nations—Constitution

COVENEY, David L.
World's fair weather watch. Flying 74:32+ Ap '64
COVENT Garden. See London—Covent Garden
COVENTRY cathedral. See Cathedrals—England
COVER crops
See also
Green manuring
Vetch
COVER design. See Book covers
COVER plants
Best ground covers to use with bulbs. E. L. Sculthorp. il House B 105:250-2 O '63
Cool green carpet under the trees. il Sunset 133:150-1 Jl '64
Ground covers for house plants. E. S. Parcher. il Horticulture 42:38 F '64
Ground covers: here are eight interesting possibilities. il Sunset 132:224-5 Mr '64
Groundcovers; with list of best groundcovers. D. Wyman. il Horticulture 43:24-7 Ja '65
Here's a hardy cover. il Sunset 130:237 Je '63
North woods ground covers. A. G. Owen. il Horticulture 41:423 Ag '63
Plant groundcovers for easy gardening. T. A. Weston. il Am Home 66:68-70 Je '63
There's variety in groundcovers. E. F. Steffek. il Pop Gard 15:34-5+ Ja '64
Try quick groundcovers where grass is slow. D. Klaber. il Pop Gard 15:70+ Jl '64
Use phlox carpeting. M. P. Kunkel. il Horticulture 41:307 Je '63
While waiting for junipers. il Sunset 132:246+ Mr '64
See also
Alpine flora
Crown vetch
Partridge berries
COVERDALE, Joan
Small boats on the move. il Yachting 114:52-3 O '63
COVERED bridges
Covered bridges of the West, by K. A. Adams. Review
Sunset il 131:68+ O '63
Detour to four covered bridges; Williamette Valley, Ore. il Sunset 132:56 F '64
Oregon still has 106 covered bridges. il Sunset 130:34-6+ Ap '63
COVERLETS
Bed rug in colonial America. M. D. Iverson. bibliog il Antiques 85:107-9 Ja '64
Bedding isn't what it used to be. il House B 106:100-7 F '64
Bedspreads woven of glass. il House & Gard 125:214-15 My '64
Cover story; bedspreads. G. O'Brien. il N Y Times Mag p 114-15 N 1 '64
Coverlet: trade-Marks of H. Tyler. L. F. Reals. il Hobbies 69:28 Mr '64
Good-morning princess; crib coverlet. il McCalls 91:112-13+ D '63
Institute answers your questions on bedspreads. Good H 157:172 Ag '63
Ready-mades rate you an A. R. W. Houseman. il Am Home 67:46-9 Mr '64
So easy, so giftable. il McCalls 92:130-1+ O '64
Storage
Place for bedspreads. il House & Gard 123: 118+ Ap '63
COVERS (philately)
Dealer's record price for a stamp error; three-penny bonanza. il Life 55:46+ N 29 '63
COVERS, Book. See Book covers
COVERS, Periodical. See Periodical covers
COVERT, Angela M. and Makuen, D. R.
Continuing challenge to the student community. Sch & Soc 91:146-7 Mr 23 '63
COVERT, E. Richard, and Schodde, S. C.
USNSA defines the student role. Sch & Soc 92:387-8 D 12 '64
COVERT, George S.
Sewage problems respect no political boundaries. Am City 78:71-3 F '63
COVICI, Pascal
Obituary
Pub W por 186:26 O 26 '64
COVINGTON, Ga.
Retire the relics; relighting historic city square. J. H. Bryan. il Am City 78:117 D '63
COW mats. See Barns and stables—Equipment
COW stanchions. See Barns and stables—Equipment
COW testing. See Cows—Testing
COW testing associations
Target: better cow testing. Farm J 88:66D O '64
COWAN, Geoffrey
And three letters home from Mississippi. Esquire 62:105-6+ S '64
COWAN, John
Flash: the Arctic. il por Vogue 144:136-41+ N 1 '64
about
John Cowan; specialist in action. il U S Camera 27:40-5+ Ag '64
COWAN, Paul
And three letters home from Mississippi. Esquire 62:105-6 S '64
COWAN, Peter. See Llewelyn-Davies, R. jt. auth.
COWAN, Robert C.
What papers should we keep? questions and answers. PTA Mag 57:35 Je '63
COWAN, Thomas A.
Decision theory in law, science, and technology. bibliog Science 140:1065-75 Je 7 '63
COWARD, Noel
Mrs Capper's birthday party: story. Ladies Home J 80:96-8 D '63
Old-friend gives the low-down on Lillie. por Life 56:129-30 My 15 '64
Pretty Polly; story. Ladies Home J 81:60-1 Ag '64
about
Hay fever. Criticism
New Yorker 40:200-1 N 21 '64
Outpatient of the year. por Time 84:82 D 4 '64
COWARD, Robert
Sound advice. Mod Phot 27:10+ F '63
COWBOYS
Cowhand. O. L. McKeen. il Am Heritage 14: 16-31 O '63
Texas trail ride; Negro cowboys. il Ebony 18:115-16+ My '63
See also
Rodeos
COWELL, Henry
Feast of fascinations by Henry Cowell. A. Cohn. il por Am Rec G 30:476-7+ F '64
Jubilee fare. O. Daniel. Sat R 46:71 Mr 30 '63
COWEN, Denis V.
Call for a dialogue in South Africa. N Y Times Mag p 19+ My 17 '64
COWEN, Robert C.
Weather computers. Nation 198:71-3 Ja 20 '64; Same abr. with title Needed, umbrella weather forecasting. Sci Digest 55:25-9 Ap '64
COWES regatta. See Regattas
COWGILL, U. M.
Visiting in perodicticus. Science 146:1183 N 27 '64
—See Hutchinson, G. E. jt. auth.
COWLES, John
Morning song, or Everthing in life is worthwhile but living; poem. Atlan 213:82 F '64
about
Midwest's nice monopolists, John and Mike Cowles. W. B. Furlong. Harper 226:64-8+ Je '63
Toot! toot! Time 82:56-7 O 11 '63
COWLES, Mike
Midwest's nice monopolists, John and Mike Cowles. W. B. Furlong. Harper 226:64-8+ Je '63
COWLES, Virginia
Phenomenon of Les parapluies de Cherbourg. Vogue 144:184-5+ N 1 '64
Private line from London. Vogue 144:36 Jl; 114+ S 1; 219-20 O 1; 293+ D '64; 145:86-7 F 1 '65
COWLEY, Malcolm
Dr Canby and his team. Sat R 47:54-5+ Ag 29 '64
Ghost story of the jazz age. Sat R 47:20-1 Ja 25 '64
Last of the lost generation. por Esquire 60: 77-9 Jl '63
Remembrance of the red romance. Esquire 61:124+ Mr; 78-9+ Ap '64
Van Wyck Brooks: a career in retrospect. Sat R 46:17-18+ My 25 '63
While they waited for Lefty. Sat R 47:16-19+ Je 6 '64
Writer as craftsman. Sat R 47:17-18 Je 27 '64
COWLEY, Robert
Ask the man who. Am Heritage 15:24-7 Ag '64
COWPER, Francis
Outward signs of inward grace. Horizon 6:33-40 Spr '64
COWRIES
Money cowry. A. G. Melvin. il Hobbies 69: 130+ D '64

COWS
Cows, why I like them! excerpt from Requiem for twelve cows. G. Rehm. il Farm J 87: 58X Ap '63
How to name a cow. H. B. Fox. il Farm J 87: 64F F '63
See also
Dairying
Heifers
Milking

Breeding
See Cattle breeding

Care
Replacements. D. C. Clanton. il Suc Farm 62:47+ Ap '64

Culling
Beef cow culling tips. Suc Farm 62:18 F '64
Now is the time to cull your cows. C. E. Meadows. il Suc Farm 62:30-1 D '64
Tips for culling your dairy herd. J. W. Bailey. Suc Farm 61:83 My '63

Diseases and pests
How to tackle herd health problems. M. L. Weldy. il Suc Farm 62:50-1+ N '64
See also
Mastitis

Feeding
Avoid sudden ration changes. Suc Farm 62: 74E Ap '64
Buy hay for its TDN? G. Lorang. il Farm J 89:44 Ja '65
Feed dairy cows more. D. Braun. il Farm J 87:34-5+ S '63
Full-feed grain to dairy cows? N. Reeder and J. Bickers. il Farm J 89:24-5+ Ja '65
High production, even when it's hot. J. Bickers. il Farm J 88:25+ Jl '64
How much winter feed for replacement heifers. Farm J 88:42H S '64
How to feed urea and cut feed costs. J. Russell. Farm J 88:50 Ap '64
In a drouth year 4000 lbs. more milk per cow. B. Hardy and H. Simons. Farm J 88:60 F '64
Life-cycle dairy feeding. N. L. Jacobson and H. H. Van Horn. il Suc Farm 62:50-1+ Ap; 42-3 My '64
Milking parlor lead-feeding. il Suc Farm 62:66 My '64
Red hot argument in dairying. D. Braun. il Farm J 88:35+ Mr '64
Replacements. D. C. Clanton. il Suc Farm 62:47+ Ap '64
Short of feed? try these ideas. B. Hardy. Farm J 87:49 N '63
Try latest ideas on feeding dairy cows; questions and answers; ed. by J. R. Borcherding. G. Werner and J. Crowley. il Suc Farm 62:46-7 Ja '64
Try their dairy ideas. J. R. Borcherding. il Suc Farm 61:38-9+ Ag '63
Ways to feed extra grain. O. Bay and D. Braun. il Farm J 87:62J Mr '63

Milk production
See Milk—Production

Testing
At 17,387 now, aiming for 18,000. R. Porterfield and J. R. Borcherding. il Suc Farm 61:66+ Mr '63
Ingham County's 500-pound club. J. R. Borcherding. il Suc Farm 61:46-7+ Ap '63
New records turn up surprises. D. Braun. Farm J 87:58A Ap '63
Target: better cow testing. Farm J 88:66D O '64

COWS, Cooling of. See Livestock, Cooling of
COWS, Sacred. See Cows in religion, folklore, etc.
COWS in religion, folklore, etc.
Contraceptives for sacred cows. Sci Am 212: 51 Ja '65
COWS teeth. See Teeth (animals)
COX, Allan, and others
Geomagnetic polarity epochs. bibliog Science 143:351-2 Ja 24 '64
Geomagnetic polarity epochs: Sierra Nevada II. bibliog Science 142:382-5 O 18 '63
Reversals of the earth's magnetic field. bibliog Science 144:1537-43 Je 26 '64
COX, B. Elton
New limits for an old conflict. il por Time 85:39 Ja 29 '65
COX, Carl T.
Filmstrips. bibliog Wilson Lib Bul 38:178-82 O '63
COX, Clifton
I survived tetanus; ed. by H. A. Johnson. Farm J 88:54G Ap '64
COX, Francis Huneeus-. See Huneeus-Cox, F.
COX, Harvey
Dialogue among pickets. Commonweal 79:245-6, 486 N 22 '63, Ja 24 '64
Facing the secular. Commonweal 79:619-22 F 21 '64
German ecumenism: politics and the dialogue. Commonweal 77:635-9 Mr 15 '63
Gospel and postliterate man. Christian Cent 81:1459-61 N 25 '64
Kafka East, Kafka West. Commonweal 80: 596-600 S 4 '64
Letter from Williamston. Christian Cent 80:1516-18 D 4 '63
New Protestant debate over sex. Redbook 123:56-7+ O '64
COX, Hiden
Morality in science: report on a crisis. J. Lear. il Sat R 46:49-54 Mr 2 '63
COX, James M.
Stamp of a heroic life. Sat R 46:43-4 O 5 '63
COX, Joseph T.
Cutting a big house down to size. Suc Farm 61:92-3 Mr '63
COX, Marcelene
Ask any woman. See issues of Ladies' home journal to May 1963
COX, Robert E.
(ed) Gleanings for ATM's. See issues of Sky and telescope
COX, William Drought
Cox's new kick. il Time 82:42 Ag 23 '63
COX, William Harold
Those Kennedy judges. il por Time 84:44+ N 6 '64
COX, William M.
Bones make the ship. Hobbies 68:122 Je '63
COX, William Sellers
Secret of the Eagle. il por Newsweek 64:69 Jl 27 '64
Tense sailor for a taut ship. B. Ottum. il por Sports Illus 21:46-8 Ag 31 '64
COXE, Donald G. M.
How can you rate your congressman? Nat R 14:525-8 Jl 2 '63
Strange case of Edgar Smith. Nat R 15:273-8 O 8 '63
COXE, Louis
Cruising; poem. Yale R 52:560 Je '63
Falls; Crash program; Friday, November 22, 1963; poems. Poetry 104:28-30 Ap '64
On seeing films of the war; poem. Yale R 54: 83 O '64
Squaring the circle; poem. New Yorker 40:26 Ag 15 '64
Time's arrow; poem. New Yorker 39:34 F 8 '64
COYA, Albert
Golf goes walkie-talkie. Pop Electr 21:70 Jl '64
COYDOGS. See Dogs
COYKENDALL, Ralf
How to cook a duck. Field & S 69:44-5+ N '64
COYLE, David Cushman
New rules for monopoly. Sat R 47:29 Ap 11 '64
COYLE, James
Rent-a-pigeon. il por Newsweek 63:42 Ja 13 '64
COYLE, Thomas J.
Parking program that benefits all. Am City 79:112 Ag '64
COYOTE hunting
Coyote hounds in Texas. D. M. Duffey. il Outdoor Life 134:118-20+ N '64
COYOTES
Are we wasting our best hunting? B. East. il Outdoor Life 131:32-5+ Mr '63
Coyote's charm. J. F. Dobie. il Audubon Mag 65:38-40 Ja '63
Mystery beasts; wolf, coyote or dog? T. Janes. il Outdoor Life 134:17-19+ Jl '64
COZUMEL ISLAND
Cozumel. K. Simon. Mlle 59:188 My '64
COZZENS, James Gould
Candida by Bernard Shaw; story. Sat Eve Post 237:50-2 Jl 25 '64
One hundred ladies; story. Sat Eve Post 237:40-3 Jl 11 '64
about
By ideology possessed. J. Hart. Nat R 16: 825-6 S 22 '64
Raise the banner again for Cozzens. J. Weidman. Life 57:9+ Ag 7 '64
CRAB apples
Crab apple. D. Wyman. il Flower Grower 50: 40-1+ Ap '63
Crabapples. H. E. Downer. il Pop Gard 14: 38-9+ Ap '63
Crab apples, attractive in flower, fruit and foliage. R. R. Thomasson. il Horticulture 41:564-5 N '63

CRAB grass
Latest word on crab grass control. Bet Hom & Gard 41:94 Ag '63
Spring attack vital in defeat of crab grass. B. C. Kilvert, jr. il Flower Grower 51:27 F '64
CRAB nebula. See Nebulae
CRABB, A. L.
Long pants for the last day; story. PTA Mag 58:27-9 D '63
Softening of Mr Reub Simmons; story. PTA Mag 59:14-16 D '64
CRABB, Cecil V. jr
Gaullist revolt against the Anglo-Saxons. bibliog f Ann Am Acad 351:15-23 Ja '64
CRABBE, John
Watts way. Am Rec G 31:92-4+ O '64
CRABS
Grabbers' crab. J. Durant. il Field & S 69:65+ O '64
See also
Cookery—Fish
CRABS eye vine
Rosary pea. Sci N L 86:268 O 24 '64
CRABTREE, Peter
Camping south of the border. por Am For 69:48-51+ My '63
CRACKS in houses. See Houses
CRACKS in walls. See Walls
CRADLE will rock: musical comedy. See Musical comedies, revues, etc.—Criticisms, plots, etc.
CRADLES
For baby now, toy storage later on. il Sunset 130:97 F '63
Her cradle is curved plywood. il Sunset 133: 128+ N '64
CRAFT, James
Refusal to act is often in public interest. Nations Bsns 52:25-6 F '64
Trends: Washington mood. Nations Bsns 52: 25-6 F; 23-4 Mr; 23-4 Ap '64
CRAFT, Robert
Stravinsky talks with Khrushchev; excerpts from Dialogues and a diary. Vogue 142: 134-5+ N 1 '63
Travel; excerpts on Brazil from Table talk, by I. Stravinsky and R. Craft. Vogue 144: 80 O 1 '64
about
Portrait of Robert Craft; with editorial comment. E. Salzman. il pors Hi Fi 14:23, 24-6 Jl '64
CRAFTS, Edward C.
Legislative needs for outdoor recreation; excerpt from address. por Am For 69:18-19+ Mr '63
Strong mandate. por Am For 69:10-11 Jl '63
CRAFTS. See Arts and crafts; Handicraft
CRAFTSMANSHIP
See also
Fisher body craftsman's guild
CRAGER, Tess M.
Those summer reading lists. Pub W 185:153-4 F 24 '64
CRAIG, Anne
What books for the young adult? por Library J 89:4103-6 O 15 '64
CRAIG, Calvin M.
Nuts to excelsior. Library J 89:4989 D 15 '64
CRAIG, Eugene A.
Psychology of creative writing. Writer 76:15-17 Ag '63
CRAIG, Gordon A.
Dulles as villain. Reporter 31:54+ S 10 '64
What the Germans are reading about Hitler. Reporter 31:36-8 Jl 16 '64
about
Finer over Craig. H. Finer. Reporter 31:8+ N 19 '64
Living legends. M. Richler. il por Vogue 145:128-9+ Ja 1 '65
CRAIG, James B.
Billions of bugs. Am For 70:42-8 F '64
Farm vacations. Am For 70:8-11+ Jl '64
Fifth American forest congress. Am For 69: 30-1 D '63
Fire prevention breakthrough. Am For 69: 36-8 Mr '63
Forester to head BLM. Am For 69:4-5+ Je '63
Meeting, 1963. Am For 69:4-5+ Ap '63
RFF resources forecast shows qualified optimism. Am For 69:16-19+ My '63
CRAIG, James W.
Conservation education, Merrill style. Am For 69:30-1 F '63
CRAIG, Lee
New era in marine electronics. Motor B 112: 31-3+ N '63
CRAIG, Lyman Creighton
Differential dialysis. bibliog Science 144:1093-9 My 29 '64
Separating the inseparable. il por Time 82: 62+ O 18 '63
CRAIG, Marcia L. and Russell, E. S.
Electrophoretic patterns of hemoglobin from fetal mice of different inbred strains. bibliog Science 142:498-9 O 18 '63
CRAIG, May
Woman writer takes a critical look at America; reprint. por U S News 56:78 Mr 2 '64
about
Maggie vs. May. Newsweek 61:23-4 Ap 8 '63
CRAIG, Nancy
Thinking washers sensing dryers. House B 105:152-3+ Mr '63
CRAIG, Ralph C.
Juniors of the Royal St Lawrence yacht club. il Yachting 114:58-9+ Jl '63
CRAIG, Roger
If at first. por Newsweek 62:74 Ag 19 '63
CRAIG, Walter E.
Excerpt from address, April 29, 1964. Cong Digest 43:279+ N '64
Excerpt from statement, February 24, 1964. Cong Digest 43:150 My '64
about
And so to court. Time 84:62 Jl 31 '64
People of the week. U S News 56:16 Mr 9 '64
Right track. il por Time 82:52-3 O 18 '63
CRAIG, William, family
Indiana's top gentle way family. il Ebony 19:102-4+ Je '64
CRAIGHEAD, John J.
Wilderness in Montana, a report. Liv Wildn 85:25-9 Wint '64
CRAIK, James
James Craik: the first White House physician. J. Luter. il Todays Health 42:46-9+ F '64
CRAIN, Stanley M. and Peterson, E. R.
Bioelectric activity in long-term cultures of spinal cord tissues. bibliog Science 141:427-9 Ag 2 '63
CRAINE, Lyle E. and Craine, Mrs L. E.
Memorandum to a network. Sat R 46:28 D 28 '63
CRAINE, Mrs Lyle E. See Craine, L. E. jt. auth.
CRAINE, W. H. See Ulrich, R. E. jt. auth.
CRAMER, Robert L.
How to do it! monster movies. U S Camera 27:68-9+ S '64
Latch on to the running gag. U S Camera 27:78-9+ Ag '64
CRAMER, Robert S.
President Kennedy talks about women and world peace. Parents Mag 38:57+ N '63
CRAMER, William C.
Excerpt from debate, August 28, 1962. Cong Digest 43:239+ O '64
Excerpt from remarks, July 2, 1964. Cong Digest 43:307+ D '64
CRAMERTON, N.C. See Company towns
CRAMPS. See Menstruation—Disorders
CRANBERG, Lawrence
Ethical code for scientists? letter. bibliog Science 141:1242; 142:1257. S 27, D 6 '63
Fast-neutron spectroscopy; with biographical sketch. Sci Am 210:21, 79-86+ Mr '64
CRANBERRIES
Cranberry growers like marketing order. Farm J 87:13 F '63
See also
Cookery—Fruit
CRANBERRY bush
One shrub for all seasons. R. H. Stokes. Flower Grower 50:41 D '63
CRANDALL, Brad
Talk man. il Time 83:80 My 1 '64
CRANDALL, C. H.
Buying a good used camera. Pop Mech 120: 118-21 Ag '63
CRANDALL, Del
Man must look up; personal tragedy of D. Crandall of the Milwaukee Braves, and how he mastered it. T. Cohane. il pors Look 27:72-4+ Ag 13 '63
CRANDALL, Delmar Wesley. See Crandall, D.
CRANDALL, Dennison R.
It's hooking-up time. Outdoor Life 131:36-7+ Ja '63
Shad are back. Outdoor Life 133:44-5+ Mr '64
Stump lot adventure. Outdoor Life 131:80-1+ Ap '63

CRANDALL, Ken
(ed) See Hilderbrand, E. B. Cougar nightmare
CRANDALL, Prudence
Canterbury tale; school for Negro girls in Connecticut, 1832-34. R. Rushmore. Reporter 28:46-7 Ap 25 '63
CRANDELL, Frank J.
He makes accidents obsolete. M. Stearns. il Pop Mech 120:101-4+ Ag '63
CRANE, David A.
Public art of city building. bibliog f Ann Am Acad 352:84-94 Mr '64
CRANE, Edward A.
Oxford & Cambridge; school board's refusal to rent a high school auditorium. por Time 81:20 F 8 '63
CRANE, Edward Matthews, 1896-1964
Obituary
Pub W 185:60-1 Ap 20 '64
CRANE, Les
Television's new bad boy. B. Carey. il pors Look 28:111-14 N 3 '64
Wasn't it fun? por Newsweek 64:80 Ag 17 '64
CRANE, Paul
Kenya's achievement. America 111:216-17 Ag 29 '64
Profumo: a class on trial. America 109:13 Jl 6 '63
Universities for all. America 110:37 Ja 11 '64
CRANE, Stephen
Farewell the plumed troop. A. Karlen. Nation 199:54-5 Ag 10 '64
CRANES (birds)
Displaced sandhill cranes. C. W. Buchheister. Audubon Mag 66:85 Mr '64
Dispossessed sandhill cranes of the Missouri River. J. W. Johnson. il Audubon Mag 65: 212-17 Jl '63
On shooting swans and cranes. C. W. Buchheister. il Audubon Mag 65:356-7 N '63
Twenty-eight whooping cranes left. B. Tufty. Sci N L 83:245 Ap 20 '63
Whoopers' bloopers in the Audubon park zoo in New Orleans. il Life 54:95-6 Ap 12 '63
Whooping crane dies. Sci N L 85:223 Ap 4 '64
Whooping crane flock diminished by six. Nat Parks Mag 37:17 Mr '63
Whooping crane lives. B. Tufty. il Sci N L 85:310 My 16 '64
Whooping crane safe. B. Tufty. il(p257) Sci N L 86:262 O 24 '64
Whooping crane: today and tomorrow. R. C. Clement. il Audubon Mag 66:74-7 Mr '64
Whooping cranes ready for long trip south. Sci N L 84:216 O 5 '63
Whooping cranes summering in Canada. Sci N L 85:363 Je 6 '64
CRANES, derricks, etc.
Cranes: high styli in the sky. il Arch Forum 118:110-13 Mr '63
How to lift 150 tons; photographs by B. Smallman. Pop Sci 184:97-9 F '64
Migrating cranes; self-mounting tower crane. il Time 83:66 Ja 24 '64
CRANIAL aneurysm. See Aneurysms
CRANIN, A. Norman
Dental care during pregnancy. Redbook 123: 46+ S '64
CRANIOTOMY. See Brain—Surgery
CRANKO, John
Style in Stuttgart. il por Time 83:56 Je 12 '64
Trials and triumphs in Stuttgart. H. Koegler. il por Dance Mag 39:37-9+ Ja '65
CRANKS and crankshafts
Crank mod. E. Rickman. il Hot Rod 17:106 O '64
Stroke it! E. Rickman. il Hot Rod 16:74-9 N '63
CRANKSHAW, Edward
Big brother is still watching. N Y Times Mag p8+ D 29 '63
Cold war of the communisms. N Y Times Mag p25+ My 26 '63
East and West enter a new phase. N Y Times Mag p 16+ Ag 30 '64
Farmer frustrates Khrushchev. N Y Times Mag p 17+ S 20 '64
Long look at Stalin, ten years after. N Y Times Mag p30+ Ap 7 '63
Neither communism nor capitalism. N Y Times Mag p36-7+ O 6 '63
Russia catch up? not for a long time. N Y Times Mag p 19+ Mr 1 '64
Split between Russia and China. Atlan 211: 60-5 My '63
Two dogmas shake the Communist world. N Y Times Mag p5+ Jl 21 '63
CRANMER, Thomas
Thomas Cranmer, by J. Ridley. Review Christian Cent 80:274 F 27 '63. E. W. Whan
CRANN, Frank. See Caprio, R. G. jt. auth.
CRANSTON, Alan
Million-dollar loser looks at campaigning. por Fortune 70:124+ N '64
about
No place to go but up. il por Newsweek 63: 30 My 25 '64
CRANWOOD race course. See Race tracks
CRAPE Jasmines
Crape jasmine. A. D. Hawkes. Horticulture 42:48 Ja '64
CRAPPIE fishing
How to con a crappie. C. Conley. il Field & S 69:55-7+ Je '64
It's time for crappies. W. Curtis. il Outdoor Life 133:26-8+ Mr '64
CRARY, A. P.
Antarctica. Bul Atomic Sci 20:27-30 Ja '64
CRASH beacon locator. See Radio in aviation
CRASH; story. See Warren, J.
CRASSULA. See Jade plants
CRATER LAKE NATIONAL PARK
Crater Lake is a spring surprise. il Sunset 130:82 My '63
Two seasons at Crater Lake. S. Twight. Nat Parks Mag 37:15 Ag '63
Volcanic ash from Mount Mazama (Crater Lake) and from Glacier Peak. H. A. Powers and R. E. Wilcox. bibliog il Science 144: 1334-6 Je 12 '64
CRATERS
Debate origin of craters. Sci N L 85:338 My 30 '64
See also
Meteorite craters
CRATERS, Moon. See Moon—Surface
CRAVEY, Claudia
Brief biography. S. Goodman. pors Dance Mag 37:52-3 Ag '63
CRAWFISH festival. See Festivals—Louisiana
CRAWFORD, Broderick
Celebrity register. C. Amory. por McCalls 91:188 O '63
CRAWFORD, H. D.
Forests and food. Am For 69:38-41+ S '63
CRAWFORD, Joan
Celebrity register. C. Amory. por McCalls 91:188 O '63
Other life of Joan Crawford. il pors Bsns W p90-2+ S 21 '63
Well-planned Crawford. R. Oulahan. il por Life 56:11-12 F 21 '64
CRAWFORD, John
Celebrity register. C. Amory. por McCalls 91:188 O '63
CRAWFORD, John S.
Close-ups; too close. il Outdoor Life 133:28-9+ F '64
CRAWFORD, Kenneth
Revolution in Dixie. por Newsweek 61:40 My 13 '63
Suicide notes. por Newsweek 61:34 Ap 22 '63
Washington. See issues of Newsweek
CRAWFORD, Marc
Ominous Malcolm X exits from the Muslims. Life 56:40-40A Mr 20 '64
Throttle the fair, the public be damned. Life 56:40-1 Ap 24 '64
CRAWFORD, Robert W.
Tapping fresh sources; excerpts from address. por Recreation 57:12-14 Ja '64
CRAWFORD, William A.
U.S. note, April 2, 1963. Dept State Bul 48: 661-2 Ap 29 '63
CRAY, Ed
Jesse Unruh: Big Daddy of California. Nation 196:199-207 Mr 9 '63
CRAY, Seymour R.
Computers get faster than ever; high-powered 6600. il por Bsns W p28+ Ag 31 '63
CRAYFISH
Carotenoids of cavernicolous crayfish. D. A. Wolfe and D. G. Cornwell. bibliog il Science 144:1467-9 Je 19 '64
Endocrine control of tanning in the crayfish exoskeleton. M. Fingerman and Y. Yamamoto. bibliog Science 144:1462 Je 19 '64
CRAYON painting. See Encaustic painting
CRAYONS
It's easy to be creative with crayons. E. M. McCabe. il Parents Mag 38:18+ F '63
CRAZY horse saloon, Paris. See Night clubs
CREAM
See also
Cookery—Cream
CREAM, Sour
Sour cream. M. Kaytor. il Look 27:102-3 Je 18 '63
See also
Cookery—Cream, Sour

CREAM cheese. See Cookery—Cheese
CREAM jugs. See Jugs
CREAM of wheat corporation
Tale of a porridge pot. M. Keiser. il Parents Mag 40:18+ Ja '65
CREAM puffs. See Pastry
CREAMER, Robert
Baseball. See issues of Sports illustrated during the baseball season
Track & field (title varies) Sports Illus 20: 66+ Ja 27; 56+ F 10; 46+ F 24 '64
—and others
1963 scouting reports. Sports Illus 18:45-66+ Ap 8 '63
CREAMER, Susan
Summer for Susan. C. S. Wren. il pors Look 27:101-4 S 24 '63
CREARY, Herman J.
Are Americans afraid to be free? Cath World 198:115-21 N '63
CREATINE
See also
Krebiozen
CREATION
Child of God's thought. C. Davis. America 111:158-9 Ag 15 '64; Reply. L. Moran. 111: 336 S 26 '64
Creation. il Life 57:16-23 D 25 '64
See also
Adam and Eve in art
Cosmogony
CREATION (literary, artistic, etc)
Act of creation, by A. Koestler. Review
Nat R 16:1019-20+ N 17 '64. A. Lejeune
New Repub 151:20-1 N 28 '64. V. Lange
Sci Am 211:145-9 N '64. G. A. Miller
Science 147:37-8 Ja 1 '65. E. R. Hilgard
Big question of creativity. E. S. Stewart. il Parents Mag 38:62-3+ Je '63
Can the public school foster creativity? R. J. Mueller. il Sat R 47:48-9+ D 19 '64
Creative color; interview, ed. by A. Rothstein. J. Szarkowski. U S Camera 26:8-9 My '63
Creative dilemma. J. Baldwin; J. W. Krutch. Sat R 47:14-17+ F 8 '64
Creative education & the special student. G. Barlow. il Sch Arts 63:29-34 Ja '64
Creative energy and fiction writing. R. McKenna. Writer 76:7-9+ Je '63
Creative writer as an image maker; excerpt from Creative writing. W. Stegner. Writer 76:24 O '63
Creativity with the new automatic? N. Rothschild. Pop Phot 53:56-7 O '63
Cry and the creation. M. DeJong. il Horn Bk 39:197-206 Ap '63
David's stonewares. K. R. Beittel. il Sch Arts 63:23-7 S '63
Depth's four dimensions. R. C. Burkhart. Sch Arts 62:30-1 Ap '63
Don't wait to write your novel. E. E. Tigue. Writer 76:25-6 S '63
Emotion in non-fiction writing. E. M. Dean. Writer 77:26-7 S '64
Eureka process; excerpt from Act of creation. A. Koestler. il Horizon 6:16-25 Autumn '64
Experience of being & becoming. M. F. Andrews. il Sch Arts 62:5-9 Mr; 22-4 Ap; 5-7 My '63 (to be cont)
Furnishing the rooms. K. Reed. Writer 77:20-1+ Mr '64
Gifted and the creative student. P. A. Witty. bibliog f Sch & Soc 92:183-5 Ap 18 '64
How to handle a creative child. R. W. Bacmeister. il Parents Mag 39:38-9+ Ja '64
Imagination, by H. Rugg. Review
Sat R 46:49 Ag 17 '63. F. Parker
Key to action. M. McMullan. il Sch Arts 63: 5-7 Mr '64
Make way for creativity; with study-discussion program, by D. B. Harris and E. S. Harris. P. Witty. bibliog il PTA Mag 57: 16-18, 35 Mr '63
My son, the safety patrol. I. Berg. il Sch Arts 63:39-40 D '63
My three-hundred-pound ballerina. H. Ware. Writer 76:7-9+ O '63
New stereotype. L. H. Chapman. il Sch Arts 62:10-11 Mr '63
On creativity. Sr Schol 82:1T F 20 '63
On sculpture. G. Stark. il Sch Arts 63:27-30 Mr '64
On words, singleness of mind, and the genius loci. M. Benary-Isbert. Horn Bk 40:202-9 Ap '64
Painting became my life. H. Rubin. il Am Artist 29:46-51+ Ja '65
Psychology of creative writing. E. A. Craig. Writer 76:15-17 Ag '63
Questions and answers; male vs. female creativity. M. Mead. Redbook 120:30+ Mr '63
Salt crystals, spider webs, and words. P. Engle. Sat R 47:10-13 Mr 14 '64
Strange business of chemistry. D. Delman. Writer 77:9-11+ Je '64
Useful genius; intelligence, creativity, and American values. K. Kreuter and G. Kreuter. il Sat R 47:64-7 O 17 '64
Way it isn't done: notes on the distress of Norman Mailer. Esquire 60:306-8 D '63
See also
English language—Composition—Creative activities
Inspiration
CREATIVE ability. See Creation (literary, artistic, etc)
CREATIVE imagination. See Imagination
CREATIVE thinking. See Thought and thinking
CREATIVE writing. See English language—Composition—Creative activities
CREATURES of the night: story. See Cave, H. B.
CRÈCHES. See Christmas cribs
CREDIMATIC international vending corporation
Push-button grocer; vending machines for frozen food. il Bsns W p62 My 4 '63
CREDIT
All about credit. il Changing T 17:25-40 Mr '63
As the cost of money rises. U S News 57:90 D 14 '64
Avoid legal tangles in using credit. N. G. P. Krausz and D. B. Hipp. Suc Farm 62:54+ S '64
Beating the Fed's old rule. Bsns W p 169 S 12 '64
Boom raises three challenges. M. Nadler. il Nations Bsns 52:31-3 My '64
Borrowers confound the credit experts. il Bsns W p49-50+ N 28 '64
Borrowing will aid business in '65; survey of leading bankers. Nations Bsns 52:34-5+ D '64
Butterflies in the boom; Italy's credit-happy economy. il Time 82:111 O 18 '63
Buying on time (cont) il Consumer Rep 28: 211-17 D '63
Checks and balances; credit check by bank officials. Newsweek 64:75 Jl 27 '64
Coming back to New York; borrowers from abroad. Bsns W p73 D 28 '63
Confident borrowers build up their debts. il Bsns W p35-6 S 26 '64
Consumer credit. R. Cissell and H. Cissell. il America 111:552-4 N 7 '64
Consumer credit: buy now, pay later? il Sr Schol 85:16 Ja 7 '65
Consumer credit goes up and up. il Bsns W p52+ O 12 '63
Cost of borrowing going up again? il U S News 55:111-12 S 23 '63
Costlier borrowing for many. U S News 54: 109 Je 17 '63
Credit: an embarrassment of riches. il Newsweek 61:73 My 20 '63
Danger signals show up in credit. Bsns W p62+ Mr 16 '63
Do you know what you pay for credit? il Changing T 18:17-18 O '64
Don't overlook these sources of money. F. Bailey, jr. Suc Farm 62:38+ Jl '64
Easier credit? dispute is on; quality of bank credit. U S News 55:127-9 O 7 '63
Economic arithmetic. New Repub 148:6 Je 15 '63
Experts foresee credit risk. il Nations Bsns 52:40-1+ Mr '64
Fed credit chiefs hold private tug-of-war. il Bsns W p29 Mr 16 '63
Fed tightens credit. Bsns W p28 Je 8 '63
Fed tightens credit just a bit. il Bsns W p94-5 Ja 19 '63
Getting along with your lender. il Suc Farm 62:39+ Ag '64
Great credit pump. C. Rieser. il Fortune 67: 122-4+ F '63
Group of ten releases report on International monetary system; statement, August 1, 1964. V. Giscard d'Estaing. Dept State Bul 51:323-5 Ag 31 '64
Importance of being in debt. il Time 84:100 O 30 '64
Know what it's costing you to borrow. B. Brantley. Suc Farm 62:39+ Je '64
Lenders rub their hands. il Bsns W p93-4 Ap 6 '63
Money box. il Fortune 68:52+ N '63
More students are studying now, paying later. R. G. Moon, jr. il Sat R 46:74-5+ Je 15 '63
No jump in the cost of money; with charts. Bsns W p30-1 Ja 2 '65
Out on the limb, will it hold? consumer credit. il Bsns W p45-6+ Mr 28 '64
Outlook on credit: rates will creep up. il Bsns W p42-3 D 28 '63

CREDIT—*Continued*
Pleasures and pitfalls of credit. B. Brantley and J. Brake. il Suc Farm 62:44-5 My '64
Rediscovery of money. M. A. Heilperin. il Fortune 71:152-3+ Ja '65
Scandal in personal bankruptcy. R. A. Phalon. il Duns R 81:35-6+ Mr '63
Scepter for king consumer; in California. il Bsns W p 106+ Mr 30 '63
Split about credit policy. U S News 54:109-10 Mr 18 '63
Still piling up debt, but slower. il Bsns W p75 Ag 22 '64
This proposal shortchanges your customers; federal credit control plan. il Nations Bsns 51:98-102 Mr '63
Too much buying of stocks on credit? il U S News 55:127+ N 18 '63
Too much money? il Fortune 70:32+ D '64
Trade credit zooms up; concerning study, prepared by M. H. Seiden. Bsns W p72 Ap 25 '64
What's on your credit record? personnel & insurance reports. il Changing T 19:33-5 Ja '65
What's worrying bankers as they look ahead. il U S News 57:106-8 N 9 '64
Why credit controls would hurt. P. W. McCracken and others. Nations Bsns 52:34-5+ D '64
Will White House get control over credit? concerning Federal reserve system. il U S News 56:83-4 My 4 '64
With inflation talk in the air, borrowing still will be easy. U S News 57:115-17 S 28 '64
See also
Debt
Discount
Farm finance
Finance companies
Instalment plan
Loans, Bank
Loans, Personal

CREDIT, Export. See Export credit

CREDIT agencies, Government. See Government lending

CREDIT cards
American offers installment credit plan. J. W. Carter. Aviation W 80:34 Mr 30 '64
Carriers flock to credit card bandwagon. J. W. Carter. Aviation W 81:30-1 Ag 31 '64
Embarrassment is wonderful. il Time 81:81 F 22 '63
Flying on the cuff. il Bsns W p 115-16 Je 27 '64
He who steals my purse steals my credit cards. Time 83:53 Je 19 '64
International markets; foreign trade credit card. A. O. Stanley. Duns R 81:57-8 Je '63
Key Athens issues include credit, fares. J. W. Carter. Aviation W 81:36 S 21 '64
Supermarket shoppers put it on the cuff. il Bsns W p 117 Je 15 '63
See also
Diners' club, incorporated

CREDIT corporations. See Finance companies

CREDIT dollar. See Money—United States

CREDIT insurance. See Insurance, Credit

CREDIT unions
Credit union security. R. Wayne. NEA J 52:48 My '63
Innovative design in texture and scale; Illinois credit union league. il Arch Rec 133:154-5 Mr '63
Steel and chrome of the credit union. E. B. Eubanks. NEA J 53:47 My '64

CREED, Virginia
Austria: winter Olympics. Travel 120:44-6 D '63

CREEGAN, Robert F.
Gabriel Marcel in Albany. Sch & Soc 92:86 F 22 '64

CREELEY, Robert
Beat Voznesensky. Nation 199:336-7 N 9 '64
For Leslie; poem. Nation 197:420 D 14 '63
Messengers: for Allen Ginsberg; poem. Nation 197:404 D 7 '63
Think what's got away. . . Poetry 102:42-8 Ap '63
Woman; Pattern; Mechanic; Walls; I keep to myself such measures. . . ; Dream; Hello; Quick-step; Variations; Chance; Window; Walking; Language; poems. Poetry 104:133-48 Je '64
about
Extension of content. A. Saroyan. Poetry 104:45-7 Ap '64
Reticences of pattern. W. Dickey. Poetry 101:421-4 Mr '63

CREHAN, Hubert
Change of Pace. Art N 63:39-41+ Ap '64

CREMATION
Cremation and change; Catholic attitude. America 110:842 Je 20 '64
Cremation: permissible; Holy Office instruction. Time 83:85 Je 12 '64

CREMIN, Lawrence A.
Is the issue clearly drawn? Sat R 47:79-80 Mr 21 '64
Schools and democracy. Sat R 46:86-7 F 16 '63

CREMONA violin. See Violin

CRENCHAW, Charles
Weekend climber. il pors Ebony 19:125-8 N '63

CREOLE petroleum corporation. See Petroleum industry and trade—Venezuela

CRÊPES. See Griddle cakes

CRÊPES Suzette. See Griddle cakes

CRESCIMBENI, Joseph, and Mammarella, Raymond
Hidden hazards in teaching. NEA J 54:31 Ja '65
—See Mammarella, R. jt. auth.

CRESPIN, Régine
Quote; unquote; interview, ed. by R. Jacobson. por Mus Am 84:22 Mr '64
about
Régine Crespin. G. L. Mayer. il Am Rec G 30:668-9 Ap '64

CRESSEY, George B.
Obituary
Sr Schol 83:4T N 8 '63

CRESTED BUTTE, Colo.
Colorado conversion; ski site switches to summer celebration. R. Auletta. il Travel 121:58-9 My '64

CRESTED irises. See Irises

CRETACEOUS period. See Geology, Stratigraphic—Cretaceous; Paleontology—Cretaceous

CRETE
Easter in Crete. D. M. Doren. il Sat R 46:34-6+ Mr 16 '63
Going places, finding things in the Cyclades and Crete. M. M. Hemingway. il House & Gard 123:24+ Je '63
Independence, honour, and ecstasy, in Crete. C. Haldeman. il Vogue 145:101-2+ Ja 15 '65

Description and travel
Crete: a photographic essay. I. Penn. Vogue 145:98-113 Ja 15 '65
Rough map of Greece: the night boat. P. L. Adams. il Atlan 213:57-62 My '64

CREVALLÉ fishing
Jack the giant killer. A. J. McClane. il Field & S 68:80-2+ Mr '64

CREW, Alfred
Triple-treatment sewage plant. Am City 79:96-8 Mr '64

CREWE, Albert V.
Red carpet. Bul Atomic Sci 19:25-6 S '63

CREWEL work
Old stitch hits the bigtime. il Life 54:49-50 Mr 15 '63
Sources of the design of early crewelwork. R. Davidson. il Antiques 86:206 Ag '64

CRIB deaths. See Infant mortality

CRIBS (beds)
Crib and a five-level child's bed. il Sunset 131:117-18 N '63

CRICHTON, Don
Brief biography. S. Goodman. por Dance Mag 38:58-9 D '64

CRICHTON, Marion Carrie
Revolt of the vegetables; drama. Plays 24:69-72 O '64

CRICK, Bernard
Politics of textbooks. Commentary 38:67-9 Jl '64

CRICK, Francis Harry Compton
On the genetic code; address, December 11, 1962. bibliog Science 139:461-4 F 8 '63

CRICKET (game)
Now it's cricket to be a pro. B. Hollowood. il N Y Times Mag p39-40+ My 26 '63
Private line from London. V. Cowles. Vogue 144:114+ S 1 '64
Sporting scene; test series: England vs. West Indies. A. Reid. il New Yorker 39:188+ O 19 '63
This is cricket; West Indian test match team in Great Britain. il Newsweek 62:63 Jl 8 '63

CRICKETS
Crickets chirp indoors with autumn's arrival. Sci N L 84:216 O 5 '63
Daily fluctuation in the blood sugar concentration of the house cricket, gryllus domesticus L. J. W. Nowosielski and R. L. Patton. bibliog il Science 144:180-1 Ap 10 '64

CRIME and criminals

Answer to the rise in crime and violence; excerpts from address, September 8, 1964. G. B. McClellan. il U S News 57:89-90 N 9 '64

Convict who became a minister. J. Robbins and J. Robbins. il Redbook 124:38-9+ D '64

Roots of evil. by C. Hibbert. Review Nation 197:394-5 D 7 '63. S. Bedford

See also

Brigands and robbers
Burglary and burglars
Counterfeits and counterfeiting
Criminal investigation
Criminal law
Embezzlement
Fraud
Justice, Administration of
Juvenile delinquency
Murder
Police
Robberies and assaults
Self defense
Sex crimes
Thieves
Trials

Identification

See Identification

International aspects

See also

International criminal police commission

Law

See Criminal law

Australia

Omerta in the Antipodes; Italian immigrant shootings. il Time 83:30 Ja 31 '64

Brazil

Law of the favelas; policeman assassinated. il Time 84:36 S 25 '64

Canada

Crime problem in Canada; how the Mounties handle it; interview, ed. by K. M. Chrysler. C. W. Harvison. il U S News 55:66-8 Jl 29 '63

Colombia

Death of black blood. Time 83:36+ My 8 '64

Killers; rural gang warfare. Newsweek 62:40 Ag 5 '63

Senseless slaughter; Aranguren massacre. il Time 82:21 Ag 23 '63

Transistor murderer. Newsweek 64:59 N 30 '64

Europe, Western

How courts in Europe deal with criminals. il U S News 58:48-9 Ja 18 '65

France

End of fantasy; arrest of The strangler. il Newsweek 64:46-7 Jl 20 '64

I am the strangler! you must believe me! Lucien Leger. E. Behr. il Sat Eve Post 237:74-5 O 10 '64

War of nerves; murder of Jean Luc Taron near Paris. Newsweek 63:30 Je 29 '64

Great Britain

Crime and punishment. Newsweek 64:38 Jl 27 '64

Guilty innocent; Harold Loughan. Time 81:25-6 Mr 1 '63

In defense of R. Hood. R. Payne. il N Y Times Mag p48+ N 17 '63

See also

London—Crime

Italy

Course in geography; a crime of honor. il Time 84:49 O 30 '64

New Mafia is deadlier. R. Neville. il N Y Times Mag p22+ Ja 12 '64

See also

Mafia

Japan

Way of chivalry; gangster-ridden nation. Newsweek 64:42 S 14 '64

See also

Kidnaping

Massachusetts

Muddy track; scandal at Berkshire Downs. il Newsweek 61:33+ Mr 18 '63

Mexico

Murdering madams; sisters González Valenzuela. il Newsweek 64:60 N 2 '64

Sisters of shame; Mexican white slavers. il Time 84:50 O 30 '64

Mississippi

Law-abiding Mississippi. Time 84:60 Ag 28 '64

New England

New England; the refined Yankee in organized crime. D. S. Strong. bibliog f Ann Am Acad 347:40-50 My '63

Russia

Crime and punishment in the Soviet Union today; questions and answers. C. Foltz, jr. il U S News 56:90-1 Mr 2 '64

Russia has Socialist crime, too. G. Feifer. il N Y Times Mag p20+ Ap 5 '64

See also

Justice, Administration of—Russia

Sicily

See also

Mafia

Southern states

New bombing terrorists of the South call themselves Nacirema: American spelled backward. G. McMillan. Life 55:39-40 O 11 '63

United States

At large and most wanted: ten dangerous men. K. Detzer. il Read Digest 84:190-2+ Mr '64

Barry fights crime, but you'd never know it from the record. J. Ridgeway. New Repub 151:9-11 O 3 '64

But listen to his canary. Life 55:4 O 18 '63

Che cosa? means what's that? M. Kempton. New Repub 149:6-7 O 12 '63

Civil rights act of 1964; respect for law; address, September 18, 1964. N. deB. Katzenbach. Vital Speeches 31:27-9 O 15 '64

Combating organized crime; symposium, ed. by G. Tyler. bibliog f il Ann Am Acad 347:1-112 My '63

Crime and politics; proclamations of Goldwaterism. E. J. Hughes. Newsweek 64:25 O 19 '64

Crime goes on and gets worse. il U S News 55:76 S 9 '63

Crime in U.S. is it getting out of hand? with charts. U S News 55:38-43 Ag 26 '63

Crime syndicate and the way it works. U S News 55:10 Ag 19 '63

Crook's tour. H. Pask. Travel 119:51+ Ap '63

Every street a jungle. Christian Cent 81:923 Jl 22 '64

Fear takes over our city parks. S. Grafton. il McCalls 91:108-11+ O '63; Same abr. with title Danger stalks our parks. Read Digest 85:114-17 Jl '64

FBI studies histories of chronic offenders. Am City 79:22 S '64

Free crime school? TV explosion. America 108:425 Mr 30 '63

Going up; FBI figures. Newsweek 64:24 S 14 '64

Good-by to Bobby One-Eye Wilcoxson. B. Clark. il Read Digest 82:63-8 F '63

How criminals solve their investment problem; crime in business. il U S News 56:74-6 Mr 30 '64

How much crime can America take? interviews. W. G. Long; W. H. Parker. il U S News 56:66-72 Ap 20 '64

I sure was scared; case of Ricky Hale and Melvin Allen Weaver. Newsweek 62:27 Jl 15 '63

Is crime running wild? with chart. il U S News 57:19-21 Ag 3 '64

Killers in prison; J. Valachi before Senator McClellan's permanent investigations subcommittee. il Time 82:33 O 4 '63

Last days of Dillinger; excerpt from The Dillinger days. J. Toland. il Look 27:79-80+ F 12 '63

Major crime up ten per cent. Christian Cent 81:982 Ag 5 '64

Robert Kennedy defines the menace. R. F. Kennedy. il N Y Times Mag p 15+ O 13 '63

Roll of dishonor; F.B.I.'s list of ten most wanted fugitives. C. Remsberg and B. Remsberg. N Y Times Mag p69 Ja 26 '64

Show biz in Washington. Nation 197:229 O 19 '63

Special supplement on crime and punishment: symposium. il Harper 228:121-36+ Ap '64; Discussion. 228:6+ Je '64

Take the handcuffs off our police! F. Sondern, jr Read Digest 85:64-8 S '64

Television: stimulant to violence. J. Ellison. Nation 197:433-6 D 21 '63

Terror in the cities. America 108:287-8 Mr 2 '63

Them are the pictures; Sam Giancana versus J. Edgar Hoover. il Newsweek 62:43-4 Jl 29 '63

Thirty-five years ago. S. D. Smith. il N Y Times Mag p96-8 O 27 '63

CRIME and criminals—United States—*Cont.*
Two roads to a deadly face-off; case of Don Carpenter and Sheriff Tarr. T. Thompson. il Life 55:17-18 N 22 '63
War on crime. America 108:848 Je 15 '63
Where is science taking us? new criminal: a report on the hip killer. L. Yablonsky. il Sat R 46:54-6 F 2 '63
Who's got Bananas? il Newsweek 64:38 N 2 '64
Will city streets ever be safe again? interview. S. R. Schrotel. il U S News 54:80-3 Ap 8 '63
Without portfolio; public apathy toward criminal acts. C. B. Luce. McCalls 91:18+ S '64
See also
Gambling
Lynching
Mafia
Molly Maguires
Negroes in the United States—Crime
New Orleans—Crime
Prisons—United States
Racketeering
United States—Federal bureau of investigation
also subhead Crime under names of cities, e.g. New York (city)—Crime

History

When crime paid. il Esquire 60:89-94 N '63

CRIME and the press
Case of trial by press. A. Lewis. il N Y Times Mag p31+ O 18 '64
Focus on chapter V; Warren commission report. Nation 199:205-6 O 12 '64
How I made a crime wave; excerpt from Autobiography of Lincoln Steffens. L. Steffens. Read Digest 85:160D+ D '64
When newsmen become newsmakers; problem of publicity before and during a trial. E. N. Griswold. Sat R 47:21-3 O 24 '64; Reply. W. O'Neil. 47:25 N 21 '64
See also
Newspaper court reporting

CRIME detection. See Criminal investigation; Identification

CRIME in literature
See also
Detective and mystery stories

CRIME novels. See Detective and mystery stories

CRIME prevention
Citizen crimebusters, one answer to city violence; Jewish citizens' patrol force in Brooklyn. il U S News 57:62-4 Jl 13 '64
First scream, then scram. il U S News 54:58-9 Ap 1 '63
Interdisciplinary attack on organized crime. G. Tyler. bibliog f Ann Am Acad 347:104-12 My '63
When silence is a crime. L. Nizer. McCalls 92:95+ O '64
When the police welcome false alarms; child molesters. G. Marten. PTA Mag 57:30-1 My '63
Without bars: some bold and some timorous experiments. G. Playfair. Harper 228:171-5 Ap '64
See also
Juvenile delinquency—Prevention
Police

CRIME syndicates. See Crime and criminals—United States

CRIMES, War. See War crimes

CRIMES aboard aircraft
Shooting determined cause in F-27 crash; near San Ramon, Calif, May 7, 1964. Aviation W 82:78-9+ Ja 4 '65

CRIMINAL behavior. See Criminal psychology

CRIMINAL identification. See Identification

CRIMINAL investigation
Air force murder case; Nancy Johnson and her son. J. Foisie. Nation 196:285-7 Ap 6 '63
Confessions from suspects; Danny Escobedo's conviction reversed. Time 84:51 Jl 3 '64
Criminalistics. P. L. Kirk. bibliog Science 140:367-70 Ap 26 '63
End of road for Hoffa? what his conviction means. il U S News 56:46-7 Mr 16 '64
Good-by to Bobby One-Eye Wilcoxson. B. Clark. il Read Digest 82:63-8 F '63
Hoffa: how they nailed him. H. Suydam. il Life 56:20-5 Mr 13 '64
Innocent's grim ordeal; murder of wife of airman Alec Johnson, Mountain Home air force base, Idaho. J. R. Phelan. il Sat Eve Post 236:62-7 F 2 '63
Only five out of 100 unsolved murder cases. Sci N L 83:120 F 23 '63
Quick, Watson the Geiger counter! neutron activation analysis. C. Remberg. il Pop Mech 119:97-100 Ap '63
Reporter at large; burglary. S. Black. il New Yorker 39:89-91+ D 14 '63
Search for the strangler; tactical patrol force of Boston. J. Iams. il Sat Eve Post 236:28+ My 18 '63
Solving crimes on paper; excerpt from Science in crime detection. N. Morland. il Sci Digest 53:12-23 Mr '63
Why was Carol killed? case of Carol Thompson. D. J. Giese. il Sat Eve Post 236:73-7 S 14 '63
Your portrait by the police; Identikit. A. Hamilton. il Sci Digest 55:31-4 Mr '64
See also
Electronics in criminal investigation, espionage, etc.
Fingerprints
Identification
Lie detectors
Photography, Legal
Radioactivation analysis
United States—Federal bureau of investigation

CRIMINAL law
Behavioral science and criminal law. E. J. Sachar. il Sci Am 209:39-45 bibliog(p 186) N '63; Reply with rejoinder. J. V. McConnell. 210:8-9 Ja '64
Control yourselves; new penal code for Poland. Newsweek 61:52+ Je 10 '63
Equal justice for all; economic equality in the criminal process. il Time 83:78 F 21 '64
How much crime can America take? interviews. W. G. Long; W. H. Parker. il U S News 56:66-72 Ap 20 '64
Inciting to suicide; a felony. Time 83:88 My 22 '64
Maryland; a law-enforcement dilemma. A. J. T. Zumbrun. bibliog f il Ann Am Acad 347:58-66 My '63
New approach to the control of organized crime. M. Ploscowe. Ann Am Acad 347:74-81 My '63
To balance the scales; rights of criminals. il Time 83:48 Mr 20 '64
Two views of Chicago; how the police chief sees it. O. W. Wilson. Harper 228:140-5 Ap '64
Uncertain criminal law: rights, wrongs, and doubts. I. R. Kaufman. il Atlan 215:61-7 Ja '65
When silence is a crime. L. Nizer. McCalls 92:95+ O '64
Wolfenden report: report of the committee on homosexual offenses and prostitution. Review
Sat R 46:31-2 My 4 '63. J. M. Murtagh
See also
Capital punishment
Criminal procedure
Obscenity (law)
Trials
Wife beating

CRIMINAL lawyers. See Lawyers

CRIMINAL liability
Defendant Ruby will meet the ghost of a long dead Scot. E. Havemann. il Life 56:30-1 F 21 '64
Law, liberty and psychiatry, by T. S. Szasz. Review
Nat R 16:201-3 Mr 10 '64. R. M. Schuchman

CRIMINAL procedure
Comrades & their courts. il Time 84:118 O 2 '64
Criminal gets the breaks. D. Gutman. il N Y Times Mag p36+ N 29 '64
New approach to criminal law. B. J. George, jr. Harper 228:183-8 Ap '64
Reform in West Germany: investigative arrest curbed. il Time 84:53 Jl 3 '64
See also
Bail
Jury

CRIMINAL psychology
Benny and his brothers. K. E. Whelan. Harper 228:166-7 Ap '64
Can a sane robber be an insane rapist? U S News 54:6 Ap 8 '63
I care, you care, he cares. J. Little. il Harper 228:169-70 Ap '64
Killer had been paroled. R. P. Crosley. Read Digest 83:105-8 O '63
Oswald killing discussed. Sci N L 84:355 D 7 '63
Violence pattern in U.S.: Check violence threats. Sci N L 84:357 D 7 '63
Where is science taking us? new criminal: a report on the hip killer. L. Yablonsky. il Sat R 46:54-6 F 2 '63
See also
Forensic psychiatry

CRIMINAL statistics
See also
Juvenile delinquency—Statistics

CRIMINALS. See Crime and criminals

CRIMMIN, Eileen
A B sea of a first cruise. Motor B 113:118+ Ap '64
Cruising tips. Motor B 111:40-1+ Ap '63
Families by the boatload. Motor B 111: 106+ Ap '63
High road, low road. Buchans take the blow road. Motor B 111:146-7 My '63
High tide of debris. Motor B 112:24-7+ Jl '63
Lake Roosevelt; sailor's luck. Motor B 114:90-4 Ag '64
Lesson taught by a shoelace. Motor B 114:54+ Jl '64
Mercer Island marathon. Motor B 112:62+ Ag '63
Musson, closeup of a champion. Motor B 114:34+ Jl '64
Northern squall eclipses southern sun. Motor B 112:106-7+ S '63
Northwest gales. See issues of Motor boating
Pieces and quiet. Motor B 111:137-9 F '63
Puget Sound. Motor B 111:30-2+ My '63
Seattle yacht club opening day. Motor B 113: 54+ My '64
Space-age boating. Motor B 113:26-8+ F '64
Staudacher; man with a mission. Motor B 115:109-11+ Ja '65
Tall in the cockpit. Motor B 113:24-5+ My '64
There oughta be a lawr. Motor B 111:147-8 Je '63
What's your line? Motor B 113:86-9+ Ja '64
Winning ways of Wee Willie. Motor B 111: 43+ My '63
—See Carver, B. jt. auth.

CRIMSON feather; drama. See Watts, F. B.

CRIPPLE CREEK mines. See Gold mines and mining—United States

CRIPPLES
Doctor on wheels. il Ebony 19:83-4+ O '64
Every kindergarten needs a Tino. M. Lang. PTA Mag 58:25 O '63
See also
Amputees
Orthopedia

Rehabilitation

See Rehabilitation

CRISIS; story. See Clark, V.

CRISLER, Fritz
Man who changed football. G. Holland. il pors Sports Illus 20:22+ F 3 '64

CRISLER, Herb
They know the wild in wildlife. I. Petite. il pors Audubon Mag 66:20-5 Ja '64

CRISLER, Lois
They know the wild in wildlife. I. Petite. il por Audubon Mag 66:20-5 Ja '64

CRISLER, Richard C. Jr
German cabarets flourish. il Theatre Arts 47:25-7 Je '63

CRIST, Raymond E.
Bolivians trek eastward. Américas 15:33-8 Ap '63
Why move a capital? Américas 15:13-17 Ag '63

CRISTELLA Marie, Sister
Speckled malaise; poem. Cath World 196: 350 Mr '63

CRITES, Stephen
All spaces and times are suns; poem. Christian Cent 81:1584 D 23 '64
New deal for the academic shuffle. Atlan 211:117-19 My '63

CRITICAL path analysis
ABCs of the critical path method; excerpts from Industrial scheduling. F. K. Levy and others. bibliog f il Harvard Bsns R 41:98-108 S '63
Contractor gets steady check on profits with new PERT-type system. W. Beller. il Miss & Roc 14:38-9+ Ja 13 '64
CPM opens a pool ten months early; West Hartford, Conn. S. Moses. il Am City 79:78-9 D '64
C.P.M.: what factors determine its success? F. A. Sando. il Arch Rec 135:211-16 Ap; 202-4 My '64
How Pert-cost helps the general manager. H. W. Paige. il Harvard Bsns R 41:87-95 N '63
Introduction to CPM. E. Van Krugel. il Arch Rec 136:337+ S '64
Inventor of the month; the computer that plans ahead; Planalog. il Sci Digest 55:52-3 Je '64

Bibliography

Interpretations of PERT. A. R. Dooley. Harvard Bsns R 42:160-2+ Mr '64

CRITICAL path method. See Critical path analysis

CRITICISM
Angry young men. America 111:150-1 Ag 15 '64; Discussion. 111:274-6, 606-7+ S 19, N 14 '64
How to cope with criticism. N. V. Peale. Read Digest 84:117-20 My '64
In defense of educationists. V. Beck. NEA J 53:16 Mr '64
Mea culpa compulsion. America 110:475 Ap 4 '64
Word. V. P. McCorry. America 111:76 Jl 18 '64
See also
Art criticism
Critics
Dramatic criticism
Literary criticism
Moving picture plays—Criticisms, plots, etc.
Television criticism

CRITICISM, Personal. See Self evaluation

CRITICS
Criticizing the critics (cont) G. Spelvin. il Theatre Arts 47:32-3 Jl '63
Critics. G. Ace. Sat R 47:13 N 28 '64
De gustibus. Hi Fi 13:41 Mr '63
Don't knock U.S. culture; adapted from Culture consumers. A. Toffler. il Life 57:96-100+ O 30 '64
Immediate experience; unfamiliar with what they are criticizing. Christian Cent 81:535 Ap 22 '64
Instant critics; TV drama critics. il Newsweek 65:61 Ja 25 '65
No tickets for Clurman. Nation 197:379 D 7 '63
On being a music critic; excerpts from Music observed. B. H. Haggin. Commentary 38:50-2 Jl '64; Reply. D. H. Heintz. 38:28 O '64
Paying guest; London's enfant terrible. Time 81:64+ Mr 22 '63
Return to civilian life; what theatregoing now means to a former critic. L. Kronenberger. il Theatre Arts 47:14-15+ F '63
Reviling the reviewers. Newsweek 64:82 Jl 27 '64
Ten nights club. S. Spaeth. il Opera N 28:6-7 Ap 11 '64
See also
Dramatic criticism
Literary criticism

CRITTENDEN, John R.
Hardened electronic systems urged. Miss & Roc 13:18-19 S 9 '63

CRITTENDEN, Pauline
Reader's choice. Travel 120:6 O '63

CRO cameras. See Cameras

CROAN, Robert J.
Mozart the dramatist. Opera N 29:35 Ja 2 '65

CROATIA
Visit to Croatia. T. De Bousson. il America 109:353 S 28 '63

CROCE, Arlene
Movies (cont) Nat R 14:123-4; 16:413-15 F 12 '63, My 19 '64
New York film festival. Nat R 16:1118-19 D 15 '64

CROCK, Muriel B.
I can lick every person in this camp! NEA J 53:52-3 N '64

CROCKER, Lionel
Realms of gold; address, May 6, 1964. Vital Speeches 30:537-9 Je 15 '64

CROCKER, T. Timothy, and others
Poliovirus: growth in non-nucleate cytoplasm. bibliog Science 145:401-3 Jl 24 '64

CROCKER art galleries. See E. B. Crocker art gallery, Sacramento, Calif.

CROCKETT, George W. Jr, and Goodman, Ernest
Legal help needed. Nation 196:inside cover Je 1 '63

CROCKETT, William J.
Foreign policy needs people, including you; remarks, January 20, 1964. Dept State Bul 50:632 Ap 20 '64

CROCKETT, Tex.
When the bubble burst in Crockett, Texas. C. Stevenson. Read Digest 85:197-8+ S '64

CROCODILES
Crocodiles in the cellar. J. Atwater. il Sat Eve Post 237:32-3 S 26 '64
Nature note. Sci N L 86:347 N 28 '64
Nobody loves a crocodile. G. Gaskill. il Read Digest 86:17-18+ Ja '65

CROCUSES
To have winter blooming crocus... il Sunset 133:158 D '64

CROCUSES, Autumn. See Autumn crocuses

CROFOOT, Helen E.
In appreciation. Nat Parks Mag 38:16 My '64

CROFUT, Bill
Folk-singing ambassadors. il pors Sr Schol 83:17 S 27 '63

CROFUT, Bill—*Continued*
Hootenanny under fire; State-department-sponsored tour of the Far East and Africa. il por Time 85:48-9 Ja 8 '65
Long trail a-winding. il por Newsweek 61:53 Ap 29 '63
CROISSANT, Rene Barter-. See Barter-Croissant, R.
CROISSANTS. See Bread
CROMAGNON man. See Man, Prehistoric
CROMBIE, A. C.
Early concepts of the senses and the mind; with biographical sketch. Sci Am 210:24, 108-16 My '64
CROMBIE, D. D.
Very-low-frequency radio waves and the ionosphere. Science 142:508+ O 25 '63
CROMIE, William J.
Great Mohole mess. Sci Digest 54:59-63 N '63
Killer whale! Read Digest 82:176-80 Mr '63
Secrets from cold storage. Natur Hist 72:20-7 O '63
CROMWELL, John
Matter of life and death. Criticism
New Yorker 39:90 O 12 '63
Opening night. Criticism
New Yorker 39:90 O 12 '63
CROMWELL, William Nelson
Panama Canal lobby of Philippe Bunau-Varilla and William Nelson Cromwell. C. D. Ameringer. Am Hist R 68:346-63 Ja '63
CRONIN, A. J.
Quo vadis? Read Digest 82:118-20+ My '63
CRONIN, Joseph M. See Fahrner, C. J. jt. auth.
CRONIN, Pat Somers
Nuns I've known. America 108:710-11 My 18 '63
CRONKITE, Walter
Terrible disappointment of Walter Cronkite; excerpts from telephone conversation, May 15, 1964. Nat R 16:435 Je 2 '64
about
Anchor's aweigh. Time 84:52 Ag 7 '64
D-day plus twenty years. H. Mitgang. il por Look 28:78-85 F 25 '64
His crime was playing it straight. R. Oulahan. Life 57:13 Ag 28 '64
On the news beat. il por Newsweek 63:74-5 Je 1 '64
Secret life of Walter (Mitty) Cronkite. L. H. Lapham. il pors Sat Eve Post 236:65-7 Mr 16 '63
Upstairs was unhappy. il por Newsweek 64:44-5 Ag 10 '64
Walter Cronkite: why won't he be himself on TV? I. Taves. il pors Look 28:74+ Ag 25 '64
CROOK, Mel
Lake George patrol. Yachting 115:96-7+ Ja '64
More power to you. See issues of Yachting
Rugged race to Nassau. il Yachting 115:46-9+ Je '64
CROP insurance. See Insurance, Agricultural
CROP insurance corporation. See Federal crop insurance corporation
CROP reports. See Agriculture—Statistics
CROP rotation. See Rotation of crops
CROPLEY, Jac A.
Making headlines. por Recreation 57:393+ O '64
Recreation out of necessity; excerpts from paper. por Recreation 57:84-5+ F '64
CROPPING. See Photographs—Trimming, mounting, etc.
CROPS
Crop cost-cutting ideas that really work. P. R. Robbins. il Suc Farm 62:34-5 D '64
Crops and soils; ed. by R. D. Wennblom and G. W. Wormley. See issues of Farm journal
Crops news (cont of) Crops and soils. See issues of Farm journal
How many crops can you afford? R. D. Wennblom. il Farm J 88:34-5+ O '64
What's new and outlook for. See issues of Successful farming
See also names of crops, e.g. Sugar
Statistics
See Agriculture—Statistics
CROPS and climate. See Plants, Effect of climate on
CROSBY, Bing
Bing and I. K. G. Crosby. il pors Good H 156:86-91+ Mr '63
Notes for a gazetteer; Crosbyana room of Crosby library, at Gonzaga university. P. Hamburger. New Yorker 39:198 O 26 '63
CROSBY, H. Ashton
Nonnuclear defense of Europe. Bul Atomic Sci 20:30-1 Ap '64
CROSBY, Harry
Become a versatile amateur! P. Caulfield. il Mod Phot 27:56-61 Ag '63
CROSBY, John
I was wrong about Paris. Ladies Home J 81:42+ My '64
So sorry! Read Digest 84:123-4 F '64
about
Great idea town; New York herald tribune columnist in London. por Newsweek 62:96 N 4 '63
Lulu, Daphne, and an uncertain sky. P. J. Smith. il Hi Fi 14:68-71 N '64
Sante Fe at seven. G. Martin. il por Opera N 28:28-31 Ap 11 '64
CROSBY, Kathryn (Grant)
Bing and I. pors Good H 156:86-91+ Mr '63
about
Mrs Bing Crosby: student nurse. S. Gordon. il pors Look 27:98-100 Mr 12 '63
CROSBY, Ken, and Durmas, Jim
We got to hang on; ed. by B. Fellows. pors Life 55:19-20 O 25 '63
CROSS, Bert
Businessmen in the news. por Fortune 68:101 Jl '63
CROSS, Gilbert
Gentle bulldozers of Peoria. Fortune 68:166-71+ Jl '63
Gourmet by the gallon. Esquire 61:34+ My '64
House the janitors built. Read Digest 82:201-4 F '63
White man looks at the Negro. Look 27:60+ D 17 '63
CROSS, Richard E.
World of the renaissance executive. il por Newsweek 62:92-4 N 18 '63
CROSS, Robert D.
What religion has meant in American history. por Cath World 197:280-7 Ag '63
William V. Shannon on the American Irish. Commonweal 79:695-6 Mr 6 '64
CROSS, Wilbur
Pets on loan. Parents Mag 38:60-1 Ap '63
Publishing the corporate book. Sat R 47:56+ Jl 11 '64
Sounds of sites. Travel 119:32-3 Mr '63
CROSS, Way of the. See Stations of the cross
CROSS and crosses
Case of the midnight Christians; controversy over cross erected in Eugene, Ore. R. P. Nelson. Christian Cent 82:22-3 Ja 6 '65
Coventry cross visits World's fair. Christian Cent 81:326 Mr 11 '64
Missing Michelangelo? discovery of painted wood crucifix. il Life 56:45-6+ F 21 '64
Rarest ivory cross. il Life 56:119-20 Je 12 '64
Unburied cross; Romanesque cross recently acquired by Manhattan's Metropolitan museum of art. il Time 83:68-9+ Je 19 '64
Why the cross? Christian Cent 81:323 Mr 11 '64
CROSS breeding. See Hybridization
CROSS-Canada automobile rally. See Automobile racing
CROSS country running. See Running
CROSS-country skiing. See Skis and skiing
CROSS country trails. See Trails
CROSS pollination. See Fertilization of plants
CROSS-stitch
See also
Samplers
CROSS TIMBERS grasslands, Tex. See Wilderness areas
CROSS ventilation. See Ventilation
CROSSCUP, Richard
What do children value? excerpts from address; June 18, 1964. por Wilson Lib Bul 39:146-50 O '64
CROSSES. See Cross and crosses
CROSSING over (genetics)
Cytological evidence for crossing-over in vitro in human lymphoid cells. J. German. bibliog il Science 144:298-301 Ap 17 '64
Hybrid resistance to parental marrow grafts: association with the K region of H-2. G. Cudkowicz and J. H. Stimpfling. bibliog il Science 144:1339-40 Je 12 '64
Recombination events in the bacterial genus nocardia. J. N. Adams and S. G. Bradley. bibliog il Science 140:1392-4 Je 28 '63
Tetrasporic embryo-sac formation in trisomic sectors of maize. M. G. Neuffer. bibliog il Science 144:874-6 My 15 '64
CROSSLEY, Robert P.
Killer had been paroled. Read Digest 83:105-8 O '63

CROSSMAN, R. H. S.
Apocalypse at Dresden. Esquire 60:149-52+ N '63; 61:126 F '64
British Labor looks at Europe. For Affairs 41:732-43 Jl '63
Polish miracle. Commentary 35:210-19 Mr '63
CROSSWORD puzzles
Fifteen letters: most popular game. J. M. Willig. il N Y Times Mag p22+ D 15 '63
CROTHERS, Bill
Young druggist's sure Rx. R. Creamer. il por Sports Illus 20:56+ F 10 '64
CROUCH, Archie R.
Christians in newborn Malaysia. Christian Cent 80:1437; 81:465-6 N 20 '63, Ap 8 '64
CROUSE, Russel
Oscar Hammerstein; a healing sort of guy. Read Digest 84:80-6 Ja '64
CROUT, George
(ed) See Catrow, G. C. Diary of George C. Catrow.
CROUT, J. R. and others
Release of metaraminol (aramine) from the heart by sympathetic nerve stimulation. bibliog Science 145:828-9 Ag 21 '64
CROVITZ, Herbert F.
Köllner effect and suppression of the view of an eye. bibliog Science 146:1329-30 D 4 '64
—and Lipscomb, D. B.
Binasal hemianopia as an early stage in binocular color rivalry. bibliog Science 139:596-7 F 15 '63
CROW Indians
Indian fair; on the Crow Indian reservation, southeastern Montana. M. Jensen. il Am For 69:20-1+ My '63
CROW shooting
Best thing about crows. C. Ford. il Field & S 69:8+ S '64
Crows a la carte. T. E. Huggler. il Outdoor Life 131:26-7+ Ja '63
We move for crows. T. Janes. il Outdoor Life 133:52-5+ My '64
CROWDER, Tinsley
Scientific publishing. Science 144:633-7 My 8 '64
CROWDS
Crowds and power, by E. Canetti. Review
Commonweal 77:544 F 15 '63. J. P. Sisk
Time il 81:103+ F 15 '63
Social standing; new science of proxemics. Newsweek 61:84 Ap 22 '63
CROWE, C. Lawson
Rights and differences: some notes for liberals. Christian Cent 81:1359-60 N 4 '64
CROWE, Cecily
Sweater from a distant place; story. Seventeen 22:118-19 F '63
CROWE, Sparkle G.
Teacher's role in politics. NEA J 53:31 O '64
CROWE, William P.
Offshore California: the Channel Islands. il Yachting 117:106-7+ Ja '65
CROWELL-Collier publishing company
Collier's affair: a rueful memoir; excerpt from personal file. P. C. Smith. Esquire 62:132-5+ S '64
Crowell-Collier holds peaceful annual meeting. Pub W 185:35 Ap 13 '64
Crowell-Collier holds stormy annual meeting. Pub W 183:69-70 Ap 15 '63
CROWER, Bruce
Indy 500 diary. Hot Rod 16:90-2+ S '63
CROWLEY, James. See Werner, G. jt. auth.
CROWN, Henry
GD: the hard road back from the brink; Convair fiasco. il Bsns W p 144-6+ D 7 '63
CROWN, James Tracy
India tomorrow. Nation 198:599-602 Je 15 '64
Party's responsibility. Nation 197:411-13 D 14 '63
CROWN jewels
Lord and the regalia. S. Hugh-Jones. il Horizon 5:92-6 My '63
CROWN publishers, incorporated
Crown denies FTC charges of deceptive pricing. Pub W 185:104 Ja 20 '64
Initial FTC decision against Crown. Pub W 186:78 Ag 24 '64
CROWN vetch
Colorful groundcover. il Pop Gard 16:69 Ja '65
CROWN Zellerbach corporation
DMSO: fact and fancy. W. B. Morse. il Am For 70:6-7+ S '64
That utilizing monster: barker chipper. W. B. Morse. il Am For 71:30-1+ Ja '65
CROWNING of King Arthur; drama. See Olfson, L.
CROWNINSHIELD, George, jr
Cleopatra's barge. C. H. Jenrich. il por Motor B 114:116-17 D '64

CROWNS
Their majesties' splendor. il Horizon 5:97-104 My '63
CROWTHER, John F.
Rationale for quantity discounts. Harvard Bsns R 42:121-7 Mr '64
CROY, O. R.
Darkroom designer; excerpt from Design by photography. Design 65:202-6 My '64
CROZIER, George
Leg up on a good heart. Sports Illus 21:28+ S 21 '64
CROZIER, Roger
Bald and the bold. il por Newsweek 64:46 D 21 '64
Wispy and worrying, but he wins. R. Lardner. il por Sports Illus 21:81-2 N 23 '64
CRUCE, B. H.
Off-street parking program. Am City 79:113-14 F '64
CRUCIBLE; drama. See Miller, A.
CRUCIBLE; opera. See Ward, R.
CRUCIFIXES. See Cross and crosses
CRUCIFIXION of Jesus Christ. See Jesus Christ—Crucifixion
CRUELTY to animals. See Animals—Treatment
CRUELTY to children
Battered-child cases. America 110:559 Ap 25 '64
Cry rises from beaten babies. il Life 54:38-9 Je 14 '63
Helping neglectful parents. J. A. Bishop. bibliog f Ann Am Acad 355:82-9 S '64
More of the same. Nation 198:339 Ap 6 '64
Parents who abuse children. V. De Francis. il PTA Mag 58:16-18 N '63
Protecting children from abuse. K. B. Oettinger. Parents Mag 39:12 N '64
Saving battered children. il Time 85:43 Ja 8 '65
Shocking price of parental anger. L. David. Good H 158:86-7+ Mr '64; Same abr. Read Digest 85:181-2+ S '64
Terror-struck children. R. Coles. New Repub 150:11-13 My 30 '64
CRUET, Jorge Perez-. See Perez-Cruet, J.
CRUETS
Antiques; silver caster and cruet stand by George Ridout. A. Winchester. il Antiques 86:166-7 Ag '64
CRUICKSHANK, Allan D.
Land of mysterious waters. il Audubon Mag 65:156-63 My '63
CRUICKSHANK, John
Charting a literary log. Sat R 46:25+ Ag 31 '63
Evil on a pedestal. Sat R 47:56 N 14 '64
CRUIKSHANK, Nelson H.
Excerpt from address, June 27, 1962. Cong Digest 42:214+ Ag '63
CRUISE, Edwina J.
Great Garbo. Seventeen 23:28 Ja '64
CRUISERS. See Yachts and yachting
CRUISERS, Fishing. See Fishing boats
CRUISES. See Cruising
CRUISING
Atlantic liners extend the sun run; Caribbean winter-cruise circuit. il Newsweek 65:68-70 Ja 11 '65
Baja California. C. West. il Yachting 116: 44-7+ O; 58-9+ N '64
Boats we meet: North Star. J. Emmett. il Yachting 115:42-3+ Mr '64
Catamaran to Tahiti; ed. by R. Choy. K. Murphy; A. Reid. il Yachting 113:36-8+ Mr; 85-7+ Ap '63
Channel cruise to glorious Devon. A. Villiers. il Nat Geog Mag 124:208-59 Ag '63
Circumnavigating Nova Scotia. Mrs A. E. Phillips, jr. il Yachting 115:38-40+ Je '64
Coast to coast cruising, and then some. S. Penington. il Motor B 114:22-3+ N '64
Come cruise California! S. West. il Motor B 111:26-9+ My '63
Come to Champlain. il Motor B 113:22-9 Ap '64
Cruise to the sea. F. Mowat. il Yachting 113: 57-9+ Je; 114:54-6+ Jl '63
Cruisemanship. V. M. Black. il Travel 120: 35-7 N '63
Cruises that click. C. Darlington. il Motor B 112:40+ S '63
Cruising in company; planning ahead for a fleet vacation. H. M. Winters. il Motor B 113:102-3+ F '64
Cruising the Chesapeake country. il Motor B 112:22-7 S '63
Cruising the Lakes on your way to the fair. il Sunset 132:70+ My '64
Cruising the Santa Barbara Channel Islands. J. Bugay. il Yachting 113:40-2+ My '63

CRUISING—*Continued*
Cruising your boat south. J. Emmett. il Yachting 114:45-7+ S; 64-6+ O '63
Delight around Denmark. W. Britton. il Motor B 111:90-2+ F; 126+ Mr '63
Down to the sea; Windjammer cruises. il Time 83:72 My 15 '64
Dwellers and voyagers. I. Anthony. il Yachting 116:43+ D '64
East of The Race and west of the Cape; leisurely tour on the Finisterre. C. Mitchell. il Sports Illus 19:46-54 Jl 22 '63
East to Abaco. L. A. Solomon. il Motor B 114:36-9+ S '64
Far side of paradise; northwest Florida. J. Gribbins. il Motor B 112:38 S '63
Fiji interlude. B. Robinson. il Yachting 115: 56-7+ F '64
First cruise. B. Meister. il Yachting 113:204-7 My '63
5:25 for St Thomas. G. Sloane. il Motor B 113: 44-5+ Ap '64
Florida-Bahamas yachting; symposium. il Yachting 114:45-62+ N '63
Going places with Esquire. Esquire 60:111 Ag '63
Group cruising, new fun afloat. il Motor B 113:48-9+ F '64
Harbors of history: the Southeast heritage cruise. il Motor B 114:21-9 S '64
Henriette V made the great circle. L. Solomon. il Motor B 112:46-7+ O; 94+ N; 76-7+ D '63
Heritage of Hiroshige. C. Mitchell. il Sports Illus 19:106-10+ D 23 '63
Home to the sea. W. C. Brewer, jr. il Motor B 113:114-15+ Ja; 24-5+ F; 52+ Mr '64
Inside the Outer Banks. F. A. Montgomery, jr. il Motor B 111:28-31+ Ap '63
Island gunkholing paradise. B. D. Barker, 3d. il Yachting 114:38-40+ D '63
Landfalls ahead! West Indies cruise on Cunard liner Franconia. O. R. Cohen. il Travel 123:48-51 Ja '65
Lure of islands. il Motor B 112:18-25 Ag '63
New England heritage cruise. B. Killam. il Motor B 111:20-7+ Ap '63
New good move for travellers; cruising the Orient. Vogue 143:66 Mr 1 '64
North Channel. K. Collins. il Yachting 115:36-8+ Mr '64
North to Antigua; from Martinique. M. P. Ryan. il Motor B 114:42-5 S '64
North to the islands. B. Robinson. il Yachting 115:68-70+ Ja '64
Northwest Passage. W. Bagley. il Yachting 113:52-3 Je '63
Offshore California: the Channel Islands. W. P. Crowe. il Yachting 117:106-7+ Ja '65
Piloted cruise to Nassau. il Yachting 115:53 F '64
Profiles; two-week cruise aboard sloop Merrywend, around Long Island Sound. M. M. Hunt. il New Yorker 40:37-40+ Ag 22; 37-8+ Ag 29; 37-40+ S 5 '64
Red tape and blue water. M. B. Petersen. il Motor B 112:26+ Ag '63
Rest from racing; cruise from Alameda up the Napa River. D. Keleher. il Yachting 115:202-4 My '64
Retire and cruise. C. Stoessel. il Motor B 113: 38-9+ Ap '64
Rideau revisited. J. G. Robinson. il Yachting 114:38-40+ Ag; 52-3+ S '63
Rideau, with four feet apiece. H. L. Brun. il Motor B 114:28-9+ Jl '64
Sailing our inland seas; Great Lakes. J. Grenard and J. Grenard. il Motor B 111: 22-3+ Je '63
Small boat in the Bahamas. B. Robinson. il Yachting 114:41-4+ N '63
Sound cruising. C. R. Meyer. il Travel 119: 38-40 Je '63
South to the Islands. D. Street. il Yachting 116:54-6+ Ag '64
Southern yachting; symposium. il Yachting 116:34-54+ N '64
There's more than one way to go to the sun. M. Gough. il House B 106:56+ Ja '64
This summer, why not Alaska? H. E. McLean. il Motor B 113:26-7+ My '64
Thousand miles of islands. J. Martenhoff. il Motor B 112:40-3 D '63
Under El Yunque; excerpt from Where the trade winds blow, a yachting guide to southern waters. B. Robinson. il Yachting 114: 48-9+ O '63
Virgin cruising. D. Phillips. il Motor B 114: 24-8 N '64
Virgin Isles adventure; Windjammer cruise on Maverick. W. M. Domin. il Travel 122: 35-8 D '64
Voyage north: from Seattle to Seward, Alaska. J. E. Randall, 2d. il Yachting 115: 47-9+ F '64
West to northwest; from Los Angeles, Cal, to Cape Flattery, Wash. C. West. il Yachting 115:58-60+ My '64
White wakes in the Bahamas. F. T. Moss. il Yachting 113:49-51+ F '63
Winter boating vacation guide. il Motor B 112:22-6+ D '63
Would you like to take a sabbatical afloat? M. MacDuffie. il Yachting 113:55-7+ Mr '63
Yankee cruises the Chesapeake. M. MacDuffie. il Yachting 116:40-2+ D '64
See also
River trips

Anecdotes, facetiae, satire, etc.

A B sea of a first cruise. E. Crimmin. il Motor B 113:118+ Ap '64
CRUISING club of America
Cruising club measurement rule. G. M. Curtis, jr. il Yachting 115:44-6+ Mr '64
CRUISING houseboats. See House boats
CRUM, M. Colyer. See Law, W. A. jt. auth.
CRUMP, N. R.
Canadianism today; address, February 20, 1963. Vital Speeches 29:394-7 Ap 15 '63
CRUSADES
Conquest of the Holy City. F. Shor. il Nat Geog Mag 124:838-55 D '63
Constantinople, A.D. 1204. America 110:274 F 29 '64
Crusader road to Jerusalem. F. Shor. il Nat Geog Mag 124:797-837 D '63
See also
Lepanto, Battle of, 1571
CRUSE, Heloise (Bowles)
Dishrags to riches: the saga of Heloise. M. Cheshire. il pors Sat Eve Post 236:58-61 Mr 2 '63
CRUSHERS, Ice. See Ice crushers
CRUST of the earth. See Earth—Surface
CRUSTACEA
Calorific values of microcrustacea. G. W. Comita and D. W. Schindler. bibliog il Science 140:1394-6 Je 28 '63
Conchostracans: living and fossil from Chihuahua and Sonora, Mexico. P. Tasch and B. L. Shaffer. bibliog Science 143:806-7 F 21 '64
Crustacea: a primitive Mediterranean group also occurs in North America. B. Maguire, jr. bibliog il Science 146:931-2 N 13 '64
See also
Eye (crustacea)
CRUSTACEA, Fossil
Conchostracans: living and fossil from Chihuahua and Sonora, Mexico. P. Tasch and B. L. Shaffer. bibliog Science 143:806-7 F 21 '64
CRUX (periodical) See Periodicals—Australia
CRUZ SAAVEDRA, Juan de la
Root-carver from Cali. A. Pardo-Tovar. il por Américas 16:35-8 N '64
CRYING
See also
Infants—Crying
Tears
CRYOGENIC research. See Low temperature research
CRYOGENICS. See Low temperatures
CRYOSURGERY. See Brain—Surgery
CRYPTOCOCCUS neoformans. See Fungi, Pathogenic
CRYSTAL, Maxwell M.
Insect fertility: inhibition by folic acid derivatives. bibliog Science 144:308-9 Ap 17 '64
CRYSTAL (glass) See Glass, Ornamental
CRYSTAL BALL CAVE. See Caves
CRYSTAL CITY, Tex.
Anglo minority. il Newsweek 61:26 Ap 29 '63
Revolt of the Mexicans. il Time 81:25 Ap 12 '63
CRYSTAL for company; story. See Frasier, K.
CRYSTAL oscillators. See Oscillators, Crystal
CRYSTAL palace. See London—Crystal palace
CRYSTAL receivers. See Radio receiving apparatus
CRYSTAL RIVER, Colo.
Up Colorado's Crystal River. il Sunset 133:43-4 Jl '64
CRYSTALLOGRAPHY
Amethyst: optical properties and paramagnetic resonance. T. I. Barry and W. J. Moore. il Science 144:289-90 Ap 17 '64
Boron-oxygen polyanion in the crystal structure of tunellite. J. R. Clark. bibliog il Science 141:1178-9 S 20 '63
Crystal formation from vapor probed; growth of silicon whiskers. il Miss & Roc 14:23 Mr 16 '64

CRYSTALLOGRAPHY—*Continued*
Crystalline deamino-oxytocin. D. Jarvis and V. du Vigneaud. bibliog il Science 143:545-8 F 7 '64
Crystallization of SE polyoma virus. W. T. Murakami. bibliog il Science 142:56-8 O 4 '63
Free radicals and reactive molecules in clathrate cavities. P. Goldberg. bibliog il Science 142:378-9 O 18 '63
Growth of oxalic acid single crystals from solution: solvent effects on crystal habit. J. L. Torgesen and J. Straussburger. bibliog il Science 146:53-5 O 2 '64
Hydrazine-water system: the water-rich eutectic. J. A. McMillan and S. C. Los. bibliog il Science 145:1307 S 18 '64
Hydrogen ion incorporation in crystals. D. McConnell. bibliog Science 141:171 Jl 12 '63
Infrared study of the OH groups in expanded kaolinite. R. L. Ledoux and J. L. White. bibliog il Science 143:244-6 Ja 17 '64
Nobel prize in chemistry awarded to crystallographer. G. A. Jeffery. Science 146:748-9 N 6 '64
Pentaborate polyanion in the crystal structure of ulexite, $NaCaB_5O_6(OH)_6.5H_2O$. J. R. Clark and D. E. Appleman. bibliog il Science 145:1295-6 S 18 '64
Planets and comets: role of crystal growth in their formation. B. Donn and G. W. Sears. bibliog il Science 140:1208-11 Je 14 '63
Shape of the recorded area in precession photographs and its application in orienting crystals. M. J. Buerger and W. A. Dollase. il Science 145:264-5 Jl 17 '64
Site of preference energy and selective uptake of transition-metal ions from a magma. R. G. Burns and W. S. Fyfe. bibliog il Science 144:1001-3 My 22 '64
Sodium chloride: modification of crystal habit by chemical agents. R. S. Ploss. bibliog il Science 144:169-70 Ap 10 '64
Sodium perxenate hexahydrate. A. Zalkin and others. bibliog il Science 142:501-2 O 25 '63
Stishovite: thermal dependence of the crystal habit. C. B. Sclar and others. bibliog il Science 144:833-5 My 15 '64
Thermochemical etching reveals domain structure in magnetite. R. E. Hanss. bibliog il Science 146:398-9 O 16 '64
Uranyl ion coordination. H. T. Evans, jr. bibliog il Science 141:154-8 Jl 12 '63
Uranyl ion coordination. J. O. Edwards and J. A. Stritar. bibliog il Science 142:1651 D 27 '63
See also
Dendrites
Dislocations in crystals
Liquid crystals

X ray studies

Crystal and molecular structure of ferrichrome A. A. Zalkin and others. bibliog il Science 146:261-3 O 9 '64
Crystal structure of weddellite. C. Sterling. bibliog il Science 146:518-19 O 23 '64
Electron microscopy of meteoritic and artificially shocked graphite. T. P. Sciacca and M. E. Lipschutz. bibliog il Science 145:1049-50 S 4 '64
Ferric tourmaline from Mexico. B. Mason and others. bibliog il Science 144:71-33 Ap 3 '64
Graphitization of organic material in a progressively metamorphised pre-Cambrian iron formation. B. M. French. bibliog il Science 146:917-18 N 13 '64
High-pressure B-type polymorphs of some rare-earth sesquioxides. H. R. Hoekstra and K. A. Gingerich. bibliog il Science 146:1163-4 N 27 '64
High-pressure metallic indium telluride: preparation and crystal structure. C. B. Sclar and others. bibliog il Science 143: 352-3 Ja 24 '64
High pressure phases of some compounds of groups II-VI. A. N. Mariano and E. P. Warekois. bibliog il Science 142:672 N 8 '63
High-pressure phase transition in tin telluride. J. A. Kafalas and A. N. Mariano. bibliog il Science 143:952 F 28 '64
High-pressure polymorphs in the silver iodide phase diagram. B. L. Davis and L. H. Adams. bibliog il Science 146:519-21 O 23 '64
High-voltage Laue X-ray photography of large single crystals. B. Paretzkin and H. S. Peiser. bibliog il Science 146:260-1 O 9 '64
Mononuclear and polynuclear chemistry of rhenium (III): its pronounced homophilicity. F. A. Cotton and others. bibliog il Science 145:1305-7 S 18 '64
Plutonium dioxide: preparation of single crystals. K. D. Phipps and D. B. Sullenger. bibliog il Science 145:1048-9 S 4 '64
Silicon oxynitride: a meteoritic mineral. C. A. Andersen and others. bibliog il Science 146:256-7 O 9 '64
X-ray diffraction study of a DNA which contains uracil. R. Langridge and J. Marmur. bibliog il Science 143:1450-1 Mr 27 '64
X-ray diffraction studies on dysprosium at high pressures. J. C. Jamieson. bibliog il Science 145:572-4 Ag 7 '64

CRYSTALS. See Crystallography

CRYSTALS, Ice. See Ice

CRYSTALS, Liquid. See Liquid crystals

CRYSTALS, Metal. See Metal crystals

CRYSTALS, Quartz. See Quartz crystals

CRYSTALS, Snow. See Snow

CSERNA, George
Architect's photographer. C. Schwalberg. il U S Camera 26:66-9+ Mr '63

CSILLIK, Bartalan
Tremorine: its peripheral action on striated muscle. bibliog Science 146:765-6 N 6 '64

CUB scouts. See Boy scouts—Cubs

CUBA
Anniversary song. il Newsweek 63:36 Ja 13 '64
Anything going to happen on May 20? Time 83:48 My 15 '64
As the Cubans see Castro. R. Hudson. Sat R 47:97-9+ O 10 '64
Call on Castro; U.S. newsmen in Cuba. il Newsweek 64:62-4 Ag 10 '64
Castro must go! G. J. Facio. Read Digest 84:109-13 F '64
Comrade Blimp; Morozov letter. Newsweek 62:50 D 16 '63
Cuba: invitation to reason. J. O'Connor. Nation 198:198-9 F 24 '64
Cuba lives by Castro's moods. R. Eder. il N Y Times Mag p 12-13+ Jl 26 '64
Cuba: lost soul, new saints. E. M. Reingold. il Newsweek 61:26-7 F 4 '63
Cuba: why Castro is feeling stronger. E. Tetlow. New Repub 151:9-10 Jl 11 '64
Cuban scene: a photographer's report. il N Y Times Mag p6-7 Je 21 '64
Diary of a visit. J. Gerassi. il Newsweek 64:38+ Ag 3 '64
Flora strikes, the deadliest ever. il Life 55: 34-43 O 18 '63
Is Castro an obsession with us? G. S. McGovern. il N Y Times Mag p9+ My 19 '63
My twenty-eight days in Communist Cuba. L. Bergquist. il Look 27:15-27 Ap 9 '63
Next step in Cuba: a letter to an island in Castro's mind. J. Tallet and C. T. Fenyvesi. Nat R 16:397-8 My 19 '64
Return to Cuba: the revolution is still alive. G. Greene. New Repub 149:16-18 N 2 '63
This is Castro's Cuba seen face to face. H. Cartier-Bresson. il Life 54:28-43 Mr 15 '63
View from Havana. il Time 84:28 Ag 14 '64
What it's like in Cuba; journeyman notes on life under Fidel Castro. B. Smith. New Repub 148:21-4 Ap 13 '63
Wooden anniversary. il Time 83:27 Ja 10 '64
See also
Agriculture—Cuba
Anti-Communist movements—Cuba
Architecture—Cuba
Art—Cuba
Communism—Cuba
Food supply—Cuba
Havana
Investments, Foreign (in Cuba)
Libraries—Cuba
Petroleum industry and trade—Cuba
Prisoners of war in Cuba
Prisons—Cuba
Russia—Armed forces—Forces in Cuba
Trials—Cuba
Water supply—Cuba

Commerce

Allied aid to Cuba: growing U.S. problem. il U S News 56:4 Mr 2 '64
Buses for Cuba. Sr Schol 84:16 Ja 31 '64
Deal that makes Castro happy; sale of British city buses. il U S News 56:13 Ja 20 '64
Dramatic flourish, empty gesture; breakdown of U.S. trade embargo on Cuba. il Time 83:23 F 28 '64
Falling apart: economic blockade of Cuba. il U S News 56:6 F 17 '64

CUBA—Commerce—*Continued*
Hole in the embargo. Time 83:33 Ja 17 '64
More help for Castro from an ally of U.S. U S News 56:8 My 18 '64
Quandary over Cuba. il Bsns W p26 F 15 '64
Trade with the reds; a bonanza for Canada. il U S News 56:64 Mr 2 '64
See also
Sugar industry and trade

Defenses

Burr under the blanket; Shut up! Cuban situation. Nat R 14:145-6 F 26 '63
Cuba: how dangerous now; with excerpt from President Kennedy's news conference, February 7, 1963. il U S News 54:58-63 F 18 '63
Cuba under the lens: no missiles but . . . il Newsweek 61:19-22 F 18 '63
Inside Cuba now: latest reports. il U S News 54:36 F 4 '63
Latest facts on Russia's Cuban base; interview. K. B. Keating. il U S News 54:43-5 F 11 '63
McNamara says no deal involved in removal of missiles from Cuba. Aviation W 78:35 Ap 1 '63
Military value of missiles in Cuba. R. Hagan and B. Bernstein. il Bul Atomic Sci 19:8-13 F '63
Most critical area in the world. Life 54:4B F 22 '63
New storm brewing over Cuba? Sr Schol 82: 15 F 27 '63
What's there. il Newsweek 61:30 F 11 '63
Whose missiles? Newsweek 63:45 My 4 '64
Why Soviets are rushing a military buildup in Cuba. U S News 54:42-3 F 11 '63

Economic conditions

After all of Cuba's troubles, what's ahead for Castro. il U S News 55:34-5 N 4 '63
As Castro's troubles multiply—. il U S News 56:55 My 25 '64
Big eyes, small pocketbook. Time 84:48 S 4 '64
Calamity island. il Newsweek 62:38+ N 4 '63
Castro and Khrushchev: the ties that bind. Panatela. il Reporter 28:38-9 Mr 14 '63
Castro tells Cubans: get down to work. il Bsns W p28-9 Ag 10 '63
Chaos in Castro's Cuba; with editorial comment. E. Behr. il Sat Eve Post 236:20-2+, 72 Je 8 '63
Close-up Cuba after five years of Castro. il U S News 56:8 Ja 13 '64
Communisms's failure in Cuba; an on-the-ground report; reprint. R. S. Knowles. il U S News 54:66-8 Je 17 '63
Cuba paints its own shade of red. il Bsns W p46-8+ Je 13 '64
Cuba, the lingering debate. il Sr Schol 82:8-11 Mr 6 '63
Cuba: the moment is now; aftermath of hurricane Flora. Nat R 15:379 N 5 '63
Cuba's lame economy. Bsns W p 126 F 16 '63
Fidel's sixth. Newsweek 65:44 Ja 18 '65
For Castro, triple trouble now. il U S News 56:66 Ap 27 '64
Reds keep Cuba going. il Bsns W p 126-8+ S 14 '63
Report from Cuba: passion for seed potatoes. J. Gerassi. il Newsweek 64:44+ Jl 27 '64
What a reporter found; after five and a half years of communism; how Cuba looks today. C. Migdail. il U S News 57:38-40 Ag 31 '64
What hurricane Flora really did to Cuba. U S News 55:8 O 28 '63

Economic policy

Five years of Castro's Cuba. T. Draper. bibliog f Commentary 37:25-37 Ja '64; Discussion. 37:3+ My '64

Economic relations

Barking at big brother. Time 85:35 Ja 15 '65
Breaching the blockade. Newsweek 63:47 F 10 '64
By sea, by air. Newsweek 64:58 S 28 '64
Cuban embargo myth. P. Geyelin. Reporter 30:18-19 Ap 23 '64
Horse-trade in Moscow. Bsns W p25-6 My 4 '63

Expropriation policy

Contested cargo; legal battle between expropriated company, C.A.V. and Cuba's Banco nacional. Time 83:71-2 Ap 3 '64
Courts can't bar seizures; suit by Banco nacional de Cuba against U.S. firm. Sr Schol 84:20+ Ap 10 '64

Foreign relations

Adopted son in revolt. Newsweek 62:51 S 16 '63
After the Cuban crisis. D. H. Wrong. Commentary 35:28-33 Ja '63
Calamity island. il Newsweek 62:38+ N 4 '63
Calling for action on Castro. il Bsns W p31-2 F 16 '63
Caribbean, troubled waters; Guantánamo crisis. il Newsweek 63:13-14 F 17 '64
Case against Castro; excerpts from report of five-nation committee of the Organization of American states. il U S News 56: 59 Mr 9 '64
Castro, Khrushchev, and Mao. T. Draper. il Reporter 29:27-31 Ag 15 '63
Castro's challenge to U.S: the real reasons. il U S News 56:38-9 F 17 '64
Castro's Cuba: a U.S. problem becomes a threat to the world. il U S News 56:51-4 F 10 '64
Castro's mysterious trip to Russia. il U S News 56:16 Ja 27 '64
Courting Comrade Castro; first visit to the Soviet Union. il Newsweek 61:43-4 My 13 '63
Cuba: between promise and decay. R. Eder. il N Y Times Mag p5+ Je 21 '64
Cuba branded aggressor. Sr Schol 84:16 Mr 13 '64
Cuba condemned; action of Organization of American states. Sr Schol 85:24 S 16 '64
Cuba: how Castro wins and U.S. loses. il U S News 56:66-8 Ap 6 '64
Cuba: our cold-shoulder policy. R. A. Falk. il Nation 199:113-17 S 14 '64
Cuba, the lingering debate. il Sr Schol 82:8-11 Mr 6 '63
Cuban intervention in Venezuela; excerpts from report. Américas 16:44 Ap '64
Deal Castro wants with U.S. C. Migdail. U S News 57:47 Ag 10 '64
Eager to coexist? il Newsweek 64:42 Ag 10 '64
Easing off; Guantánamo Bay. il Newsweek 63:34 F 24 '64
Evidence to consider; Cuban gunrunning. il Time 84:23 Jl 3 '64
Fidel in wonderland. il Time 83:18-19 Ja 24 '64
Fidel's reflections. Newsweek 61:40 Ap 1 '63
Five years of Cuban revolution. R. M. Schneider. bibliog f Cur Hist 46:26-33 Ja '64
For a free Cuba. Nat R 14:483-4 Je 18 '63
For Castro, triple trouble now. il U S News 56:66 Ap 27 '64
Friendly Fidel. il Time 84:35 Jl 17 '64
Fruits of Castro's plotting; with editorial comment. S. Alsop. il Sat Eve Post 236:75-80 Mr 16 '63
Further clarification; concerning interviews with Kennedy and Castro. J. Daniel. New Repub 149:6-7 D 21 '63
In the works: deal with Castro? U S News 54:65 Je 17 '63
Is Castro planning to shoot down U-2s? il U S News 57:12 N 23 '64
Kremlin climate; Castro's visit to Moscow. il Newsweek 63:38 Ja 27 '64
LBJ and Cuba: what comes next. U S News 55:41 D 23 '63
Ninth meeting of consultation: OAS foreign ministers vote measures against Cuba; concerning Rio treaty, with resolution and excerpts from governmental statements. il Américas 16:1-10 S '64
No time to let up on Castro. Life 57:4 Ag 7 '64
OAS approves Rio treaty measures against Castro regime; with statements, and text of final act, July 22-30, 1964. D. Rusk; L. B. Johnson. bibliog f Dept State Bul 51:174-84 Ag 10 '64
O.A.S. on Venezuela's charges against Cuba; text of act, signed on July 26, 1964. Cur Hist 48:40-4 Ja '65
Rethinking Cuba. Christian Cent 80:1191-2 O 2 '63
Sales and sanctions. Newsweek 63:42 Mr 9 '64
Task of the O.A.S. Cuba: address, July 21-24, 1964. D. Rusk. Vital Speeches 30:665-7 Ag 15 '64
United States, Cuba, and Castro, by W. A. Williams. Review
New Repub 148:23-4 Ap 20 '63. S. Shapiro
U.S. replies to Cuban charges in U.N. General assembly; statement, December 11, 1964. A. E. Stevenson. Dept State Bul 52: 24-6 Ja 4 '65
U.S. sympathizes with Cuban people in aftermath of hurricane Flora; Department statement, October 23, 1963. Dept State Bul 49: 741 N 11 '63
Unofficial envoy: an historic report from two capitals. J. Daniel. New Repub 149:15-20 D 14 '63
Variation on a theme; Castro proposes Cuban co-existence with the U.S. il Newsweek 64:49-50 Jl 20 '64
Venezuelan miracle. R. Betancourt. il Reporter 31:37-41 Ag 13 '64
We are the victors. Time 81:40+ Je 14 '63

CUBA—Foreign relations—*Continued*
What's going on in Cuba now. U S News 55:8 Jl 1 '63
When Castro heard the news. J. Daniel. New Repub 149:7-9 D 7 '63
When Khrushchev and Castro get together. il U S News 54:37-9 My 13 '63
Why Castro wants U.S. to bail him out. U S News 57:62 Jl 20 '64

History

Air will be ours; Cuban fighters tell why they expected air cover; with excerpts from radio messages. M. A. de Varona; G. Herrera. il U S News 54:33-6 F 4 '63
Cuba: issues and alternatives. W. A. Williams. Ann Am Acad 351:72-80 Ja '64
How President Kennedy upset Cuban invasion of April 1961. U S News 54:29-30+ F 4 '63

British occupation, 1762-1763

When the British captured Havana. G. de Zéndegui. il Américas 16:21-8 Mr '64

Invasion, 1961

Air will be ours; Cuban fighters tell why they expected air cover; with excerpts from radio messages. M. A. de Varona; G. Herrera. il U S News 54:33-6 F 4 '63
Anatomy of the snafu. T. Flaherty. il Life 54:80-3 My 10 '63; Same abr. with title What we learned from the Bay of Pigs. Read Digest 83:92-4 Jl '63
Bay of Pigs, by H. Johnson and others. Review
America 110:773-4 My 30 '64. E. K. Culhane
Esquire 62:74+ S '64. M. Muggeridge
New Repub 150:21-2 Je 27 '64. T. R. Fehrenbach
Newsweek il 63:106+ My 18 '64
Reporter 30:53-6 Je 18 '64. J. E. Smith
Sat R 47:41+ My 16 '64. H. Lavine
Bay of Pigs: the curtain is lifting. il U S News 54:82 Mr 18 '63
Bay of Pigs; the unanswered questions. J. E. Smith. il Nation 198:360-3 Ap 13 '64
CIA: the case builds up. F. J. Cook. il Nation 198:616-18 Je 22 '64
Cover story; Bay of Pigs disaster. Reporter 28:16+ F 14 '63
Cover-up; deaths of four U.S. flyers. Time 81:23-5 Mr 8 '63
Cuba story, wraps off. R. De Toledano. Nat R 14:288-9 Ap 9 '63
Decision for disaster; condensation. M. Lazo. il Read Digest 85:241-4+ S '64
How President Kennedy upset Cuban invasion of April 1961. U S News 54:29-30+ F 4 '63
Refugee leader blames U.S. for broken promise; excerpts from statement, April 18, 1963. J. Miró Cardona. U S News 54:65-7+ Ap 29 '63
Roberto's story; forgotten young men; with editorial comment. W. F. Rickenbacker. il Nat R 15:94, 105-6 Ag 13 '63
Secrecy boomerang; managing the news. R. Hotz. Aviation W 78:21 Mr 18 '63
Sequel to the Bay of Pigs: four U.S. pilots; they died while serving their country. B. Surface. il Life 54:44 Mr 15 '63
Specter and flashback; Four who didn't return. il Newsweek 61:25-6 Mr 11 '63
Story of Americans at the Bay of Pigs. il U S News 54:33-4 Mr 11 '63
Strange case of the CIA widows; husbands at Bay of Pigs. D. Wise and T. B. Ross. il Look 28:77-8+ Je 30 '64
Up to the others; questions about Cuba. il Time 81:19-20 Mr 15 '63
We who tried; with report by J. Dille. il Life 54:20-34+ My 10 '63

Industries

White elephants on parade. Time 83:36 Mr 6 '64
See also
Cigar industry
Sugar industry and trade

Intellectual life

Letter from Havana. M. Schleifer. Nation 198:442-5 Ap 27 '64

Invasion

See Cuba—History—Invasion, 1961

Politics and government

After the Cuban crisis. D. H. Wrong. Commentary 35:28-33 Ja '63
Cuba, the lingering debate. il Sr Schol 82: 8-11 Mr 6 '63
Cuban doctor's decision. B. Asbell. il Redbook 120:46-7+ Mr '63
Future of Castroism. D. Burks. Cur Hist 44: 78-83+ F '63
Is Cuba ripe for revolt? E. Tetlow. New Repub 148:8-9 F 23 '63
New trouble in Cuba; Castro's woes keep growing. il U S News 57:14 D 21 '64
Off-stride troika. Newsweek 63:38 Ap 13 '64
Rise and fall of Cuba; address, May 20, 1964. M. L. Simpson. Vital Speeches 30:520-2 Je 15 '64

Religious institutions and affairs

Castro vs. the witnesses. Newsweek 61:72 Mr 25 '63
See also
Catholic church in Cuba
Evangelical church in Cuba
Methodist church in Cuba
Protestants in Cuba

Social conditions

Nonstop day with Castro. il Newsweek 63: 28-9 Mr 2 '64
Tale of three classes. J. Gerassi. il Newsweek 64:42-3 Ag 10 '64

CUBA and the United States
Cuba revisited. J. A. MacKay. il Christian Cent 81:200-3 F 12 '64; Discussion. 81:402-6, 772 Mr 25, Je 10 '64
Fresh look at Cuba. J. A. Mackay. Christian Cent 81:983-7 Ag 5 '64; Discussion. 81:1308 O 21 '64
Red junket to Cuba; ed. by R. Tunley. B. Hoffmann. il Sat Eve Post 236:25-9 O 5 '63

CUBAN bases. See Guided missile bases

CUBAN blockade. See Blockade

CUBAN crisis, 1962
After Cuba: two lessons. E. Rabinowitch. Bul Atomic Sci 19:2-8 F '63
Always Cuba. Nation 198:450 My 4 '64
Artful dodging; Stennis subcommittee investigation of Cuban military buildup. Nat R 14:438 Je 4 '63
Cuba and the nuclear risk. W. Lippmann. Atlan 211:55-8 F '63
Cuba, Latin America, and communism; address, September 20, 1963. E. M. Martin. Dept State Bul 49:574-82 O 14 '63
Cuba story, wraps off. R. De Toledano. Nat R 14:288-9 Ap 9 '63
Cuban crisis: how close we were to war; excerpts from Politics of policy-making: the Kennedy years. R. Hilsman. il U S News 57:59-60 Ag 17 '64; Excerpts. Look 28:17-21 Ag 25 '64
Department replies to statements by Dr Miró Cardona, statements, April 15 and April 18, 1963. Dept State Bul 48:709-10 My 6 '63
Five years of Cuban revolution. R. M. Schneider. bibliog f Cur Hist 46:26-33 Ja '64
Further clarification; concerning interviews with Kennedy and Castro. J. Daniel. New Repub 149:6-7 D 21 '63
God bless our allies! Nation 198:61 Ja 20 '64
How Castro tried to rewrite history. il U S News 55:14 D 23 '63
I spied on Castro's Cuba; Capt. Hennagan. il Ebony 18:114-16+ Ap '63
Intelligence gap on Cuba? the Senate gets a report. il U S News 54:63-6 My 20 '63
Interdependence and the principles of self-determination and nonintervention; address, April 16, 1963. E. M. Martin. Dept State Bul 48:710-15 My 6 '63
Kenneth Keating, critic of our Cuban policy. J. Daniel. Read Digest 82:190-2+ My '63
Letter from Washington. R. H. Rovere. New Yorker 39:125-31 Mr 2 '63
Love and power in today's setting. A. J. Muste. Christian Cent 80:639-42 My 15 '63
Man in the middle: role played by diplomatic correspondent ABC's J. Scali. Newsweek 64:80-1 Ag 17 '64
Ministers of seven governments meet in Nicaragua; text of final act, April 4, 1963. Dept State Bul 48:719-21 My 6 '63
My advance view of the Cuban crisis. K. Keating. il Look 28:96+ N 3 '64
Ninety dangerous days for U.S: summary of Strike in the West, by J. Daniel and J. G. Hubbell. il U S News 54:70-2 Mr 11 '63
October, 1962 the Cuba crisis: nuclear war was hours away. il Newsweek 62:24-6 O 28 '63
Plan to free Cuba. F. L. Howley. Read Digest 83:89-92 Jl '63
Red drive in Cuba. S. Synnestvedt. bibliog f Cur Hist 45:216-22+ O '63
Refugee leader blames U.S. for broken promise; excerpts from statement, April 18, 1963. J. Miró Cardona. U S News 54:65-7+ Ap 29 '63

CUBAN crisis, 1962—*Continued*
Secretary appears on Washington reports to the people; interview, ed. by H. W. Flannery. D. Rusk. Dept State Bul 48:440-3 Mr 25 '63
Secretary Rusk addresses Advertising council; remarks, March 12, 1963; with questions and answers. D. Rusk. Dept State Bul 48: 467-75 Ap 1 '63
Secretary Rusk interviewed on GFWC television program, April 13, 1963. D. Rusk. Dept State Bul 48:698-703 My 6 '63
Secretary Rusks' news conference of February 7, 1964. D. Rusk. Dept State Bul 50:274-84 F 24 '64
Senate group says Cuban data unreliable. K. Johnsen. Aviation W 78:119+ My 20 '63
Some current issues in U.S. foreign policy; remarks, April 18, 1963; with questions and answers. D. Rusk; G. W. Ball; W. A. Harriman. Dept State Bul 48:679-98 My 6 '63
Strange aftermath of the Cuban deal. il U S News 55:51-2 N 11 '63
United Nations in crisis; Cuba and the Congo; address, February 23, 1963. R. N. Gardner. Dept State Bul 48:477-81 Ap 1 '63
United Nations: its value to the United States; statement, March 13, 1963. A. E. Stevenson. Dept State Bul 48:522-8 Ap 8 '63
United Nations role in political disputes; address, March 11, 1963. J. J. Sisco. Dept State Bul 48:529-35 Ap 8 '63
U.S. comments on Venezuelan discovery of Cuban arms cache; Department statement, November 29, 1963. Dept State Bul 49:913-14 D 16 '63
Unofficial envoy: an historic report from two capitals. J. Daniel. New Repub 149:15-20 D 14 '63
Untold story of the Cuban crisis. H. Brandon. Sat R 46:56-7 Mr 9 '63
While America slept; condensation of Strike in the West. J. Daniel and J. G. Hubbell. il Read Digest 82:60-6+ Mr '63

Anecdotes, facetiae, satire, etc.

How I signed up at $250 a month for the big parade through Havana bla-bla-bla and wound up in Guatemala with the CIA. T. Southern. Esquire 59:67-8+ Je '63
CUBAN missile sites. See Guided missile bases
CUBAN raids. See Raids
CUBAN refugees. See Refugees, Cuban
CUBAN revolutionary council
Infiltration, not invasion. Time 81:20 Je 28 '63
War in words. il Newsweek 62:34 Jl 1 '63
CUBAN SAMSITES. See Guided missile bases
CUBANS
Cuba: the girl and the slogans. A. Hoppe. il Nation 199:216-17 O 12 '64
From a Cuban journal; tr. by T. Molnar; reply. C. T. Sheldon. Nat R 14:172 F 26 '63
Report from Guantánamo: we're ready for Castro's next step. H. Handleman. il U S News 56:52-3 Mr 2 '64
This is Castro's Cuba seen face to face. H. Cartier-Bresson. il Life 54:28-43 Mr 15 '63
What it's like in Cuba; journeyman notes on life under Fidel Castro. B. Smith. New Repub 148:21-4 Ap 13 '63
CUBANS in the United States
Bitter, frustrated, divided: Cuba's refugees. M. Bracker. il N Y Times Mag p7+ Ap 21 '63
Keeping pace with the PTA; Operation simpático; Dade County, Fla. C. Marburgh. il PTA Mag 58:31-2 S '63
Miami si, Castro no. il Sr Schol 82:8-9+ My 1 '63
New command for anti-Castro Cubans? il U S News 56:21 Je 8 '64
See also
Refugees, Cuban
CUBAS, José de
Westinghouse's de Cubas; the new global executive. por Duns R 81:49 Ap '63
CUBBEDGE, Robert
False promise of Medicare. Read Digest 84: 137-41 Ap '64
CUBIC corporation
Poor man's launcher may encourage non-space nations. W. Beller. il Miss & Roc 13:43+ S 30 '63
CUBISM
Autumn at the Guggenheim. M. Kozloff. Nation 199:203-4 O 5 '64
Gallery for young people; Le Canigou of J. Gris. C. B. Johnson. il Sch Arts 62:40 My '63
Gleizes: cubism as a way of life; retrospective exhibition at the Guggenheim and the San Francisco museum. D. Robbins. il Art N 63:24-7+ S '64
Letter from Paris. Genêt. New Yorker 39: 185-6+ S 14 '63
Letter from Paris; exhibition at the Musée national d'art moderne of Ecole de Paris paintings. New Yorker 40:182+ Ap 4 '64
CUCHULAIN
Hound of Ulster, by R. Sutcliff. Review
Horn Bk 40:273 Je '64. P. Heins
CUCKOO spit; story. See Lavin, M.
CUCKOOS
Ways of a parasitic bird. K. Koffán. il Natur Hist 72:48-51 Je '63
CUCUMBERS
Make a side dish with cucumbers. Sunset 131: 147 Ag '63
Sensitivity of female inbreds of cucumis sativus to sex reversion by gibberellin. O. Shifriss and W. L. George, jr. bibliog il Science 143:1452-3 Mr 27 '64
CUDAHY, Edward A. jr
Cudahy of Cudahy packing co. por Fortune 67: 53 F '63
CUDKOWICZ, Gustavo, and Stimpfling, J. H.
Hybrid resistance to parental marrow grafts: association with the K region of H-2. bibliog Science 144:1339-40 Je 12 '64
—and others
Pluripotent stem cell function of the mouse marrow lymphocyte. bibliog Science 144: 866-8 My 15 '64
CUE for Cleopatra; drama. See Martens, A. C.
CUENCA, Manuel
Jeepney. New Yorker 40:49-50 O 24 '64
CUÉNOD, Hugues
Remembrances of an enchantress. Hi Fi 14: 36-8 Jl '64
about
Music to my ears; performance of Erik Satie's Socrate. I. Kolodin. Sat R 48:38 Ja 23 '65
Notes from our correspondents. S. Fleming. por Hi Fi 14:22+ My '64
CUÉNOD, Michel. See Reis, D. J. jt. auth.
CUEVAS, José Luis
Joy wearies me. il por Newsweek 62:72 Ag 12 '63
CUEVAS, Robert A. See Shanklin, R. G. jr, jt. auth.
CUFF, Sergeant, pseud. See Winterich, J. T.
CUFFE, James
Printing, planning and public relations. por Am City 78:102 N '63
CUFFEY, Irene
I believe; ed. by J. Alley. por Seventeen 23: 54 Mr '64
CUKOR, George
Why they let George do it. A. Seidenbaum. McCalls 92:189-90 O '64
CULBERSON, Chicita F.
Joint occurrence of a lichen depsidone and its probable depside precursor. bibliog Science 143:255-6 Ja 17 '64
CULBERTSON, Don S.
Another Tower of Babel? bibliog por Library J 88:940-3 Mr 1 '63
CULBERTSON, Ely
Great bridge battle! C. H. Goren. il por McCalls 91:36+ O '63
CULBERTSON, James T.
Painstaking robot; excerpt from Minds of robots. Sat R 47:54-5 Ap 4 '64
CULHANE, Eugene K.
Another ex-Communist. America 108:196-8 F 9 '63
Big, bad businessmen. America 110:331 Mr 14 '64
Book reviews. America 110:773-4 My 30 '64
FERES study of Latin America. America 111:345-7 S 26 '64
(comp) Mexico's youth speaks; excerpts from a poll. America 109:408 O 12 '63
Social-minded archbishop. America 109:5 Jl 6 '63
CULISETA melanura. See Mosquitoes
CULKIN, John M.
Movies, TV, and paperbacks. Sr. Schol 83:28T-29T Ja 17 '64
CULLATHER, James L.
Parish income tax. America 109:118-19 Ag 3 '63
CULLEN, Arthur E.
How to have a safe boat trip. Todays Health 41:38-41 Ag '63
CULLEN, Robert
Dolphin; poem. Commonweal 77:544 F 15 '63
CULLIGAN, Matthew Joseph
I call on Joe Culligan. P. Martin. por Esquire 59:84-6+ Mr '63

CULLING. See Cows—Culling
CULLMAN, Marguerite
How an angel picks a play; excerpt from Occupation: angel. Theatre Arts 47:66-7+ Ap '63
CULLMAN, Oscar
Do we really mean this unity talk? Christian Cent 81:38 Ja 6 '64; Reply. H. N. Richardson. 81:206-7 F 12 '64
CULLY, Kendig Brubaker
Theology as literature. Christian Cent 81: 237-8 F 19 '64
CULT, The. See Religion, Primitive
CULTER, R. Gilbert, jr
Conservation activities in the secondary school. NEA J 53:38-40 D '64
CULTIVATION of corn. See Corn—Cultivation
CULTS, Negro
See also
Black Muslim movement
CULTURAL centers
New centers for theatre-goers. R. Meyer, jr. il Travel 119:46-8 My '63
CULTURAL cooperation. See United States—Cultural relations
CULTURAL evolution. See Social change
CULTURAL exchanges. See Exchange of persons programs
CULTURAL relations
Fourth dimension of foreign policy: educational and cultural affairs, by P. H. Coombs. Review
Sat R 47:61-2 D 19 '64. W. W. Brickman
New dimensions in cultural communication; address, December 29, 1962. L. D. Battle. Dept State Bul 48:92-7 Ja 21 '63
Orient-Occident; a study in ignorance; excerpts from Encounters and celebrations. G. Fradier. il UNESCO Courier 16:4-7 Ap '63
See also subhead Cultural relations under names of continents and countries, e.g. Russia—Cultural relations
CULTURALLY deprived children. See Socially handicapped children
CULTURE
Cult of culture. C. J. McNaspy. il America 110:626-8 My 9 '64
Culture and freedom; excerpt from Freedom and culture, comp. by UNESCO. G. Arciniegas. il UNESCO Courier 16:26-32 D '63
Recent developments in culture and personality. J. J. Honigmann and R. J. Preston. bibliog f Ann Am Acad 354:153-62 Jl '64
See also
Civilization
History
CULTURE, American. See United States—Civilization; United States—Intellectual life; United States—Popular culture
CULTURE, Russian. See Russia—Intellectual life
CULTURE apparatus. See Bacteriological apparatus
CULTURE contacts. See Acculturation
CULTURE media
See also
Fungi—Culture media
CULTURE of tissues. See Tissues—Culture
CULTURE pearls. See Pearls
CULTURE tubes. See Bacteriological apparatus
CULVER, Eloise C.
Dr Carter G. Woodson; To the Freedom riders; poems. Negro Hist Bul 27:129-30 F '64
CULVERTS
Precasting culvert prevents traffic hold-up; Montclair, Calif. S. E. Scholl. il Am City 79:89 D '64
CUMAE
Ancient Cumae. R. V. Schoder. il Sci Am 209:108-21 D '63
CUMBERLAND MOUNTAINS. See Cumberland Plateau
CUMBERLAND PLATEAU
Night comes to the Cumberlands, by H. M. Caudill. Review
Harper 227:94 Ag '63. P. Pickrel
New Repub 149:22 Jl 20 '63. G. W. Johnson
CUMING, Cecile Lamalle
Why don't you go home? story. New Yorker 40:180 O 3 '64
CUMMERFORD, Edward F.
Civil rights and civil wrongs; reprint. por U S News 56:84-6 F 17 '64
CUMMING, Joseph B. jr
Art of not being thirty-seven. Esquire 60: 95+ N '63
CUMMINGS, Edward Estlin
Ten poems. New Yorker 39:22-3 Ag 24 '63
What if a much of a which of a wind; poem. Sat R 47:18 O 24 '64
about
Cummings' Daisy. L. Abel. Nation 197:420-1 D 14 '63
E. E. Cummings. H. Gregory. Commonweal 79:725-6 Mr 13 '64
Legacy of three poets. J. Jacobsen. Commonweal 78:189-92 My 10 '63
What if a much of a which of a wind. J. Ciardi. Sat R 47:18+ O 24 '64
CUMMINGS, Parke
How to make a champion out of a four-year-old. Sports Illus 18:E3-E4 Ap 29 '63
Never say no! Read Digest 83:24C Ag '63
CUMMINS, Brian
Canadian winter rally. Motor T 16:80-1 Je '64
Shell 4000-mile rally. Motor T 15:80-1 Jl '63; 16:70-3 Jl '64
Smile! your car's on TV. Motor T 15:58-61 Ap '63
Those mighty Minis! Motor T 16:64 Mr '64
CUMMINS engine company
Heavy-duty, high gear merger; White motor and Cummins engine. Bsns W p94+ O 5 '63
CUMMISKEY, Barbara
Lack of freedom defeats Cathy. . . Life 54:70 Mr 15 '63
CUNARD steamship company
New Queen. Time 82:103 N 1 '63
CUNEGUNDE; story. See Singer, I. B.
CUNEIFORM inscriptions
Birth of cuneiform; Sumerian inscriptions. il UNESCO Courier 17:13 Mr '64
CUNLIFFE, Marcus
Long gray line. Commentary 38:66-8 D '64
Modern war. Commentary 36:323-5 O '63
CUNNING little vixen; opera. See Janáček, L.
CUNNINGHAM, Eloise
Music and the Olympics; Tokyo 1964. Mus Am 84:36-7+ D '64
CUNNINGHAM, J. V.
To what strangers? what welcome? poem; excerpts. Poetry 103:281-3 F '64
Two love poems: Miramar beach; Perfect imperfection. Poetry 103:26-7 O '63
CUNNINGHAM, John K.
Construction boss. il pors Ebony 18:105-8+ Jl '63
CUNNINGHAM, Merce, dance company. See Merce Cunningham dance company
CUNNINGHAM, Phillip J.
Movie of the month. Cath World 196:387-9 Mr '63
CUNNINGHAM, Walter W.
Heather makes itself at home. Horticulture 42:18 Ja '64
CUOMO, George
Ode after reading too much didactic poetry; Later ode after reading too much imagistic poetry. Sat R 47:31 Ja 4 '64
Passing helper was his father; poem. Sat R 46:45 Mr 30 '63
Room at the bottom, room at the top; story. Sat Eve Post 236:46-51 N 2 '63
Visitant; poem. Nation 196:124 F 9 '63
CUPBOARDS
Early American hutch you can build. W. Luxenburg. il Pop Sci 184:120-1 Ja '64
Livery cupboards in New England. N. F. Little. il Antiques 84:710-13 D '63
Thomas Lincoln's corner cupboards. R. G. McMurtry. il Antiques 85:206-8 F '64
See also
Kitchen cabinets
CUPCAKES. See Cake
CUPID in command; drama. See McGowan, J.
CUPRESSUS. See Cypress
CUPS
Plastic cups invade coffee break market. Bsns W p57 F 29 '64
Stain-resistant plastic cups; Melmac. il Consumer Bul 46:31-2 O '63
CURATORS, Museum. See Museum workers
CURB parking. See Automobile parking
CURBS
Curb and gutter by extrusion. N. Donaghy. il Am City 79:25 Je '64
CURCI, Amelita Galli-. See Galli-Curci, A.
CURE; story. See Seager, A.
CURETON, R. H.
Better paving procedure. Am City 79:93 Je '64
CURIA romana. See Catholic church—Roman curia
CURING of meat. See Meat—Preservation
CURIO cabinets. See Cabinets (furniture)
CURIOSITY
Needed, a way to save curiosity. F. A. J. Ianni and L. Josephs. bibliog f Sch Life 46:23-4 N '63

CURIOSITY—*Continued*
Stairway to the stars. J. H. Glenn, jr. il NEA J 52:8+ Ap '63
Writing in the sky. M. E. Jenkins. il PTA Mag 57:2-3 Ap '63
CURLERS, Hair. See Hair curlers
CURLEY, Daniel
Posthumous son contemplates the photograph of his father; poem. America 111:559 N 7 '64
CURLEY, Rosemary
How to see the cup races. Yachting 116: 166-7 Jl '64
CURLEY, Thomas F.
Catholic novels & American culture. Commentary 36:34-42 Jl '63
CURLEY, Walter W.
Protection and insurance. por(p4153) Library J 88:4154-6 N 1 '63
CURLING
Country club set takes up curling; Chicago curling club. il Bsns W p28-9 F 16 '63
Curling, anyone? letter. J. V. Terango. Recreation 56:160 Ap '63
Games worth the candle. Sports Illus 20:8+ Ja 20 '64
CURRAGHMORE. See Ireland—Historic houses, etc.
CURRAN, Charles E.
Re-examining the church's teaching on contraception. Commonweal 81:360-2 D 4 '64
CURRAN, Joseph
Labor's mutinous mariners. A. H. Raskin. por Atlan 214:72-8 N '64
CURRANTS
See also
Ribes viburnifolium
CURRELLY, Charles Trick
Toronto treasures; universal and university; Royal Ontario museum draws a 50th anniversary show. J. S. Boggs. il Art N 61:32-4+ F '63
CURRENCY. See Money
CURRENCY convertibility
Reforming the international monetary system. R. V. Roosa. For Affairs 42:107-22 O '63
World monetary reform. H. Hazlitt. Newsweek 62:96 O 21 '63
CURRENCY question
How sound is the dollar? il Changing T 17: 19-21 D '63
Suppose the U.S. dollar were devalued. il U S News 55:32-3 Jl 29 '63
CURRENT, Richard N.
It is . . . a small college . . . yet, there are those who love it. Am Heritage 14:10-14+ Ag '63
CURRENT events
Affairs of state. S. Alsop. See issues of Saturday evening post
As in a dream; disputes between the nations of the world. Newsweek 64:42 S 28 '64
Atlantic report on the world today. See issues of Atlantic
CIA analysis. New Repub 151:3-4 S 12 '64
Contemporary affairs test. il Sr Schol 85:25-6 S 16 '64
Front page of the week. See issues of U.S. news & World report
How to help out; world's perennial hot spots. Newsweek 64:82 O 5 '64
Life on the newsfronts of the world. See issues of Life
March of events. See issues of Senior scholastic
March of the news; front page of the week. See issues of U.S. news & World report
Month in review. See issues of Current history
Overseas. Commonweal 79:496-7 Ja 31 '64
Press section; excerpts from newspapers and periodicals. See issues of Reader's digest
That was the week that was; last week's momentous events. il Newsweek 64:31-2 O 26 '64
Uncertain world; events of past week in relation to presidential election. W. Lippmann. Newsweek 64:29 O 26 '64
U.S. and world affairs annual 1963-64. il Sr Schol 83:10-42+ O 4 '63
U.S. and world affairs annual 1964-65; ed. by E. R. Floyd. il Sr Schol 85:12-39+ O 7 '64
Washington report; ed. by R. Stolley. il Life 57:25 D 18 '64; 58:32 Ja 8; 40D Ja 15; 34D Ja 22 '65
Week that was will long be with us. Life 57:4 O 30 '64
Week the dam broke; handling torrents of major news events. il Time 84:75 O 23 '64
While you were away. New Repub 149:5 S 21 '63
Study and teaching
Foreign affairs begin at home. J. F. Travers. Cath World 199:16-21 Ap '64
CURRENT RIVER
Not so gently down the stream. A. Higgins. il Sports Illus 18:34+ Ap 29 '63
Reporter at large. R. Roueché. il New Yorker 39:48-50+ Ap 6 '63
CURRENTS, Ocean. See Ocean currents
CURRICULUM. See Colleges and universities—Curriculum; Courses of study; High schools—Curriculum
CURRICULUM development, Association for. See Association for supervision and curriculum development
CURRICULUM studies. See Educational research
CURRIE, Brainerd
Dark science of conflict. il por Time 85:42 Ja 8 '65
CURRIER, Lura Gibbons, and Vaughn, E. G.
Small library: S.O.S; reprint. Wilson Lib Bul 37:775-8 My '63
CURRIER, Stephan
Angels are white; who pays the bills for civil rights? R. Cleghorn. New Repub 149:12-14 Ag 17 '63
CURRY, Jesse
Others; year after the assassination of President Kennedy. Time 84:34 N 27 '64
CURRY, Peggy Simson
Dialogue with distinction. Writer 77:11-13+ Jl '64
Invitation to the wedding; story. Good H 156:86-7 Je '63
Portrait of a naturalist. Liv Wildn 84:15-21 Sum '63; Same. Audubon Mag 65:358-63 N '63
Writers, speak now! excerpt from Creating fiction from experience. Writer 77:7-10 F '64
CURRY-LINDAHL, Kai
New theory on a fabled exodus. il Natur Hist 72:46-53 Ag '63
CURRY
Curry. V. T. Habeeb. il Am Home 66:48-9+ S '63
Fire Island curry; with recipe. il N Y Times Mag p94 Ap 21 '63
This curry buffet may surprise you. il Sunset 132:194+ Ap '64
CURSILLOS de christiandad (movement)
Cursillo conference. America 111:100 Ag 1 '64
I made a cursillo. J. McLaughlin. America 110:94-6+ Ja 18 '64
Little courses. il Time 83:61 Mr 13 '64
CURSING. See Swearing
CURTAIN and drapery fixtures
Drapery hardware. il Bet Hom & Gard 42: 24 My '64
Get the hang of pretty window dressing. il Am Home 66:20+ My '63
CURTAIN calls. See Applause
CURTAINS and draperies
Clean crisp curtains. Am Home 67:93 S '64
Cool, cool window treatments. il Bet Hom & Gard 42:66-9 Je '64
Create the ultimate in glamour with a valance and beams. il Bet Hom & Gard 41:52 S '63
Decorator's notebook. il Seventeen 22:184-5 F '63
Drapery services that simplify shopping. Bet Hom & Gard 41:129 O '63
Fiber glass fabrics modify environment. A. W. Metzger. il Arch Rec 136:219-20 N '64
For beauty at your windows. House & Gard 123:198 Ap '63
Fringe benefits; beaded curtains. J. Peter. il Look 27:41 Ag 27 '63
Get the hang of pretty window dressing. il Am Home 66:20+ My '63
Institute answers your questions on draperies. Good H 156:160 F '63
New new ready-made trimmings to wake up your windows. il House & Gard 125:154-5 F '64
Ready-mades rate you an A. R. W. Houseman. il Am Home 67:46-9 Mr '64
Sheer delight. P. Clapp. il Am Home 66:32-3 O '63
Trend to tiebacks! F. Byerly. il Bet Hom & Gard 41:64-5 Je '63
Window curtains in colonial Boston and Salem. A. Brightman. il Antiques 86:184-7 Ag '64
Wonderful ways to wake up your windows. il House & Gard 125:88-97 F '64
Woolen window curtains; eighteenth-century wool textiles. A. Brightman. il Antiques 86: 722-7 D '64
See also
Textile fabrics

CURTIN, Phyllis
Quote: unquote; interview, ed. by R. Jacobson. por Mus Am 83:45 S '63

CURTIN, Willard S.
Excerpt from address, December 19, 1963. Cong Digest 43:146 My '64

CURTIS, C. Michael
New sportswriter. Atlan 214:120+ D '64
Should tenure go? Nat R 16:864 O 6 '64
Where oh where has my little bear gone? poem. Atlan 211:138 Mr '63

CURTIS, Carl Thomas
Excerpt from address, April 5, 1962. Cong Digest 42:205+ Ag '63

CURTIS, Charlotte
Parties: who's in charge? N Y Times Mag p24 Jl 7 '63
Upper crust. il por Newsweek 64:62+ S 28 '64

CURTIS, Dal, pseud. See Dallis, N. P.

CURTIS, David
(comp) Shakespeare views the Fair; quotations. Travel 122:42-3 Ag '64

CURTIS, E. J. C. and Cantlon, J. E.
Germination of melampyrum lineare; interrelated effects of afterripening and gibberellic acid. bibliog Science 140:406-8 Ap 26 '63

CURTIS, Edwin U.
Strike that made a president. F. Russell. il por Am Heritage 14:44-7+ O '63

CURTIS, Gordon M. jr
Cruising club measurement rule. Yachting 115:44-6+ Mr '64

CURTIS, Helena
Cancer-inducing DNA; excerpt from report. Sat R 46:52 F 2 '63

CURTIS, Howard J.
Biological mechanisms underlying the aging process. bibliog Science 141:686-94; 142:540, 1261 Ag 23, N 1, D 6 '63
—and Smith, H. H.
Corn seeds affected by heavy cosmic ray particles. bibliog Science 141:158-60 Jl 12 '63

CURTIS, Joseph E.
Floodlighting solves a problem. por Recreation 56:230-2 My '63
Public gifts. por Recreation 56:61 F '63
Zoning for today's needs. por Recreation 57:16-17 Ja '64

CURTIS, Michael
Books in the news. Sat R 46:24-6+ Je 8 '63

CURTIS, Philip C.
Hot capriccios. il Time 83:60-1 My 29 '64

CURTIS, Thomas Bradford
Clouds on the economic horizon; address, October 2, 1964. Vital Speeches 31:29-30 O 15 '64
Economic security; address, September 11, 1963. Vital Speeches 30:17-21 O 15 '63
Excerpt from address, April 30, 1963. Cong Digest 42:211+ Ag '63
Excerpts from addresses, January 17 and February 4, 1963. Cong Digest 42:152+ My '63
Foreign economic policy; address, January 7, 1963. Vital Speeches 29:260-3 F 15 '63
U.S. balance of payments problems; address, July 8, 1963. Vital Speeches 29:657-62 Ag 15 '63

CURTIS, William
All out for cripples. Field & S 69:70+ O '64
It's time for crappies. Outdoor Life 133:26-8+ Mr '64
Little animal, big stink. Field & S 68:49+ Je '63
Little gray brush-popper. Field & S 68:33+ Ag '63

CURTIS publishing company
Butts reverses field to try for full $3,060,000. Pub W 185:77 F 10 '64
Culligan's round. il Newsweek 62:69-70 D 23 '63
Curtis commitment (cont) Sat Eve Post 236:90 Ap 20 '63
Curtis fight over Post reduced to twenty-six issues. Pub W 186:31-2 N 23 '64
Curtis management fight coming to a head. Pub W 186:23 O 26 '64
Curtis mutiny. il Newsweek 64:72 O 19 '64
Curtis publishing hit with $3,060,000 libel verdict. Pub W 184:45 S 2 '63
From good to bad at the Post. Time 84:61 Ag 7 '64
Getting Curtis off the spot; straight term-loan bank financing. Bsns W p96 Ag 17 '63
Grosset buys Curtis' interest in three subsidiaries. Pub W 185:133 F 24 '64
Latest Post installment. Newsweek 64:99 N 23 '64
Libel judgement against Curtis reduced to 460,000. Pub W 185:239 Ja 27 '64
Looking for a solution. Time 84:92 O 30 '64
Nhu deal. il Newsweek 62:65-6 N 25 '63
No solution at Curtis. il Time 84:69+ N 13 '64
Optimism at Curtis. il Time 82:31 D 20 '63
Philadelphia story; struggle for control. il Newsweek 64:64 N 2 '64
Rescue work at Curtis. Time 84:49 N 20 '64
Revolt at Curtis. il Time 84:85 O 16 '64
Revolt that fizzled shakes up Curtis. Bsns W p32+ O 17 '64
See also
Saturday evening post

CURTISS, Ursula
Out of the dark; story. Good H 158:83-5 F '64

CURTISS-Wright corporation
C-W extends Garrett stock plan. Aviation W 79:30 O 21 '63
Garrett asks court to prevent Curtiss-Wright purchase of stock. Aviation W 79:33 S 30 '63
Garrett opposes Curtiss offer. Aviation W 79:39 S 16 '63
Garrett, Signal oil continue merger plan. Aviation W 79:32 N 11 '63
Garrett, Signal propose to merge after Curtiss-Wright raises offer. Aviation W 79:33 O 28 '63
On the way, straight up. il Bsns W p 116+ Ag 17 '63

CURTO, Frank
Vines. Horticulture 42:34-6 D '64

CURUTCHET, Jean Marie
Better than the firing squad; life sentence. il por Time 84:35 Jl 10 '64

CURVES
Mathematical games; helical structures, from corkscrews to DNA molecules. M. Gardner. il Sci Am 208:148+ Je '63
See also
Cycloids

CUSACK, Cyril
To Padraig, newborn; poem. Commonweal 77:618 Mr 8 '63

CUSCADEN, R. R.
Spring on the railroad; poem. Sat R 48:58 Ja 30 '65

CUSH
Africa's golden past; kingdom of Kush. W. L. Hansberry and E. H. Johnson. il Ebony 20:30-2+ N '64

CUSHING, Natalie
Natalie Cushing, glimpses of a young romantic. il pors Vogue 143:36-43 Ja 15 '64

CUSHING, Richard James, cardinal
Cardinal Cushing; interview, ed. by W. M. Abbott. America 108:864-7 Je 15 '63
Cardinal Cushing remembers: twice, I saw Jack Kennedy cry; ed. by B. Kornitzer. pors Look 28:92+ N 17 '64
Change in Catholic laws? excerpts from interview. por U S News 54:19 Je 24 '63
Cushing wants church laws liberalized; interview, ed. by W. M. Abbott. Christian Cent 80:820 Je 26 '63
Eulogy to John F. Kennedy, November 24, 1963. Vital Speeches 30:100-1 D 1 '63
Public opinion in the church; excerpts from pastoral letter. Commonweal 78:426-7 Jl 12 '63

about

American in Rome. il por Newsweek 61:76 Je 24 '63
Cardinal re-endorses Birch society. Christian Cent 81:596 My 6 '64
Crusader and Cardinal. por Newsweek 64:71 O 19 '64
Cushing of Boston. J. Roddy. il pors Look 27:62-6 D 31 '63
Episcopal leadership. America 111:249 S 12 '64
From a cardinal: praise for a Protestant crusader. por U S News 57:24 O 19 '64
Moral miracle. America 110:785 Je 6 '64
Unlikely cardinal. il pors Time 84:35-40 Ag 21 '64; Same abr. with title Boston's contrary cardinal. Read Digest 85:119-23 N '64; Reply. America 111:228-9 S 5 '64

CUSHIONS
Appliqué pillows to make yourself. il House & Gard 126:94-5 Jl '64
You can lean against this bear. il Sunset 132:143 My '64

CUSHMAN, Edward L.
Management's adjustment to change. Mo Labor R 86:630-5 Je '63

CUSHMAN, George W.
Sound with your pictures. See issues of Popular photography to September 1963

CUSHMAN, Jack
Let's check the check ride. Flying 74:46-7+ Ap '64
—and Dowd, Merle
Fresh flock of fold-wing planes. Pop Mech 119:90-5+ F '63

CUSHMAN, Jerome
Folk music in the library. por Library J 88:1833-4 My 1 '63
New Orleans replies to the New republic; excerpts from letter. Library J 89:2758 Jl '64
CUSTARDS
Custard desserts with meringue. Sunset 133: 173 S '64
House & garden's summer dessert cook book. J. Platt. il House & Gard 123:185-6 My '63
CUSTIN, Mildred
Bonwit's lady boss. por Time 85:68 Ja 22 '65
Boss ladies; symposium, ed. by L. L. Tornabene. por Esquire 63:102-3+ Ja '65
Lady in charge. Newsweek 65:71 Ja 25 '65
CUSTODIAN account. See Trusts and trustees
CUSTODIANS, School. See Janitors
CUSTOM cars. See Automobiles—Design
CUSTOMER relations
New battleground, consumer interest. T. M. Hopkinson. bibliog f Harvard Bsns R 42: 97-104 S '64
To live and die for Armstrong. H. Kay. il Fortune 69:124-9+ Mr '64
CUSTOMS (tariff) See Tariff
CUSTOMS service

United States

Have you declared everything? C. Mydans. il Life 57:41+ Ag 28 '64
Red letter days: measures for avoidance of Communist propaganda. Reporter 29:20+ Jl 18 '63
Temporary relief: pre-clearance in European ports. Time 82:45 Jl 19 '63
Welcome, stranger. K. Detzer. il Read Digest 83:19-20+ S '63
CUSTOMS service and tourists
Bringing home what you buy abroad. House & Gard 125:70-2 My '64
Getting through customs. il Changing T 17: 18-20 Jl '63
Have you declared everything? C. Mydans. il Life 57:41+ Ag 28 '64

Anecdotes, facetiae, satire, etc.

Duty free. S. Corbett. il Atlan 213:124-6 Ap '64
CUT flowers. See Flowers—Cut flowers
CUT out work. See Paper work
CUTLER, Ann
Call for future doctors! Read Digest 83:35-6 O '63
New fight against sudden death. Look 28: 44-6+ D 1 '64
Shakespeare's England. Travel 121:34-40 Mr '64
CUTLER, Bruce
Long reach, strong speech. Poetry 103:387-93 Mr '64
Poetry chronicle. Poetry 102:182-3 Je '63
Sun city; poem. Poetry 104:363-4 S '64
CUTLER, Gladys B.
To a mountain creek; poem. Nat Parks Mag 37:15 F '63
Wilderness road; poem. Nat Parks Mag 37:13 N '63
CUTLERY
Good cutlery cuts kitchen chores. B. G. Wadsworth. il Parents Mag 39:144 N '64
See also
Knives
CUTOUT work. See Paper work
CUTRIGHT, Paul Russell
I gave him barks and saltpeter. bibliog Am Heritage 15:58-61+ D '63
CUTSHALL, Norman, and Osterberg, Charles
Radioactive particle in sediment from the Columbia River. bibliog Science 144:536-7 My 1 '64
CUTTER, Richard D.
Sensible way to understand teenagers. Parents Mag 40:46-7+ Ja '65
CUTTERS (boats) See Yachts and yachting
CUTTING, Glass. See Glass cutting
CUTTING boards. See Kitchen utensils
CUTTING gardens. See Gardens
CUTTING machines
See also
Pantograph
CUTTING tools
Decorative carving made easy, with a fly cutter. R. J. DeCristoforo. il Pop Mech 119: 194-6 Ap '63
Homemade tile cutter. H. P. Strand. il Pop Sci 182:120-1 F '63
See also
Knives

CUTTINGS, Plant. See Plant propagation
CUTTS, Warren G.
Phonies in beginning reading. por Sch Life 45:8-11 Ja '63
Reading; for what? Sr Schol 84:13T-14T Mr 6 '64
Reading unreadiness in the underprivileged. NEA J 52:23-4 Ap '63
Value of ITA. NEA J 53:21-2 S '64
CVEJIC, Biserka
Unrehearsed impact; interview, ed. by F. Merkling. por Opera N 27:16 F 9 '63
CYANAMIDE
Cyanamide formation under primitive earth conditions. A. Schimpl and others. bibliog il Science 147:149-50 Ja 8 '65
CYANIDES
Economical plating-waste treatment. H. E. P. Barta. il Am City 79:75-6 Ja '64
CYBERNETICS
Bionic computers. K. Gilmore. il Electr World 69:25-8+ Mr '63
Bionics: a new science looks at nature's secrets. J. R. Thomson. il Todays Health 42:44-9+ Ja '64
Bionics; report of symposium in Dayton, Ohio, March 1963. L. E. Lipetz. Science 140:1419-20+ Je 28 '63
Brains, machines, and mathematics, by M. A. Arbib. Review
Sci Am 210:130+ Je '64. J. Bronowski
Cars steered by flicks of muscles foreseen. Sci N L 85:43 Ja 18 '64
Control theory. R. Bellman. il Sci Am 211: 186-90+ S '64
Cybernated era; address, June 30, 1964. R. Theobald. Vital Speeches 30:636-40 Ag 1 '64
Cybernetics. M. Maruyama. bibliog il NEA J 53:51-4 D '64
Cybernetics of population control. H. Hoagland. Bul Atomic Sci 20:2-6 F '64
Electrochemical nerve cells under study. B. Miller. il Aviation W 78:103+ F 18 '63
Firm studying method to grow computers. Miss & Roc 14:22 Mr 16 '64
Light-beam transmitter powered by human voice; Retrometer. Sci N L 85:294 My 9 '64
Navy studying control of weapons through thinking of them. Miss & Roc 13:20 D 2 '63
New science of bionics. H. E. Klein. il Duns R 82:40-2+ Jl '63
Symposium points to more AF emphasis on hardware; engineering bionics. H. M. David. il Miss & Roc 12:34-5 Ap 1 '63
Talk via brain waves. W. MacLaurin. Sci N L 86:275 O 31 '64
Under poetic license; feedback principles applied to artificial limbs. J. Lear. Sat R 46: 87 D 7 '63; Reply with rejoinder. 47:23+ Ja 25 '64
UAC cyborg study in second phase. H. M. David. il Miss & Roc 12:41+ My 13 '63
USAF Electronics technology lab plans extensive bionics studies. Aviation W 78:109+ Je 24 '63
What is cybernetics? J. J. Honomichl. il Recreation 56:425-6 N '63
CYBULSKI, Zbigniew
Man in the green lenses. por Time 84:71 D 18 '64
CYCLADES (islands)
Going places, finding things in the Cyclades and Crete. M. M. Hemingway. il House & Gard 123:24+ Je '63
In the light of the Aegean. J. Knowles. il Horizon 6:98-104 Spr '64
Serene isles. il Life 54:54-71+ Je 14 '63
See also
Paros (island)
CYCLAMATE. See Sugar substitutes
CYCLAMENS
Cyclamen for year-round bloom. L. H. Gee. il Horticulture 41:472-3 S '63
Persian cyclamen. R. Tenent. il Horticulture 41:66 F '63
CYCLES, Biological. See Periodicity
CYCLES, Business. See Business cycles
CYCLING
Bike boom. J. Star. il Look 28:M14+ D 1 '64
Bike pike; Alverthorpe Park, Abington, Pa. J. C. Dittmar. il Recreation 57:495+ D '64
Cycling for fitness. P. D. White. il Recreation 57:405-6 O '64
Fifty-five million cyclists can't be wrong. J. G. Harmount. il Todays Health 42:32-3+ O '64
Fourteen laps; bicycle path in Central park. New Yorker 40:46-7 S 19 '64
Life guide; pedal-pushing. il Life 54:17 My 10 '63
Pedaling to health. il Time 82:42 Ag 2 '63
See also
Bicycle racing

CYCLING—*Continued*

Safety devices and measures

Basic rules for bike safety. il Good H 156: 164 Ap '63

CYCLOHEXIMIDE. See Antibiotics

CYCLOIDS

Mathematical games; curious properties of a cycloid curve. M. Gardner. il Sci Am 211: 110-12+ Jl '64

CYCLOTRON

Hillside building for a new type of accelerator; Lawrence radiation laboratory, University of California, Berkeley. il Arch Rec 134:190-2 S '63

CYLINDERS, Automobile. See Automobile engines

CYMBALARIA muralis. See Kenilworth ivy

CYNTHIA (synthetic intelligence machine) See Automatons

CYPRESS

Monterey cypress. D. L. Roberson. Horticulture 41:195 Ap '63

CYPRESS gardens. See Gardens—Florida

CYPRIPEDIUM. See Ladys slippers

CYPRUS

Air attacks on Cyprus impose new strains on NATO alliance. L. L. Doty. Aviation W 81: 20 Ag 17 '64
Ancient strife in Cyprus fires up again. il Life 56:32-32A Ja 10 '64
Anger again. Time 83:43-4 Je 12 '64
Another war worry for U.S. il U S News 56:48 Mr 23 '64
Atlantic report. Atlan 214:12+ O '64; Reply. A. A. Matsas. 214:42 D '64
Aura of doom. Newsweek 64:41 S 14 '64
Awful possibility. Newsweek 63:36 Ja 27 '64
Back of the fighting on Cyprus. il U S News 56:6 Ja 6 '64
Back to the precipice. Time 84:39 S 4 '64
Between Greeks and Turks; with report by W. Just. il Newsweek 63:36-7 Mr 23 '64
Bombing of Cyprus; with report by T. Green. il Life 57:20-5 Ag 21 '64
Boomerang? Greek Cypriot assault on St Hilarion. Newsweek 63:40+ My 11 '64
Boys in blue; U.N. peace-keeping force. il Newsweek 63:25 Mr 30 '64
Breather. Time 84:28 Ag 28 '64
Burning fuses. Newsweek 63:51 Je 15 '64
Careless smokers. il Time 84:21-2 Ag 21 '64
Crescent and cross. G. D. Kumlien. Commonweal 80:364-5 Je 12 '64
Crossed fingers. Newsweek 63:32+ Je 1 '64
Cyprus; a tormented island shakes up the West. S. Castan. il Look 28:30-5 Je 2 '64
Cyprus; address, July 3, 1964. K. B. Keating. Vital Speeches 30:695-6 S 1 '64
Cyprus eyewitness: terror and death in an island war. J. Law. il U S News 56:77-8 F 24 '64
Cyprus: is there a peaceful way out? il Sr Schol 85:10-13+ S 30 '64
Cyprus, island of hate and fear; closeup of Greeks and Turks, the deadly enemies. M. Wall. il N Y Times Mag p 13+ Mr 8 '64
Cyprus: it might be another Cuba. B. Cornwall. New Repub 151:8 Jl 11 '64
Cyprus: peeling the last artichoke. il Newsweek 63:39 F 24 '64
Cyprus problem=Makarios problem. M. Wall. il N Y Times Mag p38-9+ O 18 '64
Cyprus: sunny island with chronic ills. il Sr Schol 84:10-12 F 28 '64
Cyprus: the archbishop can't lose. C. Sterling. il Reporter 30:12-16 Je 4 '64
Cyprus, the reluctant republic. G. Gaskill. il Read Digest 82:209-11+ Je '63
Cyprus: the Turks strike back. il Newsweek 64:37-8 Ag 17 '64
Cyprus, where saints and goddesses meet. L. Rasponi. Vogue 141:162-3+ Ap 1 '63
Cyprus; who is right? is anyone? Time 83: 29 My 1 '64
Day the press halted a war; with report by L. Chelminski. il Life 56:28-35 Ap 3 '64
Death at high noon. il Time 83:23 F 14 '64
Death wish. il Newsweek 63:29 Ja 13 '64
Deceptive peace. il Time 84:30 Jl 24 '64
Digging in. New Repub 150:7-8 F 29 '64
Dilemma on Cyprus. B. Cornwall. New Repub 151:12 S 5 '64
Diplomatic jockeys. Time 83:26-7 F 28 '64
End or a beginning; Turkish intervention. il Time 84:20-1 Ag 14 '64
Enmity or enosis. Time 83:43 Ap 17 '64
Frightening logic. il Newsweek 64:40 Jl 27 '64
Fulbright's task. New Repub 150:9 My 16 '64
Fuse burns shorter. il Newsweek 64:39 Ag 10 '64
Going places, finding things in new fields for adventurous wayfarers. J. Sakol. il House & Gard 125:22+ Ja '64
Greek-Turkish tension. E. von Kuehnelt-Leddihn. Nat R 16:536 Je 30 '64
Greek vs. Turk in Cyprus. il N Y Times Mag p8-9 F 16 '64
Greeks bearing gifts; end to blockade of Kokkina. Time 84:27 S 25 '64
Here come the Van Doos; Royal 22nd regiment in Cyprus. Time 83:23 Mr 27 '64
Holding action. il Newsweek 63:42-3 Mr 16 '64
In mutual hate. Newsweek 63:27-8 Ja 20 '64
In suspension. il Newsweek 64:38+ Jl 6 '64
Into the asylum. il Newsweek 63:35-6 Mr 9 '64
Irrationality in flower. il Time 83:34 F 21 '64
Island in conflict. Sr Schol 83:18-19 Ja 17 '64
Island of hate. il Time 83:36-7 Ja 3 '64
Island of tension. il Time 83:31 Ja 10 '64
Letter from Cyprus. C. Foley. il Nat R 16:724-5 Ag 25 '64
Life on a war-torn island; eyewitness report. J. Law. il U S News 57:41-2 Ag 31 '64
Makarios: key to peace on Cyprus. U S News 57:16 Ag 24 '64
Makarios of Cyprus: he enjoys to gamble. il Newsweek 63:34-8 Mr 2 '64
Match in the hay. New Repub 150:13 Ja 18 '64
Mediterranean Cuba? Nat R 16:95+ F 11 '64
Mediterranean Taft-Hartley. Time 83:28-9 Mr 13 '64
Mr Ball leaves for London talks on Cyprus; U.S. restates position; statement, February 8, 1964. R. J. McCloskey. Dept State Bul 50:284 F 24 '64
Nationalism: a matter of pride and prejudice. Sr Schol 85:17 O 7 '64
New fish in the lake? Time 84:32 O 9 '64
No niceties. Newsweek 63:46+ Je 22 '64
NATO effort. il Newsweek 64:43 Ag 31 '64
NATO to the rescue. Time 83:32 F 7 '64
Notch tighter. Time 84:29 Ag 7 '64
On a sun-washed island, a brutal backalley war; with report by T. Green. il Life 56:24-31 F 28 '64
On the brink. il Newsweek 63:46+ F 17 '64
One sort of stability. Newsweek 63:56 Ap 20 '64
One way to learn. il Newsweek 63:47 My 18 '64
Parable of the blue beads; President Johnson's mediation effort. Time 84:24 Jl 3 '64
Peerless brinkman; Archbishop Makarios. il Newsweek 64:40 S 7 '64
Potent peace. J. A. Morris, jr. Newsweek 64: 27 D 28 '64
President Johnson discusses Cyprus situation with Prime Ministers of Turkey and Greece; exchanges of greetings, with joint communiques. L. B. Johnson; I. Inonu; G. Papandreou. Dept State Bul 51:48-50 Jl 13 '64
President Johnson expresses hope for end of strife in Cyprus; exchange of messages. C. Gursel; L. B. Johnson. Dept State Bul 50:90 Ja 20 '64
President Johnson replies to Soviet letter on Cyprus; exchange of letters, February 7 and March 4, 1964. L. B Johnson; N. S. Khrushchev. Dept State Bul 50:446-8 Mr 23 '64
Priest's war or soldier's peace? il Newsweek 64:35-6 Ag 24 '64
Protracted conflict. Nat R 16:709 Ag 25 '64
Remembrance day. Newsweek 63:47 Ap 13 '64
Scorpions in a bottle. il Time 83:31 Mr 20 '64
Search for compromise. il Time 83:29 Mr 6 '64
Self-determination. il Newsweek 63:40 Ap 27 '64
Solomon for Cyprus. il Newsweek 63:28 Je 29 '64
Tinderbox. il Newsweek 63:37 F 10 '64
Toward the vortex. Newsweek 64:52+ S 21 '64
Under Secretary Ball comments on Cyprus situation; television interview, August 9, 1964. G. W. Ball. Dept State Bul 51:301-2 Ag 31 '64
Under the Union Jack. il Newsweek 63:31 Ja 6 '64
U.S. fleet: peace keeper in the Mediterranean; sixth fleet. il U S News 56:42 Mr 16 '64
War on three fronts; new worry for U.S; with report by J. Law. U S News 57:29-30 Ag 24 '64
War or peace? Sr Schol 84:18 F 21 '64
What Americans face in Cyprus. J. Law. il U S News 56:41 F 17 '64

See also

Mining industry and finance—Cyprus
United Nations—Armed forces—Forces in Cyprus
United Nations—Cyprus

CYPRUS—*Continued*

Religious institutions and affairs

His Beatitude the President; head of Cyprus' Orthodox church. il Time 84:70+ S 18 '64

CYPRUS mines corporation

Beleaguered California miners. il Fortune 69: 67-8 My '64

Hot spot that produces plenty of cold cash. il Bsns W p 102+ O 10 '64

CYRANO de Bergerac; drama. See Rostand, E.

CYRILLIC alphabet

Eleven centuries of the Cyrillic alphabet. il UNESCO Courier 17:24-5 Mr '64

CYSTATHIONINE

Homocystinuria: absence of cystathionine in the brain. T. Gerritsen and H. A. Waisman. bibliog il Science 145:588 Ag 7 '64

Homocystinuria due to cystathionine synthetase deficiency: the mode of inheritance. J. D. Finkelstein and others. bibliog il Science 146:785-7 N 6 '64

CYSTEINE

Cysteine stimulation of glucose oxidation in thyroid tissue. J. A. Pittman and others. bibliog il Science 140:389 Ap 26 '63

Somatic instability caused by a cysteine-sensitive gene in arabidopsis. G. P. Rédei. bibliog il Science 139:767-9 F 22 '63

Succinic ester and amide of homoserine: some spontaneous and enzymatic reactions. M. Flavin and others. bibliog il Science 143:50-2 Ja 3 '64

CYSTIC fibrosis

Aerosol for breathing. il Time 82:62 N 22 '63

Boy on fire; R. Nostri creator of film World of Childrens hospital. H. Gold. il Sat Eve Post 237:28-9 S 12 '64

Clarify cystic fibrosis relationship to heart. Sci N L 86:361 D 5 '64

Curb cystic fibrosis if carriers not marry. Sci N L 86:265 O 24 '64

What parents ask about cystic fibrosis. M. J. E. Senn. il McCalls 91:77+ My '64

CYSTINE

Cystinuria: in vitro demonstration of an intestinal transport defect. S. Thier and others. bibliog il Science 143:482-4 Ja 31 '64

CYSTINURIA. See Intestines—Diseases

CYTAWA, Jerzy. See Teitelbaum, P. jt. auth.

CYTOCHROMES

Coenzyme Q: reversal of inhibition of succinate cytochrome c reductase by lipophilic compounds. S. Takemori and T. E. King. bibliog il Science 144:852-3 My 15 '64

Cytochrome content of mitochondria stripped of inner membrane structure. B. Chance and others. bibliog il Science 143:136-9 Ja 10 '64

Cytochrome function in relation to inner membrane structure of mitochondria. B. Chance and D. F. Parsons. bibliog il Science 142:1176-80 N 29 '63

Cytochrome in thiobacillus thiooxidans. J. London. bibliog il Science 140:409-10 Ap 26 '63

Cytochromes of a blue-green alga: extraction of a c-type with a strongly negative redox potential. R. W. Holton and J. Myers. bibliog il Science 142:234-5 O 11 '63

CYTOLOGY. See Cells

CYTOPLASM

Glow of youth; experiments with cytoplasm. il Newsweek 62:98 D 2 '63

Intracellular transport apparatus of phloem fibers. J. W. Mitchell and J. F. Worley. bibliog Science 145:409-10 Jl 24 '64

CYTOSINE

Tautomerism and site of protonation of 1-methylcytosine; proof by nuclear magnetic resonance spin-spin coupling. H. T. Miles and others. bibliog il Science 142:1569-71 D 20 '63

CYTOTOXINS. See Toxins and antitoxins

CZAMANSKE, Gerald K. and others

Neutron activation analysis of fluid inclusions for copper, manganese, and zinc. bibliog Science 140:401-3 Ap 26 '63

CZECHOSLOVAKIA

Atlantic report. Atlan 211:26+ Je '63; 214: 12+ N '64

See also

Airlines—Czechoslovakia

Airplane industry and trade—Czechoslovakia

Architecture—Czechoslovakia

Automobile industry and trade—Czechoslovakia

Communist party (Czechoslovakia)

Education—Czechoslovakia

Karlsbad

Munich four power agreement, 1938

Music—Czechoslovakia

Publishers and publishing—Czechoslovakia

Research—Czechoslovakia

Space research—Czechoslovakia

Theater—Czechoslovakia

World war, 1939-1945—Underground movements—Czechoslovakia

Description and travel

Now it's easier to get in; easing of travel restrictions. Sunset 133:44 S '64

Economic conditions

Disappointment in Prague; Novotny reelected. il Time 84:38 N 20 '64

Economic mess. il Time 84:60 Jl 31 '64

Gymnast. K. Ames. Newsweek 64:52+ D 7 '64

Kafka's nightmare comes true. G. Bailey. Reporter 30:15-20 My 7 '64

No time for jokes. Newsweek 63:48+ My 18 '64

Economic policy

Russia's satellites in new orbits. A. Werth. Nation 200:27-9 Ja 11 '65

Politics and government

Baiting the bosses. Newsweek 63:32 Ja 20 '64

Czechoslovakia; a dull drama. I. Duchacek. Cur Hist 44:273-80+ My '63

Understanding Kafka. il Time 83:41-2 My 15 '64

Popular culture

Letter from Prague. R. Littell. Nation 199: 171-2 S 28 '64

Religious institutions and affairs

See also

Catholic church in Czechoslovakia

CZULAK, Josef

He keeps the bacteria jumping. A. K. Klingender. il Sat R 47:51-2 My 2 '64

CZURA, Pete

Best rabbit insurance. pors Field & S 69: 94-5+ Ja '65

Blue ribbon waters. Field & S 68:62-3+ My '63

Duel with nature. Field & S 69:52-3+ Jl '64

Gun dogs. Field & S 69:130+ S '64

How to camp out and enjoy it. Todays Health 42:32-5+ Jl '64

Join the fun for pan fishing. Todays Health 42:46-50+ S '64

Nebraska's never-fail lakes. Field & S 69: 116-20 S '64

Quail shoot with a twist. Field & S 69:48-9 Je '64

Real deer sleeper. Field & S 68:104-6+ N '63

Shotgun primer. Field & S 68:42-5 Jl '63

D

DAL. See Defenders of American liberties

DAR. See Daughters of the American revolution

DASH (destroyer anti-submarine helicopter) See Helicopters—Military applications

DC restorer. See Television circuits

DCE (diversified cooperative education) See Education, Cooperative

DDT (insecticide)

Bats: sensitivity to DDT. M. M. Luckens and W. H. Davis. bibliog il Science 146:948 N 13 '64

Billions of bugs: Willapa looper project. J. B. Craig. il Am For 70:42-8 F '64

DDT: a new hypothesis of its mode of action. R. D. O'Brien and F. Matsumura. bibliog il Science 146:657-8 O 30 '64

DDT antagonism to dieldrin storage in adipose tissue of rats. J. C. Street. bibliog il Science 146:1580-1 D 18 '64

DDT build-up in forests may harm food chain. Sci N L 86:104 Ag 15 '64

Great pesticide controversy. J. Strohm and C. Ganschow. Read Digest 83:123-8 O '63

Persistence of DDT in soils of heavily sprayed forest stands. G. M. Woodwell and F. T. Martin. bibliog il Science 145:481-3 Jl 31 '64

Resistance to DDT in the mosquito fish, gambusia affinis. V. S. Bradleigh and others. bibliog il Science 139:217-18 Ja 18 '63

You can save your elms; spraying with DDT; Detroit. F. Vaydik. il Am City 78: 110-11 S '63

Injurious effects

. . . And Rachel Carson again. Am City 78:7 Je '63

Bats most sensitive of mammals to DDT. Sci N L 86:376 D 12 '64

D D T (insecticide)—Injurious effects—*Cont.*
Death of a salt pond; Cotuit, Mass. S. Cobb. Audubon Mag 65:70-2 Mr '63
Gypsy moth in New York; DDT controversy. E. W. Littlefield. il Am For 70:42-5+ Ja '64
Miss Carson goes to Congress. R. Carson. il Am For 69:20-3+ Jl '63
Tests show forty species of birds poisoned by DDT. G. J. Wallace and R. F. Bernard. Audubon Mag 65:198-202 Jl '63
When a state spray kills the state bird. A. G. Etter. il Audubon Mag 65:134-7 My '63

DDT in milk. See Milk contamination

D day invasion. See World war, 1939-1945—Campaigns and battles—Western

DESP. See National education association—Department of elementary school principals

DEW (distant early warning) See Radar defense network

D-H diet. See Diet

DMSO. See Methyl sulfoxide

DNA. See Deoxyribonucleic acid

DOP (dermo-optical perception) See Touch

DAANE, J. Dewey
Face of the Fed. por Newsweek 62:92-3 N 11 '63
Not in Martin's pocket; Fed's hard money policies. por Bsns W p 116 N 9 '63

DABBS, James McBride
Episcopalians consider Megabagdad. Christian Cent 81:302-3 Mr 4 '64
He stands at the door. Christian Cent 81:359-60 Mr 18 '64

DABBS, Stuart
Cut, long, short. U S Camera 27:78-9+ Ap '64

DABKOWSKI, H. B.
Outrigger ski sled. Pop Mech 121:152-3 F '64

DABNEY, Virginius
Has Hitler's ghost been laid? Sat R 46:16-18 Mr 9 '63
New ways to permanent files. Sat R 47:67-8 My 9; 77 N 14 '64
Richmond's quiet revolution. Sat R 47:18-19+ F 29 '64
What the GOP is doing in the South. Harper 226:86-8+ My '63

DABROWSKA, Jadwiga. See Brutkowski, S. jt. auth.

DACHAU, Germany
Has Hitler's ghost been laid? V. Dabney. il Sat R 46:16-18 Mr 9 '63
Visit to a Munich suburb. E. Wakin. America 111:235-6 S 5 '64

DACHAU concentration camp. See Concentration camps—Germany

DACHILLE, Frank, and others
Coesite and stishovite: stepwise reversal transformations. bibliog Science 140:991-3 My 31 '63

DACKO, David
Colored rulers. G. C. Turner. Negro Hist Bul 27:153 Mr '64

DACRES, James Richard
By heaven, that ship is ours! L. McKee. il por(p7) Am Heritage 16:96-8 D '64

DACRON. See Textile fabrics, Synthetic

DACRON sails. See Sails

DADAISM
Man; show of Dadaist paintings. il Newsweek 61:98-9 My 20 '63

DADDAH, Moktar Ould
Summary of address, October 14, 1963. por U N Rev 10:8 D '63

DADDARIO, Emilio Q.
Daddario unit seeking proper level of R&D aid; interview, ed. by H. M. David. por Miss & Roc 15:26 Ag 10 '64

DADDARIO, Joseph J. See Stuiver, M. jt. auth.

DADDY come home; drama. See Grieco, R.

DADE COUNTY, Fla.
Safety town trains children. il Am City 79:23 Jl '64

Education

Cooperative venture; Joint book selection committee with Miami public library. M. H. Edmonds. Wilson Lib Bul 38:689 Ap '64
In Dade County, Florida. P. L. Tornillo, jr. il NEA J 52:51-2 D '63

Politics and government

Dade County: unbossed, erratically led. T. J. Wood. bibliog f Ann Am Acad 353:64-71 My '64

Recreation

Gulf streamed recreation. A. Peavy. il Recreation 57:275+ Je '64

DADO joints. See Joints (carpentry)

DAEDALUS (periodical)
Houghton to publish hardcover Daedalus issues. Pub W 184:32 O 28 '63

DAEHLER, R. E. See Whitesell, C. D. jt. auth.

DAERLY, Pierre
Isolated people awakes to progress. Negro Hist Bul 27:77-8 Ja '64

DAETZ, G. M.
My Eskimo adventure. Outdoor Life 131:48-9+ F '63

DAFFODILS. See Narcissus

DAG Hammarskjöld library. See United Nations library

DAG Hammarskjöld Memorial Grove (proposed)
Redwood grove may honor Hammarskjold. Nat Parks Mag 37:16 D '63

DAGERMAN, Stig
From Birgitta suite; poem. by T. Vance and V. Vance. Poetry 103:231-3 Ja '64

about

Note on Stig Dagerman. T. Vance. Poetry 103:255 Ja '64

DAGGETT, Noél J.
Noél J. Daggett: a determined painter. F. Whitaker. il por Am Artist 27:42-7+ Mr '63

DAGUERREOTYPES
How they made daguerreotypes. B. Newhall. il Pop Phot 53:58+ Jl '63
More living than the memory of the man. B. Newhall. Pop Phot 55:152-3+ N '64
To force the sun to paint pictures. il N Y Times Mag p22-3 Ag 30 '64

DAHL, Roald
Life movie review. Life 57:16 D 18 '64

DAHLBERG, Edward
Wages of risk. A. Karlen. Nation 198:331-4 Mr 30 '64

DAHLBERG, Edwin L.
Edwin L. Dahlberg seeks mood in a motif; with biographical sketch. il por Am Artist 29:40-1+ F '65

DAHLGREN, George, and Simmerman, N. L.
Intramolecular catalysis of the hydrolysis of N-dimethylaminomaleamic acid. bibliog Science 140:485 My 3 '63

DAHLIA exhibits. See Flower exhibits

DAHLIAS
Before you say no to dahlias. il Sunset 130:266+ My '63
Dahlias are back in style. Horticulture 41:258 My '63
How to multiply dahlias. il Sunset 132:132 Ja '64
Little dahlias make a big show. F. F. Rockwell. il Flower Grower 50:22-3 Je '63
Wax dahlia tubers for longer life. M. F. Kirby. Flower Grower 50:19 N '63
Year of the dahlia. B. Black. il Pop Gard 15:10-12 Ap '64

DAHLQUIST, Eric
500-mph LSR car? pors Hot Rod 17:46-7+ Ag '64
Ford axle for Chevys. il Hot Rod 17:92-3 F '64

DAHOMEY
Colored rulers. G. C. Turner. Negro Hist Bul 28:36-7 N '64
Sounds in the night. Time 82:36 N 8 '63
Violence in Africa; developments in Togo, Brazzaville and Dahomey. T. P. Melady. America 109:734-5 D 7 '63

See also

Art—Dahomey

DAI, Shen-yu
Roots of Chinese ideology. bibliog f Cur Hist 45:158-64+ S '63

DAICHES, David
Breakthrough? Commentary 38:61-4 Ag '64
Dialectical Judaism. Commentary 37:75-7 Ap; 38:15 Ag '64
Doom and love. Commentary 35:537-40 Je '63
Hayim Greenberg's legacy. Commentary 38:81-2+ S '64

DAILY, Jay E.
Oil for the lamps of knowledge. por Library J 89:4483-7 N 15 '64
Search for sample books. Wilson Lib Bul 39:59-61+ S '64

DAILY, Mary A.
Everyone is a child at Christmas. por Redbook 122:6+ D '63

DAILY mail, London
Evening with Virginia Woolf. E. Irons. New Yorker 39:115-16+ Mr 30 '63

DAILY mirror, New York. See New York mirror

DAILY news, Chicago. See Chicago daily news

DAILY press, Detroit. See Detroit daily press

DAIMLER- Benz, ag. See Automobile industry and trade—Germany (Federal Republic)

DAIN, Sir Guy
Advantages of the National health service. Cur Hist 45:32-3+ Jl '63
DAIN, N. E.
Teaching and criticism; reprint. Library J 88:3538 O 1 '63
DAIRY barns. See Barns and stables
DAIRY farm management
Planning guide for dairymen. P. B. Jones and R. L. Maddex. il Suc Farm 63:30-1 Ja '65
DAIRY farming. See Dairying
DAIRY farms
At 17,387 now, aiming for 18,000. R. Porterfield and J. R. Borcherding. il Suc Farm 61:66+ Mr '63
Dairy system, convertible to beef. il Farm J 87:38-9 My '63
Down on the farm. I. Mothner. il Look 28:34-7 Ja 14 '64
See also
Dairy farm management
DAIRY herd improvement association. See Cow testing associations
DAIRY industry and trade
Dairy dispute. il Time 81:94+ Je 7 '63
How now, brown cow? A. Brynes. New Repub 148:8 Ap 20 '63
Our dairy surplus, we import a chunk of it; with editorial comment. M. Norton. Farm J 87:34, 126 My '63
Three dairy ideas for more profit. C. E. Ball. Farm J 88:50D Ja '64
See also
American dairy association
DAIRY machines
See also
Milking machines
DAIRY parlors. See Milking parlors—Equipment
DAIRY products
Milky way treats. il Suc Farm 61:64-5 N '63
Two dairy foods you cannot buy; homemade sour cream and fromage blanc. Sunset 133: 145 Jl '64
See also
Butter
Bacteriology
See also
Cheese—Bacteriology
Prices
See also
Milk—Prices
DAIRYING
As a dairyman, how do you rate? V. R. Houghaboom. Farm J 88:42F N '64
Best dairy ideas from Europe: 10,000 miles and seven countries. D. Braun. il Farm J 87:36-7+ F '63
Big farming on fifty acres: F. Steury, Adams Country, Ind. il Suc Farm 62:74H Ap '64
Dairy; ed. by D. Braun. See issues of Farm journal
Dairy news (cont of) Dairy. See issues of Farm journal
Expanding your dairy herd? L. H. Brown. il Suc Farm 61:38 My '63
Forty-one top cows as good as eighty-seven average ones. J. R. Borcherding. il Suc Farm 61:42-3 S '63
Four dairy ideas, straight from Europe. il Farm J 87:481 O '63
How Europe makes high-solids milk. D. Braun. Farm J 87:52G My '63
How 120 dairymen cut costs. il Farm J 87:38-9+ Ap '63
I got too big. C. E. Ball. il Farm J 87:33+ S '63
More cows, less work. J. R. Borcherding. il Suc Farm 62:40-1+ Je '64
What's new and outlook for. See issues of Successful farming
See also
American dairy science association
Cows—Feeding
Dairy farm management
Dairy farms
DAISIES
Daisies do tell. M. B. Williams. il Pop Gard 14:42+ Jl '63
Daisies that are different! R. C. Hands. il Horticulture 41:266-7 My '63
Daisy quiz. G. Frerichs. il Horticulture 41: 400 Ag '63
Freshen your garden with daisies. il Am Home 66:10+ Je '63
DAISY manufacturing company
Not just kid stuff; Daisy rifles. il Bsns W p88-90 Ja 25 '64
Rifle called Daisy. J. D. Brown. il Sports Illus 18:58-64+ Ap 29 '63
DAKOTA Indians
Just bad Indians; state jurisdiction over Indian affairs. New Repub 148:8 Mr 30 '63
Treaties
There are no Indians left now but me. M. Rosenberg and D. Rosenberg. il Am Heritage 15:18-23+ Je '64
DALAND, Peter
Gray-flannel émigré from the East builds an empire out West. C. Phinizy. il por Sports Illus 18:43-4+ Mr 25 '63
DALARNA. See Dalecarlia, Sweden
D'ALBE, E. M. Fournier
300,000 earthquakes a year. UNESCO Courier 16:26-9 O '63
DALE, Chester
Chester Dale: collector. N. MacNeil. il McCalls 91:120-7+ N '63
DALE, Dick
Good life of an idol. il pors Life 55:82-3 Ag 30 '63
King at twenty-four; surf guitarist. il por Newsweek 62:71 Ag 26 '63
DALE, Edgar
Educating for flexibility. por ALA Bul 57:131-4 F '63
Reasons for doing nothing. por NEA J 52: 11 N '63
DALE, Edwin L. jr
Europe; illusion of unity. New Repub 148: 14-15 F 23 '63
Europe's crisis of sovereignty. N Y Times Mag p7+ Jl 7 '63
Great unemployment fallacy. New Repub 151: 10-12 S 5 '64
How Britain does it. New Repub 148:7-8 Mr 30 '63
Subsidizing the states. New Repub 151:11-12 N 28 '64
When will it be safe to balance the budget? N Y Times Mag p 14-15+ Ja 24 '65
DALE, George
On the tender care of records. Mus Am 84:60 Ja '64
DALE, Robert
Don't let camera thieves spoil your vacation. Pop Phot 54:132-3 Ap '64
Memoirs of a contemporary cutpurse; interview, ed. by W. R. Morey. Mlle 58: 184-5+ Ap '64
DALE, Robert F.
Agricultural meteorology. Science 146:1601-2 D 18 '64
DALE, Robert G.
Battery charger uses an SCR. Electr World 72:79 S '64
DALE, Slade
Our footloose correspondents. A. Bailey. il New Yorker 40:141-2+ O 31 '64
DALE, William E. and Quinby, G. E.
Chlorinated insecticides in the body fat of people in the United States. bibliog Science 142:593-5 N 1 '63
—and others
Poisoning by DDT: relation between clinical signs and concentration in rat brain. bibliog Science 142:1474-6 D 13 '63
DALECARLIA, Sweden
Journey to Dalecarlia. E. Unnerstad. il Horn Bk 39:580-7 D '63
DALEY, Adeline
Report on rapport. NEA J 52:12-13 D '63
DALEY, Arthur
World serious, then and now. N Y Times Mag p34+ S 29 '63
DALEY, Richard Joseph
Clouter with conscience. il pors Time 81:24-35 Mr 15 '63
Last dinosaur wins again. A. Balk. il por Sat Eve Post 236:72-3 My 11 '63
Mayor Daley's Chicago. J. Dugan. il por Holiday 34:84-93+ D '63
More of everything; election results. il por Newsweek 61:32 Ap 15 '63
Political leader who's slipping. por U S News 54:19 Ap 15 '63
When marchers turned on Chicago's mayor. il por U S News 55:10 Jl 15 '63
DALEY, Robert
Fighting Yankee of Seville. Sat Eve Post 237:62-3 Ap 11 '64
Football's marvelous misfit. Sat Eve Post 237:82+ D 5 '64
Lonely champions quest for Olympic gold. Sat Eve Post 237:66-73 O 10 '64
Wild world of European sports. Sat Eve Post 236:60-1 F 16 '63
DALEY, William P.
Artist & teacher. Sch Arts 62:13-15 Mr '63
DALGLIESH, Alice
Books for young people. See issues of Saturday review
Design or content? Sat R 46:44 My 11 '63

DALGLIESH, Alice—*Continued*
Picture books. Sat R 46:58-65 N 9 '63; 47: 48-56 N 7 '64
Spreading chestnut tree. Sat R 46:53 Ag 17 '63
Wonderful silence. Sat R 48:51-2 Ja 23 '65

DALI, Salvador
Why they attack the Mona Lisa. Art N 62: 36+ Mr '63
about
Dali reapproached. New Yorker 39:23 F 15 '64
Dilly Dali; exhibition at Knoedler gallery. il Time 82:90 D 6 '63
New twist on Dali's moustache. il pors Look 28:74 D 29 '64

DALIS, Irene
Irene Dalis: villainess with charm. J. Ardoin. por Mus Am 83:44 Mr '63

DALL sheep hunting. See Mountain sheep hunting

DALLAPICCOLA, Luigi
Atonal humanist. il por Newsweek 64:90-1 N 16 '64
Music to my ears; Dallapiccola in retrospect. I. Kolodin. Sat R 47:32+ N 21 '64

DALLAS, Philip
Going places, finding things in southern Italy. House & Gard 124:24-6+ S '63

DALLAS
After tragedy, the pulpit. J. C. Evans. Christian Cent 81:29-30 Ja 1 '64
Back to Dallas; first presidential visit to Dallas since November 22, 1963. il por Newsweek 64:30-1 O 19 '64
Big day for D; Cotton bowl game, Texas vs. Navy. J. Underwood. il Sports Illus 20:16-17 Ja 13 '64
Boy, don't you know I'm on camera? M. Kempton. New Repub 150:7 F 29 '64
Dallas image unveiled; near-riot after A. Stevenson's address. J. C. Evans. Christian Cent 80:1438-40 N 20 '63
Dallas public and private, by W. Leslie. Review
Sat R 47:49 Ap 18 '64. L. Tinkle
Dallas' reaction to Dallas public and private. Pub W 185:49 Ap 20 '64
Dallas rejoinder. Nation 198:519 My 25 '64
Different look at Dallas, Texas. il U S News 56:42-6 F 3 '64
In defense of two cities. R. Moley. Newsweek 63:110 Ap 27 '64
May God forgive Dallas. il Newsweek 62:46-8 D 9 '63
Memo about a Dallas citizen. T. G. Harris. il Look 28:64+ Ag 11 '64
Memo from a Dallas citizen. J. M. Shea, jr. Look 28:88+ Mr 24 '64
Shame of Dallas. Sat R 46:26 D 28 '63
Tips; book by W. Leslie to be published soon. Pub W 185:80 F 3 '64
What kind of place is Dallas? R. Wallace. il Life 56:67-8+ Ja 31 '64
What makes Dallas different? W. Morris. New Repub 150:20-2 Je 20 '64

City planning
Dallas develops its downtown; Main place. il Am City 79:145+ O '64
Sunken superblock for Dallas. il Bsns W p30 My 30 '64
What your city needs to grow. il Nations Bsns 52:31-3+ S '64

Housing
Mews type plan for Texas development. il Arch Rec 135:148-9 Ja '64
Staggered for privacy and view; sixteen-unit row house. il Arch Rec 136:116-17 Ag '64

Music
[Musical events] (cont) il Mus Am 83:18 Mr; 21 Ap; 54 S '63; 84:20-1 Ja; 14 Mr; 24 Jl '64
See also
Dallas civic opera company

Newspapers
Comprehensive coverage; assassination of John F. Kennedy. Time 82:81-2 D 6 '63

Parades
Big bowls of glitter. il Life 56:38-45 Ja 3 '64

Police
Commission has concluded. . . major recommendations of the Warren commission. il Newsweek 64:63-4 O 5 '64
Did press pressure kill Oswald? reprint. L. Grove. il U S News 56:78-9 Ap 6 '64
Lessons to be learned; Warren commission's findings. il Time 84:50+ O 2 '64
Police in Dallas. New Repub 150:8 Ja 18 '64
Shame of Dallas, Texas. il Sat Eve Post 237:82 Ap 11 '64

Politics and government
How business failed Dallas. R. A. Smith. il Fortune 70:156-60+ Jl '64
Tussle in Texas. S. Friedman. Nation 198: 114-17 F 3 '64

Stores
But they came back same day; Neiman-Marcus disaster. il Bsns W p 15 D 26 '64
Neiman-Marcus fire: 200 firms to pay insurance. il U S News 58:10 Ja 4 '65
Neiman-Marcus flambé. il Newsweek 65:48-9 Ja 4 '65
Phoenix in Dallas; $10 million fire at Neiman-Marcus store. il Time 85:63 Ja 1 '65
Sub in the sagebrush; Neiman-Marcus department store, gimmick gifts. il Newsweek 62:96 N 11 '63

Theater
Rise of rep. il(p56-7) Time 83:61 F 14 '64

DALLAS civic opera company
Seeds of Verdi; presentation of Monteverdi's Poppea. il Time 82:69 N 22 '63
Texas roundup. J. Rosenfield. il Theatre Arts 47:23+ Mr '63
Texas triumvirate. A. Holmes. il Opera N 28:32 D 28 '63
Texas twins; Suor Angelica and Pagliacci. J. Rosenfield. Opera N 27:31 F 2 '63

DALLAS COUNTY, Ala.
Black Belt, Alabama. J. DeMuth. Commonweal 80:536-9 Ag 7 '64

DALLAS public library
Foursome for Dallas; Casa View, Preston Royal, Hampton-Illinois, and South Oak Cliff branches. W. Jones. il Library J 89: 4733-6 D 1 '64
November in Dallas. W. Jones. Library J 89:72 Ja 1 '64
$1 million book exhibit at Dallas public library. Library J 88:3575 O 1 '63
That was the day that was; opening of Casa View branch. W. Jones. Library J 89: 2752+ Jl '64

DALLEGRET, François
François Dallegret; inventions. il por Arch Forum 120:109-14 My '64

DALLEN, James
Existentialism and the Catholic thinker. Cath World 200:294-9 F '65

DALLETT, Francis James
Some Franco-American silversmiths and jewelers. Antiques 84:706-9 D '63

DALLIN, Alexander
Russia and China view the United States. bibliog f Ann Am Acad 349:153-62 S '63

DALLIS, Nicholas Peter
Psychiatrist at the drawing board. M. Wagner. il pors Todays Health 41:14-17+ Ag '63

DALMATIA
Dalmatian montage. K. Simon. Vogue 144: 8 N 15 '64
See also
Dubrovnik, Yugoslavia

DALMATIAN dogs
Uric acid transport system: apparent absence in erythrocytes of the dalmatian coach hound. A. M. Harvey and H. N. Christensen. bibliog il Science 145:826-7 Ag 21 '64

DALRYMPLE, Byron W.
Antelope hunt with Ace Reid. il Farm J 87: 42-3+ O '63
Big circle tour. pors Field & S 69:66-9+ O '64
Boat-float bucks. Field & S 69:54-5+ Jl '64
Dippy dipper. Field & S 69:58+ Je '64
Piper of the peaks. Field & S 69:49+ S '64
Pop picket pins. Outdoor Life 133:48-9+ F '64
Turkey on the wing. por Outdoor Life 132: 60-3+ S '63

DALRYMPLE, Jean
Initiation into Broadway; excerpt from September child, with introductions by J. Harris. pors Theatre Arts 47:19-21+ Ag '63
Make up your mind. por Seventeen 22:162+ S '63
Mexico's performing arts. Travel 122:44-6 Ag '64
On 55th street, the longest run of all. N Y Times Mag p84-5 D 8 '63

DALTON, William J.
Thoughts over the Pacific. America 111:383 O 3 '64

DALVEN, Rae
Note on Yannis Ritsos. Poetry 103:334 F '64
(tr) See Ritsos, Y. Night of a solitary; Immobility of the voyage; Surpassing of danger; Rainy; Ultimate landing; Honest confrontation; Heard and the unheard; Estrangement; Recollection; Moment; Architect
Theatre and lyric. Poetry 102:54-5 Ap '63
DALY, John
That's his line. Newsweek 61:80 F 4 '63
DALY, Leo A, company
From Omaha to Brazil; Midwest's biggest firm of engineer-architects. il Time 83:94 My 22 '64
DALY, Mary
Built-in bias. Commonweal 81:508-11 Ja 15 '65
DALY, Richard. See Mattison, L. jt. auth.
DALY, Sheila John
Female bearcat named Stutz. Sat Eve Post 236:60-2 Ap 13 '63
DAMADIAN, R. and Solomon, A. K.
Bacterial mutant with impaired potassium transport and methionine biosynthesis. bibliog Science 145:1327-8 S 18 '64
DAMAGES
Pay for crime victims? excerpts from address. A. J. Goldberg. U S News 56:16 F 24 '64
Pay for crime victims: second nation adopts plan. U S News 56:12 Ap 6 '64
Victims. R. Childres. Harper 228:159-62 Ap '64
See also
Liability (law)
D'AMATA, Constance J. See Hicks, S. P. jt. auth.
D'AMATO, Cus
Goodby, Cus. Sports Illus 20:14 Je 1 '64
I am a bit of a fanatic. R. H. Boyle. il por Sports Illus 19:64-5 O 21 '63
DAMAZ, Paul
Art and architecture: a new light on monastic design. Craft Horiz 23:24-5+ Ja '63
Art in Latin American architecture. Craft Horiz 23:12-39+ S '63
D'AMBOISE, Jacques
Let's make ballet a manly art; interview, ed. by P. Bunzel. pors Life 54:64-9 Je 21 '63
about
Sticking his neck out. il por Newsweek 62:82 S 30 '63
DAME Sybil and Dame Edith; story. See Zeigerman, G.
DAMES violets
Sweet scents. C. K. Mosher. il Horticulture 41:226 Ap '63
D'AMICO, Victor
Creative art education workshop. Sch Arts 62:32-4 Ap '63
about
Art barge; Summer art center at Napeague Harbor, Amagansett. New Yorker 39:33-4 S 21 '63
DAMITA Jo
Imperial crown roast of pork. il por Ebony 19:104+ Ja '64
DAMMIT dolls. See Dolls
DAMNATION of Faust; opera. See Berlioz, H.
DAMORE, Leo
Memory; story. Redbook 123:36-7 Ag '64
D'AMOUR, O'Neil C.
Catholic case. Commonweal 79:515-19 Ja 31 '64
Scholastic teacher interviews: Msgr O'Neil C. D'Amour; ed. by H. Langer. por Sr Schol 84:9T-11T Ap 10 '64
DAMPNESS in buildings
Letter to the owner of a wet basement. il House B 106:186+ Ap '64
No cure-all for wet basements. Consumer Bul 46:15 Mr '63
DAMS
Bridge Canyon Dam is not necessary; with editorial comment. S. Raushenbush. il Nat Parks Mag 38:2, 4-8 Ap '64
Dams protect and destroy; World knowledge pool investigates dams. Sci N L 85:390 Je 20 '64
How safe are our dams? E. D. Fales, jr. il Pop Sci 185:33-7+ Jl '64
Lake of Perfidy; Allegheny reservoir. New Repub 150:5 Ap 18 '64
Mighty Colorado. Pacific Southwest water plan and Bridge Canyon Dam. A. W. Smith. Nat Parks Mag 37:2+ O '63
Quiet crisis or lost cause? W. Stegner. Sat R 47:28+ S 19 '64
Senecas to be flooded out; Kinzua Dam project. Sr Schol 84:17 Mr 20 '64
U.S. undercuts own job-making goal. il Nations Bsns 51:40-1+ Jl '63
Water challenge of the
with editorial comment.
Nat Parks Mag 38:2, 4-7 J
Water vs. parks. issue o
River. J. B. Craig. Am F
See also
Dikes (engineering)
Fish ladders
Flood prevention and control

Failures
Day the dam broke; Baldwin
voir. R. Leadabrand. il Am
F '64
Day the dam burst; St Francis
W. S. Griswold. il Pop Sci 184:
'64
How safe are our dams? E. D. Fa
Pop Sci 185:33-7+ Jl '64
Oil on troubled waters; oil wells bla
Baldwin Hills Dam failure. Newsw
23 D 28 '64
There's a break in the dam! we've got
out! Baldwin Hills Dam. B. Sherida
B. Roberts. McCalls 91:91-2+ Ap '6
Why? Baldwin Hills reservoir disaste
Newsweek 62:17 D 30 '63

Fish problems
See Fish ladders

Alaska
Alaskan Dam: boon or boondoggle? Rampart Dam project. C. Callison. il Audubon Mag 65:238 Jl '63
Building the bigger dam; Rampart Dam. P. M. Tilden. Natur Hist 72:66 D '63
Indictment of Rampart Dam. C. H. Callison. Audubon Mag 66:242 Jl '64
Rampart Dam: a wildlife catastrophe for nothing? G. H. Gillelan. il Outdoor Life 134:14-15+ D '64
Rampart roulette. F. Dufresne. il Field & S 69:10-13+ Ag '64
Rampart we watch. R. Stearns. Field & S 68:12+ Ag '63
Yukon River features; Rampart Dam project. C. Callison. Liv Wildn 83:28-9 Spring '63

Canada
U.S. and Canada to tame a river. il U S News 55:44 D 30 '63

Egypt
See also
Aswan High Dam

France
Moon power over St Malo. H. Manchester. il Read Digest 84:37-8+ Je '64

Iran
Water & blood; Mohammed Reza Shah Pahlevi Dam. il Time 81:31 Mr 22 '63

Italy
After the flood, an inquest; Vaiont Dam tragedy. il Bsns W p36 O 19 '63
Death of a valley; Vaiont Dam overflows. C. McCarry. il Sat Eve Post 236:76-81 N 30 '63
Italian dam tragedy will not happen here; Vaiont Dam. Sci N L 84:260 O 26 '63
Italian flood: disaster truly biblical; Vaiont Dam. il U S News 55:6 O 21 '63
Italian government provides Vaiont Dam disaster relief. Dept State Bul 50:803-4 My 18 '64
Like Pompeii. . ; remains of Longarone, Italy. il Time 82:43 O 18 '63
There the dam stood, proud and beautiful and then. . . R. Ajemian. il Life 55:30-41 O 25 '63
Valley of death; Vaiont Dam overflows. il Newsweek 62:62+ O 21 '63

Jordan
Ask the ancients; Siq Dam and diversion system. il Time 82:70 O 25 '63

Netherlands
Clamshell dikes tame the ocean. G. B. Rubinstein. il Pop Mech 120:90-1 Jl '63
DAN, Ikuma
Mr Dan presents Mr Dan. Newsweek 64:75 Jl 20 '64
DANA, John Cotton
Think nothing of it, Mr Dana, it's only a flesh wound; quotations, ed. by C. A. Goodrum. por Library J 89:3687-8 O 1 '64
DANA, Marshall N.
Magic of water. Am For 70:8-13+ Mr '64
DANA, Robert Patrick
Winter's tale; poem. New Yorker 39:28 F 1 '64

T.
of fame. Am For 70:16+ O '64
rspectives; address. pors Am For
'63
DAN of Yale. Am For 69:10+ S '63
Aed by the American forestry asso-
to review and evaluate proposals for
ds preservation. por Am For 70:12 D

SMITH, Valerie
niscence of Hemingway. por Sat R 47:
1+ My 9 '64

E, Helen
m mad and lightning fast. Sat R 46:
2-3 Je 15 '63

NCE, Stanley
And all that jazz. Sat R 46:39+ Jl 27 '63
Chicago, Chicago. Sat R 47:45 Jl 25 '64
Ellington's My people. Sat R 46:73 S 28 '63
Harlem yesterdays. Sat R 47:74-5 S 26 '64
Jazz in Pittsburgh. Sat R 47:43+ Jl 11 '64
Meditations with a beat. Sat R 46:45 F 9 '63
Recordings reports: jazz LPs. See issues of Saturday review
Self-portrait of a Lion. Sat R 47:50 S 12 '64

DANCE agencies. See Theatrical agencies

DANCE bands. See Bands (music)

DANCE companies
American dance theater, New York state theater. D. Hering. Dance Mag 39:57+ Ja '65
Judson dance theater, Judson memorial church. J. Maskey. Dance Mag 38:20 D '64
Pearl Wheeler: a tribute; Denishawn company. J. Dougherty. il Dance Mag 39:52-4 Ja '65
See also
Sanasardo, Paul, dance company

DANCE conferences
Encore conventions. P. Draper. Dance Mag 37:69 Je '63
Experiment in learning; fourth annual summer conference of the Northeast regional ballet festival association. I. W. Clarke. il Dance Mag 38:54-5 N '64

DANCE etiquette. See Etiquette

DANCE festivals
Calendar of international summer dance events; comp. by J. Fox. il Dance Mag 38:32-7+ My '64
Calendar of summer dance events here and abroad; comp. by J. Fox. il Dance Mag 37:32-4 My '63
Campus in ferment; Connecticut college dance school and American dance festival. D. Hering. il Dance Mag 38:34-9 O '64
Ethnic accent at Los Angeles ANTA dance festival. il Dance Mag 37:14-15 S '63
Gift to a grateful New York city; Rebekah Harkness foundation dance festival; Delacorte theatre, Central park. J. Maskey. Dance Mag 37:30-1 O '63
Holiday in Athens. D. Hering. il Dance Mag 37:50-3 Jl '63
International gala, Delacorte theatre, New York. D. Hering. Dance Mag 38:29+ O '64
Jacob's Pillow revisited. J. Martin. Sat R 46:38+ Jl 27 '63
Love, work, warm night air; Rebekah Harkness foundation dance festival in Central park. il Time 82:54 S 20 '63
Lyn goes to Houston; second annual Southwestern regional ballet festival. D. Hering; W. Habich. il Dance Mag 38:52-7 Jl '64
Mirkels, major and minor; annual Southeastern regional ballet festival. D. Hering. il Dance Mag 38:58-63 Je '64
Modern dance festival in Toronto. W. Sorell. il Dance Mag 37:16+ My '63
Sense of ministry. il Time 84:42 Ag 21 '64
Shanta Rao & company; the Jacob's Pillow dancers; Claudia Cravey and Hans Meister at Jacob's Pillow. D. Hering. Dance Mag 37:60-1 O '63
Something for everybody, everything for somebody; five major European dance festivals. C. Barnes. il Dance Mag 38:36-8+ S '64
Style in Stuttgart. il Time 83:56 Je 12 '64
Taste of tomorrow; fifth Northeast regional ballet festival. D. Hering. il Dance Mag 37:48-51+ Ag '63
Triumph along the St Johns; Southeastern regional ballet festival. D. Hering. il Dance Mag 37:48-53 Je '63
Where do they come from? report on American dance festival, Connecticut college. D. Hering. il Dance Mag 37:23-5+ O '63
Wonderful old-time hoofers at Newport. L. Jay. Dance Mag 37:18-19 Ag '63
See also
Jacob's Pillow dance festival

DANCE films. See Moving pictures—Dance films

DANCE halls
Last waltz at Aragon; Chicago ballroom. il Bsns W p30-1 F 15 '64
This way to Mecca. il Newsweek 62:57-8 Jl 1 '63

DANCE institutes and workshops
Earth theatre; first presentation of the African-Caribbean-American institute of dance arts. M. Marks. Dance Mag 38:28 Ag '64

DANCE magazine
American way; Dance magazine awards presentation; symposium. il Dance Mag 38:36-41+ Je '64
Conversation with Dolores Magwood; ed. by L. Joel. D. Magwood. il Dance Mag 38:26-7 O '64
Dance magazine's 1962-1963 awards. Dance Mag 37:30-3 Ap '63; 38:32-5+ Mr '64
Golden years. R. Orthwine. Dance Mag 39:30-1 Ja '65
Wit and wisdom at the Dance magazine awards presentation; symposium. il Dance Mag 37:30-5 Je '63

DANCE music. See Phonograph records—Dance music

DANCE notation
Observer at the dance notation conference. C. Roope. il Dance Mag 38:13-15 Ag '64

DANCE of the divorced; story. See Gold, H.

DANCE parties. See Childrens parties

DANCE photography. See Photography

DANCE production
Changes I've seen. T. Shawn. il Dance Mag 37:26-7 Je '63; Reply. E. W. Sutherland. 37:28-9 Ag '63
Charles Weidman: still pioneering. J. Anderson. Dance Mag 38:32-4 S '64
Coach to Spoleto; interview, ed. by W. Sorell. J. Erdman. il Dance Mag 37:35+ My '63
Culture in Kabul; Robert Joffrey company abroad. R. Heitzig. il Dance Mag 37:28+ Ap '63
Hitting the road; tours of Goya and Matteo. H. Smith. il Dance Mag 37:29-30 D '63
Lady, you bring romance; Brooklyn schools view a Sophie Maslow demonstration. H. Smith. il Dance Mag 38:62-3 Ap '64
Lament for Broadway; '62-'63 season round-up. L. Lerman. il Dance Mag 37:24-5 Je '63
Materials of publicity: dance photographs. D. Duncan. il Dance Mag 38:37-9 D '64 (to be cont)
Meet Simon Sadoff. E. Palatsky. il Dance Mag 37:19-20 D '63
Naked in its native beauty. G. Jackson. il Dance Mag 38:32-7 Ap '64
On the gypsy circuit. See issues of Dance magazine
Revivals save the day; '62-'63 theatre round-up. L. Lerman. il Dance Mag 37:27-9 Jl '63
Saida Gerrard discusses the L.A. problem. J. Dougherty. il Dance Mag 37:16+ Mr '63
School of performing arts, N.Y. school of printing auditorium. J. Maskey. Dance Mag 38:64-5 Jl '64
Show time at Roseland. D. Duncan. il Dance Mag 38:27 D '64
Solitary athlete; Martha Graham and her company; Lunt-Fontanne theatre. D. Hering. il Dance Mag 37:54-9 D '63
They also dance who only sit. C. C. Mark. il Dance Mag 38:54-5 F '64
Third parents. D. Hering. il Dance Mag 37:60-1+ D '63
Visit to the antique world; '62-'63 theatre round-up. L. Lerman. il Dance Mag 37:24-6 Ag '63

DANCE recitals
Dance drama company, 92nd street Y. J. Maskey. Dance Mag 38:84 Je '64
Dancers studio, 92nd street Y. M. Marks. Dance Mag 38:67 Je '64
School of performing arts dance concert at High school of printing auditorium. D. Hering. Dance Mag 37:14-16 Jl '63

DANCE schools
Campus in ferment; Connecticut college dance school and American dance festival. D. Hering. il Dance Mag 38:34-9 O '64
Europe as we see it. H. De Becker. il Dance Mag 38:19+ My; 14-17 Jl '64
Everyman's African roots; Primus-Borde school of dance. D. Leddick. il Dance Mag 38:20-1 O '64
Group; New dance group. J. Maskey. il Dance Mag 39:44-9 Ja '65
Happy solution to an old puzzle; Houston's Asbury school. il Dance Mag 39:59 Ja '65
Manifold implications; A. Halprin. J. Anderson. il Dance Mag 37:44-7 Ap '63
Milestone celebration at Jacob's Pillow. R. Stevenson. il Dance Mag 38:36-7 Ag '64

DANCE schools—*Continued*
New Jersey modern dance school inspires a foundation into existence. J. N. Schwartz and E. Ubell. il Dance Mag 37:18-19 Mr '63
Pasadena playhouse. J. Dougherty. il Dance Mag 37:22-3 My '63
Reminiscences and plans: Perry-Mansfield school of theatre & dance. C. Perry. il Dance Mag 37:48-51+ Ap '63
Summer camps. W. Como. il Dance Mag 37: 60-4 Ap; 61 My '63
20th century school of dance; Philadelphia dance academy. B. Kevles. il Dance Mag 38:20-2 My '64

DANCE teachers
Contrast in climates. M. Kuni. il Dance Mag 37:18-19 Je '63
Conversation with Dolores Magwood; ed. by L. Joel. D. Magwood. il Dance Mag 38:26-7 O '64
Europe as we see it. H. De Becker. il Dance Mag 38:19+ My; 14-17 Jl '64
Kid from Kentucky; J. Stanly. il Dance Mag 37:26-8 Mr '63
Lessons with Carmelita Maracci. J. W. Knowles. il Dance Mag 38:38-41 My '64
Never too busy. R. Clark. il Dance Mag 37: 16-17 Ap '63
Pasadena playhouse. J. Dougherty. il Dance Mag 37:22-3 My '63
Professor in ballet slippers. N. S. Hey. il Dance Mag 37:48-52 My '63
Roots and wings; excerpts from address, June 2, 1963. V. Tanner. Dance Mag 37:16-17 N '63
Summer teacher meetings. il Dance Mag 37: 52-7 O '63; 38:50-5+ O '64
What makes a great teacher of classical ballet? E. V. Williams. Dance Mag 37: 20-1 Ag '63
See also
Castle, N.
National council of dance teacher organizations

Education

Dance alone is not enough. M. Chace. Dance Mag 38:46-7+ Jl '64

DANCE therapy
Dance alone is not enough. M. Chace. Dance Mag 38:46-7+ Jl '64
Power of movement with others; working with hospitalized mental patients. M. Chace. Dance Mag 38:42-5+ Je '64
World opens. L. Canino. il Dance Mag 38: 46-7 O '64

DANCERS
Acting for dancers. il Dance Mag 37:47+ Ag '63
Annual directory of dance attractions, choreographers, and lecturers. il Dance Mag 37: 65+ D '63; 38:67-70+ D '64
As I see it; American talent in Europe. H. De Becker. il Dance Mag 37:23-5 N '63
Brief biographies. S. Goodman. See issues of Dance magazine
Calendar of international summer dance events; comp. by J. Fox. il Dance Mag 38: 32-7+ My '64
Encore for twelve high-kicking housewives; former Rockettes at Radio City music hall. L. H. Lapham. il Sat Eve Post 237:72+ O 24 '64
Europe as we see it. H. De Becker. il Dance Mag 38:19+ My '64
Good big girls; Bluebells. il Time 81:78 F 15 '63
Hitting the road; tours of Goya and Matteo. H. Smith. il Dance Mag 37:29-30 D '63
I'm proud to be a gypsy. L. Leabo. il Dance Mag 38:42-3+ O '64
Impressions in paint and words. R. Banks. il Dance Mag 37:40-1 Mr '63
In the news; concerts. il Dance Mag 37:20-1 Mr '63
In the news: exodus and exchange. il Dance Mag 37:36-7 Je '63
In the news; photographs. See issues of Dance magazine
Little background on tap dancing. M. Stearns and J. Stearns. il Esquire 62:192-3+ D '64
Mata and Hari, Brooklyn academy of music. M. Marks. Dance Mag 38:21+ D '64
Musical events: development of stars of New York city ballet. W. Sargeant. New Yorker 39:149-50 S 7 '63
Naked in its native beauty. G. Jackson. il Dance Mag 38:32-7 Ap '64
Olga Zampos, Mimi Garrard, Albert Reid, Henry street playhouse. M. Marks. Dance Mag 38:84-5 Je '64
On the gypsy circuit. See issues of Dance magazine
Presstime news. See issues of Dance magazine
Program of modern dance, Judson Hall. J. Maskey. Dance Mag 38:30 Ap '64
Russia's Rockettes. il Life 56:58A-58B+ Je 26 '64
Summer convention personalities. il Dance Mag 38:81 Je '64
Tokyo dancers dig our beat. W. Como. il Dance Mag 38:45-7 Ag '64
View from the big eye; Hollywood's TV dancers. O. Maynard. il Dance Mag 39:40-3 Ja '65
Way of life; regional ballet. D. Hering. il Dance Mag 38:55-7 D '64
What the dancer should know about publicity (cont) I. Fisher. Dance Mag 37:69 F '63 (to be cont)
World's most famous kick: Rockettes. il Life 57:76-84+ D 11 '64
See also
Dancer's theatre company
also names of dancers, e.g. M. Plisetskaya

Anecdotes, facetiae, satire, etc.

How to get a job as a swing dancer in a hit Broadway show. B. Evans. il Harper 230:28-31 Ja '65

DANCER'S theatre company
Dancer's theatre company, 92nd street Y. M. Marks. Dance Mag 38:68 My '64

DANCERS' workshop of San Francisco
It's all the fault of Christopher Columbus! A. Halprin. il Dance Mag 37:38-9+ Ag '63

DANCES, School. See Student activities

DANCING
All fall down; la bostella. il Newsweek 65:55 Ja 18 '65
American dance portfolio, by J. Mitchell. Review
Dance Mag il 38:46-51 Je '64
Bill Frank, Phyllis Lamhut, Murray Louis, Henry street playhouse. J. Maskey. Dance Mag 38:32-3 Je '64
Bossa nova. il Ebony 18:103-6 Mr '63
Building cultural bridges. M. Marks. il Dance Mag 37:20-1 My '63
Calendar of international summer dance events; comp. by J. Fox. il Dance Mag 38: 32-7+ My '64
Calendar of summer dance events here and abroad; comp. by J. Fox. il Dance Mag 37:32-4 My '63
Dance concert for the performing arts. M. Marks. Dance Mag 38:139 D '64
Dance; dance of the absurd. F. Bowers. Nation 197:116-18 S 7 '63
Dance is recreation; report prepared by program department, National recreation association. il Recreation 56:71-85 F '63
Dance; Sahm-Chun-Li Korean dancers. Mus Am 84:43 F '64
Dancing commercials: 1880. il Dance Mag 38:37-9 Jl '64
Dancing enriches their retirement years; Sirovich day center in New York city. il Todays Health 41:64 Ag '63
Discothèque dancing. il Life 56:97-100+ My 22 '64
Doggerel for modern jazz dance. L. Joel. il Dance Mag 37:36-9 D '63
Everything here is chaos; preliminary report on dance at the 1964 New York world's fair. N. Lansdale. il Dance Mag 38:22-5+ Je '64
Isadora Duncan and Constantin Stanislavsky; with excerpts from letters. N. Rene. il Dance Mag 37:40-3 Jl '63
It's all the fault of Christopher Columbus! A. Halprin. il Dance Mag 37:38-9+ Ag '63
It's gone silly! J. Cole explodes on the subject of modern jazz dance. C. Cole. Dance Mag 37:35 D '63
Lincoln Center situation. E. Palatsky. il Dance Mag 37:36-8 My '63
Lotte Goslar, Lupe Serrano, Ivan Allen, Ballets Bihari, Patricia Wilde co. Delacorte theatre, New York. J. Maskey. Dance Mag 38:72-3 O '64
Merri-Mimes in The firebird, Cricket theatre. M. Marks. Dance Mag 38:71 My '64
Music: your silent partner. J. Nunlist. il Dance Mag 38:48-9+ Ag '64
My words echo thus. D. Hering. il Dance Mag 38:42-5 F '64
Naked in its native beauty. G. Jackson. il Dance Mag 38:32-7 Ap '64
Nameless new dance. F. Bowers. il Harper 229:20+ D '64
Philip; latest teen-age dance craze in Britain. Newsweek 62:78 S 16 '63
Presstime news. See issues of Dance magazine

DANCING—*Continued*
Reviews. See issues of Dance magazine
Slipping the disque. il Time 83:62 Mr 20 '64
Step by step dance to slimness. il McCalls 90:154+ Mr '63
Surplus dance theatre, Stage 73. M. Marks. Dance Mag 38:71 Ap '64
See also
Choreography
Folk dancing
Indians of Mexico—Dances
Moving pictures—Dance films
Tap dancing
Television broadcasting—Dancing

Anecdotes, facetiae, satire, etc.
They could have danced all night, and did. S. McKelway. New Yorker 39:34-5 My 25 '63

Bibliography
Dancer's bookshelf. J. Anderson. Dance Mag 38:147 D '64
Dancers' bookshelf. J. Schlottmann. Dance Mag 38:36 Jl '64
Holiday treat: dance books. il Dance Mag 37:14-15 N '63

Childrens programs
Story-time dance theatre, P.S. 33. M. Marks. Dance Mag 38:85 Je '64

Competitions
Met award winners. D. Hering. il Dance Mag 38:50 Ag '64

History
From primitive dance to minuet to slop; excerpt from Book of the dance. A. De Mille. il N Y Times Mag p30-1+ O 27 '63

Photographs
Freud, electronics, dance. A. Hughes. N Y Times Mag p92-3 O 6 '63
See also
Photography of dancing

Production and direction
See Dance production

Publicity
Materials of publicity: dance photographs. D. Duncan. il Dance Mag 38:37-9 D '64
Materials of publicity: the press book. D. Duncan. Dance Mag 39:36+ Ja '65

Study and teaching
College or career for dancers? Bennington's answer. E. Stodelle. il Dance Mag 38:40-5 S '64
College scene this summer. il Dance Mag 38:14-19 Ap '64
Contrast in climates. M. Kuni. il Dance Mag 37:18-19 Je '63
Emphasis on music. M. Dorian. il Dance Mag 38:56-7 F '64
Open letter from Matt Mattox: a complaint. M. Mattox. il Dance Mag 38:145 D '64
Roots and wings; excerpts from address, June 2, 1963. V. Tanner. Dance Mag 37:16-17 N '63
Symbiosis: Pasadena art museum and dance classes. H. Mullin and V. Potter. il Dance Mag 37:38-41 F '63

Europe, Western
As I see it; American talent in Europe. H. De Becker. il Dance Mag 37:23-5 N '63

DANCING (in religion, folklore, etc)
Apparitions in dance. O. Maynard. il Dance Mag 37:32-5+ O '63
Dance is my beloved; Indian dance. M. Sarabhai. il Dance Mag 38:54-7 Ja '64
Drama at the altar; Spencer memorial Presbyterian church, Brooklyn Heights. il Time 83:58-9 Ja 3 '64
Koreans visit World's fair festival; Sahm-Chun-Li programs. il Dance Mag 38:41 Ap '64
Sacred dance at the crossroads. W. Sorell. il Dance Mag 38:24-5 Ag '64
Three masks of the deer dancer. O. Maynard. il Dance Mag 38:34-6+ Ja '64
To carol is to dance. S. Aker. il Dance Mag 38:40-1 D '64

DANCING, African
African dancers at the fair. R. F. Thompson. il Sat R 47:37-9 Jl 25 '64
Everyman's African roots; Primus-Borde school of dance. D. Leddick. il Dance Mag 38:20-1 O '64

DANCING, Argentine
Ballet espanol Alba, Reyes, 92nd street Y. J. Maskey. Dance Mag 38:64 Je '64
Tango. S. Bernardi. il Américas 16:20-6 D '64

DANCING, Bulgarian
Koutev Bulgarian national ensemble, Philharmonic Hall. M. Marks. Dance Mag 37:68 N '63

DANCING, Canadian
Modern dance festival in Toronto. W. Sorell. il Dance Mag 37:16+ My '63

DANCING, Chinese
Foo Hsing theatre at Morosco theatre. D. Hering. Dance Mag 37:57+ F '63
Hu troupe and Katherine Liu at Judson hall. M. Marks. Dance Mag 37:57-8 Mr '63

DANCING, Haitian
Les ballets folkloriques d'Haiti at Carnegie recital hall. M. Marks. Dance Mag 37:62 F '63

DANCING, Indian (East Indian)
Blindfolded traveller in New Delhi; excerpts from Encounters and celebrations. G. Fradier. il UNESCO Courier 16:4-11 S '63
Dance is my beloved. M. Sarabhai. il Dance Mag 38:54-7 Ja '64
Eternal dance of India; with photographs by Brian Blake. N. Cameron. Horizon 5:64-73 S '63
Great discovery of royal Chhau. F. Bowers. il Dance Mag 38:40-1+ Mr' 64
Mystery and the wonder: Shanta Rao. F. Bowers. il Dance Mag 37:46-9 O '63
Stories told with the hands. G. Fradier. il UNESCO Courier 16:8-9 S '63

DANCING, Indonesian
New spirit in an ancient dance; World's fair Indonesian dancers. M. Dehn. il Dance Mag 38:16+ S '64

DANCING, Israeli
Evening of Israeli dance and music at 92nd street Y. M. Marks. Dance Mag 37:56 Mr '63
Karmon Israeli dancers at Royale theatre. D. Hering. Dance Mag 37:11+ Jl '63

DANCING, Japanese
Contrast in climates. M. Kuni. il Dance Mag 37:18-19 Je '63
See also
Hanayagi, S.

DANCING, Korean
Folk dances for today. Recreation 56:63 F '63
Koreans visit World's fair festival; Sahm-Chun-Li program. il Dance Mag 38:41 Ap '64
Sahm-Chun-Li dancers and musicians, Philharmonic Hall. J. Maskey. Dance Mag 38:67 Je '64
Sahm-Chun-Li Korean dancers & musicians at Hunter college assembly hall. M. Marks. Dance Mag 38:62 Mr '64

DANCING, Mexican
See also
Ballet folklórico of Mexico

DANCING, Philippine
Bayanihan is back. il N Y Times Mag p 108-9 My 17 '64
Happy people; Bayanihan dancers. il Newsweek 63:75 Ap 20 '64
Reviews; Bayanihan Philippine dance company at New York state theater. D. Hering. Dance Mag 38:26+ Ag '64

DANCING, Russian
Isadora Duncan and Constantin Stanislavsky; with excerpts from letters. N. Rene. il Dance Mag 37:40-3 Jl '63
Vaganova; excerpts, tr. by V. Litvinoff. Dance Mag 38:40-3 Jl; 42-4+ Ag '64

DANCING, Spanish
Antonio and the Ballets de Madrid. H. Yurchenco. Mus Am 84:57 O '64
Antonio and the Ballets de Madrid, N.Y. city center. J. Maskey. Dance Mag 38:29-30+ N '64
Cousins; Antonio's Ballets de Madrid in New York. il Newsweek 64:88-9 S 28 '64
Music to my ears; Antonio-Rosario. I. Kolodin. Sat R 47:32 O 3 '64
See also
Flamenco

DANCING in art
Art salutes the dance. J. Canaday. il N Y Times Mag p26-7 Ap 12 '64
Man in space. B. Mumaw. il Dance Mag 38:44-5 Jl '64

DANCING in moving pictures. See Moving pictures—Dancing

DANE, Benjamin. See Van Der Kloot, W. G. jt. auth.

DANE, Chase
For reading out loud! PTA Mag 58:13 N '63

DANENBERG, Elsie N.
Salt marsh garden. Horticulture 42:46-7 N '64

DANES, Margaret F.
Notice to librarians. Library J 88:2059-62 My 15 '63

DANFORTH, Mrs Charles Haskell
Smithson and the Smithsonian. Am Heritage 15:26-7 D '63
DANFORTH foundation
First winners of the Danforth award for college teachers. il Sat R 46:65 Mr 23 '63
D'ANGELO, Gianna
Scaling the heights; interview, ed. by R. D. Daniels. por Opera N 28:32 Ja 25 '64
about
Quote: unquote. E. Helm. por Mus Am 83:17 Ag '63
D'ANGELO, Lou
You can't tell an author by his cover. Sat R 47:18-19 Ag 15 '64
DANGERFIELD, George
Steamboat's charter of freedom. Am Heritage 14:38-43+ O '63
DANIEL, Charles Ezra
One-man magnet for industry. il pors Bsns W p50-2+ Ja 11 '64
DANIEL, Dorothy
Brains versus brawn; judo expert. il pors Ebony 19:83-4+ N '63
DANIEL, Glyn
History by commission. Nation 197:55-6 Jl 27 '63
Megaliths and men. Natur Hist 73:46-53 Ap '64
DANIEL, J. C.
Humpy wonder fly. Field & S 69:38-9 Ag '64
Shooting the Snake. por Field & S 68:58-61 S '63
DANIEL, James
Fallacy behind the tax cut. Read Digest 84: 77-81 F '64
Incorruptible John Williams; the conscience of the Senate. Read Digest 84:105-10 My '64
Kenneth Keating, critic of our Cuban policy. Read Digest 82:190-2+ My '63
Negro colleges: their product and promise. Read Digest 85:33-4+ D '64
Our globetrotting students. Read Digest 85: 106-10 Ag '64
Paris takes an epic bath. Read Digest 83: 174-80 Ag '63
Threats to the battle against disease. Read Digest 85:114-18 O '64
—and Hubbell, J. G.
While America slept; condensation of Strike in the West. Read Digest 82:60-6+ Mr '63
DANIEL, Jean
Ben Bella and Castro. New Repub 149:9-11 O 5 '63
Ben Bella's triumph. New Repub 149:18-20 Jl 6 '63
Boycotting Cuba; whose interest does it serve? New Repub 149:19-22 D 28 '63
Camus as journalist. New Repub 150:19-21 Je 13 '64
Can de Gaulle do it? New Repub 148:9-11 Mr 2 '63
De Gaulle and red China. New Repub 150: 9-11 F 1 '64
De Gaulle and the strike. New Repub 148:10-11 Ap 13 '63
De Gaulle's Vietnam. New Repub 149:7-9 S 14 '63
Europe; renaissance of chauvinism. New Repub 148:15-16 F 23 '63
Foreign alarm over Goldwater. New Repub 151:34+ S 19 '64
France, 1964. New Repub 150:14-17 My 2 '64
Further clarification; concerning interviews with Kennedy and Castro. New Repub 149: 6-7 D 21 '63
Judgment of Daniel. Reporter 30:10+ F 27 '64
Paris notes. New Repub 151:27-9 O 24 '64
Pierre Mendès-France. New Repub 150:9-11 F 29 '64
Sartre: fragments of an autobiography. New Repub 151:19-21 O 10 '64
Unofficial envoy. New Repub 149:15-20 D 14 '63
What de Gaulle and JFK have in common. New Repub 149:5-6 O 19 '63
When Castro heard the news. New Repub 149:7-9 D 7 '63
Why Gaston Defferre? Harper 229:85-8+ Jl '64
about
How Castro tried to rewrite history. il U S News 55:14 D 23 '63
Reporter engagé. por Newsweek 62:70 D 23 '63
What's fit to print? Reporter 30:12 Ja 2 '64; Reply with rejoinder. J. Daniel. 30:10+ F 27 '64
DANIEL, John
Pride, prejudice and wit. Nation 198:170-1 F 17 '64
DANIEL, Margaret (Truman)
What did you want most at seventeen? ed. by A. Ebert. por Seventeen 22:132-3 S '63
DANIEL, Oliver
Anarchy and order. Sat R 46:73 O 26 '63
Behind the Pilsener curtain. Sat R 46:55 D 28 '63
Dutch treat from Donemus. Sat R 47:40-1 Jl 25 '64
1895, Hindemith, 1963. Mus Am 84:58-9 Ja '64
Enlivening avant-garde. Sat R 47:50+ Mr 28 '64
Far east of Boston. Sat R 46:124 O 12 '63
Jubilee fare. Sat R 46:71 Mr 30 '63
Moderns from Louisville. Sat R 46:77+ S 28 '63
Opera conference in Hamburg. Sat R 47:40-1 Ag 22 '64
Ten from Cleveland. Sat R 47:58 N 28 '64
DANIEL, Price
Assessing the blame in the President's death; excerpts from address, December 14, 1963. por U S News 55:73 D 30 '63
DANIEL, Ralph W.
Teen-agers and school. PTA Mag 57:18-20 Ap '63
DANIEL, Robert S.
Electroencephalographic correlogram ratios and their stability. bibliog Science 145:721-3 Ag 14 '64
DANIEL, William H.
Keep on the grass! play lawn. Am Home 67: 80-1 S '64
DANIEL Boone regional library. See Columbia, Mo. public library
DANIELL, Rosemary
Bridal luncheon; poem. Atlan 214:58 Ag '64
DANIELL, Thomas
India in aquatints; exhibition at the University of Chicago. il Time 81:52 F 8 '63
DANIELL, William
India in aquatints; exhibition at the University of Chicago. il Time 81:52 F 8 '63
DANIELS, Ada M.
Parent and child. N Y Times Mag p 109-10 S 13 '64
DANIELS, Brett
Passing scene. Nat R 14:202-3, 253-4 Mr 12-26 '63
DANIELS, Clem
Mr Halfback. H. L. Masin. por Sr Schol 85:34 S 16 '64
DANIELS, Ethel
Root feeding method effective in care of trees and shrubs. Flower Grower 50:58 Ag '63
DANIELS, George
Amazing plastic ropes, they splice themselves. Pop Sci 184:142-8 Je '64
Big idea: a spray booth. por Pop Sci 183: 100-1 S '63
Buying or building docks, piers and floats. Pop Mech 120:152-7 Ag '63
How to keep your fiberglass boat young and floating. Pop Sci 185:98-100+ S '64
How to sharpen everything. Pop Sci 185: 136-40+ Ag; 174-7+ O '64
New way to save an old boat. Pop Sci 182: 127-30 F '63
New wonder products for boat repairs. Pop Sci 182:123-5+ Mr '63
Pry bars: lift five tons or pull a nail. Pop Sci 182:102-4+ Je '63
Stick with the right glue. Pop Mech 119:179-83+ F '63
Tackle it better with tape. Pop Sci 185:112-16+ Ag '64
Which shop vises do you need Pop Sci 186: 162-5+ Ja '65
DANIELS, Guy
Cat and the starling (from Krylov) poem. New Repub 151:22 Jl 25 '64
DANIELS, Jane W.
Aid through aides. por Library J 88:2194-7 Je 1 '63
DANIELS, Robert V.
Conflicts & affinities. Commentary 38:86-8 S '64
Social democratic witness. Commentary 35: 84-6 Ja '63
DANIELS, Thomas E.
Vermont Indians; summary of booklet. por Hobbies 69:112-13+ Mr '64
DANIELSON, Irvin
He says think small. R. B. Weeghman. il por Flying 74:31+ F '64
DANIELSON, Nora
March; poem. Horn Bk 39:217 Ap '63
DANIELSON, Phyllis
Aluminum maskmaking. Design 65:195 My '64
DANINOS, Pierre
Le snob-snob à l'etranger; excerpt from Snobissimo. Harper 230:119 Ja '65
Snobs of Paris. Vogue 141:124-7+ Ap 1 '63

DANISE, Giuseppe
Giuseppe Danise, January 11, 1882-January 9, 1963. R. Lawrence. por Opera N 27:13 Mr 2 '63
DANISH cookery. See Cookery. Danish
DANISH furniture. See Furniture, Danish
DANISH pastry. See Pastry
DANISH pottery. See Pottery, Danish
DANISH silver. See Silverware
DANKER, William J.
Behind the bamboo. Christian Cent 80:713 My 29 '63
Two worlds or none. Christian Cent 80:737-9 Je 5 '63
DANKLEFF, Richard
Emerson; poem. Mlle 57:164 Je '63
DANNEMORA prison. See Prisons—New York (state)
DANNHAUSER, Werner J.
Brink of moderation. Commentary 37:92-4 My '64
Goebbels's nature. Commentary 35:272-6 Mr '63
Philosophy and Judaism. Commentary 38:92-5 N '64
Terrorism. Commentary 36:90-2 Jl '63
D'ANNUNZIO, Gabriele. See Annunzio, G. d'
DANTAS, Francisco Clementino San Tiago
Letter of March 25, 1963, from Finance minister Dantas to Administrator Bell. Dept State Bul 48:558-60 Ap 15 '63
about
Brazilian brings home the bacon. il por Bsns W p82+ Mr 30 '63
Brink of bankruptcy. por Time 81:22 Mr 22 '63
New look in U.S. aid; strings attached. U S News 54:6 Ap 8 '63
People of the week. il por U S News 54:22 Mr 25 '63
DANTE ALIGHIERI
BCD triology. P. W. Schmidtchen. il por Hobbies 68:106-7 Ja '64
Dante's Divine comedy in Esperanto. il UNESCO Courier 16:32-3 Je '63
DANTO, Arthur
Santayana and the task ahead. Nation 197: 437-40 D 21 '63
DANUBE RIVER
Danube, Europe's great waterway. il UNESCO Courier 17:38-9 Jl '64
Down the Danube. M. Elsy. il Travel 120:47-51 Jl '63
Haven on the Danube. C. Mydans. il Atlan 214:178+ N '64
DANVILLE, Ill.
Welcome home, Bobby. il Ebony 19:64-6+ Je '64
DANVILLE, Va.
Danville on trial. S. Belfrage. New Repub 149:11-12 N 2 '63
Friends of Danville; white sympathizers who took action to aid Negro desegregation. A. Karro. America 110:633-5 My 9 '64
It did happen here; subpoena of the editorial staffs. R. L. Tobin. il Sat R 46:65-6 S 14 '63; Discussion. 46:49 O 12; 82 N 9 '63
Uses of violence; outrageous treatment of the American Negro. Nation 197:2-3 Jl 6 '63
DANZIG, Allison
Greatest tennis player of all time. N Y Times Mag p 19+ D 22 '63
DANZIG, David
Meaning of Negro strategy. Commentary 37: 41-6 F; 38:10 Jl '64
Rightists, racists, and separatists: a white bloc in the making? Commentary 38:28-32 Ag '64
DANZIS, Alan L.
Nonsense box. Pop Electr 19:47-8 Jl '63
DAPHNE; opera. See Strauss, R.
DA PONTE, Lorenzo
Libretto as literature. F. V. Grunfeld. il Reporter 31:37-40 D 31 '64
DAPPER, Gloria
It's what's up top that counts. Sat R 46: 48-9+ D 21 '63
School boards spokesman. Sat R 47:73+ Mr 21 '64
Spokesman for the two-year college. Sat R 47:55 D 19 '64
DARBONNE, Rodger Lee
In Xanadu, U.S.A. NEA J 53:51-2 F '64
DARDI, Virgil David
$5,000,000 swindle. il por Time 81:95 Mr 15 '63
DARGA, Klaus
Master goof in Amsterdam. L. Evans. il Sports Illus 21:48 Jl 20 '64
DARGOMYZHSKII, Aleksandr Sergeevich
Dargomyzhsky: first recordings of two operas. P. L. Miller. Am Rec G 30:838+ My '64
DARIAUX, Genevieve Antoine
Sensible woman's guide to elegance; excerpts from Elegance. Redbook 122:66-7+ Mr '64
DARIEN, Conn.
Darien's dolce vita; narcotics charges. Time 84:60 N 27 '64
How to keep teens out of trouble. R. Carson. il Parents Mag 39:48-9+ Je '64
Overprivileged; Darien, Conn. delinquents. il Newsweek 61:29 My 27 '63
Twice as big, better than new. A. W. Saburn. il Am City 78:91-3 F '63
DARIN, Bobby
Six quitters. por Esquire 62:103 S '64
DARK, Alvin Ralph
Beanball my men? we'll beanball you, Alvin vows darkly. D. Moser. il por Life 55:28-28A Jl 26 '63
Crossing the Delaware with Alvin Dark. R. Creamer. por Sports Illus 19:46-8 Ag 26 '63
Faith or works; concerning interview with Stan Isaacs. Sports Illus 21:7 Ag 17 '64
Giant issue. il por Newsweek 64:54 Ag 17 '64
Giant-sized trouble. por Time 84:44-5 Ag 14 '64
Time of trial for Alvin Dark. R. H. Boyle. il pors Sports Illus 21:26-31 Jl 6 '64
DARK, Harris Edward
Experts discuss twelve driving emergencies. Todays Health 42:38-42 Mr '64
Exploding myths about oil changes. Pop Mech 120:93-7+ N '63
One man's battle against poison. Todays Health 42:43+ Mr '64
Premium choice Travel 119:44-5 F '63
Return of the classic Cord. por Pop Mech 120:82-4+ Ag '63
Route sixty-six; boulevard to the Golden West. Todays Health 41:28-9+ Je '63
Twenty-minute safety tour can save you and/or your home. Todays Health 41:36-7+ F '63
Wonderful world of antique cars. Pop Sci 184:82-7+ Ja '64
—See Schultz, M. J. jt. auth.
DARK, Harry, and Dark, Phyl
Is your car child-safe? Todays Health 41:14-17 Jl '63
DARK, Phyl. See Dark, H. jt. auth.
DARK corners; drama. See Koven, S.
DARK glasses. See Sun glasses
DARK; story. See Updike, J.
DARKNESS
Why is the sky dark at night? B. Bliven. Read Digest 83:203-4+ Jl '63
DARKROOMS. See Photography—Studios and darkrooms
DARLING, Frances C.
Book caravan. Horn Bk 39:207-10 Ap '63
DARLING, Richard L.
School library reporter. Sch Life 46:19 N '63; 41-2 Ja; 27 Mr; 6 Je '64
School library services for the culturally deprived child. bibliog f Sch Life 46:18-20 O '63
DARLING, Robert B.
Heat from lights re-used for economy. Arch Rec 136:211-12 O '64
DARLINGTON, Alice B.
Mrs Ambassador; interview. ed. by A. M. Lingg. por Opera N 28:6 D 14 '63
DARLINGTON, Celia
Cruises that click. Motor B 112:40+ S '63
Little bird that snorted. Sat R 46:84-5 O 12 '63
Little now. Atlan 214:167-8 N '64
Matter of form(s) Atlan 212:134-7 N '63
Put yourself in the editor's chair. Writer 77:26-7 O '64
Semper paratus. Motor B 111:34-5+ Je '63
'62 club of the year: San Leandro. Motor B 111:51+ My '63
Steamboat on San Francisco Bay. Motor B 111:50+ My '63
What's up below? Motor B 113:46-8 Mr '64
DARLINGTON manufacturing company. See Deering, Milliken and company
DARLINGTONIA. See Pitcher plants
DARNBOROUGH, Anne
New sights and sounds in the classroom. UNESCO Courier 17:12-14 F '64
DARNELL, A. J. and Libby, W. F.
Indium antimonide: the metallic form at atmospheric pressure. bibliog Science 139: 1301 Mr 29 '63
—and others
Indium telluride metal. bibliog Science 141: 713-14 Ag 23 '63
DARRACH, Henry Bradford, Jr
Letter from the publisher. B. M. Auer. il por Time 82:21 S 20 '63

DARRELL, Margery
Mary McCarthy and the group. Look 28:106-8+ F 25 '64
DARRELL, Robert Donaldson
Case of the tilted stylus. Hi Fi 13:34-6+ My '63
Organs without pipes. Hi Fi 14:27-30+ Jl '64
Second look at dynagroove. Hi Fi 13:92 Ag '63
Short guide to test records. Hi Fi 13:48-51+ D '63
Sonic showcase. Hi Fi 14:90 Ja; 102 F; 95 Je; 101 Ag; 115 D '64; 15:107 F '65
Stereo reference shelf. Hi Fi 14:53-5+ D '64
Tape deck. See issues of High Fidelity
Tapes from the professionals. Hi Fi 13:48-50 Ag '63
DARROW, Charles
Play-money game that made millions; Monopoly. J. F. Wilkinson. il Sports Illus 19: 52-4+ D 2 '63
DART, Francis E.
Rub of cultures. For Affairs 41:360-71 Ja '63
DART, Richard Pousette-. See Pousette-Dart, R.
DARTMOUTH college, Hanover, N.H.
Bob Blackman and his Big Green. C. S. Wren. il Look 28:89-92+ N 3 '64
It is . . . a small college . . . yet, there are those who love it; Dartmouth college v. Woodward; with letters by R. Choate. R. N. Current. il Am Heritage 14:10-15+ Ag '63
Jesuit at Dartmouth; reflections on the problem of good and evil in education. T. V. Purcell. America 108:534-6+ Ap 20 '63
Message from the Dartmouth Christian union. T. Mitchell. Negro Hist Bul 26:186 Mr '63
School for alumni. il Time 83:50 F 7 '64
Hopkins center
Campus center designed to provide creative arts context for social activities. il Arch Rec 136:120-1 D '64
DARWIN, Charles
Tierra del Fuego; excerpts from The cloud forest. P. Matthiessen. il Américas 16:39-42 F '64
DARWIN, Erasmus
Erasmus Darwin, by D. King-Hele. Review Newsweek 63:87 F 10 '64
Man of enlightenment. M. Peckham. por Sat R 47:44-5 Mr 28 '64
Sage of Lichfield. il por Time 83:96+ F 21 '64
DAS, Nirmal K.
Chromosomal and nucleolar RNA synthesis in root tips during mitosis. bibliog Science 140:1231-3 Je 14 '63
DASHBOARDS, Automobile. See Automobiles—Dashboards
DATA processing, Electronic. See Electronic data processing
DATA processing centers
Data-processing center in the State department of education. J. E. Bean. Sch Life 46: 10-11 Jl '64
Rise of the service center. il Duns R 84:pt2 120-2+ S '64
DATA processing equipment company. See Control data corporation
DATA storage and retrieval systems. See Information storage and retrieval systems
DATA tapes
Tape-punching for bibliography: standards to be established. Pub W 185:85 Je 1 '64
DATE palm. See Palms
DATEO, George P. jr. See Roth, L. M. jt. auth.
DATES (history) See Chronology, Historical
DATING
Am I really in love? questions and answers. A. Wood. il Seventeen 23:136-7+ Je '64
Any questions, please? J. Wescott. il Seventeen 22:8 Je '63
Boy dates girl. Gay Head. See issues of Senior scholastic
Boy's advice on coping with boys; questions and answers. H. Makow. Seventeen 24:92 Ja '65
Boys and girls together; excerpt from Moving into manhood. W. W. Bauer. il Todays Health 41:54-5+ S '63
Boys and other beasts; excerpts. B. Lang. McCalls 91:68+ F; 74+ Mr; 78+ Ap '64 (to be cont)
Break-up. J. Wescott. il Seventeen 23:10 O '64
College boy counsels on boy problems; questions and answers. S. Adams. Seventeen 23: 98 Ja '64
Colleges and public decency. R. Kirk. Nat R 16:112 F 11 '64; Discussion. 16:248 Mr 24 '64
Come into my parlor; excerpt from Boys and other beasts. B. Lang. il McCalls 91:66+ Jl '64
Does a good date make a good mate? D. Sugarman and R. Hochstein. il Seventeen 23:148-9+ Ap '64
Father Carey's chickens. il Time 81:52 Mr 8 '63
Good-by, my love. J. Wescott. il Seventeen 22:22 My '63
Good manners in love; excerpts from Seventeen book of etiquette and entertaining. E. A. Haupt. Seventeen 23:26 Mr '64
How much kissing is too much kissing? questions and answers. A. Wood. il Seventeen 22:86-7+ Jl '63
How to hold a boy without hanging on; questions and answers. A. Wood. il Seventeen 22:216-17+ Ag '63
How to meet boys; excerpt from Seventeen book of etiquette and entertaining. E. A. Haupt. Seventeen 22:40 N '63
I've been dropped; questions and answers. A. Wood. il Seventeen 23:158-9+ N '64
Love on the campus. J. Poppy. il Look 27: 66-71 Ag 13 '63
Man talk: the importance of saying no. D. Newman and R. Benton. il Mlle 58:160+ Ap '64
Must dating always be a game? questions and answers. A. Wood. il Seventeen 22:154-5+ S '63
Second date; questions and answers. J. Wescott. il Seventeen 22:17 Jl '63
Secret system: how boys grade girls. A. Penname. il Seventeen 23:142-3+ N '64
Six boys discuss dating and morals; symposium. il Seventeen 23:86-9+ Jl '64
Talking it over with Gay Head; questions and answers (cont of) Boy dates girl. Gay Head. See issues of Senior scholastic
Ten-dollar understanding: brothel behavior of the college boy. J. Richardson. Esquire 62:101+ S '64
Too much sex on campus. J. L. Barron. il Ladies Home J 81:48+ Ja '64; Same abr. Read Digest 84:59-62 My '64
Whatever happened to courtship? A. Moss. Mlle 56:151+ Ap '63
When I go out on a date. J. Wescott. il Seventeen 22:38 Mr '63
Why didn't he call again? questions and answers. A. Wood. il Seventeen 22:124-5+ Mr '63
Will I ever find a boy I really love? questions and answers. A. Wood. il Seventeen 22: 156-7+ My '63
See also
Courtship
Anecdotes, facetiae, satire, etc.
New date book. D. Newman and R. Benton. il Mlle 57:82-5 Je '63
DATING, Radiocarbon. See Radiocarbon dating
DATO, Low Yat
Chinese big shots branch out. il por Fortune 70:60 D '64
DATTA, P. R. and others
Conversion of p,p′ DDT to p,p′ DDD in the liver of the rat. bibliog Science 145:1052-3 S 4 '64
DATURA
Angel trumpet. D. Holland. il Pop Gard 15: 8+ Mr '64
DAUBER wasps. See Wasps
DAUBIGNY, Charles François
Charles François Daubigny, forerunner of impressionism. R. N. Gregg. il por Antiques 85:548-51 My '64
Daubigny's gentle naturalism. il Time 83:86-7+ My 15 '64
DAUGHERTY, A. C.
Tooling up for profits; address, May 7, 1964. Vital Speeches 30:530-3 Je 15 '64
DAUGHERTY, Harry Micajah
Four mysteries of Warren Harding. F. Russell. il Am Heritage 14:4-9+ Ap '63
DAUGHERTY, John, and Daugherty, Molly
Air your knowledge. Sci Digest 55:45-7 Ja '64
Are you a cave man? Sci Digest 54:5-7 D '63
Big drip; questions and answers. Sci Digest 55:45-7 F '64
Chemistry in the raw; questions and answers. Sci Digest 56:76-8 S '64
Colorful quiz. Sci Digest 55:43-5 My '64
Do you know your weather? Sci Digest 54: 41-3 O '63
Gem of a quiz. Sci Digest 54:25-7 N '63
Hereditary quiz. Sci Digest 56:89-91 N '64
Hot and cold quiz. Sci Digest 57:83-5 Ja '65
Know your fibers and fabrics; questions and answers. Sci Digest 56:27-9 O '64
Never have enough time? Sci Digest 53:55-7 Je '63

DAUGHERTY, John, and Daugherty, Molly—*Continued*
Restful quiz. Sci Digest 55:5-7 Mr '64
Touching quiz. Sci Digest 55:5-7 Je '64
Way out quiz. Sci Digest 55:66-8 Ap '64
What do those food labels mean? questions and answers. Sci Digest 56:5-7 Ag '64
What you hear and what you don't. Sci Digest 54:87-90 S '63
What's your quake I.Q? questions and answers. Sci Digest 56:57-9 Jl '64
Wood you know? questions and answers. Sci Digest 56:93-5 D '64

DAUGHERTY, Louise G.
Working with disadvantaged parents. NEA J 52:18-20 D '63

DAUGHERTY, Molly. See Daugherty, J. jt. auth.

DAUGHTER of her own; story. See Gerber, M. J.

DAUGHTER of the chief of police; story. See Boles, P. D.

DAUGHTERS
Hunting, anyone? G. L. Voss. il Outdoor Life 131:42-3+ F '63

DAUGHTERS and mothers. See Parent-child relationship

DAUGHTERS and parents. See Parent-child relationship

DAUGHTERS of the American revolution
Daughters. M. Kempton. New Repub 148:6-7 My 4 '63
Dear Daughters. K. Crawford. Newsweek 61:29 Ap 29 '63

D'AULAIRE, Ingri Parin. See Aulaire, I. P. d'

DAUTERMAN, Carl Christian
Colossal for the medium: Meissen porcelain sculptures. Antiques 85:214-17 F '64

DAVENEL, George
Career planning for the age of automation. Parents Mag 39:74-6+ S '64

DAVENPORT, Arthur
Double buck. pors Field & S 69:30-1+ D '64
Pine tree pheasants. Field & S 68:56-7+ F '64

DAVENPORT, Beulah. See Shelton, B. C. jt. auth.

DAVENPORT, Guy
Archilochus: a sheaf of poems and fragments. Poetry 101:404-9 Mr '63
Books for Christmas. Nat R 15:532+ D 17 '63
Christmas picture books. Nat R 16:1113-14 D 15 '64
Happy birthday, Wm. Shaxper. Nat R 16:874-6 O 6 '64

DAVENPORT, Gwen
Million-dollar question: story. McCalls 91:98-9 Mr '64
Perfect wedding: story. McCalls 90:112-13 My '63

DAVENPORT, John
Economics and human values. Yale R 53:381-94 Mr '64
Free vs. the manipulated society; address, November 9, 1964. Vital Speeches 31:125-8 D 1 '64
Mr Berle's nostalgia. Fortune 67:94+ Je '63
Ugly face in Africa. Fortune 67:84+ F '63

DAVENPORT, Marcia
Revival of bel canto. Opera N 28:8-13 Ja 11 '64

DAVENPORT, Roy Kirklin
Big man in biggest building. il pors Ebony 18:84+ Ap '63

DAVERN, Jeremyn
Entrée. New Yorker 40:22-4 Je 27 '64

DAVES, Delmer
Auteur theory. A. Knight. Sat R 46:22 My 4 '63

DAVEY, Daniel, and company
Davey company selling scientific translations. Pub W 186:77 Ag 24 '64

DAVID, king of Israel
Kingly glory and ordeal; David made the Hebrews into a nation. R. Wallace. il pors Life 57:60-5 D 25 '64

DAVID, Henry
Ill-fed, clad, housed, and ill. Sat R 46:23 Ag 31 '63
Plan today for a richer tomorrow. Sat R 47:33-4 Ag 15 '64
Problems of prosperity. Sat R 47:58-9 Ja 11 '64

DAVID, Irene. See David, L. jt. auth.

DAVID, Lester
New miracles of baby surgery. Good H 156:76-7+ Ap '63
Now! many women can have the babies they want. Good H 157:79+ O '63
Shocking price of parental anger. Good H 158:86-7+ Mr '64; Same abr. Read Digest 85:181-2+ S '64
—and David, Irene
Do ministers really understand people? Good H 156:65+ Mr '63
Healing power of love. Good H 157:50+ N '63

DAVID, Paul T.
TV image. Nation 197:413-14 D 14 '63

DAVIDIA involucrata. See Dove trees

DAVIDON, William C. and others
Perils of deterrence. Bul Atomic Sci 19:28 Mr '63

DAVIDS, Richard C.
Friends, in the name of Allah. por Farm J 87:20 D '63
Grandfather to half a million kids. Farm J 88:28-9+ Jl '64
I saw Bethlehem shining. Farm J 87:32+ D '63
New York world's fair. Farm J 88:44-5+ F '64

DAVIDSOHN, Israel
Research; medicine's unfinished business. por Todays Health 41:16, 19 My '63

DAVIDSON, Angus
(tr) See Moravia, A. Escape
(tr) See Moravia, A. Loveliest thing of all
(tr) See Moravia, A. Tough nut

DAVIDSON, Basil
Africa: the face behind the mask. Horizon 5:38-59 Mr '63

DAVIDSON, Bill
Buck$ Benny rides again. Sat Eve Post 236:26-8+ Mr 2 '63
Case for and against induced labor. Good H 158:58-9+ Ja '64
Double image of Lee Remick. Sat Eve Post 236:38-9 My 18 '63
Fantastic Walt Disney. Sat Eve Post 237:66-8+ N 7 '64
Great Asian flu mystery. Sat Eve Post 236:58 Ap 27 '63
Great DMSO mystery. Sat Eve Post 237:72-4 Jl 25 '64
Great Scott. Sat Eve Post 236:88-9 N 16 '63
How Mafia killers got their man. Sat Eve Post 237:38-40 O 31 '64
How the mob controls Chicago. Sat Eve Post 236:17-27 N 9 '63
Men who rule the stars. Sat Eve Post 237:81-5 O 24 '64
New Orleans: Cosa nostra's Wall Street. Sat Eve Post 237:15-21 F 29 '64
Old S.O.B. does it again. Sat Eve Post 237:36+ My 23 '64
Oldest Fonda. McCalls 90:88-9+ My '63
Stan Freberg, his private war. Sat Eve Post 236:56-7 F 9 '63
TV's prosperous pitchmen. Sat Eve Post 236:26-7 Ag 24 '63
Thistles in paradise: truth about retirement housing. Sat Eve Post 238:19-25 Ja 16 '65
Washington; a city in trouble. Sat Eve Post 236:17-23 Jl 13 '63
—See Davidson, Muriel, jt. auth.

DAVIDSON, Bruce
Child's guide to sport in New York. il Sports Illus 20:66-75 Ap 20 '64
Sight of privacy. I. C. Lieb. il U S Camera 26:70-3 F '63

DAVIDSON, Chandler
America's dirty war. Nation 199:299-303 N 2 '64
Oil patch; roughnecks and operators on a forgotten frontier. Harper 229:41-6 Ag '64

DAVIDSON, Clarissa Start
Night lights. por Library J 28:2544-6 Je 15 '64

DAVIDSON, Homer L.
Better model control for $5.50. Pop Electr 19:66-7 S '63
Build the tune-table. Pop Electr 20:49-50 Je '64
Easy start tool. Pop Electr 20:88-9 Ja '64
Family message center. Pop Electr 21:79-81 Ag '64
Touch, it's on; touch again, it's off. Pop Sci 184:125 Ja '64

DAVIDSON, Hugh
Canadian composers: differences, contradictions, anomalies. Mus Am 83:20-1+ S '63
State of the unions. Mus Am 83:23+ O '63

DAVIDSON, J. A.
After Moncure Daniel Conway. Christian Cent 80:277 F 27 '63
Justice for Joad. Christian Cent 80:1238-9 O 9 '63
Victorian heretic. Christian Cent 81:17 Ja 1 '64

DAVIDSON, Jacqueline
Maine & American artists, 1710-1963. Am Artist 27:32-9+ D '63

DAVIDSON, Joan K.
Kids in Wrangell. Reporter 31:38-40 N 5 '64

DAVIDSON, John F.
Fantasy; poem. Christian Cent 80:458 Ap 10 '63
Tiny tempest; poem. Christian Cent 80:1046 Ag 28 '63

DAVIDSON, Margaret
Look where the laundry is. Ladies Home J 80:84 S '63
Trees: stars of Christmas. Ladies Home J 81:50-3 D '64
DAVIDSON, Marshall B.
Carl Bodmer's unspoiled West. Am Heritage 14:43-65 Ap '63
Voyage pittoresque aux Etats-unis de l'Amérique par Paul Svignine; an appreciation. Am Heritage 15:49-51+ F '64
DAVIDSON, Muriel
Are movies fit for our families? Good H 157: 94-7+ Jl '63
Deadly favor. Ladies Home J 80:53-7 N '63; Same abr. with title Abortion, the deadly favor. Read Digest 84:189-92 F '64
Let me entertain you. pors Sat Eve Post 237:72-3 My 16 '64
Shirley MacLaine sounds off. Sat Eve Post 236:30, 33 N 30 '63
Under the Lemmon skin. Ladies Home J 80:115-19 S '63
(ed) See Victor, T. Drama the cameras missed
—and Davidson, Bill
Van Johnson: back from the edge. McCalls 90:86-7+ Ag '63
DAVIDSON, Ruth
Auction notes. Antiques 86:324+ S '64
Books about antiques. See issues of Antiques
In the galleries. Antiques 86:622 N '64
In the museums. See issues of Antiques
Paintings and antiques. Antiques 84:556-61 N '63
Shop talk. See issues of Antiques
Special events. Antiques 83:224, 334+, 468+, 574+; 85:336 F-My '63, Mr '64
Summer exhibitions in Paris. Antiques 86: 195 Ag '64
DAVIDSON, Thomas
Thomas Davidson and the New life fellowship. W. S. Smith. Christian Cent 80: 642-5 My 15 '63
DAVIDSON, Treat
Bullfrog ballet filmed in flight. il Nat Geog Mag 123:790-9 Je '63
DAVIDSON, William R. See Doody, A. F. jt. auth.
DAVIE, Alan
Bienal's best; São Paulo bienal in Brazil. il Time 82:90 O 4 '63
DAVIE, Donald
Autumn imagined; Hot hands; Where depths are surfaces; Vying; Red mills; July; Battlefield; poems. Poetry 102:312-16 Ag '63
DAVIE, Earl W. and Ratnoff, O. D.
Waterfall sequence for intrinsic blood clotting. bibliog Science 145:1310-12 S 18 '64
DAVIES, Arthur Bowen
Story behind a great art event; Armory show. B. B. Perlman. il Am Artist 27:26-9+ F '63
DAVIES, David S. and Kaplan, R. A.
Activated carbon treatment. Am City 80: 78-81 Ja '65
DAVIES, John Paton, Jr
Another view of the Latin-American problem. N Y Times Mag p 15+ Ag 25 '63
Crisis of casualness in Latin America. Harper 229:12+ Ag '64
Sino-Soviet rift: an old, old story. Reporter 29:32-4+ Ag 15 '63

about

Martyrdom by diplomacy. L. J. Halle. New Repub 151:17-18 O 24 '64
Old hand speaks out. C. B. Marshall. Reporter 31:52-3 S 10 '64
DAVIES, Mandy Rice-. See Rice-Davies, M.
DAVIES, P.
Audio. Mus Am 84:57 S; 47 O; 52 N '64
DAVIES, Rhys
Friendly stove. House & Gard 124:216-17 O '63
I will keep her company; story. New Yorker 39:26-34 Ja 4 '64
Little heiress; story. New Yorker 40:31-6 Ag 29 '64
DAVIES, Richard Llewelyn-. See Llewelyn-Davies, R.
DAVIES, Robertson
Educating for the future. por Atlan 214:140-4 N '64
Northern muse. Holiday 35:10+ Ap '64
DAVIES, Ruth A.
Planning together in the instructional materials center. ALA Bul 57:158 F '63
DAVIES, W. L. and others
Antiviral activity of 1-adamantanamine (amantadine) Science 144:862-3 My 15 '64
DAVIES, Wilbur
Cooperative advertising: how to make it cooperative; summary of address. Pub W 186:20 O 26 '64

DAVILA, Pedrarias. See Pedrarias
DAVIS, Al
I don't need money, I need points. W. Bingham. il pors Sports Illus 19:27-9 N 4 '63
DAVIS, Allen F.
Social workers and the Progress party, 1912-1916. bibliog f Am Hist R 69:671-88 Ap '64
DAVIS, Anna King
Summer in the blackjack oak. Audubon Mag 66:326-7 S '64
DAVIS, Arnold M.
This month in the North (cont of) Things to do this month in the North. See issues of Popular gardening
DAVIS, B. L.
X-ray diffraction data on two high-pressure phases of calcium carbonate. bibliog Science 145:489-91 Jl 31 '64
DAVIS, Ben Arthur
Southern pointers. See issues of Flower grower
DAVIS, Bette
Lesson in survival; interview, ed. by W. Marchant. por Holiday 36:83-4+ Ag '64

about

Bette Davis' biggest victory. K. Baskette. il pors Good H 157:30+ Ag '63
DAVIS, Briant L. and Adams, L. H.
High-pressure polymorphs in the silver iodide phase diagram. bibliog Science 146:519-21 O 23 '64
DAVIS, Charles
Rich significance of baptism; excerpt from Sacraments of initiation. Cath World 199: 293-300 Ag '64
Seminary theology; excerpts. Commonweal 80:43-6 Ap 3 '64
Starting-point of Mariology; excerpt from Theology for today. Cath World 197:15-20 Ap '63
Theological asides. America 108:861; 109:98, 236, 457, 710; 110:91, 281, 514, 720; 111:42, 158-9, 353, 558, 803 Je 15, Jl 27, S 7, O 19, N 30 '63, Ja 18, F 29, Ap 11, My 23, Jl 11, Ag 15, S 26, N 7, D 19 '64
DAVIS, Charles Carroll
Biology is not a totem pole; letter. Science 141:308+ Jl 26 '63
DAVIS, Charles T.
Impressionism as a cultural impulse. bibliog Sch Arts 63:12-15 F '64
DAVIS, Christopher
Belmarch; story. Esquire 60:138-9 D '63
Silence; story. Sat Eve Post 236:48-55 N 9 '63
DAVIS, Clint
He knows. il Liv Wildn 82:20 Wint '62
DAVIS, Daniel S.
(comp) As other Presidents took the oath; excerpts from inaugural addresses. N Y Times Mag p22+ Ja 17 '65
(comp) On film. N Y Times Mag p60+ S 13 '64
DAVIS, David C.
In praise of over-the-shoulder reading. Sr Schol 83:10T-12T O 4 '63
It's this way, kid! Horn Bk 40:523-7 O '64
Who'll kill the mockingbirds? Horn Bk 39: 265-71 Je '63
DAVIS, David E. See Christian, J. J. jt. auth.
DAVIS, Donald R. and Libby, W. F.
Positive-ion chemistry: high yields of heavy hydrocarbons from solid methane by ionizing radiation. bibliog Science 144:991-2 My 22 '64
DAVIS, Douglas M.
Court tennis: the royal game. Holiday 36:158+ D '64
(ed) See Golding, W. Conversation with Golding
DAVIS, E. Dexter
Senior gardening. Horticulture 41:379 Jl '63
DAVIS, E. Louise
Big four speak. por Library J 88:2069-70+ My 15 '63
—and Allen, P. H.
(comps) New fall children's books. Library J 89:4152-87 O 15 '64
(eds) Junior books appraised. See issues of Library journal to May 1963
—and others
(eds) Junior books appraised. See issues of Library journal beginning June, 1963
(comps) New fall children's books. Library J 88:4028-66 O 15 '63
(comps) New spring juvenile books. Library J 88:1320-55 Mr 15 '63
DAVIS, Edwina
Medical language made easy. Todays Health 43:34-7 Ja '65
DAVIS, Elmer
Man of honor from Indiana. M. W. Childs. New Repub 150:25 Mr 28 '64

DAVIS, Ernie
End of the dream. por Time 81:61 My 24 '63
Ernie Davis, a man of courage. A. Wright. por Sports Illus 18:24-5 My 27 '63
—and August, Bob
I'm not unlucky. por Sat Eve Post 236:60-2 Mr 30 '63
DAVIS, Freddie
Mississippi chicken processor. il pors Ebony 18:45-6+ F '63
DAVIS, Fremont
Cameras see in the dark. Sci N L 83:135+ Mr 2 '63
DAVIS, Garry
Little man, big idea. A. Morrissett. Commonweal 78:549-50 S 20 '63
DAVIS, George H.
Management of water in arid lands. Natur Hist 73:26-33 Ag '64
DAVIS, H. Grady
Call for reconstruction. Christian Cent 81:1065 Ag 26 '64
DAVIS, Hallowell
Enhancement of evoked cortical potentials in humans related to a task requiring a decision. bibliog Science 145:182-3 Jl 10 '64
DAVIS, Harold E.
José Artigas: father of Uruguay. bibliog Américas 16:1-5 O '64
DAVIS, Jefferson
Chimp to man; kidney transplants. il por Newsweek 62:55 D 30 '63
DAVIS, Jefferson, 1808-1889
Jefferson Davis, by H. Strode. Review
Sat R 47:40 N 28 '64. W. B. Catton
Time por 84:128+ O 16 '64
DAVIS, Jefferson Columbus
I have been basely murdered. H. H. Peckham. il por Am Heritage 14:88-92 Ag '63
DAVIS, Johanna
She never does the dishes. Ladies Home J 81:64-5+ Je '64
DAVIS, John A.
Influence of Africans on American culture. bibliog f Ann Am Acad 354:75-83 Jl '64
DAVIS, John D. and Miller, N. E.
Fear and pain: their effect on self-injection of amobarbital sodium by rats. Science 141:1286-7 S 27 '63
DAVIS, John Shelton. See Johnson, C. E. jt. auth.
DAVIS, Joseph A. jr
Books in review. Natur Hist 73:4+ D '64
DAVIS, Joseph L.
Whole town's talking. NEA J 52:26-7 O '63
DAVIS, Julia, fund. See Negro literature—Collections
DAVIS, Katharine
American islomania. Mlle 57:122-3+ Je '63
Notes for flying freshmen, sailing sophomores, journeying juniors, and sight-seeing seniors. Mlle 57:309+ Ag '63
Overlooked islands. Mlle 57:106-10 My '63
DAVIS, Kenneth S.
In the name of the great Jehovah and the Continental congress! Am Heritage 14:65-77 O '63
DAVIS, Kingsley
Population; with biographical sketch. Sci Am 209:24, 62-71 bibliog(p306) S '63
DAVIS, Lambert
Copyright; excerpt from address. Pub W 184:49-50 Jl 15 '63
DAVIS, Leroy
Clergy-laity schism. Christian Cent 81:1455-6 N 25 '64
DAVIS, Lou
Flying clubs, here; U.S.A. Flying 74:54 Je '64
DAVIS, Luther C. jr
Amazon's rate of flow. Natur Hist 73:14-19 Je '64
DAVIS, Margaret B. and Deevey, E. S. jr
Pollen accumulation rates: estimates from late-glacial sediment of Rogers Lake. bibliog Science 145:1293-5 S 18 '64
DAVIS, Marie
Librarians view publishers' promotion and advertising; summary of address. Pub W 184:33-5 D 2 '63
DAVIS, Maxine
Sex problems after ten years of marriage. McCalls 90:50+ My '63
DAVIS, Melton S.
Most controversial director. N Y Times Mag p34-5+ N 15 '64
DAVIS, Meyer
Bands of gold. B. Day. il pors Sat Eve Post 236:20, 23-5 Ap 20 '63
DAVIS, Miles Dewey, 1926-
Antic arts. K. Tynan. por Holiday 33:101-3+ F '63
Jazz records. W. Balliett. New Yorker 40:194-7 Ap 25 '64
DAVIS, Murray
Shilling better than Sovereign. Motor B 113:93+ Ja '64
DAVIS, Olive Stull
My life with cancer. por Ladies Home J 81:68-9+ O '64
about
From fowl to woman? por Time 83:79 Ap 3 '64
DAVIS, Ossie
Suddenly Ossie and Ruby are everywhere. il pors Life 55:110-13 D 6 '63
DAVIS, Peter
Eastman's Walter Hendl. Mus Am 84:286-7 D '64
Experiment in Harrania. Sch Arts 63:7-10 O '63
Henze's Elegy for young lovers. Mus Am 84:45 N '64
about
Audition. New Yorker 40:29-32 Mr 28 '64
DAVIS, Philip J.
Lonesome pine foundation. Harper 229:23-4+ Ag '64
Number; with biographical sketch. Sci Am 211:28, 50-9 bibliog(p269) S '64
DAVIS, Ralph L.
Hybrid alfalfa's here, how good is it? por Suc Farm 63:72-3 Ja '65
DAVIS, Raymond, jr
Learning from neutrinos. Time 83:50 Ja 3 '64
DAVIS, Richard H.
Soviet attaché accused of improper activities; U.S. asks departure; note, July 1, 1963. Dept State Bul 49:137 Jl 22 '63
Soviet empire will face new stresses. por Nations Bsns 51:62-3 D '63
DAVIS, Robert B.
Math takes a new path. PTA Mag 57:8-11 bibliog(p36) F '63
DAVIS, Robert P.
How to defeat any gale. Motor B 112:42-3+ O '63
Letter home; story. il Motor B 112:27 D '63
New way to get your weather. por Motor B 113:40-3+ Je '64
Speaking of moorings. Motor B 113:48-51 My '64
DAVIS, Ron
Ron Davis dance theatre; Hunter college playhouse. J. Maskey. Dance Mag 38:28 Ag '64
DAVIS, Ronald L.
Stars over Texas. Opera N 29:12-15 N 14 '64
DAVIS, Rowland H.
Neurospora mutant lacking an arginine-specific carbamyl phosphokinase. bibliog Science 142:1652-4 D 27 '63
DAVIS, Roy L.
Environmental hazards. NEA J 53:68-70 Mr '64
DAVIS, Sammy
Sammy Davis; with report by T. Thompson. il pors Life 57:84A-96 N 13 '64
DAVIS, Sammy, family
Home life of Mai Britt and Golden boy. il Ebony 20:136-8+ D '64
DAVIS, Shirley
Christmas dinner with Tommy Davis. il por Ebony 19:162+ D '63
DAVIS, Stuart
Born to paint. il por Newsweek 64:75 Jl 6 '64
Epitaph in jazz. por Time 84:59 Jl 3 '64
Stuart Davis, 1894-1964. D. Suro. il Américas 17:30-1 Ja '65
Stuart Davis, 1894-1964: last interview. W. I. Homer. il por Art N 63:43+ S '64
DAVIS, Thelma F.
Local associations need up-to-date constitutions. NEA J 53:32 F '64
NEA mutual fund. NEA J 53:29-30 N '64
Scholastic teacher interview: ed. by H. Langer. por Sr Schol 85:9T-14T+ D2 '64
DAVIS, Thurston N.
Announcing the John LaFarge institute. America 110:791-3 Je 6 '64
Pope John's letter. America 108:707-10 My 18 '63
Protestants in Spain. America 108:390 Mr 23 '63
Sad surfside soliloquy. America 108:702 My 18 '63
They die for the New York times. America 109:280 S 21 '63
DAVIS, Tommy
Dodgers' Tommy-gun. H. L. Masin. por Sr Schol 84:26 Ap 17 '64
DAVIS, Velmar W. and Brantley, Bill
Corn handling. Suc Farm 62:41-5 S '64

DAVIS, W. E. jr, and Cole, L. J.
Homograft tolerance in mice: use of urethan and sublethal irradiation. bibliog Science 140:483-4 My 3 '63
DAVIS, Watson
Need information center. Sci N L 84:70-1 Ag 3 '63
Need sex desegregation. Sci N L 86:22 Jl 11 '64
New age for ancient man. Sci N L 83:154-5 Mr 9 '63
Teen science brain force. Sci N L 87:21 Ja 9 '65
DAVIS, Wayne H. See Luckens, M. M. jt. auth.
DAVIS, William E. jr, and others
Homographs in thymectomized, irradiated mice: responses to primary and secondary skin grafts. bibliog Science 145:394-5 Jl 24 '64
DAVIS, William Hammatt
Store of wisdom. Nation 199:83 S 7 '64
DAVIS, William J.
Mrs Murphy's private rights. America 109:454-6 O 19 '63
DAVIS, Willie T.
Engine temperature indicator. Electr World 71:36+ Ap '64
DAVIS, Wynn
America's greatest gamefish. Outdoor Life 134:34-7+ Jl '64
Angling. See issues of Outdoor life
For midsummer trout; let it rain. por Outdoor Life 132:30-1+ Ag '63
Look southward, angler. por Outdoor Life 133:33-5+ Mr '64
Revolution in fishing tackle. Outdoor Life 131:49-51+ Ap '63
Twenty-five top fishing holes. Outdoor Life 133:33-5+ My '64
DAVIS cup. See Tennis
DAVISON, John
Gene action mechanisms in the determination of color and pattern in the frog (rana pipiens) bibliog Science 141:648-9 Ag 16 '63
DAVISON, Peter
Conviction means loss of license; poem. Atlan 214:54 O '64
Fogged in; poem. Atlan 211:75 Ap '63
Madness in the new poetry. Atlan 215:90-3 Ja '65
Moment; poem. Atlan 212:76 N '63
New poetry. Atlan 212:82-5 D '63
True feeling leaves no memory; poem. Atlan 212:41 Jl '63
about
Five poets. J. Jacobsen. Poetry 105:203-5 D '64
DAVISON, Verne E.
Backyard survey; how bobwhites form a covey. Audubon Mag 66:52-5 Ja '64
Fruits bring eleven species to feeders. Audubon Mag 66:322-5 S '64
101 foods for cardinals. Audubon Mag 65:180-3 My '63
DAVY, Gloria
Two fine Glorias. Time 83:59 Mr 13 '64
DAWDLING. See Procrastination
DAWKINS, Cecil
Violet season; story. Redbook 121:50-1 Jl '63
DAWN, Walter
Pink-headed warbler. il Natur Hist 72:28-31 O '63
DAWN. See Sunrise
DAWN redwood. See Metasequoia
DAWS, Gavan, and Head, Timothy
Niihau: a shoal of time. Am Heritage 14:48-51+ O '63
DAWSON, Al
Five-year stalk: new record whitetail. Outdoor Life 132:32-5+ Ag '63
DAWSON, David M. and others
Lactic dehydrogenases: functions of the two types. bibliog Science 143:929-33 F 28 '64
DAWSON, E. Yale
Ecological paradox of coastal Peru. Natur Hist 72:32-7 O '63
DAWSON, John M.
Georgian setting for Delaware. Library J 88:4569-71 D 1 '63
DAWSON, John W.
Hogan said no, but Dawson said yes. G. S. Brown. il por Sports Illus 20:35-7 Ja 13 '64
DAWSON, Percy Millard
Still going strong at ninety-one. il Todays Health 42:20 Je '64
DAWSON, Raymond H.
What kind of NATO nuclear force? bibliog f Ann Am Acad 351:30-9 Ja '64
DAWSON, Ruth
Gift; poem. Mlle 59:309 Ag '64
DAWSON trail. See Canada—Description and travel
DAWYDOFF, Alex
Grounded and impounded. Flying 74:36-8+ Ja '64
DAY, Beth
Bands of gold. Sat Eve Post 236:20, 23-5 Ap 20 '63
Enjoy adventures in friendliness. Read Digest 85:175-6+ Ag '64
Living in shadow. N Y Times Mag p42+ Ap 12 '64
Minister stirs up Brooklyn Heights. N Y Times Mag p88+ Je 7 '64
—See Klaben, H. jt. auth.
DAY, Clarence
Legs vs. architects; excerpt from Crow's nest. por Library J 88:4526-7 D 1 '63
DAY, Doris
Doris Day I know; ed. by G. Christy. T. Melcher. il pors Good H 157:88-91+ O '63
In the Garden of Eden with Doris Day. il pors Look 27:138+ D 17 '63
Is there a Doris Day? R. Kahn. il pors Ladies Home J 80:62-5 Jl '63
Tomato on top is Doris. il pors Life 55:105-7 S 27 '63
DAY, Duane L.
Another Oberlin conference. Christian Cent 80:1334-5 O 30 '63
DAY, J. Edward
Ex-cabinet member opposes health care plan; interview. por Nations Bsns 51:42-3+ D '63
Day is done. Newsweek 62:24-5 Ag 5 '63
Goodbye, Mr ZIP. Time 82:11-12 Ag 2 '63
Mail-service cutback: is it blackmail? U S News 54:8 My 6 '63
DAY, John A.
Building blocks of the clouds. Natur Hist 74:36-43 Ja '65
DAY, John Stewart
Steps to the stars. H. Horn. il pors Sports Illus 20:52-8 F 3 '64
DAY, Richard
Advertising designs of Jack Kabat. Am Artist 28:56-60+ Ja '64
Balance your car's wheels. Pop Sci 185:128-30 D '64
Heidi Brandt, illustrator & painter. Am Artist 27:18-23+ D '63
DAY, Richard Ward
Happy landing; tenth principal of Phillips Exeter academy. por Newsweek 61:108 Je 24 '63
Tackling man; new headmaster of Exeter. por Time 81:59 Je 21 '63
DAY, Virgil B.
Economic growth; address, December 5, 1963. Vital Speeches 30:181-4 Ja 1 '64
DAY, William C. and Erdman, J. G.
Ionene: a thermal degradation product of β-carotene. bibliog Science 141:808 Ag 30 '63
DAY-LEWIS, C.
Party of one. Holiday 33:32+ Mr '63
Day Lewis: a style of his own. R. M. Elman. New Repub 150:26+ Mr 28 '64
In the convention. W. Dickey. Poetry 104:377 S '64
DAY among the immortals; story. See Murray, W.
DAY Beaumont grew acquainted with his pain; story. See Le Clézio, J. M. G.
DAY beds
Méridienne. C. J. Otto. il Antiques 83:675-9 Je '63
DAY camps. See Camps
DAY care for children. See Day nurseries
DAY dreams. See Daydreams
DAY in spring; story. See Stanford, D.
DAY lilies
Day after day. M. C. Ohlander. il Flower Grower 50:31 My '63
Daylilies. A. V. Holmes. il Pop Gard 14:40+ Jl '63
Day-lilies always & in all ways. il Flower Grower 51:26-7 Jl '64
Daylilies, midsummer delight. B. Black. il Pop Gard 15:71+ Jl '64
Daylilies today. R. Johnson. il Horticulture 42:22-3+ Jl '64
Daylily splendor; shows of American hemerocallis society. il Pop Gard 14:14+ Mr '63
Delightful daylilies. E. J. Purcell. il Pop Gard 15:32-3+ Ap '64
Divide crowded day-lilies for more bountiful bloom. B. Brinhart. il Flower Grower 51:45-6 Ag '64
Indispensable daylilies. R. Redding. il Pop Gard 14:36-7 Ap '63
Mrs Lester & her famous day-lilies. B. Deane. il Flower Grower 51:25+ Jl '64
Summer is the big season for day-lilies. E. J. Purcell. il Flower Grower 50:28-9+ Jl '63

DAY nurseries
Home away. il Time 84:70 Ag 7 '64
Part-time care: the day-care problem. E. M. Hosley. Ann Am Acad 355:56-61 S '64
See also
Nursery schools

DAY the river spoke; story. See Nair, K.

DAYDREAMS
Don't be ashamed of your daydreams. F. Leiber. il Sci Digest 54:14-20 Ag '63
What daydreaming reveals about your personality. J. E. Gibson. il Todays Health 41:43+ N '63

DAYHOFF, M. O. and others
Thermodynamic equilibria in prebiological atmospheres. bibliog Science 146:1461-4 D 11 '64

DAYLIGHT saving
Chaos of clocks; U.S. time snarl. Time 81:52 My 10 '63
Crazy quilt; daylight time inconsistency. il Newsweek 61:26 My 6 '63
Daylight saving is one result of international time standard. T. D. Nicholson. il Natur Hist 73:54-6 Ap '64
Time out of joint. Newsweek 63:95A+ My 11 '64

DAYLIGHTING. See Lighting

DAYLILIES. See Day lilies

DAYS and nights of Beebee Fenstermaker; drama. See Snyder, W.

DAYS and the neighbors; story. See Henderson, R.

DAYTON, Ohio
Community standards; public opinion poll to determine contemporary community standards of decency. America 110:357 Mr 21 '64

City planning

Aimed folders find their targets. il Am City 79:116+ Jl '64

Galleries and museums

Airborne museum; plans for Air force museum at Wright-Patterson air force base. il Time 84:82 N 27 '64
Soaring air museum and an earthbound one. il Fortune 70:176-7 D '64

Sanitary affairs

Clean sewers on schedule. J. A. Chifala. il Am City 78:110-11 Je '63

Streets

Everybody pitches in. W. Shartzer. il Am City 78:90-1 N '63

DAYTON brothers
Retail empire reaches across the prairie; from western Wisconsin to eastern Montana. il Bsns W p70-2+ Mr 7 '64

DAYTONA international speedway. See Speedways

DAYTON'S department store. See Minneapolis—Stores

DEACONS
Bishops, under or with the pope? J. B. Sheerin. Cath World 198:139-43 D '63
Married deacons. America 110:696+ My 23 '64
Married deacons. Newsweek 64:72 O 12 '64

DEAD bodies. See Cadavers

DEAD SEA scrolls
Essenes or zealots? excavations at Massada. il Newsweek 63:72 F 10 '64
Explaining the scrolls. Newsweek 63:67 Je 15 '64
New light on the Dead Sea scrolls. C. Roth. Commentary 37:27-32 Je '64; Reply with rejoinder. S. B. Hoenig. 38:14+ D '64

DEADLY nightshade. See Nightshade, Black

DEAF
Listen, my heart; condensation of Make a joyful sound. H. E. Waite. il Read Digest 82:297-308+ Ap '63
See also
Libraries—Work with deaf

Education

Broadening our educational horizons for the deaf; adaptation of address. L. M. Elstad. Sch Life 46:28-9 Ja '64
Educating deaf children; adaptation of address. S. R. Silverman. Sch Life 46:24-8 Ja '64
Forms of sounds as shown on oscilloscope by roulette figures. G. W. Barton, jr. and S. H. Barton. il Science 142:1455-6 D 13 '63; Reply. B. O. Pyron and F. R. Williamson, jr. 145:72-3 Jl 3 '64
International congress on education of the deaf. Sch & Soc 92:34-5 Ja 25 '64
Pictures of human sounds aid to deaf children. Sci N L 85:9 Ja 4 '64
See also
Teachers of the deaf

DEAF, Apparatus for the
See also
Hearing aids

DEAF, Moving pictures for the
New horizons for the deaf. M. J. Norwood. Sch Life 45:6-7 Ja '63

DEAF, Teachers of the. See Teachers of the deaf

DEAF-mutes
Not so deaf, not so dumb; Perdoncini schools. il Time 85:55 Ja 29 '65

DEAFNESS
I can't hear, doctor; is there any help? J. E. Landis. il Todays Health 41:24-5+ S '63
Link tooth loss, hearing; deafness after tooth extractions. F. Marley. Sci N L 86:117 Ag 22 '64
Not so deaf, not so dumb; Perdoncini schools. il Time 85:55 Ja 29 '65
Return from the deaf. M. G. Smith. il Farm J 87:70 Jl '63
See also
Hearing

DEAFNESS, Tone. See Tone deafness

DEAK and company, incorporated
World of Deaknick. il Time 83:103 Je 12 '64

DEAKIN, Gerald E.
Watch that rhapsody to a fig leaf! Dance Mag 37:48-9 N '63

DEAKIN, James
I've got a secret. New Repub 152:13-15 Ja 30 '65

DEAL, Babs H.
Chocolate cake; story. Redbook 123:56-7 Jl '64
Myth motif in modern ficton. Writer 76:12-14+ N '63
Pride; story. Redbook 123:62-3 My '64
With love from Joe; story. Redbook 122:40-1 Ja '64

DEALE, H. Vail
Campus vs. community. bibliog por Library J 89:1695-7 Ap 15 '64

DEALER relations
Brand-new industrial package. L. Blumenthal. il Duns R 82:pt2 136-8+ N '63
Magnavox goes its own golden way. S. H. Brown. il Fortune 69:112-15+ F '64

DEALERS, Art. See Art dealers

DEALERS, Automobile. See Automobile dealers

DEALERS, Farm equipment. See Farm equipment dealers

DEALERS in antiques. See Antique dealers

DEAN, Beth
Year of accomplishment. Dance Mag 37:16-17 Ag '63

DEAN, Charles O.
Phosfon controls chrysanthemum height. Horticulture 42:29 Ag '64
Practical hotbed. Horticulture 42:12 F '64

DEAN, Edith M.
Emotion in non-fiction writing. Writer 77:26-7 S '64
Know your markets. Writer 77:28-30 F '64

DEAN, Edward S.
Hoppety hypnotism. Sat R 46:46-7 S 7; 54 N 2 '63
Traps of identity. Nation 196:349-51 Ap 27 '63

DEAN, Loomis
Kitzbühel look. il Sports Illus 19:62-5 N 25 '63

DEAN, Mary, pseud.
Atrocious Christmas card. Atlan 212:132-4 O '63

DEAN, Reginald, and Geber, Marcelle
Why African babies are more intelligent. Sci Digest 56:35-40 S '64

DEAN, Robert L.
England warns its youth. America 108:253-5 F 23 '63
It's right here somewhere. America 108:404-5 Mr 23 '63

DEAN, Stephen O.
Vacuum: sputtering, desorption, and surface physics; report on annual Sherwood vacuum conference. Science 144:1251-2 Je 5 '64

DEANE, Barbara
Mrs Lester & her famous day-lilies. Flower Grower 51:25+ Jl '64

DEANE, Michael B.
Judge. New Repub 150:7 Ja 18 '64

DE ANGELI, Marguerite
700 turn out to honor author. Library J 88:4830-1 D 15 '63

DEANGELIS, Anthony
Boiling in oil. por Time 82:87A D 13 '63
Bubble bursts. il por Newsweek 62:74+ D 2 '63

DEANGELIS, Anthony—*Continued*
Commodities: soybeans and salad oil; the greatest scandal in the history of Wall Street is still going on. P. Vanderwicken. il Esquire 61:91-3+ Ap '64
Commodities: the troubled markets. il por Newsweek 63:51-4 Ja 6 '64
$46.5 million bail. Newsweek 63:28+ Ja 27 '64
Justice steps in. Time 83:75 Ja 3 '64
Nineteen million in the hole. Time 82:90+ N 29 '63
$150 million in oil, all gone! P. Mandel. il pors Life 56:90-2+ Ap 3 '64
Plea for guilty. Newsweek 65:61 Ja 18 '65
Salad oil deal still a mystery. por Bsns W p54 Ja 25 '64
Tino's bottomless tanks of oil. N. C. Miller. il pors Sat Eve Post 237:19-25 Ap 25 '64
Where genius went wrong. il por Bsns W p 164-6+ Ap 18 '64
Where's the oil? il por Newsweek 62:65-6 D 16 '63

DE ANGELIS, George
How I built my wonderful three-hoss shay. pors Pop Sci 182:37-41 Je '63

DEANS, Edwina
Mathematics. Sch Life 45:18-19 Jl '63

DEANS, College. See College deans

DEAR me, the sky is falling; drama. See Spigelgass, L.

DEARBORN, Mich.
Baby-sitting for shoppers. il Am City 79:117-18 D '64
Electronic automation fills the bill. W. B. Godette. il Am City 78:99 N '63
Ice skaters enjoy heat breaks. O. L. Hubbard and R. K. Archer. il Am City 78:86-7 D '63
Operation eyesore stops urban decay. O. L. Hubbard. il Am City 78:165-6 My '63
See also
Henry Ford museum and Greenfield Village

Housing

Precast load-bearing exterior wall. il Arch Rec 136:122-3 Ag '64
Senior-citizen housing. il Am City 79:79-80 Jl '64

Sanitary affairs

No need for emergencies. J. M. Dick. il Am City 79:103-4 My '64

DEARDEN, John
Can management information be automated? Harvard Bsns R 42:128-35 Mr '64
Case of the disputing divisions. Harvard Bsns R 42:158-9+ My '64
Profit-planning accounting for small firms. Harvard Bsns R 41:66-76 Mr '63

DEARDEN, John Francis, abp
Should you buy a new missal? America 111: 180-1 Ag 22 '64

DEARDORFF, Robert
Delightsome land. Redbook 121:66-7+ My '63
Land of the sky blue water. Redbook 123:70-1+ S '64
North of Broadway. Redbook 121:68-9+ O '63
Step by step through Milan. Travel 119:59-61 Ap '63
Step by step through Munich. Travel 119:63-7 Mr '63
Step by step through Naples. Travel 119:55-9 My '63
Step by step through Venice. Travel 120: 53-4+ Ag '63
Step by step through Zurich. Travel 120: 33-4+ Jl '63
They did the impossible, and then. N Y Times Mag p74-5+ D 6 '64
(ed) See Interview with Ingrid Bergman

DEARFIELD colony. See Weld County, Colo.

DEARING, Bruce
Three myths about the college teacher. Sat R 47:65-7 Ja 18 '64

DEARING, George Bruce
Education of humane living in an age of automation. Sch & Soc 92:305-9 O 31 '64

DEARLY beloved; story. See Kokjohn, J. E.

DEARMORE, Tom
Arkansas: squire vs. demagogue. Reporter 31: 38-42 O 22 '64

DE ARRIBA Y CASTRO, Beniamino, cardinal
Limits of charity; suggested establishment of a co-ordinating agency in Rome for social reform. America 109:476 O 26 '63

DEASON, Hilary J.
Paperbacks in an age of science. Sr Schol 83: 31T Ja 17 '64

DEASY, Mary
Fortuneteller; story. Sat Eve Post 237:50-1 My 16 '64

DEASY, Philip
Creative teaching. Commonweal 79:410 D 27 '63
Nuclear age parables. Commonweal 77:616-18 Mr 8 '63

DEATH
Death & modern man. il Time 84:92+ N 20 '64
Doctor looks at death. F. Martí-Ibáñez. Read Digest 84:145-6+ Mr '64
Fear of death. E. J. Carnell; discussion. Christian Cent 80:367-8 Mr 20 '63
How to rise above the fear of death. N. V. Peale. Read Digest 82:103-6 Ap '63
Matter of death and life; life-giving death. Christian Cent 81:291 Mr 4 '64
Meaning of death. W. Cloud. Pop Sci 183: 21-2 S '63
Mortal no: death and the modern imagination, by F. J. Hoffman. Review
Commonweal 81:76-9 O 9 '64. B. Murchland
See also
Bereavement
Children and death
Euthanasia
Longevity
Resurrection

Causes

What Americans die of; where smoking fits in; with chart. il U S News 56:62-3 F 10 '64
Where is science taking us? excerpt from Horizons in biochemistry. D. E. Koshland, jr. Sat R 46:46 Je 1 '63

DEATH (biology)
What happens when you die. O. A. Battista. Sci Digest 55:80-4 My '64
Where is science taking us? excerpt from Horizons in biochemistry. D. E. Koshland, jr. Sat R 46:46 Je 1 '63

DEATH, Apparent. See Anabiosis

DEATH and children. See Children and death

DEATH feigning by animals. See Animals—Habits and behavior

DEATH in America; story. See Hellman, R.

DEATH in literature. See Literature—Themes

DEATH of a salesman; drama. See Miller, A.

DEATH of a scientific humanist; story. See Friel, B.

DEATH penalty. See Capital punishment

DEATH rate. See Infant mortality

DEATH ray weapons. See Weapons

DEATH VALLEY, Calif.
Back roads in Death Valley. il Sunset 132: 82+ Mr '64

DEATH VALLEY-Big Pine road. See Roads—California

DEAUX, Edward B. and Gormezano, I.
Eyeball retraction: classical conditioning and extinction in the albino rabbit. bibliog Science 141:630-1 Ag 16 '63

DEBAKEY, Michael Ellis
Medicine's frontier: rebuilding the human body. G. Astor. il pors Look 28:22-9 Je 30 '64
Surgeon; Duke of Windsor's operation. il por Newsweek 64:34-5 D 28 '64

DE BALLA, Borisz
Tides of history and the age of anxiety. Cath World 197:36-43 Ap '63

DE BARY, Gerald
His dying words: don't blame the snake; it's not its fault. J. Hicks. il por Life 56:38 F 7 '64

DE BARY, William Theodore
East Asian studies: a comprehensive program. Ann Am Acad 356:63-9 N '64

DEBASE, Lucy
Why do I teach? Parents Mag 39:82 S '64

DEBATES and debating
Alumni day; Columbia college vs. Massachusetts correctional institute. Newsweek 62:34 N 25 '63
Little Giant vs. Honest Abe. il Sr Schol 85:5 O 14 '64
Suitcase set; college debaters. il Newsweek 61:96+ My 13 '63
See also
Forums (discussion and debate)

DE BECKER, Hal
As I see it. por Dance Mag 37:23-5 N '63 (to be cont)
Europe as we see it. por Dance Mag 38:19+ My; 14-17 Jl '64 (to be cont)

DE BEERS consolidated mines, limited
Girls are De Beers' best friend. il Bsns W p36 F 8 '64
King of diamonds. il Time 81:76 Mr 1 '63

DE BETHUNE, André J.
Child spacing: the mathematical probabilities. bibliog Science 142:1629-34; 144:795 D 27 '63, My 15 '64
DE BLANK, Joost, bp
Joost de Blank comes home. C. Northcott. Christian Cent 81:328 Mr 11 '64
DE BLASI, Anthony J.
How I grow tuberous begonias. Flower Grower 51:46+ Mr '64
Try the tree ponies. Horticulture 42:24-5 F '64
DEBOO, Gordon J.
Bootstrap circuits. Electr World 72:66-7 Jl '64
DE BOUSSON, Thérèse, pseud.
Visit to Croatia. America 109:353 S 28 '63
DEBRÉ, Michel
Island fling. Time 81:34-5 My 17 '63
6,000 miles from home. Time 81:29 Mr 29 '63
DE BRULER, Olive
D.C. Board of educ. confirms library position called temporary since 1962. Library J 89: 1839 Ap 15 '64
DEBT
Craps on credit; foreign gambling debts collectible in New York. Time 84:57 N 27 '64
Debt in a new environment; address, November 5, 1964. R. A. Peterson. Vital Speeches 31:149-53 D 15 '64
Do people owe too much? officials and bankers worry. il U S News 54:103-6 Ap 29 '63
How much debt can you handle? il Changing T 17:38-40 Mr '63
Is private debt too big? il U S News 56:50-2 F 17 '64
New way out of debt; Family debt counselors of Phoenix. M. T. Bloom. Read Digest 85:134-7 Ag '64
Skyrocketing private debt: why officials are worried. il U S News 57:98+ O 12 '64
Trillion in liquid assets; offset to Americans' debts? il U S News 57:134-5 O 26 '64
When a family's debt gets too big. il U S News 56:93-5 Mr 2 '64
Why debt is a growing worry. il U S News 55:90-1 Ag 26 '63
Why the growing worry over debt people owe; with statements by C. C. Balderston and J. W. Barr. il U S News 57:89-92 O 19 '64
See also
Credit
Farm finance
DEBTS, Public
National debt. G. A. Wing. il America 111: 555-7 N 7 '64

Europe

Billions that would solve dollar problem; war debts from European nations. il U S News 55:94 N 25 '63

United States

Are we looking at the wrong budget? W. W. Howard. il Reporter 28:41-2+ My 23 '63; Discussion. 28:8-9 Je 20 '63
Battle over the debt limit. Atlan 211:8+ Je '63
Break for U.S. debt manager. U S News 58: 94 Ja 25 '65
Debt in a new environment; address, November 5, 1964. R. A. Peterson. Vital Speeches 31:149-53 D 15 '64
Deficit advocates. U S News 54:15 F 11 '63
Financing seven years of deficit; with editorial comment. il Bsns W p 126+, 156 F 23 '63
Headache on debt limit too. U S News 54: 106-7 Mr 11 '63
In the red: twenty-seven out of the last thirty-three budgets have run deficits. il U S News 55:34-9 Jl 22 '63
National debt and the peril point. J. D. Stern. il Atlan 213:35-8 Ja '64; Discussion. 213:38+ Mr; 44 Ap '64
Rising issue; the public debt. Nations Bsns 52:88-92 Ag '64
Stretching out federal debts. U S News 55: 105 S 16 '63
Taxes & spending: what the people want. il Nations Bsns 51:34-5+ Ap '63
Taxes & spending: where the money goes. il Nations Bsns 51:36-7 Ap '63
U.S. borrows to help dollar. U S News 54: 98-9 Mr 4 '63
U.S. deficit shrinks by a billion. Bsns W p21 Jl 6 '63
When will it be safe to balance the budget? E. L. Dale, jr. il N Y Times Mag p 14-15+ Ja 24 '65
Will we ever pay off? H. Hazlitt. il Newsweek 63:84 Je 8 '64; Same abr. Read Digest 85:115-16 Ag '64
DEBTS, State. See State finance
DEBUS, Allen
Lillian Russell. Hobbies 69:44-5 Jl '64
DEBUSSY, Claude
Enjoy the new feast of Debussy recordings. E. Kinard. House B 105:30+ O '63
First recordings of Debussy and Hindemith works for narrator and ensemble. R. Sabin. il Am Rec G 30:926-7 Je '64
From Angel, a first-class Jeux. C. J. Luten. il Am Rec G 31:313 D '64
In Debussy, a special valedictory. H. Goldsmith. Hi Fi 14:77-8 D '64
LP overview of Debussy's seascape: La Mer. A. Chipman. il Am Rec G 30:390-3 Ja '64
Pelléas et Mélisande. Criticism
Opera N il 28:32 D 14 '63
Sat R 46:20+ Jl 6 '63
DEBUTANTES
Big weekend; debuts of Effie Taylor and Janet Auchincloss. il Time 82:30-1 Ag 30 '63
Debs. il Newsweek 64:54-5 D 21 '64
Fultz quads debut at Zeta cotillion. il Ebony 19:56-8+ Ap '64
Fun party: coming out of Fernanda Wanamaker Wetherill. il Newsweek 62:31-2 S 16 '63
Late late show: trial of seven members of after-party brawl at coming-out party of Philadelphia debutante Fernanda Wanamaker Wetherill. il Time 83:74 Ap 24 '64
My debut a horror. B. Frazier. il Life 55: 133-4+ D 6 '63
Telstar cotillion; Negro debutantes. il Ebony 18:40+ Jl '63
Wanamaker debut begins and ends up in a rampage; with report by D. Abrahamsen. il Life 55:30-7 S 20 '63
DEBYE, Peter J. W.
Peter J. W. Debye: an interview; March 5, 1964; ed. by D. R. Corson and others. por Science 145:554-9 Ag 7 '64
DECANTERS. See Bottles
DE CARLI, Paul S. and Milton, D. J.
Stishovite: synthesis by shock wave. bibliog Science 147:144-5 Ja 8 '65
—See Milton, D. J. jt. auth.
DECATUR, Stephen
Bloodshed at dawn. C. S. Forester. il por Am Heritage 15:40-5+ O '64
DECATUR, Ill.
Decatur pinpoints the problems of the aged. Am City 78:138+ My '63

Sanitary affairs

Scuba divers replace missing pipe. A. Van Praag, jr. il Am City 78:84-5 D '63

Street traffic

Survey, plan, expedite and review. J. F. Nolan. il Am City 78:85-7 Ag '63
DECAVALLES, Andonis
Poet's novel. Poetry 105:65-7 O '64
DECCA navigation
Decca to show improved system in U.S. P. J. Klass. il Aviation W 81:88-9+ S 21 '64
DECEMBER
December embers. D. E. Rose. il Horticulture 41:600-1 D '63
In December; few of the dates, memorable and not so, coming up this month (title varies) (cont) il N Y Times Mag p52 D 1 '63; 40 N 29 '64
DECENTRALIZING authority in business. See Business management and organization
DECENYLSUCCINIC acid. See Succinic acid
DECEPTIVE packaging. See Packaging
DECIMAL classification. See Classification, Decimal
DECIMAL system
100 cents to £1? Newsweek 62:63 O 7 '63
DECISION making
ABCs of the critical path method; excerpts from Industrial scheduling. F. K. Levy and others. bibliog f il Harvard Bsns R 41:98-108 S '63
Computer in the boardroom. H. E. Klein. il Duns R 84:pt2 102-3+ S '64
Decision making in the Defense department; address, April 20, 1963. R. S. McNamara. Vital Speeches 29:508-12 Je 1 '63
Decision theory in law, science, and technology. T. A. Cowan. bibliog Science 140: 1065-75 Je 7 '63; Reply. I. Kraft. 143:99-100 Ja 10 '64
Decision trees for decision making. J. F. Magee. il Harvard Bsns R 42:126-38 Jl '64
Decisions, decisions; in high places from Moses to the current President. Reporter 29:16+ Ag 15 '63

DECISION making—*Continued*
Enhancement of evoked cortical potentials in humans related to a task requiring a decision. H. Davis. bibliog il Science 145: 182-3 Jl 10 '64
Frankly speaking; candid comments of some well-known people; comp. by G. Wagner. il McCalls 91:142 Jl '64
Hierarchy of objectives. C. H. Granger. bibliog f il Harvard Bsns R 42:63-74 My '64
How to evaluate corporate strategy. S. Tilles. bibliog f Harvard Bsns R 41:111-21 Jl '63
How to use decision trees in capital investment. J. F. Magee. il Harvard Bsns R 42: 79-96 S '64
Industry's stake in education; address, January 16, 1963. C. G. Mortimer. Vital Speeches 29:270-3 F 15 '63
Make up your mind. J. Dalrymple. Seventeen 22:162+ S '63
Man-computer relationship. D. L. Johnson and A. L. Kobler; discussion. Science 139: 1231-2+ Mr 22 '63
New way to improve your decisions. J. G. Mason. il Nations Bsns 52:58-60+ Je '64
President considers timing vital to success. M. Smith. Nations Bsns 51:23-4 Je '63
ROI for new-product policy. P. A. Scheuble, jr. il Harvard Bsns R 42:110-20 N '64
Rx for profits; better decisions faster; address, November 8, 1963. L. B. Lundborg. Vital Speeches 30:146-50 D 15 '63
Think your way to success. S. Schuler. il Nations Bsns 52:88-90+ Ap '64
Troubled conscience of American business: excerpts from Myths and mythmakers in the modern economy. B. Nossiter. Harper 227:37-43 S '63; Discussion. 227:8+ N '63
See also
Choice (psychology)

DECISION; story. See Robinson, L. W.

DECISIONS, Judicial. See Judgments

DECKER, F. E. and others
Containers don't count. Esquire 59:102-3+ Ap '63

DECKER, George C.
NDEA loans to private schools. por Sch Life 45:19-21 Ap '63

DECKERT, Gordon H.
Pursuit eye movements in the absence of a moving visual stimulus. bibliog Science 143:1192-3 Mr 13 '64

DECKS
Folding deck for cartop boat. W. J. Jahoda. il Pop Mech 119:167-8 Ap '63

DECKS (outdoor rooms) See Outdoor rooms

DECKTER, Jack
Portfolio of figure drawings. il Am Artist 28:48-53+ My '64

DECLARATION of human rights. See Universal declaration of human rights

DECLARATION of independence
Universal appeal of the Declaration of independence. D. Rusk. Dept State Bul 51: 74-8 Jl 20 '64

DECLARATION of the rights of the child
Declaration of the rights of the child. U N Rev 10:32-3 D '63

DECONTAMINATION (from gases, chemicals, etc)
Decontamination of potato tubers containing cesium-137. H. J. Perkins and G. Strachan. bibliog il Science 144:59-60 Ap 3 '64
Make milk safe for children. Christian Cent 81:1132 S 16 '64
Their house was haunted by atomic ghosts; Harry Kizirian's house, Lansdowne, Pa. F. C. Appel. il Sat Eve Post 237:72-3 S 26 '64
U.S. food safe from DDT. Sci N L 85:350 My 30 '64
See also
Space vehicles—Sterilization

DECORATION and ornament
Be eclectic about wall decorations. il Am Home 67:118-20+ Jl '64
Beautiful lead pipe cinch. il Design 65:41 S '63
Fun-to-make holiday decorations for Thanksgiving. K. Bourke. il Pop Gard 14:28-9 N '63
How to create the fantasy finishes that simulate semi-precious stones. il House & Gard 126:108-9 Ag '64
Leaf silhouettes; patterns in concrete to enhance your patio. A. R. Ball. il Pop Gard 15:12-13 Ja '64
Seashells on your wall? why not! Good H 157:170 N '63
See also
Appliqué work
Arts and crafts
Candles
Christmas decorations
Design, Decorative
Embroidery
Fruit, Artificial
Glass, Ornamental
House decoration
Jewelry
Monograms
Paper, Decorative
Paper work
Silk screen printing
Stencil work
Table decoration

DECORATION and ornament, Architectural
Anonymous art; Anonymous arts recovery society. New Yorker 40:49-51 N 14 '64
Art in Latin American architecture. P. Damaz. il Craft Horiz 23:12-39+ S '63
Department of amplification; collaboration between architect and artist. H. H. Reed, jr. New Yorker 39:163 Ap 20 '63
Fantasy finishes. il House & Gard 124:126-7 Ag '63
Life guide; displays of modern art in city buildings. il Life 55:14 Ag 9 '63
Portraits of our symbol; eagles on Pennsylvania station. il N Y Times Mag p33 N 17 '63
See also
Finials
Grilles
Mural painting and decoration

DECORATIONS, Christmas. See Christmas decorations

DECORATIONS of honor
Cover; presentation of the Badge of military merit to Sergeant Elijah Churchill by General Washington. il Am Artist 29:4+ F '65
Medalurgical note of distinction. Life 54:4 Mr 8 '63
Scarlet epidemic; Legion of honor, France. il Time 82:30 D 13 '63
See also
Medal of honor (United States)
Medals

DECORATIVE design. See Design, Decorative

DECORATIVE paper. See Paper, Decorative

DECOSTE, Fredrik
Fort that went to sea! Am For 70:15 Ag '64

DÉCOUPAGE. See Paper work

DECOYS (hunting)
Decoys for doves. R. F. Burgess. il Outdoor Life 132:44-7+ D '63
Decoys of Nathan Cobb, jr. W. J. Mackey, jr. il Antiques 86:192-3 Ag '64
Goose hunt farm style. C. P. Streeter. il Farm J 87:37+ N '63
Paper-bag goose decoys. D. Jones and O. Orr. il Outdoor Life 132:139 S '63
Secrets of black brant. E. Park. il Field & S 69:21-3+ Ja '65
Toward season's end. T. Trueblood. il Field & S 69:12-13+ Ja '65

DE CRISTOFORO, R. J.
ABCs of building chests and cabinets. Pop Sci 185:116-21 N; 132-5 D '64; 186:132-6 Ja '65 (to be cont)
All-purpose table for portable tools. Pop Sci 182:146-50 Mr '63
Big idea: island shop with big-door access. por Pop Sci 183:108 S '63
Copper overcoats for saw blades. Pop Mech 120:124-5+ O '63
Decorative carving made easy, with a fly cutter. Pop Mech 119:194-6 Ap '63
DeWalt's new direct-drive table saw. Pop Sci 185:160-1 N '64
Disston's dial-a-power drill. Pop Sci 182: 153-5 Ap '63
Drill-press tool rack. Pop Mech 120:180-1 S '63
Hitch a router to your lathe! Pop Sci 183: 116-18 Ag '63
How to do lathework on your table saw. Pop Sci 182:138-41 F '63
How to saw good, like all of us should. Pop Sci 184:104-7 Je '64
Motorize your turning chisel. Pop Mech 121: 184-7 Ja '64
Multipurpose tool gets a built-in sawdust vacuum. Pop Mech 120:109-11 N '63
New twists on rotary planers. Pop Sci 183: 106-9 Jl '63
Now, automatic turning for your lathe. Pop Sci 182:168-9 F '63
Roll-away table for ping-pong. Pop Sci 183: 152-4 O '63
Sliding work holder for your table saw. Pop Mech 119:184-6 Ap '63
Table-saw doodles: could you cut them? Pop Sci 185:138-40 Jl '64
Tips for the home shop. Pop Sci 182:137 F '63
Wood sculpture with a power saw. Pop Sci 183:141-3 S '63
Woodworking joints that lock. Pop Sci 185: 162-5 O '64

DECTER, Midge
Growing old in America. Commentary 35:22-7 Ja '63
Mailer's campaign. Commentary 37:83-5 F '64
Negro & the New York schools. bibliog f Commentary 38:25-34 S '64
Peace ladies. Harper 226:48-53 Mr '63
Strangely polite Dr Strangelove. Commentary 37:75-7 My '64
DECTER, Moshe
Russian art & anti-Semitism. Commentary 36:433 D '63
Status of the Jews in the Soviet Union. For Affairs 41:420-30 Ja '63
DE CUBAS, Jose
Development aid: address, April 4, 1963. Vital Speeches 29:499-502 Je 1 '63
DE DIENES, Andre
Land of adventure. U S Camera 27:75-7+ Ag '64
DEDIJER, Vladimir
Sarajevo fifty years after. bibliog f For Affairs 42:569-84 Jl '64
DEDUCTIBLE yacht; story. See Auchincloss, L.
DEE, Johnny
New deal at Notre Dame. F. Deford. il por Sports Illus 21:28-9 D 21 '64
DEE, Ruby
Suddenly Ossie and Ruby are everywhere. il pors Life 55:110-13 D 6 '63
DEE, Sandra
Odd odyssey of Sandra Dee. C. R. Jennings. il pors Sat Eve Post 236:22-3 Je 22 '63
DEEDY, John G. Jr
Middle way. Commonweal 80:353-4 Je 12 '64
Shared time experiment. Commonweal 79: 530-2 Ja 31 '64
DEEGAN, Thomas J.
Fair's till begins to jingle. Bsns W p34 Mr 7 '64
He thumps the tub for the fair. il por Bsns W p 120-2+ Ja 25 '64
Ho hum, come to the fair. M. Mayer. Esquire 60:117+ O '63
DE EGRY, Anne
Leo de Garius fecit, 1179. Art N 62:34-7+ Ja '64
DEEN, Rosemary F.
Larkin's poetry. Commonweal 81:459 D 25 '64
DEEP RIVER, Ontario
Making headlines; North Renfrew times. J. A. Cropley. il Recreation 57:393+ O '64
DEEP sea deposits
Carbonate deposits and paleoclimatic implications in the northeast Pacific Ocean. Y. R. Nayudu. bibliog il Science 146:515-17 O 23 '64
Clay- and carbonate-accumulation rates in three south Atlantic deep-sea cores. K. K. Turekian and M. Stuiver. il Science 146: 55-6 O 2 '64
Cretaceous, paleocene,and pleistocene sediments from the Indian Ocean. Y. Herman. bibliog il Science 140:1316-17 Je 21 '63
Geochronology of marine and fluvial sediments; report on conference. E. Rona. Science 144:1595-7 Je 26 '64
Mining the bottom of the sea; excerpts from draft of general scientific framework; ed. by J. Lear. R. Revelle. il Sat R 47:60-1 O 3 '64
Miocene-pliocene boundary in the Philippines as related to late tertiary stratigraphy of deep-sea sediments. O. L. Bandy. bibliog il Science 142:1290-2 D 6 '63
Modern graywacke-type sands. C. D. Hollister and B. C. Heezen. bibliog il Science 146:1573-4 D 18 '64
Origin of oceanic manganese minerals. G. Arrhenius and others. bibliog il Science 144: 170-3 Ap 10 '64
Pleistocene epoch in deep-sea sediments. D. B. Ericson and others. bibliog il Science 146:723-32 N 6 '64
Pliocene-pleistocene boundary in deep-sea sediments. D. B. Ericson and others. bibliog il Science 139:727-37 F 22 '63
Pliocene-pleistocene boundary in deep-sea sediments. W. R. Riedel and others. bibliog il Science 140:1238-40 Je 14 '63
Pteropod ooze from Bermuda pedestal. C. Chen. bibliog il Science 144:60-2 Ap 3 '64
Pyrene and fluoranthene in manganese nodules. D. W. Thomas and M. Blumer. bibliog il Science 143:39 Ja 3 '64
Sediment cores from the Arctic and subarctic seas. D. B. Ericson and others. bibliog il Science 144:1183-92 Je 5 '64
Tellurium content of marine manganese oxides and other manganese oxides. H. W. Lakin and others. bibliog il Science 142: 1568-9 D 20 '63
Time's traces in sediment. D. B. Ericson and G. Wollin. il Natur Hist 72:52-61 F '63
DEEP sea diving. See Diving, Submarine
DEEP sea fishes. See Fishes, Deep sea
DEEP sea photography. See Photography, Submarine
DEEP-sea research vessels. See Ships, Research
DEEPE, Beverly
Self-reliance in Saigon. por Time 85:38 Ja 8 '65
DEER
Birth of two whitetails. il Natur Hist 73:30-1 Je '64
Deer war. B. East. il Outdoor Life 132:17-19+ D '63
Legacy of a French Noah; whitetail deer to Anticosti Island. J. Olsen. il Sports Illus 19:62-4+ O 7 '63
So deer to my garden. S. Grant. il Flower Grower 52:16-17 Ja '65
To unlock fighting deer, courage is the key. D. Harbour. il Audubon Mag 66:234-6 Jl '64

Collisions with automobiles

See Automobile driving—Animal hazards

Diseases and pests

New life for a blind deer. G. Carousso. il Sat Eve Post 237:77-8 My 9 '64
DEER hunting
Advice from expert bowhunters. G. H. Gillelan. il Outdoor Life 132:26+ S '63
Backwoods buck. C. Elliott. il Outdoor Life 132:48-9+ D '63
Beast of Buckless Gulch. C. Chatfield. il Outdoor Life 134:54-5+ O '64
Beware of timberline bucks. O. A. Washburn. il Field & S 69:50-1+ Je '64
Boat-float bucks. B. W. Dalrymple. il Field & S 69:54-5+ Jl '64
Bowhunting for gunners. G. H. Gillelan. il Outdoor Life 132:12-13+ Ag '63
California deer camp. F. Dufresne. il Field & S 69:36-7+ Ag '64
Deer by the dozen. T. Janes. il Outdoor Life 132:17-19+ N '63
Deer camp on wheels. L. Dietz. il Field & S 68:37-9+ D '63
Deer hunt country style. K. Shrout and B. Shrout. il Field & S 68:54-7+ O '63
Deer hunting with dad. R. Bressler. il Outdoor Life 133:60-3+ My '64
Deer in the dunes. F. H. Ames. il Outdoor Life 134:48-9+ Ag '64
Deer in your pocket. B. Cary. il Outdoor Life 132:54-5+ S '63
Deer of Thanksgiving. C. Gresham. il Outdoor Life 134:40-1+ N '64
Don't blow it. O. Lagelbauer. il Outdoor Life 132:38-9+ D '63
Double buck. A. Davenport. il Field & S 69: 30-1+ D '64
Double hat rack; ed. by B. East. P. Helser. il Outdoor life 134:24-7+ D '64
Double on deer. T. McNally. il Outdoor Life 132:40-3+ S '63
Dwarf deer in Sonora. J. O'Connor. il Outdoor Life 131:42-3+ Mr '63
Earthquake deer. E. A. Bauer. il Outdoor Life 131:56-9+ Je '63
Five-year stalk: new record whitetail. A. Dawson. il Outdoor Life 132:32-5+ Ag '63
Fog horns. G. Laycock. il Outdoor Life 131: 38-9+ Ja '63
40th buck. C. Chatfield. il Outdoor Life 132: 28-9+ Jl '63
Guides for bowhunting. G. H. Gillelan. il Outdoor Life 132:80-3 Jl '63
Horn hunters' heaven. O. A. Washburn. il Field & S 68:49-51 O '63
How I shot the no. 1 deer. E. T. McMaster. il Outdoor Life 134:17-19+ N '64
How to see a deer. H. G. Tapply. il Field & S 69:48 D '64
Hunting horse. J. O'Connor. il Outdoor Life 132:46-7+ Jl '63
Instant deer hunt; questions and answers. D. Du Bois. il Outdoor Life 134:62-4 S '64
Minnesota brush bucks. H. Bradshaw. il Field & S 69:138-41+ O '64
Mountain of mule deer. B. Jourdan. il Outdoor Life 134:40-1+ D '64
Mule deer muskets. W. Page. il Field & S 68:78-82 O '63
My last buck. C. E. Gillham. il Field & S 68:32-4+ Jl '63
Pilgrim Mountain buck. C. V. Whitney. il Field & S 68:32-4+ F '64
Problem of range. W. Page. il Field & S 69:100-5 O '64
Real deer sleeper. P. Czura. il Field & S 68:104-6+ N '63
Regulated bowhunts. G. H. Gillelan. il Outdoor Life 131:110-11+ F '63

DEER hunting—*Continued*
Secret side of Manti-La Sal. B. Behme. il Field & S 69:21-3+ D '64
Still hunt. C. Ford. il Field & S 68:6+ D '63
Take it easy. T. Trueblood. il Field & S 68: 24+ S '63
Tips for taking big game; bow hunting. G. H. Gillelan. il Outdoor Life 134:26-7+ O '64
Too good to shoot. R. Camp. il Field & S 67: 56-7+ Mr '63
Twenty best places to kill deer in the U.S; symposium. il Outdoor Life 134:44-7+ O '64
Two best ways to get a deer. B. East. il Outdoor Life 132:46-7+ N '63
What whitetails taught me; stalking of deer. D. M. Lance. il Outdoor Life 134:30-1+ N '64
Where the deer are; symposium. il Outdoor Life 132:44-7+ O '63
Where to bowhunt for deer. G. H. Gillelan. il Outdoor Life 134:12+ Ag '64
Whitetails for all. E. A. Bauer. il Outdoor Life 132:36-9+ O '63
Wild deer area opens; the Triangle. H. Wixom. il Outdoor Life 132:38-9+ Ag '63
Wisconsin's biggest day of the year. G. Laycock. il Field & S 68:60-1+ O '63
Wisdom of whitetails. D. J. Anderson. il Field & S 69:62-4+ O '64
World's biggest deer camp. W. Page. il Field & S 68:25-7 N '63
X marks the spot. M. Ellis. il Field & S 69:50-2+ S '64
DEER meat. See Venison
DEER mice. See Mice, White footed
DEERBRUSH
Colorful shrub for West Coast gardens. M. G. Schmidt. il Flower Grower 50:16-17+ O '63
DEERE and company
Green, yellow & gold. il Time 81:92+ My 24 '63
John Deere's sticks of steel. il Arch Forum 121:76-85 Jl '64
Moline's biggest bash; Saarinen-designed headquarters. il Bsns W p62-4 Je 20 '64
Plowmen's palace; new headquarters. il Time 84:64-5 Ag 7 '64
Rural mural for a tractor maker. il Fortune 70:144-7 D '64
DEERFIELD colony. See Weld County, Colo.
DEERING, Elmer C.
Bonds for educational purposes, sales, interest rates, et cetera; public schools (title varies) See issues of School life
—See Bokelman, W. R. jt. auth.
DEERING, Milliken and company
Latest on business's right to close; Darlington manufacturing company case. U S News 55:95 D 2 '63
Right to fail; Darlington manufacturing co. case before Supreme court. Newsweek 64: 66 D 21 '64
Textile mill that rolls with the whim. il Bsns W p 164+ O 26 '63
DEERWESTER, C. L.
Ultimate in a traffic-signal tower truck. Am City 78:133 S '63
DEES sisters. See Triplets
DEEVER, John
She's a big girl. Sat Eve Post 236:58-61 D 21 '63
DEEVEY, Edward S. Jr, and others
Fractionation of sulfur and carbon isotopes in a meromictic lake. bibliog Science 139:407-8 F 1 '63
—See Davis, M. B. jt. auth.
DEFAMATION. See Libel and slander
DEFEATISM. See Political psychology
DEFECTIONISTS. See Turncoats
DEFECTIVE speech. See Speech defects
DEFECTIVES
See also
Mentally handicapped children
DEFELICE, J. and others
Cosmic-ray exposure age of the Farmington meteorite from radioactive isotopes. bibliog Science 142:673-4 N 8 '63
DEFENDERS, Public. See Public defenders
DEFENDERS of American liberties (organization)
Defenders of the right. il Newsweek 61:20 F 4 '63
DEFENSE, Civil. See Civil defense
DEFENSE, Department of. See United States —Defense, Department of
DEFENSE, Self. See Self defense
DEFENSE and space group. See Burroughs corporation
DEFENSE appropriations. See United States —Armed forces—Appropriations and expenditures
DEFENSE buying. See United States—Armed forces—Procurement
DEFENSE communications agency. See United States—Defense, Department of—Defense communications agency
DEFENSE contracts. See Contracts, Government
DEFENSE economy. See War—Economic aspects
DEFENSE industries. See Munitions industries
DEFENSE information, Classified
How to play unpolitics. W. J. Coughlin. Miss & Roc 15:50 O 5 '64
Our defense secrets are for sale cheap. O. Schisgall. il Look 27:78-80 Ag 27 '63
DEFENSE intelligence agency. See United States—Defense, Department of—Defense intelligence agency
DEFENSE measures of corporations. See Corporations—Defense measures
DEFENSE mechanisms (biology)
Tremoctopus violaceus uses physalia tentacles as weapons. E. C. Jones. bibliog il Science 139:764-6 F 22 '63
DEFENSE of Taipei; drama. See Bromberg, C.
DEFENSE research and engineering, Director of. See United States—Defense research and engineering, Director of
DEFENSE science board. See United States—Defense, Department of—Defense science board
DEFENSE supply agency. See United States—Defense, Department of—Defense supply agency
DEFENSE work. See Contracts, Government
DEFERRED payment plan. See Instalment plan
DEFFERRE, Gaston
After de Gaulle, Monsieur X? por Newsweek 62:49 N 4 '63
Beginning a dialogue. il por Time 83:24 F 14 '64
Challenger talks back to President de Gaulle. H. Giniger. il pors N Y Times Mag p25+ Mr 15 '64
De Gaulle's challenger. New Repub 150:6-7 Mr 21 '64
France: a third force? E. Taylor. Reporter 30:24-6 F 27 '64
Horizon 1980. Newsweek 63:51 F 17 '64
Letter from Paris. Genêt. New Yorker 40:98+ F 22; 144-6 Mr 7 '64
Long shot bucks De Gaulle; with report by H. Moffett. il pors Life 56:71-2+ Ap 3 '64
New challenger? il por Time 82:23 D 27 '63
Preview of a candidate. il por Time 83:39-40 Ap 3 '64
Why Gaston Defferre? J. Daniel. Harper 229 85-8+ Jl '64
DEFFEYES, K. S. and others
Dolomitization: observations on the island of Bonaire, Netherlands Antilles. bibliog Science 143:678-9 F 14 '64
DEFIANCE industries, incorporated
What's in it for Eddie, Bob, and Vic? S. H. Brown. il Fortune 70:139-43+ S '64
DEFICIENCY diseases
See also
Kwashiorkor
DEFICIENCY diseases in plants
All that glitters is not gold. R. M. Carleton. il Horticulture 41:326-7 Je '63
DEFICIENT diet. See Diet, Deficient
DEFICIT spending. See Government spending policy
DEFILIPPES, Frank M.
Nucleotides: separation from an alkaline hydrolysate of RNA by thin-layer electrophoresis. bibliog Science 144:1350-1 Je 12 '64
DEFOE, Daniel
Fortunes and misfortunes of the famous Daniel Defoe. V. S. Pritchett. il Horizon 7:40-9 Wint '65
DEFONTAINE, Dorothy
Trade wind world; Florida, Bahamas, West Indies. Yachting 116:34-6+ N '64
DEFONTAINE, Ham
Gadgets & gilhickies. See issues of Yachting
DEFORD, Frank
Baseball. Sports Illus 20:84-5 Ap 6; 69-70+ Je 1; 21:49-50 Ag 3 '64
Basketball. Sports Illus 20:58+ Ap 20 '64; 22:46-7 Ja 4 '65
Big splash for bath and tennis. Sports Illus 19:36-41 S 2 '63
College basketball. Sports Illus 19:100 D 23 '63; 20:48-9 Ja 6 '64
Lacrosse. Sports Illus 20:66+ Je 8 '64
Pro basketball. Sports Illus 20:81-2+ My 4 '64

DEFORD, Frank—*Continued*
Tennis. Sports Illus 18:57-9 Mr 18; 55-7 Ap 29; 19:40-1 Jl 1 '63; 20:57-8 Mr 2; 21:93-5 S 21; 76-8 S 28 '64
(ed) See Ramsey, F. Smart moves by a master of deception
DEFORD, Miriam Allen
Psychology of mystery story writing. Writer 77:12-14 Je '64
DEFORMITIES
Abnormalities associated with a chromosome region in the mouse. L. C. Dunn; D. Bennett. bibliog il Science 144:260-7 Ap 17 '64
Bipolar planarians in a stock culture. M. M. Jenkins. bibliog il Science 142:1187 N 29 '63
Birth defects. L. W. Sauer. PTA Mag 58:13-14 D '63
Congenital anomalies induced in hamster embryos with H-1 virus. V. H. Ferm and L. Kilham. bibliog il Science 145:510-11 Jl 31 '64
Defects cause guilt sense. Sci N L 86:291 N 7 '64
Doctor is a detective. il Todays Health 42:30-1+ S '64
Egg and Doctor Grabowski. A. J. Snider. il Todays Health 41:80-1 N '63
Embryonic deformities. Sci N L 83:258 Ap 27 '63
Help for thalidomide victims; Abteilung 10, West Germany. il Time 81:63-4 Ap 26 '63
Helping hand; thalidomide children. il Newsweek 62:62 S 9 '63
Hormone-like substance may cause birth defects. Sci N L 83:111 F 16 '63
How medical progress has hastened the passing of the side show. J. Lentz. il Todays Health 42:48-51 Mr '64
Malformed by quinine. Sci N L 84:54 Jl 27 '63
My search to find the drug that crippled my baby. K. H. Schulte-Hillen. il Good H 156:94-102 My '63
New hope in the fight against deformed births. O. J. Miller and J. Ryan. il Sci Digest 54:69-73 O '63
New miracles of baby surgery. L. David. Good H 156:76-7+ Ap '63
Preventable birth defects. L. W. Sauer. PTA Mag 59:31-2 N '64
Solving the mystery of birth defects. S. S. Rosenberg. il Parents Mag 39:36-7+ Ja '64
Teratogenic effects of meclizine hydrochloride on the rat. C. T. G. King. bibliog il Science 141:353-5 Jl 26 '63
Teratogenic significance of ionic and fluid imbalances. C. T. Grabowski. bibliog il Science 142:1064 N 22 '63
Thalidomide babies' care. Sci N L 83:382 Je 15 '63
Thalidomide syndrome in monkeys. C. S. Delahunt and L. J. Lassen. bibliog Science 146:1300+ D 4 '64
We are not created equal. F. Marley. il Sci N L 84:55+ Jl 27 '63
See also
Bladder—Deformities
International conference on congenital malformations
DEFORMITIES, Cure of. See Orthopedia
DE FRANCE, Edward
I'm a culture vulture; poem. Liv Wildn 82:37 Winter '62
DE FRANCIS, Vincent
Parents who abuse children. PTA Mag 58:16-18 N '63
DEFRÈRE, Désiré
Obituary
Opera N por 29:29 D 5 '64. F. Robinson
DEFROSTERS, Windshield. See Automobiles—Windshield defrosters
DEFROSTING
See also
Refrigerators, Electric—Defrosting
DEFURIO, Anthony G.
Letters. Sch Arts 64:46 N '64
DE GÁMEZ, Tana
Alicia Alonso and the National ballet of Cuba. Dance Mag 38:30-5 Jl '64
DEGAS, Edgar
Portraits of three painters. H. Kramer. il Reporter 31:35-6 D 17 '64
DE GAULLE, Charles. See Gaulle, C. de
DE GAULLE, Yvonne Thérèse (Vendroux) See Gaulle, Y. T. V. de
DEGEEST, Hilaire, and others
Negative inotropic effect of the vagus nerves upon the canine ventricle. bibliog Science 144:1223-5 Je 5 '64
DEGENHART, Pearl
Seed mosaics. Design 64:146-7 Mr '63
DEGENERATION
Devastating defect; hepatolenticular degeneration. il Time 81:49 Mr 8 '63

DEGLER, Carl N.
Ordeal of Herbert Hoover. Yale R 52:563-83 Je '63
DEGNAN, James P.
Through a dark, glassily. Atlan 212:102+ S '63
DE GRAAFF, Jan
Why we hybridize lilies. Pop Gard 14:28-9+ S '63
DE GRABOWSKI, Christopher
Voyage of pleasure. por Motor B 113:46-9+ Ap '64
DEGRAFF, John
(comp) Yachtsman's bookshelf (cont) Yachting 114:162+ N; 122+ D '63
DE GRAMONT, Sanche
Ecumenical council. Sat Eve Post 236:86-91 F 23 '63
Nasser's hired Germans. Sat Eve Post 236:60-1+ Jl 13 '63
Triumph of Paul VI. Sat Eve Post 236:79-83 Jl 27 '63
Tshombe in wonderland. Sat Eve Post 237:83+ O 3 '64
What became of the Aga Khan? Sat Eve Post 237:30-2 D 5 '64
DEGREES, Academic
Confusion of degrees. P. Woodring. Sat R 46:59 Je 15 '63
Doctorate at Teachers college. Sch & Soc 92:185 Ap 18 '64
Drive for doctorates. il Time 82:34 D 20 '63
Earned degrees, another year, another increase. W. V. Grant. il Sch Life 45:12-13 F '63
Engineering enrollments and degrees. Sch & Soc 92:179-80 Ap 18 '64
More college degrees. Sci N L 87:50 Ja 23 '65
More teachers for business education. B. I. Blackstone. il Sch Life 45:23 My '63
Offered: a short cut to a master's degree; Yale university. U S News 56:8 Ja 27 '64
DEGREES, Honorary
Kudos (cont) il Time 81:83-5 Je 14; 60-1 Je 21; 64 Je 28 '63; 83:69 Je 5; 60 Je 12; 76+ Je 19; 62 Je 26 '64
Matter of degrees. il Newsweek 63:57 Je 22 '64
Anecdotes, facetiae, satire, etc.
Degree circus; season of kudos. W. Thompson. il Nation 198:580-1 Je 8 '64
DE GREGORY, Hugo
New Hampshire hangover. Nation 198:566 Je 8 '64
DEGROVE, John M. See Kammerer, G. M. jt. auth.
DEHAAN, Robert F.
Function of research centers. Science 140:1362 Je 28 '63
DE HIRSCH, Katrina
Reporter at large. C. Tomkins. New Yorker 39:130+ S 14 '63
DEHN, Mura
New spirit in an ancient dance. por Dance Mag 38:16+ S '64
DE HOLGUIN, Beatrice
Coconuts, tourists, and pirate gold. Américas 15:39-41 Ap '63
DEHYDRATED food. See Food—Drying
DEHYDRATED potatoes. See Potatoes, Dried
DEHYDRATING food. See Food, Dried
DEHYDRATION of fruits, vegetables, etc. See Food—Drying
DEHYDROGENASES
Allosteric properties of glutamate dehydrogenases from different sources. N. Talal and G. M. Tomkins. bibliog il Science 146:1309-11 D 4 '64
D-malate: effects on activity of L-malate dehydrogenase in developing sea urchin embryos. R. D. Billiar and others. bibliog il Science 146:1464-5 D 11 '64
Electron microscopic and biochemical studies of pyruvate dehydrogenase complex of escherichia coli. L. J. Reed and others. bibliog il Science 145:930-2 Ag 28 '64
Erythrocyte glucose-6-phosphate dehydrogenase in Caucasians: new inherited variant. T. B. Shows, jr. and others. bibliog il Science 145:1056-7 S 4 '64
Estrogen-induced 16-hydroxysteriod dehydrogenase activity in rat kidney. K. J. Ryan and others. bibliog il Science 142:243-4 O 11 '63
Fructose-1,6-diphosphate requirement of streptococcal lactic dehydrogenases. M. J. Wolin. bibliog il Science 146:775-7 N 6 '64
Glucose-6-phosphate dehydrogenase in drosophila: X-linked electrophoretic variants. W. J. Young and others. bibliog il Science 143:140-1 Ja 10 '64

DEHYDROGENASES—*Continued*
Human erythrocyte lactate dehydrogenase: four genetically determined variants. A. P. Kraus and C. L. Neely, jr. bibliog il Science 145:595-7 Ag 7 '64
Lactate dehydrogenase in pigeon testes: genetic control by three loci. W. H. Zinkham and others. bibliog il Science 144: 1353-4 Je 12 '64
Lactate dehydrogenase in testis: dissociation and recombination of subunits. W. H. Zinkham and others. bibliog il Science 142: 1303-4 D 6 '63
Lactate dehydrogenase isozymes: dissociation and recombination of subunits. C. L. Markert. bibliog il Science 140:1329-30 Je 21 '63
Lactate dehydrogenase isozymes: lability at low temperature. H. A. Zondag. bibliog il Science 142:965-7 N 15 '63
Lactate dehydrogenase variant from human blood: evidence for molecular subunits. S. H. Boyer and others. bibliog il Science 141:642-3 Ag 16 '63
Lactate dehydrogenases in human testes. A. Blanco and W. H. Zinkham. bibliog il Science 139:601-2 F 15 '63
Lactic and malic dehydrogenases in human spermatozoa. E. Goldberg. bibliog il Science 139:602-3 F 15 '63
Lactic dehydrogenase: genetic control in man. W. E. Nance and others. bibliog il Science 142:1075-7 N 22 '63
Lactic dehydrogenases: functions of the two types. D. M. Dawson and others. bibliog il Science 143:929-33 F 28 '64
Lactic dehydrogenases subfractionation of isozymes. P. J. Fritz and K. B. Jacobson. bibliog il Science 140:64-5 Ap 5 '63
Malate dehydrogenase: multiple forms in separated blastomeres of sea urchin embryos. R. O. Moore and C. A. Villee. bibliog il Science 142:389-90 O 18 '63
Malate dehydrogenases in the rusted bean leaf. R. C. Staples and M. A. Stahmann. bibliog il Science 140:1320-1 Je 21 '63
Molecular heterogeneity of enzymes: malate dehydrogenase of euglena. J. Chancellor-Maddison and C. R. Noll, jr. bibliog il Science 142:60-1 O 4 '63
Regulation of enzyme activity by specific reversal of feedback inhibition. E. Sturani and others. bibliog il Science 141:1053-4 S 13 '63
Where life is controlled; C. L. Markert's work with lactic dehydrogenase. Newsweek 65:50 Ja 11 '65
Xanthine dehydrogenase: differences in activity among drosophila strains. E. C. Keller, jr. and E. Glassman. bibliog il Science 143:40-1 Ja 3 '64
Xanthine dehydrogenase in drosophila: detection of isozymes. K. D. Smith and others. bibliog il Science 142:226-7 O 11 '63
See also
Enzymes

DE-ICERS. See Airplanes—Ice protection; Ice on rivers, lakes, etc.—Control

DEIGHTON, Lee
Publisher's viewpoint. por Sr Schol 85:12T-13T+ O 7 '64

DEINDORFER, Robert G.
(ed) See Kennedy, J. F. Private letters of John F. Kennedy

DEINOPIDAE. See Spiders

DEISS, Joseph Jay
Herculaneum: Italy's neglected treasure trove. Harper 228:55-60 Mr '64

DEITTMANN, Paul R.
All in each place. Christian Cent 81:799-801 Je 17 '64

DEJ, Gheorghe Gheorghiu-. See Gheorghiu-Dej, G.

DÉJÀ vu
Annals of medicine. B. Roueché. New Yorker 39:34-6+ Ag 17 '63

DE JONG, Bettie
Brief biography. S. Goodman. pors Dance Mag 38:40-1 N '64

DEJONG, David Cornel
Assailed from without; Born in a county-seat; poems. Poetry 104:9-11 Ap '64
August; poem. Atlan 214:74 Ag '64
Boot zonder dek; poem. Sat R 46:51 Mr 30 '63
Dangers of nature in the city; poem. Sat R 46:11 N 16 '63
Detritus; poem. Commonweal 80:476 Jl 10 '64
Home; poem. Ladies Home J 80:138 Ja '63
Keep moving forward. Writer 76:20-1 Je '63
New and selected, and a first volume. Poetry 102:125-7 My '63
Young pioneer; poem. New Repub 151:16 S 12 '64

DEJONG, Meindert
Cry and the creation. Horn Bk 39:197-206 Ap '63

DEJONG, Russell N.
MS; crippler of young adults. Todays Health 42:36-7 N '64

DE KIEWIET, C. W.
Loneliness in the beloved country. For Affairs 42:413-27 Ap '64

DEKNIGHT, Freda
Date with a dish. See issues of Ebony

DEKOCK, Duane E.
How to outsmart that six-pound bass. Farm J 87:24 S '63

DE KOONING, Elaine Marie (Fried)
Painting a portrait of the President. il Art N 63:37+ Sum '64
about
Elaine deKooning: portraits in a New York scene. L. Campbell. il por Art N 62:38-9+ Ap '63
Instant summaries. il por Time 81:68 My 3 '63
Oldest art; exhibition at New York's Graham gallery. il por Newsweek 61:105 My 13 '63
Quest for a famous likeness. il pors Life 56: 120-2 My 8 '64

DE KOONING, Willem
Art galleries. H. Rosenberg. New Yorker 38:126+ F 16 '63
De Kooning. H. Rosenberg. il pors Vogue 144:146-9+ S 15 '64
De Kooning: grand style. il pors Newsweek 65:56-7 Ja 4 '65
Strange eye and art of De Kooning. G. Dickerson. il pors Sat Eve Post 237:68-71 N 21 '64
Three more faces of Eve; exhibition at the Stone gallery, New York. V. Petersen. il Art N 63:30+ Mr '64

DELA BECKWITH, Byron
Beckwith mistrial. Sr Schol 84:17 F 28 '64
Beckwith trial. il por Newsweek 63:27 F 10 '64
Colonel's grandson. il por Newsweek 62:22-3 Jl 8 '63
Hung jury. Newsweek 63:16-17 F 17 '64
Hung jury. por Time 83:20-1 F 14 '64
Justice in Mississippi; notes on the Beckwith trial. J. Herron. Nation 198:179-81 F 24 '64
Little abnormal. il por Time 82:15-16 Jl 5 '63
Red carpet for Beckwith. J. DeMuth. New Repub 150:9 My 23 '64
Star prisoner. por Newsweek 62:28+ D 16 '63
Trial of Delay Beckwith. H. H. Martin. il por Sat Eve Post 237:77-81 Mr 14 '64
Welcome home. Newsweek 63:30 Ap 27 '64

DELACATO, Carl
Return to babyhood: maverick methods give help to brain-injured children: with report by J. Delay. il por Life 55:31+ Ag 23 '63

DELACORTE, George T.
Dell chairman receives New York city medallion. il por Pub W 186:33 O 12 '64

DELACORTE, Valerie
GBS in filmland. Esquire 62:150-1+ D '64

DELACROIX, Eugène
Delacroix: prophet in paint. K. Kuh. il Sat R 46:21-3 Je 22 '63
Duality of Delacroix. F. Cachin. il por Art N 62:38-41+ Sum '63
He had a sun in his head. il por Time 82: 50-3 Jl 26 '63
He opened the door to modern art. G. Kent. il por Read Digest 83:158-60+ D '63
La gloire. il por Newsweek 61:85 Je 3 '63
Letter from Paris; centenary exhibition in Louvre's salon Carré and Grande gallerie. Genêt. New Yorker 39:73-4 Je 29 '63
Master art and opera. R. Rushmore. il Opera N 28:28-9 Ja 4 '64
Revered, detested, romantic rebel. J. Canaday. il por N Y Times Mag p62-3 My 5 '63

DELAHUNT, C. S. and Lassen, L. J.
Thalidomide syndrome in monkeys. bibliog Science 146:1300+ D 4 '64

DELANEY, Shelagh
Blackpool: the English fun-and-chips holiday town. il Vogue 141:100-1+ Je '63
P.S. to summer; its English lunatic cheer. Vogue 144:197+ S 1 '64
Sweetly sings the donkey; story. Sat Eve Post 236:42-3 My 18 '63
about
Dead end kids. por Time 82:62 Ag 30 '63
Lion in love. Criticism
America 109:63-4+ Jl 13 '63
New Yorker 39:90+ My 4 '63
Newsweek 61:83 My 6 '63
Theatre Arts il 47:64-5 Je '63
Time por 81:76 My 3 '63

DELANO, Frank
Gabon. Travel 121:48-9 Mr '64
DELANY, Elvira
State and local developments. See occasional issues of Recreation to May 1964
DELAPLANE, Stan
Cooking on the outside (crying on the inside) Am Home 67:7 My '64
Letter from Stan Delaplane. See issues of Today's health
DELAVALLADE, Carmen
On stage. R. W. Murphy. por Horizon 5:48-9 My '63
DE LA VEGA, Aurelio
New World composers. por Américas 16:23-8 Jl '64
DELAWARE
See also
Prisons—Delaware
DELAWARE, Ohio
Elegant bay of Mrs. Buck; Overtrick wins Little brown jug. K. Rudeen. il Sports Illus 19:30-1 S 30 '63
DELAWARE. University, Newark
Georgian setting for Delaware; Hugh M. Morris library. J. M. Dawson. il Library J 88:4569-71 D 1 '63
DELAY, James
Theory works out fine for Johnny. Life 55: 34+ Ag 23 '63
DELAY devices
Electromagnetic delay lines. S. L. Silver. il Electr World 69:46-9+ F '63
Magnetostrictive delay lines. J. R. Collins. il Electr World 71:48-9 Ja '64
DELAY lines. See Delay devices
DELCENA, Louise
Louise Delcena dance company at Judson Hall. D. Hering. Dance Mag 37:13 Ag '63
DELEEUW, Louise G.
Jewels for your garden. Flower Grower 50: 34-5 Ap '63
DELEGATES, Convention. See National conventions (political)
DELEGATES to the United Nations. See United Nations—Delegates
DELEGATION of powers
Dilemma of decentralization; symposium, ed. by T. O'Hanlon. il Duns R 84:41-2+ S '64
DEL FAVA, Arlene
Case of the switchblade. por Newsweek 64: 34 Jl 27 '64
DELGADO, Jose Manuel Rodriguez
Cerebral heterostimulation in a monkey colony. bibliog Science 141:161-3 Jl 12 '63
Radio control of minds. Sci N L 84:50 Jl 27 '63
DELHOM, M. Mellanay
18th century Wedgwood horizons in a Chicago collector's home. il Hobbies 68:28-9 D '63
DELIBES, Leo
Delibes highlights from Lakmé. M. de Schauensee. il Am Rec G 30:1099 Ag '64
On records: Lakmé (excerpts) Opera N 29: 35 Ja 9 '65
DELICATE arch. See Arches, Natural
DELINQUENT chacha, esq; story. See Mehta, V.
DELINQUENT children. See Juvenile delinquency
DELINQUENT girls. See Girls, Delinquent
DELINQUENT taxes. See Tax collection
DELINQUENTS. See Juvenile delinquency
DE LISSOVOY, Peter
Comedy's cold sustenance. Nation 199:383-5 N 23 '64
Odds on freedom; gambler's choice in Georgia. Nation 198:618-21 Je 22 '64
Testing the new law: legalists, publicists, activists. Nation 199:7-10 Jl 13 '64
This little light. Nation 199:486-90 D 21 '64
Visible Ellison. Nation 199:334-6 N 9 '64
DELIUS, Anthony
Tsotsis and the Pondos; story. New Yorker 39:26-30 F 1 '64
DELIUS, Frederick
Beecham's Delius: love and understanding could do no more. R. Sabin. Am Rec G 31: 136 O '64
Reissues for the Delius centenary. H. Glass. il por Am Rec G 30:294-5 D '63
DELL publishing company
Dell injunction against popular library denied. Pub W 186:45-6 O 5 '64
Dell sues Popular library over another Harlow book. Pub W 186:298 Ag 31 '64
Dell's encyclopedia: the biggest paperback ever. il Pub W 186:62+ Ag 3 '64
Expansion plans for Dell's Harlin Quist books: paperback juveniles. Pub W 185:40-1 Je 1 '64
DELLA CASA, Lisa
Notes from our correspondents. S. Fleming. Hi Fi 14:26 F '64
Stars at home: photographs. Opera N 29:14-16 D 19 '64
DELLA ROBBIA, Giovanni. See Robbia, G. della
DELLIN, L. A. D.
Bulgaria under Soviet leadership. Cur Hist 44:281-7 My '63
DELMAN, Alice
Ancient magic of the zither. House B 105: 94-5+ Jl '63
DELMAN, David
Barrier; story. Redbook 122:62-3 Ap '64
Strange business of chemistry. Writer 77:9-11+ Je '64
Summer out of season; story. Redbook 121: 149-74 My '63
DELMAN, Maury
Tux or tackle: Winnipeg. Travel 119:26-30 My '63
DELMAS, Gladys
De Gaulle's Mexican hat dance. Reporter 30:30-2 Ap 23 '64
Mexico from the South. Atlan 213:91-4 Mr '64
Peru's new politics: the hit-or-miss approach. Reporter 29:35-8 O 24 '63
DELON, Alain
En garde, ladies: France exports a devastator. il pors Life 56:75-8 F 24 '64
DELORME, Jean
Launching Europe into space; Air liquide. il por Bsns W p66-7+ N 2 '63
DELP, Alfred
Father Delp's prison diary. Cath World 196: 364-9 Mr '63
DELPHI, Ind. public library
Cataloging by the bootstrap method. E. C. Biddle. ALA Bul 58:49-52 Ja '64; Discussion. 58:255, 261, 431-2 Ap, Je '64
DELPHINIUMS
Larkspur is better than ever. M. M. Taylor. il Pop Gard 15:8 F '64
Secret that grows delphinium. M. M. Leister. il Flower Grower 50:23+ Jl '63
DELRIN
New super-smooth metal substitute. D. Brigham. il Sci Digest 53:27-30 Mr '63
DEL RIO, James
Michigan's ghetto buster. il pors Ebony 18: 55-6+ F '63
DELTA air lines
Airline economics distorted, Delta claims. Aviation W 78:45 F 4 '63
Delta April traffic increases 25 per cent; general gain seen for carriers. J. R. Ashlock. Aviation W 78:39+ My 6 '63
First for Delta. Time 81:95 My 3 '63
DELTA plan. See Reclamation of land—Netherlands
DELTA prize novel award
Dell announces winner of first Delta novel award. Pub W 185:35 Mr 30 '64
Spk, he bggd. H. Frankel. Sat R 47:40-1 S 19 '64
DELTAS
Peoples of the deltas: see-saw battle between river and sea. A. Volker. il UNESCO Courier 17:44-7 Jl '64
DELUCCA, Daniel M.
TV searches the business soul. il pors Bsns W p99-100 Mr 28 '64
DE LUE, Donald
Rocket thrower of Donald De Lue. il Am Artist 28:78-9+ Je '64
DELUSIONS. See Medical delusions
DELVAUX, Paul
Mindscape painter. il Newsweek 62:66-7 Jl 1 '63
Poetic shock. il por Time 81:60-1 Je 28 '63
DEMAEREL, Peter
Belgium's carnival craze. Travel 121:44-6 F '64
DE MAEYER, Edward, and De Maeyer-Guignard, J.
Effects of polycyclic aromatic carcinogens on viral replication: similarity to actinomycin D. bibliog Science 146:650-1 O 30 '64
DE MAEYER-GUIGNARD, Jaqueline. See De Maeyer, E. jt. auth.
DEMAGGIO, A. E. See Lott, J. A. jt. auth.
DEMAIO, Lawrence. See Corn, M. jt. auth.
DEMAND and supply. See Supply and demand
DE MARGERIE, Bertrand
Brazil: dearth of priests. America 108:220-2 F 16 '63
DEMARS, Robert
Sex chromatin patterns and the Lyon hypothesis. bibliog Science 141:649-50 Ag 16 '63
DEMAS, Corinne
Curl up and read. Seventeen 23:39 My '64
DEMBLING, Merwin
Bill Herrick: showman with stills. Pop Phot 53:158-61+ D '63
DE MELO NETO, João Cabral
From The death and life of a Severino; poem; excerpts, tr. by E. Bishop. Poetry 103:10-18 O '63

DEMETER, Don
Player of the week; Detroit outfielder. por Sports Illus 21:124 S 7 '64

DE MILLE, Agnes
From primitive dance to minuet to slop; excerpt from Book of the dance. N Y Times Mag p30-1+ O 27 '63
Goodnight, C.B. por Esquire 61:119-31 Ja '64
Laurey makes up her mind. Dance Mag 37: 34-5 Mr '63
We take leap after leap in the dark; ed. by J. Howard. Life 55:94 N 15 '63

about

Grande dame of dance. il pors Life 55:89-90+ N 15 '63

DE MILLE, Cecil Blount
Goodnight, C.B. A. De Mille. il pors Esquire 61:119-31 Ja '64

DEMINERALIZATION of saline water. See Water, Saline

DEMINERALIZERS. See Water purifiers, Domestic

DEMING, Barbara
In the Birmingham jail. Nation 196:436-7 My 25 '63

DEMING, Frederick L.
Money men in key spots. por Newsweek 65:63 Ja 11 '65
New monetary boss will pioneer, cautiously. por Bsns W p25 Ja 9 '65
People of the week. por U S News 58:15 Ja 11 '65
Two are tapped for Treasury. por Bsns W p58 Ja 2 '65

DEMIS, D. Joseph. See Zimmer, J. G. jt. auth.

DEMLOW, James E.
So you want to be a railroad president. Hobbies 68:118-19 F '64

DEMOCRACY
Age of the rights of man; address, October 12, 1963. D. Rush. Dept State Bul 49:654-8 O 28 '63
Battle for freedom; address, July 4, 1963. R. Menzies. Vital Speeches 29:647-9 Ag 15 '63
Challenge of democracy in developing nations; address, January 26, 1964. W. W. Rostow. Dept State Bul 50:251-60 F 17 '64
Democracy and the emerging nations of Africa; address, March 14, 1963. G. M. Williams. Dept State Bul 48:541-5 Ap 8 '63
Democracy faces a global dilemma. W. H. McNeill. il N Y Times Mag p27+ N 17 '63
Democracy is inevitable. P. E. Slater and W. G. Bennis. bibliog f Harvard Bsns R 42:51-9 Mr '64
Democracy on trial in Africa. S. Drake. bibliog f Ann Am Acad 354:110-21 Jl '64
From the land of the free to the big PX. I. Kristol. il N Y Times Mag p7+ D 20 '64
Gettysburg address and our commitment to freedom; address, November 17, 1963. D. Rusk. Dept State Bul 49:842-4 D 2 '63
Human rights and democracy. P. P. Camargo. il Américas 15:33-6 My '63
Inter-continental unity: the federation of the free world; address, November 20, 1964. N. A. Rockefeller. Vital Speeches 31:132-5 D 15 '64
Liberal idea of freedom, by D. Spitz. Review Commentary 39:81-4 Ja '65. G. Kateb
Making self-government work; address, May 21, 1963. A. N. Booth. Vital Speeches 29:606-8 Jl 15 '63
Of leaders and followers; address, May 28, 1963. E. M. Clark. Vital Speeches 29:602-6 Jl 15 '63
Paradoxes of freedom, by S. Hook. Review Commentary 35:260-2 Mr '63. L. A. Coser
Party system and democracy in Africa. T. J. Mboya. For Affairs 41:650-8 Jl '63
Politics of the possible: the American scene. S. Rousseas and J. Farganis. Nation 196: 240-4 Mr 23 '63; Discussion. 197:inside cover, 93 Ag 24 '63
Prospects for democracy around the world; address. A. E. Stevenson. Vital Speeches 29:305-9 Mr 1 '63
Seventeen states vote to destroy democracy as we know it. T. B. Morgan. il Look 27: 76+ D 3 '63
Stitching the world together; toward a global democracy. P. C. Jessup. Sat R 47:17-19+ F 1 '64
Toast of democracy; address, January 22, 1963. Viscount Hailsham. Vital Speeches 29:300-3 Mr 1 '63
What you should know about democracy and why. il Sr Schol 82:16-18 Mr 6; 19-20+ Mr 13; 17-18 Mr 20; 18-20 Mr 27; 15-18+ Ap 17; 21-2+ My 1; 20+ My 8 '63

See also
Communism and democracy
Equality
Liberty
Representative government and representation
Suffrage

Study and teaching

Learning about freedom the democratic way; excerpt from Teaching and learning the democratic way. G. Noar. Sch & Soc 91:37-9 Ja 26 '63
New approach to citizenship. F. M. Hechinger. Parents Mag 38:49+ My '63

DEMOCRACY and communism. See Communism and democracy

DEMOCRACY and education. See Education and democracy

DEMOCRACY and religion. See Religion and democracy

DEMOCRATIC party
Among Democrats: who for second place? il U S News 56:35 Mr 16 '64
As Democrats see it. il U S News 57:29-31 S 7 '64
Boring Republicans. S. Alsop. il Sat Eve Post 237:16 Ap 25 '64
Business, and the party platforms. T. O'Hanlon. il Duns R 84:55-7+ O '64
Case against the Democrats. M. Moos. il N Y Times Mag p9+ Ja 12 '64
Case for democratic liberalism. J. S. Clark. Sat R 47:14-17+ Jl 11 '64
Case for the Democratic party. H. H. Humphrey. Sat R 47:21-3 O 31 '64
Consolidating Democratic gains. W. V. Shannon. Commonweal 81:317-18 N 27 '64
Counting chickens; Democrats warn themselves against overconfidence. K. Crawford. Newsweek 64:74 O 5 '64
Democratic sweep: in legislatures, too. U S News 57:10 N 16 '64
Democrats. il Time 83:14-15 Ja 17; 21-2 Ja 31; 21-2 Mr 20; 16-17 Mr 27; 23A Ap 10; 22 Ap 24; 24 My 22; 84:19 Jl 31; 18 Ag 14; 17 Ag 21; 17 Ag 28; 19A-19B S 4 '64
Democrats in a key city tell why they shifted votes; Philadelphia. il U S News 55:56-7 N 25 '63
Democrats: well on the way. il Time 82:23 O 25 '63
F.D.R. and the Democratic triumph. J. T. Patterson. Cur Hist 47:216-20+ O '64
F.D.R. vs. the Democratic party. W. Myers. il Esquire 59:115+ Mr '63
Frosty touch of age. R. Moley. Newsweek 62:80 D 23 '63
How Democrats expect to win. Nations Bsns 52:76+ Je '64
How Democrats held a congressional seat. il U S News 55:6 Ag 12 '63
Is an Austin-Boston coalition possible? E. T. Folliard. America 110:402 Mr 28 '64
Issue isn't personal. R. Moley. Newsweek 62: 64 D 30 '63
Jesse Unruh: Big Daddy of California. E. Cray. Nation 196:199-207 Mr 9 '63
Johnson as party leader. New Repub 149:7-8 D 28 '63
Johnson's Eisenhower premise. S. Rousseas. Nation 199:375-9 N 23 '64
Kennedy's strategy for the '64 election. il U S News 55:34-6 Ag 19 '63
Lincoln takeover. Time 81:24 F 22 '63
Men who will run LBJ's campaign. il U S News 57:12 S 7 '64
Mr Johnson defines his political creed; excerpts from statements. L. B. Johnson. U S News 55:114 D 9 '63
Negro & the Democratic coalition; excerpts from White and black: test of a nation. S. Lubell. Commentary 38:19-27 Ag '64
Negro minority vs. a white majority? R. De Toledano. Nat R 16:814-15 S 22 '64
New directions? Democrats loss of congressional seats to Republicans in the South. il Newsweek 64:36 N 16 '64
Newly emerging peoples; Democratic politics in New York. Reporter 29:20+ O 24 '63
Notes and comment; Kennedy in Miami. New Yorker 39:49-51 N 30 '63
One more clue to November vote. il U S News 57:40 O 12 '64
Organization: Johnson's campaign staff. Cato. Nat R 16:807 S 22 '64
Party's responsibility. J. T. Crown. Nation 197:411-13 D 14 '63
Political parties plan new strategies. il Nations Bsns 51:40-1+ D '63

DEMOCRATIC party—*Continued*
Political powerhouse in action; strategy of the Kennedy clan. J. Chamberlain. Read Digest 85:189-90 N '64
Powerful persuaders; Lady Bird's trip through the South. H. Fuller. New Repub 151:11-12 O 24 '64
Really tough test for the whip. J. N. Eller. America 111:684 N 28 '64
Right down the center. il Bsns W p25-7 Ag 29 '64
Stephen E. Smith. M. Kempton. New Repub 148:15-17 Mr 9 '63
Unruh bucks the clubs. K. Hendrick. Nation 198:472-4 My 11 '64
What unions did to help the Democrats. il U S News 57:102-4 N 9 '64
Where Democrats are rocking the boat. il U S News 56:44 Ap 6 '64
Which extremism is your extremism? Nat R 16:756-7 S 8 '64
White and black: test of a nation, by S. Lubell. Review
Nat R 16:1018-19 N 17 '64. V. Miller
Why a Democratic senator turned Republican; address, September 16, 1964. S. Thurmond. il U S News 57:83-4 S 28 '64
Why Democrats swept a Republican state; case study. il U S News 57:44-6 N 30 '64
Why I am a Republican. D. D. Eisenhower. Sat Eve Post 237:17-19 Ap 11 '64; Same abr. with title Policies I believe will strengthen this country. Read Digest 85:102-8 Jl '64
Without portfolio. C. B. Luce. il McCalls 91:16+ Ag '64
See also
Copperheads (nickname)
National conventions, Democratic
Platforms, Political
Tammany Hall

DEMODULATORS. See Modulators

DEMOGRAPHY. See Population

DEMOLAY, Order of
Racial crisis in DeMolay. R. H. Dinegar. Christian Cent 81:378 Mr 18 '64; Discussion. 81:356, 771 Mr 18, Je 10 '64

DEMOLITION of buildings. See Wrecking

DEMONOLOGY
See also
Witchcraft

DEMONS; story. See Taylor, P.

DE MORELOS, Leonardo C.
He came, he saw, he conquered. Sat R 47:36 My 30 '64

DEMOTT, Benjamin Haile
Anatomy of Playboy. Commentary 34:111-19, 35:73-4 Ag '62, Ja '63
New books (cont) Harper 226:106+ My '63; 228:106-10 Ap; 114+ Je; 229:106+ S '64
Uses of anti-Americanism. New Repub 148:22-5 Mr 9 '63
Writer as middleman. Harper 227:88+ Jl '63

DEMPEWOLFF, Richard
Those handy aerosols can be dangerous. Pop Mech 121:85-9+ Mr '64; Same abr. with title Be careful with those aerosol sprays! Read Digest 84:130-3 Ap '64

DEMPSEY, David
All the customers are always right. See occasional issues of Saturday review beginning February 16, 1963
Case of the improper imprint. Sat R 47:26-7 Je 13 '64
Literary prize game. Horizon 5:68-75 Jl '63
Mr Jenkins sees it through. Sat R 47:88+ Ag 29 '64
Offering; story. Sat Eve Post 237:44-6 Mr 28 '64
Publishing scene. See occasional issues of Saturday review beginning February 16, 1963
Why the girls scream, weep, flip. N Y Times Mag p 15+ F 23 '64

DEMPSEY, Jack
Boxing mess, and what to do about it. por Read Digest 83:85-90 O '63
about
Back in the ring; Dempsey sues Time inc. for libel. Time 83:53 Ap 10 '64
Days of wine and bloody noses; excerpt from Million dollar gate. J. Kearns and O. Fraley. il Sports Illus 20:50-4+ Ja 20 '64
He didn't know the gloves were loaded; excerpt from Million dollar gate; with editorial comment. J. Kearns and O. Fraley. il pors Sports Illus 20:4, 48-56 Ja 13 '64

DEMPSEY, Paul
Shrubs in Florida. Horticulture 42:18-21 N '64

DEMPSEY, William H. jr
Life and death. Commonweal 80:156-7 Ap 24 '64

DEMUMBRUM, L. E.
Montmorillonite-vermiculite interstratification in clays from eocene chalk soils. Science 140:187-8 Ap 12 '63

DEMUTH, Jerry
Black Belt, Alabama. Commonweal 80:536-9 Ag 7 '64
Celebrity boycott. New Repub 150:8-9 Ap 25 '64
Race in the land of Lincoln. Commonweal 78:44-6 Ap 5 '63
Red carpet for Beckwith. New Repub 150:9 My 23 '64
Summer in Mississippi; freedom moves in to stay. Nation 199:104-5+ S 14 '64
Tired of being sick and tired. Nation 198:548-51 Je 1 '64

DEMY, Jacques
Phenomenon of Les parapluies de Cherbourg. F. R. Bastide. il Vogue 144:184-5+ N 1 '64

DENBY, Edwin
Dear dance fan. Dance Mag 38:34-5 Je '64
Katz: collage, cutout, cut-up. Art N 63:42-5 Ja '65

DENDRITES
Dendrites. W. A. Tiller. bibliog il Science 146:871-9 N 13 '64
Electrolytic growth of silver dendrites. W. A. Ainsworth. bibliog il Science 146:1294-5 D 4 '64

DENDROMECON rigida. See Bush poppies

DENEMARK, George W.
Schools are not factories. NEA J 53:25-7 Mr '64

DENENBERG, R. V.
Students get the vote out. Nation 199:45-9 Ag 10 '64

DENENBERG, Victor H.
Early experience and emotional development. Sci Am 208:138-40+ Je '63
—and Whimbey, A. E.
Behavior of adult rats is modified by the experiences their mothers had as infants. bibliog Science 142:1192-3 N 29 '63
—and others
Mice reared with rats: modification of behavior by early experience with another species. bibliog Science 143:380-1 Ja 24 '64

DENEVI, Marco
Three fables without morals. Américas 16:35-8 My '64

DENGLER, Harry William
Colonial Christmas. Am For 70:6-7+ D '64
Cones for Christmas. Am For 69:8-11+ D '63
De Tocqueville of the trees. Am For 69:8-9+ Ag '63
300th anniversary; Evelyn's Silva. Am For 70:26-7+ D '64

DENGUE
Dandy fever outbreak. Sci N L 84:198 S 28 '63
Dengue types 1 and 4 viruses in wild-caught mosquitoes in south India. D. E. Carey and others. bibliog il Science 143:131-2 Ja 10 '64
Outbreak of dengue. Time 82:42 O 25 '63

DENHARD, Charles
Former ad chiefs' advice: describe the book; summary of address. por Pub W 185:54-5 F 17 '64

DENISHAWN company. See Dance companies

DENISON, Tex.
Our merchants like big garbage cans. J. Smithen. il Am City 78:23 Jl '63

DENISON college, Denison, Ia.
College campus that is Main Street. il Arch Rec 137:124-6 Ja '65

DENKER, Henry
Case of libel; dramatization of My life in court, by L. Nizer. Criticism
America 109:751 D 7 '63
Commonweal 79:194 N 8 '63
Nation 197:306+ N 9 '63
New Yorker 39:99 O 19 '63
Newsweek il 62:104 O 21 '63
Sat R 46:18 N 2 '63
Theatre Arts 48:66 Ja '64
Time 82:78 O 18 '63

DENMARK
Denmark. V. Lawford. il Vogue 144:194-211+ O 1 '64
See also
Airlines—Denmark
Copenhagen
Helsingor
Hunting—Denmark
Jews in Denmark
Libraries—Denmark
Music festivals—Denmark
Women—Denmark

DENMARK—*Continued*

Description and travel

New good move for travellers. Vogue 144: 64+ O 1 '64
Summertime trip to fairy-tale land. M. Gough. il House B 105:128+ D '63

Economic policy

Cutting back with Krag. il Time 81:34 Mr 8 '63

History

German occupation, 1940-1945

Rescue in Denmark. by H. Flender. Review Sat R 46:26+ Je 1 '63. S. Spender

Moral conditions

Danish girls. J. Star. il Look 28:43-6+ Mr 10 '64

Royal family

Storm over a royal love affair. C. Plimmer and D. Plimmer. il Redbook 121:60-1+ O '63

DENMARK and the United States
Vice President Johnson visits northern Europe; address, September 14, 1963. L. B. Johnson. Dept State Bul 49:589-92 O 14 '63

DENNIN, Carl, and Cottrell, W. F.
Extra duties. Am City 78:95 S '63

DENNING, Alfred Thompson Denning, baron
Ineffectual but innocent; Lord Denning's report. il Time 82:40-1 O 4 '63
Word of Christine; concerning the Denning report. G. Playfair. New Repub 149:11-13 D 21 '63

DENNING, Kaye
Kaye Denning: enamels. il Craft Horiz 23: 35-7 Mr '63

DENNIS, Donald D.
Cedar Crest on a cantilever. Library J 88: 4564-6 D 1 '63
Profile: Joseph L. Wheeler; with quotations. Library J 89:2941-3 Ag '64

DENNIS, Jessie McNab
Heraldry on Wedgwood creamware. Antiques 86:168-73 Ag '64
J. G. Herold and the hidden pleasures of Meissen chinoiserie; excerpts. Antiques 85: 558-64 My '64

DENNIS, Lloyd B.
Education in prison. New Repub 151:6 S 12 '64
Foot in the door. New Repub 150:5 Mr 14 '64

DENNIS, Patrick, pseud. See Tanner, E. E. 3d

DENNIS, Sandy
Any Wednesday's Sandy. il pors Look 28:100-4 Je 16 '64
Love letters of a tough critic. W. Kerr. por Life 56:113 Je 19 '64
Two in the center. il por Time 83:64-5 Mr 6 '64

DENNISON, Edward S.
Bolivia. pors Nat Geog Mag 126:314-19 S '64

DENNISON, H. Lee
Triple-benefit waterfront projects. Am City 78:110-12 Mr '63

DENNISON, Harry S.
Famous firsts: bringing brainwork to the fore. por Bsns W p54+ F 15 '64

DENNISTON, Elinore
(ed) See Roosevelt, E. Tomorrow is now

DENNY, Robert R.
Some answers about college admission. Bet Hom & Gard 42:114-16 Ap '64

DENOMINATIONAL colleges
Canadians find a solution; federation of Campion's university section with Regina campus. P. W. Nash. America 111:302-3 S 19 '64
Church-state confrontation in Maryland; suit to determine the constitutionality of tax funds for church-related colleges. I. G. Zepp, jr. Christian Cent 82:84+ Ja 20 '65
Constitutionality of tax funds for sectarian schools; church-related colleges in Maryland. Sch & Soc 91:420 D 28 '63
Federal aid and higher education. G. E. Snavely. Sch & Soc 91:86-8 F 23 '63
Legal world series; Maryland suit against the use of public funds for four church-related colleges. America 109:339 S 28 '63
On the campuses. W. L. Thorkelson. Christian Cent 81:1092-4 S 2 '64
Secular tendency in church-related colleges in Pennsylvania; excerpt from History of higher education in Pennsylvania. S. Sack bibliog f Sch & Soc 91:430+ D 28 '63
Special mission of the church-related college. E. J. McGrath. Sch & Soc 91:165-8 Ap 6 '63
See also names of denominational colleges, e.g. Drury college, Springfield, Mo.

DENOMINATIONAL publications. See Religious newspapers and periodicals

DENOMINATIONALISM. See Sects

DENOMINATIONS, Religious. See Sects

DENSITOMETERS
Foto facts; homemade densitometer. P. Farber. U S Camera 27:24+ My '64

DENSITY. See Specific gravity

DENT, Harold C.
EB school library award; Prairie Village, Kansas. por Wilson Lib Bul 39:400-1+ Ja '65

DENTAL calculi. See Calculi, Dental

DENTAL caries. See Teeth—Diseases

DENTAL fees
What doctors & dentists charge. il Changing T 17:30 S '63

DENTAL hygiene. See Teeth—Care and hygiene

DENTAL instruments and apparatus
Cleaner tools for the dentist; dental equipment blamed for cross-contamination. il Bsns W p80-2 O 5 '63

DENTAL insurance. See Insurance, Dental

DENTAL research
New ideas about preventing tooth decay. Good H 156:143 Mr '63
easier. il Todays Health 43:6-7 Ja '65

DENTAL service
See also
United States—Armed forces—Dental service

DENTAL service, Cost of. See Dental fees

DENTIFRICES
Annals of business; Crest toothpaste. B. Bliven, jr. New Yorker 39:83-4+ Mr 23 '63
Cue, too. Newsweek 64:59 Ag 10 '64
Toothpaste you can swallow; oral hygiene in space. Sci Digest 55:78-9 Je '64

Advertising

Brushing with fluoride. Time 84:82 Ag 7 '64

DENTISTRY
Closing the gap; transplanted human teeth. il Newsweek 62:75 Ag 26 '63
Don't get a toothache in Russia. Sci Digest 55:36 F '64
Inside the world of dental specialties. il Good H 157:150-1 S '63
It is no longer like pulling teeth. A. Whitman. il N Y Times Mag p44+ N 24 '63
Remarkable world of dentistry. H. Earle. il Todays Health 41:36-9+ Ap '63
Replanted teeth. Sci Am 210:72 F '64
Sad case of our good old-fashioned dentistry. S. Grafton. il McCalls 91:106-7+ N '63
Soviets lag in dental care, mission reports. Todays Health 41:87 Ap '63
Tuning in teeth; radio transmitters fitted into dummy teeth. Time 83:54 Je 26 '64
See also
Children—Preparation for medical and dental care
Dental research
Teeth

DENTISTS
It is no longer like pulling teeth. A. Whitman. il N Y Times Mag p44+ N 24 '63
My friend, the pedodontist; dentistry for children. P. W. Goldman. il N Y Times Mag p34 F 2 '64

Fees

See Dental fees

DENTITION
All about teething. E. Sunley. il Parents Mag 38:36-7+ Ag '63

DENTON, D. A. and others
Ureotelism of echidna and platypus. bibliog Science 139:1225 Mr 22 '63

DENTSU advertising, limited. See Advertising agencies

DENVER
Notes for a gazetteer. P. Hamburger. New Yorker 40:125-9 Je 20 '64

Description

U.S. city weekends. T. B. Lesure. il Travel 120:28-32+ Jl '63

Education

Denver achieves professional negotiations. R. Newlon and B. J. Lee. il NEA J 52:14-16 F '63
Denver graduates come up to PAR. J. D. Leake. NEA J 52:24-5 N '63
Denver preschool reading project: ETV plus parents' guidebook. Library J 89:4621 N 15 '64
Emily's pupils: the strength of a city; Emily Griffith opportunity school. D. Kostka. Read Digest 83:123-6 S '63

DENVER—Education—*Continued*
Parents, teachers, and early readers; your child for reading; through National educational television services. D. DuBose. il Sr Schol 83:8T-9T N 1 '63

Hospitals

Transplant triumph; first initially successful liver transplant on record. Newsweek 61:69+ My 27 '63

Libraries

See also
Denver public library

Lighting

Relighting downtown Denver. W. J. Shoemaker and J. A. Bruce. il Am City 78:93-4 D '63

Music

Denver swallow. E. B. Rogers. Opera N 28: 33 Ja 18 '64
[Musical events] (cont) Mus Am 83:17 F; 19 Mr; 14-15 My '63; 84:13 F; 17-18 My '64

Politics and government

What happened to Denver's metro. H. A. Green. Am City 79:129+ Ap '64

Social life and customs

Mile-high social life of Denver. P. Mesta. McCalls 91:26+ Mr '64

Zoo city park

Two wings for the big cats. il Am City 80: 24 Ja '65

DENVER and Rio Grande Western railroad
Steam still has a day. il Bsns W p60-2 Ag 22 '64

DENVER Broncos (football club) See Football clubs

DENVER mint. See United States—Mint

DENVER post
Thank you, Denver post, we like you too. Sat Eve Post 236:90 Ap 20 '63

DENVER public library
75th anniversary for Denver. il Wilson Lib Bul 39:218 N '64

Branches

By popular request: branch building in Denver. B. J. Rule. il Wilson Lib Bul 37: 569-70 Mr '63

DENZINGER, Katharina
Borrowed for the wedding. Mlle 56:122-4 F '63

DEODORANTS
Everyone needs a deodorant, why, when, what kind? L. D. Kirk. il Parents Mag 39:106 My '64
What to expect from your deodorant. C. Leth. Todays Health 41:13+ Je '63

DEODORIZATION
How to get rid of cooking vapors. Good H 156:167 Ap '63

DE ONIS, Juan
Brazil's Goulart skirts the abyss. N Y Times Mag p20+ Ag 18 '63

DEORSEY, Leo
Further on ethics. W. J. Coughlin. Miss & Roc 12:46 Je 10 '63

DEOXYADENOSINE
Deoxyadenosine form may give key to life. Sci N L 86:94 Ag 8 '64

DEOXYCYTIDYLIC deaminase. See Growth inhibiting substances (animals)

DEOXYRIBONUCLEASE
Deoxyribonuclease sensitivity of ribonucleic acid synthesizing system from tobacco leaves. J. G. Shaw. bibliog il Science 139: 924-5 Mr 8 '63

DEOXYRIBONUCLEIC acid
Actinomycin: correlation of structure and function of its complexes with purines and DNA. E. Reich. bibliog il Science 143:684-9 F 14 '64
Association of rapidly metabolized DNA and RNA. J. H. Cherry. bibliog il Science 146: 1066-9 N 20 '64
Basic chemistry of life seen revolutionized. Sci N L 84:377 D 14 '63
Bromine alolysis in 5-bromouracil-labeled DNA by X-ray fluorescence. L. Zeitz and R. Lee. bibliog il Science 142:1670-3 D 27 '63
5-bromodeoxyuridine: effect on myogenesis in vitro. F. Stockdale and others. bibliog il Science 146:533-5 O 23 '64
Cancer-inducing DNA; excerpt from report. H. Curtis. Sat R 46:52 F 2 '63
Cell life cycle: macromolecular aspects; report of symposium sponsored by the Biology division of the Oak Ridge national laboratory and the Division of biology and medicine of the Atomic energy commission. D. M. Prescott. Science 141:547-8 Ag 9 '63
Chromosome puffs. W. Beermann and U. Clever. il Sci Am 210:50-8 bibliog(p 156) Ap '64
Control over cell growth seen near achievement. Sci N L 83:323 My 25 '63
Delayed incorporation of tritiated thymidine into DNA. S. H. Robinson and G. Brecher. bibliog il Science 142:392-3 O 18 '63
Deoxycytidine in urine of humans after whole-body irradiation. H. K. Berry and others. bibliog il Science 142:396-8 O 18 '63
DNA can trace evolution. Sci N L 85:2 Ja 4 '64
DNA contents and chromosome Ph^1 and chromosome 21 in human chronic granulocytic leukemia. G. T. Rudkin and others. bibliog il Science 144:1229-32 Je 5 '64
DNA from bacteriophage lambda: molecular length and conformation. L. A. MacHattie and C. A. Thomas, jr. bibliog il Science 144:1142-4 My 29 '64
DNA; it calls the signals for life. W. Cloud. il Pop Sci 182:66-9+ My '63
DNA made to specification. Sci Am 210:56 Je '64
DNA pieces synthesized. F. Marley. il Sci N L 85:275 My 2 '64
DNA replication and recombination; report on symposium at annual meeting of the American society for microbiology. E. A. Adelberg. Science 146:1193-5 N 27 '64
DNA segregation in escherichia coli: observations by means of tritiated thymidine decay. S. Person and M. Osborn. bibliog il Science 143:44-6 Ja 3 '64
DNA synthesis in alveolar cells of the mammary gland: acceleration by ovarian hormones. F. Bresciani. bibliog il Science 146: 653-5 O 30 '64
DNA understanding may explain defects, cancer. il Sci N L 83:243 Ap 30 '63
DNA zipper. Sci Am 209:69 Jl '63
DNA's code; key to all life; with report by A. Hills and A. Rosenfeld. il Life 55:70-8+ O 4 '63
Diploid and endoreduplicated cells: measurements of DNA. A. G. Bell. il Science 143: 139 Ja 10 '64
Electron microscopy of single-stranded DNA: circularity of DNA of bacteriophage ϕX174. D. Freifelder and others. bibliog il Science 146:254-5 O 9 '64
Electron microscopy of the replicative form of the DNA of the bacteriophage ϕX174. A. K. Kleinschmidt and others. bibliog il Science 142:961 N 15 '63
Exploring the secrets of life. il Newsweek 61:63-6 My 13 '63
Fragment sizes produced from T5 bacteriophage DNA molecules by acid deoxyribonuclease. L. A. MacHattie and others. bibliog il Science 141:59-60 Jl 5 '63
Genetic code. M. W. Nirenberg. il Sci Am 208:80-6+ bibliog(p 190) Mr '63
Genetics: how nature reads the code. Time 82:61 N 15 '63
He stuck in his thumb and pulled out—DNA! P. Bergstrom. il Sat R 46:57-8 Mr 2 '63
Heterogeneity of DNA in density and base composition. T. Y. Cheng and N. Sueoka. bibliog il Science 141:1194-6 S 20 '63
Histone and DNA in isolated nuclei from chicken brain, liver, and erythrocytes. M. B. Sporn and C. W. Dingman. bibliog il Science 140:316-18 Ap 19 '63
How we're cracking the code of life; radio interview, ed. by C. Collingwood. S. Ochoa. il Sci Digest 56:79-83 S '64
Hydroxyurea: inhibitory effect on DNA metabolism. C. W. Young and S. Hodas. bibliog il Science 146:1172-4 N 27 '64
Loss of radioactivity from labeled DNA of primary human amnion cells. R. S. Chang and H. Vetrovs. bibliog il Science 139:1211 Mr 22 '63
Medicines of tomorrow; excerpts from Science book of modern medicines. D. G. Cooley. il Todays Health 41:38-42 N '63
Mitochondrion. D. E. Green. il Sci Am 210: 63-6+ bibliog(p 152) Ja '64
Mitomycins and porfiromycin: chemical mechanism of activation and cross-linking of DNA. V. N. Iyer and W. Szybalski. bibliog il Science 145:55-8 Jl 3 '64
Molecular approach in the systematics of higher organisms. B. H. Hoyer and others. bibliog il Science 144:959-67 My 22 '64; Discussion. Time 83:80 My 29 '64; Sci N L 85:365 Je 6 '64
New biology and the nature of man; adaptation of address, 1963. G. W. Beadle. Bul Atomic Sci 20:13-17 Mr '64
Nongenetic genetic code? Sci Am 209:49-51 Ag '63

DEOXYRIBONUCLEIC acid—*Continued*
Perspectives for the life sciences. H. J. Muller. Bul Atomic Sci 20:3-7 Ja '64; Reply with rejoinder. D. H. Elwyn. 20:36-7 O '64
Polymer similar to polydeoxyadenylate-thymidylate in various tissues of a marine crab. T. Y. Cheng and N. Sueoka. bibliog il Science 143:1442-3 Mr 27 '64
Polyoma virus genetic material in a virus-free polyoma-induced tumor. D. Axelrod and others. bibliog il Science 146:1466-9 D 11 '64
Polyoma virus: production in bacillus subtilis. K. E. Bayreuther and W. R. Romig. bibliog il Science 146:778-9 N 6 '64
Radiation action on DNA in bacteria: effect of oxygen. E. C. Pollard and P. M. Achey. bibliog il Science 146:71-3 O 2 '64
Replicating form of a single-stranded DNA virus: isolation and properties. M. Hayashi and others. bibliog il Science 140:1313-16 Je 21 '63
Replication of DNA and cell division in synchronously dividing cultures of euglena gracilis. L. N. Edmunds, jr. bibliog il Science 145:266-8 Jl 17 '64
Test tube life doubted. F. Marley. Sci N L 86:102 Ag 15 '64
Thermal inactivation of the primer in DNA-dependent synthesis of RNA in animal tissue. J. J. Furth and P. Loh. bibliog il Science 145:161-2 Jl 10 '64
Transcription in vivo of DNA from bacteriophage SP8. J. Marmur and C. M. Greenspan. bibliog il Science 142:387-9 O 18 '63
Transcription of a repressed gene: evidence that it requires DNA replication. P. Hanawalt and R. Wax. bibliog il Science 145: 1061-3 S 4 '64
Triplets unlocking code. W. Wingo. Sci N L 86:103 Ag 15 '64
Uracil: failure to restore DNA synthesis while relieving 5-fluorouracil-induced inhibition. M. Reich and H. G. Mandel. bibliog il Science 145:276-7 Jl 17 '64
What Johnny should learn before school; adaptation of address. G. W. Beadle. Sci Digest 56:28-33 N '64
X-ray diffraction study of a DNA which contains uracil. R. Langridge and J. Marmur. bibliog il Science 143:1450-1 Mr 27 '64
X-ray sensitivity and DNA synthesis in synchronous populations of HeLa cells. T. Terasima and L. J. Tolmach. bibliog il Science 140:490-2 My 3 '63

DEOXYRIBONUCLEIC virus
Circularity of the replicating form of a single-stranded DNA virus. B. Chandler and others. bibliog il Science 143:47-9 Ja 3 '64

DE PAOLIS, Alessio
Obituary
Opera N 28:36 Ap 18 '64

DEPARTMENT of elementary school principals. See National education association—Department of elementary school principals

DEPARTMENT of state bulletin. See United States—State, Department of—Bulletin

DEPARTMENT of urban affairs and housing. See United States—Urban affairs and housing, Department of (proposed)

DEPARTMENT store records. See Business records

DEPARTMENT stores
Clues for action from shopper preferences; survey of women shoppers in New York city and in Cleveland. S. U. Rich and B. Portis. il Harvard Bsns R 41:132-49 Mr '63
Giant step; acquisition of Bullock's twenty-three stores by Federated department stores. Time 84:81 Jl 24 '64
Stores; newest thinking on store design; symposium. il Arch Rec 133:159-82+ Je '63
See also
Chain stores
Charge accounts (retail trade)
Macy, R. H. and company
Mail order business
May department stores company
Retail trade
Shopping centers
also subhead Stores under names of cities, e.g. Boston—Stores

Automobile parking garages

Macy's park-and-shop; Elmhurst, N.Y. branch. il Arch Forum 120:37 Ap '64

Book departments

Department store promotions that stimulated holiday buying. il Pub W 186:30-1 D 14 '64
Dept. store Xmas promotions launched early. il Pub W 184:20-2 D 2 '63
Store subway takes patrons from shopping area to store; Leonards, Fort Worth, Tex. il Pub W 184:44-5 S 30 '63

Employees

Service with a snarl; sales clerks in Russia. il Newsweek 64:52 D 7 '64
Trying out three-way organizing; store employees unions, Gimbels-Schusters, Milwaukee. il Bsns W p90-1 Ja 19 '63

DEPATTA, Margaret
Obituary
Craft Horiz il 24:10 Jl '64. Y. Uchida

DE PAUL, Stephen
Washington front. America 111:82 Jl 25 '64

DE PAUL university, Chicago
Departure at De Paul; four new philosophy courses. il Time 84:68+ O 23 '64

DEPENDABILITY
Form and the substance. Duns R 83:35 F '64

DEPENDENTS schools, Army. See Military post schools, American

DEPENDENTS schools overseas. See American schools abroad

DE PIETRO, Albert
Circles, lines: poem. Cath World 200:177 D '64
Feeding goldfish: poem. Cath World 198:319 F '64

DE PINIÉS, Jaime
Young power in diplomacy. por Vogue 143: 91 Ap 15 '64

DEPINTO, John A. and Campbell, L. L.
Formation and degradation of cyclic dextrins by intracellular enzymes of bacillus macerans. bibliog Science 146:1064-6 N 20 '64

DEPLETION allowances
Depletion; what's at stake for thirty companies. il Fortune 67:206 Ap '63
Privileged sanctuary. Nation 198:179 F 24 '64
Should oil's 27½ per cent be cut? il Newsweek 61:66-8 Mr 4 '63
Water depletion allowance; High Plains underground water district. New Repub 148:5 F 9 '63

DEPOSIT stations, Library. See Libraries—Branches and stations

DEPOSITION (geology) See Sedimentation and deposition

DEPOTS, Railroad. See Railroads—Stations

DEPRECIATION
How to beat the high cost of auto depreciation. Bet Hom & Gard 42:40 Ap '64
Revolution in farm buildings: how to save taxes. F. Bailey, jr. Suc Farm 62:59-60 Ag '64
See also
Amortization deductions

DEPRESSED areas aid. See Economic assistance, Domestic

DEPRESSION, Business. See Business depression

DEPRESSION, Mental
Depression cure foreseen. Sci N L 87:46 Ja 16 '65
Expedition depression. Sci N L 83:107 F 16 '63
How to recognize suicidal depression. B. H. Roisum. Ladies Home J 81:26+ S '64
Pill to fight mental depression; Eutonyl. Bsns W p76+ Ap 13 '63
Pills to soothe tension. W. Wingo. Sci N L 84:178 S 21 '63
Quick lift for depression; hydroxytryptophane injection. Time 82:48 S 6 '63

DEPRIVATION, Sensory. See Sensory deprivation

DEPSIDES
Joint occurrence of a lichen depsidone and its probable depside precursor. C. F. Culberson. bibliog il Science 143:255-6 Ja 17 '64

DEPTH indicators
Kit-build depth finder. C. Conley. il Field & S 68:125-6 My '63
See also
Sonar

DEPTH of field. See Photography—Focusing

DEPTH perception. See Space perception

DEPUTY; drama. See Hochhuth, R.

DE-QUILLING a dog. See Dogs—Care

DERAIN, André
Derain: illusion and disillusion. S. C. Faunce. il Art N 63:38-9+ N '64

DE RAMUS, Betty
African art gallery seen as retribution to Negro cause. Negro Hist Bul 27:127+ F '64

DERBY porcelain. See Pottery, English

DEREK, John
Ursula major. por Newsweek 64:79B-80 Jl 20 '64

DEREMER, Bernard. See Teetor, D. jt. auth.

DERFLINGHER, Filipe
Imprisoning glass. il Pop Mech 121:137 Ja '64

DERING, Wladyslaw Alexander
Dering case; surgeon at Auschwitz. M. Ellmann. Commentary 38:19-25 Jl '64
DERINGER, Henry, jr
Henry Deringer, jr. C. G. Worman. il Hobbies 68:124-5 Ja '64
D'ERLANGER, Edwina
Star of Venus; house in Tunisia owned by Edwina and Leo D'Erlanger. L. Blanch. il pors Vogue 144:194-201+ N 1 '64
D'ERLANGER, Leo
Star of Venus; house in Tunisia owned by Edwina and Leo D'Erlanger. L. Blanch. il pors Vogue 144:194-201+ N 1 '64
DERMATOLOGY. See Skin
DERMIS. See Skin
DERMO-OPTICAL perception. See Touch
Le DERNIER sauvage: opera. See Menotti, G. C.
DE ROBERTIS, E. and others
Acetylcholine and cholinacetylase content of synaptic vesicles. bibliog Science 140:300-1 Ap 19 '63
DEROCHE, Edward F.
My parents, my teacher, and me. NEA J 52:16-17 D '63
DE ROCHEMONT, R.
Opinion, please from New York. Mlle 59:62+ S '64
DE ROO, Edward
Idaho's Coeur d'Alene country. Travel 121:42-4 My '64
DEROOS, Carolyn C. See DeRoos, R. jt. auth.
DE ROOS, Robert
Arizona: booming youngster of the West. Nat Geog Mag 123:299-343 Mr '63
Magic worlds of Walt Disney. Nat Geog Mag 124:158-207 Ag '63
Mysterious Monument Valley. Read Digest 82:134-9 Je '63
World's master caster. Sports Illus 19:30-6 Jl 8 '63
DEROOS, Roger, and DeRoos, C. C.
Angiotensin II: its effects on corticoid production by chicken adrenals in vitro. bibliog Science 141:1284 S 27 '63
DE ROSA, Lynn E.
Art with broken chalk. Design 65:76-7 N '63
DERRINGERS. See Pistols
DERSO, Alois
A. Derso, RIP. por Nat R 17:14 Ja 12 '65
Peace in their time, by E. Kelen. Review
Nat R por 16:199-200 Mr 10 '64. P. L. Buckley
DE SA, Richard, and others
Luminescent crystalline particles: an organized subcellular bioluminescent system. bibliog Science 141:1269-70 S 27 '63
DE SABLE, Jean Baptiste. See Pointe de Sable, J. B.
DE SAGER, Walter
Antiques abroad. Antiques 84:184+, 312+, 456-7 Ag-O '63
Funk family, craftsmen of Bern. Antiques 85:565-9 My '64
DESAI, Morarji
Date with Desai. Time 81:33 Mr 8 '63
DESALINIZATION. See Water purification—Desalting
DESALTING of sea water. See Sea water—Desalting
DE SANTILLANA, Giorgio
Alessandro Volta; with biographical sketch. Sci Am 212:16, 82-91 Ja '65
Birth of reason. Life 54:62+ F 8 '63
DE SAPIO, Carmine Gerard
Road back. il por Newsweek 62:27 S 2 '63
DESBIENS, Jean Paul
Reporter at large. E. Wilson. New Yorker 40:64-6+ N 21 '64
DESCENT. See Genealogy
DE SCHAUENSEE, Max
First stereo recording of Samson et Dalila. Am Rec G 30:497+ F '64
Gianninis. Opera N 28:14-16 Ap 11 '64
Great opera houses: Dublin. Opera N 27:28-31 F 23 '63
Portrait of Manon. Am Rec G 30:1100-1 Ag '64
Verdi-Shakespeare discography. Mus Am 84:14-15+ Ja '64
DESCHIN, Celia S.
Another epidemic of teen-age VD? Ladies Home J 80:30+ Ja '63
Needed: a new approach to the VD problem. PTA Mag 57:25-8 bibliog(p37) F '63
DESCHIN, Jacob
Critic's choice. Pop Phot 54:114-15+ Ja '64
[Monthly column] See issues of Popular photography
Viewpoints (cont of) Say it with your camera. See issues of Popular photography
DESCRIPTION (rhetoric)
Writing colorful descriptions. S. Cochell. Sr Schol 85:12T N 18 '64
DESCRIPTIVE writing. See Description (rhetoric)
DESEGREGATION. See Colleges and universities—Desegregation; Public schools—Desegregation
DESEGREGATION decision, 1954. See United States—Supreme court—Decisions
DESEGREGATION of libraries. See Libraries and Negroes
DESERT candles
For a spring show grow foxtail-lily. M. M. Paetzel. il Flower Grower 50:60-1 N '63
DESERT fauna
See also
Kangaroo rats
DESERT flora. See Desert vegetation
DESERT Rat (motor vehicle) See Motor vehicles
DESERT sheep hunting. See Mountain sheep hunting
DESERT strike. See War games
DESERT vegetation
Acetylene ester from aster spinosus. J. C. Spitzer and C. Steelink. bibliog Science 146:1460-1 D 11 '64
Desert is not all sand. E. McCown. il Horticulture 41:86-7 F '63
New demonstration desert garden. il Sunset 130:116-19 My '63
Oil and rubber spray makes deserts bloom. Sci N L 85:381 Je 13 '64
DESERT willow. See Pittosporum
DESERTED towns. See Abandoned towns
DESERTS
Boom in the desert; why it grows and grows. il U S News 56:46-52 My 25 '64
See also
Arid regions
Atacama Desert
Mojave Desert
Sahara Desert
DESFERAL. See Desferrioxamine-B
DESFERRIOXAMINE-B
Beware of iron. il Time 84:66 O 9 '64
DE SICA, Vittorio
How they live and die in Naples. por Horizon 5:49-59 S '63
DESIGN
Design in America; symposium. il Sat R 47:12-29 My 23 '64
Study and teaching
Approach to design. P. Johnson. il Sch Arts 62:16-20 Mr '63
Art, design: search for a new image. G. Pappas. il Sch Arts 63:19-20 O '63
Designs from rubbings. il Design 66:40-1 S '64
Dynamic design. D. Saff. il Sch Arts 64:32-7 N '64
Imagination is the product; Chicago institute of design. C. B. Hicks. il Pop Mech 121:116-20+ Ja '64
DESIGN, Architectural. See Architecture
DESIGN, Book. See Book design
DESIGN, Decorative
New designs on exhibit. G. O'Brien. il N Y Times Mag pt2 p20-1 S 29 '63
Story of design, by M. Downer. Review
Sat R il 47:52+ O 24 '64
See also
Book covers
Circus in art
Lettering
Monograms
Textile design
Animal forms
Indonesian decorative design. G. Kaler. il Hobbies 69:42-4 Ja '65
Plant forms
Fall decorative panels. R. O. Burke. il Sch Arts 63:15-16 N '63
Grow your own snack garden! il Seventeen 22:102-3+ Je '63
Study and teaching
See Design—Study and teaching
DESIGN, Industrial
Craftsman in production; symposium, ed. by J. McDevitt. il Craft Horiz 24:21-33 Mr '64
Designed by craftsmen; outstanding American contemporary designs. il Am Home 67:54-7 Jl '64
Designers honored for uses of steel. il Arch Forum 118:8 Ap '63
Exploring the mystery of design. W. D. Teague. il Sat R 47:48+ O 24 '64
Man in the trap. Time 81:74 My 3 '63

DESIGN, Industrial—*Continued*
Pair of designing Finns. R. Moss. il Horizon 5:62-7 Jl '63
Paris redesigned. Newsweek 62:75-6 S 2 '63
Twenty best industrial designs since World war II. W. D. Teague. il Sat R 47:16-19 My 23 '64
See also subhead Design under various subjects, e.g. Automobiles—Design

Exhibitions
Designs on your future; 13th triennale, Milan. E. Jablow. il Sat Eve Post 237:22-7 O 17 '64
Milan: the triennale; symposium. il Craft Horiz 24:25-41+ S '64
Triennale of Milan. il House & Gard 126:288-90 N '64
Unframed beauty; thirteenth Triennale of industrial design, in Milan; with colored photographs. Time 84:82-5 S 4 '64

Study and teaching
Education for design. H. Backlin. Craft Horiz 24:59-60 Mr '64
Motor trend's search for stylists. il Motor T 16:34-6 Ja '64
School for stylists. il Motor T 15:76-8 D '63
Take twelve paper clips. il Sci Digest 56:32-4 S '64

Italy
Milan: the triennale; Italian exhibit. il Craft Horiz 24:34-8+ S '64

United States
Milan: the triennale; United States exhibit. il Craft Horiz 24:26-33 S '64

DESIGN, Ornamental
Counterchange, for a change. il Design 66:38 S '64
DESIGN group, incorporated
Craft guild concept seen in work of Design group. il Pub W 186:68+ Ag 3 '64
DESIGN in photography. See Composition (photography)
DESIGN of automobiles. See Automobiles—Design
DESIGN research, incorporated. See New York (city)—Stores
DESIGNERS
Pair of designing Finns. R. Moss. il Horizon 5:62-7 Jl '63
Scene designers: their art and their impact. H. Hewes. il Sat R 47:26-31 D 12 '64
Some designing people. G. O'Brien. il N Y Times Mag p56-7 Ja 24 '65
World's autos wear the Italian look; Turin school of auto design. il Bsns W p56-8 N 16 '63
Worth thinking about. B. Pepis. il House & Gard 123:154-5 My '63
See also
Costume designers
Noyes, E.
DESIGNS, Architectural. See Architecture—Designs and plans; Architecture, Domestic—Designs and plans
DESILU productions
Don't laugh when you call me president. L. Ball. McCalls 90:51-2 Mr '63
DESIRE under the elms; drama. See O'Neill, E. G.
DESK furnishings
Desk-top pretties. il Seventeen 22:173 O '63
DESKS
Build this space-saving desk. il Bet Home & Gard 42:108 Mr '64
Chest-desk for a child. il Pop Sci 182:136 Mr '63
Cook needs a place; desk in kitchen. il Sunset 133:116+ O '64
Desk, hobby bench, add legs and it's also a bar. H. M. Burke, jr. il Pop Sci 184:146-8 Ap '64
Do great things for a child's desk with a tough new plastic laminate top. il Bet Hom & Gard 41:30 S '63
For belles lettres. il House & Gard 123:196-9 My '63
Home office. C. Kellogg. il Ladies Home J 80:116-18+ Ja '63
How to make room for a desk in a dinky bedroom? il Bet Hom & Gard 41:45 S '63
Now it's a sewing center, now a desk. il Sunset 132:70 Ja '64
Return of the roll-top desk. il Fortune 70:178 D '64
Right for writing. G. O'Brien. il N Y Times Mag p30-1 S 6 '64
Wall-mounted desk. C. W. Close. il Pop Sci 185:143 D '64
DES MARAIS, Philip H.
Convention year, 1964. America 111:45-7 Jl 11 '64

DES MOINES
Architecture
New work of Mies van der Rohe. il Arch Forum 119:84-5 S '63
DESMOND, Charles S.
Should it take thirty-four months for a trial? N Y Times Mag p29+ D 8 '63
DESMOND, James
Rockefeller's cool campaign. Nation 197:23-5 Jl 13 '63
Rocky wrecks the joint. Nation 197:63-5 Ag 10 '63
Starting gun in New Hampshire. Nation 198:168-9 F 17 '64
DE SOISSONS, Brian
Brighter opportunities ahead in Latin America. por Nations Bsns 51:80-2+ S '63
DE SOUZA, Eunice
Christian India. America 111:87-90 Jl 25 '64
DESOXYRIBONUCLEIC acid. See Deoxyribonucleic acid
DES PLAINES, Ill.
Tips for tired snow fighters. E. R. Warnicke. il Am City 78:76-7 F '63
D'ESSEN, Bern
How to live with animals. R. Osk. Am Home 66:90 N '63
DESSEN, Edgar
Doctor Dessen's can-do city. W. J. Monaghan. il por Todays Health 42:48-9+ N '64
D'ESSEN, Lorrain
How to live with animals. R. Osk. Am Home 66:90 N '63
DESSERTS
Big-batch salad/dessert: frozen fruit salad. N. Nichols. il Farm J 88:76 D '64
Brownie baked Alaska. il Good H 158:142 Mr '64
Cereal for dessert. C. Claiborne. il N Y Times Mag p 112 O 11 '64
Club desserts. il Bet Hom & Gard 41:93-4 N '63
Coffee mousse with strawberries. il Sunset 130:257 My '63
Come for dessert and coffee. il Good H 157:104-18 O '63
Cool dessert, fresh fruit on ice. il Sunset 133:121 Ag '64
Cool desserts. il Redbook 123:72-3+ Ag '64
Coolest trio in town. il Am Home 66:48-9+ Jl '63
Dazzling new desserts. il Bet Hom & Gard 43:79-80 Ja '65
Desserts. il Good H 157:96-9+ D '63
Desserts for that special occasion. J. Figg. il Suc Farm 62:70-1 F '64
Desserts to enjoy on your patio. il Pop Gard 15:54 N '64
Fast and fancy with fruit cocktail. il Bet Hom & Gard 42:95 Mr '64
Five desserts with coffee flavor. J. Figg. il Suc Farm 61:82-3 F '63
Four fancy ways to wind up Easter dinner. il Sunset 132:158-9 Mr '64
Happy holiday sweets. il Bet Hom & Gard 42:77-8 D '64
Harvest of holiday desserts. il McCalls 91:158-9+ N '63
Holiday goodies to serve with pride. B. M. Stover. il Parents Mag 39:61-3+ D '64
It's zuppa inglese (English soup) il Sunset 131:188 O '63
Make-ahead magic. M. Johnston. il Bet Hom & Gard 41:70-5+ S '63
Making dessert magic with eggs. il Sunset 132:194-6+ My '64
Making desserts with cereals. Sunset 130:127 F '63
Million dollar desserts. E. Ward-Hanna. il Ladies Home J 80:64-6+ S '63
New idea: start a diet club; with recipes. il Seventeen 23:146-7+ Mr '64
New sherbet-like melon dessert. R. Behnke. il Farm J 87:56-7 Jl '63
Nut desserts. il Bet Hom & Gard 43:115-16 Ja '65
Perfect finish. il Ladies Home J 81:153-6 O '64
Polka-dot desserts. il Bet Hom & Gard 41:80 My '63
Pumpkin desserts. il Bet Hom & Gard 42:87-8 O '64
Quick fruit desserts. il Farm J 88:93+ F '64
Refrigerator desserts. il Suc Farm 61:76+ O '63
Show business right at the table. il Sunset 132:118-19 My '64
Snow in summer & other molded delights. il McCalls 90:110-11+ Ag '63
Show-off desserts. il McCalls 92:134-5+ D '64
Successful recipes. il Suc Farm 61:51-2 D '63
Successful recipes; citrus desserts. il Suc Farm 62:73-4 F '64
Summer dessert cook book. J. Platt. il House & Gard 123:179+ My '63

DESSERTS—*Continued*
Sweet endings for the holidays. il McCalls 92:140-2+ N '64
Sweet magic in minutes. il Bet Hom & Gard 42:66-7 D '64
Sweet remembrances. il Am Home 67:60-1+ Mr '64
Sweet talk; with recipes. il Am Home 66:44-5+ Mr '63
These desserts are full of ginger! il Bet Hom & Gard 42:90 N '64
Three luscious desserts from eggnog. il Bet Hom & Gard 42:82 D '64
Truly the crème de la crème. C. Claiborne. il N Y Times Mag p86-7 Mr 8 '64
See also
Cake
Cheesecake
Cookery—Fruit
Cookies
Ice cream, ices, etc.
Meringue
Pie
Puddings

DESSUREAULT, Jean Marie
Canada and Latin America; remarks, February 1964. por Américas 16:36-7 Ap '64

D'ESTAING, Valéry Giscard. See Giscard d'Estaing, V.

DESTOUCHES, Louis Ferdinand
Céline: the sod beneath the skin. I. Howe. New Repub 149:19-22 Jl 20; 17-20 Ag 17 '63

DESTROYER escorts. See Warships—United States

DETACHABLE collars. See Collars

DETAILS, Architectural. See Architecture—Details

DETECTION of crime. See Criminal investigation

DETECTION of metals. See Metals—Detection

DETECTION of submarine boats. See Submarine boats—Detection

DETECTIVE and mystery stories
Casual notes on the mystery novel. R. Chandler. Writer 76:13-16+ Jl '63
Death as a game M. Innes. Esquire 63:55-6 Ja '65
Defective detectives. V. Mercier. Nation 199: 362-3 N 16 '64
Getting away with murder. E. S. Gardner. Atlan 215:72-5 Ja '65
Have typewriter, should travel. E. Lacy. Writer 77:16-17+ Ap '64
No mirrors, please! D. Gardiner. Writer 77:16-19 Ja '64
Simenon's mosaic. J. Jacobs. Reporter 32:38-40 Ja 14 '65
Strike a note, and hold it! D. J. Marlowe. Writer 76:20-1 Ag '63
Viewpoint and the mystery short story. S. Ellin. Writer 76:7-9 My '63
Writing the juvenile mystery. P. A. Whitney. Writer 76:14-18 Ap '63
See also
Television broadcasting—Crime programs

Bibliography

Criminal record. J. T. Winterich. See last issue of each month of Saturday review
I spy a mystery. L. Lerman. il Mlle 59:62-3 Jl '64
Mystery, detective, suspense (cont) J. Sandoe. Library J 88:579, 1028, 1550+, 1906, 2276, 2732-3+, 3105, 3648-50, 4239-41, 4666-7 F 1, Mr 1, Ap 1, My 1, Je 1, Jl, S 1, O 1, N 1, D 1 '63
Mystery, detective, suspense. M. K. Grant. Library J 89:658-60, 1118-19, 1626-7, 1986-7, 2368-70, 2828-9, 3036-7, 3188-9, 3777-8, 4389-90, 4826-8; 90:136-7 F 1, Mr 1, Ap 1, My 1, Je 1, Jl-S 1, O 1, N 1, D 1 '64, Ja 1 '65

Single works

Falling star. P. Moyes. Mlle 59:65-89 Jl '64
Four hours to fear. F. Lockridge and R. Lockridge. il Ladies Home J 81:78-80 My '64
Hospitality of the house; condensation. D. M. Disney. il Seventeen 23:116-19 O '64

Technique

Do-it-yourself homicide; rules for crime writing. J. Webb. Writer 76:17-20+ O '63
Party of one. M. Allingham. Holiday 34:11-15 S '63
Psychology of mystery story writing. M. A. deFord. Writer 77:12-14 Je '64
Suspense: rules and non-rules. P. Highsmith. Writer 77:9-12 N '64

DETECTORS
Facts on smell machines aired by scientists. Sci N L 84:345 N 30 '63
Inventor of the month; atomic detector for suitcase bombs. S. V. Jones. il Sci Digest 56:16 D '64
Sniffer may detect bombs on aircraft. P. J. Klass. il Aviation W 81:42+ N 16 '64
Underground traffic detectors; Palo Alto, Calif. J. Taylor. il Am City 79:140+ S '64
See also
Metals—Detection

DETECTORS, Gas. See Gas detectors

DETERGENTS. See Cleaning compositions

DETERMINED productions, incorporated
Adult juveniles. il Newsweek 62:80+ Ag 19 '63

DETERMINISM. See Free will and determinism

DETERRENCE (strategy) See Strategy

DETHIER, Vincent G.
Life on other planets. Cath World 198:245-50 Ja '64
Microscopic brains; adaptation of address. bibliog Science 143:1138-45 Mr 13 '64
Mpanda, the beggar; story. Cath World 200: 307-11 F '65

DE TOLEDANO, Ralph
Cuba story, wraps off. Nat R 14:288-9 Ap 9 '63
If it's Goldwater v. Johnson, who will win? Nat R 16:101-2+ F 11 '64
Lodge: the little man who wasn't there. Nat R 16:399-401 My 19 '64
Marginal notes; poem. Nat R 15:486 D 3 '63
Negro minority vs. a white majority? Nat R 16:814-15 S 22 '64
Poet is a poet is a what. Nat R 15:404+ N 5 '63
Records (cont) Nat R 14:204-6, 417-19; 15: 160-1, 317-18; 16:658-9+, 737-8, 920-2; 17: 71-2 Mr 12, My 21, Ag 27, O 8 '63, Jl 28, Ag 25, O 20 '64, Ja 26 '65

DETONATION waves. See Shock waves

DETONATORS
French Canada's strange revolt; role of FLQ (Quebec liberation front) L. Bergquist. il Look 27:90-4+ D 3 '63

DETROIT
Battle in Baden-Baden; IOC meeting. Sports Illus 19:6 S 16 '63
Detroit dolls up; renaissance in stodgy city. il Bsns W p 132-3+ N 23 '63
Detroit loses again; 1968 Olympics. Newsweek 62:84 O 28 '63
Detroit's total war on poverty; Community action center. il Bsns W p76-7 Ja 9 '65
Light (torch division) that failed; Olympic torch from Los Angeles to Detroit by relay of runners. H. Higdon. Sports Illus 19: 47-9 N 4 '63
You can save your elms. F. Vaydik. il Am City 78:110-11 S '63

Air pollution

Detroit's smog-shrouded mystery. P. Hillary. il Motor T 17:62-5 Ja '65

Architecture

Detroit's road of good intentions. il Arch Forum 120:18-19 Ap '64
Granite skyscraper for a Detroit loan association. il Arch Rec 133:202-4 Ap '63
New work of Mies van der Rohe. il Arch Forum 119:88-9 S '63
Yamasaki's first skyscraper; headquarters for Consolidated gas company. J. S. Hornbeck. il Arch Rec 133:143-50 My '63
Yamasaki's first tower. D. B. Carlson. il Arch Forum 118:98-113 My '63

Banks

Detroit bank restyles its lines. il Bsns W p76+ N 14 '64
Economical office tower; Detroit bank & trust company. il Arch Rec 135:153-6 My '64

Charities

See also
United foundation torch fund

Crime

Detroit vs. the Mafia: a city fights back. J. Atwater. il Sat Eve Post 237:69-73 My 30 '64
When the Mafia takes over a city. U S News 55:6 O 21 '63

Economic conditions

Boom in city that autos built; how Detroit made a comeback. il U S News 57:64-7 Jl 27 '64

Education

Detroit high school challenges nation; Central high's stepped-up program. H. J. Bims. il Ebony 19:25-8+ Ag '64
Good in a ghetto; Detroit's Central high school. il Time 84:87 O 2 '64
School bonds nixed. H. Salsinger. Sr Schol 85:1T-2T N 4 '64

DETROIT—Education—*Continued*
Suburban campus-plan school designed for future team teaching; East Hills junior high school; Bloomfield Hills. il Arch Rec 136:240-1 S '64

Galleries and museums

See also
Detroit institute of arts

Industries

When science supplants technology; with comments by prominent businessmen. T. Levitt. il Harvard Bsns R 41:14-16+ Jl '63

Libraries

See also
Detroit public library

Music

[Musical events] Mus Am 84:56 F; 19 My '64
Opera on four cylinders; Metropolitan spring tour in Detroit. A. M. Lingg. Opera N 28: 21-2 O 19 '63

Negroes

Detroit feels brunt of Negro pressure. il Bsns W p90-1 Je 29 '63
Detroit: new model in city hall. T. R. Brooks. Reporter 30:25-7 Ap 9 '64
How a big city voted on selling homes to Negroes; homeowners' rights: what Detroit law says. U S News 57:10 S 14 '64
Negro physician in Detroit. C. H. Wright. Negro Hist Bul 27:109-10 F '64
You can't live there. A. Whitaker. Negro Hist Bul 26:223-4 Ap '63

Newspapers

Detroit's newspaper troubles; seven strikes in less than nine years. U S News 57:63 Ag 3 '64
15th week in Detroit; Detroit's newspaper strike. Time 84:92 O 30 '64
How idled workers get by when a strike stops their jobs. U S News 57:120+ O 26 '64
Lesson in economics. il Time 84:73 D 4 '64
Settlement on premium pay. U S News 57:82-3 N 23 '64

Police

Detroit; a lesson in law enforcement. G. Edwards. Ann Am Acad 347:67-73 My '63

Politics and government

Detroit: new model in city hall. T. R. Brooks. Reporter 30:25-7 Ap 9 '64
Detroit's surprising mayor. T. Nicholson. Harper 227:76-8+ D '63

Prisons and reformatories

Jail addition designed for maximum security; Wayne County jail, Detroit. il Arch Rec 136: 159-61 N '64

Sanitary affairs

Burn brush without smoke. G. C. Richards and R. Schink. il Am City 78:34 S '63

Stores

New buildings at Northland in Detroit. il Arch Rec 133:166-7 Je '63

Streets

Economy street paving fills the gap. G. C. Richards and D. Behm. il Am City 78:89-91 S '63

Water supply

Eleven small water systems unite. D. A. Keylon. il Am City 78:131+ Ag '63
Intermunicipal cooperation means assured water supply; Pontiac, Mich. H. G. Parker. il Am City 79:120-1 Ap '64

DETROIT institute of arts
African art gallery fund. W. F. Wood. Negro Hist Bul 27:132 F '64
African art gallery seen as retribution to Negro cause. B. De Ramus. Negro Hist Bul 27:127+ F '64
Detroit branch, ASNLH, launches $50,000 African art drive. A. D. Coar. il Negro Hist Bul 27:99-102 F '64

DETROIT Lions (football club) See Football clubs

DETROIT public library
Couple apprehended with stolen documents in Detroit. Pub W 185:136 F 24 '65
Couple convicted in stolen documents case. Pub W 186:54 Jl 20 '64
Detroit doubles into three. R. A. Ulveling. il Library J 88:4531-4 D 1 '63
Detroit pl combines forces with FBI to solve bizarre document swindle case. Library J 89:825-6 F 15 '64
Investigate before you inveigh. R. Ulveling. il Library J 88:4693-5 D 15 '63
Metropolitan reference services: patterns, problems, solutions. K. G. Harris. il Library J 88:1606-11 Ap 15 '63
Pages on wheels. il Library J 88:4528 D 1 '63

DETROIT Red Wings (hockey team) See Hockey teams

DETROIT Tigers (baseball) See Baseball clubs

DETROIT'S Central high school. See Detroit—Education

DETTMER, Roger
Backstage battle. Mus Am 84:10-11 F '64
Doomed to disappointment. Mus Am 84:22-3+ Ja '64
Fritz Reiner, 1888-1963. Mus Am 83:272-3 D '63
Jean Martinon, new maestro in Chicago. Mus Am 83:50-2 N '63

DETWEILER, Robert
For a Christian poetics. Christian Cent 81:913 Jl 15 '64

DETZER, Karl
At large and most wanted: ten dangerous men. Read Digest 84:190-2+ Mr '64
Snapshots of a Soviet spy. Read Digest 83: 210-14 N '63
Snorkel Bob: Chicago's champion fire fighter. Read Digest 85:117-20 Ag '64
Welcome, stranger. Read Digest 83:19-20+ S '63
Whiting doesn't spare the rod. Read Digest 82:167-70+ My '63
Woodman, save that tree! Am For 70:12-15+ S '64

DEUTCH, Richard
Half of life; poem. Nation 197:302 N 9 '63
One summer night; poem. Nation 197:328 N 16 '63

DEUTERIUM
Deuterated water effects on acid ionization constants. R. B. Martin. bibliog Science 139:1198+ Mr 22 '63
Infrared study of selective deuteration of kaolinite and halloysite at room temperature. R. L. Ledoux and J. L. White. bibliog il Science 145:47-9 Jl 3 '64
Vibrational excitation in some four-center transition states. S. H. Bauer and E. L. Resler, jr. bibliog il Science 146:1045-8 N 20 '64

Physiological effects

Fully deuterated euglena gracilis. S. E. Mandeville and others. bibliog il Science 146:769 N 6 '64

DEUTSCH, Babette
Coleridge on himself. Poetry 102:128-30 My '63
Day in late August; poem. Sat R 46:52 Ap 13 '63
Lament for the makers: 1964; poem. Atlan 214:72-3 D '64
Platform verse. Poetry 102:400-2 S '63

about

Three notable collections. L. Untermeyer. Poetry 103:384-5 Mr '64

DEUTSCH, Esther
Ten hardy heathers. Flower Grower 51:26+ Ag '64

DEUTSCH, H. F.
Crystalline low molecular weight γ-globulin from a human urine. bibliog Science 141: 435-6 Ag 2 '63

DEUTSCH, Harold C.
Impact of the Franco-German entente; address, April 6, 1963; with questions and answers. Ann Am Acad 348:82-94 Jl '63

DEUTSCH, Herbert A.
Synaesthesia. New Yorker 39:20-2 Ja 25 '64

DEUTSCH, J. A.
Test of Deutsch's drive-decay theory of rewarding self-stimulation of the brain. S. S. Pliskoff and T. D. Hawkins. bibliog il Science 141:823-4 Ag 30 '63; Reply with rejoinder. J. A. Deutsch. 142:1125-6 N 29 '63

DEUTSCH, Karl W. and Wiener, Norbert
Lonely nationalism of Rudyard Kipling. Yale R 52:499-517 Je '63

DEUTSCH, Martin
Long research and the happy payoff. P. Blake. il por Life 56:88-9 Ap 3 '64

DEUTSCH, Patricia, and Deutsch, R. M.
Chicago. Redbook 122:68-9+ N '63
How Los Angeles eases racial tensions. Read Digest 85:86-90 O '64
Spirit of St Louis. Redbook 121:60-1+ Jl '63
These five were cured of overweight. Ladies Home J 80:131-2+ Ap '63
Your health (cont) Redbook 120:28 Ap; 121: 26 Je '63
—See Deutsch, R. M. jt. auth.

DEUTSCH, Ronald M.
How much health is there in health foods? Read Digest 82:57-61 My '63
—See Deutsch, P. jt. auth.
—and Deutsch, Patricia
Stroke: the killer that can be curbed. Read Digest 85:70-4 D '64

DEUTSCHE gramophon gesellschaft. See Phonograph record industry—Germany (Federal Republic)
DEUTSCHER, Isaac
Russian problems and U. S. politics. Nation 199:43-5 Ag 10 '64
Survival's favorite son. Nation 199:494-6 D 21 '64
DEUTSCHMAN, Paul
Jungle Mesabi; excerpts from report. Fortune 68:81-2+ D '63
United fruit's experiment in international partnership. Read Digest 85:146-50 O '64
DE VALERA, Eamon
President de Valera of Ireland visits United States; arrival remarks, and toast, with address to Congress, May 28, 1964. Dept State Bul 50:927-33 Je 15 '64
DE VALOIS, Dame Ninette
Ninette de Valois retires as director. C. Barnes. il pors Dance Mag 38:42-6 Mr '64
Royal ballet's most uncommon commoner. J. Martin. por Sat R 46:55-6+ Ap 27 '63
DE VALOIS, Russell L. and others
Responses of single cells in visual system to shifts in the wavelength of light. Science 146:1184-6 N 27 '64
DEVALUATION of currency. See Currency question
DEVANEY, John
Bible in the bullpen. Sat Eve Post 237:28-9 My 2 '64
How safe are the birth control pills? Redbook 120:45+ F '63
DEVANEY, Robert P.
Communicating in a high-noise environment. Electr World 72:39-41+ N '64
DE VARONA, Donna
I hit that turn, gung ho, guts out! pors Life 57:104-5 O 9 '64
Olympian at the fair. S. Gordon. il pors Look 28:98-100+ F 11 '64
DEVELOPMENT. See Evolution
DEVELOPMENT, Economic. See Economic development
DEVELOPMENT banks
Poorer nations find a new bootstrap; private development banks financing over-all economy. Bsns W p63-4+ Mr 14 '64
DEVELOPING (photography) See Photography—Developing and developers
DEVER, James A.
Play center for young imaginations. Pop Sci 183:114 Ag '63
DEVERELL, Diana
Curl up and read. Seventeen 24:115 Ja '65
DEVIANT behavior. See Behavior (psychology)
DEVIATION of the compass. See Compass
DEVIL
Word. V. P. McCorry. America 108:317-18 Mr 2 '63
DEVILFISH. See Rays (fishes)
DEVILS; drama. See Whiting, J.
DEVIL'S ISLAND
Return to Devil's Island. R. S. Smith. il Travel 122:38-42 O '64
DEVILS TOWER NATIONAL MONUMENT
Devil's Tower. D. Minney. il Travel 119:52-3 Ap '63
DEVITO, E. B.
Meat of it; poem. Good H 156:132 Mr '63
DEVLIN, Dennis
Silent voices. H. Carruth. Poetry 103:191-2 D '63
DEVLIN, John C.
Hal Borland and the voice of nature. Audubon Mag 66:175-7 My '64
Please don't feed the pigeons! Read Digest 85:12E-12F+ Ag '64
DEVLIN, Polly
John Osborne. Vogue 143:98-9+ Je '64
DEVLIN, Wende
More beat poems of a beat mother (cont) Good H 157:44 S '63; 158:32 My '64
DEVOE, Mary
(comp) Wild wisdom. Read Digest 85:24C+ O '64
DEVOE, Merrill
Ways to build stronger sales team; excerpts from How to tailor your sales organization to your markets. Nations Bsns 52:62-4+ F '64
DEVON horse show. See Horse shows
DEVONIAN period. See Paleontology—Devonian
DEVONSHIRE, dukes of
Ducal life; the Devonshires. R. Douglas-Home. il Vogue 141:156-61+ Mr 1 '63
DEVONSHIRE, England
Channel cruise to glorious Devon. A. Villiers. il Nat Geog Mag 124:208-59 Ag '63
DEVORE, Hugh
Enigma of the interim coach. il por Sports Illus 19:59 O 28 '63
DEVORE, Sy
As long as you're up, get me a Grant. il por Time 82:58 O 11 '63
DEVOTION to the Sacred Heart. See Sacred Heart, Devotion to
DEVOTIONAL medals. See Medals, Devotional
DEVOTIONS. See Prayer
DEVRIES, Arthur L. and Wohlschlag, D. E.
Diving depths of the Weddell seal. bibliog Science 145:292 Jl 17 '64
DE VRIES, Peter
Adventures of a people buff; story. New Yorker 39:28-31 F 15 '64
Conversational ball; story. New Yorker 40:33-4 Je 13 '64
Forever panting; story. New Yorker 39:169-70 S 28 '63
Our revels now are ended; story; excerpt from Reuben, Reuben. Ladies Home J 81:78-9 Mr '64
Reuben, Reuben; story. Sat Eve Post 237:38-41 Ja 18 '64
Till the sands of the desert grow cold; story. New Yorker 39:20 Ag 10 '63
about
De Vries in Westport. por Newsweek 63:94 F 17 '64
Renegade reformed; graduates of Calvin college. Christian Cent 80:815 Je 19 '63
DEW line. See Radar defense network
DEWAN, Wilfrid F.
Tradition is a living message. Cath World 197:238-45 Jl '63
DEWAR, Robert Kerr
Language of scientific reports; letter. Science 142:11 O 4 '63
DEWART, Leslie
Academic freedom and Catholic dissent. Commonweal 80:33-6 Ap 3 '64
Church in Cuba: a universal dilemma; excerpts from Christianity and revolution. Commonweal 79:67-9, 717-19 O 11 '63, Mr 13 '64
Openings for diplomacy; Cuba: catalyst of peace. Nation 196:113-15 F 9 '63
DEWEY, John
Dewey's labs. Newsweek 61:75 Je 3 '63
DEWEY, Melvil
Changing catalog rules; reprint. Library J 89:2296 Je 1 '64
DEWEY classification. See Classification, Decimal
DEWHURST, Colleen
Cleo in the park. A. Pryce-Jones. pors Theatre Arts 47:16-18 Jl '63
New York is a stage: Ballad of the sad café: a lyric horror story. I. Mothner. il pors Look 28:121-3 F 11 '64
DEWHURST, J. Frederic
Why buy growth stocks? Changing T 18:7-11 F '64
DE WILDE, Ronald, jr
Dependable rhododendrons. il Horticulture 42:26-7+ Je '64
DEWLEN, Al
How to make an idea work. Writer 76:18-19 Ag '63
DEWSON, James H. 3d
Speech sound discrimination by cats. bibliog Science 144:555-6 My 1 '64
DE WYS, Fred
How to make a monster. Design 65:19-21 S '63
DEXTER, Gerry L.
Calling all SWL DX'ers. Pop Electr 19:39-42+ S '63
DEXTRINE
Formation and degradation of cyclic dextrins by intracellular enzymes of bacillus macerans. J. A. DePinto and J. L. Campbell. bibliog il Science 146:1064-6 N 20 '64
DEYOUNG, Russell
Businessmen in the news. il por Fortune 69:45 My '64
DE YOUNG memorial museum. See M. H. De Young memorial museum, San Francisco
DEZETTEL, L. M.
Transistorized wireless intercom. Electr World 69:76-7 F '63
DHAHRAN, Saudi Arabia
Airports
Yamasaki's Dhahran airport. il Arch Rec 133:145-8 Mr '63
DHARMAPALA, Anagarika
Anagarika Dharmapala, Buddhist missionary and educator. W. Rahula. Sch & Soc 92:383-5 D 12 '64

D'HARNONCOURT, Rene
When is art modern art? N Y Times Mag p 17+ My 24 '64
DIABETES
Diabetes cases reported on the rise in U.S. Sci N L 86:137 Ag 29 '64
Diabetes mellitus in the sand rat induced by standard laboratory diets. K. Schmidt-Nielsen and others. bibliog il Science 143:689-90 F 14 '64
Diabetes on increase but control possible. Sci N L 86:376 D 12 '64
Good news for diabetics; pills. il Sci Digest 55:84 Ap '64
Hope for diabetes cure. Sci N L 86:242 O 17 '64
Hope for diabetes drug. Sci N L 85:259 Ap 25 '64
Hot on the trail of diabetes. Bsns W p 124+ N 14 '64
New diabetes test completed in one minute. Sci N L 86:200 S 26 '64
Nicotinic acid biosynthesis: control by an enzyme that competes with a spontaneous reaction. A. H. Mehler and others. bibliog il Science 145:817-19 Ag 21 '64
Please save my son! case of J. Havens. D. O. Woodbury. Read Digest 82:157-8+ F '63
Pyruvate metabolism and control: factors affecting pyruvic carboxylase activity. A. D. Freedman and L. Kohn. bibliog il Science 145:58-60 Jl 3 '64
Role heredity plays in diabetes. Good H 157:126 Jl '63
Spotting the pre-diabetic. Sci Digest 55:75 Mr '64
Survival for diabetics. Todays Health 41:88 F '63
Wanted: the other million diabetics. G. G. Greer. Bet Hom & Gard 42:19 Ap '64
See also
Insulin
Diagnosis
Detecting diabetes early. il Time 83:54 Je 26 '64
DIABETES research
Young diabetics tested on diet without insulin. Sci N L 83:239 Ap 13 '63
DIACONATE. See Deacons
DIAFINE. See Photography—Developing and developers
DIAGNOSIS
Condition critical: cause unknown. D. Murray. il Todays Health 43:48-9+ Ja '65
Doctor, what's wrong with me? E. Hill. il Sat Eve Post 237:64-6 My 2 '64
It's not always in your head. Sci Digest 56:58 N '64
Sick? let a computer do the diagnosis. S. Gibson. il Pop Electr 21:45-8+ N '64
See also
Moving pictures in medicine
Photography, Medical
Thermography
Ultrasonic waves—Medical applications
also subhead Diagnosis under names of diseases, e.g. Diabetes—Diagnosis
DIAL, Dorothy W.
Alliums for show and seasoning. Horticulture 42:18-19 F '64
DIAL (periodical)
Light and the dark. H. Kramer. New Repub 150:23+ F 15 '64
Pages from a usable past. G. Hicks. Sat R 46:17 D 21 '63
DIAL-a-movie. See Moving pictures—Moral aspects
DIAL Emmy for murder; story. See Preston, B. B.
DIAL gages. See Gages
DIAL indicators. See Gages
DIAL telephone. See Telephone, Dial
DIAL-type thermometers. See Thermometers and thermometry
DIALOGUE
Books; conversation. R. Adler. New Yorker 40:203-4 My 16 '64
Dialogue. P. Duganne. Writer 76:19-20 Ap '63
Dialogue with distinction. P. S. Curry. Writer 77:11-13+ Jl '64
Don't tell it, say it. E. Jensen. Writer 76:14-16 F '63
DIALOGUE mass. See Mass
DIALOGUE method. See Discussion
DIALOGUES of the Carmelites; opera. See Poulenc, F.
DIALYSIS
Dialysis of sleep and waking factors in blood of the rabbit. M. Monnier and L. Hösli. bibliog il Science 146:796-8 N 6 '64
Differential dialysis. L. C. Craig. bibliog il Science 144:1093-9 My 29 '64
Welcome to Kidney Towers. S. Alexander. Life 57:31 N 20 '64
See also
Kidneys, Artificial
DIAMINES
Male pill. Newsweek 61:94 Ap 15 '63
DIAMOND, C. Gerald. See Widing, J. W. jr. jt. auth.
DIAMOND, Edwin
Aqua-lung days in a watery night. Sat R 46:42 Je 22 '63
Rites of spring. Bul Atomic Sci 19:26-9 My '63
Speaking out. por Sat Eve Post 236:16+ S 28 '63
That moon trip: debate sharpens. N Y Times Mag p 10+ Jl 28 '63
What goes on in those youth cafés. McCalls 90:38+ Je '63
DIAMOND, Herbert, and Stewart, D. C.
Transplutonium. Science 141:184+ Jl 12 '63
DIAMOND, I. A. L.
Bright Diamond. M. Schumach. il por N Y Times Mag p80-1 My 26 '63
DIAMOND, James M.
Okinawa: trigger in the Pacific. Nation 198:547-8 Je 1 '64
DIAMOND, Louis K. See Hughes, D. W. O. jt. auth.
DIAMOND, Marvin
Mapping the air by sound. Time 82:52 Ag 30 '63
DIAMOND, Rachel F.
Town steps back into history and the library helps pave the way. Wilson Lib Bul 37:578-9 Mr '63
DIAMOND cave. See Caves
DIAMOND mines and mining
Now they're getting diamonds from the sea; Marine diamond. U S News 54:6 Mr 25 '63
They fish for diamonds; Marine diamond corp. A. P. Armagnac. il Pop Sci 182:85-7+ My '63
See also
De Beers consolidated mines, limited
DIAMOND trade. See Diamonds
DIAMONDBACKS. See Rattlesnakes
DIAMONDBIRDS
Australia's spotted diamondbirds. A. Keast. il Natur Hist 74:28-31 Ja '65
DIAMONDS
Bomba on the Caroni. il Newsweek 63:78-9 F 24 '64
Burning; rise in prices. il Newsweek 63:79-80 Mr 23 '64
Diamonds are a dealer's best friend. il Time 83:80+ Je 5 '64
Diamonds are not necessarily forever. A. Carthew. il N Y Times Mag p46+ O 4 '64
Diamonds for the masses; Zale jewelry co. J. McDonald. il Fortune 70:134-7+ D '64
Diamonds from the sea. Newsweek 61:76+ My 27 '63
Do-it-yourself diamonds; gem hunters at Murfreesboro, Ark. il Time 81:71 Ap 12 '63
Girls are De Beers' best friend. il Bsns W p36 F 8 '64
Origin of diamonds in the ureilites. M. E. Lipschutz. bibliog il Science 143:1431-4 Mr 27 '64
Real diamonds vs. real blue chips. C. Bird. il N Y Times Mag p69+ Ap 14 '63
X-ray detects diamonds in dyalpur meteorite. Sci Digest 53:63 Mr '63
DIAMONDS, Artificial
Diamond synthesis with Bridgman opposed-anvil apparatus. F. P. Bundy. bibliog il Science 146:1673 D 25 '64
DIAMONDS, Baseball. See Baseball fields
DIANELLA
Little goddess of the woods. il Sunset 132:291 Ap '64
DIANETICS
See also
Scientology
DIANTHUS. See Pinks
DIANTHUS barbatus. See Sweet williams
DIAPAUSE. See Insects—Development
DIAPER service. See Diapers, Infants
DIAPERS, Infants
Diaper service. M. W. Lear. McCalls 91:84-5+ Ja '64
Pinning down the facts on diapers. Good H 156:208k Ap '63
DIAPHRAGM, Artificial
Diaphragm by dacron. Newsweek 62:83-4 S 30 '63
DIARIES
Preserving the secrets of the White House. H. F. Graft. il N Y Times Mag p9+ D 29 '63
Your savings account of memories. J. Fisher. il Read Digest 82:181-3+ My '63

DIARIES—*Continued*

Quotations, maxims, etc.

Up betimes and. .; comp. by E. F. Murphy. N Y Times Mag p48 D 15 '63

DIARRHEA
Epizootic diarrhea of infant mice: identification of the etiologic agent. W. R. Adams and L. M. Kraft. bibliog il Science 141:359-60 Jl 26 '63
Infant diarrhea. I. J. Rossman. Parents Mag 39:140 Ap '64

DIARY of a madman; drama. See Gogol, N. V.

DIAS, Earl J.
Christmas starlet; drama. Plays 23:15-26 D '63
Don't tell the folks back home; drama. Plays 23:27-37 Ja '64
Tall stranger; drama. Plays 22:1-12 Mr '63
Way, way down East; drama. Plays 23:99-108 My '64

DIATOMS
Fine structure of a diatom centrosome. R. W. Drum and H. S. Pankratz. bibliog il Science 142:61-3 O 4 '63

DIAZ, Justino
Winners two; interview, ed. by A. M. Lingg. por Opera N 28:29 Ja 11 '64
Look at the future. por Mus Am 83:9 Jl '63

DIAZ ORDAZ, Gustavo
President-elect of Mexico visits President Johnson at LBJ ranch; remarks, November 12, 1964. Dept State Bul 51:806-7 D 7 '64

about

Ahead for Mexico: change in leadership. por U S News 57:20 Jl 13 '64
Bright spot in the hemisphere: a close look at Mexico. il por U S News 56:95-7 F 24 '64
Everything's O.K. on the LBJ. K. Fleming. il por Newsweek 64:34-5 N 23 '64
Glowing start. por Time 84:53 D 11 '64
Keeping steam in Mexico's boom. il por Bsns W p90+ N 28 '64
Meet the president. il por Time 84:22 Jl 3 '64
Mexico chooses stability for 1964-70. por U S News 55:83 N 18 '63
Mexico follows a solo camino. K. Botsford. il pors N Y Times Mag p20+ Ap 26 '64
1964 shoo-in for Mexico? il por Sr Schol 83:10-13 D 13 '63
President-elect. por Newsweek 64:44 Jl 13 '64
Presidential march: left, right. il por Time 82:53 N 15 '63
Presidential ritual. por Newsweek 62:56 N 18 '63
U.S.-Mexican relations: new tests for new president. por U S News 57:20 D 7 '64
Viva el candidato! R. Armstrong. il pors Sat Eve Post 237:73-7 Je 20 '64
Volkswagen president. il por Newsweek 64:60-1 D 7 '64

DICENTRA cucullaria. See Dutchmans-breeches

DICHLOROPHENOXYACETIC acid. See 2.4-D

DICK, Arthur R. See Sacktor, B. jt. auth.

DICK, James M.
No need for emergencies. Am City 79:103-4 My '64

DICKENS, Brenda C.
Why Negro history week. Negro Hist Bul 27:153-4 Mr '64

DICKENS, Charles
Christmas carol; excerpts. Sat Eve Post 237:24-31 D 19 '64

about

Christmas time! Good H 157:60-1 D '63
Dark corners of the mind: Dickens' childhood reading. H. Stone. il Horn Bk 39:306-21 Je '63
Intimate of every household. C. Mackenzie. il por Horizon 6:108-15 Sum '64
When Pickwick went to Vanity fair. A. Ashforth. il por N Y Times Mag p8+ D 22 '63

DICKENS, Monica
WLB biography. P. Edge. por Wilson Lib Bul 37:883 Je '63

DICKERSON, Adolphus Sumner
Key man of the South: the Negro minister. C. E. Lincoln. il pors N Y Times Mag p36-7+ Jl 12 '64

DICKERSON, Eddie
Why didn't they hit back? J. Robbins and J. Robbins. por Redbook 121:52-3+ Jl '63

DICKERSON, George
After the New frontier; a new lost generation. Mlle 59:158-9+ S '64
Coming on of night; poem. New Yorker 40:140 N 7 '64
Strange eye and art of De Kooning. Sat Eve Post 237:68-71 N 21 '64
Strange sower; poem. Mlle 58:72 D '63
What's dimming the city of lights? Mlle 59:104+ O '64

DICKERSON, Nancy H.
Husbands in crisis. por McCalls 90:112+ Ag '63
In the Washington swim. por McCalls 90:46+ Jl '63
Marguerite: hair stylist to Washington's leading ladies. por McCalls 90:72+ S '63
Television's princess of the press corps. B. Gottehrer. il pors Sat Eve Post 237:36-7 O 31 '64

DICKERT, Lois
They thought the war was on. McCalls 90:96-7+ Ap '63
—and Seidenbaum, Art
Rah! rah! rah! college for everybody. McCalls 91:98+ My '64
What goes on in those youth cafés. McCalls 90:38+ Je '63

DICKEY, Charley
Charged by a dove. Field & S 68:56-7+ S '63
Cottontails to spare. Outdoor Life 131:64-5+ Ap '63
Florida quail cruise. Field & S 68:31-3+ N '63
Hunting, with gun and wallet. il Esquire 60:212-13+ D '63
I learn about quail. Outdoor Life 132:28-31+ N '63
Loaded with bass. por Outdoor Life 133:64-5+ Je '64
That night before. Field & S 68:58-60+ Mr '64

DICKEY, David Dale
Railroad bird hunt. Field & S 69:59-61 Je '64

DICKEY, James
Angina; poem. New Yorker 40:30 Ag 15 '64
Being; Why in London the blind are saviors; Folk-singer of the thirties; poems. Poetry 102:281-91 Ag '63
Breath; poem. New Yorker 39:48 N 9 '63
Bums, on waking; poem. New Yorker 39:34 S 7 '63
Cherrylog road; poem. New Yorker 39:51 O 12 '63
Common grave; story. New Yorker 40:54 O 24 '64
Driver; poem. New Yorker 39:54 D 7 '63
Escape; poem. New Yorker 40:30 Jl 18 '64
Firebombing; poem. Poetry 104:63-72 My '64
First and last things. Poetry 103:316-24 F '64
Goodbye to serpents, poem. New Yorker 39:47 S 21 '63
Ice skin; poem. New Yorker 39:37 D 28 '63
Kudzu; poem. New Yorker 39:44 My 18 '63
Language of the brain. Poetry 103:187-90 D '63
Reincarnation; poem. New Yorker 40:51 Mr 7 '64
Scarred girl; poem. New Yorker 39:36 Je 1 '63
Them, crying; poem. New Yorker 40:42 My 9 '64
Theodore Roethke. Poetry 105:119-22 N '64
War wound; poem. New Yorker 40:54 S 12 '64

about

James Dickey's new book. W. Berry. Poetry 105:130-1 N '64
Oriented by instinct by stars. R. Duncan. Poetry 105:131-3 N '64

DICKEY, John Sloan
Robert Frost: teacher-at-large. Sat R 46:21-2 F 23 '63
Taste for change; address, September 23, 1963. Vital Speeches 30:24-5 O 15 '63

DICKEY, William
In the convention. Poetry 104:375-8 S '64
Islands; poem. Poetry 102:368 S '63
Native resistances; poem. Atlan 213:70 Mr '64
Poem for the Bank of America, Westlake branch. Harper 228:93 F '64
Precious stones; poem. New Yorker 39:26 Jl 20 '63
Rehabilitation; poem. Poetry 105:166 D '64
Reticences of pattern. Poetry 101:421-4 Mr '63
Things kept; poem. New Yorker 39:42 Ap 13 '63

DICKINSON, Emily
Books in the making. Pub W 187:100 Ja 4 '65
Emily Dickinson: poetry and punctuation. E. P. Stamm. il por Sat R 46:26-7+ Mr 30 '63; Reply. T. Ward. 46:25 Ap 27 '63; Rejoinder. 46:23 My 25 '63

DICKINSON, Pramuan
Thailand: I am no longer the hind legs of an elephant. UNESCO Courier 17:17+ S '64

DICKS, Russell L. See Cabot, R. C. jt. auth.

DICKSON, Alex
Accent in quality. il por Am For 70:8-9 D '64

DICTAPHONE corporation
Chuckling past a milestone. il Bsns W p38 O 19 '63
DICTATING machines
See also
Dictaphone corporation
DICTATORS
Democracy faces a global dilemma. W. H. McNeill. il N Y Times Mag p27+ N 17 '63
Speaking out; let's stop being foolish about dictators. E. O. Briggs. Sat Eve Post 236: 8+ S 14 '63
DICTATORSHIP
On tyranny, by L. Strauss. Review
Commentary 36:412-16 N '63. G. Lichtheim
DICTIONARIES
Books; my fifty years with dictionaries and grammars. E. Wilson. New Yorker 39:165-76+ Ap 20 '63
See also
English language—Dictionaries
also subhead Dictionaries and encyclopedias under various subjects, e.g. Education—Dictionaries and encyclopedias
DICTIONARIES, Childrens
Picture dictionaries; summary. Library J 88: 1725-6+ Ap 15 '63
DICTYOSTELIUM. See Myxomycetes
DIDION, Joan
American summer. Vogue 141:117+ My '63
Bosses make lousy lovers. Sat Eve Post 238: 34+ Ja 30 '65
Coming home; story. Sat Eve Post 237:50-2 Jl 11 '64
Movies. Vogue 143:24 Ja 1; 57 Mr 1; 42 Ap 1; 60 My; 42 Je; 144:35 Jl; 34 Ag 1; 106 S 1; 110 O 1; 64 N 1; 150 D '64; 145:66 Ja 1; 99 F 1 '65
Passing scene. Nat R 15:246+ S 24 '63
Silver to have and to hurl. Vogue 143:60 Ap 1 '64
World was his oyster. Nat R 16:1064-5 D 1 '64
DIEBENKORN, Richard
Art; retrospective at the Washington gallery of art. F. Getlein. New Repub 151:25-6 D 5 '64
Ethics of adversity. il por Newsweek 64:97 N 30 '64
DIEBOLD, John
ADP, the still-sleeping giant. Harvard Bsns R 42:60-5 S '64
When will your husband be obsolete? interview, ed. by P. L. Cahn. McCalls 90:64-5+ Jl '63
about
All the news that's fit to automate. il Time 82:52 Jl 5 '63
DIEBOLD, William, jr
He tried to bring France to England. Sat R 47:41-2+ Mr 7 '64
Market price of power. Sat R 47:40 Mr 28 '64
DIEBOLD, Incorporated
Waiting for new deals to click; rivals in selling vaults to U.S. bankers. il Bsns W p 140-2 Je 6 '64
DIEDERICH, Paul B.
In praise of praise. NEA J 52:58-9 S '63
DIEFENBAKER, John George
As Canada heads for showdown at the polls. il por U S News 54:48 Ap 8 '63
Canada goes to the polls. H. Bigart. il Reporter 28:29-32 Ap 11 '63
Diefenbaker falls: did he jump or was he pushed? il por Newsweek 61:33-6 F 18 '63
Diefenbaker vision. I. Sclanders. por Nation 198:387-8 Ap 20 '64
Gift from Washington. Time 81:31 Ap 5 '63
Liberals gain in Canadian elections. por Sr Schol 82:16 Ap 24 '63
Now U.S. is the issue in Canada. il por U S News 54:31-2 F 18 '63
Nuclear blowup. Newsweek 61:52 F 11 '63
Renegade in power, by P. C. Newman. Review
Newsweek por 62:62 N 25 '63
Storm over Diefenbaker. il por Time 82:34+ N 29 '63
Unfinished election in Canada. il Bsns W p27 Ap 13 '63
Washington gives Canada an election and an issue; with statement by U.S. Department of state. W. H. Hessler. Reporter 28:29-31 F 28 '63; Discussion. 28:6+ Mr 28 '63
When friends fall out. il por Time 81:32 F 8 '63
DIEFFENBACHIAS
Let's use dumbcane. K. S. Phillips. il Pop Gard 15:16-17 Ja '64
DIEGO ALVAREZ ISLAND. See Gough Island
DIEHL, Charles E.
D.C. to A.C. transistor power supply. Electr World 69:66 Je '63
DIEKHOFF, John S.
College graduate as a lifetime reader; excerpts from address. por ALA Bul 58:995-7+ D '64
How to visit a college. PTA Mag 57:20-2 Mr '63
Mind is its own place. PTA Mag 58:12-14 My '64
What's the right college for your youngster? PTA Mag 57:4-6 F '63
DIELDRIN
Dieldrin susceptibility: partial restoration in anopheles selected with a carbamate. G. P. Georghiou and R. L. Metcalf. bibliog il Science 140:301-2 Ap 19 '63
DIELSI, Frank J.
Wide-range wow & flutter meter. Electr World 71:76-8 Je '64
DIEM, Ngo-dinh-. See Ngo-dinh-Diem
DIEMERT, Helen
From wax on ice to jewelry. Sch Arts 63:5-10 My '64
DIENBIENPHU, Battle of. See Indochina, French—History—Civil war, 1946-1954
DIENER, U. L. and others
Toxin-producing aspergillus isolated from domestic peanuts. bibliog Science 142:1491-2 D 13 '63
DIENSTFREY, Harris
Doctors, lawyers & other TV heroes. Commentary 35:519-24 Je '63
New millions. Nation 199:466-7 D 14 '64
Radicalism of A. J. Muste. Commentary 37: 88-90 My '64
Tea and sympathy. Commentary 36:410-12; 37:16 N '63, Mr '64
DIEPPE raid, 1942
Dieppe: the shame and the glory, by T. Robertson. Review
America 109:141-2 Ag 10 '63. W. B. McKean
DIERS, Richard
(ed) See O'Faolain, S. On writing
DIERS, Tracy
Check your tape heads. Pop Mech 120:180-1 D '63
DIES, Martin
Liberals do believe in devils. M. S. Evans. Nat R 14:457-8 Je 4 '63
DIESEL, Rudolf
Rudolf Diesel; the man and his engine. H. G. Strepp. il pors Motor B 114:25-7+ O '64
DIESEL construction company
Building skylines is his business. il Bsns W p33-4 Jl 11 '64
DIESEL engines
Delivery truck market gets a new diesel; GMC's Toro-flow. il Bsns W p 112+ Ja 18 '64
Historic diesel pioneer presented to Smithsonian. Sci N L 85:88 F 8 '64
How a diesel engine works. W. T. Hull. il Motor B 114:28-30+ O '64
Sound of a diesel. R. P. Lister. Atlan 211: 139-41 Mr '63
DIESEL engines, Automotive
Dandy little diesel for $2,660. F. Clymer. il Pop Sci 185:98-9+ N '64
DIESEL engines, Marine
Engines. E. H. Nabb. il Yachting 115:44-5+ Ap '64
Repowering with diesel. F. T. Moss. il Motor B 114:31-2 O '64
Shape of power today. il Motor B 114:42-3+ O '64
Surveying a boat with diesel power. J. W. Smith. Motor B 114:32-3 O '64
See also
Motor ships
DIET
Are we drinking too much milk? with opposing views. W. W. Sackett, jr. Sci Digest 53:19-25 Ap '63
Beauty bulletin; the seven most-talked-about diets of the moment. il Vogue 144:180+ O 15 '64
Beauty checkout; the fat American daughter. Vogue 143:40+ F 1 '64
Bee venom tolerance in white mice in relation to diet. A. W. Benton and others. bibliog il Science 145:1448-9 S 25 '64
Believe me, you can lose weight! weekly food plan. N. Gleason. il Farm J 89:63+ Ja '65
Can diet prevent heart attacks? A. L. Blakeslee. il Sat Eve Post 237:66-7 Ja 25 '64
Champagne diet. il Vogue 142:150-1 O 1 '63
Complexion-clearing diet; excerpt from Eat and reduce. il Vogue 143:141 Je '64
Cutting calories. Time 83:64 My 15 '64
Diet full of cheer; Drinking man's diet. il Newsweek 65:54-5 Ja 11 '65
Diet: the new dos and don'ts. il Mlle 59:158-9 O '64

DIET—*Continued*
Dieters' clipboard. See issues of Seventeen
Dieting the most drastic way; effects of total starvation. il Time 83:31 Ja 24 '64
Dormitory diet. il Mlle 57:270-1 Ag '63
Eating too much? NAS-NRC recommendations. Newsweek 63:74 My 18 '64
Everyday guide to good eating. B. M. Stover. il Parents Mag 39:69-71+ bibliog(p 143) N '64
Facts on low-calorie foods. J. Anderson and E. Ward-Hanna. il Ladies Home J 80:138+ Ap '63
Fats and diet. Newsweek 64:78 Jl 13 '64
Food for the heart. il Newsweek 62:70-1 Ag 5 '63
Gourmet diet cook book. R. E. Church. il House & Gard 125:143-5+ Je '64
Gourmet's diet. il Esquire 59:92-4 Je '63
Holiday roundup for problem diets. Good H 157:205-8 D '63
Hot dog diet. M. Kaytor. il Look 27:38-9 Ag 13 '63
How to choose the right diet. W. Bar-Illan. bibliog il Sci Digest 54:32-8 Ag '63
How to dine well on 300 calories. il Ladies Home J 80:126+ Ja '63
How to dine well on 300 calories. M. J. Engel. il Ladies Home J 80:94 Mr '63
How to lose weight if you've stopped smoking. McCalls 91:40+ Je '64
How to stay on a diet; with recipes. B. A. Bullen. il Seventeen 23:176-7+ S '64
Joe Levine's crash diet. il Esquire 63:99 Ja '65
Low-calorie diet reduces only fat, not lean. Sci N L 83:345 Je 1 '63
Martinis versus pie. il Newsweek 64:75 Ag 24 '64
Modest diet that won't leave you hungry. il Redbook 124:52-5+ Ja '65
My anti-headache diet. U. Sinclair. il Harper 227:40-2 D '63
New data on diets. il Ladies Home J 82:62-5 Ja '65
New eat diet. McCalls 90:84-5+ Je '63
New idea: start a diet club; with recipes. il Seventeen 23:146-7+ Mr '64
Personality, diet link. Sci N L 84:197 S 28 '63
Psychology of dieting. H. Bruch. Ladies Home J 82:66 Ja '65
Reducing against a deadline; eating from whatever's served; the debutante diet. Vogue 141:150-1+ F 1 '63
Snack diet. A. Lake. McCalls 90:26+ Jl '63
These five were cured of overweight. P. Deutsch and R. Deutsch. il Ladies Home J 80:131-2+ Ap '63
This is dieting? turn diet fare into feasting. il Bet Hom & Gard 42:76-7+ My '64
Watch those holiday calories! Consumer Bul 47:17-18 D '64
What's your question? questions and answers. F. J. Stare. il Seventeen 22:160-1+ S '63
Who succeeds at dieting? il Sci Digest 54:65 S '63
Who wants to be a tub! Polly. il Farm J 88:90 O '46
Will my baby cost me my figure? G. C. Schauffler. Ladies Home J 80:40+ My '63
Winning the weight battle. F. Marley. il Sci N L 85:230+ Ap 11 '64
You and your diet. See issues of Good housekeeping
You can reach for these and not worry. il Sunset 130:120 F '63
Zero calorie diet. S. Alexander. il Life 55:105-8+ O 11 '63
See also
Cesium in diet
Children—Nutrition
Food fads
Food preferences
Nutrition research
Oils and fats, Edible
Strontium in diet
Sugar—Physiological effects

Anecdotes, facetiae, satire, etc.

Crashing off your diet. E. Klein and F. Giddon. Mlle 59:112-13+ My '64
I'll have a triple-decker clubhouse sandwich. J. Goodsell. il McCalls 91:103+ My '64
You too can be fat and love it. A. Buchwald. il McCalls 90:16 F '63

DIET, Deficient
Compact bone deficiency in protein-calorie malnutrition. S. M. Garn and others. bibliog il Science 145:1444 S 25 '64
Diabetes mellitus in the sand rat induced by standard laboratory diets. K. Schmidt-Nielsen and others. bibliog il Science 143:689-90 F 14 '64
Diet causes malnutrition; protein deficiency. Sci N L 83:387 Je 22 '63
Eating but still starving. R. Yoshioka. il Sci N L 83:346-7 Je 1 '63
For the child who has nothing. New Repub 151:7-9 D 19 '64
Protein synthesis enhanced in the liver of rats force-fed a threonine-devoid diet. H. Sidransky and others. bibliog il Science 146:766-8 N 6 '64
Sensitivity of visual receptors of carotenoid-depleted flies: a vitamin A deficiency in an invertebrate. T. H. Goldsmith and others. bibliog il Science 146:65-7 O 2 '64

DIET in disease
Low-sodium diets can be tasty; with recipes. B. Weathers. il Parents Mag 40:66-7+ Ja '65
Personal business; cholesterol dieting. Bsns W p 135 Je 27 '64
Without a grain of salt; excerpts. E. W. Bagg. il Todays Health 42:32-5+ My '64

DIET in exploration, shipwreck, etc.
Astronauts' breakfast. Newsweek 61:63 Ap 15 '63

DIETARY studies. See Diet; Diet, Deficient

DIETER, Kathleen
Businessmen's expectations. Duns R 83:11 Je; 84:11 S; 11 D '64

DIETHER, Jack
Another view. con. Am Rec G 29:523-4 Mr '63
Aspects of Jupiter. Am Rec G 30:936-7 Je '64
At last, Prokofieff's Second symphony. Am Rec G 30:1016-18 Jl '64
Benjamin Britten's Sechs Hölderlin-fragmente. Am Rec G 30:386-8 Ja '64
Burton Hamlet. Am Rec G 30:1092-5 Ag '64
For the quadricentennial; the tragedie of Hamlet, prince of Denmarke. Am Rec G 30:778-81+ My '64
Fresh life for an old genre. Am Rec G 31:292-5 D '64
From Angel, DGG, and Amadeo, a feast of Bruckner's church music. Am Rec G 29:850-2 Jl '63
From London, Britten's overpowering War requiem. Am Rec G 29:916-19+ Ag '63
Immoral? from Vox, Monteverdi's L'incoronazione di Poppea. Am Rec G 29:700-4+ My '63
L'incoronazione di Poppea. Am Rec G 31:410-15 Ja '65
Klemperer's Bruckner: two views. Am Rec G 29:446 F '63
Milhaud's view of Sophocles; and Bernstein's view of Milhaud; Les Choéphores. Am Rec G 30:232-4 N '63
More Mahler by Bernstein, No. 5. Am Rec G 30:664-5 Ap '64
Music since the LP. Mus Am 84:8-9 Ja '64
Not one but three new versions of Pierrot Lunaire. Am Rec G 29:643-4+ Ap '63
On RCA Victor, Britten (and others) by Bream: deeply satisfying. Am Rec G 31:216-18 N '64
Strange case of Bruckner's Eighth: five recorded performances of three different editions. Am Rec G 30:498-500 F '64
Such music as ne'er was made by bird, harp, or maiden. Am Rec G 30:582-4 Mr '64
Taming of the shrew. Am Rec G 30:36-8 S '63

DIETHYLSTILBESTROL. See Stilbestrols

DIETRICH, Marlene
Two old pros. por Time 83:44 My 29 '64

DIETS. See Diet

DIETZ, Howard
Fledermaus today. Opera N 27:25 Ap 13 '63

DIETZ, Lew
Fledermaus today. Opera N 27:25 Ap 13 '63
Mr '64
Deer camp on wheels. Field & S 68:37-9+ D '63
Old Mose of Paddy Mill Creek. Field & S 68:58-60+ My '63
Put that rifle down, babe. Field & S 69:54-6+ N '64
Stripers in the river. Field & S 68:44-5+ Ag '63

DIETZEL, Paul
Army's future is still ahead. Sports Illus 19:34 D 2 '63

DI FERRANTE, Nicola
Precipitins in the rabbit produced by protein polysaccharide from bovine nasal cartilage. bibliog Science 143:250-2 Ja 17 '64

DIFFENBACH, Shirley L.
Drawing the head & face. Sch Arts 63:39 Mr '64

DIFFERENCES, Racial. See Racial differences

DIFFERENT time, a different place; story. See Coates, R. M.

DIFFERENTIAL equations. See Equations, Differential

DIFFERENTIAL topology. See Topology

DIFFERENTIATION (biology)
Cell differentiation: some aspects of the problem. R. A. Flickinger. bibliog il Science 141:608-14 Ag 16 '63
Clonal analysis of myogenesis. I. R. Konigsberg. bibliog il Science 140:1273-84 Je 21 '63
Cytodifferentiation and its controls. C. Grobstein. bibliog il Science 143:643-50 F 14 '64
Embryological origin of muscle. I. R. Konigsberg. il Sci Am 211:61-6 Ag '64
Exovagination of newt endoderm: cell affinities altered by the mesodermal inducing factor. U. Kocher-Becker and others. bibliog il Science 147:167-9 Ja 8 '65
Histones from developing tissues of the chicken; heterogeneity. D. T. Lindsay. bibliog il Science 144:420-2 Ap 24 '64
Lethal genes and analysis of differentiation. S. Gluecksohn-Waelsch. bibliog il Science 142:1269-76 D 6 '63
Mitosis and differentiation in roots treated with actinomycin. A. K. Bal and P. R. Gross. bibliog il Science 139:584-6 F 15 '63
Protein structure and function during differentiation; report of a symposium at Federation meetings of the American society of biological chemists. W. D. McElroy. Science 140:1427-30 Je 28 '63
DIFFICULT children. See Problem children
DIFFICULT part; story. See Shyer, M. F.
DIFFRACTION
Pictures without a lens; Fresnel zone plates. il(p 17) Sci N L 87:23 Ja 9 '65
See also
Electrons—Diffraction
X rays—Diffraction
DIFFUSION
Diffusion coefficients of hydrocarbons in water: methods for measuring. D. N. Saraf and others. bibliog il Science 142:955-6 N 15 '63
Diffusion in oceans and fresh waters; report on symposium at the Lamont geological observatory. G. B. Dowling and F. C. W. Olson. Science 146:1492-3 D 11 '64
Diffusion of gases from alveolus to precapillary arteries. A. G. Jameson. bibliog il Science 139:826-8 Mr 1 '63
Fluid flow in porous media studied by a nulear magnetic resonance technique. A. Timur and I. Fatt. bibliog il Science 146:1162-3 N 27 '64
Intercellular diffusion. Y. Kanno and W. R. Loewenstein. bibliog il Science 143:959 F 28 '64
Phospholipid-sugar complexes in relation to cell membrane monosaccharide transport. P. G. LeFevre and others. bibliog il Science 143:955-7 F 28 '64
Urea: apparent carrier-mediated transport by facilitated diffusion in dogfish erythrocytes. H. V. Murdaugh and others. bibliog il Science 144:52-3 Ap 3 '64
DIFFUSION pumps. See Vacuum pumps
DIFFUSION techniques (photography)
Confusion about diffusion. C. Wright. Pop Phot 52:112-13 Ap '63
Glamor; diffusion for illusion. P. Gowland. il Pop Phot 52:8 Ap '63
DIGEORGE, Angelo M. See Pinsky, L. jt. auth.
DIGESTER gas. See Sewage gas
DIGESTER tanks. See Sewage tanks
DIGESTION
Schistosome ova: rapid separation from mouse tissue by digestion with pinguinain. E. Toro-Goyco and others. bibliog il Science 142:407 O 18 '63
See also
Enzymes
DIGESTIVE system
Diseases
How do you know it's a stomach-ache? G. Baker. il Redbook 122:26 Ja '64
See also
Diabetes
Dyspepsia
DIGESTS of books. See Books, Condensed
DIGGS, Charles, jr
Negro congressmen. Negro Hist Bul 27:114+ F '64
DI GIOVANNI, Norman Thomas
Consuming the land. Nation 198:100-1 Ja 27 '64
DIGITAL computers. See Calculating machines—Digital computers
DIGITAL equipment corporation
Computer that grows with you; DEC's PDP-6. il Bsns W p56+ Mr 14 '64
DIGITALIS
Overdose of digitalis offset by citrate salts. Sci N L 84:34 Jl 20 '63
DIGITRONICS corporation
One theme but many variations. il Bsns W p 148+ Ap 13 '63
DIHYDROXYMETHYL valeric acid
Estrone inhibition of cholesterol biosynthesis at the mevalonic acid stage. A. J. Merola and A. Arnold. bibliog il Science 144:301-2 Ap 17 '64
DIJKSTRA, Sjoukje
How to succeed by trying; world's figure-skating championship. il por Time 81:78 Mr 15 '63
DIJON, France
Reverend mayor of Dijon. il Time 83:48 Ja 31 '64
DIKEMAN, May
Peak; story. Atlan 215:55-60 Ja '65
Woman across the street; story. Atlan 212:60-5 N '63
DIKES (engineering)
Dutch against the sea; twenty-five year program: Delta plan. H. Gilroy. il N Y Times Mag p96-7 S 15 '63
DILATUSH, Tom
You can grow holly. Pop Gard 14:22-3+ N '63
DILCHER, David L.
Eocene epiphyllous fungi. bibliog Science 142:667-9 N 8 '63
DILEO, Joseph
Garden is a place to play, to learn, to grow. Pop Gard 15:32-3 Jl '64
DILIGENTI, Franco
Mystery quints of Argentina; Diligenti quintuplets. H. H. Martin. il por Sat Eve Post 237:38-43 Ja 25 '64
DILIGENTI quintuplets. See Quintuplets
DILL, Frederick J.
Dictyotene stage of meiosis in mosses. bibliog Science 144:541-3 My 1 '64
DILLARD university, New Orleans
For such a tide is moving; prefreshman program. F. G. Jennings. il Sat R 47:74-5+ My 16 '64
DILLE, John
Revolution isn't coming, it is already here. Life 57:94-5+ S 25 '64
With a quiet curse it all began. Life 54:23+ My 10 '63
DILLER, Phyllis
Rubber-faced comic. il pors Life 54:57-60 My 17 '63
DILLIARD, Irving
An immortal makes his mark. Sat R 46:22-3 Ag 17 '63
How the government grows. Sat R 48:33 Ja 16 '65
Nation and the nine. Sat R 46:39-40 Mr 9 '63
DILLINGER, John
Dillinger days, by J. Toland. Review
Time por 81:106+ Ap 5 '63
Last days of Dillinger; excerpt from The Dillinger days. J. Toland. il Look 27:79-80+ F 12 '63
Thirty years ago. W. B. Furlong. il pors N Y Times Mag p25+ Ag 9 '64
DILLINGHAM, Lowell
Looking to the mainland. il por Time 82:66+ Ag 16 '63
DILLINGHAM, Walter Francis
Patriarch to a state. il por Time 82:27 N 1 '63
DILLINGHAM corporation
Looking to the mainland. il Time 82:66+ Ag 16 '63
DILLON, Clarence Douglas
Achievements of the Inter-American development bank; statement, April 14, 1964. Dept State Bul 50:717-22 My 4 '64
Developing strength of the International monetary system; statement, September 8, 1964. Dept State Bul 51:444-8 S 28 '64
Development financing and the Alliance for progress; address, November 30, 1964. Dept State Bul 51:878-81 D 21 '64
Dillon: a tax cut will help budget; excerpts from statement, September 1, 1963. U S News 55:105 S 16 '63
European interest rates; address, May 21, 1964. Vital Speeches 30:585-8 Jl 15 '64
Excerpt from address, October 23, 1962. Cong Digest 42:78+ Mr '63
Excerpt from testimony before Committee on banking and currency, November 20, 1963. Cong Digest 43:46+ F '64
Excerpt from testimony before Committee on ways and means, February 6, 1963. Cong Digest 42:108+ Ap '63
Excerpts from addresses, February 11, March 7, 21, 1963. Cong Digest 42:141+ My '63
In sight: budget of 100 billions; summary of testimony. U S News 55:100 Ag 26 '63
Strengthening the international monetary system; statement, October 1, 1963. Dept State Bul 49:613-19 O 21 '63

DILLON, Clarence Douglas—*Continued*
Tax reduction and balanced budget; address, October 8, 1963. Vital Speeches 30:44-7 N 1 '63
about
Danger to the dollar; what Treasury wants to do about it. por U S News 55:81-2 Jl 22 '63
Treasury's Dillon; the conservative power center in Washington. J. Kraft. por Harper 226:51-6 Je '63
DILLON, George
Alcools, uncut. Poetry 105:136-7 N '64
DILLON, Howard W.
Professional internship: a program and a proposal; Ohio state university libraries. C. I. Wilson. bibliog por Library J 88:2201-5 Je 1 '63
DILLON, Jack
Jane Winston's ordeal; story. McCalls 92: 114-15 O '64
DILLON, Richard S.
Veterans hospitals: government medicine in action. Read Digest 82:49-53 Mr '63
DILLON, Wilton
Bonne année, Oncle Charles. New Repub 150: 15-16 Ja 4 '64
Wandering African intellectuals. New Repub 148:17-19 Mr 9 '63
DILTS, Peggy
(ed) Look and listen. See issues of Senior scholastic
Looking and listening. See issues of Senior scholastic
DI LUZIO, N. R. See Wooles, W. R. jt. auth.
DILWORTH, Richardson
Liberal's advice to northern Negroes; excerpts from address, January 9, 1964. U S News 56:6 Ja 20 '64
DIM light. See Electric lighting—Control
DIMAND, Maurice S.
Mongol rugs in Chinese paintings; excerpts from book. Antiques 84:714-17 D '63
DIME novels
Dime novels. C. Miller. Hobbies 69:107 N '64
DIMETHYL sulfide. See Methyl sulfide
DIMETHYL sulfoxide. See Methyl sulfoxide
DIMETHYLAMINO group
Intramolecular catalysis of the hydrolysis of N-dimethylaminomaleamic acid. G. Dahlgren and N. L. Simmerman. bibliog il Science 140:485 My 3 '63
DIMITRI Mitropoulos international music competition. See Music—Competitions
DIMMED room lights. See Electric lighting—Control
DIMMERS, Automobile. See Automobiles—Lighting
DIMMING mirrors. See Automobiles—Equipment
DIMOCK, Edward C.
Post-Gandhi preconceptions. Sat R 46:40 S 14 '63
DIMOND, A. E. and others
Pesticide research. Science 143:151-2+ Ja 10 '64
DIMOND, E. Grey
Hands and brains; letter. Science 142:445+ O 25 '63
DIMONDSTEIN book company, incorporated
Dimondstein in the suburbs finds space, quiet, efficiency. il Pub W 184:23-4 O 21 '63
DINAR. See Money—Yugoslavia
DINE, James
What is pop art? interview; ed. by G. R. Swenson. il Art N 62:25+ N '63
about
Discredited merchandise. il por Newsweek 64:94+ N 9 '64
James Dine. Child's blue wall. 1962. C. B. Johnson. il Sch Arts 63:31 S '63
DINELEY, David L.
Armor-plated and jawless Devonian fish. Natur Hist 73:48-53 Ag '64
DINER counters. See Furniture
DINERS' club, incorporated
Day there was no money; publicity stunt in Winsted, Conn. W. K. Zinsser. Reporter 29:46-8 S 12 '63
DINESEN, Isak, pseud. See Blixen, K. D.
DINGHIES. See Boats and boating
DINGMAN, C. Wesley, and Sporn, M. B.
Molecular theories of memory. bibliog Science 144:26-9 Ap 3 '64
—See Sporn, M. B. jt. auth.
DINH, Ton-that-. See Ton-that-Dinh
DINING. See Dinners and dining
DINING cars. See Railroads—Dining cars
DINING rooms
Color makes the difference! D. Popplestone. il Bet Hom & Gard 41:64-5 Ap '63
Dining needs ambiance. il House & Gard 124: 232-5 N '63
Dining rooms and centerpieces for autumn. il McCalls 92:128-33 N '64
Roses: Oliver Messel's holiday bounty. il Vogue 142:134-5 D '63
This new dining room is the former terrace. il Sunset 130:134 Mr '63
DINING tables. See Tables
DINITROPHENOL
2,4-dinitrophenol: lack of interaction with high-energy intermediates of oxidative phosphorylation. R. H. Eisenhardt and O. Rosenthal. il Science 143:476 Ja 31 '64
DINKEL, Donald H.
Light-induced inhibition of potato tuber sprouting. bibliog Science 141:1047-8 S 13 '63
DINNER music. See Music
DINNERS and dining
After the big game: dinner for ten; with recipes. il Seventeen 22:137+ O '63
Alfred Hitchcock dinner hour; with recipes. M. Kaytor. il Look 27:42-4 Ag 27 '63
Chef's trial; Lucullus circle's dinner to honor J. P. Donon. K. Lloyd. il Vogue 143: 114-15+ Ap 15 '64
Cooperative gourmet dinner. Sunset 131:248+ O '63
Country-style gourmet dinner. N. Nichols. il Farm J 87:96-7+ F '63
Danish dinner for four. il Vogue 144:214 O 1 '64
Dining with the presidents; with recipes. H. D. Bullock. il Am Home 67:58-9+ N '64
Dinner a day for November; with recipes and menus. il Good H 157:98-112 N '63
Dinner for one. C. Claiborne. il N Y Time Mag p64+ Mr 1 '64
Dinner in the great tradition, but with the work shared by four. J. Child. il House B 105:136-43+ D '63
Dinners for two under two dollars. il Redbook 123:74-5+ My '64
Dinners that wait, hurry, warm over or stretch for families on the go. B. C. Williams. il Parents Mag 39:77-9 S '64
Easter dinner for eight. M. J. Engel. Ladies Home J 80:98 Ap '63
Feast your eyes. M. Johnston. il Bet Hom & Gard 41:74-7+ Ap '63
Food to please a man. E. Ward-Hanna. il Ladies Home J 80:112-13+ O '63
For cooks who frequently are short of time. Sunset 130:228+ My '63
For last minute dinner planning. il Sunset 134:101 Ja '65
From appetizer to dessert: just 600 calories and delicious. Sunset 131:136-7 S '63
Great dinners. il Life 56:47-50+ Ja 31; 102-3+ F 21; 92-3+ Mr 27; 110-11+ Ap 24; 126-7+ My 22; 92-3+ Je 26; 57:66-7+ Jl 31; 80-4 Ag 21; 148-9+ S 18; 152-3+ O 16; 122-3+ N 13; 102-3+ D 18 '64; 58:84-5+ Ja 29 '65
Holiday dinner for six. il Vogue 144:270 D '64
How does Countess Elizabeth Oberndorff do it? il Vogue 141:176-7+ My '63
How to be a great hostess! M. Johnston. il Bet Hom & Gard 42:74-9+ F '64
How to dine well on 300 calories. il Ladies Home J 80:126+ Ja '63
How to dine well on 300 calories. M. J. Engel. il Ladies Home J 80:94 Mr '63
How to give a dinner party and have fun doing it. V. T. Habeeb. Am Home 66:60 Je '63
How to give a marvelous new kind of party! il House & Gard 124:224-31 N '63
How to win at your own dinner party. V. T. Habeeb. il Am Home 66:48-50+ Je '63
Hurry-up dinners for two. Good H 156:180d Mr '63
I'll make dinner tonight; with recipes. il Seventeen 23:158 F '64
Liston's favorite menu. D. J. Robinson. il Ebony 18:148+ Ap '63
Man's cook book. il House & Gard 124:105-10 Jl '63
Meals to impress. il Am Home 66:50-1+ Ja '63
Men who come to dinner. J. Poppy. il Look 28:M10-13 Je 30 '64
Old-fashioned corned beef & cabbage; with recipes. il McCalls. 91:110-11+ S '64
Portable picnic; elegant box dinner. il Sunset 132:146+ Mr '64
Round-the-world dinners. A. Wartenberg. il Parents Mag 38:81-4+ S '63
Shortened cocktail hour. J. A. Beard. House & Gard 124:46 N '63
Strictly home style. il McCalls 91:156-7+ N '63
Sunday dinner with the children. il Vogue 144:158 N 15 '64
Table for two. Ladies Home J 81:26 O '64; 82:17 Ja '65

DINNERS and dining—*Continued*
This year, make it an old-fashioned family reunion; pot-luck dinner. W. Bar-Illan. il Ladies Home J 81:102-4 Ag '64
Time savers & time adjusters. B. T. MacDonald. il Parents Mag 39:87+ F '64
Twenty-five ways to delight your dinner guests. il Redbook 124:96-104 N '64
Vogue's own menu; a black-tie dinner for ten. Vogue 141:162 Mr 1 '63
Vogue's own menu; a formal dinner for eight. Vogue 141:150 Ap 1 '63
Vogue's own menu: a little dinner for four friends. il Vogue 144:202 N 1 '64
Vogue's own menu; dinner for four. Vogue 144:182 S 15 '64
Vogue's own menu; dinner for six. Vogue 142:192 S 15 '63
Vogue's own menu; dinner to cool eight. Vogue 142:130 Ag 15 '63
What's for dinner? il Ladies Home J 80:132 My '63
Wine tasters' dinner; American chapter of the Confrérie des chevaliers du tastevin. M. Kaytor. il Look 27:52-5 Jl 2 '63
See also
Buffet meals
Christmas dinners
Eating
Thanksgiving dinners

DINNERSTEIN, Harvey
Four realists: a review. F. Whitaker. il Am Artist 28:54-61+ O '64

DINNERWARE. See Tableware

DINOFLAGELLATES
Plague of Florida and California; red tide. N. B. Slaton. il Sci Digest 56:9-13 N '64

DINOSAUR models. See Zoological models

DINOSAURS
Case of the vanishing monsters. J. D. Ratcliff. il Read Digest 85:254-6+ N '64
Dinosaurs of the Arctic; Iguanodon. E. H. Colbert. il Natur Hist 73:20-3 Ap '64
Fossilized stomach contents of a sauropod dinosaur. W. L. Stokes. il Science 143:576-7 F 7 '64
If you wonder about dinosaurs; Field house of natural history, Vernal State Park, Utah. il Sunset 132:35 My '64
New species of dinosaurs. il Sci N L 84:340 N 30 '63

DINUBA, Calif.
Cultural growth in capital letters! programs of cultural interests. J. Prendergast. il Recreation 57:440-1 N '64

DINWIDDIE, Jill
Queen Bee of the school; with report of sociologists, ed. by B. Villet. il pors Life 55:68-80+ O 11 '63

DINWIDDIE, Robert
Fantastic adventures of Captain Stobo. R. C. Alberts. il Am Heritage 14:65-77 Ag '63

DIOCESES
Big diocese, small diocese; theologians, trying to find theoretical norms for the right size. America 110:560 Ap 25 '64
See also
Catholic church—Dioceses

DIODE switches. See Electric switches

DIODES
Burned-out pilot-lamp indicators; bridge and zener diodes. R. L. Ives. il Electr World 69:40 Je '63
Diodes regulate power supply. R. K. Re. il Electr World 70:66 O '63
Fabulous diodes. L. E. Garner, jr. il Pop Electr 20:65-80 My '64
Four and five layer semiconductor diodes. D. E. Lancaster. il Electr World 72:61-4+ O '64
High wattage reducer; use of silicon diodes for easy power control. F. A. Parker. il Pop Electr 20:57-8 F '64
Snooperscope television. il Time 81:75 Ap 19 '63
Using zener diodes. I. Math. il Electr World 72:88 N '64
Varactor diode cuts millimeter losses. B. Miller. il Aviation W 81:78-80 D 21 '64
Zener receiver muter. I. C. Chapel. il Pop Electr 21:88 Ag '64

Testing

Diode curve-tracer & analyzer. J. Kyle. il Electr World 71:44-5+ Je '64

DIODES, Tunnel. See Tunnel diodes

DIOGENES
Great confrontations: Diogenes and Alexander. G. Highet. il por Horizon 5:10-13 Mr '63

DIONAEA muscipula. See Venus's flytraps

DIONNE, Annette, and others
Dear quints, with love from the quints; ed. by J. Brough. pors McCalls 91:60+ F '64
We were five; ed. by J. Brough. pors McCalls 91:102-5+ O; 116-19+ N '63

DIONNE family
Dear quints, with love from the quints; ed. by J. Brough. A. Dionne and others. il McCalls 91:60+ F '64
We were five; ed. by J. Brough. A. Dionne and others. il McCalls 91:102-5+ O; 116-19+ N '63

DIOR, Christian
Marvelous mission to Moscow. L. Bemelmans. Holiday 35:108+ F '64

DIORAMAS
Halloween dioramas. J. Fox. il Sch Arts 63:21-3 O '63

DIORI, Hamani
Colored rulers. G. C. Turner. Negro Hist Bul 27:17 O '63

DIOSPYROS. See Persimmons

DIPAOLO, Joseph A.
Polydactylism in the offspring of mice injected with 5-bromodeoxyuridine. bibliog Science 145:501-3 Jl 31 '64
—and Wenner, C. E.
Thalidomide: effects on Ehrlich ascites tumor cells in vitro. bibliog Science 144:1583 Je 26 '64

DIPHTHERIA
Diphtheria: onetime child-strangler. F. H. Richardson. il Todays Health 42:12+ My '64

DIPHTHERIA toxoid. See Toxins and antitoxins

DIPLOID cell. See Cells

DIPLOMACY
East-West relations today; address, February 18, 1964. G. C. McGhee. Dept State Bul 50:488-96 Mr 30 '64
Education for the new diplomacy; address, March 2, 1963. R. E. Lee. Dept State Bul 48:423-7 Mr 25 '63
How Harriman earned a dinner from Khrushchev. P. Mandel. il Life 55:28-30A Ag 9 '63
President Johnson receives chiefs of diplomatic missions; remarks with reply, December 13, 1963. L. B. Johnson; G. Sevilla-Sacasa. Dept State Bul 49:996-7 D 30 '63
Speaking out; let's stop being foolish about dictators. E. O. Briggs. Sat Eve Post 236:8+ S 14 '63
Today's challenges to diplomacy. J. P. Warburg. Bul Atomic Sci 19:2-4 N '63
See also
Ambassadors
Arbitration, International
International relations
World war, 1939-1945—Diplomatic history

DIPLOMATIC and consular service
Deadbeat diplomacy; tensions in Bonn. Time 82:42+ O 4 '63
United Nations training programme for foreign service officers from newly independent countries. D. Protitch. UN Mo Chron 1:67-71 N '64
See also
Women as foreign service employees
also Diplomatic and consular service under names of countries, e.g.Russia—Diplomatic and consular service

DIPLOMATIC etiquette
Functions of protocol in today's world; address, February 6, 1964. A. B. Duke. Dept State Bul 50:344-7 Mr 2 '64
Profiles; A. B. Duke. New Yorker 40:34-6+ Ag 15 '64
Protocol and peacekeeping; address, October 22, 1964. A. B. Duke. Dept State Bul 51:736-9 N 23 '64
Protocol and the conduct of foreign affairs; address, October 9, 1963. A. B. Duke. Dept State Bul 49:700-4 N 4 '63
See also
Precedence

DIPLOMATIC privileges and immunities
Unchecked immunity. il Time 83:68 Ap 3 '64
Wayward diplomats; abuse of diplomatic privilege in Bonn. il Newsweek 64:36 S 14 '64

DIPLOMATS
Peace in their time, by E. Kelen. Review Nat R 16:190-200 Mr 10 '64. P. L. Buckley
Where to put diplomats; new Washington problem. il U S News 55:52-3 Jl 1 '63
See also
Ambassadors
Negro diplomats
United States—Foreign service

DIPOLE orbital belts in space
Blue Scout jr. payload to gather frequency data above ionosphere. Aviation W 79:34 Ag 5 '63

DIPOLE orbital belts in space—*Continued*
Huge antenna could spot marble 1,000 miles away; looking for needles. il(p241) Sci N L 86:249 O 17 '64
MIT panel dissects West Ford at IEEE. M. Getler. Miss & Roc 14:46+ Ap 6 '64
Needles bar space view. A. Ewing. Sci N L 84:163 S 14 '63
Needles in orbit. Newsweek 61:74 Je 3 '63
Needles spread out in precise orbit. Sci N L 83:360 Je 8 '63
No danger from needles. B. Tufty. Sci N L 83:279 My 4 '63
Optical effects of the 1963 Project West Ford experiment. W. Liller. bibliog il Science 143: 437-41 Ja 31 '64
Optical effects of the West Ford belt. il Sky & Tel 26:183+ O '63
Orbital lifetime of the West Ford dipoles. H. M. Jones and others. Science 140:1173 Je 14 '63
Orbiting needles sighted. Sci N L 83:340 Je 1 '63
Project West Ford. Sky & Tel 25:311 Je '63
Second West Ford launch is successful. R. D. Hibben. il Aviation W 78:34 My 20 '63
Superior animal. J. Lear. Sat R 46:35-6 Je 1 '63
U.S. replies to Soviet charges against certain space activities; text of letter, June 6, 1963 to U.N. Secretary-General U Thant; with statemenet on Project West Ford. A. E. Stevenson. Dept State Bul 49:104-7 Jl 15 '63
West Ford dipole belt: optical detection at Palomar. A. Sandage and C. Kowal. il Science 141:797-8 Ag 30 '63
West Ford dipole belt: photometric observations. W. G. Tifft and others. il Science 141:798-9 Ag 30 '63
West Ford report notes bit-rate falloff. R. D. Hibben. Aviation W 79:95+ S 30 '63
Wired for protest; Project West Ford. Time 81:81-2 My 24 '63

DIPPERS (birds)
Dippy dipper. B. W. Dalrymple. il Field & S 69:58+ Je '64
Nature note. Sci N L 85:63 Ja 25 '64

DI PRIMA, Diane
Fuzz's progress. Nation 198:463-5 My 4 '64

DIPTERA
See also
Flies

DIRAC, P. A. M.
Evolution of the physicist's picture of nature; with biographical sketch. Sci Am 208: 36, 45-53 bibliog(p 192) My '63

DIRECT mail advertising. See Advertising, Direct mail

DIRECT mail advertising association
Mail industry fights back; legitimate mail advertisers try to halt the flow of obscenity through the mail. J. B. Halper. America 108:260-1 F 23 '63

DIRECT placement of securities. See Securities —Marketing

DIRECT selling. See Canvassing

DIRECTING (theater) See Theatrical directors

DIRECTION, Sense of. See Orientation

DIRECTION finding apparatus
See also
Radio in navigation

DIRECTIONAL discontinuity ring radiator. See Radio antennas

DIRECTORIES
See also
Telephone directories
also subhead Directories under various subjects, e.g. Theological schools—Directories

DIRECTORS. See Moving picture directors

DIRECTORS, Corporation. See Corporations—Directors

DIREITO, F. Teixeira. See Teixeira Direito, F.

DIRIGIBLES. See Airships

DIRKSEN, Everett McKinley
Excerpt from address, August 14, 1963. Cong Digest 43:15+ Ja '64
Some thoughts on destiny; excerpts from Senate debate. por Time 82:25-6 S 20 '63
Speaking out. por Sat Eve Post 237:10+ S 12 '64

about

After Senator Dirksen decided White House mail was wrong. U S News 55:16 Ag 19 '63
Annals of legislation. R. Harris. New Yorker 40:56+ Mr 28 '64
As Senator Dirksen's party role grows. . . por U S News 57:19 Jl 13 '64
Better man than his public image. J. N. Eller. America 111:7 Jl 4 '64
Dirksen breather. Time 84:37 S 18 '64
Dirksen delivers the souls. M. Kempton. New Repub 150:9-11 My 2 '64
Dirksen's way. K. Crawford. Newsweek 62: 28 Ag 12 '63
Ev & Barry show. il por Time 84:20-1 Jl 10 '64
Everett Dirksen's newest role. M. Greenfield. il Reporter 30:26-9 Ja 16 '64
Goldwater's Dirksen. K. Crawford. Newsweek 64:31 Jl 13 '64
Old Ev, the good wizard. L. Wainwright. Life 56:29 Je 5 '64
Same program, new sponsors: the return of Ev and Charlie. por U S News 54:25 Mr 11 '63
Senator Dirksen: Vandenberg of the '60s? por U S News 55:24 S 23 '63
Senator's lost time for greatness. J. N. Eller. America 109:6 Jl 6 '63
Tipping the balance on civil rights bill. pors Bsns W p20-1 My 30 '64

DIRLIK, Paul. See Byck, R. jt. auth.

DIRTADIAN, Helen
Damage to Alaskan libraries; letter. ALA Bul 58:371 My '64

DISABILITY insurance. See Insurance, Disability

DISABLED. See Handicapped

DISABLED, Employment of. See Vocational rehabilitation

DISACCHARIDASES. See Intestines—Diseases

DI SANT'AGNESE, Paul A.
German university honors U.S. scientist. por Todays Health 42:88 Ja '64

DISAPPEARING beds. See Beds

DISARMAMENT
Armers and the disarmers; report of International symposium on arms control at University of Michigan. J. D. Singer; A. Rapoport. Nation 196:174-7+ Mr 2 '63
Arms control and disarmament; transcript of the television program State department briefing: disarmament, first broadcast, January 14, 1963. Dept State Bul 48:115-27 Ja 28 '63
Arms race or disarmament? J. J. Stone. Bul Atomic Sci 20:20-4 S '64; Reply with rejoinder. D. K. Lewis. 21:29-31 Ja '65
Balanced approach to disarmament; statement, October 29, 1963. C. C. Stelle. Dept State Bul 49:793-8 N 18 '63
Begin to disarm by disarming! Christian Cent 81:4 Ja 1 '64
Beyond illusion. E. E. Best. Christian Cent 81:40-2 Ja 8 '64
Big last bang. New Repub 150:3-4 Mr 14 '64
Blunted probe; U.S. and British talks in Moscow. Newsweek 61:40 My 6 '63
Demilitarized world and how to get there. W. Millis. Sat R 47:18-22+ S 12 '64
Development of the peacekeeping capacity of the United Nations; address, April 26, 1963. R. N. Gardner. Dept State Bul 48:789-96 My 20 '63
Disarmament; address, February 25, 1964. R. A. Butler. Vital Speeches 30:331-6 Mr 15 '64
Disarmament in perspective; symposium. bibliog f Cur Hist 46:321-53+ Je '64
Disarmament picture, 1965. H. A. Jack. Christian Cent 82:104-6 Ja 27 '65
First real chance for disarmament. P. M. S. Blackett; discussion. Harper 226:12+ Ja; 8+ Mr; 6 My; 20+ Je '63
Gradual arms reduction. A. Etzioni. Bul Atomic Sci 19:30-3 O '63
Information in arms control verification. B. G. Lall. Bul Atomic Sci 20:43-5 O '64
National strategy, security, and arms control; address, October 31, 1963. W. C. Foster. Dept State Bul 49:824-9 N 25 '63
New hopes in the race for peace. Bsns W p26-7 Ja 25 '64
Our defense needs: the long view. R. L. Gilpatric. For Affairs 42:366-78 Ap '64
Peacemonger answers some questions. A. Etzioni. il N Y Times Mag p 14+ Ap 21 '63
Secretary Rusk's news conference of January 2, 1964. D. Rusk. bibliog f Dept State Bul 50:81-9 Ja 20 '64
Solving the inhuman equation; can arms control end the population crisis? G. Clark. Sat R 46:15-16+ F 16 '63
Soviet attitude toward disarmament. B. G. Bechhoefer. bibliog f Cur Hist 45:193-9 O '63
Speaking out; we can make the Russians disarm. W. P. Reuther. Sat Eve Post 236: 10+ D 7 '63
Speculations during a white night. J. F. Wharton. Sat R 46:14-17 Ap 6 '63
This month's feature: U.S. & international control of arms. Cong Digest 43:193-224 Ag '64

DISARMAMENT—*Continued*
U.S. and weapons control; symposium. bibliog f il Cur Hist 47:65-106+ Ag '64
Warsaw and Geneva. Commonweal 79:735-6 Mr 20 '64
Way to disarmament? L. B. Sohn. New Repub 148:5-6 F 23 '63
Weapons control today; symposium. bibliog f Cur Hist 47:1-46 Jl '64
World disarmament; address, June 12, 1964. J. S. Clark. Vital Speeches 30:688-92 S 1 '64
See also
Atomic weapons and disarmament
Conference of the Eighteen-nation committee on disarmament, Geneva, 1962-
Peace
United Nations—Disarmament commission
United States—Defenses

Bibliography

Arms and arms control. Cur Hist 46:354-6 Je '64
Readings on weapons control and disarmament. Cur Hist 47:109-10 Ag '64

Control and inspection

See Disarmament—Inspection

Economic aspects

Alternatives to armament expenditures; excerpts from address, December 1962. W. Leontief. il Bul Atomic Sci 20:19-21 Je '64
Coming politics of disarmament. F. J. Cook. il Nation 196:131-5 F 16 '63; Discussion. 196:inside cover Mr 9 '63
Committee to study economic impact of defense and disarmament; White House announcement, with text of memorandum, December 21, 1963. L. B. Johnson. Dept State Bul 50:120 Ja 27 '64
Congress focuses on defense cuts impact. K. Johnsen. Aviation W 80:26-7 Je 15 '64
DOD seeks disarmament impact ideas. P. J. Klass. Aviation W 79:35 Ag 12 '63
Disarmament and the developing countries. UNESCO Courier 17:26 N '64
Disarmament and the economy. B. B. Seligman. Commentary 35:369-77 My '63; Discussion. 36:196-7 S '63
Disarmament and the economy, ed. by E. Benoit and K. E. Boulding. Review
New Repub 148:25-6 Je 1 '63. E. T. Chase
Disarmament: its economic impact to be studied by Johnson panel; subject has been little explored. E. Langer. Science 143:28-30 Ja 3 '64
Economic alternatives to arms prosperity. S. Melman. bibliog f il Ann Am Acad 351:121-31 Ja '64
Economic impact of defense shifts eyed. K. Johnsen. Aviation W 79:28-9 S 30 '63
Economic impact of disarmament. il UNESCO Courier 17:22-5 N '64
Economics and politics of arms reduction; symposium. Bul Atomic Sci 20:6-23 Ap '64
Economics of arms control and disarmament; address, June 6, 1963. W. C. Foster. Dept State Bul 49:7-11 Jl 1 '63
Economics of permanent peace. O. Nathan. Bul Atomic Sci 19:21-4 Je '63
False fears of disarmament. W. D. Grampp. Harvard Bsns R 42:28-30+ Ja '64
If peace does come, what happens to business? il U S News 55:22-5 Ag 12 '63
McNamara cutback. New Repub 151:5 D 5 '64
McNamara's band. America 111:734-5 D 5 '64
Ounce of modicum. Nation 197:150 S 21 '63
Peace trend will bring better business. C. T. Stewart, jr. il Nations Bsns 52:66-8+ Je '64
Peacetime prosperity? Duns R 83:29 Je '64
Planning for prosperity; concerning reconversion of armament plants. N. Cousins. Sat R 47:32 D 5 '64
Questions and answers on the U.S. production freeze proposal. B. G. Lall. Bul Atomic Sci 20:30-4 D '64
Reconversion and automation; proposed commissions. Nation 197:191 O 5 '63
Sword and the ploughshares. il UNESCO Courier 17:14-17 N '64
What can industry do as Pentagon cuts back? il Newsweek 62:87-90 O 7 '63
Where the cutback cuts deep. D. Oberdorfer. il Sat Eve Post 237:17-21 S 12 '64
Where the cuts hurt. il Bsns W p56+ Jl 18 '64
Why cutting the budget isn't easy. il Bsns W p32-3 N 28 '64
Would disarmament mean a depression? E. Benoit. il N Y Times Mag p 16+ Ap 28 '63

Inspection

Arms control inspection tests set; Project cloud gap. J. Trainor. Miss & Roc 14:14 Je 15 '64
Cold war and weapons control. L. W. Martin. Cur Hist 47:1-5+ Jl '64
Cuba: missile episode provided new incentive for arms agreement, but left behind some impediments. D. S. Greenberg; reply with rejoinder. F. K. Berrien. Science 139:250 Ja 18 '63
Disadvantages of reliable inspection. T. C. O'Sullivan, jr. Bul Atomic Sci 19:18-19 Mr '63
Disarmament after Cuba. D. R. Inglis; discussion. Bul Atomic Sci 19:28-30 Mr '63
Disarmament police aircraft planned. K. Johnsen. Aviation W 79:36-7 O 14 '63
Games of peace. L. Norman. il Newsweek 63:56-7 Ja 27 '64
Postwar disarmament negotiations. L. Jensen. Cur Hist 46:336-40+ Je '64
Public will be unwilling to buy costly arms inspection system. R. Hawkes. Miss & Roc 15:22 Jl 13 '64
Risk and security in the age of nuclear weapons; address, December 15, 1962. W. C. Foster. Dept State Bul 48:128-34 Ja 28 '63
Safeguarded zonal disarmament. J. Orear. il Bul Atomic Sci 19:18-21 F '63
Secretary Rusk interviewed on NBC's Today program; interview, January 21, 1963, ed. by M. Agronsky and H. Downs. D. Rusk. Dept State Bul 48:202-7 F 11 '63
Step-by-step disarmament. D. R. Inglis. Cur Hist 47:88-92+ Ag '64
U.S. and U.S.S.R. exchange views on nuclear test ban; exchange of letters; with Department statement of January 20, 1963. N. Khrushchev; J. F. Kennedy. Dept State Bul 48:198-202 F 11 '63
Verification and response in disarmament agreements; excerpts from report. Bul Atomic Sci 19:44-8 Ap '63
Wasted decades: 1899-1939. F. L. Schuman. bibliog f Cur Hist 46:326-30 Je '64
Weapons control as seen abroad. C. Quigley Cur Hist 46:346-53+ Je '64

Psychological aspects

Noneconomic factors in the institutionalization of the cold war. I. L. Horowitz. bibliog f Ann Am Acad 351:110-20 Ja '64

Study and teaching

Issues of disarmament. R. Hagan. bibliog il Sr Schol 83:12T-13T N 22 '63

Arctic Regions

Arctic disarmament. Sci Am 212:48 Ja '65
Arctic disarmament. A. Rich and A. P. Vinogradov. Bul Atomic Sci 20:22-3 N '64

Europe

Gomulka proposals; freezing nuclear and thermonuclear armaments in central Europe. il Cur Hist 47:107-8 Ag '64

Great Britain

See also
Campaign for nuclear disarmament (organization)

United States

Disarmament policy and the Pentagon. B. G. Lall. Bul Atomic Sci 20:37-40 S '64
Is U.S. giving up in the arms race? with excerpts from article by S. T. Possony. il U S News 55:37-43 Ag 5 '63

DISARMAMENT agency. See United States—Arms control and disarmament agency

DISASTERS
And miracles; disaster-filled week. Newsweek 62:46 N 18 '63
Disaster in paradise. W. P. Booth and S. N. Matthews. il Nat Geog Mag 124:436-58 S '63
Fundamentals for survival; with program for discussion group, by E. G. Neisser. R. Brecher and E. Brecher. Parents Mag 38: 35-6+, 45+ Je '63
Imitating nature; catastrophies in Venezuela and Mexico. il Newsweek 64:48 S 7 '64
Is your town prepared for disaster? S. Schuler. Am Home 67:12+ O '64
See also
Explosions
Fires
Floods
Hurricanes
Relief work

DISC brakes. See Brakes, Automobile

DISC electrophoresis. See Electrophoresis

DISC jockeys
New age of radio. A. Bester. il Holiday 33: 56-65+ Je '63
Record cabinet; lady disc jockey for L'interdit, at Hotel Gotham. New Yorker 39: 42-3 O 5 '63
Stuntman of the air. il Newsweek 61:71 Mr 25 '63

DISCARDING of books. See Libraries—Book discarding
DISCHARGED prisoners. See Prisoners, Discharged
DISCIPLES of Christ
Baptists explore church union. Christian Cent 80:734 Je 5 '63
Disciples and Catholicity. R. E. Wentz. Christian Cent 81:400-1 Mr 25 '64
Disciples in Detroit; International (U.S. and Canada) convention of Christian churches. H. E. Fey. Christian Cent 81:1327-8 O 28 '64
Disciples on civil rights; International convention of Christian churches. H. E. Fey. Christian Cent 80:1326-7 O 30 '63
Faith of the President. il Newsweek 62:90 D 9 '63
Formula in flux: reformation for the Disciples of Christ? R. E. Osborn. Christian Cent 80:1163-6 S 25 '63
Worried Disciples. il Time 82:86 O 25 '63
DISCIPLINE
College morals mirror our society. G. Hechinger and F. M. Hechinger. il N Y Times Mag p22+ Ap 14 '63
Discipline problems in camp. B. H. Chetkow. Recreation 57:136-7 Mr '64
Escalation in California. N. Cousins. Sat R 48:20 Ja 30 '65
Girls and dorms; Harvard's parietal regulations. Newsweek 62:78 N 11 '63
Morals revolution on the U.S. campus. il Newsweek 63:52-6+ Ap 6 '64
Must the colleges police sex? J. T. Rule. il Atlan 213:55-8 Ap '64; Discussion. 213: 42+ Je '64
Teen-agers disciplining; codes for teen-age behavior. il Newsweek 65:38 Ja 4 '65
We respect this approach to child discipline. I. P. Buckley. Bet Hom & Gard 41:25+ Je '63
What does the code say, dear? A. P. Eliasberg. il N Y Times Mag p87+ Ap 26 '64
Your child and discipline; excerpts from Children: the challenge. R. Dreikurs and V. Soltz. il NEA J 54:32-47 Ja '65
See also
Children—Management and training
School discipline
DISCOMFORT index. See Weather—Mental and physiological effects
DISCOUNT
Administration moves on the payments gap. Bsns W p25 Jl 20 '63
Stage set for boost in Fed discount rate. Bsns W p112+ Jl 13 '63
Waging the gold war. il Time 82:76+ Jl 26 '63
DISCOUNT, Trade
Rationale for quantity discounts. J. F. Crowther. il Harvard Bsns R 42:121-7 Mr '64
DISCOUNT houses (retail trade)
Clues for action from shopper preferences; survey of women shoppers in New York city and in Cleveland. S. U. Rich and B. Portis. il Harvard Bsns R 41:132-49 Mr '63
Discounting: Mexico's newest revolution. il Bsns W p52-4+ Jl 6 '63
Fewer stores to share the pie. Bsns W p 182 N 16 '63
Fish are drowning. Newsweek 61:80 F 25 '63
Forward's march; pioneering Arango brothers at Mexico. il Time 81:83 F 8 '63
If discounters threaten, don't panic, fight back. H. W. Schwartz. Pub W 1855:40-1 Mr 30 '64
King of the discounters; Polk brothers. R. Tunley. il Sat Eve Post 236:28-9 Ap 13 '63
Retail revolution that is floundering. il U S News 54:48 F 18 '63
Round for GM. Newsweek 61:83 Mr 25 '63
Selling below cost should be prohibited. J. D. Kahn. Pub W 183:48 Ap 1 '63
What to expect in discount stores. Changing T 17:6 Ap '63
Your right to a car bargain. W. Marx. Nation 196:195-7 Mr 9 '63
See also
Gamble-Skogmo, incorporated
John's bargain stores corporation
Masters, incorporated
DISCOUNT selling. See Stocks—Marketing
DISCOURTESY. See Courtesy
DISCOVERIES in science. See Inventions; Patents; Research
DISCRIMINATION
See also
United Nations—Subcommission on prevention of discrimination and protection of minorities
DISCRIMINATION, Racial. See Race discrimination
DISCRIMINATION in education
Advanced degrees: discrimination wanes as a barrier to Negro grad students; other hurdles remain. J. Walsh. Science 141:1019-21 S 13 '63
DISCRIMINATION in employment
Anti-discrimination pact signed in Philadelphia; action of Printing industries. Pub W 184:35 O 14 '63
Business, next target for integration? J. Perry. Harvard Bsns R 41:104-15 Mr '63
Civil rights battle; northern style. il Ebony 18:96-8+ Mr '63
Civil rights: the law and the unions. A. H. Raskin. il Reporter 31:23-8 S 10 '64
Discrimination, unions and Title VII. G. R. Blakey. America 111:210-12 Ag 29 '64
Economic growth and employment opportunities for minorities, by D. L. Hiestand. Review
Commentary il 38:95-8 N '64. R. Lekachman
Expanding opportunities; New York hotel industry's anti-discrimination program. W. B. Gould. Commonweal 81:342 D 4 '64
Fatal flaw; NAACP lawsuit. Newsweek 63:21 My 4 '64
Green case closed. America 108:658-9 My 11 '63
Help unwanted; case of New York's non-union plumbers. il Newsweek 63:34-5 My 25 '64
Invisible persuader on promotions; study by American Jewish committee. il Bsns W p 154+ D 12 '64
Job-training and poverty. America 110:154 F 1 '64
Jobless on Labor day. America 109:151-2 Ag 17 '63
Labor agreements under state antidiscrimination laws; report to ABA meeting. Mo Labor R 87:1179-80 O '64
Labor union discrimination limits Negroes in apprenticeships, skilled jobs. Ebony 18:28 My '63
Managing your manpower; Negro employment problem. T. R. Brooks. Duns R 82:59-60+ Ag '63
Managing your manpower; Negro push for employment opportunities. T. R. Brooks. Duns R 83:59-60 Je '64
Market is color-blind. H. Hazlitt. Newsweek 64:94 N 23 '64
Marion Green case. B. L. Masse. America 108:285 Mr 2 '63
Negro drive for jobs; with editorial comment. il Bsns W p52-4+, 124 Ag 17 '63
Negroes attack bias in building trades. il Arch Forum 119:5+ Jl '63
Negro's search for a better job. il Newsweek 63:79-83 Je 8 '64
New definitions of job rights. Mo Labor R 87:III-IV D '64
No Negro barbers; situation in Kansas. New Repub 152:7 Ja 23 '65
No Negroes wanted; big construction job at Howard university, Washington, D.C. America 108:454 Ap 6 '63
No room at the top; discrimination against Jews. E. C. Parker. Christian Cent 81:152-4 Ja 29 '64
Only WASP's? discrimination against Jewish executives. Newsweek 63:64-6 Ja 13 '64
Plumbers dispute opens long hot summer. il Arch Forum 120:5+ Je '64
Puerto Rico; the migration reverses. A. W. Maldonado. il Nation 198:255-7 Mr 16 '64
Race and labor; Bronx plumbers' dispute. Commonweal 80:281-2 My 29 '64
Senate to shelve rights bill for weeks; waiting action on tax cut. Bsns W p28-9 F 15 '64
Signs of shame and progress. Arch Forum 119:79 S '63
Union program for eliminating discrimination. Mo Labor R 86:58-9 Ja '63
Unions feel growing pressure to take more Negroes. il U S News 56:86+ My 25 '64
Voice from the dark ages. Fortune 68:102 D '63
What helps or harms promotability? G. W. Bowman. il Harvard Bsns R 42:6-8+ Ja '64
When a Negro challenged a union. U S News 57:76 Jl 13 '64
Who gets promoted? two-year study by University of Michigan's institute for social research. E. C. Parker. Christian Cent 82: 124 Ja 27 '65
Who's to decide if a banker is biased? Bank of America picketed by CORE. Bsns W p29-30 Je 13 '64
See also
Equal pay for equal work
Negroes in the United States—Employment
United States—Fair employment practice, Committee on

DISCRIMINATION in housing
Are there really ghettos in America? interview. O. Handlin. il U S News 55:70-2 Jl 22 '63
Backlash in California: Proposition fourteen gains support. R. S. Wheeler. Nat R 16:817 S 22 '64; Reply. R. W. Smith. 16:890+ O 20 '64
Berkeley discriminates. R. S. Wheeler. Nat R 14:497 Je 18 '63
Breaking the housing barrier; dual housing market. E. Marciniak. Commonweal 77:588-91 Mr 1 '63
California housing and civil rights; proposed amendments to 1963 Rumford act. E. G. Bianchi. America 111:174 Ag 22 '64
California realtors fight fair housing; Proposition fourteen cancels the Rumford act. Christian Cent 81:1325 O 28 '64
Chicago story: after Negroes moved in, the trials of a community; excerpts from I went to see the elephant. D. J. Ingle. il U S News 55:96-7 S 16 '63
Churchmen admonish West coast realtors. Christian Cent 81:70 Ja 15 '64
City-cage; Proposition fourteen, backed by National association of real estate boards. S. Alsop. Sat Eve Post 237:14 O 10 '64
Courageous pastoral; Archbishop Joseph T. McGucken of San Francisco on Proposition fourteen. America 111:541 N 7 '64
Detroit legalizes discrimination; adopted homeowners rights ordinance. Christian Cent 81:1164 S 23 '64
Development problems; address, February 27, 1964. R. C. Weaver. Vital Speeches 30:460-3 My 15 '64
Device for division; housing intergration case, Deerfield, Ill. Time 81:24 Ap 26 '63
Fair play in housing; Catholic spokesmen offering moral leadership. America 110:356 Mr 21 '64
Housing bias. Commonweal 78:181 My 10 '63
Housing controversy; Berkeley, Calif. E. Culver. Christian Cent 80:590 My 1 '63
Housing order & its limits. C. Abrams. Commentary 35:10-14 Ja '63
Housing's prospects look a little better. il Bsns W p27-8 My 4 '63
How a big city voted on selling homes to Negroes; homeowners' rights: what Detroit law says. U S News 57:10 S 14 '64
Keeping the outsiders out. E. Richey. il Sat R 46:22-4 O 19 '63; Discussion. 46:20-1, 23 N 30 '63
Mayor moved. Nation 198:226-7 Mr 9 '64
Our middle-class ghetto; Cleveland, Ohio. J. Horwitz. il Look 28:42-3+ Ja 14 '64
Proposition fourteen, concerning the sale or rental of California real estate properties. il Time 84:23 S 25 '64
Racist proposition: California on trial. D. Bess. Nation 199:179-82 O 5 '64
Right to sell to anyone; election issue in California; Proposition fourteen. U S News 57:8 N 2 '64
Showdown in California; Proposition fourteen on the November ballot. L. Zimpel. Commonweal 81:153-5 O 30 '64
Southern city with northern problems; Louisville. H. S. Thompson. il Reporter 29:26-9 D 19 '63
Splitsville, U.S.A: urban renewal and racial segregation; Chicago's Negro ghetto. E. Richey. il Reporter 28:35-8 My 23 '63; Discussion. 29:5 Jl 4 '63
Spotlight on California; realtor-sponsored Proposition fourteen. R. M. Brown. Christian Cent 81:1202-4 S 30 '64; Reply. G. Aki. 81:1470 N 25 '64
Tumult in suburbia; Folcroft, a Philadelphia suburb. H. W. Fry. Christian Cent 80:1154 S 18 '63
Where a Negro captain lives: his problem or ours? il Look 27:36-7 D 17 '63
Where whites staged a protest march; Chicago. il U S News 55:6 S 23 '63
Who's integrating? il Newsweek 62:62 D 23 '63
See also
Negroes in the United States—Housing

DISCUS, pseud.
Music in the round. See issues of Harper's magazine

DISCUS throwing. See Weight throwing

DISCUSSION
Being wise in membership; where learners are gathered together. B. W. Overstreet. il PTA Mag 58:14-16 F '64
Getting involved; exchange of religious ideas at coffee houses. il Newsweek 63:76 Ja 20 '64
Group learning of speech sequences without awareness. D. Shapiro. bibliog il Science 144:74-6 Ap 3 '64
Talking helps; group discussion. E. J. Le Shan. Parents Mag 38:88 Ag '63
See also
Conversation

DISCUSSION groups. See Forums (discussion and debate)

DISEASE, Diet in. See Diet in disease

DISEASE carriers. See Carriers of infection

DISEASE resistance. See Immunity

DISEASES
Environmental variables in disease; subjects of symposia to be held at AAAS annual meeting, December 26-31, 1964 at Montreal. il Science 146:954-5 N 13 '64
Laugh and get sick; laughing sickness. il Sci Digest 54:73 N '63
Made of cotton? Japanese patients with skin lesions seeming to produce cotton fibers. il Newsweek 64:78-9 Jl 13 '64
Medical news of the month. M. Fishbein. See issues of McCall's
No laughing matter; laughing sickness in Tanganyika. Newsweek 62:74 Ag 26 '63
Nobel winners discover how metabolism works and what can go wrong. il Life 54:63-6+ Mr 29 '63
Promising report on cancer, heart trouble, arthritis, and other critical diseases. G. G. Greer. Bet Hom & Gard 41:48-9+ Ag '63
There's a doctor in the house. B. C. Spicer. Ladies Home J 80:49+ Je '63
Three killer diseases seen controlled in U.S; heart disease, cancer and stroke. Sci N L 86:397 D 19 '64
See also
Diagnosis
Venereal diseases
also subhead Diseases under parts of the body, e.g. Lungs—Diseases

Causes and theories of causation

How man becomes allergic to parts of himself; autoimmune diseases. il Time 83:55-6 My 1 '64
Social factors in disease. J. A. Clausen. bibliog f Ann Am Acad 346:138-48 Mr '63

DISEASES, Hereditary. See Heredity of diseases

DISEASES, Industrial
Asbestos workers live longer but get cancer. Sci N L 86:297 N 7 '64
Danger of lung cancer in asbestos workers; also of asbestosis. Sci N L 86:276 O 31 '64
Dangerous dust? biological effects of asbestos. Sci Am 211:64 D '64

DISEASES, Psychosomatic. See Medicine, Psychosomatic

DISEASES of animals. See Domestic animals—Diseases and pests

DISEASES of plants. See Plants—Diseases and pests

DISH driers, Electric. See Dishwashing and drying machines

DISH gardens. See Gardens, Miniature

DISHONESTY. See Honesty

DISHWASHING and drying machines
Dishwashers. il Changing T 18:21-2 My '64
Dishwashers are time savers. M. B. Keiser. il Parents Mag 39:12+ Ag '64
Dishwashers: the why, how, where of them. il McCalls 92:74 N '64
Pushbutton eating center; combination dining counter-dishwasher-disposal unit. il Pop Mech 120:96-8 Ag '63
Recipe for 225 more leisure hours in 1964. Am Home 66:66+ D '63
Tappan dishwasher. Consumer Bul 47:12 N '64

DISINFECTION and disinfectants
How to disinfect your buildings and truck. J. W. Bailey. Suc Farm 61:141 Mr '63
See also
Sterilization

DISK jockeys. See Disc jockeys

DISK plows. See Plows

DISLIKES. See Likes and dislikes

DISLOCATIONS
First aid; shoulder dislocation. C. J. Potthoff. il Todays Health 43:86 Ja '65

DISLOCATIONS in crystals
Dislocation movements in metals. D. Kuhlmann-Wilsdorf and H. G. F. Wilsdorf. bibliog il Science 144:17-25 Ap 3 '64
Dislocations in ice. C. E. Hayes and W. W. Webb. bibliog il Science 147:44-5 Ja 1 '65

DISMISSAL of employees. See Employees—Dismissal

DISNEY, Doris Miles
Hospitality of the house; condensation of story. Seventeen 23:116-19 O '64

DISNEY, Dorothy Cameron
(ed) Can this marriage be saved? See issues of Ladies' home journal

DISNEY, Dorothy Cameron—*Continued*
Making marriage work (cont) Ladies Home J 80:94 Ja; 18 Mr; 34 Je; 52 Jl '63
(ed) See Fischer, M. A. Long hour of birth
(ed) See Fischer, M. A. My life, my children

DISNEY, Walt
Fantastic Walt Disney. B. Davidson. il pors Sat Eve Post 237:66-8+ N 7 '64
Greatest one-man show on earth: Walt Disney. S. Birmingham. il por McCalls 91:98-101+ Jl '64; Same abr. with title Walt Disney: imagination unlimited. Read Digest 85:272-3+ N '64
Magic worlds of Walt Disney; with editorial comment by M. B. Grosvenor. R. De Roos. il pors Nat Geog Mag 14:157D, 158-207 Ag '63
Onward and upward with the arts. K. Wallace. il New Yorker 39:104+ S 7 '63
Preview of Disney's World's fair shows; past, present and future in twelve minutes; 1,500-seat carousel; around-the-world cruise; the living Lincoln. D. Cohen. il pors Sci Digest 54:8-15 D '63
Walt Disney: giant at the fair. G. Zimmermann. il pors Look 28:28-32 F 11 '64

DISNEY, Walt, productions
Fantastic Walt Disney. B. Davidson. il Sat Eve Post 237:66-8+ N 7 '64

DISNEYLAND park, Anaheim, Calif.
Dazzled in Disneyland. A. Menen. il Holiday 34:68-70+ Jl '63
Magic worlds of Walt Disney; with editorial comment by M. B. Grosvenor. R. De Roos. il Nat Geog Mag 124:157D, 158-207 Ag '63
Onward and upward with the arts. K. Wallace. il New Yorker 39:104+ S 7 '63

DISOBEDIENCE. See Obedience

DISPLACED persons

Resettlement

See Refugees—Resettlement

DISPLAY boxes. See Exhibition cases

DISPLAY of merchandise
Imaginative window displays stop passers-by and sell books. Pub W 183:57 My 20 '63
See also
Showrooms

DISPLAY offices. See Showrooms

DISPLAYS, Library. See Library exhibits

DISPLAYS, Window. See Show windows

DISPOSAL of refuse. See Refuse and refuse disposal

DISPUTES, International. See Arbitration, International

DISSENTING opinions of Quentin Whiteside IV; story. See Webb, L.

DISSERTATIONS, Academic
Books for burning; intellectually sterile Ph.D. theses. Time 85:47 Ja 8 '65
Doctoral dissertations; excerpts from address. V. Carstensen. Pub W 184:40-1 Jl 15 '63

DISTANCE measuring equipment (aircraft to ground station)
Half price DME. R. Beatty. il Flying 74:45-6+ Je '64

DISTANCE perception. See Space perception

DISTANCES

Measurement

See also
Logs (nautical instruments)
Tellurometer

DISTANCES, Astronomical. See Astronomical distances

DISTANT early warning line. See Radar defense network

DISTANT planet (ballet) See Ballets

DI STEFANO, Alfredo
Comic cops. il por Time 82:30 S 6 '63

DISTEFANO, Victor, and Borgstedt, H. H.
Reduction of dimethylsulfoxide to dimethylsulfide in the cat. bibliog Science 144:1137-8 My 29 '64

DISTEMPER
Distemper diagnosed by test on eyelid cells. Sci N L 86:152 S 5 '64

DISTILLATION
Stretching distillation towers; Union carbide corp. Bsns W p 118+ N 30 '63
See also
Water, Distilled

DISTILLERS company, limited. See Distilling industries

DISTILLING, Illicit. See Moonshining

DISTILLING industries
Bourbon sets sail. Bsns W p29 Je 8 '63
Chemical company with a whisky base; Distillers co. ltd. il Bsns W p56+ S 19 '64
Distillers co. fights back; Scotch whisky. il Fortune 68:75-6+ O '63
Drum-beating for rum; Bacardi's comeback. il Bsns W p 102-4+ O 12 '63
Pouring Scotch whisky into the portfolio. il Bsns W p 170+ N 16 '63

DISTINGUISHED service award. See American forestry association

DISTLER, Theodore A.
Quarter-century of the Society for the advancement of education. Sch & Soc 92:261 O 3 '64

DISTORTION, Audio. See Amplifiers

DISTORTION, Photographic. See Photography —Distortion

DISTRIBUTION (economics). See Marketing

DISTRIBUTION cost analysis. See Cost accounting

DISTRIBUTION of animals and plants. See Geographical distribution of animals and plants

DISTRIBUTION of goods. See Marketing

DISTRIBUTION of wealth. See Wealth, Distribution of

DISTRIBUTION stations. See Warehouses

DISTRICT judges. See Judges

DISTRICT nursing. See Nurses and nursing, Public health

DISTRICT of Columbia reformatory, Lorton, Va. See Reformatories

DISTRICTS, School. See School districts

DI SUVERO, Mark
Four sculptors, four styles. il Art N 62:36-7+ Sum '63

DITCH; story. See Bannister, E.

DITCHING of airplanes. See Airplanes—Ditching

DITKA, Mike
Chicago's honey-bear. H. L. Masin. por Sr Schol 85:20 O 14 '64

DITLEV, Hans
Musk ox; story. Sat Eve Post 236:56-65 N 9 '63

DITTMAR, James C.
Bike pike. por Recreation 57:495+ D '64

DIURETICS and diuresis
Ethacrynic acid: diuretic property coupled to reaction with sulfhydryl groups of renal cells. R. M. Komorn and E. J. Cafruny. bibliog Science 143:133-4 Ja 10 '64

DIVERS. See Diving, Submarine

DIVERS contact air lenses. See Contact lenses

DIVERSA, incorporated
For Diversa, a deal that walks; buying and selling of companies. Bsns W p72+ S 14 '63

DIVERSIFICATION in industry
Armour cuts the meat in its diet; Armour's chemicals group. il Bsns W p54+ My 9 '64
Avco made its mistakes early; converting from military to civilian work. il Bsns W p 130-1+ Ag 22 '64
Beating the up-and-down cycle; Mill moves into consumable products, electronics, and plastics. il Bsns W p90-2+ O 19 '63
Borden's green pastures. il Time 81:86+ Mr 29 '63
Cotton's king tills new fields; pushing diversification. il Bsns W p 138+ Ja 23 '65
Entrepreneurship and the depressed area. S. F. Reed. Yale R 54:31-40 O '64
Giant gets in quickstep; new product paths. il Bsns W p 136-8+ N 9 '63
How to manage a conglomerate making. S. H. Brown. il Fortune 69:154-7+ Ap '64
It's a spryer Singer. E. K. Faltermayer. il Fortune 68:144-8+ D '63
Millions under Martin Marietta's mattress. C. J. V. Murphy. il Fortune 68:134-41+ N '63; 69:76+ F '64
New kind of gusher; oil company diversification. il Time 82:59-60 Ag 2 '63
Now the transnational enterprise. D. P. Kircher. Harvard Bsns R 42:6-8+ Mr '64
Oldest corporation in the world; Stora Kopparberg Bergslags Aktiebolag. il Time 81:96+ Mr 15 '63
One way to make a pipeline grow; diversification into energy fields. il Bsns W p80+ O 26 '63
Republic seeking diversification to backstop phaseout of F-105; summary of address. M. I. Peale. Aviation W 78:113 Ja 21 '63
R&D by the numbers. il Bsns W p59-61 Ag 24 '63
Rockwell increases its thrust. il Bsns W p 146+ D 12 '64
Ruhr scrubs the grime. il Bsns W p 100-2+ O 3 '64
Unexplored assets for diversification. G. R. Conrad. Harvard Bsns R 41:67-73 S '63

DIVERSIFICATION in industry—*Continued*
Versatile production line. il Duns R 83:pt2 118-20+ Mr '64
Weaving the payoff; Textron incorporated. il Bsns W p45-6+ Je 15 '63
DIVERSIFIED cooperative education. See Education, Cooperative
DIVERTICULITIS. See Intestines—Diseases
DIVIDENDS
Cash and dividends. il Fortune 67:206+ Je '63
Cash payout keeps climbing. Bsns W p 172 N 14 '64
Company board rooms catch the holiday spirit. il Bsns W p36+ N 28 '64
For stockholders: a banner year? U S News 55:118-19 N 25 '63
More rises are in the cards. il Bsns W p74+ Ag 29 '64
Official worry: rate war for the savings dollar. il U S News 55:113-15 O 14 '63
Waiting for the mailman. il Time 82:55 Ag 30 '63

Taxation

If you own stocks: what tax changes will mean. il U S News 56:33 F 10 '64
Tax tips for stockholders; questions and answers. il Changing T 18:43-5 Ag '64
DIVIDENDS, Insurance. See Insurance, Life
DIVIDING line; story. See Fenstermaker, V.
DIVINATION
See also
Astrology
DIVINE comedy. See Dante Alighieri
DIVINE healing. See Faith cure
DIVING
Bold and fluid beauty of the human form. il Sports Illus 19:32-8 Jl 29 '63
Master switch of life. P. F. Scholander. il Sci Am 209:92-6+ bibliog(p 178) D '63
DIVING, Cliff. See Cliff diving
DIVING, Submarine
Aquanauts skin-dive to retrieve missiles. il Pop Sci 185:108-9 N '64
At home in the sea. J. Y. Cousteau. il Nat Geog Mag 125:465-507 Ap '64
Bonanza on the bottom; scuba divers on Florida beaches. Time 84:42-3 Ag 28 '64
Circulatory adaptation to diving in the freshwater turtle. J. E. Millen and others. bibliog il Science 145:591-3 Ag 7 '64
Come feed my trigger fish; collecting saltwater fish. il Time 82:31 Ag 30 '63
Drowned galleons yield Spanish gold. K. Wagner. il Nat Geog Mag 127:1-37 Ja '65
First aqualung in the U.S. J. McMillan. il Sci Digest 56:14-18 Jl '64
Fish men; twenty-nine day Cousteau experiment. il Newsweek 62:64-5 Jl 29 '63
Flippers! gin! weight belt! gin! faceplate! gin! J. Jones. il Esquire 59:124-7 Je '63
How to get started in scuba diving. E. H. Ortner. il Pop Sci 183:91-4+ Ag '63
Living sea, by J. Y. Cousteau and J. Dugan. Review
Sat R il 46:42 Je 22 '63. E. Diamond
Sci Digest il 54:28 Jl '63. D. Cohen
Long, deep dive. Kilbracken. il Nat Geog Mag 123:718-31 My '63
Man's future beneath the sea. W. Johnson. il Sr Schol 85:6-9+ Ja 7 '65
Ocean-bottom homes for skin divers; homo aquaticus. J. Y. Cousteau. il Pop Mech 120: 98-103+ Jl '63
Our man-in-sea project. E. A. Link. il Nat Geog Mag 123:712-17 My '63
Perilous pleasures of skin diving. W. R. Vath. il Todays Health 41:14-19 Je '63
Photographing the night creatures of Alligator Reef. R. E. Schroeder. il Nat Geog Mag 125:128-54 Ja '64
Portrait of homo aquaticus. J. Dugan. il N Y Times Mag p38-9+ Ap 21 '63
Race for the bottom of the sea. W. Cloud. il Pop Sci 183:35-40+ Jl '63
Refit the boat for diving. J. Joye. il Motor B 111:28-31 Mr '63
Scuba divers replace missing pipe; Decatur, Ill. A. Van Praag, jr. il Am City 78:84-5 D '63
Sea women; Korean women. il N Y Times Mag p 122-3 S 8 '63
Single-hose regulators for scuba diving. W. E. Mundell. il Consumer Bul 46:6-10 Ap; 33-5 My '63
Skin diving; one part fun, one part danger. S. James. il Read Digest 85:152-4+ Ag '64
Smaller and better eyes for the human fish; diver's contact air lenses. C. Phinizy. il Sports Illus 19:62-4 D 16 '63
Sneakers and snorkels: Fish watcher's guide to the Caribbean. F. R. Smith. il Sports Illus 20:36-8+ Ja 20 '64
Spanish gold two fathoms deep; off Florida's coast. J. Atwater. il Sat Eve Post 237:66-71 D 12 '64
Underwater furniture factory; out of Great Lakes shipwrecks. J. Grenard and J. Grenard. il Motor B 111:76-7+ Je '63
Underwater reservoir inspection. il Am City 79:34 Ja '64
See also
Archeology, Submarine

Safety devices and measures

Danger, divers below. R. P. Kingett. il Motor B 111:39-40+ Je '63

Study and training

School for frog men; Sogetram school for training frogmen. Garennes-sur-Eure, France. il Sci Digest 54:48-51 O '63
DIVING apparatus
First aqualung in the U.S. great sport of SCUBA diving. J. McMillan. il Sci Digest 56:14-18 Jl '64
How to get started in scuba diving. E. H. Ortner. il Pop Sci 183:91-4+ Ag '63
Long, deep dive. Kilbracken. il Nat Geog Mag 123:718-31 My '63
Our man-in-sea project. E. A. Link. il Nat Geog Mag 123:712-17 My '63
Scuba fire fighters; wharf fires. S. Gordon. il Look 27:M7-8 S 10 '63
Single-hose regulators for scuba diving. W. E. Mundell. il Consumer Bul 46:6-10 Ap; 33-5 My '63
Some signs of danger in the air; scuba divers. D. Barnes. Sports Illus 19:51 Jl 29 '63
See also
Bathyscaphe
DIVING bells
Deepstar for shells? A. G. Melvin. il Hobbies 68:130+ Mr '63
Race for the bottom of the sea. W. Cloud. il Pop Sci 183:35-40+ Jl '63
Sub rescues, four miles deep. S. D. Pursglove. il Pop Mech 120:69-73+ Ag '63
DIVING saucer. See Bathyscaphe
DIVING suits
Human fish acquires a brighter, tougher skin; scuba diver's colored suits. C. Phinizy. il Sports Illus 18:62-3 Ap 15 '63
DIVINI redemptoris. See Encyclicals
DIVINING rod
Dowser who finds oil wells; W. J. Nelson's doodlebug. W. Trombley. il Sat Eve Post 236:88-9 D 7 '63
Dry run for the dowsers; Life goes to a water-diviners' convention. il Life 55:143-4 O 18 '63
DIVINITY of Christ. See Jesus Christ—Divinity
DIVINITY schools. See Theological schools
DIVISION (horticulture) See Plant propagation
DIVISION of home missions of the National council. See National council of the churches of Christ in the United States of America—Division of home missions
DIVISION of powers. See Separation of powers
DIVISIONAL management. See Business management and organization
DIVORCE
Divorce in politics; its meaning in U.S. and abroad. il U S News 54:44-7 Je 3 '63
Some guide rules for divorced fathers. S. Withers. il N Y Times Mag p 103 S 29 '63
See also
Marriage

Anecdotes, facetiae, satire, etc.

What is your divorce potential? A. Buchwald. McCalls 91:86 O '63; Same abr. with title Warning all wives! Read Digest 84:129-30 F '64

Statistics

Divorce phenomenon. W. C. Ellzey. Christian Cent 80:424-6 Ap 3 '63
Divorce rate half-truth. Sci N L 84:157 S 7 '63

Mexico

How to get a quickie divorce. il Esquire 59: 94-5 F '63
Mexican divorce, will it stand up in court? G. Simons. il McCalls 91:52+ N '63
Perils of Mexican divorce. il Time 82:34 D 27 '63

United States

Children of divorce. G. B. Blaine. il Atlan 211:98-101 Mr '63
Divorce in Sun Valley. il Newsweek 63:75-6 Mr 2 '64
Divorce, New York style. P. Rowley. Nation 199:461-3 D 14 '64

DIVORCE—United States—*Continued*
Divorce phenomenon. W. C. Ellzey. Christian Cent 80:424-6 Ap 3 '63
Divorce, proper style; New York state's divorce laws. Time 81:24 Je 7 '63
Eight myths about divorce, and the facts. H. Carter. il N Y Times Mag p 17+ My 3 '64
Judgment of Solomon; child custody proceedings. E. Balcomb. Christian Cent 82: 106-10 Ja 27 '65
Picnic trial; case of Rockefeller v. Murphy concerning custody of children. il Time 84: 63 S 11 '64
Question of custody; Happy Rockefeller's suit. il Time 84:88+ O 9 '64
Slowdown for quickie divorces; Alabama's racket. il Time 83:78 My 15 '64
Who gets the child? (how the court decides) H. M. Fain. McCalls 92:85+ Ja '65
Without portfolio. C. B. Luce. McCalls 90:29+ S '63
See also
Alimony

DIVVER, Margaret
Advice to a young woman; interview. por Changing T 17:31-4 Ap '63

DIX, Marion Quin
Art for learning's sake. Sch Arts 63:36-7 Ap '64

DIX, Otto
Fame by installments. il Time 81:86 Ap 19 '63

DIXIE hotel. See New York (city)—Hotels, restaurants, etc.

DIXON, Dean
Cultural ambassador. America 108:628 My 4 '63

DIXON, Henry L. Jr
Biographical sketch. il por Negro Hist Bul 27:142 Mr '64

DIXON, James P.
Air pollution. Science 143:1349-50 Mr 20 '64

DIXON, Jeremiah
Mason & Dixon: their line and its legend. A. H. Mason and W. F. Swindler. il Am Heritage 15:22-9+ F '64

DIXON, John Davenport
War horse; poem. Christian Cent 81:9 Ja 1 '64

DIXON, Paul Rand
Annals of legislation. R. Harris. New Yorker 40:80+ Mr 21 '64
Root of the FTC's confusion. H. B. Meyers. il pors Fortune 68:114-16+ Ag '63

DIXON, Pierson
Sirens, Spartans, and Socrates. Sat R 47:32-3 Mr 28 '64

DIXON, Robert G. Jr
Reapportionment: what the Court didn't do. Reporter 31:39-41 O 8 '64

DIXON, Ill.
Everything under control in Dixon. C. K. Willett. il Am City 79:112-13 Ap '64

DIXWELL, John
Hunt for the regicides. A. Winston. il Am Heritage 16:26-9+ D '64

DIZZINESS
Dizziness: your body's warning light; ed. by L. S. Hutchison. B. H. Shuster. il Todays Health 41:50+ F '63
What makes you dizzy. T. Berland. Redbook 121:20+ O '63

DJAKARTA. See Jakarta, Indonesia

DJILAS, Milovan
Idealism of Milovan Djilas. B. Raditsa. Commentary 35:149-53 F '63

DO-it-yourself work
Build your own music; do-it-yourself music component kits. il House & Gard 125:64 Mr '64
Soldering-iron saga: building hi-fi from kits mingles triumph and tedium. R. Freas. il Am Home 66:6+ S '63

DO you know the Milky way? drama. See Wittlinger, K.

DOAN, Leland I.
Our most precious possession; address, January 10, 1963. Vital Speeches 29:344-7 Mr 15 '63

DOAR, John Michael
Changing the guard at Justice. il por Time 85:47 Ja 1 '65

DOBAY, A. C.
Cooperative purchasing. por Am City 78:134+ My '63

DOBBIN, John
Better maps with satellites. Sci N L 85:253 Ap 18 '64

DOBBINS, Cris
Ready-mixed competition. il por Bsns W p61-2+ My 23 '64

DOBIE, J. Frank
Coyote's charm. Audubon Mag 65:38-40 Ja '63
Obituary
Pub W 186:96-7 S 28 '64

DOBLE, Mrs William
Used Christmas trees. Horticulture 41:630 D '63

DOBLER, Ken
Wireless re-broadcaster. Pop Electr 22:47-9+ Ja '65

DOBZHANSKY, Theodosius
Books. Sci Am 208:169-70+ F; 13 Ap '63
Evolution, organic and superorganic. Bul Atomic Sci 20:4-8 My '64
Evolutionary and population genetics. bibliog Science 142:1131-5 N 29 '63
about
Man as nature's man. P. Hefner. Christian Cent 81:1556-9 D 16 '64
SR Anisfield-Wolf awards, 1963. A. Montagu. il por Sat R 46:22-3 Ap 13 '63

DOCASANOIC acid
Petroleum hydrocarbons: generation from fatty acid. J. W. Jurg and E. Eisma. bibliog il Science 144:1451 Je 19 '64

DOCK workers. See Longshoremen

DOCKS
Buying or building docks, piers and floats. G. Daniels. il Pop Mech 120:152-7 Ag '63
Fiberglass dock float systems. B. Cobb, jr. il Yachting 113:80-2+ Je '63
See also
Marinas
Piers

DOCKSTADER, Frederick J.
Totem poles: family trees. Natur Hist 73: 62-3 O '64

DR Faustus; drama. See Marlowe, C.

DR Jason Love and the curious equation; story. See Leasor, J.

DR Salaam; story. See Perera, P.

DOCTORAL dissertations. See Dissertations, Academic

DOCTORS. See Physicians

DOCTORS strike (Belgium) See Strikes—Belgium

DOCTRINAL theology. See Theology

DOCTRINE, Religious. See Theology

DOCUMENTARY films. See Moving pictures—Documentary films; Television broadcasting—Documentary films

DOCUMENTARY photography. See Photography, Documentary

DOCUMENTARY television programs. See Television broadcasting—Documentary programs

DOCUMENTATION
Citations in popular and interpretive science writing; letter. E. Garfield. Science 141:392 Ag 2 '63
Documentation: a synthetic science; address, 1963. F. E. Mohrhardt. bibliog il Wilson Lib Bul 38:743-9 My '64
Documentation activities of associations. M. F. Tauber. bibliog il Wilson Lib Bul 38:768-72 My '64
Documentation pitt. A. Kent. Library J 89: 206, 818+, 1202-3, 2046-7 Ja 15, F 15, Mr 15, My 15 '64
Rutgers library school reports on its own documentation research. Library J 88:1966 My 15 '63
See also
American documentation institute

Anecdotes, facetiae, satire, etc.
Devil's documentation; definitions. E. Moon. Library J 88:3035 S 1 '63

DOCUMENTATION institute, American. See American documentation institute

DOCUMENTS
Wanted: documents librarians. E. P. Fishbein. il Library J 89:2037-9 My 15 '64

Conservation and restoration
Parchment patients; Vatican's Institute for the scientific restoration of books. il Newsweek 61:90 Ap 8 '63
Protect those documents. H. W. Tribolet. Hobbies 68:110-12+ Mr '63

DOCUMENTS librarians. See Librarians

DODD, Allen R. Jr
Let chance write the script. Pop Phot 53:95+ Ag '63
Paris, et cetera, in your backyard! Pop Phot 53:100-2 O '63

DODD, Thomas Joseph
Cold war education; understanding of communism is inadequate; address, June 12, 1963. Vital Speeches 29:586-9 Jl 15 '63
Negotiating with Communists: a test case; excerpts from address, February 21, 1963. Nat R 14:184 Mr 12 '63
Your right to own a gun; will it be challenged by new restrictions? no. por Pop Mech 121:94-9+ F '64

DODD, Thomas Joseph—*Continued*

about

Case against a test ban. Senator Dodd speaks out. U S News 54:22 Mr 18 '63
Crusader from Connecticut. E. H. Methvin. por Read Digest 85:101-6 S '64
Senate test ploy. K. Crawford. Newsweek 62:28 Jl 22 '63
Will the Senator yield? Nat R 14:483 Je 18 '63

DODD, Mead and company
Anthology reflects 125 years of publishing at Dodd, Mead. Pub W 186:27-9 D 14 '64
Looking backwards with Dodd, Mead. D. Dempsey. Sat R 47:36+ D 12 '64

DODDS, William A.
Congo: Col. Dodds observes; interview, ed. by E. Deverill. por Newsweek 64:48+ N 23 '64

DODECANESE (islands)
Serene isles. il Life 54:54-71+ Je 14 '63

DODGE, Christie
Lonesome pine; poem. Horn Bk 40:321 Je '64

DODGE, David
Bali: Eden's last stand. Holiday 34:24+ D '63
Portugal's sunny shore. Holiday 33:40+ Mr '63
Visit to Sirmione. Holiday 33:28+ My '63

DODGE, Donald W.
From scrap to sculpture. por Sch Arts 64:36-7 Ja '65

DODGE, F. W, corporation
F. W. Dodge construction outlook for 1964-1965. il Arch Rec 134:141-8 O '63; 136:82a-82g O '64
$120 billion in construction in 1975; forecast. G. A. Christie. il Arch Rec 134:173-80 S '63

DODGE, Natt N.
Behind the scene at Chiricahua. Nat Parks Mag 37:10-14 Mr '63
Mountain with a heavy heart. Nat Parks Mag 38:9-10 Ap '64

DODGE, Ralph E. bp
Bishop Dodge expelled by Southern Rhodesia. Christian Cent 81:981 Ag 5 '64

DODGE division. See Chrysler corporation—Dodge division

DODGEN, Howard
Story of LBJ and a hunting incident. U S News 56:8 My 18 '64

DODGERS (baseball) See Baseball clubs

DODSON, Dan W.
Are we segregating our children? Parents Mag 38:70-1+ S '63
Schools in our rural slums. Sat R 46:75 Ap 20 '63

DODSON, Helen W. and Hedeman, E. R.
Solar minimum and the International years of the quiet sun. bibliog Science 143:237-40 Ja 17 '64
—and others
Solar activity during the first six months of the International years of the quiet sun. Science 145:1050-2 S 4 '64

DODSON, Jacob
Negro who rode with Fremont in 1847. G. M. Bergman. pors Negro Hist Bul 28:31-2 N '64

DODSON, Roy E.
Art experiences in camping. por Recreation 56:135+ Mr '63

DOELL, Ruth G. and Kretchmer, Norman
Intestinal invertase: precocious development of activity after injection of hydrocortisone. bibliog Science 143:42-4 Ja 3 '64

DOERMANN, Humphrey
Changing face of Harvard college. Sat R 46:61-3 O 19 '63

DOETSCH, Raymond N.
History of microbiology. Science 146:956 N 13 '64

DOG

Intelligence

See Animal intelligence

DOG breeding
Choosing a sire. J. Stetson. il Field & S 68:182-4 Ap '64
Off-beat dogs. J. Stetson. il Field & S 68:108+ Jl '63
Planned litterhood. J. Stetson. il Field & S 68:124+ S '63

DOG breeds. See Dogs

DOG fighting
Same old frontier; badger vs. dog fight in Nevada. Sports Illus 19:6 Ag 26 '63

DOG food
Catering to the cats and dogs. il Bsns W p64-6+ N 9 '63
Feeding the family dog. il Consumer Bul 46:12-13 My '63
Picking a pet food by reading the label. M. Murray. il Consumer Bul 48:17-18 Ja '65

DOG houses. See Kennels

DOG Monday. See Special days, weeks, and months

DOG racing
Down the straight at 40 m.p.h. il Time 85:51 Ja 22 '65
They all missed a bet on Big Red. P. B. Kyne. Sports Illus 18:E5-6 Mr 25 '63

DOG schools. See Dogs—Training

DOG shows
Best girl in the dog show. R. H. Boyle. il Sports Illus 20:40-2+ F 10 '64
Canine cavalcade; Westminster kennel club show, N.Y. J. H. Winchester. il Travel 121:42-3 F '64
How to succeed at a dog show without really cheating. H. Horn. il Sports Illus 18:35-7 F 11 '63
Top show dogs; with photographs by N. Leen; and report by P. Hunt. Life 56:56-63 F 7 '64
Westminster's winner, a whippet. il Life 56:82-3 F 21 '64

DOG sleds and sledding
Arctic trail. W. O. Pruitt, jr. il Harper 226:44-50 Je '63
On the river ice; excerpt from Two in the Far North. M. E. Murie. il Liv Wildn 82:3-8 Winter '62
Sledding for stamina; World championship sled dog derby at Laconia, N.H. J. Stetson. il Field & S 69:168-70 My '64

DOG stories. See Dogs—Stories

DOG training. See Dogs—Training

DOG trials. See Field trials (dogs)

DOG who lives at the Waldorf; story. See Brough, J.

DOGFISH
Long journey of the dogfish. W. N. Hess. il Natur Hist 73:32-5 N '64

DOGGERELS
Goodbye Burma-Shave. W. K. Zinsser. il Sat Eve Post 237:65-6 S 5 '64

DOGMATIC theology. See Theology

DOGS
Champ, the fire dog. R. Hewett. il Look 28:M13-17 My 5 '64
Dogs. D. M. Duffey. See issues of Outdoor life
Dogs (cont) V. Kraft. il Sports Illus 18:43 F 18; 99-100+ Ap 8; 52+ Je 10 '63
Dogs can be fun and safe. A. R. Roalman. il Todays Health 42:20-2 Jl '64
Gentle setters sit out their stay of execution. il Life 54:41 Mr 22 '63
Give your heart to a dog. E. R. Choate. il Atlan 214:81-4 D '64
Gun dogs; ed. by J. Stetson. See issues of Field & stream
Hobo; dog that bums rides on freight trains. S. Harris. il Look 27:93-6 Je 4 '63
Kit Carson: new New Yorker. il Look 27:50+ Mr 26 '63
Last hermit. E. W. Smith. il Field & S 67:56-8+ Ap '63
Man's best friend of the moment. il Time 83:48-9 F 21 '64
Money, votes and psychiatry are going to the dogs. M. J. Kempner. il Sports Illus 20:72+ My 11 '64
Mystery beasts; wolf, coyote or dog? T. Janes. il Outdoor Life 134:17-19+ Jl '64
Pack dog hunt. W. Bever. il Outdoor Life 133:28-31+ Ja '64
Pet to grow with; photographs. N Y Times Mag p 104 S 8 '63
Pups of Pan; Webster terrier. Sports Illus 18:10 Ap 29 '63
Responsibilities of a dog owner. B. Brown. Bet Hom & Gard 42:117 My '64
Superdog. il Newsweek 62:84+ Jl 22 '63
Top show dogs; with photographs by N. Leen; and report by P. Hunt. Life 56:56-63 F 7 '64
Where to bury a dog; excerpt from How could I be forgetting? B. H. Lampman. Read Digest 84:26B My '64
Your dog is like you. il Sci Digest 54:74-5 N '63

See also
Basset hounds
Beagles (dogs)
Dalmation dogs
Field trials (dogs)
German shorthaired pointers
Hunting dogs
Pointers (dogs)

Anecdotes, facetiae, satire, etc.

Dog that bit the circus lion; excerpt from Personality of the dog. D. Marquis. il Read Digest 85:44-7 Ag '64
First catch your dog. R. Fontaine. il Atlan 212:132+ N '63
Of ailurophiles & dogs. H. A. Dubin. il McCalls 90:40+ Jl '63
Top dog on campus. J. Paulson. il Read Digest 83:167-8 D '63

DOGS—*Continued*

Breeding

See Dog breeding

Care

ABC's of dog care. P. Czura. il Field & S 69:130+ S '64
De-quilling a dog. T. H. Wiser. il Field & S 69:94-5 D '64
This doesn't guarantee the dog will enjoy his bath. il Sunset 132:157 My '64

Diseases and pests

Dogs have royal disease. F. Marley. Sci N L 85:295 My 9 '64
Persistence of neorickettsiae helminthoeca in an endorparasite of the Pacific salmon. R. K. Farrell and others. bibliog Science 145: 162-3 Jl 10 '64
See also
Distemper
Fleas
Rabies—Immunity
Worms, Intestinal and parasitic

Feeding

Balanced diet your pet requires. il Good H 158:162-3 Je '64
See also
Dog food

Photographs

See Animals—Photographs

Stories

Largely about my dog. R. F. Young. Writer 76:13-14+ Je '63
Sweet revenge of Mr Toad Clay. R. Starnes. Field & S 68:12+ D '63

Training

Best girl in the dog show. R. H. Boyle. il Sports Illus 20:40-2+ F 10 '64
Canine U: dog school; it's harder on the owners than the dogs. L. Tyler. Am Home 67:23 Jl '64
City slicker. R. L. Brown. il Field & S 67: 10-11 F '63
Fetch. D. M. Duffey. il Outdoor Life 134:98-101 D '64
It may be too late. J. Stetson. il Field & S 68:136-7+ O '63
Lyford's puddle jumper. C. Ford. il Field & S 67:6+ Mr '63
Making of a dog. C. Ford. il Field & S 69:8+ N '64
Making of a setter. D. B. Hague. il Field & S 68:28-31 D '63
Men behind the dogs. J. Stetson. il Field & S 68:100-1+ Ag '63
Neglected training details. D. M. Duffey. il Outdoor Life 132:142-6 O '63
Pet's gazette: academies for tailwaggers. il House & Gard 125:138+ My '64
Pup or trained dog? D. M. Duffey. il Outdoor Life 134:96-9 Ag '64
Reformation of Bo. H. Babcock. il Field & S 68:60-2+ Ap '64
Retriever training clinic. L. Smits. il Field & S 67:62-3 Mr '63
Tame quail for training. G. B. Evans. il Field & S 68:90-1+ Ja '64

DOGS, Experiments on. See Animal experimentation

DOGS in police work. See Police dogs

DOGS on television programs. See Animals on television programs

DOGWOOD
Flowering dogwood for the North. H. Rohrback. il Horticulture 41:556 N '63
Grow the best dogwoods. E. S. Henderson. il Horticulture 42:30-1+ My '64
Hero of the spring. A. Nicholson. il Read Digest 82:158-64 My '63
Relatives of the flowering dogwood. H. Roca-Garcia. il Horticulture 41:165 Mr '63
This one is the evergreen dogwood. il Sunset 133:258 O '64

DOHERTY, Patricia
In this orbiting age, every household needs a globe. House B 105:158-9+ My '63

DOHNALIK, Jan
PAX: Poland's Proteus. Atlan 212:79-81 D '63

DOI, Akira
Changing population patterns in Japan. Cur Hist 46:219-22 Ap '64

DOIG, Desmond
Sikkim. Nat Geog Mag 123:398-429 Mr '63

DOISNEAU, Robert
Love on the light side. il U S Camera 26:40 O '63

DOKO, Toshiwo
Who's who in foreign business. il por Fortune 70:64 Ag '64

DOKUMENTA III, Kassel. See Art—Exhibitions

DOLAND, S.D.
Sentimental journey; H. Humphrey makes a visit. J. Lindsay. il Newsweek 64:31-3 S 21 '64

DOLCI, Danilo
Gandhi of Sicily. G. D. Kumlien. Commonweal 79:745-6 Mr 20 '64
Small candle of Danilo Dolci. A. Winston. Christian Cent 81:1109-10 S 9 '64

DOLGINS, Judith
Good man is hard to keep. Duns R 81:63-4+ My '63
Wanted: one hundred presidents. Duns R 81:36-8 Je '63

DOLIN, Anton
Olga Spessivtzeva today. pors Dance Mag 37:34-8 Ap '63

D'OLIVE, Charles
Memoirs of an ace. V. Bourjaily. il pors Esquire 62:29-32+ Ag '64

DOLL clothes
Century of doll hats. C. H. Fawcett. il Hobbies 68:38+ Ap '63

DOLL houses
Doll's drawing room of 1893. C. H. Fawcett. il Hobbies 68:36-8+ Ag '63
Miniaturia. S. A. Parvin. il Hobbies 69:116-17 Mr; 116-17 Ap '64

DOLLAR. See Money—United States

DOLLAR bills. See Paper money—United States

DOLLAR gap. See Balance of payments

DOLLASE, Wayne A. See Buerger, M. J. jt. auth.

DÖLLINGER, Ignaz
From Döllinger to Vatican II; a century too soon? J. Coulson. Commonweal 79:400-3 D 27 '63

DOLLS
All dolled up; family-doll craze. il Newsweek 62:106+ N 25 '63
American dolls: historic dolls. Mrs A. Reed. il Hobbies 69:40+ Ap '64
Barbie-doll set. Nation 198:407 Ap 27 '64
Barbie is a million-dollar doll. W. K. Zinsser. il Sat Eve Post 237:72-3 D 12 '64
Case of the teen-age doll. B. Milton. il N Y Times Mag p84+ Ap 21 '63
Corn husk dolls. J. Adams. Hobbies 68:40 F '64
Dammit all; Dammit dolls. il Newsweek 63: 68 F 3 '64
Darling last-minute little-girl gift. il Good H 157:200-1 D '63
Dollology. C. H. Fawcett. See issues of Hobbies
Dolls from nowhere. M. Howard. il Redbook 121:32 S '63
Good-bye dolly. J. L. O'Neill. il Am Home 67:23 D '64
Grandmother and her dolls. E. Gurewitsch. il Look 28:71-3 D 29 '64
Kooky dolls new campus rage. J. Peter. il Look 27:M18+ S 24 '63
Magic world of dolls; International doll library. R. O'Brien. il Read Digest 85:146-53 D '64
Most popular doll in town: Barbie. il Life 55:73-5 Ag 23 '63
Pedlar dolls. C. H. Fawcett. il Hobbies 68:37+ D '63
Raggedy Ann: still flouncy at fifty. il Life 57:4 D 18 '64
Signs of spring. E. B. Booker. il Sch Arts 62: 35-6 Ap '63
Temple of the seven dolls; belief in dolls with curative powers. C. H. Fawcett. il Hobbies 68:36+ S '63
Toys from towels. il McCalls 92:40 N '64
See also
Paper dolls

Anecdotes, facetiae, satire, etc.

Living doll. R. Wallace. il Harper 228:38-40 Ja '64

DOLL'S house; drama. See Ibsen, H.

DOLNYTSIN, Anatoli
D for Dolnytsin. Newsweek 62:40 Jl 22 '63

DOLOMITE (mineral)
Age and accumulation rate of dolomite-bearing carbonate sediments in South Australia. H. C. W. Skinner and others. bibliog Science 139:335-6 Ja 25 '63
Dolomitization: observations on the island of Bonaire, Netherlands Antilles. K. S. Deffeyes and others. bibliog il Science 143:678-9 F 14 '64
Oxygen isotope fractionation between coexisting calcite and dolomite. J. N. Weber. bibliog il Science 145:1303-5 S 18 '64

DOLOMITES
Up they claw in winter's Alpine epic; Great Lavaredo's north face. R. Brigham. il Life 54:22-5 F 15 '63

DOLORIMETERS. See Pain
DOLPHIN fishing
Fly on the ocean. F. Dufresne. il Field & S 68:34-5 Ag '63
DOLPHINS (mammals)
Anesthesia for the bottlenose dolphin, tursiops truncatus. E. L. Nagel and others. bibliog il Science 146:1591-3 D 18 '64
Deep body temperature of untethered dolphin recorded by ingested radio transmitter. R. S. Mackay. bibliog il Science 144:864-6 My 15 '64
Gamboling dolphin in a new role; my pal Flipper. il Life 54:61-4+ Je 7 '63
Pet porpoise in the pool. J. O'Reilly. il Sports Illus 19:81-2+ S 23 '63
Porpoise. New Repub 151:2 Ag 22 '64
Porpoise: wonder of the sea. D. P. Egen. il Motor B 112:40+ Jl '63
Porpoises can teach man marine diving, detection. Sci N L 84:159 S 7 '63
Porpoises, smarter than people? J. Steen. il Pop Sci 182:59-63+ Je '63
Sea intelligence; the dolphin. B. Tufty. il Sci N L 86:138-9 Ag 29 '64
Status pet; photographs by E. Ciampi; with account by F. C. Appel. Sat Eve Post 237: 22-4+ Ja 4 '64
Visual problem-solving in a bottlenose dolphin. W. N. Kellogg and C. E. Rice. bibliog il Science 143:1052-5 Mr 6 '64
Vocal mimicry in tursiops: ability to match numbers and durations of human vocal bursts. J. C. Lilly. bibliog il Science 147: 300-1 Ja 15 '65
DOLSON, Hildegarde
Heaven had better be good; excerpt from Guess whose hair I'm wearing. Harper 226: 41-4 Ap '63; Same abr. with title Where there's a will. Read Digest 83:132-4 S '63
How to travel alone, and like it. Redbook 123:65+ My '64
I love a nice liar. McCalls 90:67+ Ag '63; Same abr. Read Digest 83:83-5 N '63
Most embarrassing prisoner. Harper 228:176-8 Ap '64
DOLTON, Myrtle C.
Amazing dwarf torch lily. Horticulture 41: 160 Mr '63
August blooming vesper iris. Horticulture 41: 256 My '63
Carefree veronicas. Horticulture 41:512-13 O '63
Ixora coccinea. Horticulture 41:202 Ap '63
New spreading lantana, fountain of bloom. Horticulture 41:110 F '63
DOMAIN, Eminent. See Eminent domain
DOMAN, Glenn
Little children can learn to read; excerpts from How to teach your baby to read. PTA Mag 59:30-2 Ja '65
That's our kid; excerpt from How to teach your baby to read. PTA Mag 59:23-5+ D '64
—and others
You can teach your baby to read. Ladies Home J 80:62-3+ My '63
about
Return to babyhood; maverick methods give help to brain-injured children; with report by J. Delay. il Life 55:31+ Ag 23 '63
DOMES
Biggest dome of all, for Texas, of course; lamella trusses for roof of Houston stadium. il Bsns W p56-8+ O 5 '63
Construction of two large plastic bubbles. il Arch Rec 136:257-8 S '64
Giant Illinois dome nears completion. il Arch Forum 118:117 Mr '63
Houston's big new bubble. il Sports Illus 21:26-7 Ag 10 '64
Prestressed units form inverted dome. il Arch Rec 136:198-201 O '64
Structure of St Sophia; with editorial comment. R. L. Van Nice. il Arch Forum 118: 131-8+, 154 My '63; 121:45-9 Ag '64
Two air-supported structures for athletics; gym and indoor swimming pool, Forman school, Litchfield, Conn. il Arch Rec 135: 209-10 Mr '64
Under the big dome in Houston; Colt's new air-conditioned dome. il Newsweek 64:68-70 Ag 17 '64
University of Illinois spectacular. il Arch Rec 134:111-16 Jl '63
DOMESTIC all-cargo airlines. See Air freight service
DOMESTIC animals
See also
Domestication
Diseases and pests
Not just disease control, eradication! L. M. Palmer. il Farm J 87:38-41+ N '63
History
History of domesticated animals, by F. E. Zeuner. Review
Sci Digest il 55:61 Mr '64. D. Cohen
DOMESTIC appliances. See Electric apparatus and appliances, Domestic; Household appliances
DOMESTIC architecture. See Architecture, Domestic
DOMESTIC economic assistance. See Economic assistance, Domestic
DOMESTIC employees. See Household employees
DOMESTIC finance
Family money questions answered. See issues of Better homes and gardens
Family spending; see how it changes. il Changing T 18:43-5 Mr '64
How women feel about money. G. H. Gallup and S. Grafton. il McCalls 91:74-7+ Jl '64
Money is a family affair. Am Home 67:32+ O '64
Newlyweds, a market unto themselves. il Bsns W p98-100 N 2 '63
Pleasures of thrift; excerpt from Profession: housewife. P. McGinley. il Ladies Home J 80:26+ My '63
Queen of the family purse, or is she? finding of study by Social research, inc. il Bsns W p26-7 Ag 10 '63
See also
Budget, Household
Budget, Personal
Cost of living
Debt
Saving and savings
DOMESTIC peace corps. See Volunteers in service to America
DOMESTIC relations
See also
Divorce
Family life
Husbands
Marriage
Quarrels
DOMESTIC science. See Home economics
DOMESTIC service. See Household employees
DOMESTICATION
History of domesticated animals, by F. Zeuner. Review
Science 144:672-5 My 8 '64. R. H. Dyson, jr.
Prehistoric fauna from Shanidar, Iraq. D. Perkins, jr. bibliog il Science 144:1565-6 Je 26 '64
DOMIN, William M.
Virgin Isles adventure. Travel 122:35-8 D '64
DOMINANCE, Mixed
Self-presentation and self-termination of a conflict-producing stimulus. E. Hearst and M. B. Koresko. bibliog il Science 146:415-16 O 16 '64
DOMINIC, Sister Mary. See Mary Dominic, Sister
DOMINICAN REPUBLIC
Quisqueya, by S. Rodman. Review
Sat R 47:49 S 26 '64. D. Kurzman
Struggling forward. Time 83:28 Ap 10 '64
Tensions on Hispaniola. il Américas 15:44 Je '63
See also
Art—Dominican Republic
Communism—Dominican Republic
Fishing—Dominican Republic
Guerrillas—Dominican Republic
Hispaniola
Santo Domingo
Strikes—Dominican Republic
United Nations—Dominican Republic
Description and travel
Dawn for the Dominicans. H. Sutton. Sat R 46:34+ Ap 20 '63
Economic conditions
Limits of American power; the lesson of the Dominican Republic. A. F. Lowenthal. Harper 228:87-9+ Je '64
Foreign relations
Shock of recognition; diplomatic relations. Newsweek 62:64 N 11 '63
Trujillo: the last Caesar, by A. Espaillat. Review
Nat R 15:530-1 D 17 '63. N. Weyl
Politics and government
After Bosch. New Repub 149:4 O 5 '63
After Trujillo, a reformer with a mission. T. Szulc. il N Y Times Mag p30+ S 8 '63
Caribbean failure. Commonweal 79:64-5 O 11 '63

DOMINICAN REPUBLIC—Politics and government—*Continued*
Days of doubt in Dominican Republic. Sr Schol 83:20 O 18 '63
Democracy derailed in the Dominican Republic. il Sr Schol 83:4-7 O 25 '63
End of an experiment. il Time 82:55 O 4 '63
Fall of Juan Bosch. N. Gall. il Nation 197: 253-6 O 26 '63
Fresh start in Santo Domingo. M. Barrenechea. America 108:366-7 Mr 16 '63
Goons again. N. Gall. il Nation 198:159-61 F 17 '64
How Trujillo died. N. Gall. New Repub 148: 19-20 Ap 13 '63
If it's war in Haiti, who'll win? C. Migdail. il U S News 54:44 My 13 '63
Island divided. Sr Schol 83:6 S 20 '63
Latest revolt in Caribbean; its meaning for U.S. il U S News 55:66-7 O 7 '63
Limits of American power; the lesson of the Dominican Republic. A. F. Lowenthal. Harper 228:87-9+ Je '64
Made in U.S.A. Reporter 30:20 F 27 '64
Military run the show again. il Bsns W p36 O 5 '63
New man for the Dominicans. New Repub 148:8 Mr 2 '63
Nonintervention: a shield for Papa Doc. G. Sherman. il Reporter 28:27-9 Je 20 '63
Question mark. Time 81:29 Mr 8 '63
Return to democracy. N. A. Haverstock. il Américas 15:14-16 Mr '63
Santo Domingo: the empty showcase. D. A. Allan. il Reporter 29:28-31 D 5 '63
Shuffle to the right. il Newsweek 62:64 O 7 '63
Then there were none. Time 84:29 Jl 10 '64
Trujilloism without Trujillo. H. J. Wiarda. New Repub 151:5-6 S 19 '64
U.S.-backed reform flops as Bosch gets the bounce. S. Halper. il Life 55:49-50 O 18 '63
Why Bosch fell. V. Alba. New Repub 149: 12-14 O 12 '63
Worst of neighbors. il Time 81:39 My 10 '63

DOMINIONS, British. See Commonwealth of nations

DOMINO, Edward F. and others
Simultaneous recordings of scalp and epidural somatosensory-evoked responses in man. bibliog Science 145:1199-200 S 11 '64

DOMINO, Ruth
Word; poem. tr. by D. Hoffman and J. Mangione. Poetry 104:85 My '64

DOMKE, Herbert R.
How Pittsburgh licked the problem. Sci Digest 53:7-8 My '63

DON Carlo; opera. See Verdi, G.

DON Giovanni; opera. See Mozart, J. C. W. A.

DON Pasquale; opera. See Donizetti, G.

DON Rodrigo; opera. See Ginastera, A.

DONAGHY, Norman
Curb and gutter by extrusion. Am City 79:25 Je '64

DONAHUE, Barbara
I believe. Seventeen 22:46+ O '63
Your first job: how to get it. Seventeen 22: 78-9+ Je '63

DONAHUE, Charles
Labor relations; role of government; address, August 27, 1964. Vital Speeches 30:751-5 O 1 '64

DONAHUE, Mildred L. and Donahue, R. J.
Lowly disguise of the giant swallowtail. il Audubon Mag 66:320-1 S '64
—See Donahue, R. J. jt. auth.

DONAHUE, Ralph J. and Donahue, M. L.
Poppy mallow. Horticulture 41:416 Ag '63
—See Donahue, M. L. jt. auth.

DONAHUE, Troy
Straight from the shoulder. E. Miller. il pors Seventeen 23:140-1+ My '64

DONALD, David
Changing State of the Union. Sat R 46:48+ N 16 '63

DONALD, Frances G.
Art + math = SRO. Wilson Lib Bul 37:574-5 Mr '63

DONALDSON, E. E.
Surface physics. Science 141:364-5; 145:1471-2+ Jl 26 '63, S 25 '64

DONALDSON, Gordon
Financial goals: management vs stockholders. bibliog f Harvard Bsns R 41:116-29 My '63

DONALDSON, Lufkin and Jenrette, incorporated
Courting the big stock buyers; research-oriented brokerage house. il Bsns W p96-8+ F 22 '64

DONALDSON, Norman Vaux
Obituary
Pub W por 185:244 Ja 27 '64

DONALDSON, Sam
Second look. Liv Wildn 82:2 Wint '62

DONALDSON, Yvonne
World-record trout. il pors Look 27:80a-80b Ag 13 '63

DONAT, Alexander
Our last days in the Warsaw ghetto. Commentary 35:378-89 My '63

DONAUESCHINGEN festival. See Music festivals—Germany (Federal Republic)

DONCHIN, E. and others
Cortical evoked potentials and perception of paired flashes. bibliog Science 141:1285-6 S 27 '63

DONDES, S. See Harteck, P. jt. auth.

DONELSON, Loren
(ed) Fruits and truck crops. See issues of Farm journal

DONER, Dean
Giving; story. New Yorker 39:32-8 F 15 '64

DONGEN, Kees van
Man in a boat. por Newsweek 62:50-1 Jl 15 '63

DÖNHOFF, Marion, gräfin
Outspoken Gräfin. il por Time 82:58 S 13 '63

DONIZETTI, Gaetano
Between Rossini and Verdi. M. Bernheimer. por Sat R 46:70 O 26 '63
Donizetti, and the world of opera in Italy, Paris, and Vienna in the first half of the nineteenth century, by H. Weinstock. Review
Opera N 28:36 Ja 18 '64. J. Browning
Donizetti today. H. Weinstock. il por Opera N 29:8-12 Ja 9 '65
Don Pasquale. Criticism
New Yorker 40:234 N 21 '64
Opera N 29:18-20 Ja 9 '65
Opera N 29:24-5 Ja 9 '65
Lucia di Lammermoor. Criticism
New Yorker 40:221 O 24 '64
Opera N il 29:17-20 D 5 '64
Maria di Rohan. Criticism
Opera N 27:32 Mr 23 '63
Mary Stuart; presentation in New York. F. Merkling. Opera N 29:31 Ja 2 '65
Musical events; concert performance, Donizetti's Maria Stuarda in Philharmonic Hall, by Concert opera association. W. Sargeant. New Yorker 40:234-5 N 28 '64
On records; Don Pasquale. Opera N 29:35 Ja 9 '65
On records; Lucia di Lammermoor. Opera N 29:35 D 5 '64

DONLEAVY, J. P.
Romantic life of Alphonse A; story. Esquire 60:66 Ag '63

about

Fairy tales of New York. Criticism
Commonweal 78:20 Mr 29 '63
Ginger man; dramatization of novel. Criticism
Commonweal 79:432-3 Ja 10 '64
Nation 197:444 D 21 '63
New Repub 149:28 D 21 '63
New Yorker 39:131 D 7 '63
Newsweek 62:68 D 2 '63
Sat R 46:35 D 7 '63

DONLON, Roger Hugh C.
Beyond mere duty: a night for valor. il por Life 57:45 D 18 '64
Beyond the call. por Newsweek 64:38 D 14 '64
One who was belligerent; Medal of honor award. il por Time 84:31 D 11 '64

DONN, Bertram, and Sears, G. W.
Planets and comets: role of crystal growth in their formation. bibliog Science 140: 1208-11 Je 14 '63

DONN, William L.
Alaskan earthquake of 27 March 1964: remote seiche stimulation. bibliog Science 145:261 Jl 17 '64
—and Shaw, D. M.
Sea level and climate of the past century. bibliog Science 142:1166 N 29 '63
—and others
Propagation of air waves from nuclear explosions. bibliog Science 139:307-17 Ja 25 '63

DONNALLEY, W. F. and Ries, S. K.
Amitrole translocation in agropyron repens increased by the addition of ammonium thiocyanate. bibliog Science 145:497-8 Jl 31 '64

DONNAY, J. D. H. and Takeda, Hiroshi
Computer program for printing undeformed Fourier maps. Science 143:1162-3 Mr 13 '64

DONNELLEY, Robert G.
Family business. bibliog f Harvard Bsns R 42:93-105 Jl '64

DONNELLY, Dorothy
Origin of species; To three old ladies; poems. Poetry 101:392-4 Mr '63

about

New and selected, and a first volume. D. C. DeJong. Poetry 102:127 My '63

DONNELLY, Joseph F.
Changing of the guard. B. L. Masse. America 111:511 O 31 '64; Discussion. 111:781-2 D 12 '64
DONNELLY, Joseph P.
How can I tell I'm pregnant? Redbook 122: 38+ Mr '64
DONNELLY, R. R, and sons, company
Mighty heir to Gutenberg. il Fortune 70:132-5 N '64
DONNER, Frederic G.
Highest-paid man in industry. por U S News 54:19 My 6 '63
Two gentlemen of GM. por(p31) Duns R 82: 32 S '63
Two records: highest profit, highest pay. por U S News 56:64 My 4 '64
DONOGHUE, Roger
I killed a man. por Sat Eve Post 236:65-6 Mr 23 '63
DONOHUE, H. E. F.
Bit of gravy; story. Ladies Home J 81:82-4 Je '64
Farewell! farewell! farewell! story. Sat Eve Post 237:54-5 Ja 25 '64
(ed) See Algren, N. Nelson Algren at fifty-five
DONOHUE, Jack
Jack and his beanstalk. H. L. Masin. il Sr Schol 82:24 Mr 13 '63
DONOHUE, Stephen T.
What is an internist? Todays Health 41:48-53+ Ap '63
—See Walsh, T. F. jt. auth.
DONON, Joseph P.
Chef's trial. K. Lloyd. il por Vogue 143:114-15+ Ap 15 '64
DONOSO, José
Five Chilean poets. Américas 16:15-20 My '64
DONOVAN, Gail. See Patterson, F. jt. auth.
DONOVAN, Hedley W.
Difficulty of being fair to Goldwater. Life 57: 93-6+ S 18 '64
Letter from the publisher. B. M. Auer. il por Time 83:15 Ap 24 '64
Succession. por Newsweek 63:76 Ap 27 '64
DONOVAN, James A.
Automation of government. Sat R 47:23-4+ D 12 '64
DONOVAN, James B.
Silent years in Siberia. America 111:807 D 19 '64
Strangers on a bridge; excerpt. pors Sat Eve Post 237:30-2+ Mr 28 '64
about
American example. Newsweek 63:75-6 Mr 30 '64
Biggest fish. il por Newsweek 61:24-5 My 6 '63
Cuban prisoner exchange. B. Lindeman. il por Sat Eve Post 236:15-17+ F 2 '63
It's just as cold for a real spy. P. Mandel. Life 56:12+ Ap 17 '64
James Donovan and Castro. G. Samuels. Nation 196:299-302 Ap 13 '63
Man in Havana. New Yorker 39:22-3 Jl 6 '63
Modern Mercedarian. N. McKenty. America 111:101 Ag 1 '64
DONOVAN, John
Riverside drive. Criticism
New Yorker 39:113 F 15 '64
DONOVAN, John C.
Better skills will improve job outlook; interview. por Nations Bsns 52:66-8+ D '64
DONOVAN, John D.
Creating anti-intellectuals? Commonweal 81: 37-9 O 2 '64
DONOVAN, Patrick J.
Real Patsy; baseball manager. Sports Illus 18:11 My 20 '63
DONOVAN'S retreat; story. See Miller, J. R.
DON'T forget; story. See Kanin, G.
DON'T tell the folks back home; drama. See Dias, E. J.
DOOB, Joseph L.
Government and university research. Bul Atomic Sci 20:33 Ap '64
DOODY, Alton F. and Davidson, W. R.
Growing strength in small retailing. bibliog f Harvard Bsns R 42:69-79 Jl '64
DOOLEY, Arch. R.
Interpretations of PERT. Harvard Bsns R 42:160-2+ Mr '64
DOOLEY, D. J.
Cauldron of unholy loves. America 109:262-3, 646 S 14, N 23 '63
DOOLEY, Jim
Down. New Yorker 40:30-2 Mr 21 '64
DOOLEY, Rickard F.
Snake hunt. il pors Sci Digest 56:47-51 Ag '64
DOOLEY, Roger B.
Playwright, plays and byplay. Sat R 46:47-9 N 23 '63
When the dawn came up in Erin. Sat R 47: 44 S 26 '64
Womanless world of Edwin O'Connor. Sat R 47:34-6 Mr 21 '64
DOOLEY, Thomas Anthony
Tom Dooley writes to a young doctor; excerpt from Promises to keep, by A. W. Dooley. Read Digest 82:213-14+ F '63
DOOLEY, William
Berlin brogue; interview, ed. by F. Stevenson. por Opera N 28:32 F 29 '64
DOOLITTLE, Alice R.
Marley's ghost. NEA J 52:44-5 D '63
DOOLITTLE, Hilda
Poetry of three women. M. Swenson. Nation 196:164-6 F 23 '63
DOOLITTLE, Jerome H.
Genesis of a men's club. Esquire 63:115 Ja '65
Gentleman from Georgia goes home. Sat Eve Post 237:26-8 D 5 '64
Second Washington. Esquire 61:112-14+ My '64
DOOR fittings
Sculptured door pulls of Ted Bielefeld. J. Pugliese. il Craft Horiz 23:18-19 My '63
DOOR latches. See Latches
DOOR locks. See Locks and keys
DOOR opens, a door closes; story. See Gavin, M.
DOOR steps
Solid repairs to keep a stoop in step. J. Hand. il Pop Sci 185:142-3+ Ag '64
DOOR to door selling. See Canvassing
DOORBELLS
Tuned bells for your front door; Swiss sheep bells. W. Waltner and E. Waltner. il Pop Sci 185:161 O '64
DOORKEEPERS
But who will be concierge to the concierges? il Time 83:28 Ja 17 '64
DOORMEN concessions. See Concessions (food, etc)
DOORS
ABC's of buildings chests and cabinets; four kinds of doors. R. J. De Cristoforo. il Pop Sci 186:132-6 Ja '65
Decoration that may save a life; Vikon crash guards. Consumer Bul 46:8 O '63
Glass doors should be made of safety glass. il Consumer Bul 47:43+ My '64
How to avoid glass-door dangers. Good H 156:142 Mr '63
How to buy a storm door without getting stuck. J. H. Ingersoll. il Pop Sci 185:148-51+ O '64
How to choose aluminum storm windows and doors. il Consumer Bul 47:2+ D '64
Panel door decor. il Pop Mech 120:144-5 S '63
Paradise regained; duplicate doors of Florentine Baptistery installed in San Francisco's Protestant Episcopal Grace cathedral. il Time 84:84 D 4 '64
This wide door pivots. il Sunset 133:119 N '64
Treat your home to a new door. il Pop Mech 120:146-7 S '63
Repairing
Help for doors that stick. il Good H 156:153 F '63
DOORS, Mechanically operated
Radio-controlled garage-door openers. il Consumer Rep 28:378-82 Ag '63
$35 electric door opener. F. L. Greenwald. il Pop Mech 120:172-8 D '63
DOORS, Sliding
Sliding wall between study and bedroom. il Sunset 131:98 S '63
These panels add privacy. il Sunset 130:123 Je '63
They slide on piano wire. il Sunset 133:160 N '64
DOORWAY planting. See Landscape gardening
DOORWAYS
Five ways to enhance your back door. il Pop Gard 15:40-1 S '64
How public should the front entrance be? M. Thatcher. il House B 105:222-7 N '63
How to make a better entrance. il Pop Sci 185:116-18 S '64
Mexico's vivid doors. il Arch Forum 119: 86-90 Ag '63
Slate entry. il Pop Mech 121:135-8 Ap '64
DOORYARD gardens. See Gardens
DOPAMINE
Dopamine: its occurrence in molluscan ganglia. D. Sweeney. bibliog il Science 139:1051 Mr 15 '63

DöPFNER, Julius, cardinal
Cardinal Doepfner's views; interview, ed. by W. M. Abbott. America 108:714-15 My 18 '63
Unfinished reformation. por Time 83:66 F 7 '64
DOPPLER radar. See Radar
DOPPLER radar system. See Radar in aviation
DORAL BEACH hotel. See Miami Beach, Fla. —Hotels, restaurants, etc.
DORAN, Margaret
When conversation wanes: ask a silly question. Library J 88:1735 Ap 15 '63
DORATI, Antal
Antal Dorati; interview, ed. by S. Fleming. por Hi Fi 13:22 Je '63
Dorati in tandem, the conductor as composer. A. Cohn. il por Am Rec G 30:124 O '63
DORAZIO, Piero
Dorazio. M. Gendel. Art N 63:36+ Ja '65
DORCHESTER, Mass.
Great interlude, by F. Russell. Review Nat R 16:691-3 Ag 11 '64. J. Chamberlain
DOREN, David MacNeil
Easter in Crete. Sat R 46:34-6+ Mr 16 '63
Hiking the Holy Mountain. il Sat R 47:44-6+ Mr 14 '64
DORF, Erling
Petrified forests of Yellowstone Park; with biographical sketch. Sci Am 210:27, 106-12+ Ap '64
DORFMAN, Leon M.
Pulse radiolysis: fast reaction studies in radiation chemistry. bibliog Science 141:493-8 Ag 9 '63
DORIAN, Margery
Emphasis on music. Dance Mag 38:56-7 F '64
DORIES. See Boats and boating
DORING, Walter
End to corrosion. Motor B 111:155-7 Ap '63
DORIOT, Georges F.
Profit-minded professor. por Time 81:88+ Mr 8 '63
DORJI, Jigme
Murder in Shangri-La. Newsweek 63:58 Ap 20 '64
DORLÉAC, Françoise
Françoise Dorléac gamine fatale. il pors Vogue 144:144-5 O 1 '64
DORMAN, Purman
Contact lenses. Consumer Bul 46:10-11+ Mr '63
Eye make-up and contact lenses. Consumer Bul 47:2 My '64
DORMAN, Sonya
Fair exchange; story. Redbook 121:68-9 My '63
Old folks at home; story. Redbook 121:62-3 Je '63
Thumb does many things: poem. Sat R 48:13 Ja 16 '65
DORMANT bank accounts. See Bank deposits, Unclaimed
DORMANT buds. See Buds
DORMER windows. See Windows
DORMITORIES
Designing with deference; medical library at Harvard, and dormitories at the University of Massachusetts, Princeton, M.I.T. and Bowdoin. il Arch Rec 133:133-44 Mr '63
Dream dorm or nightmare? Women's residence at the University of Pennsylvania designed by E. Saarinen. L. Baron. il Mlle 60:109+ Ja '65
Fortress for Seattle; University of Washington in Seattle. il Arch Forum 121:140-1 Ag '64
Harvard married student apartments. il Arch Rec 134:208-9 S '63
Married students residence completed at Harvard. il Arch Rec 136:12-14 N '64
Modest dormitories for a country prep school; St Paul's school, Concord, N.H. il Arch Rec 133:125-32 Je '63
New dorms for coeds. il Arch Forum 118:86-7 Mr '63
Residence halls; Cornell college, Mt Vernon, Ia. H. Weese. il Arch Rec 133:134-5 My '63
Small units comprise residence complex for U. of Rhode Island. il Arch Rec 134:15 N '63
Trim house for girls' campus. il Arch Forum 118:88-9 Mr '63
DORN, Edward
Some questions of precision. Poetry 104:184-5 Je '64
This March afternoon; Daffodil song; Dark ceiling; poems. Poetry 103:304-5 F '64
DORNE, Albert
What is a pro? Design 65:136 Mr '64

about

Famous money-makers hit gold at Westport. il por Bsns W p38-40 D 28 '63
DORNER, Peter
Farmers: the real surplus. Nation 196:115-17+ F 9 '63
Tax cut: a dissenting view. Nation 197:171-3 S 28 '63
DORNEY, Thomas
Prayer of the church in council; poem. Commonweal 78:351 Je 21 '63
DORNWAL. See Tranquilizing drugs
DOROTHY Canfield Fisher library awards
Annual Book-of-the- month awards to honor forty-five small public libraries. Library J 89:80-1 Ja 1 '64
B-O-M expansion. Wilson Lib Bul 38:121 O '63
Minnesota library gets $5000 B-O-M club award. Pub W 185:68 F 3 '64
Questioning a question; and some of the answers. E. Moon. il Library J 88:2644-7 Jl '63
What happened after the award. C. Shaw. il ALA Bul 57:337-8 Ap '63
DOROUGH, H. Wyman, and others
Nonhydrolytic pathway in metabolism of n-methylcarbamate insecticides. bibliog Science 140:170-1 Ap 12 '63
DORPAT observatory. See Astronomical observatories—Estonia
DORROS, Sidney
Case for independent professional teachers' associations. Mo Labor R 87:543 My '64
DORSEN, Norman
Libel and the free press. Nation 198:93-5 Ja 27 '64
DORSET, Thomas Sackville, 1st earl of
Who remembers Thomas Sackville? P. W. Schmidtchen. il por Hobbies 68:106-8 My '63
DORSKIND, Albert A.
One man's method. R. L. Shayon. Sat R 47:26 Ap 25 '64
DORST, Jean
Secrets of migration; excerpt from The migrations of birds, tr. by C. Sherman. Audubon Mag 65:12-15, 102-6, 240-3+ Ja-Mr, Jl '63
DORTU, M. G.
Toulouse-Lautrec paints a portrait. Art N 62:24-7+ F '64
DORVILLIER, William J.
San Juan: the new Havana. Sat R 48:41+ Ja 2 '65
DORWARD, Mary
Missouri show; exhibition at M. Knoedler & co. New Yorker 39:26 F 23 '63
DOSIMETERS. See Radiometers
DOS PASSOS, John
Battle of San Francisco. Nat R 16:640,652 Jl 28 '64
Brazil; excerpt from Brazil on the move. Sat R 46:80-3+ O 12 '63
Most dangerous man in Brazil. Nat R 15:53-7 Jl 30 '63
Old Hem was a sport. Sports Illus 20:58-60+ Je 29 '64
Please Mr Rip Van Winkle, wake up some more. por Nat R 16:71-4 Ja 28 '64
U.S.A. revisited. Atlan 213:47-54 Ap '64
What hope for maintaining a conservative opposition? Nat R 16:907-9 O 20 '64

about

Crime of John Dos Passos. Nat R 17:51-2 Ja 26 '65
Dos, which side are you on? D. Wakefield. Esquire 59:112-14+ Ap '63
DOSTAL, Lumir
Man behind the mechanized plow. il por Bsns W p 168 O 24 '64
DOSTOEVSKII, Feodor Mikhailovich
All the depths. por Newsweek 61:92+ Ap 29 '63
Christian's dilemma. J. Collignon. il por Sat R 47:14-16 Je 27 '64
Common sense on Dostoevsky. H. Muchnic. Nation 197:34-5 Jl 13 '63
Dostoevsky, by D. Magarshack. Review New Repub 149:30-2+ S 21 '63. V. Lange
Human irritants of an immortal. I. Spector. por Sat R 46:61 S 28 '63
DOTSON, Janie
What one college freshman found; far from home. por Seventeen 24:108-9 Ja '65
DOTTER, Charles
Clearing an artery. il pors Life 57:43-4+ Ag 14 '64
DOTY, Roy, and others
Wordless workshop. See issues of Popular science monthly
Le **DOUANIER.** See Rousseau, H.
DOUATTE, Roland
Notes from our correspondents. R. McMullen. Hi Fi 14:10+ Jl '64
DOUBLE houses. See Houses, Two-family
DOUBLE jeopardy; story. See Morrow, S.

DOUBLE nine of Chih Yuan; drama. See Nolan, P. T.
DOUBLE sideband system. See Radio transmission—Double sideband system
DOUBLE standard in sexual ethics. See Sexual ethics
DOUBLE stars. See Stars, Double
DOUBLE taxation. See Taxation, Double
DOUBLE-time. See Overtime
DOUBLEDAY and company
After six years: the Doubleday merchandising plan. il Pub W 186:24-7 D 7 '64
Doubleday establishes new Catholic prize contest. Pub W 184:28 D 16 '63
Doubleday launches textbook series on minority groups' contributions. Library J 89:4618 N 15 '64
Doubleday's new series dealing with minority groups. il Pub W 186:35-6 N 2 '64
Image books anniversary: 10 million copies in ten years. il Pub W 185:67-9 F 10 '64
Retailing and overstock: the annual markdown sale; Doubleday book shop organization. Pub W 185:50 My 11 '64
School and bookstore: an experiment with surprises; Doubleday school service. Pub W 186:177-8 Jl 13 '64
DOUBLETALK; drama. See Carlino, L. J.
DOUCHING. See Woman—Health and hygiene
DOUGALL, D. K. See Gibbs, J. L. jt. auth.
DOUGAN, Mrs Ronald A.
Recipes from a good cook's notebook. por Suc Farm 62:52-3 Je '64
DOUGH
Homemade bread doughs into your freezer. il Sunset 132:154+ F '64
These people are good eating; Finnish version of gingerbreadmen. il Sunset 131:119 D '63
DOUGHERTY, Ellsworth C. and Harris, L. G.
Antarctic micrometazoa; fresh-water species in the McMurdo Sound area. bibliog Science 140:497-8 My 3 '63
—See Fatt, H. V. jt. auth.
DOUGHERTY, James E.
Christian and nuclear pacifism. Cath World 198:336-46 Mr '64
Nuclear weapons control. bibliog f Cur Hist 47:31-8+ Jl '64
DOUGHERTY, Joanna
Conference on book fairs stresses the practical. Pub W 185:20-3 My 11 '64
Distinguished contribution. Pub W 183:36 Mr 11 '63
Sixty days with a salesbook: a reviewer sells at Christmas. Pub W 185:61-2 F 3 '64
DOUGHERTY, John
Pasadena playhouse. Dance Mag 37:22-3 My '63
Pearl Wheeler: a tribute. Dance Mag 39:52-4 Ja '65
Perspective on Adolph Bolm (cont) Dance Mag 37:44-7+ F; 50-3 Mr '63
Saida Gerrard discusses the L.A. problem. Dance Mag 37:16+ Mr '63
DOUGHERTY, Richard
Case for the cop. Harper 228:129-33 Ap '64
DOUGHNUTS
For Hallowe'en. il Sunset 131:243 O '63
Square doughnuts; with recipes. R. Behnke. il Farm J 88:66-7 S '64
DOUGLAS, Lord Alfred Bruce
Bosie. by R. Croft-Cooke. Review
Esquire 62:10+ Ag '64. M. Muggeridge
Sat R il 47:48 My 16 '64
Degeneracy or decadence? S. Leslie. Nat R 15:445-6 N 19 '63
Letters of Oscar Wilde. by R. Hart-Davis. Review
New Yorker 39:155-62+ Mr 9 '63. W. H. Auden
DOUGLAS, Charles S.
Even the kitchen sink. U S Camera 27:82 Ag '64
DOUGLAS, Geddes
Other iris. Horticulture 42:20-1+ My '64
DOUGLAS, Gilean
First snow; poem. Am For 69:45 D '63
Pause in twilight; poem. Am For 70:84 O '64
DOUGLAS, Joan Carol (Martin)
Third wife for Justice Douglas. por U S News 55:16 Ag 19 '63
DOUGLAS, Patrick Sholto-. See Sholto-Douglas, P.
DOUGLAS, Paul Howard
Excerpt from debate, August 21, 1964. Cong Digest 44:17+ Ja '65
Our best chance to save the Indiana dunes. Audubon Mag 66:112-14 Mr '64
DOUGLAS, Robert H.
Transistorized audio sweep generator. Electr World 72:71-4 Ag '64
DOUGLAS, Stephen A.
Little Giant vs. Honest Abe. il Sr Schol 85:5 O 14 '64
Stephen A. Douglas letters in the State historical library. T. E. Felt. Hobbies 69:110-12+ Ag '64
DOUGLAS, Steven D. See Gilbert, P. W. jt. auth.
DOUGLAS, William Orville
America's vanishing wilderness. Ladies Home J 81:37-41+ Jl '64; Same abr. with title To preserve America's glories. Read Digest 86:146-54 Ja '65
Archeologist on an Oriental journey. Sat R 47:59 N 14 '64
Banks Island: Eskimo life on the Polar Sea. por Nat Geog Mag 125:702-35 My '64
Why we must save the Allagash. Field & S 68:24-9+ Jl '63

about

Douglas vs. Black: old friends fall out. por U S News 54:20 Je 17 '63
Greatest honor, says Justice Douglas of Audubon medal. il por Audubon Mag 65:113 Mr '63
Sequel to springtime; marriage to Joan Martin. il pors Time 82:17 Ag 16 '63
Third wife for Justice Douglas. por U S News 55:16 Ag 19 '63
DOUGLAS-HOME, Sir Alexander Frederick
Communism and peaceful coexistence; address, October 1, 1963. Vital Speeches 30:5-9 O 15 '63
Neither dead nor red. Read Digest 82:69-71 F '63
What happens to Great Britain now? interview. por U S News 54:62-5 F 4 '63
—See Johnson, L. B. jt. auth.

about

And now there's the anti-Establishment. C. Hussey. il N Y Times Mag p42+ My 3 '64
At home with Sir Alec. C. Brogan. Nat R 15:567-8 D 31 '63
Britain's new leader: what to expect. U S News 55:24 O 28 '63
British election: can Labor win? por Newsweek 64:44+ S 28 '64
British elections. R. Presthus. Nation 198:480-3 My 11 '64
Caligula's horse. A. Burnet. New Repub 149:10-11 N 2 '63
Choice Britain is making. il por U S News 57:45 O 19 '64
Dull no more. il por Time 82:35 N 1 '63; Same abr. with title Belted earl who became Prime Minister. Read Digest 84:68-72 Ja '64
Elegant anachronism vs. one-man band. S. Gruson. il pors N Y Times Mag p34+ O 11 '64
Fourteenth earl becomes a political pro. S. Gruson. il pors N Y Times Mag p32+ N 24 '63
Fox trots no minuets. il por Newsweek 63:21 F 24 '64
His ex-lordship goes for the grassroots vote. il pors Life 55:40-40A N 8 '63
Home free? Newsweek 62:52+ N 11 '63
Home in the Highlands. il pors Time 82:38 N 8 '63
Home's home run. A. Boyle. America 109:563 N 9 '63
In Britain, Home gets the job Wilson wants. il por Bsns W p 102-4+ O 26 '63
Into battle. por Time 82:30 N 22 '63
Letter from London. M. Panter-Downes. New Yorker 39:221-2+ N 9; 202+ N 30 '63; 119-20 F 15; 40:152-6 O 24 '64
Lord Home got the job; But he won't keep it long. A. Lejeune; A. Waugh. Nat R 15:438-9 N 19 '63
New strains on an old alliance. il por U S News 56:42 F 24 '64
No reason to grouse. Newsweek 63:37-8 Mr 9 '64
Other election. por Sr Schol 85:23 S 30 '64
Prime Minister meets the people. H. Massingham. New Repub 151:9-11 S 26 '64
Right honourable foreign secretary. G. Brook-Shepherd. il por Reporter 29:31-3 Jl 18 '63
Sir Alec: miracle man in Britain? il por U S News 57:19 S 14 '64
Tide turning for Britain's Tories? il por U S News 55:68 O 28 '63
U.S. stake in Britain's election. por U S News 57:55-6 O 12 '64
War of succession; Lord Home becomes Prime Minister; with excerpts from addresses. il pors Time 82:30-5 O 25 '63; Same abr. with title Belted earl who became Prime Minister. Read Digest 84:68-72 Ja '64
What will Home do at no. 10 Downing? il por Newsweek 62:31-2 O 28 '63

DOUGLAS-HOME, Robin
Ducal life; the Devonshires. Vogue 141:156-61+ Mr 1 '63
Scotland; the dour and the beautiful. Vogue 143:132-45+ Ap 15 '64
DOUGLAS-HOME, William
At home with Sir Alec. C. Brogan. Nat R 15:567-8 D 31 '63
DOUGLAS aircraft company
Battling for new jet trade; Douglas DC-9 to counter Britain's BAC-111. il Bsns W p52+ Mr 23 '63
DC-9 enters the short-range jet race. il Newsweek 65:64-6 Ja 18 '65
Douglas due to get new MORL award. Miss & Roc 15:60 N 30 '64
Douglas rejects merger offer. il Aviation W 78:28 Ap 1 '63
Douglas shows higher fiscal 1962 earnings. Aviation W 78:33 Ja 28 '63
Douglas to build DC-9 despite order lack. il Aviation W 78:40-2 Ap 15 '63
Jet fighters; short range planes. il Newsweek 61:72+ Ap 22 '63
New yardstick for defense contracts; award of X-22 contract to Bell. Bsns W p30 Je 22 '63
Spacecraft re-usability emphasized at Douglas. Miss & Roc 14:35 My 11 '64
Why aerospace needs flexible men. il Bsns W p44+ Je 22 '63
DOUGLAS fir
Diseases and pests
Engravings beneath the bark; Douglas-fir beetles. M. M. Fisher. il Natur Hist 72:54-6 Ag '63
DOUGLAS fir beetles. See Beetles
DOUGLASS, Frederick
Up-to-date Frederick Douglass; his own words. por Ebony 19:70-2+ Je '64
about
Black abolitionist. por Time 81:100+ My 24 '63
Frederick Douglass: father of the protest movement. L. Bennett, jr. il pors Ebony 18:50-2+ S '63
Frederick Douglass; reprint. B. Quarles. Negro Hist Bul 26:182+ Mr '63
DOUGLASS, Harl R.
Junior high accreditation? NEA J 53:36 O '64
DOUGLASS, James W.
Nuclear morality and eschatological realism. Cath World 198:177-84 D '63
135,000 dead. Commonweal 80:376 Je 12 '64
DOUGLASS, Suzanne
Silent treatment; Fly-by-night; poems. McCalls 91:161, 169 D '63
DOUGLASS, William C.
For whom the bell rings. Nation 198:310 Mr 30 '64
DOUKHOBORS. See Dukhobors
DOULENS, Humphrey
Memories of Dangeville. Opera N 27:34 F 9 '63
DOUMANI, George A. and Tasch, Paul
Leaiid conchostracan zone in Antarctica and its Gondwana equivalents. bibliog Science 142:591-2 N 1 '63
DOUTHIT, Ancil M.
Safe drivers cut costs, create goodwill. Am City 78:138 Je '63
—and Peek, F. B.
Purchasing manual is a must. Am City 78:89 N '63
DOVE-cotes
Poetry of birds in flight. il House B 105:104-7+ Ag '63
DOVE shooting. See Mourning dove shooting
DOVE trees
Canary Island madrone and the handkerchief tree. il Sunset 130:283-4+ My '63
DOVER, Del.
In his own backyard; State news. il Time 82:91 O 18 '63
DOVETAIL joints. See Joints (carpentry)
DOW chemical company
Bricks without straw bosses. J. Lear. il Sat R 47:45-9 F 1 '64
DOW Corning corporation
Dow Corning tailoring silicone work to meet individual needs of buyers. J. F. Judge. il Miss & Roc 14:27-8 My 18 '64
DOW-Jones averages. See Stocks—Price indexes and averages
DOWBEN, Robert M.
Muscular dystrophy. T. Berland. il por Sat Eve Post 236:40+ D 14 '63
DOWD, Douglas F.
Second thoughts on the Common market. Yale R 53:168-91 D '63
DOWD, Merle. See Cushman, J. jt. auth.
DOWDALL, Joe
Gold cup for Bardahl. Motor B 112:52-3+ S '63
Roostertails, history and the Detroit River. Motor B 111:42+ Je '63
DOWDING, Hugh Caswall Tremenheere Dowding, 1st baron
Man who won the battle of Britain. A. Lunn. Nat R 16:487-8 Je 16 '64
DOWDY, John
Excerpt from address before Dayton lawyers club, January 30, 1964. Cong Digest 43:113+ Ap '64
Mounting scandal of urban renewal. Read Digest 84:51-7 Mr '64
DOWELL, R. Lawrence. See Burks, C. S. jt. auth.
DOWEY, Edward A. Jr
Synopsis of Calvin. Christian Cent 81:1309-10 O 21 '64
DOWLING, Donald D.
New methods of care. bibliog f Ann Am Acad 355:49-55 S '64
DOWLING, George B. and Olson, F. C. W.
Diffusion in oceans and fresh waters. Science 146:1492-3 D 11 '64
DOWLING, John E.
Foveal receptors of the monkey retina: fine structure. bibliog Science 147:57-9 Ja 1 '65
DOWLING, Robert
Story of Sterling Forest. por Pop Gard 14:76-7 Jl '63
DOWN beat (periodical)
Upbeat Down beat. il Newsweek 63:56+ Je 29 '64
DOWNE, Aylward E. R.
Mosquitoes; comparative serology of four species of aedes (ochlerotatus) bibliog Science 139:1286-7 Mr 29 '63
DOWNER, Henry E.
Crabapples. Pop Gard 14:38-9+ Ap '63
DOWNES, Bruce
On being photographed by Philippe Halsman. por Pop Phot 56:22+ Ja '65
DOWNES, Edward
His hand on his heart. Opera N 28:24-6 F 22 '64
House that Wagner built. Hi Fi 14:49-52+ F '64
Tender irony. Opera N 29:24-5 Ja 2 '65
Tristan's children. Opera N 27:8-12 F 23 '63
DOWNES, Mollie Panter-. See Panter-Downes, M.
DOWNEY, Howard R.
Dewey or LC? Library J 89:2292-3 Je 1 '64
DOWNEY, Peggy
He turned the poles to gold. Sports Illus 18:E5-8 Mr 11 '63
Horseback in the classroom. Sports Illus 19:24-7 N 11 '63
Way under par in a parking lot. Sports Illus 19:16-17 Jl 15 '63
DOWNIE, George
Victory on Lake Champlain. C. S. Forester. il Am Heritage 15:11+ D '63
DOWNING, Andrew Jackson
America's Victorian homes. C. Carmer. Am Home 67:86-7 Mr '64
DOWNING, John, and Rose, Ivan
Value of ITA. NEA J 53:20+ S '64
DOWNING, Scarff
Bumpy journey to oblivion. por Sports Illus 19:28-30+ D 9 '63
DOWNS, George L.
Airline eavesdropper. Pop Electr 18:46-7 Ap '63
DOWNS, Hugh
How to see it without going. Sci Digest 55:8-12 Ap '64
Hugh Downs column. See issues of Science digest
about
Hugh Downs and the common man. V. Kelly. il pors Look 27:49-50+ D 3 '63
DOWNS, Robert B.
Small library: decline and fall. Wilson Lib Bul 37:772-4 My '63
DOWNTOWN areas. See Business districts
DOWNTOWN-Lower Manhattan association
Friend at the Chase; financial group to renew Lower Manhattan. il Bsns W p24+ D 21 '63
DOWSING. See Divining rod
DOXIADIS, Constantinos Apostolos
Profiles. C. Rand. New Yorker 39:49-50+ My 11 '63
DOYLE, Sir Arthur Conan
Sherlock Holmes and the stockbroker's clerk; dramatization. See Olfson, L.
DOYLE, L. L. and Margolis, A. J.
Intrauterine foreign body: effect on pregnancy in the rat. Science 139:833; 140:1136 Mr 1, Je 7 '63

DOYLE, Louis F.
This side idolatry. Cath World 199:182-7 Je '64
DOYLE, Paul A.
Updike's fiction: motifs and techniques. Cath World 199:356-62 S '64
DOYLE Dane Bernbach, incorporated
Met Doyle Dane's Bernbach. il Newsweek 63: 76 Je 8 '64
D'OYLY, Bridget Carte. See Carte, B. D.
D'OYLY Carte opera company
Great opera houses: the Savoy theatre. B. D. Carte. il Opera N 29:26-9 D 12 '64
Patter still matters; performances at New York city center. D. E. Scherman. Life 58: 14 Ja 8 '65
DRACHMAN, Daniel B.
Atrophy of skeletal muscle in chick embryos treated with botulinum toxin. bibliog Science 145:719-21 Ag 14 '64
DRAFT law. See Military service, Compulsory —United States
DRAFT riots, 1863
Draft marches into its 100th year. il Sr Schol 82:12-13 Mr 6 '63
DRAFTEES. See Soldiers
DRAFTING, Mechanical. See Mechanical drawing
DRAFTING room practice. See Drawing room practice
DRAFTSMEN
Two draftsmen: exhibitions at the Pan American union. R. Squirru. il Américas 16:42 Jl '64
DRAG (aerodynamics)
Slotted for smoothness. il Time 81:43 Mr 29 '63
DRAG racing. See Automobile racing
DRAGADZE, Peter
At 3½ I was under the piano. il Life 57:62+ O 2 '64
DRAGO, Joseph P.
When Americans make machines for reds; excerpts from testimony. U S News 54: 8 Ap 1 '63
DRAGON; drama. See Schwarz, E.
DRAGONETTI, Mary
Fracas; poem. Horn Bk 39:166 Ap '63
DRAGSTERS. See Automobiles, Racing
DRAHOS, Mary
Eternal Sabbath. Criticism
America 109:497-8 O 26 '63
DRAHOS, Nick
(ed) See Avery, R. Biggest bear in the East
DRAINAGE
Drainage details for buildings using standard steel components. il Arch Rec 134:149-50 D '63
Letter to the owner of a wet basement. il House B 106:186+ Ap '64
Pumping out the Punjab; world's largest irrigation project. Pop Sci 184:24+ Ja '64
What to do when a hole won't drain. il Sunset 132:266-8 My '64
See also
Sewerage
DRAINAGE, House
More Japanese ideas cross the Pacific; silent downspout. il Sunset 130:78 F '63
DRAKE, Carol Christopher
Requiem. Christian Cent 80:1580 D 18 '63
DRAKE, Daniel
Daniel Drake and his medical Baedeker; excerpts from Doctors on the frontier. R. Dunlop. il Todays Health 41:42-5+ Mr '63
DRAKE, Francis Vivian
Bomb carrier nobody can stop. Read Digest 84:153-4+ Ap '64
We're running the wrong race with Russia! Read Digest 83:49-55 Ag '63
We've got the planes, what about the men? Read Digest 92:110-14 F '63
—and Drake, Katharine
Earliest man on earth? Read Digest 84:157-61+ Ja '64
They're thinking big down under. Read Digest 85:106-12 O '64
DRAKE, Frank Donald
Littlest astronomer. Science 141:861 S 6 '63
Our weakness in space. por Sat R 48:96-9 Ja 2 '65
DRAKE, Gordon V.
Conservatives, too, have tenure. R. Kirk. Nat R 16:729 Ag 25 '64
DRAKE, John
Obeying the law. il Horizon 5:110-12 N '63
DRAKE, Katharine
Great flamingo rescue. Read Digest 84:209-11+ Je '64
—See Drake, F. V. jt. auth.
DRAKE, Robert
As old as man himself. Nat R 16:324-5 Ap 21 '64
Fountain filled with blood. Christian Cent 80:432-6 Ap 3 '63
Harrowing evangel of Flannery O'Connor. Christian Cent 81:1200-2 S 30 '64
DRAKE, St Clair
Democracy on trial in Africa. bibliog f Ann Am Acad 354:110-21 Jl '64
DRAKE university, Des Moines, Ia.
Student-faculty council revisited. P. A. Bloland. Sch & Soc 91:216-18 My 4 '63
DRAMA
Comedy and tragedy transposed; modern drama. E. D. Leyburn. Yale R 53:553-62 Je '64
Laugh now, pay later. R. Hatch. il Horizon 5:106-9 Mr '63
Metatheatre, by L. Abel. Review
Sat R 46:42 Ap 20 '63. H. Hewes
Oh mom, poor mom; epidemic of antimom plays; with report by T. Prideaux. il Life 54:93-4+ My 10 '63
So long as the theater can do miracles. T. Guthrie. il N Y Times Mag p24-5+ Ap 28 '63
Theatre of politics: the Negro. L. Abel. Nation 196:351-4 Ap 27 '63; Reply. H. F. Winslow, sr. 196:inside cover My 11 '63
What's right with the theatre; excerpt from Dramatis personae. J. M. Brown. Sat R 46:19-21 My 11 '63
See also
Dramatic criticism
Greek drama
Historical drama
Melodrama
Negro drama
Passion plays
Plots (drama, novel, etc)
Television broadcasting—Drama
Theater
Tragedy

Competitions

Playwriting contests. Theatre Arts 47:6 F; 79 Mr; 80 My; 5 Je; 5 Jl; 3 Ag; 75 O; 79 N '63; 48:6-7 Ja '64

Study and teaching

Baker v. Baylor. Time 81:42 Mr 22 '63
Reminiscences and plans; Perry-Mansfield school of theatre & dance. C. Perry. il Dance Mag 37:48-51+ Ap '63
See also
Shakespeare, W.—Study and teaching

Technique

Odets at center stage; interview, ed. by M. J. Mendelsohn. C. Odets. il Theatre Arts 47:16-19+ My; 28-30+ Je '63
Play construction; excerpt from Play's the thing. L. Langner. Writer 76:17-24 F '63
Plays that never get written. A. Pryce-Jones. Theatre Arts 47:18-19 O '63
Playwright and the contemporary world. J. Gassner. Theatre Arts 48:22-3+ Ja '64
Practice of playwriting. M. C. Chase. Writer 76:17-19 Je '63

Themes

Grinding of an axe. Theatre Arts 47:10 O '63
Half-world of American drama. M. Mannes. Reporter 28:48-50 Ap 25 '63
How pertinent is our theater? W. S. Smith. Christian Cent 81:1393-5 N 11 '64
DRAMA, Industrial. See Entertaining in sales promotion
DRAMA, Medieval
Arts; presentation of Play of Herod at The Cloisters, in New York city. C. J. McNaspy. America 109:808-9 D 21 '63
Carillons and vielles; New York Pro musica presentation of Play of Herod. Newsweek 62:51 D 23 '63
Daniel and Job. F. Merkling. il Opera N 27: 33 F 2 '63
Play of Herod; New York pro musica presentation. C. S. Susa. Mus Am 84:55-6 Ja '64
DRAMA, Negro. See Negro drama
DRAMA critics. See Critics
DRAMA festivals
Asolo theatre festival. J. Hayes. il Theatre Arts 47:30-1 Jl '63
European festivals. Theatre Arts 47:74-6 Je '63
Letter from England; Chichester festival theatre. J. Novick. Nation 196:553-5 Je 29 '63
Letter from London; Chichester festival. M. Panter-Downes. New Yorker 39:68-9 Ag 3 '63
Openings, Stratford-upon-Avon; Chichester. A. Brien. il Theatre Arts 47:26-8+ O '63

DRAMA festivals—*Continued*
Summer theater, junior branch; Old Greenwich summer youth festival. S. Schuler. il N Y Times Mag p54 Ag 4 '63
Sweden is a summer festival. G. Loney. il Theatre Arts 47:62-3+ Ap '63
What price theater? H. Hewes. Sat R 47:36 S 19 '64
See also
Shakespeare festivals

DRAMAS
Advocate. R. Noah. il Theatre Arts 47:33-64 N '63
Affair; dramatization of novel by C. P. Snow. R. Millar. il Theatre Arts 47:25-56 Mr '63
After the fall. A. Miller. il Sat Eve Post 237:32-7+ F 1 '64
Calculated risk. J. Hayes. il Theatre Arts 47:20-54 D '63
Chinese wall; tr. by J. L. Rosenberg. M. Frisch. il Theatre Arts 47:32-60 Ag '63
Chips with everything. A. Wesker. il Theatre Arts 47:33-57 O '63
Do you know the Milky way? K. Wittlinger. il Theatre Arts 47:37-60 Je '63
Four plays; Playwright and the public; Handshakers; Doctor and the patient; This I believe. W. Saroyan. Atlan 211:50-2 Ap '63
Man for all seasons. R. Bolt. il Theatre Arts 47:33-66 My '63
Ross. T. Rattigan. il Theatre Arts 47:25-58 Ap '63
Take her, she's mine. P. Ephron and H. Ephron. il Theatre Arts 47:37-70 Jl '63
Thousand clowns. H. Gardner. il Theatre Arts 48:33-64 Ja '64
Wen. S. Bellow. il Esquire 63:72-4+ Ja '65
See also
Columbus, C.—Drama
Election day—Drama
Ghost plays
Skits (drama)

Criticisms, plots, etc.

Broadway postscript. H. Hewes. See issues of Saturday review
Burst of Negro drama; with report by T. Thompson. il Life 56:62A-70 My 29 '64
Goings on about town. See issues of New Yorker
Life guide. See issues of Life
Life theater review. See issues of Life
Off Broadway. E. Oliver. See issues of New Yorker
Off-Broadway, by halves. il Time 83:70-1 Ja 3 '64
On Broadway and off; a midseason view of the current plays. J. Simon. Harper 226:98-100+ Mr '63
Openings, London. A. Brien. See issues of Theatre arts
Openings, New York (cont) A. Pryce-Jones. il Theatre Arts 47:10-13+ F; 57-9+ Mr; 10-13, 68-9 Ap; 12-15+ My; 10-13+ Je; 10-13 Jl; 10-15+ Ag; 10-13 D '63; 48:10-11+ Ja '64
Openings, Paris. J. P. Lenoir. il Theatre Arts 47:28-9+ My '63
Stage. G. Rogoff. Commoweal 80:176-7, 299-300 My 1, 29 '64
Stage. R. Gilman. See issues of Commonweal
Theater. See issues of Time
Theatre. E. Hardwick; H. Popkin. See issues of Vogue
Theatre. G. Rogoff. Nation 198:153-4 F 10 '64
Theatre. H. Clurman. See issues of Nation
Theatre. J. McCarten. See issues of New Yorker
Theater. R. Brustein. See issues of New republic
Theatre. R. Hatch. See issues of Horizon
Theatre. T. Lewis. See issues of America
Theater (cont) Nat R 14:291+, 465-7, 535-7; 15:406-7, 446-8+; 16:34-5, 289-90, 458-9, 546-7, 780-1, 982-3 Ap 9, Je 4, Jl 2, N 5-19 '63, Ja 14, Ap 7, Je 2, 30, S 8, N 3 '64
Three at the Cherry Lane. H. Clurman. Nation 198:383-4 Ap 13 '64
Time listings. See issues of Time
Week of despondency. T. F. Driver. Christian Cent 80:239-41 F 20 '63
See also
London—Theater
New York (city)—Theater
Shakespeare, W.—Plays

Single works

See name of author for full entry

Abe Lincoln in Illinois. R. E. Sherwood
Absence of a cello. I. Wallach
Advocate. R. Noah
After the fall. A. Miller
Alchemist. B. Jonson
Alfie! B. Naughton
American dream. E. Albee
Andorra. M. Frisch
Any Wednesday. M. Resnik
Arturo Ui. B. Brecht
Baal. B. Brecht
Baby want a kiss. J. Costigan
Bald soprano. E. Ionesco
Ballad of the sad café. E. Albee
Barefoot in the park. N. Simon
Beauty part. S. J. Perelman
Bed sitting room. J. Antrobus and S. Milligan
Beekman place. S. Taylor
Benito Cereno. See Old Glory, below
Blood knot. A. Fugard
Blue boy in black. E. White
Blues for Mr Charlie. J. Baldwin
Bonheur, impair et passe. F. Sagan
Brig. K. H. Brown
Burning. W. Hamilton
But for whom Charlie. S. N. Behrman
Cages. J. Carlino
Call it virtue. L. Pirandello
Candida. G. B. Shaw
Case of libel. H. Denker
Cat and the canary. J. Willard
Changeling. T. Middleton and W. Rowley
Chief thing. N. Evreinov
Child buyer. P. Shyre
Children from their games. I. Shaw
Chinese prime minister. E. Bagnold
Chips with everything. A. Wesker
Coach with the six insides. J. Erdman
Color of darkness. E. Violett
Comforter. E. A. Molloy
Corruption in the palace of justice. U. Betti
Country wife. W. Wycherley
Crucible. A. Miller
Cyrano de Bergerac. E. Rostand
Daddy come home. R. Grieco
Dark corners. S. Koven
Days and nights of Beebee Fenstermaker. W. Snyder
Death of a salesman. A. Miller
Dear me, the sky is falling. L. Spigelgass
Defense of Taipei. C. Bromberg
Deputy. R. Hochhuth
Desire under the elms. E. G. O'Neill
Devils. J. Whiting
Diary of a madman. N. V. Gogol
Do you know the Milky way? K. Wittlinger
Dr Faustus. See Tragical historie of Dr Faustus, below
Doll's house. H. Ibsen
Doubletalk. L. J. Carlino
Dragon. E. Schwarz
Dutchman. L. Jones
Dybbuk. S. Ansky
Dylan. S. Michaels
Electra. Sophocles
Emperor. H. Gressieker
Enter laughing. J. Stein
Eternal Sabbath. M. Drahos
Entertaining Mr Sloane. J. Orton
Exit the king. E. Ionesco
Fairy tales of New York. J. P. Donleavy
Firebugs. M. Frisch
First. W. Holt
Five evenings. A. Volodin
Funnyhouse of a Negro. A. Kennedy
Ginger man. J. P. Donleavy
Glass menagerie. T. Williams
Have I got a girl for you! I. Cooper
Hay fever. N. Coward
Helen. W. Gray
Her master's voice. C. Kummer
Heroine. F. Tarloff
Hey you, light man. O. Hailey
Hidden stranger. M. Maltz
Der hofmeister. B. Brecht
Hughie. E. G. O'Neill
I got shoes. F. Merlin
I was dancing. E. O'Connor
Il faut passer par les nuages. F. Billetdoux
Immoralist. A. Goetz and R. Goetz
Importance of being earnest. O. Wilde
Impromptu at Versailles. J. B. P. Molière
In the J. Robert Oppenheimer affair. H. Kipphardt
In the counting house. L. Weiner
In white America. M. B. Duberman
Incident at Vichy. A. Miller
Irish Faustus. L. Durrell
Irregular verb to love. H. Williams and M. Williams
Les jouets. G. Michel
Journey to the day. R. O. Hirson
Just wild about Harry. H. Miller
Kiss mama. G. Panetta
Knack. A. Jellicoe
Lady of the camellias. G. Cooper and T. McNally
Last analysis. S. Bellow
Last minstrel. L. Yerby
Laundry. D. Guerdon
Lesson. E. Ionesco

DRAMAS—Criticisms, plots, etc.—Single works —*Continued*
Life is a dream. P. Calderón de la Barca
Lion in love. S. Delaney
Little Eyolf. H. Ibsen
Lord Pengo. S. N. Behrman
Lorenzo. J. Richardson
Love nest. D. Washburn
Lover. H. Pinter
Lower depths. M. Gorky
Luther. J. Osborne
Luv. M. Schisgal
Maids. J. Genêt
Man and boy. T. Rattigan
Man and Superman. G. B. Shaw
Man's a man. B. Brecht
Marathon '33. J. Havoc
Marco millions. E. G. O'Neill
Le mariage de Figaro. P. A. C. Beaumarchais
Marriage of Figaro. See Le mariage de Figaro, above
Matter of life and death. J. Cromwell
Milk train doesn't stop here any more. T. Williams
Mr Grossman. S. Koven
Mr Simian. S. Kerman
Mrs Warren's profession. G. B. Shaw
Month in the country. I. S. Turgenev
More stately mansions. E. G. O'Neill
Mother Courage and her children. B. Brecht
Moumou. See Pajama tops, below
Music at midnight. F. Buchman.
My kinsman, Major Molineux. See Old Glory, below
My mother, my father and me. L. Hellman
Natural affection. W. Inge
Next time I'll sing to you. J. Saunders
Nobody loves an albatross. R. Alexander
Oh les beaux jours. S. Beckett
Oh, what a lovely war. J. Littlewood
Old Glory. R. Lowell
One flew over the cuckoo's nest. D. Wasserman
Opening night. J. Cromwell
Owl and the pussycat. B. Manhoff
P.S. I love you. L. Roman
Pajama tops. M. Green and E. Feilbert
Passage through the clouds. See Il faut passer par les nuages, above
Passion of Josef D. P. Chayefsky
Pedestrian. See World of Ray Bradbury, below
Pedestrian of the air. E. Ionesco
Persecution and assassination of Marat as performed by the inmates of the asylum of Charenton under the direction of the Marquis de Sade. P. Weiss
Peterpat. E. Rudd
Photo finish. P. Ustinov
Physicists. F. Dürrenmatt
Play. S. Beckett
Play with a tiger. D. Lessing
Poor Bitos. J. Anouilh
Poor Richard. J. Kerr
Private ear. P. Shaffer
Proxy. See Der stellvertreter, below
Public eye. P. Shaffer
Pygmalion. G. B. Shaw
Rainy day in Newark. H. Teichmann
Rattle of a simple man. C. Dyer
Ready when you are C.B.! S. Slade
Recruiting officer. G. Farquhar
Rehearsal. J. Anouilh
Right you are if you think you are. L. Pirandello
Riot act. W. Greene
Riverside drive. J. Donovan
Room. H. Pinter
Royal gambit. H. Gressieker
Royal hunt of the sun. P. Shaffer
Saint Joan. G. B. Shaw
Save me a place at Forest Lawn. L. Yerby
Saving grace. E. H. Blum
Scapin. J. B. P. Molière
School for scandal. R. B. B. Sheridan
Seize the day. M. Otis
Semi-detached. D. Turner
Severed head. I. Murdoch and J. B. Priestley
Shout from the rooftops. J. Gregg
Sign in Sidney Brustein's window. L. Hansberry
Six characters in search of an author. L. Pirandello
Slave. L. Jones
Slight ache. H. Pinter
Slow dance on the killing ground. W. Hanley
Sponge room. K. Waterhouse and W. Hall
Sponono. A. Paton and K. Shah
Spoon River. C. Aidman
Squat Betty. K. Waterhouse and W. Hall
Der stellvertreter. See Deputy, above
Strange interlude. E. G. O'Neill
Subject was roses. F. D. Gilroy
Summer of Daisy Miller. B. Greene
Tambourines to glory. L. Hughes
Tartuffe. J. B. P. Molière
Telemachus Clay. L. J. Carlino
Theatre of Peretz. I. Sheffer
Thistle in my bed. G. Powers
Three sisters. A. P. Chekhov
Tiger. M. Schisgal
Tiger, tiger, burning bright. P. S. Feibleman
Time of the key. M. Erskine
Tiny Alice. E. Albee
To the Chicago abyss. See World of Ray Bradbury, below
Toilet. L. Jones
Too much Johnson. W. Gillette
Too true to be good. G. B. Shaw
Tragical historie of Dr Faustus. C. Marlowe
Traveller without luggage. J. Anouilh
Trojan women. Euripides
Tutor. See Der hofmeister, above
Typists. M. Schisgal
Uncle Vanya. A. P. Chekhov
Veldt. See World of Ray Bradbury, below
Vicar. See Der stellvertreter, above
Victims of duty. E. Ionesco
Victor. R. Vitrac
La vida es sueño. See Life is a dream, above
Volpone. B. Jonson
Walk in darkness. W. Hairston
War and peace. A. Neumann and others
What happened. G. Stein
White House. A. E. Hotchner
Who's afraid of Virginia Woolf? E. Albee
World of Ray Bradbury. R. Bradbury
Zoo story. E. Albee

DRAMATIC art. See Acting

DRAMATIC criticism
Critics and creators. I. Brown. Sat R 46:11-13+ Ag 10 '63
Critic's credo. H. Clurman. Nation 199:120-2, 147-8 S 14-21 '64
Critics; TV or not TV. G. Spelvin. il Theatre Arts 47:64-5 Ap '63
Drama beyond the drama: first-night vigil. A. Levy. il N Y Times Mag p 12+ D 22 '63
Theater of the undiscussable. W. Sheed. Commonweal 81:454-5 D 25 '64
See also
Moving picture plays—Criticisms, plots, etc.

DRAMATIC production. See Theatrical production

DRAMATIC production (in prison) See Prison recreation

DRAMATIC readings
Broadway postscript; Hollow crown. H. Hewes. Sat R 46:25 F 16 '63
Cavalcade of kings: Hollow crown. Time 81:56 F 8 '63
Liz and Dick put iambics in the big time. T. Prideaux. Life 57:12 Jl 24 '64
Off Broadway; Brontës. E. Oliver. New Yorker 39:61-2 Ja 4 '64
Off Broadway; Paul Shyre's oral adaptation of S. O'Casey's I knock at the door. E. Oliver. New Yorker 40:88+ D 5 '64
Off Broadway; Paul Shyre's oral adaptation of S. O'Casey's Pictures in the hallway. E. Oliver. New Yorker 40:52-3 D 26 '64
Off Broadway; Place for chance. E. Oliver. New Yorker 40:134+ My 23 '64
Off Broadway; Worlds of William Shakespeare. E. Oliver. New Yorker 39:80+ D 14 '63
Openings. New York; Hollow crown. A. Pryce-Jones. Theatre Arts 47:64 Mr '63
Regal revue; Hollow crown. Newsweek 61:84 F 11 '63
Something to write home about; E. Taylor and R. Burton do a poetry reading. il Time 84:62 Jl 3 '64
Theatre; Hollow crown. H. Clurman. Nation 196:146-8 F 16 '63
Theatre: Hollow crown. J. McCarten. New Yorker 38:66 F 9 '63

DRAMATICS for children. See Childrens plays

DRAMATISTS
Playwright and the contemporary world. J. Gassner. Theatre Arts 48:22-3+ Ja '64

DRAMATISTS, American
Five playwrights talk about how they got there. L. Lerman. pors Mlle 56:170-1+ Mr '63
Where are the new playwrights? waiting. H. Clurman. il N Y Times Mag p26-7+ Je 7 '64
See also
Albee, E.
Jones, L.
O'Neill, E. G.

DRAMATISTS, English
See also
Marlowe, C.
Osborne, J.
Wesker, A.

DRAMATISTS, French
See also
Corneille, P.
Duras, M.
Genêt, J.

DRAMATISTS, German
See also
Brecht, B.
DRAMATISTS conferences. See Authors conferences
DRAMATIZATION in education
Children look at their own behavior. R. Lippitt and others. il NEA J 53:14-16 S '64
Role-playing in comparing communism to democracy. E. M. McCoy. il Sr Schol 83: 15T O 18 '63
DRAMATIZATION of history
See also
Son et lumière (sound and light)
DRANSFELD, Klaus
Kilomegacycle ultrasonics; with biographical sketch. Sci Am 208:28, 60-8 bibliog(p 183) Je '63
DRAPELA, Ernest
Identification. Recreation 57:196-7 Ap '64
DRAPER, Hal
Librarian vs. scholar-user. por Library J 89:1907-10 My 1 '64
DRAPER, L.
Highest waves ever seen; reprint. Sci Digest 56:59-61 N '64
DRAPER, Paul
Tap series. See issues of Dance magazine to September, 1963
about
Sophie Maslow dance company: Paul Draper at Delacorte theater. D. Hering. Dance Mag 37:14 Ag '63
DRAPER, Theodore
Castro, Khrushchev, and Mao. Reporter 29: 27-31 Ag 15 '63
Five years of Castro's Cuba. bibliog f Commentary 37:25-37 Ja; 12+ My '64
DRAPER, V. M.
Gone flying to Minnesota. Flying 74:28-32+ Je '64
Used aircraft pilot report; Stinson. Flying 75: 71-2+ S '64
DRAPER catalogue. See Stars—Spectra
DRAPERIES. See Curtains and draperies
DRAW poker. See Poker
DRAWERS
Cabinet with spillproof drawers. W. Luxenburg. il Pop Sci 184:148 Mr '64
Family room wall of convenient places for everything. il Bet Hom & Gard 41:56 S '63
DRAWING
Directional line drawing for senior high school students. F. Snider. il Sch Arts 64: 18-19 Ja '65
Drawing & painting after dark. J. S. Walsh. il Am Artist 27:36-41+ Mr '63
Editorial; science drawing. B. R. SerVaas. Design 66:4 S '64
Hands are for drawing. M. Smith. il Sch Arts 63:21 F '64
Kalman Aron, draughtsman. J. Lovoos. il Am Artist 28:30-5+ Mr '64
Line; excerpt from Drawing lessons from the great masters. R. B. Hale. il Am Artist 29:58-63 Ja '65
Making numerous drawings of one subject. N. Kent. il Am Artist 28:56-61+ Je '64
Quick line sketching. Design 64:109 Ja '63
Sketching tour of France. J. Nielsen. il Am Artist 28:20-5+ Ap '64
Some notes on drawing. H. Breverman. il Am Artist 28:36-41+ Ja '64
Value of independent drawing. D. R. Smiton. il Am Artist 28:52-7 N '64
See also
Architectural drawing
Brush drawing
Figure drawing
Pastel drawing
Pen drawing
Scratchboard drawing
Wash drawing

Study and teaching

Bernard Garbutt, animal draughtsman. J. Lovoos. il Am Artist 27:53-7+ F '63
Drawing. J. Stoops. il Sch Arts 63:29-31 Je '64
Drawing issue; symposium. il Sch Arts 62:2 Je '63
Expressive line and form. E. G. Snellenberger. il Design 66:42-3 S '64
Joy. M. Luman. il Sch Arts 62:5-6 Ap '63
Notes on drawing. R. Wise. il Sch Arts 63: 32-5 Je '64
Teaching drawing at the college level. B. Clements and C. Clements. il Sch Arts 63:31-2 N '63
DRAWING, Childrens. See Childrens art
DRAWING, Mechanical. See Mechanical drawing
DRAWING and quartering; story. See Kingston, J.
DRAWING instruments
Three-dimensions on the double; automatic perspective translator and perspective drafting machine. L. W. Luce. il Pop Mech 119: 114-15+ F '63
DRAWING room practice
No finger guides the roving pen; numerically controlled drafting machines. il Bsns W p 100 Mr 7 '64
DRAWINGS
Art; exhibition of drawings by G. C. Bingham at Knoedler's. H. Kramer. Nation 196: 212-13 Mr 9 '63
Art in the stroke of a pen. J. Canaday. il N Y Times Mag p20-1 Jl 26 '64
At home through the ages; excerpts from Les styles. P. Julian. il Horizon 5:80-3 Mr '63
Contemporary drawing. G. Pappas. il Sch Arts 62:44 Je '63
Drawings by George Romney at Yale. E. Sharp. il Antiques 86:598-603 N '64
Drawings of Ben Solowey. H. C. Pitz. il Am Artist 27:26-31 My '63
Drawings of Nicholas Solovinoff. L. Hanson. il Am Artist 28:28-33+ O '64
Modigliani, master draughtsman. A. Werner. il Am Artist 28:18-23+ F '64
Portfolio of drawings by Charles Schorre. il Am Artist 27:30-5 N '63
Portfolio of drawings by Paul Hogarth. N. Kent. il Am Artist 27:42-7+ Ap '63
Recently acquired European drawings; Metropolitan museum of art. Hobbies 68:92 Ag '63
Sequential drawing and the generation of visual ideas. P. Edmonston. il Sch Arts 63: 29-32 O '63
Sketching tour of France. J. Nielsen. il Am Artist 28:20-5+ Ap '64
Traveling in Europe with a sketchbook. H. C. Pitz. il Am Artist 27:30-5+ Ap '63
See also
Drawing

Exhibitions

Artists' paper work; American drawings at Guggenheim museum. il N Y Times Mag p 142-3 S 13 '64
Autumn at the Guggenheim. M. Kozloff. Nation 199:204 O 5 '64
Chicago: something ventured something gained; master drawings from the Art institute of Chicago, exhibited at Wildenstein's New York gallery. K. Kuh. Sat R 46:25-7 N 23 '63
Folio of master drawings; on view at Wildenstein's. B. O'Doherty. il N Y Times Mag p30-1 O 13 '63
Il bon disegno from Chicago; Art institute's acquisitions exhibited in New York. A. Frankfurter. il Art N 62:28-31+ N '63
Master drawings; exhibitions at the Guggenheim museum and the Wildenstein gallery in N.Y. city. B. Kaufman. Commonweal 79:411 D 27 '63
Venice, the eternal fantasy; drawings on loan from Venice's Correr museum. J. Canaday. il N Y Times Mag p70-1 O 27 '63
DRAY, Robert
Howland success! H. L. Masin. il por Sr Schol 84:22 F 28 '64
DREAMS
Accelerated dreams may prevent behavior change. Sci N L 87:40 Ja 16 '65
Alcohol and caffeine: effect on inferred visual dreaming. S. C. Gresham and others. bibliog il Science 140:1226-7 Je 14 '63
Carol's dream. il Esquire 63:58-9 Ja '65
Does poison make us dream? il Sci Digest 55:39-40 Mr '64
Sleep and wakefulness, by N. Kleitman. Review
Time il 83:44-6 F 14 '64
Sleep pattern of tooth-grinding: its relationship to dreaming. G. R. Reding and others. bibliog il Science 145:725-6 Ag 14 '64
Was Freud wrong about dreams? F. R. Schreiber and M. Herman. il Sci Digest 56: 19-23 Jl '64
See also
Daydreams
Psychoanalysis

Quotations, maxims, etc.

Realm of dreams; comp. by E. F. Murphy. il N Y Times Mag p50-1 Ja 5 '64
To sleep, perchance to analyze; comp. by R. Block. il N Y Times Mag p 10+ Ja 10 '65
DREBINGER, John
Drebby and Dan. por Newsweek 63:54 Ap 13 '64
Long seasons. por Time 83:53 Ap 10 '64

DRED Scott case
Black pawn on a field of peril. B. Catton. il Am Heritage 15:66-71+ D '63
DREDGING
Triple-benefit waterfront projects; Suffolk County, N.Y. H. L. Dennison. il Am City 78:110-12 Mr '63
See also
Lakes—Clearing
DREHER, Carl
Atomic power; the fear and the promise. Nation 198:289-93 Mr 23 '64
Big atom; solving the water shortage. Nation 197:451-4 D 28 '63; Same abr. with title A-power can end the water shortage. Sci Digest 56:57-60 Ag '64
Epochal leap to vacuum. Nation 196:330-1 Ap 20 '63
Martyrs on the moon? Harper 226:33-8 Mr '63
Science explosion. Nation 197:14-16 Jl 6 '63
Science talks about peace. Nation 197:31-3 Jl 13 '63
Two-way radio for everyman. Atlan 214:168+ N '64
What the Russians remember. Nation 196:208-10 Mr 9 '63
DREIKURS, Rudolf, and Soltz, Vicki
Your child and discipline; excerpts from Children: the challenge. NEA J 54:32-47 Ja '65
DREIS, D. David
Writing for trade magazines. Writer 77:25-6 N '64
DREISER, Theodore
Dreiser and the Tragedy. I. Howe. New Repub 151:25-8 Ag 22 '64
Stature of Theodore Dreiser. I. Howe. New Repub 151:19-21 Jl 25 '64
DRENNAN, Henry T.
Metropolitan public libraries in the sixties. bibliog Library J 89:67-70 Ja 1 '64
(ed) War on poverty. Library J 89:340-74+ S 15 '64
—and others
Full range of weapons. por Library J 89:3266-73 S 15 '64
DRESDEN
Air raids
Apocalypse at Dresden. R. H. S. Crossman. Esquire 60:149-52+ N '63; Discussion. 61:124-6 F '64
Destruction of Dresden, by D. Irving. Review
Commonweal 80:376 Je 12 '64. J. W. Douglass
Nation 198:243-4 Mr 9 '64. W. Miller
Newsweek il 63:85-6 Mr 2 '64
DRESS. See Clothing and dress; Costume
DRESS accessories
See also
Collars
DRESS design. See Costume design
DRESS designers. See Costume designers
DRESS shoes. See Shoes
DRESSED pictures. See Pictures
DRESSELHAUS, Mildred S. See Kolm, H. H. jt. auth.
DRESSER, Davis
WLB biography. R. Shor. por Wilson Lib Bul 38:202 O '63
DRESSER, William T.
Design for multiple use. Am For 70:12-15 Jl '64
DRESSING, Poultry. See Cookery—Poultry
DRESSING of game. See Game, Dressing of
DRESSING tables
If you plan a dressing room. il Sunset 131:159-60 N '63
DRESSINGS (surgery) See Surgical dressings
DRESSMAKING
Be knowing about sewing! C. D. Legg. il Farm J 88:71 Je '64
Dressmaker touches. il Farm J 87:68 S '63
Easy-care fabrics for spring sewing. C. D. Legg. il Farm J 87:86-8 Ap '63
I sewed my way through college; Aneth Marcy, Sterling college, Sterling, Kan. il Suc Farm 61:96 Mr '63
Now the sew-it-yourself boom. S. Wright. il N Y Times Mag p 19+ Mr 8 '64
Sew a shift for spring. il Ebony 18:142-3 My '63
DRESSNER, Howard R.
Get your work done faster. Nations Bsns 51:58-60+ My '63
How to handle a bigger job. Nations Bsns 51:68-71 Ag '63
DREW, Cornelius J.
Cardinal in Harlem. America 109:86 Jl 27 '63
DREW, Elizabeth Brenner
Civil-rights maze. Reporter 31:12-14 D 17 '64
Gun law that didn't go off. Reporter 31:33-5 O 8; 8 N 5 '64
Mr Passman meets his match. Reporter 31:40-3 N 19 '64
Politics of cloture. Reporter 31:19-23 Jl 16 '64
DREW, M. E.
Fragment; poem. McCalls 90:174 S '63
Pushover; poem. McCalls 91:142 F '64
DREWS, Elizabeth Monroe
Your child's intelligence: reprint. Todays Health 41:70 Jl '63
DREXEL institute of technology, Philadelphia
School of library science
Drexel library school issues five-year progress report. Library J 88:2260 Jl '63
DREXLER, Arthur
Disappearing object. Sat R 47:13-15 My 23 '64
DREXLER, Rosalyn
Tabloid universe. il por Newsweek 63:53 Mr 30 '64
Three more faces of Eve; exhibition at the Kornblee gallery, New York. L. Campbell. il Art N 63:30-1+ Mr '64
DREXLER, Sherman
Short, cool summer at the colony. pors Art N 63:37-9+ D '64
DREYFUS, Jack
Dreyfus case; with editorial comment. J. D. Brown. il por Sports Illus 20:4, 62-4+ Mr 30 '64
DREYFUS, John
IPEX: machines and techniques. Pub W 184:78+ S 9 '63
P. J. Conkwright and University press book design; excerpt. Pub W 183:78+ Mr 4 '63
DRIBERG, Tom
Member for barking. New Yorker 40:26-8 Ja 23 '65
DRICKAMER, H. G.
Pressure and electronic structure. bibliog Science 142:1429-35 D 13 '63
—See Aust, R. B; Stager, R. A. jt. auths.
DRIED bouquets. See Flowers, Dried
DRIED flowers. See Flowers, Dried
DRIED fruit. See Fruit, Dried
DRIED meat. See Meat, Dried
DRIED potatoes. See Potatoes, Dried
DRIESELL, Charles G.
Five tall strangers shoot 'em up; Davidson's basketball team. B. Ottum. il Sports Illus 20:12-13 Ja 13 '64
DRIFTERS. See Unemployables
DRIFTING of continents. See Continental drift
DRIFTWOOD
Driftwood fantasies. E. Wahleen. il Am For 69:15 My '63
Finding and finishing driftwood. Sunset 133:133-4+ N '64
Look what you can do with driftwood. D. Shiner. il Design 65:210-11 My '64
DRILL press. See Drilling and boring machinery
DRILL press vises. See Vises
DRILLING and boring (earth and rocks)
How to break the crust and come back again; needle reactor. il Time 83:75 Ja 10 '64
See also
Mohole project
DRILLING and boring (woodwork)
Big holes, little holes, now you can drill 'em all! S. M. Gallagher. il Pop Sci 185:134-6 Jl '64
DRILLING and boring machinery
Before you buy a portable drill. H. Steinberg. Am Home 67:86+ Ja '64
Big holes, little holes, now you can drill 'em all! S. M. Gallagher. il Pop Sci 185:134-6 Jl '64
Cordless drills. il Hot Rod 17:32-3 Mr '64
Cut the best of circles with a drill press. D. G. Waggoner. il Pop Sci 185:132 Ag '64
Disston variable speed drill. il Consumer Rep 29:54-5 F '64
Disston's dial-a-power drill. R. J. De Cristoforo. il Pop Sci 182:153-5 Ap '63
Drill press; also a sander, shaper, and router. il Pop Sci 183:166-7 N '63
Drills for digging deepest hole yet; Mohole equipment. il Bsns W p44+ D 19 '64
Electric drill. il Pop Sci 183:156+ D '63
Electronic drill-press drive. F. L. Greenwald. il Pop Mech 121:188-93 F '64
Greater power for a small drill. il Consumer Rep 29:516 N '64

DRILLING and boring machinery—*Continued*
How to break the crust and come back again; needle reactor. il Time 83:75 Ja 10 '64
Two new drills: tough and trigger-happy. S. M. Gallager. il Pop Sci 185:178-9 O '64
DRILLING rigs, Oil well. See Oil well drilling rigs
DRILLS (machinery) See Drilling and boring machinery
DRILLS, Air raid. See Air raids—Protective measures
DRINAN, Robert Frederic
Can public funds be constitutionally granted to private schools? address, January 9, 1963. Vital Speeches 29:273-8 F 15 '63
Counseling for Catholics. America 109:209 Ag 31 '63
Equality in education; address, November 2, 1963. Vital Speeches 30:223-4 Ja 15 '64
Excerpt from article in Boston Sunday globe, June 14, 1964. Cong Digest 43:285+ N '64
Racial balance in schools. America 110:158-60 F 1 '64
Religious freedom in Israel. America 108:456-7 Ap 6 '63
Should public funds aid parochial schools? por Parents Mag 38:70-1+ N '63
State and federal aid to parochial schools; address, April 24, 1964. Vital Speeches 30:559-62 Jl 1 '64
Television in the courtroom: no. America 112:73+ Ja 16 '65
DRINK question. See Alcoholism; Liquor problem; Temperance
DRINKING, Social. See Liquor problem
DRINKING and traffic accidents
Crash echoes across the Nation. il Life 55:22-7 Jl 19 '63
Morning after; films of driver taking sobriety tests. il Time 82:61 N 22 '63
Night of the teen-ager; debutante's party in Darien, Conn. il Time 84:61-2 O 16 '64
DRINKING customs
English drinking habits. R. Postgate. il Holiday 33:87-8+ F '63
Hosts with the most toasts; Georgian republic. R. Brigham. il Life 55:123-6 S 13 '63
Thirsty Europeans. Sci Digest 56:26 O '64
DRINKING vessels
Newly discovered Amelung tumbler at Corning museum. il Hobbies 69:76 S '64
DRINKS. See Beverages; Liquors
DRIPPS, Robert D.
Pharmacology of general anesthetic agents. Science 140:1247 Je 14 '63
DRIPSTONES. See Stalactites
DRISCOLL, Giovanna
On the death of a hermit saint; poem. Commonweal 81:449 D 25 '64
DRISCOLL, John P.
Irish film society. America 108:660 My 11 '63
DRISKILL hotel. See Austin, Tex.—Hotels, restaurants, etc.
DRIVE-in and curb services
Ultimate drive-in; San Francisco's Hilton hotel. il Time 83:50 My 29 '64
DRIVE-in moving picture theaters. See Moving picture theaters, Open air
DRIVER, Tom F.
Arthur Miller's pilgrimage. Reporter 30:46+ F 27 '64
As flies to wanton boys. Reporter 28:44-6 Mr 14 '63
Going through the motions. Reporter 29:53 N 21 '63
I know not seems. Reporter 30:43-4 My 21 '64
Man of the theater. Christian Cent 81:484-5 Ap 15 '64
Meaning of silence. Reporter 30:40+ Ap 9 '64
Spiritual diabolism of Jean Genet. Christian Cent 80:1433-5 N 20 '63
Week of despondency. Christian Cent 80:239-41 F 20 '63
What's the matter with Edward Albee? Reporter 30:38-9 Ja 2 '64
DRIVER, William J.
People of the week. por U S News 58:15 Ja 11 '65
DRIVER training courses. See Automobile driving—Study and teaching
DRIVES (money raising) See Fund raising
DRIVESHAFTS. See Automobiles—Propeller shafts
DRIVEWAYS
Building of a country road. il Sunset 132:140+ Ap '64
Make your drive and motor court interesting. il House B 105:166-7+ My '63
Planting for a turncourt. R. S. Maxwell. il Flower Grower 51:29 O '64
Solve that off-street parking problem. il Pop Gard 15:40-1 F '64
DRIVING, Automobile. See Automobile driving

DROMEDARY project. See Airplanes, Experimental
DRONE airplanes. See Airplanes, Drone
DROP forging. See Forging
DROPOUTS, College; Dropouts, High school. See Student withdrawals
DROPPING-mercury electrode. See Electrodes
DROSOPHILA
Beta-alanine utilization of ebony and non-ebony drosophila melanogaster. M. E. Jacobs and K. K. Brubaker. bibliog il Science 139:1282-3 Mr 29 '63
Chromosome puffs in drosophila induced by ribonuclease. F. M. Ritossa and R. C. Von Borstel. bibliog il Science 145:513-14 Jl 31 '64
Courtship sound production in two sympatric sibling drosophila species. I. Waldron. bibliog il Science 144:191-3 Ap 10 '64
Culture of embryonic cells of drosophila melanogaster in vitro. M. Horikawa and A. S. Fox. il Science 145:1437-9 S 25 '64
Interference between sex-ratio agents of drosophila willistoni and drosophila nebulosa. B. Sakaguchi and others. bibliog il Science 147:160-2 Ja 8 '65
Mutations: incidence in drosophila melanogaster reared on irradiated medium. M. S. Swaminathan and others. bibliog il Science 141:637-8 Ag 16 '63
Xanthine dehydrogenase: differences in activity among drosophila strains. E. C. Keller, jr. and E. Glassman. bibliog il Science 143:40-1 Ja 6 '64
Xanthine dehydrogenase in drosophila: detection of isozymes. K. D. Smith and others. bibliog il Science 142:226-7 O 11 '63
DROUGHTS
As drought became disaster. il U S News 57:8 N 23 '64
As the drought got worse and worse. il U S News 55:12 O 28 '63
Big drought of 1964: where it hit, how much it hurt; with interview with J. M. Mitchell, jr. il U S News 57:52-5 N 30 '64
Down to a trickle; eight-month-old drought in Hong Kong. Newsweek 61:48 My 27 '63
Drought: growing U.S. problem. il U S News 57:92 N 16 '64
Fire watch in a dry, dry woodland; east of the Mississippi River. C. Phinizy. il Sports Illus 19:22-4 N 4 '63
Land goes thirsty. il Bsns W p31 N 2 '63
Man-made drouth threatens Everglades National Park. V. O. Williams. il Audubon Mag 65:290-4 S '63
Parched; drought in US. il Newsweek 62:69 N 4 '63
Spring drouth hurts Northeast. B. Hardy. Farm J 87:31 Je '63
Too few ill winds for our own good. il Bsns W p 170-1 N 21 '64
When the wind blew black blizzards. A. Balk. il N Y Times Mag p98-101 N 10 '63
Wrung out; widespread drought in US. il Newsweek 64:37-8 N 23 '64
DROWNED man; story. See Brennan, M.
DROWNING
Life after drowning; case of Roger Arntsen of Norway. il Time 81:66 My 31 '63
Swimming safety. C. J. Potthoff. Todays Health 41:56 Jl '63
DROWNPROOFING. See Swimming—Safety devices and measures
DRUCKER, Peter F.
Automation is not the villain. N Y Times Mag p26-7+ Ja 10 '65
Big power of little ideas; excerpts from Managing for results: economic tasks and risk-taking decisions. Harvard Bsns R 42:6-8+ My '64
Care and feeding of the profitable product; excerpts from Managing for results: economic tasks and risk-taking decisions. Fortune 69:133-5 Mr '64
Find your company's hidden strength. Nations Bsns 52:80-2+ Mr '64
If I were a company president. Harper 228:16+ Ap '64
Japan tries for a second miracle. Harper 226:72-8 Mr '63; Same abr. Read Digest 82:181-2+ Je '63
Managing for business effectiveness. Harvard Bsns R 41:53-60 My '63
Martyrs unlimited. Harper 229:12+ Jl '64
Meet tomorrow's customer. Nations Bsns 51:102-4+ Je '63
Twelve fables of research management. Harvard Bsns R 41:103-8 Ja '63

about

Peter Drucker: troubleshooter at the top. P. Korenvaes. Duns R 84:43+ Jl '64

DRUG habit. See Narcotic habit

DRUG labels. See Labels

DRUG laws and legislation
Annals of legislation; background and history of Drug industry antitrust bill. R. Harris. New Yorker 40:48-50+ Mr 14; 75-6+ Mr 21; 46-8+ Mr 28 '64
Change ahead in rules for sale of drugs. U S News 56:6 Mr 9 '64
Drug makers vs. review; legal definitions of old and new drugs. Sci N L 86:94 Ag 8 '64
Effect of drug price drop; Colombia's new law. F. Marley. Sci N L 84:247 O 19 '63
Kefauver's last interview. B. H. Frisch. il Sci Digest 54:10-18 N '63
Laws alone can't make drugs safe. L. Lessing. il Fortune 67:122-5+ Mr '63
Safety & effectiveness; requirements of Drug amendments act, 1962. Time 83:82 Mr 13 '64
See also
Narcotic laws
United States—Food and drug administration

DRUG plants. See Botany, Medical

DRUG research. See Pharmaceutical research

DRUG trade
Bayer bounces back; Germany's Bayer farbenfabriken. Time 82:102 S 13 '63
Drug makers launch fight on prominence FDA seeks for generic names on labels. Bsns W p60 S 14 '63
Drug safety. Consumer Rep 28:134-7 Mr '63
Drugs & pills, no prescription needed. il Changing T 17:12-14 O '63
Ethical problem; low-cost drug-marketing. il Newsweek 62:78 S 23 '63
FTC's new threat is compulsory licensing; makers of tetracycline guilty of price-fixing. Bsns W p27 Ag 17 '63
FDA: drug agency answers critics by attempting to step up science, but many critical problems remain. E. Langer. Science 142:1280-2 D 6 '63
FDA: trouble-ridden medical unit gets new director after 2-year search to fill difficult position. E. Langer. Science 143:1018-19 Mr 6 '64
High cost of fair trade. J. Duscha. Reporter 30:29-30 Mr 12 '64
Human guinea pigs and the law. J. Lear; discussion. Sat R 46:58-9 F 2 '63
In the black; aid in ransoming Bay of Pigs prisoners. Time 81:16 Mr 29 '63
Kefauver's reward. Nation 198:23 Ja 6 '64
New drug story in Washington. H. H. Miller il New Repub 149:33-5 N 9 '63
Patents and pirates; Italy. il Fortune 67:94+ My '63
Pooling drug research; Interpharm GmbH & co. il Bsns W p66-8+ O 26 '63
Problems of drug development. L. Lasagna. Science 145:362-7 Jl 24 '64; Discussion. 145:1258; 146:717 S 18, N 6 '64
Producers declare war over a wonder drug; suit against McKesson & Robbins. Bsns W p26 Ag 15 '64
Psychotoxic drugs: Dodd bill passes Senate, comes to rest in the House; critics are sharpening their knives. J. Walsh. Science 145:1418-20 S 25 '64
Real voice, by R. Harris. Review
Nation 199:166-8 S 28 '64. E. Langer
New Repub 151:25-6 S 5 '64. G. W. Johnson
Tangled trail of tetracycline. il Bsns W p90-1+ D 5 '64
Tetracycline tangle; legal side-effects. il Newsweek 64:64-5 Ag 31 '64
That uneasy feeling. il Time 84:91-2 S 4 '64
Threats to the battle against disease. J. Daniel. il Read Digest 85:114-18 O '64
Untranquilized drug makers. W. Guzzardi, jr. il Fortune 68:124-8+ D '63
See also
Government investigations—Drug trade
Miles laboratories, incorporated
Richardson-Merrell, incorporated

Advertising

Case of the substituted drug. J. Lear. Sat R 47:62 N 7 '64
Drugs and doctors. Nation 199:130 S 21 '64
Ethical drug ads. America 108:520 Ap 20 '63

Laws and legislation

See Drug laws and legislation

Securities

Look at the drug stocks for the long and the short term. il Duns R 84:81-2+ Ag '64

DRUGS
Aspirin jungle. B. Inglis. Nation 197:83-6 Ag 24 '63; Reply with rejoinder. G. S. Meister. 197:inside cover S 14 '63
Body's response to drugs may depend on timing. Sci N L 83:136 Mr 2 '63
Drug for urinary infection; NegGram antibacterial drug. F. Marley. Sci N L 85:211 Ap 4 '64
Drug-of-the month club. Sci Digest 54:65 D '63
Drug to replace morphine; Win 20,228. F. Marley. Sci N L 84:131 Ag 31 '63
Drugs & pills, no prescription needed. il Changing T 17:12-14 O '63
Drugs conquer fungus; tolnaftate thiabendazole. Sci N L 86:291 N 7 '64
Drugs; how safe is safe enough? new medical director of the U.S. Food and drug administration. W. R. Young. il Life 57:37-40 Jl 3 '64
Drugs worth risk-taking. Sci N L 85:180 Mr 21 '64
God's own; pentazocine. Newsweek 62:71 S 23 '63
Impurities in pure biochemicals; letter. D. Freifelder. Science 144:1087+ My 29 '64
Medical supplies and appliances. Consumer Rep 29:240-8 D '64
Mental care program calls on communities. il Bsns W p 104-6 F 9 '63
More buck for less bang; Bofors entry into pharmaceuticals. il Bsns W p 111+ O 26 '63
New drug for heart pain and irregularity. Sci N L 84:397 D 21 '63
New drug threat possible. F. Marley. Sci N L 84:3 Jl 6 '63
Qualms on new drug routine. Bsns W p66 Mr 7 '64
So simple, so treacherous; mislabeled drugs. T. Taylor. il Sat Eve Post 237:66-7 N 28 '64
Substitute for morphine; pentazocine. F. Marley. Sci N L 84:179 S 21 '63
Theory explains drug combination therapy. Sci N L 83:184 Mr 23 '63
Thirty leading drugs buried in medical time capsule. Sci N L 84:231 O 12 '63
Threats to the battle against disease. J. Daniel. il Read Digest 85:114-18 O '64
We can avoid another drug disgrace. A. S. Flemming. Good H 156:8 Je '63
What you should know about the drugs you take. R. E. Gosselin. Read Digest 82:99-102 Mr '63
Your self (cont) il Consumer Rep 28:31-79 D '63
See also
Antibiotics
Aspirin
Atromid S
Hallucinogenic drugs
Inositol
Medicines, Patent, proprietary, etc.
Methadone
Peyote
Pharmacopoeias
United States—Food and drug administration

Advertising

See Drug trade—Advertising

Contamination

Contamination of commercial rabbit albumin preparations by bovine albumin. W. D. Linscott. il Science 142:1170-2 N 29 '63
Hidden menace in nose drops. J. Orr. il Todays Health 42:24-5 D '64
Impure drug causes early sexual maturity. Sci N L 83:152 Mr 9 '63

Laws and legislation

See Drug laws and legislation

Manufacture

Tangled trail of tetracycline. il Bsns W p90-1+ D 5 '65

Physiological effects

Action of two drugs causes deformities. Sci N L 86:100 Ag 15 '64
Activity rhythm in peromyscus: its influence on rates of recovery from nembutal. S. T. Emlen and W. Kem. bibliog il Science 142:1682-3 D 27 '63
Anemic pregnant women warned about iron drug. Sci N L 84:120 Ag 24 '63
Brunettes turn blond after taking sedative; mephenesin carbamate. Sci N L 83:280 My 4 '63
Chemical mind-changers. R. Coughlan. il Life 54:81-2+ Mr 15 '63
Chloramphenicol in blood: simple chemical estimations in patients receiving multiple antibiotics. D. W. O. Hughes and L. K. Diamond. bibliog il Science 144:296-7 Ap 17 '64

DRUGS—Physiological effects—*Continued*
Cleft palate in the mouse: a teratogenic index of glucocorticoid potency. L. Pinsky and A. M. DiGeorge. bibliog il Science 147: 402-3 Ja 22 '65
Convulsant drug action on neuronally isolated cerebral cortex. B. Grafstein. bibliog il Science 142:973-5 N 15 '63
Dangers of modern medicine. Sci Digest 55:85-6 My '64
Dissociation and recovery of a response learned under the influence of chlorpromazine or saline. L. S. Otis. bibliog il Science 143:1347-8 Mr 20 '64
Drug administration to neonatal rats: effects on later emotionality and learning. R. D. Young. bibliog il Science 143:1055-7 Mr 6 '64
Drug-induced changes in the liver endoplasmic reticulum: association with drug-metabolizing enzymes. H. Remmer and H. J. Merker. bibliog il Science 142:1657-8 D 27 '63
Drugs in pregnancy & childhood; questions and answers. M. J. E. Senn. McCalls 91: 61+ Jl '64
Drugs worth risk-taking. Sci N L 85:180 Mr 21 '64
Fear and pain: their effect on self-injection of amobarbital sodium by rats. J. D. Davis and N. E. Miller. il Science 141:1286-7 S 27 '63
Genie escapes the bottle. A. Ogle. America 110:314 Mr 7 '64
Hazards of new drugs. W. Modell. bibliog Science 139:1180-5 Mr 22 '63
7-Hydroxychlorpromazine: potential toxic drug metabolite in psychiatric patients. T. L. Perry and others. bibliog il Science 146: 81-3 O 2 '64
Isolated mammalian eye: a method for quantitative evaluation of automatic drugs. W. T. Beaver. bibliog il Science 141:1274-5 S 27 '63
Medicine headache cause. Sci N L 84:258 O 26 '63
Merrell's bitter pill; anti-cholesterol drug, MER-29. Bsns W p23 D 28 '63
New problems for surgery; excerpts from address, December 30, 1963. F. D. Moore. Science 144:388-92 Ap 24 '64
Newborn attention as affected by medication during labor. G. Stechler. bibliog il Science 144:315-17 Ap 17 '64
Of cheese and tranquilizers. Pop Sci 184:22 Ja '64
Overdose of digitalis offset by citrate salts. Sci N L 84:34 Jl 20 '63
Pharmacology of individual neurons. G. C. Salmoiraghi and F. E. Bloom. bibliog il Science 144:493-9 My 1 '64
Photochemical action spectrum of the terminal oxidase of mixed function oxidase systems. D. Y. Cooper and others. bibliog il Science 147:400-2 Ja 22 '65
Placebo. J. P. Coogan. McCalls 92:68+ O '64
Purple heart drug; young addicts. Sci N L 85:402 Je 27 '64
Side effects: a new worry for doctors; iatrogenic diseases. M. M. Hunt. il Look 27:24-6+ D 31 '63
Stress modification of drug response. B. D. Rupe and others. bibliog il Science 141: 1186-7 S 20 '63
Thalidomide: effect upon pregnancy in the rhesus monkey. J. F. Lucey and R. E. Behrman. bibliog il Science 139:1295-6 Mr 29 '63
Thalidomide heroine seeks new culprits. Sci Digest 53:32 My '63
Thalidomide remembered; research into effects of drugs on embryonic opossums. Time 84:81 S 25 '64
Three beneficial drugs may cause other disease: lupus erythematosus. Sci N L 84: 18 Jl 13 '63
Tremorine: its effect on amines of the central nervous system. A. H. Friedman and others. bibliog il Science 141:1188-90 S 20 '63
Warning on drugs and driving. Consumer Rep 28:150 Ap '63
Women warned on drugs; pain-relieving drugs dangerous during pregnancy. F. Marley. Sci N L 86:130 Ag 29 '64
Wonder drugs, cure or . .? questions and answers. L. Galton. il Pop Sci 183:98-100+ N '63

Prices

Annals of legislation; background and history of Drug industry antitrust bill. R. Harris. New Yorker 40:48-50+ Mr 14; 75-6+ Mr 21; 46-8+ Mr 28 '64
Effect of drug price drop; Colombia's new law. F. Marley. Sci N L 84:247 O 19 '63
Producers declare war over a wonder drug; suit against McKesson & Robbins. Bsns W p26 Ag 15 '64
Tetracycline tangle; legal side-effects. il Newsweek 64:64-5 Ag 31 '64

Psychological effects

Behavioral pharmacology; report on annual meeting of the Behavioral pharmacology society. B. Weiss. Science 144:730-1 My 8 '64
Drugs affect learning. Sci N L 83:285 My 4 '63
Drugs and behavior; Behavioral pharmacology society. B. Weiss. Science 140:1109+ Je 7 '63
Drugs cause more loss of memory than shock. Sci N L 84:229 O 12 '63
Psychotoxic drugs: Dodd bill passes Senate, come to rest in the House; critics are sharpening their knives. J. Walsh. Science 145:1418-20 S 25 '64

Testing

Drug safety: industry-sponsored study commission recommends expansion research activities. E. Langer. il Science 145:1284-7 S 18 '64
Drug safety meeting; drug court planned; FDA rules and research discussed. Sci N L 84:21 Jl 13 '63
Drug tests behind bars; Upjohn and Parke-Davis labs in Jackson, Mich. prison. il Bsns W p58-60+ Je 27 '64
FDA probes popular drug: bonine. Sci N L 84:94 Ag 10 '63
Loss of good drugs seen. Sci N L 83:214 Ap 6 '63
New research on a stop smoking drug. il Good H 158:161 Mr '64
Problems of drug development. L. Lasagna. Science 145:362-7 Jl 24 '64; Discussion. 145:1258; 146:717 S 18, N 6 '64
Seek drug-review panels. Sci N L 85:321 Ap 11 '64
Testing. Newsweek 63:52 Mr 9 '64
Thalidomide: effects on Ehrlich ascites tumor cells in vitro. J. A. DiPaolo and C. E. Wenner. bibliog Science 144:1583 Je 26 '64
Toxicity, the therapeutic index, and the ranking of drugs. M. A. Schneiderman and others. bibliog il Science 144:1212-14 Je 5 '64
What to take for pain. B. H. Frisch. il Sci Digest 54:22-6 D '63

DRUGSTORES
Oldest U.S. drug store; Simon Rau & co, Bethlehem, Pa. il Travel 121:33-5 Je '64

DRUKKER, Leendert
Methods & materials. See issues of Popular photography

DRUM, Ryan W. and Pankratz, H. S.
Fine structure of a diatom centrosome. bibliog Science 142:61-3 O 4 '63

DRUM (periodical) See Periodicals—South Africa

DRUMFISH fishing
We beat our drums. G. Heinold. il Outdoor Life 131:66-7+ Ap '63

DRUMM, S. L.
War on prosperity; address, September 16, 1964. Vital Speeches 31:19-22 O 15 '64

DRUMMOND, Harold
Grouping; a preliminary statement. Sch Life 45:9-10 Je '63

DRUMMOND, Mary Hazel
Decorative indoor plants: bromeliads. Horticulture 41:504-5 O '63

DRUMMOND, Richard H.
Japan's new religions and the Christian community. Christian Cent 81:1521-3 D 9 '64
Thoughts of a returned expatriate. Christian Cent 81:172-4 F 5 '64

DRUMMOND, Roscoe
GOP candidate's position papers. Sat R 47:41-2 S 19 '64
Is the government ready for the future? Sat R 47:56+ Ag 29 '64
Liberal conservative speaks Sat R 47:41-2 My 23 '64
Light on the radical right. Sat R 47:39 O 3 '64
Speaking out. por Sat Eve Post 236:8+ F 9 '63

DRUNKEN drivers. See Drinking and traffic accidents

DRUNKENNESS. See Alcoholism

DRUON, Maurice
Wonders of Leningrad. Vogue 144:224-37+ D '64

DRURY, Allen
Can the U.N. survive? Read Digest 82:142-4+ Mr '63
Dangerous game of Let's pretend. Read Digest 84:37-42 Mr '64

DRURY, Allen—*Continued*
about
Hazard of history-by-diary. L. C. Wilson. Nat R 15:529-30 D 17 '63
DRURY, Michael
How to say thank you. Read Digest 83:173+ Jl '63
Never say never. Read Digest 84:99-100 My '64
This much and more; story. Good H 157:80-3 O '63
(ed) See Connally, Mrs J. Since that day in Dallas
(ed) See Harvey, I. You can do anything when you know you're not alone
DRURY college, Springfield, Mo.
Improvement of the human character; address, November 6, 1964. R. H. Amberg. Vital Speeches 31:121-3 D 1 '64
DRY cleaning. See Cleaning
DRY cleaning industry. See Cleaning and dyeing industry
DRY cleaning machines
Coin-ops get through the wash. il Bsns W p 105-6 S 19 '64
Do-it-yourself dry cleaning. il Changing T 17:27-8 My '63
How to save with self-service dry cleaning. Bet Hom & Gard 42:30 Ap '64
Troubles of coin-ops. il Time 81:92 Ap 5 '63
DRY flies. See Fishing lures, flies, etc.
DRY goods
See also
Notions (merchandise)
DRY printing. See Xerography
DRYDEN, Hugh L.
Doctor Dryden to Academician Blagonravov; letter, July 8, 1963. Dept State Bul 49:405 S 9 '63
Dryden cites contributions of engineers; address. por Aviation W 78:67+ My 20 '63
Footprints on the moon. Nat Geog Mag 125: 356-401 Mr '64
Space age challenge to physicists; excerpts from address. Aviation W 79:21 Ag 12 '63
Why the moon is a must; interview, ed. by J. Steen. por Pop Sci 183:92-4+ S '63
about
Man who put the pace in space. il por Pop Sci 183:92+ S '63
DRYDEN, John
Master of the marble image. J. L. Clifford. por Sat R 46:32+ Ag 10 '63
DRYER, Robert L. See Smalley, R. L. jt. auth.
DRYFOOS, Orvil Eugene
Line of succession. Newsweek 61:64 Je 10 '63
DRYING (crops)
See also
Corn—Drying
Grain—Drying
DRYING (fruits, vegetables, etc) See Food—Drying
DRYING apparatus
See also
Hair dryers
DRYLOT feeding. See Cattle—Feeding
DRYROT. See Wood—Diseases and pests
DUAL distribution. See Marketing
DUAL nationality. See Citizenship
DUAL-rate contract system. See Shipping—Rates
DUANE, Pat
Flying lady of the Flying Dutchman. A. Zich. il por Sports Illus 18:43-4+ Ap 22 '63
DUBANOSKI, Richard A. See Thompson, W. R. jt. auth.
DU BAY, Theodore. See Laas, W. jt. auth.
DU BAY, William H.
Readings in Protestant catechetics. por Cath World 199:43-9 Ap '64
Who's got the hymns? America 109:158-9 Ag 17 '63
about
Cable to Rome. Nation 198:643 Je 29 '64
DuBay case. J. Leo. Commonweal 80:477-82 Jl 10 '64
In praise of Father DuBay. D. Callahan. Commonweal 80:408-9 Je 26 '64
Los Angeles, 1964. il por Newsweek 63:82 Je 29 '64
Parish priest accuses his cardinal on civil rights. S. Alexander. il por Life 56:41 Je 26 '64
Postscript on L.A. J. Leo. Commonweal 80: 529 Ag 7 '64
Priest appeals to Rome. Christian Cent 81:852-3 Jl 1 '64
Question of leadership. por Time 83:52-3 Je 26 '64

DUBBING (moving pictures) See Moving picture sound recording
DUBEAU, Normand P. See Wainerdi, R. E. jt. auth.
DUBERMAN, Martin B.
In white America; dramatization of documents. Criticism
America 109:754 D 7 '63
Commonweal 79:693 Mr 6 '64
Nation 199:254-6 O 19 '64
New Repub 149:28-9 N 16 '63
New Yorker 39:98-9 N 9 '63
DUBIN, Harry A.
Of ailurophiles & dogs. McCalls 90:40+ Jl '63
DUBLER, Dorothea
Fire with enthusiasm. Sch Arts 62:21 Mr '63
DUBLIN
Description
Fair Dublin. S. O'Faolain. il Holiday 33:72-81+ Ap '63
New good move for travellers. il Vogue 144: 38 N 15 '64
Hotels, restaurants, etc.
Dublin hotel is tightly planned. il Arch Rec 136:176 O '64
Music
Great opera houses. M. De Schauensee. il Opera N 27:28-31 F 23 '63
Theater
Dublin's lusty theater. P. Smith. il Holiday 33:119-20+ Ap '63
Great opera houses. M. De Schauensee. il Opera N 27:28-31 F 23 '63
Quarreling with Yeats: a friendly recollection. F. O'Connor. Esquire 62:157+ D '64
DUBLIN revolt. See Ireland—History—Sinn Fein rebellion, 1916
DUBOIS, Cleo Gehrke
Pickle secrets revealed! Flower Grower 50: 32 O '63
Winter protection for chrysanthemums. il Flower Grower 50:62-3 O '63
DU BOIS, Donald
How's your gamebird savvy? quiz. Outdoor Life 134:38-9 Jl '64
Instant deer hunt; questions and answers. Outdoor Life 134:62-4 S '64
DUBOIS, Graham
Just and lasting peace; drama. Plays 23: 25-34, 84 F '64
Poison ivy; drama. Plays 22:23-34 Ap '63
Road to Bethlehem; drama. Plays 23:27-35 D '63
DUBOIS, Robert L. See Laidley, R. A. jt. auth.
DU BOIS, William Edward Burghardt
Du Bois dies in Ghana. Christian Cent 80: 1092 S 11 '63
W. E. B. Du Bois: pioneer reconstruction historian. D. Walden. bibliog f Negro Hist Bul 26:159-60+ F '63
DUBOSE, Dorothy
Parents, teachers, and early readers. Sr Schol 83:8T-9T N 1 '63
DUBRIDGE, Lee A.
Physics. bibliog NEA J 52:24-8 D '63
Policy and the scientists. For Affairs 41:571-88 Ap '63
DUBROVNIK, Yugoslavia
Balkans in brief; the rector's roost. H. Sutton. il Sat R 46:48-50 Je 15 '63
Dubrovnik. M. Lawrence. il Atlan 213:126+ F '64
DUBROVNIK festival. See Music festivals—Yugoslavia
DUBUFFET, Jean
Jean Dubuffet: Chemin bordé d'herbe 1901. C. B. Johnson. il Sch Arts 62:23 F '63
DU BUY, Herman G. and others
Tetracycline fluorescence in permeability studies of membranes around intracellular parasites. bibliog Science 145:163-5 Jl 10 '64
DUCCI, Roberto
World order in the sixties. For Affairs 42:379-90 Ap '64
DUCHACEK, Ivo
Czechoslovakia: a dull drama. Cur Hist 44: 273-80+ My '63
DUCHAINE, William J.
Cedar and the backyard living boom. Am For 69:40-3 O '63
DUCHAMP, Marcel
What's happened to art? interview; ed. by W. Seitz. il por Vogue 141:110-13+ F 15 '63
DUCHAMP-VILLON, Marcel. See Duchamp, M.
DUCHIN, Peter
Mr Right. il por Esquire 59:86 F '63
DUCK as food. See Cookery—Poultry
DUCK blinds
Build yourself a man-sized blind. J. P. McGaughey. il Field & S 68:80-1 N '63

DUCK blinds—*Continued*
Destination, ducks. N. Bryant. il Outdoor Life 134:32-3+ D '64
Duck hunter's coffin. P. McLain. il Field & S 68:10-11 N '63
Formula for fidgeters. H. G. Tapply. il Field & S 68:46 D '63
DUCK calling. See Bird calling
DUCK decoys. See Decoys (hunting)
DUCK shooting
Combat those bluebird blues. B. M. Blum. il Field & S 69:32-4+ N '64
Desert duck hunting. V. L. Oertle. il Field & S 69:84-5 D '64
Destination, ducks. N. Bryant. il Outdoor Life 134:32-3+ D '64
Double for the captain. A. Parsons. il Outdoor Life 133:46-7+ Mr '64
Duck hunter's coffin. P. McLain. il Field & S 68:10-11 N '63
Duck hunters: take to the swamps. K. Botty. il Outdoor Life 132:48-9+ O '63
Duck shooting on Maine's icy ledges. D. Barnes. il Sports Illus 21:74-6+ N 30 '64
Fat duck in the fall. F. Dufresne. il Field & S 68:34-5+ N '63
Formula for fidgeters. H. G. Tapply. il Field & S 68:46 D '63
Great Bay bonanza. B. M. Blum. il Field & S 68:86-8+ D '63
I'll take those trash ducks. M. Ellis. il Field & S 68:36-7+ Ag '63
Like artillery coming in. C. Bergen. il Outdoor Life 132:44-5+ N '63
Mixed bag down East. T. Janes. il Field & S 67:74-6+ Ap '63
Outdoors. V. Bourjaily. Esquire 62:40+ S '64
Quality duck hunting. H. Titus. il Field & S 69:56-8+ My '64
Santa Claus brought waterfowl. H. Bradshaw. il Outdoor Life 135:32-3+ Ja '65
Terror on an open lake. G. Lau. il Outdoor Life 134:48-9+ Jl '64
See also
Decoys (hunting)
Game laws

Anecdotes, facetiae, satire, etc.

One hell of a duck hunt; amateur trumpeters as hunters. V. Bourjaily. il Esquire 60:98-100+ O '63
DUCKETT, Kenneth W.
Ohio land patents. Hobbies 68:110-11+ Ag '63
DUCKS
Components of recognition in ducklings. G. Gottlieb. il Natur Hist 74:12-19 bibliog(p70) F '65
Following-response initiation in ducklings: age and sensory stimulation. G. Gottlieb. bibliog il Science 140:399-400 Ap 26 '63
See also
Eider ducks
DUCKS, Wild
Black phantom. W. Jarvis. il Field & S 68:50-1+ Mr '64
Bill Huey's birds; New Mexican duck. W. B. Morse. il Am For 69:26-7+ D '63
Imprinting in nature. G. Gottlieb. bibliog Science 139:497-8 F 8 '63
More ducks to migrate down four U.S. flyways. Sci N L 84:168 S 14 '63
Operation duck rescue. E. Peller. il Audubon Mag 65:364-7 N '63
Queer ducks; Friedrich Schulz' experiments with sexual imprinting. Newsweek 64:82 S 14 '64
Ways and ways for ducks. E. A. Bauer. il Outdoor Life 134:32-5+ N '64
Where the ducks are. F. Calkins. il Field & S 69:41-3+ N '64
Wild, free days. T. Trueblood. Field & S 69:16+ D '64
See also
Cookery—Game
Duck shooting
DUCKS unlimited, Incorporated
Ducks limited. Sports Illus 19:8 Ag 19 '63
DUCKWORTH, Cleveland J.
Scholastic teacher interview; ed. by H. Langer. por Sr Schol 85:9T-10T+ O 21 '64
DUCLOUX, Walter
California gold; interview, ed. by F. Merkling. pors Opera N 28:15-16 Ap 4 '64
Return to paradise. Opera N 27:8-12 My 4 '63
DUCROT, Jerome
Ducrot's summertime pictures; with account. il por Pop Phot 53:50-7+ Ag '63
DUCTLESS glands. See Glands, Ductless
DUDA, Edward J.
Do our elms have a chance. Horticulture 42:20-1+ D '64
DUDE ranches. See Ranches

DUDEVANT, Amatine Lucile Aurore (Dupin)
See Sand, G. pseud.
DUDINSKAIA, Natal'ia
Friendly visit. J. Anderson. il pors Dance Mag 38:18-21+ N '64
DUDLEY, Rae O.
Prejudice hurts everyone. Parents Mag 38:72-3+ F '63
DUDLEY, Thomas Haines
Man who stopped the rams. W. W. Wade. il por Am Heritage 14:18-23+ Ap '63
DUDMAN, Richard
Commentary of an eyewitness. New Repub 149:18 D 21 '63
Socialism in the armed forces. New Repub 149:24-6 N 9 '63
about
Deadliest bullets. New Repub 148:7 Je 8 '63
DUDRA, Michael
Approaches to union security in Switzerland, Canada, and Colombia; excerpt from address. Mo Labor R 86:136-8 F '63
I **DUE** Foscari; opera. See Verdi, G.
DUE process of law
Justice Black and the absolute. J. Grossman. Commentary 36:244-8 S '63
Passports and due process. Commonweal 78:180 My 10 '63
See also
Right to counsel
DUECKER, Heyman C. and Lippincott, E. R.
Pressure-induced trapping phenomenon in silver iodide. bibliog Science 146:1295-7 D 4 '64
—See Lippincott, E. R. jt. auth.
DUELING
Art of the duel; essay from his translation of Pushkin's Eugene Onegin. V. Nabokov. Esquire 60:54-5 Jl '63
Bloodshed at dawn; Barron vs. Decatur. C. S. Forester. il Am Heritage 15:40-5+ O '64
DUERDEN, Richard
Bee: flowers; Circle, death, magic; Well well; Today the sun's up; poems. Poetry 105:89-93 N '64
Lit glass; poem. Nation 199:413 N 30 '64
DUERRENMATT, Friedrich. See Dürrenmatt, F.
DUFAULT, Peter Kane
Anthill in winter; poem. New Yorker 40:140 Mr 7 '64
Cock; poem. New Yorker 39:38 S 7 '63
Cows, a winter landscape; poem. New Yorker 38:36 F 16 '63
On aesthetics, more or less; poem. New Yorker 40:228 O 10 '64
Thoughts while splitting wood; poem. New Yorker 40:60 N 14 '64
DUFF, Annis
Ezra Jack Keats. Library J 88:1292-4 Mr 15 '63
DUFF, Edward
Perspectives on Paul VI. Christian Cent 80:1128-31 S 18 '63
Scandal of squalor. Commonweal 81:223-6 N 13 '64
Vatican II, session 2. Christian Cent 81:1034-7, 1057-61 Ag 19-26 '64
DUFF, Robert Clark-. See Clark-Duff, R.
DUFFERIN and Ava, Sheridan Frederick Terence Hamilton-Temple-Blackwood, 5th marquess of
Four eligible bachelors in London. E. O'Brien. por Vogue 144:142 S 15 '64
DUFFETT, Petro
Mexico's M.I.T. Sat R 46:40-2+ Ag 17 '63
DUFFEY, David Michael
Dogs. See issues of Outdoor life
Fishing the 58th parallel. pors Outdoor Life 134:50-2+ Jl '64
Sportsmen don't happen. Outdoor Life 135:64-5+ F '65
DUFFY, Edward P.
What to do when your child is sick. Parents Mag 39:44-6+ N '64
DUFFY, Joseph A.
ABA establishes award for Publisher of the year. Pub W 185:48 Ap 13 '64
ABA section. Pub W 185:119 Ja 20 '64
Call of books. Pub W 185:46 Mr 30 '64
Convention forecast: the ABA 1964. Pub W 185:45-6 My 11 '64
Lasser survey; step toward understanding. Pub W 186:61 O 5 '64
Toward excellence in bookselling. Pub W 185:90 F 3 '64
DUFOUR, Alfred P. and others
Genetics of isoniazid metabolism in Caucasian, Negro, and Japanese populations. bibliog Science 145:391 Jl 24 '64

DUFRESNE, Frank
Biggest liar in Alaska. Field & S 68:44-5+ Mr '64
Boy and the bear. Field & S 68:24-6+ Ja '64
California deer camp. Field & S 69:36-7+ Ag '64
Crisis in California. Field & S 68:12-15+ Jl '63
Dog man from Oregon. Field & S 69:52-3+ N '64
Fat duck in the fall. Field & S 68:34-5+ N '63
Fly on the ocean. Field & S 68:34-5 Ag '63
Groucho of the wilds. Read Digest 83:121-5 D '63
No. 1 Alaska guide. Field & S 69:32-4 D '64
Poke-pole fishing. Field & S 69:36 O '64
Rampart roulette. Field & S 69:10-13+ Ag '64
Salmon of Yucataw Rapids. Field & S 69: 68-9 S '64
Squaw candy. Field & S 69:8 Ag '64
Ten years better. Field & S 68:124-6+ O '63

DUFY, Raoul
Resurrected mural. il Time 84:46-7 Ag 14 '64

DUGAN, Alan
Admonitor: a pearl for arrogance; On trees; Variation on a theme by Stevens; Accommodation to Detroit; Winter's onset from an alienated point of view; poems. Poetry 102:8-11 Ap '63
about
Long reach, strong speech. B. Cutler. Poetry 103:389-91 Mr '64

DUGAN, David L.
Dedicated to youth. por Recreation 57:190 Ap '64

DUGAN, James
Mayor Daley's Chicago. Holiday 34:84-93+ D '63
Portrait of homo aquaticus. N Y Times Mag p38-9+ Ap 21 '63
—See Cousteau, J. Y. jt. auth.

DUGANNE, Phyllis
Dialogue. Writer 76:19-20 Ap '63

DUGAS, Gaile
Facts and fancies of Christmas. House & Gard 124:48+ N '63

DUGGAN, Alfred
Sword: badge of the gentleman. Holiday 34: 32+ N '63
about
Alfred Duggan: in memoriam. E. Waugh. America 111:483-5 O 24 '64

DUGGAN, Dennis
Mirror, mirror on the wall. il U S Camera 26:50-1 D '63

DUGGAN, William E.
Easy-to-make golden wreath. il Flower Grower 51:15 D '64

DUGGER, Ronnie
Home in Texas. New Repub 150:6 Mr 28 '64
Old times there are not forgiven. Nation 198: 659-60 Je 29 '64
Texas: two-fisted, three-party state. N Y Times Mag p24-5+ N 3 '63
These are the times: on being a southern liberal; excerpts from Black, white and gray. Commentary 37:40-5 Ap '64

DUGGER, Roy W.
Training for a job under MDTA. por Sch Life 45:17-22 F '63

DUGMORE, Edith
Anne Arnold's wood menagerie. Craft Horiz 24:20-3 Jl '64

DUGOUT canoes. See Canoes and canoeing

DUGUID, H. Q.
How capacitors change V.T.V.M. readings. Electr World 72:53+ O '64
Rating unknown power transformers. Electr World 72:24-5 Jl '64

DUHAMEL, Joseph S.
Time has come. America 108:608-11 Ap 27 '63

DUHÈME, Jacqueline
Artist's reverent portrait of Pope Paul's pilgrimage. il McCalls 91:113-17 Ap '64

DUHL, Leonard J.
Urbanization and human needs. Christian Cent 81:930-3 Jl 22 '64
—See Liberman, E. J. jt. auth.
about
Health planner. New Yorker 40:22-3 Jl 11 '64

DUI, Gulliver, pseud.
Ms. found in a bottle. por Wilson Lib Bul 38:401-3 Ja '64

DUIS, Frank
Junior sports jamboree. Recreation 57:359+ S '64

DUISBURG, Germany
Sinking city. il Time 82:63 O 11 '63

DU JARDIN, Rosamond (Neal)
Rosamond du Jardin dies of stroke. por Library J 88:2093-4 My 15 '62

DUK Sung Son
Gentleman's guide to barroom brawling. por Esquire 62:131 O '64

DUKE, Angier Biddle
Functions of protocol in today's world; address, February 6, 1964. Dept State Bul 50:344-7 Mr 2 '64
Protocol and peacekeeping; address, October 22, 1964. Dept State Bul 51:736-9 N 23 '64
Protocol and the conduct of foreign affairs; address, October 9, 1963. Dept State Bul 49:700-4 N 4 '63
World view of freedom's hopes and dilemmas; address, August 10, 1964. Dept State Bul 51:340-7 S 7 '64; Same with title Freedom. Vital Speeches 30:696-701 S 1 '64
about
New diplomatic Hand. il por Newsweek 65: 27-8 Ja 11 '65
New protocol chief: onetime Texas student leader. por U S News 58:15 Ja 11 '65
Profiles. E. J. Kahn, jr. por New Yorker 40:34-6+ Ag 15 '64
Washington's official hosts. J. Peter. il por Look 28:53-9 Ap 21 '64

DUKE, Benjamin C.
Educational developments in Asia; Japan's new role. Sch & Soc 91:369-71 N 30 '63

DUKE, Patty
I believe. por Seventeen 23:102 Ja '64
about
Double life of Patty Duke. A. Gillespie. il pors Good H 158:52+ Ap '64

DUKE, Paul
Foreign aid fiasco. Reporter 30:20-5 Ja 16 '64
Foreign aid: the Johnson round. Reporter 30:25-6 Mr 26 '64
G.O.P. against itself. Reporter 31:12-15 Jl 2 '64
Oddball crusade of Congressman Patman. Sat Eve Post 237:62-3 Mr 7 '64
Southern politics and the Negroes. Reporter 31:18-21 D 17 '64
Waiting game of William W. Scranton. Reporter 30:30-2 F 27 '64
—and Meisler, Stanley
Immigration: quotas vs. quality. Reporter 32: 30-2 Ja 14 '65
Is this the year for Medicare? Reporter 30: 23-6 Ap 23 '64

DUKE, Robin Chandler
Blair House. House & Gard 127:88-99 Ja '65
about
Washington's official hosts. J. Peter. il por Look 28:53-9 Ap 21 '64

DUKE gardens foundation. See Gardens—New Jersey

DUKE university, Durham, N.C.
Duke and Knight. il Newsweek 62:61 S 9 '63
New Duke. il Time 82:90-1 S 13 '63
Law school
Sizing up an unknown force. il Bsns W p 164-6+ N 14 '64
Marine biological laboratory
Ocean ship launched for research studies; Eastward. Sci N L 85:328 My 23 '64

DUKELOW, Donald A.
Have you kept your immunity up to date? Todays Health 42:8-9+ Ap '64

DUKES, Janice
Coiled wire menagerie. Design 65:190-1 My '64

DUKHOBORS
Doukhobors invade Vancouver. Christian Cent 80:228-9 F 20 '63

DULA, Robert M.
Training for military programs. Recreation 57:520 D '64

DULBECCO, Renato
Mutagenic and carcinogenic agents. Science 145:300 Jl 17 '64
Transformation of cells in vitro by viruses. bibliog Science 142:932-6 N 15 '63

DULCE, Sister
Sister Dulce. S. Seegers and K. Seegers. il por Cath World 199:230-7 Jl '64

DULK, George A. See Warwick, J. W. jt. auth.

DULLEA, Keir
Haunting new face. il pors Life 56:115-16 Je 12 '64

DULLES, Allen
Craft of intelligence. pors Harper 226:128-74 Ap '63
Our spy-boss who loved Bond. por Life 57:19 Ag 28 '64

DULLES, Allen—*Continued*
Redbook dialogue: Allen Dulles and Ian Fleming. por Redbook 123:44-5+ Je '64
Seven safeguards for dealing with reds. por Nations Bsns 51:66-7+ O '63
DULLES, Avery
Pope Paul's ecumenical perspective; address. Cath World 200:15-21 O '64
DULLES, John Foster
Dulles over Suez, by H. Finer. Review
Esquire 62:68+ S '64. M. Muggeridge
Nat R 16:915 O 20 '64. G. F. Eliot
Reporter 31:54+ S 10 '64. G. A. Craig
DULLES, John Foster, library. See Princeton university—Libraries
DULLES, John W. F.
End of reformers in Latin America. Nat R 16:24 Ja 14 '64
Keeping touch with the Goulart lobby. Nat R 16:949-51 N 3 '64
DULLES international airport. See Washington, D.C.—Airports
DULUTH zoo. See Zoological gardens
DUMAS, Alexandre, 1824-1895
Lady of the camellias; dramatization. See Cooper, G. and McNally, T.
DUMAS, Robert H.
Bookshows for seniors only. Library J 89: 1828-9 Ap 15 '64
DU MAURIER, Daphne
Glass-blowers; condensation of novel. Good H 156:63-72 F; 73-5 Mr; 86-7 Ap '63
DUMB cane (plants) See Dieffenbachias
DUMBARTON Oaks museum. See Washington, D.C.—Galleries and museums
DUMMER family
Dummer coat-of-arms. H. K. Eilers. il Hobbies 69:124-5 Ap '64
DUMMY board figures
Old dummy board figures. A. Scott and C. Scott. il Antiques 83:564-7 My '63
DUMOND, Dwight L.
Long, relentless reign of wrong. Sat R 47:47-8 My 9 '64
Reason and the limits of racism. Sat R 47: 35-6 S 12 '64
DU MONT, John S.
Powder horns and history. Antiques 84:60-2 Jl '63
DUMPING (commercial policy)
Debate over dumping. New Repub 148:5-6 My 25 '63
U.S. foreign trade: no dumping allowed. il Fortune 67:87-8+ My '63
DUMPLINGS
Dumplings international. C. Claiborne. il N Y Times Mag p56+ F 16 '64
How to make egg foam dumplings. il Sunset 134:102 Ja '65
Orange dumplings, also apple, peach, and apricot. il Sunset 132:166+ Mr '64
DUMPS, Municipal. See Municipal dumps
DUN, Angus
Spirit bloweth. New Repub 148:8 My 18 '63
DUN and Bradstreet
Assessing gilt; nation's three bond-rating services. il Time 84:58 D 25 '64
Pinpointing America: analysis of industrial markets; tables. il Duns R 84:43-50 Ag '64
DUNANT, Henry
Flag of mercy. Newsweek 62:42-4 S 16 '63
Red cross; centenary of a universal banner. H. d'Havrincourt. il por UNESCO Courier 16:20-5 Je '63
DUNBAR, Ernest
African revolt in Russia. Look 28:31-5 My 5 '64; Same abr. Read Digest 85:71-4 Ag '64
DUNBAR vocational high school. See Chicago —Education
DUNCAN, David Douglas
Paris, in photographs. McCalls 91:84-95 F '64
Paris, prisms and Picasso. il Sat Eve Post 237:24-37 Mr 7 '64
DUNCAN, Donald
Ballet '63 hits the big time. Dance Mag 37: 20-1 S '63
Kid from Kentucky. Dance Mag 37:26-8 Mr '63
On the gypsy circuits. Dance Mag 37:43-5 D '63; 38:26-7 Ja '64
Struggles of One Bull and Good Feather. Dance Mag 37:25-6 F '63
Twenty years of Oklahoma! Dance Mag 37: 32-4 Mr '63
DUNCAN, Douglas
Mantle's breaks, and yours. Pop Sci 185:100-3+ O '64
DUNCAN, Frances
Pledge of allegiance. Atlan 213:120-1 My '64
DUNCAN, Isadora
Isadora Duncan and Constantin Stanislavsky; with excerpts from letters. N. Rene. il pors Dance Mag 37:40-3 Jl '63
She danced to feeling. G. Beiswanger. Sat R 47:38 F 8 '64
DUNCAN, Jeff
Jeff Duncan dance company at Fashion institute auditorium. D. Hering. Dance Mag 37:30+ Mr '63
Jeff Duncan dance company at High school of art and design. J. Maskey. Dance Mag 38:30 F '64
DUNCAN, John J.
Award winning mall. Am City 79:74-5 N '64
DUNCAN, Leroy E. Jr, and others
Lipoprotein movement through canine aortic wall. bibliog Science 142:972-3 N 15 '63
DUNCAN, Patrick
Overthrow of apartheid. New Repub 148:9-10 Mr 9 '63
South West Africa; timetable for freedom. Nation 198:265-7 Mr 16 '64
Toward a world policy for South Africa. For Affairs 42:38-48 O '63
DUNCAN, Robert
Continent; poem. Poetry 103:28-32 O '63
Fifth sonnet. Nation 197:262 O 26 '63
Oriented by instinct by stars. Poetry 105: 131-3 N '64
Risk; poem. Poetry 101:383-6 Mr '63
Sonnet 4. Nation 197:97 Ag 24 '63
about
Scales of the marvelous. H. Carruth. Nation 199:442-4 D 7 '64
DUNCAN, Ronald
Three poems: Abelard; Practical ballad; Solitudes. Nat R 14:116 F 12 '63
DUNCAN, Vera
Gift of memory at Christmas. Hobbies 69: 28 D '64
DUNDEE, Angelo
Tigers' tiger. il por Newsweek 61:64-5 Je 17 '63
DUNDEE elementary school. See Greenwich, Conn.—Education
DUNDY, Elaine
Crane, masters, Wolfe, etc. slept here. Esquire 62:100-3+ O '64
DUNE buggies. See Motor vehicles
DUNGAREES. See Clothing and dress—Children
DUNHAM, Barrows
When thoughts are unthinkable. Nation 198:411-13 Ap 27 '64
DUNHAM, Katherine
Caribbean tourist tips. Travel 121:50-3 F '64
Seconding the motion; interview, ed. by G. Fitzgerald. Opera N 28:15 D 7 '63
This historic necessity for music; address, November 11, 1963. Mus Am 83:157-8 D '63
DUNHAM, Lowell
Scholar, novelist, and president. Américas 16:1-6 D '64
DUNHILL international, incorporated
Cigars & pipe dreams. Time 83:91-2 F 7 '64
DUNIGAN, Vincent J.
Sundown on Christianity in the Sudan. Cath World 199:245-52 Jl '64
DUNKARDS. See Church of the Brethren
DUNKERS. See Church of the Brethren
DUNLAP, Jack
Invisible man. il por Newsweek 62:43 O 21 '63
Playboy sergeant who spied for Russia. D. Oberdorfer. il por Sat Eve Post 237:40+ Mr 7 '64
DUNLAP, Justus R. See Hynek, J. A. jt. auth.
DUNLOP, Richard
Doctors on the frontier; excerpts. Todays Health 41:42-5+ Mr; 34-7+ O; 44-7+ D '63; 42:44-7+ Mr; 12-15+ Je; 12-13+ Jl; 40-3+ Ag; 42-5+ S; 40-1+ N '64
Granny had a cure for everything. Todays Health 41:30-3+ My '63
John Wesley: medical missionary in the New World. Todays Health 42:20-3+ D '64
Magic of California's golden city. Todays Health 42:32-5+ Je '64
Medical I.D. tag can save your life. Todays Health 41:8-13 Jl '63; Same abr. with title Tag that can save your life. Read Digest 83:217-19+ O '63
Probing the mysteries of light. Todays Health 41:34-9+ Mr '63
Put on your walking shoes when you visit old Charleston. Todays Health 41:44-7+ Ap '63
Something old, something new; all things special for your honeymoon. Todays Health 42:34-7+ Ap '64
Spanish doctors in the old Southwest. Todays Health 41:44-7+ F '63
—See Minette, B. jt. auth.
DUNLOP, Richard B.
Did the Romans discover America? Pop Mech 120:70-4+ Jl '63

DUNLOP, Robert H.
Lactic acids: chemistry and metabolism. Science 147:315-17 Ja 15 '65
DUNLOP rubber company, limited
Dunlop rides high. il Time 83:79 My 29 '64
DUNLOP tire and rubber corporation
Why the pressure is off wages; unemployment is high. il Bsns W p 101-2+ Mr 9 '63
DUNN, Halbert L.
Positive view of aging asks much of education. Sch Life 46:30-4 Ja '64
DUNN, Harold
What kids say about rockets. Sci Digest 54: 65-8 O '63
What kids say about science. Sci Digest 56: 67-70 O '64
DUNN, Joseph S.
Book selection: education or communication? Wilson Lib Bul 37:673+ Ap '63
DUNN, Kenneth J.
How we rewrote our social studies curriculum. Sr Schol 85:8T-9T S 16 '64
DUNN, L. C.
Transmission and population genetics of the t-region. Science 144:260-3 Ap 17 '64
DUNN, Michael
I'm no cutie-midget needing a mother; interview, ed. D. Lurie. por Life 56:50 F 14 '64
Dwarf's full-size success. pors Life 56:43-4+ F 14 '64
Small talk. il por Newsweek 62:72 N 18 '63
DUNN, Mignon
Triple threat; interview, ed. by R. D. Daniels. por Opera N 27:14 Ap 6 '63
DUNN, Thomas
Performing the Brandenburgs. por Mus Am 83:52-3 My '63
Quote: unquote; interview, ed. by P. Davis. por Mus Am 84:21 O '64
about
Compact model. il Newsweek 64:102 O 12 '64
Musical events. W. Sargeant. New Yorker 40:143-4 N 7 '64
Time of the baroqueniks; midsummer music festival at Philharmonic Hall. il por Time 82:55 Ag 9 '63
DUNN, N. C.
Garbage goes underground to beat costs. A. B. Uzzle, jr. and J. T. Jackson. Am City 79:34 Mr '64
Upside-down wells. A. B. Uzzle, jr. il Am City 79:30 My '64
DUNN international exhibit. See Art—Exhibitions
DUNNE, Finley Peter
Mr Dooley's friends; excerpts from Mr Dooley remembers. Atlan 212:77-80+ S '63
about
Montaigne with a brogue. por Time 82:64+ D 27 '63
DUNNE, Irene
What have they done to Irene Dunne. S. Birmingham. por McCalls 91:100-1+ Ag '64
DUNNE, John Gregory
British satirists are a bloody bore. Life 56: 18 Ap 24 '64
Life movie review. Life 57:21 D 4 '64
Movies. Nat R 15:536-8 D 17 '63
Movies in brief. Nat R 15:72 Jl 30 '63
Theater (cont) Nat R 15:406-7 N 5 '63
DUNNE, John P.
Help, but at a price. Motor B 114:40-1+ S '64
DUNNING, Dorothy C. and Roeder, K. D.
Moth sounds and the insect-catching behavior of bats. bibliog Science 147:173-4 Ja 8 '65
DUNNING, Harrison F.
Labor and management; excerpts from address. por Duns R 81:23-4 Ap '63
DUNPHY, William
Ecumenism in Morocco. America 11:694 N 28 '64
DUNRAVEN, Windham Thomas Wyndham-Quin, 4th earl of
America's cup. S. Leslie. Nat R 16:918-20 O 20 '64
DUN'S review
Looking backward and forward. A. M. Sullivan. il Duns R 82:3 Jl '63
DUNSFORD, John E.
Public policy on birth control. America 111: 132-4 Ag 8 '64
DUNTON, Sam
Nature and photography. Natur Hist 74:61-5 F '65
DUONG-van-Minh
Fall of the house of Ngo; with report by Beverly Deepe. il por Newsweek 62:27-31 N 11 '63
Is the U.S. better off after Vietnam coup? por Bsns W p31-2 N 9 '63
Pro-American Big Minh; the big man in Vietnam. il por U S News 55:28 N 18 '63
Revolution in the afternoon. il por (cover) Time 82:30-2 N 8 '63
DUPARC, Henri
Two interpretations of the Duparc dozen. P. L. Miller. Am Rec G 30:840+ My '64
DUPEE, Norman E.
Ornithogalum. Horticulture 42:34-5 N '64
DUPLESSIS, Maurice LeNoblet
Reporter at large. E. Wilson. New Yorker 40:146+ N 28 '64
DU PLESSIX, Francine
At the Calders. House & Gard 124:154-9+ D '63
Cooking by scent. Vogue 142:104-5 S 15 '63
Milan: a capital in search of a country. Vogue 142:152-5+ N 15 '63
P.S. to summer; its savage American joys. Vogue 144:197+ S 1 '64
DUPLEX houses. See Houses, Two-family
DUPLICATORS. See Copying processes
DUPONT, Allaire
Move over, Man o' War. W. Tower. il por Sports Illus 19:36-8 N 11 '63
Two ladies in search of the world. W. Tower. il por Sports Illus 19:26-7 O 7 '63
DU PONT, Irénée
Last of the brothers. por Newsweek 62:51-2 D 30 '63
DU PONT, Samuel Francis
Du Pont storms Charleston; excerpt from Civil war. S. Foote. il por Am Heritage 14: 28-34+ Je '63
DU PONT DE NEMOURS, E. I, and company
Du Pont's financial acumen. J. Ross-Skinner. il Duns R 81:42-4+ F '63
Giant gets in quickstep; new product paths. il Bsns W p 136-8+ N 9 '63
Last of the brothers. Newsweek 62:51-2 D 30 '63
Master technicans. il Time 84:94-8 N 27 '64
Mill grinds fine by the Brandywine. J. Bird. il Sat Eve Post 236:34+ Jl 27 '63
Research: if the shoe fits, another winner for industry. il Newsweek 63:65-6 Ap 6 '64
Synthetic rival for leather; Du Pont's Corfam. il Bsns W p34 O 5 '63
Synthetics ride hell-bent for leather. L. Lessing. il Fortune 70:172-5+ N '64
Who owns what's in your head? W. Bowen. il Fortune 70:175-8+ Jl '64
World trade; national and corporate interests; address, November 19, 1963. L. D. Copeland. Vital Speeches 30:264-7 F 15 '64
DU PONT family
Du Ponts of Delaware, by W. H. A. Carr. Review
Time il 83:134+ Ap 17 '64
DUPRE, Louis
From Augustine to Janssens. Commonweal 80:336-8+ Je 5 '64
DUPREE, Louis
Afghanistan: the canny neutral. Nation 199: 134-7 S 21 '64
Prehistoric archeological surveys and evcavations in Afghanistan: 1959-1960 and 1961-1963. bibliog Science 146:638-40 O 30 '64
DUPREY, Richard A.
Battle for the American stage. Cath World 197:246-51 Jl '63
Broadway. Cath World 197:271-2 Jl; 198:71-2 O '63
Gargoyle; a Christmas story. Cath World 198:163-7 D '63
Movie of the month. Cath World 198:327-8 F '64
Play of the month (cont) Cath World 197:143-4; 199:199-200, 327-8; 200:131-2 My '63; Je, Ag, N '64
—and Palms, C. L.
Play of the month. Cath World 198:135-6 N '63
DUPUY, R. Ernest
MacArthur: the greatest captain of his era. por U S news 56:78-9 Ap 27 '64
DUQUESNE university, Pittsburgh, Pa.
Mossie Murphy's crusade. M. Cope. il Sports Illus 18:18-20+ Ja 28 '63
DURAND, Forrest V.
Planning, a prologue to action; address. Am For 70:26-9+ N '64
DURAND, José
Julio Cortázar: storytelling giant. Américas 15:39-43 Mr '63
Octavio Paz: Mexican poet-diplomat. Américas 15:30-3 Jl '63
DURANT, Ariel
Spry old team does it again. J. Hicks. il por Life 55:89+ O 18 '63
DURANT, John
Grabbers' crab. Field & S 69:65+ O '64
DURANT, Mary
Miss Hattie's lawn party; story. Ladies Home J 81:98-100 Ap '64

DURANT, Will
Spry old team does it again. J. Hicks. il pors Life 55:89+ O 18 '63
DURANT, William C.
My years with General motors. A. P. Sloan, jr. il por Fortune 68:135-42+ S '63 (to be cont)
DURANT, Okla.
Boom town? disclosure by prisoner of buried nitroglycerin. Newsweek 63:34+ Mr 16 '64
DURANTE, Jimmy
Wild woild of Jimmy Durante. J. Reddy. por Read Digest 83:202-4+ N '63
DURAS, Marguerite
Marguerite Duras. H. Hobson. il por Theatre Arts 47:22-4+ N '63
DURATION, Intuition of. See Time perception
DURATION of life. See Longevity
DURAVIC, Steven
Curious case of krebiozen. H. Margolis. Bul Atomic Sci 20:29-31 Mr '64
DURBIN, Mrs James
What is a park? Recreation 57:387 O '64
DURDIN, Peggy
Ambassador's wife is an ambassador, too. N Y Times Mag p21+ O 4 '64
Shanghai. Sat R 48:42-3+ Ja 2 '65
DURDIN, Tillman
Chiang still dreams his dream. N Y Times Mag p 18-19+ Mr 22 '64
DURE, Leon, and Waters, Larry
Long-lived messenger RNA; evidence from cotton seed germination. bibliog Science 147:410-12 Ja 22 '65
DUREAU, A. C.
Royal fruit. Horticulture 41:330 Je '63
DÜRER, Albrecht
Albrecht Dürer. J. Canaday. il pors Horizon 6:16-31 Sum '64
DURHAM, Gloria
Skydiver. il pors Ebony 18:47-8+ O '63
DURHAM, J. W. and Caster, K. E.
Helicoplacoidae: a new class of echinoderms. bibliog Science 140:820-2 My 17 '63
DURHAM, Jack
Howard Zahniser; in memoriam; poem. Liv Wildn 85:7 Wint '64
DURHAM, Mae J.
Some thoughts about picture books. Horn Bk 39:476-84 O '63
DURHAM, Michael
End of a tale of two towns: army lights and serenity. Life 55:24-5 Jl 26 '63
How Gideon changed High court's mind. Life 56:86+ Je 12 '64
How it feels to be beat up by a rampaging mob. por Life 56:44-5 Ap 3 '64
Ollie McClung's big decision. Life 57:31 O 9 '64
DURHAM, N. C.
200 per cent more space with microfilm. B. S. Barker. il Am City 78:95-6 O '63
DURHAM COUNTY, N.C.
EB school library award. C. P. Bomar and C. Jenkins. il Wilson Lib Bul 39:397-8 Ja '65
DURHAM rule. See Insanity—Jurisprudence
DURIANS
Durlance vile. il Newsweek 61:79 Ap 1 '63
DURKEE, Stephen
What is pop art? interview; ed. by G. R. Swenson. il Art N 62:42+ F '64
DURKIN, Dolores
Should the very young be taught to read? bibliog NEA J 52:20+ N '63
DURKIN, J. T.
Four eyes on the Washington march. America 109:252 S 14 '63
DURMAS, Jim. See Crosby, K. jt. auth.
DURNIAK, John
Focus on Jay Maisel. Pop Phot 54:76-85+ Mr '64
Focus on Pete Turner. Pop Phot 52:62-71+ My '63
Focus on Zimmerman. Pop Phot 52:82-91+ Ap '63
Four afternoons with a $40,000 lens. il Pop Phot 54:66-7+ F '64
Music to shoot by. Pop Phot 53:77+ S '63
Not-so-easy art of framing. Pop Phot 55:166-7+ D '64
This book may make you mad. Pop Phot 52:72-3+ My '63

about

Changeover. B. Downes. Pop Phot 55:42 S '64
DUROCHER, Leo
Candid memoirs of Leo Durocher; ed. by E. Linn. pors Sat Eve Post 236:26-8+ My 11 '63

about

Leo: under the sunset gun. R. Cantwell. il pors Sports Illus 18:20-4 F 18 '63
Walt Alston: manager with a hair shirt. M. Durslag. il por Look 27:64+ Jl 30 '63
DUROVIC, Stevan
Another round in the krebiozen battle. il por Time 82:64 Jl 26 '63
Curious case of krebiozen. H. Margolis. Bul Atomic Sci 20:29-31 Mr '64; Reply. A. C. Ivy. 20:28 S '64
Fantastic krebiozen story. R. P. Goldman. il pors Sat Eve Post 237:15-19 Ja 4 '64
Incredible story behind a cancer cure. S. Blum. il Redbook 123:40-1+ Je '64
Krebiozen in court. il por Newsweek 64:91 N 30 '64
Krebiozen; why it hasn't been tested. Consumer Rep 28:441-3 S '63
DURRELL, Donald D.
Learning to read. Atlan 214:87-8 S '64
DURRELL, Gerald
Animals in jeopardy. Holiday 34:153-8 N '63
DURRELL, Lawrence
Portfolio; poem. Sat R 47:73 D 5 '64
Scaffoldings; Poemandres; In the margin; poems. Mlle 60:137 N '64
What-ho on the Rialto! story. Mlle 57:152-3 S '63

about

From the twosome, a quartet. E. Moon. por Sat R 46:28-9 F 23 '63
Irish Faustus. Criticism
Time il por 83:56 Ja 3 '64
Larry & Henry. por Time 81:80 Mr 1 '63
What they wrote and what they were. D. Littlejohn. Reporter 28:42+ Ap 11 '63
DÜRRENMATT, Friedrich
Physicists. Criticism
Christian Cent 80:301-2 Mr 6 '63
Commonweal 81:237-8 N 13 '64
Life il 57:89-90 N 20 '64
Nation 196:380 My 4 '63
Nation 199:340 N 9 '64
Newsweek il 64:102 O 26 '64
Sat R 47:31 O 31 '64
Time 84:67 O 23 '64
Vogue 144:152 D '64
Study in vindictiveness. W. R. Mueller. Christian Cent 81:1340+ O 28 '64
DURRWELL, F. X.
Inward law of Christian liberty; excerpt from In the redeeming Christ; toward a theology of spirituality. Cath World 197:187-92 Je '63
DURSIN, Margaret
Bat lady; story. Harper 229:71-5 O '64
DURSLAG, Melvin
Baseball. Sports Illus 21:44-5 Jl 20 '64
Coach has all the problems. Sat Eve Post 236:72-3 D 14 '63
Doctor Kildare is a doll. Sat Eve Post 236:14-15 Mr 30 '63
Pious partners of success. Sat Eve Post 236:28+ My 4 '63
Walt Alston: manager with a hair shirt. Look 27:64+ Jl 30 '63
DU SABLE, Jean Baptiste. See Pointe de Sable, J. B.
DUSCHA, Julius
Angry and old-fashioned. New Repub 149:6-7 N 30 '63
Arms and the big money men Harper 228:39-47 Mr; 59-65 Ap; 56-62 My '64
Dull part of desegregation. Reporter 29:43-6 Ag 15 '63
High cost of fair trade. Reporter 30:29-30 Mr 12 '64
Mark Hatfield, man with a tough job. Reporter 31:15-17 Jl 2 '64
Rockefeller vs Goldwater. New Repub 149:13-14 O 26 '63
DUSHANE, Graham Phillips
Seven years of progress. P. H. Abelson. Science 141:491 Ag 9 '63
DUSSELDORF
Under the trees to the Jaegerhof; municipal museum. il Sunset 133:24+ O '64
DUST
Bali high; volcanic dust and pumice. il Newsweek 62:102 N 18 '63
Meteoric dust observed. Sky & Tel 27:86 F '64
DUST, Interstellar. See Matter, Interstellar
DUST BOWL. See Great Plains
DUST jackets. See Book covers
DUST jackets, Phonograph records. See Phonograph record covers
DUST storms
When the wind blew black blizzards. A. Balk. il N Y Times Mag p98-101 N 10 '63
DUSTING. See House cleaning
DUSTING, Aerial. See Airplanes in insect control
DUSTMAN, Robert E. and Beck, E. C.
Long-term stability of visually evoked potentials in man. Science 142:1480-1 D 13 '63

DUTCH
Holland: the deftly governed. V. S. Pritchett. il Holiday 35:64-7+ Ja '64
DUTCH, Pennsylvania. See Pennsylvania Germans
DUTCH bulbs. See Bulbs
DUTCH cookery. See Cookery, Dutch
DUTCH elm disease. See Elm—Diseases and pests
DUTCH painting. See Painting, Dutch
DUTCH poetry
Down there on a visit: poetry in the Netherlands. T. Cassity. Poetry 102:38-42 Ap '63

Translations into English

Gedicht: een schoon gezicht heeft de dagbladpostiche; Avondgeluiden; Berceuse for grown-ups; Gedicht: Zan brandt de rozelaar; Oude man; tr. by H. Van Ameyden Van Duym. P. van Ostaijen. Poetry 104:170-5 Je '64
DUTCH Reformed church in South Africa. See Reformed church in South Africa
DUTCH Reformed church in the Netherlands. See Reformed church in the Netherlands
DUTCH state mines. See Mines and mineral resources—Netherlands
DUTCH visitors in the United States. See Foreign visitors in the United States
DUTCHESS COUNTY co-operative hunting area. See Hunting—United States
DUTCHMAN; drama. See Jones, L.
DUTCHMANS-breeches
Plant these more often. I. D. Jolly. il Horticulture 41:425 Ag '63
DUTIES (tariff) See Tariff
DUTIES, Childrens. See Occupations for children
DUTT, Vidya Prakash
China: jealous neighbor. bibliog f Cur Hist 44:135-40+ Mr '63
DUTTON, D'Arcy B. G. and Wood, C. W.
Stop surface spalling. Am City 79:71-3 N '64
DUTTON, E. P. and company
Soviets say contract for Solzhenitsyn novel is void. Pub W 183:48-9 F 4 '63
DUTTON, Frederick G.
Cold war between the Hill and foggy bottom. N Y Times Mag p36+ S 15 '63
DUTTON, Richard W. See Richardson, M. jt. auth.
DUTY
Watchword for 1964. Christian Cent 81:3 Ja 1 '64
Word. V. P. McCorry. America 109:200-1 Ag 24 '63
DUTY free importation
Antiques and the tariff. W. H. Van Hoesen. Antiques 85:328+ Mr '64
Bringing back your own; tax-free liquor. Newsweek 61:57 Ap 8 '63
Tax-free sales boost European carriers. E. Walford. il Aviation W 79:46-7 S 30 '63
U.K. tariff was a close call for American books; U.S. failure to implement the Florence agreement. R. H. Smith. Pub W 186:37 N 23 '64
DUVALIER, François
Dictatorship in Haiti. H. Herring. Cur Hist 46:34-7+ Ja '64
Haiti. R. D. Heinl, jr. New Repub 150:15-21 My 16 '64
Haiti, land of the big tontons. R. Eder. il pors N Y Times Mag p9+ Ja 24 '65
Haiti today. F. J. Cook. Nat R 16:312 Ap 21 '64
Haiti: where lid is about to blow. C. Migdail. il por U S News 54:65-6 My 6 '63
Haitian voodoo. il por U S News 54:42 My 20 '63
Haiti's voodoo tyrant. L. Stowe. por Read Digest 83:222-6+ N '63
If it's war in Haiti, who'll win? C. Migdail. por U S News 54:44 My 13 '63
Is Haiti next? A. A. Berle. Reporter 28:16 My 23 '63
Island divided. por Sr Schol 83:6 S 20 '63
It's hell to live in Haiti with Papa Doc; with report by B. Farrell. il por Life 54:28-35 Mr 8 '63
Life sentence. por Time 83:28 Ap 10 '64
Living dead. il Time 82:20-1 Jl 26 '63
Nonintervention: a shield for Papa Doc. G. Sherman. il Reporter 28:27-9 Je 20 '63
Nothing happened. Reporter 28:11 Je 6 '63
Now: new danger next door to Cuba. il por U S News 54:40-2 My 20 '63
Papa Doc rides out Haiti D day, but. . . por U S News 54:8 My 27 '63
There'll be another Haiti revolt soon, but. . . il por U S News 55:10 Ag 19 '63
Troubled Caribbean waters. Sr Schol 82:19 My 15 '63
Voodoo and politics. E. Mirel. Sci N L 83:299 My 11 '63
Warning to a dictator. por Time 81:26 My 3 '63
DUVALL, Evelyn Millis
Young moderns' marriage dreams. PTA Mag 57:4-7 bibliog(p36) Ap '63
DUVALL, Mrs Raymond
My husband, the ag teacher. Farm J 88:58E My '64
DUVE, Christian de
Lysosome; with biographical sketch. Sci Am 208:36, 64-72 My '63
DUVEEN brothers. See Art dealers
DUVEL, William A.
Businessmen's expectations. Duns R 82:11 S; 11 D '63; 83:11-12 Mr '64
DU VIGNEAUD, Vincent. See Jarvis, D. jt. auth.
DVOŘÁK, Antonín
Dvorak revived; Musica aeterna's Requiem. C. J. McNaspy. America 110:351-2 Mr 14 '64
Keeping up with the Kohons. J. W. Barker. il Am Rec G 30:609 Mr '64
Music to my ears; Dvorak's Requiem revived. I. Kolodin. Sat R 47:113 Mr 14 '64
Musical events; Dvořák's Requiem mass performed by Musica aeterna; conducted by F. Waldman. W. Sargeant. New Yorker 40:171-3 Mr 7 '64
New Artia debuts with a very valuable pair of records. J. W. Barker. il Am Rec G 30:126-8 O '63
On records; Stabat mater. Opera N 28:35 Ja 18 '64
Vox is doing us all a vast service. J. W. Barker. Am Rec G 29:543-5 Mr '63
DWARF apple trees; Dwarf cannas; etc. See Apple trees; Cannas; etc.
DWARF fruit trees. See Fruit trees, Dwarf
DWARF stars. See Stars, Dwarf
DWARF trees. See Trees, Dwarf
DWARFISM
Inbreeding & dwarfism. il Time 84:59-60 Ag 21 '64
DWARFS
Dwarf's full-size success; Michael Dunn. il Life 56:43-4+ F 14 '64
If you were a midget. A. Hamilton. il Sci Digest 55:30-4 Ja '64
DWELL meters
Cam-dwell meter for quick, sure auto tune-up. B. Ward. il Pop Mech 121:196-8 F '64
Simple dwell meter. T. C. Penn. il Electr World 71:43+ Je '64
DWIGHT, Edward H.
Audubon, the artist. Audubon Mag 65:20-3 Ja '63
DWIGHT, Edward Joseph, 1934?-
First Negro astronaut candidate. L. Robinson. il pors Ebony 18:71+ Jl '63
Pinpoint portrait. J. H. Roy. Negro Hist Bul 27:92 Ja '64
DWORIN, Arthur
I believe. il Seventeen 22:116 Je '63
DWORKIN, Martin, and Gibson, S. M.
System for studying microbial morphogenesis: rapid formation of microcysts in myxococcus zanthus. bibliog Science 146:243-4 O 9 '64
DWORKIN, Martin S.
Forty-six poems. Cath World 196:369 Mr '63
Modes of Greek skepticism: number three; poem. Cath World 197:113 My '63
DWORKIN, Michael Gordon
Lesson in economics. il por Time 84:73 D 4 '64
DWYER, Douglas W.
Operation sail. Yachting 115:64-6+ Ap '64
DWYER, James E.
Add radiance with holiday magic. Pop Gard 15:36-41 N '64
Discovering the wonderful world of nature. Pop Gard 15:24-7 Jl '64
DWYER, Kenneth R. See Sutton, D. C. jt. auth.
DWYER, Robert J.
I know about the Negroes and the poor. Nat R 15:517-18+; 16:83-4 D 17 '63, Ja 28 '64
Religion. Nat R 16:494 Je 16 '64
DYBBUK; drama. See Ansky, S.
DYE, David L. and Wilkinson, Maurice
Radiation hazards in space. bibliog Science 147:19-25 Ja 1 '65
DYE, Eugene N.
Travel well. See issues of Travel beginning January 1965
DYER, Charles
Rattle of a simple man. Criticism
New Yorker 39:82 Ap 27 '63
Sat R 46:23 My 4 '63
Theatre Arts il 47:10-11 Je '63
Time il 81:58 Ap 26 '63

DYER, Edward
Standards for travel credit. NEA J 53:68 F '64
DYER, Henry S.
Critical look at testing. Sat R 46:56-7 D 21 '63; 47:61 F 15 '64
DYER, John
Soybean weed killers, they really work. Farm J 87:28-9 Je '63
(ed) See Putnam, M. Why I go-it-alone with broilers
DYER, Louise Hanson-. See Hanson-Dyer, L.
DYER, W. J. H.
How the Frostbite dinghy found its future. pors Motor B 112:38+ Ag '63
DYER-BENNET, Richard
Richard Dyer-Bennet; interview. ed. by S. Fleming. por Hi Fi 13:16+ Mr '63
Mark Twain, obscenity, folk songs. R. De Toledano. Nat R 15:160-1 Ag 27 '63
Richard Dyer-Bennet: folk singer in white tie. E. Helm. por Mus Am 83:43 F '63
DYES and dyeing
Color coating for shoes. il Consumer Bul 46: 43+ N '63
Emperors' dye of the Mixtecs; Tyrian purple. P. Gerhard. il Natur Hist 73:26-31 Ja '64
Tie-dyeing your own fabrics. il Sunset 132: 72+ Ja '64
See also
Hair—Dyeing and bleaching
DYESS air force base. See Air bases
DYGERT, Ruth E.
Tanganyika. pors Nat Geog Mag 126:320-3 S '64
DYHRENFURTH, Norman Gunther
Six to the summit. por Nat Geog Mag 124: 460-73 O '63
about
Old Glory on Everest. il por Newsweek 61:52 My 13 '63
Up to the gods. il por Time 81:85 My 10 '63
DYKE, W. P.
Advances in field emission; with biographical sketch. Sci Am 210:20, 108-16+ bibliog(p 152) Ja '64
DYKEMAN, Wilma, and Stokely, James
Hopeful dialogue of the races. N Y Times Mag p 10+ Ag 11 '63
DYKES, Archie R.
Democracy, teachers, and educational decision-making Sch & Soc 92:155-6 Ap 4 '64
DYLAN, Bob
Angry young folk singer; with excerpt from II outlined epitaphs. il pors Life 56:109-10+ Ap 10 '64
Baez & Dylan; a generation singing out. R. Fariña. por Mlle 59:242+ Ag '64
I am my words. por Newsweek 62:94-5 N 4 '63
Let us now praise little men. por Time 81:40 My 31 '63
Profiles. N. Hentoff. por New Yorker 40:64-6+ O 24 '64
DYLAN; drama. See Michaels, S.
DYMSZA, Henry A. See Miller, S. A. jt. auth.
DYNACHROME films. See Photography—Films
DYNAGROOVE phonograph records. See Phonograph records
DYNAGROOVE recording system. See Phonograph records—Recording
DYNAMICS
See also
Aerodynamics
DYNAMOMETERS
Instant dyno. J. Wright. il Motor T 16:68-9 Ag '64
DYNA-SOAR (glider) See Airplanes, Experimental
DYNEL. See Textile fabrics, Synthetic
DYSART, Lawrence A.
Wanted: effective communicators; address, June 1, 1963. Vital Speeches 29:668-71 Ag 15 '63
DYSLEXIA. See Word blindness
DYSMENORRHEA. See Menstruation—Disorders
DYSON, Freeman J.
Defense against ballistic missiles. Bul Atomic Sci 20:12-18 Je '64
Mathematics in the physical sciences; with biographical sketch. Sci Am 211:30, 128-34+ S '64
DYSON, James L.
Ice age national scientific reserve. Nat Parks Mag 37:4-9 Ag '63
DYSON, Robert H. jr
On the origins of the neolithic revolution. Science 144:672-5 My 8 '64
Sciences meet in ancient Hasanlu. Natur Hist 73:16-25 O '64
Selected aspects of archaeology, 1958 to 1963. Ann Am Acad 351:181-93 Ja '64
DYSPEPSIA
Acid indigestion: myth & mysteries. il Time 84:39 Ag 28 '64
DYSPROSIUM
High pressure: effect on dysprosium. P. C. Souers and G. Jura. bibliog il Science 145: 575-7 Ag 7 '64
X-ray diffraction studies on dysprosium at high pressures. J. C. Jamieson. bibliog il Science 145:572-4 Ag 7 '64
DYSTROPHY, Muscular
Abnormal myoglobin ultraviolet spectrum in Duchenne type of progressive muscular dystrophy. K. Miyoshi and others. bibliog Science 142:490-1 O 25 '63
Drug delays course of muscular dystrophy. Sci Digest 53:46-7 Mr '63
Let them go free; ed. by M. G. Ward. G. G. Bradley. Read Digest 85:121-4 Ag '64
Muscular dystrophy. T. Berland. il Sat Eve Post 236:40+ D 14 '63
Muscular dystrophy clue. F. Marley. il Sci N L 85:183 Mr 21 '64
Muscular dystrophy prevented in lambs. Sci N L 85:79 F 1 '64
Of muscles & enzymes; possible prevention of muscular dystrophy. il Time 84:59 Ag 21 '64
DZIEWANOWSKI, M. K.
West Germany and East Europe. Cur Hist 44:208-13+ Ap '63

E

E. B. Crocker art gallery, Sacramento, Calif.
Notes for a gazetteer. P. Hamburger. New Yorker 38:86-8 F 2 '63
ECAFE. See United Nations—Economic commission for Asia and the Far East
ECE. See United Nations—Economic commission for Europe
ECLA. See United Nations—Economic commission for Latin America
ECSC. See European coal and steel community
EEC. See European economic community
EEOC. See United States—President's committee on equal employment opportunity
EFTA. See European free trade association
EIA. See Electronic industries association
E. I. Du Pont de Nemours and company. See Du Pont de Nemours, E I and company
ELDO. See European launcher development organization
EMI. See Electric and musical industries, limited
ENI (Ente nazionale idrocarburi) See Petroleum industry and trade—Italy
EOS. See Electro-optical systems, incorporated
EPC. See Educational policies commission
EPE-D (energetic particles Explorer D) See Artificial satellites—Use in research
E pluribus unum (motto) See Mottoes
EPTA (expanded program of technical assistance) See United Nations—Technical assistance program
E. R. Squibb and sons. See Squibb, E. R. and sons
ERC. See United States—National aeronautics and space adminstration—Electronics research center (proposed)
ERMA (electronic recording machine accounting) See Calculating machines
ESB (electrostimulation of the brain) See Electrophysiology
ESI. See Educational services, incorporated
ESP. See Extrasensory perception
ESRO. See European space research organization
ETS. See Educational testing service
ETV. See Television in education
ETV stations. See Television stations, Educational
E-type Charlie; story. See Benedictus, D.
EACH man in his time; story. See Epstein, S.
EAGAN, William B.
Ten retaining walls to dress up your yard. Pop Mech 119:160-2 My '63
You can make a lattice fence. il Flower Grower 50:22 Jl '63
EAGER, Edward
(tr) See Pirandello, L. Call it virtue

EAGLE, Joanna Shaw
7,000 years of Iranian art. Craft Horiz 24:34-9+ N '64
Shugen Inouye: potter. Craft Horiz 23:33-5+ N '63
EAGLE (emblem) See Emblems, National
EAGLE HARBOR, Mich.
Where copper is king. E. J. La Branche. il Travel 122:40-2 Jl '64
EAGLES
Bald eagles aren't producing enough young; summary of address, November 10, 1962. A. Sprunt, 4th. il Audubon Mag 65:32-5 Ja '63
Golden eagle report on the way. C. W. Buchheister. Audubon Mag 66:147 My '64
Old Abe the battle eagle; Wisconsin outfit's mascot during Civil war. B. Catton. il Am Heritage 14:32-3+ O '63
Old Abe, Wisconsin's Civil war eagle, was there. F. Hallam. il Audubon Mag 65:222-5 Jl '63
Regulations on golden eagle are tightened. Nat Parks Mag 37:22 Ap '63
Slaughter is tarnishing golden eagle population. Sci N L 84:328 N 23 '63
Wintering eagles on the Mississippi. O. S. Pettingill, jr. il Audubon Mag 65:342-3 N '63
Wolves and congressmen. D. Cort. il Nation 197:216-18 O 12 '63
EAKIN, Mary K.
Notes on high school book selection. Library J 89:4603-4 N 15 '64
EAKINS, Thomas
Familiar truths in clear and beautiful language. J. Canaday. il por Horizon 6:88-105 Autumn '64
Positive and negative forms in and around the figure. P. Pollack. il Pop Phot 54:66-7+ My '64
EALEY, E. H. M.
Kangaroo cave life. il Natur Hist 72:42-9 D '63
EAR
In the ear and eye, complex hi-fi gives us sound and sight. R. Campbell. il Life 54:70-2, 76B+ Je 28 '63
Inside the inner ear. il Time 83:68 Ap 10 '64
See also
Deafness
Hearing
Labyrinth (ear)
EAR (animals)
Ears of dipodomys; bannertail kangaroo rat. D. B. Webster. il Natur Hist 74:26-33 F '65
Mitoses; distribution in mouse ear epidermis. J. V. Frei and others. bibliog il Science 140:487-8 My 3 '63
EAR (insects)
Night fighters in a sonic duel; moth's use of hearing to evade bats. K. D. Roeder. il Natur Hist 73:32-9 Ja '64
EAR phones. See Earphones
EARL, Jay J.
Buy a piano you'll keep on enjoying. Pop Mech 121:124-7 F '64
EARLE, Howard
Loan program that helps you become a doctor. Todays Health 41:36-41 Jl '63
Pesticides: facts, not fear. Todays Health 41:18-23+ F '63
Recruiting tomorrow's doctors today. Todays Health 41:34-6+ N '63
Remarkable world of dentistry. Todays Health 41:36-9+ Ap '63
Self-help plan for doctorless towns. Todays Health 41:34-9 S '63
What is your brain power? Todays Health 41:50-5 O '63
EARLHAM, I.
Here's how they help out mother and dad. R. C. Davids. il Farm J 88:58B-58C N '64
EARLHAM college, Richmond, Ind.
Earlham's considerate library; Lilly library. E. I. Farber. il Library J 88:4561-4 D 1 '63
New departure: a Quaker seminary. D. E. Trueblood. Christian Cent 80:531-2+ Ap 24 '63
EARLY rising
Blessings of life before breakfast. M. M. Bitker. il Read Digest 84:56-8 Ja '64
EARLY school admissions project. See Baltimore—Education
EARNEST, Ernest
New Yorker tale; poem. Atlan 211:114 F '63
EARNINGS, Corporate. See Corporations—Finance
EARNSHAW, Donald
Locomobile. Motor T 16:78-81 D '64
Special-interest cars. Motor T 16:78 N '64
EARPHONES
Aerospace uses seen for ear microphone. B. Miller. il Aviation W 81:53-4 Jl 27 '64
Any phone goes; magnetic, dynamic, or crystal. A. Trauffer. il Pop Electr 18:56 F '63
Assemble a phone-boost. L. Garner. il Pop Electr 19:55-6+ N '63
Build the inductaphons; wireless earphone. P. Carr. il Pop Electr 18:65-8 My '63
Earphones for stereo? R. N. Angus. Mod Phot 27:90+ S '63
FM listening with no amplifier. A. Trauffer. il Pop Mech 119:140 F '63
Headphones up to date. A. Sterling. il Hi Fi 14:52-5 Ap '64
High fidelity (title varies) C. L. Osborne. Opera N 27:35 Ap 13 '63
Koss PRO-4 stereo earphones. L. Zide. il Am Rec G 29:960 Ag '63
Mono use of stereo phones having two plugs. A. Trauffer. il Electr World 71:79 My '64
Radio earphones for back seaters. H. L. Davidson. il Pop Mech 119:141 F '63
Stereo head-phones. il Consumer Rep 28:481-5 O '63
Surplus stereophones. J. H Larimore. il Pop Electr 20:100 My '64
EARRINGS
Extra big earrings; with photographs by P. Harrington. Look 27:38+ Mr 12 '63
EARTH
Geonomists, unite; study of the earth. Newsweek 62:78 S 2 '63
Planet called earth, by G. Gamow. Review
New Yorker 39:241-4 N 23 '63. J. Bernstein
Sci Digest il 54:86 S '63. H. Pryor
Scientists in collision: was Velikovsky right? E. Larrabee. Harper 227:48-50+ Ag '63; Discussion. 227:12+ O; 83-7 D '63; 228:12 Ja '64
See also
Cosmology
Magnetism, Terrestrial

Age

Fission-track ages and track-annealing behavior of some micas. R. L. Fleischer and others. bibliog il Science 143:349-51 Ja 24 '64
See also
Geological time

Crust

See Earth—Surface

Internal structure

Deep structure of continents. G. J. F. MacDonald. bibliog il Science 143:921-9 F 28 '64
Geochronology. G. R. Tilton and S. R. Hart. bibliog il Science 140:357-66 Ap 26 '63
Geologic evolution of North America. A. E. J. Engel. bibliog il Science 140:143-52 Ap 12 '63
How NSF got lost in Mohole. H. Solow. il Fortune 67:138-41+ My '63
Inhomogeneous mantle; Upper Mantle project. Sci Am 209:56 O '63
Messages from inside the earth. G. H. T. Kimble. il N Y Times Mag p 14-15+ Ap 28 '63
Moon captured by earth. W. Davis. Sci N L 83:291 My 11 '63
New earth core theory. Sci N L 85:291 My 9 '64
Relative contributions of uranium, thorium, and potassium to heat production in the earth. G. J. Wasserburg and others. bibliog il Science 143:465-7 Ja 31 '64
Russians dig to reach below earth's crust. Sci N L 84:135 Ag 31 '63
Upper Mantle project. V. V. Beloussov. il UNESCO Courier 16:12-17 O '63
See also
Mohole project

Rotation

Slowing down. Newsweek 62:103 O 21 '63
See also
Foucault's pendulum

Surface

Earth's crust measured. Sci N L 83:262, 338 Ap 27, Je 1 '63
Geology of the crust and mantle, western United States. G. A. Thompson and M. Talwani. bibliog il Science 146:1539-49 D 18 '64
See also
Earth tides
Faults (geology)
Ocean bottom

Temperature

See Earth temperature
EARTH, Photography of. See Space photography

EARTH magnetism. See Magnetism, Terrestrial

EARTH movements

Earth movements: Alaskan earthquake, 1964. M. N. Christensen and B. A. Bolt. Science 145:1207-8+ S 11 '64

See also

Mine subsidences

Seismology

EARTH pollution. See Soil pollution

EARTH science. See Geology

EARTH station, Andover, Me. See United States—National aeronautics and space administration

EARTH temperature

Geothermal heat flow in the Gulfs of California and Aden. R. P. von Herzen. bibliog il Science 140:1207-8 Je 14 '63

Relative contributions of uranium, thorium, and potassium to heat production in the earth. G. J. Wasserburg and others. bibliog il Science 143:465-7 Ja 31 '64

EARTH tides

Tides in earth studied by Columbia scientists. Sci N L 84:5 Jl 6 '63

EARTHQUAKE detectors. See Seismometers

EARTHQUAKES

California plays ostrich: the earthquake taboo. D. Cort. il Nation 199:404-6 N 30 '64

Earthquake from explosion. B. Tufty. Sci N L 85:293 My 9 '64

Earthquakes not cause of any bad weather. Sci N L 85:227 Ap 11 '64

How earthquakes were naturalized; excerpts from writings. Voltaire; T. D. Kendrick; W. C. Putnam. Sat R 47:44-5 My 2 '64

Mystery of earthquakes; where, when, what to do; interview. I. Zietz. il U S News 56:37-9 Ap 13 '64

Next big quake, where will it hit? W. Cloud. il Pop Sci 184:45-9+ Je '64

Quake prediction seen. Sci N L 84:404 D 28 '63

Shocks follow quake. B. Tufty. Sci N L 86:327 N 21 '64

What causes earthquakes, hopes for predicting them. A. Rosenfeld. il Life 56:37-8 Ap 10 '64

What's your quake I.Q? questions and answers. J. Daugherty and M. Daugherty. il Sci Digest 56:57-9 Jl '64

See also

Faults (geology)

Seismic sea waves

Seismology

Seismometers

Research

Alaska: first phase of post-quake reconstruction ending; long-term scientific program is under way. J. Walsh. Science 146:38-9 O 2 '64

Earthquake alarm. Newsweek 62:72 Ag 26 '63

Earthquake prediction; report on conference held in Tokyo. J. Oliver. Science 144:1364-5 Je 12 '64

Quake damage greater miles from origin. Sci N L 86:89 Ag 8 '64

Alaska

Alaska, a shattered giant picks up the pieces. il Sr Schol 84:6-8 Ap 24 '64

Alaska: a thorough postmortem on earthquake urged on behalf of both science, reconstruction. J. Walsh. il Science 144:515-18 My 1 '64

Alaska after the big quake; shaky jokes and too many cooks. D. Moser. il Life 56:21 My 29 '64

Alaska after the quake; a look at the future. K. M. Chrysler. il U S News 56:34-6 Ap 13 '64

Alaska aviation reacts rapidly to quake. R. G. O'Lone. il Aviation W 80:25-6 Ap 6 '64

Alaska begins to rebuild. il Sr Schol 84:17-18 Ap 17 '64

Alaska digs out. R. E. Wolf. il Am For 70:10-13+ My '64

Alaska digs out of disaster; federal aid is needed. il Bsns W p25-6 Ap 4 '64

Alaska earthquake, 27 March 1964; report on meeting. D. Landen. il Science 145:74-6 Jl 3 '64

Alaska: first phase of post-quake reconstruction ending; long-term scientific program is under way. J. Walsh. Science 146:38-9 O 2 '64

Alaska quake damages all building types. il Arch Forum 120:5 My '64

Alaska starts on way back; no outright federal grants to victims. il Bsns W p 162 Ap 11 '64

Alaskan earthquake of 27 March 1964; remote seiche stimulation. W. L. Donn. bibliog il Science 145:261 Jl 17 '64

Alaskan family's night of terror. T. P. Thomas. il Nat Geog Mag 126:142-56 Jl '64

Alaskan quake ruptured Norad links, hit alert hangars, Nikes. Aviation W 80:27 Ap 13 '64

Alaska's rise and fall. Newsweek 63:62 My 4 '64

Anchorage fights back. L. L. Woodman. il Am City 79:118-20 S; 119-21 O '64

Bad Friday. il Time 83:29 Ap 3 '64

Damage to Alaskan libraries: report from the state librarian; letter. H. Dirtadian. ALA Bul 58:371 My '64

Danger: tidal wave! S. V. Jones. il Sci Digest 56:83-7 Jl '64

Earth movements: Alaskan earthquake 1964. M. N. Christensen and B. A. Bolt. Science 145:1207-8+ S 11 '64

Earthquake rings earth. A. Ewing. Sci N L 85:227 Ap 11 '64

Earthquake! W. P. E. Graves. il Nat Geog Mag 126:112-39 Jl '64

Earthquake, tidal waves, strike Alaska; Forest service and BLM survey damage. Am For 70:12 Ap '64

Fury of the quake: 200,000 megatons; with report by A. Rosenfeld. il Life 56:26-32F+ Ap 10 '64

Future for Alaska. Nation 198:386 Ap 20 '64

Hell on Good Friday; Alaskan quake. il Newsweek 63:19 Ap 6 '64

How a stricken state met chaos. B. Lindeman. il Sat Eve Post 237:24-31 My 9 '64

Letter from Anchorage. J. Stewart. Pub W 185:21 Ap 13 '64

Long, hard road to recovery. T. R. Paden. Christian Cent 81:710+ My 27 '64

Picking up the pieces. il Newsweek 63:24 Ap 13 '64

Picking up the pieces; Good Friday earthquake in Anchorage. il Time 83:22-3 Ap 10 '64

Seven severe sickening minutes: Anchorage, Alaska. L. L. Woodman. il Am City 79:98-9+ My '64

Terra infirma. il Newsweek 63:86+ Ap 13 '64

Why Anchorage rocked. il Time 83:45-6 Ap 10 '64

Azores

Atlantic peril: earthquakes on São Jorge Azores islands. Newsweek 63:32 Mr 2 '64

Shucks! no lava; São Jorge. Time 83:29 F 28 '64

Japan

Changing scene: city of Niigata. il Newsweek 63:32 Je 29 '64

Good-luck city; Niigata. il Time 83:31 Je 26 '64

300,000 earthquakes a year. E. M. F. d'Albe. il UNESCO Courier 16:26-9 O '63

Two minutes to noon; condensation. N. F. Busch. il Read Digest 84:221-6+ Mr '64

Libya

Sunset shock; destruction of El Marj. Time 81:26 Mr 1 '63

This boy witnessed the wrath of Allah. J. Bonfante. il Life 54:36-8 Mr 8 '63

Mexico

Mexico mapped into four earthquake zones. Sci Digest 53:57 F '63

Morocco

Night the world fell down; ed. by A. Burgess. S. Martin. il Read Digest 83:64-9 Ag '63

Portugal

How earthquakes were naturalized; excerpts from writings. Voltaire; T. D. Kendrick; W. C. Putnam. Sat R 47:44-5 My 2 '64

United States

California's coming earthquake. V. H. Gaddis. il Sci Digest 54:27-34 D '63

Earthquake country, by R. Iacopi. Review Sunset il 132:116-17 My '64

See also

Earthquakes—Alaska

San Francisco—Earthquake and fire, 1906

Yugoslavia

Letter from Skopje. E. Larrabee. il New Yorker 40:131-2+ O 17 '64

Missing minarets: Skoplje. il Newsweek 62:35 Ag 12 '63

Quakes take annual toll; Skoplje earthquake. Sci N L 84:87 Ag 10 '63

Shock in Skoplje: with report by R. Chelminski. il Life 55:62A-68+ Ag 9 '63

EARTHQUAKES—Yugoslavia—*Continued*
Trembling dawn; city of Skoplje. il Time 82: 20 Ag 2 '63
Twice obliterated; Skoplje. il Newsweek 62: 36 Ag 5 '63
When a killer quake hits a city. il U S News 55:12 Ag 5 '63

EARTHQUAKES and building
Quake resistant buildings. Sci N L 85:227 Ap 11 '64
Wanted: more quake-proof buildings. K. Takeyama. il UNESCO Courier 16:30-2 O '63

EARTHS, Rare
Allotropy in some rare-earth metals at high pressures. G. J. Piermarini and C. E. Weir. bibliog il Science 144:69-71 Ap 3 '64
High-pressure B-type polymorphs of some rare-earth sesquioxides. H. R. Hoekstra and K. A. Gingerich. bibliog il Science 146:1163-4 N 27 '64
Rare-earth elements in tektites. L. Haskin and M. A. Gehl. bibliog il Science 139:1056-8 Mr 15 '63
Rare-earth metals in the sun. R. N. Watts, jr. Sky & Tel 26:328 D '63
See also
Lutetium

EARTHWORKS (archeology)
Ancient America's geometers; Poverty Point earthworks. J. Lear. il Sat R 47:53-6 O 3 '64; Discussion. 47:71-2 N 7; 86 D 5 '64

EARTHWORMS
Happy grunting grounds; inducing fish worms to surface. J. Prokop. il Am For 70:50 Ja '64
When nothing else works, try worms. S. James. il Pop Mech 121:116-17 Ap '64

EASELS
It's an easel for two. il Sunset 133:100 Jl '64

EASON, Leo A.
Want a job? ASCUS. NEA J 52:53-4 D '63

EAST, Ben
Are we wasting our best hunting? Outdoor Life 131:32-5+ Mr '63
Deer war. Outdoor Life 132:17-19+ D '63
Get the game, grab the jet. Outdoor Life 131: 13-15+ Ja '63
Great little cat. Outdoor Life 135:24-7+ Ja '65
How to catch trout on opening day. Outdoor Life 133:47-9+ Ap '64
My hare turns white. Outdoor Life 134:50-2+ D '64
They find lost men. Outdoor Life 133:33-5+ Je '64
They watched for ravens gathering. Outdoor Life 133:40-3+ Mr '64
Two best ways to get a deer. por Outdoor Life 132:46-7+ N '63
(ed) See Bear, F. My greatest trophy; tiger with an arrow
(ed) See Helser, P. Double hat rack
(ed) See Streubel, D. Biggest black ever killed

EAST, Frank D.
More truck-tire mileage. Am City 79:86-8 Jl '64

EAST, Marjorie
Economics in home economics. NEA J 52: 33-4 F '63

EAST, Sarita Kenedy
Will & two ways. Time 82:64 N 22 '63

EAST (United States) See Atlantic states

EAST AFRICA. See Africa, East

EAST AFRICAN FEDERATION (proposed)
East African Federation. C. G. Rosberg, jr. and A. Segal. bibliog f il Int Concil 543:4-72 My '63
Third largest; proposed East African Federation. il Time 81:39 Je 14 '63

EAST AFRICAN safari. See Automobile racing

EAST and West
Challenged to reconcile. I. Travers-Ball. America 109:736-7 D 7 '63
De Gaulle and Asia. Nation 198:157 F 17 '64
Developing nations of the world: necessity of working together; address, December 6, 1963. Prince Bernhard. Vital Speeches 30: 229-33 F 1 '64
Divided world of communism; interview, ed. by E. Abel. D. Rusk. Dept State Bul 48: 644-6 Ap 29 '63
East versus West, a thinking man's society. Sci Digest 53:60 Mr '63
Lonely nationalism of Rudyard Kipling. K. W. Deutsch and N. Wiener. Yale R 52:499-517 Je '63
Orient-Occident: a study in ignorance; excerpts from Encounters and celebrations. G. Fradier. il UNESCO Courier 16:4-7 Ap '63
Secretary Rusk discusses the outlook for 1964 over Japanese television; interview, December 24, 1963. D. Rusk. Dept State Bul 50: 40-6 Ja 13 '64
Squeeze play on U.S. in Asia: the Mao-Sukarno axis. il U S News 56:72-4 My 18 '64

EAST ASIA Christian conference
Asian studies in church history. G. H. Anderson. Christian Cent 80:1306 O 23 '63
For greater unity in east Asia. A. Carleton. Christian Cent 81:612+ My 6 '64

EAST BERLIN. See Berlin (East Berlin)

EAST BERLINERS. See Berliners

EAST EUROPEAN studies. See Area studies

EAST GERMAN refugees. See Refugees, German

EAST GERMANY. See Germany (Democratic Republic)

EAST HADDAM, Conn.
Charming folly restored; Goodspeed opera house. il Arch Forum 119:102-7 Ag '63
Rebirth of a relic; Goodspeed opera house. il Newsweek 62:60 Jl 1 '63

EAST HAMPTON, N.Y.
Summer place. il Time 84:46 Ag 14 '64

EAST Harlem Protestant parish
Come out of the wilderness. by B. Kenrick. Review
Christian Cent 80:431-2 Ap 3 '63. W. Stringfellow

EAST HENDRED, England
Town no scandal can shake. M. Gellhorn. Vogue 142:144-5+ N 15 '63

EAST HILLS, N.Y.
It costs less, accomplishes more. E. Johannemann. il Am City 79:15 Ap '64

EAST INDIAN authors. See Authors, Indian (East Indian)

EAST INDIAN refugees. See Refugees, Indian (East Indian)

EAST INDIANS
New crorepathis; the Marwaris. il Time 81: 77 Mr 1 '63
Peasant; College graduate; Bourgeois; Sweeper. il Newsweek 63:42-3 Je 29 '64

EAST ORANGE, N.J.
Dirty streets have no place in our cleanest city. R. P. English and others. il Am City 78:93-5 My '63

Education

Blueprint for progress: proposed one-campus school system. W. K. Richards. il Sr Schol 85:11T Ja 14 '65

EAST ORANGE, N.J. public library
ABC classification for children using school and public libraries. L. K. M. Gorski. Library J 88:4437-40 N 15 '63; Discussion. 89: 298 Ja 15 '64

EAST PACIFIC rise. See Ocean bottom

EAST PAKISTAN. See Pakistan

EAST PROVIDENCE, R.I.
Foam-equipped fire-pumper. E. Griffith. il Am City 78:149-50 F '63

EAST side. See New York (city)—Description

EAST Side house settlement, incorporated
East Side house is grateful to Antiques magazine. C. F. Smithers. il Antiques 85:34 Ja '64; 87:50 Ja '65

EAST Side house settlement winter antiques show. See Antiques—Exhibitions

EAST-West center, Honolulu. See Hawaii. University, Honolulu—Cultural center

EAST-West center press
East-West interchange through books. A. Morris. America 112:44 Ja 9 '65

EAST-West exchange agreements. See Exchange of persons programs

EAST-West relations. See International relations

EAST-West trade. See Communist countries—Commerce

EASTER
Autumnal Easter. Christian Cent 80:355 Mr 20 '63
Easter in Crete. D. M. Doren. il Sat R 46: 34-6+ Mr 16 '63
Easter in Italy; the reverent festival. G. Maddox. il Todays Health 41:40-3+ Ap '63
Easter in 1963. America 108:486 Ap 13 '63
Easter in Norilsk. America 110:404 Mr 28 '64
Fixed date for Easter a possibility. Christian Cent 80:1394 N 13 '63
How to rise above the fear of death. N. V. Peale. Read Digest 82:103-6 Ap '63
In the joyous season. M. E. Jenkins. PTA Mag 58:2-3 Mr '64
Indomitable Easter. Christian Cent 81:476 Ap 15 '64
See also
Jesus Christ—Resurrection and ascension

EASTER—*Continued*

Drama

Peppermint Easter egg. M. E. Slattery. Plays 22:35-42 Ap '63

Poetry

Resurrection. I. N. Munson. Good H 156: 73 Ap '63
Seven other last words. W. I. Elliott. Christian Cent 80:461 Ap 10 '63

EASTER baskets
My running fight with the Easter bunny. J. Coogan. il Ladies Home J 80:55-6 Ap '63

EASTER breads. See Bread

EASTER business. See Retail trade

EASTER dinners. See Dinners and dining

EASTER eggs
Dress up your eggs for Easter. H. Sibley. il Pop Mech 119:160-1 Ap '63
Easter egg fantasy; decorated eggs. il Design 65:146-8+ Mr '64
Easter egg party. B. Stover. il Parents Mag 39:75 Mr '64
Easter eggs in wonderland. V. E. Walker. il Ladies Home J 80:104+ Ap '63
Egghead ideas. il Recreation 56:176-7 Ap '63
Fun with Easter eggs. il Parents Mag 38:75 Ap '63
How to decorate Easter eggs. il Am Home 67: 26+ Mr '64
Nursery rhyme Easter eggs. il Good H 156: 112-13+ Ap '63

EASTER ISLAND
Easter Island study set to precede airfield. Sci N L 86:131 Ag 29 '64

EASTERN AI cooperatives, incorporated
Dairymen to get better sires. Farm J 87:8 Je '63

EASTERN air lines
Air shuttle soaring. il Bsns W p 130 Ap 27 '63
Blow to Eastern; merger with American turned down. Newsweek 62:56 Jl 1 '63
Eastern boosts aircraft, flight reliability. J. R. Ashlock. il Aviation W 81:37+ Ag 17 '64
Eastern president sees one-year wait before financial recovery. J. R. Ashlock. Aviation W 80:40 Ap 27 '64
Eastern seeking $60-million loan after $14.9-million loss in 1962. J. R. Ashlock. Aviation W 78:37 Mr 25 '63
Eastern shuffle aimed at ending losses. Aviation W 81:31 Jl 20 '64
Eastern's new pilot. Newsweek 62:79+ D 2 '63
Flight engineers prepare new moves in dispute with Eastern. Aviation W 79:43 S 23 '63
In & out at Eastern. Time 82:94+ N 29 '63
Industry wary of Eastern fare revisions. R. G. O'Lone. Aviation W 82:27-8 Ja 11 '65
New Eastern. Time 85:80 Ja 15 '65
Private turbulence of Eastern air lines. I. Ross. il Fortune 70:172-4+ Jl '64
TWA's Hall selected to succeed MacIntyre as Eastern's president. Aviation W 79:37-8 N 25 '63

EASTERN churches
See also
Byzantine rite
Orthodox Eastern church

EASTERN college librarians. See Conference of eastern college librarians

EASTERN EUROPE. See Europe, Eastern

EASTERN EUROPEAN fiction. See European fiction

EASTERN EUROPEANS. See Europeans

EASTERN GERMANY. See Germany (Democratic Republic)

EASTERN Orthodox church. See Orthodox Eastern church

EASTERN Orthodox church in the United States. See Orthodox Eastern church in the United States

EASTERN states farmers' exchange
GFL-ESFX propose marriage. il Farm J 88: 38+ Ja '64

EASTERN white pine. See Pine

EASTLAKE, William
Land of grace and isolation. D. Phelps. il Nation 199:225-7 O 12 '64

EASTLAND, James O.
Eastland's charge: Communists are moving into civil rights; excerpts from address, July 22, 1964. por U S News 57:4 Ag 3 '64

about

Annals of legislation. B. Harris. New Yorker 40:56+ Mr 28 '64

EASTMAN, Fred
Fred Eastman: a cultural pioneer. Christian Cent 80:516 Ap 24 '63

EASTMAN, George
U.S.A. revisited; Kodak man. J. Dos Passos. Atlan 213:52-3 Ap '64

EASTMAN, Linda A.
Linda A. Eastman. R. C. Lindquist. pors ALA Bul 57:783-5 S '63

EASTMAN, Max
Am I conservative? por Nat R 16:57-8 Ja 28 '64
Courtship among the insects. Audubon Mag 65:152-4 My '63; Same abr. with title Love among the insects. Read Digest 82:193-6 Je '63
Immortal treasures of Florence. Read Digest 85:145-51 S '64

about

Cheerful radical. il pors Time 85:67+ Ja 8 '65
Eastman's loves and revolutions. W. S. Schlamm. por Nat R 17:65-6 Ja 26 '65
Exile from socialism. J. L. Featherstone. New Repub 152:19+ Ja 16 '65
Traveling man. il por Newsweek 65:62 Ja 4 '65

EASTMAN Kodak company
Automated cameras catch the customers; instamatic cameras. il Bsns W p82 Ag 3 '63
Instamatic v. rapid. il Time 84:98 S 4 '64
It's good business; employee relations. L. L. L. Golden. Sat R 47:59 Jl 11 '64
Kodak introduces instant loading. il Pop Phot 52:45-6 My '63
Kodak's new click. il Time 81:86 Mr 8 '63
Kodak's new teaching tool. D. Vestal. il Pop Phot 54:16+ Ap '64
Kodak's photo wonderland Pop Phot 54:124-5 My '64
Negative positive. A. Asnis. U S Camera 26: 36+ D '63
New Kodak Instamatics. il Consumer Rep 28:534 N '63
Quality at Kodak. T. R. Brooks. il Duns R 81:33-5+ Je '63

EASTMAN school of music, Rochester, N.Y.
Eastman's Walter Hendl. P. Davis. Mus Am 84:286-7 D '64

EASTON, Florence
Florence Easton. A. Favia-Artsay. pors Hobbies 68:30-1 D '63

EASY chairs. See Chairs

EAT, drink, and be wary; story. See Perelman, S. J.

EATHERLY, Claude Robert
Hiroshima pilot, by W. B. Huie. Review
Esquire 62:10+ Jl '64. M. Muggeridge
Nation 198:440-2 Ap 27 '64. W. Whitman
Time pors 83:99 My 1 '64
Hiroshima pilot. il por Newsweek 64:53 D 21 '64
Will to believe. M. Kempton. New Repub 150:17-20 Ap 11 '64

EATING
Filet of hippo, anyone? Anteaters association. A. Chamberlin. il Sat Eve Post 238: 78+ Ja 30 '65
Gourmets of San Sebastian. B. Wason. il Atlan 213:117+ Je '64
Ketchup, yet! new wave in French eating habits. il Newsweek 65:36 F 1 '65
Spreads; entremets of opinion on the matter of eating for the holiday season, comp. by B. Francis. il N Y Times Mag p69-70 N 29 '64
Stupid questions about what you eat. J. Berry. il Pop Sci 185:74-5+ N '64
Thomas Jefferson, gourmet. J. H. Hazelton. il Am Heritage 15:20-1+ O '64
See also
Diet
Food

EATING, Psychology of
Behavior in hydra: inhibition of the contraction responses of hydra pirardi. N. B. Rushforth and others. bibliog il Science 145:602-4 Ag 7 '64
Eat your way out of the blues. Sci Digest 54: 60 Jl '63
Fat man's weakness. Newsweek 65:50 F 1 '65
Great balancing act: eating vs. activity. M. F. Trulson, and F. J. Stare. il Todays Health 41:35-7+ Je '63
Neuroses in nut eating. L. Morse. Duns R 83:66+ My '64
Odd food, emotion link. Sci N L 84:101 Ag 17 '63
Personality, diet link. Sci N L 84:197 S 28 '63
Why fat people keep eating. Time 84:51 Jl 24 '64

EATON, Allen
Obituary
Craft Horiz por 23:10 Ja '63

EATON, Charles C, company. See Shoes—Trade and manufacture

EATON, Charles Edward
Chores; poem. Reporter 29:45 S 26 '63
Kite; poem. Reporter 30:44 Mr 12 '64
Last page but one; poem. Reporter 29:34 D 19 '63
October; poem. Commonweal 81:166 O 30 '64
Parrot; poem. Reporter 31:60 Ag 13 '64
Stuff of life; poem. Sat R 46:42 Ap 20 '63
EATON, Ethel M.
Geraniums from seed. Horticulture 41:362 Jl '63
EATON, Jerome A.
Home-greenhouse. See issues of Flower grower
EATON, Quaintance
Carnegie and opera. Opera N 28:27-31 Mr 14 '64
Great opera houses. Opera N 28:28-33 F 8 '64; 29:28-33 Ja 9 '65
Renaissance woman. Opera N 28:26-9 Ap 18 '64
EATON, T, company, limited. See Toronto—Stores
EATON, William J.
Battle of the Great Lakes. Reporter 29:38-40 N 21 '63
EATONTOWN, N.J.
Color and texture brighten a compact shopping center. il Arch Rec 135:174-6 Je '64
EAVESDROPPING devices. See Electronics in criminal investigation, espionage, etc.
EBAN, Abba
Freedom with knowledge. UNESCO Courier 16:10-13 Jl '63
EBEL, Robert L.
Social consequences of educational testing. Sch & Soc 92:331-4 N 14 '64
EBENSTEIN, William
Totalitarianism. bibliog NEA J 53:59-62 Ap '64
EBERHARD, Tom
Wilderness whodunit. Outdoor Life 133:10+ Mr '64
EBERHART, Jonathan
F-111 gives and takes. Sci N L 86:279 O 31 '64
Five launchings at once. Sci N L 86:51 Jl 25 '64
Looking afar, from afar. Sci N L 87:10-11 Ja 2 '65
Machines reproducing. Sci N L 85:303 My 9 '64
Man's leap into space. Sci N L 86:373-4 D 12 '64
Next on moon: Surveyor. Sci N L 86:101 Ag 15 '64
Reusable rocket designed. Sci N L 86:197 S 26 '64
Space shot significance. Sci N L 86:259 O 24 '64
EBERHART, Richard
Am I my neighbor's keeper? poem. Sat R 46:37 F 2 '63
Cold white death; poem. Atlan 214:73 S '64
Death by drowning; poem. Sat R 47:35 F 8 '64
Ruby Daggett; poem. Nation 198:398 Ap 20 '64
Vision; poem. New Yorker 39:54 O 5 '63
about
Touching sacred objects. W. Stafford. Poetry 102:116-17 My '63
EBERSOLE, Mark C.
Proper and the quasi. Christian Cent 80:273 F 27 '63
EBERT, Alan
(ed) See Bancroft, A. What did you want most at seventeen?
(ed) See Burnett, C. What did you want most at seventeen?
(ed) See Daniel, M. T. What did you want most at seventeen?
(ed) See Marshall, C. What did you want most at seventeen?
(ed) See Page, P. What did you want most at seventeen?
(ed) See Rama Rau, S. What did you want most at seventeen?
EBERT, James D.
Biology on the cuff. is AIBS worth saving? Science 139:321-2 Ja 25 '63
EBLING, George, jr. See Jaslow, R. I. jt. auth.
EBOH, F. S. Okotie-. See Okotie-Eboh, F. S.
EBONY (periodical)
Ebony's ten most trusted whites. Sat R 47:86 My 16 '64
Statement from the publisher. J. H. Johnson. Ebony 18:19 S '63
EBTEHAJ, Abol Hassan
Vindication for Ebtehaj. Time 83:40 F 28 '64
EBY, Ann
We have our own home beauty shop. Parents Mag 39:84 Jl '64
EBY, Gordon M.
Gatti's first lady. Opera N 27:14-15 My 4 '63
(ed) See Sayão, B. Bidú
ECCENTRICS and eccentricities
For the British it's odd man in. B. Holloway. il N Y Times Mag p48-9+ Ja 24 '65
Irish eccentrics. M. Bence-Jones. Vogue 144:124+ O 1 '64
Yank returns to Oxford. B. Smith, jr. il Sat Eve Post 236:70+ Mr 23 '63
ECCLES, Bill
Photography behind Cuba's iron curtain. Mod Phot 27:99 Ag '63
ECCLES, Sir John Carew
Ionic mechanism of postsynaptic inhibition; adapted from address, December 10, 1963. bibliog Science 145:1140-7 S 11 '64
Synapse; with biographical sketch. Sci Am 212:16, 56-66 bibliog(p 134) Ja '65
about
Nobel medical awards. por Sci N L 84:259 O 26 '63
Nobel prize: 1963 award honors three for research on nerve functioning. M. G. F. Fuortes. por Science 142:468-70 O 25 '63
Nobels for nerves. Newsweek 62:90-1 O 28 '63
ECCLESIASTICAL architecture. See Church architecture
ECCLESIASTICAL art. See Christian art and symbolism
ECCLESIASTICAL immunity. See Privileges and immunities
ECCLESIASTICAL law
Canon law on schools. America 112:105 Ja 23 '65
Change in Catholic laws? excerpts from interview. R. Cushing. U S News 54:19 Je 24 '63
Pope's third phase: to revise the church's Code of canon law. America 108:481 Ap 13 '63
Reform of canon law. L. M. Örsy. America 109:514-17 N 2 '63
Revising canon law. J. D. Conway. Commonweal 80:143-6 Ap 24 '64; Discussion. 80:260-1, 300-1 My 22-29 '64
ECCLESIASTICAL music. See Church music
ECCLESIASTICAL polity. See Church government
ECCLESIAM Suam. See Encyclicals
ECDYSONE
Actinomycin and puromycin: effects on sequential gene activation by ecdysone. U. Clever. bibliog il Science 146:794-5 N 6 '64
Ecdysone: five biologically active fractions from Bombyx. W. J. Burdette and M. W. Bullock. bibliog il Science 140:1311 Je 21 '63
Genetics: how nature reads the code. Time 82:61 N 15 '63
ECHANOVE, Carlos A.
Palenque's explorers; excerpts. Américas 15:16-21 Ap '63
ECHEVERIA
Echeverias: variation in foliage flower form. R. C. Hands. il Horticulture 41:278-9 My '63
ECHINODERMS
See also
Embryology—Echinoderms
Sea urchins
ECHINODERMS, Fossil
Helicoplacoidea: a new class of echinoderms. J. W. Durham and K. E. Caster. bibliog il Science 140:820-2 My 17 '63
New echinoderms found. Sci N L 83:381 Je 15 '63
ECHO of love; story. See Kanin, G.
ECHO ranging. See Sonar
ECHO satellites. See Communications satellites
ECK, Richard V.
Genetic code: emergence of a symmetrical pattern. bibliog Science 140:477-81 My 3 '63
ECKELBERRY, Don
Bird painting in a tropical valley. il por Audubon Mag 66:284-9 S '64
ECKENRODE, C. J.
Librarian plays the central role. ALA Bul 58:810-11 O '64
ECKER, David W.
Programmed instruction: challenge or threat to art education? bibliog Sch Arts 63:3-6 O; 12-14 N; 8-10 D '63
ECKER, E. E. See Brenner, L. J. jt. auth.
ECKERT, Allan W.
Lure picking's fun. Field & S 68:122-3 My '63
One license: is it feasible? Field & S 67:53+ Ap '63
Wood-boring carpenter bee. Sci Digest 53:13-18 Ap '63

ECKHOFF, Harry C.
Golf course loan programs; excerpts from address, August 1963. por Recreation 57:24-5 Ja '64
Guidelines for planning a golf course. por Recreation 57:306-8 Je '64
ECKLES, B. F. See Smith, G. S. jt. auth.
ECKMAN, Charley
Here comes Cholly bop de bop bop. F. Deford. il pors Sports Illus 20:40+ F 3 '64
ECKMAN, Fern Marja
Crusade against the poor. Redbook 120:58-9+ F '63
ECKMAN, Frederick
Vocations; Retrospect; poems. Poetry 102: 161-2 Je '63
ECKRICH, Catherine
Cardinal in snowfall; poem. Cath World 200:171 D '64
ECKSTEIN, Alexander
On the economic crisis in Communist China. For Affairs 42:655-68 Jl '64
ECKSTEIN, Gustav
Shiro Tashiro: American scientist. por Sat R 46:64-6 O 5 '63
ECKSTEIN, Harry
Genesis of the National health service. bibliog f Cur Hist 45:6-11+ Jl '63
ECKSTEIN, Jerome
Jewish Aristotelian. Commentary 34:174-6. 35: 77 Ag '62. Ja '63
ECKSTEIN, Otto
Old reliable team. por Newsweek 64:84 N 30 '64
ECKSTRAND, Al
How to drive a champion drag stocker. pors Hot Rod 16:46-7+ Je '63
ECLAIRS. See Pastry
ECLIPSES
See also
Occultations

Photographs

See Astronomical photography
ECLIPSES, Lunar
Cause of the dark moon and those red sunsets. Time 83:75 Ja 10 '64
December 18th lunar eclipse preview. J. Ashbrook. il Sky & Tel 28:386-7 D '64
Early lunar eclipse notes. il Sky & Tel 27: 79 F '64
Eclipse. New Yorker 40:23-4 Ja 2 '65
January's penumbral lunar eclipse is widely viewed. il Sky & Tel 25:153-4 Mr '63
June's total lunar eclipse. Sky & Tel 27: 381 Je '64
Lunar eclipse roundup. il Sky & Tel 28:104-6 Ag '64
Measuring the earth's shadow. J. Ashbrook. il Sky & Tel 27:156-60 Mr '64
Moon eclipse December 30th. J. Ashbrook. il Sky & Tel 26:324-7 D '63
Moon eclipse observed successfully in Africa. Sci N L 86:22 Jl 11 '64
Next total eclipse of the moon. il Sky & Tel 27:320 My '64
Remarkable eclipse of the moon. il Sky & Tel 27:142-6 Mr '64
Sky reporter; total lunar eclipse on June 24th. T. D. Nicholson. il Natur Hist 73: 54-7 Je '64
Total eclipse of moon likely to be dark. Sci N L 85:376 Je 13 '64
Why was last December's lunar eclipse so dark? E. M. Brooks. il Sky & Tel 27:346-8 Je '64
ECLIPSES, Solar
Airplanes seen best for viewing eclipse. il Sci N L 84:69 Ag 3 '63
Alaska notes. L. Coe. il Sky & Tel 26:189 O '63
Astronomers visit Alaska. J. B. Irwin. il Sky & Tel 26:120-5 S '63
Don't look now; safeguards for viewing solar eclipse. il Time 82:72+ Jl 12 '63
Eclipse. il Sat R 46:41 Jl 6 '63
Eclipse. J. Updike. il Sat Eve Post 236:92 N 16 '63
Eclipse across Canada. il Sky & Tel 26:184-9 O '63
Eclipse observing from eastern Maine. C. F. Merriam. il Sky & Tel 25:91-3 F '63
Eclipse outside totality. il Sky & Tel 26:140-3 S '63
Eclipse shadow band motions, an illusion? E. Paulton. il Sky & Tel 25:328-9 Je '63
Eclipse talk, air and ground. L. J. Robinson. il Sky & Tel 26:200-3 O '63
Eclipse travel to Alaska and western Canada. L. Coe. il Sky & Tel 25:202-3 Ap '63
Glory of the sun's big show. il Life 55:14-19 Ag 2 '63
Lunar shadow on Alaska. T. D. Nicholson. il Natur Hist 72:10-17 Je '63
Memorable eclipse. Sky & Tel 26:119 S '63
Moon's shadow at July's solar eclipse. W. H. Glenn. il Sky & Tel 25:339-40 Je '63
Next May's eclipse in the Pacific. F. M. Bateson. il Sky & Tel 28:210-12 O '64
Notes and comment; view from the Bronx. New Yorker 39:19 Ag 3 '63
Notes on July eclipse expeditions. Sky & Tel 25:253 My '63
Notes on the coming solar eclipse. Sky & Tel 25:325 Je '63
Observing the eclipse in Quebec. I. K. Williamson. il Sky & Tel 25:204-5 Ap '63
On July 20 next the world will not come to an end. F. Korotkin. il Sci Digest 54:19-21 Jl '63
Partial phases of July's eclipse. il Sky & Tel 25:258-9 My '63
Photographing July's solar eclipse. P. A. Leavens. il Sky & Tel 25:216-19 Ap '63
See it now. il Newsweek 62:56 Jl 22 '63
Shadow play; July 20, 1963. il Time 82:52 Jl 19 '63
Shoot the solar eclipse! P. A. Leavens. il U S Camera 26:42-3 Jl '63
Sky during totality. W. C. Atkinson. il Sky & Tel 25:205 Ap '63
Solar eclipse from a jet. W. B. Klemperer. il Nat Geog Mag 124:784-96 N '63
Sun eclipse magnificent sight. A. Ewing. il(p 1) Sci N L 84:10 Jl 6 '63
Sun's halo. il Newsweek 62:63 Jl 29 '63
Total eclipse. il Motor B 111:144 Je '63
Total eclipse as seen in Maine. il Sky & Tel 26:126-31 S '63
When filming solar eclipse July 20 beware of your camera and eyesight! W. Lane. il Travel 120:58-60 Jl '63
ECLIPSES, Stellar
Eclipsing stars and their periods. R. Szafraniec. il Sky & Tel 28:20-1 Jl '64
See also
Stars, Double—Eclipses
ECLIPSING stars. See Stars, Variable
ECLOV, Shirley
World of difference; story. Redbook 121:153-76 O '63
ECOLE polytechnique, Paris
X=the French power elite. A. Sampson and V. Makins. il Esquire 62:70-5+ Jl '64
ECOLOGY
Aeolian zone. L. W. Swan. bibliog Science 140:77-8 Ap 5 '63
Cave ecology; symposium. T. C. Barr. Science 144:321-2 Ap 17 '64
Ecological effects of radiation. G. M. Woodwell. il Sci Am 208:40-9 Je '63
Ecological paradox of coastal Peru. E. Y. Dawson. il Natur Hist 72:32-7 O '63
Every home landscape includes a wide variety of climates in miniature. il House & Gard 123:212-14 My '63
Minimum ecological systems for man; report on conference. D. H. Calloway. Science 147: 184+ Ja 8 '65
Onward and upward with the sciences; ecology and taxonomy expeditions of the New York botanical garden. G. T. Hellman. il New Yorker 40:41-2+ My 30 '64
Our fellow immigrants. R. Froman. il Am Heritage 14:60-3+ F '63
Pick the best place for each plant. il House & Gard 123:174-7 My '63
See also
Balance of nature
Botany—Ecology
Fishes—Ecology
Marine ecology
Mountain ecology
Zoology—Ecology
ECOLOGY, Human. See Human ecology
ECONOMAKI, Chris
Profiles in racing; ed. by M. Muhleman. Motor T 15:66-71 Mr '63
ECONOMIC advisers. See Public officers
ECONOMIC assistance
Aid's blind alley. New Repub 150:3-4 Ja 4 '64
Atlantic agenda; address, March 16, 1964. W. W. Rostow. bibliog f Dept State Bul 50:578-87 Ap 13 '64
Common problems of industrial and developing countries; statement, March 25, 1964. G. W. Ball. Dept State Bul 50:634-40 Ap 20 '64
Economics of aid. A. McCormack. il Commonweal 81:227-30 N 13 '64; Reply. F. J. Kottke. 81:494-5 Ja 8 '65
Export economies between East and West. J. Levin. Yale R 52:373-84 Mr '63
Hungry nations, by W. Paddock and P. Paddock. Review
Sat R 48:53 Ja 9 '65. A. E. Burns
On self-help and foreign aid; address, April 2, 1963. F. S. Okotie-Eboh. Vital Speeches 29:502-3 Je 1 '63

ECONOMIC assistance—*Continued*
Open system in North-South relations, April 9, 1964. G. W. Ball. Dept State Bul 50:657-62 Ap 27 '64
Peace levy approach. S. Zaromb. Bul Atomic Sci 20:33-4 Ap '64
Poorer nations face a debt crisis; repaying creditors. il Bsns W p 110+ D 7 '63
Poorer nations find a new bootstrap; private development banks financing over-all economy. Bsns W p63-4+ Mr 14 '64
Pugwash XII; official statement. Bul Atomic Sci 20:45-8 Je '64
Science in less-developed countries; letter. J. B. Calhoun. Science 146:717 N 6 '64
Security and instability. O. Feinstein. Sat R 46:15-16 My 4 '63
Settling price. New Repub 150:3-4 Ap 4 '64
Why foreign aid? B. L. Masse. America 108: 637-9 My 4 '63
See also
International development association
United Nations—Special fund

ECONOMIC assistance, American
Abundance and the future of man. G. Piel. Atlan 213:84-90 Ap '64
Administration urges Congress to support $4.1 billion aid bill; statement, August 20, 1963. J. F. Kennedy. Dept State Bul 49:399 S 9 '63
After 2 billion dollars in aid: troubles for the U.S. from four dictators. il U S News 58:16 Ja 11 '65
Aid and the national interest; address, August 1, 1963. F. M. Coffin. Vital Speeches 29: 719-21 S 15 '63
Aid but not comfort. New Repub 149:3-4 N 23 '63; Reply. E. Gruening. 149:8-9 N 30 '63
Aid, investment in the future; address, April 23, 1963. U. A. Johnson. Dept State Bul 48:829-34 My 27 '63
Aid, or investment? H. Hazlitt. Newsweek 62:77 D 16 '63
Aid without strings. Commonweal 79:180-1 N 8 '63
Aid's blind alley. New Repub 150:3-4 Ja 4 '64
America and the world revolution; symposium, ed. by N. Podhoretz. Commentary 36:278-96 O '63; Discussion. 37:17-18 F '64
America's brightest opportunities. D. Rusk. Nations Bsns 51:76-8+ Je '63
Around the world, reds burn U.S. books. il U S News 57:62-3 D 21 '64
Big slashes in foreign-aid funds. U S News 55:10 D 23 '63
Blunting the ax; aid bill. Newsweek 64: 23-4 Jl 6 '64
Budget of the United States government for the fiscal year ending June 30, 1964; excerpts from budget message. J. F. Kennedy. il Dept State Bul 48:224-8 F 11 '63
Butcher's knife. Newsweek 62:22+ S 2 '63
Caricature of foreign aid; address, December 28, 1962. H. Cleveland. Dept State Bul 48: 60-5 Ja 14 '63
Chip, chip, chip. Time 82:34-5 N 15 '63
Clay report. D. Cater. Reporter 28:10+ Ap 11 '63
Clay's feat. K. Crawford. Newsweek 61:28 Ap 8 '63
Compliments from abroad; editorial in the Daily courier of Kelowna, B.C. Christian Cent 81:1133 S 16 '64
Congress hobbles aid bill. Bsns W p27-8 N 16 '63
Crackdown starts on foreign aid. U S News 55:50 D 2 '63
Crisis in foreign aid: a proposal. G. Ranis. Yale R 53:522-32 Je '64
Cut-down bill. Time 82:21 N 22 '63
Cutting report on foreign aid; Clay committee report. il Newsweek 61:17-18 Ap 1 '63
Dilemma of foreign aid. H. Hazlitt. Newsweek 63:106 Ap 20 '64
Do-it-yourself foreign aid. il Changing T 18:33-5 Je '64
Does foreign aid aid? H. Hazlitt. Newsweek 62:97 N 25 '63
Feat of Clay; findings of Clay committee. Nat R 14:265+ Ap 9 '63
First step; reduction of the foreign aid bill. Nat R 15:176-7 S 10 '63
For foreign aid: curbs and cutbacks. U S News 55:8 N 18 '63
Foreign aid. W. Lippmann. Newsweek 61:17 Ap 29 '63
Foreign aid; a bikini is better than nothing. Time 83:20 Je 19 '64
Foreign aid; a hard look. il Time 83:25 Ja 10 '64
Foreign aid; address, November 8, 1963. J. F. Kennedy. Vital Speeches 30:66-8 N 15 '63; Same with title Our obligations to the family of man. Dept State Bul 49:806-10 N 25 '63
Foreign aid and foreign policy, by H. Feis. Review
Sat R 47:25 Jl 4 '64. D. Perkins
Foreign aid and the liberal dissent. I. Frank. New Repub 152:17-22 Ja 23 '65
Foreign aid: billions in search of a good reason. C. J. V. Murphy. il Fortune 67: 126-30+ Mr '63
Foreign aid cuts. America 109:182 Ag 24 '63
Foreign aid cuts. Commonweal 78:524 S 6 '63
Foreign aid cuts jolt White House; with editorial comment. Bsns W p23, 100 Ag 31 '63
Foreign aid debate. Commonweal 78:156-7 My 3 '63
Foreign aid: debating its doom. il Time 82: 23-4 N 8 '63
Foreign aid: distinctions needed. J. Burnham. Nat R 15:560 D 31 '63
Foreign aid: down, down, down. U S News 56:23 Ja 6 '64
Foreign aid fiasco. P. Duke. il Reporter 30: 20-5 Ja 16 '64; Discussion. 30:6 F 13; 6+ F 27 '64
Foreign-aid folly. H. Hazlitt. Newsweek 62: 77 Jl 8 '63
Foreign aid has succeeded. B. Ward. il N Y Times Mag p9+ Jl 12 '64
Foreign aid: how firm a foundation? R. Calder. Reporter 28:34-6 F 28 '63
Foreign aid: how it was spent in 1962. il Time 82:16 S 27 '63
Foreign aid in trouble. W. V. Shannon. Commonweal 79:246-7 N 22 '63
Foreign aid is a good long-term policy tool. Life 54:4 Ap 12 '63
Foreign aid is like an elephant. J. Nuveen. Christian Cent 80:1463-5 N 27 '63
Foreign aid; message to Congress, March 19, 1964. L. B. Johnson. Dept State Bul 50:518-22 Ap 6 '64
Foreign aid program for 1964; statement, June 11, 1963. D. Rusk. Dept State Bul 49:19-28 Jl 1 '63
Foreign aid program; statement, April 5, 1963; with annex, fiscal year 1964 foreign assistance program. D. Rusk. Dept State Bul 48:664-72 Ap 29 '63
Foreign aid: saved by the Bell? J. Kraft. Harper 226:73-6+ F '63
Foreign aid: success or failure? O. E. Passman. Nat R 14:401-4 My 21 '63
Foreign aid: the essential factors for success; address, May 28, 1963. C. Bowles. Dept State Bul 48:939-45 Je 17 '63
Foreign aid: the hard line. il Newsweek 61:27-9 Je 3 '63
Foreign aid: the Johnson round. P. Duke. Reporter 30:25-6 Mr 26 '64
Foreign aid: the story of 98 billion dollars; interview. D. A. FitzGerald. U S News 54: 48-51 F 25 '63
Foreign aid: time for a diagnosis. il Sr Schol 84:10-12+ F 7 '64
Foreign aid today; address, May 1, 1964. D. E. Bell. Dept State Bul 50:831-5 My 25 '64
Foreign aid; what happened? Commonweal 79:268-9 N 29 '63
Foreign aidsmanship. K. Crawford. Newsweek 62:29 Jl 15 '63
Foreign assistance program; statement, March 23, 1964. D. Rusk. bibliog f Dept State Bul 50:595-601 Ap 13 '64
Fortress Americas; Clay committee policy implications. Nation 196:277 Ap 6 '63
Free-world defense and assistance programs; message to Congress, April 2, 1963. J. F. Kennedy. Dept State Bul 48:591-9 Ap 22 '63
Giving and getting; Clay report on foreign aid. New Repub 148:3-4 Ap 6 '63
History of planned generosity. A. E. Burns. Sat R 47:33-4 Ag 1 '64
How nations aided by U.S. vote in the United Nations; chart. K. Mundt. il U S News 57: 12 Ag 24 '64
Impact of foreign aid on the American economy; address, October 23, 1963. D. E. Bell. Dept State Bul 49:830-3 N 25 '63
Improving the effectiveness of U.S. assistance to international rural development; addresses, July 27, 1964. D. E. Bell; O. L. Freeman. Dept State Bul 51:376-88 S 14 '64
Investment no, aid yes? concerning views of Secretary Dillon. H. Hazlitt. Newsweek 63:84 F 17 '64
Kennedy pulls back on aid; with editorial comment. il Bsns W p26, 108 Ap 6 '63

ECONOMIC assistance, American—*Continued*
Let's stop financing socialism in Latin America. J. G. Tower. Read Digest 84:121-4 Ja '64
Let's stop sending U.S. dollars to aid our enemies. C. Stevenson. Read Digest 83:71-8 Ag '63
Letter to members of House; August 17, 1963. D. Rusk and R. S. McNamara. Dept State Bul 49:399-400 S 9 '63
Local community and world affairs; remarks, April 21, 1964. L. B. Johnson. Dept State Bul 50:746-9 My 11 '64
LBJ's own aid cut. Newsweek 63:17 Mr 30 '64
Major objectives of the foreign aid program; address, November 21, 1964. D. E. Bell. Dept State Bul 51:821-5 D 7 '64
Mansfield mission. America 108:324 Mr 9 '63
Mr Passman meets his match; foreign-aid program. E. B. Drew. Reporter 31:40-3 N 19 '64; Reply. L. Rudel. 31:6 D 17 '64
Much ado about foreign aid; Clay committee. il Sr Schol 82:19-20 Ap 17 '63
New era in foreign aid; what it will mean and where. il U S News 54:40-2 Ap 8 '63
New implications of industrial competition; address, June 10, 1964. D. E. Bell. Dept State Bul 51:205-9 Ag 10 '64
New look at coups; Mann tells U.S. policy; summary of address. T. C. Mann. U S News 56:14 Mr 30 '64
New perspectives on the United States' world relationships; address, April 29, 1963. C. Bowles. Dept State Bul 48:817-23 My 27 '63
New plan for aid abroad, JFK's version. U S News 54:8 Ap 15 '63
New setup in foreign aid? U S News 56:34 Ja 13 '64
No great loss. Nation 196:297 Ap 13 '63
Now what's wrong with the foreign-aid program? J. F. Brewer. America 108:224-7 F 16 '63
On our quarrel with success; address, June 9, 1963. J. K. Galbraith. Dept State Bul 49:52-6 Jl 8 '63
On working with history; address, June 5, 1964. W. W. Rostow. Dept State Bul 50:961-6 Je 22 '64
104-billion-dollar story; with chart. U S News 56:62 Mr 30 '64
$100,000,000,000 mistake; foreign aid program. Nat R 15:471 D 3 '63
One way to cut aid funds by two billions. U S News 55:12 N 11 '63
Planning of development. E. S. Mason. il Sci Am 209:235-6+ bibliog(p310) S '63
President appoints committee to review foreign aid programs; statement, December 26, 1963. L. B. Johnson. Dept State Bul 50:128-9 Ja 27 '64
President Johnson and Secretary Rusk urge full appropriations for foreign aid; statements, December 12 and December 14, 1963. L. B. Johnson; D. Rusk. Dept State Bul 49:999-1004 D 30 '63
President Johnson signs into law Foreign assistance act of 1963; statement, December 16, 1963. L. B. Johnson. Dept State Bul 50:26-7 Ja 6 '64
President reports on operation of foreign assistance program; letter, October 3, 1964. L. B. Johnson. Dept State Bul 51:675-7 N 9 '64
Quest for concepts; findings of Clay committee. Time 81:22 Ap 12 '63
Reply to opponents of foreign aid. D. E. Bell. il N Y Times Mag p9+ S 1 '63
Report on aid. il Time 81:14-16 Mr 29 '63
Report on foreign aid. America 108:460 Ap 6 '63
Revamping foreign aid; Clay commission's report. Commonweal 78:36 Ap 5 '63
Rich world that leans on U.S. il U S News 56:90 Je 29 '64
Same or less; money-saving features in foreign aid programs. Time 83:15 Mr 27 '64
Scratching the surface; financial dishonesty among government employees. Nation 200:1 Ja 4 '65
Secretary Rusk holds press and radio news briefing at Los Angeles. D. Rusk. Dept State Bul 48:363-4 Mr 11 '63
Secretary Rusk's news conference of November 8, 1963. D. Rusk. Dept State Bul 49:810-17 N 25 '63
Setback for aid; Clay committee report. W. V. Shannon. Commonweal 78:61-2 Ap 12 '63
Settling price. New Repub 150:3-4 Ap 4 '64
Shaping the future; address, January 9, 1964. W. W. Rostow. Dept State Bul 50:177-83 F 3 '64
Some current issues in U.S. foreign policy; remarks, April 18, 1963; with questions and answers. D. Rusk; G. W. Ball; W. A. Harriman. Dept State Bul 48:679-98 My 6 '63
Some perspectives on the current debates on aid; address, September 11, 1963. F. M. Coffin. Dept State Bul 49:514-19 S 30 '63
Spark plugs of the foreign-aid revolt. il U S News 55:16 N 25 '63
Speaking out; self-help, not help yourself. C. Bowles. Sat Eve Post 236:8+ My 18 '63
Stingy foreign aid. America 110:36 Ja 11 '64
Struggle over foreign aid. V. C. Ferkiss. America 108:488-90 Ap 13 '63
Stunning setback. Time 82:14-15 Ag 30 '63
Success of foreign aid; it must continue, address, March 3, 1964. C. Raupe. Vital Speeches 30:406-9 Ap 15 '64
This month's feature: Congress and the foreign aid program. Cong Digest 42:163-92 Je '63
Threat to AID; Ball committee proposals. Commonweal 79:472 Ja 24 '64
Tightening up, but no end to aid abroad; interview. L. D. Clay. U S News 54:43 Ap 8 '63
Tighter purse for foreign aid; Clay commission's report; with editorial comment. il Bsns W p27-8, 148 Mr 23 '63
Trade and jobs: a world view. J. Lomax. il Nation 198:365-7 Ap 13 '64
U.S. national security; address, December 10, 1963. D. E. Bell. Vital Speeches 30:167-9 Ja 1 '64
Vanities of Otto Passman. M. Kempton. New Repub 149:14-15 D 28 '63
What Johnson wants for foreign aid. il U S News 58:10 Ja 25 '65
What's ahead for foreign aid. il Bsns W p50-1 Jl 6 '63
White House holds conference on export expansion; addresses, September 17, 1963. J. F. Kennedy; D. Rusk; C. A. Herter. Dept State Bul 49:595-605 O 14 '63
Why foreign aid; address, April 24, 1963. C. Bowles. Dept State Bul 48:777-84 My 20 '63
Why foreign aid is in trouble. il U S News 55:62-5 S 9 '63
Why I am opposed to foreign aid. O. E. Passman. il N Y Times Mag p 16-17 Jl 7 '63
Witness for foreign aid. W. V. Shannon. Commonweal 80:165-7 My 1 '64
Your stake in foreign aid; address, March 6, 1964. D. Rusk. Dept State Bul 50:434-8 Mr 23 '64
See also
Food relief
United States—Agency for international development
Volunteers for international technical assistance

Anecdotes, facetiae, satire, etc.

They wonder why Congress is so slow. Nat R 16:21-2 Ja 14 '64

ECONOMIC assistance, British
Britain and the new Europe; address, April 5, 1963; with questions and answers. D. O. Gore. Ann Am Acad 348:1-14 Jl '63

ECONOMIC assistance, Communist
See also
Economic assistance, Russian

ECONOMIC assistance, Domestic
Advance guard in war on poverty; pilot program set up with aid of Ford foundation in N.C. il Bsns W p26-7 My 30 '64
Antipoverty bill passes. Christian Cent 81:1052-3 Ag 26 '64
Antipoverty plans. America 111:98 Ag 1 '64
Appalachia: the path from disaster. H. Caudill. il Nation 198:239-41 Mr 9 '64
Automation & the state. B. B. Seligman. Commentary 37:49-54 Je '64; Discussion. 38:23-4 D '64
Brand of LBJ; anti-poverty bill in the House. Newsweek 64:32+ Ag 17 '64
Challenge with a difference; anti-poverty program. S. Shriver. Sat R 47:30 D 5 '64
Characteristics of urban depressed areas; excerpt from federal aid to depressed areas. S. A. Levitan. il Mo Labor R 87:48-52 Ja '64
Close-up on poverty; O'Hara of Boston. M. Harrington. il Look 28:64-72 Ag 25 '64
Commonwealth of human responsibility; address, June 15, 1964. W. W. Wirtz. Vital Speeches 30:610-12 Ag 1 '64
Congress debates the war on poverty; book publishing's role. R. H. Smith. Pub W 186:37 Ag 10 '64
Conventional war; war on poverty. Cato. Nat R 16:482 Je 16 '64
Depressed areas built to order. B. B. VanDusen. il Nation 200:79-81 Ja 25 '65
Detroit's total war on poverty; Community action center. il Bsns W p76-7 Ja 9 '65
Do antipoverty funds aid parochial schools? charge made by American Jewish congress. Christian Cent 82:102 Ja 27 '65

ECONOMIC assistance, Domestic—*Continued*
Education: weapon against poverty; economic opportunity act of 1964. Sch Life 47:23-4 O '64
Field marshal in poverty war. il Bsns W p28-9 Mr 7 '64
First salvo; declaration of war on poverty. Nation 198:309 Mr 30 '64
Future for Alaska. Nation 198:386 Ap 20 '64
Generalissimo of the war on poverty: S. Shriver. A. H. Raskin. il N Y Times Mag p39+ N 22 '64
Here come the boys! Job corps and Volunteers in service to America programs. J. Prokop. il Am For 70:12-14+ O '64
How the antipoverty dollars will be used. U S News 57:17 D 7 '64
How the $1-billion will be split up; war on poverty. Bsns W p30 Ag 15 '64
In Hazard, Ky. D. Wakefield. Commentary 36:209-17 S '63; Reply. H. L. Sheppard. 37: 14+ Ja '64
Johnson vs poverty. C. Jencks. New Repub 150:15-18 Mr 28 '64
Latest plan: full pay for no work. il U S News 56:84 Ap 6 '64
Lead time to Utopia. Nation 199:450-1 D 14 '64
Libraries and the war on poverty; relevant federal legislative programs, chart, with introd. by G. T. Stevenson; comp. by P. Winnick. ALA Bul 59:43-8 Ja '65
LBJ's anti-poverty plan. Sr Schol 84:1T Ap 3 '64
Miner is a miner. Nation 199:423 D 7 '64
900 millions to start; who'll get the poverty dollars. il U S News 57:36-8 Ag 24 '64
On the anti-poverty bill; excerpts from testimony before House committee. G. J. Hecht. Parents Mag 39:40+ Je '64
Planning to push Appalachia. il Bsns W p44+ D 7 '63
Politics of poverty; key provisions of Lyndon Johnson's anti-poverty bill. Time 84:24-5 Ag 28 '64
Poor house; working quarters for staff of anti-poverty program. Cato. Nat R 17:15 Ja 12 '65
Poverty act report. il Sr Schol 85:1T O 14 '64
Poverty battle plan. Sr Schol 84:30+ Ap 3 '64
Poverty bill passed. Sr Schol 85:31 S 23 '64
Poverty in the House; President's poverty bill. New Repub 150:6-7 Je 13 '64
Poverty laboratory: the cost, four billions; with interview with H. M. Caudill. il U S News 56:66-71 My 11 '64
Poverty package. H. Hazlitt. Newsweek 64:72 Ag 24 '64
Poverty plan. il Time 83:14-15 Mr 27 '64
Poverty's second generation; Bootheel of Missouri. F. W. Lindecke. il Nation 199: 163-5 S 28 '64
Saving stricken cities. il Bsns W p88 N 7 '64
Scrambling for sales in war on poverty; to test and sell theories and products. Bsns W p32 Jl 11 '64
Should there be compensation for Negroes? domestic Marshall plan. W. M. Young, jr. il N Y Times Mag p43+ O 6 '63
There's already a war on poverty. il U S News 56:46 Ap 13 '64
These areas want more of your money. il Nations Bsns 52:52-4 Ag '64
This month's feature: Congress and the Appalachia program. il Cong Digest 43:289-314 D '64
This month's feature: federal public works and unemployment. Cong Digest 43:225-56 O '64
This month's feature: U.S. food surpluses & the Nation's needy, food stamp program. il Cong Digest 43:162-92 Je '64
Tragedy of Appalachia; major battlefield in Johnson's war on poverty. R. Armstrong. il Sat Eve Post 237:34-6+ Ag 22 '64
Two revolutions and a war; Economic opportunity act of 1964. T. F. Lord. Christian Cent 81:1334-6 O 28 '64; Reply. E. Walsh. 81:1595 D 23 '64
Unconditional war; adaptation of address, February 24, 1964. M. Harrington. il Wilson Lib Bul 38:834-9 Je '64
Vested interest in poverty. Nation 199:449 D 14 '64
War on poverty. H. Hazlitt. Newsweek 63:74 Ap 6 '64
War on poverty. J. Howard. NEA J 53:47-8 D '64
War on poverty bill: as it stands now. U S News 57:6 Ag 3 '64
War on poverty: impact on education. il Sr Schol 85:1T Ja 14 '65
War on poverty; symposium, ed. with introd. by H. T. Drennan. il Library J 89:3239-74+ S 15 '64. Discussion. 89:3274, 3354, 4674+ S 15, D 1 '64
War on poverty: the first shots. il Newsweek 64:71-4+ D 14 '64
What's back of fight over ARA. Nations Bsns 51:74-6+ N '63
What's become of the affluent society; interview. J. K. Galbraith. U S News 56:66-8 My 4 '64
Where $1-billion will go; LBJ's anti-poverty program. Bsns W p29-30 Mr 21 '64
Who gets the cash in the war on poverty. il U S News 56:33-5 Mr 30 '64
Who the poor are and ways to help them. Life 57:4 Jl 31 '64
Will there be any free Americans left? excerpts from letter. F. T. Taber. U S News 56:14 Je 8 '64
See also
United States—Job corps
Volunteers in service to America

ECONOMIC assistance, French
Aid trouble in France, too. Life 56:4 Ap 3 '64
Cost of grandeur; aid to North African and African territories. il Newsweek 63:41+ Mr 23 '64

ECONOMIC assistance, German
German aid to Africa. W. W. Schmokel. il Cur Hist 44:219-25 Ap '63

ECONOMIC assistance, Russian
After all of Cuba's troubles, what's ahead for Castro. il U S News 55:34-5 N 4 '63
Balance sheet of Soviet foreign aid. M. I. Goldman. For Affairs 43:349-60 Ja '65
Money from Moscow. Time 85:24 Ja 8 '65
New Communist sales pitch. il Sr Schol 82: 12-14 F 13 '63
Poor time for tin cup in Russia; Fidel Castro in Moscow. Bsns W p26 My 4 '63
Race to help Nasser. il U S News 56:70 Je 8 '64
Red bankroll: Middle eastern economic aid. il Time 85:30-1 Ja 15 '65
Reds keep Cuba going. il Bsns W p 126-8+ S 14 '63
Russian foreign aid: big headache for Khrushchev. il U S News 54:50-3 My 27 '63
Russian job that's on schedule; Nasser's High Dam. J. Law. il U S News 56:82-5 Mr 23 '64
Soviet aid: worldwide cutback. il Newsweek 62:48+ O 14 '63
Soviet dilemma. America 108:185 F 9 '63

ECONOMIC assistance in Afghanistan
Afghanistan: the canny neutral. L. Dupree. il Nation 199:134-7 S 21 '64

ECONOMIC assistance in Africa
African development; statement, February 22, 1963. W. M. Kotschnig. Dept State Bul 48:625-8 Ap 22 '63
Aid for the needy; the need for a new look. E. Huxley. Nat R 16:531-2 Je 30 '64
American aid to Africa; address, April 10, 1964; with questions and answers. E. C. Hutchinson. Ann Am Acad 354:65-74 Jl '64
Emerging nations of Africa; address, March 2, 1963. G. M. Williams. Dept State Bul 48: 457-9 Mr 25 '63
German aid to Africa. W. W. Schmokel. il Cur Hist 44:219-25 Ap '63
New patterns of African trade; address, April 1, 1964. G. M. Williams. Dept State Bul 50:664-70 Ap 27 '64
Rising Afro-Asian nations. U. A. Johnson. Dept State Bul 48:449-56 Mr 25 '63
Role of U.S. foreign assistance in Africa; address, December 8, 1964. E. C. Hutchinson. Dept State Bul 51:915-18 D 28 '64; Same. Vital Speeches 31:165-7 Ja 1 '65
What a senator saw and didn't like on African tour; excerpts from report. il U S News 54:93-4 My 20 '63

ECONOMIC assistance in Argentina
U.S. announces loans to Argentina; press release, March 28, 1963. Dept State Bul 48:617 Ap 22 '63

ECONOMIC assistance in Asia
Progress and problems in east Asia: an American viewpoint; address, September 29, 1964. W. P. Bundy. Dept State Bul 51:534-42 O 19 '64
Rising Afro-Asian nations. U. A. Johnson. Dept State Bul 48:449-56 Mr 25 '63
U.S. foreign policy in the Far East; address, June 20, 1963. U. A. Johnson. Dept State Bul 49:78-82 Jl 15 '63
See also
Colombo plan

ECONOMIC assistance in Bolivia
New success story in Latin America. il U S News 56:62-3 Je 15 '64
Solvency & self-respect; tin mines. Time 82:27 Ag 16 '63

ECONOMIC assistance in Brazil
Billion-dollar booster. Time 84:17 D 25 '64
Brazil: exploitation or aid. A. G. Frank. Nation 197:318-23 N 16 '63
Brazil gums up plans for its own rescue; inflation, strike, and political crises. il Bsns W p54-6 N 9 '63
Brazil: 2 billion dollars from U.S. and yet—. il U S News 54:44-7 Ap 1 '63
Brazilian brings home the bacon. il Bsns W p82+ Mr 30 '63
Help on an if basis. il Time 81:30 Ap 5 '63
Inflation and U.S. aid. J. W. Rowe. Reporter 30:28-30 Ap 23 '64
More aid for Brazil? il U S News 54:22 Mr 25 '63
New look in U.S. aid; strings attached. U S News 54:6 Ap 8 '63
On the road in Brazil. M. Miller. il Harper 227:65-70+ O '63
2.6 billion dollars in U.S. aid, and still— il U S News 57:44-6 D 28 '64
United States agrees to lend Brazil $50 million. Dept State Bul 51:59 Jl 13 '64
U.S. and Brazil reach understanding in economic and financial talks; exchange of letters. F. C. S. T. Dantas; D. E. Bell. il Dept State Bul 48:557-61 Ap 15 '63

ECONOMIC assistance in Cambodia
Cambodia cuts off U.S. aid. Sr Schol 83:18 Ja 17 '64
Cambodia's high-wire act. il Sr Schol 84:8-10 My 1 '64
Country that's neutral in favor of Communists. R. P. Martin. il U S News 56:80-2 Ap 27 '64
New worry for U.S. in southeast Asia. U S News 55:10 D 2 '63
Our far-flung correspondents. R. Shaplen. New Yorker 40:150+ Ap 18 '64
Problem for the U.S: handling Prince Sihanouk. U S News 56:13 Ja 6 '64
Strange case of Cambodia: a trouble area for the U.S. S. W. Sanders. il U S News 55:42-3 D 30 '63
Why Cambodia is threatening to reject U.S. aid. il U S News 55:6 N 25 '63

ECONOMIC assistance in Ceylon
Golden rule. A. Brynes. New Repub 148:20-1 Mr 9 '63
U.S. suspends aid to Ceylon. Dept State Bul 48:328 Mr 4 '63

ECONOMIC assistance in Chile
Move or else. New Repub 148:10 Je 15 '63

ECONOMIC assistance in Cuba
Money from Moscow. Time 85:24 Ja 8 '65

ECONOMIC assistance in Egypt
Colonel sends his compliments. Nat R 17:10+ Ja 12 '65
Race to help Nasser. il U S News 56:70 Je 8 '64
Russian job that's on schedule: Nasser's High Dam. J. Law. il U S News 56:82-5 Mr 23 '64
Why Nasser acts the way he does; anti-Americanism while taking U.S. aid. il U S News 58:30-1 Ja 4 '65

ECONOMIC assistance in Ethiopia
My adventures in Africa; Operation crossroads Africa. W. Peter. il Seventeen 24:70-1+ Ja '65

ECONOMIC assistance in Europe
Why western Europe cheered Kennedy. il U S News 55:32-4 Jl 15 '63

ECONOMIC assistance in Germany (Federal Republic)
Marshall plan marches on. Time 83:96+ Mr 6 '64

ECONOMIC assistance in Greece
Greek minister of coordination ends talks with U.S. officials; statement, June 7, 1963. Dept State Bul 48:970 Je 24 '63

ECONOMIC assistance in Haiti
Haiti: a case study in freedom. R. D. Heinl, jr. New Repub 150:15-21 My 16 '64
Toward the consequences. Time 81:35 F 22 '63

ECONOMIC assistance in India
Aid for Indian steel. E. H. McGrath. America 109:108 Ag 3 '63
Big country adrift; how long can aid save India? il U S News 56:64-9 Je 1 '64
Blow at Bokaro: loan for state-owned steel mill blocked. Newsweek 62:64 S 2 '63
Bokaro issue: aid for government-operated steel plant. Time 81:17 Je 28 '63
Consortium to aid India pledges $1 billion for 1964-65: communique, May 26, 1964. il Dept State Bul 50:943 Je 15 '64
Foreign-aid folly. T. Hazlitt. Newsweek 62:77 Jl 8 '63
How many strings on aid to India? D. Kirk. il Reporter 29:52-5 Ag 15 '63
India opens wider to foreign funds. il Bsns W p79-80 Ap 11 '64
Key test of U.S. aid: socialized steel for India. il U S News 54:75-6 Ap 15 '63
Need for steel. New Repub 148:9 My 25 '63
What happens to aid. H. Hazlitt. Newsweek 63:72 Je 22 '64
What's ahead for foreign aid; question of banning aid to Bokaro steel mill project. il Bsns W p50-1 Jl 6 '63
Why a steel mill for India hit a foreign-aid roadblock. il U S News 55:42 S 2 '63

ECONOMIC assistance in Indonesia
Another foreign-aid foul-up: this one by the Communists. il U S News 55:80 S 30 '63
Can another $1 per person save a country from communism? il U S News 55:86-8 Jl 29 '63
Department opposes legislation ending aid to Indonesia; statement. R. J. McCloskey. Dept State Bul 51:313 Ag 31 '64
From Washington straight; foreign aid. Cato. Nat R 14:272 Ap 9 '63
Hoodwinked. Time 82:26 O 25 '63

ECONOMIC assistance in Kenya
Communist foothold in a new African nation? U S News 56:11 Je 1 '64

ECONOMIC assistance in Korea (Republic)
Secretary comments on Korean exchange rate system reform; statement, May 3, 1964. D. Rusk. Dept State Bul 50:830 My 25 '64
Silent Sam, the pressure man. Time 81:44+ Ap 19 '63

ECONOMIC assistance in Laos
Reporter at large. R. Shaplen. il New Yorker 40:78+ Ja 16 '65

ECONOMIC assistance in Latin America
Aid abroad from U.S. unions; program of housing developments. il U S News 57:110 N 30 '64
End of reformers in Latin America. J. W. F. Dulles. Nat R 16:24 Ja 14 '64; Discussion. 16:123 F 11 '64
Europe helps out in Latin America. Bsns W p 128 Ap 13 '63
For Latin America; Inter-American cooperative institute. Commonweal 79:157 N 1 '63
Latin American odds. New Repub 150:3-4 Ja 11 '64
Organizing for progress in Latin America; address, September 17, 1964. T. C. Mann. Dept State Bul 51:479-82 O 5 '64
Why we are wrong on Latin America. Tiresias. il Nat R 16:225-6+ Mr 24 '64
See also
Alliance for progress
Inter-American development bank

ECONOMIC assistance in Mexico
No aid for the competent. New Repub 149:9 N 2 '63

ECONOMIC assistance in Puerto Rico
Commonwealth of Puerto Rico. R. Picó. bibliog il Focus 14:1-6 O '63

ECONOMIC assistance in Spain
Spain: concealed handout. L. Fernsworth. Nation 198:138-40 F 10 '64

ECONOMIC assistance in Taiwan
United States ends grant aid to Republic of China; statement, May 28, 1964. R. I. Phillips. Dept State Bul 50:934 Je 15 '64

ECONOMIC assistance in Thailand
Reporter at large. R. Shaplen. New Yorker 40:96+ Ja 16 '65

ECONOMIC assistance in the Congo
Summary of U.S. recommendations for program of aid to the Congo. Dept State Bul 48:481-4 Ap 1 '63

ECONOMIC assistance in the Dominican Republic
Limits of American power; the lesson of the Dominican Republic. A. F. Lowenthal. Harper 228:87-9+ Je '64

ECONOMIC assistance in the Ryukyu Islands
U.S. and Japan to cooperate on aid programs for Ryukyus. Dept State Bul 50:755 My 11 '64

ECONOMIC assistance in Turkey
Fetish of foreign aid. Nation 199:42-3 Ag 10 '64
Turkey's internal crisis. S. Lens. Commonweal 80:629-31 S 18 '64

ECONOMIC assistance in Venezuela
Private peace corps. Time 83:39 Mr 6 '64

ECONOMIC assistance in Viet Nam (Republic)
America's new program for Vietnam war; the way it will work. U S News 56:6 Mr 30 '64
Smiles and confusion in Vietnam. il Bsns W p50+ N 23 '63
Vietnam: test case for massive U.S. aid. il Bsns W p82-3+ S 28 '63

ECONOMIC assistance in Yugoslavia
Aid to Tito. W. D. Broderick; M. M. Mestrovic. Commonweal 77:620-1 Mr 8 '63
Billions in U.S. aid and Tito wants to bury capitalism. A. Kucherov. il U S News 55:68-9 S 16 '63

ECONOMIC census. See United States—Census

ECONOMIC change
- Bread without sweat; Ad hoc committee on the triple revolution. Christian Cent 81:451-2 Ap 8 '64
- Epochal change. A. M. Sullivan. Duns R 83: 138 My '64
- If the machine wants our jobs, let's buy it. Life 57:4 Ag 14 '64
- Momentous problem; finding a place to live. Sci N L 84:301 N 9 '63
- Triple revolution. J. Riha. America 112:162-4 Ja 30 '65
- Triple revolution; concerning report of the Ad hoc committee on the triple revolution. J. O'Gara. Commonweal 80:78 Ap 10 '64

ECONOMIC commission for Africa. See United Nations—Economic commission for Africa

ECONOMIC commissions of the United Nations. See name of commission under United Nations, e.g. United Nations—Economic commission for Africa

ECONOMIC conditions
- Business around the world. See issues of U.S. news & World report
- Common upbeat; economies of the European common market nations, Britain and the U.S. il Time 82:90 Jl 12 '63
- Confidence. D. Lawrence. U S News 57:116 D 14 '64
- Good times ahead, too, for America's key allies. U S News 56:45-7 Ja 13 '64
- International economy; a steady performance. il Time 83:66+ Ja 10 '64
- Material outlook for mankind. A. E. Burns. Sat R 47:44-6 Je 6 '64
- Mood abroad: let others worry. U S News 57: 64 Ag 24 '64
- Shift of the compass. Commonweal 80:440-1 Jl 3 '64
- World economic developments; address, November 16, 1964. G. S. Moore. Vital Speeches 31:162-5 Ja 1 '65
- World economic outlook. U N Rev 10:52-3 Jl '63

See also
- Business conditions
- Business cycles
- Business depression
- Cost of living
- Poverty
- Standard of living
- Underdeveloped areas
- *also* subhead Economic conditions under names of countries, states, cities, e.g. France—Economic conditions

ECONOMIC cooperation. See Economic planning, International; International cooperation

ECONOMIC cycles. See Business cycles

ECONOMIC development
- Abundance and the future of man. G. Piel. Atlan 213:84-90 Ap '64
- Activities planned to meet objectives of the development decade; summary of report. Thant. U N Rev 10:47-9 Jl '63
- Africa's problems and progress; address, March 1, 1964. G. M. Williams. Dept State Bul 50:501-6 Mr 30 '64
- Alliance for progress: two-year review. N. A. Haverstock. il Américas 15:2-9 Ag '63
- Anatomy of underdevelopment (cont) il UNESCO Courier 16:27-9 Mr '63
- Application of science, technology to quicken economic development; statement, September 27, 1963. U N Rev 10:28-33 N '63
- Britain and the new Europe; address, April 5, 1963; with questions and answers. D. O. Gore. Ann Am Acad 348:1-14 Jl '63
- Campaign for world literacy; Campaign against hunger and disease; Science and technology for development. U N Rev 11:31-4 Ja '64
- Challenge of democracy in developing nations; address, January 26, 1964. W. W. Rostow. Dept State Bul 50:251-60 F 17 '64
- Colonialism and the decade of development; address, February 21, 1963. J. B. Bingham. Dept State Bul 48:459-61 Mr 25 '63
- Commodity trade and economic development; statement, April 30, 1963. W. M. Blumenthal. Dept State Bul 48:844-8 My 27 '63
- Developing nations' greatest need. C. Bowles. il N Y Times Mag 15+ Ap 12 '64
- Development aid: address, April 4, 1963. J. De Cubas. Vital Speeches 29:499-502 Je 1 '63
- Economic development: some lessons of a common experience; address, August 19, 1963. W. W. Rostow. Dept State Bul 49: 422-30 S 16 '63; Same Vital Speeches 29: 712-17 S 15 '63
- Economic growth; address, December 5, 1963. V. B. Day. Vital Speeches 30:181-4 Ja 1 '64
- Economic growth in the West: comparative experience in Europe and North America, by A. Maddison. Review
  - New Repub 152:24-6 Ja 16 '65. P. Mattick
- Economic strains slow progress in many developing countries; text of introduction to Economic survey of Asia and the Far East, 1962. U N Rev 10:20-3 Mr '63
- Emerging consensus on economic and social development; statement, July 10, 1963. A. E. Stevenson. Dept State Bul 49:265-72 Ag 12 '63
- Experts see three bright years ahead; symposium. il Nations Bsns 51:41+ N '63
- Flexible formula for economic growth; Sweden's decade of progress. il Bsns W p88-9 Jl 6 '63
- Foreign aid: the essential factors for success; address, May 28, 1963. C. Bowles. Dept State Bul 48:939-45 Je 17 '63
- GATT ministers reach agreement on tariff negotiating procedures; statements, May 16 and May 17, 1963; with resolution on trade negotiations, adopted May 21, 1963. C. A. Herter. Dept State Bul 48:990-6 Je 24 '63
- Giants plan to get still bigger. il Bsns W p 100-2+ Je 6 '64
- Good friend and critic; speaking out on American issues. Bsns W p57-8+ D 14 '63
- Human resources and economic development; excerpts from United States papers prepared for UNCSAT conference. P. M. Hauser; F. H. Harbison. Mo Labor R 86:262-7 Mr '63
- International aspects of development; address, April 5, 1963. Thant. il U N Rev 10:12-14 Ap '63
- International enterprise; address, July 3, 1963. J. H. Loudon. Vital Speeches 29:677-9 S 1 '63
- International trade and economic development; statement, May 27, 1963. I. Frank. Dept State Bul 49:173-8 Jl 29 '63
- Is the long cycle why we don't grow? creeping pace of industrial growth. il Bsns W p78+ F 16 '63
- Issues before the U.N. conference. I. Frank. For Affairs 42:210-26 Ja '64
- Kennedy: cut taxes for our economic growth. il Bsns W p26-7 Mr 2 '63
- Man and nature; address, October 12, 1964. D. Rusk. Dept State Bul 51:618-21 N 2 '64
- Nationalization of takeoff; address, May 2, 1963. W. W. Rostow. Dept State Bul 48:824-9 My 27 '63
- Natural resources and international development, ed. by M. Clawson. Review
  - Am For 70:42+ S '64. B. F. Grossling
- New implications of industrial competition; address, June 10, 1964. D. E. Bell. Dept State Bul 51:205-9 Ag 10 '64
- Open system in North-South relations, April 9, 1964. G. W. Ball. Dept State Bul 50:657-62 Ap 27 '64
- OECD manpower policy for promoting economic growth; excerpt. Mo Labor R 87: 1033-4 S '64
- Pakistan: the case for technological development. A. Salam. il Bul Atomic Sci 20:2-5 Mr '64
- Pause in West Germany's boom. il Bsns W p60 Je 8 '63
- Perspective on the United Nations conference on trade and development; address, February 21, 1964. G. G. Johnson. Dept State Bul 50:410-15 Mr 16 '64
- Postwar advance of the five hundred million. M. Ways. il Fortune 70:104-9+ Ag '64
- Problems of economic development; statement, October 3, 1963. J. B. Bingham. Dept State Bul 49:712-21 N 4 '63
- Production and distribution of knowledge in the United States, by F. Machlup. Review
  - Science 140:473-4 My 3 '63. R. R. Nelson
- Russians drop a lap behind; lagging growth rate. il Bsns W p30-1 Ja 18 '64
- Scholars see trend to more security, less freedom. F. Morley. Nations Bsns 51:27-8 O '63
- S.T.P: index of prosperity. V. A. Kovda. il UNESCO Courier 16:18-23 Jl '63
- Shaping the future; address, January 9, 1964. W. W. Rostow. Dept State Bul 50: 177:83 F 3 '64; Same. Vital Speeches 30: 260-4 F 15 '64
- Slow growth is no. 1 problem: survey by campus economists. il Bsns W p39-40 D 7 '63
- Some lessons of economic development since the war; address, October 7, 1964. W. W. Rostow. Dept State Bul 51:664-9 N 9 '64
- Strategy for innovation. M. Michaelis. Bul Atomic Sci 20:19-23 Ap '64

ECONOMIC development—*Continued*
Technology and economic development. A. Briggs. il Sci Am 209:52-61 bibliog(p306) S '63
Toward the brotherhood of man; address, October 19, 1964. D. Rusk. Dept State Bul 51:650-2 N 9 '64
Trade and development; with text of joint declaration of representatives of developing countries. il U N Rev 10:35-8 D '63
Training program in development financing. il U N Rev 11:37-8 Mr '64
Trust Territory of the Pacific Islands; statements, June 5 and June 17, 1963. M. W. Goding; V. N. Santos. Dept State Bul 49:207-29 Ag 5 '63
UNESCO: Director General stakes out broader responsibilities in applying research to development. J. Walsh. Science 142:470-1 O 25 '63
U.N. economic and social council meets at Geneva; statements, July 14 and July 23, 1964. H. Cleveland; F. H. Williams. Dept State Bul 51:241-52 Ag 17 '64
United States policy in the Pacific; address, August 20, 1963. R. Hilsman. Dept State Bul 49:386-93 S 9 '63
Urban economic development. J. H. Nixon and P. H. Gerhardt. bibliog f Ann Am Acad 352:39-47 Mr '64
West debates the great growth issue. B. Ward. il N Y Times Mag p22+ O 27 '63
Why Britain slowed its boom. il Bsns W p45-6+ Mr 7 '64
Why China ends its isolation. il Bsns W p26-7 F 1 '64
Why Russia downgrades planners. Bsns W p98-100+ O 31 '64
World bank and affiliates examine pressing problems of economic development. G. D. Woods. UN Mo Chron 1:59-62 N '64
World trade and world trouble Fortune 69:107-8 My '64
See also
Development banks
Economic planning, International
United Nations—Economic commission for Africa

ECONOMIC development, Committee for. See Committee for economic development
ECONOMIC education. See Economics—Study and teaching
ECONOMIC education, Joint council on. See Joint council on economic education
ECONOMIC education workshop. See Educational workshops
ECONOMIC forecasting. See Forecasts (economics)
ECONOMIC growth. See Economic development
ECONOMIC history
See also
United States—Economic history
ECONOMIC imperialism. See Imperialism
ECONOMIC insecurity. See Social and economic security
ECONOMIC liberty. See Liberty
ECONOMIC literature. See Economics literature
ECONOMIC opportunity, Office of. See United States—Economic opportunity, Office of
ECONOMIC opportunity act, 1964. See Economic assistance, Domestic
ECONOMIC planning
Canada's planners walk a tightrope; new Economic council. il Bsns W p 146+ Mr 14 '64
Disarmament and the economy. B. B. Seligman. Commentary 35:369-77 My '63; Discussion. 36:196-7 S '63
Economic planning, European-style. W. P. Blass. bibliog f il Harvard Bsns R 41:109-20 S '63
Economy: a case for efficient planning. H. Malmgren. il New Repub 151:41-4+ N 7 '64
Fallacy of too much planning. H. Hazlitt. Read Digest 82:95-6 F '63
France: planned expansion outspeeds itself. il Bsns W p58 Mr 16 '63
How planned is our economy? J. Tobin. il N Y Times Mag p 18+ O 13 '63
Planning debate comes to the U.S. il Bsns W p 140+ My 25 '63
See also
United States—Council of economic advisors
ECONOMIC planning, International
Geneva, a center of international cooperative efforts; excerpts from an address, September 22, 1964. R. W. Tubby. Dept State Bul 51:740-7 N 23 '64
Planning of development. E. S. Mason. il Sci Am 209:235-6+ bibliog(p310) S '63
Progress and prospects in international economic cooperation; address, October 21, 1964. G. G. Johnson. bibliog f Dept State Bul 51:708-14 N 16 '64
Second thoughts on the Common market. D. F. Dowd. Yale R 53:168-91 D '63
See also
European economic community
Inter-American economic and social council
United Nations—Economic and social council
ECONOMIC policy
Economics of development. C. Clark. il Nat R 14:373-5 My 7 '63
Relationship of sound money to freedom; address, April 8, 1964. K. Brandt. Vital Speeches 30:623-8 Ag 1 '64
West debates the great growth issue. B. Ward. il N Y Times Mag p22+ O 27 '63
See also
Economic planning
Government spending policy
Industrialization
Social and economic security
also subhead Economic policy under names of countries, e.g. Russia—Economic policy
ECONOMIC progress. See Progress
ECONOMIC relations
Kennedy tries to stem the tide in Europe. il Bsns W p28-9 Je 29 '63
ECONOMIC research
See also
National bureau of economic research
ECONOMIC security. See Social and economic security
ECONOMIC statistics
Bird's-eye look at the countryside; input-output table. il Time 84:58 N 20 '64
Qui numerare incipit errare incipit; excerpts from On the accuracy of economic observations. O. Morgenstern. il Fortune 68:142-4+ O '63; Reply. J. Shiskin. 69:66 F '64
See also
Employment—Statistics
Unemployment—Statistics
ECONOMIC theory. See Economics
ECONOMICS
Abundance, threat or promise? R. Theobald. Nation 196:387-412 My 11 '63; Discussion. 196:inside cover Je 15 '63
Case against Goldwater's economics. P. Samuelson. il N Y Times Mag p28+ O 25 '64
Consumptionists. H. Hazlitt. Newsweek 64:100 O 5 '64
Economics and human values. J. Davenport. Yale R 53:381-94 Mr '64
Economics in a free society, by W. Roepke. Review
Bsns W p72+ Ap 13 '63
Nat R 14:532-3 Jl 2 '63. L. M. Hacker
Free men and free markets, by R. Theobald. Review
Sat R 46:57-8+ S 28 '63. K. Schriftgiesser; Reply. R. Theobald. 46:27 N 16 '63
Keynes formula sweeps on. G. Schwartz. il N Y Times Mag p32+ S 8 '63
Keynesian inflation. H. Hazlitt. Newsweek 62:74 Jl 15 '63
Keynesianism: retrospect and prospect, by W. H. Hutt. Review
Nat R 16:158-60 F 25 '64. M. Palyi
Paper economy, by D. T. Bazelon. Review
New Repub 148:21-3 My 25 '63. P. Green; Reply with rejoinder. D. J. Ashton. 149:29-30 Jl 13 '63
Replacing the myth of the free price-market system. E. T. Chase. Commonweal 79:288-90 N 29 '63
Tax-cut fallacies. H. Hazlitt. Newsweek 63:76 Mr 9 '64
Tax cut: the triumph of an idea. Bsns W p 180+ Ap 11 '64
Theoretical economics. S. Weintraub. bibliog f Ann Am Acad 352:152-64 Mr '64
See also
Capitalism
Consumption (economics)
Efficiency, Industrial
Employment
Free enterprise
Liquidity (economics)
Profit
Prosperity
Wealth, Distribution of

Bibliography

Books for Americans; White House library. H. Hazlitt. Newsweek 62:80 S 30 '63

History

Main currents in modern economics: economic thought since 1870, by B. B. Seligman. Review
Commentary 35:356-60 Ap '63. C. E. Ayres

Methodology

See also
Economics, Mathematical

ECONOMICS—*Continued*

Study and teaching

Arkansas schools get economics-minded. il Bsns W p 112-14 Jl 20 '63
Current revolution in economics teaching. H. L. Hurwitz. il Sr Schol 83:7T-8T S 13 '63
Economic education; address, June 18, 1964. L. C. Michelon. Vital Speeches 30:648-52 Ag 15 '64
Economics for tots to teens. Bsns W p 104 Je 13 '64
Economics in primary grades. Sch & Soc 92: 284 O 17 '64
Economics with ABCs; primary grade youngsters in Elkhart, Ind. il Bsns W p 186-8+ Mr 21 '64
Further study in economics. J. C. Hall. NEA J 52:28-9 O '63
Gingerbread lesson; experimental program to Newsweek 63:73 Mr 30 '64
teach economics in the lower grades. il
Need for economic education. J. D. Garwood. bibliog f Sch & Soc 92:289-91 O 17 '64
New economics. Library J 89:4995 D 15 '64
Not so dismal science of economics. E. G. Nourse. bibliog il NEA J 52:38-41 Mr '63
See also
Joint council on economic education

Terminology

Economics in the news. il Sr Schol 85:21 S 30; 18 O 14; 16 O 21; 20 N 4; 12 D 2; 11 D 9 '64; 16 Ja 7; 18 Ja 14 '65

ECONOMICS, Agricultural. See Agriculture—Economic aspects

ECONOMICS, Mathematical
Mathematics in the social sciences. R. Stone. il Sci Am 211:168-72+ bibliog(p270+) S '64

ECONOMICS and Christianity. See Christianity and economics

ECONOMICS and politics
Bread, butter and abstractions. J. Burnham. Nat R 16:350 My 5 '64
Businessman looks at today's big issues; excerpts from address, November 5, 1964. T. O. Yntema. il U S News 57:100-4 N 30 '64
Economics and human values. J. Davenport. Yale R 53:381-94 Mr '64
Economics and politics. S. E. Harris. Bul Atomic Sci 20:32-4 Ja '64
Economics and the quality of life; adaptation of address, December 27, 1963. J. K. Galbraith. bibliog Science 145:117-23 Jl 10 '64; Discussion. 145:876 Ag 28 '64
Gap between economist and politician. S. E. Harris. il N Y Times Mag p26+ Ap 14 '63
If people's pocketbooks decide how they vote. il U S News 57:34-5 N 2 '64

ECONOMICS and science. See Science and economics

ECONOMICS literature
Economics library selections. R. T. Jordan. Library J 88:1625-9 Ap 15 '63
Economics library selections revived by U. of Pittsburgh. Library J 89:1208+ Mr 15 '64

ECONOMIST (London)
Capitalist critique. il Time 81:68+ Je 14 '63

ECONOMISTS
Adding up the cost of economic swindling. il Bsns W p50-2 Ja 4 '64
Consumptionists. H. Hazlitt. Newsweek 64:100 O 5 '64
Doctors of development. il Time 83:86+ Je 26 '64
Goldwater's economists. pors Newsweek 64:62-4 Ag 31 '64
Man for all seasons at CBS. Bsns W p 128-8+ Ag 10 '63
Trail of dissent; nation's leading economists disagree. Newsweek 64:64+ S 7 '64
See also
Keynes, J. M. K.

ECONOMOS, James P. and Fontaine, André
You can have decent traffic courts. Read Digest 84:129-32 Ja '64

ECONOMY. See Thrift

ECONOMY in government. See Government spending policy

ECONOMY runs. See Automobile engines—Fuel consumption

ECOSYSTEMS. See Ecology

ECTOHORMONES. See Pheromones

ECUADOR
Ecuador's socio-political mosaic. E. S. Urbanski. bibliog f Cur Hist 46:19-25 Ja '64
See also
Aviation—Ecuador
Guayaquil
Quito
Transportation—Ecuador

Antiquities

See Indians of South America—Antiquities—Ecuador

Description and travel

Streetcar named Autoferro Ecuatoriano; a ride from Quito to Guayaquil. S. Meyer. il Sat R 46:94+ O 12 '63

Foreign relations

U.S. recognizes military junta as government of Ecuador; Department statement, July 31, 1963. Dept State Bul 49:282 Ag 19 '63

Politics and government

Morning after; coup d'état. Newsweek 62:49 Jl 29 '63
One for the road. Time 82:22-3 Jl 19 '63
Progress after a coup. Time 81:29-30 Mr 8 '63
Toppled tippler. Newsweek 62:49 Jl 22 '63

Social conditions

Ecuador; Peace corps volunteers. R. Brooks and E. Brooks. il Nat Geog Mag 126:338-45 S '64

ECUADORIAN fiction
Ecuador's novels and novelists. E. Uzcátegui. il Américas 16:29-34 My '64

ECUADORIAN poetry
Six Ecuadorian poets; with poems. G. R. Pérez; U. Estrella. il Américas 16:30-4 N '64

ECUMENICAL council, 2d. See Vatican council, 2d

ECUMENICAL councils. See Councils and synods

ECUMENICAL institute
Bossey's '64 program. G. Murray. Christian Cent 81:152 Ja 29 '64
Gesture in ecumenism; summer course at Bossey. H. Winter. America 111:614-19 N 14 '64

ECUMENICAL movement
After four hundred years; England's ecumenical awakening. I. Evans. Commonweal 78:222-4 My 17 '63
All in each place. P. R. Deittmann. Christian Cent 81:799-801 Je 17 '64
Baltimore unity workshop. J. J. Gallagher. America 111:138-9 Ag 8 '64
Cardinal on ecumenism; and the World council. America 110:589 My 2 '64
Catholics rejoin interfaith group; British council of Christians and Jews. Christian Cent 81:355 Mr 18 '64
Church unity and church mission, by M. E. Marty. Review
Christian Cent 81:886 Jl 8 '64. J. R. Nelson
Common burden. Commonweal 79:471-2 Ja 24 '64
Date in 1980; church unity problems in Britain. Newsweek 64:86 S 28 '64
Decree on ecumenism. E. C. Bianchi. America 111:776 D 12 '64
Dialogue at the top. D. J. O'Hanlon. America 109:231-4 S 7 '63; Reply. D. A. Walsh. 109: 441 O 19 '63
La dolce vita ecumenica. K. Bridston. Christian Cent 80:679 My 22 '63; Discussion. 80:985-6 Ag 7 '63
East-West theological dialogue; Russian churchmen in the U.S. B. Kroker. Christian Cent 80:585-6 My 1 '63
Ecumen in. il Times 83:60 Mr 13 '64
Ecumenical changes; concerning sermons. America 109:656-7 N 23 '63
Ecumenical dialogue and conversions. B. Leeming. Cath World 198:223-9 Ja '64
Ecumenical dialogue at Harvard, ed. by S. H. Miller and G. E. Wright. Review
Sat R 47:32 My 30 '64. D. A. Poling
Ecumenical goal: community, not consensus. Christian Cent 81:1389 N 11 '64
Ecumenical in Erie. R. Schaffer. Christian Cent 80:863-4 Jl 3 '63
Ecumenicity, unlimited. Christian Cent 81: 227- F 19 '64
Ecumenics and laymen in the pew. E. S. Stanton. America 109:210-12 Ag 31 '63
Ecumenics and non-Christians; new secretariat for non-Christians. bibliog America 110:753 My 30 '64
Ecumenism in Montreal. I. Beaubien. America 109:16-17 Jl 6 '63
Ecumenism in Morocco; Benedictine monks at Toumliline. W. Dunphy. America 111: 694 N 28 '64
Ecumenism in Spain. America 110:503 Ap 11 '64
Extending the dialogue. America 111:224 S 5 '64

ECUMENICAL movement—*Continued*
Geneva to Rome; resolution to establish with the Vatican a joint working committee on interfaith cooperation. il Time 85:89 Ja 29 '65
Greater dialogue; proposal to set up special bureau for relations with the Muslim world. America 111:207 Ag 29 '64
Harvest time. O. W. Wagner. Christian Cent 81:990-3 Ag 5 '64
Heirs of Abbé Couturier; Catholic-Protestant dialogue. I. Chabas. Christian Cent 82:41-3 Ja 13 '65
Hold unprecedented ecumenical service; Protestant Episcopal and Roman Catholic joint worship service. Christian Cent 81:1548 D 16 '64
Interview with Jean Guitton, the only Catholic layman at the council; ed. by J. Pelissier. J. Guitton. Cath World 196:279-84 F '63
Key figure of the World council of churches discusses Christian unity; interview, ed. by E. C. Bianchi. W. A. Visser 't Hooft. America 109:354-6 S 28 '63
Modern Protestantism: aimless or resurgent? B. E. Meland. Christian Cent 80:1494-7 D 4 '63
New Catholic image: openness to today's world. J. B. Sheerin. Cath World 198:204-7 Ja '64
New ecumenical journal. America 110:400 Mr 28 '64
New warmth between Protestants and Catholics; excerpts from Steps to Christian unity. J. A. O'Brien. Read Digest 85:101-5 O '64
Not indifferentism. America 108:486-7 Ap 13 '63
Operation understanding. America 110:178 F 8 '64
Pan-Christian summit meeting? Christian Cent 81:68 Ja 15 '64
Patriarch Maximos IV and Vatican council II; interview, ed. by E. Inglessis and E. Inglessis. Maximos IV. Cath World 198:372-9 Mr '64
Pentecostal gesture; Pope Paul's announcement of new secretariat for relations with non-Christians. America 110:757 My 30 '64
Pope Paul's other dialogue. J. Gremillion. Cath World 198:208-14 Ja '64
Problems before unity. Review
America 108:808-10 Je 1 '63; Reply. B. Leeming. 108:834-5 Je 8 '63
Reactions to Ecclesiam suam. America 111:204 Ag 29 '64
Reciprocal ecumenism. America 109:183 Ag 24 '63
Reconciliation in Rochester; work of Central committee. H. E. Fey. Christian Cent 80:1125-7 S 18 '63
Reformation Sunday. Commonweal 81:149-50 O 30 '64
Return or reconciliation? C. Davis. America 109:710 N 30 '63
Rome takes the initiative. C. Northcott. Christian Cent 82:103 Ja 27 '65
Secretariat for non-Christians. Commonweal 80:280-1 My 29 '64
Seminar in ecumenical trialogue; Greater Boston ecumenical seminar. N. Ehrenstrom. Christian Cent 81:579-81 Ap 29 '64
Seminars on ecumenics; Institute on ecumenical leadership, Boston university school of theology. L. R. Applegate. Christian Cent 81:1282 O 14 '64
Servant church. il Time 84:45-9 D 25 '64
Speaking out; ecumenical movement threatens Protestantism. H. A. Buchanan and B. W. Brown. Sat Eve Post 237:10+ O 24 '64; Reply. G. Hinson. Christian Cent 81:1592-5 D 23 '64
Toward dialogue. America 111:766 D 12 '64
Trifaith conference; Protestant-Catholic-Jewish. A. P. Klausler. Christian Cent 81:1572-3 D 16 '64
Unity, by M. Villain. Review
Cath World 199:188-9 Je '64. C. L. Palms
Vernacular for unity; concerning speech given by the president of the World Methodist council. America 109:472 O 26 '63
Visit with Cardinal Liénart; interview, ed. by W. M. Abbott. A. Liénart. il America 108:802-3 Je 1 '63
Word. V. P. McCorry. America 111:163-4, 268 Ag 15, S 12 '64
Worldly ecumenism. America 112:71 Ja 16 '65
See also
Church unity
Religious conferences
Religious cooperation

Bibliography

Ecumenical ABC's. America 109:444 O 19 '63

ECUMENICAL student conference on the Christian world mission
Holy Spirit at the 19th quadrennial. M. W. Hess. Christian Cent 81:370-2 Mr 18 '64
EDAVILLE railroad
All aboard for happy land. E. L. Barcella. il Todays Health 41:62-3+ N '63
EDDY, Edward D. jr.
Results of a liberal education; adaptation of address, 1963. Sch & Soc 92:201-3 My 2 '64
What's the use of educating women? bibliog Sat R 46:66-8 My 18 '63
EDDY, George Sherwood
Sherwood Eddy: among the saints. Christian Cent 80:421 Ap 3 '63
EDDY, Sherwood. See Eddy, G. S.
EDEL, Leon
Appreciating Pritchett. New Repub 151:26+ Ag 8 '64
Hostess with most of the great. Sat R 47:37+ Je 20 '64
Spirals of reason and fancy. Sat R 47:23-4 S 5 '64
about
Powers, Edel, Stafford win National book awards. Pub W 183:30-1 Mr 18 '63
EDELEN, Buddy
Painful path to glory. L. Shecter. il pors Sat Eve Post 237:76+ O 3 '64
Straight man in a twisty race. J. Lovesey. il por Sports Illus 20:40-2+ Je 1 '64
EDELMAN, Maurice
British-eye view of Congress. Holiday 34:54-5+ Jl '63
Doorstep to British democracy. Sat R 46:52-3 S 28 '63
Rights and permissions. P. Nathan. Pub W 183:85 Je 17 '63
EDELSACK, E. A. and others
Molecular biophysics: International summer school. Science 146:1193 N 27 '64
EDELSON, Michael
Case for carrying a camera. il U S Camera 27:58-9+ Ag '64
Keep 'em working. U S Camera 28:56-7+ Ja '65
SLR: a new seeing tool. U S Camera 27:42+ S '64
Wrong exposures for the right reasons. U S Camera 28:58-9 Ja '65
Wrong film at the right time. U S Camera 27:48-9+ Jl '64
EDELSTEIN, J. M.
Virginia Woolf in her madness. New Repub 151:15-17 D 5 '64
EDEMA
Pulmonary edema as a consequence of hypothalamic lesions in rats. R. W. Reynolds. bibliog il Science 141:930-2 S 6 '63
EDEN
Approximations of paradise. Christian Cent 81:255 F 19 '64
EDER, Richard
Cuba: between promise and decay. N Y Times Mag p5+ Je 21 '64
Cuba lives by Castro's moods. N Y Times Mag p 12-13+ Jl 26 '64
Haiti, land of the big tontons. N Y Times Mag p9+ Ja 24 '65
EDEY, Maitland A.
Should man try to save the animals? Life 55:79-82+ O 25 '63
EDGAR, Barry
On-the-move cook book. House & Gard 123:141+ Je '63
EDGAR Allan Poe awards. See Mystery writers of America
EDGE, Peggy
WLB biography (cont) Wilson Lib Bul 37:883; 38:352, 697; 39:269 Je, D '63, Ap, N '64
EDGERTON, Germeshausen and Grier, incorporated
No pain for business; bomb research and monitoring devices. Bsns W p21-2 Ag 3 '63
EDGERTON, Harold E. and others
Sonar probing in Narragansett Bay. Science 146:1459-60 D 11 '64
EDGERTON, William H.
Building construction costs. Arch Rec 137:20 Ja '65
EDGING plants. See Garden borders
EDGINGS, Garden. See Garden borders
EDGREN, H. D.
My philosophy of recreation. por Recreation 56:59-60 F '63
EDIBLE greens. See Greens, Edible
EDIBLE oils and fats. See Oils and fats, Edible
EDIE, Carolyn Andervont
Succession and monarchy: the controversy of 1679-1681. bibliog f Am Hist R 70:350-70 Ja '65
EDINA, Minn.
Roulette at the police station. H. M. Wrobleski. il Am City 78:90 Ag '63

EDINBURGH
Music
Edinburgh guests. P. Heyworth. Opera N 28:31-2 D 14 '63
See also
International festival of music and drama, Edinburgh

EDINBURGH festival of music and drama. See International festival of music and drama, Edinburgh

EDINGER, Edward F.
Inner life in an outer-space age. Sat R 46:23+ Je 1 '63

EDINGER, Lois V.
Education for world responsibility. por NEA J 53:23 S '64

EDISON, Charles
Tribute to Charles Edison. Nat R 14:395 My 21 '63

EDISON, Thomas Alva
Edison in pictures, his life, his wives, his work. il pors Sci Digest 54:6-13 Ag '63
Some of Edison's famous firsts. Look 28:102 F 25 '64
They made our world. L. Rosten. il por Look 28:100-1 F 25 '64

EDISON award. See Thomas Alva Edison award

EDISON effect. See Thermionic emission

EDITING. See Editors and editing

EDITING amateur moving pictures. See Moving pictures, Amateur—Editing

EDITORIAL projects for education, incorporated
Daring them to think. Time 81:84+ Je 7 '63

EDITORIALS
Appraising a president; reaction to Lyndon Johnson's speech before Congress. Time 82:81 D 6 '63

EDITORS and editing
Book publishers' editors describe duties, problems. il Pub W 185:26-9 Mr 23 '64
Book publishing today; interview, ed. by R. W. Apple, jr. M. Bessie. Writer 76:10-11+ F '63
Don't lick the stamp yet. B. Robinson. Writer 76:11-13+ S '63
Editor's advice on article sales. C. Peterson, jr. Writer 77:14-17 O '64
Editors regret; phrasing of rejection slips. J. Ciardi. Sat R 48:24 Ja 2 '65
Handwritten letter to a favorite aunt; art of editorial writing. G. P. Hunt. Life 56:3 Je 26 '64
Hero is not made. E. Globe. Arch Rec 135:9 Ja '64
Importance of being persistent. N. J. Stoyenoff. Writer 76:25+ My '63
Key to article sales. M. Gunther. Writer 77:12-14 Ag '64
Man with the pencil of light; newspapers of tomorrow. R. L. Tobin. il Sat R 47:138-9+ Ag 29 '64
MLA's experience; excerpts from address. G. W. Stone. Pub W 184:39-40 Jl 15 '63
Off the cuff. A. Marple. Writer 77:5-6 Ap '64
Off the cuff; questions and answers. A. Marple. Writer 77:6-8 N '64
Outlines and article writing; excerpt from Prose by professionals, ed. by T. Morris. M. Weisinger. Writer 76:12-15+ Mr '63
Over the editor's shoulder; children's books, reprint. H. L. Jones. Library J 89:4969-71 D 15 '64
Put yourself in the editor's chair; rejected articles. C. Darlington. Writer 77:26-7 O '64
Putting the Times to bed. J. Tebbel. il Sat R 47:67-8+ D 12 '64
Setting your literary goals. C. Mercer. Writer 76:10-11+ Mr '63
Something worth publishing. M. Mather. Writer 76:7-10+ S '63
Successful query letters. C. W. Casewit. Writer 76:15-17 D '63
Triple play; changes in staffs of women's magazines. Newsweek 65:48 Ja 18 '65
View from the heights; T. Catledge becomes executive editor of Sunday and daily Times. il Time 84:55-6 S 11 '64
What does a writer expect of an editor? childrens book editors. P. A. Whitney. Library J 88:3985-6 O 15 '63
See also
Journalism

Anecdotes, facetiae, satire, etc.
Ed. Christian Cent 80:1319 O 23 '63

EDMONDS, May H.
Children's libraries. Wilson Lib Bul 38:689 Ap '64

EDMONSTON, Paul
Sequential drawing and the generation of visual ideas. Sch Arts 63:29-32 O '63

EDMUNDS, Leland N. jr
Replication of DNA and cell division in synchronously dividing cultures of euglena gracilis. bibliog Science 145:266-8 Jl 17 '64

EDQVIST, Dagmar
Bulango affair; story; condensation of Black sister, tr. by J. Tate. Sat Eve Post 236:30-4 Je 22 '63

EDSALL, James V. and Edsall, M. S.
Trail-blazing a vacation. pors Outdoor Life 131:56-9+ My '63

EDSALL, John T.
Birth control; our disgraceful ignorance. Nation 196:499-503 Je 15 '63
New perspectives in biology. Science 143:267-8+ Ja 17 '64
—See Eisenberg, D. S. jt. auth.

EDSALL, Marian S.
On the trail of the voyageurs. Travel 120:42-4 Ag '63
—See Edsall, J. V. jt. auth.

EDUCATED American woman; story. See Cheever, J.

EDUCATION
Automation's challenge to education and human values; excerpts from Automation, education, and human values, ed. by William W. Brickman and Stanley Lehrer. bibliog f Sch & Soc 92:303-15 O 31 '64
Education in the year 2,000 A.D; a uniworld university, with local campuses; address, April 10, 1964. R. T. Oliver. Vital Speeches 30:399-401 Ap 15 '64
Retooling the mind. N. W. Chamberlain. Atlan 214:48-50 S '64
Teaching and the expanding knowledge. A. Szent-Györgyi. Science 146:1278-9 D 4 '64
What sort of school day is it? H. Spears. Sr Schol 85:8T N 4 '64
See also
Books and reading
Catholic church—Education
Coeducation
Communication in education
Correspondence schools and courses
Courses of study
Education of women
Foreign study
Illiteracy
Learning, Psychology of
Learning and scholarship
Liberal education
Libraries
Monitorial system of education
Moral education
Motivation (education)
Psychology, Educational
Public schools
Socially handicapped children—Education
Specialization in education
Teaching
Textbooks
also Art education; Business education; and similar headings

Aims and objectives
Age of paradox: gifted child, juvenile delinquent, merit scholar, drop-out. J. Shera. Wilson Lib Bul 39:409+ Ja '65
American agenda; evaluation of our society; address, May 1, 1963. J. W. Fulbright. bibliog Vital Speeches 29:520-6 Je 15 '63
American education week message from the White House. L. B. Johnson. il Sr Schol 85:1T N 4 '64
Bamboo and silk and the art of talking back. J. Shera. Wilson Lib Bul 37:870 Je '63
Century of the educated man; address, June 9, 1963. L. B. Johnson. Vital Speeches 29:653-5 Ag 15 '63
Challenge of education. L. B. Johnson. il Sr Schol 85:4 Ja 21 '65
Challenge to teachers; address, October 25, 1963. J. A. Perkins. Vital Speeches 30:172-6 Ja 1 '64
Conversation on education; questions and answers. R. M. Hutchins. Library J 88:2821-8 Ag '63; Reply. C. M. Hutt. 88:3776 O 15 '63
Cost of conformity; with study discussion program, by E. M. Duvall. R. Squires. bibliog PTA Mag 58:4-6, 36 Mr '64
Could you pass the third grade? M. Mayer. il Esquire 63:60-5 Ja '65
Does automation call for new solutions? V. M. Rogers. il PTA Mag 58:7-9 Je '64
Education: a decade of dilemmas; excerpts from address, July 18, 1963. S. B. Gould. ALA Bul 57:837+ O '63
Education: acceptance of responsibility; address, July 16 1964. C. Pell. Vital Speeches 30:725-7 S 15 '64
Education and the new America. by S. T. Kimball and J. E. McClellan, jr. Review
Nat R 14:285-7 Ap 9 '63. G. Wills

EDUCATION—Aims and objectives—*Continued*
Education in an industrial society, by G. H. Bantock. Review
Science 143:556-8 F 7 '64. R. J. Havighurst
Education in our changing times: address, June 2, 1963. Thant. U N Rev 10:48-50 Je '63
Education of teachers; address, February 14, 1963. J. D. Koerner. Vital Speeches 29:412-16 Ap 15 '63
Education's role in the developing nations. P. H. Coombs. il Sat R 46:29-30 Ag 17 '63
Getting the most from the newer media. W. C. Miller and A. L. Goldberg. il NEA J 53:30-1 Ap '64
Gross challenge: are we educators or baby-sitters? summary of address. C. E. Gross. Sr Schol 82:1T+ Ap 24 '63
Guest editorial by the President of the United States. L. B. Johnson. Parents Mag 39:54 S '64
High school dumping grounds. M. Venable. il Sch Arts 63:32-4 My '64
It's time. . . who shall go to college? address, March 16, 1963. E. L. Harden. Vital Speeches 29:430-4 My 1 '63
Kind of public schools we want; address. F. Keppel. Vital Speeches 29:569-72 Jl 1 '63
New mythology. M. E. Jenkins. PTA Mag 57:2-3 Mr '63
Queen Bee of the school; with report of sociologists, ed. by B. Villet. il Life 55:68-80+ O 11 '63
Road less traveled by. J. L. Brown. bibliog f Negro Hist Bul 27:144-5 Mr '64
Scholastic teacher interview; ed. by H. Langer. T. Davis. Sr Schol 85:9T-14T+ D 2 '64
Shaping educational policy, by J. B. Conant. Review
Sr Schol 85:1T-2T N 18 '64
Slowing down; reprint. J. O. Hunter. Library J 89:300 Ja 15 '64
Stairway to the stars. J. H. Glenn, jr; R. M. White. il NEA J 52:8-10 Ap '63
Strange world of our children; excerpts from address, May 1964. M. B. Mitchell. il PTA Mag 59:8-10 S '64
Ten delusions of youth; address, February 14, 1963. W. P. Shofstall. Vital Speeches 29:400-3 Ap 15 '63
To know and to do. M. Mayer. il Sat R 47:62-3+ F 15 '64
Today's challenge in education; address, February 28, 1963. M. Rafferty. Vital Speeches 29:450-4 My 15 '63
Two-year-olds are very smart. R. Gross. il N Y Times Mag p 10-11+ S 6 '64
Understanding the role of education. M. J. Thomas. Sch & Soc 91:284 O 5 '63
War on poverty; book publishing's role in adult education, job retraining; symposium; with editorial comment. il Pub W 185:38-50, 57 F 17 '64
What, then, is all this teaching for? address, April 10, 1964. P. D. Leedy. Vital Speeches 30:501-4 Je 1 '64
What's ahead in education. F. M. Hechinger. il Parents Mag 39:62-3+ S '64
Whose values should be taught? M. Birnbaum. il Sat R 47:60-2+ Je 20 '64
Why go to school. P. Goodman. New Repub 149:13-14 O 5 '63
Writing in the sky. M. E. Jenkins. PTA Mag 57:2-3 Ap '63

Anecdotes, facetiae, satire, etc.

If I could go to school again. D. Herold. Read Digest 82:270-1 My '63
It still goes on. H. F. Ellis. il Atlan 211:112-14 My '63
Report card. J. Scanlon. See issues of Saturday review

Bibliography

Books on education in the White House library. Sat R 46:51 S 21 '63
Editor's bookshelf. P. Woodring. See occasional issues of Saturday review
Foreign books for educators. W. W. Brickman. Sch & Soc 91:149-54, 381-7 Mr 23, N 30 '63
Most important books on education 1963-1964. Sat R 47:58-9 D 19 '64
New books. Sat R 46:88 F 16; 76 Ap 20; 60 Jl 20; 72 S 21; 86 N 16 '63; 47:72 Ja 18; 80 Mr 21; 71-2 Ap 18; 58 Jl 18; 67 Ag 15; 71 S 19; 67 O 17; 75 N 21 '64; 48:62 Ja 16 '65
New books in education: race, religion, and research. H. L. Hurwitz. il Sr Schol 85:18T-21T O 7 '64
New professional books: issues and approaches; paperbacks. H. L. Hurwitz. il Sr Schol 85:24T D 2 '64
Outstanding education books of 1962-1963. NEA J 52:49-51 My '63; 53:54-5 My '64
U.S. books for educators. W. W. Brickman. Sch & Soc 91:246-57, 310-20, 440-6; 92:242-50, 418-25 Sum, O 19, D 28 '63, Sum, D 26 '64

Curricula

See Courses of study

Dictionaries and encyclopedias

50th anniversary of Monroe's Cyclopedia of education. F. Cordasco. bibliog f Sch & Soc 91:123-4 Mr 9 '63

Economic aspects

Expenditures for education in relation to national income. R. M. Walker. il Sch Life 45:23 Ja '63
How to win the fight for a new school. H. Mehling. il Redbook 122:48-9+ Ja '64
Money for education. America 112:9-10 Ja 2 '65
Paying for education. C. Jencks. New Repub 150:13-16 F 1 '64
Personal business; educating junior. Bsns W p97-8 Mr 30 '63
Will Congress pay for education? C. Jencks. il New Repub 150:11-14 Ja 11 '64
See also
Colleges and universities—Finance

Federal aid

See Federal aid to education

Finance

See School finance

History

International living in the universities of the past. W. W. Brickman. Sch & Soc 92:40 F 8 '64
1964 as a centennial year in the history of education. F. Parker. Sch & Soc 92:31-2 Ja 25 '64
1963 as a centennial year in the history of education. W. C. Eells. Sch & Soc 91:41-2 Ja 26 '63
Schoolboy in Sumer; prestige of the scribe; excerpt from History of mankind. L. Woolley. il UNESCO Courier 16:14-15 Je '63
See also
Education—United States—History

International aspects

Come in, world. See issues of PTA magazine
Education for citizenship in the modern world; address, February 16, 1964. D. Rusk. Dept State Bul 50:358-64 Mr 9 '64
International study at home and abroad. S. A. Freeman. bibliog f Ann Am Acad 356:133-41 N '64
Programmed instruction abroad. P. K. Komoski. il Sr Schol 84:13T Mr 13 '64
Proposal for centers for development education. D. K. Adams. Sch & Soc 91:282-3 O 5 '63
Revolutionary social forces; address, March 27, 1963. L. H. Evans. Vital Speeches 29:454-7 My 15 '63
Student art: International school art program. il NEA J 53:31-3 Mr '64
See also
International education
International society for education through art
United Nations educational, scientific and cultural organization

International cooperation

See also
Students, Interchange of
Teachers, Interchange of

Laws

See School laws and legislation

Objectives

See Education—Aims and objectives

Periodicals

See also
NEA journal
School and society (periodical)

Philosophy

American agenda; adaptation of address. J. W. Fulbright. Sat R 46:15-17+ Jl 20 '63
Analytic philosophy and educational thought; excerpt from Foundations of education. G. F. Kneller. bibliog f Sch & Soc 91:61+ F 9 '63
Existential criticism in educational theory; adaptation from address, April, 1963. M. I. Berger. Sch & Soc 92:334-5 N 14 '64

EDUCATION—Philosophy—*Continued*
Family business in brief; traditional vs. progressive education. A. P. Eliasberg. il N Y Times Mag p39 Jl 26 '64
Improvement of the human character; address, November 6, 1964. R. H. Amberg. Vital Speeches 31:121-3 D 1 '64
Return to essentialism. Sch & Soc 91:185-6 Ap 20 '63
Searching for certitudes. P. Schrag. Commonweal 79:36-40 O 4 '63
To know and to do. M. Mayer. il Sat R 47: 62-3+ F 15 '64
To think and to feel. A. Montagu. NEA J 53:15 O '64
Upheld mirror. L. C. Eiseley. NEA J 52: 29 D '63
What the family isn't teaching. H. Taylor. Sat R 46:17-19 My 18 '63

Quotations, maxims, etc.

As school reopens; comp. by E. F. Murphy. N Y Times Mag p 145 S 13 '64
Quotes: education; comp. by E. F. Murphy. il N Y Times Mag p 102 N 24 '63

Societies

See Educational associations

Standards

Education is a national responsibility. W. S. Paley. NEA J 53:10 My '64
Revolt against educational flapdoodle just beginning. F. Morley. Nations Bsns 51:27-8 F '63
Scholastic teacher interviews: Mortimer Smith; ed. by H. Langer. M. Smith. il Sr Schol 84:9T-12T My 1 '64
Standards of excellence in the junior college; excerpt from address, June 17, 1963. F. Keppel. Sch & Soc 91:329-30 N 2 '63
Why we need national academic standards. A. C. Eurich. il Parents Mag 39:61+ F '64

State control

See Education and state

Statistics

American public school teachers, 1960-61. il NEA J 52:48-51 Ap '63
Educational figures for 1973. Sch & Soc 92: 330 N 14 '64
Educational statistics in Britain. Sch & Soc 91:209+ My 4 '63
Enrollment, teachers, and schoolhousing; highlights from the fall 1962-63 survey of public schools. C. J. Hobson and S. Schloss. Sch Life 45:14-17 Ja '63; 46:18-23 Ja '64
Facts and figures of the Americas. il Américas 15:8-9 S '63
How do the public schools of your state rank? il Parents Mag 39:16 S '64
How does your state rank in education? Parents Mag 38:79 S '63
Magnitude of the American educational establishment (1963-64) il Sat R 46:63 S 21 '63
Numbers game. Newsweek 61:56 F 4 '63
School population in England. il Sch & Soc 91:245 Sum '63
Schoolhousing in 1963: USOE survey begins next month. G. J. Collins. il Sch Life 46: 8-11 O '63
Statistic of the month. See issues of School life
See also
Junior colleges—Attendance
Private schools—Statistics
School attendance

Study and teaching

Education graduates view education and academic courses. R. C. Preston. bibliog f il Sch & Soc 92:233-7 Sum '64
Improving education as a subject of study; excerpt from American educational theory. C. J. Brauner. bibliog Sch & Soc 92:25-9 Ja 25 '64
See also
Colleges and universities—Education departments
Teachers—Education

Terminology

Information about dropouts: terms and computations. J. F. Putnam. bibliog Sch Life 45:24-9 My '63
Principles for a program of comparable information. A. R. Lichtenberger. bibliog f Sch Life 45:8-10 My '63

Africa

Africanization of higher education in Africa. Sch & Soc 92:151+ Ap 4 '64
Priorities in African education. J. A. Joyce. il Sat R 47:55-7+ Ag 15 '64
Raising number of African scientists. Sch & Soc 92:328 N 14 '64
Thousands of teachers needed in Africa. Sch & Soc 92:200 My 2 '64

Africa, West

Teaching through trial and error; NEA teach corps in Sierra Leone. L. F. Bailey. Sr Schol 84:10T-11T Ap 17 '64

Alabama

Boomerang. il Newsweek 62:24+ S 16 '63
Shameful thing. il Time 82:26-7 S 13 '63

Alaska

Alaskan school teacher. il Ebony 18:38+ O '63

Arkansas

Still separate, unequal. New Repub 150:5 Mr 28 '64
See also
Little Rock, Ark.—Education

Asia

Reports on international education; symposium. bibliog f il Sch & Soc 91:369-75, 378-9 N 30 '63
U.S. educational ideas in Asia. Sch & Soc 91:367 N 30 '63

Australia

Closing of Catholic schools in Australia. A. Foster. bibliog f Sch & Soc 91:375-7 N 30 '63
See also
Private schools—Australia

Burma

See also
Colleges and universities—Burma

California

Braden's round. Newsweek 61:54 Ap 1 '63
I was the target of a hate campaign. T. Braden. Look 27:54+ O 22 '63
Max Rafferty of California. P. Woodring; discussion. Sat R 46:60+ F 16 '63
Max's maxims. il Newsweek 63:72-3 Mr 30 '64
Revolt against educational flapdoodle just beginning. F. Morley. Nations Bsns 51:27-8 F '63
Scholastic teacher interviews: Dr Max Rafferty; ed. by H. Langer. M. Rafferty. Sr Schol 83:5T-7T+ S 20 '63
See also
San Diego, Calif.—Education
San Francisco—Education

Canada

Educating for the future. R. Davies. Atlan 214:140-4 N '64
Enlightenment on Canadian education. W. W. Brickman. Sch & Soc 91:367 N 30 '63
Parochial education abetted in Saskatchewan. Christian Cent 81:677-8 My 20 '64
Reporter at large; concerning book of letters on French Canada, by Le Frère Untel. E. Wilson. New Yorker 40:64-6+ N 21 '64

Ceylon

Schools in Ceylon. J. P. Cotter. America 109: 212-13 Ag 31 '63

China (People's Republic)

Housewife becomes literate in Communist China; testimony, tr. by D. C. Chu. L. Y. Wang. Sch & Soc 91:379-80 N 30 '63
Quality in secondary education in Communist China. E. L. Harner. Sch & Soc 91:169-70 Ap 6 '63
See also
Colleges and universities—China (People's Republic)

Colorado

See also
Denver—Education

Congo (capital Leopoldville)

UNESCO in the Congo. G. Fullerton. il UNESCO Courier 16:4-11 N '63

Connecticut

See also
Greenwich, Conn.—Education

Cuba

Castro's crash program in education. R. Popkin. il Sat R 47:64-5+ Mr 21 '64

District of Columbia

See Washington, D.C.—Education

EDUCATION—*Continued*

Egypt

Art education in Egypt. T. Abdul-Razik. il Sch Arts 63:34-8 F '64
See also
Colleges and universities—Egypt

England

See Education—Great Britain

Ethiopia

Teacher education in Ethiopia. F. Klassen. Sch & Soc 91:96-8 F 23 '63

Europe

Types of European secondary education. Sch & Soc 91:288 O 5 '63

Europe, Western

American education, a national failure, by H. G. Rickover. Review
U S News il 55:69-70 N 25 '63

Florida

Answer to dropouts: the nongraded high school; Melbourne high school, Cape Kennedy. B. F. Brown. Atlan 214:86-90 N '64
High cost of stinginess; high schools in Duval County disaccredited. Time 84:69 D 18 '64
Southern schooling. New Repub 149:4 S 28 '63

France

Ahead of the bac; baccalauréat exam questions sold to students. Newsweek 64:54 Jl 13 '64
Breaking the *bachot*; French examination questions revealed. il Time 84:53 Jl 10 '64
France's culture corps; overseas lycées. il Time 84:67-8 Ag 7 '64
Joyful school for city kids; snow classes in Alps and Pyrenees; with photographs by J. Marquis. Sports Illus 18:32-4+ Mr 25 '63
See also
Colleges and universities—France
Ecole polytechnique, Paris
Paris—Education

Georgia

Demonstration project to combat poverty. Sch Life 46:4 Ag '64
Let's make it exciting! B. McCullar. il NEA J 52:10-12 Mr '63
Schools or prisons? Sr Schol 84:2T-3T F 7 '64
Science education programs in Georgia high schools. W. M. Brogdon and C. L. Koelsche. Sch & Soc 91:195-7 Ap 20 '63

Germany (Federal Republic)

Learning who Hitler was. il Newsweek 65:53 Ja 18 '65
Schools at the crossroads. R. Plant. il Sat R 46:49-51+ Jl 20 '63

Great Britain

American education, a national failure, by H. G. Rickover. Review
Sch & Soc 92:203-4 My 2 '64. L. H. Johnson
U S News il 55:69-70 N 25 '63
Are Britain's Etons doomed to go? il Bsns W p 174-6+ S 19 '64
Britain's plan for higher education. J. S. Maclure. Sch & Soc 92:228-31 Sum '64
British government endorses the Robbins report. Sch & Soc 92:107-8 Mr 7 '64
Changes coming in British education. il Sr Schol 83:1T-2T N 15 '63
Compulsory professional teacher training in England. H. K. Hutton. bibliog f Sch & Soc 92:358-9 N 28 '64
Education minister's view of education; address, July 5, 1963. E. Boyle. Sch & Soc 92:53-8 F 8 '64
Educational statistics in Britain. Sch & Soc 91:209+ My 4 '63
Expansion and decay in British education R. Kirk. Nat R 16:28 Ja 14 '64
Minus eleven-plus; abolition of Britain's eleven-plus exam. il Time 83:71 Mr 13 '64
Newsom report in England: with text of document. Sch & Soc 92:238-9 Sum '64
School population in England. il Sch & Soc 91:245 Sum '63
Schools in England will not be neglected. Sch & Soc 92:65 F 22 '64
Soon an American revolution in Britain's schools. il U S News 55:113-15 N 11 '63
What's so wonderful about English schools? C. C. Park. Ladies Home J 82:24+ Ja '65
See also
Colleges and universities—Great Britain
London—Education
Oxford university

Hawaii

See also
Schools—Hawaii

India

Historical report from Madras. R B. Sutton. Sch & Soc 92:231-2 Sum '64
New directions for India's teacher education. J. P. Lipkin. Sch & Soc 92:293-4 O 17 '64
See also
Colleges and universities—India

Indiana

Learn to live together. R. A. Fangmeier. Christian Cent 81:410-12 Mr 25 '64
Trouble is teachers. Time 84:90 D 4 '64

Iowa

New name on the list; unsatisfactory educational conditions, Pleasantville, Ia. D. Janson. il Sr Schol 84:1T-2T Ap 10 '64
See also
Iowa. University, Iowa City
Simpson college, Indianola

Ireland

See also
Colleges and universities—Ireland

Israel

See also
Colleges and universities—Israel
Vocational education—Israel

Japan

Educational developments in Asia. B. C. Duke. Sch & Soc 91:369-71 N 30 '63
Fierce scramble. il Newsweek 61:106 Ap 15 '63
See also
Colleges and universities—Japan

Kansas

EB school library award; Prairie Village. H. C. Dent. Wilson Lib Bul 39:400-1+ Ja '65

Kenya

African studies our schools. M. T. Wangombe. NEA J 52:21-2 F '63
Kenya's curious bottleneck. Time 83:43 Ja 10 '64

Latin America

Education: backbone of the Alliance for progress. G. Betancur-Mejía. il Américas 15:2-7 S '63
Education for change; address, 1964. G. Plaza. il Américas 16:11-15 S '64
Education: passkey to the future; statement, August 4, 1963. L. D. Battle. Dept State Bul 49:411-17 S 9 '63
Facts and figures of the Americas. il Américas 15:8-9 S '63; 16:46-7 My '64
Planning for education in Latin America. R. Maheu. il Sat R 47:52-4 Ag 15 '64
Report card on ignorance. il Time 82:27 Ag 16 '63
Soul for the Alliance; Third inter-American education ministers meeting, Bogotá, Colombia. R. C. Schroeder. il Américas 15:2-6 O '63
What ever happened to Euclid? F. L. Phelps. il Américas 16:5-11 N '64

Louisiana

See also
Tulane university, New Orleans

Malaya

Peace corps volunteers praise P.E. project; Satellite communications society at Kuala Lumpur technical college. P. Hardberger. il Pop Electr 20:54-5+ Ja '64

Maryland

Armageddon in Maryland; question of state aid to church-supported colleges and schools. Newsweek 64:72 D 21 '64
Education in prison; Maryland state penitentiary. L. B. Dennis. New Repub 151:6 S 12 '64
School dropouts; summary of study. P. V. Williams. il NEA J 52:10-12 F '63
See also
Baltimore—Education
Rockville, Md.—Education
St John's college, Annapolis, Md.

Massachusetts

Double-purpose plan. L. S. Vander Werf. Sch & Soc 91:213-14 My 4 '63
See also
Harvard university
Massachusetts institute of technology, Cambridge

EDUCATION—*Continued*

Mexico

Compulsory? free? tendentious textbooks. America 108:455-6 Ap 6 '63
See also
Colleges and universities—Mexico

Michigan

When someone complains; threats of book banning. D. P. Whitmer. Sr Schol 83:27T Ja 17 '64
See also
Detroit—Education
Negro schools—Michigan

Minnesota

See also
St Paul—Education

Mississippi

Good deed, bad reason; bill providing state tuition grants to children in private schools. America 111:28 Jl 11 '64
Mississippi idea; Freedom schools. H. Zinn. il Nation 199:371-5 N 23 '64
See also
Mississippi. University

Missouri

See also
Stephens college, Columbia, Mo.

Nepal

Highest school in the world: Sir E. Hillary's latest conquests in the Himalayas. R. J. Spector. il UNESCO Courier 17:12-17 O '64

New Jersey

How we rewrote our social studies curriculum. K. J. Dunn. Sr Schol 85:8T-9T S 16 '64
See also
East Orange, N.J.—Education
Fairleigh Dickinson university, Rutherford, N.J.
New Jersey—Education, Department of

New York (state)

Balancing act; end to de facto segregation in the public schols. Newsweek 62:48 Jl 1 '63
Foreign area studies in New York schools and colleges. W. Morehouse. Sch & Soc 91: 280-2 O 5 '63
It takes only two; literacy programs in New York state. T. L. Conklin. Christian Cent 81:1474 N 25 '64
It's what's up top that counts. G. Dapper. il Sat R 46:48-9+ D 21 '63
See also
New York (city)—Education
New York state university—Teachers college at Cortland

New Zealand

Teacher, by S. Ashton-Warner. Review
Commonweal 79:410 D 27 '63. P. Deasy
Sat R il 46:45 O 5 '63. L. S. Mitchell
Time il 82:42+ S 6 '63

Nigeria

Letter from Nigeria. E. A. Ford. il Sch Life 47:5-9 N '64

North Carolina

New structure for opportunity; North Carolina fund. Sr Schol 84:14T Ap 24 '64
One-man Rand; Prof. J. Ehle raising level of education. Newsweek 63:77-8 Je 1 '64
State of learning. Time 83:41 Ja 24 '64

Northern Rhodesia

See Education—Zambia

Norway

See also
Schools—Norway

Ohio

Ohio; with new board of regents, master plan in works, state takes plunge into statewide planning. J. Walsh. il Science 145: 253-5+ Jl 17 '64; Discussion. 146:14 O 2 '64
School gusher; three wells on former baseball diamond of Edison, Ohio junior high school. I. H. Wenning. Sr Schol 84:3T My 8 '64
See also
Cleveland, Ohio—Education

Oregon

Race and education. M. A. Talney. Christian Cent 81:1568-70 D 16 '64
See also
Oregon state university, Corvallis

Pakistan

Current teacher education in Pakistan. L. H. Stoner and E. Neteland. Sch & Soc 91:174-5 Ap 6 '63
See also
Library schools and education—Pakistan

Pennsylvania

Lord helps Charly, and vice versa; Church farm school, near Pennsylvania. B. Hibbs. Read Digest 85:140-4 Ag '64
Pennsylvania: more bears than books. J. Rowell. ALA Bul 58:816+ O '64

Peru

American aid to education in Peru. L. C. Keating. Sch & Soc 92:206-8 My 2 '64
South American students ask about U.S. schools. C. C. Gill. Sch & Soc 91:193-5 Ap 20 '63

Philippines

Department welcomes amendment to Philippine war damage act; statement, with remarks by Roger Hilsman. Dept State Bul 49:301 Ag 19 '63
Education on their minds. N. Cousins. il Sat R 47:30-1+ My 23 '64
See also
Colleges and universities—Philippines

Poland

See also
Colleges and universities—Poland

Quebec (province)

See Education—Canada

Rhode Island

Church and state; textbooks for 50,000 parochial and private-school pupils. Newsweek 61:106+ Mr 25 '63

Russia

Children's crusade in reverse; Communist indoctrination of children. D. A. Lowrie. Christian Cent 81:1141-3 S 16 '64
Cutback in Russia; school age. Time 84:69 Ag 21 '64
Every child an atheist; Communist indoctrination of children. D. A. Lowrie. Christian Cent 80:776-7 Je 12 '63
Is Russia's school system so good after all? C. Foltz, jr. il U S News 56:70-1 F 3 '64
Moffetts go a-moseying; account of a Communist young pioneer camp. H. Moffett. il Life 55:100-2+ S 13 '63
Report from Russia. P. Ben. New Repub 150: 16-18 Je 13 '64
Social science: a textbook for Soviet secondary schools, by G. K. Shakhnazarov and others. Review
Sr Schol il 85:9T+ N 18 '64. H. Hurwitz
Soviet education in 1962-1963. I. Schlesinger. bibliog f Sch & Soc 91:197-8; 92:204-5 Ap 20 '63, My 2 '64
Soviet educators on Soviet education, ed. and tr. by H. B. Redl. Review
Sat R 48:61-2 Ja 16 '64. M. Greene
Soviet school reform. H. Rogger. Cur Hist 47:292-8 N '64
Soviet university. F. E. MacGregor. America 111:779-80 D 12 '64
What Ivan doesn't want; new reforms shorten schooling period. il Newsweek 64: 74-5 Ag 24 '64

South Carolina

ETV in South Carolina. S. Elam. New Repub 149:7 Ag 31 '63

Southern states

As trouble spreads: ten years of mixed schools. il U S News 55:33-5 S 16 '63
Mixed schools: as eleventh year begins. il U S News 57:37 Ag 31 '64
More speed, less deliberation; Supreme court decisions in Virginia's Prince Edward County and Atlanta. Time 83:68 Je 5 '64
Southern schooling. New Repub 149:4 S 28 '63
Wallace notwithstanding. New Repub 149: 3-4 S 21 '63; Reply with rejoinder. M. Meltsner. 149:29-30 O 12 '63
See also
Negroes in the United States—Education

Spain

See also
Colleges and universities—Spain

Sweden

See also
Colleges and universities—Sweden

Taiwan

Examination hell in Taiwan. J. T. Hatfield. Sch & Soc 91:378-9 N 30 '63

EDUCATION—*Continued*

Texas

See also
Houston, Tex.—Education
Southwest Texas state teachers college, San Marcos

Thailand

Three villages under a microscope; Bangkok institute of child study. il UNESCO Courier 17:18-20 S '64

Underdeveloped areas

Education for development; Nyasaland, Colombia, China and Egypt. F. Harbison. il Sci Am 209:140-4+ bibliog (p307) S '63
Education in the developing nations. R. Maheu; J. A. Joyce. il Sat R 47:52-7+ Ag 15 '64
Education's role in the developing nations. P. H. Coombs. il Sat R 46:29-30 Ag 17 '63
Proposal for centers for development education. D. K. Adams. Sch & Soc 91:282-3 O 5 '63

United States

Adults and their level of educational achievement. R. M. Walker. il Sch Life 45:12 Mr '63
Afterward, college for all. Time 83:42 Ja 10 '64
American agenda; adaptation of address. J. W. Fulbright. Sat R 46:15-17+ Jl 20 '63; Reply. G. P. Kuiper. 46:13 Ag 17 '63
American education, a national failure, by H. G. Rickover. Review
  Sch & Soc 92:203-4 My 2 '64. L. H. Johnson
  U S News il 55:69-70 N 25 '63
Are our children half-educated? L. H. Hodges. il Look 28:85-6 Ja 28 '64
Are we selling education short? Suc Farm 61:76 Ag '63
Art of being free. G. W. Johnson. il Atlan 213:60-4 Ja '64
Circle of futility. P. Schrag. Commonweal 79: 685-8 Mr 6 '64
Comments on Rafferty; letters to editor. Sr Schol 83:4T O 25; 6T N 8 '63
Compulsory mis-education, by P. Goodman. Review
  Reporter 31:48-9 N 5 '64. N. Hentoff
Creative revolutions; curriculum revision. F. G. Jennings. Sat R 47:63-4 Je 20 '64
Critics of the schools never die, either. C. H. Wilson. il Sat R 47:51-3+ Je 20 '64; Discussion. 47:42 Jl 18 '64
Danger from within. D. D. Eisenhower. Read Digest 82:76-82 Mr '63
Delayed independence. D. Wolfle. Science 143: 103 Ja 10 '64
Democracy and excellence in American secondary education, by H. S. Broudy and others. Review
  Sat R 47:85 My 16 '64. M. Greene
Do our schools neglect the average student? E. H. Hanson. il Parents Mag 38:61+ S '63
Education and change. il Sr Schol 84:1T Ap 17 '64
Education and politics. P. Hazelton. il Sat R 46:62-3+ Je 15 '63
Education and the new America, by S. T. Kimball and J. E. McClellan, jr. Review
  Nat R 14:285-7 Ap 9 '63. G. Wills
  Newsweek il 61:92 Mr 11 '63
Education: case for federal aid, comprehensive planning discussed as costs and enrollment rise. J. Walsh. Science 147:30-2 Ja 1 '65
Education: cultivating greater diversity. C. Jencks. il New Repub 151:33-6+ N 7 '64
Education for the cold war? R. Gross. Commonweal 80:36-9 Ap 3 '64
Education in America; ed. by P. Woodring and others. See issues of Saturday review
Education: passkey to the future; statement, August 4, 1963. L. D. Battle. Dept State Bul 49:411-17 S 9 '63
Education: President's message outlines program concentrated on aiding the disadvantaged. J. Walsh. Science 147:382-3 Ja 22 '65
Education: President's program provides more room at top. J. Walsh. Science 139: 474-5+ F 8 '63
Educational research; crisis for publishers; summaries of addresses at conference cosponsored by the U.S. office of education and the American textbook publishers institute; with editorial comment. il Pub W 187:45-59; 71 Ja 11 '65
Equal opportunity in education. M. H. Wagner. America 111:209 Ag 29 '64
Equal rights for every 10th American and every 7th child; address, August 9, 1963. H. L. Carey. Vital Speeches 29:728-30 S 15 '63
Extreme situation; dropouts return to school. P. Goodman. New Repub 149:7 O 19 '63
For better schools. D. Wolfle. Science 144:619 My 8 '64
Genuine educational frontiers. W. Van Til. il Sat R 47:66-8 Ap 18 '64
How sinister is the education establishment? D. W. Robinson. Sat R 48:56-7+ Ja 16 '65
How's your state doing in education? il Changing T 18:22-3 N '64
Improving education as a subject of study; excerpt from American educational theory. C. J. Brauner. bibliog Sch & Soc 92:25-9 Ja 25 '64
Into the century of the educated man. F. Keppel. Sat R 46:37-8 D 21 '63
Knowledge: the biggest growth industry of them all. G. Burck. il Fortune 70:128-31+ N '64
Last chance for our schools? with editorial comment. M. Mayer. il Sat Eve Post 236: 24-6+, 78 S 14 '63
Library as a way to excellence in education. P. B. Knapp. ALA Bul 57:1039-42 D '63
Magnitude of the American educational establishment (1963-65) il Sat R 46:63 S 21 '63; 47:70 N 21 '64
Mass education must face the idiot response. F. Morley. il Nations Bsns 52:29-30 F '64
Miracle ahead, by G. Gallup. Review
  Sat R 47:78-9 Mr 21 '64. E. Roper
Modern revolution in education. A. E. Traxler. Sch & Soc 92:33 Ja 25 '64
Much more remains to be done. E. Green. NEA J 53:16-17+ F '64
News and trends. See issues of NEA journal
1964: the year that was. Sr Schol 85:1T Ja 7 '65
1963: this was the year that was. il Sr Schol 83:3T Ja 10 '64
Not enough. Nation 198:1-2 Ja 4 '64
On taking education seriously. J. B. Conant. il Reporter 31:18-21 D 3 '64; Discussion. 31:6 D 31 '64
On the Anti-Poverty bill; excerpts from testimony before House committee. G. J. Hecht. Parents Mag 39:40+ Je '64
On the fringe of a golden era: the U.S. student. il Time 85:57B+ Ja 29 '65
Open society: key to an advancing America; address, October 26, 1963. L. D. Battle. Dept State Bul 49:864-9 D 2 '63
Outstanding developments in American education in 1963. W. W. Brickman. Sch & Soc 91:417 D 28 '63
Outstanding events in American education in 1964. W. W. Brickman. Sch & Soc 92:395+ D 26 '64
Party platforms on education; excerpts from platforms. il NEA J 53:14 O '64
Pat on the back; summary of address. C. P. Snow. Sr Schol 82:4T Mr 20 '63
Plea for the year-round college. E. J. McGrath. il N Y Times Mag p52+ Ap 28 '63
Popular education and democratic thought in America, by R. Welter. Review
  Sat R 46:86-7 F 16 '63. L. A. Cremin
President asks $1.5 billion for aid to education; with editorial comment. Pub W 187: 273-4, 280 Ja 25 '65
President Johnson speaks out on education; special statement for the National education association. L. B. Johnson. NEA J 53: 12-14 Ja '64
President's message on education; January 29, 1963. J. F. Kennedy. Sch Life 45:5-7+ F '63
President's program for education; summary of proposals. il Sat R 46:68-9 Mr 23 '63
Professors and pedagogues. C. Jencks. New Repub 150:28+ My 16 '64
Program to improve our schools; excerpts from Education for all children. H. G. Rickover. Ladies Home J 80:20+ O '63
Proposal for a revolution. J. P. Lyford. il Sat R 46:19-22 O 19; 25-8+ O 26 '63
Reasons for doing nothing. E. Date. NEA J 52:11 N '63
Right and the responsibility. F. Keppel. NEA J 52:15 O '63
Saving the liberal arts. P. Goodman. Commonweal 80:359-61 Je 12 '64
Scholastic teacher interviews: Francis Keppel. F. Keppel. Sr Schol 84:1T-2T+ Ap 24 '64
School: whose is it? F. Canavan. America 111: 153-6 Ag 15 '64; Reply with rejoinder. J. J. Ryan. 111:299-301 S 19 '64
School gains prove no aid needed. il Nations Bsns 52:88 F '64
Schoolmaster Rickover. C. Jencks. New Repub 148:14-16 Mr 2 '63; Discussion. 148: 15-18 Ap 27; 30-1 My 25 '63
Schools educate themselves. P. Woodring. il Sat R 47:153-5+ Ag 29 '64

EDUCATION—United States—*Continued*
Schools for the sixties. il NEA J 53:37-52 Ja '64
Schools for the sixties; concerning National education association's report with summary of recommendations. J. S. Gow, jr. Sat R 46:58-60+ O 19 '63
Schools in the news. Sat R 47:66 N 21 '64
Schools make news. Sat R 48:51 Ja 16 '65
Scientific age: the impact of science on society, by L. V. Berkner. Review
Sat R 47:72-3 N 21 '64. R. Gross
Senator Fulbright on U.S. education; excerpts from address, October 13, 1962. J. W. Fulbright. Sch & Soc 91:31+ Ja 26 '63
Shaping educational policy, by J. B. Conant. Review
PTA Mag 59:25-6 Ja '65. W. D. Boutwell
Sat R il 47:71 N 21 '64. P. Woodring
Sr Schol 85:1T-2T N 18 '64
Time 84:102 N 20 '64
Some plain talk about higher education; address, October 2, 1964. V. F. Spathelf. Vital Speeches 31:40-3 N 1 '64
Soon an American revolution in Britain's schools. il U S News 55:113-15 N 11 '63
South American students ask about U.S. schools. C. C. Gill. Sch & Soc 91:193-5 Ap 20 '63
Space and national priorities; address, October 17, 1963. J. W. Fulbright. Vital Speeches 30:41-4 N 1 '63
Speech education, a terrible responsibility. G. A. Yeomans. Vital Speeches 30:348-52 Mr 15 '64
Summer '64. il Sr Schol 85:1T-2T S 16 '64
Technology's challenge to education; symposium. Sat R 47:21-5+ D 12 '64
Top of the agenda: Johnson's comprehensive education bill. il Newsweek 65:56-7 Ja 25 '65
Triumph of the intellect. Sch & Soc 91:236-7+ Sum '63
Uncle Sam, schoolmaster. R. Moley. Newsweek 62:110 S 23 '63
Understanding the role of education. M. J. Thomas. Sch & Soc 91:284 O 5 '63
Vote of confidence. J. M. Carter. NEA J 52:15 Ap '63
War on poverty; book publishing's role in adult education, job retraining; symposium; with editorial comment. il Pub W 185:38-50, 57 F 17 '64
What ever happened to Euclid? F. L. Phelps. il Américas 16:5-11 N '64
What the family isn't teaching. H. Taylor. Sat R 46:17-19 My 18 '63
What they are doing to your children, by M. Rafferty. Review
Sat R 47:79-80 Mr 21 '64 L A Cremin
What's ahead in education. F. M. Hechinger. il Parents Mag 39:62-3+ S '64
What's happening in education? W. D. Boutwell. See issues of PTA magazine
What's happening in our schools. J. B. Kelley. America 108:547-9 Ap 20 '63
What's wrong in the schools; educator speaks out; excerpts from address, December 6, 1963. M. Rafferty. U S News 55:78-9 D 30 '63
Where the schoolhouse goes from here. H. B. Gores. Arch Rec 136:225-7 S '64
While school keeps. J. Cass. See issues of Saturday review
Why go to school. P. Goodman. New Repub 149:13-14 O 5 '63
See also
Adult education
American education week
Colleges and universities—United States
Education—Southern states
Education and democracy
Education and state
Education of women—United States
Essentialist committee for the advancement of American education
High schools
Immigrants in the United States—Education
Junior colleges
National education association
Negroes in the United States—Education
Private schools
Public schools—United States
Rural schools—United States
School laws and legislation—United States
Service men, Discharged—Education
Socially handicapped children—Education
Summer schools
United States—Army—Education
United States—Education, Office of
Vocational education

Bibliography

New books; slightly cheerful news about our schools. B. DeMott. Harper 226:106+ My '63

History

Conant, Koerner, and the history of education. W. W. Brickman. bibliog f Sch & Soc 92:135-9 Mr 21 '64
Diary of George C. Catrow; excerpts, ed. by G. Crout. G. C. Catrow. NEA J 54:29-30 Ja '65

Utah

Deliberate slowness. Newsweek 62:52-3 Jl 15 '63
Recess in Utah; teachers walkout. il Newsweek 63:77 Je 1 '64
Strikes, sanctions, and the schools. J. Scanlon. il Sat R 46:51-5+ O 19 '63; Discussion. 46:39 D 21 '63
Utah schools; demands for more state educational aid. New Repub 148:5 Ap 13 '63
See also
Utah education association

Vermont

See also
Bennington college, Bennington, Vt.

Virgin Islands

See also
Colleges and universities—Virgin Islands

Virginia

Catching up in Prince Edward. il Time 82:56 Ag 9 '63
Fundamental principle is involved. NEA J 53:16 Ja '64
See also
Richmond, Va.—Education

Washington (state)

Librarian's dream come true; Knapp school libraries project, Marcus Whitman elementary school, Richland. P. Sullivan. il NEA J 53:46-7 S '64
See also
Seattle—Education

Zambia

Founding the Department of African education in Northern Rhodesia; address, February 1962. F. Parker. il Negro Hist Bul 27:29-34 N '63

EDUCATION, Adult. See Adult education
EDUCATION, Agricultural. See Agricultural education
EDUCATION, Art. See Art education
EDUCATION, Boards of. See School boards
EDUCATION, Business. See Business education
EDUCATION, College. See College education
EDUCATION, Commissioner of. See United States—Education, Office of
EDUCATION, Comparative
Proposal for centers for development education. D. K. Adams. Sch & Soc 91:282-3 O 5 '63
See also
Comparative education society
EDUCATION, Cooperative
Chicago's answer for dropouts; Education-employment program. il Ebony 18:81-2+ O '63
Cooperative education is first-rate education. G. E. Probst. il PTA Mag 58:26-8 N '63
Expansion of cooperative education; work-study plan. Sch & Soc 91:102 F 23 '63
Indiana program of job training and work experience for students; excerpt. S. Cohen and W. C. Pyle. Mo Labor R 86:161-3 F '63
EDUCATION, Cost of. See Education—Economic aspects
EDUCATION, Elementary
Could you pass the third grade? M. Mayer. il Esquire 63:60-5 Ja '65
Economics with ABCs; primary grade youngsters in Elkhart, Ind. il Bsns W p 186-8+ Mr 21 '64
Father in the first grade. W. Stanton. il McCalls 91:82-3+ F '64
First grade and first worries; with study-discussion program, by R. Strang. M. Marston. bibliog il PTA Mag 57:14-16. 34 Ap '63
Gingerbread lesson; experimental program to teach economics in the lower grades. il Newsweek 63:73 Mr 30 '64
New views on grades. Time 84:30 D 25 '64
New way for children to learn. J. K. Lagemann. il Redbook 122:42-3+ F '64
Primer for parents of first readers. P. Parish. il N Y Times Mag p 102 S 8 '63
Reading in basic education; excerpt from address, August 1, 1962. M. Smith. Sch & Soc 91:56-9 F 9 '63
What to measure in elementary school. M. Hunter. NEA J 53:15-16 My '64

EDUCATION, Elementary—*Continued*
When the school has no grade levels. Good H 156:144-5 Mr '63
See also
Courses of study
Montessori method of education
Readiness for school

Activity programs

Have a creative corner in your room. R. C. Jennette. il Sch Arts 62:33-5 Mr '63
How we discourage creative children. J. K. Lagemann. il Redbook 120:44-5+ Mr '63

EDUCATION, Engineering. See Engineering education

EDUCATION, Experimental
Art and uncertainty. D. F. Guillaume. il Sch Arts 63:23-4 Mr '64
Double-purpose plan. L. S. Vander Werf. Sch & Soc 91:213-14 My 4 '63
Education: PSAC panel draws on experience of curriculum reform to point way to wider innovation. J. Walsh. Science 144:394-5 Ap 24 '64
Laboratory to test new educational methods. il Arch Rec 134:212-13 O '63
There's no limit to learning. J. Murphy and R. Gross. il Parents Mag 39:62-3+ F '64
Utopia and rebellion: the New college experiment; excerpt from Innovation in education. G. Watson. bibliog Sch & Soc 92:72+ F 22 '64
See also
Goddard college, Plainfield, Vt.
Progressive education

EDUCATION, Higher. See College education; Colleges and universities

EDUCATION, Liberal. See Liberal education

EDUCATION, Medical. See Medical education

EDUCATION, Military. See Military education

EDUCATION, Moral. See Moral education

EDUCATION, Museum. See Museum education

EDUCATION, Musical. See Music—Instruction and study

EDUCATION, Office of. See United States—Education, Office of

EDUCATION, Physical. See Physical education and training

EDUCATION, Primary. See Education, Elementary

EDUCATION, Progressive. See Progressive education

EDUCATION, Religious. See Religious education

EDUCATION, Rural. See Rural schools

EDUCATION, Scientific. See Scientific education

EDUCATION, Secondary
Chinese and Japanese in high school. Sch & Soc 91:288+ O 5 '63
Democracy and excellence in American secondary education, by H. S. Broudy and others. Review
Sat R 47:85 My 16 '64. M. Greene
Extended schooling versus higher education. J. F. Ohles. Sch & Soc 92:156-7 Ap 4 '64
New look at readiness; excerpt from Democracy and excellence in American secondary education. H. S. Broudy and others. bibliog Sch & Soc 91:424-30 D 28 '63
On the fringe of a golden era: the U.S. student. il Time 85:57B Ja 29 '65
Quality secondary schools of the future. O. F. Parody. Sch Life 47:23-7 N '64 (to be cont)
Secondary education for the academically untalented. Sch & Soc 92:259+ O 3 '64
What's in the wind for student activities? G. M. Van Pool. il PTA Mag 57:25-7 Ap '63
See also
High schools

EDUCATION, Social. See Social education

EDUCATION, State departments of
Data-processing center in the State department of education. J. E. Bean. Sch Life 46:10-11 Jl '64
Guidance worker in the State department of education. D. Camp. il Sch Life 46:6-9 Jl '64
Research in the State department of education. J. E. Bean. Sch Life 45:17-18 My '63

EDUCATION, Technical. See Technical education

EDUCATION, Theological. See Theological education

EDUCATION, Urban
Case for the asphalt campus. D. Boroff. il N Y Times Mag p 15+ Ap 21 '63
Slums and suburbs. Sr Schol 82:1T-3T My 1 '63
Urbanization and higher education. J. S. Pope. il NEA J 52:16-18 Mr '63

EDUCATION, Value of
Day our boy quit school, and how we got him back in! il Farm J 88:33+ My '64
Education; address, June 7, 1964. S. A. Nielsen. Vital Speeches 30:603-5 Jl 15 '64
How much is it worth to win? J. R. Gallagher. Seventeen 23:152+ My '64
It's practical to be intellectual. G. B. Leonard. NEA J 52:31 My '63
Responsibilities of the educated man; address, April 9, 1964. G. Kirk. Vital Speeches 30:471-4 My 15 '64
World you live in; your share in the future; address, June 4, 1963. B. F. Parker. Vital Speeches 29:754-6 O 1 '63
See also
College education, Value of

EDUCATION, Vocational. See Vocational education

EDUCATION and business. See Business and education

EDUCATION and church. See Church and education

EDUCATION and democracy
Democracy in relation to education; excerpt from Philosophy of education: introductory studies. P. Smith. bibliog f Sch & Soc 92:414-18 D 26 '64
Democracy, teachers, and educational decision-making. A. R. Dykes. Sch & Soc 92:155-6 Ap 4 '64
How not to integrate the schools; a personal testament. I. L. Gibel. Harper 227:57-60+ N '63; Discussion. 228:6 Ja '64
Teaching the fundamentals of international understanding; address, September 8, 1964. D Rusk. Dept State Bul 51:437-41 S 28 '64
See also
Citizenship, Education for

EDUCATION and economic problems. See School and social and economic problems

EDUCATION and industry. See Business and education

EDUCATION and social problems. See School and social and economic problems

EDUCATION and state
Bulwarks against federal control. A. W. F. Ford. Sr Schol 82:16T Mr 20 '63
Church-state confrontation in Maryland: suit to determine the constitutionality of tax funds for church-related colleges. I. G. Zepp, jr. Christian Cent 82:84+ Ja 20 '65
Federal influence distorts education; U.S. programs create imbalance in colleges. il Nations Bsns 51:31-3+ Mr '63
Good deed, bad reason; bill providing state tuition grants to children in private schools. America 111:28 Jl 11 '64
Graduate education; interest of the government; address, December 27, 1963. P. P. Muirhead. Vital Speeches 30:280-2 F 15 '64
Higher education: fourth branch of government? C. K. Arnold. il Sat R 47:60-1+ Ja 18 '64; Reply. L. H. Fountain. 47:62 Mr 21 '64
Legal world series; Maryland suit against the use of public funds for four church-related colleges. America 109:339 S 28 '63
National goals and the university. J. C. Warner. Science 142:462-4 O 25 '63
New estate. A. M. Weinberg. Bul Atomic Sci 20:16-19 F '64
Politics and higher education; address, June 10, 1964. E Hutchinson. bibliog Science 146:1139-42 N 27 '64
Public higher education and the needs of government; excerpt from address, April 29, 1963. J. K. Pollock. Sch & Soc 92:45-7 F 8 '64
Research: as the stakes go up, idea of a man in Washington considered by more universities. J. Walsh. Science 142:1043-5 N 22 '63
Scholastic teacher interviews: William G. Carr: ed. by H. Langer. W. G. Carr. il Sr Schol 83:9T-13T Ja 17 '64
State's role. America 108:853 Je 15 '63
This month's feature: Congress and aid to higher education. Cong Digest 42:35-64 F '63
See also
Church schools
Federal aid to education

EDUCATION and state in Australia
Federal aid in Australia. America 110:838 Je 20 '64

EDUCATION and state in Canada
School aid in Saskatchewan. J. J. Toth. America 110:812 Je 13 '64

EDUCATION and state in Great Britain
Letter from London; concerning Robbins report on higher education. M. Panter-Downes. New Yorker 39:58+ Ja 25 '64

EDUCATION and state in Mexico
Battle of the books. Newsweek 61:88+ F 25 '63

EDUCATION associations. See Educational associations

EDUCATION centre library, Toronto. See Toronto—Education, Board of—Education centre library

EDUCATION departments, College. See Colleges and universities—Education departments

EDUCATION-employment program. See Chicago—Education, Board of

EDUCATION for citizenship. See Citizenship, Education for

EDUCATION for family life. See Family life, Education for

EDUCATION for the arts. See Art education

EDUCATION for the handicapped. See Handicapped—Education

EDUCATION in American citizenship, National foundation for. See National foundation for education in American citizenship

EDUCATION of adults. See Adult education

EDUCATION of children

Another kind of camera. A. M. Tredup. il Horn Bk 39:30-5 F '63

Can you help your child get better grades? G. Hechinger and F. M. Hechinger. il McCalls 92:50+ O '64

Education minister's view of education; address, July 5, 1963. E. Boyle. Sch & Soc 92:53-8 F 8 '64

Foreign affairs begin at home. J. F. Travers. Cath World 199:16-21 Ap '64

Help yourself learning; special science classes in Los Angeles. il Time 81:62+ Mr 15 '63

How to prepare your child for the world of the '70s. P. L. Cahn. il McCalls 92:53+ Ja '65

How to teach your child to remember. H. Pollan. il Parents Mag 39:54-5+ Mr '64

Little brains think big. V. Cadden. il N Y Times Mag p89-90 Ap 28 '63

Night the stars fell; art of adding dimensions to a child's world. A. Gordon. il Read Digest 85:93-6 O '64

Parent's guide to children's education, by N. Larrick. Review
Sat R 46:48-9 Ag 17 '63. F. G. Jennings

Redbook dialogue; Mario Montessori and A. S. Neill discuss their famous schools and their radical approaches to child rearing. M. Montessori and A. S. Neill. Redbook 124:42-3+ D '64

Speaking out; stop pampering gifted children. B. Bettelheim. Sat Eve Post 237:8+ Ap 11 '64; Reply. C. Jencks. New Repub 150:26-8 Ap 25 '64; Rejoinder. 150:29-30 My 9 '64

Talking typewriter teacher. il Sci Digest 55:41-2 Mr '64

Three is a threshold. R. Kramer. il N Y Times Mag p 122+ O 18 '64

Two-year-olds are very smart. R. Gross. il N Y Times Mag p 10-11+ S 6 '64

UN international school. C. Holm. il Parents Mag 39:66-7+ F '64

What's happening in education; home education of children. W. D. Boutwell. PTA Mag 57:16 F '63

When do they know too much? J. Ciardi. Sat R 46:16 My 11 '63

Worlds of innocence. H. Behn. il Horn Bk 39:21-9 F '63

See also
Camping—Educational aspects
Children—Management and training
Children of migrant laborers—Education
Childrens reading
Cookery by children
Education, Elementary
Kindergarten
Montessori method of education
Music and children
Nature study
Nursery schools
Play
Preschool children
Readiness for school
Sex instruction
Social education

Anecdotes, facetiae, satire, etc.

MARY: teacher's pet; repalcement of students with learning machines, Mechanical analogue response yielders. J. Biermann and B. Toohey. Wilson Lib Bul 39:402 Ja '65

EDUCATION of girls. See Education of women

EDUCATION of librarians. See Library schools and education

EDUCATION of Negroes. See Negroes in the United States—Education

EDUCATION of princes and princesses

Miya-chama at school; education of Prince Hiro of Japan. il Newsweek 63:98 Ap 27 '64

Student princess. il N Y Times Mag p74 S 8 '63

EDUCATION of prisoners

Case of the squeezed pencils; night classes at Poplar Hill correctional camp, Maryland. L. W. Harrington. NEA J 53:24 O '64

EDUCATION of women

Access of girls and women to education in rural areas. Sch & Soc 92:328 N 14 '64

Change and challenge for the educated woman. P. Tompkins. Sat R 46:69-70+ My 18 '63

Educating women. P. Woodring. Sat R 46:61 My 18 '63

Education of women; symposium. il Sat R 46:61, 64-70+ My 18 '63; Discussion. 46:60-1 Je 15 '63

Why don't they talk? J. Comings. Sat R 46:15 Jl 6 '63; Discussion. 46:15 Ag 3 '63

Without portfolio. C. B. Luce. McCalls 92:20+O '64

See also
College graduates, Women
College students, Women

United States

Educating women. P. Woodring. Sat R 46:61 My 18 '63

Education for the mature woman; excerpt from American women, the report of the President's commission on the status of women. Sat R 46:90 N 16 '63

Education of a modern girl: with study-discussion program, by E. M. Duvall. H. Taylor. bibliog il PTA Mag 58:4-6, 36 S '63

Education of women: adaptation of report. Sch Life 46:17-19 N '63

Education of women; symposium. il Sat R 46:61, 64-70+ My 18 '63; Discussion. 46:60-1 Je 15 '63

From kitchens to careers. il Sr Schol 85:5 N 4 '64

GI bill for women? excerpt from Feminine mystique. B. Friedan. Sat R 46:68 My 18 '63

How not to waste college on girls; with study-discussion program, by M. Smart. G. Hechinger and E. M. Hechinger. il Parents Mag 39:40, 70-1+ F '64

Trained intelligence: the Nation's greatest weapon; address, June 12, 1963. A. E. Stevenson. Vital Speeches 29:581-4 Jl 15 '63

Warm-hearted guide to certain girls' schools. P. LaFarge. Harper 226:73-9 Ap '63

What's the use of educating women? E. D. Eddy, jr. bibliog il Sat R 46:66-8 My 18 '63

See also names of womens colleges, e.g. Barnard college, New York

EDUCATION week. See American education week

EDUCATIONAL acceleration

Accelerating; new Yale program. Newsweek 63:52 Ja 27 '64

Double degree at Yale. Time 83:41 Ja 24 '64

See also
Children, Gifted
High school students, Mentally superior

EDUCATIONAL achievements. See Student achievements

EDUCATIONAL administration. See School management and organization

EDUCATIONAL advertising. See School publicity

EDUCATIONAL associations

Advancing the cause of education. E. O. Melby. NEA J 52:29 F '63

Advancing the welfare of members. F. L. Hipp. NEA J 53:19-20 Ja '64

Better late than later. C. Mitchell. NEA J 52:23 D '63

Building local association strength; St Louis teachers association. il NEA J 52:39-41 D '63

Change for Albuquerque's teachers. NEA J 52:37 My '63

Denver achieves professional negotiations. R. Newlon and B. J. Lee. il NEA J 52:14-16 F '63

How local associations do it. J. A. Letorney. NEA J 53:56 Mr '64

Improving educational practices. J. E. Christenson. NEA J 53:17-18 Ja '64

Local associations chart new courses; symposium. NEA J 53:28-30 My '64

Local-state-national. L. S. Bangs. NEA J 52:26 F '63

Opportunities in professional organization. S. Stoncius. NEA J 53:60 O '64

Schools are not factories. G. W. Denemark. NEA J 53:25-7 Mr '64

Special journal feature; symposium. il NEA J NEA J 53:18-32 F '64

EDUCATIONAL associations—*Continued*
Teacher influence in politics; state of Washington. E. M. Taylor. NEA J 53:64 Ja '64
Teacher welfare in France: Mutuelle generale de l'education nationale, mutual benefit society organized by French national teachers syndicate. D. Forestier. NEA J 54:19-20 Ja '65
What's happening in education? W. D. Boutwell. PTA Mag 58:13-14 Mr '64
See also names of educational associations, e.g. American association of school administrators

EDUCATIONAL attainment
Adults and their level of educational achievement. R. M. Walker. il Sch Life 45:12 Mr '63

EDUCATIONAL conferences
Contemporary educational issues; theme of the 50th conference of Schoolmen's week. H. Huus. Sch & Soc 91:45-6 Ja 26 '63
It's a date (cont) NEA J 52:60-1 My; 63-4 S '63; 53:79+ Ja; 58-9 My; 70-1 S '64; 54:71+ Ja '65
Maps for action: third annual conference of the National council on the arts in education. M. Van Tuyl. Dance Mag 39:26-7 Ja '65
PTA goes abroad. J. Moorhead. il PTA Mag 59:20-2 D '64
See you at the conventions! Convention previews; National council for the social studies, National council of teachers of English, and National council for geographic education. il Sr Schol 83:1T+ N 22 '63
Social studies curriculum: proposals for the future; report on the 1963 Cubberley conference, Stanford university. R. E. Gross. Sr Schol 83:8T-9T O 25 '63
Technology, education, and human values; conference on technology and human values, sponsored by the Center for continuing liberal education, Pennsylvania state university. A. Trachtenberg. Sch & Soc 92:316-18 O 31 '64
See also names of educational conferences, e.g. Yale conference on the teaching of English

EDUCATIONAL cooperation
Academic common market; Committee on institutional cooperation. Time 81:41 F 22 '63
Catholicism in Ohio. New Repub 149:5 N 2 '63
Chance for shared time. J. O'Gara. Commonweal 80:110 Ap 17 '64
Church related schools; shared-time. New Repub 148:4-6 My 11 '63
New hope for weak colleges; the consortium plan. G. H. Hanford. il Sat R 48:52-3+ Ja 16 '65
Reactions to shared time. D. Iwamoto. il NEA J 53:49+ D '64
Shared time experiment. E. Wakin; T. Powell. il Sat R 47:68-9+ F 15 '64; Discussion. 47:63 Mr 21 '64
Shared time in Chicago. America 110:470 Ap 4 '64
Shared time; parochial and public schools. Commonweal 80:247-8 My 22 '64
Shared time program is worth a try. A. S. Flemming. Good H 156:48B+ F '63
See also
Colleges and universities—Cooperation

EDUCATIONAL exchanges
Advisory commission reports on exchange program. Dept State Bul 51:485 O 5 '64
Anniversary of Fulbright agreement observed at Manila. Dept State Bul 48:545 Ap 8 '63
Board of foreign scholarships reports on exchange program. Dept State Bul 49:869-70 D 2 '63
Commission urges expansion of American studies overseas; press release, July 12, 1963. Dept State Bul 49:169 Jl 29 '63
Education: passkey to the future; statement, August 4, 1963. L. D. Battle. Dept State Bul 49:411-17 S 9 '63
Educational exchange agreements signed with Australia and Ceylon. Dept State Bul 51:442-3 S 28 '64
International educational and cultural exchanges: a look back and a look ahead; address, October 24, 1963. D. Rusk. Dept State Bul 49:742-4 N 11 '63
Jointly financed exchange programs established with Austria and Sweden. Dept State Bul 49:100-1 Jl 15 '63
Open society: key to an advancing America; address, October 26, 1963. L. D. Battle. Dept State Bul 49:864-9 D 2 '63
Record-breaking educational exchange. Sch & Soc 92:373+ D 12 '64
U.S. and Australia to establish educational foundation; Department statement, August 10, 1964, with Australian announcement. R. G. Menzies. Dept State Bul 51:311-12 Ag 31 '64
U.S. and China agree to extend educational exchange program. Dept State Bul 50:755 My 11 '64
United States and Greece extend educational exchanges. Dept State Bul 50:24 Ja 6 '64
United States and Norway extend educational exchange program. Dept State Bul 50:539 Ap 6 '64
United States and Thailand sign educational exchange agreement. Dept State Bul 48:945 Je 17 '63
United States and Yugoslavia sign educational exchange agreement. Dept State Bul 51:831-2 D 7 '64
U.S. signs exchange agreements with Afghanistan and Argentina. Dept State Bul 49:410 S 9 '63
See also
Foreign students in the United States
Teachers, Interchange of

EDUCATIONAL extension. See Extension education

EDUCATIONAL films. See Moving pictures—Documentary films

EDUCATIONAL finance. See School finance

EDUCATIONAL foundations. See Foundations, Charitable and educational

EDUCATIONAL games. See Games

EDUCATIONAL guidance
Guidance in our changing world. G. J. Pine. il Sr Schol 83:9T+ N 8 '63
Teaching as counseling. A. V. Boy. il Sr Schol 83:12T N 8 '63
See also
Personnel service (education)
School children—Adjustment
School counselors
Vocational guidance

Bibliography

Resources for guidance. il Sr Schol 83:13T-14T N 8 '63

EDUCATIONAL information. See Communication in education

EDUCATIONAL laws and legislation. See School laws and legislation

EDUCATIONAL literature
Books for your professional bookshelf. H. L. Hurwitz. il Sr Schol 84:15T-16T Mr 6 '64
Educational library for the White House. W. W. Brickman. Sch & Soc 91:327 N 2 '63

EDUCATIONAL materials laboratory. See United States—Education, Office of—Educational materials laboratory

EDUCATIONAL measurement. See Educational tests and measurements

EDUCATIONAL media index
Educational media index. Wilson Lib Bul 39:5-6 S '64
Educational media index. Review
Library J 89:3108-11 S 1 '64. D. Melcher

EDUCATIONAL planning
330 million brains for a new era. R. Maheu. il UNESCO Courier 16:24-9 Jl '63
See also
International institute of educational planning

EDUCATIONAL policies commission
Afterward, college for all. Time 83:42 Ja 10 '64
Free college after H.S? Sr Schol 84:4T Ja 31 '64
Public interest in how teachers organize; report. NEA J 53:43-5 S '64; Same. il Sr Schol 85:10T-11T N 18 '64
School aid: new strategy urged by policy commission to expand federal support for education. D. S. Greenberg. Science 144:1558-9 Je 26 '64
Universal opportunity for education beyond the high school: adapted from statement. il NEA J 53:58-60 Ja '64

EDUCATIONAL psychologists. See Psychologists

EDUCATIONAL psychology. See Psychology, Educational

EDUCATIONAL records. See School reports and records

EDUCATIONAL records bureau
Meeting, 1962. A. E. Traxler. Sch & Soc 91:72 F 9 '63
Meeting, 1963. A. E. Traxler. Sch & Soc 92:33 Ja 25 '64

EDUCATIONAL research
Educational research: crisis for publishers; summaries of addresses at conference co-sponsored by the U.S. office of education and the American textbook publishers institute: with editorial comment. il Pub W 187:45-59; 71 Ja 11 '65
New center for educational research; joint operations by Harvard university and a dozen New England educational agencies. Sch & Soc 92:372 D 12 '64

EDUCATIONAL research—*Continued*
Project social studies, a report; curriculum study centers at institutions of higher education. G. R. Smith. Sch Life 45:25-7 Jl '63
Research clues. NEA J 53:62 S; 65 O; 49 N; 61 D '64; 54:67 Ja '65
Research in the State department of education. J. E. Bean. Sch Life 45:17-18 My '63
Social impact of standardized testing. D. A. Goslin. NEA J 52:20-2 O '63
USOE cooperative research. F. A. J. Ianni. Sch Life 46:28-9 O; 15-16 N; 20-1 D '63; 26-7 Mr '64
USOE cooperative research. L. S. Josephs. Sch Life 46:12-13 Je '64
See also
Colleges and universities—Research
Follow up studies (education)
Fund for the advancement of education
National education association—Research division

EDUCATIONAL research council of Greater Cleveland
Fountains of reform; curriculum change in local school systems. il Time 84:92-3 S 18 '64

EDUCATIONAL reviewer (periodical)
Survey of the political and religious attitudes of American college students. Nat R 15:279-302 O 8 '63

EDUCATIONAL segregation. See Segregation in education

EDUCATIONAL services, incorporated
Ford grant to Educational services, inc. Sch & Soc 91:154 Mr 23 '63

EDUCATIONAL sociology
See also
School and social and economic problems
Socially handicapped children—Education

EDUCATIONAL standards. See Education—Standards

EDUCATIONAL study tours. See Travel study courses

EDUCATIONAL surveys
More social studies; concerning survey by Cooperative test division of ETS. il Sr Schol Schol 84:2T-3T Ap 10 '64
Project talent. J. C. Flanagan. il NEA J 53: 8-10 Ja '64
Reader survey, highlights & insights. H. E. Hoffa. il Sch Arts 63:33-4 D '63
School health education study. E. M. Sliepcevich. NEA J 53:60-1 Mr '64
Survey of the political and religious attitudes of American college students. Nat R 15:279-302 O 8 '63
Who's the teacher? profile of the American public school teacher, by NEA research division. Sr Schol 84:4T Mr 6 '64

EDUCATIONAL television. See Television in education

EDUCATIONAL television stations. See Television stations, Educational

EDUCATIONAL testing service
College entrance exams. C. Jencks. New Repub 148:7 Ap 20 '63
Improving the tools. il Time 84:80 O 9 '64
More social studies; concerning survey by Cooperative test division of ETS. il Sr 84:2T-3T Ap 10 '64
Way to finish earlier; advanced placement students to enter American university. Time 84:41 Jl 31 '64
What makes an essay good? il Sr Schol 82: 12T-13T My 8 '63

EDUCATIONAL tests and measurements
Characteristics of entering freshmen in a teachers college. W. P. Angers and others. il Sch & Soc 91:68-9 F 9 '63
Child sorters. S. Grafton. il McCalls 90:98-101+ Ag '63
Denver graduates come up to PAR; proficiency and review tests. J. D. Leake. NEA J 52:24-5 N '63
Educational tests. L. Wolfle. Science 142:1529 D 20 '63; Discussion. 143:997; 145:533; 146: 171, 598, 1113 Mr 6, Ag 7, O 9, 30, N 27 '64
Improving public understanding of testing. T. McNulty. Sch & Soc 92:51-2 F 8 '64
Is all this testing necessary? W. D. Boutwell. PTA Mag 58:14 Ap '64
Social consequences of educational testing. R. L. Ebel. Sch & Soc 92:331-4 N 14 '64
Teacher-made tests. F. R. Link. NEA J 52: 23-5 O '63
Test uses and limitations. B. A. Thresher. il NEA J 52:16-19 O '63
Testing: if something exists, can it be measured? L. Litwack. il Sr Schol 83:11T N 8 '63
Tests can be wrong! il Parents Mag 39:64-5+ Mr '64
They shall not pass, by H. Black. Review
Sat R 46:56-7 D 21 '63. H. S. Dyer; Reply with rejoinder. H. Black. 47:61 F 15 '64
Why we need national academic standards. A. C. Eurich. il Parents Mag 39:71+ F '64
See also
Aptitude tests
Educational testing service
Examinations
Grading and marking (students)
Intelligence tests
Personality tests

Bibliography

NEA bibliography on testing. NEA J 52:21 O '63

EDUCATIONAL theory. See Education—Philosophy

EDUCATIONAL toys. See Toys

EDUCATIONAL workshops
Arkansas schools get economics-minded. il Bsns W p 112-14 Jl 20 '63
Pebbles from a workshop; concerning report of the Williamstown workshop. D. A. Pardoe. il Sr Schol 84:14T My 1 '64
Plan for teaching teachers of data processing. R. M. Knoebel. il Sch Life 46:7-10 D '63

EDWARD VII, king of Great Britain
Happy times when Edward was king. C. Connolly. il Ladies Home J 81:78+ Ja '64
King Edward the Seventh, by P. Magnus. Review
Atlan il por 213:58-61 Je '64. G. W. Johnson
Life 56:15+ My 22 '64. A. Bryant
Nat R 16:497-8 Je 16 '64. S. Leslie
Sat R il por 47:47-8 My 16 '64
Time il por 83:106+ My 22 '64

EDWARD VIII, king of Great Britain (abdicated 1936)
I have joined Arnie's army. por Sports Illus 19:20-1 N 4 '63
about
Britain's ex-king becomes a film star: action, your highness! il pors Life 57:55-6+ D 11 '64
Duke and Duchess of Windsor in Paris; with photographs by Horst. V. Lawford. Vogue 143:176-87+ Ap 1 '64
Duke's operation; just what the surgeon did. por U S News 57:12 D 28 '64
Repairing the royal aorta. il por Time 84:52 D 25 '64

EDWARD, prince of Great Britain
Hours in the life of Prince Edward Antony Richard Louis. G. Fisher and H. Fisher. il por McCalls 92:44+ Ja '65

EDWARD of Norwich, 2d duke of York
Makers of the sports page. P. Knauth. il Sports Illus 19:34-6+ S 16 '63

EDWARDS, Aaron W.
Accurate audio of frequency measurement. Electr World 70:46-7+ Ag '63
Confused fuse. Electr World 71:100 Ja '64
High-speed electronic printer. Electr World 72:46-8 D '64

EDWARDS, Art
How to irrigate your garden. il Suc Farm 62:62 Jl '64

EDWARDS, Charlotte
Where do characters come from? Writer 77: 10-12+ Mr '64
Where do you start? Writer 77:20-2+ D '64
Who says teen-agers are soft? McCalls 91: 40+ O '63

EDWARDS, Dixon
Perfect host, Civil air patrol. Flying 75:72 Ag '64
—See Vail, B. jt. auth.

EDWARDS, Geoff
I learned about flying from that. Flying 74: 56+ F '64

EDWARDS, George
Detroit; a lesson in law enforcement. Ann Am Acad 347:67-73 My '63
Merry Christmas Walter Reuther: two ex-union men as federal judges. W. Schulz. Nat R 15:484 D 3 '63
Senate problem: judgeships for two ex-union men? por U S News 55:12 N 11 '63

EDWARDS, Harlan
Prefabricated flashing for parapet walls. Arch Rec 135:209-10 My '64

EDWARDS, John O. and Stritar, J. A.
Uranyl ion coordination. bibliog Science 142: 1651 D 27 '63

EDWARDS, Lena F.
Three Negroes receive 1964 Presidential freedom medal. C. W. Thomas. por Negro Hist Bul 28:58-9 D '64

EDWARDS, M. Lowell
AMA honors engineer for his heart valve invention. il por Todays Health 42:52-3 Ja '64

EDWARDS, Margaret
Taming the young barbarian: excerpts from address, 1963. Library J 89:1819-21 Ap 15 '64

EDWARDS, Mike
Teachers in the Peace corps. Sat R 46:42-4+ Jl 20 '63
EDWARDS, Owen Dudley
They never came back. America 10:336-40 Mr 14 '64
EDWARDS, R. A.
In the bag for keeps. Am City 78:89-92 Ap '63
EDWARDS, V. C. Wynne-. See Wynne-Edwards, V. C.
EDWARDS, Vincent
Little pretty pocket book. PTA Mag 57:17 Ap '63
My battle with Ben Casey. pors Seventeen 23:130-1+ F '64
EDWARDS, Willard E.
Water-works corrosion. Am City 78:86-8 F '63
EDWARDS air force base flight test center. See Proving grounds
EDWARDS PLATEAU, Tex.
Why Texas is proud of the Edwards Plateau. O. S. Pettingill, jr. il Audubon Mag 66: 11-13 Ja '64
EELLS, George
Men, women and children; Hamlets all. Theatre Arts 48:18-21+ Ja '64
Riches or ruin for theatre? Theatre Arts 47: 27-32+ N '63
EELLS, Richard
Should business support the arts? excerpt from Corporate support of the performing arts. Mus Am 84:8-9 O '64
EELLS, Walter Crosby
1963 as a centennial year in the history of education. Sch & Soc 91:41-2 Ja 26 '63
Walter Crosby Eells, 1886-1962. E. V. Hollis. Sch & Soc 91:242 Sum '63
EELS
Slipperiest fish in the sea. V. B. Moore. il Sports Illus 18:38-41+ Je 3 '63
EELS, Electric. See Electric eels
EELWORMS. See Nematodes
EFFECT of Barney Fuller; story. See Bailey, A.
EFFECT of temperature on metals. See Metals, Effect of temperature on
EFFICIENCY
Make way for the no-problem guy. W. D. Ellis. Read Digest 82:95-7 My '63
See also
Ability
EFFICIENCY, Agricultural. See Farm management
EFFICIENCY, Household. See Home economics
EFFICIENCY, Industrial
Adding up the cost of economic swindling. il Bsns W p50-2 Ja 4 '64
Efficient economy. Time 82:85-6 Jl 12 '63
Executives tell how to meet it; symposium. il Nations Bsns 51:30-1+ Ag '63
How to cut purchasing costs. L. Blumenthal. il Duns R 83:53-4+ Mr '64
Inefficiency. D. Lawrence. U S News 56:100 Je 1 '64
Materials handling's new sophistication. il Duns R 81:pt2 S107-8+ Mr '63
Profit from the learning curve. W. B. Hirschmann. bibliog f il Harvard Bsns R 42:125-39 Ja '64
Quest for the perfect plant. il Duns R 81:pt2 S103-5+ Mr '63
Rate your company's research productivity. M. H. Hodge, jr. bibliog f il Harvard Bsns R 41:109-22 N '63
Unexplored assets for diversification. G. R. Conrad. Harvard Bsns R 41:67-73 S '63
What makes a best-managed company? J. B. Weiner. il Duns R 82:40-2+ D '63
Where you can cut costs next. S. Schuler. il Nations Bsns 51:58-60+ O '63
Why new businesses succeed. Nations Bsns 52:56+ Ap '64
You can improve your business timing. C. A. Cerami. Nations Bsns 51:94-6+ My '63
See also
Labor productivity
Work measurement
EFFICIENCY experts. See Business consultants
EFFIGY, Executions in. See Executions in effigy
EFFINGER, Rita
Early winter bird; poem. Horn Bk 39:96 F '63
EFREMOV, Georgi, and Braend, Mikael
Serum albumin: polymorphism in man. bibliog Science 146:1679-80 D 25 '64
EGAN, Cyril B.
Kind of prayer; poem. America 109:291 S 21 '63
Subway stations of the cross. America 110: 367-9 Mr 21 '64
EGAN, Daniel Francis
Junkie priest, by J. D. Harris. Review
America 110:735 My 23 '64. J. A. Gavin
EGAN, James
Five minutes from Lake Como. Atlan 213: 128+ Ap '64
Joséphine Baker chez elle. Atlan 214:130+ D '64
St Maarten: a Caribbean find. Atlan 213: 106+ Ja '64
Star boarding in the French provinces. Atlan 211:100+ Ap '63
EGAN, Mary C.
Nutrition. NEA J 53:62-4 Mr '64
EGBERT, Sherwood Harry
Studebaker comes out of a skid. il pors Bsns W p66+ Mr 9 '63
Studebaker puts on new face. por Bsns W p26 S 14 '63
EGEN, D. P.
Porpoise: wonder of the sea. Motor B 112:40+ Jl '63
EGG cases. See Eggs—Care and handling
EGG farms. See Poultry farms
EGG industry and trade
Will the egg giants push you out? D. Braun. il Farm J 87:38-9+ O '63
EGG people. See Tankas
EGG production. See Poultry—Egg production
EGG shells
Eggshell giftware; mosaic-styled designs for boxes. B. Ruff. il Design 64:157 Mr '63
You can prevent cracks. Farm J 87:52 My '63
EGGAN, Fred
Social anthropology: models, political systems, religion, and urbanization. Science 141: 1204-6 S 20 '63
EGGAR, Samantha
Girl named Sam. I. Mothner. il pors Look 28:90-3 O 20 '64
EGGERS, Hans J. See Tamm, I. jt. auth.
EGGHEADS. See Intellectuals
EGGPLANT
Royal fruit; eggplant. A. C. Dureau. il Horticulture 41:330 Je '63
See also
Cookery—Vegetables
EGGS
Cracked eggs start derby; salmonella derby infection. F. Marley. Sci N L 84:67 Ag 3 '63
Does dehy cause blood spots? G. Lorang. Farm J 88:61 Mr '64
Eggs, something to crow about! H. S. Sharpe. il Parents Mag 38:69+ Ap '63
Well-balanced egg. Time 82:79 O 11 '63
See also
Birds eggs
Cookery—Eggs
Easter eggs
Egg shells
Incubation
Poultry—Egg production

Care and handling

Automated eggs, from hen to cases. O. Bay. il Farm J 88:20-1+ Ag '64
Carts that pamper eggs. il Farm J 87:64D F '63
Easier egg gathering. il Farm J 87:64F O '63
Egg handling made easy. C. F. Marley. il Suc Farm 61:100 My '63
These home-made gadgets cut costs. il Farm J 87:62P Mr '63
Tips for packing eggs; photographs. Farm J 87:86 F '63
Warm-packed eggs stay just as fresh. Farm J 87:52 My '63

Grading and standardization

Quality eggs? you're kidding! Farm J 88: 34L Jl '64

Marketing

New fresh frozen product; may change egg markets. il Farm J 87:10 Mr '63
New middleman co-op; marketing of eggs. L. M. Palmer. Farm J 87:69-70 Ap '63
Now color helps sell eggs; bottled eggs. D. Seim and D. Braun. il Farm J 87:26-7+ Je '63
One-day eggs may shake up markets. Farm J 88:51 Ja '64
Through college on egg money. G. C. Lorang. il Farm J 87:40H Jl '63
EGGS, Bottled. See Eggs—Marketing
EGGS, Frozen
New fresh frozen product: may change egg markets. il Farm J 87:10 Mr '63
EGGS of insects. See Insects—Eggs
EGLIN air force base, Fla. See Proving grounds

EGLINGTON, Archibald William Montgomerie, 13th earl of
When knighthood's flower wilted; excerpt from The knight and the umbrella. I. Anstruther. il Sports Illus 20:88-90+ My 18 '64

EGLINTON, Geoffrey, and others
Hydrocarbons of biological origin from a one-billion-year-old sediment. bibliog Science 145:263-4 Jl 17 '64

EGO. See Self

EGOFF, Sheila A. and Hagler, R. A.
Look northward! Library J 88:4421-8 N 15 '63

EGOROV, Boris
Capitalist's guide to drinking. Esquire 61:99 Ja '64

EGREMONT, George O'Brien Wyndham, 3d earl of
In the glow of the perfect patron. P. Quennell. il por Horizon 5:62-71 Mr '63

EGRETS
Our cattle egret is also an elephant egret. A. O. Gross. il Audubon Mag 66:218-21 Jl '64
White egrets of Sagiyama. T. Tanaka. il Audubon Mag 65:298-305 S '63

EGRI, Lajos
Where does a story begin? Writer 77:15 N '64

EGYPT
Atlantic report. Atlan 213:12+ Mr '64
See also
Aerospace industries—Egypt
Airlines—Egypt
Airplanes—Egypt
Colleges and universities—Egypt
Costume—Egypt
Economic assistance in Egypt
Education—Egypt
Food supply—Egypt
Geology—Egypt
Giza
Nile River
Paleontology—Egypt
Socialism—Egypt
Space research—Egypt
Suez Canal
United Arab Republic

Antiquities

Across eternal Egypt. F. L. Lucas. il Holiday 35:66-75+ Je '64
Egypt's antiquities. S. Fields. il Travel 123: 30-5 Ja '65
First engineer; sacred tomb of Imhotep. il Newsweek 65:72 Ja 18 '65
King Tut's golden hoard. J. Stewart-Gordon. il Read Digest 84:198-204 Ap '64
Science classic: why they dig. H. Carter. il Sci Digest 53:11-15 Je '63
Search for the first intellectual; hidden tomb of Imhotep. il Time 85:58 Ja 15 '65
Siege warfare in Pharaonic Egypt. A. R. Schulman. il Natur Hist 73:12-21 Mr '64
Tutankhamen, by C. Desroches-Noblecourt. Review
Art N il 62:32-3+ Ja '64. K. Levin
Tutankhamun's golden trove. C. D. Noblecourt. il Nat Geog Mag 124:624-46 O '63
See also
Abu Simbel, Temples of
Rosicrucian Egyptian, Oriental museum and art gallery. San Jose, Calif.

Civilization

Behind Cleopatra. D. Cohen. il Sci Digest 53:5-10 Je '63

Defenses

Free-booters: German scientists hired by the Egyptians to help build weapons. New Repub 148:6 Ap 6 '63
Nasser's hired Germans; Israelis fight to stop missiles being built. S. de Gramont. il Sat Eve Post 236:60-1+ Jl 13 '63
Rockets in Egypt; German technicians in Egypt's military factory 333. Newsweek 61: 50+ Ap 15 '63
Trouble for 333; Egypt's military factory. Time 81:34+ Ap 5 '63

Description and travel

Across eternal Egypt. F. L. Lucas. il Holiday 35:66-75+ Je '64
Nile cruise. il Travel 120:45-9 O '63
Pre-Europe. C. J. McNaspy. America 111:115-16 Ag 1 '64

Economic conditions

If Khrushchev tries to bail out Nasser... il U S News 56:63-4+ My 25 '64
Once again Nasser's dream of empire. il U S News 54:75 Mr 18 '63
Progress in the Nile. il Time 84:83 Jl 17 '64
Situation desperate. Newsweek 65:24+ Ja 4 '65

Economic policy

Atlantic report. Atlan 211:36+ My '63

Foreign relations

Atlantic report. Atlan 211:36+ My '63
Base motives? Newsweek 63:38 Mr 9 '64
Down with Nasser? Time 82:34 S 27 '63
Egypt, the Soviet Union and Israel. New Repub 150:11-12 Je 6 '64
Everyone's delighted. Time 81:26 My 31 '63
Nasser's decade. A. Sherman. Commentary 36:151-7 Ag '63
Nasser's kaleidoscope. New Repub 150:9 F 22 '64
Nasser's way. Commonweal 78:181 My 10 '63
Rameses' nemeses. Newsweek 61:46-7 My 27 '63

Israel

Bomb shop in the Nile: target Israel. T. Prittie. Atlan 214:37-40 Ag '64

Jordan

Quick change. Time 82:41 O 11 '63

Russia

Khrushchev's tour: no great triumph. il U S News 56:14 Je 1 '64
Postmortem; Khrushchev's tour. J. A. Morris, jr. il Newsweek 63:30+ Je 1 '64
Visit to the Land of the Sphinx; Khrushchev in Egypt. J. A. Morris, jr. il Newsweek 63:41 My 25 '64

United States

Sea & tympany; Nasser's speech at Port Said. Time 85:34-5 Ja 1 '65
Why Nasser acts the way he does. il U S News 58:30-1 Ja 4 '65

Yemen

Inside story; Egyptians v. royalists, with report by J. A. Morris, jr. il Newsweek 61:56+ Je 24 '63

History

Africa's golden past; kingdom of Kush. W. L. Hansberry and E. H. Johnson. il Ebony 20:30-2+ N '64
Battle of Tel el Kebir. il Esquire 60:98-103 N '63
Indianization of the Egyptian administration under British rule. R. L. Tignor. bibliog f Am Hist R 68:636-61 Ap '63
Then Antony met Cleopatra. R. Payne. il N Y Times Mag p26-7+ Je 2 '63
See also
Hyksos

Historiography

Ancient Egypt: a survey of current historiography. M. Lichtheim. bibliog f Am Hist R 69:30-46 O '63

Invasion, 1956

Dulles over Suez, by H. Finer. Review
Esquire 62:68+ S '64. M. Muggeridge
Nat R 16:915 O 20 '64. G. F. Eliot

Kings and rulers

See also
Hyksos

Native races

See also
Nubians

Politics and government

Nasser's decade. A. Sherman. Commentary 36:151-7 Ag '63

Social conditions

Camel driver. il Time 81:22-6 Mr 29 '63

EGYPT and England. See England and Egypt

EGYPTIAN Coptic church. See Copts

EGYPTIAN farmers in the United States. See Foreign visitors in the United States

EGYPTIAN humor. See Humor, Egyptian

EGYPTIAN language
See also
Hieroglyphics

EHLE, John
One-man Rand. por Newsweek 63:77-8 Je 1 '64

EHMANN, W. D. and Setser, J. L.
Zirconium and hafnium in stone meteorites. bibliog Science 139:594-5 F 15 '63

EHRENBURG, Il'ia
Curtain half lifted. por Time 84:140+ N 13 '64
Mirror on the highway. por Newsweek 64: 104+ N 16 '64

EHRENBURG, Il'ia
Soviet autobiography. T. Frankel. Commentary 35:179-82+ F '63
Survival's favorite son. I. Deutscher. Nation 199:494-6 D 21 '64
EHRENSTROM, Nils
Seminar in ecumenical trialogue. Christian Cent 81:579-81 Ap 29 '64
EHRLICH, Alice
Flower painting. Sch Arts 63:5-7 D '63
EHRLICH, Blake
Notre Dame: a pageant of 800 years. N Y Times Mag p26-7+ My 5 '63
EHRLICH, Eugene
Speed reading. NEA J 52:45-6 Ap '63
EHRLICH, Paul R.
Population biology. G. L. Webster. bibliog Science 139:236+ Ja 18 '63
—and Holm, R. W.
Patterns and populations. bibliog Science 137: 652-7; 139:238-42 Ag 31 '62, Ja 18 '63
EHRLING, Sixten
Sink or swim. F. P. Gill. Mus Am 84:56 F '64
EHRMAN, Lee
Crossing species produces strange life forms. Sci Digest 53:70-6 Mr '63
Cytoplasmic sterility in drosophila paulistorum which is ultimately dependent on nuclear genes. bibliog Science 145:159, 1460 Jl 10, S 25 '64
EHRMANN, Hans
Jooss, conquistadores, and the wheel of fortune. Dance Mag 38:32-4 N '64
EICHELBAUM, Stanley
Actor's workshop of San Francisco. Theatre Arts 47:34-6+ Je '63
EICHENBERG, Fritz
Graphic arts: USA. Pub W 185:114-16 F 3 '64
EICHER, George
Giving fish a go sign. il pors Bsns W p 198-200 Ap 18 '64
EICHLER, Myron
Psychological changes associated with induced hyperammonemia. bibliog Science 144:886-8 My 15 '64
EICHMANN, Adolf
Eichmann case. R. H. Glauber. Christian Cent 80:681-2 My 22 '63
Eichmann in Jerusalem, by H. Arendt. Review
Commentary 36:201-8 S '63. N. Podhoretz; Discussion. 37:6+ F; 16+ My '64
Nat R il por 16:1007-12 N 17 '64. M. Geltman; Discussion. 16:1130+ D 29 '64
Nat R por 15:154-7 Ag 27 '63. E. van den Haag; Discussion. 15:207, 251, 367 S 10-24, O 22 '63
New Repub 148:23-33 Je 15 '63. B. Bettelheim. Discussion. 148:29-31 Je 29; 149: 28-30 Jl 20 '63
New Yorker 39:17 Jl 20 '63
Newsweek il por 61:94-5 Je 17 '63
Time por 81:100 My 24 '63
Reporter at large. H. Arendt. New Yorker 38:40-2+ F 16; 39:40-2+ F 23; 40-2+ Mr 2: 48-50+ Mr 9; 58-60+ Mr 16 '63; Correction of Mr 9 issue. 39:108 Ap 27 '63
EICHMANN trial
Eichmann in Jerusalem, by H. Arendt. Review
Commonweal 78:429-30 Jl 12 '63. A. E. Mayhew
Nat R il 16:1007-12 N 17 '64. M. Geltman; Discussion. 16:1130+ D 29 '64
Nat R 15:154-7 Ag 27 '63. E. van den Haag; Discussion. 15:207, 251, 367 S 10-24, O 22 '63
New Repub 148:23-33 Je 15 '63. B. Bettelheim; Reply with rejoinder. M. A. Musmanno. 148:29-31 Je 29 '63
Reporter at large. H. Arendt. New Yorker 38:40-2+ F 16: 39:40-2+ F 23; 40-2+ Mr 2: 48-50+ Mr 9; 58-60+ Mr 16 '63; Correction of Mr 9 issue. 39:108 Ap 27 '63
EIDELBERG, E. and others
Neurobiology: interdisciplinary discussions of the nervous system. Science 144:1478+ Je 19 '64
EIDER ducks
When the eiders flew. C. E. Gillham. il Field & S 68:60-2+ F '64
EIELSON, Rodney S.
Sins of the parents. por McCalls 92:48+ Ja '65
EIFFEL tower
Cashing in on its seventy-five years. il Bsns W p30-1 My 16 '64
Grand old landmark. il Sunset 130:72+ Ap '63
High dive; suicide toll. Newsweek 61:52 My 20 '63
Letter from Paris; seventy-fifth anniversary of Tour Eiffel. Genêt. New Yorker 40:176 My 16 '64
New man conquers Mt Eiffel; tower climbed like a mountain. il Life 56:108+ Je 5 '64

8mm films. See Moving picture films; Photography—Films
EIGHTEEN-nation disarmament conference. See Conference of the Eighteen-nation committee on disarmament, Geneva, 1962-
EIGHTEEN; story. See Hughes, H.
EIGHTEENTH of August; story. See Templeton, E.
EIGNER, Larry
Six poems. Poetry 103:227-30 Ja '64
EILAT. See Elath, Israel
EILER, Jim Paul
Breeding ground. Theatre Arts 47:9 D '63
EILERS, Hazel Kraft
At the sign of the crest. See issues of Hobbies
EILSHEMIUS, Louis Michel
Eilshemius, the unique; exhibition at Manhattan's Balin-Traube gallery. il Time 81:84 Mr 15 '63
Spirit-painter supreme. il Newsweek 61:103 Mr 25 '63
EIMBINDER, Jerry
Domestic replacements for foreign semiconductors. Electr World 70:26-8 Jl '63
Replacements for non-standard domestic transistors. Electr World 70:36+ S '63
EIMERL, Sarel
Behold, it was good. Reporter 30:52+ Ja 16 '64
Direct approach. Reporter 28:56-7 F 28 '63
From imp to blimp. Reporter 31:55-6 D 3 '64
Gentle despots. Reporter 29:46+ D 19 '63
Many-faced terror. Reporter 30:42+ Ap 23 '64
Moral murder? Reporter 28:44-6 Je 6 '63
Most marvelous party. Reporter 31:62+ Ag 13 '64
One man's treasures. Reporter 28:64-5 Mr 28 '63
Tragicomedy in five acts. Reporter 29:64-5 Ag 15 '63
EIMON, Pan Dodd
(ed) City tells its story. See issues of American city
EINAUDI, Giulio
Strange songs of Spain find friends. W. M. Abbott. America 108:216 F 16 '63
EINSTEIN, Albert
Bearing of philosophy on the history of science; address, December 29, 1963. A. Grünbaum. bibliog Science 143:1406-12 Mr 27 '64
Einstein: an intimate memoir; ed. by J. P. Blank. T. L. Bucky. il pors Harper 229:43-8 S '64
Einstein letter that started it all. R. E. Lapp. il por N Y Times Mag p 13+ Ag 2 '64
EINSTEIN, Lewis
Aging of Justice Holmes. F. Biddle. New Repub 151:19-22 D 19 '64
EINSTEIN theory. See Relativity (physics); Space and time
EIRE. See Ireland
EISCH, Erwin
Glass by Erwin Eisch. H. Littleton. il por Craft Horiz 23:14-17 My '63
EISCHENS, R. P.
Infrared spectroscopy and catalysis research. bibliog Science 146:486-93 O 23 '64
EISELEY, Loren C.
Endure the night. Atlan 211:75-8 Je '63
Francis Bacon. bibliog Horizon 6:32-47 Wint '64
In the beginning was the artifact. Sat R 46:52 D 7 '63
No secret formula for making scientists. N Y Times Mag p66+ O 18 '64
Uncompleted man. Harper 228:51-4 Mr '64
Upheld mirror. por NEA J 52:29 D '63

about

WLB biography. L. Ash. Wilson Lib Bul 38: 875+ Je '64
EISEMAN, Florence, incorporated
Out of the rocker; handsomest children's clothes in the U.S. il Time 84:58+ N 27 '64
EISENBERG, Arlene
(ed) See Williams, N. L. Q. Africa's uphill struggle for maturity
—and Eisenberg, Howard
Child care created by mother. Ladies Home J 81:56-7+ Je '64
Christian war on anti-Semitism. Look 28: 48+ Je 2 '64
Why clergymen are against school prayer. Redbook 124:38-9+ Ja '65
You can get your money back. Read Digest 84:131-2+ F '64
EISENBERG, David S. and Edsall, J. T.
Spectrophotometric titrations of human serum albumin and reduced carboxymethylated albumin. bibliog Science 142:50-1 O 4 '63

EISENBERG, Howard
(ed) See Williams, N. L. Q. Africa's uphill struggle for maturity
—See Eisenberg, A. jt. auth.

EISENBERG, Larry
Mighty Matterhorn; story. Harper 229:64-5 Ag '64

EISENBERG, Leon
Can emotions be changed? excerpts from address. Sci Digest 56:14-18 S '64

EISENBERG, Norman
Cabinet for connoisseurs. Hi Fi 13:42-3 My '63
High fidelity newsfronts. See issues of High fidelity

EISENBUD, Merril, and Petrow, H. G.
Radioactivity in the atmospheric effluents of power plants that use fossil fuels. Science 144:288-9 Ap 17 '64

EISENDRATH, David B. Jr
Bargains from Uncle Sam's bookstore. Pop Phot 52:84-6+ My '63
Color clinic. See issues of Popular photography
Midway in the optics revolution. Pop Phot 54:59+ Ap '64

about

How to split a second. C. Smith. il Pop Phot 52:58-60+ F '63

EISENHARDT, Rudolf H. and Rosenthal, Otto
2,4-dinitrophenol: lack of interaction with high-energy intermediates of oxidative phosphorylation. bibliog Science 143:476 Ja 31 '64

EISENHOWER, Dwight David
As Ike sees the candidates now; summary of interview, ed. by C. Brown. U S News 56:14 Ap 20 '64
Berlin wall; what Ike would have done; excerpts from address. por U S News 56:14 Ap 13 '64
Danger from within. por Read Digest 82:76-82 Mr '63
Eisenhower on Lincoln; excerpts from TV discussion with Bruce Catton. Sr Schol 82:23-4 F 6 '63
Emancipation proclamation centennial, statement. por Ebony 18:21 S '63
Epidemic of friendship. por Read Digest 83:132-8 N '63
Excerpt from letter, March 5, 1964. Cong Digest 43:148 My '64
Excerpt from letter to Representative C. A. Halleck, March 26, 1963. Cong Digest 42:140 My '63
Future of the Republican party. pors Sat Eve Post 238:21-5 Ja 30 '65
George Catlett Marshall; address. por Atlan 214:41-3 Ag '64
Ike on government in business; excerpts from address, December 9, 1964. por U S News 57:61 D 21 '64
Ike's view: FDR policy prolonged the war; summary of interview, ed. by E. T. Folliard. por U S News 58:12 Ja 4 '65
Ike's view: Kennedy regime has sorry record; excerpts from statement, June 13, 1963. U S News 54:19 Je 24 '63
Is government too big? what Ike and LBJ say; excerpts from address, June 8, 1964. U S News 56:16 Je 22 '64
Let's be honest with ourselves. por Sat Eve Post 236:23-5 O 19; 26-7 O 26 '63; Same abr. Read Digest 83:61-8 D '63
Picture of the Republican party; address July 15, 1964. Vital Speeches 30:645-7 Ag 15 '64
Republican choice: where Eisenhower stands; summary of interview. por U S News 56:20 Je 22 '64
Six qualities that make a president. por Time 81:28 Je 14 '63
Spending into trouble. pors Sat Eve Post 236:15-16 My 18 '63; Same abr. with title We are spending ourselves into trouble. Read Digest 83:60-8 Jl '63
Terrible disappointment of Walter Cronkite; excerpts from telephone conversation, May 15, 1964. Nat R 16:435 Je 2 '64
When the highest office changes hands. por Sat Eve Post 236:15 D 14 '63
Why a Mandate for change; excerpts from address, June 10, 1963. Pub W 183:34-5 Je 24 '63
Why I am a Republican. por Sat Eve Post 237:17-19 Ap 11 '64; Same abr. with title Policies I believe will strengthen this country. Read Digest 85:102-8 Jl '64

about

Bleating of sheep. M. Kempton. New Repub 150:15-18 Je 20 '64
Books. R. H. Rovere. New Yorker 39:235-8 N 16 '63
Call to political duty. Sat Eve Post 236:90 Ag 10 '63
Can Barry Goldwater be stopped? il por Newsweek 63:27-31 My 18 '64
Cold crusade. A. Rosenthal. Nation 196:361-4 Ap 27 '63
Crusade in America. G. G. Kirstein. Nation 197:349-50 N 23 '63
D-day plus twenty years. H. Migang. il pors Look 28:78-85 F 25 '64
D-day reminder of the best of Ike. L. Wainwright. Life 56:29 Je 19 '64
Ecce Ike. W. F. Buckley, jr. por Nat R 15:487-8+ D 3 '63
Eisenhower administration: a self-portrait. O. Handlin. il por Atlan 212:67-72 N '63; Reply. M. M. Rabb. 213:44 Mr '64
Eisenhower as man, Eisenhower as mystique. W. D. Burnham. Commonweal 79:408-9 D 27 '63
Eisenhower on Eisenhower. C. Forbes. Christian Cent 81:18 Ja 1 '64
Eisenhower: what did he want? D. Cater. Reporter 29:59-60 N 21 '63
Epistles from the Eisenhower age. M. Kempton. Commentary 35:232-8 Mr '63
For the record; Eisenhower vs. McCarthy over Conant to Germany. W. F. Buckley, jr. Nat R 16:188 Mr 10 '64
From former President Eisenhower: an O.K. for test-ban treaty, if—. por U S News 55:24 S 9 '63
Grappling with succession & disability. Time 83:21 Je 5 '64
Hard way to the middle course. E. D. Canham. Sat R 46:42-3 N 9 '63
How JFK and Ike compare as golfers. il pors U S News 55:24 Ag 5 '63
Ike on Ike. il por Newsweek 62:107-8+ N 11 '63
Ike plan cometh. J. J. Kilpatrick. il por Nat R 16:483-6 Je '64; Reply. 16:521+ Je 30 '64
Ike sheds some light. W. V. Shannon. Commonweal 79:682-3 Mr 6 '64
Ike takes a stand. il por Newsweek 63:40 Je 8 '64
Impact of Eisenhower. S. Alsop. por Sat Eve Post 236:14 N 9 '63
Is this the Ike who launched 1,000 ships? Newsweek 63:24 Je 22 '64
Johns Hopkins to publish Eisenhower papers. Pub W 185:57 Ja 6 '64
Neutralist. E. J. Hughes. Newsweek 63:13 Je 1 '64
Notes for a gazetteer. P. Hamburger. New Yorker 40:84+ Ap 4 '64
Ordeal of power, by E. J. Hughes. Review
New Repub 148:25-6 Ap 27 '63. W. A. Korns
New Yorker 39:195-6+ Mr 16; 119 My 11 '63 R. H. Rovere
Newsweek por 61:104 Mr 18 '63
Reporter 28:58+ Mr 28 '63. J. P. Roche
Sat R 46:85-6 Mr 16 '63. H. Brandon
Party of Ike. E. J. Hughes. Newsweek 63:15 My 4 '64
Peripatetics. por Newsweek 64:70-1 O 5 '64
President Eisenhower's summing-up. Sat Eve Post 236:108 N 16 '63
Reading, writing and history. B. Catton. Am Heritage 15:109-10 F '64
Republican campaigner; the Eisenhower role for '64. por U S News 55:26 O 21 '63
Ribbons and bibbons. M. Kempton. New Repub 149:13-16 N 30 '63; Reply. R. Rovere. 149:29 D 14 '63
Role Ike sees: and his views on Goldwater. U S News 56:16 Je 1 '64
Sell the TVA? W. F. Buckley, jr. Nat R 15:472 D 3 '63
Sic transit gloria. K. Crawford. Newsweek 64:35 Jl 27 '64
Straight down the middle? views on coming election and Republican party. il por Time 83:19-20 Je 5 '64
TV zooms in on GOP. Bsns W p32+ F 22 '64
Truman and Eisenhower: their administrations and campaigns. V. Albjerg. il Cur Hist 47:221-8 O '64
Valet's view; with excerpts from Ordeal of power, by E. J. Hughes. il por Time 81:17-19 Mr 22 '63
Visit to Gettysburg. N. Cousins. Sat R 47:18-19 Jl 11 '64
Visitors; White House visit. il Newsweek 61:28 Je 24 '63

EISENHOWER, Mamie Geneva (Doud)
Mamie Eisenhower's longest day, D-day; interview, ed. by P. Mesta. por McCalls 91:69+ Je '64
What three presidents say about their wives; excerpt from Woman in the White House. M. Means. il por Good H 157:59+ Ag '63

EISENHOWER, Milton
Epilogue to a failure: excerpts from Wine is bitter. Time 82:20 Jl 26 '63

EISENHOWER, Milton—*Continued*
Furious footnote; excerpts from Wine is bitter. por Newsweek 62:42 Jl 29 '63
Inside story of an amazing Cuba deal; excerpts from Wine is bitter. por U S News 55:23 Jl 29 '63
Third scientific revolution; excerpts from address, May 6, 1964. Sci N L 85:322+ My 23 '64
EISENMAN, David P.
Room acoustics for stereo. Hi Fi 13:50-3+ F '63
EISENSTAEDT, Alfred
Scarred face of Verdun. il Life 56:68-83 Je 5 '64
EISENSTEIN, Sergei Mikhailovich
Shame and glory in the movies. A. Berson and J. Keller. il Nat R 16:17-21 Ja 14 '64; Correction. 16:124 F 11 '64
EISLER, Colin
Genius as snob. Nation 198:75-6 Ja 20 '64
EISLER, Hanns
Eisler on Schoenberg; interview, ed. by W. Lowenfels. por Sat R 46:33-4 Ag 31 '63
EISLER, Michael
Moving art. Sch Arts 64:34-6 D '64
EISMA, E. See Jurg, J. W. jt. auth.
EISMAN, Eugene R
Space project that makes sense. Sci Digest 55:56-60 Mr '64
EISMAN, Lucille
Fun with herbs. Pop Gard 14:41+ Ap '63
Sweet potatoes from scratch. Horticulture 41:383 Jl '63
EISMAN, Marian
How to get along with children. Parents Mag 39:116 N '64
EISNER, Elliot W.
Evaluating children's art. Sch Arts 63:20-2 S '63
Paradigm for teaching the visual arts. Sch Arts 63:29-31 My '64
EISNER, Jack
More photo fun. il Pop Mech 121:138-9 Ja '64
Thanksgiving cutouts. Pop Mech 120:152-4 N '63
EISNER, Joseph
Plainview emphasizes site. Library J 89:4724-6 D 1 '64
EISNER, Thomas
Catnip: its raison d'être. bibliog Science 146:1318-20 D 4 '64
—and others
Adhesiveness of spider silk. bibliog Science 146:1058-61 N 20 '64
Cyanogenic glandular apparatus of a millipede. bibliog Science 139:1218-20 Mr 22 '63
EISS, Albert F.
Teaching junior high school science. NEA J 52:54-6 O '63
EJECTION devices (space vehicles) See Space vehicles—Ejection devices
EKEBERG, Gladys W.
Lincoln's mothers; poem. Christian Cent 81:174 F 5 '64
EKINS, Herbert Roslyn
Yesterday's globe-trotter. por Time 82:53 O 25 '63
EKLUND, Carl R.
Antarctic skua; with biographical sketch. Sci Am 210:30+, 94-8+ bibliog(p 152) F '64
EKLUND, Henning
Fresh water: temperature of maximum density calculated from compressibility. bibliog Science 142:1457-8 D 13 '63
EKSTROM, Ruth B. and Cliff, Norman
Parents' feelings about college costs. Sch & Soc 91:99-100 F 23 '63
EKTACHROME films. See Photography—Films
EL AL Israel airlines. See Airlines—Israel
ELAM, Lee
Low-cost calf shelter. il Suc Farm 61:88 O '63
ELAM, Stanley
ETV in South Carolina. New Repub 149:7 Ag 31 '63
Union or guild? organizing the teachers. Nation 198:651-3 Je 29 '64
ELAND hunting
What a beautiful morning. W. Page. il Field & S 68:46-7+ Mr '64
EL-ANI, Arif S. See Ani, A. S.
ELASMOBRANCHII
Methylurea and acetamide: active reabsorption by elasmobranch renal tubules. B. Schmidt-Nielsen and L. Rabinowitz. bibliog il Science 146:1587-8 D 18 '64
ELASTIC hose. See Hosiery
ELASTIC textile fibers. See Textile fibers. Elastic
ELASTOMERS. See Rubber, Artificial
ELATH, Israel
Israel's resort on the Red Sea. Sunset 131:38 O '63
EL-BASSIOUNY, M. Y. See Bassiouny, M. Y.
ELDER
Elderberry bush. H. Roca-Garcia. il Horticulture 41:458 S '63
ELDER craftsmen shop. See New York (city) —Stores
ELDERBERRY. See Elder
ELDERFIELD, Robert C.
Chemistry: pure and applied. Science 142:72-3 O 4 '63
ELDERS, Joycelyn
New day, new doctor. il pors Ebony 19:27-30+ Ap '64
EL DORADO, Kan.
Centralized purchasing system. G. L. Schrader. il Am City 78:108-9 S '63
ELDRED, Earl. See Bridgman, C. F. jt. auth.
ELDREDGE, Inman F.
Nation of faith and works. Am For 69:11 Je '63
ELDRIDGE, Donald A.
More on campus mores. Sat R 47:57-9+ Je 20 '64
ELECTION day
Drama
Election day in Spooksville. R. K. Rybak. Plays 24:29-39 O '64
Mr Bates goes to the polls. N. B. Reay. Plays 24:76-8 N '64
ELECTION day in Spooksville; drama. See Rybak, R. K.
ELECTION districts
Redistricting by computer. Sci Am 210:57 Mr '64
See also
Apportionment (election law)
ELECTION expenses. See Campaign funds
ELECTION forecasts. See Political forecasts
ELECTION frauds. See Elections—Corrupt practices
ELECTION laws
See also
Literacy tests (election law)
Voters, Registration of
United States
Either Court or Constitution is wrong on election rules. F. Morley. il Nations Bsns 51:27-8 My '63
Mississippi politics. R. Moley. Newsweek 63:92 Ap 6 '64
ELECTIONS
'63 elections take world spotlight. Sr Schol 82:21-2 My 15 '63
See also
Voting
Corrupt practices
Fraud! fraud! A. B. Callow, jr. il N Y Times Mag p60+ S 27 '64
How to beat a voting machine and a drive to make it honest; voting frauds in Chicago. il U S News 54:63 Ap 8 '63
Operation eagle eye; New York's honest ballot association vs. vote-stealing. Nat R 16:940-2 N 3 '64
Operation eagle-eye; Republican poll-watchers. New Repub 151:4-5 O 24 '64
Where listed voters outnumber the people. U S News 55:10 Jl 1 '63
Algeria
Synonyms for democracy. Time 84:64 O 2 '64
Argentina
New deal now in Argentina? U S News 55:51 Jl 22 '63
Puff the magic Perón. Newsweek 62:49 Jl 22 '63
We can go home. Time 82:22 Jl 19 '63
Australia
Landslide down under. Time 82:44 D 6 '63
Two nations that are staying conservative. U S News 55:10 D 16 '63
Bolivia
Bolivian style. New Repub 150:5 Je 13 '64
New mandate. Time 83:50 Je 12 '64
British Guiana
Can Jagan hold on? C. C. Moskos, jr. New Repub 150:10-11 Mr 21 '64
Cheddi's last stand. il Time 84:37 D 18 '64
Nothing but losers. Newsweek 64:42 D 21 '64
Canada
Canada goes to the polls. H. Bigart. il Reporter 28:29-32 Ap 11 '63
Canada: victory for the Liberals. Newsweek 61:50+ Ap 22 '63
Canadian election. Nation 196:129 F 16 '63

ELECTIONS—Canada—*Continued*
Canadian elections. M. Gayn. Nation 196:319-21 Ap 20 '63
Canadian elections. N. McKenty. America 108:602 Ap 27 '63
Conservative prairies. G. B. Mather. Christian Cent 80:686 My 22 '63
Down with a bump goes the Dief. New Repub 148:10 Ap 20 '63
Four-way split; melancholy prospect. il Time 81:36 Mr 15 '63
Good news in Canada; Lester Pearson's near victory. Life 54:4 Ap 19 '63
John George's chorus. Newsweek 61:57 Mr 18 '63
Liberals gain in Canadian elections. il Sr Schol 82:16 Ap 24 '63
New leader. il Time 81:33-7 Ap 19 '63; Same abr. with title Lester Pearson: Canada's new leader. Read Digest 83:130-4 Ag '63
Now U.S. is the issue in Canada. il U S News 54:31-2 F 18 '63
Pearson comes out on top. Bsns W p37 Ap 20 '63
Pearson heads new Canadian regime. Christian Cent 80:516 Ap 24 '63
Unfinished election in Canada. il Bsns W p27 Ap 13 '63
Washington gives Canada an election and an issue; with statement by U.S. Department of state. W. H. Hessler. Reporter 28:29-31 F 28 '63

Chile

Christian & democratic; Eduardo Frei to be president. il Time 84:27 S 11 '64
Momentous contest. P. Zottele. Christian Cent 81:1246+ O 7 '64
New power at the polls. il Time 81:37 Ap 19 '63
Stopping short; Reform or revolution, how six Chileans chose. il Newsweek 64:44+ S 14 '64

Czechoslovakia

Disappointment in Prague; Novotny re-elected. il Time 84:38 N 20 '64

France

Letter from Paris; candidate against de Gaulle. Genêt. New Yorker 40:98+ F 22 '64

Germany (Federal Republic)

Bit of a jolt. Time 84:31 O 9 '64

Ghana

One party, four walls. Time 83:26+ F 14 '64

Great Britain

Another Tory setback; Dundee by-election. Time 82:47 N 29 '63
Britain: narrowing the margin: Leyton and Nuneaton by-elections. il Newsweek 65:27 F 1 '65
Britain, too, has an election. il U S News 57:67 S 28 '64
Choosing up sides. A. Cooke. il Vogue 144:148-9+ O 15 '64
Election prospects in Britain. M. Cooper. America 11:81 Jl 25 '64
Election sweepstakes; bet on the balloting. il Newsweek 64:42-3 S 7 '64
Fry, lechery, fry; Stratford-on-Avon by-election. Newsweek 62:43 Ag 26 '63
Great bore. C. Brogan. Nat R 16:1015-16+ N 17 '64
Grey to black for the Tories. il Time 83:43 Ap 17 '64
Harold Wilson's dilemma. A. Lejeune. Nat R 16:970 N 3 '64
How white backlash struck in Britain. il U S News 57:67 O 26 '64
Labor takes reins. Sr Schol 85:23 O 28 '64
Labor's love won, by a conservative edge. il Newsweek 64:56+ O 26 '64
Letter from London. M. Panter-Downes. New Yorker 40:202+ S 19; 152-6 O 24 '64
Loss of Luton. il Time 82:39 N 15 '63
Man bites Hogg; St Marylebone by-election. Time 82:30 D 13 '63
Omen on Avon; by-election. Time 82:30 Ag 23 '63
Other election. il Sr Schol 85:23 S 30 '64
Private line from London. V. Cowles. Vogue 144:219-20 O 1 '64
Signs of things to come. H. G. Nicholas. il Reporter 31:20-1 N 5 '64
Taxicab majority. il Time 84:32+ O 23 '64
Three in four; Tory victory in by-elections. il Newsweek 63:51 My 25 '64
Three out of four for the Tories; by-elections. il Time 83:29 My 22 '64
Tory times. il Newsweek 62:49 N 18 '63
U.S. stake in Britain's election. il U S News 57:55-6 O 12 '64
Up to the wire. il Newsweek 63:53 Ap 20 '64
What has Hamlet done for you lately? Stratford-upon-Avon campaign. Time 82:21 Ag 16 '63
See also
Political parties—Great Britain

Greece, Modern

Back to the polls. Newsweek 63:30 Ja 13 '64
Back to the polls. Time 83:30 Ja 10 '64
Hubris doesn't win. il Time 82:45 N 15 '63
Slap for the center; municipal elections. Time 84:32 Jl 17 '64

Guatemala

First step back. Newsweek 63:60 Je 8 '64

India

A Nehru back in politics. Time 84:38 D 4 '64
Critics return; by-election victories. Time 81:29 Je 7 '63

Iran

Iran: remolding a nation nearer to the heart's desire. H. B. Bloomer. il Reporter 30:32-6 Ja 16 '64
New Majlis. il Time 82:33 S 27 '63
Royal reformer: Iran's shah gets a mandate. U S News 55:16 S 30 '63
Shah's revolution. New Repub 149:11 O 5 '63

Ireland

Election fervor. H. F. Woodhouse. Christian Cent 81:1570 D 16 '64

Italy

At last! il Newsweek 65:39 Ja 11 '65
Between left & right. il Time 81:26 My 10 '63
Communist by any other name. il Time 84:37 D 4 '64
Elections in Italy. M. Painelle. America 108:712-13 My 18 '63
Italian elections. B. Renton. Nation 196:414 My 18 '63
Italian elections: even worse than before. C. Sterling. il Reporter 28:22-5 My 23 '63
Italy: a new village around an old fountain. E. M. Borgese. Nation 196:327-9 Ap 20 '63
Italy's new president: the next stop. America 112:67 Ja 16 '65
Leftists gain in Italy. il Bsns W p 122-3 My 4 '63
Lurching left? il Newsweek 61:47 My 13 '63
Il motorino. il Newsweek 61:43+ Ap 22 '63
Off & running. il Time 81:30 F 22 '63
Opening for the left. J. Burnham. Nat R 14:400 My 21 '63
Pope John and Communist gains. Marcello. America 108:896 Je 29 '63
Red votes end Italian impasse. Bsns W p22 Ja 2 '65
Trend to the left. G. D. Kumlien. Commonweal 78:244-5 My 24 '63
Victory, of sorts, in Sicily. Time 81:29 Je 21 '63
Warning signal: Communist gains. Newsweek 64:48+ D 7 '64
Where did all those Communists come from? F. Canavan. America 108:703 My 18 '63
Worst way: election of president. il Time 85:20-1 Ja 8 '65

Japan

Ballots and boom. Newsweek 62:58 D 2 '63
Contented yawn. il Newsweek 62:54-6 N 25 '63
Defeat of the Socialists. New Repub 148:8-9 My 4 '63
Vote of confidence for Ikeda. Time 82:46 N 29 '63

Korea (Republic)

Back to normal. Time 82:44 D 6 '63
General Park's victory. T. Oka. New Repub 149:10-11 O 26 '63
Slim mandate. il Time 82:40 O 25 '63
South Korea elects Park as president. Sr Schol 83:16 N 1 '63
Tired of turmoil. Newsweek 62:60 D 9 '63

Latin America

Surprises all over. Time 83:29-30 Mr 27 '64

Malaysia

Confrontation at the polls. il Time 83:32 My 8 '64
Growing danger. New Repub 150:9-10 My 16 '64

Morocco

Experimenting with elections. Time 81:37 My 24 '63

Netherlands

Dutch elections. America 108:791 Je 1 '63

ELECTIONS—*Continued*

New Guinea

See Elections—Territory of Papua and New Guinea

New Zealand

Two nations that are staying conservative. U S News 55:10 D 16 '63

Nigeria

Model breaks down. il Time 85:18-19 Ja 8 '65
What Britain joined; tribalism threatens Federation. Newsweek 65:38 Ja 11 '65

Northern Rhodesia

First prime minister. Time 83:24 Ja 31 '64

Pakistan

Guided victory; Ayub Khan re-elected. Newsweek 65:38 Ja 18 '65
Sorry beginning. Time 85:26+ Ja 15 '65

Panama

Expected surprise; presidential elections. Newsweek 63:54 My 25 '64
More votes than crowds; presidential election. Time 83:27 My 22 '64
Someone to love. il Time 83:39 My 1 '64

Papua

See Elections—Territory of Papua and New Guinea

Paraguay

Dictator by popular request. Time 81:35 F 22 '63

Peru

On the road. Newsweek 61:66 Je 24 '63
To the polls, again. il Time 81:26 Je 7 '63

Philippines

Uncle Sam's other island. il Time 82:34 N 22 '63

Puerto Rico

Successor to Munoz: R. S. Vilella. Sr Schol 85:20 N 18 '64

Sicily

See Elections—Italy

Somalia

Indelibles; ink to discourage indefatigable repeat voters. il Time 83:37 Ap 10 '64

Spain

Voter no. forty-one does his duty. il Time 82:45 N 15 '63

Taiwan

Chiang is beaten. New Repub 150:9 My 16 '64

Territory of Papua and New Guinea

Bigfella elekson. Sr Schol 84:22 Ap 10 '64
Don't eat the candidate. il Newsweek 63:40 Mr 9 '64
Stone age election. il Time 83:40 F 28 '64

United States

After the election. E. Roper. Sat R 47:12 N 28 '64
After the elections; both parties take stock. il Sr Schol 85:8-11 D 2 '64
And what about the next Congress? il U S News 57:39 O 19 '64
Around and about politics. il Newsweek 64:42 N 9 '64
Backlash and Christian faith. R. R. Parsonage. Christian Cent 81:1300-2 O 21 '64
Campaign, some of the issues, extremism & the ADA; symposium, with editorial comment. il Nat R 16:953-68 N 3 '64
Changing U.S. electorate. S. Lubell. il Fortune 70:132-5+ Jl '64
Class of 1958. K. Crawford. Newsweek 61:38 My 20 '63
Comfort and concern; election returns. il Newsweek 62:31-3 N 18 '63
Congress race: running hard to stand still. il Bsns W p53-4+ O 10 '64
Democratic sweep: in legislatures, too. U S News 57:10 N 16 '64
Election issue: who's against JFK most? il U S News 55:15 Ag 19 '63
Elections. il Time 82:36 N 15 '63
Figures: 1964 statistics. Time 84:39 N 13 '64
From abroad: congratulations and expectations. il Newsweek 64:47 N 16 '64
How to watch the election. il Newsweek 64:27-9 N 2 '64
How your right to vote was won. A. Balk. Todays Health 42:52-4 F '64
Ins and outs at State houses. il Newsweek 64:40-2 N 9 '64
Is JFK weaker politically? How the voting went in important areas. il U S News 55:43-6 N 18 '63
Long recount; election of Minnesota's governor. il Newsweek 61:27-8 Mr 11 '63
Lost brigade; defeat of Goldwater partisans. Reporter 31:12 N 19 '64
LBJ's record majority; with comment on the world's news fronts. il Sr Schol 85:18-19 N 18 '64
Major congressional contests. il Sr Schol 85:19 S 23 '64
Major state contests; governorship elections. il Sr Schol 85:18 S 23 '64
Minnesota winner, recount court picks Rolvaag. U S News 54:16 Ap 1 '63
Nature of the choice. Christian Cent 81:1027-8 Ag 19 '64
Negro vote. Newsweek 63:32 My 18 '64
Now there are two Senators Kennedy; Other Senate races; House: new ball game. il Newsweek 64:35-9 N 9 '64
One place where Republicans gained; gubernatorial contests. U S News 57:12 N 16 '64
Outlook for new lineup in the 89th Congress. il U S News 57:32-3 N 2 '64
Peace at the polls. R. Hagan. Nation 196:83-91 F 2 '63
Political almanack for the year 1964. il U S News 56:46-7 Mr 9 '64
Politics in a pluralist democracy: studies of voting in the 1960 election, by L. S. Dawidowicz and L. J. Goldstein. Review
Commentary 38:87-9 O '64. D. P. Moynihan
President may help elect Congress he won't like. J. Craft. il Nations Bsns 52:23-4 Ap '64
Proud name and a proud family grieve as the G.O.P. loses two of its finest; scarce winners stand tall amid the Republican rubble. il Life 57:40-3 N 13 '64
Racial issues: what the voters decided; other issues. U S News 57:6 N 16 '64
Reading the returns. W. D. Burnham. Commonweal 79:271-4 N 29 '63
Republican South. K. Crawford. Newsweek 64:42 N 16 '64
Result: few surprises; 1963 state and local elections. Sr Schol 83:20-1 N 22 '63
Senate elections of '64: where Republicans hope to win. il U S News 54:44-5 Je 10 '63
Some facts you may not know about elections. Todays Health 42:55+ F '64
Story of eighty-seven votes that made history; congressional election in Texas. il U S News 56:46-50 Ap 6 '64
Voter discontent. D. Lawrence. U S News 55:136 N 18 '63
Watch these races. il Nations Bsns 52:82-3 Ap '64
What election issues mean. il Nations Bsns 52:88-9+ Jl '64
What happens to your ballot on Election day? A. Balk. il Todays Health 42:32-5+ N '64
What the voters said. Nat R 15:425 N 19 '63
When Republicans take a closer look at election returns; with statements by leaders on future of party. U S News 57:41-2 N 23 '64
Why I won; why I lost; candidates' own analysis. U S News 57:129-30+ N 16 '64; Correction. 57:16 N 23 '64
Will '64 election be a surprise? il U S News 54:42-4 Mr 11 '63
Winner by decision; Minnesota's gubernatorial election. Newsweek 61:27 Ap 1 '63
Year of the Democrat. il Newsweek 64:35-6 N 16 '64

See also

Candidates, Political
National conventions (political)
Nominations for office
Presidential campaigns
Presidential candidates
Presidents—United States—Election
Primaries
Public opinion polls
Senators—Election
Suffrage—United States
Voting

Venezuela

Betancourt goes double or nothing. Bsns W p 114+ N 30 '63
Red terror vs. an election: on-the-spot report from Venezuela. D. B. Richardson. il U S News 55:78 D 2 '63
Repudiating Castro. il Time 82:36 D 13 '63
Si, amigo, ballots beat bullets in Venezuela. il Sr Schol 84:13-15 F 7 '64
Siege before election; campaign of terror by F.A.L.N. il Time 82:34 N 29 '63
Terror fails to stem Venezuela's vote. il Life 55:42-4 D 13 '63

ELECTIONS—Venezuela—*Continued*
Test in Caracas. Reporter 29:12 D 19 '63
Truce and consequences. il Newsweek 62:53-4 D 9 '63
Where U.S. won and Castro lost in Latin America. D. B. Richardson. il U S News 55:92-4 D 16 '63
Will the terrorists get Betancourt? R. Peter. Nat R 15:482 D 3 '63

Zanzibar

Deadlocked magic. Time 82:26 Jl 26 '63

ELECTIONS and business conditions. See Business—Political aspects

ELECTORAL college
Action is needed to preserve election stability. F. Morley. Nations Bsns 51:29-30 D '63
Electoral college: the obsolete filter. D. A. Meyer and M. Nathan, jr. Nation 199:396-9 N 30 '64
Electoral reform would make your vote more important. F. Morley. il Nations Bsns 51:25-6 S '63
If president-elect should die—. il U S News 57:44 N 9 '64
It could happen here. K. Crawford. Newsweek 61:33 Je 17 '63
Presidential election dispute of 1876. Sr Schol 85:7 D 2 '64
Reforming the college. il Time 81:21 Je 21 '63
'64 election: suppose the South does revolt. il U S News 54:44-5 Je 24 '63
Time for election reform is now. F. Morley. il Nations Bsns 52:25-6 D '64
Voting system adds to election uncertainty. F. Morley. il Nations Bsns 52:27-8 S '64

ELECTRA (airplane) See Airplanes

ELECTRA; drama. See Sophocles

ELECTRIC alarms
Automatic systems for safety. H. Holcomb. il Motor B 112:34-6 N '63
Build panic alarm. R. E. Pafenberg. il Pop Electr 20:37-9+ My '64
Electronic dispatching gets 100 per cent response. il Am City 79:36 Ag '64
Freeze alarm to save your car and pipes; electronic alarm. R. M. Benrey. il Pop Sci 184:96+ F '64

ELECTRIC and musical industries, limited
Beatle business; record sales. il Time 84:112 O 2 '64

ELECTRIC apparatus and appliances
Beauty is just a b-zzz-zzz away! il Am Home 67:18+ Jl '64
See also
Electric apparatus industry

Care

Lamp cleaner, a new magician; Broadway maintenance corp. il Am City 79:113 N '64

Exhibitions

Electronic parts show. W. A. Stocklin. Electr World 72:6 Ag '64

Marketing

Building a faster track from factory to home; GE's controversial sales plan. il Bsns W p45-6 F 16 '63

ELECTRIC apparatus and appliances, Cordless
Cordless battery-powered appliances. il Consumer Bul 47:26-7 F '64
Cordless tools & appliances. il Changing T 18:39-41 F '64; Same abr. with title Gadgets that run by themselves. Read Digest 85:155-6 O '64
Look at those new cordless appliances. il Good H 158:164 Ap '64
Power without cords. il Time 81:80 Ap 26 '63

ELECTRIC apparatus and appliances, Domestic
Appliance makers rejoicing. il Bsns W p 109-10+ Je 20 '64
Beat the heat with hot-weather helpers. J. Holmstrand. il Suc Farm 61:56 Ag '63
Big hand for the hostess. il Ladies Home J 81:118 D '64
Blend it round the clock. il McCalls 91:76+ N '63
Cook in the cool of the day, eat in the cool of the evening; cool-cooking electric skillet. il McCalls 90:94-5+ Jl 63
Cooking with electrical appliances. il House & Gard 126:208-11 S '64
Cordless mixer that didn't go far; Sunbeam Cordless. il Consumer Rep 29:5-6 Ja '64
Electric fry pans. il Consumer Rep 29:280-3 Je '64
Electric knife sharpeners. il Consumer Rep 28:478-80 O '63
Electric mixers. il Consumer Bul 46:12-16+ S '63
Few pointers about griddles. il Redbook 121:74-5+ Je '63
Going abroad to live, or stay for a time? American-made household appliances. Consumer Bul 47:39 My '64
Good housekeeping buying guide for small appliances. il Good H 157:166-7 N '63
Help yourself to Christmas; keep everything serving-ready. il McCalls 92:140-1 D '64
Home cooking. il Redbook 122:64-5+ Ja '64
How to put those gift appliances right to work! H. A. Dawson. il Bet Hom & Gard 42:16+ D '64
If you had twenty-one wishes. Good H 158:132+ F '64
Latest in covered cooking. il Bet Hom & Gard 41:92-3 Je '63
McCall's dandy dictionary of handy helpers. il McCalls 90:106-7 F '63
Magnetic force in the kitchen; all-purpose appliance uses spinning magnet. il Bsns W p63 My 30 '64
Mixer with extras and a high price; Mixboy. il Consumer Rep 29:316 Jl '64
My top ten appliances. V. T. Habeeb. Am Home 66:77-8 N '63
New skillets are better. il McCalls 91:38+ Mr '64
New strategy: try to beat the clock. il Bsns W p50-1 F 1 '64
Portable electric food mixers. il Consumer Rep 28:228-33 My '63
Sharp! electric slicing knife and electric sharpener. il McCalls 92:76 N '64
Small appliances; hard-working helpers. J. Figg. Suc Farm 62:104-5+ Ap '64
Split-second gourmet with a blender. il Good H 158:176-8+ Mr '64
What's new in kitchen equipment? N. Craig. il House B 105:40+ My '63
What's new in small appliances? Bet Hom & Gard 42:98 N '64
When should you replace a major kitchen appliance? R. Charles. Parents Mag 38:63-6+ Ap '63
Wonderful world of appliances. E. M. McCabe. il Parents Mag 38:32+ Je '63
World tour of cool, quick cooking. il Bet Hom & Gard 41:72-7 Je '63
Your home (cont) il Consumer Rep 28:88-217 D '63
See also
Electric stoves
Electric toasters
Laundry equipment
Washing machines

Care

Use and care of household appliances (cont) Consumer Rep 28:273-8 D '63

Repairing

Appliance warranties & service. il Changing T 18:42-5 Ja '64

Safety devices and measures

Guarding against electric shock (cont) Consumer Rep 28:380-4 D '63

ELECTRIC apparatus industry
Appliance makers rejoicing. il Bsns W p 109-10+ Je 20 '64
Household revolution; Italian refrigerators and washing machines. il Time 82:64 Ag 2 '63
Price trends and the postwar market for appliances. J. C. Daugherty. il Mo Labor R 86:1259-65 N '63
Two in every home. il Time 83:93 F 28 '64

ELECTRIC arc
How to make a Jacob's ladder. H. P. Strand. il Pop Sci 184:110-11 F '64

ELECTRIC auto-lite company
Ford road takes a surprise turn; merger with Electric autolite co. il Bsns W p 152+ S 14 '63
Prestolite builds a new world. Bsns W p63-4+ D 14 '63

ELECTRIC batteries
Battery-powered lights. H. Friedman. il Pop Phot 54:112-13+ Mr '64
Battery reliability ensures continued use. M. L. Yaffee. il Aviation W 80:49+ Je 1 '64
How to pick the right battery! H. Friedman. il Pop Phot 54:115+ Ap '64
Modern batteries; primary and secondary batteries. J. R. Collins. il Electr World 70:34-6+ O '63
Packaged power packs new punch. H. G. McEntee. il Pop Sci 184:80-3+ Je '64
Portable power probe. R. Miller. il U S Camera 26:62-5+ Je '63
See also
Thermopiles

History

Babylon battery. W. G. Salm. il Pop Electr 21:51-2 Jl '64

ELECTRIC blankets, coverlets, etc.
Electric blankets. il Changing T 19:13-14 Ja '65
Electric blankets. il Consumer Bul 47:22-6 Ja '64
How to care for electric blankets. Bet Hom & Gard 42:118 Je '64
On electric blankets. il Consumer Bul 48:19-22 Ja '65

ELECTRIC blenders. See Electric apparatus and appliances, Domestic

ELECTRIC broilers
Portable electric broilers. il Consumer Rep 28:347-51 Jl '63

ELECTRIC cables
Shielded cables. W. H. Buchsbaum. il Electr World 72:36-8+ N '64

ELECTRIC capacitance
Capacitance nomogram. F. D. Gross. il Electr World 72:31 D '64
RC filter chart. R. K. Re. il Electr World 70:25 Jl '63

ELECTRIC capacitors
A.C. negative-resistance devices R. P. Turner. bibliog il Electr World 70:50-1+ Jl '63
Bargains by the bagful. O. P. Ferrell. il Pop Electr 20:49-52 F '64
C bridge. F. A. Parker. il Pop Electr 19:65-6+ N '63
Capacitance transducer systems. S. L. Silver. il Electr World 72:38-40+ S '64
Capacitor former for electronic flash units. M. S. Lieberman. il Electr World 70:54-6 D '63
How capacitors change V.T.V.M. readings. H. Q. Duguid. il Electr World 72:53+ O '64
Modern capacitors. J. R. Collins. il Electr World 69:42-4+ My '63

Testing

Capacitor value checker. A. A. Mangieri. il Electr World 72:44-5+ Jl '64

ELECTRIC circuit breakers
When protection doesn't protect. il Bsns W p 112+ Jl 18 '64

ELECTRIC circuit testers
TI, Fairchild aiming at circuit tester market. M. Getler. Miss & Roc 13:38-9 S 16 '63

ELECTRIC circuits
Development of an electrical raceway for laboratory application. B. F. Winckowski. il Arch Rec 134:235-6 S '63
See also
Electronic circuits
Impedance (electricity)
Radio circuits
Television circuits
Vacuum-tube circuits

ELECTRIC clocks. See Clocks, Electric

ELECTRIC clothes dryers. See Clothes dryers

ELECTRIC coffee pots. See Coffee pots, percolators, etc.

ELECTRIC coils
Using slug-tuned coils. J. Tartas. il Electr World 71:48-50 Ap '64
See also
Radio coils

ELECTRIC conductivity
Electroconductive polymers. J. H. Lupinski and K. D. Kopple. bibliog il Science 146:1038-9 N 20 '64
Electrokinetic behavior of ion-exchange resin. D. H. Freeman and G. Scatchard. il Science 144:411 Ap 24 '64
Electrolytic conductance of sea water: effect of calcium carbonate dissolution. K. Park. bibliog il Science 146:56-7 O 2 '64
Negative temperature coefficient of resistance in bismuth I. P. C. Souers and G. Jura. bibliog il Science 143:467-9 Ja 31 '64
Semiconducting region of ytterbium. P. C. Souers and G. Jura. bibliog il Science 140:481-3 My 3 '63
See also
Superconductivity

ELECTRIC conductors
What is skin effect? J. Tusinsk. il Electr World 69:80-1 Je '63
See also
Semiconductors

ELECTRIC connectors
Jacks in box; patching different connectors together. J. A. Fred. il Pop Electr 20:68 Mr '64
New connectors and techniques. il Electr World 70:80-2 Jl '63

ELECTRIC control
Better model control for $5.50. H. L. Davidson. il Pop Electr 19:66-7 S '63
Build the Multi-Trol. R. Wilson. il Pop Electr 20:40-2 My '64
How to select electric motors and controls. W. J. Fletcher. il Suc Farm 62:44-5 F '64
Noiseless remote switching. C. W. Martel. il Electr World 71:60 Mr '64
See also
Voltage regulators

ELECTRIC cooking
See also
Electric broilers

ELECTRIC cords
Cheater cord de luxe; TV control box. J. A. Fred. il Pop Electr 19:73 O '63
Trouble lights and extension cords. il Consumer Bul 48:37-40 F '65

ELECTRIC current rectifiers
Controlled-rectifier gate circuits. il Electr World 69:84-5 Je '63
Electronics enters appliance field; silicon controlled rectifier. Sci Digest 55:46-7 Je '64
Experiments with a chemical rectifier. C. Green. il Pop Electr 22:71-2 Ja '65
Gate turnoff controlled rectifier. D. L. Pippen. il Electr World 72:46+ Ag '64
High wattage reducer; use of silicon diodes for easy power control. F. A. Parker. il Pop Electr 20:57-8 F '64
Low-cost SCR motor speed control. il Pop Electr 21:67-8 D '64
New electronic control begins to take hold. il Bsns W p68+ O 24 '64
New SCR developments. D. Lancaster. il Electr World 72:25-7+ D '64
SCR automotive ignition system. B. Ward. il Electr World 72:44-5+ N '64
SCR; silicon controlled rectifiers; new applications in the home. L. Stern. il Electr World 70:27-30+ O '63
SCR tester. T. E. Hopkins. il Electr World 71:56 Ja '64

ELECTRIC currents
Conserved current; vector current. Sci Am 208:82 Ap '63
See also
Electric current rectifiers
Electric measurements
Hall effect
Short circuits

Grounding

Operation pickup Mk II; building 6- and 12-volt positive, 6-volt negative ground systems. C. E. Ruoff. il Pop Electr 19:47-8+ O '63

ELECTRIC currents, Direct
Clip-on D.C. current probe. A. Bergh and others. il Electr World 72:41-3+ S '64

ELECTRIC discharges through gases
See also
Plasma (ionized gases)

ELECTRIC dishwashers. See Dishwashing and drying machines

ELECTRIC distribution
Find the faults first; electric distribution maintenance, Naperville, Ill. J. O. Turner. il Am City 79:94 N '64

Grounding

Underground power distribution cuts costs, promotes city growth: Jacksonville Beach, Fla. H. Brantley. il Am City 80:93-4 Ja '65

ELECTRIC drills. See Drilling and boring machinery

ELECTRIC drills, Portable. See Drilling and boring machinery

ELECTRIC eels
Eel electroplaques: spike electrogenesis without potassium activation. Y. Nakmura and others. bibliog il Science 146:266-8 O 9 '64
Electrophorus adenosine triphosphatase; sodium-activated exchange after N-ethyl maleimide treatment. S. Fahn and others. bibliog il Science 145:283-4 Jl 17 '64

ELECTRIC engineering
Inventing ways to make things; Western electric's Engineering research center at Princeton. il Bsns W p 120+ Ap 20 '63

ELECTRIC engineers
Electronics field engineers around the world. C. J. Olson. il Electr World 70:42-3+ S '63
Instrument calibration and repair technician; electronics technicians and engineers. G. C. Gedney and F. M. Winterburg. il Electr World 70:28-9 Ag '63

ELECTRIC equipment
See also
Audio-visual aids

ELECTRIC equipment industry
Big money question; six suppliers overcharged; Philadelphia electric and UGI. il Bsns W p 176+ Ap 18 '64
Britain: how Bloom withered. il Fortune 70:53-4+ O '64
Climbing toll for the price-fixers. il Bsns W p96-8+ Ag 29 '64
Damaging suit. Time 83:98+ Je 12 '64

ELECTRIC fans
Return of the rubber-blade; Samson-Monroe products. il Consumer Rep 29:270 Je '64
Sweet summer breezes. il McCalls 91:126 Jl '64
ELECTRIC fences. See Fences, Electric
ELECTRIC field
Electric fields across water-nitrobenzene interfaces. M. Blank and S. Feig. bibliog il Science 141:1173-4 S 20 '63
ELECTRIC filters
Ripple-filter design chart. A. L. Teubner. il Electr World 70:31 O '63
See also
Radio filters
ELECTRIC fishes. See Electric organs in fishes
ELECTRIC fishing devices. See Fishing—Implements and appliances
ELECTRIC flashlights. See Flashlights, Electric
ELECTRIC flashlights. See Flashlights, Electric
ELECTRIC floor washers. See Floor machines
ELECTRIC fry pans. See Electric apparatus and appliances, Domestic
ELECTRIC furnaces, Foundry. See Furnaces, Foundry
ELECTRIC fuses
Confused fuse. A. W. Edwards. Electr World 71:100 Ja '64
Short circuits and fuses. B. Francois. il Motor B 111:37-8+ Mr '63
Ten ways to blow a fuse. C. Smith. il Pop Phot 52:57 Ja '63
ELECTRIC generators
Amps for camps. P. Geraci. il Pop Sci 184:112-15 My '64
Avco aims MHD generator at space role. R. D. Hibben. il Aviation W 80:62+ Ap 27 '64
Boost for fossil fuels; magnetohydrodynamic power generation. Sci Am 210:68+ F '64
Emergency power. Am Home 66:81-3 N '63
GE seeking practical MHD space system. M. L. Yaffee. il Aviation W 81:55+ Jl 13 '64
Installing a marine generating plant. C. Kucyn. il Motor B 112:38-9+ N '63
Light-controlled power supply. il Pop Electr 20:53-5+ F; 21:70-2 S '64
Machine that makes your lights go on. il Sci Digest 55:63-5 Ja '64
Martin generates continuing MPD power. M. L. Yaffee. il Aviation W 80:65+ Ja 6 '64
More electric power; magnetohydrodynamic generation. Sci N L 85:390 Je 20 '64
New magnet provides more efficient way to convert heat directly into electricity. Bsns W p54 Ja 19 '63
New MHD generator may aid in harnessing of nuclear heat. Bsns W p 122 Ap 11 '64
New system announced for generating electricity; magnetoplasmadynamic generator. il Sci N L 85:22 Ja 11 '64
Representative space vehicle thermionic generator systems. Aviation W 80:58-9 Je 8 '64
Superconducting magnet teamed with generator. Sci N L 83:70 F 2 '63
You can take it with you; midget gasoline generator. il Pop Mech 121:162 Ja '64
See also
Thermionic converters

Control

Instruments for engines that generate power. E. R. Sauder. il Am City 79:121-2 S '64
ELECTRIC generators, Alternating current
All about alternators. J. V. Poticny. il Motor B 111:34-5+ Mr '63
Alternators: selection and installation. W. J. Hector. il Electr World 69:70-3 Je '63
Getting to know your alternator. M. J. Schultz. il Pop Mech 119:174-9+ Mr '63
What you should know about alternators. E. Robberson. il Yachting 113:40-2+ F '63
ELECTRIC generators, Electrostatic
Lighting in your living room; Van de Graaff generator. H. Walton. il Pop Sci 185:142-5 N '64
ELECTRIC grinders. See Grinding machines
ELECTRIC hair dryers. See Hair dryers
ELECTRIC heaters
Portable electric heaters. il Changing T 17:17-18 N '63
ELECTRIC heating
Big shift to electric heat. H. Steinberg. il Am Home 67:82+ Mr '64
Electric home heating. W. Fletcher. il Suc Farm 61:52 N '63
Heat conservation in the electrically-heated house. E. R. Ambrose. il Arch Rec 135:7+ mid-My '64
See also
Heating, Infrared
ELECTRIC inductance. See Inductance
ELECTRIC industries
In electrical manufacturing, the word is rationalize; European electrical industry. G. Burck. il Fortune 68:110-15+ S '63
See also
Electric apparatus industry
also names of electric industry companies, e.g. Westinghouse electric corporation

Wages and hours

Wage chronology: Commonwealth Edison co. of Chicago, 1962-63. il Mo Labor R 86:1184-6 O '63
ELECTRIC insect trap. See Insect traps
ELECTRIC instruments
Polarity indicators provide an end to shoreside shock. H. Mendelson. il Motor B 112:43+ N '63
ELECTRIC insulation. See Insulation (electric)
ELECTRIC irons
Steam irons: their care and keep. E. Taylor. il Good H 156:173 F '63
Steam-spray irons. il Consumer Rep 29:56-9 F '64
ELECTRIC knives. See Knives
ELECTRIC lamps
Battery-powered lights. H. Friedman. il Pop Phot 54:112-13+ Mr '64
Benevolent light bulb. D. Moraes. House & Gard 124:248-9 N '63
Big light in a little package; miniature high-intensity lamps. J. H. Ingersoll. il Pop Sci 186:151 Ja '65
Burned-out pilot-lamp indicators. R. L. Ives. il Electr World 69:40 Je '63
Buy light, not just bulbs. il Consumer Bul 47:43+ O '64
Galaxy of lights. G. O'Brien. il N Y Times Mag p54-5 Ag 11 '63
Hi-Lighter. B. G. Wels. il Pop Electr 21:46 S '64
Hobby lamp, potent and portable. il House & Gard 123:193 Ap '63
How new movie lights stack up! M. A. Matzkin. il Mod Phot 28:94-5+ Ja '64
How to buy a table lamp. il House & Gard 123:202-5 My '63
Lamp cleaner, a new magician; Broadway maintenance corp. il Am City 79:113 N '64
Lamp tops radio. A. Trauffer. il Pop Electr 19:62 Ag '63
Light brigade; house owner's guide to bulbs. il House & Gard 126:230-1 S '64
Light bulbs, what you don't know. il Changing T 18:32-4 Mr '64
Little giant; Tensor corp. mini-lamps. il Newsweek 65:60 Ja 18 '65
Little lamp that grew up; miniature, high intensity lamp. il Bsns W p64+ D 19 '64
Man-in-the-moon; childs night light. M. H. Slutz. il Pop Mech 120:132 D '63
Movie lights better for stills? M. A. Matzkin. il Mod Phot 29:78-9+ Ja '65
New light; it's a glowing bubble. il Sunset 130:161-2 My '63
New lighting advances. il Am City 78:124+ O '63
Novelty lamps. A. Trauffer. il Pop Mech 121:161 F '64
Some light on the subject of miniature high-intensity lamps. il Consumer Bul 47:6-9 D '64
Understanding burn-out; vacuum tube and pilot lamp filaments. L. Vicens. il Pop Electr 20:69 Mr '64
X-line nite light. L. F. Hudson. il Pop Electr 21:57-8 Ag '64
See also
Electric lighting

History

Battle of the bulbs. H. F. Kutschbach. il Pop Electr 21:44-5+ Ag '64
ELECTRIC lamps, Flashing
Build this automatic safety flasher. L. Garner. il Pop Electr 19:56-7 S '63
Do-nothing box. C. W. Campbell. il Pop Electr 20:68 Ja '64
Electronic candles dance and glow. J. H. Taylor. il Pop Electr 21:49-52 N '64
Nonsense box. A. L. Danzis. il Pop Electr 19:47-8 Jl '63
Spookin' light. J. H. Taylor. il Pop Electr 21:67-9 S '64
ELECTRIC lamps, Flashlight
AG-1 flash. D. L. Miller. il Mod Phot 29:74-5+ Ja+ '65
Big light from small sources. B. Pierce. il Pop Phot 52:62-3+ Ja '63
Big little flash. J. Wolbarst. il Mod Phot 28:78-9+ Ja '64

ELECTRIC lamps, Flashlight—*Continued*
Brilliant flash times your engine; xenon flash lamps. R. Berney. il Pop Sci 183:164-7 O '63
Can flash synchronization be added to a used camera? A. C. Muller. Mod Phot 28:108 D '64
Competitor for the laser; flash tube, Enetron. il Pop Sci 184:19 Ja '64
Electronic flash; is it the perfect portable light source? R. M. Benrey. il Pop Phot 55:154-5+ N '64
Flash for your garden. J. J. Simpkins. Flower Grower 50:65 My '63
Guide to help you end the confusion in floodlamp sources. N. Rothschild. Pop Phot 52:134-6 Ja '63
How to get the most out of an AG-1 bulb. C. W. Kennedy. il Pop Phot 55:154-7+ D '64
Light side of picture taking; selecting flash bulbs. il Consumer Bul 47:2+ Ap '64
Lowdown on portable electronic flash units. T. Karp. il Mod Phot 28:82-7 Ja '64
Photoflashes: a potential new tool for control of insect populations. R. J. Barker and others. bibliog il Science 145:1195-7 S 11 '64
Pocketable speedlight. R. Kinne. il Pop Phot 54:62-7+ Mr '64
Repeating flash you can build; electronic flash. R. M. Benrey. il Pop Sci 185:132-6+ O '64
Roundup: new lights. A. Francekevich. il Pop Phot 52:58-61+ Ja '63
Seven new speedlights: how do they stack up? S. Nathan. il U S Camera 27:43-5 Mr '64
Simple slave strobe sync. N. Sheffield, jr. il Pop Electr 20:59-61+ My '64
Slave photoflash. il Electr World 73:68 Ja '65
What's what light A. Trauffer. il Pop Electr 19:62 Jl '63
ZJ photoflash slave. B. Ward. il Pop Electr 18:39-40 Je '63

ELECTRIC lamps, Fluorescent
Fluorescent city, U.S.A: Rockville, Conn. L. B. Flaherty, jr. il Am City 78:124 Ap '63
Fluorescent light for car, camp, or boat. il Pop Sci 184:146 F '64
Fluorescents instead of ornaments: Saginaw, Mich. E. H. Potthoff, jr. and M. E. Peacock. il Am City 79:126+ O '64
How to trouble-shoot fluorescent lights. Bet Hom & Gard 42:92 Jl '64
Wall-to-wall illumination. J. Hand. il Pop Sci 184:150-2 Ap '64

ELECTRIC lamps, Incandescent
Battle of the bulbs. H. F. Kutschbach. il Pop Electr 21:44-5+ Ag '64
Electronic candles dance and glow. J. H. Taylor. il Pop Electr 21:49-52 N '64
Light dimmers for home and industry; controls for incandescent lamps. F. M. Wolff. il Electr World 71:25-9+ My '64

ELECTRIC lamps, Mercury vapor
Mercury city, U.S.A: Winsted, Conn. A. J. Cannavo. il Am City 78:121 Mr '63
Pittsburgh pushes for more mercuries. F. C. Poorman. il Am City 79:131 O '64

ELECTRIC lamps, Neon
Nonsense box. A. L. Danzis. il Pop Electr 19:47-8 Jl '63

ELECTRIC light bulbs. See Electric lamps

ELECTRIC light fixtures. See Lighting fixtures

ELECTRIC lighting
Design your own custom lighting. N. Seney. il Bet Home & Gard 42:30+ Je '64
Fine art of lighting. il House & Gard 124:250-3 N '63
Lighting hospital patient rooms; excerpts from Lighting for hospital patient rooms, study by U.S. Public health service. Arch Rec 134:192-3 N '63
New lights for special places. il Bet Hom & Gard 42:103 F '64
New look at light. il Ladies Home J 81:137-40+ Mr '64
Wall-to-wall illumination. J. Hand. il Pop Sci 184:150-2 Ap '64
See also
Electroluminescence

Control

Automatic controls can cut lighting costs. W. P. Chapman. il Arch Rec 133:192-3 My '63
Dim your lights at home, too. H. Stockert. il Pop Mech 119:154-7+ F '63
For drama at night, dim the lights. D. X. Manners. il House B 105:124-5 F '63
Light dimmers for home and industry. F. M. Wolff. il Electr World 71:25-9+ My '64
Multipurpose electronic control: lamp dimmer. D. Lancaster. il Electr World 73:36-7 Ja '65
Self-regulating lighting controller. E. P. Nawracaj and F. Forman. il Pop Electr 22:67-8 Ja '65
Watch those watts; dimmed room lights. R. E. Pafenberg. il Pop Electr 18:71 Mr '63

ELECTRIC lighting sets
Emergency household lamp. R. L. Winklepleck. il Pop Electr 18:55-7 My '63
Emergency lighting; EV-R-LERT system of Maintenance company, of Long Island City. New Yorker 39:19 Jl 20 '63

ELECTRIC lines
Development of an electrical raceway for laboratory application. B. F. Winckowski. il Arch Rec 134:235-6 S '63
Loss figures for 300-ohm twin-lead. M. L. Nelson. il Electr World 73:30 Ja '65
Plan power inter-tie; proposed Pacific Northwest-Southwest high voltage direct current line. Sci N L 86:85 Ag 8 '64
Vogue for ever higher voltage; extra-high voltage. il Bsns W p47-8+ Ap 13 '63
Whose lands are these? R. Moley. Newsweek 61:104 Mr 11 '63
See also
Linemen

Grounding

See Electric distribution—Grounding

ELECTRIC measurements
New approach to high-frequency measurements. B. Ferrous. il Electr World 72:41-3+ Ag '64
See also
Electric meters
Electric units
Inductance
Potentiometers
Strain gages

ELECTRIC meters
Add-on S-meter. R. L. Winklepleck. il Pop Electr 18:48-50 F '63
Converting meter scales. B. Apperson. il Electr World 71:74 Mr '64
Design of simple Q meter. D. H. Sandrock. il Electr World 72:84-6 S '64
Economy CB S-meter. M. Miller. il Pop Electr 20:50-1 Ap '64
Meter protection circuit. A. A. Mangieri. il Electr World 73:48-9 Ja '65
Multiple meter test set. R. E. Pafenberg. il Pop Electr 19:59 O '63
VHF grid-dip meter. E. H. Marriner. il Pop Electr 20:59-61+ Ja '64
See also
Ammeters
Electric measurements
Meter reading
Phasemeter
Voltohmmeters
Wattmeters

ELECTRIC mixers. See Electric apparatus and appliances, Domestic

ELECTRIC motors
How to select electric motors and controls. W. J. Fletcher. il Suc Farm 62:44-5 F '64
New motor makes news by going slow; Enercon. H. Luckett. il Pop Sci 182:57-60 Mr '63
Variable-speed motor is brushless. il Pop Sci 182:190 Mr '63

Control

Motor speed control. il Electr World 72:102 N '64

ELECTRIC motors, Alternating current
Motor speed control. il Electr World 72:102 N 4 '64

ELECTRIC mowers. See Lawn mowers

ELECTRIC organ. See Organ

ELECTRIC organs in fishes
Electric location by fishes. H. W. Lissmann. il Sci Am 208:50-9 bibliog(p 188) Mr '63

ELECTRIC oscillators. See Oscillators

ELECTRIC outlets. See Electric wire and wiring

ELECTRIC ovens
Adaptable auxiliary oven; Caloric 320. Consumer Rep 29:109-10 Mr '64
Range with a self-cleaning oven; General electric range. il Consumer Rep 29:231 My '64

ELECTRIC plants
See also
Electric power
Hydroelectric plants

ELECTRIC plants, Municipal
Bethanyites get a bargain; Bethany, Ill. il Am City 78:77 Ag '63
Power costs drop; Kingman, Kan. il Am City 79:124+ Ap '64

ELECTRIC plugs. See Electric wire and wiring

ELECTRIC popcorn poppers. See Corn poppers

ELECTRIC power
Build the AUX-9; 9-volt power supply. T. H. Charters. il Pop Electr 21:65-7+ O '64
Grid; transmission grid for Far West project. Newsweek 64:57+ Ag 10 '64
Growing market for nuclear kw. il Fortune 68:172-6+ Jl '63
High-voltage power transmission. L. O. Barthold and H. G. Pfeiffer. il Sci Am 210: 38-47 bibliog(p 150) My '64
Hybrid bridge power supplies. J. Marshall. il Electr World 69:82-3 Je '63
Kilowatts for tomorrow. H. Manchester. Read Digest 83:29-30+ N '63
Look out, America, here comes Granby. E. Hill. il Sat Eve Post 237:64-5 Ap 4 '64
Low-cost solid-state power supply. G. A. Lehmann. il Electr World 70:92-3 O '63
MAPPing a new power network; nation's biggest power pool. il Bsns W p30 Ag 31 '63
Minature regulated power supply. J. P. Shields. il Electr World 71:74-5 F '64
Perpetual transistor power package. L. E. Greenlee. il Pop Electr 20:53-5+ My '64
Power plan for the future; one system to serve whole U.S. il U S News 57:64-5 D 28 '64
Regulated transistorized power supplies. J. R. Collins. il Electr World 69:40-2 Mr '63
Semiconductors for power supplies. F. W. Gutzwiller. il Electr World 72:27-30+ N '64
Unusual D.C. to D.C. supply. R. L. Winklepleck. il Electr World 71:62-3 My '64
Westward ho! plan for the world's largest electric power complex. Time 84:111A O 2 '64
See also
Hydroelectric plants
Hydroelectric power
Voltage regulators

Transmission

See Electric transmission

Africa

New energy resources. Sci N L 83:101 F 16 '63

Brazil

Darkness in Rio. il Time 81:45 My 24 '63

Italy

Headaches of nationalization. il Time 85:64 Ja 8 '65

Latin America

Facts and figures of the Americas. il Américas 16:48 S '64

United States

See Electric power

ELECTRIC power lines. See Electric lines
ELECTRIC power production
Electrical device implantation in animals studied. H. M. David. il Miss & Roc 13:18 Jl 22 '63
GE lab uses rodent to power transmitter. Aviation W 79:30 Jl 15 '63
No rush to nuclear plants. il Bsns W p 100+ F 8 '64
Yep, you're a human dynamo. A. Zuckerman. il Pop Mech 121:132 Mr '64
ELECTRIC power production from bacteriological action
Amazing bug battery. D. S. Halacy, jr. il Pop Electr 20:41-4+ F '64
ELECTRIC power production from chemical action
See also
Fuel cells
ELECTRIC power transmission. See Electric transmission
ELECTRIC precipitators
Electrostatic precipitators can solve the fly-ash problem in municipal incinerators. A. B. Walker. il Am City 79:148+ S '64
ELECTRIC railroads, Toy. See Railroads, Toy
ELECTRIC ranges. See Electric stoves
ELECTRIC razors. See Razors
ELECTRIC rectifiers. See Electric current rectifiers
ELECTRIC refrigerators. See Refrigerators. Electric
ELECTRIC relays
See also
Electronic relays
ELECTRIC resistance
A.C. negative-resistance devices. R. P. Turner. bibliog il Electr World 70:50-1+ Jl '63
Delta-Y transformation nomogram. A. L. Teubner. il Electr World 71:31 F '64
Electrical and thermal measurements with Bridgman anvils. R. S. Kirk and R. J. Vaišnys. bibliog il Science 143:1436-7 My 27 '64
High-field galvanomagnetic properties of metals. W. A. Reed and E. Fawcett. bibliog il Science 146:603-10 O 30 '64
High pressure: effect on dysprosium. P. C. Souers and G. Jura. bibliog il Science 145: 575-7 Ag 7 '64
Power & resistor charts. R. Jones. il Electr World 72:33 S '64
Racial differences in skin resistance. L. C. Johnson and N. L. Corah. bibliog il Science 139:766-7 F 22 '63
RC filter chart R. K. Re. il Electr World 70: 25 Jl '63
Tunnel diode high-resistance checker. C. D. Todd. il Electr World 69:86-8 Je '63
Ytterbium; effect of pressure and temperature on resistance. R. A. Stager and H. G. Drickamer. bibliog il Science 139:1284 Mr 29 '63
See also
Impedance (electricity)
ELECTRIC resistors
Bargains by the bagful. O. P. Ferrell. il Pop Electr 20:49-52 F '64
Fixed resistors. J. R. Collins. il Electr World 70:44-6+ S '63
Making resistors with math; noninductive Möbius resistor. il Time 84:49 S 25 '64
Making special resistors. R. Jones. il Electr World 70:96 N '63
Parallel-resistor chart. L. W. Brindley. il Electr World 70:31 N '63
Resistor power calculator. R. K. Re. il Electr World 69:37 Je '63
Resistor power-rating nomogram. J. Kyle. il Electr World 71:29 Ap '64
See also
Strain gages
Thermistors
ELECTRIC resonance. See Resonance
ELECTRIC sanders. See Floor machines
ELECTRIC saws. See Saws
ELECTRIC service, Rural
How a subsidized business thrives; rural electric cooperatives. il Nations Bsns 52:36-7+ O '64
Lights go on in the Yaak River Valley. il Time 82:31 O 18 '63
See also
United States—Rural electrification administration
ELECTRIC shavers. See Razors
ELECTRIC shock
Amnesic and punishing effects of electroconvulsive shock. J. L. McGaugh and M. C. Madsen. bibliog il Science 144:182-3 Ap 10 '64
Guarding against electric shock (cont) Consumer Rep 28:380-4 D '63
Polarity indicators provide an end to shoreside shock. H. Mendelson. il Motor B 112: 43+ N '63
Retrograde amnesia from conditioned competing responses; electroconvulsive shock. D. J. Lewis and H. E. Adams. Science 141: 516-17 Ag 9 '63; Reply. C. J. Dye. bibliog 143:973 F 28 '64
ELECTRIC shock treatment. See Shock therapy
ELECTRIC signs
Unspectacular Douglas Leigh. J. F. Fixx. il Sat R 47:54-5 Jl 11 '64
ELECTRIC skillets. See Electric apparatus and appliances, Domestic
ELECTRIC slicing knives. See Knives
ELECTRIC soldering gun. See Soldering apparatus
ELECTRIC sparks
See also
Lichtenberg figures
ELECTRIC standards
Units and standards of electrical measure. F. K. Harris. il Electr World 72:29-32+ Ag '64
ELECTRIC stoves
Cleaner, better electric ranges. il Consumer Bul 47:33-8 D '64
Cook it where you want to eat it; portable electric ranges. N. Craig. il House B 105: 102-3 Ag '63
High-oven ranges. il Consumer Rep 29:116-20 Mr '64
Hotpoint's hazard and Hotpoint's defense; high-oven ranges. il Consumer Rep 29:268-9 Je '64
How to buy a range in 1965. V. T. Habeeb. il Am Home 68:56-7 Ja '65
Little ranges that go far. il McCalls 91:63 Jl '64

ELECTRIC stoves—*Continued*
Now: ranges that think! il Bet Hom & Gard 41:106-7 Mr '63
See also
Electric ovens

ELECTRIC switches
Dim your lights at home, too. H. Stockert. il Pop Mech 119:154-7+ F '63
Dynaquad touch control. il Pop Electr 19:40 Jl '63
Electronic scanning simplifies telemetry. L. G. Sands. il Electr World 72:36-7+ Jl '64
Electronic switch for your oscilloscope. S. E. Bammel. il Electr World 17:38-9+ F '64
Fluid switches studied for use in computers. Sci N L 84:34 Jl 20 '63
Hi-fi shutoff; time-delay switch. R. Wilensky. il Pop Electr 18:50-1+ Je '63
Latest advances in touch control. C. E. Atkins. il Electr World 69:34-7+ My '63
Light-activated switch. H. McEntee. il Pop Sci 184:128-9+ Ja '64
Light dimmer & power-tool control. D. Lancaster. il Electr World 72:46-7+ Jl '64
More switched outlets for hi-fi. R. L. Conhaim. il Pop Electr 19:67 O '63
Movie projectionist's friend. J. R. Oswald. il Pop Electr 20:90 Ja '64
New light-operated switch; Raysistor, photocell with self-contained light source. D. E. Whateley. il Electr World 70:47+ N '63
Noiseless remote switching. C. W. Martel. il Electr World 71:60 Mr '64
Organ kit uses diode switching; electronic organ. il Electr World 72:75 D '64
Remote volume control; Raysistor, a photocell with self-contained light. C. W. Martel. il Electr World 72:62 Jl '64
Shock-avoider switch box. F. P. Fritz. il Pop Mech 120:188-9 S '63
Touch, it's on; touch again, it's off; electronic switch. H. L. Davidson. il Pop Sci 184:125 Ja '64
What is your choice in wall switches? il Sunset 130:139-40 Je '63
What's what light. A. Trauffer. il Pop Electr 19:62 Jl '63
Wide choice in wall switches. il Good H 158:208+ Ap '64

ELECTRIC toasters
Automatic toasters. il Consumer Bul 46:6-9 Mr '63
Talented new toasters. il McCalls 91:52 My '64

ELECTRIC tools, Portable
Carving wood with power. P. McCafferty. il Pop Sci 182:142-5 Mr '63
How to pick a portable. Bet Hom & Gard 42:20 Ja '64
New portable all-jobs tool. H. B. Comstock. il Pop Sci 184:130-3 My '64
Popular science buyer's guide to home shop tools. il Pop Sci 183:155-6+ D '63
Power tools for boatmen. F. M. Paulson. il Field & S 69:90-2+ N '64
Powered rasps. W. C. Lammey. il Pop Mech 120:184-9 O '63
What's new in shop tools. il Suc Farm 61:102 F '63
Which power tools for you? il Bet Hom & Gard 42:119-20+ My '64
Workshop. il Consumer Rep 29:276-91 D '64
See also
Black and Decker manufacturing company

Control

Speed control boxes to make power tools more versatile. il Consumer Rep 29:394-5 Ag '64

Safety devices and measures

To shock-test power tools. Sunset 130:139-40 My '63

ELECTRIC toothbrush. See Toothbrushes

ELECTRIC toys
Build the Blipper. N. Smith. il Pop Electr 21:51-2 S '64
Electric cannon fires BBs. R. L. Clough, jr. il Pop Mech 120:162-3 N '63
Electric toys. il Consumer Rep 29:534-7 N '64

ELECTRIC transformers
Constant-voltage transformer operation. T. Jaski. il Electr World 71:40-1 Ap '64
Four and five layer semiconductor diodes. D. E. Lancaster. il Electr World 72:61-4+ O '64
Inexpensive D.C.-variable inductor. R. P. Turner. il Electr World 71:79 F '64
New look in transformers. J. R. Collins. il Electr World 71:36-8 Mr '64
Output-transformer chart. il Electr World 70:57 D '63
Rating unknown power transformers. H. Q. Duguid. il Electr World 72:24-5 Jl '64
Repairing miniature I.F. transformers. G. McKinney. il Electr World 71:85 Je '64
Transformer winding quiz. R. P. Balin. il Pop Electr 21:65+ D '64
You can transform this transformer. H. P. Strand. il Pop Mech 121:188-92 Ja '64
See also
Tesla coils

ELECTRIC transmission
D.C. on the wires; use of mercury-arc valves. il Time 84:50 Jl 31 '64
High-voltage power transmission. L. O. Barthold and H. G. Pfeiffer. il Sci Am 210:38-47 bibliog(p 150) My '64
Progress made in sending electricity without wire. Sci N L 85:216 Ap 4 '64
Vogue for ever higher voltage; extra-high voltage. il Bsns W p47-8+ Ap 13 '63
See also
Electric lines
Hydroelectric plants

ELECTRIC typewriters. See Typewriters, Electric

ELECTRIC units
Units and standards of electrical measure. F. K. Harris. il Electr World 72:29-32+ Ag '64

ELECTRIC utilities
Power partnerships get popular; Southwest's private and public. il Bsns W p42+ S 26 '64
See also
American and foreign power company
American electric power company
Consolidated Edison company of New York
Electric plants, Municipal
Pacific gas and electric company

Advertising

Study in motivation. Nation 196:83 F 2 '63

Employees

See also
Electric utilities—Wages and hours

Government ownership

Power industry vs. rural co-ops: a growing fight. il U S News 54:83-5 Ap 29 '63
There's no stopping REA, or is there? H. Kay. il Fortune 67:118-21+ F '63

Rates

How we reduced electric rates; Ames, Ia. W. Schlagel. il Am City 78:136+ N '63

Securities

Still more room for a rise? il Bsns W p90-2 S 5 '64

Wages and hours

Earnings in electric and gas utility systems, July 1962. F. L. Bauer. il Mo Labor R 86:530-3 My '63

ELECTRIC voltage regulators. See Voltage regulators

ELECTRIC waffle irons. See Waffle irons

ELECTRIC washing machines. See Washing machines

ELECTRIC watches. See Watches

ELECTRIC water heaters. See Water heaters

ELECTRIC waves
See also
Microwaves

ELECTRIC welding
Arc welding basics. A. Youngquist. il Pop Mech 121:144-7+ Ja; 173-7+ F '64

ELECTRIC welding equipment
Selecting arc-welding equipment. W. R. Anderson. il Suc Farm 62:32 O '64

ELECTRIC wire and wiring
Are you safe with your electric plugs? il Consumer Bul 47:17-18 Ag '64
Automatic wiring checkouts. S. Bond. il Electr World 73:46-7 Ja '65
Chassis design for labs; wired units for experimentation and circuit study. J. W. Essex. il Electr World 70:91-2 S '63
Does the house need rewiring? il Changing T 17:37-8 Ag '63
Farmstead wiring. W. H. Peterson. il Suc Farm 61:36-7+ S '63
Handling resistance ignition wire. C. E. Cohn. il Pop Electr 21:52 N '64
How's your wiring? with safety check list. Suc Farm 62:12 Mr '64
Three-prong plug for two-prong outlets. il Consumer Rep 29:364 Ag '64
Using hook-up wire. J. Tartas. il Electr World 72:36-8 D '64
See also
Automobiles—Electric wiring
Electricity in the home

Safety devices and measures

775,000 volts with bare hands. A. Hamilton. il Sci Digest 55:35-8 Ja '64

ELECTRIC workers
Electronics lab technician: his role in industry. C. Glickstein. il Electr World 70:40-2+ N '63
Instrument calibration and repair technician; electronics technicians and engineers. G. C. Gedey and F. M. Winterburg. il Electr World 70:28-9 Ag '63
Radicians at the DEW line. W. A. Stocklin. il Electr World 71:48-9+ My '64
See also
Electric utilities—Wages and hours
International brotherhood of electrical workers
Linemen
ELECTRICAL rocket engines. See Rocket engines
ELECTRICITY
Progress made in sending electricity without wire. Sci N L 85:216 Ap 4 '64
See also
Fuel cells
Hall effect
High voltages
Impedance (electricity)
Magnetism

Experiments

How to make a Jacob's ladder. H. P. Strand. il Pop Sci 184:110-11 F '64
Snap, crackle, pop! il Sci Digest 54:90 N '63

History

Ten minute history of electricity. il Sci Digest 54:74-6 Jl '63
ELECTRICITY, Animal. See Electrophysiology
ELECTRICITY, Static
Shocking situation; shock problem in offices with wall-to-wall carpeting. Time 83:46 Ja 3 '64
ELECTRICITY, Terrestrial. See Magnetism, Terrestrial
ELECTRICITY cooperatives. See Cooperative associations
ELECTRICITY in medicine. See Electrotherapy
ELECTRICITY in the home
Downstairs no upstairs; limiter system; economical electricity in Northern Ireland. B. Friel. New Yorker 39:82+ Ag 24 '63
See also
Electric wire and wiring
ELECTRICITY on boats. See Boats—Electric equipment
ELECTRICITY on the farm
Farmstead wiring. W. H. Peterson. il Suc Farm 61:36-7+ S '63
ELECTROBIOLOGY. See Electrophysiology
ELECTROCARDIOGRAPHY
Death in the cockpit; Royal Canadian air force's ECG program. Time 83:72 F 21 '64
Electrocardiographic studies of free-swimming sharks. P. W. Gilbert and S. D. Douglas. bibliog il Science 140:1396 Je 28 '63
Messages from your heart: the electrocardiogram. J. Lentz. il Todays Health 41:26-7+ Je '63
Reaction time as a function of the cardiac cycle in young adults. J. E. Birren and others. bibliog il Science 140:195-6 Ap 12 '63
Unborn baby's heart rate. F. Marley. Sci N L 85:245 Ap 18 '64
What EKG tells the doctor about your heart. J. D. Ratcliff. Read Digest 82:91-4 Je '63
ELECTROCHEMISTRY
See also
Electrolysis
Electroplating
ELECTROCORTICOGRAMS
Long-term stability of visually evoked potentials in man. R. E. Dustman and E. C. Beck. il Science 142:1480-1 D 13 '63
ELECTROCUTION
First electrocution. A. Beichman. Commentary 35:410-13 My '63
ELECTRODES
Recharging made fast; GE's new cell uses third electrode. Bsns W p60 O 5 '63
Sodium perxenate and xenon (II) diflouride reduction at the dropping-mercury electrode. B. Jaselskis. bibliog il Science 146: 263-4 O 9 '64
Your choice of electrodes for 180 AMP A.C. welders. il Pop Mech 121:148-9 Ja '64
ELECTRODES, Glass
Phosphate glass electrode with good selectivity for alkaline-earth cations. A. H. Truesdell and A. M. Pommer. bibliog il Science 142:1292-4 D 6 '63
ELECTRODIAGNOSIS
See also
Electrocardiography

ELECTROENCEPHALOGRAMS. See Electroencephalography
ELECTROENCEPHALOGRAPHY
Activating and synchronizing centers in cat brain: electroencephalograms after lesions. A. Camacho-Evangelista and F. Reinoso-Suárez. bibliog il Science 146:268-70 O 9 '64
Alcohol and caffeine: effect on inferred visual dreaming. S. C. Gresham and others. bibliog il Science 140:1226-7 Je 14 '63
Behavioral and electroencephalographic arousal to contrasting novel stimulation. N. M. Weinberger and D. B. Lindsley. bibliog il Science 144:1355-7 Je 12 '64
Bilateral differences in the human occipital electroencephalogram with unilateral photic driving. N. L. Freedman. bibliog il Science 142:598-9 N 1 '63
Brain monitor operates inside astronaut helmet. Sci N L 84:133 Ag 31 '63
Electroencephalograms of sharks. P. W. Gilbert and others. bibliog il Science 145:949-51 Ag 28 '64
Electroencephalographic correlates of binocular rivalry in man. R. W. Lansing. bibliog il Science 146:1325-7 D 4 '64
Electroencephalographic correlogram ratios and their stability. R. S. Daniel. bibliog il Science 145:721-3 Ag 14 '64
Electroencephalographic data: reduction by wave-width analysis. W. J. MacIntyre and others. bibliog il Science 144:1357-8 Je 12 '64; Reply with rejoinder. R. M. Chapman. 146:671 O 30 '64
Electroencephalographic desynchronization in irradiated rats with transected spinal cords. G. P. Cooper and D. J. Kimeldorf. il Science 143:1040-1 Mr 6 '64
Electroencephalographic responses to ionizing radiation. J. Garcia and others. bibliog il Science 140:289-90 Ap 19 '63
Electronarcosis and evoked cortical responses. A. Sances, jr. and others. bibliog il Science 141:733-5 Ag 23 '63
Implanted electrodes; cable coupler for elimination of movement artifact. D. Sutton and J. M. Miller. il Science 140:988-9 My 31 '63
Influence of methodology on electroencephalographic sleep and arousal: studies with reserpine and etryptamine in rabbits. W. G. Steiner and others. bibliog il Science 141:53-5 Jl 5 '63
Intracellular potentials of cortical neurons during focal epileptogenic discharges. E. S. Goldensohn and D. P. Purpura. bibliog il Science 139:840-2 Mr 1 '63
Let me dial your cardiogram; Dataphone-computer combination. il Time 84:51 Jl 24 '64
Prolonged immobilization of the body: changes in performance and in the electroencephalogram. J. P. Zubek and L. Wilgosh. bibliog Science 140:306-8 Ap 19 '63
Sleep tendencies: effects of barometric pressure. W. B. Webb and H. Ades. il Science 143:263-4 Ja 17 '64
Spontaneous electrical activity in the brains of diapausing insects. L. M. Schoonhoven. il Science 141:173-4 Jl 12 '63
Synchronous sensory bombardment of young rats: effects on the electroencephalogram. W. Heron and H. Anchel. il Science 145: 946-7 Ag 28 '64
Variations in alpha voltage of the electroencephalogram and time perception. J. Anliker. bibliog il Science 140:1307-9 Je 21 '63
Wave of psychosis; characteristic brain-wave pattern. il Newsweek 62:68 O 7 '63
ELECTROLUMINESCENCE
Electroluminescence: theory and practice. L. W. Strock. il Electr World 73:23-6+ Ja '65
New luminescent screen. Sci N L 83:142 Mr 2 '63
Tiny electron light shines without heat. Sci N L 83:185 Mr 23 '63
Variety of techniques holds promise. C. D. LaFond and R. Pay. il Miss & Roc 15:31-2+ O 5 '64
ELECTROLYSIS
Chemiluminescence resulting from electrochemically generated species. D. M. Hercules. bibliog il Science 145:808-9 Ag 21 '64
New life for electrolytics. J. T. Doster. il Pop Electr 20:68 Mr '64
Polarity indicators provide an end to shoreside shock. H. Mendelson. il Motor B 112: 43+ N '63
ELECTROLYTIC capacitors. See Electric capacitors
ELECTROLYTIC process of water purification. See Water purification

ELECTROMAGNETIC waves
Expanding spectrum. J. L. Chapman. il Harper 229:70-4+ Jl '64
Millimeter waves hold aerospace promise. B. Miller. il Aviation W 81:70-1+ Ag 24 '64
Plasmas in solids. R. Bowers. il Sci Am 209: 46-53 bibliog(p 186) N '63

ELECTROMAGNETISM
Atomic retaliation jeopardized: EMP effects. W. Davis. Sci N L 84:293+ N 9 '63
Cosmic electromagnetic radiation. E. M. Hafner. bibliog il Science 145:1263-71 S 18 '64
Electronic equipment to protect U.S. defense; preventing harmful effects by EMP. Sci N L 86:180 S 19 '64
Radio observation of the electromagnetic emission from warm clouds. J. D. Sartor. bibliog il Science 143:948-50 F 28 '64
Release of EMP data urged. H. M. David. Miss & Roc 13:23-4 S 30 '63
Soviets may have ultimate ABM; possibility of de-activating U.S. missiles in silos. Miss & Roc 13:14-15 S 16 '63; Discussion. 13: 54 S 16; 9 S 30; 9 O 7 '63; Pop Sci 183:19 D '63
Treaty debate underscores lack of electromagnetic data. Miss & Roc 13:19 S 23 '63
See also
Faraday effect

ELECTROMAGNETISM in medicine
Doughnut-like device aids circulation study; measuring blood electromagnetically. Sci N L 86:201 S 26 '64
Magnetic man. il Newsweek 61:90-1 My 13 '63

ELECTROMAGNETS
Inside industry. H. E. Klein. il Duns R 81: 69-70+ F '63

ELECTROMETERS
Muscle-equivalent environmental radiation meter of extreme sensitivity. J. Kastner and others. bibliog il Science 140:1100-1 Je 7 '63
Versatile vibrating-reed electrometer delivered to NASA. il Miss & Roc 15:51 S 14 '64

ELECTROMYOGRAPH
Navy studying control of weapons through thinking of them. Miss & Roc 13:20 D 2 '63

ELECTRON beams. See Electrons—Beans

ELECTRON diffraction. See Electrons—Diffraction

ELECTRON light. See Electrons—Beams

ELECTRON microscope and microscopy
Advances in electron microscopy. K. Gilmore. il Electr World 70:21-4+ Jl '63
Cellulose acetate membranes: electron microscopy of structure. R. Riley and others. bibliog il Science 143:801-3 F 21 '64
Electron beam technique makes, inspects semiconductor microcircuits. P. J. Klass. il Aviation W 79:80-1+ S 23 '63
Electron microscope autoradiography of bacteria labeled with iodine-125. N. O. Kuhn and C. G. Harford. bibliog il Science 141: 355-6 Jl 26 '63
Electron microscopes: committee in House urges reinstatement of former tariff on foreign models. E. Langer. Science 139:892-3 Mr 8 '63
Electron microscopes: duty on foreign models restored by House; action in Senate is uncertain. E. Langer. il Science 145:1164-5 S 11 '64
Electron microscopy of single-stranded DNA: circularity of DNA of bacteriophage ΦX174. D. Freifelder and others. bibliog il Science 146:254-5 O 9 '64
Electron microscopy: proteins in experimental pathology; report of symposium at annual meeting of the Federation of American societies for experimental biology. G. W. Richter. Science 141:834-5 Ag 30 '63
Electron microscopy: quantitative techniques; report on symposium. C. E. Hall. Science 145:1467-9 S 25 '64
Electron microscopy; report of meeting of the Electron microscope society. F. W. C. Boswell and G. D. Pappas. il Science 142:686-8 N 8 '63
Electron microscopy; report on symposium of the Biophysical society. M. Beer. Science 144:431 Ap 24 '64
Electronic seeing eye; scanning electron microscope. il(p289) Sci N L 84:292 N 9 '63
Fluorescent, electron microscopic, and immunoelectrophoretic studies of labeled antibodies. K. C. Hsu and others. bibliog il Science 142:1471-3 D 13 '63
Fly's tongue in 3-D. il Life 56:69-70+ My 1 '64
Nerve fibers and terminals: electron microscopy after nauta staining. R. W. Guillery and H. J. Ralston. bibliog il Science 143: 1331-2 Mr 20 '64
New in pathology: a giant jigsaw puzzle. il Todays Health 41:74 Ag '63
Origin of the electron microscope. M. M. Freundlich. bibliog il Science 142:185-8 O 11 '63
Osmiophilic reagents: new cytochemical principle for light and electron microscopy. J. S. Hanker and others. bibliog il Science 146:1039-43 N 20 '64
Ultramicrotome: a simple, easily constructed instrument. M. R. Clevenger. il Science 142: 241-2 O 11 '63
X-ray hazard from electron microsopes; letter. V. A. Phillips and J. A. Hugo. Science 143:1120-1 Mr 13 '64; Reply. F. W. Pauli. 144:1178 Je 5 '64

ELECTRON radiography. See Radiography

ELECTRON tubes
See also
Vacuum tubes

Grids
Receiving tube grid current. A. Szilasi. il Electr World 69:50-1+ F '63

ELECTRONARCOSIS. See Electronic anesthesia

ELECTRONIC aids to navigation
Omega, last word in electronic navigation. A. N. Garden. il Yachting 113:172+ Je '63

ELECTRONIC alarms. See Electric alarms

ELECTRONIC anesthesia
Electronic anesthesia. W. H. Buchsbaum. il Electr World 70:27-9 S '63
Out like a light. il Newsweek 63:66 Mr 23 '64

ELECTRONIC apparatus and appliances
All stations are go! L. Smith. il Hot Rod 16:102-3 D '63
CB buyer's guide. il Pop Electr 21:59-75 Ag '64
CB equipment buyer's guide. il Pop Electr 19:65-92+ Ag '63
Electronics world lab tested. See issues of Electronics world
Frog's-eye view. il Newsweek 61:49 Ap 1 '63
How to identify surplus gear. K. Greenberg. il Pop Electr 20:66-8 Ja '64
Innovation, junior-size. Time 83:88 Je 5 '64
Lowdown on portable electronic flash units. T. Karp. il Mod Phot 28:82-7 Ja '64
Man-made frog's eye. il Time 81:45 Mr 29 '63
New avionic products. See issues of Aviation week & space technology
Procrastinator's companion; picking the winner electronically. R. C. Apperson, jr. il Pop Electr 20:88 Ap '64
Say aah: new inspection device, Flexiscope. il Pop Sci 183:75-6 S '63
Snooperscope television. il Time 81:75 Ap 19 '63
What's coming tomorrow from today's telephones. il U S News 56:60-4 Mr 9 '64
See also
Audio-visual aids
Calculating machines
Guided missiles—Electronic equipment
Translating machines
Traveling wave tubes

Exhibitions
Parts show moves to N.Y; Electronic parts distributors show. W. A. Stocklin. Electr World 72:8 N '64

Noise
AF research aircraft zero in on tracking system noise. M. L. Yaffee. il Aviation W 79: 78-9+ N 11 '63
Sound. J. Wesson. U S Camera 27:32-3 Mr '64

Radiation effects
Effects of radiation on electronic components. E. Tromanhauser. il Electr World 70:76-7 Jl '63
Transient radiation effects on avionics systems. Aviation W 79:97 Ag 19 '63

Testing
Automatic electronic testing. K. Gilmore. il Electr World 71:25-8+ Ja '64
Technique predicts reliability of avionics before initial system design work begins. P. J. Klass. il Aviation W 80:76-7+ Ja 6 '64
Test duplication cut with data exchange; Interservice data exchange program. B. Miller. il Aviation W 79:87+ Jl 15 '63

ELECTRONIC apparatus industry and trade
Case of the dubious deferral: with discussion. D. F. Hawkins. il Harvard Bsns R 41: 162-4+ My '63
Growth, at a price, for transistors. Bsns W p 102+ Ap 6 '63

ELECTRONIC apparatus industry and trade—*Continued*
Stanford: boom in electronics in the San Francisco Bay area was ignited down on the farm. J. Walsh. Science 143:1305-7 Mr 20 '64
See also
Digitronics corporation
Electronics as a profession
Litton industries, incorporated
Philips of Eindhoven companies
Teledyne, incorporated

Advertising

Another numbers game; misuse of power-output figures. W. A. Stocklin. Electr World 70:8 S '63

Wages and hours

Employment and occupational outlook in electronics. J. F. Fulton and R. B. Flanders. il Mo Labor R 86:1026-32 S '63

France

Bull at the altar; deal with Machines Bull. Fortune 70:59-60+ S '64
GE and Bull. Newsweek 64:65 Ag 3 '64
GE and Gen. de Gaulle; General electric co. to buy Compagnie des Machines Bull. Newsweek 63:88+ Ap 27 '64
Gored Bull; Compagnie des Machines Bull. Time 83:90-1 F 14 '64
Machines Bull hits bearish times; La compagnie des Machines Bull. il Bsns W p58+ Ja 25 '64
Machines Bull's computer crisis; France's proud business-machine firm. T. R. Bransten and S. H. Brown. il Fortune 70:154-5+ Jl '64

Great Britain

Britain seeks stimulus for advanced R&D. P. J. Klass. il Aviation W 81:92-3+ S 7 '64
British emphasize thin-film microcircuits. il Aviation W 81:97+ S 14 '64
Many specialties mark avionic producers. il Aviation W 81:115-16+ S 7 '64

Italy

See also
Olivetti

Japan

Sony's purposeful dreams. il Fortune 70:83-4+ Jl '64

United States

Another numbers game; misuse of power-output figures. W. A. Stocklin. Electr World 70:8 S '63
Competition tightens for avionics dollars. P. J. Klass. il Aviation W 80:225-7+ Mr 16 '64
Competition to tighten in semiconductors. B. Miller. il Aviation W 79:56-9+ S 23 '63
Electronic parts show. W. A. Stocklin. Electr World 72:6 Ag '64
$15.1-billion electronics market in 1963. W. A. Stocklin. il Electr World 69:8 Ap '63
Higher profit margin called avionics need; address. D. H. Putnam. il Aviation W 81:105+ O 26 '64
Industry. See issues of Missiles and rockets to March 5, 1963
Looking beyond our problems. W. A. Stocklin. Electr World 72:6 S '64
Microcircuit users seek expanded role. B. Miller. il Aviation W 81:107-9+ S 14 '64
Microcircuitry production growth outpaces applications. B. Miller. il Aviation W 81:76-7+ N 16 '64
Microcircuits stimulate avionic changes. B. Miller. il Aviation W 78:237-8+ Mr 11 '63
New Year & the old. W. A. Stocklin. Electr World 71:10 Mr '64
R&D: new awareness in Congress of stimulus of federal research stirs envy of areas like Boston. J. Walsh. Science 139:1273-5 Mr 29 '63
Sperry gyro gets new spin; Information & communications div. il Bsns W p45-6 O 12 '63
Test duplication cut with data exchange; Interservice data exchange program. B. Miller. il Aviation W 79:87+ Jl 15 '63
See also
Litton industries,incorporated

ELECTRONIC cables. See Electric cables

ELECTRONIC calculating machines. See Calculating machines

ELECTRONIC cameras. See Cameras

ELECTRONIC circuits
Adaptive computer utilizes microcircuits. B. Miller. il Aviation W 80:87-9+ My 11 '64
AF pushes work on IC exploitation. M. Getler. Miss & Roc 15:22-3 N 23 '64
Avionics demands spur microcircuit sales. B. Miller. il Aviation W 79:63-5+ D 23 '63
Beyond the transistor. il Time 83:89-90 F 7 '64
Bootstrap circuits. G. J. Deboo. il Electr World 72:66-7 Jl '64
British emphasize thin-film microcircuits. il Aviation W 81:97+ S 14 '64
Building a profit circuit out of antique tubes. il Bsns W p 118-19 N 21 '64
Circuit weight slashed in advanced Minuteman. R. Pay. il Miss & Roc 14:35 Mr 2 '64
Design seen as interim solution to circuit irradiation. M. Getler. Miss & Roc 14:37-8 Mr 2 '64
Device speeds special microcircuit masks. P. J. Klass. il Aviation W 82:67+ Ja 25 '65
Electron beam technique makes, inspects semiconductor microcircuits. P. J. Klass. il Aviation W 79:80-1+ S 23 '63
Feasibility of digital microcircuits tested. B. Miller. il Aviation W 80:83-6, 89 F 10 '64
Frequency multiplication & division. L. E. Frenzel, jr. il Electr World 70:53-6 S '63
Graphite masking technique developed for thin-film circuits. M. Getler. Miss & Roc 14:35-6 Ap 27 '64
In-line vacuum ups thin film output. M. Getler. il Miss & Roc 12:35-6 Ap 22 '63
Integrated circuits. L. Solomon. il Electr World 72:27-32 S '64
Micro electronics, state of the art; integrated circuits improving in quality, dropping in cost. il Miss & Roc 14:50-2+ F 3 '64
Microcircuit plant to serve in-house need. P. J. Klass. il Aviation W 80:66-9 Mr 9 '64
Microcircuit radiation problems probed. B. Miller. il Aviation W 79:93-4+ Ag 19 '63
Microcircuit technique uses gold support. P. J. Klass. il Aviation W 81:98-9+ N 9 '64
Microcircuit technology shows versatility; equipments shown at National aerospace electronics conference. P. J. Klass. il Aviation W 80:59+ Je 1 '64
Microcircuit users seek expanded role. B. Miller. il Aviation W 81:107-9+ S 14 '64
Microcircuitry production growth outpaces applications. B. Miller. il Aviation W 81:76-7+ N 16 '64
Microcircuits stimulate avionic changes. B. Miller. il Aviation W 78:237-8+ Mr 11 '63
Microcircuits survive Van Allen belt. Aviation W 79:101 Ag 19 '63
Navy expands microcircuitry program. P. J. Klass. il Aviation W 79:89-90 Jl 1 '63
New facility is designed for microcircuits. P. J. Klass. il Aviation W 79:114-15+ S 16 '63
New Motorola plant produces semiconductor microcircuits. il Aviation W 80:57 Mr 30 '64
New product, old problem. Bsns W p63 Ap 4 '64
Panel appraises outlook for microcircuits. P. J. Klass. il Aviation W 80:79+ Ap 6 '64
Plumbing the microwave circuit. R. C. Apperson, jr. il Electr World 71:23-5 Je '64
RCA makes new type of small microcircuit. Aviation W 78:104 F 11 '63
Science of vanishing electronics; integrated circuits. L. Stern. il Sci Digest 55:44-7 Je '64
Shrunken circuits. il Time 83:51 Ap 3 '64
Snap-in breadboard. L. Vicens. il Pop Electr 19:54-5 Jl '63
Study forecasts microcircuitry growth. B. Miller. il Aviation W 78:84+ F 25 '63
Super microcircuit chips appear feasible. P. J. Klass. il Aviation W 81:77+ D 14 '64
Thin-film transistor research pressed. B. Miller. il Aviation W 78:68-9+ F 4 '63
USAF seeks new microcircuit techniques. P. J. Klass. il Aviation W 78:81+ Je 17 '63
Use of infrared testing technique grows. P. J. Klass. il Aviation W 80:82+ My 4 '64
See also
Calculating machines—Circuits
Guided missiles—Electronic equipment
Printed circuits
Transistor circuits
Vacuum-tube circuits

Quality control

Electrolytic growth of silver dendrites. W. A. Ainsworth. bibliog il Science 146:1294-5 D 4 '64

ELECTRONIC clocks. See Clocks, Electronic

ELECTRONIC conductors. See Semiconductors

ELECTRONIC cooking
Four-minute cake; microwave ovens. Bsns W p94+ S 12 '64
Two-minute oven. il Time 82:95-6 O 25 '63

ELECTRONIC data processing
ADP, the still-sleeping giant. J. Diebold. il Harvard Bsns R 42:60-5 S '64

ELECTRONIC data processing—*Continued*
Automatic information processing in western Europe. G. Salton. bibliog Science 144:626-32 My 8 '64
Bendix gives up on computers; sale of Computer div. to CDC. Bsns W p36 Mr 9 '63
Buying computers by the dozen; desk-sized Monrobot XI. Bsns W p45-6 Jl 20 '63
Charity that got help; fund accounting system for World council of churches. Bsns W p64 O 24 '64
Committee will study use of ADP; automatic data processing. Miss & Roc 15:15 S 28 '64
Computer services for schools; UPDATE, Iowa program introducing automation of clerical tasks. Sch & Soc 91:274+ O 5 '63
Computers may tip the scale of justice. il Bsns W p45-6 Ag 22 '64
Data-processing subsystem to refine air force's 473L Pentagon complex. R. Pay. il Miss & Roc 15:26-7 Ag 17 '64
Data-processing subsystem aids Zeus development. M. Getler. Miss & Roc 14:32 Ja 20 '64
Data processing's role in city government. E. F. R. Hearle. Am City 79:140+ My '64
Data system used in production control; ADA system. H. D. Watkins. il Aviation W 79:62+ Ag 26 '63
Decision theory in law, science, and technology. T. A. Cowan. bibliog Science 140:1065-75 Je 7 '63; Reply. I. Kraft. 143:99-100 Ja 10 '64
Electronics: new force in hospital design. J. Falick. il Arch Forum 120:90-1 Ap '64
Estimating bids by computer; Estimat. il Bsns W p80+ N 23 '63
Figures in a flash; Ampex's videofile system. il Time 84:80-1 Ag 21 '64
473L to aid in worldwide USAF control. B. Miller. il Aviation W 81:49+ Ag 3 '64
Impact of office automation in the Internal revenue service. R. W. Riche and J. R. Alliston. il Mo Labor R 86:388-93 Ap '63
Kicking the ostrich; ALA preconference institute on data processing. Library J 89:2949-52 Ag '64; Reply. R. M. Dougherty. 89:3520+ O 1 '64
Make data processing work for you; uses in Euclid, Ohio. A. B. Baldwin. il Am City 79:105-6 F '64
Making money? find out by mail. C. W. Gifford. il Farm J 87:22-3+ Ag '63
Millennium for decision makers; Lockheed aircraft corp. il Bsns W p54+ Ag 10 '63
Office technology: the big leap forward. K. August. il Duns R 84:pt2 118-19+ S '64
1.2 seconds per bill; Los Angeles County's electronic data-processing system. J. R. Quinn. il Am City 78:105 My '63
Planning for instructional improvement; Curriculum testing project of George Peabody college for teachers. W. S. Graybeal. NEA J 52:22 O '63
Poet is a computer; reprint. il Sci Digest 55:70-1 F '64
Production's new brew; remote data-gathering systems. H. E. Klein. il Duns R 82:38-40+ O '63
Revolution in office work; meaning for jobs, business. il U S News 54:84-6+ My 13 '63
State computer analyzes city traffic; Green Bay, Wis. M. L. Bacon, jr. il Am City 79:84-5 D '64
Steel company's date with a data machine; total systems concept. Bsns W p 142+ My 4 '63
Total information service in Chicago schools. Sch & Soc 91:328 N 2 '63
Univac for the defense; automation can save a lawyer time. Newsweek 62:55 D 16 '63
Versatile passkey to communication; new standard communications code for data transmission. il Bsns W p 128+ Je 15 '63
Wanted: 500,000 men to feed computers. S. L. Englebardt. il Pop Sci 186:106-9 Ja '65
Who really started World war 1? W. S. Bacon. il Pop Electr 20:40-2+ Ap '64; Same abr. with title Computer tells who started World war 1. Sci Digest 56:44-7 Jl '64
You can't beat electronic data processing; Roseville, Minn. R. W. Turnlund. il Am City 78:97-8 Jl '63
See also
Data processing centers
Data tapes
Programming languages (calculating machines)

Study and teaching

Plan for teaching teachers of data processing. R. M. Knoebel. il Sch Life 46:7-10 D '63

ELECTRONIC engineers. See Electric engineers
ELECTRONIC equipment. See Electronic apparatus and appliances; Electronic apparatus industry and trade
ELECTRONIC equipment, Miniature. See Miniature electronic equipment
ELECTRONIC flash bulbs. See Electric lamps, Flashlight
ELECTRONIC flash photography. See Photography, Flashlight
ELECTRONIC flash units. See Electric lamps, Flashlight
ELECTRONIC industries association
EIA defines high fidelity. W. A. Stocklin. Electr World 69:6 Mr '63
Pros and cons of wideband response N. Eisenberg. il Hi Fi 14:39-42+ My '64
ELECTRONIC jewelry. See Jewelry
ELECTRONIC listening devices. See Electronics in criminal investigation, espionage, etc.
ELECTRONIC love; opera. See Kosma, J.
ELECTRONIC measurements
See also
Oscillographs
Testing instruments
ELECTRONIC medical apparatus. See Medical instruments and apparatus
ELECTRONIC monitoring. See Electronics in criminal investigation, espionage, etc.
ELECTRONIC music. See Music, Electronic
ELECTRONIC organ. See Organ
ELECTRONIC ovens
Four-minute cake; microwave ovens. Bsns W p94+ S 12 '64
Two-minute oven. il Time 82:95-6 O 25 '63
ELECTRONIC pacemaker. See Medical instruments and apparatus
ELECTRONIC printing machine. See Printing machinery
ELECTRONIC reading machines. See Reading machines
ELECTRONIC relays
Electronic time-delay relays. L. E. Frenzel, jr. il Electr World 72:44-5 D '64
ELECTRONIC service
Radio & TV news. See issues of Electronics world
ELECTRONIC service shops
Radio & TV news. See issues of Electronics world
See also
National alliance of television and electronic service associations
ELECTRONIC stoves
See also
Electronic cooking
ELECTRONIC switches. See Electric switches
ELECTRONIC technicians. See Electric workers
ELECTRONIC test instruments. See Testing instruments
ELECTRONIC thermometers. See Thermometers and thermometry
ELECTRONIC timers. See Timing devices
ELECTRONIC traffic signal control. See Traffic signals—Control
ELECTRONIC vacuum pumps. See Vacuum pumps
ELECTRONIC watches. See Watches
ELECTRONICS
Carl and Jerry. J. T. Frye. See issues of Popular electronics
Color codes chart. il Electr World 70:35-6 Ag '63
Electronic instrumentation for oil exploration. L. E. Frenzel. jr. il Electr World 70:27-30+ D '63
Electronics in the home. W. A. Stocklin. Electr World 70:8 O '63
Human factors in electronics; 5th national symposium, San Diego Calif, May, 1964. W. E. Woodson and M. Freitag. Science 145:418+ Jl 24 '64
Now anyone can understand electronics. il Sci Digest 54:59-62 Ag '63
Recent developments in electronics. See issues of Electronics world
What life will be like when the machines take over; interview. S. Ramo. il U S News 54:64-8 Je 24 '63
See also
Electroencephalography
Electronic aids to navigation
Miniature electronic equipment
National electronics conference

Anecdotes, facetiae, satire, etc.

She wore a red germanium. L. F. Ide. il Pop Electr 22:58-9+ Ja '65
Wonderful world of lids. C. Moon. il Pop Electr 21:69-70+ D '64

ELECTRONICS—*Continued*

Bibliography

New literature (title varies) See issues of Missiles and rockets

Pop'tronics bookshelf. See issues of Popular electronics

Military applications

Electronics priority given to A-ICBM, ASW, command & control. il Miss & Roc 14:113+ Mr 30 '64

Nomenclature

New nomenclature; standard prefixes. E. G. Louis. il Pop Electr 19:71 S '63

Photographic applications

See Electrophotography

Study and teaching

Going native the electronics way; Eskimos, Alaskan Indians, training in New York. il Bsns W p52-3 F 29 '64

San Francisco's PALS starts them young. A. Corona and R. Corona. il Pop Electr 19:55-6 D '63

ELECTRONICS, Medical. See Medical electronics

ELECTRONICS as a profession

Going native the electronics way; Eskimos, Alaskan Indians, training in New York. il Bsns W p52-3 F 29 '64

Jobs of the future; reprint. P. Haase and F. Lynn. il Sci Digest 56:20-4 N '64

See also

Electric workers

ELECTRONICS engineers. See Engineers

ELECTRONICS in criminal investigation, espionage, etc.

Are they listening in on you? E. D. Fales, jr. il Pop Sci 186:96-9+ Ja '65

Bug thy neighbor. il Time 83:55-6 Mr 6 '64; Same abr. Read Digest 84:143-5 Je '64

Invaders; rapid erosion of privacy. il Newsweek 63:81-2 Mr 9 '64

Invasion of privacy; excerpts from Naked society. V. Packard. Atlan 213:55-61 F '64

Moscow bughouse; microphones planted inside walls of U.S. embassy in Moscow. Time 83:28 My 29 '64

Russia's U-2: hidden microphones in U.S. embassy walls. il U S News 56:6 Je 1 '64

Snoopers: use of snooping gadgets by federal agencies. Newsweek 65:23-4 F 1 '65

Ubiquitous bugs and our privacy. Life 56:4 Je 12 '64

Walls do have ears; electronic art of listening in. V. Packard. il N Y Times Mag p23+ S 20 '64

Walls have ears; wall microphones discovered in U.S. embassy in Moscow. il Newsweek 63:32 Je 1 '64

When walls have ears, call a debugging man; business counter-espionage experts use electronic listening devices. il Bsns W p 154+ O 31 '64

See also

Wire tapping

ELECTRONICS in photography

Where is electronics leading photography? E. Nanas. il Pop Phot 54:78-9+ F '64

ELECTRONICS in traffic control

Electronic genie speeds traffic through 1,001 lights; Toronto. G. McCaffrey. il Pop Sci 185:76-7+ S '64

Electronics de-irritate on intersection; Austin, Tex. W. H. Klapproth. il Am City 78:86-7 Jl '63

Electronics recorder speeds bus travel; Chicago. il Am City 78:109 F '63

ELECTRONICS industry and trade. See Electronic apparatus industry and trade

ELECTRONICS research

Boston center finds Capitol critics; with editorial comment by W. J. Coughlin. W. Beller. il Miss & Roc 12:18-19, 50 Ap 22 '63

ELECTRONICS research center. See United States—National aeronautics and space administration—Electronics research center

ELECTRONICS world (periodical)

Special issue. W. A. Stocklin. Electr World 70:6 Ag '63

ELECTRONS

Bent chemical bonds. W. H. Flygare. bibliog il Science 140:1179-85 Je 14 '63

Fleeting particles form each second in everyone; hydrated electrons. il Sci N L 83:147 Mr 9 '63

Hydrated electron. E. J. Hart. bibliog il Science 146:19-25 O 2 '64

Hydrated electron: production and role in photobiology. G. W. Swenson and others. bibliog il Science 141:1042-3 S 13 '63

Large electron pulses in hydrocarbons. A. H. Samuel and others. bibliog Science 144:839 My 15 '64

Photochemical generation of the hydrated electron. L. I. Grossweiner and others. bibliog il Science 141:805-6 Ag 30 '63

Photochemical production of the solvated electron in ethanol. L. I. Grossweiner and others. bibliog il Science 141:1180 S 20 '63

Pressure and electronic structure. H. G. Drickamer. bibliog il Science 142:1429-35 D 13 '63

Wet electron. Sci Am 208:82-3 Ap '63

See also

Fermi surfaces

Plasma (ionized gases)

Positrons

Beams

Beam that can cut anything. il Sci Digest 53:4-5 F '63

Electron beam readout shows potential. B. Miller. il Aviation W 80:107-10 Ap 13 '64

Diffraction

Low-energy electron diffraction; improved experimental methods provide new information on the structure of surfaces of solids. A. U. MacRae. bibliog il Science 139:379-88 F 1 '63

Emission

Advances in field emission. W. P. Dyke. il Sci Am 210:108-16+ bibliog(p 152) Ja '64

See also

Thermionic emission

ELECTRO-OPTICAL systems, incorporated

EOS research to better ion engines. J. F. Judge. il Miss & Roc 12:28-9 Ap 22 '63

Surface tension is energy source; EOS ion rocket systems. R. Hawkes. il Miss & Roc 15:24-6 S 7 '64

ELECTROOPTICS

Electro-optics; report, comp. by C. D. LaFond. il Miss & Roc 14:23-31+ Je 1 '64

ELECTROOSMOSIS

Synaptic learning due to electroosmosis: a theory. J. B. Ranck, jr. bibliog il Science 144:187-9 Ap 10 '64

ELECTROPHORESIS

Blood brothers: man and ape. il Newsweek 63:52 Mr 2 '64

Disc electrophoresis of hymenoptera venoms and body proteins. R. O'Connor and others. bibliog il Science 145:1320-1 S 18 '64

Electrophoretic patterns of hemoglobin from fetal mice of different inbred strains. M. L. Craig and E. S. Russell. bibliog il Science 142:398-9 O 18 '63

Immuno-osmophoresis, a rapid and sensitive method for evaluating viruses. H. W. J. Ragetli and M. Weintraub. bibliog il Science 144:1023-4 My 22 '64

Nucleotides: separation from an alkaline hydrolysate of RNA by thin-layer electrophoresis. F. M. DeFilippes. bibliog il Science 144:1350-1 Je 12 '64

Protein purification by elution convection electrophoresis. S. Raymond. bibliog il Science 146:406-7 O 16 '64

Separation of microsomal RNA into five bands during agar electrophoresis. R. Bachvaroff and P. R. B. McMaster. bibliog il Science 143:1177-9 Mr 13 '64

ELECTROPHORUS. See Electric eels

ELECTROPHOTOGRAPHY

Future techniques; electrically-charged picture-taking system. J. Reidy. U S Camera 26:12+ D '63

Human bone marrow distribution shown in vivo by iron-52 and the positron scintillation camera. H. O. Anger and D. C. Van Dyke. bibliog il Science 144:1587-9 Je 26 '64

ELECTROPHYSIOLOGY

Adaptation in stretch receptor neurons of crayfish. S. Nakajima. bibliog il Science 146:1168-70 N 27 '64

Antidromic inhibition accompanied by ventral root positivities. R. Werman. bibliog il Science 143:824-5 F 21 '64

Conduction of the action potential in the frog ventricle. W. G. Van Der Kloot and B. Dane. bibliog il Science 146:74-5 O 2 '64

Control of the brain. R. Coughlan. il Life 54:90-2+ Mr 8 '63

Eel electroplaques: spike electrogenesis without potassium activation. Y. Nakamura and others. bibliog il Science 146:266-8 O 9 '64

Electric pleasure. Newsweek 61:60 My 20 '63

Electrical activity of the nervous system. M. A. B. Brazier. bibliog Science 146:1423-8 D 11 '64

Electrical device implantation in animals studied. H. M. David. il Miss & Roc 13:18 Jl 22 '63

ELECTROPHYSIOLOGY—*Continued*
Electrical transmission at an excitatory synapse in a vertebrate brain. E. J. Furshpan. bibliog il Science 144:878-80 My 15 '64
Electrochemical coupling in potentiation of muscular contraction. A. Sandow and others. bibliog il Science 143:577-9 F 7 '64
Electroconvulsive threshold elevation: from daily stimulation of adrenalectomized animals. C. F. Essig and others. bibliog il Science 140:828-9 My 17 '63
Electronic junctions between teleost spinal neurons: electrophysiology and ultrastructure. M. V. L. Bennett and others. bibliog il Science 141:262-4 Jl 19 '63
Excitation and conduction in nerve: quantitative analysis; address, December 11, 1963. A. F. Huxley. bibliog il Science 145:1154-9 S 11 '64
Getting under your skin; power from the bodies of rats. Time 82:40 Jl 26 '63
Inhibitory postsynaptic potentials in grasshopper muscle. P. N. R. Usherwood and H. Grundfest. bibliog il Science 143:817-18 F 21 '64
Intercellular electrical coupling at a forming membrane junction in a dividing cell. R. F. Ashman and others. bibliog il Science 145: 604-5 Ag 7 '64
Intracellular perfusion of Chilean giant squid axons. I. Tasaki and M. Luxoro. bibliog il Science 145:1313-15 S 18 '64
Intracellular regulatory mechanisms. H. E. Umbarger. bibliog il Science 145:674-9 Ag 14 '64
Ionic basis of nervous conduction; address, December 11, 1963. A. L. Hodgkin. bibliog il Science 145:1148-54 S 11 '64
Ionic mechanism of postsynaptic inhibition; adapted from address, December 10, 1963. J. C. Eccles. bibliog il Science 145:1140-7 S 11 '64
Nerve fibers and terminals: electron microscopy after nauta staining. R. W. Guillery and H. J. Ralston. bibliog il Science 143: 1331-2 Mr 20 '64
Non-electric catfish respond to electricity. Sci N L 84:52 Jl 27 '63
Nucleus of the trapezoid body: dual afferent innervation. J. M. Harrison and R. Irving. bibliog il Science 143:473-4 Ja 31 '64
Olfactory discrimination: electrophysiological spatiotemporal basis. M. M. Mozell. bibliog il Science 143:1336-7 Mr 20 '64
Rat's body electricity powers radio signals. Sci N L 84:116 Ag 24 '63
Reaction time as a function of the cardiac cycle in young adults. J. E. Birren and others. bibliog il Science 140:195-6 Ap 12 '63
Separation of transducer and impulse-generating processes in sensory receptors. W. R. Loewenstein and others. bibliog il Science 142:1180-1 N 29 '63
Signal analysis of evoked potentials recorded from cats during conditioning. E. R. John and others. bibliog il Science 141:429-31 Ag 2 '63
Simultaneous studies of firing patterns in several neurons. G. L. Gerstein and W. A. Clark. bibliog il Science 143:1325-7 Mr 20 '64
Skin impedance and phase angle as a function of frequency and current. R. Plutchik and H. R. Hirsch. bibliog il Science 141:927-8 S 6 '63
Skin resistance levels and galvanic skin response: unilateral differences. P. A. Obrist. bibliog Science 139:227-8 Ja 18 '63
See also
Brain waves
Electric organs in fishes
Electroencephalography
Electronic anesthesia
Medical electronics

Apparatus

Auditory nuclei: distinctive response patterns to white noise and tones in unanesthetized cats. D. Galin. bibliog il Science 146:270-2 O 9 '64

ELECTROPHYSIOLOGY of plants
Electrical resistance of cell membranes of avena coleoptiles. N. Higinbotham and others. bibliog il Science 143:1448-9 Mr 27 '64

ELECTROPLATING
Electroplating component has many uses. il Aviation W 80:93-7+ F 10 '64

ELECTRORETINOGRAPHY
Flicker fusion frequency of electroretinogram in light-adapted goldfish at various temperatures. I. Hanyu and M. A. Ali. bibliog il Science 140:662-3 My 10 '63
Mangabey *x* and *b* wave electroretinogram components: their dark-adapted luminosity functions. A. E. Jones and others. bibliog il Science 146:1486-7 D 11 '64
Rat electroretinogram: evidence for separate processes governing b-wave latency and amplitude. R. A. Cone and J. R. Platt. bibliog il Science 144:1016-19 My 22 '64

ELECTROSTATIC generators. See Electric generators, Electrostatic

ELECTROSTATIC loudspeakers. See Loud speaking apparatus

ELECTROSTATIC precipitators. See Electric precipitators

ELECTROSTATIC printing. See Xerography

ELECTROSTIMULATION of the brain. See Electrophysiology

ELECTROTHERAPY
Wired for health; electro-clotting and electro-pacing. il Time 84:82 Jl 10 '64
See also
Shock therapy

ELEGANCE. See Fashion

ELEGANT, Robert S.
Between East and West: a Rumanian visit. Newsweek 62:33-4 Ag 5 '63

ELEKTRA; opera. See Strauss, R.

ELEMENTARY education. See Education, Elementary

ELEMENTARY particles. See Particles (nuclear physics)

ELEMENTARY school buildings. See School buildings

ELEMENTARY school children. See School children

ELEMENTARY school counselors. See School counselors

ELEMENTARY school libraries. See School libraries

ELEMENTARY school newspapers. See College and school journalism

ELEMENTARY school teachers. See Teachers

ELEMENTARY school teaching. See Teaching

ELEMENTS, Chemical. See Chemical elements

ELEPHANT hunting
Double take on elephant. J. M. Barker. il Outdoor Life 132:32-5+ N '63
Elephant. J. O'Connor. il Outdoor Life 134: 56-9+ S '64
My first elephant hunt. N. Contini. il Seventeen 23:86-7+ Ja '64
My last safari. R. Ruark. il Sat Eve Post 236:76-81 Ap 27 '63

ELEPHANT seals
How to milk a seal. A. Hills. il Life 56:39-40+ Mr 27 '64
Life underwater. il Newsweek 63:57 Mr 9 '64

ELEPHANTS
Alas, poor elephas! he's losing class. Time 82:32 D 13 '63
Buddhist elephant worship. L. E. Springer. il Hobbies 68:51 S '63
Lysergic acid diethylamide: its effects on a male Asiatic elephant. L. J. West and others; reply. P. D. Harwood. Science 139: 684-5 F 15 '63
Ma's helping trunk. il Life 54:113-14 Mr 8 '63
Placenta of the Indian elephant, elephas indicus. R. A. Cooper and others. bibliog il Science 146:410-12 O 16 '64

ELEPHANTS, Fossil
Archaeologists discover headless elephants; Europe. Sci N L 83:104 F 16 '63

ELESKA, Elena
Andean handicrafts. M. de Ortega. il por Américas 15:29-32 Je '63

ELEVATORS
Elevatoring high-rise apartment buildings. G. R. Strakosch. il Arch Rec 135:191-2+ Je '64
Going down. Newsweek 62:53 D 23 '63
Hillside lifts for people and cargo. il Sunset 133:145-6 N '64
Up you go, by incline elevator. il Sunset 130:102+ F '63
See also
Otis elevator company

ELEVATORS, Grain. See Grain elevators

1109 Klingenstein; story. See Rogin, G.

ELF owls. See Owls

ELFANT, Robert F. See Charap, S. H. jr. auth.

ELFIN, Mel
Great air-fare snare. Reporter 30:36-8 Mr 12 '64
School aid: can Dean Keppel call the class to order? Reporter 28:32-5 Mr 14 '63

ELGER, Thomas Gwyn
Some lunar studies by T. G. Elger. G. Fielder. il por Sky & Tel 25:248-51 My '63

EL HAFEZ, Amin. See Hafez, A.

ELIADE, Mircea
Mircea Eliade and the dialectic of the sacred, by T. J. J. Altizer. Review
Christian Cent 81:179-80 F 5 '64. E. J. Jurji
ELIAS, Eileen
Big questions little ones ask. Parents Mag 39:38-9+ Jl '64
ELIAS, Rosalind
Quiet type; interview, ed. by J. W. Freeman. por Opera N 28:33 F 29 '64
ELIASBERG, Ann Pringle
Parent and child (cont) N Y Times Mag p61-3 Je 9; 34 Jl 14; 94 O 13; 28 D 22 '63; 87+ Ap 26; 79-80 My 17; 42 Je 21; 39 Jl 26; 112+ N 1; 87-8 D 13; 38 D 20 '64
ELIASBERG, Louis E.
Mr Coin collector: he has them all. il por Look 28:54-5 D 29 '64
EL INGA excavations. See Excavations (archeology)
ELIOT, Alexander
Buddy and the Bruegel. Vogue 145:132-3+ F 1 '65
Manslaughter born of a fixed race. Sports Illus 21:104-8+ O 5 '64
Speaking out. por Sat Eve Post 237:12+ Ag 22 '64
ELIOT, George Fielding
Battle saga in the great tradition. Nat R 14:161 F 26 '63
Diplomat and warrior in tandem. Nat R 16:827-9 S 22 '64
Diplomatic folly. Nat R 16:915 O 20 '64
France and her army. Nat R 15:27 Jl 16 '63
Sword of unlimited war. Nat R 15:198+ S 10 '63
ELIOT, Martha M.
Let's get behind the bold new program to combat mental retardation in children! por Parents Mag 38:38 Ap '63
ELIOT, Thomas Stearns
Greatness in moderation. J. F. Nims. por Sat R 46:25-7 O 19 '63
In memoriam: T. S. Eliot. F. Sweeney. America 112:120-1 Ja 23 '65
Journey to simplicity. H. Hewes. il Sat R 48:53-4 Ja 23 '65
Last trip to East Coker. Christian Cent 82:68 Ja 20 '65
Letter to a foreign friend; tr. by N. Valaorites. G. Seferis. Poetry 105:50-9 O '64
Notes and comment. New Yorker 40:25 Ja 16 '65
Obituary
Pub W 187:69-70 Ja 11 '65
On the death of T. S. Eliot; poems. Commonweal 81:576 Ja 29 '65
Reading Eliot today. F. Kermode. Nation 197:263-4 O 26 '63
Seven-year shaman. H. Kenner. por Nat R 16:113-14 F 11 '64
T. S. Eliot. C. Aiken. il pors Life 58:92-3 Ja 15 '65
T. S. Eliot. por Time 85:86-7 Ja 15 '65
Thomas Stearns Eliot: 1888-1965. J. Ciardi. por Sat R 48:34-6 Ja 23 '65
T. S. Eliot 1888-1965. R. Whittemore. New Repub 152:28 Ja 16 '65
T. S. Eliot 1888-1965. pors Newsweek 65:70-1 Ja 18 '65
T. S. Eliot, RIP. H. Kenner. por Nat R 17:63-4 Ja 26 '65
ELISABETH, consort of Francis Joseph I, emperor of Austria
Franz Josef: a Habsburg marriage. L. Bemelmans. Holiday 35:68-9+ Ja '64
ELISOFON, Eliot
Greatest story ever told. il Life 56:54-67 Mr 27 '64
Nile. il U S Camera 27:40-7 My '64
People from paradise. J. Morris. il U S Camera 27:34-7 Jl '64
ELIZABETH I, queen of England
Other Elizabeth. E. Jenkins. il por Opera N 28:8-13 Mr 7 '64
ELIZABETH II, queen of Great Britain
Friendly royal sisters. il Look 28:91-3 S 22 '64
Great expectations. por Newsweek 62:44+ S 30 '63
Guns boom in Fiji, pipes skirl down under: gentlemen, the Queen. il por Life 54:53-4 Mr 22 '63
Help! the Queen is coming. D. Connelly. il Life 54:12 F 15 '63; Same abr. with title Queen is coming! Read Digest 83:192C-192D+ Ag '63
Queen Elizabeth II. R. T. Elson. il pors Life 56:75-84+ Mr 6 '64
Queen wins the heart of New Zealand; photographs. O. Atkins. Sat Eve Post 236:26-9 Ap 27 '63
Vogue's notebook; tour in New Zealand and Australia; photographs. Vogue 141:44-5 My '63
Weight of St. Edward's crown; photographs. N Y Times Mag p 10-11 Je 2 '63
Welcome arrival; birth of her fourth child. il Newsweek 63:44 Mr 23 '64
When the Queen has a baby. R. Lecler. il por Good H 158:86-7+ F '64

Visit to Canada, 1964

Canada, U.S. drift toward unity; with editorial comment. il por Bsns W p24-5, 192 O 17 '64
Morning after. Time 84:43 O 23 '64
Mounties at work. il por Newsweek 64:61 O 19 '64
Queen & the chill. il por Time 84:53 O 16 '64
Queen's tour: ceremony and controversy. il por U S News 57:24 O 19 '64
Royal visit. C. Cochrane. Christian Cent 81:1381 N 4 '64
Uncertain welcome; visit to Canada. Time 84:39 O 9 '64
ELIZABETH, N.J.
New government+centralized purchasing=increased efficiency. S. H. Stone. il Am City 78:102-3 Ap '63

Riots

Black rage in New Jersey. Time 84:19 Ag 21 '64
White boycott; racial violence in Paterson and Elizabeth, N.J. Newsweek 64:27+ Ag 24 '64
ELIZABETHAN period. See Great Britain—History—Elizabethan period
ELIZALDE, R. M.
Operation Badajoz; Spain's TVA. Am For 69:24-7 F '63
ELIZONDO, E. L.
European receiving-tube numbering system. Electr World 70:74 N '63
ELK
Baby elk of White River Forest. D. Harbour. il Audubon Mag 66:35 Ja '64
Needed: a permanent refuge for California's tule elk. M. A. Rock. il Nat Parks Mag 38:8-11+ Je '64
Struggle in Owens Valley; conservation of tule elk. A. A. Amaral. il Am For 70:26-7+ Ag '64
Too many elk. T. Trueblood. il Field & S 68:36-9+ Jl '63
World's smallest elk and the rarest. il Sunset 130:24+ My '63
ELK hunting
Bugle call for a bull elk. E. A. Bauer. il Field & S 68:21-3+ Ag '63
Bulls of Oyster Creek. E. A. Bauer. il Outdoor Life 134:48-51+ S '64
Elk hunt in Virginia? ed. by G. H. Gillelan. T. Somerville. il Outdoor Life 135:42-3+ Ja '65
Elk in the tall timber. N. H. Jensen. il Field & S 69:40-2+ S '64
Elk on the roof. W. J. MacRae. il Outdoor Life 134:48-9+ N '64
I had trouble with elk. T. Howell. il Outdoor Life 134:50-3+ O '64
Medicine for elk and moose. J. O'Connor. il Outdoor Life 132:60-4 Ag '63
Now is the time. T. Trueblood. il Field & S 68:16+ Ja '64
Saddlebag safari. C. Elliott. il Outdoor Life 132:40-3+ N '63
ELKAYAM, Oshra
Oshra and Kazuko and companies at 92nd street Y. J. Maskey. Dance Mag 38:62 Mr '64
ELKHART, Ind.

Education

Economics with ABC's. il Bsns W p 186-8+ Mr 21 '64
ELKHART, Ind, public library
Elkhart corners space. R. E. Kellogg. il Library J 88:4543-4 D 1 '63
ELKIN, Stanley
Boswell steps out; story. Esquire 62:64-9 Jl '64
Miss Taylor and family: an outside view. Esquire 62:118-20+ N '64
Realism and fantasy. J. Ciardi. Sat R 47:6 Ag 15 '64
Transient; story. Sat Eve Post 237:54-60 Ap 25 '64
ELKIND, M. M. and others
Actinomycin D: suppression of recovery in X-irradiated mammalian cells. bibliog Science 143:1454-7 Mr 27 '64
ELKOFF, Marvin W.
American painter as a blue chip. Esquire 63:36-42+ Ja '65
Everybody knows his name. Esquire 62:59-64+ Ag '64
Playing off Keefe; story. Esquire 61:80-1+ Je '64

ELLE (periodical) See Periodicals—France

ELLEDGE, Eugene. See Brooks, M. jt. auth.

ELLEN, Paul, and Powell, E. W.
Timing behavior after lesions of zona incerta and mammillary body. bibliog Science 141:828-30 Ag 30 '63

ELLENBOGEN, Eileen
Vinaigrettes. Antiques 83:214-17 F '63

ELLENBOGEN, Henry
Space age electronics; address, June 16, 1964. Vital Speeches 30:662-5 Ag 15 '64

ELLENDER, Allen Joseph
Casebook of a southern senator. D. Schoenbrun. il por Esquire 60:104-8+ S '63
That new-fangled thing called voting. J. W. Anderson. New Repub 150:8 Mr 28 '64
What's wrong in Africa; a new report. por U S News 54:10 Mr 18 '63

ELLER, J. N.
Washington front. See issues of America

ELLER, Vernard
Depravity or sin? Christian Cent 80:1440 N 20 '63

ELLIN, Stanley
Viewpoint and the mystery short story. Writer 76:7-9 My '63

ELLINGSON, Marnie
Cinderella girl; story. McCalls 91:112-13 O '63
Last bite of buttercups; story. McCalls 92:96-7 N '64
Plumber who stayed for dinner; story. McCalls 90:96-7 F '63

ELLINGSON, Steve
Gate-leg dining table. Pop Mech 121:170-2 Ap '64

ELLINGTON, Duke
Duke in India; interview, tr. from a tape recording by S. Dance. pors Sat R 47:66-7 Ja 11 '64

about

Duke. R. De Toledano. Nat R 16:658-9+ Jl 28 '64
Duke at sixty-four. por Newsweek 62:71 Ag 26 '63
Duke's ball. Newsweek 63:84 Ap 13 '64
Duke's day. por Time 83:60 Je 5 '64
Durable Duke. N. Hentoff. Reporter 30:45-8 My 7 '64
Ellington, after four decades, a new luster. J. S. Wilson. il pors Hi Fi 13:106 Ap '63
Ellington era; with discography. M. Williams. il por Sat R 46:59-60 N 16 '63
Jazz concerts. W. Balliett. New Yorker 40:100-2 Ap 11 '64
Jazz records. W. Balliett. New Yorker 39:179-83 O 26 '63; 97-101 Ja 25 '64
Major phases of the latest Ellington. J. S. Wilson. por Hi Fi 14:114 Ap '64
Mid-month recordings; the enduring Ellington. M. Williams. il por Sat R 46:96 Mr 16 '63
Wa-wa-wa: jazz bands. New Yorker 39:25-7 Je 1 '63

ELLINGTON, George
Ballet girls in New York a century ago; excerpts from Women of New York. Dance Mag 38:31-3+ Ja '64

ELLINGTON, Mercedes
Show business' newest Ellington. il pors Ebony 19:67-71+ D '63

ELLIOTT, Alan J. A.
Scientists abroad. UNESCO Courier 16:65-6 Jl '63

ELLIOTT, Alfred
Playground leaders workshop. por Recreation 57:179 Ap '64

ELLIOTT, C. H.
Long-term benefits of a shoppers' mall. Am City 79:91-2 Mr '64

ELLIOTT, Carl
Elliott inquiry: chairman's loss in Alabama primary raises doubt about future of investigation. D. S. Greenberg. Science 144:1319-20 Je 12 '64
Sweeping probe of research spending; with editorial comment. por Bsns W p26-7, 152 S 21 '63

ELLIOTT, Charles
Backwoods buck. Outdoor Life 132:48-9+ D '63
For the finest fishing plan a hunting trip. Outdoor Life 134:48-9+ O '64
How not to clobber a gobbler. Outdoor Life 133:54-5+ Mr '64
Monarch of wolf creek. Outdoor Life 131:48-9+ Mr '63
Pronghorn crawl. Outdoor Life 132:48-9+ S '63
Saddlebag safari. pors Outdoor Life 132:40-3+ N '63
Those bizarre bass. por Outdoor Life 131:62-3+ My '63
Touch of wilderness. por Outdoor Life 133:56-7+ My '64
Where the bass never quit. pors Outdoor Life 133:42-3+ F '64
(ed) See Lane, J. F. Lost sheep

ELLIOTT, Charles
Taiwan's best-selling pirates. Life 55:8 N 15 '63

ELLIOTT, George P.
Childhood of a leader. Nation 199:118-19 S 14 '64
Coming of age on the Carob plantation; excerpt from Brown fountain pen. Commentary 35:390-6 My '63
Delusions. Commentary 37:78-81 Je; 38:6+ D '64
Free criminal. Commentary 37:78-80 Mr '64
Hurtsog, Hairtsog, heart's hog? Nation 199:252-4 O 19 '64
Men with their faces on. Nation 199:201 O 5 '64

about

Critic selects his own society. E. Capouya. por Sat R 47:25-6 Ap 4 '64

ELLIOTT, Henry Wood
Seals are about gone. J. Van Nostrand. il por Am Heritage 14:10-17+ Je '63

ELLIOTT, J. H.
Great confrontations V: Cortes and Montezuma. Horizon 5:92-6 N '63

ELLIOTT, James P. Jr
Garden in the making. Flower Grower 51:20-1 S '64

ELLIOTT, Lawrence
Busiest pilot in the bush. Read Digest 82:255-7+ My '63
Canada's 100-billion-dollar potash pile. Read Digest 84:144-6+ My '64
Triumph of Janis Babson; excerpts from Little girl's gift. Read Digest 82:275-86+ Je '63
—See Finan, J. jt. auth.

ELLIOTT, Leona
Henry Kaiser. Sci Digest 53:58-65 My '63

ELLIOTT, Maxine
My aunt Maxine, by D. Forbes-Robertson. Review
Newsweek por 63:95 My 4 '64
Sat R 47:30 My 2 '64. G. Oppenheimer

ELLIOTT, William I.
Elegy for Louis C. Marsh. Christian Cent 80:393 Mr 27 '63
Garden of now; poem. Christian Cent 80:270 F 27 '63
Grief in transit: for J.F.K; poem. Christian Cent 81:1454 N 25 '64
Ichthus; poem. Christian Cent 81:485 Ap 15 '64
Seven other last words; poem. Christian Cent 80:461 Ap 10 '63
What creature; poem. Christian Cent 81:1617 D 30 '64

ELLIOTT, William Yandell
Ends and means. il por Newsweek 62:65 Ag 5 '63

ELLIOTT-automation, limited
In automation, a British empire. il Bsns W p82+ Jl 25 '64

ELLIOTT KEY. See Florida Keys

ELLIS, Dean
Art: sacred & profane; interview, ed. by E. W. Watson. il por Am Artist 27:30-5+ Je '63

ELLIS, Frank
Bureaucracy and Frank Ellis. J. Ciardi. Sat R 47:14-15 Je 13 '64
Still in defense. J. Ciardi. Sat R 47:13 Jl 11 '64

ELLIS, H. F.
It still goes on. Atlan 21:112-14 My '63
Majoring in resistance. Atlan 214:104-6 S '64
Not valid in Macao. New Yorker 40:218+ O 31 '64
Shall we, for God's sake, join the ladies? New Yorker 40:142-4 My 23 '64
Spy-ban pact; story. New Yorker 39:48-9 S 28 '63
Trouble with Florence. Atlan 212:108-9 S '63
Wild music. New Yorker 39:58-60 Jl 6 '63

ELLIS, John Tracy
American layman: his roots, his trials, his future. Commonweal 79:171-2 N 1 '63
Facing the black facts. por Newsweek 63:55 F 10 '64

ELLIS, L. F.
Books. A. J. Liebling. New Yorker 39:217-18+ O 19 '63

ELLIS, Mel
Fishermen's special. Field & S 68:140-3+ My '63
Ghost pike of Manitoba. Field & S 67:120-2 Mr '63
Grass is always greener. Field & S 69:28-30+ Ag '64
I'll take those trash ducks. Field & S 68:36-7+ Ag '63

ELLIS, Mel—*Continued*
Muskie myths exploded. Field & S 69:50-1+ Jl '64
Now you shoot! Field & S 69:46-8+ N '64
Storm fish. por Field & S 67:10-11 Mr '63
X marks the spot. Field & S 69:50-2+ S '64
ELLIS, Richard A. and Abel, J. H. jr
Intercellular channels in the salt-secreting glands of marine turtles. bibliog Science 144:1340-2 Je 12 '64
ELLIS, W. P.
Strain-induced birefringence in fluoride films on uranium dioxide. bibliog Science 144: 1570-2 Je 26 '64
ELLIS, Weldon T.
Dangerous intersection. Sat R 46:31 Ag 24 '63
ELLIS, William D.
Make way for the no-problem guy. Read Digest 82:95-7 My '63
ELLIS, William S.
As New Hampshire goes, so goes who? N Y Times Mag p 12+ F 2 '64
Base in Maine called Blotner. Harper 229:26+ S '64
First rebels on the labor front. Nation 200: 8-10, inside cover+ Ja 4, 25 '65
Loneliest governor. Reporter 28:45 Ap 25 '63
Red trawlers: encroaching fishermen. Nation 197:346-8 N 23 '63
Reviving Passamaquoddy. Nation 199:10-12 Jl 13 '64
Space crescent. Nation 199:211-16, 239-43, 275-7+ O 12-26 '64
Trouble with Maine. Nation 196:527-9 Je 22 '63
ELLISON, Arthur
Ski doctor. il por Newsweek 61:60 F 4 '63
ELLISON, Gaylord D. and Konorski, J.
Separation of the salivary and motor responses in instrumental conditioning. bibliog Science 146:1071-2 N 20 '64
ELLISON, Jerome
Alcoholics anonymous; dangers of success. Nation 198:212-14 Mr 2 '64
Our quaint political folkways. Nation 197: 323-5 N 16 '63
Television: stimulant to violence. Nation 197: 433-6 D 21 '63
ELLISON, Margaret
Flamin' Mamie's bouffant belles. G. Rogin. il por Sports Illus 20:30-2+ Ap 20 '64
ELLISON, Ralph
Harlem is nowhere; excerpt from Shadow and act. Harper 229:53-7 Ag '64
On becoming a writer; excerpt from Shadow and act. Commentary 38:57-60 O '64
Visible Ellison. P. De Lissovoy. Nation 199: 334-6 N 9 '64
Visible man. por Newsweek 62:81 Ag 12 '63
ELLMANN, Mary
Dering case. Commentary 38:19-25 Jl '64
ELLORA cave temples. See Cave temples
ELLSBERG, Helen
New old worlds to conquer. Mlle 59:106-8+ Je '64
ELLSWORTH, Ralph E.
Another chance for centralized cataloging; reprint. il por Library J 89:3104-7 S 1 '64
Changing role of the university library; address, October 1962. por Library J 88:1405-11 Ap 1 '63
Library buildings of Britain and Europe. Library J 88:4529-30 D 1 '63
Shortcomings of LAD; letter to the editor. ALA Bul 57:692-3; 58:9 S '63, Ja '64
about
National organization or a private club? E. Moon. Library J 88:1429 Ap 1 '63
ELLSWORTH, Ray
RCA Victor Porgy and Bess. Am Rec G 30:196-8 N '63
ELLSWORTH, Rex Cooper
Cowboy who'd be king. W. Tower. il por Sports Illus 18:22-4+ F 25 '63
Pious partners of success. M. Durslag. il Sat Eve Post 236:28+ My 4 '63
Their hats are in the ring. W. Tower. il por Sports Illus 20:26-32 My 4 '64
ELLYETT, Clifton D. and Keay, C. S. L.
Meteors: an unexpected increase in 1963. bibliog Science 146:1458 D 11 '64
ELLZEY, W. Clark
Divorce phenomenon. Christian Cent 80:424-6 Ap 3 '63
ELM
Diseases and pests
Can Dutch elm disease be controlled? H. G. Mattoon. il Horticulture 41:274-5 My '63
Chemical retards spread of Dutch elm disease; sodium N-methyl dithiocarbamate. Sci N L 87:8 Ja 2 '65
Embattled elms. il Time 81:46+ My 10 '63
Shot in the trunk; Dutch-elm disease. Newsweek 62:50 O 28 '63
Tree program restricts elm losses; Grosse Point Park, Mich. R. A. Sloane. il Am City 79:165-6 O '64
We can save our elms. C. B. Hicks. il Pop Mech 121:122-5+ Ap '64
You can save your elms; spraying with DDT; Detroit. F. Vaydik. il Am City 78:110-11 S '63
See also
Elm bark beetles
Elm leaf beetles
ELM bark beetles
Do our elms have a chance. E. J. Duda. il Horticulture 42:20-1+ D '64
ELM leaf beetles
How we saved our shade; killing elm leaf beetles with Sevin; Colusa, Calif. J. Miller. il Am City 78:24 S '63
ELMAN, Philip
Hard-to-find quality. New Repub 149:5 O 12 '63
ELMAN, Richard M.
Beckett's testament. Commonweal 80:416-18 Je 26 '64
Institution of blacklisting. New Repub 151:17-18+ D 5 '64
Legacy of Louis MacNeice. New Repub 149: 19-21 O 26 '63
Song in friendship. Commonweal 78:252 My 24 '63
(ed) See Singer, I. B. Interview
ELMHURST, Ill.
One place to call. R. T. Palmer. il Am City 79:101 O '64
EL MOLO (native race) See Kenya—Native races
ELMORE, Daniel D. sr
High school diploma at seventy-two. il pors Ebony 19:125-6+ Ag '64
EL MOROCCO. See Night clubs
EL MORRO NATIONAL MONUMENT
New Mexico's stone autograph album. W. F. Heald. il Nat Parks Mag 37:10-12 F '63
ELOPERS; story. See Powell, D.
EL PASO, Tex.
We corral our street vehicles. R. Hickok. il Am City 78:112-13 Je '63
Airports
Head for The Pass. C. Wolfe. il Flying 75:41-3 S '64
Hospitals
Plan for vertical expansion. il Arch Rec 136: 184-6 O '64
Sanitary affairs
How to cut street-cleaning costs. R. Hickok. il Am City 79:90-1 Jl '64
EL PASO natural gas company
Record rebate. Newsweek 62:82 D 2 '63
ELSA (operatic character) See Characters in opera
ELSIE de Wolfe award. See American institute of interior designers
ELSINORE. See Helsingor, Denmark
ELSINORE, LAKE
Lake Elsinore's resurrection. B. Ruskauff. il Motor B 113:52+ My '64
ELSON, John T.
Catholic church battles its old guard. Life 55:114-51+ O 18 '63
ELSON, Robert T.
Queen Elizabeth II. Life 56:75-8+ Mr 6 '64
With this man it's think, think, think. Life 55:27-9 Jl 5 '63
ELSTAD, Leonard M.
Broadening our educational horizons for the deaf; adaptation of address. Sch Life 46: 28-9 Ja '64
ELSY, Mary
Down the Danube. Travel 120:47-51 Jl '63
ELTEN, Germany (Federal Republic)
Heim ins Reich; Elten returned to Germany. Newsweek 62:35-6 Ag 12 '63
ELTON, Godfrey Elton, 1st baron
Englishman's audit of Rhodes scholars. Harper 228:98-100+ My '64
ELUTION convection electrophoresis. See Electrophoresis
ELVSTROM, Paul
Paul Elvstrom on racing and the Olympics; interview. il pors Yachting 116:27-8+ Ag '64
ELY, David
Captain's boar hunt; story. Sat Eve Post 237: 44-5 Mr 21 '64
Human factor; story. Sat Eve Post 236:80-4 N 16 '63
ELY, Donald P.
What's in a name? NEA J 53:57-8 D '64
ELYTIS, Odysseus
Axion esti: The genesis; poem, excerpt, tr. by E. Keeley and G. Savidis. Poetry 105: 1-14 O '64

ELYTIS, Odysseus—*Continued*
Axion esti: This then is I; Six and one regrets for the sky: The sleep of the brave; poems, excerpts, tr. by R. Whitman. Poetry 105:21-3 O '64
about
Genesis: a commentary. E. Keeley. Poetry 105:16-20 O '64

EMANCIPATION of women. See Woman—Equal rights

EMANCIPATION proclamation
Commemoration of 100th anniversary of Emancipation proclamation. H. Taylor, jr. Negro Hist Bul 26:183-5 Mr '63
Emancipation centennial address: January 6, 1963. S. Z. Westerfield. Negro Hist Bul 26:208-9 Ap '63
Emancipation proclamation, a turning point in our history. C. H. Wesley. Negro Hist Bul 26:158+ F '63
Emancipation proclamation; address, January 13, 1963. S. Reese. Vital Speeches 29:283-6 F 15 '63
Emancipation reconsidered; adaptation of address, February 12, 1963. E. A. Toppin. bibliog Negro Hist Bul 26:233-6 My '63
Historical basis of emancipation, 1963; address. H. N. Meyer. Negro Hist Bul 27:4-6 O '63
Libraries and Emancipation centennial. E. J. Josey. Negro Hist Bul 26:219-21 Ap '63
Lincoln and the Emancipation proclamations. H. L. Hurwitz. Sr Schol 82:8T-10T F 13 '63
Mr Lincoln's Proclamation, by F. Donovan. Review
Sat R il 47:30-1 Ag 1 '64. W. B. Catton
Second emancipation; address, June 16, 1963. J. H. Robinson. Vital Speeches 29:610-13 Ag 1 '63
White House Emancipation proclamation centennial by the President of the United States of America; a proclamation. J. F. Kennedy. Negro Hist Bul 26:195 Mr '63

EMANS, Elaine V.
Cat-and-dog rain; poem. Farm J 88:78 Ap '64
For a daughter discovering books; poem. Horn Bk 39:273 Je '63
Question after ten years; poem. McCalls 90:197 Ap '63
Song for unspoken words. Farm J 88:69 Je '64

EMBARGO
See also
Blockade

EMBASSIES (buildings)
Castro pulls the eagle's tail; retaliatory seizure of U.S. embassy in Havana. il U S News 55:23 Ag 5 '63
Chevy Chasers. il Newsweek 61:32 Je 10 '63
German factory graces embassy row in Washington. il Fortune 70:178 O '64
Great Britain plans new embassy in Rome. il Arch Rec 135:12-13 Mr '64
Moscow bughouse: United States embassy. Time 83:28 My 29 '64
Open diplomacy; Roosevelt House, New Delhi. il Time 81:60-1 Ap 12 '63
Opening nights; new U.S. embassies. il Time 83:60 My 29 '64
Russia's U-2: hidden microphones in U.S. embassy walls. il U S News 56:6 Je 1 '64
Sinewy drum for Dublin; U.S. embassy. il Arch Forum 121:144-7 Ag '64
Those do-it-yourself spontaneous riots; anti-American demonstrations. il Time 84:27-8 D 18 '64
Undiplomatic diplomatic move; seizure of U.S. embassy building. il Sr Schol 83:7 S 20 '63
U.S. discovers microphones in walls of embassy at Moscow: statement, May 19, 1964. G. M. Gentile. Dept State Bul 50:933 Je 15 '64
Walls have ears; wall microphones discovered in U.S. embassy in Moscow. il Newsweek 63:32 Je 1 '64
Where to put diplomats: new Washington problem. il U S News 55:52-3 Jl 1 '63

EMBASSIES (United States) See United States—Diplomatic and consular service

EMBASSY pictures corporation
Supercolossal, well, pretty good, world of Joe Levine. K. Hamill. il Fortune 69:130-2+ Mr '64

EMBERLEY, Edward Randolph
Meet Ed Emberley; ed. by I. Stokvis and others. il por Library J 88:3991-5 O 15 '63

EMBEZZLEMENT
Corrupt society. F. J. Cook. Nation 196:470-2 Je 1 '63
Death for hot sweaters; cases in Russia. Time 82:23-4 Ag 23 '63
From a family of bound feet; Dolly Gee. il Time 83:26 Ja 10 '64
Home is the sailor; Arthur Keller general manager of Mainbocher, falsifies accounts. il Newsweek 63:33-4 My 11 '64
Misunderstood; conviction of Secretary-General of Italian atomic energy commission. il Newsweek 64:50 N 16 '64
Scratching the surface; financial dishonesty among government employees. Nation 200:1 Ja 4 '65

EMBLEMS
Art and communication; exhibition at Musée Guimet. P. Schneider. il Art N 63:48+ My '64
Who's got the button? almost everybody; civil rights emblem. il Time 82:15 Ag 9 '63

EMBLEMS, National
Antiques; American eagle on glass tumblers, etc. A. Winchester. il Antiques 85:180-1 F '64
Portraits of our symbol; eagles on Pennsylvania station. il N Y Times Mag p33 N 17 '63

EMBOLISM
Attack on embolisms; heart-lung machine saves patients. Newsweek 64:92+ N 9 '64
Embolism rise requires anticoagulant drugs. Sci N L 84:248 O 19 '63
Tilting out of trouble; resuscitation of a skindiving student. Time 82:60 Ag 30 '63

EMBOSSED stationery. See Stationery

EMBOSSING
Embossing, the new easy way to make holiday decorations. P. Hyde. il House B 105:244-7+ N '63
Hammer crafting sheet metal. W. E. Burton. il Pop Mech 119:140-2 Ap '63

EMBROIDERY
Embroider these gay spice-chart linens. il Am Home 67:12+ Ap '64
Flame stitching makes your needle fly like magic. il House & Gard 123:152-3 Ap '63
German and Italian embroidery of the middle ages; excerpts from Pictorial history of embroidery. M. Schuette and S. Müller-Christensen. il Craft Horiz 24:23-7+ N '64
Kate Auerbach's stitchery. A. Adams. il Craft Horiz 23:32-3 Jl '63
Kitchen wall embroidery. il Am Home 66:12 S '63
Letter from London; exhibition of medieval embroideries at Victoria and Albert museum. M. Panter-Downes. New Yorker 39:209 N 30 '63
Needleworks of art. V. P. Guild. il Good H 156:120-1+ Ap '63
On stitchery. N. Krevitsky. il Craft Horiz 23:18-20+ N '63
Opus anglicanum; English embroiderers loan exhibition at the Victoria & Albert museum, London. A. Frankfurter. il Art N 62:22-5+ D '63
Stitchery. M. K. Kight. il Sch Arts 63:32-3 S '63
Stitchery & the retarded child. B. McMillin. il Sch Arts 63:18-19 Ja '64
Stitchery; the quartet. P. Burkhart. il Sch Arts 62:21-2 F '63
Sweden's striking embroidery. il Good H 157:134-5 O '63
Touch of traditional elegance for your home. il Redbook 120:82-5+ Ap '63
See also
Crewel work
Samplers

Study and teaching

Decorative wall hangings. D. B. Van Dommelen. il Sch Arts 62:7-9 Ap '63
Stitchery. Mrs D. W. Heidt. il Design 66:18-20 S '64

EMBRYOLOGY
Embryology: report of International embryological conference. V. Hamburger. Science 142:1367 D 6 '63
See also
Differentiation (biology)
Placenta

Birds

Actinomycin D: specific inhibitory effects on the explanted chick embryo. N. W. Klein and L. J. Pierro. bibliog il Science 142:967-9 N 15 '63
Egg and Doctor Grabowski. A. J. Snider. il Todays Health 41:80-1 N '63
First tiny heartbeat of bird in egg recorded. Sci N L 85:329 My 23 '64
Inhibition of growth of chick embryo by inhibition of deoxycytidylate deaminase. J. S. Roth and others. bibliog il Science 142:1473-4 D 13 '63
Messenger RNA utilization during development of chick embryo lens. R. B. Scott and E. Bell. bibliog il Science 147:405-7 Ja 22 '65

EMBRYOLOGY—Birds—*Continued*
Osteoclasts: organization in chick embryo bone. M. L. Tanzer and R. D. Hunt. bibliog il Science 141:1270-2 S 27 '63
Possible cytoplasmic change in an immunologically competent tissue of the chicken. B. Glick. il Science 142:485-6 O 25 '63
Ribosomal RNA in the developing chick embryo. M. A. Lerner and others. bibliog il Science 141:1187-8 S 20 '63
Teratogenic significance of ionic and fluid imbalances. C. T. Grabowski. bibliog il Science 142:1064 N 22 '63

Echinoderms

D-malate: effects on activity of L-malate dehydrogenase in developing sea urchin embryos. R. D. Billiar and others. bibliog il Science 146:1464-5 D 11 '64
Malate dehydrogenase: multiple forms in separated blastomeres of sea urchin embryos. R. O. Moore and C. A. Villee. bibliog il Science 142:389-90 O 18 '63

Mammals

Abnormalities associated with a chromosome region in the mouse. L. C. Dunn; D. Bennett. bibliog il Science 144:260-7 Ap 17 '64
Antibody formation in embryos. M. F. La Via and others. bibliog il Science 140:1219-20 Je 14 '63
Congenital malformations in hamster embryos after treatments with vinblastine and vincristine. V. H. Ferm. bibliog il Science 141: 426 Ag 2 '63; Reply. J. G. Armstrong and others. 143:703 F 14 '64
Development of mouse eggs in diffusion chambers. D. L. Bryson. bibliog il Science 144:1351-3 Je 12 '64
Electrophoretic patterns of hemoglobin from fetal mice of different inbred strains. M. L. Craig and E. S. Russell. bibliog il Science 142:398-9 O 18 '63

Mollusks

Ribonucleic acids of the ilyanassa embryo. J. R. Collier. bibliog il Science 147:150-1 Ja 8 '65

EMBURY, Aymar, 2d
Living with antiques. Antiques 84:154-7 Ag '63
EMBURY, Barbara
Curl up and read. Seventeen 23:22 F '64
EMEL'IANOV, Vasilii Semenovich
Atomic power and disarmament. Bul Atomic Sci 19:16-20 O '63
On the eve of the third Conference on the peaceful uses of atomic energy. UN Mo Chron 1:84-6 Jl '64
EMERALD LAKE, British Columbia
Emerald encore. E. F. Mertens. il Am For 69:4-6 Jl '63
EMERGENCIES. See First aid in illness and injury
EMERGENCY communications systems
One place to call; Elmhurst, Ill. R. T. Palmer. il Am City 79:101 O '64
Telephones give split-second emergency response; Allentown, Pa. G. M. Monahan. il Am City 79:111 S '64
EMERGENCY exits. See Airplanes—Safety devices and measures
EMERGENCY landing, Airplanes. See Airplanes—Landing
EMERGENCY lighting. See Electric lighting sets
EMERGENCY medical service. See Medical service
EMERGENCY powers. See Presidents—United States—Powers and duties
EMERICK, Robert S.
Infrared units for space heating. Arch Rec 133:201-2 My '63
EMERSON, Alfred E.
Termites. New Yorker 39:23 Ja 18 '64
EMERSON, Gloria
I was the world's most scared skydiver. por Read Digest 82:86-90 Mr '63
New way to cut out smoking. Read Digest 83:100-4 O '63
EMERSON, Harrington
Famous firsts: high priest of efficiency. por Bsns W p 100+ Je 22 '63
EMERSON, Ralph Waldo
Mama, they've begun again! B. Bliven. il por Am Heritage 16:12-16+ D '64
Sage of Concord. P. W. Schmidtchen. il por Hobbies 69:106-7 D '64
Two Concord men in a boat. F. Tilden. por Nat Parks Mag 38:8-10 Jl '64
EMERSON, Randall
Hong Kong heartbeat. Travel 122:43-4 O '64
EMERSON, Roy
Another long chorus of waltzing Matilda. F. Deford. il por Sports Illus 21:93-5 S 21 '64
Bright shine on an old shoe. F. Deford. il por Sports Illus 21:38+ S 7 '64
Outcasts are counted in. J. Lovesey. il por Sports Illus 21:22+ Jl 13 '64
Swag man. Newsweek 64:70+ O 12 '64
EMERSON electric manufacturing company
Emerson offers a solution to nozzle problem. il Miss & Roc 13:31 D 23 '63
EMHART manufacturing company
American hardware marries for love. il Bsns W p 144+ My 16 '64
EMIGRATION and immigration law. See Immigration and emigration law
EMILIANI, Cesare
Precipitous continental slopes and considerations on the transitional crust. bibliog Science 147:145-8 Ja 8 '65
EMILIE, Sister Mary. See Mary Emilie, Sister
EMILY Griffith opportunity school. See Denver—Education
EMINENT domain
Bulldozers at your door. S. Z. Searles. Read Digest 83:83-7 S '63
Castro pulls the eagle's tail; retaliatory seizure of U.S. embassy in Havana. il U S News 55:23 Ag 5 '63
It's a hard way to lay pipe; Colonial pipeline co. il Bsns W p37-8 D 21 '63
No property is safe from condemnation. E. D. Fales, jr. Am Home 66:16+ Mr '63
Personal business; condemnation of property. Bsns W p 105 Je 29 '63
Swiss resistance movement; U.S. embassy building, Havana. Time 82:26+ Ag 2 '63
EMISSION of electrons. See Electrons—Emission
EMLEN, Stephen T. and Kem, William
Activity rhythm in peromyscus; its influence on rates of recovery from nembutal. bibliog Science 142:1682-3 D 27 '63
EMLEY, Grace. See Ray, O. S. jt. auth.
EMMA Willard school. See Private schools
EMMAUS, Pa.
New lighting a real bargain. O. T. Iobst. il Am City 78:131 O '63
EMMET, Christopher
Canadians answer a question. America 108: 563 Ap 20 '63
Common market crisis. America 108:333-5 Mr 9 '63
EMMETT, J. A.
Accessories for boatmen. Outdoor Life 133: 62-3+ F '64
Boating. See issues of Outdoor life
Boating trends for 1964. Outdoor Life 133: 56-60+ F '64
New boats for 1965. Outdoor Life 135:56-9+ Ja '65
New trailers for 1965. Outdoor Life 135:60-1 Ja '65
Outdoor life boating, 1964-1965. Outdoor Life 133:52-5 F '64; 135:52-5+ Ja '65
EMMETT, Jim
(ed) Boating. See issues of Outdoor life
Boats for fishing. Outdoor Life 131:52-5+ F '63
Boats we meet. il Yachting 115:42-3+ Mr '64
Boats we meet; Serenity. Yachting 116:60-2+ Jl '64
Cruising your boat south. Yachting 114:45-7+ S; 64-6+ O '63
Going South. Yachting 116:64+ O '64
Latest boating trends. Outdoor Life 131:56+ F '63
New or old, is she your first boat? Do-it-yourself: suggestions. Yachting 115:52+ Ap '64
Okeechobee waterway. Yachting 114:132-3 D '63
Switch to power. por Yachting 113:71-3+ Ap; 50-3+ My '63
EMMONS, W. Stuart
Old bookworm keeps turning slowly. il Bsns W p81-2+ S 12 '64
EMMYS. See Academy of television arts and sciences
EMORY university, Atlanta, Ga.
New broom for Emory. Time 82:36+ Jl 19 '63
EMOTIONAL stability
Personal business; troubled teenager. Bsns W p 173-4 O 17 '64
EMOTIONS
Burns affect emotions. E. Mirel. Sci N L 83:179 Mr 23 '63
Can emotions be changed? excerpts from address. L. Eisenberg. Sci Digest 56:14-18 S '64
Power of emotion; capturing emotions in photographs. J. Morris. il U S Camera 26: 76-7+ F '63

EMOTIONS—*Continued*
Try letting yourself go! H. Van Horne. Read Digest 84:48-50 Mr '64
See also
Anger
Anxiety
Hate
Love
Psychoanalysis
Temper
EMOTIONS and food. See Eating, Psychology of
EMPATHY
Empathy unlimited. E. Pearson. Writer 76:25-6 F '63
EMPEROR; drama. See Gressieker, H.
EMPEROR penguins. See Penguins
EMPERORS. See Kings and rulers
EMPEROR'S new robes; drama. See Foley, M. A.
EMPHYSEMA
Bronchitis or emphysema? Sci N L 84:211 O 5 '63
Cigarette, emphysema link. Sci N L 85:70 F 1 '64
Emphysema, a growing menace. il Changing T 18:15-16 Ap '64
Emphysema in lung macrosections correlated with smoking habits. A. E. Anderson, jr. and others. bibliog il Science 144:1025-6 My 22 '64
Diagnosis
Free emphysema tests given to congressmen. Sci N L 84:57 Jl 27 '63
Wind on the Hill; mobile unit tests congressmen. il Time 82:42 Ag 2 '63
EMPIRICISM, Logical. See Logical positivism
EMPLOYEE incentives. See Incentives in industry
EMPLOYEE morale
How taxpayers pick up the check for picnics; boosting defense plant morale. Bsns W p25 Jl 25 '64
To live and die for Armstrong. H. Kay. il Fortune 69:124-9+ Mr '64
Who are your motivated workers? M. S. Myers. il Harvard Bsns R 42:73-88 Ja '64
You can keep morale high. N. Stewart. Nations Bsns 51:70-2+ Mr '63
EMPLOYEE recreation. See Industrial recreation
EMPLOYEE savings. See Saving and savings
EMPLOYEE seniority. See Seniority, Employee
EMPLOYEE thefts. See Stealing
EMPLOYEE vacations. See Vacations, Employee
EMPLOYEES
Back to the guild? il Newsweek 61:62 Je 3 '63
Legal hurdle for job-hoppers. Bsns W p95 Je 1 '63
See also
Job satisfaction
Labor turnover
Office workers
Personnel management
also subhead Employees under various subjects, e.g. Automobile factories—Employees
Dismissal
Eleven ways to lose a job. il Changing T 17:41-2 Je '63
Length of service
See Seniority, Employee
Promotion
Invisible persuader on promotions; study by American Jewish committee. il Bsns W p 154+ D 12 '64
What helps or harms promotability? G. W. Bowman. il Harvard Bsns R 42:6-8+ Ja '64
Who do you promote? symposium. Duns R 83:50-2+ My '64
Rating
Positive program for performance appraisal. A. F. Kindall and J. Gatza. Harvard Bsns R 41:153-4+ N '63
Split roles in performance appraisal. H. H. Meyer and others. Harvard Bsns R 43:123-9 Ja '65
Selection
See Employment systems
Training
Apprenticeship and skill training, a trial balance; excerpts from testimony before Subcommittee on employment and manpower, October 24, 1963. F. F. Foltman. bibliog f Mo Labor R 87:28-35 Ja '64
Better skills will improve job outlook; interview. J. C. Donovan. il Nations Bsns 52:66-8+ D '64
Blue collar elite. T. R. Brooks. il Duns R 83: pt2 121-2+ Mr '64
Bringing engineers up to date. G. A. W. Boehm. il Fortune 67:120-1+ My '63
Can industry harness the elusive engineer? H. E. Klein. il Duns R 83:48-9+ My '64
Challenge of change; address, November 18, 1963. L. H. Hodges. Vital Speeches 30:107-11 D 1 '63
Church and poverty; Job training center at Lansing, Mich. America 111:250 S 12 '64
Does automation call for new solutions? V. M. Rogers. il PTA Mag 58:7-9 Je '64
Here's do-it-yourself unemployment cure; South Carolina committee for technical education. il Nations Bsns 51:62-8 S '63
How challenge can be met. il Nations Bsns 51:32-3+ Je '63
How to create a salesman. L. Morse. il Duns R 82:46-7+ D '63
IBM's growth power. il Duns R 82:33-5+ Jl '63
Increase in job mobility. T. R. Brooks. Duns R 84:51E-52 S '64
Indiana program of job training and work experience for students; excerpt. S. Cohen and W. C. Pyle. Mo Labor R 86:161-3 F '63
Integrated approach to technical staffing. E. D. Phelps and W. Gallagher. il Harvard Bsns R 41:122-9 Jl '63
Learning new jobs before old ones fade; United auto workers. il Bsns W p 114+ Ap 11 '64
Meeting of the minds that train industry; company training directors conference. il Bsns W p56+ Je 20 '64
Michigan on the move; Michigan Catholic conference's job-training project. America 110:244 F 22 '64
National apprenticeship program: unfinished business. D. E. Christian. bibliog f il Mo Labor R 87:625-32 Je '64
New federal program trains those leaving farms; Manpower development and training act. F. Bailey, jr. Suc Farm 61:92 F '63
New training law in Great Britain. Mo Labor R 87:III-IV Ag '64
No room at the bottom; paid work and school study programs. L. Velie. il Read Digest 84:169-70+ Ap '64
Older workers' performance in industrial retraining programs. E. Weinberg. bibliog f il Mo Labor R 86:935-9 Ag '63
Original schoolmaster. Duns R 82:3 D '63
Packing up an Armour packing plant, Sioux City. Bsns W p80+ Jl 20 '63
Programming harmony; Relationship improvement program. il Bsns W p 142+ Ap 18 '64
Public policies and programs. M. F. Riche. bibliog f Mo Labor R 87:143-8 F '64
Retraining and the South. J. E. Williams. il Mo Labor R 87:657-9 Je '64
Retraining fills a gap; Toledo branch, Ohio state employment service. il Bsns W p 164 Ap 20 '63
Retraining in West Virginia. H. A. Gibbard. Mo Labor R 87:661-2 Je '64
Retraining the jobless. P. Hirsch. New Repub 148:8-9 Je 22 '63
Retraining's brave promise. F. C. Porter. New Repub 148:14-16 Ap 13 '63; Reply. R. Carey. 148:37 My 4 '63
Second chance for George. L. Velie. Read Digest 82:61-5 Je '63
Second chance for ninety men in Norfolk. J. W. Canan. il Reporter 31:34-6 Jl 16 '64
Self-help in Philadelphia; Rev. L. Sullivan's Opportunities industrialization center. H. Lees. il Reporter 31:15-17 D 17 '64; Discussion. 32:12 Ja 28 '65
Sending a plant back to school; St Maries plywood co. Bsns W p65-6 N 28 '64
Statistics on apprenticeship and their limitations. P. Groom. bibliog f il Mo Labor R 87:391-5 Ap '64
Strategies for using programed instruction. J. R. Murphy and I. A. Goldberg. bibliog f il Harvard Bsns R 42:115-32 My '64
TV teachers: leading a company into space. il Bsns W p60-1+ Ag 29 '64
TV teachers: training plant bosses statewide; South Carolina companies. il Bsns W p64+ Ag 29 '64
Train the job-hunter to fit the job. il Changing T 19:21-3 Ja '65
Trainees favor on-the-job. Bsns W p60+ Je 29 '63
When job retraining helps: Armour's training program. Bsns W p50 N 16 '63

EMPLOYEES—Training—*Continued*
Wife, six children and no job. B. Asbell. il Redbook 121:46-7+ Ag '63
See also
Apprentices

EMPLOYEES, Reporting to
What can you tell employees? Leff report. L. L. L. Golden. Sat R 46:50 Ag 10 '63; Reply. B. Liss. 46:49 O 12 '63

EMPLOYEES, Transfer of
In the realty business in spite of themselves; transferred employees homes. il Bsns W p58-9 Ag 10 '63
Interplant transfers in the automobile industry. P. Taft. Mo Labor R 86:276-8 Mr '63
Shanghaied technicians. Nation 196:435 My 25 '63

EMPLOYEES as stockholders
Lure of stock options tempts insurance men. il Bsns W p76+ O 3 '64

EMPLOYEES benefit plans
Health and insurance benefits for salaried employees. A. H. Anderson and W. F. Hahn. Mo Labor R 86:1266-74 N '63

EMPLOYEES representation in management
When unions are put on boards of directors; West Germany. il U S News 58:74-5 Ja 11 '65

EMPLOYER-employee relations. See Industrial relations; Personnel management

EMPLOYMENT
Abundance, threat or promise? R. Theobald. Nation 196:387-412 My 11 '63; Discussion. 196:inside cover Je 15 '63
Account of American labor in 1964. P. Groom. Mo Labor R 87:1385-92 D '64
Automation; we can handle it. T. G. Harris. il Look 29:58-62 Ja 12 '65
Basic principle of the free world; address, November 29, 1962. A. Ames. Vital Speeches 29:248-50 F 1 '63
Challenge of leisure; address, February 17, 1964. D. Rockefeller. Vital Speeches 30:379-81 Ap 1 '64
Comprehensive manpower and employment planning. Mo Labor R 87:III-IV Je '64
Employment impact of changing defense programs. J. F. Fulton. bibliog f il Mo Labor R 87:508-16 My '64
Employment projections to 1975. il Mo Labor R 86:240-8 Mr '63
For the class of '63; job outlook now. W. W. Wirtz. il U S News 54:74-5 Ap 29 '63
How jobs, wages are shifting; with chart. U S News 55:95-6 S 30 '63
January employment: a record. U S News 56:105 F 17 '64
Job outlook for the class of '64. il U S News 56:88-9 My 11 '64
Jobs after high school. il Changing T 18:20-3 Mr '64; Same with title Good jobs for high-school graduates. Read Digest 85:130-3 Jl '64
Jobs for the future; symposium. il Nations Bsns 51:31-41+ Je '63
Keynesian system, by D. M. Wright. Review Nat R 14:239-41 Mr 26 '63. W. Roepke
Labor force and employment in 1963. S. S. Holland. il Mo Labor R 87:645-53 Je '64
More jobs coming twice as fast. il Nations Bsns 52:31-3+ Je '64
Not so daffy; need for new civilian industries. Nation 196:318 Ap 20 '63
Poverty and profits; symposium; with editorial comment. bibliog f Harvard Bsns R 42:6-8+ S '64
Taxes & spending: how investment creates jobs. il Nations Bsns 51:40-1+ Ap '63
Training for jobs. H. Hazlitt. Newsweek 64:71 Je 6 '64
Triple revolution. G. W. Johnson. New Repub 150:38-9 Ap 11 '64
U.S. jobs: gains for minorities. U S News 56:96 Mr 16 '64
Where the jobs are. L. Velie. Read Digest 86:102-6 Ja '65
See also
Age and employment
Applications for positions
Disarmament—Economic aspects
Part time employment
Self employed
Student employment
Unemployment
Unemployment—United States
Woman—Employment
Youth—Employment

Government guaranty

For a guaranteed income. M. D. Reagan. il N Y Times Mag p20+ Je 7 '64; Reply. H. Hazlitt. Newsweek 63:78 Je 29 '64

Stability

See Employment systems—Guaranty of employment

Statistics

Concentration of industrial empolyment. S. S. Small. il Mo Labor R 87:997-1001 S '64
Employment paradox. America 109:67 Jl 20 '63
Employment; tables. See issues of Monthly labor review
Geographic changes in U.S. employment from 1950 to 1960. S. P. Manor. il Mo Labor R 86:1-10 Ja '63
Geographic mobility and employment status, March 1962-March 1963. S. Saben. il Mo Labor R 87:873-81 Ag '64
Marital and family characteristics of workers, March 1962. J. Schiffman. il Mo Labor R 86:24-36 Ja '63
Marital and family characteristics of workers, March 1963. V. C. Perrella. il Mo Labor R 87:149-60 F '64
New jobs fatten incomes. Bsns W p76-7 Ja 26 '63
Outlook and trends in civil aviation employment. S. H. Luskin. il Mo Labor R 86:1290-6 N '63
Prevalence of disabilities in the work force. D. K. Lewis. il Mo Labor R 87:1002-8 S '64
Revision of establishment employment statistics, 1963. D. Hinton. il Mo Labor R 86:1194-5 O '63
Self-employment in the United States, 1948-62. J. E. Bregger. il Mo Labor R 86:37-43 Ja '63
Work experience of the population in 1962. S. Saben. il Mo Labor R 87:18-27 Ja '64
Worker absence due to illness. il Mo Labor R 87:1181-3 O '64
See also
Unemployment—Statistics

Germany (Federal Republic)

J.F.K. needs Adenauer's problem: *überbeschäftigung*. J. Bell. il Life 54:8 Je 7 '63

United States

See Employment

EMPLOYMENT, Agricultural. See Farm labor

EMPLOYMENT, Supplementary. See Supplementary employment

EMPLOYMENT agencies
Finding jobs coast-to-coast; Snelling and Snelling. il Time 83:92 F 7 '64
How to steal an engineer. J. H. York. il Sci Digest 55:27-9 My '64
White-collar Negroes; Hallmark employment agency in New York city. il Newsweek 63:86+ Mr 23 '64
See also
National employment association
United States—Employment service

EMPLOYMENT discrimination. See Discrimination in employment

EMPLOYMENT management. See Personnel management

EMPLOYMENT systems
Business goes on a manhunt. L. Stessin. il N Y Times Mag p37+ N 8 '64
Employers rush the girls' schools; government agencies and industries combing the women's colleges for recruits. il Bsns W p 116+ My 18 '63
Guide to using psychological tests. R. S. Barrett. Harvard Bsns R 41:138-46 S '63
Home recruiting lures the grads; Toledo's Operation native son. il Bsns W p62-3 Ja 9 '65
How to get men you want. G. S. Odiorne. il Nations Bsns 52:70-2+ Ja '64
How to hire key people. E. Raudsepp. il Nations Bsns 51:54-9 S '63
How to steal an engineer. J. H. York. il Sci Digest 55:27-9 My '64
Industry rushes for Negro grads. il Bsns W p78-80+ Ap 25 '64
Is nepotism so bad? D. W. Ewing. il Harvard Bsns R 43:22-6+ Ja '65
Managing your manpower; how employers are preparing for the civil rights act. T. R. Brooks. Duns R 84:57+ N '64
On recruiting federal officials. J. J. Corson. Science 144:663-4 My 8 '64
Personnel selection in academic institutions; letter. M. B. Shimkin. Science 143:637 F 14 '64
See also
Applications for positions
Discrimination in employment

Guaranty of employment

Approach to automation: the Kaiser plan. A. H. Raskin. il N Y Times Mag p20-1+ N 3 '63
Automation: road to lifetime jobs? A. H. Raskin. Sat R 47:14-16+ N 28 '64
Backlog syndrome. E. R. Gomersall. il Harvard Bsns R 42:105-15 S '64

EMPLOYMENT systems—Guaranty of employment—*Continued*
Steelworkers talk a tough line. Bsns W p 160 S 26 '64
Taking the sting out of de-hiring; Martin Marietta hired a consultant to help place and relocate key men. Bsns W p78 Ja 2 '65
Testing the Glidden decision. Duns R 81:46 Mr '63
That empty chair by the featherbed. L. Velie. Read Digest 82:97-102 Ap '63
Union agenda for security. J. Seidman. Mo Labor R 86:636-44 Je '63
UMW seeks job security, safety. Bsns W p68 Ja 4 '64
Wage and employment guarantees in major agreements. A. H. Anderson. il Mo Labor R 87:1287-90 N '64
When the rank-and-file balks; demands for job security. Bsns W p68+ O 19 '63
Who has total security? with editorial comment. il Bsns W p45-6, 192 O 17 '64
Why Wichita said no; rejection of new contract between the Boeing co. and the International assn. of machinists. il Bsns W p 106 Ap 27 '63
See also
Employment—Goverment guaranty
EMPRESS tree. See Paulownia
EMRICH, Duncan
(ed) See Cass, L. On report, gentlemen! army officers. 1813
EMRICH, Ruth
Art project: burlap hangings. Sch Arts 64:33 D '64
EMRICK, Ernestine Hoff
Flight of faith; poem. Christian Cent 80:744 Je 5 '63
EMULSION paint. See Paint
ENAMEL and enameling
Ceramics and enameling art. il Design 65:38-40 S '63
Copper enameling on clay. N. Spiridigliozzi. il Sch Arts 64:38 N '64
Enamels and glass. il Craft Horiz 24:74-82 My '64
English enamels; metal mounts. G. Kaler. il Hobbies 69:42-4+ Jl '64
Kaye Denning: enamels. il Craft Horiz 23:35-7 Mr '63
Schreiber collection of enamels. G. Kaler. il Hobbies 69:42+ Mr; 42+ Ap; 42+ My; 42-3+ Je '64
Seventeenth-century French enameled watches in the Walters art gallery. P. Verdier. il Antiques 84:686-90 D '63
Untracht on enamels. O. Untracht. il Craft Horiz 23:28-31+ Jl '63
See also
Cloisonné
Ferro corporation
ENAMEL and enameling (paints, etc) See Paint
ENAMELS. See Enamel and enameling
ENCAMPMENT for citizenship
Encampment for citizenship. I. Mothner. il Look 27:57+ Jl 16 '63
ENCAP (mulch) See Mulching
ENCAUSTIC painting
Instant-encaustic tool. il Design 65:64 N '63
Painted with melted crayons; lovely candle is wax-on-wax decorated. il Design 65:65 N '63
ENCEPHALITIS
Virus-containing leukocytes in polioencephalitis. E. Nelson and others. bibliog il Science 139:499-501 F 8 '63
ENCEPHALITIS, Epidemic. See Sleeping sickness
ENCEPHALITIS virus
Animal-borne viruses; encephalitis virus among Seminole Indians. F. Marley. Sci N L 86:69 Ag 1 '64
Serological evidence of arbovirus infection in the Seminole Indians of southern Florida. T. H. Work. bibliog il Science 145:270-2 Jl 17 '64
ENCEPHALOMYELITIS
Allergic encephalomyelitis: a hyperacute form. S. Levine and E. J. Wenk. bibliog il Science 146:1681-2 D 25 '64
Allergic encephalomyelitis: rapid induction without the aid of adjuvants. S. Levine and E. J. Wenk. bibliog il Science 141:529-30 Ag 9 '63
Methotrexate; suppression of experimental allergic encephalomyelitis. M. W. Brandriss. il Science 140:186-7 Ap 12 '63
ENCEPHALOMYELITIS virus
Venezuelan equine encephalitis virus from south Florida. R. W. Chamberlain and others. bibliog il Science 145:272-4 Jl 17 '64
Venezuelan equine encephalitis virus in Veracruz, Mexico, and the use of hamsters as sentinels. W. F. Scherer and others. Science 145:274-5 Jl 17 '64
ENCHANTED room; story. See Grubb, D.
ENCKELL, Ralph
International co-operation year. UN Mo Chron 1:71-4 D '64
ENCKE'S comet. See Comets
ENCLOSURES, Loudspeaker. See Loud speaking apparatus—Cabinets
ENCOUNTER (periodical)
Down with dogma. il Newsweek 62:66 N 25 '63
Happy encounter. Newsweek 63:89 My 11 '64
ENCOUNTER on a summer night; story. See Shevchenko, T. G.
ENCOURAGEMENT
See also
Praise
ENCYCLICALS
Apostles of peace; need for widespread study, discussion and interpretation of the encyclical Pacem in terris. America 108:898-9 Je 29 '63
Back of the changes in Vatican policy; Pacem in terris. il U S News 54:60-1 Ap 29 '63
Break with the past; Mater et magistra and Pacem in terris. M. Novak. Commonweal 78:372-5 Je 28 '63
Cardinal Suenens; explanation of Pacem in terris. Commonweal 78:268 My 31 '63
Cooling off the Pope; translation of Pope John's encyclical Pacem in terris (Peace on earth) challenged. Newsweek 61:91 My 27 '63
Declaration of interdependence; encyclical Peace on earth; with excerpts. N. Cousins. il Sat R 46:18-20 My 4 '63
Development and awareness; concerning the encyclical Ecclesiam suam. R. W. Hanning. il Commonweal 80:634-7 S 18 '64
Dialogue in Pope Paul's encyclical. J. B. Sheerin. Cath World 200:4-7 O '64
Dialogue of salvation; Pope Paul VI's first encyclical, Ecclesiam suam. America 111:176 Ag 22 '64
Divini redemptoris to Pacem in terris. F. S. Meyer. Nat R 14:406 My 21 '63
Ecclesiam suam; Pope Paul's first encyclical. Commonweal 80:561 Ag 21 '64
Encyclical's impact; Pacem in terris. America 110:565 Ap 25 '64
Encyclical's impact; reactions to Pacem in terris. America 108:632 My 4 '63
Future is ours; Pacem in terris. Life 54:4 Ap 26 '63
Gus Hall and the Pope; Communist notes on Pacem in terris. America 109:550+ N 9 '63
His church; Pope Paul VI's first encyclical Ecclesiam suam. Newsweek 64:76 Ag 24 '64
Homnibus bonae voluntatis; encyclical Pacem in terris. J. Burnham. Nat R 14:353 My 7 '63
John XXIII appeals for world peace; Pacem in terris. Christian Cent 80:517 Ap 24 '63
John XXIII: surprising pontiff. Christian Cent 80:567 Ap 24 '63
Language of encyclicals. America 108:825 Je 8 '63
Letter from Europe; report on reactions to de Gaulle, nuclear arms and Pacem in terris. A. Boyle. America 108:668-9 My 11 '63
Light to the nations; Pacem in terris? America 108:604 Ap 27 '63
Lively papacy; John XXIII's Pacem in terris. E. J. Hughes. Newsweek 61:19 Ap 22 '63
Living encyclical; Pacem in terris to be studied by the Center for the study of democratic institutions. America 110:857-8 Je 27 '64
New encyclical; a question of perspective; Pacem in terris. W. Herberg. il Nat R 14:364-5 My 7 '63; Reply. J. Elligett. 14:469 Je 4 '63
On translating encyclicals. America 108:732 My 25 '63
Pacem in terris. Commonweal 78:123-4 Ap 26 '63
Pacem in terris. M. Ascoli. Reporter 28:20-1 My 23 '63; Discussion. 28:8 Je 20 '63
Pacem in terris a year later. J. Cogley. Commonweal 80:356-7 Je 12 '64
Pacem in terris: an opening to the left? V. C. Ferkiss. Cath World 198:100-8 N '63
Pacem in terris, Ecclesiam Suam and communism. C. Wallace. Cath World 200:231-8 Ja '65
Pacem in terris: for all humanity; with excerpts. il Newsweek 61:21-2 Ap 22 '63

ENCYCLICALS—*Continued*
Pacem in terris; international conference to revive the discussion of the encyclical. J. Cogley. Commonweal 80:639 S 18 '64
Pacem in terris, magna charta for peace. J. B. Sheerin. Cath World 197:148-51 Je '63
Pacem in terris; possible misunderstandings. America 108:518 Ap 20 '63
Peace on earth. J. Cogley. Commonweal 78: 158-9 My 3 '63
Politics and Catholic freedom, by G. Wills. Review
Commonweal 80:607-9 S 4 '64. D. Callahan
Pope John calls for world unity; encyclical Pacem in terris (Peace on earth) il Sr Schol 82:16 Ap 24 '63
Pope John: the astonishing Catholic pontiff; and why he stirred the world; Pacem in terris. J. Roddy. il Look 27:18-29 Jl 2 '63
Pope John's essay on inequality; Mater et magistra. B. L. Masse. America 108:368-71 Mr 16 '63
Pope John's letter; interpretation of Pacem in terris. T. N. Davis. America 108:707-10 My 18 '63
Pope John's vision; concerning the encyclical Mater et magistra. P. Pavan. il Commonweal 81:231-4 N 13 '64
Pope of the dialogue; John XXIII. B. Ward. Atlan 212:54-7 S '63
Pope Paul on the church; concerning the encyclical Ecclesiam suam. M. Novak. il Commonweal 80:631-4 S 18 '64
Pope's formula for world peace. il U S News 54:25 Ap 22 '63
Slavic heritage; encyclical Magnifici eventus. America 108:797 Je 1 '63
Things old and new in Pacem in terris. J. C. Murray. America 108:612-14 Ap 27 '63
This problem of bigness; excerpt from Justice for all. B. L. Masse. America 111: 128-30 Ag 8 '64
Toward peace and justice; Pacem in terris. H. Schomer. Christian Cent 80:703-6 My 29 '63
Venture in ambivalence; Ecclesiam suam. Christian Cent 81:1051-2 Ag 26 '64
What we are for; summary of new encyclical on world peace. John XXIII. il Time 81:60+ Ap 19 '63

ENCYCLOPAEDIA Britannica
Myth of the Britannica, by H. Einbinder. Review
Christian Cent 81:273-6 F 26 '64. M. Frakes
Commonweal 79:757-8 Mr 20 '64. G. Wagner
Nation 198:303-4 Mr 23 '64. R. Hatch
Newsweek il 63:78 F 3 '64
Sat R 47:57 F 22 '64. D. M. Glixon
Science 144:665-6 My 8 '64. D. J. de S. Price
1963 edition reflects EB'S biggest revision yet. Pub W 183:40 F 25 '63
Rule, Britannica! D. Dempsey. Sat R 46:24-5 My 18 '63

ENCYCLOPAEDIA Britannica, incorporated
Building word power. il Bsns W p36 S 19 '64
EB press expands in trade, text, juvenile books. Pub W 184:36-7 D 30 '63
Encyclopaedia Britannica will buy G. & C. Merriam. il Pub W 186:36-7 S 21 '64
It's official: EB buys G. & C. Merriam. Pub W 186:23-4 O 26 '64
Meeting of minds; Encyclopaedia Britannica buys the Merriam-Webster dictionaries. il Time 84:100 S 18 '64
Staff upheaval followed by uncertainty at EB press. Pub W 185:76 F 10 '64
Temporary injunction halts Merriam sale; McGraw bids. Pub W 186:44-5 O 5 '64
25th volume; purchase of G. & C. Merriam co. Newsweek 64:92 S 21 '64

ENCYCLOPAEDIA Britannica press. See Encyclopaedia Britannica, incorporated

ENCYCLOPAEDIA Britannica school library awards
EB award: jubilation and responsibilities; Bremerton school district, Washington. E. M. Morrison. Wilson Lib Bul 38:85 S '63
EB school library awards: 1964. il Wilson Lib Bul 39:397-401+ Ja '65
Ten school systems named for library awards. Pub W 185:69 F 3 '64
Three school systems win library awards. Pub W 185:132 F 24 '64

ENCYCLOPEDIA international
Grolier launches new Encyclopedia international. Pub W 183:32 Mr 18 '63
New encyclopedia. New Yorker 39:41-2 Mr 16 '63

ENCYCLOPEDIA of photography
First look at a monumental encyclopedia. D. Vestal. il Pop Phot 54:136-7 My '64

ENCYCLOPEDIAS
Arius through diathermy; childrens encyclopedias. E. Rudin. Library J 88:4826 D 15 '63; Discussion. 89:902 F 15 '64
Books for young people; facts and ideas. A. Dalgliesh. il Sat R 46:40-1 Mr 23 '63
Books of facts and fascination lead to learning; Book of knowledge. M. B. Keiser. il Parents Mag 39:38+ S '64
Dell's encyclopedia: the biggest paperback ever. il Pub W 186:62+ Ag 3 '64
Encyclopedias. W. T. Johnston. il Consumer Bul 47:2+ Ja '64
Rare Tibetan encyclopedia of Buddhism; acquisition of Yale university library. Wilson Lib Bul 38:378 Ja '64
Reader's encyclopedia of American literature, ed. by M. J. Herzberg. Review
Sat R 46:32 Mr 23 '63. G. Hicks
See also
Columbia encyclopedia

END of a season; story. See Loeser, K.

END of the world
Trumpeter of doomsday; Millerites. H. A. Larrabee. il Am Heritage 15:34-7+ Ap '64

ENDERS, John F.
Enders, vaccine pioneer. Sci N L 83:195 Mr 30 '63
Non-physician scientist to receive AMA award. Sci N L 83:360 Je 8 '63

ENDOCRINE glands. See Glands, Ductless

ENDOCRINOLOGY
Endocrine control of growth; report of symposium sponsored by the Division of comparative endocrinology of the American society of zoologists. L. I. Gilbert. Science 139:928-9 Mr 8 '63
Endocrine control of tanning in the crayfish exoskeleton. M. Fingerman and Y. Yamamoto. bibliog Science 144:1462 Je 19 '64
Endocrines, behavior, and population. J. J. Christian and D. E. Davis. bibliog il Science 146:1550-60 D 18 '64

ENDORSEMENTS in advertising. See Advertising—Testimonials

ENDOTOXINS. See Toxins and antitoxins

ENDRES, Michael E.
So it's parochialism. America 110:823-5 Je 13 '64

ENDRIN
Case against endrin. Newsweek 63:69 My 18 '64
Chemical controversy; search for cause of dead fish in Mississippi and Missouri Rivers. Time 83:72+ Je 19 '64
Death on the Atchafalaya. J. Ridgeway. New Repub 150:13-14 Ap 25 '64
Don't go near the water; use of endrin in Louisiana. New Repub 150:5 Ap 11 '64
Endrin in Memphis. New Repub 150:4-5 My 2 '64
More dead fish. New Repub 151:7 Jl 25 '64
No dead endrin? Newsweek 64:84 Jl 13 '64
What killed the fish in the Mississippi River? il U S News 56:52 My 4 '64
You're the guinea pig. New Repub 150:3-4 My 23 '64

ENEMY; story. See Chidester, A.

ENERCON motor. See Electric motors

ENERGIZERS. See Stimulants

ENERGY. See Force and energy

ENERGY, Vital. See Vital force

ENERGY conversion systems corporation
New motor makes news by going slow; Enercon. H. Luckett. il Pop Sci 182:57-60 Mr '63

ENFORCEMENT of law. See Law enforcement

ENG, Rita
Slick clinic. Writer 76:10-12 Je '63

ENGAGEMENT rings. See Rings

ENGAGEMENTS, Marriage
I broke my engagement. il Good H 157:12+ O '63
Persian courtship; excerpts from Persia revisited. A. S. Mehdevi. Harper 228:48-53 Je '64

ENGAN, Toralf
Man who jumps with the devil. J. Lovesey. il pors Sports Illus 20:42-5 Ja 27 '64

ENGAWA. See Porches

ENGEL, A. E. J.
Geologic evolution of North America. bibliog Science 140:143-52 Ap 12 '63
—See Engel, C. G. jt. auth.
—and Engel, C. G.
Composition of basalts from the Mid-Atlantic Ridge. bibliog Science 144:1330-3 Je 12 '64
Igneous rocks of the East Pacific rise. bibliog Science 146:477-85 O 23 '64

ENGEL, Celeste G. and Engel, A. E. J.
Basalts dredged from the northeastern Pacific Ocean. bibliog Science 140:1321-4 Je 21 '63
—See Engel, A. E. J. jt. auth.
ENGEL, Leonard
Cholesterol: guilty or innocent? N Y Times Mag p29+ My 12 '63
Death comes to a cancer virus? N Y Times Mag p25+ N 8 '64
We could save 40,000 babies a year. N Y Times Mag p31+ N 17 '63
ENGEL, Mary Jane
How to dine well on 300 calories. Ladies Home J 80:94 Mr '63
Little kitchen, big party. Ladies Home J 80:102-3+ S '63
ENGEL, Michael M.
Palette notes. Design 65:138, 183 Mr-My '64
ENGEL, Niels
New chemical theory. Sci N L 85:403 Je 27 '64
ENGEL, Ralph E.
How to make your lawn better than it is. House B 105:217-19 S '63
ENGEL, Tinka D.
Your child. Redbook 121:36 My '63
ENGELBERG, Joseph. See Hinegardner, R. T. jt. auth.
ENGELHARD, Charles W.
Presentation of independence gift; statement at Lusaka, Zambia, October 26, 1964. Dept State Bul 51:723 N 16 '64
ENGELHARD, Mrs Charles
What the beautiful people are doing. il pors Vogue 143:48-51 F 15 '64
ENGELHARDT, N. L. Jr
Resource centers: educators' new focal point; interview. Arch Rec 134:210-11 O '63
ENGELHARDT, Tom
America goes to the convention. il America 108:550-1 Ap 20 '63
ENGELS, John
Angler; poem. Reporter 29:58 Ag 15 '63
De pere: feeding a child, 5:30 A.M; Poem on the death of the gardener's wife. Poetry 101:399-401 Mr '63
Domesticity; poem. Reporter 31:29 D 31 '64
Five poets. Poetry 102:402-5 S '63
For a christening; poem. Reporter 28:51 Ap 25 '63
Miss Addleman revisited; poem. Commonweal 80:232 My 15 '64
Resurrection from the county home gardens; poem. Reporter 30:43 Je 18 '64
ENGELSMAN, Ralph G.
Your family's insurance needs. Parents Mag 38:74-5+ S '63
ENGH, Jeri
St Paul's social studies institute. Sr Schol 85:10T-11T Ja 14 '65
ENGINE, engine number nine; story. See Fineman, M.
ENGINEER corps. See United States—Army—Corps of engineers
ENGINEERING
See also
Morrison-Knudsen, company
Piles and pile driving
also Marine engineering; Structural engineering; and similar headings

Exhibitions

Significant forms at engineering scale. il Arch Rec 136:16-17 S '64

Study and teaching

Engineering as a full partner in the university; excerpt from address, October 13, 1963. H. T. Heald. Sch & Soc 91:84-6 F 23 '63
Training for new engineering areas. Sch & Soc 92:150 Ap 4 '64
See also
Engineering education
ENGINEERING, Ethics of. See Engineers, Professional ethics for
ENGINEERING as a profession
Career decisions of very able students. R. C. Nichols. il Science 144:1315-19 Je 12 '64; Discussion. 144:1535; 145:533-4 Je 26, Ag 7 '64; Wilson Lib Bul 39:489+ F '65
ENGINEERING colleges
See also names of engineering colleges, e.g. Illinois institute of technology, Chicago
ENGINEERING contracts
See also
Roads—Contracts
ENGINEERING education
Concerning the engineers. J. G. Parr. Sat R 46:42-3 S 7 '63
Depletion allowance; grant to M.I.T. to retrain seasoned engineers. Time 81:88 My 3 '63
Fine new art of educating engineers; science vs. design. il Bsns W p 142+ Mr 28 '64
Industrial universities; company-financed schooling. il Time 84:44+ Ag 28 '64
University education and applied science. H. G. Booker. Science 141:486+ Ag 9 '63
See also
Ecole polytechnique, Paris
Massachusetts institute of technology, Cambridge
ENGINEERING models
See also
Roads—Models
ENGINEERING research
Dryden cites contributions of engineers; address. H. L. Dryden. Aviation W 78:67+ My 20 '63
Inventing ways to make things; Western electric's Engineering research center at Princeton. il Bsns W p 120+ Ap 20 '63
1963-1964 science review. Sci N L 84:391; 86:392 D 21 '63, D 19 '64
ENGINEERING societies
See also
American society of civil engineers
ENGINEERING students
Engineering enrollments. W. V. Grant. il Sch Life 45:28 Je '63
Engineering enrollments and degrees. Sch & Soc 92:179-80 Ap 18 '64
ENGINEERING teachers
Who should teach engineering? letter. M. B. Richardson. Science 143:916 F 28 '64; Discussion. 144:245 Ap 17 '64
ENGINEERS
Can industry harness the elusive engineer? H. E. Klein. il Duns R 83:48-9+ My '64
Consulting engineers, how to select them. Am City 79:7 My '64
Consulting engineers launch campaign to promote job opportunities abroad. Arch Rec 133:23 Ja '63
Engineers: plans for playing broader national role include National academy of engineering. J. Walsh. Science 144:980-2 My 22 '64
Fellowship expansion: presidential plan criticized at hearing before House science, space committee. D. S. Greenberg. Science 139:392-3 F 1 '63
Goddard's technical manpower. R. W. Hutchison. il Electr World 71:62-3 Je '64
Manpower: academy study presents proposals for better utilization of scientists and engineers. D. S. Greenberg. Science 145:252-3 Jl 17 '64
Mystery duo: engineers behind the Soviet space effort. Newsweek 62:73 N 25 '63
U.S. science-technology manpower is 2.7 million. Sci N L 84:137 Ag 31 '63
See also
Engineering as a profession
Engineering education
Engineers unions
Women as engineers

Salaries

Engineer income up eight per cent in two years. il Miss & Roc 13:37 Jl 15 '63

Supply and demand

Aid to the U.S. D. Wolfle. Science 139:803 Mr 1 '63
Demand for engineers at new low. W. A. Stocklin. Electr World 71:6 My '64
Engineering grads find high-paying jobs easily. Sci N L 86:217 O 3 '64
How to steal an engineer. J. H. York. il Sci Digest 55:27-9 My '64
Manpower: activist administration finds Congress hard to convince on bigger investment in people. J. Walsh. Science 139:815-17 Mr 1 '63
Scientists and engineers, 1960-70; supply and demand. H. V. Stambler. il Mo Labor R 86:1275-82 N '63
Single office proposed to combat shortage of scientists and engineers. H. M. David. il Miss & Roc 15:21 O 5 '64
Technical personnel shortage. Electr World 70:75 D '63
That manpower shortage. W. J. Coughlin. Miss & Roc 15:46 Jl 13 '64
ENGINEERS, Negro. See Negro engineers
ENGINEERS, Professional ethics of
Ethical code for scientists? letter. L. Cranberg. bibliog Science 141:1242 S 27 '63; Discussion. 142:916, 1257 N 15, D 6 '63
ENGINEERS unions
Dilemma for engineers: union or professional society? excerpt from Professional or employee-oriented: dilemma for engineering unions. G. Strauss. Mo Labor R 87:1026-8 S '64
See also
National marine engineers' beneficial association
ENGINES
Common-sense engine care. W. J. Fletcher. il Suc Farm 62:43 Ag '64

ENGINES—*Continued*
Engines: what makes them run? il Sci Digest 54:61-3 O '63
See also
Diesel engines
Gas and oil engines
Marine engines

ENGLAND, John, bp
Charter for laymen, 1822. G. Traynor. Commonweal 81:418-21 D 18 '64

ENGLAND
Inside England 1964. J. Gunther. il Look 28: 19-26 Ap 7 '64
One man's guide to England. R. Abel. Sat R 47:72 Ja 4 '64
See also
Architecture, Domestic—England
Bath
Blackpool
Colleges and universities—England
Cornwall
Country estates—England
Devonshire
English
Fishing—England
Gardens—England
Hampstead
Lake district
Libraries—England
Liverpool
Music—England
Music festivals—England
New Forest
Oxford
Scilly Islands
Sherwood Forest
Shopping centers—England
Sports—England
Stratford-on-Avon
Water supply—England

Antiquities
See also
Stonehenge

Description and travel
As I was going to St Ives. J. M. Brinnin. il Atlan 211:118+ Je '63
It isn't far from London. M. Gough. il House B 105:172+ O '63
Letter from London; concerning report: South East study. M. Panter-Downes. New Yorker 40:113-14+ Ap 4 '64
Look, luv, quick, it's Westminster! J. Kruger. il Mlle 59:334 Ag '64
Personal business; exploring England's countryside. Bsns W p 129-30 Jl 11 '64
Spring comes to England; photographs. E. Haas. Look 27:68-77 My 21 '63
Travel's picture portfolio. Travel 123:52-7 Ja '65
See also
Architecture, Domestic—England

Education
See Education—Great Britain

Historic houses, etc.
Barnums of old blighty. L. Martin and S. Martin. il Sat R 46:49-50+ Mr 16 '63
Castle tomorrow; L. Chadwick remodels Lypiatt Park. J. Russell. il Vogue 142: 126-33 Ag 1 '63
Ducal life; the Devonshires. R. Douglas-Home. il Vogue 141:156-61+ Mr 1 '63
In the glow of the perfect patron. P. Quennell. il Horizon 5:62-71 Mr '63
Leith Hill Place, home of Wedgwoods and Darwins. C. V. Wedgwood. il Antiques 83: 438-43 Ap '63

History
See Great Britain—History

Money
See Money—Great Britain

Public health
See Public health—Great Britain

Reconstructions
See Great Britain—Reconstruction

Religious institutions and affairs
News of the Christian world (cont) Christian Cent 80:246+, 347-8, 722+, 789-90, 938-40, 1034, 1150+, 1279, 1529-30; 81:28, 283-4, 526, 678, 866+, 1066+, 1154-5, 1314, 1475, 1540; 82:29-30 F 20, Mr 13, My 29, Je 12, Jl 24, Ag 21, S 18, O 16, D 4 '63, Ja 1, F 26, Ap 22, My 20, Jl 1, Ag 26, S 16, O 21, N 25, D 9 '64, Ja 6 '65
Urge to merge; Anglican and Methodist churches. Newsweek 61:46 F 4 '63
See also
Catholic church in England
Church of England
Methodist church in England

Social history
Extraordinary life and times of George Selwyn, by O. Sherwin. Review
Newsweek il 63:84+ Ja 20 '64
Pleasures of Bath in the eighteenth century. I. Origo. il Horizon 7:4-15 Wint '65

Social life and customs
England. K. W. Purdy. Atlan 211:118+ F '63
Hawthorne discovers the English. W. G. Carleton. Yale R 53:395-414 Mr '64
Neighbours, by H. Bracey. Review
Newsweek il 64:81+ Ag 24 '64
Private line from London. V. Cowles. Vogue 144:293+ D '64
Two scenes of English life. C. Sigal. Commentary 38:55-7 Jl '64
See also
Victorian period

Unemployment
See Unemployment—Great Britain

ENGLAND, Church of. See Church of England

ENGLAND and Egypt
Indianization of the Egyptian administration under British rule. R. L. Tignor. biblog f Am Hist R 68:636-61 Ap '63

ENGLAND and Ireland
Great hunger, by C. Woodham-Smith. Review
Nat R 14:499 Je 18 '63. F. D. Cohalan
Reporter il 28:50-2 Ap 25 '63. D. P. Moynihan

ENGLAND and Nepal
Ayo Gorkhali! R. Hughes. il N Y Times Mag p34-5+ O 18 '64

ENGLAND and Scotland
Letter from Edinburgh. A. Reid. il New Yorker 40:103-4+ O 24 '64

ENGLAND and the United States
America the what? Newsweek 61:44+ F 11 '63
Citizen Churchill's view of us; quotations. W. Churchill. il N Y Times Mag p29 Ap 14 '63
Opinion, please, from New York. A. Pryce-Jones. Mlle 59:38+ Je '64
Visit to the United Kingdom; joint communique, June 30, 1963. J. F. Kennedy and H. Macmillan. Dept State Bul 49:132-3 Jl 22 '63
Whilst he still lives amongst us; W. Churchill's convictions about Anglo-American friendship. Q. Hogg. il Life 57:49-50+ D 11 '64
See also
Americans in England

ENGLE, Anita
3,000 years of glass-making; excerpts from cracked about glass. UNESCO Courier 17: 20-7 F '64

ENGLE, Clair
Call from California. il por Newsweek 63:22 Mr 9 '64
Clair's health. il por Newsweek 63:19 F 3 '64
Senator Salinger? Newsweek 64:28 Ag 10 '64
Silent senator. il por Newsweek 63:28 Ap 27 '64

ENGLE, Donald L.
Try a foundation. Mus Am 84:12-13 Jl '64

ENGLE, Doreen
If you don't want to buy it, rent it! Am Home 66:23 N '63

ENGLE, Lois P. See Gibbons, R. J. jt. auth.

ENGLE, Paul
Ending; poem. New Yorker 40:34 Ag 1 '64
Home for Christmas; excerpt from An old-fashioned Christmas. Redbook 124:35+ D '64
In a bar near Shipuya station, Tokyo; Taichung, Taiwan, Republic of China; poems. Poetry 105:185-7 D '64
Opinion, please: from Iowa City. Mlle 59:34+ O '64
Runaway; poem. Ladies Home J 82:20 Ja '65
Salt crystals, spider webs, and words. Sat R 47:10-13 Mr 14 '64
Word and the poet; poem. Sat R 47:40 D 12 '64

ENGLE, Ralph L. Jr. See Nachman, R. L. jt. auth.

ENGLEBARDT, Stanley L.
Wanted: 500,000 men to feed computers. Pop Sci 186:106-9 Ja '65

ENGLEHART, Gordon
Wallace in Indiana. Nation 198:451-3 My 4 '64

ENGLEMAN, Finis E.
Adult education, dimensions and necessities; excerpt from address, February 15, 1963. por Sch Life 45:8-13 F '63
ENGLEWOOD, N.J.
Education
Englewood and the northern dilemma. G. Walker. Nation 197:7-10 Jl 6 '63
Negroes
Englewood, New Jersey: visitors in the classroom. S. Klaw. il Reporter 29:14-17 Jl 4 '63
Where a state is breaking up the neighborhood schools. il U S News 55:64-5 Ag 19 '63
ENGLISH, Raymond, 1917-
Britain in the 'sixties. Yale R 52:481-98 Je '63
ENGLISH, Raymond P. and others
Dirty streets have no place in our cleanest city. Am City 78:93-5 My '63
ENGLISH, S. P. jr
(ed) See Acosta, G. Lions beat them all
ENGLISH, W. David, and Kidwell, R. L.
Azeotrope of isopropyl alcohol and isopropyl borate. bibliog Science 139:341-2 Ja 25 '63
ENGLISH
Anatomy of Britain, by A. Sampson. Review
New Yorker 39:169-74+ My 11 '63. A. J. Liebling
British family, 1964. J. Morschauser. il Look 28:26-9 Ap 7 '64
Freeze; personal view of Britain's coldest winter. N. Mostert. Reporter 28:39-40 Mr 14 '63
Opinion, please from London. A. Alvarez. il Mlle 58:99-100 N '63
Visiting Englishmen are no roses. G. Steinem. il N Y Times Mag p63-4 Mr 29 '64
See also
Londoners
ENGLISH authors. See Authors, English
ENGLISH automobiles. See Automobiles, Foreign
ENGLISH CHANNEL
Channel cruise to glorious Devon. A. Villiers. il Nat Geog Mag 124:208-59 Ag '63
Latest plan for a Channel crossing; bridge-and-tunnel combination. il U S News 55:14 Jl 8 '63
ENGLISH CHANNEL tunnel (proposed)
Chunnel. Newsweek 62:76 S 30 '63
Chunnel, a new Channel tunnel idea. J. H. Winchester. il Sci Digest 55:21-6 Ja '64
Chunneling choice. Time 83:24 F 14 '64
Chunneling under the streak. il Time 82:32 S 27 '63
English Channel tunnel. Sci N L 85:218-19 Ap 4 '64
Official O.K. for Channel tunnel. il U S News 56:6 F 17 '64
Survey for tunnel to link Britain, France. Sci N L 86:120 Ag 22 '64
Under the Channel by tunnel. I. Ross. il Read Digest 85:35-6+ Jl '64
ENGLISH composition. See English language—Composition
ENGLISH cookery. See Cookery, English
ENGLISH country estates. See Country estates
ENGLISH departments, College. See Colleges and universities—English departments
ENGLISH drama
See also
London—Theater
ENGLISH fiction
Wall and the jungle: the early novels of Evelyn Waugh. A. B. Kernan. Yale R 53: 199-220 D '63
ENGLISH furniture. See Furniture, English
ENGLISH glass. See Glassware
ENGLISH history. See Great Britain—History
ENGLISH holly. See Holly
ENGLISH humor. See Humor, English
ENGLISH in Tanganyika
White sultan. C. Miller. il Sat Eve Post 236:80+ Ap 20 '63
ENGLISH in the United States
British brain explains the brain drain. B. Lovell. N Y Times Mag p 13+ Mr 22 '64
English secretaries must have nous: British secretaries in New York. L. W. Robinson. il N Y Times Mag p 16+ D 20 '64
Fabian abroad. S. Kauffmann. New Repub 148:28-30 Je 22 '63
Return of the Redcoats. P. S. Catling. Esquire 61:74+ Je '64
They kept the old flag flying; the British colony of Hollywood. G. Bocca. il Horizon 5:74-81 S '63
ENGLISH in Uganda
White man's burden. Newsweek 63:37 Ja 6 '64

ENGLISH language
American language, by H. L. Mencken. Review
Newsweek 62:93 D 16 '63
Loss for words. M. Pei. il Sat R 47:82-4 N 14 '64; Discussion. 47:63 D 12 '64; 48: 75-6 Ja 9 '65
Wanted: effective communicators; address, June 1, 1963. L. A. Dysart. Vital Speeches 29:668-71 Ag 15 '63
Who is behind the assault on English? L. Barnett. Horizon 5:33-48 Jl '63
See also
Slang
Words
Alphabet
See Alphabet
Anecdotes, facetiae, satire, etc.
Manner of speaking. J. Ciardi. Sat R 46:12 Je 8 '63
Quest for lavishes ghast. M. Spark. il Esquire 62:216+ D '64
Business English
For better business writing. J. S. Fielden. bibliog f Harvard Bsns R 43:164-6+ Ja '65
What do you mean I can't write? J. Fielden. il Harvard Bsns R 42:144-8+ My '64
Composition
English composition; symposium. il NEA J 53:14-22 N '64
English saints & sinners: freshmen at Univ. of Michigan & Univ. of California. Sr Schol 85:2T N 11 '64
Freshman term paper. A. M. Alston and E. Wilcox. il Wilson Lib Bul 37:858-9 Je '63
How to make words say something. W. H. Armstrong. Bet Hom & Gard 41:108-9 Mr '63
Improvement of student writing. R. Slow. il Sch & Soc 91:175-7 Ap 6 '63
In praise of praise. P. B. Diederich. il NEA J 52:58-9 S '63
Project English: improving written composition. J. Mersand. Sr Schol 83:13T O 11 '63
Why Johnny can't write. N. Cousins. Sat R 46:20 Je 8 '63
Why nobody can't write good. J. Fischer. Harper 228:16+ F '64; Discussion. 228:6+ Ap '64
See also
Style, Literary
Creative activities
Creative writing and school achievement. K. Yamamoto. bibliog f il Sch & Soc 91:307-8 O 19 '63
Every morning in Cairo; teaching creative writing at American university. J. Stuart. il Sr Schol 84:9T-10T My 8 '64
Eye for writing; excerpts from Stop, look, and write! H. Leavitt and D. Sohn. il Sr Schol 85:18T-19T D 2 '64
From Alice to Animal farm: getting students to appreciate and write satire. S. Cochell. il Sr Schol 85:10T S 16 '64
Monologues: something new for creative writing. S. Cochell. il Sr Schol 83:10T O 25 '63
Picture window: view as textbook for English composition. E. P. Schafer. NEA J 54:18 Ja '65
Steel and quicksilver. M. Garthwaite. Horn Bk 40:212-14 Ap '64
Teaching of writing. K. Boyle. NEA J 53:11-12 Mr '64
They didn't have to tell the truth. J. M. Neugeboren. NEA J 53:21-2 N '64
Dialects
Here's your Jenny Lee to London's odd dickey birds! D. Gunston. Travel 119:51-2+ F '63
See also
Pidgin English
Dictionaries
Desk dictionaries. A. W. Read. il Consumer Rep 28:547-50 N '63; Discussion. 28:510; 29:96-7 N '63, F '64
Dictionaries. Consumer Rep 29:267-72 D '64
Johnson's dictionary: a modern selection, ed. by E. L. McAdam, jr. and G. Milne. Review
Sat R 46:52-3 Mr 23 '63. R. Halsband
Time 81:M28+ Mr 29 '63
Loss for words. M. Pei. il Sat R 47:82-4 N 14 '64
Merriam's mirror of the language: Webster third revisited. S. Solomon. Sr Schol 83: 9T-10T S 13 '63
Offspring of Webster's Third; collegiate edition. E. Strainchamps. Sat R 46:68 Ap 20 '63
Smaller dictionaries. A. W. Read. Consumer Rep 29:145-7 Mr '64

ENGLISH language—Dictionaries—*Continued*
Spellbinder; Webster's third edition. Newsweek 62:71 S 2 '63
Standard is a trademark. J. Sledd. Consumer Rep 28:551-2 N '63
Ten bony nutlets; Webster's seventh new collegiate dictionary. E. Rudin. Library J 89:1288 Mr 15 '64
That dictionary or the dictionary? Webster's third new international. A. W. Read. Consumer Rep 28:488-92 O '63; Discussion. 29: 96-7 F '64
Tips: all-new Standard college dictionary. Pub W 184:46 Ag 12 '63
Your leisure. Consumer Rep 28:344-6 D '63

Euphemism

In B—D with Mrs Grundy. P. Fryer. il Horizon 6:66-9 Spr '64

Gender

Magic word game. N. Perrin. Vogue 142:124+ S 1 '63

Grammar

Nonetheless. G. Ace. Sat R 48:20 Ja 9 '65
Watch your language! excerpts from More language that needs watching. T. M. Bernstein. Read Digest 82:253-5 Je; 83:39+ N '63
Wrong way to improve schools. R. Kirk. Nat R 15:196 S 10 '63

Pronunciation

Babel-mapper. Newsweek 61:94-5 Mr 11 '63
Plants most likely to be mispronounced. House B 106:120+ Ja '64

Study and teaching

Coming revolution in teaching English. A. Schiller. il Harper 229:82-4+ O '64
English=communication; summary of address. F. Rinker. Sr Schol 84:1T-2T F 28 '64
Five rules for sequence. J. R. Squire. NEA J 53:14-16 N '64
How they teach English these days. il Changing T 17:12-14 F '63
Improvement of English instruction: adaptation of address. R. C. M. Flynt. Sch Life 46: 5-9 Ag '64
Individualizing instruction with paperbacks. D. H. Moscow. il NEA J 53:21-2 Ap '64
Language arts. H. K. Mackintosh. Sch Life 45:16-18 Jl '63
Look, ma, I'm writin'! Time 84:37 Ag 14 '64
Madison avenue methods: teaching ideas that work; Harlem, N.Y. junior high school. S. R. Selby. il Sr Schol 85:7T O 14 '64
New wave; English curriculum center, University of Nebraska. il Newsweek 61:90 My 27 '63
Peripatetic reviewer. E. Weeks. Atlan 215: 124+ Ja '65
Phase programming; Central high school, Columbus, Ohio. R. Marsh. il Sr Schol 83: 7T N 15 '63
Project English: a report to the profession. J. Mersand. il Sr Schol 83:15T-16T S 20 '63
Project English; with list of institutions, directors, and subjects. Sch Life 46:6 O '63
Raising the level of literacy; Project English; adaptation of address, March 7, 1964. J. E. Fogarty. bibliog Sch Life 46:4-6 Je '64
Reading by rainbow; system of color-coding sounds. il Time 83:59-60 Je 12 '64
Reading in basic education; excerpt from address, August 1, 1962. M. Smith. Sch & Soc 91:56-9 F 9 '63
What programming can do for English. W. E. Hoth. il Sr Schol 84:14T Mr 13 '64
Why Johnny can't write. N. Cousins. Sat R 46:20 Je 8 '63
Why nobody can't write good. J. Fischer. Harper 228:16+ F '64; Discussion. 228:6+ Ap '64
Why they don't teach good like they should. Time 83:68 Mr 13 '64
See also
English language—Composition
English language—Grammar
National council of teachers of English
Yale conference on the teaching of English

Terms and phrases

Abecedarian book; excerpts. C. W. Ferguson. PTA Mag 59:15 N '64
Couth to uncouth and vice versa; words are changing. B. Evans. il N Y Times Mag p22+ N 10 '63
Hail to the cliche; Associated press computer assesses use of clichés. R. L. Tobin. Sat R 48:65-6 Ja 9 '65
I mean, after all; some of our common expressions and phrases. E. W. Smith. il Redbook 121:15 Jl '63
To coin a phrase. Newsweek 61:88 F 25 '63
Word to the word-wise. H. B. Jacobs. il N Y Times Mag p 18 Jl 26 '64
Words that are ours. B. W. Overstreet. il PTA Mag 59:10-11 Ja '65
See also
Slogans

Anecdotes, facetiae, satire, etc.

Asian English; not English English or American English. T. Vittachi. il N Y Times Mag p52+ O 6 '63

Textbooks

High school English textbooks, by J. J. Lynch and B. Evans. Review
Nation 198:242-3 Mr 9 '64. J. P. McCall
Sr Schol 84:10T-11T F 7 '64. W. Jovanovich

ENGLISH language arts. See Language arts
ENGLISH language in the United States. See English language
ENGLISH law. See Law—Great Britain
ENGLISH literature
Opinion, please from London. A. Alvarez. il Mlle 58:99-100 N '63
See also
Authors, English
English poetry

History

William Hazlitt, by H. Baker. Review
Reporter 28:50+ Ja 17 '63. G. Steiner; Reply with rejoinder. V. Anderson. 28: 8+ F 28 '63

Jewish authors

Jewish writing in England. D. Jacobson. Commentary 37:46-50 My '64; Reply. B. Glanville. 38:20+ S '64
Zangwill in retrospect. J. Gross. Commentary 38:54-7 D '64

Study and teaching

No lollipop. F. Hascall. Horn Bk 39:86-91 F '63
No picnic in the beginning; teaching in a Harlem junior high. S. R. Selby. il Sr Schol 84:10T-11T Ap 24 '64
Two project English programs: cultural riches, and cultural poverty. J. Mersand. il Sr Schol 83:7T N 1 '63
Wrong way to improve schools. R. Kirk. Nat R 15:196 S 10 '63
See also
Shakespeare, W.—Study and teaching

Textbooks

High school English textbooks, by J. J. Lynch and B. Evans. Review
Sr Schol 84:10T-11T F 7 '64. W. Jovanovich

ENGLISH money. See Money—Great Britain
ENGLISH mosaic; story. See Warner, S. T.
ENGLISH music. See Music, English
ENGLISH painting. See Painting, British
ENGLISH philosophy. See Philosophy, English
ENGLISH poetry
In the convention. W. Dickey. Poetry 104:375-8 S '64
Poets old and young. C. Kizer. Poetry 102: 393-9 S '63
Pretense on Parnassus. R. Graves. il Horizon 5:81-5 My '63
Some British poets. G. Baro. Poetry 102:193-8 Je '63
Uses of typology. H. Carruth. Poetry 101: 424-6 Mr '63
See also
Poets, English
ENGLISH poets. See Poets, English
ENGLISH portraits. See Portraits, British
ENGLISH scientists. See Scientists, British
ENGLISH silver. See Silverware
ENGLISH sparrows. See Sparrows
ENGLISH springer spaniel national championship. See Field trials (dogs)
ENGLISH springer spaniels. See Spaniels
ENGLISH stage company. See London—Theater
ENGLISH statesmen. See Statesmen
ENGLISH students. See British students
ENGLISH villages. See Villages
ENGLISH visitors in the United States. See Foreign visitors in the United States
ENGLISH walnut trees. See Walnut trees
ENGLISH yew. See Yew
ENGLISHMEN. See English

ENGLUND, J. W. and others
Transistorized FM-stereo demodulator. Electr World 72:34-5+ D '64
ENGRAVING
See also
Callot, J.
Lithography
ENGRAVINGS
See also
Lithographs
ENKELAAR, Carol
(ed) See Schillebeeckx, E. Procreation and human dignity
ENLARGING (photography) See Photography—Enlarging
ENLARGING meter. See Photography—Apparatus and supplies
ENLISTMENT. See United States—Army—Recruiting and enlistment
ENLOE, Cortez F. jr
Other end of the line. Motor B 114:39+ Ag '64
Powerboat skippers show the way. Yachting 115:59-61+ Ap '64
ENNIS, H. L. and Lubin, M.
Cycloheximide: aspects of inhibition of protein synthesis in mammalian cells. bibliog Science 146:1474-6 D 11 '64
ENNIS, Merlin
Travel far and near; the African poison test. Natur Hist 74:67-9 F '65
ENNIS, Thomas E.
Vietnam: land without laughter. Cur Hist 46:101-6 F '64
ENNUI. See Boredom
ENOCH, Kurt, and Frase, R. W.
Book distribution in the USSR. bibliog ALA Bul 57:518-23 Je '63
ENOCH Pratt free library, Baltimore
Challenge and opportunity; excerpts from address, October 12, 1963. E. Castagna. il Library J 89:1825-7 Ap 15 '64
Library, asylum, platform for uninhibited leaps; address, February 15, 1963. K. Shapiro. il Wilson Lib Bul 37:661-9 Ap '63
Pratt's service to students. J. R. T. Stevens. il Wilson Lib Bul 39:384-8 Ja '65
Scanty information on student use. R. Ake. Library J 88:4707-8 D 15 '63
Shakespeare in Maryland. D. Sinclair. il Wilson Lib Bul 39:480-1 F '65
Up to our ears in students, or, Something's got to give; excerpts from address, May 2, 1963. E. Castagna. Library J 88:2422-3 Je 15 '63
Wealthier by the world; foreign librarians in Enoch Pratt free library. E. Castagna. il Wilson Lib Bul 39:48-50 S '64
ENOLASE. See Enzymes
ENOMOTO, Isami
Four ceramists of Hawaii. J. Lovoos. il por Am Artist 27:66-73+ Je '63
ENOVID. See Contraceptives
ENQUIRER. See National enquirer
ENQUIRER, Cincinnati. See Cincinnati enquirer
ENRICHED food. See Food, Enriched
ENRICO Fermi atomic power plant. See Atomic power plants
ENRICO Fermi award. See Fermi award
ENRIGHT, Elizabeth
Out of darkness; story. Redbook 123:50-1 O '64
ENRIGHT, Evelyn
When and how to use a decorator. Redbook 122:56-7+ F '64
ENROLLMENT, College. See Colleges and universities—Attendance; Junior colleges—Attendance
ENROLLMENT, Private school. See Private schools
ENROLLMENT, School. See School attendance
ENSIGNS. See Flags
ENSLEY, F. Gerald
Church unity is a growing thing. Christian Cent 81:10-12 Ja 1 '64
Ensley heads new Methodist group. Christian Cent 81:902 Jl 15 '64
Negro heads Iowa Methodists. P. B. Mather. Christian Cent 81:1044 Ag 19 '64
ENSLIN, Theodore
Presentiment; poem. Nation 196:274 Mr 30 '63
ENSOR, James, baron
Ensor as etcher. il Time 82:80 O 11 '63
ENSTROM, Rudolph J.
Up from the basement; R. J. Enstrom corp. il por Newsweek 63:70-1 Ja 20 '64
ENTER laughing; drama. See Stein, J.
ENTEROCOCCI. See Streptococci
ENTERPRISE (aircraft carrier) See Aircraft carriers, Atomic powered
ENTERPRISE, Free. See Free enterprise

ENTERTAINERS
Let's nix the sickniks; seamy comics and singers with sloppy manners. R. Ruark. il Sat Eve Post 236:38-9 Je 29 '63
See also
Comedians
Negro entertainers

Political activities

Is it wise for entertainers to take part in political campaigns? pro and con discussion. il Sr Schol 84:6-7 My 1 '64
ENTERTAINING
All set for fun. il Seventeen 23:144-5 O '64
Are you entertaining more and enjoying it less? D. B. Thompson. Am Home 67:38 N '64
Cocktails at 21; Bliss party for boxholders to celebrate the eightieth anniversary of the Opera house. il Opera N 28:12-13 D 14 '63
Coffeehouse party. il Ladies Home J 80:107-8 N '63
Convention plans and memories. P. Mesta. il McCalls 81:18+ Ag '64
Cook-along party. M. J. Engel. il Ladies Home J 81:145-6+ Mr '64
Dinner & games: the more the merrier. C. Brock. il Good H 158:166+ Mr '64
Diplomats entertain. M. Cartwright. il Negro Hist Bul 26:187-8 Mr '63
Diplomats entertain; problem of crashing. M. Cartwright. il Negro Hist Bul 26:216-18 Ap '63
Drama beyond the drama: first-night vigil. A. Levy. il N Y Times Mag p 12+ D 22 '63
Entertain under the stars; with recipes. il McCalls 90:118-19+ Je '63
Entertaining calls for some crystal-clear thinking. il Am Home 67:56-7 My '64
Entertaining fourth meal. il Redbook 120:72-3+ Mr '63
Entertaining is easy, in eleven different places. il House B 105:70-1+ Jl '63
Etiquette of bridal showers. Good H 158:166 My '64
Fine full life; Edith Head entertains. J. Peter and M. Kaytor. il Look 27:56-9 F 26 '63
Gilt-edged investments for entertaining. il House & Gard 124:194-9 O '63
Give a shower of roses and dainty tea treats for your favorite bride-to-be; with recipes. il Am Home 67:58-9+ My '64
Give the party they gave in the White House. il House B 105:212-13+ O '63
Good food tops off an evening. N. Nichols. il Farm J 87:75+ O '63
Have you the courage to be elegant? il House & Gard 124:217 N '63
Hello Halloween! M. J. Engel. il Ladies Home J 80:80-2 O '63
Holiday open house. il Ladies Home J 81:121+ D '64
Hospitality from the heart; Hawaiian parties. il House & Gard 126:64-9 Jl '64
Hostess notebook. C. Brock. See issues of Good housekeeping
Hostess party cues. M. R. Beasley. Am Home 66:25 Ja '63
Hostmanship and the kind of parties men like to give and go to; symposium. il House & Gard 124:96-102 Jl '63
H&G's new kind of party moves into summer. il House & Gard 125:114-17 Je '64
House beautiful wishes you most entertaining Christmas. il House B 105:133-67+ D '63
How to give a marvelous new kind of party! il House & Gard 124:224-31 N '63
How to give a successful party; excerpt from Seventeen book of etiquette and entertaining. E. A. Haupt. Seventeen 22:40 Jl '63
How to give the prettiest parties in town. H. Bell. il House B 105:182-4 D '63
How to keep a party log. il House & Gard 125:112-17 F '64
How to put the gracious gloss on hospitality. M. Gough. il House B 105:96-7+ Jl '63
If you plan a tea, here are menu ideas. il Sunset 131:130+ Jl '63
If you want something to happen make it! with recipes. il Seventeen 23:150-3+ O '64
It's party time. il Seventeen 23:45-65+ Jl '64
Keeping yacht club juniors interested. A. C. Hubert. il Motor B 112:50-1+ D '63
Make every meal a party meal. il Pop Gard 15:62-3 Jl '64
Marvelous food at Messel's. V. Riis-Hansen. il Vogue 142:136+ D '63
Master menu cook book. P. Harvey. il House & Gard 124:273+ N '63
Most likely to succeed at your next teen-age bash. Am Home 67:73-4 S '64

ENTERTAINING—*Continued*
Notes for the hostess. D. Bryan. See issues of House & garden incorporating Living for young homemakers
One great party with enough ideas to spark a dozen. il House & Gard 126:224-9+ N '64
107 ways to be a happy hostess. il Good H 158:102-19 Je '64
Painless parties for in-betweens. M. Gross. il Parents Mag 39:40-1+ D '64
Parties in full bloom; with menus. il Good H 157:66-88 Jl '63
Parties: who's in charge? C. Curtis. il N Y Times Mag p24 Jl 7 '63
Parties. . .; with recipes. il Seventeen 22: 51-2+ Jl '63
Party planning. Recreation 57:360+ S '64
Partying the oriental way. il Good H 156: 118-21+ Mr '63
Perfect parties; with menus and recipes. M. Johnston. il Bet Hom & Gard 41:68-79+ N '63
Perle Mesta's party notebook. P. Mesta. See issues of McCall's
Portable pleasures and easy-to-carry props can add flair to your entertaining off bounds. il House & Gard 123:132-8 Je '63
Pre-teen supper search. il Good H 157:120 Ag '63
Prize safari party. C. Paxman. il Seventeen 22:180 My '63
Quiz your palate with a wine-tasting party. il House & Gard 123:178+ My '63
Round the world parties; for a world of fun. il Seventeen 23:148-51 F '64
Service with a style. C. Brock. il Good H 156: 158 Ap '63
Seventeen reasons to give a party! il Seventeen 22:132-3 O '63
Shower the bride-to-be with gifts. il Seventeen 22:134-5 My '63
Sounds like fun! with recipes. M. Powell. il Seventeen 24:90-1+ Ja '65
Staging strategy for a beautiful party in one room. il House & Gard 125:162-5 My '64
Sunday afternoon record party for twenty-four; with recipes. il Seventeen 22:134+ O '63
Teen-age party in the White House. il Look 28:22-3 Mr 10 '64
This is the U.N. at play. S. Massie and R. Massie. il Sat Eve Post 236:54-7 Mr 30 '63
To the aid of the party. J. Wescott. il Seventeen 23:13 Jl '64
Toast to Victor Goodhost; excerpts from I try to behave myself. P. Bracken. il Ladies Home J 81:20+ Ja '64
Today's most popular parties. il House & Gard 126:196-201 O '64
U.N. parties are hard to digest. J. Bingham. il N Y Times Mag p 16+ Je 2 '63
Visit your own home; how to put your future guests at ease. H. Morrison. Am Home 67: 28 N '64
We gave a tasting party. I. Ray. il Farm J 87:78 D '63
What makes a party. Vogue 142:109+ D '63
Where's the party: let's crash it! R. Wallace. il Life 55:62-4+ Jl 5 '63; Same abr. Read Digest 83:131-5 O '63
Why not give an opera in the garden? L. Wilcox. il House B 105:112-13+ Je '63
Why not invite the whole neighborhood! il Am Home 66:20 Jl '63
See also
Afternoon teas
Buffet meals
Business entertaining
Catering
Childrens parties
Dinners and dining
Lawn parties
Menus
Suppers
Table decoration
Table setting
ENTERTAINING, Government. See Government entertaining
ENTERTAINING in sales promotion
Bert Lahr and the beauties; show to introduce the latest fabrics of Milliken. J. Anderson. il Dance Mag 38:24-5 S '64
Industry dons sock and buskin; industrial shows. A. Levy. Reporter 31:44+ S 10 '64
New line bows, old rumor spiked; Ford and Philco festivities in New York for dealers. il Bsns W p54-6+ My 30 '64
Show biz for big biz. il Newsweek 62:72-4 S 9 '63
ENTERTAINING Mr Sloane; drama. See Orton, J.
ENTERTAINMENT industry
Season's reasons. L. Lerman. il Mlle 58:128-31 N '63
ENTERTAINMENTS. See Amusements
ENTHOVEN, Alain Charles
Reason, morality and defense policy. America 108:461-5, 494-7, 597-8 Ap 6-13, 27 '63
U.S.-Soviet agreement possible on war definition, Enthoven says; summary of address. Aviation W 78:39 F 18 '63
Whizziest kid. il por Time 81:18-19 Je 28 '63
ENTIS, Ann
Children in clay. Design 64:200-1 Je '63
ENTOMOLOGICAL research
No war on bugs. New Repub 149:6 N 2 '63
ENTRANCE age, School. See School age
ENTRANCE drives. See Driveways
ENTRANCE halls. See Halls
ENTRANCE requirements, College. See Colleges and universities—Entrance requirements
ENTRANCES (doorways) See Doorways
ENTRICAN, Harry J.
Many uses of solder. Electr World 70:65 Jl '63
ENTWISTLE, Basil. See Roots, J. M. jt. auth.
ENURESIS. See Urine—Incontinence
ENVELOPES (philately) See Covers (philately)
ENVIRONMENT
Behavior: confinement, adaptation, and compulsory regimes in laboratory studies. J. L. Kavanau. bibliog Science 143:490 Ja 31 '64; Reply, with rejoinder. J. D. Hawkins. 145: 1460-2 S 25 '64
Cause for concern; man manipulates himself in tampering with his environment; excerpt from report. Sat R 46:53 F 2 '63
Descending spiral of ugliness. A. Heckscher. il Recreation 56:315-16+ S '63
Environmental hazards. R. L. Davis. il NEA J 53:68-70 Mr '64
Health for peace and vice versa; address, September 27, 1963. H. Cleveland. Dept State Bul 49:676-81 O 28 '63
Obsolete assumptions; excerpts from address, March 1963. S. L. Udall. il Recreation 56: 359-61 O '63
See also
Adaptation (biology)
Ecology
Heredity
Man—Influence of environment
ENVIRONMENTAL engineering
Environmental control in hospital design. A. Greenberg. il Arch Rec 136:202-6 O '64
Third of a building for mechanical services; Texas instruments plant, Dallas. il Fortune 70:211 N '64
ENVIRONMENTAL laboratories. See Testing laboratories
ENZOOTIC Sendai virus. See Viruses
ENZYMES
Actinomycin: inhibition of cortisone-induced synthesis of hepatic gluconeogenic enzymes. G. Weber and others. bibliog il Science 142: 390-2 O 18 '63
Alpha-ketoglutaric semialdehyde: a metabolic intermediate. R. M. M. Singh and E. Adams. bibliog il Science 144:67-8 Ap 3 '64
Antigens and enzymes made insoluble by entrapping them into lattices of synthetic polymers. P. Bernfeld and J. Wan. bibliog il Science 142:678-9 N 8 '63
Apocatalase of catalase-negative staphylococci. J. Jensen and M. O. Hyde. bibliog il Science 141:45-6 Jl 5 '63
Catalase hybrid enzymes in maize. L. Beckman and others. bibliog il Science 146:1174-5 N 27 '64
Citrate cleavage enzyme in livers of obese and nonobese mice. M. S. Kornacker and J. M. Lowenstein. bibliog il Science 144: 1027-8 My 22 '64
Correlation of structure and function in enzyme action; excerpts from address. D. E. Koshland, jr. bibliog il Science 142:1533-41 D 20 '63
Detective story. il Newsweek 64:82-3 Ag 17 '64
Double-stranded ribonucleic acid formation in vitro by MS 2 phage-induced RNA synthetase. C. Weissmann and P. Borst. bibliog il Science 142:1188-91 N 29 '63
Drug-induced changes in the liver endoplasmic reticulum: association with drug-metabolizing enzymes. H. Remmer and H. J. Merker. bibliog il Science 142:1657-8 D 27 '63
Enolase multiple molecular forms in fish muscle. H. Tsuyuki and F. Wold. bibliog il Science 146:535-7 O 23 '64
Enzymatic alteration of nucleic acid structure. P. R. Srinivasan and E. Borek. bibliog il Science 145:548-53 Ag 7 '64
Enzymatic dissection of the mammalian ovary. H. S. Grob. bibliog il Science 146: 73-4 O 2 '64

ENZYMES—*Continued*
Enzymatic formation of adrenaline and other catechols from monophenols. J. Axelrod. bibliog il Science 140:499-500 My 3 '63
Enzyme changes in flight muscle correlated with aging and flight ability in the male housefly. M. Rockstein and K. F. Brandt. bibliog il Science 139:1049-51 Mr 15 '63
Enzyme regulation in mammalian tissues; report on international symposium. G. Weber. Science 144:195-7 Ap 10 '64
Enzyme regulation in mammalian tissues; report on international symposium at the Indiana university school of medicine. G. Weber. Science 146:1489-92 D 11 '64
Erythrocyte acid phosphomonoesterase and glucose-6-phosphate dehydrogenase deficiency in Caucasians. F. A. Oski and others. bibliog il Science 139:409-11 F 1 '63
Erythrocytes; 5-adenylic acid deaminase requirement for ammonia or monovalent metal ion. A. Askari. bibliog il Science 141:44-5 Jl 5 '63
Feedback control of purified deoxycytidylate deaminase. G. F. Maley and F. Maley. bibliog il Science 141:1278-9 S 27 '63
Formation and degradation of cyclic dextrins by intracellular enzymes of bacillus macerans. J. A. DePinto and L. L. Campbell. bibliog il Science 146:1064-6 N 20 '64
Genetic alteration of adenylic pyrophosphorylase in salmonella. G. P. Kalle and J. S. Gots. bibliog il Science 142:680-1 N 8 '63
Glycogen deposition in the liver induced by cortisone: dependence on enzyme synthesis. O. Greengard and others. bibliog il Science 141:160-1 Jl 12 '63
Hormone-induced esterase in mouse kidney. C. R. Shaw and A. L. Koen. bibliog il Science 140:70-1 Ap 5 '63
Induction of several adaptive enzymes by actinomycin D. F. Rosen and others. bibliog il Science 146:661-3 O 30 '64
Intracellular regulatory mechanisms. H. E. Umbarger. bibliog il Science 145:674-9 Ag 14 '64
Is memory a matter of enzyme induction? C. E. Smith; discussion. Science 139:1090-2+ Mr 15 '63
Laboratory of molecular biology, Cambridge. V. K. McElheny. Science 145:36-8 Jl 3 '64
Lactate dehydrogenase isozymes: lability at low temperature. H. A. Zondag. bibliog il Science 142:965-7 N 15 '63
Machine tools of life. il Time 81:85 Ap 5 '63
Man, a bundle of enzymes. R. Yoshioka. il Sci N L 84:234-5+ O 12 '63
New enzyme discovery. Sci N L 85:405 Je 27 '64
Nicotinic acid biosynthesis: control by an enzyme that competes with a spontaneous reaction. A. H. Mehler and others. bibliog il Science 145:817-19 Ag 21 '64
Phenoloxidase system of the blowfly, callisphora erythrocephala. C. E. Sekeris and D. Mergenhagen. bibliog il Science 145:68-9 Jl 3 '64
Potentiation by adrenaline of a proteolytic activity associated with purified myosin. P. Gordon and R. Zak. bibliog il Science 140:294-5 Ap 19 '63
Protein-digesting enzymes; proteolytic enzymes. H. Neurath. il Sci Am 211:68-79 bibliog(p 154) D '64
Rhodopsin: an enzyme. D. G. McConnell and D. G. Scarpelli. Science 139:848 Mr 1 '63
Schistosome ova: rapid separation from mouse tissue by digestion with pinguinain. E. Toro-Goyco and others. bibliog il Science 142:407 O 18 '63
Semipermeable microcapsules. T. M. S. Chang. il Science 146:524-5 O 23 '64
Staphylolytic enzyme from chalaropsis: mechanism of action. D. J. Tipper and others. bibliog il Science 146:781-2 N 6 '64
Thalidomide: effects on enzymes of glutamic acid metabolism in mice. E. Hirschberg and others. bibliog il Science 143:1343-4 Mr 20 '64
Thermal inactivation of the primer in DNA-dependent synthesis of RNA in animal tissue. J. J. Furth and P. Loh. bibliog il Science 145:161-2 Jl 10 '64
Transcription of a repressed gene: evidence that it requires DNA replication. P. Hanawalt and R. Wax. bibliog il Science 145:1061-3 S 4 '64
Where is science taking us? excerpt from Horizons in biochemistry. D. E. Koshland, jr. Sat R 46:46 Je 1 '63
Wound-healing process linked to new enzyme. Sci N L 85:79 F 1 '64
See also
Amylase
Catalase
Cholinacetylase
Cholinesterase
Coenzymes
Dehydrogenases
Esterases
Galactosidases
Phosphorylases
Proteinases
Ribonuclease
Uricase
also names of enzymes, e.g. Ceruloplasmin

Nomenclature

Critique of certain parts of the 1961 report of the Commission on enzymes; letter on Commission on enzymes of the International union of biochemistry recommendations. W. M. Clark. Science 141:995-6+ S 13 '63

EOCENE period. See Geology, Stratigraphic—Eocene; Paleontology—Eocene

EPERNAY, Mark, pseud.
Allston Wheat's crusade. Harper 226:53-7 My '63
Let us now appraise famous men. Esquire 60:128-30+ O '63
Sad state of the Department of state: the hog-wild machine. Esquire 60:102-3+ S '63

EPHRON, Henry. See Ephron, P. jt. auth.

EPHRON, Phoebe, and Ephron, Henry
Take her, she's mine: text. Theatre Arts 47:37-70 Jl '63

EPHRUSSI, Boris. See Imsande, J. jt. auth.

EPIDEMIC encephalitis. See Sleeping sickness

EPIDEMICS
Meet our medical FBI; excerpts from To save your life. N. D. Spingarn. il Parents Mag 38:78-9+ O '63
See also
Black death
Cholera
Influenza
Rubella
Typhoid fever

EPIDERMIS. See Skin

EPILEPSY
Battle for understanding. R. White. il Sat Eve Post 236:62-4 Je 8 '63
Cellular mechanisms in experimental epileptic seizures. H. Matsumoto and C. A. Marsan. bibliog il Science 144:193-4 Ap 10 '64
Chemically induced epileptiform seizures in the cat. S. P. Grossman. bibliog il Science 142:409-11 O 18 '63
Electric wires in brain aid epilepsy surgery. Sci N L 83:281 My 4 '63
I wish I could sign my name to this article. I'm tired of living a lie. Good H 158:84-5+ Ap '64
Possessed: epileptic seizures. Newsweek 63:66 Mr 23 '64
What most people don't know about epilepsy. S. M. Linde. bibliog il Todays Health 42:38-41+ Jl '64

EPILEPTICS
Education for epileptics. Sci N L 84:51 Jl 27 '63
Epileptics on the job. il Todays Health 42:41 Jl '64
I wish I could sign my name to this article. I'm tired of living a lie. Good H 158:84-5+ Ap '64
Need better epilepsy laws. F. Marley. Sci N L 85:375 Je 13 '64

EPIMEDIUMS
Enchanting epimedium. E. L. Scultorp. il House B 106:239-40 My '64

EPIPHANY
Word. V. P. McCorry. America 110:28; 112:86 Ja 4 '64, Ja 16 '65

EPIPHYLLUMS
Colorful Christmas plants. C. Hodgson. il Horticulture 41:602-3 D '63
Orchid cactus, exotic of the cactus world. E. M. Schroeder. il Horticulture 41:415 Ag '63

EPIPHYTES. See Air plants

EPISCIAS
Episcias: African violet cousins. G. Arthur. il Horticulture 42:24 Ja '64

EPISCOPAL church. See Protestant Episcopal church

EPISCOPAL theological school, Cambridge, Mass.
Seminar in ecumenical trialogue; Greater Boston ecumenical seminar. N. Ehrenstrom. Christian Cent 81:579-81 Ap 29 '64

EPISCOPUS, pseud
X. Rynne, gloom, doom and council. America 110:224-5 F 15 '64

EPISTLES. See Bible—New Testament—Epistles
EPOXY adhesives
Easy mixes epoxy. K. Murray. il Motor B 111:113 Je '63
White glues. il Consumer Rep 29:385 Ag '64
EPOXY compounds
New epoxy stops leaks. J. Joseph. il Pop Sci 183:107-9+ Ag '63
Useful sealants & adhesives. B. Cobb, jr. Yachting 115:178-9 Je '64
EPOXY resins. See Resinous products
EPPERT, Ray R.
Why American companies are going abroad; interview. por U S News 56:64-7 F 10 '64
about
Businessmen for LBJ; Ford and Eppert. por U S News 56:22 Je 8 '64
EPPLEY, Garrett G.
Park and recreation administrator. por Recreation 57:194-5+ Ap '64
EPSILON. See Mesons
EPSTEIN, Aaron
Is it cheaper to ship books by common carrier? Pub W 186:50-2 Ag 10 '64
EPSTEIN, Brian
Beatle man; manager for Beatles. New Yorker 39:23-4 D 28 '63
Building the Beatle image. V. Packard. il Sat Eve Post 237:36 Mr 21 '64
Cool brain behind the bonfire. G. Cameron. il por Life 57:62+ Ag 28 '64
George, Paul, Ringo, and John: the Beatles in the United States. il por Newsweek 63:54-7 F 24 '64
EPSTEIN, David, and Epstein, Rafael
Snowflake Bentley's magnificent obsession. Read Digest 83:182-6 D '63
EPSTEIN, Jack
Operation understanding. NEA J 53:22-4 Mr '64
EPSTEIN, Sir Jacob
Jacob Epstein, sculptor, by R. Buckle. Review
Commentary 37:84+ My '64. H. Kramer
EPSTEIN, Jason
Children's hero; the genteel conspiracy. Wilson Lib Bul 38:156-60 O '63
Civilization as a process; culture as banal repetition; address, May 27-29, 1963. ALA Bul 57:664-7 Jl '63
Good bunnies always obey; books for American children. Commentary 35:112-22 F '63
EPSTEIN, Joseph
Beerbohm revival. New Repub 150:32-3 Je 27 '64
Hutchins in Chicago. New Repub 151:24-6 N 28 '64
Two southern liberals. Commentary 38:73-4+ D '64
EPSTEIN, Julius
Guide to be used. Nat R 16:916-18 O 20 '64
EPSTEIN, Lee
Design protection. Craft Horiz 24:9-10 Mr '64
EPSTEIN, Rafael. See Epstein, D. jt. auth.
EPSTEIN, Seymour
Each man in his time; story. Redbook 124:82-3 N '64
Eye of the beholder; story. Redbook 122:145-68 F '64
Quality and opinion. Writer 76:7-9+ Jl '63
Touchstone in writing fiction. Writer 77:9-11+ O '64
EQUAL employment opportunity commission. See United States—President's committee on equal employment opportunity
EQUAL pay for equal work
Equal pay act of 1963: text. Mo Labor R 86:947 Ag '63
Equal-pay bill. America 108:700-1 My 18 '63
Equal pay for women. Commonweal 78:293-4 Je 7 '63
Equal pay for women: its effect. U S News 56:91-2 Je 15 '64
Equal pay law: how it will work. il U S News 54:10 Je 24 '63
Fairer wages for the fair sex; Fair labor standards act. il Bsns W p74 Je 6 '64
Funny thing happened to her on the way to the bank. M. A. Guitar. Mlle 59:179+ S '64
On equal pay for women. U S News 56:115-17 Mr 23 '64
EQUAL rights for women. See Woman—Equal rights
EQUAL time rule (television) See Television laws and regulations
EQUALITY
After desegregation, what next? R. Wilkins. il Ebony 18:64-5 S '63
Black and white reality; a British observer's view; reprint. P. Worsthorne. il U S News 55:62-3 Jl 1 '63
Can laws make men equal? a minister's answer; sermon, September 13, 1963. W. R. Courtenay. il U S News 55:113-16 N 18 '63
Equality theory insults the uncommon man. F. Morley. Nations Bsns 52:27-8 Ap '64
Human inequality; reprint. V. Royster. U S News 55:128 O 14 '63
It's timely to consider still another inequality. F. Morley. il Nations Bsns 52:27-8 My '64
Justice and love in the racial crisis. L. D. Kliever. Christian Cent 81:1055-7 Ag 26 '64
Pride of color; reprint. D. Lawrence. U S News 57:88 Ag 10 '64
Rousseau's message for our world today. L. G. Machado. il UNESCO Courier 16:21-3 Mr '63
Should there be compensation for Negroes? parity, not preference. K. Haselden. il N Y Times Mag p43+ O 6 '63
Uneven road to equality. W. Johnson. Sat R 47:53+ My 9 '64
See also
Democracy
Liberty
Race relations
Quotations, maxims, etc.
Quotes: equality; comp. by H. Helfer. il N Y Times Mag p43 O 25 '64
EQUALIZER (sound) See Sound—Apparatus
EQUATIONS, Differential
Evolution of an active mathematical theory. A. M. Gleason. bibliog il Science 145:451-7 Jl 31 '64
EQUESTRIAN statues. See Statues
EQUILIBRIUM (physiology)
See also
Labyrinth (ear)
EQUINE encephalomyelitis virus. See Encephalomyelitis virus
EQUIPMENT, Municipal. See Municipal equipment
EQUIPMENT, Music. See Music rooms and equipment
EQUIPMENT and supplies, Sickroom. See Medical supplies
EQUIPMENT industries
See also
Machine tool industry and trade
EQUIPMENT renting. See Rental services
ERALP, Orhan
Position of Turkey. UN Mo Chron 1:10-12 O '64
ERANTHIS. See Winter aconites
ERBSEN, Claude E.
Torpedoes and concerts. Américas 15:35-8 Ag '63
ERDMAN, J. Gordon. See Day, W. C; Mulik, J. D; Schwendinger, R. B. jt. auths.
ERDMAN, Jean
Coach to Spoleto; interview, ed. by W. Sorell. por Dance Mag 37:35+ My '63
Coach with the six insides; dramatization of Finnegans wake, by J. Joyce. Criticism Nation 196:147-8 F 16 '63
EREMURUS. See Desert candles
ERHARD, Ludwig
Germany's Erhard talks about trade, tariffs, the U.S. dollar; interview, ed. by K. Lachmann and A. Zanker. por U S News 56:62-4 Je 8 '64
Place of Germany in the alliance of free nations; address, June 11, 1964. Vital Speeches 30:582-5 Jl 15 '64
President and Chancellor Erhard reaffirm commitment to U.S.-German cooperation within free-world community; joint communique, December 29, 1963; with exchanges of remarks, December 28 and December 29, 1963. Dept State Bul 50:74-80 Ja 20 '64
—See Johnson, L. B. jt. auth.
about
Adenauer gets heir apparent. por Bsns W p36 Ap 27 '63
At last, clearly in charge. por Time 84:34-5 Jl 24 '64
Atlantic report. Atlan 213:32+ F '64
Change at the top in West Germany. il por U S News 55:22 O 14 '63
Changing cornerstones. Newsweek 63:44 F 24 '64
Deadly friends. Newsweek 64:58+ O 12 '64
Der Dicke takes over. il por Time 82:35-6 O 25 '63
Diplomacy at LBJ ranch; Erhard visit. il por U S News 56:26 Ja 6 '64
Doing dandy. il por Time 83:24 Ja 24 '64
Domestic war. il por Newsweek 64:38-9 Jl 27 '64
Enter: the ten-gallon era; visit to LBJ ranch. il pors Life 56:20-7 Ja 10 '64
Erhard finally moves toward the summit. A. J. Olsen. il pors N Y Times Mag p20+ My 5 '63

ERHARD, Ludwig—about—Continued
Erhard vs Brandt. Newsweek 63:44 Mr 16 '64
Feather for Ludwig's cap. por Time 81:36 My 17 '63
Foam rubber lion? A. Schalk. Commonweal 79:368-70 D 20 '63
From Adenauer to Erhard; changeover in West Germany. il por Sr Schol 83:12-15+ N 15 '63
Gaullist Adenauer challenges Erhard. A. J. Olsen. il pors N Y Times Mag p 11+ Jl 26 '64
German miracle under debate. por Bsns W p 108+ My 11 '63
Germany: the Adenauer era ends. il por Newsweek 61:52-4 Mr 6 '63
Germany without Adenauer: what it will be like. il por U S News 55:80-1 O 21 '63
Germany's Erhard: ready to take over, but. . . por U S News 54:19 F 18 '63
Going, going. il por Newsweek 62:32+ O 28 '63
Heart of Europe: West Germany. il pors Time 82:30-4 N 1 '63
Herr Bundeskanzler comes to see us. A. J. Olsen. il pors N Y Times Mag p24+ Je 7 '64
Lion vs. the bull. Newsweek 63:36 Je 1 '64
Ludwig Erhard: a new ruler for Germany. J. P. O'Donnell. il pors Sat Eve Post 236: 93-5 O 19 '63
Mapping a new course. por Bsns W p93-4+ O 12 '63
Missing whip. Newsweek 62:27-8 D 23 '63
Onkel Ludi at the helm. il pors Newsweek 62:52-4+ O 7 '63
Our West German friends. Sat Eve Post 237: 80 Ja 25 '64
Professor is ready. R. Brigham. il pors Life 55:59-60+ S 6 '63; Same abr. with title Erhard, Germany's new chancellor. Read Digest 83:119-22 N '63
Special relations. por Newsweek 62:24 D 30 '63
Squeeze play. por Newsweek 65:28+ F 1 '65
Sweet success. il por Time 81:29 My 3 '63
Time of the sphinx. il por Time 82:27 S 27 '63
Waiting for the call. il por Time 81:31 F 15 '63
West Germany's next chancellor. T. Prittie. New Repub 148:11-12 My 11 '63
When Erhard takes over in Germany. il por U S News 54:20 My 6 '63
Who's next? por Time 81:43 Mr 15 '63
Will Germany now edge closer to U.S? Kennedy and the Germans. il por U S News 54:62-3 Je 24 '63

ERICAS. See Heaths (plants)

ERICKSON, Anna
Auction! excerpt. J. Brough. McCalls 90:112-13+ Ap '63

ERICKSON, Carl O.
Meteorological satellites. Science 143:612-13 F 7 '64

ERICKSON, Edgar L.
Sessional papers: an epilogue to an epilogue. Library J 88:2208-9 Je 1 '63

ERICKSON, Kenneth
Parents who care, more or less. PTA Mag 58:25-7 Je '64

ERICKSON, Lila
Not a care in the world? pors Farm J 87: 52-3+ Jl '63

ERICSON, David B. and Wollin, Goesta
Time's traces in sediment. Natur Hist 72: 52-61 F '63
—and others
Pleistocene epoch in deep-sea sediments. bibliog Science 146:723-32 N 6 '64
Pliocene-pleistocene boundary in deep-sea sediments. bibliog Science 139:727-37 F 22 '63
Sediment cores from the Arctic and subarctic seas. bibliog Science 144:1183-92 Je 5 '64

ERICSON, Edward L.
Military recreation: a family affair. por Recreation 56:373-4 O '63
T for travel. por Recreation 57:506-7 D '64

ERICSON, Eric E.
Rockwell collection of Carder's Steuben. Hobbies 68:28-9+ My '63

ERICSSON, Leif. See Leif Ericsson

ERIE, Pa.
Ecumenical in Erie. R. Schaffer. Christian Cent 80:863-4 Jl 3 '63

ERIE, LAKE
Lake Erie niche for gulls; ring-billed gulls nesting on Mohawk Island. R. S. Palmer. il Natur Hist 73:48-51 N '64

ERIE forge and steel corporation
Hard-hit Erie forge tries a pay cut ploy. Bsns W p50 S 14 '63
Pay cut ratified, 1,200 jobs saved. U S News 55:87 O 28 '63

ERIGBAAGTSA Indians. See Indians of South America—Brazil

ERIKSEN, Stuart P. and Kulkarni, A. B.
Methanol in normal human breath. bibliog Science 141:639-40 Ag 16 '63

ERIN, Nuri
American business overseas; address, April 8, 1963. Vital Speeches 29:497-9 Je 1 '63

ERKINS, Robert A.
He's forever chasing rainbows; Snake River trout ranch; Buhl, Idaho. F. J. Taylor. il por Sat Eve Post 236:70-1 N 30 '63

ERLENMEYER-KIMLING, L. and Jarvik, L. F.
Genetics and intelligence: a review. bibliog Science 142:1477-9; 144:80 D 13 '63, Ap 3 '64

ERLER, Fritz
Basis of partnership. For Affairs 42:84-95 O '63

ERMINES. See Weasels

ERNEST observes; story. See Rogin, G.

ERNST, Jimmy
Younger Ernst. F. Getlein. New Repub 148: 35-6 Mr 23 '63

ERNST, Max
Landmarks of modern art. K. Kuh. il Sat R 46:51 My 11 '63
Max Ernst. J. Russell. il pors Vogue 144:168-73+ S 1 '64

ERNST, Morris L.
Speaking out. por Sat Eve Post 237:8+ Mr 7 '64

ERNST, Paul
Flight grounded; story. Good H 157:74-5 N '63
Real thing; story. Redbook 124:119-42 D '64
To my daughter Carol; story. Redbook 122: 151-74 Mr '64

ERNST, Stanton G.
Pieces of the puzzle. Nat Parks Mag 37:20-1 Ap '63

ERNST in civilian clothes; story. See Gallant, M.

EROS (periodical)
Eros convicted of obscenity. Pub W 183:44 Je 24 '63
Publisher of Eros loses obscenity appeal. Pub W 186:52 N 16 '64
Publisher of Eros sentenced to five years. Pub W 184:41 D 30 '63
Twenty-eight errors of Eros. Newsweek 61:75 Je 24 '63
Two definitions of obscenity. il Time 81:44 Je 21 '63

EROSION
Disappearing U.S. Sci Am 211:58 O '64
Erosion and deposition of Italian stream valleys during historic time. S. Judson. bibliog il Science 140:898-9 My 24 '63
Steel wall saves a road; Contra Costa County, Calif. V. W. Sauer. il Am City 78:8 N '63

EROSION prevention and control
Use jute until root appears; Harrison County Industrial Seaway, Miss. il Am City 79:49 Ap '64
See also
Terraces (agriculture)

EROTIC literature
Hungry generation; works of young Indian poets. il Time 84:44 N 20 '64
Knock on the door; censorship strikes a librarian at home. W. L. Purcell. Library J 88:526+ F 1 '63; Reply. D. A. Seager. 88: 1492 Ap 1 '63
Love and the lyricist. W. Allen. New Repub 149:21-3 N 30 '63
On the Orient excess. R. Payne. il Sat R 46: 24-5 Jl 6 '63
Speaking out; eroticism, sex and love. J. B. Priestley. Sat Eve Post 236:10+ Ap 27 '63

ERROR of judgment; story. See Meade, W.

ERRORS
Desk-pounding useless. W. Wingo. Sci N L 85:36 Ja 18 '64

ERRORS, Popular
How much health is there in health foods? R. M. Deutsch. Read Digest 82:57-61 My '63
Myths we live by; excerpts from address. L. Rosten. Redbook 122:35+ Ja '64
Sense and nonsense about nutrition. F. J. Stare. Harper 229:66-70 O '64; Same abr. with title Sense and nonsense about the food we eat. il Read Digest 86:58-62 Ja '65
Superstitious side of eating. G. Maddox. il Todays Health 41:48-51+ D '63; Same abr. with title Twenty-one diet fallacies. Sci Digest 56:57-61 O '64

ERRORS, Typographic
Tied up in nots. Christian Cent 81:287 F 26 '64

ERSKINE, Milton
Time of the key. Criticism
America 109:397 O 5 '63

ERVIN, Samuel James, 1896-
Excerpt from debate, February 5, 1962. Cong Digest 42:49+ F '63
Excerpt from remarks, July 16, 1963. Cong Digest 42:269+ N '63
Excerpts from address, February 20, 1964. Cong Digest 43:144, 149+ My '64
With George & Sam on Capitol hill. il Time 82:11-12 Jl 26 '63

ERWIN, Gloria
Education's newest magic lantern. Sr Schol 84:28T-29T Mr 20 '64

ERWIN, Henry
World record flight. il pors Ebony 18:85-6 Ag '63

ERWIN, Joseph, and Bloch, K. E.
Biosynthesis of unsaturated fatty acids in microorganisms. bibliog Science 143:1106-12 Mr 6 '64

ERXLEBEN, Al
From surplus a bargain computer. Pop Electr 18:42-4 Je '63
Wind, weather and waldorf salad. Pop Electr 21:36-7 Jl '64

ERYSIPHE polygoni. See Fungi, Pathogenic

ERYTHROBLASTOSIS
Womb transfusion. Newsweek 62:68 O 7 '63

ERYTHROCYTES
Erythrocytes: 5'-adenylic acid deaminase requirement for ammonia or monovalent metal ion. A. Askari. bibliog il Science 141:44-5 Jl 5 '63
Reticulocyte protein synthesis: response of ribosome fractions to polyuridylic acid. I. B. Weinstein and others. bibliog il Science 140:314-16 Ap 19 '63
Staphylococcal alpha-hemolysin: detection on the erythrocyte membrane by immunofluorescence. A. S. Klainer and others. bibliog il Science 145:714-15 Ag 14 '64
Urea: apparent carrier-mediated transport by facilitated diffusion in dogfish erythrocytes. H. V. Murdaugh and others. bibliog il Science 144:52-3 Ap 3 '64
Uric acid transport system: apparent absence in erythrocytes of the dalmatian coach hound. A. M. Harvey and H. N. Christensen. bibliog il Science 145:826-7 Ag 21 '64

ERYTHROMYCIN
Action of erythromycin on protoplasts in vivo. L. B. Guze and G. M. Kalmanson. bibliog il Science 146:1299-300 D 4 '64
Erythromycin: mode of action. A. D. Wolfe and F. E. Hahn. bibliog il Science 143:1445-6 Mr 27 '64

ERYTHROPOIESIS
Erythropoietin production following gamma irradiation and hemorrhage in dogs. N. Pesic and others. bibliog il Science 143:49-50 Ja 3 '64

ESCALATOR clause (wages) See Wages—Cost of living adjustments

ESCANABA, Mich. Carnegie public library
Positive approach; student problem; letter to the editor. H. R. Courtright. Library J 89: 1172 Mr 15 '64

ESCAPE capsules, Airplane. See Airplanes—Escape devices

ESCAPE devices (space vehicles) See Space vehicles—Escape devices

ESCAPE! story. See Butters, D. G.

ESCAPE; story. See Moravia, A.

ESCAPES
Berlin: the great tunnel thriller; with report by L. Hall and R. Chelminski. il Life 57: 57-9+ O 16 '64
East Germany; freedom tunnel. Time 84:41 O 16 '64
Escape secrets of World war II; excerpt from Official secret. C. Hutton. il Pop Sci 184:69-73+ Ja '64
Gay life; fifty-seven escape through tunnel in Berlin. Newsweek 64:52 O 19 '64
Great jail break; Charles F. Wilson escapes from Winson Green prison, England. Time 84:23 Ag 21 '64
Great jail break; train robber Charles F. Wilson escapes from English prison. Newsweek 64:37 Ag 24 '64
Long walk home; Charles Klusmann escapes from Pathet Lao stronghold. il Time 84:40 S 11 '64
Mysterious Pentagon; escape of Lt. C. F. Klusmann from Pathet Lao. il Newsweek 64:33 S 14 '64

ESCAPES from death. See Survival (after airplane accidents, shipwrecks, etc)

ESCARRE, Aureli M.
Abbot of Montserrat. America 110:330-1 Mr 14 '64; Reply. V. de la Serna. 110:498 Ap 11 '64
Of many things; abbot of Montserrat condemns lack of freedom in Spain. T. N. Davis. America 110:28 Ja 11 '64

ESCH, Harald
Bee beep. il por Time 81:54 My 31 '63

ESCHATOLOGY
See also
Limbo

ESCHERICHIA coli
Amino acid code alcaligenes faecalis. J. J. Protass and others. il Science 143:1174-6 Mr 13 '64
Bacterial mutant with impaired potassium transport and methionine biosynthesis. R. Damadian and A. K. Solomon. bibliog il Science 145:1327-8 S 18 '64
DNA segregation in escherichia coli: observations by means of tritiated thymidine decay. S. Person and M. Osborn. bibliog il Science 143:44-6 Ja 3 '64
Effect of bromination on the biological activities of transfer RNA of escherichia coli. C. T. Yu and P. C. Zamecnik. bibliog il Science 144:856-9 My 15 '64
Electron microscopic and biochemical studies of pyruvate dehydrogenase complex of escherichia coli. L. J. Reed and others. bibliog il Science 145:930-2 Ag 28 '64
Erythromycin: mode of action. A. D. Wolfe and F. E. Hahn. bibliog il Science 143:1445-6 Mr 27 '64
Inhibition of bacterial growth by drugs of the morphine series. E. J. Simon. bibliog il Science 144:543-4 My 1 '64
Interferon-like viral inhibitor in rabbits after intravenous administration of endotoxin. M. Ho. bibliog il Science 146:1472-4 D 11 '64
Mitomycin C: effect on ribosomes of escherichia coli. H. Suzuki and W. W. Kilgore. bibliog il Science 146:1585-7 D 18 '64
Overlap of photoreactivation and liquid holding recovery in escherichia coli B. A. Castellani and others. bibliog il Science 143:1170-1 Mr 13 '64
Phenethyl alcohol synergism with mitomycin C, porfiromycin, and streptonigrin. J. R. White and H. L. White. bibliog il Science 145:1312-13 S 18 '64
Phenotypic repair of RNA-bacteriophage mutants by streptomycin. R. C. Valentine and N. D. Zinder. bibliog il Science 144:1458-9 Je 19 '64
Protein structure relationships revealed by mutational analysis. C. Yanofsky and others. bibliog il Science 146:1593-4 D 18 '64
Replication of the RNA of bacteriophage R17. M. L. Fenwick and others. bibliog il Science 146:527-30 O 23 '64
Ribonucleic acid synthesis in protoplasts of escherichia coli: inhibition by actinomycin. D. B. Mach and E. L. Tatum. bibliog il Science 139:1051-2 Mr 15 '63
Specificity of potassium-activated phosphodiesterase of escherichia coli. M. F. Singer and G. Tolbert. bibliog il Science 145:593-5 Ag 7 '64
Thymine dimers and inhibition of DNA synthesis by ultraviolet irradiation of cells. R. B. Setlow and others. bibliog il Science 142:1464-6 D 13 '63
Ultraviolet sensitivity of escherichia coli containing heat-inducible λ prophages. M. Lieb. bibliog il Science 145:175-6 Jl 10 '64

ESCHSCHOLTZIA californica. See California poppies

ESCOBAR, Alberto
Ciro Alegría's worlds. Américas 15:7-10 F '63

ESCOBAR, Marisol. See Marisol (Marisol Escobar)

ESCORIAL
Dogma shaped in stone. il Time 82:58-9 S 27 '63

ESCORTED tours. See Travel

ESCURIAL. See Escorial

ESERINE
Eserine and amphetamine: interactive effects on sleeping time in mice. C. D. Barnes and F. H. Meyers. bibliog il Science 144: 1221-2 Je 5 '64

ESFANDIARY, F. M.
Middle East paradox, the beggar rich. N Y Times Mag p22+ N 3 '63

ESHKOL, Levi
U.S. and Israel exchange views on matters of mutual interest; exchange of greetings, with joint communique, June 2, 1964. Dept State Bul 50:959-60 Je 22 '64

about

Eshkol in Nazareth. New Repub 150:10 Ap 4 '64
Israel's Eshkol: U.S. visit worries Arabs. il por U S News 56:22 Je 15 '64
Trouble in Zion. il por Newsweek 64:29-30 D 28 '64

ESHLEMAN, Clayton
Seppuku; Koreans; Second; February 25; Ascent; poems. Poetry 103:359-63 Mr '64

ESHLEMAN, Clayton—*Continued*

about

Poems, books of poems, and character. J. Langland. Poetry 103:256 Ja '64

ESKENAZI, Gerald

Getting the picture. N Y Times Mag p 101 Ap 19 '64

ESKIMO pies; story. See Somerlott, R.

ESKIMOS

Always be thankful when you catch whales; tape recorders captivate the igloo market. S. Steiner. il Horizon 6:64-5 Sum '64

Banks island: Eskimo life on the Polar Sea. W. O. Douglas. il Nat Geog Mag 125: 702-35 My '64

Eskimo north. H. Innes. il Holiday 35:88-93+ Ap '64

Eskimos get the make-up message. D. Connelly. il Life 56:17+ Ja 31 '64

Reporter at large; First conference of the Arctic coöperatives at Frobisher Bay. E. Iglauer. New Yorker 39:188+ N 23 '63

See also

Arctic exploration

Art

Murder in stone; soapstone carvings. il Sci Digest 54:5-7 S '63

Nature of Indian and Eskimo artifacts. C. Miles. il Hobbies 69:112-14 D '64

One-of-a-kind Eskimo art. il Design 65:128-9 Ja '64

Seal oil and soapstone. il Horizon 5:120 Mr '63

Crime

Murder in stone; soapstone carvings. il Sci Digest 54:5-7 S '63

Food

Fallout in the food chain; contaminated caribou diet of Nunamiut Eskimos. il Time 82: 63 S 13 '63

Health and hygiene

Resurrection of the Eskimoes. il UNESCO Courier 17:12-13 Ap '64

Origin

Eskimos and Aleuts: their origins and evolution. W. S. Laughlin. bibliog il Science 142:633-45 N 8 '63

ESKIMOTOR. See Motor vehicles

ESKOW, Gerald W.

New breed in transportation. G. R. Rosen. por Duns R 83:pt2 100-2+ Je '64

ESKUALDUNAK. See Basques

ESOPHAGEAL speech. See Speech

ESPALIERS. See Plants, Training of; Trees, Training of

ESPAILLAT, Manuel Tavares. See Tavares Espaillat, M.

ESPAILLAT, Rhina P.

O tempora; poem. Ladies Home J 80:93 Mr '63

ESPERANTO

How many Esperantists? letter to the editor. UNESCO Courier 17:33 F '64

Second language for all. E. D. Allen. UNESCO Courier 15:33 D '62; Discussion. 16:33 Mr; 33 My; 31-2 Je; 33 N '63

World language? letter. E. C. Pollock. Sat R 48:43 Ja 9 '65

ESPINOSA, E. and others

Sex-associated differences in serum proteins of mice. bibliog Science 144:417-18 Ap 24 '64

ESPIONAGE

Craft of intelligence. A. Dulles. il Harper 226: 128-74 Ap '63

Great western spy net; G. Wynne and O. Penkovsky. il Time 81:35 My 17 '63

Greatest plot in history: how the reds stole the A-bomb, by R. De Toledano. Review

Bul Atomic Sci 20:29-30 F '64. H. P. Green

Nat R 15:200-1 S 10 '63. W. A. Rusher

Include the women. il Time 84:34 D 11 '64

Leaks at the top? case of G. M. Wynne and O. V. Penkovsky. Newsweek 61:44 My 13 '63

Redbook dialogue: Allen Dulles and Ian Fleming. A. Dulles; I. Fleming. il Redbook 123:44-5+ Ja '64

Snag in the net; case against Soviet spy, Aleksandr Sokolov and accomplice dropped. il Time 84:29 O 9 '64

Spies in Moscow: more than meets the eye; G. Wynne and O. Penkovsky. il Newsweek 61:41 My 20 '63

Spying: the second oldest profession. W. S. Walker. il Sat R 46:30-1+ My 25 '63

Theresa & Miss X; Skripov and Australian intelligence. Time 81:32+ F 15 '63

U.S. businessman faces the Soviet spy. J. E. Hoover. Harvard Bsns R 42:140-6+ Ja '64

Water on the brain. Nation 197:63 Ag 10 '63

Who's spying for whom? world puzzle and a shake-up. il U S News 55:54-5 Jl 29 '63

You were expecting maybe James Bond? Israeli-Egyptian espionage. Time 83:33 Je 5 '64

See also

Electronics in criminal investigation, espionage, etc.

Spies

Wire tapping

Anecdotes, facetiae, satire, etc.

Sex and spying. R. Fontaine. il Atlan 213:118+ F '64

ESPIONAGE, Industrial. See Spies, Industrial

ESPY, Willard R.

Little books. New Yorker 40:40 Ap 18 '64

ESQUIRE (periodical)

Dis-establishmentarian; sharp look at the Washington press corps. Newsweek 63:46-7 Mr 30 '64

Esquire books celebrates 25th anniversary; book division of Esquire magazine. il Pub W 185:36 Ap 13 '64

Esquire's third-fourth annual dubious achievements awards for 1963-1964. il Esquire 61:61-7 Ja '64; 63:91-7 Ja '65; Reply to Ja '64 issue. A. Gingrich. 61:12 Mr '64

How much can you tell a magazine about its cover? A. Gingrich. Esquire 61:6 Je '64

In the shadow of the unforeseen. A. Gingrich. Esquire 61:6 F '64

Thirty years hath Esquire. A. Gingrich. il Esquire 60:8+ O '63

Thirty years of Esquire. il Newsweek 62:88 D 16 '63

Will the real July issue of Esquire please stand? A. Gingrich. il Esquire 60:6 Ag '63

Anecdotes, facetiae, satire, etc.

Harvard Lampoon parodies Esquire; symposium. il Mlle 57:37-99 Jl '63

How to crack Esquire. M. Holland. Esquire 62:90 D '64

Caricatures and cartoons

Harvard Lampoon parodies Esquire; symposium. il Mlle 57:37-99 Jl '63

ESQUIRE literary symposium

Lively and responsive weekend at Princeton. A. Gingrich. Esquire 60:6+ Jl '63

Sixth Esquire symposium. A. Gingrich. Esquire 62:6 Jl '64

ESQUIVEL, Oscar Chaves

Land reform in Costa Rica. Américas 15:11-15 F '63

ESSAYS

Excitement of travelling with a civilized companion; travel essays. F. Stark. Vogue 143:148-9+ Je '64

Competitions

Twentieth century culture in the Americas: general rules for the Américas essay contest. Américas 15:1 Jl '63

Writing awards. Sr Schol 84:20-2+ My 15 '64

ESSENTIALISM (education) See Education—Philosophy

ESSENTIALIST committee for the advancement of American education

Essentialism and American education. W. W. Brickman. Sch & Soc 91:185 Ap 20 '63

ESSEX, Hiram E.

Medical progress depends on animal research. Todays Health 42:18+ N '64

ESSEX, James W.

Chassis design for labs. Electr World 70:91-2 S '63

ESSIG, C. F. and others

Electroconvulsive threshold elevation: from daily stimulation of adrenalectomized animals. bibliog Science 140:828-9 My 17 '63

ESSO literary prize

Industrial prize for Colombian novelists. E. Sánchez O. il Américas 16:31-2 S '64

The ESTABLISHMENT. See Great Britain—Politics and government

ESTABLISHMENT; revue. See Musical comedies, revues, etc.—Criticisms, plots, etc.

ESTABROOK, R. W. See Chance, B. jt. auth.

ESTATE planning

Executive investor; portfolio problems of the typical executive. il Duns R 83:99-100+ Ja '64

Personal business. Bsns W p 141-2 Mr 9 '63; 73-4 Ja 2 '65

What you should know about estate planning. il Good H 157:158 S '63

ESTENSSORO, Victor Paz. See Paz Estenssoro, V.
ESTERASES
Affinity and phosphorylation constants for the inhibition of esterases by organophosphates. A. R. Main. bibliog il Science 144:992-3 My 22 '64
Esterase inhibitors as pesticides. J. E. Casida. bibliog il Science 146:1011-17 N 20 '64
ESTERDAY, Bjorn J.
Washington front. America 109:505 N 2 '63
ESTEROW, Milton
Ambulatory Arthur Schwartz. Mus Am 83:16-17 O '63
Erich Leinsdorf: musician of the year. Mus Am 83:16-19 D '63
James McCracken: career in three acts. Mus Am 83:18 My '63
To talk of many things. Mus Am 83:58 Ap '63
ESTERQUEST, Ralph T.
Esterquest report published on N.Y.'s Medical library resources; summary. Library J 88:1498 Ap 1 '63
ESTES, Billie Sol
Billie's guilty again. Newsweek 61:24 Ap 8 '63
Corrupt society. F. J. Cook. Nation 196:485-96 Je 1 '63
Other cheek. il por Newsweek 61:18 F 4 '63
Verdict in Texas. Time 81:29 Ap 5 '63
Visit with Billie Sol Estes. K. Fleming. il pors Newsweek 64:85-6 O 12 '64
ESTES, Howell M.
New reliability goals: excerpts from address. Aviation W 80:21 Ja 13 '64
ESTES, Jane
Rise of his rage to learn. Life 57:80+ D 4 '64
ESTES, Nolan, and others
Fringe benefits for teachers. NEA J 53:24-5 S '64
ESTES, Raymond L.
Some spring secrets. il Outdoor Life 131:72-3+ Ap '63
ESTES, Wayne
Shoot-'em-up Wayne! H. L. Masin. il por Sr Schol 85:24 Ja 21 '65
ESTHER Kreindel the second; story. See Singer, I. B.
ESTHETICS. See Aesthetics
ESTIMATES
Estimating bids by computer; Estimat. il Bsns W p80+ N 23 '63
See also
Building—Estimates
ESTONIA
See also
Astronomical observatories—Estonia
ESTRADIOL
Estradiol: evidence for its direct effect on hypothalamic neurons. R. D. Lisk and M. Newlon. bibliog il Science 139:223-4 Ja 18 '63
ESTREICHER, Karol
Six centuries of the University of Cracow. Sch & Soc 92:337-9 N 14 '64
ESTRELLA, Ulises
Six Ecuadorian poets. Américas 16:34 N '64
ESTROGENS
Estrogen administered neonatally affects adult sexual behavior in male and female rats. S. Levine and R. Mullins, jr. bibliog il Science 144:185-7 Ap 10 '64
Estrogen-induced 16-hydroxysteroid dehydrogenase activity in rat kidney. K. J. Ryan and others. bibliog il Science 142:243-4 O 11 '63
Estrone inhibition of cholesterol biosynthesis at the mevalonic acid stage. A. J. Merola and A. Arnold. bibliog il Science 144:301-2 Ap 17 '64
Feminine behavior in neonatally castrated and estrogen-treated male rats. H. H. Feder and R. E. Whalen. bibliog il Science 147:306-7 Ja 15 '65
Glycogen-containing cells of estrogen-induced renal tumors of the hamster. J. A. Arcadi. bibliog il Science 142:592-3 N 1 '63
Setback for birth-control pills; possible cause of breast cancer. Bsns W p32 O 26 '63
Suppression of the development of female mating behavior by estrogen administered in infancy. R. E. Whalen and R. D. Nadler. il Science 141:273-4 Jl 19 '63
Truth about female hormones. S. A. Kaufman. Ladies Home J 82:22-3 Ja '65
ESTRUATION
Estrous synchrony in mice: alteration by exposure to male urine. H. M. Marsden and F. H. Bronson. il Science 144:1469 Je 19 '64
Heat-control hormones look good. Farm J 88:50 F '64
5-methoxytryptophol: effect on estrus and ovarian weight. W. M. McIsaac and others. bibliog il Science 145:63-4 Jl 3 '64
ESTUARIES
Estuaries; report on Conference on estuaries. G. H. Lauff. Science 146:553-4 O 23 '64
ESTY, John C. Jr
Draft becomes an issue. Nation 198:109 F 3 '64
Draft: many threatened, few chosen. N Y Times Mag p 13+ O 20 '63
We don't need the draft. Nation 196:151-4 F 23 '63
ETCHING
Acetate etchings. il Design 64:106-8+ Ja '63
Etchings of Sigmund Abeles. S. Hurwitz. il Am Artist 28:58-63+ S '64
See also
Callot, J.
ETERNAL life. See Immortality
ETERNAL Sabbath; drama. See Drahos, M.
ETHANE
Conversion of p,p' DDT to pp' DDD in the liver of the rat. P. R. Datta and others. bibliog il Science 145:1052-3 S 4 '64
ETHANOL
Ethanol accumulation in the rumen after overfeeding with readily fermentable carbohydrate. M. J. Allison and others. bibliog il Science 144:54-5 Ap 3 '64
Photochemical production of the solvated electron in ethanol. L. I. Grossweiner and others. bibliog il Science 141:1180 S 20 '63
Rhizomorph production by armillaria mellea induced by ethanol and related compounds. A. R. Weinhold. bibliog il Science 142:1065-6 N 22 '63
ETHER (of space)
Michelson-Morley experiment. R. S. Shankland. il Sci Am 211:107-14 N '64
ETHERINGTON, Edwin Deacon
Amex: a new face and form. il por Bsns W p91-2+ Je 8 '63
Fire brigade. por Newsweek 61:75-6 Mr 11 '63
Young Ted Etherington's AMEX. T. A. Wise. il por Fortune 71:166-70+ Ja '65
ETHICAL drug trade. See Drug trade
ETHICAL education. See Moral education
ETHICAL nihilism
Moral nihilism. Christian Cent 81:691 My 27 '64
ETHICS
Brain, morals, and politics. A. Szent-Györgyi. Bul Atomic Sci 20:2-3 My '64
Divergent ethics; Protestant and Catholic in America. America 111:686-7 N 28 '64
Ethics and science, by H. Margenau. Review
Sci N L 86:287 O 31 '64
Ethics of the scientific age. W. Heitler. Bul Atomic Sci 20:21-3 O '64
Foundations of morality, by H. Hazlitt. Review
Nat R 17:25-6 Ja 12 '65. E. M. von Kuehnelt-Leddihn
Idea of perfection. I. Murdoch. Yale R 53:342-80 Mr '64
Moral decay and renewal. J. W. Gardner. Sat R 46:18+ D 14 '63
Morality and beyond, by P. Tillich. Review
Commonweal 80:123-4 Ap 17 '64. B. Murchland
Morals revolution; address, May 4, 1964. W. I. Nichols. Vital Speeches 30:539-42 Je 15 '64
Power of the positive no! N. V. Peale. Read Digest 84:49-52 F '64
Whatever became of personal ethics? L. Kronenberger. Horizon 5:60-1 Mr '63
Worship and ethics: a study in rabbinic Judaism, by M. Kadushin. Review
Commentary 38:78+ D '64. M. Fox
See also
Business ethics
Cheating in schoolwork
Christian ethics
Christian life
Communist ethics
Compromise
Integrity
Journalistic ethics
Justice
Literature and morals
Medical ethics
Moral attitudes
Moral conditions
Political ethics
Responsibility
Scientists. Professional ethics for
Sexual ethics
Social ethics
Student ethics
Teachers ethics
Television broadcasting—Moral aspects
War, Ethics of
ETHICS and law. See Law and ethics
ETHIONINE. See Butyric acid

ETHIOPIA
Atlantic report. Atlan 212:14+ Ag '63
Ethiopia: at the edge of today. P. R. Webb. il Newsweek 64:42-3 Jl 27 '64
King of kings; Ethiopia's frontier conflict with Somalia. New Repub 150:8 F 29 '64
Shades of the Mad Mullah; Somali-Ethiopian border fighting. il Newsweek 63:48 Ap 13 '64
See also
Economic assistance in Ethiopia
Education—Ethiopia
Public health—Ethiopia

Description and travel

If you like paradox, you'll love Ethiopia. M. Gough. il House B 105:126+ Ap '63
Travel notes. R. Joseph. il Esquire 60:78+ N '63

Foreign relations

Display of affection. il Time 82:25-6 O 11 '63
Emperor of Ethiopia visits United States; texts of an exchange of toasts between President Kennedy and the Emperor, October 1, 1963 and a joint communique October 2, 1963. J. F. Kennedy; Haile Selassie I, emperor of Ethiopia. Dept State Bul 49: 674-5 O 28 '63

ETHIOPIA and the United States
Selassie's message to the Negro. A. Morrison. il Ebony 19:29-32+ D '63

ETHIOPIA in literature
Meeting with a stranger, by D. Bradley. Review
Negro Hist Bul 28:37 N '64. G. C. Turner

ETHIOPIAN art. See Art, Ethiopian

ETHNIC minorities. See Minorities

ETHNIC types
African chief explains tribalism. S. O. Adebo. il N Y Times Mag p26-7+ Mr 1 '64
See also
Race

ETHNOLOGY
Origin of races: a new theory; excerpt from The origin of races. C. S. Coon; reply with rejoinder. O. L. Haught. Sat R 46:57-8 F 2 '63
Origin of races, by C. S. Coon. Review
Nat R 14:33-5 Ja 15 '63. N. Weyl; Reply. R. DeMille. 14:129 F 12 '63
Sat R 46:41 Je 22 '63. M. Mead
See also
Racial differences

Aleutian Islands

Eskimos and Aleuths: their origins and evolution. W. S. Laughlin. bibliog il Science 142: 633-45 S 8 '63

Latin America

Science in action; on ethnological tactics; among the Kuikuru of central Brazil and the Amahuaca of eastern Peru. R. L. Carneiro. Natur Hist 73:58-9+ Ag '64

ETHNOMUSICOLOGY. See Music and race

ETHRIDGE, Mark Foster
Back in action. Newsweek 62:51 Ag 26 '63
Friendly arrangement. por Time 82:36 Ag 23 '63

ETHYLENE
Ethylene production in fading vanda orchid blossoms. E. K. Akamine. bibliog il Science 140:1217-18 Je 14 '63

ETHYLENE oxide
Ethylene oxide sterilization of tissue culture media. B. L. Brown and R. Fuerst. bibliog il Science 142:1654-5 D 27 '63
Fountain of youth found for flowers. Sci N L 85:104 F 15 '64
Now, 70-hour roses. Sci Digest 53:81 My '63

ETHYLENEDIAMINE tetraacetic acid
Phosphorylase α activity in uterine muscle: stimulation by ethylenediaminetetraacetic acid. H. P. Schane and S. L. Leonard. bibliog il Science 140:811-12 My 17 '63

ETIQUETTE
Basic rules of holiday etiquette. il Good H 157:179 D '63
Boy takes girl to concert. Polly. il Farm J 87: 75 Je '63
Etiquette for the wedding guest. Good H 156: 162 My '63
Gracious living. A. Vanderbilt. See issues of McCall's to May 1964
Guider; A. Vanderbilt. il Time 81:67 Mr 1 '63
Hints on etiquette; excerpts from Hints on etiquette and the usages of society. Aywyos. Read Digest 83:192F N '63
How to cope with the social tangle; excerpt from I try to behave myself. P. Bracken. il Ladies Home J 81:26+ Mr '64
Mysterious East: advice to businessmen. il Time 82:73 Ag 16 '63
Nice to be with: in public; excerpt from Seventeen book of etiquette and entertaining. E. A. Haupt. Seventeen 22:28 O '63
Oteliaquette at Chapel Hill. Time 82:45-6 Jl 19 '63
Saying I'm sorry is not enough. R. W. Bacmeister. il Parents Mag 38:60-1+ Mr '63
Seventeen book of etiquette and entertaining; excerpts. E. A. Haupt. Seventeen 22:136-9+ Mr; 60-1 Ap '63
Social graces and disgraces; with study-discussion program, by C. Smallenburg and H. Smallenburg. M. W. Piers. bibliog il PTA Mag 59:7-9, 35-6 D '64
Table manners that take you anywhere; excerpt from Seventeen book of etiquette and entertaining. E. A. Haupt. Seventeen 22: 282+ Ag '63
Talking it over with Gay Head: table manners. Gay Head. Sr Schol 85:34 N 18 '64
Toast to Victor Goodhost; excerpts from I try to behave myself. P. Bracken. il Ladies Home J 81:20+ Ja '64
What does the code say, dear? A. P. Eliasberg. il N Y Times Mag p87+ Ap 26 '64
What price, good manners? M. A. Guitar. il Am Home 67:30 S '64
When you eat at restaurants; excerpt from Seventeen book of etiquette and entertaining. E. A. Haupt. Seventeen 23:73 S '64
When you go to proms and dances; excerpt from Seventeen book of etiquette and entertaining. E. A. Haupt. Seventeen 22:28 My '63
Who'll take the hi-road? C. Fadiman. Read Digest 82:78-80 Ap '63
See also
Courtesy
Diplomatic etiquette
Precedence

Anecdotes, facetiae, satire, etc.

Etiquette, the social whirl, & all that jazz. P. Bracken. il Ladies Home J 80:38+ D '63

ETKIN, William
Metamorphosis-activating system of the frog. bibliog Science 139:810-14 Mr 1 '63

ETO, Kimio
Eto & the koto. il por Time 85:48 Ja 8 '65

ETON college. See Public schools (endowed)—England

ETRURIANS. See Etruscans

ETRUSCAN vases. See Vases, Etruscan

ETRUSCANS
Etruscan culture, land and people, by A. Boëthius and others. Review
Art N il 63:42-3+ Mr '64. M. Gendel
Etruscan enigma. A. Menen. il Holiday 34: 46-51+ S '63

ETRYPTAMINE
Influence of methodology on electroencephalographic sleep and arousal: studies with reserpine and etryptamine in rabbits. W. G. Steiner and others. bibliog il Science 141: 53-5 Jl 5 '63

ETTELDORF, Raymond
Council and curia. America 109:234-5, 540+ S 7, N 9 '63
Greatness of Pope John. America 108:884-6 Je 22 '63

ETTENBERG, Eugene M.
Morton Goldsholl, art director of the year. Am Artist 28:22-7+ S '64
Pratt graphic art center. Am Artist 28:34-8+ My '64

ETTER, Alfred G.
When a state spray kills the state bird. Audubon Mag 65:134-7 My '63

ETTINGER, Richard Prentice
New award, fellowships made for science writing. Pub W 184:66 N 11 '63

ETTLINGER, G. and Morton, H. B.
Callosal section: its effect on performance of a bimanual skill. bibliog Science 139:485-6 F 8 '63

ETZIONI, Amitai
Gradual arms reduction. Bul Atomic Sci 19: 30-3 O '63
Multilateral force: Germany's finger on the atom. Nation 199:208-11 O 12 '64
Multilateral force or farce? debate. por N Y Times Mag p25+ D 13 '64
No short cut to progress. Sat R 47:18-19 Jl 18 '64
Peacemonger answers some questions. N Y Times Mag p 14+ Ap 21 '63
When scientists testify. Bul Atomic Sci 20: 23-6 O '64

EUBANKS, E. Burton
Steel and chrome of the credit union. NEA J 53:47 My '64

EUBANKS, Ralph Travis
Leadership and the sane society; address, March 24, 1963. Vital Speeches 29:478-80 My 15 '63
EUBANKS, Thelma M.
Negro teacher. Negro Hist Bul 27:113 F '64
EUCHARIST. See Catholic church—Eucharist; Lords Supper
EUCHARISTIC congresses
Bombay's spiritual spectacular. il Time 84: 92 D 4 '64
Catholic congress in Bombay; International eucharistic congress. P. G. Altbach. Christian Cent 82:116+ Ja 27 '65
Eucharistic congress in Bombay. W. Congdon. America 111:805-6 D 19 '64
Eucharistic congress threatened; scheduled for Bombay, India. Christian Cent 81:1134 S 16 '64
India: the Eucharistic congress; opposition by the All-India Hindu Mahasabha. V. Koilpillai. il Christian Cent 81:1444 N 18 '64
Lisbon's wrath; missionary magazine suspended for discussing papal visit. America 111:730 D 5 '64
Meaning of Bombay. V. S. Kearney. America 111:767 D 12 '64
New man at Bombay; 38th International eucharistic congress. America 111:649 N 21 '64
Protest in Portugal. America 112:33 Ja 9 '65
EUCLID
Geometry. M. Kline. il Sci Am 211:60-9 bibliog(p269) S '64
EUGÈNE, prince de Savoie-Carignan
Prince Eugen of Savoy, by N. Henderson. Review
Time il por 85:74+ Ja 22 '65
EUGENE, Ore.
Case of the midnight Christians; concrete cross, with neon tubing, erected on city-owned property. R. P. Nelson. Christian Cent 82:22-3 Ja 6 '65
Notes for a gazetteer. P. Hamburger. New Yorker 39:95-9 Je 1 '63
EUGENE Onegin; opera. See Tchaikovsky, P. I.
EUGENICS
Human future. F. Osborn. Sci N L 86:54-5+ Jl 25 '64
Science's touchiest subject. B. H. Frisch. il Sci Digest 54:34-9 N '63
See also
Prenatal influences
Sterilization of defectives, criminals, etc.
EUGLENA gracilis. See Algae
EUPHEMISM
Words, words, words. Newsweek 63:95-6+ Je 8 '64; Same abr. with title Never call a spade a spade. Read Digest 85:133-4 O '64
See also subdivision Euphemism under names of languages, e.g. English language—Euphemism
EURATOM. See European atomic energy community
EURICH, Alvin C.
Higher education in the 21st century. Atlan 211:51-5 Je '63
Look at higher education: teaching methods of the future; address, January 15, 1963. Vital Speeches 30:28-32 O 15 '63
Why we need national academic standards. Parents Mag 39:61+ F '64
EURICH, Nell
Querelle des femmes. Sat R 46:64-5+ My 18 '63
EURIPIDES
Trojan women; tr. by E. Hamilton. Criticism
Nation 198:58-9 Ja 13 '64
New Repub 150:30 F 1 '64
New Yorker 39:70 Ja 11 '64
Newsweek 63:61 Ja 6 '64
EURODISC (record company) See Phonograph record industry—Germany (Federal Republic)
EUROPE
Geographic terminology of Europe. G. E. Pearcy. il Dept State Bul 48:330-8 Mr 4 '63
Triumph of the technocrats? the death of the old Europe. D. Littlejohn. Commonweal 81: 512-15 Ja 15 '65
Winds of change. il Time 84:39-40 S 18 '64
See also
Debts, Public—Europe
Disarmament—Europe
Music festivals—Europe
Negroes in Europe
Waterways—Europe

Boundaries

Changing face of Europe. J. W. Morris. il Sr Schol 85:14T-15T N 11 '64

Civilization

Going home to Europe; excerpt from Guide to Christian Europe. C. J. McNaspy. Cath World 197:126-32 My '63

Description and travel

Europe enjoyed: the grand tour today. W. Sansom. il Holiday 37:38-51+ Ja '65
Traveling in Europe with a sketchbook. H. C. Pitz. il Am Artist 27:30-5+ Ap '63

Economic policy

Europe brews trouble for U.S. companies. il Nations Bsns 52:38-9+ N '64

Economic relations

Russia and Europe. Z. Brzezinski. For Affairs 42:428-44 Ap '64

History

Going home to Europe; excerpt from Guide to Christian Europe. C. J. McNaspy. Cath World 197:126-32 My '63
See also
European war, 1914-1918

Bibliography

Articles and other books received; northern Europe, comp. by O. J. Falnes. See issues of American historical review

1789-1815

Revolutionary-Napoleonic era: how much of a watershed? excerpts from Longmans general history of Europe. F. L. Ford. bibliog f Am Hist R 69:18-29 O '63

20th century

Chaotic heritage. W. E. Leuchtenburg. il Life 56:84+ Je 5 '64
Fall of the dynasties, by E. Taylor. Review
Am Heritage 14:108-9 Ap '63
Last years of splendor. E. Kern. il Life 55: 71-88 N 22 '63
Vials of wrath were ready to break. E. Kern. il Life 56:46-61 Ja 3 '64
When England offered everything to France; excerpt. P. Reynaud. il Sat R 46:26-8 Mr 16 '63

Intellectual life

Letter from Paris; excerpts from news conference. A. Malraux. New Yorker 40:188+ Ap 18 '64

Maps

Map of Europe (cont) Sr Schol 83:24 O 4 '63; 85:28 O 7 '64

Nationalism

Europe warned against resurgent nationalism. Christian Cent 81:876 Jl 8 '64
Residual nationalism: a rising threat to projected European union. B. Bolles. bibliog f Ann Am Acad 348:102-9 Jl '63

Politics

Europe's road to Potsdam, by W. Jaksch. Review
Nat R 16:542+ Je 30 '64. O. von Habsburg
New Europe. W. Lippmann. Newsweek 63:23 Je 8 '64
Russia and Europe. Z. Brzezinski. For Affairs 42:428-44 Ap '64
See also
Munich four power agreement, 1938
United States of Europe (proposed)

Population

Europe's initial population explosion. W. L. Langer. bibliog f Am Hist R 69:1-17 O '63

Social history

Last years of splendor. E. Kern. il Life 55: 71-88 N 22 '63
EUROPE, EASTERN
Along the iron curtain: how people feel, what they say. A. Kucherov. il U S News 55:37-42 Ag 19 '63
Balance of world power at the start of a new year. il U S News 58:32-3 Ja 4 '65
Barrier that divides the world; iron curtain. il Sr Schol 84:7 Mr 6 '64
Don't underestimate Europe. J. C. Harsch. il N Y Times Mag p32-3+ N 29 '64
Dynamics of progress in central Europe; address, November 11, 1964. G. C. McGhee. Dept State Bul 51:870-6 D 21 '64
East Europe; symposium. bibliog f il Cur Hist 44:257-304+ My '63
East Europe's second chance. V. E. Mares. bibliog f il Cur Hist 47:272-9+ N '64
Eastern Europe; stirrings. il Time 82:18-19 Ag 16 '63
Faces of the satellites. P. Schuster. il Life 55:102-14 N 15 '63
May day troubles. America 110:663 My 16 '64
New directions. New Repub 150:8 My 2 '64
Russia's Europe; shifting satellites. A. Werth. il Nation 198:644-6 Je 29 '64

EUROPE, Eastern—*Continued*
Satisfaction in silence; meeting of Communist leaders. il Time 85:24 Ja 29 '65
Soviet empire will face new stresses. R. H. Davis. Nations Bsns 51:62-3 D '63
United States and eastern Europe; address June 14, 1963. E. Anderson. Dept State Bul 49:87-92 Jl 15 '63
Weight of empire; burden for S. Khrushchev. Newsweek 63:37 Mr 9 '64
See also
Airlines—Europe, Eastern
Banks and banking—Europe, Eastern
Communism—Europe, Eastern
Foreign visitors in Eastern Europe
Hunting—Europe, Eastern
Opera—Europe, Eastern
Space research—Europe, Eastern

Commerce

East-West trade: the iron curtain eighteen years later; address, November 11, 1964. R. B. Wright. Dept State Bul 51:815-20 D 7 '64
Thaw in the cold war encourages East-West trade. F. Morley. il Nations Bsns 51:27-8 N '63

Defenses

How strong is the Soviet bloc? R. F. Staar. bibliog f il Cur Hist 45:209-15 O '63
See also
Warsaw pact, 1955

Description and travel

Down the Danube. M. Elsy. il Travel 120:47-51 Jl '63

Economic conditions

Focus on Europe. il Sr Schol 83:34 O 4 '63
How the other half lives. Time 83:65 Ja 24 '64
Is Russia losing East Europe? C. Foltz, jr. il U S News 56:48-54 Ap 20 '64
Khrushchev's hidden weakness; captive nations; with editorial comment. R. M. Nixon. il Sat Eve Post 236:23-9, 88 O 12 '63
Moscow's satellites; in and out of orbit. A. Shub. il N Y Times Mag p22-3+ Mr 15 '64
Winter of communism's discontent. A. Shub. il Reporter 30:29-31 Ja 2 '64

Economic policy

Conditions in eastern Europe; statement, March 10, 1964. W. A. Harriman. Dept State Bul 50:485-7 Mr 30 '64
See also
Council for mutual economic assistance

Economic relations

Russia's satellites in new orbits. A. Werth. Nation 200:27-9 Ja 11 '65

Foreign relations

Creeping together; U.S.-Soviet bloc relations. Newsweek 63:34+ F 10 '64

History

Forgotten people, by S. Freidin. Review
Sat R 46:92 Mr 16 '63. H. C. Wolfe

Bibliography

Articles and other books received; eastern Europe, comp. by C. Morley. See issues of American historical review

Intellectual life

Who's afraid of Franz Kafka? intellectual ferment behind the iron curtain. Time 83:42-3 Ap 17 '64

Politics

Eastern Europe: a region in ferment; address, October 13, 1964. G. C. McGhee. Dept State Bul 51:716-21 N 16 '64
Khrushchev's European allies. J. F. Brown. New Repub 148:18-20 Mr 30 '63

Social conditions

Big changes, too, in eastern Europe. il U S News 55:47 Ag 12 '63
World in change: a trip through eastern Europe. E. Griffiths. il Newsweek 62:36-8+ O 28 '63; Same abr. Read Digest 84:119-24 Ap '64

Social life and customs

Tough time for puritans behind the iron curtain. C. Grenier. il N Y Times Mag p 14-15+ My 24 '64

EUROPE, EASTERN, and the United States. See Europe and the United States

EUROPE, WESTERN
This was the summer that was. il Time 82:20-1 S 6 '63
West Europe, 1964; symposium. bibliog f Cur Hist 47:321-61+ D '64
Western unity. America 108:250 F 23 '63
See also
Advertising—Europe, Western
Aeronautics, Military—Europe, Western
Aerospace industries—Europe, Western
Agriculture—Europe, Western
Airlines—Europe, Western
Airplane industry and trade—Europe, Western
Automobile industry and trade—Europe, Western
Automobile touring—Europe, Western
Ballet—Europe, Western
Book industries and trade—Europe, Western
Camping—Europe, Western
Camps—Europe, Western
Communism—Europe, Western
Dancing—Europe, Western
Economic assistance in Europe
Education—Europe, Western
Forests and forestry—Europe, Western
Hotels, taverns, etc.—Europe, Western
Housing—Europe, Western
Investments, Foreign (by Europe)
Investments, Foreign (in Europe)
Labor and laboring classes—Europe, Western
Labor laws and legislation—Europe, Western
Land—Europe, Western
Libraries—Europe, Western
Medicine—Europe, Western
Munitions industries—Europe, Western
Music—Europe, Western
Music festivals—Europe, Western
Opera—Europe, Western
Parks—Europe, Western
Price regulation by government—Europe, Western
Public opinion—Europe, Western
Public works—Europe, Western
Publishers and publishing—Europe, Western
Research—Europe, Western
Restaurants—Europe, Western
Road traffic—Europe, Western
Shopping and shoppers—Europe, Western
Socialism—Europe, Western
Socialist parties—Europe, Western
Space research—Europe, Western
Sports—Europe, Western
Tariff—Europe, Western
Tourist trade—Europe, Western
Trade unions—Europe, Western

Armed forces

Heart of Europe: West Germany. il Time 82:30-4 N 1 '63
See also
United States—Armed forces—Forces in Europe

Bibliography

Books in the news. M. Curtis. il Sat R 46:24-6+ Je 8 '63

Capital (proposed)

Lake Europa, a new capital for a united Europe, by J. M. Miller. Review
Arch Rec il 133:50 Je '63

Civilization

Cultural pluralism in the United States and in the projected European union; address, April 5, 1963; with questions and answers. S. K. Padover. Ann Am Acad 348:25-33 Jl '63
Fifth Europe. E. A. Mowrer. il Horizon 5:4-9 Mr '63

Climate

Europe's wildest winter. G. Kent. il Read Digest 83:198-201+ S '63

Commerce

Calculated risks; trade with eastern Europe and the Soviet Union. Time 84:103 S 11 '64
East-West: the new trade winds; expansion of trade with the Soviet bloc; with report by E. Griffiths. il Newsweek 62:38-40 Ag 19 '63
East-West trade: the iron curtain eighteen years later; address, November 11, 1964. R. B. Wright. Dept State Bul 51:815-20 D 7 '64
Europeans as beef eaters; what's in it for U.S. il U S News 56:96 Je 15 '64
Europe's competitive threat will ease; U.S. businessmen will get break from shift in balance of payments. C. A. Cerami. il Nations Bsns 51:34-5+ Mr '63
Germany's Erhard talks about trade, tariffs, the U.S. dollar; interview, ed. by K. Lachmann and A. Zanker. L. Erhard. U S News 56:62-4 Je 8 '64
One world or many? H. Hazlitt. Newsweek 62:95 O 7 '63
Rougher going on trade. il Bsns W p27-8 F 9 '63

EUROPE, Western—Commerce—*Continued*
Trade; the key to Atlantic maturity; address, May 17, 1964. A. Ribicoff. Vital Speeches 30:514-16 Je 15 '64
Will foreign cars share in the U.S. boom? il U S News 57:125-6 O 19 '64
See also
European free trade association

Defenses

Alliance: whose Grand design? il Newsweek 61:17-19 F 11 '63
And where is France? il Newsweek 62:58 O 7 '63
Arms and stability in Europe, by A. Buchan and P. Windsor. Review
New Repub 150:22-4 Ja 11 '64. H. Malmgren
At least they're speaking; France and allies. Time 81:38 Ap 19 '63
Atlantic defense. A. Buchan; L. Muray. New Repub 152:11-15 Ja 9 '65
Atlantic relationships and nuclear problems: a French view. F. de Rose. For Affairs 41:479-90 Ap '63
Britain and Europe: the lesson of Skybolt. R. Steel. Commonweal 77:507-9 F 8 '63
Common market stimulus; Monnet's sanction of European nuclear defense force. Commonweal 78:87-8 Ap 19 '63
Cuba crisis and nuclear arms; why de Gaulle goes his own way; reprint. C. B. Luce. U S News 54:64-5 F 18 '63
Defense; the dilemma & the design. il Time 81:22+ F 15 '63
Diminishing the danger of surprise attack in Europe. B. G. Lall. Bul Atomic Sci 20:31-4 Mr '64
Disintegrating alliance. R. Steel. Commonweal 78:127-9 Ap 26 '63
Europe looks for a solution; new answers to military and economic problems; with report by E. Griffiths. il Newsweek 61:34-6 Je 3 '63
European security; interrelation of political, military, and economic factors. L. B. Sohn. Bul Atomic Sci 20:16-18 D '64
Evolution of western defense. P. Stehlin. For Affairs 42:70-83 O '63
Exercise big lift: opening a 5,700-mile air bridge to Europe; with analysis by M. S. Johnson. M. L. Stone and T. J. O'Halloran. il U S News 55:36-9 N 4 '63
Exploding alliances; NATO powers. Christian Cent 80:195 F 13 '63
France puts new strain on NATO but is expected to aid arms output. C. Brownlow. Aviation W 78:41 F 18 '63
Heart of Europe: West Germany. il Time 82:30-4 N 1 '63
It's April in Paris; chestnuts in blossom; SEATO and NATO consultations. Newsweek 61:37 Ap 22 '63
Letter from Europe; report on reactions to de Gaulle, nuclear arms and Pacem in terris. A. Boyle. America 108:668-9 My 11 '63
McNamara details nuclear yields; average tactical nuclear weapon in western Europe. R. S. McNamara. Miss & Roc 15:12 S 28 '64
Marriage of inconvenience. L. Gelber. For Affairs 41:310-22 Ja '63
Merchant mission; mending defenses. il Newsweek 61:33 Mr 4 '63
Merchant navy; missile-carrying ships. Newsweek 61:47-8 Mr 25 '63
Merchant of Nassau; with editorial comment. D. Healey. New Repub 148:9-10 Mr 16 '63
Mixed-manned force: whom to believe? Newsweek 61:37-8 Je 17 '63
More fingers on the trigger? Life 54:4 Mr 22 '63
MLF, a west European view. W. Young. Bul Atomic Sci 20:19-21 N '64
Multilateral force: an appraisal. J. Newhouse. Bul Atomic Sci 20:13-18 S '64
Multilateral force: Germany's finger on the atom. A. Etzioni. il Nation 199:208-11 O 12 '64
MLF: modified or out. New Repub 151:8 N 14 '64
Nassau reconsidered: what can America and Britain do now? A. Buchan. New Repub 148:21-3 Mr 2 '63
New start for the Alliance. E. V. Rostow. il Reporter 28:23-9 Ap 25 '63
Nonnuclear defense of Europe. H. A. Crosby. Bul Atomic Sci 20:30-1 Ap '64
NATO and Nukes: keeping up appearances. il Newsweek 61:33-4 Je 3 '63
NATO's nuclear dilemma. H. A. Kissinger. il Reporter 28:22-33+ Mr 28 '63; Discussion. 28:6+ Ap 25; 8+ My 9 '63; Bul Atomic Sci 20:18-20 S '64
Nuclear policy and French intransigence. M. W. Hoag. For Affairs 41:286-98 Ja '63
Off collision course; NATO ministerial meeting. il Time 84:18-19 D 25 '64
On the fence with MLF. Time 81:30+ Je 7 '63
Organizing western defense. K. U. von Hassel. For Affairs 43:209-16 Ja '65
Partners and allies. B. Alastair. For Affairs 41:621-37 Jl '63
Practice of partnership. D. Acheson. For Affairs 41:247-60 Ja '63
President Kennedy holds talks with Prime Minister of Italy; joint communique, January 17, 1963. J. F. Kennedy and A. Fanfani. Dept State Bul 48:164 F 4 '63
Pressure from Washington. New Repub 150:11-12 Mr 7 '64
Razor's edge; French, American and British plans. Time 84:36-7 D 11 '64
Reading de Gaulle's mind. R. Aron. New Repub 148:12-13 My 4 '63
Report from London: the Western alliance. W. Young. Bul Atomic Sci 19:44+ My '63
Taking stock of Europe's nuclear defenses. H. W. Baldwin. il Reporter 28:29-34 Ap 25 '63
Three on a horse; the Britons' real feelings toward the multilateral force. Time 81:33 Je 14 '63
Today's impasse, tomorrow's solution. R. Aron. New Repub 148:13-14 Je 1 '63
Tory bind; Washington's campaign for a mixed-crew surface force. D. Healey. New Repub 148:14-15 Je 22 '63
Toward a new dimension in the Atlantic partnership; address, October 27, 1963. D. Rusk. Dept State Bul 49:726-31 N 11 '63
Trading off; British strategy on multilateral force. il Newsweek 64:48 Jl 20 '64
Trap offered de Gaulle; with reply, by T. W. Stanley. P. M. Gallois. Bul Atomic Sci 19:24-30 O '63
U.S. and Europe: the argument over defense. M. S. Johnson. il U S News 54:43 Je 3 '63
U.S. demands return on NATO funding. C. Brownlow. Aviation W 80:28-30 F 3 '64
U.S.-French thaw stirs fears for NATO. L. L. Doty. Aviation W 81:20 D 28 '64
We want a Europe able to defend itself. Life 54:4 F 15 '63
Western defense. America 108:824 Je 8 '63
What it takes to protect Europe. Bsns W p 172 O 26 '63
What price conventional capabilities in Europe? B. Brodie. il Reporter 28:25-9+ My 23 '63
Who will defend Europe? J. Burnham. Nat R 14:190 Mr 12 '63
Why de Gaulle cannot win. L. J. Halle. N Y Times Mag p9+ Je 2 '63
Why western Europe cheered Kennedy. il U S News 55:32-4 Jl 15 '63
Withdrawal from Europe? an illusion. D. Acheson. il N Y Times Mag p7+ D 15 '63
See also
North Atlantic treaty organization

Description and travel

Case for the passé resort. J. P. Harman. il Travel 121:48-50+ Je '64
Europe for those who like the quiet inns close to the cities. R. Joseph. Esquire 59:36+ F '63
Europe in the fall; with reproductions of paintings. R. Joseph. Esquire 62:124-7 S '64
Europe: on $5 an hour? H. L. Hurwitz. il Sr Schol 85:10T-11T Ja 7 '65
Europe's winter wonders. J. Fanelli. il Travel 122:32-8 N '64
Inside Europe aboard Yankee; cruise on a ketch. I. Johnson and E. Johnson. il Nat Geog Mag 126:157-95 Ag '64
Let's travel in autumn. il Mlle 59:181-3 S '64
Let's travel to Europe. Mlle 56:106+ Mr '63
Let's travel to Europe; package tours. il Mlle 59:167-8 O '64
Main Street, Europe. il Travel 119:19-22 Ap '63
She travels the fastest. J. Howard. Mlle 56:70+ F '63
Speaking out; no, I don't want to go to Europe. S. Jackson. Sat Eve Post 237:8+ Je 6 '64
Travel notes. R. Joseph. Esquire 62:24+ S '64
Traveling the new Europe. il Holiday 35:117-22 Ja '64
Velvet Europe; the Continent's winter playgrounds. F. Morton. il Holiday 35:38-53 Ja '64
See also
Tourist trade—Europe, Western

Economic conditions

Better solace; Twentieth century fund report. Time 84:82 Jl 17 '64

EUROPE, WESTERN—Economic conditions—*Continued*
Boom in west Europe and where it is headed; interview. K. Lachmann. il U S News 57:38-9+ N 2 '64
Danger signs appear in Europe's boom. il U S News 57:64-6 Ag 3 '64
Depoliticalization in Europe. J. Burnham. Nat R 16:1096+ D 15 '64
Don't underestimate Europe. J. C. Harsch. il N Y Times Mag p32-3+ N 29 '64
Economic growth in the West, by A. Maddison. Review
Sat R 47:30 Ag 8 '64. S. Chase
Europe goes shopping; increasing Americanization of taste. il Bsns W p58-60+ My 18 '63
Europe's boom goes on, but— il U S News 55:68 Ag 26 '63
Europe's boom slows down; where it's heading next. il U S News 57:116-18 O 5 '64
Europe's pangs of prosperity. Duns R 81:37 F '63
Focus on Europe. il Sr Schol 83:34 O 4 '63
For Europe: year of crisis ahead? il U S News 58:25-7 Ja 4 '65
High cost of living. il Time 85:76 Ja 29 '65
Inflation in Europe. H. Hazlitt. il Newsweek 63:98 My 18 '64
Inflation spiral over the Continent. il Newsweek 63:59-61 Je 1 '64
Is Europe's boom in trouble? il U S News 57:85 N 16 '64
Look at the force behind Europe's boom. il U S News 54:79-80 Ap 1 '63
Neocapitalism. il Time 84:103 O 30 '64
New Europe. T. J. O'Halloran. il U S News 56:48-51 Ja 13 '64
Old Europe's young again and fretting. R. Lubar. il Fortune 67:86-91+ F '63
Outlook report: business future for U.S. and Europe. il U S News 56:88-90 Ap 13 '64
Le plan. Time 81:76 Mr 1 '63
Price of prosperity. il Time 83:89 Mr 20 '64
When inflation sours. H. Hazlitt. Newsweek 63:84 Je 15 '64
Where inflation fails to boost stocks. il Bsns W p 150+ Ap 11 '64
Why western Europe is booming again. il U S News 55:36-7 Jl 8 '63
Worry shifts to Europe; with editorial comment. il Bsns W p81-2, 156 Je 27 '64
You'll feel impact of change in Europe. Nations Bsns 51:84-5 F '63
See also
Loans, Foreign

Economic integration

Parallel roles of business and diplomacy in an era of expanding frontiers; address, May 19, 1964. G. C. McGhee. Dept State Bul 51:18-25 Jl 6 '64

Economic policy

Britain's failure at Brussels: the economic consequences. il Newsweek 61:74-5+ F 11 '63
Economic growth in the West, by A. Maddison. Review
Sat R 47:30 Ag 8 '64. S. Chase
Europe juggles to keep prices down, growth up. il Bsns W p 166+ D 5 '64
Europe looks for a solution; new answers to military and economic problems; with report by E. Griffiths. il Newsweek 61:34-6 Je 3 '63
European security; interrelation of political, military, and economic factors. L. B. Sohn. Bul Atomic Sci 20:16-18 D '64
Planning debate comes to the U.S. il Bsns W p 140+ My 25 '63
See also
Budget—Europe, Western
European economic community

Economic relations

After Brussels. A. Shonfield. For Affairs 41:721-31 Jl '63
After de Gaulle's thunder. il Fortune 67:65-6+ Ap '63
Community economic relations with associated African states and other countries. J. J. van der Lee. Ann Am Acad 348:15-24 Jl '63
Europe's boom slows down; where it's heading next. il U S News 57:116-18 O 5 '64
In gear again. Time 84:24 N 6 '64
Pilgrims' progress; economic integration. Time 83:24 Ja 24 '64
Tariffs aren't the only problem; EEC restrictions. il Bsns W p76+ S 7 '63

United States

Critical look at U.S. from Europe. il U S News 55:43 Ag 19 '63

Economic union

See European economic community

Foreign relations

ABC of MLF. A. Fontaine. il Reporter 31:10-14 D 31 '64
Alliance: whose Grand design? il Newsweek 61:17-19 F 11 '63
Allied disunity and German politics. G. Bailey. il Reporter 31:14-16 D 31 '64
As Europe turns left. il U S News 54:62-4 Ap 29 '63
Can de Gaulle shape Europe to his mold? Bsns W p82-3+ Ja 26 '63
Communist China and western Europe. O. M. Lee. bibliog f Cur Hist 47:143-8+ S '64
Europe without America. W. Lippmann. Newsweek 61:17 F 18 '63
For France, the power of isolation. il Newsweek 61:38+ F 18 '63
Hold fast. P. H. Spaak. For Affairs 41:611-20 Jl '63
In Europe, growing doubts about U.S. il U S News 55:66-7 S 16 '63
Isolationist Europe; the odds on a turn away from U.S. il U S News 54:56-8 Ap 8 '63
New & obscure destination; de Gaulle's veto of Britain's admission to the Common market. il Time 81:22+ F 8 '63; Same abr. with title De Gaulle corners the market. Read Digest 82:65-70 Ap '63
Peace as motion. Commonweal 79:416-17 Ja 10 '64
Polycentrism and western policy. G. F. Kennan. For Affairs 42:171-83 Ja '64
Size-up of de Gaulle; interview, ed. by A. J. Meyers. R. Aron. il U S News 54:68-72 Ap 22 '63; Same abr. with title Frenchman explains de Gaulle. Read Digest 83:79-82 Jl '63
U.S. failing in Europe? J. Fromm and F. M. Painton. il U S News 54:48-52 Mr 25 '63
We too are independent. W. F. Buckley, jr. Nat R 16:526 Je 30 '64
Who will defend Europe? J. Burnham. Nat R 14:190 Mr 12 '63

Russia

Strength of the projected union vis-à-vis Russia; address, April 5, 1963. F. C. Barghoorn. Ann Am Acad 348:54-64 Jl '63

United States

Basis of partnership. F. Erler. For Affairs 42:84-95 O '63
Clues to trans-Atlantic distrust. M. Gordey. il N Y Times Mag p25+ Je 9 '63
Crisis in the western alliance; American and British views. H. J. Morgenthau; G. Hutton. Commentary 35:185-98 Mr '63
Why Europe fears us; excerpt from Great debate, tr. by E. Pawel. R. Aron. Atlan 214:47-52 D '64

Industries

Battle for the kitchen; Europe's industries. P. Siekman. il Fortune 69:108-11+ Ja '64
Business still booms, but with a difference. il Bsns W p 110-14+ Ap 4 '64
Case of the multiplant manufacturer; excerpts from European problems in general management. R. C. K. Valtz. il Harvard Bsns R 42:12-16+ Mr '64
Europe's industries. il Fortune 68:96-101+ Ag; 110-15+ S '63 (to be cont)
Personal business; U.S. businessmen in Europe, to mix business with pleasure. Bsns W p 107-8 My 30 '64
Those American managers don't impress Europe; excerpts from Americanization of Europe. E. A. McCreary. Fortune 70:138-9+ D '64
Trouble on the tapes; Italy's Olivetti and France's Machines Bull. il Time 83:88 Je 5 '64

Intellectual life

Fifth Europe. E. A. Mowrer. il Horizon 5:4-9 Mr '63
From Europe: trends in culture. il U S News 54:73 Ap 8 '63
Obstacles to European unification. T. V. Kalijarvi. Ann Am Acad 348:46-53 Jl '63

Moral conditions

See also
Prostitution

Politics

Basis of partnership. F. Erler. For Affairs 42:84-95 O '63
De Gaulle's pursuit of grandeur; excerpt from American foreign policy. D. Brandon. Cath World 199:224-9 Jl '64
Depoliticalization in Europe. J. Burnham. Nat R 16:1096+ D 15 '64
Europe looks for a solution; new answers to military and economic problems; with report by E. Griffiths. il Newsweek 61:34-6 Je 3 '63

EUROPE, WESTERN—Politics—*Continued*
Europe: storm signals; defiant de Gaulle threatens western unity; with reports by E. Weintal, L. Norman and A. de Borchgrave. il Newsweek 64:40-2+ N 30 '64
European security; interrelation of political, military, and economic factors. L. B. Sohn. Bul Atomic Sci 20:16-18 D '64
European unity: appearance and reality. il Newsweek 63:35 Mr 9 '64
Europe's crisis of sovereignty. E. L. Dale, jr. il N Y Times Mag p7+ Jl 7 '63
Letter from Europe; report on reactions to de Gaulle, nuclear arms and Pacem in terris. A. Boyle. America 108:668-9 My 11 '63
New effort to build Europe. P. H. Spaak. For Affairs 43:199-208 Ja '65
New Europe, by G. Lichtheim. Review
Commentary 35:446-50 My '63. O. Gass
Post-bourgeois Europe. G. Lichtheim. Commentary 35:1-9 Ja '63
Round I to the General; Sparks across the channel. il Time 81:30-1 F 15 '63
Shadows over Latin Europe. E. J. Hughes. Newsweek 61:23 My 20 '63
Supreme choice: Britain and Europe, by D. Middleton. Review
Newsweek 61:98 My 6 '63
Tensions within the Alliance. R. R. Bowie. For Affairs 42:49-69 O '63
What preoccupies the Europeans. W. Lippmann. Newsweek 64:15 D 21 '64
Will European union bring about merged national goals? address, April 5, 1963; with questions and answers. D. Lerner. Ann Am Acad 348:34-45 Jl '63
Wrong Europe. C. Bourdet. Nation 196:191-5 Mr 9 '63
See also
Atlantic community

Popular culture

Obstacles to European unification. T. V Kalijarvi. Ann Am Acad 348:46-53 Jl '63

Social conditions

People are turning Europe into one big country; while politicians argue. il U S News 55:44-7 Ag 12 '63
Post-bourgeois Europe. G. Lichtheim. Commentary 35:1-9 Ja '63

Social life and customs

Europe for climbers; photographs. R. Fréson. Esquire 61:49-59 F '64
Now voyager, a little attention to ways and means. R. Joseph. il Esquire 61:60-5 F '64
Where the action is in Europe. K. D. Fishman. il Mlle 58:139-99 Mr '64

Union (proposed)

Atlantic and European unity; address, May 9, 1964. D. Rusk. Dept State Bul 50:810-15 My 25 '64
Atlantic partnership; address, January 15, 1964. A. Segni. Vital Speeches 30:258-60 F 15 '64
Effect of the projected European union on NATO; address, April 5, 1963. W. R. Tyler. Dept State Bul 48:648-52 Ap 29 '63
Europe and the Atlantic alliance; address, June 24, 1964. W. W. Rostow. Dept State Bul 51:38-43 Jl 13 '64; Same. Vital Speeches 30:617-20 Ag 1 '64
Europe; illusion of unity; renaissance of chauvinism; reaction in Britain. E. L. Dale, jr; J. Daniel; D. Healey. New Repub 148: 14-16 F 23 '63
Europe moves toward unity. G. L. Weil. bibliog f Cur Hist 47:321-5+ D '64
European communities. H. A. Schmitt. bibliog f il Cur Hist 45:257-63+ N '63
European unity: appearance and reality. il Newsweek 63:35 Mr 9 '64
Four designs for tomorrow's Europe. H. J. Morgenthau. il N Y Times Mag p 18+ My 17 '64
Idea of Europe: View from France. America 108:392-3 Mr 23 '63
New effort to build Europe. P. H. Spaak. For Affairs 43:199-208 Ja '65
New Europe: implications for the United States; symposium; ed. by J. C. Charlesworth. bibliog f Ann Am Acad 348:1-163 Jl '63
People are turning Europe into one big country; while politicians argue. il U S News 55:44-7 Ag 12 '63
President Kennedy visits Europe; texts of joint communiques released at Bonn, Birch Grove house, Sussex, and Rome, with major addresses and remarks, June 23-July 2, 1963. J. F. Kennedy. Dept State Bul 49:114-28 Jl 22 '63
Visit to Italy; address, July 2, 1963. J. F. Kennedy. Dept State Bul 49:134-7 Jl 22 '63
See also
Western European union

EUROPE, WESTERN, and the United States. See Europe and the United States

EUROPE and France
Future of political unity in western Europe; address, April 6, 1963; with questions and answers. H. Kohn. Ann Am Acad 348:95-101 Jl '63

EUROPE and Germany
Some American thoughts on current issues; address, July 16, 1964. G. C. McGhee. Dept State Bul 51:138-44 Ag 3 '64

EUROPE and the United States
American culture? qu'est-ce que c'est? L. F. Hannon. il N Y Times Mag p 10+ F 16 '64
Cracked alliance. L. J. Halle. New Repub 148: 17-20 F 23 '63
Defense against Gaullist isolationism. J. P. Warburg. Ann Am Acad 351:24-9 Ja '64
Demands of power. R. Aron. New Repub 148: 12-13 Mr 30 '63
Europe nervously watches our election. D. W. Brogan. il N Y Times Mag p 15+ O 4 '64
For an Atlantic future. T. Sommer. For Affairs 43:112-25 O '64
Future of political unity in western Europe; address, April 6, 1963; with questions and answers. H. Kohn. Ann Am Acad 348:95-101 Jl '63
Grand Design revisited: a legacy with life. J. Kraft. Harper 228:104+ F '64
Projected European union and American international prestige. Q. Wright. bibliog f Ann Am Acad 348:132-40 Jl '63
Secretary Rusk interviewed on BBC's Encounter program, May 10, 1964. D. Rusk. Dept State Bul 50:816-22 My 25 '64
Today's challenges to diplomacy. J. P. Warburg. Bul Atomic Sci 19:2-4 N '63
USIA: building bridges of peace in a changing world; address, December 8, 1964. C. T. Rowan. Dept State Bul 51:906-12 D 28 '64
World perspectives, 1964. G. Kirk. For Affairs 43:1-13 O '64

EUROPEAN athletes. See Athletes

EUROPEAN atomic energy community
U.S. and Euratom to cooperate on fast neutron reactors; Department announcement, May 27, 1964. Dept State Bul 50:941-3 Je 15 '64

EUROPEAN authors. See Authors, European

EUROPEAN business men. See Business men

EUROPEAN coal and steel community
Coal and steel community policies for averting unemployment; excerpt from testimony, June 21, 1963. K. Braun. il Mo Labor R 86: 1139-44 O '63
Steel outlook sours in Europe; overcapacity and competition. il Bsns W p96+ Ap 6 '63
Turnabout; European coal and steel community raises tariffs. Newsweek 62:75 D 16 '63
Uncommon authority; Common market's tariff raised. Time 83:84 Ja 17 '64

EUROPEAN common market. See European economic community

EUROPEAN conference of churches
Church at sea; European conference of churches held on MS Bornholm. Christian Cent 81:1326 O 28 '64
Continental ecumenism; Conference of European churches. G. Murray. Christian Cent 80:278 F 27 '63
Ecumenism at sea. America 111:583 N 14 '64

EUROPEAN cookery. See Cookery, European

EUROPEAN council for nuclear research. See European organization for nuclear research

EUROPEAN economic community
Adenauer sizes up de Gaulle; interview, ed. by K. Lachmann. K. Adenauer. U S News 54:31 F 11 '63
Advance toward unity. Commonweal 79:416 Ja 10 '64
After Brussels. A. Shonfield. For Affairs 41:721-31 Jl '63
After Brussels. E. Taylor. Reporter 28:29-32 F 14 '63
After de Gaulle's thunder. il Fortune 67:65-6+ Ap '63
America gets an unexpected break. H. S. Reuss. Harper 226:37-42 My '63; Reply. M. G. Johnson. 227:6+ Jl '63
Atlantic disunity and de Gaulle. Sat Eve Post 236:74 F 16 '63
Atlantic partnership: a vital force in motion; address, April 28, 1963. G. C. McGhee. Dept State Bul 48:771-5 My 20 '63
Atlantic report. Atlan 211:18+ My '63
Bad start for Geneva trade talks. Bsns W p 124 My 2 '64

EUROPEAN economic community—*Continued*
Beyond the Common market. Nat R 15:137-8 Ag 27 '63
Big bang; French ultimatum on agricultural organization. Newsweek 64:53-4 N 2 '64
Blackballing Britain's bid. il Bsns W p96-8+ Ja 26 '63
Blessing in disguise; British popular reactions for de Gaulle's veto. D. W. Brogan. America 108:262-3+ F 23 '63
Blow to European unity: Britain gets a no; with editorial comment. il Bsns W p23-4, 100 F 2 '63
Britain starts pushing at home. il Bsns W p 120+ F 16 '63
Britain, the Common market, and the challenge to western unity. B. M. Russett. il Cath World 196:299-305 F '63
Britain's failure at Brussels: the economic consequences. il Newsweek 61:74-5+ F 11 '63
Broadest trade talks, and slowest; Kennedy round at Geneva. il Bsns W p30-2 My 9 '64
Burial rites. Newsweek 61:32-3 F 4 '63
Business still booms, but with a difference. il Bsns W p 110-14+ Ap 4 '64
Can de Gaulle shape Europe to his mold? Bsns W p82-3+ Ja 26 '63
Chemicals: the reluctant competitors. G. Burck. il Fortune 68:148-53+ N '63
Chicken war puts new strains on unity; EEC curbs on poultry; with editorial comment. Bsns W p25-6, 132 Ag 10 '63
Chicken-war stew; United States and the Common market. P. Hendry. Reporter 29:30+ N 7 '63
Clearing the air for GATT; preliminary talks in Washington. il Bsns W p27 Mr 14 '64
Coming to terms with the Common market. P. Forbath. il Reporter 28:24+ Je 20 '63
Common market: a Noël from France? il Newsweek 62:21 D 30 '63
Common market; address, January 30, 1963. H. Macmillan. Vital Speeches 29:332-3 Mr 15 '63
Common market and space program; address, June 17, 1963. J. M. Gavin. Vital Speeches 29:591-4 Jl 15 '63
Common market and the Kennedy round. il Sr Schol 84:9-11 Ap 24 '64
Common market at the crossroads; address, March 20, 1963. A. K. Watson. Vital Speeches 29:397-400 Ap 15 '63
Common market clash; de Gaulle's threats. Time 82:16 D 20 '63
Common market crisis. C. Emmet. America 108:333-5 Mr 9 '63
Common market moves ahead. Bsns W p96 D 26 '64
Common market must resolve basic contradictions. F. Morley. il Nations Bsns 52:27-8 N '64
Common market: now 'Le package deal'? il Newsweek 62:70-3+ D 16 '63
Common market stimulus. Commonweal 78:87-8 Ap 19 '63
Community economic relations with associated African states and other countries. J. J. van der Lee. Ann Am Acad 348:15-24 Jl '63
Crisis point. Time 82:88 N 22 '63
Deadlock, or deathblow? il Time 81:34 My 17 '63
Dealing with a new Europe; with editorial comment. il Bsns W p46-54, 88 Jl 4 '64
Decision at dawn. il Newsweek 64:46 D 28 '64
DeGaulle and the future of the western alliance. Sr Schol 82:6-9+ Mr 27 '63
De Gaulle's double no, single yes. A. Rothberg. Christian Cent 80:334-5 Mr 13 '63
De Gaulle's new Europe: meaning to Britain, U.S. il U S News 54:66-7 F 4 '63
Diplomats flutter in market sputter. il Life 54:28-9 F 15 '63
Doubts about the EEC. H. Hazlitt. Newsweek 62:78 Jl 22 '63
Economic courtships. Time 83:98+ F 28 '64
Europe & the United States; tr. by R. McInerny. R. Aron. Commentary 38:54-60 Ag '64
Europe brews trouble for U.S. companies. il Nations Bsns 52:38-9+ N '64
Europe; illusion of unity; renaissance of chauvinism; reaction in Britain. E. L. Dale, jr; J. Daniel; D. Healey. New Repub 148:14-16 F 23 '63
Europe juggles to keep prices down, growth up. il Bsns W p 166+ D 5 '64
Europe, too, can have a farm problem; Kennedy Round of transatlantic tariff cuts. il Sr Schol 85:10-13 Ja 7 '65
European cold war; threat to Common market. Nat R 16:639 Jl 28 '64
European common market; symposium. bibliog f il Cur Hist 45:257-303 N '63
EEC: a federation in the making; address, August 12, 1963. A. F. Lowenfeld. Dept State Bul 49:372-7 S 2 '63
European economic community; address, March 2, 1963. W. Hallstein. Vital Speeches 29:364-9 Ap 1 '63
EEC antitrust action. Duns R 81:53-4 Mr '63
EEC drags its feet. Bsns W p28-9 Mr 2 '63
European integration and American foreign policy; address, February 9, 1963. A. Chayes. Dept State Bul 48:318-22 Mr 4 '63
Europe's new farm problem. Bsns W p 116 Jl 20 '63
Europe's uncommon market comes alive. E. O. Hauser. il Read Digest 85:140-4 Jl '64
Exploding alliances; NATO powers. Christian Cent 80:195 F 13 '63
First round of the Kennedy round. il Newsweek 63:78-82 My 11 '64
Focus on the Common market. il Sr Schol 83:35 O 4 '63
For the West: hopes rise after days of gloom. il Bsns W p26-8 Ja 19 '63
Franco's Spain and the new Europe. R. Alan; reply with rejoinder. W. A. Miele. Commentary 35:164-5 F '63
French foreign policy; address, November 3, 1964. M. Couve de Murville. Vital Speeches 31:101-5 D 1 '64
From Paris: a no for Britain. il Sr Schol 82:15-16 F 13 '63
Future of Germany; address, January 13, 1964. S. von Braun. Vital Speeches 30:365-9 Ap 1 '64
Geneva trade talks; Common market and U.S. Nat R 14:441 Je 4 '63
Getting set for Kennedy round. il Bsns W p 125-6 Ap 13 '63
Government pattern: can we breach EEC's wall? Bsns W p93-4 Je 15 '63
Growing slower. Time 82:91 N 8 '63
Herter's uphill struggle. Atlan 211:10 Je '63
Holland: gateway to Europe? transportation center of Common market. il Duns R 84:44-5+ Jl '64
Implications for U.S. of breakdown in U.K.-EEC negotiations; text of letter to Senator Paul H. Douglas, February 15, 1963. G. W. Ball. Dept State Bul 48:412-15 Mr 18 '63
In Common market: new optimism, cooperation. U S News 56:45 Ja 13 '64
In the not so united Europe; French milk strike. E. Taylor. Reporter 31:12+ O 8 '64
International markets; significance of Africa. A. O. Stanley. Duns R 81:59-62 F '63
International markets; what we can expect in our world trade position in 1963. A. O. Stanley. Duns R 81:51-3+ Ja '63
International outlook. Bsns W p 165 S 14 '63
International outlook; U.S. relations with EEC. Bsns W p65 Ag 31 '63
Is EEC splitting at the seams? Franco-German rivalry. il Bsns W p 16-17 D 21 '63
Is Europe still a good business bet? il Bsns W p88-91 F 9 '63
Kennedy round, progress and promise; address, July 17, 1963. W. T. Gossett. Dept State Bul 49:291-6 Ag 19 '63
Kennedy-round talks get down to business. Bsns W p30 N 21 '64
Kennedy tries to stem the tide in Europe. il Bsns W p28-9 Je 29 '63
Light in Brussels. Newsweek 63:32+ Ja 6 '64
Macmillan at Rome. M. Painelle. America 108:265-6 F 23 '63
More flies in the EEC ointment; inflationary pressures and financial squeeze. il Bsns W p58+ N 23 '63
Myth about the Common market? E. Griffiths. il Newsweek 62:61-2+ Ag 12 '63
New & obscure destination; de Gaulle's veto of Britain's admission to the Common market. il Time 81:22+ F 8 '63; Same abr. with title De Gaulle corners the market. Read Digest 82:65-70 Ap '63
Normalcy. D. Lawrence. U S News 54:100 F 11 '63
On the move? il Newsweek 61:40 Ap 15 '63
Paradise re-examined. il Time 81:83 F 15 '63
Paris-Bonn axis. T. Prittie. New Repub 148:8-9 F 9 '63
Political evolution of Europe; news conference, January 14, 1963. C. de Gaulle. Vital Speeches 29:230-5 F 1 '63
Politics of German wheat. D. Schoenbaum. Nation 197:447-9 D 28 '63
Question at issue; address, January 29, 1963. M. Couve de Murville. Vital Speeches 29:333-4 Mr 15 '63
Question of exceptions; Kennedy round of tariff-cutting talks. Time 84:66 N 20 '64
Remember the alcazar; vote against Spain's joining Common market. Nat R 16:307 Ap 21 '64

EUROPEAN economic community—*Continued*
Report on an uneasy Common market. W. Roepke. Nat R 16:195-6 Mr 10 '64
Revenge is bitter. Newsweek 61:38+ Mr 11 '63
Revolt of Europe; with editorial comment. E. Griffiths. il Sat Eve Post 236:13-21, 76 Mr 9 '63
Rift in West: how serious. il U S News 54:29-30 F 11 '63
Rougher going on trade. il Bsns W p27-8 F 9 '63
Round I to the General; Sparks across the channel. il Time 81:30-1 F 15 '63
Second thoughts on the Common market. D. F. Dowd. Yale R 53:168-91 D '63
Secretary Rusk appears on Meet the press; transcript of interview, January 27, 1963. D. Rusk. Dept State Bul 48:244-50 F 18 '63
Seeds of agreement; ministerial meeting in Brussels. il Time 82:62 D 27 '63
Setting stage for GATT; U.S. battled EEC on ground rules. Bsns W p27-8 My 25 '63
Shaping the big stick; European Common market's anticartel policy. Newsweek 61:71 Ap 29 '63
Six move toward union. C. Sterling. Reporter 32:25+ Ja 14 '65
Sobering lesson on trade. Bsns W p 112 Je 1 '63
Spain outside the door. Time 83:40+ Ap 3 '64
Strength of the projected union vis-à-vis Russia; address, April 5, 1963. F. C. Barghoorn. Anr Am Acad 348:54-64 Jl '63
Tariff men do their homework. il Bsns W p49+ Mr 21 '64
Tariffs aren't the only problem; EEC restrictions. il Bsns W p76+ S 7 '63
Tarnished ideal; report of negotiations between Britain and the Common market. Newsweek 61:45 Mr 18 '63
Ten commandments; common policy. Time 83:97-8 Ap 24 '64
Triumph for Europe; common market for cereals. il Time 84:19 D 25 '64
Triumph over politics. il Time 82:82-3 S 6 '63
U.S. and EEC hold talks on poultry import fees; statement, May 31, 1963, and announcement, June 7, 1963. C. A. Herter. Dept State Bul 48:996-7 Je 24 '63
United States and the European economic community; address, June 3, 1963. P. H. Trezise. Dept State Bul 48:971-6 Je 24 '63
U.S. failing in Europe? J. Fromm and F. C. Painton. il U S News 54:48-52 Mr 25 '63
U.S. investments in France. R. Grenier. il Reporter 28:23-4+ Je 6 '63
U.S. raises duty on four articles imported from EEC countries; proclamation, December 4, 1963. L. B. Johnson. Dept State Bul 49:969-70 D 23 '63
United States trade policies; address, October 3, 1963. A. Chayes. Vital Speeches 30:47-51 N 1 '63
United States trade relations with the new Europe: the challenge and the opportunities; address, January 10, 1963. D. MacArthur, 2d. Dept State Bul 48:174-9 F 4 '63
Ups and downs of tariffs. Sr Schol 83:10-11 S 27 '63
Victory of an idea. Time 83:76 Ja 3 '64
What de Gaulle sees ahead. il U S News 54:55 F 11 '63
What happens to Great Britain now? interview. Earl of Home. il U S News 54:62-5 F 4 '63
What next for the Common market? R. Grenier. Reporter 28:24-6 F 28 '63
What the chicken war means. Farm J 87:110 S '63
Where Britain can turn; views from Europe. U S News 54:67-8 F 4 '63
Where Europe is headed now. A. Zanker. il U S News 54:50-2 Je 3 '63
Who gets to farm? Farm J 88:106 Ja '64
Why de Gaulle blocked Britain; a German view. U S News 54:10 Mr 11 '63
Will farmers be sold out? C. P. Streeter. Farm J 88:39+ Ja '64
Year of special importance; 1963, a crucial time; address, October 2, 1963. P. H. Spaak. Vital Speeches 30:37-41 N 1 '63
Yielding a bit; agreement to meeting of Britain and the Common market. Newsweek 62:41-2 Jl 22 '63

EUROPEAN fiction
Ideology and the private vision; fiction from Eastern Europe. E. Pawel. Nation 197:301-3 N 9 '63
Return of Europe's Jews. E. Roditi. Commentary 36:63-8 Jl '63

EUROPEAN folk art. See Folk art

EUROPEAN free trade association
After Brussels. A. Shonfield. For Affairs 41:721-31 Jl '63
Britain and the European community. A. D. Monroe. Cur Hist 45:271-5+ N '63
Britain in EFTA's doghouse. il Bsns W p31 N 28 '64
Britain makes trouble for EFTA. Time 85:76+ Ja 29 '65
Changing cornerstones. Newsweek 63:44 F 24 '64
Common market must resolve basic contradictions. F. Morley. il Nations Bsns 2:27-8 N '64
Europe: a major role for EFTA; letter from Geneva. M. A. Heilperin. il Fortune 69:61-2+ Mr '64
Hard bargaining and many concessions bring Outer seven pact to end tariffs. Bsns W p74 My 18 '63
Outsiders. Time 81:25 Mr 1 '63

EUROPEAN hazelbushes. See Filbert trees

EUROPEAN institute of business administration, Fontainebleau. See Business education

EUROPEAN intervention in Mexico, 1861-1867. See Mexico—History—European intervention, 1861-1867

EUROPEAN launcher development organization
Cooperation keynotes meeting; third spaceflight symposium. W. Beller. Miss & Roc 12:14-15 My 27 '63
Europe builds multilateral space effort. il Aviation W 81:100-1+ Jl 6 '64
European Comsat plan advances. F. G. McGuire. il Miss & Roc 15:12-13 N 9 '64
ELDO participants report brisk pace. Miss & Roc 13:21 O 14 '63
ELDO third-stage model test scheduled. W. C. Wetmore. il Aviation W 79:73-4+ D 16 '63
First Blue Streak arrives in Australia for ELDO use. B. W. Poirier. il Miss & Roc 13:35 Ag 19 '63
First ELDO Europa 1 booster hardware begins automated static testing program. il Aviation W 81:124-6 S 7 '64
First flight of ELDO booster T/M components due next August. F. G. McGuire. il Miss & Roc 15:26-7 N 2 '64

EUROPEAN literature
Critique in brief; series of Columbia essays on modern writers. G. Hicks. Sat R 47:19-20 D 19 '64
European literary scene. R. J. Clements. il Sat R 47:28-9 Jl 11; 26-7 Ag 8; 38-9 S 12; 34-5 O 3; 30 N 21; 24-5 D 26 '64; 48:24-5 Ja 30 '65

EUROPEAN megaliths. See Megalithic monuments

EUROPEAN men. See Men

EUROPEAN organization for nuclear research
Our far-flung correspondents; CERN (Conseil européen pour la recherche nucléaire) J. Bernstein. New Yorker 40:164+ D 12 '64
Particle accelerators at CERN. V. K. McElheny. il Science 144:983-6 My 22 '64

EUROPEAN painting. See Painting, European

EUROPEAN space agency (proposed)
Cooperation keynotes meeting; third spaceflight symposium. W. Beller. Miss & Roc 12:14-15 My 27 '63

EUROPEAN space research organization
Access to international brainpower accrues from cooperative projects; NASA-ESRO collaboration. il Miss & Roc 13:149-50 N 25 '63
Cooperation keynotes meeting; third spaceflight symposium. W. Beller. Miss & Roc 12:14-15 My 27 '63
Cooperative space research agency. V. K. McElheny. Science 144:275-7 Ap 17 '64
Europe builds multilateral space effort. il Aviation W 81:100-1+ Jl 6 '64
European Comsat plan advances. F. G. McGuire. il Miss & Roc 15:12-13 N 9 '64
ESRO facility to buy U.S. equipment. W. Beller. il Miss & Roc 15:24-5 O 19 '64
ESRO plans satellites in 1967-68. Aviation W 80:31 Ap 27 '64

EUROPEAN visitors in the United States. See Foreign visitors in the United States

EUROPEAN war, 1914-1918
Chaotic heritage. W. E. Leuchtenburg. il Life 56:84+ Je 5 '64
First World war. il Life 56:42-60B Mr 13; 62-78+ Mr 20; 58-74+ Ap 17; 66-83+ My 8; 68-88+ My 22; 68-83 Je 5 '64 (to be cont)
How it all began. Newsweek 64:36 Ag 31 '64
Illustrated history of the first World war, by A. J. P. Taylor. Review
Newsweek il 63:88 Ap 6 '64
Lasting echoes of the Kaiser's war. R. Graves. il N Y Times Mag p 16-17+ My 17 '64

EUROPEAN war, 1914-1918—*Continued*
Of arms and the man. J. O'Gara. Commonweal 80:134 Ap 24 '64
Price we paid for war. G. F. Kennan. il Atlan 214:50-4 O '64
Sarajevo; the end of innocence. E. Stillman. il Horizon 6:4-6+ Sum '64
Swordbearers; supreme command in the first World war, by C. Barnett. Review
Nat R il 16:610+ Jl 14 '64. T. A. Lane
Reporter 31:42+ Jl 16 '64. R. P. Knapp, jr
Teaching about the great world wars; symposium, ed. by H. L. Hurwitz. il Sr Schol 85:6T-10T+ N 11 '64
Their world was ending, but few knew it. H. W. Baldwin. il N Y Times Mag p7-9+ Jl 26 '64
War that changed the world. il Sr Schol 85:6-7 N 11 '64

Aerial operations

Air war. il Life 56:62-78+ Mr 20 '64
Memoirs of an ace: C. D'Olive. V. Bourjaily. il Esquire 62:29-32+ Ag '64
When the airplane became a lethal weapon. J. B. Benge, jr. il Esquire 62:33-40 Ag '64

American participation

See European war, 1914-1918—United States

Bibliography

New perspectives on the great wars. H. L. Hurwitz. il Sr Schol 85:18T-19T N 11 '64

Blockades

British official histories of the blockade of the central powers during the First World war. M. C. Siney. bibliog f Am Hist R 68:392-401 Ja '63

Campaigns and battles

Big push, by B. Gardner. Review
Am Heritage 14:110-11 Ap '63
Far-flung battlefronts. il Life 56:66-83+ My 8 '64
Into the Argonne. il Life 56:78-81 My 22 '64
Over the top under fire. il Life 56:48-60B Mr 13 '64
See also
Belleau Wood, Battle of, 1918
Verdun, Battle of, 1916

Africa

Bush fox of Africa. E. Kern. il Life 56:87-8+ My 8 '64

Austro—Italian front

Guns in the Alps. il Life 56:74-5 My 8 '64

Russia

Eastern front. il Life 56:76-83 My 8 '64

Turkey and the Near East

Seesaw in the Middle East. il Life 56:69-71 My 8 '64

Western

1914-1918: bloody years. E. Dunbar. il Look 28:51-63 Ag 11 '64

Causes

Vials of wrath were ready to break. E. Kern. il Life 56:59-61 Ja 3 '64
What caused the great world wars? H. L. Hurwitz. il Sr Schol 85:6T-10T N 11 '64

Diplomatic history

See also
European war, 1914-1918—Causes

Economic aspects

British official histories of the blockade of the central powers during the First World war. M. C. Siney. bibliog f Am Hist R 68:392-401 Ja '63

Naval operations

War at sea. il Life 56:58-74+ Ap 17 '64
See also
Great Britain—Navy
Jutland, Battle of, 1916

Peace and mediation

See also
Peace conference, 1919, Versailles

Personal narratives

Carry on, carry on; excerpts from Margin released. J. B. Priestley. Atlan 211:64-70 F '63
Irish Mail and the Kaiser's war. S. M. Meyer. New Yorker 39:74-7 D 21 '63
1914-1918: bloody years. E. Dunbar. il Look 28:51-63 Ag 11 '64
Over the top: the ordeal in France; excerpts from Reminiscences of General Douglas MacArthur. D. MacArthur. il Life 56:66-74+ Ja 24 '64

Relief work

See also
American relief administration

Science

See War and science

Submarine operations

Deadly prowlers. il Life 56:60-3 Ap 17 '64
Q-ships and raiders. E. Kern. il Life 56:74+ Ap 17 '64

France

Dare call it treason, by R. M. Watt. Review
Am Heritage 14:111 Ap '63
Horror of the western front. il Life 56:44-60B Mr 13 '64
Pétain of Verdun, of Vichy, of history. H. Giniger. il N Y Times Mag p94-5+ N 15 '64
See also
European war, 1914-1918—Campaigns and battles
France—Army

Italy

See also
European war, 1914-1918—Campaigns and battles—Austro-Italian front

United States

Doughboys: the story of the AEF, 1917-1918, by L. Stallings. Review
Sat R il 46:28 Jl 6 '63. M. S. Watson
Over the top: the ordeal in France; excerpts from Reminiscences of General Douglas MacArthur. D. MacArthur. il Life 56:66-74+ Ja 24 '64
When gentlemen prepared for war. F. Russell. il Am Heritage 15:24-7+ Ap '64
Yanks are coming at last. il Life 56:68-88+ My 22 '64

EUROPEAN war, 1939-1945. See World war, 1939-1945

EUROPEAN war in art
After Sarajevo; excerpts from American heritage history of World war I. il Horizon 6:7-13 Sum '64

EUROPEAN wireworms. See Wireworms

EUROPEANS
Faces of the satellites. P. Schutzer. il Life 55:102-14 N 15 '63
How to make love in five languages; excerpts from How to marry a millionaire. D. Lilly. il McCalls 91:94-5 Je '64
People are turning Europe into one big country; while politicians argue. il U S News 55:44-7 Ag 12 '63
Slow melting; national barriers and prejudices. il Newsweek 64:37 Ag 3 '64

EUROPEANS in Africa
White man holds on in Africa; photographs. N Y Times Mag p26-9 N 8 '64

EUROPEANS in Algeria
New dilemmas for the *pieds noirs*. P. Braestrup. il N Y Times Mag p28+ My 26 '63

EUROPEANS in Kenya
Do white men have a future in Africa? T. J. Mboya. il N Y Times Mag p24-5+ D 8 '63

EUROSPACE
Cooperation with Europe. W. J. Coughlin. Miss & Roc 15:46 Jl 6 '64
Eurospace members represent twelve nations. Aviation W 81:113 Jl 6 '64
Eurospace outlines plans for joint aerospace transporter. F. G. McGuire. Miss & Roc 15:32-3 N 23 '64

EUTHANASIA
Let the hopelessly ill die? U S News 55:18 Jl 1 '63
Right to life, by N. St John-Stevas. Review
Commonweal 80:156-7 Ap 24 '64. W. H. Dempsey, jr
Sacredness of life. W. M. Abbott. America 108:328 Mr 9 '63
Tragedy at Liege; Vandeput's thalidomide baby. J. Gallahue. il Look 27:72-4+ Mr 12 '63; Discussion. 27:16 Ap 23 '63

Anecdotes, facetiae, satire, etc.

Freedom to die. F. Canavan. America 110:33 Ja 11 '64

EVALUATION (psychology) See Values (psychology)

EVALUATION of works of art. See Art—Valuation

EVANGELICAL and Reformed church. See United church of Christ

EVANGELICAL church in Cuba
Church endures in Cuba. Christian Cent 80:702 My 29 '63

EVANGELICAL church in Germany
Conscience in East Germany; Weissensee declaration. Time 82:60 Jl 19 '63
West Germany. F. Luepsen. Christian Cent 80:472-4 Ap 10 '63
EVANGELICAL Lutheran church. See Lutheran church in the United States
EVANGELICALS, National association of. See National association of Evangelicals
EVANGELISTA, A. Camacho-. See Camacho-Evangelista, A.
EVANGELISTIC work
Billy Graham's own story; God is my witness. B. Graham. il McCalls 91:122-5+ Ap; 118-19+ My; 62+ Je '64
Bold mission in South Africa. Christian Cent 80:1070 S 4 '63
Convert decline. J. A. O'Brien. America 109: 382 O 5 '63; Reply. D. Howard. 109:470 O 26 '63; Rejoinder. 109:646 N 23 '63
Crusader in the Coliseum; B. Graham. il Time 82:53 S 6 '63
France prepares for Billy Graham. Y. Chabas. Christian Cent 80:614-15 My 8 '63
Nostalgia is betrayal. F. D. Lueking. Christian Cent 81:461-2 Ap 8 '64
Texas to Tokyo; Baptist evangelical rally. il Newsweek 61:61 Ap 29 '63
Vision in the valley; Campbell's Creek revivalist S. Campbell. il Newsweek 63:82-3 Je 29 '64
Vivid portrait of the famous revivalist; Billy Graham. H. H. Martin. il Sat Eve Post 236: 17-23 Ap 13 '63
EVANS, A. Murray
Ameiotic alternation of generations: a new life cycle in the ferns. bibliog Science 143: 261-3 Ja 17 '64
EVANS, Bergen
Couth to uncouth and vice versa. N Y Times Mag p22+ N 10 '63
Milk, beads, thongs, and the spiral nebulae. Atlan 214:126-7 Jl '64
Now everyone is hip about slang. N Y Times Mag p22+ Mr 22 '64
EVANS, Bill
Jazz. W. Balliett. New Yorker 39:158-61 S 21 '63
EVANS, Bob
How to get a job as a swing dancer in a hit Broadway show. Harper 230:28-31 Ja '65
EVANS, C. R. See Robertson, A. D. J. jt. auth.
EVANS, Daniel Jackson
Dan Evans, that's who. il por Time 84:40 N 13 '64
EVANS, Evan C. 3d
Polar transport of calcium in the primary root of zea mays. bibliog Science 144: 174-7 Ap 10 '64
EVANS, George Bird
Blackwater paradise. Field & S 69:29-31+ N '64
Quail recall pen. il Field & S 69:120-1+ N '64
Tame quail for training. Field & S 68:90-1+ Ja '64
EVANS, Geraint
Welsh Knight; interview. ed. by B. Fischer-Williams. por Opera N 29:13 Ja 23 '65
EVANS, Gordon Heyd
New military strategy. bibliog f Cur Hist 47:77-80+ Ag '64
World of nuclear plenty. Bul Atomic Sci 19:26-30 F '63
EVANS, Howard E.
Clustering wasps, and why they cluster. il Audubon Mag 65:236-7 Jl '63
Predatory wasps. Sci Am 208:145-50+ Ap '63
EVANS, Howard T, jr
Uranyl ion coordination. bibliog Science 141: 154-8 Jl 12 '63
EVANS, Illtud
After four hundred years. Commonweal 78: 222-4 My 17 '63
C. C. Martindale, S.J. 1879-1963. America 108: 466-7 Ap 6 '63
EVANS, J. C.
Fund raising through refreshment operations. Recreation 56:233+ My '63
EVANS, J. Claude
Dallas image unveiled. Christian Cent 80:1438-40 N 20 '63
Methodist students in quadrennial session. Christian Cent 82:114-16 Ja 27 '65
Playboy philosophy. Cath World 200:42-8 O '64
Texan looks at a Texan looking at a Texan. Christian Cent 81:1296 O 21 '64
EVANS, J. V. and Whitlock, J. H.
Genetic relationship between maximum hematocrit values and hemoglobin type in sheep. bibliog Science 145:1318 S 18 '64
EVANS, John W.
Motions in the solar atmosphere. Sky & Tel 25:321-5 Je '63
EVANS, Joseph E.
Prize and the risk. U S News 54:120 My 20 '63
EVANS, Larry
Chess. Sports Illus 21:48 Jl 20 '64
EVANS, Luther
Mayhem under power. Yachting 114:20-1+ D '63
EVANS, Luther H.
Revolutionary social forces; address, March 27, 1963. Vital Speeches 29:454-7 My 15 '63
Some neglected aspects of education in an age of automation. Sch & Soc 92:310-11 O 31 '64
EVANS, M. Stanton
Collective insecurity. Nat R 15:201-3 S 10 '63
Computerized convention? Nat R 16:608-9 Jl 14 '64
Conservatives marshal the data. Nat R 16:496-7 Je 16 '64
Goldwater, Rockefeller, and the Young Republicans. Nat R 15:97-100+ Ag 13 '63
Image is all. Nat R 15:309-10 O 8 '63
Liberals do believe in devils. Nat R 14:457-8 Je 4 '63
Patriotism: a Freudian dissection. Nat R 16: 281-3 Ap 7 '64
Public enemy. Nat R 17:70-1 Ja 26 '65
Publishing scene. Nat R 16:981 N 3 '64
Sudden magnificence of William W. Scranton. Nat R 16:269-70+ Ap 7 '64
What to look for on November 4. Nat R 16: 965-7 N 3 '64
EVANS, Oliver
Melting pot in the Bayous. Am Heritage 15:30-2+ D '63
Pad in Brooklyn Heights. Nation 199:15-16 Jl 13 '64
EVANS, Patricia
Teen-age beauty with brains. il pors Ebony 19:77-80+ Ag '64
EVANS, Rowland, jr
Insiders. il por Newsweek 64:71 Jl 27 '64
Invisible men who run Congress. Sat Eve Post 236:13-17 Je 8 '63
Pennsylvania Avenue politics. New Repub 148:19-20 F 2 '63
Whither the Republicans? Reporter 28:32-4 F 28 '63
—and Novak, R. D.
Birmingham: keeping our fingers crossed. New Repub 151:17-18 Ag 8 '64
Can Johnson get Congress moving? Sat Eve Post 237:34+ Ap 4 '64
Men around Goldwater. Sat Eve Post 237: 32-4 O 24 '64
Showdown in California: big crisis for Goldwater. Sat Eve Post 237:15-19 My 30 '64
Unmaking of a president. Esquire 62:90-2+ N '64
EVANS, W. D. Emrys
British English teacher in the Bronx. Sat R 47:54-5+ Jl 18 '64
EVANS, Walker
Collectors' items; photographs. Mlle 57:182-5+ My '63
EVAPORATION
Evaporation enhancement by protein films. L. K. James, jr. and D. J. O. Berry. bibliog il Science 140:312-14 Ap 19 '63
Sea-to-air transport of surface active material. D. C. Blanchard. bibliog il Science 146:396-7 O 16 '64
EVAPORATORS
Now, a drink from the sea. T. Willets. il Motor B 113:90-1+ Ja '64
EVARTS, John
Hans Rosbaud, 1895-1962. Mus Am 83:21 F '63
EVELYN, John
300th anniversary; Evelyn's Silva. H. W. Dengler. il por Am For 70:26-7+ D '64
EVEN the devil gets lonesome; story. See Rohde, B.
EVENARI, Michael
Stones that make the desert bloom. il Sci Digest 54:67-8 Ag '63
EVENING and continuation schools
See also
Adult education
EVENING bulletin, Philadelphia. See Bulletin, Philadelphia
EVENING clothes. See Clothing and dress
EVENING grosbeaks. See Grosbeaks
EVENING mail (New York) See New York evening mail
EVEREST, A. Wallace
Amateur telescope maker A. W. Everest dies. R. E. Cox. il por Sky & Tel 25:213 Ap '63

EVEREST, MOUNT
American and Geographic flags top Everest. M. M. Payne. il Nat Geog Mag 124:157-157C Ag '63
American triumphs atop Mt Everest. il U S News 54:16 Je 3 '63
Commando raid on Everest. W. W. Sayre. il Life 54:58-66+ Mr 22 '63
Everest; the American expedition is studying itself under stress as part of its scientific mission. J. Walsh. Science 140:620-1 My 10 '63
First traverse; West ridge. T. F. Hornbein. and W. F. Unsoeld. il Nat Geog Mag 124:508-13 O '63
How we climbed Everest. B. C. Bishop. il Nat Geog Mag 124:474-507 O '63
Mass attack on the mighty peak; American Mount Everest expedition, 1963, with report by J. R. Ullman. il Life 55:68-7+ S 20 '63
Old Glory on Everest. il Newsweek 61:52 My 13 '63
One way to live. il Newsweek 63:78-9 Mr 30 '64
Point of no return; U.S. climbers rendezvous on Mt Everest. il Time 81:64 My 31 '63
Six to the summit. N. G. Dyhrenfurth. il Nat Geog Mag 124:460-73 O '63
Up to the gods; expedition, headed by N. Dyhrenfurth. il Time 81:85 My 10 '63
EVERETT, Beverly
Family farm has a future if. . . por Farm J 87:80+ Ap '63
EVERETT, Glenn D.
Goldwater on church and state. Christian Cent 81:987-9 Ag 5 '64
EVERGLADE kites. See Kites (birds)
EVERGLADES
Everglades skimmers. P. Redford. il Motor B 112:44-5+ D '63
Moods of the Everglades. J. Speiser. il Nat Parks Mag 38:12-15 Ag '64
See also
Ten Thousand Islands
EVERGLADES NATIONAL PARK
Everglades must not vanish. A. W. Smith. Nat Parks Mag 38:2 F '64
Everglades Nike site. Nat Parks Mag 38:15 D '64
Houseboat in the Everglades. M. Hunn. il Motor B 114:33-5+ N '64
Invasion of the Everglades. Nat Parks Mag 38:17-18 S '64
Man-made drouth threatens Everglades National Park. V. O. Williams. il Audubon Mag 65:290-4 S '63
Two national preservations threatened by proposed refueling station. Nat Parks Mag 38:16 Mr '64
Water problem in Everglades National Park. P. M. Tilden. il Nat Parks Mag 38:4-9 F; 8-11 Mr '64 (to be cont)
EVERGREEN review (periodical)
D.A. seizes Evergreen review, Grove press sues. Pub W 185:31-2 My 11 '64
Federal court orders Evergreen review released. Pub W 185:67 Je 22 '64
Nassau County, N.Y. drops appeal on Evergreen review. Pub W 185:48-9 Je 29 '64
EVERGREENS
Dwarf evergreens. H. M. Bergman. il Horticulture 42:28-30 Ja '64
Geography of evergreens. il House & Gard 125:156-7+ F '64
How big will it grow? R. C. Hands. Horticulture 41:247 My '63
Trimming and training evergreens. il Bet Hom & Gard 42:28 Je '64
See also names of evergreen trees and shrubs, e.g. Yew
EVERHART comet. See Comets
EVERITT, Helen
Packaged Pilgrims. Harper 230:115-18 Ja '65
EVERLASTING flowers
Everlastings, flowers for dry arrangements to sow in your garden now. C. B. Norris. il Pop Gard 14:90-1 My '63
See also
Strawflowers
EVERLY, Jack C.
He makes alfalfa his high-profit crop. Suc Farm 62:42-3 Jl '64
He uses silos year-round. Suc Farm 62:38 Ap '64
Oats make me as much money as corn. Suc Farm 61:40-1 Jl '63
EVERLY, Robert
Most-wanted pool features. Am City 80:84-6 Ja '65
EVERS, Charles G.
Marine art of Charles G. Evers. E. Metzl. il Am Artist 27:28-33+ Mr '63
EVERS, Medgar W.
Why I live in Mississippi; interview, ed. by F. H. Mitchell. pors Ebony 18:143-8 S '63
about
. . . And the bells toll; Bishop Gill on the assassination of M. W. Evers. T. E. Gill. America 108:894 Je 29 '63
Beckwith trial. il Newsweek 63:27 F 10 '64
Colonel's grandson. il Newsweek 62:22-3 Jl 8 '63
End and a beginning. il(p31) Newsweek 61:32-3 Je 24 '63
He said he wouldn't mind dying if . . . M. Evers. il Life 54:34-7 Je 28 '63
In memoriam. il por Ebony 18:142 S '63
Life & death in Jackson. il por Time 81:17-18 Je 21 '63
Martyr to an immoral system. Life 54:4 Je 28 '63
Negroes walk to freedom; murder lies on a nation's conscience. il Life 55:32-3 Jl 5 '63
Trail of blood: a Negro dies. il por Life 54:28-9 Je 21 '63
Trial of Delay Beckwith. H. H. Martin. il Sat Eve Post 237:77-81 Mr 14 '64
Voice in Jackson; Bishop R. O. Gerow on assassination of M. W. Evers. R. O. Gerow. America 108:894 Je 29 '63
EVERS, Medgar W, family
Fund; Evers scholarship fund for Evers children. New Yorker 39:21 Ag 31 '63
EVERS, Myrlie
He said he wouldn't mind dying if . . por Life 54:34-7 Je 28 '63
EVERSOLE, Finley
Art and sacrament. Christian Cent 81:393-6 Mr 25 '64
Truthful ugliness. Christian Cent 80:1611-12 D 25 '63
EVERSON, R. G.
Late news flashes; poem. Atlan 214:139 N '64
EVERSON, William K.
Sixty-year saga of the horse opera. N Y Times Mag p74-5 Ap 14 '63
EVERTS, Connor
Artist & teacher. Sch Arts 62:21-3 Je '63
EVERYBODY adored Cara; story. See Head, A.
EVERYONE gets somewhere; story. See Gerber, M. J.
EVERYTHING neat and tidy; story. See Friel, B.
EVETT, Robert
Hindemith early and late. New Repub 148:26-8 Ap 6 '63
Passing out money among artists. New Repub 150:9-10 Ja 18 '64
EVIAN spa. See Health resorts, watering places, etc.
EVICTION
Bulldozers at your door. S. Z. Searles. Read Digest 83:83-7 S '63
EVIDENCE (law)
Hoffa trial. F. J. Cook. il Nation 198:415-39 Ap 27 '64
Laws of probability; new test of circumstantial evidence. Time 85:42 Ja 8 '65
Long nightmare of a police witness: Artie Schlitz. B. Lindeman. il Sat Eve Post 236:71-2+ N 2 '63
New break for criminals? voluntary out-of-court admissions and confessions. U S News 56:16 Je 1 '64
Price of getting involved; Hector Mangual. T. Armbrister. il Sat Eve Post 237:81-5 S 26 '64
Search & seizure; be sure it's legal. Time 83:80 My 15 '64
Strange case of Edgar Smith. D. G. M. Coxe. il Nat R 15:273-8 O 8 '63
See also
Confession (law)
Self incrimination
Witnesses
EVIDENCE, Expert
See also
Writing—Identification
EVIL eye
Evil eye. J. Bryan, 3d. il Holiday 35:58-9+ My '64
EVIS manufacturing company
Case history of a winner. Nations Bsns 51:79 My '63
EVOLUTION
Anthropology of the credit card; evolution of man. J. Lear. Sat R 47:45-7 Ap 4 '64
Apish origins of human tension. J. E. Pfeiffer. Harper 227:55-60 Jl '63
Blood brothers; man and ape. il Newsweek 63:52 Mr 2 '64
DNA can trace evolution. Sci N L 85:2 Ja 4 '64
Early relatives of man. E. L. Simons. il Sci Am 211:50-62 bibliog(p 142) Jl '64
Evolution of behavior; report of a symposium at Philadelphia meeting of the AAAS. G. W. Barlow. Science 139:851-2 Mr 1 '63

EVOLUTION—*Continued*
Evolution, organic and superorganic. T. Dobzhansky. Bul Atomic Sci 20:4-8 My '64; Reply. C. Hartshorne. 20:38 O '64
Evolutionary and population genetics. T. Dobzhansky. bibliog Science 142:1131-5 N 29 '63
Flowers, insects, and evolution; Ruby Range fossils. H. F. Becker. il Natur Hist 74:38-45 bibliog(p70) F '65
Man as nature's man. P. Hefner. Christian Cent 81:1556-9 D 16 '64
On choosing our future. L. J. Halle. New Repub 149:14-17 Ag 31 '63
Polar bear on way to sea. Sci N L 84:146 S 7 '63
Rat man's distant cousin. Sci N L 84:146 S 7 '63
Science and the new humanism; excerpts from address. H. Hoagland. bibliog Science 143:111-14 Ja 10 '64; Discussion. 143:1121-3; 144:1293 Mr 13, Je 12 '64
Why is man? excerpt from Animal species and evolution. E. Mayr. Sat R 46:48 My 4 '63
Wisdom of evolution, by R. J. Nogar. Review Sci Digest 55:44 F '64. B. H. Frisch
See also
Adaptation (biology)
Genetics
Life (biology)
Man—Origin and antiquity
Phylogeny
Plants—Evolution
EVOLUTION, Social. See Social change
EVREINOV, Nikolai Nikolaevich
Chief thing. Criticism
New Yorker 39:88+ My 11 '63
EVTUSHENKO, Evgenii Aleksandrovich
Babi Yar; tr. by M. Hayward; Irreconcilable; tr. by G. Reavey; poems. pors Life 54:32-3 Ap 19 '63
Heirs of Stalin; poem. tr. by G. Reavey. Sat Eve Post 236:60 Ag 10 '63
Precocious autobiography; excerpt, tr. by A. R. MacAndrew; with introduction by A. W. Dulles. por Sat Eve Post 236:45-8+ Ag 10 '63
Prologue; poem. tr. by G. Reavey. Sat Eve Post 236:62 Ag 10 '63
Russian art & anti-semitism; debate. Commentary 36:434 D '63
about
Consider me a Communist; a portrait of Evtushenko on stage and off. M. Gordey. Harper 227:51-2+ O '63
Cry out, Russian poet! with editorial comment, and with report by D. E. Scherman. il pors Life 54:4, 30-7 Ap 19 '63
Evtushenko's return. Newsweek 62:63 O 7 '63
Kind of revolt. H. Carruth. Nation 197:165-6 S 21 '63
Man with Olena's legs. por Time 82:47 O 4 '63
Platform verse. B. Deutsch. Poetry 102:400-2 S '63
Poet and politics. Newsweek 61:50 Ap 15 '63
Poet-hero of the young at heart; with excerpt from Precocious autobiography, by M. Kalb. por Sat R 46:20-1 Ag 10 '63
Poet is a poet is a what. R. De Toledano. Nat R 15:404+ N 5 '63
Poetry and policy. il por Newsweek 61:37 Mr 4 '63
Polonius or Laertes? por Newsweek 62:74B Ag 5 '63
That strange time. il por Time 81:30 Ap 12 '63
Wolves: Communist critics crackdown. Time 81:40 Ap 19 '63
EWEN, Edward T.
Mummy case to Ben Casey. N Y Times Mag p42+ Ag 25 '63
Poet, actor, painter: cabbie. N Y Times Mag p36+ O 27 '63
Revolution on the razor's edge. N Y Times Mag p58+ O 6 '63
EWES. See Sheep
EWING, Alex
Robert Joffrey ballet in Leningrad. Dance Mag 37:40-2 D '63
EWING, Ann
Astronomy. Sci N L 84:10 Jl 6 '63
Fusion control closer; burnout achieved in experiments. Sci N L 86:115 Ag 22 '64
Quasars are crazy. Sci N L 86:106 Ag 15 '64
Time: one-way street. Sci N L 86:99 Ag 15 '64
EWING, David W.
Is nepotism so bad? Harvard Bsns R 43:22-6+ Ja '65
Knowledge of an executive. bibliog f Harvard Bsns R 42:91-100 Mr '64
Russians yearn for the managerial mind. Harper 230:67-72 Ja '65
Tension can be an asset. bibliog f Harvard Bsns R 42:71-8 S '64
EWING, John H.
Friendly president; Abercrombie & Fitch. New Yorker 39:24 Je 1 '63
EWING, Maurice L. and others
Space controversy: Senate committee to hear scientists on moon program, statement of eight scientists. Science 140:1078 Je 7 '63
—See Grott, J. J. jt. auth.
EWING, S. A. See Burroughs, W. jt. auth.
EWING, Stephen
High flying hobby! il pors Ebony 20:111-12+ D '64
EXACT and very strange truth; novel. See Piazza, B.
EXAMINATIONS
Essay exam: probing the iceberg; excerpts from address. R. W. Winks. il Sr Schol 85:12T-13T O 21 '64
Harvard test ban? Newsweek 62:32 D 16 '63
How to score better on tests. D. Huff. Bet Hom & Gard 41:106+ F '63
It's what's up top that counts. G. Dapper. il Sat R 46:48-9+ D 21 '63
Minus eleven-plus; abolition of Britain's eleven-plus exam. il Time 83:71 Mr 13 '64
Testing is a big part of teaching. D. Leuchtenburg. il NEA J 53:55-6 O '64
When in doubt, bull. Time 82:78 D 13 '63
See also
College entrance examination board
Colleges and universities—Entrance requirements
Educational tests and measurements
Anecdotes, facetiae, satire, etc.
Final final exam; a sentimental education. D. Newman and R. Benton. Esquire 60:70-2 S '63
Imaginary advice to students on taking examinations. W. C. Trow. Sch & Soc 91:124-5 Mr 9 '63
Time to study. D. Kuester. il Harper 226:31-4 Je '63
EXAMINER, San Francisco. See San Francisco examiner
EXCAVATIONS
See also
Street openings
EXCAVATIONS (archeology)
Digging for pictures. W. Golding. Holiday 33:86-7+ Mr '63
Early man in the Andes; El Inga, Ecuador. W. J. Mayer-Oakes. il Sci Am 208:116-22+ My '63
See also
Archeology
Herculaneum
Pompeii
Sybaris
Troy
also subhead Antiquities under names of continents, countries, states, cities, etc. e.g. Iran—Antiquities
EXCELLENCE. See Leadership
EXCEPTIONAL children. See Children, Exceptional
EXCESS profits tax
Boeing seeks settlement in profits cases. K. Johnsen. Aviation W 82:29 Ja 25 '65
GOP unit seeks renegotiation phase-out. K. Johnsen. Aviation W 80:33-4 Ap 27 '64
Supreme court refuses to hear appeal in Boeing renegotiation. K. Johnsen. Aviation W 80:30 My 11 '64
EXCHANGE, Foreign. See Foreign exchange
EXCHANGE of houses. See Houses, Exchange of
EXCHANGE of persons programs
Barghoorn affair and educational exchange. W. W. Brickman. Sch & Soc 92:63 F 22 '64
Gabriel Marcel in Albany. R. F. Creegan. Sch & Soc 92:86 F 22 '64
Gresham's law in Soviet-American exchange. Bul Atomic Sci 20:2-3 Je '64
Need to explore inner space; address, July 2, 1964. L. D. Battle. Dept State Bul 51:110-19 Jl 27 '64
Red carpet. A. V. Crewe. Bul Atomic Sci 19:25-6 S '63
Roads to international understanding; address, January 15, 1963. C. D. Norrell. Dept State Bul 48:214-17 F 11 '63
Scholar as pawn; arrest of Professor Barghoorn in Russia. il Time 82:27 N 22 '63
Soviet aims in astronomy and space research; reprint. B. Lovell. Bul Atomic Sci 19:36-9 O '63
Soviet-American exchanges, tit-for-tat goodwill. S. S. Rosenfeld. Science 143:1413-17 Mr 27 '64

EXCHANGE of persons programs—*Continued*
Soviet Union rebuked on climate of fear. Christian Cent 80:1490-1 D 4 '63
U.S.-Japan cooperative science program. N. P. Neureiter. Bul Atomic Sci 21:39 Ja '65
Value of exchange. G. T. Seaborg. Bul Atomic Sci 19:25 S '63
When exchange is not really exchange. E. Broda. Bul Atomic Sci 20:23-5 N '64
Will the swaps keep on? Barghoorn incident. il Bsns W p28-9 N 23 '63
Yankee come here. Newsweek 62:42+ S 9 '63
See also
Educational exchanges
Students, Interchange of
Teachers, Interchange of

EXCHANGE of political prisoners. See Political prisoners, Exchange of

EXCHANGE students. See Students, Interchange of

EXCHANGES
See also
Chicago board of trade
London metal exchange
Stock exchange

EXCHANGES, Educational. See Educational exchanges

EXCHANGES, Literary and scientific
New U.S.-Rumanian accord includes books. Pub W 185:52 Je 29 '64
See also
Smithsonian institution—Science information exchange
United States book exchange, incorporated

EXCISE tax
Another kind of tax relief in '65? U S News 56:125-6 F 24 '64
Crazy like an uncut excise tax. M. Viorst. New Repub 151:10-11 Jl 11 '64
End of a nuisance? il Time 84:99-100 S 18 '64
Excise cut can pack big wallop; if companies pass the savings on to customers. il Bsns W p70+ Ja 16 '65
Excise taxes come on the firing line; Ways & means hearings. il Bsns W p26-7 Je 20 '64
Excise taxes: to raise money or lower sales? Sr Schol 85:18 Ja 14 '65
In the works: new tax cuts: repeal of all retail excises, repeal or reduction of some manufacturers' and service excises. U S News 57:89-91 N 23 '64
LBJ favors delay in excise-tax cut. U S News 56:103 Je 15 '64
Next tax cut: excises. Bsns W p36 Ap 25 '64
Next tax cut: the target and the time. U S News 56:101-2 My 11 '64
Washington desk. J. R. Slevin. Duns R 83:5-6 Mr '64

EXCLUSIVE agencies
Can franchises keep their flavor? Tastee Freez failure. Bsns W p62+ N 2 '63
Fortunes in franchising. N. Buckley. il Duns R 83:36-7+ Ap '64
Franchising, new scope for an old technique. W. P. Hall. il Harvard Bsns R 42:60-72 Ja '64
Profits for mom & pop; franchised shops. il Time 81:90+ My 24 '63
Small town greets the discounters; Tempo discount centers. il Bsns W p90+ O 3 '64

EXCLUSIVE brethren. See Plymouth brethren

EXCURSIONS
Americana rail cruises. L. Martin. il Travel 121:48-9 My '64
How to see the Cup races; America's cup excursion boats. il Motor B 114:44 Ag '64
World of white. R. L. Nelson. il Audubon Mag 66:92-6 Mr '64

EXCURSIONS, School. See School excursions

EXCUSES
Compleat alibier. F. Calkins. il Field & S 69:54-5+ O '64

EXECUTIONS and executioners
Execution of Charles I. C. V. Wedgwood. il Horizon 6:41 Sum '64
Warning to renegades: Haiti's first public execution in thirty years. Time 84:44+ N 27 '64
Young man, be an executioner. G. Walker. Esquire 60:62-3 Ag '63
See also
Capital punishment

EXECUTIONS in effigy
Burnt effigies. J. Ciardi. Sat R 47:13 Ag 22 '64

EXECUTIVE ability
Executives need this skill. L. R. Sayles. il Nations Bsns 52:48-50 Ag '64
Get your work done faster. H. R. Dressner. il Nations Bsns 51:58-60+ My '63
Make your time more productive. A. Uris. il Nations Bsns 51:98+ Ap '63
Think things through. S. Schuler. il Nations Bsns 51:86-8 Ag '63

EXECUTIVE departments (United States) See United States—Executive departments

EXECUTIVE jets. See Airplanes, Business

EXECUTIVE mansions. See Governors mansions

EXECUTIVE planes. See Airplanes, Business

EXECUTIVE power
See also
Presidents—United States—Powers and duties

EXECUTIVE program in business administration. See Columbia university

EXECUTIVE responsibility. See Responsibility

EXECUTIVE service corps. See International executive service corps

EXECUTIVE suicide. See Suicide

EXECUTIVES
American vs. European management philosophy. O. H. Nowotny. bibliog f il Harvard Bsns R 42:101-8 Mr '64
Conflict: the vital corporate ingredient. G. S. Odiorne. il Duns R 83:51-2+ Mr '64
Corporation at war with itself. W. E. Moore. il Duns R 81:58-60 Ap '63
Corrupt society. F. J. Cook. Nation 196:474-5 Je 1 '63
Difference in being president. T. R. Brooks. il Duns R 84:33-4 D '64
Etiquette of the executive lunch. R. F. Shepard. Esquire 60:142-3+ N '63
Executive investor; sixteen rapidly growing industries. il Duns R 85:103-4+ Ja '65
Executive sideline: timber; rewards of tree farming. il Duns R 85:39-40+ Ja '65
Executive trends. See issues of Nation's business
Executives, wives, and trouble; Presidents' panel report. W. R. Roberts. il Duns R 85:34-5+ Ja '65
Free the man who's boxed in. N. Stewart. Nations Bsns 52:82-4+ Jl '64
Great opportunities ahead; successful businessman of 1975; symposium. Nations Bsns 52:28-9+ Ja '64
Hard look at middle management. il Duns R 83:49-50+ Mr '64
How bosses really feel. il Bsns W p58 Mr 2 '63
How to cope with problem executives. S. Schuler. il Nations Bsns 52:78-80+ S '64
Human dilemmas of leadership. A. Zaleznik. Harvard Bsns R 41:49-55 Jl '63
If I were a company president. P. F. Drucker. Harper 228:16+ Ap '64; Reply. R. S. Taplinger. 228:12+ Je '64
Intellectual and the market place. G. J. Stigler. Nat R 15:473-4+ D 3 '63
Job of being president. Duns R 81:26-7+ Mr '63
Make yourself a better manager. J. G. Mason. il Nations Bsns 52:80-2 F '64
Mirror worship. Duns R 82:37 O '63
Mysterious management committee. S. Nicholson. il Duns R 81:57-9+ My '63
New breed in transportation. G. R. Rosen. il Duns R 83:pt2 100-2+ Je '64
Nine at the summit; most powerful men in Dallas. Fortune 70:161 Jl '64
Personal business; contract for your job. Bsns W p 139 S 7 '63
Pink slips and chief executives. L. Wolman. il Duns R 81:47-8+ F '63
Poisons of corporate infighting. G. S. Odiorne. Duns R 83:39-40+ F '64
Power to see ourselves. P. J. Brouwer. Harvard Bsns R 42:156-62+ N '64
President and corporate planning. M. L. Mace. Harvard Bsns R 43:49-62 Ja '65
Psyches at the top. Newsweek 63:83 Je 22 '64
Role of the manager in industry; address, November 2, 1964. W. T. Ingram. Vital Speeches 31:94-6 N 15 '64
Six enemies of executive output. J. A. Patton. il Duns R 81:33-4+ Mr '63
Thinking small. il Time 81:22 Mr 22 '63
Those American managers don't impress Europe; excerpts from Americanization of Europe. E. A. McCreary. Fortune 70:138-9+ D '64
Three at the top. il Time 84:59 D 25 '64
Truth about executive stress. M. R. Feinberg. il Duns R 84:34-6+ Ag '64
Turn anger into an asset. H. Levinson. il Nations Bsns 52:82-4+ My '64
What future managers will need; symposium. il Nations Bsns 51:69-73 Jl '63
Where is the organization man? L. W. Porter. bibliog f il Harvard Bsns R 41:53-61 N '63

EXECUTIVES—*Continued*
Young executives. W. Guzzardi, jr. il Fortune 69:96-9+ Je; 70:146-8+ Jl; 161-4+ S; 140-3+ O '64
See also
Business conferences
Business management and organization
Corporations—Directors
Women as executives

Health and hygiene

See Men—Health and hygiene

Photographs

See also
Photography of executives

Qualifications

Changing American executive; symposium. Duns R 83:38-40+ Ja '64
Dis-organization man. J. B. Weiner. il Duns R 83:32-4+ Ap '64
Executive motivation: what is the spur? J. F. Olesky. il Duns R 42:3+ N '64
Executive trouble abroad. F. N. Parks. Duns R 82:35-6+ Ag '63
Few grey flannels for brass. il Bsns W p 143+ N 2 '63
Find the pivot man. J. G. Mason. il Nations Bsns 52:80-2+ D '64
Growing problem of executive obsolescence; address. L. J. Weigle. Duns R 83:38-9+ Ap '64
How men get ahead. R. M. Powell. il Nations Bsns 52:56-8+ Mr '64
How to get to the top of the creative tree; excerpt from Confessions of an advertising man. D. Ogilvy. Vogue 142:82-5+ O 15 '63
How to measure maturity. M. R. Feinberg. Nations Bsns 51:40-1+ F '63
How to spot comers. N. Stewart. il Nations Bsns 51:82-4+ N '63
Knowledge of an executive. D. W. Ewing. bibliog f Harvard Bsns R 42:91-100 Mr '64
This test spots leaders. C. A. Cerami. Nations Bsns 52:68-70+ My '64
Three types of executive personality. R. W. Wallen. Duns R 81:54-6+ F '63
What helps or harms promotability? G. W. Bowman. il Harvard Bsns R 42:6-8+ Ja '64
What is the manager? H. Sonthoff. bibliog f Harvard Bsns R 42:24-6+ N '64
What it takes to be successful; symposium. il Nations Bsns 51:66-8+ Je '63
What it takes to stay on top; findings of a team of consultants and psychologists. il Nations Bsns 51:104-6 O '63
What it takes to take charge. J. G. Mason. il Nations Bsns 51:76-8+ D '63
Who do you promote? symposium. Duns R 83:50-2+ My '64

Rating

Fallacy in measuring management. E. C. Schleh. il Duns R 82:49-50+ N '63

Retirement

See Retirement from business, etc.

Salaries, allowances, etc.

Biggest salaries get bigger. il Bsns W p81-2+ My 23 '64
Detroit's highest tribute. Time 81:100 My 3 '63
Executive compensation by 1970. A. Patton. il Harvard Bsns R 42:137-46 S '64
Executive compensation: the new wave. W. Bowen. il Fortune 70:176-8+ N '64
Executives: how far, how fast, how much? D. Haymes. il Duns R 84:46-8+ O '64
For executives, cash is the sweetest deal. il Bsns W p 108-9 S 5 '64
General motors bonus system: an indispensable incentive. A. P. Sloan, jr. Fortune 69: 125+ Ja '64
Gleaming year for big brass. il Bsns W p32 Ap 4 '64
Highest-paid man in industry. U S News 54:19 My 6 '63
Nice year for the top brass. il Bsns W p28 Ap 13 '63
Overseas pay. Newsweek 62:71 S 9 '63
Paychecks ride the profit wave; with tables. Bsns W p85-6+ My 18 '63
Personal business; stock options are better than cash. Bsns W p 183 My 18 '63
Stock options at the crossroads. J. C. Baker. Harvard Bsns R 41:22-4+ Ja '63
Stock options lose a lot of luster. Bsns W p 104+ Mr 14 '64
Upturn in executive compensation; survey prepared by McKinsey & company. A. Patton. il Harvard Bsns R 41:133-7 S '63
Utility stock options: executive incentive v. public interest. L. Metcalf. il Nation 199: 151-4 S 28 '64
When deferred compensation doesn't pay. G. H. Foote. Harvard Bsns R 42:99-106 My '64
Where pay is best for top executives. U S News 58:14 Ja 11 '65
Who got the big pay in U.S. companies. il U S News 54:63-5 My 13 '63
Who takes home the biggest paychecks; with chart. U S News 56:61-4 My 4 '64

Selection and appointment

Britain; shaking the Old Boy network. Time 83:96+ My 22 '64
Executive: how far, how fast, how much? D. Haymes. il Duns R 84:46-8+ O '64
How to pick a president. R. N. McMurry. il Duns R 82:57-8+ O '63
Middle management enigma. Duns R 82:29 Jl '63
Where to find new leaders. J. L. Schultz. il Nations Bsns 52:38-9+ O '64

Supply and demand

Beat the manager shortage. Nations Bsns 52:14 S '64
Business goes on a manhunt. L. Stessin. il N Y Times Mag p37+ N 8 '64
Good man is hard to find. J. Dolgins. il Duns R 81:63-4+ My '63
Most wanted men in industry; survey by the Association of executive recruiting consultants. N. Buckley. il Duns R 83:49-50+ F '64
These trends will change your job. Nations Bsns 51:86+ Ap '63
Wanted; one hundred presidents. J. Dolgins. il Duns R 81:36-8 Je '63

Training

B-schools for Britain; concerning Lord Franks plan. Bsns W p84+ D 7 '63
Breakthrough in organization development; symposium. bibliog f il Harvard Bsns R 42: 133-55 N '64
Broader education at the top. Bsns W p202 N 21 '64
Business peace corps. il Newsweek 62:72 S 30 '63
Case of the earmarked executives; case study of junior boards of directors; with excerpt from European problems in general management, by E. P. Learned and others. F. J. Aguilar. il Harvard Bsns R 41:6-8+ N '63
Executive training by meeting the best; MIT's Sloan program. il Bsns W p46-7 Ap 6 '63
GE's college is back in session; Management research & development institute at Crotonville, N.Y. il Bsns W p78+ F 8 '64
Growing problem of executive obsolescence; address. L. J. Weigle. Duns R 83:38-9+ Ap '64
Helping business talk to the natives. Bsns W p 120+ My 16 '64
Management development is a game. R. J. House. bibliog f il Harvard Bsns R 41:130-43 Jl '63
Refreshment on the rock; policymakers from business firms at Arden house. il Time 84:67 Ag 7 '64
T-groups for organizational effectiveness. C. Argyris. bibliog f il Harvard Bsns R 42:60-74 Mr '64
To the top, fork in hand; weekly dinners at Oakland university. Bsns W p78+ O 17 '64
Trilingual business education; European institute of business administration, Fontainebleau. il Fortune 69:51-2+ F '64
Upgrading courses for lady brass; UCLA management seminars. Bsns W p 156+ N 16 '63
What one top company wants; excerpts from address. J. J. Scanlon. Nations Bsns 52: 68+ Ap '64
What's ahead for business education; symposium. il Nations Bsns 52:40-1+ Ap '64
Why businessmen go back to school; university-run management development programs. il Bsns W p47-8+ Ap 27 '63
See also
Industrial management—Study and teaching

EXECUTIVES as stockholders
Companies' stocks; as their officials size them up. il U S News 57:100-2 O 19 '64
Executives and their stocks: buying and selling both rise. il U S News 55:70-2 Jl 29 '63
Executives and their stocks: now they're buying again. il U S News 54:101-3 Mr 4 '63

EXECUTIVES as stockholders—*Continued*
Should management own more stock? J. J. Friedman. il Duns R 81:52-3 My '63
Stock options: tighter rules? U S News 54: 105-6 Mr 11 '63
Tightening tax laws on stock options. Bsns W p74 Mr 2 '63
See also
Executives—Salaries, allowances, etc.
EXECUTIVES seminars. See Seminars
EXECUTIVES wives. See Wives
EXEGESIS. See Bible—Criticism, interpretation, etc.
EXEMPTION from taxation. See Taxation, Exemption from
EXERCISE
Atlas was right all along; isometrics. il Life 56:47-8 Ap 17 '64
Beauty: new legs to stand on. D. A. Robinson. il Ladies Home J 81:80-3 N '64
Chair-borne exercises. il Vogue 141:64-5 Je '63
Comforting truth about exercise. il Ladies Home J 80:134+ Ap '63
Counteracting effects of physical exercises performed during prolonged perceptual deprivation. J. P. Zubek. bibliog il Science 142:504-6 O 25 '63
Cycling for fitness. P. D. White. il Recreation 57:405-6 O '64
Do exercises work? il Seventeen 23:128-9 Mr '64
Eleven minutes a day; systems of Royal Canadian air force. il Time 81:66-7 Mr 1 '63
Exercise and heart disease. S. A. Levine. il Atlan 212:42-5 Jl '63
Exercise and heart trouble. il Sci Digest 55: 88 My '64
Exercise at any age. Time 83:72 F 21 '64
Exercise important in reducing heart disease. Sci N L 84:40 Jl 20 '63
Exercise now for better skiing later. il Todays Health 42:20-2 Ja '64
Exercises for a younger, prettier face; excerpt from Facial isometrics. C. E. Patterson. il McCalls 92:112 Ja '65
Experiment in fitness; Eastchester, N.Y. V. D. Bellew. Recreation 57:281-2 Je '64
Facial isometrics, by C. E. Patterson. Review
Time il 85:43 Ja 29 '65
Far out Far Eastern exercise; ancient Chinese calisthenics. H. B. Jacobs. il Sat Eve Post 236:68-9 My 18 '63
Fit to kill; getting into top shape for hunting. E. M. Orlick. il Outdoor Life 134:46-7+ S '64
Five minutes a day to keep fit. C. K. Morris. il Farm J 88:72 Ja '64
Get into shape for skiing. il Seventeen 22:74+ N '63
Hips, hips away! il Seventeen 22:136-7 S '63
How slim you look! il Good H 157:119-21 O '63
How to exercise without moving a muscle, by V. Obeck. Review
Sat R 47:60+ O 24 '64. H. Frankel
How to have a better figure. il Redbook 120:75-82 Mr '63
How to move inches, without moving an inch. il Mlle 57:110-11+ Je '63
How to reshape your post-baby figure. Farm J 88:78 Ja '64
How to take the dull edge off winter; all-family fitness program. il Bet Hom & Gard 43:40-1 Ja '65
Inactivity complicates fat child's problem. il Todays Health 41:78+ D '63
Keep in shape with the marines; women. il McCalls 91:124-5+ O '63
Leg up on a good heart; vigorous exercise good for one's heart. G. Crozier. il Sports Illus 21:28+ S 21 '64
Long stretch. G. Peterson. il Mlle 59:314-15 Ag '64
Mlle's own beauty adviser. il Mlle 58:117-21 F '64
Me and my XBX. J. Howard. il Life 55:17 N 8 '63
Muscles are his business. R. Stonewall. il Ebony 20:147-50 D '64
One, two, three, oof! do-it-yourself instruction booklet. il Newsweek 62:76 S 2 '63
Paragon traveller exercises aloft; ten isometric exercises. il Vogue 144:30+ Jl '64
Peggy's exercises. il McCalls 90:162 My '63
Physical fitness for everyone. S. Musial. Parents Mag 39:38 N '64
Project: you; figure. B. Clerke. il Ladies Home J 80:73-6 Mr '63
Promotion of grace; new swerve in exercise. Vogue 144:138 D '64
Rag-doll exercises. D. A. Robinson. il Ladies Home J 81:82-3 Ap '64
Safe, sensible approach to exercise. il Good H 158:155 Mr '64
Sensible ways to keep fit. bibliog il Changing T 18:44-6 N '64
Shape a swim-suit figure. il Seventeen 22: 128-9 My '63
Shape terrific; how to get it, how to keep it. il Vogue 143:120+ F 15 '64
Shape-up; East Side gymnasium for Manhattan's upper crust. il Newsweek 64:92 D 14 '64
Slim half dozen lazy, lying-down exercises. V. Obeck. il McCalls 92:118-19 O '64
Step by step dance to slimness. il McCalls 90:154+ Mr '63
These five were cured of overweight. P. Deutsch and R. Deutsch. il Ladies Home J 80:131-2+ Ap '63
To exercise or not to exercise? J. J. Lentz. il Todays Health 41:28-9+ Mr '63
Top form for teens; physical-fitness pamphlets, vim (for girls) and vigor (for boys) il Newsweek 63:93 My 11 '64
Union of two worlds; Olympic games. E. O. Reischauer. il Sports Illus 19:50-4 D 23 '63
What the beatiful people are doing. il Vogue 143:48-57 F 15 '64
What's a dancer doing at Mr Kenneth's? H. Smith. il Dance Mag 39:22-3 Ja '65
Without moving a muscle. il Time 83:38-9 Ja 31 '64
You get trimmer every day! il Seventeen 23:104-5 Je '64
Youth and fitness, where do we stand? il Sr Schol 82:8-9+ F 13 '63
See also
Physical education and training
Walking
EXERCISE big lift. See Military maneuvers
EXERCISE delawar. See Military maneuvers
EXERCISE Hawk star. See Military maneuvers
EXERCISE polar siege. See Military maneuvers
EXERCISES, Spiritual. See Spiritual exercises
EXERCISES, Yoga. See Yoga
EXERCISING machines
Who uses mechanical devices for the toning of muscles? people. il Vogue 142:126-7 N 15 '63
EXHAUST gases. See Automobile engines—Exhaust
EXHAUST systems
See also
Automobile engines—Exhaust
EXHIBITION cases
Many-sided showcase. il Bsns W p54 Ag 24 '63
Unusual fixtures sell paperbacks in Holland. il Pub W 183:26-7 Ap 8 '63
EXHIBITIONS
Are trade shows worth it? L. Blumenthal. il Duns R 83:39-40+ Je '64
Canada looks south; trade fair in Philadelphia. il Bsns W p 178-80 N 16 '63
Capsule history of world's fairs. A. Karlen. Holiday 36:68-9 Jl '64
Century of exhibitions went from Crystal palace to crystal ball. il Look 28:92 F 11 '64
China peddles wares; trade fair in Tokyo. il Bsns W p68-9 Ap 25 '64
Coins and medals for fairs and expositions. C. French. Hobbies 69:102 S '64
Come to the fair. A. M. Lingg. il Opera N 28:8-14 Ap 4 '64
Delights of the Swiss fair; Swiss national exposition, Lausanne '64. A. Stagg. il House & Gard 126:234-7+ O '64
Dreamland; Start your own business exposition at Coliseum, New York. New Yorker 38: 26-7 F 9 '63
Expositions, exhibits and today's museums; relationship between world's fairs and museums. G. Reekie. il Natur Hist 73:20-9 Je '64
Fair game. T. L. Christie. il Sat R 47:48+ Mr 14 '64
Flying trade show. il Bsns W p76+ D 12 '64
Glance at the past, a preview of '64. il Sr Schol 84:6-7 Ap 3 '64
Golden era of fairs. il Life 56:53-4+ My 1 '64
IPEX: machines and techniques; London exhibition, July 16 to 27, 1963. J. Dreyfus. il Pub W 184:78+ S 9 '63
Mexico's show window; National home fair, at Juarez. il Bsns W p68-9 S 26 '64
National scene. See issues of Hot rod
Our man in Lausanne; Swiss national exposition. New Yorker 40:23-5 Jl 25 '64
SR/1965 world travel calendar. R. E. Meyer, jr. il Sat R 48:47-8+ Ja 2 '65
Selling a city to itself; Los Angeles' industrial fair and congress. il Bsns W p54-5 Mr 14 '64

EXHIBITIONS—*Continued*
Setting a style for Texas. il Bsns W p 132+ Ag 15 '64
Slalom; event at National ski fair, sponsored by White rose tea. New Yorker 39:24 F 15 '64
Spectacle that astonished Salonica; international trade fair. D. Wharton. Read Digest 83:113-16 S '63
Swiss build a thinking man's fair. O. Tanner. il Arch Forum 121:92-9 Jl '64
Visit to the World's fair of 2014. I. Asimov. il N Y Times Mag p20+ Ag 16 '64; Reply. New Yorker 40:39 S 12 '64
Westprint '64; items of book industry interest. L. D. Osborne. il Pub W 186:102-4+ Jl 6 '64
See also
Audio fairs
Book exhibits
New York (city)—Worlds fair, 1939-1940
New York (city)—Worlds fair, 1964
Seattle—Century 21 exposition, 1962
also subhead Exhibitions under various subjects, e.g. Photography—Exhibitions
EXHIBITIONS, Traveling
Iran: light vs. darkness; traveling show of Persian art. J. Brzostoski. il Art N 63:39-41+ Sum '64
Sales & distribution; flying fair promotes U.S. goods in Europe. Duns R 84:93 O '64
Seven millenniums under one roof. il Time 84:58-60 Jl 17 '64
Traveling study collections: museums into the classroom, Seattle. F. Cochran. Sr Schol 85:21T Ja 21 '65
See also
Smithsonian institution—Traveling exhibition service
Anecdotes, facetiae, satire, etc.
I brought Chagall to America. K. Kellen. Esquire 62:60+ D '64
EXHIBITS
Kit for a fast display; Exhibitkit. il Bsns W p84 Mr 2 '63
See also special types of exhibits, e.g. Book exhibits
EXHIBITS, Industrial
TWA goes on the road to get suppliers. il Bsns W p 138+ Ja 26 '63
EXILES
Exiled revolutionaries and the French political police in the 1850's. H. C. Payne and H. Grosshans. bibliog f Am Hist R 68:954-73 Jl '63
Paris exiles: Vietnamese political exiles. H. B. Lamb. il Nation 197:65-8 Ag 10 '63
See also
Expatriation
EXISTENTIALISM
Christianity and existentialism, by W. Earle and others. Review
Christian Cent 82:111 Ja 27 '65. R. Luecke
Creative fidelity, by G. Marcel. Review
America 110:320 Mr 7 '64. D. A. Drennen
Existential and Christian. A. E. Mayhew. Commonweal 80:152-3 Ap 24 '64
Existential criticism in educational theory; adaptation from address, April, 1963. M. I. Berger. Sch & Soc 92:334-5 N 14 '64
Existentialism and the Catholic thinker. J. Dallen. Cath World 200:294-9 F '65
Existentialism; with report by F. Kappler. il Life 57:86-96+ N 6 '64
Search for a method, by J. P. Sartre, tr. by H. E. Barnes. Review
Sat R 46:38-9 Je 22 '63 A. Bloch
What is existentialism? by W. Barrett. Review
Newsweek 63:84+ Mr 2 '64
EXIT the king; drama. See Ionesco, E.
EXITS, Emergency. See Airplanes—Safety devices and measures
EXNER, Frederick B.
Filth we breathe. Sci Digest 53:11 My '63
EXNER, Virgil Max, 1909-
Introducing the 1964 Duesenberg, Packard, Stutz and Mercer! D. Bartley. il Esquire 60:200-3 D '63
EXNER, Virgil Max, jr
Introducing the 1964 Duesenberg, Packard, Stutz and Mercer! D. Bartley. il Esquire 60:200-3 D '63
EXOBIOTA. See Life on other planets
EXODUS. See Bible—Old Testament—Exodus
EXOSPHERE. See Atmosphere, Upper
EXOTHERMIC brazing. See Brazing
EXOTHERMIC reactions. See Chemical reactions
EXOTOXIN. See Toxins and antitoxins
EXPANDED program of technical assistance. See United Nations—Technical assistance program
EXPANDING universe. See Universe
EXPANSION, House. See Houses, Remodeled
EXPANSION of industry. See Industrial expansion
EXPATRIATION
Artist as blimp. W. Sheed. Commonweal 78: 245-6 My 24 '63
New faces in the expatriate colony. E. Gilbert. il N Y Times Mag p30+ D 8 '63
EXPENDITURES, Family. See Domestic finance
EXPENDITURES, Municipal. See Municipal finance
EXPENDITURES, Personal. See Budget, Personal
EXPENDITURES, State. See State finance
EXPENSE accounts (business)
As Congress takes a hand in expense-account rules. U S News 54:112+ Ap 22 '63
Big beef stew; effect of expense account cuts. il Newsweek 61:72 Mr 11 '63
Bistros up in arms; vs IRS rules. Bsns W p29 Mr 30 '63
Corrupt society. F. J. Cook. Nation 196:476-7 Je 1 '63
Dear diary: $26.73 for . . . Bsns W p 102+ F 23 '63
Easing expense accounts. il Time 82:77 Jl 5 '63
Easing the bite. Newsweek 62:74+ Jl 8 '63
Expense-account fiasco; its effects. il U S News 54:39-41 Mr 11 '63
Expense-account meals: what the rules really are. il U S News 54:96+ Mr 4 '63
Expense-account party at home. il U S News 55:46 Jl 29 '63
Expense-account socialism. Nation 196:278 Ap 6 '63
Here are those new rules on expense accounts. il U S News 54:50-1 Ap 8 '63
Latest word on expense accounts. U S News 55:105 S 30 '63
Mortimer Caplin: the man who takes your money. B. Herndon. il Sat Eve Post 236: 70+ Ap 13 '63
Now it's official: tax guide for expense accounts. il U S News 55:98-100 Jl 8 '63
Prove it and you're O.K; IRS regulation of expense account expenditures. Time 81:76 Ap 5 '63
Pulling the tax punch; new regulations. il Bsns W p34 Ap 6 '63
Take your wife on your next business trip? Bet Hom & Gard 43:24-5 Ja '65
Tax men get another earful on expense-account rules. il U S News 54:109-12 My 20 '63
What expense-account curbs are doing to business. il U S News 54:41-2 F 4 '63
What expense-account rules are doing now to business. il U S News 55:101-3 S 9 '63
What expense-account rules are doing to conventions. il U S News 54:113-16 Ap 8 '63
What you can and cannot do on an expense account. il U S News 54:54-7 Ap 15 '63
Who said two drinks? Nation 197:3 Jl 6 '63
With a business gleam in his eye; IRS rules on expense accounts. il Newsweek 61:67 Ap 8 '63
See also
Business entertaining
Anecdotes, facetiae, satire, etc.
Fiction as strange as fact: death of another salesman; excerpts from address, March 18, 1963. T. R. Groom. il U S News 54:51-3 Ap 22 '63
EXPERIENCE
See also
Pragmatism
EXPERIENCE (religion)
Aldersgate and 1963; J. Wesley's experience of the warmed heart. G. Kennedy. Christian Cent 80:677-8 My 22 '63
Fire next time, by J. Baldwin. Review
Nat R il 14:408-14+ My 21 '63. G. Wills; Discussion. 14:507 Je 18 '63
John Wesley and Aldersgate 1963. P. B. Mather. Christian Cent 80:1581-3 D 18 '63
EXPERIMENT in international living (organization)
My most exciting summer ever: in Europe! W. Birnie. il Seventeen 23:116-17+ Je '64
They experiment in international living. D. S. Strotzel. il Parents Mag 39:37+ Ap '64; Same abr. with title Winning the peace is a family job. Read Digest 84:205-7+ Ap '64
EXPERIMENTAL aircraft association
Airplane in the basement, homemade airplanes. il Time 85:30-1 Ja 8 '65
Experimental aircraft association. R. Bach. Flying 75:78-9 Ag '64
Fresh flock of fold-wing planes. J. Cushman and M. Dowd. il Pop Mech 119:90-5+ F '63

EXPERIMENTAL airplanes. See Airplanes, Experimental

EXPERIMENTAL animals. See Laboratory animals

EXPERIMENTAL education. See Education, Experimental

EXPERIMENTAL music. See Music

EXPERIMENTAL neuroses. See Neuroses, Experimental

EXPERIMENTAL psychology. See Psychology, Experimental

EXPERIMENTAL schools. See Schools. Experimental

EXPERIMENTATION on man. See Medical research—Experimentation on man

EXPERIMENTS
See also
Biology—Experiments

EXPERTISING in art. See Art—Expertising

EXPERTS. See Specialists

EXPERTS (in business) See Business consultants

EXPLODING wire phenomena
AF adopts new EBW buy approach. J. F. Judge. il Miss & Roc 15:34+ Ag 10 '64
Exploding bridgewire critics answered. il Miss & Roc 12:43 My 27 '63
EBW field needs systems approach. J. F. Judge. il Miss & Roc 14:30-1+ Ja 27 '64
Makers seeking answers to unknowns of exploding bridge wire. R. Pay. Miss & Roc 14:32-3 Mr 23 '64; Reply. D. Powell. 14:5 My 4 '64
Reliable exploding bridgewire remains to be developed. V. J. Menichelli. il Miss & Roc 13:34+ D 16 '63

EXPLORATION, Submarine. See Diving, Submarine

EXPLORATIONS
Admiral Peary and all that; exhibition at American museum of natural history. il Sci Digest 54:28-33 N '63
See also
America—Discovery and exploration

EXPLORER (artificial satellites) See Artificial satellites—Use in research

EXPLORERS
Great adventures with National geographic. Review
Nat Geog Mag il 124:728-33 N. '63. M. B. Grosvenor

EXPLORERS, French
See also
Perrot, N.

EXPLORERS, Spanish
Conquistadors in North American history, by P. Horgan. Review
Reporter 28:52+ Ap 25 '63. W. T. Hagan
Ephemeral Amazon kingdom; dark deeds of Lope de Aguirre. R. J. Sender. il Américas 15:28-32 My '63; Reply. A. B. Mason. 15:48 S '63
Spanish doctors in the old Southwest. R. Dunlop. il Todays Health 41:44-7+ F '63

EXPLORERS club
Ballroom explorers. New Yorker 40:36 My 23 '64

EXPLORER'S hall. See National geographic society—Explorer's hall

EXPLOSIONS
Did a comet collide with the earth in 1908? Tungus meteorite expedition. K. P. Florenskii. il Sky & Tel 26:268-9 N '63
Frozen moment at Indianapolis. il Life 55: 44A N 15 '63
Handle gas with care to avoid explosions. Sci N L 84:313 N 16 '63
Hellish Halloween; Indianapolis coliseum gas explosion. il Newsweek 62:40+ N 11 '63
Ice show's finale; explosion in Indianapolis' state fairgrounds coliseum. il Time 82:25 N 8 '63
Meaning of an explosion; Gorgopotamos bridge. il Time 84:46 D 11 '64
Message from sixty-one Cygni; Tungus blast. il Time 83:48+ Ap 3 '64
See also
Bombs
Mine accidents and explosions

EXPLOSIVE bonding. See Welding

EXPLOSIVE detectors. See Detectors

EXPLOSIVE forming of metals
Explosions join metals. E. Hall. il Sci N L 85:378-9 Je 13 '64

EXPLOSIVE ordnance research. See Ordnance research

EXPLOSIVE welding. See Welding

EXPLOSIVES
Detonation-wave phenomena. D. D. Abernathy. Science 146:1635 D 25 '64
Explosive welding with nitroguanidine. L. D. Sadwin. bibliog il Science 143:1164+ Mr 13 '64
Nobel's old company: still dynamite. il Bsns W p60+ D 12 '64
See also
Detonators

Safety devices and measures
Keeping danger at arm's length; Hercules powder mixes and tests explosive rocket fuels. il Bsns W p77 Ag 10 '63

EXPORT credit
Calculated risks; trade with eastern Europe and the Soviet Union. Time 84:103 S 11 '64
Department opposes restriction of credit to Communist nations; statement, November 21, 1963. G. W. Ball. Dept State Bul 49:935-6 D 16 '63

EXPORT credit insurance. See Insurance, Credit; Insurance, Investment guaranty

EXPORT controls
Soviet-bloc market: so big and yet so far. il Bsns W p53-4 O 19 '63

EXPORT-import bank of Washington
Export-import bank feels Congress' pinch. Bsns W p29 Ag 10 '63
Innocent bystander. Bsns W p 112 Ag 24 '63

EXPORT trade. See Commerce

EXPOSICIÓN editorial del continente americano. See Book fairs

EXPOSITIONS. See Exhibitions

EXPOSURE (photography) See Photography—Exposure

EXPOSURE calculator. See Photography—Exposure

EXPOSURE meters
Ad libs. P. Farber. il U S Camera 26:32-3 Mr '63
Ad libs; use the 3A. P. Farber. U S Camera 26:14-15 Jl '63
Amateur scientist; telescope for a home observatory and a light meter. F. Aime. il Sci Am 209:124-6 Ag '63
Amazing new exposure meters. R. M. Benrey. il Pop Sci 185:84-7+ S '64
Beseler Topcon Super D: behind-the-lens meter system. D. Gerritt. il U S Camera 26:62-3+ O '63
Best answer yet: behind-the-lens meters for 8mm movie cameras. B. Sherman and M. A. Matzkin. il Mod Phot 27:98-9+ N '63
C is for care with Cds. C. W. Kennedy. il Pop Phot 56:150+ Ja '65
Confused about CdS vs. selenium exposure meters? T. Karp. il Mod Phot 27:64-5+ Jl '63
Creative color. A. Rothstein. U S Camera 26:8+ F '63
Durst Analite. B. Pierce. il Pop Phot 52: 110-11 Ap '63
Exposure methods & meters. P. Farber. il U S Camera 27:50-3+ Je '64
Fast meter reading. C. Wright. Pop Phot 52:92-3 Mr '63
How Beseler Topcon put the meter in the mirror. T. Baba and H. Keppler. il Mod Phot 27:109-10 O '63
Inexpensive CdS meters. M. Morrison il U S Camera 27:48-9+ D '64
Lenses for meters? B. Sherman and H. Keppler. il Mod Phot 28:75 Jl '64
Logetronic's Focatron, an image-sharpness meter. C. Wright. il Pop Phot 52:88-9 My '63
Meter angle error? H. Keppler. il Mod Phot 28:74 Jl '64
Meters for available darkness. R. T. Hammarlund. il U S Camera 26:66-9 F '63
Modern's 1963-1964 exposure meter directory. D. L. Miller. Mod Phot 27:82-3 Jl '63; 28: 66-7 Jl '64
New! low-price clip-on meter with choice of three angles. C. Wright. il Pop Phot 55:97 Jl '64
1964-1965 directory and buying guide. il Pop Phot 56:52C-64C Ja '65
Primer on exposure meters. B. Pierce. il Pop Phot 54:68-73+ Je '64

L'EXPRESS. See Paris—Newspapers

EXPRESS companies
See also
American express company

EXPRESS highways
Fight to tame the urban freeway takes a positive new turn. D. Canty. il Arch Forum 119:68-73 O '63
Interstate highway system. R. G. Knox. il Motor T 15:118-21 N '63
Interstate highways: a progress report; with map. Changing T 18:23-5 Je '64
Most drivers don't know how to drive safely on a freeway, do you? Bet Hom & Gard 42:131 My '64
New science of driving; freeway driving. A. Hamilton. il Sci Digest 55:86-90 F '64

EXPRESS highways—*Continued*
Open roads. il Time 81:61 Ap 12 '63
Progress report on the Nation's superhighways. il U S News 54:96-7 My 27 '63
Sixteen lanes plus mass transit; Chicago's Dan Ryan expressway. R. F. Nusbaum. il Am City 79:14 Ja '64
Superhighways: now there are 17,000 miles; interstate-highway system. il U S News 57:44-5 Ag 31 '64
View from the road: a highway redesigned for the drama of driving; excerpts from View from the road. D. Appleyard and others. il Arch Forum 119:74-7 O '63
EXPRESSIONISM (art)
Van Gogh and expressionism. B. Kaufman. Commonweal 81:110-11 O 16 '64
EXPRESSWAY centers, incorporated
Truck stop goes fancy; Toledo 5. il Bsns W p 108-9+ Mr 16 '63
EXPROPRIATION
Big steal abroad. il U S News 55:57-9 D 2 '63
See also
Cuba—Expropriation policy
EXSTROPHY. See Bladder—Deformities
EXTENDED range film. See Photography—Films
EXTENDED vacation. See Vacations, Employee
EXTENSION cords. See Electric cords
EXTENSION education
Extended schooling versus higher education. J. F. Ohles. Sch & Soc 92:156-7 Ap 4 '64
EXTENSION service. See United States—Federal extension service
EXTERIOR decorator; drama. See Boiko, C.
EXTERIOR house decoration. See House decoration, Exterior
EXTERIOR: with figure; story. See O'Hara, J.
EXTERMINATION of cockroaches. See Cockroaches—Extermination
EXTERMINATION of fishes. See Fishes—Extermination
EXTERMINATION of mosquitoes. See Mosquitoes—Extermination
EXTINCT animals. See Animals, Extinct
EXTINCTION of animals. See Animals, Extinct
EXTINCTION of man. See Man—Survival
EXTORTION
Kiss, tape, and tell; charge against J. and C. Heneghan. il Newsweek 62:42 O 7 '63
EXTRA high voltage transmission. See Electric transmission
EXTRACTION apparatus
Continuous extraction during treatment with ultrasound. J. A. Lott and A. E. DeMaggio. bibliog il Science 139:825-6 Mr 1 '63
EXTRACTORS. See Extraction apparatus
EXTRACURRICULAR activities. See Student activities
EXTRADITION
Breaking a tradition in favor of democracy; case of P. Jiménez. il Time 82:20-1 Ag 23 '63
Britain: law or justice? case of Antony Enahoro. Newsweek 61:40+ Ap 22 '63
Where the crooks can't go; U.S. and Brazil exchange. Time 84:44 N 27 '64
EXTRAS (opera) See Operatic production
EXTRASENSORY perception
ESP is NG, says AF. Sci Digest 54:59-60 Jl '63
Now a seer helps stalk the Boston strangler. P. Mandel. il Life 56:49-50 Mr 6 '64
Psychic powers of Sam Benson. J. Robbins and J. Robbins. Read Digest 86:119-22 Ja '65
Why some scientists believe in telepathy. il Good H 158:167 My '64
EXTRATERRESTRIAL material. See Matter, Interstellar
EXTREMISM (political science) See Right and left (political science)
EYCK, F. Gunther
Benelux countries. Cur Hist 47:355-61 D '64
Benelux in the Common market. bibliog f Cur Hist 45:295-301 N '63
EYDE, Richard H. See Stern, W. L. jt. auth.
EYE
In the ear and eye, complex hi-fi gives us sound and sight. R. Campbell. il Life 54:70-2, 76B+ Je 28 '63
Isolated mammalian eye: a method for quantitative evaluation of autonomic drugs. W. T. Beaver. bibliog il Science 141:1274-5 S 27 '63
Lens development: fiber elongation and lens orientation. J. L. Coulombre and A. J. Coulombre. bibliog il Science 142:1489-90 D 13 '63
Light adaptation kinetics: the influence of spatial factors. W. S. Battersby and I. H. Wagman. bibliog il Science 143:1029-31 Mr 6 '64
What's in an eye? il U S Camera 26:18 D '63
Why of the eye; excerpt from Ambidextrous universe. M. Gardner. il Sat R 47:67 N 7 '64
See also
Cornea
Lacrimal organs
Pupil (eye)
Retina
Sight
Accommodation and refraction
Adaptation to chromatic aberration by the human visual system. J. C. Hay and others. bibliog il Science 141:167-9 Jl 12 '63
Care and hygiene
Beware: hidden threat to young eyes. G. G. Greer. Bet Hom & Gard 42:36 S '64
Beware of eclipse eyes. Field & S 68:32 Je '63
Eye injuries. C. J. Potthoff. Todays Health 41:64 Mr '63
How good are school eye tests? V. Sande. Redbook 121:130 S '63
Why eyes require a regular checkup. il Good H 157:124-5 Jl '63
See also
National society for the prevention of blindness
Diseases and defects
California doctor spreads eye infection. Sci N L 83:345 Je 1 '63
Found: drug that cures a blinding virus. il Life 55:78+ S 6 '63
Long time no see. Mrs J. Thurber. il Ladies Home J 81:50-1+ Jl '64
Tracking down the enemies of vision. R. L. Masland. il Todays Health 41:52-7 N '63
See also
Blindness
Cataract
Conjunctivitis
Glaucoma
Trachoma
Movements
Averaged brain activity following saccadic eye movement. K. Gaarder and others. bibliog il Science 146:1481-3 D 11 '64
Control mechanisms of the eye. D. H. Fender. il Sci Am 211:24-33 bibliog(p 142) Jl '64
Eye fixation aspect of attention to visual stimuli in infant chimpanzees. G. Berkson and F. L. Fitz-Gerald. bibliog il Science 139:586-7 F 15 '63
Eyeball retraction: classical conditioning and extinction in the albino rabbit. E. B. Deaux and I. Gormezano. bibliog il Science 141:630-1 Ag 16 '63
Pursuit eye movements in the absence of a moving visual stimulus. G. H. Deckert. bibliog il Science 143:1192-3 Mr 13 '64
Protection
Beware of summer glare. A. Nelson. il Sci Digest 54:63-6 Ag '63
Don't look now; safeguards for viewing solar eclipse. il Time 82:72+ Jl 12 '63
How to watch next week's eclipse: don't burn your eyes. il Life 55:41+ Jl 12 '63
See also
Eye—Care and hygiene
Surgery
Built-in eyeglasses; regrinding the lens of the eye. Pop Sci 184:22+ Ja '64
Can you see, my son, can you really see? cataracts removed from five Rotolo brothers; with report by J. Bonfante. il Life 57:32-41 N 20 '64
Into the eye with ultrasound. il Time 84:96 O 2 '64
New light for the blind. il Sci Digest 54:52 N '63
Ultrasound used to save eye of eight-year-old boy. Sci N L 86:217 O 3 '64
See also
Eye banks
EYE (amphibia)
Unit responses in the frog's tectum to moving and nonmoving visual stumuli. U. Grüsser-Cornehls and others. bibliog il Science 141:820-2 Ag 30 '63
Vision in frogs. W. R. A. Muntz. il Sci Am 210:110-15+ Mr '64; Reply with rejoinder. D. J. Merrell. 210:10+ My '64
EYE (animals)
Incredible eyes of animals. J. George. il Audubon Mag 67:20-3 Ja '65
See also
Sight (animals)
EYE (crustacea)
Ultraviolet eye; horseshoe crab. Sci Am 210:62+ Ap '64

EYE (Insects)
Dynamics of motion perception in the desert locust. J. Thorson. bibliog il Science 145:69-71 Jl 3 '64
Visual responses in the eye of the dragon fly. M. G. F. Fuortes. il Science 142:69-70 O 4 '63
EYE, Evil. See Evil eye
EYE banks
Race against blindness; ham radio operators and eye surgeons join forces. M. Gunther. il Sat Eve Post 237:36-7 My 30 '64
They can see again. J. K. Lagemann. Read Digest 84:217-18+ F '64
Triumph of Janis Babson; excerpts from Little girl's gift. L. Elliott. Read Digest 82:275-86+ Je '63
EYE makeup. See Cosmetics; Make-up
EYE melanin. See Melanin
EYE of the beholder; story. See Epstein, S.
EYE protection. See Eye—Protection
EYEBROWS
How to shape your eyebrows. il Ladies Home J 81:85 Jl '64
EYEGLASSES
Franklin look; half-moon spectacles. il Time 84:53 S 4 '64
Look pretty in glasses. il Seventeen 23:160-1+ S '64
Mom! mom! I can see! highpowered spectacles for legally blind. T. Irwin. il Sat Eve Post 236:71-2 My 25 '63
New glasses darken as sky brightens. Sci N L 85:184 Mr 21 '64
See also
Contact lenses
Sun glasses
EYELASHES, Artificial
How to apply false eyelashes. il Ladies Home J 81:127 N '64
Lashed up. il Time 83:49 F 21 '64
EYELIDS
Measurement of the conditioned eyelid reflex. H. S. Pennypacker. bibliog il Science 144:1248-9 Je 5 '64
EYER, Ronald
Aloha, out there. Mus Am 84:56-7 F '64
Minas Christian, conductor Evansville philharmonic, Indiana. Mus Am 83:11 My '63
Weaver of German opera. Opera N 27:8-13 F 2 '63
EYES. See Eye
EYESIGHT. See Sight
EYRING, Henry M.
Doctor Eyring president of A.A.A.S. in 1965. Sci N L 85:3 Ja 4 '64
Henry Eyring, president-elect. C. J. Christensen. por Science 143:826-8 F 21 '64
EYSENCK, H. J.
Measurement of motivation; with biographical sketch. Sci Am 208:38, 130-4+ My '63
EYSTER, Warren
Homecoming of the children; story. Sat Eve Post 237:44-5 O 3 '64
EYZIES, Les, excavation. See France—Antiquities

F

FAA. See United States—Federal aviation agency
FAO. See Food and agriculture organization of the United Nations
FBI. See United States—Federal bureau of investigation
FCC. See United States—Federal communications commission
FCIA. See Foreign credit insurance association
FCIC. See Federal crop insurance corporation
FDA. See United States—Food and drug administration
FDIC. See Federal deposit insurance corporation
FEIA. See Flight engineers international association
FEPC. See United States—Fair employment practice, Committee on
FFA. See Future farmers of America
FHA. See United States—Federal housing administration
FHA loans. See United States—Federal housing administration
FHLBB. See United States—Federal home loan bank board
FID. See International federation for documentation
FLES (foreign languages in the elementary school) See Languages, Modern—Study and teaching
FLN (Front de libération nationale) See Algeria—Politics and government
FM. See Radio frequency modulation
FM radio stations. See Radio stations, Frequency modulation
FM receivers. See Radio receiving apparatus—Frequency modulation receivers
FM-stereo antennas. See Radio antennas
FMC corporation
Antitrusters suffer a setback; FMC corp. merger with Avisco. Bsns W p88 Ag 10 '63
Giant that makes almost anything; FMC corp. to absorb American viscose. il Bsns W p58+ Mr 9 '63
FMCS. See United States—Federal mediation and conciliation service
FOR. See Fellowship of reconciliation
FOUR. See Federation of union representatives
FPA. See Foreign policy association
FPC. See United States—Federal power commission
FRB. See United States—Federal reserve board
FTC. See United States—Federal trade commission
F. W. Woolworth company. See Woolworth, F. W. and company
FABELA, Isidro
Mexico looks to the North. Atlan 213:95-8 Mr '64
FABER, Doris
I'm not against it, but—. N Y Times Mag p58+ O 27 '63
FABER, Harold
Presidential firsts, mosts and almosts. N Y Times Mag p 16+ My 24 '64
FABIAN society
Thomas Davidson and the New life fellowship. W. S. Smith. Christian Cent 80:642-5 My 15 '63
FABIANI, Aurelio
In this corner: Aurelio Fabiani; interview, ed. by F. Stevenson. Opera N 28:16-17 N 16 '63
FABLES
Adam's image. R. T. Reilly. America 108:746-8 My 25 '63
Four fables from Poland; tr. by K. Syrop. S. Mrozek. il Mlle 57:158-61 My '63
Glass in the field; excerpts from Fables for our time. J. Thurber. Read Digest 82:168C Mr '63
Man from the moon. T. Ungerer. il Holiday 36:76-83 D '64
New fable of the grasshopper and the ant. J. Ciardi. il McCalls 90:100-1 My '63
Old story well told; commentary on William Golding's Lord of the flies. W. R. Mueller. Christian Cent 80:1203-6 O 2 '63; Reply. V. Eller. 80:1440 N 20 '63
Three fables without morals. M. Denevi. il Américas 16:35-8 My '64
See also
Parables
FABRAY, Nanette
One battle I had to win; ed. by R. Hochstein. por Good H 156:88 My '63
FABRIC wall coverings. See Wall coverings
FABRICANT, Noah D.
What science has learned about varicose veins. Todays Health 41:35+ Ap '63
FABRICS. See Textile fabrics
FABRICS, Tire. See Tire fabrics
FACADES
Arch form as a facade motif; Inwood Manor, Houston, Tex. il Arch Rec 136:118-19 Ag '64
FACE, ElRoy
Fork ball and Roy Face. T. C. Brody. Sports Illus 18:24 Je 24 '63
FACE
About face. il Redbook 121:70-1+ S '63
Exercises for a younger, prettier face; excerpt from Facial isometrics. C. E. Patterson. il McCalls 92:112 Ja '65
I shall not look upon his like again; a few exceptions. M. Brandel. il Horizon 6:96-7 Spr '64
Look first at the face. Gowland. il Pop Phot 55:22+ N '64
See also
Beauty, Personal
FACE; story. See Sorensen, V.
FACE flies. See Flies
FACES, Stone. See Rock profiles
FACIAL expression
Evolution of facial expression. R. J. Andrew. bibliog il Science 142:1034-41 N 22 '63
Smiles of men and monkeys. Sci Am 210:56+ Ja '64

FACIAL surgery. See Surgery, Facial
FACIALS. See Skin—Care and hygiene
FACIO, Gonzalo J.
Castro must go! Read Digest 84:109-13 F '64
FACKENHEIM, Emil L.
Kant and Judaism. Commentary 36:460-7 D '63
On the eclipse of God. Commentary 37:55-60 Je; 38:26-7 D '64
FACKLAM, Margery A.
We traded security for happiness. por Redbook 120:6+ Mr '63
FACT (periodical)
Couch & the stump; Fact questionnaire. Time 84:73 O 9 '64
Goldwater's health; poll of psychiatrists. America 111:469 O 24 '64
Matter of Fact. Christian Cent 81:351, 476-7 Mr 11, Ap 15 '64
FACTORIES
New profits from new plants. il Duns R 81: pt2 S92-4+ Mr '63
Special report on industrial facilities; symposium. il Duns R 83:pt2 98-110+ Mr '64
Ten plants win factory awards. il Arch Rec 133:14-15+ Je '63
See also
Automobile factories
Foundries
Design
Allocating facilities with CRAFT. E. S. Buffa and others. il Harvard Bsns R 42:136-47+ Mr '64
Dividends from design. il Duns R 83:pt2 116-18+ Mr '64
Machine factory with a woodland setting. il Arch Rec 134:126-7 D '63
Nervi gives a factory the grace of a bridge; Cartiere Burgo's new mill in Mantua. il Arch Forum 121:110-13 Jl '64
Quest for the perfect plant. il Duns R 81:pt2 S103-5+ Mr '63
Rice university conference develops five factory projects. S. L. Pittman. il Arch Rec 134:115-20 D '63
Toms chocolate company; Ballerup, Denmark. il Arch Rec 137:158-61 Ja '65
Torrington Nivelles; factory in Belgium. il Arch Rec 137:153-5 Ja '65
Two-level scheme for food processing. il Arch Rec 134:132-4 D '63
Expansion
Critical decision: to build or modernize. J. B. Weiner. il Duns R 83:pt2 100-2+ Mr '64
Foreign branches
See Branch factories, Foreign
Grounds
See also
Industrial districts
Location
See Location in business and industry
Maintenance and repair
Maintenance: the wasted dollars. N. Buckley. Duns R 83:pt2 123-4+ Mr '64
You can cut your upkeep costs. S. Schuler. il Nations Bsns 52:94-6 My '64
Remodeling
Critical decision: to build or modernize. J. B. Weiner. il Duns R 83:pt2 100-2+ Mr '64
FACTORIES, Automatic. See Machinery, Automatic
FACTORY (magazine)
Ten plants win factory awards. il Arch Rec 133:14-15+ Je '63
FACTORY management
What bothers the boss in a Soviet factory. il Bsns W p45-6 Jl 13 '63
See also
Industrial management and organization
Production control
Subcontracting
FACTORY tours. See Industrial tours
FACTORY waste. See Trade waste
FACULTIES, College. See College professors and instructors
FACULTY relationships. See Colleges and universities—Administration
FADE out-fade in; musical comedy. See Musical comedies, revues, etc.—Criticisms, plots, etc.
FADER, Bruce
How to stop noise. Am City 79:103-5 Je '64
FADER, Shirley Sloan
Where did you go? home; what did you do? nothing. House B 106:42+ Mr '64
FADIMAN, Clifton
I know whatcha mean. Read Digest 82:229-30 My '63
Party of one (cont) Holiday 33:11+ F; 14+ Je; 34:10+ Ag; 12+ N '63; 36:12+ Jl '64
Reading I've liked. See issues of Holiday
Tinker's itch. Read Digest 82:19-20+ Mr '63
Wayward reader. Holiday 36:26+ N '64; 37: 33-4 Ja '65
Who'll take the hi-road? Read Digest 82:78-80 Ap '63
FADIMAN, William
Talk of Hollywood. Sat R 46:76-7 N 9 '63
FADOS
Sound of saudade: Portugal's melancholy fado; with discography. O. B. Brummell. il Hi Fi 14:106-10 O '64
You ain't been blue. Time 83:68+ F 7 '64
FADS
Beatles' secret. Reporter 30:16+ F 27 '64
Going, going, gonk; new craze in England. il Newsweek 64:106+ O 19 '64
Good cocktail; Ninja craze in Japan. il Newsweek 64:31+ Ag 3 '64
Kooky dolls new campus rage. J. Peter. il Look 27:M18+ S 24 '63
Mad fad for stir-crazy students; squeezing a piano through a hole. il Life 54:43-5 Mr 8 '63
Piano lesson; piano wrecking. il Time 81:64 Mr 1 '63
Teen scene. See issues of Seventeen
What the Beatles prove about teen-agers; interview. D. Riesman. il U S News 56:88 F 24 '64
What's Beatle. Seventeen 23:100 Ag '64
See also
Food fads
FAGAN, Edward R.
Field, philosophy, & esthetics. Sch Arts 63: 24-8 My '64
FAGER, E. W. and McGowan, J. A.
Zooplankton species groups in the North Pacific. bibliog Science 140:453-60 My 3 '63
FAGERLIE, Joan
Monies of antiquity. Natur Hist 73:20-5 Ja '64
FAGG, William
Royal ease along the Niger. Horizon 5:51 Mr '63
FAGIN, Bryllion
New look of Mr Chips. Sat R 46:57 Jl 20 '63
FAGIN, Henry
Urban transportation criteria. Ann Am Acad 352:141-51 Mr '64
FAGIN, Patricia E.
United Nations tour guide supervisor. il pors Ebony 18:34-8 Ag '63
FAGINI, Virginia
Little girl grows up. pors Esquire 62:208-9 D '64
FAHER, John L. See Terry, W. D. jt. auth.
FAHEY, James J.
Story behind the book; interview. Writer 76:17-18 S '63
about
Bluejacket's tale. il por Newsweek 62:88+ Jl 22 '63
FAHEY, Jed William
Apples; poem. Horn Bks 40:418-19 Ag '64
FAHEY, John L. and Goodman, Howard
Antibody activity in six classes of human immunoglobulins. bibliog Science 143:588-90 F 7 '64
—See Mishell, R. I. jt. auth.
FAHN, Stanley, and others
Electrophorus adenosine triphosphatase: sodium-activated exchange after N-ethyl maleimide treatment. bibliog Science 145: 283-4 Jl 17 '64
FAHRNER, Carl J. and Cronin, J. M.
Grouping by sex. NEA J 52:16-17 My '63
FAIGELE the idiotke; story. See Charyn, J.
FAILURE. See Success
FAIN, Harry M.
Who gets the child? (how the court decides) McCalls 92:85+ Ja '65
FAINA, Carlo
New chemical hybrid; Italy's Montecatini and Royal Dutch/Shell oil combine. il por Bsns W p70-3 Ja 11 '64
FAINTING
Parlor game of fainting no lark for players. Sci N L 84:57 Jl 27 '63
Why people faint. J.-E. Brown. il Todays Health 41:18-19+ Ag '63
You faint when you can't run. il Sci Digest 54:85 O '63
FAIR, C. M.
Open letter to the Le Goarnics; poem. New Yorker 39:32 Je 1 '63
FAIR campaign practices committee
For a clean campaign. Christian Cent 81: 789 Je 17 '64

FAIR day's work; story. See Monsarrat, N.
FAIR employment practice committee. See United States—Fair employment practice, Committee on
FAIR employment practices. See Discrimination in employment
FAIR exchange; story. See Dorman, S.
FAIR labor standards act. See Labor laws and legislation—United States
FAIR LAWN, N.J. free public library
Fair Lawn, N.J. public library circulates teaching machines. il Library J 88:3818 O 15 '63
FAIR play. See Sportsmanship
FAIR trade laws. See Price maintenance by industry; Price regulation by government
FAIRBANKS, Douglas, 1909-
Who killed chivalry? por McCalls 92:117+ N '64
FAIRBANKS, Henry G.
Diem and the Buddhists. Commonweal 78: 452-4 Jl 26 '63
Facing hard facts in Vietnam. Cath World 199:89-95 My '64
Setback in Vietnam. Commonweal 77:593-5 Mr 1 '63
FAIRBANKS, Rollin J.
On clinical pastoral training. Christian Cent 80:556-9 Ap 24 '63
FAIRBANKS Whitney corporation
Unmusical chairs. Time 81:86+ F 15 '63
Why the hell? resignation of David Karr. Newsweek 61:70+ F 18 '63
FAIRBROTHER, Nan
Secret gardens. Vogue 144:256-7+ D '64
FAIRCHILD, Edmund Wade
Miracle on Twelfth street. W. Sullivan. il Sat R 47:48-9+ F 8 '64
FAIRCHILD, John Burr
Pace-setters; interview. por Mlle 59:280-1 Ag '64
about
All the fit that's news to print. G. Greene. il pors Sat Eve Post 237:77-81 Ap 11 '64
FAIRCHILD, Louis Edgar
Miracle on Twelfth street. W. Sullivan. il Sat R 47:48-9+ F 8 '64
FAIRCHILD camera and instrument corporation
Do-it-yourself reruns. il Bsns W p 186+ Ap 18 '64
FAIRCHILD recording equipment corporation
Sound ideas. L. Zide. Am Rec G 30:150-1 O '63
FAIRCHILD stratos corporation
Fairchild reveals Republic stock buy. Miss & Roc 14:17 Je 29 '64
When Americans make machines for reds; excerpts from testimony. J. P. Drago. U S News 54:8 Ap 1 '63
FAIRCHILD tropical garden, Coconut Grove, Fla.
Fairchild tropical garden. J. Popenoe. il Horticulture 42:32-3+ D '64
FAIRFAX family
Fairfax coat-of-arms. H. K. Eilers. il Hobbies 68:120-1+ F '64
FAIRFAX COUNTY, Va.
See also
Reston, Va.
Education
New revolution on the Potomac; impact of the paperback revolution. R. J. Hurley. Sr Schol 82:13T Mr 13 '63
FAIRFAX COUNTY, Va, public library
Fairfax County library storm shifts from film to book protests. Library J 88:2462 Je 15 '63
National library week brings film furor to Fairfax County. Library J 88:2216-17 Je 1 '63
FAIRFIELD, Roy P.
Peace corps training at Ohio university. Sch & Soc 92:339-41 N 14 '64
FAIRLEIGH Dickinson university, Rutherford, N.J.
Reading lab: Rx for better reading. J. Sullivan. il Sr Schol 83:20T-21T O 4 '63
FAIRLY, Kenneth. See Martin, H. jt. auth.
FAIRLY, Ron
Player of the week; Dodgers first baseman. por Sports Illus 21:66 Jl 27 '64
FAIRMOUNT park, Philadelphia. See Philadelphia—Parks and playgrounds
FAIRS
Alpine view of U.S.A; American fair at Jelmoli department store. il Bsns W p30-1 Mr 7 '64
Dancing at every wedding; Hanover fair, West Germany. il Time 81:112+ My 17 '63
Fine day at Glenties. B. Friel. Holiday 33: 22+ Ap '63
SR/1965 world travel calendar. R. E. Meyer, jr. il Sat R 48:47-8+ Ja 2 '65
See also
Audio fairs
Book fairs
Exhibitions
Science fairs
FAIRVIEW PARKS, Ohio
Four-way program of sewer rehabilitation. E. J. Baugh. il Am City 79:117 Mr '64
FAIRY plays
Single works
Jack and the magic beanstalk; dramatization of story. A. Thane. Plays 24:55-64 Ja '65
Little Snow White. W. King. Plays 23:79-82 Ja '64
Magic telephone. H. L. Miller. Plays 23:65-9 F '64
Magic well. E. Leuser. Plays 22:91-5 My '63
Thankful elf. G. Chaloner. Plays 23:73-7 N '63
Toinette and the elves; dramatization of story by S. Coolidge. A. Thane. Plays 23:59-68 D '63
Twelve dancing princesses; dramatization of Grimms' fairy tale. A. Thane. Plays 24: 37-46, 54 N '64
FAIRY rings
Novel method for fairy ring control. R. M. Carleton. il Flower Grower 51:54 Ap '64
FAIRY tales
Acid test. M. Garthwaite. Horn Bk 39:408-11 Ag '63
Enchanted centenary of the brothers Grimm. E. Bowen. il N Y Times Mag p28-9+ S 8 '63
On fairy-stories. J. R. R. Tolkien. Horn Bk 39:457 O '63
On three ways of writing for children; reprint. C. S. Lewis. Horn Bk 39:459-69 O '63
FAIRY tales of New York; drama. See Donleavy, J. P.
FAISAL, king of Saudi Arabia. See Feisal
FAITH, Sister Mary. See Mary Faith, Sister
FAITH
Cross and the switchblade; ed. by J. Sherrill and E. Sherrill. D. Wilkerson. il Good H 157:49-53+ Jl '63
Dilemma for Americans; address, August 22, 1964. H. C. Case. Vital Speeches 30:715-17 S 15 '64
From whence cometh our light. J. Moorhead. PTA Mag 59:2-3 D '64
Letter on the parish ministry; reply to an earnest inquirer. P. L. Berger. Christian Cent 81:547-50 Ap 29 '64; Discussion. 81:936 Jl 22 '64
Man the believer. S. H. Miller. Christian Cent 81:1167-8 S 23 '64
My search for faith; ed. by J. Poppy. B. Sternberg. il Look 28:78-82+ Mr 10 '64
Naturalist's path to faith. D. C. Peattie. Read Digest 83:61-5 O '63
Outside the camp; excerpt from Passion. K. A. Olsson. Christian Cent 80:264-7 F 27 '63
Paul Tillich's concept of faith; condensation of Faith without belief. R. Smith. Cath World 200:162-3+ D '64
Reason in religion, by N. F. S. Ferré. Review. Christian Cent 81:115-16 Ja 22 '64. W. Gray
Theology is not American. N. F. S. Ferré; discussion. Christian Cent 80:244 F 20 '63
What Luther meant by faith alone. M. W. Hess. Cath World 199:96-101 My '64
Why I believe there is a God; symposium (cont) Ebony 18:86 F '63
Word (cont) V. P. McCorry. America 108:596; 109:220-1 Ap 20, Ag 31 '63
FAITH and order, World conference on. See World conference on faith and order
FAITH and order conference. See Religious conferences
FAITH and order movement. See World council of churches
FAITH cure
Catholic and reformed; study on confession and spiritual healing. America 111:471 O 24 '64
How religion helps to heal; what doctors & clergy report. A. J. Snider. il Sci Digest 56:6-13 Jl '64
FAITH trees
Faith tree. M. S. Lewis. Horticulture 41:107 F '63
FAKE; story. See Gary, R.
FALCO, Louis
Brief biography. S. Goodman. pors Dance Mag 37:54-5 Jl '63
FALCONBRIDGE nickel mines, limited
Mining new markets for nickel. il Bsns W p62-4+ S 5 '64

FALCONER, Vera
Films and filmstrips. Sr Schol 85:30T S 23; 6T O 21; 8T-9T O 28; 14T N 18 '64; 19T Ja 21 '65
FALCONRY
Falconry sport allowed. B. Tufty. Sci N L 86:95 Ag 8 '64
He hunts with the wild falcon. R. B. Berry. il Sat Eve Post 237:62-5 Je 20 '64
Makers of the sports page. P. Knauth. il Sports Illus 19:36+ S 16 '63
Paean to a winged hunter. B. Gilbert. il Sports Illus 18:50-5 F 4 '63
FALCONS
About: falcons. B. Gilbert. il N Y Times Mag p38+ D 8 '63
He hunts with the wild falcon. R. B. Berry. il Sat Eve Post 237:62-5 Je 20 '64
FALES, Daniel C.
Look out for harbor pirates! Yachting 116: 52-3+ Jl '64
1,600 miles on a windjammer. por Pop Sci 185:74-7+ Ag '64
—and Fales, E. D. jr
Don't let faulty flashing flood your home. Pop Sci 185:152-6 O '64
Get off the ground on scaffolding. Pop Sci 185: 130-4 S '64
FALES, Dean A. Jr
Hosmer family furniture. Antiques 83:548-9 My '63
Two Essex County clocks. Antiques 84:80-1 Jl '63
FALES, Edward D. Jr
Are they listening in on you? Pop Sci 186: 96-9+ Ja '65
Crash! are small cars death traps? Pop Sci 185:50-3+ Ag '64
Danger on the runway: how birds cause crashes. Pop Sci 183:90-3+ N '63
Dry run on wells. Am Home 66:42+ S '63
How safe are our dams? Pop Sci 185:33-7+ Jl '64
How to get a good body-repair job. Pop Sci 183:45-9+ S '63
How to get towed without getting took. Pop Sci 183:33-7+ Ag '63
I rode the jet freight to Shannon. por Pop Sci 185:52-5+ Jl '64
I rode with the avalanche patrol. Pop Sci 182:112-14+ F '63
New facts about skidding. Pop Sci 184: 58-61+ Mr '64
No property is safe from condemnation. Am Home 66:16+ Mr '63
Ol' Man River meets his match. Pop Sci 183:48-53+ Jl '63
1,000 days in frozen space. Pop Sci 182:42-4 Je '63
Ordeal of Snowcloud one. por Pop Sci 185: 56-61+ D '64
Seven deadly skids. Pop Sci 185:59-61+ N '64
Should you use chemicals? where? how? Pop Sci 184:120-1+ F '64
Snow convoy! Pop Sci 184:69-74+ F '64
Strange highway forces that louse up your driving. Pop Sci 184:94-7+ My '64
Time bombs in the Mississippi. Pop Sci 182: 124-30+ Ap '63
Try a teamwork association. Am Home 66: 22+ Ap '63
Weather by the minute. Yachting 114:40-2+ Jl '63
What do they think of pay TV? Pop Sci 183:75-8+ Jl '63
Why can't I get help? Am Home 66:25 N '63
—See Fales, D. C. jt. auth.
FALICK, James
Electronics: new force in hospital design. Arch Forum 120:90-1 Ap '64
FALK, Charles W.
Our polluted water sports; poem. Am For 70:70 O '64
FALK, Elizabeth
I believe; ed. by A. Armstrong. por Seventeen 22:38 Jl '63
FALK, Ray
Babes and arms. Sat R 46:91 Mr 16 '63
FALK, Richard A.
Cuba: our cold-shoulder policy. Nation 199: 113-17 S 14 '64
Nonrecognition; the diplomatic trap. Nation 198:457-60 My 4 '64
FALK, Sam
Here come the couples. il N Y Times Mag p40+ N 24 '63
One photographer's New York. il N Y Times Mag p36-7 Mr 1 '64
FALKLAND ISLANDS
Kelpers of the Falklands. il Newsweek 64:65 S 21 '64
FALL, Bernard B.
Dienbienphu: battle to remember. N Y Times Mag p21+ My 3 '64
Grain of rice is worth a drop of blood. N Y Times Mag p 10-12+ Jl 12 '64
How much time do we have in Vietnam? New Repub 150:10-11 F 22 '64
New faces, more chaos. Nation 197:380-2 D 7 '63
Our friend Diem. New Repub 149:24+ O 19 '63
Our options in Vietnam. Reporter 30:17-22 Mr 12 '64
Peking strikes South. bibliog f Cur Hist 45: 151-7 S '63
Talk with Ho Chi Minh. New Repub 149:19-22 O 12 '63
Teacher and world affairs. NEA J 53:38 My '64
Truth about the war U.S. is losing; interview. por U S News 57:58-62 S 28 '64
Vietnam hawks and doves. New Repub 152: 7-8 Ja 16 '65
What de Gaulle actually said about Vietnam. Reporter 29:39-41 O 24; 6+ D 19 '63
Who's who in Vietnam? New Repub 151:10-12 O 17 '64
Why the French mistrust us. N Y Times Mag p6+ S 6 '64
FALL. See Autumn
FALL daffodils. See Sternbergia
FALL of Rome. See Rome—History
FALL planting. See Gardening
FALLA, Manuel de
Argentine Atlantis. G. Knepler. Opera N 28: 27 S 28 '63
FALLACI, Oriana
Oriana's world. por Newsweek 64:56-7 Ag 17 '64
FALLACIES, Food. See Errors, Popular
FALLAW, Wesner
Religious education bookshelf. Christian Cent 80:1170-1 S 25 '63
Why not three-year colleges? Christian Cent 81:601-2 My 6 '64
FALLEDER, Arnold
New musicals. Sat R 48:61-2 Ja 30 '65
FALLING objects
Spiraling spheres. Sci Am 210:71 F '64
FALLING star; story. See Moyes, P.
FALLON, E. H.
Should farmers own food chains? Farm J 88:54-5 D '64
FALLOUT, Radioactive. See Radioactive fallout
FALLOUT shelters. See Atomic bomb shelters
FALLS (accidents) See Accidents
FALNES, Oscar J.
(comp) Articles and other books received; Northern Europe. See issues of American historical review
FALSE imprisonment
Innocent's grim ordeal; murder of wife of airman Alec Johnson, Mountain Home air force base, Idaho. J. R. Phelan. il Sat Eve Post 236:62-7 F 2 '63
Wrong man behind the bars. J. Howard. il Life 56:57-8+ My 15 '64
FALSE lashes. See Eyelashes, Artificial
FALSE summer; story See Heiremans, L. A.
FALSTAFF; opera. See Verdi, G.
FALTER, Mary Elizabeth
How to live with the four seasons. House & Gard 126:28+ S '64
Notes of a happy housekeeper. See issues of House & garden
FALTERMAYER, Edmund K.
Future of American express. Fortune 69:158-9+ Ap '64
Is labor's wage push more bark than bite? Fortune 69:100-3+ Je '64
It's a spryer Singer. Fortune 68:144-8+ D '63
National: a pacesetter in steel. Fortune 69: 96-103+ F '64
Next turn in taxes. Fortune 70:104-7+ D '64
Paper world of Karl Landegger. Fortune 70:168-71+ N '64
Squeeze in American motors' road. Fortune 70:154-7+ S '64
Who are the American poor? Fortune 69: 118-19+ Mr '64
FAME
Fame is a funny thing. G. Moore. il Look 28: 77+ S 22 '64
FAMILY
Don't fence him in. Newsweek 63:85 F 10 '64
Love, O love, O careful love. J. H. Adams. il America 109:481-4 O 26 '63; Discussion. 109: 658-9; 110:1, 149 N 23 '63, Ja 4, F 1 '64
New type of family needed today. Sci N L 83:168 Mr 16 '63
What the family isn't teaching. H. Taylor. Sat R 46:17-19 My 18 '63
What's happening to the American family; interview. M. Mead. il U S News 54:48-50 My 20 '63

FAMILY—*Continued*
Word (cont) V. P. McCorry. America 112:63-4 Ja 9 '65
See also
Birth control
Divorce
Family life
Kinship
Matriarchy

FAMILY, Size of
Are smaller families coming back in style? W. Best. il Parents Mag 39:64-5+ N '64
Baby puts a strain on marriage. C. Chilman. il Parents Mag 38:48-9+ Je '63
Busiest mothers in the world; parents of large families. N. M. Lobsenz. il Redbook 122:64-5+ Ap '64
Cult of fertility? Catholic preference for larger families. Newsweek 64:50 Ag 17 '64
Doing the fair with fourteen kids; the Rocks and their family. il Life 57:81-3 Jl 24 '64
Happy miracle in Lima, Ohio; Axe family. A. E. Farrell. il Good H 157:86-7+ S '63
Human future. F. Osborn. Sci N L 86:54-5+ Jl 25 '64
My life, my children; ed. by D. C. Disney. M. A. Fischer. il Ladies Home J 80:56-8+ D '63
Please stop telling me that I have to have a baby. J. Seabaugh. Redbook 121:6+ My '63
Three sets of twins in three years. S. James and R. W. Goldfarb. il Redbook 121:58-9+ My '63

FAMILY allowances

United States

Guaranteed income; concerning report of the Ad hoc committee on the triple revolution. New Repub 150:4-5 Ap 4 '64

FAMILY budget. See Budget, Household

FAMILY business. See Family corporations

FAMILY camping. See Camping

FAMILY camps. See Camps

FAMILY conversation. See Conversation

FAMILY corporations
All in the family. il Time 84:112+ N 13 '64
Family business. R. G. Donnelley. bibliog f il Harvard Bsns R 42:93-105 Jl '64
Pot of gold, Quebec family style; Beauchemin family's complex of companies. il Bsns W p 146+ N 28 '64

FAMILY counseling. See Counseling

FAMILY doctors. See Physicians

FAMILY enterprises. See Family corporations

FAMILY excursions. See Excursions

FAMILY farm operating agreements. See Father-son farm operating agreements

FAMILY finance. See Domestic finance

FAMILY history. See Genealogy

FAMILY income. See Income

FAMILY life
Anti-bias coffee klatsch; interracial home visit day. il Ebony 18:67-8+ Ap '63
Can three generations live together? B. M. Silverman. Parents Mag 38:43+ Ap '63
Cancer taught me to be brave. il Good H 158:12+ Mr '64
Child care created by mother. A. Eisenberg and H. Eisenberg. il Ladies Home J 81:56-7+ Je '64
Disturbed family test. Sci N L 83:179 Mr 23 '63
Family in health and illness; some neglected areas. C. E. Vincent. bibliog f Ann Am Acad 346:109-16 Mr '63
Family life weakens; statistics. Christian Cent 80:821 Je 26 '63
Grace at table. J. Richards. Read Digest 83: 114-16 Ag '63
How America lives. B. H. Hoffman. il Ladies Home J 80:24+ Ap '63
How to live with a swing-shift husband. R. Worthington. il Parents Mag 39:50-1+ O '64
More children, the more love. B. K. Tucker. Bet Hom & Gard 41:105 Mr '63
Nice to be with: in your home; excerpt from Seventeen book of etiquette and entertaining. E. A. Haupt. Seventeen 22:118 D '63
Our Johnny-come-lately baby. P. Buck. il Parents Mag 38:52-3+ D '63
Party for all ages. M. Shearer. il House B 105:160-3 D '63
Recreation and family needs; excerpts from Helping the family in urban society. R. S. Tefferteller. Recreation 56:423-4 N '63
Sentimental trap; excerpts from Profession: housewife. P. McGinley. Ladies Home J 80: 20+ N '63
Taming the neighborhood bully; with program for discussion group, by M. Smart. S. H. Strait. il Parents Mag 38:44-5+, 140 Ap '63
We found more time for each other. B. B. Lawler. Redbook 121:6+ Je '63
What makes a good father. S. Blum. il Redbook 122:38-9+ Ja '64
What's happening to the American family; interview. M. Mead. il U S News 54:48-50 My 20 '63
When my husband lost his job; interview, ed. by H. Lees. K. Lober. il McCalls 90:68+ My '63
Where did you go? home; what did you do? nothing. S. S. Fader. House B 106:42+ Mr '64
Word. V. P. McCorry. America 110:56 Ja 11 '64
See also
Children
Love
Parent-child relationship

Anecdotes, facetiae, satire, etc.

How to lose a good night's sleep. S. Rothman. Read Digest 83:25-6 Ag '63
Man next door. B. Hillis. See issues of Better homes and gardens
There's a man in the house. H. Miller. See issues of Ladies' home journal to June 1963

Caricatures and cartoons

It's all in the family. S. Berenstain and J. Berenstain. See issues of McCall's

FAMILY life, Education for
Apprenticeship for marriage; a startling proposal. M. Mead. Redbook 121:14+ O '63
Critical look at family life courses; with study-discussion program, by E. M. Duvall. E. S. Force. bibliog il PTA Mag 58:18-20. 36 Ap '64
Family living, can it be taught? L. Strong. il N Y Times Mag p89-90 O 20 '63
Grooming a future bride. J. R. Komaiko. il Parents Mag 39:42-3+ Ja '64

FAMILY limitation. See Birth control

FAMILY man; story. See Hutter, D.

FAMILY movement, Christian. See Christian family movement (organization)

FAMILY names. See Names, Personal

FAMILY planning. See Birth control

FAMILY portraits. See Portraits

FAMILY quarrels. See Quarrels

FAMILY records
Family facts on file. K. Kuperstock. Parents Mag 38:54+ Jl '63
How to use your family check list. R. A. Golden. Suc Farm 61:109-10 Ap '63
Those important papers: what to keep and where. il Changing T 17:15-16 Ag '63

FAMILY recreation. See Recreation

FAMILY reunions
Christmas in July. il Ebony 19:94-6+ S '64

FAMILY rooms. See Living rooms

FAMILY talk. See Conversation

FAMILY therapy. See Mental illness—Therapy

FAMILY vacations. See Vacations

FAMINES
Will world famine hit during the '70s? U S News 57:14 S 14 '64

Ireland

Great hunger, by C. Woodham-Smith. Review
Am Heritage 14:104-6 F '63. B. Catton
Commentary 36:389-93 N '63. S. Marcus
Commonweal 78:51-2 Ap 5 '63. L. T. King
Nat R 14:499 Je 18 '63. F. D. Cohalan
Nation 196:269-71 Mr 30 '63. S. O'Faolain
Reporter il 28:50-2 Ap 25 '63. D. J. Moynihan
Sat R il 46:34-5 Mr 23 '63. C. FitzGibbon
Time 81:104+ Ap 12 '63

Japan

On the frontier; island of Hokkaido. Newsweek 64:46 D 7 '64

FAMOUS artists schools, incorporated
Famous money-makers hit gold at Westport. il Bsns W p38-40 D 28 '63

FAMOUS men. See Great men

FAMOUS photographers school
Famous photographers school shows how. il U S Camera 27:46-7 F '64
U.S. mail: campus for cameras. M. R. Weiss. il Sat R 47:58-9 Je 13 '64

FAMOUS women. See Women, Famous

FANATICISM
Hoover's warning: be alert to fanatics; excerpts from address, December 4, 1963. J. E. Hoover. U S News 55:14 D 16 '63

FANCHER, Betsy
Den mother to the clubwomen. Sat Eve Post 236:60-1 Mr 9 '63

FANCHER, H. Brainard
Space; its relationship to economic growth; address, May 14, 1964. Vital Speeches 30:542-4 Je 15 '64

FANCY dress. See Costume

FANDEL, John
Poets and mystics. Commonweal 79:309-10 D 6 '63
Triptych: the transmogrified; poem. Commonweal 79:407 D 27 '63

FANELLI, John
Europe's winter wonders. Travel 122:32-8 N '64

FANFANI, Amintore
—See Kennedy, J. F. jt. auth.

about

Il motorino. il por Newsweek 61:43+ Ap 22 '63
Off & running. il por Time 81:30 F 22 '63
Signor Fanfani's self-made bed. A Leone-Moats. il por Nat R 14:404-5 My 21 '63

FANGMAN, John. See Whalen, W. J. jt. auth.

FANNING, James
Plant palette for winter windows. House & Gard 124:192-3+ D '63
Servicing the year-round window. House & Gard 126:194-5+ D '64
What wonders science and devotion have worked with lilies. House & Gard 126:252-5+ O '64

FANS
Fans of sorrow. E. Oldham. il Hobbies 68:28-9 Je; 26-8 Jl '63

FANS, Baseball. See Baseball fans

FANS, Electric. See Electric fans

FANS, Ventilating. See Ventilators

FANTASTICKS; musical comedy. See Musical comedies, revues, etc.—Criticisms, plots, etc.

FANTASY
See also
Fairy tales

FANTASY finishes. See Decoration and ornament. Architectural

FANTEL, Hans H.
A's to your Q's about stereo. Pop Sci 186:102-5 Ja '65
Audio (cont of) High fidelity. Opera N 29:35 Ja 23 '65
Audio: low-cost stereo. Opera N 29:33 N 14 '64
Audio: medium-priced stereo. Opera N 29:33 D 12 '64
Audio: the all-out system. Opera N 29:34 D 26 '64
High fidelity. Opera N 28:32 S 28; 38 N 16; 35 D 14; 34 D 28 '63; 35 Ja 11; 34 Ja 25; 35 F 8; 35 F 22; 36 Mr 7; 33 Mr 28; 34 Ap 4; 35 Ap 18; 29:29 S 26 '64
Slim silhouette speaker systems. Pop Electr 19:41-6 Jl '63

FANTINI, Mario, and Weinstein, Gerald
Stars, smiles, and the hidden curriculum. Sr Schol 85:14T S 30 '64

FANTZ, Robert L.
Pattern vision in newborn infants. bibliog Science 140:296-7 Ap 19 '63
Visual experience in infants: decreased attention to familiar patterns relative to novel ones. bibliog Science 146:668-70 O 30 '64

FAR EAST
See also
Americans in the Far East
Asia, Southeastern
Foreign visitors in the Far East
Libraries—Far East
Moving pictures—Far East
Sports—Far East
United Nations—Economic commission for Asia and the Far East

Description and travel

Going places, finding things in the Far East: Japan, Hong Kong, Bangkok. D. Walker. il House & Gard 124:26+ Ag '63
Half a world half a day away. F. R. Smith. il Sports Illus 19:86-93 D 23 '63
Pacific/Orient '63; scrutiny of the bounty. R. Joseph. il Esquire 60:42-53 Ag '63
Travel notes. R. Joseph. Esquire 60:25-9 Ag '63
Well traveled camera. H. Keppler. il Mod Phot 28:22+ D '64

History

Portuguese Sancho Panza in the Far East. A. J. Saraiva. il UNESCO Courier 16:14-19 Ap '63

Social life and customs

Mysterious East: advice to businessmen. il Time 82:73 Ag 16 '63

FAR EASTERN studies. See Area studies

FAR WEST. See West

FARADAY effect
Faraday rotation on decametric radio emissions from Jupiter. J. W. Warwick and G. A. Dulk. bibliog il Science 145:380-3 Jl 24 '64

FARAGO, Ladislas
Patton family sues to stop Farago biography. Pub W 185:58-9 Je 15 '64
Patton heirs withdraw objection to Farago book. Pub W 186:51 Jl 6 '64

FARAN, James J. jr
How to buy a tuba. Horizon 5:97-9 N '63

FARAWAY places; story. See Jordan, E. H.

FARB, Peter
Monarch: jeweled traveler of the skies. Read Digest 83:70-4 S '63

FARBENINDUSTRIE, I.G. See Interessengemeinschaft farbenindustrie aktiengesellschaft

FARBER, Charles
Prosthesia; poem. Nation 196:336 Ap 20 '63

FARBER, Evan Ira
Earlham's considerate library. Library J 88:4561-4 D 1 '63

FARBER, Leslie H.
I'm sorry, dear; excerpt from Ways of the will. Commentary 38:47-54 N '64

FARBER, Manny
Fading movie star. Commentary 36:55-60 Jl '63

FARBER, Norma
Another part of the island; poem. Sat R 47:35 S 26 '64
Same glad tidings; poem. Horn Bk 40:636-9 D '64

FARBER, Paul R.
Ad libs. See issues of U.S. camera & travel to December 1963
Automated photographer. U S Camera 27:48-9+ S '64
Black light for brilliant color. U S Camera 27:38-9+ Ag '64
Color vision: an experiment. U S Camera 27:50-1+ Ja '64
Cross-polarized color. U S Camera 27:38-9+ Jl '64
Darkroom delirium. il U S Camera 27:72-5 N '64
Exposure methods & meters. il U S Camera 27:50-3+ Je '64
Foto facts. See issues of U.S. camera & travel
Hypo-sniffer-outer. U S Camera 27:54-5+ D '64
Light sieves of photography. U S Camera 28:44-5+ Ja '65
Methods & materials. por U S Camera 27:16+ Ja '64
New FR paper makes color prints in seventeen minutes. U S Camera 27:38-9+ Mr '64
New product report; Fotoval. U S Camera 27:60+ Mr '64
Paper negative. U S Camera 27:60-1+ O '64
Pinhole camera. U S Camera 26:58-9+ Ap '63
Primer for old hands. U S Camera 26:59-61+ My '63
Rapid vs Instamatic loading. U S Camera 27:18+ N '64
Sedentary safari in 3-D. U S Camera 26:62-3+ Mr '63
Spill pix. U S Camera 27:60-1+ Ap '64
Split development. U S Camera 26:72-3+ Je '63
Strictly for strobe-o-philes. U S Camera 26:48-51 F '63
Tic, tac, toe of composition. U S Camera 27:54-5+ F '64
Unsharp positive. il U S Camera 26:56-7+ D '63

FARBEROW, Norman L. and Shneidman, E. S.
Can we stop suicides? Todays Health 41:59+ D '63

FARBSTEIN, Leonard
Tempest in a glass tea. il por Newsweek 63:31 My 25 '64

FARE tokens. See Tokens

FARELL, Mary Jane
Other side of point count. C. Goren. il Sports Illus 21:56-7 Jl 27 '64

FARES, Airline. See Airlines—Fares

FARES, Taxicab. See Taxicabs—Fares

FAREWELL, Neal C.
Repairman bites back. Atlan 213:127 Je '64

FAREWELL! farewell! farewell! story. See Donohue, H. E. F.
FAREWELL to April; story. See Chapin, V.
FARGANIS, James. See Rousseas, S. jt. auth.
FARIBAULT, Marcel
Can French Canada stand alone? Atlan 214:135-9 N '64
FARIÑA, Richard
Baez & Dylan; a generation singing out. Mlle 59:242+ Ag '64
Field near the cathedral at Chartres; poem. Mlle 57:78 My '63
Monterey fair. Mlle 58:188+ Mr '64
FARKAS, Harold M.
Bumper crop from little trees. Pop Gard 15:26-7 Ap '64
FARLAND, Joseph Simpson
Making friends. America 109:182 Ag 24 '63
about
Ambassador in motion. il por Time 82:31 S 6 '63
Orange is squeezed; a report on one failure in Panama. M. Kempton. New Repub 150:15-18 Ja 25 '64
Panama: the crisis we could have avoided. C. W. Hall. il Read Digest 84:84-9 Ap '64
FARLEY, Catherine
My son Nobody. Redbook 121:38 My '63
FARLEY, Edward
Cutting the tie. Christian Cent 81:767 Je 10 '64
FARLEY, James A.
Creed for a time of danger; excerpts from address. Read Digest 83:49-52 Jl '63
Expanding pattern of American law; address, May 2, 1964. Vital Speeches 30:497-9 Je 1 '64
Troubled international waters; address, March 15, 1963. Vital Speeches 29:389-91 Ap 15 '63
Two magic words. Read Digest 84:167-8 Ap '64
FARLEY, Robert J.
Dean departs from Ole Miss. R. Cleghorn. Reporter 29:42 O 24 '63
FARM boys
Day our boy quit school, and how we got him back in! il Farm J 88:33+ My '64
What I think about while plowing. R. D. Haney. il Farm J 87:58Z Ap '63
FARM building finance. See Farm finance
FARM buildings
Get the most from building dollars. W. J. Fletcher. il Suc Farm 61:48-9 Ap '63
Make buildings pay their way. W. J. Fletcher. il Suc Farm 61:64-5 Mr '63
Planning for the future. W. J. Fletcher. il Suc Farm 61:70-1+ F '63
Revolution in farm buildings. il Suc Farm 62:53+ Ag '64
Roofing and sliding. W. J. Fletcher. il Suc Farm 61:34-5 Jl '63
What you should know about framing and pole-type construction. W. J. Fletcher. il Suc Farm 61:40-1 Je '63
See also
Barns and stables
Calf pens
Foundations
Swine farrowing crates and pens
Swine houses

Depreciation

See Depreciation

Heating and ventilation

Controlled environment, what it is and what it does for hogs, poultry, dairy and beef. il Farm J 87:40-2 My '63
Labor-free lambing; environmental control. D. Hagen. Farm J 87:52L My '63

Renting

How to finance farm buildings. B. Brantley. il Suc Farm 62:55+ Ag '64
FARM buildings, Prefabricated. See Buildings, Prefabricated
FARM bureau federation. See American farm bureau federation
FARM bureaus. See American farm bureau federation
FARM chores
Now, get ready for cold weather. J. W. Bailey. Suc Farm 61:85 Ag '63
FARM corporations. See Farms, Incorporated
FARM electrification. See Electricity on the farm
FARM equipment
Home-made and handy; photographs. See issues of Farm journal
Tips for selecting cattle handling equipment. B. W. Robinson. il Suc Farm 62:71 Mr '64
See also
Agricultural machinery
Farm tools
Swine farms—Equipment
FARM equipment dealers
You and your dealer. D. L. Schwitters. Suc Farm 63:68 Ja '65
FARM finance
Changing credit needs. D. Hanson. Suc Farm 61:8 O '63
How to finance farm buildings. B. Brantley. il Suc Farm 62:55+ Ag '64
How to use life insurance in your farm business. C. W. Gifford. il Farm J 88:42B+ Ap '64
How you can have more peace of mind when it's time to borrow money. L. Lane. Farm J 88:86+ Mr '64
Seven things your banker looks for. O. Bay. Farm J 87:36L Ag '63
Six danger signals for your farm loan. Farm J 88:44H D '64
Watch those unpaid bills! il Suc Farm 62:94 N '64
What's this: loans you never pay off? R. E. Geyer. Suc Farm 62:43+ N '64
When and where to invest off the farm. B. Brantley and others. il Suc Farm 62:52+ N '64
Where should you spend money on your farm? J. E. Kadlec and J. H. Atkinson. il Suc Farm 62:52+ O '64
Your banker's sizing you up. L. Lane. Farm J 88:72 Ap '64
Your nonfarm assets; what are they worth? il Suc Farm 61:35 O '63
FARM forestry. See Forest management; Woodlots
FARM houses. See Farmhouses
FARM income. See Agriculture—Economic aspects
FARM insurance. See Insurance, Agricultural
FARM journal
First eighty-five years. C. P. Streeter. il Farm J 87:4 Mr '63
First what's new, then how to do. C. P. Streeter. Farm J 87:4 S '63
Friends. C. P. Streeter. Farm J 88:4 Ap '64
Now: power farming news. C. P. Streeter. Farm J 87:4 O '63
We make some changes. C. P. Streeter. Farm J 87:4 Ag '63
Why it's your magazine. C. P. Streeter. Farm J 87:4 Ap '63
FARM kitchens. See Kitchens
FARM labor
California farm labor. A. Ogle. America 111:799+ D 19 '64
Congress extends braceros program. Christian Cent 81:5 Ja 1 '64
Fate of P.L. 78. Commonweal 78:316 Je 14 '63
Hired men who take an interest. Farm J 88:44D Je '64
How to get and keep hired help. R. E. Geyer. Suc Farm 62:35 Mr '64
How to keep good hired help. J. Bickers. il Farm J 87:34-5+ D '63
Man with a hoe, 1964; excerpts. P. Jacobs. Commentary 38:26-9 Jl '64
See also
Migrant labor
FARM land. See Land
FARM leases. See Leases
FARM legislation. See Agricultural laws and legislation
FARM life
Family farm has a future if. . . B. Everett. il Farm J 87:80+ Ap '63
Good-by, little boy! H. G. Green. il Read Digest 83:79-82 S '63
How to cope with company. E. Pearson. il Farm J 87:29+ Jl '63
How we get dad in on the fun. M. Felkner. Farm J 87:77+ Ap '63
Let a little nonsense in! symposium. Farm J 88:61+ Ja '64
Letters from farm women. See issues of Farm journal
Not a care in the world? L. Erickson. il Farm J 87:52-3+ Jl '63
Surprise! D. E. Pogue. Farm J 88:43 Ag '64
Things do happen to you! M. Longwell. il Farm J 87:59-60 Je '63
This life is to share. M. Longwell. il Farm J 88:71+ Ap '64
See also
City and country
Country life
Farm women
Ranch life
FARM machinery. See Agricultural machinery

FARM management
Do you plan your farm changes backward? C. E. French and R. B. Wilson. il Suc Farm 61:70D S '63
Double-duty hog lagoon. C. F. Marley. il Suc Farm 61:104 Ap '63
Expanding your dairy herd? L. H. Brown. il Suc Farm 61:38 My '63
Farm as well as you know how. D. Hanson. Suc Farm 61:6 N '63
For the feeding season: fourteen ways to boost your profit. C. Peterson, jr. and B. Suter. il Suc Farm 61:48-9+ N '63
Forty-one top cows as good as eighty-seven average ones. J. R. Borcherding. il Suc Farm 61:42-3 S '63
How many crops can you afford? R. D. Wennblom. il Farm J 88:34-5+ O '64
How 120 dairymen cut costs. il Farm J 87:38-9+ Ap '63
How to rent a better farm. H. Pike. il Suc Farm 61:36+ O '63
How you can make more profit this year. Suc Farm 62:39+ F '64
I got too big. C. E. Ball. il Farm J 87:33+ S '63
Ideas from a small western feeder. G. Bevard. il Suc Farm 61:54 O '63
Let's have two-man family farms. H. Pike. Farm J 87:44A S '63
Look what top management can do for rough land. R. J. Reiman and L. E. Zeman. il Suc Farm 62:44-5+ N '64
More cows, less work. J. R. Borcherding. il Suc Farm 62:40-1+ Je '64
Useful winter ideas. B. Brantley. il Suc Farm 61:36 F '63
You can learn from their mistakes. H. Guither. Suc Farm 61:32+ F '63
See also
Dairy farm management
Farm records
Farms, Small
Poultry farm management
FARM materials handling. See Materials handling
FARM mechanization. See Agricultural machinery
FARM ownership
Down on the farm. I. Mothner. il Look 28:34-7 Ja 14 '64
What, me buy a farm? R. Starnes. Field & S 69:20+ Je '64
FARM policy. See Agricultural administration—United States
FARM ponds. See Ponds
FARM prices. See Farm produce—Prices
FARM produce
Wheat, and what else? U.S. crops to Russia. il Bsns W p34+ N 9 '63
See also
Crops
Surplus products, Agricultural
Marketing
Can farmers control food chains? Bsns W p25 D 19 '64
From farm to supermarket to you. I. Wolfert. il Read Digest 85:124-9 N '64
How to make a national market; address, October 1, 1963. W. W. Rostow. Dept State Bul 49:667-73 O 28 '63
Should farmers own food chains? with editorial comment. E. H. Fallon. Farm J 88:54-5, 94 D '64
Will we return to the free market? D. Paarlberg. Suc Farm 61:45 Je '63
See also
Vegetables—Prepackaging
Prices
Across the editor's desk. D. Hanson. Suc Farm 61:10 My '63
Europe's new farm problem. Bsns W p 116 Jl 20 '63
Hard sell at right price. D. Hanson. Suc Farm 62:8 Ja '64
You can get higher prices. C. W. Gifford. Farm J 89:23+ Ja '65
See also subhead Prices under names of farm produce, e.g. Wheat—Prices
FARM records
Making money? find out by mail. C. W. Gifford. il Farm J 87:22-3+ Ag '63
Where does all that money go? L. Lane. Farm J 88:67+ N '64
FARM resorts. See Farms
FARM subsidies. See Agricultural administration—United States
FARM tenancy
How to rent a better farm. H. Pike. il Suc Farm 61:36+ O '63
What's ahead in farm leases? F. J. Reiss. Suc Farm 61:24 N '63
Why tenants don't stay with farming. H. Guither. Suc Farm 61:22 Ap '63
FARM terracing. See Terraces (agriculture)
FARM tools
Plan your farm service center; with tool list. O. A. Kimmel. il Suc Farm 63:45+ Ja '65
FARM tours
Best dairy ideas from Europe; 10,000 miles and seven countries. il Farm J 87:36-7+ F '63
FARM tractors. See Tractors
FARM vacations. See Vacations
FARM waterways. See Channels
FARM women
Be yourself first; ed. by L. Lane. A. L. Rutledge. Farm J 87:73+ O '63
Changing role of today's farm wife. il Suc Farm 62:67+ F '64
How much do you know about your farm business? try this quiz. F. M. Sims. Farm J 87:104 F '63
How to be a better business partner. L. Lane. il Farm J 87:92-4+ Mr '63
I recommend rock-sitting. H. Virden. il Farm J 88:61 S '64
I should put my wife on the payroll. H. Pike. il Suc Farm 62:105+ Mr '64
I took a vacation at home. A. Z. Chapin. il Suc Farm 62:75+ My '64
I'm glad I married that gal. M. Parks. il Farm J 88:85+ F '64
It's good to finish something! ed. by M. Longwell. D. Warnick. il Farm J 87:47 Ag '63
I've learned to say no. J. Fithian. il Farm J 87:85 My '63
Letters from farm women. See issues of Farm journal
October week that was. il Farm J 88:77 O '64
Perils and rewards of a rancher's wife. P. Letellier. il Suc Farm 62:49+ Jl '64
Shepherd is a lady. il Ebony 19:68-70+ Jl '64
Should you marry a farmer? questions. il Farm J 87:55 Jl '63
Sometimes I lead a double life. B. Lehman. il Farm J 87:55+ S '63
Three jobs you need to tackle. G. Dieken. Farm J 87:67 N '63
Vice presidents in the apron. il(p 1) Farm J 89:102 Ja '65
When mom goes over the hill. M. Felkner. il Farm J 88:71+ My '64
Wives help with farm work. R. R. Gogerty. il Suc Farm 61:53 N '63
Your banker's sizing you up. L. Lane. Farm J 88:72 Ap '64
FARM woodlands. See Woodlots
FARM workshops. See Workshops
FARMED-out work. See Subcontracting
FARMER, Art
Jazz records. W. Balliett. New Yorker 40:194-7 Ap 25 '64
Man with a horn. por Newsweek 61:78 Mr 4 '63
FARMER, E. A.
Check water storage against peak loads. Am City 78:87-9 My '63
FARMER, Gene
Heroes, legends and myths. Life 56:87-8+ My 22 '64
Stalked and cussed at, de Gaulle has a case. Life 54:34 Mr 1 '63
FARMER, Guy
Labor experts urge new policies; interview. por Nations Bsns 51:66-8+ Ap '63
FARMER, James
Demonstrations will spread; interview. por U S News 56:67-9 F 24 '64
Pace-setters; interview. por Mlle 59:282 Ag '64
We cannot afford to fail. N Y Times Mag p27+ S 29 '63
about
Fair. New Yorker 40:39 My 2 '64
James Farmer of CORE. por Negro Hist Bul 27:160-1 Ap '64
FARMER, John J.
Rise and fall of Jersey City. Reporter 31:47-9 Ag 13 '64
FARMER, Victor C.
Infrared absorption of hydroxyl groups in kaolinite. bibliog Science 145:1189-90 S 11 '64
FARMER-hunter relations
Hunter and the landowner. A. Lincoln, jr. Am For 70:40 Ag '64
Hunters on your farm? know your legal rights. N. G. P. Krausz. Suc Farm 62:36 O '64

FARMER-hunter relations—*Continued*
No more free hunting? A. Grahame. il Outdoor Life 131:14-15+ F '63
Recreation, farming's giant new crop. R. C. Davids. il Farm J 87:40-1+ F '63
Red carpet for pheasant hunters. H. Titus. il Field & S 68:47-9+ S '63
Why I let them hunt on my place. R. Gogerty. il Farm J 88:42G N '64

FARMERS
Case of the disappearing farmer. il Sr Schol 83:16-18+ S 20 '63; Reply. H. Mitchell. 84:18 Ap 24 '64
Cash in on campsites. J. Bickers. il Farm J 88:28-9+ Je '64
Death in Bonduel: ethics of farmers' boycott of livestock sales. America 11:344 S 26 '64
Farewell to the small farm; excerpt from Farms and farming in an urban age. E. Higbee. il Read Digest 84:176-80 Mr '64
Farmers' plight deepens. Christian Cent 80:573-4 My 1 '63
Farmers vote for freedom; wheat referendum. J. Strohm. Read Digest 83:95-9 S '63
How to get your money's worth out of social security. G. B. Whitman and B. Brantley. il Suc Farm 61:45-56 F '63
Milking'n sugaring; good combination. W. H. Hardy. il Farm J 88:23 O '64
New federal program trains those leaving farms; Manpower development and training act. F. Bailey, jr. Suc Farm 61:92 F '63
School that just about guarantees a job. D. James. Farm J 87:44H S '63
Soybeans have been good to me. il Farm J 87:22 O '63
Where can we go? what can we do? B. Asbell. il Redbook 122:52-3+ Mr '64
Which one went to college? J. D. Boyd. il Farm J 88:39+ F '64
Why we take a dozen vacations a year. E. Pearson. Farm J 87:36B Ag '63
You can learn from their mistakes. H. Guither. Suc Farm 61:32+ F '63
See also
Negro farmers
Peasantry
Strikes—United States—Farmers

Political activities

Fewer farmers, but here's what the farm vote can do. il U S News 55:75-6 Jl 1 '63
How farmers will vote, and why. C. W. Gifford. il Farm J 88:29+ N '64
How will farmers vote? D. R. Murphy. New Repub 150:6 My 2 '64
Social services for farmers. D. Hanson. Suc Farm 62:10 Ap '64
What farmers think of their future; present farm program; address, June 11, 1963. C. P. Streeter. Vital Speeches 29:600-2 Jl 15 '63

Public relations

See Agriculture—Public relations

FARMERS clubs. See Clubs

FARMERS cooperative associations. See Cooperative associations—United States

FARMERS' educational and co-operative union of America
Pat on the back; meeting at Carnegie Hall. il Time 81:18 Mr 29 '63

FARMERS home administration. See United States—Farmers home administration

FARMERS retirement. See Retirement from business, etc.

FARMERS test plots. See Field experiments (agriculture)

FARMERS wives. See Farm women

FARMHOUSES
Home for today's farm family. J. Holmstrand. il Suc Farm 62:68-9 F '64
Their house is in order. R. Martens. il Farm J 88:102-3 Mr '64
This farm for sale? E. P. Gorsline. Farm J 87:89+ Mr '63
Ways to grow with a bungalow. R. Martens. il Farm J 87:26-7 Ag '63

FARMHOUSES, Remodeled. See Houses, Remodeled

FARMING. See Agriculture

FARMS
Family farm has a future if. . . B. Everett. il Farm J 87:80+ Ap '63
Family farm here to stay. D. Hanson. Suc Farm 62:8 F '64
Recreation crop. Time 81:55 Mr 22 '63
Recreation, farming's giant new crop. R. C. Davids, il Farm J 87:40-1+ F '63
See also
Dairy farms
Farm management
Poultry farms
Swine farms

FARMS, Incorporated
Facts and fallacies about farm corporations. D. W. Hubbard. Suc Farm 61:61+ Mr '63

FARMS, Small
Hundred acres is enough for me. R. E. Geyer and B. Brantley. il Suc Farm 61:54-5 N '63

FARMS, Worn-out
Shadows of a deserted farm. J. P. Jackson. il Am For 69:8+ Ap '63

FARMSTEAD feeding. See Livestock self feeders

FARNBACH, Irene. See Gerlach, V. S. jt. auth.

FARNBOROUGH air show. See Aviation—Exhibitions

FARNHAM, Eleanor
Youth vs. VD. PTA Mag 58:37 O '63

FARNHAM, Moulton H.
Good name, better than precious ointment. Motor B 113:20-3 F '64
Hands and berths. Motor B 111:47+ F '63
I.O.D.'s, the big little class. Motor B 113:80-3+ Ja '64
Navigating the Bermuda race. Yachting 115:41-3+ Je '64

FARNHAM, Wallace D.
Weakened spring of government: a study in nineteenth-century American history. bibliog f Am Hist R 68:662-80 Ap '63

FARNSWORTH, Clyde A.
Sleuth with 6 million clients. N Y Times Mag p 11+ F 2 '64

FARNSWORTH, Dana L.
Way to stay healthy: a doctor's advice to businessmen; address, April 2, 1963. U S News 55:72-4 Ag 26 '63

about

Hallucinogenic drug cult. N. Gordon. il Reporter 29:35-43 Ag 15 '63; Discussion. 29:8 S 26 '63
Strange case of the Harvard drug scandal. A. T. Weil. Look 27:44+ N 5 '63

FARQUHAR, George
Recruiting officer. Criticism
New Yorker 39:117-18 F 15 '64

FARR, Finis
Jeff, it's up to you! excerpts from Black champion. Am Heritage 15:64-77 F '64

FARRAR, Straus and company. See Farrar, Straus and Giroux (publishers)

FARRAR, Straus and Giroux (publishers)
Farrar, Straus becomes Farrar, Straus and Giroux. Pub W 186:89 S 28 '64

FARRAR family
Farrar coat-of-arms. H. K. Eilers. il Hobbies 68:126-7+ Jl '63

FARRELL, A. E.
Happy miracle in Lima, Ohio. Good H 157:86-7+ S '63

FARRELL, Barry
Guns, black magic, torture are what doc prescribes. Life 54:32-5 Mr 8 '63
Life TV review. Life 56:17 My 8 '64

FARRELL, Charles David
Charlie's seventh heaven. A. Wright. il pors Sports Illus 18:36+ Ap 15 '63

FARRELL, Dick
Losing twenty games isn't easy. L. Merchant. pors Sat Eve Post 236:58-61 Je 8 '63

FARRELL, James Thomas
Updating an old favorite. H. Frankel. por Sat R 47:32-3+ Je 20 '64

FARRELL, R. Keith, and others
Persistence of neorickettsiae helminthoeca in an endoparasite of the Pacific salmon. bibliog Science 145:162-3 Jl 10 '64

FARRELL, Robert E.
French nuclear, space work moves toward major goals. Aviation W 80:270-2+ Mr 16 '64

FARRELL, W. Ranger
Sound isolation between teaching spaces. Arch Rec 134:229-32 O '63

FARRELL, William
Craftsman & teacher. pors Sch Arts 63:28-30 N '63

FARRIERY. See Horseshoeing

FARRINGTON, Josephine
Walking tour of Greater St Louis. por Wilson Lib Bul 38:855-9 Je '64

FARROW, Mia
Mia. por Newsweek 65:31+ Ja 4 '65
Mia Farrow: an actress in search of a character. S. Gordon. il pors Look 28:72-6 D 1 '64

FARROW, Richard G.
Helping the child who comes into conflict with the law. Ann Am Acad 355:90-7 S '64

FARROWING crates and pens. See Swine farrowing crates and pens

FARROWING of swine. See Swine

FARSON, Richard E. and others
Praise reappraised. Harvard Bsns R 41:61-6 S '63

FASAL, John H.
Hysteresis-loop plotter. bibliog Electr World 69:29-31+ My '63

FASCHING. See Carnival

FASCISM

Argentina

Terrorists at work. R. Peter. Nat R 16:638 Jl 28 '64

Germany

Early Goebbels diaries 1925-1926, ed. by H. Heiber. Review
Commentary 35:272-6 Mr '63. W. J. Dannhauser
Forty years ago. S. D. Smith. il N Y Times Mag p46+ N 3 '63
Germans against Hitler, by T. Prittie. Review
Time il 84:104 S 4 '64
Hitler and the Deutsche arbeiterpartei. R. H. Phelps. bibliog f Am Hist R 68:974-86 Jl '63
Hitler: the legend that failed. H. Trevor-Roper. Holiday 36:35+ O '64
Literature of the holocaust. A. Alvarez. Commentary 38:65-9 N '64
On Nazism, de Gaulle, Russia, the future; interview, ed. by O. Schisgall. K. Adenauer. Look 27:27-9 D 17 '63
Rise and fall of the Third Reich, by W. L. Shirer. Review
Christian Cent 79:1510-12 D 12 '62. J. W. Montgomery; Reply. W. Kliewer. 80:179-80 F 6 '63
What we didn't know. M. Hofmann. Sat R 46:13+ D 21 '63

Germany (Federal Republic)

Familiar whiffs. Time 83:36 F 7 '64
Hitler: the legend that failed. H. Trevor-Roper. Holiday 36:35+ O '64
Nazi skeletons. Newsweek 61:34+ Mr 4 '63

Italy

Brutal friendship, by F. W. Deakin. Review
Reporter 28:50+ My 23 '63. M. Salvadori
Fascism for export: Italy and the United States in the twenties. A. Cassels. bibliog f Am Hist R 69:707-12 Ap '64

United States

Fascism for export: Italy and the United States in the twenties. A. Cassels. bibliog f Am Hist R 69:707-12 Ap '64
Few words concerning this picture: American Nazi party headquarters. N. Podhoretz. il Esquire 59:68-9 Mr '63

FASCIST propaganda. See Propaganda, Fascist

FASHION
Alta moda, Italian style; spring and summer collections. il Time 85:42 Ja 29 '65
Bare market; evening gowns with transparent tops. il Newsweek 63:67 Je 22 '64
Can you top this? women's topless bathing suits. il Newsweek 64:72-3 Jl 6 '64
Dressed for action. il Newsweek 63:68 Je 15 '64
Fashion pace-setter; Mrs C. Wrightsman. H. Markel. il Good H 156:38-40+ Je '63
Fashions. O. E. Schoeffler. Esquire 59:43 Je '63
Follow the fashion or leave the country. F. Sagan. Vogue 141:120+ Mr 1 '63
Gilding the lily. il Time 82:58-61 N 8 '63
Heim line; Paris fall fashion showings. il Newsweek 62:46 Ag 5 '63
Net gain: fishnet clothes. il Time 84:74 D 11 '64
Pretty Parisian profusion of pants. il Life 57:42-3 D 11 '64
Rush to leather. il Vogue 141:56-63 F 15 '63
Sensible woman's guide to elegance; excerpts from Elegance. G. A. Dariaux. il Redbook 122:66-7+ Mr '64
Shift ahoy! il Time 82:45 Jl 19 '63
Spirit of style. P. Stout. il Sat R 47:45-7+ O 24 '64
Stars pick the Paris plums. il Life 54:82A-87 Mr 8 '63
Taking the plunge; the bosom fashionable again. il Newsweek 62:97 D 2 '63
See also
Clothing and dress
Costume design
Hairdressing

History

See also
Clothing and dress—History

FASHION designers. See Costume designers

FASHION industry. See Clothing industry

FASHION photography. See Photography, Fashion

FASHION shows
Fashion fair Americana; Ebony's traveling show. il Ebony 18:195-8+ S '63
Fashion fair with a Spanish flair; Ebony's annual fashion fair. il Ebony 19:135-6+ S '64
How coat maker takes its show on the road. il Bsns W p52-3 Ap 27 '63
Rites of new fashion. il Newsweek 62:48-51 Ag 12 '63
So young, so young; with report by H. Moffet. il Life 57:43-6+, 52 S 4 '64
Talk, the clothes, the glitter at the New York openings; backstage notes. il Vogue 141:136-45+ Mr 1 '63
Truly completely marvelous; spring collections. il Time 81:56+ F 15 '63
Young and wild; Parisian lines. il Newsweek 64:78 Ag 17 '64

Caricatures and cartoons

Haute couture. Saxon. New Yorker 40:58-63 O 10 '64

FASHIONABLE society. See Upper classes

FAST, Betty
Enjoy your stay at ALA. ALA Bul 57:413+ My '63

FAST, Howard
Scotland for outsiders. por Esquire 61:69+ F '64

FAST Dan; story. See Fox, W. P.

FAST day menus. See Lenten menus

FASTENINGS
Fastener for every purpose. il Bsns W p 164-6 My 16 '64
See also
Zippers

FASTENINGS (hardware)
Wall fasteners for every purpose. il Good H 157:156 S '63

FASTENINGS (machinery)
For driving fasteners into hard masonry; Shure-Set fastening kit. il Consumer Rep 29:414-15 S '64
What holds your boat together? G. P. Manning. il Motor B 111:39-41+ Mr '63
See also
Staples and stapling machines

FASTING
Add two pounds daily. Sci N L 83:403 Je 29 '63
Fast, fast, fast. il Newsweek 61:94-5 Ap 15 '63
Meat on Friday? America 111:589+ N 14 '64
Reducing formula: starve! Sci Digest 54:52-3 O '63
Woman who stopped eating. il Sci Digest 55:81-2 Ap '64
See also
Lent

FASTS and feasts
Stars of San Gennaro; four singers on a holiday in Little Italy; photographs. Opera N 28:13-15 N 16 '63
See also
Epiphany
Ramadan

FAT
Adipose tissue; ability to respond to nerve stimulation in vitro. J. W. Correll. bibliog il Science 140:387-8 Ap 26 '63
Body composition: relative in vivo determinations from potassium-40 measurements. J. E. Christian and others. bibliog il Science 140:489-90 My 3 '63
Brown fat may be key to space survival; hibernating glands. Sci N L 83:390 Je 22 '63
Brown fat: thermogenic effect during arousal from hibernation in the bat. R. L. Smalley and R. L. Dryer. bibliog il Science 140:1333-4 Je 21 '63
Chlorinated insecticides in the body fat of people in the United States. W. E. Dale and G. E. Quinby. bibliog il Science 142:593-5 N 1 '63
Excess body fat. Sci N L 83:372 Je 15 '63
Fatness of the total body as estimated from measurements on the eviscerated carcass. G. C. Pitts and G. Hollifield. bibliog il Science 141:718-19 Ag 23 '63
Homeostasis of the nonfat components of migrating birds. E. P. Odum and others. bibliog il Science 143:1037-9 Mr 6 '64
Thermoregulatory and adaptive behavior of brown adipose tissue. R. E. Smith. bibliog il Science 146:1686-9 D 25 '64
See also
Corpulence

FATAL accidents. See Accidents

FATEHPUR SIKRI, India
Fatehpur Sikri. il Arch Forum 119:118-23 N '63

FATHER and son; story. See Senesi, M.

FATHER-child relationship. See Parent-child relationship

FATHER Christmas. See Santa Claus

FATHER-daughter relationship. See Parent-child relationship
FATHER-son farm operating agreements
I pay my rent in hogs. W. Messerly. il Suc Farm 61:50 Mr '63
Partners work long hours. il Suc Farm 62:8 Ap '64
They formed a partnership. il Suc Farm 62:67 Ag '64
FATHER-son relationship. See Parent-child relationship
FATHERS
I'm a bachelor father. R. Gogerty. Farm J 88:26 My '64
Reducing the risks for expectant fathers. J. Cook. il N Y Times Mag p 19 Jl 5 '64
364 other days with father. S. Withers. il N Y Times Mag p56 Je 16 '63
What makes a good father. S. Blum. il Redbook 122:38-9+ Ja '64
See also
Stepparents

Anecdotes, facetiae, satire, etc.

Fathers don't stand a chance. W. Stanton. il Good H 156:54+ F '63
FATHERS-in-law
You do marry the family. E. M. Stern. il Parents Mag 39:70-1+ Ap '64
FATIGUE
Ergonomics and the worker. T. R. Brooks. Duns R 82:55-6 Jl '63
Performance and the tired businessman; causes and effects of fatigue. H. J. Johnson. il Duns R 85:45-6+ Ja '65
Pitfalls of fatigue. Parents Mag 39:131 Je '64
Why so many of us are tired. J. B. K. Smith and R. Mines. il Sci Digest 53:87-91 My '63
See also
Relaxation
FATT, Helene V. and Dougherty, E. C.
Genetic control of differential heat tolerance in two strains of the nematode caenorhabditis elegans. bibliog Science 141:266-7 Jl 19 '63
FATT, I. See Timur, A. jt. auth.
FATT, Irving. See Hill, R. M. jt. auth.
FATTY acids. See Acids, Fatty
FAUBUS, Orval Eugene
Arkansas: squire vs. demagogue. T. Dearmore. il por Reporter 31:38-42 O 22 '64
Can Win win? por Time 84:38 O 16 '64
Coming up: a two-party fight in Arkansas. por U S News 56:20 My 4 '64
Showdown in Arkansas: Win Rockefeller vs. Orval Faubus. B. H. Bagdikian. il pors Sat Eve Post 237:75-7 S 19 '64
Winthrop Rockefeller against Orval Faubus. P. J. Owens. New Repub 150:6-7 Ap 25 '64
FAUCETS. See Plumbing
FAUCHEUX, Alvin J. jr
Six quitters. por Esquire 62:103 S '64
FAULK, John Henry
Destruction in a little black book. G. Seldes. por Sat R 47:34-5 N 14 '64
Fighting the blacklist. por Newsweek 64:105-6 N 16 '64
Ordeal of John Henry Faulk. J. P. Blank. il pors Look 27:80-2+ My 7 '63
FAULKNER, D. J.
Current studies of the Magellanic clouds. Sky & Tel 26:69-73 Ag '63
FAULKNER, Douglas
Hot colors of cold fish. U S Camera 26:76-9+ O '63
FAULKNER, Ray, and others
This is ceramics; excerpts from Art today. Design 65:22-5+ S '63
FAULKNER, William
Colonel Sartoris and Mr Snopes. N. Hale. Vogue 142:112-13+ Ag 1 '63
Curse & the hope. il pors Time 84:44-8 Jl 17 '64
Death of William Faulkner. H. Rudd. il por Sat Eve Post 236:32-4+ Jl 13 '63
Faulkner country; with excerpts from novels. il pors Life 55:46B-53 Ag 2 '63
Faulkner without fanfare. R. N. Linscott. Esquire 60:36+ Jl '63
My brother Bill, by J. Faulkner. Review
Sat R 46:31-2 S 21 '63. G. Hicks
Time il por 82:110 S 13 '63
Reivers: William Faulkner's valediction. W. R. Mueller. Christian Cent 80:1079-81 S 4 '63
William Faulkner, by C. Brooks. Review
Nat R por 16:324-5 Ap 21 '64. R. Drake
Young man, old man. A. Kazin. por Reporter 29:36-40 D 19 '63
FAULL, Harry A.
Pomona sets a pattern. Am City 79:77-8 Ja '64
FAULTS (geology)
California's coming earthquake; tension in San Andreas fault. V. H. Gaddis. il Sci Digest 54:27-34 D '63
Fault's movement causes winery damage. Sci N L 86:345 N 28 '64
Guinea fracture zone in the equatorial Atlantic. D. C. Krause. bibliog il Science 146:57-9 O 2 '64
Mystery of earthquakes; where, when, what to do; interview. I. Zietz. il U S News 56:37-9 Ap 13 '64
Our restless earth. M. M. Miller. il Nat Geog Mag 126:140-1 Jl '64
Terra infirma. il Newsweek 63:86+ Ap 13 '64
Troublesome fault; Atlantic fault. Sci Am 209:69-70 N '63
Why Anchorage rocked. il Time 83:45-6 Ap 10 '64
FAUMAN, Gordon
Day of the duners. il Motor T 15:64-7 O '63
FAUNCE, Sarah C.
Derain: ilusion and disillusion. Art N 63:38-9+ N '64
FAUNTROY, Walter E.
Why I believe there is a God. por Ebony 18:80 Mr '63
FAURE, Edgar
France's Faure. H. de Turenne. il pors N Y Times Mag p29+ Ap 26 '64
FAURE, Robert
International ski scandal; with editorial comment. J. Lovesey. il por Sports Illus 19:9. 16-17+ D 16 '63
FAUST, Alfred Luke
Three sisters. Atlan 211:72-6 My '63
FAUST, Irvin
Madras rumble; story. Sat Eve Post 237:44-7 N 14 '64
FAUST; opera. See Gounod, C. F.
Il FAUT passer par les nuages; drama. See Billetdoux, F.
FAUX bois. See Wood finishing
FAVELL, Gene
Wall of gem points. C. Miles. il por Hobbies 69:112+ S '64
FAVIA-ARTSAY, Aida
Historical records. See issues of Hobbies
FAVORS, Party. See Party favors
FAVREAU, Guy
Quebec lieutenant. Newsweek 63:45 F 3 '64
FAVRETTI, Rudy J.
Germinating very fine seeds. Horticulture 42:52-5+ Mr '64
FAWCETT, Clara H.
Dollology. See issues of Hobbies
FAWCETT, E. See Reed, W. A. jt. auth.
FAWCETT, John
Urban renewal, our investment in tomorrow. Am City 78:100-2 N '63
FAWCETT, Temple
Team teaching & art teaching from the inside. Sch Arts 62:18-20 F '63
FAY, Albert
Two Texans shoot it out with a pair of 5.5s. H. Whall. il por Sports Illus 19:52-4 S 16 '63
FAY, Ernest
Two Texans shoot it out with a pair of 5.5s. H. Whall. il por Sports Illus 19:52-4 S 16 '63
FAY, Marion
Why so few women doctors? Todays Health 41:46-9+ Je '63
FAYE'S comet. See Comets
FAYETTE COUNTY, Tenn.
Fayette fraud. Nation 199:62 Ag 24 '64
Students get the vote out. R. V. Denenberg. il Nation 199:45-9 Ag 10 '64
FAYOL, Henri
Famous firsts: discoveries from looking inward. por Bsns W p 152+ Je 6 '64
FEAR
Are parents responsible for childhood fears? F. H. Richardson. il Todays Health 42:8+ O '64
Battlements of terror; fear as a deterrent? S. A. Coblentz. Christian Cent 81:1329-31 O 28 '64
Big, bad fears of childhood. J. E. Allen and F. H. Allen. il Parents Mag 39:62-3+ Mr '64
Children's fears and phobias; with study discussion program. by R. Strang, H. H. Comly. bibliog il PTA Mag 58:7-9. 35 Mr '64
Fear itself: an athropologist's view. G. D. Berreman. Bul Atomic Sci 20:8-11 N '64
I enjoy myself most when I'm scared. I. A. R. Wylie. Read Digest 82:77-80 Je '63
Minister's mail. J. F. Newton. Read Digest 85:119-21 O '64
Nuclear threat harms children. J. Viorst. il Sci N L 83:106-7 F 16 '63

FEAR—*Continued*
What parents ask about children's fears. M. J. E. Senn. il McCalls 90:74+ Ap '63
See also
Anxiety

FEAST of lights. See Hanukkah (Feast of lights)

FEASTER, Carl V. See Turcotte, E. L. jt. auth.

FEATHER, Leonard
Jazz conquers Japan. por Ebony 19:127-8+ O '64

FEATHER RIVER
Autumn camping on the Feather. il Sunset 133:69+ O '64
Muddy waters. Nat R 14:268 Ap 9 '63
Say your good-byes to Bidwell Bar; Feather River country. il Sunset 131:20-2+ N '63

FEATHERBEDDING (industrial relations)
Back to woodburners? Nat R 14:347 My 7 '63
Basis for bargaining; Rosenman report on railroads. Newsweek 61:75-6 My 27 '63
Beyond the last mile. il Time 82:13-16 Jl 26 '63
Deciding on the featherbed; railroad featherbedding fight. il Bsns W p67 S 28 '63
End of the line? il Newsweek 62:64 Jl 15 '63
End to featherbedding? T. R. Brooks. Commonweal 78:301-3 Je 7 '63
Federal fetters for featherbedders; fictional committee meeting in House of representatives. L. K. Randall. il Harvard Bsns R 41: 82-97 Ja '63
History of a law. H. Hazlitt. Newsweek 62:75 S 16 '63
It's bogus; but is it featherbedding? (cont) A. H. Brown. Nat R 14:127 F 12 '63
Lumps in the featherbed. Newsweek 61:76 Mr 18 '63
New round of stalemate; dispute between the railroad industry and the unions. B. J. Widick. Nation 197:68-70 Ag 10 '63
Next trouble spots: railroads and steel? il U S News 54:35-6 Mr 18 '63
One for the roads. il Time 81:92+ Mr 15 '63
Padding the payrolls; superfluous workers in Latin America. Time 81:96+ Je 7 '63
Rail bill: does it solve anything? il Newsweek 62:67 S 9 '63
Rail board offers peace plan; guidelines for settlement dispute over railroad work rules. Bsns W p 172 My 18 '63
Rail firemen: fight flares again; feather bedding on Southern railway. U S News 58:71-2 Ja 11 '65
Railroad strike: what are the chances? il U S News 54:43-4 My 27 '63
Red light ahead. Newsweek 62:36+ Jl 29 '63
Seesaw to settlement. Newsweek 62:55-6 Ag 26 '63
Showdown ahead on the railroads; strike or end of featherbedding? U S News 54:101 Mr 18 '63
Showdown in the rail dispute; how deadline pressure built up. U S News 55:84 Jl 29 '63
Showdown over featherbedding. il Sr Schol 83:14-16+ S 27 '63
Speaking out; the country needs featherbedding. A. H. Raskin. Sat Eve Post 236:10+ O 12 '63
That empty chair by the featherbed. L. Velie. Read Digest 82:97-102 Ap '63
Timetable; chronology of the railroad featherbedding battle. Time 82:16 Jl 19 '63
Tracks clear for railroad cutback? il Sr Schol 82:22 Mr 27 '63
Until August 29. Newsweek 62:23 Ag 5 '63
Until July 29; no railroad strike. il Newsweek 62:66 Jl 22 '63
Will it be compulsory arbitration on the railroads? il U S News 55:78-80 Jl 1 '63
Will unions lose rail dispute? il U S News 55:89-91 Ag 5 '63
Working on the railroads as featherbedding goes. il U S News 55:82-3 Jl 15 '63

FEATHERS
Astaxanthin in the cedar waxwing. A. H. Brush and K. Allen. bibliog il Science 142: 47-8 O 4 '63

FEATHERSTONE, Joseph L.
Did the church fail? Commonweal 79:649-51 F 28 '64
Exile from socialism. New Repub 152:19+ Ja 16 '65

FEBRUARY
In February; few of the dates, memorable and not so, coming up this month (title varies) (cont) il N Y Times Mag p 16 F 2 '64
Something's got to be done about February! il Changing T 17:46 F '63

FECHNERS law
Psychophysics of perceived intensity: a theoretical basis for Fechner's and Stevens' laws. D. M. MacKay. bibliog il Science 139:1213-16 Mr 22 '63

FECUNDITY. See Fertility, Human

FEDER, Abe H.
New light. New Yorker 40:24-5 D 26 '64

FEDER, Harvey H. and Whalen, R. E.
Feminine behavior in neonatally castrated and estrogen-treated male rats. bibliog Science 147:306-7 Ja 15 '65

FEDERAL agencies, boards, bureaus, commissions, etc. of the United States government. See name of agency, board, bureau, commission, etc. under United States, e.g. United States—Federal maritime commission

FEDERAL aid. See Art and state; Federal and municipal relations; Federal and state relations; Grants-in-aid; Libraries and state; Subsidies; *also* subhead Federal aid under various subjects, e.g. Medical research—Federal aid

FEDERAL aid to education
Administration offers another school bill; controversy renewed on parochial aid. Christian Cent 80:196 F 13 '63
Aid to church-connected schools? R. Kirk. Nat R 16:1146 D 29 '64
Aid to education. America 110:35-6 Ja 11 '64
Aid to education: a better deal. W. L. Miller. il Reporter 30:20-3 Ap 23 '64
Aid to schools: what the President wants. il U S News 58:35 Ja 18 '65
Aiding the schools. Commonweal 81:499-500 Ja 15 '65
Ambitious program for the 88th Congress. H. G. Sackett. NEA J 52:32 F '63
American council on education: conference designed to illuminate the ins and outs of grantsmanship. J. Walsh. Science 140:1383 Je 28 '63
Beyond the school question. J. O'Gara. Commonweal 78:15 Mr 29 '63
Bill for education. New Repub 148:6-7 Je 15 '63
Candor needed on federal aid to education. Christian Cent 81:1484 D 2 '64
Categorical aid. America 111:9 Jl 4 '64
Changing opinion on federal aid; excerpt from Federal aid to private schools. L. R. Ward. Cath World 199:167-74 Je '64
Christian discord over aid to schools. J. B. Sheerin. Cath World 199:4-7 Ap '64
Church and state: AFT vs. NEA over federal aid to parochial schools. Sr Schol 85:6T D 2 '64
Church-related schools. New Repub 148:4-5 Mr 2; 4-6 My 11 '63; Discussion. 148:30-1 Mr 16 '63
Citizens for educational freedom. J. R. Brown. America 110:194-6 F 8 '64; Reply. E. M. O'Keefe. 110:299 Mr 7 '64
College architecture; the economics and aesthetics. W. McQuade. il Fortune 67:148-50 My '63
Congress: a broad expansion of National defense education act passes relatively unnoticed. J. Walsh. Science 146:383-4 O 16 '64
Congress and school construction. H. C. F. Arnold. il Arch Rec 135:18 F '64
Congress and the colleges. Sr Schol 83:1T N 8 '63
Congress: new study shows federal education budget of $2.2 billion, $613 million of it for research. J. Walsh. Science 141:29-31 Jl 5 '63
Congress winds up session. Sr Schol 83:16 Ja 10 '64
Constitutionality of tax funds for sectarian schools; church-related colleges in Maryland. Sch & Soc 91:420 D 28 '63
Control of schools. America 110:247-8, 305 F 22, Mr 7 '64
Crack in the ice; NEA resolutions on federal support for public education. America 109: 127 Ag 10 '63
Dear Mr President; letter. G. J. Hecht. Parents Mag 38:55+ F '63
Decision for the sixties; concerning the pamphlet, Public funds for parochial schools. Christian Cent 80:899 Jl 17 '63
Digest of 1961 state reports on vocational education. P. Groom. il Mo Labor R 86:1162-5 O '63
Dilemma of federal aid. Time 81:84+ Ap 12 '63
Disbursement of federal aid by the Office of education, 1962-63. R. M. Walker. Sch Life 46:15 Mr '64
Domestic brain drain; imbalance of research funds. Newsweek 63:52 Mr 2 '64
Economics of training the unemployed; manpower development and training act of 1962. L. A. Cornelsen. il Sch Life 47:17-18 O '64
Education bill. Time 85:19 Ja 22 '65
Education: case for federal aid, comprehensive planning discussed as costs and enrollment rise. J. Walsh. Science 147:30-2 Ja 1 '65

FEDERAL aid to education—*Continued*
Education funds voted: who gets the money and how. il U S News 55:6 D 23 '63
Education in State of Union message; President's budget message. il NEA J 52:4 F '63
Education in the party platforms; Republican and Democratic statements. P. Woodring. Sat R 47:51-2 O 17 '64
Education legislation: deadlock on vocational education broken; landmark college aid bill passed. J. Walsh. Science 142:1556-8 D 20 '63
Education: President's message outlines program concentrated on aiding the disadvantaged. P. Walsh. Science 147:382-3 Ja 22 '65
Education stalemate. C. Jencks. New Repub 148:6 F 9 '63
Education: weapon against poverty; economic opportunity act of 1964. Sch Life 47:23-4 O '64
Educational leadership. D. Wolfle. Science 143:767 F 21 '64
ETV grants go to five agencies. Sch Life 46:39 O '63
Eventually, a tax subsidy for college education? U S News 56:96 F 17 '64
Federal aid and Catholic schools; symposium. il Commonweal 79:501-42 Ja 31 '64; Discussion. 79:633-4, 664-5; 80:150-1 F 21-28, Ap 24 '64
Federal aid and higher education. G. E. Snavely. Sch & Soc 91:86-8 F 23 '63
Federal aid bill. America 108:819 Je 8 '63
Federal aid controversy. America 111:204 Ag 29 '64
Federal aid for higher education; church-related institutions. E. H. Rutkowski. Commonweal 79:40-3 O 4 '63
Federal aid for parochial and private schools. W. S. Vincent. Sch & Soc 92:355-7 N 28 '64
Federal aid, 1963. America 108:190 F 9 '63
Federal aid picture. America 111:682 N 28 '64
Federal aid plank; Democratic party's statement. America 111:244 S 12 '64
Federal aid: third round. Commonweal 77:631-2 Mr 15 '63
Federal aid to colleges: boon or bane? P. Friggens. Read Digest 84:139-43 Ja '64
Federal aid to education; address, March 13, 1963. J. A. Howard. Vital Speeches 29:434-7 My 1 '63
Federal aid? will there be government control? and to whom will federal funds be paid? J. M. Hanlon. America 110:418-19 Mr 28 '64
Federal aid's Scylla and Charybdis. Christian Cent 82:99-100 Ja 27 '65
Federal funds for education. il Sat R 46:81 F 16 '63
Federal government and the universities. K. W. Mildenberger. Ann Am Acad 356:23-9 N '64
Federal handouts may get skimpier. Bsns W p45-6 My 16 '64
Federal influence distorts education; U.S. programs create imbalance in colleges. il Nations Bsns 51:31-3+ Mr '63
Forty first-rate universities. D. Wolfle. Science 144:1413 Je 19 '64; Reply. C. A. MacKenzie. 145:314 Jl 24 '64
$4.6 billion baby; President Kennedy's aid-to-education bill. Newsweek 61:86-7 F 11 '63
Free exercise of religion? J. O'Gara. Commonweal 81:472 Ja 8 '65
Germaneness of the U.S. Congress; federal grants for construction of medical and dental schools. Sat Eve Post 236:100 O 19 '63
Going up fast; Office of education, budget to be doubled. Time 85:50 Ja 15 '65
Goldwater on church and state. G. D. Everett. Christian Cent 81:987-9 Ag 5 '64
Good cause, bad argument. Commonweal 78:35 Ap 5 '63; Discussion. 78:166-9, 329 My 3, Je 14 '63
Graduate aid; poll of educators suggests that needs vary widely in scientific disciplines. D. S. Greenberg. Science 140:35-7 Ap 5 '63
Graduate education; interest of the government; address, December 27, 1963. P. P. Muirhead. Vital Speeches 30:280-2 F 15 '64
Higher education as a national resource: a proposed federal program; text of document, January 17, 1963. Sch & Soc 91:218-21 My 4 '63
Higher education facilities act of 1963. il Sch Life 46:13-22 My '64
Higher education: fourth branch of government? C. K. Arnold. il Sat R 47:60-1+ Ja 18 '64; Reply. L. H. Fountain. 47:62 Mr 21 '64
Housecleaning needed. America 108:218-19 F 16 '63
Housing act and higher education. L. G. Burns. bibliog f Sch & Soc 91:211-12 My 4 '63
Is there really a crisis in U.S. schools? il U S News 54:43-5 My 20 '63
Kennedy program. Sr Schol 82:1T-2T F 13 '63
Kennedy's latest plan for aid to schools. il U S News 54:60 F 11 '63
Landmark; major new program of Federal aid to education. Newsweek 62:71 D 23 '63
Legislators who move school bills in Congress. il NEA J 53:42-3 Ap '64
LBJ fills in his design. il Bsns W p25-6 Ja 16 '65
LBJ's school budget. Sr Schol 84:1T F 7 '64
Mass education must face the idiot response. F. Morley. il Nations Bsns 52:29-30 F '64
Much more remains to be done. E. Green. NEA J 53:16-17+ F '64
NDEA loans to private schools. G. C. Decker. il Sch Life 45:19-21 Ap '63
NSF: new program aims to speed process for transforming good institutions into excellent ones. D. S. Greenberg. Science 144:154-5 Ap 10 '64
Needed: one voice. America 108:287 Mr 2 '63
New education bill. F. Canavan. America 112:108-9+ Ja 23 '65
New education laws. W. D. Boutwell PTA Mag 59:33-4 N '64
New effort for federal aid to education. R. H. Smith. Pub W 183:44 F 25 '63
New leadership in education. Life 58:4 Ja 29 '65
New obstructionism; college aid bill. America 109:784 D 21 '63
New schools in federally affected areas. il Sch Life 47:14-15 O '64
Next steps in federal aid. R. H. Wyatt. NEA J 53:35-6 Mr '64
One big gulp; twenty-four part federal aid bill. Time 81:49 F 8 '63
Other side of the coin. O. J. Murdick. il America 111:230-2 S 5 '64; Reply. F. D. Rabaut. 111:365 O 3 '64
Paying for education. C. Jencks. New Repub 150:13-16 F 1 '64
Policy and legacy. J. Walsh. Science 142:1152-3 N 29 '63
Poverty and parochial schools; federal grants to Catholic schools. B. L. Masse. America 112:101 Ja 23 '65
President Johnson speaks out on education; special statement for the National education association. L. B. Johnson. NEA J 53:12-14 Ja '64
President Kennedy and education. W. W. Brickman. Sch & Soc 92:93 Mr 7 '64
President on education. Reporter 32:18+ Ja 28 '65
President signs college aid bill. Christian Cent 81:4 Ja 1 '64
President's choice. America 111:732 D 5 '64
President's message on education; January 29, 1963. J. F. Kennedy. Sch Life 45:5-7+ F '63
President's message on education; excerpts. L. B. Johnson. Wilson Lib Bul 39:440+ F '65
Protestant call to action; concerning editorial in Christianity and crisis. J. O'Gara. Commonweal 79:270 N 29 '63
Public funds for parochial schools? by G. La Noue. Review
Commonweal 78:184 My 10 '63. J. O'Gara
Public higher education and the needs of government; excerpt from address, April 29, 1963. J. K. Pollock. Sch & Soc 92:45-7 F 8 '64
Public schools need federal aid. Christian Cent 81:390 Mr 25 '64
Question of image; problem of aid for parochial schools. J. O'Gara. Commonweal 81:558 Ja 29 '65
Rejects parochial school tax aid. Christian Cent 80:765 Je 12 '63
Religion, orthodoxy, public schools. C. M. Whelan. America 108:640-3 My 4 '63
Religious neutrality. J. J. Regan. America 110:74-6 Ja 18 '64
School aid: can Dean Keppel call the class to order? M. Elfin. il Reporter 28:32-5 Mr 14 '63
School aid makes it at last. Bsns W p32 Ag 24 '63
School aid: new strategy urged by policy commission to expand federal support for education. D. S. Greenberg. Science 144:1558-9 Je 26 '64
School aid: what LBJ and Goldwater believe: excerpts from statements. L. B. Johnson; B. M. Goldwater. U S News 57:15 S 28 '64
School gains prove no aid needed. il Nations Bsns 52:88 F '64
Schools and churches. New Repub 148:3-5 Mr 23 '63; Discussion. 148:28-31 Ap 6 '63

FEDERAL aid to education—*Continued*
Science and federal programs: the continuing dialogue; adapted from address, April 28, 1964. J. A. Shannon. Science 144:976-8 My 22 '64
Seeks income tax aid for college students. Christian Cent 80:877 Jl 10 '63
Senator's plan to end religious issue in school aid; excerpts from address, May 20, 1963. A. Ribicoff. il U S News 54:100-2 Je 3 '63
Separate but interacting. H. E. Fey. Christian Cent 81:231-2 F 19 '64; Reply. 81:293-4 Mr 4 '64
Shaping educational policy. D. Wolfle. Science 146:1117 N 27 '64
Shift in opinion; Gallup poll. America 108:245 F 23 '63
Should public funds aid parochial schools? pro and con discussion. R. F. Drinan; R. L. Hunt. Parents Mag 38:70-1+ N '63
Space in Houston; NASA's arrival bringing new skills and interests to Nation's petrochemical center. D. S. Greenberg. Science 140:618-19 My 10 '63
Speaking out; a liberal calls for aid to church schools. R. M. Hutchins. Sat Eve Post 236: 6+ Je 8 '63; Discussion. Christian Cent 80:819-20, 1141 Je 26, S 18 '63
Speaking out; why we need more federal aid for our schools. S. McMurrin. Sat Eve Post 236:6+ Mr 23 '63
State aid Down Under and at home. America 109:546 N 9 '63
State and federal aid to parochial schools; address, April 24, 1964. R. F. Drinan. Vital Speeches 30:559-62 Jl 1 '64
Statements on education by the Democratic and Republican presidential candidates. L. B. Johnson; B. M. Goldwater. il NEA J 53:12-13 O '64
Straws in the wind. America 108:386 Mr 23 '63
Students and taxes. America 110:838 Je 20 '64
Summary of the administration's bill for education. Sch Life 45:27-8 F '63
T.R.B. from Washington; Catholics and schools. New Repub 148:2 F 16 '63; Discussion. 148:4-5 Mr 2; 31 Mr 9; 39 Mr 23 '63
Tax credits for education. V. C. Blum. il America 110:669-72 My 16 '64; Reply. J. F. Morse. 110:855 Je 27 '64; Rejoinder. 111:97 Ag 1 '64
Teacher-opinion poll. il NEA J 52:76 O '63
This month's feature: Congress and aid to higher education. Cong Digest 42:35-64 F '63
This month's feature: 88th Congress and higher education. Cong Digest 42:225-56 O '63
Tuition deductions? Time 81:39 My 31 '63
Utah schools; demands for more state educational aid. New Repub 148:5 Ap 13 '63
Vocation education act of 1963. il Sch Life 46:3-12 Mr '64
We will not put. America 108:700 My 18 '63; Reply. J. R. Price. 108:873 Je 22 '63
What government can and can't do. il Nations Bsns 51:34-5+ Je '63
What's happening in education? education package presented to Congress by the late President Kennedy. W. D. Boutwell. PTA Mag 58:17-18 F '64
What's happening in education? education under President Johnson's administration. W. D. Boutwell. PTA Mag 59:17 D '64
What's happening in education? new education bills. W. D. Boutwell. PTA Mag 58:13 Ap '64
What's happening in education? new education plan proposed. W. D. Boutwell. PTA Mag 57:11-12 Ap '63
Where the Democrats and the Republicans stand on school aid. G. J. Hecht. Parents Mag 39:42+ O '64
While school keeps. J. Cass. Sat R 46:46 Ag 17 '63
Who gets the billions in LBJ's school plan. il U S News 58:66-7 Ja 25 '65
Whose common good. America 110:184 F 8 '64
Why you oppose aid to education (the inside story) Nat R 14:349 My 7 '63
Will Congress pay for education? C. Jencks. il New Repub 150:11-14 Ja 11 '64
See also
Medical education—Federal aid
Student loans

FEDERAL aid to science. See Research—Federal aid

FEDERAL and municipal relations
Administrative and fiscal considerations in urban development. W. Z. Hirsch. bibliog f Ann Am Acad 352:48-61 Mr '64
Cure for sick cities. C. Case. Sat R 46:12-14 F 9 '63
Federal aid? Indianapolis says, Uncle, go home! P. Friggens. Read Digest 82:266-8+ Je '63
Growing echo in the states' vaults; with editorial comment. il Bsns W p 112+, 202 S 19 '64
How Washington would control your city. Nations Bsns 51:94+ O '63
Local leaders tire of federal ties; survey conducted by Senate subcommittee on intergovernmental relations. il Nations Bsns 52: 36-7+ F '64
Phoenix unreborn; federal aid and urban-renewal. R. L. Gilbert, jr. Reporter 29:48-9 N 21 '63
States blunt federal grab for cities. il Nations Bsns 51:108-10+ Ap '63
View from the bridge: politics no picnic on banks of pollution; strong federal agency is likely. E. Langer. Science 142:566-7 N 1 '63
Why Boston is puzzled by a federal economy move. il U S News 57:84-6 N 23 '64

FEDERAL and provincial relations (Canada)
Now secession talk in Canada's biggest province. il U S News 54:60-1 Ap 1 '63
Will Canada break up? a story of tensions. il U S News 57:56-7 N 2 '64

FEDERAL and state relations
Administration's way of helping Negro. il Bsns W p25 My 11 '63
Angry language; interim report considers cutting off federal funds for Mississippi. Newsweek 61:25-6 Ap 29 '63
Before the showdown: Wallace's views; excerpts from statement. G. C. Wallace. U S News 54:19 Je 17 '63
Birmingham and the law. New Repub 148:3-4 My 25 '63
Can the state live on crumbs? federal-state fiscal relations. J. Anderson. il Sat R 48: 31-2+ Ja 9 '65
Civil rights: federal responsibility; address, November 14, 1964. W. L. Taylor. Vital Speeches 31:143-6 D 15 '64
Defense lag; address, August 10, 1964. B. M. Goldwater. Vital Speeches 30:676-8 S 1 '64
Federal intrusions anger states; providing outdoor-recreation opportunities. H. Titus. Field & S 68:20+ D '63
Federal viewpoint on combating organized crime. H. J. Miller, jr. bibliog f Ann Am Acad 347:93-103 My '63
Federalism and civil rights, by B. Marshall. Review
America 112:22-3 Ja 2 '65. A. A. North
New Repub 151:17-18 O 31 '64. A. M. Bickel
Fifty states with one big problem, money. il Sr Schol 82:8-10 F 6 '63
Funds for the states; Heller plan. Commonweal 81:436-7 D 25 '64
Government has no free money; interview. D. J. Mays. Nations Bsns 52:37+ F '64
Government's hidden dimension. E. S. Muskie. Sat R 47:18-22 Ap 18 '64
Growing echo in the states' vaults; with editorial comment. il Bsns W p 112+, 202 S 19 '64
High court: its growing impact; with excerpts from majority and dissenting opinions. il U S News 56:34-7 Je 29 '64
How Supreme court is changing U.S; with interviews with C. S. Hyneman and P. B. Kurland. il U S News 58:56-62 Ja 18 '65
How to put the states back in business. E. G. Brown. Harper 229:98+ S '64
How to win against prosperity; GOP campaign. Bsns W p 16-17 Ag 1 '64
Ideological heroin. Christian Cent 81:1355-6 N 4 '64
Is the government ready for the future? R. Drummond. Sat R 47:186-7 Ag 29 '64
Is Washington too powerful? R. Kirk; E. F. Goldman. il N Y Times Mag p22+ Mr 1 '64
Johnson Congress: what it will do. il Nations Bsns 52:32-3+ D '64
Johnson's economics; quotations from statements on major economic issues. L. B. Johnson. il Bsns W p47-8+ O 31 '64
Labor agreements under state antidiscrimination laws; report to ABA meeting. Mo Labor R 87:1179-80 O '64
Local leaders tire of federal ties; survey conducted by Senate subcommittee on intergovernmental relations. il Nations Bsns 52: 36-7+ F '64
Massive federal spending; concentration of national power; address, May 3, 1963. H. F. Byrd. Vital Speeches 29:514-20 Je 15 '63
Mississippi; suggested cut-off of federal funds. New Repub 148:3-4 Ap 27 '63
No-strings aid for the states? A. L. Otten and C. B. Seib il Reporter 32:33-5 Ja 28 '65

FEDERAL and state relations—*Continued*
Our quaint political folkways. J. Ellison. Nation 197:323-5 N 16 '63
Provincialism and constitutionalism: the role of the states in foreign area studies. W. Morehouse. bibliog f Ann Am Acad 356:119-25 N '64
Reaction's refuge; proposed constitutional amendments. K. Crawford. Newsweek 61:31 Je 3 '63
Rights of the states; address, December 8, 1963. L. Collins. Vital Speeches 30:369-73 Ap 1 '64
See here, General Kennedy; federal government empowered to use state militia and federal troops for law enforcement in states. Time 84:45-6 Jl 10 '64
Seventeen states vote to destroy democracy as we know it. T. B. Morgan. il Look 27:76+ D 3 '63
Share-the-tax-revenue plan; domestic economic policy. R. L. Heilbroner. il N Y Times Mag p8+ D 27 '64
Speaking out; the Supreme court is defying the people. E. M. Dirksen. Sat Eve Post 237:10+ S 12 '64
State governments better shape up; the Heller plan. Life 57:4 D 18 '64
States blunt federal grab for cities. il Nations Bsns 51:108-10+ Ap '63
States get a warning on the price of bias; administration's civil rights programs. Bsns W p23-4 Ja 9 '65
Subsidizing the states; the Heller plan. E. L. Dale, jr. New Repub 151:11-12 N 28 '64; Discussion. 151:29 D 12; 29-30 D 19; 29-30 D 26 '64
Two concepts of law. Fortune 68:91-2 Ag '63
Uncle Sam is really needed; federal role in local affairs is necessary. M. D. Reagan. il N Y Times Mag p31+ S 13 '64
U.S. troops in Alabama; Governor, President, and the law; telegrams, text of law. G. Wallace; J. F. Kennedy. U S News 54:40-1 My 27 '63
U.S. voting map: a year of change. il Newsweek 61:28-30 Mr 25 '63
Virtue grounded in principle still prevails at grass roots. F. Morley. Nations Bsns 51:25-6 Ag '63
Walks and walkers; murder of William Moore. Nation 196:385 My 11 '63
West and its public lands; address, February 6, 1964. S. L. Udall. Vital Speeches 30:297-301 Mr 1 '64
Where High court put federal standards on state rules. U S News 54:30 Ap 1 '63
Where money from Washington is being turned down. il U S News 56:76-9 Mr 16 '64
Why bail out the states? the Heller plan. C. Jencks. New Repub 151:8-10 D 12 '64; Discussion. 151:28-9 D 26 '64
Why local government serves best; interview. J. A. Love. il Nations Bsns 51:38-9+ S '63
Why not enforce the law? Nation 196:413 My 18 '63
Withholding federal funds: a weapon in the Rights fight? U S News 54:8 Ap 29 '63
See also
Centralization in government
State rights
FEDERAL art project
WPA and after. il Newsweek 62:66 Ag 5 '63
FEDERAL buildings. See Public buildings
FEDERAL city club. See Washington, D.C.—Clubs
FEDERAL courts. See Courts—United States
FEDERAL crop insurance. See Insurance, Agricultural
FEDERAL crop insurance corporation
Report on 1964 policies. Suc Farm 62:10 F '64
FEDERAL debt (United States) See Debts, Public—United States
FEDERAL deposit insurance corporation
Flesh & blood. Time 83:88+ My 1 '64
FEDERAL electric corporation
Radicians at the DEW line. W. A. Stocklin. il Electr World 71:48-9+ My '64
FEDERAL employees. See Government employees
FEDERAL expenditures. See United States—Appropriations and expenditures
FEDERAL furniture. See Furniture, American
FEDERAL government
Government's hidden dimension. E. S. Muskie. Sat R 47:18-22 Ap 18 '64
Inter-continental unity: the federation of the free world; address, November 20, 1964. N. A. Rockefeller. Vital Speeches 31:132-5 D 15 '64
New lamps for old? centralism; address, November 11, 1964. L. Bushnell. Vital Speeches 31:112-14 D 1 '64
Non rule in America. D. T. Bazelon. bibliog f Commentary 36:438-45 D '63
What a southern conservative thinks. J. J. Kilpatrick. Sat R 47:15-18 Ap 25 '64; Discussion. 47:27-8 My 16; 24 Je 6 '64
See also
Centralization in government
Democracy
Federal and state relations
United States—Politics and government
FEDERAL grants. See Grants-in-aid
FEDERAL hazardous substances labeling act. See Labels
FEDERAL judges. See Judges
FEDERAL medicine. See Medical service, State
FEDERAL prisons. See Prisons—United States
FEDERAL reserve banks
Costlier borrowing for many. U S News 54:109 Je 17 '63
Fed credit chiefs hold private tug-of-war. il Bsns W p29 Mr 16 '63
Fight over the Federal reserve. il Time 83:85 F 14 '64
Money to burn; case of missing Treasury bonds, Federal reserve bank of San Francisco. Newsweek 61:25 Ap 8 '63
Now it's the money managers who are under fire. il U S News 54:94-5 Ap 1 '63
Patman hits a raw nerve. Bsns W p68 F 8 '64
Split about credit policy. U S News 54:109-10 Mr 18 '63
Will White House get control over credit? concerning Federal reserve system. il U S News 56:83-4 My 4 '64
Wright Patman's well-heeled windmills. G. Carr. New Repub 150:11-12 F 8 '64
See also
United States—Federal reserve board
FEDERAL reserve system. See Federal reserve banks
FEDERAL urban renewal program. See Urban renewal
FEDERALISM. See Federal government
The FEDERALIST
State of our understanding. W. Kendall. Nat R 15:491-4 D 3 '63
FEDERATED department stores, incorporated
Giant step; acquisition of Bullock's twenty-three stores. Time 84:81 Jl 24 '64
FEDERATION internationale de documentation. See International federation for documentation
FÉDERATION internationale des jeunesses musicales. See Musical societies
FEDERATION of American scientists
FAS endorses test ban; backs policy with facts. Sci N L 84:104 Ag 17 '63
FAS: for further arms control; statement. Bul Atomic Sci 19:46 N '63
FAS statement on biological and chemical warfare. Bul Atomic Sci 20:46-7 O '64
FEDERATION of American societies for experimental biology
Meeting, 1963. R. D. Dripps. Science 140:1247 Je 14 '63
FEDERATION of Malaysia. See Malaysia
FEDERATION of Republican women. See Political clubs and associations
FEDERATION of societies to aid lepers and fight leprosy, Brazil. See Leprosy and lepers
FEDERATION of Tanganyika, Uganda and Kenya. See East African Federation (proposed)
FEDERATION of union representatives
David Dubinsky: why his throne is wobbling. P. Jacobs; discussion. Harper 226:12+ F '63
FEDORENKO, Nikolai Trofimovich
Soviet Union and African countries; address, April 10, 1964; with questions and answers. Ann Am Acad 354:1-8 Jl '64
about
Professor. New Yorker 39:37-8 My 4 '63
FEEBLE-minded children. See Mentally handicapped children
FEED grain plan. See Agricultural administration—United States
FEED grinders and grinding
Everybody gets the discount; new satellite push button feed mill. B. Hardy. il Farm J 89:26-7+ Ja '65
FEED handling
Aflatoxin B_1: chemical identity and biological activity. S. B. Chang and others. bibliog il Science 142:1191-2 N 29 '63
Compact feed center. W. J. Fletcher. il Suc Farm 62:86 F '64
Expanding? which way to mechanize. W. J. Fletcher and C. Peterson, jr. il Suc Farm 61:54-5+ Ap '63

FEED handling—*Continued*
How to plan a beef feeding layout. P. B. Jones and R. L. Maddex. il Suc Farm 62:38-41 O '64
Jim Speery keeps 'em rolling. il Suc Farm 62:33 Ja '64
One stop grain handling, hog feeding. R. E. Geyer. il Suc Farm 61:32-3+ Je '63
Using augers and elevators. il Suc Farm 62:47 O '64

FEED mixers and mixing
Everybody gets the discount; new satellite push button feed mill. B. Hardy. il Farm J 89:26-7+ Ja '65

FEED supplements, Antibiotic. See Antibiotic feed supplements

FEEDBACK control. See Automatic control

FEEDER airlines. See Local service airlines

FEEDERS (birds)
Catering to birds. J. Peter. il Look 28:124 Ap 21 '64
Game-bird savers. W. C. Lammey. il Pop Mech 121:158-61+ Ja '64
In feeders, variety is the spice of bird life. E. Heacock. il Audubon Mag 66:390-4 N '64
Open house for birds. il House & Gard 124:249 O '63
These are all for the birds. il Sunset 130:110+ F '63
Three bird feeders for you to build; with diagrams. Flower Grower 50:13 O '63
Welcome the winter birds. J. K. Terres. il Pop Gard 14:26-7+ N '63

FEEDERS (livestock) See Calf self feeders

FEEDING and feeding stuffs
Crack down on cattle feeding costs. D. Malena and others. il Suc Farm 62:44-5+ O '64
Ebb of winter. J. P. Jackson. il Am For 70:14-15+ Mr '64
Green-chopping cuts his costs. il Suc Farm 61:64 Ag '63
How to avoid hay shortage. C. D. McGrew and J. R. Staubus. Suc Farm 62:74A Ap '64
Now: a supplement with no oil meal. il Farm J 88:34 Je '64
Three months' milk down the drain! S. Churchill. Farm J 88:47 F '64

See also
Calves—Feeding
Cattle—Feeding
Corn
Cows—Feeding
Dog food
Feed handling
Feed mixers and mixing
Forage plants
Hay
Poultry—Feeding
Ralston purina company
Sheep—Feeding
Silage
Sorghum
Swine—Feeding
Urea

Contamination by drugs and pesticides

Here's the latest on pesticides in hay. Farm J 88:29 Ag '64

Grain

Feed grain program. F. Bailey, jr. Suc Farm 61:45 Ap '63
In a drouth year 4000 lbs. more milk per cow. B. Hardy and H. Simons. Farm J 88:60 F '64
Short of feed? try these ideas. B. Hardy. Farm J 87:49 N '63

Pelleted feed

Feed alfalfa pellets to dairy cows? B. Hardy. Farm J 87:40F Jl '63
Pelleting saves feed during finishing. D. Seim. Farm J 88:48 My '64

Phosphorus content

Phosphorus for beef cattle. A. D. Tillman. il Suc Farm 62:102 Mr '64

FEEDING stations for birds. See Feeders (birds)

FEEDLOTS, Cattle. See Cattle self feeders

FEELINGS. See Emotions

FEELY machines. See Simulators

FEENEY, Leonard
Slaves of Leonard Feeney. il Time 85:45 Ja 1 '65

FEENEY, Mary E.
Three-M muddle. Library J 89:2960-2 Ag '64

FEES, Airport. See Airports—Finance

FEES, Legal. See Cost (law)

FEET. See Foot

FEFFER and Simons, incorporated
W. S. Hall & co. to merge with Feffer and Simons. Pub W 184:33-4 D 30 '63

FEHRENBACH, T. R.
CIA and the Cuban invasion. New Repub 150: 21-2 Je 27 '64

FEHSENFELD, Bob
People in a trap; Negro protest movement, Cambridge, Md. S. Alsop. il Sat Eve Post 237:12 Je 6 '64

FEIBELMAN, W. A.
Monochromatic photographs of the Orion nebula. il Sky & Tel 27:154-5 Mr '64

FEIBLEMAN, James K.
Magic to meditation. Sat R 46:37-8 F 16 '63
Uses of thinking. Sat R 46:18-19+ Mr 2 '63
Words to mirror the world. Sat R 46:37-8 Je 22 '63

FEIBLEMAN, Peter S.
Enduring life of the Pueblo Indians. Holiday 34:58-9+ Ag '63
New York's Spanish restaurants. Holiday 34: 104-5+ D '63
Tiger, tiger, burning bright. Criticism Theatre Arts il(p 12) 47:66 F '63

FEIFER, George
Art for Marx' sake. N Y Times Mag p 12-13+ D 20 '64
Crime in Moscow. Sat Eve Post 237:36-7+ My 9 '64
It's hard to get into Moscow U. N Y Times Mag p44-5+ N 22 '64
Moscow: a day in the people's court. Reporter 30:29+ My 21 '64
Now Moscow debates its manners. N Y Times Mag p28+ Ag 23 '64
Red and the black: racism in Moscow. Reporter 30:27-8 Ja 2 '64
Russia has socialist crime, too. N Y Times Mag p20+ Ap 5 '64
Sasha's creed: Russia right or wrong. N Y Times Mag p9+ Ap 28 '63
Soviet fathers and sons. New Repub 148:11-13 Je 1 '63
—See Gottlieb, L. jt. auth.

about

Author. M. K. Harvey. por Sat R 47:27 Je 27 '64

FEIFFER, Jules
Feiffer. See issues of New republic
Matter of conscience. Commentary 38:52-4 D '64
New Horatio Alger series starring L.B.J. Life 56:10+ Je 5 '64
Nixon and the fat lady. Commentary 37:86-8 My '64
You are his target. G. Millstein. il por Sat Eve Post 237:38+ O 3 '64
You should have caught me at the White House. Holiday 33:66-7 Je '63

about

Seek, seek, seek. por Time 81:84 Je 28 '63

FEIG, Steven. See Blank, M. jt. auth.

FEIGHAN, Michael A.
Challenge to representative self-government; address, January 23, 1964. Vital Speeches 30:304-7 Mr 1 '64
Immigration: quotas vs. quality. P. Duke and S. Meisler. il Reporter 32:30-2 Ja 14 '65

FEIGHT, J. J. See Knake, E; Shurleff, M. jt. auths.

FEIGNER, Eddie
Man with a golden arm. il por Time 82:41 Ag 23 '63

FEILBERT, Ed. See Green, M. jt. auth.

FEIN, Mark
Madam's mark. il por Time 84:34 N 20 '64
Tale of Manhattan. il por Newsweek 64:27 D 7 '64

FEIN, Rashi
Economics of the Nation's health. New Repub 149:7-9 N 9 '63

FEINBERG, Gerald, and Goldhaber, Maurice
Conservation laws of physics; with biographical sketches. Sci Am 209:20, 36-45 bibliog(p 156) O '63

FEINBERG, Mortimer R.
How to measure maturity. Nations Bsns 51: 40-1+ F '63
Manager vs. the self image. Duns R 83:55-6+ F '64
Parent and child. N Y Times Mag p93 O 13 '63
Truth about executive stress. Duns R 84:34-6+ Ag '64

FEININGER, Andreas
Different way of seeing things; excerpt from World through my eyes. il N Y Times Mag p24-5 N 10 '63
Large camera. See issues of Modern photography

FEININGER, Andreas—*Continued*

about

Feininger; photographs from The world through my eyes. H. Keppler. Mod Phot 28:70-1 F '64

Feininger's eye on the world. M. R. Weiss. il Sat R 46:56-8 D 7 '63

FEINSTEIN, Harold
Bumper crop. il por Newsweek 64:72 S 14 '64
Critic's choice. J. Deschin. il Pop Phot 54:114-5+ Ja '64

FEINSTEIN, Herbert
(ed) See Horne, L. Lena Horne speaks freely on race, marriage, stage

FEINSTEIN, Irwin K.
Mastering modern math. PTA Mag 59:19-22 bibliog(p37) S '64

FEINSTEIN, Otto
Disarmament: economic effects. bibliog f Cur Hist 47:81-7 Ag '64
Security and instability. Sat R 46:15-16 My 4 '63

FEISAL, king of Saudi Arabia
Acting for the king. por Newsweek 63:47 Ap 13 '64
Arabian nights tale launches 1,001 fights. il pors Life 54:42 Mr 22 '63
Brother act. por Newsweek 63:34 Ja 13 '64
Crown prince. por Newsweek 64:50+ N 16 '64
Faisal modernizes but with caution. D. Z. Schmidt. il pors N Y Times Mag p38+ N 1 '64
Our Yemen policy: pursuit of a mirage. P. Horton. il por Reporter 29:29-34 O 24 '63
Out of the Arabian nights into the 20th century. il por U S News 55:83-4 N 25 '63
Reformer replaces a big spender. por U S News 56:16 Ap 13 '64
Where a friend of the West runs things now. por U S News 57:20 N 16 '64

FEISS, Julian W.
Minerals; with biographical sketch. Sci Am 209:26, 128-36 bibliog(p307) S '63

FEITELSON, B. J.
Relocation of big mains. Am City 79:108-10 Mr '64

FEITEN, James B. See Hays, D. F. jt. auth.

FELBER, Linda
I believe. por Seventeen 23:177 N '64

FELD, Bernard T.
Nonproliferation of nuclear weapons. Bul Atomic Sci 20:2-6 D '64

FELDBRILL, Victor
Victor Feldbrill, conductor Winnipeg symphony, Canada. E. Helm. por Mus Am 83:13 My '63

FELDMAN, Harold
Oswald and the FBI. Nation 198:86-9 Ja 27 '64

FELDMAN, Irving
Artist and model; poem. Poetry 102:155-60 Je '63
Double; poem. New Yorker 40:52 S 26 '64
Learning poems. Commentary 37:76-7 Ja '64
Little lullaby. New Yorker 40:51 S 12 '64
Portrait de femme, after Picasso; poem. New Yorker 40:188 Ap 25 '64
Scene of a summer morning; poem. New Yorker 40:26 Ag 8 '64

FELDMAN, Morton
Feldman and Brown. Mus Am 83:33-4 N '63

FELDMAN, Myer
Man to see on business issues. por Bsns W p50+ Jl 13 '63

FELDMAN, William H.
Veterinary medicine advances human medicine; excerpts from address. Todays Health 41:12+ N '63

FELDSPAR
Maskelynite: formation by explosive shock. D. J. Milton and P. S. De Carli. bibliog il Science 140:670-1 My 10 '63

FELIG, Philip, and others
Protein-bound iodine in serum of rats breathing 99 percent oxygen. bibliog Science 145:601 Ag 7 '64

FELIPE de Jesus, Saint
Felipe. J. A. Magner. America 108:584+ Ap 20 '63

FELISCH, Hans Schwab-. See Schwab-Felisch, H.

FELIX, Christopher
Modern spy extends his arena. N Y Times Mag p24+ Je 9 '63

FELIX, Robert H.
Community mental health center, a new concept. Arch Rec 134:162-4 N '63

FELKEL, Herbert
Mother's day thoughts. Hobbies 68:55 My '63

FELKNER, Myrtle
How we get dad in on the fun. Farm J 87:77+ Ap '63
When mom goes over the hill. Farm J 88:71+ My '64

FELLIG, Arthur
They tried to match Weegee. il Pop Phot 53:68-9+ Jl '63
What did Weegee do? il Pop Phot 52:56-7 F '63

FELLINI, Federico
Disturber of the peace: interview, ed. by G. Bachmann. pors Mlle 60:152-3+ N '64
Dizzy doings on a set; making of movie, 8½. il pors Life 55:95-7 Jl 19 '63
La dolce far niente. il por Time 81:46 Mr 1 '63
Fellini's La dolce italia. J. J. Navone. Commonweal 77:639-41 Mr 15 '63
Free. New Yorker 39:19-20 Jl 6 '63
From ½ through 8½. H. Alpert. il N Y Times Mag p20-1 Jl 21 '63
What Fellini thinks Mastroianni thinks about women. Vogue 142:50-1+ Ag 15 '63

FELLOWES, Daisy
Daisy Fellowes. J. Pope-Hennessy. por Vogue 143:148-9+ My '64

FELLOWS, Bob
Tornado danced like a dust devil. Life 57:51+ O 16 '64
(ed) See Crosby, K. and Dumas, J. We got to hang on

FELLOWS, Edwin J. See Tedeschi, D. H. jt. auth.

FELLOWSHIP of reconciliation
Churchmen defend the F.O.R; tax-exempt status. Christian Cent 80:733 Je 5 '63
Faith without works? Commonweal 78:238 My 24 '63
F.O.R. wins its tax appeal. Christian Cent 81:877 Jl 8 '64
Revenue service revokes F.O.R.'s tax status. Christian Cent 80:357-8 Mr 20 '63
What price peace? Newsweek 61:28-9 My 27 '63

FELONY. See Criminal law

FELSENSTEIN, Walter
Midas across the wall; Komische oper. por Time 82:70+ O 18 '63

FELSON, Benjamin
Hearts too good to die. Esquire 61:160 My '64

FELT, Harry Donald
Vietnam victory in three years? por U S News 54:16 F 11 '63

FELT, Thomas E.
Stephen A. Douglas letters in the State historical library. Hobbies 69:110-12+ Ag '64

FELTRINELLI, Giangiacomo
Giangiacomo Feltrinelli: Italian publisher-bookseller pioneers to new book markets. P. J. Rosenwald. il por Pub W 185:56-60 F 3 '64
Total recall. il por Newsweek 63:59 Ap 27 '64

FEMININE mystique; story. See Cousins, M.

FEMINISM. See Woman—Equal rights; Woman—Social and moral questions

FEMUR
Femoral expansion in aging women: implications for osteoporosis and fractures. R. W. Smith, jr. and R. R. Walker. bibliog il Science 145:156-7 Jl 10 '64

FEN, Sing-nan
Mary S. Peake, 1823-62. bibliog f Sch & Soc 91:171-2 Ap 6 '63

FENCES (receivers of stolen property) See Stealing

FENCES
Back up your planting. J. B. Brimer. il Flower Grower 50:30-1 S '63
Design yourself a colorful, different kind of fence. il Bet Hom & Gard 41:57 S '63
Fence for you to build. il Flower Grower 50:53 Je '63
Fences. C. B. Lees. il Horticulture 42:30-3 N '64
Fences; a portfolio of ideas for gardens. J. R. Rebhan. il Pop Gard 14:68-71 My '63
Four fine fences. il Bet Hom & Gard 42:31+ Mr '64
Four fine fences. il Bet Hom & Gard 41:42+ Je '63
How are you fixed for privacy? il Bet Hom & Gard 41:68-9 My '63
I'm against fences! E. H. Logsdon. il Farm J 89:50H Ja '65
Landscape with fences. il Pop Gard 15:35-8 Mr '64
More Japanese ideas cross the Pacific sodegaki or sleeve fence. il Sunset 130:77 F '63
Plant a fence. il House & Gard 125:154-7 Mr '64
Playful and colorful. il Sunset 130:102-3 Je '63

FENCES—*Continued*
Rail fences. T. S Buie. il Am For 70:44-6 O '64
Role of the garden screen-fence. il Sunset 132:173 My '64
Screens and fences are for adornment too! il Am Home 67:32+ Mr '64
These fences do not fence you in. il Sunset 131:60-1 Ag '63
They used lumber in slender strips. il Sunset 132:116 Ap '64
This garden court keeps changing; portable, free-standing screens. il Sunset 133:145 O '64
This long fence gives privacy, and it's a garden art display. il Sunset 130:230-1 Mr '63
To make a bamboo fence: you simply tie it together. il Sunset 131:100-1 N '63
What you should know about the law on fences. H. W. Hannah. Suc Farm 62:10 O '64
You can make a lattice fence. W. B. Egan. il Flower Grower 50:22 Jl '63

FENCES, Electric
Electric fence charger. L. E. Greenlee. il Pop Electr 21:57-60+ D '64

FENCING
En garde! U.S. collegiate fencing. il Time 83:82 Ap 3 '64
Squeak! you got me; plunger-tipped foils make fencing safe for small musketeers. il Life 57:133-4 O 2 '64
See also
Dueling

FENDELL, Bob
Fiberglass futures. Motor T 16:96-101+ N '64

FENDER, Derek H.
Control mechanisms of the eye; with biographical sketch. Sci Am 211:14, 24-33 bibliog(p 142) Jl '64

FÉNELON, François de
Fénelon: Christian educator. M. W. Hess. Christian Cent 82:16-17 Ja 6 '65

FENICHEL, Carl
Approach to the severely disturbed child; League school, Brooklyn. H. S. Arnstein. il por N Y Times Mag p 119-20 O 6 '63

FENNELL, Desmond
Goodbye to summer. Nat R 14:273-8 Ap 9 '63

FENNELL, Raven, and Storm, Bruce
Printmaking. Sch Arts 64:27-9 N '64

FENNELLY, Catherine
Staffordshire on American tables: the Collamore evidence. Antiques 84:75-9 Jl '63

FENNELLY, Donald J.
On the judging of mince pies. Harvard Bsns R 42:77-86 N '64

FENNER, Mildred Sandison
Editor's notebook. See issues of NEA journal

FENNER, Phyllis
Bringing books to children. Library J 88:4823-5 D 15 '63
Three cheers for children's book week. Horn Bk 39:486-9 O '63

FENSTERMAKER, Vesle
Dividing line; story. Redbook 123:54-5 Jl '64

FENTON, Frank
Why is it all so lousy? Esquire 59:46+ F '63

FENTON, Richard
Olympic training in southern California. Yachting 115:44-5+ Je '64

FENTON, Ronald S.
Where we stand with water desalting. UNESCO Courier 17:28-31 Jl '64

FENWICK, Charles G.
Books. Américas 16:38 Jl '64
International law: old and new. por Américas 15:26-9 S '63

FENWICK, M. L. and others
Replication of the RNA of bacteriophage R17. bibliog Science 146:527-30 O 23 '64

FENWICK, Sara I. and Batchelor, L. L.
Library service for the teacher. pors ALA Bul 57:129-30 F '63

FENYVESI, Charles T. See Tallet, J. jt. auth.

FEODOROV, Leonid
Exarch Leonid Feodorov, by P. Mailleux. Review
America 111:52 Jl 11 '64. M. F. Meyers

FEOKTISTOV, Konstantin
See also
Space flight—Manned flights—Komarov-Yegorov-Feoktistov flight, 1964

FERBER, Edna
Kind of magic. por McCalls 90:82-5+ Ag; 92-3+ S; 91:106-7+ O; 128-9+ N '63
about
Glimpses of a half-century. por Time 82:90 S 6 '63

FERDINAND, Sister Mary. See Mary Ferdinand, Sister

FERDON, Edwin N. jr
Polynesian origins. bibliog Science 141:499-505; 142:1255-6 Ag 9, D 6 '63

FERGASON, James L.
Liquid crystals. Sci Am 211:76-82+ Ag '64

FERGUSON, Charles A.
Language study and the Middle East. Ann Am Acad 356:76-85 N '64

FERGUSON, Charles W.
Abecedarian book; excerpts. PTA Mag 59:15 N '64

FERGUSON, D. E. See Chetham-Strode, A. jt. auth.

FERGUSON, Donald C. and Fisher, A. E.
Behavior disruption in cebus monkeys as a function of injected substances. bibliog Science 139:1281-2 Mr 29 '63

FERGUSON, Eugene S.
Origins of the steam engine; with biographical sketch. Sci Am 210:20, 98-107 bibliog(p 152) Ja '64

FERGUSON, Gerald
Gerald Ferguson: art director of a science magazine. C. Weiss. il por Am Artist 27:42-7+ Je '63

FERGUSON, John H.
Blood clotting: enzymic activation. Science 144:1159 My 29 '64

FERGUSON, Joseph T.
Ohio puts the personal touch. por Am City 78:113-14 Mr '63

FERGUSON, Ken
Ontario's Bruce: blue heart of the Great Lakes. Motor B 114:42-3+ Jl '64
Trailer down to New Orleans. Motor B 113:84-5+ Ja '64
Trailer your boat and tent to Florida. Motor B 12:36-9 D '63

FERGUSON, Lawrence L.
Social scientists in the plant. Harvard Bsns R 42:133-43 My '64

FERGUSON library, Stamford, Conn.
Ferguson library entrance ramp commended by architecture group. il Library J 88:4603 D 1 '63

FERKISS, Victor C.
After colonialism: the shock of what freedom means. Commonweal 79:464 Ja 17 '64
Breakdown in the Congo. Commonweal 81:325-8 N 27 '64
Myth of Communist solidarity. Cath World 199:159-66 Je '64
Pacem in terris: an opening to the left? Cath World 198:100-8 N '63
Pressures on South Africa. Commonweal 79:591-4 F 14 '64
Struggle over foreign aid. America 108:488-90 Ap 13 '63

FERLACH, Austria
Co-op works for craftsmen; Cooperative of master gunmakers of Ferlach. il Bsns W p24-5 D 28 '63

FERLINGHETTI, Lawrence
Seven poets and a playwright. D. Stuart. Poetry 104:261-2 Jl '64

FERM, Deane William
Time has come. bibliog f Christian Cent 81:903-6 Jl 15 '64

FERM, Vergil H.
Congenital malformations in hamster embryos after treatment with vinblastine and vincristine. bibliog Science 141:426 Ag 2 '63
—and Kilham, Lawrence
Congenital anomalies induced in hamster embryos with H-1 virus. bibliog Science 145:510-11 Jl 31 '64

FERMENTATION
See also
Enzymes

FERMI award
Atomic energy award to Oppenheimer. Sr Schol 82:19 My 1 '63
Brotherly spirit. il Newsweek 62:54 D 16 '63
Doctor Oppenheimer honored. Sci N L 83:243 Ap 20 '63
Fermi award: Rickover honored: selection signals some changes. J. Walsh. Science 146:1149-50 N 27 '64
Fermi prize: J. Robert Oppenheimer named to receive annual AEC award. H. Bethe. Science 140:161-3 Ap 12 '63
Fermi prize money: congressional committee takes steps to assume control of annual $50,000 award. D. S. Greenberg. Science 143:1305 Mr 20 '64; Reply. D. O. Walter. 144:796 My 15 '64
Honors for Oppenheimer; but security cloud remains. il U S News 55:26 D 16 '63
Oppenheimer play. Nat R 14:307+ Ap 23 '63
Oppie's comeback. Newsweek 61:28-9 Ap 15 '63
Rehabilitation? case of R. J. Oppenheimer. Nation 196:317 Ap 20 '63

FERMI award—*Continued*
Tangled drama and private hells of two famous scientists. R. Coughlan. il Life 55:87A-94+ D 13 '63
Warless world? presentation of medal to J. R. Oppenheimer. Sci N L 84:375 D 14 '63

FERMI surfaces
Fermi surface of metals. A. R. Mackintosh. il Sci Am 209:110-20 Jl '63
High-field galvanomagnetic properties of metals. W. A. Reed and E. Fawcett. bibliog il Science 146:603-10 O 30 '64

FERMOR, Patrick Leigh
Rock monasteries of Cappadocia; excerpt from A time to keep silence. Horizon 6:66-73 Wint '64

FERMOR, Sophia
Background of a conversation piece. E. Gaines. il Antiques 85:578-9 My '64

FERNAND Point's Restaurant de la Pyramide, Vienne. See Restaurants—France

FERNANDES, Helio
Prickliest pundit. por Time 82:62-3 Ag 9 '63

FERNÁNDEZ, Julio César
Henri Bergson's message. Américas 15:10-12 Ag '63
Phantom war of 1804. Américas 15:23-8 Je '63

FERNANDEZ, Justo
Mexican empire builder. il por Bsns W p 142-4 Je 20 '64

FERNANDEZ, Manuel A.
Fernandez wins 1963 Reynolds student prize. il por Arch Rec 133:29 Mr '63

FERNANDINA BEACH, Fla.
Florida casts its bread; marine welcome station and 40-yacht marina. il Bsns W p98-9 F 16 '63

FERNANDO, Quintus, and others
Metal chelates in analytical chemistry. Science 143:491-2+ Ja 31 '64

FERNELIUS, Byrne C.
Recruitment factors. Recreation 57:527 D '64

FERNOW, Bernhard Eduard
Fernow, the man who brought forestry to America. C. E. Randall. por Am For 70:14-16+ Ap '64

FERNS
Ameiotic alternation of generations: a new life cycle in the ferns. A. M. Evans. bibliog il Science 143:261-3 Ja 17 '64
Gibberellins: their effect on antheridium formation in fern gametophytes. B. R. Voeller. bibliog il Science 143:373-5 Ja 24 '64
How to grow ferns from spores. il Sunset 131:164 Ag '63
I discovered ferns. H. V. P. Wilson. il Flower Grower 50:38-40+ Mr '63
Marsilea vestita; conversion of the water form to the land form by darkness and by far-red light. J. J. Gaudet. bibliog il Science 140:975-6 My 31 '63
Native ferns. il Sunset 130:204+ Je '63
Squirrel's-foot and bear's-foot. il Sunset 132:264 Je '64
There's variety in indoor ferns. E. F. Steffek. il Pop Gard 14:38-9+ Mr '63
See also
Bird's-nest ferns

FERNSWORTH, Lawrence
Spain: concealed handout. Nation 198:138-40 F 10 '64
Spanish tragedy. Christian Cent 81:1563 D 16 '64

FERRAGALLO, Roger
Every surface has pattern or texture. Sch Arts 63:8-11 Je '64

FERRÉ, Léo
Malady of Paris. por Time 83:100 My 22 '64

FERRE, Luis A.
Science and religion; address, December 18, 1963. Vital Speeches 30:277-9 F 15 '64

FERREDOXIN
Anaerobic formate oxidation: a ferredoxin-dependent reaction. W. J. Brill and others. bibliog il Science 144:297-8 Ap 17 '64
Chemical go-between. Sci N L 83:275 My 4 '63

FERRELL, Jeanne, and Ferrell, Kay
Our point of view of you, Jimmy Wescott. Seventeen 23:42 Ja '64

FERRELL, Kay. See Ferrell, J. jt. auth.

FERRELL, Oliver P.
Bargains by the bagful. Pop Electr 20:49-52 F '64

FERRELL, Orran L.
Loan program that helps you become a doctor. H. Earle. il pors Todays Health 41:36-41 Jl '63

FERREN, John
Middle East squiggle. il por Newsweek 63:56 Ap 13 '64

FERRER, Terry
Rosemary Park: new president of Barnard. Sat R 46:66-8 Ap 20 '63

FERRETS
Our rarest mammal? C. L. Homolka. il Audubon Mag 66:244-6 Jl '64
Pop goes the ferret! B. Gilbert. il Sports Illus 21:98-102+ D 7 '64

FERRICHROME. See Peptides

FERRIES, Charles
Skier on a slope to glory. R. Terrell. il por Sports Illus 18:30-4+ Mr 11 '63

FERRIES
Farewell to the ferry. C. B. Mitchell. il Am Heritage 15:38-49 Ap '64
Ferryboat farewell; Chesapeake Bay ferries. D. W. Ross. il Travel 119:41-3 Ap '63
Foil-borne ferry approved by coast guard. W. H. Koelbel. il Motor B 111:72+ F '63
New route to Alaska; Marine highway. il Travel 119:64 Ap '63
Now a new "highway" to Alaska by sea; Marine highway. K. M. Chrysler. il U S News 54:70-2 Je 24 '63
On air; aboard the Albatross, hydrofoil ferry. American hydrofoil lines. New Yorker 39:19-20 Ag 31 '63
You can still ferry across the Columbia. il Sunset 132:39-40 Ap '64

FERRIL, Thomas Hornsby
New path; poem. Sat R 46:37 F 9 '63
Swallows; poem. Atlan 213:89 F '64
What prudent stewardship? poem. Atlan 214:89 O '64

FERRINI, Vincent
Seven poets and a playwright. D. Stuart. Poetry 104:259-61 Jl '64

FERRIS, Elmer W.
Roses from seed. Horticulture 41:276-7 My '63

FERRIS, Helen
Mrs Roosevelt and children's books. Library J 89:2149-51+ My 15 '64

FERRIS, John
Angelic voice. Opera N 29:26-7 Ja 30 '65
Just how dependable are hog cycles and ratios? Suc Farm 61:55 Mr '63
Man at the Center. Opera N 29:11-13 Ja 16 '65
O ciel! Opera N 28:6-7 Mr 7 '64
Scrap of paper. Opera N 29:6-7 Ja 9 '65

FERRIS, Wayne R. See Zaitlin, M. jt. auth.

FERRITIN
Invertebrate ferritin: occurrence in mollusca. K. M. Towe and others. bibliog il Science 142:63-4 O 4 '63

FERRO, Hellén
New novel in Mexico: a look at Juan Rulfo. Américas 16:40-1 O '64

FERRO corporation
All frit, no fret. il Time 83:92 Ap 24 '64

FERROCARRIL Chihuahua al Pacifico. See Railroads—Mexico

FERROELECTRICITY
Spectroscopy of solids in the far-infrared. M. Tinkham. bibliog il Science 145:240-7 Jl 17 '64

FERROSILITE
Ferrosilite ($FeSiO_3$): synthesis at high pressures and temperatures. D. H. Lindsley and others. bibliog il Science 144:73-4 Ap 3 '64

FERROUS, Bob
New approach to high-frequency measurements. Electr World 72:41-3+ Ag '64

FERROUS sulfate poisoning. See Iron poisoning

FERRY, Alan. See Koella, W. P. jt. auth.

FERRY, Charles A.
George Romney gone bust. New Repub 150:12-15 Ja 25 '64

FERRY, W. H.
What price peace? Bul Atomic Sci 19:19-23 S '63

FERRY, William M.
God with us; poem. Christian Cent 80:1604 D 25 '63

FERRYBOATS. See Ferries

FERSH, Seymour
Materials for teaching about Asia. Sr Schol 83:14T S 27 '63

FERSTER, Charles B.
Arithmetic behavior in chimpanzees; with biographical sketch. Sci Am 210:24, 98-104+ My '64

FERTIG, Lawrence
Who are the unemployed? Read Digest 85:115-16 S '64

FERTIG, Wendell
They fought alone, by J. Keats. Review
Time por 82:72+ Ag 23 '63

FERTILITY, Human
Hormones for fertility. il Time 84:66 O 9 '64
Immune to sperm. il Newsweek 62:80 O 21 '63
New advance in female fertility. I. Taves. il Look 28:91-4+ My 19 '64
Now! many women can have the babies they want. L. David. il Good H 157:79+ O '63

FERTILITY, Plant. See Plants, Sex in
FERTILITY control. See Birth control
FERTILITY of soils. See Soil fertility
FERTILIZATION, Artificial. See Artificial insemination, Human
FERTILIZATION of plants
Evolutionary mechanisms in pollination biology. H. G. Baker. bibliog il Science 139:877-83 Mr 8 '63
Gross-pollination of an orchid; Showy lady's-slipper. H. L. Gibson. il Natur Hist 73:42-3 Ap '64
How science aids our overworked bees. J. W. Poling. il Audubon Mag 65:280-3 S '63
See also
Pollen
FERTILIZER factories
Women crash another field; Svenska salpeterverken, Koping, Sweden. Bsns W p 120 Ag 22 '64
FERTILIZER industry and trade
Fertilizer makes the green grow. il Bsns W p21 Ag 1 '64
Fertilizing the oil business. il Time 82:92 S 20 '63
Head start on red trade; ICI pushing for deals with Russia. il Bsns W p 100+ My 9 '64
Oil's new play: fertilizers; mergers of oil companies with fertilizer companies. Bsns W p28 Ag 17 '63
Spreading fertilizer. il Time 83:73-4 Ja 3 '64
See also
Arizona biochemical company
Wages and hours
Wages in fertilizer plants, April 1962. C. M. O'Connor. il Mo Labor R 86:164-7 F '63
FERTILIZER spreaders
Fertilizer hook-ups that save trips; photographs. Farm J 87:40-1 Mr '63
Have you heard? B. C. Kilvert, jr. il Flower Grower 51:40-1 S '64
Lawn spreaders. il Consumer Rep 28:127-30 Mr '63
Manure odor? plow it under! B. Hardy. il Farm J 88:28-9 D '64
FERTILIZERS and manures
Best way to buy fertilizer? R. Hagen. Farm J 88:44F D '64
Don't forget secondary elements. Suc Farm 61:96 F '63
Feed to keep healthy. P. F. Frese. il Pop Gard 15:56 Ap '64
Fertilize pastures! six reasons why. L. E. Zeman. il Suc Farm 61:46-7 Ag '63
Folklore of steer manure. il Sunset 130:214-18 Je '63
Give old plants a new lease on life. il Pop Gard 14:43 F '63
Good time to apply fertilizer. Suc Farm 61:91 O '63
How range fertilization pays off. Suc Farm 61:82 Je '63
How to figure fertilizer for your garden. il Farm J 88:58F My '64
How to find a market for manure. D. Braun. Farm J 87:80 F '63
How to get soil bank acres back in corn. Farm J 88:45 Ap '64
How to: stretch your fertilizer dollars. L. E. Zeman. il Suc Farm 61:50-1+ O '63
Lawn fertilizing. Horticulture 42:28 Mr '64
Make compost out of comfrey. V. L. Heitmann. il Horticulture 41:456 S '63
Manure odor? plow it under! B. Hardy. il Farm J 88:28-9 D '64
Report on slurry fertilizer. il Suc Farm 61:40 Mr '63
Seventy-five bu. more corn with $15 worth of fertilizer. O. Bay. Farm J 87:46 F '63
Unhappy record of composting. Am City 78:7 D '63
Unlocking soil grow power (cont) il Suc Farm 61:72-3+ F; 70-1+ Mr; 50-1 Ap '63
What to know about plant food. Bet Hom & Gard 42:26 Je '64
See also
Green manuring
Lawns
Nitrates
Peat
Analysis
New fertilizer labels: what they mean. il Suc Farm 62:18 Je '64
Handling
Easy way to handle manure: pump it. L. M. Palmer. il Farm J 88:22-3+ Jl '64
Ideas for handling bulk fertilizer. il Suc Farm 62:58 My '64
Preservation and storage
Build a compost pile now. R. C. Hands. il Horticulture 41:535+ O '63
Composting; its role in European refuse disposal. E. F. Spitzer. il Am City 79:102-5 O '64
Spray applications
How to get the most from a feeding program. B. Hering. il Pop Gard 15:58-9 My '64
New way to apply fertilizer: by air; interview. P. J. Stangel. il Suc Farm 62:38+ Je '64
Spreaders
See Fertilizer spreaders
FESSAS, Phaedon, and Loukopoulos, Dimitris
Alpha-chain of human hemoglobin: occurrence in vivo. bibliog Science 143:590-1 F 7 '64
FESTIVAL International du son. See Audio fairs
FESTIVAL of composers of western Poland. See Musical festivals—Poland
FESTIVAL of two worlds, Spoleto. See Festivals—Italy; Music festivals—Italy
FESTIVAL orchestra society
Musical events; concert performed by Festival orchestra of New York. W. Sargeant. New Yorker 40:143-4 N 7 '64
FESTIVALS
Festivals are communication. Am City 79:144+ My '64
Festivals of the arts. il Am Artist 27:65-9 Ap '63; 28:59-64 Ap '64
Life guide. See issues of Life
1964: a year-long jamboree for wanderers. H. Sutton. il Sat R 47:33-5+ Ja 4 '64
SR/1964-1965 world travel calendar. R. E. Meyer, jr. il Sat R 47:45-50 Ja 4 '64; 48:47-8+ Ja 2 '65
See also
Carnival
Celebrations
Drama festivals
Moving picture festivals
Music festivals
Processions
Shakespeare festivals
Australia
On the go; Moomba festival, Melbourne. L. Barry. il Pop Phot 56:14+ Ja '65
Belgium
Belgium's carnival craze. P. DeMaerel. il Travel 121:44-6 F '64
Brazil
Festival in Penedo. M. Ramos. il Américas 15:32-4 N '63
California
Danish days begin September 20; Solvang's annual festival. il Sunset 131:26 S '63
Fishing fleet parades in Los Angeles harbor. il Sunset 131:34+ S '63
Colorado
Colorado conversion; ski site switches to summer celebration. R. Auletta. il Travel 121:58-9 My '64
Europe, Western
Europe's winter wonders. J. Fanelli. il Travel 122:32-8 N '64
Florida
Poetry, a lively art indeed! Hollywood, Fla. annual poetry night. P. J. Heneghan and J. Justice. il Recreation 57:504-5 D '64
India
Grand salaam. R. Joseph. il Esquire 59:84-7 Je '63
Italy
Happy ending in Spoleto; world première of Nureyev's Raymonda. Newsweek 64:75 Jl 20 '64
Louisiana
Crawfish capital celebrates. il Bsns W p30-1 Ap 25 '64
Maryland
Banner festival. Travel 122:29 Jl '64
Spain
Fiesta of Pamplona. R. Trout. il Atlan 211:142+ Mr '63
Tennessee
Dream of spring; Dogwood arts festival, Knoxville, Tenn. A. Black. il Recreation 56:62-3 F '63

FESTIVALS—*Continued*

Texas

Crop that never fails us; sixth Autumn trials festival, Winnsboro; ed. by J. D. Boyd. C. Spivey. il Farm J 88:36-7+ N '64
Stetsons and sausage at home on the range. il Bsns W p30-1 N 14 '64

United States

Life guide (cont) il Life 54:6 F 15; 16 Mr 8; 10 Ap 12; 25 Ap 19; 12 Ap 26; 20 My 3; 17 My 10 '63
Summer festivals. J. Ciardi. Sat R 46:12-13 O 5; 14 O 12; 12+ O 19 '63

Washington (state)

Seafair: August fun and foolery in Seattle. il Sunset 131:18+ Ag '63

Wyoming

Cheyenne's seven wild and woolly days in July; Frontier days celebration. il Bsns W p22-3 Ag 3 '63
Notes for a gazetteer; Cheyenne frontier days festival. P. Hamburger. New Yorker 39: 152+ N 16 '63

FETAL erythroblastosis. See Erythroblastosis

FETH, G. C.
Nonlinear magnetics and superconductivity. Science 145:838 Ag 21 '64

FETUS
Fetal death from nicotinamide-deficient diet and its prevention by chlorpromazine and imipramine. I. Fratta and others. bibliog il Science 145:1429-30 S 25 '64
Fetal homeostasis; report on first of a projected series of conferences on fetal homeostasis. R. M. Wynn. Science 146:1080+ N 20 '64
How your unborn baby is nourished. V. Apgar. Redbook 124:24-5+ Ja '65
Ontogeny of the immune response. A. M. Silverstein. bibliog Science 144:1423-8 Je 19 '64
Unborn baby's movements. C. L. Buxton. Redbook 123:32+ Ag '64

FEUER, Cy
Broadway's hottest producers. il por Bsns W p90-1 F 2 '63

FEUER, Lewis S.
Dilemma of the Soviet intellectual. N Y Times Mag p 13+ Ag 18 '63
From freedom's herald to prophet in chains; excerpt from The scientific intellectual. Sat R 46:42-3 Jl 6 '63
Jews in the Soviet Union. New Repub 149: 11-12 N 30 '63

FEUERLICHT, Roberta Strauss
God and man at Flushing Meadow. Reporter 31:54+ Ag 13 '64
Murder that started World war I. Sat Eve Post 237:80-1+ Je 27 '64

FEUERMANN, Emanuel
In memoriam: Emanuel Feuermann (1902-1942) J. Lyons. Am Rec G 30:228 N '63

FEVER
See also
Dengue

FEVER ticks. See Ticks

FEY, Harold E.
Clear light on church-state relations. Christian Cent 80:735-6 Je 5 '63
N.C.C. reorganizes. Christian Cent 80:1602-4 D 25 '63
Radical reconciler. Christian Cent 81:211 F 12 '64
Russians visit the U.S. Christian Cent 80: 326-7 Mr 13 '63
Separationists confer. Christian Cent 81:166-7 F 5 '64
Statesman of stature. Christian Cent 81:938 Jl 22 '64

about

Announcement. F. Hoskins. Christian Cent 81:134 Ja 29 '64
Announcement. K. Haselden. Christian Cent 81:1078 S 2 '64
In newness of life. M. E. Marty. Christian Cent 81:1071 Ag 26 '64
Switch at Century. Time 83:77 Mr 20 '64

FEYOCK, Jack
Technical books and their sale examined at Denver ABA meeting; summary of address. por Pub W 184:31 N 11 '63

FIALKA, Ladislav
Prague pantomime theatre, Philharmonic Hall. J. Maskey. Dance Mag 38:28-9 O '64

FIAT company. See Automobile industry and trade—Italy

FIBEL, Lewis R.
Getting ahead; questions and answers. See issues of Popular science monthly

FIBER board
Fancy hardboard. M. Banister. il Pop Mech 120:173-8 N '63
Putting waste to work. il Bsns W p 137-8 Mr 23 '63

FIBER glass. See Glass fibers

FIBER glass boats. See Boats—Materials

FIBER optics
Experiment in fiber optics. R. E. Pafenberg. il Pop Electr 19:41-4+ Ag '63
Focus on fiber optics. H. E. Klein. il Duns R 81:75-6+ My '63
Sceptron; a sound-operated fiber-optic brain cell. L. S. Balandis. il Electr World 69: 36-7+ Mr '63

FIBER tipped pens. See Pens

FIBERGLASS. See Glass fibers

FIBERGLASS boatbuilding. See Boatbuilding

FIBERGLASS cars. See Automobiles—Materials

FIBERS
See also
Glass fibers

FIBICH, Felix
Judith and Felix Fibich and company, the Brooklyn museum. J. Maskey. Dance Mag 38:74 Ap '64

FIBICH, Judith
Judith and Felix Fibich and company, the Brooklyn museum. J. Maskey. Dance Mag 38:74 Ap '64

FIBRINOGEN
Paracrystalline forms of fibrinogen. C. Cohen and others. bibliog il Science 141:436-8 Ag 2 '63

FIBROBLASTS. See Cells

FIBROSIS, Cystic. See Cystic fibrosis

FICHTER, George S.
Green turtles: tasty treasures of the sea. Read Digest 82:212C-212D+ F '63

FICHTER, Joseph H.
Church attendance. America 108:832-4 Je 8 '63
Father Fichter at Harvard. America 111:647 N 21 '64

FICHTNER, Joseph A.
Our local dialogue. Cath World 196:285-91 F '63

FICKLE goddess; story. See Plagemann, B.

FICTION
Big bite. N. Mailer. Esquire 59:23-4+ Je '63
Books. M. Muggeridge. Esquire 63:24+ Ja '65
Exercise in extremity. R. Kiely. Nation 196: 549-50 Je 29 '63
Fiction, the publisher's Cinderella-child. L. Meyer. Pub W 184:53-4 S 23 '63
Modern novel in Britain and the United States, by W. Allen. Review
Sat R 47:35 Je 20 '64. H. T. Moore
New kitsch. C. Hemley. Sat R 47:36-7 D 5 '64
Off the cuff. A. Marple. Writer 76:5-6 Jl '63
Setting your literary goals. C. Mercer. Writer 76:10-11+ Mr '63
Sex, crime, and, to a lesser extent, sports; excerpt from Now, Barrabas. W. Jovanovich. il Sat R 47:14-17+ Jl 18 '64
Teenage novel. V. J. MacQuown; V. Westphal. Library J 89:1832-5 Ap 15 '64
Vanishing novel. H. Kubly. Sat R 47:12-15+ My 2 '64
We represent the library's interest: 19th century fiction of US and Britain; Tom Fool publishing company, Allagash, Me. Library J 89:4871 D 15 '64
What's missing in the novel. L. Marshall. Sat R 46:15-16 F 9 '63
See also
Characters in literature
Christmas stories
Detective and mystery stories
Negroes in literature
Plots (drama, novel, etc)
Politics in literature
Realism in literature
Science fiction
Sex in literature
Short stories
Temperance in literature
also American fiction; Indian fiction (East Indian) etc; *also* subhead Fiction under various subjects, e.g. Baseball—Fiction

Advertising

See Books—Advertising

Appreciation and interpretation

See Literature—Appreciation and interpretation

Bibliography

Fiction. W. B. Hill. America 108:678-80; 109: 682-3+; 110:635+; 111:717-19+ My 11, N 23 '63, My 9, N 28 '64

FICTION—Bibliography—*Continued*
Instant guide to quality reading; recent novels of quality. T. Foote. Life 56:8+ Je 26 '64
Survey of recent fiction. Commentary 36:488-92+ D '63
Competitions
Four organizations join in fiction award program. Pub W 185:43 Je 1 '64
Rights and permissions; Novel award program. P. Nathan. Pub W 185:62 Je 1 '64
Rights and permissions; William Heinemann, ltd, Corgi books and Columbia pictures corporation offering award in England. P. Nathan. Pub W 186:68 N 16 '64
Three publishers and movie company join in literary talent search; Novel award program. Library J 89:2571 Je 15 '64
Psychology
See Literature—Psychology
Technique
Advice can be dangerous. W. Brown. Writer 78:19-21 Ja '65
And where do you get your ideas? R. W. Wells. Writer 77:24-5+ Ja '64
Background as plus-value. G. Amoury. Writer 76:19-20+ S '63
Background vs. setting. D. J. Marlowe. Writer 76:12-13+ F '63
Beginning and the middle of your story. F. A. Rockwell. Writer 76:13-16+ O '63
Category novel. I. Moore. Writer 77:9-13 S '64
Coconut on top. F. E. Randall. Writer 77:15-17 Ag '64
Contrast. B. Roer. Writer 77:23-4 Je '64
Control of character. R. Savage. Writer 76: 7-9 Ag '63
Creative energy and fiction writing. R. McKenna. Writer 76:7-9+ Je '63
Crossing the river of time. M. J. Waldo. Writer 76:7-9 Ap '63
Don't lick the stamp yet. B. Robinson. Writer 76:11-13+ S '63
Don't start with too much. K. Kay. Writer 76:10-13 Ap '63
Don't wait to write your novel. E. E. Tigue. Writer 76:25-6 S '63
Eighteen checkpoints for your story. J. Z. Owen. Writer 77:11-15 Ap '64
Empathy unlimited. E. Pearson. Writer 76: 25-6 F '63
Expand or contract? E. Lee. Writer 76:18-20+ D '63
Fifty self-starters for fiction writers; excerpts from Writing short stories for pleasure and profit. M. Gavin. Writer 77:11-13+ F '64
Four rules for the short story. S. W. Taylor. Writer 76:7-9 F '63
Fresh fresh fresh eye. M. Williams. Writer 76:13-14+ Ag '63
How to make an idea work A. Dewlen. Writer 76:18-19 Ag '63
How to plot your story. E. S. Fox. Writer 76:21-4+ D '63
How to write a novel. S. Cloete. Writer 77: 9-10 Jl '64
I remember Androcles. E. Jensen. Writer 77:7-10 Ap '64
I would not coddle the child. J. Beatty and P. Beatty. il Horn Bk 40:149-52 Ap '64
If it's shocking, will it sell? E. G. Patterson. Writer 76:17-19 Jl '63
Irving Wallace bends some rules; interview, ed. by M. Manheim. I. Wallace. Writer 78:12-15+ Ja '65
Is fiction here to stay? address, June 4, 1963. M. Cousins. Writer 77:9-15 Ja '64
It pays to write confession stories. H. Withrow. Writer 77:17-21 F '64
Largely about my dog. R. F. Young. Writer 76:13-14+ Je '63
Meanwhile, back at the plot. . . . W. Walden. Sat R 48:19-20 Ja 2 '65
My three-hundred-pound ballerina. H. Ware. Writer 76:7-9+ O '63
New venture, a new beginning. D. Walker. Writer 77:9-11+ Ag '64
Novelist and his theme. T. C. Turner. Writer 76:12-14+ D '63
Novelist's dilemma. R. G. Kelly. Writer 76: 7-9+ Mr '63
Of style and the stylist. E. Cameron. Horn Bk 40:25-32 F '64
Off the cuff; questions and answers. A. Marple. Writer 77:6-8 Je '64
On words, singleness of mind, and the genius loci. M. Benary-Isbert. Horn Bk 40:202-9 Ap '64
Oysters and a novelist's art. J. Wain. New Repub 151:23-4 Ag 8 '64
Plausibility. V. Thiessen. Writer 76:21-3+ O '63
Plot blueprints. F. A. Rockwell. Writer 77: 16-21 My '64
Psychology of creative writing. E. A. Craig. Writer 76:15-17 Ag '63
Quality and opinion. S. Epstein. Writer 76: 7-9+ Jl '63
Setting and background in the novel. M. Stewart. Writer 77:7-9 D '64
Something worth publishing. M. Mather. Writer 76:7-10+ S '63
Tell me more. W. Wolfe. Writer 77:17-18 S '64
That certain feeling. G. Taber. Writer 77: 14-16 F '64
Touchstone in writing fiction. S. Epstein. Writer 77:9-11+ O '64
Trouble with trouble. R. A. Knowlton. Writer 76:15-16+ Je '63
Use threefold magic; build suspense into your story. J. Z. Owen. Writer 77:18-20+ O '64
Variety is the spice of writing. R. Armor. Writer 76:18-9 N '63
View from upstairs porch. S. F. Ciulla. Writer 76:9-11 N '63
What about flashbacks? E. S. Fox. Writer 77:16-18 N '64
What is a secret? G. H. Freitag. Writer 77:26-7 Mr '64
When the writer comes of age. B. J. Chute. Writer 76:10-14 My '63
Where do you start? C. Edwards. Writer 77: 20-2+ D '64
Where does a story begin? L. Egri. Writer 77:15 N '64
Writers, speak now! excerpt from Creating fiction from experience. P. S. Curry. Writer 77:7-10 F '64
Writing the episodic novel. R. White. Writer 77:9-12 My '64
You write what you are. N. M. Stewart. Writer 76:25 Ap '63
See also
Characterization
Description (rhetoric)
Detective and mystery stories—Technique
Dialogue
Fiction in periodicals and newspapers
Short stories
Themes
See Literature—Themes
FICTION, Religious. See Religious literature
FICTION contests. See Fiction—Competitions
FICTION for children. See Childrens literature
FICTION in libraries. See Libraries—Fiction collections
FICTION in periodicals and newspapers
New look in Adventure. A. Norton. Writer 77:26-7 F '64
Slick clinic. R. Eng. Writer 76:10-12 Je '63
Those magic one-liners. E. Jensen. Writer 78:9-11 Ja '65
When Redbook looks for stories. B. Blakemore. Writer 77:26 D '64
Writing the episodic novel. R. White. Writer 77:9-12 My '64
FICUS. See Figs
FIDDLEHEAD greens. See Greens, Edible
FIDDLER on the roof: musical comedy. See Musical comedies, revues, etc.—Criticisms, plots, etc.
FIDDLERSBURG preacher; story. See Warren, R. P.
FIDELIAN, Brother
Christian schools, secular subjects. Commonweal 81:566-8+ Ja 29 '65
FIDELIO; opera. See Beethoven, L. van
FIDELIS, Sister Maria. See Maria Fidelis, Sister
FIDELITY bonds. See Insurance, Surety and fidelity
FIEDLER, Arthur
Let them listen, they may love it. Am Home 67:18+ S '64
Younger than springtime. il por Time 83:69 Je 26 '64
FIEDLER, Leslie A.
Race, the dream & the nightmare; excerpts from Waiting for the end. Commentary 36: 297-304 O '63
FIEDLER, Lore
New Jersey's Green Acres program. Am For 70:40-2 Je '64
FIEGHT, J. J. See Shurtleff, M. jt. auth.
FIELD, Betty
Out islands are in. Vogue 141:132-4+ F 15 '63
FIELD, Carolyn
Children's libraries. Wilson Lib Bul 37:885 Je '63
Criteria and the individual. Horn Bk 40:527-9 O '64
Library 21: what was its meaning? Library J 88:831 F 15 '63

FIELD, Edward
Tulips and addresses; poem. New Yorker 39: 47 Ap 27 '63
about
Sly natural. G. Conover. Nation 197:303-4 N 9 '63

FIELD, Elinor Whitney
Chapters from Horn book history. Horn Bk 39:327-30 Je '63

FIELD, Erastus Salisbury
Eighth wonder of Erastus Field. F. B. Robinson. il Am Heritage 14:12-17 Ap '63
Erastus Salisbury Field and the sources of his inspiration. M. C. Black. il Antiques 83:201-6 F '63

FIELD, Jane Taylor
What the books don't tell you. NEA J 53:58-9 O '64

FIELD, Marshall, 1893-1956
Marshall Field III, by S. Becker. Review
New Repub 151:22-3 Jl 11 '64. J. Luskin.

FIELD, Marshall, Jr
Second city empire. il por Newsweek 63:88 My 11 '64

FIELD, Rosamond
Pumpkin; poem. Nation 198:401 Ap 20 '64

FIELD, Shirley Anne
On screen. R. Gutwillig. por Horizon 5:36-7 Mr '63

FIELD, Winston
Another tea party? Newsweek 63:53-4 Ap 27 '64

FIELD, Magnetic. See Magnetic field

FIELD and stream fishing contest. See Fishing—Competitions

FIELD emission
Advances in field emission. W. P. Dyke. il Sci Am 210:108-16+ bibliog(p 152) Ja '64

FIELD enterprises, incorporated
Second city empire. il Newsweek 63:88 My 11 '64

FIELD enterprises educational corporation
Field enterprises sues Childrens press. Pub W 184:247 Ag 26 '63
New firms seek astronaut story rights. A. P. Alibrando. Aviation W 79:28-9 Jl 15 '63
Publisher drops offer for astronauts' stories. Pub W 184:28 Jl 22 '63
Scrubbed on the pad; concerning publicizing personal stories of astronauts. Time 82:40 Jl 19 '63
Unfair competition charged in encyclopedia suit; suit against Publishers company, inc, of Washington. Pub W 186:50 N 16 '64

FIELD experiments (agriculture)
Test-plot farming pays off. R. J. Reiman. il Suc Farm 62:36-7 Je '64

FIELD glasses
Clear views on your binoculars. R. J. Reichert and E. Reichert. il Audubon Mag 66: 115-17 Mr '64
Get the most out of your binoculars. E. Robberson. il Yachting 115:57-9+ Mr '64
More phony binocular advertising. il Consumer Bul 46:27 Ag '63
Prism binoculars; Japanese glasses. il Consumer Bul 47:30-3 Ap; 30-4 My '64
Your leisure (cont) Consumer Rep 28:301-4 D '63

FIELD service, American. See American field service

FIELD sports. See Track athletics

FIELD trials (dogs)
Back-course mystery. D. M. Duffey. il Outdoor Life 134:138-40+ S '64
Casey and his cougar run over California. V. Kraft. il Sports Illus 19:67-8 N 25 '63
English springer national trial. D. M. Duffey. il Outdoor Life 133:138-40+ Mr '64
Finding new fun in the fields. V. Kraft. il Sports Illus 18:52+ Je 10 '63
Golden retriever trial. D. M. Duffey. il Outdoor Life 131:94-7 Ja '63
Gun dogs; ed. by J. Stetson. See issues of Field & stream
National retriever championship. D. M. Duffey. il Outdoor Life 135:134-8 F '65
One lady who gives a Continental; field trials for pointing dogs. V. Kraft. Sports Illus 18:43 F 18 '63
Rise of goldens. J. Stetson. il Field & S 68: 96-7 D '63
Shooting dog championship. D. M. Duffey. il Outdoor Life 131:122-5 Je '63; 133:164-6+ My '64
U.S. chicken championship. D. M. Duffey. il Outdoor Life 131:128-30+ F '63

FIELD trips, Educational. See School excursions

FIELD trips, Geological. See Geology—Study and teaching

FIELD trips, Historical. See History—Study and teaching

FIELD trips, Nature study. See Nature study

FIELDEN, John
What do you mean I can't write? Harvard Bsns R 42:144-8+ My '64

FIELDEN, John S.
For better business writing. bibliog f Harvard Bsns R 43:164-6+ Ja '65

FIELDER, Gilbert
Some lunar studies by T. G. Elger. Sky & Tel 25:248-51 My '63

FIELDING, Byron
De facto segregation. NEA J 53:11-14 My '64

FIELDING, Gabriel, pseud. See Barnsley, A. G.

FIELDING, Henry
Henry Fielding: the journey through Gin Lane. J. H. Plumb. il por Horizon 6:74-83 Wint '64

FIELDING-JONES, Frances
Camp season's coming. Parents Mag 38:68-9+ Mr '63

FIELDING'S progress; story. See Rogin, G.

FIELDS, James Thomas
Parnassus corner, by W. S. Tryon. Review
Atlan 214:131-2 Jl '64
Pub W il por 184:26-30 Jl 29 '63. J. T. Winterich
Time por 82:116+ O 11 '63

FIELDS, Stanley
Egypt's antiquities. Travel 123:30-5 Ja '65

FIENE, Ernest
Cover. il Am Artist 28:4+ Je '64

FIFIELD, Vi
Time to write. Writer 77:28-9 O '64

FIFTH avenue, New York. See New York (city)—Streets

FIFTH street gym, Miami Beach, Fla. See Gymnasiums

FIFTY books of the year exhibit. See Book exhibits

FIGHTER planes. See Airplanes, Military

FIGHTING (psychology)
Acetophenazine and fighting behavior in mice. W. R. Knight and others. bibliog il Science 141:830-1 Ag 30 '63
Behavior: persistence of shock-induced aggression. R. E. Ulrich and W. H. Craine. bibliog il Science 143:971-3 F 28 '64
Classroom incident; symposium. NEA J 53: 55-6 D '64
Should boys be taught to fight back? J. A. Moran. il Parents Mag 39:44-5+ Je '64
To unlock fighting deer, courage is the key. D. Harbour. il Audubon Mag 66:234-6 Jl '64

FIGHTING, Hand-to-hand
Gentleman's guide to barroom brawling. C. Basilio; A. Rocca; Duk Sung Son. il Esquire 62:128-31 O '64

FIGHTING fishes
Visual reinforcement in Siamese fighting fish. T. I. Thompson. bibliog il Science 141:55-7 Jl 5 '63

FIGS
Strangler fig, native epiphyte. V. N. Argo. il Natur Hist 73:26-31 N '64

FIGUEROA, John
On seeing the reflection of Notre Dame in the Seine; poem. America 112:165 Ja 30 '65

FIGURAL aftereffects
Measurement of a visual motion aftereffect in the rhesus monkey. T. R. Scott and D. A. Powell. bibliog il Science 140:57-9 Ap 5 '63

FIGURE drawing
Draftsmanship as dissection; Balthus. T. B. Hess. il Art N 62:34-5+ D '63
Figure sketching in watercolor. S. Sutherland. il Am Artist 27:50-3+ O '63
Go for action. R. Thresher. il Recreation 62: 12-14 Je '63
People and the second grade. P. Greenberg. il Sch Arts 64:17-21 S '64
Portfolio of figure drawings; with commentary. J. Deckter. il Am Artist 28:48-53+ My '64
Sunday painters; excerpts from My eye is in love. F. Franck. il Harper 227:32+ O '63
See also
Human figure in art

FIGURE heads. See Figureheads of ships

FIGURE over the town; story. See Goyen, W.

FIGURE skating. See Skating

FIGUREHEADS of ships
Figureheads the glory of the prow. E. A. Stackpole. il Motor B 112:48-9+ D '63

FIGURES of speech
Opinion, please. E. Janeway. Mlle 59:190 Ag '64
Thank you, William Shakespeare! G. Wright. Read Digest 85:82 Ag '64

FIGURINES
Poetry in porcelain; some figures in the collection of Mrs Lesley G. Sheafer. il Antiques 84:302-3 S '63
Rococo retrospective; exhibition of Bustelli figurines at Bavarian national museum, Munich. il Time 82:40-1 Ag 30 '63
FIJI
British in Capricorn. H. Sutton. il Sat R 47:30+ My 16 '64
Fiji interlude. B. Robinson. il Yachting 115:56-7+ F '64
Guns boom in Fiji, pipes skirl down under; gentlemen, the Queen. il Life 54:53-4 Mr 22 '63
Inkling of happiness. N. L. Greenfield. Redbook 122:6+ Mr '64
See also
United Nations—Fiji
FIJIANS
Plea to the Fijians. N. Cousins. il Sat R 47:14-15 Jl 25 '64
FILA dough. See Pastry
FILAMENTS
Polaris cases wound in Nebraska. J. F. Judge. il Miss & Roc 14:30+ My 4 '64
FILAMENTS, Plastic
Filament winding; report. il Miss & Roc 13:22-3+ Ag 12 '63
FILAS, Francis L.
Book review. America 110:52-3 Ja 11 '64
Problem in teen-age sex education. America 111:594-5+ N 14 '64
FILBERT trees
Hazelbushes: European and Turkish. C. P. Holway. il Horticulture 42:31 Ja '64
Hazelnuts and filberts. L. H. MacDaniels. il Horticulture 42:44-5+ O '64
FILENE'S sons company. See Boston—Stores
FILES and filing (documents, etc)
ALA filing rules to be revised. Library J 88:1638+ Ap 15 '63
ALA to revise rules for filing catalog cards: your help needed. il Library J 88:1738 Ap 15 '63
File those sounds. A. Zuckerman. il Pop Phot 55:82+ O '64
Revision of ALA filing rules. Wilson Lib Bul 37:632+ Ap '63
Top-notch filing system. il Suc Farm 61:32 D '63
What papers should we keep? questions and answers. R. C. Cowan. PTA Mag 57:35 Je '63
FILES and rasps
Powered rasps. W. C. Lammey. il Pop Mech 120:184-9 O '63
Roller rest for precision filing. H. Walton. il Pop Sci 184:140-3 Ap '64
Things you never knew about files. il Pop Sci 184:172-3 Ja '64
FILHO, Adonians
Speaking of Brazil. Américas 15:34-6 F '63
FILIBUSTERING in legislation. See United States—Congress—Senate—Rules and practice
FILIPACCHI, Daniel
Hi pals; Salut les copains. Newsweek 62:65 Jl 29 '63
FILIPINOS
Reporter at large; Peace corps in the Philippines. R. Shaplen. New Yorker 39:50-2+ S 28 '63
FILLER, John
John Filler. pors Esquire 60:27-31 Jl '63
FILLERS, Wood. See Filling materials
FILLETS, Fish. See Fish fillets
FILLING (earthwork)
Our landfill plays favorites; Westchester County, N.Y. C. E. Pound. il Am City 79:85-6 Ja '64
This landfill has real togetherness; Maryville, Tenn. H. E. Best. il Am City 78:27 F '63
FILLING materials
How to get a smooth start with wood. il Bet Hom & Gard 41:122-3 O '63
FILLING stations. See Automobile service stations
FILLMORE, Millard
Forgotten man of the White House. il Sr Schol 85:5 Ja 7 '65
Millard Fillmore, thirteenth President 1850-1853. F. Freidel. il por Nat Geog Mag 127:110-13 Ja '65
FILM adaptations
Based on the best seller by. . . S. Peck. il N Y Times Mag p44-5 S 13 '64
Big money writers; books turned into movies. R. Schickel. il Life 57:58-60+ Jl 31 '64
Big novel syndrome. A. Knight. Sat R 46:18 Ag 31 '63
Everybody blows up! Two hours to doom and Fail-safe. D. E. Scherman. il Life 54:49-50 Mr 8 '63
Films; on spectaculars and books. D. Macdonald. Esquire 59:48+ Mr '63
Friends and enemies within. il Newsweek 61:98 Mr 11 '63
Rights and permissions. P. Nathan. See issues of Publishers' weekly
Wonderland of subsidiary rights. P. Nathan. Sat R 46:58-9+ D 14 '63
FILM censorship. See Moving picture censorship
FILM clubs. See Moving picture clubs
FILM conferences. See Moving picture industry—United States
FILM festival, Cannes. See Cannes international film festival
FILM festivals. See Moving picture festivals
FILM-maker's cooperative. See Moving picture industry—United States
FILM projection. See Moving picture projection
FILM propaganda. See Moving pictures—Propaganda films
FILM societies. See Moving picture societies
FILM strips
Bill Herrick: showman with stills. M. Dembling. il Pop Phot 53:158-61+ D '63
Creative color. A. Rothstein. U S Camera 27:8+ N '64
Films and filmstrips. V. Falconer. Sr Schol 85:30T S 23; 6T O 21; 8T-9T O 28; 14T N 18 '64; 19T Ja 21 '65
Preview: films and filmstrips 1964-65. V. M. Falconer. il Sr Schol 84:9T My 15 '64
Story & color on film. Sister Mary Laurus. il Sch Arts 63:17-18 N '63
See also
Libraries and film strips
Shakespeare, W.—Film strips
FILM washing. See Photography—Fixing
FILMS
Cell guidance by alterations in monomolecular films. M. D. Rosenberg. bibliog il Science 139:411-12 F 1 '63
Crystal films; report of conference at Philco scientific laboratory, Blue Bell, Pa. M. H. Francombe. Science 141:364 Jl 26 '63
In-line vacuum ups thin film output. M. Getler. il Miss & Roc 12:35-6 Ap 22 '63
Strain-induced birefringence in fluoride films on uranium dioxide. W. P. Ellis. bibliog il Science 144:1570-2 Je 26 '64
Thin-film transistor research pressed. B. Miller. il Aviation W 78:68-9+ F 4 '63
Thin films: nucleation, growth, and structure; report on first symposium of Thin film division of the American vacuum society. C. A. Neugebauer. Science 146:1604-5 D 18 '64
See also
Photography—Films
FILMS, Metallic
In-line vacuum ups thin film output; Tantalum film. M. Getler. il Miss & Roc 12:35-6 Ap 22 '63
FILMS, Photographic. See Photography—Films
FILMS from books. See Film adaptations
FILMSTRIPS. See Film strips
FILTER paper electrophoresis. See Electrophoresis
FILTER plants
Big improvement in operation. J. Skorupski. il Am City 79:78-9 Ap '64
Chicago's struggle for clean water. il Bsns W p 127-8 O 24 '64
More wells weren't the answer; Belton, Honea Path, Anderson County, S.C. J. L. Gassaway. il Am City 79:107-8 Ap '64
Old filters provide new storage; Philadelphia. il Am City 79:116-17 My '64
Piecemeal water-improvement plan; Kenosha, Wis. O. F. Nelson. il Am City 78:88-9 Ag '63
Zeta potential cleans a difficult water; Gouveneur, N.Y. il Am City 79:96-8 S '64
FILTERS, Air. See Air filters
FILTERS, Automobile. See Air filters, Automobile
FILTERS, Cigarette. See Cigarette filters
FILTERS, Electric. See Electric filters
FILTERS, Light. See Light filters
FILTERS, Radio. See Radio filters
FILTERS and filtration
Pool filters bow to a catch-basin cleaner; method used in Appleton, Wis. R. W. Bues. il Am City 79:25 F '64
Swimming pool filters. S. Hedwall. il Recreation 56:418-20 N '63
See also
Sewage disposal—Filtration
Water purification

FILTERS and filtration (biological products)
Novel filter for biological materials. R. L. Fleischer and others. bibliog il Science 143:249-50 Ja 17 '64
FILTERS and filtration (chemistry)
Fibrous filters as particle-size analyzers. M. D. Silverman and W. E. Browning, jr. bibliog il Science 143:572-3 F 7 '64
Prediction of ultrafiltration membrane performance. W. E. Clark; reply with rejoinder. C. J. Van Oss. Science 139:1123-6 Mr 15 '63
FINAL report; story. See Maxwell, W.
FINAN, James, and Elliott, Lawrence
Mayor is no angel. Read Digest 83:154-7 Jl '63
FINANCE
New trends in the financial markets; address, December 12, 1963. D. Rockefeller. Vital Speeches 30:267-9 F 15 '64
Shopping center for money. il Time 84:111C O 2 '64
See also
Bonds
Church finance
Credit
Farm finance
Inflation (finance)
Interest
Investment companies
Investments
Silver as money
State finance
Stock exchange
also subhead Finance under various subjects, e.g. Airlines—Finance

Statistics

Facts and figures of the Americas. il Américas 15:42-3 Jl '63; Correction. 15:48 S '63

Arab states

Kuwait; Wall Street of the Middle East. R. Hewins. il Nation 198:234-6 Mr 9 '64

Brazil

Brink of bankruptcy. Time 81:22 Mr 22 '63
On the edge of the abyss. il Time 83:32 Ja 3 '64
Printing-press economy. il Fortune 67:63-4+ Mr '63
When inflation runs wild. C. T. Stewart, jr. il Nations Bsns 53:78-82 Ja '65

Canada

See also
Banks and banking—Canada
Budget—Canada

Europe, Western

Very delicate question. il Time 81:90 Mr 22 '63
See also
Budget—Europe, Western

France

Coping with an old foe. Time 82:34 S 20 '63

Germany (Federal Republic)

Capital crisis. il Newsweek 62:64 D 23 '63
Germany's financial coronaries. H. Nickel and R. Sheehan. il Fortune 69:130-1+ Je '64

Great Britain

Citadel of the Commonwealth; the City. il Time 84:107-8 D 11 '64
Needs for planned incomes; address, October 26, 1964. H. Wilson. Vital Speeches 31:66-7 N 15 '64
Sterling performance. Newsweek 61:77-8 Mr 25 '63
$3 billion bail bond. il Time 84:33 D 4 '64
Why Britain slowed its boom. il Bsns W p45-6+ Mr 7 '64
With an eye on tomorrow. il Time 81:32 Ap 12 '63
See also
Budget—Great Britain
Great Britain—Appropriations and expenditures
Money—Great Britain

Israel

Place to make money. Time 81:94 My 10 '63

Italy

What the doctor ordered. M. A. Heilperin. il Fortune 70:60+ O '64

Japan

International markets; Japan frees the yen. A. O. Stanley. Duns R 81:67 Ap '63
See also
Stock exchange—Tokyo

New Hampshire

New Hampshire's lottery: private vice and public virtue. D. F. Ford. il Reporter 30:32-4 Ja 2 '64
Why a state adopts a lottery; New Hampshire sweepstakes. il Bsns W p62-4 My 11 '63

Russia

How to hunt dollars; Russia's balance-of-payments problems. il Time 82:68 Ag 9 '63

United States

Blast at U.S. fiscal policy. Bsns W p29 Je 15 '63
Clichés cost us our shirts; misuse of the term, federal funds. H. J. Taylor. Read Digest 84:165 Ja '64
Dearer money. il Fortune 69:32+ Ap '64
Exporting inflation. H. Hazlitt. Newsweek 62:78 S 9 '63
Fallacy behind the tax cut. J. Daniel. Read Digest 84:77-81 F '64
Financial assets: how they grew. U S News 57:78-9 S 7 '64
Free vs. the manipulated society; address, November 9, 1964. J. Davenport. Vital Speeches 31:125-8 D 1 '64
How real is the drain on dollars? il Bsns W p43-4+ S 5 '64
Inflation and statism. H. Hazlitt. Newsweek 63:73 Mr 2 '64
J.F.K. deficit: all of it or else? Life 54:4 My 10 '63
Kennedy comes home to trouble. il U S News 55:29-30 Jl 15 '63
Lasting prosperity? il Fortune 70:27-8+ Jl '64
Long cycle: hidden force in the economy. B. G. Hickman. il Duns R 82:48-9+ D '63
Looking for scapegoats. H. Hazlitt. Newsweek 63:69 Ja 13 '64
Misery with the dollar or happiness? Life 55:4 Ag 2 '63
Missing $11 billion. H. Hazlitt. Newsweek 63:92 Mr 16 '64
Money on the move. il Fortune 67:44+ Ap '63
More tax cuts coming. il Nations Bsns 52:38-41+ My '64
Old fashioned? Farm J 87:136 F '63
Rigging interest rates. H. Hazlitt. Newsweek 64:76 Jl 13 '64
Right remedy but late and little. Bsns W p 144 Ja 26 '63
Shackled dollar. Fortune 70:108 S '64
Taxes & spending. il Nations Bsns 51:32-41+ Ap '63
Tightening up. il Time 81:89 Je 14 '63
U.S. dollar; keeping up confidence. Newsweek 63:79 Mr 16 '64
Use and abuse of economic policy. A. Sproul. Sat R 48:36+ Ja 9 '65
Verdict on money and credit; report evaluated by Heller committee. Bsns W p98+ Ap 27 '63
Why future recessions will be mild; symposium. il Nations Bsns 51:52+ N '63
World monetary order. H. Hazlitt. Newsweek 63:92 Ap 27 '64
Worrying about money, but making it. il Time 82:59 Ag 2 '63
Your partner; the federal government; address, September 25, 1963. C. R. Sligh, jr. Vital Speeches 30:51-4 N 1 '63
Your stake in financial fights. U S News 54:99-100 Mr 4 '63
See also
Banks and banking—United States
Bonds, Government
Budget—United States
Debts, Public—United States
Federal reserve banks
Inflation (finance)
Money—United States
Silver as money
State finance
Taxation—United States
United States—Appropriations and expenditures
United States—Federal reserve board
United States—General accounting office
United States—Treasury department
FINANCE, Highway. See Roads—Finance
FINANCE, International
Alternatives to key currencies. J. C. Murphy. Yale R 53:61-75 O '63
Bailing out the British pound. il Newsweek 64:73-4+ D 7 '64
Balance of payments; special message to Congress, July 18, 1963. J. F. Kennedy. Dept State Bul 49:250-9 Ag 12 '63
Beleaguered pound and the threatened dollar. M. J. Rossant. il Reporter 32:30+ Ja 28 '65

FINANCE, International—*Continued*
Borrowers from abroad see Wall Street first. il Bsns W p94+ Ap 27 '63
Budget of the United States government for the fiscal year ending June 30, 1965; with excerpts from Budget message of the President. il Dept State Bul 50:218-22 F 10 '64
Capital complications; Europeans to rely more on their own capital markets. il Fortune 69:75-6 Ap '64
Cheap-money mania. H. Hazlitt. Newsweek 64:69 D 21 '64
Conflicting goals. Time 83:79 My 29 '64
Europe warily eyes the dollar. Bsns W p32+ Ag 17 '63
European interest rates; address, May 21, 1964. C. D. Dillon. Vital Speeches 30:585-8 Jl 15 '64
Facing up to the fiscal facts of life. Newsweek 62:100-2+ O 14 '63
Gold war. il Time 85:77-8 Ja 15 '65
Heroic defense; faltering British pound. il Time 84:99-100 D 4 '64
How Europe fills the capital void. il Bsns W p47-8+ Ap 11 '64
How to stay liquid. Bsns W p48+ S 5 '64
How we hope Europe foils inflation. il Bsns W p82-3 F 15 '64
If you're puzzled about gold; answers to some key questions. il U S News 58:96-7 Ja 25 '65
International monetary fund: its work and its future. M. D. Goldstein. il Dept State Bul 49:465-76 S 23 '63
Keeping U.S. dollars at home; President's proposed interest equalization tax. il Bsns W p 19-22 Jl 27 '63
Let the dollar drift? concerning the Brookings institution report. H. Hazlitt. Newsweek 62:64 Ag 26 '63
Money watchers; Beirut bankers. Time 85: 22-3 Ja 8 '65
New touch of caution; with editorial comment. il Bsns W p27-8, 154 N 28 '64
New York is where the money is. il Bsns W p68-70 Ag 3 '63
Next threat: world money squeeze. il Bsns W p64+ Jl 27 '63
President moves to facilitate use of foreign currencies. Dept State Bul 49:204 Ag 5 '63
Push to sell bonds in foreign currency. il Bsns W p88-9 Mr 30 '63
Reforming the international monetary system. R. V. Roosa. For Affairs 42:107-22 O '63
Strengthening the international monetary system; remarks and statements, September 30-October 4, 1963. J. F. Kennedy; C. D. Dillon; G. W. Ball. Dept State Bul 49:610-23 O 21 '63
Taking the fun out of currency speculation. il Bsns W p 132+ Mr 14 '64
Trade and jobs: a world view. J. Lomax. il Nation 198:365-7 Ap 13 '64
What drags the balance down. il Bsns W p55-8+ Jl 27 '63
With the pound saved, labor pushes ahead; with editorial comment. il Bsns W p28-9, 172 D 5 '64
World monetary order. H. Hazlitt. Newsweek 63:92 Ap 27 '64
World monetary reform. H Hazlitt. Newsweek 62:96 O 21 '63
World money reform. H. Hazlitt. Newsweek 64:74 S 7 '64
See also
Balance of payments
Inter-American development bank
International bank for reconstruction and development
International bank of economic cooperation
International development association
International monetary fund
Investments, Foreign

FINANCE, Local. See Local finance

FINANCE, Municipal. See Municipal finance

FINANCE, Personal
How's your financial IQ? il Am Home 66:27+ S '63
Scandal in personal bankruptcy. R. A. Phalon. il Duns R 81:35-6+ Mr '63
See how much you're worth. il Changing T 18:13-15 Ag '64
See also
Budget, Personal

FINANCE, School. See School finance

FINANCE, State. See State finance

FINANCE committee, Senate. See United States—Congress—Senate—Committees

FINANCE companies
Aiming at $2-million and under. il Bsns W p 151-2 N 21 '64
Captive finance companies. V. L. Andrews. il Harvard Bsns R 42:80-92 Jl '64
Department store that sells money. il Bsns W p45-6+ My 23 '64
How long a rope for captives? il Bsns W p93-4 Jl 13 '63
PCA loans for college. D. Hagen and J. Bickers. il Farm J 87:24 N '63
See also
Associates investment company
General acceptance corporation

Securities

Investing in lending. il Fortune 69:239-40+ Ap '64

FINANCIAL analysts. See Investments—Advisers

FINANCIAL news. See Newspapers—Financial news

FINANCIAL shopping centers. See Finance

FINANCIAL statements
Those special items. il Fortune 70:77-8+ Ag '64

FINANCIERS. See Capitalists and financiers

FINCH, Elfreda W.
Designs to surround a home. Flower Grower 51:24-7 N '64
Simple bouquets from garden flowers. il Flower Grower 51:38-9 Jl '64
Sun & rock lovers. Flower Grower 50:36-7+ Ag '63

FINCH, Hardy
Books for younger readers. Sr Schol 82:11T Ap 17 '63
History heads the list. Sr Schol 85:22T O 7 '64
How to buy them when you need them. Sr Schol 83:24T Ja 17 '64
(comp) Spring reading roundup. Sr Schol 82:18T-19T Mr 13 '63

FINCHES
Forest bird becomes a city dweller; siskin. R. G. Clearwater. Audubon Mag 66:256-7 Jl '64
Songbirds sensitive; chaffinches. Sci N L 84: 134 Ag 31 '63

FINCHUM, R. N.
Fidelity and crime insurance for schools. por Sch Life 45:16-17 Je '63

FINDERS, View. See View finders

FINDING by the referee; story. See Potter, J.

FINDING of lost articles. See Lost articles

FINDLAY, John W.
300-foot radio telescope at Green Bank. Sky & Tel 25:68-75 F '63

FINDLAY, Ohio
Civic celebrations don't just happen. W. J. Carlin. il Am City 78:109+ Ap '63

FINE, Donald J.
Mostly about paperbacks: a little light, a little heat; excerpt from American reading public. Pub W 184:26-7 O 14 '63

FINEBERG, S. Andhil
Plight of Soviet Jews. Christian Cent 81:429-31 Ap 1 '64

FINEMAN, Morton
Are you ready for Egyptland? story. Sat Eve Post 238:56-8 Ja 30 '65
Bless Charlie; story. Sat Eve Post 237:54-7 O 31 '64
Engine, engine number nine; story. Sat Eve Post 237:42-6 D 5 '64

FINER, Herman
Finer over Craig. Reporter 31:8+ N 19 '64

FINES (penalties)
No-traffic jam; Webberville, Mich. Newsweek 61:21-2 Ap 29 '63

FINES, Library. See Libraries—Fines

FINES, Trade union. See Trade unions—Dues, fees, etc.

FINGER painting
Homemade finger paints. il Design 64:192-3 Je '63
New ways with finger paint; portraiture and literal landscape. R. Fridenstein. il Design 65:108-9 Ja '64

FINGERET, Rose W.
Aids for the reader with changing vision. por ALA Bul 58:792-4 O '64

FINGERMAN, Milton, and Yamamoto, Yoshihiro
Endocrine control of tanning in the crayfish exoskeleton. bibliog Science 144:1462 Je 19 '64

FINGERNAILS. See Nails (anatomy)

FINGERPRINTS
Identifying fingerprints. J. D. Corrington. il Natur Hist 72:6-4 My '63

FINGERS
Finger and thumb injuries. C. J. Potthoff. Todays Health 41:62 Ap '63

FINIALS
Add finials to gates and fences. il Pop Gard 15:47 Mr '64
FINISHING, wood. See Wood finishing
FINISHING materials
Finishes that stop soil before it starts. M. Bender. House B 106:134-5+ Mr '64
How to simulate tortoise shell. il House & Gard 124:162-4 S '63
New epoxy coating waterproofs shower walls. J. H. Ingersoll. Pop Sci 182:138-9+ Je '63
FINISHING schools. See Private schools
FINK, G. R.
Gene-enzyme relations in histidine biosynthesis in yeast. bibliog Science 146:525-7 O 23 '64
FINK, L. Kenneth. See Hurley, R. J. jt. auth.
FINK, Louis C.
ABC's of a field trip: attitude, behavior and clothing. Audubon Mag 66:124-5, 190 Mr-My '64
FINKEL, Donald
Negative; Sonic boom; Father; Husband; Bachelor; For Noah, my son, sleeping; Bones; poems. Poetry 101:387-91 Mr '63
Paz in English. Poetry 104:382-5 S '64
Stranger; poem. Atlan 211:73 F '63
FINKELSTEIN, James D. and others
Homocystinuria due to cystathionine synthetase deficiency: the mode of inheritance. bibliog Science 146:785-7 N 6 '64
FINKELSTEIN, Louis
Cajori: the figure in the scene. Art N 62:38-41+ Mr '63
Rabbi's tribute; John XXIII. America 108:859 Je 15 '63
Tworkov: radical pro. Art N 63:32-5+ Ap '64
FINKELSTEIN, Martin S. and Uhr, J. W.
Specific inhibition of antibody formation by passively administered 19S and 7S antibody. bibliog Science 146:67-9 O 2 '64
FINKLEY, Mary Jane
Harlem's antique collector. il pors Ebony 18:105-6+ Ap '63
FINLAND
Letter from Finland. J. Bainbridge. il New Yorker 40:141-2+ O 3 '64
See also
Airlines—Finland
Architecture—Finland
Architecture, Domestic—Finland
Forests and forestry—Finland
Lapland
Theater—Finland

Foreign relations

Finland's success: looking East, living West; with report by S. Hagerty. il Newsweek 63:39 My 11 '64

Industries

Miles of mink; bound for U.S; Finnish mink farm. il Bsns W p 128-30 D 19 '64

Politics and government

Atlantic report. Atlan 211:14+ Mr '63

Social conditions

Atlantic report. Atlan 211:14+ Mr '63
FINLAND and the United States
Vice President Johnson visits northern Europe; address, September 7, 1963. L. B. Johnson. Dept State Bul 49:585-8 O 14 '63
See also
Americans in Finland
FINLAYSON, A. J.
Aromatic biosynthesis and metabolism. Science 142:981-2 N 15 '63
FINLEY, Charles O.
Checkmate for Charlie. Sports Illus 20:10 Ja 27 '64
Happiness is being somewhere else. F. Graham, jr. il pors Sat Eve Post 237:73-7 Ap 4 '64
Louisville sluggers? Kansas City Athletics. il por Newsweek 63:58-9 Ja 20 '64
Strikeout? Newsweek 63:76 Ja 27 '64
What every team needs; purchase of Kansas City Athletics by C. O. Finley. il por Time 83:30 Ja 24 '64
FINLEY, M. I.
Silent women of Rome. Horizon 7:56-64 Wint '65
Year one. Horizon 6:4-17 Wint '64
FINN, David
Businessman and his critics; excerpt. Sat R 47:60-2+ S 12 '64
FINN, Firmin
Heart on the hill. il por Newsweek 62:80 Jl 22 '63
FINN, Jack. See Arquilla, E. R. jt. auth.
FINN, James
James Baldwin's vision. Commonweal 78:447-9; 79:76-7 Jl 26, O 11 '63
On Cyril Connolly. Commonweal 81:125-7 O 23 '64
Play of the month. Cath World 200:323-4 F '65
Uses of Genet. Commonweal 80:86-8 Ap 10 '64
FINN, James D.
Franks had the right idea. NEA J 53:24-7 Ap '64
FINNAIR. See Airlines—Finland
FINNEGAN, Bob
Picture post card. See issues of Hobbies
FINNEGAN, Elizabeth
Adventures in the vegetable kingdom. Parents Mag 39:50-1+ My '64
FINNEY, Albert
Actor Finney: he needs the Everests. il pors Newsweek 62:56-9 O 28 '63
Albert Finney. A. Williamson. il pors Theatre Arts 47:30-2+ O '63
Enthusiastic actors dig a classic! E. Miller. il pors Seventeen 22:114-15 F '63
Finney, the flesh and the devil. il pors Look 27:76+ N 19 '63
Thirst for greatness. T. Prideaux. il pors Life 55:125-6 O 11 '63
FINNEY, Charles G.
Isabell the inscrutable. Harper 228:51-8 Ap '64
FINNEY, John W.
Astronauts can't be automated. N Y Times Mag p24-5+ My 5 '63
Creating the hydrogen bomb. New Repub 151:24-5+ O 17 '64
Is the AEC obsolete? Reporter 31:44-6 N 19 '64
Second canal? New Repub 150:21-4 Mr 28 '64; Same abr. with title Biggest building job of all time. Sci Digest 56:33-7 Jl '64
Tandem to the moon? Reporter 29:36 O 10 '63
FINNISH cookery. See Cookery, Finnish
FINNISH fur industry. See Finland—Industries
FINNO-Ugrian languages
See also
Ural-Altaic languages
FINNS
Letter from Finland. J. Bainbridge. il New Yorker 40:141-2+ O 3 '64
FINOT, Paul
Tea and goatee. Newsweek 63:80 Mr 9 '64
FIR
Most unusual fir in the world? il Sunset 130:254+ Mr '63
Tree of Christmas. K. Bowe. il Am For 69:16-17+ D '63
FIRE
Fire, source of fear. B. Tufty. il Sci N L 83:90-1 F 9 '63
FIRE alarms
Don't be panic-sold on fire alarms. C. L. Walker. il Read Digest 82:89-92 Ap '63
Hand-written fire communications; Montebello, Calif. J. N. Hale. il Am City 79:12 Mr '64
How good are home fire alarms? Good H 156:149 F '63
Two-city fire dispatching; El Segundo and Hawthorne, Calif. il Am City 79:28 F '64
What happens if you push a fire alarm. Good H 157:166 O '63
See also
Electric alarms
FIRE apparatus, Motor
Fire engine to fight flames seventy-four floors high. il Newsweek 62:69 Jl 22 '63
Fires and fire engines. B. Finnegan. il Hobbies 68:118-19+ Mr '63
Foam-equipped fire-pumper; East Providence, R.I. E. Griffith. il Am City 78:149-50 F '63
Have 90-foot aerial platform, will fight fires; Poughkeepsie, N.Y. I. D. Merrick. il Am City 79:23 Jl '64
Mightiest fire engine. P. Mandel. il Life 56:23-4 Mr 20 '64
This truck will answer any emergency; new rescue and salvage unit; Littleton, Colo. J. A. Easton. il Am City 79:22 S '64
FIRE arms. See Firearms
FIRE boats. See Fireboats
FIRE buff clubs. See Clubs
FIRE departments
Self-employed fire chief. il Ebony 18:59-60+ Mr '63
See also
Fire alarms
Firemen
also subhead Fire department under names of cities, e.g. Chicago—Fire department
FIRE eating
Burning questions. R. G. G. Price. il Atlan 214:122+ O '64
FIRE engines. See Fire apparatus, Motor

FIRE escapes
Obeying the law; photographic patterns made by a fire escape. J. Drake. Horizon 5:110-12 N '63
FIRE extinguishers
Out of the fire, into worse trouble. Consumer Rep 29:413 S '64
What you should know about fire extinguishers. D. X. Manners. il House B 105:186-7+ My '63
FIRE fighting. See Fire protection
FIRE flies. See Fireflies
FIRE inspection. See Fire protection
FIRE insurance. See Insurance, Fire
FIRE insurance companies. See Insurance companies
FIRE insurance rates. See Insurance, Fire—Rates
FIRE ISLAND
Fire Island: a possible national seashore. V. B. Moore. il Nat Parks Mag 37:4-9 F '63
FIRE ISLAND NATIONAL SEASHORE
Curbing Fire Island speculation. Nat Parks Mag 38:15 D '64
Fire Island. P. M. Tilden. Natur Hist 73:65-6 D '64
Fire Island: a possible national seashore. V. B. Moore. il Nat Parks Mag 37:4-9 F '63
Sketch of the newly created Fire Island National Seashore. il Nat Parks Mag 38:16 N '64
FIRE logs. See Fireplaces—Fuel
FIRE making
Do you really know how to build a fire? A. W. Bealer, 3d. il House B 106:28+ F '64
How to keep the home fire burning. Bet Hom & Gard 42:143 N '64
New twist in fire starters. W. Haussamen. il Outdoor Life 131:116 Ap '63
FIRE or ice; story. See Hickler, H. W.
FIRE prevention. See Fire protection
FIRE protection
Fire prevention, the key to low fire losses; Beverly Hills, Calif. C. C. Benford. il Am City 78:35 N '63
Fire, source of fear. B. Tufty. il Sci N L 83:90-1 F 9 '63
For a safer Christmas. Consumer Bul 46:25 D '63
How to prevent church fires. il Consumer Bul 47:37-8 O '64
Keep gasoline away from heating appliances. il Consumer Bul 47:43 S '64
Learning to control runaway fires. il Todays Health 41:51 F '63
Life guide; fire museums. il Life 56:21 Mr 20 '64
Notes of a happy housekeeper; six point program of fire safety. M. E. Falter. il House & Gard 127:26+ Ja '65
Scuba fire fighters; wharf fires. S. Gordon. il Look 27:M7-8 S 10 '63
Snorkel Bob: Chicago's champion fire fighter. K. Detzer. il Read Digest 85:117-20 Ag '64
Ways to fireproof your Christmas. Suc Farm 62:41 D '64
See also
Fire alarms
Fire apparatus, Motor
Fire extinguishers
Forest fire protection
Helicopters in fire protection

Laws and regulations

War on the fire felons; address. B. Holleman. Am For 70:29+ F '64

Study and teaching

Shock cure for fires. il Bsns W p30-1 Mr 14 '64
FIRE vortex. See Vortex motion
FIRE works. See Fireworks
FIREARMS
Bang, bang you're dead; mail-order weapons. J. Ridgeway. New Repub 148:6 F 16 '63
Cannon to the right of us. New Repub 150:5 Je 20 '64
Christmas tree, 1964. W. Page. il Field & S 69:54-60 D '64
Firearms. See issues of Hobbies
Gentlemen, choose your weapons. il Esquire 62:118-19 O '64
Getting the range. J. O'Connor. See issues of Outdoor life
Guns. Consumer Rep 29:338-42 D '64
Shooting. J. O'Connor. See issues of Outdoor life
Shooting; ed. by W. Page. See issues of Field & stream
Where Johnny gets his gun. J. Anderson. Read Digest 83:138-40 Jl '63
Womanly art of self-defense. S. Alexander. Life 57:29 O 23 '64
Your leisure. Consumer Rep 28:353-6 D '63
See also
Air guns
Cartridges
Pistols
Revolvers
Rifles
Shooting
Shotguns

Care

Care in the field. W. Page. il Field & S 68:54-8 D '63
Hints for the proper care and cleaning of antique firearms. W. R. Orbelo. Hobbies 69:125+ S '64

Collectors and collecting

Shopwalk; shop in New York for gun collectors. C. Curtis. Sports Illus 18:E1-E2+ Ap 1 '63

Laws and regulations

Anti-gun extremists are at it again. R. Starnes. Field & S 68:12+ Ap '64
Arms and the law. Sports Illus 19:15 D 9 '63
Be strong, carry a gun. New Repub 149:7 D 14 '63
Case for registering guns. T. Batman. Sat R 47:18 Ag 1 '64; Discussion. 47:19+ Ag 22 '64
Don't wait, buy a gun now! J. Ridgeway. New Repub 150:9-10 Je 6 '64
Firearms and the citizen; pro and con discussion. Sr Schol 83:17 D 13 '63
For a strong America; article II, the Bill of rights. Field & S 68:10-11 Ap '64
Fun with guns in the United States Senate. J. Ridgeway. New Repub 150:6-7 F 22 '64
Gentle thoughts on murder. F. Canavan. America 110:503 Ap 11 '64
Get your gun from the army. S. Meisler. il Nation 198:568-71 Je 8 '64
Gun law that didn't go off; the Dodd bill. E. B. Drew. il Reporter 31:33-5 O 8 '64; Discussion. 31:6+ N 5 '64
Gun owners should switch to the offense. A. Grahame. Outdoor Life 132:10-11+ N '63
In the works: tighter laws on gun sales. il U S News 55:4 D 9 '63
Plot to disarm Washington; Sullivan law. R. Starnes. Field & S 68:18+ S '63
Rifles: target for control? il Newsweek 64:21-3 D 28 '64
Right to bear arms. il Newsweek 62:70-1 D 9 '63
Speaking out; too many people have guns. J. V. Lindsay. Sat Eve Post 237:12+ F 1 '64
Traffic in guns: a forgotten lesson of the assassination. C. Bakal. Harper 229:62-8 D '64
What other nations do about guns. il U S News 55:71 D 23 '63
You might call it CBS distorts. R. Starnes. Field & S 69:20+ S '64
Your right to own a gun; pro and con discussion. R. Starnes; T. J. Dodd. il Pop Mech 121:94-9+ F '64

Safety devices and measures

Sportsmen don't happen. D. M. Duffey. il Outdoor Life 135:64-5+ F '65
Tips for handling guns. B. Clede. il Suc Farm 62:126+ Mr '64

Sights

Best power in the scope? J. O'Connor. il Outdoor Life 131:98-102 F '63
Marlin-realist scopes. Outdoor Life 134:160 O '64
More from four; 4X scope. W. Page. il Field & S 68:54-6+ N '63
Moves by Bausch & Lomb. Field & S 69:130 My '64
New B.&L. scopes. J. O'Connor. Outdoor Life 132:111 S '63
Sighting in for big game. J. O'Connor. il Outdoor Life 132:70+ S '63
See also
Telescopic sights
FIREARMS industry and trade
Co-op works for craftsmen; Cooperative of master gunmakers of Ferlach. il Bsns W p24-5 D 28 '63
See also
Olin Mathieson chemical corporation—Winchester-Western division
Plainfield machine company
FIREBALLS. See Meteors

FIREBOATS
Chicago fire department jets around. R. J. Quinn. il Am City 79:89 Jl '64
FIREBUGS; drama. See Frisch, M.
FIREFLIES
Belly dance of a glow-worm. Sci Digest 55:7 Mr '64
Luring love lights. Time 83:75 Ja 10 '64
Pest-eating insects: excerpt from Beneficial insects. L. A. Swan. bibliog f il Audubon Mag 66:314-19 S '64
FIREMEN
Scuba fire fighters; wharf fires. S. Gordon. il Look 27:M7-8 S 10 '63
Training
Backbone fire training has a few new wrinkles; Baltimore, Md. J. J. Killen. il Am City 78:89-91 Jl '63
Overcoming smoke inhalation. il Am City 78: 26 D '63
FIREMEN, Railroad. See Railroads—Employees
FIREMEN and oilers, International brotherhood of. See International brotherhood of firemen and oilers
FIREMEN'S union. See International brotherhood of firemen and oilers
FIREPLACE accessories
See also
Dummy board figures
FIREPLACES
Christmas is where the hearth is. il Am Home 66:25-31 D '63
Concrete fireplace and stone fireplace. il Arch Rec 135:134-5 F '64
Fireplaces are furniture. G. O'Brien. il N Y Times Mag p 154-5 Ap 7 '63
How to plug in a fireplace. il Sunset 132:160+ My '64
Massive fireplace in stone, concrete. il Sunset 132:122 Je '64
Place of the fire. il Sunset 133:92-9 N '64
Pre-fab fireplace can be its heart. il House B 105:98-9+ F '63
So I built my own fireplace. D. Huff. il Pop Sci 183:129-31+ N '63
Southwest tradition: the corner fireplace. il Sunset 131:120+ S '63
Fuel
Logs; Village firewood cooperative in New York. New Yorker 40:20-1 F 22 '64
FIREPLACES, Outdoor
See also
Barbecue grills
FIREPROOFING of wood
Fireproofing from the Dead Sea; Israeli bromine. il Time 84:33 D 25 '64
FIRES
But they came back same day; Neiman-Marcus disaster. il Bsns W p 15 D 26 '64
Neiman-Marcus fire: 200 firms to pay insurance. il U S News 58:10 Ja 4 '65
People to burn; fire hazards in nursing homes. Christian Cent 82:67 Ja 20 '65
Phoenix in Dallas; $10 million fire at Neiman-Marcus store. il Time 85:63 Ja 1 '65
Start from scratch; rebuilding after Bel Air fire. L. Spigelgass. il Ladies Home J 80:50+ D '63
Surviving fire effects of nuclear detonations. A. Broido. Bul Atomic Sci 19:20-3 Mr '63
We learned the hard way about fire in the house. P. Wylie. Read Digest 84:157-8+ Je '64
When Chicago burned; with drawings by A. R. Waud. R. Keeler. Am Heritage 14: 54-61 Ag '63
See also
Arson
Brush fires
Forest fires
Photographs
Photos record a tower of horror; Rio de Janeiro office building. Life 55:35-8 Jl 12 '63
FIRES at sea. See Ships—Fires and fire protection
FIRES in ships. See Ships—Fires and fire protection
FIRESTONE, Richard W.
Why. New Yorker 40:20-1 Ag 8 '64
FIRESTONE tire and rubber company
Getting a grip when you slip; spiked tires. il Bsns W p24-5 D 7 '63
Rubber battle at Indy; Firestone fires up! G. Moore. il Motor T 16:55-7 Mr '64
FIRETHORNS
Plant pyracantha to brighten winter drabness. I. McLendon. il Horticulture 41:130-1 Mr '63
FIREWALLS, Automobile. See Automobiles—Fires and fire protection
FIREWORKS
Explosions for freedom. B. Tufty. il Sci N L 83:406-7 Je 29 '63
One-hour blast; fireworks displays. il Newsweek 64:63 Jl 6 '64
Safe and sane. Time 84:67 Jl 3 '64
FIRING of employees. See Employees—Dismissal
FIRMS, Architectural. See Architectural firms
FIRST, Helen G.
Curl up and read. See issues of Seventeen to July 1963
FIRST aid for animals. See Veterinary first aid
FIRST aid in illness and injury
Antidotes for poisoning and drug overdoses. Good H 156:146 Mr '63
First aid. C. J. Potthoff. See issues of Today's health
First aid for athletic injuries. Todays Health 42:49 O '64
Health and first-aid guide for summer. G. G. Greer. il Bet Hom & Gard 42:22+ Jl '64
Medical assistance. B. L. Jones. il Motor B 111:41+ Je '63
Medical I.D. tag can save your life. R. Dunlop. il Todays Health 41:8-13 Jl '63; Same abr. with title Tag that can save your life. Read Digest 83:217-19+ O '63
Medical supplies for the camper. il Consumer Rep 28:243-5 My '63
Time for a quick review: first aid. il Changing T 17:26 My '63
See also
Respiration, Artificial
Resuscitation
Splints (surgery)
FIRST amendment to the Constitution. See United States—Constitution—Bill of rights
FIRST chamber dance quartet. See Ballet companies
FIRST committee of the General assembly. See United Nations—Political and security committee
FIRST communion
Gigi's first communion. C. Morrison. il Look 28:20-5 Ag 11 '64
FIRST day; story. See Kaufman, S.
FIRST; drama. See Holt, W.
FIRST gift, first love; story. See Knowlton, R. A.
FIRST ladies. See Presidents—United States—Wives
FIRST love; story. See Lee, L.
FIRST national bank of Boston. See Boston—Banks
FIRST national city bank of New York. See New York (city)—Banks
FIRST night parties. See Entertaining
FIRST principles. See Philosophy
FISCH, Gerald G.
Stretching the span of management. bibliog f Harvard Bsns R 41:74-85 S '63
FISCHER, Alfred G. See Honjo, S. jt. auth.
FISCHER, Andrew J.
Father of ten looks to the future; ed. by J. Bird. Sat Eve Post 237:23 My 2 '64
Our life will never be the same; ed. by J. Bird. pors Sat Eve Post 236:25-44 N 16 '63
We aren't going to live in a fishbowl; ed. by J. Bird. por Ladies Home J 80:59 D '63
FISCHER, Andrew J, family
Dear quints, with love from the quints; ed. by J. Brough. A. Dionne and others. il McCalls 91:60+ F '64
Father of ten looks to the future; ed. by J. Bird. A. J. Fischer. Sat Eve Post 237:23 My 2 '64
Our life will never be the same; ed. by J. Bird. A. J. Fischer. il Sat Eve Post 236:25-44 N 16 '63
Quintuplet story; symposium. il pors Ladies Home J 80:55-74 D '63
FISCHER, Carl
Soft focus cat. il U S Camera 27:56-7 Mr '64
FISCHER, Carl H.
Federal control threatens pension plan growth; interview. por Nations Bsns 52:56-8+ N '64
FISCHER, Clare
Clare Fischer: the Pan-American way. R. F. Thompson. por Sat R 47:46-7 N 28 '64
FISCHER, Harry
Swinging art dealers: the Marlborough boys in New York. J. Russell. il por Vogue 143: 102-5+ Ja 1 '64
FISCHER, John
Editor's easy chair. See issues of Harper's magazine
What women can do for peace. Harper 226: 14+ Ap '63; Same abr. Read Digest 82:55-9 Je '63

FISCHER, John H.
Boycotts and bargaining; excerpts from address, February 1964. Sr Schol 84:4T Mr 20 '64
Desegregating city schools. PTA Mag 59:10-13 D '64
Our schools: battleground of conflicting interests; adapted from address, February 18, 1964. Sat R 47:66-7+ Mr 21 '64
Scholastic teacher interview; ed. by H. Langer. por Sr Schol 85:8T-13T+ S 23 '64

FISCHER, Mary Ann (Brady)
Fischer quints at home; ed. by J. Bird. por Sat Eve Post 237:18-27 My 2 '64
Long hour of birth; ed. by D. C. Disney. por Sat Eve Post 236:31 N 16 '63
My life, my children; ed. by D. C. Disney. Ladies Home J 80:56-8+ D '63
What a year it has been! ed. by J. Bird. pors Sat Eve Post 237:25-31 S 26 '64

FISCHER, Muriel
Where hats are made. Sat Eve Post 236:64-7 Ap 6 '63

FISCHER, Richard B.
Ambassador of birdlife. il Audubon Mag 67:26-31 Ja '65

FISCHER, Robert James
Amazing Bobby Fischer. P. Lyon. il por Holiday 33:125-9+ My '63
Amazing victory streak of Bobby Fischer. il Sports Illus 20:14-15 Ja 13 '64
Bobby Fischer; best in chess? R. O'Brien. il por Sat R 46:22-3 Ap 27 '63; Same abr. with title America's wizard of chess. Read Digest 82:221-2+ My '63
Have pawn, will travel. L. H. Lapham. il pors Sat Eve Post 237:18-19 F 8 '64
One-track mastermind; with report by J. Howard. il pors Life 56:97-8+ F 21 '64

FISCHER, W. A. and others
Infrared surveys of Hawaiian volcanoes. bibliog Science 146:733-42 N 6 '64

FISCHER-WILLIAMS, Barbara
(ed) See Evans, G. Welsh Knight

FISCHER quintuplets. See Quintuplets

FISCHLER, Stan
Hockey in the slapstick style. Sports Illus 18:E3-4 F 11 '63

FISCHMAN, Walter Ian
Friar who saved 5,000 Jews. Look 28:66+ D 1 '64
Jewels that crawl. Sat Eve Post 236:68 My 11 '63

FISCOR, Gyula. See Neuffer, M. G. jt. auth.

FISH, Byron
Washington state; America's scenic storeroom. Read Digest 82:151-6 Mr '63

FISH, Canned. See Canned food

FISH, Frozen
Some better news on frozen fish. Consumer Rep 28:101-2 Mr '63

FISH, Smoked
Botulism: the killer who came to dinner. T. Berland. il Sat Eve Post 237:71-3 Mr 7 '64
End to the smoked-fish scare? U S News 55:16 N 11 '63
Freezing to be safe; Great Lakes fishing industry. il Bsns W p36 N 9 '63
Moving in on a menace; botulism research. Bsns W p 132+ Ja 25 '64
Mystery of the botulism-poisoned fish; Great Lakes smoked fish. Consumer Rep 29:84 F '64
Squaw candy. F. Dufresne. il Field & S 69:8 Ag '64
To bagelville and beyond. H. Sutton. Sat R 47:36+ N 21 '64

FISH and chips. See Cookery, English

FISH and wildlife service. See United States—Fish and wildlife service

FISH as food
All about fish. il Redbook 120:70-1+ Mr '63
Fishmen angle for two Fridays. il Bsns W p74-5+ F 15 '64
Inexhaustible riches from the sea. G. A. W. Boehm. il Fortune 68:132-7+ D '63; Same abr. Read Digest 84:111-15 Ap '64
Wine & fish. J. A. Beard. House & Gard 123:150+ Mr '63
See also
Cookery—Fish
Fishes—Preservation

FISH chowder. See Chowder

FISH culture
Here's a push-button fish trap. il Sunset 130:30+ Je '63
He's forever chasing rainbows; Snake River trout ranch; Buhl, Idaho. F. J. Taylor. il Sat Eve Post 236:70-1 N 30 '63
How to keep big fish in your pond. O. Bay. Farm J 87:48J O '63
Is your trouble too many fish? R. K. Davis. Farm J 88:34J Jl '64

FISH extermination. See Fishes—Extermination

FISH fillets
How to fillet sole and salmon. il House & Gard 123:162-4 Mr '63

FISH flies. See Fishing lures, flies, etc.

FISH flour
Fish flour: administration's interest has not been matched by funds for needed research. D. S. Greenberg. Science 139:891-2 Mr 8 '63
Fracas over fish flour. D. S. Greenberg. il Sat Eve Post 236:34-5 N 23 '63
New foods and new hopes. il Newsweek 61:51 Je 17 '63

FISH hawks. See Ospreys

FISH industry and trade
Americans at sea. Nation 199:103 S 14 '64
Feast and a famine. il Bsns W p 116-18 S 14 '63
Fishmen angle for two Fridays. il Bsns W p74-5+ F 15 '64
Freezing to be safe; Great Lakes fishing industry. il Bsns W p36 N 9 '63
Great big little fish; Peru head of world's fishing business. Time 85:31 Ja 1 '65
Great tuna war; commercial seiners vs sport fishermen. F. T. Moss. il Field & S 68:10-12+ Je '63
Moving in on a menace; botulism research. Bsns W p 132+ Ja 25 '64
Mystery of the botulism-poisoned fish; Great Lakes smoked fish. Consumer Rep 29:84 F '64
Nothing for the birds; poaching by foreign fishermen. Newsweek 62:33-4 S 16 '63
Red trawlers: encroaching fishermen. W. S. Ellis. il Nation 197:346-8 N 23 '63
War at sea. il Time 82:98-107 O 11 '63

FISH ladders
Giving fish a go sign. il Bsns W p 198-200 Ap 18 '64

FISH lines. See Fishing tackle

FISH meal
Industry overboard; Peru's biggest industry. Time 83:38 My 8 '64

FISH noises. See Sound production by fishes

FISH ponds. See Ponds

FISH products. See Marine resources

FISH protection
Better fishing for a nickel; letters to legislators. W. Davis. Outdoor Life 131:86+ Ap '63

FISH tagging
Platinum tuna. M. R. Rascovich. il Field & S 68:50-3+ Ap '64

FISHBACK, Margaret
Never listless; poem. Am Home 67:70 Je '64
Quiet interlude; poem. Am Home 67:101 O '64

FISHBEIN, Elise P.
Wanted: documents librarians. por Library J 89:2037-9 My 15 '64

FISHBEIN, I. Leo
Nature and mental health. Audubon Mag 66:25 Ja '64

FISHBEIN, Morris
Medical news of the month. See issues of McCall's

FISHBEIN, William N. and Carbone, P. P.
Hydroxyrurea: mechanism of action. bibliog Science 142:1069-70 N 22 '63

FISHER, Adrian S.
U.S. discusses freeze proposal in disarmament committee; statement, April 16, 1964. bibliog f Dept State Bul 50:756-9 My 11 '64
U.S. makes proposals for safeguards for peaceful nuclear activities and for bomber destruction; statements, March 5 and March 19, 1964. bibliog f Dept State Bul 50:641-5 Ap 20 '64

FISHER, Aileen
Christmas tablecloth; drama. Plays 23:45-8, 58 D '63
Our 49th state; drama. Plays 23:83-95 Ja '64
Special edition; drama. Plays 22:61-8 My '63
Voice of liberty; drama. Plays 23:57-64, 96 Ap '64
What happened on Clutter street; drama. Plays 24:47-52 O '64
Why the sleepy Dormouse; drama. Plays 23:75-8, 84 F '64
Writing children's verse. Writer 76:21-4 Ap '63
—and Rabe, Olive
Johnny Appleseed's vision; drama. Plays 24:65-8 Ja '65
Rocket to freedom; drama. Plays 23:53-8, 76 My '64

FISHER, Alan E.
Chemical stimulation of the brain. Sci Am 210:60-8 Je '64
—See Ferguson, D. C. jt. auth.
FISHER, David
What you can do about your aching back. McCalls 90:45 Ap '63
FISHER, David E.
Ages of the Sikhote alin iron meteorite. bibliog Science 139:752-3 F 22 '63
FISHER, Eddie
Funny thing happened on the way to decorum. il Time 83:56 Ja 3 '64
Mr Fisher is open. J. Richardson. Esquire 60:158+ D '63
FISHER, Frederick E.
Modern lighting sells itself. Am City 79: 111+ D '64
Upgrading a second-rate snow program. Am City 79:108-9 O '64
FISHER, Geoffrey Francis, baron Fisher of Lambeth. See Fisher of Lambeth, G. F. F.
FISHER, Graham, and Fisher, Heather
Hours in the life of Prince Edward Antony Richard Louis. McCalls 92:44+ Ja '65
Teen-age princes and princesses. Seventeen 23:122-3+ Je '64
FISHER, Hans, and others
Avian atherosclerosis: retardation by pectin. bibliog Science 146:1063-4 N 20 '64
FISHER, Heather. See Fisher, G. jt. auth.
FISHER, Herbert O.
Small speedster. New Yorker 38:23-4 F 2 '63
FISHER, Homer, jr. See Steele, H. E. jt. auth.
FISHER, Isabelle
What the dancer should know about publicity (cont) Dance Mag 37:69 F '63
FISHER, James
Briton traces the origin of our national park idea. Audubon Mag 65:334-41 N '63
FISHER, John
Your savings account of memories. Read Digest 82:181-3+ My '63
FISHER, Joseph P.
Nuns in the wide, wide world. America 110: 282-3 F 29 '64
FISHER, Leicester W.
Business outlook is good, over all: interview. por U S News 56:54-6 Mr 2 '64
Indications of bull market; interview. por U S News 54:41-3 Ap 22 '63
FISHER, M. F. K.
Oldest man; story. New Yorker 40:62-6 D 5 '64
Second time around; story. New Yorker 39: 30-40 Ja 18 '64
FISHER, Marjory M.
Engravings beneath the bark. Natur Hist 72: 54-6 Ag '63
FISHER, Nelle
Nelle Fisher, Bruce King, and assisting dancers at Judson Hall. D. Hering. Dance Mag 37:22 F '63
FISHER, Roger
Slicing up the Cuban problem. New Repub 148:13-15 Je 15 '63
FISHER, Waldo R. and Gurin, Samuel
Structure of lipoproteins: covalently bound fatty acids. bibliog Science 143:362-3 Ja 24 '64
FISHER, William H.
Great art of public relations. Sch & Soc 92: 47 F 8 '64
FISHER body craftsman's guild
Model car champs. il Sr Schol 83:31 O 18 '63
FISHER brothers
Fabulous brothers. il Time 82:68 Ag 16 '63
FISHER of Lambeth, Geoffrey Francis Fisher, baron
World council. G. Murray. Christian Cent 80: 472 Ap 10 '63
FISHERIES
See also
Fish culture
Fish industry and trade
Fishery research
International North Pacific fisheries commission

International aspects

Force de flap; question of French lobster boats in Brazilian waters. il Time 81:30-1 Mr 8 '63
King crab fishing agreement with Japan becomes effective; remarks, November 25, 1964; with text of U.S. note D. Rusk and R. Takeuchi. Dept State Bul 51.892-3 D 21 '64
Lobster war; Franco-Brazilian dispute. Newsweek 61:56 Mr 11 '63
North Pacific fishery conference held at Tokyo; statement, September 10, 1963. J. F. Kennedy. Dept State Bul 49:519 S 30 '63
Tuna tussle; Ecuador vs. American tuna boat association. Time 81:25-6 Je 7 '63
U.S. and Japan reach agreement to govern king crab fishing. Dept State Bul 51:829 D 7 '64
U.S. and U.S.S.R. sign agreement on fishing operations off Alaska. Dept State Bul 52:14 Ja 4 '65

Law

See Fishery laws and legislation

Japan

Fishing, not for fun. il Bsns W p32-3 Je 29 '63

United States

See also
United States—Fish and wildlife service
FISHERMEN
Great tuna war; commercial seiners vs sport fishermen. F. T. Moss. il Field & S 68:10-12+ Je '63
FISHERMEN'S fiesta. See Festivals—California
FISHERY laws and legislation
Bill prohibits fishing by foreign vessels in U.S. territorial waters; statement, May 20, 1964, with Department statement, regarding application to Japan. L. B. Johnson. Dept State Bul 50:936 Je 15 '64
Decision in Oregon. T. Trueblood. il Field & S 69:10-12+ N '64
Fishing laws; United States and Canada (title varies) (cont) Field & S 67:18+ Ap; 68:18+ My '63; 20+ Ap; 69:22-3+ My '64
Fishing seasons (cont) Outdoor Life 131:8+ Ap; 10+ My; 30+ Je '63; 133:30+ Ap; 176+ My '64
No tuna today; fishing off Ecuador. Newsweek 61:54 Je 17 '63
Teeth without jaws; new bill. Newsweek 63:39 My 18 '64
What to do in a pinch. F. Calkins. il Field & S 68:44-6+ N '63
FISHERY research
Dreamy new era for fish; experiments with LSD-25. R. H. Boyle. Sports Illus 20:50+ Mr 30 '64
Gone fishing; oceanographic ships, Albatross IV. il Newsweek 61:60 Je 17 '63
New look into the sea. R. H. Boyle. il Sports Illus 20:58-62+ Mr 9 '64
FISHES
Famous game fish no one can catch. il Life 56:52-7 Je 26 '64
Horrors of the deep. il Sci Digest 56:11-13 S '64
Oxygen lack kills fish. Sci N L 85:365 Je 6 '64
Push from behind moves fish forward. Sci N L 86:313 N 14 '64
Smell, sex and survival in animals. K. Von Frisch. il Sci Digest 53:65-72 F '63
Tropical fish take the profit hook. il Bsns W p84+ N 14 '64
See also
Electric organs in fishes
Fishing
Hearing in fishes
Poisonous fishes
Sense organs—Fishes
Teeth (fishes)
also headings beginning Fish; *also* names of fishes, e.g. Carp

Anatomy

See also
Phosphorescence

Diseases and pests

Persistence of neorickettsiae helminthoeca in an endoparasite of the Pacific salmon. R. K. Farrell and others. bibliog Science 145:162-3 Jl 10 '64
Plague of Florida and California; red tide. N. B. Slaton. il Sci Digest 56:9-13 N '64
Red tide. il Newsweek 61:98 My 27 '63
See also
Cancer in fishes

Ecology

Fishes and climates. C. L. Smith. il Natur Hist 73:34-9 F '64
Hot tips from the tank men. D. Shaw. il Field & S 68:58-9+ F '64

Extermination

Getting rid of the bad guys; chemical warfare against predator fish. W. S. Griswold. il Pop Sci 184:110-12+ Ap '64
Green River fiasco. P. M. Tilden. Natur Hist 72:63 Je '63

FISHES—Extermination—*Continued*
Is our native underwater life worth saving? R. R. Miller. bibliog il Nat Parks Mag 37: 4-9 My '63

Habits and behavior

How to find fish with your boat. W. W. Hunter. il Field & S 68:50-3 Je '63
My quarry eye to eye; excerpts from Fisherman's fall. R. Haig-Brown. il Sports Illus 21:84-6+ O 19 '64
Symbiotic behavior among fishes from temperate ocean waters. F. H. McCutcheon and A. E. McCutcheon. bibliog il Science 145: 948-9 Ag 28 '64

Migration

Giving fish a go sign. il Bsns W p 198-200 Ap 18 '64
Long journey of the dogfish. W. N. Hess. il Natur Hist 73:32-5 N '64
Migration in Maine; brook trout. P. J. Fournier. il Natur Hist 73:46-9 O '64
Noisy fish tracked by team of scientists; sonar-equipped fish. il Sci N L 86:261 O 24 '64

Physiology

Cholinergic substance in the caudal neurosecretory storage organ of fish. H. Kobayashi and others. bibliog il Science 141: 714-16 Ag 23 '63
Electrophysiologic indications of the osmoregulatory role of the teleost urophysis. K. Yagi and H. A. Bern. bibliog il Science 142:491-3 O 25 '63
Enolase: multiple molecular forms in fish muscle. H. Tsuyuki and F. Wold. bibliog il Science 146:535-7 O 23 '64
Ostracittoxin: an ichthyotoxic stress secretion of the boxfish, ostracion lentiginosus. D. A. Thomson. bibliog Science 146:244-5 O 9 '64
Spawning of starfish: action of gamete-shedding substance obtained from radial nerves. H. Kanatani. bibliog il Science 146: 1177-9 N 27 '64

Preservation

Ammonia for speedy preservation of fish. Sci N L 84:265 O 26 '63
Ammonia: possible use for preserving fish. V. Subrahmanyan and others. bibliog il Science 142:233-4 O 11 '63

Reproduction

Hermaphroditism in Bahama groupers. C. L. Smith. il Natur Hist 73:42-7 Je '64

Stories

Exit, laughing. E. Zern. See issues of Field & stream

FISHES, Deep sea
Come feed my trigger fish; collecting salt-water fish. il Time 82:31 Ag 30 '63

FISHES, Effect of temperature on
Secrets of the frigid fish; Antarctic fish, Dissostichus mawsoni. Sci Digest 55:38 Mr '64

FISHES, Extinct
See also
Coelacanths

FISHES, Fossil
Armor-plated and jawless Devonian fish. D. L. Dineley. il Natur Hist 73:48-53 Ag '64
Fishes and climates. C. L. Smith. il Natur Hist 73:34-9 F '64

FISHES, Photography of. See Photography of fishes

FISHES, Tagging of. See Fish tagging

FISHES, birds, and sons of men; story. See Ford, J. H.

FISHING
All out for banzai! il Time 84:80-1 Jl 10 '64
Angling. W. Davis. See issues of Outdoor life
Angling's charmed circle; with editorial comment. L. Wulff. il Esquire 61:6, 96-7+ My '64
Colorado jackpot. J. Olsen. il Sports Illus 19:52-9 S 2 '63
Famous game fish no one can catch. il Life 56:52-7 Je 26 '64
Fishing aplenty for the disabled. F. White. il Todays Health 42:50-1+ S '64
Fishing (cont) il Sport Illus 18:42-3 Ja 28; 50 My 27; 19:64-5 O 21 '63
Fishing; ed. by A. J. McClane. See issues of Field & stream
Fly fishing, cheap and easy. B. Warner. il Field & S 68:52-5 Mr '64
Gist of it; digest of the outdoor news; ed. by H. Moore. See issues of Outdoor life
Hot tips from the tank men. D. Shaw. il Field & S 68:58-9+ F '64
How to find fish with your boat. W. W. Hunter. il Field & S 68:50-3 Je '63
In praise of fishing; excerpts from Fishing for fun, and to wash your soul. H. Hoover. il Read Digest 82:243-4+ Ap '63
Monofilament hates people. H. Babcock. il Field & S 68:40-2+ My '63
Sportsman's notebook. H. G. Tapply. See issues of Field & stream
Troublesome trifles. T. Trueblood. il Field & S 68:24+ Ap '64
Water temperature: key to fishing. T. Trueblood. il Field & S 69:16+ Jl '64
We took to the great outdoors with baby. E. Hayes. il Parents Mag 39:46-7+ Je '64
Where to go fishing, vacationing, hunting all over the world (title varies) P. A. Parsons. See issues of Outdoor life
World-record trout. il Look 27:80a-80b Ag 13 '63
World's master caster; J. Tarantino. R. De Roos. il Sports Illus 19:30-6 Jl 8 '63
See also
Airplanes in hunting and fishing
Salt water fishing
Smelt fishing
Trout fishing

Accidents and injuries

Bait-box voyage. Newsweek 61:40 Je 24 '63

Anecdotes, facetiae, satire, etc.

Peripatetic reviewer. E. Weeks. Atlan 213: 132+ My '64

Competitions

High cost of not catching swordfish. D. Barnes. il Sports Illus 21:46-7 Jl 20 '64
1962-1963 winners; Field & stream fishing contest. Field & S 67:18+ Mr; 32+ Ap '63; 68:14+ Mr; 90+ Ap '64
1,236 red-hot fishermen; All-England fishing championship. C. Fletcher. il Field & S 68:40-3+ N '63

Implements and appliances

Far cry from Izaak Walton. il Fortune 68: 134-5 D '63
Hooked. Newsweek 63:63-4 My 18 '64
Proper rod balance. W. Davis. il Outdoor Life 132:92-3 N '63
Sonic fish dog; Lo-K-Tor. T. Trueblood. il Field & S 69:27-9+ Jl '64
Southern comfort for the Arctic angler. H. Sibley. il Pop Mech 121:155 F '64
Things I could kick myself for. T. Trueblood. il Field & S 67:16+ F '63
To catch a tired fish: monster trawl. Time 84:51 D 4 '64
Trueblood kicks again. T. Trueblood. il Field & S 68:16+ Jl '63
See also
Fishing tackle

Law

See Fishery laws and legislation

Alaska

Everything else but. W. Page. il Field & S 67:37-9+ Mr '63
Hidden lakes; airplane trip. D. Hill. Flying 75:47+ Jl '64
Salmon for everyone. E. A. Bauer. il Outdoor Life 135:40-3+ F '65

Arctic Regions

Fiery fish. G. Laycock. il Outdoor life 131:64-7+ Je '63
Promise of the North. T. Trueblood. il Field & S 69:24+ Je '64

Argentina

Landlocks deluxe. B. Warner. il Field & S 69:37-9+ My '64
Rio Muy Grande. B. Warner. il Field & S 69: 27-9+ D '64

Arizona

Arizona's fish and fun spot: Apache-land. B. Minette and R. Dunlop. il Todays Health 41:22-5+ O '63
Fishing on the fly. E. A. Bauer. il Outdoor Life 132:17-19+ Jl '63

Arkansas

Bull bass are my hobby. S. Welch. il Outdoor Life 132:36-9+ Jl '63
Unique new fishing lake; White Oak, Ark. R. Tinsley. il Outdoor Life 134:38-9+ O '64

Bahama Islands

Duel with a hammerhead. G. Heinold. il Outdoor Life 131:8-9+ Ja '63
How to bag bonefish. G. Heinold. il Outdoor Life 134:14-15+ N '64

FISHING—Bahama Islands—*Continued*
Where the fish are. F. T. Moss. il Motor B 114:29-32+ N '63
White wakes in the Bahamas. F. T. Moss. il Yachting 113:49-51+ F '63

Bermuda

Remarkable wahoo. J. Olsen. il Sports Illus 19:80-2+ S 30 '63

British Honduras

Bay of Pigs. G. X. Sand. il Field & S 67:54-5 Mr '63

California

Boil! R. S. Mikkelsen. il Outdoor Life 134:46-7+ Jl '64
Get 'em while they're cold. V. L. Hoss. il Outdoor Life 131:70-1+ Je '63
Glow in the dark; for steelhead, fire flies. L. Green. il Outdoor Life 132:40-3+ O '63
Gold for fishermen. V. L. Hoss. il Outdoor Life 133:54-7+ Ap '64
Hog-wild chinooks. F. H. Ames. il Outdoor Life 132:50-2+ D '63
In Mill Creek the rainbows grow fat and sassy. il Sunset 133:18+ O '64
It's a happy place for fishermen: McCloud River. il Sunset 131:38+ S '63
It's time for crappies. W. Curtis. il Outdoor Life 133:26-8+ Mr '64
Keep moving. J. Freeman. il Outdoor Life 132:48-9+ N '63
Loaded with bass. C. Dickey. il Outdoor Life 133:64-5+ Je '64
Maytime is shad time. L. R. Green. il Outdoor Life 131:82-4+ My '63
Minor league steelhead. J. Freeman. il Field & S 68:114-17+ F '64
New steelhead thrills. D. F. Brown. il Outdoor Life 134:42-3+ D '64
Owens; never-fail trout river. J. Mears. il Field & S 67:31-3+ Mr '63
Steelhead action on the Scott. il Sunset 131:53-4 N '63
Steelhead fly fishing. T. Trueblood. il Field & S 68:16+ O '63
Strong-arm steelheads. F. H. Ames. il Outdoor Life 135:34-5+ Ja '65
Tall tule bass. F. H. Ames. il Outdoor Life 133:40-1+ Ja '64
They're all having luck; Bidwell Lake. il Sunset 132:83-4+ My '64
Trapped in Devil's Hole. K. E. Oveson. il Outdoor Life 132:50-1+ S '63
Try northern California for fishing at its best. M. Kane. il Todays Health 42:46-51+ My '64
Tule dippers. H. Hayden. il Field & S 68:54-5+ F '64
West Coast stompede. L. R. Green. il Outdoor Life 131:30-1+ Mr '63
Wet-fly casting for steelhead; Klamath River. il Sunset 133:18 S '64
What makes Hot Creek hot? J. Mears. il Outdoor Life 134:32-5+ S '64
When winter storms roil the rivers, try the Smith for steelhead. il Sunset 132:19 Ja '64
Yellow streak. B. Beebe. il Outdoor Life 132:48-9+ Jl '63

California, Gulf of

Fly on the ocean. F. Dufresne. il Field & S 68:34-5 Ag '63
Magic fish trap. C. M. Kreider. il Outdoor Life 133:36-7+ F '64

California, Lower

Pickup camper paradise. R. Cannon. il Field & S 67:70-3+ Ap '63

Canada

Fisherman's guide to the Maritimes. A. J. McClane. il Field & S 69:126-8+ Je '64
Fishermen's special: Algoma wilderness. M. Ellis. il Field & S 68:140-3+ My '63
Fishing the 58th parallel. D. M. Duffey. il Outdoor Life 134:50-2+ Jl '64
Fishing was wild. A. W. Prince. il Outdoor Life 131:45-7+ Je '63
For great fishing, try Canada. H. Bradshaw and V. Bradshaw. il Suc Farm 61:67 Je '63
Ghost pike of Manitoba. M. Ellis. il Field & S 67:120-2 Mr '63
Great new lake; St Lawrence fishway. T. Janes. il Outdoor Life 131:24-7+ Mr '63
Greatest rainbow trip. B. McPherson. il Outdoor Life 133:40-3+ My '64
Grilse of the Upsalquitch. B. S. Wright. il Field & S 67:68-9 Ap '63
How to net a fish. W. Davis. il Outdoor Life 134:76-7 D '64
Hudson Bay and back by canoe. D. Jarden. il Outdoor Life 132:36-9+ S '63
Hunters' holiday. W. Page. il Field & S 68:38-40 Ag '63
Kayak merry-go-round. J. Clark. il Field & S 69:32-5 Ja '65
Lake trout lore. A. J. McClane. il Field & S 69:70-4 D '64
Land of ekaluk aluk. A. J. McClane. il Field & S 68:46-8+ Je '63
Muskie on his back. J. C. Chapralis. il Field & S 69:70-1+ S '64
My favorite guide; Johnny Burns. J. Cornelius. il Field & S 68:46-7+ My '63
My no. 1 fishing spot. H. Andrews. il Outdoor Life 132:24-7+ Jl '63
New land of strange trout. E. A. Bauer. il Field & S 68:35-7+ Ap '64
New landlock salmon water. M. Terziev. il Outdoor Life 134:20-3+ Jl '64
New road to Rocky Mountain trout. E. A. Bauer. il Outdoor Life 131:68-71+ My '63
Old-fashioned trout trip. R. Bailey. il Outdoor Life 133:36-9+ Je '64
Quebec's newest road to fishing. E. R. Thornton. il Field & S 69:46-9+ Jl '64
Rescue! E. R. Thornton. il Field & S 67:34-6+ Mr '63
River of records. B. White. il Field & S 68:122-4+ Je '63
River to the Arctic. B. Warner. il Field & S 68:78-80+ Ja '64
Salmon of Yucataw Rapids. E. Dufresne. il Field & S 69:68-9 S '64
Technique for Northerns. J. O. Cartier. il Field & S 67:62-5+ Ap '63
Topside togue. A. J. McClane. il Field & S 67:29-31+ F '63
Trail-blazing a vacation. J. V. Edsall and M. S. Edsall. il Outdoor Life 131:56-9+ My '63
Trailer trek to Timagami. F. M. Paulson. il Field & S 68:64+ Ap '64
Trophy brook trout. A. J. McClane. il Field & S 68:82-5 N '63
Two weeks for steelhead. J. Freeman. il Field & S 67:48-51+ F '63
We ran the blackwater. R. E. Landsburg. il Outdoor Life 132:40-3+ Ag '63
Where northerns come big. G. Laycock. il Outdoor Life 134:44-5+ Ag '64
Whitefish magic. J. Brooks. il Outdoor Life 132:30-1+ Jl '63
Wild thyme fish. A. J. McClane. il Field & S 68:66-9 D '63

Chile

Something for a rainy day. G. Laycock. il Outdoor Life 135:44-7+ Ja '65

Colorado

Bright Angel brownies. C. Fletcher. il Field & S 69:42-3 D '64
Rocky Mountain springtime; photographs by M. Kauffman. Sports Illus 18:38-41 Mr 25 '63

Connecticut

Christmastide fish. F. McKinley. il Outdoor Life 132:36-7+ D '63

Costa Rica

Budget safari. il Time 83:88 Ap 10 '64

Dominican Republic

In the land of Oh-by-Jingo. V. Heilner. il Field & S 69:110-13 N '64

England

1,236 red-hot fishermen; All-England fishing championship. C. Fletcher. il Field & S 68:40-3+ N '63

Florida

Backwater bass. W. Blassingame. il Field & S 68:38-40+ Ap '64
Battle with a heavyweight. G. Heinold. il Outdoor Life 133:10-11+ Ja '64
Battling barracuda. G. Heinold. il Outdoor Life 134:26-7+ S '64
Big snook is disaster. W. Jacqmar. il Outdoor Life 131:40-1+ F '63
Blue water bargain. G. Casey. il Outdoor Life 133:60-3+ Je '64
Chaos in heaven. W. Blassingame. il Field & S 68:38-9+ Ja '64
Convict fish. G. Heinold. il Outdoor Life 135:14-15+ F '65
Far-flung Atlantic bonito. G. Heinold. il Outdoor Life 134:10-11+ D '64
Fly rod tarpon. J. Brooks. il Field & S 67:34-5 F '63
Jack the giant killer. A. J. McClane. il Field & S 68:80-2+ Mr '64
Mayhem in the mangroves (cont) A. J. McClane. il Field & S 67:62-7 F '63
Millions of dam fish. W. Blassingame. il Outdoor Life 133:34-5+ Ja '64

FISHING—Florida—*Continued*
New rig for balao salt water sensation. G. Robey. il Outdoor Life 131:44-5+ Ja '63
Sailfish for excitement. G. Heinold. il Outdoor Life 134:30-1+ O '64
Slugging red snapper. G. Heinold. il Outdoor Life 132:22+ S '63
Southern pier fishing. G. Heinold. il Outdoor Life 135:14-15+ Ja '65
Sport with pompano. G. Heinold. il Outdoor Life 132:22+ O '63
Strike of lightning. J. Brooks. il Outdoor Life 135:20-3+ Ja '65
Tarpon are sissies. J. A. Knight. il Field & S 69:30-1+ Ja '65
Trail of the tarpon. D. M. Newell. il Field & S 68:56-7+ Mr '64
We fought a fresh-water monster. E. Nowak, jr. il Outdoor Life 133:48-9+ Ja '64
When the shad come home from the sea; reproductions of paintings by F. Golden; with account by D. Barnes. Sports Illus 20:40-51 Mr 16 '64
Where the bass never quit. C. Elliott. il Outdoor Life 133:42-3+ F '64
Where the fish are. W. Davis. il Outdoor Life 132:54-6 Ag '63
Where to catch snook. G. Heinold. il Outdoor Life 132:12+ N '63

Georgia

Those bizarre bass. C. Elliott. il Outdoor Life 131:62-3+ My '63

Hawaii

Around your feet swims 'oama. il Sunset 133:22 Jl '64

Idaho

Cold weather trout. T. Trueblood. il Field & S 67:22+ Mr '63
Heavy devils of Hell's Canyon. C. Ormond. il Outdoor Life 133:58-9 My '64
How to con a crappie. C. Conley. il Field & S 69:55-7+ Je '64
Where the outdoor experts go. K. N. Anderson. il Todays Health 41:44-7+ S '63

Iowa

Outdoors. V. Bourjaily. Esquire 61:57+ Je '64

Ireland

Travel notes; joy of living in Ireland. R. Joseph. Esquire 59:24+ Ap '63

Jamaica

Jamaican holiday. A. J. McClane. il Field & S 68:138-41+ Mr '64

Kenya

Malindi: a place of deep water. N. Adams. il Sports Illus 18:78-84+ Je 17 '63
Trolling for tramcars. W. Page. il Field & S 68:43-5 D '63

Labrador

Lifting the lid on Labrador. E. Buck. il Am For 70:28-31+ Ag '64

Louisiana

Bussey is best; it's bassy. G. Gresham. il Outdoor Life 133:76-7+ Ap '64
Choupique by the sackful. L. Dietz. il Field & S 68:42-3+ Mr '64

Maine

Allagash story; wilderness trout trip. T. Janes. il Outdoor Life 134:32-3+ Ag '64
Fishing's forgotten spot. B. L. Spiller. il Field & S 67:96-8+ F '63
Hide-and-seek perch. A. J. McClane. il Field & S 68:106-9 O '63
Last of the skitterers. B. Geagan. il Field & S 69:38-40+ Jl '64
Place for everything; go out for bass, come back with duck. A. W. Prince. il Outdoor Life 134:52-3+ S '64
Stripers in the river. L. Dietz. il Field & S 68:44-5+ Ag '63
Tips for summer landlocks. W. Davis. il Outdoor Life 134:56+ Jl '64
Trout from still waters. E. W. Smith. il Field & S 68:58-9+ O '63
Weatherproof fishing. H. F. Blaisdell. il Outdoor Life 133:44-5+ Je '64

Maryland

Budget marlin. Time 82:51-2 Ag 16 '63
Potomac bass float trip. D. Carpenter. il Am For 69:24-6 Ag '63
Promised land of bass. T. Janes. il Outdoor Life 131:76-7+ Je '63

Massachusetts

Best ways to bluefish. G. Heinold. il Outdoor Life 134:10-11 Ag '64

Michigan

Everybody's doing it. J. B. Cleason. il Outdoor Life 133:30-1+ F '64
Perch are running. J. B. Gleason. il Outdoor Life 133:66-8+ My '64
Perfect trout stream. J. B. Gleason. il Outdoor Life 132:50-2+ Jl '63
Storm fish. M. Ellis. il Field & S 67:10-11 Mr '63

Minnesota

Autumn jackpot. H. Bradshaw. il Outdoor Life 132:44-7+ S '63
Blizzard bass. B. Cary. il Outdoor Life 133:60-1+ Ap '64
Snowmobile lakers. H. Bradshaw. il Field & S 69:27-9+ Ja '65
Why waste winter? D. W. Larson. il Outdoor Life 133:24-7+ Ja '64

Mississippi

Fish the midnight eel. R. E. Price. il Outdoor Life 132:36-7+ Ag '63
Grabbling for those crazy Mississippi cats. H. Peterson. il Sports Illus 20:58-60+ Je 15 '64
October bass explosion. R. E. Price. il Outdoor Life 132:56-9+ O '63

Missouri

Bull bass are my hobby. S. Welch. il Outdoor Life 132:36-9+ Jl '63

Montana

Beartooth adventure. E. A. Bauer. il Outdoor Life 133:48-51+ Je '64
Best all-round trout fly; muddler minnow. J. Brooks. il Outdoor Life 132:64-5+ O '63
Big fish lake, a sequel. D. A. Burk. il Field & S 69:44 O '64
Fly fishing in lakes. A. J. McClane. il Field & S 69:86-9 N '64
Found: bass bonanza. E. A. Bauer. il Outdoor Life 131:24-7+ F '63
Gallatin glissade. J. Clark. il Field & S 68:21-3+ Jl '63
Mighty trout of the Mighty Mo. J. Brooks. il Outdoor Life 131:56-9+ Ap '63
Wilderness reward. T. Trueblood. il Field & S 67:47-9+ Ap '63

Nebraska

Blue ribbon waters. P. Czura. il Field & S 68:62-3+ My '63
Nebraska's never-fail lakes. P. Czura. il Field & S 69:116-20 S '64

Nevada

Hiking in for golden trout. il Sunset 131:36+ Ag '63

New England

Fifty-six minutes to paradise; southern New England. W. R. Miller. il Flying 75:42-4 Ag '64

New Hampshire

Go light for mackerel. G. Heinold. il Outdoor Life 133:12+ Ap '64
Great Bay bonanza. B. M. Blum. il Field & S 68:86-8+ D '63
Remote ponds near home. N. Bryant. il Outdoor Life 131:76-7+ My '63
Trout after dark. N. Bryant. il Outdoor Life 132:44-5+ Jl '63

New Jersey

Delaware shad. C. Conley. il Field & S 68:61-3 Mr '64
First day blues. C. Conley. il Field & S 68:40-1+ Jl '63
Fly rod in the surf. P. McLain. il Field & S 69:58-61 O '64

New Mexico

New Mexico's high country. R. Tinsley. il Travel 122:48-9 S '64

New York (state)

Casting's fun, but can you catch trout? W. Jacqmar. il Outdoor Life 131:17-19+ Mr '63
Day Alfandre fought geronimo. F. T. Moss. il Outdoor Life 133:70-3+ Ap '64
For midsummer trout: let it rain. W. Davis. il Outdoor Life 132:30-1+ Ag '63
I am a bit of a fanatic. R. H. Boyle. il Sports Illus 19:64-5 O 21 '63
It's hooking-up time. D. R. Crandall. il Outdoor Life 131:36-7+ Ja '63
Obliging porgy. G. Heinold. il Outdoor Life 132:10-11+ Ag '63
Pulling the plug that killed a great shad stream; Delaware River. J. S. Martin. Sports Illus 18:50 My 27 '63

FISHING—New York (state)—*Continued*
Shad are back. D. R. Crandall. il Outdoor Life 133:44-5+ Mr '64
Some spring secrets. R. L. Estes. il Outdoor Life 131:72-3+ Ap '63
Stripers in the Hudson. A. Glowka. il Outdoor Life 134:20-3+ Ag '64
Tiger of Lake Chautauqua. E. P. Clarkson. il Motor B 112:82+ Jl '63
Warden's way. D. Knight. il Field & S 69:46-7+ Je '64

Newfoundland

New hotspot for tuna. V. C. Heilner. il Field & S 69:144-6 My '64

North Carolina

Another gorge to fish. H. L. Lawrence. il Outdoor Life 133:78-82 Ap '64
Big red drum. G. Heinold. il Outdoor Life 132:64-5+ S '63
Touch of wilderness. C. Elliott. il Outdoor Life 133:56-7+ My '64

Norway

Best single salmon pool anywhere; Norway's Malangsfoss pool. il Sports Illus 21:64-7 Ag 17 '64

Ohio

How to fish the weeds. E. A. Bauer. il Outdoor Life 134:28-31+ Ag '64
We fish the ice at night. E. A. Bauer. il Outdoor Life 131:16-19+ Ja '63

Oklahoma

New winter favorite. G. E. Gurley. il Outdoor Life 135:72-4 F '65

Oregon

Decision in Oregon. T. Trueblood. il Field & S 69:10-12+ N '64
Fishing's fine for ninety miles. il Sunset 132:90 My '64
Mail-run adventure. J. Clark. il Outdoor Life 134:44-5+ Jl '64
Oregon. T. Bacon. il Flying 75:43-4+ Jl '64
Oregon's September madness. B. Behme. il Field & S 68:41-3 S '63
They give you the jumps. J. V. Wormer. il Outdoor Life 133:56-9 Mr '64
Wickiup browns. D. Murphey. il Field & S 69:49-51+ Ag '64

Panama

Mob of marlin in the bays of Panama. J. Olsen. il Sports Illus 18:62-8+ Ap 22 '63
Panama paradise. A. J. McClane. il Field & S 68:52-3+ O '63

Pennsylvania

Bass for the asking. S. R. Slaymaker, 2d. il Outdoor Life 132:24-7+ N '63
Broken stream revives; Brodhead Creek, Monroe County, Pa. J. Hayes. il Outdoor Life 131:52-5+ Je '63
Fish catches man; trout fishing. C. K. Fox. Esquire 59:44+ Ap '63
Hatch matching made easy. S. R. Slaymaker, 2d. il Outdoor Life 133:66-7+ Ap '64
Miracle of Whites Creek. J. Hayes. il Outdoor Life 134:24-7+ N '64
New fishing for Easterners; Erie's spring rainbow run. J. Hayes. il Outdoor Life 131:40-1+ Mr '63

Rhode Island

Fishing tidal rivers. G. Heinold. il Outdoor Life 131:20+ Je '63

Scotland

Fisherman's tour of Scotland. J. Brooks. il Outdoor Life 131:28-31+ Ja '63

South Carolina

Singing rivers and a sea of mud. E. White. il Sports Illus 19:66-8+ D 16 '63

Southern states

For a warm opening day. W. Davis. il Outdoor Life 133:70+ Mr '64
Look southward, angler. W. Davis. il Outdoor Life 133:33-5+ Mr '64

Surinam

How to eat a piranha before it eats you. G. McKay. il Sports Illus 18:48-50 Mr 11 '63

Tennessee

All about... ah... brim. C. Vinson. il Outdoor Life 131:82-3+ Ap '63
Big trout on the little T. H. L. Lawrence. il Field & S 68:42-3+ Ja '64
Dynamite on Doe Creek. J. Rutherfoord. il Field & S 69:84-6+ Ja '65
Trout find of the year. E. A. Bauer. il Outdoor Life 131:36-9+ Mr '63

Texas

Float into the past. R. Tinsley. il Outdoor Life 132:17-19+ Ag '63
Grand awakening. R. Tinsley. il Outdoor Life 131:50-3+ Mr '63
LCRA spells fish! R. Tinsley. il Travel 121:56-8 F '64
Pothole catfish. R. Tinsley. il Outdoor Life 131:78-80+ Je '63
Summer's hottest fishing. R. Tinsley. il Field & S 68:48-9+ Jl '63
Texas two-bit fishing. G. Getner. il Field & S 67:158-61+ Ap '63

United States

Are you a sap for the ribbon cutters? destruction of fishing streams through highway building. A. Grahame. il Outdoor Life 131:10-12+ Je '63; Reply with rejoinder. R. M. Whitton. 132:4+ S '63
Fish the flat water. G. B. Gordon. il Outdoor Life 133:50-1+ My '64
Great new lake; St Lawrence fishway. T. Janes. il Outdoor Life 131:24-7+ Mr '63
Hats off to the cats. R. Tinsley. il Outdoor Life 134:42-3+ N '64
How to catch big stripers. F. T. Moss. il Field & S 68:54-7+ My '63
Join the fun for pan fishing. P. Czura. il Todays Health 42:46-50+ S '64
Life guide; trout fishing. il Life 54:14 Ap 26 '63
My favorite striper hotspots. G. Heinold. il Outdoor Life 133:16+ Je '64
Perch that is a bass. W. Davis. il Outdoor Life 134:54-6 Ag '64
Planning a float trip. J. A. Emmett. il Outdoor Life 131:12+ Ap '63
Pockets full of trout. W. Davis. il Outdoor Life 133:70+ My '64
Shooting-preserve fishing. A. MacBain. il Field & S 67:182-3 Ap '63
Summer fishing eastern streams. R. Warner. il Field & S 68:92-4+ Jl '63
Technique for Northerns. J. O. Cartier. il Field & S 67:62-5+ Ap '63
Top fish and where to catch them; symposium. il Outdoor Life 131:60-3+ Ap '63
Trouting, where? D. Carpenter. il Am For 69:22-3+ Mr '63
Twenty-five top fishing holes. W. Davis. il Outdoor Life 133:33-5+ My '64
Two weeks for steelhead. J. Freeman. il Field & S 67:48-51+ F '63
Wing dam walleyes. H. Bradshaw. il Field & S 68:10-11 My '63
Your fishing and hunting routes to the World's fair; symposium. il Field & S 68:41-8+ Ap '64

Utah

Fishing Utah by camper. B. Behme. il Field & S 68:36-9+ F '64
Where trout bite on marshmallows; Panguitch Lake. il Sunset 131:46 O '63

Vermont

April trout look down. H. F. Blaisdell. il Outdoor Life 131:72+ Ap '63
Big bugs bug big pike. H. F. Blaisdell. il Outdoor Life 134:42-3+ S '64
Smelt have me hooked. H. F. Blaisdell il Outdoor Life 131:30-1+ F '63

Virgin Islands

Virgin Islands discovery. J. Brooks. il Outdoor Life 135:62-3+ F '65

Virginia

Bomb range bass. K. Osborne. il Field & S 69:43-5+ S '64
How to outsmart cobia. G. Heinold. il Outdoor Life 134:10-11+ Jl '64
Rocks of the Roanoke River. J. Rutherfoord. il Field & S 69:52-5+ My '64
Surfing for channel bass. G. Heinold. il Outdoor Life 133:10+ My '64

Washington (state)

Most underfished river in the U.S; Yakima River. W. W. Hunter. il Outdoor Life 132:24-7+ Ag '63
Ten years better; Grand Coulee Dam transformed Grant County, Wash. F. Dufresne. il Field & S 68:124-6+ O '63
Trolling deep at Lake Crescent. il Sunset 133:36+ Ag '64
When the kings run. W. W. Hunter. il Outdoor Life 133:56-7+ Je '64

FISHING—*Continued*

Western states

Go West; flying to fishing and hunting areas. J. Gartner. il Flying 75:38-49+ Jl '64
Nothing like it. J. Zumbo. il Outdoor Life 134:28-31+ D '64
Rainbows of Flaming Gorge. H. Wixom. il Field & S 69:100-2+ Jl '64

Wisconsin

Five days for muskies. E. A. Bauer. il Outdoor Life 131:76-9+ Ap '63
Grass is always greener. M. Ellis. il Field & S 69:28-30+ Ag '64
Muskie myths exploded. M. Ellis. il Field & S 69:50-1+ Jl '64
Potluck on the Red Cedar. G. Laycock. il Field & S 68:112-14+ S '63
Trouble-shoot for trout. H. Wixom. il Outdoor Life 133:48-51+ Mr '64

Wyoming

Beartooth adventure. E. A. Bauer. il Outdoor Life 133:48-51+ Je '64
Day at Saratoga; deer and trout in one day. W. Page. il Field & S 69:35-7 N '64
For the finest fishing plan a hunting trip. C. Elliott. il Outdoor Life 134:48-9+ O '64
Shooting the Snake. J. C. Daniel. il Field & S 68:58-61 S '63

FISHING, Deep sea. See Salt water fishing

FISHING, Winter
Christmastide fish. F. McKinley. il Outdoor Life 132:36-7+ D '63
Everybody's doing it. J. B. Gleason. il Outdoor Life 133:30-1+ F '64
Finding fish in winter. H. G. Tapply. il Field & S 68:44 Ja '64
Homemade auger speeds ice fishing. H. Bradshaw. il Pop Sci 184:154 F '64
How to prime an ice hole. H. G. Tapply. il Field & S 68:66 F '64
Ice fisherman's favorite. W. Davis. il Outdoor Life 135:76+ F '65
Ice fishing, it's the greatest. H. Bradshaw. il Suc Farm 61:116 F '63
It's hooking-up time. D. R. Crandall. il Outdoor Life 131:36-7+ Ja '63
Lakers at 30 below. B. Cary. il Outdoor Life 135:40-1+ Ja '65
New ice-fishing ideas; Michigan's rainbows. H. F. Zeman. il Outdoor Life 135:48-9+ F '65
New vacation trend: winter fishing. W. Davis. il Outdoor Life 133:68-70 Ja '64
Patient madmen of Sheepshead Bay. A. Zich. il Sports Illus 18:18-23 F 4 '63
Smelt have me hooked. H. F. Blaisdell. il Outdoor Life 131:30-1+ F '63
Snowmobile lakers. H. Bradshaw. il Field & S 69:27-9+ Ja '65
We fish the ice at night. E. A. Bauer. il Outdoor Life 131:16-19+ Ja '63
Why waste winter? D. W. Larson. il Outdoor Life 133:24-7+ Ja '64

FISHING boat captains. See Shipmasters

FISHING boats
Boats for fishing. J. A. Emmett. il Outdoor Life 131:52-5+ F '63
Fishermen reel in a U.S. flier; with report by H. Lavallee. il Life 55:49-52 S 13 '63
46' custom sportfisherman. il Motor B 112:54 O '63
Growing Soviet threat on the high seas; Russia's trawlers. il U S News 56:13 F 3 '64
Last of the hook boats; sponge boats. R. C. Weller. il Yachting 114:126+ Ag '63
Last of the old hookers. il Yachting 113:154 F '63
Offshore sportfisherman. il Yachting 114:50-1 O '63
What red spy fleet is doing off U.S. il U S News 55:8 S 9 '63

Chartering

Charter in the islands. il Motor B 112:41-4 S '63
Fishing boat captain. il Ebony 18:43-5 O '63
New sport: captain-fishing. V. Kraft. il Sports Illus 19:26-30+ S 2 '63

Design

Designed for sportfishing. Lijack. il Yachting 114:57+ Jl '63
Sportfisherman plus! N. Beckner. il Yachting 116:57+ Ag '64

Equipment

Cruisingman's guide to a fisherman's boat. B. Wisner. il Motor B 113:34-5+ My '64

FISHING boats, Remodeled
Yachtsman's dreamboat; Coastal Queen, remodeled diesel-powered oyster buy-boat. H. Bloomfield. il Yachting 114:57-9+ O '63

FISHING clubs
Gone fishing. il Fortune 69:144-8 My '64

FISHING flies. See Fishing lures, flies, etc.

FISHING guides. See Guides

FISHING industry. See Fish industry and trade

FISHING lake; story. See Spencer, E.

FISHING licenses. See Licenses

FISHING lines. See Fishing tackle

FISHING lures, flies, etc.
Amazing trout bug. H. G. Tapply. il Field & S 67:80 Ap '63
Bass bugs made easy. D. Scott. il Outdoor Life 134:52 Ag '64
Best bet for bass. R. Tinsley. il Field & S 67:60-1+ Ap '63
Best flies for big trout. A. J. McClane. il Field & S 69:88-94 Je '64
Best lures for early trout. W. Davis. il Outdoor Life 131:54+ Mr '63
CQ fish; electronic lure. B. Billick. il Pop Electr 20:45-7 Je '64
Change of pace. A. J. McClane. il Field & S 69:96-9 S '64
Deadliest fly; nymph fishing. W. Davis. il Outdoor Life 131:86+ My '63
Do it with nail polish; protect fresh-water lures in salt water. H. G. Tapply. il Field & S 69:46 Ja '65
Dropper-fly dope. H. G. Tapply. il Field & S 68:70 My '63
Fine art of midging. W. Davis. il Outdoor Life 132:54-6 Jl '63
Fine points for fly casters. W. Davis. il Outdoor Life 133:70-2 Je '64
Fishing with a stripteaser; piece of fish belly. H. G. Tapply. il Field & S 68:62 S '63
Five deadly walleye lures. W. Davis. il Outdoor Life 134:118+ S '64
Flies for sophisticated trout. T. Trueblood. il Field & S 68:24+ My '63
Fly fishing for smallmouths. A. J. McClane. il Field & S 68:88-90+ Je '63
Glow in the dark; for steelhead, fire flies. L. Green. il Outdoor Life 132:40-3+ O '63
Humpy wonder fly. J. C. Daniel. il Field & S 69:38-9 Ag '64
Ice flies for panfish jigging. D. Shiner. il Pop Mech 119:160-4 F '63
Kit of basic lures. W. Davis. il Outdoor Life 132:118+ O '63
Leaves from my notebook. W. Davis. il Outdoor Life 134:90-2 N '64
Live baits or artificials? W. Davis. il Outdoor Life 134:120-2 O '64
Lure picking's fun. A. W. Eckert. il Field & S 68:122-3 My '63
Miracle marabous. B. Zwirz. il Field & S 67:54-5 Ap '63
My eye on the tying of a dry fly. P. Miller. il Life 54:14 My 10 '63
New rig for balao salt water sensation. G. Robey. il Outdoor Life 131:44-5+ Ja '63
Reverse fly. J. Novick. il Field & S 68:90-1 S '63
Rig a jig. C. A. Barnes. il Outdoor Life 134:62-3 O '64
Rough and ready feather merchants; Feather River trading co. Rough and Ready, Calif. T. Trueblood. il Field & S 68:43-5+ My '63
Skaters' waltz. J. Brooks. il Field & S 69:60-1+ My '64
Sneaky art of fooling fish. H. Bradshaw. il Pop Sci 184:150-5 Mr '64
That old-fashioned wet fly. A. J. McClane. il Field & S 69:116-19 O '64
Those deadly blondes. J. Brooks. il Outdoor Life 132:24-7+ D '63
Tricks for opening day. A. J. McClane. il Field & S 67:104-6+ Ap '63
Trout flies: a starter's dozen. H. G. Tapply. il Field & S 69:66 Je '64

FISHING outfits. See Fishing—Implements and appliances

FISHING records
New world record fish. il Field & S 68:54-5 Je '63

FISHING reels. See Fishing tackle

FISHING rods. See Fishing tackle

FISHING stories
How to hide the truth. T. Trueblood. il Field & S 67:26+ Ap '63

FISHING tackle
Americana of angling; America's oldest maker of fine fishing tackle. H. Blaisdell. il Field & S 69:46-7+ My '64
Canandaigua can-can. T. Janes. il Outdoor Life 134:40-3+ Jl '64

FISHING tackle—*Continued*
Cast-and-carry fishing. H. G. Tapply. il Field & S 68:50 Jl '63
Choosing bait and spinning lines. W. Davis. il Outdoor Life 133:84+ Ap '64
Fish tough. F. McKinley. il Outdoor Life 134: 28-31+ Jl '64
Fishing and boating. Consumer Rep 29:342-8 D '64
How to choose a fishing rod. T. Trueblood. il Field & S 68:24+ Mr '64
How to fish the surf. G. Heinold. il Outdoor Life 131:16+ My '63
Ideal rod. W. Davis. il Outdoor Life 133: 78-80 F '64
Latest bait reels. W. Davis. il Outdoor Life 131:68+ Ja '63
Light-tackle fad. A. J. McClane. il Field & S 68:70-3+ Ag '63
Low-down fly line. T. Trueblood. il Field & S 69:24+ My '64
Matching fly rod and line. H. G. Tapply. il Field & S 67:64 Mr '63
Monofilament hates people. H. Babcock. il Field & S 68:40-2+ My '63
New reels, they take the fumbling out of fishing. H. Bradshaw. il Pop Sci 185:122-5+ Ag '64
New world for fly fisherman. L. Green. il Outdoor Life 133:22-3+ F '64
Poke-pole fishing. F. Dufresne. Field & S 69:36 O '64
Reel problems. A. J. McClane. il Field & S 69:84-7+ Ag '64
Revolution in fishing tackle. W. Davis. il Outdoor Life 131:49-51+ Ap '63
Rigs that take fish. W. Davis. il Outdoor Life 132:70-1 D '63
Spinning; closed-face reels. A. J. McClane. il Field & S 69:94-8 My '64
Spinning open-face reels. A. J. McClane. il Field & S 68:76-81 F '64
Spinning reels. il Consumer Rep 29:284-7 Je '64
Tackle tells the tale. B. Wisner. il Motor B 114:46-7+ S '64
Ten on-the-spot fixes for your fishing reels. H. Bradshaw. il Pop Sci 184:150-3 Je '64
What is light tackle? W. Davis. il Outdoor Life 135:86-8 Ja '65
Your leisure. Consumer Rep 28:352-3 D '63

FISHING tournaments. See Fishing—Competitions

FISHING with bow and arrow
Bowfishing time. G. H. Gillelan. il Outdoor Life 133:26+ Ap '64
Stump lot adventure; snapping turtles. D. R. Crandall. il Outdoor Life 131:80-1+ Ap '63
What to hunt now. G. H. Gillelan. il Outdoor Life 131:38+ My '63

FISHMAN, Jack
My darling Clementine; condensation. Read Digest 84:201-4+ Ja '64; Excerpts. Life 54: 88-90+ Je 7; 84-6+ Je 14 '63

FISHMAN, Joshua A.
Academic social compact. Sch & Soc 92:29-31 Ja 25 '64
Administrator in higher education as an educational leader; excerpt from address. Sch & Soc 91:304-6 O 19 '63

FISHMAN, Katharine Davis
Open road for women. Mlle 59:110-11+ Je '64
Where the action is in Europe. Mlle 58:189-99 Mr '64

FISHMAN, William H. See Sie, H. G. jt. auth.

FISHPONDS. See Fish culture

FISHWAYS. See Fish ladders

FISHWICK, Marshall William
Dark thoughts in the Black Forest. Sat R 46:19-20+ Mr 9 '63
Diagnosing the American dream. Sat R 46: 8-11 D 21 '63
Everything nailed down is coming loose: condensation of address. Sat R 46:11-14 Je 29 '63
Evolution of monsters: adapted from Faust revisited. Sat R 46:32+ S 14 '63
Making of a hero. Sat R 47:12-15 Ag 1 '64

FISHWORMS. See Earthworms

FISK, Alex A.
Timeless sport. Recreation 57:517+ D '64

FISKE, Virginia M.
Serotonin rhythm in the pineal organ: control by the sympathetic nervous system. bibliog Science 146:253-4 O 9 '64

FISLI, Ruth
How our library runs a school-wide book club. Sr Schol 82:21T Mr 13 '63

FISSION, Atomic. See Nuclear fission

FISSIONABLE materials. See Radioactive substances

FISTER, George M.
Speaking out. por Sat Eve Post 236:8+ F 23 '63
Truth treatment for critics of American medicine. por Todays Health 41:6+ F '63

FITCH, Charles Marden
Bright perennial rock pink. Horticulture 41: 196 Ap '63
Rhododendrons that stay small. Flower Grower 50:53-5 Ap '63

FITCH, Frank W. and Anders, Edward
Organized element; possible identification in orgueil meteorite. bibliog Science 140:1097-100 Je 7 '63

FITCH, James Marston
African notebook. Horizon 6:48-59 Autumn '64
Church of the Autostrada. Arch Forum 121: 100-9 Jl '64
Phoenix cities of Poland. Horizon 6:52-9 Spr '64

FITCH, Robert E.
Common sense sex code. Christian Cent 81: 1233-5 O 7 '64; Excerpts. Time 84:91 O 16 '64
Extremism in the defense of... Christian Cent 82:11-15 Ja 6 '65
New Protestant debate over sex. Redbook 123:105-6 O '64
Sexplosion. Christian Cent 81:136-8 Ja 29 '64
Shakespeare and man's salvation. Christian Cent 81:486-8 Ap 15 '64

FITHIAN, Janet
How common stocks fit our savings program. por Suc Farm 62:71+ Ag '64
I've learned to say no. por Farm J 87:85 My '63

FITNESS, Physical. See Health

FITNESS is the fashion; drama. See Martens, A. C.

FITTED sheets. See Sheets

FITTING out boats. See Boats—Care; Motor boats—Care

FITTS, Dudley
Between the sirens and the muse. Sat R 47:34-6 My 2 '64
(tr) See Lucian. Conservation at the Styx
(tr) See Martial. Any author to any friend
(tr) See Martial. To Ligurinus, relentlessly a poet

about

Aristophanes in American. X. J. Kennedy. Poetry 102:56-60 Ap '63

FITZ, Grancel
Grancel Fitz's last trophy. pors Outdoor Life 132:56-9+ S '63
Top trophy of North America? por Outdoor Life 133:17-21+ F '64

about

Outdoor life publishes new Grancel Fitz book: How to measure and score big-game trophies. Outdoor Life 132:59+ S '63

FITZGERALD, C. P.
China: new alternatives. Nation 197:155-7 S 21 '63
Sino-Soviet balance sheet in the underdeveloped areas. bibliog f Ann Am Acad 351: 40-9 Ja '64

FITZGERALD, D. A.
Foreign aid: the story of 98 billion dollars; interview. por U S News 54:48-51 F 25 '63

FITZGERALD, Ed
Planned action sequence. U S Camera 27: 66-7 Jl '64

FITZGERALD, Edmund B.
Industry and the technological revolution; address, June 4, 1964. Vital Speeches 30: 659-62 Ag 15 '64

FITZGERALD, Ella
Ella and others. M. Williams. Sat R 47:51 N 28 '64
She who is Ella. por Time 84:86+ N 27 '64

FITZ-GERALD, Frances L. See Berkson, G. jt. auth.

FITZGERALD, Francis Scott Key
Letters to an only daughter; excerpts from Letters of F. Scott Fitzgerald. McCalls 91:100-1+ O '63
Love to all of you, of all generations: letters. por Esquire 60:86-90+ Jl '63

about

Bigger than the Ritz. por Time 82:120+ O 18 '63
F. Scott Fitzgerald: the dimension of greatness. D. Littlejohn. Commonweal 79:198-9 N 8 '63
Fitzgerald attends my Fitzgerald seminar. V. Bourjaily. il por Esquire 62:110-11+ S '64
Ghost story of the jazz age. M. Cowley. il por Sat R 47:20-1 Ja 25 '64

FITZGERALD, Francis Scott Key—about—*Cont.*
Scott Fitzgerald; excerpt from Moveable feast. E. Hemingway. il pors Life 56:80+ Ap 10 '64
Scott Fitzgerald's America. J. Hart. Nat R 15:443-4 N 19 '63
Summer with F. Scott Fitzgerald. L. G. Hearne. il pors Esquire 62:160-5+ D '64
That summer in Paris, by M. Callaghan. Review
New Yorker 39:139-42+ F 23 '63. E. Wilson; Reply. M. Hemingway. 39:160+ Mr 16 '63
Will the real Scott Fitzgerald please stand up and be counted? A. Gingrich. Esquire 62:8+ D '64

FITZGERALD, G.
(ed) See Dunham, K. Seconding the motion

FITZGERALD, George R.
Mining the precious ore. America 109:292+ S 21 '63

FITZGERALD, Gerald
Path of roses. Opera N 29:24-5 D 12 '64

FITZGERALD, James H.
Critic in court. il por Newsweek 65:74 F 1 '65

FITZGERALD, John Francis
How J.F.K's. grandfather fought the grandfather clause. H. N. Meyer. por(p25) Negro Hist Bul 27:27 N '63

FITZGERALD, L. D. Vesey-. See Vesey-Fitzgerald, L. D.

FITZGERALD, Neil C.
Steps; poem. America 108:829 Je 8 '63

FITZGERALD, R. Bernard
Creative music teaching in the elementary school. NEA J 53:42-3 D '64

FITZGERALD, Robert
What's a dancer doing at Mr Kenneth's? H. Smith. il pors Dance Mag 39:22-3 Ja '65

FITZGERALD, Zelda
Far side of Zelda Fitzgerald; paintings. por Esquire 62:158-9 D '64

FITZGERALD family
Italian blood. New Yorker 38:23-4 F 16 '63
Kennedy's Irish kin. il Life 55:69-75 Jl 5 '63

FITZGIBBON, Constantine
Again the issue of German guilt. N Y Times Mag p 17+ Ag 18 '63
How grim was their island. Sat R 46:34-5 Mr 23 '63
Life movie review. Life 57:15 Ag 7 '64

FITZGIBBON, William
Fine art of keeping one's head. Read Digest 83:62-5 S '63

FITZINGER frogs. See Frogs

FITZMYER, Joseph A
Book reviews. America 109:597-8 N 9 '63
Gospel truth. America 110:844-6, 111:119 Je 20, Ag 8 '64

FITZPATRICK, Aileen
Something proud; poem. McCalls 90:171 Je '63

FITZPATRICK, George D. See Baumhart, R. jt. auth.

FITZPATRICK, Robert J.
Gain in Spain. America 111:656-8 N 21 '64

FITZROYA patagonica. See Alerces

FITZSIMMONS, James Edward
Jim's sunny day. Sports Illus 19:10 Ag 5 '63
Sunny Jim bows and turns himself out to pasture. il por Life 54:44 Je 28 '63
Sunny Jim's lament. R. Riger. il por Esquire 60:83-6 Ag '63
Time to go. il por Newsweek 61:64 Je 17 '63

FITZSIMMONS, M. A.
Tragedy of Trotsky. Commonweal 79:598-600 F 14 '64

5 A.M. jazz; musical comedy. See Musical comedies, revues, etc.—Criticisms, plots, etc.

FIVE dollar-a-day guidebooks. See Guidebooks

FIVE evenings; drama. See Volodin, A.

500-pound club. See Clubs

FIVE minutes before sleep; story. See Wertenbaker, W.

FIX, John
Never bedevil a devil fish! Motor B 114:93+ N '64
Pulchritudinous pest. Motor B 112:47+ D '63
River that nearly girdles the globe. Motor B 114:40-1 N '64

FIXES, Basketball. See Bribery

FIXES, Football. See Bribery

FIXING (photography) See Photography—Fixing

FIXLER, Michael
Bernard Berenson of Butremanz. Commentary 36:135-43 Ag '63

FIXTURES, Bathroom. See Bathroom fixtures

FIXX, James F.
(ed) As others see us. Sat R 47:31-3+ O 24; 35-7 N 7; 31-3 N 28; 43-4 D 12 '64; 48:33-4 Ja 2; 41-2 Ja 30 '65
Asking the wrong questions. Sat R 47:26 N 7 '64
Books in communications. See second issue of each month of Saturday review
Case of the unknown library. Sat R 47:45-6 Ap 11 '64
High cost of writing. Sat R 47:53+ Je 13 '64
Journalists behind bars. Sat R 46:54-5+ Mr 9 '63
Personal touch. Sat R 47:146-7 Ag 29 '64
Quarterbacking a nation's news. Sat R 46:48-9 Ag 10 '63
Should every student travel abroad? Sat R 46:46+ F 16 '63
Unspectacular Douglas Leigh. Sat R 47:54-5 Jl 11 '64
Who cares what the boss thinks? Sat R 46:14-15 D 28 '63
Year of the great migration. Sat R 47:78-9 F 15 '64

FIZDALE, Robert
Quote: unquote; interview, ed. by R. Jacobson. por Mus Am 83:16 Ag '63

FJELDSTED, Margaret
Right turn in California? New Repub 152:18 Ja 16 '65

FLACKS, Richard
Seminars on peace issues. Sr Schol 83:14T N 22 '63

FLAG salute
Pledge of allegiance. F. Duncan. il Atlan 213:120-1 My '64

FLAG signals. See Signals and signaling

FLAGELLA
Bending waves of the posterior flagellum of ceratium. C. J. Brokaw and L. Wright. bibliog il Science 142:1169-70 N 29 '63

FLAGELLATES
Synthesis of α-linolenic acid by leishmania enrietti. E. D. Korn and C. L. Greenblatt. bibliog il Science 142:1301-3 D 6 '63
See also
Noctiluca

FLAGELLATES, Fossil
Fossil coccoliths in limestone examined by electron microscopy. S. Honjo and A. G. Fischer. bibliog il Science 144:837-9 My 15 '64

FLAGELLO, Ezio
Holding the line; interview, ed. by F. Merkling. por Opera N 27:14 Mr 30 '63
Multi-talented Ezio Flagello. M. de Schauensee. Am Rec G 29:870 Jl '63

FLAGLER, Henry Morrison
Whitehall. J. T. Maher. il pors Ladies Home J 82:99-103 Ja '65

FLAGLER, J. M.
Letter from Sendagaya. New Yorker 40:58+ Jl 25; 86+ Ag 15 '64
Tokyo takes on the Olympics. Read Digest 85:185-8 Jl '64

FLAGLER park. See West Palm Beach, Fla.—Parks and playgrounds

FLAGS
Banner year for banners. il Horizon 6:60-5 Spr '64
Banners. il Craft Horiz 24:30-3 N '64
Flags for space. P. Zich. il Sch Arts 63:43 N '63
New flags fly every other week in Washington. il U S News 54:26 Mr 11 '63
Pennant or burgee? W. H. Koelbel. il Motor B 114:72+ Jl '64
What's in a flag? everything. R. Payne. il N Y Times Mag p20+ Ag 30 '64

Canada

Flag by committee. il Time 84:31 N 6 '64
Maple leaf forever. Nation 198:547 Je 1 '64
Maple leaves forever; new national flag. il Newsweek 63:42 Je 1 '64
New Canadian flag; new bitterness, too. il U S News 57:6 D 28 '64
New flag. il Sr Schol 85:18 Ja 7 '65
Rallying round a flag; design for a national flag. Time 83:33 My 29 '64
Searching for unity. il Time 84:48 S 18 '64
Their own flag at last. il Time 84:17 D 25 '64
This is a good flag; red-and-white maple-leaf flag approved. il Newsweek 64:32 D 28 '64
Trooping the colors; proposed new flag. Newsweek 64:58 N 16 '64
Two peoples under one flag; controversy over new national flag. B. Hutchison. il N Y Times Mag p29+ Ag 23 '64

United States

Flags; when and how to fly them. C. F. Chapman. il Motor B 113:97-104 Ja '64
Flying Old Glory at home. il Sunset 131:56-9+ Jl '63

FLAGS—United States—*Continued*
O say can you see; abstract expressionist flags sold by Betsy Ross flag and banner company. il Newsweek 65:78 Ja 11 '65

Anecdotes, facetiae, satire etc.

Flag and I. B. Brower. il Esquire 63:67-9+ Ja '65

FLAGSTAD, Kirsten
Art of Kirsten Flagstad. B. H. Haggin. New Repub 148:27 Mr 9 '63
Da capo; recordings. S. Smolian. Am Rec G 29:814 Je '63
In memoriam, 1895-1963; Kirsten Flagstad's farewell performance. P. L. Miller. por Am Rec G 29:613 Ap '63
Kirsten Flagstad: an appreciation. G. Pluck. pors Hobbies 68:30-1 F '64
Kirsten Flagstad, 1895-1962. E. Helm. pors Mus Am 83:81 Ja '63
Memory of Flagstad; Strandenaes portrait and fund for Metropolitan. il Opera N 28: 6-7 F 1 '64

FLAGSTAFF, Ariz.
For putrescibles only. L. D. Hueppelsheuser. il Am City 80:18 Ja '65

FLAGYL. See Metronidazole

FLAHERTY, Ann
Life movie review. Life 57:15 Ag 28 '64

FLAHERTY, Daniel L.
Books for Lenten reading. America 108:304-5 Mr 2 '63
Chat with the publishers. America 108:256-7 F 23 '63
Emphasis on books. America 110:258-9 F 22 '64
Fanfare for fall. America 109:428-30 O 12 '63
Look at the fall books. America 111:414-15 O 10 '64
Object lesson for optimists. America 109:148 Ag 17 '63
Paperbacks in school. America 111:523+ O 31 '64
Stranger than fiction. America 110:772 My 30 '64
What price ETV? America 108:491-3, 760 Ap 13, My 25 '63

FLAHERTY, Leo B. Jr
Fluorescent city, U.S.A. Am City 78:124 Ap '63

FLAHERTY, Tom
Anatomy of the snafu. Life 54:80-3 My 10 '63; Same abr. with title What we learned from the Bay of Pigs. Read Digest 83:92-4 Jl '63
Big $$$ in the fast draft. Life 54:15 Mr 22 '63
Gas grenade in the face; a sniper's bullet in the arm. Life 56:25-9 Ja 24 '64
Long voyage in inner space. Life 54:119-20 My 17 '63
Why the big eye made the big deal: this was done for dollars. Life 57:88 Ag 28 '64

FLAHERTY, Vincent X.
Most unforgettable character I've met. Read Digest 82:115-19 Je '63

FLAHIVE, Robert F.
They're writing till it hurts us. NEA J 52: 57 S '63

FLAIANO, Ennio
In New York. Vogue 144:30+ N 1 '64

FLAMBEAU RIVER
Tale of two rivers. E. Swift. il Am For 70:32-5+ Je '64

FLAME stitching. See Embroidery

FLAME vortex. See Vortex motion

FLAMEFLOWERS. See Tigerflowers

FLAMENCO
Flamenco. il Vogue 144:122-31 O 15 '64
Los Morenos, 92nd street Y. J. Maskey. Dance Mag 38:32 Je '64
Olé and all that flamenco. P. K. Brooks. il Sat R 47:30-1 O 3 '64

FLAMING (cookery) See Cookery

FLAMINGO flowers
Anthuriums. K. Berggrav. il Horticulture 42: 22-3+ S '64

FLAMINGOS
Freeing flamingos from anklets of death. J. G. Williams. il Nat Geog Mag 124:934-44 D '63
Great flamingo rescue; Lake Magadi, Tanganyika. K. Drake. il Read Digest 84:209-11+ Je '64
Wild flamingoes on parade. S. Sprunt, jr. il Audubon Mag 65:352-5 N '63

FLAMM, E. J. and Lingenfelter, R. E.
Neutron and proton dosages in the upper atmosphere from solar flare radiation. bibliog Science 144:1566-9 Je 26 '64
—See Lingenfelter, R. E. jt. auth.

FLAMM, W. G. See Birnstiel, M. L. jt. auth.

FLAMMARION, Camille
First lady of French astronomy. F. Baldet. il por Sky & Tel 25:77 F '63

FLAMMARION, Gabrielle (Renaudot)
First lady of French astronomy. F. Baldet. il por Sky & Tel 25:77 F '63

FLAMSTEED, John, 1646-1719
Not observed or existing. J. Ashbrook. il Sky & Tel 26:80-1 Ag '63

FLANAGAN, John C.
Project talent. NEA J 53:8-10 Ja '64

FLANAGAN, Joseph E. Jr
Water supply and pollution control. Science 145:840+ Ag 21 '64

FLANAGAN, Theodore R. and Langille, A. R.
Phenol in quackgrass associated with dalapon. bibliog Science 140:179-80 Ap 12 '63

FLANDERS, Ralph E.
Celestial mechanics of unemployment. Duns R 82:65+ O '63

FLANNER, Janet
Letter from Paris. See issues of New Yorker

FLANNERY, Harry W.
Italy: problem for Pope Paul. Cath World 197:372-9 S '63

FLANNERY, Kent V. See Coe, M. D. jt. auth.

FLAPS, Airplane
Peruvians study rotating-cylinder flap. D. A. Brown. il Aviation W 81:70-1 D 7 '64

FLARE stars. See Stars, Variable

FLARES, Solar. See Solar flares

FLASH floods. See Floods

FLASH units. See Electric lamps, Flashlight

FLASHBULBS. See Electric lamps, Flashlight

FLASHING
Don't let faulty flashing flood your home. D. C. Fales and E. D. Fales. il Pop Sci 185:152-6 O '64
How to know if your roof flashing is going bad. il Bet Hom & Gard 42:121+ O '64
How to use stainless steel for flashing. il Arch Rec 134:201-2 N '63
Prefabricated flashing for parapet walls. H. Edwards. il Arch Rec 135:209-10 My '64

FLASHING electric lamps. See Electric lamps, Flashing

FLASHLIGHT batteries. See Storage batteries

FLASHLIGHT electric lamps. See Electric lamps, Flashlight

FLASHLIGHT photography. See Photography, Flashlight

FLASHLIGHTS, Electric
Great flashlight scandal; junk floods the market. il Changing T 17:45-6 Ap '63
Is there a no battery flashlight? il Consumer Bul 47:11 S '64
Science of a dynamic advertisement. Consumer Bul 47:16-17 My '64
Two-cell flashlights. il Consumer Bul 47:28-30 Jl '64
Your flashlight and other batteries; should they be recharged? il Consumer Bul 46: 32-5 S '63

FLASKS. See Bottles

FLATHEAD Indians. See Salish Indians

FLATOW, Herb
Confessions of a color slide judge. U S Camera 27:30+ D '64
Tough guy with a soft heart; interview, ed. by B. Mason. il U S Camera 27:62-5+ Ja '64

FLATS. See Apartments

FLATS, etc (horticulture)
Care of seedlings. F. F. Rockwell and E. C. Grayson. Flower Grower 50:70-1 Mr '63
Home greenhouse. J. Eaton. il Flower Grower 51:57-8 Mr '64
Indoor seed sowing. R. Kersey. il Flower Grower 51:48-9+ Ja '64
Sow your own seed. il Pop Gard 16:14-17 F '65
Start seeds indoors. P. C. Geraci. il Pop Gard 14:74-8 F '63
Transplanting seedlings indoors. R. Kersey. il Flower Grower 51:38-9+ F '64

FLATT, Ernie
Ernie Flatt in action. E. Palatsky. il pors Dance Mag 38:42-5 D '64
Success and unpredictability for Ernie Flatt. il por Dance Mag 37:49 Jl '63

FLATTED saxophone; story. See O'Hara, J.

FLATTERY
I love a nice liar. H. Dolson. McCalls 90:67+ Ag '63; Same abr. Read Digest 83:83-5 N '63

FLATULENT indigestion. See Dyspepsia

FLATWARE, Stainless steel. See Tableware, Stainless steel

FLAUGHER, Ronald L. See Nunnally, J. C. jt. auth.

FLAVIN, Martin, and others
Succinic ester and amide of homoserine: some spontaneous and enzymatic reactions. bibliog Science 143:50-2 Ja 3 '64
FLAVINS
Flavin sensitized photoreactions: effects of 3-(p-chlorophenyl)-1,1-dimethylurea. P. Homann and H. Gaffron. bibliog il Science 141:905-7 S 6 '63
FLAVIUS Josephus. See Josephus, F.
FLAVONOIDS
Citrus flavonoid complex: chemical fractionation and biological activity. L. Freedman and A. J. Merritt. bibliog il Science 139:344-5 Ja 25 '63
FLAVOR of food. See Food
FLAVORING essences
See also
Seasonings
FLAX
Gay little winter bloomer; Indian flax. Sunset 134:122 Ja '65
FLEAK, Dorothy H. See Lucioli, C. E. jt. auth.
FLEAS
Square pegs and round holes and getting rid of fleas. D. M. Duffey. il Outdoor Life 131:144-5 Ap '63
FLEAY, David
Strange animals of Australia. Nat Geog Mag 124:388-411 S '63
FLECK, Richard
Rambling through the Never Summers. Nat Parks Mag 38:10-12 F '64
Die FLEDERMAUS; opera. See Strauss, J.
FLEGAL, Georgia Anne
Gigi's first communion. C. Morrison. il Look 28:20-5 Ag 11 '64
FLEISHER, Leon
Quote-unquote; interview, ed. by C. S. Susa. por Mus Am 84:105 D '64
FLEISCHER, R. L. and Price, P. B.
Tracks of charged particles in high polymers. bibliog Science 140:1221-2 Je 14 '63
Uranium contents of ancient man-made glass. bibliog Science 144:841-2 My 15 '64
—and others
Fission-track ages and track-annealing behavior of some micas. bibliog Science 143:349-51 Ja 24 '64
Novel filter for biological materials. bibliog Science 143:249-50 Ja 17 '64
FLEMING, Sir Alexander
Germ killer discovered twice. Todays Health 42:10 D '64
FLEMING, Anne (Charteris)
The Ian Flemings. R. Harling. il por Vogue 142:222-7+ S 1 '63
FLEMING, D. F.
(ed) Changing cold war. Ann Am Acad 351:1-179 Ja '64
Epilogue. Ann Am Acad 351:180 Ja '64
New Europe and the cold war. bibliog f Ann Am Acad 348:141-55 Jl '63
Turn toward peace. bibliog f Ann Am Acad 351:157-69 Ja '64
FLEMING, Dan B. Jr
Teacher's view inside Congress. NEA J 53:69-72 Ja '64
FLEMING, Donald
Meaning of mental illness. Atlan 214:72-6 Jl '64
FLEMING, Frances. See Hodges, E. D. jt. comp.
FLEMING, Ian
Hamburg: more rather James Bond adventures. Vogue 141:98-9+ Je '63
Redbook dialogue: Allen Dulles and Ian Fleming. por Redbook 123:44-5+ Je '64
about
Books. M. Muggeridge. Esquire 62:36+ D '64
Education of presidents. R. Kirk. Nat R 15:308 O 8 '63
The Ian Flemings. R. Harling. il pors Vogue 142:222-7+ S 1 '63
Ian goldfinger. por Newsweek 63:73 Ap 6 '64
Man with the golden Bond. il por Time 84:22-3 Ag 21 '64
Obituary
Pub W por 186:79 Ag 24 '64
Our spy-boss who loved Bond. A. Dulles. il por Life 57:19 Ag 28 '64
Sorry to have troubled you. por Newsweek 64:37 Ag 24 '64
Spectacular cult of Ian Fleming. G. Bocca. il por Sat Eve Post 236:66-8 Je 22 '63
FLEMING, James R. and Johnson, J. A.
Wheat gibberellins. bibliog Science 144:1021-2 My 22 '64
FLEMING, John F.
Rare book dealer sues Silver estate. Pub W 186:24-5 Ag 17 '64
FLEMING, Peter
Party of one. Holiday 35:14+ Ja '64
FLEMING, Rodney R.
How sweepers really perform. bibliog Am City 79:113-15 My '64
Plows and plans for successful snow-fighting. bibliog Am City 79:75-7+ Ag '64
Water reuse by design. bibliog Am City 78:106-8 O '63
When and how to use water meters. Am City 79:110-12 Je '64
FLEMING, Roscoe
Big beef on the range. New Repub 150:10 Mr 7 '64
FLEMING, Shirley
Noisy bantling in old New York. Hi Fi 13:82-9 O '63
Notes from our correspondents. Hi Fi 14:26+ F; 22+ My; 20+ Je; 12+ Jl; 51+ O; 24+ N '64; 15:22+ Ja '65
(ed) See Bachauer, G. Gina Bachauer
FLEMING, Thomas J.
Busy social life of germs. Life 55:19-20 D 13 '63
Crisis in Catholic schools. Sat Eve Post 236:19-25 O 26 '63
Enigma of General Howe. Am Heritage 15:6-11+ F '64
G. Washington meets a test. Am Heritage 14:56-9+ F '63
Kennedy the Catholic. Nation 198:571-2 Je 8 '64
One small candle; condensation. Read Digest 83:207-12+ D '63
Why do we neglect the useful art of memorizing? Read Digest 82:271+ Ap '63
FLEMING, Warren R. See Stanley, J. G. jt. auth.
FLEMINGS
Lingua belgica. il Time 81:34 Je 7 '63
FLEMISH, The. See Flemings
FLEMISH language
Atlantic report. Atlan 211:18+ My '63
FLEMMING, Arthur S.
In my opinion. . . por Good H 156:46 Ap; 76 My; 8 Je; 157:10 Jl; 41+ Ag; 72+ O '63
FLESCH, Gerald D. See Svec, H. J. jt. auth.
FLESHLER, Morton. See Hoffman, H. S. jt. auth.
FLETCHER, Colin
Backpacking the Grand Canyon. pors Field & S 68:33-7+ Mr '64
Bright Angel brownies. Field & S 69:42-3 D '64
D-day plus twenty years. Read Digest 84:112-15 Je '64
I've rediscovered walking. Read Digest 82:139-41 Mr '63
Lightning strikes on Bugaboo Spire. Read Digest 82:49-54 Je '63
1,236 red-hot fishermen. Field & S 68:40-3+ N '63
FLETCHER, James Chipman
Changing U of U. Newsweek 64:68-9 D 7 '64
FLETCHER, William J.
How to select electric motors and controls. Suc Farm 62:44-5 F '64
FLETTNER rotor ships. See Rotor ships
FLEXIBLE shafting. See Shafting, Flexible
FLEXIBLE wood. See Veneers and veneering
FLEXISCOPE. See Electronic apparatus and appliances
FLEXNER, Eleanor
Little way. America 112:77-8 Ja 16 '65
FLEXNER, Josefa B. and others
Memory in mice as affected by intracerebral puromycin. bibliog Science 141:57-9 Jl 5 '63
FLEXNER, Stuart
Man who corrupted California. Esquire 61:82-3+ Mr '64
FLICK, Elmer
Day when all the sentiment stands still; Cooperstown on Hall of fame day. por Sports Illus 19:56-7 Ag 19 '63
Elmer the Great. Newsweek 61:84 F 11 '63
FLICK, Friedrich
Flick's fortunes. il por Time 82:78 Jl 26 '63
FLICKER phenomena
Electroencephalographic correlates of binocular rivalry in man. R. W. Lansing. bibliog il Science 146:1325-7 D 4 '64
FLICKERS
Summer in the blackjack oak. A. K. Davis. Audubon Mag 66:326-7 S '64
FLICKINGER, Reed A.
Actinomycin D effects in frog embryos: evidence for sequential synthesis of DNA-dependent RNA. bibliog Science 141:1063-4 S 13 '63
Cell differentiation: some aspects of the problem. bibliog Science 141:608-14 Ag 16 '63
Der FLIEGENDE Holländer; opera. See Wagner, R.

FLIEGERS, Serge
(ed) See Montini, G. B. Nephew's portrait of Pope Paul
(ed) See Rainier III, prince of Monaco. Memoirs of Monaco
FLIES
Enzyme changes in flight muscle correlated with aging and flight ability in the male housefly. M. Rockstein and K. F. Brandt. bibliog il Science 139:1049-51 Mr 15 '63
Giant polytene chromosomes in hypodermal cells of developing footpads of dipteran pupae. J. M. Whitten. bibliog il Science 143:1437-8 Mr 27 '64
Promise her anything; courtship techniques. Newsweek 61:56 Mr 4 '63
Stretch receptor-like organs in the fly larva: their possible role in growth regulation. J. M. Whitten. bibliog il Science 143:260-1 Ja 17 '64
Tanning in the adult fly: a new function of neurosecretion in the brain. G. Fraenkel and C. Hsiao. bibliog Science 141:1057-8 S 13 '63; Reply. E. Thomsen. 143:973 F 28 '64
See also
Blowflies
Drosophila
Fruit flies
Extermination
Good advice on how to control flies. il Good H 157:123 Jl '63
Latest ways to kill face flies. il Farm J 88:32 Je '64
Make best use of back rubbers for beef. H. J. Stockdale. il Suc Farm 61:46 Jl '63
New ways to kill flies; SIMAX, containing Ciodrin. il Farm J 87:54+ My '63
FLIES, Artificial. See Fishing lures, flies, etc.
FLIGHT
Crazy way to fly; Kremer prize flight of a man-powered aircraft. P. Hamill. il Sat Eve Post 237:62-3+ F 8 '64
See also
Birds—Flight
Gliding and soaring
Insects—Flight
Navigation, Aerial
Space flight
FLIGHT advisory weather service. See United States—Weather bureau
FLIGHT engineers. See Airplane crews
FLIGHT engineers international association
American engineers cancel strike vote following mediation request. Aviation W 79:45 S 16 '63
American engineers still ask pilot rating. Aviation W 79:47 S 9 '63
American, flight engineers agree in principle on proposed contract. Aviation W 81:42 O 26 '64
FEIA seeks injunction against American airlines in dues dispute. Aviation W 78:41 My 13 '63
Flight engineers prepare new moves in dispute with Eastern. Aviation W 79:43 S 23 '63
FLIGHT grounded; story. See Ernst, P.
FLIGHT recorders. See Aeronautic instruments
FLIGHT records. See Aviation records
FLIGHT research center. See United States—National aeronautics and space administration—Flight research center
FLIGHT simulators
American designs and builds crew training aids. il Aviation W 80:35 Mr 9 '64
Animated light displays portray Boeing 727 systems for training. il Aviation W 80:80 Ja 6 '64
Eastern's digital simulator facilitates flight training. K. J. Stein. il Aviation W 80:98-103 Ja 27 '64
Jet flying, two feet up; Link trainers. A. Ewing. il Sci N L 84:374 D 14 '63
Simulation grows in support analysis. Aviation W 81:47+ mid-D '64
Test complex simulates Polaris re-entry heat. J. N. Steinmetz, jr. il Miss & Roc 14:24-5 Ja 6 '64
V/STOL aircraft studied in simulator. D. A. Brown. il Aviation W 79:78-84 Jl 1 '63
XV-5A flight reproduced by simulator. C. M. Plattner. il Aviation W 78:79+ Ja 21 '63
See also
Space flight simulators
FLINN, P. A. and others
Mössbauer effect for surface atoms: iron-57 at the surface of π Al_2O_3. bibliog Science 143:1434+ Mr 27 '64
FLINT, Emily
(tr) See Amor, I. Dealer's view
(tr) See Casanova, P. G. Mexico looks to the future
FLINT, Richard Foster
Status of the pleistocene Wisconsin stage in central North America. bibliog Science 139:402-4 F 1 '63
FLINT, Mich.
Lavish skinflint. Newsweek 62:24 Jl 1 '63
Mr Flint. Time 81:19 Je 28 '63
FLINT implements and weapons. See Stone implements and weapons
FLIP (ship) See Ships, Research
FLIRTING. See Sexual ethics
FLOAT glass. See Glass
FLOAT planes. See Seaplanes
FLOAT with the current; story. See Frasier, K.
FLOATING bridges. See Bridges, Pontoon
FLOATING gardens of Mexico. See Xochimilco, Mexico
FLOATING instrument platforms. See Ships, Research
FLOATING meteorological stations. See Meteorological stations
FLOATS. See Rafts
FLOCK, K. D.
Bear that almost made me infamous. Am For 70:20-1+ D '64
Response of man to raw challenge. Am For 70:34-5 Jl '64
FLOCK (fibers)
How to fit fine tools to a case; you do it with flock! H. Walton. il Pop Sci 185:130-1+ N '64
FLOGGING. See Corporal punishment
FLOKOS, Nicholas
Allegiance to Aphrodite; poem. Mile 57:227 My '63
FLOM, Merton C. and others
Contour interaction and visual resolution: contralateral effects. bibliog Science 142:979-80 N 15 '63
FLOOD insurance. See Insurance, Flood
FLOOD lighting. See Light projection; Photography—Lighting
FLOOD plains, Utilization of. See Land utilization
FLOOD prevention and control
Ask the ancients; Siq Dam and diversion system, Jordan. il Time 82:70 O 25 '63
President asks additional funds for U.S.-Mexico flood project. Dept State Bul 51:544 O 19 '64
United States
Down the drain. New Repub 148:5 Ap 13 '63
See also
Mississippi River—Regulation
FLOODLIGHTING. See Light projection
FLOODS
Floods! floods!! floods!!! M. Pardé. il UNESCO Courier 17:54-9 Jl '64
Italy
After the flood, an inquest; Vaiont Dam tragedy. il Bsns W p36 O 19 '63
Death of a valley; Vaiont Dam overflows. C. McCarry. il Sat Eve Post 236:76-81 N 30 '63
Italian dam tragedy will not happen here; Vaiont Dam. Sci N L 84:260 O 26 '63
Italian flood: disaster truly biblical; Vaiont Dam. il U S News 55:6 O 21 '63
Like Pompeii. . . ; remains of Longarone, Italy. il Time 82:43 O 18 '63
There the dam stood, proud and beautiful and then. . . . R. Ajemian. il Life 55:30-41 O 25 '63
Valley of death; Vaiont Dam overflows. il Newsweek 62:62+ O 21 '63
United States
Air lift to flood area gains momentum. il Aviation W 82:20+ Ja 11 '65
As killer floods hit five states. il U S News 54:16 Mr 25 '63
Avalanche of rain; destruction and tragedy over the West coast. il Time 85:28 Ja 1 '65
Boy caught in a man-killing flood; Great Falls, Mont. il Life 56:38-9 Je 19 '64
Civil air operators active in flood area. H. D. Watkins. il Aviation W 82:94-5+ Ja 18 '65
Dam is busted; disaster at Great Falls, Mont. il Newsweek 63:30+ Je 22 '64
Day the dam broke; Baldwin Hills reservoir. R. Leadabrand. il Am For 70:30-3+ F '64
Day the dam burst; St Francis Dam, Calif. W. S. Griswold. il Pop Sci 184:88-91+ Mr '64
Flood tragedy; Pacific Northwest. il Sr Schol 85:23 Ja 14 '65

FLOODS—United States—*Continued*
Helicopters, fixed-wing aircraft supplying flood-bound areas in West. il Aviation W 82:22-4 Ja 4 '65
Lovely land laid waste by weather; with report by H. Wingo. il Life 58:20-7 Ja 8 '65
One of those things. il Newsweek 61:25 Mr 18 '63
Twin furies; five-state flood belt. il Newsweek 65:18 Ja 4 '65
Weather, mud, slush challenge airlife crews. H. D. Watkins. Aviation W 82:21 Ja 11 '65
When a tropical storm hit the Far West. il U S News 58:8 Ja 4 '65
When floods hit the West coast; $1-billion damages. il Bsns W p 19-20 Ja 2 '65

FLOOR coverings
Confused about floor coverings? J. Holmstrand. il Suc Farm 62:106-7 Mr '64
Fake tiling, fake caning. il Vogue 142:136-7+ O 15 '63
Making an oil-cloth floor-covering for Pres. Andrew Johnson's home. H. Wandrus. il Hobbies 68:54+ Jl '63
Room-makers. il Vogue 142:56+ O 15 '63
What to know about smooth-surface floors. Bet Hom & Gard 41:24 F '63
See also
Rugs and carpets
Tiles, Floor

FLOOR leaders in Congress. See United States—Congress

FLOOR machines
Floor washer-dryers. il Consumer Rep 28: 438-40 S '63
New floor-care tools are better. il McCalls 91:38 Ap '64
Portable sanders. il Consumer Bul 47:27-31 S '64
Water-powered floor washer: Dolphin II. Consumer Rep 29:109 Mr '64

FLOOR trading. See Stock exchange

FLOOR waxes. See Waxes

FLOORING
Parquet, beautiful and easy! il Bet Hom & Gard 42:111 Ap '64

FLOORS
Casters for book trucks, what type is best for carpeted floors? G. T. Piez. il ALA Bul 57:787-9 S '63
Floors are to walk on. il Parents Mag 38:65-8+ Je '63
He combined two new ideas; SPF hogs and slotted floors. il Suc Farm 61:33 My '63
Skid-proof floors. J. L. Parker. Farm J 87:55 F '63
What slotted floors will and won't do for you. A. H. Jensen and J. A. Hoefer. il Suc Farm 61:66-7 F '63
What's new for your floors? F. Byerly. il Bet Hom & Gard 41:70-3 F '63
See also
Boats—Floors
Calf pens—Floors
Floor coverings

Care
Axles and cones: Butcher polish company, Malden, Mass. New Yorker 40:28-9 Ja 16 '65
Caring for your floors; with guide to stain and spot removal. Suc Farm 62:108 Mr '64
Floor care time-savers. B. G. Wadsworth. Parents Mag 38:19 Je '63
Quick tips for floors. il Bet Hom & Gard 42: 94-5 Je '64
Waxed beauty for hardwood floors. Good H 156:1801 Mr '63

FLOORS, Brick
Floor patterns for your patio. il Pop Gard 14:40-3 N '63
If white shows on brick or tile. Sunset 133: 98 Jl '64

FLOORS, Concrete
Slats pay for themselves in six months. D. Wolf. il Farm J 87:34-5+ F '63
Trouble-free industrial concrete floor. C. B. Wigton, jr. il Arch Rec 136:193-4 Jl '64

FLOORS, Tile
Decorative vinyl flooring. il House & Gard 123:116 Ap '63
If white shows on brick or tile. Sunset 133: 98 Jl '64

FLOORS, Wood
Wood floors: how to keep them in the prime. House & Gard 127:20-1 Ja '65

FLORAL decoration. See Flowers, Arrangement of

FLORAL painting. See Flowers in art

FLORENCE
Art
Florence: a five day tour. D. Holden. il Am Artist 28:48-54+ Ap '64
Immortal treasures of Florence. M. Eastman. il Read Digest 85:145-51 S '64
Churches
Church of the Florentine businessmen. il Fortune 67:133-7 Je '63
Description
Florence: a five day tour. D. Holden. il Am Artist 28:48-54+ Ap '64
Trouble with Florence. H. F. Ellis. Atlan 212:108-9 S '63
Galleries and museums
See also
Uffizi gallery
Music
Great opera houses. M. J. Matz. il Opera N 27:29-31 Mr 23 '63

FLORENCE agreement. See Duty free importation

FLORENCE Eiseman incorporated. See Eiseman, Florence, incorporated

FLORENSKII, Kirill P.
Did a comet collide with the earth in 1908? Sky & Tel 26:268-9 N '63

FLORENTINE May festival. See Music festivals—Italy

FLORES, Antonio Carrillo
Mexico and the Indian. Américas 16:9-16 F '64

FLORES, Ralph
Couple who wouldn't die. T. Whiteside. il pors Sat Eve Post 236:56-65 Je 22 '63
Fit survive. il por Newsweek 61:27 Ap 8 '63
How long people can last without food. il por U S News 54:20 Ap 8 '63

FLORICULTURE
Down-to-earth advice to the new gardener. E. McKeegan. il Flower Grower 51:42-3 My '64
Garden for all America. il Flower Grower 51: 54-5 Ja '64
Garden for three seasons: spring, summer and fall. M. C. Ohlander. il Flower Grower 51:32-3 Jl '64
Highlights of spring planting. E. McDonald. il Pop Gard 15:31-4 Mr '64
Hill-top gardening. R. Raeder. il Horticulture 41:79 F '63
H&G's gardener's month. See issues of House & garden
Midwest pointers. R. M. Carleton. See issues of Flower grower
Northern pointers. H. V. Wilson. See issues of Flower grower
Quick and easy tips. il Pop Gard 14:40-1 My '63
Report from the South; symposium. Flower Grower 50:24-5 Ap '63
Rose by any other name is different. il Changing T 18:33-4 Ag '64
Southern pointers. See issues of Flower grower
Spring check-up. il Pop Gard 15:16 Ap '64
Time to take cuttings. F. F. Rockwell and E. C. Grayson. il Flower Grower 50:47 Jl '63
West Coast pointers. R. E. Atkinson. See issues of Flower grower
Which is better spring or fall planting? R. D. Roe. il Horticulture 41:506 O '63
See also
Annuals (plants)
Bulbs
Flowers
Gardening
Greenhouses

FLORIDA
Before you move to Florida look both ways! E. T. Kienz. Consumer Bul 47:6-9 F '64
Trade wind world. D. DeFontaine. il Yachting 116:34-6+ N '64
What's new when you get there. R. F. Burnham. il Motor B 112:34-7+ S '63
See also
Architecture, Domestic—Florida
Aviation—Florida
Birds—Florida
Biscayne Bay
Booksellers and bookselling—Florida
Botany—Florida
Dade County
Education—Florida
Everglades
Everglades National Park
Festivals—Florida
Fishing—Florida
Forests and forestry—Florida
Fort Jefferson National Monument
Gardens—Florida

FLORIDA—See also—*Continued*
Hunting—Florida
Law—Florida
Marquesas Keys
Roads—Florida
St Johns River
Ten Thousand Islands
Unemployment—Florida
Water supply—Florida
Zoology—Florida

Climate

Winter weather in the palm belt. W. S. Kals. il Yachting 116:42-3+ N '64

Description and travel

Far side of paradise; northwest Florida. J. Gribbins. il Motor B 112:38 S '63
Florida-Bahamas yachting; symposium. il Yachting 114:45-62+ N '63
Florida dream. S. Birmingham. il Holiday 34:62-81 D '63
Florida rides a space-age boom. B. Thielen. il Nat Geog Mag 124:858-903 D '63
Florida springtime. L. Harris. il Travel 120:26-30 S '63
Four faces of Florida. K. N. Anderson. il Todays Health 42:22-5+ N '64
From tip to top in Florida. G. Bourke. See issues of Travel
Golden cities of the Gold Coast. H. Sutton. il Sat R 46:39-40+ F 16 '63
Guide to vacationing in Florida. Esquire 62:36-36C+ N '64
Holiday tour of the Sunshine state. il Bet Hom & Gard 41:117-20 N '63
Where and what to shoot in Florida. S. Teller. il U S Camera 27:70-1+ Ja '64

Historic houses, etc.

Whitehall. J. T. Maher. il Ladies Home J 82:99-103 Ja '65

History

Tragic dream of Jean Ribaut; flag of France on America's South Atlantic coast. S. Harris. il Am Heritage 14:8-15+ O '63

Legislature

And a peanut broker; new seats to be filled. il Newsweek 61:28 Mr 4 '63
Bell-ringer; Eddie Gong. il Newsweek 61:36 Mr 25 '63
Florida's sinner safari; Johns committee. E. Peter, jr. New Repub 148:13-15 Ap 27 '63
Footnote on Florida. A. Lewis. New Repub 148:9 My 11 '63

Parks and reserves

Africa's wild veldt moves in on Florida; Busch gardens, in Tampa. il Bsns W p 180-2 N 7 '64
Trailer your boat and tent to Florida. K. Ferguson. il Motor B 112:36-9 D '63
Underwater America; John Pennekamp Coral Reef State Park. H. Sutton. il Sat R 47:39-40 D 12 '64

Politics and government

Astounding results; gubernatorial election. il Time 84:41-2 N 13 '64
Coming up: Daddy Warbucks for president; use of comic strips in election campaign. il New Repub 150:10 Ap 25 '64
See also
Florida—Legislature

Race problems

After dark in St Augustine. M. Waldron. il Nation 198:648-51 Je 29 '64
Anarchy in St Augustine. L. Goodwyn. il Harper 230:74-81 Ja '65
Old slave market. Nation 198:594 Je 15 '64

Religious institutions and affairs

News of the Christian world (cont) Christian Cent 80:474-6, 892-3 Ap 10, Jl 10 '63

Social conditions

Still another list; investigation of homosexuality in the teaching profession in Florida. Nation 198:615 Je 22 '64

FLORIDA agricultural and mechanical university, Tallahassee
Best band in the land. il Ebony 19:172-8 N '63

FLORIDA Atlantic university, Boca Raton
Good-by to Suntan U. il Newsweek 64:88 N 16 '64
Staffing a computer based library. E. Heiliger. il Library J 89:2738-9 Jl '64

FLORIDA BAY
Thousand miles of islands. J. Martenhoff. il Motor B 112:40-3 D '63

FLORIDA CANAL. See Florida Ship Canal project

FLORIDA East Coast railway
Back of the dynamite. Nation 198:254 Mr 16 '64
Blowup; Florida East Coast railway labor war. il Newsweek 63:67-8 F 24 '64
Court dents longest rail deadlock. Bsns W p 104+ D 12 '64
FBI enters case; explosions. il Sr Schol 84:18 Mr 20 '64
Florida rail strike halted. Bsns W p52 N 16 '63
Florida ry. hits a new roadblock; court orders to abandon cost-saving changes in work rules and pay rates. Bsns W p98 Mr 7 '64
Florida's railroad war; a few sticks of dynamite. R. G. Sherrill. il Nation 198:227-30 Mr 9 '64
Moonport stalled by rail strike. il Bsns W p64+ F 15 '64
New impasse in rail dispute. U S News 56:67 Ja 6 '64
One way to run a railroad and meet work-rule problems. il U S News 55:67-9 S 2 '63
Rail strike and the moon shot. U S News 55:86 O 28 '63
Rail strike that reaches into space. il Bsns W p46+ O 26 '63
Railroad that defies the unions. T. Armbrister. il Sat Eve Post 237:84-9 F 22 '64
Thirteen-month rail strike heats up. il U S News 56:116 F 24 '64
Where rail workers are on strike and trains are running. il U S News 54:93-6 Mr 11 '63

FLORIDA EVERGLADES. See Everglades

FLORIDA Indians. See Seminole Indians

FLORIDA KEYS
Elliott Key; unique marina park. H. Modavis. il Yachting 116:54+ N '64
Reporter at large; northernmost Keys, proposed as Islandia National Monument. B. Roueché. New Yorker 40:37-8+ D 26 '64

FLORIDA land boom. See Real estate business

FLORIDA SHIP CANAL project
Cross-Florida Canal. E. J. Long. il Am For 70:16-19+ Je '64

FLORIDA state university, Tallahassee
Triumph or trimonster? Time 82:91 S 13 '63

FLORINSKY, Michael T.
Change and stability in the Soviet Union. Cur Hist 45:205-8+ O '63
Trends in the Soviet economy. Cur Hist 47:266-71 N '64

FLORISTS
Florist who has a business diploma; San Francisco's Podesta Baldocchi. il Bsns W p56-8+ Je 29 '63

FLORIT, Ermenegildo, abp
Archbishop Florit and the laity; interview. ed. by W. M. Abbott. America 108:836-7 Je 8 '63

FLORMAN, Samuel C.
Wrong way on the 8:10. N Y Times Mag p72+ My 12 '63

FLOTATION equipment. See Boats and boating—Safety devices and measures

FLOUNDER fishing
Early season fishing. G. Heinold. il Outdoor Life 131:8+ Mr '63
Winter flounder fishing. G. Heinold. il Outdoor Life 133:12+ Mr '64

FLOUR
On all the shelves at once; Gold Medal Wondra. il Bsns W p 127-8 O 5 '63

FLOUR, Fish. See Fish flour

FLOUR beetles
Temperature dependence of wing abnormality in tribolium confusum. J. V. Slater and others. il Science 140:408-9 Ap 26 '63

FLOUR industry and trade
At the belt; price-fixing charges against the twelve millers. Time 83:86+ My 8 '64

FLOUR mills
See also
General mills, incorporated

FLOUR sculpture. See Modeling

FLOW meters
Laser flowmeter measures gases, fluids. P. J. Klass. il Aviation W 82:75-7 Ja 11 '65
See also
Venturi tubes

FLOW of matter. See Rheology

FLOWER, Sir Newman
Obituary
Pub W 185:35 Mr 23 '64

FLOWER arrangements. See Flowers, Arrangement of

FLOWER beds, Raised. See Landscape gardening

FLOWER borders. See Garden borders

FLOWER boxes, planters, etc.
Accent on containers. il Pop Gard 14:46-7 N '63
Big redwood planter is demountable. il Sunset 131:102 S '63
Brick planter made without mortar. S. Pott. il Pop Mech 120:149 O '63
Cape basket. L. B. Pearson. il Flower Grower 51:65-6 Ja '64
Cookout bar and planter. W. C. Leckey. il Pop Mech 120:120-5 Jl '63
Cultural requirements of container-grown plants. H. Teuscher. il Horticulture 41:138-9 Mr '63
Double-barreled planter. D. Shiner. il Design 65:214 My '64
Easy-to-build planter box. il Pop Gard 16:18 F '65
Fall crop of planters. G. O'Brien. il N Y Times Mag p88-9+ O 13 '63
Five flower boxes for your porch or patio. J. Brimer. il Pop Sci 185:108-9 Jl '64
Hand-crafted plant containers. il Sunset 131:112-14 O '63
How to have a changeable terrace with free wheeling flower beds. il House & Gard 124: 152-5 S '63
Imaginative miniature garden. L. H. Gee. il Horticulture 41:322-3 Je '63
Indoor scenery for greenery. il Life 54:59-60+ My 10 '63
Ladies of Hilo hang flowers high. il Sunset 130:154+ My '63
More than meets the eye. il Sunset 132:257 Mr '64
Patio planter for waterlilies. C. A. Barquist. il Pop Gard 14:56 My '63
Plant window boxes for sun or shade. il Pop Gard 15:10+ My '64
Planters for year-round gardeners. il House & Gard 126:26-7 D '64
Pots for plants. G. Taloumis. il Flower Grower 50:32-5 Jl '63
Stage plants dramatically. W. Radcliffe. il Flower Grower 50:42-4 N '63
These boxes are handsome and easily made. il Sunset 130:138 Ap '63
Ways to use big concrete containers. il Sunset 130:177 F '63
Window boxes on Boston's Beacon Hill. G. Taloumis. il Pop Gard 14:42-5+ My '63
FLOWER exhibits
American exhibits at England's famous Chelsea flower show. S. Saunders. il Pop Gard 14:6+ My '63
Camellia shows. Horticulture 41:71 F '63
Flower festival at Bath, England. J. Clements. il Horticulture 41:220-1 Ap '63
Flower shows. il Horticulture 41:156-9+ Mr '63
Flower shows and garden tours (cont) il House & Gard 123:170-1 Mr '63; 125:207-9 Mr '64
Garden events. See issues of Flower grower
Garden events [in month] (title varies) See issues of Sunset
Go to the show and take your dahlias too. F. J. Knocke. il Flower Grower 51:34+ Ag '64
Have fun, competing in a flower show. B. Black. il Pop Gard 14:18-19+ My '63
Hints on exhibiting house plants. W. H. Hull, jr. il Horticulture 41:457 S '63
Impressions of Chelsea. B. Nichols. il Pop Gard 15:64-5 Ja '64
Letter from Paris; Floralies internationales. Genêt. New Yorker 40:170-1 My 16 '64
Major spring flower shows. Pop Gard 14:8 Mr '63
1963 almanac of flower shows and garden tours. il House & Gard 123:170-1 Mr '63
Plant society news; dates to remember. Pop Gard 14:81+ Ap '63
Tulips in the Skagit country. il Sunset 132:26 Ap '64
See also
Horticultural exhibitions
FLOWER gardening. See Floriculture
FLOWER gardens. See Gardens
FLOWER grower (periodical)
Weathervane. R. G. Miner. Flower Grower 50:6 D '63; 51:8 Mr '64
Weathervane; fiftieth anniversary of Flower grower. R. G. Miner. Flower Grower 51:8 Ja '64
FLOWER painting. See Flowers in art
FLOWER photography. See Photography of flowers, plants, trees, etc.
FLOWER pots
Flower pot patio bells. il Design 64:217 Je '63
Pots; in several shapes and sizes. G. Taloumis. il Horticulture 42:20-1 Mr '64
FLOWER seeds. See Flowers—Seed
FLOWER shows. See Flower exhibits
FLOWER stands
New importance of plant stands. il House B 105:122-3+ F '63
FLOWERING cherry. See Oriental flowering cherry
FLOWERING crab apples. See Crab apples
FLOWERING dogwood. See Dogwood
FLOWERING maples
Grow abutilon. E. T. Manos. il Horticulture 41:618 D '63
FLOWERING of plants. See Plants, Flowering of
FLOWERING onions. See Alliums
FLOWERING shrubs. See Shrubs
FLOWERING trees
Dress up your yard with lovely spring-flowering trees. G. Harshbarger. il Am Home 66:6+ Mr '63
Force branches for an early spring. il Horticulture 42:43 F '64
Stylish streets wear flowering trees. G. Taloumis. il Flower Grower 50:55-7 My '63
Summer propagation; flowering trees and shrubs. R. G. Coggeshall. il Horticulture 42: 40-1 Je '64
See also
Franklinia
Goldenrain trees
FLOWERS, Nancy
Majestic workboats of a Portuguese lagoon. il Natur Hist 74:20-5 F '65
FLOWERS
Flowers & shade. H. K. Morse. il Flower Grower 50:48-9+ Mr '63
Flowers that bloom in the spring. M. Compton. il Horticulture 41:166-7 Mr '63
How to put color in your landscape. il House & Gard 125:156-9+ My '64
I like local varieties. M. Payne. il Pop Gard 14:104 My '63
More new flowers for you in '65. Farm J 89:83 Ja '65
New and novelty flowers; 1964. Horticulture 42:20-3+ F '64
New flowers for '64. L. Donelson. il Farm J 88:80-1 Ja '64
New flowers for your yard. L. Donelson. il Farm J 89:75 Ja '65
New flowers to chirp about. T. A. Weston and G. Harshbarger. il Am Home 66:42-3+ Ja '63
Novelty flowers and vegetables for your 1964 garden. il Horticulture 42:20-3 Ja '64
There's a place in every garden for tall growing flowers. P. Headley. il Horticulture 41:206-7 Ap '63
They're actually this big-and bigger! new giants of the garden world. il Bet Hom & Gard 42:54-5 My '64
This is my favorite. See issues of Popular gardening & living outdoors
What are flowers for? J. W. Krutch. House & Gard 125:150-1 Mr '64
See also
Alpine flora
Annuals (plants)
Color of flowers
Floriculture
Flowers as gifts
Leis
Perennials
State flowers
Wild flowers
also names of flowers, e.g. Day lilies
All America selections
See Plants—All America selections
Cut flowers
Fountain of youth found for flowers. Sci N L 85:104 F 15 '64
See also
Flowers, Arrangement of
Photographs
Color from your garden brightens the indoors. J. J. Simpkins. Flower Grower 50:71 Ag '63
Quotations, maxims, etc.
Poetry of flowers; photographs by R. Block. N Y Times Mag p24-5 My 24 '64
Truth & poetry; ed. by H. V. Wilson. Flower Grower 50:67 Je '63
Seed
Germinating very fine seeds. R. J. Favretti. il Horticulture 42:52-5+ Mr '64
FLOWERS, Arrangement of
Arrangements of a master! Japanese flower master, Sofu Teshigahara. il Bet Hom & Gard 43:50-3 Ja '65
Basic aids for flower arranging. il Good H 157:130 Jl '63

FLOWERS, Arrangement of—*Continued*
Beauty and the abstract. H. V. Wilson. il Flower Grower 50:22-4+ D '63
Before you start your arrangement, take five basic steps. D. Biddle. il Pop Gard 14:12 Mr '63
Bring the springtime indoors. il Am Home 67:4 My '64
Easy summer bouquets for your patio. M. A. Roche. il Pop Gard 15:76-7 Jl '64
Fill your house with flowers. il Pop Gard 14:26-7 Jl '63
Flower designs; impressions from Scandinavia. B. Hubbard and H. C. Schwartz. il Am Home 66:34-5 Mr '63
Flower festival at Bath, England. J. Clements. il Horticulture 41:220-1 Ap '63
Fresh flowers vs. phony posies. F. B. Hunt. il Horticulture 41:96 F '63
How to bring summer indoors. il Horticulture 42:36-7 Ag '64
How to make successful flower arrangements. E. Yuasa. il House B 106:92-113+ Ag '64
How to make your philodendron bloom. il Pop Gard 15:22 Ja '64
How to use flowers from the field. il Farm J 88:81 S '64
Let's arrange chrysanthemums. V. T. Bayles. il Pop Gard 15:42-3 S '64
Line; living plant material. M. C. Cole. il Flower Grower 50:51 My '63
Look what flowers can do for a room! E. Craster and F. Huttenlocher. il Bet Hom & Gard 42:50-3 Ag '64
Make a splash with flowers. R. Martens. il Farm J 87:66-7 Jl '63
Matter of arrangement; excerpt from Garden open today. B. Nichols. Pop Gard 14:28+ Jl '63
New dimensions. R. E. Carr. il Flower Grower 50:34-5+ Ag '63
One good arrangement deserves another! E. D. Craster. il Bet Hom & Gard 41:60-5 Ag '63
Parties in full bloom; with menus. il Good H 157:66-88 Jl '63
Passion for flowers: Baronne Geoffroy de Waldner and her French garden; with account by V. Lawford. il Vogue 144:260-9, 275-6+ D '64
Projects a man can do for his flower arranger. il Bet Hom & Gard 42:100-1 Mr '64
See what a few branches can do. il Bet Hom & Gard 41:86 My '63
Simple bouquets from garden flowers. E. Finch. il Flower Grower 51:38-9 Jl '64
Simplicity with chrysanthemums; photographs. R. Carr. Flower Grower 50:48-9 O '63
Smart arrangements with spring flowers; photographs. Suc Farm 61:80-1 Ap '63
Some basic techniques for good arrangements. R. Carr. il Flower Grower 51:50-1 Jl '64
Sow them, grow them and arrange them. il Pop Gard 15:8-9 Ja '64
Sunshine in November; easy-to-arrange mums M. C. Cole. il Am Home 67:10 N '64
These say spring is really here. il Sunset 130: 168+ F '63
Unusual ways with lilliputian bouquets. D. L. Brightbill. il Am Home 66:9 Jl '63
What's wrong with flower arranging? C. B. Lees. il Horticulture 42:46-9 Ap '64
See also
Bouquets
Flowers, Dried
Roses, Arrangement of
Vases

FLOWERS, Artificial
Bouquets of tissue paper. P. E. Roberts. il Design 64:153+ Mr '63
Flowering of fake flowers; polyethylene greenery. S. Kohn. il N Y Times Mag p54+ Ag 23 '64
Fresh flowers vs. phony posies. F. B. Hunt. il Horticulture 41:96 F '63
Quick-to-make paper flowers. il Sunset 130: 148 My '63
Ring your room in roses. il McCalls 91:110-11 D '63

FLOWERS, Dried
Decorating with dried flowers; excerpts from New ways with dried flowers. R. Gannon. il Design 64:150-2 Mr '63
Dried flowers and potpourri. il House & Gard 125:102-3+ Je '64
Fun with summer flowers. M. Perry. il Flower Grower 51:30-1 Ag '64
Little things make my life interesting; ed. by R. Martens. A. Kracht. il Farm J 87: 106-7 F '63
Press plants for permanence. L. M. Andrews. il Horticulture 41:577 N '63
Pressed-flower art. A. D. B. Marsh. il Am Home 67:124 Jl '64
Pressed petunias. J. L. Russell, jr. Pop Gard 14:21 Jl '63
Put a leaf on your letters. il Sunset 133:82 Ag '64
Thoughts on drying flowers in silica. D. L. Zakon. il Horticulture 41:470-1 S '63
Win blue ribbons with dried herbs. A. H. Williamson. il Horticulture 42:26-7 F '64

FLOWERS, Everlasting. See Everlasting flowers

FLOWERS, Fragrant. See Gardens, Fragrant

FLOWERS, Names of. See Botany—Nomenclature

FLOWERS, Pressed. See Flowers, Dried

FLOWERS, Wild. See Wild flowers

FLOWERS as food
Flower recipes for garden gourmets. D. L. Roberson. il Horticulture 41:174-5 Mr '63
Rose recipes. D. L. Roberson. il Horticulture 41:313 Je '63

FLOWERS as gifts
Flowers to unwrap; H&G designs of flowers for delivery anywhere in the U.S. il House & Gard 126:166 D '64

FLOWERS in art
Floreat Philadelphia; exhibition of flower paintings in Philadelphia museum. H. Clifford. il Art N 62:30-1+ My '63
Flower painting. A. Ehrlich. il Sch Arts 63: 5-7 D '63

FLOWERS in house decoration. See Plants in house decoration

FLOWERS in literature
Why Nero Wolfe likes orchids. R. Stout. il Life 54:108 Ap 19 '63

FLOWERS of sorrow; story. See Hazzard, S.

FLOWMETERS. See Flow meters

FLOYD, Barry
Federal Republic of Nigeria. bibliog Focus 15:1-6 O '64

FLOYD, Carlisle
Susannah. Criticism
New Yorker 39:150-2 My 11 '63

FLOYD, Elizabeth R.
Blurred images. Sr Schol 84:8-9 F 28 '64

FLOYD, John B.
Was the Secretary of war a traitor? W. A. Swanberg. il pors Am Heritage 14:34-7+ F '63

FLOYD, Wayne
Coat hanger chandelier. il Design 65:154 Mr '64

FLU. See Influenza

FLUGELHORN. See Musical instruments

FLUID amplifiers. See Amplifiers

FLUID control. See Hydraulic control

FLUID dynamics
Flowage differentiation. S. Bhattacharji and C. H. Smith. bibliog il Science 145:150-3 Jl 10 '64
Probable energy control by fluids unveiled. Sci N L 85:403 Je 27 '64

FLUID mechanics. See Hydromechanics

FLUID sensors. See Aeronautic instruments

FLUIDS
Freezing-point depression: new method for measuring ultramicro quantities of fluids. D. J. Prager and R. L. Bowman. bibliog il Science 142:237-9 O 11 '63

FLUIDS, Brake. See Brake fluids

FLUMES
Last of the lumber flumes? Broughton flume, Washington. il Sunset 133:52 N '64

FLUORESCENCE
Fluorescent gems from Davy Jones's locker. P. A. Zahl. il Nat Geog Mag 124:260-71 Ag '63
See also
Antibodies, Fluorescent
Mössbauer effect

FLUORESCENCE spectra. See Spectrum—Fluorescence spectra

FLUORESCENT antibodies. See Antibodies, Fluorescent

FLUORESCENT flies. See Fishing lures, flies, etc.

FLUORESCENT lamps. See Electric lamps, Fluorescent

FLUORESCENT lighting. See Electric lamps, Fluorescent

FLUORESCENT paint. See Paint, Luminous

FLUORIDATION. See Water supply—Fluoridation

FLUORIDES
Bonding in xenon fluorides and halogen fluorides. K. S. Pitzer. bibliog il Science 139: 414-15 F 1 '63
Chlorine pentafluoride. D. F. Smith. Science 141:1039 S 13 '63

FLUORIDES—*Continued*
Documenting the case against fluoridation. J. Lear. il Sat R 47:85-92 Ja 4 '64; Same abr. Sci Digest 55:34-9 Ap '64; Discussion. Sat R 47:49-53 F 1; 24-31 F 15; 51-3 Mr 7; 47-9 My 2; 44 Ag 1 '64
Fluoride: its effects on two parameters of bone growth in organ culture. W. R. Proffit and J. L. Ackerman. bibliog il Science 145:932-4 Ag 28 '64
Fluoride's checkered past. J. Lear. Sat R 47:90-1 Ja 4 '64
Inorganic fluorine chemistry; report on symposium. L. Stein. Science 143:1058-60 Mr 6 '64
Krypton difluoride: preparation and handling. D. R. MacKenzie. bibliog Science 141:1171 S 20 '63
Krypton fluoride; preparation by the matrix isolation technique. J. J. Turner and G. C. Pimentel. bibliog Science 140:974-5 My 31 '63
Krypton tetrafluoride: preparation and some properties. A. V. Grosse and others. bibliog il Science 139:1047-8 Mr 15 '63
Protactinium fluorides, the new class, $MPaF_6$. L. B. Asprey and R. A. Penneman. bibliog il Science 145:924 Ag 28 '64
Raoult's law study of vanadium pentafluoride in uranium hexafluoride. R. C. Shrewsberry and B. Musulin. bibliog il Science 145:1452-4 S 25 '64
Strain-induced birefringence in fluoride films on uranium dioxide. W. P. Ellis. bibliog il Science 144:1570-2 Je 26 '64
Thermochemical properties of xenon difluoride and xenon tetrafluoride from mass spectra. H. J. Svec and G. D. Flesch. bibliog il Science 142:954-5 N 15 '63
Xenon fluorides; fluorine-19 nuclear magnetic resonance spectra. A. C. Rutenberg. bibliog il Science 140:993-4 My 31 '63
Xenon hexafluoride complexes. H. Selig. bibliog Science 144:537 My 1 '64
Xenon hexafluoride: preparation of pure form and melting point. I. Sheft and others. bibliog Science 145:701-2 Ag 14 '64
Xenon oxyfluoride. D. F. Smith. bibliog il Science 140:899-900 My 24 '63
Xenon tetrafluoride: fluorine-19 high-resolution magnetic resonance spectrum. T. H. Brown and others. bibliog Science 140:178 Ap 12 '63
Xenon tetrafluoride: heat of formation. S. R. Gunn and S. M. Williamson. bibliog Science 140:177-8 Ap 12 '63
Xenon tetrafluoride: reaction with aqueous solutions. S. M. Williamson and C. W. Koch. bibliog il Science 139:1046-7 Mr 15 '63
See also
Vinyl fluoride

FLUORINE
Xenon difluoride and the nature of the xenon-fluorine bond. P. A. Agron and others. bibliog il Science 139:842-4 Mr 1 '63
Xenon fluorosilicate and related compounds. A. F. Clifford and G. R. Zeilenga. bibliog Science 143:1431 Mr 27 '64

FLUOROURACIL
Potentiation of 5-fluorouracil inhibition of Flexner-Jobling carcinoma by glucose. S. S. Kung and others. bibliog il Science 141:627-8 Ag 16 '63

FLUSH tanks. See Plumbing
FLUSHERS, Street. See Street cleaning apparatus
FLUSHING, Street. See Street cleaning
FLUSHING Meadow Park marina. See Marinas

FLUTE
Baroque flute. S. Baron. il Mus Am 83:30 Jl '63

FLUTE music
See also
Phonograph records—Flute music

FLUTE players
See also
Steig, J.

FLUTE solo with figured bass; story. See Simon, M. L.
FLUTTER meters. See Radio instruments
FLY catching plants. See Insectivorous plants
FLY cutters. See Cutting tools
FLY tying. See Fishing lures, flies, etc.

FLYGARE, W. H.
Bent chemical bonds. bibliog Science 140:1179-85 Je 14 '63

FLYING. See Flight
FLYING automobiles. See Airplanes, Light—Automobile combinations
FLYING boats. See Seaplanes
FLYING bridge. See Navigating bridge
FLYING clubs. See Aviation clubs
FLYING Dutchman; opera. See Wagner, R.
FLYING foxes. See Bats
FLYING jeep. See Airplanes, Military—United States

FLYING machines
Look at the new flying machines. W. Langewiesche. il Read Digest 84:85-9 Je '64

FLYING pole dances. See Indians of Mexico—Dances

FLYING saucers
Ufology; new report debunks belief that unidentified flying objects are buzzing the earth. il Newsweek 62:44 Ag 5 '63
World of flying saucers, by D. H. Menzel and L. G. Boyd. Review
Sci Digest il 54:64 S '63. D. Cohen

FLYING schools. See Aviation schools
FLYING squirrels. See Squirrels
FLYING start; story. See Warner, S. T.
FLYING submarine. See Submarine boats—Airplane combination

FLYING Tiger line, incorporated
Cargo lines want in; demand a share of mail business. il Bsns W p 120+ Ap 25 '64
Who'll fly the freight? il Bsns W p58+ O 12 '63

FLYNN, Elizabeth Gurley
End of the rebel girl. il por Time 84:41 S 18 '64

FLYNN, John
He's the greatest since Jim Thorpe. Life 55:47-9 O 25 '63
U.S. bombers are blasted in Vietnam. Life 57:50-1 N 13 '64
Young civilian tries to win the fight on the people front. Life 57:40-5 N 27 '64

FLYNN, John P. See MacDonnell, M. F. jt. auth.

FLYNN, John Thomas
John T. Flynn, RIP. Nat R 16:345-6 My 5 '64
Obituary
Pub W 185:65 Ap 27 '64

FLYNT, Ralph C. M.
Improvement of English instruction; adaptation of address. por Sch Life 46:5-9 Ag '64

FLYWAYS, Migration. See Birds—Migration

FLYWHEELS
Horsepower havoc! E. Rickman. il Hot Rod 16:76-9+ Ag '63
How about a heavy wheel? R. Huntington. il Hot Rod 16:46-7+ F '63

FOA, Bruno
Italy's stake in the Common market. Cur Hist 45:289-94+ N '63

FOA, Joseph V.
Where is science taking us? por Sat R 47:68-9 N 7 '64

FOAM plastics. See Plastics
FOAM rubber. See Rubber, Sponge
FOCUSING. See Photography—Focusing

FOEHR, Lee
Talk's not cheap anymore; poem. Ladies Home J 80:120 Mr '63

FOERSTER, Bernd
What to teach about architecture. Sch Arts 62:24-6 My '63

FOETUS. See Fetus

FOG
Fog piloting. H. S. Holcomb. il Yachting 115:214 My '64
Pea souper. A. W. Moffat. il Yachting 115:147 F '64
Taking the curse out of fog. F. T. Moss. il Yachting 116:48-50+ Ag '64

FOGARTY, Anne
City apartment unified by the snap of black and white. il House & Gard 125:90-3 Ja '64

FOGARTY, John E.
Raising the level of literacy; adaptation of address, March 7, 1964. bibliog por Sch Life 46:4-6 Je '64
State and federal support of libraries; excerpt from address, July 13, 1963. ALA Bul 57:772-3 S '63
about
Political good fortune of medical research. M. Viorst. por Science 144:267-70 Ap 17 '64

FOGGING of glass. See Glass—Fogging
FOIL, Aluminum. See Aluminum foil
FOILS, Fencing. See Fencing

FOISIE, Jack
Air force murder case. Nation 196:285-7 Ap 6 '63

FOLDBOATS. See Boats and boating

FOLDES, Joseph
$ in color post cards. Pop Phot 55:70-1 Jl '64
Four new color films. U S Camera 26:64-5 S '63

FOLDES, Joseph—*Continued*
Informal portraits in your livingroom. U S Camera 27:82-3 Mr '64
Pocket studio. U S Camera 26:56+ N '63
Roll film. See issues of U.S. camera to July 1963
Un-miniature ultra-miniature. U S Camera 26:68-9+ N '63
Which viewing system for you? U S Camera 27:66-9 F '64
Wide angle lenses. U S Camera 26:52-7+ S '63

FOLDING beds. See Beds

FOLDING boats. See Boats, Rubber

FOLDING chairs. See Chairs

FOLDING ladders. See Ladders

FOLDING paper. See Paper work

FOLDING shelves. See Shelves

FOLDING tables. See Tables

FOLEY, Brian
First annual British international drag festival. il Hot Rod 18:50-6 Ja '65

FOLEY, Charles
Letter from Cyprus. Nat R 16:724-5 Ag 25 '64

FOLEY, Daniel F.
American legion; address, January 6, 1964. Vital Speeches 30:311-13 Mr 1 '64
American legion of today; address, November 9, 1963. Vital Speeches 30:121-2 D 1 '63
Independence day 1964; address, July 4, 1964. Vital Speeches 30:634-6 Ag 1 '64

FOLEY, Grover
Liberty of love. Christian Cent 81:826-9 Je 24 '64
Religionless religion. Christian Cent 80:1096-9, 1472 S 11, N 27 '63

FOLEY, Henry A.
To a poet; poem. America 108:372 Mr 16 '63

FOLEY, Jasena Rappleye
People who work in glasshouses. Antiques 83:557-9 My '63

FOLEY, Leo A.
Last of the giants. America 112:160-2 Ja 30 '65

FOLEY, Marie Agnes
Emperor's new robes; drama. Plays 23:41-51 Mr '64

FOLEY, P. J. See Lavery, J. J. jt. auth.

FOLEY, Paul
Whatever happened to women's rights? Atlan 213:3-5 Mr '64; Same abr. with title Women's rights and what they don't do about them. Read Digest 84:227+ My '64

FOLEY, William L.
Citizens on the alert. por Recreation 57:14-15 Ja '64

FOLGER Shakespeare library, Washington, D.C.
Cloud-blankets of words; report. Library J 88:2445 Je 15 '63
Folger Shakespeare library; reprint. H. W. Hewlett. il Wilson Lib Bul 38:630-5 Ap '64

FOLIAGE. See Leaves; Plants, Ornamental

FOLIAR fertilization. See Fertilizers and manures—Spray applications

FOLIC acid
Insect fertility: inhibition by folic acid derivatives. M. M. Crystal. bibliog il Science 144:308-9 Ap 17 '64
Severe childood disease treated with folic acid. Sci N L 85:73 F 1 '64

FOLIES-Bergère (New York visit) See Vaudeville

FOLIES-Bergère, Paris. See Paris—Theater

FOLK art
Antiques; examples of American folk art. A. Winchester. il Antiques 84:50-1 Jl '63
Byfield stones; our earliest American sculpture? L. W. Watkins. il Antiques 84:420-3 O '63
Country cousins. B. Plumb. il N Y Times Mag p36-7 Ag 2 '64
Experiment in Harrania: revival of Egyptian folk art. P. Davis. il Sch Arts 63:7-10 O '63
Focus on folk art. M. C. Cole. il Flower Grower 50:16-19 D '63
Folk art for big city folk; Museum of early American folk arts. B. O'Doherty. il N Y Times Mag p36-7 S 22 '63
Putting folk art to good use. Sunset 133:126 N '64
Setting for American folk art in old remodeled barns. il House B 105:138-9 Ap '63

FOLK dancing
Nuance makes the difference. il Dance Mag 38:48-51 Ap '64
Reporter at large; dancers in May: P.S. 31 in Park fête in Central park. L. Ross. il New Yorker 40:35-8+ Jl 18 '64
Reviews: folk. H. Yurchenco. Mus Am 84:55 Ja '64

FOLK drama
See also
Pastoral drama

FOLK drama, Brazilian
Folk theater in northeastern Brazil. A. Suassuna. il Américas 16:18-23 N '64

FOLK drama, Chinese
Double nine of Chih Yuan. P. T. Nolan. Plays 23:78-84, 96 O '63

FOLK drama, German

Single works

Rumpelstiltskin. A. Thane. Plays 22:53-63 Ap '63

FOLK literature
Folk-tale collections. E. S. Ross. Horn Bk 39:490-1 O '63

FOLK literature, Haitian
Bouqui and Malice, a folk tale of Haiti. E. C. Tate. Negro Hist Bul 26:176-7 F '63

FOLK literature, Indonesian
Storytelling in Java. P. B. McVickar. il Horn Bk 40:596-601 D '64

FOLK literature, Serbian
This is the Christmas. R. Sawyer. Horn Bk 40:666-73 D '64

FOLK literature, Turkish
Folk tales in Turkey. B. K. Walker and A. Uysal. Horn Bk 40:42-6 F '64

FOLK medicine. See Medicine, Popular

FOLK museums
Here's an unmusty museum; Lane County pioneer museum, Eugene, Ore. il Sunset 132:65 Ap '64
Plan a stop-off in Yreka; Siskiyou County museum, Calif. il Sunset 132:79 Mr '64
Surprise south of Visalia; Tulare County museum, Calif. il Sunset 133:62 N '64
See also
Shelburne museum, Shelburne, Vt.

FOLK music
Folk music in New York (title varies) H. Yurchenco. Mus Am 83:226+ Ja; 34 F; 40 My '63; 84:263 D '64
Folk singers and their fans. S. Castan. il Look 27:49-50+ Ag 27 '63
Folk song frenzy. il N Y Times Mag p66-7 O 20 '63
Just playin' folks; photographs by J. Launois. Sat Eve Post 237:24-9 My 30 '64
Reviews: folk. H. Yurchencko. il Mus Am 84:55 Ja; 47 Mr; 42-3 N '64
See also
Phonograph records—Folk music

FOLK music, American
Fourth man makes the trio tick; Kingston trio. il Bsns W p56-8 F 23 '63
Hootenanny for young leaders; folk-singing evening for college students, Washington, D.C. P. Mesta. il McCalls 90:18+ Je '63
I hear America singing or leaves of grass revisited, like. J. Shepherd. Mlle 59:243+ Ag '64
Nashville sound; Country music festival. il Time 84:76+ N 27 '64
Take a boy like me; New Christy minstrels. il Time 81:40 Mr 29 '63

FOLK singers. See Singers

FOLK singing. See Singing

FOLK song festivals. See Music festivals

FOLK songs
Bookshelf of the blues. L. Cohn. il Sat R 47:49+ Je 13 '64
Folk music around the world a basic library collection; with discography. H. Yurchenco. il Library J 88:1838-40 My 1 '63
Gitars, folk songs, and halls of ivy. A. Shaw. Harper 229:33-4+ N '64
Long trail a-winding; S. Addiss and B. Crofut. il Newsweek 61:53 Ap 29 '63
See also
Ballads

FOLK songs, American
Basic library of U.S. folk music; with discography. I. Silber. il Library J 88:1835-8 My 1 '63
Controversy in song; Chad Mitchell trio. il Sr Schol 82:18 My 8 '63
Folk singers and their fans. S. Castan. il Look 27:49-50+ Ag 27 '63
It's been good to know him; W. Guthrie. N. Hentoff. Reporter 32:48-9 Ja 14 '65
Leadbelly songbook; the ballads, blues, and folksongs of Huddie Ledbetter. ed. by M. Asch and A. Lomax. Review
Sat R 46:57 Je 15 '63. L. Cohn
Listen to the folk singers! il Read Digest 82:39-40+ F '63
New beat: topical folk singers, their songs. B. Rollin. Vogue 144:60+ S 1 '64
Profiles; B. Dylan. N. Hentoff. New Yorker 40:64-6+ O 24 '64
Rag peddler; M. Morath. Time 81:42 F 22 '63

FOLK songs, American—*Continued*
Still small voice. F. Taylor. il Mus Am 83: 12-13 F '63
They hear America singing. il Time 82:53+ Jl 19 '63
See also
Negro songs
FOLK songs, Peruvian
Songs of Andean pastures. S. Q. Jara. il Américas 15:37-9 My '63
FOLK songs, Portuguese
See also
Fados
FOLK tales. See Folk literature
FOLKLORE
See also
Animal lore
Literature, Primitive
Mythology
Japan
Good cocktail; Ninja warriors. il Newsweek 64:31+ Ag 3 '64
FOLKLORE, Negro
What is Negro folklore? R. Clark. Negro Hist Bul 27:40-1 N '63
FOLLETT, Mary Parker
Famous firsts: sibyl of a modern science. il pors Bsns W p 196+ N 21 '64
FOLLIARD, Edward T.
Escorting Mona Lisa to America. por Nat Geog Mag 123:838-47 Je '63
Washington front. See occasional issues of America
(ed) See Eisenhower, D. D. Ike's view: FDR policy prolonged the war
FOLLIS, Betty
Making history live. Sr Schol 85:17T N 11 '64
FOLLOW up studies (education)
College records of mediocre high school graduates. Sch & Soc 92:350+ N 28 '64
Follow-up of freedom schools; Mississippi project. Sch & Soc 93:3-4 Ja 9 '65
Whither the college graduate? Sch & Soc 92:64-5 F 22 '64
FOLSOM, Marion B.
Health, education and welfare: the first decade. Cur Hist 45:87-91+ Ag '63
How to pay the hospital. Atlan 211:79-82 Je '63
Where unemployment hits hardest. Sat R 47: 21-6 Ja 11 '64
FOLSOM, T. R. and others
Variation of cesium in the ocean. bibliog Science 144:538-9 My 1 '64
FOLTMAN, Felician F.
Apprenticeship and skill training, a trial balance; excerpts from testimony before subcommittee on employment and manpower, October 24, 1963. bibliog f Mo Labor R 87:28-35 Ja '64
FOLTZ, William J.
Malagasy: patterns and prospects. bibliog f Cur Hist 46:163-8+ Mr '64
FOME-COR corporation
Kit for a fast display; Exhibitkit. il Bsns W p84 Mr 2 '63
FOMIN, Aleksandr S.
Cuban crisis: how close we were to war; excerpts from Politics of policy-making: the Kennedy years. R. Hilsman. il U S News 57:59-60 Ag 17 '64; Excerpts. Look 28:19-21 Ag 25 '64
FONDA, Henry
Oldest Fonda. B. Davidson. por McCalls 90: 88-9+ My '63
FONDA, Jane
Lady Jane. A. Aronowitz. il pors Sat Eve Post 236:22-5 Mr 23 '63
U.S. Jane conquers Paris. il pors Life 56:75-6 Ja 10 '64
FONDA, Peter
Peter Fonda on his own. E. Miller. pors Seventeen 22:208-9+ Ag '63
FONDILLER, Harvey V.
Films at the fair. Pop Phot 55:88-91+ Ag '64
Flaherty seminar. Pop Phot 54:112-13 F '64
How to break in. Pop Phot 54:107+ F '64
Make sound-money. Pop Phot 55:81 O '64
Movies to learn from: see these, edit better. Pop Phot 55:84-5+ S '64
Shopping guide to tape recorders for the field. Pop Phot 53:51-6+ S '63
Space films by people who can't go. Pop Phot 52:96+ F '63
Tape the unheard. Pop Phot 55:83 O '64
There's action in stills. Pop Phot 53:90-3 Ag '63
Where to study film-making. Pop Phot 53: 98-9+ O '63
FONER, S. N.
Free radicals and unstable molecules. bibliog Science 143:441-50 Ja 31 '64
FONG, Katheryn
I believe; ed. by D. Taylor. por Seventeen 23:78 Ag '64
FONTAINE, André
ABC of MLF. Reporter 31:10-14 D 31 '64
Boating. Sports Illus 18:41 Ja 28 '63
Government-business team that works. Read Digest 83:111-14 D '63
Remarkable story of the dropouts and the college students. McCalls 91:36+ Mr '64
Trading stamps, who gets what? Read Digest 82:66-9 Je '63
—See Economos, J. P. jt. auth.
FONTAINE, Everett O.
People and places of the Milam era; excerpts from address, 1964. pors ALA Bul 58:363-71 My '64
FONTAINE, Frank
Celebrity register. C. Amory. por McCalls 90:158 Ag '63
FONTAINE, Joan
Celebrity register. C. Amory. por McCalls 90:158 Ag '63
FONTAINE, Pat
Celebrity register. C. Amory. por McCalls 90:158 Ag '63
FONTAINE, Robert
Efficiency expert; drama. Plays 24:77-82 O '64
First catch your dog. Atlan 212:132+ N '63
My son, the rebel. Atlan 211:115-17 Je '63
Off the cuff. Writer 77:5-6 D '64
Sex and spying. Atlan 213:118+ F '64
Suit like new; story. Sat Eve Post 236:50-4 Je 15 '63
Supermarket blues; drama. Plays 24:83-6 D '64
Why don't you try the piano instead? Atlan 214:124+ O '64
FONTANNE, Lynn
Stage-struck: the romance of Alfred Lunt & Lynn Fontanne; excerpts. M. Zolotow. il pors Look 28:92-9+ D 15 '64
They glory in a rustic, high-style hideaway. il pors Life 55:76-8 Jl 26 '63
FONTEYN, Dame Margot
Fonteyn, the enchantress. S. Hugh-Jones. Vogue 142:64-7 S 15 '63
Hottest little team in show biz. il pors Life 54:107-8 My 24 '63
Margot Fonteyn. por Dance Mag 37:31 Ap '63
Not quite it; Royal ballet at Metropolitan opera house. il Time 81:43-4 My 10 '63
Nureyev: top male dancer who quit the Soviets dazzles the West. R. Schickel. il por Look 27:26-8+ Jl 16 '63
People are talking about. . . por Vogue 141: 84-5 Ap 15 '63
FOOD
Bringing home the hippo; African wildlife as food. E. Huxley. il N Y Times Mag p 134-7 N 29 '64
Family food shopper. See occasional issues of Parents' magazine & better homemaking to August 1964
Flavor, the secret of good cooking. M. Johnston and P. McBride. il Bet Hom & Gard 42:66-7+ Mr '64
Food forum. E. Weston. il McCalls 92:26 O; 46 N; 52 D '64; 28 Ja '65
Foods. Consumer Rep 29:136-57 D '64
Gastronomy for the bold. R. Calder. il UNESCO Courier 16:21-5+ F '63
Keeping up to date; with news about food. il Farm J 88:86 My '64
Round little peg in a big square kitchen; excerpt from The Margaret Rudkin Pepperidge farm cookbook. M. Rudkin. il McCalls 90:122-3+ S '63
Something really good to eat; Vogue's address book of special shops for special foods in New York. Vogue 143:63+ My '64
Stupid questions about what you eat. J. Berry. il Pop Sci 185:74-5+ N '64
These foods are news! (cont) Bet Hom & Gard 41:112 Mr '63
To bagelville and beyond. H. Sutton. Sat R 47:36+ N 21 '64; Discussion. 47:33 D 12 '64
Your household (cont) il Consumer Rep 28: 218-39+ D '63
See also
Diet
Dinners and dining
Eating
Flowers as food
Hunger
Indians of North America—Food
Meals
Nutrition
Nutrition problems
Space flight—Food problems
United States—Army—Commissariat
also names of food, e.g. Meat

FOOD—*Continued*

Advertising

Objectionable advertising of foods and beverages. A. Mullins. il Consumer Bul 46:35-7 N '63

Decontamination

See Decontamination (from gases, chemicals, etc)

Drying

Exploded foods cook fast, save time. Sci N L 85:229 Ap 11 '64
How to dry apricots at home. il Sunset 132: 177 Je '64

Exhibitions

Vice President Johnson to open food exposition at Amsterdam. Dept State Bul 49:594 O 14 '63

Irradiation

See Food, Effect of radiation on

New sources

See Food supply—New sources

Preservation

See Food preservation and preservatives

Prices

Do you really save on those weekend food specials? il Changing T 17:30 Ap '63
Food distribution changes and the CPI. E. D. Hoover and M.S. Stotz. il Mo Labor R 87:58-64 Ja '64
Government keeps food prices high. il Nations Bsns 52:38-9+ Je '64
How to make your dollars go further. E. Peterson. il Suc Farm 62:79+ S '64
Mystery of rising food prices. il U S News 56:80-1 Mr 16 '64
Now it's the food industry under fire. il U S News 57:98-9 Jl 20 '64
Segregated food at the supermarket. J. Ridgeway. New Repub 151:6-7 D 5 '64
Some good news for shoppers. U S News 54: 8 F 18 '63
Time & money in the kitchen; convenience foods: economy or extravagance? il Changing T 17:34 F '63
Why food prices keep on rising. il U S News 56:35-7 Ap 20 '64
See also subhead Prices under names of foods, e.g. Meat—Prices

Psychology

See Eating, Psychology of

Ready-to-cook food

Christmas time savers! il Bet Hom & Gard 42:66-7 D '64
General foods is five billion particulars. il Fortune 69:114-17+ Mr '64
Instant cook. L. Stilwill. il Ladies Home J 81:132 Ja '64
Make it with packaged potatoes. Am Home 67:78 Ap '64
Pleasures of convenience foods. L. Stilwill. il Ladies Home J 80:133 N '63
Spend & save. il Ladies Home J 81:106-8+ Je '64
These foods are news! Bet Hom & Gard 41:112 Mr '63; 42:105 Ap '64

Smoking

Handy meat smoker; Abu smoke box. C. Conley. il Field & S 68:77 D '63

Storage

How to store staples. il House B 105:82+ My '63
Let's talk about food; question of cooling food before placing in refrigerator; ed. by P. L. White. Todays Health 42:21+ N '64

Study and teaching

Food expert teachers at Cornell. il Ebony 18:73-4+ Ag '63

FOOD, Canned. See Canned food

FOOD, Compressed
Astronauts' breakfast. Newsweek 61:63 Ap 15 '63

FOOD, Concentrated
Concentrate on the future. M. Kaytor. il Look 27:50+ Ap 23 '63

FOOD, Cooling of
How to keep food and drink cold. N. Craig. il House B 106:102-6 Jl '64

FOOD, Cost of. See Food—Prices

FOOD, Dried
Dry soup mixes. il Consumer Rep 28:225-7 My '63
Freeze-dried market begins to thaw; dehydrating food. Bsns W p68 Mr 16 '63
Go lightly into the wilderness; freeze-dry method of processing foods. D. Connelly. il Sports Illus 18:20-1 Je 24 '63
New lightweight, portable outdoor foods; freeze-dry process. D. Connelly. il House B 106:114+ Ag '64
Some freeze-dried food better than canned. Sci N L 85:191 Mr 21 '64
See also
Food—Drying

FOOD, Effect of radiation on
Atomic food preservation destroys vitamin C. Sci N L 83:216 Ap 6 '63
GIs test irradiated chow; radiation-processed food. Bsns W p88 Mr 2 '63
Hardy germ holds up nuclear food processing; organism that causes botulism. il Todays Health 42:60 Mr '64
Irradiated food tested. Sci N L 86:247 O 17 '64
Neatest trick since canning. E. Nanas. il Sat Eve Post 236:64-5 Je 1 '63
Perishables you can store on the shelf. il Bsns W p 120+ O 10 '64
Zap! you're preserved. Newsweek 62:71-2 S 9 '63

FOOD, Enriched
Three meals in your pocket; Nu-V energy food bar. C. Conley. il Field & S 68:111 O '63

FOOD, Frozen
Adventures in home cooking. S. Spitzer. il Holiday 34:99-104 S '63
Be meals ahead with your freezer. D. B. Marsh. il Good H 156:92-107+ Mr '63
Boil-in-the-bag for home freezing; Scotchpak. il Consumer Rep 28:260 Je '63
Freezing & canning cookbook; excerpts. N. Nichols. il Farm J 87:101-5+ Mr '63
Frozen foods cook book. il House & Gard 125:155+ Ap '64
Hearty main dishes to freeze ahead; with recipes. il Farm J 87:54+ Jl '63
Heat-and-eat potato dishes from the freezer; with recipes. D. Groves. il Farm J 88:82-4 O '64
Instant cook. L. Stilwill. il Ladies Home J 80:161-2 O '63
It's a breeze with a freezer; with recipes. il McCalls 91:62+ Ag '64
Magic of mixes. N. C. Wood. il Ladies Home J 80:90-1+ Ap '63
Meals from the freezer; with recipes. J. Figg. il Suc Farm 62:54-5 Jl '64
Nuisance item proves a big profit-maker; McKinsey study of frozen foods. il Bsns W p 116+ Mr 14 '64
Three-course dinners; TV-dinners. Consumer Rep 28:412 S '63
See also
Eggs, Frozen
Freezers
Freezing of food
Poultry, Frozen

FOOD, Irradiated. See Food, Effect of radiation on

FOOD, Smoked
Fish, fowl and smoke; art of cooking with smoke. R. Cantwell. il Sports Illus 19:52-5 O 28 '63

FOOD, Synthetic. See Food substitutes

FOOD additives
Joke: bread is made from wheat. Sci Digest 54:54 O '63
Valuable pamphlet on chemicals in foods. Consumer Bul 46:14 Je '63
What do those food labels mean? questions and answers. J. Daugherty and M. Daugherty. Sci Digest 56:5-7 Ag '64

FOOD adulteration and inspection
See also
Food laws and legislation

FOOD allergies. See Allergy

FOOD and agriculture organization of the United Nations
Africans and Asians; outstanding at World's food congress. M. Cartwright. il Negro Hist Bul 27:6-10 O '63
Battle against hunger. Commonweal 78:364 Je 28 '63
Battle against hunger. il U N Rev 10:14-15 Mr '63
Can forestry help? World food congress. J. Prokop. il Am For 69:7+ Jl '63
FAO council meets in Rome. UN Mo Chron 1:85 N '64
FAO lists title in World intelligence service; new edition of catalog. Pub W 185:53-4 Ap 20 '64
Food and Prof. Toynbee; World food congress. America 108:875 Je 22 '63
Food enough. America 109:34 Jl 13 '63
Forests and food. H. D. Crawford. il Am For 69:38-41+ S '63

FOOD and agriculture organization of the United Nations—*Continued*
Freedom from hunger campaign. il U N Rev 11:26-8 F '64
Global attack on hunger. il U N Rev 10:12-14 Je '63
Half the world is hungry; Third world food survey. B. Tufty. il Sci N L 83:371 Je 15 '63
How many starving millions? C. Clark. Nat R 16:522 Je 30 '64
Hunger and sacrifice; World food congress. Christian Cent 80:875-6 Jl 10 '63
Hunger round the world: 10,000 die every day. il Newsweek 61:43-4+ Je 17 '63
Mathematics of hunger. C. Bakal. il Sat R 46:16-19 Ap 27 '63
More food for southeast Asia. R. Calder. Bul Atomic Sci 19:31-2 Mr '63
Need to solve problems of hunger and malnutrition; address. B. R. Sen. U N Rev 10:35-6+ N '63
No more room; population report. Newsweek 61:36 F 4 '63
Operation Nordeste; Brazil's bold programme in the hunger campaign. J. de Castro. il UNESCO Courier 16:24-31 My '63
Our half hungry world. B. R. Sen. Parents Mag 39:32+ Ag '64
Solving world food problem. il U N Rev 10: 39-41 Jl '63
Toasted breadcrumbs of the future; address, June 3, 1963. H. Cleveland. Dept State Bul 49:13-17 Jl 1 '63
United States to be host to World food congress. Dept State Bul 48:583-4 Ap 15 '63
Visit to FAO. H. Clepper. il Am For 70:12-15 Ja '64
World food congress meets at Washington; welcoming remarks, June 4, and address, June 5, 1963. J. F. Kennedy; O. L. Freeman. Dept State Bul 49:58-68 Jl 8 '63
World food programme. A. H. Boerma. UN Mo Chron 1:72-6 N '64
World hunger. Commonweal 78:4 Mr 29 '63
See also
Food relief

FOOD and drug administration. See United States—Food and drug administration

FOOD as carrier of infection. See Food poisoning

FOOD as gifts
Christmas gifts from your kitchen. il Ebony 20:170+ D '64
Christmas is for giving; sweet-tooth gifts; with recipes. il Suc Farm 62:52+ D '64
Gift from your kitchen. Sunset 131:134-5 D '63
Instant Christmas. il McCalls 91:116-19 D '63

FOOD chain stores. See Chain stores

FOOD columns. See Newspapers—Sections, columns, etc.

FOOD concessions. See Concessions (food, etc)

FOOD consumption
More meat, less wheat. Sci N L 85:109 F 15 '64

FOOD containers. See Containers

FOOD contamination
Fallout dangers in food: what is being done? Good H 157:147-8 S '63
Fallout, food, and man; report of symposium at meeting of Federation of American societies for experimental biology. M. S. Read and H. S. Olcott. Science 140:1341-2+ Je 21 '63
Fallout in our food. il Consumer Rep 28:190-3 Ap '63
Food: NAS-NRC report cites microbiological hazards in new types of processing. J. Walsh. Science 147:132-4 Ja 8 '65
More fallout in foods. Sci N L 83:219 Ap 6 '63
Radiation and food: is action needed? C. L. Comar. Bul Atomic Sci 19:37-40 Mr '63
See also
Cesium in diet
Milk contamination
Strontium in diet

FOOD fads
Just how healthy are health foods? G. G. Greer. Bet Hom & Gard 41:92 Mr '63
Superstitious side of eating. G. Maddox. il Todays Health 41:48-51+ D '63; Same abr. with title Twenty-one diet fallacies. Sci Digest 56:57-61 O '64

FOOD fair stores, incorporated
You have to change to grow. il Bsns W p48-9+ Mr 2 '63

FOOD fallacies. See Errors, Popular

FOOD for peace program. See Food relief

FOOD freezers. See Freezers

FOOD habits of animals. See Animals—Food

FOOD handling
See also
Food technology

FOOD in exploration, shipwreck, etc. See Diet in exploration, shipwreck, etc.

FOOD industry and trade
Catering to the cats and dogs. il Bsns W p64-6+ N 9 '63
Chain squeeze; power of big food; with editorial comment. D. Smith. il Nation 198:642, 646-8 Je 29 '64
Dinner in ninety seconds. W. Bar-Illan. Sci Digest 56:73-80 Ag '64
Food distribution changes and the CPI. E. D. Hoover and M. S. Stotz. il Mo Labor R 87:58-64 Ja '64
Gourmet foods fill the supermarket cart. il Bsns W p47-8+ D 5 '64
How to bake a cake by automation; Kitchens of Sara Lee. il Duns R 82:51 D '63
Let's keep politics out of the pantry. C. G. Mortimer. il Look 29:80+ Ja 26 '65
LBJ urges a new study on role of food chains. Bsns W p97 F 8 '64
Off the fat of the land; low-calorie products. il Time 82:67 Ag 9 '63
Science streamlines food to meet new desires. Sci N L 84:281 N 2 '63
Supermarket chain that isn't a chain; Midwest food wholesaler. il Bsns W p80-2+ Ag 22 '64
Taste for Yankee food. il Time 84:66+ N 20 '64
Yes, let's find out. il Farm J 88:130 My '64
See also
Food, Frozen
General foods corporation
Staley, A. E, manufacturing company

Accounting

New textbook for supermarkets. il Bsns W p 156+ O 26 '63

United States

Now it's the food industry under fire. il U S News 57:98-9 Jl 20 '64

FOOD labels. See Labels

FOOD laws and legislation
Contents anonymous; Michigan comminuted meat law. Consumer Rep 28:414-15 S '63
Total health; address, November 30, 1964. W. H. Chase. Vital Speeches 31:177-81 Ja 1 '65
See also
United States—Food and drug administration

FOOD machinery and chemicals corporation. See FMC corporation

FOOD mixers, Electric. See Electric apparatus and appliances, Domestic

FOOD mixes
Alas, poor Betty; failure of General mills in Britain. Time 81:96 My 24 '63
Dry soup mixes. il Consumer Rep 28:225-7 My '63
Good things that come from small packages. il Redbook 121:70-1+ Je '63
I was a cooking snob. E. L. Lipshutz. Farm J 88:54 Jl '64
Magic of mixes. N. C. Wood. il Ladies Home J 80:90-1+ Ap '63
Watermelon cake; angel-food mix; with recipe. il Seventeen 23:238-9+ Ag '64

FOOD packaging. See Packaging

FOOD poisoning
Beware of summer food poisoning. il Changing T 18:13-15 Jl '64
Eggs salmonella. Newsweek 62:59 Jl 22 '63
Salmonella increasing as a cause of food poisoning. Consumer Bul 46:36-7 Je '63
Typhoid from canned meat unlikely in U.S. Sci N L 85:375 Je 13 '64
See also
Botulism

FOOD preferences
Food taboos. G. Schultz. il Todays Health 42:28-32 F '64
How to make a boy say wow! with recipes. il Seventeen 22:166-9+ Ap '63
Predictors of human food consumption. F. J. Pilgrim and J. M. Kamen. bibliog il Science 139:501-2 F 8 '63

FOOD preservation and preservatives
Dinner in ninety seconds. W. Bar-Illan. Sci Digest 56:73-80 Ag '64
Freezing & canning cookbook; excerpts. N. Nichols. il Farm J 87:101-5+ Mr; 94-7+ Ap '63
How to feed millions. W. Davis. Sci N L 83:131 Mr 2 '63
Long life for food; controlled atmosphere. Time 81:66 F 15 '63
New ways to preserve food. Good H 157: 147 Ag '63
See also
Fishes—Preservation
Food, Effect of radiation on

FOOD processing. See Food preservation and preservatives

FOOD production. See Food supply

FOOD regulation. See Food laws and legislation

FOOD relief

Closing the hunger gap; US Food for peace program. New Repub 152:6-7 Ja 30 '65

Common enemy of mankind: manifesto. il U N Rev 10:23 Ap '63

Department supports extension of Public law 480; statement, February 28, 1964. W. A. Harriman. Dept State Bul 50:507-9 Mr 30 '64

Food for peace; recommendations by Friends committee on national legislation. Christian Cent 81:1420 N 18 '64

Food for peace ships $1.5 billion in commodities in fiscal 1963. Dept State Bul 49:403 S 9 '63

Food subsidy for city folk; food stamp plan. il Bsns W p 164 Ap 11 '64

For the child who has nothing. New Repub 151:7-9 D 19 '64

From the people of the United States. il Newsweek 61:45 Je 17 '63

Here's the way the nationwide foodstamp program will work. U S News 57:12 Ag 24 '64

Hunger and sacrifice; World food congress. Christian Cent 80:875-6 Jl 10 '63

Latest idea: U.S. feed the world; expansion of Food for peace program. il U S News 57:43 D 28 '64

Mathematics of hunger. C. Bakal. il Sat R 46:16-19 Ap 27 '63

President calls for public support of freedom-from-hunger campaign; letter to James G. Patton, with text of proclamation. J. F. Kennedy. Dept State Bul 48:254-5 F 18 '63

President reports to Congress on Food for peace program. Dept State Bul 50:683-4 Ap 27 '64

President sends Food for peace report to Congress; accompanying memorandum, September 21, 1964. R. W. Reuter. Dept State Bul 51:678-80 N 9 '64

President signs bill extending Food for peace program; statement, October 8, 1964. L. B. Johnson. Dept State Bul 51:677-8 N 9 '64

Program that's working; Food for peace program. D. Hanson. Suc Farm 62:22 D '64

Rusty bells of hope. H. Bowser. Sat R 46:24 Je 22 '63

Seeks restructured overseas relief; Public law 480. Christian Cent 81:453 Ap 8 '64

Senate extends Food for peace program. Christian Cent 81:1260 O 14 '64

This month's feature: U.S. food surpluses & the Nation's needy, food stamp program. il Cong Digest 43:162-92 Je '64

World food congress meets at Washington; welcoming remarks, June 4, and address, June 5, 1963. J. F. Kennedy; O. L. Freeman. Dept State Bul 49:58-68 Jl 8 '63

World food programme. A. H. Boerma. UN Mo Chron 1:72-6 N '64

See also

American relief administration

Christian rural overseas program

Food and agriculture organization of the United Nations

Latin America

Feeding the children; Food for peace program. Time 81:23 Mr 1 '63

Food for peace. J. F. Wood. il Américas 15:1-6 My '63

Operation niños. G. Kroloff. il Sch Life 46:9-11 Je '64

Operation ninos. il Todays Health 42:58-61 S '64

Russia

Toast to President Hoover. N. Cousins. Sat R 46:30 N 9 '63

FOOD research

Today's research for babies' future. M. B. Keiser. il Parents Mag 39:20+ N '64

FOOD sections in newspapers. See Newspapers—Food sections

FOOD stamp plan. See Food relief

FOOD stores

See also

Chain stores

Great Atlantic and Pacific tea company

Grocery stores

Safeway stores, incorporated

Supermarkets

Winn-Dixie stores, incorporated

FOOD substitutes

Apple pie without apples; with recipes. J. R. Sibbald. il Am Heritage 15:114 Ap '64

Key to hunger problem: synthetic food. Sci N L 83:387 Je 22 '63

FOOD supplements. See Nutrition

FOOD supply

Battle against hunger. il U N Rev 10:14-15 Mr '63

Food and people. A. McCormack. Commonweal 80:79-82 Ap 10 '64; Reply. R. J. Allen. 80:237 My 15 '64

Food enough. America 109:34 Jl 13 '63

Food gap: calories around the world. il Newsweek 63:39 Ja 20 '64

Food stockpiling urged. Sci N L 83:139 Mr 2 '63

Food surplus inadequate. Sci N L 83:77 F 2 '63

Gastronomy for the bold. R. Calder. il UNESCO Courier 16:21-5+ F '63

Half the world is hungry; Third world food survey. B. Tufty. il Sci N L 83:371 Je 15 '63

Hunger in the free world; address, November 17, 1964. O. L. Freeman. Vital Speeches 31:190-2 Ja 1 '65

Hunger round the world: 10,000 die every day. il Newsweek 61:43-4+ Je 17 '63

Lagging food. Time 84:103 O 9 '64

Man, land and food, by L. R. Brown. Review U S News il 56:28-31 Ja 6 '64

Mathematics of hunger. C. Bakal. il Sat R 46:16-19 Ap 27 '63

Our half hungry world. B. R. Sen. Parents Mag 39:32+ Ag '64

Pope of the needy. America 108:453-4 Ap 6 '63

Requisites of abundance; address, March 9, 1964. H. Cleveland. Dept State Bul 50:550-5 Ap 6 '64

To give thanks. America 109:619 N 16 '63

World's food must triple. Sci N L 86:79 Ag 1 '64

See also

Famines

Food and agriculture organization of the United Nations

Surplus products, Agricultural

New sources

Cultivation of tilapia. C. F. Hickling. il Sci Am 208:143-8+ My '63

Food for the future. E. Hall. il Sci N L 85:10-11 Ja 4 '64

Political aspects

Let's keep politics out of the pantry. C. G. Mortimer. il Look 29:80+ Ja 26 '65

Statistics

Facts and figures of the Americas. il Américas 15:42-3 F '63

Alaska

When the eiders flew. C. E. Gillham. il Field & S 68:60-2+ F '64

Asia, Southeastern

More food for southeast Asia. R. Calder. Bul Atomic Sci 19:31-2 Mr '63

Brazil

Operation Nordeste: Brazil's bold programme in the hunger campaign. J. de Castro. il UNESCO Courier 16:24-31 My '63

China (People's Republic)

Grain of rice is worth a drop of blood. B. B. Fall. il N Y Times Mag p 10-12+ Jl 12 '64

Cuba

Cuba now: shortages everywhere, even food rations can't be met. il U S News 54:47-8 My 27 '63

Egypt

Too much & too little; acute food shortage. Time 84:78 D 18 '64

India

Accent on food. V. Koilpillai. Christian Cent 81:1252-4 O 7 '64

Fear of famine. Newsweek 64:38 Ag 10 '64

Feeding the famished. il Newsweek 64:50 N 23 '64

Hunger and worry plague India. Christian Cent 81:1053 Ag 26 '64

Hunger takes center of Indian news. Christian Cent 81:981 Ag 5 '64

India's battle for food. H. Maddick. bibliog il Cur Hist 44:160-6+ Mr '63

Not enough food for too many people. C. Bowles. il N Y Times Mag p7+ S 6 '64

Socialism and famine. H. Hazlitt. Newsweek 64:67 Ag 31 '64

Too many people, too little food. Time 84:24+ Jl 31 '64

Italy

Food and revolution. J. Burnham. Nat R 14:490 Je 18 '63

Russia

Necessary admission; growing bread shortage. Newsweek 62:61 N 11 '63

FOOD supply—Russia—*Continued*
Socialism and famine. H. Hazlitt. Newsweek 64:67 Ag 31 '64
Why Khrushchev needs to buy wheat. il U S News 55:43 O 14 '63

Underdeveloped areas
Food. N. S. Scrimshaw. il Sci Am 209:72-80 S '63
Forests and food. H. D. Crawford. il Am For 69:38-41+ S '63
Hungry nations, by W. Paddock. Review Sci N L 87:13 Ja 2 '65. B. Tufty

United States
Food supply keeps pace. Sci N L 86:247 O 17 '64
Foods of the future. J. Marks. il Suc Farm 63:85+ Ja '65
Poison sprays and health: the facts show this. il U S News 56:50-2 My 4 '64

Viet Nam (Democratic Republic)
Grain of rice is worth a drop of blood. B. B. Fall. il N Y Times Mag p 10-12+ Jl 12 '64

FOOD technology
Food: NAS-NRC report cites microbiological hazards in new types of processing. J. Walsh. Science 147:132-4 Ja 8 '65
Science keeps chili hot and celery crunchy. Sci N L 85:360 Je 6 '64

FOOD values
Calorific values of microcrustacea. G. W. Comita and D. W. Schindler. bibliog il Science 140:1394-6 Je 28 '63
Facts on low-calorie foods. J. Anderson and E. Ward-Hanna. il Ladies Home J 80:138+ Ap '63
Food and your health: new guide to the ideal intake. il U S News 56:67 My 18 '64
Let's talk about food; ed. by P. L. White. See issues of Today's health
New Better homes and gardens basic calorie chart. D. G. Cooley. Bet Hom & Gard 42:58-9+ Ag '64
Pure maple syrup: nutritive value. A. L. Leaf. bibliog il Science 143:963-4 F 28 '64
Staff of life is sturdy. B. Tufty. Sci N L 85:387 Je 20 '64
Well-fed men not soft. Sci N L 83:388 Je 22 '63
See also
Nutrition

FOOD vendors. See Vending machines

FOOD warmers
Food warmers and their lamps; eighteenth century types. L. W. Watkins. il Antiques 86:174-8 Ag '64
Keeping warm food warm, and hot food hot. il Sunset 133:70-1 Jl '64

FOOD yeast. See Yeasts

FOODEN, Jack
Rhesus and crab-eating macaques: intergradation in Thailand. bibliog Science 143:363-5 Ja 24 '64

FOOLS and jesters
King's amusement; tr. by J. W. Freeman. A. Maurois. il Opera N 29:8-13 D 12 '64

FOOT, Sir Hugh
Whites in Africa. Sat R 47:10-12 Jl 25 '64

FOOT, Hugh, baron Caradon. See Caradon, H. F.

FOOT
Anatomy for the ballet teacher; ed. by W. Como. R. Gelabert. il Dance Mag 38:65-7 Mr; 67-9 Ap '64
Feet of a bird. P. Draper. Dance Mag 37:49 S '63
Pretty hands, pretty feet. L. D. Kirk. il Parents Mag 38:38 O '63
Right care for children's feet. il Good H 157:164 O '63
Why do we torture our feet? S. A. Mix. il il Todays Health 42:56-7+ My '64

Care and hygiene
Don't let your feet defeat you. L. D. Kirk. il Parents Mag 38:46 F '63
Foot notes for summer. il Redbook 121:66-7+ Ag '63
Put spring in your step. il Seventeen 23:171 Mr '64
What you can do about your aching feet; interviews. E. L. Ralston; W. M. Scholl; A. Helfand. McCalls 90:46 Ap '63

FOOT-and-mouth disease
New research program on foot-and-mouth virus. Sci N L 83:137 Mr 2 '63

FOOT bridges. See Bridges, Foot

FOOT stools. See Stools

FOOTBALL
Accomplished but doubting Dutchman. J. Underwood. il Sports Illus 19:20-2+ Ag 19 '63
All-American saint; Columbia quarterback A. Roberts. E. Linn. il Sat Eve Post 237:72-3 N 21 '64
Always leave them limp; New York Giants vs. Pittsburgh Steelers at Yankee stadium. il Time 82:40 D 27 '63
Apropos; Wally Butts-Bear Bryant affair. Sports Illus 18:13 My 27 '63
Ara go bragh; Notre Dame's victories. il Newsweek 64:72 N 2 '64
Ara the beautiful; Notre Dame's coach. il Time 84:84-6+ N 20 '64
Ara's new era; Notre Dame's new leader. W. B. Furlong. il Sat Eve Post 237:72-5 N 28 '64
Arkansas takes over at the top; Razorbacks vs. Nebraska in Cotton bowl. D. Jenkins. Sports Illus 22:17 Ja 11 '65
Army's future is still ahead. Sports Illus 19:34 D 2 '63
Balm for a gloomy Bear; settlement of libel actions against the Saturday evening post. Time 83:51 F 14 '64
'Bama's big, bold bid in the week that was. J. Underwood. il Sports Illus 21:24-7 N 23 '64
Battle of the bucks; payment for players. il Time 84:68+ D 11 '64
Bears upend the Giants; Chicago takes NFL title. T. Maule. il Sports Illus 20:10-17 Ja 6 '64
Bears vs. Giants, two quarterbacks decide. il Newsweek 62:57 D 30 '63
Big day for D; Cotton bowl game, Texas vs. Navy. J. Underwood. il Sports Illus 20:16-17 Ja 13 '64
Big five; college football. Time 82:50 N 22 '63
Big ones are yet to come. M. Hyman. Sports Illus 19:60+ D 2 '63
Big-time football. Sat R 46:26 D 28 '63
Bowl exposure is growing longer; television coverage of all eight major bowl games. D. Jenkins. il Sports Illus 21:64-9 D 21 '64
Bowl heroes enjoy the season's last hurrahs. K. Rudeen. il Sports Illus 20:44-6 Ja 13 '64
Catch, and crash goes Notre Dame! University of Southern California victory. J. Underwood and J. Tobin. il Sports Illus 21:26-9 D 7 '64
Century cover boon; Time cover jinx and Notre Dame's defeat. Christian Cent 81:1575 D 16 '64
Chip off the old Doc; Felix Anthony Blanchard III. T. Cohane. il Look 28:99-102+ D 1 '64
College football; Army-Navy. il Time 82:48 D 13 '63
College football 1964. D. Jenkins. il Sports Illus 21:36-44+ S 21 '64
College football 1963. il Sports Illus 19:30-45+ S 23 '63
College football; restoration of Notre Dame's football image. il Time 54:58 O 30 '64
Colts with a kick. il Time 84:87 O 9 '64
Cut 'em off at forward pass; W. Hayes of Ohio state. W. B. Furlong. il Sports Illus 21:30-3 O 19 '64
Day for optimists. il Time 85:34 Ja 8 '65
Dotted linemen; pro contracts. il Newsweek 65:56 Ja 18 '65
Dramatic moment; case of W. Butts vs. Curtis publishing company. il Sports Illus 19:26-7 Ag 26 '63
Duke's day; University of Texas vs. Navy. il Time 83:56 Ja 10 '64
Enigma of the interim coach; H. Devore of Notre Dame. il Sports Illus 19:59 O 28 '63
Everybody throw? il Newsweek 62:38 D 23 '63
Fabulous in defeat; Orange bowl game, Texas vs. Alabama. J. Underwood. il Sports Illus 22:14-17 Ja 11 '65
First of all, take your eye off the ball. il Esquire 62:79-85 O '64
Football. See issues of New Yorker
Football and the college. N. Cousins. Sat R 46:36 S 28 '63; Reply. J. J. De Boer. 46:29 O 19 63
Football: another business that's really booming; prosperity for the professionals. il U S News 55:103-4+ N 18 '63
Football's hot corner; with charts. T. Maule. il Sports Illus 19:34-41 O 21 '63
Football's week. See issues of Sports illustrated published during football season
$4.13 call; conspiracy to fix the 1962 Georgia-Alabama football game. Newsweek 61:95 Ap 15 '63
Georgia tech's football Yellow Jackets: Southern stingers. T. Cohane. il Look 27:151-4 O 22 '63
Getting their kicks; place-kickers. il Newsweek 64:62 N 16 '64
Grand parade of the bowls; eight major bowl games. D. Jenkins. il Sports Illus 19:30-5 D 23 '63

FOOTBALL—*Continued*
Green Bay blocks to win. M. H. Sharnik. il Sports Illus 21:76-9+ S 7 '64
Gridiron on the grid. Nation 196:299 Ap 13 '63
Hundred plays in a hundred-plus degrees; Oklahoma Sooners beat Southern California. D. Jenkins. il Sports Illus 19:49-51 O 7 '63
I swore I would quit football. R. Mix. il Sports Illus 19:62-71 S 16 '63
If, at first; Rensselaer polytechnic institute, Troy, N.Y. Newsweek 62:74+ N 18 '63
Is there a Dr Tashiro on the field? founder of Mohawk Valley Falcons. il Sports Illus 19:46-50 O 28 '63
It's not the money, it's the vindication; with editorial comment. R. H. Boyle. il Sports Illus 19:5, 46-7 S 2 '63
Jolly Roger; college football. il Time 82:92-4+ O 18 '63
Just one more game to go; Notre Dame and U.S.C; with report by J. R. McDermott. il Life 57:101-8+ D 11 '64
Light man to do the heavy work; Nebraska fullback F. Solich. T. Brody. il Sports Illus 21:54-5 N 2 '64
Look out, Mister Roberts; Columbia's leading rusher. A. Wright. il Sports Illus 21:34+ N 9 '64
Madness is a game on Sunday. L. Rosten. il Look 27:68-74 D 3 '63
Measured in merthiolate. il Time 82:73 N 8 '63
Midsummer night's dream of autumn; All-America bowl game of the American football coaches association. D. Jenkins. il Sports Illus 19:44-5 Jl 8 '63
Monsters and me. T. McDonald. il Sports Illus 21:58-65 Jl 27; 39-42+ Ag 3 '64
Name of the game; Georgia vs. Alabama. Sat Eve Post 236:82 Ap 27 '63
New coat of paint on the old Kentucky home; University of Kentucky football team victorious over Mississippi and Auburn. L. Van Hoose. il Sports Illus 21: 58-9 O 12 '64
New way to get rich quick, in football. il U S News 58:64-5 Ja 18 '65
Nightmarish ending for Spook Murphy's dream; Memphis state Tigers lose to Ole Miss. D. Jenkins. il Sports Illus 21:64-5 S 28 '64
1963-1964 football forecast. T. Cohane. il Look 27:56-7+ S 10 '63; 28:58-63 S 8 '64
Notre Dame in a tussle at the top. il Sports Illus 21:22-3 N 23 '64
Oklahoma-Texas football feud. T. Cohane. il Look 27:85-7+ O 8 '63
Open letter to a college president; Vernon Alden of Ohio U. D. Kazmaier. Sports Illus 19:57-8 O 14 '63
Out to win big in the city of Memphis; Memphis State Tigers. G. S. Brown. il Sports Illus 19:77-9 N 25 '63
Phenomenon of professional football. B. L. Masse. America 109:548 N 9 '63
Pitt wins (boss's orders) Chancellor Litchfield vs. J. Michelosen. J. Underwood. il Sports Illus 19:22-6+ O 28 '63
Poor get rich and the rich go broke; big upsets in college football. M. Hyman. il Sports Illus 21:68+ O 19 '64
Practice makes ulcers; preseason exhibitions. Time 84:80+ S 4 '64
Pro football goes boom! il Read Digest 83:184-8+ N '63
Profit and loss on a long, crucial weekend; college football championships settled. J. Underwood. il Sports Illus 19:69-70 D 9 '63
Roar of the Tiger is Iacavazzi; Princeton v. Yale. T. C. Brody. il Sports Illus 21:68+ N 23 '64
Roses for Wolverines, blues for Buckeyes. J. Underwood. Sports Illus 21:65-7 N 30 '64
Sad Sam; New York Giants v. Washington Redskins. il Newsweek 64:104 O 5 '64
Saturday's silent heroes; Gallaudet college football. M. Silva. il Life 57:59-60+ N 6 '64
Saturday's tough ones (title varies) Sports Illus 19:94 S 23; 67 S 30; 55 O 7; 60 O 14; 52 O 21; 62 O 28; 55 N 4; 63 N 11; 59 N 18; 83 N 25; 63 D 2 '63; 21:107 S 21; 71 S 28; 60 O 12; 70 O 19; 62 O 26; 59 N 2; 52 N 9; 68 N 16; 71 N 30 '64
Scandalous notes; Georgia's Wally Butts comments on notes made during telephone call to Alabama's Bear Bryant. D. Jenkins. il Sports Illus 18:24-5+ Ap 8 '63
Setting for greatness at Philadelphia; Army-Navy football game. D. Jenkins. il Sports Illus 19:32-4+ D 2 '63
Settled out of court; Alabama vs Georgia. J. Underwood. il Sports Illus 19:20-5 S 30 '63
Sharp change in the game; pro-type platooning. D. Jenkins. il Sports Illus 21:28-31 N 16 '64
Show biz U; half-time shows at college games. il Newsweek 64:68-9 N 9 '64
Showdown for a quarterback; Pitt's F. Mazurek vs Navy's R. Staubach. M. Cope. il Sat Eve Post 237:28-9 O 17 '64
Some Arkansas proof of the law of gravity; Texas Longhorns vs Arkansas Razorbacks. D. Jenkins. il Sports Illus 21:60-1 O 26 '64
Some little men who think they are Packers; Wittenberg university football team. T. C. Brody. il Sports Illus 21:65-6 N 16 '64
Special kind of brute with a love of violence; linebacker D. Butkus of Illinois. D. Jenkins. il Sports Illus 21:30-2+ O 12 '64
Stitch in time is the Army's best weapon; quarterback R. Stichweh. D. Jenkins. il Sports Illus 21:73-4 O 5 '64
Story of a college football fix; Georgia versus Alabama. F. Graham, jr. il Sat Eve Post 236:80-3 Mr 23 '63; Discussion. Sports Illus 18:18-21 Mr 25 '63; Time 81:51 Mr 29 '63; Newsweek 61:51 Ap 1 '63
Taste for honey; Chicago Bears against New York Giants. il Time 83:56-7 Ja 10 '64
Texas makes it look simple; University of Texas vs Oklahoma; photographs by N. Leifer. Sports Illus 19:22-5 O 21 '63
Trial that has the South seething; college football fix: Georgia versus Alabama. D. Jenkins. il Sports Illus 19:18-21 Ag 5 '63
Trojan horse; Notre Dame vs. Southern California. il Time 84:68 D 4 '64
Two yards and the clock; 1963 Army-Navy game. D. Jenkins. Sports Illus 19:59-60 D 16 '63
Upstarts hit judgment day; Auburn, Illinois and Baylor teams lost. il Sports Illus 19: 28-9 N 18 '63
Very hard look at football; 1963 silver anniversary award winners compare the game today with the 1938 version. R. Lardner. il Sports Illus 19:38-40+ D 2 '63
Wake up the echoes! undefeated Notre Dame. D. Jenkins. il Sports Illus 21:20-3 N 2 '64
Warren McVea goes thisaway and thataway; first Negro to play football for University of Houston. M. Herskowitz. il Sports Illus 21:48-9 N 9 '64
Where we stand in college football. il Look 27:94+ N 5; 82+ N 19 '63
Who loves Harvard? Dartmouth vs Harvard. A. Wright. il Sports Illus 19:14-17 N 4 '63
Who's who among the undesirables; professional football. C. E. Morton. il Atlan 212:99 Ag '63
Winning took a Giant adjustment; New York Giants vs Cleveland Browns. T. Maule. il Sports Illus 19:56-7 N 4 '63
See also
American football league
Football players
National football league
Rugby football
Soccer

Accidents and injuries

See Sports—Accidents and injuries

Anecdotes, facetiae, satire, etc.

Everybody up for the kickoff; excerpt from Boys and other beasts. B. Lang. il McCalls 92:64+ N '64
Pro football gets its shrine. Christian Cent 80:1187 S 25 '63

Caricatures and cartoons

Mordant eye on pro football. T. Ungerer. Sports Illus 21:32-6 N 16 '64

Photographs

See Sports—Photographs

Quotations, maxims, etc.

Quotes: football; comp. by E. F. Murphy. N Y Times Mag p 140 N 8 '64

Rules

Double sub trouble: NCAA football substitution rules. Sports Illus 19:14 N 11 '63
Points for perfection; pro football. il Time 84:104 N 13 '64
Sharp change in the game; pro-type platooning. D. Jenkins. il Sports Illus 21:28-31 N 16 '64
War on ferocity; injuries in pro football. W. Bingham. il Sports Illus 19:18-23 N 11 '63

Study and teaching

Day of the game: excerpt from Run to daylight; ed. by W. C. Heinz. V. Lombardi. il Sports Illus 19:94-104+ S 9 '63

FOOTBALL, Childrens
Peewees go bigtime. il Life 55:55-8+ N 15 '63
FOOTBALL bands. See Bands, College
FOOTBALL clubs
Any time, any place. il Time 84:43 N 6 '64
Ball game that never was; Baltimore Colts vs. Buffalo Bills. T. Maule. Sports Illus 21:74-6 N 16 '64
Bears upend the Giants; Chicago takes NFL title. T. Maule. il Sports Illus 20:10-17 Ja 6 '64
Big, booming business of pro football. T. J. Murray. il Duns R 84:38-40+ S '64
Big Brown boom; Cleveland Browns. T. Maule. il Sports Illus 19:16-19 O 7 '63
Big man who wasn't there; Green Bay Packers vs Detroit Lions. T. Maule. il Sports Illus 19:76+ S 30 '63
Browns win big in the East. T. Maule. il Sports Illus 21:22-5 D 21 '64
Buffalo stands for the Bills. E. Shrake. il Sports Illus 21:32-3 O 5 '64
Charley's formula worked; three-way tie in the Eastern conference of the National football league. T. Maule. il Sports Illus 19:64-6+ D 2 '63
Cold comfort; controversy over Bears-Giants championship game. Sports Illus 20:5 Ja 20 '64
College star with a slow fuse ignites the fireproof Rams; rookie quarterback B. Munson. T. Maule. il Sports Illus 21:97-9 O 5 '64
Colts rule the West again; beat the Green Bay Packers. T. Maule. il Sports Illus 21: 34-5+ O 26 '64
Cowboys can ride high on better defense. T. Maule. il Sports Illus 19:47-52 S 9 '63
Don Trull queues up and counts his money; Houston Oilers quarterback. E. Shrake. il Sports Illus 21:16-19 Ag 17 '64
Down go the Packers; Chicago Bears defeat Green Bay Packers. T. Maule. il Sports Illus 19:28-31 N 25 '63
Eight top teams. il Newsweek 62:79 S 16 '63
Eyes and ears of the N.Y. Giants; Em Tunnell. il Ebony 19:58-60+ D '63
Football punts into new territory; Toledo Tornadoes. il Bsns W p 124+ N 7 '64
Giant story; New York Giants win Eastern division championship. T. Maule. il Sports Illus 19:22-9 D 23 '63
Gigantic midget among giant men; A. Karras, tackle for Detroit Lions; photographs by M. E. Newman; with account by T. Maule. Sports Illus 21:46-52 N 30 '64
Green Bay may be little, but football is a giant; last of pro football's old home-town teams; with paintings by R. Weaver. Sports Illus 21:44-9 N 2 '64
Green Bay: the Packers' town. E. Waldron. Holiday 34:68-9+ N '63
Half a game out and one to go; St Louis Cardinals beat Cleveland Browns. E. Shrake. il Sports Illus 21:16-19 D 14 '64
How the Colts met triumph, and disaster; ed. by T. Maule. D. Shula. il Sports Illus 22:24-9 Ja 11 '65 (to be cont)
How the Packers do it; Green Bay's boom in pro football. il Bsns W p52-4+ S 21 '63
How the West has won; West vs. East. E. Shrake. il Sports Illus 21:35-6+ N 23 '64
How they racked up the great Tittle. il Life 57:141-2 O 2 '64
I don't need money, I need points; Al Davis, coach of Oakland Raiders. W. Bingham. il Sports Illus 19:27-9 N 4 '63
In the AFL, guile and go should win for the Chargers; San Diego Chargers. E. Shrake. il Sports Illus 21:26-7 D 21 '64
It's not magic, says Tittle; Giants' quarterback. W. N. Wallace. il N Y Times Mag p48+ N 10 '63
Jimmy Brown's own story. . .football bruisers I've bumped into; excerpts from Off my chest. J. Brown and M. Cope. il Look 28: 104-12+ O 20 '64
Jimmy Brown's own story . . . my case against Paul Brown; excerpts from Off my chest. J. Brown and M. Cope. il Look 28:62-4+ O 6 '64
Joe Schmidt: king of the red doggers; linebacker of Detroit Lions. I. R. McVay. il Look 27:62+ S 24 '63
Just like papa played. G. S. Halas of the Chicago Bears. il Time 82:92 D 6 '63
Kiss the guy or tackle him? M. Cope. il Sat Eve Post 236:76-7 O 26 '63
Left tackle: lineman R. Brown of New York Giants. W. N. Wallace. il N Y Times Mag p 137-41+ N 8 '64
Makings of a new pro dynasty; Baltimore Colts. T. Maule. il Sports Illus 21:40-4 O 12 '64
Mo and Baby Face; Cleveland Browns' win the National football league championship. il Newsweek 65:58-9 Ja 11 '65
NFL playoff: sizing up the big game. il Newsweek 64:37 D 28 '64
New monsters. il Newsweek 62:94 D 2 '63
Not much defense, but two long-ball hitters; G. Collins and P. Warfield of Cleveland Browns. T. Maule. il Sports Illus 21:64+ O 19 '64
Plan that worked; Cleveland Browns vs New York Giants. T. Maule. il Sports Illus 19: 16-19 O 21 '63
Players are not just people. T. Maule. il Sports Illus 18:22+ Ap 29 '63
Points for perfection; pro football. il Time 84:104 N 13 '64
Poorly packed for a Chicago trip; College All-Stars vs Green Bay Packers. D. Jenkins. il Sports Illus 19:16-17 Ag 12 '63
Pro football 1964. T. Maule. il Sports Illus 21: 44-66 S 7 '64
Pro football's profit explosion. S. Mahoney. il Fortune 70:153-5+ N '64
Pros open up full blast. T. Maule. il Sports Illus 19:28-9 S 23 '63
Return of the Romans. il Newsweek 64:52 S 7 '64
Reverse plays; National football league season. il Newsweek 64:64 N 9 '64
Road to the title in the West; ed. by T. Maule. D. Shula. il Sports Illus 22:42-4+ Ja 18 '65
Run to a title; San Diego Chargers vs. Boston Patriots in AFL championship. G. Rogin. il Sports Illus 20:8-11 Ja 13 '64
Runaway Colts; Baltimore dominates N.F.L. E. Linn. il Sat Eve Post 237:79-83 D 12 '64
Shining hour for Golden Boy; Chicago Bears vs Green Bay Packers. T. Maule. il Sports Illus 21:22-5 S 21 '64
Sporting scene; scouting St Louis Cardinals vs Redskins in preparation for New York Giants vs Cardinals. H. W. Wind. il New Yorker 39:162+ D 14 '63
Tastemakers are fed up; New York Giants no longer status symbol. H. Horn. il Sports Illus 21:88-91 D 7 '64
Team on trial. B. August. il Sat Eve Post 236:86-8 N 23 '63
Toe that lost its touch; P. Hornung of Green Bay Packers. D. Jenkins. il Sports Illus 21: 30-2+ N 30 '64
Too many Chiefs made too many touchdowns; Kansas City Chiefs vs Denver Broncos. D. Jenkins. il Sports Illus 19:26-8+ S 16 '63
Tough Cookie marches to his own drummer; Cookie Gilchrist of Buffalo Bills. E. Shrake. il Sports Illus 21:70-2+ D 14 '64
Two flags for the Cardinals? baseball Cardinals and the football Cardinals pennant winners. E. Shrake. il Sports Illus 21:20-3 N 9 '64
Two men named Brown; Cleveland Browns. il Newsweek 62:88 O 28 '63
Two pro football leagues must meet; football world series. D. Jenkins; T. Maule. il Sports Illus 19:24-6+ D 16 '63
Two tied at the top; Cleveland Browns and New York Giants. T. Maule. il Sports Illus 19:22-5 D 9 '63
Upset of the mighty; Cleveland Browns defeat Baltimore to win NFL title. T. Maule; E. Shrake. il Sports Illus 22:8-19 Ja 4 '65
Vikings on the move; now the NFL's toddlers run with the big men. E. Shrake. il Sports Illus 21:20-5 S 28 '64
Wahoo! Wahoo! Wahoo! Jets middle linebacker, E. McDaniel. E. Shrake. il Sports Illus 21:66+ O 26 '64
War in the East, impatience in the West. T. Maule. Sports Illus 19:65 O 14 '63
Winning took a Giant adjustment; New York Giants vs Cleveland Browns. T. Maule. il Sports Illus 19:56-7 N 4 '63
With the Packers, a stumble is not a bad fall. T. Maule. il Sports Illus 19:55-6 D 16 '63
Workhorse Texas Bull; running back of Chicago Bears. J. Olsen. Sports Illus 19: 52-4 O 14 '63
Y. A. Tittle is the best policy; New York Giants quarterback. T. Maule. il Sports Illus 19:64-6 N 18 '63
Zero of the Lions; amateur quarterback in professional football game; excerpt from Paper Lion. G. Plimpton. il Sports Illus 21:96-102+ S 7; 26-8+ S 14 '64
FOOTBALL clubs, Professional. See Football clubs
FOOTBALL coaches. See Physical directors
FOOTBALL fans. See Sports fans
FOOTBALL fields
Old mower now stripes ball fields. il Pop Sci 183:159 O '63

FOOTBALL gambling. See Gambling
FOOTBALL hall of fame. See Football players
FOOTBALL photography. See Photography of sports
FOOTBALL players
Ball game that never was; Baltimore Colts vs. Buffalo Bills. T. Maule. Sports Illus 21:74-6 N 16 '64
Beef, bones and Hershey bars; Penn-Texas all-star high school game. R. H. Boyle. il Sports Illus 21:18-20+ Ag 10 '64
Bench jockeys who can also ride; Green Bay Packers. T. Maule. Sports Illus 19:68-70 N 11 '63
Big Brown boom; Cleveland Browns. T. Maule. il Sports Illus 19:16-19 O 7 '63
Big man in any league; Northern Illinois quarterback G. Bork. G. Brown. il Sports Illus 19:54-6 N 11 '63
Big man who wasn't there; Green Bay Packers vs Detroit Lions. T. Maule. il Sports Illus 19:76+ S 30 '63
Bowl heroes enjoy the season's last hurrahs. K. Rudeen. il Sports Illus 20:44-6 Ja 13 '64
Bumpy journey to oblivion; Princeton vs Rutgers in lightweight football. S. Downing. il Sports Illus 19:28-30+ D 9 '63
Collectors. il Time 85:72 Ja 15 '65
College football 1963. il Sports Illus 19:30-45+ S 23 '63
College football 1964. D. Jenkins. il Sports Illus 21:36-44+ S 21 '64
Cowboys can ride high on better defense. T. Maule. il Sports Illus 19:47-52 S 9 '63
Era shaped by war; Sports illustrated silver anniversary awards. R. Cantwell. il Sports Illus 21:36-8+ N 30 '64
Fabulous in defeat; Orange bowl game, Texas vs. Alabama. J. Underwood. il Sports Illus 22:14-17 Ja 11 '65
Fastest human in spikes, or cleats; Bob Hayes of Florida A&M. T. C. Brody. il Sports Illus 21:58-60 D 14 '64
Football's grind and glitter. L. Schiller. il Sat Eve Post 236:32-7 O 5 '63
Football's hot corner; with charts. T. Maule. il Sports Illus 19:34-41 O 21 '63
Hail again the likes of Alex Wojciechowicz! M. Hyman. Sports Illus 19:61 S 30 '63
Harvard's egghead quarterback; J. McCluskey. il Ebony 20:129-30+ D '64
High-heeled recruiter and a mama's boy. M. Stuhldreher. il Sports Illus 19:72-6 S 23 '63
Hornung and Karras fired. il Life 54:38 Ap 26 '63
Is that you up there Johnny Blood? pro football's Hall of fame. G. Holland. il Sports Illus 19:18-20+ S 2 '63
Jimmy Brown's own story. . .football bruisers I've bumped into; excerpts from Off my chest. J. Brown and M. Cope. il Look 28:104-12+ O 20 '64
Jolly Roger; college football. il Times 82:92-4+ O 18 '63
Just call me football's greatest scout. M. Cope. Sports Illus 19:32-4+ S 30 '63
Life guide; football: where to seek the hotshots. il Life 55:19 O 11 '63
Look 1964 All America. T. Cohane. il Look 28:116-20+ D 15 '64
Mr Big of the bonus baby war. il Life 58:56D-57 Ja 15 '65
Mixture of mind, muscle, maturity. T. Maule. il Sports Illus 22:10-13 Ja 4 '65
Most likely to succeed. Newsweek 62:66 Jl 29 '63
1963 All America. T. Cohane. il Look 27:126-30+ D 17 '63
1963 All-American H.S. football squad. il Sr Schol 84:30 F 7 '64
1962 All-American H.S. football squad. H. L. Masin. il Sr Schol 82:32 F 6 '63
Oklahoma-Texas football feud. T. Cohane. il Look 27:85-7+ O 8 '63
On the line. H. L. Masin. il Sr Schol 83:28 N 22 '63
One wonderful conch is this Mira. J. Underwood. il Sports Illus 19:96-102+ S 23 '63
Players are not just people. T. Maule. il Sports Illus 18:22+ Ap 29 '63
Pro football 1964. T. Maule. il Sports Illus 21:44-66+ S 7 '64
Pro football 1963; reproductions of paintings. B. Peak. Sports Illus 19:35-45 S 9 '63
Pro football roundup. il Ebony 19:70-2+ N '63
Pro football's mightiest player. A. Poinsett. il Ebony 19:32-4+ Ja '64
Return of the Romans. il Newsweek 64:52 S 7 '64
Rookie and the vet. il Ebony 20:56-8+ Ja '65
Scouting reports. il Sports Illus 21:46-58+ S 21 '64
Scouting reports (cont) M. Hyman and others. il Sports Illus 19:47-60+ S 23 '63
See how they run; drawings by R. Handville. J. Olsen. Sports Illus 19:42-51 O 14 '63
Shadow over pro football. T. Maule. il Sports Illus 18:10-11 Ja 28 '63
Siren song; pro football at draft time. Time 82:48 D 13 '63
Six most wanted boys in America! players from high school gridirons. H. L. Masin. il Sr Schol 83:34 S 27 '63
Sudden abundance of big lines in the Big ten. D. Jenkins. il Sports Illus 19:50+ N 4 '63
Sunday's human targets. M. Cope. il Sat Eve Post 236:70+ D 21 '63
Super All-American (cont) H. L. Masin. il Sr Schol 83:28 Ja 10 '64; 85:22 Ja 7 '65
Texas makes it look simple; University of Texas vs Oklahoma; photographs by N. Leifer. Sports Illus 19:22-5 O 21 '63
They met the challenges of a changing era; Sports illustrated silver anniversary award. R. Cantwell. il Sports Illus 19:64-6 N 11 '63
Three arms reach for fame; college All-star game. il Sports Illus 21:12-15 Ag 17 '64
Tittle fading back. I. Shaw. il Esquire 63:31-4+ Ja '65
Tough Cookie marches to his own drummer; Cookie Gilchrist of Buffalo Bills. E. Shrake. il Sports Illus 21:70-2+ D 14 '64
Very big head getting smaller; USC end. J. Underwood. il Sports Illus 19:42-4+ O 21 '63
Very hard look at football; 1963 silver anniversary award winners compare the game today with the 1938 version. R. Lardner. il Sports Illus 19:38-40+ D 2 '63
Vikings on the move; now the NFL's toddlers run with the big men. E. Shrake. il Sports Illus 21:20-5 S 28 '64
Vintage year for pro rookies. il Sports Illus 21:32-5 D 7 '64
Wake up the echoes! undefeated Notre Dame. D. Jenkins. il Sports Illus 21:20-3 N 2 '64
Warren McVea goes thisaway and thataway; first Negro to play football for University of Houston. M. Herskowitz. il Sports Illus 21:48-9 N 9 '64
Was this their freedom ride? Negro All-stars of the AFL boycott All-star game in New Orleans. R. Mix. Sports Illus 22:24-5 Ja 18 '65
When the pros play the game in mud time; with photographs by N. Leifer. Sports Illus 19:30-5 N 4 '63
Who loves Harvard? Dartmouth vs Harvard. A. Wright. il Sports Illus 19:14-17 N 4 '63
Why pro football must live with sin. T. Cohane. il Look 27:64-71 Jl 2 '63
Zero of the Lions; amateur quarterback in professional football game; excerpt from Paper Lion. G. Plimpton. il Sports Illus 21:96-102+ S 7; 26-8+ S 14 '64
See also names of football players, e.g. C. Johnson

Recruiting

Lures for rookies. Sports Illus 19:18+ D 9 '63
McVea went thataway; high school halfback Warren McVea to University of Houston. Sports Illus 21:8-9 Jl 27 '64
Proposition from the pros; decision to end premature signing of college football players. Sports Illus 22:7 Ja 25 '65
FOOTBALL pools. See Gambling—Great Britain
FOOTBALL scouting
As the pros see them; top prospects. il Time 82:65 N 29 '63
College football: where the money will go; Time's pro-picked All-America. il Time 84:50-1 N 27 '64
Just call me football's greatest scout. M. Cope. Sports Illus 19:32-4+ S 30 '63
Pro football 1964. E. Shrake. il Sports Illus 21:70-5 S 7 '64
Pro football 1964. T. Maule. il Sports Illus 21:48-66+ S 7 '64
Pro football scouting reports. T. Brody. il Sports Illus 19:64-8 S 9 '63
Pro football scouting reports. T. Maule. il Sports Illus 19:54-6+ S 9 '63
Scouting reports. il Sports Illus 21:46-58+ S 21 '64
Scouting reports (cont) M. Hyman and others. il Sports Illus 19:47-60+ S 23 '63
Six most wanted boys in America! players from high school gridirons. H. L. Masin. il Sr Schol 83:34 S 27 '63
Sporting scene; scouting St Louis Cardinals vs Redskins in preparation for New York Giants vs Cardinals. H. W. Wind. il New Yorker 39:162+ D 14 '63

FOOTBALL uniforms. See Uniforms, Sports
FOOTE, Emerson
Ex-chain-smoker's exit. Time 84:87 S 25 '64
Good advertising. Nation 199:207-8 O 12 '64
FOOTE, George H.
When deferred compensation doesn't pay. Harvard Bsns R 42:99-106 My '64
FOOTE, L. E.
Long, long trail rewound. Am For 70:38-41 My '64
FOOTE, Paul D.
Majority opinion: right or wrong? letter. Science 142:341 O 18 '63
Noise; letter. Science 143:101 Ja 10 '64; Same. Consumer Bul 47:17-18 Jl '64
FOOTE, Raymond
Pine woods; poem. Horn Bk 40:320 Je '64
FOOTE, Shelby
Du Pont storms Charleston; excerpt from Civil war. Am Heritage 14:28-34+ Je '63
FOOTE, Stella
Montana centennial train brings the Wild West to the East. Hobbies 69:90+ My '64
FOOTE, Timothy
Importance of being Malin. Esquire 60:109 O '63
Instant guide to quality reading. Life 56:8+ Je 26 '64
FOOTE, Cone and Belding
Way for some to go. Time 82:92 S 20 '63
FOOTHILL college planetarium. See Planetariums
FOOTNOTES. See Annotations
FOOTSTOOLS. See Stools
FOOTWEAR, Rubber, plastic, etc. See Shoes, Rubber, plastic, etc.
FOR a special occasion; story. See Kaplan, M.
FOR Benny, much loved; story. See Bongartz, R.
FOR I have wept; story. See Stein, G.
FOR one golden moment; story. See West, J.
FORAGE crops. See Forage plants
FORAGE plants
Hybrid forages for farmstead feeding. il Farm J 88:42-3 Mr '64
Management ideas for forage annuals. Suc Farm 62:37 My '64
Nitrate build-up in grasses. Suc Farm 62:134 Mr '64
Unlocking forage profits. il Suc Farm 63:28-9+ Ja '65
See also
Alfalfa
Legumes
Pastures
Sainfoin
Vetch
FORAIN, Jean Louis
Forain: genius at the periphery. il Art N 62:43+ Ap '63
FORAKIS, Peter
Art galleries; exhibitions of pop art, and abstract expressionism at Janis, Pace and De Nagy galleries. R. M. Coates. New Yorker 39:107-10 Ja 18 '64
FORAMINIFERA
Ebb and flow; visit to world's only marine tidal aquarium, in Living foraminifera laboratory, at Museum of natural history. New Yorker 39:43-4 O 12 '63
Neglected amoebas in culture. J. J. Lee and H. Freudenthal. il Natur Hist 72:54-61 D '63
Oxygen isotopic composition of some right- and left-coiled foraminifera. A. Longinelli and E. Tongiorgi. il Science 144:1004 My 22 '64
Shell growth and structure of planktonic foraminifera. A. W. H. Bé and L. Lott. bibliog il Science 145:823-4 Ag 21 '64
Tiny drifters of the sea. J. J. Lee and H. Freudenthal. il Natur Hist 73:44-5 O '64
FORAMINIFERA, Fossil
Aquitanian planktonic foraminifera from Erben Guyot. O. L. Bandy. bibliog il Science 140:1402-3 Je 28 '63
Ice age started early. il Sci N L 86:341 N 28 '64
FORBATH, Peter
Coming to terms with the Common market. Reporter 28:24+ Je 20 '63
FORBES, Aleck
UN international school. C. Holm. il por Parents Mag 39:66-7+ F '64
FORBES, Crosby
Eisenhower on Eisenhower. Christian Cent 81:18 Ja 1 '64
FORBES, John Murray
Little known abolitionist. por Negro Hist Bul 26:210-11 Ap '63
FORBES, Kathryn
Mama and the roomer. Read Digest 82:228E-228F Ap '63
FORBES, Robert H.
Here comes skyhook logging! Am For 71:10-13+ Ja '65
Vertical logging. Am For 70:30-2 Ja '64
FORBES, Will
Sub-35. Pop Phot 53:58-60 Ag '63
—See Harrison, H. jt. auth.
FORCE, Elizabeth S.
Critical look at family life courses. PTA Mag 58:18-20 bibliog(p36) Ap '64
FORCE (violence) See Violence
FORCE, Vital. See Vital force
FORCE and energy
Can science offset the population explosion? excerpt from address. A. M. Weinberg. il Sci Digest 53:17-22 F '63
Conservation laws of physics. G. Feinberg and M. Goldhaber. il Sci Am 209:36-45 bibliog(p 156) O '63
Machine simulates muscles in operation; conversion of chemical into mechanical energy. M. L. Yaffee. il Aviation W 81:64-5 Ag 31 '64
New power on the production line. H. E. Klein. il Duns R 83:43-5+ F '64
See also
Impact
Motion
Quantum theory
Vital force
FORCED labor. See Labor, Compulsory
FORCED landings. See Airplanes—Landing
FORCELLA, Enzo
Italian socialism chooses the things that are possible. New Repub 149:13-14 N 16 '63
Pope Paul VI. New Repub 149:7-9 Jl 6 '63
FORCEPS deliveries. See Childbirth
FORCING (plants)
Make spring come early. il Pop Gard 15:21 Ja '64
Order bulbs for forcing. F. F. Rockwell and E. C. Grayson. il Flower Grower 50:65 Ag '63
Put spring in a bottle. L. Burgess. il Flower Grower 50:26-7 N '63
FORD, Anne
Lively ones. il por Newsweek 65:52 Ja 11 '65
FORD, Archie W.
Bulwarks against federal control. Sr Schol 82:16T Mr 20 '63
Dilemma of federal aid. por Time 81:84+ Ap 12 '63
FORD, Barbara E.
Something for a day in spring; poem. America 108:469 Ap 6 '63
FORD, Charles B.
Struck by lightning. Yachting 115:63-5+ Je '64
FORD, Charlotte
Lively ones. il por Newsweek 65:52 Ja 11 '65
Miss Charlotte Ford. por Vogue 141:142-3 My '63
FORD, Corey
Do you talk double-take? Read Digest 85:101-2 N '64
Don't do it now! Read Digest 82:33-4+ F '63
Down will come kitty. Field & S 67:6+ F '63
I can't get away with anything. Read Digest 85:17+ D '64
Is nature getting neurotic? Read Digest 82:15-16+ My '63
Lower forty. See issues of Field & stream
My life as a squirrel. Read Digest 84:227-8+ Je '64
Thanks just the same. Read Digest 82:15-16+ Ap '63
Who's they? Read Digest 83:169-70 Ag '63
Why do I look so familiar? Read Digest 85:19-20+ Ag '64
Winter leaves me cold. Sports Illus 18:E5-8 F 4 '63; Same abr. Read Digest 83:131-3 D '63
FORD, Daniel F.
Nation's primary primary. Reporter 30:37-9 F 27 '64
New Hampshire's lottery: private vice and public virtue. Reporter 30:32-4 Ja 2 '64
Only war we've got. Nation 199:66-8 Ag 24 '64
Planes over Saigon: wings tear off. Nation 199:3-5 Jl 13 '64
Puritan sweepstake. New Repub 150:5-6 Ap 25 '64
With the redskins of Vietnam. Nation 199:29-31 Jl 27 '64
FORD, Edmund A.
Letter from Nigeria. Sch Life 47:5-9 N '64
FORD, Edsel
Bequest; poem. McCalls 90:185 My '63
Honorable mention to the last runner; poem. McCalls 92:146 O '64
FORD, Ford Madox
No place to go after the parade. G. Hicks. Sat R 47:37-8 My 16 '64

FORD, Franklin L.
Revolutionary-Napoleonic era: how much of a watershed? excerpts from Longmans general history of Europe. bibliog f Am Hist R 69:18-29 O '63

FORD, Gerald R.
As Republicans look ahead to 1966; interview. por U S News 58:40-1 Ja 18 '65
Excerpt from testimony, April 23, 1964. Cong Digest 43:274+ N '64
Piecing together the evidence. il por Life 57: 42-50A O 2 '64
What can save the G.O.P? por Fortune 71: 140-1+ Ja '65

about

Ford and Long: new leaders in the 89th. por Newsweek 65:20 Ja 18 '65
Image maker. Reporter 32:22+ Ja 28 '65
In the House: a new Republican image. por U S News 58:36-7 Ja 18 '65
New minority leader. por Time 85:20-1 Ja 15 '65

FORD, Henry. 1863-1947
Fifty years ago. S. D. Smith. il N Y Times Mag p62-4 F 16 '64
Ford: decline and rebirth 1933-1962, by A. Nevins and F. E. Hill. Review
Newsweek il por 62:73 Ag 5 '63
Time il por 82:66 Ag 2 '63

FORD, Henry, 1917-
How Henry Ford II sees the outlook in autos; interview. pors U S News 55:72-5 Ag 19 '63
How high are profits? address, March 5, 1964. Vital Speeches 30:433-6 My 1, 64; Same abr. with title How high is up? Read Digest 85: 227-30+ S '64; Excerpts. por U S News 56: 55 Mr 23 '64
Strike in autos? Henry Ford's answer; excerpt from address, June 22, 1964. por U S News 57:77-8 Jl 6 '64
Taxes and prosperity; address, July 8, 1963. Vital Speeches 29:717-19 S 15 '63; Excerpts. U S News 55:16 Jl 22 '63
Technological exploration; address, January 15, 1964. Vital Speeches 30:246-9 F 1 '64

about

Businessmen for LBJ: Ford and Eppert. por U S News 56:22 Je 8 '64
Challenge from Ford. Newsweek 63:68 Je 29 '64
Ford & an Austin. il Time 82:36 Ag 16 '63
Ford, Ward, and Graham; civilization vs self-love. W. F. Buckley, jr. Nat R 15:143 Ag 27 '63
Ford's forest. C. F. Sutherland, jr. il pors Am For 69:18-19+ S '63

FORD, Jesse Hill
Cave; story. Atlan 212:73-8 D '63
Fishes, birds, and sons of men; story. Atlan 211:60-3 Ap '63
Look down, look down; story. Atlan 213:76-80 Je '64
To the open water; story. Atlan 214:82-5 N '64
Trial; story. Atlan 213:59-62 Ap '64

FORD, John
Autumn of John Ford. P. Bogdanovich. il por Esquire 61:102-4+ Ap '64
Autumn of John Ford. S. Peck. il por N Y Times Mag p 124+ N 29 '64

FORD, John C. and Kelly, Gerald
Will the church's teaching on birth control change? excerpt from Contemporary moral theology. Cath World 198:87-93 N '63

FORD, Kenneth W.
Magnetic monopoles; with biographical sketch. Sci Am 209:30, 122-5+ bibliog(p 180) D '63

FORD, Norman D.
Retire by climate. Travel 121:28-32+ Ja '64
Retirement hotels. Travel 119:36-40 Ap '63

FORD, O'Neil
Setting a style for Texas. il pors Bsns W p 132+ Ag 15 '64

FORD, Walter B.
60-cycle repulsion coil-resonance engine. Pop Electr 20:41-5+ Mr '64

FORD, Whitey
Player of the week; pitcher of New York Yankees. por Sports Illus 20:73 Je 22 '64
Repair of a pitching arm. il Time 84:95 N 20 '64

FORD, William A. and Stika, A. J.
Gas utilities earn dividends. Am City 78: 89-90 F '63

FORD foundation
B.M.O.C; special program in education. Newsweek 63:45 Ja 6 '64
Conscience of educational foundations. W. W. Brickman. Sch & Soc 92:199 My 2 '64
Dance; grants to ballet companies. R. Krokover. Mus Am 84:54-5 Ja '64
$ for humanities. Sr Schol 82:1T F 6 '63
Dollars to Deutschland; $2,000,000 project to expand the artistic, educational and cultural resources of Berlin. Mus Am 83:19 F '63
Ford foundation aids Negro colleges. Christian Cent 81:925 Jl 22 '64
Ford foundation grants $2 million for publication of historical papers. Library J 89:4493 N 15 '64
Ford foundation's ballet grants. J. Martin. il Sat R 47:47-8+ Mr 28 '64; Discussion. 47:68-9 Ap 25 '64
Ford foundation's mid-Manhattan greenhouse. il Fortune 70:177-8 O '64
Ford grant to Educational services, inc. Sch & Soc 91:154 Mr 23 '63
Ford grants $750,000 for translation center; at University of Texas, Austin. Pub W 187: 65 Ja 11 '65
Ford in its future; grants to New York city ballet and the School of American ballet. Time 82:37 D 27 '63
Ford purchases. Am Artist 27:6 Mr '63
Fording ahead; Special program in education grants. Newsweek 64:73 Jl 6 '64
Foreign affairs scholarships for minorities. Sch & Soc 92:24 Ja 25 '64
Foundation and the arts; address, November 11, 1963. W. M. Lowry. Mus Am 83:156-7 D '63
From the editor; grants for artistic and cultural development in New York, and no investment in recordings. J. Lyons. Am Rec G 30:180 N '63
Giving out & getting richer. Time 85:52 Ja 15 '65
Historic bonanza for ballet in America: 7.7 million in grants from Ford foundation. Dance Mag 38:3-4 Ja '64
Howard university to conduct Foreign affairs scholars program; statement, October 9, 1963. D. Rusk. Dept State Bul 49:684 O 28 '63
In the year of our Ford; grants to encourage the art of film. il Time 83:96+ Ap 3 '64
Lifetime sabbaticals. Duns R 83:46 Ja '64
Mr Ford's busy billions. B. Hibbs. il Sat Eve Post 236:68-72 Mr 16 '63
New NET programming. Sr Schol 83:1T O 18 '63
Novelists in the theater; grants to established writers. R. Gilman. Commonweal 78:20-2 Mr 29 '63
Open letter: about the Ford foundation's SAB program of services to ballet students and teachers. O. Maynard. Dance Mag 38: 22-4 Jl '64
Passing out money among artists. R. Evett. New Repub 150:9-10 Ja 18 '64; Reply. E. Winer. 150:30-1 F 1 '64
Private war on poverty; $2,485,000 grant to the Pittsburgh, Pa. public school system. America 112:153 Ja 30 '65
Seed money; Special program in education. il Time 84:68-9 Jl 3 '64
Sing unto the Ford a new song; awards to stimulate the choral medium. Sat R 48:50+ Ja 30 '65
$266,900,000: private give-away, done by three men. A. Talmey. Vogue 141:102 Je '63
Two-time winners; grants to Brown, Brandeis, and the University of Southern California. Time 84:30 D 25 '64
Urban renewal for people. D. B. Carlson. il Arch Forum 120:86-9 Ja '64

See also

Center for advanced study in the behavioral sciences
Fund for the advancement of education
Fund for the Republic
Resources for the future, incorporated

FORD instrument company
Thermionic cell generates A-C power. W. Beller. il Miss & Roc 12:18-19 F 11 '63

FORD motor company
All right, Walter; UAW's Ford settlement. Newsweek 64:80-1 S 28 '64
Arjay way; new Ford president. il Newsweek 61:77-8+ Ap 22 '63
At the Daytona speedway derby; stockcar racing. il Newsweek 63:75-8 F 24 '64
Automated caveman gets a rear-end drive; Ford pavillion Magic skyway. il Pop Sci 184:91-2 Ja '64
Car of the year; the 1964 Fords. C. Nerpel. il Motor T 16:32-62 F '64
Detroit back in race; Indianapolis 500. il Bsns W p96-7+ My 25 '63
Fifty years ago. S. D. Smith. il N Y Times Mag p62-4 F 16 '64
Ford: decline and rebirth 1933-1962, by A. Nevins and F. E. Hill. Review
Time il 82:66 Ag 2 '63
Ford road takes a surprise turn: merger with Electric autolite co. il Bsns W p 152+ S 14 '63

FORD motor company—*Continued*
Ford sells hot bundle to Britain; Rootes buys Fairlane. il Bsns W p32 N 2 '63
Ford shifts top men. Bsns W p36 Ap 13 '63
Ford soups up its youth drive; folk-jazz wing dings at colleges. il Bsns W p32-4 Ja 4 '64
Ford turns the Mustang loose. il Bsns W p 152+ Ap 18 '64
Ford watches Chevy go by. il Bsns W p30-1 Mr 16 '63
Ford's bid for a better year. il Bsns W p47-8+ S 28 '63
Ford's week. il Newsweek 64:82 N 9 '64
Ford's young one; Mustang. il Time 83:92-102 Ap 17 '64
Friden with style; new president of Ford motor co. Time 81:104+ Ap 19 '63
Henry's wonderful Tin Lizzie. il Newsweek 62:67 Ag 12 '63
Introduction to the '65 cars. il Motor T 16: 48-53 N '64
Mustang a new breed out of Detroit. il Newsweek 63:97-101 Ap 20 '64
Mustang, for those who think young. D. Bartley. il Esquire 61:86-8 My '64
Mustang twins move up. il Time 85:67-8 Ja 22 '65
New line bows, old rumor spiked; Ford and Philco festivities in New York for dealers. il Bsns W p54-6+ My 30 '64
New ones, 1965. il Motor T 16:36-41 O '64
New shape at Ford. il Time 82:95-6 S 13 '63
On sale: 4 million Ford shares. U S News 55: 95-6 N 4 '63
Philco gets the T-Bird look; success of the Ford-Philco merger. il Bsns W p45-6+ Ag 17 '63
'64 cars. il Motor T 15:64-73 N '63
Special-interest cars; classic Thunderbird; 1955-57. S. Keys. il Motor T 16:81 N '64
Special-interest cars; Model T Ford. R. A. Mogge. il Motor T 16:77 N '64
Sports car for everyman; Ford's new Mustang.. R. Grossman. il Sports Illus 20: 38-40+ Ap 20 '64
Stray Mustang. il Newsweek 63:80 Mr 16 '64
There they go again; U.A.W. workers at Ford launch their own strike. Time 84:110 N 13 '64
Troubles not over in autos. U S News 57:105 N 9 '64
Turbine in a truck; experimental gas turbine truck. il Bsns W p28 O 31 '64
Twenty-five years with Mercury. il Motor T 15:40-3 O '63
U.S. tractors plow some global fields. il Bsns W p 174+ O 24 '64
Wage chronology: Ford motor co; 1959-64. H. West. il Mo Labor R 87:1039-50 S '64
What savings pay at GM, Ford. U S News 54:75 F 4 '63
What's Ford up to for '63½? R. Brock. il Hot Rod 16:48-51 F '63
What's new at the Ford motor company. J. Whipple. il Pop Sci 185:76-9 O '64
World's fair ride proved on test track; Ford's Magic skyway. il Pop Sci 183:69 N '63

Lincoln-Mercury division

Family car gets back its frills. il Bsns W p 100-2 Ja 9 '65

FORD motor company, limited, Dagenham, England
Battle of Dagenham. Newsweek 61:76+ Mr 18 '63
British Ford unions hit. Bsns W p 162 Ap 20 '63

FORD museum. See Henry Ford museum and Greenfield Village, Dearborn, Mich.

FORDHAM, Alfred J.
Woody plant seeds. Horticulture 42:18-20+ S '64

FORECASTS
Boastradamus; Criswell predicts. Newsweek 62:56 Jl 15 '63
Changing careers in a changing world; with charts. il Sr Schol 83:8-11 N 8 '63; Reply. J. H. Bivins. 84:32 F 7 '64
If you scare easily. Am City 79:7+ O '64
Newsgram. See issues of U.S. news & World report
Opinion, please from New York: predictions on affairs of state for 1965. H. Salisbury. il Mlle 60:13-14 Ja '65
School of tomorrow will never overflow. il Sci N L 85:263 Ap 25 '64
Science forecast for 1964-1965. W. Davis. il Sci N L 84:402-3; 86:402-3 D 28 '63, D 26 '64
Science of being almost certain. G. A. W. Boehm. il Fortune 69:104-7 F '64
Technology, prediction, and disorder. A. Wohlstetter. il Bul Atomic Sci 20:11-15 O '64
Trouble with technological forecasting; letter. M. S. Peterson. Science 144:795-6 My 15 '64
World of the future. N. N. Semenov. il(cover) Bul Atomic Sci 20:10-15 F '64
See also
Agricultural forecasts
Business forecasting
Political forecasts
Weather forecasts

Anecdotes, facetiae, satire, etc.

Glare into the future. F. P. Tullius. New Yorker 40:24-5 Jl 11 '64

FORECASTS (economics)
Another peak, but by a hair. il Bsns W p53-4 F 2 '63
Are they wrong even when they're right? economic indicators. Bsns W p90 My 4 '63
Business roundup; eighteen month forecast. il Fortune 69:27-8+ Ja '64
Canada's boom lies year away. il Bsns W p22-3 D 28 '63
Charting the way to stable growth. il Bsns W p 162+ O 31 '64
Economic forecast: sounder growth. J. Backman. Nations Bsns 51:74-7 Ag '63
$50 billion worth of good news; survey of U.S. economic prospects for 1964-65. il Life 56:13 Ja 10 '64
Forecast paints rosy picture. il Bsns W p83-4 Je 15 '63
Going into next year at a gallop. il Bsns W p27-9 S 19 '64
How good will business get? il U S News 57:87-90 Jl 13 '64
How much longer? longest peacetime expansion; with editorial comment. il Bsns W p23-5, 158 Mr 28 '64
How they see the work ahead; economists' round table. il Bsns W p26-8 Ja 9 '65
How will you fare in '65? with charts. Changing T 19:7-12 Ja '65
In '64, a batch of new highs; with charts. Bsns W p 15-17 D 28 '63
Is recession inevitable? interview ed. by G. R. Rosen. H. C. Wallich. Duns R 84:30-1+ Ag '64
More expansion likely in 1964. Nations Bsns 51:106-7 N '63
More gains next year, and clear to 1970. il Bsns W p 128+ O 3 '64
More push for plant; latest Commerce-SEC report. il Bsns W p27-8 Mr 16 '63
Nation and world face sweeping changes; study of Technical military planning operation. il Nations Bsns 52:23-5+ Ja '64
1964: looks good, also dangerous; with charts. il Changing T 18:7-12 Ja '64
On the level; Fortune's forecast for the next eighteen months. il Fortune 71:27-8+ Ja '65
Outlook for the boom: rises and risks; symposium. il Nations Bsns 52:31-41+ Mr '64
Pace is firm but not so fast. il Bsns W p25-6 N 14 '64
Preview of change: from now to 1980; interview. L. Cherne. il Nations Bsns 53:50-2+ Ja '65
Preview of your markets in '75. il Nations Bsns 52:66-70+ N '64
Prosperous times for all in year 2000. Sci N L 83:105 F 16 '63
Second half of the 60s; symposium. il Nations Bsns 52:36-41+ S '64
Set for a fifth fat year; with charts. il Bsns W p 11-13 Ja 2 '65
Seven forces will block inflation. J. Backman. il Nations Bsns 52:38-9+ Ap '64
Sighting higher; consensus of leading economic forecasters; with editorial comment. il Bsns W p29-31, 204 Ap 20 '63
Stimulus and restraint. il Fortune 68:31-2 Ag '63
Stock market trends to watch. M. Nadler. Nations Bsns 52:90+ D '64
Washington business outlook. See issues of Nation's business
Washington desk. J. R. Slevin. Duns R 84:5-6 D '64
What will bring back prosperity? symposium. il U S News 54:40-7 F 18 '63
What's ahead by year 2000. il Nations Bsns 52:86-7 Je '64
See also
Business forecasting

FORECLOSURE of mortgages. See Mortgages

FOREIGN agents in the United States. See Foreign propagandists in the United States

FOREIGN aid. See Economic assistance; Economic assistance, American

FOREIGN area studies. See Area studies

FOREIGN banks in the U.S. See Banks and banking—United States—Foreign banks

FOREIGN bodies (surgery)
Swallowed safety pins; medical tools designed around powerful magnets. Sci N L 85:21 Ja 11 '64
FOREIGN born. See United States—Foreign population
FOREIGN branch factories. See Branch factories, Foreign
FOREIGN cookery. See Cookery, International
FOREIGN correspondents. See Reporters and reporting
FOREIGN credit insurance. See Insurance, Credit
FOREIGN credit insurance association
FCIA program broadened. A. O. Stanley. Duns R 81:54-5 Mr '63
FOREIGN exchange
P.L. 480 currency available for sale to U.S. tourists in Cairo. Dept State Bul 48:173 F 4 '63
See also
Currency convertibility
Money
FOREIGN expansion of business. See Business—Foreign expansion
FOREIGN investments. See Investments, Foreign
FOREIGN investments in the United States. See Investments, Foreign (in United States)
FOREIGN language films. See Moving pictures—Foreign language films
FOREIGN languages. See Languages, Modern
FOREIGN languages in the elementary school. See Languages, Modern—Study and teaching
FOREIGN legion. See France—Army—Foreign legion
FOREIGN loans. See Loans, Foreign
FOREIGN missions. See Missions
FOREIGN office (Great Britain) See Great Britain—Foreign office
FOREIGN policy association
Great decisions program. R. C. Mastrude. il Sr Schol 83:12T D 6 '63
FOREIGN propagandists in the United States
Israel lobby. Newsweek 62:24 Ag 12 '63
Their men in Washington. F. J. Cook. il Nation 198:311-30 Mr 30 '64
FOREIGN relations. See International relations
FOREIGN relations, Senate committee. See United States—Congress—Senate—Committees
FOREIGN service (United States) See United States—Foreign service
FOREIGN service, Women in. See Women as foreign service employees
FOREIGN shoppers and shopping. See Shopping and shoppers
FOREIGN station wagons. See Station wagons, Foreign
FOREIGN students in Bulgaria
African students at iron curtain schools flee a hateful epithet: *cherni maimuni.* J. Bonfante. Life 54:19 Mr 15 '63
Segregation in Sofia. il Newsweek 61:42 F 25 '63
U.S. exploring ways to help African students leaving Bulgaria. Dept State Bul 48:375 Mr 11 '63
FOREIGN students in China (People's Republic)
African student in red China; excerpts. E. J. Hevi. Harper 228:63-6+ Ja '64; Same abr. Read Digest 84:139-40+ Mr '64
FOREIGN students in Communist countries
Troubles in the big red schoolhouses. il Sr Schol 82:6 Mr 6 '63
FOREIGN students in Europe
Those student tours to Europe: what really goes on. G. Bocca. il McCalls 90:92-3+ Jl '63
FOREIGN students in France
5,000 Vietnamese students study, in Paris. M. Clos. il N Y Times Mag p38-9+ D 6 '64
How to survive the Sorbonne. T. R. Bransten. il Mlle 59:100-2+ Je '64
FOREIGN students in Japan
Exchange of postdoctoral students with Japan; letter. K. E. Chernetski. Science 146:597 O 30 '64
FOREIGN students in Russia
African lesson for the Russians. Life 56:4 Ja 3 '64
African revolt in Russia. E. Dunbar. il Look 28:31-5 My 5 '64; Same abr. Read Digest 85:71-4 Ag '64
African students in Russia: racial discrimination as it exists in the U.S. is unknown. J. C. Kennedy. Commonweal 78:161-3 My 3 '63
Amerikanets in a Moscow school. S. Shabad. il N Y Times Mag p44+ Je 9 '63; Reply with rejoinder. B. Jones. p2+ Jl 7 '63
Anger in Red square; demonstration protesting racial discrimination by African nations. il Sr Schol 83:17 Ja 10 '64
Girl trouble. New Repub 150:9 Ja 11 '64
Good-by, Lumumba U; African students leave Russia. il Newsweek 63:80+ F 10 '64
Now, race riots in Moscow's Red square; blacks in Russia: world's loneliest men. il U S News 55:5 D 30 '63
Red and black; African students demonstration in Moscow. il Newsweek 62:28 D 30 '63
Red and the black: racism in Moscow. G. Feifer. il Reporter 30:27-8 Ja 2 '64
We too are people; African students vs. Soviet police. il Time 82:20-1 D 27 '63
FOREIGN students in the United States
Americanization of Axel. R. Starnes. Field & S 69:10-11+ Ja '65
Big week with a Watusi. L. Wainwright. Life 57:23 Jl 17 '64
Blurred images: what misconceptions do foreign students have about the U.S. and vice versa? New York herald tribune forum discussion. E. R. Floyd. il Sr Schol 84:8-9 F 28 '64
Do not bring foreign students, unless. . . C. M. Pak. il Sat R 47:62-3+ Ag 15 '64; Discussion. 47:53 S 19; 57 N 21 '64
Finding jobs for foreign students. D. O'Shea. America 108:558-62 Ap 20 '63
Foreign student enrollment rises sharply. Christian Cent 80:925 Jl 24 '63
Foreign student: his problems, his impact; Latin American students. D. Heft. il Américas 16:17-21 F '64
Foreign students in America: problems, progress, and prospects; address, April 24, 1963. L. D. Battle. Dept State Bul 48:752-8 My 13 '63
Foreign teens view the U.S. New York herald tribune forum discussion. il Sr Schol 82:14-15 My 8 '63
Helping foreign students. H. Bischoff. America 109:566-8 N 9 '63
I believe; Nigerian at Barnard college. Seventeen 22:90-1 My '63
I think in English; boy from Norway discovers America. S. Lystrup. il Seventeen 22:112-13+ O '63
IIE to assist in aiding African students who left Bulgaria; Department statement. Dept State Bul 48:448 Mr 25 '63
Mo is Sa'aid's nickname at Cornell. il Newsweek 61:59-62+ Ap 22 '63
Reporter at large; African scholarship program of American universities. K. T. Kinkead. New Yorker 40:51-2+ My 23 '64
Saburo's native land. C. B. Gross. il Read Digest 82:107-9 F '63
Social contacts of foreign students with Americans; excerpt from Attitudes and social relations of foreign students in the United States. C. Selltiz. bibliog Sch & Soc 91:261-6 Sum '63
While school keeps. J. Cass. Sat R 46:54 Jl 20 '63
See also
National association of foreign student advisers
FOREIGN study
Junior year abroad? Newsweek 64:55 Jl 13 '64
Kalamazoo college's foreign study program. Sch & Soc 92:219 Sum '64
Our globetrotting students. J. Daniel. il Read Digest 85:106-10 Ag '64
Personal business; European summer study programs for college students. Bsns W p113 Ap 27 '63
Should every student travel abroad? J. F. Fixx. il Sat R 46:46+ F 16 '63
FOREIGN subsidiaries. See Corporations—Foreign subsidiaries
FOREIGN teachers in the United States
African studies our schools; Kenyan education officer observing education in America. M. T. Wangombe. NEA J 52:21-2 F '63
Bringing the world to the classroom. P. H. Binzen. il Sat R 47:60-2+ Ap 18 '64
Numbers of Africans on assistance programs increases. il Sch Life 47:3-4 N '64
FOREIGN trade. See Commerce; United States—Commerce
FOREIGN visitors in Australia
Shore leave a la Russe; Russia's whaling fleet in Melbourne. il Bsns W p30-1 My 23 '64
FOREIGN visitors in Austria
My most exciting summer ever: in Europe! Experiment in international living. W. Birnie. il Seventeen 23:116-17+ Je '64
FOREIGN visitors in China
Conversation in Peking. R. Terrill. Christian Cent 82:47-50 Ja 13 '65
Tourism for ugly imperialists. il Time 84:30-1 Jl 31 '64

FOREIGN visitors in Cuba
Castro's U.S. guests. il Time 82:31-2 Ag 9 '63
Long way home; U.S. students defiance of State department travel ban. il Time 82:30 S 6 '63
Raucous caucus room; House committee on un-American activities hearings on students, rebels, and hangers-on who had journeyed to Castro's Cuba in defiance of State department ban. il Newsweek 62:30+ S 23 '63
Red junket to Cuba; ed. by R. Tunley. B. Hoffman. il Sat Eve Post 236:25-9 O 5 '63
RSVP: and fifty-nine came. Newsweek 62:47 Jl 15 '63
U.S. students in Cuba: a discredit to U.S.? C. Migdail. U S News 57:10 Ag 24 '64
U.S. students in Cuba: how far left? W. Schulz. Nat R 15:229 S 24 '63

FOREIGN visitors in Eastern Europe
One look at Russia was enough; visits of Italian Communist workers to Russia and satellite states. il U S News 57:51 N 30 '64

FOREIGN visitors in Europe
Europe: on $5 an hour? H. L. Hurwitz. il Sr Schol 85:10T-11T Ja 7 '65
How Europe changed me. il Seventeen 23:150-1+ N '64
Letter from the publisher; Time sponsors news tour of Europe for U.S. businessmen. B. M. Auer. il Time 82:28-9 N 15 '63
Speaking out; no, I don't want to go to Europe. S. Jackson. Sat Eve Post 237:8+ Je 6 '64
Wealthy American bum. R. Kirk. Nat R 14: 198 Mr 12 '63; Reply. R. W. Blair. 14:333 Ap 23 '63
Where to go in '64; visit U.S.A. tour through Europe, 1961. M. Sutton. il Am For 70: 16-19+ Ja '64
Who lost an American? by N. Algren. Review
Reporter 28:46-7 Je 20 '63. H. Kramer

FOREIGN visitors in Far East
Half a world half a day away. F. R. Smith. il Sports Illus 19:86-93 D 23 '63

FOREIGN visitors in France
Candy goes to France. il Seventeen 23:178 O '64
How to be at home abroad. P. Langeweische. il House B 105:148-9+ Mr '63

FOREIGN visitors in Germany
Nobel prize winner's triumph in Europe. il Ebony 20:40-2+ N '64

FOREIGN visitors in Ghana
Piper's village; American visitor in Ghana's rain forest. Akosua. Reporter 29:38-42 S 26 '63

FOREIGN visitors in India
American specialist abroad. E. B. Bohanon. Horn Bk 40:642-5 D '64

FOREIGN visitors in Italy
Penultimate chapel. M. E. Marty. Christian Cent 81:1511 D 2 '64

FOREIGN visitors in Japan
Fun and merry talks along the Mitsubishi concert circuit. J. Lowenthal. il Mus Am 84:60-1 O '64
Our far-flung correspondents; American visitors in Japan. C. Frankel. New Yorker 39:74+ My 25 '63

FOREIGN visitors in Mexico
Conversation with Francisco. D. W. Bazil. Christian Cent 80:366-7 Mr 20 '63
Saint's day; Oaxaca, Mexico, and nearby Indian village. A. Marriott. New Yorker 39: 111+ O 19 '63

FOREIGN visitors in Poland
Paul in Poland; pop singer P. Anka; ed. by E. Miller. il Seventeen 23:160-1+ Ap '64

FOREIGN visitors in Russia
Big brother is still watching. E. Crankshaw. il N Y Times Mag p8+ D 29 '63
Capitalist critique; Economist of London editors. il Time 81:68+ Je 14 '63
Capitalistic invasion; R. Thomson's audience with Khrushchev. il Time 81:54 F 22 '63
Conversing with Russians; American peace groups and members of Sane visiting the Soviet Union. S. Gottlieb. Bul Atomic Sci 21:35-6 Ja '65
Good-by Mr Barghoorn, pleasant journey. il Newsweek 62:37-8 N 25 '63
Impressive power of Soviet libraries reported by U.S. delegates to Russia. Library J 88: 528-9 F 1 '63
Industrial research leaders return from Soviet Union; White House announcement with remarks by President Johnson. Dept State Bul 52:12-13 Ja 4 '65
My Russian journey; teacher of history, Salt Lake City, Utah. E. L. Grossen. il Sr Schol 84:12T Ap 17 '64
Nikita & the capitalists; American executives on a European tour. il Time 82:38-9 N 15 '63
Our footloose correspondents. V. Perera. New Yorker 39:144+ Ap 27 '63
Planting new ideas; a report on a visit to Soviet farms. O. L. Freeman. Bul Atomic Sci 19:44-5 D '63
Prairie schooner rolls into Moscow. R. Brigham. il Life 57:121-3 N 6 '64
Return of the professor. Nat R 15:469 D 3 '63
Tit-for-tat Russians call Yale prof a spy. il Life 55:48-9 N 22 '63
Two American teens in Russia. N. Holmes. il Seventeen 23:208-9+ Ag '64
Why Soviets arrested a Yale professor. U S News 55:18 N 25 '63

FOREIGN visitors in South Africa
Jim Crow South African style. il Ebony 19: 123-4+ My '64

FOREIGN visitors in Spain
Letter home. J. Jones. Esquire 60:28+ D '63

FOREIGN visitors in the Congo
Every time I come here, things are a little more difficult; letter. A. J. Meyers. il U S News 54:61 F 4 '63

FOREIGN visitors in the Netherlands
People to people. R. Rothstein. il U S Camera 27:62 Ap '64

FOREIGN visitors in the United States
Art of welcoming visitors from abroad. M. Tree. il House & Gard 126:242-3 N '64
Cold shoulder; visit of Russian writers to Yale. il Time 84:61 D 11 '64
Contribution of women in a changing world; address, April 20, 1963. K. Louchheim. Dept State Bul 48:801-5 My 20 '63
Cowboys and Indians; visit to the U.S. by managers of a dude ranch in France. New Yorker 39:35-6 S 28 '63
Dissidents confounded; movement protesting the visit of Russian churchmen to Austin. H. Kilpatrick. Christian Cent 80:466-8 Ap 10 '63
East-West theological dialogue; Russian churchmen in the U.S. B. Kroker. Christian Cent 80:585-6 My 1 '63
English in New England. C. Brossard. il Look 28:84-5+ My 5 '64
Europeans flood in. il Bsns W p92 Je 6 '64
Face to face; Italian tourists, employees of Marzotto firms. New Yorker 39:33-4 Je 8 '63
Fifty-fifty vision; impressions of V. P. Nekrasov. Newsweek 61:37 F 4 '63
Foreign country. il Time 84:56 Ag 14 '64
Friends, in the name of Allah; Egyptian farmers in the United States. R. C. Davids. il Farm J 87:20 D '63
How do we look to these foreign tourists? R. Littell. Read Digest 82:233-4+ Ap '63
How to have guests from abroad; Americans-at-home program. il Changing T 18:13-14 D '64
Letter from Paris; tourists from France. Genêt. New Yorker 40:124-6 My 30 '64
Opinion, please; an Englishman's impressions of the consumer's role in America. M. Bradbury. Mlle 60:40+ D '64
People to people. R. Rothstein. il U S Camera 27:62 Ap '64
Plea for graciousness; visit of Christians from Russia. Christian Cent 80:323 Mr 13 '63
Russian churchmen visit United States. Christian Cent 80:228 F 20 '63
Russian with the $100 bill; Russian church leaders at National council of churches' general board meeting. il Time 81:58 Mr 8 '63
Russians visit the U.S. Russian church delegation in Denver. H. E. Fey. Christian Cent 80:326-7 Mr 13 '63
Sikh discovers America. J. S. Rekhi. il Nat Geog Mag 126:558-90 O '64
Sophie en Amérique. il Seventeen 23:177 O '64
Students at last Kennedy reception; Berlin high school students. Sr Schol 83:18 D 13 '63
Wealthier by the world; foreign librarians in Enoch Pratt free library. E. Castagna. il Wilson Lib Bul 39:48-50 S '64
Where to go in '64; visit U.S.A. tour through Europe, 1961. M. Sutton. il Am For 70: 16-19+ Ja '64
Why should I travel when I'm already here? A. Sinclair. il Mlle 56:138-9+ Ap '63
See also
Hiroshima maidens

Anecdotes, facetiae, satire, etc.

Advice to a nervous visitor. W. Golding. Holiday 34:42-3+ Jl '63

FOREIGN visitors in Yugoslavia
Letter from Belgrade. J. Wechsberg. New Yorker 39:125-6+ S 21 '63
My friend, the Titoist. A. Schalk. Commonweal 80:542-4 Ag 7 '64

FOREIGN words and phrases. See French language—Foreign words and phrases

FOREIGNERS in Argentina. See Argentina—Foreign population
FORELL, George W.
Ecumenical goal: community, not consensus. Christian Cent 81:1389 N 11 '64
FOREMAN, Carl
Something worth fighting for; interview, ed. by H. Alpert. por Sat R 46:16-18 D 28 '63
FOREMAN, Percy
Casus Belli. il por Time 83:34+ Mr 27 '64
Get Percy Foreman. T. Martin and P. O'Bryan. il pors Sat Eve Post 237:40+ N 14 '64
FORENSIC photography. See Photography, Legal
FORENSIC psychiatry
Psychiatry's threat to civil liberties. T. S. Szasz. il Nat R 14:191-3 Mr 12 '63; Discussion. 14:295 Ap 9 '63
FORER, Lois G.
No place for the rabble. Horizon 6:4-7+ Spr '64
FOREST conservation
Conservation platform for American forestry; text. Am For 70:3-16 F '64
Job ahead for AFA. M. K. Goddard and R. R. Widner. Am For 69:6-7+ D '63
New look at Penn's woods. V. C. Miles and G. V. Holmberg. il Am For 70:38-40 S '64
Redwood totem. H. Gilliam. il Nation 199:91-3 S 7 '64
See also
Forest fire protection
FOREST ecology
Trapped by heredity. Sci N L 83:285 My 4 '63
FOREST fire patrol
Fire watch in a dry, dry woodland; east of the Mississippi River. C. Phinizy. il Sports Illus 19:22-4 N 4 '63
FOREST fire patrol, Aerial
Fertilizer fights fire near San Bernardino. Sci N L 86:88 Ag 8 '64
Ontario's aerial fire fighters. J. Montagnes. il Am For 69:22-3+ My '63
PBY water bombers battle forest fires in Quebec. D. A. Brown. il Aviation W 81:66-8+ Ag 3 '64
Rugged prep school for smoke jumpers. F. A. Tinker. il Pop Mech 119:134-7+ F '63
FOREST fire protection
Fire prevention breakthrough; Fire control simulator. J. B. Craig. il Am For 69:36-8 Mr '63
Hot fires in Chile. N. Frederick. il Am For 70:28-9+ Mr '64
Peaceful warpath. J. C. Hunt. il Am For 70:36-8+ Mr '64
Wildfires in Alaska. D. E. Hess and others. il Am For 70:24-7+ F '64
See also
Forest fire patrol
Forest fire patrol, Aerial
United States—Forest fire fighters service
United States—Forest service
FOREST fires
Bird worth a forest fire; saving the Kirtland's warbler. L. Line. il Audubon Mag 66:370-5 N '64
Crazy blazes. C. E. Randall. Am For 69:8+ Jl '63
Darkness at noon; Massachusetts, May 19, 1780. J. Ashbrook. bibliog Sky & Tel 27:219 Ap '64
Fire crisis in Brazil; state of Paraná. M. S. Lowden. il Am For 71:42-4+ Ja '65
Fire ecology of the giant sequoias; controlled fires one solution to survival. R. J. Hartesveldt. il Natur Hist 73:12-19 bibliog(p67) D '64
Fire! photo story. G. Laycock. Field & S 68:30-1 Jl '63
Great Paraná fire. G. Meek. il Américas 15:38-40 D '63
Holocaust; devastation of Parana, Brazil. il Time 82:42 S 20 '63
Law and the liability of the public forester. J. W. Giles. Am For 69:31+ Mr '63; Reply. L. F. Marion. 69:2 Je '63
Sky fire: how science fights it. F. B. Quigg. il Am For 69:12-15+ O '63
Thread of evidence. P. Hutchinson. il Am For 69:30-1+ Jl '63
See also
Arson
Forest fire patrol, Aerial
United States—Forest fire fighters service
FOREST land
AFA's third landownership study; Tarheel territory. K. B. Pomeroy. il Am For 69:16:19+ O '63
Expanding use of industrial forest land; excerpts from address, January 1963. J. F. Shanklin. il Recreation 57:18-19+ Ja '64
FOREST Lawn memorial-park. See Cemeteries
FOREST management
Design for multiple use. W. T. Dresser. il Am For 70:12-15 Jl '64
Economics of sustained yield forestry in Sweden. T. Streyffert. il Am For 69:36-8+ Jl '63
Farm forests are bonus crops. R. W. Neelands and R. R. Reynolds. il Am For 69:9+ Je '63
Ford's forest. C. F. Sutherland, jr. il Am For 69:18-19+ S '63; Reply. S. G. Fontanna. 69:84 N '63
King on the mountain: editorial. Am For 69:11 Ag '63
Maine's farm woodlands. B. Geagan. il Am For 69:34-6 S '63
More on the Johnson fortune: Lady Bird's pine lands and her tenants; backlands of Alabama. il U S News 56:43-5 My 4 '64
Small woodlands are a big problem, what can AFA do? K. B. Pomeroy. Am For 70:55 Mr '64
Two views on the Seattle watershed; timber management, yes! A. E. Thompson. il Am For 69:8+ N '63
See also
Forest ownership
New England forestry foundation, Boston
FOREST ownership
AFA's North Carolina land ownership study; new light on small woodlands. J. G. Yoho and R. O. McMahon. il Am For 69:32-4+ N '63
FOREST planting
Forests of New Zealand. E. R. Yarham. il Am For 70:36-9+ Jl '64
See also
Reforestation
Tree planting
FOREST products
Why a national forest products week? B. West. il Am For 69:44+ N '63
See also
Lumber industry and trade
Wood products industry
FOREST products laboratory. See United States—Forest products laboratory
FOREST rangers. See United States—Forest service
FOREST recreation
Why recreation depends on taxation; reprint. E. Swift. Am For 71:32-3 Ja '65
FOREST research. See Forestry research
FOREST reserves. See State parks and reserves
FOREST service (United States) See United States—Forest service
FOREST soils
Root of the matter. Am For 70:7 Ag '64
FOREST taxation. See Forests and forestry—Taxation
FOREST workers. See Foresters
FORESTATION. See Reforestation
FORESTER, C. S.
Bloodshed at dawn. Am Heritage 15:40-5+ O '64
Victory on Lake Champlain. Am Heritage 15:4-11+ D '63; Reply with rejoinder. E. C. Beer. 15:94 Ap '64
FORESTER, Leslie R.
How would you like to live next door to you? Am Home 67:52-3+ O '64
FORESTERS
Confessions of a dirt forester. C. W. Wylie. il Am For 70:28-30+ Ap '64
See also
Fernow, B. E.
Guthrie, J. D.
FORESTIER, Denis
Teacher welfare in France. NEA J 54:19-20 Ja '65
FORESTRY, Industrial. See Forest management
FORESTRY building. See Portland, Ore.— Galleries and museums
FORESTRY camps
Forestry's role in youth conservation. W. G. Magnuson. Am For 70:12-14 Ag '64
FORESTRY laws and regulations
On the land and water fund front. J. B. Craig. Am For 70:46 My '64
FORESTRY merit badge. See Boy scouts
FORESTRY research
Growth of American forestry research and education. R. J. Preston. il Am For 70:36-7+ D '64
World's tallest tree farm; follow-up for the future. E. A. Hofsted. il Am For 70:22-5+ S '64
See also
Pulp and paper research institute of Canada
Wood research
FORESTRY schools and education
Forestry education; key to resource management; concerning the Dana-Johnson study. J. A. Zivnuska. Am For 70:20+ F '64; Reply. J. A. O'Callaghan. 70:2 Ag '64

FORESTRY societies
Texas forestry association's 50th anniversary; the green gold of Texas; with Congratulatory message from the President of the United States. E. Wagoner. il Am For 70:26-9+ S '64
See also
North Carolina forestry association

FORESTS, National. See National forests

FORESTS, Petrified. See Petrified forests

FORESTS, Private. See Forest management

FORESTS, School. See School forests

FORESTS, State
Vermont ski trails. N. Ashby. il Am For 70:50-2 F '64

FORESTS and forestry
Forests and food. H. D. Crawford. il Am For 69:38-41+ S '63
See also
Forest fires
Lumbering
Tree breeding
Woodlots
Woods

Economic aspects

Economics of sustained yield forestry in Sweden. T. Streyffert. il Am For 69:36-8+ Jl '63

International aspects

American forestry abroad. H. S. Kernan. Am For 70:38-9+ Ap '64

Laws and regulations

See Forestry laws and regulations

Societies

See Forestry societies

Study and teaching

Conservation education, Merrill style; Merrill, Wisc. public schools. J. W. Craig. il Am For 69:30-1 F '63
30,000 boys and a merit badge; Boy scout forestry merit badge. R. Sheldon. il Am For 70:21+ My '64
See also
Forestry schools and education
School forests

Taxation

Don't burn the barn down, Mr Dillon. Am For 69:13+ Mr '63
Private forestry united. Am For 69:11 Ap '63
Why recreation depends on taxation; reprint. E. Swift. Am For 71:32-3 Ja '65

Alaska

Wildfires in Alaska. D. E. Hess and others. il Am For 20:24-7+ F '64

Australia

Letter from Australia. M. D. Passmore. Am For 70:64 Je '64

Burma

Notes of a traveling forester; Burma and Thailand. N. T. Mirov. il Am For 69:4-5+ F '63

California

City boys and forestry. R. Leadabrand. il Am For 69:8-9 S '63
Redwood parks in peril. J. B. Craig. il(cover) Am For 70:8 Ap '64; Discussion. 70:64 Je '64

Canada

Spraying program uses new techniques; controlling outbreak of spruce budworms, New Brunswick. D. A. Brown. il Aviation W 80:88-9+ My 18 '64
They know their target. D. B. Huyck. il Am For 71:18-21+ Ja '65

Chile

Hot fires in Chile. N. Frederick. il Am For 70:28-9+ Mr '64

Europe, Western

From the Connecticut to the Rhine; tour by foresters, industry representatives and conservation leaders. E. R. Foster and H. F. R. Mason, jr. il Am For 69:20-2 Ap '63

Finland

Suomi, land of forests. E. R. Yarham. il Am For 69:16-19+ F '63

Florida

Visit to Eglin. F. E. Hornaday. il Am For 70:19-21 Ag '64

France

Forests of France and their wildlife. G. Olivier. il Audubon Mag 66:28-31 Ja '64

Great Britain

Arboretum et fruticetum Britannicum. The trees and shrubs of Britain, by J. C. Loudon. Review
Am For il 69:8-9+ Ag '63. H. W. Dengler

Hawaii

Forests, a natural defense against seismic waves. C. D. Whitesell and R. E. Daehler. il Am For 70:38-9 N '64

Honduras

Beetle explosion in Honduras; southern pine beetle. J. A. Beal and others. il Am For 70:31-3 N '64

Ireland

Forestry in Ireland. W. E. Sullivan. il Am For 70:31 Ap '64

Jamaica

Timber from Jamaican ore pits. E. J. Long. il Am For 69:22-5 S '63

Java

Notes of a traveling forester. N. T. Mirov. il Am For 69:39+ Jl '63

Maine

Maine asks for a chance on the Allagash; editorial. J. B. Craig. Am For 69:10-11 O '63
Maine's farm woodlands. B. Geagan. il Am For 69:34-6 S '63

Mexico

Forests by jet; Mexican seed-collecting program. C. Peet. il Am For 70:48-50 O '64

Michigan

Cedar and the backyard living boom. W. J. Duchaine. il Am For 69:40-3 O '63
Lake states research inspected. K. B. Pomeroy. il Am For 70:33 Ja '64

Mississippi

Heresy of Isaac Houston Bass. H. H. Leard. il Am For 69:20-1+ S '63

New England

See also
New England forestry foundation, Boston

New Jersey

New Jersey's Green Acres program. L. Fiedler. il Am For 70:40-2 Je '64

New Zealand

Forests of New Zealand. E. R. Yarham. il Am For 70:36-9+ Jl '64

North Carolina

AFA's North Carolina land ownership study; new light on small woodlands. J. G. Yoho and R. O. McMahon. il Am For 69:32-4+ N '63
AFA's third landownership study; Tarheel territory. K. B. Pomeroy. il Am For 69:16-19+ O '63
Forester's notebook. K. B. Pomeroy. il Am For 69:68 My '63

Norway

Norway hosts 10th Northern forest congress. R. E. Marsh. il Am For 69:24-7+ My '63

Pennsylvania

New look at Penn's woods. V. C. Miles and G. V. Holmberg. il Am For 70:38-40 S '64

Puerto Rico

Our smallest national forest. N. Ashby. il Am For 69:30-1+ S '63

Scandinavia

Norway hosts 10th Northern forest congress. R. E. Marsh. il Am For 69:24-7+ My '63

Somalia

Somali foresters, jacks-of-all-trades. D. E. Clark. il Am For 69:21+ D '63

Southern states

Foot that rocks the cradle. il Am For 70:18-19 O '64

Sweden

Economics of sustained yield forestry in Sweden. T. Streyffert. il Am For 69:36-8+ Jl '63
Forestry: a way of life; address. R. E. Marsh. il Am For 70:36-8+ Ag '64
Swedish view of American forestry. H. F. R. Mason, jr. and E. R. Foster. il Am For 70:30-1+ Mr '64

FORESTS and forestry—*Continued*

Texas

Texas forestry association's 50th anniversary; the green gold of Texas; with Congratulatory message from the President of the United States. E. Wagoner. il Am For 70: 26-9+ S '64

Thailand

Notes of a traveling forester; Burma and Thailand. N. T. Mirov. il Am For 69:4-5+ F '63

United States

Cradle of forestry. il Am For 70:18-20 My '64
Defender of the forestry profession: editorial. A. G. Hall. Am For 69:13 S '63
Fernow, the man who brought forestry to America. C. E. Randall. Am For 70:14-16+ Ap '64
Forester's notebook. K. B. Pomeroy. Am For 69:3+ F '63; 70:35 Ap '64
Forestry in the federal budget, fiscal year ending June 30, 1965. Am For 70:6 Mr '64
Forests resources report. Am For 70:40+ Mr '64
Job ahead for AFA. M. K. Goddard and R. R. Widner. Am For 69:6-7+ D '63
Swedish view of American forestry. H. F. R. Mason, jr. and E. R. Foster. il Am For 70:30-1+ Mr '64
Transitions in forestry; address, March 26, 1963. E. Swift. Am For 69:22-3+ Je '63
Washington lookout. A. G. Hall. See issues of American forests
What does it take? sharing United States forestry experience with the world's peoples. T. Gill. Am For 70:11 Ja '64
Why conservationists are missing a big bet! S. S. Chase. il Am For 70:14-16 My '64
See also
American forest congress
Forest conservation
National forests
United States—Forest service

Viet Nam (Republic)

Forests of Viet-Nam. H. S. Kernan. il Am For 70:31+ Je '64

Washington (state)

Two views on the Seattle watershed. A. E. Thompson; J. R. Heath. il Am For 69:8-9+ N '63

Western states

Big mop up; Columbus day storm. J. C. Hunt. il Am For 70:10-13+ Ap '64

Wisconsin

Lake states research inspected. K. B. Pomeroy. il Am For 70:33 Ja '64

FOREVER panting; story. See De Vries, P.

FORGACS, Chaim. See Stein, G. jt. auth.

FORGASH, Morris
Roll and rock of containerization in transport economics. Ann Am Acad 345:115-21 Ja '63

FORGE, Andrew
Bacon: the paint of screams. Art N 62:38-41+ O '63

FORGE presses. See Presses

FORGERIES, Art. See Forgery of works of art

FORGERY
How document detectives catch crooks. J. R. Berry. il Pop Sci 184:120-2+ Ap '64
Most embarrassing prisoner. H. Dolson. Harper 228:176-8 Ap '64
Solving crimes on paper; excerpt from Science in crime detection. N. Morland. il Sci Digest 53:12-23 Mr '63
See also
Literary forgeries and mystifications

FORGERY of works of art
Aesthetics of snobbery; excerpt from Act of creation. A. Koestler. Horizon 7:50-3 Wint '65
For the ring of crystal. N. Kent. Am Artist 28:3+ Mr '64

FORGETTING. See Memory

FORGING
Boone forge; Burnsville, N.C. photographs. Travel 122:39-41 Ag '64
Drop forge goes automatic; Chambersburg impacter. il Bsns W p83-4+ O 17 '64
Forged metal in Germany; excerpts from Neue schmiedeformen, tr. by H. Wegener. E. Roth. il Craft Horiz 24:12-17+ Ja '64
Forging shop turns its back on suppliers; Cameron iron works. il Bsns W p 194-6+ My 18 '63

FORGIVENESS
Forgive the little children. J. Wellington. il PTA Mag 58:12-14 Je '64

FORGIVING; story. See Hazzard, S.

FORM (art)
Expressive line and form. E. G. Snellenberger. il Design 66:42-3 S '64

FORMAN, Bernard I.
Our own space project. Recreation 56:286 Je '63

FORMAN, Fred. See Nawracaj, E. P. jt. auth.

FORMAN, James
Weapons: dollar and ballot; interview. por U S News 56:69-71 F 24 '64

about

South's war against Negro votes. J. Poppy. por Look 27:38+ My 21 '63
With new civil-rights law; how Negroes see the future. il por U S News 56:38-9 Je 29 '64

FORMATES
Thermal reduction of bicarbonate to formate. I. C. Hisatsune and K. O. Hartman. bibliog il Science 145:1455-6 S 25 '64

FORMENTOR prize
Formentor and International publishers prizes awarded. Pub W 185:42 My 18 '64

FORMIC acid
Anaerobic formate oxidation: a ferredoxin-dependent reaction. W. J. Brill and others. bibliog il Science 144:297-8 Ap 17 '64

FORMICA company
World's fair house. il Good H 158:100-13+ My '64

FORMICHINI, Dino
Miranda's match; interview, ed. by F. Stevenson. por Opera N 27:15 Ap 13 '63

FORMOSA. See Taiwan

FORMS, Municipal. See Municipal government—Forms, blanks, etc.

FORMS, Natural. See Natural forms

FORMS and blanks, Business. See Business—Forms, blanks, etc.

FORMS of address
Now Moscow debates its manners. G. Feifer. il N Y Times Mag p28+ Ag 23 '64

FORMULA writing. See Fiction

FORNOFF, W. E.
Computer puts a plus in inventory control. Am City 79:90-1 N '64

FORREST, Richard I.
I learned about flying from that! Flying 74: 56 Ap '64

FORRESTAL, James
James Forrestal, by A. A. Rogow. Review
Commonweal 80:303 My 29 '64. D. Killeen
Nat R 16:281-3 Ap 7 '64. M. S. Evans
New Repub 150:26-7 F 29 '64. C. B. Marshall
Reporter 30:52+ F 27 '64. W. H. Hessler
Sat R por 47:54-5 F 22 '64. E. M. Yoder, jr
Time il por 83:70-1+ Ja 31 '64

FORRETTE, John E.
Spectroscopy. Science 141:442-3 Ag 2 '63

FORSCHER, Bernard K.
Chaos in the brickyard; letter. Science 142: 339 O 18 '63

FORSCHER, Marty
Committee for a sane policy in automation; interview, ed. by H. Shaman. Pop Phot 55:39+ O '64

FORSHEY, Gerald
Divided flocks in Jackson. Christian Cent 80:1469-71 N 27 '63

FORSLING, C. L.
Ravelling watersheds; grazing lands must be restored. Am For 69:12-14+ F '63

FORST, Don
When a fugitive turns to fight. Sat Eve Post 236:44-5 O 19 '63

FORSTER, E. M.
Living legends. A. Brien. il por Vogue 145: 124-5+ Ja 1 '65
Mr Forster of King's. S. Campbell. por Mlle 59:80-1+ Je '64
Modern Mr Forster. G. A. Harrison. New Repub 150:15-16 Ja 11 '64
Old Man at King's. S. Hynes. Commonweal 79:635-8 F 21 '64

FORSTER, Robert
Provincial noble: a reappraisal. bibliog f Am Hist R 68:681-91 Ap '63

FORSYTH, George H.
Island of faith in the Sinai wilderness. por Nat Geog Mag 125:82-106 Ja '64

FORSYTH, Gordon
Cost of the National health service. Cur Hist 45:19-24+ Jl '63

FORSYTHE, Eve
Bad year of marriage. Redbook 123:62-3+ Ag '64

FORSYTHE, Virginia
Parents across the sea. Read Digest 82:137-9 F '63

FORSYTHIAS
Best forsythias. D. Wyman. il Horticulture 42:38-9+ Mr '64
Forsythia; shrub that all gardeners enjoy. il Flower Grower 51:48-9+ Mr '64
FORT, Harriet
Uncle Hobey; story. Seventeen 22:210-11 Ag '63
FORT DIX. See Military training camps
FORT HOOD, Tex. See Military training camps
FORT JEFFERSON NATIONAL MONUMENT
Two national preservations threatened by proposed refueling station. Nat Parks Mag 38:16 Mr '64
FORT KNOX
Fort Knox wins first Conservation special award. il Am For 69:35 Ag '63
FORT LAUDERDALE, Fla.

Harbor

Resort port booms; Port Everglades. il Bsns W p78-80 N 16 '63
FORT ORD, Calif. See Military training camps
FORT SANTA ELENA
Fort that went to sea! F. Decoste. Am For 70:15 Ag '64
FORT SIMCOE STATE HISTORICAL PARK. See Washington (state)—Parks and reserves
FORT SMITH, Ark.
Go-getters of Fort Smith, Ark. il Fortune 69:120-1 Ap '64
FORT TICONDEROGA
In the name of the great Jehovah and the Continental congress! K. S. Davis. il Am Heritage 14:65-77 O '63
Ticonderoga, key to a continent. J. M. Lape. il Antiques 84:57-9 Jl '63
FORT WORTH, Tex.

Politics and government

Councilmen are smart. J. L. Brownlee. il Am City 78:105-6 Je '63
Two-way radio. J. I. Koski. il Am City 79:151-2 My '64

Sanitary affairs

Hand sweeping loses. C. M. Thelin. il Am City 78:20 Jl '63
Inter-city water-sewerage agreements. P. Holley. il Am City 79:73-5 D '64

Stores

Private subway; Leonards. il Time 81:44 F 22 '63
Store subway takes patrons from shopping area to store; Leonards. il Pub W 184:44-5 S 30 '63
White on white. il Arch Forum 119:96-9 Jl '63

Water supply

Inter-city water-sewerage agreements. P. Holley. il Am City 79:73-5 D '64
FORT WORTH opera association
U.S. calendar. Opera N 29:31 D 5 '64
FORT WORTH public library
First for Fort Worth: Southwest branch. D. A. Holcomb. il Library J 88:4555-7 D 1 '63
FORTENBERRY, Frances
Wild game, its care and cooking. Suc Farm 61:81 N '63
FORTIFICATION
Fascinating U.S. forts. P. Geraci. il Travel 122:24-30 Jl '64
FORTINBERRY, Barbara
Courage is a private affair; story. Vogue 142: 68-71 S 15 '63
FORTNUM and Mason, limited. See London—Stores
FORTS. See Fortification
FORTUNE, T. Thomas
Early career of T. Thomas Fortune, 1879-1890. S. M. Scheiner. bibliog por Negro Hist Bul 27:170-2 Ap '64
FORTUNE telling
Carmen and the tarots. W. Starkie. il Am Rec G 31:4-9 S '64
Onward and upward with the arts. H. Suyin. il New Yorker 39:38-40+ D 28 '63
Planets, palms, and numbers. H. Stackpole. il Mlle 60:50-1+ Ja '65
FORTUNETELLER; story. See Deasy, M.
FORUMS (discussion and debate)
College colloquies. R. Kirk. Nat R 14:366 My 7 '63
Mice or men in the space age? round-table discussion from 1964 Williamsburg student burgesses. il Sr Schol 84:12-13+ Ap 24 '64
Over and out; Village vanguard series of Speak outs. New Yorker 40:29-31 D 19 '64
Today's youth, tomorrow's leaders; round-table discussion from 1963 Williamsburg student burgesses. il Sr Schol 82:16-17 Mr 27 '63
See also
Center for the study of democratic institutions, Santa Barbara, Calif.
New York herald tribune forum for high schools
Seminars
La FORZA del destino; opera. See Verdi, G.
FOSBURGH, Pieter
Naturalist's book list. Natur Hist 73:6+ Ag '64
FOSDICK, Harry Emerson
Inner peace and how to find it; reprint. Read Digest 83:110-13 Jl '63
FOSKETT, D. J.
Information retrieval in the social sciences. bibliog por Wilson Lib Bul 38:755-62 My '64
International federation for documentation. Library J 89:4478-80 N 15 '64
FOSMIRE, Frederick R. and Tryk, H. E.
Word association: common and original response. bibliog Science 139:415-16 F 1 '63
FOSSE, Bob
Bob Fosse. por Dance Mag 37:32 Ap '63
FOSSEN, Dag
From razor blades to rockets. Pop Sci 183: 126-7 O '63
FOSSIL fishes; insects; etc. See Fishes, Fossil; Insects, Fossil; etc.
FOSSIL forests. See Petrified forests
FOSSIL man. See Man, Prehistoric
FOSSIL microorganisms. See Micropaleontology
FOSSIL plants. See Paleobotany
FOSSILS. See Paleontology
FOSTER, Ashley
Closing of Catholic schools in Australia. bibliog f Sch & Soc 91:375-7 N 30 '63
FOSTER, Elmer R. and Mason, H. F. R. jr
From the Connecticut to the Rhine. Am For 69:20-2 Ap '63
—See Mason, H. F. R. jr. jt. auth.
FOSTER, Frank P.
Warning against a physical fitness mania. N Y Times Mag p 15+ F 9 '64
FOSTER, G. Allen
John Scobell, Union spy in Civil war; excerpts from Eyes and ears of the Civil war. il Ebony 19:135-8+ D '63
Woman who saved the Union navy. Ebony 19:48-50+ Jl '64
FOSTER, G. W. jr
North and West have problems, too. Sat R 46:69-72+ Ap 20 '63
FOSTER, Gertrude B.
Ever hear of the first-aid plant? House B 105:100+ Jl '63
Grow flavorful herbs in your garden or kitchen window. Am Home 66:41+ Mr '63
Twelve most useful herbs, and how to grow them. House B 106:182-3+ Ap '64
FOSTER, Hugh G.
Infinite Zero. Holiday 33:131-3+ Mr '63
FOSTER, Irene
Three women; story. Good H 157:94-5 O '63
FOSTER, Jim
(ed) See Owens, C. How to build a Grand national stock car racer
FOSTER, John
How isotopes aid medicine in tracking down your ailments. Todays Health 42:40-5+ My '64
FOSTER, John S.
Meet Johnny Foster; reprint. D. M. Wilkes. il pors Sci Digest 54:30-7 S '63
FOSTER, Julian M.
Scarlett O'Hara's millions. F. Knebel. il por Look 27:39-40+ D 3 '63
FOSTER, Luther Hilton
Luther Foster of Tuskegee. J. Scanlon. il por Sat R 47:76+ My 16 '64
FOSTER, William C.
Economics of arms control and disarmament; address, June 6, 1963. Dept State Bul 49:7-11 Jl 1 '63
Eighteen-nation disarmament committee recesses 1964 session; statement, September 17, 1964. bibliog f Dept State Bul 51:524-7 O 12 '64
Eighteen nation disarmament conference reconvenes at Geneva; statement, June 9, 1964. Dept State Bul 50:1004-7 Je 29 '64
Excerpt from interview, August 1, 1963. Cong Digest 43:214+ Ag '64
National strategy, security, and arms control; address, October 31, 1963. Dept State Bul 49:824-9 N 25 '63
Nuclear test ban issue; statement, February 12, 1963. Dept State Bul 48:398-402 Mr 18 '63

FOSTER, William C.—*Continued*
Risk and security in the age of nuclear weapons; address, December 15, 1962. Dept State Bul 48:128-34 Ja 28 '63
U.S. calls for exploration of freeze concept; statement, January 31, 1964. Dept State Bul 50:350-2 Mr 2 '64
U.S. outlines cutoff and verification provisions to halt production of fissionable materials for nuclear weapons use; statements, June 18 and June 25, 1964. Dept State Bul 51:123-7 Jl 27 '64
U.S. proposes curb on spread of nuclear weapons; statement, February 6, 1964. Dept State Bul 50:376-9 Mr 9 '64

about

Mr Foster leaves for disarmament conference at Geneva. Dept State Bul 50:163 F 3 '64
William C. Foster named to head delegation to disarmament talks; White House statement, January 10, 1964. Dept State Bul 50:119 Ja 27 '64

FOSTER home care
Child waits; film produced by the Federation of Protestant welfare agencies, inc. il Ebony 18:89-90+ Mr '63
Foster-home problem. R. Haitch. Nation 196: 279-81, 306-8 Ap 6-13 '63
New methods of care. D. D. Dowling. bibliog f Ann Am Acad 355:49-55 S '64
Unmet and future needs. E. E. Glover and J. H. Reid. bibliog f Ann Am Acad 355: 16-17 S '64

FOSTER parents
Foster-family care: has it fulfilled its promise? M. Lewis. bibliog f Ann Am Acad 355:31-41 S '64
Needed: parents pro tem. M. Weston. il N Y Times Mag p96 Ap 21 '63
Why can't Susan stay? G. B. Hughes. il Parents Mag 39:60-1+ O '64
Why I'm raising other people's children. E. G. Reid. Parents Mag 38:78+ S '63

FOSTER parents' plan, incorporated
Parents across the sea. V. Forsythe. Read Digest 82:137-9 F '63
Year we rediscovered Christmas. C. L. Yellin. Redbook 124:10+ D '64

FOTOVAL. See Photography—Printing processes

FOUCAULT'S pendulum
Amateur scientist; how to photograph air currents in color and build an accurate Foucault pendulum. R. Walan. il Sci Am 210:132-3+ F '64

FOULKE, Adrienne
(tr) See Aragon, L. Power of the king... Picasso
(tr) See Bodin, S. Bettina's Nile diary
(tr) See Cocteau, J. To the young of 2000 A.D.

FOUNDATION for contemporary performance arts
Artists for artists; exhibition at Allan Stone gallery. New Yorker 39:32-4 Mr 9 '63
Paintings for sale: profits for performers. il Dance Mag 37:44-5 Mr '63
Pictures from modern masters to aid music and dance. il Art N 61:44 F '63

FOUNDATION for education in American citizenship, National. See National foundation for education in American citizenship

FOUNDATION for religious education
New kind of sisters' school. M. McGrory. America 111:206 Ag 29 '64

FOUNDATION garments
Accent is on foundations. il Ebony 19:117+ Jl '64
Best silhouette. H. Obolensky. il Redbook 122:50-1+ Ja '64
Curving the curple. il Time 82:79 O 11 '63
Girdles: better care=longer wear. il Good H 158:6 My '64
Take a fashion lesson; do's, don'ts and dressing room decorum. il Seventeen 23:67 O '64
Take a fashion lesson; sports wardrobe. il Seventeen 23:206 My '64
See also
Brassieres

FOUNDATION planting. See Landscape gardening

FOUNDATIONS
Footings and foundations. W. J. Fletcher. il Suc Farm 61:48-9 My '63
What belongs in a foundation investigation. D. M. Greer. il Arch Rec 133:190-2 Je '63
See also
Piles and pile driving

FOUNDATIONS, Charitable and educational
Foundations: aristocrats of philanthropy. il Sr Schol 85:9-10 D 9 '64
Foundations as a tax dodge. F. J. Cook. Nation 196:321-5 Ap 20 '63; Reply. J. Williams. 196:inside cover My 18 '63
Foundations as fronts; channeling CIA funds. Nation 199:102 S 14 '64
Foundations in business report. U S News 55:104-5 O 28 '63
Foundations: Patman maintains pressure for tighter regulation of tax-exempt organizations. J. Walsh. Science 145:559-61 Ag 7 '64
Foundations: Patman plugs away at theme that growth, operations of tax exempts call for scrutiny. J. Walsh. Science 142:370-2 O 18 '63
Grantsmanship. J. O'Reilly. Mlle 58:90-1+ D '63
Growth of foundations' wealth and activities. R. H. Smith. Pub W 185:109 Ja 20 '64
Heat on foundations; abuses of tax exemption. Bsns W p38 S 19 '64
Heat on Hunt; investigation of tax-exempt foundations. Newsweek 64:23-4 S 14 '64
I'm amazed; finances of foundations. Newsweek 64:61-2 Ag 24 '64
It's a gift! contributions to parks and recreation. il Recreation 57:20+ Ja '64
Leisure of the theory class. M. Mayer. Esquire 59:16+ Mr '63
Maiden ladies; housing for unmarried daughters of the aristocracy in Germany and Denmark. N. S. Hazelton. New Yorker 39:162+ S 21 '63
New ventures for private philanthropy. J. G. Harrar. il N Y Times Mag p29+ Je 9 '63
Patman hits funds; excerpts from report. W. Patman. Sr Schol 82:1T-2T Ja 30 '63
Patman shoots again. Bsns W p 146+ O 26 '63
Role of the foundations. G. M. Beckmann. Ann Am Acad 356:12-22 N '64
Theological seminary receives large gift. Christian Cent 80:1569 D 18 '63
Tighter tax rules for foundations? U S News 57:76 Ag 3 '64
Try a foundation; assistance to young musical artists. D. L. Engle. Mus Am 84:12-13 Jl '64
While school keeps; Citizens' scholarship foundation. J. Cass. Sat R 46:84 F 16 '63
See also names of foundations, e.g. Norton Simon foundation

Anecdotes, facetiae, satire, etc.

Lonesome pine foundation. P. J. Davis. Harper 29:23-4+ Ag '64

FOUNDATIONS, Subaqueous. See Piles and pile driving

FOUNDLINGS
Abandoned child. A. Henley. il McCalls 91: 126-7+ My '64

FOUNDRIES
Clean, quiet foundry almost runs itself; Sloan valve company foundry, Melrose Park, Ill. il Bsns W p52-3 Ap 13 '63

Wages and hours

Earnings in iron and steel foundries, November 1962. F. W. Mohr. il Mo Labor R 86: 1045-7 S '63

FOUNDRY furnaces. See Furnaces, Foundry

FOUNDRY practice
See also
Continuous casting
Steel castings

FOUNDRY workers
See also
Foundries—Wages and hours

FOUNTAIN, Lawrence H.
NIH and Fountain; part of problem is that an atmosphere of suspicion has enveloped the relationship. D. S. Greenberg. por Science 140:1076-8 Je 7 '63

FOUNTAIN pens
They don't make fountain pens, or library paste, or hardly anything that way any more. R. P. Smith. il McCalls 90:194+ S '63
See also
Parker pen company

FOUNTAINS
Create magic with water. il Pop Gard 15:50-1 My '64
$H_2\$$; money-tossing vogue. S. D. Kohn. il N Y Times Mag p 121-2 S 13 '64
Pooled assets; how to dispose of coins thrown into New York fountains. il Newsweek 64: 62 Ag 17 '64
Winners announced in fountain competition; design of a monumental fountain to be in Philadelphia. il Arch Rec 137:14 Ja '65

FOUQUET, Nicolas
Minister's fatal showplace. W. H. Hale. il por Horizon 5:76-83 Jl '63

FOUR-day week. See Hours of labor

480; novel. See Burdick, E.

4-H clubs
Grandfather to half a million kids; C. Anderson in Korea. R. C. Davids. il Farm J 88:28-9+ Jl '64

4-H clubs—*Continued*
Six 4-H club members win National health awards. il Todays Health 42:72 Mr '64
What will your kids do for a living? B. Rollins. il Farm J 87:58S-58T Ap '63
FOUR hours to fear; story. See Lockridge, F. and Lockridge, R.
FOUR hundred and twenty; story. See Mehta, V.
FOUR is a lovely number; story. See Hintze, N. A.
FOUR-wheel-drive campers. See Automobiles—Gearing
FOURNIER, John H.
Measure for measure. Flying 75:82 S '64
FOURNIER, Paul J.
Can animals talk? Field & S 69:52-4+ Je '64
Find that deer. Field & S 69:71-2+ O '64
Migration in Maine. Natur Hist 73:46-9 O '64
FOURSQUARE gospel. See International church of the foursquare gospel
FOURTEEN hundred and ninety-two
And what else happened in 1492? il Sr Schol 83:5 O 11 '63
Before Columbus came. G. Baquero. il Américas 15:35-9 O '63
FOURTEENTH amendment. See United States—Constitution—Amendments
FOURTH amendment to the Constitution. See United States—Constitution—Bill of rights
FOURTH bride; story. See Streeter, E.
FOURTH of July
Biggest Fourth of July salute; Rebild National Park, Denmark. C. W. Hall. il Read Digest 85:145-6 Jl '64
Bombs bursting in air! W. Stanton. il McCalls 91:71+ Jl '64
Explosions for freedom. B. Tufty. il Sci N L 83:406-7 Je 29 '63
The Fourth; Jefferson's replacement library for LC. R. Stokes. Library J 88:2648 Jl '63
Let freedom ring! bell-ringing ceremonies in Los Angeles. B. Stephens. Recreation 57:308 Je '64
Mrs Anderson addresses Bulgarian people on U.S. Independence day. E. Anderson. Dept State Bul 51:78 Jl 20 '64
FOWL. See Poultry
FOWLE, Leonard M.
Marblehead's 74th. Yachting 114:51+ S '63
—and Hodges, M. J.
Organizing a junior sailing program. Sports Illus 18:35-8 Je 24 '63
—See Barker, B. D. 3d, jt. auth.
FOWLER, Henry Hamill
Trying to lure foreign investors to these shores. il Bsns W p94 My 2 '64
FOWLER, Henry Watson
On the fringe. H. Frankel. Sat R 47:40 Mr 21 '64
FOWLER, June
Informal meals for warm weather serving. D. J. Robinson. il pors Ebony 18:100+ Ag '63
FOWLER, Robert M.
Impact of American business. Atlan 214:119-23 N '64
FOWLER, William A.
Way of galaxy. il por Time 81:58+ F 8 '63
FOWLER, William B. and Samios, N. P.
Omega-minus experiment. Sci Am 211:36-45 O '64
FOWLES, John
Marriage, passion, love; excerpts from Aristos. Vogue 144:114-15 N 15 '64
FOWLIE, Wallace
Four poets and two dramatists. Poetry 104:187-92 Je '64
French poetry today. Poetry 104:322-8 Ag '64
Machines and the poetic imagination. Poetry 101:292-4 Ja '63
Method of Sainte-Beuve. Poetry 103:183-4 D '63
(tr) See Char, R. Chanson des etages; Post-scriptum à lettera amorosa; Sept parcelles de Luberon; Les parages d'Alsace
(tr) See Grosjean, J. Graduel; Hiver
(tr) See Jouve, P. J. Ténèbre; A la beauté
(tr) See Renard, J. C. Poèmes (extraits)
FOWLING
See also
Falconry
FOX, Allan S. See Horikawa, M. jt. auth.
FOX, Austin McCracken
New kid in school. Library J 88:3254-7 S 15 '63
FOX, Charles K.
Early conservation and the golden era of trout fishing; excerpts from This wonderful world of trout. Am For 70:38-41+ Ja '64
Fish catches man. Esquire 59:44+ Ap '63
FOX, Dorothea Magdalene
Thornton W. Burgess recalls a ninety-year romance with nature. Audubon Mag 66:312-13 S '64
FOX, Edward S.
How to plot your story. Writer 76:21-4+ D '63
Let's build a story. Writer 77:17-20+ Je '64
What about flashbacks? Writer 77:16-18 N '64
FOX, Edward Whiting
France of Charles de Gaulle. Cur Hist 47:332-8+ D '64
FOX, Frederic
Pater patriae as pater familias. Am Heritage 14:32-7+ Ap '63
FOX, Harland, and Kerpen, M. C.
Special retirement provisions in industry; excerpt from Corporate retirement policy and practices. Mo Labor R 87:781-5 Jl '64
FOX, Howard B.
Hymenocallis ovata. Horticulture 42:25 Ja '64
FOX, Josephine
(comp) Calendar of summer dance events here and abroad. Dance Mag 37:32-4 My '63; 38:32-7+ My '64
(ed) See St Denis, R. Divine moment
FOX, Joyce
Halloween dioramas. Sch Arts 63:21-3 O '63
FOX, Lester
Recreation harvest. Recreation 57:21-4 Ja '64
Recreation site finders. Recreation 56:92-3 F '63
—See Roth, B. A. jt. auth.
FOX, Marvin
Assimilating the law. Commentary 37:72-4 Je '64
Exploring the Jewish mind. Commentary 35:86-9 Ja '63
Jews, temporal & timeless. Commentary 35:353-6 Ap '63
Moral reason. Commentary 38:78+ D '64
Rabbi and the heretic. Commentary 36:174-6 Ag '63
FOX, Matthew M.
Box; will it revolutionize TV? P. O'Neil. il por Life 57:43-4+ Jl 17 '64
FOX, Richard Kyle
Bible of the barbershop. M. Weisbord. il por Sports Illus 18:54-61 F 18 '63
FOX, Sidney Martin
Missing microbes. Newsweek 63:70 Ja 20 '64
FOX, Tom
Pool. Sports Illus 20:58-61 Mr 23 '64
FOX, Virgil
Virgil Fox; interview, ed. by S. Fleming. por Hi Fi 13:30 Ag '63

about

Virgil Fox plays the Philharmonic Hall organ at Lincoln Center. R. Kammerer. por Am Rec G 29:958-9 Ag '63
FOX, William
Basement science: what happens when a do-it-yourself scientist looks to Washington for support. D. S. Greenberg. por Science 146:621-3 O 30 '64; Discussion. 146:1251-2; 147:109-10 D 4 '64, Ja 8 '65
FOX, William Price
Fast Dan; story. Harper 228:79-84 My '64
Have you ever rode the Southern? story. Sat Eve Post 236:38-41 Jl 13 '63
Moonshine light, moonshine bright: story. Sat Eve Post 236:46-52 Mr 16 '63
FOX hunting
All equal but the fox; Banwen hunt club, Wales. il Newsweek 62:46 N 18 '63
Beast with the high I.Q; American red fox. J. George. il Read Digest 85:231-2+ O '64
Favored sport of Jacqueline; color photographs; with account by D. Phillips. M. Hawkins. Sat Eve Post 236:24-8+ F 23 '63
Florida fox hunt. D. M. Duffey. il Outdoor Life 135:116-18+ Ja '65
How to hunt foxes. E. A. Bauer. il Outdoor Life 133:24-7+ F '64
No tallyho. E. Chaze. Life 54:19 Mr 8 '63
Rampart of pedigree. H. Horn. il Sports Illus 18:62-70 F 11 '63
They come a-running. F. R. Martin. il Outdoor Life 133:32-3+ Ja '64
FOX LAKE, Wis.
Self-help plan for doctorless towns. H. Earle. il Todays Health 41:34-9 S '63
FOX squirrel hunting. See Squirrel hunting
FOXBORO company
Foxboro takes industry's measure. il Bsns W p 146+ O 3 '64
FOXCROFT school, Middleburg, Va. See Private schools
FOXE, John
Elect nation, by W. Haller. Review
Christian Cent 81:912 Jl 15 '64. C. S. Meyer

FOXES
Beast with the high I.Q; American red fox. J. George. il Read Digest 85:231-2+ O '64
Foxes like mice on menu, find birds less tasty. Sci N L 86:121 Ag 22 '64
Little gray brush-popper. W. Curtis. il Field & S 68:33+ Ag '63
See also
Fox hunting
FOXGLOVES
Foxgloves: quick and easy from seed. M. C. Ohlander. il Flower Grower 51:37 Jl '64
FOXHALL, William B.
How architects practice interior design. Arch Rec 136:89+ N '64
How one large office uses construction cost estimates. Arch Rec 135:106+ My '64
Mental hospitals. Arch Rec 134:161 N '63
FOXTAIL lilies. See Desert candles
FOXY; musical comedy. See Musical comedies, revues, etc.—Criticisms, plots, etc.
FOY, Fred C.
Are we gaining or guessing abroad? address, March 27, 1963. Vital Speeches 29:421-5 My 1 '63
FOYERS. See Halls
FOYLE, William Alfred
Obituary
Pub W 183:59 Je 17 '63
FOYT, A. J.
Driver in a tight corner. B. Ottum. il pors Sports Illus 20:78-80+ Je 1 '64
Firecracker 400. M. Muhleman. il por Motor T 16:70-5 S '64
Magnificent and the macabre. B. Ottum. il por Sports Illus 20:24-9 Je 8 '64
Riding it out. por Newsweek 64:53 Ag 3 '64
FOYT, Tony
Hard, lonely life of a champion driver. B. Libby. il por Sat Eve Post 236:42-3 N 2 '63
FOZZY, Paula
Two views of nuclear power: AEC, industry. Bul Atomic Sci 19:37-8 Je '63
FRACTURES
Femoral expansion in aging women: implications for osteoporosis and fractures. R. W. Smith, jr. and R. R. Walker. bibliog il Science 145:156-7 Jl 10 '64
Fracture of pelvic bone. C. J. Potthoff. Todays Health 41:64 N '63
Rib fracture. C. J. Potthoff. Todays Health 42:62 N '64
Ski doctor. il Newsweek 61:60 F 4 '63
FRACTURES (geology) See Faults (geology)
FRADIER, Georges
Blindfolded traveller in New Delhi; excerpts from Encounters and celebrations. UNESCO Courier 16:4-11 S '63
Orient-Occident; a study in ignorance; excerpts from Encounters and celebrations. UNESCO Courier 16:4-7 Ap '63
FRAENKEL, G. and Hsiao, Catherine
Tanning in the adult fly; a new function of neurosecretion in the brain. bibliog Science 141:1057-8 S 13 '63
FRAENKEL, Heinrich. See Manvell, R. jt. auth.
FRAENKEL-CONRAT, Heinz
Genetic code of a virus; with biographical sketch. Sci Am 211:18, 46-54 bibliog(p 142) O '64
FRAGER, Malcolm
Oh, Vladimir! oh, Malcolm! il por Time 81:46 Je 21 '63
FRAGONARD, Jean Honoré
Curve of the sea shell. il Time 84:74 S 11 '64
Rococo master in Williamstown. Art N 63:44+ S '64
FRAGOSO, Eleanor
Manolete; poem. America 111:780 D 12 '64
FRAGRANT gardens. See Gardens, Fragrant
FRAIBERG, Selma H.
Chores that children like. Parents Mag 39:58-9+ Ap '64
Life and times with a two-year-old. Parents Mag 38:54-5+ D '63
What teen-agers don't know about sex. Parents Mag 38:35+ Jl '63
When a child is failing in school. Parents Mag 39:54-6+ My '64
FRAIN, Andy
Obituary
Sports Illus 20:20+ Ap 6 '64
FRAIR, Wayne
Blood group studies with turtles. bibliog Science 140:1412-14 Je 28 '63
FRAKES, Margaret
Episcopal dichotomy. Christian Cent 81:1390-2 N 11 '64
Goad to excellence. Christian Cent 81:273-6 F 26 '64
Methodists at Pittsburgh. Christian Cent 81:662-4 My 20 '64
Methodists in session. Christian Cent 81:694-5 My 27 '64
FRALEY, Oscar. See Kearns, J. jt. auth.
FRALEY, Pierre C. and Ubell, Earl
Science writing: a growing profession. Bul Atomic Sci 19:19-22 D '63
FRAMES for pictures. See Picture frames
FRAMING (building)
A for a holiday house; Stowe, Vt. G. O'Brien. il N Y Times Mag p60-1 Mr 29 '64
Apartment framing to resist wind; nine systems in steel and concrete. R. M. Gensert. il Arch Rec 133:160-4 Ja '63
Building basics every man should know. il Pop Mech 120:148-9 S '63
Design considerations for horizontal space frames; excerpts from paper. il Arch Rec 136:152-5 Ag '64
Logistics of vertical transport. il Fortune 67:89-95 Mr '63
Versatile structures for apartment framing; notes on wind-resistant behavior of various concrete wall and column arrangements. R. M. Gensert. il Arch Rec 135:178-9 Je; 136:185-8 Jl '64 (to be cont)
FRAMINGHAM, Mass.
Gardens
Challenge; New England wild flower preservation society campaigns to preserve the Garden in the woods. B. B. Paine. il Horticulture 42:32-5 O '64
FRANCE, Pierre Mendès-. See Mendès-France, P.
FRANCE
De Gaulle builds a new France. D. Cook. il Sat Eve Post 236:24-8+ N 23 '63
France: a return to greatness? il Newsweek 63:40-3+ F 10 '64
France, 1964; Americanization in spite of General de Gaulle. J. Daniel. New Repub 150:14-17 My 2 '64
France 1965; address, December 31, 1964. C. de Gaulle. Vital Speeches 31:212-13 Ja 15 '65
Future of France; address, December 31, 1963. C. de Gaulle. Vital Speeches 30:197-8 Ja 15 '64
Paris notes. J. Daniel. New Repub 151:27-9 O 24 '64
Searching for France. D. Littlejohn. Commonweal 79:161-5 N 1 '63
Two decades; concerning de Gaulle's speech on the twentieth anniversary of the liberation of Paris. il Time 84:42+ S 4 '64
Year of silent cannons; concerning major policy speech of de Gaulle. il Time 83:29 Ja 10 '64
See also
Advertising—France
Aerospace industries—France
Agricultural administration—France
Agriculture—France
Airlines—France
Airplane industry and trade—France
Airplanes, Military—France
Americans in France
Antibes
Astronomical observatories—France
Atomic power—France
Automobile industry and trade—France
Ballet—France
Bastille day
Birth rate—France
Books and reading—France
Brittany
Censorship—France
Cévennes
Colleges and universities—France
Crime and criminals—France
Dijon
Education—France
Electronic apparatus industry and trade—France
Finance—France
Forests and forestry—France
Government ownership—France
Hotels, taverns, etc.—France
Housing—France
Investments, Foreign (in France)
Jews in France
Labor laws and legislation—France
Liquor traffic—France
Lourdes
Marriage law—France
Medical service—France
Mégève, France
Moving picture industry—France
Music—France
Music festivals—France
National parks and reserves—France
Negroes in France

FRANCE—*See also—Continued*
Newspapers—France
Opera—France
Perigord
Periodicals—France
Political campaigns—France
Provence
Public health—France
Public opinion—France
Publishers and publishing—France
Radio broadcasting—France
Railroads—France
Restaurants—France
Road traffic—France
Saint-Tropez
Secret service—France
Space research—France
Sports—France
Strikes—France
Television broadcasting—France
Tourist trade—France
Trials—France
Vienne
Waterways—France

Antiquities

Cave man gets a new look; Les Eyzies, France, excavation; reprint. W. Sullivan. il Sci Digest 57:58-60 Ja '65
Solutrean culture. P. E. L. Smith. il Sci Am 211:86-94 Ag '64

Army

Army up in arms. D. Thomson. Nation 196: 232-3 Mr 16 '63
De Gaulle and the French army: a crisis in civil-military relations, by E. S. Furniss, jr. Review
Sat R 47:28+ Ap 4 '64. H. Lehrman
France and her army. G. F. Eliot. Nat R 15: 27 Jl 16 '63
From Napoleon's fall to de Gaulle. A. Werth. il Sat R 46:44-5 Je 22 '63

Foreign legion

From Camerone to Aubagne, the decline of the Legion. il Newsweek 61:50-1 My 13 '63

Bibliography

French books for children. S. B. Vogel. Library J 88:4428-33 N 15 '63

Civilization

Bohemian versus bourgeois, French society and the French man of letters in the nineteenth century, by C. Graña. Review
Commentary 38:88-90 S '64. J. G. Weightman
What's dimming the city of lights? tr. by B. Kerr. G. Bertil. Mlle 59:105+ O '64

Commerce

What next for the Common market? R. Grenier. Reporter 28:24-6 F 28 '63

Defenses

Alliance: whose grand design? il Newsweek 61:17-19 F 11 '63
Atlantic defense; de Gaulle has ideas of his own. L. Muray. New Repub 152:14-15 Ja 9 '65
Atomic Don Quixote. Newsweek 62:70-1 O 21 '63
Big mirage; independent nuclear force. New Repub 148:11 Ap 20 '63
De Gaulle rejects unarmed Polaris, reaffirms independent force plan. Aviation W 78:39 Ja 21 '63
De Gaulle speaks: the answer is no; with report by E. Weintal. Newsweek 62:29-30 Ag 12 '63
De Gaulle vs. NATO. Newsweek 62:32 Jl 1 '63
De Gaulle's double no, single yes. A. Rothberg. Christian Cent 80:334-5 Mr 13 '63
France earmarks $5.4 billion for nuclear force development. Aviation W 81:31 N 23 '64
France: the hard facts of nuclear life; with reports by L. Collins and E. Weintal. il Newsweek 61:39-40 Ap 15 '63
France's nuclear sword; nuclear-armed supersonic bombers. il Bsns W p34+ F 23 '63
French army officials criticize air force try for tactical role. Aviation W 82:28 Ja 25 '65
French logic vs. computers. T. D. White. Newsweek 61:24 F 11 '63
French may alter strike forces by including strategic missiles. Aviation W 79:37 N 18 '63
French missile force confirmed. Aviation W 81:25 N 16 '64
French study air-launched missile to augment Polaris-type weapons. R. E. Farrell. Aviation W 78:34 F 4 '63
From Devil's Island to Cape de Gaulle. il Time 85:25 Ja 8 '65
General de Gaulle: pro and con. America 108:628 My 4 '63
Government by disdain. R. Aron. New Repub 148:7-8 F 2 '62; Correction. 148:31 F 23 '63
N for nothing? French quest for an H-bomb. il Newsweek 61:67 Ap 22 '63
Nuclear timetable. Newsweek 61:47+ My 13 '63
Operational Polaris-type French sub fleet ten years away. F. G. McGuire. Miss & Roc 13:18 N 18 '63
SA 330 reflects French mobility concept. il Aviation W 79:46-7 Jl 29 '63
Sud-aviation at work on family of five rockets. il Miss & Roc 13:25 Jl 8 '63
Sud planning twin-turbine assault helicopter; ducted fans possible. il Aviation W 78:34 Ap 15 '63
Unmelted ice. Newsweek 61:40 Ap 29 '63
What France is out to get. R. Kleiman. il Read Digest 84:100-4 Ja '64

Description and travel

Down the Seine. V. S. Pritchett. il Holiday 34:62-7+ N '63
Gastronomic tour of France. W. Root. il House B 105:150-1+ Mr '63
Picturesque Perigord. M. Gardner. il Travel 122:28-31+ Ag '64
Romanesque runaround. A. C. Schmidt. il Reporter 32:36-8 Ja 14 '65
Sketching tour of France. J. Nielsen. il Am Artist 28:20-5+ Ap '64

Economic conditions

Balancing act; fight against inflation. Newsweek 61:72+ Mr 11 '63
Certain malady. Time 81:33 Ap 12 '63
Changes in France signal bigger sales by U.S. il Nations Bsns 52:76 S '64
De Gaulle's France: grandeur but not enough plumbing. il U S News 57:70-1 Ag 24 '64
France: planned expansion outspeeds itself. il Bsns W p58 Mr 16 '63
Le grand quartermaster. Newsweek 62:50-1 S 23 '63
Letter from France; the technocratic age. B. de Jouvenel. Bul Atomic Sci 20:27-9 O '64
Letter from Paris. Genêt. New Yorker 39: 184 S 14 '63
See also
Wages—France

Economic policy

De Gaulle's war against inflation. il Bsns W p62+ S 21 '63
France: rigid controls keep the lid on inflation. Bsns W p 124 Jl 11 '64
French new deal. V. E. Mares. bibliog f Cur Hist 45:276-82+ N '63
French slap at U.S. investment. Bsns W p 149 O 24 '64
Growth without inflation. New Repub 149:8 S 28 '63

Economic relations

After Brussels. E. Taylor. Reporter 28:29-32 F 14 '63
De Gaulle's new Europe: meaning to Britain, U.S. il U S News 54:66-7 F 4 '63
French have a stake in both Vietnams. Bsns W p86 S 28 '63
Political evolution of Europe; news conference, January 14, 1963. C. de Gaulle. Vital Speeches 29:230-5 F 1 '63
Question at issue; address, January 29, 1963. M. Couve de Murville. Vital Speeches 29: 333-4 Mr 15 '63

Foreign relations

Alliance: whose grand design? il Newsweek 61:17-19 F 11 '63
Atlantic report. Atlan 213:24+ Ja; 14+ My '64
Behind De Gaulle's veiled threats. E. Taylor. il Reporter 31:30+ N 19 '64
Bridge builder. Time 83:22 Ja 17 '64
Can de Gaulle shape Europe to his mold? Bsns W p82-3+ Ja 26 '63
Crystallization of Gaullism. Nat R 14:97 F 12 '63
Cursing de Gaulle is not a policy. S. Hoffmann. Reporter 30:38-41 Ja 30 '64
Decisions of France; address, February 24, 1964. H. Alphand. Vital Speeches 30:328-31 Mr 15 '64
De Gaulle and Asia. Nation 198:157 F 17 '64
De Gaulle and the future of the western alliance. Sr Schol 82:6-9+ Mr 27 '63
De Gaulle at Trier: the oracle speaks. E. Taylor. il Reporter 30:25-7 Je 18 '64
De Gaulle charts a collision course. il Bsns W p 130+ N 14 '64
De Gaulle keeps the pot bubbling. il Newsweek 63:37 My 11 '64

FRANCE—Foreign relations—*Continued*
De Gaulle pushes global ambitions. il Bsns W p23-4 Ja 11 '64
De Gaulle speaks: the answer is no; with report by E. Weintal. Newsweek 62:29-30 Ag 12 '63
De Gaulle, the seducer. J. Burnham. Nat R 14:232 Mr 26 '63; Reply. O. von Habsburg. 14:424 My 21 '63
De Gaulle: today China, tomorrow. . . Newsweek 63:31 F 3 '64
De Gaulle's bid to red China. J. B. Sheerin. Cath World 198:332-4 Mr '64
De Gaulle's bold gambits. A. Werth. Nation 198:339-42 Ap 6 '64
De Gaulle's double no, single yes. A. Rothberg. Christian Cent 80:334-5 Mr 13 '63
De Gaulle's France on the road to neutralism; tr. by J. Burnham; discussion. Nat R 14: 171-2 F 26 '63
De Gaulle's pursuit of grandeur; excerpt from American foreign policy. D. Brandon. Cath World 199:224-9 Jl '64
De Gaulle's Romanian gambit. E. Taylor. il Reporter 31:41-3 Ag 13 '64
De Gaulle's world view. A. Werth. Nation 198:195-7 F 24 '64
Detente and French policy; address, October 22, 1963. M. H. Alphand. Vital Speeches 30: 55-7 N 1 '63
Europe: storm signals; defiant de Gaulle threatens western unity; with reports by E. Weintal, L. Norman and A. de Borchgrave. il Newsweek 64:40-2+ N 30 '64
France and war: a 150-year record. il U S News 56:43 F 17 '64
France of Charles de Gaulle. E. W. Fox. Cur Hist 47:332-8+ D '64
France under de Gaulle; a former premier speaks out; interview, ed. by A. J. Meyers. G. Mollet. il U S News 55:126-7 O 14 '63
Franco-German axis: an end or beginning? il Newsweek 61:29+ F 4 '63
French foreign policy; address, October 29, 1963. M. Couve de Murville. Vital Speeches 30:72-5 N 15 '63
French foreign policy; address, November 3, 1964. M. Couve de Murville. Vital Speeches 31:101-5 D 1 '64
French people and de Gaulle. M. Gordey. il For Affairs 42:546-58 Jl '64
French recipe for folly. E. J. Hughes. Newsweek 62:15 Jl 15 '63
Friction with our fractious friends. Newsweek 63:27 Ja 20 '64
Future of Europe. America 108:218 F 16 '63
Gaullism. E. J. Hughes. Newsweek 64:23 N 30 '64
Gaullist explosion. W. Lippmann. Newsweek 61:11 F 4 '63
Gaullist revolt against the Anglo-Saxons. C. V. Crabb, jr. bibliog f Ann Am Acad 351: 15-23 Ja '64
General de Gaulle: pro and con. America 108:623 My 4 '63
General takes the stage again. il Newsweek 64:33 Jl 13 '64
Government by disdain. R. Aron. New Repub 148:7-8 F 2 '63; Correction. 148:31 F 23 '63
He may be right about China but wrong about Europe. L. J. Halle. New Repub 150:16-18 F 22 '64
How de Gaulle sees things. J. Burnham. Nat R 16:863 O 6 '64
In splendor he shakes up the world; de Gaulle's conference announcing new neutralist course. H. Moffett. il Life 56:18-27 F 14 '64
Letter from Paris. Genêt. New Yorker 40:58+ D 26 '64
Lifting the rug; de Gaulle's drive for a French-led Europe. Newsweek 63:31-2 Mr 2 '64
Minuet of the powers. il Newsweek 64:46+ N 9 '64
Nationalism; strength of France; address, April 28, 1964. M. Couve De Murville. Vital Speeches 30:487-90 Je 1 '64
New & obscure destination; de Gaulle's veto of Britain's admission to the Common market. il Time 81:22+ F 8 '63; Same abr. with title De Gaulle corners the market. Read Digest 82:65-70 Ap '63
No. one problem for Johnson. Nat R 16:1002 N 17 '64
NATO meets; divided and disordered. Newsweek 62:25-6 D 23 '63
One man? General de Gaulle. Nation 196:109 F 9 '63
Patching up the Atlantic alliance. Bsns W p 132 Ap 27 '63
Pebbles in the pond. il Time 83:26-30 F 7 '64
Pinpricks by de Gaulle. il Newsweek 63: 40+ Mr 16 '64
Placing General de Gaulle. R. Aron. New Repub 148:8-9 Mr 16 '63
Remembering Rac. S. Alsop. Sat Eve Post 237:19 Je 27 '64
Repeat performance; de Gaulle press conference. Newsweek 64:36 Ag 3 '64
Report from Washington: watching de Gaulle. H. Brandon. Sat R 47:14 F 22 '64
Rift in West: how serious. il U S News 54: 29-30 F 11 '63
Road to Moscow: de Gaulle and the Kremlin. C. Cate. il Atlan 212:65-71 Ag '63
Spirit of nationalism. Commonweal 77:503 F 8 '63
Stalked and cussed at, de Gaulle has a case. G. Farmer. il Life 54:34 Mr 1 '63
Standing alone; is de Gaulle right again? excerpt. P. L. Graham. Newsweek 61:34-5 F 25 '63
To NATO's brink; French position. Time 84: 54 N 13 '64
Voices of silence. E. Taylor. Reporter 30:12 F 13 '64
What de Gaulle really wants. M. Gordey. il Look 28:38-42+ My 19 '64
What de Gaulle sees ahead. il U S News 54: 55 F 11 '63
What France is out to get. R. Kleiman. il Read Digest 84:100-4 Ja '64
What of the grand design? R. Aron. New Repub 148:8-9 F 16 '63
What's de Gaulle up to? M. Ascoli. Reporter 30:22-3 F 27 '64
Why de Gaulle is challenging U.S; interview. M. C. de Murville. il U S News 56:70-5 Mr 16 '64

Algeria

Ben Bella's approach misfires in Algeria. Bsns W p65+ O 19 '63
Evian treaty; Ben Bella laughing at de Gaulle? G. Laffly. il Nat R 15:392-5 N 5 '63
One-man rule in Algeria. C. Sterling. il Reporter 29:32+ O 10 '63

Asia

New confrontation? il Newsweek 62:28-9 D 30 '63

Asia, Southeastern

De Gaulle on Vietnam. R. Steel. Commonweal 80:141-3 Ap 24 '64
France's stake in South Asia. il U S News 56:64 Je 29 '64

China (People's Republic)

About-face in Paris. Newsweek 63:44 F 24 '64
C'est moi, de Gaulle. Nat R 16:97 F 11 '64; Reply. V. Petrov. 16:205 Mr 10 '64
Chiang lets de Gaulle get off the hook. U S News 56:8 F 24 '64
Chinese checkers; projected recognition of red China. Time 83:25 Ja 31 '64
Cold slap; France will soon recognize red China. Time 83:23-4 Ja 24 '64
De Gaulle and China. J. O'Gara. Commonweal 79:618 F 21 '64
De Gaulle and red China. J. Daniel. New Repub 150:9-11 F 1 '64
De Gaulle recognizes Peking. E. M. von Kuehnelt-Leddihn. Nat R 16:152 F 25 '64
De Gaulle, red China and the U.N. Sat Eve Post 237:76 F 29 '64
De Gaulle's Chinese folly. Life 56:4 Ja 31 '64
Embassy row. il Newsweek 63:36-7 Mr 9 '64
France does what comes naturally. K. H. Miller. New Repub 151:13 S 5 '64
France nods to red China. Sr Schol 84:5 F 14 '64
France takes the plunge: recognition of red China. Bsns W p26 F 1 '64
France's bow to China; recognition of Communist China. il Bsns W p27-8 Ja 25 '64
Gaullist grand design. America 110:184-5 F 8 '64
In defense of Charles de Gaulle. J. Grigg. il N Y Times Mag p 14+ F 23 '64
Paris and Peking. E. J. Hughes. Newsweek 63:17 F 10 '64
Put up or shut up. J. Burnham. Nat R 16: 150 F 25 '64
Recognizing China. New Repub 150:5 F 1 '64
Round one to Peking. Time 83:37 F 21 '64
Sighting in on de Gaulle; newspaper comment. Time 83:60 F 7 '64
To lead or to follow. Nation 198:109 F 3 '64
What does de Gaulle intend to do? recognition of Communist China. Christian Cent 81:163 F 5 '64
What's de Gaulle up to in Asia? il Sr Schol 84:16-20 Mr 6 '64
Why de Gaulle recognized red China; summary of news conference. C. de Gaulle. U S News 56:12 F 10 '64

FRANCE—Foreign relations—*Continued*

Germany (Federal Republic)

Aftermath of a Common market veto. il Sr Schol 82:5 F 20 '63
Calculated chill. Newsweek 64:50+ S 28 '64
Common market: a Noël from France? il Newsweek 62:21 D 30 '63
Franco-German accord. il Sr Schol 82:21 F 6 '63
Old frontier; Franco-German cooperation treaty. il Newsweek 62:32-3 Jl 15 '63
Putting the squeeze on Germany. il Newsweek 64:45 N 23 '64
Reconciliation at Rambouillet. Time 85:24 Ja 29 '65
Squeeze play. il Newsweek 65:28+ F 1 '65
Strictly protocol; Chancellor L. Erhard's visit to de Gaulle. Newsweek 62:58+ D 2 '63
Unvisit. Time 82:26 Jl 12 '63

Great Britain

Blow to European unity: Britain gets a no; with editorial comment. il Bsns W p23-4, 100 F 2 '63
One more wedge between Britain and France. U S News 54:10 Mr 18 '63
When England offered everything to France; excerpt. P. Reynaud. il Sat R 46:26-8 Mr 16 '63

Iran

Charles at the Peacock Throne. il Time 82:36+ O 25 '63
Tour de (third) force. Newsweek 62:34 O 28 '63

Latin America

De Gaulle saddles up for South America. Bsns W p30 S 19 '64
De Gaulliver's travel: good-will tour to Latin America. il Time 84:66 O 2 '64
Grandstand play down Mexico way. il Life 56:24-5 Mr 27 '64
Home with trumpet & spurs; de Gaulle home after tour of South America. il Time 84:38 O 23 '64
On the long, hot road with General de Gaulle; tour of South America. il Newsweek 64:76+ O 5 '64
Why de Gaulle is making his big tour; to Latin America. il U S News 57:27 O 5 '64

Mexico

Big day in Mexico. K. Crawford. Newsweek 63:34 Mr 23 '64
De Gaulle to Mexico. Sr Schol 84:32 Ap 3 '64
De Gaulle's Mexican hat dance. G. Delmas. Reporter 30:30-2 Ap 23 '64
Latins together; de Gaulle's visit to Mexico. Newsweek 63:38+ Mr 23 '64
This is now being done; de Gaulle's official visit. il Time 83:28 Mr 27 '64
Tour de force: de Gaulle in Mexico. il Newsweek 63:33-4 Mr 30 '64
What did de Gaulle's invasion achieve? il U S News 56:14 Mr 30 '64

Russia

Heaven-sent wedge? Newsweek 61:37+ Mr 4 '63
Paris loves Moscow? Newsweek 63:41-2 Ap 13 '64

Spain

De Gaulle and Franco. New Repub 149:13-14 D 14 '63
New chums. Newsweek 63:50 Je 15 '64

United States

Case pro and con de Gaulle. L. Markel. il N Y Times Mag p 19+ Ja 10 '65
De Gaulle: just who he is and what's back of him. il U S News 57:24-6 D 28 '64
De Gaulle: trouble from an ally. U S News 57:31-2 D 7 '64
Détente cordiale? Time 83:42 Je 12 '64
France and the U.S: talking again? Newsweek 62:41 O 14 '63
France and the western alliance; address, October 29, 1963. J. W. Fulbright. Vital Speeches 30:75-8 N 15 '63
France: the hard facts of nuclear life; with reports by L. Collins and E. Weintal. il Newsweek 61:39-40 Ap 15 '63
In France, a whispering campaign against U.S; and some shouts. U S News 54:69 F 4 '63
International outlook; de Gaulle shakes a big stick at U.S. policies. Bsns W p81-2 F 9 '63
Letter from Paris; Franco-American rift. Genêt. New Yorker 40:155-8 Mr 21 '64
Letter from Paris; summary of address. G. Pompidou. New Yorker 40:143-4 Mr 7 '64
Meeting of two minds. M. Ascoli. Reporter 28:22-3 F 28 '63
Memories that irk de Gaulle. il U S News 56:57 Mr 30 '64
Politics of glory. M. Harrington. il Commonweal 77:613-16 Mr 8 '63
Reading de Gaulle's mind. R. Aron. New Repub 148:12-13 My 4 '63
U.S. puzzle: what's de Gaulle up to? U S News 56:36 Je 22 '64
What de Gaulle and JFK have in common. J. Daniel. New Repub 149:5-6 O 19 '63
Why the French mistrust us. B. B. Fall. il N Y Times Mag p6+ S 6 '64
Words, words, words. Newsweek 61:40 Ap 8 '63

Viet Nam (Republic)

De Gaulle's Vietnam. J. Daniel. New Repub 149:7-9 S 14 '63
Showdown in Vietnam; all-out fight ahead? il Bsns W p28-9 F 8 '64
What de Gaulle actually said about Vietnam. B. Fall. Reporter 29:39-41 O 24 '63; Reply with rejoinder. C. Wolf, jr. 29:6+ D 19 '63
Why the brush-off? Nation 197:149 S 21 '63
Why U.S. is losing in Vietnam, an inside story; interview. S. T. Williams. il U S News 57:62-4+ N 9 '64

Historic houses, etc.

Romantic realities. F. P. Keyes. il Travel 121:48-50 Ap '64

History

See also
World war, 1939-1945—France

Bibliography

Articles and other books received; comp. by B. F. Hyslop. See issues of American historical review

1789-1815

Bonaparte in Egypt, by J. C. Herold. Review
Time il 81:124+ Ap 19 '63

Revolution

Paris in the terror: June 1793-July 1794, by S. Loomis. Review
Reporter 30:42+ Ap 23 '64. S. Eimerl

February revolution, 1848

Changing outlines of 1848. P. Amann. bibiog f Am Hist R 68:938-53 Jl '63
Exiled revolutionaries and the French political police in the 1850's. H. C. Payne and H. Grosshans. bibliog f Am Hist R 68:954-73 Jl '63

July revolution, 1830

Crowd in the French revolution of 1830. D. H. Pinkney. bibliog f Am Hist R 70:1-17 O '64

Second empire, 1852-1870

Exiled revolutionaries and the French political police in the 1850's. H. C. Payne and H. Grosshans. bibliog f Am Hist R 68:954-73 Jl '63

European war, 1914-1918

See European war, 1914-1918—France

German occupation, 1940-1945

Day Paris was liberated; August 25, 1944. L. Collins and D. Lapierre. il N Y Times Mag p23-5+ Ag 23 '64
Pétain of Verdun, of Vichy, of history. H. Giniger. il N Y Times Mag p94-5+ N 15 '64

Industries

Bearish about Bull. Newsweek 63:62+ Mr 2 '64
Boss is a money man; Rhone-Poulenc, France's chemical and textile giant. il Bsns W p80+ Jl 18 '64
Bravo for Libby; biggest of European canneries at Vauvert. il Newsweek 64:78+ O 19 '64
Bubbling with ideas; champagne industry. il Bsns W p30-2 N 16 '63
Business is bubbling; Source Perrier. il Time 83:77 Ja 3 '64
Crystal anniversary; Baccarat, celebrating its 200th. il Newsweek 63:79 Je 15 '64
Launching Europe into space; Air liquide. il Bsns W p66-7+ N 2 '63
Michelin the mysterious; Compagnie générale des établissements Michelin. Newsweek 62:68+ S 9 '63
Schneider affair. il Time 82:108 O 11 '63
See also
Cattle industry and trade
Coal mines and mining—France
Steel industry and trade—France

FRANCE—*Continued*

Intellectual life

See also
French literature

Nobility

Crown and the aristocracy in renaissance France. J. R. Major. bibliog f Am Hist R 69:631-45 Ap '64
Provincial noble: a reappraisal. R. Forster. bibliog f Am Hist R 68:681-91 Ap '63

Parliament

Letter from Paris. Genêt. New Yorker 39:72 Je 29 '63

Politics and government

After five years, de Gaulle still towers. S. R. Graubard. il N Y Times Mag p 12+ D 15 '63
Again the assassins. il Newsweek 61:36+ F 25 '63
Après de Gaulle. Time 81:24 My 31 '63
Après moi? moi! il Time 82:41 O 4 '63
Atlantic report. Atlan 211:22+ F '63; 213:14+ My '64
Beginning a dialogue; presidential campaign. il Time 83:24 F 14 '64
Brotherhood; inner Gaullist mysteries. Time 82:26+ Jl 5 '63
Challenger talks back to President de Gaulle. H. Giniger. il N Y Times Mag p25+ Mr 15 '64
Charles de Gaulle, grand master of France. Read Digest 82:101-6 F '63
De Gaulle's challenger. New Repub 150:6-7 Mr 21 '64
De Gaulle's non! a year later. L. J. Halle. il N Y Times Mag p 14-15+ Ja 12 '64
De Gaulle's world view. A. Werth. Nation 198:195-7 F 24 '64
De Gaulle's would-be assassins. R. Barrat. Commonweal 77:663-4 Mr 22 '63
Focus on France; photographs. N Y Times Mag p28-9 Ap 7 '63
France: a third force? E. Taylor. Reporter 30:24-6 F 27 '64
France changes, but not Frenchmen. A. Maurois. il N Y Times Mag p33+ N 24 '63
France of Charles de Gaulle. E. W. Fox. Cur Hist 47:332-8+ D '64
France under de Gaulle; a former premier speaks out; interview, ed. by A. J. Meyers. G. Mollet. il U S News 55:126-7 O 14 '63
France's ban-the-bombers. S. Gervis. Nation 197:91-3 Ag 24 '63
France's Faure; power behind the Gaullist scene. H. de Turenne. il N Y Times Mag p29+ Ap 26 '64
Gaullist view. A. Rothberg. Christian Cent 80:1427-9 N 20 '63
General who is king; Charles de Gaulle. il Bsns W p90-1+ My 9 '64
Ghost from the past; proposed Socialist and Communist electoral alliance. il Time 82:46 N 15 '63
Guessing game. Newsweek 63:42 Ap 27 '64
If it happened to de Gaulle. . . il Time 82:37 D 6 '63
Letter from Paris. Genêt. New Yorker 39:60+ Ag 17 '63; 40:58+ D 26 '64
Letter from Paris; Gaullist price-stabilization project. Genêt. New Yorker 39:156+ S 28 '63
Long shot bucks de Gaulle; with report by H. Moffett. il Life 56:71-2+ Ap 3 '64
More reflections on Gaullist France. G. M. Pepper. Nat R 15:239-40 S 24 '63
New challenger? il Time 82:23 D 27 '63
New French politics. R. C. Macridis. Yale R 52:352-65 Mr '63
New left Marxism. G. Lichtheim. Commentary 35:239-43 Mr '63
Politics of glory. M. Harrington. il Commonweal 77:613-16 Mr 8 '63
Preview of a candidate: G. Defferre. il Time 83:39-40 Ap 3 '64
Three for the mantle; de Gaulle's successor. il Newsweek 61:53 Je 17 '63
Toujours de Gaulle. America 110:73 Ja 18 '64
Why Gaston Defferre? J. Daniel. Harper 229:85-8+ Jl '64

See also
Communist party (France)
Elections—France
France—Parliament
Presidents—France
Socialist party (France)

Population

Youngest daughter. America 108:185 F 9 '63

Relief work

They give a donkey; Secours catholique, the Catholic charities of France, sponsors small-scale projects in Africa. America 108:701 My 18 '63

Religious institutions and affairs

France prepares for Billy Graham. Y. Chabas. Christian Cent 80:614-15 My 8 '63

Social conditions

Nicean standoff; Algerian gangs. Time 84:42 S 11 '64

See also
Peasantry—France

Social life and customs

Baron Edmond de Rothschild's party; Mont d'Arbois hotel above Mégève. F. de Langlade. il Vogue 141:162-5 Mr 15 '63
Oyster and the book. E. Clark. Yale R 52:366-72 Mr '63
Personal touch: De Gaulle's influence on society. il Time 81:32-3 Mr 8 '63
Waltz of les Gaullistes. P. Viansson-Ponté. il Esquire 62:104-6+ O '64

Treaties

Dream comes true for two old rivals. il U S News 54:19 F 4 '63
Franco-German treaty of reconciliation. Cur Hist 44:237-9+ Ap '63
Impact of the Franco-German entente; address, April 6, 1963; with questions and answers. H. C. Deutsch. Ann Am Acad 348:82-94 Jl '63
Shadows on the success of Der Alte. D. Schorr. Reporter 28:27-8 F 28 '63

Underground organizations

See World war, 1939-1945—Underground movements—France

FRANCE (ship) See Ocean liners

FRANCE and Europe. See Europe and France

FRANCE and the United States
A l'américaine. il Newsweek 63:48+ My 25 '64
Detente and French policy; address, October 22, 1963. M. H. Alphand. Vital Speeches 30:55-7 N 1 '63
See also
Americans in France

FRANCEKEVICH, Al
Crash course in color. il Pop Phot 53:45-57+ Jl '63
Francekevich on portraiture. il Pop Phot 53:132-5+ N '63
How to use Polacolor with speedlight & flashbulbs. Pop Phot 52:61 Mr '63
In the darkroom. See issues of Popular photography
One-light setups. il Pop Phot 52:43-5+ Ja '63
Roundup: new lights. il Pop Phot 52:58-61+ Ja '63
Two new color films: Kodachrome-X. Pop Phot 52:18-19+ Mr '63

FRANCHI, Sergio
Present incumbent. por Time 83:66 Ap 3 '64

FRANCHISE system (business) See Exclusive agencies

FRANCILLON, Jacques Jacquet-. See Jacquet-Francillon, J.

FRANCIS of Assisi, Saint
Paintings of the life of St Francis in Assisi, by L. Tintori and M. Meiss. Review
Art N 63:52+ O '64. J. H. Beck

FRANCIS Joseph I, emperor of Austria
Fall of the House of Habsburg, by E. Crankshaw. Review
Reporter 29:46+ D 19 '63. S. Eimerl
Franz Josef: a Habsburg marriage. L. Bemelmans. Holiday 35:68-9+ Ja '64
Last years of splendor. E. Kern. il pors Life 55:76-7 N 22 '63

FRANCIS Joseph II, prince of Liechtenstein
Happy have-not. il por Time 82:30 Ag 23 '63

FRANCIS Ferdinand, archduke of Austria
Local, personal affair. C. G. Pepper. il Newsweek 64:37-8 Jl 13 '64
Murder that started World war I. R. S. Feuerlicht. il por Sat Eve Post 237:80-1+ Je 27 '64
Sarajevo fifty years after; consequences of the assassination of the archduke. V. Dedijer. bibliog f For Affairs 42:569-84 Jl '64
Sarajevo revisited, fifty years after. J. A. Barry. il por N Y Times Mag p 12-13+ Je 28 '64

FRANCIS, Brendan
(comp) Spreads. N Y Times Mag p69-70 N 29 '64

FRANCIS, Clarence
Lincoln Center and corporate support. por Mus Am 84:10 O '64

FRANCIS, Henry S. jr
Some views concerning the development of Mount McKinley National Park. Nat Parks Mag 37:18-19 S '63
FRANCIS A. Countway library of medicine, Boston
Opening the chambered nautilus; evaluation of uncataloged material. L. Ash. il Library J 89:2040-3 My 15 '64
FRANCISCO, Don
Bad Bascom. Hot Rod 16:48-51+ Jl '63
Bonneville wrap-up. Hot Rod 17:80-6+ Ja '64
Bonneville's most unusual streamliner. Hot Rod 16:48-53+ Mr '63
Cheetah; new GT prowler. il Hot Rod 17: 70-5+ Mr '64
Chevy on a stick. il Hot Rod 16:80-3+ Ag '63
Chevys in the Indy lineup. il Hot Rod 16:34-9+ O '63
Class A terror. il Hot Rod 16:82-4+ D '63
Go get 'em Corvair. il Hot Rod 16:32-5+ S '63
Handlebar hustler. Hot Rod 16:94-8 Ap '63
Harley-Davidson's salt shakers. Hot Rod 17: 48-51 Ag '64
Hayden Proffitt's stock car secrets. il Hot Rod 16:32-7 Mr '63
Jet age. Hot Rod 18:36-43+ Ja '65
Little Chevy makes a lot o' jeep. Hot Rod 16:76-81 My '63
Mickey-go-round. il Hot Rod 16:108-10 F '63
New thunder for an old bird. il Hot Rod 16: 42-5+ F '63
Rod alert! Hot Rod 17:46-51+ D '64
Spirit of America. il Hot Rod 16:26-33 O '63
Tune-up tips: Ford's 427. Hot Rod 16:71-5 Ag '63
FRANCISCO, Dorothy G.
Everybody's lonesome. Parents Mag 38:136 Ap '63
FRANCISCUS, James
Mr Novak cuts class; ed. by E. Miller. pors Seventeen 23:140-1+ S '64
about
Can Mr Novak keep the teachers happy? S. Gordon. il pors Look 28:111-13+ O 6 '64
FRANCK, Frederick
Art and anti-art; concerning drawings of Vatican council II. C. J. McNaspy. America 108:419-20 Mr 23 '63
Sunday painters; excerpts from My eye is in love. Harper 227:32+ O '63
FRANCK, James
James Franck, 1882-1964. E. Rabinowitch. por Bul Atomic Sci 20:16-20 O '64
FRANCO, Francisco
After twenty-five years, Franco is still a sphinx. P. Hofmann. il pors N Y Times Mag p21+ Ap 19 '64
Atlantic report. Atlan 214:24+ O '64
Franco and Pope Paul. Christian Cent 80: 995-6 Ag 14 '63; Discussion. 80:1276 O 16 '63
Franco to the cortes; reference to Catholic dissatisfaction with his authoritarian rule. America 111:80 Jl 25 '64
Misdirected fire. America 111:100 Ag 1 '64
Next miracle country. F. Painton. il por U S News 54:71-5 My 20 '63
Spain emerges from isolation. R. M. Smith. Cur Hist 47:345-9+ D '64
Spain's long, hard look at tomorrow. il por Sr Schol 82:9-11 Mr 20 '63
Twenty-five years ago in Madrid. il por Newsweek 63:42-3 Ap 13 '64
Voter no. forty-one does his duty. il por Time 82:45 N 15 '63
FRANCO Colombo, incorporated. See Music publishing
FRANCO-ENGLISH war, 1755-1763. See United States—History—French and Indian war, 1755-1763
FRANCO-GERMAN entente. See France—Treaties
FRANCOEUR, Robert T.
Approach to the problem of birth control. Commonweal 81:104 O 16 '64
On love. Commonweal 79:489-90 Ja 24 '64
Price we pay. Commonweal 79:538-42 Ja 31 '64
FRANÇOIS, Andre
Hardy St Moritz; paintings. Sports Illus 22:34-8 Ja 25 '65
FRANCOIS, Bill
Short circuits and fuses. Motor B 111:37-8+ Mr '63
Why's and how's of raw and pre-recorded tape. U S Camera 26:78-9 Mr '63
—See Buckwalter, L. jt. auth.
FRANCOIS, William
West Virginia: the first front. Reporter 30: 21-2 F 13 '64
FRANCOMBE, M. H.
Crystal films. Science 141:364 Jl 26 '63
FRANEY, Pierre
Howard Johnson's new flavor; food management program. il por Bsns W p 109-10+ O 19 '63
FRANK, Andrew Gunder
Brazil: exploitation or aid. Nation 197:318-23 N 16 '63
Brazil in perspective; the Goulart ouster. Nation 198:408-11 Ap 27 '64
FRANK, Gerold
Deed defended. Commentary 37:6+ Ja '64
Milton Berle. McCalls 91:94-7+ Mr '64
Thirty-nine. McCalls 90:90-1+ Ap '63
FRANK, Harriet, jr
And baby makes three; story. McCalls 90:88-9 Ag '63
FRANK, Isaiah
Foreign aid and the liberal dissent. New Repub 152:17-22 Ja 23 '65
International trade and economic development; statement, May 27, 1963. Dept State Bul 49:173-8 Jl 29 '63
Issues before the U.N. conference. For Affairs 42:210-26 Ja '64
FRANK, Stanley
Reassuring facts about the breast cancer controversy. Good H 158:96-7+ My '64
FRANK M. Chapman memorial hall of North American birds. See American museum of natural history, New York
FRANKE, Paul
Honest profession; interview, ed. by Q. Eaton. por Opera N 28:12 Ap 18 '64
FRANKE, Walter H.
Labor market experience of unemployed older workers. Mo Labor R 86:282-4 Mr '63
FRANKEL, Charles
Four illusions that beset us. N Y Times Mag p31+ S 22 '63
Is it ever right to break the law? N Y Times Mag p 17+ Ja 12 '64
Our far-flung correspondents. New Yorker 39:74+ My 25 '63; 40:136+ Je 6 '64
FRANKEL, Haskel
Hemisphere honors for fiction. Sat R 46:28-9 Jl 20 '63
On the fringe. See issues of Saturday review
FRANKEL, Max
China: what we know and don't know. N Y Times Mag p5-7+ Ag 2 '64
Communists in gray flannel suits. New Repub 151:7-8 O 31 '64
Intelligent woman's guide to politics in the Kremlin. McCalls 92:56+ N '64
Reform yes, revolution no. New Repub 151: 7-8 D 12 '64
Russia, revisited, is still a mystery. N Y Times Mag p34-5+ S 15 '63
Russian-Chinese struggle over who will bury us? Sat Eve Post 236:30+ Ap 13 '63; Same abr. with title Bitter feud that splits the Communist world. Read Digest 83:138-44 Ag '63
You can't go home to Weissenfels. N Y Times Mag p20-1+ Ja 10 '65
FRANKEL, Theodore
German whitewash. Commentary 36:401-2+; 37:12+ N '63, Mr '64
Soviet autobiography. Commentary 35:179-82+ F '63
FRANKEL, Tobi
Where Santa comes by troika. McCalls 92:62 D '64
FRANKENHEIMER, John
Criticism as creation. Sat R 47:12-13 D 26 '64
about
Big—bang bagatelle. il por Newsweek 63:112 Ap 20 '64
On screen. C. R. Jennings. por Horizon 5:34-5 Mr '63
FRANKENSTEIN, Alfred
Celebration at seventy; Szigeti's Prokofiev. Hi Fi 13:56-7 My '63
Rispetti e strambotti reappears. Hi Fi 14:64 Je '64
Schoenberg, from Pelléas to Genesis. Hi Fi 13:68-9 D '63
Stravinsky and San Francisco. Theatre Arts 47:22+ Mr '63
FRANKENTHALER, Helen
Two famous painters' collection. il por Vogue 143:88-91+ Ja 15 '64
FRANKFORT, Ind.
No weak spots. J. B. Wilson. il Am City 78:153+ My '63
FRANKFORT, Ky.
Notes for a gazetteer. P. Hamburger. New Yorker 40:159-60+ O 10 '64
FRANKFORT ON THE MAIN
Germans park and buy; Main-Taunus-Zentrum regional shopping center on outskirts of Frankfort. il Bsns W p58-60+ Ag 15 '64

FRANKFORT on the Main—*Continued*

City planning

Frankfurt: a big, three-dimensional grid for varied, flexible growth. il Arch Forum 121: 202-3 Ag '64

FRANKFURT book fair. See Book fairs

FRANKFURTER, Alfred M.
Big collecting in a small democracy. Art N 63:20-3+ S '64
Bologna-Rome-France: the classic ideal. Art N 61:35-7+ F '63
Il bon disegno from Chicago. Art N 62:28-31+ N '63
Carpaccio emerges an adventurous conservative. Art N 62:20-4+ S '63
Caviare? New York's newest museum. Art N 63:33-4+ Mr '64
Museum evaluations. Art N 63:26-9+ D '64; 24-7+ Ja '65
Opus anglicanum. Art N 62:22-5+ D '63

FRANKFURTER, Felix
Trips to Felix. G. Kanin. por Atlan 213:55-62 Mr '64; Same abr. with title Conversations with Felix. Read Digest 84:116-20 Je '64

FRANKFURTERS
Frankfurters. il Consumer Rep 29:428-31 S '64
Hot dog diet. M. Kaytor. il Look 27:38-9 Ag 13 '63
Sizzling hot dog barbecue. il Pop Gard 15:42 My '64
See also
Cookery—Meat

FRANKIEWICZ, Heinz
Textbook factory; Volk und wissen publishing company, East Berlin. H. Roske. Atlan 212:90-4 D '63

FRANKL, Viktor E.
Will to meaning. Christian Cent 81:515-17 Ap 22 '64

FRANKLAND, Mark
Khrushchev faces a Khrushchevian dilemma. N Y Times Mag p21+ My 12 '63

FRANKLIN, Adele
Christmas records for the young, 1964. Sat R 47:68-70 D 5 '64

FRANKLIN, Aretha
Swingin' Aretha. il pors Ebony 19:85+ Mr '64

FRANKLIN, Ben A. See Shuster, A. jt. auth.

FRANKLIN, Benjamin
Autobiography of Benjamin Franklin: the Puritan experimenter in life and art. D. Levin. Yale R 53:258-75 D '63
Man who invented himself. L. Leary. il Sat R 47:33 My 30 '64
Poor Richard's master: rich in accomplishments. il Sr Schol 83:7 Ja 17 '64
Thrift vs. borrowing, which way to good times? with excerpts from book by P. A. Samuelson. il por U S News 54:37-9 Mr 4 '63

FRANKLIN, H. H. car club. See Automobile clubs

FRANKLIN, Hardy
Day in Bedford Stuyvesant. E. Moon. il pors Library J 89:3689-93 O 1 '64
Joiner and goer; service to Bedford Stuyvesant area. K. Molz. il por Wilson Lib Bul 38:349-51 D '63

FRANKLIN, Hugh
Madeleine L'Engle. por Horn Bk 39:356-60 Ag '63

FRANKLIN, John Hope
John Hope Franklin at Cambridge; interview. il pors Ebony 18:160-2+ S '63

FRANKLIN, Kenneth L.
Gravitational forces and effects. Natur Hist 72:12-19 O; 44-51 N '63
Radio waves from Jupiter; with biographical sketch. Sci Am 211:14, 34-42 bibliog(p 142) Jl '64

FRANKLIN, Peter
Pour le sport. Flying 74:47+ Mr '64

FRANKLIN, Robert
Making parenthood possible. Redbook 124:50+ N '64

FRANKLIN, Robert D.
Game of chicken; reprint. por Library J 89:3918-19 O 15 '64

FRANKLIN, Stephen
English touch: Victoria. Holiday 35:74-5+ Ap '64

FRANKLIN, Virginia
Hell breaks loose in Paradise. il pors Life 54:73-82+ Ap 26 '63

FRANKLIN, Wendell
Breakthrough in Hollywood. il pors Ebony 19:82-4+ D '63

FRANKLIN automobile company
Special-interest cars: Franklin. D. Earnshaw. il Motor T 16:78 N '64

FRANKLIN book programs, incorporated
Bradford Wiley chairman of Franklin book programs. Pub W 186:33 O 19 '64
Franklin book program for the U.S.? F. Jennings. Sat R 47:43 D 19 '64
Franklin training program starts next month; first of Franklin book programs' seminars. Pub W 186:88 S 28 '64
Franklin's first ten years of global publishing aid. R. H. Smith. Pub W 184:34 S 30 '63
Name changed to Franklin book programs. Pub W 185:34 Mr 2 '64
Oil for the lamps of knowledge. J. E. Daily. il Library J 89:4483-7 N 15 '64
Search for sample books. J. E. Daily. il Wilson Lib Bul 39:59-61+ S '64
Shah of Iran honors head of Franklin book programs. Pub W 186:32 N 30 '64
Ten years of Franklin publications. D. C. Smith, jr. ALA Bul 57:507-12 Je '63
U.S. training program set for overseas publishers. Pub W 186:151 Jl 13 '64

FRANKLIN D. ROOSEVELT LAKE. See Grand Coulee power and reclamation project

FRANKLIN Delano Roosevelt memorial. See Washington, D.C.—Monuments, statues, etc.

FRANKLIN institute, Philadelphia
Franklin medal to Seaborg. Sci N L 84:242 O 19 '63

FRANKLIN medal. See Franklin institute, Philadelphia

FRANKLIN publications, incorporated. See Franklin book programs, incorporated

FRANKLIN reversal; drama. See Boiko, C.

FRANKLINIAS
Franklinia. R. R. Thomasson. il Pop Gard 15:54 S '64
Franklinia, as a landscape plant. R. C. Hands. Horticulture 41:466 S '63
Still worth shouting about. il Flower Grower 50:47 Ag '63

FRANKLIN'S trees. See Franklinias

FRANKS, Maurice R.
Reform for the union movement? three writers suggest ways. por U S News 54:88-9 Je 24 '63

FRANKS, Oliver Shewell Franks, baron
B-schools for Britain. por Bsns W p84+ D 7 '63

FRANSETH, Jane
Research in grouping: a review. Sch Life 45:5-6 Je '63

FRANTZ, Forrest H. sr
Exalted pot. Pop Electr 21:71-2+ D '64
Hi-fi speaker system for $7.61. Pop Electr 20:61-3 Mr '64

FRANTZ, Laurent B.
Pacifica and the FCC: dangerous precedent. Nation 197:359-61 N 30 '63

FRANZ, Henry
Glass-ware patents by Henry Franz. A. G. Peterson. il Hobbies 68:82-3 F '64

FRANZBLAU, Abraham N.
Psychiatrist looks at Tiny Alice. Sat R 48:39 Ja 30 '65

FRANZEN, Ulrich
Seven new houses by Ulrich Franzen. il Arch Rec 134:127-42 N '63
Ulrich Franzen: architecture in transition. il por Arch Forum 118:139-45 My '63

FRAREY, Carlyle J.
Report of the committee on ALA publishing to the council. ALA Bul 58:630-1 Jl '64

FRARY, Mildred P.
Cooperative materials selection in a large city system. ALA Bul 57:155-6 F '63
School responsibility. Library J 89:3387-9 S 15 '64

FRASCONI, Antonio
Frasconi the printmaker. F. Getlein. New Repub 150:28-9 F 29 '64
Frasconi work is exhibited; he designs new U.S. stamp. P. A. Bennett. il Pub W 184:86+ Jl 1 '63
Portraits in wood; exhibition, Baltimore museum of art. il por N Y Times Mag p45 N 3 '63
Wizard of the woodcut. il por Time 82:60-1 D 20 '63

FRASE, Robert W. See Enoch, K. jt. auth.

FRASER, Dawn
Dawn keeps churning along. W. Tower. il pors Sports Illus 20:26-8+ F 17 '64

FRASER, Donald M.
Congress in the atomic age; interview, ed. by R. Steel. pors Sr Schol 82:16-18 F 20 '63

FRASER, H. J.
Mining new markets for nickel. il por Bsns W p62-4+ S 5 '64

FRASER, Sir Hugh
Man who snatched away a meal. por Time 84:36-7 N 6 '64

FRASER, Ian Forbes
International exchange. Wilson Lib Bul 39:415+ Ja '65

FRASER, Kathleen
How Tuesday began; poem. New Yorker 39:143 O 26 '63

FRASER, Kathleen—*Continued*
In praise of lust; poem. Nation 198:350 Ap 6 '64
Mattress mender; poem. New Yorker 39:201 O 12 '63

FRASER, Ronald
Clock watching genius; reprint. Sat R 47: 56-7 O 3 '64

FRASIER, Kathryn
Crystal for company; story. Seventeen 22: 116-17 N 63
Float with the current; story. Seventeen 22: 226-7 Ag '63
Who means more to you? story. Seventeen 23:164-5 N '64

FRATERNAL societies. See Benefit societies

FRATERNAL twins. See Twins

FRATERNITIES. See College fraternities; Negro fraternities

FRATTA, Italo, and others
Fetal death from nicotinamide-deficient diet and its prevention by chlorpromazine and imipramine. bibliog Science 145:1429-30 S 25 '64

Die **FRAU** ohne schatten; opera. See Strauss, R.

FRAUD
Airlines planning ticket swindle defense. J. W. Carter. Aviation W 80:26-9 Mr 23 '64
Annals of finance; Ira Haupt & co. affair. J. Brooks. New Yorker 40:160+ N 14 '64
Back home in handcuffs. il Newsweek 63:78 My 4 '64
Bankruptcy by ballot; A. A. Natin of Argentina. il Time 84:94 Jl 10 '64
Bankruptcy caper; case of Joseph Pagano. Newsweek 61:31 Je 10 '63
Beware of garden gyps (cont) B. Black. il Pop Gard 14:52+ Ap '63
Beware! the woods are full of tree quacks. J. M. Haller. il Pop Sci 184:127-9+ My '64
Beware! these frauds are aimed at you. il Good H 157:170 O '63
Billie's guilty again. Newsweek 61:24 Ap 8 '63
Bite; dental clinic in Hoboken, N.J. Newsweek 61:34-5 My 27 '63
Carrier concern mounting over rising ticket frauds and thefts. Aviation W 80:41 My 11 '64
Caveat emptor; pseudo liquidating. Time 83: 82-3 Ja 17 '64
Commodities: soybeans and salad oil; the greatest scandal in the history of Wall Street is still going on. P. Vanderwicken. il Esquire 61:91-3+ Ap '64
Companies Birrell left behind. il Bsns W p96+ My 2 '64
Corrupt society. F. J. Cook. Nation 196:485-96 Je 1 '63
Country slicker: J. E. Lofland. il Newsweek 62:28-9 Jl 8 '63
Donors warned against missionary swindlers. Christian Cent 80:796 Je 19 '63
Don't be panic-sold on fire alarms. C. L. Walker. il Read Digest 82:89-92 Ap '63
Federal jury indicts four over Calories don't count. Pub W 185:30 Mr 23 '64
$5,000,000 swindle; case of V. D. Dardi. il Time 81:95 Mr 15 '63
Fly now, pay never; stolen airlines tickets. Newsweek 63:80+ Mr 16 '64
Four against the Bank of England; condensation. A. H. Kings. il Read Digest 85: 195-200+ Ag '64
Frauds against the aged. Consumer Rep 28: 131 Mr '63
Giant jailed; F. Goergen, president of Henschel works, West Germany. il Time 83:89 My 8 '64
Greatest con man of all; S. Osman. J. Bryan, 3d. il Holiday 36:46+ D '64
Growing old in America: frauds, quackery, swindle the aged and compound their troubles. E. Langer. Science 140:470-2 My 3 '63
Hoffa again; question of Teamsters pension fund. Newsweek 61:26 Je 17 '63
How to get took in New York city. P. Mandel. il Life 56:97-8+ Je 19 '64
In wake of Haupt failure; second thoughts on commodities dealing. Bsns W p 128 D 7 '63
Lessons from the Haupt affair. Fortune 69: 74+ Ja '64
Mystique of paper. Nation 197:426-7 D 21 '63
Old shell game takes to the air; cashing in phony airline tickets. il Bsns W p 132+ Je 13 '64
$150 million in oil, all gone! soybean oil swindle. P. Mandel. il Life 56:90-2+ Ap 3 '64
100-million-dollar mystery? attempt to aid Ira Haupt and co. by New York stock exchange. il U S News 55:109-10 D 16 '63
Scandal in salad oil gets bigger every day; with editorial comment. il Bsns W p32+, 160 D 14 '63
Soviet shadow economy; vast illegal network of undercover dealings. J. M. Hochstein. il Reporter 30:27-31 Ap 9 '64
Spectacular rogue, by E. P. Hoyt. Review Newsweek 62:82-3 Jl 8 '63
Sure, we cheated; pétanque at Marseilles. Newsweek 61:51 F 11 '63
They took her for a $20,000 ride; fast-talking real-estate promoters. il Changing T 18:17-22 Ja '64
Ticket theft ring suspected in New York. W. H. Gregory. Aviation W 81:37+ N 23 '64
Tighter security for ticket stock urged. J. W. Carter. Aviation W 80:42 My 18 '64
Tino's bottomless tanks of oil; salad oil swindle. N. C. Miller. il Sat Eve Post 237: 19-25 Ap 25 '64
What happens to tax returns. U S News 56: 93-4 F 10 '64
What you should know about slick deals by mail. F. Bailey, jr. Suc Farm 62:54 F '64
When is a bargain not a bargain? Consumer Bul 46:23-4 O '63
Where genius went wrong; crude oil scandal. il Bsns W p 164-6+ Ap 18 '64
See also
Advertising, Fraudulent
Impostors and imposture
Insurance—Fraudulent claims
Politics, Corruption in
Quacks and quackery
Securities, Fraudulent
Trials (fraud)

FRAUDS, Literary. See Literary forgeries and mystifications

FRAUDULENT conveyances
When there's gold in bankruptcy. il Bsns W p52+ My 23 '64

FRAUDULENT voting. See Elections—Corrupt practices

FRAUENDORFER, Max
Himmler's adjutant. Newsweek 61:46+ F 11 '63

FRAYN, Michael
Youth on the prow, and marmalade at the helm; reprint. Vogue 141:86 My '63

FRAZER, John E.
Remarkable house of Tata. Read Digest 82: 248-52 Ap '63

FRAZIER, Alexander
Broadening the experience of the culturally disadvantaged. por ALA Bul 58:523-6 Je '64
Curriculum changes and the librarian; excerpts from address, October 1964. por Wilson Lib Bul 39:389-91 Ja '65
Learning in groups: some considerations. Sch Life 45:7-9 Je '63

FRAZIER, Brenda
My debut a horror. pors Life 55:133-4+ D 6 '63

FRAZIER, E. Franklin
New role of the Negro woman. por Ebony 18:88 S '63

FRAZIER, Elroy
510-pound strongboy. il pors Ebony 19:103-8 My '64

FRAZIER, James, Jr
Detroit acclaims James Frazier. C. W. Thomas. por Negro Hist Bul 28:28 N '64

FRAZIER, Jefferson
Smart southern politics. New Repub 148:5 F 23 '63

FRAZIER, John W.
Biggest bridge ever. Read Digest 85:266-70 N '64

FRAZIER, Robert B.
Lodge is Oregon's bride by mail. New Repub 150:9-10 My 9 '64

FRAZIER, Willard
Green thumb; story. Good H 157:68-9 Ag '63

FREAKS (animals) See Abnormalities (animals)

FREAS, Ralph
Faithful sound. Esquire 60:59+ N '63; 61:46+ Mr; 24+ My; 62:58+ S; 68+ N '64
Listen here! See issues of American home to July 1964
Shopping the home entertainment circuit. Am Home 67:85-7 D '64

FREBERG, Stan
Commercials for God. Time 82:50 Jl 12 '63
Stan Freberg, his private war. B. Davidson. por Sat Eve Post 236:56-7 F 9 '63

FRECHETTE, Alfred L.
Tetanus protection is important. Horticulture 42:15 D '64

FRECHTMAN, Bernard
(tr) See Sartre, J. P. Making of a writer; excerpt from The words

FRECKER, Jack E.
Operational amplifier. Electr World 70:52-4+ Jl; 48-9+ Ag '63

FRED Miller theater. See Milwaukee—Theater

FREDERIC G. Melcher book award
Melcher award for a work of religious liberalism. Pub W 185:107 Ja 20 '64
FREDERICK II, emperor of the Holy Roman empire
Makers of the sports page. P. Knauth. il por(p 34) Sports Illus 19:36+ S 16 '63
FREDERICK Augustus, duke of York and Albany
Notes and comment. New Yorker 39:19 Jl 6 '63
FREDERICK, Ellen
Passion flower. Horticulture 42:41 Ja '64
FREDERICK, Karl T.
AFA honors two solid citizens. il por Am For 69:34-5 O '63
Obituary
Am For por 69:7+ Mr '63
FREDERICK, Nan
Hot fires in Chile. Am For 70:28-9+ Mr '64
FREDERICK, Pauline
One battle I had to win; ed. by R. Hochstein. por Good H 156:86-7 My '63
FREDERICK A. Praeger, incorporated. See Praeger, Frederick A. incorporated
FREDERICKS, J. Wayne
American policy in Africa; address, July 7, 1964. Dept State Bul 51:197-203 Ag 10 '64
Nations in the making in Africa; address, October 23, 1963. Dept State Bul 49:783-6 N 18 '63
Our policy toward Africa; address, July 18, 1963. Dept State Bul 49:284-90 Ag 19 '63; Same. Vital Speeches 29:699-702 S 1 '63
United States supports economic cooperation in Africa; statement, February 25, 1964. Dept State Bul 50:510-13 Mr 30 '64
FREDERICKSON, William, jr
Blueprint for organization. por Recreation 57:410-14 O '64
FREDERIKA Louise, consort of Paul I, king of the Hellenes
Foolish display. il por Time 82:30+ Jl 19 '63
King wants to travel. por Time 81:29 Je 21 '63
Row over royalty. il por Time 84:32-3 O 9 '64
FREDETTE, Alfred
Expression through observation. Sch Arts 64:22 O '64
FREDRICK, Jerome F.
Dental caries: a new look. Science 147:419-21 Ja 22 '65
FREE choice; story. See Brennan, M.
FREE churches. See Congregationalism
FREE coupons. See Coupons
FREE enterprise
Abundance, threat or promise? R. Theobald. Nation 196:387-412 My 11 '63; Discussion. 196:inside cover Je 15 '63
American free enterprise system; address, November 21, 1963. E. F. Scoutten. Vital Speeches 30:269-73 F 15 '64
Are we gaining or guessing abroad? address, March 27, 1963. F. C. Foy. Vital Speeches 29:421-5 My 1 '63
Dream businessmen are losing. Fortune 68:92 S '63
Economic development through private enterprise. E. G. Collado. For Affairs 41:708-20 Jl '63
Economics of the free society, by W. Roepke. Review
Bsns W p72+ Ap 13 '63
Nat R 14:532-3 Jl 2 '63. L. M. Hacker
Fallacy of too much planning. H. Hazlitt. Read Digest 82:95-6 F '63
Fifth freedom, economic freedom; address, February 7, 1963. R. R. Gros. Vital Speeches 29:465-8 My 15 '63
Four other freedoms; address, April 7, 1964. G. F. Getty, 2d. Vital Speeches 30:499-501 Je 1 '64
Free enterprise; address, April 28, 1964. A. H. Newcomb. Vital Speeches 30:730-4 S 15 '64
Hidden face of free enterprise: the strange economics of the American businessman, by J. R. Bunting. Review
Bsns W il p 164+ Je 6 '64
Ideological debate dividing businessmen. il Bsns W p201-2 S 12 '64
In defense of corporations. G. L. Phillippe. Duns R 81:52-3+ F '63
Intellectual and the market place. G. J. Stigler. Nat R 15:473-4+ D 3 '63
Mind of the businessman. B. L. Masse. America 111:296-8 S 19 '64
Myth of the American way. K. Watson. Christian Cent 80:328-30 Mr 13 '63
One man's crusade for everybody's freedom. F. J. Taylor. Read Digest 84:139-42 Je '64
Our greatest source of strength. W. H. Judd. Read Digest 85:61-70 N '64
Postwar advance of the five hundred million. M. Ways. il Fortune 70:104-9+ Ag '64
Power of free choice; address, December 3, 1963. C. G. Mortimer. Vital Speeches 30:214-16 Ja 15 '64
Survey finds: public support for business growing. Nations Bsns 51:114-16+ N '63
Toward the brotherhood of man; address, October 19, 1964. D. Rusk. Dept State Bul 51:650-2 N 9 '64
U.S. living standard leads world. il Nations Bsns 52:66-9 S '64
War on prosperity; address, September 16, 1964. S. L. Drumm. Vital Speeches 31:19-22 O 15 '64
Where federal action is not needed. Sat Eve Post 237:78 Je 6 '64
You can shape business climate; symposium. il Nations Bsns 51:61-4 Jl '63
See also
Competition
FREE-fall anchor system. See Anchors
FREE lance writing. See Authorship
FREE library of Philadelphia. See Philadelphia—Free library
FREE press. See Freedom of the press
FREE press, Detroit. See Detroit free press
FREE radicals. See Radicals (chemistry)
FREE speech
Banning the campus speaker. W. W. Van Alsyne. Nation 196:267-8+ Mr 30 '63
Bloomington blooper. Nation 198:338 Ap 6 '64
Breaking the silence. Commonweal 78:4 Mr 29 '63; Reply. 78:249-50 My 24 '63
Catholic university reversal. C. D. Kean. Christian Cent 80:565 Ap 24 '63
Dissent, si; dissenter, no; discussion. Nation 196:inside cover F 16 '63
Goldfish bowl; ban on Catholic theologians. America 108:329 Mr 9 '63
Heresy in Ohio. Nation 196:519 Je 22 '63
Hoosier witch hunt. N. R. Hanson. il Nation 196:443-4 My 25 '63; Discussion. 196:inside cover. 529 Je 22 '63
House vs. the Spirit of '76. Nation 197:62 Ag 10 '63
India follows the U.S. Time 84:54+ O 23 '64
Libel and the free press; appealing of judgement from Alabama Supreme court by New York times. N. Dorsen. il Nation 198:93-5 Ja 27 '64
Mind is its own place. J. S. Diekhoff. il PTA Mag 58:12-14 My '64
Then how about Koch? Nation 198:206-7 Mr 2 '64
Uninvited; speakers in a student-sponsored lecture series at Catholic university. Commonweal 77:608-9 Mr 8 '63
Vigilance is needed. J. Sellers. Christian Cent 80:617 My 8 '63
Violation of Arthur. W. F. Buckley, jr. Nat R 14:271 Ap 9 '63
When & where to speak. il Time 84:68-9 D 18 '64
When is a ban not a ban? theologians prevented from speaking in the archdiocese of Dublin. America 110:153 F 1 '64
See also
Academic freedom
FREE trade and protection
Talking free trade on autos; U.S. and Canada negotiate. Bsns W p24 O 10 '64
Unions veer toward protectionism. Bsns W p 124+ N 9 '63
FREE trade area, European. See European free trade association
FREE verse
How free is free verse? J. Ciardi. Sat R 47:14-15 Mr 21 '64; Same. Writer 77:15-16 Je '64
FREE will and determinism
Free will, again. H. D. Aiken. Commentary 37:79-82 F '64
Uncle Tom and predestination. D. Chaput. Negro Hist Bul 27:143 Mr '64
Word (cont) V. P. McCorry. America 110:240 F 15 '64
FREED, Jerome J.
Cell culture perfusion chamber: adaptation for microscopy of clonal growth. bibliog Science 140:1334-5 Je 21 '63
FREED, Richard
Barbirolli's vintage fifths. Sat R 47:62 N 28 '64
Haydn quake, second tremor. Sat R 47:49+ Ja 25 '64
Heritage by mail. Sat R 47:47-8 Jl 25 '64
Klemperer in 3/4 time. Sat R 46:46 F 9 '63
New this month on tape. Sat R 46:63+ Ap 27 '63
Recordings reports: miscellaneous LPs. See last issue of each month of Saturday review (comp) Recommended recordings. Sat 47:71-3 D 5 '64

FREED, Richard—*Continued*
Reissues: limited and unlimited. Sat R 46: 49+ My 25 '63
Scherchen on discs. Sat R 47:65 O 31 '64
Shakespeare on LP. Sat R 47:60-1+ My 16 '64
Wonderful world of Johann Strauss. House B 105:270-3 N '63
FREED, Rita
Swinging lady with the red hatbox from Allentown, Pa. S. Nathan. il por U S Camera 26:60-1+ D '63
FREEDGOOD, Seymour
Avon: the sweet smell of success. Fortune 70:108-13+ D '64
Big dogs, little dogs, and the air cargo bone. Fortune 70:122-9+ O '64
88,000 golden acres waiting for the dust to settle. Fortune 68:142-7+ N '63
Hotels: time to stop and rest. Fortune 68: 162-5+ Jl '63
Man who has everything, in Wilson, Ark. Fortune 70:143-7+ Ag '64
Mormonism: rich, vital, and unique. Fortune 69:136-9+ Ap '64
$100 million in rags. Fortune 67:151-4+ My '63
What happened at Burlington when the king dropped dead. Fortune 69:104-11+ Je '64
FREEDLEY, George
New York public library's Theatre collection. por Wilson Lib Bul 38:636-9 Ap '64
FREEDMAN, Aaron D. and Kohn, Leonard
Pyruvate metabolism and control: factors affecting pyruvic carboxylase activity. bibliog Science 145:58-60 Jl 3 '64
FREEDMAN, D. G. and Keller, Barbara
Inheritance of behavior in infants. bibliog Science 140:196-8 Ap 12 '63
FREEDMAN, Elisha C.
City life is best, says Hartford firm. Am City 79:106 Ag '64
FREEDMAN, Frances
Lighthouse; new assistant editor appointed; Wilson library bulletin. il Wilson Lib Bul 38:430 Ja '64
FREEDMAN, Louis, and Merritt, A. J.
Citrus flavonoid complex: chemical fractionation and biological activity. bibliog Science 139:344-5 Ja 25 '63
FREEDMAN, Margaret R.
People on a pleasure hunt. Sat R 46:41 N 23 '63
FREEDMAN, Morris
Bats. Atlan 212:138-9 D '63
FREEDMAN, Nelson L.
Bilateral differences in the human occipital electroencephalogram with unilateral photic driving. bibliog Science 142:598-9 N 1 '63
FREEDMAN, Ronald. See Berelson, B. jt. auth.
FREEDMAN, Sanford J. See Held, R. jt. auth.
FREEDMAN, Toby, and Lindner, G. S.
Must tomorrow's man look like this? from address. Pop Sci 183:77-80+ N '63
FREEDOM. See Liberty
FREEDOM, Intellectual. See Intellectual liberty
FREEDOM academy (proposed)
Let's demand this new weapon for democracy. E. H. Methvin. Read Digest 82:75-81 My '63
FREEDOM from hunger campaign. See Food relief
FREEDOM marches. See Civil rights demonstrations
FREEDOM of information. See Information, Freedom of
FREEDOM of opinion. See Public opinion
FREEDOM of religion. See Religious liberty
FREEDOM of speech. See Free speech
FREEDOM of teaching. See Academic freedom
FREEDOM of the press
Baptist editor survives attack; Baptist pastors vs editor of the Arkansas Baptist newsmagazine. Christian Cent 81:1582 D 23 '64
Can newspapermen refuse to disclose sources? H. F. Pilpel. Pub W 184:245 Ag 26 '63
Censorship begins at home; results of letters to the editor on Women strike for peace. M. J. Estren. Nat R 15:209-10 S 10 '63
Do newsmen have special rights in court? R. L. Tobin. Sat R 46:59-60 Ap 13 '63; Reply. J. C. Crumlish, jr. 46:49+ Je 8 '63
Evening bulletin test case. R. L. Tobin. Sat R 46:55 My 11 '63
It did happen here; subpoena of the editorial staffs in Danville, Va. R. L. Tobin. il Sat R 46:65-6 S 14 '63; Discussion. 46:49 O 12; 82 N 9 '63
Libel and the free press; appealing of judgement from Alabama Supreme court by New York times. N. Dorsen. il Nation 198:93-5 Ja 27 '64
Liberty, ltd. Christian Cent 80:1355-6 N 6 '63
New York times's vital victory; Alabama libel case. R. L. Tobin. Sat R 47:69-70 Ap 11 '64; Discussion. 47:61 My 9; 52 Je 13 '64
Should the offended try the offender? il Time 83:48 Ap 10 '64
Victory for a free press. Sat Eve Post 237:78 Ap 4 '64
See also
Censorship
Free speech
Government and the press
Information, Freedom of
Libel and slander
Television broadcasting—Trials
FREEDOM schools
Follow-up of freedom schools; Mississippi project. Sch & Soc 93:3-4 Ja 9 '65
Freedom schools, North and South. C. Mabee. il Reporter 31:30-2 S 10 '64
Mississippi idea. H. Zinn. il Nation 199:371-5 N 23 '64
Summer in Mississippi; freedom moves in to stay. J. DeMuth. il Nation 199:104-5+ S 14 '64
Their text is a civil rights primer; Ruleville, Miss. school. P. Watters. il N Y Times Mag p 10-11+ D 20 '64
FREEDOM singers. See Negro songs
FREEDOM; story. See Sandburg, H.
FREEDOM to read. See Intellectual liberty
FREEDOM to travel. See Travel regulations
FREEDOMLAND, USA. See Amusement parks
FREEDOM'S journal. See Negro press
FREEHAFER, Edward G.
Public relations: everybody's business. por Wilson Lib Bul 38:534-5 Mr '64
FREEMAN, David H. and Scatchard, George
Electrokinetic behavior of ion-exhange resin. Science 144:411 Ap 24 '64
FREEMAN, Donald
Donna Reed: fire and ice. Sat Eve Post 237:22-3 Mr 28 '64
I think I'm gaining on myself. Sat Eve Post 237:68-70 Ja 25 '64
Nonsensical world of Dr Seuss. McCalls 92: 115+ N '64
FREEMAN, Ernie
Portrait of an antiquer. R. R. Olney. il pors Flying 74:32+ Ja '64
FREEMAN, Fulton
New hand across the border. il por Time 83:40 F 21 '64
FREEMAN, Gaylord A. jr
Tax device to stem the outflow of gold; letter. Fortune 68:94 S '63
FREEMAN, Grace Beacham
My father and the big camellia. Redbook 122: 6+ Ap '64
FREEMAN, James Dillet
Anteroom; poem. Sat R 47:38 S 12 '64
Go tell the beloved; poem. McCalls 90:124 F '63
Tell me you love me; poem. McCalls 91:196 Ap '64
Wanderer in wondershire; poem. McCalls 91: 131 Jl '64
FREEMAN, Jean Todd
Bridling; poem. Ladies Home J 81:92 S '64
In memoriam; poem. McCalls 91:134 S '64
Iron gates; story. Redbook 123:60-1 S '64
Look out for sharks; story. Redbook 123:48-9 Ag '64
More than a memory; story. Redbook 123:38-9 Je '64
Second chance; story. Redbook 122:44-5 F '64
Writing the commercial short story. Writer 77:10-15+ D '64
FREEMAN, Jim
Keep moving. por Outdoor Life 132:48-9+ N '63
Minor league steelhead. por Field & S 68:114-17+ F '64
Two weeks for steelhead. pors Field & S 67:48-51+ F '63
FREEMAN, John
Ginger man. por Newsweek 65:62 Ja 25 '65
FREEMAN, John W.
Idyllic retreat. Opera N 28:24-5 F 8 '64
Measure for measure. Opera N 27:24-5 Mr 23 '63
Mixed bouquet. Opera N 27:28-9 F 9 '63
(ed) On records. See issues of Opera news
FREEMAN, Monroe E. and Hersey, D. F.
Keeping up with current research: Science information exchange. Science 141:119 Jl 12 '63
FREEMAN, Orville Lothrop
Excerpt from testimony before the Committee on agriculture of the U.S. house of representatives, June 11, 1963. Cong Digest 43: 174+ Je '64
Hunger in the free world; address, November 17, 1964. Vital Speeches 31:190-2 Ja 1 '65

FREEMAN, Orville Lothrop—*Continued*
Improving the effectiveness of U.S. assistance to international rural development; address, July 27, 1964. Dept State Bul 51:383-8 S 14 '64
Planting new ideas; a report on a visit to Soviet farms. Bul Atomic Sci 19:44-5 D '63
Successful farming interviews Secretary Freeman. por Suc Farm 61:63+ F '63
Work horses in the sky. por Flying 74:24 My '64
World food congress meets at Washington; address, June 5, 1963. Dept State Bul 49:61-8 Jl 8 '63
about
Farmers face their toughest choice. J. Bird. il por Sat Eve Post 236:74-6 My 18 '63
Hard row to hoe. il por Time 81:21-5 Ap 5 '63
Wheat vote; against Freeman's program. il Time 81:13-14 My 31 '63
FREEMAN, Roger A.
Urban financing, difficult but not desperate. Am City 79:7+ Mr '64
FREEMAN, Stephen A.
International study at home and abroad. bibliog f Ann Am Acad 356:133-41 N '64
FREEMASONS
Fez and games; Shriners convention in New York. il Newsweek 64:45 Ag 3 '64
Patients nobody wanted; Shriners' burns-treatment program. A. Lake. il Sat Eve Post 237:87-91 D 5 '64
Racial crisis in DeMolay. R. H. Dinegar. Christian Cent 81:378 Mr 18 '64; Discussion. 81:356, 771 Mr 18, Je 10 '64
Racial crisis in DeMolay; with editorial comment. R. H. Dinegar. Christian Cent 81:356, 378 Mr 18 '64
Shriners; ninetieth annual convention. New Yorker 40:26-7 Ag 1 '64
Who are those Arabs? Shriners in Manhattan. il Time 84:44-5 Jl 31 '64
FREEMASONS, Negro
Pioneers in protest; Prince Hall; founder of first Negro chapter of Masons. L. Bennett, jr. il Ebony 19:88-9+ Ap '64
FREER, Coburn
Running out to spring; poem. Atlan 214:56 Ag '64
FREEWAYS. See Express highways
FREEZE-drying process. See Food, Dried
FREEZER food plans. See Food, Frozen
FREEZERS
Defroster devices for refrigerators and freezers; new electrical hazard. il Consumer Bul 47:9-11 My '64
General electric Americana refrigerator-freezer. il Consumer Bul 47:19-21 Ag '64
Get the most from your family freezer. B. G. Wadsworth. Parents Mag 38:86 Jl '63
Make that freezer pay its way. il Changing T 17:22-4 D '63
Refrigerator-freezer combinations. il Consumer Bul 46:6-15 Jl '63
Two-door refrigerator-freezers. il Consumer Rep 29:368-75 Ag '64
FREEZING
Applejack technique: new application of an old approach to solute concentration. H. M. Habermann. il Science 140:292 Ap 19 '63
Freezing and viability of tetrahymena pyriformis in dimethylsulfoxide. S. W. Hwang and others. bibliog il Science 144:64-5 Ap 3 '64
Undercooling of liquids. D. Turnbull. il Sci Am 212:38-46 bibliog(p 134) Ja '65
FREEZING (therapy) See Cold—Therapeutic applications
FREEZING of food
Are you up to date with freezing? S. R. Meidinger. Bet Hom & Gard 42:109-11 O '64
Be meals ahead with your freezer. D. B. Marsh. il Good H 156:92-107+ Mr '63
Deepest freeze; liquid nitrogen to snap-freeze foods. Bsns W p92 Ag 15 '64
Freezer tips for the holidays. Am Home 66:84 N '63
Future dimension for food. M. Davidson. il Ladies Home J 81:114 Je '64
See also
Fruit—Preservation
FREGEAU, Jerome H.
Nucleon structure. Science 141:548-9+ Ag 9 '63
FREGOSI, Jim
Star on the wrong team. F. Deford. il por Sports Illus 20:69-70+ Je 1 '64
FREI, Eduardo
Aims of Christian democracy; excerpt from Religion, revolution, and reform, ed. by F. B. Pike and W. V. D'Antonio. Commonweal 81:63-6 O 9 '64
President Frei on U.S. capitalism; reprint. America 111:285 S 19 '64
about
And now to toil. il por Time 84:35 N 20 '64
Chile: an example of U.S. troubles in Latin America. il por U S News 57:77-80 N 9 '64
Chile enters a new era. D. W. Bray. Cur Hist 48:21-5+ Ja '65
Chile: revolution of good intentions. M. Wyman. Nation 199:320-1+ N 9 '64
Chile: the last, best hope. L. Gross. il pors Look 28:80+ Je 2 '64
Chile's goal: a doubled income. il U S News 57:76 S 21 '64
Chile's leader: pro-American leftist. por U S News 57:21 S 21 '64
Good news from South America. Life 57:4 S 18 '64
Moderate wins. il por Sr Schol 85:30 S 23 '64
Momentous contest. P. Zottele. Christian Cent 81:1246+ O 7 '64
New hope for Chile? il por Sr Schol 85:12-15 O 21 '64
FREI, Emil, 3d, and Freireich, E. J.
Leukemia; with biographical sketches. Sci Am 210:24, 88:96 bibliog(p 150+) My '64
FREI, J. V. and others
Mitoses; distribution in mouse ear epidermis. bibliog Science 140:487-8 My 3 '63
FREI, Otto
People of East Berlin. Atlan 212:118-21 D '63
FREIBERG, Stanley K.
Gethsemane; poem. Christian Cent 80:393 Mr 27 '63
FREIDEL, Frank
Private record of a public servant. Sat R 47:41-2 O 17 '64
Profiles of the Presidents. Nat Geog Mag 126:642-87; 127:80-121 N '64, Ja '65 (to be cont)
FREIDSON, Eliot
Medical care and the public; case study of a medical group. Ann Am Acad 346:57-66 Mr '63
FREIER, Phyllis, and Webber, W. R.
Radiation hazard in space from solar particles. bibliog Science 142:1587-92 D 20 '63
FREIFELDER, David, and others
Electron microscopy of single-stranded DNA: circularity of DNA of bacteriophage ΦX174. bibliog Science 146:254-5 O 9 '64
FREIGHT airplanes. See Airplanes, Freight
FREIGHT and freightage
Unraveling the freight rate mess; transportation bill. Bsns W p56+ F 8 '64
Who carries what commodities. il Duns R 81:pt2 S118-19 Je '63
See also
Air freight service
Railroads—Freight service
Shipping
Trucking
FREIGHT cars. See Railroads—Freight cars
FREIGHT handling
See also
Loading and unloading
FREIGHT rates. See Railroads—Rates; Shipping rates
FREIGHT vessels
ECAFE proposals for construction of standard coasting vessels. il U N Rev 10:40 Mr '63
Great leap overboard; Communist China's Yüeh Chin. Time 81:34 My 10 '63
Hijackers ashore; Venezuela's hijacked freighter Anzoátegui. Time 81:23 Mr 1 '63
It takes more than ships; oceangoing barge of Matson company. il Bsns W p68-70+ Jl 6 '63
Phantom raiders; Spanish freighter Sierra Aranzazu, attacked off Cuba. Time 84:36 S 25 '64
Tramps reap the harvest; Russian demand for ships to carry Canadian wheat. Bsns W p28 S 28 '63
See also
Ore carriers
Tank ships

Food service

Feasting aboard freighters; with recipes. S. Bary. il Travel 122:39-42 N '64
FREILING, Edward C.
Theoretical basis for logarithmic correlations of fractionated radionuclide compositions. Science 139:1058-9 Mr 15 '63
FREIMANN, Frank M.
Magnavox goes its own golden way. S. H. Brown. il por Fortune 69:112-15+ F '64
FREIREICH, Emil J. See Frei, E. 3d, jt. auth.
FREISER, Leonard H.
Information retrieval for students. Library J 88:1121-3, 3251-3 Mr 15, S 15 '63

FREITAG, George H.
Lions are loose; story. Atlan 214:50-2 Jl '64
Tune on a bass drum; story. Atlan 211:89-90 F '63
What is a secret? Writer 77:26-7 Mr '64
FREITAG, M. See Woodson, W. E. jt. auth.
FREMANTLE, Anne
At the heart of the quattrocento. Commonweal 77:649-51 Mr 15 '63
Country auction; story. New Yorker 39:53-7 O 19 '63
In the wake of the prophet. Reporter 30:46-7 Mr 26 '64
Letter from Paris. Commonweal 80:210-12 My 8 '64
Renewal: Easter at the Cloisters. N Y Times Mag p20-1 Ap 14 '63
FREMLING, Calvin R.
Mayfly distribution indicates water quality on the upper Mississippi River. bibliog Science 146:1164-6 N 27 '64
FREMON, Suzanne. See Cohen, E. jt. auth.
FREMONT, John C.
Negro who rode with Fremont in 1847. G. M. Bergman. Negro Hist Bul 28:31-2 N '64
FRENCH, B. V. K.
Indoor horn for TV-FM reception. bibliog Electr World 70:50-1+ D '63
FRENCH, Bevan M.
Graphitization of organic material in a progressively metamorphosed Precambrian iron formation. bibliog Science 146:917-18 N 13 '64
FRENCH, Charles
Coin quiz. See issues of Hobbies
Numismatics. See issues of Hobbies
FRENCH, Charles E. and Wilson, R. B.
Do you plan your farm changes backward? Suc Farm 61:70D S '63
FRENCH, Diana
(ed) See Jack, M. Left for dead
FRENCH, Harriet F. See Balaban, V. jt. auth.
FRENCH, Roderick
Primitive ecumenical catechism. Christian Cent 80:1505-8 D 4 '63
Young African Christians speak. Christian Cent 80:242-3 F 20 '63
FRENCH
Carnage à trois; jealousy in France. Newsweek 63:38 Mr 23 '64
France changes, but not Frenchmen. A. Maurois. il N Y Times Mag p33+ N 24 '63
FRENCH and Indian war, 1755-1763. See United States—History—French and Indian war 1755-1763
FRENCH art. See Art, French
FRENCH authors. See Authors, French
FRENCH automobiles. See Automobiles, Foreign
FRENCH CANADA. See Quebec (province)
FRENCH CANADIAN literature
Reporter at large; an American's notes on Canadian culture. E. Wilson. New Yorker 40:64-6+ N 21 '64
FRENCH CANADIANS
Angry French Canadians. il Sat Eve Post 236:20 Ap 6 '63
Angry welcome for a Queen; French revolt that threatens Canada. R. Sherrod. il Sat Eve Post 237:19-23 O 10 '64
Canada: a house dividing? il Sr Schol 84:8-10+ Ap 10 '64
Fissionable material; raids by Army for the liberation of Quebec. il Newsweek 63:42+ Mr 9 '64
French Canada's strange revolt; role of FLQ (Quebec liberation front) L. Bergquist. il Look 27:90-4+ D 3 '63
In French Canada, vive la difference. il Bsns W p64-5+ O 12 '63
Pearson's progress; Canada after a year of Liberal government. W. H. Hessler. il Reporter 30:24-9 Mr 12 '64
Quebec guerrillas; Canada faces secession. R. E. Spencer. il Nation 198:283-6 Mr 23 '64
Quebec's quiet revolution. C. de Mestral. Christian Cent 81:1268-70 O 14 '64
Rise of the separatists; raids by Quebec liberation army. Time 83:39 Mr 6 '64
Separatists in Quebec; Canada's confederation in danger. W. F. Butcher. Christian Cent 80:742-4 Je 5 '63
Trying to blast a nation apart; Le Front de liberation quebecois (FLQ) il Bsns W p 100+ Je 1 '63
Two peoples under one flag; controversy over new national flag. B. Hutchison. il N Y Times Mag p29+ Ag 23 '64
See also
Quebec (province)
FRENCH chain stores. See Chain stores
FRENCH coal miners. See Coal miners
FRENCH CONGO. See Congo (capital Brazzaville)
FRENCH cookery. See Cookery, French
FRENCH drama
American Negro in post-war French drama. A. Cismaru. Negro Hist Bul 27:79-80 Ja '64
FRENCH dressing. See Salads
FRENCH economic assistance. See Economic assistance, French
FRENCH exiles. See Exiles
FRENCH foreign legion. See France—Army—Foreign legion
FRENCH furniture. See Furniture, French
FRENCH GUIANA
From Devil's Island to Cape de Gaulle. il Time 85:25 Ja 8 '65
See also
Devil's Island
FRENCH in the United States
M. Laporte. New Yorker 39:37-8 Ap 20 '63
FRENCH intervention in Mexico, 1861-1867. See Mexico—History—European intervention, 1861-1867
FRENCH language
Parlez-vous franglais? pidgin French-English. il Time 82:80 N 29 '63
Foreign words and phrases
Parlez-vous franglais? by R. Etiemble. Review
New Yorker 40:104+ F 22 '64. Genêt
Terms and phrases
Travel well. C. Rule. il Travel 121:53 Mr '64
FRENCH literature
Books. F. Steegmuller. New Yorker 39:114-16 Ja 18 '64
French poets and novelists, by H. James. Review
Nation 198:377-9 Ap 13 '64. G. Brée
See also
Authors, French
FRENCH manuscripts. See Manuscripts, French
FRENCH opera. See Opera, French
FRENCH painting. See Painting, French
FRENCH poetry
French poetry today. W. Fowlie. Poetry 104:322-8 Ag '64
Translations into English
Ballade of the ladies of time past; tr. by R. Wilbur. F. Villon. Poetry 105:81-2 N '64
Chanson des etages; Post-scriptum à lettera amorosa; Sept parcelles de Luberon; Les parages d'Alsace. tr. by W. Fowlie. R. Char. Poetry 104:278-95 Ag '64
Femme noire; tr. by C. Guenther. L. S. Senghor. Reporter 29:41 D 5 '63
Graduel; Hiver, tr. by W. Fowlie. J. Grosjean. Poetry 104:296-309 Ag '64
Poèmes (extraits) tr. by W. Fowlie. J. C. Renard. Poetry 104:310-21 Ag '64
Ténèbre; A la beauté, tr. by W. Fowlie. P. J. Jouve. Poetry 104:273-7 Ag '64
FRENCH posters. See Posters
FRENCH press conferences. See Press conferences
FRENCH revolution. See France—History—Revolution
FRENCH RIVIERA. See Riviera
FRENCH students
Fiction
See French students in literature
FRENCH students in literature
Looking at youth's problems; concerning The new aristocrats, by M. de Saint Pierre; American view; French view. C. J. Burlage; G. Callies. America 108:230-2+ F 16 '63
FRENCH TOGOLAND. See Togo
FRENCH visitors in the United States. See Foreign visitors in the United States
FRENCH WEST AFRICA
French-speaking West Africa. A. R. Zolberg. bibliog f Cur Hist 45:347-54 D '63
On African socialism, by L. S. Senghor, tr. from the French by M. Cook. Review
Sat R 47:47 Je 6 '64. C. Miller
See also
Senegal
FRENCH WEST INDIES. See West Indies, French
FRENCH wine. See Wine
FRENCH women. See Women—France
FRENK, S. See Maturana, H. R. jt. auth.
FRENZEL, Louis E. Jr
Electronic instrumentation for oil exploration. Electr World 70:27-30+ D '63
Electronic time-delay relays. Electr World 72:44-5 D '64
Frequency multiplication & division. Electr World 70:53-6 S '63
Voltage regulator design. Electr World 71:52-4+ My '64

FREQUENCY, Radio. See Radio frequency
FREQUENCY allocation, Radio. See Radio frequency allocation
FREQUENCY allocation, Television. See Television frequency allocation
FREQUENCY-deviation meters. See Radio instruments
FREQUENCY measurement
Precise measurement of radio frequencies. J. R. Johnson. il Electr World 72:47-50 Ag '64
FREQUENCY modulation. See Radio frequency modulation
FREQUENCY modulation receivers. See Radio receiving apparatus—Frequency modulation receivers
FREQUENCY signal generators. See Signal generators
FREQUENCY standards
Frequency & time standards. G. E. Hudson. il Electr World 72:20-3 Ag '64
High-stability crystal frequency standards. I. Math. il Electr World 72:44-5 Ag '64
FRERICHS, Gisela
Daisy quiz. Horticulture 41:400 Ag '63
FRESCO painting. See Frescoes
FRESCOES
Lost treasures are seen again; wall paintings in remote churches, Yugoslavia. il Life 54:52-61 Ap 12 '63
FRESE, Paul F.
All-America winners for 1965, annuals. Pop Gard 16:41-3 Ja '65
Annuals. Pop Gard 15:24-5 My '64
(comp) Bulb planting guide for fall. Pop Gard 15:62-3 S '64
Half dozen ways to use roses in your garden. Pop Gard 14:24-5 S '63
Iris; the tall bearded. Pop Gard 14:30-2 My '63
Lawn maintenance. Pop Gard 15:52-8 Ap '64
Lawn making made easy. Pop Gard 15:27-9 Mr '64
New annuals for 1964. Pop Gard 15:52-4 Ja '64
Newcomers for 1964. Pop Gard 15:43-5+ F '64
FRESE, Robert E.
Board member of CU resigns. Consumer Rep 28:510 N '63
FRESH air charity
Something special in vacations. J. K. Lagemann. il Read Digest 82:222-3+ Je '63
FRESH water algae. See Algae
FRESH water fauna
Antarctic micrometazoa; fresh-water species in the McMurdo Sound area. E. C. Dougherty and L. G. Harris. bibliog il Science 140:497-8 My 3 '63
FRESHMEN. See College students
FRESNEL diffraction. See Diffraction
FRESNO, Calif.
Hot-patch box saves cold cash. M. J. Carozza. il Am City 78:9 Jl '63
How Fresno upgraded parking-meter service. M. J. Carozza and N. O. Jefford. il Am City 78:117+ N '63
Men and machines cut one-third off sweeping bill. A. Stenman. il Am City 79:111-12 Mr '64

Streets

We trade concrete for right-of-way. M. J. Carozza. il Am City 78:130-1 Je '63
FRESNO COUNTY, Calif, free library
California: demonstrated success. A. F. Reilly. il Library J 89:1683-7 Ap 15 '64
FRÉSON, Robert
Europe for climbers. il Esquire 61:49-59 F '64
Focus on Robert Freson. C. Reynolds. il por Pop Phot 54:74-81+ Je '64
FREUD, Sigmund
Books. L. Mumford. New Yorker 40:155-6+ My 23 '64
Meaning of mental illness. D. Fleming. Atlan 214:72-6 Jl '64
They made our world. L. Rosten. por Look 29:80-2 Ja 12 '65
FREUDENTHAL, Hugo. See Lee, J. J. jt. auth.
FREUDISM. See Psychoanalysis
FREUND, J. M.
Clique, clique, clique! Seventeen 23:148-9 O '64
FREUND, Paul A.
To amend, or not to amend, the Constitution. N Y Times Mag p33+ D 13 '64
Religion in the schools. por Time 84:59 D 11 '64
FREUND, Rudolf
Rudolf Freund, scientific illustrator. H. C. Pitz. il por Am Artist 28:20-5+ My '64
FREUND, Tibor
Motion in painting: a new art form. il Am Artist 28:46-50+ N '64
FREUNDLICH, Martin M.
Origin of the electron microscope. bibliog Science 142:185-8 O 11 '63
FREY, Donald Nelson
Mustang twins move up. por Time 85:67-8 Ja 22 '65
FREY, J. R. and others
Immunological tolerance induced in animals previously sensitized to simple chemical compounds. bibliog Science 144:853-4 My 15 '64
FREY, John E.
Recorded reviews. por Wilson Lib Bul 39:333-4 D '64
FREY, Marguerite (Kurth)
Toddlers can be taught more than you think. Parents Mag 38:56-7+ My '63; Same abr. with title Children can be taught life, early. Read Digest 83:95-6 Jl '63
FREYBERG, Sir Bernard
My most unforgettable character. R .C. Queree. por Read Digest 85:164-6+ N '64
FREYMAN, Leonard
A+ for our lay readers. NEA J 53:19-20 N '64
FREYRE, Gilberto
Ethnic democracy: the Brazilian example. Américas 15:1-6 D '63
Pride of miscegenation. por Time 81:28 Ap 26 '63
Which is the real Brazil? Américas 16:10-15 Ap '64
FRIAR, Kimon
George Seferis. Sat R 46:16-20 N 30 '63
FRIARS
Guilty friars. Newsweek 62:46 Jl 15 '63
FRIBOURG, Michel
Continental's coup. il por Newsweek 63:65 F 3 '64
FRIBOURG, René
Lived with. New Yorker 39:29-30 My 25 '63
Sale of the century. il Newsweek 62:58 Jl 8 '63
Versailles in Manhattan; R. Fribourg collection. il Time 81:72 Mr 8 '63
FRIBOURG, René, collection. See Art—Private collections
FRICHTEL, Mary Lee
Day at the polls. New Repub 148:9 Je 15 '63
FRICK, Ford
Crossroads; commissioners of baseball. Sports Illus 21:13 N 16 '64
Never on Sunday? Sports Illus 21:11 S 21 '64
FRICKER, John
Building boom in foreign bizjets. Flying 74:38-9+ Je '64
Pilot report. Flying 74:42-3+ Mr '64
FRICSAY, Ferenc
Da capo; recordings. S. Smolian. Am Rec G 29:815 Je '63
FRIDENSTEIN, Ruth
New ways with finger paint. Design 65:108-9 Ja '64
Straw and burlap creations. Design 65:194 My '64
FRIED, Alexander
Jacques Singer, conductor, Portland symphony, Oregon. Mus Am 83:9 My '63
FRIED, Irving M.
Prospects for psychoacoustics. Hi Fi 13:48-50+ Ap '63
FRIED, Joseph P. and Kurtz, H. I.
Article ideas: from manuscript to magazine. Writer 77:16-19+ D '64
FRIED, Morton H.
Ethnic minorities around the world. Science 139:1304-5 Mr 29 '63
FRIEDAN, Betty
Fraud of femininity; excerpts from The feminine mystique. McCalls 90:81+ Mr '63
GI bill for women? excerpt from Feminine mystique. Sat R 46:68 My 18 '63
Have American housewives traded brains for brooms? Ladies Home J 80:24+ Ja '63
Woman: the fourth dimension. Ladies Home J 81:48-55 Je '64
You're a freak if you have a brain; interview, ed. by J. Howard. por Life 55:87-8 N 1 '63

about

Angry battler for her sex. il pors Life 55:84-6 N 1 '63
FRIEDBERG, Felix, and Hayden, G. A.
Gamma irradiation of polypeptides: transformation of amino acids. bibliog Science 140:825-6 My 17 '63
FRIEDBERG, Maurice
Politics, poetry, and prose. Sat R 47:40+ My 16 '64
State of Soviet Jewry. Commentary 39:38-43 Ja '65
FRIEDEBERG, Pedro
Mexico and points East; drawings, with introductory note. por Horizon 6:52-7 Sum '64

FRIEDEL, R. A. and Sharkey, A. G. Jr
Alkanes in natural and synthetic petroleums: comparison of calculated and actual compositions. bibliog Science 139:1203-5 Mr 22 '63
FRIEDEN, Earl
Chemistry of amphibian metamorphosis; with biographical sketch. Sci Am 209:30+, 110-18 bibliog(p 187) N '63
FRIEDENBERG, Daniel M.
Ambassador Smith's Cuban report. Commonweal 77:622-4 Mr 8 '63
Land lords and the American process. New Repub 149:21-4 O 19 '63
Man's fate; poem. New Repub 148:20 My 11 '63
Notes on Israel. Commonweal 81:381-5 D 11 '64
FRIEDENBERG, Edgar Z.
Educationists. Commentary 36:260-4 S '63
Ideology of school withdrawal; summary of address, December 1962. Commentary 35: 492-500 Je '63
Modern high school: a profile. Commentary 36:373-80 N '63
FRIEDLAENDER, Leny Noske-. See Noske-Friedlaender, L.
FRIEDLAND, Louis L.
Organized labor and the city boss. bibliog f Ann Am Acad 353:40-51 My '64
FRIEDLANDER, S. K.
Surface contamination. Science 145:1076 S 4 '64
FRIEDMAN, Alexander H. and others
Tremorine: its effect on amines of the central nervous system. bibliog Science 141:1188-90 S 20 '63
FRIEDMAN, Arnold P.
What to do about headaches; interview. por U S News 57:92-4+ O 26 '64
FRIEDMAN, B. H.
Art for the New York Hilton. Craft Horiz 23:8-15+ Jl '63
FRIEDMAN, Bruce Jay
Black angels; story. Esquire 62:133 D '64
Interview; story. Esquire 62:81 Jl '64
Mission; story. Sat Eve Post 237:46-7 Mr 7 '64
Radical innocent. N. Algren. Nation 199:142-3 S 21 '64
FRIEDMAN, Bruno
Lasers: 100 million messages on a beam of light. UNESCO Courier 17:15-19 F '64
FRIEDMAN, Herbert
Battery-powered lights. Pop Phot 54:112-13+ Mr '64
How to keep your tape recorder in shape. Pop Phot 55:76+ O '64
How to live with low-cost portables. Pop Phot 55:77 O '64
How to pick the right battery! Pop Phot 54:115+ Ap '64
Walkie-talkie as a photo accessory. Pop Phot 55:78+ O '64
Where is science taking us? por Sat R 47:44-5 Jl 4 '64
X-ray astronomy; with biographical sketch. Sci Am 210:18, 36-45 Je '64
FRIEDMAN, Herman
Antibody plaque formation by normal mouse spleen cell cultures exposed in vitro to RNA from immune mice. bibliog Science 146:934-6 N 13 '64
Inhibition of antibody plaque formation by sensitized lymphoid cells: rapid indicator of transplantation immunity. bibliog Science 145:607-9 Ag 7 '64
FRIEDMAN, Jack J.
Long steady rise of air freight. Duns R 81: pt2 S120-1+ Je '63
Should management own more stock? Duns R 81:52-3 My '63
FRIEDMAN, Lawrence M.
Today, I dominate pugilism and prosody; tomorrow, perhaps, the world. Nat R 15:305-6 O 8 '63
FRIEDMAN, Martin
Adolph Gottlieb: private symbols in public statements. Art N 62:32-5+ My '63
Is sculpture a step-child? a colloquy. Art N 63:40-2+ S '64
FRIEDMAN, Maurice
(tr) See Buber, M. Interpreting Hasidism
FRIEDMAN, Meyer
They ran the heart study. il pors Bsns W p50-1+ D 12 '64
FRIEDMAN, Milton
Goldwater view of economics. N Y Times Mag p35+ O 11 '64
Right face. il por Newsweek 63:73 Ja 13 '64
Theorizing for Goldwater? por Bsns W p 106+ N 23 '63
FRIEDMAN, Norman
Expostulation and reply; poem. Nation 198: 246 Mr 9 '64
In conflict with love; poem. Nation 199:468 D 14 '64
FRIEDMAN, Paul
Psychiatrist examines suicide, questions and answers; excerpts from Encyclopedia of mental health. Todays Health 41:56-9+ D '63; Correction. 42:87 Ja '64
FRIEDMAN, Ralph
New office to spur Alliance investment. Bsns W p85-6 Mr 30 '63
FRIEDMAN, Ruby
Pine trees; poem. Am For 69:49 O '63
FRIEDMAN, Saul
Rand corporation and our policy makers. Atlan 212:61-8 S '63
Tussle in Texas. Nation 198:114-17 F 3 '64
FRIEDMAN, Stan, family
They cared enough to give the most. W. Trombley. il Ladies Home J 81:32+ Ap '64
FRIEDMAN-KIEN, Alvin E. and others
Milker's nodules: isolation of a poxvirus from a human case. bibliog Science 140: 1335-6 Je 21 '63
FRIEDMANN, John
Challenge of urbanization. bibliog NEA J 53: 42-5 N '64
Metropolitan form and social choice. Bul Atomic Sci 20:30-2 My '64
FRIEDRICH, Otto
There are 00 trees in Russia. Harper 229: 59-65 O '64
FRIEL, Brian
Death of a scientific humanist; story. New Yorker 40:58-62 N 14 '64
Downstairs no upstairs. New Yorker 39:82+ Ag 24 '63
Everything neat and tidy; story. New Yorker 40:39-42 Ap 11 '64
Fine day at Glenties. Holiday 33:22+ Ap '63
Giant of Monaghan. Holiday 35:89+ My '64
Ginger hero; story. Sat Eve Post 236:58-63 My 18 '63
Illusionists; story. Sat Eve Post 236:56-62 Ap 6 '63
Labors of love. Atlan 211:130-2 Ap '63
Walk to that exit. Holiday 34:48+ N '63
Widowhood system; story. New Yorker 40:29-36 S 5 '64
FRIEND, Jacob L.
Notes on China's ancient calendar. Sky & Tel 26:329 D '63
FRIEND from Nebraska; story. See Sire, G. and Sire, J.
FRIEND of a friend; story. See Cousins, M.
FRIENDLINESS. See Kindness
FRIENDLY, Alfred, 1911-
African Bushman art treasures. Nat Geog Mag 123:848-65 Je '63
Army's language school. Sat R 46:72-3 F 16 '63
Gitlow will show you how to shuffle. New Repub 150:9 My 23 '64
Perfect haircut. Esquire 59:76-7+ Ap '63
War that should never end. NEA J 53:21 D '64

about

Friendly pool. Time 81:68 Mr 15 '63
FRIENDLY, Fred W.
Bulldozer. por Newsweek 63:56 Mr 16 '64
D-day plus twenty years. H. Mitgang. il Look 28:78-85 F 25 '64
On the town meeting. il Newsweek 62:81 Jl 22 '63
Reason-why man. por Time 83:62+ Mr 13 '64
FRIENDLY ISLANDS. See Tonga (islands)
FRIENDS, Society of
Exporting the American idea: Quaker technology among the Senecas. A. Wallace. Sat R 46:54-6 Ap 6 '63
New departure: a Quaker seminary. D. E. Trueblood. Christian Cent 80:531-2+ Ap 24 '63
Ordeal of William Penn. F. Biddle. il Am Heritage 15:30-3+ Ap '64
See also
Friends committee on national legislation
FRIENDS committee on national legislation
Food for peace; recommendations. Christian Cent 81:1420 N 18 '64
FRIENDS of Covent Garden
Covent Garden's friends; imitation of Metropolitan opera guild. P. J. Smith. Opera N 29:29 D 19 '64
FRIENDS of French opera, Incorporated
Music to my ears; concert version of La Juive. I. Kolodin. Sat R 47:23+ Mr 28 '64
Musical events; concert version of Halévy's La juive. W. Sargeant. New Yorker 40:175-6 Mr 21 '64

FRIENDS of Sammy; story. See Stanton, W.
FRIENDSHIP
On friendship between women. J. West. Holiday 35:13-17 Mr '64
Party of one. C. Fadiman. Holiday 33:14+ Je '63
What makes a girl my best friend. il Farm J 87:117 F '63
See also
Playmates
FRIENDSHIP bracelet; drama. See Clapp, P.
FRIENDSHIP; story. See Randall, F. E.
FRIESEN, Abram J. D. and others
Identification of acetylcholine in sympathetic ganglia by chemical and physical methods. bibliog Science 145:157-9 Jl 10 '64
FRIGGENS, Paul
Bad news for brother rat. Read Digest 86: 126-9 Ja '65
Change rides the range. Read Digest 85:182-4+ Ag '64
Federal aid? Indianapolis says, Uncle, go home! Read Digest 82:266-8+ Je '63
Federal aid to colleges: boon or bane? Read Digest 84:139-43 Ja '64
Free land! the saga of the homesteaders. Read Digest 82:98-102 My '63
Sam Shepard's faith. PTA Mag 58:18-20+ Mr '64; Same abr. with title Is the Negro equal in intelligence and ability? Read Digest 84: 83-7 Mr '64
They challenge our top students. PTA Mag 57:4-7 My '63; Same abr. with title Here's a new kind of summer school. Read Digest 82:157-8+ Je '63
FRIML, Rudolf
Pox on Broadway; ed. by M. Schumach. N Y Times Mag p54+ S 15 '63
FRINGE benefits. See Non-wage payments
FRIOU, George J. and Teague, P. O.
Spontaneous autoimmunity in mice: antibodies to nucleoprotein in strain A/J. bibliog Science 143:1333-4 Mr 20 '64
FRISCH, Bruce H.
A-bomb on New York's doorstep. il Sci Digest 54:29-35 O '63
Detergent mess. Sci Digest 54:72-8 S '63
First it was IGY, now it's IQSY. Sci Digest 53:46 My '63
Gasolines: is there any difference? Sci Digest 54:37-41 Jl '63
Kefauver's last interview. Sci Digest 54:10-18 N '63
(ed) See Heezen, B. Ocean's maps and earth theories revolutionized by latest findings
FRISCH, Max
Chinese wall; text, tr. by J. L. Rosenberg. Theatre Arts 47:32-60 Ag '63
about
Andorra; tr. by G. Tabori. Criticism
New Repub 148:28-9 Mr 9 '63
New Yorker 38:114 F 16 '63
Newsweek por 61:60 F 25 '63
Sat R 46:29 Mr 2 '63
Time 81:75 F 22 '63
Firebugs. Criticism
New Repub 148:29 Mr 9 '63
New Yorker 39:114 F 23 '63
Newsweek 61:60 F 25 '63
Sat R 46:29 Mr 2 '63
Time 81:75 F 22 '63
Max Frisch: the sage of Bahnhofstrasse. A. Pryce-Jones. il por Theatre Arts 47:22-3+ Ag '63
FRISCH, Otto von
Enigmatic lizard. il Natur Hist 72:46-51 O '63
FRISSELL, Toni
Love's warm instant: the embrace. il Life 55:150-6 D 6 '63
Splendor of a great family: the Vanderbilts; photographs. Life 57:50-65 Ag 14 '64
FRISTROM, R. M.
Scavenger probe sampling: a method for studying gaseous free radicals. bibliog Science 140:297-300 Ap 19 '63
FRISVOLD, Sandra
Curl up and read. Seventeen 23:24 N '64
FRITS
All frit, no fret. il Time 83:92 Ap 24 '64
FRITSCH, Arnold R. See Seaborg, G. T. jt. auth.
FRITSCHE, Jeannette
I believe. Seventeen 22:67 Mr '63
FRITTERS
Fritter away. il McCalls 91:148-9 Ap '64
Time to fritter; with recipes. C. Claiborne. il N Y Times Mag p82 My 17 '64
FRITZ, Emanuel
Damned if we do, damned if we don't! por Am For 69:34-5 F '63
FRITZ, Frank P.
Hot-series test box. Pop Mech 119:191-3+ Mr '63
FRITZ, Jean
Cinderella summer; story. Seventeen 23:84-5 Jl '64
Merry Christmas, Mr Longfellow; story. Seventeen 22:78-9 D '63
Mr America. Atlan 214:125-9 D '64
Nice girl for Christmas; story. Seventeen 23:76-7 D '64
World without end; story. Redbook 122:66-7 N '63
FRITZ, P. J. and Jacobson, K. B.
Lactic dehydrogenases; subfractionation of isozymes. bibliog Science 140:64-5 Ap 5 '63
FROGGATT, J. D.
British economy. Cur Hist 46:291-5+ My '64
FROGS
Amphibian cell culture: permanent cell line from the bullfrog (rana catesbeiana) K. Wolf and M. C. Quimby. bibliog il Science 144:1578-80 Je 26 '64
Bullfrog ballet filmed in flight. T. Davidson. il Nat Geog Mag 123:790-9 Je '63
Frogs of spring are springing for their lives. B. Heilman. il Sports Illus 18:46-8+ Ap 1 '63
Gene action mechanisms in the determination of color and pattern in the frog (rana pipiens) J. Davison. bibliog il Science 141: 648-9 Ag 16 '63
Poison arrow frog collection. Hobbies 68: 115+ Je '63
Tadpoles developing in egg short-cut evolution; Fitzinger frogs. Sci N L 83:248 Ap 20 '63
See also
Tree frogs and tree toads
Development
See Amphibia—Development
FROGS eye. See Eye (amphibia)
FROGS legs. See Frogs
FROM Dublin's fair city; story. See Glennon, M.
FROMAN, Robert
Bootlegger. New Yorker 39:176+ S 14 '63
Great-granddad's last battle. Read Digest 83:25-6+ D '63
Our fellow immigrants. Am Heritage 14:60-3+ F '63
Wanted: ten million amateur scientists: excerpts from Wanted: amateur scientists. Pop Sci 184:82-5+ Ap '64
FROMBOLUTI, Omero
Wall: mosaic tiles. K. Sawyer. il por Craft Horiz 23:20-3+ My '63
FROME, Michael
Aruba's one-man resources department. Am For 70:24-6+ Jl '64
Capsule history of the income tax. Holiday 35:66-7 My '64
Enjoying the national forests. Holiday 35: 131-6 Je '64
Enjoying the Rockies. Holiday 34:93-100 Ag '63
Kind of special breed. por Am For 70:4-5+ Ja '64
Let's rescue our roadsides now! Am For 69: 10-11+ N '63
Nature's pageantry on the Potomac. Am For 69:16-21+ N '63
Our Indian crafts. Holiday 34:179-84 D '63
Why I love the Smokies. Am For 70:8-9 O '64
FROMM, Erich
Creators and destroyers. Sat R 47:22-5 Ja 4 '64
Speaking out. por Sat Eve Post 237:8+ Jl 25 '64
about
Neo-Freudianism & Erich Fromm. E. Z. Friedenberg; reply. C. Landesman. Commentary 35:78 Ja '63
Visit with Dr Erich Fromm. C. Brossard. pors Look 28:50+ My 5 '64
FROMME, Allan
Our ability to love. Redbook 121:44-5+ Ag '63
FROMMER, Arthur
Europe plain & simple; Europe on $5 a day. il por Time 82:61 Jl 26 '63
FROMMER, Gabriel P. and Livingston, R. B.
Arousal effects on evoked activity in a nonsensory system. bibliog Science 139:502-4 F 8 '63
FROMMER-Pasmantier publishing corporation
Arthur Frommer changes distributor, sets up new line. Pub W 183:57 Je 17 '63
FROMMES, Stephen P. See Weber, A. F. jt. auth.
FRONDIZI, Arturo
Freedom to maneuver. Time 81:36 Mr 15 '63

FRONER, Robert R.
Bank night. Newsweek 64:73 S 21 '64
FRONT doors. See Doorways
FRONT-drive cars. See Automobiles—Design
FRONT seat on the roller coaster; story. See Lanham, E.
FRONT street theater, Memphis. See Memphis, Tenn.—Theater
FRONTIER airlines, incorporated
Frontier airlines pushes sales campaign. il Aviation W 78:43 My 20 '63
Turboprop Convairs cut Frontier's costs. il Aviation W 81:41-2 N 9 '64
FRONTIER and pioneer life

Kentucky

World of Daniel Boone. R. P. Warren. Holiday 34:162+ D '63

United States

Doctors of the frontier. G. Groh. il Am Heritage 14:10-11+ Ap '63
Doctors on the frontier; excerpts. R. Dunlop. il Todays Health 41:34-7+ O; 44-7+ D; 42:44-7+ Mr; 12-15+ Je; 12-13+ Jl; 40-3+ Ag; 42-5+ S; 40-1+ N '64
Frontier photographer; excerpts from following the frontier. F. Tilden. il Am Heritage 15:22-35 O '64
No place for a lady; condensation of Cripple Creek days. M. B. Lee. il Read Digest 84: 255-60+ My '64
White Indians; excerpt from Quiet crisis. S. L. Udall. il Field & S 68:32-3+ D '63
See also
Cowboys
Homesteads
Pioneers

Anecdotes, facetiae, satire, etc.

Pioneering; letter. P. L. Petrakis. Science 142:1019 N 22 '63
FROSCH, Robert A.
Underwater sound: deep-ocean propagation. bibliog Science 146:889-94 N 13 '64
FROSLID, E. Kenneth
Froslid's protest; concerning NY world's fair 64 on license plates. New Yorker 39:28 F 8 '64
FROST, Dianne
Fog; poem. Horn Bk 39:94 F '63
FROST, Douglas L.
Madrid; poem. Commonweal 81:129 O 23 '64
FROST, Douglas V.
Metric system of measurement; letter. Science 140:1138+ Je 7 '63
FROST, Gregory
What Russian girls are like. N Y Times Mag p 16-17+ Ja 24 '65
FROST, Harold M. See Landeros, O. jt. auth.
FROST, Joan Van Every
What are we all here for? por Library J 89: 4979-80 D 15 '64
FROST, Lesley
Our family Christmas. Redbook 122:45+ D '63
FROST, Malcolm H.
BMI work, outlook; summary of report. por Pub W 184:71-2+ O 14 '63
FROST, Richard
To hell with revising, I'm writing a new poem; poem. Harper 228:21 F '64
FROST, Robert
Away; poem. Sat R 46:19 F 23 '63
Fearless wisdom of Robert Frost. Vogue 141: 118-19 Mr 15 '63
Stopping by woods on a snowy evening; poem. por Newsweek 61:90 F 11 '63
Stopping by woods on a snowy evening; Road not taken; Sound of the trees; Excerpt. Death of the hired man; poems. por Am For 69:5 Mr '63
To prayer I go; excerpt from Letters of Robert Frost to Louis Untermeyer; with comment by R. Kahn. pors Sat Eve Post 236:47-56+ S 14 '63

about

Affectionately, Rob. por Newsweek 64:75-6 Ag 31 '64
Beginning. S. F. Morse. Poetry 104:253-7 Jl '64
Classicism of Robert Frost. J. F. Nims. il pors Sat R 46:22-3+ F 23 '63
Ever yours, Robert. il por Time 82:102+ S 20 '63
Frost books donated to N.Y.U. library. Pub W 185:105-6 Ja 20 '64
Frost: courage is the virtue that counts most. Newsweek 61:90-1 F 11 '63
Frost's personal library goes to NYU, not to library named in his honor. Library J 89:594 F 1 '64
Gift outright. A. MacLeish. Atlan 213:50-2 F '64
Insight into the human soul. por Sr Schol 82: 21 F 13 '63
Kennedy speaks at Frost library dedication; summary of address, October 26, 1963. J. F. Kennedy. il Wilson Lib Bul 38:317 D '63
Legacy of three poets. J. Jacobsen. Commonweal 78:189-92 My 10 '63
Lover's quarrel with the world. por Time 81:84 F 8 '63
Memory of Robert Frost and his influence. F. G. Melcher. Pub W 183:98 F 11 '63
Not unlike job. P. Schlueter. Christian Cent 81:1216-17 S 30 '64
Obituary notes; some prices paid for Mr Frost's work in recent years. Pub W 183:96-7 F 11 '63
Off the cuff. A. Marple. Writer 76:5-6+ My '63
Our own remembrance of Robert Frost. G. P. Hunt. Life 54:3 F 8 '63
Poet & the public man. il por Time 84:127 D 11 '64
Poetry and power. J. F. Kennedy. il Atlan 213:53-4 F '64
Prose he did not write. K. G. Chapin. New Repub 152:16-17 Ja 2 '65
Robert Frost: a momentary stay. I. Howe. New Repub 148:23-8 Mr 23 '63
Robert Frost: a reminiscence. R. Kahn. Nation 196:121 F 9 '63
Robert Frost: best-printed U.S. author, and his printer, Spiral press. P. A. Bennett. il Pub W 185:82-6+ Mr 2 '64
Robert Frost confronts Khrushchev. F. D. Reeve. por(cover) Atlan 212:33-9 S '63
Robert Frost, 1874-1963. C. R. Anderson. pors Sat R 46:16-20 F 23 '63
Robert Frost, 1875-1963. Reporter 28:20 F 28 '63
Robert Frost; his last poem. pors Life 54:46-7 F 8 '63
Robert Frost in Russia, by F. D. Reeve. Review
Newsweek il por 63:91 Ap 6 '64
Robert Frost, RIP. H. A. Kenny. Nat R 14:100 F 12 '63
Robert Frost: teacher-at-large. J. S. Dickey. il por Sat R 46:21-2 F 23 '63
Robert Frost: To earthward. J. Ciardi. Sat R 46:24 F 23 '63
Spirals of reason and fancy. L. Edel. il por Sat R 47:23-4 S 5 '64
Stamp of a heroic life. J. M. Cox. il por Sat R 46:43-4 O 5 '63
Strength of Robert Frost. A. Kazin. Commentary 38:49-52 D '64
FROST
Frost recedes north. Sci N L 83:235 Ap 13 '63
FROST protection
Before winter comes. B. Black. il Pop Gard 14:18-21+ N '63
Heat your orchard with stovepipe. B. Fowler. il Farm J 88:54N Ap '64
Save fruit trees from winter damage. E. C. Richardson. Suc Farm 61:75 N '63
FROSTBITE
Tips for your home and family. Todays Health 41:77 N '63
What to do about frostbite. Parents Mag 38: 139 D '63
FROSTINGS. See Icings
FROTA-PESSOA, O. and others
Christmas factor: dosage compensation and the production of blood coagulation factor IX. bibliog Science 139:348-9 Ja 25 '63
FROZEN desserts. See Desserts; Ice cream, ices, etc.
FROZEN eggs; Frozen fish; etc. See Eggs, Frozen; Fish, Frozen; etc.
FROZEN food vending machines. See Vending machines
FROZEN ground
Frozen ground rich in treasures; permafrost research. Sci N L 84:327 N 23 '63
Particle sorting by repeated freezing and thawing. E. E. Corte. bibliog il Science 142:499-501 O 25 '63
Permafrost; report on 1st international conference on permafrost. K. B. Woods and G. A. Leonards. il Science 143:1060-1 Mr 6 '64
Underground cold war; conference of Western and Soviet permafrost experts at Purdue. il Time 82:75 N 22 '63
FRUCHTER, Norman
Echoes of an evolutionary. Nation 199:169-70 S 28 '64
Radical vision. Nation 198:349-51 Ap 6 '64

FRUCTOSE
Fructose-1,6-diphosphate requirement of streptococcal lactic dehydrogenases. M. J. Wolin. bibliog il Science 146:775-7 N 6 '64
FRUGOLI, Diana M. See Gifford, R. O. jt. auth.
FRUIT
Delicate art of peeling fruit at the table. il House & Gard 124:40-1+ S '63
Growth, maturation, and senescence in fruits. J. B. Biale. bibliog il Science 146:880-8 N 13 '64
Guests serve themselves from the fruit tower. il Sunset 131:104+ Jl '63
New fruits and vegetables for '65. il Farm J 89:38H Ja '65
Straight talk about fruit myths. il Good H 156:161 My '63
Try a gift from the tropics: strange and wonderful fruits. il McCalls 92:84+ D '64
Unusual fruits. G. L. Slate. il Horticulture 42:26-7+ Ap '64
Unusual fruits you may want to try. Good H 156:165 Ap '63
See also
Cookery—Fruit
Spray residue on fruits, vegetables, etc.
also names of fruit, e.g. Bananas

Packing

One bad apple can't spoil this pack. il Farm J 88:44F Je '64

Picking

Mechanized date picker out-dates hand method. Sci N L 86:87 Ag 8 '64

Preservation

How to freeze and can fresh plums. Sunset 133:114-15 Jl '64
How up to date are your freezing and canning? questions and answers. Farm J 87:62 Je '63
See also
Canning and preserving

Storage

Chemical halts fruit decay. Farm J 87:52J My '63
See also
Apples—Storage
FRUIT, Artificial
Onions, lemons, peppers, apples. il Sunset 132:159-60 Ap '64
FRUIT, Candied. See Confectionery
FRUIT, Canned
Fast and fancy with fruit cocktail. il Bet Hom & Gard 42:95 Mr '64
Garden on your shelf. il McCalls 92:140-2+ O '64
Look what you can do with cling peaches hot or cold! il Bet Hom & Gard 41:94 F '63
FRUIT, Dried
Dried fruits packed with flavor. il Am Home 67:56-7+ Ja '64
FRUIT cake. See Cake
FRUIT culture
Fruit-truck news (cont of) Fruits and truck crops. See issues of Farm journal
Fruits and truck crops; ed. by L. Donelson. See issues of Farm journal
Physiological studies on fruit development by means of ovule transplantation in vivo. V. L. Moosad Melnick and others. bibliog il Science 145:609-11 Ag 7 '64
Twenty new fruits and vegetables. L. Donelson. il Farm J 87:64B-64C F '63
What U.S. fruit growers can learn from Europe. J. C. Snyder. il Farm J 87:77 Mr '63
See also
Apple trees
Citrus fruits
Fruit
Grafting
also names of fruits, e.g. Pears
FRUIT desserts. See Desserts
FRUIT drinks. See Beverages
FRUIT farms

Equipment

New shakers speed up fruit harvesting. il Farm J 88:34F Jl '64
FRUIT flies
Dreaded fruit fly returns to Florida. Sci N L 84:41 Jl 20 '63
See also
Drosophila
FRUIT handling
Bulk bins for everything. B. Fowler. il Farm J 87:40B-41 O '63
See also
Apples—Handling
FRUIT industry
See also
Citrus fruit industry
United fruit company
FRUIT juices
Fruit juice. il McCalls 90:126-7+ My '63
Tempting uses of soup and juices. Good H 156:221 Ap '63
FRUIT juices, Frozen
See also
Minute maid company
FRUIT-O-MATIC. See Vending machines
FRUIT picking. See Fruit—Picking
FRUIT salads. See Salads
FRUIT syrup. See Syrups
FRUIT trees
It's a one-tree orchard. il Sunset 130:183 F '63
New for '63. Pop Gard 14:89-90 F '63
New natural growth promoting substance in young citrus fruit. R. A. Khalifah and others. bibliog il Science 142:399-400 O 18 '63
Save fruit trees from winter damage. E. C. Richardson. Suc Farm 61:75 N '63
Shop now for these fruit, nut trees. Sunset 130:172 F '63
These trees give you shade and also give you a crop. Sunset 133:176 Jl '64
Two ways to make orchards pay more. B. Hardy. il Farm J 88:44B+ D '64
See also
Grafting
Landscape gardening
Pomegranates

Pruning

See Pruning

Spraying

See Spraying and dusting
FRUIT trees, Dwarf
Dwarf citrus. R. E. Atkinson. il Flower Grower 51:16-17 D '64
New way to train dwarf trees. G. Lorang. il Farm J 88:50F+ Ja '64
Spray that dwarfs trees; B-9. G. Lorang. Farm J 88:54 Mr '64
Tiny fruit trees grown for pick-'em-yourself. Sci N L 84:152 S 7 '63
FRUIT vending machines. See Vending machines
FRUITS. See Fruit
FRUITS, Citrus. See Citrus fruits
FRUITS, vegetables, etc. in decoration
Christmas decorating with fruit. il Sunset 133:70 D '64
Witty centerpieces from the fruits of the harvest. il Am Home 66:34-5 N '63
FRUMKIN, Gene
Man preserved in stone; King of daydreams; poems. Poetry 104:18-19 Ap '64
Now yesterday's fine words are uninhabited; poem. Sat R 47:70 Ap 25 '64
about
First and last things. J. Dickey. Poetry 103:316-18 F '64
FRY, Edward F.
Art. Nation 198:512-14 My 18 '64
FRY, John R.
United Presbyterians: prophecy vs. tradition. Christian Cent 80:1235-7 O 9 '63
FRY, Thornton
Mathematicians in industry, the first seventy-five years. Science 143:934-8 F 28 '64
FRYE, Alton
Military danger. Atlan 212:46-50 Ag '63
FRYE, John T.
Carl and Jerry. See issues of Popular electronics
Mac's electronics service. See issues of Electronics world to April 1963
FRYE, William R.
U Thant at the U.N. 10 A.M. to 8 P.M. N Y Times Mag p 18-19 O 20 '63
FRYER, Peter
In B—D with Mrs Grundy. Horizon 6:66-9 Spr '64
FRYING
Fried pastry idea. il Sunset 130:178+ Mr '63
Out of the frying pan. il McCalls 90:126-7+ Ap '63
Sautéing and frying. il House & Gard 125:147-8 F '64
FRYING pans. See Skillets
FRYMAN, L. R. and Albright, J. L.
Check your milking machine, it may be stealing profits. Suc Farm 62:94+ Mr '64
FUCHS, Bernie
When it's three and two. il Sports Illus 20:42-3 Ap 13 '64
FUCHS, Lawrence H.
Religious vote: when, why and how much? Cath World 200:285-93 F '65
FUCHS, Victor R.
Fallacies and facts about automation. N Y Times Mag p27+ Ap 7 '63

FUCHSBERG, Jacob D.
Brief for the jury in civil cases. N Y Times Mag p34+ Mr 1; 4+ Mr 22 '64
FUCHSIAS
Fuchsias. M. Moriarty. il Horticulture 41:570 N '63
Fuchsias outdoors. J. Machado. il Horticulture 42:30-2 Ag '64
Gardener's month. il House & Gard 123:160-3+ Je '63
How to grow fuchsias as shrubs. il Sunset 131:158-9 Ag '63
It's about time to prune your fuchsias. il Sunset 132:226+ Mr '64
Some opinions on the new fuchsias. Sunset 130:292 Ap '63
FUDENBERG, Betty Roof. See Fudenberg, H. H. jt. auth.
FUDENBERG, H. Hugh, and Fudenberg, B .R.
Antibody to hereditary human gamma-globulin (Gm) factor resulting from maternal-fetal incompatibility. bibliog Science 145: 170-1 Jl 10 '64
—and Hirschhorn, Kurt
Agammaglobulinemia: the fundamental defect. bibliog Science 145:611-12 Ag 7 '64
—See Aladjem, F. jt. auth.
FUEL
Energy. S. A. Schurr. il Sci Am 209:110-44+ bibliog(p307) S '63
See also subhead Fuel under various subjects, e.g. Airplane engines—Fuel
FUEL cells
Amazing bug battery; biocells. D. S. Halacy, jr. il Pop Electr 20:41-4+ F '64
Battery reliability ensures continued use. M. L. Yaffee. il Aviation W 80:49+ Je 1 '64
Cool fuel cell. Sci Am 208:78 Je '63
Energy unlimited? il Newsweek 62:50 O 28 '63
Fabulous fuel cell. W. G. Salm. il Pop Electr 21:47-50+ S '64
For space and under the sea. il Bsns W p 114+ N 7 '64
Fuel cell readied for orbital test. il Miss & Roc 13:34+ Ag 26 '63
Fuel cells: electricity in a promising new package. L. Buckwalter and B. Francois. il Pop Mech 119:102-6+ Mr '63
Gemini fuel cell readied for GT-2 flight, now scheduled for September. M. Getler. il Miss & Roc 14:29-32+ Je 8 '64
GE's Gemini/bios fuel cell progresses. il Miss & Roc 15:35 N 2 '64
Hydrocarbon fuel cells may power tracking sites. W. Beller. il Miss & Roc 12:26+ Ap 29 '63
New diesel fuel cell. il Pop Mech 120:30 Jl '63
New fuel cell to convert energy; chemicals into electricity. Bsns W p78 My 4 '63
New fuel cells surpass air force requirements. il Sci N L 84:263 O 26 '63
Space power from fuel cells. W. Von Braun. il Pop Sci 185:80-1+ Ag '64
Will this some day run your car? il Sci Digest 54:72 Ag '63
FUEL gages. See Gages
FUEL injection systems. See Airplane engines—Fuel feeding
FUEL oil tanks. See Oil tanks
FUEL pumps
Injector with a brain. B. Greene. il Hot Rod 16:34-5+ Jl '63
Keep the fuel flowing. M. J. Schultz. il Pop Mech 119:158-63+ Je '63
FUEL research
See also
Rockets—Fuel
FUEL supply
Energy. S. H. Schurr. il Sci Am 209:110-14+ bibliog(p307) S '63
Food stockpiling urged. Sci N L 83:139 Mr 2 '63
FUEL tanks, Motor boat. See Motor boats—Fuel tanks
FUENTES, Carlos
Last rites for a fat cat. H. R. Lane. Nation 198:558-60 Je 1 '64
FUENTES, Miguel Ydígoras. See Ydígoras Fuentes, M.
FUERST, Robert. See Brown, B. L. jt. auth.
FUGARD, Atholl
Blood knot. Criticism
America 110:552 Ap 18 '64
Nation 198:334-5 Mr 30 '64
New Yorker 40:110+ Mr 14 '64
Newsweek 63:97 Mr 16 '64
Time 83:73 Mr 13 '64
Vogue 143:62 My '64
FUGATE, Gerald B.
Where are you going? America 110:673-5 My 16 '64
FUGAZY, William Denis
Boxing mess: why I want to get out. pors Sat Eve Post 236:28-30+ Ap 6 '63
FUGITIVE slaves. See Slavery—United States—Fugitive slaves
FUJI, MOUNT
Fuji, the ever-changing mountain. L. Barry. il Pop Phot 54:24+ My '64
FUJI-HAKONE NATIONAL PARK. See National parks and reserves—Japan
FUJINAGA, Motosaku
Cultured prawns; the kuruma prawn. il Time 81:43+ Mr 29 '63
FUJITA, Fuji
Notes from abroad. Hi Fi 13:22+ Ag '63
FUJIWARA opera company. See Opera—Japan
FUJIYAMA. See Fuji, Mount
FULBRIGHT, James William
American agenda; evaluation of our society; address, May 1, 1963. bibliog Vital Speeches 29:520-6 Je 15 '63; Sat R 46:15-17+ Jl 20 '63
American character; address, December 5, 1963. Vital Speeches 30:164-7 Ja 1 '64
Cold war; address, April 5, 1964. bibliog f Vital Speeches 30:422-7 My 1 '64
Dangerous delusions. por Sat R 47:24-5+ O 24 '64
Excerpt from testimony before Committee on banking and currency, November 21, 1963. Cong Digest 43:50+ F '64
Foreign policy, old myths and new realities; address, March 25, 1964. Vital Speeches 30:388-94 Ap 15 '64; Excerpts, Newsweek 63:18 Ap 6 '64; Summary. por Time 83:23-4 Ap 3 '64
France and the western alliance; address, October 29, 1963. Vital Speeches 30:75-8 N 15 '63; Summary. por U S News 55:26 N 11 '63
Senator Fulbright on U.S. education; excerpts from address, October 13, 1962. Sch & Soc 91:31+ Ja 26 '63
Space and national priorities; address, October 17, 1963. Vital Speeches 30:41-4 N 1 '63
Speaking out; let's talk sense about Cuba. por Sat Eve Post 237:8+ My 16 '64

about

Chinks in Fulbright's armor. Christian Cent 81:509 Ap 22 '64
Democratic dialogue. K. Crawford. Newsweek 63:32 Ap 13 '64
Foreign affairs debate: are our policies turning obsolete? with editorial comment. por Bsns W p28-9, 120 Ap 4 '64
Fulbright and myths. Commonweal 80:101-2 Ap 17 '64
Fulbright criticizes foreign policy. Christian Cent 81:452-3 Ap 8 '64
Fulbright on de Gaulle. K. Crawford. Newsweek 62:49 N 11 '63
Fulbright proposal. America 110:500-1 Ap 11 '64
Fulbright's progress. Nation 198:357 Ap 13 '64
Growing foreign-policy row: two top Democrats urge changes. por U S News 56:19 Ap 6 '64
Hard line policy pays off. por U S News 56: 6 Ap 13 '64
Israel lobby. Newsweek 62:24 Ag 12 '63
Letter from Washington. R. H. Rovere. New Yorker 40:149-55 Ap 11 '64
Myths and realities: the debate over U.S. foreign policy; with quotations. por Sr Schol 84:8-11 My 8 '64
New myths for old. W. W. Shannon. Commonweal 80:102-3 Ap 17 '64
Reshaping policy. Commonweal 80:75-6 Ap 10 '64
Secretary Rusk's news conference of March 27, 1964. D. Rusk. Dept State Bul 50:570-6 Ap 13 '64
Senate's scholarly dissenter. Bsns W p29 Ap 4 '64
Senator and Castroism. Life 56:2 Ap 10 '64
Senator Fulbright. T. Coffin. por Holiday 36:34-7+ S '64
Senator Fulbright's new foreign policy. H. J. Morgenthau. Commentary 37:68-71 My '64
Senator speaks out. W. Lippman. Newsweek 63:19 Ap 13 '64
Space: Senator Fulbright steps into lunar landing controversy. D. S. Greenberg. Science 142:470 O 25 '63
Ultimate self-interest. il pors Time 85:14-18 Ja 22 '65
U.S. policy: old myths, mixed voices. il por Newsweek 63:17-18 Ap 6 '64
We and they. New Repub 150:3-4 Ap 18 '64
FULFORD, Roger
She wore a crown and a widow's cap. Sat R 48:46 Ja 23 '65
FULL day's wages; story. See Sackett, K. E.

FULLER, Mrs Charles
Wondrous house formerly a Baptist church. V. Lawford. il Vogue 143:164-73+ F 1 '64
FULLER, Edmund
Corridor; story. Good H 156:80-1 My '63
FULLER, Ethel Romig
All Adam's children; poem. Christian Cent 81:517 Ap 22 '64
Attention, all tourists; poem. Christian Cent 80:909 Jl 17 '63
FULLER, Helen
Kennedy's problem: could he get more from Congress? New Repub 148:12-14 Mr 9 '63
Man to watch at the Democratic convention. Harper 229:47-52 Ag '64
Powerful persuaders. New Repub 151:11-12 O 24 '64
FULLER, Hoyt W.
Negro writer in the United States. Ebony 20:126-8+ N '64
Our far-flung correspondents. New Yorker 39: 35-6+ Ja 4 '64
Rise of the Negro militant. Nation 197:138-40 S 14 '63
FULLER, Jack
Photogoplane. U S Camera 26:42 Ap '63
FULLER, John G.
Heyday of the documentary. Sat R 47:172 Ag 29 '64
Trade winds. See issues of Saturday review
FULLER, John Langworthy. See Huff, S. D. jt. auth.
FULLER, John Leopold
Poets old and young. C. Kizer. Poetry 102: 395 S '63
FULLER, Reginald H.
Mixed bag. Christian Cent 80:1241-2 O 9 '63
New Testament bookshelf. Christian Cent 80:271-3 F 27 '63
FULLER, Richard Buckminster
Notes on the future. Sat R 47:43-4+ Ag 29; 26-7 S 19; 26 O 3 '64

about

Bucky Fuller's firsthand God. Christian Cent 81:447 Ap 1 '64
Comprehensive man. por Newsweek 62:66-7 Ag 5 '63
Dymaxion American. il pors Time 83:46-51 Ja 10 '64
Inventor of the month. S. V. Jones. por Sci Digest 56:62 O '64
FULLER, Roy
Veterans and recruits. S. F. Morse. Poetry 102:330-1 Ag '63
FULLER, S. B.
Negro businessman speaks his mind; interview. pors U S News 55:58-61 Ag 19 '63
FULLER-SANDYS, Stuart
Breaking the rules. il por Time 81:40 My 17 '63
FULLERTON, Garry
UNESCO in the Congo. UNESCO Courier 16: 4-11 N '63
FULLMER, Gene
Smile on the face of the Tiger; Dick Tiger, Gene Fullmer fight in Africa. J. Olsen. il pors Sports Illus 19:12-19 Ag 19 '63
FULTON, John
Fighting Yankee of Seville. R. Daley. il pors Sat Eve Post 237:62-3 Ap 11 '64
FULTON, John Oxie
Time on whose hands? Read Digest 85:73-5 O '64
FULTON, Reid S.
By books possessed. il por Newsweek 62:74 Ag 12 '63
FULTON, Robert
Steamboat's charter of freedom; Gibbons v. Ogden. G. Dangerfield. il por Am Heritage 14:41-3+ O '63
FULTON, Robert Brank
Grounds for hope in Birmingham. Christian Cent 81:1012-13 Ag 12 '64
FULTON, Mo.
Don't get caught water-short. J. L. Worley. il Am City 78:133-4 Jl '63
FULTON fish market. See New York (city)—Markets
FULTZ quadruplets. See Quadruplets
FULWYLER, M. J. See Van Dilla, M. A. jt. auth.
FUND for education concerning world peace through world law
Grenville Clark at eighty. M. K. Harvey. Sat R 46:17 F 16 '63
FUND for the advancement of education
It's what's up top that counts. G. Dapper. il Sat R 46:48-9+ D 21 '63
New education grants. Sr Schol 83:2T Ja 10 '64
FUND for the Republic
Foundations as a tax dodge. F. J. Cook. Nation 196:323-5 Ap 20 '63
Funds and furor; anniversary convocation. il Newsweek 61:56-7 F 4 '63
Whither the world? two day gathering at New York city's hotel Americana. il Bsns W p30-1 Ja 26 '63
See also
Center for the study of democratic institutions, Santa Barbara, Calif.
FUND raising
Art of fund-raising. L. L. L. Golden. Sat R 47:45 Ag 8 '64
Especially for Christmas: fund-raising ideas for churches & clubs; excerpts from McCall's book of fund-raising ideas. M. F. Chester and R. Marek. il McCalls 92:88 N '64
Fund-raisers' fair. il Good H 157:144 S '63
Fund raisers for freedom. il Ebony 18:120-2+ O '63
Fund raising through refreshment operations. J. C. Evans. Recreation 56:233+ My '63
Life goes to Jackie Robinson's jam session: $15,000 for civil rights. il Life 55:79-81 Jl 5 '63
NAACP Freedom spectacular; all-star TV show. il Ebony 19:57-8+ Jl '64
One plan to control fund raising abuses; Los Angeles system. il Good H 156:164 My '63
Out of the ashes; funds for rebuilding burned Negro churches. il Newsweek 64:72 O 12 '64
Passing the collective hat; money for community and charitable services. Bsns W p92 My 2 '64
Peddling their papers for charity; Old newsboys day in St Louis. il Bsns W p 134-5 D 5 '64
Penny-by-penny; Branford, Conn. community house. J. Trepasso. il Recreation 57:500-1 D '64
Personal business. Bsns W p 123 O 5 '63
Sales plans for club fund raising. Good H 157:155 S '63
Trading stamps? no, thanks! fund raising for church. Christian Cent 81:388-9 Mr 25 '64
See also
American association of fund-raising counsel
Campaign funds
United foundation torch fund
FUNDAMENTAL particles. See Particles (nuclear physics)
FUNDAMENTALISM
Love, hatred and politics. Christian Cent 80: 1423-4 N 20 '63
Secular fundamentalism. America 108:733 My 25 '63
FUNDERBURK, Earl C.
Two expanded NEA insurance plans. NEA J 52:60 Mr '63
FUNDS-flow analysis. See Corporations—Finance
FUNERAL directors. See Undertakers and undertaking
FUNERAL rites and ceremonies
Evening funeral masses. America 108:188 F 9 '63
Funeral of the year; J. MacDonald. il Newsweek 65:22-3 F 1 '65
In Texas a policeman and an assassin are laid to rest too. T. Thompson. il Life 55: 52B-52E D 6 '63
In time of sorrow: the gift of your presence. S. Shubin. Read Digest 84:240-2 Je '64
Ways of death; concerning three books on funeral industry. J. Brooks. Consumer Rep 29:40-3 Ja '64
See also
Cremation
Kennedy, J. F.—Funeral rites and ceremonies
FUNERAL services. See Funeral rites and ceremonies
FUNERALS, Cost of
American way of death, by J. Mitford. Review
America 109:285 S 21 '63
Nat R 15:362-4 O 22 '63. F. Russell; Discussion. 15:455-6 N 19 '63
New Repub 149:29-30 Ag 31 '63. J. Ridgeway
Newsweek 62:84 S 9 '63
Reporter 29:48-50 S 26 '63. K. S. Lynn
Sat R 46:21-2 Ag 31 '63. D. Cort; Discussion. 46:37 S 28 '63
American way of death; condensation. J. Mitford. il Good H 158:69-82 F '64
Burial business hears voices; concerning J. Mitford's American way of death. Bsns W p80+ N 9 '63
Business of dying. il Time 82:68+ S 20 '63; Same abr. Read Digest 84:144-6 Ja '64
Funeral furor. Christian Cent 80:1259 O 16 '63
Furor over funerals; why the cry of scandal? bibliog il Changing T 17:7-12 N '63
High cost of dying, by R. M. Harmer. Review
Newsweek 61:87 Je 3 '63

FUNERALS, Cost of—*Continued*
New York to probe funeral gouging; Bureau of consumer frauds and protection. Christian Cent 80:1538 D 11 63
Outrage over the death business; with report by P. Blake. il Life 55:98B-105+ S 20 '63
Speaking out; Americans don't want fancy funerals. J. Mitford. Sat Eve Post 236:8+ N 23 '63
To die is gain. America 109:278 S 21 '63
Ways of death; concerning three books on funeral industry. J. Brooks. Consumer Rep 29:40-3 Ja '64
Why the cost of dying is so high. U S News 55:10 N 18 '63
See also
Undertakers and undertaking

FUNERARY figures. See Tomb figures

FUNGI
Aflatoxin B_2: chemical identity and biological activity. S. B. Chang and others. bibliog il Science 142:1191-2 N 29 '63
Carcinogenic mold; aflatoxin. Sci Am 211:60 N '64
Ceratocystis infection in sweet potato: its effect on proteins, isozymes, and acquired immunity. D. J. Weber and M. A. Stahmann. bibliog il Science 146:929-31 N 13 '64
Fungi and yeasts: chemistry and biochemistry. J. O. Lampen. Science 142:603 N 1 '63
Fungi; plants that are parasites. il Sci Digest 54:71-2 N '63
Microscopic plant traps and kills tiny pests; acaulopage pectospora. Sci N L 83:153 Mr 9 '63
Mycotoxins: aflatoxin isolated from penicillium puberulum. F. A. Hodges and others. bibliog Science 145:1439 S 25 '64
Nematode-trapping fungi. D. Pramer. bibliog il Science 144:382-8 Ap 24 '64
Nematode-trapping fungi: evaluation of axenic healthy and galled roots as trap inducers. D. W. Iffland and P. V. Allison. bibliog il Science 146:547-8 O 23 '64
Nutritional relationships among certain filamentous fungi and a marine nematode. S. P. Meyers and others. bibliog il Science 141:520-2 Ag 9 '63
Sporangium discharge in pilobolus: a photographic study. R. M. Page. bibliog il Science 146:925-7 N 13 '64
Staphylolytic enzyme from chalaropsis: mechanism of action. D. J. Tipper and others. bibliog il Science 146:781-2 N 6 '64
See also
Basidiomycetes
Lichens
Mushrooms
Mycology
also names of fungi. e.g. Mycorhiza

Culture media

Fungi of lichens. V. Ahmadjian. il Sci Am 208:122-30+ F '63
Growth of the cellular slime mold polysphondylium pallidum in a simple nutrient medium. M. Sussman. bibliog il Science 139: 338 Ja 25 '63

FUNGI, Fossil
Eocene epiphyllous fungi. D. L. Dilcher. bibliog il Science 142:667-9 N 8 '63
Fossils of tiny fungus found in Tennessee. Sci N L 85:26 Ja 11 '64

FUNGI, Pathogenic
Blood substance kills disease-causing fungus. Sci N L 85:73 F 1 '64
Conjunctiva contains factor inhibiting growth of candida albicans. P. J. Kozinn and others. bibliog il Science 146:1479-80 D 11 '64
Drug conquer fungus; ringworm and athlete's foot. Sci N L 86:291 N 7 '64
Microsporum nanum: first recorded isolation from animals in the United States. G. R. Bubash and others. bibliog il Science 143:366-7 Ja 24 '64
Pigeons and cryptococcosis; letter. J. D. Schneidau, jr. Science 143:525 F 7 '64
Plaster cast transmits TB-like fungus disease; coccidioidomycosis. Sci N L 83:377 Je 15 '63
Resistance to erysiphe polygoni of red clover infected with bean yellow mosaic virus. L. N. King and others. bibliog il Science 146:1054-5 N 20 '64
Rhizomorph production by armillaria mellea induced by ethanol and related compounds. A. R. Weinhold. bibliog il Science 142:1065-6 N 22 '63
Toxin-producing aspergillus isolated from domestic peanuts. U. L. Diener and others. bibliog il Science 142:1491-2 D 13 '63

FUNGICIDES
New chemical makes sprays work better. Farm J 88:54 F '64
Rout pests and disease early. R. L. Hering. il Pop Gard 16:46-7 Ja '65
Sneak up now on spring's pests. Sunset 130: 174 F '63
Your boat in A.D. 2063; Calignum. H. A. Calahan. il Motor B 111:26-7+ Mr '63

FUNGUS diseases. See Fungi, Pathogenic

FUNK, Mathäus
Funk family, craftsmen of Bern. W. De Sager. il Antiques 85:565-9 My '64

FUNK, Robert W
Logic and the logos. Christian Cent 81:1175-7 S 23 '64

FUNK, Wilfred John
Abaft the word (cont) Motor B 111:62+ Ap; 56 My; 112:58 Ag '63
It pays to increase your word power. See issues of Reader's digest

FUNKE, Lewis
Always in the wings, the shakes. N Y Times Mag p20+ My 17 '64
What time does the bus leave? Theatre Arts 47:61-3+ Je '63

FUNNIES. See Comics (books, strips, etc)

FUNNY girl; musical comedy. See Musical comedies, revues, etc.—Criticisms, plots, etc.

FUNNYHOUSE of a Negro; drama. See Kennedy, A.

FUNSTON, Keith
Quiet rebellion moves into the open por Bsns W p 120 Je 20 '64

FUORTES, M. G. F.
Nobel prize: 1963 award honors three for research on nerve functioning. Science 142: 468-70 O 25 '63
Visual responses in the eye of the dragon fly. Science 142:69-70 O 4 '63
—and Nelson, P. G.
Strychnine: its action on spinal motoneurons of cats. bibliog Science 140:806-8 My 17 '63

FUR, Artificial
Why you can't call fake fur a fake. Consumer Bul 47:24-5 F '64

FUR coats, wraps, etc.
New fur bravura. il Vogue 142:160-71 O 1 '63

FUR farming
Miles of mink; bound for U.S; Finnish mink farm. il Bsns W p 128-30 D 19 '64

FUR seal. See Seals (animals)

FUR trade
Relics from the rapids. S. F. Olson. il Nat Geog Mag 124:412-35 S '63
West of William H. Ashley, ed. by D. L. Morgan. Review
Am Heritage 15:81-3 Je '64. B. Catton
See also
Fur farming

FURASH, Edward E.
Businessmen review the space effort. Harvard Bsns R 41:14-16+ S '63

FURCOLO, Foster
From dazzling to fizzling. Time 84:27 O 23 '64
Mess thickens. por Newsweek 64:38 O 26 '64

FURLONG, William Barry
Ara's new era. Sat Eve Post 237:72-5 N 28 '64
Babes in a swampland. Sports Illus 19:66-70+ O 21 '63; Same abr. with title Most successful swamp in America. Read Digest 84:164-7+ F '64
Bloody but unbowed: the golf buff. N Y Times Mag p24-5+ My 19 '63
Cut 'em off at forward pass. Sports Illus 21: 30-3 O 19 '64
He's a great pair of golfers. N Y Times Mag p 14+ S 1 '63
Man behind the golfer. N Y Times Mag p72+ O 11 '64
Mary queen of Scots started it. N Y Times Mag p44+ Ag 18 '63
Midwest's nice monopolists, John and Mike Cowles. Harper 226:64-8+ Je '63
New stage in baseball's cold war. N Y Times Mag p36+ My 12 '63
Sad day for baseball. Sports Illus 21:26-7+ S 21 '64
Sounds of history. N Y Times Mag p72+ Mr 22 '64
They call him the greatest on ice. N Y Times Mag p36+ F 23 '64
Third world of the turf. Sat Eve Post 236: 74-6 S 21 '63
Thirty years ago. N Y Times Mag p25+ Ag 9 '64
Truth about medication errors in hospitals. Good H 157:76-7+ N '63
What's the truth about those flu shots? Good H 158:73+ Ap '64

FURNACES
Water-spray humidifier for a warm-air furnace. A. N. Anderson. il Pop Sci 186:156-7 Ja '65
See also
Oil burners
Solar furnaces

FURNACES, Foundry
Forging shop turns its back on suppliers; Cameron iron works. il Bsns W p 194-6+ My 18 '63

FURNAS, Clifford C.
Renewal of the professional man; address, November 7, 1963. Vital Speeches 30:144-6 D 15 '63

FURNAS, J. C.
They are bringing back the chestnut tree. Read Digest 82:129-32 Ap '63
Vandals in the library. Read Digest 84:175-6+ Ja '63

FURNESS library. See Helen Kate Furness free library, Wallingford, Pa.

FURNISHINGS, Household. See Household furnishings

FURNITURE
Bright-on-a-budget; furniture with a long future; furnishing a one-room apartment. il House & Gard 124:208-9 O '63
Britain goes modern. G. O'Brien. il N Y Times Mag p88-9 Mr 8 '64
Buying furniture? know your wood. il Changing T 17:13-14 Ag '63
Decorator's notebook: shop, look and listen. il Seventeen 23:163+ Mr '64
Distinctive character of the work of Lannuier. L. W. Pearce. il Antiques 86:712-17 D '64
Enchanting rooms that fool the eye. il House & Gard 125:106-13 Ap '64
Four simple small-shop low-cost projects you can build. D. Jordan. il Bet Hom & Gard 42:38-9 Ja '64
Fun furniture; useful pieces for party time. il Am Home 67:56-7 N '64
Furniture, antique vs. reproduction. Am Home 67:90 O '64
Furniture finds under $50. il House & Gard 125:182-3 My '64
Furniture glossary. il Am Home 67:126 N; 110 D '64; 68:78 Ja '65
Furniture in the raw. G. O'Brien. il N Y Times Mag p44-5+ Je 2 '63
Furniture that likes children. B. G. Wadsworth and N. Pierce. il Parents Mag 40:55-7 Ja '65
Furniture with a future. il House & Gard 125:54-5 Mr; 192-3 Ap; 166-7 Je; 126:228-9 S; 232-3 O; 282-3 N; 190-1 D '64
Guide to buying wood furniture. il Good H 157:160-1 O '63
Home; 1963-1964. G. O'Brien. il N Y Times Mag pt2 p 15-23+ S 29 '63; pt2 p 15-23+ S 27 '64
How to buy upholstered furniture. C. Murphy. il Redbook 121:80-1+ O '63
How to give modern furniture traditional flavor. il House & Gard 123:126-9 F '63
Idea furniture under $100. il Bet Hom & Gard 41:82 Jl '63
Modern classics. G. O'Brien. il N Y Times Mag p88-90 O 27 '63
Modern, mass produced. G. O'Brien. il N Y Times Mag p38-9 Jl 28 '63
New jobs for canework. G. O'Brien. il N Y Times Mag p 100-1 Ap 21 '63
Now on the home front; campaign furniture. G. O'Brien. il N Y Times Mag p82-3+ Mr 15 '64
100 ideas under $100. il Bet Hom & Gard 41:10+ Jl '63; 42-28-59 Jl '64
Pushbutton eating center; combination dining counter-dishwasher-disposal unit. il Pop Mech 120:96-8 Ag '63
Redbook's guide to eighteenth century furniture. J. Macurdy. il Redbook 122:82-90 N '63
Seven page portfolio of new furniture. il Good H 158:113-19+ Ap '64
Small pieces for small places. il House B 105:66+ O '63
Starter furniture for young marrieds. il House B 105:132-9+ Je '63
Taste of tradition. il McCalls 90:114-21 Ap '63
What's new in furnishings and housewares. R. Martens and J. Gillies. il Farm J 88:84-5 Mr '64
Wood furniture problems. E. Taylor. il Good H 157:226 O '63
See also
Office furniture
Upholstery
Woodworking
also names of pieces of furniture, e.g. Chairs; Tables; etc.

Care

Furniture repairs you can do. il Good H 157:143 Ag '63
How to take the hard work out of upkeep. Bet Hom & Gard 41:42 N '63

Design

Buying with the power to discern. il Bsns W p58-60 Ag 31 '63
How to be a happy, healthy oldster; furniture requirements of older people. House & Gard 124:112+ S '63
Living with modern antiques. G. O'Brien. il N Y Times Mag p52-3 Je 14 '64
New furniture with a go-with-everything look. F. Heard. il House B 105:216-19 O '63
New leisure furniture heads for the sun. il House & Gard 123:138-45+ Ap '63
Rare quality on the open market; sequent group. il House B 105:228-31 N '63
Some designing people. G. O'Brien. il N Y Times Mag p56-7 Ja 24 '65
Sources of the empire style. R. H. Randall, jr. il Antiques 83:452-3 Ap '63

Refinishing

Refinishing furniture. il Consumer Bul 47:9-13 Mr; 27-9 Ap '64
Restoring old furniture. D. Carlos. il House & Gard 125:50+ Ap '64

Anecdotes, facetiae, satire, etc.

Things my wife drags home! J G. Hubbell. il Read Digest 84:125-8 My '64

FURNITURE, American
Aaron Roberts and the southeastern Connecticut cabinetmaking school; report on H. Bulkeley's discoveries. H. Comstock. il Antiques 86:437-41 O '64
All-American furniutre. il Am Home 67:56-9 O '64
American & beautiful. R. W. Houseman. il Am Home 66:30-5+ Ap '63
American federal furniture in Argentina. V. Carreño. il Antiques 84:283-7 S '63
American triangular turned chair? S. D. Ripley. il Antiques 85:104-6 Ja '64
Diversity in Connecticut blockfront. H. Comstock. il Antiques 84:63-7 Jl '63
Ebenezer Hartshorne, cabinetmaker. R. H. Randall, jr and M. McElman. il Antiques 87:78-9 Ja '65
Federal furniture: a Philadelphia heritage. il House & Gard 125:198-9 Ap '64
Fine Federal furniture attributed to Portsmouth. C. E. Buckley. il Antiques 83:196-200 F '63
Furniture of New Hampshire; bird's-eye view from 1725-1825. C. E. Buckley. il Antiques 86:56-61 Jl '64
Furniture with the sweet taste of variety. F. Heard. il House B 105:158-61+ Ap '63
History in houses; the Noah Webster House at Greenfield Village. G. G. Gibson. il Antiques 85:196-201 F '64
Hosmer family furniture. D. A. Fales, jr. il Antiques 83:548-9 My '63
Meeks family of cabinetmakers. J. N. Pearce and others. il Antiques 85:414-20 Ap '64
New antiques; excerpts. G. Grotz. il House B 105:252-5+ N '63
New leisure furniture heads for the sun. il House & Gard 123:138-45+ Ap '63
Philadelphia empire furniture by Antoine Gabriel Quervelle. R. C. Smith. il Antiques 86:304-9 S '64
Recent museum accessions in American furniture. R. Davidson. il Antiques 86:472+ O '64
Redbook's guide to early American furniture. J. Macurdy. il Redbook 121:76-84 Jl '63
Shaker revival; restoration at Pleasant Hill, Ky. il Look 28:56-61 D 1 '64
Shop talk. R. Davidson. il Antiques 84:226+; 85:256+; 86:234+ S '63, Mr. S '64
Some Connecticut case furniture. F. K. Barbour. il Antiques 83:434-7 Ap '63

History

John F. Watson: first historian of American decorative arts. F. Sommer. il Antiques 83:300-3 Mr '63

FURNITURE, Argentine
American federal furniture in Argentina. V. Carreño. il Antiques 84:283-7 S '63

FURNITURE, Arrangement of
Apartment where change is the rule. il House & Gard 123:146-51 Ap '63
Foolproof decorating for beginners. il McCalls 92:120-3 O '64
How to give an average apartment a made-to-order look. M. Gough. il House B 105:102-5+ F '63
How to give pianos and organs the place they deserve. il House & Gard 123:164-7 Ap '63
How to make an old house look as fresh as tomorrow. il House & Gard 123:134-41 My '63
Is there a truly comfortable corner in your house? il House B 105:170-2 Mr '63
Living with antiques; New York apartment. P. Warren. il Antiques 83:326-9 Mr '63

FURNITURE, Arrangement of—*Continued*
Manhattan pied-à-terre. il House & Gard 125:154-5 My '64
Mrs Guest and Monsieur Boudin. il Vogue 141:148-9+ Ap 1 '63
New stacking furniture inspired by an old culture. C. S. Murray. il House B 105:166-9 Mr '63
Personal, and portable. G. O'Brien. il N Y Times Mag p58-9 Je 9 '63
Staging strategy for a beatiful party in one room. il House & Gard 125:162-5 My '64
Two-by-twos. il House & Gard 123:118-21 Mr '63
Wrongs made right. il Bet Hom & Gard 41:26+ F '63

FURNITURE, Austrian
See also
Biedermeier style

FURNITURE, Bermudian
New furniture in the Bermuda tradition. F. Heard. il House B 106:162-5 Mr '64

FURNITURE, Biedermeier. See Biedermeier style

FURNITURE, Built in
Bookshelf sewing center. il Pop Mech 121:146-8 Ap '64
Built-in look. G. O'Brien. il N Y Times Mag p40-1 My 31 '64
Fold-away bedroom. il Pop Mech 121:166-70 Mr '64
Four terrific projects you can build. F. R. Glass. il Bet Hom & Gard 41:54-5 Mr '63
Handsome built-ins now flank the old problem fireplace. il Sunset 130:176+ My '63
Handy built-ins for the bedroom area. R. Martens. il Farm J 87:58-60 S '63
How to stretch space for storing clothes. il House B 105:192-5 S '63
Sculptured house of concrete block. il Arch Rec 133:70-3 mid-My '63
This built-in beats four big problems. il Bet Hom & Gard 42:19 Mr '64
See also
Beds, Built in

FURNITURE, Childrens
Child-size closet, display board, and desk. il Bet Hom & Gard 41:27 S '63
Child's garden of bookshelves. il House & Gard 123:208-9 Ap '63
Keeping it simple. G. O'Brien. il N Y Times Mag p54-5 Ja 5 '64
Young-eyed look at new children's furniture. il House & Gard 125:178-9 Ap '64
See also
Cradles
Desks

FURNITURE, Convertible
Basic best buys, every one of them an inspired solution to a vital need; with editorial comment. il House & Gard 124:171, 172-83+ O '63
How to benefit from the intensive use of objects. il House B 105:88-93 Jl '63
Make room for an extra bed. il Good H 156:108-15 Mr '63
New stacking furniture inspired by an old culture. C. S. Murray. il House B 105:166-9 Mr '63
Party on the go. C. Kellogg. il Ladies Home J 80:99-101 N '63

FURNITURE, Danish
Designs from Denmark. G. O'Brien. il N Y Times Mag p50-1 F 16 '64

FURNITURE, Dutch
Some early Dutch furniture. il Antiques 84:439-41 O '63

FURNITURE, English
English furniture exports to America, 1697-1830. E. T. Joy. il Antiques 85:92-8 Ja '64
Furniture from the Rotch bequest to the Victoria and Albert museum. J. F. Hayward. il Antiques 83:560-3 My '63
George Hepplewhite, English cabinet-maker. E. H. Bjerkoe. il Hobbies 69:90-2 Jl '64
Shop talk. R. Davidson. il Antiques 85:148+ F '64
Thomas Sheraton. E. H. Bjerkoe. il Hobbies 69:90-1 Ag '64

FURNITURE, French
Paintings and antiques; New York apartment of E. A. Bragaline. R. Davidson. il Antiques 84:556-61 N '63
Redbook's guide to French provincial furniture. J. Macurdy. il Redbook 122:82-90 Mr '64
Shop talk. R. Davidson. Antiques 85:492+ My '64
Straighter Bourbon; Louis XIII furniture. il Time 85:64-6 Ja 15 '65
Three French kings helped to remodel a stable-garage. il House & Gard 123:106-11 F '63

FURNITURE, German
Rhenish cabinet of the eighteenth century. R. C. Smith. il Antiques 87:68-72 Ja '65

FURNITURE, Greek
Lost Greek look retrieved; how the Nicholas Goulandrises had the furniture of the fifth century B.C. re-created for their new Athens flat. il Vogue 141:118-23+ F 15 '63

FURNITURE, Metal
Modular metal lab furniture is tailored to specific jobs. P. Kirk. il Arch Rec 133:173-4+ Ja '63

FURNITURE, Outdoor
Do-it-yourself projects. P. J. Peart. il Pop Gard 15:42 Ja '64
Everything you need for family picnics. il Parents Mag 39:55-8+ Jl '64
Furniture for relaxing. il Pop Gard 15:38 Ap '64
Furniture you can leave out all year. il House B 105:114-17+ Je '63
Furniture you can make. il Pop Gard 15:43 Mr '64
Garden furniture; with shopping guide. C. Squire. il Pop Gard 14:50-5 My '63
Good care for outdoor furniture. Good H 158:168 My '64
In a kitchen, patio, family room-this furniture fits. J. Holmstrand. il Suc Farm 62:50-1 Je '64
Move outdoors with carefree new furniture. il Good H 158:126-33 Je '64
New leisure furniture heads for the sun. il House & Gard 123:138-45+ Ap '63
Patio furniture in redwood. P. McCafferty. il Pop Sci 184:147-51 My; 120-3 Je '64
Sculptured look in garden seats. W. Radcliffe. il Flower Grower 51:58-9 Ja '64
Selecting summer furniture. Bet Hom & Gard 41:114 Je '63
Set a mood with patio furniture. il Pop Gard 16:20 Ja '65
Sprucing outdoor furniture. Sunset 132:181-2+ My '64
Summer weekend project. A. L. Breakstone. il Pop Gard 15:10-11 Jl '64
These outdoor chairs swivel. il Sunset 130:162 Ap '63
Things to go out in the summer shine. il Vogue 141:182-3 My '63
Victorian summer. J. Peter. il Look 27:49 Jl 2 '63
We call them sun tables. il Sunset 133:64-5 Jl '64
See also
Benches
Garden ornaments
Tables

FURNITURE, Painted
Portuguese painted chairs. R. C. Smith. il Antiques 83:680-3 Je '63

FURNITURE, Portuguese
Portuguese painted chairs. R. C. Smith. il Antiques 83:680-3 Je '63

FURNITURE, Remodeled
Bright new ideas in furniture restyling. il Bet Hom & Gard 43:48-9 Ja '65
Complete picture-steps to easy and elegant furniture restyling. il Bet Hom & Gard 41:56-9 Mr '63
Reviving tired furniture. il Bet Hom & Gard 41:43 S '63

FURNITURE, Spanish
Handwrought imported furniture is in the grand Spanish tradition. J. Peter. il Look 27:74-5 N 19 '63
Redbook's guide to Spanish furniture. J. Macurdy. il Redbook 123:82-90 O '64

FURNITURE, Steel. See Furniture, Metal

FURNITURE, Swiss
Funk family, craftsmen of Bern. W. De Sager. il Antiques 85:565-9 My '64

FURNITURE, Wicker
Wicker moves in. G. O'Brien. il N Y Times Mag p54-5 Ag 25 '63

FURNITURE design. See Furniture—Design

FURNITURE factories

Employees

See also
Furniture industry and trade—Wages and hours

FURNITURE industry and trade
Fine time for furniture. il Time 84:76+ Jl 17 '64
Heading for new high. Bsns W p31 Ap 18 '64
See also
American walnut manufacturers association
Kroehler manufacturing company

Wages and hours

Earnings in wood household furniture, July 1962. G. L. Stelluto. il Mo Labor R 86:814-16 Jl '63

FURNITURE makers. See Cabinetmakers

FURSHPAN, E. J.
Electrical transmission at an excitatory synapse in a vertebrate brain. bibliog Science 144:878-80 My 15 '64

FURST, Betty
Space for the basic urge to be ornery. Recreation 56:163 Ap '63
FURST, Robert E.
Design of a high-quality transistor power amplifier. Electr World 71:34-5+ F '64
—and Zide, Larry
Transistors for music. Electr World 71:48-50 Mr '64
FURTADO, Celso
Brazil: what kind of revolution? For Affairs 41:526-35 Ap '63
Development of Brazil; with biographical sketch. Sci Am 209:28, 208-12+ bibliog (p308+) S '63
FURTH, J. J. and Loh, Patricia
Thermal inactivation of the primer in DNA-dependent synthesis of RNA in animal tissue. bibliog Science 145:161-2 Jl 10 '64
FURTHER education; story. See Wain, J.
FURTWÄNGLER, Wilhelm
Furtwängler file. R. Lawrence. Sat R 47:66 O 31 '64
In memoriam: Wilhelm Furtwängler. C. J. Luten. pors Am Rec G 31:14-17 S '64
Wilhelm Furtwängler, a luminous probing. A. Rich. por Hi Fi 14:47-9+ S '64
FUSCO, E. Miles
How far have we gone? Mod Phot 27:40 Ag '63
FUSCO, Gene C.
Preparing the city child for his school. bibliog f por Sch Life 46:5-8 My '64
Teachers and parents work together in depressed neighborhoods. Sr Schol 84:13T-14T Ap 24 '64
FUSCO'S restaurant, New York. See New York (city)—Hotels, restaurants, etc.
FUSES, Electric. See Electric fuses
FUSION reaction. See Nuclear fusion
FUSON, Ben W.
Fifteen years later. Sat R 48:23 Ja 2 '65
FUTCH, David
Will Italian democracy survive? Nat R 15:152-3 Ag 27 '63
FUTURE
As a famed historian sees the world of the future; interview, ed. by J. Fromm. A. J. Toynbee. il U S News 56:78-82 Mr 30 '64
Can we learn from other planets? excerpt from Of men and galaxies. F. Hoyle. il Sat R 47:63-7 N 7 '64
Creating man's future; goals for a world of plenty. B. Ward; R. L. Heilbroner; W. Reuther. il Sat R 47:27-9+ Ag 29 '64
Face of the future; quotations by Americans aged eighteen to twenty-five. il Look 29:72-4+ Ja 12 '65
Future-mindedness. K. Nott. Commentary 36:49-54 Jl '63
Future that nobody knows? reprint. D. Lawrence. U S News 58:96 Ja 11 '65
Grandchilden. D. Lawrence. il U S News 56:116+ My 18 '64
Hail automation, hail peace. N. Cousins. Sat R 47:20 Ja 18 '64
Into the world of the future. N. Semenov. il UNESCO Courier 16:58-63 Jl '63
Inventing the future, by D. Gabor. Review Science 144:278 Ap 17 '64. R. M. MacIver
It is one world or no world. A. J. Toynbee. il N Y Times Mag p28+ Ap 5 '64
Just seven years from now: coming changes in America. il U S News 55:62-5 D 2 '63
Notes on the future. R. B. Fuller. Sat R 47:43-4+ Ag 29; 26-7 S 19; 26 O 3 '64
Priorities of the future; address. A. E. Summerfield. Vital Speeches 29:334-6 Mr 15 '63
Since World war I: what fifty years have brought and what another fifty years may bring. il U S News 57:38-43 Jl 6 '64
Tomorrow is now; excerpts from Foreword, ed. by E. Denniston. E. Roosevelt. Ladies Home J 80:39-45 S '63
What the future holds for America; as the President's idea men see it; symposium. il U S News 56:40-4+ Je 22 '64
See also
Forecasts
Nineteen hundred and eighty-four
Two thousand (year)

Anecdotes, facetiae, satire, etc.

Last night. N. Mailer. Esquire 60:151+ D '63
FUTURE clubs. See Clubs
FUTURE farmers of America
Youth heads California future farmers. il Ebony 19:49-50+ D '63
FUTURE life
See also
Immortality
Limbo
FUTURE physicians clubs
Call for future doctors! A. Cutler. Read Digest 83:35-6 O '63
Future physician's clubs attract teen-agers to the medical profession. H. Bradshaw and V. Bradshaw. il Todays Health 42:54-7 Ja '64
FUTURE teachers of America
FTA summer experience; Northern Illinois university. E. M. Anglin and J. H. King. NEA J 53:31 My '64
FUTURISM
Consistent inconsistency of Joseph Stella. E. C. Baker. il Art N 62:46-7+ D '63
FYFE, William S. See Burns, R. G. jt. auth.

G

GA. See Gibberellic acid
GAC. See General acceptance corporation
GAF. See General aniline and film corporation
GAO. See United States—General accounting office
GATT. See General agreement on tariffs and trade
G. and C. Merriam company. See Merriam, G. and C. company
G&N (guidance and navigation) See Space vehicles—Control systems
GCA (ground control approach) See Airplanes—Landing
GDI. See General drive-in corporation
GE. See General electric company
GEM. See Ground effect machines
GI bill of rights. See Service men, Discharged—Education
GLF. See Cooperative grange league federation exchange
GM. See General motors corporation
GNP. See Gross national product
GOP (Grand old party). See Republican party
G. P. Putnam's sons. See Putnam's, G. P, sons
G-penicillin. See Penicillin
GSA. See United States—General services administration
GAARDER, Kenneth, and others
Averaged brain activity following saccadic eye movement. bibliog Science 146:1481-3 D 11 '64
GABEL, Émile
Freedom of information. America 109:133-5 Ag 10 '63
GABELLA, W. F.
Smooth landing on smooth water. Flying 74:47+ Je '64
GABER, Norman H.
Book marking analysis. por Library J 89:1503-7 Ap 1 '64
Development and testing of a new book marking system. Library J 89:1911-13 My 1 '64
GABIN, Jean
Playing to the crowd. il por Newsweek 63:38 My 11 '64
GABIS, Stanley T.
Leadership in a large manager city: the case of Kansas City. bibliog f Ann Am Acad 353:52-63 My '64
GABON
Autocrat insurance. il Time 83:35 Ap 24 '64
But why U.S? attacks on the U.S. embassy. Newsweek 63:53 Mr 23 '64
Colored rulers. G. C. Turner. Negro Hist Bul 27:177 Ap '64
De Gaulle to the rescue. il Time 83:29 F 28 '64
Gabon. F. Delano. il Travel 121:48-9 Mr '64
Gabon; Peace corps volunteers. J. F. Murphy, jr. il Nat Geog Mag 126:324-9 S '64
More growing pains. Newsweek 63:42 Mr 2 '64
Sure cure for sterility. Time 83:37 Mr 20 '64
See also
Iron mines and mining—Gabon
Lambaréné
GABON and the United States
See also
Americans in Gabon
GABOR, Dennis
Perils of leisure. Horizon 5:102-9 N '63
GABRIEL, Sister Marie Louis
Vatican and Jewry. Cath World 198:157-62 D '63
GADDIS, Vincent H.
California's coming earthquake. Sci Digest 54:27-34 D '63

GADES, Antonio
Brief biography. S. Goodman. pors Dance Mag 38:52-3 Ag '64
Flamenco: olé! pors Vogue 144:124-31 O 15 '64
GADGETS
Mail-order items for the gadgeteer. Consumer Bul 47:10 S '64
What's your gadget IQ? il Am Home 67:80+ D '64
GADSDEN, Ala.
Respecting people and titles. Christian Cent 81:229 F 19 '64
GAFFRON, Carole
Time for silence; story. Redbook 121:48-9 Ag '63
GAFFRON, Hans. See Homann, P. jt. auth.
GAGAKU. See Music, Japanese
GAGE, Grace
Why I'm glad I'm in a home. por Farm J 88:69 F '64
GAGE, Marvin H.
Caution!! heed the directions. Horticulture 41:252 My '63
GAGE, Merrell
Sculpture of Merrell Gage. D. Watson. il por Am Artist 27:60-5+ Je '63
GAGE family
Gage coat-of-arms. H. K. Eilers. il Hobbies 68:126 Je '63
GAGES
Aircraft radioisotope oil/fuel gaging. il Aviation W 80:77 My 4 '64
Dial indicator. V. Wheelwright. il Hot Rod 17:50-1+ Je '64
4x magnifying thickness gauge. E. R. Haan. il Pop Mech 120:174-5 Ag '63
Nucleonic sensor to gage spacecraft fuel. B. Miller. il Aviation W 80:74-5+ My 4 '64
Shotgun gauges. J. O'Connor. il Outdoor Life 133:132+ My '64
Tire gauges. Consumer Bul 48:16 Ja '65
Vacuum tester for $2. il Farm J 87:60B N '63
Zero-G liquid gage based on absorption of infrared radiation by gases; Molimetric liquid gaging system. R. D. Hibben. il Aviation W 81:56-7+ D 14 '64
See also
Indexing (machine work)
Strain gages
GAGLIARDO, Ruth Garver
Frederic Melcher and children's books. ALA Bul 57:549-52 Je '63
GAGLIARDO, Ruth Garver, School library scholarship. See Library science—Scholarships and fellowships
GAGS (Jokes) See Humor
GAINES, Edith
Collectors' notes. See issues of Antiques
Interim collection. Antiques 84:592-5 N '63
Living with antiques. Antiques 84:162-4 Ag '63
GAINES, Ervin J.
Confusion, criticism, and dissent great new Minneapolis librarian. Library J 89:2564 Je 15 '64
Intellectual freedom. ALA Bul 57:711-12, 817-18, 1009-10; 58:17-18, 87-9, 177, 345-7, 453-4, 595-6, 675-6, 767-8, 983-4; 59:17-18 S-O, D '63-Mr, My-O, D '64-Ja '65
GAINESVILLE, Fla.

Police

How to train a motorcycle squad. C. A. Roberts. il Am City 79:99 F '64
GAINHAM, Sarah
Political cabarets. Atlan 212:95-9 D '63
GAINS tax. See Income tax—Capital gains tax
GAITHER, James W. and others
Should vocational guidance be junked? NEA J 52:30-2 D '63
GAITSKELL, Hugh Todd Naylor
Letter from London. M. Panter-Downes. New Yorker 38:94+ F 2 '63
GAL, M. See Mokady, R. jt. auth.
GALACTIC systems
Age of our galaxy. Sky & Tel 27:287 My '64
Astronomers see galaxy better tilted upright; Andromeda galaxy. il Sci N L 86:53 Jl 25 '64
B stars and galactic exploration. R. M. Petrie. il Sky & Tel 26:330-4 D '63
Biggest blast; explosion in M-82. il Newsweek 62:101 O 7 '63
Brightest galaxies. Sci Am 208:76-7 My '63
Brightest things in the universe. Sci Digest 54:41 Jl '63
Cataclysm in Messier 82. il Sky & Tel 26:261-2; 27:344 N '63, Je '64
Chronology of the galaxy. D. D. Clayton. bibliog il Science 143:1281-6 Mr 20 '64
Collapse of the galaxy. il Sky & Tel 25:252 My '63
Compact galaxies. Sky & Tel 28:131-2 S '64
Compact galaxies found. Sci N L 86:21 Jl 11 '64
Deep-sky wonders. W. S. Houston. See issues of Sky and telescope
Distant supernova remnant. Sci Am 209:59-60 O '63
Dwarf galaxies. P. W. Hodge. il Sci Am 210:78-86 My '64
Evolution of galaxies. T. L. Page. bibliog il Sky & Tel 29:4-10 Ja '65 (to be cont)
Evolution of galaxies; report on twelfth congress of the International astronomical union. T. Page. bibliog il Science 146:804-6+ N 6 '64
Exploding galaxies. A. R. Sandage. il Sci Am 211:38-47 N '64
Exploding galaxy M82: evidence for the existence of a large-scale magnetic field. A. R. Sandage and W. C. Miller. bibliog il Science 144:405-9 Ap 24 '64
Explosion in M82? Sky & Tel 26:22 Jl '63
Finding the fastest galaxy: 3C-147. Time 83:46 Ap 10 '64
Galactic magnetism. Sci Am 211:46 Jl '64
Globular cluster Omega Centauri. J. Saunders. il Sky & Tel 26:133-7 S '63
Huge galactic explosion. il(p209) Sci N L 84:215 O 5 '63
Hydrogen in galaxies. M. S. Roberts. il Sci Am 208:94-100+ Je '63
Hypernova? Sci Am 209:67 Jl '63
Jeans' criterion of gravitational instability. S. S. Huang. il Sky & Tel 26:77-9 Ag '63
Local group of galaxies; reprint. G. O. Abell. il Sky & Tel 27:21 Ja '64
Local system of stars. O. Struve. il Sky & Tel 25:78-81 F '63
Machines in heavens source of radio waves. Sci N L 83:200 Mr 30 '63
Near the edge. il Newsweek 62:60 D 30 '63
Oldest rocks found; half the age of Milky way galaxy. il Sci N L 87:7 Ja 2 '65
Our galaxy: its structure and evolution; summary of address. J. H. Oort. Sky & Tel 28:266-7 N '64
Pregalactic stars. Sci Am 208:65-6 F '63
Pulsing quasar. Time 83:73 My 8 '64
Radio map of the Andromeda galaxy. J. M. MacLeod. bibliog il Science 145:389-91 Jl 24 '64
Radio map of the Andromeda galaxy. J. M. MacLeod. bibliog il Science 145:389-91 Jl 24 '64; Reply. H. C. Arp. 145:952 Ag 28 '64
Sculptor and Fornax dwarf galaxies. P. W. Hodge. il Sky & Tel 28:336-9 D '64
Sodium lines in galaxies. Sky & Tel 26:197 O '63
Twinkle, twinkle 3C-273. Time 81:85-6 Ap 5 '63
Very remote radio galaxies. Sky & Tel 25:311 Je '63
Visual impressions of galaxies. J. H. Mallas. il Sky & Tel 27:376-8 Je '64
Way of a galaxy. il Time 81:58+ F 8 '63
See also
Magellanic clouds

Spectra

Finding the fastest galaxy: 3C-147. Time 83:46 Ap 10 '64
GALACTOSE
Galactose metabolism by rat liver tissue: influence of age. S. Segal and others. bibliog il Science 142:1311-13 D 6 '63
GALACTOSEMIA
Blue-red test for trouble. Time 84:106 N 27 '64
GALACTOSIDASES
Galactosidase action on human blood group B active escherichia coli and ox red cell substances. G. F. Springer and others. bibliog il Science 146:946-7 N 13 '64
β-Galactosidase: inactivation of its messenger RNA by ultraviolet irradiation. P. A. Swenson and R. B. Setlow. bibliog il Science 146:791-4 N 6 '64
Neurospora β-galactosidase: evidence for a second enzyme. W. K. Bates and D. O. Woodward. bibliog il Science 146:777-8 N 6 '64
GALAMISON, Milton A.
Backlash. New Yorker 40:25-8 My 30 '64
Hooky. il por Newsweek 63:62 F 17 '64
GALANOS, James
Galanos. E. Merriam. il por Sat Eve Post 236:54+ O 26 '63
Girl with the Galanos air. il por Holiday 33:74-9 Je '63
Socko American pair. il Life 54:75-7+ Mr 1 '63
Talk, the clothes, the glitter at the New York openings; backstage notes. il por Vogue 141:142-5+ Mr 1 '63

GALANT, Henry C.
France; a comprehensive health plan. bibliog f Cur Hist 44:351-8+ Je '63
GALANTER, Marc
Dissent on Brother Daniel. Commentary 36:10-17 Jl '63
GALANTINES. See Cookery—Poultry
GALÁPAGOS ISLANDS
See also
Zoology—Galapagos Islands
GALAX
Charming and useful galax. E. L. Sculthorp. il House B 105:284-5 N '63
GALAXIES. See Galactic systems
GALAXY (Milky way) See Milky way
GALAZKA, Jacek M.
(tr) See Lec, S. More unkempt thoughts
GALBRAITH, Catherine A.
Mother doesn't do much. Atlan 211:47-52 My '63
GALBRAITH, Georgie Starbuck
First lines on a new leaf; poem. McCalls 90:177 S '63
It isn't the principle of the thing; poem. McCalls 91:143 Ja '64
Long way; poem. Ladies Home J 80:108f S '63
Love's season is brief; poem. McCalls 91:226 O '63
Meteorological note; poem. McCalls 90:156 Je '63
Only in life; poem. McCalls 92:184 O '64
Somewhat envious portrait; poem. McCalls 90:146 Jl '63
Stolen day; poem. McCalls 90:128 Mr '63
Storm; poem McCalls 90:142 Ag '63
Three phases of Eve; poem. Ladies Home J 80:132 Ja '63
GALBRAITH, John Kenneth
Book project in India; summary of address. Pub W 185:45-7 Je 22 '64
Campus rules on sex; excerpts from letter. por U S News 55:18 N 25 '63
Economics and the quality of life; adaptation of address, December 27, 1963. bibliog Science 145:117-23 Jl 10 '64
Experiment in India. Sat R 47:20-3 Ag 15 '64
Let us begin: an invitation to action on poverty. Harper 228:16+ Mr '64
Life book review. Life 56:13 Mr 27 '64
On our quarrel with success; address, June 9, 1963. Dept State Bul 49:52-6 Jl 8 '63
Scotch in Canada; excerpts from Scotch. Harper 228:35-40 Je; 229:79-84 Jl; 77-80 Ag '64
Warring on poverty; summary of address. Sr Schol 84:4T F 7 '64
What's become of the affluent society; interview. por U S News 56:66-8 My 4 '64

about

Other side of affluence. por Bsns W p 190+ Ap 18 '64
Truants' return. il por Newsweek 62:76 O 7 '63
What we don't know might kill us. E. Capouya. Sat R 47:26-7 Mr 28 '64
GALBRAITH, John Kenneth, family
Open diplomacy; Roosevelt House, New Delhi. il Time 81:60-1 Ap 12 '63
GALBRAITH, Thomas Galloway Dunlop
Britain's scandalous spy case. C. Brogan. il Nat R 14:195-6+ Mr 12 '63
GALBRAITH, Virginia
Japan's position in world trade. bibliog f Cur Hist 46:207-11+ Ap '64
GALE, Eleanor
We had the sense to stay poor. por Redbook 124:8+ N '64
GALE, John
John's other wife. Motor B 111:45-6+ F '63
GALE, Joseph
How the Great Swamp of New Jersey was saved. Nat Parks Mag 37:10-14 Ag '63
GALE, Selma R.
Hand extended. ALA Bul 58:777-80 O '64
GALEN Martini, Sister. See Martini, G.
GALENA, Ill.

Historic houses, etc.

Parnell House in Galena. il Hobbies 68:55 S '63
GALERIES Lafayette (store) See Paris—Stores
GALES. See Storms
GALILEE
Galilee is still Galilee. C. Northcott. Christian Cent 80:645 My 15 '63
GALILEE, SEA OF
Land of Jesus. il Vogue 142:98-101 D '63
GALILEI, Galileo
Majesty of the cosmos; excerpt from Dialogue on the great world systems. por UNESCO Courier 17:26 My '64

about

Galileo gala; sky show and exhibit at Hayden planetarium. New Yorker 39:28-30 F 8 '64
Galileo Galilei; a new vision of the universe. C. Maccagni. il por UNESCO Courier 17:24-5+ My '64
Galileo Galilei, 1564-1642. C. A. Ronan. il pors Sky & Tel 27:72-8 F '64
Galileo in Padua; reprint. R. Suter. il Sky & Tel 27:99-100 F '64
Galileo's first records of Jupiter's satellites; reprint. J. Meeus. il Sky & Tel 27:105-6 F '64
Galileo's visits to Rome; reprint. W. J. Miller. il Sky & Tel 27:101-5 F '64
Man who looked to the stars. I. B. Cohen. il pors N Y Times Mag p 19-20+ F 9 '64
One Galileo case is enough. J. J. Langford. Cath World 200:205-10 Ja '65
Our heritage from Galileo Galilei; address, May 21, 1964. R. E. Gibson. il Science 145:1271-6 S 18 '64; Discussion. 146:997-8 N 20 '64
With a simple telescope Galileo mapped the true orbit of Venus. T. D. Nicholson. il Natur Hist 73:46-8 My '64
GALIN, David
Auditory nuclei: distinctive response patterns to white noise and tones in unanesthetized cats. bibliog Science 146:270-2 O 9 '64
GALL, Norman
Dominican Republic: the goons again. Nation 198:159-61 F 17 '64
Fall of Juan Bosch. Nation 197:253-6 O 26 '63
How Trujillo died. New Repub 148:19-20 Ap 13 '63
Letter from Peru. Commentary 37:64-9 Je '64
GALLAGER, Sheldon M.
Shop talk. See issues of Popular science monthly
GALLAGHER, Barney
Confidential. il por Newsweek 63:74-5 My 25 '64
GALLAGHER, Cornelius
Excerpt from article. Cong Digest 43:220+ Ag '64
GALLAGHER, D. Nora
Adelphi's accent on grace. Library J 88:4558-61 D 1 '63
GALLAGHER, Dan
Conversation corner; New York repertoire workshop. L. Joel. Dance Mag 37:18 F '63
GALLAGHER, Francis J.
Books to be noted; biography. America 108:684-6; 109:673-4; 110:640-2; 111:708-10+ My 11, N 23 '63, My 9, N 28 '64
GALLAGHER, J. Joseph
Baltimore unity workshop. America 111:138-9 Ag 8 '64
GALLAGHER, J. P.
Nuclear power for Piquads. Am City 79:71-2 Jl '64
GALLAGHER, J. Roswell
Emotional life of the teen-ager. PTA Mag 58:26-8 bibliog(p37) F '64
How much is it worth to win? por Seventeen 23:152+ My '64
GALLAGHER, Joseph V.
After the council: back to school? Cath World 200:28-33 O '64
Book of the month. Cath World 200:185-6 D '64
Challenge of Christian freedom. Cath World 197:223-30 Jl '63
Pastoral liturgy. Cath World 197:330-2 Ag '63
GALLAGHER, Leo
That old hotel in Paradise. il Nat Parks Mag 38:4-7 Ja '64
GALLAGHER, Leonard V. and Old, B. S
Continuous casting of steel. Sci Am 209:74-88 bibliog(p 178) D '63
GALLAGHER, Robert S.
Ban the Pooh! Reporter 29:62 D 5 '63
God's little helpers. Reporter 30:24-6 Je 4 '64
Labor's love lost. Reporter 30:47-8 Mr 26 '64
—and Semple, Ronald
Life and times of Tony Pro. Reporter 29:37-40 S 12 '63
GALLAGHER, Thomas
My night as a police officer. Read Digest 82:173-4+ Je '63
GALLAGHER, William. See Phelps, E. D. jt. auth.
GALLAHUE, John
Tragedy at Liege. Look 27:72-4+ Mr 12 '63
GALLANGO, M. L. See Arends, T. jt. auth.
GALLANT, Barbara
How beautiful can you get? pors Mlle 57:124-5 Je '63
GALLANT, Mavis
Autobiography; story. New Yorker 39:31-8 F 1 '64
Careless talk; story. New Yorker 39:41-7 S 28 '63

GALLANT, Mavis—*Continued*
Circus; story. New Yorker 40:38-40 Je 20 '64
Ernst in civilian clothes; story. New Yorker 39:54-8 N 16 '63
Ice wagon going down the street; story. New Yorker 39:54-62 D 14 '63
Unmarried man's summer; story. New Yorker 39:54-60 O 12 '63
GALLATIN NATIONAL FOREST. See National forests
GALLAUDET college, Washington, D.C.
Saturday's silent heroes; Gallaudet college football. M. Silva. il Life 57:59-60+ N 6 '64

GALLBLADDER

Diseases

Gall bladder diseases. I. J. Rossman and C. J. Schein. Parents Mag 39:133-4 O '64
GALLEGOS, Rómulo
Scholar, novelist, and president. L. Dunham. il pors Américas 16:1-6 D '64
GALLER, David
Consistencies; poem. Commonweal 81:168 O 30 '64
Hand; Root; Self-hatred; Bow; poems. Poetry 103:236-40 Ja '64
Shadow; poem. Commonweal 79:463 Ja 17 '64
Tyutchev and Tomlinson. Poetry 101:418-20 Mr '63
Use of anthologies. Poetry 103:261-5 Ja '64
GALLERY of modern art, New York
Caviare? New York's newest museum. A. Frankfurter. il Art N 63:33-4+ Mr '64
Hartford modern: what's in a name. il Newsweek 63:64-5 Mr 23 '64
Hartford's gallery; opening of Huntington Hartford's gallery of modern art. New Yorker 40:32-3 Mr 21 '64
Home for wholesome art. il Life 56:65-6 Ap 3 '64
Huntington Hartford's ivory tower. M. Grosser. Nation 198:402-3 Ap 20 '64
New museum in New York; Huntington Hartford gallery of modern art. N. Lansdale. il Am Artist 29:55-7+ F '65
New York's modern merry-go-round; Huntington Hartford's gallery of modern art. K. Kuh. il Sat R 47:25-7 Mr 21 '64
One man's taste; Huntington Hartford's Gallery of modern art. il Time 83:62-3 Mr 27 '64
Philanthropic philistine. D. Peerman. Christian Cent 81:706-7 My 27 '64
Square on the Circle. F. Getlein. New Repub 150:36-7 Ap 11 '64
GALLERY of modern art, Washington, D.C. See Washington, D.C.—Galleries and museums
GALLERY passport, limited
Something of value; guided tours. il Newsweek 61:92+ My 6 '63
GALLEYS, Boat. See Boats—Equipment
GALLICO, Paul William
Silent miaow; story. McCalls 92:100-1 O '64
WLB biography. M. L. Holton. por Wilson Lib Bul 38:797 My '64
GALLI-CURCI, Amelita
Galli-Curci, 1883-1963. J. Ardoin. por Mus Am 84:72 Ja '64
Galli-Curci today; photographs. F. Robinson. Opera N 28:13-15 S 28 '63
Obituary
Opera N por 28:34 F 22 '64
GALLIEN-Lartigue, O. and Goldwasser, E.
Hemoglobin synthesis in marrow cell culture: the effect of rat plasma on rat cells. Science 145:277-9 Jl 17 '64
GALLIGAN, William
Idaho's instant goat hunt. por Outdoor Life 131:72-5+ Je '63
GALLIPOLI campaign, 1915. See European war, 1914-1918—Campaigns and battles—Turkey and the Near East
GALLIUM
Crystal structures at high pressures of metallic modifications of compounds of indium, gallium, and aluminum. J. C. Jamieson. bibliog il Science 139:845-7 Mr 1 '63
GALLIUM arsenide diodes. See Diodes
GALLO, Joey
My life inside the mob; ed. by Q. Reynolds. S. Slater. il pors Sat Eve Post 236:38-43+ Ag 24 '63
GALLO gang. See Gangs
GALLOIS, Pierre M.
Trap offered de Gaulle. Bul Atomic Sci 19:24-7 O '63
GALLOWAY Methodist church. See Jackson, Miss.—Churches
GALLSTONES. See Calculi, Biliary
GALLUP, George
Do polls tell the story? interview. pors U S News 57:52-4+ O 5 '64
George Gallup looks at tomorrow's customer; interview. por Nations Bsns 52:68-70+ Mr '64
—and Grafton, Samuel
How women feel about money. McCalls 91:74-7+ Jl '64
Ten biggest mistakes in any woman's budget. McCalls 91:46+ Ag '64
GALLUP polls. See Public opinion polls
GALOSHES. See Shoes, Rubber, plastic, etc.
GALPHIN, Bruce M.
Judge Pye and the hundred sit-ins. New Repub 150:8-9 My 30 '64
Pop literature of the radical right. New Repub 151:22-5 O 10 '64
To break the silent heart. Sat R 48:51 Ja 9 '65
When a Negro is on trial in the South. N Y Times Mag p 17+ D 15 '63
GALTON, Lawrence
Desperate gamble: organ transplants. Pop Sci 185:94-6+ D '64
Great debate over pests and pesticides. N Y Times Mag p34+ Ap 14 '63
Medical science reaches for the impossible. Pop Sci 186:114-18 Ja '65
New canal, dug by atom bombs. N Y Times Mag p24-5+ S 20 '64
6,000,000 pints of blood is not enough. N Y Times Mag p38+ Mr 29 '64
Under the weather? Pop Sci 184:88-90+ Ja '64
Will space research pay off on earth? N Y Times Mag p29+ My 26 '63
Wonder drugs, cure or. . ? Pop Sci 183:98-100+ N '63
World is getting thirstier. N Y Times Mag p94+ S 27 '64
GALTON, Michael
Generalized Shwartzman reaction in the pregnant golden hamster. bibliog Science 139:923-4 Mr 8 '63
GALUN, Rachel, and Kindler, S. H.
Glutathione as an inducer of feeding in ticks. bibliog Science 147:166-7 Ja 8 '65
—and others
Feeding response in aedes aegypti: stimulation by adenosine triphosphate. bibliog Science 142:1674-5 D 27 '63
GALVANI, Luigi
Alessandro Volta. G. De Santillana. il por Sci Am 212:82-91 Ja '65
GALVANIZING
Hot-dip galvanizing. il Pop Mech 119:190-2 Ap '63
GALVAO, Henrique
Price of the Azores; tr. from the Portuguese by G. Rabassa. Nation 197:432-3 D 21 '63
about
Lone crusader. Nation 197:446-7 D 28 '63
UN and Captain Galvao. Nation 197:377-8 D 7 '63
GALVESTON

City planning

From pirate's haven to magic harbor. il Bsns W p68 Ag 22 '64
GALVIN, John A. T.
$21 million mystery man. il por Time 81:20 Mr 22 '63
GAMACHE, Mary Fitzgerald
Summer forecast; family fun. Parents Mag 38:60-1+ Je '63
GAMAREKIAN, Edward. See Stumpf, K. L. jt. auth.
GAMBELL, Saint Lawrence Island
Alaska village in sight of Siberia. il Sunset 133:8 Jl '64
GAMBIA
Bride for Senegal? New Repub 149:9 Jl 13 '63
See also
United Nations—Gambia
GAMBLE-Skogmo, incorporated
Small town greets the discounters; Tempo discount centers. il Bsns W p90+ O 3 '64
GAMBLERS
Battle of the hottest sticks; World's pocket billiards tournament; with drawings by D. Gorsline. Sports Illus 18:32-7 F 25 '63
Gambling; why? with photographs by P. Fusco. G. Zimmermann. Look 27:21-35 Mr 12 '63
Noblest hustlers; shooting pool for big money. J. Richardson. Esquire 60:94+ S '63
Winners often lose. B. Surface. il N Y Times Mag p96-8+ Ap 19 '64
GAMBLING
Bank night, biggest payoff at Roosevelt raceway. Newsweek 64:73 S 21 '64
Bush-league scandal. Time 81:45 Ap 26 '63
Christians and the gambling mania. L. M. Starkey, jr. Christian Cent 80:267-70 F 27 '63

GAMBLING—*Continued*
Come into the parlor; off-track betting, in New York. il Newsweek 62:96+ N 4 '63
Craps on credit; foreign gambling debts collectible in New York. Time 84:57 N 27 '64
Detroit; a lesson in law enforcement. G. Edwards. Ann Am Acad 347:67-73 My '63
Gambler's world series. E. Asinof. il Sat Eve Post 236:72-4 N 30 '63
Gentlemen, place your bets; casino is in Nevada state prison. il Newsweek 62:25 Jl 1 '63
Happiness is Mr Lynch's office; Roosevelt raceway, Westbury, L.I. J. Willig. il N Y Times Mag p50+ O 18 '64
Hicks picks; London's Daily mail sports editor picks the races in print. Newsweek 62:49 Jl 8 '63
Hornung and Karras fired. il Life 54:38 Ap 26 '63
Horse player Havemann rides again. E. Havemann. Life 54:15 Ap 12 '63
Horse sense; largest win in parimutuel history. il Newsweek 63:58 My 11 '64
Horseplayer wins $81,000. il Ebony 19:124-6+ Jl '64
How to raise money without really trying. il Time 81:29 Ap 5 '63
Hypothetical sport. Newsweek 61:61 F 11 '63
Illegal gambling casinos in the USA: where the law ends. S. Grafton. il Look 28:124-5+ O 20 '64
It's bye! bye! blackjack. D. E. Scherman. il Sports Illus 20:18-20+ Ja 13 '64; Same abr. Read Digest 84:223-6 Je '64
Judgement day; suspension of P. Hornung and A. Karras. il Newsweek 61:84 Ap 29 '63
Legalized gambling: the dreams and the realities; New York city's proposal to legalize off-track betting. M. R. Wessel. Nation 200:46-8 Ja 18 '65
Maryland; a law-enforcement dilemma. A. J. T. Zumbrun. bibliog f il Ann Am Acad 347:58-66 My '63
No more alligator shoes; casinos closed down in Hot Springs, Ark. il Newsweek 63:102 Ap 20 '64
Off-track betting: the outlook in New York, Nevada, Britain. U S News 55:10+ N 18 '63
100-year spree at Saratoga; with report by M. Smith. il Life 55:52B-61 Jl 26 '63
Pick a number from 000 to 999. F. Powledge. il N Y Times Mag p35+ D 6 '64
Players are not just people. T. Maule. il Sports Illus 18:22+ Ap 29 '63
Playing the ponies with a pair of experts. P. D. Willis. il Harper 228:48-50 Mr '64; Same abr. Read Digest 84:240-1+ My '64
Professor who breaks the bank. P. O'Neil. il Life 56:80-2+ Mr 27 '64
Quack medicine; proposal to license off-track betting. Nation 197:151 S 21 '63
Seek repeal of gambling law. W. Peabody. Christian Cent 81:1091 S 2 '64
Seven men on four horses; winners on a long shot at New York's Roosevelt raceway. il Time 84:43 My 8 '64
Showdown in Arkansas: no dice in Hot Springs. J. Skow. il Sat Eve Post 237:78-9 S 19 '64
Sixty-five miles from home; Hot Springs, Ark. Nation 198:282 Mr 23 '64
State as bookie; legalized gambling. Sports Illus 22:5 Ja 4 '65
Third world of the turf. W. B. Furlong. il Sat Eve Post 236:74-6 S 21 '63
True crisis; corruption in sports. J. Underwood. il Sports Illus 18:16-19+ My 20 '63
Who will get policy baron's fortune? H. Bims. il Ebony 19:116-18+ O '64
Why pro football must live with sin. T. Cohane. il Look 27:64-71 Jl 2 '63
See also
Book making (betting)
Lotteries
Pinball machines
Probabilities

Laws and regulations

Off and running in state lottery; New Hampshire sweepstakes. il Bsns W p34-5 S 12 '64
Off-track betting, from the horse's mouth; voting by New Yorkers. J. M. Willig. il N Y Times Mag p55+ N 3 '63

Psychology

Gambling fever; winner lose all. D. C. Disney. Ladies Home J 80:18 Mr '63
Gambling; why? with photographs by P. Fusco. G. Zimmermann. Look 27:21-35 Mr 12 '63

Taxation

Intolerable squeeze; relationship between states and racing. A. Hammond. il Sports Illus 18:34-6+ My 6 '63
When horses pay off, the tax collector wins. U S News 54:11 Mr 11 '63

Grand Bahama Island

Bonanza in the Bahamas. il Newsweek 64:88-9+ O 26 '64
Offshore Eden. Time 83:31 Ap 3 '64

Great Britain

Britain goes on a gambling spree. I. Ross. il Read Digest 84:93-7 Ap '64
British life, it's a gamble. G. Gorer. il N Y Times Mag p 10+ S 1 '63
Election sweepstakes; bet on the balloting. il Newsweek 64:42-3 S 7 '64
In Britain, gambling is a growth industry. il Bsns W p29-31 S 14 '63
Poor Charlie; clerk wins fortune in soccer pool. Newsweek 63:26 Mr 30 '64

Russia

Betting, Soviet style; at Moscow races. il Bsns W p32-3 F 23 '63

United States

Case for a national lottery. E. Silberling. il McCalls 90:68+ S '63
New England; the refined Yankee in organized crime. D. S. Strong. bibliog f Ann Am Acad 347:40-50 My '63

GAMBUSIA
Resistance to DDT in the mosquito fish, gambusia affinis. V. S. Bradleigh and others. bibliog il Science 139:217-18 Ja 18 '63

GAME
Hunters do not reduce quail and game supply. Sci N L 84:201 S 28 '63
See also
Cookery—Game
Venison

GAME, Dressing of
Deer in a dishpan; special butchering method. L. L. Rue, 3d. il Outdoor Life 132:50-2 N '63
How to field-dress a deer. H. G. Tapply. il Field & S 68:48 N '63

GAME birds
Game-bird savers. W. C. Lammey. il Pop Mech 121:158-61+ Ja '64
See also
Duck shooting

GAME calls. See Animal calling

GAME hour; story. See Bail, J.

GAME laws
Bowhunting laws. G. H. Gillelan. il Outdoor Life 131:34+ Ap '63
Field & stream 1964 hunting forecast, small & big game. il Field & S 69:73-80 O '64
Hunting in our national parks? A. W. Smith. Audubon Mag 65:6-9 Ja '63
Hunting seasons (cont) Outdoor Life 132:12+ S; 12+ O '63; 134:10+ S; 16+ O '64
1963 Field & stream hunting forecast and game laws. il Field & S 68:41-8 O '63
No way to duck. Sports Illus 22:8 Ja 25 '65
What to do in a pinch. F. Calkins. il Field & S 68:44-6+ N '63
See also
Animals, Predatory—Bounties
Birds—Protection

GAME preserves
At home on the range; Dixie lily ranch. H. Sutton. il Sat R 46:30+ N 16 '63
He manages his farm for crops and wildlife; D. Schultz, Shelby County, Ia. C. Mayhugh. il Suc Farm 61:82+ N '63
Home, home on the preserve. il Time 82:66 N 29 '63
Hunting, with gun and wallet. C. Dickey. il Esquire 60:212-13+ D '63
Needs for the future; New York state. A. MacBain. il Field & S 68:104+ Jl '63
Place to hunt; Dutchess County co-operative hunting area. T. Janes. il Outdoor Life 134:33-5+ O '64
Preserve shooting. A. MacBain. See issues of Field & stream to April 1964
Private shooting preserves; list prepared by the Sportsman's service bureau of New York city. Esquire 60:93+ D '63
Quality duck hunting. H. Titus. il Field & S 69:56-8+ My '64
Too many elk. T. Trueblood. il Field & S 68:36-9+ Jl '63
Upland shooting down on Florida's Gold Coast. V. Kraft. il Sports Illus 18:52+ Mr 4 '63
Wild pigs' wild ride. il Life 54:51-2 Je 28 '63
Wildlife management in the national parks; Leopold committee report. il Am For 69:32-5+ Ap '63; Same. Nat Parks Mag 37:11-16 Ap '63; Discussion. Am For 69:11 Ap '63; Nat Parks Mag 37:11 Ap '63

GAME protection
Leopold report appraised. il Liv Wildn 83: 20-4 Spring '63
Wildlife management in the national parks. A. S. Leopold and others. il Audubon Mag 65:166-71+ My '63
See also
Game laws
Wildlife conservation
GAME tables. See Tables
GAMER, Eleanor E.
National parks of Japan. Nat Parks Mag 37:8-11 Jl '63
GAMES
Anyone can play. il Am Home 67:28+ Je '64
Brain-busting; new trend toward harder games. il Time 82:44+ D 13 '63
Confessions of a stoop ball champion. G. Rogin. Sports Illus 20:75-6+ Ap 20 '64
Dinner & games: the more the merrier. C. Brock. il Good H 158:166+ Mr '64
Family game; the Kennedys. New Yorker 39:35-6 Ap 27 '63
For adults: games and tables. J. Peter. il Look 28:79 O 20 '64
Fun and games for everyone. il House & Gard 124:186-7 D '63
Games that make children think. R. M. Goldenson. il Parents Mag 39:58-9+ Je '64
Games that teach fair play. R. W. Bacmeister. il Recreation 56:196-7 Ap '63
Games the entire family can play. Good H 157:171 D '63
Games! the whole family wins. E. Craster. il Bet Hom & Gard 43:42-3+ Ja '65
How to keep the kids happy on a trip. E. Beaver. il Bet Hom & Gard 42:93-4 Jl '64
How to liberate Latvia; game called Victory over communism. Newsweek 65:54-5 Ja 18 '65
It's your move! board games. il Recreation 57:238-9 My '64
Life of the party! il Bet Hom & Gard 43:113 Ja '65
Making money with games. C. R. Graham. il Sci Digest 53:48-53 F '63
My favorite party games; excerpt from My favorite things. D. Rodgers. il McCalls 91: 34+ S '64
Pass go and retire; Monopoly. R. Bongartz. il Sat Eve Post 237:26-7 Ap 11 '64
Pits & pebbles; kalah. il Time 81:67 Je 14 '63
Play-money game that made millions; Monopoly. J. F. Wilkinson. il Sports Illus 19:52-4+ D 2 '63
Put-down: the great summer game from Esquire. R. H. Smith. Pub W 184:31 Jl 22 '63
Rousing game for lively youngsters. C. Brock. il Good H 158:220 My '64
Selling goods through games; use of games in supermarkets. L. Morse. Duns R 84:49 Jl '64
Space ball. H. Bradshaw and V. Bradshaw. il Pop Sci 182:110-11 F '63
Summer is for fun. il Seventeen 22:118 Je '63
There's fun for everyone when you vacation at home. il Pop Gard 15:28-31 Jl '64
Two travel games for children. Sunset 130: 59 Je '63
War games for the kids this Christmas. W. H. Honan. New Repub 151:8-9 D 19 '64
What children learn from play. B. Bettelheim. il Parents Mag 39:48-9+ Jl '64
With a hop, skip, and jump; symposium. il Recreation 57:175-7 Ap '64
See also
Anagrams
Backgammon
Billiards
Blackjack (game)
Chess
Pinatas
Poker
Recreation for the aged
Shuffleboard
Skittles
Sports
Word games
GAMES; story. See Webber, H.
GAMES, Mathematical. See Mathematical recreations
GAMES of chance. See Gambling
GAMES of the new emerging forces. See Asiad (games)
GAMETOPHYTES
Differentiation in fern gametophytes treated with purine and pyrimidine analogs. V. Raghavan. bibliog il Science 146:1690-1 D 25 '64
Gibberellins: their effect on antheridium formation in fern gametophytes. B. R. Voeller. bibliog il Science 143:373-5 Ja 24 '64
GAMEZ, Tana de
Position of the artist in Cuba today. Art N 63:36-9+ S '64
GAMMA globulin
Allotypic specificities of A- and B-chains of rabbit gamma globulin. G. W. Stemke. bibliog il Science 145:403-5 Jl 24 '64
Antibodies to genetic types of gamma globulin after multiple transfusions. J. C. Allen and H. G. Kunkel. bibliog il Science 139:418 F 1 '63
Antibody to hereditary human gamma-globulin (Gm) factor resulting from material-fetal incompatibility. H. H. Fudenberg and B. R. Fudenberg. bibliog il Science 145:170-1 Jl 10 '64
Antigenic determinants in fragments of gamma globulin from rabbit serum. J. W. Goodman. bibliog il Science 139:1292-3 Mr 29 '63
Dependence of a Gm(b) antigen on the quaternary structure of human gamma globulin. S. H. Polmar and A. G. Steinberg. bibliog il Science 145:928-9 Ag 28 '64
Gamma globulin affinity for normal human tissue of the central nervous system. C. D. Allerand and M. D. Yahr. bibliog il Science 144:1141-2 My 29 '64
Gamma globulin antigenic types defined by heavy chain determinants. R. E. Ballieux and others. bibliog il Science 145:168-70 Jl 10 '64
Gamma globulin: unmasking of hidden antigenic sites on light chains. R. L. Nachman and R. L. Engle, jr. bibliog il Science 145: 167-8 Jl 10 '64
Gamma-globulins: quantitative relationships in human serum and nonvascular fluids. W. B. Chodirker and T. B. Tomasi, jr. bibliog Science 142:1080-1 N 22 '63
Hereditary globulin factors and immune tolerance in man. A. G. Steinberg and J. A. Wilson. bibliog il Science 140:303-4 Ap 19 '63
Hybridization of half molecules of rabbit gamma globulin. A. Nisonoff and J. L. Palmer. bibliog il Science 143:376-9 Ja 24 '64
Lymphoid organs and normal gamma-globulin in the rat. S. B. Andersen and F. Bierring. bibliog il Science 144:1219-20 Je 5 '64
Polypeptide chains of human gamma-globulin: cellular localization by fluorescent antibody. G. M. Bernier and J. J. Cebra. bibliog il Science 144:1590-1 Je 26 '64
Polypeptide chains of rabbit gamma globulin. P. A. Small, jr. and others. bibliog il Science 142:393-4 O 18 '63
Rubella virus: neutralizing antibody in commercial gamma globulin. G. M. Schiff and others. bibliog il Science 142:58-60 O 4 '63
See also
Agammaglobulinemia
GAMMA rays
Fission product gamma activity with northerly winds and with southerly winds. C. J. Brasefield. bibliog il Science 142:952-3 N 15 '63
Gamma irradiation of polypeptides: transformation of amino acids. F. Friedberg and G. A. Hayden. bibliog il Science 140:825-6 My 17 '63
Ozone formation in air exposed to cobalt-60 gamma radiation. Z. I. Kertesz and G. F. Parsons. bibliog il Science 142:1289-90 D 6 '63
Synergistic effect of 5-bromodeoxyuridine and gamma rays on chromosomes. F. K. S. Koo. bibliog il Science 141:261-2 Jl 19 '63
See also
Mössbauer effect
GAMOW, George
Science milestone; Niels Bohr: the man who explained the atom. por Sci Digest 53:71-8 My '63
GAN (island) See Maldive Islands
GANDAR, Laurence
South Africa's voice of opposition. por Time 85:37-8 Ja 8 '65
GANDHI, Indira
Daughter. il por Time 83:30+ My 1 '64
GANDHI, Mohandas Karamchand
John Haynes Holmes; discoverer of Gandhi; excerpt from Rabbi and minister. C. H. Voss. Christian Cent 81:603-6 My 6 '64
Reporter at large. H. R. Isaacs. New Yorker 40:83-4+ D 12 '64
They made our world. L. Rosten. por Look 28: 60-1 Ag 25 '64
GANGE, John
Mix of fact and myth. Nation 199:63-6 Ag 24 '64
Southeast Asian cockpit. Ann Am Acad 351: 58-71 Ja '64
GANGLIONIC nervous system. See Nervous system, Sympathetic

GANGRENE
Case of gangrene. Newsweek 62:80 O 14 '63
GANGS
All in the family; Gallo gang and Profaci gang. Newsweek 62:20 D 23 '63
Chicago; shades of Capone. V. W. Peterson. Ann Am Acad 347:30-9 My '63
Cross and the switchblade; ed. by J. Sherrill and E. Sherrill. D. Wilkerson. il Good H 157:49-53+ Jl '63
Death down a dark street; L. Marsh. D. Peerman. Christian Cent 80:166-7 F 6 '63
Death of a youth worker; L. Marsh. G. Samuels. il Sat Eve Post 236:74-6 Ap 6 '63
It's better than beating up old ladies with bicycle chains; Merseyside gangs in Liverpool turn to rock 'n' roll. il Time 83:73 Mr 20 '64
No more rumbles; summary of Youth on the streets. S. Bernstein. Sr Schol 83:2T+ O 11 '63
Report of a Harlem gang that preys on whites. U S News 56:10 My 18 '64
Reporter at large; girls' gang in Brownsville section of east Brooklyn. R. Rice. il New Yorker 39:153-4+ O 19 '63
GANGSTERS. See Crime and criminals—United States
GANLEY, Rosemary Burns
Spacing births. America 110:366-7 Mr 21 '64
GANNAWAY, Woody
Amateur scientist. Sci Am 211:118-24+ Jl '64
GANNETS
Bass Rock gannets; Sula bassana. B. Nelson. il Natur Hist 73:32-41 Ap '64
Birds of the sea. A. Sprunt, 4th. il Motors B 112:54+ N '63
Most prosperous bird colony; Guano Islands. H. S. Ullmann. il Audubon Mag 65:150-1 My '63
GANNON, Robert
After sixty-four years, the prisoner comes home. Sat Eve Post 237:38+ Mr 14 '64
Big-brother 7074 is watching you. Pop Sci 182:86-8+ Mr '63
Giant spraymobiles. Pop Sci 184:64-7+ Mr '64
How to be a sidewalk superintendent. Pop Sci 185:122-5+ O '64
Stratoscope II: sky-high and starry-eyed. Pop Sci 182:86-90+ F '63
Stupid questions about alcohol. Pop Sci 184: 70-3+ Mr '64
Tools for space mechanics. Pop Sci 184:114-15+ Ap '64
Weightless workshop. pors Pop Sci 182:112-13+ Ap '63
What really happened to the Thresher. Pop Sci 184:102-9+ F '64; Same abr. Read Digest 84:111-16 My '64
Who says flying is for the birds? Pop Sci 183:52-3 Ag '63
Why sports records are being broken: science or supermen? Pop Sci 182:58-62+ My '63
GANNON, Ruth
Decorating with dried flowers: excerpts from New ways with dried flowers. Design 64: 150-2 Mr '63
GANNON, Thomas M.
Kennedy memorabilia. America 111:304-6 S 19 '64
GANS, Carl
Vertebrate hard tissues. Science 144:323-4 Ap 17 '64
—and Bonin, J. J.
Acoustic activity recorder for burrowing animals. bibliog Science 140:398 Ap 26 '63
GANS, Herbert J.
Access survey; from the social scientist's viewpoint. bibliog por Wilson Lib Bul 38: 336-41+, 623-5 D '63, Ap '64
Planning and power. Commentary 35:176-9 F '63
Poverty problem. Commentary 38:64-6 Jl; 12+ D '64
Round pegs, square holes. New Repub 149:23-5 Jl 20 '63
GANSCHOW, Cliff. See Strohm, J. jt. auth.
GANTNER, Edna
Chrysanthemums. Pop Gard 15:30-1+ My '64
GANTNER, Herman
Something for the birds. Flower Grower 51: 21 O '64
GANTT, Harvey
Integration with dignity; with editorial comment. G. McMillan. il por Sat Eve Post 236:15-21, 80 Mr 16 '63
New semester, a new Negro student. il por U S News 54:15 F 11 '63
New term, new South. il por Newsweek 61:29 F 11 '63
GANTT, Henry Laurence
Famous firsts: charting a way to democracy. por Bsns W p44+ Ja 11 '64
GANTT, W. Horsley
Outlook for national medicine. bibliog f Cur Hist 44:321-5+ Je '63
GANZ, Leo. See Sekuler, R. W. jt. auth.
GAOLS. See Prisons
GAPOSCHKIN, Cecilia Payne-. See Payne-Gaposchkin, C.
GARA, Larry
Academic freedom at Grove City. J. P. Park. Christian Cent 80:928-9 Jl 24 '63
GARAGE doors, Mechanically operated. See Doors, Mechanically operated
GARAGES
Convert the garage and add a car shelter to gain living space on the street side. il Sunset 130:108-11 Ap '63
Five steps from big garage to handsome home. il Am Home 66:92 N '63
Garages & carports; guide for planning, designing, building. il Changing T 18:13-14 F '64
Horrors! a handsome garage. E. Goble. Arch Rec 133:9 F '63
Increase your living space. il Ladies Home J 80:114 Mr '63
Kitchen in a carport. M. Davidson. il Ladies Home J 80:106-7 Mr '63
Low-cost garage structure shows design finesse; Bellevue hospital center, N.Y. il Arch Rec 135:164-6 Ja '64
More than a place to park. il Pop Sci 183: 160-2 O '63
Parking by computer. Time 83:94 My 22 '64
Parking program that benefits all. T. J. Coyle. il Am City 79:112 Ag '64
Parking: the crisis is downtown. il Arch Forum 118:100-9 F '63
Paul Rudolph designs a place to park in downtown New Haven. il Arch Rec 133:145-50 F '63
Stretching space with a garage. il Bet Hom & Gard 42:62-3+ F '64
There's space for a shop and the car. il Bet Hom & Gard 42:34 Mr '64
Thirteen stories of parking pleasure; Lafayette, La. J. R. Bertrand. il Am City 79: 113 Jl '64
Two outdoor projects to make your summer more successful. D. Jordan. il Bet Hom & Gard 42:48-9 Ag '64
GARAGES, Municipal
Designed to work hard; sanitation garage, Hempstead, N.Y. W. J. Landman. il Am City 79:106-7 Mr '64
Every detail received attention in expandable city maintenance center; Greensboro, N.C. T. Z. Osborne. il Am City 79:110-12 My '64
Garage full of ideas; Lake Forest, Ill. G. L. Watson and H. R. Von Huben. il Am City 78:71-3 Jl '63
Parking: the crisis is downtown. il Arch Forum 118:100-9 F '63
Pittsburgh expands its parking program. M. A. Neale. il Am City 80:109 Ja '65

Heating and ventilation

Ventilating Boston's underground garage. il Arch Rec 136:172-5 D '64
GARAGIOLA, Joe
They led the league in gags; ed. by D. Anderson. pors Sat Eve Post 236:62-3 S 14 '63
Yogi of the Yankees; ed. by D. Anderson. Read Digest 85:110-13 Jl '64

about

Garagiola's way. por Newsweek 64:40 D 28 '64
Joe to behold! H. L. Masin. il por Sr Schol 83:24 S 20 '63
GARBAGE. See Refuse, Utilization of; Refuse and refuse disposal
GARBAGE bags. See Refuse receptacles
GARBAGE cans. See Refuse receptacles
GARBAGE collection and disposal. See Refuse and refuse disposal
GARBAGE trucks. See Refuse collection trucks
GARBARINO, John A.
Reporter at large. R. Harris. New Yorker 40: 101-3+ S 12 '64
GARBELL, Maurice A.
Sea that spills into a desert; with biographical sketch. Sci Am 209:16, 94-100 bibliog(p 140) Ag '63
GARBO, Greta
La dolce Greta. Newsweek 61:89 Mr 11 '63
Great Garbo. E. J. Cruise. il Seventeen 23: 28 Ja '64
GARBUS, Joel. See Weinbach, E. C. jt. auth.
GARBUTT, Bernard
Bernard Garbutt, animal draughtsman. J. Lovoos. il por Am Artist 27:53-7+ F '63

GARCIA, Carlos Restelli
Stubborn man; stubborn car. J. Star. il pors Look 27:21-7 S 24 '63
GARCIA, Helen Roca-. See Roca-Garcia, H.
GARCIA, J. and others
Electroencephalographic responses to ionizing radiation. bibliog Science 140:289-90 Ap 19 '63
Sensitivity of the head to X-ray. bibliog Science 144:1470-2 Je 19 '64
GARCIA, Julian Grimau. See Grimau Garcia, J.
GARCIA, Mo
Letter from the publisher. B. M. Auer. por Time 84:25 N 27 '64
GARCIA DEL SOLAR, Lucio
Young power in diplomacy. por Vogue 143:88 Ap 15 '64
GARCIA LORCA, Federico
Tenses of the truth. por Time 83:138+ Ap 17 '64
GARCIA-MORA, Manuel R.
Panama Canal controversy; address, March 16, 1964. Vital Speeches 30:412-16 Ap 15 '64
GARCÍA TERRÉS, Jaime
Jaime García Terrés and the *lista negra*. F. H. Wardlaw. Harper 230:16+ Ja '65
GARD, Leonard M.
Nuclear explosions: some geologic effects of the Gnome shot. Science 139:911-14 Mr 8 '63
GARDA, LAKE
Visit to Sirmione. D. Dodge. il Holiday 33:28+ My '63
GARDELS, Keith. See Herman, R. jt. auth.
GARDEN, A. Newell
Omega. Yachting 113:172+ Je '63
GARDEN, Mary
Remembrances of an enchantress. H. Cuenod. il por Hi Fi 14:36-8 Jl '64
GARDEN architecture. See Arbors
GARDEN barrows. See Wheelbarrows
GARDEN benches. See Benches
GARDEN borders
Beauty in a May garden. il Horticulture 41:260-1 My '63
Beauty up front. J. R. Rebhan. il Flower Grower 50:32-3+ S '63
Edging plants that are different and easy. D. Klaber. il Pop Gard 15:34 Ap '64
Edgings save work. il Pop Gard 15:19 Mr '64
Elegance of silver. P. Headley. il Horticulture 42:52-3 Je '64
Foliage and texture in the garden. P. Shedesky. il Horticulture 41:376-7 Jl '63
For summer color, five successful border plans. il Sunset 130:262-4 My '63
Keep your lawn trim and neat. P. F. Frese. il Pop Gard 15:55 Ap '64
Update your perennial borders. J. Fanning. il Pop Gard 16:24-5 F '65
When you restyle your flower border. J. R. Rebhan. il Pop Gard 14:38-9 F '63
GARDEN carts. See Carts
GARDEN catalogs. See Catalogs, Seed and plant
GARDEN centers

Caricatures and cartoons

Garden center. Stevenson. New Yorker 39:38-41 My 18 '63
GARDEN chess. See Chess
GARDEN CITY, N.Y.
Noteworthy features of new incinerator. B. J. Gorman. il Am City 79:94-5 Jl '64
GARDEN club of North Carolina. See Garden clubs
GARDEN clubs
Clippings from clubs and societies. See issues of Horticulture to January 1964
Garden club world. D. Biddle. See issues of Popular gardening & living outdoors to May 1964
North Carolina's enchanted garden; Elizabethan garden. R. Landolina. il Horticulture 41:170-1 Mr '63
They changed the face of this country. H. Hull. il Flower Grower 51:56-7 Ja '64
What fun it is to garden; garden therapy program of Rock Spring garden club, Arlington County, Va. F. Colbert. il Pop Gard 14:57+ S '63
See also
Horticultural societies
GARDEN design
Basic garden layout. J. B. Brimer. il Flower Grower 52:43-4 Ja '65
French parterre garden back yard style. il Pop Gard 15:44-5 Jl '64
Garden lives its second life; remodeled. il Sunset 133:62-3 S '64
Important factor in plants: texture. H. S. Ortloff. il Horticulture 41:82 F '63
Tailor your lot for lots of living. il Pop Gard 15:10-11 F '64
Why a garden needs more than plants. E. L. Sculthorp. il House B 106:80-7 Ag '64
GARDEN equipment. See Garden tools, equipment and supplies
GARDEN exhibits
1963 almanac of flower shows and garden tours. il House & Gard 123:170-1 Mr '63
See also
Flower exhibits
GARDEN fences. See Fences
GARDEN frauds. See Fraud
GARDEN furniture. See Furniture, Outdoor
GARDEN gates. See Gates
GARDEN hose
Irrigator's friend; handy hose cart. il Sunset 133:108 S '64
GARDEN houses, shelters, etc.
Build a canopy for shade and storage. R. A. Henry, jr. il Pop Gard 15:50-3 S '64
Enjoy the comfort of a screen house. il Pop Gard 15:52-3 My '64
Handy garden house you can build. il Pop Sci 182:173 Ap '63
Lawn cabana. M. L. Olds. il Pop Mech 120:131-2 Ag '63
Meet the retreat; new ways to get away from it all. C. Besinger. il House B 105:49-59 Jl '63
Our garden house has many uses. C. Lisle. il Flower Grower 51:14+ D '64
Place for everything; storage in the garden and patio. J. H. Ingersoll. il Pop Gard 14:49-55 S '63
Play pavilion for at-home recreation. il Arch Rec 134:152 Ag '63
Projects you can build and enjoy this summer. il Bet Hom & Gard 42:56-9 Je '64
We design a gardener's workshop for the fair. il Am Home 67:5 Ap '64
See also
Arbors
Lath houses
GARDEN in the woods. See Framingham, Mass.—Gardens
GARDEN lamps. See Lamps
GARDEN lighting. See Gardens—Lighting
GARDEN literature
Books are gardening tools. D. S. Manks. il Horticulture 41:522-3 O '63
GARDEN of Eden. See Eden
GARDEN ornaments
Beauty and the good life outdoors; garden accessories. il Am Home 67:4 Jl '64
For barbecue fun; ideas for better living outdoors. R. M. Peters. il Pop Gard 14:50 Jl '63
Treasures to track down. il Flower Grower 51:40-1 Jl '64
See also
Fountains
GARDEN pools
Birds will come if there's water. A. F. W. Vick, jr. il Horticulture 42:22-3 Je '64
Build good design into your garden pool. J. B. Brimer. il Flower Grower 50:22-3 Mr '63
Construct a water-lily pool. il Flower Grower 50:52 Ag '63
Garden pools; how, what, and where. il Bet Hom & Gard 42:45 Je '64
How to add interest in front of a wall. il Sunset 131:152 O '63
How to keep algae out of your pool. B. B. Paine. il Flower Grower 50:42-4 S '63
I find enchantment in my water-lily pool. J. Hillstrom. il Flower Grower 51:24-6 Mr '64
Pools to grace a garden. B. C. Kilvert, jr. il Flower Grower 50:48-51 Ag '63
Water adds coolness to the garden. M. F. Bunting. il Horticulture 41:318-19 Je '63
See also
Water gardens
Water lilies
GARDEN rocket. See Dames violets
GARDEN rooms. See Rooms
GARDEN seats. See Furniture, Outdoor
GARDEN shelters. See Garden houses, shelters, etc.
GARDEN soils. See Gardening—Soil preparation
GARDEN sprinklers. See Sprinklers
GARDEN stakes and staking
Galvanized pipe as a tree stake. il Sunset 131:291 O '63
Many uses of bamboo. il Flower Grower 50:34-6 Je '63
Plant supports. il Sunset 132:230 Mr '64
GARDEN steps
Flower grower's home garden notebook. J. B. Brimer. il Flower Grower 51:33-4 O '64

GARDEN steps—*Continued*
In this old Portland garden, a handsome new pathway. il Sunset 131:161 Jl '63
Portfolio of garden steps. C. B. Lees. il Horticulture 42:28-32 S '64
Steps and steppingstones. il Pop Gard 15:32-5 S '64
Steps down are inviting. il Sunset 133:97 Jl '64

GARDEN supplies. See Garden tools, equipment and supplies

GARDEN therapy
What fun it is to garden; Edison school Arlington County, Va. F. Colbert. il Pop Gard 14:57+ S '63

GARDEN tools, equipment and supplies
Baker's dozen. L. Van de Boe. Pop Gard 15:16 Jl '64
Basic tools help save more time. il Flower Grower 50:46-7 Mr '63
Choose the right tool; then use it right. B. C. Kilvert, jr. il Flower Grower 51:50-5 Mr '64
Cut lawn and garden work. il Suc Farm 61:28 Je '63
Good old chicken wire. M. M. Leister. il Flower Grower 50:20 Ag '63
Good tools speed lawn making. il Pop Gard 15:74 Mr '64
Grass shears. il Consumer Bul 47:16-18 Mr '64
Hand tools are powerful too. il Pop Gard 15:6 F '64
Hand tools still high on list of gardening aids. B. C. Kilvert, jr. il Flower Grower 50:43-4 Je '63
Have you heard? B. C. Kilvert, jr. See issues of Flower grower
How to reduce your garden cleanup time by 75 per cent; new blower-vacuum. il House B 106:170-3+ Ap '64
It's a folding soil sifter. il Sunset 131:262 N '63
Lawn and garden equipment. Consumer Bul 29:304-12 D '64
Lawn spreaders. il Consumer Rep 28:127-30 Mr '63
Make use of peat bale slats. B. C. Kilvert, jr. Flower Grower 50:21 Ag '63
Making of a garden is much easier if you just rent power. il Sunset 133:108-13 N '64
Many uses for a shower curtain. B. C. Kilvert, jr. il Flower Grower 51:50 My '64
Power to spare: tips on tools for better turf. B. C. Kilvert, jr. il Flower Grower 51:42-4 Ap '64
Reduce maintenance. il Pop Gard 14:42-3 Mr '63
Sharp tools mean less work. M. R. Beasley. il Pop Gard 15:68 Ja '64
Short cuts to easy gardening. il Pop Gard 15:40-3 Jl '64
Stop! look! listen! B. C. Kilvert, jr. Flower Grower 50:30+ Jl '63
Tools every gardener needs. il Good H 158:163 My '64
See also
Hedge clippers
Hoes
Lawn sweepers
Spraying and dusting apparatus
Tractors

Care

Five point plan for fall. J. H. Ingersoll. il Pop Gard 15:32-5 N '64
Long life for power equipment. il Pop Gard 15:59 Ap '64
Power tools need care now. il Horticulture 42:46-7 O '64
Rough weather ahead. il Flower Grower 50:30-2 O '63

Storage

Best storage ideas we've seen. il Bet Hom & Gard 41:7+ Ap '63
See also
Garden houses, shelters, etc.

GARDEN tours
All the world's a garden. M. Perry. il Flower Grower 51:20-1 N '64
Clippings from clubs and societies. See issues of Horticulture to January 1964
Flower-lovers' ramble: garden tour through Europe. il Life 55:65-70 Ag 2 '63
Places where spring seems lovelier. M. Gough. il House B 105:118+ Mr '63
Weathervane (cont) R. G. Miner. il Flower Grower 50:16 Jl; 6 O '63; 51:6 F; 8 O '64

GARDEN tractors. See Tractors

GARDEN umbrellas. See Umbrellas

GARDEN walks
Beat a path to a pretty front garden. il Am Home 67:8 Jl '64
Floating concrete pad. il Sunset 130:100 F '63
How to resurface a garden walk. il Sunset 132:145-6+ Ap '64
Sneak paths. il Sunset 132:308 My '64
Steps and steppingstones. il Pop Gard 15:32-5 S '64

GARDEN walls
Add the natural beauty of a stone retaining wall to your garden. il Bet Hom & Gard 41:48 S '63
All around the place. J. Milton. il Pop Gard 14:30 Ap '63
Rock pile to garden wall. J. Lawson. il Pop Gard 15:24-5 Ap '64
Sun & rock lovers. E. W. Finch. il Flower Grower 50:36-7+ Ag '63
Walls worth their weight in stone; photographs. Flower Grower 50:32-3 Je '63

GARDEN work rooms. See Garden houses, shelters, etc.

GARDENING
All around the place. J. Milton. Pop Gard 14:21+ My; 10-11 Jl; 13 S '63; 15:73 My; 78 Jl; 69 S '64
And soon it will be spring. Changing T 18:6 F '64
Answers to your garden questions; about trees, shrubs, and flowers. Suc Farm 62:104-5 F '64
Are you a better gardener than your spouse? J. P. Roche; M. A. Roche. Pop Gard 15:10-11 Ja '64; Reply. F. N. Kenny. 15:6+ My '64
Bare-root planting. il Sunset 134:130-1 Ja '65
Basic principles of planting. Pop Gard 14:33 Mr '63
Before you leave on vacation. G. Taloumis. il Pop Gard 14:65+ Jl '63
Beginner's guide to fall planting. E. McDonald. il Pop Gard 14:33-6 S '63
Best plants; symposium. See issues of Flower grower to July 1964
Confessions of a scavenger; excerpts from Joy of a small garden. J. Gillespie. House & Gard 123:217-20 My '63
Do as farmers do. B. A. Roth and L. Fox. il Pop Gard 14:22-3 My '63
Fall gardening in New England. E. M. Marshall. il Flower Grower 50:23 O '63
Flower grower's four seasons 1965. il Flower Grower 51:23-30 D '64
Flower grower's 1964 garden year. il Flower Grower 50:25-32 D '63
For the pure joy of it. D. Warren. il Horticulture 41:401 Ag '63
Fruit-truck news (cont of) Fruits and truck crops. See issues of Farm journal
Gardening in the Midwest. B. F. Vance. il Pop Gard 14:16 My; 20 Jl; 18 S; 16 N '63
Gardening on a dime. D. E. Stebbins. il Horticulture 41:308-9 Je '63
Good ideas all over the lot. S. S. Baker. il Pop Sci 182:105 Je '63
Good ideas for gardeners. il Sunset 132:273+ My '64
Have a fun garden. E. C. Polatin. House B 105:130-1 S '63
High mountain gardening. il Sunset 130:314 My '63
Highlights of spring planting. E. McDonald. il Pop Gard 15:31-4 Mr '64
H&G's gardener's month. See issues of House & garden
How to garden like an expert. B. Brinhart. il Pop Gard 14:52-3 Mr '63
How to plant just about anything. il Bet Hom & Gard 42:32+ Ap '64
Invitation, mystery, surprise; the gardens at Stour. R. Churchill. il Vogue 143:152-3+ Mr 1 '64
It took a tractor to turn my gardening chores into a joy ride. E. McHutchison. il Flower Grower 51:30-1 F '64
Know these gardening safety tips. Good H 158:163 My '64
Midwest pointers. R. M. Carleton. See issues of Flower grower
[Month] gardening where you live! See issues of Better homes and gardens
[Month] in your garden. See issues of Sunset
My garden has roses, gladiolus, dahlias. . . J. E. Goodson. Flower Grower 51:15-17 Ja '64
New plantings need fall care. L. C. Grove. il Bet Hom & Gard 42:30 O '64
Northern pointers. H. V. Wilson. See issues of Flower grower
Now is the time! See issues of Horticulture to February 1964
Off-duty joys of gardening. W. A. Buck. House B 105:194-7 Mr '63
Pick the best place for each plant. il House & Gard 123:174-7 My '63
Plan now for spring. il Pop Gard 15:58-61 S '64
Planting ideas that make for easy upkeep. G. Taloumis. il Pop Gard 14:44-5+ Mr '63

GARDENING—*Continued*
Pop Gardener says. H. R. O'Brien. See issues of Popular gardening
Preparing a garden for cold weather. il Good H 157:168-9 O '63
Quick and easy tips. See issues of Popular gardening & living outdoors
Regional gardening; symposium. See issues of Popular gardening & living outdoors
Report from the South; symposium. Flower Grower 50:24-5 Ap '63
Senior gardening. E. D. Davis. il Horticulture 41:379 Jl '63
Short cuts to easy gardening. il Pop Gard 15:40-3 Jl '64
Southern pointers. See issues of Flower grower
Spring planting in the fall in California. il Sunset 131:260-4 O '63
Terrific garden ideas! il Bet Hom & Gard 41: 101 Ap '63
There's always time for gardening. E. Lindeman. il Pop Gard 15:6-7 Ap '64
These men really get a kick out of gardening. H. Mason and R. O'Harra. il Bet Hom & Gard 41:68-71 Mr '63
This month in the Midwest (cont) B. F. Vance. Pop Gard 14:18 F; 24 Mr; 24 Ap '63
This month in the North (cont of) Things to do this month in the North. A. M. Davis. See issues of Popular gardening
This month in the Northwest (cont of) Things to do this month in the Northwest. D. Collins. See issues of Popular gardening
This month in the South (cont of) Things to do this month in the South. C. J. Hudson, jr. See issues of Popular gardening
This month in the Southwest (cont of) Things to do this month in the Southwest. R. D. Westcott. See issues of Popular gardening
Tips for string savers. R. Rodgers. il Pop Gard 14:24-5+ F '63
Twelve steps to easy gardening. J. Threlkeld. Pop Gard 15:24-5 Mr '64
Weathervane. R. G. Miner. Flower Grower 51:8 My; 6 Je '64
Weathervane; letter to the editors. M. De Vitalis. Flower Grower 51:6+ Ap '64
Weathervane; the Englishman's devotion to gardening. R. G. Miner. Flower Grower 50: 6 N '63
Weekend garden checklist. Pop Gard 14:64 Jl '63
West Coast pointers. R. E. Atkinson. See issues of Flower grower
What can a gardener do on vacation? il House & Gard 123:114-17 Je '63
What to do in [month] See issues of Horticulture
What type of gardener are you? E. L. Sculthorp. House B 105:207-8 Ap '63
What's in store for gardeners. Changing T 17:6 F '63
See also
Bulbs
Catalogs, Seed and plant
Childrens gardens
Floriculture
Garden therapy
Gardens
Horticulture
Lawns
Mulching
Plants
Seedlings
Transplanting
Watering of gardens, lawns, etc.

Anecdotes, facetiae, satire, etc.

All that mulch and no petunias. J. L. O'Neill. il Am Home 67:10 My '64
Green grows my kudzu. P. Mandel. il Life 54:80+ My 31 '63
Is nature getting neurotic? C. Ford. il Read Digest 82:15-16+ My '63

Bibliography

Books. E. C. Hall. Pop Gard 15:44+ N '64
Books for Christmas. Flower Grower 50:10 D '63
Books for Christmas giving. E. C. Hall. il Pop Gard 14:50+ N '63
Garden reference books; analysis of the best of them. G. H. M. Lawrence. Horticulture 42:40-2 Ap '64
Good books for gardeners. il Changing T 17:15-17 My '63
Some new books. See issues of Popular gardening
See also
Garden literature

Competitions

Garden club yearbook (cont) il Horticulture 41:486 S '63

Equipment and supplies

See Garden tools, equipment and supplies

Planting plans and tables

Every home landscape includes a wide variety of climates in miniature. House & Gard 123:212-14 My '63
How does Disneyland do it? il Sunset 132: 224-5 Je '64
How to enjoy spring in midwinter. il Sunset 133:182+ S '64
How to make our mild winters work for you; lesson from Arizona for Californians. il Sunset 133:250-2+ O '64
See also
Garden design

Soil preparation

Here's how to improve your problem soil. M. S. Anderson. Am Home 67:82-3 My '64
Soil air essential for good plant growth. B. Brinhart. il Horticulture 41:92-3 F '63
We tested our soil. H. S. Witty. il Flower Grower 51:44-5+ Mr '64

Study and teaching

Gardeners under glass; gardening courses at Brooklyn. M. A. Guitar. il N Y Times Mag p62+ My 12 '63
Start them young; Hilltop gardening program. F. D. Cavinder. il Pop Gard 14:72+ F '63

GARDENING, Indoor. See Greenhouses
GARDENING, Landscape. See Landscape gardening
GARDENING, Vegetables. See Vegetable gardening
GARDENS
Cutting garden. R. C. Hands. il Horticulture 41:404-5 Ag '63
Designing and planting your atrium garden. A. M. Kofranek. il Am Home 66:77-8 S '63
Garden is a place to play, to learn, to grow. J. DiLeo. il Pop Gard 15:32-3 Jl '64
In a tiny garden. J. W. Hatcher. Pop Gard 14:56-7 Mr '63
New flowers to chirp about. T. A. Weston and G. Harshbarger. il Am Home 66:42-3+ Ja '63
Plan an easy-upkeep garden. il Pop Gard 15:24-28+ Ja '64
Secret gardens. N. Fairbrother. il Vogue 144: 256-7+ D '64
Take-home ideas by the gardenful; Julimar farm exhibit at the Worlds fair. il House & Gard 126:246-9 N '64
Think of your garden as an outdoor room. il House B 105:90-5 Je '63
What you can learn from a city garden. il House B 106:188-9 Mr '64
Wildflowers; gardens for people who don't like to garden. il Vogue 141:28 Mr 1 '63
You can be secluded in your own garden. il Am Home 67:50-1 O '64
See also
Church gardens
City gardens
Gardening
Roof gardens
Water gardens

Color

Beauty in a May garden. il Horticulture 41: 260-1 My '63
Chartreuse enchantment. R. K. Stroh. il Flower Grower 50:24-5 Je '63
Color me! il Flower Grower 50:24-7 Jl '63
Color schemes that bloom! H. Mason and others. il Bet Hom & Gard 42:46-9 Je '64
Combinations that click. J. D. Walters. il Flower Grower 50:42-3+ Ag '63
Elegance of silver. P. Headley. il Horticulture 42:52-3 Je '64
Fall color. C. P. Holway. il Horticulture 41: 574-5 N '63
For more color use interplanting. M. C. Ohlander. il Flower Grower 50:38-9 N '63
Frost gray foliage for cool contrast. il Pop Gard 15:46-7 Jl '64
Garden for all America. il Flower Grower 51:54-5 Ja '64
How to enjoy spring in midwinter. il Sunset 133:182+ S '64
My golden spring. C. Lisle. il Flower Grower 51:24-5 S '64
On having the blues; excerpt. B. Nichols. il Pop Gard 14:46-7 My '63
Perennials. M. Costigan. il Pop Gard 15: 30-1+ Ap '64
Perennials for color through August. D. E. Stebbins. il Horticulture 41:224-5 Ap '63
Plan for winter color in your garden. R. C. Hands. Horticulture 42:43 O '64
Trees & shrubs for all season color. F. F. Rockwell and E. C. Grayson. il Flower Grower 50:45+ O '63

GARDENS—Color—Continued
Woman's touch. B. Nichols. il Pop Gard 15:6 Mr '64
See also
Color of flowers

History

Shakespeare and the garden. F. C. Coulter. il Pop Gard 15:14+ S '64

Lighting

Glowing lights in your garden. il Sunset 133: 146-7 Ag '64
Lighting for living outdoors. A. S. Green. il Pop Gard 14:37-44 S '63
Lights for your garden. H. V. Wilson. il Flower Grower 50:8+ N '63
Low voltage lighting: easy to install and flexible. il Sunset 131:82 Ag '63
More living with lights. il Flower Grower 51:33-6 Ap '64

Alabama

Bellingrath gardens. il Travel 119:47-9 Mr '63

California

California, what a way to live! il McCalls 90:62-3 Jl '63
For California gardeners; why not grow your vegetables in special places? il Sunset 130: 228-9 Mr '63
How does your garden look from the roadside? il Sunset 133:242-3 N '64
It has a green future. il Sunset 133:154 Jl '64
It's just for someone who likes plants. il Sunset 133:102-5 O '64
Rule-breaker planted this unusual garden. il Sunset 132:282+ My '64
These photographs show a garden growing up; private garden in Orinda. il Sunset 132: 100-1 Je '64
Year-around California garden: it's as good looking in November as it is in May. il Sunset 131:260-1 N '63

Connecticut

What a team, what a garden: Elda and Walter Haring, Greenwich. B. Black. il Flower Grower 51:28-9+ Je '64

England

Going places, finding things in English gardens, in and around London. R. Harling. il House & Gard 123:40-1+ My '63
Invitation, mystery, surprise; the gardens at Stour. R. Churchill. il Vogue 143:152-3+ Mr 1 '64
Savill gardens. il Flower Grower 51:20-1 D '64

Florida

Babes in a swampland; Cypress gardens. W. B. Furlong. il Sports Illus 19:66-70+ O 21 '63; Same abr. with title Most successful swamp in America. Read Digest 84: 164-7+ F '64
Superswamp; Cypress gardens. R. Bongartz. il Sat Eve Post 236:78-81 N 23 '63
See also
Fairchild tropical garden, Coconut Grove, Fla.

France

Passion for flowers: Baronne Geoffroy de Waldner and her French garden; with account by V. Lawford. il Vogue 144:260-9, 275-6+ D '64
See also
Versailles—Gardens

Hawaii

Over the mountains from Honolulu; Haiku gardens in Oahu. il Sunset 131:16 S '63

Hong Kong

Three private gardens in Hong Kong. S. Stewart. il Pop Gard 14:36-7 Jl '63

Iowa

Welcome to our garden. G. Harshbarger. il Flower Grower 51:30-1+ Mr '64

Ireland

Reader's choice: Japanese gardens of Kildare. R. Austin. Travel 120:6 N '63

Italy

Horrors of Bomarzo; interview, ed. by M. L. B. Ambrosini. G. Borghese. il Harper 228: 66-71 Ap '64
Italy. G. Taloumis. il Horticulture 43:36-7 Ja '65
Italy, where people garden for fun. M. Roche. il House & Gard 123:162-3+ Ap '63

Louisiana

Reader's choice. P. Crittenden. Travel 120:6 O '63

Massachusetts

Garden of good ideas; Tredinnock, Great Barrington, Mass. G. Wright. il Flower Grower 51:22-5 Ag '64
Great past, greater future. M. C. Ohlander. il Flower Grower 51:46-9+ Ap '64

Netherlands

Holland in bloom. J. H. Winchester. il Travel 119:28-30 F '63
Salute to the Hollanders and their bulbs. T. A. Weston. il Am Home 66:27-9 O '63

New Jersey

Excitement under glass; Duke gardens foundation greenhouses in Somerville. il House & Gard 127:118-23+ Ja '65
Our garden is a family affair. R. Van Doren. il Flower Grower 50:22-5+ S '63

New York (state)

Garden of many moods. H. Aul. il Flower Grower 50:20-1 My '63
Sorcery of green: Mrs William S. Paley and her American garden. il Vogue 144:258-9 D '64
Story of Sterling Forest. R. Dowling. il Pop Gard 14:76-7 Jl '63
Tulips old and new at Sterling Forest. C. Lewis. il Horticulture 42:26-7+ My '64

North Carolina

North Carolina's enchanted garden; Elizabethan garden. R. Landolina. il Horticulture 41:170-1 Mr '63

Pennsylvania

See also
Philadelphia—Gardens

Scotland

Scotland's gardens. D. L. McFadden. il Pop Gard 14:32-3+ Ap '63

South Africa

Gardening in South Africa. S. E. Knight. il Pop Gard 14:63-4 Mr '63

Sweden

Sweden's king, a royal gardener. M. Perry. il Flower Grower 52:32-4 Ja '65

United States

Life guide: autumn gardens. il Life 55:9 S 20 '63
Twentieth century look of a gardener's garden. C. Calkins. il House B 105:160-3 My '63
See also subhead Gardens under names of cities, e.g. Seattle—Gardens

Virginia

Springtime in Virginia. il Pop Gard 14:10 Ap '63; 15:13 Ap '64

Washington, D.C.

Bouquet for the White House garden. M. Perry. il Flower Grower 50:17 Jl '63
Weathervane. R. G. Miner. il Flower Grower 50:6 Ag '63
White House garden. M. Perry. il Flower Grower 50:24-33 Ag '63

GARDENS, Bird. See Bird gardens
GARDENS, Childrens. See Childrens gardens
GARDENS, Church. See Church gardens
GARDENS, City. See City gardens
GARDENS, Fragrant
Fragrance that grows and grows and grows. il Flower Grower 50:44-5 Ap '63
Laced pinks are for every garden. A. T. Robinson. il Horticulture 41:124-5 Mr '63
Sweet scents. C. K. Mosher. il Horticulture 41:226 Ap '63
Winter fragrance. H. V. Wilson and L. Bell. il Flower Grower 51:39+ Ja '64
GARDENS, Indoor
Corner of a warm winter garden. il Ladies Home J 81:140 Ja '64
Garden in a nutshell. il House & Gard 126: 192-5+ S '64
How to live with spring ten months a year. C. C. Calkins. il House B 105:157-63+ Mr '63
In San Francisco small showcase gardens. il Sunset 133:158 Jl '64
Three ways to create a garden room for all seasons. il Am Home 68:84-5 Ja '65
GARDENS, Italian
See also
Gardens—Italy

GARDENS, Japanese
Garden gate and wall in the Japanese manner. il Sunset 130:286 Ap '63
Garden? Japanese garden, Ryoanji, at Brooklyn botanic garden. New Yorker 39:27-9 S 7 '63
Japan is nearer than you think! photographs. M. Perry. Flower Grower 50:26-7 Je '63
Mirror of the Orient. R. S. Maxwell. il Pop Gard 15:28-31 N '64
Total sculpture; garden at Chase Manhattan plaza. New Yorker 39:46 D 14 '63
Zen grows in Brooklyn. il Newsweek 61:69 Je 10 '63
GARDENS, Miniature
Carrot-top dish garden. W. Radcliffe. il Pop Gard 16:51 Ja '65
Imaginative miniature garden. L. H. Gee. il Horticulture 41:322-3 Je '63
See also
Terrariums
GARDENS, Protection of. See Plants, Protection of
GARDENS, Rock
Earth-cradling rocks give us some of our loveliest gardens. il House & Gard 123:146-9 Mr '63
Hints on rock gardening. T. H. W. Langley. il Horticulture 41:204-5 Ap '63
How to enhance the natural beauty of rock. E. L. Sculthorp. il House B 106:176-9+ Ap '64
Turn boulders into beauty. il Pop Gard 15: 8 S '64
We go idea-collecting in Northwest rock gardens. il Sunset 131:246-8+ N '63
See also
Landscape gardening
GARDENS, Roof. See Roof gardens
GARDENS, Water. See Water gardens
GARDENS, Wild
Woodland garden. J. Hersey. il Horticulture 41:510-11 O '63
GARDINER, Dorothy
No mirrors, please! Writer 77:16-19 Ja '64
GARDINER, Gerald Austin
Labor's lord high chancellor. pors Time 84: 86 N 13 '64
GARDINER, Robert, D. L.
World's fair fare. New Yorker 40:36-7 Ap 4 '64
GARDINIER, David E.
(comp) Articles and other books received; Africa. Am Hist R 70:304-5 O '64
GARDIPEE, Charles R.
Handicapped child. bibliog f Ann Am Acad 355:121-7 S '64
GARDNER, D. Bruce
Child and the society; excerpt from Development in early childhood: the preschool years. Sch & Soc 92:157-61 Ap 4 '64
GARDNER, Dwayne E.
Educational specifications for the school library. por ALA Bul 58:114-15 F '64
GARDNER, Erle Stanley
Getting away with murder. Atlan 215:72-5 Ja '65
Mad strangler of Boston. Atlan 213:49-56 My '64
about
Writing lawyer of Rancho del Paisano. B. Hibbs. il por Read Digest 83:160-2+ Ag '63
GARDNER, Frank M.
Luton's literary supermarket. Library J 88: 4545-7 D 1 '63
To fill the empty mind; excerpts from address. por Library J 89:3681-6 O 1 '64
GARDNER, Herb
Thousand clowns; text. Theatre Arts 48:33-64 Ja '64
GARDNER, John W.
Future of the university. Sat R 46:46 N 2 '63
Know yourself! excerpt from address, January 21, 1963. Read Digest 83:72-4 N '63
Moral decay and renewal. Sat R 46:18+ D 14 '63
On men and moral values; excerpt from Self-renewal: the individual and the innovative society. Read Digest 84:167-8 Mr '64
Self-development; excerpts from Self-renewal: the individual and the innovative society. Science 143:641 F 14 '64
$266,900,000: private give-away, done by three men. A. Talmey. por Vogue 141:103 Je '63
GARDNER, Margaret
Picturesque Perigord. Travel 122:28-31+ Ag '64
GARDNER, Martin
Bewitched, bothered or befuddled? excerpt from Scientific American book of mathematical puzzles & diversions. Read Digest 85:21-2+ S '64
Mathematical games. See issues of Scientific American
Want to be fuddled? excerpt from Mathematical puzzles. Read Digest 83:37-8+ O '63
Why librarians dislike Oz; reprint. Library J 88:834-6 F 15 '63
Why of the eye; excerpt from Ambidextrous universe. Sat R 47:67 N 7 '64
GARDNER, Paul
Enid Bagnold, the articulate sprite. Theatre Arts 48:17+ Ja '64
GARDNER, Paul M. See Bensley, J. H. jt. auth.
GARDNER, Paul V.
Great glass from American collections. Antiques 85:190-5 F '64
GARDNER, Philip
Architecture roundup. Christian Cent 81: 434-5 Ap 1 '64
Corbu show in Chicago. Christian Cent 80: 832 Je 26 '63
New directions in church design. Christian Cent 81:424-8 Ap 1 '64
GARDNER, Richard K.
Richard K. Gardner to edit ALA-ACRL book selection journal. por Library J 88:2653-4 Jl '63
GARDNER, Richard N.
Cooperation in outer space. For Affairs 41: 344-59 Ja '63
Development of the peacekeeping capacity of the United Nations; address, April 26, 1963. Dept State Bul 48:789-96 My 20 '63
18th General assembly: a testing ground of hopes and opportunities; address, September 11, 1963. Dept State Bul 49:501-8 S 30 '63
Fifteenth anniversary of Universal declaration of human rights; address, December 8, 1963. bibliog f Dept State Bul 50: 20-4 Ja 6 '64; Same with title International promotion of human rights. Vital Speeches 30:207-9 Ja 15 '64
Human rights and foreign policy; excerpts from In pursuit of world order. Sat R 47: 23-5+ S 19 '64
Human rights: some next steps; address, August 5, 1963. Dept State Bul 49:320-2 Ag 26 '63
Needed: a stand-by U.N. force. N Y Times Mag p 12+ Ap 26 '64
Outer space; problems of law and power; address, August 10, 1963. Dept State Bul 49:367-71 S 2 '63
Politics of population. Sat R 46:10-12+ S 7 '63
Politics of population: a blueprint for international cooperation; address, May 4, 1963. Dept State Bul 48:906-14 Je 10 '63
Space meteorology and communications: a challenge to science and diplomacy; address, April 19, 1963. Dept State Bul 48:740-6 My 13 '63
Statement, February 18, 1963. Dept State Bul 48:358-60 Mr 11 '63
United Nations financial crisis; address, March 12, 1963. Dept State Bul 48:535-40 Ap 8 '63
United Nations in crisis; Cuba and the Congo; address, February 23, 1963. Dept State Bul 48:477-81 Ap 1 '63
GARDNER, Robert
Judge tells how to deal with under-age hoods. por U S News 55:44-5 Ag 26 '63
Speaking out. por Sat Eve Post 236:10+ Je 22 '63
GARDNER, Romaine L.
St Martin's day? Commonweal 81:458-9 D 25 '64
GARDNER, Trevor
Lonely warrior. R. Hotz. Aviation W 79:21 O 14 '63
Obituary
Miss & Roc 13:29 O 7 '63
GARDNER, W. R. and Nieman, R. H.
Lower limit of water availability to plants. bibliog Science 143:1460-2 Mr 27 '64
GARFIELD, Eugene
Citations in popular and interpretive science writing; letter. Science 141:392 Ag 2 '63
Science citation index, a new dimension in indexing. bibliog Science 144:649-54 My 8 '64
GARFIELD, James Abram
Murder most foul. A. Robertson. il pors Am Heritage 15:90-104 Ag '64
GARGAN, Edward T.
Tocqueville and the problem of historical prognosis. bibliog f Am Hist R 68:332-45 Ja '63
GARGAN, William
William Gargan's finest role; esophageal speech. C. B. Wall. por Read Digest 83:49-54 S '63
GARGOYLE; a Christmas story. See Duprey, R. A.

GARIS, Howard R.
My father was Uncle Wiggily. R. Garis. il por Sat Eve Post 237:64-6 D 19 '64
GARIS, Roger
My father was Uncle Wiggily. por Sat Eve Post 237:64-6 D 19 '64
GARLAND, Charles Talbott
National capitalism; address, October 15, 1964. Vital Speeches 31:109-12 D 1 '64
GARLAND, Judy
There'll always be an encore. por McCalls 91:54-7+ Ja; 64+ F '64

about

Judy and Mickey reunited. il pors Life 55:47+ Jl 19 '63
Liza Minnelli: Judy's daughter bows in. S. Castan. il por Look 27:51-4 My 21 '63
Momma's girl; J. Garland's daughter. N. Poirier. por Sat Eve Post 236:30-1 O 5 '63
Question mark. pors Newsweek 62:70 N 4 '63
Second generation, Garland style. Sr Schol 84:14 Ja 31 '64
TV troubles of Judy Garland. R. W. Lewis. il pors Sat Eve Post 236:92-5 D 7 '63
Two old pros. Time 83:44 My 29 '64
GARLAND family
Garland coat-of-arms. H. K. Eilers. il Hobbies 68:120-1 S '63

GARLANDS. See Leis
GARLIC
Garlic. D. Reay. il Horticulture 41:228 Ap '63
GARLITS, Don
Don Garlits' speed secrets. R. Brock. il pors Hot Rod 17:28-35+ N '64
Fame and terror at 200 MPH. M. Kram. il pors Sports Illus 21:26-8+ Ag 31 '64
GARMENT trades. See Clothing industry
GARMENT workers
See also
International ladies' garment workers' union
GARN, Stanley M. and others
Compact bone deficiency in protein-calorie malnutrition. bibliog Science 145:1444 S 25 '64
Compact bone in Chinese and Japanese. bibliog Science 143:1439-40 Mr 27 '64
Gonadal dosages in investigative radiography. bibliog Science 143:1039-40 Mr 6 '64
Molar size sequences and fossil taxonomy. bibliog Science 142:1060 N 22 '63
GARNER, Fradley H.
Secrecy behind the Nobel prizes. Sci Digest 56:30-7 O '64
GARNER, James
James Garner makes the scene; ed. by E. Miller. por Seventeen 23:122-3+ O '64
GARNER, John Nance
What is Cactus Jack up to now? F. X. Tolbert. il pors Sat Eve Post 236:26, 29 N 2 '63
GARNER, Lou
Assemble a phone-boost. Pop Electr 19:55-6+ N '63
Transistor topics. See issues of Popular electronics
GARNET, Highland
Nay-sayer of the Negro revolt. L. Bennett, jr. il pors Ebony 19:66-8+ S '64
GARNETS
Garnet ratios and provenance in the glacial drift of western New York. G. G. Connally. bibliog il Science 144:1452-3 Je 19 '64
Those rubies are really garnets. il Sunset 130:58+ My '63
GARNETT, David
John's royal wife. N Y Times Mag p 104-6 Ap 5 '64
One man's treasures. S. Eimerl. Reporter 28:64-5 Mr 28 '63
GARNISHES
Bumper crop of garnishes. il Am Home 68:60-2+ Ja '65
Sampler of garnishes. il Redbook 124:92-5 N '64
GARRA, Martha Ludes
Summer perennials. Horticulture 42:30-3 Je '64
GARRARD, Mrs Robert
Doctors' wives tackle the suicide problem. M. Benson. il por Todays Health 42:60-3 My '64
GARRATY, John A.
Marbury v. Madison: case of the missing commissions. Am Heritage 14:6-9+ Je '63
(ed) Supreme court. Am Heritage 14:4-9+ Je; 10-15+ Ag; 38-43+ O; 15:66-71+ D '63; 44-8+ F; 52-5+ Ap '64
GARRETSON, Robert C.
Future challenges marketing. Harvard Bsns R 41:168-70+ N '63

GARRETT, Charlotte (Wilson)
Drawn to that time; poem. Poetry 101:253-4 Ja '63
GARRETT, George
Proposition; poem. Mlle 58:42 Ja '64
Shards for her; poem. Mlle 57:121 Ag '63
GARRETT, Henry E.
Racial mixing could be catastrophic; interview. por U S News 55:92-3 N 18 '63
GARRETT, W. E.
Mountaintop war in remote Ladakh. il Nat Geog Mag 123:664-87 My '63
GARRETT, William N.
Shade for beef cattle. Suc Farm 61:67 Ag '63
GARRETT corporation
C-W extends Garrett stock plan. Aviation W 79:30 O 21 '63
Garrett asks court to prevent Curtiss-Wright purchase of stock. Aviation W 79:33 S 30 '63
Garrett opposes Curtiss offer. Aviation W 79:39 S 16 '63
Garrett, Signal oil continue merger plan. Aviation W 79:32 N 11 '63
Garrett, Signal propose to merge after Curtiss-Wright raises offer. Aviation W 79:33 O 28 '63
GARRICK, Michael D. and others
Tryptophan synthetase from neurospora: a modification in the reaction scheme. bibliog Science 145:491-2 Jl 31 '64
GARRIGAN, Owen W.
Interventions of man in nature. por Cath World 196:292-8 F '63
Origin of life on the earth. Cath World 198:281-7 F '64
GARRIGUE, Jean
Adam tree; When shall we set sail for happiness, Baudelaire; French country circus; poems. Poetry 104:335-8 S '64
Note to La Fontaine; poem. New Yorker 40:171 Mr 21 '64
Of history more like myth; poem. New Yorker 39:44 S 28 '63
Three poems; Of Provence and the river Var; How I loved; On the legend of a dancer. Poetry 103:33-6 O '63
Written in London after a protest parade; poem. New Repub 149:20 Jl 13 '63
You know; poem. New Yorker 39:24 Jl 27 '63
GARRISON, Guy
Wisconsin: a working model. por Library J 89:1680-2 Ap 15 '64
GARRISON, James
Case of the crusading DA. Newsweek 61:26 F 18 '63
GARRISON, Jim
Vice man cometh. J. Phelan. il pors Sat Eve Post 236:67-71 Je 8 '63
GARRISON, Lloyd
Adolua tries to bind up the wounds. N Y Times Mag p25+ My 12 '63
Now Angola: study of a rebel. N Y Times Mag p 12-13+ F 16 '64
Portrait of Nkrumah as dictator. N Y Times Mag p 15+ My 3 '64
White mercenaries on a rabbit hunt. N Y Times Mag p30-1+ N 15 '64
GARRISON, Warren M. and others
Radiation-chemical oxidation of peptides in the solid state. bibliog Science 146:250-2 O 9 '64
GARRISON, William Lloyd
I will be heard. il Newsweek 61:97-8 F 25 '63
Leaders of the first freedom movement. L. Bennett, jr. il por Ebony 19:68-70+ Ag '64
Liberator, by J. L. Thomas. Review
Time por 81:80+ Mr 1 '63
GARRISON, Winfred Ernest
W. E. Garrison at ninety; tributes by his friends. Christian Cent 81:1614-15 D 30 '64
GARRITY, John
New grip on the game. G. S. Brown. il Sports Illus 19:53 D 16 '63
GARRITY, John T.
Top management and computer profits. Harvard Bsns R 41:6-8+ Jl '63
GARRO, Elena
Before the Trojan war; story. Américas 16:28-31 O '64
GARRY, Ralph
Television; address, January 27, 1964. Vital Speeches 30:273-7 F 15 '64
GART, Murray
Green and fertile field for the Goldwater rush. Life 55:32-3 N 1 '63
GARTERS
Other means of support; plastic garter grips. Consumer Rep 30:7 Ja '65
GARTH, David
Boy meets girl. por Seventeen 23:79+ Ja '64
GARTH, Midi
Midi Garth and company, 92d street Y. M. Marks. Dance Mag 38:25+ Ja '64

GARTHOFF, Raymond L.
Manual of Soviet strategy. Reporter 28:34+ F 14 '63
Sino-Soviet military relations. bibliog f Ann Am Acad 349:81-93 S '63
GARTHWAITE, Marion
Acid test. Horn Bk 39:408-11 Ag '63
Steel and quicksilver. Horn Bk 40:212-14 Ap '64
GARTNER, John
Go West. Flying 75:38-49+ Jl '64
GARTON, William W.
Simpson's catalytic action. Library J 89:4758-60 D 1 '64
GARVAN, Anthony N. B.
Culture change and the planner. Ann Am Acad 352:33-8 Mr '64
GARVER, Juliet
Howling success; drama. Plays 24:15-24 Ja '65
My fair Linda; drama. Plays 22:1-13 My '63
GARVEY, William D. and Griffith, B. C.
Scientific information exchange in psychology. Science 146:1655-9 D 25 '64
GARVIN, James E. See Slavin, R. G. jt. auth.
GARWOOD, John D.
Need for economic education. bibliog f Sch & Soc 92:289-91 O 17 '64
GARY, Beverly
Bride in Boystown. Mlle 57:290-1+ Ag '63
GARY, Bill
Big noise is jazz-tap. W. Como. il pors Dance Mag 37:20-1 N '63
GARY, Romain
Fake; story. Ladies Home J 80:78-80 N '63
Humanist; story. Sat Eve Post 236:58-60 O 26 '63
I know a place in Paris. Holiday 37:54-7+ Ja '65
Oldest story ever told; story. Esquire 60:144-7 D '63
Ski bum; story. Ladies Home J 81:76-8 O '64
GARY, Ind.
Negroes
Gary's rank-and-file reaction; white backlash. V. Hoffman and J. Strietelmeier. il Reporter 31:28-9 S 10 '64; Reply. K. R. Mitchell. 31:6 S 24 '64
U.S. court victory for neighborhood schools. U S News 56:50 Mr 16 '64; Same abr. with title What is a segregated school? Read Digest 84:128-9 Je '64
GARZIO, Angelo
German salt glazing. il Craft Horiz 23:20-2 Mr '63
GAS, Natural
Big find in a small country; Dutch strike it rich. il U S News 54:79-81 My 20 '63
Embarrassment of riches. Groningen gas field, Holland. Newsweek 61:65-6 Mr 4 '63
Europe turns to new source of power; natural gas under the North Sea. il U S News 57:110+ S 21 '64
Exploring the big bubble; quest for natural gas. il Time 85:66 Ja 1 '65
Gas battle; world's second largest natural gas deposit. Time 82:110+ N 15 '63
Holland strikes it rich in natural gas. J. H. Winchester. il Read Digest 85:83-6 Ag '64
Look what's cooking with natural gas! F. Cameron. Read Digest 83:204C+ O '63
Looking for the sixpence; search in Europe's North Sea. il Time 83:92 My 1 '64
Oil in the bush. il Time 83:99 Ap 10 '64
Record rebate. Newsweek 62:82 D 2 '63
See also
Gas industry—Regulation
Pipe lines
California gas race starts over. Bsns W p98+ Jl 27 '63
Las Vegas, N.M. gets natural gas. il Am City 79:96 D '64
One way to make a pipeline grow; diversification into energy fields. il Bsns W p80+ O 26 '63
Pipelines through the swamp; Mississippi delta. il Bsns W p 116-18 Jl 18 '64
Watching 2,600 miles of pipeline grow. il Fortune 67:100-9 F '63
GAS and oil engines
Baby engine does big jobs; gas engine. S. M. Gallager. il Pop Sci 185:170-2 O '64
Gas-fueled engine cuts pumping costs 58 per cent; Glendale, Ariz. il Am City 79:145 F '64
Rotary engines take to water; Wankel. il Pop Mech 119:138-9 Mr '63
Stern drive. A. S. Woodle. il Esquire 59:45-6+ My '63
Wankel. K. W. Purdy. il Atlan 215:109-10 Ja '65
See also
Marine engines
Anecdotes, facetiae, satire, etc.
Some day I'll understand you, Mary Ann. D. Van Keuren. il Motor B 115:92-3 Ja '65
Cooling
Case for fresh-water cooling. il Motor B 113:42-3+ Mr '64
Lubrication
Oil, your engine's lifeblood. B. Simpson. Motor B 113:188-9 My '64
Starting
Snap starting. Suc Farm 63:61 Ja '65
GAS and oil engines, Inboard
Engines. E. H. Nabb. il Yachting 115:44-5+ Ap '64
Inboard engines 64-65. il Motor B 113:134-7+ Ja '64; 115:130-5+ Ja '65
Piggyback propulsion. S. F. Manning. il Motor B 114:44+ O '64
Shape of power today. il Motor B 114:40-1+ O '64
Cleaning
Acid cleaning; inboard engines. L. V. Andrews. il Motor B 113:44+ Mr '64
GAS and oil engines, Outboard
Astern in '65. il Motor B 114:36-8+ O '64
Engines. E. H. Nabb. il Yachting 115:44-5+ Ap '64
Extras for outboards. F. M. Paulson. il Field & S 68:138-40+ Ap '64
From motors to boats. il Yachting 114:69 N '63
Handy guide to the '63 outboards. il Pop Sci 182:126-7 Mr '63
How the engineers put sizzle in the '65s. J. Roe. Pop Sci 185:80-4 N '64
How to choose; outboard or inboard-outboard? J. A. Emmett. il Outdoor Life 133:118-21 Mr '64
How to go boating with hardly any water; tilt mechanisms. W. Swegle. il Pop Sci 185:94-6 Jl '64
Inside the '64 outboards. il Motor B 112:48-9+ O '63
Inside today's outboards. H. Holcomb. il Motor B 114:34-5+ O '64
Low cost auxiliary fuel for your outboard. K. F. Hildebrand. il Pop Mech 119:140-1 Mr '63
New motors. il Outdoor Life 131:56-9 F '63
New outboard motors for fishing. Outdoor Life 134:12+ O '64
1964 lineup of new boats and motors. F. M. Paulson. il Field & S 68:27-34 Ja '64
1964 motors. il Yachting 114:75-7 O '63
1965 motor buyer's guide. il Field & S 69:44 Ja '65
Onward the outboard. F. M. Paulson. il Field & S 69:64-9 D '64
Outboard for '64. il Pop Mech 120:104-6+ O '63
Outboard motors, 1965. il Yachting 116:61-3 O '64
Outboard motors 64-65. il Motor B 113:146-9 Ja '64; 115:142-5 Ja '65
Outboard wells for the small auxiliary. R. W. Carrick. il Yachting 117:77-9+ Ja '65
Outboards for fishing feature 1964 lines. Outdoor Life 132:124-5 O '63
Outboards for 1964. F. M. Paulson. il Field & S 68:70-4 D '63
Outdoor life boating, 1964-1965. J. A. Emmett. il Outdoor Life 133:52-60+ F '64; 135:52-5+ Ja '65
Roundup: littlest motors astern. H. Holcomb. il Motor B 113:36-7+ My '64
Sailor takes to outboards. R. N. Bavier, jr. il Yachting 114:60-1+ Jl '63
Care
Learn to trouble shoot. J. A. Emmett. il Outdoor Life 134:80-2 Jl '64
Outboard motor and salt water. B. Whittier. il Yachting 113:56-7+ My '63
Ignition
Caring for the electrical system. B. Whittier. il Yachting 113:62-3+ Je '63
Testing
Jim Roe pre-tests the '64 outboards. J. Roe. il Pop Sci 183:106-11+ N '63
One-of-a-kind outboard: Jim Roe tests the Homelite four-cycle. J. Roe. il Pop Sci 183:136-9+ S '63
GAS appliances
Two in every home. il Time 83:93 F 28 '64
GAS as fuel
See also
Gas, Natural
GAS chromatography. See Chromatographic analysis
GAS clothes dryers. See Clothes dryers

GAS companies
See also
El Paso natural gas company
Pacific gas and electric company

Employees

See also
Gas companies—Wages and hours

Wages and hours

Earnings in electric and gas utility systems, July 1962. F. L. Bauer. il Mo Labor R 86:530-3 My '63

GAS companies, Municipal
Gas utilities earn dividends; five small cities in Illinois with natural-gas systems. W. A. Ford and A. J. Stika. il Am City 78:89-90 F '63

GAS detectors
Gas detection aboard boats. P. Williams. il Motor B 112:78+ N '63

GAS engines. See Gas and oil engines

GAS explosions. See Explosions

GAS gages. See Gages

GAS gangrene. See Gangrene

GAS industry

Consolidations and mergers

Justice gets some sharper teeth; Supreme court decisions reversing mergers approved by regulatory agencies. Bsns W p29-30 Ap 11 '64

Regulation

Gassing game. J. Ridgeway. New Repub 150:4-5 My 9 '64
See also
United States—Federal power commission

Securities

Executive investor; provocative look at the pipeliners of natural gas. il Duns R 84:139-40+ O '64

GAS lamps
New-old era. il Time 84:55 N 20 '64

GAS leaks, Detection of. See Gas detectors

GAS motors. See Gas and oil engines

GAS poisoning. See Gases, Asphyxiating and poisonous

GAS stations. See Automobile service stations

GAS stoves
Free-standing gas ranges. il Consumer Bul 46:6-11 My '63
How to buy a range in 1965. V. T. Habeeb. il Am Home 68:56-7 Ja '65
Now: ranges that think! il Bet Hom & Gard 41:106-7 Mr '63

GAS turbines
Coal-fired gas turbine may cut electricity cost. Sci N L 85:8 Ja 4 '64
Small turbines planned by Lycoming for diversity of uses. M. L. Yaffee. il Aviation W 81:38-9+ Jl 20 '64

GAS turbines, Aircraft
Allison plans regenerative engine family. M. L. Yaffee. il Aviation W 80:60-1+ Mr 2 '64
Allison turboprops to be installed on four Frontier airlines Convairs. Aviation W 79:39 N 25 '63
BS.100 VTOL powerplant readied for bench testing; turbofan engine. il Aviation W 81:86-9 S 7 '64
Canadair completes CL-84 VTOL design. D. E. Fink. il Aviation W 79:70-1+ N 25 '63
Continental T65 passes fifty-hr. PFRT. D. A. Anderton. il Aviation W 78:79+ F 18 '63
Convair will proceed with Dart refit kits. Aviation W 81:43 N 9 '64
Cruise fan engine effort pushed by GE; for proposed CX-HLS. J. R. Ashlock il Aviation W 80:70-1+ My 11 '64
Fairchild offers enlarged F-27; twin-turboprop. E. H. Kolcum. Aviation W 81:41 S 14 '64
Flying jeep; OV-10A, also referred to as LARA or COIN. H. Shuldiner. il Pop Sci 185:45-7+ D '64
Garrett uprates T76 engine to 660 shp. for COIN aircraft. C. M. Plattner. il Aviation W 81:92-3+ Ag 24 '64
GE seeks company pilot views in defining CF700 engine loan, overhaul programs; turbofan powerplant. D. A. Brown. il Aviation W 80:98-9+ Ap 6 '64
Growth versions of PT6 being developed. D. A. Brown. Aviation W 81:79 N 2 '64
Khrushchev admits turboprop problems. Aviation W 80:82 Ja 13 '64
Leading international gas turbines; specifications. Aviation W 78:213+ Mr 11 '63; 80:205+ Mr 16 '64
Lear liner specifications, costs detailed. D. A. Brown. il Aviation W 80:29-30 Je 29 '64
Shortcut to engine design; scaled powerplants. J. S. Butz, jr. il Flying 74:49+ My '64
Small turbines planned by Lycoming for diversity of uses. M. L. Yaffee. il Aviation W 81:38-9+ Jl 20 '64
Swiss charter expanding turboprop fleet; Globe air ag. E. Walford. il Aviation W 81:34+ Ag 31 '64
Testing causes changes in Turbo Skyvan. il Aviation W 81:146-9 S 7 '64
TWA develops vane straightener. Aviation W 79:30 S 2 '63
Turbine aircraft load factors in scheduled service; tables. Aviation W 81:57 S 14 '64
Turbine aircraft 1962-1963 operating and traffic statistics; tables. Aviation W 78:48-9 Mr 18 '63; 81:32 Jl 27; 60-1+ S 14 '64
Turbine engine parts policy is criticized. Aviation W 79:35 Jl 1 '63
Turbine power adds to Beaver capability. D. A. Brown. il Aviation W 82:84-5+ Ja 11 '65
Turbine-powered Buffalo built for short, rough fields. D. A. Brown. il Aviation W 80:84-6+ My 25 '64
Turbomeca planning lightplane turbine. W. C. Wetmore. il Aviation W 79:66-7+ Ag 5 '63
Turbo-Porter displays exceptional STOL performance. D. A. Brown. il Aviation W 81:84-9 O 5 '64
Turboprop Convairs cut Frontier's costs. il Aviation W 81:41-2 N 9 '64
240 airframe bolstered for Dart engine. D. A. Brown. il Aviation W 81:41+ S 28 '64
U.S. gas turbine engines; specifications (cont) Aviation W 78:197+ Mr 11 '63; 80:203-4 Mr 16 '64
Use dictates 727 engine fixes. Aviation W 82:35 Ja 18 '65
Wagner W-18 will use high lift devices. H. D. Watkins. il Aviation W 81:66-8+ Jl 27 '64
See also
Helicopter engines

Design

J93 viewed as basis for SST powerplant. il Aviation W 79:32-3 S 16 '63
JT8D engine uses full-length fan duct. D. E. Fink. il Aviation W 79:52-3+ O 14 '63
RM-8 detail design pushed by Flygmotor; to power Sweden's next manned weapons system. W. C. Wetmore. il Aviation W 79:48-9+ N 18 '63

Statistics

Turbine aircraft operating expenses, dollars per revenue hour; table. Aviation W 79:73 O 7 '63
Turbine equipment operation; table. Aviation W 79:83 O 7 '63
Turbine powered aircraft capacities (tons) in scheduled airline service; table. Aviation W 79:85 O 7 '63

Testing

Pratt & Whitney testing basic version of CX-HLS powerplant. il Aviation W 81:17 Jl 20 '64

GAS turbines, Automotive
America's first turbine car. A. Rothenberg. il Look 27:28+ Je 4 '63
Big test. il Time 81:90 My 10 '63
Chrysler Turboflite experimental. il Motor T 15:34-5 My '63
Comeback in Detroit. J. C. Jones. il Sat Eve Post 236:74-6 My 25 '63
Emotion key to turbine. E. Hall. Sci N L 85:228 Ap 11 '64
500-mph LSR car? J-79 turbo-jet car. E. Dahlquist. il Hot Rod 17:46-7+ Ag '64
Gas turbine car feasible. Sci N L 85:219 Ap 4 '64
Gas turbine supertruck loves drivers and gas. Sci N L 86:361 D 5 '64
On the road; Chrysler's turbine-powered car. il Newsweek 62:50-1 D 30 '63
PM drives Chrysler's new gas turbine. il Pop Mech 120:26-9 Jl '63
Test-driving a jet; Chrysler's new turbine engine. il Bsns W p74-6+ Mr 28 '64
That's the jet. il Newsweek 62:94+ N 11 '63
Turbine drive. Newsweek 61:84-6 My 13 '63
Turbine in a truck; experimental gas turbine truck. il Bsns W p28 O 31 '64
Wh-o-o-o-sh, here come the turbines! B. Greene. il Hot Rod 16:74-7 Jl '63

GAS turbines, Marine
Rooster tales. D. Naef. il Hot Rod 17:106-7 My '64
Shape of tomorrow's power? il Motor B 114:39+ O '64

GAS turbines, Marine—*Continued*
Small turbines planned by Lycoming for diversity of uses. M. L. Yaffee. il Aviation W 81:38-9+ Jl 20 '64
GAS warfare. See Gases in warfare
GAS wells. See Gas, Natural
GASCAR, Pierre
Full circle. R. Howard. Nation 198:400-2 Ap 20 '64
GASEOUS indigestion. See Dyspepsia
GASES
Gases; molecules in motion. Sci Digest 54:79-81 D '63
Scavenger probe sampling: a method for studying gaseous free radicals. R. M. Fristrom. bibliog il Science 140:297-300 Ap 19 '63
See also
Atmosphere
Carbon dioxide
Plasma (ionized gases)
also names of gases, e.g. Helium
GASES, Asphyxiating and poisonous
For safe silos. Suc Farm 61:15 S '63
One man's meat; use of toxic gases. New Repub 148:5 Mr 23 '63
Poison gas? Egyptian planes against Yemeni royalists. Newsweek 62:42 Jl 22 '63
See also
Carbon monoxide
Chemical warfare
Tear gas
GASES, Liquefied
Making products flow to the customers; shipment of solids and gases in liquid form. il Bsns W p68-70 My 2 '64
GASES, Rare
Chemistry of noble gas compounds. H. H. Hyman. bibliog il Science 145:773-83 Ag 21 '64
Chemistry of the noble gases. H. Selig and others. il Sci Am 210:66-77 bibliog(p 150) My '64
Fluorine compounds of xenon and radon. C. L. Chernick and others; discussion. Science 138:75, 1350; 139:242+, bibliog 672-3 O 12, D 21 '62, Ja 18, F 15 '63
Noble gas compounds; report of conference at Argonne national laboratory, April 1963. H. H. Hyman. Science 141:61-3 Jl 5 '63; Reply. L. C. Allen. 141:116 Jl 12 '63
Noble gases in sea water. R. Bieri and others. bibliog il Science 146:1035-7 N 20 '64
Out of thin air. il Time 81:92+ Je 7 '63
See also
Krypton
Xenon
GASES in warfare
Gas for gas warfare. A. Harrigan. Nat R 14:283+ Ap 9 '63
Now, an argument over gas warfare. U S News 56:8 My 4 '64
See also
Chemical warfare
GASKILL, Gordon
Cyprus, the reluctant republic. Read Digest 82:209-11+ Je '63
Dinghy cruise to Turkey. Yachting 115:48-50+ Mr '64
How I learned to be an expert bargainer. Read Digest 82:228-9+ Mr '63
Nobody loves a crocodile. Read Digest 86:17-18+ Ja '65
South Africa's king of diamonds. Read Digest 84:197-8+ My '64
Spitsbergen: oasis in the Arctic. Read Digest 84:224-6+ F '64
GASLIGHT square. See St Louis
GASNER, Beverly
Nina upstairs; story. McCalls 92:64-73 Ja '65
GASOLINE
Gasolines: is there any difference? B. H. Frisch. il Sci Digest 54:37-41 Jl '63
Selecting the gasoline best for your car. il Good H 156:147 F '63
Story of gasoline. J. D. Soltis and C. H. Beckham. il Motor T 16:106-9 N; 50-3 D '64; 17:58-61 Ja '65
See also
Automobile engines—Fuel

Additives

Gasoline additives. Sci Digest 54:39 Jl '63
Gasoline additives, here's what they do. Suc Farm 63:52 Ja '65
Grain alcohol in gasoline? Sci N L 84:178 S 21 '63

Anti-knock and anti-knock mixtures

Fuel lead found in ocean from auto engines burning antiknock gasoline. Sci N L 84:405 D 28 '63
Regular gas: use at your own risk? il Consumer Rep 28:114-15 Mr '63

Prices

Gasoline price wars; what to expect next. U S News 55:8 N 18 '63

Statistics

Facts and figures of the Americas: gasoline production in Latin America 1955-1962. Américas 16:45 F '64

Storage

Keep gasoline away from heating appliances. il Consumer Bul 47:43 S '64

Taxation

How to save gas tax money on a boat or an off-road vehicle. Sunset 130:63-4 Je '63
GASOLINE, Solid
It's solid gasoline. il Life 55:49-50 O 11 '63
GASOLINE engines. See Gas and oil engines
GASOLINE fume detectors. See Gas detectors
GASOLINE generators. See Electric generators
GASOLINE lanterns. See Lanterns
GASOLINE pumps
Gas stations cut the guesswork; electronic metering systems. il Bsns W p 116+ Ja 16 '65
GASOLINE substitutes
See also
Automobile engines—Fuel
GASOLINE supplements. See Gasoline—Additives
GASOLINE tank trucks. See Tank trucks
GASPÉ, Quebec
Ring around the Gaspé. B. Thielen. il Holiday 35:22+ Ap '64
GASPERI, Alcide de
Alcide De Gasperi. E. A. Carrillo. America 111:156-8 Ag 15 '64
GASPERINI, Brunella
Summer by the sea; story. Sat Eve Post 236:52-3 Jl 13 '63
GASS, Oscar
America and the world revolution; ed. by N. Podhoretz. Commentary 36:278-96 O '63
Britain after world power. New Repub 148:18-20 Je 8; 23-6 Je 22; 22-4+ Je 29 '63
Europe renewed and transformed. Commentary 35:446-50 My '63
Politics of the dead center. New Repub 148:21-6 F 9 '63
Russia: Khrushchev and after. bibliog f Commentary 36:353-63 N '63 (to be cont)
Soviet economic developments. bibliog f Commentary 37:54-68 F; 38:13-15 Jl '64
Vietnam, resistance or withdrawal? bibliog f Commentary 37:37-45 My '64
GASSAWAY, J. L.
More wells weren't the answer. Am City 79:107-8 Ap '64
GASSER, Henry
All about framing. Design 64:204-9+ Je '63
Capture winter in oils. il Design 64:124-5+ Ja '63
Career of John R. Grabach. Am Artist 28:38-43+ Mr '64
GASSET, José Ortega y. See Ortega y Gasset, J.
GASSETT, William H.
We are still in a growth economy; interview. por U S News 55:48-9 S 16 '63
GASSNER, John
Playwright and the contemporary world Theatre Arts 48:22-3+ Ja '64
Who's afraid of Virginia Woolf? on LP. Sat R 46:39-40+ Je 29 '63
GAST, Paul W. and others
Isotopic composition of lead and strontium from Ascension and Gough Islands. bibliog Science 145:1181-5 S 11 '64
GASTER, Theodor H.
Dead Sea scandal. Sat R 48:30-1 Ja 30 '65
Translating the Bible. Commentary 36:305-11 O '63
GASTON III, Phoebus, count of Foix
Makers of the sports page. P. Knauth. il por(p35) Sports Illus 19:41-3 S 16 '63
GASTRIC acidity. See Stomach—Acidity
GASTRIC juice
Gastric content of fasted primates: a survey. D. A. Brodie and R. W. Marshall. bibliog il Science 141:174-5 Jl 12 '63
Humoral factor from the brain which activates gastric motility. N. C. Jefferson and others. Science 144:58-9 Ap 3 '64
GASTRIC ulcers. See Peptic ulcers
GASTRO camera. See Medical instruments and apparatus
GASTROENTERITIS of swine. See Swine—Diseases and pests
GASTRONOMY. See Food

GASTROPODS
Linear polymerization of a gastropod hemocyanin. R. M. Condie and R. B. Langer. bibliog il Science 144:1138-40 My 29 '64

GATE-leg tables. See Tables

GATECRASHING of parties. See Entertaining

GATELL, Frank Otto
Spoils of the bank war: political bias in the selection of pet banks. bibliog f Am Hist R 70:35-58 O '64

GATES, Arthur I.
Today's better teaching methods. Todays Health 42:60-1 Ja '64

GATES, Elgin T.
Africa's new big-game utopia. por Field & S 69:43-5+ My '64

GATES
Gateways to outdoor living. il Am Home 66: 19-20 Je '63
Handmade tiles decorate this garden gate. il Sunset 130:196 F '63
Welcome-mat gates. il Pop Gard 15:44-5 Mr '64

GATES, Hydraulic
Little gates built big; sluice gates at New York city's Jamaica pollution-control project. il Am City 79:118 Ap '64

GATEWAY arch. See St Louis—Monuments, statues, etc.

GATSOS, Nikos
Amorgós; poem, tr. by E. Keeley. Poetry 105:24-31 O '64

about

Translator's notes on proper names; Amorgós: a commentary. E. Keeley. Poetry 105:31-5 O '64

GATTI, Carlo
New kind of event; tr. by M. J. Matz. Opera N 29:14-15 Ja 23 '65

GATTIS, David A.
Transistor ignition. Pop Sci 184:106-9+ Mr '64

GATZA, James. See Kindall, A. F. jt. auth.

GAUBIS, Anthony
I'm not very optimistic; interview. por U S News 55:50-1 S 16 '63

GAUDET, John J.
Marsilea vestita; conversion of the water form to the land form by darkness and by far-red light. bibliog Science 140:975-6 My 31 '63

GAUDI Y CORNET, Antonio
Gaudí. J. J. Sweeney. il Vogue 141:78-81+ Je '63

GAUGH, H. F.
Music at Indiana U. Mus Am 84:12-14 Ap '64

GAUGUIN, Paul
Gauguin, by H. Perrruchot. Review
Time il pors 83:120 My 15 '64
Strange life of Paul Gauguin. G. Kent. il por Read Digest 83:188-93 O '63
Yellow Christ. C. B. Johnson. il Sch Arts 63:22-3 D '63

GAULLE, Charles de
As de Gaulle sees world issues now; excerpts from news conference, July 23, 1964. por U S News 57:10 Ag 3 '64
Encore, non; summary of TV address. Time 81:31 Ap 26 '63
France 1965; address, December 31, 1964. Vital Speeches 31:212-13 Ja 15 '65
Future of France; address, December 31, 1963. Vital Speeches 30:197-8 Ja 15 '64
Political evolution of Europe; news conference, January 14 1963. Vital Speeches 29:230-5 F 1 '63
Vision of Charles de Gaulle; writings and remarks. Time 81:23 F 8 '63
Why de Gaulle recognized red China; summary of news conference. por U S News 56:12 F 10 '64
World today as de Gaulle sees it; news conference, July 29, 1963. por U S News 55: 62-3 Ag 12 '63

about

Adenauer sizes up de Gaulle; interview, ed. by K. Lachmann. K. Adenauer. U S News 54:31 F 11 '63
After Brussels. E. Taylor. Reporter 28:29-32 F 14 '63
After five years, de Gaulle still towers. S. R. Graubard. il pors N Y Times Mag p 12+ D 15 '63
Again the assassins. il Newsweek 61:36+ F 25 '63
Après moi? moi! il por Time 82:41 O 4 '63
Atlantic disunity and de Gaulle. Sat Eve Post 236:74 F 16 '63
Atlantic report. Atlan 211:22+ F '63; 213: 24+ Ja '64
Behind de Gaulle's veiled threats. E. Taylor. il Reporter 31:30+ N 19 '64
Big day in Mexico. K. Crawford. Newsweek 63:34 Mr 23 '64
Can de Gaulle do it? J. Daniel. New Repub 148:9-11 Mr 2 '63
Can de Gaulle shape Europe to his mold? pors Bsns W p82-3+ Ja 26 '63
Case pro and con de Gaulle. L. Markel. il N Y Times Mag p 19+ Ja 10 '65
C'est moi, de Gaulle. Nat R 16:97 F 11 '64; Reply. V. Petrov. 16:205 Mr 10 '64
Challenger talks back to President de Gaulle. H. Giniger. il N Y Times Mag p25+ Mr 15 '64
Charles de Gaulle, grand master of France. Read Digest 82:101-6 F '63
Common market: a Noël from France? il Newsweek 62:21 D 30 '63
Common market crisis. C. Emmet. America 108:333-5 Mr 9 '63
Complete war memoirs of Charles de Gaulle, 1940-1946. Review
Esquire 62:16+ N '64. M. Muggeridge
Count of Paris. E. von Kuehnelt-Leddihn. Nat R 15:102 Ag 13 '63
Crisis in the western alliance; American and British views. H. J. Morgenthau; G. Hutton. Commentary 35:185-98 Mr '63
Crystallization of Gaullism. Nat R 14:97 F 12 '63
Cuba crisis and nuclear arms; why de Gaulle goes his own way; reprint. C. B. Luce. U S News 54:65 F 18 '63
Cursing de Gaulle is not a policy. S. Hoffmann. por Reporter 30:38-41 Ja 30 '64
Day Paris was liberated. L. Collins and D. Lapierre. il pors N Y Times Mag p23-5+ Ag 23 '64
Dealing with de Gaulle; Dean Acheson tells how. U S News 54:22 Mr 25 '63
Dean Acheson speaks out again: target is President de Gaulle; summaries of addresses. D. G. Acheson. U S News 55:15 S 30 '63
De Gaulle. E. Spears. pors Look 27:68-70+ My 7 '63
De Gaulle and the French army: a crisis in civil-military relations, by E. S. Furniss, jr. Review
Sat R 47:28+ Ap 4 '64. H. Lehrman
De Gaulle and the future of the western alliance. Sr Schol 82:6-9+ Mr 27 '63
De Gaulle and the strike. J. Daniel. New Repub 148:10-11 Ap 13 '63
De Gaulle at Trier: the oracle speaks. E. Taylor. il Reporter 30:25-7 Je 18 '64
De Gaulle builds a new France. D. Cook. il pors Sat Eve Post 236:24-8+ N 23 '63
De Gaulle by twilight. L. J. Halle. New Repub 148:10-14 F 9 '63
De Gaulle charts a collision course. il Bsns W p 130+ N 14 '64
De Gaulle in Oceania. Nation 199:22-3 Jl 27 '64
De Gaulle: just who he is and what's back of him. il por U S News 57:24-6 D 28 '64
De Gaulle keeps the pot bubbling. il Newsweek 63:37 My 11 '64
De Gaulle on Vietnam. R. Steel. Commonweal 80:241-3 Ap 24 '64
De Gaulle pushes global ambitions. il Bsns W p23-4 Ja 11 '64
De Gaulle recognizes Peking. E. M. von Kuehnelt-Leddihn. Nat R 16:152 F 25 '64
De Gaulle rejects unarmed Polaris, reaffirms independent force plan. Aviation W 78:39 Ja 21 '63
De Gaulle speaks: the answer is no; with report by E. Weintal. pors Newsweek 62: 29-30 Ag 12 '63
De Gaulle takes a trip. Newsweek 61:40+ My 6 '63
De Gaulle, the seducer. J. Burnham. Nat R 14:232 Mr 26 '63; Reply. O. von Habsburg. Nat R 14:424 My 21 '63
De Gaulle to Mexico. Sr Schol 84:32 Ap 3 '64
De Gaulle: today China, tomorrow. Newsweek 63:31 F 3 '64
De Gaulle: trouble from an ally. por U S News 57:31-2 D 7 '64
De Gaulle vs. America: who's going to run NATO? U S News 56:20 My 11 '64
De Gaulle's bid to red China. J. B. Sheerin. Cath World 198:332-4 Mr '64
De Gaulle's bold gambits. A. Werth. Nation 198:339-42 Ap 6 '64
De Gaulle's D day. Newsweek 64:36 Ag 24 '64
De Gaulle's France: grandeur but not enough plumbing. il por U S News 57:70-1 Ag 24 '64
De Gaulle's France on the road to neutralism; tr. by J. Burnham; discussion. Nat R 14: 171-2 F 26 '63
De Gaulle's labor policy on trial: what the French strikes are about. il U S News 54:90-1 Ap 1 '63
De Gaulle's Mexican hat dance. G. Delmas. Reporter 30:30-2 Ap 23 '64

GAULLE, Charles de—about—*Continued*
De Gaulle's new Europe: meaning to Britain, U.S. il U S News 54:66-7 F 4 '63
De Gaulle's non! a year later. L. J. Halle. il por N Y Times Mag p 14-15+ Ja 12 '64
De Gaulle's pursuit of grandeur; excerpt from American foreign policy. D. Brandon. Cath World 199:224-9 Jl '64
De Gaulle's reasons. A. Werth. Nation 199: 422 D 7 '64
De Gaulle's Romanian gambit. E. Taylor. il por Reporter 31:41-3 Ag 13 '64
De Gaulle's world view. A. Werth. Nation 198:195-7 F 24 '64
De Gaulle's would-be assassins. F. Barrat. Commonweal 77:663-4 Mr 22 '63
Disenchantment of General de Gaulle. F. Canavan. America 111:123 Ag 8 '64
Dream comes true for two old rivals. il por U S News 54:19 F 4 '63
El Macho comes to call; first trip to Latin America. Time 83:40 Mr 13 '64
Enigmatic fascination of Charles de Gaulle; tr. by R. Howard. F. Mauriac. il pors Vogue 144:174-9 S 1 '64
Europe: storm signals; defiant de Gaulle threatens western unity; with reports by E. Weintal, L. Norman and A. de Borchgrave. il por Newsweek 64:40-2+ N 30 '64
Exploding alliances; NATO powers. Christian Cent 80:195 F 13 '63
Face watching; de Gaulle's return to public life. il por Time 83:33 Je 5 '64
Flower potshot; third known attempt on de Gaulle's life. Newsweek 64:36+ S 14 '64
France: a return to greatness? il pors Newsweek 63:40-3+ F 10 '64
France: a third force? E. Taylor. Reporter 30:24-6 F 27 '64
France nods to red China. Sr Schol 84:5 F 14 '64
France of Charles de Gaulle. E. W. Fox. Cur Hist 47:332-8+ D '64
France under de Gaulle; a former premier speaks out; interview, ed. by A. J. Meyers. G. Mollet. por U S News 55:126-7 O 14 '63
French people and de Gaulle. M. Gordey. il For Affairs 42:546-58 Jl '64
Friend explains de Gaulle. por U S News 55:36 Jl 15 '63
Fulbright on de Gaulle. K. Crawford. Newsweek 62:49 N 11 '63
Fulbright target: de Gaulle; summary of address, October 29, 1963. J. W. Fulbright. U S News 55:26 N 11 '63
Gaullism. E. J. Hughes. Newsweek 64:23 N 30 '64
Gaullism today. W. Lippmann. Newsweek 61:25 Je 24 '63
Gaullist explosion. W. Lippmann. Newsweek 61:11 F 4 '63
Gaullist revolt against the Anglo-Saxons. C. V. Crabb, jr. bibliog f Ann Am Acad 351:15-23 Ja '64
Gaullist view. A. Rothberg. Christian Cent 80:1427-9 N 20 '63
General and the miners. E. Taylor. il Reporter 28:14-18 Ap 11 '63
General takes the stage again. il por Newsweek 64:33 Jl 13 '64
General who is king. il pors Bsns W p90-1+ My 9 '64
Government by disdain. R. Aron. New Repub 148:7-8 F 2 '63; Correction. 148:31 F 23 '63
Le grand quartermaster. Newsweek 62:50-1 S 23 '63
Grandstand play down Mexico way. il por Life 56:24-5 Mr 27 '64
Guessing game. por Newsweek 63:42 Ap 27 '64
He may be right about China but wrong about Europe. L. J. Halle. New Repub 150:16-18 F 22 '64
He who says no; obstacle to appeasement with the Soviet bloc. Nat R 15:88-9 Ag 13 '63
How de Gaulle came out in showdown with miners. il U S News 54:105-6 Ap 15 '63
How de Gaulle handles his labor problems. por U S News 54:100 Mr 18 '63
How de Gaulle rates with the home folks. por U S News 54:19 F 18 '63
How de Gaulle sees things. J. Burnham. Nat R 16:863 O 6 '64
If it happened to de Gaulle. . . il Time 82: 37 D 6 '63
If the war in Vietnam can't be won is neutralization an answer? il Newsweek 63: 44-5 F 17 '64
If you're puzzled about gold; answers to some key questions. il U S News 58:96-7 Ja 25 '65
In defense of Charles de Gaulle. J. Grigg. il pors N Y Times Mag p 14+ F 23 '64
In France, a whispering campaign against U.S; and some shouts. por U S News 54:69 F 4 '63
Inner-directed general. Nation 196:82 F 2 '63
King and his court, by P. Viansson-Ponté, tr. by E. P. Halperin. Review
Sat R por 48:48-9 Ja 9 '65. A. Werth
Latins together; visit to Mexico. Newsweek 63:38+ Mr 23 '64
Let's relax about Europe. S. Alsop. por Sat Eve Post 238:16 Ja 16 '65
Letter from Paris. Genêt. New Yorker 39: 133-4+ D 7 '63; 40:98+ F 22; 155-8 Mr 21; 90+ My 2; 90 Je 27; 58+ D 26 '64
Letter from Paris; de Gaulle, Gaullism and Gaullists. Genêt. New Yorker 39:60+ Ag 17 '63
Letter from Paris; Gaullist price-stabilization project. Genêt. New Yorker 39:156+ S 28 '63
Life of one man; fresh attempt on de Gaulle's life. il Time 81:27-8 F 22 '63
Magic on the Meuse; tour of northeastern France. Time 81:30 My 3 '63
Man of strong opinions. Newsweek 62:22 D 30 '63
Meeting of two minds. M. Ascoli. Reporter 28:22-3 F 28 '63
Memories that irk de Gaulle. il pors U S News 56:57 Mr 30 '64
More reflections on Gaullist France. G. M. Pepper. por Nat R 15:239-40 S 24 '63
Napoleon? ce n'est pas moi. New Repub 148:7 F 16 '63
New & obscure destination; de Gaulle's veto of Britain's admission to the Common market. il pors Time 81:22+ F 8 '63; Same abr. with title De Gaulle corners the market. Read Digest 82:65-70 Ap '63
New French politics. R. C. Macridis. Yale R 52:352-65 Mr '63
New start for the Alliance. E. V. Rostow. il Reporter 28:23-9 Ap 25 '63
No. one problem for Johnson. Nat R 16:1002 N 17 '64
Normalcy. D. Lawrence. U S News 54:100 F 11 '63
One man? General de Gaulle, the 1963 scapegoat. Nation 196:109 F 9 '63
Operation royal. Time 83:33 Ap 24 '64
Other de Gaulle. M. Harrington. Commonweal 79:419-21 Ja 10 '64
Pebbles in the pond. il pors Time 83:26-30 F 7 '64
Perfect plan to kill de Gaulle. C. Plimmer and D. Plimmer. il Read Digest 82:101-6 Je '63
Pinpricks by de Gaulle. il por Newsweek 63: 40+ Mr 16 '64
Placing General de Gaulle. R. Aron. New Repub 148:8-9 Mr 16 '63
Portrait of de Gaulle's Anglo-Saxons. G. Gorer. il N Y Times Mag p28+ My 12 '63
Prophet heard from; press conference. il por Time 84:20 Jl 31 '64
Put up or shut up. J. Burnham. Nat R 16: 150 F 25 '64
Remembering Rac. S. Alsop. por Sat Eve Post 237:19 Je 27 '64
Repeat performance. Newsweek 64:36 Ag 3 '64
Report from Washington; watching de Gaulle. H. Brandon. Sat R 47:14 F 22 '64; Reply. J. M. Conlon. 47:43 Ap 11 '64
Revolt of Europe; with editorial comment. E. Griffiths. il pors Sat Eve Post 236:13-21, 76 Mr 9 '63
Rift in West: how serious. il por U S News 54:29-30 F 11 '63
Ring-around-the-rockets; France and the test ban treaty. il por Time 82:19-20 Ag 9 '63
Road to Moscow: de Gaulle and the Kremlin. C. Cate. il por Atlan 212:65-71 Ag '63
Round I to the General; Sparks across the channel. il por Time 81:30-1 F 15 '63
Rusk warns allies: do more for defense. U S News 55:26 N 11 '63
Shadows on the success of Der Alte. D. Schorr. Reporter 28:27-8 F 28 '63
Sighting in on de Gaulle. Time 83:60 F 7 '64
Size-up of de Gaulle; interview, ed. by A. J. Meyers. R. Aron. il pors U S News 54:68-72 Ap 22 '63; Same abr. with title Frenchman explains de Gaulle. Read Digest 83: 79-82 Jl '63
So that tomorrow will be like today; tour of Picardy. il Time 83:24 Je 19 '64
Squeeze play. por Newsweek 65:28+ F 1 '65
Stalked and cussed at, de Gaulle has a case. G. Farmer. il Life 54:34 Mr 1 '63
Standing alone; is de Gaulle right again? excerpt. P. L. Graham. Newsweek 61:34-5 F 25 '63
This is now being done; official visit to Mexico. il pors Time 83:28 Mr 27 '64
To the new generation. Time 82:34 O 18 '63
Too poor to bow. il por Time 84:92+ Ag 28 '64

GAULLE, Charles de—about—*Continued*
Toujours de Gaulle. America 110:73 Ja 18 '64
Tour de force; de Gaulle in Mexico. il pors Newsweek 63:33-4 Mr 30 '64
Tour de (third) force. Newsweek 62:34 O 28 '63
Traveling tall; visit to Athens. il por Time 81:32 My 24 '63
Troubles of a trouble maker. Bsns W p88 Ag 1 '64
Two decades. il por Time 84:42+ S 4 '64
U.S. puzzle: what's de Gaulle up to? U S News 56:36 Je 22 '64
Vive Papa Charles. Newsweek 63:49 Ap 6 '64
Voices of silence. E. Taylor. Reporter 30:12 F 13 '64
Waltz of les Gaullistes. P. Viansson-Ponté. il pors Esquire 62:104-6+ O '64
Warrior's rest. Time 81:39 Je 14 '63
What de Gaulle actually said about Vietnam. B. Fall. Reporter 29:39-41 O 24 '63; Reply with rejoinder. C. Wolf, jr. 29:6+ D 19 '63
What de Gaulle really wants. M. Gordey. il pors Look 28:38-42+ My 19 '64
What de Gaulle sees ahead. il U S News 54:55 F 11 '63
What did de Gaulle's invasion achieve? il pors U S News 56:14 Mr 30 '64
What to do about de Gaulle? H. Moffett. il pors Life 58:37-8+ Ja 8 '65
What's de Gaulle up to? M. Ascoli. Reporter 30:22-3 F 27 '64
What's de Gaulle up to in Asia? pors Sr Schol 84:16-20 Mr 6 '64
Why de Gaulle cannot win. L. J. Halle. il N Y Times Mag p9+ Je 2 '63
Why de Gaulle is challenging U.S.; interview. M. C. de Murville. il por U S News 56:70-5 Mr 16 '64
Wrong Europe. C. Bourdet. Nation 196:191-5 Mr 9 '63
Year of special importance: 1963, a crucial time; address, October 2, 1963. P. H. Spaak. Vital Speeches 30:37-41 N 1 '63
Yielding a bit; agreement to meeting of Britain and the Common market. Newsweek 62:41-2 Jl 22 '63

Visit to Latin America, 1964

As you would greet me. il Time 84:53-4 O 16 '64
Balance sheet. il por Newsweek 64:66 O 26 '64
Cruising comfortably; Latin American trip. il por Time 84:36 O 9 '64
De Gaulle saddles up for South America. por Bsns W p30 S 19 '64
De Gaulle's visit to Latin America. J. P. O'Neill. America 111:507 O 31 '64
De Gaulliver's travels. il por Time 84:66 O 2 '64
Grand voyageur; de Gaulle to tour South America. Time 84:24-5 S 25 '64
La grandeur; tour of the southern hemisphere. il Newsweek 64:52 S 28 '64
Home with trumpet & spurs. il por Time 84:38 O 23 '64
On the long, hot road with General de Gaulle. il por Newsweek 64:76+ O 5 '64
Slightly tarnished; visit to Argentina. Newsweek 64:61 O 19 '64
Sort of triumph; tour of South America. Newsweek 64:68 O 12 '64
What French salesman de Gaulle was selling in Latin America. il U S News 56:100 Ap 6 '64

GAULLE, Yvonne Thérèse (Vendroux) de
Silent first lady of France. E. Behr. il por Sat Eve Post 237:64-5 Ja 18 '64

GAULT, William Campbell
Off the cuff. Writer 77:7-8 S '64
There is only you. Writer 76:25 O '63

GAUSTAD, Edwin S.
Building a basic theological library. Christian Cent 80:560-2 Ap 24 '63
Dialogue, anyone? Christian Cent 80:1030 Ag 21 '63

GAUTIER, Felisa Rincón de
One battle I had to win; ed. by R. Hochstein. por Good H 156:89 My '63
Unbeatable mayor of San Juan. il pors Life 57:65-6+ S 25 '64

GAUTIER, T. N.
Ionosphere and radio propagation in the lower frequencies. Science 143:1197+ Mr 13 '64

GAVER, Jessyca Russell
Absence makes the heart grow. Read Digest 85:100-1 Jl '64
How to be happy the second time around! McCalls 90:54+ Ap '63
Rewards; poem. McCalls 90:145 Mr '63
Teens want to help. Parents Mag 38:60+ O '63; Same abr. with title To Claudia with love. Read Digest 83:215-16 O '63

GAVER, Mary Virginia
What next in school libraries? bibliog f por ALA Bul 58:123-7 F '64

about

Library services on three levels recommended in New Jersey report. Library J 90:88 Ja 1 '65
School library book catalog. Wilson Lib 38:713-14 My '64

GAVIN, James M.
Common market and space program; address, June 17, 1963. Vital Speeches 29:591-4 Jl 15 '63

GAVIN, Marian
Door opens, a door closes; story. Redbook 124:66-7 N '64
Fifty self-starters for fiction writers; excerpts from Writing short stories for pleasure and profit. Writers 77:11-13+ F '64

GAVIN, William F.
Intelligent liberal student's guide to world literature. Nat R 16:64 Ja 28 '64
Seminar in modern journalistic thought: final examination. Nat R 16:959 N 3 '64
Uncle Cornpone greets the press. Nat R 16:867 O 6 '64

GAVRILOV, N. F. and Bagrova, I. IU.
Libraries in the USA; official Soviet report. ALA Bul 57:341-4 Ap '63

GAVRON, Daniel
Masada dig. Commentary 38:52-6 O '64

GAY, Clyde F.
Gay of John Hancock. por Fortune 70:43 D '64

GAY, Peter
Annals of childhood. Sat R 46:73-4 Mr 23 '63

GAY Head, pseud.
Boy dates girl. See issues of Senior scholastic
Talking it over with Gay Head; questions and answers (cont of) Boy dates girl. See issues of Senior scholastic

GAYDN, Ernst
Get a good knife. Outdoor Life 132:54-5+ N '63

GAYLOR, Judith
Chic U.S. resorts. Travel 120:44-9 N '63

GAYN, Mark
Canadian elections. Nation 196:319-21 Ap 20 '63

GAYSEK, Marlene
Teen-agers on an art binge. B. Leavitt. il pors Look 27:M13-14+ S 24 '63

GAZPACHO. See Soups

GBADEYAN, Samuel
Big chickens of James and Samuel. P. Conklin. Reporter 28:30-1 Je 20 '63

GBENYE, Christophe
Backed by red China: leftist chief of Congo rebels. il por U S News 57:22 D 14 '64

GEAGAN, Bill
Cross and doublecross. Outdoor Life 133:42-3+ Ja '64
Last of the skitterers. Field & S 69:38-40+ Jl '64
Maine's farm woodlands. Am For 69:34-6 S '63
Red paint people. Hobbies 68:115-16 Ap '63
Woodland caribou comes home to Maine. Nat Parks Mag 38:8-9 My '64

GEARING
See also
Automobiles—Gearing
Clutches (machinery)
Indexing (machine work)

GEBER, Marcelle. See Dean, R. jt. auth.

GEBHARD, Bruno
Is there too much secrecy in medicine? Ladies Home J 80:38 Jl '63

GEBHARD, Patricia
School for ninety-day wonders. por Library J 88:2198-200 Je 1 '63

GECKOS. See Lizards

GEDDA, Nicolai
Quote . . . unquote. J. Ardoin. por Mus Am 83:19 Jl '63

GEDDES, Andrew
Local organization for recruitment. ALA Bul 58:825-6 O '64

GEDDES, Donald Porter
Obituary
Pub W 183:35 Mr 11 '63

GEDDES, Joan Bel
Gardens, children and the good old summertime. Pop Gard 15:22-3 Jl '64

GEDNEY, Grover C. and Winterburg, F. M.
Instrument calibration and repair technician. Electr World 70:28-9 Ag '63

GEE, Louise Holford
Cyclamen for year-round bloom. Horticulture 41:472-3 S '63
Imaginative miniature garden. Horticulture 41:322-3 Je '63

GEERLINGS, Gerald K.
Cooling your house with free air. Pop Sci 183:99-101 Jl '63

GEESE
Little brother of the snow. W. B. Morse. il Am For 69:28-9+ F '63
Scotch guards; Dumbarton's goose patrol. il Life 55:39-40 Jl 5 '63
See also
Cotton goosing
GEESE, Wild
Giant Canada goose believed extinct, alive. Sci N L 83:245 Ap 20 '63
Goof hunter's bible. N. Riley. il Outdoor Life 132:34-5+ D '63
Goose hunt farm style. C. P. Streeter. il Farm J 87:37+ N '63
Goose hunting is getting better. G. Laycock. il Suc Farm 62:108-9 O '64
Goose that carries a knife; super-winged goose. R. B. Aitken. il Field & S 69:10-13 D '64
Hunters follow where the wild goose leads. il Bsns W p26-7 D 19 '64
New kind of pond. B. A. Roth. Farm J 87: 64D O '63
Now you shoot! M. Ellis. il Field & S 69:46-8+ N '64
Secrets of black brant. E. Park. il Field & S 69:21-3+ Ja '65
Slaughter at Swan Lake. D. McKinley. Audubon Mag 66:144-5 My '64; Discussion. 66: 270; 67:5-7 S '64, Ja '65
Snows of Ile aux Grues. N. Karas. il Field & S 69:51-3+ O '64
Very special goose; black brant. E. Park. il Outdoor Life 133:50-2+ Ja '64
Washtub honkers. B. Carver and E. Crimmin. il Field & S 67:12-13 Ap '63
What every goose hunter should know. E. A. Bauer. il Field & S 68:23-5+ D '63
GEESE decoys. See Decoys (hunting)
GEHL, Mary A. See Haskin, L. jt. auth.
GEHLBACH, Frederic R.
Biological visit to McKittrick Canyon. il Nat Parks Mag 37:4-7 Mr '63
GEHLEN, Reinhard
Triple double. il Time 82:26 Jl 19 '63
GEHMAN, Richard
Alexander H. Cohen: bigger than Barnum. Theatre Arts 47:20-2+ O '63
Letter to a young article writer. Writer 76: 15-17 N '63
Little war can be a lot of fun. Sports Illus 22:36-41 Ja 4 '65
Man who owns Paradise. Sat Eve Post 236:66+ Ap 27 '63
about
Man of many words. il por Newsweek 62: 52-3 Jl 22 '63
GEHRIG'S disease. See Sclerosis
GEIB, M. Eugenia
Miscellaneous mayhem. Opera N 28:24-6 Ja 18 '64
GEIER, Woodrow
How headlines saved Nashville. Christian Cent 81:335-6 Mr 11 '64
GEIGER, Abraham
Abraham Geiger and liberal Judaism, comp. by M. Wiener. Review
Commentary 35:172-4 F '63. A. Hertzberg
GEIGER, Don
Tree watching; poem. Atlan 214:49 Ag '64
Voice, the poet, and the poem. Poetry 101: 275-8 Ja '63
GEIGER-Müller counters
Geiger counter; how to detect radioactivity. il Sci Digest 54:81-2 D '63
GEIS, Gilbert, and Bittle, W. E.
Dream that faded. N Y Times Mag p47+ D 6 '64
GEISEL, Theodor Seuss
Speaking out. por Sat Eve Post 237:6+ N 28 '64
about
He makes c-a-t spell big money. il pors Bsns W p72-3 Jl 18 '64
Nonsensical world of Dr Seuss. D. Freeman. il McCalls 92:115+ N '64
GEISER, David T.
FCC and 11 meters: a CBer's view. Pop Electr 20:59-60+ Je '64
How you can get a license to operate a student experimental radio station. Pop Electr 19:69-70+ S '63
Hum interference in car radios. Electr World 70:80 D '63
12-foot transformer for CB. Pop Electr 18: 90 Mr '63
GEISER, Elizabeth A.
If you want a book, any book. Pub W 186: 50-3 D 14 '64
GEISHAS
Girls. T. Prideaux. il Life 57:98 S 11 '64
New Japan. R. Blackmon. Vogue 144:135-7 Ag 15 '64
Secret of the porcelain veil: a Japanese geisha's make-up. il Vogue 144:252-5 D '64
GEISMAR, Maxwell
Jack London today. New Repub 151:29-31 N 14 '64
Wings of the dove: or, False gold; excerpt from Henry James and the Jacobites. Atlan 212:93-8 Ag '63
GEISTER, Janet M.
Trends in nursing as they affect library services. por ALA Bul 58:812-14 O '64
GELABERT, Raoul
Anatomy for the ballet teacher; ed. by W. Como See issues of Dance magazine
GELATIN
Unflavored gelatine and the family that made it famous. E. M. McCabe. il Parents Mag 39:16+ Ap '64
GELATIN salads. See Salads
GELATT, Esther
(ed) See Callas, M. Maria Callas
GELATT, Roland
Last French composer? Reporter 28:52-4+ Mr 28 '63
Music makers. See issues of High fidelity to October 1963
Notes from our correspondents. Hi Fi 14:24+ F '64
Record notes. See occasional issues of The reporter to August 15, 1963
Tunnel under the Alps. Reporter 28:36-8 Ap 11 '63
GELB, Lawrence D. and Lerner, A. M.
Reovirus hemagglutination: inhibition by N-acetyl-D-glucosamine. bibliog Science 147: 404-5 Ja 22 '65
GELBER, Lionel
Marriage of inconvenience. For Affairs 41: 310-22 Ja '63
GELBOIN, Harry V. and Klein, Michael
Skin tumorigenesis by 7,12-dimethylbenz(a) anthracene: inhibitions by actinomycin D. bibliog Science 145:1321-2 S 18 '64
GELDZAHLER, Henry
Los Angeles: the second city of art. Vogue 144:42+ S 15 '64
Movies. Vogue 144:38 Ag 15; 76 S 15; 100 O 15 '64
GELLER, Andrew
Houses that unsquare the cube. F. R. Smith. il pors Sports Illus 19:40-5 Jl 29 '63
GELLER, Evelyn
WLB biography (cont) Wilson Lib Bul 38: 572+; 39:187+ Mr, O '64
about
Evelyn Geller joins Bowker co. as SLJ editor beginning May 11, 1964. por Library J 89:2167-8 My 15 '64
GELLER, Irving
Conditioned anxiety and punishment effects on operant behavior of goldfish (carassius auratus) bibliog Science 141:351-3 Jl 26 '63
GELLER, S. and others
Superconducting indium antimonide. bibliog Science 140:62 Ap 5 '63
GELLERMAN, Saul W.
Strike threat will decline. Nations Bsns 51: 36-7+ Jl '63
GELLHORN, Alfred, and Benjamin, William
Insulin action in alloxan diabetes modified by actinomycin D. bibliog Science 146:1166-8 N 27 '64
GELLHORN, Martha
I have monkeys on my roof. Ladies Home J 81:26+ Jl '64
Is there a new Germany? Atlan 213:69-76 F '64
Tanganyika: African new frontier. Atlan 212: 40-5 S '63
Town no scandal can shake. Vogue 142:144-5+ N 15 '63
about
German students reply to Martha Gellhorn; tr. by B. Ostendorf. G. Schmidt; H. Bauer; L. Zimmer. Atlan 213:74+ My '64
GELLIS, Sydney S.
Doctor is a detective. il por Todays Health 42:30-1+ S '64
GELMAN, Harry
Russia, China, and the underdeveloped areas. bibliog f Ann Am Acad 349:130-42 S '63
GELS. See Colloids
GELSENKIRCHEN, Germany (Federal Republic)
City theater. G. E. K. Smith. il Arch Rec 134:192-4 O '63
GELTMAN, Max
Hannah Arendt and her critics. Nat R 16: 1007-12, 1160 N 17, D 29 '64

GEM carving. See Carving (art industries)
GEM international, incorporated
Will it go in Britain? first suburban shopping center. il Bsns W p86-9 Ja 9 '65
GEMINI project. See Space flight—Manned flights
GEMMILL, Henry
Dual image? reprint. U S News 56:96+ F 10 '64
GEMS
Beautiful investments. il Fortune 68:264 Jl '63
Gem of a quiz. J. Daugherty and M. Daugherty. il Sci Digest 54:25-7 N '63
Gems and minerals. H. D. Brown. See issues of Hobbies
Holiday handbook of precious stones. M. Pollack. il Holiday 33:153-8 Mr '63
Jewelry and gemstones. G. V. Axon. il Consumer Bul 47:12-15 My '64
See also
Amethysts
Diamonds
Jewelry
GENAILLE, Richard A.
Low-pass audio filters for increased talk-power. Electr World 70:47-9 S '63
GENAUER, Emily
Can this be art? Ladies Home J 81:151-5 Mr '64
GENDEBIEN, Olivier, and Jerome, John
Whizz-quiz on cars. Vogue 142:114-19+ N 1 '63
GENDEL, Milton
Art news from Rome (cont) Art N 62:48+ Sum '63; 63:44-5+ Sum '64
Hugger-mugger in the giardini. Art N 63: 32-5+ S '64
Italy: pre-, pro- and post-Roman. Art N 63: 34-6+ Ja '65
Michelangelo year opens in Rome. il Art N 63:26-8 Ap '64
New treasures uncovered in old Rome. Art N 62:34-5+ Sum '63
Royal Etruscan birthday. Art N 63:42-3+ Mr '64
GENEALOGY
Personal business; family history. Bsns W p 185 N 16 '63
Want a coat of arms? trace your family tree? il Life 54:103-8 My 3 '63
We are all descended from grandfathers! grandfathers of the candidates. O. Jensen. il Am Heritage 15:4-13+ Je '64
GENEEN, Harold S.
One man's $1-billion company; ITT. il pors Bsns W p80-2+ My 4 '63
GENERAL acceptance corporation
Finance company all your own. il Bsns W p59-60+ Je 13 '64
GENERAL accounting office. See United States—General accounting office
GENERAL advisory committee to the Atomic energy commission. See United States—Atomic energy commission
GENERAL agreement on tariffs and trade
Atlantic partners. New Repub 148:3-4 Je 8 '63
Bad start for Geneva trade talks. Bsns W p 124 My 2 '64
Breakthrough; GATT negotiations on variable tariff cuts. Newsweek 63:68+ Mr 9 '64
Broadest trade talks, and slowest; Kennedy round at Geneva. il Bsns W p30-2 My 9 '64
Clearing the air for GATT: preliminary talks in Washington. il Bsns W p27 Mr 14 '64
Coming to terms with the Common market. P. Forbath. il Reporter 28:24+ Je 20 '63
Common market and the Kennedy round. il Sr Schol 84:9-11 Ap 24 '64
Disappointing start; the Kennedy round. Time 83:107 My 15 '64
EEC drags its feet. Bsns W p28-9 Mr 2 '63
GATT and the Kennedy round. il Newsweek 61:78-80 My 20 '63
GATT asked for advisory opinion on U.S.-EEC poultry dispute; letter to Eric Wyndham White, October 16, 1963. C. A. Herter. Dept State Bul 49:751-2 N 11 '63
GATT at Geneva. America 108:824-5 Je 8 '63
GATT contracting parties draft articles on trade and development; text of articles. Dept State Bul 51:922-5 D 28 '64
GATT contracting parties meet at Geneva. Dept State Bul 50:423 Mr 16 '64
GATT contracting parties to hold ministerial meeting in May. Dept State Bul 48:418 Mr 18 '63
GATT ministers open Kennedy round of trade negotiations; remarks, May 4, 1964; with declaration adopted by ministers May 6, 1964. C. A. Herter. Dept State Bul 50:878-80 Je 1 '64
GATT ministers reach agreement on tariff negotiating procedures; statements, May 16 and May 17, 1963; with a resolution on trade negotiations, adopted May 21, 1963. C. A. Herter. Dept State Bul 48:990-6 Je 24 '63
Geneva: agreed on the shell of an egg. il Newsweek 61:61 Je 3 '63
Geneva talks on trade. America 108:706 My 18 '63
Getting set for Kennedy round. il Bsns W p 125-6 Ap 13 '63
Guide for trade talks; CED report. Bsns W p 148 Je 13 '64
Haves and have-nots. H. Miller. New Repub 150:6-7 Mr 28 '64
Major aircraft import duty cuts seen. L. L. Doty. Aviation W 81:30 N 23 '64
Mr Blumenthal holds trade talks in three Latin American countries. Dept State Bul 51:369 S 14 '64
Policies for trade and development. R. M. Stern. bibliog f il Int Concil 548:3-63 My '64
President names additional public advisers for trade negotiations. Dept State Bul 51: 313 Ag 31 '64
President names Public advisory committee on trade negotiations. Dept State Bul 50:457 Mr 23 '64
President proclaims protocol for Spain's accession to GATT; proclamation, September 6, 1963. J. F. Kennedy. Dept State Bul 49: 550-1 O 7 '63
Public hearings announced for 1964 GATT trade negotiations; announcement, with notice of proposed trade agreement negotiations and articles to be considered for negotiation by President Kennedy, and notice of public hearings by Sidney Picker, jr, October 21, 1963. il Dept State Bul 49: 745-51 N 11 '63
Recent trade agreements made effective. Dept State Bul 48:145 Ja 28 '63
Rougher going on trade. il Bsns W p27-8 F 9 '63
Setting stage for GATT; US. battled EEC on ground rules. Bsns W p27-8 My 25 '63
Sobering lesson on trade. Bsns W p 112 Je 1 '63
Tariff men do their homework. il Bsns W p49+ Mr 21 '64
Tariffs aren't the only problem; EEC restrictions. il Bsns W p76+ S 7 '63
Technical representatives named for trade negotiations. Dept State Bul 51:517 O 12 '64
Trade developments and trade policy; statement, November 21, 1963. S. Z. Westerfield, jr. Dept State Bul 50:101-4 Ja 20 '64
Trade in the Pacific area; address, February 3, 1964. R. Hilsman. Dept State Bul 50: 293-8 F 24 '64
Trade talks begin in Geneva; names of the U.S. delegates. Dept State Bul 49:72 Jl 8 '63
U.S. and EEC delegations discuss forthcoming GATT negotiations; joint communique, March 6, 1964. Dept State Bul 50:458 Mr 23 '64
Views invited on GATT relations with Spain and U.A.R; Department announcement, January 14, 1963; with notice of public hearings. Dept State Bul 48:183-5 F 4 '63
When steel seeks help from Uncle Sam; steel's case against imports. il Bsns W p80-1 F 15 '64
White House holds conference on export expansion; address, September 17, 1963. C. A. Herter. Dept State Bul 49:601-5 O 14 '63
World trade; address, May 7, 1964. N. A. Rockefeller. Vital Speeches 30:494-7 Je 1 '64
See also
United States—Commercial treaties and agreements
GENERAL aniline and film corporation
Awakening a giant. Time 85:63-4 Ja 1 '65
Clearing way to sell aniline; war-seized company. Bsns W p 16 D 26 '64
Deal cuts General aniline knot. Bsns W p29 Mr 9 '63
GAF goes public; stock to be offered to the public. Newsweek 64:45-6 D 28 '64
General aniline goes private. I. Ross. il Fortune 68:127-9+ S '63
General aniline's fate; Justice dept. and Swiss interhandel. Bsns W p38 O 19 '63
What am I bid? Newsweek 61:79 Mr 18 '63
GENERAL assembly of the national council. See National council of the churches of Christ in the United States of America
GENERAL assembly of the United Nations. See United Nations—General assembly
GENERAL builders corporation
That crazy Latvian. il Newsweek 63:73-4 Mr 9 '64; Same abr. Read Digest 85:25-6 Jl '64

GENERAL commission on chaplains and armed forces personnel
Condemn compulsory chapel; for cadets and midshipmen. Christian Cent 81:1388 N 11 '64

GENERAL drive-in corporation
Movie screens get back some silver; shopping center theaters. il Bsns W p41-2+ Ag 31 '63

GENERAL dynamics corporation
F-111 subcontracts monitored closely. E. J. Bulban. Aviation W 79:55+ Ag 26 '63
GD reports improved results; common stock dividends possible. Aviation W 80:89 F 24 '64
How the Pentagon is run: what TFX fight shows; with excerpts from statement by R. S. McNamara. il U S News 54:54-7 Ap 22 '63
McNamara assails critics of TFX award. G. C. Wilson. Aviation W 78:26-9 Mr 18 '63
Pentagon blasts back at the TFX probers. il Bsns W p29-30 Mr 23 '63
Phasing out the air force? contract for TFX. Nat R 14:223-4 Mr 26 '63
Pounding it out; TFX fighter-plane contract. il Newsweek 62:53-4 Ag 5 '63
Rescue. il Time 83:80 Je 5 '64
$7-billion contract that changed the rules. R. A. Smith. il Fortune 67:96-101+ Mr; 110-11+ Ap '63
TFX award stirs storm. Bsns W p25 Mr 9 '63
TFX board selected Boeing four times; investigation of General dynamics-Grumman contract by Senate investigations subcommittee, with excerpts from hearing. G. C. Wilson. Aviation W 78:22-4 Mr 4 '63
TFX plane: what the fight is about. il U S News 54:61-3 Mr 25 '63
Tactical fighters; TXF hearing. Reporter 28:12 Ap 11 '63

Convair division

GD: the hard road back from the brink; Convair fiasco. il Bsns W p 144-6+ D 7 '63

GENERAL education. See Liberal education

GENERAL electric company
Abridging free speech; decision against General electric by NLRB. H. Hazlitt. Newsweek 65:49 Ja 4 '65
Bringing engineers up to date. G. A. W. Boehm. il Fortune 67:120-1+ My '63
Building a faster track from factory to home; GE's controversial sales plan. il Bsns W p45-6 F 16 '63
Can GE follow steel's path? Joint study committees. Bsns W p35 Ag 3 '63
Case for Boulwarism. H. R. Northrup. bibliog f il Harvard Bsns R 41:86-97 S '63
Competition aims to improve kitchen design. Arch Rec 136:352 S '64
Corrupt society; price-rigging by GE. F. J. Cook. Nation 196:456-65 Je 1 '63
Different way to deal with unions; GE with IUE. il U S News 55:120-1 O 7 '63
Electric's new general. Time 82:104+ O 18 '63
Executive investor; some intriguing aspects of General electric. Duns R 84:87 S '64
GE aerospace sales down 20 per cent from peak. Aviation W 81:21 D 28 '64
G.E. and a community. Commonweal 81:61 O 9 '64
GE and Bull. Newsweek 64:65 Ag 3 '64
GE and Gen. de Gaulle; General electric co. to buy Compagnie des Machines Bull. Newsweek 63:88+ Ap 27 '64
GE develops satellite command unit. il Miss & Roc 12:34 F 4 '63
GE develops single-reversal TWT. il Miss & Roc 13:34 Ag 5 '63
General electric embarks on testing nuclear space power system dynamic components. J. F. Judge. il Miss & Roc 14:26-8 F 17 '64
GE shifts herald harder consumer sell. il Bsns W p88 O 12 '63
GE tries for two feet in the door; dickering with Italy's Olivetti for Europe's computer market. Bsns W p 112+ Ag 15 '64
GE tries new tack on prices; one price for turbines. Bsns W p30 My 25 '63
General electric wins biosatellite contract. Aviation W 79:33 Ag 26 '63
GE working on tunnel-cathode tube. C. D. LaFond. il Miss & Roc 12:22-3 F 11 '63
GE's college is back in session; Management research & development institute at Crotonville, N.Y. il Bsns W p78+ F 8 '64
GE's space division thrives in adversity. il Bsns W p39-40 D 19 '64
Glitter of real estate lures industry dollars. il Bsns W p32+ Mr 2 '63
IUE chief accuses GE; charge of Boulwarism. il Bsns W p71-2+ S 28 '63
IUE raps Local 301's GE pact; conversion from incentive to hourly pay. Bsns W p56 O 17 '64
Is GE policy fair to labor? NLRB examiner says no. Bsns W p73 Ap 6 '63
Is incentive pay headed for shelf? automation vs incentive worker. il Bsns W p51-2 Je 27 '64
Low-pressure potassium vapor powers two-stage turbine at GE. J. F. Judge. il Miss & Roc 15:23-4 Ag 3 '64
Machines Bull's computer crisis; France's proud business-machine firm. T. R. Bransten and S. H. Brown. il Fortune 70:154-5+ Jl '64
Management ways of General electric. J. Thackray. il Duns R 82:28-30+ N '63
NLRB calls GE unfair; failed to bargain in good faith. Bsns W p 116 D 19 '64
New boss at GE. Newsweek 62:86 O 21 '63
New challenges to IBM; computers by Honeywell and GE. il Bsns W p30 D 7 '63
New fuel cell to convert energy; chemicals into electricity. Bsns W p78 My 4 '63
New speech limit on employers? U S News 54:107-8 Ap 15 '63
150,000 at GE share $110-million payout. Bsns W p80+ Mr 16 '63
Paris-Milan express. Time 84:60 Jl 31 '64
Portable TV that's light, inexpensive, and pretty good. il Consumer Rep 28:430-1 S '63
Power reactor makers launch business drive. Bsns W p43-4+ Mr 14 '64
Social scientists in the plant. L. L. Ferguson. il Harvard Bsns R 42:133-43 My '64
Where pressure is rising against the union shop. il U S News 54:105-6 Ap 22 '63
Why GE is joining Olivetti. il Bsns W p 140+ S 12 '64
Wonderful world of appliances. E. M. McCabe. il Parents Mag 38:32+ Je '63

GENERAL federation of women's clubs
Secretary Rusk interviewed on GFWC television program, April 13, 1963. D. Rusk. Dept State Bul 48:698-703 My 6 '63
Women's vote; how will it go? McCalls 91:70+ Mr '64

GENERAL foods corporation
General foods is five billion particulars. il Fortune 69:114-17+ Mr '64
Nuisance item proves a big profit-maker; McKinsey study of frozen foods. il Bsns W p 116+ Mr 14 '64

GENERAL instrument corporation
Diode rings in a Dixie belle. il Bsns W p70 Ap 4 '64

GENERAL mills, incorporated
Alas, poor Betty; failure in Britain. Time 81:96 My 24 '63
On all the shelves at once; Gold Medal Wondra. il Bsns W p 127-8 O 5 '63

GENERAL motors corporation
Alfred Sloan's success story. C. Kaysen. New Repub 150:21-3 F 29 '64
Auto bargaining takes on a new complexion. il Bsns W p92+ N 7 '64
Betting on a short one; with editorial comment. il Bsns W p25-7, 156 O 3 '64
Big smoke screen in Daytona; Chevrolet engines. K. Rudeen. Sports Illus 18:36-8 Mr 4 '63
Breaking the logjam. il Bsns W p23-4 O 10 '64
Car design and public safety; Corvair criticized for design flaws. J. Ridgeway. il New Repub 151:9-11 S 19 '64; Reply. H. E. Campbell. 151:38 O 3 '64
Detroit: out on one strike. Bsns W p28-9 O 31 '64
Fairs: builders of dreams; General motors new Futurama ride. A. Rothenberg. il Look 28:90+ F 11 '64
Flexible world of GM's planning. il Bsns W p 136-8+ O 5 '63
Ford watches Chevy go by. il Bsns W p30-1 Mr 16 '63
Full disclosure: stockholder relations. L. L. L. Golden. Sat R 46:56 O 12 '63
GM and the Negro; Detroit NAACP prepares for demonstrations. il Bsns W p36 Ap 18 '64
General motors bonus system: an indispensable incentive. A. P. Sloan, jr. Fortune 69:125+ Ja '64
GM jolts steelmen; stockpiling steel. il Bsns W p28 F 23 '63
GM strike end is near. Bsns W p96+ O 24 '64
GM strike: prototype for more conflict. B. J. Widick. il Nation 199:349-52 N 16 '64
Going continental. il Time 85:73A Ja 29 '65
Great GM mystery. H. Wolff. bibliog f Harvard Bsns R 42:164-6+ S '64
Hair tonic and dignity; UAW strike against General motors. il Newsweek 64:86+ O 12 '64

GENERAL motors corporation—*Continued*
High cost of uncertainty; GM stockpiling steel. Bsns W p 100 Mr 2 '63
Highest-paid man in industry. U S News 54: 19 My 6 '63
How General motors did it. R. Sheehan. il Fortune 67:96-111+ Je '63
How GM will expand this year and next. U S News 56:9 Mr 30 '64
How world's biggest profit makes jobs. il Nations Bsns 52:40-1+ Jl '64
Introduction to the '65 cars. il Motor T 16: 54-61 N '64
Is this to be the year of a big strike in autos? issue of UAW with GM. il U S News 56:93-5 Mr 16 '64
Kadett vs. VW. Newsweek 62:81-2 D 2 '63
Little things behind a big strike. il U S News 57:89-91 O 12 '64
Many happy returns; record nine-month profits. Time 84:111-12 N 13 '64
Mr General Motors. Newsweek 63:73 Ja 27 '64
My years with General motors. A. P. Sloan, jr. il Fortune 68:135-42+ S; 145-8+ O; 167-70+ N; 149-52+ D '63; 69:123-6+ Ja; 123-6+ F '64; Reply. P. F. Drucker. 70: 130+ Jl '64
Negroes take aim at GM. il Bsns W p32+ Jl 20 '63
New ones, 1965. il Motor T 16:24-36 O '64
New road opens; pre-bargaining study committee. il Newsweek 61:68+ Ap 29 '63
No racing for GM. Newsweek 63:90+ My 25 '64
$1,459,000,000 for GM. Newsweek 61:68+ F 11 '63
Only local disputes left to settle at GM. il Bsns W p89 O 31 '64
People want to buy automobiles. il Newsweek 61:67-8+ F 25 '63
Profit phenomenon. il Time 81:75 F 8 '63
Real issue in the auto strike: demand for union power. il U S News 57:91-2 O 5 '64
Right not to work; United auto workers against General motors. il Time 84:111 O 2 '64
Round for GM. Newsweek 61:83 Mr 25 '63
'64 cars. il Motor T 15:74-91 N '63
Sort of ending; United auto workers reach a national agreement with General motors. Time 84:104 O 16 '64
Special-interest cars; vintage Chevrolet. D. Steele. il Motor T 16:76 N '64
Strategist of success. Time 83:62-4 Ja 24 '64
Union problem: what is there to strike about? il U S News 57:80-1 Jl 20 '64
Wage chronology: General motors corp. 1961-63. il Mo Labor R 86:1170-83 O '63
Walkout in Detroit; UAW strike. Newsweek 64:93-4 O 5 '64
What happens when a big strike drags on. U S News 57:70-2 N 2 '64
What makes GM go. T. R. Brooks. il Duns R 82:30-2+ S '63
What savings pay at GM, Ford. U S News 54:75 F 4 '63
What's new at General motors. J. Whipple. il Pop Sci 185:80-5 O '64
Will this be the no. 1 show? Futurama ride. il Sci Digest 55:13-19 Ap '64
Your right to a car bargain. W. Marx. Nation 196:195-7 Mr 9 '63

AC spark plugs division

Special library convinces management that the library is not a luxury. H. S. Sharp. Library J 88:1107-8 Mr 15 '63

Allison division

Allison plans regenerative engine family. M. L. Yaffee. il Aviation W 80:60-1+ Mr 2 '64

Buick motors division

Making Buick fans of golfers; Buick Open, Grand Blanc, Mich. il Bsns W p30-1 Je 15 '63

Cadillac motor car division

Automotive milestones; history of the Cadillac V-16, 1930-1940. N. F. Uhlir. il Motor T 17:78-83 Ja '65
Cadillac kicks up its heels; adds sportier models. il Bsns W p98+ Ag 17 '63

Truck and coach division

Delivery truck market gets a new diesel; GMC's Toro-flow. il Bsns W p 112+ Ja 18 '64

GENERAL motors training center, Tarrytown, N.Y.
College of mechanical knowledge. A. Markovich. il Pop Sci 184:76-8 Mr '64
GENERAL practitioners. See Physicians

GENERAL precision equipment corporation
Shrinking computers; tiny all-transistorized LGP-21 computer. Bsns W p 106 Ap 6 '63

Link division

Profit in make-believe; Link simulators. il Time 81:86 Je 21 '63

GENERAL reinsurance corporation
Insuring the insurers. il Bsns W p 125-6+ My 18 '63
GENERAL services administration. See United States—General services administration
GENERAL telephone and electronics corporation
How a company keeps going despite strike, sabotage; General telephone company of Florida. il U S News 55:77+ Ag 26 '63
Sabotage in Tampa; strike against the General telephone co. of Florida. il Time 82: 65-6 Ag 16 '63
GENERALS
MacArthur: the greatest captain of his era. R. E. Dupuy. il U S News 56:78-9 Ap 27 '64
Man on horseback; war heroes as presidents, with reproductions of paintings. E. M. Halliday. Am Heritage 15:10-23 Ag '64
Merit will be rewarded. il Newsweek 64:19 Jl 6 '64
Pentagon shift: generals who moved up. il U S News 57:12 Jl 6 '64
Three top soldiers. il Time 84:16 Jl 3 '64
GENERALS, German. See Germany—Army—Officers
GENERATION. See Reproduction
GENERATORS, Electric. See Electric generators
GENERATORS, Signal. See Signal generators
GENEROSITY
See also
Giving
GENES
Actinomycin and puromycin: effects on sequential gene activation by ecdysone. U. Clever. bibliog il Science 146:794-5 N 6 '64
Albinism and water escape performance in the mouse. H. D. Winston and G. Lindzey. bibliog il Science 144:189-91 Ap 10 '64; Reply with rejoinder. G. W. Meier and D. P. Foshee. 147:307-8 Ja 15 '65
Cell differentiation: some aspects of the problem. R. A. Flickinger. bibliog il Science 141: 608-14 Ag 16 '63
Dispensable and indispensable genes in neurospora. J. Morrow. bibliog il Science 144:307-8 Ap 17 '64
Evolving genes and proteins; report on symposium, September 17 and 18, 1964. V. Bryson and H. J. Vogel. Science 147:68-71 Ja 1 '65
First linkage of a species antigen in the genus streptopelia. W. J. Miller. bibliog il Science 143:1179-80 Mr 13 '64
Gene action mechanisms in the determination of color and pattern in the frog (rana pipiens) J. Davison. bibliog il Science 141: 648-9 Ag 16 '63
Genes without chromosomes. W. Cloud. Pop Sci 183:21 N '63
Inherited variant of erythrocyte carbonic anhydrase in Micronesians from Guam and Saipan. R. E. Tashian and others. bibliog il Science 140:53-4 Ap 5 '63
Lethal genes and analysis of differentiation. S. Gluecksohn-Waelsch. bibliog il Science 142:1269-76 D 6 '63
Mutant gene that changes protein composition and increases lysine content of maize endosperm. E. T. Mertz and others. bibliog il Science 145:279-80 Jl 17 '64
Operon: on its third anniversary. G. S. Stent. bibliog Science 144:816-20 My 15 '64
Partial gene duplication. Sci N L 84:84 Ag 10 '63
Sensitivity of female inbreds of cucumis sativus to sex reversion by gibberellin. O. Shifriss and W. L. George, jr. bibliog il Science 143:1452-3 Mr 27 '64
Sequential gene action in the establishment of lysogeny. M. Levine and H. O. Smith. bibliog il Science 146:1581-2 D 18 '64
Somatic instability caused by a cysteine-sensitive gene in arabidopsis. G. P. Rédei. bibliog il Science 139:767-9 F 22 '63
Transcription of a repressed gene: evidence that it requires DNA replication. P. Hanawalt and R. Wax. bibliog il Science 145: 1061-3 S 4 '64
See also
Genetics
Heredity of diseases
GENESCO, incorporated
Computer ships the shoes; Genesco's automatic shipping sorter. il Bsns W p96-7+ Jl 11 '64

GENESIS, Book of. See Bible—Old Testament —Genesis
GENÊT, pseud. See Flanner, J.
GENÊT, Jean
Case of Jean Genet. il por Time 82:114+ O 11 '63
Evil and the ecstasy. L. S. Roudiez. por Sat R 46:38-9 O 26 '63
Evil on a pedestal. J. Cruickshank. Sat R 47:56 N 14 '64
Genet. il pors Vogue 143:172-3 My '64
Look for Genet. A. Chester. Commentary 37:63-7 Ap '64
Maids. Criticism
New Yorker 39:143-4+ N 23 '63
Saint Genet, by J. P. Sartre. Review
New Yorker 39:234-8+ N 9 '63. R. Adler
Solitude of Jean Genet. V. Lange. New Repub 149:23-6 N 23 '63
Spiritual diabolism of Jean Genet. T. F. Driver. Christian Cent 80:1433-5 N 20 '63
Uses of Genet. J. Finn. Commonweal 80:86-8 Ap 10 '64
Visions out of orbit. H. Hewes. Sat R 46:39 O 26 '63
GENETIC research
Acid phosphatases of human red cells: predicted phenotype conforms to a genetic hypothesis. L. Lai and others. bibliog il Science 145:1187-8 S 11 '64
GUU means valine; first break in genetic code. Sci Am 211:82+ S '64
Genetic code supported. Sci N L 86:83 Ag 8 '64
Life activity observed. Sci N L 87:37 Ja 16 '65
Molecular approach in the systematics of higher organisms. B. H. Hoyer and others. bibliog il Science 144:959-67 My 22 '64; Discussion. Time 83:80 My 29 '64; Sci N L 85:365 Je 6 '64
Operon: on its third anniversary. G. S. Stent. bibliog Science 144:816-20 My 15 '64
GENETICS
Again, Lysenko. Sci Digest 57:45-6 Ja '65
Antibody to hereditary human gamma-globulin (Gm) factor resulting from maternal-fetal incompatibility. H. H. Fudenberg and B. R. Fudenberg. bibliog il Science 145:170-1 Jl 10 '64
Behavior genetics and individuality understood; excerpts from discussions at symposiums. J. Hirsch. bibliog il Science 142: 1436-42 D 13 '63
Coding ambiguity in cell-free extracts of chlamydomonas. R. Sager and others. bibliog il Science 140:304-6 Ap 19 '63
Essays of a humanist, by J. Huxley. Review
Sci Am 211:135-8 O '64. A. E. Mirsky; Reply with rejoinder. J. Huxley. 212: 6-9 Ja '65
Evolutionary and population genetics. T. Dobzhansky. bibliog Science 142:1131-5 N 29 '63
Exploring the secrets of life. il Newsweek 61:63-6 My 13 '63
Future of man. H. Downs. Sci Digest 56:43-5 O '64
Genes outside the chromosomes. R. Sager. il Sci Am 212:70-9 bibliog(p 134) Ja '65
Genetic code. M. W. Nirenberg. il Sci Am 208:80-6+ bibliog(p 190) Mr '63
Genetic code: emergence of a symmetrical pattern. R. V. Eck. bibliog il Science 140: 477-81 My 3 '63
Genetic code of a virus. H. Fraenkel-Conrat. il Sci Am 211:46-54 bibliog(p 142) O '64
Genetic control of differential heat tolerance in two strains of the nematode caenorhabditis elegans. H. V. Fatt and E. C. Dougherty. bibliog il Science 141:266-7 Jl 19 '63
Genetic control of hemerythrin specificity in a marine worm. C. Manwell. bibliog il Science 139:755-8 F 22 '63
Genetic control of hemoglobin synthesis. W. E. Nance. bibliog il Science 141:123-30 Jl 12 '63
Genetic differences in antibody production to determinant groups on insulin. E. R. Arquilla and J. Finn. bibliog il Science 142: 400-1 O 18 '63
Genetic effects. L. Pauling. Bul Atomic Sci 19:30-2 S '63
Genetic regulatory mechanisms at the population level in man. P. A. Parsons. bibliog Science 146:924-5 N 13 '64
Genetic relationship between maximum hematocrit values and hemoglobin type in sheep. J. V. Evans and J. H. Whitlock. bibliog il Science 145:1318 S 18 '64
Genetic studies on the mixed leukocyte reaction. B. Bain and L. Lowenstein. bibliog il Science 145:1315-16 S 18 '64
Genetics and intelligence: a review. L. Erlenmeyer-Kimling and L. F. Jarvik. bibliog il Science 142:1477-9 D 13 '63; Reply with rejoinder. E. E. Daniel. 144:80 Ap 3 '64
Genetics and the human race. W. C. Boyd. bibliog il Science 140:1057-64 Je 7 '63
Genetics at Cologne. V. K. McElheny. il Science 146:904-7 N 13 '64
Hemoglobin solubility and α-chain structure in crosses between two inbred mouse strains. J. J. Hutton and others. bibliog il Science 143:252-3 Ja 17 '64
Histamine: differences in amount available for release in lungs of guinea pigs susceptible and resistant to acute anaphylaxis. S. H. Stone and others. bibliog il Science 146:1061-2 N 20 '64
Histone biology and chemistry; report on first World conference on histone biology and chemistry. J. Bonner and P. O. P. Tso. Science 141:651+ Ag 16 '63
How we're cracking the code of life; radio interview, ed. by C. Collingwood. S. Ochoa. il Sci Digest 56:79-83 S '64
Improvement of man; excerpts from address. R. E. Cooke. il Time 83:81 My 22 '64
Intelligence and genetic trends; letter. H. B. Newcombe. bibliog Science 141:1104-6+ S 13 '63; Reply with rejoinder. W. Wolfensberger. 142:1620-1 D 27 '63
Ionizing radiation: effect on genetic transcription. E. C. Pollard. bibliog il Science 146:927-9 N 13 '64
Lactate dehydrogenase in pigeon testes; genetic control by three loci. W. H. Zinkham and others. bibliog il Science 144:1353-4 Je 12 '64
Lactic dehydrogenase: genetic control in man. W. E. Nance and others. bibliog il Science 142:1075-7 N 22 '63
New biology and the nature of man; adaptation of address, 1963. G. W. Beadle. Bul Atomic Sci 20:13-17 Mr '64
Nongenetic genetic code? Sci Am 209:49-51 Ag '63
On the genetic code; address, December 11, 1962. F. H. C. Crick. bibliog Science 139: 461-4 F 8 '63
Perspectives for the life sciences. H. J. Muller. Bul Atomic Sci 20:3-7 Ja '64; Reply with rejoinder. D. H. Elwyn. 20:36-7 O '64
Rationale for a universal genetic code. R. T. Hinegardner and J. Engelberg. il Science 142:1083-5 N 22 '63; Reply with rejoinder. C. R. Woese. bibliog 144:1030-1 My 22 '64
Streptomycin and the genetic code. Sci Am 211:44-6 Jl '64
Transfer of genetic information; concerning a symposium at AAAS meeting. J. Abelson. Science 139:774-6 F 22 '63
Triplets unlocking code. W. Wingo. Sci N L 86:103 Ag 15 '64
Yeast genetics conference; report on conference on yeast genetics and related biochemical problems. R. C. Von Borstel. Science 142:1594 D 20 '63
See also
Chromosomes
Crossing over (gentics)
Dwarfism
Genes
Heredity
International conference of genetics
Research
See Genetic research
GENEVA, Switzerland
City of lost causes. il Time 81:24-5 Mr 1 '63
Description
New good move for travellers. Vogue 143: 72 Ap 1 '64
Music
Alpine moods. D. A. Mackinnon. il Opera N 29:30 D 26 '64
Geneva contretemps. D. A. Mac Kinnon. il Opera N 28:32-3 Ap 4 '64
[Musical events] Mus Am 83:15 Je '63
Notes from abroad. C. Nobs. Hi Fi 13:26 S '63
GENEVA conference on the discontinuance of nuclear tests. See Conference on the discontinuance of nuclear weapons tests, Geneva, 1958-1961
GENEVA conference on the peaceful uses of atomic energy. See International conference on the peaceful uses of atomic energy, 3d, Geneva, 1964
GENEVA disarmament conference. See Conference of the Eighteen-nation committee on disarmament, Geneva, 1962-

GENGHIS Khan. See Jenghis Khan
GENGOZIAN, Nazareth
Transplantation of rat bone marrow in irradiated mice: effect of exposure rate. bibliog Science 146:663-4 O 30 '64
GENIUS
Devourers of genius. H. Bowser. Sat R 47:34 F 22 '64
See also
Creation (literary, artistic, etc)
Great men
GENNARO, Peter
Conversation with Peter Gennaro; ed. by L. Joel. por Dance Mag 38:18-19 Ag '64
GENOA
Description
Simon's city; photographs by A. Rosenberg. Opera N 29:14-16 Ja 30 '65
Stores
New building abroad; remodeled boutique. il Arch Forum 118:102-3 Je '63
GENOCIDE
Destruction of the European Jews, by R. Hilberg. Review
Christian Cent 80:680 My 22 '63. D. Peerman
GENOTYPE and phenotype
Prezygotic selection in ABO blood groups. E. Matsunaga and Y. Hiraizumi; discussion. Science 137:861-2; bibliog 139:406-7 S 14 '62. F 1 '63
GENOVAR, Christine
St Augustine's oldest store museum. Hobbies 68:51+ D '63
GENOVESE, Catherine
Murder they heard. S. Milgram and P. Hollander. il Nation 198:602-4 Je 15 '64
GENOVESE, Eugene D.
One-tenth in urban bondage. Nation 200:38-9 Ja 11 '65
GENOVESE, Vito
Boss of all bosses. por Time 82:50+ N 1 '63
GENSERT, Richard M.
Apartment framing to resist wind. Arch Rec 133:160-4 Ja '63
High-rise apartment structures of steel. Arch Rec 136:206-9 N '64
Versatile structures for apartment framing. Arch Rec 135:178-9 Je; 136:185-8 Jl '64 (to be cont)
GENTAMICIN. See Antibiotics
GENTELE, Göran
Northern exposure; interview, ed. by A. M. Lingg. por Opera N 29:13 Ja 30 '65
GENTIANS
Gentians for your garden. D. Klaber. il Horticulture 41:606-7; 42:16-17 D '63-Ja '64
GENTILE, G. Marvin
U.S. discovers microphones in walls of embassy at Moscow; statement, May 19, 1964. Dept State Bul 50:933 Je 15 '64
GENTILE Jewesses; story. See Spark, M.
GENTLE executioner; story. See Piazza, L. G.
GENTLEMEN, be seated! opera. See Moross, J.
GEOCHEMISTRY
Biogeochemistry; report of symposium under auspices of National research council and Scientific committee on oceanic research. R. G. Bader and F. F. Koczy. Science 142: 74+ O 4 '63
Chemical examination of a core from Lake Zeribar, Iran. G. E. Hutchinson and U. M. Cowgill. il Science 140:67-9 Ap 5 '63
See also
Mineralogy
GEOCHRONOLOGY. See Geological time
GEODESY
Geodesy by satellite. R. R. Newton. bibliog il Science 144:803-8 My 15 '64
Geologic evolution of North America. A. E. J. Engel. bibliog il Science 140:143-52 Ap 12 '63
Get geodetic accuracy using shotgun blast. Sci N L 84:8 Jl 6 '63
See also
Artificial satellites—Mapping applications
Geographical positions
GEODETIC satellites. See Artificial satellites—Mapping applications
GEODUCKS. See Clams
GEOGRAPHICAL distribution of animals and plants
Exponential values for the species-area relation. P. D. Kilburn. bibliog il Science 141:1276 S 27 '63
GEOGRAPHICAL models. See Relief maps
GEOGRAPHICAL names. See Names, Geographical
GEOGRAPHICAL positions
Bermuda gone north, satellites discover. Sci N L 86:249 O 17 '64
GEOGRAPHICAL societies
See also
National geographic society
GEOGRAPHY
Study and teaching
Modern geography curriculums. C. F. Kohn and others. il NEA J 54:58-60 Ja '65
See also
National council for geographic education
GEOGRAPHY, Political. See Geopolitics
GEOLOGICAL chemistry. See Geochemistry
GEOLOGICAL excursions. See Geology—Study and teaching
GEOLOGICAL laboratories. See Research laboratories
GEOLOGICAL specimens
Rock-headed and glassy-eyed; rock-hounds at Prineville, Ore. and bottle collectors in Florida or out West. H. Sutton. il Sat R 47:26-7 D 19 '64
GEOLOGICAL survey (United States) See United States—Geological survey
GEOLOGICAL time
Coral clock. Sci Am 208:78+ My '63
Fossil microorganisms: possible presence in precambrian shield of western Australia. C. G. A. Marshall and others. bibliog il Science 144:290-2 Ap 17 '64
Geochronology. G. R. Tilton and S. R. Hart. bibliog il Science 140:357-66 Ap 26 '63
Geochronology of marine and fluvial sediments; report on conference. E. Rona. Science 144:1595-7 Je 26 '64
Geologic evolution of North America. A. E. J. Engel. bibliog il Science 140:143-52 Ap 12 '63
Geological eras; reading the story of the earth's past; reprint. il Sci Digest 55:62-4 F '64
Pleistocene epoch in deep-sea sediments. D. B. Ericson and others. bibliog il Science 146:723-32 N 6 '64
Rubidium-strontium isochron study of the Grenville front near Lake Timagami, Ontario. J. A. Grant. bibliog il Science 146: 1049-53 N 20 '64
See also
Earth—Age
Radioactive dating
Radiocarbon dating
GEOLOGY
Earth science today; excerpts from address. P. E. Cloud, jr. Science 144:1428-31 Je 19 '64
Nuclear explosions: some geologic effects of the Gnome shot. L. M. Gard. il Science 139: 911-14 Mr 8 '63
See also
Faults (geology)
Sedimentation and deposition
Submarine geology
Volcanoes
History
Crises in the history of life; mass extinctions of animals by natural catastrophe. N. D. Newell. il Sci Am 208:76-92 bibliog(p 185) F '63
God, man, and geology. Newsweek 62:48 D 23 '63
Study and teaching
Geological jaunt; Fort Tryon park. New Yorker 40:35 My 9 '64
Aden, Gulf of
Geothermal heat flow in the Gulfs of California and Aden. R. P. von Herzen. bibliog il Science 140:1207-8 Je 14 '63
Alaska
Pleistocene marine microfauna in the Bootlegger Cove Clay, Anchorage, Alaska. R. A. M. Schmidt. bibliog il Science 141: 350-1 Jl 26 '63
Potassium-argon and lead-alpha ages of plutonic rocks, Bokan Mountain area, Alaska. M. A. Lanphere and others. bibliog il Science 145:705-7 Ag 14 '64
Aleutian Islands
Anangula: a geologic interpretation of the oldest archeologic site in the Aleutians. R. F. Black and W. S. Laughlin. bibliog il Science 143:1321-2 Mr 20 '64
Antarctic Regions
Cretaceous fossils collected at Johnson Nunatak, Antarctica. J. C. Behrendt and T. S. Laudon. bibliog il Science 143:353-4 Ja 24 '64
Leaiid conchostracan zone in Antarctica and its Gondwana equivalents. G. A. Doumani and P. Tasch. bibliog il Science 142:591-2 N 1 '63

GEOLOGY—Antarctic Regions—*Continued*

Polar geology; report on symposium at the annual meeting of AAAS. A. Mirsky. Science 143:1196-7 Mr 13 '64

Arctic Regions

Genesis of the Arctic Ocean Basin. E. R. King and others. bibliog il Science 144: 1551-7 Je 26 '64

Polar geology; report on symposium at the annual meeting of AAAS. A. Mirsky. Science 143:1196-7 Mr 13 '64

Sediment cores from the Arctic and subarctic seas. D. B. Ericson and others. bibliog il Science 144:1183-92 Je 5 '64

Arizona

Dome-shaped volcanic gas vents in Arizona. R. A. Laidley and R. L. DuBois. il Science 145:153-4 Jl 10 '64

Australia

Age and accumulation rate of dolomite-bearing carbonate sediments in South Australia. H. C. W. Skinner and others. bibliog Science 139:335-6 Ja 25 '63

Fossil microorganisms: possible presence in precambrian shield of western Australia. C. G. A. Marshall and others. bibliog il Science 144:290-2 Ap 17 '64

Bonaire

Dolomitization: observations on the island of Bonaire, Netherlands Antilles. K. S. Deffeyes and others. bibliog il Science 143: 678-9 F 14 '64

California

Basaltic cone suggests constructional origin of some guyots; Mono Lake, Calif. M. N. Christensen and C. M. Gilbert. bibliog il Science 143:240-2 Ja 17 '64

Geomagnetic polarity epochs: Sierra Nevada II. A. Cox and others. bibliog il Science 142:382-5 O 18 '63

California, Gulf of

Geothermal heat flow in the Gulfs of California and Aden. R. P. von Herzen. bibliog il Science 140:1207-8 Je 14 '63

Canada

Coesite and shocked quartz from Holleford Crater, Ontario, Canada. T. E. Bunch and A. J. Cohen. bibliog il Science 142:379-81 O 18 '63

Connecticut

Submergence of the Connecticut coast. A. L. Bloom and M. Stuiver. bibliog il Science 139:332-4 Ja 25 '63

Vegetation, climate, and coastal submergence in Connecticut. P. B. Sears. bibliog il Science 140:59-60 Ap 5 '63

Egypt

Shells rewrite geologic history of ancient Nile Valley. Sci Digest 53:57-8 F '63

Hawaii

Volcanic squeeze measured in Hawaii. Sci N L 85:200 Mr 28 '64

Illinois

Illinoian and Wisconsin (Farmdale) drifts recently exposed at Rockford, Illinois. M. M. Leighton and J. A. Brophy. bibliog il Science 139:218-21 Ja 18 '63

Iran

Chemical examination of a core from Lake Zeribar, Iran. G. E. Hutchinson and U. M. Cowgill. il Science 140:67-9 Ap 5 '63

Preliminary pollen studies at Lake Zeribar, Zagros mountains, southwestern Iran. W. van Zeist and H. E. Wright, jr. bibliog il Science 140:65-7 Ap 5 '63

Italy

Erosion and deposition of Italian stream valleys during historic time. S. Judson. bibliog il Science 140:898-9 My 24 '63

Kentucky

Kope formation (Upper Ordovician): Ohio and Kentucky. M. P. Weiss and W. C. Sweet. bibliog il Science 145:1296+ S 18 '64

Michigan

Biological remnants in a Precambrian sediment; White Pine Mine, Mich. W. G. Meinschein and others. bibliog Science 145:262-3 Jl 17 '64

Clues to life's origin: discovery of biological chemicals in Precambrian shale at White Pine Mine, Mich. A. Ewing. Sci N L 86:67 Ag 1 '64

Hydrocarbons of biological origin from a one-billion-year-old sediment; White Pine Mine, Mich. G. Eglinton and others. bibliog Science 145:263-4 Jl 17 '64

Middle western states

Status of the pleistocene Wisconsin stage in central North America. R. F. Flint. bibliog il Science 139:402-4 F 1 '63

Minnesota

Graphitization of organic material in a progressively metamorphosed Precambrian iron formation. B. M. French. bibliog il Science 146:917-18 N 13 '64

New Jersey

Submergence of the New Jersey coast. M. Stuiver and J. J. Daddario. bibliog il Science 142:951 N 15 '63

North America

Geochronology. G. R. Tilton and S. R. Hart. bibliog il Science 140:357-66 Ap 26 '63

Geologic evolution of North America. A. E. J. Engel. bibliog il Science 140:143-52 Ap 12 '63

Ohio

Kope formation (Upper Ordovician): Ohio and Kentucky. M. P. Weiss and W. C. Sweet. bibliog il Science 145:1296+ S 18 '64

Oklahoma

Lead isotope variation with growth zoning in a galena crystal. R. S. Cannon, jr and others. bibliog il Science 142:574-6 N 1 '63

Ontario

Rubidium-strontium isochron study of the Grenville front near Lake Timagami, Ontario. J. A. Grant. bibliog il Science 146: 1049-53 N 20 '64

Oregon

Des Chutes River country. H. D. Brown. il Hobbies 69:118 S '64

Philippines

Miocene-pliocene boundary in the Philippines as related to late tertiary stratigraphy of deep-sea sediments. O. L. Bandy. bibliog il Science 142:1290-2 D 6 '63

Sicily

Erosion and deposition of Italian stream valleys during historic time. S. Judson. bibliog il Science 140:898-9 My 24 '63

Southwestern states

Environment and man in arid America. H. E. Malde. bibliog il Science 145:123-9 Jl 10 '64

Tanganyika

Stratigraphy of beds I through IV, Olduvai Gorge, Tanganyika. R. L. Hay. bibliog il Science 139:829-33 Mr 1 '63

Tennessee

Eocene epiphyllous fungi. D. L. Dilcher. bibliog il Science 142:667-9 N 8 '63

Texas

Gravity and magnetic anomalies of the Sierra Madera, Texas, dome. J. R. Van Lopik and R. A. Geyer. bibliog il Science 142:45-7 O 4 '63

United States

Study earth's history and magnetic personality. Sci N L 87:56 Ja 23 '65

Undersea history of America. M. C. McKenna. il Sat R 47:54-7 Je 6 '64

Utah

Polygonal fracture and fold systems in the salt crust, Great Salt Lake Desert, Utah. F. W. Christiansen. il Science 139:607-9 F 15 '63

Virginia

Pleistocene sea levels, southeastern Virginia. R. Q. Oaks, jr. and N. K. Coch. bibliog il Science 140:979-83 My 31 '63

GEOLOGY, Stratigraphic

Geological eras; reading the story of the earth's past; reprint. il Sci Digest 55:62-4 F '64

Miocene-pliocene boundary in the Philippines as related to late tertiary stratigraphy of deep-sea sediments. O. L. Bandy. bibliog il Science 142:1290-2 D 6 '63

GEOLOGY, Stratigraphic—*Continued*
Potassium-argon and lead-alpha ages of plutonic rocks, Bokan Mountain area, Alaska. M. A. Lanphere and others. bibliog il Science 145:705-7 Ag 14 '64
Submergence of the New Jersey coast. M. Stuiver and J. J. Daddario. bibliog il Science 142:951 N 15 '63
See also
Paleontology

Cretaceous

Cretaceous fossils collected at Johnson Nunatak, Antarctica. J. C. Behrendt and T. S. Laudon. bibliog il Science 143:353-4 Ja 24 '64

Eocene

Eocene epiphyllous fungi. D. L. Dilcher. bibliog il Science 142:667-9 N 8 '63

Miocene

Chinoptilolite: a new occurrence in North Carolina phosphorite. T. P. Rooney and P. F. Kerr. il Science 144:1453 Je 19 '64
River drowned under bay. E. Hall. Sci N L 84:86 Ag 10 '63

Ordovician

Kope formation (Upper Ordovician): Ohio and Kentucky. M. P. Weiss and W. C. Sweet. bibliog il Science 145:1296+ S 18 '64

Permian

Leaiid conchostracan zone in Antarctica and its Gondwana equivalents. G. A. Doumani and P. Tasch. bibliog il Science 142:591-2 N 1 '63

Pleistocene

Geometry of Bermuda calcareous dune cross-bedding. F. T. Mackenzie. il Science 144:1449-50 Je 19 '64
Older man; longer pleistocene. Sci Am 208:69-70 F '63
Pleistocene epoch in deep-sea sediments. D. B. Ericson and others. bibliog il Science 146:723-32 N 6 '64
Pleistocene sea levels, southeastern Virginia. R. Q. Oaks, jr. and N. K. Coch. bibliog il Science 140:979-83 My 31 '63
Pliocene-pleistocene boundary in deep-sea sediments. D. B. Ericson and others. bibliog il Science 137:727-37 F 22 '63
Start of the pleistocene. Sci Am 208:76+ Mr '63

Pliocene

Pliocene-pleistocene boundary in deep-sea sediments. D. B. Ericson and others. bibliog il Science 139:727-37 F 22 '63
Pliocene-pleistocene boundary in deep-sea sediments. W. R. Riedel and others. bibliog il Science 140:1238-40 Je 14 '63

Precambrian

Ancient granite gneiss in the Black Hills, South Dakota. R. E. Zartman and others. bibliog il Science 145:479-81 Jl 31 '64
Graphitization of organic material in a progressively metamorphosed Precambrian iron formation. B. M. French. bibliog il Science 146:917-18 N 13 '64

GEOLOGY, Structural
Continental drift and the origin of mountains. E. Orowan. bibliog il Science 146:1003-10 N 20 '64
Flowage differentiation. S. Bhattacharji and C. H. Smith. bibliog il Science 145:150-3 Jl 10 '64
Geology of the crust and mantle, western United States. G. A. Thompson and M. Talwani. bibliog il Science 146:1539-49 D 18 '64
Pattern of uplifted islands in the main ocean basins. J. T. Wilson. bibliog il Science 139:592-4 F 15 '63

GEOMAGNETISM. See Magnetism, Terrestrial

GEOMETRY
Geometry. M. Kline. il Sci Am 211:60-9 bibliog(p269) S '64
See also
Topology

Problems, exercises, etc.

Fold paper to learn geometry. R. Yoshioka. il Sci N L 83:138-9 Mr 2 '63

Problems, Famous

See also
Pythagorean proposition

GEOMETRY, Projective
Geometry. M. Kline. il Sci Am 211:60-9 bibliog(p269) S '64

GEOPHONE
He makes accidents obsolete. M. Stearns. il Pop Mech 120:101-4+ Ag '63

GEOPHYSICAL apparatus
See also
Gravimeters

GEOPHYSICAL prospecting. See Prospecting—Geophysical methods

GEOPHYSICAL research
1963-1964 science review. Sci N L 84:391-2; 86:393-4 D 21 '63, D 19 '64

GEOPHYSICS
Geological aspects of high-pressure research. F. R. Boyd. bibliog il Science 145:13-20 Jl 3 '64
Stress differences and the reference ellipsoid. J. A. O'Keefe and W. M. Kaula. bibliog il Science 142:382 O 18 '63
See also
Earth—Internal structure
Prospecting—Geophysical methods

Study and teaching

University organization for geophysics education; excerpts from address, April 1964. W. A. Baum. Science 146:619-21 O 30 '64

GEOPOLITICS
Geopolitics and foreign relations. G. E. Pearcy. il Dept State Bul 50:318-30 Mr 2 '64

GEORGE, B. J. jr
New approach to criminal law. Harper 228:183-8 Ap '64

GEORGE, David Lloyd, 1st earl Lloyd George of Dwyfor. See Lloyd George of Dwyfor, D. L. G.

GEORGE, Homer
One man's battle against poison. H. E. Dark. il Todays Health 42:43+ Mr '64

GEORGE, Jean
April magic in the ocean deeps. Read Digest 82:107-11 Ap '63
Beast with the high I.Q. Read Digest 85:231-2+ O '64
Catfish, super-snooper of the deep. Read Digest 85:21-2+ Jl '64
Here come the robins! Read Digest 84:217-20 Mr '64
Incredible eyes of animals. Audubon Mag 67:20-3 Ja '65
Sociable sea gull. Read Digest 83:108-13 Ag '63
That astounding creator, nature. Read Digest 84:96-9 Ja '64

GEORGE, W. L. jr. See Shifriss, O. jt. auth.

GEORGE, William G.
Phylogenetic riddle. Natur Hist 72:44-7 F '63
Rarely seen songbirds of Peru's high Andes. Natur Hist 73:26-9 O '64

GEORGE, Lake, N.Y.
Lake George patrol. M. Crook. il Yachting 115:96-7+ Ja '64

GEORGE C. Marshall research library. See Virginia military institute, Lexington

GEORGE Outram and company, limited. See Outram, George, and company, limited

GEORGE Peabody college for teachers, Nashville, Tenn.
George Peabody college for teachers. M. O. Donley. il NEA J 53:73-6 Mr '64
Planning for instructional improvement. W. S. Graybeal. NEA J 52:22 O '63

GEORGE Washington bridge. See Hudson River bridges

GEORGE Washington high school. See New York (city)—Education

GEORGES-PICOT, Jacques
Suez sails on without its canal; Compagnie financiere de Suez. il por Bsns W p60-2+ F 22 '64

GEORGETOWN university, Washington, D.C.
Sit-in at Georgetown. F. E. Kearns. Commonweal 78:94+ Ap 19 '63; Discussion. 78:250-2 My 24 '63

GEORGHIOU, G. P. and Metcalf, R. L.
Dieldrin susceptibility: partial restoration in anopheles selected with a carbamate. bibliog Science 140:301-2 Ap 19 '63

GEORGI, Charlotte
(comp) Business books of 1963. por Library J 89:1026-32 Mr 1 '64

GEORGIA
Progress goes marching through Georgia. B. Hibbs. il Sat Eve Post 236:69-73 F 16 '63
See also
Booksellers and bookselling—Georgia
Courts—Georgia
Education—Georgia
Fishing—Georgia
Law—Georgia
Okefenokee national wildlife refuge

History

Georgia's famous trees. M. Hunn. il Am For 70:42-5 N '64

GEORGIA—*Continued*

Legislature

Court says all votes must weigh the same; reapportionment of congressional districts. Bsns W p27 F 22 '64
Georgia redraws its political map; congressional districts. Bsns W p34 F 29 '64
Georgia's Negro senator. L. Bennett, jr. il Ebony 18:25-8+ Mr '63
Redrawing the lines; Georgia's congressional districts. il Time 83:19-20 F 28 '64

Politics and government

It's nearly all white in the South. P. Watters. il New Repub 150:11-12 Je 13 '64

Race problems

Odds on freedom; gambler's choice in Georgia. P. De Lissovoy. il Nation 198:618-21 Je 22 '64
Progress goes marching through Georgia. B. Hibbs. il Sat Eve Post 236:69-73 F 16 '63
Senselessness in Georgia; killing of Lemuel Penn. Time 84:18 Ag 14 '64
White tears in Georgia; Atlanta restaurateur refuses to desegregate. il Time 84:18-19 Ag 21 '64

Religious institutions and affairs

News of the Christian world (cont) Christian Cent 80:252 F 20 '63

GEORGIA, Russia

Social life and customs

Hosts with the most toasts. R. Brigham. il Life 55:123-6 S 13 '63

GEORGIA. University, Athens
Education in Georgia, by C. Trillin. Review Commonweal 80:61-4 Ap 3 '64. L. F. X. Mayhew
Lonely years of Hamilton Holmes. A. Wexler. il Ebony 19:101-2+ N '63
Reporter at large; admission of Negro students. C. Trillin. New Yorker 39:30-4+ Jl 13; 32-6+ Jl 20; 34-6+ Jl 27 '63

GEORGIA institute of technology, Atlanta
Georgia tech's football Yellow Jackets: Southern stingers. T. Cohane. il Look 27: 151-4 O 22 '63

GEORGIEV, Ivan Assen Hristov
Name that tune. Time 83:37 Ja 3 '64
Price to pay. por Newsweek 63:32 Ja 6 '64
Tomorrow is forever. Newsweek 63:31 Ja 13 '64

GEOS (artificial satellite) See Artificial satellites—Mapping applications

GEOTHERMAL energy. See Steam, Natural

GEOTHERMAL measurements. See Earth temperature

GEOTHERMAL wells. See Water, Underground

GEOTROPISM (botany)
Geotropism: its orienting force. A. H. Westing. bibliog il Science 144:1342-4 Je 12 '64

GERACI, Phil
Amps for camps. Pop Sci 184:112-15 My '64
Cross country camping. Travel 119:31-3+ My '63
Fascinating U.S. forts. Travel 122:24-30 Jl '64
How to put a wall tent on wheels. Pop Sci 185:126-8 Jl '64
Invisible CAT pilots dread. Pop Mech 121: 104-7+ Ap '64
New garden tractors: more heft more hustle. Pop Sci 184:129-33 Ap '64
Silencing your stereo system. Pop Sci 184:100-3 Je '64
World's safest airport. Pop Sci 186:110-13 Ja '65

GERACI, Philip C.
Start seeds indoors. Pop Gard 14:74-8 F '63

GERANIUMS
All are fragrant but some you must pinch. il Sunset 132:260+ Ap '64
Fill your house with geraniums. M. Orans. il Pop Gard 15:21+ N '64
Geraniums from seed. C. O. Wisham. il Flower Grower 50:42 D '63
Geraniums from seed. E. M. Eaton. il Horticulture 41:362 Jl '63
Grandma's geraniums are fashionable again. P. Headley. il Horticulture 41:312 Je '63
If you fancy pelargoniums. il Sunset 130:277 Ap '63
Make a tree geranium. G. Taloumis. il Flower Grower 50:28 N '63
Scented geraniums grow indoors and out. R. James. il Flower Grower 51:40-2 F '64
Trailing ivy-leaved geraniums. M. Moriarty. il Horticulture 41:126-7 Mr '63
Tree geraniums. R. W. Woodbury. il Pop Gard 15:16 F '64

GERARD, David E.
Mirror, mirror on the wall. por Library J 90:192-5 Ja 15 '65

GERARD, Larry
135-bushel corn with plow-plant. Suc Farm 61:56-7 My '63
One man grows 30,000 bushels of corn. Suc Farm 62:50-1 Mr '64
They grew 200-bushel corn! can you? Suc Farm 61:72-3+ Mr '63
Which minimum tillage system for you? Suc Farm 61:56-7 Ap '63

GERBER, H. J.
Metalworking tips. Pop Sci 182:143 F '63
Short cuts and tips for machine-shop workers. Pop Sci 186:158-9 Ja '65

GERBER, John
Captain is back on deck. C. Goren. il Sports Illus 21:63 Ag 31 '64

GERBER, Merrill Joan
Cost depends on what you reckon it in; story. Mlle 56:182-3 Ap '63
Daughter of her own; story. Redbook 122:36-7 Ja '64
Everyone gets somewhere; story. Redbook 123:74-5 O '64
Latitude; story. New Yorker 40:24-7 Ag 8 '64
Many are cold; story. Redbook 123:48-9 My '64
Night out; story. Redbook 124:60-1 N '64
Stop here, my friend; story. Redbook 124:64-5 D '64
We know that your hearts are heavy; story. New Yorker 39:42-52 Ap 20 '63

GERBER, Paul
Tumors induced in hamsters by simian virus 40; persistent subviral infection. bibliog Science 140:889-90 My 24 '63
Virogenic hamster tumor cells: induction of virus synthesis. bibliog Science 145:833 Ag 21 '64

GERBER, Rudolph J.
Religious studies on campus. America 111: 292-5 S 19 '64

GERBER, Sophia P.
Making cartoons out of people. Sci Digest 53: 27-34 F '63

GERBER products company
Manna for Gerber. il Newsweek 63:68 Je 1 '64
Today's research for babies' future. M. B. Keiser. il Parents Mag 39:20+ N '64

GERBER scientific instrument company
No finger guides the roving pen; numerically controlled drafting machines. il Bsns W p86 Mr 28 '64

GERBERAS
Rewarding gerberas. C. Wylie. il Horticulture 41:332 Je '63

GERBERDING, William
Teacher sweats it out. il pors Life 58:56-65 Ja 22 '65

GERBERICH, J. Raymond
Your child's intelligence; reprint. Todays Health 41:11 Je '63

GERBILS
Four months without water. Sci Digest 53:50 My '63

GERBNER, George
Education in newspaper advertisements. Sch & Soc 92:363-5 N 28 '64

GERDTS, William H.
American painting collection of Henry Melville Fuller. Antiques 86:66-71 Jl '64
American painting in the collection of James H. Ricau. Antiques 86:578-82 N '64
American sculpture: the collection of James H. Ricau. Antiques 86:291-8 S '64
Nineteenth-century still-life painting in New Jersey. Antiques 86:718-21 D '64
Painting of Thomas Moran: sources and style. Antiques 85:202-5 F '64

GERHARD, Peter
Emperors' dye of the Mixtecs. Natur Hist 73: 26-31 Ja '64

GERHARD, Roberto
Meaning of the rats. por Time 83:80 Ap 10 '64

GERHARDT, Elena
Historical records. A. Favia-Artsay. por Hobbies 67:31 F '63
On records; Elena Gerhardt. por Opera N 28:35 Ja 25 '64
Work of a very great artist. P. L. Miller. Am Rec G 31:107 O '64

GERHARDT, Paul H. See Nixon, J. H. jt. auth.

GERIATRICS. See Aged

GERKEN, Eva
Ambition lost. Opera N 27:28-9 F 2 '63
Elsa of Brabant. Opera N 28:12 F 1 '64
Sequels. Opera N 29:24-5 D 19 '64

GERLACH, Lee
For Peter; poem. Poetry 102:305 Ag '63

GERLACH, Vernon S. and Farnbach, Irene
How to teach library skills without really being there. Library J 89:921-2 F 15 '64

GERLE, Robert
Quote: unquote; interview, ed. by M. Brozen. por Mus Am 83:16 Je '63
GERM cells. See Cells
GERM free animals
Animals without germs. J. Viorst. il Sci N L 84:42-3 Jl 20 '63
Germfree animals and biological research. M. Pollard. bibliog il Science 145:247-51 Jl 17 '64
Germ-free isolators. P. C. Trexler. il Sci Am 211:78-80+ Jl '64
Nitrogen mustard: diminution of toxicity in axenic mice. L. P. White and E. F. Claflin. bibliog il Science 140:1400-1 Je 28 '63
Why germfree animals? K. N. Anderson. il Todays Health 41:30-3 Ag '63
GERM free surgery. See Surgery, Aseptic and antiseptic
GERM warfare. See Biological warfare
GERMAN, James
Cytological evidence for crossing-over in vitro in human lymphoid cells. bibliog Science 144:298-301 Ap 17 '64
GERMAN apprentices. See Apprentices
GERMAN art. See Art, German
GERMAN athletes. See Athletes
GERMAN atrocities. See World war, 1939-1945—Atrocities
GERMAN authors. See Authors, German
GERMAN automobiles. See Automobiles, Foreign
GERMAN castles. See Castles
GERMAN composers. See Composers, German
GERMAN cookery. See Cookery, German
GERMAN Evangelical church. See Evangelical church in Germany
GERMAN fiction
Nerve of Günter Grass. G. Steiner. Commentary 37:77-80 My '64
GERMAN furniture. See Furniture, German
GERMAN historians. See Historians, German
GERMAN internment camps. See Concentration camps—Germany
GERMAN invasion of Poland. See World war, 1939-1945—Poland
GERMAN language
Army of words. M. Walser. Holiday 36:24+ O '64
Sprechen sie what? intrusion of foreign expressions. Newsweek 62:68+ O 21 '63

Study and teaching

Impact of World war I on the American high school; excerpt from Shaping of the American high school. E. A. Krug. bibliog f Sch & Soc 92:161-71 Ap 4 '64
GERMAN literature
Voice from the future. K. Boyle. il Holiday 36:12+ O '64
See also
Authors, German
GERMAN mail order business. See Mail order business
GERMAN measles. See Rubella
GERMAN opera. See Opera, German
GERMAN pottery. See Pottery, German
GERMAN propaganda. See Propaganda, German
GERMAN refugees. See Refugees, German
GERMAN reunification question. See Germany—Union (proposed)
GERMAN scientists. See Scientists, German
GERMAN shepherd police dogs. See Police dogs
GERMAN shorthaired pointers
Ludwig's fountain; University of California, Berkeley; photographs. T. Bronstein. Look 27:50a-50c My 21 '63
Shakedown of a breed. D. M. Duffey. il Outdoor Life 132:98-102 Ag '63
GERMAN students
German students reply to Martha Gellhorn; tr. by B. Ostendorf. G. Schmidt; H. Bauer; L. Zimmer. Atlan 213:74+ My '64
Is there a new Germany? M. Gellhorn. il Atlan 213:69-76 F '64; Discussion. 213:42+ Ap '64
Pfiff's in what you can't see; university students in Germany today. R. Hoffmann. il Mlle 60:118-21+ D '64
GERMAN students in the United States. See Foreign students in the United States
GERMAN visitors in the United States. See Foreign visitors in the United States
GERMAN war criminals. See World war, 1939-1945—War criminals
GERMAN wine. See Wine

GERMAN youth movement. See Youth movement—Germany
GERMANIUM
Crystal structures at high pressures of metallic modifications of silicon and germanium. J. C. Jamieson. bibliog il Science 139:762-4 F 22 '63
New dense form of solid germanium. F. P. Bundy and J. S. Kasper. bibliog il Science 139:340-1 Ja 25 '63
GERMANIUM transistors. See Transistors
GERMANS
Adipose society: West Germany. il Time 82:29 Jl 19 '63
Again the issue of German guilt. C. Fitzgibbon. il N Y Times Mag p 17+ Ag 18 '63; Discussion. p4 S 1 '63
Appointment with hate. E. Wiesel; discussion. Commentary 35:348-50 Ap '63
German democracy; a reporter's notebook. G. Samuels. il N Y Times Mag p 17+ Ja 5 '64
German students reply to Martha Gellhorn; tr. by B. Ostendorf. G. Schmidt; H. Bauer; L. Zimmer. Atlan 213:74+ My '64
German tradition; with photographs by Arnold Newman. Holiday 36:66-73 O '64
Is there a new Germany? M. Gellhorn. il Atlan 213:69-76 F '64; Discussion. 213:42+ Ap '64
Passing of work-obsessed Germany. T. Prittie. il N Y Times Mag p41+ Ap 21 '63
Secret people. V. S. Pritchett. il Holiday 36:46-55+ O '64
See also
Berliners
GERMANS in Pennsylvania. See Pennsylvania Germans
GERMANS in the United States
What America means to me. F. Jaensch. Good H 156:62+ Je '63
GERMANTOWN. See Philadelphia
GERMANY
Germany: symposium; with editorial comment. il Holiday 36:12+, 44 O '64
See also
Airplanes, Military—Germany
Fascism—Germany
Jews in Germany
World war, 1939-1945—Germany

Army

Officers

Men who tried to kill Hitler; excerpts, ed. by J. Naar. R. Manvell and H. Fraenkel. il Look 28:50-2 D 15 '64
When the big one (Hitler) got away; Generals' plot to kill Hitler. S. D. Smith. il N Y Times Mag p86-8+ My 24 '64

Foreign relations

Austria

See also
Austro-German customs union (proposed)

Great Britain

Appeasers, by M. Gilbert and R. Gott. Review
Nat R 15:403-4 N 5 '63. A. Lejeune

United States

Hitler's image of the United States. G. L. Weinberg. bibliog f Am Hist R 69:1006-21 Jl '64

History

Arguments of blood. A. M. Maughan. il Holiday 36:56-7+ O '64
Germany's search for identity. H. A. Schmitt. bibliog f Cur Hist 47:326-31 D '64
Old warrior looks back; ed. by D. Schorr. K. Adenauer. il Sat Eve Post 236:96-9 O 19 '63
Putting a country together again. L. L. Snyder. Sat R 46:34-5 D 28 '63
Remembrance: 25th anniversary of Kristallnacht (Night of crystal) il Time 82:33 N 22 '63

Bibliography

Articles and other books received; Germany, Austria, and Switzerland, comp. by A. H. Price. See issues of American historical review

1871-

From Adenauer to Erhard; changeover in West Germany. il Sr Schol 83:13-15+ N 15 '63

20th century

Enigma of Germany. N. R. Clifford. Commonweal 81:363-6 D 4 '64

1933-1945

Reichstag fire, by F. Tobias. Review
Nation 198:272-4 Mr 16 '64. H. Koningsberger

GERMANY—*Continued*

Intellectual life

See also
German literature

National socialist movement

See Fascism—Germany

Politics and government

German diary. G. Lichtheim. Commentary 38:42-9 S '64

Propaganda

See Propaganda, German

Reichstag fire

See Reichstag fire

Religious institutions and affairs

German ecumenism: politics and the dialogue. H. Cox. Commonweal 77:635-9 Mr 15 '63
Saviors of honor. il Time 84:62-3 Jl 24 '64
See also
Catholic church in Germany

Union (proposed)

Again the issue of the two Germanys. T. Prittie. il N Y Times Mag p 10+ Ag 16 '64
Berlin's new outlook. L. R. Colitt. Nation 197:236-8 O 19 '63
Dynamics of progress in central Europe; address, November 11, 1964. G. C. McGhee. Dept State Bul 51:870-6 D 21 '64
German question. W. Lippmann. Newsweek 62:15 S 2 '63
Germany's search for identity. H. A. Schmitt. bibliog f Cur Hist 47:326-31 D '64
Herr Erhard goes to Washington. New Repub 150:13-15 Je 27 '64
Hurt, bothered & bewildered. Time 85:31 Ja 15 '65
Killing a myth; West German debate over reunification. Newsweek 62:46 S 9 '63
Projected European union and the question of German unity. K. H. Kappstein. Ann Am Acad 348:73-81 Jl '63
Some American thoughts on current issues; address, July 16, 1964. G. C. McGhee. Dept State Bul 51:138-44 Ag 3 '64
Speaking out; Berlin: let's stop courting disaster. C. Pell. Sat Eve Post 237:8-9 F 8 '64
Three western powers reaffirm desire for German reunification; declaration of France, the United Kingdom and the United States. Dept State Bul 51:44-5 Jl 13 '64
Unsolved German settlement. F. W. Neal. bibliog f Ann Am Acad 351:148-56 Ja '64

War guilt

See World war, 1939-1945—Causes

GERMANY (Democratic Republic)
Inside Ulbricht's empire: with report by R. S. Elegant. Newsweek 61:42+ F 18 '63
Journey through the land of eloquent silence: East Germany revisited, by J. Wechsberg. Review
Sat R 47:43 O 10 '64. H. C. Wolfe
Joy, not jubilation. il Time 84:56 O 2 '64
See also
Architecture—Germany (Democratic Republic)
Astronomical observatories—Germany (Democratic Republic)
Berlin
Berlin (East Berlin)
Colleges and universities—Germany (Democratic Republic)
Jews in Germany
Leipzig
Opera—Germany (Democratic Republic)
Prisoners—Germany (Democratic Republic)
Publishers and publishing—Germany (Democratic Republic)
Trade unions—Germany (Democratic Republic)
Weissenfels
Youth—Germany (Democratic Republic)

Army

Why the border guards defect. M. Mara. il Atlan 212:100-2 D '63

Economic conditions

East Germany: quiet revival. K. Ames. il Newsweek 64:46-7 N 23 '64
East Germany revisited: change at a snail's pace. R. A. Haeger. il U S News 58:54-6 Ja 11 '65
New look at life behind the iron curtain. A. Kucherov. il U S News 54:96-7 Ap 22 '63
Reds' pet satellite looks west. il U S News 57:84 Ag 17 '64
Stalemate in Germany; sixth congress of the Socialist unity party. T. Prittie. New Repub 148:10-11 F 2 '63
They have given up hope. il Time 82:38+ D 6 '63

Economic relations

Booty at the back door. M. Madden. Nation 199:84-5 S 7 '64

Industries

What Ulbricht doesn't know. K. Wismach. Atlan 212:114-17 D '63

Politics and government

East Germany revisited: change at a snail's pace. R. A. Haeger. il U S News 58:54-6 Ja 11 '65
Stalinist rule in East Germany. C. G. Anthon. Cur Hist 44:265-72+ My '63
See also
Berlin question, 1945-

Religious institutions and affairs

Dateline: East Germany. Christian Cent 81:1422 N 18 '64
News of the Christian world (cont) Christian Cent 80:411-12, 718+, 989, 1414+, 1450; 81:219-20, 468-9, 943-4, 1573-4 Mr 27, My 29, Ag 7, N 13-20 '63, F 12, Ap 8, Jl 22, D 16 '64
Seeds behind the wall; journey to East Berlin. D. Callahan. Commonweal 78:275+ My 31 '63
See also
Christians in Germany
Evangelical church in Germany

Treaties

Sign of the times; Russia and East Germany sign treaty of friendship, mutual assistance, and cooperation. il Newsweek 63:44+ Je 22 '64
Sop for Walter; friendship pact between East Germany and the Soviet Union. Time 83:26 Je 19 '64
Soviet-East German friendship treaty; text. Cur Hist 47:363-4+ D '64

GERMANY (Federal Republic)
Adenauer era: events and the man; photographs. A. J. Olsen. N Y Times Mag p 16-17 O 13 '63
Again the issue of German guilt. C. Fitzgibbon. il N Y Times Mag p 17+ Ag 18 '63; Discussion. p4 S 1 '63
Germany: the Adenauer era ends. il Newsweek 61:48-9+ My 6 '63
Heart of Europe. il Time 82:30-4 N 1 '63
Role of Germany in the evolution of world politics; address, September 18, 1963. W. W. Rostow. Dept State Bul 49:536-42 O 7 '63
West Germany; symposium. bibliog f il Cur Hist 44:193-239+ Ap '63
What is the new Germany? V. Dabney; M. Fishwick. il Sat R 46:16-20+ Mr 9 '63
See also
Aeronautics, Military—Germany (Federal Republic)
Aerospace industries—Germany (Federal Republic)
Africa and Germany (Federal Republic)
Agricultural administration—Germany (Federal Republic)
Airlines—Germany (Federal Republic)
Airplane industry and trade—Germany (Federal Republic)
Airplanes, Military—Germany (Federal Republic)
Airports—Germany (Federal Republic)
Architecture—Germany (Federal Republic)
Astronomical observatories—Germany (Federal Republic)
Automobile industry and trade—Germany (Federal Republic)
Aviation—Germany (Federal Republic)
Ballet—Germany (Federal Republic)
Berlin
Berlin (West Berlin)
Colleges and universities—Germany (Federal Republic)
Dachau
Duisburg
Düsseldorf
Economic assistance in Germany (Federal Republic)
Education—Germany (Federal Republic)
Employment—Germany (Federal Republic)
Fascism—Germany (Federal Republic)
Finance—Germany (Federal Republic)
Foreign visitors in Germany
Frankfort on the Main
Gelsenkirchen
Government ownership—Germany (Federal Republic)
Gütersloh
Hamburg

GERMANY (Federal Republic)—See also—*Cont.*
Hotels, taverns, etc.—Germany (Federal Republic)
Housing—Germany (Federal Republic)
Insurance, Health—Germany (Federal Republic)
Jews in Germany
Justice, Administration of—Germany (Federal Republic)
Kassel
Labor and laboring classes—Germany (Federal Republic)
Libraries—Germany (Federal Republic)
Mannheim
Medicine—Germany (Federal Republic)
Munich
Music festivals—Germany (Federal Republic)
Music—Germany (Federal Republic)
Newspapers—Germany (Federal Republic)
Opera—Germany (Federal Republic)
Phonograph record industry—Germany (Federal Republic)
Political parties—Germany (Federal Republic)
Public welfare—Germany (Federal Republic)
Publishers and publishing—Germany (Federal Republic)
Railroads—Germany (Federal Republic)
Research—Germany (Federal Republic)
Rhine River
Ruhr Valley
Secret service—Germany (Federal Republic)
Space research—Germany (Federal Republic)
Strikes—Germany (Federal Republic)
Textbooks—Germany (Federal Republic)
Theater—Germany (Federal Republic)
Trade unions—Germany (Federal Republic)
Trials—Germany (Federal Republic)
Ulm
Youth—Germany (Federal Republic)

Armed forces

Multilateral force: Germany's finger on the atom. A. Etzioni. il Nation 199:208-11 O 12 '64
Multilateral muddle. Nation 199:319-20 N 9 '64

Army

What kind of host? Newsweek 63:30 Je 29 '64

Civilization

German diary. G. Lichtheim. Commentary 38:42-9 S '64
Germany's new historians. G. Mann. il Nation 198:572-6 Je 8 '64
Secret people. V. S. Pritchett. il Holiday 36:46-55+ O '64

Commerce

Ambassador from Krupp. il Time 82:82 Jl 5 '63
No pipeline for Moscow. T. Prittie. New Repub 148:9-10 Ap 6 '63
Sheep didn't jump; export of large-bore steel pipe to the Soviet Union. Newsweek 61:32 Ap 1 '63
Staunch old fist in NATO dike. Life 54:4 Mr 29 '63
Window to the East. Newsweek 62:46 Jl 29 '63

Commercial treaties and agreements

Looking eastward; trade pact with Poland. Time 81:43 Mr 15 '63
Window to the East; trade pact with Poland. Newsweek 61:45 Mr 18 '63

Defenses

Discussions held at Washington with German defense minister; joint statement of the Departments of state and defense, February 27, 1963. Dept State Bul 48:444 Mr 25 '63
Rusk warns allies: do more for defense. U S News 55:26 N 11 '63

Description and travel

Germany's high point offers a great Alps view; Garmisch-Partenkirchen. il Sunset 132:27-8+ Je '64
Smiling land. W. Sansom. il Holiday 36:58-63+ O '64
Travel in Germany; with list of hotels and restaurants. R. Postgate. il Holiday 36:131-8 O '64
See also
Rhine River

Economic conditions

Germans seek bigger voice in the West. il Bsns W p 108+ O 3 '64
Germany: the Adenauer era ends. il Newsweek 61:48-9+ My 6 '63; Same abr. with title Up from the rubble. Read Digest 83:121-2 N '63
Germany's economic dilemma, by P. M. Boarman. Review
New Repub 151:24-6 D 26 '64. A. Campbell
Plagued by plenty. Time 83:93 Ap 3 '64
West Germany's economic miracle. W. Struve. Cur Hist 44:231-6+ Ap '63

Economic policy

Chickens and votes. A. Brynes. New Repub 149:14-15 O 26 '63
German miracle under debate. Bsns W p 108+ My 11 '63
Germany and the Common market. W. W. Schmokel. bibliog f Cur Hist 45:283-8 N '63
Germany's economic future; address, April 29, 1963. F. Berg. Vital Speeches 29:506-8 Je 1 '63
Politics of German wheat. D. Schoenbaum. Nation 197:447-9 D 28 '63
West German Council of economic experts. Mo Labor R 87:431 Ap '64
West Germany's economic miracle. W. Struve. Cur Hist 44:231-6+ Ap '63

Economic relations

Great danger for the world, unless LBJ acts forcefully; German's view. U S News 57:104 D 14 '64

Foreign relations

Adenaullism; Adenauer urges support for the European Third force that De Gaulle envisions. Time 84:32 Jl 17 '64
At last, clearly in charge. il Time 84:34-5 Jl 24 '64
Big idea: look after Germany first. il Newsweek 61:51 Je 10 '63
Changing cornerstones. Newsweek 63:44 F 24 '64
Exclusive Senior scholastic interview. W. Brandt. Sr Schol 83:16+ N 15 '63
Farewell to Der Alte. A. Horne. Nat R 15:350-1 O 22 '63
Foam rubber lion? A. Schalk. Commonweal 79:368-70 D 20 '63
For an Atlantic future. T. Sommer. For Affairs 43:112-25 O '64
From Adenauer to Erhard; changeover in West Germany. il Sr Schol 83:12-15+ N 15 '63
Future of Germany; address, January 13, 1964. S. von Braun. Vital Speeches 30:365-9 Ap 1 '64
Germans seek bigger voice in the West. il Bsns W p 108+ O 3 '64
Germany gives rise to vast uncertainties. H. J. Morgenthau. il N Y Times Mag p21+ S 8 '63
Germany in world politics. H. Kohn. bibliog f Cur Hist 44:202-7+ Ap '63
Germany without Adenauer: what it will be like. il U S News 55:80-1 O 21 '63
New diplomacy. il Newsweek 64:38 Ag 24 '64
Place of Germany in the alliance of free nations; address, June 11, 1964. L. Erhard. Vital Speeches 30:582-5 Jl 15 '64
Stalemate in Germany; West German apathy. T. Prittie. New Repub 148:11 F 2 '63
U.S. and Germany reaffirm agreement on East-West problems; joint communique, June 12, 1964. L. B. Johnson and L. Erhard. Dept State Bul 50:992-4 Je 29 '64
Weighing the advantages; Soviet-American détente. H. Brandon. Sat R 46:16+ N 2 '63

Arab states

Worst-kept secret; German-Israeli arms deal. Newsweek 65:28 F 1 '65

Europe, Eastern

West Germany and East Europe. M. K. Dziewanowski. il Cur Hist 44:208-13+ Ap '63

Europe, Western

Germany and the Common market. W. W. Schmokel. bibliog f Cur Hist 45:283-8 N '63
West German policy in West Europe. A. S. Nanes. Cur Hist 44:214-18+ Ap '63

France

Adenauer: still a major figure in world affairs. U S News 57:19 N 23 '64
Aftermath of a Common market veto. il Sr Schol 82:5 F 20 '63
Atlantic report. Atlan 214:12+ Ag '64
Franco-German accord. il Sr Schol 82:21 F 6 '63
Gaullist Adenauer challenges Erhard; should West Germany move closer to France or to the United States? A. J. Olsen. il N Y Times Mag p 11+ Jl 26 '64
Mongoose and cobra. Newsweek 61:33-4 F 25 '63
Old frontier; Franco-German cooperation treaty. il Newsweek 62:32-3 Jl 15 '63

GERMANY (Federal Republic)—Foreign relations—France—*Continued*
On nazism, de Gaulle, Russia, the fuuture; interview, ed. by O. Schisgall. K. Adenauer. Look 27:27-9 D 17 '63
Paris-Bonn axis. T. Prittie. New Repub 148: 8-9 F 9 '63
Putting the squeeze on Germany. il Newsweek 64:45 N 23 '64
Reconciliation at Rambouillet. Time 85:24 Ja 29 '65
Squeeze play. il Newsweek 65:28+ F 1 '65
Strictly protocol; Chancellor L. Erhard's visit to de Gaulle. Newsweek 62:58+ D 2 '63
Unvisit. Time 82:26 Jl 12 '63

Israel

Ben-Gurion's guest; former West German Defense Minister Franz-Josef Strauss. Newsweek 61:52 Je 10 '63
Nasser's German scientists. T. Prittie. New Repub 148:12-13 Ap 20 '63
Visitor's welcome. il Time 81:30 Je 7 '63
Worst-kept secret; German-Israeli arms deal. Newsweek 65:28 F 1 '65

Russia

On nazism, de Gaulle, Russia, the future; interview, ed. by O. Schisgall. K. Adenauer. Look 27:27-9 D 17 '63

United States

Discussions held at Washington with German defense minister; joint statement of the Departments of state and defense, February 27, 1963. Dept State Bul 48:444 Mr 25 '63
Gaullist Adenauer challenges Erhard; should West Germany move closer to France or to the United States? A. J. Olsen. il N Y Times Mag p 11+ Jl 26 '64
Herr Erhard goes to Washington. New Repub 150:13-15 Je 27 '64
President and Chancellor Erhard reaffirm commitment to U.S.-German cooperation within free-world community; joint communique, December 29, 1963; with exchanges of remarks, December 28 and December 29, 1963. L. Erhard; L. B. Johnson. Dept State Bul 50:74-80 Ja 20 '64
President Kennedy visits Europe; texts of joint communiques released at Bonn, Birch Grove house, Sussex, and Rome, with major addresses and remarks, June 23-July 2, 1963. J. F. Kennedy. Dept State Bul 49:114-28 Jl 22 '63
Special relations. Newsweek 62:24 D 30 '63
Will Germany now edge closer to U.S? Kennedy and the Germans. il U S News 54:62-3 Je 24 '63

Industries

Bayer bounces back; Germany's Bayer farbenfabriken. Time 82:102 S 13 '63
Decision from the grave; electronics empire of Robert Bosch. Time 84:85-6 Ag 7 '64
Dream motor steps out; NSU werke. il Bsns W p48+ O 12 '63
Flick's fortunes. il Time 82:78 Jl 26 '63
Perilous swaying; Stinnes' cash-shy empire, West Germany. Time 82:111+ O 18 '63
Ruhr scrubs the grime. il Bsns W p 100-2+ O 3 '64
Surprise bid; Rheinische Stahlwerke makes a bid to purchase Henschel. Time 84:84 Jl 24 '64
Tribute to the German photo industry. P. Stackpole. U S Camera 27:28-9+ Ag '64
See also
Aerospace industries—Germany (Federal Republic)
Airplane industry and trade—Germany (Federal Republic)
Automobile industry and trade—Germany (Federal Republic)
Krupp works, Essen
Phonograph record industry—Germany (Federal Republic)
Photographic apparatus industry and trade
Trusts, Industrial—Germany (Federal Republic)

Intellectual life

Stirrings in West Germany. N. Birnbaum. Commentary 37:53-8 Ap '64
See also
Berlin (West Berlin)—Intellectual life

Politics and government

Adenauer gets heir apparent. Bsns W p36 Ap 27 '63
Adenauer years. H. Abosch. Nation 197:28-31 Jl 13 '63
Allied disunity and German politics. G. Bailey. il Reporter 31:14-16 D 31 '64
Atlantic report (cont) Atlan 211:14+ F; 212: 20-3 Jl '63; 213:32+ F; 214:12+ Ag '64; 215: 24+ Ja '65
Back-seat driver. il Newsweek 62:67-8 O 21 '63
Change at the top in West Germany. il U S News 55:22 O 14 '63
Deadly friends. Newsweek 64:58+ O 12 '64
Der Dicke takes over. il Time 82:35-6 O 25 '63
Division among democrats. New Repub 150: 9-10 Mr 14 '64
Domestic war. il Newsweek 64:38-9 Jl 27 '64
Dropping the pilot. New Repub 149:8 O 12 '63
End of the Adenauer era. C. G. Anthon. il Cur Hist 44:193-201 Ap '63
Erhard vs. Brandt. Newsweek 63:44 Mr 16 '64
Erhard's gauntlet. Newsweek 61:42+ Mr 25 '63
Farewell to Der Alte. A. Horne. Sat R 15:350-1 O 22 '63
From Adenauer to Erhard; changeover in West Germany. il Sr Schol 83:12-15+ N 15 '63
German democracy; a reporter's notebook. G. Samuels. il N Y Times Mag p 17+ Ja 5 '64
Germany gives rise to vast uncertainties. H. J. Morgenthau. il N Y Times Mag p21+ S 8 '63
Germany without Adenauer: what it will be like. il U S News 55:80-1 O 21 '63
Germany's Erhard: ready to take over, but... il U S News 54:19 F 18 '63
Going, going. il Newsweek 62:32+ O 28 '63
Great legacy from Adenauer. Life 55:4 O 25 '63
Herr Bundeskanzler comes to see us. A. J. Olsen. il N Y Times Mag p24+ Je 7 '64
Hexed ministry. Newsweek 63:34 F 3 '64
Himmler's adjutant. Newsweek 61:46+ F 11 '63
Kingmaker? il Newsweek 63:26+ Mr 30 '64
Leader of the opposition; Adenauer's disapproval of Erhard. Newsweek 64:48+ N 16 '64
Mapping a new course; Chancellor Erhard. Bsns W p93-4+ O 12 '63
Missing whip. Newsweek 62:27-8 D 23 '63
Old man won't let go. T. Prittie. New Repub 148:9-10 Ap 27 '63
Onkel Ludi at the helm. il Newsweek 62:52-4+ O 7 '63
Qualified triumph. il Newsweek 63:40 Mr 2 '64
Reawakening on the Rhine. S. Muller. Bul Atomic Sci 20:2-6 S '64; Reply. F. H. Tucker. 20:22 D '64
Socialists gaining. Time 84:34+ D 4 '64
Sweet success. il Time 81:29 My 3 '63
Thirteenth shake; Adenauer-Erhard feud. il Newsweek 61:46 Mr 18 '63
Waiting for the call. il Time 81:31 F 15 '63
West Germany's next chancellor. T. Prittie. New Repub 148:11-12 My 11 '63
When Erhard takes over in Germany. il U S News 54:20 My 6 '63
Willy Brandt's third Germany. G. Bailey. il Reporter 30:33-6 F 13 '64
See also
Berlin question, 1945-
Fascism—Germany (Federal Republic)
Political parties—Germany (Federal Republic)

Popular culture

Stirrings in West Germany. N. Birnbaum. Commentary 37:53-8 Ap '64

Reconstruction

Onkel Ludi at the helm. il Newsweek 62:52-4+ O 7 '63

Religious institutions and affairs

News of the Christian world (cont) Christian Cent 80:757-8, 1012, 1248+, 1385; 81: 154-6, 650-2, 1091-2, 1152-4, 1346 Je 5, Ag 14, O 9, N 6 '63, Ja 29, My 13, S 2, 16, O 28 '64
See also
Catholic church in Germany (Federal Republic)

Social conditions

Appointment with hate. E. Wiesel; discussion. Commentary 35:348-50 Ap '63

Social life and customs

Eclipse of princes. il Time 81:32+ Ap 26 '63

Treaties

Dream comes true for two old rivals. il U S News 54:19 F 4 '63
Franco-Germany treaty of reconciliation. Cur Hist 44:237-9+ Ap '63

GERMANY (Federal Republic)—Treaties—*Cont.*
Impact of the Franco-German entente; address, April 6, 1963; with questions and answers. H. C. Deutsch. Ann Am Acad 348:82-94 Jl '63
Shadows on the success of Der Alte. D. Schorr. Reporter 28:27-8 F 28 '63
GERMANY (Federal Republic) and Israel. See Israel and Germany
GERMANY, EASTERN. See Germany (Democratic Republic)
GERMANY, WESTERN. See Germany (Federal Republic)
GERMANY and Europe. See Europe and Germany
GERMINATION
Germination of melampyrum lineare; interrelated effects of afterripening and gibberellic acid. E. J. C. Curtis and J. E. Cantlon. bibliog il Science 140:406-8 Ap 26 '63
Long-lived messenger RNA: evidence from cotton seed germination. L. Dure and L. Waters. bibliog il Science 147:410-12 Ja 22 '65
Woody plant seeds. A. J. Fordham. il Horticulture 42:18-20+ S '64
GERMS. See Microorganisms, Pathogenic
GERNSBACK, Hugo
Barnum of the space age. P. O'Neil. il pors Life 55:62-4+ Jl 26 '63
This above all, to thine own tube be true. il por Time 83:65 Mr 6 '64
GERONIMO park, Ariz. See Baseball fields
GERONTOLOGY. See Aging
GEROW, Richard O. bp
Voice in Jackson. America 108:894 Je 29 '63
GERRARD, Saida
Saida Gerrard discusses the L.A. problem. J. Dougherty. il pors Dance Mag 37:16+ Mr '63
GERRISH, Benjamin
Benjamin Gerrish, brazier. R. H. Randall, jr. il Antiques 85:320-1 Mr '64
GERRITSEN, Theo, and Waisman, H. A.
Homocystinuria: absence of cystathionine in the brain. bibliog Science 145:588 Ag 7 '64
GERRITT, David
Beseler Topcon Super D. U S Camera 26:62-3+ O '63
GERRITZ, E. M.
Advanced placement. NEA J 54:22+ Ja '65
GERRY, Roger G.
Living with antiques: East meets West on Long Island. il Antiques 87:80-4 Ja '65
GERRYMANDER
See also
Apportionment (election law)
GERSH, Gabriel
Arab world in ferment: the scorpion and the frog. Commonweal 79:217-20 N 15 '63
Big small country. Commonweal 80:113-16 Ap 17 '64
Israel after fifteen years. Christian Cent 80:487-9 Ap 17 '63
Israel's Negev comes to life. Christian Cent 81:169-71 F 5 '64
Living in a nice place to visit. Sat R 47:37 O 17 '64
Nasser's brand of socialism. Christian Cent 81:962-5 Jl 29 '64
State of the Sicilian civilian. Sat R 47:33+ Je 6 '64
Turkey in crisis. Christian Cent 80:231-3 F 20 '63
GERSHMAN, Isaac
Shoe-leather school. il por Newsweek 65:50 Ja 4 '65
GERSHON-COHEN, Jacob
New medical device spots hidden diseases; thermograph camera. R. P. Goldman. il por Sat Eve Post 236:44-6+ S 28 '63
GERSHOY, Leo
Best of all possible monarchies. Sat R 47:32 Ja 18 '64
GERSHWIN, George
Other side of the canvas: Gershwin's paintings. W. Sullivan. il por Sat R 46:18-19 Je 8 '63
RCA Victor Porgy and Bess. R. Ellsworth. il por Am Rec G 30:196-8 N '63
Trunkful of tunes. Newsweek 63:48 Mr 2 '64
GERSHWIN, Ira
Trunkful of tunes. Newsweek 63:48 Mr 2 '64
GERSTEIN, G. L. and Clark, W. A.
Simultaneous studies of firing patterns in several neurons. bibliog Science 143:1325-7 Mr 20 '64
GERSTENKORN, H.
Moon captured by earth. W. Davis. Sci N L 83:291 My 11 '63
GERSTER, Georg
Threatened treasures of the Nile. il Nat Geog Mag 124:586-621 O '63
GERSTMAN, Maria K.
What makes a good art teacher? Sch Arts 64:31-2 S '64
GERSTNER, G. A.
Maximum-minimum approach to civil-defense communications. por Am City 78:131-2 N '63
GERTLER, Diane B.
Nonpublic high schools: fall 1963 enrollment and 1962-63 graduates. Sch Life 47:32-5 O '64
Statistics of nonpublic schools. por Sch Life 46:31-6 O '63
GERTLER, Menard M.
How to predict your heart attack and prevent it: excerpts from You can predict your heart attack and prevent it. Read Digest 84:51-5 Ja '64
GERVAIS, André Pierre
Reporter at large. J. Wechsberg. il New Yorker 39:140+ My 18 '63
GERVIS, Stephanie
France's ban-the-bombers. Nation 197:91-3 Ag 24 '63
Gray spring in Hazard. Commonweal 78:220-2 My 17 '63
Paris problem. Esquire 61:86-8+ F '64
Stevenson at the U.N. Commonweal 77:591-3 Mr 1 '63
GESELL, Gerhard Alden
Georgia's Vinson: battling the Pentagon. U S News 55:16 S 30 '63
Pentagon jumps into the race fight. il U S News 55:49-50 Ag 19 '63
GESELL Institute of child development
What parents ask most about children. J. H. Pollack. il Todays Health 41:24-7+ F '63
GESNERIACEAE. See Achimenes
GESSNER, George John
I gave them all. il por Time 83:21 Je 19 '64
GESSNER, Robert
Handwriting on the screen. Sat R 47:36 O 10 '64
GETLEIN, Frank
Art. See issues of New republic
In Herblock, the world is almost exclusively political. Commonweal 81:332-4 N 27 '64
GETNER, Gus
Texas two-bit fishing. por Field & S 67:158-61+ Ap '63
GETTELL, Richard Glenn
Academic, social, and spiritual program at Mount Holyoke college. Sch & Soc 92:270-2 O 3 '64
GETTY, George F, 2d
Four other freedoms; address, April 7, 1964. Vital Speeches 30:499-501 Je 1 '64
GETTY, Jean Paul
Rich man's story. por Newsweek 61:67 Je 3 '63
GETTY, Russell E.
New hope for public land watersheds. por Am For 70:14-19 D '64
GETTYSBURG, Pa.
Gettysburg and Vicksburg: the battle towns today. R. P. Jordan. il Nat Geog Mag 124:4-57 Jl '63
Notes for a gazetteer. P. Hamburger. New Yorker 40:83-4+ Ap 4 '64
GETTYSBURG, Battle of, 1863
General Reynolds and Dear Kate; reprint. M. R. Maloney. il Am Heritage 15:62-5 D '63
Gettysburg: great turning point. B. Catton. il N Y Times Mag p9+ Je 30 '63
Gettysburg 1963. B. Roberts. il U S Camera 26:74-7+ Ag '63
Notes for a gazetteer. P. Hamburger. New Yorker 40:83-4+ Ap 4 '64
Page one news: account written a century ago. Time 82:70 Jl 12 '63
Prelude to Gettysburg. R. P. Jordan. il Nat Geog Mag 124:14-21 Jl '63
Recharge at Gettysburg. R. Wallace. il Life 55:14+ Jl 5 '63
Suppose Lee had won at Gettysburg. il U S News 55:60-1 Jl 8 '63
Task remaining; celebration of centennial. il Newsweek 62:18-19 Jl 15 '63
GETTYSBURG address. See Lincoln, A.
GETZ, Stan
Bossa nova nova. il Time 84:46 Jl 31 '64
Jazz records. W. Balliett. New Yorker 39:118-22 Ap 6 '63
GEUM. See Avens
GEURINK, Robert J.
Southern honor. Commonweal 81:476-7 Ja 8 '65
GEWECKE, Gordon
Built to fit the site. Am City 78:120-1 Je '63
GEYELIN, Philip
Cuban embargo myth. Reporter 30:18-19 Ap 23 '64
Irksome Panama wrangle. Reporter 30:14-17 Ap 9 '64
GEYER, Richard A. See Van Lopik, J. R. jt. auth.

GEYER, Richard E.
Can you farm without debt today? Suc Farm 62:74 My '64
Coming, better agricultural jobs without college. Suc Farm 62:88 Ap '64
How to get and keep hired help. Suc Farm 62:35 Mr '64
One stop grain handling, hog feeding. Suc Farm 61:32-3+ Je '63
What's this: loans you never pay off? Suc Farm 62:43+ N '64
—and Brantley, Bill
Hundred acres is enough for me. Suc Farm 61:54-5 N '63
GEYSER, Albert
Geyser wins appeal. Christian Cent 80:701 My 29 '63
GEYSERS
Old Faithful's winter plume. D. L. Coe. il Nat Parks Mag 37:8-9 Mr '63
Steam means trouble in Lassen's Section thirty-six. P. Hyde. il Nat Parks Mag 37:4-6 Je '63
GHALI, Boutros Boutros-. See Boutros- Ghali, B.
GHANA
Subversion, inc; Bureau of African affairs. Newsweek 61:50 My 20 '63
See also
Elections—Ghana
Foreign visitors in Ghana
Law—Ghana
Theater—Ghana
Trials—Ghana
Constitution
Fruits of redemption. Time 83:25 Ja 31 '64
Economic conditions
Ghana's industrial revolution. il Ebony 19:154-60+ My '64
Foreign relations
Atlantic report. Atlan 213:28+ My '64
Fighting fantasy. Newsweek 63:54 F 17 '64
From U.S. to Ghana: millions; from Ghana to U.S: insults. il U S News 56:40 F 24 '64
Ghana: a charismatic nation. L. Tiger. bibliog f Cur Hist 45:335-40 D '63
Mobs assail U.S. in Ghana. Sr Schol 84:18 F 21 '64
Reluctant hero speaks his mind; with letter. il Ebony 19:164 Ap '64
Industries
Ghana's industrial revolution. il Ebony 19:154-60+ My '64
Politics and government
Atlantic report. Atlan 213:28+ My '64
Cribbing from Moscow. Time 83:27 Ja 17 '64
Dealing with enemies. il Time 81:38 Ap 26 '63
Ghana: a charismatic nation. L. Tiger. bibliog f Cur Hist 45:335-40 D '63
Ghana: communism's new foothold in Africa. D. Reed. il Read Digest 85:202-7+ Jl '64
Loyalties in the emerging nations. G. W. Shepherd, jr. Christian Cent 80:206-7 F 13 '63
Nkrumah tightens the reins. il Sr Schol 84:11-13+ Mr 20 '64
Osagyefo thinks deep. T. Sterling. il Reporter 31:30-2 N 5 '64
Portrait of Nkrumah as dictator. L. Garrison. il N Y Times Mag p 15+ My 3 '64
Verdict overruled. Newsweek 62:34 D 23 '63
GHEDINI, Francesco
(ed) See Loren, S. Secrets of Sophia
GHEORGHIU-DEJ, Gheorghe
Fathers & sons. il Time 83:27 My 8 '64
Rumania's Gheorghiu-Dej: another rebel red? por U S News 57:22 Jl 20 '64
GHIAUROV, Nicolai
New Chaliapin? il por Newsweek 64:90-1 N 9 '64
GHIBERTI, Lorenzo
Paradise regained. il Time 84:84 D 4 '64
GHOSE, Zulfikar
Artist and lover; poem. Atlan 213:95 Je '64
Marriages; poem. Yale R 53:233 D '63
GHOST plays
Reggie the ghost. M. Hall. Plays 24:65-8, 82 O '64
GHOST stories
Single works
One of the dead. W. Wood. il Sat Eve Post 237:42-3 O 31 '64
GHOST towns. See Abandoned towns
GHOST writing. See Authorship—Collaboration
GHOSTS
Come back, Nell Gwyn; NBC show, The stately ghosts of England. il Newsweek 65:70 Ja 18 '65
Notes for a gazetteer; Natchez, Miss. P. Hamburger. New Yorker 39:110-14 Mr 2 '63
Caricatures and cartoons
Sinking spell. E. Gorey. Holiday 35:68-71 My '64
GHURKAS
Ayo Gorkhali! R. Hughes. il N Y Times Mag p34-5+ O 18 '64
GIACOBINI, Ezio, and others
Isolated neuron preparation for studies of metabolic events at rest and during impulse activity. bibliog Science 140:74 Ap 5 '63
GIACOMETTI, Alberto
Champ of the prize winners. il pors Life 56:90-1+ My 29 '64
GIALLELIS, Stathis
Determined dreamer. il por Sr Schol 84:7 F 28 '64
One chance in a million. E. Miller. il pors Seventeen 22:124-5+ S '63
Success with 30¢ to spare. R. Oulahan. por Life 56:115-16 Mr 6 '64
GIANNATTASIO, Francesco, and Turner, D. E.
Center moves left. America 108:606-8 Ap 27 '63
GIANNI Schicchi; opera. See Puccini, G.
GIANNINI, Vittorio
Hovhaness and Giannini symphonies: a complete success. A. Cohn. Am Rec G 30:853-4 My '64
GIANNINI controls corporation
Pure fluid guidance advances through research at Giannini. R. Pay. il Miss & Roc 13:28+ D 9 '63
GIANNINI family
Gianninis; musical Philadelphia family. M. De Schauensee. il Opera N 28:14-16 Ap 11 '64
GIANT at the window; story. See Hurlbut, K.
GIANT pandas. See Pandas
GIANT swallowtails. See Butterflies
GIANTS (baseball) See Baseball clubs
GIAP, Vo-nguyen-. See Vo-nguyen-Giap
GIARDELLO, Joey
Comeuppance for Joey. Sports Illus 21:15 N 2 '64
Last chance. por Newsweek 62:69 D 9 '63
Long ago. il Time 82:71 Jl 5 '63
Match made in the jungle. M. Gross. il pors Sat Eve Post 237:76-8 O 24 '64
Mighty desirable fellow. J. Underwood. il pors Sports Illus 20:30-2+ My 18 '64
You can't keep a bad boy down. M. Sharnik. il pors Sports Illus 19:18-19 D 16 '63
GIARDINA, Teresa
Poor connection; story. Mlle 57:63-5 Je '63
GIARMAN, Nicholas J. and Roth, R. H.
Differential estimation of gamma-butyrolactone and gamma-hydroxybutyric acid in rat blood and brain. bibliog Science 145:583-4 Ag 7 '64
GIBB, Walter M.
Walk on the wild side. Atlan 211:132-4 Ap '63
GIBBERELLIC acid
Amateur scientist; extraction of growth-promoting substances from cantaloupe. R. C. Caggiano. il Sci Am 211:100-3 Ag '64
Germination of melampyrum lineare; interrelated effects of afterripening and gibberellic acid. E. J. C. Curtis and J. E. Cantlon. bibliog il Science 140:406-8 Ap 26 '63
New way to use GA. B Fowler. Farm J 89:50F Ja '65
Plant morphology: its control in proserpinaca by photoperiod, temperature, and gibberellic acid. A. Wallenstein and L. S. Albert. bibliog il Science 140:998-1000 My 31 '63
GIBBERELLINS
Gibberellin: effect on diffusible auxin in fruit development. K. K. S. Sastry and R. M. Muir. bibliog il Science 140:494-5 My 3 '63
Gibberellin production in pea seeds developing in excised pods: effect of growth retardant AMO-1618. B. Baldev and others. bibliog il Science 147:155-7 Ja 8 '65
Gibberellins: their effect on antheridium formation in fern gametophytes. B. R. Voeller. bibliog il Science 143:373-5 Ja 24 '64
Growth response of the d-5 and an-1 mutants of maize to some kaurene derivatives. M. Katsumi and others. bibliog il Science 144:849-50 My 15 '64
Sensitivity of female inbreds of cucumis sativus to sex reversion by gibberellin. O. Shifriss and W. L. George, jr. bibliog il Science 143:1452-3 Mr 27 '64
Wheat gibberellins. J. R. Fleming and J. A. Johnson. bibliog il Science 144:1021-2 My 22 '64
GIBBINGS, T. H. Robsjohn-. See Robsjohn-Gibbings, T. H.

GIBBON, Edward
Decline and fall revisited. W. H. Chamberlin. por Sat R 47:18-19 Ag 8 '64
Pope, the bishops, and Edward Gibbon. O. Hastings. il Reporter 31:22-5 D 31 '64
GIBBONS, Euell
Stalking the weed eater. D. L. Goodrich. il por Sat Eve Post 237:22-3 Jl 25 '64
GIBBONS, Eugene F. and Peters, J. H.
Don't wait for stoppages. Am City 79:79-81 N '64
GIBBONS, Glenn
400-foot pier fabricated on shore. Am City 78:185 S '63
GIBBONS, Harold
Aides quit, but Hoffa stays in driver's seat. por Bsns W p94+ D 14 '63
If Hoffa stumbles. Reporter 30:12+ Ja 16 '64
Limit of devotion. por Newsweek 62:75-6 D 16 '63
Revolt against Jimmy. Time 82:29 D 13 '63
Stakes in the struggle against Hoffa. L. Velie. Read Digest 84:92-6 Mr '64
GIBBONS, Ronald J. and Engle, L. P.
Vitamin K compounds in bacteria that are obligate anaerobes. bibliog Science 146:1307-9 D 4 '64
GIBBONS, Russell W.
Backlash and the Catholic vote. Christian Cent 81:1303-5 O 21 '64
Rebellion in steel. Commonweal 81:540-2 Ja 22 '65
GIBBONS, Thomas
Steamboat's charter of freedom; Gibbons v. Ogden. G. Dangerfield. il por Am Heritage 14:38-43+ O '63
GIBBONS, William J.
Book of the month. Cath World 199:50-2 Ap '64
Food for thought. America 108:202 F 9 '63
Interventions in nature. Cath World 197:2-3 Ap '63
Report on fertility research. Cath World 197: 44-50 Ap '63
GIBBONS
New zoo act; siamangs at Bronx zoo. il Life 54:47-8+ Ap 5 '63
GIBBS, Barbara
Merwin as translator. Poetry 101:353-5 F '63
GIBBS, C. L. and Ricchiuti, N. V.
Activation heat in muscle: method for determination. bibliog Science 147:162-3 Ja 8 '65
GIBBS, Joy L. and Dougall, D. K.
Growth of single plant cells. bibliog Science 141:1059 S 13 '63
GIBBS, William Francis
Mightiest fire engine. P. Mandel. il Life 56:23-4 Mr 20 '64
Profiles. W. Sargeant. por New Yorker 40:49-50+ Je 6 '64
GIBBS and Cox, incorporated
Profiles; W. F. Gibbs. W. Sargeant. New Yorker 40:49-50+ Je 6 '64
GIBEL, Inge Lederer
How not to integrate the schools; a personal testament. Harper 227:57-60+ N '63
GIBEON. See Palestine—Antiquities
GIBNEY, Harriet H.
Accidents don't just happen. Parents Mag 38:88-9+ O '63
GIBOR, A. and Granick, S.
Plastids and mitochondria: inheritable systems. bibliog Science 145:890-7 Ag 28 '64
GIBRALTAR
Most happy colony. il Time 84:64-5 O 2 '64
Spain's Gibraltar. L. R. Tschirky. il Travel 120:38-9 S '63
See also
United Nations—Gibraltar
GIBSON, Althea
Brussels sprouts italiano. il por Ebony 18: 120+ Jl '63
GIBSON, George W.
More return from your film dollar. Harvard Bsns R 41:162-3+ Jl '63
GIBSON, Gerald G.
History in houses. Antiques 85:196-201 F '64
GIBSON, H. Lou
Cross-pollination of an orchid. il Natur Hist 73:42-3 Ap '64
GIBSON, John E.
Science looks at liquor. Todays Health 41:84-6 F '63
Science looks at tobacco; questions and answers. Todays Health 42:33+ F '64
What daydreaming reveals about your personality. Todays Health 41:43+ N '63
GIBSON, Manley B.
Legacy. Sports Illus 20:8+ Je 29 '64
GIBSON, R. E.
Our heritage from Galileo Galilei; address May 21, 1964. Science 145:1271-6 S 18 '64
GIBSON, Sally M. See Dworkin, M. jt. auth.
GIBSON, Scott
DX'ing Jupiter! Pop Electr 21:41-3+ Ag '64
Sick? let a computer do the diagnosis. Pop Electr 21:45-8+ N '64
GIBSON Lee, incorporated
Throw away the collar; paper collars and dickies. il Bsns W p67-8+ S 7 '63
GIBSON refrigerator sales corporation
Troubled town; question of closing Gibson refrigerator Greenville plant. Newsweek 61: 74+ My 20 '63
GIDAL, Peter
Beauty; poem. Horn Bk 39:417 Ag '63
GIDDIS, Albert, and Maggi, Louis
Radio telescopes: past, present & future. Electr World 72:19-23+ Jl '64
GIDDON, Franklin. See Klein, E. jt auth.
GIDE, André Paul Guillaume
Immoralist; dramatization. See Goetz, A. and Goetz, R.
about
Gide's Hamlet. J. O'Brien. Reporter 31:38-9 Jl 16 '64
New look at Andre Gide. G. Greene. Commonweal 79:376-7 D 20 '63
Quest for Gide. H. Peyre. Nation 197:395+ D 7 '63
Strait was the gate to art. L. LeSage. por Sat R 46:39-40 N 16 '63
GIDEON, Clarence Earl
And the Court said unto Gideon. por Time 82:53 O 18 '63
Annals of law. A. Lewis il New Yorker 40: 144+ Ap 25; 125-6+ My 2; 150+ My 9 '64
Bar behind bars. Time 83:88+ My 22 '64
Ex-con overturns the law: with report by M. Durham. il pors Life 56:83-4+ Je 12 '64
Gideon's trumpet, by A. Lewis. Review
Newsweek il por 63:89-90 Je 22 '64
Sat R 47:28 Je 27 '64. W. B. Butler
GIDEONSE, Hendrik D.
Conant report; is enlightened debate possible? Sat R 47:56-7+ S 19 '64
GIDNEY, Robert S.
Banker to his own flesh and blood. C. Aucoin. New Yorker 40:125-6+ Ap 18 '64
GIESE, Donald John
Open house for young hoods. Read Digest 84:125-9 Ap '64
Why was Carol killed? Sat Eve Post 236: 73-7 S 14 '63
GIESSEN university. See Colleges and universities—Germany (Federal Republic)
GIFFEN, Daniel H.
Louisiana state museum. Hobbies 68:52 N '63
GIFFEN, Jane C.
Living with antiques. Antiques 86:72-6 Jl '64
GIFFORD, Frank
Always leave them limp; New York Giants vs. Pittsburgh Steelers at Yankee stadium. il Time 82:40 D 27 '63
GIFFORD, Henry
Master of pain. Poetry 105:196-7 D '64
GIFFORD, Philip C. See Scougall, S. jt. auth.
GIFFORD, Richard O. and Frugoli, D. M.
Silica source in soil solutions. bibliog Science 145:386-8 Jl 24 '64
GIFFORD, Selene
Educating the American Indian. Sch Life 47:10-12 N '64
GIFT boxes. See Christmas boxes
GIFT cards. See Greeting cards
GIFT of tongues
Against glossolalia. Time 81:84 My 17 '63
And there appeared to them tongues of fire; M. Phillips. il Sat Eve Post 237:30-2+ My 16 '64
Blue tongues. Time 81:52 Mr 29 '63
No noisy gongs; research by Lutheran medical center of Brooklyn, N.Y. America 111: 173-4 Ag 22 '64
Speaking in tongues: the high church heresy. D. Bess. Nation 197:173-7 S 28 '63
Taming the tongues: Rev. A. Herbert Mjorud, promoter of glossolalia. Time 84:64+ Jl 10 '64
Tongue speaking, by M. T. Kelsey. Review
Christian Cent 81:1243-4 O 7 '64. D. Yu
GIFT wrapping. See Wrapping of packages
GIFTED children. See Children, Gifted
GIFTED college students. See College students, Mentally superior
GIFTS
Better life with father. il Esquire 59:114-17 Je '63
Case history of a favor. Christian Cent 81: 415 Mr 25 '64
For me? M. A. Rodgers. il Redbook 124:31+ Ja '65
For the benefit of? conditions under which artists should donate their work. T. B. Hess. Art N 62:23 Ap '63

GIFTS—*Continued*
Presents for rooms and board. il Vogue 142: 178 N 15 '63
Shower the bride-to-be with gifts. il Seventeen 22:134-5 My '63
See also
Christmas gifts
Food as gifts
Giving
Plants as gifts
Wedding gifts
also subhead Gifts, or Gifts, legacies, etc. under various subjects, e.g. Cities and towns—Gifts, legacies, etc.

Taxation

Personal business; estate and gift tax planning. Bsns W p 135 F 23 '63

GIFTS, Spiritual
And there appeared to them tongues of fire; Charismatic renewal movement. M. Phillips. il Sat Eve Post 237:30-2+ My 16 '64

GIFTS for children
Put it in the child's name? stocks, bonds, bank accounts. il Changing T 17:38-40 Ap '63
See also
Christmas gifts for children
Toys

GIFTS for the New Year; drama. See Miller, H. L.

GIFTS from children
Love & merry Christmas. C. Blunt. il Parents Mag 39:35+ D '64

GIFTS in business
Business of giving; corporate gift giving to contacts and customers. il Time 84:100+ D 4 '64
Unusual business gifts; Be my guest. J. B. Weiner. Duns R 82:61 N '63

GIGNOUX, Dominique M. P.
Inventor of the month. S. V. Jones. por Sci Digest 55:52 My '64

GIL, David
David Gil's Bennington potters. N. Nelson. il Craft Horiz 24:34-5 Mr '64

GILA monsters
Gila monster. Sci N L 86:98 Ag 15 '64

GILBERT, Arthur
Opening the religious press. America 108:336 Mr 9 '63
Penalty for witness. America 110:620 My 9 '64

GILBERT, Bil
About: falcons. N Y Times Mag p38+ D 8 '63
Exploring, ugh! Sports Illus 20:72-6+ Ja 27 '64
Minks, shrews and men in a winter swamp. Sports Illus 18:38-42+ Mr 18 '63
Owl in the playpen. Sat Eve Post 237:72+ Jl 11 '64
Paean to a winged hunter. Sports Illus 18:50-5 F 4 '63
Pop goes the ferret! Sports Illus 21:98-102+ D 7 '64
Vanishing knave of clubs. Sat Eve Post 237:68+ Je 20 '64

GILBERT, C. M. See Christensen, M. N. jt. auth.

GILBERT, Dorothy R.
Angola border; poem. Christian Cent 80:581 My 1 '63
At the Brooklyn docks; poem. New Yorker 39:55 Ja 25 '64
Freighters at night; poem. New Yorker 39: 136 D 7 '63

GILBERT, Edward M.
When a fugitive turns to fight. D. Forst. il pors Sat Eve Post 236:44-5 O 19 '63

GILBERT, Edwin
New faces in the expatriate colony. N Y Times Mag p30+ D 8 '63

GILBERT, G. R.
Simple hum-bucking circuit. Electr World 70:77 Ag '63

GILBERT, George
Bring on the oldies. U S Camera 27:16+ Je '64
Down memory lane. U S Camera 27:36-7+ Ja '64
Focusing systems for SLRs. U S Camera 27:42-3+ D '64
How slow is your slow shutter? U S Camera 26:78-9+ N '63
Light, portable tape recorders capture live sound. U S Camera 26:22-3+ Ag '63
New product report: Agfa contrast no. 6. U S Camera 27:61-3+ Mr '64
Shakespeare on photography. U S Camera 27:15 Ja '64
Fifteen tips from the pros. il U S Camera 27:54-5+ Mr '64

GILBERT, H. E.
Beyond the last mile. il por Time 82:13-16 Jl 26 '63

GILBERT, Jack
Plundering of Circe; poem. Atlan 211:71 My '63

GILBERT, James
International aerobatics. por Flying 74:40-2+ F '64

GILBERT, John
Audience swam for their lives; excerpts from YM-YWHA-sponsored symposium on The state of American poetry today, ed. by J. Scully. Nation 198:244-5+ Mr 9 '64

GILBERT, Lawrence I.
Endocrine control of growth; report of symposium sponsored by the Division of comparative endocrinology of the American society of zoologists. Science 139:928-9 Mr 8 '63
—See Chino, H; Schneiderman, H. A. jt. auths.

GILBERT, Perry W. and Douglas, S. D.
Electrocardiographic studies of free-swimming sharks. bibliog Science 140:1396 Je 28 '63
—and others
Electroencephalograms of sharks. bibliog Science 145:949-51 Ag 28 '64

GILBERT, Richard L. Jr
New wild West. Esquire 60:138-9+ O '63
Phoenix unreborn. Reporter 29:48-9 N 21 '63

GILBERT and Sullivan operas
City Center Savoyards. M. Bernheimer. Sat R 47:61-2 Ap 11 '64
Patter still matters; D'oyly Carte opera troupe. D. E. Scherman. Life 58:14 Ja 8 '65
Satire and sopranos. il Seventeen 23:58 N '64
Take advantage of the Gilbert and Sullivan recording boom. E. Kinard. House B 105: 30+ Mr '63
See also
D'Oyly Carte opera company

GILBERTO, Astrud
Bossa nova nova. il por Time 84:46 Jl 31 '64
Girl from Ipanema. Newsweek 64:47 Ag 3 '64

GILCHRIST, Carlton
Tough Cookie marches to his own drummer. E. Shrake. il por Sports Illus 21:70-2+ D 14 '64

GILDEA, Ray Y. Jr, and Taylor, Alice
Rwanda and Burundi. bibliog Focus 13:1-6 F '63

GILDEA, Robert L.
Confusion on church and state. Christian Cent 80:1381-2 N 6 '63

GILDEN, R. V. and Tokuda, S.
Antibody quality after sequential immunization with related antigens. bibliog Science 140:405-6 Ap 26 '63

GILDER, Rosamond
European theatres revisited. Theatre Arts 47:68-70 N '63

GILELS, Emil
Evolution of Emil. il por Time 84:67 D 18 '64

GILES, John Warren
Bear facts. Am For 69:26 Jl '63
Law and the liability of the public forester. Am For 69:31+ Mr '63
Libel, slander and religion. Christian Cent 80:1331-3 O 30 '63
Perils of the sea, who's liable? Motor B 111: 44 Mr '63
Skipper: just how liable are you? Motor B 113:248+ Ja '64

GILES, Robert
Austerity in Ohio. Reporter 29:39-42 N 7 '63

GILES, Warren Crandall
Honest Warren Giles: he always strives to please. G. Holland. por Sports Illus 18: 32-4+ Je 10 '63

GILI, Terence A.
Tails out of school. U S Camera 26:50-1+ N '63

GILIEN, Ted
Ted Gilien; a vigorous painter. J. Lovoos. il por Am Artist 27:24-9 D '63

GILKEY, Langdon
Is God dead? Christian Cent 82:18-19 Ja 6 '65

GILL, Brendan
Books. New Yorker 40:235-44 D 12 '64
Current cinema. See issues of New Yorker

GILL, Clark C.
South American students ask about U.S. schools. Sch & Soc 91:193-5 Ap 20 '63

GILL, Frank
Lost weekend. Mus Am 84:20-1 Jl '64

GILL, Richard
Imagination of disaster. Sat R 47:10-13+ S 5 '64

GILL, Robert L.
Negro in the Supreme court, 1954-64; address, 1964. bibliog por Negro Hist Bul 28:51-2+ D '64 (to be cont)

GILL, Thomas E. bp
. . . And the bells toll. America 108:894 Je 29 '63

GILL, Tom
What does it take? Am For 70:11 Ja '64

GILL, William Jerome
Art from nobody knows where. Sat Eve Post 237:56-8 F 8 '64
GILL, Artificial. See Respiratory apparatus
GILLELAN, G. Howard
Archery. See issues of Outdoor life
Deer mirrors: nine states test them to cut road kill. por Outdoor Life 135:24-6+ F '65
My wild Spanish goat. por Outdoor Life 135: 58-61+ F '65
Rampart Dam: a wildlife catastrophe for nothing? Outdoor Life 134:14-15+ D '64
(ed) See Somerville, T. Elk hunt in Virginia?
GILLENSON, Lewis W.
Manhattan principal at work. Sat R 47:77-9+ My 16 '64
GILLESPIE, Alfred
Double life of Patty Duke. Good H. 158:52+ Ap '64
Frenzied world of Phil Silvers. Good H 158: 30-2+ Ja '64
GILLESPIE, Janet
Confessions of a scavenger; excerpts from Joy of a small garden. House & Gard 123:217-20 My '63
GILLESPIE, John Birks
Man behind the horn. A. Morrison. il pors Ebony 19:143-4+ Je '64
GILLESPIE, Susan
Boy in a boater; story. New Yorker 40:207-8 N 14 '64
GILLESPIE, Vernon, Jr
Captain Gillespie goes out after the Vietcong. L. Hall. il pors Life 57:32-5 N 27 '64
GILLETT, C. A.
Mr Gillett's farm bureau talk; summary of address, December 9, 1963. Am For 70:62 Ja '64
GILLETT, G. Elizabeth
Maxfield Parrish at ninety-three. Sat R 47:129-30 Mr 14 '64
GILLETTE, Arthur
Holiday cure for bored teen-agers. UNESCO Courier 16:24-7 Ap '63
Voluntary workcamping. Américas 15:13-18 O '63
GILLETTE, William
Too much Johnson; adapted by B. Shevelove. Criticism
New Yorker 39:74+ Ja 25 '64
GILLETTE company
Blade battle. il Time 85:78 Ja 29 '65
Gillette faces the stainless-steel dragon. W. Guzzardi, jr. il Fortune 68:158-61+ Jl '63
Gillette goes stainless. Time 82:79 S 6 '63
Steel that shaves the world; Sweden's Sandvik steel supplies stainless to Gillette. il Bsns W p63-4+ O 5 '63
Well fixed for blades. Newsweek 63:67 Je 22 '64
GILLEY, Fred T.
Wood to launch a president. Am For 71:2-3+ Ja '65
GILLEY, Leonard
At the end; poem. Christian Cent 81:965 Jl 29 '64
Now, and later: fifty megaton; poem. Christian Cent 81:77 Ja 15 '64
GILLHAM, C. E.
Chachalaca. Field & S 68:54-5+ S '63
Dog gods wept. Field & S 68:58-60 Je '63
My last buck. Field & S 68:32-4+ Jl '63
Mystery ram of Dead Mountain. Field & S 67:14+ Ap '63
Oh, I'll never go there anymore. pors Field & S 67:50-2+ Ap '63
$10 turkey. Field & S 67:26-8+ F '63
When the eiders flew. Field & S 68:60-2+ F '64
GILLHAM, J. K.
Polymer structure: cross-linking of a polybenzimidazole. bibliog Science 139:494-5 F 8 '63
GILLIAM, Harold
Redwood totem. Nation 199:91-3 S 7 '64
GILLIAM, Lila Williamson
Mixer-made meat loaf. Farm J 88:79 N '64
Tortes: the conversation-piece dessert. Farm J 88:68-9 D '64
GILLIARD, E. Thomas
Evolution of bowerbirds. Sci Am 209:38-46 bibliog(p 140) Ag; 10+ D '63
GILLIATT, Penelope
Hollywood nursery. Harper 226:87-90 Je '63
Putting down the queen's teens. Nation 199: 227-9 O 12 '64
GILLIES, John
Justice, southern style. Christian Cent 81: 112-14 Ja 22 '64
GILLIGAN, Francis J.
Gilligan's law. America 111:224 S 5 '64
GILLIGAN, Thomas R.
Postmortem. por Newsweek 64:26+ S 14 '64
Unanimous decision. il Time 84:25-6 S 11 '64
GILLILAND, Willard R, family
Living memorial in strangers' eyes. Time 82:60 Ag 30 '63
GILLIS, Don
Meanwhile, back at the ranch. Opera N 28: 8-11 F 22 '64
GILLIS, Leon
Prairie schooner rolls into Moscow. R. Brigham. il pors Life 57:121-3 N 6 '64
GILLMOR, Margaret Albrecht
How to succeed as a working mother. Parents Mag 38:58-9+ Mr '63
Short cuts in baby care. Parents Mag 39:36-7+ Ag '64
GILLMORE, Margalo
Four flights up; excerpts. McCalls 91:84-7+ Mr '64
GILLMORE, W. F. See Goldstein, R. M. jt. auth.
GILMAN, Richard
Critic as taxpayer. New Repub 149:25-7 N 30 '63
Embattled criticism. Commentary 36:325-7+ O '63
Epitaph for Lincoln Center. Commonweal 80: 89-91 Ap 10 '64
Fact of mortality. Commonweal 79:337-8 D 13 '63
Intellect and its enemies. New Repub 149: 19-22 Jl 13 '63
Movie of the month (cont) Cath World 197: 207-8, 335-6 Je, Ag '63
Padlock on the Living theatre. Commonweal 79:182 N 8 '63
Stage. See issues of Commonweal
Svevo: news from the past. New Repub 149: 19-23 N 2 '63
Why Mailer wants to be president. New Repub 150:17-20+ F 8 '64
Youth of an author. New Repub 148:25-7 Ap 13 '63
GILMORE, Bob
Solid advice about ready-mixed concrete. Pop Sci 185:142-3+ Jl '64
Stilts for fun. Pop Sci 184:144-5 Ap '64
GILMORE, C. P.
City on fire. Sat Eve Post 236:83-7 S 7 '63
Color TV in pieces. por Pop Mech 121:194-5 F '64
Color TV: is it finally worth the money? Pop Sci 183:80-3+ Ag '63
Hurricane killers learn where to aim. Pop Mech 119:114-18+ Mr '63
I was shot down by an American jet. Pop Mech 121:108-13+ Mr '64
Junket on a Chinese junk. Pop Mech 120: 102-6+ S '63
Laser goes to work. Pop Sci 183:80-4+ D '63
Sky cameras. Pop Sci 183:116-21+ O '63
So we land on the moon, then what? Pop Sci 183:59-61+ D '63
Stay-putnik. Pop Sci 182:68-71 Mr '63
This is hi-fi? Pop Sci 182:72-5+ Mr '63
Those things you can't help doing. Pop Sci 184:90-2+ F '64
Will science find a safer cigarette? Pop Sci 185:60-1+ Jl '64
Wiring people for life. Pop Sci 185:66-8+ Ag '64
—and Luckett, Hubert
Low-down on hi-fi stereo. pors Pop Sci 183: 82-9+ S '63
Low-down on hi-fi stereo tuners. Pop Sci 185:102-5+ S '64
GILMORE, Ken
Advances in electron microscopy. Electr World 70:21-4+ Jl '63
Automatic electronic testing. Electr World 71:25-8+ Ja '64
Bionic computers. Electr World 69:25-8+ Mr '63
Electronics in banking. Electr World 69:29-32+ Ap '63
Integrated amplifier-speaker. Electr World 71:32-5+ Mr '64
Optical scanners; machines that read. Electr World 72:33-7+ O '64
GILMORE, Kenneth O.
Highway robbery in Massachusetts. Read Digest 85:83-7 D '64
Let's clean up this highway mess. Read Digest 85:86-92 N '64
—and Methvin, E. H.
REA, a case study of bureaucracy run wild. Read Digest 83:81-7 D '63
GILMORE, Tamara
Rise of Russian women. pors Sci Digest 54: 8-14 S '63
GILMORE, Volt
Volt Gilmore wins annual Travel award. il pors Travel 119:38-40 My '63

GILOT, Françoise
Living with a legend. J. Jacobs. Reporter 31:52+ D 3 '64
—and Lake, Carlton
Pablo Picasso's love: la femme-fleur; excerpt from Life with Picasso. por Atlan 214:79-84+ Ag '64

GILPATRIC, Roswell Leavitt
Cut in defense costs? what a top official says; summary of address, October 1963. U S News 55:16 N 4 '63
Expert looks at the joint chiefs. N Y Times Mag p 11+ Mr 29 '64
Gilpatric explains Defense decision policy. Aviation W 78:32 F 11 '63
Our defense needs. For Affairs 42:366-78 Ap '64
Strangelove? Seven days? not likely. N Y Times Mag p 15+ My 17 '64

about

Cut of twenty-five per cent in defense costs? por U S News 56:16 Mr 30 '64
Effort urged to ease effect of DOD shifts. K. Johnsen. Aviation W 79:31 N 11 '63
Gilpatric's records are new TFX issue. G. C. Wilson. Aviation W 79:27-8 N 11 '63
Senate TFX probers split on Gilpatrick. G. C. Wilson. Aviation W 79:27-9 N 25 '63

GILPIN, Laura
Austerity of the desert pervades her home and her work. il House B 105:144-5+ Ap '63

GILROY, Frank D.
Gilroy is here. por Time 83:43 Je 19 '64
Subject was roses. Criticism
America 110:853 Je 20 '64
Life 56:17 Je 19 '64
Life il pors 57:71-3 S 4 '64
Nation 198:611 Je 15 '64
New Yorker 40:86 Je 6 '64
Newsweek 63:69 Je 8 '64
Sat R 47:44 Je 13 '64
Time il 83:75 Je 5 '64
Vogue 144:30 Ag 1 '64

GILRUTH, Robert R.
Making of an astronaut. por Nat Geog Mag 127:122-44 Ja '65

GILSDORF, Gordon
Good woods; poem. Commonweal 80:602 S 4 '64

GILSON, W. E.
Differential respirometer of simplified and improved design. Science 141:531-2 Ag 9 '63

GIMENO, Carlos Mendoza. See Mendoza Gimeno, C.

GIN
Another in gin? Tanqueray English gin. il Newsweek 64:94+ O 12 '64

GIN rummy. See Rummy (game)

GINASTERA, Alberto
Concerto of quality: Ginastera's new violin concerto. I. Kolodin. Sat R 46:47 O 19 '63
Don Rodrigo. Criticism
Américas il 16:35-8 O '64
From the Argentine. A. Cohn. il por Am Rec G 31:397 Ja '65
On to surrealism; Violin concerto played by New York philharmonic. Time 82:75 O 18 '63

GINGER (spice)
These desserts are full of ginger! il Bet Hom & Gard 42:90 N '64

GINGER hero; story. See Friel, B.

GINGER man; drama. See Donleavy, J. P.

GINGERBREAD
Mama's gingerbread. il McCalls 92:136-7+ O '64
Successful recipes. il Suc Farm 61:71-2 N '63

GINGERICH, Karl A. See Hoekstra, H. R. jt. auth.

GINGERICH, Owen
Laboratory exercises in astronomy, special classification. Sky & Tel 28:80-2 Ag '64
Laboratory exercises in astronomy, the moon's orbit. Sky & Tel 27:220-1 Ap '64
Laboratory exercises in astronomy, the rotation of Saturn and its rings. Sky & Tel 28:278-9 N '64
Spiral galaxy of astronomers. Sky & Tel 25:132-4 Mr '63

GINGRICH, Arnold
Publisher's page. See issues of Esquire

about

Predicts puritan revolution. Christian Cent 81:1076-7 S 2 '64
Puritan revolution. America 111:224 S 5 '64

GINGRICH, Joe R. See Meyer, R. E. jt. auth.

GINIGER, Henry
Algerian aftermath. N Y Times Mag p32+ Mr 22 '64
Challenger talks back to President de Gaulle. N Y Times Mag p25+ Mr 15 '64
France's no. 2 mar N Y Times Mag p24+ Ja 5 '64
Pétain of Verdun, of Vichy, of history. N Y Times Mag p94-5+ N 15 '64

GINKGO
Ancient trees for modern gardens. E. S. Henderson. il Horticulture 41:448-9 S '63

GINN and company
Random house sells Blaisdell to Ginn. Pub W 184:44 Ag 5 '63

GINNA, Robert Emmett
Mercurial Mercouri. Sat Eve Post 236:24-5 My 25 '63

GINSBERG, Allen
Back on the open road for boys. A. Glaser. il pors Esquire 60:48-9+ Jl '63
Ginsberg's new poems. A. R. Ammons. Poetry 104:186-7 Je '64
Search for passion. J. Scully. Nation 197:329-30 N 16 '63

GINSBERG, H. L.
Hebrews & Hellenes. Commentary 36:333-6, 426+ O, D '63

GINSBERG, Louis
Gauges and gadgets; poem. McCalls 90:155 F '63
Swan; poem. Commonweal 79:129 O 25 '63

GINSBURG, Benjamin
Bronze mounts and a new label. Antiques 83:459 Ap '63

GINSBURG, Mirra
(tr) See Lagin, L. Glass of water
(tr) See Singer, I. B. Taibele and Hurmizah

GINSBURGH, Robert N.
Challenge to military professionalism. bibliog f For Affairs 42:255-68 Ja '64; Excerpts. por U S News 56:93 F 17 '64

GINSENG
America's oddest export: mysterious ginseng root. il Pop Mech 120:32 Ag '63
Man plant's return. H. L. Lawrence. il Natur Hist 73:34-7 My '64

GINZBERG, Eli
An expert tells how the draft can be changed; interview. por U S News 56:54-7 Ja 27 '64
How poor are American Negroes? New Repub 149:23-4+ O 12 '63
Negro's problem is the white's. N Y Times Mag p 14+ F 9 '64

GINZBURG, Ralph
Ginzburg passes. America 108:895 Je 29 '63
Knock on the door; censorship strikes a librarian at home. W. L. Purcell. Library J 88:526+ F 1 '63
Publisher of Eros loses obscenity appeal. Pub W 186:52 N 16 '64
Publisher of Eros sentenced to five years. Pub W 184:41 D 30 '63
Two definitions of obscenity. il por Time 81:44 Je 21 '63

GIONO, Jean
Prison of Jean Giono. M. Chapsal. Reporter 29:30-1 Jl 4 '63

GIORCELLI, Franco G. See Cigna, A. A. jt. auth.

GIORDAN, Alma Roberts
Green-eyed to the shallow-footed; poem. Commonweal 79:600 F 14 '64
Honeymoon is over; poem. McCalls 91:160 Je '64

GIORDANO, Umberto
Andrea Chénier. Criticism
Opera N il 27:14-15 Mr 2 '63
Opera N 27:17-20 Mr 2 '63
Opera N il 27:25-6 Mr 2 '63
On records; Andrea Chenier. Opera N 29:27 O 17 '64
On records; Andrea Chénier. J. W. Freeman. Opera N 27:35 Mr 2 '63

GIORDMAINE, J. A.
Interaction of light with light. Sci Am 210:38-49 bibliog(p 156) Ap '64

GIOVANNI, Norman Thomas di
Letter from Piemonte. New Repub 151:15-18 S 12 '64
Sullenness under the sun. Nation 196:287-9 Ap 6 '63

GIPPNER, Erika
At the marketplace; story. Atlan 213:85-8 Mr '64

GIPSY moths
Battle of the sexes; New Jersey pest control. Nat Parks Mag 38:18 S '64
Death scent for gypsies; carbaryl. il Time 84:55 Jl 17 '64
Gypsy moth in New York; DDT controversy. E. W. Littlefield. il Am For 70:42-5+ Ja '64

GIPSY music
Ballet, violins and shish kebab! Bihari. E. Caroll. il Dance Mag 37:27-8 D '63

GIRAFFES

Capture

See Animals—Capture

GIRARD, Alexander
Rural mural for a tractor maker. il Fortune 70:144-7 D '64
GIRARD, André
Painting on light. C. J. McNaspy. America 110:613-14 My 2 '64
GIRDERS
Cantilevered office in California Valley. il Arch Forum 118:120-1 Ap '63
GIRDLER, Reynolds
18,000,000 books nobody reads. Sat R 46:71+ Ap 13 '63
GIRDLES. See Foundation garments
GIRL athletes. See Women as athletes
GIRL everybody noticed; story. See Robinson, B.
GIRL in the curio shop; story. See Stanton, W.
GIRL next door; story. See Rackowe, A.
GIRL overhead; story. See Wallace, J. F.
GIRL scouts
Books; four new Girl scout handbooks. R. Adams. Esquire 61:38+ F '64
Conservation in a Girl scout camp; Rockwood National Girl scout camp, Potomac, Md. L. Knox. il Nat Parks Mag 37:14-16 N '63
Girl scouts promote all-new handbooks. il Pub W 184:43-5 S 9 '63
Girl scouts together; convention of the Girl scout national council. Newsweek 62:96 N 4 '63
GIRL who came to supper; musical comedy. See Musical comedies, revues, etc.—Criticisms, plots, etc.
GIRL who said no; story. See Heimer, M.
GIRL with the goat-cart; story. See Hale, N.
GIRLS
Any questions, please? J. Wescott. il Seventeen 22:8 Je '63
Are you the new kind of girl who fits in the new kind of world? M. M. Hunt. Seventeen 22:86-7+ O '63
Charmers; Italian and American. L. Barzini. il Vogue 143:57-8+ Ja 15 '64
From a boy's point of view. J. Wescott. il Seventeen 24:15 Ja '65
Girl-watching. D. Shulman. il Seventeen 22: 92-3+ Je '63
Grooming a future bride. J. R. Komaiko. il Parents Mag 39:42-3+ Ja '64
Growing up beautiful. il Redbook 120:76-7 Ap '63
How good a flirt are you? Seventeen 22:24 F '63
Likes of me for the likes of you; what boys like about girls. J. Wescott. Seventeen 22:16 O '63
Secret system: how boys grade girls. A. Penname. il Seventeen 23:142-3+ N '64
Speaking out; little girls are too sexy too soon. C. Shupp. Sat Eve Post 236:12+ Je 29 '63
Teen-age girl and the book market. K. Corinth. il Pub W 186:18-21 Ag 17 '64
Teen-age girls love horses, and what to do about it. il Changing T 17:45-7 N '63
Tomboy. B. M. Silverman. il Parents Mag 39: 50-1 Ag '64
Way we feel. Seventeen 22:143 Je '63
When your daughter wants to hunt. R. Starnes. il Field & S 67:12-14+ F '63
Why the girls scream, weep, flip. D. Dempsey. il N Y Times Mag p 15+ F 23 '64
Young living; questions and answers. A. Wood. See issues of Seventeen
See also
Adolescence
Camp fire girls
Daughters
Debutantes
Runaway boys and girls
Woman
Youth
GIRLS, Delinquent
New open door policy for wayward girls. H. Lees. il Ladies Home J 80:26+ S '63
People versus Baby. G. Samuels. il N Y Times Mag p40-1+ Ja 17 '65
See also
Gangs
GIRLS, Education of. See Education of women —United States
GIRLS, Short. See Stature
GIRLS clubs
Integrated club. B. Baum. il Parents Mag 38:62-3+ N '63
Our point of view of you, Jimmy Wescott; with reply by J. Wescott. J. Ferrell and K. Ferrell. il Seventeen 23:42-3 Ja '64
See also
Camp fire girls
GIRLS in books; drama. See Miller, H. L.
GIRLS of Killíni; story. See Vivante, A.
GIRLS of slender means; story. See Spark, M.
GIRLS rooms. See Childrens rooms
GIRLS schools. See Private schools
GIROUX, Robert
Farrar, Straus becomes Farrar, Straus and Giroux. Pub W 186:89 S 28 '64
GIRSON, Rochelle
Mutations in the body politic. Sat R 47:74-86+ Ag 29 '64
GISCARD D'ESTAING, Valéry
Group of ten releases report on International monetary system; statement, August 1, 1964. Dept State Bul 51:323-5 Ag 31 '64
about
France: rigid controls keep the lid on inflation. por Bsns W p 124 Jl 11 '64
Sincere budget. por Time 84:25 S 25 '64
GISH, Dorothy
Sixty years in show business. I. C. Kuhn. Nat R 14:504-5 Je 18 '63
GITT, Josiah W.
Pride of York County. il por Newsweek 65: 56-7 Ja 11 '65
GITTELSOHN, Roland B.
Changing dimensions of faith. Sat R 47:39-40+ Mr 7 '64
Where religion and science meet. Sat R 46: 23-4+ Mr 23 '63
World to make real. Sat R 47:26+ Ag 1 '64
GITTINGS, John
China's military strategy. Nation 200:43-6 Ja 18 '65
GITZO combine titrex. See Photography—Printing processes
GIUFFRE, Jimmy
Jazz concerts; Performing arts concert at Town Hall. W. Balliett. New Yorker 39: 97-9 Mr 2 '63
What is jazz? Newsweek 62:53 S 2 '63
GIULIANO, Salvatore
Profiles; the Mafia. N. Lewis. New Yorker 39:45-6+ F 15 '64
GIUSTI, George
George Giusti, graphic designer. F. Johnson. il por Am Artist 28:46-51+ D '64
GIVE her back; story. See O'Faoláin, J.
GIVE her love on a cloudy day; story. See Albee, G. S.
GIVING
Cassie and Beth discover the joy of sharing. il Good H 157:48+ D '63
English philanthropy, 1660-1960, by D. Owen. Review
New Repub 152:24+ Ja 30 '65. A. Welsh
For me? M. A. Rodgers. il Redbook 124:31+ Ja '65
Joy of giving. J. C. Cornelius. Read Digest 84:65-7 Ja '64
Man in Missouri; D. A. Mallory's donations to Buffalo, Mo. schools. Time 81:102-3 My 17 '63
Multiplying your dollars; Thanksgiving offerings help finance the feeding of needy persons overseas. Christian Cent 81:1453 N 25 '64
Profession: philanthropy; J. D. Rockefeller. III. il Bsns W p80-2+ Ja 16 '65
Put something in the pot. il Ebony 18:94-5 Mr '63
See also
Charities
Christmas gifts
Church finance
Tithes
GIVING blood; story. See Updike, J.
GIVING; story. See Doner, D.
GIZA, Egypt
Dandy day in the desert; photographs. Travel 122:39-41 D '64
GLACIAL epochs
Great infra-Cambrian ice age. W. B. Harland and M. J. S. Rudwick. il Sci Am 211:28-36 bibliog(p 116) Ag '64
Ice age national scientific reserve; with editorial comment. J. L. Dyson. il Nat Parks Mag 37:2, 4-9 Ag '63
Ice age started early. il Sci N L 86:341 N 28 '64
What caused the cold? il Time 83:50 Ja 24 '64
GLACIAL geology
Garnet ratios and provenance in the glacial drift of western New York. G. G. Connally. bibliog il Science 144:1452-3 Je 19 '64
Great infra-Cambrian ice age. W. B. Harland and M. J. S. Rudwick. il Sci Am 211:28-36 bibliog(p 116) Ag '64
Here is glacial polish; glacier-polished rock. il Sunset 132:57 Je '64

GLACIAL geology—*Continued*
Illinoian and Wisconsin (Farmdale) drifts recently exposed at Rockford, Illinois. M. M. Leighton and J. A. Brophy. bibliog il Science 139:218-21 Ja 18 '63
Microfossils in Wisconsinan loess and till from western Illinois and eastern Iowa. R. L. Jones and others. bibliog il Science 140:1222-4 Je 14 '63
Status of the pleistocene Wisconsin stage in central North America. R. F. Flint. bibliog il Science 139:402-4 F 1 '63

GLACIER NATIONAL PARK
Glacier: the park with everything. E. A. Bauer. il Field & S 69:39-41 Je '64
Winding trail to Sperry Glacier. il Sunset 131:34+ Jl '63
See also
Waterton-Glacier International Peace Park

GLACIER PEAK
Volcanic ash from Mount Mazama (Crater Lake) and from Glacier Peak. H. A. Powers and R. E. Wilcox. bibliog il Science 144:1334-6 Je 12 '64

GLACIERS
Chronology of a small glacier in eastern British Columbia, Canada. J. R. Bray. Science 144:287 Ap 17 '64
Glacier geophysics. B. Kamb. bibliog il Science 146:353-65 O 16 '64
Ice movement of valley glaciers flowing into the Ross Ice Shelf, Antarctica. C. W. Swithinbank. bibliog il Science 141:523-4 Ag 9 '63
Northern glacier advancing rapidly; Otto Fiord glacier, Ellesmere Island. Sci N L 85:73 F 1 '64

GLACIOLOGY. See Ice

GLADE, William P.
Wisconsin: Latin America's neighbor. Américas 15:34-7 Jl '63

GLADIOLUS
Creating gladiolus. D. A. Wise. il Horticulture 41:430 Ag '63
Dig gladiolus corms and store over the winter; photographs. Flower Grower 51:48 O '64
Gladiolus: All-America winners for 1965. P. F. Frese. il Pop Gard 16:11 F '65
Try gladiolus? don't hesitate. Sunset 132:182-3 F '64

GLADSTONE, Bernard
How to stay alive on a ladder. Pop Mech 120:166-9 Ag '63
Set-and-forget sprinkler systems. Pop Mech 120:150-6 Jl '63

GLAESSNER, Philip
Development financing and the Alliance for progress; statement, December 2, 1964. Dept State Bul 51:881-4 D 21 '64

GLAMOR. See Beauty, Personal

GLANDS
Intercellular channels in the salt-secreting glands of marine turtles. R. A. Ellis and J. H. Abel, jr. bibliog il Science 144:1340-2 Je 12 '64
Melatonin synthesis in the pineal gland: control by light. R. J. Wurtman and others. bibliog il Science 142:1071-3 N 22 '63
Melatonin synthesis in the pineal gland: effect of light mediated by the sympathetic nervous system. R. J. Wurtman and others. bibliog il Science 143:1328-30 Mr 20 '64
Rectal glands of marine and fresh-water sharks: comparative histology. M. Oguri. bibliog il Science 144:1151-2 My 29 '64
See also
Mammary glands
Pituitary body

GLANDS, Ductless
Life-giving balancing act. R. Campbell. il Life 55:68-81 N 8 '63
See also
Thymus gland
Thyroid gland

GLANDS, Lacrimal. See Lacrimal organs

GLANDS, Salivary. See Salivary glands

GLANDS, Sebaceous. See Sebaceous glands

GLANVILLE, Brian
Global madness of soccer. Holiday 35:116+ Mr '64
Roses in Burnt Oak; story. Mlle 59:76-7 Je '64
Twins; story. Sat Eve Post 237:56-8 Ja 25 '64
about
Sporting life. por Newsweek 63:74-5 Mr 23 '64

GLANVILLE-HICKS, Peggy
My beautiful Greek house, handmade for $2,000. Vogue 141:14+ Ap 1 '63

GLANZ zoomatel lense. See Lenses, Photographic

GLASER, Alice
Back on the open road for boys. Esquire 60:48-9+ Jl '63
Indian-head nickel: some words with himself. Esquire 61:58+ Mr '64

GLASER, Barney G.
Comparative failure in science. bibliog Science 143:1012-14 Mr 6 '64

GLASER, Joe
Three prime safety ingredients. por Yachting 114:54-5+ Ag '63

GLASER, Milton
Bowl of orange for a pick-me-up. il Sports Illus 21:40-7 D 14 '64

GLASGAL, Ralph
Checking stereo separation and phase. Electr World 70:37+ O '63

GLASGOW, Mary
Scholastic expands language-teaching aids. il por Pub W 185:33 Mr 30 '64

GLASHAN, John
London street scene. il Holiday 36:50-1 S '64
Shakespeare exposed. Holiday 35:58-63 Je '64
Three contemporary allegories. il Holiday 34:70-5 N '63

GLASKY, Alvin J. and others
Interferons: selectivity and specificity of action in cell-free systems. bibliog Science 144:1581-3 Je 26 '64

GLASS, Herbert
Beethoven's Christus am Oelberg. Am Rec G 29:860-2 Jl '63
La Cenerentola. Am Rec G 31:196-8 N '64
Hotter's third and best Winterreise. Am Rec G 29:561-3 Mr '63
Die Meistersinger. Am Rec G 31:26-8+ S '64

GLASS, Marvin
Inventing toys is no mere child's play. il pors Bsns W p40-1+ D 21 '63

GLASS
Amazing modern glass. il UNESCO Courier 17:28-9 F '64
Auto change no one will notice; float glass windows in GM cars. il Bsns W p52+ S 5 '64
Chemical strengthening of glass. J. S. Olcott. bibliog il Science 140:1189-93 Je 14 '63
Glass changes color; photochromic glass. Sci N L 85:84 F 8 '64
Glass revolution; float glass. il Newsweek 64:87 N 23 '64
Glories of glass. A. Pryce-Jones. House & Gard 123:152-3 My '63
New glasses darken as sky brightens. Sci N L 85:184 Mr 21 '64
Photochromic glass: it darkens in light, clears in darkness. E. Nanas. il Pop Phot 54:38+ My '64
Photochromic silicate glasses sensitized by silver halides. W. H. Armistead and S. D. Stookey. bibliog il Science 144:150-4 Ap 10 '64
President calls for review of tariffs on glass products. Dept State Bul 50:697 My 4 '64
Thickness of large glass lights crucial. il Arch Rec 135:172 Ja '64
Through a glass darkly; photochromic glass. il Time 83:36+ Ja 31 '64
Through a glass that darkens; reversible photochromic glass. Sci Am 210:59 Mr '64
See also
Glassware
Tektites

Decoration

New adventures with glass: decorating kiln-fired glass. M. L. Scarpino. il Sch Arts 64:34-5 Ja '65

Fogging

Anti-fog liquids and cloths. il Consumer Bul 46:43+ O '63

GLASS, Decorated. See Glass, Ornamental

GLASS, Optical
Techniques tomorrow. B. Sherman. Mod Phot 27:10-11 O '63

GLASS, Ornamental
Imprisoning glass. il Pop Mech 121:137 Ja '64
Poetry in glass. il Design 65:207-9 My '64
Poetry in three dimensions; Poetry in crystal exhibition at Steuben's. J. Ciardi. il Sat R 46:22-5 Ap 20 '63
Revival in glass. E. Sverbeyeff. il N Y Times Mag p 104-5 S 20 '64
Sculptured glass. il Design 66:34-5 S '64

GLASS, Safety
Glass doors should be made of safety glass. il Consumer Bul 47:43+ My '64

GLASS, Stained. See Glass painting and staining

GLASS, Structural
Glass screen shields glass wall from sun. il Arch Rec 133:210-11 Mr '63
New FHA requirements for glass. il Arch Rec 133:165 Ja '63

GLASS, Volcanic. See Obsidian

GLASS-blowers; novel. See Du Maurier, D.

GLASS blowing and working
Amateur scientist; blowing glass for the amateur laboratory. C. L. Stong. il Sci Am 210:129-30+ My '64
Glass blowing in the classroom. C. F. Gunther. il Sch Arts 64:29-32 Ja '65
Offhand glass blowing. D. Smith. il Craft Horiz 24:22-3+ Ja '64

GLASS construction
Faceted facade in Texas headquarters. il Arch Forum 118:123 Ap '63
In Texas the glass box goes 3-D; Tennessee building. il Arch Forum 119:124-31 S '63

GLASS cutting
Cut the best of circles with a drill press. W. G. Waggoner. il Pop Sci 185:132 Ag '64
How to make a glass-cutting board. il Pop Sci 183:132 N '63

GLASS doors. See Doors

GLASS electrodes. See Electrodes, Glass

GLASS etching
Engraving on glass. L. Lew. il Recreation 62:11 Je '63
Sculptured glass. il Design 66:34-5 S '64

GLASS fabrics
Bedspreads woven of glass. il House & Gard 125:214-15 My '64

GLASS fiber cars. See Automobiles—Materials

GLASS fibers
Aerojet moves into basic glass. J. F. Judge. il Miss & Roc 12:34-5 Mr 18 '63
Building a stock fiberglass cruiser. B. Cobb. jr. il Yachting 117:70-2+ Ja '65
Drop anchor at the fair. il Recreation 57:59 F '64
Fiber glass fabrics modify environment. A. W. Metzger. il Arch Rec 136:219-20 N '64
Fiberglass seats cut transportation costs. il Am City 78:116 Ap '63
Fiberglass; use of fiberglass-reinforced plastic for boats. G. M. Irvine, jr. il Motor B 114:22-7 D '64
Glass buckets; photographs. L. Smith. Hot Rod 17:38-9 O '64
How fair is a flip with the flexible pole? il Life 54:36 F 22 '63
Laboratory designed in fiber glass and plastics. il(p209) Sci N L 83:210 Ap 6 '63
Material with 33,000 uses. il Time 84:59 Jl 31 '64
Reinforced plastic forms produce sharply detailed concrete facade. il Arch Rec 135:182-? Je '64
Sixteen extra inches in fiberglas. S. James. il Pop Mech 120:114-15 S '63

GLASS fibers, Optical. See Fiber optics

GLASS houses
Wrapped up in itself. il House & Gard 123: 156-61+ My '63

GLASS industry
Glass by Erwin Eisch. H. Littleton. il Craft Horiz 23:14-17 My '63
See also
Corning glass works, Corning, N.Y.
Glass manufacture
Pilkington brothers, limited
Steuben glass, incorporated

GLASS jewelry. See Jewelry

GLASS manufacture
Crystal anniversary; Baccarat, celebrating its 200th. il Newsweek 63:79 Je 15 '64
Joel Myers and Blenko glass. J. Myers. il Craft Horiz 24:36-7 Mr '64
New strength in glass; float process. il Fortune 70:110-13 Ag '64
People who work in glasshouses. J. R. Foley. il Antiques 83:557-9 My '63
See also
Corning glass works, Corning, N.Y.
Glass blowing and working

History

Ancient glass. R. H. Brill. il Sci Am 209:120-30 bibliog(p 188) N '63
New England glass company: some discoveries. M. F. Rogers, jr. il Antiques 86:77-81 Jl '64
Pressed-and-blown glass. A. G. Peterson. il Hobbies 68:84-5 N; 82 D '63
Search for New Bremen and the glass of John Frederick Amelung. I. N. Hume. il Antiques 85:310-13 Mr '64
3,000 years of glass-making; excerpts from cracked about glass. A. Engle. il UNESCO Courier 17:20-7 F '64
Toledo's glass heritage; New England glass company. il Hobbies 68:53 O '63

GLASS marbles. See Marbles

GLASS menagerie; drama. See Williams, T.

GLASS MOUNTAIN. See Volcanoes

GLASS of water; story. See Lagin, L.

GLASS painting and staining
Edgar Miller; a versatile artist & craftsman. L. Bruner. il Am Artist 27:38-43+ My '63
Enamels and glass. il Craft Horiz 24:74-82 My '64
Glass on glass. B. J. Bramlett. il Sch Arts 62:39 Ap '63
Glory of glass. C. J. McNaspy. America 111: 462-4 O 17 '64
Marc Chagall's big year; stained-glass window in the United Nations Secretariat building and ceiling for the Paris Opéra. il Life 57:70-7 D 4 '64
Modern-day boom in an Old World art; stained-glass production. il Bsns W p 186-8+ O 17 '64
Restless glass; work of G. Meistermann. il Time 81:68-9 Mr 29 '63
Stained glass. H. Collins. il Sch Arts 63:35-8 D '63
Stained glass; 400 years in one family. P. Almasy. il UNESCO Courier 16:17-20 My '63
Stained glass is now a craft almost anyone can try. il Sunset 130:102-9 Mr '63
Stained glass; project of fifth and sixth graders. E. Radin. il Sch Arts 63:14-15 D '63

GLASS walls. See Walls, Glass

GLASS wax. See Cleaning compositions

GLASSCO, John Grant
Streamlining Canada's bureaucracy. por Bsns W p 100+ Mr 28 '64

GLASSES for the eyes. See Eyeglasses

GLASSFORD, Pelham D.
Bonus march. J. D. Weaver. il por Am Heritage 14:18-23+ Je '63

GLASSMAN, Edward. See Keller, E. C. jr, jt. auth.

GLASSWARE
All kinds of glassware. il Changing T 18:15-16 D '64
Atterbury's basket weave pattern. A. G. Peterson. il Hobbies 68:80-1 Mr '63
Atterbury's fern, lily and mirror patterns. A. G. Peterson. il Hobbies 67:78-9 F '63
Atterbury's prism and reeded patterns and selected nonpattern item. A. G. Peterson. il Hobbies 68:80-1 Ap '63
Baccarat. J. P. Boore. il Hobbies 69:82-5+ Mr; 82-4 Ag '64
Beilby glasses. R. J. Charleston. il Antiques 83:320-3 Mr '63
Carnival glass. M. T. Hartung. Hobbies 68: 90 F '64
Cup that cheers. il House & Gard 124:28-9 O '63
Empress pattern glass. A. G. Peterson. il Hobbies 69:87 D '64
English heroes honored in glass. T. H. Marsh. il Hobbies 68:86 My '63
Evolution of the medicine glass. G. Griffenhagen. il Hobbies 68:84-5+ Ja '64
Glass by Erwin Eisch. H. Littleton. il Craft Horiz 23:14-17 My '63
Glass reproductions. A. G. Peterson. Hobbies 68:84 My '63
Glass terminology. T. H. Marsh. Hobbies 69: 85+ O '64
Glass-ware patents by Henry Franz. A. G. Peterson. il Hobbies 68:82-3 F '64
Glass-ware patents of David Barker. A. G. Peterson. il Hobbies 69:66-7 Ag '64
Glassware patents of Daniel Bennett. A. G. Peterson. il Hobbies 68:82-3 Je '63
Glass-ware patents of John Bryce. A. G. Peterson. il Hobbies 69:74-5 S '64
Glass-ware patents of Washington Beck. A. G. Peterson. il Hobbies 69:82-3 O '64
Glass-ware patents; William King. A. G. Peterson. il Hobbies 69:72 Ja '65
Glass-ware prices way back when. T. H. Marsh. il Hobbies 69:78-9+ S '64
Glasswares by Apsley Pellatt. H. Wakefield. il Antiques 87:85-8 Ja '65
Glories of glass. A. Pryce-Jones. House & Gard 123:152-3 My '63
Great glass from American collections; pieces in Smithsonian exhibition assembled for sixth International congress on glass. P. V. Gardner. il Antiques 85:190-5 F '64
How far that little candle throws its beam; hands in glassware. T. H. Marsh. il Hobbies 69:84-5 Ja '65
Loop & dart with round ornaments pattern. B. G. Kaye. il Hobbies 68:84-5 Ag '63
Louis C. Tiffany, rebel in glass, by R. Koch. Review
Nation 199:469-70 D 14 '64. R. Howard
New England glass company: some discoveries. M. F. Rogers, jr. il Antiques 86:77-81 Jl '64
New York: glass of Czechoslovakia and Italy. P. Perrot. il Craft Horiz 24:42-7+ S '64

GLASSWARE—*Continued*
Notes on some types of American art glass. R. C. Barret. il Antiques 85:671-8 Je '64
Politics and the glass-maker. T. H. Marsh. il Hobbies 69:82-3 Jl; 74-5 Ag '64
Pressed glass; ten most popular patterns. il Am Home 66:71 Je '63
Royalty in glass; Queen Victoria golden jubilee plates. T. H. Marsh. il Hobbies 68:84-5 Jl '63
Sandwich glass. J. Peter. il Look 27:78-9 Je 18 '63
Search for New Bremen and the glass of John Frederick Amelung. I. N. Hume. il Antiques 85:310-13 Mr '64
Some English glass from colonial Virginia. I. N. Hume. il Antiques 84:68-71 Jl '63
Waterford glass. R. Kovel and T. Kovel. Hobbies 68:77+ My '63
See also
Corning glass center, Corning, N.Y.

Collectors and collecting

Glass souvenirs of the Grand tour. R. Charleston. il Antiques 83:665-9 Je '63
Rockwell collection of Carder's Steuben. E. E. Ericson. il por Hobbies 68:28-9+ My '63

Exhibitions

19th century cameo glass on exhibit. Hobbies 68:77 Je '63
Toledo's glass heritage; exhibition at the Toledo museum of art. il Hobbies 68:53 O '63

GLASSWARE, Ancient
Ancient glass. R. H. Brill. il Sci Am 209:120-30 bibliog(p 188) N '63
Birth of glass; excerpt from History of mankind. L. Woolley. il UNESCO Courier 16:18-19 Je '63
History revealed in ancient glass. R. W. Smith. il Nat Geog Mag 126:346-69 S '64
3,000 years of glass-making; excerpts from cracked about glass. A. Engle. il UNESCO Courier 17:20-7 F '64
Uranium contents of ancient man-made glass. R. L. Fleischer and P. B. Price. bibliog il Science 144:841-2 My 15 '64

GLASSWARE manufacture. See Glass manufacture

GLAUBER, Robert H.
Eichmann case. Christian Cent 80:681-2 My 22 '63
Shock treatment. Christian Cent 81:769-70 Je 10 '64

GLAUCOMA
Blindness you can prevent. A. Safir. Parents Mag 39:132-3 Je '64
Gains against glaucoma. il Newsweek 63:90 Je 8 '64
Movies through eye help study of vision. Sci N L 84:104 Ag 17 '63
Taste sensitivity to phenylthiourea in glaucoma. B. Becker and W. R. Morton. bibliog il Science 144:1347-8 Je 12 '64
Tracking down the enemies of vision. R. L. Masland. il Todays Health 41:52-7 N '63
Your eyes: their two worst enemies: cataracts and glaucoma. il Changing T 17:17-18 D '63

GLAUCOMYS sabrinus. See Squirrels

GLAUCONITE
Glauconite from the Precambrian belt series, Montana. R. A. Gulbrandsen and others. bibliog il Science 140:390-1 Ap 26 '63

GLAVES, Bob
Look, but don't touch. Flying 75:34-5 Jl '64

GLAZE, Andrew
Glory: poem. Sat R 47:21 Mr 14 '64

GLAZER, Nathan
Good society; excerpts from lecture. Commentary 36:226-31+ S '63
Herbert H. Lehman of New York. Commentary 35:403-9 My '63
Liberalism and the Negro. Commentary 37:25-42 Mr '64
Negro independence. Commentary 38:77-9 O '64
Negroes & Jews: the new challenge to pluralism. Commentary 38:29-34 D '64
Puerto Ricans. Commentary 36:1-9 Jl '63

GLAZER, Sidney
(comp) Articles and other books received: Near East. See issues of American historical review

GLAZES and glazing
Natzler glazes. O. Natzler. il Craft Horiz 24:24-7+ Jl '64
See also
Frits

GLAZUNOV, A. K.
From the Bolshoi: the first complete Raymonda. R. Sabin. il Am Rec G 30:1034 Jl '64

GLEASON, Andrew M.
Evolution of an active mathematical theory. bibliog Science 145:451-7 Jl 31 '64

GLEASON, Jackie
Great Gleason: TV's vast waistband. J. Reddy. por Read Digest 82:132-6 F '63
June Taylor dancers open with tap. Dance Mag 37:42-3 Je '63

GLEASON, John B.
Everybody's doing it. Outdoor Life 133:30-1+ F '64
I eat words, and rabbits. Outdoor Life 132:38-9+ N '63
Perch are running. Outdoor Life 133:66-8+ My '64
Perfect trout stream. Outdoor Life 132:50-2+ Jl '63

GLEASON, Norma
Believe me, you can lose weight! por Farm J 89:63+ Ja '65

GLEASON, Philip
Catholic intellectualism again. America 112:112-19 Ja 23 '65
Pluralism and the new pluralism. America 110:308-12 Mr 7 '64

GLEASON, Ralph J.
This year at Monterey. Sat R 46:118-19 O 12 '63

GLEASON, Robert W.
Anticlericalism, American style. Christian Cent 80:419-20 Ap 3 '63

GLEASON, Teddy
I don't request. il por Newsweek 63:62 Mr 2 '64

GLEASON, Thomas W.
New dock boss barks, but will he bite? por Bsns W p75+ Jl 27 '63
On the waterfront. Newsweek 62:61 Jl 29 '63

GLEAZER, Edmund J. Jr
Community college growth described at ATPI meeting; summary of address. Pub W 186:35-6 O 19 '64
Spokesman for the two-year college. G. Dapper. por Sat R 47:55 D 19 '64

GLEE clubs. See Choral groups and societies

GLEITMAN, Henry
Place-learning. Sci Am 209:116-22 O '63
—and Jung, Louise
Retention in rats: the effect of proactive interference. bibliog Science 142:1683-4 D 27 '63

GLEIZES, Albert
Albert Gleizes: underrated cubist. K. Kuh. il Sat R 47:32-3 O 31 '64
Autumn at the Guggenheim. M. Kozloff. Nation 199:203-4 O 5 '64
Gleizes: cubism as a way of life. D. Robbins. il por Art N 63:24-7+ S '64

GLEKEL, Newton
Mobile libraries in the park proposed by New York businessman. il Library J 88:2856 Ag '63

GLEN CANYON
Lake Powell is being filled. L. Corbeau. il Motor B 112:44-6 Ag '63

GLEN CANYON DAM
Glen Canyon Dam complex receives award from A.S.C.E. il Arch Rec 135:53 Ap '64
Glen Canyon recommended for ASCE award. il Am City 79:116 Mr '64

GLEN CANYON NATIONAL RECREATION AREA. See National parks and reserves—United States

GLENCOE, Ill.
Personal touch to preventive maintenance. R. H. Goodin. il Am City 79:47 Ja '64

Education

Restoration of report cards; symposium, ed. by P. J. Misner; with study-discussion program, by D. B. Harris and E. S. Harris. bibliog il PTA Mag 58:10-12, 36 F '64

GLENDALE, Calif.

Hospitals

Psychiatric clinic for a general hospital. il Arch Rec 134:182-4 N '63

GLENDALE people; story. See O'Hara, J.

GLENDENING, Fred
Tests tougher sealants at signalized intersections. Am City 79:109 Ap '64

GLENESK, William Bell
Brooklyn cleric and Fanny keep news media scrambling. Library J 89: 1575 Ap 1 '64
Drama at the altar; Spencer memorial Presbyterian church, Brooklyn Heights. il por Time 83:58-9 Ja 3 '64
Minister stirs up Brooklyn Heights. B. Day. por N Y Times Mag p88+ Je 7 '64
Rebel in a Brooklyn pulpit. S. Castan. il pors Look 27:59-60+ Mr 26 '63

GLENN, John Herschel, 1921-
Stairway to the stars. por NEA J 52:8+ Ap '63
Why astronauts sold their personal stories; interview. pors U S News 55:77-8 S 30 '63

about

Astronaut's progress; countdown in Ohio. R. L. Maher. il por Nation 198:131-3 F 10 '64
Astrowives in Ohio. il por Time 83:17-18 Mr 27 '64
Glenn in orbit. Nation 198:111 F 3 '64
In orbit. il por Time 83:13-14 Ja 24 '64
Inside the inner ear. il Time 83:68 Ap 10 '64
Into orbit. il por Newsweek 63:18 Ja 27 '64
John Glenn: aftermath of a bad year. J. Robbins and J. Robbins. il pors Redbook 124:44-5+ Ja '65
John Glenn gives up space to launch himself in politics; with report by L. Wainwright. il pors Life 56:36-36B Ja 31 '64
Notes and comment. New Yorker 39:21 F 1 '64
One used astronaut. por Newsweek 64:70-1 Ag 3 '64
Scrubbed. por Newsweek 63:25-6 Ap 13 '64
Scrubbed; Glenn withdraws from Ohio's primary. il por Time 83:23A Ap 10 '64
Shooting for the moon. Reporter 30:16+ Ja 30 '64
Sorrowful year. W. J. Coughlin. Miss & Roc 12:72 F 25 '63
Was John Glenn injured in space? H. Shuldiner. il pors Pop Sci 186:55-9+ Ja '65
What made John Glenn run? with editorial comment. H. H. Martin and D. Oberdorfer. il pors Sat Eve Post 237:21-5, 90 F 22 '64
Writing in the sky. M. E. Jenkins. PTA Mag 57:2-3 Ap '63

GLENNON, Maurade
From Dublin's fair city; story. Mlle 59:298-9 Ag '64

GLENTIES, Ireland
Fine day at Glenties. B. Friel. Holiday 33:22+ Ap '63

GLICK, Bruce
Possible cytoplasmic change in an immunologically competent tissue of the chicken. Science 142:485-6 O 25 '63

GLICK, J. Leslie, and Cohen, W. D.
Nocturnal changes in exidative activities of rat liver mitochondria. bibliog Science 143:1184-5 Mr 13 '64

GLICKSTEIN, Cyrus
Advances in ultrasonics. Electr World 71:25-6 F; 39-41 Mr '64 (to be cont)
Are you a potential electronics technical writer? Electr World 69:58-60+ My '63
Electronics lab technician: his role in industry. Electr World 70:40-2+ N '63

GLICKSTEIN, M. and others
Lateral geniculate nucleus and cerebral cortex: evidence for a crossed pathway. bibliog Science 145:159-61 Jl 10 '64
—See Miller, J. jt. auth.

GLIDDEN company
Glidden goes for less width but more depth. il Bsns W p60-2+ Mr 30 '63

GLIDERS (aeronautics)
Dornier is developing paraglider rocket. W. C. Wetmore. il Aviation W 80:65+ Ja 13 '64
First manned flight of Gemini-type glider called proof of feasibility. W. E. Wilks. il Miss & Roc 16:31 Ja 4 '65
Five-month test of Gemini paraglider paves way for operational development. C. M. Plattner. il Aviation W 79:60-1+ D 16 '63
Glider may be post-Apollo guinea pig. R. Hawkes. il Miss & Roc 12:26-7 F 11 '63
M-2 flight successes spur interest in lift reentry. R. Hawkes. il Miss & Roc 13:14-15 S 9 '63
NASA favors gliding parachutes for land recovery of spacecraft. Aviation W 81:61 D 14 '64
NASA re-entry paraglider nears first flight test. il Miss & Roc 12:16-17 My 13 '63
NASA tesifies that Rogallo wing is probably dead in Gemini program: Rogallo wing paraglider. H. M. David. Miss & Roc 14:21 F 24 '64
New parachutes float spacecraft to earth; Cloverleaf. Sci N L 87:25 Ja 9 '65
Para-sail drop tests with full-scale Gemini capsules due. R. D. Hibben. il Aviation W 81:50-2+ Ag 31 '64
Parasail to be proposed for Gemini. R. Pay. il Miss & Roc 15:22-3 Ag 31 '64
Plane that isn't; M-2 and HL-10. il Sci Digest 56:inside back cover O '64
Sailing like the birds; sailplane. E. Hall. il Sci N L 85:135+ F 29 '64
Sailplane trip difficult. Sci N L 84:219 O 5 '63

GLIDING and soaring
Silent wings; world soaring championships. il Time 81:66 Mr 8 '63

GLIMCHER, Melvin J.
Under poetic license; feedback principles applied to artificial limbs. J. Lear. por Sat R 46:87 D 7 '63

GLINKA, Mikhail Ivanovich
Coachmen's music. F. Grunfeld. Reporter 29:56+ O 10 '63
Record and a book: Mikhail Ivanovich Glinka. J. W. Barker. por Am Rec G 30:298-9+ D '63

GLIXON, David M.
Best of references. Sat R 46:36-7+ Mr 23 '63
On checking references. Sat R 47:57 F 22 '64
Reader's adviser, tenth edition. Pub W 186:34-5 S 21 '64
Road map to the fields of learning. Sat R 47:37-9+ Mr 21 '64

GLOAG, Julian
Celebration of a happy childhood. Sat R 47:36+ N 14 '64

GLOBE (Boston)
Zuppa soup, etc. C. W. Morton. il Atlan 213:120 Ap '64

GLOBE air ag. See Airlines—Switzerland

GLOBES
How to display and sell globes. Pub W 184:106 Ag 19 '63
In this orbiting age, every household needs a globe. P. Doherty. il House B 105:158-9+ My '63

GLOBES, Astronomical
Precision globes of Mars. J. A. Roth. il Sky & Tel 27:19 Ja '64

GLOBKE, Hans
Globke saga. Newsweek 62:41 Jl 22 '63

GLOBULAR clusters. See Stars—Clusters

GLOBULINS
Antibody activity in six classes of human immunoglobulins. J. L. Fahey and H. Goodman. bibliog il Science 143:588-90 F 7 '64
Antigen-binding activity of 6S subunits of β_2-macroglobulin antibody. K. Onoue and others. bibliog il Science 146:404-5 O 16 '64
Binding of an alpha globulin to hyaluronate-protein in pathological synovial fluids. J. Sandson and D. Hamerman. bibliog il Science 146:70-1 O 2 '64
Crystalline low molecular weight γ-globulin from a human urine. H. F. Deutsch. bibliog il Science 141:435-6 Ag 2 '63
Differences in the amino acid composition of a third rabbit antibody. M. E. Koshland and others. bibliog il Science 143:1330-1 Mr 20 '64
Macroglobulin from human plasma which forms an enzymatically active compound with trypsin. J. W. Mehl and others. bibliog il Science 145:821-2 Ag 21 '64
Structural differences between two types of heavy chain disease proteins and myeloma globulins of corresponding types. K. Takatsuki and E. F. Osserman. bibliog il Science 145:499-500 Jl 31 '64
Subclasses of human γ_2-globulin based on differences in the heavy polypeptide chains. W. D. Terry and J. L. Fahey. bibliog il Science 146:400-1 O 16 '64
See also
Gamma globulin

GLOBULINS in the blood. See Serum globulins

GLOMUS tissue. See Tissues

GLORIA; story. See Bongartz, R.

GLORIOSA. See Glory lilies

GLORIOUS failure; story. See Mills, H. B.

GLORIOUS sun; story. See Letton, J.

GLORY bowers
Clerodendrum, a shrub for southern gardens. A. Miller. il Pop Gard 14:25 My '63

GLORY lilies
Gloriosa: the climbing lily. Horticulture 42:53 Ja '64

GLOSSBRENNER, Alfred S.
Personalities. por Time 82:96 O 25 '63

GLOSSOLALIA. See Gift of tongues

GLOSTER, Jesse E.
Insurance among Negroes prior to the Civil war. bibliog Negro Hist Bul 27:42-3 N '63

GLOVER, E. Elizabeth, and Reid, J. H.
Unmet and future needs. bibliog f Ann Am Acad 355:9-19 S '64

GLOVER, Everett D. See Sippel, R. F. jt. auth.

GLOVES
To keep your hand in. il Time 83:42 My 8 '64
Well-dressed hands. H. Obolensky. il Redbook 122:82-3+ Ap '64

GLOVIER, Pauline
Cloisonné teapots. il(p 1) Hobbies 69:30 O '64
GLOW worms. See Fireflies
GLOWKA, Arthur
Stripers in the Hudson. Outdoor Life 134:20-3+ Ag '64
GLOXINIAS
Colorful gloxinia. B. Thompson. il House B 105:120-1+ F '63
Want gloxinias like those on our cover? il Bet Hom & Gard 42:132 N '64
GLUBB, John Bagot
Military mecca. M. Khadduri. por Sat R 47: 48-9 F 15 '64
GLUCK, Christoph Willibald
On records; Iphigénie en Tauride. Opera N 27:32 My 4 '63
Vox reissues its justly famous Orphée. M. de Schauensee. Am Rec G 29:872 Jl '63
GLUCK, Louis, and others
Experimental cardiac hypertrophy: concentrations of RNA in the ventricles. bibliog Science 144:1244-5 Je 5 '64
GLUCK, Louise
Delivering; poem. Mlle 58:72 D '63
GLUCOSE
Autonomic mediation of the effect of raised arterial glucose upon free fatty acids. C. J. Goodner and W. A. Tustison. bibliog il Science 146:770-2 N 6 '64
Glucose transfer from adenosine diphosphate-glucose to starch in preparations of waxy seeds. O. E. Nelson and C. Y. Tsai. bibliog il Science 145:1194-5 S 11 '64
Potentiation of 5-fluorouracil inhibition of Flexner-Jobling carcinoma by glucose. S. S. Kung and others. bibliog il Science 141: 627-8 Ag 16 '63
Trachoma agent: glucose utilization by purified suspensions. R. A. Ormsbee and E. Weiss. bibliog il Science 142:1077-8 N 22 '63
GLUE
Gluing isn't what it used to be; with chart. D. X. Manners. House B 105:98-9+ Jl '63
Roll on the glue. K. Murray. il Pop Sci 184: 109 Ja '64
Stick with the right glue. G. Daniels. il Pop Mech 119:179-83+ F '63
White glues. il Consumer Rep 29:385 Ag '64
See also
Adhesives
Cements, Adhesive
GLUE, Epoxy. See Epoxy adhesives
GLUE sniffing
Glue sniffing. W. C. Burgess. PTA Mag 58: 15-17 Mr '64
Glue sniffing solution seen in new chemical. Sci N L 85:344 My 30 '64
GLUECK, Eleanor (Touroff)
Five signs on the highroad. N. Gordon. il por Sat R 46:49-52 Ap 6 '63
GLUECK, Grace
Clubs, clubs, and more clubs. N Y Times Mag p44 Ap 7 '63
It's the thought that counts. N Y Times Mag p98+ D 1 '63
Now his is hers. N Y Times Mag p 45+ S 20 '64
Statistics, N.Y. N Y Times Mag p29+ Je 23 '63
Thoughts that count. N Y Times Mag p 121-2 D 13 '64
GLUECK, Nelson
Shards of history. il por Time 82:50-60 D 13 '63
GLUECKSOHN-WAELSCH, Salome
Lethal genes and analysis of differentiation. bibliog Science 142:1269-76 D 6 '63
GLUING. See Glue
GLUSHANOK, Peter
Every lens has a personality. Pop Phot 51: 112+ D '62
GLUSHKO, Valentin Petrovich
Mystery duo, engineers behind the Soviet space effort. Newsweek 62:73 N 25 '63
GLUTAMATE. See Monosodium glutamate
GLUTAMATE dehydrogenases. See Dehydrogenases
GLUTAMIC acid
Thalidomide: effects on enzymes of glutamic acid metabolism in mice. E. Hirschberg and and others. bibliog il Science 143:1343-4 Mr 20 '64
GLUTATHIONE
Glutathione as an inducer of feeding in ticks. R. Galun and S. H. Kindler. bibliog il Science 147:166-7 Ja 8 '65
GLUTTONS (animals) See Wolverines
GLYCERIDES
Four fats in the blood: which cause heart attacks? il Time 83:66-7 Je 19 '64
New drug lowers fats in blood stream: effect of Astromid S on triglycerides. Sci N L 85:40 Ja 18 '64
Triglycerides may be key in coronary disease. Sci Digest 53:45-6 F '63

GLYCOGEN
Glycogen-containing cells of estrogen-induced renal tumors of the hamster. J. A. Arcadi. bibliog il Science 142:592-3 N 1 '63
Glycogen deposition in the liver induced by cortisone: dependence on enzyme synthesis. O. Greengard and others. bibliog il Science 141:160-1 Jl 12 '63
Glycogen synthetase: its response to cortisol. H. G. Sie and W. H. Fishman. bibliog il Science 143:816 F 21 '64
Hypothermia, asphyxia, and cardiac glycogen in guinea pigs. J. S. Miller, jr. and others. bibliog il Science 144:1226-7 Je 5 '64
GLYCOPEPTIDES. See Peptides
GLYN, Caroline
I believe. por Seventeen 23:117 Jl '64
GLYNDEBOURNE festival. See Music festivals—England
GLYPHS. See Hieroglyphics
GMITRO, Carol
Hosteler's handbook Mlle 59:194-6 My '64
GNEISS
Analysis of variance of migmatite composition II: comparison of two areas. R. F. Ward and S. L. Werner. bibliog il Science 143:1032-3 Mr 6 '64
Analysis of variance of the composition of a migmatite. R. F. Ward and S. L. Werner. bibliog il Science 140:978-9 My 31 '63
GNOSTICISM
Another disciple is heard from; concerning The Gospel of Philip. il Time 81:57-8 Mr 8 '63
GNOTOBIOTICS. See Biological research
GO-kart racing. See Karting
GO-karts. See Karts (midget cars)
GOA
Goa: a case of indigestion. S. Rajan. Reporter 31:22 Jl 2 '64
GOAL seeking. See Aspiration level
GOAL values. See Values (psychology)
GOALS, National. See United States
GOAT hunting
Idaho's instant goat hunt. W. Galligan. il Outdoor Life 131:72-5+ Je '63
My wild Spanish goat; Catalina Island bow hunt. G. H. Gillelan. il Outdoor Life 135: 58-61+ F '65
See also
Rocky Mountain goat hunting
GOATS

Photographs

See Animals—Photographs
GOATS, Photography of. See Photography of animals
GOBERMAN, Max
Haydn renascence continues. R. C. Marsh. il por Hi Fi 13:78-9 N '63
Music makers. R. Gelatt. Hi Fi 13:67 Mr '63
GOBIES
Fish out of water? they like it that way; mudskippers. Sci N L 86:377 D 12 '64
GOBLE, Emerson
Behind the Record. See issues of Architectural record
GOD
Anselm: fides quaerens intellectum, by K. Barth. Review
New Yorker 39:203-6+ O 12 '63. J. Updike
Bishop of Woolwich speaks for the growing edge of Christian thought in America as well as Europe. D. Auchincloss. il Horizon 5:8-9 S '63
Christian belief in God, by D. Jenkins. Review
Christian Cent 82:18-19 Ja 6 '65. L. Gilkey
Future of God. J. Lear. il Sat R 47:173-5+ Ag 29 '64
God and the Bishop of Woolwich; excerpt from Honest to God; with reply by M. Ramsey. J. A. T. Robinson. il Horizon 5:4-7+ S '63
God's presence and absence; Africa's primitive religious cults. J. V. Taylor. Christian Cent 81:1136-8 S 16 '64
Honest to God, by J. A. T. Robinson. Review
Commonweal il 80:573-4+ Ag 21 '64. T. Merton
On the eclipse of God. E. L. Fackenheim. Commentary 37:55-60 Je '64; Discussion. 38:24+ D '64
Prospect for mankind. R. B. Fuller. Sat R 47: 26 O 3 '64
Why I believe there is a God; symposium (cont) Ebony 18:86 F; 80 Mr '63
Word (cont) V. P. McCorry. America 108: 623-4; 110:750 Ap 27 '63, My 23 '64

GOD—Continued
World belongs to God; address, May 19, 1963. D. Lyons. Vital Speeches 29:542-4 Je 15 '63
See also
Atheism
Creation
Holy Spirit
Natural theology
Theology
Trinity
GOD, Grace of. See Grace (theology)
GOD bless Captain Freddy and Private Ming! story. See Charyn, J.
GODBOUT, Oscar
Outdoor upsmanship. Read Digest 84:24D Je '64
GODDARD, George W.
Aerial reconnaissance R&D boost urged; excerpts from address. por Aviation W 80: 85-91 Ja 6; 86 Mr 6 '64
GODDARD, Maurice K.
Use of the dithyramb as a tool in small watershed management. Am For 69:29 Jl '63
—and Widner, R. R.
Job ahead for AFA. por Am For 69:6-7+ D '63
GODDARD, Robert Hutchings
How Lindbergh gave a lift to rocketry; excerpts from This high man: a biography of Dr Robert H. Goddard. M. Lehman. il pors Life 55:115-18+ O 4 '63
Robert H. Goddard. D. Wolfle. Science 146: 1639 D 25 '64
GODDARD college, Plainfield, Vt.
Goddard at twenty-five. Newsweek 61:88-9 Ap 8 '63
GODDARD space flight center. See United States—National aeronautics and space administration—Goddard space flight center
GODDEN, Rumer
Battle of the Villa Fiorita; novel. Sat Eve Post 236:48-9 O 5; 60-4 O 12; 62-3 O 19 '63
Bread. House & Gard 123:136-7+ Ap '63
Imaginary correspondence. Horn Bk 39:369-75 Ag '63
New blaze of India. Vogue 144:194-5+ D '64
Words make the book. Ladies Home J 81:32+ Ja '64; Same. Writer 77:14-17 Jl '64
GODE, Alexander
Computer for translating. Sci N L 83:374 Je 15 '63
GODETTE, W. B.
Electronic automation fills the bill. por Am City 78:99 N '63
GODING, M. Wilfred
Trust Territory of the Pacific Islands; opening statement, June 5 and closing statement, June 17, 1963. Dept State Bul 49: 207-19, 222-9 Ag 5 '63
Trust Territory of the Pacific Islands; statement, May 28, 1964. Dept State Bul 50:1007-18 Je 29 '64
GODOY, Ricardo Pérez. See Pérez Godoy, R.
GOD'S will; story. See Ugalde, M. de
GODSOE, William D.
Family unity and fitness too; reprint. Recreation 56:478 D '63
GOEBBELS, Joseph
Early Goebbels diaries 1925-1926, ed. by H. Heiber. Review
Commentary 35:272-6 Mr '63. W. J. Dannhauser
GOEBEL, Heinrich
Battle of the bulbs. H. F. Kutschbach. il por Pop Electr 21:44-5+ Ag '64
GOELLER, Carl
Greeting card market today. Writer 76:28-30 Mr '63
GOELLER, Friedrich B.
Auxiliary power by rule of thumb. Motor B 115:98-9 Ja '65
GOERG, Alfred J.
Bears with a handgun. pors Outdoor Life 135:28-31+ Ja '65
GOERGEN, Fritz Aurel
Giant jailed. il por Time 83:89 My 8 '64
GOETHE, Johann Wolfgang von
Goethe: a psychoanalytic study, by K. R. Eissler. Review
Commonweal 79:326-8 D 6 '63. K. Stern
Sat R por 46:29-30 Jl 20 '63. R. Plant
Limit to rapture. G. Paulding. Reporter 28: 62-3 F 14 '63
Voila un homme! P. W. Schmidtchen il por Hobbies 69:106-7 N '64
GOETT, Harry J.
Guest editorial. por Electr World 71:50 Je '64
GOETZ, Augustus, and Goetz, Ruth
Immoralist; dramatization of novel by A. Gide. Criticism
Commonweal 79:283-4 N 29 '63
GOETZ, Ronald
Baptist breakthrough. Christian Cent 81:1145 S 16 '64
GOETZ, Ruth. See Goetz, A. jt. auth.
GOFF, Georgena
Culture for the savages. por Redbook 120:6+ Ap '63
GOFFE, William
Hunt for the regicides. A. Winston. il pors Am Heritage 16:26-9+ D '64
GOGARTY, Oliver St John
Times I've seen: Oliver St John Gogarty, by U. O'Connor. Review
Newsweek 63:76+ Mr 30 '64
Sat R 47:43 Ap 4 '64. P. Colum
GOGERTY, Rex R.
Why I let them hunt on my place. Farm J 88:42G N '64
Wives help with farm work. Suc Farm 61:53 N '63
GOGH, Vincent van
Sweet and powerful. Newsweek 63:56 Ap 13 '64
Van Gogh and expressionism. B. Kaufman. Commonweal 81:110-11 O 16 '64
GOGOL', Nikolaĭ Vasil'evich
Diary of a madman; dramatization of story. Criticism
New Yorker 40:130+ Ap 25 '64
Real life on the edge of dreams. E. J. Simmons. por Sat R 47:29-30 Ag 22 '64
GOGOLAK, Charlie
Go, go, Gogolaks! R. Wallace. il pors Life 55:127-8 N 8 '63
GOGOLAK, Peter
Go, go, Gogolaks! R. Wallace. il pors Life 55:127-8 N 8 '63
GOHEEN, Robert F.
Liberal arts; address, January 26, 1963. Vital Speeches 29:318-20 Mr 1 '63
GOING ahead; story. See Williams, J.
GOING away; story. See Bingham, S.
GOING away; story. See Randal, V.
GOING steady; drama. See Nolan, P. T.
GOINS, William M.
Capital music maker. il pors Ebony 18:91-2+ Jl '63
GOLAY, Frank H.
Southeast Asia: an economist's viewpoint. Ann Am Acad 356:70-5 N '64
GOLD, Arthur
Quote: unquote; interview, ed. by R. Jacobson. por Mus Am 83:16 Ag '63
GOLD, Ben
Fair sailing. Motor B 113:110+ Ja '64
GOLD, Don
Choosing records for children. Ladies Home J 81:45-6 D '64
In God she trusts. Ladies Home J 80:66-7 N '63
GOLD, Ed
Just read the emergency instructions. Am City 79:22 Ag '64
GOLD, Herbert
Boy on fire. Sat Eve Post 237:28-9 S 12 '64
Caruso the truck driver; story. Sat Eve Post 237:56-8 Ap 4 '64
Dance of the divorced; story. Sat Eve Post 237:68-73 My 23 '64
Nobody's mad at Murphy. N Y Times Mag p42+ D 13 '64
Ring-a-ding resort. Sat Eve Post 236:22-3 Mr 30 '63
Survivors. Reporter 28:44-8 F 14 '63
What we must save: space. Horizon 6:120 Wint '64
about
Author. J. Poppy. por Sat R 46:46 Ap 20 '63
GOLD, Ivan
Big puff. Nation 198:462-3 My 4 '64
GOLD, John
(ed) See Boyden, A. How could it have happened again?
GOLD, T.
Ranger moon pictures: implications. bibliog Science 145:1046-8 S 4 '64
GOLD, Victor
Bounce high the head beams, Governor. Nat R 16:492 Je 16 '64
How the West was rapproched. Nat R 16:911 O 20 '64
Unthinkables. Nat R 14:278+ Ap 9 '63
GOLD, William Jay
Vulgar boatmen. Life 54:8+ My 17 '63
GOLD
Capsule history of gold. G. Kahn. Holiday 33:72-3 My '63
End of the gold age; controls on India's private gold holdings. Newsweek 61:40 F 4 '63
Sun-colored metal; new collection of pre-Columbian art at World's fair. il Time 83: 76-7 Je 12 '64
See also
Alchemy

GOLD—*Continued*

Therapeutic use

Gilding the veins. America 111:648 N 21 '64
Gold prevents adhesions; use of electrostatically charged leaves in surgery or medicine. F. Marley. il Sci N L 86:211 O 3 '64

GOLD as money
Beleaguered pound and the threatened dollar. M. J. Rossant. il Reporter 32:30+ Ja 28 '65
Cover coming off. Newsweek 65:68+ Ja 25 '65
Cross of gold. Reporter 29:20+ S 12 '63
Dollar and the international monetary system. J. W. Angell; reply with rejoinder. E. N. Adams. Science 140:1141-2+ Je 7 '63
Dollar: national and international bulwark; address, April 22, 1963. A. Hayes. Vital Speeches 29:490-3 Je 1 '63
Fighting the flow; Some questions & answers about gold. Time 85:66-7 Ja 22 '65
Foreign scapegoats; report by congressional Joint economic committee. H. Hazlitt. Newsweek 63:80 Ap 13 '64
Gold problem; a banker's view; reprint. F. N. Goodrich. U S News 54:116 Ap 22 '63
Gold talk. il Nat R 14:393-4 My 21 '63
Gold: the talk gets tough. Nat R 15:224 S 24 '63
Gold war. il Time 85:77-8 Ja 15 '65
Golden hoard; question of how much gold the world has. Time 84:85 Ag 7 '64
Good as gold. Newsweek 62:59-60 Jl 29 '63
If you're puzzled about gold: answers to some key questions. il U S News 58:96-7 Ja 25 '65
In search of a monetary constitution. ed. by L. B. Yeager. Review
 Nat R 14:459-60+ Je 4 '63. M. Palyi
No gold at all? H. Hazlitt. Newsweek 65:69 F 1 '65
Push to sell bonds in foreign currency. il Bsns W p88-9 Mr 30 '63
Red gold funnels to the West. Bsns W p31 O 19 '63
Suddenly, new worry about the dollar. il U S News 55:31 Jl 15 '63
Suppose the U.S. dollar were devalued. il U S News 55:32-3 Jl 29 '63
Taking the fun out of currency speculation. il Bsns W p 132+ Mr 14 '64
U.S. braces for drain on its gold: 25 per cent gold cover on U.S. money supply. il Bsns W p26-8 Ja 16 '65
U.S. improves balance-of-payments positions; increases gold holdings; statement; with report by Secretary Dillon. L. B. Johnson. Dept State Bul 51:752-3 N 23 '64
Waging the gold war. il Time 82:76+ Jl 26 '63
Warning bell rings; Congress to remove or reduce the 25 per cent gold cover. Bsns W p 148 Ja 23 '65
Wilting dollar. Nat R 14:521-2 Jl 2 '63
Yankee dollar. M. Mayer. Sat Eve Post 237:28-30 Ja 18 '64

GOLD coins. See Coins
GOLD cup regatta. See Motor boat racing
GOLD dollar. See Money—United States
GOLD in your garden; drama. See Asbrand, K.
GOLD Medal Wondra. See General mills, incorporated
GOLD mine at Jeremiah Flats; drama. See Anderson, R. A.
GOLD mines and mining

Russia

That Russian gold. il Time 83:107-8 My 15 '64

South Africa

African gold loses glitter; Consolidated gold fields of South Africa, ltd. Bsns W p30 Je 1 '63

United States

Digging for gold over one mile deep; Homestake mine. J. Liston. il Pop Sci 185:68-71 N '64
Early mining achievement. H. D. Brown. il Hobbies 68:124-5 Je '63
Era of discovery. P. M. Tilden. il Natur Hist 72:58-64 Ag '63
Gold digs; Homestake mine. il Newsweek 63:85+ My 25 '64
No place for a lady; condensation of Cripple Creek days. M. B. Lee. il Read Digest 84:255-60+ My '64

GOLD mining in art. See Art—Themes
GOLD prospecting. See Prospecting
GOLD reserves. See Gold as money
GOLD standard. See Gold as money

GOLDBERG, Albert
L.A.'s golden age. Opera N 29:22-3 S 26 '64

GOLDBERG, Albert L. See Miller, W. C. jt. auth.

GOLDBERG, Arthur Joseph
Arthur J. Goldberg talks to teens. por Seventeen 22:104+ Je '63
Constitutional right to publish; excerpts from address, May 1, 1963. U S News 54:120 My 13 '63
Court sits, in the center of the storm. por N Y Times Mag p30+ N 8 '64
Creative use of leisure time; address, November 11, 1963. Mus Am 83:161 D '63
Equal justice for the poor, too. N Y Times Mag p24+ Mr 15 '64
Excerpt from statement, April 12, 1962. Cong Digest 43:236+ O '64
Mr President, you aren't sufficiently informed; excerpts from interviews, ed. by T. G. Harris. por Look 28:58 N 17 '64
Pay for crime victims? excerpts from address. U S News 56:16 F 24 '64
Speaking of the split; excerpts from address. por Time 82:17-18 Ag 23 '63

about

In High court: when Goldberg says yes, White says no. por U S News 54:65 My 27 '63
Nightmare for oil marketers; Sun oil case. Bsns W p66 Ja 19 '63

GOLDBERG, Beverly R.
Park provides a living monument. Recreation 56:313-14 S '63

GOLDBERG, Dorothy
Island of time; condensation of Creative woman. por Redbook 121:52-3+ My '63

GOLDBERG, Elias
Elias Goldberg paints a picture. L. Campbell. il por Art N 62:42-5+ N '63

GOLDBERG, Erwin
Lactic and malic dehydrogenases in human spermatozoa. bibliog Science 139:602-3 F 15 '63

GOLDBERG, Harvey
Masked civil war. Nation 197:3-7 Jl 6 '63
Le parti d'intelligence? Nation 199:496-9 D 21 '64

GOLDBERG, Hyman
Prudence Penny. pors Sat Eve Post 236:40+ D 7 '63

about

My son the cook. il por Time 82:96+ O 4 '63
Prudence; concerning Prudence Penny cooking column in the Mirror. New Yorker 39:36-7 S 14 '63

GOLDBERG, Irving A. See Murphy, J. R. jt. auth.

GOLDBERG, Joe
Cecil Taylor and the new tradition. Sat R 46:42-3 F 9 '63

GOLDBERG, Leo
Space astronomy; summary of address. por Sky & Tel 28:264-6 N '64

GOLDBERG, Michael
Michael Goldberg paints a picture. W. Berkson. il pors Art N 62:42-5+ Ja '64

GOLDBERG, Paul
Free radicals and reactive molecules in clathrate cavities. bibliog Science 142:378-9 O 18 '63

GOLDBERG, Rube
Rube (A) to Rube (B). il Newsweek 63:87 My 4 '64
To make them laugh. il por Time 83:66 My 1 '64

GOLDBERG, Stanley
On laws that govern the growth of science. Science 140:639-41 My 10 '63

GOLDBERG, Vicki
Mondrian is a paper napkin. Horizon 5:90-1 My '63

GOLDE, Roger A.
Practical planning for small business. bibliog f Harvard Bsns R 42:147-55+ S '64

GOLDEN, Charles Franklin, bp
Easter in Jackson. J. K. Mathews. Christian Cent 81:478-80 Ap 15 '64

GOLDEN, Francis
When the shad come home from the sea. il Sports Illus 20:40-8 Mr 16 '64

GOLDEN, Harry
Dime was our passport. Travel 122:50-2 S '64
Last of the personal journalists? (cont) Sat R 46:48 F 9 '63

GOLDEN, James L.
Moments to remember; last four years; address, May 29, 1964. Vital Speeches 30:570-2 Jl 1 '64
Political speaking since the 1920's; address, August 20, 1963. bibliog Vital Speeches 29:763-7 O 1 '63

GOLDEN, John
Initiation into Broadway; excerpt from September child, with introduction by J. Harris. il Theatre Arts 47:19-21+ Ag '63
GOLDEN, L. L. L.
Public relations. See second issue of each month of Saturday review
Time out for a troubled neighbor. Sat R 47: 28-9 Jl 4 '64
GOLDEN, Martin
Selective calling for two-way radio. Electr World 69:41-4+ Je '63
GOLDEN, Roy A.
How to use your family check list. Suc Farm 61:109-10 Ap '63
Paying guests on the farm? check your liabilities! Suc Farm 62:36 Ag '64
GOLDEN boy; musical comedy. See Musical comedies, revues, etc.—Criticisms, plots, etc.
GOLDEN door resort. See Health resorts, watering places, etc.
GOLDEN eagles. See Eagles
GOLDEN evenings; story. See Stanton, W.
GOLDEN key award. See Rewards, prizes, etc.
GOLDEN retrievers
Gorgeous golden. D. M. Duffey. il Outdoor Life 133:120-2+ Je '64
Rise of goldens. J. Stetson. il Field & S 68: 96-7 D '63
GOLDENBERG, Carl
Canada's labor umpire faces first rhubarb. por Bsns W p 100+ O 24 '64
GOLDENRAIN trees
Eye-catcher, the goldenrain. il Sunset 131: 162 Jl '63
GOLDENSOHN, Eli S. and Purpura, D. P.
Intracellular potentials of cortical neurons during focal epileptogenic discharges. bibliog Science 139:840-2 Mr 1 '63
GOLDENSON, Loreen
Roar, Republicans, roar! Seventeen 23:63 O '64
GOLDENSON, Robert M.
Games that make children think. Parents Mag 39:58-9+ Je '64
Guide to play and playthings. Parents Mag 39:62-3+ O '64
GOLDFADER, Ed
Vanishing Americans. il por Newsweek 63:88 F 24 '64
GOLDFARB, Robert W. See James, S. jt. auth.
GOLDFARB, Ronald
Crime, wealth and justice. New Repub 151:15-16 Ag 22 '64
Declaring a war on injustice. New Repub 152:15-17 Ja 16 '65
Ensuring fair trials. New Repub 150:11-14 F 29 '64
Great bail scandal. New Repub 150:14-17 Je 6 '64
James V. Bennett's prisons. New Repub 151: 5 S 12 '64
TV and the Supreme court. Commonweal 81:150-1 O 30 '64
GOLDFISH
Flicker fusion frequency of electroretinogram in light-adapted goldfish at various temperatures. I. Hanyu and M. A. Ali. bibliog il Science 140:662-3 My 10 '63
GOLDHABER, Maurice
Omega minus. New Yorker 40:39-40 Mr 7 '64
GOLDHABER, Maurice—See Feinberg, G. jt. auth.
GOLDHABER, Paul
Heparin enhancement of factors stimulating bone resorption in tissue culture. bibliog Science 147:407-8 Ja 22 '65
GOLDHURST, William
Martinet or martyr. Horizon 5:42-8 S '63
GOLDIE, Grace Wyndham
Goldie's gang. Newsweek 61:86 Ap 29 '63
GOLDILOCKS at graveside; story. See Shaw, I.
GOLDING, Morton J.
Bruise-proofing your playground. Pop Mech 120:88-90+ S '63
GOLDING, William
Advice to a nervous visitor. Holiday 34:42-3+ Jl '63
Conversation with Golding; interview, ed. by D. M. Davis. New Repub 148:28-30 My 4 '63
Copernicus: a universe revealed. Holiday 35: 56-61+ Ja '64
Digging for pictures. Holiday 33:86-7+ Mr '63
Party of one. Holiday 33:10+ Ap; 34:12+ D '63; 35:12+ My '64

about

Appeal of Golding. L. M. Grande; reply with rejoinder. F. E. Kearns. Commonweal 77: 569-71 F 22 '63
Building a monument. G. Steiner. Reporter 30:37-9 My 7 '64
–Golding's view of man. J. M. Egan; discussion. America 108:242+ F 23 '63
–Is Golding Calvinistic? a more optimistic interpretation of the symbolism found in Lord of the flies. America 109:18-20 Jl 6 '63
–Lord of the flies. R. Gutwillig. il Vogue 141: 154-7+ My '63
–Lord of the flies goes to college; symposium. New Repub 148:27-8 My 4 '63
Old story well told; commentary on William Golding's Lord of the Flies. W. R. Mueller. Christian Cent 80:1203-6 O 2 '63; Reply. V. Eller. 80:1440 N 20 '63
Reader's choice. W. Barrett. Atlan 213:135-6 My '64
Salinger and Golding: conflict on the campus. F. E. Kearns; discussion. America 108:242+ F 23 '63
GOLDMAN, A. Bruce
Photographer is a rabbi. C. Schwalberg. il por U S Camera 26:66-9+ O '63
GOLDMAN, Albert
Comedy of Lenny Bruce. Commentary 36: 312-17 O '63
Listening to jive talk. New Repub 151:34-6 N 28 '64
Predicament of the Jewish musician. Commentary 35:102-11; 36:74 F, Jl '63
Television. New Repub 150:27-8 F 22; 31+ Ap 11; 34-5 Je 13 '64
Trial of Lenny Bruce. New Repub 151:13-14 S 12 '64
GOLDMAN, Bernard
Bronzes of Luristan. Natur Hist 73:12-21 My '64
GOLDMAN, Eric F.
Can public men have private lives? N Y Times Mag p 13+ Je 16 '63
Is Washington too powerful? N Y Times Mag p22+ Mr 1 '64
Making of foreign policy; television interview, January 11, 1964. Dept State Bul 50:164-76 F 3 '64
Summer Sunday; excerpt from Incident in Coatesville. Am Heritage 15:50-3+ Je '64

about

People of the week. por U S News 56:20 F 17 '64
GOLDMAN, Jordan
Banish freeze-and-fry home heating. Pop Mech 120:172-7+ O '63
Jet propulsion. Motor B 111:50-1+ F '63
GOLDMAN, Marshall I.
Balance sheet of Soviet foreign aid. For Affairs 43:349-60 Ja '65
Economic controversy in the Soviet Union. For Affairs 41:498-512 Ap '63
GOLDMAN, Michael
Crack; poem. New Yorker 40:57 O 10 '64
Lime umbrella; poem. New Yorker 39:38 Je 8 '63
Resistance to music; Skill; Caverned from the storm; poems. Poetry 103:251-2 Ja '64
Sense of crisis; poem. Atlan 213:73 My '64
Three poems: Journeys; Dawn: embarking for Sicily; Head of state. Yale R 53:234-6 D '63
GOLDMAN, Phyllis
Try winter aconite. Horticulture 41:539 O '63
GOLDMAN, Phyllis W.
Parent and child. N Y Times Mag p34 F 2; 83-4 Mr 8; 79-80 Ap 12; 58+ Je 14; 47-8 Je 28; 94+ N 29 '64; 58 Ja 10 '65
—See Goldman, R. P. jt. auth.
GOLDMAN, Robert P.
Dial a psychiatrist. Sat Eve Post 236:41-2 N 23 '63
Dope invades the suburbs. Sat Eve Post 237: 19-25 Ap 4 '64
Fantastic krebiozen story. Sat Eve Post 237: 15-19 Ja 4 '64
5,600,000 of us are mentally retarded. N Y Times Mag p31+ N 22 '64
Instant happiness. Ladies Home J 80:67-71 O '63
New medical device spots hidden diseases. Sat Eve Post 236:44-6+ S 28 '63
—and Goldman, P. W.
Parent and child. N Y Times Mag p87-8 Mr 15; 26 S 6 '64
GOLDMARK, John
Birchers lose. P. Jacobs. New Repub 150:5 F 8 '64
Fair verdict. Nation 198:110 F 3 '64
Fallout from the Times. Time 84:44 D 18 '64
Limits of political invective. por Time 83:58 Ja 31 '64
Ordeal in Okanogan. G. Bassett. Nation 197: 454-6 D 28 '63
Vindication. Newsweek 63:26 F 3 '64

GOLDMARK, Sally
Birchers lose. P. Jacobs. New Repub 150:5 F 8 '64
Fallout from the Times. Time 84:44 D 18 '64
Limits of political invective. por Time 83:58 Ja 31 '64
Ordeal in Okanogan. G. Bassett. Nation 197: 454-6 D 28 '63
Vindication. Newsweek 63:26 F 3 '64
GOLDOVSKY grand opera theater
Tosca on the road; at Queens college. A. M. Lingg. Opera N 28:33 Ja 4 '64
GOLDRATH, Bert
Boating. Sports Illus 18:52-4 Mr 18 '63
Polaroid camera means business. U S Camera 27:22+ Je '64
Sliding up a damp chute. Field & S 68:46-7 Jl '63
There's a way to ride a river; conquering the wild, white Rogue. Pop Mech 119:104-6 My '63
GOLDREICH, Arthur
Escape artists. por Time 82:25 Ag 30 '63
GOLDREICH, Gloria
Street of the prophets; story. Commentary 38:55-60 N '64
GOLDRING, Sidney, and others
Caudate-induced cortical potentials: comparison between monkey and cat. bibliog Science 139:772 F 22 '63
GOLDSCHMIDT, Arthur
Development of the U.S. South; with biographical sketch. Sci Am 209:28, 224-30+ bibliog(p310) S '63
GOLDSHOLL, Morton
Morton Goldsholl, art director of the year. E. M. Ettenberg. il por Am Artist 28:22-7+ S '64
GOLDSMITH, Arthur
Bargains in great photographs. Pop Phot 55: 58-61+ D '64
Seven steps to good composition. Pop Phot 53:137-53+ D '63
GOLDSMITH, Harris
Anthology of pianism from a more poetic age. Hi Fi 14:66-7 F '64
Beethoven and Brahms with a master's stamp. Hi Fi 14:124-6 O '64
Brahms piano concertos in fruitful collaborations. Hi Fi 13:70-1 Mr '63
For Schubert, dissimilar excellences. Hi Fi 14:70-1 Ap '64
For Schumann, a sonic replacement; for Rubinstein, artistic vindication. Hi Fi 13: 71-2 Ag '63
From among the symphonic treatises of Anton Bruckner. Hi Fi 13:67-8 D '63
From the legacy of Clara Haskil, Chopin and Falla. Hi Fi 13:77-8 N '63
In Debussy, a special valedictory. Hi Fi 14:77-8 D '64
New revelations of the Choral Fantasia. Hi Fi 14:67-8 S '64
On two recital discs, debut of a new Czech pianist. Hi Fi 13:74-5 Ap '63
With the Philadelphians in 1941, Toscanini's Schubert Ninth. Hi Fi 13:125-6 O '63
GOLDSMITH, John R.
Air pollution and health. Science 145:184-6 Jl 10 '64
Air pollution and medical research. Science 141:832-4 Ag 30 '63
GOLDSMITH, Timothy H. and others
Sensitivity of visual receptors of carotenoid-depleted flies: a vitamin A deficiency in an invertebrate. bibliog Science 146:65-7 O 2 '64
GOLDSMITHING
See also
Jewelry
GOLDSTEIN, Bernard, and Indik, B. P.
Unionism as a social choice: the engineers' case. bibliog f Mo Labor R 86:365-9 Ap '63
GOLDSTEIN, E. R. and others
Collagenolytic activity of intact and necrotic connective tissue. bibliog Science 146:942-4 N 13 '64
GOLDSTEIN, Harry
Photography at Tucson high. il por U S Camera 27:50-1+ Mr '64
GOLDSTEIN, Herbert
Planning for the educable mentally retarded. NEA J 53:34-5 My '64
GOLDSTEIN, J. L. See Joslyn, M. A. jt. auth.
GOLDSTEIN, Marvin H. See Wedeen, R. P. jt. auth.
GOLDSTEIN, Mortimer D.
International monetary fund: its work and its future. Dept State Bul 49:465-76 S 23 '63
GOLDSTEIN, Richard M.
Radar observations of Jupiter. bibliog Science 144:842-3 My 15 '64
—See Carpenter, R. L. jt. auth.
—and Gillmore, W. F.
Radar observations of Mars. Science 141: 1171-2 S 20 '63
GOLDSTEIN, S. J. Jr
Radio astronomy. Science 146:1605-6 D 18 '64
GOLDSTEIN, Walter
Teaching about the United Nations. bibliog Sr Schol 83:11T N 22 '63
GOLDWASSER, E. See Gallien-Lartigue, O. jt. auth.
GOLDWATER, Barry Morris
Barry Goldwater talks about liberals and liberalism; excerpts from address, June 27, 1963. pors U S News 55:44-5 Jl 8 '63
Busing for racial balance is wrong; excerpts from address, October 16, 1964. U S News 57:97 N 2 '64
Campaign issues: Goldwater opens his drive: address, September 3, 1964. por U S News 57:92-5 S 14 '64; Same with title Peace through strength. Vital Speeches 30:743-6 O 1 '64
Candidate's creed; excerpts from acceptance speech. Time 84:18 Jl 24 '64
Candidates spell out the issues. por N Y Times Mag p23+ N 1 '64
Defense lag; address, August 10, 1964. Vital Speeches 30:676-8 S 1 '64
Economic realities; address, January 15, 1964. Vital Speeches 30:234-7 F 1 '64
Excerpt from address, August 25, 1960. Cong Digest 42:203+ Ag '63
Excerpt from address, April 18, 1964. Cong Digest 43:237+ O '64
Excerpt from address, January 15, 1963. Cong Digest 42:235+ O '63
Exclusive interview: Goldwater speaks his mind. pors U S News 57:46-9+ D 21 '64
Failure of our foreign policy; address, October 21, 1964. Vital Speeches 31:36-8 N 1 '64; Excerpts. U S News 57:96-7 N 2 '64
Foreign policy; some thoughts of the nominee. New Repub 151:14 Jl 25 '64
From party leaders: Republican future; excerpts from news conference. por U S News 57:68 N 16 '64
Goldwater defense philosophy; excerpts from Where I stand. Aviation W 81:11 Ag 31 '64
Goldwater defines conservatism; interview. pors N Y Times Mag p25+ N 24 '63
Goldwater on foreign policy; excerpts from address, September 9, 1964. U S News 57:118 S 21 '64
Goldwater on Goldwater: where he stands on issues; English transcript of an interview published in Der Spiegel. por U S News 57: 70-2 Jl 20 '64
Goldwater: Republicans will cut taxes, reduce debt; excerpts from address, September 8, 1964. por U S News 57:117 S 21 '64
Goldwater speaks; quotations, ed. by F. Knebel. pors Look 28:81-2+ Ap 21 '64
Goldwater's economics; interview. il por Bsns W p 176-8+ S 26 '64
Goldwater's opening gun; victory will be ours; address, July 16, 1964. pors U S News 57:92-6 Jl 27 '64; Same with title Republican national convention. Vital Speeches 30:642-4 Ag 15 '64
Growing political issue; America's atomic strength; excerpts from statements. por U S News 57:8 Ag 24 '64
Interview with Goldwater; ed. by B. Bradlee. por Newsweek 62:37 O 21 '63
Let me assure you; key remarks from address. Time 84:14 Ag 21 '64
Letters to a daughter. por Ladies Home J 81:64-5+ O '64
My case for the Republican party, 1964. por Sat R 47:21-3+ O 17 '64
My proposals for a can-win foreign policy. por Life 56:30B-30D Ja 17 '64
School aid: what LBJ and Goldwater believe; excerpt from statement. U S News 57:15 S 28 '64
Some new views of Senator Goldwater; summary of statements. por U S News 57:10 Ag 3 '64
Speaking out. por Sat Eve Post 236:10+ Ap 13 '63
Statements on education by the Democratic and Republican presidential candidates. por NEA J 53:12-13 O '64
Taking a stand on issues: Goldwater's own words; excerpts from statements and addresses. por U S News 55:44-6 Jl 15 '63
Test ban treaty; only an illusion of peace; address, September 1963. Vital Speeches 29:767-8 O 1 '63
Views on the future of the U.S. in space; statement. por Miss & Roc 15:16-18 O 26 '64
We have a challenge to security; excerpts from address, August 13, 1963. por (p55) U S News 55:66-7 Ag 26 '63

GOLDWATER, Barry Morris—*Continued*
Where does Goldwater stand? interview. pors U S News 55:34-41 S 2 '63
Where I stand on farming; questions and answers. por Farm J 88:32-3+ O '64
Why Goldwater said no to civil-rights bill; address, June 18, 1964. U S News 56:67-8 Je 29 '64
Will to be strong; address, September 23, 1964. Vital Speeches 31:5-7 O 15 '64
World problems and national security; address, April 25, 1963. Vital Speeches 29: 482-6 Je 1 '63

about

Abandoning the middle of the road. Bsns W p 148 Jl 25 '64
Across the Nation: the story of the '64 election; with charts. il U S News 57:38-44 N 16 '64
Aerospace politics. Nation 199:262 O 26 '64
After the deluge. K. Crawford. Newsweek 64: 37 S 28 '64
After the fall: to the mainstream? Newsweek 64:31-2 N 9 '64
After the primaries. R. Moley. Newsweek 63:92 Je 22 '64
Ahead for Goldwater: struggle for leadership. il por U S News 57:20 N 16 '64
Air force candidate Goldwater. R. D. Senter. New Repub 151:8 S 5 '64
Alien reviews the election. E. v. Kuehnelt-Leddihn. Nat R 16:1058 D 1 '64
All sorts of roads. il Time 82:24 N 1 '63
Ambassador Lodge running strong. il por Newsweek 63:21-5 Mr 23 '64
Anatomy of the Goldwater boom. T. Wicker. il pors N Y Times Mag p7+ Ag 11 '63; Discussion. p 16+ Ag 25 '63
And still, Goldwater can win. F. S. Meyer. Nat R 15:528 D 17 '63
Another campaign issue: wealth of candidates. il U S News 57:14 Ag 24 '64
Answers for conservatives; questions and answers. W. F. Buckley, jr. por Nat R 16: 145-6+ F 25 '64; Discussion. 16:293 Ap 7 '64
Antidote to extremism; concerning acceptance speech. Christian Cent 81:955-6 Jl 29 '64
As high school students see it. il Sr Schol 85:11 O 28 '64
As '64 campaign gets going. il por U S News 57:31-2 Jl 20 '64
As Republicans close ranks. il por U S News 57:34-5 Ag 24 '64
As the campaign got rougher. por U S News 57:11 O 19 '64
As the race ends: who'll win? il pors U S News 57:25-31 N 2 '64
Atlantic report; Goldwater's views. Atlan 214:6+ S '64; Discussion. 214:48+ N '64
Back to the wars. Newsweek 64:20+ Jl 6 '64
Backdown on the farm. Time 84:33 O 30 '64
Backlash may do it. M. Ryskind. Nat R 16: 968 N 3 '64
Backlash on November 3. America 111:651 N 21 '64
Backlash vote is G.O.P. pitfall. Life 57:4 Jl 24 '64
Barry and the defectors. il pors Newsweek 64: 23 Ag 3 '64
Barry and the pilots. Nation 199:235 O 19 '64
Barry at bay; Peripatetics; discussion of campaign issues with Eisenhower. por Newsweek 64:69-71 O 5 '64
Barry fights crime, but you'd never know it from the record. J. Ridgeway. New Repub 151:9-11 O 3 '64
Barry fights the Court. A. M. Bickel. New Repub 151:9-11 O 10 '64
Barry Goldwater, by E. McDowell. Review Nat R 16:656-7 Jl 28 '64. W. A. Rusher
Barry Goldwater on space: GOP candidate wants military, not civilians, to run space program. E. Langer. Science 145:470-1 Jl 31 '64
Barry in space. Nation 199:103 S 14 '64
Barry on the beam. Nation 199:130 S 21 '64
Barry vs. LBJ: the fireworks start. il por U S News 57:31-2 S 14 '64
Barry's chances against LBJ. il U S News 56:31-3 Je 22 '64
Barry's economic crusade. J. Tobin. New Repub 151:13-16 O 24 '64
Barry's holy mission. New Repub 151:2 Jl 25 '64
Barry's iron curtain. Newsweek 64:31-2 O 19 '64
Barry's remote control. Reporter 31:20+ S 24 '64
Barry's summit. Newsweek 65:15 Ja 4 '65
Barry's war. Newsweek 63:18 Ja 27 '64
Battle of San Francisco. J. Dos Passos. Nat R 16:640, 652 Jl 28 '64
Behind the Goldwater phenomenon. H. Brandon. Sat R 47:6+ Jl 11 '64
Bell for round one. Nat R 16:94-5 F 11 '64
Big kazoo. Nation 198:62 Ja 20 '64
Big new face of the G.O.P; Republican convention. il pors Life 57:20-32B Jl 24 '64
Big scare vs the issues. Farm J 88:114 N '64
Bit short. il por Newsweek 63:28 Ap 27 '64
Bleating of sheep. M. Kempton. New Repub 150:15-18 Je 20 '64
Block Goldwater movement in the GOP. il por Newsweek 62:19-20 Jl 22 '63
Blowing Barry's horn. S. Meisler. il por Nation 197:48-9 Jl 27 '63
Bolters seldom eat. M. Kempton. New Repub 151:4-5 Ag 22 '64
British politics and Goldwater. A. Lejeune. Nat R 16:770 S 8 '64
Business, and the party platforms. T. O'Hanlon. il por Duns R 84:55-7+ O '64
Businessmen's vote: it's going to be a tough decision. il por Bsns W p23-5 S 5 '64
California primary. Nation 198:593 Je 15 '64
Campaign. New Repub 151:3-4 O 3 '64
Campaign and candidates: letters to the editor. Christian Cent 81:1276-7+ O 14 '64
Campaign and the candidates. F. Knebel. il Look 28:23-5 N 3 '64
Campaign report from the East: if the people were voting for president now. il U S News 57:37-8 S 21 '64
Campaign report: on the road with the candidates. il por U S News 57:124-5 O 12 '64
Campaign: what does it all add up to? with editorial comment. S. Alsop. por Sat Eve Post 237:71-3, 76 O 31 '64
Campaigner Goldwater. S. Alsop. por Sat Eve Post 237:16 O 3 '64
Can anyone stop Goldwater now? il por Newsweek 63:23-4+ Je 15 '64
Can Barry Goldwater be stopped? il por Newsweek 63:27-31 My 18 '64
Can Goldwater win? with editorial comment. S. Alsop. il pors Sat Eve Post 237:13-15, 86 Ag 8 '64
Can Goldwater win in 64? S. Alsop. il pors Sat Eve Post 236:19-25 Ag 24 '63; Discussion. 236:4 S 28 '63
Can Rockefeller stop Goldwater? por U S News 55:34 Jl 29 '63
Can the GOP survive Goldwater? R. Wilson. il Look 28:20-1 Jl 14 '64
Candidate. Nat R 16:632 Jl 28 '64
Candidate's dilemma. H. Brandon. Sat R 47: 16+ O 17 '64
Carping about a candidate. Time 83:36 Je 19 '64
Case against Goldwater's economics. P. Samuelson. il N Y Times Mag p28+ O 25 '64
Cell 772, or Life among the extremists. W. Morris. Commentary 38:31-9 O '64
CAP and TVA: Barry's fine distinction. D. Oberdorfer. Reporter 31:36-8 S 10 '64
Choice not an echo; Cow Palace climacteric. il pors Newsweek 64:18-22 Jl 27 '64
Cinched nomination. il Time 84:19-24 Jl 17 '64
Civil rights, government money, and the vote in the South. il U S News 57:41-2 O 19 '64
Civil rights: the White House meeting. Newsweek 64:15 Ag 3 '64
Clear choice. Nation 199:81 S 7 '64
Clear choice. E. Moon. il Library J 89:3926-7 O 15 '64; Discussion. 89:4232+, 4448+, 4872+ N 1-15, D 15 '64
Clear choice. por Newsweek 63:15-16 Ja 13 '64
Close look at a puzzled candidate. C. Mohr. il pors N Y Times Mag p 11+ My 17 '64
Close look at the South and LBJ's home state. il U S News 57:45-6 O 12 '64
Close-up of the Republican presidential candidate. il pors Sr Schol 85:10-11 S 23 '64
Column right. Newsweek 65:55-6 Ja 11 '65
Coming showdown. H. Brandon. Sat R 47:16-17 Ag 15 '64
Common cause. il por Newsweek 63:19-20 Mr 2 '64
Communism & corruption; campaign issues. Time 84:28-9 O 30 '64
Conservatism and the Goldwater consensus. F. S. Meyer. Nat R 15:386+ N 5 '63
Counterattack at Colorado. W. H. Carroll. Nat R 14:494-5 Je 18 '63
Countrywide report on election race. il por U S News 57:39-42 S 28 '64
Covering the candidate. il Newsweek 64:71-2 Jl 20 '64
Crime and politics. E. J. Hughes. Newsweek 64:25 O 19 '64
Crisis at the Cow palace. S. Alsop. il pors Sat Eve Post 237:17-21 Jl 11 '64
Cutting bait? il por Newsweek 62:28+ S 30 '63
Dangerous delusions. J. W. Fulbright. Sat R 47:24-5+ O 24 '64
Dialogue begins. Nat R 16:50-1 Ja 28 '64

GOLDWATER, Barry Morris—about—*Cont.*
Did Goldwater lose? D. Bernd. New Repub 151:8-10 D 5 '64
Different campaign. K. Crawford. Newsweek 64:36 Jl 20 '64
Difficulty of being fair to Goldwater. H. Donovan. il pors Life 57:93-6+ S 18 '64
Diluted Goldwater. K. Crawford. Newsweek 62:32 Ag 19 '63
Does Ike like Barry? il por Newsweek 62:18 O 28 '63
Down in the dumps. il por Time 83:37 My 15 '64
Draft Goldwater move starts, its meaning. il pors U S News 54:42-5 Ap 29 '63
Dream come true, with comments by W. Lippmann. Reporter 31:7-8 Jl 2 '64
Dream world of Goldwater. W. Lippmann. Newsweek 64:13 Ag 3 '64
Each is sure the triumph of the other will wreck the party; California primary. T. H. White. il por Life 56:26-31 My 29 '64
Easygoing man behind the image. K. Wheeler and W. Lambert. il pors Life 57:88-90+ O 23 '64
Election. Nat R 16:999-1001 N 17 '64
Election decided in mid-July. E. T. Folliard. America 111:587 N 14 '64
Emotional campaign will test voters' judgment. P. Lisagor. por Nations Bsns 52:23-4 S '64
End of an era. il por Newsweek 65:23-4 Ja 25 '65
Extremism in defense of the Democratic party. C. B. Luce. Nat R 16:719-21 Ag 25 '64
Extremism: letters to the editor. Christian Cent 81:1306-7 O 21 '64
Factor X for '64: stay-at-homes. il U S News 57:32-3 Ag 17 '64
Fasten your seat belts. M. Ascoli. Reporter 29:22 N 7 '63; Reply. S. McCalmont. 29:8+ D 5 '63
Fastest gun. il por Newsweek 63:20-1 Ja 20 '64
Fear & the facts. il Time 84:15-19 S 25 '64
Finger of fate? il por Time 82:24-5 N 8 '63
Finger of fate? Senator Goldwater's foray into New Hampshire. Newsweek 62:37-8 N 11 '63
Fingers crossed. il por Newsweek 63:45 Je 8 '64
Flank attacks. Newsweek 63:58 Je 22 '64
Focus on Nov. 3. Nat R 16:344, 390, 520-1, 855, 899, 943 My 5-19, Je 30, O 6-20, N 3 '64
For Goldwater, there's no more freewheeling. por Bsns W p30-2 O 5 '63
Foreign alarm over Goldwater. J. Daniel. New Repub 151:34+ S 19 '64
FDR's 1932 platform suits Goldwater for '64. U S News 55:6 S 23 '63
From Britain; reaction to Goldwater. J. M. Cameron. Commonweal 80:563-4 Ag 21 '64
From Washington straight. Cato. Nat R 16: 906 O 20 '64
Getting across to the voters. il Bsns W p32-3 S 19 '64
Go with Goldwater? K. Crawford. Newsweek 61:25 F 4 '63
God, guilt and Goldwater. W. Stringfellow. Christian Cent 81:1079-83 S 2 '64; Discussion. 81:1338-9 O 28 '64
Goldwater. Nat R 14:519 Jl 2 '63
Goldwater: a close look at a damned cowboy. C. Mohr. il pors Sat Eve Post 237:16-19 Ag 8 '64
Goldwater air campaign nears 70,000 mi. il Aviation W 81:67+ N 2 '64
Goldwater: an effort to evaluate the effects that his election might have on scientific activity. D. S. Greenberg. Science 145:685-7 Ag 14 '64; Discussion. 146:171+ O 9 '64
Goldwater: an English view. M. Muggeridge. Commentary 38:81-4 O '64
Goldwater and Rockefeller. J. O'Gara. Commonweal 78:472 Ag 9 '63
Goldwater and the John Birch society. W. F. Buckley, jr. Nat R 15:430 N 19 '63
Goldwater and the race issue. Nat R 15:45-6+ Jl 30 '63
Goldwater and the Republican party. Bsns W p 148 Je 13 '64
Goldwater and the Soviet Union. W. F. Buckley, jr. Nat R 16:56 Ja 28 '64
Goldwater and the state. Commonweal 80:495 Jl 24 '64
Goldwater appeal: not only nuts and kooks. T. Wicker. il N Y Times Mag p9+ Je 21 '64
Goldwater bandwagon. M. Ascoli. Reporter 30: 10+ Je 18 '64; Discussion. 31:8 Jl 16 '64
Goldwater begins work on platform. Christian Cent 81:69 Ja 15 '64
Goldwater blitz described by a fellow senator. U S News 57:22 Jl 20 '64
Goldwater challenges the four-party system. J. M. Burns. il por N Y Times Mag p7+ Je 28 '64
Goldwater country. J. J. Kilpatrick. por Nat R 14:281-2 Ap 9 '63
Goldwater endorses school prayers. Christian Cent 81:1292 O 21 '64
Goldwater enters race for presidency. il por U S News 56:19 Ja 13 '64
Goldwater for president? a drive is launched. por U S News 54:25 Ap 22 '63
Goldwater for president; is it conceivable? is it feasible? W. F. Buckley, jr; L. B. Bozell. Nat R 14:312-13+ Ap 23 '63
Goldwater for therapy. W. V. Shannon. Commonweal 81:30-1 O 2 '64
Goldwater gold; Barry's finances. il Time 84: 19 Ag 14 '64
Goldwater in Illinois. R. T. Cooper. New Repub 151:10-13 O 31 '64
Goldwater in New York. il por Newsweek 63:29-30 My 25 '64
Goldwater in '64. Nat R 16:570+ Jl 14 '64
Goldwater in the European mirror. J. Burnham. Nat R 16:1140 D 29 '64
Goldwater in the old confederacy. il por Newsweek 64:25-6 S 28 '64
Goldwater movement. W. Lippmann. Newsweek 62:13 Ag 5 '63; Reply. Nat R 15:223 S 24 '63
Goldwater: next president? il pors U S News 57:29-41 Jl 27 '64
Goldwater? no! Christian Cent 81:851 Jl 1 '64; Discussion. 81:933-5 Jl 22 '64
Goldwater on church and state. G. D. Everett. Christian Cent 81:987-9 Ag 5 '64
Goldwater on extremists. R. Moley. Newsweek 62:76 Jl 29 '63
Goldwater on missiles. W. Wingo. Sci N L 86: 35 Jl 18 '64
Goldwater out front: will he be blocked? il pors U S News 55:41-3 Jl 15 '63
Goldwater, Pentagon clash on defense; with editorial comment. J. Trainor. Miss & Roc 15:12, 46 Ag 17 '64
Goldwater people; symposium. il Look 28: 52-4+ N 3 '64
Goldwater resorts to military moderates. G. C. Wilson. Aviation W 81:21 S 28 '64
Goldwater, Rockefeller, and the Young Republicans. M. S. Evans. por Nat R 15:97-100+ Ag 13 '63
Goldwater seeks a new coalition. A. K. Campbell and S. Sacks. il por N Y Times Mag p22+ Ag 23 '64
Goldwater; Southwest political story. F. Knebel. il por Look 27:36-7 O 8 '63; Discussion. 27:18+ N 19 '63
Goldwater statement on nuclear weapons: an analysis. Aviation W 81:27 Ag 24 '64
Goldwater: the home stretch. F. S. Meyer. Nat R 16:447 Je 2 '64
Goldwater, the romantic regression. H. J. Morgenthau. Commentary 38:65-8 S '64
Goldwater: the world reacts. Newsweek 64:36-7 Jl 27 '64
Goldwater threat. W. Lippmann. Newsweek 64:13 Jl 6 '64
Goldwater vs. LBJ; '64 choice? il por U S News 56:35-7 Je 15 '64
Goldwater vs. moon shot. W. Wingo. Sci N L 86:77 Ag 1 '64
Goldwater view of economics. M. Friedman. il N Y Times Mag p35+ O 11 '64
Goldwater: yes or no? symposium by Protestant theologians. Christian Cent 81:879-83 Jl 8 '64
Goldwaterism. E. J. Hughes. Newsweek 64:17 Jl 27 '64
Goldwaterite revolution. W. D. Burnham. Commonweal 80:531-5 Ag 7 '64; Discussion 80:610-14 S 4 '64
Goldwater's bombshell. Nation 199:393 N 30 '64
Goldwater's boosters and Goldwater himself. E. T. Folliard. America 108:661 My 11 '63
Goldwater's chances. New Repub 150:5-6 Ja 11 '64
Goldwater's chances now. il por U S News 57: 27-31 Ag 3 '64
Goldwater's decision. R. Moley. Newsweek 63:78 Ja 13 '64
Goldwater's Dirksen. K. Crawford. Newsweek 64:31 Jl 13 '64
Goldwater's economists. il Newsweek 64:62-4 Ag 31 '64
Goldwater's education. R. Moley. Newsweek 62:116 O 7 '63
Goldwater's faith. il por Time 84:56 Ag 28 '64
Goldwater's foreign policy: let's hear more. il por(cover) Life 55:4 N 1 '63; Reply. B. M. Goldwater. 56:30B-30D Ja 17 '64
Goldwater's good deeds in Arizona; attitude towards integration. New Repub 151:9-10 Ag 22 '64
Goldwater's hour. il pors Bsns W p23-5 Jl 18 '64
Goldwater's law: poverty and social welfare. New Repub 150:4 F 1 '64

GOLDWATER, Barry Morris—about—*Cont.*

Goldwater's managers. R. Moley. Newsweek 63:100 Ap 13 '64

Goldwater's military views. Nation 199:14 Ag 10 '64

Goldwater's nine. C. Mohr. il pors N Y Times Mag p28-9 S 13 '64

Goldwater's problem and the G.O.P. Life 56: 4 Je 19 '64

Goldwater's South? K. Crawford. Newsweek 64:34 Ag 17 '64

Goldwater's staff. R. Moley. Newsweek 64:88 Ag 24; 80 Ag 31 '64

Goldwater's thirty days. Commonweal 79: 585 F 14 '64

GOP candidate's position papers. R. Drummond. por Sat R 47:41-2 S 19 '64

GOP in San Francisco: Alabama casts twenty votes for. . . Delegates: a grand old party. il Newsweek 64:16-21 Jl 20 '64

GOP opens with a pair. por Bsns W p36 My 4 '63

GOP's Goldwater: busting out all over; Listening post: a head for Rockefeller but a heart for Goldwater. por Newsweek 61:28-32 My 20 '63

GOP's unmerry Christmas. E. J. Hughes. Newsweek 64:9 D 28 '64

Great defoliator. Christian Cent 81:847 Je 24 '64

Guidebook (conservative) New Repub 150: 4 F 29 '64

He could phenomenon. Time 84:20-1 Ag 7 '64

Heads off. New Repub 150:2+ Je 20 '64

He's rolling along like a tumbleweed; with report by R. B. Stolley. il pors Life 55:22-3+ Jl 12 '63

Hi-ho New Hampshire! Barry goes galloping in; with reports by P. O'Neil and M. Gart. il pors Life 55:28-35 N 1 '63

High noon in the Cow Palace. C. McWilliams. por Nation 199:23-7 Jl 27 '64

His chief targets: McNamara and reds; GOP campaign. il Bsns W p 18-19 Ag 1 '64

His own kind of campaign. il por Bsns W p 122-4+ Jl 25 '64

How dependable are America's long-range missiles? Goldwater vs. McNamara. il U S News 56:6 Ja 20 '64

How farmers will vote, and why. C. W. Gifford. il Farm J 88:29+ N '64

How Goldwater got his strength. il pors U S News 57:29-32 Jl 13 '64

How Goldwater won in California. B. Stout. por Reporter 31:17-19 Jl 2 '64

How good are U.S. missiles, is Goldwater right? U S News 56:44-5 Ja 27 '64

How Kennedy sizes up Goldwater's chances; excerpts from news conference, October 9, 1963. J. F. Kennedy. U S News 55:6 O 21 '63

How not to stop Barry. Cato. Nat R 14:489 Je 18 '63

How to tell jokes and influence voters. G. Ace. Sat R 47:21 Mr 14 '64

How to win against prosperity; GOP campaign. Bsns W p 16-17 Ag 1 '64

I paint the candidates; with portraits. N. Rockwell. Look 28:50-3 O 20 '64

I welcome Hubert. il por Newsweek 64:29-30 S 7 '64

Ideologist, not a conservative. Christian Cent 81:789 Je 17 '64

If Barry goes to White House: what labor can expect. U S News 57:76-7 Jl 27 '64

If Goldwater gets it. New Repub 150:3-4 Je 13 '64

If it's Goldwater v. Johnson, who will win? R. De Toledano. por Nat R 16:101-2+ F 11 '64; Reply. F. Meyers. 16:248 Mr 24 '64

I'll live with it. por Newsweek 64:28 N 16 '64

Images & oratory. il por Time 84:42 O 2 '64

In front, and getting farther. il por Time 82: 22-3 S 27 '63

In home stretch: can Scranton make it? il pors U S News 56:31-3 Je 29 '64

In the home stretch: can Goldwater still make it? il por U S News 57:35-8 O 19 '64

In the peace pipe room. Newsweek 64:68 N 16 '64

In the red light: a history of the Republican convention in 1964. N. Mailer. il Esquire 62:83-9+ N '64

In the thick of it; four-day swing through western and midwestern states. il Time 84:30+ S 18 '64

In the West, fear is uppermost. P. R. Wieck. New Repub 151:11-12 Ag 22 '64

In U.S. heartland: how candidates shape up. il U S News 57:43-6 S 28 '64

Inadmissible default. P. Lehmann. Christian Cent 81:908-9 Jl 15 '64

Into the heartland. il por Newsweek 64:33-4 O 12 '64

Into the '64 campaign homestretch. Sr Schol 85:8-11 O 28 '64

Is Goldwater moving left? Nat R 15:335+ O 22 '63

Is it to be Goldwater? here are latest trends. il por U S News 56:36-7 My 18 '64

Is LBJ slipping? il Nat R 16:902-4 O 20 '64

Itchy-finger image. Time 84:15 S 25 '64

It's called Goldwater country; but who's leading? il U S News 57:68-9 O 5 '64

It's up to the undecideds. D. F. O'Neil. por Nat R 16:193-4 Mr 10 '64

Jet bandwagon; Goldwater's scorecard. il por Newsweek 62:33-4 O 7 '63

JFK in Goldwater country; what he found out. il U S News 55:49-50 O 7 '63

Johnson or Goldwater, two scientists explain their choice. G. B. Kistiakowsky; E. Teller. Science 146:380-2 O 16 '64

Karl Hess; Goldwater finds his Sorenson. M. Kempton. New Repub 151:10-14 Ag 8 '64

Key men on the Goldwater team. il U S News 56:20 Je 22 '64

Khrushchev takes a hand. Nat R 16:678-9 Ag 11 '64

K7UGA will get the ham vote. A. Whitman. por N Y Times Mag p64+ S 13 '64

Kickoff. il por Time 84:20-1 S 11 '64

Landside view. J. Burnham. il Nat R 16:317-18 Ap 21 '64

Left hook. Nat R 15:7+ Jl 16 '63

Lessons of the nomination drive. W. A. Rusher. Nat R 16:641-3 Jl 28 '64

Letter from London. M. Panter-Downes. New Yorker 40:67 Ag 1 '64

Letter from Paris. Genêt. New Yorker 40: 82 Je 27 '64

Letter from San Francisco. R. H. Rovere. il New Yorker 40:77-80+ Jl 25 '64

Letter from Washington. R. H. Rovere. New Yorker 39:113-20 N 2 '63; 40:178+ Mr 21 '64; 193-8 My 16; 111-18 Je 13; 102-7+ Ag 22; 235-8+ N 14; 161-2 D 19 '64

Listening post: how the pros see the election. por Newsweek 64:20-2 Ag 31 '64

Looking up. W. F. Rickenbacker. Nat R 16: 354 My 5 '64

Los Angeles did it. K. Crawford. Newsweek 63:38 Je 15 '64

Losers. por Newsweek 64:27 N 9 '64

LBJ vs. Goldwater, a study in contrasts. por U S News 57:32-4 S 7 '64

Lyndon Johnson: will he win? story the polls tell. il U S News 57:44-7 S 7 '64

Man on the bandwagon. il pors Time 83:31-2+ Je 12 '64

Man to beat. il por Time 83:21-2 My 8 '64

Man who. J. O'Gara. Commonweal 80:530 Ag 7 '64

Men behind Goldwater. R. G. Spivack. il Look 28:45+ N 3 '64

Mind of Barry Goldwater. R. Kirk. por Nat R 15:149-51 Ag 27 '63

Minds of Barry Goldwater. R. H. Rovere. Harper 229:37-42 S '64

Missiles and men. Nat R 16:51-2 Ja 28 '64

Mom and pop; Goldwater-Smith ticket. Reporter 29:24 N 21 '63

Myth America contest. Time 83:19 My 29 '64

NR and Goldwater. Nat R 16:9 Ja 14 '64

Neither an echo nor a choice. M. Ascoli. Reporter 31:22-3 O 8 '64

New conservative manifesto. T. G. Harris. il Look 28:19-23 D 29 '64

New Hampshire poll: write-in fever gains. il por(cover) Newsweek 63:18-21 Mr 9 '64

New men. New Repub 151:3-5 Jl 25 '64

New, new guard of the GOP. V. E. Lewis and H. Chambers. Nation 199:85-8 S 7 '64

New political map of America. F. S. Meyer. Nat R 16:687 Ag 11 '64

New statesmen; opponents. Nat R 15:179 S 10 '63

Night Barry Goldwater lost. M. Kempton. New Repub 150:4-6 Mr 21 '64

1964 election. E. Weeks. Atlan 214:49 O '64

1964 religious issue. Christian Cent 81:1227-8 O 7 '64

No fudge. il por Newsweek 64:27-8 Ag 31 '64

Non-candidate. Nation 198:517 My 25 '64

Northern California story. J. Caravan. Nat R 16:448 Je 2 '64

Now, the Jenkins case: meaning to the campaign. il U S News 57:55-6 O 26 '64

Odds against Goldwater. E. J. Hughes. Newsweek 62:21 N 4 '63

Odds against Goldwater. T. Wicker. il N Y Times Mag p 18+ N 10 '63

Ohio and Governor Rhodes. W. F. Rickenbacker. il Nat R 16:61-4 Ja 28 '64

One man's stand; civil rights bill. pors Time 83:18 Je 26 '64

One who isn't? por Time 81:30 Ap 19 '63

Only the senator can stop it now. M. McGrory. America 109:69 Jl 20 '63

Our defense: a crucial issue for candidates. Life 57:10 S 25 '64

GOLDWATER, Barry Morris—about—*Cont.*

Ozward & onward. il por Time 84:18-19 Jl 31 '64
Party control. R. Moley. Newsweek 64:76 Ag 3 '64
Party of Ike. E. J. Hughes. Newsweek 63:15 My 4 '64
Party realignment, letters to the editor. Reporter 29:8 D 5 '63
Paydirt? warnings about morality. por Newsweek 64:33-4 O 26 '64
Peddler's grandson. por(cover) Time 84:22+ Jl 24 '64
Pen pal for Dean. Time 85:17 Ja 8 '65
Perils of under-simplification. J. Burnham. Nat R 16:766 S 8 '64
Picking Barry. K. Crawford. Newsweek 62:37 S 23 '63
Platform built for Barry. il Newsweek 64:22+ Jl 20 '64
Play against Goldwater; private property and civil rights bill. W. F. Buckley, jr. Nat R 15:13 Jl 16 '63
Political campaign goes into high gear. U S News 57:21 S 21 '64
Political fundamentalism in profile. L. J. Averill. Christian Cent 81:1009-12 Ag 12 '64; Discussion. 81:1147 S 16 '64
Political mood of U.S. now. il por U S News 57:54-63 Ag 24 '64
Pop extremists. A. Frankfurter. Art N 63:19+ S '64
Presidential '64: rewriting the political rulebook. il por Sr Schol 85:8-11+ S 16 '64
Principles and heresies; why Goldwater can defeat Johnson. F. S. Meyer. Nat R 16:581 Jl 14 '64
Project White. W. F. Buckley. Nat R 16:634-5 Jl 28 '64
Race riots: Goldwater boon. F. Knebel. il Look 28:34+ S 22 '64
Realignment of parties? W. Lippmann. Newsweek 64:15 Jl 20 '64
Rebirth of news. Nat R 16:636 Jl 28 '64
Reflections on California. Nat R 16:477-9 Je 16 '64
Reporter at large. R. Harris. New Yorker 40:101-3+ S 12 '64
Reporter at large. R. H. Rovere. New Yorker 40:201-4+ O 3 '64
Republican party and the conservative movement; symposium. Nat R 16:1053-6+ D 1 '64
Rippling Goldwater. K. Crawford. Newsweek 63:27 Je 29 '64
Rockefeller vs Goldwater. J. Duscha. New Repub 149:13-14 O 26 '63
Runaway Republicans. M. Ascoli. Reporter 31:26-7 Ag 13 '64
Russian diplomat's question. S. Alsop. Sat Eve Post 237:16 O 17 '64
San Francisco is next. il por Bsns W p23-4 Je 6 '64
Scent of gold water. Newsweek 62:36-7 S 23 '63
Scranton's move. H. Brandon. Sat R 47:7-8 Jl 4 '64
Secretary Rusk interviewed on issues and answers, July 26, 1964. D. Rusk. Dept State Bul 51:231-7 Ag 17 '64
Sell TVA? how much would it bring? il U S News 55:50 N 11 '63
Sell the TVA? W. F. Buckley, jr. Nat R 15:472 D 3 '63
Senator finds the trail is icy. R. Ajemian. il por Life 56:31-3 Mr 6 '64
Senator Goldwater and the backbiters. W. F. Buckley, jr. Nat R 17:16+ Ja 12 '65
Senator Goldwater and the Negro. M. Greenfield. Reporter 31:27-8 O 8 '64
Senator Goldwater as editors see him. U S News 57:6 Jl 27 '64
Senator Keating explains his stand; excerpts from news conference, August 18, 1964. K. B. Keating. U S News 57:33 Ag 31 '64
Shopping trip. G. Ace. Sat R 47:8 Je 6 '64
Showdown in California. Reporter 30:10 My 21 '64
Showdown in California: big crisis for Goldwater; with editorial comment. R. Evans and R. Novak. il por Sat Eve Post 237:15-19, 74 My 30 '64
Sick, sick, sick. K. Crawford. Newsweek 64:32 Ag 31 '64
Some facts of history. iy Time 84:19 Jl 10 '64
Something's wrong theme: concerning B. Goldwater's speech at the Illinois state fair in Springfield. il por Time 84:24 Ag 28 '64
Somewhat nonconformist. il por Time 82:18 S 6 '63
Sound of footsteps. Time 82:17 N 22 '63
Sparkless campaign. K. Crawford. Newsweek 64:41 S 21 '64
Spawning season for G.O.P. delegates. Life 56:4 My 8 '64
Speaking out; Goldwater is wrong on civil rights. A. Lewis. Sat Eve Post 237:12+ S 26 '64
Speaking out: we want our politicians to be hypocrites. W. F. Buckley, jr. Sat Eve Post 237:8+ O 17 '64
Special Goldwater section; symposium. il pors Sat Eve Post 237:19-34+ O 24 '64
Stamping out peace; his attitude toward peace and war. J. O'Gara. Commonweal 81:6 S 25 '64
Straight down the middle? il por Time 83:19-20 Je 5 '64
Strauss heads scientists. Sci N L 86:235 O 10 '64
Straws in the south wind. New Repub 151:13 Ag 22 '64
Students' choice. por Sr Schol 85:1T O 28 '64
Study in contrasts. H. Brandon. Sat R 47-12+ O 31 '64
Suite 3505. W. A. Rusher. por Nat R 16:683-6 Ag 11 '64
T.R.B. from Washington; nobody but us whites. New Repub 151:2 S 26 '64
T.R.B. from Washington; why not Goldwater? New Repub 149:2 S 21 '63
Tally. New Yorker 40:20-3 Ag 15 '64
Tamper with an image? R. Moley. Newsweek 62:116 N 25 '63
Terrible disappointment of Walter Cronkite; excerpts from telephone conversation, May 15, 1964. D. D. Eisenhower; W. Cronkite. Nat R 16:435 Je 2 '64
Theorizing for Goldwater? Bsns W p 106+ N 23 '63
There was plenty of give and take. il por Newsweek 64:19-20 Ag 24 '64
This president thing. il pors Time 81:26-31 Je 14 '63
Thorns from Barry. il por Newsweek 63:20 F 24 '64
Tick-tock of the campaign clock. il por Newsweek 64:29-30 S 21 '64
Time to hear from Goldwater; summary of statement. N. A. Rockefeller. Life 55:4 Jl 26 '63
To the Grove. il por Newsweek 64:19-20 Ag 10 '64
Together again. Newsweek 65:20-1 F 1 '65
Tribute to Barry. Cato. Nat R 16:682 Ag 11 '64
Twenty-four hours in the life of Barry Goldwater. por McCalls 91:46+ Ja '64
Two Goldwaters. S. Meisler. il Nation 197:256-9 O 26 '63
Two key decisions: Rocky's and GOP's. il por Newsweek 61:23-4 My 6 '63
Uncle Lyndon. S. Alsop. Sat Eve Post 237:16 O 24 '64
Unionists counter Goldwater gains. U S News 57:69 Ag 10 '64
Union's war on Goldwater; AFL-CIO plans its strategy. il U S News 57:73-4 Ag 17 '64
Up in New Hampshire. il por Newsweek 63:65 F 17 '64
Varieties of disaster. Commonweal 80:384-5 Je 19 '64
Victory at San Francisco: how Goldwater did it. il U S News 57:42-4 Jl 27 '64
View from defeat. E. J. Hughes. Newsweek 63:20-1 Je 15 '64
View from the Tower. Christian Cent 81:1262-3 O 14 '64
Vile campaign. W. F. Buckley, jr. Nat R 16:853-6+ O 6 '64
Voices of moderation: days following the Republican convention; quotations. Nat R 16:675-6 Ag 11 '64
Walden West; seclusion at Bohemian Grove. il por Time 84:21 Ag 7 '64
Way out West. G. A. Harrison. New Repub 149:15-22 N 23 '63
We support Goldwater. Nation 196:386 My 11 '63
Were the kingmakers caught napping? E. T. Folliard. America 110:840 Je 20 '64
West's backlash. E. J. Hughes. Newsweek 64:13 Ag 10 '64
Westward ho! il por Time 82:30 O 18 '63
What mom wrought. W. F. Buckley, jr. Nat R 16:715 Ag 25 '64
What price peace? il por Newsweek 64:30 Ag 17 '64
What-was-said gap. Time 84:15 Ag 21 '64
What we owe to Barry. Nation 199:347-8 N 16 '64
When the chips are down. F. S. Meyer. Nat R 16:319 Ap 21 '64
Where Barry stands. Time 82:13 Ag 2 '63
Where both candidates stand on the big issues: with editorial comment. il por Bsns W p64-6+, 192 O 10 '64
Who's for Barry? What's he for? il New Repub 149:3-5 Jl 20 '63

GOLDWATER, Barry Morris—about—*Cont.*
Who's really for LBJ? R. Moley. Newsweek 64:126 O 12 '64
Whose Republican party? C. Joyner. New Repub 150:10-11 Je 13 '64
Why a Democratic senator turned Republican; address, September 16, 1964. S. Thurmond. il pors U S News 57:83-4 S 28 '64
Why Goldwater is gaining ground. il por U S News 56:31-3 Ap 27 '64
Why he is losing. H. Hazlitt. Newsweek 64:94 O 26 '64
Why Kennedy, Goldwater are going to the voters now. il por U S News 55:43-4 S 16 '63
Why LBJ will win. New Repub 151:3-4 O 31 '64
Will Goldwater sweep the South? il por U S News 57:41-2 Ag 10 '64
Will it be Goldwater, Rockefeller, or—? poll of Republican leaders in fifty states. il pors U S News 55:46-8 O 7 '63
Winning side, by R. De Toledano. Review Nat R por 15:570 D 31 '63. J. G. Tower
Words across the sea. il por Time 84:31 S 4 '64
Wraps are off; Rockefeller vs Goldwater. por Newsweek 62:41 Jl 29 '63
Wrong approach. il por Time 84:23 O 9 '64
Yippee! il pors Newsweek 63:18-19 Je 29 '64
Zeroing in. por Newsweek 62:18 Ag 12 '63
Zowie, wham, boom: supporters' ideas for campaign. Nat R 16:899-900 O 20 '64

Anecdotes, facetiae, satire, etc.

Tears for the grand old party. C. B. Luce. il Nat R 16:529-30+ Je 30 '64

GOLDWATER, Barry Morris, family
LBJ's wealth grows as an issue; both candidates are millionaires. il Bsns W p32 Ag 22 '64

GOLDWATER, Josephine (Williams)
Senator's pioneer mother talks about Barry and herself. R. B. Stolley. il pors Life 55: 24-7 Jl 12 '63

GOLDWATER, Leonard J.
Doctor comments. Art N 62:37+ O '63

GOLDWATER, Margaret Johnson
Another campaign issue: wealth of candidates. il U S News 57:14 Ag 24 '64
Lonely lady behind Barry. N. Robertson. il por Sat Eve Post 237:36 O 24 '64
Mrs Goldwater: quiet campaigner. il por U S News 57:22 O 19 '64
Norman Rockwell paints from the life of Peggy Goldwater. il pors McCalls 92:104-5 N '64
Woman behind Barry Goldwater. A. Toffler. il pors Good H 158:58+ My '64

GOLDWATER, Robert
An exciting ride in the van. Sat R 46:19 Ag 17 '63

GOLDWYN, A. J.
Advance of automation: its implications for library education; report. por Library J 88:2640-3 Jl '63

GOLDWYN, Samuel
Just above water: Albatross's maiden voyage on the Port Washington, L.I.-Wall Street run. il por Time 82:59 Jl 26 '63

GOLDY, Daniel L.
Daniel L. Goldy named national export expansion coordinator. Dept State Bul 50:56 Ja 13 '64

GOLENIEWSKI, Michal
How many Soviet spies in U.S. agencies? summary of statement, March 2, 1964. U S News 56:10 Mr 16 '64

GOLF
Am in pro-am. A. Wright. il Sports Illus 18: 48-53 Ja 28 '63
Arnie's earnings. il Time 82:63 Jl 12 '63
Artist must chart his course. L. Gustavson. il Am Artist 27:54-9+ Je '63
Because it isn't there: frostbite golf. il Newsweek 61:61 F 11 '63
Bloody but unbowed: the golf buff. W. B. Furlong. il N Y Times Mag p24-5+ My 19 '63
Bob Hope in the road to golf. E. Linn. il Sat Eve Post 236:28-30+ N 9 '63
Bold way to play tough trap shot. J. Nicklaus. il Sports Illus 19:73 N 25 '63
Champagne Tony has a winning look. G. S. Brown. Sports Illus 18:26-8+ Mr 25 '63
Consider the lie before hitting the wedge. J. Nicklaus. il Sports Illus 19:96 D 23 '63
East succumbs to a western craze. A. Wright. il Sports Illus 19:86-91 N 25 '63
Fascinating world of galleries; Wonderful world of golf, with photographs by H. Power. Sports Illus 18:38-45 F 11 '63
Getting a line, without cheating. J. Nicklaus. il Sports Illus 20:53 Mr 9 '64
Give every shot a cockeyed look. J. Nicklaus. il Sports Illus 20:49 F 17 '64
Golf. A. Palmer. Esquire 62:18-19+ Jl; 56-7 S; 54+ D '64
Golf gets its first southpaw hero. A. Wright. il Sports Illus 18:28+ My 27 '63
Hit the shot right, and get bite. J. Nicklaus. il Sports Illus 20:92 Ap 13 '64
Hitting man's golfer. Time 83:55 F 21 '64
Hold that trap; world series of golf. il Time 82:66 S 20 '63
I got a touch like a blacksmith; Yogi Berra in Pinehurst, N.C. G. Holland. il Sports Illus 19:28-30+ N 11 '63
I have joined Arnie's army. Duke of Windsor. il Sports Illus 19:20-1 N 4 '63
I won $100,000 and a pair of moldy salmon. J. Nicklaus. il Sports Illus 19:26-7+ D 9 '63
If a Texas portent holds true, watch out for Big Billy; contender in U.S. Open. G. S. Brown. il Sports Illus 20:81-2+ My 18 '64
If you see a snake, hit it; Bella Vista and La Hacienda golf clubs, Mexico. il Sports Illus 19:20-2+ Ag 26 '63
Life I lead. J. Nicklaus. il Sports Illus 20: 80-6+ My 11; 44-6+ My 18; 52-4+ My 25; 46-8+ Je 1 '64
Little flaw that is not a flaw. J. Nicklaus. il Sports Illus 21:44 N 9 '64
Longer clubs won't help a tall golfer. J. Nicklaus. il Sports Illus 20:64 Mr 16 '64
Money for the meek. Time 83:63 F 14 '64
More jack for Jack. Time 81:96 My 17 '63
My game and yours. A. Palmer. il Sports Illus 19:28-42 Jl 15; 28-33 Ag 5; 40-5 Ag 12 '63
Neglected shot to keep you out of trouble. J. Nicklaus. il Sports Illus 21:64 O 6 '64
Off at L.A. with a clink, clank. A. Wright. il Sports Illus 20:42-3 Ja 13 '64
Palmer gets fit to fight again. E. Havemann. il Sports Illus 18:22-5 Je 3 '63
Palmer speaks out; PGA policy. Sports Illus 20:7 F 24 '64
Player in paradise. A. Wright. il Sports Illus 18:22-4+ Mr 18 '63
Plight of the bumblebee; U.S.G.A. rules. il Time 81:50 F 22 '63
Pro golfer's candid story; excerpts from Golfers' gold. T. Lema and G. S. Brown. il Sports Illus 20:62-6+ Mr 23; 30-2+ Mr 30; 45-6+ Ap 6 '64
Ready for war at Augusta; Palmer vs. Player vs. Nicklaus. A. Wright. il Sports Illus 18: 36-9 Ap 1 '63
Room for a fourth? il Newsweek 61:85 Ap 22 '63
Secrets of the short game. J. Barber and G. S. Brown. il Sports Illus 18:32-40 F 18; 50-3 F 25 '63
Six-million golfers can't be wrong. il Bsns W p 106-8+ S 14 '63
Stars don't reign, but confusion does. G. S. Brown. il Sports Illus 20:48-50 F 10 '64
Take time to find out how the land lies. J. Nicklaus. il Sports Illus 20:47 Ja 6 '64
Three big ones talk about golf; interviews, ed. by C. Price. J. Nicklaus; A. Palmer; G. Player. il Sat Eve Post 236:66+ Ap 13 '63
To avoid choking up, try choking down. J. Nicklaus. il Sports Illus 19:66 D 9 '63
Tough way to make 100 grand. Time 84:70 D 4 '64
Welcome to the club; All-America team picked by Golf magazine. il Time 84:51 D 25 '64
When the tension builds up slow down. J. Nicklaus. il Sports Illus 20:56 Mr 23 '64
Young Jack, the mighty master. A. Wright. il Sports Illus 18:26-31 Ap 15 '63
See also
Caddies (golf)
Golf courses
Putting
Swing (golf)

Equipment

Club holder for a golf cart. J. Sherman. il Pop Sci 184:154 My '64

Study and teaching

Fairway woods: swing hard and be fearless; ed. by E. Shrake. B. Rawls. il Sports Illus 21:18-20+ Ag 3 '64
How to keep swinging in the rain. J. Nicklaus. il Sports Illus 19:74 S 9 '63
Knee action for a power play. J. Nicklaus. il Sports Illus 19:46 S 16 '63
Let me help your game; ed. by A. Wright. C. Harmon. il Sports Illus 20:38-47 Ap 27; 70-6 My 4 '64
Swing is simple. A. Palmer. il Sports Illus 19:18-30 Jl 22 '63
Winning shots. A. Palmer. il Sports Illus 19:24-30 Jl 29 '63

GOLF—*Continued*

Tournaments

After the avalanche; K. Venturi wins the U.S. Open. il Time 83:44 Je 26 '64
Amateur hour in pro sports; U.S. Open golf championship at Congressional country club, Washington, D.C. B. Gilbert. il Sport Illus 20:78-82+ Je 15 '64
Arnold Palmer gets stumped right out of the tournament. il Life 55:34B-34C Jl 5 '63
Augusta; where Georgia retaliates for Sherman's march. D. Jenkins. il Sports Illus 20: 94-6+ Ap 6 '64
Big Jay has his day; 1963 Open championship. A. Wright. il Sports Illus 19:16-21 Jl 1 '63
Brinkmanship; Tony Lema wins Cleveland Open. il Time 84:80 Jl 10 '64
Champion conquers a Kansas sea breeze; B. McIntire wins Women's amateur. A. Wright. Sports Illus 21:56-7 Ag 31 '64
Chief; 28th Masters tournament. il Newsweek 63:72 Ap 27 '64
Children's hour; P.G.A. championship. il Time 82:53 Ag 2 '63
Congressional: where a small splash will cost big money. A. Wright. il Sports Illus 20: 38-42 Je 15 '64
Deane of the amateurs wins again; National amateur public links championship at Detroit. G. S. Brown. il Sports Illus 19:90+ S 23 '63
Dream match produces a dream round; B. Hogan vs. S. Snead on Shell's wonderful world of golf. A. Wright. il Sports Illus 20: 54-6+ Je 8 '64
For goodness' sake, hold on; Titleholders championship. il Time 83:56+ My 8 '64
Good time to obey a mother-in-law; PGA championship, Dallas. ed. by G. Brown. J. Nicklaus. il Sports Illus 19:44-5 Ag 5 '63
Ham and the knife; British Open. G. S. Brown. il Sports Illus 19:10-11+ Jl 22 '63
High time for all at the Bourbon Open; Bardstown, Ky. B. Surface. il Sports Illus 18:60-2 Je 10 '63
Horror to play in but great to watch; U.S. Open preview; portfolio of paintings. Sports Illus 20:32-7 Je 15 '64
Hot finish; U.S. Open. il Newsweek 63:62-3 Je 29 '64
Hottest man in a furnace; Professional golfers' association championship. A. Wright. il Sports Illus 19:16-17 Jl 29 '63
Humbling game; T. Lema wins the British Open. il Time 84:72-3 Jl 17 '64
I changed my game to win the Masters; ed. by G. S. Brown. J. Nicklaus. il Sports Illus 18:18-23 Ap 22 '63
Key to the Masters. J. Nicklaus. il Sports Illus 20:30-3 Ap 6 '64
Making Buick fans of golfers; Buick Open, Grand Blanc, Mich. il Bsns W p30-1 Je 15 '63
Master. il Time 81:92-3 Ap 19 '63
Master to top them all; A. Palmer. A. Wright. il Sports Illus 20:18-27 Ap 20 '64
Matter of pride at endsville; Cajun-country tournament. G. S. Brown. il Sports Illus 21: 22-7 N 30 '64
New darling of the galleries; Women's amateur golf championship. R. Lardner. il Sports Illus 19:14-15 S 2 '63
No picnic; tournament spectators. il Newsweek 61:54 F 4 '63
No substitute for swinging; T. Lema wins New York's thunderbird classic. il Time 83: 46+ Je 19 '64
Nobody loses at the Poor boy open; Waco Turner open. E. Shrake. il Sports Illus 20: 28-31 My 11 '64
Old cat-o'-nine-tails; Walker cup matches. Time 81:64 My 31 '63
Old club offers a new challenge; National Open at The country club, Brookline, Mass; ed. by G. S. Brown. J. Nicklaus. il Sports Illus 18:46-53 Je 17 '63
Old man and the tee; 1963 U.S. Open. Newsweek 62:63 Jl 8 '63
Old man brings back a great day. M. Smith. il Life 54:35+ Je 21 '63
Old pro; U.S. Open champion. il Time 82:68+ Jl 5 '63
One for the left; 1963 British Open. il Time 82:50 Jl 19 '63
Pair of pained plutocrats gave TV a show; world series of golf. G. S. Brown. il Sports Illus 19:20-1 S 16 '63
Pity the poor short hitters; Masters tournament. E. Shrake. il Sports Illus 20:28-9 Ap 13 '64
Poor Ken hits it rich again; U.S. Open championship in Washington; with editorial comment. A. Wright. il Sports Illus 20:6, 12-19 Je 29 '64
Pro tour begins as rabbits chase kings. A. Wright. il Sports Illus 22:26-8 Ja 18 '65
Saint gets revenge on King Tut; U.S. amateur championship. A. Wright. il Sports Illus 21:72-4 S 28 '64
Shoot for a million; Masters at Augusta, Ga. M. M. McCormack. il Sports Illus 20:34+ Ap 6 '64
Spain sent a two-man armada; Canada cup tournament in France. H. Longhurst. il Sports Illus 19:18-20 N 4 '63
Sporting scene; four major events. H. W. Wind. il New Yorker 40:182+ N 7 '64
Sporting scene; Masters championship. H. W. Wind. il New Yorker 40:178+ My 16 '64
Sporting scene; Masters tournament. H. W. Wind. New Yorker 39:117-18+ Ap 20 '63
Sporting scene; National Open at country club, Brookline, Mass. H. W. Wind. New Yorker 39:44+ Jl 6 '63
Sporting scene, United States Open championship. H. W. Wind. il New Yorker 40:78+ Jl 11 '64
Sporting scene; Walker cup matches. H. W. Wind. il New Yorker 39:58+ Je 15 '63
Superchamps in deep trouble; Crosby tournament. il Sports Illus 20:18-23 Ja 27 '64
Take that, you people's choice; Masters tournament. il Time 83:65 Ap 24 '64
This one is fun, but the Open is torture; Masters; excerpt from Golfers' gold. T. Lema and G. S. Brown. il Sports Illus 20:45-6+ Ap 6 '64
Three for first. il Newsweek 62:62 Jl 1 '63
Tony Lema: touring golf pro and his wife. G. Astor. il Look 28:121-6 My 5 '64
Triumph against all odds in Las Vegas. A. Wright. il Sports Illus 18:30-3 My 13 '63
Triumph for two swingers; Canada cup for the U.S. A. Wright. il Sports Illus 21:24-6 D 14 '64
Victorious crusade in the valley of sin; British Open. J. Lovesey. il Sports Illus 21:16-19 Jl 20 '64
What more could anyone ask? Canada cup. Time 82:73-4 N 8 '63
When Mickey Wright did nothing wrong; LPGA tournament in Texas. G. S. Brown. il por Sports Illus 21:84-5 N 23 '64
Where duffers fall for the aloha push; Canada cup matches at Royal Kaanapali golf course. G. S. Brown. il Sports Illus 21: 59-60+ N 30 '64
Winning a barrel of beer money; first $200,000 Carling world golf championship. A. Wright. il Sports Illus 21:32-5 S 7 '64
With the help of St Jude; Professional golfers association championship. Time 84: 42-3 Jl 31 '64
Word for the T-bird was 'ouch'; Thunderbird classic. G. S. Brown. il Sports Illus 18:16-17+ Je 24 '63
You aren't going to believe this, but... Bobby Nichols won the PGA championship at Columbus, Ohio. A. Wright. il Sports Illus 21:48-9 Jl 27 '64
Young Sam wins while old Mac sues; PGA seniors' tournament in Palm Beach Gardens. E. Shrake. Sports Illus 20:52+ Mr 2 '64

GOLF, Indoor
Computer golf; Golf-O-Tron. il Time 82:56 N 22 '63
Golf moves indoors, lifesize and real; Golf-O-Tron. il Bsns W p54-5 Ag 31 '63

GOLF balls
Golf ball: a panegyric. C. Price. Esquire 62: 171+ D '64

GOLF clubs. See Country clubs

GOLF clubs (sticks)
Amateur scientist; dynamics of a golf club. L. A. Graham. il Sci Am 210:131-3+ Ja '64
Fine adjustment for the finicky player. J. Nicklaus. il Sports Illus 22:49 Ja 4 '65
Good time to take a nip, not a divot. J. Nicklaus. il Sports Illus 19:63 N 18 '63
Longer clubs won't help a tall golfer. J. Nicklaus. il Sports Illus 20:64 Mr 16 '64
Make your putter suit your game. J. Nicklaus. il Sports Illus 22:49 Ja 11 '65
Many merits of the longest iron. J. Nicklaus. il Sports Illus 21:49 Jl 20 '64
New grip on the game. G. S. Brown. il Sports Illus 19:53 D 16 '63
Sporting scene; Braemar seven-club professional tournament, Turnberry, Scotland. H. W. Wind. il New Yorker 40:182+ N 7 '64

GOLF courses
After dinner golf. il Esquire 62:138-9 N '64
Amateur hour in pro sports; U.S. Open golf championship at Congressional country club, Washington, D.C. B. Gilbert. il Sports Illus 20:78-82+ Je 15 '64

GOLF courses—*Continued*
Bogeyman; golf architect R. T. Jones. il Newsweek 63:62+ Je 15 '64
Champion conquers a Kansas sea breeze; B. McIntire wins Women's amateur. A. Wright. Sports Illus 21:56-7 Ag 31 '64
Championship in a royal barnyard; French view of golf. P. E. Ress. il Sports Illus 19:58-60 O 21 '63
Compact golf; par-three courses. il Time 81: 56+ Ap 26 '63
Congressional: where a small splash will cost big money. A. Wright. il Sports Illus 20:38-42 Je 15 '64
Golf course loan programs; excerpts from address, August 1963. H. C. Eckhoff. Recreation 57:24-5 Ja '64
Green ex-pastures; land in Cleveland County, N.C. Time 81:26 Ap 12 '63
Guidelines for planning a golf course. H. C. Eckhoff. il Recreation 57:306-8 Je '64
He golfs on the farm. il Suc Farm 61:70B S '63
High time for all at the Bourbon Open; Bardstown, Ky. B. Surface. il Sports Illus 18:60-2 Je 10 '63
Key to the Masters. J. Nicklaus. il Sports Illus 20:30-3 Ap 6 '64
Old club offers a new challenge; National Open at The country club, Brookline, Mass; ed. by G. S. Brown. J. Nicklaus. il Sports Illus 18:46-53 Je 17 '63
Real golf. il Newsweek 65:58 Ja 25 '65
Recreation in the coal mines; Wee-Ma Tuk Hills, Ill. il Pop Mech 121-222 Ap '64
Sandy trap for a million golfers; photographs; with report by G. S. Brown. Sports Illus 20:26-37 Ja 13 '64
Six-million golfers can't be wrong. il Bsns W p 106-8+ S 14 '63
Sketchbook of the great masters. R. Wells. il Esquire 59:104-8 Ap '63
Sporting scene; National Open at country club, Brookline, Mass. H. W. Wind. New Yorker 39:44+ Jl 6 '63
Sporting scene; north to the links of Dornoch; Scottish courses. H. W. Wind. il New Yorker 40:96+ Je 6 '64
Verdant investment; North Hills golf club, Manhasset, N.Y. il Fortune 70:134-8 S '64
When a golf course turns on you; reproductions of paintings. R. Osborn. Sports Illus 21:36-45 Ag 31 '64
Where duffers fall for the aloha push; Canada cup matches at Royal Kanaapali golf course. G. S. Brown. il Sports Illus 21: 59-60+ N 30 '64
Wickedness at Wykagyl. Sports Illus 21:5 Jl 20 '64
Young Sam wins while old Mac sues; PGA seniors' tournament in Palm Beach Gardens. E. Shrake. Sports Illus 20:52+ Mr 2 '64

Lighting

Golf-course lighting. il Am City 79:135 Mr '64
Ski or golf at night; Wheeling, W.Va. E. E. Gaylor. il Am City 80:114 Ja '65

GOLF fans. See Sports fans

GOLF-O-TRON. See Golf, Indoor

GOLF players
Life I lead. J. Nicklaus. il Sports Illus 20: 80-6+ My 11; 44-6+ My 18; 52-4+ My 25; 46-8+ Je 1 '64
Way to avoid a fatal case of the bends; good posture. J. Nicklaus. il Sports Illus 20:76 My 25 '64

GOLF tees. See Tees

GOLF trophies. See Trophies, Sport

GOLFERS
Amateur hour in pro sports; U.S. Open golf championship at Congressional country club, Washington, D.C. B. Gilbert. il Sports Illus 20:78-82+ Je 15 '64
Arnold Palmer: tycoon on the tee. T. O'Hanlon. il Duns R 83:39-40+ Mr '64
Board, books and birdies; golfers for U.S. colleges. D. Jenkins. il Sports Illus 18: 43-4+ My 20 '63
Bob Hope in the road to golf. E. Linn. il Sat Eve Post 236:28-30+ N 9 '63
British went out in the noonday sun; Ryder cup golf matches. A. Wright. il Sports Illus 19:53-4 O 21 '63
Championship in a royal barnyard; French view of golf. P. E. Ress. il Sports Illus 19:58-60 O 21 '63
Fatalist with finesse: Gary Player. G. Zimmermann. il Look 27:105-6+ Je 18 '63
Form fore and aft; women golfers, photographs. Sports Illus 18:18-19 F 18 '63
Good looks and good golf on the ladies' tour. G. S. Brown. il Sports Illus 18:32-7 Je 3 '63
High kind of Low life. D. Jenkins. il Sports Illus 21:56-60+ Jl 6 '64
Hogan said no, but Dawson said yes. G. S. Brown. il Sports Illus 20:35-7 Ja 13 '64
How JFK and Ike compare as golfers. il U S News 55:24 Ag 5 '63
Key to the Masters. J. Nicklaus. il Sports Illus 20:32-3 Ap 6 '64
Little Chi Chi's other side. D. Jenkins. il Sports Illus 21:34-6+ Ag 10 '64
Man behind the golfer. W. B. Furlong. il N Y Times Mag p72+ O 11 '64
Mary queen of Scots started it; women golfers. W. B. Furlong. il N Y Times Mag p44+ Ag 18 '63
Masters; photographs. P. Turner. Sports Illus 18:26-35 Ap 1 '63
Off at L.A. with a clink, clank. A. Wright. il Sports Illus 20:42-3 Ja 13 '64
Payday on the senior circuit. R. Creamer. il Sports Illus 18:22-3 F 11 '63
Pity the poor short hitters; Masters tournament. E. Shrake. il Sports Illus 20:28-9 Ap 13 '64
Poor Ken hits it rich again; U.S. Open championship in Washington; with editorial comment. A. Wright. il Sports Illus 20:6, 12-19 Je 29 '64
Pro golfer's candid story; excerpts from Golfers' gold. T. Lema and G. S. Brown. il Sports Illus 20:62-6+ Mr 23; 30-2+ Mr 30; 45-6+ Ap 6 '64
Pro tour begins as rabbits chase kings. A. Wright. il Sports Illus 22:26-8 Ja 18 '65
Ready for war at Augusta; Palmer vs. Player vs. Nicklaus. A. Wright. il Sports Illus 18:36-9 Ap 1 '63
Shoot for a million; Masters at Augusta, Ga. M. M. McCormack. il Sports Illus 20:34+ Ap 6 '64
Sketchbook of the great masters. R. Wells. il Esquire 59:104-8 Ap '63
Spain sent a two-man armada; Canada cup tournament in France. H. Longhurst. il Sports Illus 19:18-20 N 4 '63
Sporting scene; left-handed golfer winning British Open championship. H. W. Wind. il New Yorker 39:52+ Ag 3 '63
Sporting scene; Masters tournament. H. W. Wind. New Yorker 39:117-18+ Ap 20 '63
Sporting scene; Walker cup matches. H. W. Wind. il New Yorker 39:58+ Je 15 '63
Sporting scene; Women's world amateur team championship, Saint-Germain-en-Laye golf club, outside Paris. H. W. Wind. il New Yorker 40:188-92 N 7 '64
Stars don't reign, but confusion does. G. S. Brown. il Sports Illus 20:48-50 F 10 '64
Superchamps in deep trouble; Crosby tournament. il Sports Illus 20:18-23 Ja 27 '64
When a golf course turns on you; reproductions of paintings. R. Osborn. Sports Illus 21:36-45 Ag 31 '64
When the tension builds up slow down. J. Nicklaus. il Sports Illus 20:56 Mr 23 '64
Young Jack, the mighty master. A. Wright. il Sports Illus 18:26-31 Ap 15 '63
See also names of golfers, e.g. A. Palmer

Anecdotes, facetiae, satire, etc.

How to be happy though compulsive. A. Gingrich. Esquire 62:6 S '64

GOLIA, Ludvik Peric-. See Peric-Golia, L.

GOLIGHTLY, Carole, and Byrne, Donn
Attitude statements as positive and negative reinforcements. Science 146:798-9 N 6 '64

GOLIN, Milton
Science boosters unlimited. Todays Health 41:50-1+ My '63

GÓMARA, Francisco López de
City of the living god; excerpts from Cortés: the life of the conqueror by his secretary, tr. by L. B. Simpson. Am Heritage 15:67-79 Ap '64

GOMATOS, Peter J. and Tamm, Igor
Base composition of the RNA of a reovirus variant. bibliog Science 140:997-8 My 31 '63
—See Langridge, R. jt. auth.

GOMBRICH, Ernst H.
Exhibitionship. Atlan 213:77-8 F '64

GOMER, Joseph
Joseph and Mary Gomer, missionaries. M. H. Miller. por Negro Hist Bul 26:163-4 F '63

GOMER, Mary
Joseph and Mary Gomer, missionaries. M. H. Miller. Negro Hist Bul 26:163-4 F '63

GOMERSALL, Earl R.
Backlog sydrome. Harvard Bsns R 42:105-15 S '64

GOMES DOS SANTOS, Ferdinando, abp
Social-minded archbishop. E. K. Culhane. America 109:5 Jl 6 '63

GÓMEZ-SICRE, José
Art safari. Américas 16:12-17 N '64
Contrast in São Paulo. Américas 15:18-22 D '63
Córdoba's biennial comes to Washington. Américas 15:16-19 F '63
Meeting in Madrid. Américas 15:30-9 S '63
GOMORRAH. See Sodom and Gomorrah
GONADOTROPIC hormones. See Hormones, Sex
GONATAS, N. K. See Shy, G. M. jt. auth.
GONDWANALAND. See Continental drift
GONGS
Gongs. L. E. Springer. il Hobbies 69:53 Mr '64
GONORRHEA
Gonorrhea. Consumer Rep 28:499 O '63
Trouble with gonorrhea. Time 81:49 Mr 8 '63
GONSALVES, James
Crown; poem. America 110:411 Mr 28 '64
GONSER, U. and others
Mössbauer effect in hemoglobin with different ligands. bibliog Science 143:680-1 F 14 '64
GONZAGA university, Spokane, Wash.
Notes for a gazetteer: Crosbyana room of Crosby library. P. Hamburger. New Yorker 39:198 O 26 '63
GONZALES, Pancho. See Gonzales, R. A.
GONZALES, Richard Alonzo
Great Gonzalez. W. Brinkley. por Holiday 34:85-90+ Jl '63
Legend dies on the court. W. Bingham. por Sports Illus 19:18-19 Jl 8 '63
GONZALES, Veronica
Open skies for Negro girls. il pors Ebony 18:43-6+ Je '63
GONZALEZ, Arturo F. Jr
Cave-in! Pop Sci 183:43-8+ D '63
Chips are down in the islands of the sun. Sat R 47:69+ O 10 '64
Day in the life of a pro-football doctor. Todays Health 42:22-5+ O '64
Moppet market. Reporter 30:40+ Je 18 '64
South Vietnam's 40 megacycle intercom. Pop Electr 18:41-5+ Ap '63
Unsung hero of Vietnam: the G.I. medic. Todays Health 41:26-9 O '63
What a perfectly lovely smashup. Sci Digest 56:26-31 S '64
Who really wins the Indianapolis. Sci Digest 55:8-13 My '64
Worldwide disease busters: the navy medics. Todays Health 42:36-8+ S '64
GONZALEZ, Julio
Landmarks of modern art. K. Kuh. il Sat R 46:56 F 16 '63
GONZALEZ LUQUE, Guillermo
My most unforgettable character. Read Digest 83:264-6+ N '63
GONZALEZ ROBLES, Luis
Meeting in Madrid: joint exhibit of Spanish and New World artists. J. Gómez-Sicre. il por Américas 15:30-9 S '63
GOOD, Carter V.
Methodology of educational research and scholarship. Sch & Soc 91:140-4 Mr 23 '63
GOOD, Glendon R.
Manhattan opera company. Hobbies 69:30-1+ O '64; 32 Ja '65
GOOD, Paul
Bowl of gumbo for Curtis Bryant. Reporter 31:19-22 D 31 '64
GOOD and evil
See also
Conscience
GOOD and evil in literature. See Literature and morals
GOOD-bye possums; story. See Phelan, R. C.
GOOD day for Miss Tillie; story. See Murray, W.
GOOD housekeeping (periodical)
Fine romance, with no kisses; excerpts from address, April 14, 1964. W. H. Nichols. Writer 77:18-19 Jl '64
GOOD housekeeping institute
Just what is Good housekeeping institute? Good H 158:6 Ja '64
GOOD humor corporation
Ice cream taster; seven-year-old Lloyd Jose; photographs. Look 27:81+ Mr 12 '63
GOOD manners. See Courtesy
GOOD night, Mister Mulcahy, good night; story. See Maher, J. T.
GOOD taste. See Aesthetics
GOOD will
Anecdotes, facetiae, satire, etc.
Thanks just the same. C. Ford. il Read Digest 82:15-16+ Ap '63
GOODALE, Jane C.
Qualifications for adulthood. il Natur Hist 72:10-17 Ap '63
GOODALL, Jane
My life among wild chimpanzees. il pors Nat Geog Mag 124:272-308 Ag '63
about
Chimp girl. il pors Sci Digest 55:74-7 My '64
GOODE, J. H. See Liacopoulos, P. jt. auth.
GOODE, Ruth. See Miller, B. F. jt. auth.
GOODENOUGH, Ward H.
Arms control and behavioral science; excerpts from address, September 2, 1963. bibliog Science 144:821-4 My 15 '64
GOODFIELD, June
Tunnel of Eupalinus; with biographical sketch. por Sci Am 210:18, 104-10+ Je '64
GOODFRIEND, Arthur
How an idealist won a two-front war. M. K. Sanders. Harper 226:111 Je '63
GOODFRIEND, Lewis S. and Cardinell, R. L.
Planning for quieter, sound-conditioned homes. Arch Rec 133:29+ mid-May '63
GOODFRIEND, Theodore L. and others
Antibodies to bradykinin and angiotensin; a use of carbodiimides in immunology. bibliog Science 144:1344-6 Je 12 '64
GOODHART, Arthur Lehman
Common law; address, May 22, 1963. Vital Speeches 29:589-91 Jl 15 '63
GOODLAD, John I.
Changing curriculum of America's schools. Sat R 46:65-7+ N 16 '63
GOODMAN, Andrew
Limpid shambles of violence. il pors Life 57: 32-34B Jl 3 '64
GOODMAN, David A. See Whitehead, S. C. jt. auth.
GOODMAN, Ernest. See Crockett, G. W. jr, jt. auth.
GOODMAN, George J. W.
Our man in Saigon. Esquire 61:57-60+ Ja '64
GOODMAN, Howard. See Fahey, J. L. jt. auth.
GOODMAN, Joel W.
Antigenic determinants in fragments of gamma globulin from rabbit serum. bibliog Science 139:1292-3 Mr 29 '63
GOODMAN, Marie White
Fish & fish mates. Parents Mag 38:71-4+ Mr '63
GOODMAN, Marjorie J.
NACS: can college stores cope with the paperback boom? summary of address. por Pub W 184:16-21 D 16 '63
GOODMAN, Mary Ellen
Good character is made, not born. Parents Mag 39:54-5+ O '64
V.D. menace; prevention is better than cure. por Parents Mag 39:143-5 F '64
GOODMAN, Mitchell
England's own South Sea Islands. House B 105:48+ N '63
Maine idea. Redbook 123:64-5+ Jl '64
Provence. Atlan 214:110-12 Ag '64
Voyage to the foam-white isles and wine-dark seas of Greece. House B 105:100-1+ F '63
West coast of Mexico. Esquire 60:28+ S '63
GOODMAN, Paul
Children of Birmingham. Commentary 36: 242-4 S '63
Columbia's unorthodox seminars. Harper 228:72-5+ Ja '64
Disturber of the peace: Paul Goodman; interview, ed. by E. Auchincloss and N. Lynch. por Mlle 58:104-5+ F '64
Extreme situation. New Repub 149:7 O 19 '63
Haiku; Firefly; poems. Poetry 102:304 Ag '63
Intelligence, rebellion, interest. H. Carruth. Poetry 104:44-5 Ap '64
New deal for the arts. Commentary 37:68-71 Ja '64
Saving the liberal arts. Commonweal 80:359-61 Je 12 '64
Television. New Repub 148:24-6 F 23; 35-7 Mr 2; 28-30 Mr 16; 26-8 Mr 30; 32-4 Ap 13; 25-7 Ap 20; 26-8 My 18; 24+ My 25 '63
Why go to school? New Repub 149:13-14 O 5 '63
about
Goodman and the TV networks. D. Brinkley. New Repub 148:39 Mr 23 '63; Reply. R. Howard. 148:30 Ap 27 '63
On Paul Goodman. G. Steiner. Commentary 36:158-63 Ag '63
One of the lucky. D. Levertov. Nation 196: 310 Ap 13 '63
Village anarchist. N. Hentoff. Reporter 29:54-5 Jl 18 '63
GOODMAN, Ralph
Will Lever bros. lose all? Nation 196:138-9 F 16 '63

GOODMAN, Ryah Tumarkin
Night will never fall; poem. Horn Bk 40:209 Ap '64
GOODMAN, Saul
Brief biographies. See issues of Dance magazine
Dancing along with Mitch. Dance Mag 37:30-3+ S '63
Meet Una Kai. Dance Mag 37:19-21+ O '63
GOODMAN, Sidney
Like half-forgotten dreams; exhibition at Manhattan's Terry Dintenfass gallery. il Time 81:75 Mr 8 '63
They paint; you recognize. il por Time 83:74-5+ Ap 3 '64
GOODMAN, Walter
Battle against cancer. Ladies Home J 81:37-9+ Ag '64
Deciphering the cigarette code. New Repub 151:14 D 5 '64
Striking changes in the way Protestants & Catholics feel about each other. Redbook 122:62-3+ Mr '64
What our future doctors will do about wonder drugs, abortion, medical care for the aged and the high cost of illness. Redbook 121:54-5+ My '63

about

Lie detectors don't lie, but. N Y Times Mag p 12-13+ Ja 24 '65
GOODNER, C. J. and Tustison, W. A.
Autonomic mediation of the effect of raised arterial glucose upon free fatty acids. bibliog Science 146:770-2 N 6 '64
GOODNIGHT, Clarence J.
Arachnid behavior. Science 144:82 Ap 3 '64
GOODRICH, B. F. company
Annals of business; trade secrets in development of space suits issue in Goodrich vs D. W. Wohlgemuth case. J. Brooks. New Yorker 39:37-8+ Ja 11 '64
B. F. Goodrich building largest segmented case. il Miss & Roc 13:31-2 Ag 12 '63
Legal hurdle for job-hoppers. Bsns W p95 Je 1 '63
Traffic builders and confidence destroyers; bait advertisement in Reader's digest. Consumer Rep 29:269-70 Je '64
GOODRICH, David L.
Girls take the cue. Sat Eve Post 237:24-7 Ap 18 '64
Miracle on a mountain. Sat Eve Post 237:22-7 S 12 '64
Stalking the weed eater. Sat Eve Post 237:22-3 Jl 25 '64
Will the real Miss Rheingold stand out? Sat Eve Post 236:48+ N 16 '63
GOODRICH, Frederick N.
Gold problem; a banker's view; reprint. U S News 54:116 Ap 22 '63
GOODRICH, Shirley G.
Enchanted child. Ladies Home J 80:58 O '63
GOODRUM, Charles A.
Dog census. Atlan 211:82-5 Mr '63
(ed) See Dana, J. C. Think nothing of it, Mr Dana, it's only a flesh wound
GOODSELL, Jane
Cook's tour; poem. McCalls 92:178 O '64
How do I love him? well, it's like this; poem. McCalls 92:160 D '64
If I had anyone to get mad at, I'd scream. Good H 158:48+ Ap '64
I'll have a triple-decker clubhouse sandwich. McCalls 91:103+ My '64
It's perfectly simple, but so am I. Ladies Home J 80:22 Je '63
Low finance. Ladies Home J 80:42 Ap '63
Myth of the pampered housewife. Read Digest 85:64-6 Jl '64
'Tis the season to be frantic; poem. McCalls 91:134 D '63
GOODSON, Joan E.
My garden has roses, gladiolus, dahlias . . . Flower Grower 51:15-17 Ja '64
GOODSON, Mark
Lords of fun and games. G. Rogin. il por Sports Illus 18:52-60 Je 24 '63
GOODSPEED opera house, East Haddam, Conn. See Opera houses
GOODWILL Industries
Goodwill recreation program; Dayton, Ohio. R. A. Steinbrunner. il Recreation 57:408-9 O '64
GOODWIN, Dick
On the occasion of what was to have been his 47th birthday; poem. New Yorker 40:30 Jl 11 '64
GOODWIN, Irwin. See Simmons, H. jt. auth.
GOODWIN, Polly
Polly Goodwin receives the Constance Lindsay Skinner award. M. B. King. il por Pub W 186:108-10 Jl 13 '64
GOODWYN, Larry
Anarchy in St Augustine. Harper 230:74-81 Ja '65
GOODYEAR, Joseph
Trail blazers for moon explorers. Pop Mech 119:128-31+ F '63
GOODYEAR tire and rubber company
Blimp covers boat race, goes joyriding in its PR role. il Bsns W p40 Ap 20 '63
Good year for Goodyear. G. Moore. il Motor T 16:74-7 F '64
Goodyear's battle to stay on top. il Bsns W p 106-8+ D 14 '63
Where rubber reigns. il Time 82:110+ D 6 '63
GOOEY ducks. See Clams
GOOKIN, Sylvester R.
Second hundred years are the hardest. Motor B 113:84-5+ My '64
GOONEYS. See Albatrosses
GOOSE hunting. See Geese, Wild
GOOSE shooting. See Geese, Wild
GOOSEBERRIES
Gooseberry, innocent outlaw; carrier of white pine blister rust. R. L. Hawk. il Horticulture 41:366-7 Jl '63
GOOTLIEB, Liza
(tr) See Perventsev, A. A. Bourgeois manners for the Bolshevik masses
GOPHERS
Toothy; sheathing that resists gnawing by gophers. il Newsweek 62:56 Jl 8 '63
GORDEY, Michel
Clues to trans-Atlantic distrust. N Y Times Mag p25+ Je 9 '63
Consider me a Communist; a portrait of Evtushenko on stage and off. Harper 227:51-2+ O '63
French people and de Gaulle. For Affairs 42:546-58 Jl '64
What de Gaulle really wants. Look 28:38-42+ My 19 '64
(ed) See Khrushchev, N. S. Behind the Russian-Chinese split
GORDIMER, Nadine
Party of one. Holiday 34:12+ Jl '63
Stranger in town; story. Harper 229:108-10 N '64
GORDON, Arthur
Know the right moment. Read Digest 83:135-7 Ag '63
Night the stars fell. Read Digest 85:93-6 O '64
Parent's thoughts on good manners. Bet Hom & Gard 42:112-13 N '64
Rewards of caring. Read Digest 83:81-4 O '63
Search. Read Digest 82:137-8 Ap '63
Welcome, we need you. Read Digest 84:167-8 Je '64
(ed) See Blanton, S. Can we learn not to hate?
(ed) See Jordan, C. W. E. Painted in darkness
GORDON, Caroline
Katherine Anne Porter and the ICM. Harper 229:146-8 N '64
GORDON, Cyrus H.
Decipherment of Minoan. Natur Hist 72:22-31 N '63
GORDON, Dane R.
Justice and the death penalty. Christian Cent 80:955 Jl 31 '63
GORDON, Edward
Freedom to teach and to learn. PTA Mag 58:4-7 O '63
GORDON, Elizabeth
There's more than one reason for going to Zurich. House B 106:99+ Jl '64
—and Yuasa, Eiko
Discover tempura: a non-greasy way of frying in deep fat. House B 105:126-7+ F '63
GORDON, Ethel Edison
Holiday dance; story. Redbook 122:58-9 D '63
Remember; story. Redbook 120:48-9 Mr '63
Small cause for alarm; story. Ladies Home J 80:101 Je '63
Someone to share; story. Redbook 123:34-5 Je '64
Summer husband; story. Redbook 124:111-38 Ja '65
GORDON, Galvy
Paperback pilot project. Library J 89:191-2 Ja 15 '64
Thoughts for trustees about total service. Library J 88:3024-6 S 1 '63
GORDON, George B.
Fish the flat water. Outdoor Life 133:50-1+ My '64
GORDON, Ira J.
What nursery schools can and cannot do. PTA Mag 58:10-12 bibliog(p35) S '63
GORDON, Irwin
Reporter at large; dancers in May: P.S. 31 in Park fête in Central park. L. Ross. New Yorker 40:35-8+ Jl 18 '64

GORDON, James Stewart-. See Stewart-Gordon, J.

GORDON, Jesse E.
Snooping and testing; letter. New Repub 152: 28-30 Ja 9 '65

GORDON, John F.
Two gentlemen of GM. por(p31) Duns R 82:32 S '63
Two records: highest profit, highest pay. por U S News 56:64 My 4 '64

GORDON, Julia W.
Grouping and human values; excerpt from address. Sch Life 45:10-15 Jl '63

GORDON, Kermit
Excerpt from testimony before Committee on ways and means, February 18, 1963. Cong Digest 42:122+ Ap '63
Excerpt from testimony before Joint economic committee, January 29, 1963. Cong Digest 42:143+ My '63
How much should government do? Sat R 48: 25-7+ Ja 9 '65

about

Deficit advocates. U S News 54:15 F 11 '63
Kermit Gordon, eleventh cabinet member. por Newsweek 65:13 Ja 4 '65
Kermit Gordon; the President's affable no man on the budget. por Newsweek 63:66-7 Ja 27 '64
Lyndon's budgeteer. il por Time 84:76 Jl 24 '64
Man with a $100-billion budget. il pors Bsns W p 100+ Jl 20 '63
Tax cuts & Puritans. por Time 81:16-17 F 8 '63
U.S. will tighten up spending. por Bsns W p75-6+ O 5 '63

GORDON, Larry
Art-o-focus. L. Barry. il Pop Phot 55:136-7 D '64

GORDON, Lincoln
Terms of trade and the Brazilian balance of payments; address, January 29, 1963. Dept State Bul 48:284-93 F 25 '63

GORDON, Michael. See Green, P. C. jt. auth.

GORDON, Milton M.
Recent trends in the study of minority and race relations. bibliog f Ann Am Acad 350: 148-56 N '63

GORDON, Noah
Five signs on the highroad. Sat R 46:49-52 Ap 6 '63
Hallucinogenic drug cult. Reporter 29:35-43 Ag 15 '63

GORDON, Paul
How to buy a good used piano. por Bet Hom & Gard 42:104-6 Mr '64
—and Zak, Radovan
Potentiation by adrenaline of a proteolytic activity associated with purified myosin. bibliog Science 140:294-5 Ap 19 '63

GORDON, Philip W.
Winds of change; I talked with God this morning; poems. Negro Hist Bul 27:129 F '64

GORDON, Richard
How to solve math problems with a square. Pop Sci 182:132-5 Ap '63

GORDON, Richard M.
Armor vincit omnia; poem. New Repub 149: 22 Jl 6 '63

GORDON, Ruth
Trouble with Christmas; story. McCalls 91: 82-3 D '63

GORDON, Ruth McKee
Adam; poem. Christian Cent 80:365 Mr 20 '63
Lazarus to the bitter; poem. Christian Cent 81:732 Je 3 '64
Short sermon on Matthew 19:26; poem. Christian Cent 80:1262 O 16 '63

GORDON, W. J. J.
Mrs Schyler's plot; story. Atlan 211:90-3 Je '63
Nobel prize winners; story. Atlan 212:77-82 N '63

GORDON WALKER, Patrick
Labor party's defense and foreign policy. For Affairs 42:391-8 Ap '64
Labour's shadow diplomacy; interview. ed. by G. Brook-Shepherd. Reporter 30:37-40 F 13; 8 Mr 12 '64

about

Battle of Leyton hall. por Time 85:24-5 Ja 22 '65
Britain: narrowing the margin. il por Newsweek 65:27 F 1 '65
Leyton affair. il por Time 85:23 Ja 29 '65
Rusk's opposite number in Britain: how pro-U.S? U S News 57:14 N 2 '64

GORDON, Walter L.
Changing scene in Canada; address, April 20, 1964. Vital Speeches 30:450-2 My 15 '64

GORDON, William E.
Arecibo ionospheric observatory. bibliog Science 146:26-30 O 2 '64

GORDON research conferences
Gordon research conferences. W. G. Parks. Science 139:1066-76+ Mr 15 '63
Gordon research conferences: program for 1964. W. G. Parks. Science 143:1203+ Mr 13 '64
Winter Gordon research conferences; program. W. G. Parks. Science 146:1195-6 N 27 '64

GORDONSTOWN school. See Public schools (endowed)—Scotland

GORDY, Walter. See Snipes, W. C. jt. auth.

GORE, Albert Arnold
To rule space: law or might? N Y Times Mag p23+ N 10 '63
U.S. withdraws proposal on Angola opposed by Afro-Asian group; statement, December 18, 1962. Dept State Bul 48:105-6 Ja 21 '63

about

Oak Ridge searches for its future. por Bsns W p77-8 Ja 23 '65
One who worries them. por Time 82:28 O 25 '63
Pulling the rug from stock options. por Bsns W p 104+ Ja 11 '64

GORE, Arthur Kattendyke Strange David Archibald, 8th earl of Arran. See Arran, A. K. S. D. A. G.

GORE, Daniel
Anachronistic wizard: the college reference librarian. por Library J 89:1688-92, 2258, Ap 15, Je 1 '64
Neglected topic: the cost of classification. por Library J 89:2287-91 Je 1 '64
Subject cataloging: some considerations of costs. Library J 89:3699-703 O 1 '64

GORE, David Ormsby, 5th baron Harlech. See Harlech, D. O. G.

GORE, Gary
Symbolism in university press jacket design. Pub W 187:92-4 Ja 4 '65

GORE, Julian Ormsby
Four eligible bachelors in London. E. O'Brien. por Vogue 144:141 S 15 '64

GORE, Lesley
Your music is your mirror. por Seventeen 24:24 Ja '65

about

Making it big. por Newsweek 61:70 Je 24 '63

GORE, Lillian L.
What is a good nursery school? bibliog por Sch Life 45:18-22 Je '63

GOREAU, Thomas F.
Mass expulsion of zooxanthellae from Jamaican reef communities after hurricane Flora. bibliog Science 145:383-6 Jl 24 '64

GOREN, Charles Henry
Bridge. See issues of Sports illustrated
Cards. Sports Illus 20:90-1 Ap 6 '64
Goren's new formula; ed. by J. Olsen. pors Sports Illus 20:32-8+ F 17; 24-8+ F 24; 32-4+ Mr 2; 28-30+ Mr 9; 52-3+ Mr 16 '64
[Monthly column on bridge] See issues of McCall's
Slam-bang slams. por McCalls 91:72+ Ap '64
Sure cure for hard luck. McCalls 91:28+ Mr '64

about

Fifty-two characters who found authors. McCalls 91:34+ F '64

GORER, Geoffrey
British life, it's a gamble. N Y Times Mag p 10+ S 1 '63
Portrait of de Gaulle's Anglo-Saxons. N Y Times Mag p28+ My 12 '63

GORES, Harold
Where the schoolhouse goes from here. Arch Rec 136:225-7 S '64

about

Gores of E.F.L. notes changing standards for size and location of big city schools. Arch Rec 135:23 Mr '64

GOREY, Edward
Sinking spell. il Holiday 35:68-71 My '64

GOREY, Hays
Motor sports. Sports Illus 19:46-8+ Ag 19 '63; 21:66-7 O 12; 72-4 O 26 '64
Ugliest, cheapest and best in the world. Sports Illus 21:24-5 N 9 '64

GORILLAS
Fifi; si! Bobo? no! il Time 84:57 Ag 14 '64

GORILLAS—*Continued*
Jambo, first gorilla raised by its mother in captivity. E. M. Lang. il Nat Geog Mag 125:446-53 Mr '64
Mountain gorilla, by G. B. Schaller. Review
Sci Digest il 54:32 Jl '63
Time il 82:55 Jl 5 '63
Mountain gorilla displays; chest-beating. G. B. Schaller. il Natur Hist 72:10-17 Ag '63
Year of the gorilla, by G. B. Schaller. Review
New Yorker 40:96+ Jl 18 '64. N. Bliven
Reporter 30:45-6 Je 4 '64. G. Weales

Photographs

See Animals—Photographs

GORKY, Arshile
Gorky, when the going was rough. il Art N 62:27+ Ap '63
Mystery of Arshile Gorky: a personal account. M. Osborn. il pors Art N 61:42-3+ F '63
GORKY, Maxim
Lower depths; tr. by A. Szogyi. Criticism
Nation 198:404 Ap 20 '64
New Yorker 40:95-7 Ap 11 '64
GORMAN, Bernard J.
Noteworthy features. Am City 79:94-5 Jl '64
GORMAN, Katherine
Candlelight; poem. Cath World 198:294 F '64
Nightmare; poem. Commonweal 80:503 Jl 24 '64
GORMAN, Paul Albert
Gorman of Western electric. por Fortune 69: 39 F '64
GORME, Eydie
Steve Lawrence, a guy from Brooklyn. R. Atcheson. il pors Sat Eve Post 237:30-1 Je 27 '64
GORMEZANO, I. See Deaux, E. B. jt. auth.
GORR, Rita
Music to my ears; Gorr's Dalila. I. Kolodin. Sat R 47:35+ O 31 '64
GORRELL, Frank
Pope Paul and the council. New Repub 151:28+ Jl 25 '64
GORSKI, Lorraine K. M.
ABC classification... Library J 88:4437-40 N 15 '63
GORSKI, Roman S.
Trees; poem. Am For 70:48 D '64
GORSLINE, Ethlyn Paige
This farm for sale? Farm J 87:89+ Mr '63
Why save the cream? Farm J 88:81 Mr '64
GORZ, André
Call for intellectual subversion. Nation 198: 534-7 My 25 '64
GORZ, H. J. See Haskins, F. A. jt. auth.
GOSLAR, Lotte
Lotte Goslar's world of clowns; Jacob's Pillow. D. Hering. Dance Mag 38:29 Ag '64
GOSLIN, David A.
Social impact of standardized testing. NEA J 52:20-2 O '63
GOSPEL songs. See Negro songs
GOSPELS. See Bible—New Testament—Gospels
GOSS, Bert C.
Paradox in government-industry relations: peace at top, strife at bottom; address, June 5, 1964. Vital Speeches 30:555-8 Jl 1 '64
There oughtn't to be a law; deterioration of American self-reliance; address, October 24, 1963. Vital Speeches 30:81-4 N 15 '63
GOSSAGE, Howard
Mavericks on Madison avenue. P. B. Bart. Sat R 46:60+ D 14 '63
GOSSELIN, Robert E.
What you should know about the drugs you take. Read Digest 82:99-102 Mr '63
GOSSETT, William T.
Kennedy round, progress and promise; address, July 17, 1963. Dept State Bul 49: 291-6 Ag 19 '63
GOSSIP
See also
Rumor
GOSSNER, Simone Daro
Comets' wanderings end eventually in dissipation into space. Natur Hist 72:52-3 O '63
Sky reporter. See issues of Natural history incorporating Nature magazine
GÖTEBORG

Music

Northern lights. O. Wallgren. Opera N 28:33 Mr 7 '64
Stora tunes. H. Lundbergh. il Opera N 28:32 Ja 4 '64
Swedish nightingales. O. Wallgren. il Opera N 29:30 D 26 '64
GOTHA missal. See Missals
GOTHAM book mart. See Booksellers and bookselling—New York (state)

GOTS, Joseph S. See Kalle, G. P. jt. auth.
GOTT, Vincent L. and others
Heparin bonding on colloidal graphite surfaces. bibliog Science 142:1297-8 D 6 '63
GOTTEHRER, Barry
Television's princess of the press corps. Sat Eve Post 237:36-7 O 31 '64
GÖTTERDÄMMERUNG; opera. See Wagner, R.
GOTTESFELD, E.
WLB biography. Wilson Lib Bul 37:599 Mr '63
GÖTTINGEN university. See Colleges and universities—Germany (Federal Republic)
GOTTLIEB, Adolph
Adolph Gottlieb: private symbols in public statements. M. Friedman. il por Art N 62: 32-5+ My '63
Bienal's best; São Paulo bienal in Brazil. il por Time 82:90 O 4 '63
Older. il por Newsweek 63:82 F 24 '64
GOTTLIEB, Dan, and Gottlieb, Diane
Does the FCC have AT&T's number? New Repub 148:17-19 Ap 6 '63
GOTTLIEB, Diane. See Gottlieb, Dan, jt. auth.
GOTTLIEB, Gilbert
Components of recognition in ducklings. Natur Hist 74:12-19 bibliog(p70) F '65
Following-response initiation in ducklings: age and sensory stimulation. bibliog Science 140:399-400 Ap 26 '63
Imprinting in nature. bibliog Science 139: 497-8 F 8 '63
GOTTLIEB, Linda, and Feifer, George
Yankee fans in Yerevan. Reporter 30:36-7 Ja 16 '64
—and Gottlieb, Paul
How to see India; be young. Mlle 56:136-7+ F '63
GOTTLIEB, Paul. See Gottlieb, L. jt. auth.
GOTTLIEB, Robert
Scrutiny bound. New Repub 149:21-4+ D 7 '63
GOTTLIEB, Robert J.
Classic comments. See issues of Motor trend
Ten best American classics. Motor T 15:112-15 N '63
GOTTLIEB, Sanford
Conversing with Russians. Bul Atomic Sci 21:35-6 Ja '65
GOTTLIEB, Sylvia B.
Liberals and the labor movement. Mo Labor R 87:134-5 F '64
GOTTSCHALK, Louis
En garde, Vanguard! recording of Gottschalk's A night in the tropics. H. Shanet. Sat R 47:118 Mr 14 '64; Discussion. 47:58 Ap 11; 69 Je 27 '64
First complete recording of Gottschalk's symphony, A night in the tropics. R. Kammerer. por Am Rec G 30:102-3 O '63
GOTTSCHO, Samuel H.
Our glamorous weeds. il Audubon Mag 65: 226-31 Jl '63
GOUCHER college, Baltimore
Broad stairs, stone walls and courtyard form handsome gateway to rural campus. il Arch Rec 134:117-24 Jl '63
Clouds and umbrellas; new $2,000,000 college center. Mus Am 83:15 F '63
GOUGET, Charles W.
We take the puzzle out of grape pruning. Pop Gard 14:46+ Mr '63
GOUGH, Marion
Color that makes tradition come alive. House B 105:134-47 Mr '63
Decorator's diary. See issues of House beautiful
How to leave home and like it. See issues of House beautiful
If you like paradox, you'll love Ethiopia. House B 105:126+ Ap '63
Places where spring seems lovelier. House B 105:118+ Mr '63
Wonders of the wilderness. House B 106:115+ Ag '64
GOUGH ISLAND
Isotopic composition of lead and strontium from Ascension and Gough Islands. P. W. Gast and others. bibliog il Science 145:1181-5 S 11 '64
GOULANDRIS, Mrs Nicholas
Lost Greek look retrieved. il pors Vogue 141:118-23+ F 15 '63
GOULART, João
President Goulart to President Johnson; letter, December 13, 1963. Dept State Bul 50: 48-9 Ja 13 '64

about

As the dust settles in Brazil. A. A. Berle. Reporter 30:27-8 Ap 23 '64; Discussion. 30: 6+ My 21 '64
Brazil and Chile. New Repub 150:5-6 Ap 11 '64
Brazil: giant in chains. il por Sr Schol 82: 10-13+ My 8 '63

GOULART, João—about—*Continued*
Brazil in perspective; the Goulart ouster. A. G. Frank. il por Nation 198:408-11 Ap 27 '64
Brazil in quandary. J. J. Johnson. Cur Hist 48:9-15+ Ja '65
Brazil's Goulart: power for the sake of what? il por Newsweek 61:48-50+ Mr 11 '63
Brazil's Goulart skirts the abyss. J. De Onis. il por N Y Times Mag p20+ Ag 18 '63
Cabinet maker. il por Time 81:21 Je 28 '63
Country that saved itself. C. W. Hall. il Read Digest 85:133-58 N '64
Country where inflation is the way of life. D. B. Richardson. por U S News 55:67-9 Ag 12 '63
Goodbye to Jango. il Time 83:26-7 Ap 10 '64
Goulart audit. il por Time 83:36+ My 1 '64
Goulart forced out. il por Sr Schol 84:18-19 Ap 17 '64
Goulart goes over brink in Brazil. il por Bsns W p27 Ap 4 '64
Goulart's gone, but Brazil's problems stay. il por Newsweek 63:37-8 Ap 13 '64
Goulart's legacy. R. Peter. por Nat R 16:358 My 5 '64
How close the reds came to taking over Brazil. il por U S News 56:65 Ap 27 '64
Now with Castro turned back; a new start for Brazil. il U S News 56:73-4 Ap 20 '64
Quickstep to the left. por Newsweek 63:54 Mr 23 '64
Revolution. D. B. Richardson. il por U S News 56:31-3 Ap 13 '64
Revolution in Brazil, by I. L. Horowitz. Review
Nat R por 16:949-51 N 3 '64. J. W. F. Dulles
Seven days in April. Nat R 16:308 Ap 21 '64
Spirit of '32. il por Time 83:30 Ap 3 '64
When executives turned revolutionaries. P. Siekman. il Fortune 70:147-9+ S '64
Where did everybody go? Continental congress of solidarity with Cuba. por Time 81:30 Ap 5 '63
GOULASH. See Stew
GOULD, Alan J.
Again, the Olympic challenge. Nat Geog Mag 126:488-513 O '64
GOULD, Charles L.
Let's face up to the truth; address, July 21, 1964. Vital Speeches 30:701-4 S 1 '64
GOULD, Flo, and Kerckhoff, R. K.
What makes a good neighborhood? PTA Mag 57:19-21 My '63
GOULD, Glenn
Bach by Gould: incomparably the most fascinating. R. Sabin. por Am Rec 31:211-12 N '64
Fugue; private showing of G. Gould's Anatomy of fugue. New Yorker 39:47-50 D 7 '63
Glenn Gould: a poet and a seeker. R. Sabin. il por Am Rec G 30:292-3 D '63
Secure in the universe; Bach's modern interpreters. il por Time 83:67 Ja 3 '64
Strauss and the electronic future. Sat R 47: 58-9+ My 30 '64
Zany genius of Glenn Gould. A. Bester. por Holiday 35:149-54+ Ap '64
GOULD, Jack
Cactus Jack. il por Time 82:58 O 11 '63
GOULD, Joan
Why women make great crews; and we do! Yachting 116:56-7+ O '64
GOULD, Joe
Profiles. J. Mitchell. il New Yorker 40:61-2+ S 19; 53-4+ S 26 '64
Squash & stretch. M. Klonsky. il por Esquire 60:162-3+ D '63
GOULD, John
Lottery, the Puritan and the devil. N Y Times Mag p 16+ My 19 '63
GOULD, Laurence McKinley
Laurence McKinley Gould, president-elect. H. Odishaw. por Science 139:612-14 F 15 '63
GOULD, Samuel B.
Education: a decade of dilemmas; excerpts from address, July 18, 1963. por ALA Bul 57:837+ O '63
Welding fifty-eight schools into one big university. il por Bsns W p92-100+ O 17 '64
GOULD, William B.
Expanding opportunities. Commonweal 81:342 D 4 '64
GOULD, William S. Baring-. See Baring-Gould, W. S.
GOULDTHORPE, Ken
(ed) See Chapman, E. Big tickle puts the scream too high
GOULET, Denis
Economic progress and Brazilian nationalism. Cath World 198:314-19 F '64
GOULET, Robert
Gangway for Goulet. D. J. Hamblin. il pors Life 54:86-8+ Ap 26 '63
Go-go-go of Robert Goulet. G. Millstein. pors Sat Eve Post 236:24-5 Ap 27 '63
Robert Goulet goes to Hollywood. R. Hochstein. il pors Good H 157:30+ S '63
GOUNOD, Charles François
Faust. Criticism
New Yorker 39:128+ N 16 '63
Opera N 28:17-23 Ja 4 '64
On records; Faust. Opera N 28:36 Ja 4 '64
GOURAS, P. and Carr, R. E.
Primate retinal responses: slow changes during repetitive stimulation with light. bibliog Science 145:413-14 Jl 24 '64
GOURDS
Gourds; how to grow, harvest, and cure them. D. T. Stuart. il Pop Gard 14:73+ My '63
House for Jenny-wren. M. Adams. il Flower Grower 50:49 Je '63
I have the feeling we're being watched; gourd people. il Am Home 67:10+ O '64
Lagenarias are unusual. J. H. Andrew, jr. il Horticulture 41:230-1 Ap '63
GOURMET clubs. See Clubs
GOURMET food industry. See Food industry and trade
GOURMETS. See Eating
GOUVENEUR, N.Y.
Zeta potential cleans a difficult water. il Am City 79:96-8 S '64
GOVERNMENT. See Nations; State, The
GOVERNMENT, Resistance to
Plot that flopped: CUSA for Conservatism-USA, secret organization. P. Swank. il Look 29:28-9 Ja 26 '65
See also
Revolutions
GOVERNMENT agencies. See United States—Executive departments
GOVERNMENT aid. See Grants-in-aid; Subsidies
GOVERNMENT aid to business
Industrial aid bonds: boon or bane? Duns R 81:pt2 S100 Mr '63
See also
Government lending
Industry and state
GOVERNMENT airplanes. See Airplanes, Government
GOVERNMENT and art. See Art and state
GOVERNMENT and labor. See Labor laws and legislation
GOVERNMENT and science. See Science and state
GOVERNMENT and the press
Administration news practices investigated. Aviation W 78:27 Mr 25 '63
Alaskan air commander disputes official version of Soviet flights. L. Booda. Aviation W 78:30 Ap 1 '63
All the news that manages to fit. A. Krock. Nat R 14:189 Mr 12 '63
And a time for ecclesiastes. Reporter 32:12 Ja 14 '65
Baker case: news that will not stay managed? il U S News 56:43-5 F 24 '64
Can you manage the news? il Bsns W p90-2 Mr 2 '63
Cracks in image mirror irritate Kennedy fans. M. Smith. il Nations Bsns 51:23-4 Ap '63
Don't swallow everything. il Time 81:51 Mr 29 '63
Electronic conscience. Reporter 28:16+ Ap 25 '63
Few anguished questions. M. Ascoli. Reporter 28:22 Ap 25 '63; Discussion. 28:6 My 23 '63
Foreign policy and the people's right to know; address, May 5, 1964. R. J. Manning. Dept State Bul 50:868-77 Je 1 '64
Foreign policy in the open society; statement, March 25, 1963. R. J. Manning. Dept State Bul 48:575-9 Ap 15 '63
Fourteen clues to Washington news. R. Baker. il N Y Times Mag p31+ Ap 7 '63
From Washington straight. Cato. Nat R 14: 189 Mr 12 '63
From Washington straight: use of backgrounder technique in President L. Johnson's relations with the press. Cato. Nat R 17:15 Ja 12 '65
From Washington straight; W. Jenkins story. Cato. Nat R 16:984 N 3 '64
Furor over managed news. il U S News 54: 103 Ap 8 '63
How free is the German press? F. E. Hirsch. Cur Hist 44:226-30+ Ap '63
How much management of the news? il Newsweek 61:59-63 Ap 8 '63
How news is managed by officials in Washington. il U S News 54:38-42 Ap 15 '63

GOVERNMENT and the press—*Continued*
If a government begins to deceive; excerpts from address, April 24, 1963. I. Maier. U S News 54:10 My 6 '63
I've got a secret: President Johnson and the press. J. Deakin. New Repub 152:13-15 Ja 30 '65
JFK termed brilliant in managing the news. U S News 54:10 Mr 11 '63
Johnson woos press. il Bsns W p34+ F 8 '64
Journalism and foreign affairs; address, March 13, 1964. R. J. Manning. Dept State Bul 50:541-9 Ap 6 '64; Same with title Press and the government. Vital Speeches 30:453-7 My 15 '64
Kennedy parties and managed news. il U S News 54:6 Mr 4 '63
Letter from Washington. R. H. Rovere. New Yorker 39:163-9 Mr 30 '63
Lighter mood hits Washington; quotations. L. B. Johnson. U S News 56:47-8 My 11 '64
LBJ and the press. K. Crawford. Newsweek 63:18 F 17 '64
Managed news. W. Lippmann. Newsweek 61:23 Ap 15 '63
Managed news; our peacetime censorship. H. W. Baldwin. Atlan 211:53-9 Ap '63; Same abr. Read Digest 82:109-14 Je '63
Management of news. L. Markel. il Sat R 46:50-1+ F 9 '63; Discussion. 46:51+ Mr 9; 31 Mr 16 '63
Managing the news. R. Horchler. Commonweal 77:659-62 Mr 22 '63
Mismanaging the news. Sat Eve Post 237:80 Mr 7 '64
Mr Kennedy's management of the news. A. Krock. Fortune 67:82+ Mr '63; Excerpts. Nat R 14:182 Mr 12 '63
Mr Manning interviewed on News and comment; ed. by H. K. Smith. R. J. Manning. Dept State Bul 48:500-3 Ap 1 '63
Never say lie; grilling by the House information subcommittee on managed news. Time 81:81 Ap 5 '63
News management. K. Crawford. Newsweek 61:33 Mr 11 '63
News management (cont) Reporter 30:14+ F 27 '64
News management is still a live issue. J. Magmer. Cath World 197:180-6 Je '63
News managers. B. H. Bagdikian. Sat Eve Post 236:17-19 Ap 20 '63
Official spokesman for managed news. il U S News 54:14 Ap 1 '63
On the slanting of the news. H. S. Taylor. il Nat R 16:489-90 Je 16 '64
Pentagon news leaks. Aviation W 78:28 Ap 1 '63
President and the press corps, what to expect. il U S News 56:15 Ap 20 '64
Reflections on the Bob and John show. W. Rogers, jr. New Repub 148:10-11 F 23 '63
Secrecy boomerang; managing the news. R. Hotz. Aviation W 78:21 Mr 18 '63
Service chiefs must detail news contacts. Aviation W 80:20-1 Je 8 '64
Sour trumpet. R. Hotz; discussion. Aviation W 78:118 Ja 28 '63
Strictly off the record, gentlemen! M. McGrory. America 108:356 Mr 16 '63
To the editor. D. Quinn. Nat R 14:380 My 7 '63
Traitor to my class; move from Washington, D.C. to Florida. F. Knebel. il Look 28:32+ Ag 25 '64
Trial by press release. Nation 199:83 S 7 '64
Ultimate weapon; excerpts from address. H. Brucker. Time 81:65 My 3 '63
Uproar over news leaks and lie detectors. il U S News 54:8 Ap 15 '63
Viet beat; Pentagon's Operation candor in Vietnam. il Newsweek 64:76 S 7 '64
Vietnam: fact and fiction. Nation 196:169 Mr 2 '63
War that should never end. A. Friendly. NEA J 53:21 D '64
What is managed news, dad? Time 81:37 Mr 1 '63
Why American political reporting is better than England's. D. E. Butler. Harper 226:14+ My '63

Anecdotes, facetiae, satire, etc.

Day the news managers quit; fable of the New frontier. W. S. Just. Reporter 28:36-7 My 9 '63
Notes and comment; managed news. New Yorker 39:33 My 4 '63

GOVERNMENT appropriations and expenditures
See also
United States—Appropriations and expenditures

GOVERNMENT automobiles. See Automobiles, Government

GOVERNMENT banking. See Postal savings banks

GOVERNMENT bonds. See Bonds, Government

GOVERNMENT buildings. See Public buildings

GOVERNMENT contracts. See Contracts, Government

GOVERNMENT corporations
Rand: R&D nonprofit pioneered a new kind of organization, served as a model for others. J. Walsh. Science 144:1112-14+ My 29 '64

GOVERNMENT documents. See Documents

GOVERNMENT employees
AF officers to bolster Apollo management. W. J. Normyle. Aviation W 81:22 Ag 24 '64
Conservation careers in government. J. H. Caldwell. Nat Parks Mag 37:17-18 N '63
Federal agencies put a checkrein on jobs. il Bsns W p42+ D 7 '63
Federal civil service bargaining; concerning Executive order. M. S. Wortman, jr. Mo Labor R 87:659-60 Je '64
Federal employee bargaining unit determinations. H. J. Lahne and E. H. Ghearing. il Mo Labor R 87:763-6 Jl '64
Federal scientist-administrator. E. S. Uyeki and F. B. Cliffe, jr. bibliog il Science 139:1267-70 Mr 29 '63
Goddard's technical manpower. R. W. Hutchison. il Electr World 71:62-3 Je '64
Government jobs overseas. il Changing T 18:34-5 Ja '64
Government workers getting organized. il Bsns W p72 F 9 '63
On recruiting federal officials. J. J. Corson. Science 144:663-4 My 8 '64
Principal NASA, AEC and weather bureau procurement personnel. Miss & Roc 15:188+ N 30 '64
Scramble for jobs on Capitol hill. U S News 57:16 N 23 '64
U.S. seen ahead in using scientists in government. Sci N L 85:351 My 30 '64
See also
American federation of government employees
Bureaucracy
Civil service
Conflict of interests (Public office)
Misconduct in office
Negro government employees
Postal employees
Public officers
Public service
Strikes—United States—Government employees
United States—Congress—Employees

Anecdotes, facetiae, satire, etc.

One day in the life of James Hoover. J. Hoover. New Yorker 39:76+ Ag 17 '63

Appointment, qualifications, tenure, etc.

Case of Mr Henning. New Repub 152:5 Ja 9 '65
New appointments. il Time 85:16 Ja 8 '65
Snooping in the park: investigatory techniques. J. Ridgeway. New Repub 152:9-10 Ja 16 '65
Snoops; private lives and public service. J. Ridgeway. New Repub 151:13-17 D 19 '64 Discussion. 152:22 Ja 2: 28-30 Ja 9: 35-6 Ja 30 '65
Why invade privacy? security interviews. Christian Cent 81:1579 D 23 '64

Pensions

See Civil service pensions

Salaries, allowances, etc.

Federal executive salaries. D. Wolfle. Science 144:15 Ap 3 '64
Federal pay: in the competition for professionals, government faces salary gap, other problems. J. Walsh. Science 143:229-30 Ja 17 '64
Federal pay may fatten. Bsns W p96 Je 6 '64
Federal salaries in 1959. J. Lyman. Science 141:6+ Jl 5 '63
How much it pays to work for the government. il U S News 57:49-50 Jl 20 '64
Measures of federal salaries; 1789-1965. A. Sackley; J. Griest. bibliog f il Mo Labor R 87:1143-54 O '64
Penny pincher. il Newsweek 64:39 N 30 '64
Salaries and benefits under the Federal classification act. Mo Labor R 87:1155-64 O '64
U.S. pay: up by 764 millions; with charts. U S News 57:8-9 Ag 17 '64
See also
Public officers—Salaries, allowances, etc.

Training

Careers in government. il Sr Schol 85:20+ N 11 '64
Impact of office automation in the Internal revenue service. R. W. Riche and J. R. Alliston. il Mo Labor R 86:388-93 Ap '63

GOVERNMENT entertaining
Ball at the White House; photographs. N Y Times Mag p 12-13 F 23 '64
Culture at the White House. il U S News 54:71 Ap 8 '63
First state social by the Chief. il Life 56: 32-32A Ja 24 '64
Give the party they gave in the White House. il House B 105:212-13+ O '63
I believe; White House boarder; ed. by F. R. Schreiber. W. L. Smith. il Seventeen 23:196-7 S '64
Johnsons in the White House. il Look 28: 15-21 Mr 10 '64
Kennedy parties and managed news. il U S News 54:6 Mr 4 '63
My day at the White House; one of the presidential scholars. S. Clark. il Seventeen 23:30+ S '64
New record for V.I.P. hosting. P. Lisagor. il N Y Times Mag p30+ S 29 '63
100 years after Lincoln set the slaves free; integrated White House party. il U S News 54:8 F 25 '63
Start of the social season. il Time 82:25-6 S 13 '63
There's a new social style at the White House. il U S News 56:60-1+ F 17 '64
Thomas Jefferson, gourmet. J. H. Hazelton. il Am Heritage 15:20-1+ O '64
Treat & a treatment; President Johnson's informal parties for Congress. Time 83:16-17 Mr 6 '64
When LBJ outdanced the diplomats; excerpts from report. D. McCardle. il U S News 56:14 F 24 '64
When the President says: ten more for lunch. M. Hunter. il N Y Times Mag p26-7 S 20 '64
When the White House honored teen-age scholars. il U S News 56:10 Je 22 '64

Anecdotes, facetiae, satire, etc.

Thank you, Madam President; dancing at the White House. E. J. Kahn, jr. New Yorker 40:103-4+ My 2 '64

GOVERNMENT ethics. See Political ethics
GOVERNMENT guarantee of foreign investments. See Insurance, Investment guaranty
GOVERNMENT helicopters. See Helicopters, Government
GOVERNMENT investigations
Administration news practices investigated. Aviation W 78:27 Mr 25 '63
Booked for travel; colloquy and pillory: hearings on a new budget for the Travel service. H. Sutton. Sat R 46:44-5+ S 21 '63
Business loans that went sour; SBA under fire. il U S News 56:50 Mr 9 '64
Charade; congressmen's expense accounts. Newsweek 61:24-5 Ap 22 '63
Coming: new look at business regulation. Nations Bsns 51:102-3+ S '63
Gadget; radio and TV rating services. il Newsweek 61:80 Ap 8 '63
High price of silence. W. J. Coughlin. Miss & Roc 15:46 N 23 '64
Home in Texas; J. Stanford, executive secretary of the Texas Communist party. R. Dugger. New Repub 150:6 Mr 28 '64
Iceberg; machinations of investor-owned utilities. Nation 199:206 O 12 '64
Incorruptible John Williams; the conscience of the Senate. J. Daniel. Read Digest 84: 105-10 My '64
Investigating Washington; how far will it go? U S News 55:66 D 2 '63
Lone-wolf guardian of federal morality. H. B. Meyers. il Fortune 69:126-9+ Je '64
Mess in Washington? with interview with J. J. Williams. il U S News 55:36-8+ N 25 '63
No-notice checks recommended for curbing cockpit violations. W. Wright. Aviation W 79:40 Jl 1 '63
Now the whiz kids are tackling the U.S. navy. il U S News 55:59-60 N 25 '63
Pests and poisons; R. Carson before Senate investigative subcommittee. Newsweek 61: 86 Je 17 '63
Puzzle: who knows who looks at TV? investigation by House commerce investigating subcommittee. il U S News 54:44-7 Ap 8 '63
Show biz in Washington. Nation 197:229 O 19 '63
Still another list; investigation of homosexuality in the teaching profession in Florida. Nation 198:615 Je 22 '64
Their men in Washington. F. J. Cook. il Nation 198:311-30 Mr 30 '64
Too many government investigations! O. Schisgall. Read Digest 82:135-8 Mr '63
See also
Loyalty investigations
United States—President's commission to investigate the assassination of President Kennedy

Aerospace industries

Probe focuses on NASA-JPL relationship. D. E. Fink. Aviation W 80:29 Ap 27 '64

Airlines

Congress, CAB eye Riddle operations. R. H. Cook. Aviation W 79:47+ D 16 '63

Anecdotes, facetiae, satire, etc.

Intelligent liberal student's guide to world literature; concerning McCarthy era. W. F. Gavin. Nat R 16:64 Ja 28 '64

Baker case

As the Baker case inquiry gets going. il U S News 55:10 N 11 '63
As the Baker case unfolds. U S News 56:6 Ja 27 '64
Background music; Bobby Baker case. il Newsweek 63:21 F 10 '64
Baker business. Cato. Nat R 16:649 Jl 28 '64
Baker case again; a bagful of new charges. il U S News 57:49-50 D 14 '64
Baker case; concerning testimony before the Senate rules committee. Sr Schol 84:22 F 7 '64
Baker case: news that will not stay managed? il U S News 56:43-5 F 24 '64
Baker defense. Newsweek 62:28 D 16 '63
Baker issue. K. Crawford. Newsweek 63:28 Ap 6 '64
Baker rides again. Newsweek 63:26-7 Mr 23 '64
Baker's dozen. Cato. Nat R 16:224 Mr 24 '64
Bakers $470 tax on $82,000 income; unanswered questions. U S News 56:10 Ap 13 '64
Bobby Baker blossoms. M. Kempton. New Repub 151:7-8 Jl 4 '64
Bobby Baker case. Commonweal 80:77 Ap 10 '64
Bobby Baker case: infighting goes on. U S News 56:11 Ap 6 '64
Bobby Baker case: sure campaign issue. U S News 57:12 Jl 20 '64
Bobby Baker cover-up. Sat Eve Post 237:88 Ap 25 '64
Bobby Baker story: Senate unfolds chapter one; hearing of the Senate rules committee. il U S News 55:31 D 30 '63
Bobby Baker's affairs. M. Kempton. New Repub 150:6-8 F 8 '64
Bobby Baker's nonappearance on TV. Sat Eve Post 237:86 Mr 21 '64
Bobby Baker's silence; back to the Fifth. A. M. Bickel. New Repub 150:9-10 Mr 21 '64
Bobbybaking on the Potomac: coincidences; where to? Cato. Nat R 16:1142 D 29 '64
Bobby's busyness. il Time 83:19-20 Ja 31 '64
Bobby's high life. il Time 82:26-7 N 8 '63
Carole talks. il Newsweek 65:23 F 1 '65
Cash-and-carry; Mrs Novak before Senate rules committee. Newsweek 62:13 D 30 '63
Closing the books on Baker. E. Knoll and L. Stern. il Reporter 30:17-20 Ap 9 '64
Conflict of interests; question of reopening the Bobby Baker case. il Time 83:23 Je 5 '64
Deliveryman. Nation 198:545 Je 1 '64
$11,025 to $2 million. il Newsweek 63:15-16 F 3 '64
End of Bobby Baker? Commonweal 80:497 Jl 24 '64
Enterprisers. K. Crawford. Newsweek 63:28 F 3 '64
Fast rise of Bobby Baker; with excerpts from testimony before Senate rules committee by D. B. Reynolds, and statement by L. B. Johnson. il U S News 56:55-9 F 3 '64
Favors for Bobby Baker, Jimmy Hoffa's union? U S News 56:14 Ap 27 '64
First Baker witness; G. Novak before Small business committee. Time 82:18 D 27 '63
Give-and-take. il Newsweek 63:17-18 Ja 27 '64
Hoffa's name in Baker hearing; excerpts from testimony. D. B. Reynolds U S News 56:86 F 3 '64
Hopscotch. Newsweek 63:19 Mr 30 '64
How Baker turned access into an asset. Bsns W p30-1 F 8 '64
How Bobby Baker made some more money; summary of testimony. T. D. Webb, jr; F. E. Law. U S News 56:8 F 17 '64
How business sometimes is done in Washington. il U S News 57:30-1 D 21 '64

GOVERNMENT investigations—Baker case—*Continued*
In the Baker case now: a forgery claim. U S News 56:14 Mr 23 '64
Influence and loans: latest on Bobby Baker; when LBJ stepped in. U S News 56:8 Mr 16 '64
Jenkins in January. il Newsweek 64:24 D 21 '64
Joyless probe for the Senate? il Bsns W p32-3 N 9 '63
Kickback charges in the Baker case. il U S News 57:12 S 14 '64
Milking time. Newsweek 63:19 Ap 6 '64
Missile secrets; and Bobby Baker case. U S News 57:14 O 12 '64
New light on Bobby Baker's activities. il U S News 56:6 Mr 2 '64
Off again. Time 84:24 D 18 '64
One, four, five, six and out. il Newsweek 63:18 Mr 2 '64
Out of the bag. Newsweek 63:16 Ja 20 '64
Parties & payments. il Time 84:32-3 D 11 '64
Pleasure worth the price; Magic stock deals. Time 83:23 F 7 '64
Rulesmanship; proposal for renewed Baker investigation. Newsweek 64:36 S 21 '64
Senate inquiry into sugar & spices. il Newsweek 62:32-3 N 11 '63
Senate shocks a Senate prober. C. Phillips. il N Y Times Mag p20+ Ag 9 '64
Senator Williams, public eye. F. W. Collins. il N Y Times Mag p 18+ F 9 '64
Senators decide not to investigate senators. il U S News 56:8 My 25 '64
Silent witness. il Time 83:17-21 Mr 6 '64
Speaking out; they can't cover up for Bobby Baker. H. Scott. Sat Eve Post 237:8+ My 9 '64
Still alive. il Newsweek 63:22+ Mr 9 '64
Still unanswered in the Baker case. U S News 56:40 Mr 30 '64
Strange case of Bobby Baker; investigation by Senate rules committee. il U S News 56:40-2 F 10 '64
Suite F-80, inc. M. Kempton. New Repub 149:8-9 D 28 '63
That lingering aroma; case of contractor McCloskey. Time 84:21 S 11 '64
$35,000 misunderstanding. Nation 199:451-2 D 14 '64
Those confidential files. Nation 198:178 F 24 '64
Tracking Baker. Newsweek 62:30-1 N 18 '63
Unanswered questions of the Bobby Baker case. il U S News 56:42-3 Mr 9 '64
Vicissitudes of politics. Nation 197:427 D 21 '63
When the Baker case erupted again; draft report on Senate's investigation. U S News 56:8 Je 1 '64
White House leak; attempt to discredit testimony of a key witness. il Newsweek 63:15 F 17 '64
Who, us? Senate rules committee report. Newsweek 63:19 Je 1 '64
Who's a liar? reopened inquiry. il Newsweek 64:24-5 D 14 '64
Will the lid stay clamped? Time 83:26 Ap 3 '64

Boxing

My cooperation; Senate investigation of the Liston-Cassius Clay fight. il Newsweek 63:60-1 Ap 6 '64
Sonny & co; Liston case hearings. Time 83:33+ Ap 10 '64
Sparring. Newsweek 63:63 Ap 13 '64
Taking stock of Sonny Liston: Senate subcommittee investigation of Liston-Clay fight. R. H. Boyle. il Sports Illus 20:24-7 Ap 6 '64

Drug trade

Annals of legislation; background and history of Drug industry antitrust bill. R. Harris. New Yorker 40:48-50+ Mr 14; 75-6+ Mr 21; 46-8+ Mr 28 '64
Merrell's bitter pill; anti-cholesterol drug, MER-29. Bsns W p23 D 28 '63
New drug; is government supervision adequate? M. Mintz. il Reporter 28:46-9+ Mr 28 '63; Discussion. 28:11 My 9 '63
Real voice, by R. Harris. Review
Nation 199:166-8 S 28 '64. E. Langer
Sat R 47:45 S 5 '64. J. Lear

Government contracts

Admiral viewed Boeing TFX as one plane. Aviation W 78:28-9 Ap 8 '63
Another news manager. K. Crawford. Newsweek 61:29 Ap 1 '63
Blackburn memo criticizes TFX decision. A. W. Blackburn. Aviation W 78:79-83 Je 3 '63
Collision in Washington: McNamara vs. the Congress; hearings on TFX contract. Newsweek 61:25-6 Mr 25 '63
Congressional critics eye DOD civilians. G. C. Wilson. Aviation W 78:22-3 Je 3 '63
Crackdown on employee welfare programs sought. H. M. David. Miss & Roc 15:27-8 S 14 '64
Critical report on Tyco probe spurs USAF research scrutiny. Aviation W 80:20 Mr 23 '64
Dammed comic opera. il Time 81:23 Ap 12 '63
Double standard; TFX deal. Newsweek 61:27 Mr 11 '63
Editorial; TFX. R. Hotz. Aviation W 78:21 My 13 '63
Experts rebut McNamara; back Boeing's use of titanium for F-111. G. C. Wilson. Aviation W 79:36 Jl 1 '63
F-111 probe shifts to differing evaluations. G. C. Wilson. il Aviation W 78:24-5 Mr 25 '63
Fight over TFX; McNamara's side of the case. U S News 54:18+ Ap 8 '63
Fighting Bob; investigation of contract for TFX fighter plane. il Time 81:16 Mr 22 '63
Former key TFX official attacks choice. G. C. Wilson. Aviation W 78:32-3 My 27 '63
Ganging up on McNamara; with editorial comment. J. Greene. Nation 196:257, 264-6 Mr 30 '63
GAO urges stricter invention report rule. K. Johnsen. il Aviation W 82:101+ Ja 25 '65
General dynamics defends F-111 design. Aviation W 78:104+ My 20 '63
General dynamics rejects plan for TFX flying prototype contest. G. C. Wilson. Aviation W 78:27-9 My 13 '63
Gilpatric's records are new TFX issue. G. C. Wilson. Aviation W 79:27-8 N 11 '63
Grumman's variable sweep wing work cited. il Aviation W 78:105 My 20 '63
Hanging judge; Sen. John McClellan's investigation of the TFX contract. K. Crawford. Newsweek 61:35 My 27 '63
High cost of failure; TFX investigations. il Newsweek 61:22 Ap 8 '63
How the Pentagon is run: what TFX fight shows; with excerpts from statement by R. S. McNamara. il U S News 54:54-7 Ap 22 '63
Justice considers GAO pricing claims. K. Johnsen. Aviation W 82:24-5 Ja 11 '65
Korth defends TFX choice, hears charge he used raw judgment. G. C. Wilson. il Aviation W 79:19-21 Jl 8 '63
Lost point; subcommittee hearings on the award of the TFX fighter-plane contract. il Newsweek 61:20 Ap 1 '63
McClellan dubious about legality of Rubel procurement proposals. G. C. Wilson. Aviation W 78:37 Je 10 '63
McClellan says Pentagon civilians abused powers. Aviation W 78:29 Ap 15 '63
McClellan to press Korth conflict probe. G. C. Wilson. Aviation W 79:26-7 O 21 '63
McNamara assails critics of TFX award. G. C. Wilson. Aviation W 78:26-9 Mr 18 '63
McNamara explains TFX award decision. R. S. McNamara. Aviation W 78:81+ Mr 25 '63
McNamara gives report on assets. il U S News 54:95-6 Ap 1 '63
McNamara tries to steer TFX questions. G. C. Wilson. Aviation W 78:26-8 Ap 1 '63
McNamara used rough judgement on TFX. G. C. Wilson. Aviation W 78:24-5 My 6 '63
McNamara's $1-billion TFX saving hypothetical. Aviation W 78:32 My 27 '63
Navy scores DOD civilians' X-22A role. G. C. Wilson. Aviation W 78:32-3 Je 17 '63
Pentagon blasts back at the TFX probers. il Bsns W p29-30 Mr 23 '63
Pentagon changes spark an uproar. il U S News 54:21 My 20 '63
Pentagon teams prepare McNamara on TFX. G. C. Wilson. Aviation W 78:23 Ap 29 '63
Performance edge stressed in TFX quiz. G. C. Wilson. Aviation W 78:28-30 Ap 15 '63
Phasing out the air force? contract for TFX. Nat R 14:223-4 Mr 26 '63
Pitfalls of publicity; TFX contract. W. V. Shannon. Commonweal 78:126-7 Ap 26 '63
Politics in the arms business? with excerpts from Congressional record. il U S News 54:40-3 My 13 '63
President's role in TFX award disclosed. E. H. Kolcum. Aviation W 79:34-6 Ag 26 '63
Senate probers scrutinize Korth letters; with statement by F. Korth, October 19, 1963. G. C. Wilson. Aviation W 79:22-4 O 28 '63
Senate TFX probers split on Gilpatric. G. C. Wilson. Aviation W 79:27-9 N 25 '63

GOVERNMENT investigations—Government contracts—*Continued*
$7 billion contract that changed the rules. R. A. Smith. il Fortune 67:96-101+ Mr; 110-11+ Ap '63
Shifts that stem from TFX feud. Bsns W p34 Ag 24 '63
Still fighting; R. McNamara before the Joint defense procurement subcommittee. il Time 81:26-7 Ap 5 '63
Strawberry business; air force memorandum leak. Newsweek 61:26 Ap 15 '63
TFX; a feud boils up; with editorial comment. il Bsns W p 19-20. 116 My 11 '63
TFX award stirs storm; GD-Grumman over Boeing. Bsns W p25 Mr 9 '63
TFX board selected Boeing four times; investigation of General dynamics-Grumman contract by Senate investigations subcommittee, with excerpts from hearing. G. C. Wilson. Aviation W 78:22-4 Mr 4 '63
TFX chief would drop thrust reversers. D. E. Fink. Aviation W 79:38 Ag 5 '63
TFX: Congress fumes and fusses but seems to recognize that the decision wasn't a bad one. D. S. Greenberg. Science 139:1271-2 Mr 29 '63
TFX fight: there's still a split at the Pentagon. U S News 54:10 Ap 15 '63
TFX plane: what the fight is about. il U S News 54:61-3 Mr 25 '63
TFX probe to focus on possible conflict in Gilpatric, Korth roles. G. C. Wilson. Aviation W 79:27-8 S 9 '63
TFX probers fly a new route; Pentagon conflicts of interest. Bsns W p33 N 23 '63
Tactical fighters; TFX hearing. Reporter 28: 12 Ap 11 '63
Tyco probe spurs AF contracting reform. G. C. Wilson. Aviation W 79:40-1 D 16 '63
Welcome aboard. Nation 196:217 Mr 16 '63
Why not call McNamara? McClellan subcommittee investigation into the fighter plane (TFX) contract. New Repub 148:6 My 18 '63
Witnesses challenge McNamara on TFX. G. C. Wilson. Aviation W 78:26-7 Ap 8 '63
X-22 report is rebuff to DOD civilians. R. G. O'Lone. Aviation W 80:32-3 F 17 '64
Zuckert defends F-111 winner selection. G. C. Wilson. Aviation W 78:301 Mr 11 '63
Zuckert TFX rough judgment charged. D. E. Fink. Aviation W 79:29-30 Ag 12 '63

Government funded research

Congress and science: inquiries into R&D are currently quiet. D. S. Greenberg. Science 143:661-2 F 14 '64
Congress plans investigation of government-funded research. H. M. David. Miss & Roc 13:15 Ag 19 '63
Congress views science; NSF education programs under investigation. Sci N L 84:308 N 16 '63
Daddario committee: hearings to be held on overhead support and geographical distribution. D. S. Greenberg. Science 144:155 Ap 10 '64
Elliott committee: basic research fares well as House group hears thirty-eight on federal support of science. D. S. Greenberg. Science 142:1443-4 D 13 '63
Elliott committee: final reports issued as fifteen-month investigation of federal research comes to end. D. S. Greenberg. Science 147:131-2 Ja 8 '65
Elliott committee: first report should quell fears that inquiry has anti-scientific orientation. D. S. Greenberg. Science 143:791 F 21 '64
Elliot committee: latest study calls for improvement in data on scientific manpower problems. D. S. Greenberg. Science 146:234 O 9 '64
Elliott inquiry: chairman's loss in Alabama primary raises doubt about future of investigation. D. S. Greenberg. Science 144: 1319-20 Je 12 '64
From Washington: R and D on Capitol hill. H. Margolis. Bul Atomic Sci 20:33-7 My '64
Grant system: Elliott committee finds flaws, diversity in study of practices of federal agencies. D. S. Greenberg. il Science 145:795-8 Ag 21 '64
House panel to begin scrutiny of government-funded basic research. H. M. David. il Miss & Roc 15:14 S 28 '64
House R&D subcommittee told federal funding reaching peak. H. M. David. Miss & Roc 13:18 O 21 '63
Investigation: House unanimously approves comprehensive inquiry into federal support of research. D. S. Greenberg. il Science 141: 1161-4 S 20 '63
Investigation: mixed motivations led to House decision to probe government support for research; with editorial comment. D. S. Greenberg. Science 141:1245, 1261-4 S 27 '63
New overseers for federal science. J. Walsh. Science 142:210 O 11 '63
Prodigious inventory-taking. P. H. Abelson. Science 143:1127 Mr 13 '64
Sweeping probe of research spending; with editorial comment. Bsns W p26-7, 152 S 21 '63
Washington ramble: news in brief on investigations, accelerators, anger in NSF, and other matters; with editorial comment. D. S. Greenberg. Science 142:919, 940-1 N 15 '63

Guided missile industry

Senate report urges new missile buying approach. H. M. David. Miss & Roc 14:15 Ap 6 '64

Insurance companies

Lloyd's settles a Florida claim. Bsns W p74 Je 8 '63

Lobbying

Ethics of lobbying; Philippine war claims. Commonweal 78:236-7 My 24 '63
Washrooms of power: those anonymous propaganda peddlers. M. Kempton. New Repub 149:9-13 Ag 3 '63

Packaging

Packagers take a hint from the Hart bill. il Bsns W p47 N 23 '63

Ranger project

Ranger: oversight subcommittee asks why NASA doesn't prevail on JPL to rigidize projectwise. J. Walsh. Science 144:824-6 My 15 '64

Steel industry and trade

Nobody makes a row; steel price hearings. il Bsns W p27-8 Ap 27 '63

Stock exchange

Big board is under fire; special study of the securities markets. il Bsns W p23-4 Jl 20 '63
For Wall Street: tighter rules, fewer secrets; special study of securities markets. il Bsns W p23-5 Ap 6 '63
Modernizing the market; concerning SEC report. il Time 82:71-2 Jl 26 '63
Neither all bad nor all good; Cohen report on the Nation's securities markets. il Newsweek 62:64-7 Ag 19 '63
Question of skill, not scandal. Fortune 68: 92 Ag '63
SEC reforms to help, not hamstring. il Newsweek 61:75-6+ Ap 15 '63
Skeptical SEC eye on Wall Street. il Newsweek 62:55-6+ Jl 29 '63
Stock-market study. U S News 55:102 Ag 19 '63
Taking stock; findings of SEC study. il Time 81:91-2 Ap 12 '63
What Congress is told about the stock market. il U S News 54:67-8 Ap 15 '63
What's wrong in stock exchanges: official study. U S News 55:95 Jl 29 '63

Television industry

Ambush at Omaha Pass. K. Woodward. il Nation 196:373-5 My 4 '63
Crime shows on TV: a federal crackdown coming? excerpts from report by Senate subcommittee on juvenile delinquency. il U S News 57:49-50 N 9 '64

Trade unions

Will the law ever get Hoffa? H. Bigart. il Sat Eve Post 236:68-71 Mr 30 '63

GOVERNMENT labor policy. See United States—Labor policy
GOVERNMENT lending
How an LBJ associate got a U.S. loan. U S News 58:12 Ja 11 '65
Peeling off a slice of U.S. holdings; sale to investors of federal-held loans. il Bsns W p 130+ Mr 9 '63
GOVERNMENT lotteries. See Lotteries
GOVERNMENT officials. See Public officers
GOVERNMENT owned contracts. See Contracts, Government
GOVERNMENT owned patents. See Patents, Government owned

GOVERNMENT ownership
Grabbers; expropriation of foreign enterprises. il Time 81:88 Mr 29 '63
See also
Electric utilities—Government ownership
Industry and state
Railroads and state
Socialism

Argentina

Triumph for nationalism. Time 82:36 N 22 '63

Ceylon

U.S. suspends aid to Ceylon. Dept State Bul 48:328 Mr 4 '63

France

France roils the oilmen: state-owned, Union general des petroles. Bsns W p30 Je 29 '63

Germany (Federal Republic)

Denationalizing; stock of VEBA (Vereinigte elektrizitäts und bergwerks) to be sold to the public. Time 83:100 Ap 10 '64

Great Britain

Struggle for steel; debate over nationalization. il Time 85:70 Ja 22 '65

Italy

Headaches of nationalization. il Time 85:64 Ja 8 '65
Using his head. Time 82:62 D 27 '63

Latin America

Latins ease threats to U.S. mining; pressure for nationalization of foreign mining operations. Bsns W p 16-17 D 26 '64

Syria

Sliding-scale socialism. Newsweek 65:66 Ja 18 '65
Tuneful takeover; 115 firms wholly or partly nationalized. il Time 85:31 Ja 15 '65

GOVERNMENT pensions. See Civil service pensions

GOVERNMENT public relations. See Public relations

GOVERNMENT publications
Bargains from Uncle Sam's bookstore. D. B. Eisendrath, jr. Pop Phot 52:84-6+ My '63
Government aids to consumers (cont) Consumer Rep 28:80-7 D '63
Government grab-bag. Holiday 36:182-3 D '64
How to get publications from the U.S. Department of agriculture. Consumer Bul 46:22 D '63
Primary scientific publication and the federal government. B. W. Adkinson. bibliog Science 140:613-17 My 10 '63
Science in government; U.S. government organization manual. H. Pryor. Sci Digest 56:46-7 O '64
Stocking fillers from Uncle Sam's mail order list. J. Horn. il Parents Mag 38:122-3 D '63
Way of life; most frequently requested books and pamphlets. Christian Cent 82:127 Ja 27 '65
See also
Congressional record
Great Britain—Government publications

Bibliography

Congressional documents relating to foreign policy. See issues of Department of state bulletin
Publications of the Department of state. See issues of Department of state bulletin
Source material; comp. by D. Wasson. See issues of Foreign affairs

GOVERNMENT publicity
Foreign policy in the open society; statement, March 25, 1963. R. J. Manning. Dept State Bul 48:575-9 Ap 15 '63
From Washington straight. Cato. Nat R 14:104 F 12 '63
Hard sell in Washington. J. Tebbel. Sat R 47:51+ Jl 11 '64
Mr Manning interviewed on News and comment; ed. by H. K. Smith. R. J. Manning. Dept State Bul 48:500-3 Ap 1 '63
Something newsy; investigation of Hamilton Wright organization by Senate foreign relations committee. il Newsweek 62:27-8 Jl 22 '63
They've got a secret. Nat R 14:97+ F 12 '63
See also
Government and the press
Press conferences

GOVERNMENT purchasing. See Purchasing, Government

GOVERNMENT records. See Records

GOVERNMENT regulation of business. See Industry and state

GOVERNMENT regulation of industry. See Export controls; Industry and state

GOVERNMENT research
Better distribution of R&D funds sought. K. Johnsen. il Aviation W 81:101+ N 16 '64
Group warns Hornig on killing programs. Aviation W 80:63 Mr 30 '64
Individual R&D productivity is declining: summary of address. J. H. Rubel. Aviation W 78:37 Mr 18 '63
See also
Research—United States

GOVERNMENT restaurants. See Restaurants, Government

GOVERNMENT secrets. See Official secrets

GOVERNMENT security regulations. See Security classification (government documents)

GOVERNMENT service. See Civil service; Public officers

GOVERNMENT spending policy
About those spending cuts—. il U S News 56:74 Ja 20 '64
Another way to measure government spending; with charts. il U S News 54:70-1 My 27 '63
Big brother state. H. Hazlitt. Newsweek 64:78 S 14 '64
Big government, big spending; warning from Senator Byrd; excerpt from address, August 31, 1963. H. F. Byrd. U S News 55:50-1 S 9 '63
Blast at U.S. fiscal policy. Bsns W p29 Je 15 '63
Budget cuts would boost economy. R. Newcomb. Nations Bsns 51:38-9+ My '63
Budget sets a new style; with editorial comment. il Bsns W p23-4, 136 Ja 25 '64
Built-in boost for spending; Johnson's pressure for cuts. il Bsns W p25 D 14 '63
Changes planned in government spending. il U S News 56:90-2 F 3 '64
Committee to study economic impact of defense and disarmament; White House announcement, with text of memorandum, December 21, 1963. L. B. Johnson. Dept State Bul 50:120 Ja 27 '64
Congress focuses on defense cuts impact. K. Johnsen. Aviation W 80:26-7 Je 15 '64
Congress vs. spenders. il Bsns W p25-6 F 23 '63
Cutting up the arms budget. Nation 198:21 Ja 6 '64
Defense cutbacks. Nation 199:422 D 7 '64
Defense cutbacks hit professionals. il Bsns W p74-5 F 8 '64
Desperate drive to cut defense spending. C. J. V. Murphy. il Fortune 69:94-7+ Ja '64
Disarmament: its economic impact to be studied by Johnson panel; subject has been little explored. E. Langer. Science 143:28-30 Ja 3 '64
Economical year. R. Hotz. Aviation W 80:21 Ja 6 '64
Economy drive greeted with mixed emotions. J. Craft. il Nations Bsns 52:23-4 Mr '64
Effort urged to ease effect of DOD shifts. K. Johnsen. Aviation W 79:31 N 11 '63
False fears of disarmament. W. D. Grampp. Harvard Bsns R 42:28-30+ Ja '64
Federal budget hides big spending. il Nations Bsns 51:100-1+ D '63
Fiscal policy to head off recession; 1965 package. Bsns W p80 Ja 2 '65
From all sides now, a cry for a lid on federal spending. il U S News 55:102-4 S 30 '63
Government and the economy. il Sr Schol 84:14-15+ Mr 6; 14-15+ Mr 20 '64
Government expenditures; address, September 15, 1964. A. Parker. Vital Speeches 31:15-19 O 15 '64
Headed for still loftier heights: public works spending. il Bsns W p 187-8+ O 19 '63
Hitting a fiscal target. il Bsns W p23-4 O 31 '64
Hitting the target. Time 83:23-4 Ja 10 '64
How pump priming would change—. U S News 56:30 Ja 20 '64
Immorality in Washington: excerpt from address, September 5, 1963. E. P. Neilan. Farm J 87:134 O '63
Impact of possible DOD cut studied. H. M. David. Miss & Roc 13:18 D 9 '63
Issues as business sees them; symposium. il Nations Bsns 52:84-6 Ap '64
Local leaders tire of federal ties; survey conducted by Senate subcommittee on intergovernmental relations. il Nations Bsns 52:36-7+ F '64
LBJ looks ahead to more red ink. il U S News 58:73-4 Ja 4 '65
LBJ's first three months: spending hits a record. il U S News 56:95-6 Ap 13 '64
Massive federal spending; concentration of national power; address, May 3, 1963. H. F. Byrd. Vital Speeches 29:514-20 Je 15 '63
MURA accelerator: compromise for the Mid-West. D. S. Greenberg. bibliog Science 143:450-2 Ja 31 '64

GOVERNMENT spending policy—*Continued*
NIH: budget hits $1-billion mark for first time, but no one seems to be in a mood for celebration. D. S. Greenberg. Science 144: 392-3 Ap 24 '64
Old-fashioned all right. il Farm J 87:100 D '63
One budget that keeps growing. il U S News 57:77-8 Jl 13 '64
Paradise by deficit. H. Hazlitt. Newsweek 65:68 Ja 18 '65
Peace trend will bring better business. C. T. Stewart, jr. il Nations Bsns 52:66-8+ Je '64
Penny saved. New Repub 150:5-6 Ja 4 '64
President reaffirms high space priority. Aviation W 78:28 Ja 21 '63
Primer on government spending, by R. L. Heilbroner and P. L. Bernstein. Review Sat R 46:21-2 Je 1 '63. E. C. Bursk
Raising the roof. Time 83:23 Je 5 '64
Six deficits in a row? Senator Byrd sounds warning; excerpts from address, January 30, 1964. H. F. Byrd. U S News 56:12 F 10 '64
Sound, not fury. W. J. Coughlin. Miss & Roc 14:46 Ja 6 '64
Speaking out; fear threatens our prosperity. W. W. Heller. Sat Eve Post 236:8+ N 9 '63
Spend or save? D. Lawrence. U S News 56: 104 Mr 9 '64
Spending and taxes. Bsns W p204 My 18 '63
Spending into trouble; with editorial comment. D. D. Eisenhower. Sat Eve Post 236: 15-19, 82 My 18 '63; Same abr. with title We are spending ourselves into trouble; without editorial comment. Read Digest 83: 60-8 Jl '63
Spending pressures raise inflation danger. il Nations Bsns 52:30-1+ Ja '64
Strategy for American security; symposium. il Sat R 46:10-17 My 4 '63
Tax cut comes first; concerning Kennedy's State of the Union and budget messages. il Bsns W p23-6 Ja 19 '63
Tax plan: Wall Street is wary. il Bsns W p64-5 F 2 '63
Thrift vs. borrowing, which way to good times? with excerpts from book by P. A. Samuelson. il U S News 54:37-9 Mr 4 '63
Udall takes his stand. M. K. Udall. New Repub 150:10-11 Ja 18 '64
Unemployment remedies; changing military technology to civilian economy. Sci N L 85:246 Ap 18 '64
Unfinished business. D. Lawrence. U S News 57:144+ N 16 '64
Way to cut spending and still spend as much. U S News 56:95 Mr 30 '64
When do we get rid of budget deficits? D. Lawrence. U S News 56:96 Ja 20 '64
When surplus isn't all roses. il Bsns W p 150+ N 14 '64
When the Pentagon saves; that's a gang of nickels. il Newsweek 63:63-4+ Mr 9 '64
Where spending is due for a real rise. il U S News 54:48-9 Je 17 '63
Where the cutback cuts deep. D. Oberdorfer. il Sat Eve Post 237:17-21 S 12 '64
Where the money goes; figures released by the Friends committee on national legislation; reply. H. D. Kehm. Christian Cent 80:216 F 13 '63
Who are the big spenders? what the record shows. U S News 57:74-6 Ag 3 '64
See also
United States—Appropriations and expenditures
United States—Economic policy
GOVERNMENT surplus. See Surplus products
GOVERNORS
Bad words and good words down South; concerning inaugural addresses. Sat Eve Post 236:74 F 16 '63
Confrontation in the Statehouse. il Time 85: 22-3 Ja 15 '65
Law and order; responsibility of governors. America 108:796 Je 1 '63
Rub-a-dub-dub; U.S. governors visit to Japan. il Newsweek 62:57 N 4 '63
So long, Chub; gubernatorial nominations. il Time 84:37 S 18 '64
See also
Southern governors conference
GOVERNORS (machinery)
See also
Automobiles—Speed governors
GOVERNORS conference, 1963
Governors size up '64 race. il U S News 55: 50 Ag 5 '63
Politics: Rocky and the GOP win the Governors conference. il Newsweek 62:20+ Ag 5 '63
Politics vs. government. R. Moley. Newsweek 62:76 Ag 5 '63
Rocking their boat. il Time 82:12 Ag 2 '63
Rocky sells hard, governors aren't buying. il Life 55:20-3 Ag 2 '63
Rocky wrecks the joint. J. Desmond. Nation 197:63-5 Ag 10 '63
GOVERNORS conference, 1964
Bleating of sheep. M. Kempton. New Repub 150:15-18 Je 20 '64
D-day at Cleveland. Nation 198:614 Je 22 '64
Farce at Cleveland. R. Moley. Newsweek 63: 92 Je 29 '64
G.O.P. has its convention prematurely. il Life 56:47-48A Je 19 '64
Heads off. New Repub 150:2+ Je 20 '64
GOVERNORS mansions
Louisiana; million-dollar mansion. il Newsweek 61:16 F 4 '63
Mr Brown builds a dream house; governor's mansion, California. il Time 81:18 F 8 '63
GOW, J. Steele, jr
Schools for the sixties. Sat R 46:58-60+ O 19 '63
GOWING, Lawrence
Turner's pictures of nothing. Art N 62:30-3+ O '63
Unfathomable Goya. Art N 62:24-7 Ja '64
GOWLAND, Peter
Glamor. See issues of Popular photography
GOWNS, Academic. See Academic costume
GOYA, Carola
Hitting the road. H. Smith. il por Dance Mag 37:29-30 D '63
GOYA Y LUCIENTES, Francisco José de
Goya. il por Newsweek 62:72-3 D 23 '63
Letter from London. M. Panter-Downes. New Yorker 39:66-7 Ja 25 '64
Unfathomable Goya; loan show at the Royal academy, London. L. Gowing. il Art N 62: 24-7 Ja '64
GOYCO, E. Toro-. See Toro-Goyco, E.
GOYEN, William
Figure over the town; story. Sat Eve Post 236:48-53 Ap 27 '63
GOZZI, Carlo
Riddle of Turandot. P. J. Smith. Opera N 29:24-5 Ja 16 '65
GRABACH, John R.
Career of John R. Grabach. H. Gasser. il por Am Artist 28:38-43+ Mr '64
GRABOWSKI, Casimer Thaddeus
Teratogenic significance of ionic and fluid imbalances. bibliog Science 142:1064 N 22 '63
about
Egg and Doctor Grabowski. A. J. Snider. il por Todays Health 41:80-1 N '63
GRACE Patricia, consort of Rainier III, prince of Monaco
Grace of Graustark; hour-long telecast, A look at Monaco. il pors Time 81:42 F 22 '63
Grace of Kelly. R. Massie. il pors Sat Eve Post 236:18-19 Je 8 '63
Memoirs of Monaco; ed. by S. Fliegers. Rainier III. il pors McCalls 90:81-5+ Ap '63
Princess Grace: a new role. J. Hamilton. il pors Look 27:64-70 F 12 '63
GRACE, Joseph Peter, 1913-
Great challenge of Latin America; address, May 23, 1963. Vital Speeches 29:613-16 Ag 1 '63
—and others
Excerpt from memorandum, February, 1963. Cong Digest 42:87+ Mr '63
about
Alliance that is making little progress. por U S News 54:40+ F 25 '63
Unfinished job at W. R. Grace. C. Rieser. il por Fortune 68:108-13+ Ag '63
GRACE, W. R, and company
CAB must rule on Panagra ownership. Aviation W 78:42 Ja 21 '63
Huge plant scorns distance; Nitrogen products division of Grace. il Bsns W p 150 Mr 28 '64
Unfinished job at W. R. Grace. C. Rieser. il Fortune 68:108-13+ Ag '63
GRACE (theology)
Nature and grace, by K. Rahner. Review Cath World 199:255-6 Jl '64. J. V. Gallagher
Personal development through grace; excerpt from Pastoral catechetics. B. Cooke. il Cath World 199:371-8 S '64
Word. V. P. McCorry. America 109:399-400, 440-1; 111:116 O 5-12 '63, Ag 1 '64
GRACE line, incorporated
Grace line revives under its Mr Mac. il Bsns W p 172-4+ Ap 11 '64
See also
Grace, W. R, and company
GRACIOUSNESS. See Kindness
GRADING and marking (students)
Evaluating children's art. E. W. Eisner. il Sch Arts 63:20-2 S '63

GRADING and marking (students)—*Continued*
Grading, a serious matter. W. B. Maxson. NEA J 53:56-7 O '64
New views on grades. Time 84:30 D 25 '64
Pursuit of non-excellence. M. Bennett. Sat R 47:53 Je 20 '64
Saving the liberal arts. P. Goodman. Commonweal 80:359-61 Je 12 '64
See also
Ungraded classes

GRADING of swine. See Swine—Grading and standardization

GRADUATE business schools. See Business education

GRADUATE school of business administration. See Harvard university—Graduate school of business administration

GRADUATE schools. See Colleges and universities—Graduate work

GRADUATE students
Drive for doctorates. il Time 82:34 D 20 '63
Fellowship expansion presidential plan criticized at hearing before House science, space committee. D. S. Greenberg. Science 139:392-3 F 1 '63
Graduate aid; poll of educators suggests that needs vary widely in scientific disciplines. D. S. Greenberg. Science 140:35-7 Ap 5 '63
Manpower or mind power. P. H. Abelson. Science 139:79 Ja 11 '63; Discussion. 139:798+; 140:211 Mr 1, Ap 12 '63
Proper public accounting for science. P. H. Abelson. Sat R 46:51-2 F 2 '63

GRADUATE work. See Colleges and universities—Graduate work

GRADUATES, College. See College graduates

GRADUATES; story. See Alexander, R. W.

GRADUATION addresses. See Baccalaureate addresses

GRAEBNER, Norman A.
Can a nuclear world war be avoided? Ann Am Acad 351:132-9 Ja '64

GRAEF, Hilda
Play that indicts Pope Pius XII. Cath World 197:380-5 S '63

GRAEL, Barry Alan
Cowardish and Rodgersy. Newsweek 62:58 D 30 '63

GRAF, Herbert
Staging Otello. Opera N 27:8-11 Mr 23 '63

GRAF Spee (warship) See World war, 1939-1945—Naval operations

GRAFF, Henry F.
Decease of the log cabin legend. N Y Times Mag p8+ Je 30 '63
From Tippecanoe to Scranton, too. N Y Times Mag p 11+ Jl 5 '64
Heartbeat away. Am Heritage 15:81-7 Ag '64
Life with father, the President. N Y Times Mag p 10-11+ Jl 14 '63
Man who loses. N Y Times Mag p36+ N 15 '64
(comp) Presidency; by the presidents; excerpts from writings and addresses. N Y Times Mag p 18-19+ Ap 12 '64

GRAFF, M. M.
Fall bulbs. il Horticulture 42:14-16 Ag '64
Spring bulb make-up kit. House & Gard 124:204-5+ S '63

GRAFSTEIN, Bernice
Convulsant drug action on neuronally isolated cerebral cortex. bibliog Science 142:973-5 N 15 '63

GRAFT, Henry F.
Preserving the secrets of the White House. N Y Times Mag p9+ D 29 '63

GRAFT. See Politics, Corruption in

GRAFTING
Art of grafting. H. F. Stoke. il Pop Gard 14:54+ Mr '63
Budding. E. F. Steffek. il Pop Gard 14:68+ Jl '63
It's a one-tree orchard. il Sunset 130:183 F '63
It's easy to graft cactus. il Sunset 132:234+ Je '64
New trees without missing a crop. G. Lorang. il Farm J 87:79 Mr '63
Plant propagation by grafting. J. S. Wells. il Horticulture 41:80-1 F '63

GRAFTING (surgery) See Transplantation of organs, tissues, etc.

GRAFTON, Ernestine
Iowa: cross-county service. Wilson Lib Bul 38:283-4+ N '63

GRAFTON, Samuel
Best of times to be an adolescent. PTA Mag 58:7-8 My '64
Best-read city in the U.S.A: Pasadena. McCalls 90:48+ Ap '63
Child sorters. McCalls 90:98-101+ Ag '63
Cruel crowd. McCalls 92:87+ Ja '65
Fear takes over our city parks. McCalls 91:108-11+ O '63; Same abr. with title Danger stalks our parks. Read Digest 85:114-17 Jl '64
Illegal gambling casinos in the USA: where the law ends. Look 28:124-5+ O 20 '64
Sad case of our good old-fashioned dentistry. McCalls 91:106-7+ N '63
Tense generation. Look 27:17-23 Ag 27 '63; Same abr. Read Digest 83:61-6 N '63
Twisted age. Look 28:36-40+ D 15 '64
Would you want an atomic power plant near you? McCalls 91:228-9 O '63
—See Gallup, G. jt. auth.

GRAGG, Charles I.
Whose fault was it? Harvard Bsns R 42:107-10 Ja '64

GRAHAM, Arthur
Fresh voices; interview, ed. by P. Moed. por Opera N 28:28 Mr 7 '64

GRAHAM, Athol
Race against death. F. Miller. il por Read Digest 83:140-6 O '63

GRAHAM, Augusta
Huzzle-coos with our children. PTA Mag 59:26-8 bibliog(p34) D '64
Refuge for mom. PTA Mag 58:23 Ap '64

GRAHAM, Benjamin
How to handle your money now; interview. por U S News 55:66-70 Ag 5 '63

GRAHAM, Billy
Billy Graham's own story; God is my witness. pors McCalls 91:122-5+ Ap; 118-19+ My; 62+ Je '64
Time for moral courage. Read Digest 85:49-52 Jl '64
about
Billy Graham heeds his old call and prays. il por Life 55:26-7 Ag 30 '63
Billy Graham today. pors Newsweek 62:74-5 S 2 '63
Billy won't run for president. Christian Cent 81:197 F 12 '64
Celebrity register. C. Amory. por McCalls 91:62 F '64
Crusader and Cardinal. por Newsweek 64:71 O 19 '64
Crusader in the Coliseum. il por Time 82:53 S 6 '63
France prepares for Billy Graham. Y. Chabas. Christian Cent 80:614-15 My 8 '63
From a cardinal: praise for a Protestant crusader. por U S News 57:24 O 19 '64
New face in politics? Billy Graham attracts notice. por U S News 54:19 My 13 '63
Vivid portrait of the famous revivalist: Billy Graham. H. H. Martin. il pors Sat Eve Post 236:17-23 Ap 13 '63

GRAHAM, C. R.
Making money with games. Sci Digest 53:48-53 F '63

GRAHAM, Don
Go shopping for pictures. il U S Camera 26:10-11+ S '63

GRAHAM, Dorothea
Sports fitness camps. por Recreation 57:280-1 Je '64

GRAHAM, Ed
Innocent abroad on the baseball diamonds. Sports Illus 18:64-70 Mr 18 '63
On the trail of a hero. por Sports Illus 19:50-5 Ag 26 '63

GRAHAM, Elizabeth
Heroes; story. Seventeen 22:82-3 Jl '63
Sisters; story. Ladies Home J 80:56-7 Ja '63

GRAHAM, Frank, Jr
Get the lawyers out of the ring. Sat Eve Post 236:70+ Jl 13 '63
Happiness is being somewhere else. Sat Eve Post 237:73-7 Ap 4 '64
Our underdogs at Innsbruck. Sat Eve Post 237:22-7 F 1 '64
Relief to royalty on hope, hash and Corn. Sports Illus 18:E7-E8+ Ap 15 '63
Return of the mahatma. Sat Eve Post 236:66-8 Mr 9 '63
Story of a college football fix. Sat Eve Post 236:80-3 Mr 23 '63
This car's dying on us. Sat Eve Post 236:22-4 Je 1 '63

GRAHAM, Grace
Function of schools in a changing society; excerpt from Public school in the American community. Sch & Soc 91:257-60 Sum '63

GRAHAM, Henry H.
Glory of the season, winter. Am For 69:28-9 D '63

GRAHAM, J. A. Maxtone
Miss Lonelyhearts. B. C. Esquire 60:114 S '63

GRAHAM, Jackson
Army lakes float U.S. boatmen. Motor B 112:34+ Ag '63

GRAHAM, Janet
Careless; poem. McCalls 91:199 O '63
Won't anyone look at our slides? McCalls 92: 168 N '64
GRAHAM, John M. 2d
English porcelain collection at Williamburg. Antiques 87:73-7 Ja '65
GRAHAM, Jory, and Poling, James
Help is a warm puppy. Ladies Home J 80:28+ N '63
GRAHAM, Katharine Meyer
Top of the week. por Newsweek 62:11 S 30 '63
GRAHAM, Lee
Women don't like to look at women. N Y Times Mag p48+ My 24 '64
GRAHAM, Louis A.
Amateur scientist. Sci Am 210:131-3+ Ja '64
GRAHAM, Martha
Dance; program at New York's Lunt-Fontanne theater. J. A. Ardoin. il por Mus Am 83:42 N '63
Evening with Martha Graham and her dance company, Philharmonic Hall. D. Hering. Dance Mag 38:32 Je '64
Freud, electronics, dance. A. Hughes. il por N Y Times Mag p92-3 O 6 '63
Graham's triumph. il pors Theatre Arts 47: 18-19 N '63
In the news. por Dance Mag 37:38 O '63
Martha Graham. New Yorker 39:46-7 O 19 '63
Martha Graham's London season. J. Martin. il Sat R 46:68-9 S 28 '63
Phaedral case. il por Newsweek 62:68 O 28 '63
Rites in the cave of the heart. il por Time 82:81 O 25 '63
Solitary athlete; Martha Graham and her company; Lunt-Fontanne theatre. D. Hering. il pors Dance Mag 37:54-9 D '63
Stage works by Paul Hindemith at Juilliard concert hall. M. Marks. Dance Mag 37:13+ My '63
GRAHAM, Philip Leslie
Standing alone; is de Gaulle right again? excerpt. Newsweek 61:34-5 F 25 '63

about

Discontented man. por Time 82:62 Ag 9 '63
Ford, Ward, and Graham; civilization vs self-love. W. F. Buckley, jr. Nat R 15: 143 Ag 27 '63
Obituary
Art N 62:19 S '63. A. Frankfurter
Philip L. Graham, 1915-1963. por Newsweek 62:13 Ag 12 '63
Tradition: a legacy. il por Newsweek 62:30-1 Ag 19 '63
GRAHAM, Robert A.
Books to be noted; world scene. America 109: 664-5+ 110:648-50; 111:698+ N 23 '63, My 9, N 28 '64
Bus the children? America 110:160-1 F 1 '64
Civil rights in the church. America 109:257-60 S 14 '63
John LaFarge, S.J; first anniversary of his death. America 111:695-6 N 28 '64
Pius XII and the Nazis. America 111:742-3; 112:2 D 5 '64, Ja 2 '65
Return to theocracy. America 111:70-2 Jl 18 '64
GRAHAM, Sheilah
Celebrity register. C. Amory. por McCalls 91:62 F '64
From nowhere to everywhere. por Time 83: 41-2 My 29 '64
GRAHAM, Shirl O.
Indophenol blue as a chromogenic agent for identification of halogenated aromatic hydrocarbons. bibliog Science 139:835-6 Mr 1 '63
GRAHAM, Virginia
Celebrity register. C. Amory. por McCalls 91:62 F '64
GRAHAM, William Franklin. See Graham, B.
GRAHAM, Zeldine
Race against death. F. Miller. il por Read Digest 83:140-6 O '63
GRAHAME, Arthur
Are you a sap for the ribbon cutters? Outdoor Life 131:10-12+ Je; 132:6 S '63
No more free hunting? por Outdoor Life 131: 14-15+ F '63
Sportsmen honor Arthur Grahame. il por Outdoor Life 134:90 Ag '64
GRAHAME, Kenneth
Reluctant dragon: dramatization. See Thane, A.
GRAIN
Five ways to cut grain losses. L. E. Zeman and W. H. Johnson. Suc Farm 61:30 Jl '63
See also
Barley
Oats

Diseases and pests

Are there thieves in your grain bin? L. E. Zeman. il Suc Farm 61:56-7+ N '63
Small grain diseases; how to control them. M. Shurtleff and J. J. Feight. il Suc Farm 62:46-7+ Ag '64

Drying

Excessive heat lowers quality of grain. Suc Farm 61:65 O '63

Prices

Decision at dawn; grain-price agreement. il Newsweek 64:46 D 28 '64

Storage

Are there thieves in your grain bin? L. E. Zeman. il Suc Farm 61:56-7+ N '63
Farm managers see new trends in grain storage. Suc Farm 62:69 S '64
Maintaining quality of stored grain. G. Shove and F. Andrew. il Suc Farm 61:43 Jl '63
See also
Corn—Storage

Transportation

Where are the boxcars? Newsweek 62:90+ N 25 '63
GRAIN alcohol. See Alcohol
GRAIN elevators
On-farm elevator for your grains. J. Russell. il Farm J 87:32-3+ Jl '63
GRAIN in photography. See Photography—Grain
GRAIN trade
Grain gambit: U.S. grain deal with Great Britain. Newsweek 63:91 Ap 27 '64
Sixty-six shiploads; question of shipments for Austria. Time 82:16-17 Jl 26 '63
United States and United Kingdom conclude grains agreement; statement, April 16, 1964. C. A. Herter. Dept State Bul 50:703-4 My 4 '64
U.S. states position on question of unified EEC grains price; statement, July 3, 1964. C. A. Herter. Dept State Bul 51:119 Jl 27 '64
Vanishing grain; twenty-four million bushels between United States and Austria. Newsweek 62:42-3 Jl 29 '63
Will farmers be sold out? C. P. Streeter. Farm J 88:39+ Ja '64
See also
Cargill, incorporated
Continental grain company
Wheat trade
GRAINGER, J. H.
Fear of passion. Nation 196:339-42 Ap 27 '63
GRAISON, Phyllis
When we say good-by; story. Redbook 121: 147-74 S '63
GRALNICK, Alexander
Psychiatry; danger signals of a breakdown; interview. Sci Digest 55:20-4 Je '64
GRAMATKY, Hardie
Little Toot. N. Kent. Am Artist 29:4+ Ja '65
Little Toot's twenty-fifth birthday. il Horn Bk 40:518-19 O '64
GRAMBLING college, Grambling, La.
Looking for a challenger; sprint relay team. il Time 83:94+ My 15 '64
GRAMMAR, Comparative and general
Books; my fifty years with dictionaries and grammars. E. Wilson. New Yorker 39:165-76+ Ap 20 '63
GRAMMAR, English. See English language—Grammar
GRAMONT, Sanche de. See De Gramont, S.
GRAMPP, William D.
False fears of disarmament. Harvard Bsns R 42:28-30+ Ja '64
GRANADA, Spain
See also
Alhambra
GRANBERG, W. J.
Where Latin's still alive. Travel 122:28-31 O '64
World without women. Travel 122:36-9 Jl '64
GRANBY, Vt.
Look out, America, here comes Granby. E. Hill. il Sat Eve Post 237:64-5 Ap 4 '64
GRAND, P. M.
Rodin: genius with giblets. Art N 62:24-8 My '63
Wood jewels from ancient Gaul. Art N 63: 26-9 My '64
GRAND BAHAMA
Bali H'ai, a Shangri-lo? H. Sutton. il Sat R 47:24-5 Ja 18 '64
GRAND BAHAMA ISLAND
See also
Gambling—Grand Bahama Island

GRAND CANYON
Grand Canyon. il Sunset 133:76-89 O '64
GRAND CANYON NATIONAL PARK
Backpacking the Grand Canyon. C. Fletcher. il Field & S 68:33-7+ Mr '64
War clouds over the Colorado; Marble Canyon case. A. W. Smith. Nat Parks Mag 37:2 Ap '63
Water vs. parks, issue on lower Colorado River. J. B. Craig. Am For 70:3+ Ap '64
GRAND CENTRAL terminal, New York. See New York (city)—Stations
GRAND COULEE
Grand Coulee: monument to an ancient river. C. M. Ouellette. il Nat Parks Mag 38:12-15 S '64
GRAND COULEE power and reclamation project
Lake Roosevelt; sailor's luck. E. Crimmin. il Motor B 114:90-4 Ag '64
Notes for a gazetteer; Grand Coulee Dam country. P. Hamburger. New Yorker 39: 198-200+ O 26 '63
GRAND FALLS, Ariz.
Grand Falls are an Arizona Desert surprise. il Sunset 130:76+ Ap '63
GRAND JUNCTION, Colo.
Light for a world-famous small-city downtown. J. M. Lacy. il Am City 79:115 D '64
Shopper's park. J. M. Lacy. il Am City 78: 73-5 D '63
Shopping park shrinks accidents by 80 per cent. J. M. Lacy. il Am City 79:142 O '64
GRAND jury
See also
Indictments
GRAND opera. See Opera
GRAND opera singers. See Singers
GRAND prix of endurance race. See Automobile racing
GRAND prix of Mexico. See Automobile racing
GRAND RAPIDS, Mich.

Education

Training for mentally handicapped children; Children's retreat and training school. il Arch Rec 133:182-3 My '63

Hospitals

County hospital programed for service. il Arch Rec 134:168-9 N '63
Therapy center for a private institution. il Arch Rec 134:166-7 N '63

Water supply

Water on tap for city growth. D. E. Hazelswart. il Am City 78:92-4 S '63
GRAND TETON NATIONAL PARK
Getting closer to nature in the Tetons. G. Rogers. il Am For 69:12-14+ My '63
Marten and I. F. A. Blackburn. il Nat Parks Mag 38:11-14 Ap '64
GRAND tour. See Travel
GRAND TURK
Li'l orphan islands. T. J. King. il Travel 122: 61-2+ N '64
GRAND VALLEY state college, Mich.
College plan a cluster pattern. il Arch Rec 137:127-34 Ja '65
GRANDE, Luke M.
Appeal of Golding. Commonweal 77:457-9, 570-1 Ja 25, F 22 '63
Gabriel Fielding, new master of the Catholic classic? Cath World 197:172-9 Je '63
Lag in some schools. America 108:438-9 Mr 30 '63
Who said: ripeness is all? poem. Harper 230: 73 Ja '65
GRANDE salle of the Place des arts, Montreal. See Concert halls
GRANDFATHERS. See Grandparents
GRANDMA'S funeral; story. See Telpaz, G.
GRANDPARENTS
Down will come kitty. C. Ford. il Field & S 67:6+ F '63
Homework for doting grandparents. H. Puner. il Parents Mag 40:40-1+ Ja '65
Look at today's grandparents. P. W. Goldman. il N Y Times Mag p58+ Je 14 '64
Notes of a four-year-old grandfather. J. Canaday. il N Y Times Mag p61+ Ja 17 '65
We are all descended from grandfathers! grandfathers of the candidates. O. Jensen. il Am Heritage 15:4-13+ Je '64

Anecdotes, facetiae, satire, etc.

Grandmothers get all the breaks! R. Hochstein. il Good H 158:53-4 Mr '64
GRANDSTANDS
Wood to launch a president. F. T. Gilley. il Am For 71:2-3+ Ja '65
GRANDVIEW, Mo.
Cement-stabilized aggregate wins. L. W. Weller. il Am City 78:75-7 N '63
GRANGE
Foot in the door; Munn v. Illinois. C. P. Magrath. il Am Heritage 15:44-8+ F '64
GRANGER, Charles H.
Hierarchy of objectives. bibliog f Harvard Bsns R 42:63-74 My '64
GRANGER, Gale A. and Weiser, R. S.
Homograft target cells: specific destruction in vitro by contact interaction with immune macrophages. bibliog Science 145:1427-9 S 25 '64
GRANGER, Lester B.
If I were young today. por Ebony 18:72 Ap '63
GRANICK, S. See Gibor, A. jt. auth.
GRANNY from Killarney; drama. See Martens, A. C.
GRANPA and the Atlantic Ocean; story. See Woodbury, D. O.
GRANT, Bob, and Boykin, J. E.
Those silly shingles. Pop Mech 121:141-3 Mr '64
GRANT, Bruce
Love and Gabriella Smith; story. Mlle 56: 150 Mr '63
Sukarno: regional bully. Nation 198:111-14 F 3 '64
GRANT, Campbell
California's legacy of Indian rock art. Natur Hist 73:32-41 Je '64
GRANT, Cary
Archie Leach. pors Ladies Home J 80:50-3+ Ja; 23-4+ Mr; 86-7+ Ap '63

about

Cary Grant, Audrey Hepburn. il pors Look 27:87-90+ D 17 '63
How many titles of these Cary Grant movies can you name? il pors Ladies Home J 80: 46 Mr '63
Unlikely role for hairy Cary. il por Life 57: 99-100 D 18 '64
GRANT, Daniel R.
Metropolitics and professional political leadership: the case of Nashville. Ann Am Acad 353:72-83 My '64
GRANT, Donald
UN: peace and politics. Nation 199:1-2 Jl 13 '64
Vietnam: alternative to disaster. Nation 198: 521-3 My 25 '64
GRANT, Duncan
Letter from London; 80th birthday exhibition at the Wildenstein gallery. M. Panter-Downes. New Yorker 40:162-3 D 12 '64
GRANT, Frederick C.
His familiar and welcome message. Life 57:110-11 D 25 '64
GRANT, George H.
Mystery of the freak sea. Read Digest 83: 200-4 O '63
GRANT, Gregor
Motor sports. Sports Illus 20:65-6+ My 11 '64
GRANT, James A.
Rubidium-strontium isochron study of the Grenville front near Lake Timagami, Ontario. bibliog Science 146:1049-53 N 20 '64
GRANT, James P.
India, Mideast will strengthen U.S. hand. por Nations Bsns 51:68+ D '63
GRANT, John E.
Colors of prophecy. Nation 200:91-2 Ja 25 '65
GRANT, Joseph S. jr
Our man in Saigon. il pors Ebony 18:121-2+ Je '63
GRANT, Leora E.
Alaskan school teacher. il pors Ebony 18:38+ O '63
GRANT, Lillian
Prophecy in white; poem. McCalls 92:157 O '64
GRANT, Mary
Body's internal balances: what can go wrong. Life 55:85-6+ N 8 '63
GRANT, Mary Kent
Mystery, detective, suspense. Library J 89: 658-60, 1118-19, 1626-7, 1986-7, 2368-70, 2828-9, 3036-7, 3188-9, 3777-8, 4389-90, 4826-8; 90:136-7 F 1, Mr 1, Ap 1, My 1, Je 1, Jl-S 1, O 1, N 1, D 1 '64, Ja 1 '65
GRANT, Megan
What you can do about an underachiever. Parents Mag 38:56-7+ Mr '63
GRANT, Michael
High art of portraiture on Roman coins. Horizon 5:33-41 S '63
GRANT, R. P. and others
Biomedical science in Europe. bibliog Science 146:493-501 O 23 '64
GRANT, Sherman
So deer to my garden. Flower Grower 52:16-17 Ja '65

GRANT, Ulysses Simpson
—And then Grant took command; excerpt from Centennial history of the Civil war. B. Catton. il pors N Y Times Mag p26-7+ Ap 26 '64
At last Lincoln found a general; excerpt from Centennial history of the Civil war. B. Catton. il por N Y Times Mag p34-5+ N 24 '63
GRANT, W. Vance
Earned degrees, another year, another increase. Sch Life 45:12-13 F '63
GRANT, William F. See Harney, P. M. jt. auth.
GRANTON, E. Fannie
Lady in black. por Ebony 19:81-2+ F '64
GRANTS-in-aid
Government has no free money; interview. D. J. Mays. Nations Bsns 52:37+ F '64
Having it both ways. New Repub 148:6-7 My 11 '63
Winds of change; amendment to deny federal funds to any state in which the program discriminates against American citizens on the basis of race, creed or color. Nation 196:414 My 18 '63
GRAPE industry. See Viticulture
GRAPES
Grapes for the home vineyard. G. L. Slate. il Horticulture 41:208-9 Ap '63
Great grapes; superb 1964 vintage expected in France. il Newsweek 64:96 S 21 '64
We take the puzzle out of grape pruning. C. W. Gouget. il Pop Gard 14:46+ Mr '63
See also
Cookery—Fruit
GRAPH theory. See Topology
GRAPHIC arts
Books about books and graphic arts. C. B. Grannis. Pub W 184:70-4+ D 2 '63
New intaglio technique. S. Hammer. il Am Artist 27:34-9+ F '63
Of rabbit glue & beauty. il Time 84:82 S 4 '64
Penrose annual: new trends in design, map-making, automation; with editorial comment. C. B. Grannis. Pub W 186:57, 59-61 Ag 3 '64
See also
Printing

Exhibitions

Graphic arts: USA; exhibition in Soviet Union, 1963. F. Eichenberg. il Pub W 185: 114-16 F 3 '64

Study and teaching

Pratt graphic art center. E. M. Ettenberg. il Am Artist 28:34-8+ My '64
GRAPHIC arts technical foundation
GATF adds educational texts, reviews technical advances. Pub W 185:80+ Je 1 '64
LTF convention votes change in name, scope, location. Pub W 183:90 My 6 '63
Technical foundation meets, examines research projects. Pub W 185:84 Ap 6 '64
GRAPHIC methods
See also
Critical path analysis
GRAPHITE
Carbon: a new crystalline phase. R. B. Aust and H. G. Drickamer. bibliog il Science 140:817-19 My 17 '63
Electron microscopy of meteoritic and artificially shocked graphite. T. P. Sciacca and M. E. Lipschutz. bibliog il Science 145:1049-50 S 4 '64
GRAPHOLOGY
Does your handwriting give you away? J. R. Berry. il Pop Sci 182:104-7+ Ap '63
Graphology game. il Christian Cent 82:95 Ja 20 '65
GRASERS. See Light amplifiers
GRASES, Pedro
Andrés Bello, cultural liberator. Américas 16:1-4 N '64
GRASHOW, James
Portfolio of woodcuts by James Grashow. N. Kent. il Am Artist 28:26-9+ Ja '64
GRASS, Günter
Writers in Berlin. Atlan 212:110-13 D '63

about

Nerve of Günter Grass. G. Steiner. Commentary 37:77-80 My '64
GRASS clippers. See Garden tools, equipment and supplies
GRASS seed. See Grasses—Seed
GRASS shears. See Garden tools, equipment and supplies
GRASS silage. See Silage
GRASS waterways. See Channels
GRASSES
Don't pamper the lawn this spring. il Changing T 18:15-16 Mr '64
Getting rid of Bermuda in ivy. Sunset 132: 245 Mr '64
Lawn problem? we solved it with zoysia. M. H. Hunn. il Flower Grower 51:24 My '64
Many varieties of Kentucky bluegrass. R. W. Schery. il Horticulture 41:568-9 N '63
Miracle of grass. J. W. Krutch. House & Gard 123:112-13+ Je '63
New bluegrass has many assets for home lawns. il Flower Grower 51:18-19 S '64
Now you can control quackgrass. E. Knake and J. J. Feight. Suc Farm 62:61 S '64
Phenol in quackgrass associated with dalapon. T. R. Flanagan and A. R. Langille. bibliog il Science 140:179-80 Ap 12 '63
Special grass for special purposes. il Flower Grower 50:50 Mr '63
Twelve great grasses, and how to manage them. L. E. Zeman. il Suc Farm 62:54-7+ Ap '64
Zoysia grass lawn for the cool coast. il Sunset 130:220-1 Je '63
See also
Hay
Lawns
Sorghum

Diseases and pests

Grass-killing disease. Sci N L 86:11 Jl 4 '64
See also
Lawns—Diseases and pests

Seed

Dont' waste your grass seed $'s. il Consumer Bul 47:2+ S '64
Sow grass seed now. il Horticulture 41·440 S '63

Silage

See Silage

Translocation

See Plants—Translocation
GRASSHOPPER; story. See Rackowe, A.
GRASSHOPPERS
High-living grasshopper found in California. Sci N L 86:120 Ag 22 '64

Control

Tiros v. locusts; Britain's Anti-locust research center. Time 81:60 Ap 26 '63
GRASSLANDS, National. See Wilderness areas
GRATERS. See Kitchen utensils
GRATITUDE
How to say thank you. M. Drury. Read Digest 83:173+ Jl '63
Two magic words. J. A. Farley. Read Digest 84:167-8 Ap '64
GRATUITIES. See Tipping
GRAU, Shirley Ann
Keepers of the house; story. Ladies Home J 81:92-4 Ja '64
Mood and revelation in the South. R. Coles. New Repub 150:17-19 Ap 18 '64
Tips. Pub W 185:41 Mr 30 '64
GRAUBARD, Stephen R.
After five years, de Gaulle still towers. N Y Times Mag p 12+ D 15 '63
GRAVE robberies. See Tomb robberies
GRAVEL
What gravel can do for a terrace. il Bet Hom & Gard 42:102 S '64
GRAVENSON, Linda
Schools for your special interests. Holiday 36:139-42 N '64
GRAVES, Arthur Harmount
Doctor Graves' contribution. W. Leighton. por Am For 69:2 My '63
GRAVES, C. Edward
Transfiguration in wilderness. Liv Wildn 82: 9-10 Winter '62
GRAVES, Eleanor
Battle plan for the feast. Life 57:151-2 S 18; 105-6 D 18 '64; 58:87-8 Ja 29 '65
Fancy fish in brown paper; battle plan for the feast. Life 57:125-6 N 13 '64
Life World's fair review. Life 57:12 Jl 10 '64
Little hens on a spit. Life 57:80-4 Ag 21 '64

about

Editor who cooks up the Great dinners. G. P. Hunt. por Life 56:3 Ap 24 '64
GRAVES, Elizabeth Minot
Adult children's books. Commonweal 78:253-4 My 24 '63
Selected list of children's books. Commonweal 78:254-63; 81:203-11 My 24 '63, N 6 '64
—See Bishop, C. H. jt. auth.

GRAVES, Frank X.
Paterson, N.J. mayor bans The children of Sanchez. Library J 88:1128 Mr 15 '63

GRAVES, John
Overlap land, gringo and Mexican meet in the Rio Grande Valley. Holiday 35:74-5+ Mr '64
Rice university: the pangs of change. Holiday 35:76-7+ Je '64

GRAVES, Robert
Apple garden; At best, poets; Measure of casualness; Time of waiting; Expect nothing; She is no liar; Pearl; New moon through glass; poems. Atlan 212:66-7 O '63
Bank account; poem. McCalls 91:151 Je '64
Corner knot; poem. New Yorker 39:44 Mr 23 '63
Hearth; poem. New Repub 151:20 O 3 '64
Herself to herself; poem. Sat R 46:28 S 28 '63
Last poem. New Yorker 40:39 Je 6 '64
Lasting echoes of the Kaiser's war. N Y Times Mag p 16-17+ My 17 '64
Myrrhina; poem. Poetry 103:182 D '63
Poet in a valley of dry bones. Horizon 5:84-8 Mr '63
Poetry's false face. Horizon 5:42-7 N '63
Poet's investigation of science. Sat R 46:82-8 D 7 '63
Pretense on Parnassus. Horizon 5:81-5 My '63
Real women. Ladies Home J 81:151-5 Ja '64
Redbook dialogue. por Redbook 121:58-9+ S '63
St Valentine's day; poem. Atlan 213:94 F '64
T. E. Lawrence and the riddle of S.A. Sat R 46:16-17 Je 15 '63
Three poems: Rain of brimstone; Non cogunt stellae; Song: sword and rose. New Repub 150:21 Ap 11 '64
Why of the weather; poem. Sat R 46:36 Ap 13 '63
Why read poetry? Holiday 35:10+ F '64

about

First and last things. J. Dickey. Poetry 103: 318-19 F '64
Muse at MIT. por Newsweek 61:90-1 My 27 '63
Prodigious old lion of letters; with quotations, ed. by J. Howard. il pors Life 54:57-8+ Je 28 '63

GRAVES, William P. E.
Earthquake! Nat Geog Mag 126:112-39 Jl '64
Tokyo, the peaceful explosion. Nat Geog Mag 126:445-87 O '64
Washington, the city freedom built. Nat Geog Mag 126:735-81 D '64

GRAVES. See Cemeteries; Tombs

GRAVESTONES. See Sepulchral monuments

GRAVIMETERS
New instruments study earth's internal make-up. Sci N L 86:280 O 31 '64

GRAVITATION
Amateur scientist; simulating gravitational fields with droplets of water on a soap bubble. G. Yob. il Sci Am 211:134-7 D '64
Anti-G drug research described. W. C. Wetmore. Aviation W 81:24 S 21 '64
Dallas conference on super radio sources. L. C. Green. il Sky & Tel 27:80-4 F '64
Geotropism: its orienting force. A. H. Westing. bibliog il Science 144:1342-4 Je 12 '64
Gravitation, science's big riddle. H. Hellman. il Sci Digest 55:57-64 My '64
Gravitational forces and effects. K. L. Franklin. il Natur Hist 72:12-19 O; 44-51 N '63
Gravity and magnetic anomalies of the Sierra Madera, Texas, dome. J. R. Van Lopik and R. A. Geyer. bibliog il Science 142:45-7 O 4 '63
Jean's criterion of gravitational instability. S. S. Huang. il Sky & Tel 26:77-9 Ag '63
Math plus Mach equals far-out gravity; Hoyle-Narlikar theory. il Time 83:63 Je 26 '64
Satellite gravity measurements. Sci Am 210: 60-1 Ja '64
Scientists walk on walls. il Sci N L 85:213 Ap 4 '64
Sperry Rand proposes cabling technique to simulate gravity. Aviation W 81:124-5+ S 14 '64
Stress differences and the reference ellipsoid. J. A. O'Keefe and W. M. Kaula. bibliog il Science 142:382 O 18 '63
Universe's most mysterious force. A. Ewing. il Sci N L 86:298-9 N 7 '64
Wild atomic reactions. Sci N L 85:83 F 8 '64
See also
Gravimeters
Specific gravity
Weightlessness

GRAVITY free state. See Weightlessness

GRAVITY meters. See Gravimeters

GRAVY. See Sauces

GRAY, David
Our new automated world. por Recreation 56:401-2 N '63

GRAY, Francine du Plessix. See Du Plessix, F.

GRAY, Harold E.
Co-pilot at Pan Am. pors Newsweek 64:69-70 Jl 20 '64

GRAY, Jack L.
Nova Scotia's sailor artist. S. T. Spicer. il por Motor B 113:116-17+ Ja '64

GRAY, James
Sense and sensitivity. Sat R 46:24 Mr 2 '63

GRAY, Jesse
Harlem goes to war against the slumlords. R. K. Massie. il por Sat Eve Post 237: 71-5 F 29 '64
Rent strike; concerning Community council on housing. New Yorker 39:19-20 Ja 25 '64
Rent strike; in Harlem. il por Newsweek 62: 17-18 D 30 '63

GRAY, John S.
Physiologist looks at engineering. Science 140:464-6 My 3 '63

GRAY, Joseph H.
It's all mews to her. Hobbies 68:54-5 Mr '63

GRAY, Margaret
Candle of understanding. Wilson Lib Bul 37: 575-6 Mr '63

GRAY, Maxim T.
Niagara's enchanted forest; excerpts. Recreation 57:526 D '64

GRAY, Milner, and Armstrong, Ronald
Lettering for the public image. Design 64: 120-3 Ja '63

GRAY, Peter
Look at me. New Yorker 39:133-4+ Mr 23 '63

GRAY, Phyllis A.
Commerce converts a warehouse. Library J 89:4730-2 D 1 '64

GRAY, Ralph
From sun-clad sea to shining mountains. por Nat Geog Mag 125:542-89 Ap '64
How to be an economy-tour millionaire. NEA J 52:53-6 F '63

GRAY, Wallace
From the peaks. Christian Cent 81:115-16 Ja 22 '64
Helen. Criticism
America 112:149 Ja 23 '65

GRAY, Wood
(comp) Articles and other books received: United States. See issues of American historical review

GRAY foxes. See Foxes

GRAY hair. See Hair

GRAY squirrels. See Squirrels

GRAY whales. See Whales

GRAYBEAL, William S.
Planning for instructional improvement. NEA J 52:22 O '63

GRAYLING fishing
Wild thyme fish. A. J. McClane. il Field & S 68:66-9 D '63

GRAYSON, Cary T.
Colonel's folly and the President's distress. Am Heritage 15:4-7+ O '64

GRAYSON, Esther C. See Rockwell, F. F. jt. auth.

GRAYSON, Louise
I have some real misgivings. PTA Mag 58:9 My '64

GRAZ, Austria

Music

Graz old and new. C. N. Welsh. Opera N 28:29 O 19 '63
Graz schlag. C. N. Welsh. Opera N 27:33 Mr 2 '63

GRAZIER, Margaret Hayes
Beginning with assignments. ALA Bul 57: 154-5 F '63
What happens in the school library. por ALA Bul 58:104-8 F '64

GRAZING
Red clover may cause lamb birth decline. Sci N L 86:84 Ag 8 '64
See also
Pastures
Stock ranges

GRAZING fees
Well done, Mr Secretary! with editorial comment. J. Prokop. il Am For 69:8-9+ Mr '63

GRAZING lands. See Stock ranges

GRAZIOSE, Louis
Graziose the grateful; interview, ed. by F. Stevenson. por Opera N 29:6-7 D 5 '64

GRAZIOSI, Paolo
Images of the infidels. il Horizon 7:90-3 Wint '65

GREAT ABACO ISLAND. See Bahama Islands

GREAT Atlantic and Pacific tea company
Grandma changes. il Newsweek 63:67-8 Je 29 '64
Making change at A.&P. Time 81:86 Mr 22 '63
New crowd minds store for the tea company. il Bsns W p88-90+ Je 13 '64
New men for A&P's top rungs. Bsns W p32 Je 20 '64
Pinching 500,000,000,000 pennies. il Fortune 67:104-9+ Mr '63
Remodeling the A&P. il Bsns W p36 Mr 23 '63
We of A.&P; executives switch jobs. Time 81:107 Ap 19 '63

GREAT BASIN NATIONAL PARK (proposed)
See National parks and reserves—United States

GREAT BAY, N.H.
Oyster stew; problem of water pollution. P. Hirsch. New Repub 150:7-8 Ja 4 '64

GREAT BEAR LAKE
Temperature regime of deep lakes. L. Johnson. bibliog il Science 144:1336-7 Je 12 '64

GREAT books program. See Adult education—Great books program

GREAT books program, Junior. See Junior great books program

GREAT BRITAIN
Britain before the elections. T. Prittie. il Atlan 213:79-83 My '64; Reply. F. Bennett. 214:24 Jl '64
Britain 1963: looking inward. il Newsweek 62:42+ S 30 '63
John Bull X-rays himself. B. Ward. il N Y Times Mag p8+ Jl 14 '63
See also
Advertising—Great Britain
Aerospace industries—Great Britain
Airlines—Great Britain
Airplane industry and trade—Great Britain
Airplanes, Military—Great Britain
Airports—Great Britain
Arbitration, Industrial—Great Britain
Astronomical observatories—Great Britain
Automobile industry and trade—Great Britain
Aviation—Great Britain
Ballet—Great Britain
Banks and banking—Great Britain
Book industries and trade—Great Britain
Budget—Great Britain
Camping—Great Britain
Censorship—Great Britain
Chemical industries—Great Britain
Colleges and universities—Great Britain
Commonwealth of nations
Communism—Great Britain
Crime and criminals—Great Britain
Education—Great Britain
Education and state in Great Britain
Electronic apparatus industry and trade—Great Britain
England
Finance—Great Britain
Gambling—Great Britain
Government ownership—Great Britain
Hotels, taverns, etc.—Great Britain
Industrial management—Great Britain
Jazz music—Great Britain
Jews in Great Britain
Labor and laboring classes—Great Britain
Law—Great Britain
Libraries—Great Britain
Liquor traffic—Great Britain
Medicine—Great Britain
Money—Great Britain
Natural resources—Great Britain
Negroes in Great Britain
Newspapers—Great Britain
Opera—Great Britain
Paper money—Great Britain
Police—Great Britain
Postal service—Great Britain
Prices—Great Britain
Public health—Great Britain
Public opinion—Great Britain
Public schools (endowed)—Great Britain
Publishers and publishing—Great Britain
Railroads—Great Britain
Schools—Great Britain
Science—Great Britain
Secret service—Great Britain
Space research—Great Britain
Strikes—Great Britain
Tariff—Great Britain
Taxation—Great Britain
Television broadcasting—Great Britain
Theater—Great Britain
Tourist trade—Great Britain
Trade unions—Great Britain
Transportation—Great Britain
Trials—Great Britain
Unemployment—Great Britain
Women—Great Britain
Yachts and yachting—Great Britain
Youth—Great Britain
Zoology—Great Britain

Antiquities
Digging for pictures. W. Golding. Holiday 33:86-7+ Mr '63

Appropriations and expenditures
Time clocks coming? maintenance of royal residences. il Bsns W p56 Jl 20 '63
See also
Budget—Great Britain

Armed forces
British emphasize integration of services. H. J. Coleman. Aviation W 78:38-9 Ja 21 '63

Anecdotes, facetiae, satire, etc.
It was a mere scratch. C. W. Morton. il Atlan 215:108-9 Ja '65

Appropriations and expenditures
£1,000 per dog per year. Time 84:40+ S 4 '64

Forces in Malaysia
Borneo, Britain's South Vietnam; British troops and Sukarno guerrillas. R. Hughes. il N Y Times Mag p9+ Jl 19 '64

History
Battle of Tel el Kebir. il Esquire 60:98-103 N '63

Army
Anemic red line. il Newsweek 63:28-9 Ja 20 '64
Shortage of 'eroes. Time 83:35 F 7 '64

Scotch regiments
Scots on parade; Black Watch in New York; photographs. N Y Times Mag p 106 S 15 '63

Cabinet
Familiar and unfamiliar: some faces of labor; the Wilson government. il Newsweek 64:51 N 2 '64
In Britain, Home gets the job Wilson wants. il Bsns W p 102-4+ O 26 '63

Caricatures and cartoons
Business in Britain: again, the dole. N Y Times Mag p 162 Ap 7 '63

Civilization
Britain's new state of mind. J. Mander. Harper 228:76-80 Ap '64
It's U to be LMC. B. Hollowood. il N Y Times Mag p37+ N 29 '64

Colonies and dominions
See Commonwealth of nations

Commerce
Buses for Cuba. Sr Schol 84:16 Ja 31 '64
Common market; address, January 30, 1963. H. Macmillan. Vital Speeches 29:332-3 Mr 15 '63
Deal that makes Castro happy; sale of British city buses. il U S News 56:13 Ja 20 '64
European economic community; address, March 2, 1963. W. Hallstein. Vital Speeches 29:365-9 Ap 1 '63
How U.S. beef is selling in Britain. il U S News 57:66 Jl 6 '64
London's bridges building up; rise in British exports. il Time 82:109 N 15 '63
On borrowed time. il Fortune 71:89-90+ Ja '65
Red trade, red aid? Sr Schol 84:22-3 Mr 6 '64
Rift in West: how serious. il U S News 54:29-30 F 11 '63
Two for the money; British firms close trade deals with Russia. Newsweek 61:81 My 13 '63
What happens to Great Britain now? interview. Earl of Home. il U S News 54:62-5 F 4 '63
What next for the Common market? R. Grenier. Reporter 28:24-6 F 28 '63
Where Britain can turn: views from Europe. U S News 54:67-8 F 4 '63
Why de Gaulle blocked Britain; a German view. U S News 54:10 Mr 11 '63

History
English furniture exports to America, 1697-1830. E. T. Joy. il Antiques 85:92-8 Ja '64

South Africa
Maybe Lord Home has a heart; promises to halt British shipment of weapons. New Repub 149:7 Ag 17 '63

Commercial treaties and agreements
United States and United Kingdom conclude grains agreement; statement, April 16, 1964. C. A. Herter. Dept State Bul 50:703-4 My 4 '64

GREAT BRITAIN—*Continued*

Constitution

See also
Great Britain—Kings and queens

Defenses

Aerial white elephant? Newsweek 62:46+ N 18 '63
Britain 1965; address, December 16, 1964. H. Wilson. Vital Speeches 31:201-8 Ja 15 '65
Britain to spend billion on Polaris. Miss & Roc 12:13 Ap 15 '63
Britain will pay normal costs plus 5 per cent for U.S. Polaris missiles. Aviation W 78: 31 Ap 15 '63
Britain's strategic role. A. S. Nanes. bibliog f Cur Hist 46:269-74 My '64
British aim: atomic force at cut rates. il U S News 57:12 N 9 '64
British emphasize integration of services. H. J. Coleman. Aviation W 78:38-9 Ja 21 '63
British planning Blue Steel replacement. H. J. Coleman. Aviation W 78:29 F 25 '63
British stress science in defense shuffle. H. J. Coleman. Aviation W 79:327+ Jl 22 '63
Drive mounts to avert U.K. defense cuts. H. J. Coleman. Aviation W 82:22-3 Ja 18 '65
Great Britain: the bomb again. New Repub 150:8-9 F 22 '64
Honest brokers in the nuclear muddle. L. W. Martin. il Reporter 30:20-4 Ja 2 '64
Into the pool; British nuclear deterrent. il Time 84:22 D 18 '64
Macmillan upheld on Polaris accord. Aviation W 78:28 F 11 '63
Move to force U.K. cutback debate fails. H. J. Coleman. il Aviation W 82:26-7 Ja 25 '65
Nassau reconsidered: what can America and Britain do now? A. Buchan. New Repub 148:21-3 Mr 2 '63
President Kennedy holds talks at Nassau with Prime Minister Macmillan; joint communique and statement on nuclear defense systems, December 21, 1962. J. F. Kennedy and H. Macmillan. Dept State Bul 48:43-5 Ja 14 '63
Pressure from Washington; question of joining multilateral nuclear force. New Repub 150:11-12 Mr 7 '64
Review of U.K. defense efforts ordered. Aviation W 81:35 O 26 '64

Description and travel

Britain that Shakespeare knew. L. B. Wright. il Nat Geog Mag 125:613-65 My '64
Traveling with Mlle: Britain by car. K. Davis. il Mlle 57:153-5 O '63

Diplomatic and consular service

Mr Ambassador. J. Kraft. Harper 227:101+ D '63

Economic conditions

Atlantic report. Atlan 214:20+ D '64
Britain after world power; toward social democracy. O. Gass. New Repub 148:22-4+ Je 29 '63
Britain at bay; fifteen-per-cent surcharge on imports. America 111:591 N 14 '64
Britain: can the £ now save itself? Life 57: 6 D 11 '64
Britain's crisis in efficiency. il Bsns W p82-4 D 26 '64
Britain's long winter of discontent; confidence in government shaken. il Bsns W p20-1 D 19 '64
Britain's North-South problem. A. Burnet. New Repub 148:17-18 My 11 '63
British economy. J. D. Froggatt. Cur Hist 46:291-5+ My '64
British foreign policy, 1945-1961, by F. S. Northedge. Review
 New Repub 148:23-6 Je 22 '63. O. Gass
Can Britain come back? il Duns R 82:36-7+ N '63
Can Tories get in under the wire? il Bsns W p 107-8 Ag 22 '64
Crisis continues. Time 84:37 D 11 '64
Halfhearted economy. il Time 84:60-1 D 25 '64
In Britain, Home gets the job Wilson wants. il Bsns W p 102-4+ O 26 '63
Living it up; British bank rate raised. Time 83:95 Mr 6 '64
Pathology of affluence. T. Morris. Nation 197: 390-2 D 7 '63
Portrait of Britain in the fat years. il N Y Times Mag p 12+ Ap 28 '63
$3 billion bail bond. il Time 84:33 D 4 '64
Tory chances brighten. il Bsns W p21-2 My 11 '63
Trouble for the pound. Time 84:90 S 25 '64
Wilson swings the ax; remedies for balance-of-payments crisis; with editorial comment. il Bsns W p24-5, 168 O 31 '64
With pound on mend, Britain hunts cure. Bsns W p27 Ja 23 '65

See also
Budget—Great Britain
Prices—Great Britain
Taxation—Great Britain
Wages—Great Britain

Economic history

Making of the English working class, by E. P. Thompson. Review
 Commentary 38:69-71 Jl '64. B. B. Seligman

Economic policy

After Brussels. A. Shonfield. For Affairs 41:721-31 Jl '63
Backbench revolt. Time 83:40 Ap 3 '64
Brain trusters step up in Britain. il Bsns W p 142+ N 14 '64
Britain starts pushing at home. il Bsns W p 120+ F 16 '63
Britain's dynamic rebuilder. il Bsns W p 100-2+ D 7 '63
British Labor looks at Europe. R. H. S. Crossman. For Affairs 41:732-43 Jl '63
Crisis continues. Time 84:37 D 11 '64
Labor starts off with sound and fury. il Bsns W p28-9 N 14 '64
Letter from London. M. Panter-Downes. New Yorker 39:175-80 My 4 '63
On borrowed time. il Fortune 71:89-90+ Ja '65
Raising the rate; increased bank rate. Newsweek 63:70 Mr 9 '64
U.S. comments on British measures to strengthen economy; statements, by Department of state and by Treasury, October 26, 1964. Dept State Bul 51:714-15 N 16 '64
Watchdog the action; Labor government's program. Time 84:96 N 6 '64
Wilson's attempt to export a problem. Life 57:4 N 6 '64
With the pound saved, labor pushes ahead; with editorial comment. il Bsns W p28-9, 172 D 5 '64

Economic relations

Britain makes trouble for EFTA. Time 85:76+ Ja 29 '65
Britain's economy looks to Europe. A. D. Monroe. il Cur Hist 46:263-8+ My '64
Burial rites. Newsweek 61:32-3 F 4 '63
Common market crisis. C. Emmet. America 108:333-5 Mr 9 '63
Europe; illusion of unity; renaissance of Chauvinism; reaction in Britan. E. L. Dale, jr; J. Daniel; D. Healey. New Repub 148: 14-16 F 23 '63
Inertia of folly. Nation 198:205 Mr 2 '64
Where Britain can turn: views from Europe. U S News 54:67-8 F 4 '63

Arab states

Little stick. Newsweek 62:27 D 23 '63

Cuba

God bless our allies! Nation 198:61 Ja 20 '64

France

After Brussels. E. Taylor. Reporter 28:29-32 F 14 '63
De Gaulle's new Europe: meaning to Britain, U.S. il U S News 54:66-7 F 4 '63
Political evolution of Europe; news conference, January 14, 1963. C. de Gaulle. Vital Speeches 29:230-5 F 1 '63
Question at issue; address, January 29, 1963. M. Couve de Murville. Vital Speeches 29: 333-4 Mr 15 '63

Russia

Easy terms for Russia. Newsweek 64:94 S 21 '64
For the lamps of London. Newsweek 61:42 F 25 '63

Executive departments

How will labor attack research for building? British construction industry. Arch Rec 136: 304+ N '64

Foreign office

Whitehall elephant. il Time 83:28 Ja 10 '64

Foreign relations

Atlantic report. Atlan 213:14+ Ja '64
Back on the beat. New Repub 150:12-13 Ja 18 '64
Britain 1965; address, December 16, 1964. H. Wilson. Vital Speeches 31:201-8 Ja 15 '65

GREAT BRITAIN—Foreign relations—*Cont.*
Britain's moment in the Middle East, by E. Monroe. Review
New Repub 150:19-20 F 1 '64. R. H. Nolte
Britain's new leader: what to expect. U S News 55:24 O 28 '63
Britain's strategic role. A. S. Nanes. bibliog f Cur Hist 46:269-74 My '64
British defense policy under Labor. A. Verrier. For Affairs 42:282-92 Ja '64
British foreign policy, 1945-1961, by F. S. Northedge. Review
New Repub 148:23-6 Je 22 '63. O. Gass.
British policy and the United States. R. Maudling. Atlan 212:61-4 D '63
British Prime Minister visits Washington; exchange of greetings, December 7, 1964; with joint communique. H. Wilson; L. B. Johnson. Dept State Bul 51:902-4 D 28 '64
Common market; address, January 30, 1963. H. Macmillan. Vital Speeches 29:332-3 Mr 15 '63
Foreign affairs; address, November 26, 1963. R. A. Butler. Vital Speeches 30:139-41 D 15 '63
Hands across the sea. H. Brandon. Sat R 47:6 Mr 21 '64
Is it to be a little England? il U S News 57:36-8 D 14 '64
It's the uncommon Commonwealth; Britain's overseas commitments. P. Worsthorne. il N Y Times Mag p 12+ Mr 8 '64
Labor party's defense and foreign policy. P. C. G. Walker. For Affairs 42:391-8 Ap '64
Labour's shadow diplomacy; interview. ed. by G. Brook-Shepherd. P. G. Walker. il Reporter 30:37-40 F 13 '64
Letter from London. M. Panter-Downes. New Yorker 40:152-6 O 24 '64
Problems of the future; address, June 16, 1964. R. A. Butler. Vital Speeches 30:578-82 Jl 15 '64
Roots of British foreign policy. S. J. Hurwitz. Cur Hist 46:296-9+ My '64
Speaking out; England's place in the sun. S. Lloyd. Sat Eve Post 236:6+ Mr 2 '63; Excerpts. U S News 54:26 Mr 11 '63
Sticky wickets; Labor government policies. il Time 84:21 N 6 '64
Still the Trojan horse. A. Burnet. New Repub 148:8-9 F 2 '63
What happens to Great Britain now? interview. Earl of Home. il U S News 54:62-5 F 4 '63
Whatever became of SuperMac? A. Lejeune. Nat R 14:159 F 26 '63
See also
Great Britain—Foreign office

China (People's Republic)

British lions; Hong Kong and Communist China. I. Stewart. New Repub 151:14-15 S 5 '64

Europe, Western

Britain and Europe: the lesson of Skybolt. R. Steel. Commonweal 77:507-9 F 8 '63

France

Blessing in disguise; British popular reactions to de Gaulle's veto. D. W. Brogan. America 108:262-3+ F 23 '63
One more wedge between Britain and France. U S News 54:10 Mr 18 '63
What de Gaulle sees ahead. il U S News 54:55 F 11 '63
When England offered everything to France; excerpt. P. Reynaud. il Sat R 46:26-8 Mr 16 '63

Germany

Appeasers, by M. Gilbert and R. Gott. Review
Nat R 15:403-4 N 5 '63. A. Lejeune

Italy

Macmillan at Rome. M. Painelle. America 108:265-6 F 23 '63

South Africa

Atlantic report. Atlan 213:34+ Ap '64
South Africa and the world: some maxims and axioms. P. Mason. For Affairs 43:150-64 O '64
Stop South Africa now. New Repub 150:3-4 My 16 '64

United States

Anglo-American alliance. R. N. Berkes. bibliog f Cur Hist 46:275-81+ My '64
Anglo-American relations; address, May 22, 1963. D. O. Gore. Vital Speeches 29:551-3 Jl 1 '63
Britain and Europe: the lesson of Skybolt. R. Steel. Commonweal 77:507-9 F 8 '63
Britain and the US. New Repub 151:3-4 D 19 '64
British Prime Minister holds talks with President Johnson; communique, February 13, 1964. L. B. Johnson and A. F. Douglas-Home. Dept State Bul 50:336-7 Mr 2 '64; Same. Cur Hist 46:304-5 My '64
Fox trots no minuets; Mr Johnson's talks with Sir Alex Douglas-Home. il Newsweek 63:21 F 24 '64
If Wilson wins, Socialist plans for Britain. il U S News 54:19 Ap 15 '63
New strains on an old alliance. il U S News 56:42 F 24 '64
Relationship of Britain and United States; address, April 1, 1963. H. Wilson. Vital Speeches 29:418-21 My 1 '63
Scrapping of Skybolt. W. S. Just. il Reporter 28:19-21 Ap 11 '63
U.S. and Britain: LBJ calls the tune. il U S News 57:25-6 D 21 '64
U.S. and U.K. sign agreements on sale of Polaris missiles; announcement, letter from Secretary Rusk, and text of agreement, April 6 and April 9, 1963. Dept State Bul 48:759-64 My 13 '63
U.S. stake in Britain's election. il U S News 57:55-6 O 12 '64
What de Gaulle sees ahead. il U S News 54:55 F 11 '63
Whilst he still lives amongst us; W. Churchill's convictions about Anglo-American friendship. Q. Hogg. il Life 57:49-50+ D 11 '64

Government publications

Sessional papers: an epilogue. J. Weatherford. Library J 88:1630-1 Ap 15 '63; Reply. E. L. Erickson. 88:2208-9 Je 1 '63

History

Roots of British foreign policy. S. J. Hurwitz. Cur Hist 46:296-9+ My '64
See also
Great Britain—Kings and queens

Bibliography

Articles and other books received; British Commonwealth and Ireland, comp. by L. H. Carlson. See issues of American historical review

Historiography

British history, 1870-1914, reconsidered: recent trends in the historiography of the period. J. Clive. bibliog f Am Hist R 68:987-1009 Jl '63

Tudors, 1485-1603

Just a book of psalms! P. W. Schmidtchen. il Hobbies 69:106-7+ O '64

Elizabethan period, 1558-1603—Bibliography

English history, 1558-1640: a bibliographical survey. P. Zagorin. bibliog f Am Hist R 68:364-84 Ja '63

Seventeenth century—Bibliography

English history, 1558-1640: a bibliographical survey. P. Zagorin. bibliog f Am Hist R 68:364-84 Ja '63

Stuarts, 1603-1714

See also
Charles I, king of Great Britain

1714-1837

See also
United States—History—Revolution

1760-1789

When the British captured Havana. G. de Zéndegui. il Américas 16:21-8 Mr '64

Victorian period, 1837-1901

British history, 1870-1914, reconsidered: recent trends in the historiography of the period. J. Clive. bibliog f Am Hist R 68:987-1009 Jl '63

Industries

Britain's North-South problem. A. Burnet. New Repub 148:17-18 My 11 '63
Great Britain. J. T. Coppock. bibliog il Focus 14:1-6 Je '64
Playing guinea pig; Britain's Glacier metals co, ltd. il Bsns W p 166+ N 7 '64
See also
Candy industry and trade
Imperial chemical industries, limited
Pilkington brothers, limited
Steel industry and trade—Great Britain

Intellectual life

Fly and the fly-bottle, by V. Mehta. Review
Nat R 15:63-4 Jl 30 '63. A. Lejeune
To divorce art from money-making. K. Tynan. il N Y Times Mag p35+ D 1 '63

GREAT BRITAIN—*Continued*

Kings and queens

Happy times when Edward was king. C. Connolly. il Ladies Home J 81:78+ Ja '64
Succession and monarchy: the controversy of 1679-1681. C. A. Edie. bibliog f Am Hist R 70:350-70 Ja '65
See also
Great Britain—Royal family

Medical research council

See Medical research council (Great Britain)

Moral conditions

Anticlimax; the Denning report. Newsweek 62:51 O 7 '63
Britain's Cliveden set: back in the headlines. il U S News 55:64-5 Jl 15 '63
Cauldron of unholy loves. D. J. Dooley. America 109:262-3 S 14 '63; Discussion. 109:252, 441-2, 538-9, 646 S 14, O 19, N 9, 23 '63
Doctor Stephen Ward returns. R. West. Esquire 62:138+ S '64
Dolce vita in a colder climate. M. Muggeridge. il Esquire 60:96-7+ N '63
Is Britain becoming a sick nation? Profumo scandal. U S News 55:10 Jl 8 '63
John Bull & John Profumo. J. Gross. Commentary 36:144-50 Ag '63
Moral post-mortem. il Time 82:20-1 Ag 16 '63
New pornocracy. il Newsweek 62:35-6 Jl 8 '63
Notes and comment; M. A. Clarke and Frederick Augustus, duke of York. New Yorker 39:19 Jl 6 '63
Pall on Profumory; Ward-Keeler-Profumo scandal. C. Northcott. Christian Cent 80: 1023 Ag 21 '63
Personal report on Britain's biggest scandal. L. Bergquist. il Look 27:81-6 Jl 30 '63
Probe or peepshow? Denning inquiry. il Newsweek 62:48+ S 23 '63
Profumo: a class on trial. P. Crane. America 109:13 Jl 6 '63
Profumo affair. C. Brogan. Nat R 14:528-9+ Jl 2 '63
Profumo affair. J. M. Cameron. Commonweal 78:445-6 Jl 26 '63
Psychological case? Denning report. il Time 82:26 S 27 '63
Sagacious end of the affair; Denning report. Life 55:4 O 11 '63
Sexual revolution. America 108:526 Ap 20 '63; Reply. R. F. Charles. 108:625-6 My 4 '63
State of British morals. A. Burnet. New Repub 149:11-12 S 21 '63
SuperMac rides out the storm. A. Lejeune. Nat R 15:189-90 S 10 '63
There'll always be an. . . il Time 81:25 Je 21 '63
This happy breeding. Time 81:24 Mr 22 '63
What would Queen Victoria say? Profumo scandal. B. Hollowood. N Y Times Mag p7+ Je 30 '63
Word of Christine; concerning the Denning report. G. Playfair. New Repub 149:11-13 D 21 '63
See also
Prostitution

National health service

Britain: health costs mount. il U S News 57: 44-5 S 21 '64
Cacoëthes praescribendi; overprescribing doctors. Time 84:50 Ag 7 '64
Government and medicine in Britain; symposium. bibliog il Cur Hist 45:1-40+ Jl '63
Why family doctors in Britain are in revolt; with interview with G. Biss. il U S News 55:63-6 N 4 '63

National institute of oceanography

See National institute of oceanography

Navy

Keeping a blockade. il Life 56:64-5 Ap 17 '64
See also
Jutland, Battle of, 1916

Parliament

Fine art of insult. C. Hussey. il N Y Times Mag p57+ Ja 5 '64
Sir Edwin Sandys and the Parliament of 1604. T. K. Rabb. bibliog f Am Hist R 69:646-70 Ap '64

House of commons

Child of the House; W. Churchill's final farewell. il Time 84:33 Ag 7 '64
Great old man's last trip to Commons. A. Moorehead. il Life 57:30-1 Ag 7 '64
Letter from London; debate in Commons on nationalization of steel industry. M. Panter-Downes. New Yorker 40:198-200 N 21 '64
Letter from London; opening session of the House of commons. M. Panter-Downes. New Yorker 39:202+ N 30 '63
Letter from London; question of building a new block of offices for the Commons. M. Panter-Downes. New Yorker 40:96+ Je 13 '64
Seizing the heights; opening of the first session of Parliament. il Newsweek 64:46+ N 16 '64
Sessional papers: an epilogue. J. Weatherford. Library J 88:1630-1 Ap 15 '63; Reply. E. L. Erickson. 88:2208-9 Je 1 '63

Peerage

Call me mister! the peers request. C. Hussey. il N Y Times Mag p 18+ Ag 25 '63
Communist peer. Newsweek 61:36-7 Je 3 '63
Doffed coronet; peers now able to relinquish their inherited titles for life. Newsweek 62:34 Ag 12 '63
Out of the ghetto; new Peerage act. il Time 82:29 Ag 9 '63

Politics and government

Amery refuses to quit under labor fire. H. J. Coleman. Aviation W 81:25-6 Ag 10 '64
Anatomy of Britain, by A. Sampson. Review
New Yorker 39:169-74+ My 11 '63. A. J. Liebling
And now there's the anti-Establishment. C. Hussey. il N Y Times Mag p42+ My 3 '64
Atlantic report (cont) Atlan 211:20+ Ap; 212:26+ S '63; 213:14+ Ja; 214:11-12+ Jl; 20+ D '64
Battle of Leyton hall. Time 85:24-5 Ja 22 '65
Benefit of the doubt. il Time 84:23 D 25 '64
Britain: if labor wins. il Fortune 69:51-2+ Je '64
Britain in the 'sixties. R. English. Yale R 52:481-98 Je '63; Reply H. Brogan. 53:149-60 O '63
Britain: Wilson's close shave. il Sr Schol 85: 12-16 D 9 '64
Britain's new state of mind. J. Mander. Harper 228:76-80 Ap '64
Britain's political style is not like ours. A. Hacker. il N Y Times Mag p22+ S 20 '64
Britain's politics, and Britain's future. il N Y Times Mag p 10-11 O 20 '63
British elections. R. Williams. Nation 199: 154-7 S 28 '64
British elections: gentlemen vs. experts. R. Presthus. Nation 198:480-3 My 11 '64
Brown paper. il Newsweek 64:50 N 9 '64
Conservative enemy: a program for radical reform in the sixties, by C. A. R. Crosland. Review
Commentary 36:178-80 Ag '63. L. A. Coser; Discussion. 37:12 Ja '64
Crisis over Christine. E. Behr. il Sat Eve Post 236:77-85 Jl 13 '63
Eighteen-hour day of a British backbencher. L. Stone. il N Y Times Mag p32-3+ Ja 10 '65
Harold Wilson's Britain. N. MacKenzie. Harper 228:73-6+ F '64
Harold Wilson's hour. C. Sterling. il Reporter 31:17-20 N 5 '64
Home in the Highlands. il Time 82:38 N 8 '63
Home's home run. A. Boyle. America 109: 563 N 9 '63
Honest brokers in the nuclear muddle. L. W. Martin. il Reporter 30:20-4 Ja 2 '64
Ins and outs; Wilson's first week in power. il Newsweek 64:50+ N 2 '64
Into battle. il Time 82:30 N 22 '63
Is it to be a little England? il U S News 57: 36-8 D 14 '64
Labor landslide: municipal elections. Newsweek 61:50+ My 20 '63
Labor takes action. il Sr Schol 85:9-10 N 11 '64
Letter from London (cont) A. Lejeune. Nat R 14:159; 16:770, 1144 F 26 '63, S 8, D 29 '64
Letter from London. M. Panter-Downes. New Yorker 39:175-80 My 4 '63; 40:60-2 Ja 2 '65
Leyton affair. il Time 85:23 Ja 29 '65
Little England. J. Mander. Commentary 35: 139-45 F '63
Mac the Slack. il Newsweek 62:29 Jl 1 '63
Macmillan's seven years. il Newsweek 62:60 O 21 '63
Making of a prime minister. W. V. Shannon. Commonweal 79:121-3 O 25 '63
MLF & other problems. G. Lichtheim. Commentary 39:65-8 Ja '65
No easy out. il Newsweek 63:30 Ja 13 '64
No reason to grouse. Newsweek 63:37-8 Mr 9 '64
100-to-1 shot gets nod in Britain, stirs up a row. il Life 55:42-42A O 25 '63

GREAT BRITAIN—Politics and government —*Continued*
Other Birmingham; color question in politics. il Newsweek 63:25-6 Mr 30 '64
Poet and prime minister; Sir A. Douglas-Home's Communist opponent in general election. S. Hynes. Commonweal 81:84-5 O 16 '64
Political test faced by aviation ministry in fall election. Aviation W 81:138-9+ S 7 '64
Politics in Britain. T. P. Peardon. Cur Hist 46:282-6+ My '64
Poll fever; election forecasts. New Repub 150:9 Ap 11 '64
Quoodle talks. il Newsweek 63:36 Ja 27 '64
Rising generation in Britain. R. Kirk. Nat R 17:24 Ja 12 '65
Science policy shapes up as issue in coming British election. J. Maddox. il Science 143: 1146-8 Mr 13 '64
Score so far; Wilson and his government. il Newsweek 24+ D 28 '64
Signs of things to come. H. C. Nicholas. il Reporter 31:20-1 N 5 '64
Sir Alec takes over. N. Birnbaum. Nation 197: 316-18 N 16 '63
Slender hold; first test of narrow majority for Wilson government. Newsweek 64:46 N 23 '64
Socialist who will call the signals in Britain now. il U S News 57:24 O 26 '64
State of affairs. H. Brandon. Sat R 48:14-15 Ja 2 '65
Still the Trojan horse. A. Burnet. New Repub 148:8-9 F 2 '63
Strange death of Tory England. J. Mander. Commentary 38:41-5 D '64
That cad, Profumo. A. Burnet. New Repub 149:6 Jl 6 '63
They're off; question of general election. Time 81:29 My 3 '63
Tories coming up. Time 84:29 Ag 28 '64
Tory tragedy. R. Moley. Newsweek 62:84 Jl 8 '63
Under increasing fire: Britain's Wilson. U S News 57:19 D 7 '64
We want work; sac Mac, sac Mac. il Newsweek 61:33-4 Ap 8 '63
Why Tory hopes are rising. A. Burnet. New Repub 151:8-9 O 10 '64
Wilson: Labor's gray mystery; will these men run Britain? il Newsweek 61:42-4+ Ap 15 '63; Same abr. with title Harold Wilson: Britain's question mark. Read Digest 83: 109-13 O '63
Wilson's problem: staying in control. il Bsns W p 150-2+ O 24 '64
See also
Conservative party (Great Britain)
Elections—Great Britain
Great Britain—Cabinet
Great Britain—Kings and queens
Great Britain—Parliament
Great Britain—Prime ministers
Labor party (Great Britain)
Political campaigns—Great Britain
Political parties—Great Britain
Socialism—Great Britain

Popular culture

British experiment in art for the masses; Center 42. D. Thompson. New Repub 151: 7-8 N 21 '64

Prime ministers

Dull no more. il Time 82:35 N 1 '63; Same abr. with title Belted earl who became Prime Minister. Read Digest 84:68-72 Ja '64
If Macmillan is forced out. il U S News 55:17 Jl 1 '63
Letter from London; incoming prime minister. M. Panter-Downes. New Yorker 39: 221-2+ N 9 '63
Letter from London; opening session of the House of commons. M. Panter-Downes. New Yorker 39:202+ N 30 '63
Lord Home got the job. A. Lejeune. Nat R 15:438 N 19 '63
Off and running. Newsweek 62:48 N 4 '63
Quoodle or a fink? method of choosing a prime minister. il Time 83:36 F 7 '64
Tory succession: a London letter. G. Lichtheim. Commentary 36:468-72 D '63
War of succession: Lord Home becomes Prime Minister; with excerpts from addresses. il Time 82:30-5 O 25 '63; Same abr. with title Belted earl who became Prime Minister. Read Digest 84:68-72 Ja '64
What will Home do at no. 10 Downing? il Newsweek 62:31-2 O 28 '63

Prime ministers conference

See Prime ministers conferences

Race problems

Other Birmingham. il Newsweek 63:25-6 Mr 30 '64
Race trouble in Birmingham, England, too. il U S News 56:102-4 Mr 23 '64
See also
Negroes in Great Britain

Reconstruction

Planned migration. Time 83:24 Mr 27 '64

Religious institutions and affairs

Date in 1980; church unity problems. Newsweek 64:86 S 28 '64
See also
Catholic church in Great Britain
Church and state in Great Britain
England—Religious instiutions and affairs

Riots

Getting a head; fighting Mods and Rockers. il Newsweek 63:34+ Je 1 '64
What a giggle; teen-age gangs vandalism in Clacton, England. Newsweek 63:46 Ap 13 '64
Youthful riots: how U.S. and Britain differed. U S News 56:11 Ap 13 '64

Royal family

Hours in the life of Prince Edward Antony Richard Louis. G. Fisher and H. Fisher. il McCalls 92:44+ Ja '65
Letter from London; exhibition: Royal children at Owen's gallery at Buckingham palace. M. Panter-Downes. New Yorker 39:208 N 30 '63
Princess Anne grows older. C. Plimmer and D. Plimmer. il Redbook 120:58-9+ Ap '63
Queen Elizabeth II. R. T. Elson. il Life 56:75-84+ Mr 6 '64
Royal population explosion. il Look 28:94-5 S 22 '64
Succession and monarchy: the controversy of 1679-1681. C. A. Edie. bibliog f Am Hist R 70:350-70 Ja '65
What is Prince Philip really like? B. H. Hoffman. il Ladies Home J 80:60-1+ Je '63
When the Queen has a baby. R. Lecler. il Good H 158:86-7+ F '64

Social conditions

Anatomy of Britain, by A. Sampson. Review New Yorker 39:169-74+ My 11 '63. A. J. Liebling
Born to rule. A. Campbell. New Repub 150: 21+ My 2 '64
Britain in the 'sixties. R. English. Yale R 52:481-98 Je '63; Reply. H. Brogan. 53:149-60 O '63
How the British react to affluence. il Bsns W p44 Ja 19 '63
Pathology of affluence. T. Morris. Nation 197:390-2 D 7 '63

Social life and customs

Afterthoughts on the Beatles. A. Brien. Mlle 59:239+ Ag '64
Bringing up children: the American vs. the British way. E. Wintour. Harper 229:58-63 Ag '64; Discussion. 229:11-12 O '64
English drinking habits. R. Postgate. il Holiday 33:87-8+ F '63
Happy times when Edward was king. C. Connolly. il Ladies Home J 81:78+ Ja '64
My three pubs. G. Fielding. il Harper 228: 24+ Ja '64
So sorry! J. Crosby. il Read Digest 84:123-4 F '64
Yank's-eye view of British logic. R. Pearson. il Read Digest 82:117-19 Mr '63

GREAT BRITAIN and the United States. See England and the United States
GREAT crown rumble; story. See Speicher, J. F.
GREAT horned owls. See Owls
GREAT LAKES
Charting the Great Lakes for yachtsmen. F. R. Shumway. Motor B 113:98+ F '64
Cruising the Lakes on your way to the fair. il Sunset 132:70+ My '64
From a Great Lady to the Great Lakes. il Motor B 112:23 Ag '63
Great Lakes circle drive. il Bet Hom & Gard 42:121-4 Je '64
Receding waters. il Newsweek 64:56-7 Ag 10 '64
Sailing our inland seas. J. Grenard and J. Grenard. il Motor B 111:22-3+ Je '63
Seas of sweet water. il Motor B 111:20-1 Je '63
Seventeen flyways over the Great Lakes. J. P. Perkins. il Audubon Mag 66:294-9 S '64
When water runs short in the Great Lakes. il U S News 57:98-100 S 28 '64

GREAT LAKES colleges association
Science and the small college: to compete with the universities, colleges decide to hang together. J. Walsh. Science 142:564-6 N 1 '63
GREAT LAKES cruising club. See Boat clubs
GREAT LAKES fishing industry. See Fish industry and trade
GREAT LAKES REGION
U.S. requests three IJC studies on water levels and pollution; texts of letters. W. R. Tyler; D. Rusk. Dept State Bul 51:598-600 O 26 '64
See also
Water supply—Great Lakes Region
GREAT LAKES-St Lawrence waterway. See St Lawrence Seaway
GREAT LAKES shipping. See Inland water transportation
GREAT men
America's 100 most influential Negroes. il Ebony 18:228-32 S '63
Great men great events. il UNESCO Courier 17:33 O '64
Let us now appraise famous men. M. Epernay. il Esquire 60:128-30+ O '63
What men have done for love. J. T. Freeman. il Ladies Home J 80:88-9+ Ja '63
See also
Leadership
GREAT NECK, N.Y.
This sewage plant gains friends. W. F. Cosulich and T. Keevan. il Am City 78:78-80 N '63
GREAT outdoors: story. See Stanton, W.
GREAT PLAINS
Faces from the past; Okies, victims of the Dust Bowl. R. M. Ketchum. il Am Heritage 14:32-3 Ag '63
When the wind blew black blizzards. A. Balk. il N Y Times Mag p98-101 N 10 '63
GREAT ST BERNARD PASS
Snowplow, go home! il Pop Sci 182:98-9 F '63
Tunnel under the Alps. R. Gelatt. Reporter 28:36-8 Ap 11 '63
GREAT SALT LAKE
Salt migration to the northwest body of Great Salt Lake, Utah. T. C. Adams. bibliog Science 143:1027-9 Mr 6 '64
GREAT SLAVE LAKE railway
Tracks into the wilds. il Bsns W p 190+ S 12 '64
GREAT SMOKY MOUNTAINS
Why I love the Smokies. M. Frome. il Am For 70:8-9 O '64
GREAT SMOKY MOUNTAINS NATIONAL PARK
Cades Cove and Chief Mountain: symbols of our restless earth. H. S. Sharp. il Nat Parks Mag 37:8-10 S '63
Nibbling here and there. Nat Parks Mag 37:19 N '63
Trail is a trail, or is it? P. M. Tilden. il Nat Parks Mag 37:2 S '63
GREAT SWAMP national wildlife refuge. See Wildlife sanctuaries
GREAT universal stores, limited
Sears of Britain, and more. il Bsns W p 118-20+ F 8 '64
GREAT women. See Women, Famous
GREAVES, Fielding Lewis
Peace in our time. N Y Times Mag p 16+ Ap 14 '63
GREBANIER, Bernard
Rest is still silence. Sat R 47:56-7 Ja 11 '64
GREBE, Henry C, and company. See Boat building
GREBES
Detergents, deadly hazard to water birds. R. W. Nero. il Audubon Mag 66:26-7 Ja '64
El GRECO
Greek of Toledo. il Sat R 46:38 Mr 9 '63
GRECO, José
José Greco and his company at Brooklyn academy of music. M. Marks. Dance Mag 38:21+ Mr '64
Jose Greco and his Spanish ballet at Lewisohn stadium. D. Hering. Dance Mag 37:28+ S '63
GREECE

Antiquities

See Greece, Ancient—Archeology
GREECE, Ancient
Greece (cont) il Life 54:60-9+ F 8; 60-73 Mr 8; 78-93 Ap 5; 62-77 My 3; 54-71+ Je 14; 55:52-67 Jl 19 '63
See also
Athens, Greece
Cyclades
Parthenon
Sparta
Sports—Greece, Ancient
Temples—Greece, Ancient

Archeology

Dream of marble, a symphony of light. R. Warner. il N Y Times Mag p78-9+ Ap 26 '64
From the silent earth, by J. Alsop. Review
New Repub 150:19-21 Ap 25 '64. B. Knox
Newsweek 63:112+ Mr 16 '64
Sanctuary of Artemis at Brauron. J. Papadimitriou. il Sci Am 208:110-16+ bibliog(p 183) Je '63
See also
Samos, Greece

Civilization

See Civilization, Greek

History

Before the Bible; the common background of Greek and Hebrew civilizations, by C. H. Gordon. Review
Commentary 36:333-6 O '63. H. L. Ginsberg; Reply with rejoinder. C. H. Gordon. 36:424+ D '63
Sanctuary of Artemis at Brauron. J. Papadimitriou. il Sci Am 208:110-16+ bibliog(p 183) Je '63
See also
Alexander the Great
Marathon, Battle of, 490 B.C.

Persian wars, 500-449, B.C.

Persia's hordes march in to crush the Greeks, assailed by the might of Xerxes. il Life 54:80-7 Ap 5 '63

Peloponnesian war, 431-404, B.C.

War that everybody lost. il Life 54:88-93 Ap 5 '63

Social life and customs

See also
Olympic games
GREECE, Modern
Storms threaten an ancient nation. il Sat Eve Post 236:24-9 Je 15 '63
See also
Agriculture—Greece, Modern
Airlines—Greece, Modern
Athens
Athos, Mount
Copper mines and mining—Greece, Modern
Crete
Cyclades
Elections—Greece, Modern
Hotels, taverns, etc.—Greece, Modern
Ioannina
Mykonos (island)
Paros (island)
Restaurants—Greece, Modern
Syros (island)
Tourist trade—Greece, Modern

Commercial treaties and agreements

Cotton textile agreements concluded with Greece; Department announcement; with text of U.S. note, July 17, 1964. G. G. Johnson. il Dept State Bul 51:290-2 Ag 24 '64

Description and travel

Exploring Grecian villages. M. Benedict. il Travel 119:41-4 Je '63
Rough map of Greece (cont) P. L. Adams. Atlan 211:27-33 Ja; 73-7 Mr; 212:54-8 Jl '63; 213:73-8 Ap '64
Voyage to the foam-white isles and wine-dark seas of Greece. M. Goodman. il House B 105:100-1+ F '63

Foreign relations

Is U.S. aid to Greece paying off? il U S News 56:6 Mr 16 '64

Great Britain

Royalty under fire. New Repub 149:12 Jl 20 '63

Industries

Americans bearing gifts; Salonika industrial development plan. il Time 83:99 My 22 '64

Politics and government

Goodbye again. il Time 82:25 D 20 '63
King wants to travel. il Time 81:29 Je 21 '63
Long live the King. il Time 83:29 Mr 13 '64
Masked civil war. H. Goldberg. il Nation 197:3-7 Jl 6 '63
Never serious, quite critical. New Repub 149:8 N 2 '63
Old man in a hurry; G. Papandreou. Newsweek 62:49-50 N 18 '63
Queen and I; Queen Frederika and Premier Karamanlis. il Newsweek 61:46+ Je 24 '63
Queen of trumps. Newsweek 62:33 Jl 1 '63
Time of change. il Newsweek 63:40 Mr 2 '64
Under the knife. il Time 83:28 F 28 '64
See also
Elections—Greece, Modern

GREECE, Modern—*Continued*

Royal family

Storm over a royal love affair. C. Plimmer and D. Plimmer. il Redbook 121:60-1+ O '63

GREEK Americans

Our Octagonal world; condensation. A. Thompson. il Read Digest 82:279-99 My '63

GREEK ARCHIPELAGO. See Aegean Islands

GREEK civilization. See Civilization, Greek

GREEK coins. See Coins

GREEK cookery. See Cookery, Greek

GREEK drama

Showplace of the spirit. il Life 54:63 F 8 '63

Theatre and lyric. R. Dalven. Poetry 102:54-5 Ap '63

See also

Aeschylus

GREEK literature

See also

Greek drama

GREEK mythology. See Mythology, Greek

GREEK Orthodox church. See Orthodox Eastern church

GREEK Orthodox church in the United States. See Orthodox Eastern church in the United States

GREEK philosophy. See Philosophy, Greek

GREEK poetry

Contemporary Greek. D. S. Carne-Ross. Poetry 101:283-6 Ja '63

Genesis: a commentary. E. Keeley. Poetry 105:16-20 O '64

Translations into English

From Mythistorema; excerpts from poems. G. Seferis. Life 56:76+ Ja 17 '64

Greek number. Poetry 105:1-14+ O '64

Night of a solitary; Immobility of the voyage; Surpassing of danger; Rainy; Ultimate landing; Honest confrontation; Heard and the unheard; Estrangement; Recollection; Moment; Architect; tr. by R. Dalven. Y. Ritsos. Poetry 103:306-15 F '64

GREEK sculpture. See Sculpture, Greek

GREEK valerian. See Jacobs ladder

GREEK vases. See Vases, Greek

GREEKS

Cyprus, island of hate and fear; closeup of Greeks and Turks, the deadly enemies. M. Wall. il N Y Times Mag p 13+ Mr 8 '64

GREEKS in the United States

Koula; excerpt from Forever old, forever new. E. Kimbrough. il Ladies Home J 81:87+ N '64

One chance in a million; story of S. Giallelis: from Greek village to stardom. E. Miller. il Seventeen 22:124-5+ S '63

Tax law sparks a modern odyssey; Greek shipowners leaving U.S. il Bsns W p43-4 Ap 6 '63

GREEKS in Turkey

Ordeal in the Phanar. B. Thompson. Christian Cent 82:72 Ja 20 '65

U.S. expresses regret regarding expulsion of Greeks from Istanbul; statement, September 11, 1964. A. E. Stevenson. Dept State Bul 51:564-5 O 19 '64

GREELEY, Andrew M.

Authority in the church. Commonweal 80:515-16 Jl 24 '64

Church attendance among college graduates. Cath World 197:95-9 My '63

Counter-reformation comes to an end. Reporter 29:56+ N 21 '63

Entering the mainstream. Commonweal 81:33-7 O 2 '64

Four views of Rome. Reporter 31:64+ S 24 '64

How to get a red hat. Reporter 30:44 F 13 '64

New breed. America 110:706-9 My 23 '64

U.S. Catholicism: growth or decline? America 111:480-3 O 24 '64

GREELEY, Arthur V.

When are cesarean sections needed? Redbook 123:42+ O '64

GREELEY, Colo.

Casual elegance in a shopping center; Garden kitchen restaurant. il Arch Rec 136:210-11 S '64

Off-street parking program. B. H. Cruce. il Am City 79:113-14 F '64

GREEN, Arthur S.

Hardest working water in the world. Am For 70:28-30 Je '64

Lighting for living outdoors. Pop Gard 14:37-44 S '63

GREEN, Charles

Companion 6-meter transmitter. Pop Electr 21:53-7 S '64

Experimenter's L bridge. Pop Electr 22:61-3+ Ja '65

Experiments with a chemical rectifier. Pop Electr 22:71-2 Ja '65

Second American revolution. bibliog por Negro Hist Bul 27:103-5 F '64

Simple superhet for 6. Pop Electr 18:58-61 Ap '63

Two-meter simple superhet. Pop Electr 19:43-6+ S '63

Two-tube superhet for 80 meters. Pop Electr 20:45-8+ Ja '64

GREEN, Charlie

Some little men who think they are Packers. T. C. Brody. il Sports Illus 21:65-6 N 16 '64

GREEN, David E.

Mitochondrion; with biographical sketch. Sci Am 210:19, 63-6+ bibliog(p 152) Ja; 10+ Ap '64

GREEN, Edith

Much more remains to be done. NEA J 53:16-17+ F '64

about

Congress: new study shows federal education budget of $2.2 billion, $613 million of it for research. J. Walsh. Science 141:29-31 Jl 5 '63

GREEN, F. Pratt

Advice to those visiting England; poem. New Yorker 40:107 My 2 '64

Plastic begonia; poem. New Yorker 39:127 Ap 20 '63

GREEN, Frank

Summer to remember. Sch Arts 64:14-16 S '64

GREEN, H. A.

What happened to Denver's metro. Am City 79:129+ Ap '64

GREEN, H. Gordon

Good-by, little boy! Read Digest 83:79-82 S '63

Rooster who served the Lord. Read Digest 83:47+ N '63

GREEN, Harold P.

Greatest plot. Bul Atomic Sci 20:29-30 F '64

Q-clearance: the development of a personnel security program. Bul Atomic Sci 20:9-15 My '64

GREEN, J. P. See Carlini, E. A. jt. auth.

GREEN, John C.

Information explosion, real or imaginary? Science 144:646-8 My 8 '64

GREEN, Julian

Intellectual's journal, in the French tradition. D. Littlejohn. Commonweal 81:393 D 11 '64

Lonely Mr Green. R. Sale. New Repub 151:25-6 S 26 '64

GREEN, Larry R.

Glow in the dark. por Outdoor Life 132:40-3+ O '63

Maytime is shad time. por Outdoor Life 131:82-4+ My '63

New world for fly fisherman. pors Outdoor Life 133:22-3+ F '64

Striped fever. Outdoor Life 133:44-5+ My '64

West Coast stompede. Outdoor Life 131:30-1+ Mr '63

GREEN, Louis C.

Dallas conference on super radio sources. Sky & Tel 27:80-4 F '64

GREEN, Marion D.

Opening the cockpit doors. il por Time 81:24 My 3 '63

GREEN, Martin

Other Lawrence. Commonweal 81:346-8 D 4 '64

GREEN, Mawby, and Feilbert, Ed

Pajama tops; adaptation of Moumou, by J. de La Traz. Criticism

Newsweek 61:66 Je 10 '63

GREEN, Monet

Who's there? story. Ladies Home J 80:108-10 Je '63

GREEN, Philip

A. A. Berle; new myths for old. New Repub 148:21-3 Je 22 '63

Alternatives to overkill: dream and reality. Bul Atomic Sci 19:23-6 N '63

Giant step forward. New Repub 148:21-3 My 25; 149:30 Jl 13 '63

GREEN, Philip S.

Field-effect transistor. Electr World 70:66+ S '63

GREEN, Phillip C. and Gordon, Michael

Maternal deprivation: its influence on visual exploration in infant monkeys. Science 145:292-4 Jl 17 '64

GREEN, Richard

How to build & fly your own 1909 Bleriot. il Esquire 61:66-8 F '64

GREEN, Shields

Five brave Negroes with John Brown at Harpers Ferry. il Negro Hist Bul 27:164-9 Ap '64

GREEN, Stanley
Richard Rogers: serious popular or popular serious. Mus Am 83:10-11 F '63
GREEN, Timothy
Fifth of a village, gone in an instant. Life 55:42 S 20 '63
High honor for a shy genius. Life 57:41-2 Ag 7 '64
In his village the man lives on. Life 54:28 Je 14 '63
Little Harold knocks at No. ten. Life 54:37-8 Ap 12 '63
O Long of Life drinks camel milk and runs on oil. Life 54:50+ My 3 '63
They crown their country with a bowl-shaped hairdo. Life 56:30 Ja 31 '64
Villager cries out: how many more of us will die? Life 56:29 F 28 '64
GREEN, Tom
Tighten the tiny ones too. Hot Rod 16:74-7 S '63
GREEN, Vernon
Iceman cometh! Recreation 57:416-17 O '64
GREEN, William J. 3d
Evergreen. por Newsweek 63:23 My 11 '64
GREEN BAY
Blue-water cruise on Green Bay. F. M. Paulson. il Field & S 68:30-2+ Ag '63
GREEN BAY (city), Wis.
Green Bay may be little, but football is a giant; last of pro football's old home-town teams; with paintings by R. Weaver. Sports Illus 21:44-9 N 2 '64
Green Bay: the Packers' town. E. Waldron. Holiday 34:68-9+ N '63
How the Packers do it; Green Bay's boom in pro football. il Bsns W p52-4+ S 21 '63
State computer analyzes city traffic. M. L. Bacon, jr. il Am City 79:84-5 D '64
GREEN BAY Packers (football club) See Football clubs
GREEN duck company
Buttons pick the victor; political buttons. il Bsns W p34 Jl 25 '64
GREEN giant company
V.I. pea. il Time 81:82+ F 22 '63
GREEN manuring
Green manuring improves soil. H. G. Mattoon. il Horticulture 41:450 S '63
See also
Vetch
GREEN RIVER
Is our native underwater life worth saving? R. R. Miller. bibliog il Nat Parks Mag 37:4-9 My '63
GREEN sand. See Glauconite
GREEN shoe manufacturing company
Stepping out through the growing years. E. M. McCabe. il Parents Mag 38:18+ O '63
GREEN thumb; story. See Frazier. W.
GREEN turtles. See Turtles, Green
GREEN vegetables. See Vegetables
GREENACRE, James A.
Recent observation of lunar color phenomena. Sky & Tel 26:316 D '63
GREENAWAY, Kate, medal. See Kate Greenaway medal
GREENBERG, Alfred
Air-conditioning design guides for laboratory facilities. Arch Rec 135:197-201 My '64
Air conditioning of auditorium-type buildings. bibliog Arch Rec 135:205-8 Mr '64
Air conditioning of television studios. Arch Rec 135:180-1 Je '64
Environmental control in hospital design. Arch Rec 136:202-6 O '64
Library air-conditioning design. Arch Rec 135:173-4 F '64
GREENBERG, Clement
Famous art critic's collection. Vogue 143:92-5 Ja 15 '64
GREENBERG, Daniel S.
Burning question: tobacco and politics. Reporter 30:34-5 Ja 30 '64
Cuba: missile episode provided new incentive for arms agreement, but left behind some impediments. Science 138:670; 139:250 N 9 '62, Ja 18 '63
Fracas over fish flour. Sat Eve Post 236:34-5 N 23 '63
Government's marriage to science. New Repub 151:23-4 S 26 '64
Pork barrel science. New Repub 152:22 Ja 23 '65
Problems of NIH: an examination of how other federal agencies handle congressional relations. Science 140:1194-5; 141:763 Je 14, Ag 30 '63
When pure science meets pure politics. Reporter 30:39-41 Mr 12 '64
GREENBERG, Frank
To pray or not to pray, is that the question? PTA Mag 58:22-5+ F '64
GREENBERG, Hayim
Hayim Greenberg's legacy. D. Daiches. Commentary 38:81-2+ S '64
GREENBERG, Herbert M. See Mayer, D. jt. auth.
GREENBERG, Jack
N.A.A.C.P. lawyer answers some questions. N Y Times Mag p 16+ Ag 18 '63
That decade and the next. New Repub 151:24-7 D 19 '64
GREENBERG, Ken
How to identify surplus gear. Pop Electr 20:66-8 Ja '64
Tuning up on the new 460-Mc. police frequencies. Pop Electr 20:56-8+ My '64
GREENBERG, Pearl
Gyotaku Japanese fish printing. Sch Arts 63:21-2 Je '64
Mosaic wall of N.Y.C. por Sch Arts 63:5-7 S '63
People and the second grade. Sch Arts 64:17-21 S '64
Role of the art consultant. Sch Arts 63:21-3 Ap '64
Sand art. Sch Arts 64:5-9 D '64
Urban art program. Sch Arts 64:7-9 N '64
GREENBERG, Syd
Books for sneaks. il por U S Camera 27:66-7 Je '64
What's in an eye? il U S Camera 26:18 D '63
GREENBERGER, Martin
Computers of tomorrow. Atlan 213:63-7 My '64
GREENBLATT, Charles L. See Korn, E. D. jt. auth.
GREENBLATT, Lynn
(comp) There was an old man from. N Y Times Mag p 120 D 13 '64
GREENBLATT, Nat
I was dancing the cha-cha, there was an ominous thud. Life 57:100+ D 4 '64
GREENE, Andrew F. and Mascarenhas, J. P.
Coenzyme Q: intracellular distribution in rhodospirillum rubrum. bibliog Science 144:1455-6 Je 19 '64
GREENE, Bertram
Summer of Daisy Miller: dramatization of Daisy Miller, by H. James. Criticism
New Yorker 39:126+ Je 8 '63
Theatre Arts 47:11+ Ag '63
GREENE, Bette
Imbeciles who are geniuses. Sci Digest 56:16-21 Ag '64
GREENE, Bob
Up on two wheels. See issues of Hot rod
GREENE, Frank
Tests that can cinch a better job; ed. by J. Joseph. Pop Sci 185:66-7+ Jl '64
GREENE, Gael
All the fit that's news to print. Sat Eve Post 237:77-81 Ap 11 '64
College girls talk about chastity. McCalls 90:107+ S '63
Spinster's survival kit. Mlle 57:90+ Je '63
GREENE, George
First installment of Sartre's autobiography. Commonweal 81:75-6 O 9 '64
New insurgency. Commonweal 80:239-41 My 15 '64
New look at Andre Gide. Commonweal 79:376-7 D 20 '63
Wars of Wyndham Lewis. Commonweal 80:195-7 My 8 '64
GREENE, Graham
Beauty; story. Esquire 59:60 Ap '63
Nightmare republic. New Repub 149:18-20 N 16 '63
Return to Cuba. New Repub 149:16-18 N 2 '63
Root of all evil; story. Sat Eve Post 237:56-8 Mr 7 '64
about
Graham Greene, ed. by R. O. Evans. Review
Commonweal 79:727-9 Mr 13 '64. T. P. McDonnell
Novelist whitewashes Castro regime. Christian Cent 80:1457-8 N 27 '63
Our man in Havana. Criticism
Newsweek il 62:50 Jl 15 '63
GREENE, Howard M
Teacher of the President. NEA J 53:19 My '64
GREENE, Janet
Be careful. New Repub 152:8 Ja 23 '65
GREENE, Jerry
Ganging up on McNamara. Nation 196:264-6 Mr 30 '63
Tug-of-war: military budget. Nation 196:117-20 F 9 '63
GREENE, Laura
Singing saleswoman. il pors Ebony 19:143-4+ Ap '64
GREENE, Lee S.
(ed) City bosses and political machines. bibliog f Ann Am Acad 353:1-121 My '64

GREENE, Maxine
Education as a professional concern. Sat R 47:85 My 16 '64
They speak for themselves. Sat R 48:61-2 Ja 16 '65
GREENE, Milton
Some very winning Europeans; photographs. Life 55:132-43 D 20 '63
about
Screen test in Polacolor. J. Morris. il por U S Camera 27:40-1 Mr '64
GREENE, Morris
Library in the great game of politics. por Wilson Lib Bul 38:539-41 Mr '64
GREENE, Otis
Breakthrough in Hollywood. il pors Ebony 19:82-4+ D '63
GREENE, Patterson
Professional theatre on campus. Theatre Arts 47:62-3+ F '63
GREENE, Paul M. and Smith, K. U.
Maturation of performance with space-displaced vision. bibliog Science 141:727-8 Ag 23 '63
GREENE, Stephen
Decorum and independence. M. Kozloff. Nation 198:561-3 Je 1 '64
Painter of presences. il Time 81:74-5 Ap 12 '63
GREENE, Wallace Martin, 1907-
Beyond the way-out horizon. por Time 82:37 O 4 '63
People of the week. U S News 56:20 Ja 13 '64
Top marine with space-age ideas. por U S News 55:30 O 7 '63
GREENE, Will
Riot act. Criticism
New Yorker 39:137 Mr 16 '63
Newsweek 61:69 Mr 18 '63
Theatre Arts 47:73 My '63
GREENEVILLE, Tenn.
We do our own utility billing. M. C. Butler. il Am City 78:101-2 S '63
GREENEWALT, Crawford H.
Too many antitrust trials? yes, says Du Pont chief; excerpts from address, August 13, 1963. por U S News 55:21 Ag 26 '63
GREENFIELD, Edward
Art of Maria Callas. Hi Fi 14:42-6+ Mr '64
Method and manner of Elisabeth Schwarzkopf. Hi Fi 14:60-4+ N '64
Notes from our correspondents. Hi Fi 15: 30+ Ja; 30+ F '65
GREENFIELD, Meg
Atlantic City. Reporter 31:12+ S 10 '64
Everett Dirksen's newest role. Reporter 30: 26-9 Ja 16 '64
Fine art of president-baiting. Reporter 31:29-33 S 24 '64
Interregnum on the Hill. Reporter 29:19-20 D 19 '63
Man who leads the southern senators. Reporter 30:17-21 My 21 '64
New York: the Keating record. Reporter 31: 33-6 O 22 '64
Prosciutto and Mrs Mellon: Washington's society pages. Reporter 30:32-6 Mr 12 '64
Science goes to Washington. Reporter 29:20-6 S 26 '63; Same. Science 142:361-7 O 18 '63
Senator Goldwater and the Negro. Reporter 31:27-8 O 8 '64
GREENFIELD, Noelle Lamont
Inkling of happiness. por Redbook 122:6+ Mr '64
GREENFIELD VILLAGE. See Henry Ford museum and Greenfield Village, Dearborn, Mich.
GREENGARD, Olga, and others
Glycogen deposition in the liver induced by cortisone; dependence on enzyme synthesis. bibliog Science 141:160-1 Jl 12 '63
GREENHOUSE plants
Home greenhouse. J. Eaton. il Flower Grower 51:45-6 Je '64
Moving plants outdoors. Mrs W. H. Hull, jr. il Horticulture 42:36-7+ Je '64
GREENHOUSES
All-season house permits close biological studies; biotrones. Sci N L 83:120 F 23 '63
Build a greenhouse that runs itself. C. Ackerson. il Pop Gard 15:36-7 Ja '64
Controlled atmosphere for greenhouses. L. Donelson. il Farm J 87:62D Mr '63
Flowers all year. N. Coon. il Horticulture 41: 526-7 O '63
Greenhouse from a kit. il Flower Grower 51: 22-3 N '64
Greenhouses: our readers love them! il Flower Grower 51:28-9 S '64
Home greenhouse. F. F. Rockwell; E. C. Grayson; J. Eaton. See issues of Flower grower
How to live with spring ten months a year. C. C. Calkins. il House B 105:157-63+ Mr '63
In your greenhouse this month. R. M. Peters. See issues of Popular gardening to July-August 1963
New ideas for plastic greenhouses. J. Bickers. il Farm J 88:32-3 N '64
Orchids. A. Mifsud. il Horticulture 42:34-5 Jl '64
Right greenhouse for you. il Pop Gard 15:18-20 N '64
$300 builds backyard greenhouse. il Farm J 87:47 S '63
Two new ideas cut greenhouse costs. il Farm J 87:58BB Ap '63
Under glass. il Time 83:55 Mr 27 '64
See also
Cold frames
GREENHOUSES, Miniature
Compact gardens. J. Peter. il Look 27:62d Ap 23 '63
GREENLAND
Helicopter potential cited for Greenland. il Aviation W 79:49+ S 9 '63
Ice age survival. Newsweek 62:44-5 S 9 '63
Land of silence, fascination and beauty; excerpt from Arctic Riviera. L. Koch. il Natur Hist 72:46-55 Mr '63
Old man and the glacier. J. Liston. il Pop Sci 185:106-9+ O '64
GREENLEE, Lyman E.
Electric fence charger. Pop Electr 21:57-60+ D '64
Perpetual transistor power package. Pop Electr 20:53-5+ My '64
Signal stethoscope. Pop Electr 19:59-61+ Jl '63
GREENS, Edible
Edible weeds. M. Kaytor. il Look 27:34-5 Je 4 '63
Fiddlehead fern cookery; with recipes. H. Hinds. il Horticulture 41:328 Je '63
Salad greens for your garden. D. L. Roberson. il Horticulture 41:222-3+ Ap '63
Salads. il Am Home 66:62+ Jl '63
Turn over a new leaf this summer; with recipes. H. Mills. il Redbook 123:60-3 Je '64
Why wait for spinach? N. Smith. il Field & S 68:48-9+ My '63
See also
Chard
GREENSAND. See Glauconite
GREENSBORO, N.C.
Computer that pays its way. C. M. Conway. il Am City 79:102-3 S '64
Every detail received attention in expandable city maintenance center. T. Z. Osborne. il Am City 79:110-12 My '64
GREENSBURG, Kan.
Biggest well pays off in tourist coin. C. Hertlein. il Am City 79:28 Ag '64
GREENSPAN, C. M. See Marmur, J. jt. auth.
GREENSTEIN, Fred I.
Changing pattern of urban party politics. bibliog f Ann Am Acad 353:1-13 My '64
GREENSTEIN, Jesse L.
Quasi-stellar radio sources. Sci Am 209:54-62 bibliog(p 178) D '63
Solar and stellar magnetism. Science 142:686 N 8 '63
GREENVILLE, Mich.
Troubled town; question of closing Gibson refrigerator Greenville plant. Newsweek 61: 74+ My 20 '63
GREENVILLE, S.C.
Music
[Musical events] il Mus Am 83:14 My '63
GREENWALD, F. L.
Home portraits. U S Camera 26:74-5 N '63
GREENWALD, Frank L.
Electronic drill press drive. Pop Mech 121: 188-93 F '64
Keep those lifters quiet! Pop Sci 185:90-3 S '64
Make a fan-fold umbrella light. Pop Sci 185: 132-4 N '64
Multiply radio battery life. Pop Mech 120:192 S '63
$35 electric door opener. Pop Mech 120:172-8 D '63
What to do if your car is hard to start. Pop Sci 185:104-7 N '64
What you should know about engine timing. Pop Sci 186:124-7 Ja '65
GREENWALD, Herbert
Artist's biggest market. Design 64:162-6+ Mr '63
GREENWALD, Howard M.
Ordeal of an innocent man. Sat Eve Post 236:82+ O 5 '63
GREENWAY, John
Conversations with the stone age. Sat R 47: 21-3 F 15 '64

GREENWAY, Lauder
Out of many. Opera N 28:6-7 S 28 '63

GREENWICH, Conn.
One plant replaces four. W. B. Van Riper. il Am City 79:110-12 O '64
Residue tells the story. G. A. Hawkins. il Am City 78:104-6 S '63

Education

Elementary team teaching in operation. il Arch Rec 134:199-202 O '63
Intellectual leap; Montessori revival at Whitby school. il Newsweek 61:106+ Je 24 '63
Montessori in the slums; Whitby school. il Time 84:53-4 Jl 10 '64
Team teaching at Dundee. H. J. Langer. il Sr Schol 82:5T-6T+ F 27 '63
What's happening in education? team teaching. W. D. Boutwell. PTA Mag 57:25-6 My '63

GREENWICH, Conn, library
Administrator's view; library promotion. J. W. Bryant. il Wilson Lib Bul 39:464-7 F '65
Art + math = SRO. F. G. Donald. il Wilson Lib Bul 37:574-5 Mr '63
Like diamonds from Tiffany's. J. W. Bryant. il Library J 89:199-201 Ja 15 '64

GREENWICH observatory. See Astronomical laboratories—Great Britain

GREENWICH VILLAGE, New York. See New York (city)—Greenwich Village

GREENWOOD, Miss.
Locked out; drive to register Negro voters. Newsweek 61:30 Ap 15 '63
Mind on freedom; right to vote. il Newsweek 61:25-6 Ap 8 '63
Red carpet for Beckwith. J. DeMuth. New Repub 150:9 My 23 '64
Voting in Greenwood. Commonweal 78:61 Ap 12 '63
Yankee, go home. il Time 81:26 Ap 12 '63

GREER, David M.
What belongs in a foundation investigation. Arch Rec 133:190-2 Je '63

GREER, Edith S.
Academically talented. por Sch Life 45:9-12 Mr '63

GREER, Gordon G.
How to stay young and look great. Bet Hom & Gard 41:84-8 Jl '63
Just what are the most common dental problems? Bet Hom & Gard 41:34 Je '63
Plain talk about family health. See issues of Better homes and gardens
Promising report on cancer, heart trouble, arthritis, and other critical diseases. Bet Home & Gard 41:48-9+ Ag '63
What is psychotherapy? Bet Hom & Gard 41:88 Ap '63

GREER, Scott
Patterns of conquest; poem. Poetry 101:247 Ja '63

GREER, Scott Allen
Far from the heavenly city. Nation 200:87-8 Ja 25 '65
—and Minar, D. W.
Political side of urban development and redevelopment. Ann Am Acad 352:62-73 Mr '64

GREETING cards
Greeting card market today. C. Goeller. Writer 76:28-30 Mr '63
Greetings in macaroni. F. M. Major. il Design 64:194 Je '63
Making your own gift tags. il Sunset 131:112 D '63
What makes a good sentimental greeting? D. K. Quinn. Writer 77:21-4+ O '64
See also
Christmas cards
Hallmark cards, incorporated

GREGG, Davis W.
What you should know about buying life insurance; interview. por U S News 55:94-102 O 7 '63

GREGG, James R.
How's your eye-Q? Sr Schol 84:14T Ap 10 '64
Ten tips on taking your camera traveling. U S Camera 27:64 O '64

GREGG, Jess
Shout from the rooftops. Criticism
New Yorker 40:100+ N 7 '64

GREGG, Richard N.
Charles François Daubigny, forerunner of impressionism. Antiques 85:548-51 My '64

GREGO, Hal
Hal Grego jazz ballets, Brooklyn academy of music. J. Maskey. Dance Mag 38:72 Ap '64

GREGOR, A. James
Heredity and intellect. Nat R 16:287-9 Ap 7 '64

GREGOR, Arthur
Reply to a friend in New England; poem. New Yorker 40:170 S 12 '64
Shadowplay; poem. New Yorker 39:122 S 21 '63
Spirits, dancing; poem. New Yorker 40:148 N 21 '64

GREGORIAN calendar. See Calendar

GREGORY, Dick
Comedy's cold sustenance. P. De Lissovoy. Nation 199:383-5 N 23 '64
Gregory came to town. P. J. Owens. New Repub 150:10-11 Mr 28 '64
Locked out; drive to register Negro voters. Newsweek 61:30 Ap 15 '63
Mississippi airlift. Newsweek 61:30+ Mr 11 '63
Two worlds of Dick Gregory. T. B. Morgan. por Holiday 36:125-30+ D '64
Yankee, go home. il por Time 81:26 Ap 12 '63

GREGORY, Gene Adrian
Gregorys of Saigon. por Newsweek 62:40+ S 23 '63

GREGORY, Horace
E. E. Cummings. Commonweal 79:725-6 Mr 13 '64

about

Door in the desert. T. Weiss. Poetry 105:134-5 N '64
Poems split from granite. por Time 85:94 Ja 29 '65
Prospect of delight. M. L. Rosenthal. Reporter 31:50+ S 10 '64

GREGORY, John R.
Directory of 8mm zoom cameras. U S Camera 27:66-73+ Mr '64
Four closeups of movie projection. U S Camera 26:78-9+ My '63
Synchronization. U S Camera 26:72-3 O '63
What is this thing called stereo? U S Camera 26:30+ D '63

GREGORY, Virginia
Art instruction in a summer program. Recreation 56:275 Je '63

GREHAN, Farrell
America's wild beauties; excerpts from Odyssey book of American wildflowers. il Life 56:60-3 Ap 3 '64

GREIFF, Victor
Lizard to grow in the garden. il Flower Grower 50:80 Ag '63
—See O'Leary, W. A. jt. auth.

GREINER, Larry E. See Barnes, L. B. jt. auth.

GRELL, Rhoda F. and Valencia, J. I.
Distributive pairing and aneuploipy in man. bibliog Science 145:66-7 Jl 3 '64

GRELLA, George
James Bond: culture hero. New Repub 150:17-18+ My 30 '64

GREMILLION, Joseph
Pope Paul's other dialogue. por Cath World 198:208-14 Ja '64

GREMLEY, William
Time to consolidate? America 112:12-14 Ja 2 '65

GRENADA
Grenada. D. Beal. Mlle 59:188+ My '64

GRENARD, Jack. See Grenard, Jane, jt. auth.

GRENARD, Jane, and Grenard, Jack
Sailing our inland seas. Motor B 111:22-3+ Je '63
Underwater furniture factory. il Motor B 111:76-7+ Je '63

GRENIER, Cynthia
Tough time for puritans behind the iron curtain. N Y Times Mag p 14-15+ My 24 '64

GRENIER, John
Grenier plan for the G.O.P. J. Ter Horst. Reporter 31:24-6 O 8 '64

GRENIER, Mildred
When you write for tots. Writer 77:24 Ap '64

GRENIER, Richard
U.S. investments in France. Reporter 28:23-4+ Je 6 '63
What next for the Common market? Reporter 28:24-6 F 28 '63
(ed) See Bardot, B. Positivement, Mlle Sagan
(ed) See Sagan, F. Absolument, Mlle Bardot

GRENNAN, Sister Jacqueline
St Joan of Webster Groves. por Time 81:59 Je 21 '63
Sister J: secret weapon; with statements. il pors Life 57:53-4+ O 23 '64

GRÈS, Mme
Vogue's eye view of Madame Grès. E. Charles-Roux. il por Vogue 144:97-9 S 15 '64

GRESHAM, Grits
Bussey is best; it's bassy. por Outdoor Life 133:76-7+ Ap '64
Deer of Thanksgiving. Outdoor Life 134:40-1+ N '64

GRESHAM, Samuel C. and others
Alcohol and caffeine: effect on inferred visual dreaming. bibliog Science 140:1226-7 Je 14 '63
GRESHAM family
Gresham coat-of-arms. H. K. Eilers. il Hobbies 69:122-4 Jl '64
GRESSIEKER, Hermann
Emperor; tr. by G. White. Criticism
America 108:650 My 4 '63
Theatre Arts il 47:10-11+ Je '63
Royal gambit. Criticism
America 108:595 Ap 20 '63
New Yorker 39:85 Ap 27 '63
GREVATT, Ren
Artist as businessman. Hi Fi 13:32-4+ Je '63
GREY, Hugh
Cross-country editor. por Field & S 67:36-7+ F '63
One-man snow scooter. Field & S 67:143-4 Ap '63
GREY advertising, incorporated
How an ad agency hits the $100-million mark. il Bsns W p58-60+ Ja 23 '65
GREY Owl (Ojibway Indian)
Grey Owl: mysterious genius of nature lore. R. Cantwell. il por Sports Illus 18:112-14+ Ap 8 '63
GREY Towers. See Pennsylvania—Historic houses, etc.
GREYHOUND corporation
Greyhound bids for a new outlet. Bsns W p25 F 29 '64
Sign of the dog. il Time 81:82+ Ap 26 '63
Travel: go Greyhound, and leave the profits to them. il Newsweek 63:68-70 Je 22 '64
View from the top of the Greyhound bus. il Bsns W p85+ N 16 '63
Wage chronology: Western Greyhound lines, 1954-63. W. Fridie. il Mo Labor R 87:178-86 F '64
GREYHOUND racing. See Dog racing
GREYHOUNDS
Hi Joe, where are you? racing greyhound stolen. J. Lovesey. il Sports Illus 22:20-1 Ja 25 '65
GRIBBIN, John H.
Work-study program. por Library J 89:568-9+ F 1 '64
GRIBBIN, Lenore S.
Keep or discard? recommended form letter for public relations use. Library J 89:1193 Mr 15 '64
GRIBBINS, Joseph
Far side of paradise. Motor B 112:38 S '63
Forests, lakes and black-eyed peas. Motor B 111:30-1+ Je '63
In the wake of Daniel Boone. il Motor B 113:38-9+ Je '64
GRID dip meters. See Electric meters
GRID floors. See Bridges—Floors
GRIDDLE cakes
Around the world with delectable dessert pancakes. V. T. Habeeb. il Am Home 67:58-9+ Ja '64
Better batter, lotta butter: specialized pancake palaces. Time 82:59+ Jl 26 '63
Come for pancakes on Shrove Tuesday. il Sunset 132:130 F '64
Cooking Danish and Swedish pancakes. Sunset 133:175-6 N '64
Five girls and a gourmet: crêpes; with recipes. il Seventeen 22:160+ N '63
He likes to cook; pancakes. L. K. Rudd. il Bet Hom & Gard 41:80 Ap '63
It's a three-layer apricot pancake. il Sunset 130:236 Ap '63
It's an Austrian pancake torte. il Sunset 130:216 My '63
Pancakes are fancy fare. G. Maddox. il Todays Health 41:40-3+ O '63
Pancakes, plain and fancy. il Redbook 121:72-3+ Je '63
Pancakes plus; crepes. C. Claiborne. il N Y Times Mag p66 My 12 '63
Pancakes; waffles. il Suc Farm 61:64+ S '63
These filled pancakes are blintzes. il Sunset 130:204+ Mr '63
Thin crêpe and the plump crêpe. il Sunset 130:222+ My '63
GRIDDLES. See Kitchen utensils
GRIDDLES, Electric. See Electric grills
GRIDIRON club
Washington's greatest spoof: the Gridiron dinner. D. M. Allen. il Read Digest 84:51-2+ Ap '64
GRIDLEY, Peter
Color from B&W. Mod Phot 27:58-9 F '63
Make your prints shine! U S Camera 26:97 Ap '63
GRIDS (electronics) See Electron tubes—Grids
GRIECO, Rose
Daddy come home. Criticism
America 108:592+ Ap 20 '63
GRIEF. See Bereavement
GRIER, Eldon
Canadian chronicle. P. Webb. Poetry 104:386-8 S '64
GRIERSON, Ruth, and Grierson, Stan
Home fit for a kingfisher! por Audubon Mag 66:300-1 S '64
GRIERSON, Stan. See Grierson, R. jt. auth.
GRIEVANCE procedures
Grievance procedures in major contracts. R. T. Selby and M. L. Cunningham. il Mo Labor R 87:1125-30; 1269-72 O-N '64
UAW's own court sums up; review board. Bsns W p73-4 Je 15 '63
GRIEVE, Christopher Murray
Hugh MacDiarmid: hailing us all. C. Kizer. Poetry 102:177-81 Je '63
Poet and prime minister. S. Hynes. Commonweal 81:84-5 O 16 '64
GRIFFARD, C. D. and Peirce, J. T.
Conditioned discrimination in the planarian. Science 144:1472-3 Je 19 '64
GRIFFENHAGEN, George
Evolution of the medicine glass. Hobbies 68:84-5+ Ja '64
World's fanciest pill bottles; adaptation of address. Todays Health 42:42-5+ D '64
GRIFFES, Charles T.
Label comes back: Griffes on EMS. P. L. Miller. Am Rec G 29:451 F '63
GRIFFIN, C. W. Jr
Air around us. Reporter 31:39-43 S 10 '64
Morning at Marathon. Sat R 47:49-50 N 14 '64
Specialists diagnose the stricken American city. Sat R 46:22-4 Ag 3 '63
311 East 100th. Reporter 31:54+ O 22 '64
Ugly American. Reporter 30:53-4+ Ja 30 '64
GRIFFIN, Emilie
Theater. Nat R 15:446-8+ N 19 '63
GRIFFIN, Gwyn
Significant experience; story. Sat Eve Post 236:48-50 S 21 '63
GRIFFIN, John Howard
Black like me. il por Ebony 19:37-8+ My '64
WLB biography. R. Montgomery. por Wilson Lib Bul 37:802 My '63
GRIFFIN, Junius
Last word from Soul city. N Y Times Mag p62+ Ag 23 '64
GRIFFIN, Marjorie
Consultants' column (cont) por Library J 88:1126, 2650+ Mr 15, Jl '63
GRIFFIN, Merv
Merv Griffin; star by day. V. Kelly. il pors Look 27:73-6 F 12 '63
GRIFFITH, Alice B.
Library handbook standards. por Wilson Lib Bul 39:475-7 F '65
GRIFFITH, Andy
Andy Griffith: sheriff of Mayberry. C. Morrison. il pors Look 27:80a-80e Ap 9 '63
I think I'm gaining on myself. D. Freeman. il pors Sat Eve Post 237:68-70 Ja 25 '64
GRIFFITH, Belver C. See Garvey, W. D. jt. auth.
GRIFFITH, Charles E.
Obituary
Pub W 186:39 S 7 '64
GRIFFITH, Earl
Foam-equipped fire-pumper. Am City 78:149-50 F '63
GRIFFITH, Emile
All week long the word was Griffith. R. H. Boyle. il por Sports Illus 18:24-5+ Je 17 '63
King David and the Black Bull. H. Horn. il por Sports Illus 20:18-21 Je 22 '64
GRIFFITH, F. H.
Old mechanical banks. See issues of Hobbies
GRIFFITH, Hugh
Squire Hugh. por Time 82:38 D 27 '63
GRIFFITH, Sam
Obituary
Yachting 114:119 Ag '63. L. Evans
Rough race for Sam's sake. H. Whall. il Sports Illus 20:22-3 F 17 '64
GRIFFITH, Samuel B. 2d
Communist China's capacity to make war. For Affairs 43:217-36 Ja '65
Glorious military thought of comrade Mao Tse-tung. For Affairs 42:669-74 Jl '64
GRIFFITH, William E.
European communism and the Sino-Soviet schism. bibliog f Ann Am Acad 349:143-52 S '63
Quebec in revolt. For Affairs 43:29-36 O '64
GRIFFITHS, Eldon
Mr K's turn toward Stalinism. Sat Eve Post 236:70-3 Je 1 '63
Myth about the Common market? Newsweek 62:61-2+ Ag 12 '63
Revolt of Europe. Sat Eve Post 236:13-21 Mr 9 '63
World in change: a trip through eastern Europe. Newsweek 62:36-8+ O 28 '63; Same abr. Read Digest 84:119-24 Ap '64

GRIFFITHS, G. Findley
Acme steel's three years of hell. il por Bsns W p 140+ Jl 11 '64
GRIFFITHS, Martha W.
Lady of the House looks into taxes; with editorial comment. por Bsns W p28-9, 180 My 23 '64
GRIFFITHS, Peter
Cruel to lepers; Prime Minister's attack on member for Smethwick. il Time 84:53 N 13 '64
GRIGG, Sir John Edward Poynder
Cold war will not end in our time. N Y Times Mag p7+ F 2 '64
In defense of Charles de Gaulle. N Y Times Mag p 14+ F 23 '64
There is no weakening of the cold war spirit. N Y Times Mag p22+ S 27 '64
GRIGGS, D. T. and Blacic, J. D.
Quartz: anomalous weakness of synthetic crystals. bibliog Science 147:292-5 Ja 15 '65
GRIGGS, Lee
Rough creed: there's no success without suffering. Life 57:42 S 11 '64
Skating. Sports Illus 18:49 Mr 4 '63
—and Lozano, R. D.
Boxing. Sports Illus 20:66-7 Mr 16 '64
GRIGSBY, William G.
Housing and slum clearance: elusive goals. bibliog f Ann Am Acad 352:107-18 Mr '64
GRIJALVA RIVER
Exploring, ugh! B. Gilbert. il Sports Illus 20: 72-6+ Ja 27 '64
GRILLES
Grille sections to use for that air of mystery. il House B 105:278-82 N '63
More Japanese ideas cross the Pacific; window grille. il Sunset 130:79 F '63
Mysterious allure of grilles. C. Besinger. il House B 105:248-51+ N '63
GRILLET, Alain Robbe-. See Robbe-Grillet, A.
GRILLING. See Broiling
GRILLO, Joann
Winners two; interview, ed. by R. D. Daniels. por Opera N 28:29 Ja 11 '64
GRILLS, Barbecue. See Barbecue grills
GRIMAU GARCIA, Julián
Death at dawn. por Time 81:36+ Ap 26 '63
He died a Communist. Newsweek 61:39-40 Ap 29 '63
GRIMES, Tammy
Illusive, elusive Miss Tammy Grimes. L. H. Lapham. il pors Sat Eve Post 237:60-3 Ap 4 '64
Tammy Grimes: blithe spirit. V. Kelly. il pors Look 28:87-91 Mr 10 '64
GRIMM, Harold J.
Simple, sincere, salty. Christian Cent 80: 1030 Ag 21 '63
GRIMM, Jacob
Grimm tale. H. R. Meisels. Wilson Lib Bul 39:165-7 O '64
GRIMM, Robert D.
Tunnel diode receiver. Pop Electr 18:62-5+ Je '63
GRIMM, Wilhelm
Grimm tale. H. R. Meisels. Wilson Lib Bul 39:165-7 O '64
GRIMM brothers
Enchanted centenary of the brothers Grimm. E. Bowen. il N Y Times Mag p28-9+ S 8 '63
Happily ever after with the brothers Grimm. G. Kent. il Read Digest 86:167-9+ Ja '65
GRIMMICH, William
Inro art. Hobbies 68:28 N '63
GRINBERG, Miguel
Seven Argentine poets. Américas 16:16-19 O '64
GRINDING
See also
Sand blast
GRINDING machines
Grind anything anywhere. W. E. Burton. il Pop Mech 121:188-91 Mr '64
Hand grinder; high-speed shaping tool. il Pop Sci 183:182+ D '63
It's no longer just grind, grind at Norton. il Fortune 68:118-23+ Ag '63
See also
Feed grinders and grinding
GRINDING wheels
Grinding a part from start to finish; abrasive machining. il Bsns W p76 F 9 '63
GRINER, Ned
Craftsman & teacher. il pors Sch Arts 63:28-9 S '63
GRINS. See Smiles
GRIPENBERG, G. A.
Recollections of Pius XII. America 110:539+ Ap 18 '64
GRIPPE, Peter
Four sculptors, four styles. il Art N 62:37+ Sum '63
GRIPPE. See Influenza
GRIS, Charles Edouard Jeanneret-. See Le Corbusier
GRIS, Juan
Gallery for young people; Le Canigou. C. B. Johnson. il Sch Arts 62:40 My '63
Landmarks of modern art. K. Kuh. il Sat R 46:30 Je 1 '63
GRISCOM, Ludlow
Memorable days with Ludlow Griscom. C. Wellman. por Audubon Mag 66:247-9 Jl '64
GRISHAM, Jim
Fullbacks in motion. H. L. Masin. por Sr Schol 85:44 N 11 '64
GRISSETT, Anne
New technique with a familiar medium. Sch Arts 62:15 Je '63
GRISSOM, Virgil
If it goes wrong I'll be responsible. pors Life 56:118+ Je 5 '64
GRIST, Reri
Absolutely priceless. por Time 82:64 N 15 '63
Individualists; Mlle's annual Merit awards. por Mlle 58:76 Ja '64
Quote: unquote; interview, ed. by M. Brozen. por Mus Am 83:24 O '63
GRISWOLD, Alfred Whitney
Awful good man. por Newsweek 61:57 Ap 29 '63
Building years of a Yale man. W. McQuade. il Arch Forum 118:88-93 Je '63
Great builder dies. por Arch Forum 118:87 Je '63
Mr Whitney Griswold and his successor. Nat R 14:350 My 7 '63
Obituary
Pub W 183:58 Ap 29 '63; Editorial comment. 183:59 Ap 29 '63
Wise and witty fighter is dead; with editorial comment. il por Life 54:4, 34-5 My 3 '63
Witty reformer. il por Time 81:46 Ap 26 '63
GRISWOLD Erwin N.
Griswold on church-state; excerpts from address. America 108:374-5 Mr 16 '63
When newsmen become newsmakers. Sat R 47:21-3 O 24 '64
GRISWOLD, S. Smith
New hope for Californians. Sci Digest 53: 8-11 My '63
GRISWOLD, Wesley S.
Ranger 6. Pop Sci 184:77-9+ Ja '64
GRITZNER, Florence A.
Instant newspaper. Sr Schol 84:13T My 1 '64
GRIVAS, George
In suspension. il Newsweek 64:38+ Jl 6 '64
Letter from Cyprus. C. Foley. il Nat R 16: 724-5 Ag 25 '64
GRIZZLY bear hunting. See Bear hunting
GRIZZLY bears. See Bears
GRIZZLY bears, Photography of. See Photography of animals
GROAT, H. Theodore
College students are going west. Sch & Soc 91:352-4 N 16 '63
GROB, Howard S.
Enzymatic dissection of the mammalian ovary. bibliog Science 146:73-4 O 2 '64
GROBMAN, Arnold
Biology is changing, too. Sat R 46:67-9+ S 21 '63
GROBMAN, Hulda
Student performance in new high school biology programs. bibliog Science 143:265-6 Ja 17 '64
GROBSTEIN, Clifford
Cytodifferentiation and its controls. bibliog Science 143:643-50 F 14 '64
GROCERY chains. See Chain stores
GROCERY store products company
Pantry food for special diet needs. il Parents Mag 39:40+ Mr '64
GROCERY stores
My father's grocery store. P. M. Angle. il Am Heritage 14:34-7+ Ag '63
GROCERY trade
See also
Great Atlantic and Pacific tea company
Safeway stores, incorporated
Strikes—United States—Grocery trade
Supermarkets
Winn-Dixie stores, incorporated
GRODZINS, Morton M.
Obituary
Bul Atomic Sci por 20:15-16 My '64
Pub W 185:35 Mr 23 '64
GROENHOFF, Hans
Flying photographer. Flying 75:24 Jl '64
GROFF, Patrick J.
New books for the slum child. Wilson Lib Bul 38:345-8 D '63
Transformation of a poet: John Ciardi. Horn Bk 40:153-8 Ap '64

GROGAN, Ewart Scott
White and black, old and new: Uhuru for all? por Newsweek 62:42-3 D 16 '63
GROH, George
Doctors of the frontier. Am Heritage 14: 10-11+ Ap '63
GROLIER, incorporated
Change of name for Grolier's British firm. Pub W 186:92 S 28 '64
Grolier buys three reference divisions from British firm. Pub W 185:32 Ap 6 '64
Grolier launches new Encyclopedia international. Pub W 183:32 Mr 18 '63
GROLIER encyclopedia. See Encyclopedia international
GROMAIRE, Marcel
Loner. il Newsweek 62:73 Ag 19 '63
GROMBACH, John V.
Oldest show on earth. Todays Health 42:20-1+ O '64
GROMYKO, Andreĭ Andreevich
Gromyko at the U.N; excerpts from address, September 19, 1963. Bul Atomic Sci 19:43+ N '63
about
How far can U.S. trust Gromyko? por U S News 55:15 Ag 19 '63
Two kinds of reds to call on Kennedy. por U S News 55:24 S 23 '63
GRONOUSKI, John Austin
Mail service; address, September 10, 1964. Vital Speeches 30:755-7 O 1 '64
about
Change in the Cabinet; emphasis is still on youth. por U S News 55:26 S 23 '63
Hyphenated general. il por Newsweek 62:29-30 S 23 '63
Postmaster who licked stamps. il por Time 82:27-8 S 20 '63
GRONOWICZ, Antoni
Death haunted their houses. Sat R 46:37-8 D 28 '63
GROOM, Theodore R.
Fiction as strange as fact: death of another salesman; excerpts from address, March 18, 1963. por U S News 54:51-3 Ap 22 '63
GROOME, Harry C. Jr
How to criticize advertising. Sat R 46:54 O 12 '63
GROOMING, Personal. See Beauty, Personal; Toilet
GROOMS. See Weddings
GROOT, Johan J.
Palynological investigation of a core from the Biscay abyssal plain. bibliog Science 141:522-3 Ag 9 '63
—and Ewing, M. L.
Suspended clay in a water sample from the deep ocean. Science 142:579 N 1 '63
GROOVER, James R.
Visions as the boatman sees them. Motor B 111:48-9 F '63
GROPIUS, Walter
Gropius addresses convocation at Williams; excerpts from address. Arch Rec 134:10 N '63
Tradition and continuity in architecture; address. por Arch Rec 135:131-6 My; 133-40 Je; 136:151-6 Jl '64
about
Gropius' 80th birthday marked by old friends and students. il por Arch Rec 134:10 Jl '63
GROPP, Arthur E.
Books. Américas 16:40-1 Ja '64
GROS, Robert R.
Fifth freedom, economic freedom; address, February 7, 1963. Vital Speeches 29:465-8 My 15 '63
GROSBEAKS
Evening grosbeak. J. K. Terres. il Pop Gard 81:12 F '65
GROSCH, Daniel S.
Insect fecundity and fertility: chemically induced decrease. bibliog Science 141:732-3 Ag 23 '63
GROSE, Peter
Ordinary life of Americans in Saigon. N Y Times Mag p26-7+ S 27 '64
Portrait of the distant candidate. N Y Times Mag p 13+ My 10 '64
Taylor tries a new start in Vietnam. N Y Times Mag p 12-13+ Ag 9 '64
Vietcong's shadow government in the South. N Y Times Mag p 10-11+ Ja 24 '65
GROSECLOSE, Elgin. See Harnischfeger, W. jt. auth.
GROSJEAN, Jean
Graduel; Hiver: poems, with English tr. by W. Fowlie. Poetry 104:296-309 Ag '64
GROSKOPF, W. R. and others
Amino acid composition of hemerythrin in relation to subunit structure. bibliog Science 141:166-7 Jl 12 '63
GROSS, Alfred A.
Accepting the deviate. Christian Cent 80:1107 S 11 '63
GROSS, Alfred O.
Our cattle egret is also an elephant egret. il Audubon Mag 66:218-21 Jl '64
GROSS, Calvin Edward
Gross challenge: are we educators or babysitters? summary of address. por Sr Schol 82:1T+ Ap 24 '63
about
Instant integration? Newsweek 62:54 D 30 '63
Personal attention. New Yorker 39:15-16 Je 29 '63
Public schools; civilizing the blackboard jungle. il pors Time 82:86-8+ N 15 '63
Too many pupils; too many problems. il pors Newsweek 62:55-8 S 16 '63
GROSS, Charles G. See Chorover, S. L. jt. auth.
GROSS, Charles H.
But we're providing liquidity; floor trading. por Newsweek 62:56 Jl 29 '63
GROSS, Cordelia Baird
Saburo's native land. Read Digest 82:107-9 F '63
GROSS, Courtlandt S.
Lockheed chairman says industry has problems but remains sound. Aviation W 79:113-14+ N 11 '63
GROSS, Elizabeth H.
Children's hero; in quest of value. Wilson Lib Bul 38:162-4 O '63
GROSS, Ernest A.
First step to what? Reporter 29:30-2 S 12 '63
GROSS, Frank D.
Capacitance nomogram. Electr World 72:31 D '64
Music/speech discriminator. Electr World 69: 36-8+ Ap '63
Semiconductor heat sink design chart. Electr World 73:28-9 Ja '65
GROSS, Jacquelyn
As the slum goes, so goes the Alliance. N Y Times Mag p 12-13+ Je 23 '63
GROSS, Jerome
Thermal denaturation of collagen in the dispersed and solid state. bibliog Science 143: 960-1 F 28 '64
GROSS, John
Jewish chronicle and others. Commentary 36: 387-9 N '63
John Bull and John Profumo. Commentary 36:144-50 Ag '63
Zangwill in retrospect. Commentary 38:54-7 D '64
GROSS, Leonard
Who cares? Look 28:17-19 S 8 '64; Same abr. with title: Is there a Samaritan in the neighborhood? Read Digest 85:106-10 N '64
GROSS, M. Grant, and others
Varved marine sediments in a stagnant fjord. bibliog Science 141:918-19 S 6 '63
GROSS, Marthe
Painless parties for in-betweens. Parents Mag 39:40-1+ D '64
GROSS, Mason W.
Facts, values and libraries; excerpts from address, July 16, 1963. por ALA Bul 57: 829-36 O '63
Useful, ornamental, and benign; address, January 19, 1963. Vital Speeches 29:314-18 Mr 1 '63
GROSS, Michael
Take a bow: Michael Gross. il Pub W 184: 22-8 D 30 '63
GROSS, Milt
Folklore of kinetic man. H. Kenner. Nat R 15:238-9 S 24 '63
GROSS, Milton
Match made in the jungle. Sat Eve Post 237:76-8 O 24 '64
Scholarship for Barry. Sat Eve Post 236:20-3 F 23 '63
(ed) See Kaufax, S. I'm only human
(ed) See Patterson, F. I want to destroy Clay
GROSS, Paul M.
Fifth estate in the seventh decade; excerpts from address, December 28, 1963. Science 143:13-20; 144:1087 Ja 3, My 29 '64
R&D, and the relations of science and government; statement before a congressional subcommittee. Science 142:645-50 N 8 '63
GROSS, Paul R. See Bal, A. K. jt. auth.
GROSS, Richard E.
Social studies curriculum: proposals for the future. por Sr Schol 83:8T-9T O 25 '63
—and Allen, D. W.
Stop playing blindman's buff. Sr Schol 83: 9T-12T O 11 '63

GROSS, Ronald
Education for the cold war? Commonweal 80:36-9 Ap 3 '64
Two-year-olds are very smart. N Y Times Mag p 10-11+ S 6 '64
Uses of leisure. Commonweal 78:185-7 My 10 '63
Value of what knowledge? Sat R 47:72-3 N 21 '64
—See Murphy, J. jt. auth.
GROSS, Sarah Chokla
Collectors, speak up; reprint. Library J 89:202-4 Ja 15 '64
Theatre library association and Broadside. Wilson Lib Bul 38:664 Ap '64
GROSS, Selma Woodrow
Creative magic for the senior citizen. por Recreation 57:234-5 My '64
GROSS, Sidney
Gross and Rosset speak on paperbacks at Adclub. Pub W 183:50 F 4 '63
GROSS, Suzanne
Antiphon I; poem. Commonweal 80:42 Ap 3 '64
Chionoptera; poem. Commonweal 81:424 D 18 '64
GROSS national product
ABC and GNP. il Changing T 18:43-5 Ap '64
Future challenges marketing. R. C. Garretson. il Harvard Bsns R 41:168-70+ N '63
GNP: scorecard of progress. Sr Schol 85:16 O 21 '64
Growth mania. H. Hazlitt. Newsweek 61:88 Mr 18 '63
In '64, a batch of new highs; with charts. Bsns W p 15-17 D 28 '63
National wealth of the United States in the postwar period. by R. W. Goldsmith. Review
Commentary 35:268-72 Mr '63. D. T. Bazelon
New way to tell whether budgets are too big? il U S News 56:71-2 Ja 6 '64
Plan or no plan or un-plan? economic planning in Canada; address, June 3, 1963. W. E. McLaughlin. Vital Speeches 29:636-9 Ag 1 '63
Skyrocketing private debt: why officials are worried. il U S News 57:98+ O 12 '64
Stimulus and restraint. il Fortune 68:31-2 Ag '63
Target: $1-trillion a year; Twentieth century fund study. il Bsns W p 102-4 My 2 '64
Trend of business. J. Phillips. il Duns R 82:8-9 D '63
GROSSBERG, Sidney E.
Human influenza A viruses: rapid plaque assay in hamster kidney cells. bibliog Science 144:1246-7 Je 5 '64
GROSSE, Aristid V.
High-temperature research. bibliog Science 140:781-9 My 17 '63
Viscosity and self-diffusion of liquid metals. bibliog Science 145:50-1 Jl 3 '64
—See Kirschenbaum, A. D.; Streng, A. G. jt. auths.
—and others
Krypton tetrafluoride: preparation and some properties. bibliog Science 139:1047-8 Mr 15 '63
GROSSE POINTE, Michigan
Rich, rich Grosse Pointe. S. Birmingham. il Holiday 35:60-5+ My '64
GROSSE POINTE PARK, Mich.
Tree program restricts elm losses. R. A. Sloane. il Am City 79:165-6 O '64
GROSSE POINTE SHORES, Mich.
Expressway dirt builds ski slopes. T. K. Jefferis. il Am City 79:28 Jl '64
GROSSEN, Earl L.
My Russian journey. Sr Schol 84:12T Ap 17 '64
GROSSER, Axel
Master printer tells how. E. Meyers. il Mod Phot 27:86-91 N '63
Visit with Axel Grosser. A. Francekevich. Pop Phot 55:28 D '64
GROSSER, Maurice
Art (cont) Nation 198:402-3, 543-4 Ap 20, My 25 '64
GROSSER, Morton
Loom; story. New Yorker 40:72-4 Ag 1 '64
GROSSET and Dunlap, incorporated
Grosset buys Curtis' interest in three subsidiaries. Pub W 185:133 F 24 '64
Grosset's promotion plan offers free display aids. il Pub W 185:26-7 Mr 16 '64
GROSSFELD, Muriel
Individualists; Mlle's annual Merit awards. il por Mlle 58:74-5 Ja '64
GROSSHANS, Henry. See Payne, H. C. jt. auth.
GROSSI, Héctor
Author's purpose. Américas 15:37-8 F '63
GROSSLING, B. F.
Natural resources and international development. Am For 70:42+ S '64
GROSSMAN, H. J.
How to keep industry. Am City 78:122 S '63
GROSSMAN, Harold J.
Wines of America. Am Home 66:6+ O '63
GROSSMAN, James
Justice Black and the absolute. Commentary 36:244-8 S '63
GROSSMAN, Jerome
Peace crowd. Nation 198:66-8 Ja 20 '64
GROSSMAN, Mary Louise
Rebirth in the South. Sports Illus 20:43-4+ Mr 30 '64
GROSSMAN, N. M.
(comp) 1964 used camera buying guide. Mod Phot 27:66-98 D '63
GROSSMAN, Robert
Sports car for everyman. Sports Illus 20:38-40+ Ap 20 '64
GROSSMAN, Sebastian P.
Chemically induced epileptiform seizures in the cat. bibliog Science 142:409-11 O 18 '63
GROSSMAN, Shelly
Spring on a Florida river. il Sports Illus 20:38-42 Mr 30 '64
GROSSWEINER, Leonard I.
Photosensitization in solids. Science 146:88-90 O 2 '64
—and others
Photochemical generation of the hydrated electron. bibliog Science 141:805-6 Ag 30 '63
Photochemical production of the solvated electron in ethanol. bibliog Science 141:1180 S 20 '63
GROST, Michael
Prodigy. por Newsweek 64:79 O 12 '64
GROSVENOR, Donna Kerkam. See Grosvenor, G. M. jt. auth.
GROSVENOR, Elsie May Bell
Romance of the Geographic. G. H. Grosvenor. il pors Nat Geog Mag 124:516-85 O '63
GROSVENOR, Gilbert Hovey
Romance of the Geographic. pors Nat Geog Mag 124:516-85 O '63
GROSVENOR, Gilbert M. and Grosvenor, D. K.
Miniature Monaco. il Nat Geog Mag 123:546-73 Ap '63
GROSVENOR, Melville Bell
Birds about us. Nat Geog Mag 126:552-7 O '64
From the ends of the earth to the edge of the future. Nat Geog Mag 124:728-33 N '63
Last full measure. Nat Geog Mag 125:307-55 Mr '64
World's tallest tree discovered. il Nat Geog Mag 126:1-9 Jl '64
GROSZ, George
From hell to holocaust. il por Time 82:90-1+ O 4 '63
Threepenny artist. H. Kramer. il Reporter 29:57+ O 24 '63
GROTON. See Private schools
GROTZ, George
New antiques; excerpts. House B 105:252-5+ N '63
GROUND control approach system. See Airplanes—Landing
GROUND covers. See Cover plants
GROUND cypress. See Faith trees
GROUND effect machines
Aeroboatmobiles! il Life 56:32-4 Ja 3 '64
Aerohydroski uses lift from skis, wings. M. L. Yaffee. il Aviation W 81:72-3+ O 26 '64
Air-cushion passenger vehicle shows promise. il Am City 79:106+ N '64
Air Dart wins first hovercraft race. il Pop Sci 185:78-9 Ag '64
Amateur scientist; aerodynamics of air-supported vehicles. R. W. Moffat. il Sci Am 210:135-8 Ja '64
Assault on an air cushion; Bell aero-system's hydroskimmer. il Time 84:104+ O 9 '64
Boost in Hovercraft support seen. il Aviation W 81:137 S 7 '64
Buy it, build it; ride on air! V. L. Oertle. il Pop Sci 183:54-5+ Jl '63
Coast guard emerging with GEM control. Aviation W 81:45 O 26 '64
For watery missions; air-cushion amphibious craft; navy's Hydroskimmer. il Bsns W p 137 O 19 '63
Giant spraymobiles; hovercraft, hydroskimmer. R. Gannon. il Pop Sci 184:64-7+ Mr '64
GEM trials sought for two areas in U.S. J. W. Carter. Aviation W 81:50 O 19 '64
Hovercraft missile transporter seen. M. Getler. il Miss & Roc 15:18+ Ag 17 '64
It goes, but just what is it? il Bsns W p56 N 7 '64
Leading international ground effect machines; specifications. Aviation W 78:209 Mr 11 '63; 80:215 Mr 16 '64
Republic testing VA-3 for navy, developing larger GEM vehicles. il Aviation W 81:57+ Ag 17 '64

GROUND effect machines—*Continued*
Ride on a cushion of air; Carabao hovercraft. E. Hall. il Sci N L 85:91 F 8 '64
Seaplane rating aids Hydroskimmer pilot. L. Booda. il Aviation W 79:68-72 D 2 '63
Take the air train. il Newsweek 62:108 O 7 '63
Thames sightseeing boat gets a permit to fly; Hoverbus. il Pop Sci 184:94-5 F '64
VA-3 air cushion vehicle to begin tests at Republic; hovercraft. il Aviation W 80:83 Mr 2 '64
Your ticket to air cushion travel; Hovercraft. T. Holloway. il Sci Digest 53:64-70 Ap '63
GROUND meat. See Cookery—Meat
GROUND squirrels
Pop picket pins. B. W. Dalrymple. il Outdoor Life 133:48-9+ F '64
GROUND water. See Water, Underground
GROUNDCOVERS. See Cover plants
GROUNDING (electricity) See Electric currents —Grounding; Electric distribution—Grounding
GROUNDS for divorce; story. See Shaw, A.
GROUP behavior
Clique, clique, clique! J. M. Freund. il Seventeen 23:148-9 O '64
Cruel crowd. S. Grafton. il McCalls 92:87+ Ja '65
More risks taken when in group. Sci N L 83:281 My 4 '63
Teacher and group processes. J. Luft. il NEA J 52:12-14 Ap '63
What makes kids run wild? with group-discussion program, by C. W. Mattuck. C. Chilman. il Parents Mag 39:35+, 72 Ja '64
GROUP development training laboratory. See National training laboratory in group development
GROUP discussion. See Discussion
GROUP instruction. See Teaching
GROUP leadership. See Leadership
GROUP morale. See Social psychology
GROUP psychology. See Groups (sociology)
GROUP psychotherapy
Strength in numbers. il Time 81:38 F 8 '63
GROUPE, Vincent. See Bergs, V. V. jt. auth.
GROUPERS
Fish named Ulysses; excerpt from The living sea. J. Y. Cousteau and J. Dugan. il Read Digest 83:188-92+ S '63
Hermaphroditism in Bahama groupers. C. L. Smith. il Natur Hist 73:42-7 Je '64
Warsaw grouper is man-sized fish. il Field & S 68:107 Mr '64
GROUPING, Homogeneous. See Ability grouping in education
GROUPING by ability. See Ability grouping in education
GROUPS (sociology)
Young grandees on tour. G. Bocca. il Sat R 46:58-60 Mr 16 '63
GROUSE shooting
Education of ruff. T. Trueblood. il Field & S 69:53-6+ S '64
Ghost town grouse. H. L. Lawrence. il Outdoor Life 135:70-1+ F '65
Guarantee your grouse. J. O. Cartier. il Field & S 68:62-3+ O '63
Know your grouse. T. Trueblood. il Field & S 68:44-6 S '63
Midwinter bird hunt. E. A. Bauer. il Outdoor Life 131:32-5+ F '63
Railroad bird hunt. D. D. Dickey. il Field & S 69:59-61 Je '64
GROVE, Gene
Paula Prentiss. Sat Eve Post 237:68-9 F 8 '64
GROVE, Sir George
On the fringe. H. Frankel. Sat R 47:40 Mr 21 '64
GROVE, Larry
Did press pressure kill Oswald? reprint. por U S News 56:78-9 Ap 6 '64
GROVE, Walt
Honest thief; story. Redbook 121:60-1 My '63
Mary Ann, I love you; story. Redbook 121: 115-32 Ag '63
One month, during the summer; story. Sat Eve Post 236:62-3 Je 29 '63
GROVE CITY, Pa.
Modern lighting sells itself. F. E. Fisher. il Am City 79:111+ D '64
Upgrading a second-rate snow program. F. E. Fisher. il Am City 79:108-9 O '64
GROVE CITY college, Grove City, Pa.
Academic freedom at Grove City. J. P. Park. Christian Cent 80:928-9 Jl 24 '63
GROVER, Charles F.
Can you swim well enough to survive? Motor B 112:34-5+ Jl '63
GROVES, Leslie Richard
Fight over the A-bomb. F. Knebel and C. W. Bailey. Look 27:19-23 Ag 13 '63
GROWTH
Growth pattern changing. D. F. Nolan. Sci N L 86:166 S 12 '64
Knots in leucothrix mucor. T. D. Brock. bibliog il Science 144:870-2 My 15 '64
Man grows bigger if not better. H. L. Shapiro. il N Y Times Mag p 13+ D 15 '63
Radiation counter helps ascertain human growth. Sci N L 85:9 Ja 4 '64
Secret of growth sought. Sci N L 86:158 S 5 '64
See also
Children—Growth and development
Maturity
Regeneration (biology)
GROWTH (plants)
Chronic gamma radiation affects the distribution of radial increment in pinus rigida stems. G. M. Woodwell and L. N. Miller. bibliog il Science 139:222-3 Ja 18 '63
Control of growth in plant cells. F. C. Steward. il Sci Am 209:104-13 O '63
Gibberellin: effect on diffusible auxin in fruit development. K. K. S. Sastry and R. M. Muir. bibliog il Science 140:494-5 My 3 '63
Great influences on plant growth (cont) il House & Gard 123:100-5 F; 144-9 Mr; 154-9 Ap; 174-7 My '63
Growth, maturation, and senescence in fruits. J. B. Biale. bibliog il Science 146:880-8 N 13 '64
Index to next spring's growth. V. Argo. il Natur Hist 73:52-6 Ja '64
Mystery of spring. R. M. Carleton. il Todays Health 41:18-19+ Ap '63
Tenacious butternut. W. M. Harlow. il Am For 69:37 S '63
See also
Geotropism (botany)
Spiral growth and movement
GROWTH, Economic. See Economic development
GROWTH hormones. See Hormones
GROWTH inhibiting substances (animals)
Cycloheximide: aspects of inhibition of protein synthesis in mammalian cells. H. L. Ennis and M. Lubin. bibliog il Science 146:1474-6 D 11 '64
Growth-inhibiting agents from mercenaria extracts: chemical and biological properties. M. R. Schmeer. bibliog il Science 144:413-14 Ap 24 '64
Inhibition of growth of chick embryo by inhibition of deoxycytidylate deaminase. J. S. Roth and others. bibliog il Science 142:1473-4 D 13 '63
GROWTH inhibiting substances (bacteria)
Inhibition of bacterial growth by drugs of the morphine series. E. J. Simon. bibliog il Science 144:543-4 My 1 '64
GROWTH inhibiting substances (fungi)
Toxohormone inhibitory effect on the growth of an unstable strain of yeast. V. Callao and others. bibliog il Science 142:1668-9 D 27 '63
GROWTH inhibiting substances (plants)
Differentiation in fern gametophytes treated with purine and pyrimidine analogs. V. Raghavan. bibliog il Science 146:1690-1 D 25 '64
Gibberellin production in pea seeds developing in excised pods: effect of growth retardant AMO-1618. B. Baldev and others. bibliog il Science 147:155-7 Ja 8 '65
Natural plant growth regulators; report on International conference on plant growth regulation. N. P. Kefford. il Science 142: 1495-8+ D 13 '63
Phosfon controls chrysanthemum height. C. O. Dean. Horticulture 42:29 Ag '64
Spray dwarfs trees; B-9. G. Lorang. Farm J 88:54 Mr '64
Volatile growth inhibitors produced by aromatic shrubs. C. H. Muller and others. il Science 143:471-3 Ja 31 '64; Reply with rejoinder. P. V. Wells. 14:889-90 My 15 '64
See also
2,4-D
GROWTH of children. See Children—Growth and development
GROWTH of cities and towns. See Cities and towns—Growth
GROWTH promoting substances
See also
Ecdysone
Nucleasides
GROWTH promoting substances (fungi)
Zinc stimulation of RNA and protein synthesis in rhizopus nigricans. W. S. Wegener and A. H. Romano. bibliog il Science 142: 1669-70 D 27 '63

GROWTH promoting substances (plants)
Chemicals speed crop growth. Suc Farm 61:6 F '63
Natural plant growth regulators; report on International conference on plant growth regulation. N. P. Kefford. il Science 142: 1495-8+ D 13 '63
New natural growth promoting substance in young citrus fruit. R. A. Khalifah and others. bibliog il Science 142:399-400 O 18 '63
See also
Gibberellic acid
Gibberellins
2,4-D
GROWTH stocks. See Stocks
GRUBB, Davis
Enchanted room; story. Good H 156:84-5 Mr '63
GRUBER, Howard E. and Weltman, M.
Growth of self-reliance. Sch & Soc 91:222-3 My 4 '63
—and others
Moon illusion: an event in imaginary space. bibliog Science 139:750-2 F 22 '63
GRUBER, Samuel H. See Nelson, D. R. jt. auth.
GRUEN, John
Metropolitan forum; reprint. Opera N 28:33 D 21 '63
GRUEN, Victor
Full speed ahead on a dead-end road; excerpt from Heart of our cities. Horizon 6: 66-71 Sum '64
Who is to save our cities? Harvard Bsns R 41:107-15 My '63
GRUENBERG, Selma
Seen profiles. Sch Arts 63:8-9 N '63
GRUENBERGER, Fred J.
Measure for crackpots. Science 145:1413-15 S 25 '64
GRUENING, Ernest
Aid program: a senatorial dissent. New Repub 149:8-9 N 30 '63
Excerpt from address, July 19, 1962. Cong Digest 42:83+ Mr '63
Lonely wonders of Katmai. pors Nat Geog Mag 123:800-31 Je '63
Why the Alianza may fail. New Repub 148: 11 Mr 30 '63
about
People of the week. por U S News 55:16 N 25 '63
GRUENINGER, Walter F.
Phonograph records. See issues of Consumer bulletin
GRUENLER, Royce Gordon
Additions to the debate. Christian Cent 80: 1240 O 9 '63
Laugh or perish! Christian Cent 80:204-5 F 13 '63
GRUMBACH, Doris
Art of teaching: some minor heresies. por Cath World 200:22-7 O '64
On women novelists. Commonweal 80:198-200 My 8 '64
GRUMMAN aircraft engineering corporation
F-111 subcontracts monitored closely. E. J. Bulban. Aviation W 79:55+ Ag 26 '63
Grumman sales expected to rise. Aviation W 78:94-5 My 27 '63
Grumman tries to break 4-rpm limit. H. M. David. Miss & Roc 12:35+ Ap 15 '63
LEM subcontracting advanced. Aviation W 78:37 F 4 '63
Pentagon blasts back at the TFX probers. il Bsns W p29-30 Mr 23 '63
$7-billion contract that changed the rules. R. A. Smith. il Fortune 67:96-101+ Mr; 110-11+ Ap '63
TFX award stirs storm. Bsns W p25 Mr 9 '63
TFX board selected Boeing four times; investigation of General dynamics-Grumman contract by Senate investigations subcommittee, with excerpts from hearing. G. C. Wilson. Aviation W 78:22-4 Mr 4 '63
GRÜNBAUM, A.
Bearing of philosophy on the history of science; address, December 29, 1963. bibliog Science 143:1406-12 Mr 27 '64
GRUNBERG, Burt
World's best people-peeper. il U S Camera 28: 46-7 Ja '65
GRUNDFEST, H. See Usherwood, P. N. R. jt. auth.
GRUNEWALD, Donald
Reapportionment. New Repub 151:10-11 D 26 '64
GRUNFELD, Frederic V.
Beethoven is better than ever. Reporter 30: 42-4 Mr 12 '64
Coachmen's music. Reporter 29:56+ O 10 '63
Colossal nightingale. Reporter 29:52-5 D 5 '63
Crash at the start. Reporter 30:36-8 Je 4 '64
Honeymoon in a monastery. Reporter 28:33-6 Je 6 '63
Id in march time. Reporter 31:45-6+ O 8 '64
Libretto as literature. Reporter 31:37-40 D 31 '64
Life on four records. Reporter 31:31-3 Jl 2 '64
Revolt of the brasses. Reporter 29:48+ Jl 18 '63
Der stellvertreter: the play that caused a storm. Reporter 30:46+ Ja 30 '64
What the boys in the Bach room will have. Reporter 31:47-8+ N 19 '64
You may be deaf, Ludwig, but I'm not! Reporter 32:51-3 Ja 28 '65
GRUNWALD, Henry Anatole
Address from the class of 1944 to the class of 1963. Horizon 5:86-9 My '63
From Eden to the nightmare. Horizon 5:72-9 Mr '63
Quality of life behind the Soviet statistics. Fortune 69:146-7+ Mr '64
GRUNWALD, Joseph
Why not invest in Latin America? Harvard Bsns R 41:123-8 N '63
GRUSHKIN, Philip
At a price that allows us to publish the book; address. Pub W 183:96-8 Mr 4 '63
GRUSON, Sydney
Anatomy of Britain's Labor party. N Y Times Mag p 17+ Ap 19 '64
Elegant anachronism vs. one-man band. N Y Times Mag p34+ O 11 '64
Fourteenth earl becomes a political pro. N Y Times Mag p32+ N 24 '63
12,000,000 who vote Tory. N Y Times Mag p 17+ O 4 '64
Unless we lead, all will falter. N Y Times Mag p22+ D 8 '63
Wilson stirs up a whirlwind. N Y Times Mag p34+ D 6 '64
about
Separate papers. por Newsweek 61:91 Ap 22 '63
GRÜSSER-CORNEHLS, Ursula, and others
Unit responses in the frog's tectum to moving and nonmoving visual stimuli. bibliog Science 141:820-2 Ag 30 '63
GRUVER, William J.
Can your school afford the new science programs? por Sch Life 46:5-7 Ja '64
GSTAAD, Switzerland
Coming up chic. il Time 81:66 Mr 1 '63
GUADALAJARA, Mexico
Second city. H. Sutton. Sat R 47:27-8 Mr 7 '64
GUADALCANAL, Battle of, 1942-1943
Guadalcanal twenty years after. L. W. Batten, 3d. Yale R 52:418-26 Mr '63
GUADALUPE MOUNTAINS
Looping the Guadalupes. W. F. Heald. il Travel 120:34-6 O '63
GUADALUPE NATIONAL PARK (proposed)
See National parks and reserves—United States
GUADELOUPE
Pick a pair of perfect islands. E. Bedell. il Sat R 47:74-5+ O 10 '64
GUADELOUPE ISLAND
Vive Papa Charles; de Gaulle visit. Newsweek 63:49 Ap 6 '64
GUAM
Atlantic report. Atlan 212:22+ Ag '63
GUANIDINE
Poliovirus: guanidine dependence and loss of neurovirulence for monkeys. B. Loddo and others. il Science 145:945-6 Ag 28 '64
GUANINE
Guanine: formation during the thermal polymerization of amino acids. C. Ponnamperuma and others. bibliog il Science 143:1449-50 Mr 27 '64
GUANO
Most prosperous bird colony: Guano Islands. H. S. Ullmann. il Audubon Mag 65:150-1 My '63
GUANOSINE
Tautomerism and protonation of guanosine. H. T. Miles and others. bibliog il Science 142:1458+ D 13 '63
GUANTÁNAMO naval base. See Navy yards and naval stations
GUARANI Indians. See Indians of South America
GUARANÍ language. See Paraguay—Languages
GUARANTY. See Warranty
GUARANTY of employment. See Employment systems—Guaranty of employment
GUARD duty. See United States—Army—Guard duty

GUARDIAN and ward
Guardianship: every child's right. I. Weissman. bibliog f Ann Am Acad 355:134-9 S '64
GUARNERIUS violin. See Violin
GUATEMALA
Changing conditions in Guatemala. C. A. Hauberg. bibliog f Cur Hist 44:106-10+ F '63
See also
Communism—Guatemala
Indians of Central America—Antiquities—Guatemala
Natural resources—Guatemala
Tourist trade—Guatemala
United States—Foreign relations—Guatemala

Antiquities

See Indians of Central America—Antiquities—Guatemala

Description and travel

Going places, finding things in new fields for adventurous wayfarers. J. Sakol. il House & Gard 125:22+ Ja '64
Guatemala's highlands in the shadow of volcanoes. il Sunset 130:53-4 Mr '63

Economic conditions

Atlantic report. Atlan 211:12+ Ap '63
Booming toward elections. il Time 84:30-1 N 6 '64

Industries

Guatemala. R. E. Chardon. bibliog il Focus 13:1-6 My '63

Politics and government

Aiming at Arévalo. Newsweek 61:48 Ap 8 '63
Atlantic report. Atlan 211:12+ Ap '63
Democracy in Latin America; Peralta's coup. Commonweal 78:59 Ap 12 '63
Military fells democracy in Guatemala. il Sr Schol 82:19 Ap 17 '63
Pingpong game is over. Time 81:28-9 Ap 12 '63
To the death: Peralta corp. Newsweek 61:54+ Ap 15 '63
What price anti-communism. New Repub 148:7-8 Ap 13 '63
See also
Elections—Guatemala

Social conditions

Atlantic report. Atlan 211:12+ Ap '63
GUAYAQUIL
River port that became a seaport; Puerto Marítimo. A. H. Beard, jr. il Américas 15:17-19 My '63
GUAYMAS, Mexico
Guaymas is splendid in October. il Sunset 131:50+ O '63
GUBBINS, Harold E.
Reader's choice. Travel 119:39 Mr '63
GUBERNAT, Mary Buchannan
Mary Gubernat retires. il por Recreation 58:35 Ja '65
GUBERNATORIAL campaigns. See Political campaigns
GUBERNATORIAL candidates. See Candidates, Political
GUBERNATORIAL elections. See Elections—United States
GUELLAL, Cherif
Africa vis-à-vis the western powers; address, April 10, 1964; with questions and answers. Ann Am Acad 354:9-21 Jl '64
GUENTHER, Charles
Note on Léopold Sédar Senghor. Poetry 103:199 D '63
(tr) See Senghor, L. S. Femme noire
(tr) See Senghor, L. S. Midnight elegy; For kôra
GUERDON, David
Laundry; tr. by H. Richardson. Criticism
Nation 196:255 Mr 23 '63
New Yorker 39:114+ F 23 '63
Newsweek 61:52 Mr 4 '63
GUERIN, Ann
Life movie review. Life 57:28 S 25; 15 O 23 '64
GUÉRIN, Camille
Birth of a new vaccine. il por UNESCO Courier 17:10-11+ Ap '64
GUERIN, Wilfred L.
Tithing: toward a clarification. America 108:354-5 Mr 16 '63
GUERNSEY, Lee, and Taylor, Alice
Alliance for progress. bibloig Focus 14:1-6 Ap '64
GUERRILLA warfare
Guerrilla trainer; southeast Asian jungles. il Ebony 19:47-8+ Ap '64
Plea for realism in southeast Asia. R. Hilsman. il N Y Times Mag p26+ Ag 23 '64
U.S. guerrillas: with knife & strangling wire. il Time 81:24-31 My 24 '63

Bibliography

Books on guerrilla warfare, fifteen years overdue. E. Larrabee. Harper 228:120-3 My '64
GUERRILLAS

Algeria

Cuba of Africa. il Time 82:37-8 O 18 '63

Asia, Southeastern

Is U.S. fighting reds in the wrong place? il U S News 55:8 Ag 12 '63

China

Guerrilla war hits red China. R. P. Martin. il U S News 54:40-1 Mr 4 '63
Next: large-scale uprisings; interview. C. K. Chiang. il U S News 54:41-4 Mr 4 '63

Colombia

Backlands violence is almost ended; Operation Marquetalia. il Time 83:35 Je 26 '64

Congo (capital Leopoldville)

Jeunesse. il Time 83:26 F 14 '64

Cuba

Castro's Cuba: a U.S. problem becomes a threat to the world. il U S News 56:51-4 F 10 '64
Hit, run, and rue. Newsweek 61:19 Ap 1 '63

Dominican Republic

Dead rebels in the hills. Time 83:32 Ja 3 '64

Haiti

Going badly for Papa Doc. Time 84:35-6 Ag 28 '64

Iran

Next big blowup, Iran? J. Law. il U S News 54:82 Mr 25 '63
See also
Raids

Iraq

All quiet in the Zagros Mountains; cease-fire for Kurdish rebellion. Time 83:38 F 21 '64

Laos

Laos peace broken by red moves. il Sr Schol 82:16-17 My 8 '63
Laos: the war that never stops; Communist takeover of Laos. J. A. Rose. il Sat Eve Post 236:78+ Ag 24 '63

Latin America

Changing role. il Time 84:61 N 13 '64
Watch on the wild ones. Newsweek 65:38 F 1 '65

Malaya

Visiting team from terror tech; Indonesian guerrilla force. il Time 84:35 S 4 '64

Panama

Training to meet Castro threat; photo report. U S News 54:98-100 Mr 25 '63
U.S. training antiguerrillas. il U S News 54:50 Mr 18 '63

Philippines

They fought alone, by J. Keats. Review
Time 82:72+ Ag 23 '63

Venezuela

Return of the F.A.L.N. Time 84:36 Jl 24 '64

Viet Nam (Democratic Republic)

And here is the enemy. H. Moffett. il Life 56:25-7 F 14 '64
And now the rains. il Time 83:26 My 29 '64
Captain's last letters from Vietnam; excerpts. E. G. Shank, jr. il U S News 56:46-9 My 4 '64; Life 56:34B-34D+ My 8 '64; Discussion. 56:30 Je 5 '64
Close-up of the Vietcong in their jungle. G. Penchenier. il N Y Times Mag p27+ S 13 '64
Elusive Viet Cong. J. A. Rose. New Repub 148:19-26 My 4 '63
For U.S: it's war with one arm; firsthand report on red sanctuary in Laos. S. W. Sanders. il U S News 57:46-8 Jl 20 '64
Letter from Saigon. R. Shaplen. New Yorker 40:37-8+ Jl 11 '64
Other government; North Viet Nam's Radio liberation. Time 83:29-30 Ja 31 '64
Other side of the hill. Newsweek 63:32+ My 4 '64
Our options in Vietnam. B. B. Fall. il Reporter 30:17-22 Mr 12 '64

GUERRILLAS—Viet Nam (Democratic Republic)—*Continued*
Papering it over; battle of Binhgia. il Time 85:26 Ja 15 '65
Pinprick war. il Time 81:40-1 My 17 '63
Portrait of two soldiers: the Vietnamese; the Vietcong. D. Halberstam. il N Y Times Mag p 11+ Ja 5 '64
Rallying of hearts? il Newsweek 62:38+ N 25 '63
South Vietnamese raiders extending war. L. Booda. il Aviation W 80:16-19 Ap 6 '64
This is our enemy; Vietcong guerrilla. S. Karnow. il Sat Eve Post 237:19-25 Ag 22 '64
Vietnam hangs on U.S. determination. C. J. V. Murphy. il Fortune 69:159+ My '64
War of revolution. America 111:34 Jl 11 '64
Weapons for bush war; Vietnamese guerrilla war. il Bsns W p 106+ N 16 '63
Who is the real enemy in Vietnam? il U S News 56:33-5 Je 1'64
Why it's so hard to beat the Communists in Vietnam; McNamara-Taylor mission. R. P. Martin. il U S News 55:56-7 O 7 '63
With the redskins of Vietnam. D. F. Ford. Nation 199:29-31 Jl 27 '64

Viet Nam (Republic)

American special forces in action in Viet Nam. H. Sochurek. il Nat Geog Mag 127:38-65 Ja '65
Bad day in the Delta. Time 83:22 Ja 24 '64
Bandits to battalions. il Time 83:33 Ap 24 '64
Bugle's blare. il Newsweek 62:58+ D 9 '63
Bureaucrats' war over Vietnam. J. Kraft. Harper 228:108+ My '64
Death in the delta, intrigue in the cafés. Time 83:46 Ap 17 '64
Fighting priest of South Vietnam. D. Chapelle. il Read Digest 83:194-200 Jl '63
$486 per chopper. Time 84:46 O 16 '64
Fresh stir of hope in Vietnam. Bsns W p36 Mr 21 '64
Harsh challenge to Johnson: hotter war in Vietnam. il U S News 55:104 D 9 '63
I'm hit! I'm hit! I'm hit! with editorial comment. J. A. Rose. il Sat Eve Post 236:34-47, 84 Mr 23 '63
In Asia's hot war: more trouble for U.S. il U S News 55:58 S 2 '63
In Vietnam it's more than guns. il Bsns W p82-3+ Ag 1 '64
In Vietnam war: U.S. casualties, U.S. valor; What it's like when red guerrillas attack. U S News 56:8 Ap 27 '64
Inheritor of a wretched war; General Westmoreland in Saigon. J. Langguth. il N Y Times Mag p27+ N 15 '64
Is there a way out for U.S. in Vietnam? il U S News 56:42-4 F 17 '64
Little war, far away and very ugly; with photographs by A. Okamura. Life 56:34-43 Je 12 '64
Makeshift killers; rocket-carrying Hueys in South Viet Nam. il Time 81:34-5 Je 7 '63
Military man sizes up a war U.S. is losing. M. S. Johnson. il U S News 56:40-1 Mr 16 '64
National unity and stepped-up war. il Time 83:29 F 14 '64
New turn in a fifteen-year war: the real story of Vietnam. il U S News 56:50-2 Mr 23 '64
One mission too many; Major Charles Kelly shot. Time 84:40 Jl 10 '64
Opportunities missed. il Time 83:23 Ja 17 '64
Pinprick war. il Time 81:40-1 My 17 '63
Rallying of hearts? il Newsweek 62:38+ N 25 '63
Red breakthrough in Vietnam. S. W. Sanders. il U S News 57:84 O 26 '64
South Viet Nam. M. Gart. Time 82:19 D 20 '63
South Vietnam: the break-even point. il Newsweek 62:57 D 2 '63
South Vietnamese raiders extending war. L. Booda. il Aviation W 80:16-19 Ap 6 '64
Strange war the U.S. is not winning. R. P. Martin. il U S News 55:48-50 S 30 '63
Toward the showdown? il Time 84:23-7 Ag 7 '64
Trouble in the hills; rebellious Rhade warriors. il Time 84:57 O 2 '64
Truth about the war U.S. is losing; interview. B. B. Fall. il U S News 57:58-62 S 28 '64
Unexpected guts. il Time 83:28 Je 26 '64
U.S. bungle in Vietnam? the inside story. R. P. Martin; S. W. Sanders. il U S News 57:56-8 S 14 '64
Vietnam facts hidden? Republican leaders say yes. il U S News 56:19 My 4 '64
Vietnam: test case for massive U.S. aid. il Bsns W p82-3+ S 28 '63
Vietnam: what now? New Repub 151:3-4 D 5 '64
War and death, like eating and making love; excerpts from diary. R. K. McCabe. il Newsweek 62:39 Jl 15 '63
War heats up. Time 82:42 D 6 '63
We can't win, but we need not lose. J. A. Rose. New Repub 149:15-18 O 12 '63
What Johnson faces in South Vietnam. S. Castan. il Look 28:19-30 Ja 28 '64
When foul is fair; deadly fake weapons. il Newsweek 64:39 Ag 24 '64
When you are the hunted. R. Starnes. Field & S 68:14+ Ja '64
With army in charge, war speeds up in Vietnam. R. P. Martin. il U S News 55:51-2 N 25 '63

GUESS who this is; story. See Jaffe, R.

GUEST, Barbara
Fay Lansner: deliberate contraries. Art N 62:36-7+ D '63
Poems, books of poems, and character. J. Langland. Poetry 103:257-8 Ja '64
Return of the muses; Fan poems. Poetry 105:174-8 D '64

GUEST, Lucia
Their dream is not to be nervous; interview, ed. by G. Illig. Mlle 60:164-5+ N '64

GUEST, M. Mason, and others
Red blood cells: change in shape in capillaries. bibliog Science 142:1319-21 D 6 '63

GUEST, William S.
Why are Americans in Vietnam? an admiral's letter to his sons. por U S News 57:132-3 O 19 '64

GUEST, Mrs Winston F.
Mrs Guest and Monsieur Boudin. il por Vogue 141:148-9+ Ap 1 '63

GUEST houses
Charm of a houseboat, without the motion; dockhouse on Lake Placid, N.Y. il House B 106:64-7 Jl '64

GUEST ranches. See Ranches

GUESTS
Art of having (or being) a house guest. M. Shearer. il House B 106:92-5+ Jl '64
Candid thoughts on the care and feeding of overnight guests; excerpts from Profession: housewife. P. McGinley. Ladies Home J 80:43+ Jl '63
Fun for the hostess, too! weekend guests. L. Sloane. il Am Home 67:24 Je '64
How to cope with company. E. Pearson. il Farm J 87:29+ Jl '63
Your baby can be a welcome visitor. M. Bernath. il Parents Mag 39:38-9+ D '64
See also
Entertaining

Anecdotes, facetiae, satire, etc.

Weekend guests from "we're so glad you could come" to "we're so sorry you have to go" and vice versa; excerpts. W. K. Zinsser. il McCalls 90:92-3+ Ag '63

GUESTS, Government. See Government entertaining

GUETZLAFF, Gordon J.
Magic of Christmas. por Recreation 56:411-12 N '63

GUEVARA, Ernesto
Cuba; a revisit with Che Guevara; interview, ed. by L. Bergquist. pors Look 27:26-7 Ap 9 '63
about
Che's explosive return. il por Newsweek 64:43 D 21 '64
Five years of Castro's Cuba. T. Draper. bibliog f Commentary 37:25-37 Ja '64; Discussion. 37:8+ My '64
U.S. replies to Cuban charges in U.N. General assembly; statement, December 11, 1964. A. E. Stevenson. Dept State Bul 52:24-6 Ja 4 '65
White elephants on parade. Time 83:36 Mr 6 '64

GUGGENHEIM, Alicia (Patterson) See Patterson, A.

GUGGENHEIM, Peggy
Mrs Guggenheim collection. S. Price. il pors N Y Times Mag p 16-17+ Ja 17 '65
Poor Peg's treasure. il por Time 85:52-5 Ja 22 '65

GUGGENHEIM, Peggy, collection. See Art—Private collections

GUGGENHEIM, Solomon R., foundation. See Solomon R. Guggenheim foundation

GUGGENHEIM, Solomon R., museum, New York. See Solomon R. Guggenheim museum, New York

GUGGENHEIM family
Seed money: the Guggenheim story, by M. Lomask. Review
Newsweek il 63:89-90 Je 29 '64

GUGGENHEIM international award. See Art—Competitions

GUGGINO, Jack L.
Computer that earns a profit. Am City 79:102-3 Mr '64

GUI, Vittorio
Master of melos. Hi Fi 13:35-6+ Je '63

GUIANA, BRITISH. See British Guiana

GUIANA, FRENCH. See French Guiana

GUIDANCE. See Counseling; Educational guidance; Personnel service (education); Vocational guidance

GUIDANCE systems, Missile. See Guided missiles—Control

GUIDANCE systems for space vehicles. See Space vehicles—Control systems

GUIDEBOOKS
Arthur Frommer changes distributor, sets up new line; $5-a-day books. Pub W 183:57 Je 17 '63
Asia A to Z, by R. S. Kane. Review
Travel il 121:53 Ja '64 K. Gardner
Better books for traveling. E. Kiester, jr. il Redbook 120:32+ F '63
Discriminating guide for Negro tourists. Newsweek 61:96 My 20 '63
Europe plain & simple: Europe on $5 a day. il Time 82:61 Jl 26 '63
Gourmets go home; Guide Michelin to West Germany. Newsweek 63:46 My 25 '64
Life guide; invasion plans for tourists. il Life 54:19+ Je 7 '63
Mobil travel guides feature annual ratings. il Pub W 183:51-2 Je 17 '63
Plus ça change. . .Guide Michelin and Hôtel de la Côte-d'or. Newsweek 63:69 Mr 30 '64
State guides for summer tourists. il Changing T 17:35-7 Je '63
Three stars or none, quelle différence! Guide Michelin to France. P. E. Schneider. il N Y Times Mag p20+ Jl 19 '64

Bibliography

New York in fair time; evaluation of city guide books. J. Brooks. il Consumer Rep 29:199-201 Ap '64
Traveling by book. E. Kiester, jr. il Redbook 122:42+ Mr '64

GUIDED missile bases
America's top ten targets. J. H. Winchester. il Sci Digest 54:54-8 N '63
Castro's missiles: new worry for U.S. il U S News 56:34 My 4 '64
Cuba: how dangerous now; with excerpt from President Kennedy's news conference, February 7, 1963. il U S News 54:58-63 F 18 '63
Cuban crisis: how close we were to war; excerpts from Politics of policy-making: the Kennedy years. R. Hilsman. il Look 28:17-21 Ag 25 '64
Extent of Cuban missile threat revealed; photo-intelligence briefing by Defense Secretary Robert S. McNamara and John Hughes. Aviation W 78:31 F 11 '63
Further clarification; concerning interviews with Kennedy and Castro. J. Daniel. New Repub 149:6-7 D 21 '63
Intelligence; ballistic missile base construction in Cuba. K. B. Keating. Reporter 29:6 S 12 '63; Discussion. 29:8+ O 10 '63
Intelligence gap on Cuba? the Senate gets a report. il U S News 54:63-6 My 20 '63
Minuteman's new home on the Montana range. il Fortune 68:124-9 Ag '63
New Mexico: underground air force; Atlas complex no. 4, near Roswell, N.Mex. B. Kocivar. il Look 27:M5-7 O 8 '63
Ninety dangerous days for U.S; summary of Strike in the West, by J. Daniel and J. G. Hubbell. il U S News 54:70-2 Mr 11 '63
Secret caves of Cuba; loaded with IRBMs and submarine facilities. Sat Eve Post 236:72 Mr 30 '63
Soviet pullout and what stayed behind. il U S News 54:6 Mr 25 '63
Soviets press technical modernization of military services. il Aviation W 78:92-5 Mr 11 '63
Telegraphing Khrushchev: surface-to-air missiles. S. Alsop. il Sat Eve Post 237:14 Mr 7 '64

Photographs

New Defense department photos show rapid disassembly of Soviet missile sites in Cuba. Aviation W 78:54-7 F 18 '63
Recon photos reveal Soviet anti-aircraft buildup in Cuba. Aviation W 78:28-31 F 18 '63

GUIDED missile crews
How it feels to hold the nuclear trigger; with report by R. B. Stolley. il Life 57:34-41 N 6 '64
How the modern Minuteman guards the peace. J. Atwater. il Sat Eve Post 236:65-9 F 9 '63
Loneliness of the missile attendant. M. Morgan. il Esquire 62:50-3+ Jl '64

GUIDED missile flight simulator. See Flight simulators

GUIDED missile industry
German firm plans missile exports. F. G. McGuire. Miss & Roc 13:21 D 16 '63
Missile row in Britain; cost of guided missile contracts. il Bsns W p54 Ag 8 '64
Profile of an industry; with editorial comment. W. Beller. il Miss & Roc 13:22+, 70 O 28; 24-6 D 2; 30-2 D 16 '63
Rocket test team boss; Aerojet-General's W. Sprattling, jr. il Ebony 19:46-8+ My '64
See also
Government investigations—Guided missile industry
Strikes—United States—Guided missile industry

GUIDED missile models
Army gives new Lance details. D. C. Breasted il Miss & Roc 13:18 O 28 '63

GUIDED missiles
Air force defends Minuteman program. F. G. McGuire. Miss & Roc 12:18 My 13 '63
America's invisible arsenal. il U S News 56:68-71 My 18 '64
Army emphasizes close support missiles. G. Alexander. il Aviation W 80:157-8 Mr 16 '64
Atomic arsenal; concerning testimony of Secretary McNamara on nuclear test ban treaty before the Senate foreign relations, Senate armed forces and Joint atomic energy committees. il Time 82:11-15 Ag 23 '63; Same abr. with title Our awesome atomic arsenal. Read Digest 83:67-71 N '63
Boelkow designs two missiles, turbofan hot-cycle helicopter. W. C. Wetmore. Aviation W 81:19 D 7 '64
British report shows big increase in U.S. strategic missile strength. Miss & Roc 15:12 N 23 '64
Challenge met in Minuteman management. R. Twiss. il Miss & Roc 13:6 Jl 22 '63
Chilly future; R. McNamara's exposition of defense policies before the House armed services committee. il Time 81:15-16 F 8 '63
Committee accepts ICBM reliability. H. M. David. Miss & Roc 14:17-18 Ap 27 '64
Cut in ICBM buying lowers request. il Miss & Roc 14:15-16 Ja 27 '64
Decade of deadly birds. il Time 83:25 My 22 '64
Defense withholds advanced ICBM funds. Aviation W 79:26-7 N 11 '63
DOD decides to cancel LASV; CLAM still under study. J. Trainor. Miss & Roc 15:16 Jl 13 '64
DOD has new warhead plan. J. Trainor. Miss & Roc 14:15 Ap 27 '64
DOD preparing crucial bid for MMRBM funds. Miss & Roc 14:21 Ap 27 '64
Egypt shows SA-2, other missiles in parade. il Aviation W 79:30-1 Ag 5 '63
End of the manned bomber. R. D. Senter. New Repub 148:19-20 F 9 '63
First photos show Sandal emplaced. il Aviation W 80:24-5 Mr 9 '64
First photos show test firing of Redeye missile. il Aviation W 78:33 Mr 18 '63
Fixes planned for Minuteman deficiencies. Aviation W 80:26-7 F 3 '64
Former RAF Thors made into boosters. W. E. Wilks. il Miss & Roc 14:31-2 Ap 6 '64
Fortress America; latest in defense ideas. il U S News 54:56-60 Mr 25 '63
French plan surface-to-surface missiles. Aviation W 81:25 Ag 10 '64
French to show off 66-ft. rocket. il Miss & Roc 12:21+ My 27 '63
Goldwater and the bomber-gap. R. D. Senter. New Repub 150:10-12 Ja 25 '64
Goldwater defense philosophy; excerpts from Where I stand. B. Goldwater. Aviation W 81:11 Ag 31 '64
Growing debate: can U.S. stay ahead of Russia in armed might? il U S News 56:8 Ap 27 '64
How dependable are America's long-range missiles? Goldwater vs. McNamara. il U S News 56:6 Ja 20 '64
How good are U.S. missiles, is Goldwater right? U S News 56:44-5 Ja 27 '64
How it feels to hold the nuclear trigger; with report by R. B. Stolley. il Life 57:34-41 N 6 '64
If lightning struck a missile. . . Bsns W p60 Mr 7 '64
In Goldwater-McNamara dispute: what two generals say about missiles. il U S News 56:19 Ap 6 '64
IRBM work aids French space hopes. B. Poirier. il Miss & Roc 12:55 Ap 29 '63

GUIDED missiles—*Continued*
Johnson stresses army missile strength. G. C. Wilson. il Aviation W 80:33-4 F 10 '64
Last stand of the big bomber; debate between McNamara and LeMay. J. Atwater. il Sat Eve Post 237:13-17 Je 20 '64
Leading international missiles; specifications. Aviation W 80:198-9 Mr 16 '64
Limited Redeye production ordered. il Miss & Roc 14:16 Ap 20 '64
Look at America's missile arsenal. il U S News 54:66-8 Mr 18 '63
McNamara details defense buying, R&D; summary of testimony before House armed services committee. R. S. McNamara. Aviation W 78:27-30 F 4 '63
McNamara views strategic aircraft role; excerpt from testimony presented to the House armed services committee, January 30, 1963. R. S. McNamara. Aviation W 78:67+ F 11 '63
McNamara voices some optimism over Nike-X, tells Minuteman plans. H. Taylor. Miss & Roc 14:20-1 F 3 '64
Military value of missiles in Cuba. R. Hagan and B. Bernstein. il Bul Atomic Sci 19:8-13 F '63
Missile that will carry men; to fit Titan II ICBM for the Gemini spacecraft. il Bsns W p 136-8 O 12 '63
Missiles and men. Nat R 16:51-2 Ja 28 '64
Missiles and rockets astrolog; current status of U.S. missile and space programs. See occasional issues of Missiles and rockets
Missiles and rockets' world missile/space encyclopedia, 1963-1964. il Miss & Roc 13:35-7+ Jl 29 '63; 15:39-46+ Jl 27 '64
MMRBM again facing major barriers. Aviation W 80:29 Mr 2 '64
MMRBM faces new budget slash. H. M. David. Miss & Roc 14:14 F 17 '64
MMRBM shows some signs of life. H. M. David. Miss & Roc 13:17 Ag 26 '63
New basing concept prime factor in future ICBM system design. G. Alexander. Aviation W 80:27-8 Ap 27 '64
New missile concepts stress environment. I. Stone. il Aviation W 78:141-3+ Mr 11 '63
New missiles get left-handed okay; SRAM, extended range Asroc, and ARM I. J. Trainor. Miss & Roc 15:15 O 26 '64
New tactical missile contracts expected to yield billions for industry. il Miss & Roc 14:54-6 Mr 30 '64
Non-nuclear anti-satellite system in making. J. Trainor. Miss & Roc 14:12-13 My 11 '64
Pentagon says U.S. leads. il Sr Schol 84:18 My 1 '64
President Kennedy holds talks at Nassau with Prime Minister Macmillan; joint communique and statement on nuclear defense systems, December 21, 1962. J. F. Kennedy and H. Macmillan. Dept State Bul 48:43-5 Ja 14 '63
Redeye missile intercepts unmanned QF-9G. il Aviation W 80:28 Ap 20 '64
Re-entry tests led to Nike X decision. Aviation W 78:36-7 F 11 '63
Senate doubles House cut in MMRBM budget. Miss & Roc 14:16 Mr 2 '64
Sergeant shoots off. H. O. Johansen. il Pop Sci 182:101-3+ F '63
Soviet claim of Polaris equivalent questioned; summary of report of Institute for strategic studies, London. Aviation W 79:77+ D 2 '63
Soviet missile parade features anti-ICBM, wheeled carriers. il Aviation W 81:26-8 N 16 '64
Soviets display five new missiles in Red square anniversary parade. il Miss & Roc 15:16-18 N 16 '64
Soviets display missile arsenal in Moscow. il Aviation W 78:52-7 My 20 '63
Soviets parade missile inventory; refinements are evident in new ground handling equipment. il Aviation W 78:30-2 My 13 '63
Soviets press technical modernization of military services. il Aviation W 78:92-5 Mr 11 '63
Soviets unveil new air defense missile in SA-2, SA-3 family. il Aviation W 79:28-9 N 18 '63
Strangelove country. Nation 198:451 My 4 '64
Telegraphing Khrushchev; surface-to-air missiles. S. Alsop. il Sat Eve Post 237:14 Mr 7 '64
Teller criticizes DOD handling of LASV. Aviation W 81:65+ Ag 17 '64
That visceral feeling. W. J. Coughlin. Miss & Roc 15:46 Ag 31 '64
TMRBM, based on Minuteman II, studied as replacement for MMRBM; transportable medium range ballistic missile. J. Trainor. Miss & Roc 15:16 O 12 '64
Trap offered de Gaulle; with reply, by T. W. Stanley. P. M. Gallois. Bul Atomic Sci 19:24-30 O '63
USAF, DOD spar over advanced ICBMs. I. Stone. il Aviation W 80:143-5+ Mr 16 '64
USAF wages space, weapon fund battles. L. Booda. il Aviation W 78:76-9 Mr 11 '63
U.S. drones and target missiles; specifications. Aviation W 80:209 Mr 16 '64
U.S. missiles; specifications (cont) Aviation W 78:187-8 Mr 11 '63; 80:191-2 Mr 16 '64
U.S. negotiator says Russians lead in medium-range missiles. Aviation W 81:22-3 Jl 27 '64
U.S. pressure delays NATO target buy. L.L. Doty. Aviation W 81:23 N 2 '64
U.S. Soviet strengths detailed; with editorial comment. J. Trainor. Miss & Roc 14:14, 46 Ap 20 '64
Use foreseen for surplus Minutemen. Miss & Roc 16:34 Ja 25 '65
Where the birds are. il Time 83:24 Ja 10 '64
Who's ahead in missile race; what a British survey shows. il U S News 55:52-3 N 18 '63
With Titan II now in place: 790 U.S. missiles ready for action. U S News 56:4 Ja 6 '64
Worry over U.S. defense: a Maginot line of missiles? il U S News 56:38-41 Mr 9 '64

Accidents and explosions

Close call in Silo ten. J. Joseph. il Pop Sci 185:85-8+ N '64

Atomic power plants

Tory 2-C reactor to test maximum power. E. J. Bulban. il Aviation W 80:75-6+ Ap 13 '64

Control

AF to begin work on master guidance system. Miss & Roc 13:16 S 9 '63
Circuit weight slashed in advanced Minuteman. R. Pay. il Miss & Roc 14:35 Mr 2 '64
G&C military systems; defense developments put new stress on selectivity, mobility. il Miss & Roc 13:39-40 O 7 '63
Improved Polaris fire-control system going to sea duty shortly. M. Getler. il Miss & Roc 13:32-3 N 4 '63
Math model trouble-shoots Minuteman. Miss & Roc 12:40 F 25 '63
MMRBM guidance, C&C may go on. Miss & Roc 13:15 Ag 5 '63
Navy presses for new missile. J. Trainor. Miss & Roc 14:14 Ap 6 '64
Pure-fluid guidance advances through research at Giannini. R. Pay. il Miss & Roc 13:28+ D 9 '63
Star tracker boosts MMRBM accuracy. B. Miller. il Aviation W 80:99+ Ap 27 '64

Cost

Joint chiefs fight MMRBM fund slash. Aviation W 79:26 Ag 26 '63
Minuteman cost-cutting aims outlined. R. Twiss. il Miss & Roc 12:40+ Je 24 '63
Zierdt says propellants cost too much. J. F. Judge. Miss & Roc 12:35-6 F 11 '63

Crews

See Guided missile crews

Defenses

Agena is retrofitted for Midas. il Aviation W 79:32 D 2 '63
Air force proposes improved defense against sub-launched missiles. J. Trainor. il Miss & Roc 14:17 F 10 '64
Another gap? Newsweek 61:58 Ap 29 '63
Anti-missile dilemma. R. D. Senter. New Repub 148:6-7 Mr 9 '63
Anti-satellite Polaris being developed. Aviation W 81:18-19 S 28 '64
Atomic retaliation jeopardized; EMP effects. W. Davis. Sci N L 84:293+ N 9 '63
Cold war race for a missile killer; foolproof anti-missile missiles. S. D. Pursglove. il Pop Mech 121:122-5+ Ja '64
Data-processing system aids Zeus development. M. Getler Miss & Roc 14:32 Ja 20 '64
Death of Nike-Zeus. E. Ubell and S. H. Loory. il Sat Eve Post 236:15-19 Je 1 '63
Defense against ballistic missiles. F. J. Dyson. Bul Atomic Sci 20:12-18 Je '64
Defense plan lists avionic guidelines. P. J. Klass. il Aviation W 78:227-9 Mr 11 '63
DOD emphasizes Nike-X anti-missile. Aviation W 78:143 Mr 11 '63
DOD plans $125-million anti-ICBM effort; ARPA's Project defender. il Aviation W 80:31 Ja 20 '64
Electronic equipment to protect U.S. defense; preventing harmful effects by EMP. Sci N L 86:180 S 19 '64

GUIDED Missiles—Defenses—*Continued*
Goldwater on missiles. W. Wingo. Sci N L 86:35 Jl 18 '64
G&C military systems; defense developments put new stress on selectivity, mobility. il Miss & Roc 13:39-40 O 7 '63
Investigation planned of ICBM penaids. Aviation W 82:67 Ja 18 '65
Johnson stresses army missile strength. G. C. Wilson. il Aviation W 80:33-4 F 10 '64
McNamara voices some optimism over Nike-X, tells Minuteman plans. H. Taylor. Miss & Roc 14:20-1 F 3 '64
Martin co. will develop Sprint missile for new Nike X system. Aviation W 78:35 Mr 25 '63
Missile site radar paces Nike-X. J. Trainor. Miss & Roc 14:14-15 My 25 '64
New A-ICBM city defense studied. M. Getler. Miss & Roc 16:13 Ja 18 '65
Nike X decision possible in '64; cost-effectiveness is weighed. Aviation W 81:19 Jl 20 '64
Nike-X fate keyed to DOD study. J. Trainor. Miss & Roc 14:14-15 My 18 '64
Nike X keeps high-priority R&D status; cost, uncertainties cited. Aviation W 80: 25 F 3 '64
Prospects slim for Mach 3 interceptor. P. J. Klass. Aviation W 78:71+ Ap 15 '63
Radar systems guard ICBM bases. R. Lindsey. il Miss & Roc 12:33-4 Mr 11 '63
Release of EMP data urged. H. M. David. Miss & Roc 13:23-4 S 30 '63
Satellite killer. New Repub 151:7 O 3 '64
Senate rejects Nike Zeus production. Aviation W 78:27 Ap 22 '63
Shillelagh firing shown in first photos. il Aviation W 78:23 Mr 25 '63
Slowdown urged on missile defense system. Sci N L 86:35 Jl 18 '64
Soviets may have ultimate ABM; possibility of de-activating U.S. missiles in silos. Miss & Roc 13:14-15 S 16 '63; Discussion. 13:54 S 16; 9 S 30; 9 O 7 '63; Pop Sci 183:19 D '63
Soviets press technical modernization of military services. il Aviation W 78:92-5 Mr 11 '63
Soviets revert to ICBM emphasis. F. G. McGuire. Miss & Roc 13:18 D 2 '63
Sprint anti-missile tests to begin. Aviation W 80:144 Mr 16 '64
Strategic office stresses product refinement moves. il Miss & Roc 14:65-6+ Mr 30 '64
Studies of penetration aids broadening. B. Miller. il Aviation W 80:73+ Ja 20 '64
Study aids case for Nike-X; with editorial comment. J. Trainor. Miss & Roc 16:12, 46 Ja 4 '65
Test ban testimony released. Miss & Roc 14: 19+ Mr 30 '64
Test ban would not cut defense budget. G. C. Wilson. Aviation W 79:26-7 Ag 19 '63
That attack from space. R. D. Senter. New Repub 148:17-19 My 4 '63; Reply with rejoinder. P. Siedman. 148:30 Je 8 '63
Treaty debate underscores lack of electromagnetic data. Miss & Roc 13:19 S 23 '63
USSR can't salvo ICBM's. J. Trainor. Miss & Roc 15:14 Ag 10 '64
USSR displays new missiles for air defense. il Aviation W 80:73 Je 1 '64
U.S. missile might, can we count on our hole cards? W. Cloud. il Pop Sci 184:70-3+ My '64
Why LASV is needed. W. J. Coughlin. Miss & Roc 14:46 Ap 27 '64
See also
Ballistic missile early warning system
Radar defense network

Design

Mark 11A hardened against air bursts. M. L. Yaffee. il Aviation W 81:50-1+ Ag 24 '64
Navy studies deterrent force for 1980s. E. J. Bulban. Aviation W 80:91+ Je 8 '64

Detection

Infrasonic detection technique may serve as ICBM warning. P. J. Klass. Aviation W 80:31 Ja 13 '64
MIDAS concept showing promise. H. M. David. Miss & Roc 14:19 F 3 '64
New missile warning satellite succeeds. D. E. Fink. Aviation W 80:33 F 3 '64
Submerged transponders would fix missile impact points. R. Pay. il Miss & Roc 14: 18+ Mr 16 '64

Electronic equipment

Microcircuits boost Minuteman capability. B. Miller. il Aviation W 79:70-1+ O 28 '63
Phoenix missile computer data revealed. B. Miller. il Aviation W 80:54-5 F 24 '64

Launching

August gun; navy gun launches Martlet missile. il Newsweek 62:54 Jl 15 '63
Carrier tests qualify KD2B-1 for production. il Aviation W 78:104-5 Ap 8 '63
Eastern range's 1965 schedule shows sustained activity level. G. Alexander. Aviation W 82:49 Ja 4 '65
First Athena may be fired in August. Miss & Roc 13:18 Jl 8 '63
Gun launches show A-ICBM potential. il Miss & Roc 13:18-19 Jl 1 '63
HIBEX tests begin this year. J. Trainor. il(p 1) Miss & Roc 15:10 Ag 31 '64
Low-latitude noctilucent cloud of 2 November 1963. A. B. Meinel and C. P. Meinel. il Science 143:38 Ja 3 '64; Reply. A. Margoshes. 144:1158 My 29 '64
Mark 46 ASW torpedo to be operational next summer; launch from aircraft, helicopters or surface ships. il Miss & Roc 15:15 D 21 '64
Minuteman II may be operational in 1965. il Miss & Roc 15:17 O 5 '64
Missile cuts loose in space; photographs of Titan II separating from its first-stage booster Life 56:82-3 Ja 24 '64
Pershing crews graduate with launches. L. Booda. il Aviation W 79:100-1+ D 16 '63
Pershing firing rate being boosted. J. Trainor. il Miss & Roc 15:17 N 9 '64
Pershing, launcher system field-tested. il Aviation W 78:90 Ap 22 '63
Polaris A-3 launch tube production at Westinghouse: a step-by-step report. il Miss & Roc 15:14-15 D 7 '64
Sergeant shoots off. H. O. Johansen. il Pop Sci 182:101-3+ F '63
USAF expresses confidence in Atlas system. Aviation W 80:23 My 25 '64
U-2s gathering data on missile exhausts. il Aviation W 79:53+ N 18 '63

Launching from airplanes

AF adopts new EBW buy approach. J. F. Judge. il Miss & Roc 15:34+ Ag 10 '64
Carrier tests qualify KD2B-1 for production. il Aviation W 78:104-5 Ap 8 '63
French study air-launched missile to augment Polaris-type weapons. R. E. Farrell. Aviation W 78:34 F 4 '63
Future tactical missiles may draw on Bullpup technology J. Judge. il Miss & Roc 14:32-3 Ap 13 '64
I flew with TAC's top gun. K. V. Brown. il Pop Mech 120:118-22+ O '63
Industry to get SRAM RFP's soon; three-phase program for the Short-range attack missile. J. Trainor. Miss & Roc 16:12 Ja 11 '65
Kennedy sees navy's Walleye, Shrike. F. G. McGuire. Miss & Roc 12:21 Je 17 '63
Low-cost missile has dual capability. W. S. Beller. il Miss & Roc 15:34-5 D 14 '64
McNamara says Skybolt would have been $2-billion waste. Miss & Roc 12:13 F 4 '63
McNamara views strategic aircraft role; excerpt from testimony presented to the House armed services committee, January 30, 1963. R. S. McNamara. Aviation W 78: 67+ F 11 '63
Modular data system designed for Shrike. il Aviation W 81:71-2 Ag 17 '64
Navy adopts new ASW avionics approach. P. J. Klass. il Aviation W 79:64+ Jl 8 '63
Navy is emerging as major developer of air-launched missiles. M. Yaffee. il Aviation W 80:148-9+ Mr 16 '64
Phoenix missile computer data revealed. B. Miller. il Aviation W 80:54-5 F 24 '64
Redeye nearing tactical prototype stage. H. D. Watkins. il Aviation W 81:20-1 O 5 '64
Scrapping of Skybolt. W. S. Just. il Reporter 28:19-21 Ap 11 '63
Shrike program being pushed by navy. F. G. McGuire. il Miss & Roc 12:15 My 6 '63
Single source procurement yields further Bullpup cost savings. M. Getler. il Miss & Roc 15:18+ Ag 3 '64
USAF stresses YF-12A interceptor role; air-to-air missile system. il Aviation W 81:16-17 O 5 '64
Walleye weapon plans. Aviation W 79:34 Ag 5 '63

Launching from ships

Asroc test in nuclear series is revealed. Aviation W 80:30 F 10 '64
B-3 Polaris expected to be operational in '70. R. Lindsey. il Miss & Roc 15:28+ Ag 24 '64
For U.S. allies a Polaris fleet in disguise? il U S News 54:8 Mr 18 '63

GUIDED missiles—Launching from ships —*Continued*
MLF demonstration ship picked; USS Biddle. J. Trainor. Miss & Roc 14:14 Mr 2 '64
Navy presses for new missile; ship-to-shore missile. J. Trainor. Miss & Roc 14:14 Ap 6 '64
On-the-deck intercept capability sought for advanced navy missile. C. Brownlow. Aviation W 82:17-18 Ja 11 '65
Stand-off weapon for Seahawk ships is sole big missile development seen; Asroc. il Miss & Roc 15:65-9 S 21 '64
3-T successor develops slowly. J. Trainor. Miss & Roc 15:10 N 2 '64
Twenty-five Polaris ships proposed for NATO force. Aviation W 80:29 F 3 '64
U.S. urges Polaris-armed ships for multilateral nuclear force. Aviation W 78:28 Mr 4 '63
World's first automatic guided missile launcher; Mark II. S. V. Jones. il Sci Digest 55:26-7 Mr '64

Launching from submarine boats

Aerojet methods help boost Polaris range. Miss & Roc 12:35 F 25 '63
Air force proposes improved defense against sub-launched missiles. J. Trainor. il Miss & Roc 14:17 F 10 '64
Anti-satellite Polaris being developed. Aviation W 81:18-19 S 28 '64
Anti-sub rocket; SUBROC. il Life 55:49-51+ D 13 '63
Britain will pay normal costs plus 5 per cent for U.S. Polaris missiles. Aviation W 78:31 Ap 15 '63
Improved launch system for Polaris. R. Lindsey. il Miss & Roc 13:27-8 D 2 '63
Improved Polaris fire-control system going to sea duty shortly. M. Getler. il Miss & Roc 13:32-3 N 4 '63
Keeping the U.S. ahead in undersea warfare; Subroc. il U S News 55:10 D 16 '63
Macmillan upheld on Polaris accord. Aviation W 78:28 F 11 '63
McNamara says DOD is pushing Polaris B3. Miss & Roc 14:16 F 24 '64
Missile leaps from sea to kill at thirty miles; Subroc. il Pop Sci 184:96-7 Mr '64
Navigating under the sea. il Bsns W p 148-50+ Mr 16 '63
Navy evaluates underwater range plans. Miss & Roc 15:15 O 19 '64
Navy seeks approval for Polaris follow-on. D. C. Breasted. il Miss & Roc 13:18 N 4 '63
New, improved Polaris A-3. il Time 82:64 N 8 '63
Operational Polaris-type French sub fleet ten years away. F. G. McGuire. Miss & Roc 13:18 N 18 '63
Operational test phase nears for Subroc. M. L. Yaffee. il Aviation W 79:33-5 D 9 '63
Polaris B-3 program moving ahead. Miss & Roc 16:13 Ja 11 '65
Polaris line. J. Burnham. Nat R 14:107 F 12 '63
Polaris power: the new strategy for defending Europe. il U S News 54:8 F 4 '63
Polaris sub prowls the sea. R. Brigham. il Life 54:22-31 Mr 22 '63
Poseidon a further developed B-3. Miss & Roc 16:12 Ja 25 '65
Poseidon has $2-billion price tag; formerly Polaris B-3. J. Trainor. Miss & Roc 16:10-11 Ja 25 '65
Proposed fourth-generation Polaris would use state-of-art technology. R. Lindsey. Miss & Roc 14:20-1 Ja 13 '64
Sub killer; Subroc. il Newsweek 62:54-5 D 16 '63
Submerged sub fires Polaris A-3. il Aviation W 79:32 N 4 '63
Subroc anti-submarine missile readied for navy operational evaluation. il Aviation W 79:104-5 D 16 '63
Subroc faces operational tests. il Miss & Roc 13:12-14 D 9 '63
Underneath in the Ethan Allen. il Time 81:22 Mr 15 '63
U.S. destructive power underscored; Polaris singled out. Miss & Roc 16:15 Ja 18 '65

Launching pads

Four hours in a Titan II blockhouse. W. Cloud. il Pop Sci 183:54-7+ Ag '63
Martin method cuts silo repair time. W. E. Wilks. il Miss & Roc 13:32-3 S 2 '63

Launching sites

Big white room assembly raises ICBM reliability. il Miss & Roc 12:46 My 27 '63
Flying the Montana missile line. K. W. Anderson. il Flying 74:38-40+ Mr '64
Radar systems guard ICBM bases. R. Lindsey. il Miss & Roc 12:33-4 Mr 11 '63
Titan II sites get pop-up antennas. M. Getler. il Miss & Roc 12:18+ Mr 11 '63

Lightning hazards

AF conducting lightning tests. il Miss & Roc 15:17 Ag 24 '64

Manufacture

How to spin a rocket. il Life 56:33-5 Mr 13 '64
Military asks more of contractors. il Miss & Roc 12:34-40 My 20 '63
Phasing out the long-range missiles. il Bsns W p 196-8+ Ap 20 '63
Polaris A-3 launch tube production at Westinghouse: a step-by-step report. il Miss & Roc 15:14-15 D 7 '64
Single source procurement yields further Bullpup cost savings. M. Getler. il Miss & Roc 15:18+ Ag 3 '64

Materials

Air force admits big potential for boron filament structures. W. Beller. il Miss & Roc 14:22-3 Je 15 '64
Beryllium picked for structural job. J. F. Judge. il Miss & Roc 14:34+ Ap 6 '64
How to spin a rocket. il Life 56:33-5 Mr 13 '64
Minuteman carrier insulation sprayed. il Aviation W 78:94-5 Ap 1 '63
New missile concepts stress environment. I. Stone. il Aviation W 78:141-3+ Mr 11 '63
New pyrolytic graphite formation method evaluated. W. Wright. il Aviation W 78:94-5+ Ap 8 '63
Polaris cases wound in Nebraska. J. F. Judge. il Miss & Roc 14:30+ My 4 '64
Text complex simulates Polaris re-entry heat. J. N. Steinmetz, jr. il Miss & Roc 14:24-5 Ja 6 '64

Propulsion

AEC confident of Tory II-C design; for LASV propulsion. W. E. Wilks. il Miss & Roc 14:26-7 Ap 20 '64
Failure to flight-test Tory could kill Pluto. Miss & Roc 14:18 Ap 27 '64
Future tactical missiles may draw on Bullpup technology. J. Judge. il Miss & Roc 14:32-3 Ap 13 '64
Pluto nuclear ramjet project to be dropped. Miss & Roc 14:16 My 4 '64

Recovery

First Athena may be fired in August. Miss & Roc 13:18 Jl 8 '63
Project GLOW to aid ABRES program. Miss & Roc 14:27 Mr 2 '64

Symbols

New Department of defense standard rocket, missile, probe designations. il Aviation W 79:70-1 Jl 8 '63

Terminology

New Department of defense standard rocket, missile, probe designations. il Aviation W 79:70-1 Jl 8 '63

Testing

Air force will fly new Titan 2 fuel pump. Aviation W 80:41 Mr 30 '64
Army's Lance undergoes extensive pre-firing evaluation. C. Brownlow. il Aviation W 81:58-9+ N 30 '64
Atlas accuracy improves as test program is completed. G. Alexander. il Aviation W 78:54-5+ F 25 '63
Don't look up, there's a missile there. il Time 82:37 O 4 '63
French conduct re-entry tests. C. Brownlow. Aviation W 79:34 Jl 15 '63
Get ready to duck; ballistic missile firings over populated areas. il Bsns W p74+ My 25 '63
Japan begins missile development tests. Aviation W 79:34 Jl 15 '63
Mark 6 nose cone, Titan 2 mated in Vandenberg test. il Aviation W 79:22-3 Jl 29 '63
Martin facility testing ablatives. W. Beller. il Miss & Roc 15:35-6 Ag 24 '64
Mauler feasibility study tempo is quickening. Miss & Roc 14:15 My 4 '64
Minuteman shock-resistance testing scheduled for next year. W. E. Wilks il Miss & Roc 15:27-8+ S 28 '64
New pyrolytic graphite formation method evaluated. W. Wright. il Aviation W 78:94-5+ Ap 8 '63
Operational test phase nears for Subroc. M. L. Yaffee. il Aviation W 79:33-5 D 9 '63
Pershing overland firings near completion. D. C. Breasted. il Miss & Roc 13:37 O 14 '63
Polaris A2 parts rejection slashed. R. Lindsey. il Miss & Roc 12:33-4 Ap 8 '63

GUIDED missiles—Testing—*Continued*
Stringent missile reliability test set. Miss & Roc 14:11 Mr 16 '64
Subroc anti-submarine missile readied for navy operational evaluation. il Aviation W 79:104-5 D 16 '63
Subroc faces operational tests. il Miss & Roc 13:12-14 D 9 '63
Time bomb in a hole. R. B. Stolley. il Life 55:9+ O 11 '63
USAF fires last R&D Titan 2. Aviation W 80:29 Ap 20 '64
USAF had thirteen straight Atlas failures. Aviation W 80:27 Ap 20 '64

Tracking

AF research aircraft zero in on tracking system noise. M. L. Yaffee. il Aviation W 79:78-9 N 11 '63
Electronic jungle goes to sea. il Sci Digest 55:51 Ja '64
First AMR tracking ship begins checkout. G. Alexander. il Aviation W 78:28-9 My 6 '63
Floating spacecraft tracking stations. R. LaCoste. il Electr World 72:17-19+ Ag '64
Spadats network relies on varied sensors. P. J. Klass. il Aviation W 78:89+ F 18 '63
Star tracker boosts MMRBM accuracy. B. Miller. il Aviation W 80:99+ Ap 27 '64
Three companies in competition for new AFMTC missile tracker. M. Getler. il Miss & Roc 14:22-5 My 4 '64

Transportation

Army tests Pershing-Chinook compatibility; photographs. Aviation W 78:84-5 F 4 '63
Minuteman carrier insulation sprayed. il Aviation W 78:94-5 Ap 1 '63
New missile concepts stress environment. I. Stone. il Aviation W 78:141-3+ Mr 11 '63

GUIDED missiles, Atomic powered
AEC confident of Tory II-C design. W. E. Wilks. il Miss & Roc 14:26-7 Ap 20 '64
Canada to accept nuclear arms. Aviation W 78:38 My 20 '63
Failure to flight-test Tory could kill Pluto. Miss & Roc 14:18 Ap 27 '64
New A-ICBM city defense studied. M. Getler. Miss & Roc 16:13 Ja 18 '65
Pluto cancellation or cutback threatened. K. Johnsen. Aviation W 80:28-9 Ja 13 '64
Pluto nuclear ramjet project to be dropped. Miss & Roc 14:16 My 4 '64
Sprint shape shown at AUSA meeting. J. Trainor. il Miss & Roc 15:11-12 N 23 '64
Why LASV is needed. W. J. Coughlin. Miss & Roc 14:46 Ap 27 '64

Testing

Asroc test in nuclear series is revealed. Aviation W 80:30 F 10 '64
Atoms v. gunpowder; the Pershing. il Time 81:25 My 3 '63

GUIDERI, Giancarlo. See Aiello, E. jt. auth.

GUIDES
Guides for bowhunting. G. H. Gillelan. il Outdoor Life 132:80-3 Jl '63
My favorite guide; Johnny Burns. J. Cornelius. il Field & S 68:46-7+ My '63
No. 1 Alaska guide: Andy Simons. F. Dufresne. il Field & S 69:32-4 D '64

GUIDES, Road. See Road maps, guides, etc.

GUIDES, United Nations. See United Nations—Employees

GUIGNARD, Jaqueline De Maeyer-. See De Maeyer-Guignard, J.

GUILBERT, Yvette
That was Yvette, by B. Knapp and M. Chipman. Review
Time por 84:118+ N 27 '64

GUILD, June Purcell
South unfair to Negro citizens. Negro Hist Bul 26:256+ My '63

GUILLAUME, David F.
Art and uncertainty. Sch Arts 63:23-4 Mr '64

GUILLEMIN, Victor, jr
Mathematics for pratically everybody. Harper 227:98-9 Ag '63

GUILLERY, R. W. and Ralston, H. J.
Nerve fibers and terminals: electron microscopy after nauta staining. bibliog Science 143:1331-2 Mr 20 '64

GUILLET, Alma C.
Friend of Central park. New Yorker 39:34-5 Mr 9 '63

GUILT
Guilt is good for you. Sci Digest 55:45 Ap '64
Our guilt for the world's evil. A. Miller. il N Y Times Mag p 10-11+ Ja 3 '65
Tyranny of guilt feelings; excerpt from The anarchy of feeling. A. Schneiders. Cath World 198:40-5 O '63
Uses of guilt. J. Collignon. il Sat R 47:26-7+ O 31 '64

GUINEA
Atlantic report. Atlan 211:34+ F '63
Guinea returns. Newsweek 61:40+ Je 3 '63
Guinea's first five years. D. Hapgood. bibliog f Cur Hist 45:355-60 D '63
Trouble in Erewhon. il Time 82:34 D 13 '63
See also
Airlines—Guinea
Communism—Guinea
Conakry

Foreign relations

Guinea's first five years. D. Hapgood. bibliog f Cur Hist 45:355-60 D '63
Ugly American in dark Africa. W. D. Patterson. il Sat R 46:18-20+ Je 22 '63

GUINEA, PORTUGUESE. See Portuguese Guinea

GUINEA and the United States
Our far-flung correspondents; visit of American Negro to Conakry, Guinea. H. Fuller. New Yorker 39:35-6+ Ja 4 '64
Ugly American in dark Africa. W. D. Patterson. il Sat R 46:18-20+ Je 22 '63

GUINN, V. P. and Wainerdi, R. E.
Nuclear activation analysis. Science 147:415-16+ Ja 22 '65

GUINNESS, Sir Alec
Alec Guinness as Dylan. Am Rec G 30:1143-4 Ag '64
Catching up with the evasive Sir Alec. il pors Life 56:61-2+ Je 5 '64
Gamut of Guinness. S. Peck. il pors N Y Times Mag p 18 F 2 '64
Love letters of a tough critic. W. Kerr. por Life 56:114 Je 19 '64
Strolling player. New Yorker 39:30-1 F 8 '64

GUINNESS, Desmond
Shopping; an Irish eye for value. Holiday 33:106+ Ap '63
Young, lyric Irish life of the Desmond Guinnesses at Leixlip castle and its folly. V. Lawford. il pors Vogue 144:144-55+ N 15 '64

GUINNESS, Mrs Desmond
Young, lyric Irish life of the Desmond Guinnesses at Leixlip castle and its folly. V. Lawford. il pors Vogue 144:144-55+ N 15 '64

GUINNESS, Mrs Loel
Connoisseurs. por Vogue 141:116-17 Mr 1 '63

GUION, Connie
Reconciled. New Yorker 39:30-2 My 18 '63

GUIRAO, Miguelina. See Stevens, S. S. jt. auth.

GUITAR, Mary Anne
Annulment; masquerade for divorce? McCalls 92:84+ Ja '65
Antioch college; ivory tower on a muddy road. Mlle 56:154-7+ Ap '63
College smoking; how come nobody's stopped? Mlle 59:268-9+ Ag '64
Funny thing happened to her on the way to the bank. Mlle 59:179+ S '64
Gardeners under glass. N Y Times Mag p62+ My 12 '63
Good gracious! living in the Decibel arms. N Y Times Mag p55-6+ D 1 '63
I want to be an amateur. Mlle 57:152+ O '63
Journalism of tomorrow. Mlle 56:162-3+ Mr '63
Knitted brows on the subway. Mlle 58:169-71+ Ap '64
Not for finks. N Y Times Mag p50+ N 24 '63
Parent and child. N Y Times Mag p 102-3 S 15 '63; 79-80 My 3; 47-8 Ag 16; 109 O 25; 24 D 27 '64
What price, good manners? Am Home 67:30 S '64
Whatever happened to my castle? Am Home 67:40 O '64

GUITAR
Eloquent guitar. il House & Gard 123:12+ Mr '63
Legend behind the guitar. M. Mayer. il N Y Times Mag p36+ F 16 '64

GUITAR music
See also
Phonograph records—Guitar music

GUITARISTS
See also
Williams, J.

GUITEAU, Charles
Murder most foul. A. Robertson. il pors Am Heritage 15:90-104 Ag '64

GUITHER, Harold
How to buy insurance on your livestock. Suc Farm 62:32 Ap '64
Making these tax mistakes? Farm J 89:38F Ja '65

GUITHER, Harold—*Continued*
Why tenants don't stay with farming. Suc Farm 61:22 Ap '63
You can learn from their mistakes. Suc Farm 61:32+ F '63
—and Walker, Don
Mind your hog farm visiting manners! Suc Farm 61:112+ F '63
—See Mueller, A. G. jt. auth.
GUITTON, Jean
Interview with Jean Guitton, the only Catholic layman at the council; ed. by J. Pelissier. Cath World 196:279-84 F '63
GULBRANDSEN, R. A. and others
Glauconite from the Precambrian belt series, Montana. bibliog Science 140:390-1 Ap 26 '63
GULF and Western industries, incorporated
Tidy new package of auto parts. il Bsns W p 148+ Je 27 '64
GULF OF CALIFORNIA. See California, Gulf of
GULF oil corporation
Fertilizing the oil business. il Time 82:92 S 20 '63
GULF states
Glorious Gulf states. il Bet Hom & Gard 42:109-12 F '64
GULF STREAM
River that nearly girdles the globe. J. Fix. il Motor B 114:40-1 N '64
GULLANDER, W. P.
Excerpt from statement, March 5, 1963. Cong Digest 42:247+ O '63
GULLANS, Charles
Five poets. T. Cassity. Poetry 103:197-8 D '63
GULLIVER (astrorobot) See Automatons
GULLÓN, Ricardo
Diary of a newly married poet. Américas 16:11-15 Mr '64
GULLS
Antarctic skua. C. R. Eklund. il Sci Am 210: 94-8+ bibliog(p 152) F '64
Birds of the sea. A. Sprunt, 4th. il Motor B 112:45+ S '63
Feathered bomber. G. Laycock. il Field & S 69:35+ D '64
Fulton fish market: with photographs by L. Bernstein. Natur Hist 73:26-9 D '64
Lake Erie niche for gulls; ring-billed gulls nesting on Mohawk Island. R. S. Palmer. il Natur Hist 73:48-51 N '64
Seaside freeloader. D. L. Allen. il Field & S 68:49+ Ap '64
Shell menace; egg shell removal by black-headed gulls. N. Tinbergen. il Natur Hist 72:28-35 Ag '63
Sociable sea gull. J. George. il Read Digest 83:108-13 Ag '63
GULP-in-the-mouth love; story. See Sansom, W.
GUM (store) See Moscow—Stores
GUMAER, Harry T.
Junior high accreditation? NEA J 53:37 O '64
GUMM, Ben L.
Visuals and language arts. Sr Schol 85:10T Ja 21 '65
GUMP, Richard
Gump's: one of a kind. il por Bsns W p46-8+ D 21 '63
GUMP, S. and G. company. See San Francisco—Stores
GUMS (anatomy)
Diseases
Far worse than an aching tooth; periodontal disease. F. A. Arnold, jr. il Todays Health 42:56-9+ F '64
GUMS and resins
Electrokinetic behavior of ion-exchange resin. D. H. Freeman and G. Scatchard. il Science 144:411 Ap 24 '64
New soluble gum stable. Sci N L 83:148 Mr 9 '63
GUN racks
Gun and bow rack. D. Rudolph. il Pop Mech 119:159 F '63
Quick and easy gun rack. J. Krill. il Outdoor Life 133:16 My '64
GUN sights. See Firearms—Sights
GUN slings. See Hunting outfits
GUN tackers. See Staples and stapling machines
GUNDERSON, Doris V.
First-grade reading under scrutiny. Sch Life 47:19-20 O '64
GUNEWARDENE, Sir Senerat
Ceylonese gall. America 109:444-5 O 19 '63
GUNFIGHT at the Sure Enough; story. See White, R.
GUNN, Stuart R. and Williamson, S. M.
Xenon tetrafluoride; heat of formation. bibliog Science 140:177-8 Ap 12 '63
GUNNERA
Its leaves are four to eight feet across. il Sunset 130:270-1 Ap '63
GUNPOWDER, Smokeless
Picking your powder. J. O'Connor. il Outdoor Life 132:72-6 Jl '63
GUNRACKS. See Gun racks
GUNS. See Ordnance
GUNS (small arms) See Shotguns
GUNSMITHING
See also
Firearms industry and trade
GUNSTON, David
Here's your Jenny Lee to London's odd dickey birds! Travel 119:51-2+ F '63
Not just fish 'n' chips. Travel 121:63-5 F '64
When flight was silent. UNESCO Courier 16: 28-32 S '63
GUNTHER, Charles F.
Glass blowing in the classroom. Sch Arts 64:29-32 Ja '65
GUNTHER, Helen
Self-help in Appalachia. Sr Schol 85:11T O 21 '64
GUNTHER, John
Inside England 1964. Look 28:19-26 Ap 7 '64
Inside the twentieth century. por Look 29: 26-8+ Ja 12 '65
Secret life of Nina Khrushchev. McCalls 90: 52-3+ Jl '63
GUNTHER, Max
Astounding laser. Sat Eve Post 237:68-71 O 24 '64
Cracking the groen-ups' coed. Sat Eve Post 237:34-5 Je 20 '64
It's a club on wheels. N Y Times Mag p68+ N 1 '64
Key to article sales. Writer 77:12-14 Ag '64
Quicksand, nature's terrifying death trap. Read Digest 85:140-4 D '64
Race against blindness. Sat Eve Post 237: 36-7 My 30 '64
Weekends, U.S.A: what ever happened to fun? excerpt from The weekenders. McCalls 91:70-1+ Je '64
Why a northern town fights school integration. Sat Eve Post 237:66-7 S 19 '64
GUPPY, Nicholas
Alexander Calder. Atlan 214:53-60 D '64
GUPTA, Sisir
India and the Soviet Union. bibliog f Cur Hist 44:141-6 Mr '63
GURDJIEFF, Georges Ivanovich
Solving the human enigma. E. Seaver. por Sat R 46:27-8 My 18 '63
GURIN, David
Camellias outdoors in the North. Horticulture 42:44-5 N '64
Key to the villas miserias. Nation 199:199-201 O 5 '64
GURIN, Samuel. See Fisher, W. R. jt. auth.
GURKHAS. See Ghurkas
GURLEY, George E.
New winter favorite. Outdoor Life 135:72-4 F '65
GURNEY, Dan
How hot is the Mustang? pors Pop Sci 184: 55-8+ My '64
GURNEY, J. Thomas
Loss of freedom; address, May 18, 1964. Vital Speeches 30:566-70 Jl 1 '64
GÜRSEL, Cemal
General Gursel to President Johnson; letter, December 25, 1963. Dept State Bul 50:90 Ja 20 '64
GUSS, Carolyn
New instructional materials for teaching poetry. NEA J 53:57 My '64
GUSSOW, Mel
Laugh at this Negro but darkly. Esquire 62:94-5+ N '64
GUSTAD, John W.
On improving college teaching. NEA J 53: 37-8 Mr '64
GUSTAFSON, Philip F. and others
Environmental radiation: measurements of dose rates. bibliog Science 145:44-7 Jl 3 '64
GUSTAVSON, Lealand
Artist must chart his course. il Am Artist 27:54-9+ Je '63
GUSTAVUS VI, king of Sweden
Sweden's king, a royal gardener. M. Perry. il por Flower Grower 52:32-4 Ja '65
GUSWELLER, James A.
Profiles: Church of St Matthew and St Timothy. R. Rice. il por New Yorker 40:42+ Ag 1; 37-8+ Ag 8 '64
GUTERMAN, Simeon L.
Social sciences in two-year colleges. Sch & Soc 91:200 Ap 20 '63
GÜTERSLOH, Germany (Federal Republic)
Notes from abroad. K. Blaukopf. Hi Fi 13: 26+ Ap '63
GUTH, Dorothy L.
Shirt shrift. New Yorker 40:141-2 Mr 28 '64
GUTH, Francis. See Guth, J. jt. auth.

GUTH, Jenny, and Guth, Francis
Munich: International handcrafts fair. Craft Horiz 24:20-4 S '64
Venice: the biennale. Craft Horiz 24:48 S '64
GUTHEIM, Frederick
Alvar Aalto today. Arch Rec 133:135-50 Ap '63
Evolution of a city. Nation 198:74-5 Ja 20 '64
Letter from Washington. Nation 198:126-7 F 3 '64
Traffic in towns. Arch Rec 135:78+ Je '64
Where man and nature conspire. Nation 200:88-9 Ja 25 '65
GUTHRIE, A. B. Jr
Great Rockies. Holiday 34:28-41 Ag '63
Three poems; Twin Lakes hunter; Island; Twin Lakes winter. Harper 228:63 My '64
GUTHRIE, Sir Giles
Piloting BOAC out of the storm. il por Bsns W p 124+ S 19 '64
GUTHRIE, John Dennett
John Dennett Guthrie, Pinchot pioneer. por A. Ringland. il Am For 69:23+ F '63
GUTHRIE, Sir Tyrone
Can TV be saved? por Esquire 60:211+ D '63
Close-up of Ireland's basic problem. N Y Times Mag p22+ Ja 19 '64
If a theater is to prosper. N Y Times Mag p7+ Jl 28 '63
New and hopeful role for repertory. N Y Times Mag p32-3+ N 10 '63
So long as the theater can do miracles. N Y Times Mag p24-5+ Ap 28 '63
Ten favorites from Shakespeare. N Y Times Mag p 18-19 Mr 15 '64
Why bother with the bard? Seventeen 23:148-9+ S '64

about

Giant of Monaghan. B. Friel. por Holiday 35:89+ My '64
Starting from scratch. por Theatre Arts 47:9 Ag '63
Tyrone Guthrie: the artist as man of the theatre. R. Hatch. il por Horizon 5:35-41 N '63
GUTHRIE, Woody
It's been good to know him. N. Hentoff. Reporter 32:48-9 Ja 14 '65
GUTIERREZ-OLIVOS, Sergio
Science influences foreign relations; excerpts of remarks, October 5, 1964. Sci N L 86:258 O 24 '64
GUTMAN, Daniel
Criminal gets the breaks. N Y Times Mag p36+ N 29 '64
GUTMAN, John
Nothing but contempt. Opera N 28:8-11 Ap 11 '64
Singers' opera. Opera N 27:8-12 Mr 2 '63
GUTTERS
Curb and gutter by extrusion. N. Donaghy. il Am City 79:25 Je '64
GUTTERS (roof)
It's the time to check gutters. il Sunset 131:144+ O '63
GUTTERSEN, Alston G.
Programing mental health facilities. Arch Rec 134:165 N '63
GUTTES, Edmund, and Guttes, Sophie
Thymidine incorporation by mitochondria in physarum polycephalum. bibliog Science 145:1057-8 S 4 '64
GUTTES, Sophie. See Guttes, E. jt. auth.
GUTTMACHER, Alan F.
Overcoming infertility; excerpts from Planning your family. Parents Mag 39:46-7+ Ag '64
Sterilization; facts and arguments. Nation 198:344-7 Ap 6 '64
Tragedy of the unwanted chlid. por Parents Mag 39:43+ Je '64
GUTTMAN, Irving
Quote: unquote. F. Campbell. por Mus Am 83:22 N '63
GUTTMANN, Edith
My most unforgettable character. Read Digest 83:117-22 Ag '63
GUTWILLIG, Robert
Lord of the flies. Vogue 141:154-7+ My '63
On screen. Horizon 5:36-7 Mr '63
Six days in Alabama: a journal. Mlle 57:116-17+ S '63
GUTZLER, Mark, pseud. See Mannes, M.
GUTZWILLER, F. W.
Semiconductors for power supplies. Electr World 72:27-30+ N '64
GUY, Jim
IQ of a blue. Outdoor Life 132:52-3+ Ag '63
GUYER, Donna Dickey
Pointers for poets. Writer 77:27+ D '64
GUYER, Paul Q.
These beef specialists answer your twenty-one most asked questions. por Suc Farm 61:46-7 My '63
GUYS, Constantin
Master art and opera. R. Rushmore. il Opera N 28:16 D 28 '63
GUZE, Lucien B. and Kalmanson, G. M.
Action of erythromycin on protoplasts in vivo. bibliog Science 146:1299-300 D 4 '64
Persistence of bacteria in protoplast form after apparent cure of pyelonephritis in rats. bibliog Science 143:1340-1 Mr 20 '64
GUZELIS, Helen
Fragrance of lavender. Horticulture 41:279 My '63
GUZIE, Tad W.
Vernacular isn't everything. America 109:164-5 Ag 17 '63
GUZMAN, Ramon M.
From septic tanks to secondary treatment. Am City 78:103-4 N '63
GUZZARDI, Walter, Jr
Gillette faces the stainless-steel dragon. Fortune 68:158-61+ Jl '63
Optimistic world of Edgar Kaiser. Fortune 67:90-7+ Ap '63
Untranquilized drug makers. Fortune 68:124-8+ D '63
Young executives. Fortune 69:96-9+ Je; 70:146-8+ Jl; 161-4+ S; 140-3+ O '64
GWIN, Bridget
Fancies; poem. Horn Bk 39:530 O '63
GWIN, William McKendree
Operator and the emperors; with portfolio. L. Thomas. il por Am Heritage 15:4-23+ Ap '64
GYI, Ni Ni
Burma: family in transition. UNESCO Courier 17:12-16 S '64
GYMKHANA. See Motor boat racing
GYMNARCHUS
Electric location by fishes. H. W. Lissmann. il Sci Am 208:50-9 bibliog(p 188) Mr '63
GYMNASIUMS
Clean sweep in Olympics; National gymnasium and annex, Tokyo. il Arch Forum 121:158-61 Ag '64
Dingy, sprightly home of the good ones; Fifth street gym in Miami Beach. T. Maule. il Sports Illus 20:70-2+ Ap 6 '64
Outdoor gym keeps 'em slim; West Palm Beach, Fla. B. York. il Am City 79:29 Ja '64
Two air-supported structures for athletics; gym and indoor swimming pool, Forman school, Litchfield, Conn. il Arch Rec 135:209-10 Mr '64
GYMNASTICS
Can we improve our Olympic chances? G. Kaywell. il Dance Mag 37:52-7 N '63
Gymnastics workshop, Fairfax County, Va. il Recreation 57:232-3 My '64
Lithe envoys to our Latin neighbors; women's U.S. gymnastic team. il Sports Illus 18:28-32 My 6 '63
Olympic ogre: a quite grim tale; gymnastics in the US. D. McDonagh. il Dance Mag 38:35-7+ N '64
GYNECOLOGY. See Woman—Diseases
GYÖRGYI, Albert Szent-. See Szent-Györgyi, A.
GYORKI, John R.
Selecting a suitable heat sink. Electr World 69:46-8 Je '63
Transistor voltage regulator. Electr World 70:74-5 Jl '63
GYPSIES in France
Play gypsy, dance gypsy. J. Morris. il U S Camera 27:63-7 Ap '64
GYPSUM panels. See Paneling
GYPSUM wallboard. See Wallboard
GYPSY moths. See Gipsy moths
GYROPLANES. See Autogiros
GYROSCOPE
Agena-D satellites will test Nortronics attitude-stabilization gyro. C. D. LaFond. il Miss & Roc 13:34-5 Jl 1 '63
Frictionless free-fall gyro spins indefinitely. Sci N L 83:149 Mr 9 '63
G&C advanced techniques; the wide-ranging search for tougher, lighter gyroscopes in space. il Miss & Roc 13:68-9+ O 7 '63
Inertial system uses electrostatic gyros. P. J. Klass. il Aviation W 79:87-9 S 30 '63
New chore for the laser beam. Bsns W p64 Jl 6 '63
New gyros being sought for MORL. M. Getler. il Miss & Roc 16:31-3 Ja 11 '65
Their own star for guidance; electrically suspended gyroscope for Polaris submarines. il Bsns W p 124+ Ap 20 '63
GYROSCOPIC instruments
Bottled star; Honeywell's electrically suspended gyro. il Time 81:46 My 10 '63
Gimbal-less design may reduce gyro cost. il Aviation W 79:100+ S 9 '63

GYROSCOPIC instruments—*Continued*
New gyro uses mercury isotope mixture. P. J. Klass. il Aviation W 79:88-9+ Ag 12 '63
Ring laser device performs rate gyro-angular sensor functions. P. J. Klass. il Aviation W 78:98-9+ F 11 '63
Twin gyros proposed for vehicle attitude. Aviation W 79:81 S 16 '63
See also
Automatic pilot (airplanes)
Inertial guidance systems

H

HDI. See Human development institute, incorporated, Atlanta
HHFA. See United States—Housing and home finance agency
H. H. Franklin car clubs. See Automobile clubs
HMBPA. See Hexamethylene propionamide
HOT (hyperbaric oxygen therapy) See High-pressure oxygenation
HPO. See High-pressure oxygenation
HPO therapy. See High-pressure oxygenation
HUAC (House un-American activities committee) See United States—Congress—House of representatives—Committees
H. W. Wilson company. See Wilson, H. W., company
HAAG, John
Symbiotics; poem. Yale R 54:238-40 D '64
HAAGEN-SMIT, A. J.
Control of air pollution; with biographical sketch. Sci Am 210:18, 24-31 bibliog(p 152) Ja '64
HAAKE, Alfred P. Jr
Long-term outlook is good. Nations Bsns 52: 108+ Je '64
HAAN, E. R.
Double-spiral candlestick. Pop Mech 119:140-1+ My '63
4x magnifying thickness gauge. Pop Mech 120:174-5 Ag '63
I built this wood lathe for $10.67. Pop Mech 120:170-2 Ag '63
Oil burner tune-up. Pop Mech 120:186-90 N '63
Uplift for tired chairs. Pop Mech 121:171-2 F '64
HAAN, Ronald
Newsboys' revolt. por Time 83:51 Je 26 '64
HAAR, Charles M.
Latin America's troubled cities. For Affairs 41:536-49 Ap '63
HAARETZ. See Newspapers—Israel
HAAS, Ernst
Spring comes to England. il Look 27:68-77 My 21 '63
HAAS, Robert K.
Obituary
Pub W 186:78 Ag 24 '64
HAASE, Peter, and Lynn, Frank
Jobs of the future; reprint. Sci Digest 56:20-4 N '64
HAASS, Herman C. A.
Lady-killer; Hoch murder cases. A. I. Schutzer. il Am Heritage 15:36-9+ O '64
HABANA. See Havana
HABE, Hans
Walk in darkness; dramatization. See Hairston, W.
HABER, Audrey, and Kalish, H. I.
Prediction of discrimination from generalization after variations in schedule of reinforcement. bibliog Science 142:412-13 O 18 '63
HABER, Leo
Let's play A & R man. Hi Fi 14:63-4 D '64
HABERER, Robert
To act as an artist. Sch Arts 64:17-19 O '64
HABERMANN, Helen M.
Applejack technique: new application of an old approach to solute concentration. Science 140:292 Ap 19 '63
HABGOOD, H. W.
Gas chromatography, the art and the science. Science 139:579-80 F 15 '63
HABIT
Anecdotes, facetiae, satire, etc.
Hold that habit! H. A. Smith. il Read Digest 83:231-3 Jl '63
HABIT (costume) See Religious orders—Habit
HABIT; story. See Cheever, J.
HABITABLE worlds. See Life on other planets
HABITAT, Animal. See Zoology—Ecology
HABITATIONS, Animal. See Animals—Habitations
HABITS, Nervous. See Nervous habits
HABSBURG, House of. See Hapsburg, House of
HACHETTE. See Publishers and publishing—France
La HACIENDA golf club. See Country clubs
HACK, Martin H.
Signal detection in the rat. bibliog Science 139:758-60 F 22 '63
HACKER, Andrew
Academic freedom; how much is there? N Y Times Mag p25+ Je 7 '64
Again the issue of the welfare state. N Y Times Mag p9+ Mr 22 '64
America follows the middle of the road. N Y Times Mag p21+ My 5 '63
Are there too many lawyers in Congress? N Y Times Mag p 14+ Ja 5 '64
Britain's political style is not like ours. N Y Times Mag p22+ S 20 '64
Do corporations have a social duty? N Y Times Mag p21+ N 17 '63
How to carry New York. Commentary 38:68-70 Ag '64
Inquiry into the new conservatism. N Y Times Mag p7+ F 16 '64
One man, one vote, yes or no? N Y Times Mag p31+ N 8 '64
What kind of nation are we? N Y Times Mag p23+ D 8 '63
What's the mainstream? who is in it? N Y Times Mag p5+ S 6 '64
HACKER, Harold
New York: Pioneer revisited; report. Wilson Lib Bul 38:271-5 N '63
HACKER, Louis M.
Economist in the grand tradition. Nat R 14: 532-3 Jl 2 '63
HACKETT, Alice Payne
Best sellers of 1963 as sold to the U.S. trade Pub W 185:78-81 Ja 20 '64
Do you remember... Sat R 47:109-25 Ag 29 '64
(comp) Forty years of best-sellers. Sat R 47: 92+ Ag 29 '64
Hardcover best sellers of 1964 in the U.S. book trade. Pub W 187:68-71 Ja 18 '65
HACKETT, Blanche
Miniature hotels in the sky. Recreation 56: 269-70 Je '63
HACKETT, Buddy
Buddy and the Bruegel. A. Eliot. il pors Vogue 145:132-3+ F 1 '65
HACKETT, David L.
Tryout in Harlem. New Repub 148:38 Ap 13 '63
HACKETT, Joan
On the brink. por Time 81:80 Ap 12 '63
HACKETT, Robert A.
Harness racing. Sports Illus 21:51-2 Ag 24 '64
HACKETT, Walter
(ed) See Wilde, O. Canterville ghost
HACKFORD, Robert R.
Colonial press expansion, new equipment to meet industry needs. por Pub W 186:58-61 D 7 '64
HACKSAWS. See Saws
HADAS, Moses
What we remember. Reporter 30:45-6 Ap 9 '64
about
Lectures on the phone: telelectures. il por Time 82:37 Jl 19 '63
Tea and goatee. por Newsweek 63:80 Mr 9 '64
HADDAD, Gladys
Attempt at abstracts. Sch Arts 62:20 My '63
HADDAD, William Frederick
Jew in sheik's clothing? il por Time 83:23 My 22 '64
Tempest in a glass tea. il por Newsweek 63: 31 My 25 '64
HADDON craftsmen, Incorporated
Haddon's big expansion program: diversification, better service. il Pub W 186:58-9 Ag 3 '64
HADDON HEIGHTS, N.J.
Neighborhood showpiece. il Am City 78:153 F '63
HADEN, Mary Jane
Junior gallery. Sch Arts 63:4-7 Je '64
HADERER, Rudolph, bootmaker. See Shoes—Trade and manufacture
HADLEY, Leila
Parent and child. N Y Times Mag p47-8 F 23 '64
HADRIAN'S villa. See Tivoli, Italy—Hadrian's villa
HAEFF, Andrew V. and Knox, Cameron
Perception of ultrasound. Science 139:590-2 F 15 '63

HAEKKERUP, Per
Scandinavia's peace-keeping forces for U.N. For Affairs 42:675-81 Jl '64
HAESLOOP, Betty
Flight of the Honey bees. Flying 74:48-9+ F '64
el HAFEZ, Amin
Cure for sick brothers. il por Time 83:28 My 1 '64
Pacifier. Newsweek 63:36+ My 4 '64
HAFNER, Everett M.
Cosmic electromagnetic radiation. bibliog Science 145:1263-71 S 18 '64
HAFNIUM
Phase transformation at high temperatures in hafnia and zirconia. W. L. Baun. bibliog il Science 140:1330-1 Je 21 '63
Zirconium and hafnium in stone meteorites. W. D. Ehmann and J. L. Setser. bibliog il Science 139:594-5 F 15 '63
HAGAN, Roger
Issues of disarmament. bibliog Sr Schol 83: 12T-13T N 22 '63
Peace at the polls. Nation 196:83-91 F 2 '63
—and Bernstein, Bart
Military value of missiles in Cuba. Bul Atomic Sci 19:8-13 F '63
HAGAN, William T.
Invaders and invaded. Reporter 28:52+ Ap 25 '63
HAGE, Elizabeth B.
Prince George's headquarters. Library J 89: 4722-4 D 1 '64
HAGEDORN, George G.
Excerpt from statement submitted to Joint economic committee, February 15, 1963. Cong Digest 42:123+ Ap '63
HAGEN, Dick, and Bickers, Jack
New partners; slats and loafing stalls. Farm J 87:30-1+ D '63
HAGEN, Ernest
Personal experiences of an old New York cabinetmaker; ed. by E. A. Ingerman. Antiques 84:576-80 N '63
HAGEN, John P.
Navigating the gravity wells of interplanetary space. Sat R 47:48-51 Ap 4 '64
HAGEN, Mary
Turn left at Spring Creek. Am For 70:30-1+ S '64
HAGEN, Uta
Firm sense of role. il pors Time 81:82 My 10 '63
HAGER, Mary Grant
Michelangelo. Life 57:69+ Jl 17 '64
HAGER, Walter E.
Challenges to public higher education. Sch & Soc 91:200-1 Ap 20 '63
HAGERSTOWN, Md.
Report from Hagerstown; first largescale closed circuit television network exclusively designed for classroom instruction. Sat R 47:63 Ap 18 '64
HAGGIN, B. H.
New records in review. See issues of Yale review
On being a music critic; excerpts from Music observed. Commentary 38:50-2 Jl '64
Records. See issues of New republic
HAGIA SOPHIA. See Istanbul—Santa Sophia
HAGIOGRAPHY. See Saints
HAGIWARA, Susumu, and others
Membrane properties of barnacle muscle fiber. bibliog Science 143:1446-8 Mr 27 '64
HAGLER, Ronald A. See Egoff, S. A. jt. auth.
HAGLUND, Bertil
National parks of Sweden. Am For 70: 26-9+ My '64
HAGMAIER, George
Movie of the month. Cath World 196:327-8 F '63
HAGUE, Douglas B.
Making of a setter. Field & S 68:28-31 D '63
HAGUE, Raoul
Slow emergence of star sculpture. G. Nordland. il por Art N 63:30-2+ O '64
HAGUE, The

International court of justice

See International court of justice, The Hague

Music

Notes from our correspondents. L. Noske-Friedlaender. Hi Fi 14:26+ Mr '64
HAGUE philharmonic orchestra
Musical events. W. Sargeant. New Yorker 39:155-6 My 25 '63
HAHM, Pyong Choon
Korea's mendicant mentality? For Affairs 43:165-74 O '64
HAHN, Emily
Escape. New Yorker 39:125-6+ N 2 '63
I, the grapevine. . . . Vogue 141:140-1+ Ap 15 '63
Raymond. New Yorker 40:30-6 Ag 22 '64
Reporter at large. New Yorker 39:110+ Ap 27 '63; 40:131-2+ S 19 '64
Surrounding hills. New Yorker 40:184+ D 5 '64
Theresa; story. New Yorker 39:39-43 Ap 13 '63
Yankee Barbarian at the Shogun's court. Am Heritage 15:60-3+ Je '64
(ed) See Roosevelt, T. My dear Selous
HAHN, Fred E. See Wolfe, A. D. jt. auth.
HAHN, Vera D.
Decorating newsletter. Am Home 68:38 Ja '65
HAHNLOSER, Arthur
Art of collecting. il por Time 83:74-7 Mr 13 '64
HAIDER, Manfred, and Lindsley, D. B.
Microvibrations in man and dolphin. bibliog Science 146:1181-3 N 27 '64
—and others
Attention, vigilance, and cortical evoked-potentials in humans. bibliog Science 145:180-2 Jl 10 '64
HAIFA, Israel
Israel's three cities. D. Pryce-Jones. Commentary 35:52-5 Ja '63
HAIG-BROWN, Roderick
Death of the salmon. Atlan 213:57-9 Ja '64
Fall defined; excerpt from Fisherman's autumn. Atlan 212:69-70 S '63
Man tames the wilderness. Atlan 214:149-50+ N '64
My quarry eye to eye; excerpts from Fisherman's fall. il por Sports Illus 21:84-6+ O 19 '64
HAIKU. See Japanese poetry
HAIL
How to shoot down hail. P. Van Den Berg. il Sci Digest 53:42-5 My '63
Nature note: big, bad hailstones. Sci N L 86:63 Jl 25 '64
HAIL insurance. See Insurance, Hail
HAILE Selassie I, emperor of Ethiopia
Emperor of Ethiopia visits United States; texts of an exchange of toasts between President Kennedy and the Emperor, October 1, 1963, and a joint communique October 2, 1963. Dept State Bul 49:674-5 O 28 '63
Haile Selassie I, addresses General assembly; summary of address, October 4, 1963. por U N Rev 10:4-5 N '63

about

Conquering Lion. Newsweek 62:47-8 O 14 '63
Display of affection. il por Time 82:25-6 O 11 '63
Emperor tries to unite Africa. J. Walz. il pors N Y Times Mag p 18+ Mr 8 '64
Ethiopia: at the edge of today. P. R. Webb. il por Newsweek 64:42-3 Jl 27 '64
Haile Selassie; an old leader with a new role. por U S News 55:22 O 14 '63
King of kings. New Repub 150:8 F 29 '64
Lion of Judah returns to conquer. il pors Life 55:44-44A O 18 '63
Selassie's message to the Negro. A. Morrison. il pors Ebony 19:29-32+ D '63
HAILEY, Oliver
Hey you, light man! Criticism
Commonweal 77:664 Mr 22 '63
New Yorker 39:134 Mr 9 '63
Newsweek 61:86 Mr 11 '63
HAILMAN, Jack P. See Klopfer, P. H. jt. auth.
HAILSHAM, Quintin McGarel Hogg, 2d viscount. See Hogg, Q. M.
HAINES, Aubrey B.
(ed) See Rogers, G. Her school was the stage
HAINES, Francis
How the Indian got the horse. Am Heritage 15:16-21+ F '64
HAINES, Fred
Art in court; city of angels vs. Scorpio rising. Nation 199:123-5 S 14 '64
HAINES, Frederick J.
Blinker minder. Pop Electr 18:61-4 Mr '63
Build a turnstile for stereo. Pop Electr 19:68-9 N '63
HAINES, Gerald
And you shall be heard. por Negro Hist Bul 28:12 O '64
HAINES, John
On the road; poem. Nation 196:348 Ap 27 '63
South wind; poem. Nation 196:378 My 4 '63
This dark water; poem. Poetry 103:242-3 Ja '64
HAINES, Richard
Paintings of Richard Haines. J. Lovoos. il por Am Artist 27:50-7+ Ap '63
HAIR
Count silver an asset. D. A. Robinson. il Ladies Home J 82:55-7 Ja '65
Native ornament: glorious hair. il Vogue 143: 58-65 Ja 15 '64

HAIR—*Continued*
Strontium-90 in hair. B. J. Hopkins and others. bibliog il Science 139:1064-5 Mr 15 '63
See also
Baldness
Hairdressing
Wigs

Care

Bulletin on the new savvy sève of hair. Vogue 143:70+ Ja 15 '64
Children's hair care tips. Parents Mag 38: 143 Mr '63
Going on about summer hair. Vogue 143:104+ Je '64
Hair: a brush-up course. B. Clerke. il Ladies Home J 80:110-12 S '63
How women ruin their hair. il Redbook 121: 72-3+ O '63
Shine lady? il Mlle 58:136-7 N '63

Dyeing and bleaching

Color her beautiful. A. Rostenberg, jr. and G. Kass. il Todays Health 42:14-17+ Ag '64; Same abr. with title Chemistry of hair coloring. Sci Digest 56:68-74 D '64
Color me anything. Newsweek 62:55 Ag 19 '63
GH's common-sense guide to hair coloring. Good H 156:116-17+ Mr '63
Hair dyes and tints. L. Allen. Todays Health 41:8+ O '63
Hairstyles newly cued to color. il McCalls 91:78-9+ Ja '64
Notes on color. il Mlle 59:100-1 O '64
Would you like to color your hair? C. D. Legg. il Farm J 87:87-8 N '63
Your summer hairdo, do it up brown. il Mlle 56:162-3 Ap '63

HAIR combs. See Combs

HAIR curlers
Dear Haircurl: help! baffled curler-users write their editor. W. K. Zinsser. il Life 55:25+ O 18 '63

HAIR cutting. See Haircutting

HAIR dressing. See Hairdressing

HAIR dryers
Beauty gifts. il Seventeen 23:147 D '64
Hair dryers. il Consumer Rep 28:520-3 N '63
Portable hair dryers. il Consumer Bul 46: 10-13 D '63

HAIR identification. See Identification

HAIR preparations
Shine lady? il Mlle 58:136-7 N '63

HAIR seals. See Seals (animals)

HAIR transplantation. See Transplantation of organs, tissues, etc.

HAIR work. See Hairwork

HAIRCUTTING
Going on about summer hair. Vogue 143:104+ Je '64
Luck with your locks, young John. M. Acoca. il Life 54:16 My 24 '63
New beauty slant for summer: hair cut on the bias. J. T. Stark. il Look 28:M8+ Je 16 '64
New smasher; the cockney clip. Mlle 56:164-5 il Ap '63
Shaggy child story. R. Drake. il Redbook 123: 58-61+ Ag '64
Suzy Parker has her first short haircut. il Vogue 143:118-21 Je '64
Wash-and-wear hair to take to camp. il Vogue 141:203 My '63

HAIRDO. See Hairdressing

HAIRDRESSING
Adorable do's for little-girl hair. il Good H 156:76-9+ F '63
Alexandre the great. K. Whitehorn. il Ladies Home J 80:148-53 N '63
All ironed out; ironing method to straighten hair. il Newsweek 65:53 Ja 11 '65
All wet and un-set and pretty as can be: summer hairdos. il Seventeen 22:62-3+ Je '63
Ann-Margret tries new hair styles. il Seventeen 22:156-7 Ap '63
Baubles, bangles and bangs. il Ebony 19:151-2+ D '63
Be a Christmas beauty. il McCalls 92:68+ D '64
Beauty bulletin; hair. il Vogue 145:92-7 Ja 15 '65
Beauty: four hairdos. A. Taylor. il N Y Times Mag p99 D 6 '64
Beauty on a summer wave. D. R. Robinson. il Ladies Home J 81:60-1 My '64
Cool look for warmest month. il Ebony 19:119-20+ Ag '64
Cool styles for cool weather. il Ebony 19: 149-50+ N '63
Curls are back. il McCalls 91:110-11+ Mr '64
Down-to-dark holiday hairdos. il Good H 157:210 D '63
Early Barbra Streisand; teenage preoccupation with hairstyles. Newsweek 64:104+ N 2 '64
Fall hairdos for day or night. il Ebony 19: 152-3 O '64
Four guest editors hitch a ride on the beauty-go-round. il Mlle 59:318-19 Ag '64
Genius hairdos for double exposure. B. Clerke. il Ladies Home J 80:148-50+ O '63
Get set for summer. B. Clerke. il Ladies Home J 80:66-7+ My '63
Hair news: a short story. D. A. Robinson. il Ladies Home J 81:80-2 O '64
Hairdo of the month. See issues of Seventeen
Hairdos across the country; Mr Ramon of Garrison-Ramon, New York. il Seventeen 23:133 Ja '64
Hairdos by the world's top fashion designers. il McCalls 90:112-13 S '63
Hairdos for Christmas. il Ebony 20:158+ D '64
Hairdos in a snap. il Mlle 57:262-3 Ag '63
Hairstyles newly cued to color. il McCalls 91:78-9+ Ja '64
Have wash & wear hair with a new pool cut; instructions for wash-and-wear hair. il McCalls 90:138+ Je '63
Head that fits the Paris designer's dream. il Vogue 141:166-7 Mr 15 '63
High-fashion hairdos for the holidays. il Ebony 19:93-6 Ja '64
His and hers; bald beauty in Paris, in London, shaggy, shoulder-length coiffures. il Newsweek 64:64 Ag 10 '64
Honeymoon hairdos. il McCalls 90:181 My '63
Hot weather collection of young hairdos. il Good H 157:104-5+ Ag '63
How do you like my new hairdo? il Seventeen 22:96-7+ D '63
How to buy a hairdresser. il Seventeen 22: 34-5 N '63
How to do everything with your type of hair. il Seventeen 23:152-3 Ap '64
How to handle a new hairdresser. il Redbook 121:68-9+ Jl '63
I can't do a thing with my hair; five can-dos. il Mlle 57:94-8 O '63
Kenneth club. il Vogue 142:52-5 Jl '63
Look-alike do's; same set and style for you and your small fry. il Good H 158:94-7+ F '64
Look pretty in glasses. il Seventeen 23:160-1+ S '64
March hair styles: lion to lamb like. il Ebony 19:143-5 Mr '64
Mrs Leonard Holzer and the Paris she stopped cold. il Vogue 144:146-7 O 1 '64
Model hairdos. il Seventeen 23:166+ Mr '64
Monti gilds twenty Mlles. A. Hoene. il Mlle 57:264-7 Ag '63
Narrowing search for marvellous hair. il Vogue 141:108-9+ Mr 15 '63
Negro beauty culturist goes eastern. F. L. Spellmon. il Negro Hist Bul 28:15 O '64
New day-into-night dos. il Mlle 58:86-9 Ja '64
New hair lifts. il Look 28:M12-M13 D 1 '64
New hair styles for summer. il Redbook 121:62-5 My '63
New hairdos, marvelously manageable; Paris previews high-fashion hairstyles. il McCalls 91:102-5+ S '64
New highlights for your hair. R. Drake. il Redbook 122:72-5+ Mr '64
New Tom Jones. il Ebony 19:172-4 My '64
New ways to minimize facial faults. R. Drake. il Redbook 122:62-3 Ja '64
New year; a new you. il Seventeen 24:58-9 Ja '65
New year, new hair style. L. D. Kirk. il Parents Mag 39:20 Ja '64
Off to school with a pretty new hairstyle. L. D. Kirk. il Parents Mag 39:94+ Ag '64
Oliver haircut. il Vogue 141:74-5 F 15 '63
Our fair lady. D. A. Robinson. il Ladies Home J 81:85-8+ Ja '64
Overteased hair: beginning of the end. E. Harris. il Look 27:26-8+ Jl 30 '63
Peggy's hairdos. il McCalls 90:162 My '63
Portrait perfect hairdoes. il Seventeen 22:174-7+ Ag '63
Prettiest hairdo you ever had. il Seventeen 23:184-7+ Ag '64
Pretty girl, pretty girl, where have you been? il Mlle 58:176-9 Ap '64
Pretty spring hair styles for girls four to twelve. L. D. Kirk. il Parents Mag 38: 142 Mr '63
Pretty up your hairdo: three ways with one set. il Good H 157:80-9+ N '63
Quick-switch styles: wiglets change casuals to formals. il Ebony 20:158+ N '64
Redbook's guide to the new hair styles. R. Drake. il Redbook 123:84-92 S '64

HAIRDRESSING—*Continued*
Return of the romantic hairdos. B. Clerke. il Ladies Home J 80:64-7 Ja '63
Revolt against fancy hairdos. S. Kirtland. il Look 27:34-9 Jl 30 '63
Saucy coifs for Valentine's day. il Ebony 19:114-16 F '64
Shaggy Englishman story; British long hairs. A. Carthew. il N Y Times Mag p 18+ S 6 '64
Shape a pretty face. il Seventeen 22:146-7 My '63
Shoulder-length glamor. il Ebony 20:83-4 Ja '65
Six favorite models and their favorite hairdos. il McCalls 92:34+ Ja '65
Sleek and straight and hide an eye; New York's Dees sisters. il Life 56:53-4+ My 8 '64
Special hairdos for hats. il Ebony 19:112+ S '64
Stress is on the tresses; current styles especially prepared for Ebony. il Ebony 19:207-9 Je '64
Sultry sidelong look. il McCalls 90:110-11+ Ap '63
Summer hairdos, the permanent solution. Mlle 56:166 Ap '63
Theory of the coiffured lasses. il Horizon 5:118-19 Mr '63
There's a new look in hairdos. il Seventeen 23:150-1+ Ap '64
Thirty-one easiest hairdos ever! il Good H 158:120-30+ Ap '64
Tip sheet on hair for autumn from twelve of the world's top hairdressers. il Vogue 142:84-7 Ag 15 '63
Twenty-six great classic hairdos. il Good H 156:122-32+ Ap '63
Valentine hairdo to win his heart. il Good H 156:172 F '63
Versatile styles for medium length hair. il Ebony 19:122-3 Jl '64
Vogue's eye view: a haircut whizzed with charm. il Vogue 141:55 F 15 '63
What the Beatles have done to hair; teenaged British boys. il Look 28:58-9 D 29 '64
Wig waggery; hair-styling for men. J. Wescott. il Seventeen 23:22 Ap '64

HAIRPIECES. See Wigs

HAIRSTON, William
Walk in darkness; dramatization of novel by H. Habe. Criticism
New Yorker 39:99 N 9 '63

HAIRWORK
Journey to Dalecarlia. E. Unnerstad. il Horn Bk 39:580-7 D '63

HAISLIP, Martha
For flowers. Flower Grower 51:32+ Ag '64
Fragrant old rose remains a favorite. Flower Grower 51:28-9 Mr '64

HAIST, Grant
Are you serendipitacious? U S Camera 26:18+ Ap '63
Cure for single-shotitis. U S Camera 27:38-9+ My '64
Do you see faces? I do! U S Camera 27:36 F '64

HAITCH, Richard
Foster-home problem. Nation 196:279-81, 306-8 Ap 6-13 '63
Twenty-fifth child. Nation 197:238-41 O 19 '63

HAITI
Can Haiti be helped? R. L. Mirabeau. Nation 196:416-18 My 18 '63
Flora strikes, the deadliest ever. il Life 55:34-43 O 18 '63
Haiti; a case study in freedom. R. D. Heinl, jr. New Repub 150:15-21 My 16 '64
Haiti and the CIA; Case of Andrew Adams. Nation 200:22-3 Ja 11 '65
Invasion in miniature; Haitian exiles attempt. Time 82:27 Ag 16 '63
Nightmare republic. G. Greene. New Repub 149:18-20 N 16 '63
Return of the exiles. Time 84:36 Jl 24 '64
U.S. urges Security council to await OAS action on Haiti; statement, May 9, 1963. C. W. Yost. Dept State Bul 48:958-9 Je 17 '63
Visit to Haiti. J. Meslay. America 109:374-5 O 5 '63
Warning to renegades: Haiti's first public execution in thirty years. Time 84:44+ N 27 '64
See also
Airports—Haiti
United Nations—Haiti

Economic conditions

Haiti; last act of a tragicomedy. B. Rice. Harper 226:65-6+ My '63
Haiti: where lid is about to blow. C. Migdail. il U S News 54:65-6 My 6 '63
Now: new danger next door to Cuba. il U S News 54:40-2 My 20 '63

Foreign relations

Papa Doc's democracy. il Newsweek 61:52+ My 20 '63

Politics and government

After Duvalier. Nation 196:385 My 11 '63
And now there are none; attempt to overthrow Duvalier. Newsweek 64:60 N 23 '64
Beautiful, cruel, explosive, Haiti. T. Szulc. il N Y Times Mag p26-7+ Je 9 '63
Calm and peaceful. Newsweek 61:52 My 27 '63
Continued deterioration. il Time 81:32 My 17 '63
Cul de Sac; F. Duvalier vs C. and H. Barbot. Newsweek 62:49 Jl 29 '63
Dictatorship in Haiti. H. Herring. Cur Hist 46:34-7+ Ja '64
Eyes on Haiti. Nation 196:277 Ap 6 '63
Final encounter; Cantave's defeat. Newsweek 62:65 O 7 '63
Guessing game; Haitian exiles invasion. Newsweek 62:48 Ag 19 '63
Haiti: alternatives to tyranny. A. Burt. il Nation 200:10-12 Ja 4 '65
Haiti, land of the big tontons. R. Eder. il N Y Times Mag p9+ Ja 24 '65
Haiti; last act of a tragicomedy. B. Rice. Harper 226:65-6+ My '63
Haiti today. F. J. Cook. Nat R 16:312 Ap 21 '64
Haiti: where lid is about to blow. C. Migdail. il U S News 54:65-6 My 6 '63
Haiti's voodoo tyrant. L. Stowe. Read Digest 83:222-6+ N '63
Hell of Haiti. R. Alexander. Nation 196:98-9 F 2 '63
If it's war in Haiti, who'll win? C. Migdail. il U S News 54:44 My 13 '63
Innocence saves no one. New Repub 149:8 Ag 17 '63
Is there any hope for Haiti? T. Armbrister. il Sat Eve Post 236:78-81 Je 15 '63
Island divided. Sr Schol 83:6 S 20 '63
It's hell to live in Haiti with Papa Doc; with report by B. Farrell. il Life 54:28-35 Mr 8 '63
Life sentence; Duvalier's presidency. Time 83:28 Ap 10 '64
Living dead. il Time 82:20-1 Jl 26 '63
Nonintervention: a shield for Papa Doc. G. Sherman. il Reporter 28:27-9 Je 20 '63
Nothing happened. Reporter 28:11 Je 6 '63
Outraged & helpless. il Time 81:40 My 24 '63
Papa & his boy. il Time 81:21 My 31 '63
Papa Doc squirms. New Repub 148:10-11 My 11 '63
Perón of voodooism. New Repub 148:10 Je 1 '63
Republic of terror. Newsweek 61:58 My 6 '63
Tensions on Hispaniola. il Américas 15:44 Je '63
There'll be another Haiti revolt soon, but... il U S News 55:10 Ag 19 '63
Ton-ton alumnus. il Newsweek 61:48-9 Je 3 '63
U.S. pushes drive to oust Haiti's czar. Bsns W p27 My 11 '63
Voodoo terror; with account by J. Barnes. il Newsweek 61:54+ My 13 '63
Warning to a dictator. Time 81:26 My 3 '63
What is called democracy. il Time 83:36 Je 26 '64
Worst of neighbors. il Time 81:39 My 10 '63
See also
Communism—Haiti

Relief work

AID closes mission in Haiti. Dept State Bul 49:297 Ag 19 '63

Religious institutions and affairs

Life in Haiti: voodoo and the church. J. Breda. il Commonweal 78:241-4 My 24 '63
See also
Voodooism

Social conditions

Beautiful, cruel, explosive, Haiti. T. Szulc. il N Y Times Mag p26-7+ Je 9 '63

HAITI and the United States
Dictatorship in Haiti. H. Herring. Cur Hist 46:34-7+ Ja '64

HAITIAN-American meat and provision company
It's magic; Bobby Baker's financial affairs. il Newsweek 62:31 N 25 '63

HAITIAN dancing. See Dancing, Haitian

HAITIAN poetry
Five Haitian poets; with poems. M. A. Lubin. il Américas 17:16-21 Ja '65

HAL Roach studios. See Moving picture studios

HALABY, Najeeb E.
Travel at 1,800 miles an hour? why? when? interview. por U S News 55:52-8 D 23 '63; Same abr. Read Digest 84:88-91 Mr '64

about

Supersonic hot seat. B. Kocivar. il pors Look 28:93-5+ My 5 '64

HALACY, D. S. Jr
Amazing bug battery. Pop Electr 20:41-4+ F '64
Our heartless friends, the robots. Pop Electr 18:39-44+ My '63
Run your radio on solar power. Pop Sci 185:138-9 N '64

HALAS, George Stanley
All the strings. il por Newsweek 63:71 Ja 13 '64
Just like papa played. G. S. Halas of the Chicago Bears. il por Time 82:92 D 6 '63

HALASZ, George
Superstitions of Mr Molnar, and how he got rid of them. Sat R 47:6+ O 24 '64

HALBERSTAM, David
Getting the story in Vietnam. Commentary 39:30-4 Ja '65
Portrait of two soldiers. N Y Times Mag p 11-13 Ja 5 '64
Ugliest American in Vietnam. Esquire 62:114-17+ N '64

about

Our man in Saigon; with introd. by D. Schoenbrun. G J. W. Goodman. il por Esquire 61:57-60+ Ja '64

HALDANE, John Burdon Sanderson
Always a good show. il pors Time 84:81-2 D 11 '64

HALDEMAN, Charles
Independence, honour, and ecstasy, in Crete. Vogue 145:101-2+ Ja 15 '65

HALDEMAN, Robert G. See Langer, S. H. jt. auth.

HALE, Bruce
Miami's picks: Slick and Rick. J. Underwood. il Sports Illus 20:18-19 Ja 20 '64

HALE, Frank W.
Salmon Portland Chase: rhetorician of abolition. bibliog Negro Hist Bul 26:165-8 F '63

HALE, Helene
Hawaii's top woman politician. il pors Ebony 18:51-2+ Ap '63

HALE, Nancy
Colonel Sartoris and Mr Snopes. Vogue 142: 112-13+ Ag 1 '63
Girl with the goat-cart; story. New Yorker 39:55-6 N 30 '63
In a word; story. New Yorker 39:80 Jl 27 '63

HALE, Nathan
Last days and valiant death of Nathan Hale: excerpts from Documentary life of Nathan Hale; ed. by G. D. Seymour. il por Am Heritage 15:50-1 Ap '64

HALE, Nathan Cabot
Reappraisal of anatomical study. Am Artist 29:48-53+ F '65

HALE, Robert Beverly
Line; excerpt from Drawing lessons from the great masters. Am Artist 29:58-63 Ja '65

HALE, Roger Duke
Obituary
Am For por 69:2 Je '63

HALE, William Harlan
Minister's fatal showplace. Horizon 5:76-83 Jl '63

HALES, Stephen
Parson's gift to medicine. por Todays Health 41:66 Ag '63

HALESIA. See Silver-bell trees

HALÉVY, Fromental
La Juive. Criticism
Opera N il 27:29 My 4 '63

HALEY, Alex
In Uncle Tom are our guilt and hope. N Y Times Mag p23+ Mr 1 '64
Man who wouldn't quit. Read Digest 82:54-9 Mr '63

HALEY, George
Man who wouldn't quit. A. Haley. il Read Digest 82:54-9 Mr '63

HALEY, J. Evetts
Fine art of president-baiting. M. Greenfield. Reporter 31:29-33 S 24 '64
Texan looks at a Texan looking at a Texan. J. C. Evans. Christian Cent 81:1296 O 21 '64

HALEY, Sir William John
New thunderer. il por Time 83:48-9 My 8 '64
Onward and upward with the arts: Third programme. V. Mehta. New Yorker 39: 100+ My 18 '63

HALF dollars. See Money—United States

HALF-frame cameras. See Cameras

HALFORD, Russ
What's your average. U S Camera 27:56-7+ Ap '64

HALFTONE process. See Photoengraving

HALIDES
See also
Silver halides

HALIFAX, Nova Scotia
Cruise to the sea. F. Mowat. il Yachting 114:54-6+ Jl '63

HALKA: opera. See Moniuszko, S.

HALL, A. Jim
One plant tomato. Horticulture 41:141+ Mr '63

HALL, Albert C.
Future of military space; excerpts from address. Aviation W 80:17 F 10 '64
Military space program; address, February 5, 1964. Vital Speeches 30:361-5 Ap 1 '64; Excerpts. Aviation W 80:17 F 10 '64

about

Increasing importance of space acknowledged in new DOD post. Aviation W 79:31 Jl 15 '63

HALL, Albert G.
Defender of the forestry profession: editorial. Am For 69:13 S '63
Washington lookout. See issues of American forests

HALL, Ann
Victorian side-saddles. Hobbies 69:54 N '64

HALL, Cecil E.
Electron microscopy: quantitative techniques. Science 145:1467-9 S 25 '64

HALL, Clarence W.
Biggest Fourth of July salute. Read Digest 85:145-6 Jl '64
Country that saved itself. Read Digest 85: 133-58 N '64
Panama: the crisis we could have avoided. Read Digest 84:84-9 Ap '64
Poison in print and how to get rid of it. Read Digest 84:94-8 My '64
Remarkable Kadoorie brothers of Hong Kong. Read Digest 82:273-8 My '63
They discover America. Read Digest 82:81-6 Je '63
Up from the ashes, a great cathedral rises. Read Digest 82:197-200+ Je '63

HALL, David
CRI: a sonic showcase for the American composer. por Library J 88:1826-9 My 1 '63

HALL, Dick
Invisible man on the mound. R. Creamer. por Sports Illus 18:41-2 Je 24 '63

HALL, Donald
Christmas snow; story. New Yorker 40:30-6 D 26 '64
Jealous lovers; poem. New Yorker 39:52 Mr 16 '63
Stump; Wells; Assassin; Internal and external forms; Grave, the mine; poems. Poetry 104:93-8 My '64

HALL, Edward T.
Social standing; new science of proxemics. Newsweek 61:84 Ap 22 '63

HALL, Elizabeth C.
Books. Pop Gard 15:44+ N '64
Books for Christmas giving. Pop Gard 14: 50+ N '63

HALL, Floyd D.
Eastern's new pilot. por Newsweek 62:79+ D 2 '63
New breed in transportation. G. R. Rosen. por Duns R 83:pt2 100-2+ Je '64
TWA's Hall selected to succeed MacIntyre as Eastern's president. Aviation W 79:37-8 N 25 '63

HALL, Frances
Day of discovery; poem. America 111:559 N 7 '64
Deep summer; poem. America 111:44 Jl 11 '64
Perception of autumn; poem. America 111: 255 S 12 '64
Sound the trumpets; poem. America 110:140 Ja 25 '64

HALL, Francis D.
Pitfalls of intentional community. Christian Cent 80:1000-2 Ag 14 '63

HALL, Gus
Gus Hall and the Pope. America 109:550+ N 9 '63
Inviting Communists to speak at colleges: address, 1962. W. F. Buckley, jr il Nat R 15: 343-5+ O 22 '63
Pacem in terris, Ecclesiam Suam and communism. C. Wallace. Cath World 200:231-8 Ja '65
When a Communist has talked about it (cont) H. Overstreet and B. W. Overstreet. il PTA Mag 57:12-14 F; 10-12 Mr '63

HALL, H. Tracy, and others
High pressure polymorphism in cesium. bibliog Science 146:1297-9 D 4 '64
HALL, J. Curtis
Further study in economics. NEA J 52:28-9 O '63
HALL, Jack
Learn to swim in twenty min. il pors Ebony 18:93-4+ Ap '63
HALL, Jack (labor leader)
Aloha a la sinistra. L. V. Cott. il Nat R 15:57-8 Jl 30 '63
Hawaii's unions get mainland look. il por Bsns W p86+ S 7 '63
HALL, James B.
Poetry chronicle. Poetry 104:47-52 Ap '64
HALL, Jane
Craftsmen of the southeastern states. Craft Horiz 23:38-9+ N '63
HALL, Jean
Why Negro history week. Negro Hist Bul 27:155 Mr '64
HALL, Joyce C.
Greetings. New Yorker 40:26-7 Je 20 '64
HALL, Lee
Britain: a rousing election hush. Life 57:40-40B O 9 '64
Captain Gillespie goes out after the Vietcong. Life 57:32-5 N 27 '64
Man who, with all his mind and heart, loved India. Life 56:32-42B Je 5 '64
We will build a wall of dedicated men. Life 54:33-4 Mr 29 '63
—and Chelminski, Rudolph
Perilous route dug by a tough platoon of moles. Life 57:60A-60B O 16 '64
HALL, Margaret
Cherries of Sir Cleges; dramatization of an Old English tale. Plays 24:73-6 D '64
Reggie the ghost; drama. Plays 24:65-8, 82 O '64
HALL, Mary Harrington
Maria Mayer: the Marie Curie of the atom. McCalls 91:38+ Jl '64
HALL, Maybelle
Children for rent by the hour. McCalls 90:90-1+ Ag '63
HALL, Mazie
Language shop; drama. Plays 24:49-54 Ja '65
HALL, Norman
Photokina story. U S Camera 27:16-17+ N '64
HALL, Paul
Labor's mutinous mariners. A. H. Raskin. por Atlan 214:72-8 N '64
HALL, Peter
Avoiding a method. por Theatre Arts 47:24-5 Ag '63
Living figures. por Opera N 29:6-9 N 14 '64
Play that never was. il Time 82:37 Ag 2 '63
HALL, Prince
Pioneers in protest. L. Bennett, jr. il pors Ebony 19:88-9+ Ap '64
HALL, R. C.
Pisgah Forest in 1912. Am For 70:34-7+ S '64
HALL, Robert C.
Occupational plans of student borrowers under NDEA. Sch Life 45:26-9 Ja '63
HALL, Robert E.
Book on birth control. Parents Mag 38:38 S '63
Church and the pill. Nation 199:191-3 O 5 '64
HALL, Stephen King-. See King-Hall, S.
HALL, Tim
Upon realization of the poet's duty: poem. Atlan 212:59 S '63
HALL, W. S, and company
W. S. Hall & co. to merge with Feffer and Simons. Pub W 184:33-4 D 30 '63
HALL, William P.
Franchising, new scope for an old technique. Harvard Bsns R 42:60-72 Ja '64
HALL, Willis. See Waterhouse, K. jt. auth.
HALL effect
Hall effect. J. R. Collins. il Electr World 69:39-42+ Ap '63
HALL marks
Just what is a hallmark? Good H 157:167 O '63
HALL-Mills murder case. See Murder
HALL of fame, Baseball. See National baseball hall of fame and museum
HALL of fame, Conservation. See North American conservation hall of fame and museum
HALL of fame, Football. See Football players
HALL of fame for great Americans. See New York university—Hall of fame for great Americans
HALL of North American birds. See American museum of natural history, New York
HALL of science. See New York (city)—Worlds fair, 1964—Hall of science
HALLAM, Florence
Old Abe, Wisconsin's Civil war eagle, was there. Audubon Mag 65:222-5 Jl '63
HALLDEN, Naomi A. and others
Radium-226 in human diet and bone. bibliog Science 140:1327-9 Je 21 '63
HALLE, Louis J.
Any number can play nuclear chicken. N Y Times Mag p33+ N 8 '64
Appraisal of Kennedy as world leader. N Y Times Mag p7+ Je 16 '63
Armies of ignorance. New Repub 149:16-17 D 7 '63
Cracked alliance. New Repub 148:17-20 F 23 '63
De Gaulle by twilight. New Repub 148:10-14 F 9 '63
De Gaulle's non! a year later. N Y Times Mag p 14-15+ Ja 12 '64
He may be right about China but wrong about Europe. New Repub 150:16-18 F 22 '64
Kennan and the great debate. New Repub 150:25-8 My 16 '64
Martyrdom by diplomacy. New Repub 151:17-18 O 24 '64
On choosing our future. New Repub 149:14-17 Ag 31 '63
Peace in our time? New Repub 149:16-19 D 28 '63
Reconsidering our foreign policy. New Repub 148:13-15 Mr 23 '63
Rostow: the intellectual Fortinbras. New Repub 151:21-3 Jl 25 '64
Walk through Warsaw. New Repub 151:15-18 O 3 '64
Walter Lippmann: the philosopher as journalist. New Repub 149:17-20 Ag 3 '63
What's eating us? New Repub 151:17-20 S 19 '64
Why de Gaulle cannot win. N Y Times Mag p9+ Je 2 '63
World: a sense of history. New Repub 151:92-5+ N 7 '64
World challenge to Mr Johnson. N Y Times Mag p 17+ Ap 5 '64
Wrangle over strategy. New Repub 150:19-21 Ja 18 '64
HALLECK, Charles A.
Caught in crossfire; Halleck on civil rights. por U S News 55:24 N 11 '63
Fighting 89th. por Newsweek 65:18-19 Ja 18 '65
Republican feud spreads to Congress. por U S News 57:33 D 28 '64
Same program, new sponsors: the return of Ev and Charlie. por U S News 54:25 Mr 11 '63
HALLENBURG, J. K.
Man-made aquifer taps a stream. Am City 79:161-2+ Je '64
HALLER, Anthony, family
Hallers make a house come alive! E. Gilrain. il pors Bet Hom & Gard 41:48-51 My '63
HALLER, George L.
Information revolution. por Sci Digest 55:69-73 My '64
HALLER, John M
Beware! the woods are full of tree quacks. Pop Sci 184:127-9+ My '64
HALLIBURTON, John
Unexpected. Outdoor Life 134:64-6+ O '64
HALLIDAY, Brett, pseud. See Dresser, D.
HALLIDAY, E. M.
Curses, foiled again! Am Heritage 15:12-23 D '63
Man on horseback. Am Heritage 15:10-23 Ag '64
Nature's God and the founding fathers. Am Heritage 14:4-7+ O '63
HALLIDAY, Patrick
Audio trends in Britain. Electr World 70:64+ D '63
European color-TV developments. Electr World 70:66-7 Jl '63
How Britain tracks TV pirates. Electr World 69:68 Je '63
Tubes clue to air crashes. Electr World 71:83 Ja '64
HALLIDAY, William R.
Cave of the Crystal Balls. il Nat Parks Mag 39:13 Ja '65
Features and significance of the Mount Saint Helens cave area. il Nat Parks Mag 37:11-14 D '63
HALLIGAN, John T.
Attempt at censorship. Library J 88:4002-3 O 15 '63
HALLIWELL, Dean W.
Shall we have another? Library J 89:2957-60 Ag '64
HALLMARK cards, incorporated
Greetings. New Yorker 40:26-7 Je 20 '64
Hallmark story. D. Powills. il Hobbies 69:118-19 Jl '64

HALLMARK employment agency. See Employment agencies
HALLMARKS. See Hall marks
HALLORAN, Claire
Six poems. Sat R 46:27 S 21 '63
HALLORAN, Terrence W.
Prayer for these times. America 109:161 Ag 17 '63
HALLOWEEN
Halloween dioramas. J. Fox. il Sch Arts 63:21-3 O '63
Halloween tricks. K. Murray. il Pop Sci 185:173 O '64
Hello Halloween! M. J. Engel. il Ladies Home J 80:80-2 O '63
Tips for trick'r treat night. Bet Hom & Gard 42:141 O '64
Turning Halloween into a hallowed evening. Christian Cent 80:1261 O 16 '63
See also
Ghost stories—Single works

Drama

Hometown Halloween. M. Hark and N. McQueen. Plays 23:31-41 O '63
Something new for Halloween. D. Newman. Plays 23:73-7 O '63

Poetry

Halloween hoodlums: go home! O. Nash. il Ladies Home J 81:66-7 O '64
HALLOWEEN cookery. See Cookery, Ornamental
HALLOWEEN costumes. See Costume
HALLOWEEN masks. See Masks (for the face)
HALLOWEEN parties. See Entertaining
HALLOWEEN suppers. See Suppers
HALLOWELL, Sally R.
Annunciation; poem. America 110:363 Mr 21 '64
HALLOYSITE
Infrared study of selective deuteration of kaolinite and halloysite at room temperature. R. L. Ledoux and J. L. White. bibliog il Science 145:47-9 Jl 3 '64
HALLS
Entrancing entrances. il McCalls 91:62-9 Ja '64
Festive garnish for hall and buffet. il House & Gard 124:130-1 D '63
Here's a lesson in hallways. il Sunset 130: 140 Mr '63
How to make a narrow hallway interesting. il Sunset 132:110-12 Mr '64
HALLSTEIN, Walter
European economic community; address, March 2, 1963. Vital Speeches 29:364-9 Ap 1 '63
HALLSTROM, Sir Edward John Lees
Me white kangaroo. il por Life 54:49-52+ Ap 26 '63
HALLUCINATIONS. See Illusions and hallucinations
HALLUCINOGENIC drugs
Getting alienated with the right crowd at Harvard. M. Mayer. Esquire 60:73+ S '63; Reply with rejoinder. R. Alpert and T. Leary. 61:42+ Je '64
Hallucinogenic drug cult. N. Gordon. il Reporter 29:35-43 Ag 15 '63; Discussion. 29:6+ S 12; 8 S 26 '63
Hallucinogenic drugs. F. Barron and others. il Sci Am 210:29-37 bibliog(p 156) Ap '64
Instant mysticism. il Time 82:86-7 O 25 '63
LSD and all that. il Time 81:72+ Mr 29 '63
No illusions; psilocybin tests at Harvard. il Newsweek 61:92-3 Je 10 '63
Strange case of the Harvard drug scandal. A. T. Weil. il Look 27:38+ N 5 '63
Who will run your nervous system? A. Watts. New Repub 151:15-16 N 28 '64
Your guide to mind drugs. R. Mines. il Sci Digest 55:67-9 Ja '64
See also
Lysergic acid diethylamide
HALOGENS
Bonding in xenon fluorides and halogen fluorides. K. S. Pitzer. bibliog il Science 139: 414-15 F 1 '63
HALOS (meteorology)
Unusual lunar halo photograph. il Sky & Tel 27:335 Je '64
HALOTHANE
Gas & the liver. il Time 81:49-50 Mr 22 '63
Halothane's hazards. Newsweek 62:76 Jl 15 '63
Impurity in halothane anesthetic. E. N. Cohen and others. bibliog il Science 141: 899 S 6 '63; Reply. W. A. Sexton and W. G. Hendrickson. 142:621-2 N 8 '63
HALPER, John B.
Mail industry fights back. America 108:260-1 F 23 '63
HALPER, Sam
U.S.-backed reform flops as Bosch gets the bounce. Life 55:49-50 O 18 '63
HALPERIN, David
Witches' brew; excerpt. Sr Schol 82:14-15+ My 15 '63
HALPERIN, Irving
Postscript to death. Commonweal 79:713-15 Mr 13 '64
HALPERIN, Morton H.
Bomarc for Canada. New Repub 148:6-7 Mr '63
HALPERIN, Walter
Morphogenetic studies with partially synchronized cultures of carrot embryos. bibliog Science 146:408-10 O 16 '64
HALPERN, A. M.
Emergence of an Asian Communist coalition. bibliog f Ann Am Acad 349:117-29 S '63
HALPERN, Ben
From prejudice to genocide. Commentary 38: 84-7 O '64
HALPERN, Harry
Excerpt from testimony, May 27, 1964. Cong Digest 43:281+ N '64
HALPERN, Jack
South Africa: enclaves of trouble. Nation 197:49-52 Jl 27 '63
HALPERN, Seymour
Excerpt from address, January 9, 1963. Cong Digest 43:20-1 Ja '64
HALPERT, Edith Gregor
Mme Don Ton. por Time 84:82 N 27 '64
HALPIN, James H. See Rice, N. S. jt. auth.
HALPRIN, Ann
It's all the fault of Christopher Columbus! por Dance Mag 37:38-9+ Ag '63
Manifold implications. J. Anderson. il pors Dance Mag 37:44-7 Ap '63
HALSBAND, Robert
A. L. Rowse: a study in versatility. Sat R 47:57 Ja 11 '64
First word. Sat R 46:52-3 Mr 23 '63
HALSEY, Hugh
What to do about morning sickness. Redbook 124:24+ D '64
HALSMAN, Philippe
World of elegant women. il McCalls 91:94-9 O '63

about

Human document. M. R. Weiss. il Sat R 47: 100-2 O 10 '64
On being photographed by Philippe Halsman. B. Downes. Pop Phot 56:22+ Ja '65
HALSTEAD, Ward C.
What is your brain power? H. Earle. il Todays Health 41:50-5 O '63
HALVERSON, Rolf. See Castagna, E. jt. auth.
HALVERSTADT, Hal
American jewelry, 1963. Craft Horiz 23:23-34+ Mr '63
HAM, Mary Louise
Christmas in October? Horticulture 42:18-19 O '64
HAM, Norman D.
Helicopter, where now? Flying 74:32+ F '64
HAM, Richard G.
Albumin replacement by fatty acids in clonal growth of mammalian cells. bibliog Science 140:802-3 My 17 '63
HAM
Simplifying the terminology about hams. House B 106:58 My '64
See also
Cookery—Meat
HAM radio stations. See Radio stations, Amateur
HAM television stations. See Television stations, Amateur
HAMADA, Shōji
Hamada, a Japanese folk potter. il pors Am Artist 28:50-1 F '64
HAMAKER, John W. and others
Picolinic acid derivative: a plant growth regulator. Science 141:363 Jl 26 '63
HAMALIAN, Leo
Baghdad between revolutions. Nation 199: 423-5 D 7 '64
—See LeCompte, G. jt. auth.
HAMAMELIS virginiana. See Witch hazel
HAMBLEN, Donald N.
Things just take a little more effort. por Look 28:40 My 5 '64
Toughest marine. C. S. Wren. il pors Look 28:36-40 My 5 '64
HAMBLETONIAN race. See Harness racing
HAMBLIN, Dora Jane
Big mouth+massive wit+soul of a daffodil=Zero. Life 57:108+ D 4 '64
Carlo and Sophia. Life 57:80-9 S 18 '64
Case of the talking trunk. Life 57:86A-86B+ N 27 '64
Comic catapults to higher stage. Life 56: 100-2+ Mr 20 '64

HAMBLIN, Dora Jane—*Continued*
Gangway for Goulet. Life 54:86-8+ Ap 26 '63
Go on, frighten us to death, we love it! Life 55:40 Ag 30 '63
Hardly anybody knows him. Life 57:133-4+ O 16 '64
History's biggest literary whodunit. Life 56: 69-70+ Ap 24 '64; Same with title Who wrote Shakespeare? Read Digeest 85:95-9 Jl '64
In nineteen lands instant America. il Life 55:67-8+ Ag 30 '63
Life movie review. Life 58:10 Ja 22 '65
Lucrative paradise for grave robbers. Life 57:118-20+ N 20 '64
Mark (ye) (the) Twain. Life 57:13 Jl 10 '64
Mrs Kennedy's decisions shaped all the solemn pageantry. Life 55:48-9 D 6 '63
Problems and pavilions. Life 56:50+ Ja 17 '64
Those mad, merry vicars of England. Life 58:76-8+ Ja 29 '65
—and Jarvis, Wilbur
Girl behind a frozen scream. Life 54:68B-73+ Ap 12 '63
HAMBRECHT, Margaret
Second sight; poem. Mlle 59:204 S '64
Winter living; poem. Mlle 58:72 D '63
HAMBROS bank, limited. See London—Banks
HAMBURG
Reform along the Raper. il Time 83:42-3 Je 12 '64

Description

Editor's report: Deutschland duo. M. M. Davis. il(p54) Travel 122:61-2 S '64
Hamburg: more rather James Bond adventures. I. Fleming. Vogue 141:98-9+ Je '63
Letter from Hamburg. D. Richie. Nation 197: 96-8 Ag 24 '63

Music

Great opera houses: Hamburg. H. Koegler. il Opera N 28:26-8 D 14 '63
[Musical events] (cont) Mus Am 83:14-15 Je '63; 84:24 Ja; 26 S '64
Notes from abroad (cont) K. Blaukopf. Hi Fi 13:24+ Ag; 26+ S '63
Visiting fireman; interview, ed. by J. W. Freeman. R. Lieberman. il Opera N 27:14 Ap 13 '63

Theater

Goethe go home. il Time 83:56 Ja 3 '64
HAMBURG-American line
Coal for the fleet that had to die. L. J. R. Cecil. bibliog f Am Hist R 69:990-1005 Jl '64
HAMBURG state opera. See Opera houses
HAMBURGER, Michael
In the convention. W. Dickey. Poetry 104:377-8 S '64
HAMBURGER, Philip
Notes for a gazetteer. See occasional issues of New Yorker
Progress report. New Yorker 39:38-40 Mr 30 '63
HAMBURGER, Viktor
Embryology. Science 142:1367 D 6 '63
HAMBURGERS. See Cookery—Meat
HAMER, Elizabeth E.
Everybody's library. por Library J 90:49-55 Ja 1 '65
Washington report: from the Library of Congress. ALA Bul 57:499-500, 638-9, 825-6 Je-Jl, O '63
LC creates assistant librarian's post. Library J 88:753 F 15 '63
—and McCormick, Adoreen
Washington report: from the Library of Congress. ALA Bul 57:1017-19; 58:24-5, 97-8, 184-6, 356-8, 464-6, 602-4, 682-4, 773-4, 988; 59:23 D '63-Mr, My-O, D '64-Ja '65
HAMER, Fannie Lou
Tired of being sick and tired. J. DeMuth. por Nation 198:548-51 Je 1 '64
HAMER, Martin J.
One, two, three, O'Leary; story. Atlan 211: 72-5 Ap '63
Sarah; story. Atlan 213:52-6 Ja '64
HAMERMAN, David. See Sandson, J. jt. auth.
HAMILL, Harold L.
Recent developments in library service to students; excerpts from address, March 1964. ALA Bul 58:489-96 Je '64
HAMILL, Katharine
Squeeze on shopping centers. Fortune 68: 116-18+ S '63
Supercolossal, well, pretty good, world of Joe Levine. Fortune 69:130-2 Mr '64
HAMILL, Pete
But they make marriage contracts with girls who wear contacts. N Y Times Mag p59-60+ D 6 '64
Crazy way to fly. Sat Eve Post 237:62-3+ F 8 '64
Day in the life of a pediatrician. Sat Eve Post 237:69-73 D 19 '64
Doctors go on strike. Sat Eve Post 237:79-83 My 16 '64
Explosion in the movie underground. Sat Eve Post 236:82+ S 28 '63
First, I am a woman. Sat Eve Post 237: 60-3 F 15 '64
Floyd's fight to save his pride. Sat Eve Post 237:76-8 Je 27 '64
Good-bye Brooklyn, hello fame. Sat Eve Post 236:22-3 Jl 27 '63
Great British train robbery. Sat Eve Post 237:30-2+ S 19 '64; Same abr. with title Britain's great train robbery. Read Digest 85:134-9 D '64
Jean Seberg. Sat Eve Post 236:22-3 Je 15 '63
Lord Jim. Sat Eve Post 237:24-9 N 21 '64
My fair Julie. Sat Eve Post 236:68-9 D 21 '63
Politics is my life. Sat Eve Post 237:82-5 O 10 '64
Square world of Claudia Cardinale. Sat Eve Post 237:62-3 F 29 '64
Stardom and boredom of Catherine Spaak. Sat Eve Post 237:58-60 My 2 '64
When the client is a candidate. N Y Times Mag p30-1+ O 25 '64
—and Lee, Frank
Last voyage of the Lakonia. Sat Eve Post 237:72-5 F 1 '64
HAMILTON, Alexander
Alexander Hamilton and the Constitution, by C. Rossiter. Review
Nat R por 16:407-8 My 19 '64. V. Miller; Correction. 16:552 Je 30 '64
Number 7: Alexander Hamilton's secret attempts to control American foreign policy, by J. Boyd. Review
Sat R por 47:22-3 N 28 '64. E. Wright
Time por 84:95+ D 18 '64
Perspective on the founders. V. Miller. por Nat R 14:117-19 F 12 '63
HAMILTON, Andrew
California's old man of the mountains. Read Digest 83:168C+ O '63
Cannon's successor. New Repub 150:5 My 23 '64
Computer that helps rebuild lives. Sci Digest 56:19-23 S '64
Do you need eight hours sleep? Sci Digest 56:24-7 Jl '64
If you were a midget. Sci Digest 55:30-4 Ja '64
I'm going to kill myself. Sci Digest 54:57-63 S '63
Is team teaching for your child? PTA Mag 58:4-6 My '64; Same abr. with title Team teaching; how good is it? Read Digest 84: 169+ My '64
Mad, mad, mad, mad physicist. PTA Mag 59:12-14+ Ja '65; Same abr. with title Professor Miller's mighty magic. Read Digest 86:155-8+ Ja '65
Mystery of the biological clocks. Sci Digest 56:21-6 O '64
Negro: how he's different. Sci Digest 54: 6-11 O '63
New science of driving. Sci Digest 55:86-90 F '64
775,000 volts with bare hands. Sci Digest 55: 35-8 Ja '64
Sharks: sense and nonsense. Sci Digest 54: 53-6 Jl '63
Your portrait by the police. Sci Digest 55: 31-4 Mr '64
HAMILTON, Charles
Fat boy of England. D. W. Brogan. il Harper 226:80-1 Ap '63
HAMILTON, Daniel S.
Neither a wall nor a sieve. Christian Cent 81:308+ Mr 4 '64
HAMILTON, Dwight L.
Hawaii's trees of stone. Nat Parks Mag 38:15-17 Ja '64
HAMILTON, Edith
(tr) See Euripides. Trojan women

about

Heritage of Edith Hamilton: 1867-1963. J. M. Brown. il por Sat R 46:16-17 Je 22 '63
Obituary
Pub W 183:125 Je 10 '63
HAMILTON, Edna
Seventh spring, remembering; poem. McCalls 90:136 Ap '63
HAMILTON, Ernest R.
It looks like a school. Am City 79:98-100 O '64
HAMILTON, George Heard
Holiday for fine arts. Sat R 46:45-6+ D 7 '63

HAMILTON, George Heard—*Continued*
Holiday package of paintings in print. Sat R 47:56-62 D 5 '64
Line on the illogical. Sat R 47:32-3 Ap 25 '64

HAMILTON, Harry
Washington front. America 111:508 O 31 '64

HAMILTON, Horace
Before dawn; poem. New Yorker 39:62 N 30 '63
Epigone; poem. Sat R 47:31 O 10 '64

HAMILTON, L. D.
Fallout and countermeasures. Bul Atomic Sci 19:36-40 S '63

HAMILTON, Lawrence S.
Ecological perspective on urban sprawl. Am For 69:38-40+ Je '63

HAMILTON, Lee D.
City under the ice cap. Am City 78:100-2 Jl '63

HAMILTON, Randy H.
First Asian metro plan conference. Am City 79:118 N '64

HAMILTON, T. Stewart
Modern medicine requires qualified nurses; excerpt from address. por Todays Health 41:76 Ag '63

HAMILTON, Terrell H. and others
Species abundance: natural regulation of insular variation. bibliog Science 142:1575-7; 146:1075 D 20 '63, N 20 '64

HAMILTON, Thomas Hale
Citizen views the legislature; address, August 21, 1963. Vital Speeches 30:26-8 O 15 '63

HAMILTON, W. F. and others
Atmospheric iodine abates smog ozone. Science 140:190-1 Ap 12 '63

HAMILTON, Wallace
Burning. Criticism
New Yorker 39:80 D 14 '63

HAMILTON, Walter C. and others
Geometry of the perxenate ion. bibliog Science 141:532-4 Ag 9 '63

HAMILTON, Warren
Origin of high-alumina basalt, andesite, and dacite magmas. bibliog Science 146:635-7 O 30 '64

HAMILTON, William
Coming home from Birmingham. Christian Cent 80:1302-3 O 23 '63
There is no God and Jesus is his son. Christian Cent 80:1208 O 2 '63

HAMILTON, William J. Jr
Success story of the opossum. Natur Hist 72: 16-25 F '63

HAMILTON standard division. See United aircraft corporation—Hamilton standard division

HAMILTON-TEMPLE-BLACKWOOD, Sheridan Frederick Terence, 5th marquess of Dufferin and Ava. See Dufferin and Ava, S. F. T. H.-T.-B.

HAMILTON Wright organization, incorporated
Something newsy; investigation of Hamilton Wright organization by Senate foreign relations committee. il Newsweek 62:27-8 Jl 22 '63

HAMLET (literary character) See Shakespeare, W.—Characters

HAMLET; drama. See Shakespeare, W.—Plays

HAMLIN, Arthur T.
Robert G. Vosper, ALA president-elect. ALA Bul 58:698-701 S '64

HAMLIN, G. Homer
More than just a marina. Am City 79:82-4 Ja '64

HAMLIN, William O.
Substituting silicon for germanium transistors. Electr World 72:39-41+ D '64

HAMLYN, Paul
One of a new breed: Paul Hamlyn of London. P. Rosenwald. il por Pub W 183:41-5 F 4 '63

HAMMARLUND, Roger T.
Dynamic distortions by A. Kane. U S Camera 26:49-55+ Ap '63
Meters for available darkness. U S Camera 26:66-9 F '63
New product report. U S Camera 27:94 Ap '64
Technical report; XR film. U S Camera 26: 45-8 My '63

HAMMARSKJÖLD, Dag
Clues to the Hammarskjold riddle; excerpts from Markings, ed. by O. Clausen. pors N Y Times Mag p 10+ Je 28 '64
Markings; excerpts, tr. by L. Sjöberg and W. H. Auden. Vogue 144:192-3 O 1 '64
Poems from Markings; tr. by L. Sjöberg and W. H. Auden. Harper 229:104 S '64

about

Books. B. Urquhart. New Yorker 40:232-4+ O 31 '64
Congo: a calculated confusion. J. Stolle. Nation 196:252-4 Mr 23 '63
Final negotiations. por Newsweek 64:112-112A O 19 '64
God's plenipotentiary. Newsweek 62:51-2 N 4 '63
Hammarskjöld and holiness; with excerpts from Markings. H. P. Van Dusen. Christian Cent 81:1596-7 D 23 '64
Hammarskjold: the last haiku. C. Anderson. New Repub 151:23-4 N 14 '64
In abstract memoriam; United Nations memorial. il Time 83:68 Je 19 '64
Invisible man. por Time 84:110 O 23 '64
Letdown at the UN. J. Kraft. Harper 230: 84+ Ja '65
Looking ahead; address, January 7, 1964. Thant. Vital Speeches 30:226-9 F 1 '64; Same. U N Rev 11:9-11+ F '64
New Secretary-General. H. J. Morgenthau. Commentary 35:62-5 Ja '63
Secret life of Dag Hammarskjöld. J. Lindberg. il pors Look 28:66-8+ Je 30 '64

HAMMARSKJÖLD, Dag, memorial grove. See Dag Hammarskjöld memorial grove (proposed)

HAMMELIS. See Witch hazel

HAMMER, Armand
By the forelock. il por Newsweek 64:91 O 12 '64
Venture capital from inside the stock family. por Bsns W p66+ Mr 23 '63

HAMMER, Darrell P.
Tattered banners of Soviet ideology. New Repub 150:13-14 Mr 14 '64

HAMMER, Richard
Report from a Spanish Harlem fortress. N Y Times Mag p22+ Ja 5 '64

HAMMER, Sid
New intaglio technique. il por Am Artist 27: 34-9+ F '63

HAMMERS
Things you never knew about hammers. il Pop Sci 184:152+ Ja '64

HAMMERSTEIN, Oscar, 1895-1960
Oscar Hammerstein; a healing sort of guy. R. Crouse. por Read Digest 84:80-6 Ja '64

HAMMOND, Albert
Intolerable squeeze. Sports Illus 18:34-6+ My 6 '63

HAMMOND, Charles R.
He's got the whole world in his hands; collecting chemical elements. A. P. Armagnac. il Pop Sci 182:82-4 Je '63

HAMMOND, George S.
Organic photochemistry. Science 145:1469-71 S 25 '64
—and Turro, N. J.
Organic photochemistry. bibliog Science 142: 1541-53 D 20 '63

HAMMOND, Jay S.
Menace to American hunting? por Outdoor Life 131:34-5+ My '63

HAMMOND, Mac
In memory of V. R. Lang; poem. Poetry 104: 221 Jl '64

HAMMOND, P. R.
1,4-benzoquinone tetracarboxylic acid dianhydride, $C_{10}O_8$; a strong acceptor. bibliog Science 142:502 O 25 '63

HAMMOND, Philip C.
Rose-red city of Petra. Natur Hist 73:14-25 F '64

HAMNER, K. C. See Hoskizaki, T. jt. auth.

HAMNER, W. G.
Brackish water becomes fresh. Am City 78: 115-16 Mr '63

HAMNER, William M.
Diurnal rhythm and photoperiodism in testicular recrudescence of the house finch. bibliog Science 142:1294-5 D 6 '63

HAMPCO. See Haitian-American meat and provision company

HAMPDEN, Walter, memorial library. See Walter Hampden memorial library

HAMPSTEAD, England
Rural England, right in London. il Sunset 131:17 O '63

HAMPTON, P. M.
Intricate Hardy-Cross mazes bow to a computer. Am City 79:107-8 S '64

HAMS (radio) See Radio operators, Amateur

HAMSTERS
Generalized Shwartzman reaction in the pregnant golden hamster. M. Galton. bibliog il Science 139:923-4 Mr 8 '63

HANAWALT, Philip, and Wax, Richard
Transcription of a repressed gene: evidence that it requires DNA replication. bibliog Science 145:1061-3 S 4 '64

HANAYAGI, Suzushi
Suzushi Hanayagi at Fashion institute. M. Marks. Dance Mag 37:60 Je '63

HANBACK, Jacqueline
Clay modeled birds. Sch Arts 64:33 S '64

HANCOCK, John
John Hancock's copy of "New England judged". P. W. Schmidtchen. il por Hobbies 68:106+ Jl '63
HANCOCK park, Los Angeles. See Los Angeles—Parks and playgrounds
HAND, Jackson
Antique cobbler's bench. Pop Mech 120:162-4 Jl '63
Big idea: horseshoe shaped shop for saving steps. por Pop Sci 183:117-18 S '63
Do lawn sweepers earn their keep? Pop Sci 184:142-4+ My '64
Good ideas for your outdoor living room. Pop Sci 185:110-14 Jl '64
House paints. por Pop Sci 185:126-9 S '64
Interior paints. Pop Sci 186:160-2 Ja '65
Invisible darkroom. Pop Sci 184:152-3+ F '64
Natural exterior finishes. Pop Sci 185:158-9+ O '64
New plastic-mending cements. Pop Sci 182: 169-71 My '63
New seesaw Shopsmith speeds tool changing. Pop Sci 183:114-17+ N '63
Now you can afford a wall-hung toilet. Pop Sci 185:120-2 S '64
Snow at the turn of a switch. Pop Sci 182: 98-101+ Mr '63
Snow melters: say good-bye to shoveling? Pop Sci 184:120-1+ F '64
Solid repairs to keep a stoop in step. Pop Sci 185:142-3+ Ag '64
Storm and screen combinations. Pop Mech 120:134-7+ O '63
Those speed-work stapling tools. Pop Sci 184:138-41 Je '64
Twenty-five tips on shopping for lawn mowers. Pop Mech 119:74-7 My '63
Twenty tips for snowblower buyers. Pop Mech 120:96-100 D '63
Wall-to-wall illumination. Pop Sci 184:150-2 Ap '64
When a single-lever faucet drips. Pop Mech 119:136-8 My '63
Yard cart you can push or tow. Pop Sci 183: 94-7+ Jl '63
HAND, Lloyd Nelson
New protocol chief: one time Texas student leader. por U S News 58:15 Ja 11 '65
HAND
Laborers warned: take care of hands. Sci N L 83:104 F 16 '63
Pretty hands, pretty feet. L. D. Kirk. il Parents Mag 38:38 O '63
Show of hands. R. Condon. il Holiday 36:12+ S '64
Show of hands; detection of disease. il Time 83:84 Mr 13 '64
See also
Fingers
Palmistry
Surgery
Applause for China; restoration of a severed human hand. il Time 82:48 N 8 '63
HAND bags. See Handbags
HAND care. See Hand
HAND kissing. See Kissing
HAND luggage. See Luggage
HAND puppets. See Puppets and puppet plays
HAND tools. See Tools
HAND weaving. See Weaving
HANDBAGS
Need a good handbag? check this first. Good H 157:165 N '63
HANDBOOKS
See also
Libraries—Handbooks, manuals, etc.
HANDEDNESS. See Left- and right-handedness
HÄNDEL, Georg Friedrich
Choral music of George Frideric Handel. J. W. Barker. Am Rec G 31:24-5+ S '64
G. F. Handel's Rodelinda. J. Maclain. il Am Rec G 31:404-7 Ja '65
Handel's Rodelinda, Giulio Cesare, and some arias too. C. L. Osborne. il Hi Fi 14:90-2+ N '64
Handel's Water music, newly, and handsomely, afloat. A. Rich. il Hi Fi 14:67-8 Ag '64
Maurice Abravanel conducts the first recording of Handel's oratorio: Samson. J. W. Barker. il Am Rec G 30:396-9 Ja '64
Music to my ears: Foss Messiah given in the Mozart instrumentation. I. Kolodin. Sat R 48:63 Ja 9 '65
On records; Giulio Cesare. Opera N 29:34 Ja 2 '65
On records; Samson. Opera N 29:35 D 26 '64
Samson from Handel. E. Salzman. il Hi Fi 14:65-6 Ja '64
Saul. J. W. Barker. il Am Rec G 29:844-6+ Jl '63
HANDEL and Haydn society
Hooray for the Lord! 150th anniversary. il Time 85:46 Ja 1 '65
HANDELMAN, Philip
Sea-going dragnet. Yachting 114:130 D '63
HANDGUNS. See Pistols
HANDICAPPED
Prevalence of disabilities in the work force. D. K. Lewis. il Mo Labor R 87:1002-8 S '64
Stubborn man; stubborn car. J. Star. il Look 27:21-7 S 24 '63
Worker absence due to illness. il Mo Labor R 87:1181-3 O '64
See also
Blind
Libraries—Work with the handicapped
Mentally handicapped
Recreation for the handicapped
Apparatus and appliances
Aids for quads and respos. G. Laurie. bibliog f il ALA Bul 58:785-9 O '64
Computerized eating; arm-aid for the paralyzed. il Newsweek 64:104 S 21 '64
Education
They go to college in wheel chairs; University of Illinois' unique Rehabilitation-education division. G. E. Maxwell. il Todays Health 42:26-9+ Jl '64
What fun it is to garden; Edison school Arlington County, Va. F. Colbert. il Pop Gard 14:57+ S '63
Employment
See Vocational rehabilitation
Rehabilitation
See Rehabilitation
HANDICRAFT
Arts & crafts corner. il Recreation 56:138, 176-7, 487; 57:75, 199, 424 Mr-Ap, D '63, F, Ap, O '64
Elder craftsmen shop. M. Lyon. il Craft Horiz 24:22+ N '64
How to get carried away in great style. il Am Home 67:48-9+ My '64
It's good to finish something! ed. by M. Longwell. D. Warnick. il Farm J 87:47 Ag '63
Projects a man can do for his flower arranger. il Bet Hom & Gard 42:100-1 Mr '64
Smart, personal, and rewarding gifts from the darkroom. J. Von Miklos. il Pop Phot 51:72-5+ D '62
See also
Arts and crafts
Paper work
Shellwork
HANDICRAFT in schools
See also
Weaving
HANDLER, Milton, and Robinson, S. D.
Supreme court vs. corporate mergers. Fortune 71:164-5+ Ja '65
HANDLER, Philip
Where is science taking us? por Sat R 46:49 My 4 '63
HANDLIN, Oscar
Are there really ghettos in America? interview. por U S News 55:70-2 Jl 22 '63
Eisenhower administration: a self-portrait. Atlan 212:67-72 N '63
Gullibility of the neutrals. Atlan 211:41-7 Mr '63
Is integration the answer? Atlan 213:49-54 Mr; 45 Je '64
Libraries and learning. Atlan 213:96+ Ap '64
Shaped in the wilderness: the Americans; excerpts. por Atlan 211:94-106 Je '63
HANDLING of feed. See Feed handling
HANDLING of fruit. See Fruit handling
HANDS, Richard C.
Build a compost pile now. Horticulture 41: 535+ O '63
Catalogs coming. Horticulture 41:612-15 D '63
Colorful foliage for your window sill. Horticulture 41:102 F '63
Cutting garden. Horticulture 41:404-5 Ag '63
Daisies that are different! Horticulture 41: 266-7 My '63
Drifts of daffodils. Horticulture 41:314 Je '63
In many shades, fall asters. Horticulture 41: 558-9 N '63
It's easy to grow annuals from seed. Horticulture 41:144-5 Mr '63
Lycoris for something different and interesting. Horticulture 41:452-3 S '63

HANDS. See Hand
HANDWORK. See Handicraft
HANDWRITING. See Graphology; Penmanship; Writing
HANDWRITING experts. See Writing—Identification
HANDY, Jamison
Industry dons sock and buskin. A. Levy. Reporter 31:48-9 S 10 '64
HANEY, Fred
My most unforgettable character. Read Digest 84:98-102 Je '64
HANEY, George E.
Problems and trends in migrant education. por Sch Life 45:5-9 Jl '63
HANEY, Richard D.
What I think about while plowing. Farm J 87:58Z Ap '63
HANFMANN, George M. A.
Digs expose ancient Lydian capital. Natur Hist 72:18-27 D '63
Golden Sardis. Horizon 5:82-9 S '63
HANFORD, George H.
New hope for weak colleges. Sat R 48:52-3+ Ja 16 '65
HANFORD, Roy E.
Where is science taking us? por Sat R 47:54 Mr 7 '64
HANFORD laboratories, Richland, Wash.
Battelle: new contractor's role at AEC lab means diversification for Hanford, growth for institute. J. Walsh. Science 145:905-7 Ag 28 '64
HANGEN, Welles
Pakistan at bay. New Repub 148:13-15 Mr 30 '63
HANGERS, Clothes. See Clothes hangers
HANGING baskets. See Plants, Potted
HANGING judge; opera. See Lockwood, N.
HANGING lamps. See Lamps
HANGING of pictures. See Pictures, Hanging of
HANIGHEN, Frank
Obituary
Nat R 16:55 Ja 28 '64. S. La Follette
HANIWA. See Terra cottas, Japanese
HANKE, Lewis
Conquest and the cross; summary of address. Am Heritage 14:4-19+ F '63
HANKER, Jacob S. and others
Osmiophilic reagents: new cytochemical principle for light and electron microscopy. bibliog Science 146:1039-43 N 20 '64
HANKINSON, Cyril
Noblesse oblige. por Newsweek 61:34+ Ap 8 '63
HANKINSON, Norman
View from the middle. New Yorker 40:45-51 S 21 '64
HANLE, R. A.
Summer cooling for church sanctuaries. Arch Rec 134:157-9 Jl '63
HANLEY, John C.
Missing persons; poem. Commonweal 78:172 My 3 '63
HANLEY, Keenan
Hanley jet propelled iconoclast. il por Motor B 113:86+ Mr '64
HANLEY, William
Slow dance on the killing ground. Criticism
Commonweal 81:485-6 Ja 8 '65
Life 58:10 Ja 15 '65
Nation 199:523-4 D 28 '64
New Repub 152:32 Ja 23 '65
Newsweek 64:84+ D 14 '64
Sat R 47:24-5 D 19 '64
Time 84:73 D 11 '64
Vogue 145:27 Ja 15 '65
HANLON, James M.
Federal aid? America 110:418-19 Mr 28 '64
HANLON, Lorraine
I believe; champion figure skating; ed. by J. Ellenzweig. pors Seventeen 23:213 F '64
HANNA, Elaine Ward-. See Ward-Hanna, E.
HANNA, Helen
Miracle of spring; drama. Plays 23:71-6, 95 Mr '64
HANNA, John, and Wegner, Grace
Sold out! Motor B 114:124-5 Jl '64
HANNA, Lavone
Quest for peace. Sr Schol 85:16T+ N 11 '64
HANNA for hope; story. See Cavanaugh, A.
HANNAH, Arlene. See Riessman, F. jt. auth.
HANNAH, H. W.
What you should know about the law on fences. Suc Farm 62:10 O '64
HANNAH, Paul F.
Government buying erodes management. bibliog f Harvard Bsns R 42:53-62 My '64
HANNAH, Theodore M.
Restoreth thy relic radio. Pop Electr 20:31-5+ My '64
Television servicing, Soviet style. Electr World 71:78-80 Ja '64
HANNIFIN, Jerry
A-11: new U.S. jet is fastest and highest. Life 56:26-7 Mr 13 '64
—and Murphy, C. J. V.
We're losing the supersonic transport race. Fortune 69:118-22+ F '64
HANNIGAN, Ed
As I see it. See issues of U.S. camera
HANNIGAN, Margaret C.
Reader with mental and emotional problems. bibliog por ALA Bul 58:798-803 O '64
HANNING, Robert W.
Development and awareness. Commonweal 80:634-7 S 18 '64
Origins of the church-state problem. Commonweal 81:395-6 D 11 '64
HANNON, Leslie
American culture? qu'est-ce que c'est? N Y Times Mag p 10+ F 16 '64
England's puckish prelate. Sat Eve Post 236:74+ My 4 '63
HANO, Arnold
G.A.P. loves the Hillbillies. N Y Times Mag p30+ N 17 '63
Je-ne-sais-quoits or horseshoes? N Y Times Mag p96+ S 13 '64
When the traveler gets ahead of sound. N Y Times Mag p21+ My 17 '64
(ed) See Benny, Joan. My dad, Jack Benny
HANOVER, Germany (Federal Republic)

Music

Adventures in Germany. D. Stevens. il Opera N 27:32-3 Ap 6 '63
HANSBERGER, Robert V.
Action in Idaho. il por Time 82:78+ D 20 '63
Idaho woodsman makes the chips fly; lumbering industry. il por Bsns W p 144+ O 12 '63
HANSBERRY, Lorraine
This complex of womanhood. por Ebony 18:88 S '63

about

Obituary
Nat R 17:54 Ja 26 '65
Sign in Sidney Brustein's window. Criticism
America 111:758 D 5 '64
Commonweal 81:197 N 6 '64
Nation 199:340 N 9 '64
New Yorker 40:93 O 24 '64
Newsweek 64:101 O 26 '64
Sat R 47:31 O 31 '64
Time il 84:67 O 23 '64
HANSBERRY, William Leo
Africa's golden past. il pors Ebony 19:28-30+ O '64
HANSBERRY, William Leo, and Johnson, E. H.
Africa's golden past. Ebony 20:30-2+ N '64; 86-92 Ja '65
HANSEN, Carl F.
School crisis in the Nation's capital; interview. por U S News 54:62-8 Mr 11 '63

about

Blight in the Nation's capital. il por U S News 54:37-9 F 18 '63
Rumblings in D.C. Sr Schol 82:2T-4T Mr 20 '63
HANSEN, Fred
Exercise in physics. il Time 84:71 Jl 3 '64
HANSEN, Ib
Horse-happy Hansen. il Look 28:99-101 Mr 24 '64
HANSEN, Joseph
Freeway country; poem. Harper 227:72 Jl '63
HANSEN, Osmund Holm-. See Holm-Hansen, O.
HANSEN, Paul E.
Flying fotographer. Flying 74:56 My '64
Portrait of dragonfly driver. Flying 74:46-7+ My '64
HANSEN, Vagn Riis-. See Riis-Hansen, V.
HANSEN, W. Lee
Medic! (did someone cry wolf?) New Repub 149:13-14 N 9 '63
HANSEN'S disease. See Leprosy and lepers
HANSON, Bill
In air and light. il Sch Arts 63:34-5 Ap '64
John fights the Civil war. il Sch Arts 62:7-10 Je '63
HANSON, Dick
Across the editor's desk. See issues of Successful farming
HANSON, Don
Portable tripod. Outdoor Life 132:67 O '63

HANSON, Earl H.
Do our schools neglect the average student? Parents Mag 38:61+ S '63
There's no magic formula for learning to r-r-r-r-read. Parents Mag 38:56-7+ F '63
What does marriage do to teaching? NEA J 52:8-10+ N '63
HANSON, Howard
C major chord: a dialogue with H. Hanson; interview, ed. by J. W. Freeman. por Opera N 28:8-12 N 16 '63
Everyone must have an island; excerpts from address. Recreation 56:449 D '63
Place of creative arts; address, September 16, 1963. Vital Speeches 30:87-90 N 15 '63
about
Merry Mount. Criticism
Opera N il 28:8-12 N 16 '63
Other Puritans. G. Ashford. Opera N 29:31 Ja 23 '65
HANSON, Lester
Drawings of Nicholas Solovioff. Am Artist 28:28-33+ O '64
HANSON, Norwood Russell
Hoosier witch hunt. Nation 196:443-4 My 25 '63
Last of the red hot cats. pors Flying 74: 46-7+ F '64
Politics and the polls. Nation 199:331-2 N 9 '64
HANSON, Pauline
In oracles of listening; poem. Poetry 101:333-7 F '63
HANSON, Suzanne
Paper sculpture for all ages. Design 66:10-12 N '64
HANSON, W. C. and others
Iodine-131 in the thyroids of North American deer and caribou: comparison after nuclear tests. bibliog Science 140:801-2 My 17 '63
HANSON, Wallace, and Wolfe, B. T.
Your electronic flash exposure made easy. Mod Phot 28:52-3 Jl '64
HANSON, Wendy
(ed) See Visconti, L. Leopard
HANSON-DYER, Louise
Music makers. R. Gelatt. por Hi Fi 13:69 F '63
HANSS, Robert E.
Thermochemical etching reveals domain structure in magnetite. bibliog Science 146: 398-9 O 16 '64
HANSSEN, Win
Color-coded seats prevent delay. por Am City 78:95 Ag '63
HANUKKAH (Feast of lights)
For Hanukkah, the festival of lights. il Am Home 67:24 D '64
HANYU, Isao, and Ali, M. A.
Flicker fusion frequency of electroretinogram in light-adapted goldfish at various temperatures. bibliog Science 140:662-3 My 10 '63
HAPGOOD, David
Africa: the mutinous armies. Nation 198:209-12 Mr 2 '64
Africa's new elites. Harper 227:43-9 D '63; 228:11 Mr '64
Competition for Africa's students. Reporter 29:41-2 S 12; 12 O 10 '63
Guinea's first five years. bibliog f Cur Hist 45:355-60 D '63
HAPGOOD, Elizabeth Reynolds
(tr) See Schwarz, E. Dragon
HAPPILY ever after; story. See Bittle, C. R.
HAPPINESS
Editor's notebook. M. S. Fenner. NEA J 53: 84 F '64
Happiness is a journey. L. J. Hurley. Farm J 88:43+ Jl '64
Heaven had better be good; excerpt from Guess whose hair I'm wearing. H. Dolson. il Harper 226:41-4 Ap '63; Same abr. with title Where there's a will. Read Digest 83: 132-4 S '63
In the joyous season. M. E. Jenkins. PTA Mag 58:2-3 Mr '64
Is everybody happy? J. Ciardi. Sat R 47:18 Mr 14 '64
One sure way to happiness; excerpt from Love, hate, fear, anger and the other lively emotions. J. Callwood. Read Digest 85:93-6 N '64
Pursuit of happiness. P. S. Buck. Seventeen 22:112+ D '63
Speaking out; we have no right to happiness. C. S. Lewis. Sat Eve Post 236:10+ D 21 '63
Through happiness with slide rule and calipers. J. W. Krutch. Sat R 46:12-15 N 2 '63; Discussion. 46:29+ N 23; 30+ D 7 '63
We traded security for happiness. M. A. Facklam. il Redbook 120:6+ Mr '63
What makes you happy. il Sci Digest 54:36-40 O '63
What makes you happy? accent on the affirmative. il Changing T 17:31-4 N '63
See also
Pleasure
HAPSBURG, House of
Doom hovered over the Danube. H. C. Wolfe. Sat R 47:46 Mr 21 '64
Franz Josef: a Habsburg marriage. L. Bemelmans. Holiday 35:68-9+ Ja '64
HAPTOGLOBINS
Haptoglobin binding capacity of certain abnormal hemoglobins. R. L. Nagel and H. M. Ranney. bibliog il Science 144:1014-15 My 22 '64
HARAPPA culture
Harappa culture: new evidence for a shorter chronology. D. P. Agrawal. bibliog il Science 143:950-2 F 28 '64
HARARY, Isaac. See Lewis, H. jt. auth.
HARBAUGH, Dave
Interview with KN3NOB. il Pop Electr 18: 82-3 Mr '63
HARBAUGH, William H.
Growth of the Republican party. bibliog f Cur Hist 47:199-204+ O '64
HARBERT, Ruth
Movie report. See issues of Good housekeeping
HARBISON, Frederick H.
Education for development; with biographical sketch. Sci Am 209:26, 140-4+ bibliog(p307) S '63
High-level manpower development. Mo Labor R 86:265-7 Mr '63
HARBOR pilots. See Pilots and pilotage
HARBOR police. See Police boats
HARBORS
High tide of debris. E. Crimmin. il Motor B 112:24-7+ Jl '63
See also subhead Harbor under names of cities, e.g. Rotterdam—Harbor
HARBOUR, Dave
Baby elk of White River Forest. Audubon Mag 66:35 Ja '64
To unlock fighting deer, courage is the key. Audubon Mag 66:234-6 Jl '64
HARBRON, John D.
De Gaulle's Canadian beachhead. Commonweal 80:256-7 My 22 '64
HARCOURT, Brace and World, incorporated
Harcourt's new dept. for research and technology. il Pub W 186:91 S 28 '64
HARD, Walter
Pleasant rumor; In wartime; Timepiece; poems. Life 55:114+ O 11 '63
about
Vivid Vermont poet. il pors Life 55:113+ O 11 '63
HARD of hearing See Deafness
HARDACRE, Carol
Our teacher sees with her hands. S. Gordon. il pors Look 27:116a-116e Ap 23 '63
HARDBERGER, Phil
Peace corps volunteers praise P.E. project. Pop Electr 20:54-5+ Ja '64
HARDBOARD. See Fiber board
HARDEN, Edgar L.
It's time . . . who shall go to college? address, March 16, 1963. Vital Speeches 29: 430-4 My 1 '63
HARDENING
New technique for strengthening ceramics. Sci N L 83:216 Ap 6 '63
HARDENING of the arteries. See Arteriosclerosis
HARDER, Paul
Kialoa II. Yachting 115:62-3+ My '64
Mountain sailing. il Yachting 113:54-5+ Je '63
HARDIN, Wayne
Setting for greatness at Philadelphia; Army-Navy football game. D. Jenkins. il por Sports Illus 19:32-4+ D 2 '63
HARDINESS in plants. See Plants—Hardiness
HARDING, Florence (Kling) De Wolfe
Four mysteries of Warren Harding. F. Russell. il pors Am Heritage 14:4-9+ Ap '63
HARDING, H. F.
What are your ultimate objectives? address, September 6, 1963. Vital Speeches 29:757-60 O 1 '63
HARDING, Vincent
Beginning in Birmingham. Reporter 28:13-19 Je 6 '63
Toward the other shore. Reporter 29:27-31 O 10 '63
HARDING, Walter
Camper in the back yard. Horizon 6:32-9 Autumn '64
HARDING, Warren Gamaliel
All for the love of a lady. C. B. Luce. il por McCalls 91:20+ N '63

HARDING, Warren Gamaliel—*Continued*
Four mysteries of Warren Harding. F. Russell. il pors Am Heritage 14:4-9+ Ap '63
Letters from Constant. il por Time 84:27 Jl 17 '64
Ohio court enjoins use of Harding letters. Pub W 186:32 Ag 10 '64

HARDNESS of water. See Water—Hardness

HARDWARE
New ideas in home hardware. il Sunset 130: 155-6 Ap '63
See also
Casters, glides, etc (hardware)
Curtain and drapery fixtures

Exhibitions

What's new at the hardware show; spectacle at New York's Coliseum. il Pop Sci 183: 30-2+ D '63

HARDWARE man; story. See O'Hare, J.

HARDWICK, Elizabeth
Movies. Vogue 144:62 N 15 '64; 145:25 Ja 15 '65
Theatre. Vogue 143:20 Ja 1; 54 Mr 1; 40 Ap 1; 62 My; 144:30 Ag 1; 66 N 1 '64
(comp) Twenty-one great writers on the U.S.A; excerpts from literary works. Vogue 141:114-15+ F 1 '63

HARDWOOD cuttings. See Plant propagation

HARDY, Bill, and Lorang, Glenn
Easier cleaning for cages. Farm J 87:22-3+ Je '63

HARDY, Emma
Dearest Emmie, by C. J. Weber. Review
Time por 82:64 D 27 '63

HARDY, Françoise
Bonjour ennui. F. Nourissier. Vogue 142:71 Ag 1 '63
Hooray for the Yé-Yé girls. il pors Life 56: 44 My 29 '64
Vogue's eye view. por Vogue 142:57 Ag 1 '63

HARDY, Neal J.
FHA defaults cause no alarm. U S News 54: 95-6 F 11 '63

HARDY, Thomas
Dearest Emmie, by C. J. Weber. Review
Time por 82:64 D 27 '63

HARE, David
Gallery for young people. C. B. Johnson. il Sch Arts 64:45 N '64

HARE, F. Kenneth
Canadian dean. New Yorker 39:23-4 D 21 '63

HARE, P. Edgar
Amino acids in the proteins from aragonite and calcite in the shells of mytilus californianus. bibliog Science 139:216-17 Ja 18 '63

HARE hunting. See Rabbit hunting

HARE lip. See Harelip

HARELIP
My baby was different. il Good H 156:10+ F '63; Same abr. Read Digest 83:147-50 Ag '63

HARFORD, Carl G. See Kuhn, N. O. jt. auth.

HARGESHEIMER, Fred
Mastah Freddy's modest miracle. J. Reddy. il pors Sat Eve Post 238:68+ Ja 30 '65

HARGIS, Billy James
Gospel according to Billy. il por Newsweek 64: 77 Ag 24 '64
Midnight ride of Hargis and Walker; Operation midnight ride. Christian Cent 80:262 F 27 '63
Nameless one. Christian Cent 80:1039 Ag 21 '63

HARGRAVE, Lawrence
Science milestone. J. Rhea. il por Sci Digest 53:79-86 F '63

HARGROVE, Katharine
And sweet the wood; poem Cath World 196: 363 Mr '63
Lessons of a CP camp. America 109:738-40 D 7 '63

HARI, Eugene
Mata and Hari at 92nd street Y. M. Marks. Dance Mag 38:29-30 F '64

HARIJANS. See Untouchables

HARING, Bernard
Responsible parenthood, tr. by M. Ilford. Commonweal 80:323-8 Je 5 '64
Rethinking the sacrament of matrimony; excerpt from The Johannine council. por Cath World 197:359-65 S '63

HARK, Mildred
Christmas bear; drama. Plays 23:69-74, 96 D '63
Visit to the White House; drama. Plays 24: 83-95 Ja '65
—and McQueen, Noel
Hometown Halloween; drama. Plays 23:31-41 O '63
Life for mother; drama. Plays 22:43-52 My '63
Lincoln umbrella; drama. Plays 23:55-63 F '64
Mind your P's and Q's; drama. Plays 22:44-50 Mr '63
Not fit for man or beast; drama. Plays 23: 59-68 Ja '64
Portrait of an American; drama. Plays 23: 13-22 My '64
Quiet Christmas; drama. Plays 24:15-28 D '64
Turkey gobblers; drama. Plays 23:29-41 N '63

HARKEY, Ira, Jr
In a madhouse's din. il por Newsweek 62:48 Jl 8 '63

HARKINS, Paul Donal
Colonel Van and General Harkins. Nation 197:230 O 19 '63

HARKNESS, Bernard
Choose fragrant lilacs. Am Home 67:10+ S '64

HARKNESS, Kenneth A.
New emblem may save your life. Suc Farm 61:9 Jl '63

HARKNESS ballet company. See Ballet companies

HARL, Neil E.
New retirement plan. Suc Farm 61:39+ O '63

HARLAN, John Marshall
Can courts cure everything? excerpts from an address, August 13, 1963. por U S News 55:49 Ag 26 '63
Judicial usurpation; address, August 13, 1963. Vital Speeches 29:706-8 S 15 '63; Excerpts. por U S News 55:49 Ag 26 '63
Speaking of the split; excerpts from address. por Time 82:17-18 Ag 23 '63
What the Court said about congressional districts; excerpts from statement. por U S News 56:33 Mr 2 '64

about

Birth of Jim Crow; Plessy v. Ferguson. C. V. Woodward. por Am Heritage 15:52-5+ Ap '64
Dissenter. por Time 84:51+ Jl 3 '64
Dissenter Harlan critical of fellow justices. por U S News 55:26 O 28 '63
Voice for personal liberty. por U S News 54: 21 Je 10 '63

HARLAND, W. Brian, and Rudwick, M. J. S.
Great infra-Cambrian ice age; with biographical sketches. Sci Am 211:10, 28-36 bibliog(p 116) Ag '64

HARLECH, David Ormsby Gore, 5th baron
Anglo-American relations; address, May 22, 1963. Vital Speeches 29:551-3 Jl 1 '63
Britain and the new Europe; address, April 5, 1963; with questions and answers. Ann Am Acad 348:1-14 Jl '63
East-West relations; address, January 22, 1964. Vital Speeches 30:286-8 F 15 '64

about

Changing of the guard; British ambassador to be replaced. Time 85:32 Ja 15 '65
Mr Ambassador. J. Kraft. Harper 227:101+ D '63

HARLEM. See New York (city)—Harlem

HARLEM riot, 1964. See New York (city)—Riots

HARLEM youth opportunities unlimited, incorporated
Harlem's violent mood. E. Dunbar. il Look 28:29+ Jl 28 '64
People vs. politicians: defeat in Harlem. W. Klein. Nation 199:27-9 Jl 27 '64; Reply. W. M. Young, jr. 199:inside cover S 7 '64
Teen-agers who want to help. J. W. Levin. il N Y Times Mag p52 F 9 '64

HARLING, Robert
Going places, finding things in English gardens, in and around London. House & Gard 123:40-1+ My '63
The Ian Flemings. Vogue 142:222-7+ S 1 '63

HARLOW, Dana E.
Call to action. Recreation 57:108-10 Mr '64

HARLOW, Jean
Harlow: an intimate biography, by I. Shulman. Review
Esquire 62:14+ O '64. M. Muggeridge
Reporter 31:37+ Jl 2 '64. G. Weales

HARLOW, Lewis A.
Filter capacitor replacement, think ahead. Pop Electr 20:79-80 Je '64
Fix your own TV. Pop Mech 121:192-5 Ap '64
Have a policy about music lessons. House B 105:68+ Mr '63
How to choose the right mike. Pop Sci 182: 152-4 F '63
Piano, Julie, lasts a long time. House B 105:164-5+ D '63
Recording tapes, which to buy, and why. Pop Sci 184:126-7+ Ja '64
Russian in two hours. Sci Digest 54:45-8 N '63
TV's best guarded secret. Pop Electr 19:49-50 Ag '63

HARLOW, Neal
Newes of the new founde worlde; address, October, 1962. por Library J 88:2189-93 Je 1 '63
Present is not what it was. bibliog por Library J 89:2527-32 Je 15 '64
Thinking of a plan; excerpts from address, November, 1961. por Library J 88:3161-3 S 15 '63

HARLOW, William M.
Tenacious butternut. Am For 69:37 S '63
Tree ring extremes. Am For 69:27 Mr '63

HARMAN, Jeanne Perkins
Case for the passé resort. Travel 121:48-50+ Je '64

HARMON, Claude
Let me help your game; ed. by A. Wright. pors Sports Illus 20:38-47 Ap 27; 70-6 My 4 '64

HARMON, Frederick
Toward more trade. Américas 16:31-5 Ap '64

HARMON, George
How to tell a Baptist from a Methodist in the South. Harper 226:58-63 F '63

HARMON, Jack
Bioastronautics and space. Science 147:314-15 Ja 15 '65

HARMON, Jeanne Perkins
European camps for kids. Travel 119:43-50 Je '63

HARMON, Leon D.
Neuromimes: action of a reciprocally inhibitory pair. bibliog Science 146:1323-5 D 4 '64
—and Snell, F. M.
Biophysics. Science 146:276+ O 9 '64
about
Machine that reads writing. S. V. Jones. por Sci Digest 55:52-3 F '64

HARMOUNT, James Godfrey
Days are busy for only woman open-heart surgeon. Todays Health 41:31 Jl '63
Fifty-five million cyclists can't be wrong. Todays Health 42:32-3+ O '64
Keeping harmony in the family. Todays Health 42:78-9 F '64

HARMS, Ernest
My association with Kandinsky. Am Artist 27:36-41+ Je '63

HARNER, Evelyn L.
Quality in secondary education in Communist China. Sch & Soc 91:169-70 Ap 6 '63

HARNESS racing
Elegant bay of Mrs Buck; Overtrick wins Little brown jug. K. Rudeen. il Sports Illus 19:30-1 S 30 '63
Emperor in harness; B. Haughton. M. Kram. il Sports Illus 20:44+ Je 15 '64
Fair time at an old coal mine; Hambletonian race, Du Quoin, Ill. R. Hackett. il Sports Illus 19:28-33 Ag 26 '63
Harness racing. P. Ryan. il Sports Illus 19: 70-2 O 14 '63
Horse they called crazy; Ayres, favorite for trotting's Triple crown. P. Ryan. il Sports Illus 21:52+ Ag 3 '64
If it moves, said George, they'll bet on it; trotting races at night. B. Ottum. il Sports Illus 21:30-2+ Jl 27 '64
Matchless match; Speedy Scot and Overtrick. Sports Illus 19:8 O 7 '63
Scot, the Lad and black-market blood; America wins in Roosevelt international. P. Ryan. il Sports Illus 21:58-9 Ag 31 '64
They all are aiming at Ayres; Hambeltonian, foremost trotting event. R. A. Hackett. il Sports Illus 21:51-2 Ag 24 '64
Trotting's wondrous Scot; Speedy Scot at Hambletonian race. K. Rudeen. il Sports Illus 19:22-3 S 9 '63
Vicar won on three legs; Little Brown Jug race, Delaware, Ohio. P. Ryan. il Sports Illus 21:100-2 O 5 '64
Winner from the wrong side of the barn; Ayres wins Hambletonian race. P. Ryan. il Sports Illus 21:54+ S 14 '64

HARNEY, Patricia M. and Grant, W. F.
Biochemical anomaly in flower extracts of interspecific hybrids between lotus species. bibliog Science 142:1061 N 22 '63

HARNEY, Paul
Part-time pro. por Time 85:50 Ja 22 '65

HARNISCHFEGER, Walter, and Groseclose, Elgin
Excerpt from testimony, February 25, 1963. Cong Digest 42:181+ Je '63

HARNWELL, Gaylord P.
Substance of the university; address, September 6, 1963. Vital Speeches 29:756-7 O 1 '63
about
Old Ben's new Penn. il por Time 82:58+ Ag 23 '63

HARP
Listen to the sound of the harp. L. Wilcox. il House B 105:202-3+ O '63

HARPER, Janet
Great aunt; poem. Sat R 47:31 Ag 8 '64
Urban renewal: Chicago; poem. Sat R 46:31 D 21 '63

HARPER, John D.
Profitless prosperity; address, May 23, 1963. Vital Speeches 29:566-9 Jl 1 '63

HARPER, Marion, 1916-
Marketing the poverty programs. Sat R 47: 65-6 My 9 '64
Too rich, too soft, too surfeited? Sat R 46: 68+ Ap 13 '63
about
Mavericks on Madison avenue. P. B. Bart. Sat R 46:60+ D 14 '63
To the top at last. por Time 82:102 O 18 '63
Under Marion Harper's big tent. S. H. Brown. il por Fortune 69:128-32 My '64
What makes Marion Harper run. il por Newsweek 63:63-6 Mr 30 '64

HARPER and Row, publishers, incorporated
Harper's five per cent bonus discount for non-returned books. Pub W 186:30 O 12 '64

HARPSICHORD
Man with a mission. il Newsweek 61:60 F 18 '63

HARPSICHORD music
From the Landowska notebooks; tr. by D. Restout and R. Hawkins. W. Landowska. il Hi Fi 14:48-52+ D '64
See also
Phonograph records—Harpsichord music

HARRAR, J. George
New ventures for private philanthropy. N Y Times Mag p29+ Je 9 '63
about
$266,900,000: private give-away, done by three men. A. Talmey. por Vogue 141:103 Je '63

HARRELL, D. Tudor
(comp) New Year customs. Hobbies 68:28 Ja '64

HARRIERS (dogs)
Harrier. J. Stetson. il Field & S 69:112-13 Ag '64

HARRIGAN, Anthony
Case for gas warfare. Nat R 14:283+ Ap 9 '63
Letter from Vietnam. Nat R 17:59 Ja 26 '65
Quebec revolution. Cath World 199:109-15 My '64

HARRIMAN, William Averell
Appraisal of Khrushchev by Harriman. N Y Times Mag p 10+ Ag 25 '63
Conditions in eastern Europe; statement, March 10, 1964. Dept State Bul 50:485-7 Mr 30 '64
Department of state questions Freedom academy proposal; statement, February 20, 1964. Dept State Bul 50:462-4 Mr 23 '64
Department supports extension of Public law 480; statement, February 28, 1964. Dept State Bul 50:507-9 Mr 30 '64
Department supports legislation to implement coffee agreement; statement, February 25, 1964. Dept State Bul 50:459-62 Mr 23 '64
Development financing and the Alliance for progress; address, December 2, 1964. Dept State Bul 51:884-7 D 21 '64
Mr Rusk and Mr Harriman discuss nuclear test ban treaty; interview on television, July 28, 1963; ed. by M. Agronsky. Dept State Bul 49:240-5 Ag 12 '63
Negotiating a limited treaty for banning nuclear tests; address, July 31, 1963. Dept State Bul 49:278-82 Ag 19 '63
Some current issues in U.S. foreign policy; remarks, April 19, 1963; with questions and answers. Dept State Bul 48:693-8 My 6 '63
Strengthening the Alliance for progress; statement, November 13, 1963. Dept State Bul 49:937-45 D 16 '63
United States, Canada and leadership in international cooperation; address, July 25, 1964. Dept State Bul 61:237-41 Ag 17 '64
United States policy and Africa; address, August 18, 1964. Dept State Bul 51:330-3 S 7 '64
about
Back from exile. por Newsweek 61:32+ My 13 '63
Harriman: another job to do in Moscow. il pors U S News 55:14 Jl 22 '63
Harriman's job again: to save Laos. il por U S News 54:19 My 6 '63
How Harriman earned a dinner from Khrushchev. P. Mandel. il pors Life 55:28-30A Ag 9 '63
Is a U.S. deal with Russia near? il por U S News 55:27-9 Jl 22 '63

HARRIMAN, William Averell—about—*Cont.*
Laos, Cuba, and two visitors to Moscow. il por Newsweek 61:39-40 My 6 '63
Mr Harriman comes home. M. McGrory. America 109:129 Ag 10 '63
Old crocodile on the New frontier. J. Kraft. il pors Sat Eve Post 236:66-7 S 14 '63
People of the week. por U S News 54:22 Mr 18; 26 Ap 22 '63
Test ban: a rosy glow on the horizon. il por Newsweek 62:45 Jl 29 '63
Top Kremlinologist at work. C. Phillips. il pors N Y Times Mag p9+ Jl 14 '63
Tough trainman. K. Crawford. Newsweek 61:38 Mr 18 '63
Who is conning whom? J. Burnham. Nat R 15:101 Ag 13 '63
Will they take Ave? W. F. Buckley, jr. Nat R 15:51 Jl 30 '63

HARRINGTON, Joseph
Search for a man; story. Redbook 122:123-50 Ja '64

HARRINGTON, LaMar
First annual western craft competition. Craft Horiz 24:12-19 Jl '64

HARRINGTON, Lloyd W.
Case of the squeezed pencils. NEA J 53:24 O '64

HARRINGTON, Michael
Close-up on poverty. Look 28:64-72 Ag 25 '64
Facts are in. Nation 198:582-3 Je 8 '64
New lost generation: jobless youth. N Y Times Mag p 13+ My 24 '64
New parabolist. Reporter 28:50-2 F 14 '63
New Soviet man? Commonweal 78:39-42 Ap 5 '63
Other de Gaulle. Commonweal 79:419-21 Ja 10 '64
Politics of glory. Commonweal 77:613-16 Mr 8 '63
Unconditional war; adaptation of address, February 24, 1964. por Wilson Lib Bul 38:834-9 Je '64

about

Poverty & passion. por Time 83:25 F 7 '64

HARRINGTON, Milton E.
Harrington of Liggett & Myers. por Fortune 70:45 S '64

HARRIS, A. S.
Sitka spruce, Alaska's new state tree. por Am For 70:32-5 Ag '64

HARRIS, Albert J.
Three kinds of reading. Todays Health 42:14 F '64

HARRIS, Andrew
Deerfield, a Negro ghost town in Weld County, Colorado. Negro Hist Bul 27:38 N '63
Teacher and principal. Negro Hist Bul 27:198 My '64

HARRIS, Charles S.
Adaptation to displaced vision: visual, motor, or proprioceptive change? bibliog Science 140:812-13 My 17 '63

HARRIS, Chauncy D.
U.S.S.R. resources: agriculture. bibliog f Focus 13:1-6 Ja '63
U.S.S.R. resources for heavy industry. bibliog Focus 13:1-6 Mr '63

HARRIS, Christie
My heroine helped me. Horn Bk 40:361-3 Ag '64
Never underestimate an Indian village. Horn Bk 39:156-61 Ap '63

HARRIS, Dale and Harris, Elizabeth
Affluent child. PTA Mag 58:27-9 bibliog(p36) Mr '64
Organization child. PTA Mag 57:22-4 bibliog (p35) Ap '63
—and Weisbord, M. R.
Who are your child's heroes? Parents Mag 38:50-2+ Je '63

HARRIS, Dale B. See Laird, J. E. jt. auth.

HARRIS, Donald
Long journey South. J. Wechsler. por Redbook 122:68-9+ Ap '64

HARRIS, Eleanor
New York's mighty Moses. Look 27:94-5+ Mr 26 '63
Overteased hair: beginning of the end. Look 27:26-8+ Jl 30 '63
(ed) See Allen, M. L. What can we do about America's unwed teen-age mothers?

HARRIS, Elizabeth. See Harris, D. jt. auth.

HARRIS, Elizabeth T.
On giving oneself away. Harper 229:99-101 D '64

HARRIS, Forest K.
Units and standards of electrical measure. Electr World 72:29-32+ Ag '64

HARRIS, Frank
Frank account. por Newsweek 62:98+ O 28 '63
Importance of being Frank. S. Kauffmann. New Repub 149:23-7 D 28 '63

HARRIS, Frank E. See Rein, R. jt. auth.

HARRIS, Fred
Basic Bud. il Time 84:27-8 O 9 '64

HARRIS, Helen
Good loud holler. il por NEA J 52:36-7 Mr '63
Herblock's golden key. J. Star. il pors Look 27:62+ F 26 '63

HARRIS, Herbert
Riddle of the labor vote. Harper 229:43-9 O '64
Why labor lost the intellectuals. Harper 228:79-80+ Je '64

HARRIS, Jed
Confessions of a Broadway alchemist; excerpt from Watchman, what of the night? (cont) por Theatre Arts 47:22-4+ F '63
Introduction to September child. por Theatre Arts 47:19-21 Ag '63

HARRIS, John Benton
Equipment; the means to the end. il U S Camera 26:47-9 O '63

HARRIS, John F.
Colonel John F. Harris: head sixth United States army medical services; news release por Negro Hist Bul 28:57 D '64

HARRIS, Julie
Promise! what a lovely word. pors Seventeen 22:138+ O '63
A saint is a saint, you know. B. Brower. pors Sat Eve Post 237:22-3 D 5 '64

HARRIS, Katherine G.
Metropolitan reference services; patterns, problems, solutions. por Library J 88:1606-11 Ap 15 '63

HARRIS, Larry G. See Doughtery, E. C. jt. auth.

HARRIS, Leonard
Grass roots touring. Theatre Arts 47:26-8+ Ag '63
New season, New York. Theatre Arts 47:11-15+ O '63

HARRIS, Linda
Ordeal of Linda Harris. T. Irwin. il pors Good H 158:42+ F '64

HARRIS, Lou
Florida springtime. Travel 120:26-30 S '63

HARRIS, Louis, 1921-
Backlash issue. Newsweek 64:24+ Jl 13 '64
Big GOP test in the West. Newsweek 63:23 Mr 23 '64
Concerns of the Nation 1965. Newsweek 65:20 Ja 11 '65
Harris calls the election, by sex, place, race, religion. Newsweek 64:28-9 N 2 '64
Newsweek poll: the women's vote. Newsweek 64:32 S 21 '64
Polltaker's Oregon report. por Newsweek 63:28 My 25 '64
'64: the GOP could win, if. Newsweek 62:25-7 Ag 26 '63

HARRIS, MacDonald
Koto students; story. Sat Eve Post 236:54-8 Ap 13 '63

HARRIS, Marion
Six comediennes. J. Walsh. pors Hobbies 68:32-4+ Ag; 30-4 S '63

HARRIS, Mark
Government as patron of the arts. N Y Times Mag p35+ S 13 '64
My father's son; excerpt from introduction to Friedman & son. Commentary 35:199-209 Mr '63

about

Choose something like a star. J. Ciardi. Sat R 47:16 Ja 11 '64

HARRIS, Marvin
Heritage of blood and dust. Sat R 47:29-30 My 2 '64

HARRIS, Richard
Annals of legislation. New Yorker 40:48-50+ Mr 14; 75-6+ Mr 21; 46-8+ Mr 28 '64
Reporter at large (cont) New Yorker 40:101-3+ S 12 '64

about

Imperial kiss. por Newsweek 64:98+ N 30 '64

HARRIS, Robert Davis, Jr
South at prayer; poem. Negro Hist Bul 26:232 My '63

HARRIS, Rolf
Bouncing kangaroo. por Newsweek 62:50 Jl 8 '63

HARRIS, Roy
Musical events; performance of Ninth symphony by Philadelphia orchestra. W. Sargeant. New Yorker 38:77-8 F 9 '63

HARRIS, S. Richard
Dam' bear ain't there! pors Outdoor Life 134:20-3+ N '64

HARRIS, Seymour E.
Economics and politics. Bul Atomic Sci 20:32-4 Ja '64
Gap between economist and politician. N Y Times Mag p26+ Ap 14 '63

HARRIS, Seymour E.—*Continued*
Kennedy and the liberals. New Repub 148:15-16 Je 1 '63
National health insurance? Cur Hist 45:110-14 Ag '63
about
Face of the Fed. il Newsweek 62:93 N 11 '63
HARRIS, Sherwood
Coast to coast in twelve crashes. Am Heritage 15:46-9+ O '64
Tragic dream of Jean Ribaut. Am Heritage 14:8-15+ O '63
HARRIS, Townsend
Yankee Barbarian at the Shogun's court. E. Hahn. il por Am Heritage 15:60-3+ Je '64
HARRIS-Intertype corporation
Debut in composing room. il Bsns W p 133-4 Ap 25 '64
Harris-Intertype acquires Sheridan co. for $6,346,000. Pub W 185:39 My 18 '64
Harris-Intertype computers made especially for type composition. il Pub W 185:62-5 Ap 6 '64
Special computer for printers. il Bsns W p 102 Mr 7 '64
HARRIS polls. See Public opinion polls
HARRIS quadruplets. See Quadruplets
HARRISON, Alfred C. Jr
Family game. New Yorker 39:35-6 Ap 27 '63
HARRISON, Benjamin
Benjamin Harrison papers; reprint. M. Wright. Hobbies 69:110-11+ Ja '65
HARRISON, Forrest W. and McLoone, E. P.
Educational expenditures. Sch Life 46:21-3 O '63
HARRISON, G. B.
Words to pray with? America 110:508-10 Ap 11 '64
HARRISON, George M.
Clarification of transportation-policy goals. Ann Am Acad 345:22-31 Ja '63
HARRISON, Gilbert A.
Berkeley: does that banner still wave? New Repub 151:7-8 D 19 '64
Modern Mr Forster. New Repub 150:15-16 Ja 11 '64
That massive, hidden apparatus. New Repub 150:19-21 Je 27 '64
Way out West. New Repub 149:15-22 N 23 '63
HARRISON, Howard, and Forbes, Will
Bargains from the dime store. Pop Phot 52:64-7 Mr '63
HARRISON, J. Clement
Another battle of the books. por Library J 88:1946-9 My 15 '63
HARRISON, J. M. and Irving, R.
Nucleus of the trapezoid body: dual afferent innervation. bibliog Science 143:473-4 Ja 31 '64
HARRISON, James B.
Movies. Christian Cent 81:276, 807 F 26, Je 17 '64
HARRISON, Jay S.
Karajan and the Nine. Mus Am 83:44+ N '63
New York music scene. Mus Am 83:24-9 N; 178+ D '63; 84:30-6 Ja; 22-6 F; 24-30 Mr; 34-41 Ap; 28-35 My; 32-7 Jl '64
New York state theater; the building. Mus Am 84:7 My '64
Schnabel & Beethoven. Mus Am 83:274+ D '63
Thirty-two by Kempff. Sat R 47:70-1 N 14 '64
(ed) See Reiner, F. Return of Reiner
about
On top of the news. por Mus Am 83:26 S '63
HARRISON, John
John Harrison's million-dollar clock. H. Helfer. il por Sci Digest 55:62-4 Mr '64
HARRISON, Katherine
Charge: witchcraft; unique petition. Hobbies 69:92 Jl '64
HARRISON, Rex
My fair lady's dream comes true. S. Gordon. il pors Look 28:60-2+ F 25 '64
RH. A. Seidenbaum. il pors McCalls 92:98-9+ O '64
Rex Harrison and his own fair lady. J. Hamilton. il pors Look 27:72-4+ Je 18 '63
HARRISON, Robert
Public lives: Confidential magazine; reflections in tranquillity by the former owner, Robert Harrison, who managed to get away with it. T. K. Wolfe. il por Esquire 61:87-90+ Ap '64
HARRISON, Selig S.
Troubled India and her neighbors. For Affairs 43:312-30 Ja '65
World of Lyndon B. Johnson. New Repub 149:13-14 D 7 '63
HARRISON, Tom
Wild men of Borneo. Newsweek 63:47 Je 1 '64
HARRISON, Wallace K.
City and the arts; address, November 11, 1963. Mus Am 83:151-3 D '63
Home at last. il Newsweek 64:100 S 21 '64
HARRISON, William
Man of passion; story. Sat Eve Post 236:52-6 N 2 '63
HARRISON, William Henry
William Henry Harrison, ninth President 1841. F. Freidel. il pors Nat Geog Mag 127:94-7 Ja '65
HARRISON LAKE
Resort and wilderness meet at Harrison. il Sunset 131:22+ Jl '63
HARRISVILLE, Roy A.
Biblical potpourri. Christian Cent 81:1464-6+ N 25 '64
HARRITY, Richard
Again, they are readying the convention halls; excerpts from Two party system. Look 28:22-30+ Jl 14 '64
Twentieth century; excerpts from What's happened to the 20th century? Look 29:16-25 Ja 12 '65
Two parties & how they came about; excerpts from Two party system. Look 28:48-59 Jl 14 '64
—See Martin, R. G. jt. auth.
—and Martin, R. G.
Khrushchev: the red riddle. Look 27:34-6+ N 19 '63
HARROVER, Roy P.
Airport for jets and pistons. Arch Rec 134:165-72 O '63
HARRY S. Truman library, Independence, Mo.
Ramble in the past with Mr Truman. L. Wainwright. Life 56:29 Ap 24 '64
Walk through history with Harry Truman; with editorial comment. J. McCarthy. il Holiday 34:55, 56-61+ N; 96-7+ D '63
HARSCH, Joseph C.
Don't underestimate Europe. N Y Times Mag p32-3+ N 29 '64
HARSHBARGER, Gretchen
Our outdoor bonsai. il Flower Grower 51:20-1 Mr '64
Welcome to our garden. il por Flower Grower 51:30-1+ Mr '64
HART, Edwin J.
Hydrated electron. bibliog Science 146:19-25 O 2 '64
Radiation chemistry: aqueous media. Science 141:195-6+ Jl 12 '63
HART, Henry C.
India after the Chinese attack. bibliog f Ann Am Acad 351:50-7 Ja '64
HART, Howard
For Maria Therese; poem. Cath World 199:187 Je '64
This afternoon; poem. Cath World 199:42 Ap '64
HART, Howard R. Jr, and Schmitt, R. W.
Superconductivity. Science 143:57-8+ Ja 3 '64
HART, J. Truman
Luminous figures: influence of point of fixation on their disappearance. bibliog Science 143:1193-4 Mr 13 '64
HART, Jack
Cam timing for street and strip. il Hot Rod 17:74-7 D '64
Driver's compartment. Hot Rod 17:98-9 F '64
How stock is stock? Hot Rod 17:46-9 Je '64
1963 drag racing rules. Hot Rod 16:76-9 F '63
'64 drug rules. Hot Rod 17:84-5+ F '64
Stock hop. por Hot Rod 17:84-7 O '64
HART, James D.
Of infinite remembrance; excerpts from address, October 18, 1963. Library J 89:1179-83 Mr 15 '64
HART, James S.
Woven paintings. Design 65:162-3 Mr '64
HART, Jeffrey
By ideology possessed. Nat R 16:825-6 S 22 '64
C. S. Lewis: 1898-1963. Nat R 16:240+ Mr 24 '64
Hemingway's code. Nat R 16:450-2 Je 2 '64
In praise of Chesterton. Yale R 53:49-60 O '63
On the altar of equality. Nat R 16:540-1 Je 30 '64
Scott Fitzgerald's America. Nat R 15:443-4 N 19 '63
Seriousness of Evelyn Waugh. Nat R 16:1152-3 D 29 '64
Snow season. Nat R 15:356+ O 22 '63
HART, Jerrems C.
Show your prints. U S Camera 26:91 F '63
HART, Jerry
Flying bridge view of the out islands. Yachting 116:46-8+ N '64
HART, John. See Nesbitt, H. H. J. jt. auth.

HART, Philip
Artur Schnabel, a legend reëmergent. Hi Fi 13:65-8+ N '63
Fritz Reiner. Opera N 28:29 D 14 '63
High quality classics at half price. Hi Fi 13:96 S '63
Launching a career. Mus Am 84:10-11 Jl '64
Reiner in Chicago. Hi Fi 14:42-6 Ap '64

HART, Philip A.
Excerpt from statement, July 3, 1963. Cong Digest 42:276+ N '63
Truth in packaging. Nation 196:542-3 Je 29 '63

about

He's no ogre. por Newsweek 62:65 S 2 '63
New chairman and a new senator. por U S News 55:13 S 2 '63
No crusades. Time 82:17 Ag 30 '63
Packagers take a hint from the Hart bill. il Bsns W p47 N 23 '63

HART, Richard
Brush up your Shakespeare! Wilson Lib Bul 38:653-5 Ap '64

HART, S. R. See Tilton, G. R. jt. auth.

HART, Schaffner and Marx
Made to measure. il Time 84:77-8 Jl 3 '64

HART, Virginia S.
Manpower training in Navajo land. Sch Life 45:26-9 Mr '63

HARTACK, Bill
Fourth communion. il por Time 83:58 My 8 '64
I say what I think. il por Newsweek 63:86-7 Je 8 '64
Whatever happened to Bill Hartack? J. Olsen. por Sports Illus 18:12-15+ Je 24 '63

HARTECK, P. and Dondes, S.
Radiation chemistry of the fixation of nitrogen. bibliog Science 146:30-5 O 2 '64
—and others
Ozone: decomposition by ionizing radiation. bibliog Science 147:393-4 Ja 22 '65

HARTESVELDT, Richard J.
Fire ecology of the giant sequoias. Natur Hist 73:12-19 bibliog(p67) D '64

HARTFORD, Huntington
Dreamer with checkbook in hand. il por Bsns W p30+ My 2 '64
Far-out side of Paradise. H. Sutton. il Sat R 46:52+ Mr 16 '63
Hartford modern: what's in a name. il por Newsweek 63:64-5 Mr 23 '64
Hartford's gallery. New Yorker 40:32-3 Mr 21 '64
Huntington Hartford: a most unusual client. P. M. Herrera. il por Arch Forum 120:112-13 Mr '64
Man who owns Paradise. R. Gehman. por Sat Eve Post 236:66+ Ap 27 '63
Millionaire art buff takes on the bad guys. B. O'Doherty. Life 57:12+ N 27 '64
Philanthropic philistine. D. Peerman. Christian Cent 81:706-7 My 27 '64

HARTFORD, Conn.

City planning

Downtown's dramatic comeback. D. B. Carlson. il Arch Forum 120:98-9 F '64
Hartford shows what can be done; urban renewal funds from federal government and local businesses. il Bsns W p72-4+ D 7 '63
Insuring the growth of Hartford: Constitution Plaza. il Arch Rec 135:178-87 Mr '64
Under the knife, or all for their own good. il(p64) Time 84:71 N 6 '64

Hotels, restaurants, etc.

Hotel takes part in downtown renewal. il Arch Rec 136:166-7 O '64

Industries

Hartford shows what can be done; urban renewal funds from federal government and local businesses. il Bsns W p72-4+ D 7 '63

Music

[Musical events] Mus Am 84:22 Ap '64

Newspapers

Older than the country; Courant. il Time 83:46 Mr 13 '64
Two centuries of the Hartford courant. H. Brucker. il Sat R 47:62-4 My 9 '64

Sanitary affairs

TV sewer inspection. R. H. Brindley. il Am City 79:87-9 Ja '64

HARTFORD, Huntington, collection. See Gallery of modern art, New York

HARTFORD seminary foundation
Toward a more scholarly ministry; Hartford seminary's new curriculum. P. L. Berger. Christian Cent 80:524-7 Ap 24 '63

HARTIGAN, Grace
Gallery for young people. C. B. Johnson. il Sch Arts 63:36 O '63

HARTKE, Vance
Excerpt from address before Conference of business executives, January 21, 1963. Cong Digest 42:147+ My '63

HARTLEY, Ellen. See Hartley, W. jt. auth.

HARTLEY, Janet W.
Virology. Science 145:728 Ag 14 '64
—and Rowe, W. P.
New papovavirus containing Shope papilloma. bibliog Science 143:258-60 Ja 17 '64

HARTLEY, Raymond
What you can do for your country. Seventeen 23:62+ N '64
Your help is wanted in politics. Seventeen 23:132-3+ S '64

HARTLEY, William, and Hartley, Ellen
Redbook's 1964 guide to family vacations. Redbook 122:51-8 Ap '64
School with teacherless classrooms. Pop Mech 120:128-30 O '63

HARTLINE, Peter H. See Rawson, K. S. jt. auth.

HARTMAN, Carl G.
One hundred unanswered questions about the start of human life. McCalls 91:69+ S '64

HARTMAN, Geoffrey H.
Heroics of realism. Yale R 53:26-35 O '63

HARTMAN, K. O. See Hisatsune, I. C. jt. auth.

HARTMANN, Erich
Over the bounding main again; photographs. Sat Eve Post 237:64-9 Jl 11 '64

HARTMIRE, Wayne C. jr
Farm workers on the fringe. Christian Cent 81:959-62 Jl 29 '64

HARTNETT, Al
New fuel for IUE power struggle. por Bsns W p 118 O 5 '63

HARTRY, Arlene L. and others
Planaria: memory transfer through cannibalism reexamined. bibliog Science 146:274-5 O 9 '64

HARTSHORNE, Ebenezer
Ebenezer Hartshorne, cabinetmaker. R. H. Randall, jr and M. McElman. il Antiques 87:78-9 Ja '65

HARTSHORNE, Nathaniel
Big hand, little hand. Parents Mag 39:60-1+ S '64
Captain Really and the fabulous stairmounter. Harper 228:46-9 F '64
Ordeal of Lash Calhoun. Harper 228:43-4 My '64

HARTSOE, Charles E.
Anatomy of a congress. por Recreation 56:307 S '63

HARTUNG, Marion T.
Carnival glass. Hobbies 68:90 F '64

HARTUNG, Philip T.
Following the films. See issues of Senior scholastic
New movies (cont of) Movie reviews. See occasional issues of Senior scholastic
Screen. See issues of Commonweal

HARTWELL, Wayne M.
That toddlin' town also reads. por Library J 88:2426-9 Je 15 '63

HARTZ, Frederic M.
Library boards: administrative or advisory? por Library J 88:733-5 F 15 '63

HARTZOG, George B. jr.
Tomorrow's guardians: excerpts from address, February 15, 1964. por Recreation 57:165 Ap '64

about

High winds blow through the parks. A. W. Smith. Nat Parks Mag 37:2+ D '63
Man in the middle. J. Prokop. il pors Am For 70:34-6+ My '64

HARVAN, George
Rocks or faces? J. Durniak. il Pop Phot 52:61-3 F '63

HARVARD business school. See Harvard university—Graduate school of business administration

HARVARD club, New York. See New York (city)—Clubs

HARVARD fatal highway collisions project. See Traffic accidents

HARVARD Lampoon. See College and school journalism

HARVARD student agencies, incorporated. See College students—Employment

HARVARD university
Bigger and better parietals? Nat R 15:427-9 N 19 '63

HARVARD university—*Continued*
Changing face of Harvard college. H. Doermann. il Sat R 46:61-3 O 19 '63
Le Corbusier designs for Harvard. il Arch Rec 133:151-8 Ap '63
First of the month; excerpt from letter in the Harvard alumni bulletin on whether President Kennedy should resign from Harvard's Board of overseers. C. Amory. Sat R 46:6 My 4 '63
$5-million search for answers; Harvard to begin a ten-year study, financed by IBM. il Bsns W p84+ Jl 4 '64
Girls and dorms; Harvard's parietal regulations. Newsweek 62:78 N 11 '63
Harvard seminar for freshmen. Sch & Soc 91:208 My 4 '63
Harvard test ban? Newsweek 62:82 D 16 '63
How Harvard does it. L. L. L. Golden. Sat R 46:76 S 14 '63
Morals on campus. Christian Cent 80:1426 N 20 '63
Music at Harvard yesterday and today; with reports by P. Campbell and R. Wilson. H. Rogers; D. Hughes. il Mus Am 83:6-9 Je '63
Peripatetic reviewer. E. Weeks. Atlan 213: 114-15 Ja '64
Profiles; center of a new world. C. Rand. il New Yorker 40:43-8+ Ap 11; 57-8+ Ap 18; 55-6+ Ap 25 '64
Strange case of the Harvard drug scandal. A. T. Weil. il Look 27:38+ N 5 '63
Students and sex. Newsweek 62:71 N 18 '63
TAC designs new geology labs for Harvard. il Arch Rec 135:240 Ja '64

Carpenter center for the visual arts

First U.S. building by Corbu completed. il Arch Rec 133:10 Mr '63
Hand & the head; Visual arts center. il Time 81:72-5 Mr 8 '63
Le Corbusier at Harvard. W. Von Eckardt. New Repub 149:27-9 Jl 6 '63; Reply. S. Zetterbeg. 149:38-9 Ag 31 '63
Le Corbusier at Harvard: a disaster, or a bold step forward? imaginary debate. il Arch Forum 119:104-7 O '63
Le Corbusier completes his first U.S. building. il Arch Forum 118:78-81 Mr '63

Center for cognitive studies

Kids and computers; summary of address. J. Bruner. Sr Schol 83:3T N 22 '63

Graduate school of business administration

Harvardmen vs. big business. R. Nason. il Duns R 83:41-2+ Ja '64
Tailoring the B-school to new business world. il Bsns W p72-4+ Ja 19 '63

Graduate school of education

Harvard touch. Time 81:50 F 8 '63
Harvard's thirty-one-year-old dean. Time 83: 44+ Mr 20 '64

Harvard medical school

Young and daring; Peter Bent Brigham hospital. il Newsweek 61:55 F 11 '63

Libraries

Credo reconsidered; excerpts from Libraries and universities. P. Buck. il Library J 89:4295-300 N 1 '64
Fund-raising goal of $6 million set for Kennedy memorial library. Library J 89:210 Ja 15 '64
Kennedy library. E. Rudin. Library J 89:300 Ja 15 '64
Kennedy library fund established; would be open to all the people. Library J 89:335 Ja 15 '64
Opening the chambered nautilus; evaluation of uncataloged material for Francis A. Countway library. L. Ash. il Library J 89: 2040-3 My 15 '64
Shakespeare in the Harvard Theatre collection; Houghton library. H. D. Willard. il Wilson Lib Bul 38:640-4 Ap '64

HARVARD university press
Harvard's press marks half century of publishing. J. T. Winterich. il Pub W 183:14-21 Ap 22 '63

HARVESTING machinery
Machine speeds cabbage harvest. J. Bickers. il Farm J 87:50C D '63
New: hydrostatic drive for combines. il Farm J 89:47 Ja '65
Now, a machine that picks lettuce. il Farm J 87:44C S '63
Save that crop with combine know-how. D. O. Hull and W. J. Fletcher. il Suc Farm 62: 52-3 S '64
See also
Corn harvesting machinery

HARVEY, Alice M. and Christensen, H. N.
Uric acid transport system: apparent absence in erythrocytes of the dalmatian coach hound. bibliog Science 145:826-7 Ag 21 '64

HARVEY, Clyde
Gideon's echoes. Time 85:39+ Ja 29 '65

HARVEY, Frank
Child of the hurricane; story. Good H 157: 66-7 Ag '63
Instant camper on a pickup Pop Sci 184: 122-3 My '64

HARVEY, Irene
You can do anything when you know you're not alone; ed. by M. Drury. por McCalls 90:100-3+ S '63; Same abr. Read Digest 84:71-6 F '64

HARVEY, Jean Charles
Reporter at large. E. Wilson. New Yorker 40:184-9 N 28 '64

HARVEY, John
Special librarian: his characteristics and education; address, December 13, 1963. bibliog por Library J 89:4283-7 N 1 '64

HARVEY, Laurence
Boy prince. il por Time 82:84+ D 6 '63

HARVEY, Mary Kersey
Author. Sat R 46:39 F 2; 86 Mr 16 '63; 47:58 F 22 '64
Author: G. Feifer. Sat R 47:27 Je 27 '64
Author: G. Vidal. Sat R 47:32 Je 6 '64
Glenn Olds, innovator at Springfield. Sat R 47:67 F 15 '64
Grenville Clark at eighty. Sat R 46:17 F 16 '63

HARVEY, Mose L.
Inside report: how real is the Russia-China break? por U S News 56:64-9 Je 15 '64

HARVEY, Peggy
Hamburger cook book. House & Gard 127: 137+ Ja '65
Master menu cook book. House & Gard 124:273+ N '63

HARVEY aluminum, incorporated
Using tax-exempts to build business; aluminum mill in Lewisport, Ky. il Bsns W p45-6+ D 14 '63

HARVILL, Robert S.
Lore from a gemstone carving genius. D. J. Cipnic. il por Pop Mech 121:124-7+ Mr '64

HARVISON, Clifford W.
Crime problem in Canada: how the Mounties handle it; interview, ed. by K. M. Chrysler. por U S News 55:66-8 Jl 29 '63

HARWELL, Richard, and Hilyard, S. W.
One-hundred-dollar understanding. bibliog pors Library J 88:1937-40 My 15 '63

HARYOU. See Harlem youth opportunities unlimited, incorporated

HASANLU excavations. See Iran—Antiquities

HASBARGEN, Paul R. and Zeman, L. E.
How much hay do you need? Suc Farm 63:28-9+ Ja '65

HASCALL, Florence
No lollipop. Horn Bk 39:86-91 F '63

HASELDEN, Clyde L.
Lafayette in sequence. Library J 88:4577-9 D 1 '63

HASELDEN, Elizabeth Lee
Miracle on Chrystie st. Christian Cent 80: 1308 O 23 '63

HASELDEN, Kyle
Baptists in travail. Christian Cent 80:672-4 My 22 '63
Doctor Will. Christian Cent 80:174 F 6 '63
11 a.m. Sunday is our most segregated hour. N Y Times Mag p9+ Ag 2 '64
Fusion at Oberlin. Christian Cent 80:422-3 Ap 3 '63
Should there be compensation for Negroes? N Y Times Mag p43+ O 6 '63
Too busy to hate. Christian Cent 80:392-3 Mr 27 '63

about

Announcement; concerning K. Haselden's appointment as editor. F. Hoskins. Christian Cent 81:358 Mr 18 '64

HASELKORN, Robert
Actinomycin D as a probe for nucleic acid secondary structure. bibliog Science 143: 682-4 F 14 '64

HASENCLEVER, Walter
Writers in Berlin. Atlan 212:110-13 D '63

HASH
So nice to come home to hash. il McCalls 91:120-1 F '64

HASIDISM
I-thou & I-it. Time 82:49 Jl 12 '63
Interpreting Hasidism; tr. by M. Friedman. M. Buber. Commentary 36:218-25 S '63
Martin Buber's Hasidism. G. Scholem; discussion. Commentary 33:161-3 F '62; 37: 18-20 F '64

HASKELL, Douglas
Agony of Golding's new hero. Life 56:12+ Ap 24 '64

HASKELL, Douglas—*Continued*
Lost New York of the Pan American airways building. Arch Forum 119:106-11 N '63
Seventy-five years of change, mostly unpredicted. Arch Forum 121:72-80 Ag '64
HASKELL, Theodore J.
Hand labor is dead. Am City 78:79-80 Ap '63
HASKETT, Thomas R.
Audio level clippers & limiters. Electr World 71:51-4+ F '64
Broadcast band DX getting started. Pop Electr 21:53-6+ N '64
—and Blount, J. D.
Radio & TV interference. Electr World 71: 39-41 My; 40-1+ Je '64
HASKIL, Clara
From the legacy of Clara Haskil, Chopin and Falla. H. Goldsmith por Hi Fi 13:77-8 N '63
HASKIN, Glenn
Let's have a circus. Recreation 56:186-8 Ap '63
HASKIN, Larry, and Gehl, M. A.
Rare-earth elements in tektites. bibliog Science 139:1056-8 Mr 15 '63
HASKINS, Caryl P.
How guard our diversity in science? Science 140:141 Ap 12 '63
Interfaces between science and public policy; excerpts from address, March 1964. Science 144:801 My 15 '64
Scientific enigma of Communist China; excerpts from Scientific revolution and world politics. por Sat R 47:58-60 Je 6 '64

about

Meeting; Carnegie institution of Washington. New Yorker 39:31-3 Je 8 '63
HASKINS, F. A. and Gorz, H. J.
Glucosides of coumarinic and o-coumaric acids in the tonka bean. bibliog Science 139: 496-7 F 8 '63
HASKINS, John F.
Cache at Stone-fortress-hill. Natur Hist 72: 30-9 F '63
HASKINS, Sam
Year's best glamor book. J. M. Zanutto. il Pop Phot 52:70-5 Ap '63
HASLEMERE festival. See Music festivals—England
HASLUCK, PAUL
Australia and southeast Asia. For Affairs 43:51-63 O '64
U.S. New Zealand, and Australia reaffirm ties of friendship; remarks, July 17, 1964. Dept State Bul 51:196-7 Ag 10 '64
HASSAN II, king of Morocco
Clash in the Sahara. il Sr Schol 83:7-9+ N 22 '63
First of the newtime spenders; buying spree in New York. il por Time 81:33 Ap 12 '63
Friend in Washington. il por Time 81:37-8 Ap 5 '63
His Majesty Hassan II, king of Morocco; rarely photographed royal court of Morocco. C. Beaton. il pors Vogue 144:224-31 S 1 '64
King's headache. il por Time 81:29-30 Je 7 '63
Man who came to dinner. il por Time 81:27-8 Mr 22 '63
Moroccan monarch meets the press; N.B.C.-TV. Christian Cent 80:484 Ap 17 '63
Reflections on the Barbary Coast. R. Kirk. Nat R 15:442 N 19 '63
Road from Morocco: easy lies the head; with report by A. Deming. por Newsweek 61:31 Ap 1 '63
Visit from a King. M. Cartwright. il pors Negro Hist Bul 26:245-6 My '63
Visiting Moroccan monarch. por Sr Schol 82: 27 Ap 3 '63
HASSAN, Ihab
New frontiers in American literature; excerpts from address, April 24, 1964. Wilson Lib Bul 39:248-52 N '64
HASSEL, Kai Uwe von
Détente through firmness. For Affairs 42: 184-94 Ja '64
Organizing western defense. For Affairs 43:209-16 Ja '65
HASTIE, Cornelius
Quiet revolution. J. F. Warner. il Sat R 47:80-1+ My 16 '64
HASTIE, Sandra MacGregor
(tr) See Neruda. P. Four love poems
HASTIE, William Henry
Top judge. A. Morrison. il pors Ebony 19:111-12+ Mr '64
HASTINGS, Baird
Letter from Richard Wagner. Opera N 28:4 N 16 '63
HASTINGS, John E. F.
Canada's health programs. bibliog f Cur Hist 44:326-32+ Je '63
HASTINGS, Osbert
Paul VI and the bishops. Reporter 29:23-5 D 19 '63
Pope, the bishops, and Edward Gibbon. Reporter 31:22-5 D 31 '64
HAT my mother bought me; story. See Brooks, T. E.
HAT trade
See also
Millinery
HATA, Laurence
Hata time in Honolulu. L. Barry. il por Pop Phot 55:36 D '64
HATCH, Anita, and others
Long-term isolation stress in rats. bibliog Science 142:507 O 25 '63
HATCH, Jane (Maddox)
WLB biography (cont) Wilson Lib Bul 37: 712 Ap '63
HATCH, John
Congo: hostages, mercenaries and the CIA. Nation 199:452-5 D 14 '64
HATCH, Robert
Adult prodigy. Horizon 5:84-91 Jl '63
American teachers association pushes activity in two vital areas; commission for improvement of teacher competency initiated. Negro Hist Bul 27:150-2 Mr '64
Case against the Britannica. Nation 198:303-4 Mr 23 '64
Dapper wayfarer. Harper 229:129-32 O '64
Films. See issues of Nation
Theatre. See issues of Horizon
Tyrone Guthrie: the artist as man of the theatre. Horizon 5:35-41 N '63
HATCHER, Andrew Thomas
Andrew Hatcher makes good; first Negro associate White House press secretary. S. Booker. il pors Ebony 18:69-70+ O '63
HATCHER, Joan W.
In a tiny garden. Pop Gard 14:56-7 Mr '63
HATCHIE refuge, Tenn. See Bird sanctuaries
HATCHING. See Incubation
HATE
Can we learn not to hate? ed. by A. Gordon. S. Blanton. Good H 156:73+ F '63
Do they really hate to hate? W. F. Buckley, jr. Nat R 15:559 D 31 '63
Fearmongers; with report by B. Bettelheim. il Life 56:71-8+ F 7 '64
Speaking out; hate knows no direction. R. E. McGill. Sat Eve Post 236:8+ D 14 '63
HATFIELD, J. Tennis
Examination hell in Taiwan. Sch & Soc 91: 378-9 N 30 '63
HATFIELD, Lee
Poetry chronicle. P. Petrie. Poetry 102:50 Ap '63
HATFIELD, Mark Odom
Our foreign policy; address, May 27, 1964. Vital Speeches 30:533-5 Je 15 '64
Program of faith; address, July 13, 1964. Vital Speeches 30:652-4 Ag 15 '64

about

Keynoter Hatfield, the image-maker. il pors Life 56:62A-62B+ Je 26 '64
Mark Hatfield, man with a tough job. J. Duscha. por Reporter 31:15-17 Jl 2 '64
Mark the man. il por Newsweek 63:15-16 F 17 '64
Projecting the image. il por Time 83:20 Je 5 '64
HATHA yoga. See Yoga
HATOFSKY, Julius
Hatofsky: emerging expressionist. C. S. Silver. il por Art N 62:50-1+ F '64
HATRED. See Hate
HATS
Century of doll hats. C. H. Fawcett. il Hobbies 68:38+ Ap '63
Five gallon; LBJ hats. il Newsweek 63:68 F 10 '64
Hat to change your mind about hats; 1963 turban. il Vogue 141:100-7 Mr 15 '63
Hats from paper junk. P. Sanders. il Design 65:152-3+ Mr '64
Mail-order chic; Sears's best-selling hats. il Life 56:57+ Mr 20 '64
Old hat; today's fashion. il Time 81:76+ Ap 5 '63
Who's who in holiday hats; make-believe millinery. il McCalls 92:126-7+ D '64
See also
Headgear
Millinery

Anecdotes, facetiae, satire, etc.

Hats. M. A. Rodgers. il Redbook 121:15 My '63
HATS, Doll. See Doll clothes
HATTERSLEY, Ralph S
Form & content in color. Pop Phot 55:84-91 Jl '64

HATTERSLEY, Ralph S.—*Continued*
Psychology of people-pictures. Pop Phot 53: 167-82 N '63
Repairing spots and scratches on the small negative. il Pop Phot 55:140-1+ N '64
Some Atget Paris pictures. Pop Phot 55:24+ O '64
Weston's picture is about freedom, yours and mine. Pop Phot 55:70-1+ S '64
HATTIESBURG, Miss.
Hattiesburg: toward reconciliation. L. Minear. Christian Cent 81:1115-16 S 9 '64
One-sided lighting story. C. F. Pittman, jr. il Am City 79:104 Jl '64
HAUBERG, C. A.
Changing conditions in Guatemala. bibliog f Cur Hist 44:106-10+ F '63
HAUGE, Gabriel
Accent on the individual. Sat R 47:48 Ja 11 '64
HAUGHTON, Billy
Emperor in harness. M. Kram. il por Sports Illus 20:44+ Je 15 '64
HAUNTED houses. See Ghosts
HAUPERT, John S.
Israel. bibliog Focus 14:1-6 Mr '64
HAUPT, Enid A.
Seventeen book of etiquette and entertaining; excerpts. Seventeen 22:136-9+ Mr; 60-1 Ap; 28 My; 130-1 Je; 40 Jl; 282+ Ag; 28 O; 40 N; 118 D '63; 23:26 Mr; 26 Ap; 32 My; 32 Je; 16 Jl; 42 Ag; 73 S; 32 N '64
HAUPT, Ira, and company
Annals of finance. J. Brooks. New Yorker 40:160+ N 14 '64
Boiling in oil. Time 82:87A D 13 '63
Bubble bursts. il Newsweek 62:74+ D 2 '63
Commodity blow-up shuts big brokerage. il Bsns W p96+ N 30 '63
Housekeepers; practices of brokerage firms. Fortune 69:242+ Ap '64
In wake of Haupt failure; second thoughts on commodities dealing. Bsns W p 128 D 7 '63
Lessons from the Haupt affairs. Fortune 69: 74+ Ja '64
100-million-dollar mystery? attempt to aid Ira Haupt and co. by New York stock exchange. il U S News 55:109-10 D 16 '63
Rescue operation. il Newsweek 62:80+ D 9 '63
Scandal in salad oil gets bigger every day; with editorial comment. il Bsns W p32+, 160 D 14 '63
Spreading the losses. il Time 82:109-10 D 6 '63
Tino's bottomless tanks of oil; salad oil swindle. N. C. Miller. il Sat Eve Post 237: 19-25 Ap 25 '64
Where genius went wrong; crude oil scandal. il Bsns W p 164-6+ Ap 18 '64
HAUPTMANN, Gerhart
Gerhart Hauptmann, dramatist of the oppressed. K. Ruhrberg; reply. E. Locher. UNESCO Courier 16:33 Mr '63
HAURWITZ, B.
Atmospheric tides. bibliog Science 144:1415-22 Je 19 '64
HAUSER, Ernest O.
Artist in concrete. Read Digest 84:208-11+ F '64
Europe's uncommon market comes alive. Read Digest 85:140-4 Jl '64
Italy's innocent Communists. Read Digest 83: 193-5+ N '63
Michelangelo's magnificent mirror of man. Read Digest 84:176-80+ My '64
HAUSER, Huc H.
Back-seat playroom for your VW. Pop Mech 119:176-7 F '63
HAUSER, Margaret. See Gay Head, pseud.
HAUSER, Philip M.
How population explosion is changing the U.S; interview. por U S News 57:58-63 Ag 31 '64
Man and more men: the population prospects; reprint. Bul Atomic Sci 20:4-8 Je '64
Population and labor force. Mo Labor R 86:262-4 Mr '63
HAUSER, Rita
Law of letters. Sat R 46:56-7 F 9 '63
HAUSNER, Gideon
Reporter at large; Eichmann trial. H. Arendt. New Yorker 38:40-2+ F 16; 39:40-2+ Mr 2; 58-60+ Mr 16 '63
HAUSNER, H. H. See Bonis, L. J. jt. auth.
HAUSSAMEN, Walter
How to make old-fashioned jerky. Outdoor Life 133:129 F '64
HAUSSMANN, Georges Eugène, baron
Man who destroyed Paris. W. Von Eckardt. il por Horizon 5:50-75 My '63
HAUTZIG, Esther
Ezra Jack Keats. Horn Bk 39:364-8 Ag '63
HAVANA
Guided tour around Havana, courtesy Fidel; And courtesy Nikita: supply line thrives. il Life 54:40-40B F 8 '63
When the British captured Havana. G. de Zéndegui. il Américas 16:21-8 Mr '64
Description
Havana. M. Hemingway. il Sat R 48:40-1+ Ja 2 '65
HAVARD, William C.
From bossism to cosmopolitanism: changes in the relationship of urban leadership to state politics. bibliog f Ann Am Acad 353:84-94 My '64
HAVASU LAKE
Water is a deep blue-green and you fish for bass, crappie. il Sunset 131:64+ O '63
HAVASU LAKE national wildlife refuge. See Wildlife sanctuaries
HAVE I got a girl for you! drama. See Cooper, I.
HAVE you ever rode the Southern? story. See Fox, W. P.
HAVEMANN, Ernest
Big risk for pipe smokers. Sports Illus 20: 32-4+ Ap 13 '64
Darryl Zanuck: last of the movie moguls. McCalls 91:134-5+ O '63
Defendant Ruby will meet the ghost of a long dead Scot. Life 56:30-1 F 21 '64
Horse player Havemann rides again. por Life 54:15 Ap 12 '63
Judge they have to tell it to. Sports Illus 21:38+ N 16 '64
Only girl who acts with her back and front, too. Life 54:85-6+ F 22 '63
Palmer gets fit to fight again. Sports Illus 18:22-5 Je 3 '63
People's choice for L.B.J.'s V.P. Life 57:68-70+ Ag 14 '64
Pitchers make snails look fast so throw the ball! Life 55:17 S 6 '63; Same abr. with title So throw the ball! Read Digest 84: 116-18 Ap '64
Scientists search for the answers to a touchy and puzzling question, why? Life 56:76+ Je 26 '64
Storm center of justice. Life 56:108-10+ My 22 '64; Same abr. with title Warren court. Read Digest 85:130-5 S '64
Too much leisure. Life 56:76-80+ F 14; 84-6+ F 21 '64; Same abr. with title Leisure, the great new challenge. Read Digest 85: 125-8 Ag '64
Twenty-four hours in the life of Steve McQueen. McCalls 91:138-9+ Ap '64
Worried man with a frightening filly. por Sports Illus 19:16-17 Jl 22 '63
HAVEMANN, Robert
Silencing a Socrates. il por Time 83:23-4 Mr 27 '64
HAVENS, Jim
Please save my son! D. O. Woodbury. por Read Digest 82:157-8+ F '63
HAVENS, Shirley
Bruce Joffe's private library. il Library J 88:2066-8 My 15 '63
HAVERFORD college, Haverford, Pa.
Science building for small liberal arts college. il Arch Rec 136:162-4 N '64
HAVERSIAN systems. See Bone
HAVERSTICK, Iola
Servants, saints, and sinners. Sat R 46:35 Mr 23 '63
HAVERSTOCK, Nathan A.
Alliance for progress. Américas 15:2-9 Ag '63
Return to democracy. Américas 15:14-16 Mr '63
Volunteers for progress. Américas 15:2-10 Jl '63
HAVIGHURST, Robert J.
Education for contemporary society. Science 143:556-8 F 7 '64
HAVILAND, Virginia
Children's libraries. Wilson Lib Bul 38:487 F '64
Lively art of picture books. Library J 89: 4110-11 O 15 '64
about
Virginia Haviland resigns for permanent post at LC. Library J 89:338 Ja 15 '64
HAVLENA, Joan. See Werboff, J. jt. auth.
HAVOC, June
Marathon '33. Criticism
America 110:147-8 Ja 25 '64
Commonweal 79:461-2 Ja 17 '64
Nation 198:58 Ja 13 '64
New Repub 150:25 Ja 11 '64
New Yorker 39:58+ Ja 4 '64
Newsweek il por 63:61 Ja 6 '64
Sat R 47:52 Ja 11 '64
Time il 83:70 Ja 3 '64
Vogue 143:22 F 15 '64

HAVRINCOURT, Hubert d'
Red cross; centenary of a universal banner. UNESCO Courier 16:20-5 Je '63

HAWAII
50th state, at five, goes mainland. W. J. Lederer. il N Y Times Mag p24+ Ag 16 '64
Henry Kaiser: new project, Hawaii-Kai. L. Elliott. il Sci Digest 53:58-65 My '63
Seduction and challenge of Hawaii. A. Heckscher. House & Gard 126:52+ Jl '64
T.R.B. from Hawaii. New Repub 151:2 Ag 22 '64

See also
Airlines—Hawaii
Architecture—Hawaii
Architecture, Domestic—Hawaii
Botany—Hawaii
Communism—Hawaii
Fishing—Hawaii
Forests and forestry—Hawaii
Geology—Hawaii
Hotels, taverns, etc.—Hawaii
Kauai (island)
Libraries—Hawaii
Maui (island)
Mauna Kea
Niihau (island)
Oahu (island)
Political campaigns—Hawaii
Strikes—Hawaii
Theater—Hawaii
Tourist trade—Hawaii
Wages—Hawaii
Zoology—Hawaii

Climate

Weather diversity can be the gardener's best friend. il House & Gard 126:78-9 Jl '64

Description and travel

Aloha on a budget. F. Somers. il Redbook 121:36+ Ag '63
Confessions of a Hawaii fancier. H. Sutton. il Sat R 47:50-2+ O 10 '64
Going places, finding things in Hawaii. J. Wilson. il House & Gard 126:4+ Jl '64
Hawaii. E. Scully. il U S Camera 27:74-5+ Mr '64
I'm in love with our 50th state. F. Sparks. il Read Digest 85:125-8 O '64
Motorambling in Hawaii. T. B. Lesure. il Travel 122:26-9+ D '64
On the beach at Honaunau. R. A. Apple. il Ladies Home J 80:66-7+ Je '63
Personal business: winter vacation in Oahu. Bsns W p81-2 F 2 '63
Teen travel talk. T. A. Porter. il Seventeen 24:20+ Ja '65
Travel notes. R. Joseph. Esquire 62:19-20+ Ag '64
Visit to Hawaii's new Polynesian center. il Sunset 132:30+ Mr '64

Industries

Executive investor; values in Hawaii. il Duns R 82:77-9 Jl '63
Island princes bow to new ways; Hawaii's Big five companies. il Bsns W p56-8+ Ap 11 '64
Potential in the Pacific. il Time 84:111B O 2 '64

Japanese raids

See Pearl Harbor, Attack on, 1941

Parks and reserves

On Hawaii, a visit to the City of Refuge National Park. il Sunset 133:42+ N '64
On the beach at Honaunau. R. A. Apple. il Ladies Home J 80:66-7+ Je '63

Religious institutions and affairs

Aloha has many meanings. A. E. P. Wall. America 111:148 Ag 15 '64
Church for teen-agers. il Time 82:57 D 6 '63
News of the Christian world (cont) Christian Cent 80:374 Mr 20 '63

Social life and customs

Lovely lesson I learned in Hawaii. D. Walker. House & Gard 126:112-13+ Jl '64

HAWAII. University, Honolulu

Cultural center

Advisory commission to survey Hawaii's East-West center. Dept State Bul 49:684 O 28 '63
Dialogue between cultures. S. W. Bartlett. il Sat R 47:44-7+ Jl 18 '64
Educational miracle. N. Cousins. il Sat R 47:20+ Mr 21 '64
Governor of Hawaii confers on East-West center. Dept State Bul 50:976 Je 22 '64
Larsen report on the East-West center recommendations. Sat R 47:46 Jl 18 '64
Where the twain get together; East-West center. il Bsns W p34-5 N 28 '64

HAWAII NATIONAL PARK
Hawaii's trees of stone. D. L. Hamilton. il Nat Parks Mag 38:15-17 Ja '64

HAWAIIAN art. See Art, Hawaiian

HAWAIIAN cookery. See Cookery, Hawaiian

HAWAIIAN house decoration. See House decoration, Hawaiian

HAWAIIAN ISLANDS national wildlife refuge. See Wildlife sanctuaries

HAWAIIAN seals. See Seals (animals)

HAWES, Elizabeth
Window; poem. New Yorker 40:94 S 12 '64

HAWES, Gene R.
Colleges of America's upper class. Sat R 46:68-71 N 16 '63
—See Keller, G. C. jt. auth.

HAWES, Josiah Johnson
More living than the memory of the man. B. Newhall. Pop Phot 55:152-3+ N '64

HAWES, Lloyd E.
Adam and Eve in the decorative arts. Antiques 84:278-82 S '63

HAWES, Marion Emsley
Accent on the individual reader. Wilson Lib Bul 38:70+ S '63

HAWK, Richard L.
Gooseberry, innocent outlaw. Horticulture 41:366-7 Jl '63
Nut which isn't a nut. Horticulture 41:528 O '63

HAWK MOUNTAIN line. See Wanamaker, Kempton and southern railroad

HAWKES, Alex D.
Pony-tail plant. Horticulture 41:143 Mr '63
Try a bird's nest fern. Horticulture 42:10-11 Ja '64

HAWKES, Jacquetta
Awakening of the mind; excerpt from History of mankind. UNESCO Courier 16:8-10 Je '63
Dawn of art; excerpt from History of mankind. UNESCO Courier 16:11-13 Je '63

HAWKES, Joan
How to win arguments with your parents. Seventeen 22:120-1+ N '63
Looking ahead to college and careers. See issues of Seventeen

HAWKES, John
Heart demands satisfaction; story, excerpt from Second skin. Vogue 143:72-3 Ja 15 '64

HAWKING. See Falconry

HAWKINS, Augustus Freeman
Gus Hawkins, fifth Negro congressman. H. J. Massaquoi. il pors Ebony 18:38-40+ F '63

HAWKINS, Brooks
Cruising the Connecticut. il Motor B 113:30-1+ Ap '64
Ides of October. Motor B 114:45+ O '64

HAWKINS, Coleman
Jazz notes. E. Larrabee. Harper 229:117 S '64
School of Hawkins. M. Williams. Sat R 47:46-7 Jl 11 '64

HAWKINS, David F.
Case of the dubious deferral. Harvard Bsns R 41:162-4+ My '63

HAWKINS, Edler Garnett
Church catches up. C. W. Thomas. por Negro Hist Bul 28:19-20 O '64
Presbyterians' choice. por Newsweek 63:82 Je 1 '64
Presbyterians elect Negro moderator. Christian Cent 81:725 Je 3 '64

HAWKINS, George A.
Residue tells the story. Am City 78:104-6 S '63

HAWKINS, Gerald S.
Callanish, a Scottish Stonehenge. Science 147:127-30 Ja 8 '65
Secret of Stonehenge. Harper 228:96-9 Je '64

HAWKINS, Marshall
Favored sport of Jacqueline. il Sat Eve Post 236:24-7 F 23 '63

HAWKINS, Quail
Promoting, planning and producing book fairs. Pub W 186:171-5 Jl 13 '64

HAWKINS, Robert
(tr) See Landowska, W. From the Landowska notebooks

HAWKINS, T. Daryl. See Pliskoff, S. S. jt. auth.

HAWKINS, William
Marian Anderson says farewell. Mus Am 84:8-11 S '64

HAWKS
Lookouts for hawk flights in Pennsylvania. O. S. Pettingill, jr. il Audubon Mag 66:272+ S '64

HAWKS—*Continued*
Paean to a winged hunter. B. Gilbert. il Sports Illus 18:50-5 F 4 '63
See also
Falcons
Kites (birds)
Nighthawks
Ospreys
HAWLEY, Claude E.
Campaign '64. bibliog Sr Schol 84:8T-10T Mr 6 '64
HAWLEY, Henry
Neoclassicism in Italian pictures. Antiques 86:316-19 S '64
Vincennes-Sèvres porcelain at the Cleveland museum of art. Antiques 85:322-5 Mr '64
HAWORTH, Jill
I've lost my English accent; ed. by E. Miller. pors Seventeen 24:68-9+ Ja '65
HAWORTH, Leland John
Doctor Haworth named new science foundation head. Sci N L 83:213 Ap 6 '63
NSF: new director has ordered small but significant steps aimed at improving operations. D. S. Greenberg. Science 141:1017-18 S 13 '63
Science foundation; Leland Haworth of Atomic energy commission named as successor to Alan T. Waterman. D. S. Greenberg. por Science 139:1272 Mr 29 '63
HAWTHORN books, incorporated
Prentice-Hall sells Hawthorn books. Pub W 187:66 Ja 11 '65
HAWTHORNE, Gladys
Library moving made easy. ALA Bul 57:671 Jl '63
HAWTHORNE, Nathaniel
My kinsman, Major Molineux; dramatization. See Lowell, R. Old Glory
about
Hawthorne discovers the English. W. G. Carleton. Yale R 53:395-414 Mr '64
HAWTHORNE plant. See Western electric company
HAY, Jacob
Over the Blue Ridge. Holiday 35:22+ My '64
Pennsylvania Dutch. Holiday 36:40-1+ Ag '64
Portaling; story. Sat Eve Post 237:40-3 N 21 '64
HAY, John
Our alliance with nature; excerpt from address, delivered on acceptance of John Burroughs medal, April 6, 1964. Audubon Mag 66:395-8 N '64
HAY, John C. and others
Adaptation to chromatic aberration by the human visual system. bibliog Science 141:167-9 Jl 12 '63
HAY, Richard L.
Stratigraphy of beds I through IV, Olduvai Gorge, Tanganyika. bibliog Science 139:829-33 Mr 1 '63
HAY, Sara Henderson
Witch; poem. Sat R 46:44 Ap 20 '63
HAY
Buy hay for its TDN? G. Lorang. il Farm J 89:44 Ja '65
Six tons of hay per acre. L. E. Zeman. il Suc Farm 61:34-5 Je '63
HAY fever
Aaa-chooo! list of do's and don'ts. Newsweek 64:75 Ag 24 '64
Hypnosis helps hay fever. Sci N L 85:306 My 16 '64
Tips for your home and family. Todays Health 41:69-70 S '63
HAY fever: drama. See Coward, N.
HAY handling
Faster baling, less backwork. il Farm J 88:26-7 Je '64
Harvest hay by the calendar. W. F. Hueg, jr. and L. E. Zeman. il Suc Farm 62:44-5 Je '64
HAY making. See Hay handling
HAY making machinery
Big year for new hay balers. G. W. Wormley. il Farm J 88:64+ F '64
HAYASHI, M. and others
Replicating form of a single-stranded DNA virus: isolation and properties. bibliog Science 140:1313-16 Je 21 '63
HAYATSU, Ryoichi
Orgueil meteorite: organic nitrogen contents. bibliog Science 146:1291-3 D 4 '64
HAYBITTLE, John
Ethics for the scientist. Bul Atomic Sci 20:23-4 My '64
HAYDEN, C. Gervin
Hard-sell fair. Nation 197:275-8 N 2 '63
HAYDEN, Carl
Nation's Capitol revealed as never before. Nat Geog Mag 125:1-3 Ja '64
about
If something happened to the President. il por U S News 55:37 D 16 '63
McCormack and Hayden: no plan to quit. por U S News 55:12 D 23 '63
Men in line for the presidency now. por U S News 55:14 D 2 '63
HAYDEN, George A. See Friedberg, F. jt. auth.
HAYDEN, Holden
Tule dippers. Field & S 68:54-5+ F '64
HAYDEN, Imogene
Hand of the gardener. Horticulture 42:46+ F '64
HAYDEN, Jay G.
Was T.R. a drunk? Am Heritage 15:82-3 O '64
HAYDEN, Melissa
Melissa Hayden, on stage and off; excerpts. pors Dance Mag 37:48-51 D '63
HAYDEN planetarium. See Planetariums
HAYDN, Franz Joseph
DGG's Paukenmesse, the perfect compromise. H. Glass. il Am Rec G 30:1036 Jl '64
Flawless performance of a Haydn masterpiece; Missa Solemnis. H. Glass. Am Rec G 29:873 Jl '63
Gloria in excelsis Deo: the Haydn Masses; with discography. H. C. R. Landon. il Hi Fi 14:56-9+ D '64
Haydn quake, second tremor. R. Freed. il Sat R 47:49+ Ja 25 '64
Haydn renascence continues. R. C. Marsh. il Hi Fi 13:78-9 N '63
Haydn's Bear and Haydn's Hen, the right scores make all the difference. H. C. R. Landon. il por Hi Fi 14:89-90 N '64
In memoriam: Fritz Reiner's last recording. J. Diether. Am Rec G 31:141 O '64
Janigro: Haydn's Sturm und drang symphonies. J. W. Barker. Am Rec G 30:610+ Mr '64
Joseph Haydn: eighteenth century gentleman and genius, by G. A. Griesinger and A. C. Dies. Review
Sat R 46:30-1 Jl 20 '63. E. Winternitz
On records; Mass in time of war. Opera N 29:34 Ja 2 '65
Simultaneously, no less than nine different Haydn concerti. J. W. Barker. Am Rec G 30:850-1 My '64
Three by Kurt Redel, unabashed admiration. H. Glass. il Am Rec G 30:576-7 Mr '64
Westminster's Somogyi: a most auspicious debut. J. W. Barker. il Am Rec G 30:318 D '63
HAYDUK, S. Hobbs. See Uzmann, J. R. jt. auth.
HAYES, Alfred
Dollar: national and international bulwark; address, April 22, 1963. Vital Speeches 29:490-3 Je 1 '63
HAYES, Alfred S.
What is a language laboratory? Sat R 46:70-1 F 16 '63
HAYES, Bob
How fast is the fastest man alive? J. Underwood. il pors Sports Illus 20:26-9 My 18 '64
HAYES, C. E. and Webb, W. W.
Dislocations in ice. bibliog Science 147:44-5 Ja 1 '65
HAYES, Carlton J. H.
Gentleman and scholar. America 111:280 S 19 '64
HAYES, Eva
We took to the great outdoors with baby. Parents Mag 39:46-7+ Je '64
HAYES, Helen
I bid adieu to things. il pors Life 55:99-101+ N 1 '63
In memory of Mary. por Newsweek 62:104-5 O 21 '63
HAYES, Jim
Broken stream revives. Outdoor Life 131:52-5+ Je '63
Miracle of Whites Creek. Outdoor Life 134:24-7+ N '64
New fishing for Easterners. Outdoor Life 131:40-1+ Mr '63
HAYES, Jim, family
We took to the great outdoors with baby. E. Hayes. il Parents Mag 39:46-7+ Je '64
HAYES, Joseph
Asolo theatre festival. Theatre Arts 47:30-1 Jl '63
Calculated risk; text. Theatre Arts 47:20-54 D '63
HAYES, King T. Jr
Thought for Brotherhood week; poem. Negro Hist Bul 26:238 My '63
HAYES, Richard
Eugene O'Neill: the tragic in exile. Theatre Arts 47:16-17+ O '63

HAYES, Robert Lee
Fastest human in spikes, or cleats. T. C. Brody. il Sports Illus 21:58-60 D 14 '64
Fight for a fraction. il por Time 83:78+ Mr 13 '64
Start's the thing. por Time 81:66+ Je 28 '63
HAYES, Rutherford Birchard
Hayes: the diary of a president, 1875-1881, ed. by T. H. Williams. Review
Newsweek por 63:98D-99 My 11 '64
President who hurt Negroes most. C. L. Sanders. il pors Ebony 19:110-12+ My '64
HAYES, Samuel L. and Woods, D. H.
Are SBICs doing their job? Harvard Bsns R 41:6-8+ Mr '63
HAYES, Vincent de Paul
Books to be noted; religion. America 108: 680+ My 11 '63
HAYES, Woody
Cut 'em off at forward pass. W. B. Furlong. il por Sports Illus 21:30-3 O 19 '64
HAYFLICK, Leonard, and others
Human diploid cell strains. Science 143:976 F 28 '64
HAYLING, Robert
Anarchy in St Augustine. L. Goodwyn. il Harper 230:74-81 Ja '65
HAYLOCK, E. F.
Britain's challengers. Motor B 114:24-7 Ag '64
British lose Beaverbrook trophy. Motor B 112:53+ N '63
Run for his money. Motor B 113:92+ Ja '64
Smooth surfride to Torquay. Motor B 114: 46-7+ O '64
Wanted badly, a second Cup boat! Motor B 112:52+ N '63
HAYMAN, John L. Jr, and Johnson, J. T. Jr
Research on the context of instructional television. Sch Life 45:8-11 Ap '63
HAYMES, Donas
Executive: how far, how fast, how much? Duns R 84:46-8+ O '64
HAYNE, William Hamilton
Sea lyric; excerpt. Motor B 112:19 Jl '63
HAYNES, C. Vance, Jr
Fluted projectile points: their age and dispersion. bibliog Science 145:1408-13 S 25 '64
HAYNES, Frank
Frontier photographer; excerpts from Following the frontier. F. Tilden. il Am Heritage 15:22-35 O '64
HAYNES, Julian, and Burnett, A. L.
Dedifferentiation and redifferentiation of cells in hydra viridis. bibliog Science 142:1481-3 D 13 '63
HAYS, Brooks
Who makes decisions in Washington. pors Nations Bsns 53:40-1+ Ja '65
HAYS, Donald F. and Felten, J. B.
Cavity formation in thin films of viscous liquids. Science 141:1174-5 S 20 '63
HAYS, Wayne L.
New stew. il por Newsweek 62:32 N 25 '63
HAYSTACK antenna. See Radio antennas
HAYWARD, John F.
Furniture from the Rotch bequest to the Victoria and Albert museum. Antiques 83:560-3 My '63
HAYWARD, Max
(tr) See Babel, I. Two stories
(tr) See Evtushenko, E. Babi Yar
(tr) See Solzhenitsyn, A. One day in the life of Ivan Denisovich
HAYWARD, Pamela
Leland Haywards of Haywire house. V. Lawford. il pors Vogue 143:124-7+ F 15 '64
HAYWARD, Roger
Amateur scientist: tests with rolling balls. Sci Am 211:102-6 Ag '64
HAYWOOD, C. Robert
Advanced placement. NEA J 54:23-4 Ja '65
HAYWOOD, Charles Foster
Revolt of the professors. R. Cleghorn. New Repub 148:5-6 F 2 '63
HAZARD, E. I. and others
Resistance to the chemical sterilant, apholate, in aedes aegypti. Science 145:500-1 Jl 31 '64
HAZARD, John W.
Why buy growth stocks? Changing T 18:7-11 F '64
HAZARD, Leland
Are we committing urban suicide? Harvard Bsns R 42:152-4+ Jl '64
Mahatma Gandhi was wrong. Atlan 214:45-9 Jl '64
Our national goals: the hard choices. Harvard Bsns R 41:22-4+ My '63
HAZARD, Ky.
Gray spring in Hazard. S. Gervis. Commonweal 78:220-2 My 17 '63
In Hazard. D. Wakefield. Commentary 36: 209-17 S '63

HAZEL, Robert
Death in Oregon; poem. Nation 197:184 S 28 '63
Run of three. J. M. Morrison. Poetry 101:280-1 Ja '63
HAZEL nut trees. See Filbert trees
HAZELSWART, D. E.
Water on tap for city growth. Am City 78: 92-4 S '63
HAZELTON, Jean Hanvey
Thomas Jefferson, gourmet. Am Heritage 15: 20-1+ O '64
HAZELTON, Nika Standen
Going places, finding things in north Norway. House & Gard 125:23+ Je '64
House & garden's Scandinavian cook book. House & Gard 125:137+ F '64
House & garden's Swiss cook book. il House & Gard 124:169+ S '63
Maiden ladies. New Yorker 39:162+ S 21 '63
HAZELTON, Paul
Education and politics. Sat R 46:62-3+ Je 15 '63
HAZELTON, Roger
Holy Spirit and religion. Christian Cent 82:73-4 Ja 20 '65
Ministry as servanthood. Christian Cent 80: 521-4 Ap 24 '63
HAZLETON, Pa.
Doctor Dessen's can-do city. W. J. Monaghan. il Todays Health 42:48-9+ N '64
Hope in Appalachia. il Time 83:25 Je 5 '64
HAZLITT, Henry
Business tides. See issues of Newsweek
Capitalism without horns. Nat R 14:200-1 Mr 12 '63
Fallacy of too much planning. Read Digest 82:95-6 F '63
Left statisticians at play. Nat R 16:27 Ja 14 '64
Progressive taxation. por Newsweek 61:88 My 13 '63
Publishing scene. Nat R 16:366-7 My 5 '64
Two birthdays. Nat R 16:1138-9 D 29 '64
Will we ever pay off? por Newsweek 63:84 Je 8 '64; Same abr. Read Digest 85:115-16 Ag '64
HAZLITT, William
William Hazlitt, by H. Baker. Review
Reporter 28:50+ Ja 17 '63. G. Steiner; Reply with rejoinder. V. Anderson. 28: 8+ F 28 '63
HAZO, Samuel
Art and the liturgy. Cath World 199:286-92 Ag '64
Dying under drilling; poem. Harper 229:63 Ag '64
Jackass as hero; poem. Sat R 46:44 D 14 '63
Poet's cult. Commonweal 79:130-2 O 25 '63
Poets of retreat. Cath World 198:33-9 O '63
Something left for right now; poem. Commonweal 79:483 Ja 24 '64
Year I reached the years of God; poem. Commonweal 78:10 Mr 29 '63
HAZZARD, Shirley
Comfort; story. New Yorker 40:52-4 O 24 '64
Flowers of sorrow; story. New Yorker 40: 52-4 O 17 '64
Forgiving; story. Ladies Home J 81:62-3 Ag '64
In one's own house; story. Mlle 57:99-100 O '63
Leave-taking; story. New Yorker 39:20-3 Jl 13 '63
Place in the country; story. New Yorker 39: 30-40 Je 15 '63
HAZZARD, Walt
Mental Hazzard. H. L. Masin. il por Sr Schol 84:26 F 21 '64
HEACOCK, Esther
In feeders, variety is the spice of bird life. il Audubon Mag 66:390-4 N '64
HEACOCK, Raymond L.
Scientific instruments in space exploration bibliog Science 142:188-95 O 11 '63
HEAD, Ann
Everybody adored Cara; story. Redbook 120: 160-90 Ap '63
HEAD, Edith
Body by MacLaine, in originals by Edith Head. C. R. Jennings. il Sat Eve Post 236:24-9 N 30 '63
HEAD, Harold
Threat in South Africa. New Repub 149:54-5 N 9 '63
HEAD, Matthew, pseud. See Canaday, J.
HEAD, Murdock
Thinksville. por Newsweek 63:109-10 Mr 16 '64
HEAD, Timothy. See Daws, G. jt. auth.
HEAD
See also
Face

HEAD against the wall; story. See Moravia, A.
HEAD-raiser; story. See Loeser, K.
HEADACHE
Best migraine preventive. Sci N L 85:114 F 22 '64
Drug prevents headache; migraine. Sci N L 84:39 Jl 20 '63
Help for the headache prone. J. D. Wassersug. il Parents Mag 39:139+ Ap '64
Is migraine a myth? Sci Digest 54:29 Ag '63
Man against migraine. il Newsweek 63:94 Je 15 '64
Migraine headache seen caused by heredity. Sci N L 85:391 Je 20 '64
My anti-headache diet. U. Sinclair. il Harper 227:40-2 D '63
New troops march on headaches; tension and migraine research. Bsns W p72+ Je 20 '64; Same with title New attack on headaches. il Sci Digest 56:75-8 N '64
What parents ask about migraine headaches in children. M. J. E. Senn. McCalls 92:43+ Ja '65
What to do about headaches; interview. A. P. Friedman. il U S News 57:92-4+ O 26 '64
What you can do about your aching head. M. J. O'Neill. McCalls 90:40 Ap '63
HEADBOARDS. See Beds
HEADGEAR
Sport inspires some dashing haberdashery. J. Campbell. il Sports Illus 18:32-3 F 4 '63
HEADLAM, Stewart
Stewart Headlam and the Christian Socialists. W. S. Smith. Christian Cent 80:201-4 F 13 '63
HEADLEY, Paul
Elegance of silver. Horticulture 42:52-3 Je '64
Grandma's geraniums are fashionable again. Horticulture 41:312 Je '63
There's a place in every garden for tall growing flowers. Horticulture 41:206-7 Ap '63
HEADLIGHTS, Automobile. See Automobiles—Lighting
HEADPHONES. See Earphones
HEADS of state
Key men of key nations; biographical sketches. pors Sr Schol 83:14-15 O 4 '63
Who's who around the world. il Sr Schol 85:38-9 O 7 '64
Wives
First ladies of the world; photographs. N Y Times Mag p28-9 Je 14 '64
HEALD, Henry T.
Engineering as a full partner in the university; excerpt from address, October 13, 1962. Sch & Soc 91:84-6 F 23 '63
Right to knowledge; excerpt from address, July 12, 1964. Sch & Soc 92:376-9 D 12 '64
$266,900,000: private give-away, done by three men. A. Talmey. por Vogue 141:102 Je '63
HEALD, Weldon F.
Appreciation of Yellowstone National Park. Mag 38:4-7 D '64
California's methuselah trees. Am For 70:34-5 Mr '64
Charm-laden Lake Chelan. Travel 119:51-2 Je '63
Colorado River of the West; excerpt from Inverted mountains. Nat Parks Mag 37:4-9 O '63
Lively Lassen. Travel 122:46-7 N '64
Looping the Guadalupes. Travel 120:34-6 O '63
McKenzie River trip. Travel 122:31-3 Jl '64
Methuselah of trees: the bristlecone pine. il Audubon Mag 66:50-1 Ja '64
Nevada's state parks. Travel 120:40-2 S '63
New Mexico's stone autograph album. Nat Parks Mag 37:10-12 F '63
Sierra wolverine. Nat Parks Mag 38:8-9 O '64
Sky forest of the ancients. Am For 70:34-5+ N '64
Snakes are interesting. il Audubon Mag 65:218-21 Jl '63
West Texas wonderland. Travel 119:45-6 Mr '63
—See May, R. H. jt. auth.
HEALEY, Denis
Europe: reaction in Britain. New Repub 148:16 F 23 '63
Merchant of Nassau. New Repub 148:9-10 Mr 16 '63
NATO muddle. New Repub 149:8-9 N 23 '63
Tory bind. New Repub 148:14-15 Je 22 '63
HEALEY, James H.
Six challenges for tomorrow's manager. Duns R 84:60-1+ O '64
HEALEY, James S.
Salt spray and sperm whales. Wilson Lib Bul 37:565-8 Mr '63
HEALING, Divine. See Faith cure
HEALTH
Americans can walk. il U S News 54:64 F 25 '63
Are you giving houseroom to health hazards? E. M. Wylie. Am Home 66:14+ Ap '63
Family in health and illness; some neglected areas. C. E. Vincent. bibliog f Ann Am Acad 346:109-16 Mr '63
Five husbands who might have lived. A. Lake. McCalls 92:126-7+ N '64
For fitness build health. Sci N L 84:11 Jl 6 '63
Happy town where hearts stay healthy; Roseto, Pa. R. K. Massie. il Sat Eve Post 237:76-7+ O 10 '64
How to stay young and look great. G. G. Greer. Bet Hom & Gard 41:84-8 Jl '63
Key to health: your heredity; interview. ed. by F. R. Schreiber. R. J. Williams. Sci Digest 53:30-9 Ap '63
Marching orders; fitness of the White House staff. Newsweek 61:22 F 18 '63
Men, women and health. il Sci Digest 55:83-4 Ap '64
Moderation, men! Newsweek 61:74 F 4 '63
New discoveries about your health; meeting of the American medical association. il U S News 57:14 D 14 '64
Nip-ups, anyone? fitness of White House staff. il Time 81:27 F 15 '63
Physical fitness on the New Frontier. il U S News 54:10 F 18 '63
Physical fitness; report of progress. J. F. Kennedy. il Look 27:82-3 Ag 13 '63
Plain talk about family health. G. G. Greer. See issues of Better homes and gardens
Seven paths to fitness. W. W. Bauer. Todays Health 41:13+ Ap '63
Social change and medical organization in the United States; a sociological perspective. T. Parsons. bibliog f Ann Am Acad 346:21-33 Mr '63
To keep children fit and hardy; with study-discussion program, by D. B. Harris and E. S. Harris. W. W. Bauer. bibliog il PTA Mag 58:14-16, 36 O '63
Today's health news. A. L. Blakeslee. See issues of Today's health
Warning against a physical fitness mania. F. P. Foster. il N Y Times Mag p 15+ F 9 '64
When should you call the doctor? P. Deutsch and R. Deutsch. il Redbook 120:26 Ap '63
Who needs physical fitness? Sci Digest 56:80-1 Jl: 54 N '64
Your health. See issues of Redbook
See also
Children—Care and hygiene
Mental hygiene
Public health
Sleep
Woman—Health and hygiene
Anecdotes, facetiae, satire, etc.
Fit for what? A. King. il McCalls 90:46+ F '63
HEALTH, Mental. See Mental hygiene
HEALTH and weather. See Weather—Mental and physiological effects
HEALTH attitudes. See Attitudes
HEALTH benefit plans. See Insurance, Health
HEALTH centers
Clinics and offices for a county center. il Arch Rec 135:206 Ap '64
Community mental health center, a new concept. R. H. Felix. Arch Rec 134:162-4 N '63
HEALTH clinics
Six clinics. il Arch Forum 120:90-7 F '64
Two-level clinic for community service. il Arch Rec 135:204-5 Ap '64
HEALTH education
Health education; symposium. il NEA J 53:57-71 Mr '64
See also
Health exhibits
HEALTH, education and welfare, Department of. See United States—Health, education and welfare. Department of
HEALTH examinations. See Physical examinations
HEALTH exhibits
Second hospital health museum in U.S. complete; exhibits in the Reading, Pa. hospital's Health center. il(p225) Sci N L 83:230 Ap 13 '63
HEALTH insurance. See Insurance, Health
HEALTH machines. See Quacks and quackery
HEALTH resorts, watering places, etc.
Big chief many baths; spring beneath southern California's San Jacinto Mountains. il Time 81:64 My 24 '63
Calorie castle; Sun Spa Hollywood, Fla. M. M. Davis. il Travel 121:54-5 Mr '64
Europe's fine spas are for those who seek health, not a cure. C. Rule. Travel 122:53 S '64

HEALTH resorts, watering places, etc.—*Cont.*
Evian's nine-day cure; famous French spa. il Bsns W p 104-5+ Jl 6 '63
Girl behind a Golden Door; Escondido, Calif. B. La Fontaine. il Sports Illus 21:68-72+ N 2 '64
Luxe way to stop smoking: Golden door, Escondido. il Vogue 142:173-4+ S 15 '63
New good move for travellers; California's Palm Springs. Vogue 144:201 O 15 '64
Spas: goo, golf and games; with list of western Europe's historic health resorts. A. Waugh. il Sports Illus 20:88-92+ My 25 '64
This year in Marienbad; watering places in West Germany. il Time 82:24 Ag 16 '63
Travel well. C. Rule. il Travel 120:50-1 N '63
Travel well; Baden-Baden. C. Rule. il Travel 121:47-8 Ja '64
See also
Bad Gastein, Austria
Montecatini Terme, Italy
Samaden, Switzerland
Saratoga Springs, N.Y.

HEALTH service. See Medical service

HEALTH superstitions. See Medical delusions

HEALTH workers
Job preview for medical explorer scouts. il Todays Health 41:37 N '63

Training

Housewives in mental health. J. Viorst. il Sci N L 86:234-5 O 10 '64

HEALY, Ann Kirtland
I'll remember you always! NEA J 53:66 D '64

HEALY, Kent T.
Problem: rational and effective allocation of resources. Ann Am Acad 345:39-46 Ja '63

HEALY, Paul F.
(ed) See Neilan, E. P. How to get better government

HEANEY, Audrey
What photography did to me! U S Camera 26:58-9+ F '63

HEAR no evil, speak no evil; drama. See Murray, J.

HEARD, Alexander
New approach to campaign finances. N Y Times Mag p50+ O 6 '63
What's all this about a power structure in U.S? interview. por U S News 55:58-60 Jl 1 '63

HEARD, Frances
Furniture with the sweet taste of variety. House B 105:158-61+ Ap '63

HEARD, Gerald
Can this drug enlarge man's mind? Horizon 5:28-31+ My '63

HEARING
Auditory discrimination by the cat after neonatal ablation of temporal cortex. D. P. Scharlock and others. bibliog il Science 141:1197-8 S 20 '63
Auditory flutter-driving of visual flicker. T. Shipley. bibliog il Science 145:1328-30 S 18 '64
Auditory nuclei: distinctive response patterns to white noise and tones in unanesthetized cats. D. Galin. bibliog il Science 146:270-2 O 9 '64
Key to hearing may be in sending system. Sci N L 86:261 O 24 '64
Lateralization of sounds at the unstimulated ear opposite a noise-adapted ear. E. C. Carterette and others. bibliog il Science 147:63-5 Ja 1 '65
Mrs G effect; human perception of static electrical fields. Newsweek 63:52 Ja 20 '64
Now hear this; difference in hearing between an American and a Mabaan. il Newsweek 61:80 My 6 '63
Sound advice; your recorded voice. R. N. Angus. Mod Phot 27:18+ Je '63
Sound-evoked potentials in neocortex of unanesthetized opossum. P. C. Nieder and W. Randall. bibliog il Science 144:429-30 Ap 24 '64
Speakers' and listeners' processes in a word-communication task. S. Rosenberg and B. D. Cohen. bibliog il Science 145:1201-3 S 11 '64
What you hear and what you don't. J. Daugherty and M. Daugherty. il Sci Digest 54:87-90 S '63
See also
Deafness

Testing

Electronic devices spot hearing troubles. Sci N L 87:8 Ja 2 '65

HEARING aids
Electronic ear designed for totally deaf. Sci Digest 53:73 Ap '63
Hearing aids. il Consumer Bul 47:30-4 Mr '64
Not so deaf, not so dumb; Perdoncini schools. il Time 85:55 Ja 29 '65
Should you wear a hearing aid? G. E. Maxwell. il Todays Health 42:26-9+ Ag '64

HEARING in fishes
Psychophysics and hearing in fish. W. N. Tavolga. il Natur Hist 73:34-41 Mr '64

HEARLE, E. F. R.
Data processing's role in city government. Am City 79:140+ My '64

HEARNE, Laura Guthrie
Summer with F. Scott Fitzgerald. Esquire 62: 160-5+ D '64

HEARST, Eliot, and Koresko, Minnie B.
Self-presentation and self-termination of a conflict-producing stimulus. bibliog Science 146:415-16 O 16 '64

HEARST, James
Unearned gift; poem. America 111:775 D 12 '64

HEARST, Stephen
Flags are not enough: Widening gap; excerpts from TV script; ed. by A. Cooke. UNESCO Courier 17:26-9+ Je '64

HEART
Biosynthesis of norepinephrine in isolated canine heart. C. A. Chidsey and others. bibliog il Science 139:828-9 Mr 1 '63
Bradykinin: vascular relaxant, cardiac stimulant. D. Montague and others. bibliog il Science 141:907-8 S 6 '63
Calcium-activated adenosine triphosphatase localization in cultured beating heart cells. H. Lewis and I. Harary. bibliog il Science 141:47-8 Jl 5 '63
Cardiovascular concomitants of the conditioned emotional response in the monkey. W. C. Stebbins and O. A. Smith, jr. bibliog il Science 144:881-3 My 15 '64
Circulatory adaptation to diving in the freshwater turtle. J. E. Millen and others. bibliog il Science 145:591-3 Ag 7 '64
Electronic dog aids in heart research. il Todays Health 41:60 Ap '63
Experimental cardiac hypertrophy: concentrations of RNA in the ventricles. L. Gluck and others. bibliog il Science 144:1244-5 Je 5 '64
Heart action potential: dependence on external calcium and sodium ions. R. K. Orkand and R. Niedergerke. bibliog il Science 146:1176-7 N 27 '64
Leg up on a good heart; vigorous exercise good for one's heart. G. Crozier. il Sports Illus 21:28+ S 21 '64
Negative inotropic effect of the vagus nerves upon the canine ventricle. H. DeGeest and others. bibliog il Science 144:1223-5 Je 5 '64
Oxidation of carbon-14-labeled endogenous lipids by isolated perfused rat heart. J. C. Shipp and others. bibliog il Science 143: 371-3 Ja 24 '64
Primitive heart in the echinoid strongylocentrotus purpuratus. R. A. Boolootian and J. L. Campbell. bibliog il Science 145:173-5 Jl 10 '64
Release of metaraminol (aramine) from the heart by sympathetic nerve stimulation. J. R. Crout and others. bibliog il Science 145:828-9 Ag 21 '64
Respiration of heart muscle as affected by oxygen tension. W. J. Whalen and J. Fangman. bibliog il Science 141:274-5 Jl 19 '63
Take it how easy? il Time 83:52 Ja 31 '64

Diseases

Can diet prevent heart attacks? A. L. Blakeslee. il Sat Eve Post 237:66-7 Ja 25 '64
Cardiacs on the job. il Newsweek 61:88-9 Mr 11 '63
Cardiovascular disease: report of conference on Psychophysiologic aspects of cardiovascular disease. G. Saslow. Science 142: 601+ N 1 '63
Coffee and your heart. Sci Digest 54:55 O '63
Conquering heart disease. il U S News 56:54-7 My 11 '64
Coronary candidates. il Newsweek 62:63 N 4 '63
Crucial twenty-four hours. Sci Digest 56:53 Ag '64
Electrocardiographic notching in rats deficient in essential fatty acids. W. O. Caster and P. Ahn. bibliog il Science 139:1213 Mr 22 '63
Episode; excerpts. E. Hodgins. McCalls 91: 74-7+ Ja; 46+ F; 60+ Mr; 102+ Ap; 72+ My '64
Excitement risks heart. Sci N L 86:244 O 17 '64
Exercise and heart disease. S. A. Levine. il Atlan 212:42-5 Jl '63
Exercise and heart trouble. il Sci Digest 55:88 My '64

HEART—Diseases—*Continued*
Five of a kind; valve and septal defects of Negro family. il Time 82:48 S 6 '63
Happy town where hearts stay healthy; Roseto, Pa. R. K. Massie. il Sat Eve Post 237:76-7+ O 10 '64
Heart attack; what to do in an emergency. il Consumer Bul 46:2+ O '63
Heart defects caused by diminished oxygen. Sci N L 85:377 Je 13 '64
Heart disease attacks inactive, indolent men. Sci N L 83:178 Mr 23 '63
Heart disease deaths level off in Britain. Sci N L 84:169 S 14 '63
Hearts too good to die. B. Felson. Esquire 61:160 My '64
How to avoid a heart attack. J. Stamler. Sci Digest 54:43-7 S '63
How to have a heart attack; address. R. C. Bates. il Todays Health 41:54 Ag '63
How to help your heart. P. D. White. il Parents Mag 39:121-5 My '64
How to predict the next heart attack. Bsns W p34 O 26 '63
How to predict your heart attack and prevent it; excerpts from You can predict your heart attack and prevent it. M. M. Gertler. Read Digest 84:51-5 Ja '64
How to stop a heart attack before it starts. Sci Digest 56:71-2 O '64
If you have a heart-attack personality. U S News 57:16 D 7 '64
Inherited faulty protein clue to heart disease. Sci N L 84:211 O 5 '63
Medicine: be glad you're a woman, you'll live longer. H. B. Sprague. Ladies Home J 81:43 O '64
Myocardial infarction: a response to social interaction among chickens. H. L. Ratcliffe and R. L. Snyder. bibliog il Science 144:425-6 Ap 24 '64
New hope in fight on heart disease. il Bsns W p47-8 D 12 '64
Oh, doctor I need you now. L. Wainwright. Life 57:29 D 11 '64
One man's stress. Time 82:62 S 27 '63
Potassium vs. sodium; new heart disease treatment. Sci N L 86:309 N 14 '64
President's heart. Asklipios. Esquire 62:89-92+ Ag '64
Reduction of cardiac stores of nonepinephrine in experimental heart failure. J. F. Spann, jr. and others. bibliog il Science 145:1439-41 S 25 '64
Reserpine; its effect on silver-stained structures of the heart. T. Cooper and others. bibliog il Science 141:526-7 Ag 9 '63
Stress linked to heart. Sci N L 86:18 Jl 11 '64
Study offers hope to angina pectoris victims. Sci N L 85:57 Ja 25 '64
They ran the heart study. il Bsns W p50-1+ D 12 '64
U.S. sums it up: quit smoking; Surgeon General's report. il Bsns W p42-4+ Ja 18 '64
What doesn't cause heart attacks. Sci Digest 55:81-2 F '64
When a stroke hits. il Newsweek 65:50 F 1 '65
Who gets heart attacks? Sci Digest 54:81 Jl '63
Who is the coronary man? five-year study at Western electric. Bsns W p30-1 F 16 '63
Your heart has nine lives: nine steps to heart health, by A. L. Blakeslee and J. Stamler. Review
Newsweek 62:84+ D 16 '63
See also
United States—President's commission on heart disease, cancer and stroke

Diagnosis

Platinum electrodes help diagnose heart defects. Sci N L 83:121 F 23 '63
Your heart and your future; excerpts from Your heart has nine lives. A. Blakeslee and J. Stamler. il Todays Health 42:23-5+ Jl '64
See also
Electrocardiography

Murmurs

Heart murmurs in children. E. T. Wilkes. Parents Mag 39:103+ Ja '64
If your child has an innocent heart murmur. G. G. Greer. Bet Hom & Gard 42:14 My '64
When a heart murmur is serious. Good H 156:155 Je '63
Your child's health; heart murmurs. L. W. Sauer. PTA Mag 58:17-18 Ja '64

Rhythm

See Heart beat

Surgery

AMA honors engineer for his heart valve invention. il Todays Health 42:52-3 Ja '64
Blood shunt technique. Sci N L 85:15 Ja 4 '64
Girl with a hole in her heart; case of D. Morgan. P. Pierce. il Ebony 20:27-8+ D '64
Heart stopper; dislocated aortic valve. Newsweek 61:59 F 4 '63
Heart valve replaced in baby first time. Sci N L 85:217 Ap 4 '64
Induction of papillary growths in the heart. S. Rodbard and others. bibliog il Science 143:1341-2 Mr 20 '64
Infants' heart disorder helped by rare surgery. Sci N L 85:137 F 29 '64
Miracle for Amanda; case of Amanda Chiang Dao. T. Wilson. McCalls 91:52+ Je '64
Ordeal of Dorothy Pulver; dislocated aortic valve. T. Morris. il Redbook 122:58-9+ Mr '64
Surgery inside oxygen chamber saves blue babies. il Todays Health 41:44+ Ag '63
Transposition corrected. Time 82:66 N 1 '63
Urges repair of infant hearts in first six months. il Sci Digest 53:43-5 F '63
Wandering bullet. il Time 84:52-3 D 25 '64
We gave Diane back her life; first blue baby operation. W. J. Potts. il Read Digest 85:97-100 N '64

HEART, Artificial
Artificial heart outlook. Sci N L 86:396 D 19 '64
Half-heart replacement. il Time 82:50 N 8 '63
Heparin bonding on colloidal graphite surfaces. V. L. Gott and others. bibliog il Science 142:1297-8 D 6 '63

HEART, Transplantation of. See Transplantation of organs, tissues, etc.

HEART beat
Blood for fight or flight; distinction between effects of anger and fear. il Time 84:76 N 6 '64
Heart rate changes after reinforcing brain stimulation in rats. W. J. Meyers and others. bibliog il Science 140:1233-5 Je 14 '63; Reply. R. B. Malmo. 144:1029-30 My 22 '64
Heart rate: differential effects of hypothalmic and septal self-stimulation. J. Perez-Cruet and others. bibliog il Science 140:1235-6 Je 14 '63; Reply. R. B. Malmo. 144:1029-30 My 22 '64
Off-beat hearts get back in step; with tiny pacemaking devices. Sci N L 84:232 O 12 '63
Reversible cold block of the specialized cardiac tissues of the unanesthetized dog. J. W. Lister and others. bibliog il Science 145:723-4 Ag 14 '64
Shock treats heart flutter. Sci N L 84:131 Ag 31 '63

HEART block
New timers for faulty hearts. J. D. Ratcliff. il Read Digest 83:169-70+ N '63

HEART demands satisfaction; story. See Hawkes, J.

HEART disease. See Heart—Diseases

HEART diseases in animals. See Animals—Diseases and pests

HEART-lung machines
Lamb experiment may help save human babies; alive in an artificial womb. il Life 57:37-8 Ag 28 '64
Thump of life; the heart-lung resuscitator. il Time 85:29 Ja 8 '65

HEART massage. See Cardiac resuscitation

HEART murmurs. See Heart—Murmurs

HEART of America farm power show. See M and W gear company

HEART of gold; story. See Lavin, M.

HEART-of-the-daybreak; story. See Cope, J.

HEART of the house; story. See Randall, F. E.

HEART pump. See Heart, Artificial

HEART valves, Artificial. See Heart—Surgery

HEARTBEAT away; story. See St Johns, A. R.

HEARTWORMS. See Worms, Intestinal and parasitic

HEAT
Hot and cold quiz. J. Daugherty and M. Daugherty. il Sci Digest 57:83-5 Ja '65
How to melt ice with ice. il Sci Digest 55:76-9 Mr '64
See also
Earth temperature
High temperatures
Hot weather
Thermionic converters

Convection

Shadow of the invisible. il Sci Digest 55:19 Mr '64

Physiological effects

Genetic control of differential heat tolerance in two strains of the nematode caenorhabditis elegans. H. V. Fatt and E. C. Dougherty. bibliog il Science 141:266-7 Jl 19 '63

HEAT—Physiological effects—*Continued*
Hot-weather target: your heart. D. G. Cooley. il Todays Health 41:21-7 Jl '63
Keeping cool. C. J. Potthoff. Todays Health 41:56 Ag '63
Thermal denaturation of collagen in the dispersed and solid state. J. Gross. bibliog il Science 143:960-1 F 28 '64
Ultraviolet sensitivity of escherichia coli containing heat-inducible λ prophages. M. Lieb. bibliog il Science 145:175-6 Jl 10 '64
Uniform can be a death trap; football uniforms and heatstroke cases. R. Lardner. il Sports Illus 19:41-4+ N 25 '63
Weather and athletes. il Todays Health 41:82 S '63

Transmission

Semiconductor heat sink design chart. F. D. Gross. il Electr World 73:28-9 Ja '65
HEAT, Body. See Temperature, Animal and human
HEAT, Waste. See Waste heat
HEAT control valve. See Automobile engines—Valves
HEAT exchangers
Milk heats wash water. E. Welch. il Farm J 87:59 Mr '63
HEAT in animals. See Estruation
HEAT recovery evaporators. See Evaporators
HEAT resistant alloys
Refractory metal weld developed. il Aviation W 79:85 Jl 8 '63
Tantalum-tungsten alloy used in Agena vehicle. J. F. Judge. il Miss & Roc 13:28, 31 Jl 8 '63
HEAT sink. See Heat—Transmission
HEAT transmission
Selecting a suitable heat sink. J. R. Gyorki. il Electr World 69:46-8 Je '63
See also
Heat exchangers
HEATERS
Camp heaters cook, warm you, give light. il Pop Sci 183:130 Jl '63
Low-cost heat. C. Conley. il Field & S 68:103 F '64
See also
Electric heaters
HEATERS, Solar. See Solar heaters
HEATERS, Water. See Water heaters
HEATH, Aloise B.
Politics and mortal sin. Nat R 16:1147-50 D 29 '64
Spare me the rods. Nat R 15:562-6 D 31 '63
HEATH, Anna Lenington
Much ado about ants; drama. Plays 24:61-6 D '64
HEATH, Edward Richard George
Backbench revolt. Time 83:40 Ap 3 '64
Britain's dynamic rebuilder. il por Bsns W p 100-2+ D 7 '63
HEATH, J. Ray
Two views on the Seattle watershed; recreation management, no! Am For 69:9+ N '63
HEATH, James Edward
Reptilian thermoregulation: evaluation of field studies. bibliog Science 146:784-5 N 6 '64
HEATH, John Kingsley-. See Kingsley-Heath J.
HEATH, Wallace G.
Thermoperiodism in sea-run cutthroat trout (salmo clarki clarki) bibliog Science 142:486-8 O 25 '63
HEATHERS
Good soil mates. il Flower Grower 51:46-7 Ja '64
Heather makes itself at home. W. W. Cunningham. il Horticulture 42:18 Ja '64
Ten hardy heathers. E. Deutsch. il Flower Grower 51:26+ Ag '64
HEATHKIT depth sounder. See Depth indicators
HEATHORN, R. J.
Ultimate teaching machine. Harper 226:52 Ap '63
HEATHS (plants)
Good soil mates. il Flower Grower 51:46-7 Ja '64
HEATING
Banish freeze-and-fry home heating; zone heating. J. Goldman. il Pop Mech 120:172-7+ O '63
Britain edges out of the ice age; advertising campaign for central-heating systems. A. Carthew. il N Y Times Mag p60+ D 13 '64
Central heating and cooling of college campuses. il Arch Rec 134:162-4 Ag '63
Heat from lights re-used for economy. R. B. Darling. il Arch Rec 136:211-12 O '64
How to gain new comfort at home with conditioned climate. il House & Gard 127:132-5 Ja '65
How to get the most heat for your money. Bet Hom & Gard 42:26+ N '64
Mistaken ideas about heating. A. M. Watkins. Bet Hom & Gard 41:120-1 O '63
What to do if your heating system quits. M. J. Schultz. il Am Home 67:76+ Ja '64
What you should know about heating your home. A. M. Watkins. Am Home 67:86+ S '64
See also
Electric heating
Solar heating
HEATING, Infrared
Heat lamps soothe winter bus patrons; Cleveland, Ohio. T. W. McNally. il Am City 78:113 D '63
Ice skaters enjoy heat breaks; Dearborn, Mich. O. L. Hubbard and R. K. Archer. il Am City 78:86-7 D '63
Infrared units for space heating. R. S. Emerick. il Arch Rec 133:201-2 My '63
HEATING equipment
Heating checkup your home may need. il Good H 157:165 O '63
See also
Electric heaters
Oil burners
Radiators
HEATON, Leonard D.
Boss of the army's medical team. W. R. Vath. il pors Todays Health 41:24-9 D '63
HEATON, Peter J. Henniker-. See Henniker-Heaton, P. J.
HEAVNER, Theodore J. C.
Viet-Nam situation; address, August 25, 1963. Dept State Bul 49:393-8 S 9 '63
HEAVYWEIGHT boxers. See Boxers
HEBBLETHWAITE, Frank P.
Books. Américas 15:41 D '63
HÉBERT, Anne
Villes en marche: poem. Atlan 214:145 N '64
Reporter at large. E. Wilson. New Yorker 40:74+ N 21 '64
HEBES
Introducing the speedy hebes. il Sunset 134:134-5 Ja '65
HEBREW language

Alphabet

ISO technical committee produces Hebrew transliteration standard. Library J 88:4601 D 1 '63
New global standard for the transliteration of Hebrew into the Latin or Roman alphabet. Wilson Lib Bul 38:321 D '63
HEBREW manuscripts. See Manuscripts, Hebrew
HEBREW prophets. See Prophets
HEBREW religion. See Judaism
HEBREW university, Jerusalem. See Colleges and universities—Israel
HEBRIDES
See also
Skye, Isle of
HECHINGER, Fred Michael
Antidotes for incompetence. Sat R 47:21-2+ D 12 '64
Book burners. Reporter 28:42+ Je 6 '63
City schools, a mixed report card. N Y Times Mag p24+ Je 14; 2+ Jl 5 '64
Doctor Conant's bombshell. Reporter 29:44-6 S 26 '63
Failure, a new beginning. Reporter 29:52+ Jl 18 '63
Flowering of a campus hybrid. N Y Times Mag p36-7+ S 13 '64
Foreign languages stage a comeback. Sat R 46:64-6+ F 16 '63
New approach to citizenship. Parents Mag 38:49+ My '63
Preferential treatment for Negroes? Reporter 31:22-4 D 3 '64
Readin', ritin', and Rafferty. Reporter 30:46-8 Ap 9 '64
What's ahead in education. Parents Mag 39:62-3+ S '64
—See Hechinger, G. jt. auth.
HECHINGER, Grace
Getting to know your baby. Parents Mag 39:36-7+ Jl '64
Parent and child. N Y Times Mag p99 Ap 14; 52 Je 2 '63; 71-2 Ja 12; 61+ Mr 1; 50 Ag 9 '64
—and Hechinger, F. M.
Can you help your child get better grades? McCalls 92:50+ O '64
College morals mirror our society. N Y Times Mag p22+ Ap 14 '63
How not to waste college on girls. Parents Mag 39:70-1+ F '64
No cheers for the rah-rah riot. N Y Times Mag p33+ My 26 '63
Serious epidemic of automania. N Y Times Mag p 18+ Ag 11 '63

HECHLER, Ken
Teacher's view inside Congress. D. B. Fleming, jr. il NEA J 53:69-72 Ja '64
HECHT, Anthony
Hill; poem. New Yorker 40:36 F 29 '64
HECHT, Ben
Audiences are too acquiescent; excerpts from Gaily, gaily. Theatre Arts 47:14-15+ Jl '63
Chicago style. por Newsweek 63:77 Ap 27 '64
Obituary
Pub W 185:64 Ap 27 '64
HECHT, George Joseph
Dear Mr President; letter. Parents Mag 38:55+ F '63
On the anti-poverty bill; excerpts from testimony before House committee. Parents Mag 39:40+ Je '64
HECHT, Nancy A.
Centuries-old pleasure of auctions. Am Home 67:94 My '64
HECHT, Roger
Intelligence and care. Poetry 104:181-3 Je '64
HECHT company. See Baltimore—Stores; Washington, D.C.—Stores
HECK, J. Parker
Women's clubs help cities to advance street lighting. Am City 79:114-15 S '64
HECKEL, Erich
Shadow of the Bridge; beginnings of modern German art. il Time 82:44 Ag 2 '63
HECKMAN, Donald
Month's jazz. Am Rec G 29:904-5, 970-2; 30:80-3, 157-9, 266-8, 540-1 Jl-N '63, F '64
HECKSCHER, August
Bookmaking and changing standards and tastes; address to AIGA Fifty books dinner. Pub W 183:22-4 My 6 '63
Descending spiral of ugliness. por Recreation 56:315-16+ S '63
Heckscher urges President to carry out Kennedy's program for advisory arts panel. Arch Rec 135:10 Ap '64
Keynote address delivered to symposium sponsored by Manhattan school of music, November 11, 1963. Mus Am 83:150-1 D '63
Mystery in our history. Sat R 47:36-7 S 12 '64
President and the arts. Sat R 46:6+ D 14 '63
Report to the President; excerpts. Arch Forum 119:55 Ag '63
Seduction and challenge of Hawaii. House & Gard 126:52+ Jl '64

about

Art in politics. por Newsweek 61:85 Je 17 '63
President Kennedy receives Heckscher report on art and government. Arch Rec 134:10 Ag '63
HECTOR, Robert
Broadway on ice; the obsolete industry. Nation 198:267-9 Mr 16 '64
HECTOR, William J.
Alternators: selection and installation. Electr World 69:70-3 Je '63
HEDDEN, Jack
Cruise of a lifetime. Yachting 114:54-6+ O '63
HEDEMAN, E. Ruth. See Dodson, H. W. jt. auth.
HEDGE, C. E. and Walthall, F. G.
Radiogenic strontium-87 as an index of geologic processes. bibliog Science 140:1214-17 Je 14 '63
HEDGE clippers
Hedge trimmers. il Consumer Rep 29:322-5 Jl '64
HEDGES
Black raspberries for an edible hedge. I. C. Brown. il Horticulture 41:62 F '63
Flower grower's home garden notebook. J. B. Brimer. il Flower Grower 51:21-2 Je '64
Hedges. il Horticulture 42:24-7 O '64
Two good reasons to hedge with blueberries. I. Brown. il Flower Grower 52:18 Ja '65
HEDIGER, H.
Camouflaged still-fishing. Natur Hist 72:18-21 Je '63
HEDING, Henrik
Radioactive myoinositol: incorporation into streptomycin. bibliog Science 143:953-4 F 28 '64
HEDJAZ

Railroads

See Railroads—Arabia
HEDLUND, Oscar
Ingmar Bergman, the listener. Sat R 47:47-9+ F 29 '64
HEDLUND, Reuben L. See Thomas, T. M. jt. auth.
HEDMAN, Frank
Notes from our correspondents. Hi Fi 14:28+ F '64
HEDRICH, Jack
Very best in patio privacy. Bet Hom & Gard 42:28 Ap '64
HEDWALL, Stan
Swimming pool filters. Recreation 56:418-20 N '63
HEELS (shoes) See Shoes
HEER, Friedrich
Future needs the past. Christian Cent 81:635-8 My 13 '64
Need for confession. Commonweal 79:656-60 F 28 '64
HEEZEN, Bruce
Ocean's maps and earth theories revolutionized by latest findings; ed. by B. H. Frisch. Sci Digest 53:4-12 Ap '63
Reviews. Natur Hist 72:4+ O '63
HEEZEN, Bruce C. See Hollister, C. D. jt. auth.
HEFFERLINE, Ralph F. and Perera, T. B.
Proprioceptive discrimination of a covert operant without its observation by the subject. bibliog Science 139:834-5 Mr 1 '63
HEFFERNAN, Helen. See Alexander, W. M. jt. auth.
HEFFERNAN, John Paul
Mercy takes to flight. Todays Health 41:30-4+ Ap '63
HEFFNER, Richard
Very educational; dismissal of WNDT-TV's general manager. il por Newsweek 61:86 Ap 29 '63
HEFFRON, Paul T.
Toward new solutions of old church-state problems. Commonweal 81:169-70 O 30 '64
HEFINGER, Jeanne
Choicest co-ed. por Esquire 60:77 S '63
HEFNER, Hugh M.
Infinite number of monkeys; researchers for Playboy philosophy series. Christian Cent 80:1063 Ag 28 '63
Two definitions of obscenity. il por Time 81:44 Je 21 '63
Urbunnity; Playboy club. il pors Newsweek 63:48-9 Ja 6 '64
HEFNER, Philip
Man as nature's man. Christian Cent 81:1556-9 D 16 '64
HEFT, David
Foreign student. Americas 16:17-21 F '64
HEGE, Ruth
My clothes were blood-soaked, but I never moved; ed. by B. Lindeman. pors Sat Eve Post 237:84-5 O 3 '64
HEGEL, Georg Wilhelm Friedrich
On tyranny, by L. Strauss. Review
Commentary 36:412-16 N '63. G. Lichtheim
HEGEMAN, Stewart
What tape to choose? Hi Fi 13:41-4 Ag '63
HEGGE, Bob
Got a light? il Hot Rod 17:52-3 Ag '64
When a clutch lets go! il Hot Rod 16:105 O '63
HEGYELI, Andrew
Temperature dependence of the activity of the antitumor factor in the common clam. bibliog Science 146:77-8 O 2 '64
—and others
Preparation of retine from human urine. Science 142:1571-2 D 20 '63
HEIBERG, Louise Cromwell
From the first Mrs MacArthur; an account of rivalry between two famous generals; reprint. B. Beale. por U S News 56:20 My 4 '64
HEIDEGGER, Martin
Authenticity and other persons. F. G. Sturm. Christian Cent 80:340-2 Mr 13 '63
Later Heidegger. Christian Cent 80:511 Ap 17 '63
Later Heidegger and theology, ed. by J. M. Robinson and J. B. Cobb, jr. Review
Christian Cent 80:1273-4 O 16 '63. S. Laeuchli
HEIDELBERG arm. See Prosthesis
HEIDELBERG catechism. See Catechisms
HEIDELBERGER, Charles. See Kaufman, H. E. jt. auth.
HEIDT, Mrs Donald W.
Stitchery. Design 66:18-20 S '64
HEIFERS
Feed lot. C. Peterson, jr. il Suc Farm 62:46 Ap '64
Good heifers live longer. Suc Farm 63:78D Ja '65
Graded heifers make a hit. D. Hagen. Farm J 88:42F S '64
How much winter feed for replacement heifers. Farm J 88:42H S '64
HEIFETZ, Arthur
Boy vs. girl; story. Seventeen 23:74-5 Ja '64
My New York. Seventeen 23:144-5+ F '64

HEIFETZ, Jascha
Big two; Heifetz and Piatigorsky. il por Time 84:88 O 2 '64
Conversation with Jascha Heifetz; interview, ed. by S. Chotzinoff. por Holiday 34:89-94+ S '63
HEIGHT of man. See Stature
HEIL, B. H.
Division of chemical literature of the American chemical society. Science 143:1236-7 Mr 13 '64
HEILBRON, Bertha L.
Phantom cities in a promised land. Am Heritage 14:52-7 Je '63
HEILBRONER, Robert L.
Free thought. Commentary 36:331-3 O '63
Grand acquisitor. Am Heritage 16:20-5+ D '64
New horizons in economics. Sat R 47:31-2+ Ag 29 '64
Share-the-tax-revenue plan. N Y Times Mag p8+ D 27 '64
What it's like to be underdeveloped; excerpt from The great ascent. Read Digest 82:21+ F '63
HEILIG, Morton L.
Feely is here. L. H. Lapham. il Sat Eve Post 237:28-9 Ap 18 '64
HEILIGER, Edward
Staffing a computer based library. Library J 89:2738-9 Jl '64
HEILMAN, Barbara
Cool fireball named Roberts. Sports Illus 20:31-4+ F 10 '64
Out of the park on a half swing. Sports Illus 18:85+ Ap 8 '63
Track & field. Sports Illus 18:60+ Je 17 '63
HEILMAN, Paul M.
Liberation of Cuba; address. Vital Speeches 29:391-4 Ap 15 '63
HEILNER, Van Campen
In the land of Oh-by-Jingo. Field & S 69:110-13 N '64
New hotspot for tuna. Field & S 69:144-6 My '64
HEILPERIN, Michael A.
Europe: a major role for EFTA; letter from Geneva. Fortune 69:61-2+ Mr '64
Rediscovery of money. Fortune 71:152-3+ Ja '65
Skeleton that didn't rattle. Fortune 68:104 D '63
—and Lubar, Robert
It's an international farm mess now. Fortune 67:134-7+ My '63
HEIMER, Mel
Beauty; story. McCalls 90:70-1 Je '63
Girl who said no; story. McCalls 90:82-3 Mr '63
World apart; story. McCalls 91:140-1 N '63
HEIN, Fred V.
Reading, 'riting, 'rithmetic, and revaccination. Todays Health 41:14 S '63
School days should be healthy days. Todays Health 42:90 S '64
HEINDEL, Richard H.
World worries for education. Sat R 47:77-8 Ja 4 '64
HEINE, Jutta
Dash of style for track and field. R. Terrell. il pors Sports Illus 18:12-15 Ja 28 '63
Marlene Dietrich in a track suit. il pors Newsweek 61:59 F 25 '63
HEINEMAN, Ben W.
Many-tracked mind on trains and society; interview, ed. by Bruce Paisner. pors Life 57:64+ D 4 '64

about

Heavenly way to run a railroad. A. Steinberg. il Read Digest 82:175-80 My '63
Man who likes commuters. il pors Life 57:61-2 D 4 '64
New breed in transportation. G. R. Rosen. por Duns R 83:pt2 100-2+ Je '64
HEINEMAN, James H, incorporated
Heineman, inc. to bring out first list. Pub W 184:36 Jl 29 '63
HEINEMANN, Arthur
Amy; story. McCalls 92:112-13 N '64
Thank you, Peg Carpenter, for your many kindnesses; story. Sat Eve Post 237:60-2 D 5 '64
HEINITZ, Thomas
Britten's War requiem. Sat R 46:63 F 23 '63
Other side. See last issue of each month of Saturday review
HEINL, Robert Debs, Jr
Haiti. New Repub 150:15-21 My 16 '64
HEINLEIN, Robert A.
All aboard the Gemini. Pop Mech 119:112-16+ My '63
HEINOLD, George
Big red drum. Outdoor Life 132:64-5+ S '63
Pollock are powderkegs. Outdoor Life 131:78-9+ My '63
Salt water. See issues of Outdoor life
We beat our drums. Outdoor Life 131:66-7+ Ap '63
HEINOLD, Laura
Salt water (cont) por Outdoor Life 131:16+ Ap '63
HEINS, Paul
Hound of Ulster; review. Horn Bk 40:273 Je '64
HEINSOHN, Tommy, and Ottum, Bob
Of charley horses and little old ladies. pors Sports Illus 21:38-40+ O 26 '64
HEINZ, Jack
Those annoying farmers: impossible but not really serious. Harper 227:61-4+ Jl '63
HEINZ, Wilfred Charles
After twenty years: the GI's war fades away. Sat Eve Post 237:22-30+ D 12 '64
Golden boy is back. Life 57:70-2+ Ag 28 '64
Stan Musial's last day. Life 55:96-8 O 11 '63
(ed) See Lombardi, V. Day of the game
HEINZELMANN, Gertrud
Priesthood and women; tr. by W. Kramer. Commonweal 81:504-8 Ja 15 '65
HEIPLE, Clark
Lost wax sculpture for high schools. Sch Arts 63:36-7 Je '64
HEIREMANS, Luis A.
False summer; story. Américas 15:30-4 O '63
HEIRLOOM; story. See Randall, F. E.
HEIRLOOMS
Living with antiques; heirlooms in a New York apartment. A. Embury, 2d. il Antiques 84:154-7 Ag '63
See also
Antiques
HEISDORF and Nelson farms, incorporated
Science takes over the henhouse. il Bsns W p70-2 Mr 16 '63
HEITLER, W.
Ethics of the scientific age. Bul Atomic Sci 20:21-3 O '64
HEITMAN, Sidney
Odyssey of an obsolete hero. Sat R 46:47 D 14 '63
HEITMANN, Verla L.
Make compost out of comfrey. Horticulture 41:456 S '63
HEITZIG, Rupert
Culture in Kabul. Dance Mag 37:28+ Ap '63
HEJAZ. See Hedjaz
HEJHALL, Roy C.
Transistorized six-meter converter. Electr World 71:46-7 F '64
—and Thorpe, Darrell
Selecting high-frequency transistors. Electr World 72:50-2+ S '64
HEKTOEN, Faith H.
Teacher's image in children's literature. Sr Schol 83:13T O 4 '63
HELBICH, Hans Martin
Conference with Khrushchev. F. Luepsen. Christian Cent 80:1012 Ag 14 '63
HELD, Al
Al Held paints a picture. I. Sandler. il pors Art N 63:42-5+ My '64
HELD, John, Jr
Sheiks and shebas, dance no more. F. Russell. il Horizon 5:118-19 Jl '63
HELD, Richard, and Freedman, S. J.
Plasticity in human sensorimotor control. bibliog Science 142:455-62 O 25 '63
—and Rekosh, Jerold
Motor-sensory feedback and the geometry of visual space. bibliog Science 141:722-3 Ag 23 '63
HELD, Virginia
But does it work. Reporter 28:55-7 My 23 '63
HELDMAN, Gladys
Busiest voice in a busy, busy clan. B. La Fontaine. il pors Sports Illus 20:38-40+ Je 22 '64
HELEN, Sister
Trinity caters to taste. Library J 88:4573-6 D 1 '63
HELEN James John, Sister
Toward the open college. Commonweal 79:33-6, 196-7 O 4, N 8 '63
HELEN; drama. See Gray, W.
HELEN Kate Furness free library, Wallingford, Pa.
Trustee's role; freedom to read. H. A. Johnson. ALA Bul 57:631-3 Jl '63
HELFAND, Arthur
What you can do about your aching feet; interview. McCalls 90:46 Ap '63
HELFER, Harold
John Harrison's million-dollar clock. Sci Digest 55:62-4 Mr '64
(comp) Just average. N Y Times Mag p46 O 18 '64
(comp) Not so vital statistics. N Y Times Mag p90 D 1 '63; 40 S 13 '64
(comp) Quotes: equality. N Y Times Mag p43 O 25 '64

HELFFERICH, F. and Peterson, D. L.
Accurate chromatographic method for sorption isotherms and phase equilibria. bibliog Science 142:661-2 N 8 '63
HELICHRYSUM bracteatum. See Strawflowers
HELICOPTER airlines
See also
New York airways
New York airways, incorporated

Federal aid

CAB defies Congress on helicopter aid. G. C. Wilson. il Aviation W 80:34-5 My 11 '64
CAB helicopter subsidy campaign. Aviation W 81:29 N 30 '64
CAB rulings reflect helicopter policy. Aviation W 79:38 S 9 '63
Expansion seen saving helicopter service. J. R. Ashlock. Aviation W 81:34-5 Ag 24 '64
Helicopter lines fight for life. il Bsns W p64+ N 21 '64
Senate backs Boyd in approving $4.3-million helicopter subsidy. Aviation W 81:32 Ag 10 '64
Senate backs helicopter subsidies. Aviation W 79:43+ N 4 '63
Senate probe of helicopter subsidy due. Aviation W 81:34 Jl 13 '64
HELICOPTER engines
Hindustan to build Alouette 3, engine; turbine helicopters. Aviation W 79:29 D 9 '63
Hughes XV-9A to verify hot cycle system in flight tests. il Aviation W 80:60-2+ Je 22 '64
Service experience leads to T58 changes. D. A. Anderton. il Aviation W 78:48-9+ Ap 29 '63
Turbomeca planning lightplane turbine. W. C. Wetmore. il Aviation W 79:66-7+ Ag 5 '63
HELICOPTER flying. See Helicopters—Piloting
HELICOPTER industry and trade

International aspects

Vertol, Bölkow agree to exchange data. Aviation W 79:32 Jl 15 '63

United States

See also
United aircraft corporation—Sikorsky aircraft division
HELICOPTER models
Hughes develops configuration for hot gas cycle helicopter. il Aviation W 79:33 Jl 15 '63
HELICOPTER pilots

Training

Anyone for a backward takeoff. B. Mauldin. il Sports Illus 18:68-76+ My 6 '63
HELICOPTER speed records. See Aviation records
HELICOPTER taxi service. See Air taxi service
HELICOPTERS
Agusta-Bell shows reliability in Swiss Alps. E. Walford. il Aviation W 80:69-71 Mr 30 '64
Bell 204B offers stability and quietness. D. A. Brown. il Aviation W 78:84-8+ Ap 29 '63
Bölkow planning to flight test Bo 46 lead-lag rotor helicopter. Aviation W 78:29 Ja 28 '63
Copters in the future to change our lives. Sci N L 87:27 Ja 9 '65
He says think small. R. B. Weeghman. il Flying 74:31+ F '64
Helicopter potential cited for Greenland. il Aviation W 79:49+ S 9 '63
Helicopter, where now? N. D. Ham. il Flying 74:32+ F '64
Helicopters facing V/STOL competition. D. A. Anderton. il Aviation W 78:255-7+ Mr 11 '63
Larger, more powerful version of Do. 32E planned by Dornier. Aviation W 80:25 Mr 30 '64
Leading international rotary-wing aircraft; specifications. Aviation W 78:217 Mr 11 '63; 80:212 Mr 16 '64
Mi-6 incorporates detailed refinements; Soviet helicopter. il Aviation W 81:86-9 Ag 24 '64
On top of the news; Peoria's Journal star helicopter in news-gathering. il Flying 74:77 F '64
Production of Omega BS-12-D3S awaits court merger approval. Aviation W 79:108 N 11 '63
They call him Mr Helicopter. A. Dawydoff. il Flying 74:30+ F '64
Transport helicopter has detachable van; YCH-54A Skycrane. Sci N L 86:136 Ag 29 '64
Turbine-powered, 10-place Bell 204B enters commercial helicopter market. il Aviation W 78:100 Ja 21 '63
U.S. rotary-wing aircraft; specifications. Aviation W 78:205 Mr 11 '63; 80:211 Mr 16 '64
Up from the basement; R. J. Enstrom corp. il Newsweek 63:70-1 Ja 20 '64
See also
Autogiros
Heliports
Rotors
Sight-seeing helicopters

Accidents

N.Y. helicopter crash investigation speeded. Aviation W 79:39-40 O 21 '63
Oil ports on V-107-2 plugged by metal shavings, CAB told. Aviation W 80:45 Ja 20 '64

Agricultural applications

See Helicopters in agriculture

Armaments

Bell OH-4A's heavy armament adds weight but holds performance in firepower test. E. J. Bulban. il Aviation W 80:68-9+ Ap 6 '64
Bell UH-1Bs fitted with traversing turret. il Aviation W 78:32 Ja 21 '63

Chartering

Canadian mining boom boosts charter work. Aviation W 80:37 Je 1 '64

Control

Kaman UH-2A demonstrates all-weather capability, maneuverability for navy roles. D. A. Brown. il Aviation W 78:80-1+ Ap 8 '63

Design

Hughes develops configuration for hot gas cycle helicopter. il Aviation W 79:33 Jl 15 '63
Pilot report; room for one more; the Hughes 300. G. J. Schlaeger. il Flying 74:36-7 Je '64
Sikorsky CH-53A passes mockup review. D. E. Fink. il Aviation W 78:85+ Ap 15 '63
Single-place Dornier helicopter folds for transport. W. C. Wetmore. il Aviation W 78:160-1+ Je 10 '63
XH-51A reaches 160 mph. in flight tests. il Aviation W 78:90-1+ My 13 '63

Electronic equipment

Kaman UH-2A demonstrates all-weather capability, maneuverability for navy roles. D. A. Brown. il Aviation W 78:80-1+ Ap 8 '63
Navy may buy minimum helicopter navaid. B. Miller. il Aviation W 81:79+ O 5 '64

Equipment

See also
Aeronautic instruments

Landing

Suction cups tested in helicopter landings. Aviation W 78:73 Mr 18 '63

Military applications

Air assault development. W. Wright. il Aviation W 80:54-5+ F 17 '64
All UH-1s to be modified after Vietnam use reveals weakness. Aviation W 80:23 Je 8 '64
Approval is near on German UH-1D buy. C. Brownlow. il Aviation W 81:82-4 D 21 '64
Army attack helicopter plans reoriented. L. Booda. Aviation W 78:27 My 6 '63
Army completes LOH flight test program. Aviation W 81:24 Jl 13 '64
Army continues push for more helicopters. G. C. Wilson. il Aviation W 81:16-17 N 30 '64
Army evaluates Kaman UH-2 for tactical escort. il Aviation W 80:59 Mr 9 '64
Army high-speed VTOL efforts pushed. il Aviation W 80:16-18 Je 8 '64
Army receives Hughes OH-6A for testing. C. M. Plattner. il Aviation W 80:72-3+ F 3 '64
Army seeks greater mobility in added air capability. G. C. Wilson. il Aviation W 78:84-5+ Mr 11 '63
Army to seek attack helicopter proposals. G. C. Wilson. il Aviation W 78:26-7 F 18 '63
Bell demonstrates new design for tactical helicopter. E. J. Bulban. il Aviation W 79:30-2 S 23 '63
Bell, Hiller LOH modifications shown. il Aviation W 79:86-7 S 9 '63
Bell LOH uses fewer, larger components. E. J. Bulban. il Aviation W 80:104-5+ F 17 '64

HELICOPTERS—Military applications—*Cont.*
Bell OH-4A's heavy armament adds weight but holds performance in firepower test. E. J. Bulban. il Aviation W 80:68-9+ Ap 6 '64
Bell Sioux Scout tests attack helicopter concepts. il Aviation W 79:66-7 N 4 '63
Boelkow designs two missiles, turbofan hot-cycle helicopter. W. C. Wetmore. Aviation W 81:19 D 7 '64
Crash tests used to study survival in helicopter impact. D. E. Fink. il Aviation W 78:112-13+ Ap 22 '63
Delay expected in German VTOL decision. C. Brownlow. Aviation W 80:59+ Ap 6 '64
DASH will be operational in November. L. Booda. Aviation W 79:32-3 Jl 1 '63
FAA, Sikorsky test program speeds CH-3C USAF delivery. D. A. Brown. il Aviation W 80:30-2 Ja 6 '64
Firm Super Frelon orders await French type approval. il Aviation W 78:96-7+ Je 10 '63
First Hiller OH-5A delivered for army LOH evaluation. C. M. Plattner. il Aviation W 80:64-5+ Ja 20 '64
Helicopter-rifleman partnership demonstrated in army exercise; Hawk star. G. C. Wilson. Aviation W 80:17-18 Je 29 '64
Helicopters facing V/STOL competition. D. A. Anderton. il Aviation W 78:255-7+ Mr 11 '63
Improved drone helicopter model being developed for navy system. D. A. Brown. Aviation W 81:99+ Ag 24 '64
Kaman UH-2A demonstrates all-weather capability, maneuverability for navy roles. D. A. Brown. il Aviation W 78:80-1+ Ap 8 '63
Larger rotor boosts YUH-1D performance. Aviation W 78:88 Ap 29 '63
Lockheed to market rigid roter XH-51A. G. C. Wilson. il Aviation W 81:44-5 D 28 '64
Makeshift killers; rocket-carrying Hueys in South Viet Nam. il Time 81:34-5 Je 7 '63
Marine CH-53A buy to hit $200 million. G. C. Wilson. Aviation W 81:31-2 N 16 '64
Marine CH-53A enters flight test at Sikorsky plant. il Aviation W 81:28-9 N 23 '64
Military helicopter orders increasing; Great Britain. il Aviation W 81:151+ S 7 '64
Modification of Sikorsky S-61F helicopter proposed for stowed-rotor V/STOL study. D. A. Brown. il Aviation W 82:50-1+ Ja 18 '65
National V/STOL program recommended. Aviation W 80:61 Mr 30 '64
Navy building helicopter-attack vessels. W. Wright. il Aviation W 79:114-16 Ag 5 '63
Navy helicopter avionics system concepts producing spillover benefit. B. Miller. il Aviation W 81:42-3+ Ag 10 '64
Navy uses UD-46 in evaluation of vertical resupply concept. il Aviation W 81:72-3 Ag 10 '64
New army air division to make key test of helicopter's role. G. C. Wilson. Aviation W 78:31-2 Ja 28 '63
New missile site helicopter bids sought; requirements are eased. Aviation W 78:33 Ja 21 '63
Next war: massed helicopters? il U S News 56:62-3 Ap 20 '64
Quang Long battle typifies aircraft use. Aviation W 80:103 Ap 13 '64
Revisions in German helicopter criteria may eliminate S-61R. W. C. Wetmore. Aviation W 81:18 N 2 '64
Rotor study proposals requested for army heavy lift helicopter. Aviation W 81:21 Ag 31 '64
SA 330 reflects French mobility concept. il Aviation W 79:46-7 Jl 29 '63
Service experience leads to T58 changes. D. A. Anderton. il Aviation W 78:48-9+ Ap 29 '63
Sikorsky CH-53A passes mockup review. D. E. Fink. il Aviation W 78:85+ Ap 15 '63
Stand-off weapon for Seahawk ships is sole big missile development seen; DASH. il Miss & Roc 15:65-9 S 21 '64
Sud planning twin-turbine assault helicopter; ducted fans possible. il Aviation W 78:34 Ap 15 '63
VTOL research seeks gains for combat. D. Brown. il Aviation W 80:243-7+ Mr 16 '64
Vietnam war proving helicopter's value as weapon, army contends. Aviation W 80:104+ Ap 20 '64
West German helicopter decision may be delayed until November. Aviation W 80:37 My 18 '64
XH-51A reaches 160 mph. in flight tests. il Aviation W 78:90-1+ My 13 '63

Piloting

Anyone for a backward takeoff? B. Mauldin. il Sports Illus 18:68-76+ My 6 '63

Power supply

Flight by microwave; Raytheon co.'s first public demonstration of an aircraft powered by radio energy. Time 84:38+ N 6 '64
Flying on the beam; Raytheon copter. il Newsweek 64:90 N 9 '64

Radar equipment

See Radar in aviation

Radio control

Flight by microwave; Raytheon co.'s first public demonstration of an aircraft powered by radio energy. Time 84:38+ N 6 '64
Flying on the beam; Raytheon copter. il Newsweek 64:90 N 9 '64

Speed

Speed records claimed. Aviation W 79:57 N 18 '63

Testing

Army receives Hughes OH-6A for testing. C. M. Plattner. il Aviation W 80:72-3+ F 3 '64
Bell UH-1 makes IFR landings, takeoffs. Aviation W 81:22 D 7 '64
Crash tests used to study survival in helicopter impact. D. E. Fink. il Aviation W 78:112-13+ Ap 22 '63
Hughes XV-9A to verify hot cycle system in flight tests. il Aviation W 80:60-2+ Je 22 '64
Marine CH-53A enters flight test at Sikorsky plant. il Aviation W 81:28-9 N 23 '64
MT flight test; Hughes 269-A helicopter. C. Nerpel. il Motor T 15:34-9 Je '63
OH-4A finishes contractor tests. Aviation W 79:21 S 2 '63

HELICOPTERS, Amphibious
New copter at the fair. il Sci Digest 56:53-6 Jl '64
Westland to build SRN-5; Gnome to be standard Hovercraft engine. il Aviation W 78:83 My 6 '63

HELICOPTERS, Freight
Helicopters will get big hardware transport test. D. Henderson. il Miss & Roc 15:27 Ag 31 '64
How'd they get a car up there? Utah's Castle Rock. il Pop Sci 184:89-90 Ap '64
NY shippers study helicopters for cargo. Aviation W 81:44-5 Ag 17 '64
S-64 flying crane shows adaptability for varied loads. il Aviation W 78:72-3 Je 24 '63

HELICOPTERS, Government
Now, for JFK: ten copters, four jets, two yachts, big cars. il U S News 55:60-1 Jl 22 '63
Travel fleets of two Presidents. il U S News 55:65 S 16 '63

HELICOPTERS, Jet propelled
French firm static-tests jet-flap rotor. W. C. Wetmore. il Aviation W 81:57+ D 21 '64

HELICOPTERS, Military. See Helicopters—Military applications

HELICOPTERS, Russian. See Helicopters

HELICOPTERS, Sight-seeing. See Sight-seeing helicopters

HELICOPTERS in agriculture
Ag-copters. il Flying 74:32 My '64
Helicopters invading agricultural market. D. A. Brown. il Aviation W 79:112-13+ N 25 '63

HELICOPTERS in fire protection
Hook-and-ladder helicopters. E. Tozer. il Pop Sci 184:114-16 F '64

HELICOPTERS in insect control
Billions of bugs; Willapa looper project. J. B. Craig. il Am For 70:42-8 F '64

HELICOPTERS in lumbering
Helicopters fly logs. Sci N L 83:196 Mr 30 '63

HELICOPTERS in medical service
It's doc's whirly bird that catches the germ. il Life 54:99-100 Mr 22 '63

HELICOPTERS in police work
Hovering helicops; New York's aerial police. D. Robinson. il N Y Times Mag p 102-4 Ap 19 '64

HELICOPTERS in rescue work
Air lift to flood area gains momentum. il Aviation W 82:20+ Ja 11 '65
Boy caught in a man-killing flood; Great Falls, Mont. il Life 56:38-9 Je 19 '64
Civil air operators active in flood area. H. D. Watkins. il Aviation W 82:94-5+ Ja 18 '65
Helicopters, fixed-wing aircraft supplying flood-bound areas in West. il Aviation W 82:22-4 Ja 4 '65
Portrait of dragonfly driver. P. E. Hansen. il Flying 74:46-7+ My '64
Rescue! E. R. Thornton. il Field & S 67:34-6+ Mr '63
Rescue by copter and bo'sun's chair. H. Wingo. il Life 58:26-7 Ja 8 '65

HELICOPTERS in rescue work—*Continued*
Rescue on the rocks; airborne posse saves lives in High Sierras. W. S. Griswold. il Pop Sci 184:74-5+ Mr '64
Trapped in Devil's Hole. K. E. Oveson. il Outdoor Life 132:50-1+ S '63
Weather, mud, slush challenge airlift crews. H. D. Watkins. Aviation W 82:21 Ja 11 '65
See also
United States—Air force—Air rescue service

HELICOPTERS in surveying. See Surveying, Aerial

HELICOPTERS in traffic regulation
Portrait of a dragonfly driver; broadcasting daily traffic reports over Los Angeles. P. E. Hansen. il Flying 74:46-7+ My '64

HELIO aircraft corporation
Helio's Stallion designed for light military transport use. R. D. Hibben. il Aviation W 80:92-3+ Je 1 '64

HELIOGRAPHERS. See Camera clubs

HÉLION, Jean
Helion paints the impossible; exhibition at Huntington Hartford's gallery of modern art, New York. L. Bell. il Art N 63:36-7+ N '64
Painter of elsewhere; exhibition at Huntington Hartford's gallery of modern art in Manhattan. il por Newsweek 64:105-6+ N 23 '64

HELIOS. See Artificial satellites—Astronomical applications

HELIPORTS
Building owners fight rooftop heliport. J. R. Ashlock. il Aviation W 78:36-7 My 27 '63
Helicopter tests roof landing; Pan Am heliport. J. W. Carter. il Aviation W 80:27-8 Je 1 '64
Heliport quandary. W. J. Kendall. il Flying 74:26-9+ F '64
Pan Am heliport foes plan court battle. J. W. Carter. Aviation W 82:39 Ja 25 '65
Pan Am's pad: helistop for New York airways. il Newsweek 63:80 My 25 '64

HELITZER, Waring and Wayne, incorporated
Moppets and money. P. Korenvaes. Duns R 82:55 D '63

HELIUM
Canning sunstuff beneath the plains. J. Alexander. il Sat R 46:61 O 5 '63
GAO charges windfall on helium program. Bsns W p29 Ja 26 '63
Helium difluoride: possible preparative techniques based on nuclear transmutations. G. C. Pimentel and others. bibliog Science 143:674 F 14 '64
New method for recovering helium. il Miss & Roc 12:48+ Ap 29 '63
New possible compounds: helium difluoride. Sci N L 85:133 F 29 '64
Strange air in space. Sci N L 87:6 Ja 2 '65

HELIUM, Liquid
Quantized vortex rings in superfluid helium. F. Reif. il Sci Am 211:116-22 bibliog(p 156) D '64

HELIX. See Curves

HELLER, Carl G. and Clermont, Yves
Spermatogenesis in man; an estimate of its duration. bibliog Science 140:184-6 Ap 12 '63

HELLER, Joseph
So they say; interview. por Mlle 57:234-5 Ag '63

HELLER, Jules
Problems 1963: malaise in wonderland; address. Sch Arts 62:25-7 Mr '63

HELLER, Larry
Nest of hornets; story. Seventeen 22:134-5 N; 98-9 D '63

HELLER, Walter Wolfgang
At his death, he was a good orthodox economist; excerpts from interviews, ed. by T. G. Harris. por Look 28:54+ N 17 '64
Excerpt from testimony before Joint economic committee, January 28, 1963. Cong Digest 42:118+ Ap '63
No more depressions? interview. pors U S News 56:58-63 Je 29 '64
Speaking out. por Sat Eve Post 236:8+ N 9 '63
Tax reduction; address, May 20, 1963. Vital Speeches 29:561-4 Jl 1 '63
Walter Heller's word for 1964: prosperous; interview, ed. by H. Rowen. por Newsweek 62:46 D 30 '63
about
Business outlook: Burns vs. Heller. por U S News 57:63 S 7 '64
Deficit advocates. U S News 54:15 F 11 '63
More tax cuts coming. il pors Nations Bsns 52:38-41+ My '64
Thrift vs. borrowing, which way to good times? with excerpts from book by P. A. Samuelson. il por U S News 54:37-9 Mr 4 '63
Tough act to follow. Time 84:30-1 N 20 '64
Trail of dissent. Newsweek 64:64+ S 7 '64
Walter Heller, Mr Tax Cut. T. G. Harris. il pors Look 27:81-2+ Je 18 '63
Washington desk. J. R. Slevin. Duns R 84:5 Ag '64

HELLMAN, C. Doris
New star of 1572 is still exploding. Sat R 47:39-43 Jl 4 '64

HELLMAN, Geoffrey T.
Onward and upward with the arts (cont) New Yorker 39:46-8+ Je 8 '63
Onward and upward with the sciences. New Yorker 40:41-2+ My 30; 91-8+ D 5 '64
Profiles (cont) New Yorker 40:59-60+ O 17 '64
Vogue's in its heaven. New Yorker 38:121-4 F 16 '63
What is happening to our young people? New Yorker 39:100+ Mr 2 '63
What's being worn at Le pavillon? New Yorker 39:140+ Mr 9 '63

HELLMAN, H.
Gravitation, science's big riddle. Sci Digest 55:57-64 My '64
Ready, aim, wait! Sci Digest 54:35-9 D '63

HELLMAN, Lillian
Land that holds the legend of our lives. Ladies Home J 81:56-7+ Ap '64
Sophronia's grandson goes to Washington. Ladies Home J 80:78-80+ D '63; 81:82 Mr '64
My mother, my father and me; dramatization of How much? by B. Blechman. Criticism
Nation 196:334 Ap 20 '63
New Yorker 39:108 Mr 30 '63
Newsweek 61:85 Ap 8 '63
Reporter 28:48 Ap 25 '63
Sat R 46:27 Ap 27 '63
Theatre Arts 47:69-70 My '63
Time 81:56 Ap 5 '63

HELLMAN, Louis
Speaking out. por Sat Eve Post 237:8+ N 21 '64

HELLMAN, Robert
Death in America; story. Commentary 36:381-3 N '63

HELLMUTH, Jerome
Wolf in the family. por Sat Eve Post 236:38-9 O 12 '63

HELLO, Dolly. See Songs, American

HELLO, Dolly! musical comedy. See Musical comedies, revues, etc.—Criticisms, plots, etc.

HELLSTRÖM, K. E.
Growth inhibition of sarcoma and carcinoma cells of homozygous origin. bibliog Science 143:477-8 Ja 31 '64

HELLWIG, C. Alexander
Cytology. Science 140:1106+ Je 7 '63

HELM, Everett
Bartók on stage. Hi Fi 14:74-7+ N '64
Crisis in European festivals. Mus Am 84:10-11 Mr '64
European diary. Mus Am 84:17-18 Mr '64
Kirsten Flagstad, 1895-1962. Mus Am 83:81 Ja '63
Letter from Europe. Mus Am 83:38-9 S; 22 O; 271+ D '63; 84:16 F; 27-8 Ap '64
Life and times of Ralph Kirkpatrick. Mus Am 83:34+ Ja '63
Man with a mask. Hi Fi 13:54-6+ D '63
Pittsburgh's Steinberg. Mus Am 83:24 Ag '63
Rabbits from a hat. Mus Am 84:16-17 O '64
Universal musician. por Hi Fi 14:36-8+ My '64

HELM, MacKinley
Never on Wednesdays. Atlan 212:116 Jl '63

HELMER, William J.
New York's middle-class homosexuals. Harper 226:85-92 Mr '63

HELMHOLTZ, Hermann von
Origins of psychoacoustics; with editorial comment. S. J. London. pors Hi Fi 13:43, 44-7+ Ap '63

HELMS, Julia B.
Art classes for aphasic children. Sch Arts 63:35-6 Ja '64

HELOU, Charles
Charles the Sweet. Newsweek 64:44 Ag 31 '64

HELPFULNESS. See Service

HELSER, Paul
Double hat rack; ed. by B. East. pors Outdoor Life 134:24-7+ D '64

HELSINGOR, Denmark
Elsinore. H. Bendix. Mlle 58:127 F '64

HELSINKI
Letter from Finland. J. Bainbridge. il New Yorker 40:141-2+ O 3 '64

Music

[Musical events] Mus Am 83:80 Ja '63

Stores

Phone Helsinki 12-181 for all you need: 103-year-old Stockmann's. il Bsns W p60-2+ O 31 '64

HELSLEY, C. E. See Stehli, G. jt. auth.

HELWIG, John, jr
My most unforgettable character. Read Digest 84:129-33 My '64

HELXINE soleiroli. See Babys tears

HEMAGGLUTINATION. See Blood—Agglutination

HEMAGGLUTININ
Arbovirus hemagglutinin inhibitor in acetone-extracted serums from normal chickens. P. Holden and others. il Science 147:169-70 Ja 8 '65

HEMATITE
Magnetite: preferred orientation on the basal plane of partially reduced hematite. R. O. Keeling, jr. and D. A. Wick. bibliog il Science 141:1175-6 S 20 '63

HEMATOLOGY. See Blood

HEMATOPORPHYRIA
Night people; case of porphyria cutanea tarda. il Time 81:43 Je 21 '63

HEME
Terminal oxidation in the regulation of heme biosynthesis. J. Onisawa and R. F. Labbe. bibliog il Science 140:1326-7 Je 21 '63

HEMENWAY, David Allen
My trip to the IAU meeting. Sky & Tel 28: 260-3 N '64

HEMENWAY, John T.
Foundation for the future. por Am For 70: 19-21 N '64

HEMENWAY, Robert
Late show; story. New Yorker 39:46-9 N 9 '63
Stories. New Yorker 40:62-6+ N 7 '64

HEMEROCALLIS. See Day lilies

HEMERYTHRIN. See Pigments (biology)

HEMI engine. See Automobile engines

HEMINGWAY, Ernest
Paris: excerpts from Moveable feast. pors Life 56:60-79 Ap 10 '64
Scott Fitzgerald; excerpt from Moveable feast. Life 56:80+ Ap 10 '64

about

Fifty pounds of Hemingway. il por Newsweek 63:67 Ja 6 '64
Haunted house of Ernest Hemingway. S. Belfrage. il Esquire 59:66-7 F '63
Hemingway as his own fable. A. Kazin. por Atlan 213:54-7 Je '64
Hemingway (the boatman) C. Meyer. il pors Motor B 114:21-3+ Jl '64
Hemingway's code. J. Hart. Nat R 16:450-2 Je 2 '64
Look back, a look ahead; ed. by H. Markel. M. Hemingway. il por Good H 156:32-4+ F '63
Need for watering places. B. DeMott. Harper 228:114+ Je '64
Old Hem was a sport. J. Dos Passos. il Sports Illus 20:58-60+ Je 29 '64
Paris: a little incident in the rue de l'Odéon. K. A. Porter. Ladies Home J 81:54-5 Ag '64
Paris and Hemingway in the spring. S. Kauffmann. New Repub 150:17-18+ My 9 '64; Reply. T. Sturak. 150:29 Je 6 '64
Postcards from Paris. G. Paulding. il Reporter 30:40+ Je 4 '64
Reminiscence of Hemingway. V. Danby-Smith. il por Sat R 47:30-1+ My 9 '64
That summer in Paris, by M. Callaghan. Review
New Yorker 39:139-42+ F 23 '63. E. Wilson; Reply. M. Hemingway. 39:160+ Mr 16 '63
Time il 81:106 Mr 15 '63
Torrents of spring. il por Newsweek 63:102 My 11 '64
When papa was Tatie. il por Time 83:98+ My 8 '64
Who's who at the lost & found. N. Algren. Nation 198:560-1 Je 1 '64
Young man, old man. A. Kazin. Reporter 29: 33-6 D 19 '63

HEMINGWAY, Mary (Welsh)
Look back, a look ahead; ed. by H. Markel. pors Good H 156:32-4+ F '63
Sentimental safari. pors Life 54:88-92+ Ap 19 '63

about

Fifty pounds of Hemingway. il por Newsweek 63:67 Ja 6 '64

HEMINGWAY, Mary Moon
Going places, finding things in Israel. House & Gard 126:19+ Ag '64
Going places, finding things in the Cyclades and Crete. House & Gard 123:24+ Je '63
Havana. Sat R 48:40-1+ Ja 2 '65

HEMIPTERA
See also
Water scorpions

HEMLEY, Cecil
New kitsch. Sat R 47:36-7 D 5 '64
(tr) See Singer, I. B. Three tales

about

Author. M. K. Harvey. por Sat R 46:39 F 2 '63

HEMLOCK loopers
Billions of bugs: Willapa looper project. J. B. Craig. il Am For 70:42-8 F '64

HEMMING, Roy
Building your own record library. Sr Schol 83:25 D 13 '63; 84:48 F 14 '64
DISCussions. See issues of Senior scholastic
Records and tapes. Sr Schol 82:10T Ap 17; 11T My 8 '63
Scholastic magazines' basic music library. Sr Schol 83:25 D 13 '63

HEMOCHROMATOSIS
De-fusion man. il Newsweek 62:57 S 2 '63

HEMOCYANIN
Linear polymerization of a gastropod hemocyanin. R. M. Condie and R. B. Langer. bibliog il Science 144:1138-40 My 29 '64

HEMOGLOBIN
Abnormal hemoglobin studies in Taiwan aborigines. R. Q. Blackwell and J. T. H. Huang. bibliog Science 139:771 F 22 '63
Alpha-chain of human hemoglobin: occurrence in vivo. P. Fessas and D. Loukopoulos. bibliog il Science 143:590-1 F 7 '64
Amino acids: incorporation into α-and β-chains of hemoglobin by normal and thalassemic reticulocytes. J. D. Heywood and others. bibliog il Science 146:530-1 O 23 '64
Bohr effect; absence in a molluscan hemocyanin. J. R. Redmond. bibliog il Science 139:1294-5 Mr 29 '63
Electrophoretic patterns of hemoglobin from fetal mice of different inbred strains. M. L. Craig and E. S. Russell. bibliog il Science 142:398-9 O 18 '63
Genetic control of hemoglobin synthesis. W. E. Nance. bibliog il Science 141:123-30 Jl 12 '63
Genetic relationship between maximum hematocrit values and hemoglobin type in sheep. J. V. Evans and J. H. Whitlock. bibliog il Science 145:1318 S 18 '64
Haptoglobin binding capacity of certain abnormal hemoglobins. R. L. Nagel and H. M. Ranney. bibliog il Science 144:1014-15 My 22 '64
Hemoglobin $G_{Coushatta}$: a new variant in an American Indian family. R. G. Schneider and others. bibliog il Science 143:697-8 F 14 '64
Hemoglobin loci: mice classified for their Hb and Sol alleles. R. A. Popp. bibliog il Science 140:893-4 My 24 '63
Hemoglobin: molecular changes during anuran metamorphosis. C. D. Trader and others. bibliog il Science 139:918-19 Mr 8 '63
Hemoglobin molecule. M. F. Perutz. il Sci Am 211:64-76 N '64
Hemoglobin polymorphism: its relation to sickling of erythrocytes in white-tailed deer. H. Kitchen and others. bibliog il Science 144:1237-9 Je 5 '64
Hemoglobin solubility and α-chain structure in crosses between two inbred mouse strains. J. J. Hutton and others. bibliog il Science 143:252-3 Ja 17 '64
Hemoglobin synthesis in marrow cell culture: the effect of rat plasma on rat cells. O. Gallien-Lartigue and E. Goldwasser. il Science 145:277-9 Jl 17 '64
Hemoglobins A and F: formation in thalassemia and other hemolytic anemias. P. A. Marks and E. R. Burka. bibliog il Science 144:552-3 My 1 '64
Mosaic hemoglobin types in a pair of cattle twins. C. Stormont and others. bibliog il Science 145:600-1 Ag 7 '64
Mössbauer effect in hemoglobin with different ligands. U. Gonser and others. bibliog il Science 143:680-1 F 14 '64
Spectra of deoxygenated hemoglobin in the Soret Region. R. Benesch and others. bibliog il Science 144:68-9 Ap 3 '64
Stoichiometry of hemoglobin reactions. A. Schejter and others. bibliog il Science 141: 784-8 Ag 30 '63
X-ray analysis of hemoglobin. M. F. Perutz. bibliog il Science 140:863-9 My 24 '63; Reply. G. S. Eadie and G. R. Gale. 142:343 O 18 '63

HEMOLYTIC disease. See Erythroblastosis
HÉMON, Louis
Reporter at large. E. Wilson. New Yorker 40:94+ N 21 '64
HEMOPHILIA
Dogs have royal disease. F. Marley. Sci N L 85:295 My 9 '64
Hemophilias; report on International conference on hemophilia. E. Lechler and H. R. Roberts. Science 144:1043-4 My 22 '64
Heredity & clotting factors. il Time 82:41+ D 27 '63
Red cross research aims to help hemophiliacs. Sci N L 84:105 Ag 17 '63
They cared enough to give the most. W. Trombley. il Ladies Home J 81:32+ Ap '64
They live on borrowed blood. R. Massie. Sat Eve Post 236:32-4 My 4 '63
What stopped the bleeding? case of F. Wallace. il Time 81:63 Ap 26 '63
HEMORRHAGE
Erythropoietin production following gamma irradiation and hemorrhage in dogs. N. Pesic and others. bibliog il Science 143: 49-50 Ja 3 '64
Hemorrhagic shock: metabolic effects; report of workshop at Rockefeller institute. F. A. Simeone. Science 141:536+ Ag 9 '63
HEMORRHAGE, Cerebral. See Cerebral hemorrhage
HEMORRHAGIC fever
Casualties in a jungle war; Bolivian hemorrhagic fever. il Time 82:48+ Jl 19 '63
HEMORRHOIDS
Ailment nobody mentions. J. D. Ratcliff. Read Digest 85:77-80 S '64
Hidden dangers of pile remedies. T. Berland. Todays Health 42:50-1 F '64
HEMPHILL, Frazier Erich
One man's battle against rabies; Alaska. C. McClain. il Todays Health 42:56-9+ D '64
Savior of Alaska's vital sled dogs. il pors Ebony 19:118-20+ D '63
HEMPSTEAD, N.Y.
Designed to work hard. W. J. Landman. il Am City 79:106-7 Mr '64
Hempstead versus jets; Idlewild airport. il Bsns W p93-4 D 7 '63
HEMSLEY, Stuart
Archy is shocked again; poem. Atlan 213: 124 F '64
Corn yield rise linked to music; poem. Atlan 211:134 Ap '63
Notes on a male aedes aegypti whose terminalium failed to rotate; poem. Atlan 214: 107 Ag '64
Poem: When I was a lad I served a term. Atlan 214:166 N '64
Short ballad of indifferent performers. Atlan 212:104 Ag '63
HEN-and-chickens. See Houseleeks
HEN houses. See Poultry houses
HENAULT, Marie J.
Saving of Father Urban. America 108:290-2 Mr 2 '63
HENDERSON, Danna
Helicopters will get big hardware transport test. Miss & Roc 15:27 Ag 31 '64
HENDERSON, Earl E.
Traveling classrooms. NEA J 52:57 F '63
HENDERSON, Edwin B.
Washington who's who. Negro Hist Bul 26: 190-5 Mr '63
HENDERSON, Ernest
Personalities. por Time 82:76 S 27 '63
Wonderland economics of Sheraton corp. J. Thackray. il por Duns R 83:32-4+ Je '64
HENDERSON, Everett S.
Ancient trees for modern gardens. Horticulture 41:448-9 S '63
Easy vegetable gardening. Horticulture 41:270 My; 310-11 Je '63
Grow the best dogwoods. Horticulture 42:30-1+ My '64
Mockorange for fragrance. Pop Gard 16:40 Ja '65
HENDERSON, Harold
Alan Walker in South Africa. Christian Cent 80:1410+ N 13 '63
HENDERSON, John
Seasickness. por Motor B 111:42-3+ Ap '63
Sun tan safely. Motor B 114:52+ Jl '64
HENDERSON, John D.
New ALA officer. ALA Bul 57:660+ Jl '63
HENDERSON, Lois T.
Should I try to be a writer? Writer 77:21-3 Ap '64
Teen-age ambassadors of understanding. Read Digest 83:181-4 S '63
HENDERSON, Mervin
International micro midget championships. Hot Rod 17:70-3 D '64
HENDERSON, R. L.
Marina lighting; excerpt from address, June 11, 1962. Am City 78:91-2 Ag '63
HENDERSON, Robert
Days and the neighbors; story. New Yorker 40:44-7 Ap 25 '64
Go it, tortoise. New Yorker 39:39-40 S 28 '63
Leonardo Da Vinci traffic jam. New Yorker 40:24-6 Ag 15 '64
Spring and Mrs Malloy; story. Sat Eve Post 236:64-6 O 26 '63
Storeroom; story. New Yorker 39:32-5 S 7 '63
HENDERSON, Skitch
Quote . . . unquote. R. Jacobson. por Mus Am 83:19 Jl '63
HENDL, Walter
Eastman's Walter Hendl. P. Davis. por Mus Am 84:286-7 D '64
HENDLER, Richard W.
Protein biosynthesis some alternative considerations on the current hypothesis. bibliog Science 142:402-5 O 18 '63
HENDRICK, Kimmis
Unruh bucks the clubs. Nation 198:472-4 My 11 '64
HENDRICKS, Bartlett
Bush in the hand. Audubon ~~Mag~~ 65:116-19 Mr '63
HENDRICKS, Sterling B.
Metabolic control of timing. bibliog Science 141:21-7 Jl 5 '63
HENDRICKSON, John R. and Weber, W. A.
Lichens on Galápagos giant tortoises. Science 144:1463 Je 19 '64
HENDRICKSON, Robert M.
Needless agony of smallpox. Todays Health 41:22-3+ Mr '63
Second deadliest poison. Todays Health 41: 56-9+ O '63
HENDRIX, James W.
Sterol induction of reproduction and stimulation of growth of pythium and phytophthora. bibliog Science 144:1028-9 My 22 '64
HENDRON, Henry
Man who spoke to Lincoln. il pors Ebony 18:79-82+ F '63
HENDRY, John
Graduation. Sch Arts 63:3 Je '64
HENDRY, Peter
Chicken-war stew; United States and the Common market. Reporter 29:30+ N 7 '63
HENEGHAN, Joseph I.
Kiss, tape, and tell. il por Newsweek 62:42 O 7 '63
HENEGHAN, Patrick J. and Justice, June
Poetry, a lively art indeed! por Recreation 57:504-5 D '64
HENGSBACH, Franz, bp
Work ahead. America 110:15 Ja 4 '64
HENKES, Robert
Painting toward intuition. Sch Arts 62:11-13 F '63
HENLE, Fritz
Twin lens. See issues of Popular photography
about
Focus on Fritz Henle. H. M. Kinzer. il por Pop Phot 55:142-9+ N '64
HENLE, R. J.
Do we have Catholic colleges? America 109: 298-9 S 21 '63
HENLEY, Arthur
Abandoned child. McCalls 91:126-7+ My '64
Curious transformation of Laurie. Sat Eve Post 237:83+ O 17 '64
HENLEY, Elizabeth
Lines from an Oregon garden; poem. Ladies Home J 80:56 Ap '63
HENLEY, Ralph
Washington ski time. Travel 123:36-7 Ja '65
HENNAGAN, Thomas L.
I spied on Castro's Cuba. il pors Ebony 18: 114-16+ Ap '63
HENNEBERGER, Richard M. Jr. and Bush, Howard
What it costs to clean a digester. Am City 78:105 Mr '63
HENNESEY, James J.
Church in America. America 111:448-9+ O 17 '64
HENNESSY, James Pope-. See Pope-Hennessy, J.
HENNESSY, William G. and Sharf, F. A.
Benjamin Champney and the American Barbizon, 1850-1857. Antiques 84:566-9 N '63
HENNEY, Henry R. Jr. and Storck, Roger
Ribosomes and ribonucleic acids in three morphological states of neurospora. bibliog Science 142:1675-6 D 27 '63
HENNIKER-HEATON, Peter J.
Selling your poetry. Writer 77:18-20 Ap '64
HENNING, John F.
Excerpt from statement, July 24, 1963. Cong Digest 43:80+ Mr '64

HENNING, John F.—*Continued*

about

Case of Mr Henning. New Repub 152:5 Ja 9 '65
Headache for LBJ: Wirtz-Meany clash. il por U S News 58:13 Ja 4 '65

HENNING, Paul
Golden hillbillies. R. W. Lewis. il por Sat Eve Post 236:30+ F 2 '63

HENNING, William
Walpole Island. Travel 120:43-6 Jl '63

HENNINGSMOEN, Kari E. See Spjeldnaes, N. jt. auth.

HENRI, comte de Paris
Count of Paris. E. von Kuehnelt-Leddihn. Nat R 15:102 Ag 13 '63

HENRI, Robert
Art galleries; exhibition: Robert Henri and his circle at American academy of arts and letters. R. M. Coates. New Yorker 40:69 Ja 2 '65

HENRI Bendel (store) See New York (city)—Stores

HENRY IV, king of France
Henry of Navarre. by H. Pearson. Review Sat R por 47:32 Ja 18 '64. L. Gershoy

HENRY, Aaron
Aaron Henry and his friends. R. A. Woodley. New Repub 151:6-7 O 10 '64

HENRY, Carl L.
Photocell circuits for experiments. Pop Electr 19:47-9 S '63
Speed service with simple instruments. Pop Electr 20:43-5 Ap '64

HENRY, David
Cherries for fruit and flowers. Horticulture 41:294-5 My '63
How hardy are hardy chrysanthemums? Horticulture 41:444-5 S '63
Mahonias, striking during every season. Horticulture 41:542 O '63
Plant propagation, by runners and offsets. Horticulture 41:411 Ag '63
Reporter at large. K. T. Kinkead. New Yorker 40:51-2+ My 23 '64

HENRY, E. William
What to expect next in television; interview. por U S News 57:48-52 Jl 6 '64

about

From FCC chief, plain talk to broadcasters. por U S News 55:30 O 7 '63
Green shoot. por Time 81:72+ My 24 '63
People of the week. por U S News 54:23 My 27 '63

HENRY, George
Jim Crow South African style. il pors Ebony 19:123-4+ My '64

HENRY, John M.
(comp) I saw it in the paper. See issues of McCall's

HENRY, Joseph
Professor Henry and his philosophical toys; with note by Mrs C. H. Danforth. M. Blow. il por Am Heritage 15:24-9+ D '63

HENRY, Jules
Books. Sci Am 211:129-30+ Jl '64

HENRY, Laurin L.
How to watch the White House. Nations Bsns 52:34-5+ N '64

HENRY, Mary Gibson
Lady botanist. New Yorker 39:17-18 Jl 27 '63
Yes, tall oaks from little acorns grow. C. Peet. il pors Am For 69:24-7 O '63

HENRY, Mary Roblee
Africa: the new grand tour. Vogue 142:56-63+ Jl '63
Going places, finding things in Morocco. House & Gard 125:26+ F '64
Morocco from A to Z. Vogue 144:40+ S 1 '64
Play on cheeses. House & Gard 125:48+ My '64

HENRY, O. pseud. See Porter, W. S.

HENRY, Rene A. Jr
Build a canopy for shade and storage. Pop Gard 15:50-3 S '64

HENRY, Vera
Getting to know your characters. Writer 77:23-5 Ag '64

HENRY, Walt
VHF listener. Pop Electr 20:52-6+ Mr '64

HENRY, William Mellors
Man who doesn't take sides. il por Time 84:39 D 25 '64

HENRY Draper catalogue. See Stars—Spectra

HENRY V; drama. See Shakespeare, W.—Plays

HENRY Ford museum and Greenfield Village, Dearborn, Mich.
Henry Ford museum receives rare 18th century porcelain. il Hobbies 67:82 F '63
History in houses: the Noah Webster House at Greenfield Village. G. G. Gibson. il Antiques 85:196-201 F '64

HENRY Francis Dupont Winterthur museum
In the museums; new China trade room at Winterthur. R. Davidson. il Antiques 83:330+ Mr '63
Living with antiques. J. A. H. Sweeney. il Antiques 85:542-7 My '64
Sculpture at Winterthur. F. H. Sommer. il Antiques 85:182-4 F '64

HENRY, John (ballad) See Ballads, American

HENSKE, Judy
Big girl in town. por Newsweek 61:90 My 20 '63

HENSON, Josiah
Uncle Tom's Canadian cabin. L. Johnson. il por Hobbies 68:124-5 S '63

HENSON, Matthew Alexander
Ahdoolo! condensation. F. Miller. il por Read Digest 82:263-9+ F '63

HENSON, Ray D.
Due process on the USSR docket. Sat R 47:26-7 Je 27 '64

HENTOFF, Nat
Analyzing the kick. Reporter 28:56+ Ap 25 '63
Black backlash. Commonweal 80:443-5 Jl 3 '64
Chaos in welfare. Commonweal 80:522-3 Jl 24 '64
Cool, like blocked. Nation 198:298-300 Mr 23 '64
Don't be an over-indulgent father. Parents Mag 39:60-2+ Je '64
Dropout from what? Reporter 31:48-9 N 5 '64
Durable Duke. Reporter 30:45-8 My 7 '64
Gospel as gimmick. Reporter 29:46-7 Ag 15 '63
Harlem sounds. Reporter 31:41-2 D 3 '64
It's been good to know him. Reporter 32:48-9 Ja 14 '65
Jacobins of jazz. Mlle 57:268-9+ Ag '63
Jazz and race. Commonweal 81:482-4 Ja 8 '65
Jazz recordings. Atlan 211:137 Ap; 212:138+ N '63; 213:138 Ap '64
Liberals hissed. Reporter 31:46+ O 22 '64
Paying the new jazz dues. Nation 198:635+ Je 22 '64
Plenty of horn. Reporter 30:39-40 Ja 2 '64
Pressures for change in our courts. Commonweal 78:331-2 Je 14 '63
Profiles. New Yorker 40:64-6+ O 24 '64
Record notes. See occasional issues of The reporter to May 23, 1963
Rhetoric and relevance. Nation 198:663-5 Je 29 '64
Village anarchist. Reporter 29:54-5 Jl 18 '63
Young folks. Reporter 31:58-9 Ag 13 '64

about

Raising their voices. por Newsweek 64:48 D 21 '64

HENZE, Hans Werner
Henze's Elegy for young lovers. P. Davis. il Mus Am 84:45 N '64
Hour of Henze; excerpts from Elegy for young lovers. I. Kolodin. il Sat R 47:63 S 26 '64
Lucky Hans. por Time 81:48+ My 24 '63
Music to my ears; a Henze premiere: Fifth symphony. I. Kolodin. Sat R 46:33 Je 1 '63
On DGG, Henze's Elegy for young lovers. G. L. Mayer. il por Am Rec G 31:200-1+ N '64

HEPARIN
Heparin enhancement of factors stimulating bone resorption in tissue culture. P. Goldhaber. bibliog il Science 147:407-8 Ja 22 '65
Heparinic acids: determination of equivalent weights and sulfate to carboxyl ratios. K. E. Kuettner and A. Lindenbaum. bibliog il Science 144:1228-9 Je 5 '64

HEPATIC pathology. See Liver—Diseases

HEPATICAS
Bloodroot: hepatica. I. D. Jolly. il Horticulture 41:463 S '63

HEPATITIS
Lurking risks of transfusion. K. Wheeler. il Life 54:70-2+ F 15 '63
When AMA doctors met. Sci N L 83:402 Je 29 '63

HEPATITIS, Infectious

Vaccines

Hepatitis vaccine search carried to the Congo. Sci N L 85:344 My 30 '64

HEPATITIS virus
Cytochemical assay of interferon produced by duck hepatitis virus. E. A. Sueltenfuss and M. Pollard. bibliog il Science 139:595-6 F 15 '63
Grant made for study of hepatitis viruses in blood. Sci N L 85:217 Ap 4 '64
Most elusive virus. Bsns W p 112 Mr 28 '64

HEPATOLENTICULAR degeneration
Fifty cent test may thwart disease: detection of Wilson's disease. Bsns W p98 Mr 9 '63
Mental disorder test: Wilson's disease. il Sci N L 83:163 Mr 16 '63

HEPATOMAS. See Tumors
HEPBURN, Audrey
Audrey Hepburn in Givenchy hats: My fair lady to the life; photographs. C. Beaton. Vogue 144:118-21 Ag 15 '64
AH; making of My fair lady. A. Seidenbaum. il pors McCalls 92:96-8+ O '64
Cary Grant, Audrey Hepburn. il pors Look 27:87-90+ D 17 '63
Follow a star. H. Perry. il pors Seventeen 24:79+ Ja '65
My fair lady's dream comes true. S. Gordon. il pors Look 28:60-2+ F 25 '64
Who says it's a dog's life? il pors Good H 158:82-3 Mr '64
HEPBURN, Katherine
To Lawrence Langner. Theatre Arts 47:11 My '63
HEPPLEWHITE, George
George Hepplewhite, English cabinet-maker. E. H. Bjerkoe. il Hobbies 69:90-2 Jl '64
HEPPLEWHITE furniture. See Furniture, English
HEPTACHLOR in milk. See Milk contamination
HEPWORTH, Barbara
In abstract memoriam; United Nations memorial to D. Hammarskjöld. il por Time 83:68 Je 19 '64
Searching eye of a sculptress. il pors Life 57:73+ S 18 '64
HEPWORTH, Philip
Norwich on the square. Library J 88:4548-50 D 1 '63
HER master's voice; drama. See Kummer, C.
HERALD, Miami. See Miami herald
HERALD tribune, New York. See New York herald tribune
HERALD tribune fresh air fund. See Fresh air charity
HERALDRY
Arms race; sail-order coat-of-arms business. il Newsweek 64:92+ S 28 '64
At the sign of the crest. H. K. Eilers. See issues of Hobbies
Heraldry on Wedgwood creamware; with glossary. J. M. Dennis. il Antiques 86: 168-73 Ag '64
Want a coat of arms? trace your family tree? il Life 54:103-8 My 3 '63
HERAS, Joaquín Gutiérrez
Music in transition; tr. by J. Norman. Atlan 213:112-14+ Mr '64
HERAVI, Ali Reza
Young power in diplomacy. por Vogue 143: 89 Ap 15 '64
HERB teas. See Tea
HERBERG, Will
Limits of papal authority. Nat R 16:730-2+ Ag 25 '64
Religion (cont) por Nat R 14:364-5; 15:61, 104-5, 188-9 My 7, Jl 30-Ag 13, S 10 '63
HERBERS, John
Communique from the Mississippi front. N Y Times Mag p34-5+ N 8 '64
Critical test for the nonviolent way. N Y Times Mag p5+ Jl 5 '64
HERBERT, A. P.
Paddington bows to Westminster. N Y Times Mag p70-1+ N 3 '63
HERBERT, Henry George Charles Alexander Herbert, viscount
Four eligible bachelors in London. E. O'Brien. por Vogue 144:142-3 S 15 '64
HERBERT, J. See Michael, R. P. jt. auth.
HERBERT, Mary (Sidney) countess of Pembroke. See Pembroke, M. S. H.
HERBERT, Victor
Madeleine. Criticism
Opera N il por 28:6-7 Ja 25 '64
HERBICIDES
Amitrole translocation in agropyron repens increased by the addition of ammonium thiocyanate. W. F. Donnalley and S. K. Ries. bibliog il Science 145:497-8 Jl 31 '64
Diuron looks good on winter wheat. Suc Farm 62:69 O '64
Herbicides: combination enhances selectivity. S. R. Colby and G. F. Warren. bibliog il Science 141:362 Jl 26 '63
Pellets save the good, kill the bad trees. Sci N L 87:56 Ja 23 '65
Phenol in quackgrass associated with dalapon. T. R. Flanagan and A. R. Langille. bibliog il Science 140:179-80 Ap 12 '63
Picolinic acid derivative: a plant growth regulator; tordon. J. W. Hamaker and others. il Science 141:363 Jl 26 '63
Plant sprays safer. Sci N L 84:147 S 7 '63
Simazine: degradation by soil microorganisms. D. D. Kaufman and others. bibliog il Science 142:405-6 O 18 '63
See also
Weeds—Chemical control

Injurious effects
cis-3-chloroacrylic acid: a new cotton defoliant and crop desiccant. R. A. Herrett and A. N. Kurtz. bibliog il Science 141:1192-3 S 20 '63
HERBLOCK, pseud. See Block, H. L.
HERBS
Cooking with herbs and spices. Am Home 66:68+ Mr '63
For flavor and fragrance grow herbs. D. Schroeder. il Horticulture 41:464-5 S '63
Fun with herbs. L. Eisman. il Pop Gard 14: 41+ Ap '63
Garden in a window. D. Wallace. Am Home 68:26 Ja '65
Grow flavorful herbs in your garden or kitchen window. G. B. Foster. il Am Home 66:41+ Mr '63
Growing herbs outside the kitchen door. il Sunset 130:232-3 Je '63
Herbs and spices: the secret key to flavor; with recipes. V. T. Habeeb. il Am Home 66:42-3+ Mr '63
Herbs are for flavor and fragrance. M. W. Bear. il Horticulture 42:18-19+ Ag '64
Herbs from garden to kitchen. il Ladies Home J 81:133-7 My '64
Herbs in the teapot. D. E. Stebbins. il Horticulture 41:402 Ag '63
Herbs on your gift packages. A. H. Williamson. il Horticulture 42:30-1 D '64
Herbs: their ancient influences on mankind. M. Carleton. il Todays Health 42:32-7 Mr '64
Know-how of herbs. M. W. Muenscher. Bet Hom & Gard 42:75 D '64
Plant now, feast later. H. S. Witty. il Flower Grower 50:53+ My '63
Twelve most useful herbs, and how to grow them. G. Foster. il House B 106:182-3+ Ap '64
Which is which? McCalls 91:90+ My '64
Win blue ribbons with dried herbs. A. H. Williamson. il Horticulture 42:26-7 F '64
Your own dried herbs and seeds. il Sunset 131:176 Ag '63
See also
Comfrey
Garlic
Ginsberg
Ginseng
Lavender
HERBS, Medicinal. See Botany, Medical
HERBSTREIT, Jack W.
Radio meteorology. Science 147:76-8 Ja 1 '65
HERCOLANI, Laudomia, princess
Princess Laudomia Hercolani. pors Vogue 143:150-3 My '64
HERCULANEUM
Herculaneum; Italy's neglected treasure trove. J. J. Deiss. il Harper 228:55-60 Mr '64
HERCULES, David M.
Chemiluminescence resulting from electrochemically generated species. bibliog Science 145:808-9 Ag 21 '64
HERCULES powder company
Keeping danger at arm's length. il Bsns W p77 Ag 10 '63
Resourceful computer application keeps Hercules plant on schedule. J. F. Judge. il Miss & Roc 15:28+ Jl 13 '64
Thouron of Hercules powder. il Fortune 67: 51 Mr '63
HERCULON. See Textile fibers, Synthetic
HERDEG, Walter
Sun; excerpt from Sun in art. Natur Hist 72:38-47 Ap '63
HERDER correspondence (periodical)
Welcome, colleague and competitor! Christian Cent 80:1601 D 25 '63
HEREDITY
Additive inheritance of serum cholesterol level in mice. J. H. Bruell. il Science 142: 1664-5 D 27 '63
Catalase abnormality in a Caucasian family in the United States. E. W. Baur. bibliog il Science 140:816-17 My 17 '63
Cholesterol similarities shown in study of twins. Sci N L 86:248 O 17 '64
Erythrocyte glucose-6-phosphate dehydrogenase in Caucasians: new inherited variant. T. B. Shows, jr. and others. bibliog il Science 145:1056-7 S 4 '64
Hereditary globulin factors and immune tolerance in man. A. G. Steinberg and J. A. Wilson. bibliog il Science 140:303-4 Ap 19 '63
Hereditary quiz. J. Daugherty and M. Daugherty. il Sci Digest 56:89-91 N '64
Heredity vs. environment a surprising new answer. J. Kaplan and Mrs J. Kaplan. il Sci Digest 56:59-62 D '64

HEREDITY—*Continued*
Human erythrocyte lactate dehydrogenase: four genetically determined variants. A. P. Kraus and C. L. Neely, jr. bibliog il Science 145:595-7 Ag 7 '64
Inheritance of avoidance conditioning in mice: a diallel study. R. L. Collins. bibliog il Science 143:1188-90 Mr 13 '64
Inheritance of behavior in infants. D. G. Freedman and B. Keller. bibliog il Science 140:196-8 Ap 12 '63
Key to health: your heredity; interview, ed. by F. R. Schreiber. R. J. Williams. Sci Digest 53:30-9 Ap '63
Myoglobin: inherited structural variation in man. S. H. Boyer and others. bibliog il Science 140:1228-31 Je 14 '63
Somatic inheritance of habituation of responses to light in planarians. R. A. Westerman. bibliog il Science 140:676-7 My 10 '63
Stupid questions about heredity. M. Mann. il Pop Sci 183:97-9+ O '63
Will the child be normal? R. C. Baumiller. America 110:220-1 F 15 '64
See also
Chromosomes
Eugenics
Evolution
Genetics
Prenatal influences

HEREDITY of disease
Christmas factor: dosage compensation and the production of blood coagulation factor IX. O. Frota-Pessoa and others. bibliog il Science 139:348-9 Ja 25 '63
Stupid questions about heredity. M. Mann. il Pop Sci 183:97-9+ O '63
See also
Amaurotic family idiocy

HERE'S love; musical comedy. See Musical comedies, revues, etc.—Criticisms, plots, etc.

HERESY
Four faces of heresy. H. R. Trevor-Roper. il Horizon 6:8-17 Spr '64
On heresy, by K. Rahner. Review
Cath World 200:53-4 O '64. G. J. Aylward

HERING, Doris
Aurora and lesser companions. Dance Mag 37:19-23+ Jl '63
Land of long-legged butterflies. Dance Mag 37:46-7+ My '63
Met opera ballet thinks big. Dance Mag 37: 35-9+ Jl '63
Regional ballet, USA. See issues of Dance magazine
Reviews. See issues of Dance magazine
Taste of tomorrow. Dance Mag 37:48-51+ Ag '63
Tickets for the bug man. Dance Mag 37:52-3 F '63
Triumph along the St Johns. por Dance Mag 37:48-53 Je '63
Where do they come from? Dance Mag 37: 23-5+ O '63

HERING, Robert L.
Cameras & gardens. Pop Gard 15:34-5 Jl; 79 S '64; 16:14 Ja '65
Dormant garden care. Pop Gard 16:44-5+ Ja '65
Get rid of snow the easy way. Pop Gard 15:13-15 N '64
Leaves are for keeping. Pop Gard 15:28-9 S '64
Photographically speaking. See issues of Popular science monthly
Water; make it work for you. Pop Gard 15: 55-7 My '64
Why the new 8mm movie cameras never miss. Pop Sci 185:96-100 Ag '64

HERLIHY, James Leo
Astral body of a U.S. mail truck; story. Mlle 56:106-7 F '63

HERLINGER, Ria
Five designers, five approaches. P. Adler. il por Craft Horiz 24:43-4 Mr '64

HERMAN, Hamilton
AMF expects its R&D to yield new divisions. il pors Bsns W p 134-6+ My 4 '63

HERMAN, Melvin. See Schreiber, F. R. jt. auth.

HERMAN Miller, incorporated. See Miller, Herman, incorporated

HERMAN, Robert
Planning the season. pors Opera N 28:8-11 Mr 14 '64

HERMAN, Robert, 1914-, and Gardels, Keith
Vehicular traffic flow; with biographical sketches. Sci Am 209:28, 35-43 D '63

HERMAN, Sidney S. and Mihursky, J. A.
Infestation of the copepod acartia tonsa with the stalked ciliate zoothamnium. bibliog Science 146:543-4 O 23 '64

HERMAN, Steven G. See Telford, A. D. jt. auth.

HERMAN, Theodore
Trends in Chinese agriculture. bibliog f Cur Hist 45:165-72 S '63

HERMAN, Woody
Jazz records. W. Balliett. New Yorker 39:124-8 O 12 '63

HERMAN, Yvonne
Cretaceous, paleocene, and pleistocene sediments from the Indian Ocean. bibliog Science 140:1316-17 Je 21 '63

HERMANN, Helen
Recipe for raising a good cook. Parents Mag 39:55+ Ja '64

HERMANN, Robert
New boom in birth control. Sci Digest 54: 5-9 Jl '63

HERMAPHRODITE brig. See Sailing vessels

HERMAPHRODITISM
Hermaphroditism in Bahama groupers. C. L. Smith. il Natur Hist 73:42-7 Je '64

HERMENEUTICS, Biblical. See Bible—Hermeneutics

HERMITS
See also
Recluses

HERNÁNDEZ, Amalia
Because Amalia wanted to dance. A. Rankin. il por Theatre Arts 47:60-3 O '63; Same abr. with title Born to dance. Read Digest 83: 234-40 O '63
Doña Amalia's Ballet folklórico de Mexico. D. Duncan. il pors Dance Mag 37:38-42 N '63
Mother of them all. il por Newsweek 62:75 N 25 '63

HERNÁNDEZ, Francisco J.
Highway to progress. Américas 15:22-7 Ap '63

HERNÁNDEZ, Miguel
Elegy for Ramón Sijé; The unending lightning; poems, tr. by E. Honig. Poetry 101: 325-8 F '63

HERNÁNDEZ RUEDA, Lupo
Books. M. Valldeperes. il Américas 16:39-40 N '64

HERNDON, Booton
Mortimer Caplin: the man who takes your money. Sat Eve Post 236:70+ Ap 13 '63

HERNON, Joseph M. jr
Use of the American Civil war in the debate over Irish home rule. bibliog f Am Hist R 69:1022-6 Jl '64

HERO worship
Hero worship in science. Sci N L 84:134 Ag 31 '63
Making of a hero. M. W. Fishwick. il Sat R 47:12-15 Ag 1 '64
My children's heroes; celebrities childhood idols and their children's. G. Walker. il Good H 156:84-5+ Je '63
Why the girls scream, weep, flip. D. Dempsey. il N Y Times Mag p 15+ F 23 '64

HEROES
Making of a hero. M. W. Fishwick. il Sat R 47:12-15 Ag 1 '64
Man on horseback; war heroes as presidents, with reproductions of paintings. E. M. Halliday. Am Heritage 15:10-23 Ag '64
What is courage? P. Streit. il N Y Times Mag p30-1+ N 24 '63
Who are your child's heroes? with program for discussion group, by E. G. Neisser. D. B. Harris and M. R. Weisbord. il Parents Mag 38:35-6+, 50-2+ Je '63
See also
Great men
Hero worship

Anecdotes, facetiae, satire, etc.

What they might have said: gallery of heroes unfortunately omitted from leading histories. R. Rosenblum. il Am Heritage 14: 94-8 Ap '63

HEROES in literature. See Characters in literature

HEROES; story. See Graham, E.

HEROIN
Dope ring cracked. Sr Schol 84:18 Mr 20 '64

HEROINE; drama. See Tarloff, F.

HEROLD, Don
Come as you are? Read Digest 85:159-60 Ag '64
If I could go to school again. Read Digest 82:270-1 My '63

HEROLD, J. Christopher
Great confrontations: Napoleon and Alexander. Horizon 5:28-32 S '63
Our great favourite, Miss Austen. Horizon 6:41-8 Spr '64
Solitary wanderer. bibliog Horizon 6:94-103 Sum '64

HEROLD, Johann Gregor
J. G. Herold and the hidden pleasures of Meissen chinoiserie; excerpts. J. M. Dennis. il Antiques 85:558-64 My '64
HERON, W. and Anchel, H.
Synchronous sensory bombardment of young rats: effects on the electroencephalogram. Science 145:946-7 Ag 28 '64
HERON, William T.
AAAS affiliate. Science 140:321+ Ap 19 '63
HERONS
See also
Egrets
HERPES simplex virus
5-iodo-2'-deoxyuridine: relation of structure to its antiviral activity. N. Camerman and J. Trotter. bibliog il Science 144:1348-50 Je 12 '64
Found: drug that cures blinding virus. il Life 55:78+ S 6 '63
Therapeutic antiviral action of 5-tri-fluoromethyl-2'-deoxyuridine in herpes simplex keratitis. H. E. Kaufman and C. Heidelberger. bibliog il Science 145:585 Ag 7 '64
Vaccine for cold sores. Time 84:62 S 18 '64
Virus clue to cancer. Sci N L 86:163 S 12 '64
HERREID, C. F. 2d
Temperature regulation and metabolism in Mexican freetail bats. bibliog Science 142:1573-4 D 20 '63
HERRERA, Felipe
Inter-American economic relations; address, April 2, 1964. Vital Speeches 30:427-32 My 1 '64
Opportunities and obstacles in Latin America; address, December 5, 1962. Vital Speeches 29:242-5 F 1 '63
HERRERA, Gonzalo
Air will be ours; Cuban fighters tell why they expected air cover; with excerpts from radio messages. U S News 54:34-6 F 4 '63
Story of Americans at the Bay of Pigs. il U S News 54:33-4 Mr 11 '63
HERRERA, Philip
Philadelphia: how far can renewal go? Arch Forum 121:180-93 Ag '64
HERRETT, Richard A. and Kurtz, A. N.
cis-3-chloroacrylic acid: a new cotton defoliant and crop desiccant. bibliog Science 141: 1192-3 S 20 '63
HERRICK, Bill
Bill Herrick: showman with stills. M. Dembling. il pors Pop Phot 53:158-61+ D '63
HERRICK, John B.
Feed lot health mucosal complex. Suc Farm 61:108 O '63
Feed lot health: report on liver abscess. Suc Farm 61:84 N '63
Feed lot problem coccidiosis. Suc Farm 61: 86 S '63
Get a calf from every beef cow. Suc Farm 61:8 S '63
Virus diarrhea. Suc Farm 62:32 N '64
HERRICK, Virgil
Curriculum thinking and planning; excerpt from address, November 2, 1962. Sch & Soc 91:83 F 23 '63
HERRING, Hubert
Dictatorship in Haiti. Cur Hist 46:34-7+ Ja '64
Peru in serious trouble. Cur Hist 44:95-9+ F '63
HERRING gulls. See Sea gulls
HERRINGTON, R. M.
SPO officer voices confidence in future of Titan III program; remarks. Miss & Roc 12: 13 Mr 18 '63
HERRMAN, G. E.
Aluminum; light, white, versatile. Motor T 15:108-11 N '63
HERRNSTEIN, R. J. and Loveland, D. H.
Complex visual concept in the pigeon. Science 146:549-51 O 23 '64
HERRON, Jeannine
Justice in Mississippi; notes on the Beckwith trial. Nation 198:179-81 F 24 '64
Underground election. Nation 197:387-9 D 7 '63
HERRON, Michael M.
How to make jumbo contacts. U S Camera 26:44-5 Jl '63
Night exposures. U S Camera 26:60-1 S '63
HERSCHBERGER, Ruth
(tr) See Mayakovsky, V. Talk with a tax collector
HERSCHEL, William
Lunar eruption in 1783? B. M. Middlehurst. il por Sky & Tel 28:83-4 Ag '64
HERSEY, David F. See Freeman, M. E. jt. auth.
HERSEY, Jean
How to cultivate birds in your garden. House & Gard 124:250-1+ O '63
Suppose you want hundreds; excerpt from Woodland garden from scratch. Horticulture 41:410 Ag '63
Swiss chard. Flower Grower 50:33+ Mr '63
Terrariums. Flower Grower 50:24-5+ N '63
Woodland garden. Horticulture 41:510-11 O '63
HERSEY, John
Child buyer; dramatization. See Shyre, P.
Life for a vote. Sat Eve Post 237:34-8+ S 26 '64
Test of heart and mind. Life 57:62-4+ S 4 '64
HERSEY, M. Leonard
Aides to the aids to navigation. Motor B 114: 89+ Jl '64
Control points. See issues of Yachting
Cooperating on charts. Yachting 115:142 F '64
Predicted log navigation system. Yachting 114:50-2+ Ag '63
Social register for yachts. Motor B 114:54-6+ O '64
HERSH, Burton
Capsule history of the Olympic games. Holiday 36:68-75 N '64
Parachuting for pleasure. Holiday 34:115+ D '63
HERSHEY, Lenore
Echoes of heroes. McCalls 91:46+ Jl '64
Other Burton. McCalls 92:86+ Ja '65
HERSHEY, Pa.
Pool cover peels back. il Am City 79:28 D '64
HERSKOWITZ, Mickey
Baseball. Sports Illus 18:59-61 Mr 11 '63
College football. Sports Illus 21:48-9 N 9 '64
HERST, Herman, Jr
Stamps. See issues of Hobbies
HERTER, Christian Archibald
Atlantica. For Affairs 41:299-309 Ja '63
GATT asked for advisory opinion on U.S.-EEC poultry dispute; letter to Eric Wyndham White, October 16, 1963. Dept State Bul 49:751-2 N 11 '63
GATT ministers open Kennedy round of trade negotiations; remarks, May 4, 1964. Dept State Bul 50:878-9 Je 1 '64
GATT ministers reach agreement on tariff negotiating procedures; statements, May 16 and May 17, 1963. Dept State Bul 48: 990-5 Je 24 '63
Role of agriculture in trade expansion; address, March 30, 1964. bibliog f Dept State Bul 50:671-5 Ap 27 '64
Trade negotiations and the OECD statement, January 31, 1963. Dept State Bul 48:298-301 F 25 '63
United States and United Kingdom conclude grains agreement; statement, April 16, 1964. Dept State Bul 50:703-4 My 4 '64
U.S. and EEC hold talks on poultry import fees; statement, May 31, 1963. Dept State Bul 48:996-7 Je 24 '63
White House holds conference on export expansion; address, September 17, 1963. Dept State Bul 49:601-5 O 14 '63
about
Coming to terms with the Common market. P. Forbath. il Reporter 28:24+ Je 20 '63
Herter's uphill struggle. Atlan 211:10 Je '63
Setting stage for GATT. por Bsns W p27-8 My 25 '63
HERTLEIN, Carl
Biggest well pays off in tourist coin. Am City 79:28 Ag '64
HERTZ, David B.
Risk analysis in capital investment. bibliog f Harvard Bsns R 42:95-106 Ja '64
HERTZ, Richard C.
Rising tide of Negro-Jewish tensions. por Ebony 20:117-18+ D '64
HERTZ corporation
Hertz tries cut-rate field. Bsns W p 106 Mr 14 '64
It's Hertz itself in the driver's seat. S. Mahoney. il Fortune 68:118-23+ O '63
Still in the driver's seat. Time 83:91 Mr 13 '64
HERTZBERG, Arthur
Church, state, and the Jews. Commentary 35:277-88; 36:194-5 Ap, S '63
Modern Jewish dilemmas. Commentary 35: 172-4 F '63
Writing Jewish history. Commentary 36: 256-7 S '63
HERTZBERG, Hazel W.
Grasping the drama of a culture. NEA J 52: 44-6 F '63
HERTZBERG, Lee B.
Extra-feature two-way radio. Am City 78: 144+ O '63
HERTZSPRUNG-Russell diagram. See Astronomy—Charts, diagrams, etc.
HERZBERGER, Max Jacob
Techniques tomorrow. B. Sherman. Mod Phot 28:52+ N '64

HERZEN, Richard P. von
Geothermal heat flow in the Gulfs of California and Aden. bibliog Science 140:1207-8 Je 14 '63
HERZFELD, Norman Krause
What's wrong with Commonweal. Commonweal 80:293-6 My 29 '64
HERZOG, Arthur
Inquiry into the peace movement. N Y Times Mag p 17+ My 19 '63
Lowdown on the high hotel business. N Y Times Mag p 18+ Je 23 '63
Report on a think factory. N Y Times Mag p30+ N 10 '63
Specter haunts the American Communist party. N Y Times Mag p54+ O 25 '64
HERZOG visits Chicago; story. See Bellow, S.
HESBURGH, Theodore Martin
Science is amoral; need scientists be amoral, too? Sat R 46:55-6 Mr 2 '63
This New generation. America 109:383-4 O 5 '63
This side of the vision. por Time 81:88 My 3 '63
about
Notre Dame's Irish dander rises over a movie. il por Life 57:68+ D 18 '64
Vicious circles of Father Hesburgh. Christian Cent 80:1015 Ag 14 '63
HESCHEL, Abraham Joshua
Protestant renewal: a Jewish view. Christian Cent 80:1501-4 D 4 '63
HESELTINE, Philip
For Warlock, or Heseltine; letter. R. L. Beckhard. Sat R 47:55 D 26 '64
HESS, Dennis E. and others
Wildfires in Alaska. por Am For 24-7+ F '64
HESS, Eckhard H.
Imprinting in birds. bibliog Science 146:1128-39 N 27 '64
—and Polt, J. M.
Pupil size in relation to mental activity during simple problem-solving. bibliog Science 143:1190-2 Mr 13 '64
—See Klinghammer, E; Polt, J. M. jt. auths.
HESS, Eugene L. and others
Sonic energy effects in bovine serum albumin solutions. bibliog Science 143:1176-7 Mr 13 '64
HESS, H. H.
Manned lunar landing defended. Science 140:1173-4 Je 14 '63
HESS, Karl
Karl Hess; Goldwater finds his Sorenson. M. Kempton. New Repub 151:10-14 Ag 8 '64
HESS, Lilo
Assassins in your garden. il Sci Digest 54:11-13 Jl '63
HESS, M. Whitcomb
Angelus in April; poem. Cath World 197:35 Ap '63
Browning and Kierkegaard as heirs of Luther. Christian Cent 80:799-801 Je 19 '63
Depicter of American democracy. Christian Cent 81:1457-8 N 25 '64
Fénelon: Christian educator. Christian Cent 82:16-17 Ja 6 '65
Holy Spirit at the 19th quadrennial. Christian Cent 81:370-2 Mr 18 '64
Key to William Blake. Christian Cent 80:1027-8 Ag 21 '63
Out yonder: poem. Cath World 197:245 Jl '63
Toynbee dilemma. Christian Cent 81:8-9 Ja 1 '64
What Luther meant by faith alone. Cath World 199:96-101 My '64
HESS, Thomas B.
Disrespectful hand-maiden. Art N 63:38-9+ Ja '65
Phony crisis in American art. Art N 62:24-8+ Sum '63
Pollock: the art of a myth. Art N 62:39-41+ Ja '64
Steel mistletoe. Art N 61:46-7+ F '63
HESS, Walter N.
Long journey of the dogfish. Natur Hist 73:32-5 N '64
HESSIANS in the American revolution. See United States—History—Revolution—German mercenaries
HESSLER, William H.
Pearson's progress. Reporter 30:24-9 Mr 12 '64
Washington gives Canada an election and an issue. Reporter 28:20-31 F 28 '63
What killed Forrestal? Reporter 30:52+ F 27 '64
HESTER, James M.
Human challenge; address, September 2, 1964. Vital Speeches 30:746-9 O 1 '64
HETERODYNE frequency meters. See Radio instruments
HETEROGRAFTS. See Transplantation of organs, tissues, etc.
HETEROTRANSPLANTATION. See Transplantation of organs, tissues, etc.
HETLAND, Norm
Foot-loose mongoose; excerpt. Sr Schol 82:13 My 15 '63
HETZEL, Fred
Fred sails in the sunset. H. L. Masin. por Sr Schol 85:22 D 9 '64
HEUBLEIN, incorporated
Bottled bartender. il Time 85:64 Ja 1 '65
Heublein bottles a new blockbuster; vodka martini. Bsns W p76 My 9 '64
HEUCHERA sanguinea. See Coral bells
HEUSINGER, Adolf Ernst
Heusinger of the Fourth Reich, by C. R. Allen, jr. Review
Nation 198:124-6 F 3 '64. H. Pol
HEUSKEN, Henry C. J.
Yankee Barbarian at the Shogun's court. E. Hahn. il Am Heritage 15:90-7 Je '64
HEUTTE, Frederic
Norfolk botanical garden. Horticulture 42:26-7 S '64
HEUVEL, William Vanden
Prince Edward County situation. por NEA J 53:12+ Mr '64
HEVI, Emmanuel John
African student in red China; excerpts. Harper 228:63-6+ Ja '64; Same abr. Read Digest 84:139-40+ Mr '64
HEWES, Gordon W.
Hominid bipedalism: independent evidence for the food-carrying theory. bibliog Science 146:416-18 O 16 '64
HEWES, Henry
American theatre '64: its problems and promise. Sat R 47:27-9+ F 22 '64
Broadway postscript. See issues of Saturday review
Scene designers: their art and their impact. Sat R 47:26-31 D 12 '64
Visions out of orbit. Sat R 46:39 O 26 '63
HEWINS, Ralph
Kuwait; Wall Street of the Middle East. Nation 198:234-6 Mr 9 '64
HEWITT, Catherine Mary
General Reynolds and Dear Kate; reprint. M. R. Maloney. il por Am Heritage 15:62-5 D '63
HEWITT, Elizabeth
Reader's choice. Travel 121:26 F '64
HEWITT, Jean
Food (cont) N Y Times Mag p47 Je 23 '63; 49 Ja 5; 77 Ja 12; 75 My 24; 45 My 31; 100 Je 7; 41 Jl 26; 112+ S 13; 147 N 15; 92+ D 6 '64
HEWITT, William, A.
Moline's biggest bash; Saarinen-designed headquarters. il Bsns W p62-4 Je 20 '64
HEWLETT, Horace W.
Folger Shakespeare library; reprint. Wilson Lib Bul 38:630-5 Ap '64
HEWLETT, Roger S. See Anderson, D. jt. auth.
HEXAMETHYLENE propionamide
Hydrogen atom thermal parameters; for N,N'-hexamethylenebispropionamide. L. H. Jensen and M. Sundaralingam. bibliog il Science 145:1185-7 S 11 '64
HEXAMETHYLENEBISPROPIONAMIDE. See Hexamethylene propionamide
HEXTER, J. H.
Loom of language and the fabric of imperatives: the case of Il principe and Utopia. bibliog f Am Hist R 69:945-68 Jl '64
HEY, Nigel S.
Professor in ballet slippers. Dance Mag 37:48-52 My '63
HEY you, light man! drama. See Halley, O.
HEYDE, Werner
Cheating justice; suicide of Heyde. Time 83:37 F 21 '64
Fifth man. por Newsweek 64:44 F 24 '64
HEYDEN, Doris
(tr) See Bernal, I. Treasure of Teotihuacán
HEYDENRYK, Henry
Profiles. J. Brooks. por New Yorker 39:49-50+ Ap 27 '63
HEYDRICH, Reinhard
Reporter at large; Eichmann trial. H. Arendt. New Yorker 39:40-2+ F 23 '63
HEYE, Hellmuth Guido Alexander
What kind of host? Newsweek 63:30 Je 29 '64
HEYES, Frank C.
Blitzen wins race from Chicago. Yachting 114:54+ S '63
Lake Michigan's Boat of the year. por Yachting 114:35-7+ D '63
Mackinac race. Motor B 111:26-7+ Je '63
HEYMAN, Ken
Lion learns to roar. il N Y Times Mag p 132 O 6 '63

HEYMEN, Ken—*Continued*
Mind and eye at work. il Pop Phot 55:34-9+ Ag '64
Russian 500-mm mirror reflex lens. por Pop Phot 54:104-5+ Ja '64
about
Ken Heyman. il U S Camera 26:60-5 F '63
HEYMANN, Hans G.
Lessons of history; address, October 1, 1964. Vital Speeches 31:82-5 N 15 '64
HEYWOOD, J. David, and others
Amino acids: incorporation into α- and β-chains of hemoglobin by normal and thalassemic reticulocytes. bibliog Science 146:530-1 O 23 '64
HEYWOOD, Stanley J.
Still stand the embattled farmers; address, February 22, 1963. Vital Speeches 29:408-12 Ap 15 '63
HEYWORTH, Peter
Listening to Schoenberg. Hi Fi 13:51-4+ Ag '63
Shostakovich without ideology. Hi Fi 14:96-100+ O '64
HI-FI systems. See High fidelity sound systems
HIBBARD, Emerson. See Behrman, R. E. jt. auth.
HIBBEN, Frank C.
Elusive Mrs Gray. por Field & S 67:66-7+ Ap '63
So you don't like venison. Field & S 68:38-40+ O '63
Two rams for the money. Field & S 68:56-7+ Je '63
HIBBEN, Sheila
Obituary
New Yorker 40:183-4 Mr 7 '64
HIBBING, Minn.
Virtually every snowflake... J. H. Rough. il Am City 78:71-3 Ag '63
HIBBS, Albert
Can a chipmunk teach the new math on TV? R. Atcheson. il pors Sat Eve Post 238:26-7 Ja 16 '65
HIBBS, Ben
Bill Scranton: champion of states' rights and states' responsibilities. Read Digest 84:103-8 Ap '64
Boyhood on the prairie; adaptation of address. Read Digest 85:111-13 N '64
California builds big for education. Read Digest 83:164-6+ Jl '63
Lord helps Charly, and vice versa. Read Digest 85:140-4 Ag '64
Mr Ford's busy billions. Sat Eve Post 236:68-72 Mr 16 '63
Progress goes marching through Georgia. Sat Eve Post 236:69-73 F 16 '63
Where the boys are at home on the range. Read Digest 82:112-17 Ap '63
Writing lawyer of Rancho del Paisano. Read Digest 83:160-2+ Ag '63
(ed) See Romney, G. How businessmen can serve their country
HIBERNATION
Brown fat: thermogenic effect during arousal from hibernation in the bat. R. L. Smalley and R. L. Dryer. bibliog il Science 140:1333-4 Je 21 '63
Brown fat; thermogenic effector of arousal in hibernators. R. E. Smith and R. J. Hock. bibliog il Science 140:199-200 Ap 12 '63
Hibernating animals: how they survived winter. il Sci Digest 53:52 My '63
Potassium and sodium content of tissues of hamsters and ground squirrels during hibernation. J. S. Willis. bibliog il Science 146:546-7 O 23 '64
Secret of hibernation. B. Tufty. il Sci N L 84:262+ O 26 '63
Thermoregulatory and adaptive behavior of brown adipose tissue. R. E. Smith. bibliog il Science 146:1686-9 D 25 '64
HICCUP
What ails that, hic, phrenic nerve? O. A. Battista. il Sci Digest 55:27-9 Ja '64
HICKENLOOPER, Bourke B.
Case against a crash program; excerpts from report. por U S News 54:90 Je 10 '63
about
Hickenlooper's revolt. K. Crawford. Newsweek 63:27 Je 1 '64
HICKERSON, Mary G.
Senior citizens in suburbia. Recreation 56:220 My '63
HICKEY, James T.
New Lincoln financial note. Hobbies 68:110-11+ F '64
HICKLER, David H.
Pilots of Japan. Flying 75:80 Ag '64
HICKLER, Holly White
Fire or ice; story. Good H 157:56-7 Jl '63
Since last time; story. Redbook 120:60-1 Ap '63
HICKLING, Charles F.
Cultivation of tilapia. Sci Am 208:143-8+ My '63
HICKMAN, Bert G.
Long cycle: hidden force in the economy. Duns R 82:48-9+ D '63
about
Is the long cycle why we don't grow? creeping pace of industrial growth. por Bsns W p78+ F 16 '63
HICKOK, Ross
How to cut street-cleaning costs. Am City 79:90-1 Jl '64
We corral our street vehicles. Am City 78:112-13 Je '63
HICKORY house. See New York (city)—Hotels, restaurants, etc.
HICKS, Betty
PIREPS wanted. Flying 74:44-5+ My '64
HICKS, Clifford B.
And was it a silent spring? Pop Mech 119:85-8+ Je '63
Anyone for skittles? Pop Mech 121:156-7 Mr '64
Growing corn to music. Pop Mech 119:118-21+ My '63
Incredible Gateway arch. il Pop Mech 120:86-90+ D '63; Same abr. Read Digest 84:169-70+ Mr '64
Why are twins so special? Todays Health 41:18-21+ D '63
HICKS, Edward
America's greatest primitive painter. M. Vaughan. il por Read Digest 84:126-31 Mr '64
HICKS, Elija M. jr, and others
Spandex elastic fibers. bibliog Science 147:373-9 Ja 22 '65
HICKS, Granville
Authors and academicians. Sat R 45:18 D 15 '62; 46:19 F 9 '63
Literary horizons. See issues of Saturday review
Requiem for the famous son. Sat R 46:31-2 S 21 '63
Signatures to the significance of the self. Sat R 47:67-70+ Ag 29 '64
HICKS, Jim
Don't let my children know, she said, I'll tell them tonight at bedtime. Life 57:42-42A D 4 '64
His dying words: don't blame the snake; it's not its fault. Life 56:38 F 7 '64
Many a slip 'twixt earth and moon, and measles too. Life 57:36A Ag 14 '64
Mystery of the ship of fear. Life 56:47-9 Je 5 '64
Spry old team does it again. Life 55:89+ O 18 '63
HICKS, John V.
Silver rose; poem. Mlle 58:42 Ja '64
Where you begin like rivers; poem. Mlle 56:44 F '63
HICKS, Peggy Glanville-. See Glanville-Hicks, P.
HICKS, Samuel P. and D'Amato, C. J.
Low dose radiation of the developing brain. bibliog Science 141:903-5 S 6 '63
HICKS, Steacy D.
Tides, the scientific view. Motor B 112:23+ Jl '63
HICKS family
Hicks coat-of-arms. H. K. Eilers. il Hobbies 68:126-7 Ag '63
HIDALGO lyceum. See Mexico—Intellectual life
HIDDEN signs; story. See Melo, J. V.
HIDDEN stranger; drama. See Maltz, M.
HIDDEN treasure. See Treasure trove
HIDES and skins
See also
Leather
HIDUMIUM RR 58. See Aluminum alloys
HIEBER, Caroline E.
Paperbacks for college-bound students. bibliog por Library J 89:185-90 Ja 15 '64
HIEROGLYPHICS
Cleopatra & Ptolemy gave Champollion his missing clue. il UNESCO Courier 17:10-11 Mr '64
Toward a universal non-language. D. Shea. il N Y Times Mag p62+ N 22 '64
Walking Rosetta stone. Sci Digest 54:63 D '63
HIERONYMUS, T. A.
Should pay to store corn and soybeans. Suc Farm 61:33 S '63
HIGAN cherry tree. See Oriental flowering cherry

HIGASHIMURA, Takenobu, and others
Dosimetry of atomic bomb radiation in Hiroshima by thermoluminescence of roof tiles. bibliog Science 139:1284-5 Mr 29 '63
HIGBEE, Edward
Farewell to the small farm: excerpt from Farms and farming in an urban age. Read Digest 84:176-80 Mr '64
French paysan is angry. N Y Times Mag p20+ O 27 '63
Now the non-farmer asks for parity. N Y Times Mag p 15+ Je 2 '63
HIGBEE company. See Cleveland, Ohio—Stores
HIGDON, Hal
Boy wonder of Illinois politics. Reporter 30:29-31 My 7 '64
How to make yourself fall-safe. Todays Health 42:72-6 Ap '64
Olympic games. Sports Illus 19:47-9 N 4 '63
On the run from dogs and people. Sports Illus 18:76-80+ Ap 15 '63
Stars, but no bench warmers. Reporter 31:58 O 22 '64
Ten mountains almost anyone can climb. Todays Health 42:38-41+ O '64
What about insurance for dental care? Todays Health 42:52-3+ S '64
HIGGINBOTHAM, Don
American historians and the military history of the American revolution. bibliog f Am Hist R 70:18-34 O '64
HIGGINS, Alice
Horse shows (cont) Sports Illus 18:55 Mr 11; 58-9 Je 17; 19:58 N 4; 92+ N 25 '63; 20:69-70+ Je 15 '64
Not so gently down the stream. Sports Illus 18:34+ Ap 29 '63
HIGGINS, Beth
Library plant and seed sources. Horticulture 41:586 N '63
HIGGINS, Marguerite
Saigon summary. America 110:18-21 Ja 4 '64
Ugly Americans of Vietnam. America 111:376-82 O 3 '64
—See Lisagor, P. jt. auth.
HIGGINS, Michael
Happy life and dutiful death of the Midwest designer-craftsmen. Craft Horiz 23:52-3 Mr '63
HIGGINSON, Thomas Wentworth
Dear preceptor, by A. M. Wells. Review
Nation 197:95-6 Ag 24 '63. A. Laing
Sat R por 46:44 O 5 '63. E. P. Stamm
Rebel with many causes. J. Stanley. New Repub 149:22-4 Jl 13 '63
HIGGS, Robert
Robert Higgs: an Ozark watercolorist; with biographical sketch. il por Am Artist 28:40-1+ Je '64
HIGGS, William L.
Lawyer leaves Mississippi. B. Carter. il Reporter 28:33-5 My 9 '63; Discussion. 28:6 Je 6 '63
HIGH, Robert King
Florida red-head. Nation 198:520 My 25 '64
HIGH altitude, influence of. See Altitude, Influence of
HIGH-altitude sickness. See Altitude, Influence of
HIGH ASWAN DAM. See Aswan High Dam
HIGH blood pressure. See Hypertension
HIGH commissioner for refugees. See United Nations—High commissioner for refugees
HIGH cost of living. See Cost of living
HIGH energy particles. See Particles (nuclear physics)
HIGH explosives. See Explosives
HIGH fidelity (periodical)
Reissues: introducing a new department. Hi Fi 14:39 Ja '64
HIGH fidelity amplifiers. See Amplifiers
HIGH fidelity cabinets. See Cabinets (furniture)
HIGH fidelity shows. See Audio fairs
HIGH fidelity sound systems
Audio: the all-out system. H. Fantel. Opera N 29:34 D 26 '64
Basic guide to high-fidelity sound. il Good H 158:162 Mr '64
Build a hi-fi volume compressor expander. R. H. Russell. il Pop Electr 21:41-5+ O '64
EIA defines high fidelity. W. A. Stocklin. Electr World 69:6 Mr '63
Heath Hi-fi TV kit. H. Luckett. il Pop Sci 182:96-8 My '63
Hi-fi house is wired for sound top to bottom: Westport, Conn. home of L. Godowsky. J. Peter. il Look 28:M12 F 25 '64
Hi-fi loudspeaker cones. C. L. McShane. il Electr World 69:38-40+ F '63
Hi-fi showcase. See issues of Popular electronics to April 1963
Hi-fi, stereo buying guide for families with children. C. Sinclair and D. Lachenbruch. il Parents Mag 38:75+My '63
Hi-fi system to fit your budget. il House & Gard 124:165-7 S '63
Hi fi that doubles as furniture. C. Calkins. il House B 105:232-4 N '63
High fidelity (title varies) (cont) C. L. Osborne. Opera N 27:34 F 2; 35 F 16 '63
High fidelity equipment reports. See issues of High fidelity
High fidelity ill defined. Hi Fi 13:45 F '63
High fidelity newsfronts. See issues of High fidelity
High fidelity reaches its majority. I. Berger. il Sat R 48:55 Ja 30 '65
High fidelity stereo sound, with separate components. il Consumer Bul 46:21-6 N '63
How to assemble hi-fi parts for better performance and trouble-free life. R. Freas. il Am Home 66:6+ Je '63
How to get started building hi-fi kits. J. R. Thomson. il Pop Sci 183:138-40 N '63
It's easy to extend your hi fi to the garden. House B 105:44 Je '63
Kits for home assembly. L. Marcus. il Hi Fi 13:44-7+ Je '63
Listen here. R. Freas. il Am Home 67:38 Mr '64
Listen here; hi-fi in parts. R. Freas. il Am Home 66:4+ Ap '63
Low-down on hi-fi stereo. C. P. Gilmore and H. Luckett. il Pop Sci 183:82-9+ S '63
Low-down on hi-fi stereo tuners. C. P. Gilmore and H. Luckett. il Pop Sci 185:102-5+ S '64
Make your hi-fi system work harder: add a tape recorder. R. Freas. il Am Home 66:12+ O '63
Multiplex muse; a critical listing of new hardware for listening. J. M. Conly. Reporter 31:42+ D 17 '64; Reply with rejoinder. W. H. Thomas. 32:8 Ja 14 '65
New products:1964. N. Eisenberg. il Hi Fi 14:101-5 O '64
Portfolio of stereo décor; with editorial comment. J. Anderson. il Hi Fi 14:37, 38-45 F '64
Putting hi-fi in its place. G. O'Brien. il N Y Times Mag p 106-7 S 8 '63
Self-protecting transistor hi-fi amplifier. N. Kramer and R. Japenga. il Electr World 71:32-3+ Je '64
Soldering-iron saga: building hi-fi from kits mingles triumph and tedium. R. Freas. il Am Home 66:6+ S '63
Still wanted: a definition of high fidelity. Consumer Rep 28:121 Mr '63
Summertime: and the listenin' is easier through high fidelity equipment. R. Freas. il Am Home 66:6+ Jl '63
This is hi-fi? C. P. Gilmore. il Pop Sci 182:72-5+ Mr '63
Trim a hi-fi man's tree with accessories and add-ons. Am Home 66:22+ D '63
Two music systems any man would envy. il House & Gard 124:86-91 Jl '63
See also
Phonograph—High fidelity sound systems

Anecdotes, facetiae, satire, etc.

Component id and the package ego. D. Lachenbruch. il Hi Fi 13:64-5+ S '63

Bibliography

Audio bookshelf. I. Berger. Sat R 47:60 Ja 25 '64
Stereo reference shelf. R. D. Darrell. il Hi Fi 14:53-5+ D '64

Control

Audio: the tone controls. H. Fantel. Opera N 29:34 Ja 9 '65
Build hi-fi interlock. C. J. Ulrick. il Pop Electr 21:49-51 Ag '64

Repairing

On call with an audio doctor. L. Marcus. il Hi Fi 13:61-4 N '63

Terminology

High fidelity; a glossary for baffled buffs. House & Gard 125:18+ F '64

Testing

Fallaciousness of formulas. Hi Fi 13:53 N '63
Hi-fi lab check. See issues of Popular electronics to September 1964
High fidelity measurements, science or chaos? E. Villchur. il Electr World 72:33-5+ Ag '64
HIGH frequency sound waves. See Ultrasonic waves
HIGH-intensity lamps. See Electric lamps
HIGH jumping. See Jumping

HIGH-oven ranges. See Electric stoves

HIGH PLAINS, Tex, water district. See Water districts

HIGH POINT college, High Point, N.C.
On the road; course on Civil war and the reconstruction. il Newsweek 62:52 Jl 22 '63

HIGH pressure. See Pressure

HIGH-pressure oxygenation
High pressure chamber to save blue babies. Sci Digest 53:31 My '63
High-pressure treatment. il Life 56:98+ Ap 10 '64
Infant's cause of death: hyaline membrane disease; case of Patrick Bouvier Kennedy. il Time 82:33 Ag 16 '63
Lifesaving wonders of high-pressure oxygen. J. D. Ratcliff. Read Digest 85:77-81 Jl '64
Medicine's miracle chamber; high-pressure oxygen chamber. S. M. Spencer. il Sat Eve Post 237:70-2 S 19 '64
New way to give a patient the air; hyperbaric oxygen chambers. il Bsns W p64+ F 29 '64
Oil stops static sparks. Sci N L 86:243 O 17 '64
Operating under pressure. il Time 81:44+ F 15 '63
Pressure chamber used for tetanus patients. Sci N L 86:120 Ag 22 '64
Rocket case for surgery; pressure chamber. F. Marley. il Sci N L 84:195 S 28 '63
Under pressure; Boston's Children's hospital medical center. il Newsweek 61:58-9 F 18 '63
Under pressure; surgical operations in hyperbaric chambers. il Time 84:72 O 16 '64

HIGH school athletics. See School athletics

HIGH school buildings. See School buildings

HIGH school dropouts. See Student withdrawals

HIGH school education, Value of. See Education, Value of

HIGH school football players. See Football players

HIGH school graduates
College records of mediocre high school graduates. Sch & Soc 92:350+ N 28 '64
Employment of high school graduates and dropouts in 1963. V. C. Perrella. il Mo Labor R 87:522-9 My '64
Employment of high school graduates and dropouts in 1962. J. Schiffman. il Mo Labor R 86:772-9 Jl '63
Fifty hints for 1963 grads. H. Miller. Ladies Home J 80:24 Je '63
Jobs after high school. il Changing T 18: 20-3 Mr '64; Same with title Good jobs for high-school graduates. Read Digest 85: 130-3 Jl '64
Pittsburgh polls its graduates. S. R. March. NEA J 53:27 Mr '64
Statistic of the month. W. V. Grant. il Sch Life 46:7 Ag '64

HIGH school libraries
Booklists: bugaboo or boon? Shoreline high school, Seattle. P. V. Coffey. il Wilson Lib Bul 37:855-6 Je '63
Case of the missing bishop: Kensington high school library, Buffalo, N.Y. D. Pierman. il Wilson Lib Bul 37:580 Mr '63
Catcher in the library. S. L. Kennerly. il Library J 89:1822-4 Ap 15 '64
Closed-circuit TV in the school library. A. Apfel. ALA Bul 57:259-60 Mr '63
Libraries for technical education programs. W. J. Brooking and M. H. Mahar. bibliog il Sch Life 47:9-13 O '64
Pre-college library; high school library, Bellflower, Calif. S. Ziskind. il Wilson Lib Bul 37:856-8 Je '63; Reply. M. Lewis. 38:35 S '63
Resource centers: educator's new focal point; interview. N. L. Engelhardt, jr. il Arch Rec 134:210-11 O '63
School library reaches out to classroom and curriculum; Bridgeton high school, N.J. H. M. Wilcox. il Library J 88:1104-5 Mr 15 '63
Widening a world; program providing cultural opportunities in Hebbronville, Tex. P. B. Sexton. Wilson Lib Bul 38:852-4 Je '64

Paperback books

See School libraries—Paperback books

HIGH school orchestras. See School orchestras

HIGH school scholarships. See Scholarships and fellowships

HIGH school students
Boy dates girl. G. Head. See issues of Senior scholastic
Classroom incident; excerpts from Critical incidents in teaching, ed. by R. J. Corsini and D. D. Howard. NEA J 53:33-4 S '64
Do cars and school studies mix? il Good H 157:150-1 S '63
Freshness of the headlong years; with photographs by Farrell Grehan. Life 55:66-79 S 27 '63
Modern high school; a profile. E. Z. Friedenberg. Commentary 36:373-80 N '63; Reply. S. Israel. 37:19 Ap '64
On the fringe of a golden era: the U.S. student. il Time 85:56-57A+ Ja 29 '65
Profile of the twelfth-grader. Library J 89: 4138 O 15 '64
Queen Bee of the school; with report of sociologists, ed. by B. Villet. il Life 55:68-80+ O 11 '63
Talking it over with Gay Head; questions and answers (cont of) Boy dates girl. Gay Head. See issues of Senior scholastic
What students think of teachers; with study-discussion program, by E. M. Duvall. W. W. Wattenberg. bibliog il PTA Mag 58: 4-6, 36-7 Ja '64
See also
Institute of student opinion
Scholastic research center
Student activities

Adjustment

Nice to be with at school; excerpt from Seventeen book of etiquette and entertaining. E. A. Haupt. Seventeen 23:42 Ag '64

Caricatures and cartoons

Jonathan and Milly. D. Kvietys. See issues of Seventeen to August 1964

Clothing

See Clothing and dress

Dating

See Dating

Employment

See Student employment

Rating

Too many tests for high-school students? il Good H 156:154-5 Je '63

Smoking

See Smoking

HIGH school students, Interchange of. See Students, Interchange of

HIGH school students, Married
Heading off those risky teen marriages. S. Welton. il Parents Mag 39:47+ Mr '64
High school marriages. Sch & Soc 92:259 O 3 '64
If your teen wants to marry. . ; ed. by M. Longwell. J. A. Nimrod. il Farm J 88:54-5 Je '64
Teen-age marriage craze. J. Anderson. il Ladies Home J 80:66-7+ Mr '63; Discussion. 80:28 Je '63

HIGH school students, Mentally superior
Academically talented. E. S. Greer. il Sch Life 45:9-12 Mr '63
Advanced placement: completion of some college work while still in high school. E. M. Gerritz; C. R. Haywood. il NEA J 54:22-4 Ja '65
Brilliant student can be popular, if. . . A. J. Tannenbaum. il PTA Mag 57:4-6 Je '63
Identification, motivation, and training of talented students; report. A. W. Astin. Sch & Soc 92:186-9 Ap 18 '64
Nourishing of excellence; Presidential scholars. il Time 83:59 Je 12 '64
Secondary education for the academically untalented. Sch & Soc 92:259+ O 3 '64
Teen-agers distrust brilliant students. Sci Digest 53:25 F '63
Television and the superior student. R. J. Nelson and J. W. M. Rothney. il Sch & Soc 92:385-7 D 12 '64
They challenge our top students: Mark Twain summer institute, Clayton, Mo. P. Friggens. il PTA Mag 57:4-7 My '63; Same abr. with title Here's a new kind of summer school. Read Digest 82:157-8+ Je '63
Toughest high school in the United States; Bronx high school of science. G. White. il Ladies Home J 80:69+ Ap '63
We're not doing right by the gifted. C. W. Woolcock. il NEA J 52:31-2 N '63

HIGH school students, Negro. See Negro students

HIGH school students as automobile drivers. See Automobile drivers

HIGH school teachers. See Teachers

HIGH school textbooks. See Textbooks

HIGH schools
Big, comprehensive high school at low cost. il Arch Rec 135:156-7 F '64

HIGH schools—*Continued*
Compact school uses courts for circulation. il Arch Rec 135:160-1 F '64
Controlled environment for team teaching. il Arch Rec 135:162-4 F '64
Flexible environment for learning; Andrews, Tex. senior high school. il Arch Rec 133: 168-73 My '63
High school of the future; excerpt from The changing curriculum of the American high school. K. Wiles. Sch & Soc 91:32-6 Ja 26 '63
How alive is your high school? M. Mayer. il Seventeen 22:120-3+ F '63
Impact of World war I on the American high school; excerpt from Shaping of the American high school. E. A. Krug. bibliog f Sch & Soc 92:161-71 Ap 4 '64
Modern high school; a profile. E. Z. Friedenberg. Commentary 36:373-80 N '63; Reply. S. Israel. 37:19 Ap '64
Our best high schools. Atlan 214:74-8 O; 86-90 N; 90-4 D '64; 215:83-6 Ja '65
Quality secondary schools of the future. O. F. Parody. Sch Life 47:23-7 N '64 (to be cont)
School-within-a-school concept for Roanoke. il Arch Rec 135:158-9 F '64
Twenty-five outstanding high schools. Ladies Home J 80:128 Ap '63
What should high schools accomplish? with study-discussion program, by C. Smallenburg and H. Smallenburg. R. W. Tyler. bibliog il PTA Mag 59:22-4, 36-7 N '64
What's going on in schools & colleges. See issues of Changing times
See also
Education, Secondary
Junior high schools

Curriculum

Answer to dropouts; the nongraded high school; Melbourne high school, Cape Kennedy. B. F. Brown. Atlan 214:86-90 N '64
Changing curriculum of America's schools. J. I. Goodlad. il Sat R 46:65-7+ N 16 '63
Crackling excitement in school corridors; team teaching at Wayland, Mass. with report by E. J. Anderson. il Life 54:78-84+ Mr 22 '63
Good-by to homework; new plan to finish out-of-class work during school day at Marshall high school, Portland, Ore. il Newsweek 65:39 Ja 4 '65
High school of the future; excerpt from The changing curriculum of the American high school. K. Wiles. Sch & Soc 91:32-6 Ja 26 '63
Recent developments affecting the secondary school curriculum; excerpt from the American secondary school curriculum. L. H. Clark and others. bibliog f Sch & Soc 92:402-13 D 26 '64
Vocational education: in the high school? P. Woodring. Sat R 47:47-8 Ag 15 '64; Discussion. 47:52-3 S 19 '64
See also
Colleges and universities—Entrance requirements

Summer sessions

See Summer schools

HIGH schools, Private. See Private schools
HIGH SIERRAS. See Sierra Nevada, Calif.
HIGH society. See Upper classes
HIGH speed photography. See Photography, High speed
HIGH spirits; musical comedy. See Musical comedies, revues, etc.—Criticisms, plots, etc.
HIGH-steel workers. See Building workers
HIGH-temperature alloys. See Heat resistant alloys
HIGH temperatures
Beta-carotene: thermal degradation. I. Mader. bibliog il Science 144:533-4 My 1 '64
Calcite-dolomite-magnesite stability relations in solutions at elevated temperatures. P. E. Rosenberg and H. D. Holland. bibliog il Science 145:700-1 Ag 14 '64
Chemical kinetics in shock tubes. S. H. Bauer. bibliog il Science 141:867-79 S 6 '63
Dynamic reflectance spectroscopy; a new thermal technique. W. W. Wendlandt. bibliog il Science 140:1085-7 Je 7 '63
Heat adaptation and ion exchange in bacillus megaterium spores. G. Alderton and others. il Science 143:141-3 Ja 10 '64
High-temperature research. A. V. Grosse. bibliog il Science 140:781-9 My 17 '63
Shock waves and high temperatures. M. McChesney. il Sci Am 208:109-19 bibliog (p 185) F '63
Stishovite: thermal dependence of the crystal habit. C. B. Sclar and others. bibliog il Science 144:833-5 My 15 '64
Upper temperature limit of life. E. S. Kempner. bibliog il Science 142:1318-19 D 6 '63
X-ray diffraction studies on tin at high pressure and high temperature. J. D. Barnett and others. bibliog il Science 141:1041-2 S 13 '63
Xenon tetrafluoride; heat of formation. S. R. Gunn and S. M. Williamson. bibliog Science 140:177-8 Ap 12 '63
HIGH vacuum. See Vacuum
HIGH voltage power lines. See Electric lines
HIGH voltages
Con Ed switches plan; hydro power from Labrador. Bsns W p43 Ja 11 '64
Vogue for ever higher voltage; extra-high voltage. il Bsns W p47-8+ Ap 13 '63
HIGHBUSH cranberries. See Cranberry bush
HIGHER education. See College education; Colleges and universities; Junior colleges
HIGHER education facilities act, 1963. See School laws and legislation—United States
HIGHER horizons program. See New York (city)—Education
HIGHET, Gilbert
Books. See issues of Horizon
Can we save cohort? Horizon 6:119 Wint '64
Dynasty. Vogue 143:95+ F 15 '64
Great confrontations: Diogenes and Alexander. Horizon 5:10-13 Mr '63
Lucretius. Horizon 6:28-32 Spr '64
Red dawn. Vogue 141:131+ Ap 1 '63
HIGHLANDS, SOUTHERN. See Appalachian Region
HIGHLIGHTS for children (periodical)
Child's-eye view. il Newsweek 61:106 Mr 25 '63
HIGHSMITH, Patricia
Suspense: rules and non-rules. Writer 77:9-12 N '64
HIGHWAY, Pan American. See Pan-American highway
HIGHWAY access. See Roads—Intersections
HIGHWAY accidents. See Traffic accidents
HIGHWAY beautification. See Roadside improvement
HIGHWAY contracts. See Roads—Contracts
HIGHWAY engineering
Are you a sap for the ribbon cutters? destruction of fishing streams through highway building. A. Grahame. il Outdoor Life 131:10-12+ Je '63; Reply with rejoinder. R. M. Whitton. 132:4+ S '63
Highway robbery. J. Wright. il Sat Eve Post 236:19-23 N 30 '63
Labor and material requirements: highway construction, 1958 and 1961. J. C. Wakefield. il Mo Labor R 86:394-8 Ap '63
Let's clean up this highway mess. K. O. Gilmore. Read Digest 85:86-92 N '64
Street construction and maintenance. See issues of American city
Uncorking a bottleneck; modernizing Pennsylvania turnpike. il Bsns W p 106 S 21 '63
HIGHWAY finance. See Roads—Finance
HIGHWAY law
Ancient right of cows. il Time 83:68+ Je 12 '64
HIGHWAY lighting. See Roads—Lighting
HIGHWAY maintenance equipment. See Municipal equipment
HIGHWAY models. See Roads—Models
HIGHWAY signs. See Road signs
HIGHWAYS. See Roads; Streets
HIGINBOTHAM, N. and others
Electrical resistance of cell membranes of avena coleoptiles. bibliog Science 143:1448-9 Mr 27 '64
HIKING. See Walking
HILBURN, Earl D.
Ranger design and management criticized. Aviation W 80:63-4 My 11 '64
HILDEBRAND, Keith F.
Low cost auxiliary fuel tank for your outboard. Pop Mech 119:140-1 Mr '63
HILDEBRANDT, Dieter
Wedding guest crosses the wall. N Y Times Mag p36-7+ N 22 '64
HILDEGARDIS, Sister. See Hewitt, C. M.
HILDEMANN, W. H. See Vredevoe, D. L. jt. auth.
HILDERBRAND, E. Boyd
Cougar nightmare; ed. by K. Crandall. pors Outdoor Life 132:20-3+ Jl '63
HILDRETH, Barbara Parsons
Thought for Thanksgiving; poem. McCalls 91:162 N '63
HILGARD, Ernest R.
Creativity: the juxtaposition and integration of disparate categories. Science 147:37-8 Ja 1 '65

HILL, Dave
If you really want to sell. Writer 76:23-4 Je '63
HILL, Dick
Hidden lakes. Flying 75:47+ Jl '64
HILL, Evan
American doctor: death of a legend in an era of miracles. Sat Eve Post 236:30+ Je 15 '63
Doctor, what's wrong with me? Sat Eve Post 237:64-6 My 2 '64
How successful are college marriages? Redbook 123:58-9+ My '64
Look out, America, here comes Granby. Sat Eve Post 237:64-5 Ap 4 '64
We can't afford bashful trustees. por Library J 88:731-2 F 15 '63
We can't afford it. Read Digest 86:123-5 Ja '65
HILL, George W.
Don Eugenio shows the way. Read Digest 82:245-6+ Je '63
Latin America's most explosive problem. Read Digest 85:169-70+ S '64
HILL, Graham
Cool win in a crowded Glen. B. Ottum. il por Sports Illus 21:28-9 O 12 '64
Hill country. Newsweek 64:68 O 19 '64
This car's dying on us. F. Graham, jr. il pors Sat Eve Post 236:22-4 Je 1 '63
HILL, Henry Berry-. See Berry-Hill, H.
HILL, Herbert
Excerpt from testimony, May 7, 1963. Cong Digest 43:86+ Mr '64
HILL, Hyacinthe
In memoriam: William Stanley Braithwaite; poem. Negro Hist Bul 26:218 Ap '63; Same abr. 27:23 O '63
HILL, Janet
Libraries in London and New York. Sr Schol 85:25T O 7 '64
HILL, Lister
Excerpt from address, January 15, 1964. Cong Digest 43:77+ Mr '64
about
Political good fortune of medical research. M. Viorst. por Science 144:267-70 Ap 17 '64
HILL, Lucienne
(tr) See Anouilh, J. Traveller without luggage
HILL, Morton
Booksellers warned on smut following priest's fast. Pub W 184:28-9 N 4 '63
HILL, Nola MacElmon
McGinney's tavern in Nova Scotia. Antiques 84:179-81 Ag '63
HILL, Pat
Peruvian tapestry warp. Craft Horiz 23:22-6+ Jl '63
HILL, Ricardo
To rehabilitate or to punish? Américas 15: 12-16 My '63
HILL, Richard M. and Fatt, Irving
Oxygen uptake from a reservoir of limited volume by the human cornea in vivo. bibliog Science 142:1295-7 D 6 '63
—See Barlow, H. B. jt. auth.
HILL, Sidney Berry-. See Berry-Hill, S.
HILL, Victor
Case of the smoked mink. New Repub 150: 8 Ap 11 '64
TV addenda. Atlan 213:126-7 Ap '64
HILL, W. I. Scott-. See Scott-Hill, W. I.
HILL, Wilhelmina
Social studies. Sch Life 45:19-20 Jl '63
HILL, William
Betting with Bill; world's biggest bookie. por Time 82:109-10 N 15 '63
HILL, William B.
Books to be noted; fiction. America 108:678-80; 109:682-3+; 110:635+; 111:717-19+ My 11, N 23 '63, My 9, N 28 '64
HILL of the comadres; story. See Rulfo, J.
HILLARY, Sir Edmund
Highest school in the world. R. J. Spector. il UNESCO Courier 17:12-17 O '64
HILLARY, Louise
How we discovered America. il por Redbook 121:60-1+ Je '63
HILLARY, Phil
Detroit's smog-shrouded mystery. Motor T 17:62-5 Ja '65
HILLBILLIES. See Mountaineers (southern states)
HILLEN, K. H. Schulte-. See Schulte-Hillen, K. H.
HILLER, Carl E.
Main St. Sch Arts 64:25-8 S '64
HILLER, David W.
Go! said the navy; crunch! case of cutter 322. P. Mandel and R. Kennedy. il Life 55:17+ O 4 '63
HILLIARD, Raymond M.
Massive attack on illiteracy; excerpts from address, July 13, 1963. por ALA Bul 57:1034-8 D '63
about
Illiteracy; the key to poverty! B. Asbell. McCalls 91:96-7+ F '64
HILLIER, Richard L.
Bard in paper. por Library J 89:193-8 Ja 15 '64
HILLIG, William E.
Winter flying weather in Florida. por Flying 74:52+ F '64
HILLIS, Burton
Man next door. See issues of Better homes and gardens
HILLMAN, Donald
New look at urea for dairy cows. Suc Farm 62:48-9 S '64
HILLMAN, Eugene
Prior mission of the church. por Cath World 198:238-44 Ja '64
HILLMAN, Rosemary
In defense of the five-year-old. Sat R 46: 76+ N 16 '63
HILLMAN, William S.
Photoperiodism: an effect of darkness during the light period on critical night length. bibliog Science 140:1397-8 Je 28 '63
HILLS, Alicia
Animals can tell time, but how? Life 54:41-2+ My 31 '63
How to milk a seal. Life 56:39-40+ Mr 27 '64
—and Rosenfeld, Albert
Fabulous prizes for learning how to spell. Life 55:77-8+ O 4 '63
HILLS, L. Rust
How to rent a yacht on the Riviera. Esquire 59:95-6+ Ap '63
Structure of the American literary establishment. il Esquire 60:41-3 Jl '63
HILLSIDE architecture
Atrium adds an indoor garden to a northern house. il Arch Rec 133:118-21 mid-My '63
Better approach, and this house looks forty years younger. il House B 105:178-9 S '63
Bring it down to a useful level. il House B 105:180-1+ S '63
Builder's house solves a site problem. A. C. Borg. il Am Home 66:36-7 Ap '63
California house is a real cliff-hanger. il Pop Sci 185:50-1 Jl '64
Casual simplicity for a small country house. il Arch Rec 133:175-8 Mr '63
City house with a limitless view. il House & Gard 125:178-81 My '64
Cliff-climbing house. il House & Gard 127: 102-9 Ja '65
Compact saddle-roofed house that exploits a difficult site. il Arch Rec 135:157-60 My '64
Cross-shaped hilltop house provides wide variety of outlook. il Arch Rec 135:179-82 Ap '64
Formal house that exploits a sloping site. il Arch Rec 134:169-72 S '63
Good life in the tree tops. il Sunset 130: 234+ Mr '63
Hillside house for an artist. il Arch Rec 134:195-8 O '63
Hobby gardener enjoys himself in Topanga Canyon. il Sunset 130:278-9 Ap '63
Home that combines a fresh approach to tradition and contemporary design. il Arch Rec 133:66-9 mid-My '63
House a wife built to please her husband. il House & Gard 124:80-3 Jl '63
How to have your own space platform. C. Besinger. il House B 105:128-31+ Je '63
How to rescue land lost on a slope. C. Calkins. il House B 105:174-7+ Ap '63
How to step up the loveliness of an already lovely spot. C. Besinger. il House B 106: 78-81+ Jl '64
Hug the street, face the other way; Sherman Oaks, Calif. il Sunset 132:118 Mr '64
Ideas for space in a budget house. il Arch Rec 133:171-4 Mr '63
Lakeside house combines traditional atmosphere with contemporary design. il Arch Rec 135:120-3 mid-My '64
Like a camera it focuses on the view. A. C. Borg. il Am Home 66:24-7 Je '63
Like the prow of a ship. il House & Gard 123:122-9+ Mr '63
Lot of living space on a precipitous site. il Arch Rec 133:177-80 Ap '63
Many-winged house on a big wooded lot has excellent zoning and quiet privacy. il Arch Rec 133:86-9 mid-My '63
On a wooded California slope with a view. il Arch Rec 135:150-3 Ja '64
Problem: extra-narrow, sloping site. il Am Home 66:36-7 My '63

HILLSIDE architecture—*Continued*
Problem: steep hillside, one lonely tree. A. C. Borg. il Am Home 66:28-31 My '63
Slope-holding fact sheet. il Am Home 66:101-2 My '63
Small wonder on a mountain. il House & Gard 125:118-21 Ap '64
Stilted living: Los Angeles stilt-houses. il Newsweek 65:36 Ja 4 '65
This house holds up the hill; home in Los Angeles. il Sunset 132:106-7 Mr '64
Tree-top retreat for two. il House & Gard 125:116-17 Ap '64
When floor level isn't ground level, the cure is a deck. D. X. Manners. il House B 105:176-7+ S '63
Zoned, flexible house for a gently sloping site. il Arch Rec 133:159-62 My '63

HILLSON, Henry T.
Manhattan principal at work. L. W. Gillenson. il pors Sat R 47:77-9+ My 16 '64; Discussion. 47:47 Je 20 '64

HILLSTROM, Judith
I find enchantment in my water-lily pool. Flower Grower 51:24-6 Mr '64

HILO, Hawaii
Forests, a natural defense against seismic waves. C. D. Whitesell and R. E. Daehler. il Am For 70:38-9 N '64

HILSMAN, Roger, 1919-
Australia's strategic position; address, January 25, 1964. Dept State Bul 50:243-50 F 17 '64
Challenge to freedom in Asia; address, June 14, 1963. Dept State Bul 49:43-50 Jl 8 '63
Cuban crisis: how close we were to war; excerpts from Politics of policy-making: the Kennedy years. U S News 57:59-60 Ag 17 '64; Excerpts. Look 28:17-21 Ag 25 '64
Do we have a chance to win? interview, ed. by R. Carroll. por Newsweek 64:45 S 21 '64
New Chinese adventuring threatens Asia. por Nations Bsns 51:66-8 D '63
Philippines, a new era; address, May 23, 1963. Dept State Bul 48:897-900 Je 10 '63
Plea for realism in southeast Asia. N Y Times Mag p26+ Ag 23 '64
Statement on U.S. Asian policy; excerpts from address, August 20, 1963. Cur Hist 46:112+ F '64
Trade in the Pacific area; address, February 3, 1964. Dept State Bul 50:293-8 F 24 '64
United States policy in the Pacific; address, August 20, 1963. Dept State Bul 49:386-93 S 9 '63
United States policy toward Communist China; address, December 13, 1963. Dept State Bul 50:11-17 Ja 6 '64; Same. Vital Speeches 30:203-7 Ja 15 '64
Yung Lo encyclopedia presented to Library of Congress. Dept State Bul 49:740 N 11 '63
about
Secret mission of Lieutenant Hilsman. J. G. Hubbell. il pors Read Digest 84:137-8+ F '64
Washington's war. por Time 82:32-3 O 4 '63

HILTON, Conrad Nicholson
By golly! il pors Time 82:66-8+ Jl 19 '63
In nineteen lands instant America. D. J. Hamblin. il pors Life 55:67-8+ Ag 30 '63
Mr Hilton opens a hotel. R. Steinberg. il por Sat Eve Post 236:68-9 N 2 '63
Omnipresent one. Christian Cent 80:1483 N 27 '63

HILTON hotels corporation
In nineteen lands instant America. D. J. Hamblin. il Life 55:67-8+ Ag 30 '63
Mr Hilton opens a hotel. R. Steinberg. il Sat Eve Post 236:68-9 N 2 '63

HILYARD, Stevens W. See Harwell, R. jt. auth.

HIMALAYAS
Mountaintop war in remote Ladakh. W. E. Garrett. il Nat Geog Mag 123:664-87 My '63
See also
Badrinath
Everest, Mount

HIMMELFARB, Milton
In the community (cont) Commentary 35:66-70, 424-8; 36:249-51 Ja, My, S '63; 37:64-7 Ja; 72-4 My; 38:69-73 S '64; 39:69-74 Ja '65
Jewish sentiment. Commonweal 79:524-7 Ja 31 '64

HIMMLER, Heinrich
Reporter at large: Eichmann trial. H. Arendt. New Yorker 39:40-2+ Mr 2; 48-50+ Mr 9 '63

HIMSWORTH, E. W.
Advanced techniques of losing races. Yachting 115:52-3+ My '64
Sailsmanship. Yachting 113:46-7+ My '63

HINCHLIFF, William Emerson
Ask the young man who owns one. . .hundred. Sr Schol 85:26T D 2 '64
Challenge to leadership; summary of address, March 1962. por Library J 88:728-31 F 15 '63
Paperbacks in public libraries. Sr Schol 82: 12T Mr 13 '63
about
California librarians protest Santa Barbara library situation. Library J 88:4597-8 D 1 '63
Library board issues statement on Santa Barbara situation. Library J 88:3813-14 O 15 '63
Santa Barbara librarian resigns after clash with deputy. Library J 88:3182-4 S 15 '63; Reply. 88:4104 N 1 '63

HINDAWI, I. J. and Altshuller, A. P.
Plant damage caused by irradiation of aldehydes. bibliog Science 146:540-2 O 23 '64

HINDEMITH, Paul
News of the day; interview, tr. by A. M. Lingg. pors Opera N 28:8-11 F 1 '64
about
As a tree bears fruit. por Time 83:55 Ja 10 '64
First recordings of Debussy and Hindemith works for narrator and ensemble. R. Sabin. il Am Rec G 30:926-7 Je '64
Furtwängler radio performances on DGG. Am Rec G 30:570-1+ Mr '64
Hindemith at the Philharmonic: new Organ concerto. M. Bernheimer. Sat R 46:78 My 11 '63
Hindemith early and late. R. Evett. New Repub 148:26-8 Ap 6 '63
Hindemith, 1895-1963. O. Daniel. il por Mus Am 84:58-9 Ja '64
Inspired Hindemith; Oistrakh at his greatest. H. Glass. Am Rec G 29:874 Jl '63
Long Christmas dinner. Criticism
Opera N 27:33 Ap 13 '63
Sat R 46:53 Mr 30 '63
Malipiero and Hindemith by the Stuyvesants: magnificent. J. Lyons. Am Rec G 30:1041 Jl '64
Music. B. Boretz. Nation 198:104-6 Ja 27 '64
Musical events; concert performed by Philharmonic at Lincoln Center. W. Sargeant. New Yorker 39:95 Ap 27 '63
News of the day (Neues vom Tage) Criticism
Opera N il 28:8-11 F 1 '64
Obituary
Newsweek 63:72 Ja 13 '64
On records; Mathis der Maler. C. J. Luten. Opera N 27:35 F 16 '63
Requiem by, and for, Paul Hindemith. R. Sabin. por Am Rec G 30:756-8 My '64
Universal musician. E. Helm. il pors Hi Fi 14:36-8+ My '64

HINDI language
Bureaucracy by doublespeak; Hindi becomes India's official language. il Time 85:25A+ Ja 29 '65
English and Hindi official. V. Koilpillai. Christian Cent 80:867 Jl 3 '63

HINDS, Alfred George
Reward from a robbery rap. il por Time 84: 51 Ag 14 '64

HINDS, Hal
Fiddlehead fern cookery. Horticulture 41:328 Je '63
Know the toadstools. Horticulture 41:460-2 S '63

HINDS, T. E. and others
Seed discharge in arceuthobium: a photographic study. bibliog Science 140:1236-8 Je 14 '63

HINDU dancing. See Dancing, Indian (East Indian)

HINDU KUSH
Fight for the land of Hindu Kush; with report by J. Burke. il Life 55:18-27 Ag 9 '63

HINDU sculpture. See Sculpture, Indian (East India)

HINDUS
See also
India—Hindu-Moslem relations

HINE, Al
Under cover. Ladies Home J 81:20+ O '64

HINE, Daryl
Wasp; poem. New Yorker 39:48 S 14 '63

HINEGARDNER, Ralph T. and Engelberg, Joseph
Rationale for a universal genetic code. Science 142:1083-5; 144:1031 N 22 '63, My 22 '64

HINES, C. O.
Magnetopause: a new frontier in space. bibliog Science 141:130-6 Jl 12 '63

HINES, Cal
WLB biography. Wilson Lib Bul 38:297 N '63

HINES, Earl
Jazz concerts; third of Jazz on Broadway series at Little theatre. W. Balliett. New Yorker 40:159-62 Mr 14 '64
Profiles. W. Balliett. por New Yorker 40:39-42+ Ja 2 '65

HINES, Hugh
Good recreation management; address. Recreation 56:88-90+ F '63
HINES, Jerome
Boris boom. il por Time 81:46 Ap 5 '63
Three American tsars. A. M. Lingg. por Opera N 27:25-7 Ap 6 '63
HINES, John Elbridge, bp
Talk with 'PB'; interview, ed. by K. Woodward. por Newsweek 65:70 F 1 '65
about
Ecclesiastical lightning rod. il por Time 84: 87-8 O 23 '64
HINES, Ted
WLB biography. Wilson Lib Bul 37:713, 882 Ap, Je '63
HINES, Theodore C.
Fifty-fifth time. Library J 89:2954-6 Ag '64
Mile-high conference. Library J 88:2842-4 Ag '63
Programmed learning and in-service training in libraries. bibliog ALA Bul 58:719-24 S '64
Programed materials. Library J 88:2055-8+ My 15 '63
Science citation index. por Library J 89:2735-7 Jl '64
HINES, William
Snafu among the stars? Sat R 47:31+ My 9 '64
HINGLEY, Ronald
(tr) See Solzhenitsyn, A. One day in the life of Ivan Denisovich
HINGTGEN, J. N. and Aprison, M. H.
Behavioral response rates in pigeons: effect of α-methyl-m-tyrosine. bibliog Science 141: 169-71 Jl 12 '63
HINKS, Roger
Man through his art: music; excerpts. UNESCO Courier 17:23-4 Je '64
HINKSON, Charles E.
Last gun of the confederacy. Read Digest 82: 256-8+ Ap '63
HINSON, Glenn
Ecumenism: threat or hope? Christian Cent 81:1592-5 D 23 '64
HINTON, Harold C.
China: a dragon rampant. Commonweal 77: 531-4 F 15 '63
Peculiar partnership. Commonweal 79:91-4 O 18 '63
HINTZE, Naomi A.
Four is a lovely number; story. Redbook 123:56-7 My '64
Not because you are good; story. Redbook 122:153 Ap '64
HIPP, D. B. See Krausz, N. G. P. jt. auth.
HIPP, Frederick L.
Advancing the welfare of members. NEA J 53:19-20 Ja '64
HIPPOCAMPUS. See Cerebral cortex
HIPPOCRATIC oath. See Oaths
HIPPOPOTAMUS
Eureka! its twins; baby hippos at St Louis zoo. il Life 54:84+ My 10 '63
HIRABAYASHI, Kazuko
Oshra and Kazuko and companies at 92nd street Y. J. Maskey. Dance Mag 38:62 Mr '64
HIRAI, Atsushi. See Hirai, T. jt. auth.
HIRAI, Tokuzo, and Hirai, Atsushi
Tobacco mosaic virus: cytological evidence of the synthesis in the nucleus. bibliog Science 145:589-91 Ag 7 '64
HIRAKI, Shinji
Sewing up the game. il Time 83:90 My 8 '64
HIRED help. See Household employees
HIRED men. See Farm labor
HIRING. See Employment systems
HIROHITO, emperor of Japan
As Japan changes, so does the emperor. A. M. Rosenthal. il pors N Y Times Mag p 13+ My 19 '63
Emperor. il pors Life 57:45-8 S 11 '64
HIROSHIMA
Candle of understanding; Hiroshima-Honolulu sister city week. M. Gray. il Wilson Lib Bul 37:575-6 Mr '63
Children of the A-bomb. comp. by A. Osada: tr. by J. Dan and R. Sieben-Morgen. Review
Christian Cent 80:1108-9 S 11 '63. S. Klein
Dangerous intersection; value of experiences of Hiroshima and Nagasaki. W. T. Ellis. Sat R 46:31 Ag 24 '63
Hiroshima 1964. N. Cousins. il Sat R 47:24-7 Ap 18 '64
Hiroshima revisited. Christian Cent 80:971 Ag 7 '63
HIROSHIMA maidens
Orphans and the maidens; report from Hiroshima. N. Cousins. il Sat R 47:20-2 Ap 25 '64
HIRSCH, Donald Earl
Who owns what's in your head? W. Bowen. il Fortune 70:175-8+ Jl '64
HIRSCH, Felix E.
How free is the German press? Cur Hist 44: 226-30+ Ap '63
HIRSCH, Henry R. See Plutchik, R. jt. auth.
HIRSCH, Jerry
Behavior genetics and individuality understood. bibliog Science 142:1436-42 D 13 '63
HIRSCH, Katrina de. See De Hirsch, K.
HIRSCH, Phil
How the Swedes do it. New Repub 149:9 Jl 20 '63
If your town smells, stop breathing. New Repub 150:7-8 Mr 14 '64
Oyster stew. New Repub 150:7-8 Ja 4 '64
Retraining the jobless. New Repub 148:8-9 Je 22 '63
Those pesticides. New Repub 149:6 Ag 17 '63
HIRSCH, Philip R. and others
Thyrocalcitonin: hypocalcemic hypophosphatemic principle of the thyroid gland. bibliog Science 146:412-13 O 16 '64
HIRSCH, Tibor
How a rave-notice travelog was made. il Pop Phot 52:94-5+ F '63
HIRSCH, Werner Z.
Administrative and fiscal considerations in urban development. bibliog f Ann Am Acad 352:48-61 Mr '64
HIRSCHBERG, Erich, and others
Thalidomide: effects on enzymes of gluatmic acid metabolism in mice. bibliog Science 143:1343-4 Mr 20 '64
HIRSCHFELD, Charles
Brooks Adams and American nationalism. bibliog f Am Hist R 69:371-92 Ja '64
HIRSCHFIELD, Robert S.
After the Vice President? Nation 198:25-8 Ja 6 '64
Unprecedented succession. Nation 197:414-15 D 14 '63
Warren court. Nation 198:527-9 My 25 '64
HIRSCHHORN, Kurt, and others
Immune response and mitosis of human peripheral blood lymphocytes in vitro. bibliog Science 142:1185-7 N 29 '63
HIRSCHHORN, Kurt. See Bach, F; Fudenberg, H. H. jt. auths.
HIRSCHHORN, Rochelle, and others
Acid phosphatase-rich granules in human lymphocytes induced by phytohemagglutinin. bibliog Science 147:55-7 Ja 1 '65
HIRSCHMAN, Albert O.
How policy is made. Américas 15:39-41 Ag '63
HIRSCHMAN, Jack
Note on Malka Tussman. Poetry 102:406 S '63
One finger from the seasons; poem. Poetry 102:97-9 My '63
(tr) See Tussman, M. H. Spoil; Play without words; By an abandoned house
HIRSCHMANN, Winfred B.
Profit from the learning curve. bibliog f Harvard Bsns R 42:125-39 Ja '64
HIRSH, Selma
Negro: why whites fear him. Sci Digest 54:12-15 O '63
HIRSHBERG, Al
Hard sell in boom land. Life 57:67-8+ N 13 '64
Long search of Laurie Van Buren. Good H 157:64-5+ Jl '63
Sacrifice of Jill Rosean. Good H 158:52+ Je '64
Wonderful legacy of Dr Bob McCarthy. Good H 156:68-9+ Mr '63
HIRSHHORN collection. See Art—Private collections
HIRSON, Roger O.
Journey to the day. Criticism
Sat R 46:35 D 7 '63
HIRUMI, Hiroyuki, and Maramorosch, Karl
Insect tissue culture: use of blastokinetic stage of leafhopper embryo. bibliog Science 144:1465-7 Je 19 '64
HIRZEL, Austin Courtenay
Ballet boy at the Met. Dance Mag 37:36-7+ S '63
HIS excellency; story. See O'Hara, J.
HIS friend Vanka; story. See Karmel-Wolfe, H.
HISATSUNE, I. C. and Hartman, K. O.
Thermal reduction of bicarbonate to formate. bibliog Science 145:1455-6 S 25 '64
HISCOCK, Eric
Long voyage ends. il por Yachting 113:48-50+ Mr '63
HISPANIOLA
Dominican Republic; Haiti. Américas 16:43 O '64
In Haiti, terrible tyranny; interview, ed. by C. Migdail. J. Bosch. U S News 54:40 My 20 '63
Troubled Caribbean waters. Sr Schol 82:19 My 15 '63
HISPANO-AMERICAN fiction. See Latin American fiction

HISS, Alger
Assault on Whittaker Chambers. W. F. Buckley, jr il Nat R 16:1098-100 D 15 '64

HISTADRUT. See Trade unions—Israel

HISTAMINE
Histamine: differences in amount available for release in lungs of guinea pigs susceptible and resistant to acute anaphylaxis. S. H. Stone and others. bibliog il Science 146:1061-2 N 20 '64

HISTIDINE
Gene-enzyme relations in histidine biosynthesis in yeast. G. R. Fink. bibliog il Science 146:525-7 O 23 '64
Phosphohistidine. P. D. Boyer. bibliog il Science 141:1147-53 S 20 '63

HISTONES
Histone and DNA in isolated nuclei from chicken brain, liver, and erythrocytes. M. B. Sporn and C. W. Dingman. bibliog il Science 140:316-18 Ap 19 '63
Histone biology and chemistry; report on first World conference on histone biology and chemistry. J. Bonner and P. O. P. Tso. Science 141:651+ Ag 16 '63
Histone staining with ammoniacal silver. M. M. Black and H. R. Ansley. bibliog il Science 143:693-5 F 14 '64
Histones from developing tissues of the chicken: heterogeneity. D. T. Lindsay. bibliog il Science 144:420-2 Ap 24 '64
Histones: species and tissue specificity. A. Neidle and H. Waelsch. bibliog il Science 145:1059-61 S 4 '64
Intranuclear site of histone synthesis. M. L. Birnstiel and W. G. Flamm. bibliog il Science 145:1435-7 S 25 '64

HISTORIANS
Great mutation; address. C. Bridenbaugh. Am Hist R 68:315-31 Ja '63
Historian and history. A. Schlesinger, jr. For Affairs 41:491-7 Ap '63
Historian of power and elevation can serve a nation in troubled days. A. Nevins. Horizon 5:101 S '63
Modest proposal to meet an urgent need: proposals for a national center for historical scholarship; address. J. P. Boyd. bibliog f Am Hist R 70:329-49 Ja '65

HISTORIANS, American
Education of historians in the United States. W. S. Holt. Am Hist R 68:402-6 Ja '63

HISTORIANS, German
Germany's new historians. G. Mann. il Nation 198:572-6 Je 8 '64

HISTORIANS, Russian
Soviet second thoughts on tsarist colonialism. L. R. Tillett. bibliog f For Affairs 42:309-19 Ja '64

HISTORIC house museums
Louisiana; rewarding addendum to a trip through Scandinavia. H. Lundbergh. il House & Gard 125:210-13 My '64
Saluting the Hillforest historical foundation at Aurora, Ind. il Hobbies 69:52 Mr '64
Voices from the past; old Edison phonographs at the Thomas A. Edison home in Fort Myers, Fla. il Hobbies 68:50 Ap '63
See also
Henry Francis du Pont Winterthur museum

HISTORIC houses, etc.
Antiques' travel guide. See issues of Antiques
Historic houses, landmarks, and museums. See issues of Antiques
See also
Literary landmarks
also subhead Historic houses, etc. under names of countries, states, cities, etc. e.g. Quincy, Mass.—Historic houses, etc.

Conservation and restoration

See Architecture—Conservation and restoration

HISTORIC trails. See Trails

HISTORIC trees. See Trees, Historic

HISTORICAL change. See Change

HISTORICAL chronology. See Chronology, Historical

HISTORICAL drama
Dark brilliance; Spanish canvas of Don Carlo. K. McDonald. il Opera N 28:24-5 Mr 7 '64
Other Elizabeth; her strategy with Philip II. E. Jenkins. il Opera N 28:8-13 Mr 7 '64
See also
Television broadcasting—Drama

HISTORICAL fiction
I would not coddle the child. J. Beatty and P. Beatty. il Horn Bk 40:149-52 Ap '64

HISTORICAL literature
Past recaptured; address, November 10, 1962. E. G. Vining. Library J 88:826-7+ F 15 '63
Special heritage; place of the Negro in young people's books. A. Dalgliesh. Sat R 47:44 Ag 15 '64

HISTORICAL museums
See also
Henry Ford museum and Greenfield Village, Dearborn, Mich.
Milan, Ohio, historical museum

HISTORICAL research
Past recaptured; address, November 10, 1962. E. G. Vining. Library J 88:826-7+ F 15 '63

HISTORICAL societies
History like cheese improves with age; Marathon County historical society and its museum. J. L. Stoutenburgh, jr. il Hobbies 69:52-3 Ap '64
See also
Long Island historical society

HISTORIOGRAPHY. See History—Historiography

HISTORY
History lesson. M. E. Jenkins. PTA Mag 58:2-3 Ja '64
Johan Huizinga and the task of cultural history. R. L. Colie. bibliog f Am Hist R 69:607-30 Ap '64
Sorry state of history. J. H. Plumb. il Horizon 5:97-100 S '63
World: a sense of history. L. J. Halle. il New Repub 151:92-5+ N 7 '64
See also
Current events
Fourteen hundred and ninety-two
Historians

Bibliography

Blueprints for Leviathan: American style, by R. F. Nichols. Review
Am Heritage il 14:98-101 Ag '63. B. Catton
History (cont) J. J. O'Connor. America 108: 686-7; 109:670+ My 11, N 23 '63
N 23 '63, My 9, N 28 '64
Reading, writing, and history. B. Catton. See issues of American heritage

Historiography

Historian as artist. A. M. Schlesinger, jr. Atlan 212:35-41 Jl '63
Many mansions; address, December 29, 1963. C. Brinton. Am Hist R 69:309-26 Ja '64
Trevelyan: the muse or the museum? J. Clive. Nation 196:143-5 F 16 '63

Philosophy

Theology of history, by H. U. von Balthasar. Review
Commonweal 79:82-3 O 11 '63. J. Ratté
Tides of history and the age of anxiety. B. De Balla. Cath World 197:36-43 Ap '63

Psychological aspects

Baggage of the past. J. LaFarge. Sat R 46: 23-5 Mr 16 '63

Sources

Sounds of history; recorded voices of 8,000 celebrities in National voice library. W. B. Furlong. il N Y Times Mag p72+ Mr 22 '64

Study and teaching

Bridge to the past; visits to historic places. E. F. Hunter. il Parents Mag 38:64-6+ Mr '63
Essay exam: probing the iceberg; excerpts from address. R. W. Winks. il Sr Schol 85:12T-13T O 21 '64
New Ph.D. plan to train scholar-teachers in history; Harvard university. Sch & Soc 92: 222 Sum '64
See also
United States—History—Study and teaching

Textbooks

See also
World history—Textbooks

HISTORY, Ancient
See also
Civilization, Ancient
Hittites
Sumerians

Bibliography

Articles and other books received; comp. by T. R. S. Broughton. See issues of American historical review

HISTORY, Military. See Military history

HISTORY, Modern
Reflections on modern history, by H. Kohn. Review
Commentary 37:92-4 My '64. W. J. Dannhauser
See also
Nineteen hundred and five
Twentieth century

HISTORY, Universal. See World history
HISTORY and science. See Science and civilization
HIT-and-run drivers. See Automobile drivers
HITACHI limited. See Japan—Industries
HITCH, Charles J.
Programming's role in defense; excerpts from address. Aviation W 81:17 O 12 '64
about
Hitch's office has new significance. por Miss & Roc 12:77-8 Mr 25 '63
Planners for the Pentagon; with editorial comment. il por Bsns W p75-6+. 144 Jl 13 '63
HITCH hiking. See Hitchhiking
HITCHCOCK, Alfred
Redbook dialogue: Alfred Hitchcock and Dr Fredric Wertham. pors Redbook 120:70-1+ Ap '63
about
Alfred Hitchcock dinner hour; with recipes. M. Kaytor. il pors Look 27:42-4 Ag 27 '63
In charge. New Yorker 39:36-7 Mr 30 '63
Man behind the body. J. D. Weaver. Holiday 36:85-6+ S '64
Screens and screams. R. L. Shayon. Sat R 46:44 Ap 20 '63
Truffaut: author of book about Hitchcock. New Yorker 40:45-6 O 31 '64
HITCHENS, Gordon
Chicago's midwest film festival grows up. Pop Phot 53:97+ O '63
Sunday on the river. Pop Phot 54:134-5+ My '64
HITCHENS, Ivon
Modest master of Sussex. il Time 82:53 Ag 9 '63
HITCHES. See Knots and splices
HITCHHIKING
Diary of a hitchhike across the Sahara; Peace corps girls; with report by B. Kral. il Life 56:92-4+ Ap 17 '64
Le stop. il Time 83:61-2 My 15 '64
HITLER, Adolf
Appeasers, by M. Gilbert and R. Gott. Review
Nat R 15:403-4 N 5 '63. A. Lejeune
Brutal friendship, by F. W. Deakin. Review
Reporter 28:50+ My 23 '63. M. Salvadori
Time il por 81:118+ Ap 19 '63
Forty years ago. S. D. Smith. il pors N Y Times Mag p46+ N 3 '63
Hitler and the Deutsche arbeiterpartei. R. H. Phelps. bibliog f Am Hist R 68:974-86 Jl '63
Hitler reviewed. pors Newsweek 63:43 Mr 16 '64
Hitler: the legend that failed. H. Trevor-Roper. Holiday 36:35+ O '64
Hitler's image of the United States. G. L. Weinberg. bibliog f Am Hist R 69:1006-21 Jl '64
In defense of Hitler. Newsweek 63:82-3 My 18 '64
Men who tried to kill Hitler; excerpts, ed. by J. Naar. R. Manvell and H. Fraenkel. il Look 28:50-2 D 15 '64
Plot that almost changed history. il por U S News 57:52-3 Jl 27 '64
Survivors; widows and children of the chief plotters. J. Naar and R. Palm. il Look 28:54+ D 15 '64
Twenty-five years ago: Hitler strikes. H. W. Baldwin. il N Y Times Mag p 11-13+ Ag 30 '64
What the Germans are reading about Hitler. G. A. Craig. Reporter 31:36-8 Jl 16 '64
When the big one (Hitler) got away. S. D. Smith. il pors N Y Times Mag p86-8+ My 24 '64
HITLERISM. See Fascism—Germany
HITREC, Joseph
Tea with Ivo Andric. Reporter 28:47-9 My 23 '63
Touch of iconomania. Harper 229:20+ Jl '64
HITTITES
Lost civilization emerges from the past. E. Laroche. il UNESCO Courier 16:14-20 F '63
HJELMQVIST, Bengt
Levels of organization: public librarianship in Sweden. por Library J 88:4306-11 N 15 '63
HO-chi-Minh
And meanwhile what's happening up north? il por Time 83:31-2 My 8 '64
Behind the shooting war: a shift in policy for Ho chi Minh? por U S News 57:12 Ag 17 '64
Face of the enemy: Ho and his followers. il por Newsweek 63:28-9 Je 8 '64
Reunifying Vietnam. New Repub 149:3-5 S 14 '63
Who killed Diem and why? V. L. Borin. il Nat R 16:441-6 Je 2 '64
HO, Monto
Interferon-like viral inhibitor in rabbits after intravenous administration of endotoxin. bibliog Science 146:1472-4 D 11 '64
HO-thong-Minh
Negotiating with the North. New Repub 149: 18-19 O 12 '63
HOA, Augustin Nguyen Loc
Fighting priest of South Vietnam. D. Chapelle. il por Read Digest 83:194-200 Jl '63
HOADLEY, Thomas
Hoadley's test case in Indiana. J. Neugeboren. New Repub 149:14 S 21 '63
Hoosier witch hunt. N. R. Hanson. il Nation 196:443-4 My 25 '63
HOAG, Alden B.
Dissent from despair. N Y Times Mag p21+ Ap 5 '64
HOAG, Arthur A.
Experiences with cooled color emulsions. Sky & Tel 28:332-4 D '64
HOAG, Malcolm W.
Nuclear policy and French intransigence. For Affairs 41:286-98 Ja '63
HOAG, Paul F.
Lure of soldiers' letters. Hobbies 68:110-12 My '63
HOAG, Ralph L.
Training for teachers of the deaf. por Sch Life 45:18-20 Ja '63
HOAGLAND, Hudson
Cybernetics of population control. Bul Atomic Sci 20:2-6 F '64
Science and the new humanism; excerpts from address. bibliog Science 143:111-14 Ja 10 '64
HOAIMY, Viet Nam
Miracle at Hoaimy. il Time 83:26 My 1 '64
HOARDING
My life as a squirrel. C. Ford. il Read Digest 84:227-8+ Je '64
HOAXES
Hiroshima pilot, by W. B. Huie. Review
Time il 83:99 My 1 '64
How to get into Princeton; Oznot is not. Time 83:88 Ap 24 '64
Lying stones of Dr Johann Bartholomew Adam Beringer, by M. E. Jahn and D. J. Woolfe. Review
Sci Digest il 54:64 D '63. D. Cohen
Zoo story: chimpanzee's paintings hung. Time 83:71 F 21 '64
HOBAN, Russell
Meaning for a middleweight. il Holiday 36: 151-2+ N '64
HOBART, George F.
Birds and the beasts were there. Nat R 14: 485 Je 18 '63
HOBBES, Thomas
Rationalism in politics, by M. Oakeshott. Review
New Repub 148:21-6 F 9 '63. O. Gass
HOBBIES
Hobbies à la carte. J. Reck. il Pop Mech 119:118-19 Ap '63
Homemade money. J. L. Block. il Good H 157:30-2+ Jl '63
Is this the winter you do something different? il Bet Hom & Gard 42:30-7 Ja '64
Make way for a hobby corner. il Seventeen 22:82+ Je '63
Trees are my hobby. J. R. Rarick. il Horticulture 41:122 Mr '63
See also
Collectors and collecting
Handicraft
Postage stamps—Collectors and collecting

Bibliography

On the off-beat bookshelf. H. Frankel. Sat R 47:36-7 Ap 18 '64
Paperback bookshelf. Changing T 17:11-12 Ag '63
HOBBING, Enno
Young man, be a banker. Esquire 59:150-6 My '63
HOBBS, Cecil
(comp) Articles and other books received; south Asia. See issues of American historical review
HOBBS, Edward C.
Ticket to the game. Christian Cent 81:639-41 My 13 '64
HOBBS, Robert M.
Do-it-yourself bighorns. Outdoor Life 132:20-3+ D '63
HOBBS, Robert W.
Trim tabs. Yachting 115:44-5+ F '64
HOBBS, Whit
Let's stop kicking the kids around; excerpts from address. Read Digest 85:79-81 Ag '64

HOBBY horses. See Toys
HOBBY parks. See Parks
HOBSON, Carol Joy, and Schloss, Samuel
Enrollment, teachers, and schoolhousing; highlights from the fall 1962-63 survey of public schools. Sch Life 45:14-17 Ja '63; 46:18-23 Ja '64
HOBSON, Harold
Marguerite Duras. Theatre Arts 47:22-4+ N '63
HOBSON, Karl
Wheat shortage ahead? Farm J 88:16 Ja '64
HOBSON, Wilder
Amen corner. See issues of Saturday review to May 16, 1964
In memoriam. I. Kolodin. Sat R 47:49 Je 13 '64
Obituary
Newsweek por 63:71 Je 8 '64
HOCH, Johann, pseud.
Lady-killer. A. I. Schutzer. il Am Heritage 15:36-9+ O '64
HOCH, L. Clinton
Is it over, over there? interview, ed. by J. B. Weiner. por Duns R 83:pt2 108-10+ Mr '64
HOCH, Paul H.
State care. Atlan 214:82-5 Jl '64
HOCH murder cases. See Murder
HOCHBERG, Julian
Depth perception loss with local monocular suppression: a problem in the explanation of stereopsis. bibliog Science 145:1334-6; 146:800 S 18, N 6 '64
HOCHHUTH, Rolf
Danish rabbi speaks; concerning Hochhuth's play, The deputy. America 110:30 Ja 11 '64
Deputy controversy. Christian Cent 81:507-8 Ap 22 '64; Discussion. 81:861-2 Jl 1 '64
Deputy in Paris. America 110:9 Ja 4 '64
Deputy. Criticism
America 108:730-1 My 25 '63
America 109:70 Jl 20 '63
America 109:187 Ag 24 '63
America 109:570-3+ N 9 '63
America 110:139-40 Ja 25 '64
America 110:304-5 Mr 7 '64. Discussion. 110:499 Ap 11 '64
America 110:341-2 Mr 14 '64; Reply. 110:620 My 9 '64
America 110:400 Mr 28 '64
America 110:495-6 Ap 4 '64
Cath World 197:380-5 S '63
Cath World 199:135-6 My '64
Christian Cent 80:980-1 Ag 7 '63
Christian Cent 80:1269-70 O 16 '63
Christian Cent 81:349 Mr 11 '64
Christian Cent 81:507-8 Ap 22 '64
Commonweal 79:647-62 F 28 '64
Commonweal 79:749-51 Mr 20 '64
Commonweal 80:174-6 My 1 '64
Life 56:28D Mr 13 '64
Nation 197:287-8 N 2 '63
Nation 198:277-8 Mr 16 '64
Nation 198:270-2 Mr 16 '64; Discussion. 198:inside cover Mr 30 '64
New Repub 150:23-5 Mr 14 '64; Reply with rejoinder. L. Abel. 150:30 Ap 4 '64
New Yorker 39:54+ D 28 '63
New Yorker 40:118 Mr 7 '64
Newsweek 61:65 Mr 11 '63
Newsweek il por 63:78-9 Mr 2 '64
Newsweek il 63:78-9 Mr 9 '64
Reporter 30:46+ Ja 30 '64
Reporter 30:40+ Ap 9 '64
Sat Eve Post il por 237:36, 39+ F 29 '64
Sat R 47:16 Mr 14 '64
Sat R il 47:41-2 Mr 21 '64
Time il 82:85-6 N 1 '63
Time il 83:50 Mr 6 '64
U S News il 56:60 Mr 16 '64
Vogue 143:54 Ap 15 '64
Footnote to The deputy dispute: Jews of Rome, the Nazis and the Vatican. C. Mydans. Life 56:21 My 1 '64
Nothing more unjust; Pope Paul's allusion to the attacks upon Pope Pius XII in The deputy. America 110:68-9 Ja 18 '64
Pius defended; English version of Der stellvertreter. Newsweek 62:97 O 7 '63
P.O.A.U. on trial; tempest over Der stellvertreter. Christian Cent 80:1124 S 18 '63
Rolf Hochhuth: equivocal Deputy. E. Alexander. il America 109:416-18+ O 12 '63; Discussion. 109:518-20, 648, 691 N 2, 23-30 '63
Rolf Hochhuth's The deputy: symposium. Commonweal 79:647-62 F 28 '64; Discussion. 80:46+, 119-21 Ap 3, 17 '64
See or read it first! Christian Cent 81:294 Mr 4 '64
377 copies of Deputy sold at Hochhuth party. il por Pub W 185:50 Mr 16 '64
HOCHMAN, M. A.
Autumn trail trip in Rocky Mountain National Park. Nat Parks Mag 39:16-19 Ja '65
HOCHMAN, Sandra
Not having a child; poem. Poetry 104:230-1 Jl '64
Six poets. J. Woods. Poetry 104:109-10 My '64
HOCHSTEIN, Joseph M.
Soviet shadow economy. Reporter 30:27-31 Ap 9 '64
HOCHSTEIN, Rollie
Confessions of a happy homemaker. Good H 157:50+ O '63
Grandmothers get all the breaks! Good H 158:53-4 Mr '64
Man that I marry. Good H 156:86-9 F '63
(ed) One battle I had to win. Good H 156:86-9 My '63
Quick look at instancy. House & Gard 126:60-1 S '64
Robert Goulet goes to Hollywood. Good H 157:30+ S '63
—See Sugarman, D. jt. auth.
HOCK, Raymond J. See Smith, R. E. jt. auth.
HOCKEY
Border warfare: West Point vs. Royal military college of Canada. il Sports Illus 18:22-3 Mr 11 '63
Champions who had no chance; Montreal Canadiens defeat New York Rangers. T. C. Brody. il Sports Illus 20:56+ Mr 30 '64
Disaster on the ice; American amateur hockey team at Stockholm. Sports Illus 18:8 Mr 18 '63
Hockey. See issues of Sports illustrated
Hockey in the slapstick style. S. Fischler. il Sports Illus 18:E3-4 F 11 '63
Howie Young: hockey's abominable iceman. D. Anderson. il pors Sat Eve Post 237:30-1 F 22 '64
Mayhem on skates. S. Young. Holiday 35:194+ Ap '64
New face on the face-off; new rule says: that there must be no physical contact. Sports Illus 21:15 S 28 '64
They call him the greatest on ice; Detroit's G. Howe. il N Y Times Mag p36+ F 23 '64
Well-mannered mesomorph. Time 84:50 D 25 '64
See also
National hockey league
HOCKEY players
Elusive 545th: G. Howe. il Time 82:55 N 22 '63
Go, Bobby! go, to beat the magic 50; left winger of the Black Hawks, B. Hull. W. Leggett. il Sports Illus 22:14-17 Ja 25 '65
Puck's worst boy Howie Young. il Newsweek 61:96 Mr 25 '63
See also
Hull, B.
HOCKEY referees. See Umpires (sports)
HOCKEY teams
Bad penny shines again; T. Lindsay of the Red Wings. D. Anderson. Sports Illus 22:50-1 Ja 18 '65
Bald and the bold; Detroit Red Wings. il Newsweek 64:46 D 21 '64
Champions who had no chance; Montreal Canadiens defeat New York Rangers. T. C. Brody. il Sports Illus 20:56+ Mr 30 '64
Dregs from the cup that enriches: Toronto Maple Leafs postseason play for the Stanley cup. R. MacLeod. il Sports Illus 18:51-2 Ap 29 '63
High voltage on the Detroit ice; Red Wings. A. W. Schardt. il Sports Illus 18:24-32 Ja 28 '63
How do you stop a Red Wing? shoot; third straight Stanley cup for Maple Leafs. T. C. Brody. Sports Illus 20:89-90+ My 4 '64
Howe: the who, what and why of the Red Wings. M. Kram. il Sports Illus 20:30-2+ Mr 16 '64
Mannerly kind of murder; Chicago Black Hawks vs Toronto Maple Leafs. K. Rudeen. il Sports Illus 18:53-4 Mr 25 '63
Now it's alley fights on the ice; Black Hawks vs Maple Leafs. H. Weiskopf. il Sports Illus 19:36-7 D 23 '63
Question of honor; amateurs for Olympics. R. Creamer. il Sports Illus 20:58-61 Ja 27 '64
'Ray for Reay; Chicago Black Hawks. il Newsweek 62:78-9 D 16 '63
Rich bounty of mutiny; Chicago's hockey players. il Sports Illus 19:72-4 D 2 '63
Sporting scene. H. W. Wind. il New Yorker 40:133-4+ Ap 11 '64
They hurt when he hit them; Toronto Maple Leafs vs Montreal Canadiens. D. Anderson. Sports Illus 18:E5-6+ Mr 4 '63

HOCKEY teams—*Continued*
They must stay mad to win; Chicago's Black Hawks. il Sports Illus 20:10-15 F 3 '64
Who's sorry now? Chicago Black Hawks. il Time 81:62 Mr 1 '63
Why bookies have ulcers; Toronto Maple Leafs vs. Detroit Red Wings. Time 83:56 My 8 '64
Wispy and worrying, but he wins; R. Crozier of the Red Wings. R. Lardner. il Sports Illus 21:81-2 N 23 '64

HOCKING, Elton
Foreign language teaching. NEA J 54:12-14 Ja '65

HOCKING, James H.
Do you know how to walk? Recreation 56:219 My '63

HOCKING, William Ernest
Freedom to hope. Sat R 46:12-15+ Je 22 '63

about

Author. por Sat R 46:13 Je 22 '63

HOCKINSON, Joel
Fire watch in a dry, dry woodland; east of the Mississippi River. C. Phinizy. il Sports Illus 19:22-4 N 4 '63

HOCKS, Paula
After a tale from Hoffman; poem. Nation 199: 144 S 21 '64

HODAS, Sadie. See Young, C. W. jt. auth.

HODEIR, André
Critic as composer. M. Williams. por Sat R 47:59 Mr 28 '64

HODGE, Charlie
Travels with Charlie. il Newsweek 63:61 Ap 6 '64

HODGE, Melville H. Jr
Rate your company's research productivity. bibliog f Harvard Bsns R 41:109-22 N '63

HODGE, Paul W.
Dwarf galaxies; with biographical sketch. Sci Am 210:24, 78-86 My '64
Sculptor and Fornax dwarf galaxies. Sky & Tel 28:336-9 D '64

HODGENS, Richard M.
Movies. Nat R 16:1026-7 N 17 '64

HODGES, A. T. See Williams, G. jt. auth.

HODGES, Elizabeth D.
Censorship of textbooks; what can the library committee do? NEA J 52:25-6 My '63
—and Fleming, Frances
(comps) Selecting materials for children and young adults. NEA J 54:69-70+ Ja '65

HODGES, F. Allen, and others
Mycotoxins: aflatoxin isolated from penicillium puberulum. bibliog Science 145:1439 S 25 '64

HODGES, Gil
Gil Hodges: most nice guy in baseball. G. Astor. il pors Look 28:98A-100+ Jl 14 '64

HODGES, Jenny
Look, ma, I'm skiing! por Motor B 112:32-3+ Jl '63

HODGES, Luther Hartwell
Are our children half-educated? Look 28:85-6 Ja 28 '64
Are we flunking economics? address, January 15, 1963. Vital Speeches 29:286-8 F 15 '63
Challenge of change; address, November 18, 1963. Vital Speeches 30:107-11 D 1 '63
Excerpt from testimony, February 6, 1963. Cong Digest 42:112+ Ap '63
Member of the Cabinet looks at LBJ; excerpts from news conference, April 28, 1964. U S News 56:53 My 18 '64
Policy goals become less elusive. Ann Am Acad 345:14-21 Ja '63
Right to choose. Sat R 46:18+ Ap 13 '63

HODGES, Mary Jane. See Fowle, L. M. jt. auth.

HODGINS, Eric
Episode; excerpts. McCalls 91:74-7+ Ja; 46+ F; 60+ Mr; 102+ Ap; 72+ My '64
Mr Blandings' nightmare. por Time 83:42 Mr 6 '64

HODGKIN, Alan Lloyd
Ionic basis of nervous conduction; address, December 11, 1963. bibliog Science 145:1148-54 S 11 '64
Nobel medical awards. por Sci N L 84:259 O 26 '63
Nobel prize: 1963 award honors three for research on nerve functioning. M. G. F. Fuortes. por Science 142:468-70 O 25 '63
Nobels for nerves. Newsweek 62:90-1 O 28 '63

HODGKIN, Dorothy Crowfoot
Chemistry-minded mother. por Time 84:41 N 6 '64
Nobel prize in chemistry awarded to crystallographer. G. A. Jeffery. por Science 146: 748-9 N 6 '64
Nobel prize winners. il Sci N L 86:295 N 7 '64

HODGKINSON, Anthony W.
Bang, bang, you're dead. New Repub 150: 28+ Ap 25 '64
Of, by, for kids; summary of statements. Sr Schol 83:4T-5T Ja 17 '64

HODGSON, Charles
Colorful Christmas plants. Horticulture 41: 602-3 D '63
Fanciful world of topiary. Horticulture 41: 578-9 N '63

HODGSON, Godfrey
Arise, Sir George Meany. New Repub 149:11 Jl 20 '63

HOEFER, J. A. See Jensen, A. H. jt. auth.

HOEFFDING, Oleg
Sino-Soviet economic relations, 1959-1962. bibliog f Ann Am Acad 349:94-105 S '63

HOEFLICH, Sherman Clark
Sherman Hoeflich. H. C. Pitz. il por Am Artist 28:32-7+ F '64

HOEHENER, Margrit E.
Foods with a foreign flavor. See issues of Good housekeeping

HOEKSTRA, Henry R. and Gingerich, K. A.
High-pressure B-type polymorphs of some rare-earth sesquioxides. bibliog Science 146: 1163-4 N 27 '64

HOELDERLIN, Johann Christian Friedrich
Benjamin Britten's Sechs Hölderlin-fragmente. J. Diether. il por Am Rec G 30:386-8 Ja '64

HOENE, Anne
Monti gilds twenty Miles. Mlle 57:264-7 Ag '63

HOES, Laurence Gouverneur
Monroe doctrine: dead or alive? il por U S News 54:20 My 13 '63

HOES
Indispensable tools. P. W. Dempsey. Pop Gard 14:73 F '63

HOEVEN, Charles B.
Excerpt from debate, April 7, 1964. Cong Digest 43:181+ Je '64

HOFER, A. A. and Lautenschlager, E.
Hampered vinyl polymerization by embedding biological objects. Science 146:69 O 2 '64

HOFF, Laurie
Fog; poem. Horn Bk 40:95 F '64

HOFF, Philip A.
Democrat who took Vermont. R. Tunley. il pors Sat Eve Post 236:82+ N 23 '63
Loneliest governor. W. S. Ellis. Reporter 28:45 Ap 25 '63

HOFFA, Harlan
Reader survey. Sch Arts 63:33-4 D '63
Team teaching & art teaching from the outside. Sch Arts 62:18-20 F '63
Two faces of research. Sch Arts 63:20 Je '64

HOFFA, James Riddle
Hoffa on the AFL-CIO; interview, ed. by R. Vermillion. por Newsweek 62:87 N 25 '63

about

Act II in Hoffa trial. por Bsns W p 102+ Jl 18 '64
Aides quit, but Hoffa stays in driver's seat. por Bsns W p94+ D 14 '63
Behind the plot to assassinate Robert Kennedy. C. R. Mollenhoff. il por Look 28:49-50+ My 19 '64
Bonding troubles for Hoffa; underwriters refuse security. Bsns W p72 F 2 '63
Can Hoffa hold on? il Bsns W p92+ Ja 11 '64
Can they find courage to fight? il Bsns W p28-9 Mr 14 '64
Dream come true. Time 83:16 Ja 24 '64
Eight years. Newsweek 63:28 Mr 23 '64
End of road for Hoffa? what his conviction means. il pors U S News 56:46-7 Mr 16 '64
For Hoffa: money problems, too. U S News 56:97 My 11 '64
Happy Hoffa. por Newsweek 63:68 Ja 27 '64
Hoffa again; plan to achieve a common expiration date for teamster contracts. Nation 197:379 D 7 '63
Hoffa again; question of Teamsters pension fund. Newsweek 61:26 Je 17 '63
Hoffa beats back dissidents. por Bsns W p47 My 4 '63
Hoffa forever? J. O'Gara. Commonweal 78: 240 My 24 '63; Reply. J. F. Flynn. 78:401 Jl 5 '63
Hoffa found guilty; two counts of jury tampering. Sr Schol 84:19 Mr 20 '64
Hoffa, Hegel, and Hoffer. N. Cousins. Sat R 46:26 Ap 20 '63
Hoffa: how they nailed him. H. Suydam. il pors Life 56:20-5 Mr 13 '64
Hoffa hunt; bonding companies. por Newsweek 61:36 F 11 '63
Hoffa indicted in loan fraud. Bsns W p 101 Je 8 '63
Hoffa: new strong man of U.S. labor. por U S News 54:46 My 13 '63

HOFFA, James Riddle—about—*Continued*
Hoffa reaches out; latest contract demands. por Bsns W p47-8 N 16 '63
Hoffa the pure. M. Kempton. New Repub 150:16-18 Ja 18 '64
Hoffa trial. F. J. Cook. il por Nation 198:415-39 Ap 27 '64
Hoffa wins again. T. Brooks. por Reporter 28:34-5 My 23 '63
Hoffa's funds. Newsweek 63:36 My 25 '64
Hoffa's goal: nationwide contract. U S News 55:98 S 9 '63
Hoffa's name in Baker hearing; excerpts from testimony. D. B. Reynolds. U S News 56:86 F 3 '64
Hoffa's newest enemy: a law's fine print. Bsns W p47-8+ Ap 4 '64
Hoffa's throne totters. por Bsns W p32 Mr 7 '64
How Hoffa got Hoffa. L. Velie. Read Digest 85:101-6 D '64
Huh! Hoffa's demands for nationwide labor contract. por Newsweek 62:87-8 N 18 '63
If Hoffa stumbles. Reporter 30:12+ Ja 16 '64
Insider's chilling story of Hoffa's savage kingdom; with report by E. G. Partin. il por Life 56:42-6+ My 15 '64
Is Hoffa finished? A. H. Raskin. Reporter 30:22-4 Mr 26 '64
Is Hoffa washed up? U S News 56:114-15 Mr 23 '64
James R. Hoffa: the prosecution rests. R. Cooper. New Repub 151:6-7 Ag 8 '64
Jimmy & the jury. Time 81:30 My 17 '63
Jolt for Jimmy; found guilty of jury tampering. Time 83:25-6 Mr 13 '64
Jury tampering in Tennessee. C. R. Mollenhoff. il por Look 27:79-82 My 21 '63
Life and times of Tony Pro. R. S. Gallagher and R. Semple. Reporter 29:37-40 S 12 '63
Limit of devotion. por Newsweek 62:75-6 D 16 '63
Long chase through the courts. M. Kempton. New Repub 150:6-7 Mr 14 '64
Managing your manpower; J. Hoffa's leverage technique. T. R. Brooks. Duns R 83:61-4 F '64
More power to you, Jimmy. Nat R 15:425+ N 19 '63
More trouble for teamsters. U S News 54:89 Je 17 '63
My private war with Hoffa. T. Coffey. il por Sat Eve Post 237:68-70 Ja 4 '64
Now Hoffa has the power to call a nationwide strike. U S News 56:94-5 Ja 27 '64
On trial in Chicago. R. Cooper. New Repub 150:13-14 Je 6 '64
One more time; attempts to sway jurors. por Newsweek 61:35 My 20 '63
Pattern for truckers; trucking industry's new contract. il por Bsns W p 105-6+ Ja 25 '64
People of the week. por U S News 54:20 Ap 15 '63
Power of James R. Hoffa. A. H. Raskin. il por Atlan 213:39-45 Ja '64
Power play; concerning interview for David Brinkly's journal. Newsweek 61:48 Ap 1 '63
Real corruption. Time 83:28 Mr 20 '64
Revolt against Hoffa? T. R. Brooks. Commonweal 79:385-6 D 27 '63
Revolt against Jimmy. Time 82:29 D 13 '63
Seventh case against Hoffa and record to date. U S News 54:8 My 20 '63
Somebody got him. Time 84:22 Ag 7 '64
Stakes in the struggle against Hoffa. L. Velie. por Read Digest 84:92-6 Mr '64
There's no revolt. il por Newsweek 64:59-60 Ag 31 '64
Trial by press release. Nation 199:83 S 7 '64
Two down, one to go; Justice dept. vs teamsters chief Hoffa. il por Bsns W p62-3 Ag 1 '64
Verdict on Hoffa. il por Newsweek 63:30-1 Mr 16 '64
Vincible Jimmy. Newsweek 64:30 Ag 10 '64
What the judge said to Hoffa. U S News 56:114 Mr 23 '64
What's next for the teamsters? il por U S News 57:66-8 Ag 10 '64
When Hoffa gets the power he wants; demand for a contract between trucking industry and teamsters union. por U S News 55:121 N 18 '63
Where union stands on Hoffa. U S News 57:68 Ag 31 '64
Will pension trial bring Hoffa's ouster? por Bsns W p53-4 Ap 25 '64
Will the law ever get Hoffa? H. Bigart. il pors Sat Eve Post 236:68-71 Mr 30 '63
Witness for the prosecution; trial on charges of jury tampering. Time 83:25 F 28 '64

HOFFER, Bernie K.
Long, long ago. Sat R 47:6+ O 17 '64

HOFFER, Eric
Erich Hoffer: secular preacher. Christian Cent 80:727 My 29 '63
Eric Hoffer's true beliefs. G. Wills. Nat R 14:502+ Je 18 '63
Negro is prejudiced against himself. N Y Times Mag p27+ N 29 '64; Same. por U S News 57:48-52 D 28 '64
Philosopher of the misfits. por Time 81:M36+ Mr 15 '63

HOFFHINE, Martha
Made with toothpicks. Design 65:212-13 My '64

HOFFLEIT, Dorrit
Meteoriticists meet in Canada. por Sky & Tel 27:15-16 Ja '64
Summer at Maria Mitchell observatory. por Sky & Tel 27:274-5 My '64

HOFFMAN, Barry
Red junket to Cuba; ed. by R. Tunley. por Sat Eve Post 236:25-9 O 5 '63

HOFFMAN, Bernard
Photography's elite of the future? J. Deschin. il Pop Phot 52:16+ Je '63

HOFFMAN, Betty Hannah
How America lives. Ladies Home J 80:24+ Ap '63
I'm going to get a job! Ladies Home J 80:107-8 S '63
Masculinity: what is it? Ladies Home J 80:96+ Ja '63
What is Prince Philip really like? Ladies Home J 80:60-1+ Je '63

HOFFMAN, Daniel
As I was going to Saint Ives; poem. New Yorker 39:28 Jl 13 '63
Deliverance; poem. Poetry 102:310-11 Ag '63
Natural history; poem. Nation 196:352 Ap 27 '63
(tr) See Domino. R. Word

HOFFMAN, David
Safety in the airlanes. J. O'Gara. Commonweal 79:586 F 14 '64

HOFFMAN, Frank O.
Improve your profits day by day! Harvard Bsns R 41:59-67 Jl '63

HOFFMAN, Gloria
Color action at night. U S Camera 26:48-9+ Ag '63

HOFFMAN, Howard S.
Amateur scientist. Sci Am 208:159-60+ Je '63
—and Fleshler, Morton
Startle reaction: modification by background acoustic stimulation. bibliog Science 141:928-30 S 6 '63

HOFFMAN, Martin
Reflections on narcotics addiction. Yale R 54:17-30 O '64

HOFFMAN, Paul G.
Police Birchites: the blue backlash. Nation 199:425+ D 7 '64
United Nations nobody knows. Sat R 46:10-12+ D 28 '63
War on want. UN Mo Chron 1:92-8 Je '64

HOFFMAN, Roman
Latin America: the church meets the challenge of change. Cath World 197:164-71 Je '63

HOFFMANN, Rita
Can women take medicine? Mlle 57:127-9+ S '63
Happily ever after. Mlle 59:140-3 My '64
Island paradox. Mlle 57:140-2+ O '63
Pfiff's in what you can't see. Mlle 60:118-21+ D '64
Return of the prodigal. Mlle 58:116+ D '63
Swept with confused alarms: psychological climate on campus. Mlle 58:260-1+ Ag '64
Wine-tasting jobs and others not so dull. Mlle 58:112-13+ F '64
You've taught me more than any teacher. Mlle 59:134-7 O '64

HOFFMANN, Stanley
Cursing de Gaulle is not a policy. Reporter 30:38-41 Ja 30 '64

HOFFMANN, Victor, and Strietelmeier, John
Gary's rank-and-file reaction. Reporter 31:28-9 S 10 '64

HOFFORD, James L.
Movies. Christian Cent 81:462-3 Ap 8 '64

HOFMANN, Hans
Achievement of Hans Hofmann. F. Bultman. il por Art N 62:43-5+ S '63
Art galleries; exhibition at Museum of modern art. H. Rosenberg. New Yorker 39:100+ N 2 '63
Hans Hofmann; exhibition at the Museum of modern art, New York. B. Kaufman. Commonweal 79:205-7 N 8 '63
Old man crazy about painting. il por Newsweek 62:88+ S 16 '63

HOFMANN, Klaus
Machine tools of life. il por Time 81:85 Ap 5 '63

HOFMANN, Margret
What we didn't know. por Sat R 46:13+ D 21 '63

HOFMANN, Paul
After twenty-five years, Franco is still a sphinx. N Y Times Mag p 21+ Ap 19 '64
HOFMANNSTHAL, Hugo von
Four German poets. L. Mueller. Poetry 101: 290 Ja '63
Most ingenious paradox. J. W. Stedman. il Opera N 27:24-7 F 16 '63
Der HOFMEISTER; drama. See Brecht, B.
HOFSTADTER, Richard
Antitrust in America; excerpts from The business establishment, ed. by E. F. Cheit. Commentary 38:47-53 Ag; 28 N '64
Paranoid style in American politics; adaptation of address, November 1963. Harper 229: 77-82+ N '64
HOFSTED, Eugene A.
World's tallest tree farm; follow-up for the future. Am For 70:22-5+ S '64
HOFSTRA college, Hempstead, N.Y.
Backlash. New Yorker 40:25-8 My 30 '64
HOG cholera
Minute men putting curb on cholera. L. D. Mark. Suc Farm 62:43+ Ap '64
Vaccines
Spray vaccine for hog cholera? J. Russell. Farm J 87:32 Je '63
HOG feeders. See Swine—Feeding
HOG houses. See Swine houses
HOG ISLAND, Bahama Islands
Earthly delights in Paradise; photographs. J. Zimmerman. il Sat Eve Post 236:62-5 Ap 27 '63
Far-out side of Paradise. H. Sutton. il Sat R 46:52+ Mr 16 '63
HOGAN, Ben
Ben's back. por Newsweek 61:98 Je 24 '63
Dream match produces a dream round. A. Wright. il por Sports Illus 20:54-6+ Je 8 '64
HOGAN, Dan E.
Cut across the media. Library J 89:4981-4 D 15 '64
HOGAN, Daniel E. Jr
Lestoil: the road back. il por Bsns W p 118+ Je 15 '63
HOGAN, John W.
Adding VU meter to tape recorder. Electr World 72:104 O '64
HOGARTH, Arthur Paul
Connecticut Valley, where American industry began; drawings. Fortune 68:116-23 D '63
about
Age bursting with spectacle and excitement; reproduction of paintings. Life 56:60-7 Ap 24 '64
Portfolio of drawings by Paul Hogarth. N. Kent. il por Am Artist 27:42-7+ Ap '63
HOGE, Carson
Switch to slurry seal. por Am City 79:104-5 Mr '64
HOGE, Ralph O.
Inventor takes the kick out of shooting: Hydro-Coil. D. Barnes. il Sports Illus 19: 89+ S 9 '63
HOGG, Algernon
Passing scene. Nat R 14:375-7 My 7 '63
HOGG, Quintin McGarel
Toast of democracy; address, January 22, 1963. Vital Speeches 29:300-3 Mr 1 '63
Whilst he still lives amongst us. por Life 57:49-50+ D 11 '64
about
Cambridge's revenge: dons say Hailsham threatens U.S. support, block honorary degree for him. D. S. Greenberg. Science 140:282-3 Ap 19 '63
Hailsham again stirs them up. P. Worsthorne. il pors N Y Times Mag p 11+ Ag 11 '63
Hailsham vs. Cambridge: British science minister will get degree. E. Langer. Science 140:795 My 17 '63
Hoggwash? il por Newsweek 62:65 D 9 '63
Out of the ghetto; new Peerage act. il por Time 82:29 Ag 9 '63
Science policy shapes up as issue in coming British election. J. Maddox. il por Science 143:1146-8 Mr 13 '64
U.S.-Britain: battle of the brains; British scientists to U.S. Sr Schol 82:23 Mr 27 '63
HOGG, Victor H.
Abrams planetarium in Michigan. Sky & Tel 27:336-8 Je '64
HOGGAN, David Leslie
In defense of Hitler. por Newsweek 63:82-3 My 18 '64
HOGNOSED snake. See Snakes

HOGROGIAN, Nonny
Nonny Hogrogian. E. Geller. por Library J 89:4610-11 N 15 '64
HOHENBERG, John
How to spot a newsman. Sat R 46:55 Je 8 '63
HOHENHEIM, Theophrastus Bombast von. See Paracelsus
HOIBY, Lee
Music to my ears; Hoiby on Turgenyev's Natalia Petrovna. I. Kolodin. Sat R 47:68 O 24 '64
Natalia Petrovna. Criticism
Mus Am il 84:25-6 N '64
New Yorker 40:190-2 O 17 '64
HOILES, Raymond Cyrus
According to Hoiles. V. G. Sauter. New Repub 150:5 F 22 '64
Making money by making enemies. il por Time 81:94+ Ap 19 '63
HOISTING machinery
Big idea: a rail hoist for heavy stuff. A. Lindsley. il Pop Sci 183:106-7 S '63
Self-dumping hoist for a hillside; traveling hoist. il Pop Sci 183:112-13 Ag '63
HOLBEIN, Hans, the younger
Holbein: master draughtsman. A. Werner. il por Am Artist 29:42-7+ F '65
HOLBO, Paul S.
Cold war drift in Latin America. bibliog f Cur Hist 44:65-72+ F '63
HOLBROOK, Clyde A.
Religious scholarship and the Court. Christian Cent 80:1076-8 S 4 '63
HOLBROOK, David
Look, ma, I'm writin'! por Time 84:37 Ag 14 '64
HOLBROOK, Stewart H.
Blue jeans; reprint. Am For 70:2 N '64
about
Forest giant. J. Stevens. Am For 70:3 N '64
Man who wrote like an angel. J. B. Craig. por Am For 70:31 O '64
Obituary
Pub W 186:41 S 21 '64
HOLBROOK, Weare
Wring cycle. Read Digest 83:189-90+ D '63
HOLCMAN, Jan
Petri in retrospect. Sat R 46:55-6 My 25 '63
Unhomogenized Smetana. Sat R 46:63 Mr 30 '63
about
In re Holcman. H. L. Anderson. Sat R 46:62 My 25 '63
HOLCOMB, Dorothy A.
First for Fort Worth. Library J 88:4555-7 D 1 '63
HOLCOMB, Hank
Automatic systems for safety. Motor B 112: 34-6 N '63
Inside today's outboards. Motor B 114:34-5+ O '64
Roundup: littlest motors astern. Motor B 113: 36-7+ My '64
Water pressure abroad; ten steps to choosing the right system; questions and answers. Motor B 113:42-3 My '64
HOLD-ups. See Robberies and assaults
HOLDEN, David
At cross-purposes in the sands of Yemen. Reporter 28:37+ F 14 '63
Baghdad: coup by consent. Reporter 29:30-2 D 19 '63
Hungary: renaissance after revolt. Sat Eve Post 237:38+ Ap 25 '64
HOLDEN, Donald
Florence: a five day tour. Am Artist 28:48-54+ Ap '64
Start in art. Design 65:168-70+ Mr '64
HOLDEN, Lansing C.
Yukon mink. Field & S 68:35 F '64
HOLDEN, Preston, and others
Arbovirus hemagglutinin inhibitor in acetone-extracted serums from normal chickens. Science 147:169-70 Ja 8 '65
HOLDEN, William
Two birds bet a million on a club in the bush. R. Coughlan. il por Sports Illus 18:84-8+ My 20 '63
HOLDER, Geoffrey
Night they killed the bossa nova. Sat R 46: 77-9+ O 12 '63
HOLDER, William G.
Cancellation scrutiny. Aviation W 82:90 Ja 4 '65
HÖLDERLIN, Friedrich
Four German poets. L. Mueller. Poetry 101: 288-90 Ja '63
HOLDERNESS, Esther
History repeats; poem. Christian Cent 80:710 My 29 '63
Variations on a theme; poem. Christian Cent 81:672 My 20 '64

HOLDING companies
Fundamental instrument; Istituto per la ricostruzione industriale. Time 83:86 Mr 27 '64
Funds again merging with holding groups; practice of swapping shares. Bsns W p 109-10 My 9 '64
Man with many eyes; Argus corporation of Canada. il Time 81:81-2 F 8 '63
Rapid-American trouble hinted by McCrory shift. Bsns W p 168 My 18 '63
See also
B.S.F. company
Compar corporation
Diversa, incorporated
Interpublic group of companies, incorporated
Marine midland corporation
Quadri-science, incorporated
Savings and loan associations—Holding companies
HOLDING devices (machine work)
Anchors for radial-saw work. E. M. Love. il Pop Sci 182:132 Je '63
Compound slide rest for your wood lathe; accessory for metal turning. W. E. Burton. il Pop Mech 119:190-4+ F '63
How to make a sliding tool-rest for precision grinding. W. G. Waggoner. il Pop Sci 185: 144-5 Jl '64
Pistol-grip hold-down. H. R. Clark. il Pop Mech 119:187-8 F '63
Roller rest for precision filing. H. Walton. il Pop Sci 184:140-3 Ap '64
Sliding work holder for your table saw. R. J. DeCristoforo. il Pop Mech 119:184-6 Ap '63
HOLIDAY, Billie
Billie Holiday: triumphant decline. M. Williams. por Sat R 47:68+ O 31 '64
Jazz records. W. Balliett. New Yorker 39:86-9 Ag 24 '63
HOLIDAY (periodical)
Holiday annual restaurant awards (title varies) (cont) il Holiday 34:76-7 Jl '63
Holiday life. Newsweek 62:40-1 Jl 1 '63
HOLIDAY dance; story. See Gordon, E. E.
HOLIDAY inns of America, incorporated
Single standard for travelers. il Bsns W p 114+ N 16 '63
HOLIDAY meals. See Meals
HOLIDAYS
See also
Festivals
Vacations
also names of holidays, e.g. Bastille day
HOLINESS
Holiness in the dialogue. America 108:601 Ap 27 '63
Protestant sanctity. E. C. Bianchi. America 111:106-8 Ag 1 '64
HOLINESS churches
See also
Pentecostal churches
HOLLAND, Arthur J.
Mayor moved. Nation 198:226-7 Mr 9 '64
Movers and voters. il por Newsweek 63:28+ Mr 9 '64
HOLLAND, Barbara
Loved look; story. Redbook 122:44-5 Ja '64
New boy in town; story. Good H 157:72-3 S '63
Question of honor; story. Good H 158:80-1 Mr '64
Temptation; story. Good H 158:50-1 Ja '64
HOLLAND, Dan
Shot in the dark. il Field & S 69:38-41+ D '64
HOLLAND, David
Flight of the bats. Nat Parks Mag 38:8-10+ Ja '64
HOLLAND, Gerald
Young blood in a lively old tradition. Sports Illus 19:20-2+ Jl 15 '63
HOLLAND, H. D. See Rosenberg, P. E.
HOLLAND, Henrietta Fort
(ed) See Moore, M. Marianne Moore speaks
HOLLAND, James R.
Photographer on campus. U S Camera 27: 66-7+ D '64
HOLLAND, Jerome H.
Jerome Brud Holland wins Sports illustrated award. por Negro Hist Bul 27:57-8 D '63
HOLLAND, Lee
Homer and the dragon. Américas 16:28-32 Ja '64
HOLLAND, Michael
How to crack Esquire. Esquire 62:90 D '64
HOLLAND. See Netherlands
HOLLAND festival. See Music festivals—Netherlands
HOLLANDAISE sauce. See Sauces
HOLLANDER, Edward D.
Measures of workers' wealth and welfare. Mo Labor R 86:674-5 Je '63
HOLLANDER, John
Poetry chronicle. M. Swenson. Poetry 102: 118-19 My '63
Right wave; poem. Poetry 102:371 S '63
That old hack magic. Esquire 59:70-1+ Mr '63
HOLLANDER, Lorin
I wear my hair short. por Seventeen 22:330-2+ Ag '63
Prodigies. M. Mayer. por Esquire. 61:106-7+ My '64
HOLLANDER, Paul. See Milgram, S. jt. auth.
HOLLANDER, Zander
(ed) Outboard fitting out. Yachting 113:88-90+ Ap '63
HOLLANDERS. See Dutch
HOLLEMAN, Boyce
War on the fire felons; address. Am For 70:29+ F '64
HOLLEMON, Adeline E.
I killed crooked horn. por Outdoor Life 133: 68-9+ Ap '64
HÖLLERER, Walter
Writers in Berlin. Atlan 212:110-13 D '63
HOLLEY, Edward G.
Houston list. Library J 88:959-61 Mr 1 '63
Neglect of the greats. bibliog por Library J 88:3547-51 O 1 '63
HOLLEY, Phil
Inter-city water-sewerage agreements. Am City 79:73-5 D '64
HOLLIFIELD, Guy. See Pitts, G. C. jt. auth.
HOLLINGER, James R. and Mulligan, J. E.
Build the shotgun sound snooper. Pop Electr 20:51-4+ Je '64
HOLLINGS, Ernest Frederick
Which way South Carolina? Christian Cent 80:165 F 6 '63
HOLLINGSWORTH, Alvin C.
Teaching art to the gifted in a New York high school. il por Am Artist 28:68-73+ Je '64
HOLLINGSWORTH, Hansel H.
Child-caring institution on the move. bibliog f Ann Am Acad 355:42-8 S '64
HOLLINGWORTH, Clare
Lady pundit. por Newsweek 61:64 Je 10 '63
HOLLINSHEAD, Ariel C. See Wheeler, W. B. jt. auth.
HOLLIS, C. Caroll
Lincoln rejects a bodyguard. Nation 198:173-4 F 17 '64
HOLLIS, Ernest V.
Walter Crosby Eells, 1886-1962. Sch & Soc 91: 242 Sum '63
HOLLISTER, Charles D. and Heezen, B. C.
Modern graywacke-type sands. bibliog Science 146:1573-4 D 18 '64
HOLLISTER, William G.
Homes that nurture intellect. PTA Mag 57: 8-10 bibliog(p36) My '63
HOLLO, Anselm
Air, to dream in; Age: four; My ancestors; poems. Nation 199:338 N 9 '64
Anonymous; poem. Nation 197:396 D 7 '63
HOLLOMON, John Herbert
Brain mines of tomorrow. por Sat R 46:46-7 My 4 '63
about
Bricks without straw bosses. J. Lear. il Sat R 47:45-9 F 1 '64
Civilian technology; program to boost industrial research heavily slashed in House. D. S. Greenberg. Science 140:1380-2 Je 28 '63
HOLLOW crown (dramatic reading) See Dramatic readings
HOLLOWAY, George
Controversy on film; address, May 1962. por Library J 88:513-15 F 1 '63
HOLLOWAY, Nancy
Nancy Holloway. il pors Ebony 20:33-4+ Ja '65
HOLLOWAY, Stephen M. See Segal, E. F. jt. auth.
HOLLOWAY, Trevor
Your ticket to air cushion travel. Sci Digest 53:64-70 Ap '63
HOLLOWOOD, Bernard
Britain's new wave of satire ebbs. N Y Times Mag p 17+ Ja 26 '64
For the British it's odd man in. N Y Times Mag p48-9+ Ja 24 '65
It's U to be LMC. N Y Times Mag p37+ N 29 '64
Now it's cricket to be a pro. N Y Times Mag p39-40+ My 26 '63
This is the satire that is. N Y Times Mag p 13+ Jl 7 '63
What would Queen Victoria say? N Y Times Mag p7+ Je 30 '63
HOLLY
Hollies. M. M. Taylor. il Horticulture 41:604 D '63

HOLLY—*Continued*
Holly culture on the West coast. J. S. Wieman. il Horticulture 41:408 Ag '63
Holly identification: leaf shape. R. B. Clark. il Horticulture 42:22-3+ D '64
You can grow holly. T. Dilatush. il Pop Gard 14:22-3+ N '63

HOLLY mahonias
Mahonias, striking during every season. D. Henry. il Horticulture 41:542 O '63

HOLLY osmanthus. See Osmanthus

HOLLYWOOD, Calif.
How are things in panicsville? B. Schulberg. il Life 55:79-82+ D 20 '63; Same abr. with title Hollywood, where are you? Read Digest 84:68-72 Mr '64
Stars in your eyes. M. Ross. il Travel 119: 38-40+ F '63
Survival kit. il Time 83:39 Ja 24 '64

Architecture

Vest-pocket skyscraper in Hollywood. il Arch Forum 120:114-17 Ap '64

Social life and customs

Talk of Hollywood. W. Fadiman. Sat R 46: 76-7 N 9 '63

HOLLYWOOD museum
Vagabond camera; film industry's cultural and educational center. W. Lane. il Travel 123:62-3 Ja '65

HOLLYWOOD studio club
Sometimes the dream comes true. J. Taylor. il Seventeen 23:66-7 Mr '64

HOLM, Bernard J.
(comp) Articles and other books received; medieval. See issues of American historical review

HOLM, Celeste
UN international school. pors Parents Mag 39:66-7+ F '64

HOLM, Richard W.
Population biology. G. L. Webster. bibliog Science 139:236+ Ja 18 '63
—See Ehrlich, P. R. jt. auth.

HOLM-HANSEN, Osmund
Algae: nitrogen fixation by Antarctic species. Science 139:1059-60 Mr 15 '63

HOLMAN, Libby
Re-racinated. il por Newsweek 64:85 S 14 '64

HOLMAN, William R.
Mishandled, but a landmark. por Library J 88:4698-700 D 15 '63

HOLMBERG, Allan R.
Miracle at Vicos. L. Stowe. il Read Digest 82: 222-6+ Ap '63

HOLMBERG, George V. See Miles, V. C. jt. auth.

HOLMBERG, Lars
Antlered grotesque; stag beetle. Natur Hist 73:56-9 F '64

HOLMBLAD, E. C.
Ready, willing, and able: the handicapped worker. Todays Health 42:11 D '64

HOLMES, Alvhid V.
Daylilies. Pop Gard 14:40+ Jl '63

HOLMES, Brooke
Two American teens in Russia. N. Holmes. il por Seventeen 23:208-9+ Ag '64

HOLMES, Deborah A. and Zabriskie, George
Cybernetic caveman. Nation 199:194-6 O 5 '64

HOLMES, Dyer Brainerd
Mercury gone, Holmes going; with editorial comment by W. J. Coughlin. Miss & Roc 12:10, 54 Je 17 '63
Moon minus one. Newsweek 61:68 Je 24 '63
New man for the moon. Time 82:11 Ag 2 '63
Some earthier problems. Time 81:21 Je 21 '63

HOLMES, Hamilton
Lonely years of Hamilton Holmes. A. Wexler. il pors Ebony 19:101-2+ N '63
Reporter at large. C. Trillin. New Yorker 39:30-4+ Jl 13; 32-6+ Jl 20; 34-6+ Jl 27 '63

HOLMES, John
Between thousand and thousands; poem. Poetry 101:265-71 Ja '63
Two of a kind; poem. Sat R 46:32 F 9 '63

HOLMES, John Haynes
John Haynes Holmes: discoverer of Gandhi; excerpt from Rabbi and minister. C. H. Voss. Christian Cent 81:603-6 My 6 '64
Obituary
Christian Cent 81:510 Ap 22 '64

HOLMES, John W.
Canada in search of its role. For Affairs 41: 659-72 Jl '63
Diplomacy of a middle power. por Atlan 214:106-8+ N '64

HOLMES, Marjorie
Do you dare to be honest in marriage? Todays Health 42:58-9 Ap '64
Good-by, Christmas tree. McCalls 92:180 D '64
Real intimacy in marriage. Todays Health 42:18-21 Ap '64
Why women can't talk to their husbands; Why men don't talk to their wives. Todays Health 42:28-33+ Ap '64

HOLMES, Nancy
Two American teens in Russia. Seventeen 23: 208-9+ Ag '64

HOLMES, Oliver Wendell, 1841-1935
Aging of Justice Holmes. F. Biddle. New Repub 151:19-22 D 19 '64
An immortal makes his mark. I. Dilliard. por Sat R 46:22-3 Ag 17 '63
Bettabilitarian. il por Newsweek 64:124+ O 5 '64
Holmes and the life of the law. F. Biddle. New Repub 149:24-6 Ag 17 '63
Mr Holmes makes his mark. E. Latham. Nation 197:36-8 Jl 13 '63

HOLMES, Peter
Two American teens in Russia. N. Holmes. il por Seventeen 23:208-9+ Ag '64

HOLMES, Robert F.
Opportunity knocks for local forest lands. Audubon Mag 66:278 S '64

HOLMES, Theodore
Portrait of a woman; Sea; In the deep woods; poems. Poetry 101:238-41 Ja '63

HOLMES, William A.
One thing worse than this. Christian Cent 80:1555-6 D 11 '63

HOLMES comet. See Comets

HOLMSTRÖM, Bengt
Work simplification in Swedish public libraries. por Library J 88:4312-15 N 15 '63

HOLROYD, Jack
Hard life. il Outdoor Life 133:65-5+ My '64

HOLROYD, Richard A. and Taub, I. A.
Ionic intermediates and energy transfer in radiation chemistry. Science 142:1196-7 N 29 '63

HOLST, Gustav
Reflections on Gustav Holst's The hymn of Jesus. M. Serbin. il Am Rec G 29:512-14 Mr '63

HOLSTEIN, Ruth
Status of women. NEA J 52:68 N '63

HOLT, Chrys
Up, up, by the hair she goes. il pors Life 56:89-90 Ap 17 '64

HOLT, David Earl
Visitors from far out. por Library J 89:566-7 F 1 '64

HOLT, Henry
Skirmishes with a publisher; excerpts from Owl among colophons: a survey of American book publishing. C. A. Madison. por Sat R 46:24-5 N 16 '63

HOLT, Howard B.
Are school boards necessary? Sch & Soc 91: 349-50 N 16 '63

HOLT, John Roy
Decentralization and new equipment boost work output. Am City 79:31 Ag '64

HOLT, W. Stull
Education of historians in the United States. Am Hist R 68:402-6 Ja '63

HOLT, Will
Broadway postscript; World of Kurt Weill in song. H. Hewes. Sat R 46:33 Ag 10 '63
First. Criticism
New Yorker 40:129 O 31 '64

HOLTER, Ruth
Protecting the preemie. Parents Mag 38: 46-7+ Ap '63

HOLTON, Mary Louise
WLB biography. Wilson Lib Bul 37:803; 38: 80, 353, 797 My, S, D '63, My '64

HOLTON, Raymond W. and Myers, Jack
Cytochromes of a blue-green alga: extraction of a c-type with a strongly negative redox potential. bibliog Science 142:234-5 O 11 '63

HOLWAY, Chester
Big, bold exuberant perennials. Horticulture 41:164 Mr '63
Fall color. Horticulture 41:574-5 N '63
Hazelbushes: European and Turkish. Horticulture 42:31 Ja '64

HOLY Ghost. See Holy Spirit

HOLY Office. See Catholic church—Congregation of the Holy Office

HOLY places
Galilee is still Galilee. C. Northcott. Christian Cent 80:645 My 15 '63

HOLY rollers. See Church of God

HOLY See. See Vatican

HOLY Sepulcher, Church of. See Jerusalem—Church of the Holy Sepulcher

HOLY Shroud
Shroud, by J. Walsh. Review
America 110:52-3 Ja 11 '64. F. L. Filas

HOLY Spirit
Holy Spirit and religion. R. Hazelton. Christian Cent 82:73-4 Ja 20 '65

HOLY Spirit—*Continued*
Systematic theology, by P. Tillich. Review Christian Cent 81:518-19+ Ap 22 '64. D. D. Williams
Word. V. P. McCorry. America 108:816; 110:686 Je 1 '63, My 16 '64
See also
Pentecost
Trinity

HOLY Trinity monastery, Zagorsk. See Monasteries

HOLY week
Spirit of Holy week. America 108:457 Ap 6 '63
Poetry
Poems for Holy week. Christian Cent 81:392 Mr 25 '64

HOLYOAKE, Keith Jacka
U.S, New Zealand, and Australia reaffirm ties of friendship; remarks, July 17, 1964. Dept State Bul 51:195 Ag 10 '64

HOLZ, Peter
Johannesburg planetarium. Sky & Tel 27:20-1 Ja '64

HOLZER, Mrs Leonard
Mrs Leonard Holzer and the Paris she stopped cold. pors Vogue 144:146-7 O 1 '64

HOLZHAUER, Jean
Doing daddy in. Commonweal 79:100-2, 429-30 O 18 '63, Ja 10 '64
Sidestepping. Commonweal 80:124 Ap 17 '64

HOMAN, Arthur Lee
Leadership and world society. Sr Schol 83:11T S 27 '63

HOMAN, Wayne E.
USC focuses on the Pennsylvania Dutch. U S Camera 27:30-1+ Ap '64

HOMANN, Peter, and Gaffron, Hans
Flavin sensitized photoreactions: effects of 3-(p-chlorophenyl)-1,1-dimethylurea. bibliog Science 141:905-7 S 6 '63

HOME, Alexander Frederick Douglas-Home, 14th earl of. See Douglas-Home, A. F.

HOME, Robin Douglas-. See Douglas-Home, R.

HOME, William Douglas-. See Douglas-Home, W.

HOME
Gentle art of staying home. il Am Home 67:37-41 Je '64
See also
Family life

HOME accidents. See Accidents

HOME and the school. See School and the home

HOME bars. See Bars and barrooms

HOME building materials. See Building materials

HOME care hospital service. See Hospitals—Home care program

HOME decoration. See House decoration

HOME economics
Before the weekend. H. Colman. il Am Home 67:20 Je '64
Dilemmas of a househusband. R. Varga. Sat R 48:100-3 Ja 2 '65
Dishrags to riches: the saga of Heloise. M. Cheshire. il Sat Eve Post 236:58-61 Mr 2 '63
Home, sweet, livable, soilable home. il House B 106:120-1 Mr '64
Hostess hints, before and after the party. il Bet Hom & Gard 42:109 D '64
How to whittle down your weekend housekeeping. il House & Gard 123:130-1 Je '63
Keeping house with Emily Taylor. E. Taylor. See issues of Good housekeeping
Keeping up to date. il Farm J 87:51 Ag; 72 N '63; 88:42+ Ag '64
Live pretty please. J. L. O'Neill. Am Home 66:77-8 D '63
Make work lighter for summer living. B. G. Wadsworth. il Parents Mag 39:138 Je '64
Mama, you're pretty inside; housekeeping from a bed. G. H. Land. il Redbook 123:12+ S '64
Myth of the pampered housewife. J. Goodsell. il Read Digest 85:64-6 Jl '64
Notes of a happy housekeeper. M. E. Falter. See issues of House & garden
127 bright ideas for busy wives; ways to make the most of your time and energy. il Good H 156:103-26 My '63
Smart housekeeping for very busy gals. B. Strawn. Bet Hom & Gard 42:78+ Ap '64
Summer-izing. J. Holmstrand and J. Figg. il Suc Farm 61:47-9 Je '63
They're for home ec! statements; ed. by Polly. il Farm J 88:78 S '64
Things you ought to remember but probably don't. il Changing T 18:46 Ja '64
What does she do all day? record of a typical day. il Changing T 19:24-8 Ja '65
See also
Budget, Household
Good housekeeping institute
House cleaning
Housewives
Kitchens
Moving
Storage in the home
Extension work
It's extension's move. Farm J 88:82 Jl '64
Study and teaching
Economics in home economics. M. East. NEA J 52:33-4 F '63
Home economics can be a bridge between the home and the school. G. G. Jenkins and K. R. Conafay. il NEA J 52:21-3 D '63

HOME economics workers
Community approach to the home: homemaker service. J. T. McDowell. bibliog f Ann Am Acad 355:62-8 S '64
Homemaking help in a crisis; program in Palo Alto, Calif. M. C. Martin. il Parents Mag 39:52-4+ Jl '64

HOME equipment. See Household appliances; Houses—Equipment

HOME files. See Files and filing (documents, etc)

HOME freezers. See Freezers

HOME furnishings. See Household furnishings

HOME furnishings show. See Household furnishings—Exhibitions

HOME grounds
House in the homescape; city gardens; excerpts from Ladies' home journal book of landscaping and outdoor living. R. Pratt. il Ladies Home J 80:103-4 Mr '63
How to keep your yard neat without really trying. W. F. Bruning. il Pop Sci 183:102-4 Jl '63
How to take the hard work out of upkeep. Bet Hom & Gard 41:33-4+ N '63
Plan a year-round picture window garden. J. K. Abbs. il Pop Gard 16:29-30 Ja '65
Really live at home this summer! il Bet Hom & Gard 41:48-61 Je '63
This year's planning means next year's pleasure. J. Fanning. il Pop Gard 15:30-1+ S '64
This young family lives from lot line to lot line. H. Mason. il Bet Hom & Gard 41:52-3 My '63
See also
Back yards
Care
Rough weather ahead. il Flower Grower 50:30-2 O '63

HOME industries. See Cottage industries

HOME insurance. See Insurance—All risk policies

HOME is the sailor; story. See Ware, L.

HOME libraries. See Libraries, Private

HOME life. See Family life

HOME life, Education for. See Family life, Education for

HOME loan bank board. See United States—Federal home loan bank board

HOME loans. See Loans, Personal

HOME made furniture. See Furniture

HOME management. See Home economics

HOME missions, National council of churches. See National council of the churches of Christ in the United States of America—Division of home missions

HOME morale. See Family life

HOME movies; musical comedy. See Musical comedies, revues, etc.—Criticisms, plots, etc.

HOME nursing. See Nurses and nursing

HOME offices. See Offices

HOME ownership
Before you buy a house, look at the landscape. J. Fanning. il Pop Gard 15:55-7 Jl '64
Buying a house, is the price right? il Changing T 18:30-2 N '64
Buying on time (cont) il Consumer Rep 28:211-17 D '63
Choosing a house that looks good; and will look good ten years from now. il Changing T 17:23-4 O '63
Closing costs: a booby trap for unwary home-buyers. M. T. Bloom. il Read Digest 83:138-42 D '63
Complete guide to shopping a new house. Bet Hom & Gard 42:29-30+ My '64

HOME ownership—*Continued*
Costs besides a down payment in buying a home. il Good H 158:166 F '64
Federal housing chief indorses home-improvement program. R. C. Weaver. House B 105: 31 S '63
Good news for house buyers. il Changing T 18:7-10 Mr '64
House isn't just a home, it's a piggy bank. T. G. Harris. il Look 28:28+ Ja 14 '64
How to handle the finances for your custom-built home. H. Steinberg. Am Home 66:42-3 N '63
How to take the questions out of buying or selling a house. Bet Hom & Gard 41:117-20 Mr '63
How to trade your house for a new one. Bet Hom & Gard 41:79 Jl '63
If you really knew how little it takes to have a better house. il Bet Hom & Gard 42:26+ Ja '64
In the realty business in spite of themselves; transferred employees homes. il Bsns W p58-9 Ag 10 '63
It takes a heap o' red tape: hazards and headaches in buying a house; letter. Consumer Rep 28:318-19 Jl '63
It's a good time to buy a house. il Changing T 17:7-10 Ap '63
It's time to slam the door on home-improvement swindlers. A. M. Watkins. Am Home 66:38-9+ My '63
Personal business; executive house-hunting Bsns W p 109 My 2 '64
Personal business; house-hunting. Bsns W p 129-30 Ap 25 '64
Personal business; mortgage rates. Bsns W p 149 My 25 '63
Roof of one's own; excerpts from Profession: housewife. P. McGinley. Ladies Home J 80:26+ O '63
Selling a house female-style. J. L. O'Neill. Am Home 67:16+ Ja '64
Start from scratch; rebuilding after Bel Air fire. L. Spigelgass. il Ladies Home J 80: 50+ D '63
This farm for sale? E. P. Gorsline. Farm J 87:89+ Mr '63
What you can expect in a builder's house today. Bet Hom & Gard 41:20 S '63
When should you buy a home? Bet Hom & Gard 42:88 Ja '64
Where's the ceiling on new houses? J. McDonald. il Fortune 67:128-32+ Je '63
You and your home. House & Gard 123:18-19 Ap; 210-11 My; 124:166+ O; 36+ N '63
Your second home: financing and insurance tips. il Am Home 67:18 Ap '64
See also
Insurance, Mortgage
Mortgages

Anecdotes, facetiae, satire, etc.

Cottage for sale. A. Buchwald. il McCalls 91: 44 Je '64

HOME playgrounds. See Playgrounds, Home
HOME remedies. See Medicine
HOME safety devices and measures. See Safety devices and measures
HOME study
College student in residence. M. R. Feinberg. il N Y Times Mag p93 O 13 '63
Hard day's night of today's students. E. J. LeShan. il N Y Times Mag p 104+ S 27 '64
How to learn more, get better grades. Polly. il Farm J 87:76-7 S '63
Students grade homework. L. Buder. il N Y Times Mag p82+ My 26 '63
What parents think of homework. G. Langdon and I. W. Stout. il NEA J 52:9-11 D '63
Who does Johnny's homework? with study-discussion program, by D. B. Harris and E. S. Harris. E. G. Buffie and H. G. Shane. bibliog il PTA Mag 58:30-2, 36 Ja '64

Anecdotes, facetiae, satire, etc.

Education comes to a Boyle. H. Boyle. Read Digest 85:240B N '64

HOME study courses. See Correspondence schools and courses
HOME work. See Home study
HOME workshops. See Workshops
HOMECOMING; story. See Mayer, T.
HOMECOMING of the children; story. See Eyster, W.
HOMEMAKER-housekeeper service. See Visiting housekeepers
HOMEMAKERS. See Housewives
HOMEMAKING. See Home economics

HOMEOSTASIS
Man's dependence on the earthly atmosphere, ed. by K. E. Schaefer. Review
Nation 196:330-1 Ap 20 '63. C. Dreher
HOMER
Penelope and the poet; excerpt from Home is the hunter. H. MacInnes. il Horizon 6:118-20 Sum '64
HOMER, Arthur Bartlett
Bethlehem's shifting stars. il por Time 82: 86+ N 8 '63
Out for a bigger steel bite. il por Bsns W p82-3+ F 16 '63
Surprise from the boss. por Newsweek 62:92 N 11 '63
HOMER, Louise
Her own dear self. F. Robinson. il pors Opera N 28:27-9 Ja 18 '64
HOMER, Sidney
Bull in the bond market. por Fortune 71:104 Ja '65
HOMER, William Innes
Stuart Davis, 1894-1964: last interview. Art N 63:43+ S '64
HOMER, Winslow
Inland Winslow Homer; Mountainville paintings at Storm King art center. il Time 82: 66 Jl 12 '63
HOMES for retired musicians and singers. See Old age homes
HOMESICKNESS. See Nostalgia
HOMESTAKE mine. See Gold mines and mining—United States
HOMESTEAD, Fla.
Budget school offers pleasant environment. il Arch Rec 134:218-19 O '63
HOMESTEAD, Pa.
Second battle of Homestead. J. G. Colangelo, jr. il Reporter 29:29-31 Jl 18 '63
HOMESTEADS
Free land! the saga of the homesteaders. P. Friggens. il Read Digest 82:98-102 My '63
HOMETOWN Halloween; drama. See Hark, M. and McQueen, N.
HOMEWORK. See Home study
HOMING instinct. See Orientation
HOMMEL, Friedrich
Dedication of the House; opening of the rebuilt Bavarian state opera house. Mus Am 84:24-6 Ja '64
HOMO aquaticus. See Diving, Submarine
HOMO habilis. See Man, Prehistoric
HOMOCYSTINE
Homocystinuria: an enzymatic defect. S. H. Mudd and others. bibliog il Science 143: 1443-5 Mr 27 '64
HOMOCYSTINURIA. See Cystathionine
HOMOGENEOUS grouping. See Ability grouping in education
HOMOGRAFTS. See Transplantation of organs, tissues, etc.
HOMOLKA, Charles L.
Our rarest mammal? Audubon Mag 66:244-6 Jl '64
HOMOSERINE. See Aminohydroxybutyric acid
HOMOSEXUALITY
City side; homosexuality in New York. Newsweek 62:42 D 30 '63
Clergy shatter another taboo; Council on religion and the homosexual. Christian Cent 81:1581 D 23 '64
Crime of deviation; New York state proposal to exempt homosexuality from prosecution as a crime. Newsweek 64:90 D 7 '64
Homosexual men and women; interview, ed. by F. R. Schreiber. C. B. Wilbur. Sci Digest 55:55-65 Ap '64
Homosexuality as crime in North Carolina. A. M. Bickel. New Repub 151:5-6 D 12 '64; 152:5 Ja 9 '65
Homosexuality in America; with reports by P. Welch and E. Havemann. il Life 56:66-74+ Je 26 '64
Homosexuality: sin or disease? W. Overholser. Christian Cent 80:1099-101 S 11 '63; Discussion. 80:1304 O 23 '63
Letters of Oscar Wilde, by R. Hart-Davis. Review
New Yorker 39:155-62+ Mr 9 '63. W. H. Auden
New York's middle-class homosexuals. W. J Helmer. Harper 226:85-92 Mr '63
Out of the briar patch; heavy sentence on a homosexual. il Time 84:54 D 25 '64
Snooping in the park; investigatory techniques. J. Ridgeway. New Repub 152:9-10 Ja 16 '65
Speaking frankly on a once taboo subject. I. Bieber. il N Y Times Mag p75+ Ag 23 '64
Third sex. il Newsweek 63:76 Je 1 '64
Wolfenden report: report of the Committee on homosexual offenses and prostitution. Review
Christian Cent 80:1107 S 11 '63. A. A. Gross

HONAN, William H.
Peaceful use of terror. New Repub 148:19-22 Ap 27 '63
Toys and boys and Christmas. New Repub 149:7-8 D 21 '63
War games for kids this Christmas. New Repub 151:8-9 D 19 '64

HONDA, Masatake, and Arnold J. R.
Effects of cosmic rays on meteorites. bibliog Science 143:203-12 Ja 17 '64

HONDA, Soichiro
How the Thunder herd boss brought a Honda boom to U.S. il por Newsweek 64:66-8 Jl 6 '64

HONDA motor company, Japan. See Motorcycle industry and trade

HONDA motorcycles. See Motorcycles

HONDURAS
See also
Forests and forestry—Honduras
Technical assistance in Honduras
Tegucigalpa

Politics and government

Another government is missing. il Time 82:32-3 O 11 '63
Honduras revolt: another blow to U.S. il U S News 55:6 O 14 '63
Wrecking the Alliance? Newsweek 62:54+ O 14 '63

HONDURAS, BRITISH. See British Honduras

HONECK, Richard
After sixty-four years, the prisoner comes home. R. Gannon. il pors Sat Eve Post 237:38+ Mr 14 '64

HONEGGER, Arthur
Jeanne d'Arc au bûcher. Criticism
New Yorker 39:121-2 O 12 '63

HONEST thief; story. See Grove, W.

HONESTY
Honesty and dishonesty. S. Blum. il Redbook 124:46-8+ D '64
Honesty doesn't come naturally. C. Chilman. il Parents Mag 38:44-6+ Ag '63
Manner of speaking. J. Ciardi. Sat R 46:14-15 N 23 '63
Nobody is honest; business theft. Newsweek 61:78-9 Ap 29 '63
Quest for honesty. D. Callahan. Commonweal 80:137-40 Ap 24 '64; Reply with rejoinder. D. P. Gray. 80:262-3 My 22 '64
Thin gray line. M. Mannes. McCalls 91:53+ Ja '64; Same abr. Read Digest 84:61-3 Ap '64
See also
Cheating in schoolwork
Integrity
Sincerity

Quotations, maxims, etc.

Best policy? comp. by E. F. Murphy. N Y Times Mag p 116 D 1 '63

HONESTY (plant)
Honesty. B. Rivera. il Horticulture 41:605 D '63

HONEY
See also
Cookery—Honey

HONEY bees. See Bees

HONEY bird; story. See Cloete, S.

HONEY locust
Honey-locust, and no thorns. il Sunset 130:226-7 Je '63

HONEYMOON
How the bride stayed beautiful all through the honeymoon. il McCalls 90:98-9+ My '63
Something old, something new; all things special for your honeymoon. R. Dunlop. il Todays Health 42:34-7+ Ap '64

HONEYMOON present; story. See Nichols, R.

HONEYSUCKLES
Well-mannered honeysuckles. B. C. Kilvert, jr. il Horticulture 41:136-7 Mr '63

HONEYWELL, incorporated
'Pattern' planning procedure; Planning assistance through technical evaluation of relevance numbers. P. J. Klass. il Aviation W 81:56-9 D 28 '64; 82:54-5+ Ja 4 '65

HONG KONG
British lions; Hong Kong and Communist China. I. Stewart. New Repub 151:14-15 S 5 '64
Down to a trickle; eight-month-old drought. Newsweek 61:48 My 27 '63
Fragrant harbor. Time 84:40 S 4 '64
Hong Kong, and interchurch aid. G. Murray. Christian Cent 80:1471-2 N 27 '63
Life and death of Precious Plum Flower. K. L. Stumpf and E. Gamarekian. il Sat Eve Post 237:66+ Ap 4 '64
Parched colony. Time 81:37 My 24 '63
Sea gypsies of China. W. Menard. il Natur Hist 74:12-21 Ja '65
Six acres of vice. Newsweek 61:38 F 4 '63
See also
Architecture—Hong Kong
Children—Hong Kong
Clothing industry—Hong Kong
Gardens—Hong Kong
Hospitals—Hong Kong
Hotels, taverns, etc.—Hong Kong
Medicine—Hong Kong
Textile industry—Hong Kong
Water supply—Hong Kong

Commerce

Why both sides like Hong Kong. il U S News 58:50 Ja 18 '65
Wooing & growing. il Time 83:96+ Mr 13 '64

Commercial treaties and agreements

U.S. and Hong Kong announce cotton textile agreement. il Dept State Bul 51:517-18 O 12 '64

Description

Hong Kong. M. Sheraton. il Mlle 56:98+ Ap '63
Hong Kong: the new Shanghai. R. Hughes. il Sat R 48:43+ Ja 2 '65
Personal business. Bsns W p 139-40 N 2 '63
That very photogenic harbor. L. Barry. il Pop Phot 55:20+ S '64

Economic conditions

Why both sides like Hong Kong. il U S News 58:50 Ja 18 '65

Housing

Housing: one way to fight reds in Asia. R. P. Martin. il U S News 55:64-7 O 28 '63

Relief work

Project concern; somebody has to care. il Ladies Home J 80:52 Ap '63

Social conditions

Return to the frontier. E. Chang. il Reporter 28:38-41 Mr 28 '63

Social work

Remarkable Kadoorie brothers of Hong Kong. C. W. Hall. il Read Digest 82:273-8 My '63

Water supply

Lament in a dry climate. R. Starnes. Field & S 68:12+ F '64

HONIG, Edwin
Arrears; poem. New Repub 148:22 Mr 30 '63
Cuba in mind; poem. Nation 196:147 F 16 '63
From The weather's criminal; poem. Sat R 46:47 S 21 '63
(tr) See Hernández, M. Elegy for Ramón Sijé; The unending lightning

HONIG, Joel
Careers in music. Opera N 29:7 D 12 '64
Prokofiev. Opera N 29:34 D 26 '64

HONIGMANN, John J. and Preston, R. J.
Recent developments in culture and personality. bibliog f Ann Am Acad 354:153-62 Jl '64

HONING
Lap-honing makes edges supersharp. il Pop Sci 182:105 My '63

HONJO, Susumu, and Fischer, A. G.
Fossil coccoliths in limestone examined by electron microscopy. bibliog Science 144:837-9 My 15 '64

HONOLULU

Airports

No aloha, no hello-a; Honolulu international airport. il Newsweek 61:86 Ap 15 '63

Hotels, restaurants, etc.

Restaurant on the beach at Waikiki. il Arch Rec 136:214-15 S '64

Housing

Designed for sun and trade winds; Queen Emma gardens. il Arch Rec 136:126-8 Ag '64

Library of Hawaii

Candle of understanding; Hiroshima-Honolulu sister city week. M. Gray. il Wilson Lib Bul 37:575-6 Mr '63

Music

Aloha, out there. R. Eyer. Mus Am 84:56-7 F '64
Cosi in Hawaii. L. Winters. Opera N 27:26 My 4 '63

Newspapers

Matter of motive; newspaper strike. il Time 82:40 Jl 19 '63

HONOLULU symphony orchestra
Aloha, out there. R. Eyer. Mus Am 84:56-7 F '64
Island-hopping. il Newsweek 61:63 Mr 18 '63
HONOMICHL, Jack J.
What is cybernetics? Recreation 56:425-6 N '63
HONOR
See also
Dueling
Sportsmanship
HONOR awards for design excellence. See United States—Public housing administration
HONOR thy father-in-law; story. See Robinson, B.
HONORA, Sister Mary. See Mary Honora, Sister
HONORARY degrees. See Degrees, Honorary
HONORS courses. See Colleges and universities—Honors courses
HONORS lists. See Titles of honor and nobility
HOOD, Frederick E.
Yachting interviews; ed. by B. D. Barker, 3d. por Yachting 114:48-50 Jl '63
HOOD, James A.
Negro dissenters; two students speak out against leaders. U S News 55:14 Jl 22 '63
Two students. por Newsweek 62:30+ Ag 26 '63
HOOD, James F. See Rennels, E. G. jt. auth.
HOOD, Ted
Sailing to victory with a needle and thread. H. Whall. il por Sports Illus 20:52-4 F 10 '64
When business is a breeze. il pors Bsns W p94-6+ S 26 '64
HOODS, Academic. See Academic costume
HOOFT, Willem Adolf Visser 't. See Visser 't Hooft, W. A.
HOOK, Sidney
Challenging study: challenge of communism. N Y Times Mag p25+ O 13 '63
Enlightenment at dawn; regular network stations vs. closed circuit. por Sat R 47:48-9+ Jl 18 '64
Freedom to learn but not to riot. N Y Times Mag p8-9+ Ja 3 '65
Liberalism and the Negro. Commentary 37:25-42 Mr '64
HOOKE, Nina Warner
Glimpse of Eden. por Sat Eve Post 237:30-1 N 14 '64
HOOKED rugs. See Rugs and carpets
HOOPER, Bayard
Editor of our new section, the Life review. G. P. Hunt. por Life 57:3 Jl 10 '64
HOOPES, Amy
Caricatured in burlap. Design 65:58-9 N '63 86:588-91 N '64
HOOPES, Donelson F.
John Singer Sargent and decoration. Antiques
HOOPES, Ned
Why a book fair? Sr Schol 84:4T+ F 14 '64
HOOPES, Roy
National service corps. Seventeen 22:50 Ap '63
HOOSE, Herman
Ready-marked pavements. Am City 78:117 Ag '63
HOOVER, Helen
Deer track, wolf track. Aubudon Mag 66:110-11 Mr '64
Forest family of Mrs Helen Hoover; excerpts from Long-shadowed forest. Sat R 47:52-4 Ap 4 '64
Wilderness trail: summer. Liv Wildn 83:3-4 Spring '63
HOOVER, Herbert Clark
Emancipation proclamation centennial, statement. por Ebony 18:21 S '63
From Herbert Hoover on his 90th birthday. Read Digest 85:143-4 S '64; Same abr. with title American virtue as seen at ninety. Life 57:4 Ag 21 '64
Herbert Hoover in his own words; selections from his writings; comp. by L. P. Lochner. por N Y Times Mag p 15 Ag 9 '64
In praise of fishing; excerpts from Fishing for fun, and to wash your soul. por Read Digest 82:243-4+ Ap '63
President Hoover and his friends; excerpts from On growing up, ed. by W. Nichols. PTA Mag 57:17 Je '63
about
American epic. R. Moley. Newsweek 63:108 Je 8 '64
Esteemed sportsman. Sports Illus 21:13 N 2 '64
Faces from the past. R. M. Ketchum. por Am Heritage 16:30-1 D '64
He fed the hungry. America 111:503 O 31 '64
He won over defeat. R. Moley. Newsweek 64:108 N 9 '64
Herbert Hoover. New Repub 151:4-5 O 31 '64
Herbert Hoover, 1874-1964. il por Newsweek 64:40-1 N 2 '64
Herbert Hoover 1874-1964; with account by N. MacNeil. il pors Life 57:71-2+ O 30 '64
Herbert Hoover, engineer. F. E. Terman. pors Science 147:125-7 Ja 8 '65
Herbert Hoover, ninety. Nat R 16:714 Ag 25 '64
Herbert Hoover, RIP. E. Lyons. Nat R 16:946 N 3 '64
Herbert Hoover's boyhood home. il Sunset 130:73 Je '63
Hoover: a memorable career. il pors Sr Schol 85:17-18 N 4 '64
Hoover as scapegoat. H. Hazlitt. Newsweek 64:74 Ag 17 '64
Humanitarian. il pors Time 84:34-5 O 30 '64
Obituary
Sat Eve Post 237:86 N 7 '64
Ordeal and triumph of Herbert Hoover; excerpt from Herbert Hoover, a biography. E. Lyons. por Read Digest 85:161-2+ D '64
Ordeal of Herbert Hoover. C. N. Degler. Yale R 52:563-83 Je '63
Public servant to the world. il pors U S News 57:15 N 2 '64
Quaker requiem. P. B. Mather. Christian Cent 81:1446 N 18 '64
Science honored Hoover. B. Tufty. Sci N L 86:277 O 31 '64
Toast to President Hoover. N. Cousins. Sat R 46:30 N 9 '63
HOOVER, Herbert W. Jr
Hoover's well-vacuumed world. P. Siekman. il por Fortune 69:143-6+ Je '64
HOOVER, James
One day in the life of James Hoover. New Yorker 39:76+ Ag 17 '63
HOOVER, John Edgar
Enforcing the law: interview with J. Edgar Hoover. por U S News 57:36-40 D 21 '64
FBI and civil rights: J. Edgar Hoover speaks out; excerpts from news conference. por U S News 57:56-8 N 30 '64
FBI chief speaks up; summary of news conference. Sr Schol 85:21-2 D 2 '64
Hoover's warning: be alert to fanatics; excerpts from address, December 4, 1963. por U S News 55:14 D 16 '63
J. Edgar Hoover speaks out on reds in the Negro movement; excerpts from testimony before House subcommittee. por U S News 56:33 My 4 '64
U.S. businessman faces the Soviet spy. Harvard Bsns R 42:140-6+ Ja '64
Vital role in building a stronger America. PTA Mag 57:18 F '63
What J. Edgar Hoover says about pressure groups; excerpts from address, November 24, 1964. U S News 57:45 D 7 '64
When a child is missing. Parents Mag 38:67+ Mr '63
about
Cooling the controversy. il Time 84:30 D 11 '64
Faith of the FBI. R. Moley. Newsweek 61:88 Mr 4 '63
Forty years as FBI chief; no interest in retiring. por U S News 56:20 My 18 '64
Hoover-King meeting. il Newsweek 64:22+ D 14 '64
Hoover the vulgarian. Nation 199:394 N 30 '64
J. Edgar Hoover. Commonweal 81:341 D 4 '64
J. Edgar Hoover and the FBI. il pors Newsweek 64:21-6 D 7 '64
J. Edgar Hoover case. W. V. Shannon. Commonweal 81:375-6 D 11 '64
Knives sharpening. Nat R 16:1094 D 15 '64
Let him go. Nation 198:499 My 18 '64
Life imitates Art. Time 84:73 D 18 '64
Must J. Edgar go on and on? L. Wainwright. Life 56:25 My 22 '64
Next: a national police force? il por U S News 57:44-6+ D 7 '64
Next Mr Hoover. Nation 196:131 F 16 '63
Off Hoover's chest; with excerpts from press conference. por Newsweek 64:29-30 N 30 '64
Off the chest & into the fire. por Time 84:31 N 27 '64
Reds make new bid for U.S. youth. il Nations Bsns 52:38-9+ D '64
Still time for Hoover to retire in honor. Christian Cent 81:1483 D 2 '64
HOOVER, Kathleen
Nature's harmonist. Opera N 28:8-13 Ja 4 '64
Wagner's Ring. Opera N 28:7 D 14 '63
HOOVER, Mary Bidgood
Don't be afraid to act like a parent. Parents Mag 40:52-4+ Ja '65

HOOVER, Mary Bidgood—*Continued*
Parent's guide to sex education. bibliog Parents Mag 39:60-3+ Ap '64
Your child (cont) Redbook 120:40 F; 15 Ap; 121:40 Je '63
—See Mayer, G jt. auth.
HOOVER company
Hoover's well-vacuumed world. P. Siekman. il Fortune 69:143-6+ Je '64
Sweeping the world. il Time 82:100 N 1 '63
HOPE Namgyal, maharani of Sikkim
To be a princess; ed. by M. V. Thayer. pors McCalls 90:86-91+ S '63
We started off with nettle soup. McCalls 90: 170 S '63

about

American queen: the new Maharani of Sikkim. il por U S News 55:26 D 16 '63
Denjong Gyalmo, formerly Hope Cooke, now queen of Sikkim. por Vogue 144:142-3 O 1 '64
From debutante to the deities. il por Time 82:33 D 13 '63
I went to the wedding at Sikkim. N. W. Ross. Vogue 141:114-15+ Je '63
In the high Himalayas an American becomes a royal princess. N. W. Ross. il pors Sat Eve Post 236:20-5 My 11 '63
Royalty. New Yorker 40:45-7 O 3 '64
Wedding of two worlds. L. E. Battaglia. il pors Nat Geog Mag 124:708-27 N '63
Where there's Hope. il por Time 81:30 Mr 29 '63
Yankee queen. il por Newsweek 62:44 D 16 '63
HOPE, Bob
Around the world with Bob Hope. J. Reddy. por Read Digest 82:140-4 Je '63
Bob Hope wins tenth annual Travel award. il pors Travel 121:36-8 Je '64
Fish don't applaud. il por Time 82:67 O 25 '63
Holiday Hope. il Time 85:51 Ja 8 '65
Hope: all kinds of a nut about sports. J. Olsen. il pors Sports Illus 18:64-8+ Je 3 '63
HOPE
Freedom to hope. W. E. Hocking. Sat R 46:12-15+ Je 22 '63
HOPE (ship) See Hospital ships
HOPEWELL mounds. See Mounds and mound builders
HOPF, Hans
Hearty hero; interview, ed. by A. M. Lingg. por Opera N 28:16 D 14 '63
HOPF, Harry Arthur
Famous firsts: man who asked the right questions. por Bsns W p74-5 Ag 31 '63
HOPI Indians
Navajo country. il Sunset 131:60-71 S '63
See also
Pueblo Indians
HOPKINS, B. J. and others
Strontium-90 in hair. bibliog Science 139: 1064-5 Mr 15 '63
HOPKINS, Jerry
Courage vs. cancer. Good H 156:36+ Ap '63
HOPKINS, Katharine
Studies in success. Sr Schol 84:27T Mr 20 '64
HOPKINS, Percy E.
Grievance committee: medicine's conscience in action. Todays Health 42:88 Mr '64
HOPKINS, Robert E.
Critic in court. il por Newsweek 65:74 F 1 '65
HOPKINS, Robert S.
Micronesia. bibliog Focus 13:1-6 Je '63
HOPKINS, T. E.
SCR tester. Electr World 71:56 Ja '64
HOPKINS, Terence Kilbourne
Uganda: the politics of compromise. Cur Hist 46:169-74+ Mr '64
HOPKINS, Minn.
Know when to holler for help. R. Brubacher. il Am City 79:92-3 My '64
HOPKINSON, Francis
Patriot and a poet: Hopkinson and Burns songs. P. L. Miller. por Am Rec G 29:632-3 Ap '63
HOPKINSON, Tom M.
New battleground, consumer interest. bibliog f Harvard Bsns R 42:97-104 S '64
HOPKIRK, Paddy
Rallying fast, Paddy's wagon beat them all. P. E. Ress. il por Sports Illus 20:48-50 F 3 '64
HOPPE, Art
West Coast Buchwald. por Newsweek 61:75 Je 24 '63
HOPPE, Arthur
Cuba: the girl and the slogans. Nation 199: 216-17 O 12 '64
HOPPER, DeWolf
Seventy-five years ago: Casey at the bat. A. Austin. il por N Y Times Mag p51+ Je 9 '63
HOPPER, Edward
American light: Edward Hopper; retrospective exhibition. F. Getlein. New Repub 152: 27 Ja 9 '65
Art galleries; retrospective exhibition at the Whitney. R. M. Coates. New Yorker 40:166+ O 24 '64
Hopper: painter of thou shalt not; exhibition at Whitney museum, N.Y. L. Campbell. il Art N 63:42-5+ O '64
Instants in time. il Newsweek 64:100 D 7 '64
Prints of Edward Hopper. C. Zigrosser. il por Am Artist 27:38-43+ N '63
HOPPER, Hedda
Through a keyhole darkly. il por Time 81:52+ F 15 '63
You can't fool an old bag like me; with excerpts from Whole truth and nothing but. pors Life 54:87-8 Ap 12 '63
HOPPER, Stanley R.
Christianity and literature bookshelf. Christian Cent 80:1466-8 N 27 '63
HORAE (books of hours) See Hours, Books of
HORAN, Claude
Four ceramists of Hawaii. J. Lovoos. il por Am Artist 27:66-73+ Je '63
HORCHATAS. See Beverages
HORCHER'S (restaurant) See Madrid—Hotels, restaurants, etc.
HORCHLER, Richard
After you, Alphonse. Commonweal 79:214 N 15 '63
Managing the news. Commonweal 77:659-62 Mr 22 '63
HORGAN, Paul
Black snowflakes; story. Sat Eve Post 236: 30-1 Mr 30 '63
Citizen of New Salem; condensation. Read Digest 84:234-6+ F '64
Evening the score. il Horizon 6:49-51 Spr '64
Rain in Laredo; story. Sat Eve Post 236:44-5 Jl 13 '63
HORIKAWA, Masakatsu, and Fox, A. S.
Culture of embryonic cells of drosophila melanogaster in vitro. Science 145:1437-9 S 25 '64
HORIZON indicators. See Aeronautic instruments
HORMONE creams. See Cosmetics
HORMONE fattening of cattle. See Cattle—Hormone fattening
HORMONES
Actinomycin D and the response to parathyroid hormone. H. Rasmussen and others. bibliog il Science 144:1019-21 My 22 '64
Circadian periodicity in the concentration of prolactin in the rat hypophysis. R. H. Clark and B. L. Baker. bibliog il Science 143:375-6 Ja 24 '64; Reply with rejoinder. J. D. Palmer. 145:296 Jl 17 '64
Control of growth and development in insects; excerpts from address, December 28, 1962. H. A. Schneiderman and L. I. Gilbert. bibliog il Science 143:325-33 Ja 24 '64
Crystalline deamino-oxytocin. D. Jarvis and V. du Vigneaud. bibliog il Science 143:545-8 F 7 '64
Growth hormone factor in weight control. Sci N L 85:153 Mr 7 '64
Hormonal activation of the insect brain. S. D. Beck and N. Alexander. bibliog il Science 143:478-9 Ja 31 '64
Hormone excretion patterns in breast and prostate cancer are abnormal. E. Stern and others. bibliog il Science 145:716-19 Ag 14 '64
Hormone gives girls boost in height. Sci Digest 53:33 My '63
Hormone-induced esterase in mouse kidney. C. R. Shaw and A. L. Koen. bibliog il Science 140:70-1 Ap 5 '63
Hormones for fertility. il Time 84:66 O 9 '64
Hypoglycemia; a potent stimulus to secretion of growth hormone. J. Roth and others. bibliog il Science 140:987-8 My 31 '63
Juvenile hormone activity: effects of isoprenoid and straight-chain alcohols on insects. W. S. Bowers and M. J. Thompson. bibliog il Science 142:1469-70 D 13 '63
Life-giving balancing act. R. Campbell. il Life 55:78-9 N 8 '63
Lobuloalveolar differentiation in mouse mammary tissues in vitro. R. R. Ichinose and S. Nandi. bibliog il Science 145:496-7 Jl 31 '64
New hormone; lipotropic hormone. Sci Am 210:62+ My '64
New pituitary hormone; lipotropin. Sci N L 85:197 Mr 28 '64
Norepinephrine synthesis form tyrosine-C^{14} in isolated perfused guinea pig heart. S. Spector and others. bibliog il Science 139: 1299-301 Mr 29 '63

HORMONES—*Continued*
Now a hormone that melts away fat; lipotropin. S. Spillman. Sci Digest 57:71-4 Ja '65
Salamander hormones clue to human growth. Sci N L 85:150 Mr 7 '64
Sialic acid concentrations in the pituitary glands of normal and ovariectomized rats. E. G. Rennels and J. F. Hood. bibliog il Science 144:416-17 Ap 24 '64
Tanning in the adult fly: a new function of neurosecretion in the brain. G. Fraenkel and C. Hsiao. bibliog Science 141:1057-8 S 13 '63; Reply. E. Thomsen. 143:973 F 28 '64
Thyroid hormones: control of terminal oxidation. J. R. Bronk. bibliog il Science 141:816-18 Ag 30 '63
Transport of neurohormones from the corpora cardiaca in insects. B. Johnson and B. Bowers. bibliog il Science 141:264-6 Jl 19 '63
What parents ask about hormones. M. J. E. Senn. McCalls 90:56+ Je '63
See also
ACTH
Ecdysone
Estrogens
Oxytocin
Vasopressin
Stilbestrols

HORMONES, Plant
See also
Gibberellic acid

HORMONES, Sex
DNA synthesis in alveolar cells of the mammary gland: acceleration by ovarian hormones. F. Bresciani. bibliog il Science 146:653-5 O 30 '64
Gonadal dosages in investigative radiography. S. M. Garn and others. bibliog il Science 143:1039-40 Mr 6 '64
Hormones and sexual behavior. W. C. Young and others. bibliog il Science 143:212-18 Ja 17 '64
Many uses of sex hormonal therapy. il Good H 158:130-1 Ja '64
Medieval hormone chemistry; Chinese compendium of pharmaceutical preparations written in 1596. Sci Am 210:68 F '64
New advance in female fertility. I. Taves. il Look 28:91-4+ My 19 '64
Truth about female hormones. S. A. Kaufman. Ladies Home J 82:22-3 Ja '65
See also
Progesterone

HORN, Carl Carlsson von
Hard-luck Horn. il por Newsweek 62:40 S 9 '63
Harried are the peacemakers. Time 81:30+ Je 21 '63

HORN, Francis H.
Five years for college? NEA J 53:40-1 N '64

HORN, Helen, and Slater, Mary
New horizon for classroom painting. Sch Arts 64:39-41 O '64

HORN, Huston
Beetle does float. Sports Illus 19:58-62+ Ag 19 '63; Same abr. with title Beetle that runs like a car. Read Digest 85:210-14 Jl '64
Boxing (cont) Sports Illus 19:42-5 Jl 1 '63
Pro football. Sports Illus 21:88-91 D 7 '64
Steps to the stars. Sports Illus 20:52-8 F 3 '64

HORN, Jacqueline
Stocking fillers from Uncle Sam's mail order list. Parents Mag 38:122-3 D '63

HORN, Kahn-Tineta
Mohawk beauty with a mission. C. Brossard. il pors Look 28:91-4 Ja 28 '64

HORN (musical instrument)
See also
Tuba (musical instrument)

HORN (signal) See Horns (signals)

HORN book magazine
Anniversary. R. H. Viguers. Horn Bk 40:457 O '64
Chapters from Horn book history (cont) Horn Bk 39:92-3, 207-10, 327-30, 412-15 F-Ag '63
Horn book magazine: 40th anniversary this month. Wilson Lib Bul 39:107 O '64

HORN of plenty; drama. See Miller, H. L.

HORNADAY, Fred E.
Visit to Eglin. Am For 70:19-21 Ag '64

HORNBEIN, Thomas F. and Unsoeld, W. F.
First traverse. pors Nat Geog Mag 124:508-13 O '63

HORNE, Alistair
Farwell to Der Alte. Nat R 15:350-1 O 22 '63

HORNE, Katharyn
Brief biography. S. Goodman. pors Dance Mag 37:42-3 F '63

HORNE, Lena
Lena Horne speaks freely on race, marriage, stage; interview, ed. by H. Feinstein. pors Ebony 18:61-7 My '63

HORNE, Marilyn
Music to my ears; recital in Philharmonic Hall. I. Kolodin. Sat R 47:46-7 My 9 '64
Take the low road. por Newsweek 63:103 Ap 27 '64

HORNE, Roderick
Why I prefer backlighting. il Pop Phot 52:52-5 Ja '63
about
How our cover pictures were made. il pors Pop Phot 52:78 Ja '63

HORNED grebes. See Grebes

HORNED owls. See Owls

HORNER, Harry
Sounding the depths; interview, ed. by A. M. Lingg. por Opera N 28:33 Ja 25 '64

HORNER, Richard Elmer
Solutions to cost overruns recommended. Aviation W 79:91+ O 28 '63

HORNIG, Donald F.
Horning outlines U.S. space mandate; interview, ed. by W. Beller. por Miss & Roc 14:34-5 Ap 20 '64
Ranger VIII; briefing for Johnson brings out high level chit chat on various aspects of space. Science 145:563-5 Ag 7 '64
Research comes first; excerpt from address. Sci N L 86:226 O 10 '64
U.S. science entering new era; interview. por Nations Bsns 52:40-1+ Je '64
about
JFK's new science advisor. por Sci N L 84:327 N 23 '63
New boss for U.S. research. Bsns W p34 N 16 '63
New quarterback; President Kennedy's new science adviser. il por Newsweek 62:98B-99 N 25 '63
Out of the catalyst into the fire. por Bsns W p72+ D 14 '63
Research competition: as budgetary pressures grow, Congress reveals concern about scientific choices. D. S. Greenberg. il por Science 143:1149-51 Mr 13 '64
Wiesner successor: Donald Hornig, Princeton chemistry head, named to take over top science posts. D. S. Greenberg. Science 142:939 N 15 '63

HORNS (signals)
Two-mile boat horn. L. Buckwalter. il Pop Mech 120:178-9 Ag '63

HORNS, Powder. See Powder horns

HORNSBY, Rogers
Last days of Rogers Hornsby. B. Surface. il pors Sat Eve Post 236:72+ Je 15 '63

HORNSTEIN, Erika von
Young Germans. Atlan 212:122-3+ D '63

HORNUNG, Clarence P.
Antique autos; new collection of prints: Gallery of the American automobile. il por Library J 88:2630-3 Jl '63
Portfolio of antique automobiles. il por Am Artist 27:54-7+ O '63

HORNUNG, Paul
Back in bounds. por Newsweek 63:54-5 Mr 30 '64
Best year of their lives. Sports Illus 19:6 S 2 '63
Gold for the golden boy. il por Time 82:66 S 20 '63
Golden boy is back. W. C. Heinz. pors Life 57:70-2+ Ag 28 '64
Judgement day. il por Newsweek 61:84 Ap 29 '63
Shining hour for Golden Boy. T. Maule. il pors Sports Illus 21:22-5 S 21 '64
Toe that lost its touch. D. Jenkins. il por Sports Illus 21:30-2+ N 30 '64

HOROSCOPES. See Astrology

HOROWITZ, Al
Chess corner. See issues of Saturday review

HOROWITZ, David
Victims of anomie. Nation 198:606-8 Je 15 '64

HOROWITZ, Irving Louis
Noneconomic factors in the institutionalization of the cold war. Ann Am Acad 351:110-20 Ja '64

HOROWITZ, Milton W.
Instructor flunks a test. Flying 75:24-7 S '64

HOROWITZ, Vladimir
Horowitz collection. R. Kammerer. por Am Rec G 30:14-16 S '63
Piano that sings. H. Kupferberg. il Atlan 213:128+ My '64

HORROR films. See Moving pictures—Horror films

HORROR television programs. See Television broadcasting—Horror programs

HORS d'oeuvres. See Appetizers

HORSE and two goats; story. See Narayan, R. K.

HORSE at Islamabad villa; story. See Shaw, D.

HORSE breeding
Cowboy who'd be king; owner of world's largest racing stable. W. Tower. il Sports Illus 18:22-4+ F 25 '63

HORSE naming contests. See Competitions

HORSE power. See Horsepower (mechanics)

HORSE race betting. See Gambling; Gambling—Russia

HORSE racing
And still champion; Kelso wins Aqueduct stakes. Time 84:90 S 18 '64
Betting, Soviet style; at Moscow races. il Bsns W p32-3 F 23 '63
Big day for optimists; Kentucky derby. il Time 81:84 My 10 '63
Big spill; Santa Anita Derby. il Sports Illus 18:16-20 Mr 11 '63
Big three looked mighty small; Carry Back's comeback in Cleveland. W. Tower and W. Leggett. il Sports Illus 19:16-17 Ag 26 '63
Bug boy rides like an old hand; apprentice jockey M. Venezia. J. Olsen. il Sports Illus 22:26-8+ Ja 25 '65
Candy Spots wins in the classic manner; Preakness race. W. Tower. il Sports Illus 18:22-3 My 27 '63
Carry Back comeback? il Newsweek 62:56 Ag 12 '63
Centennial summer; thoroughbred racing in Saratoga Springs. il Newsweek 62:55 Ag 19 '63
Cinderella v. Old Moneybags; Gun Bow beats Kelso at Aqueduct. il Time 84:86 O 9 '64
Dancer dazzles old Kentucky. W. Tower. il Sports Illus 20:22-7 My 11 '64
Dancer, the Scoundrel, and Mr Moon. W. Tower and W. Leggett. il Sports Illus 20:24-7 Ap 13 '64
Derby star rises; rating the leading Kentucky Derby colts. W. Tower. il Sports Illus 20:16-19 Mr 9 '64
Derby victory prance; Chateaugay. W. Tower. il Sports Illus 18:24-9 My 13 '63
DuPonts, win and place; in the Laurel international. W. Tower. Sports Illus 19:67 N 18 '63
Fourth communion; Kentucky Derby. il Time 83:58 My 8 '64
Hard times at Calumet. il Time 83:46-7 Mr 27 '64
Harness racing. See issues of Sports illustrated
Headlong horse race; Siena's Palio. il Holiday 37:58-63 Ja '65
Here the sport is going sour; ed. by W. Tower. E. B. Ryan. il Sports Illus 20:34-8 Je 8 '64
He's a freak; Gun Bow. il Time 84:80 S 4 '64
Horse racing. W. Tower. See issues of Sports illustrated
Intolerable squeeze; relationship between states and racing. A. Hammond. il Sports Illus 18:34-6+ My 6 '63
It was sire and son day at Saratoga. W. Tower. Sports Illus 21:92-3+ S 7 '64
It's the world's favorite sport. Sports Illus 20:32-8+ Je 8 '64
Judge they have to tell it so; G. Schilling. E. Havemann. il Sports Illus 21:38+ N 16 '64
Life guide; steeplechases. il Life 56:15+ Mr 6 '64
Misters Big; favorites for the Kentucky Derby. il Time 81:78-9 Mr 15 '63
Move over, Man o' War; Kelso top U.S. thoroughbred. W. Tower. il Sports Illus 19:36-8 N 11 '63
Moving toward a day in May; Kentucky Derby candidates: Candy Spots and Never Bend. il Sports Illus 18:18-19 Mr 4 '63
Old Hat struts some new stuff; beats favored Miss Cavandish. W. Tower. il Sports Illus 21:56 Ag 10 '64
100-year spree at Saratoga; with report by M. Smith. il Life 55:52B-61 Jl 26 '63
One more to make it nine; Triple crown for Northern Dancer. W. Tower. il Sports Illus 20:30-1 Je 8 '64
Pious partners of success. M. Durslag. il Sat Eve Post 236:28+ My 4 '63
Playing the ponies with a pair of experts. P. D. Willis. il Harper 228:48-50 Mr '64; Same abr. Read Digest 84:240-1+ My '64
Pleasure of keeping fast company; highlights of world's big races between May 1st and last of June. M. R. Werner. Sports Illus 19:44 Jl 15 '63
Protruding proboscis; Gun Bow outfought Kelso. W. Tower. il Sports Illus 21:68-70 O 12 '64
Psychiatrist; jockey S. Brooks. il Time 81:93 Ap 19 '63
Quadrangle fits nicely in a racing oval; Derby threat to Hill Rise and Northern Dancer. W. Tower. il Sports Illus 20:66-8+ Ap 27 '64
Quadrangle splashes ahead. W. Tower. il Sports Illus 21:60-2 Ag 31 '64
Q&A; Quadrangle wins Belmont stakes. il Time 83:79 Je 12 '64
Race track. A. Minor. See issues of New Yorker
Rich get richer; Woodward stakes. Time 82:71 O 4 '63
Romantic realities. F. P. Keyes. il Travel 121:48-50 Ap '64
Saratoga Springs. R. Kelley. il Travel 120:50-2 Ag '63
Seven doped horses; cases in England. Sports Illus 19:6 Jl 22 '63
Sport of governors. il Time 83:102 F 28 '64
Sporting scene; Saratoga Springs, N.Y. R. Angell. New Yorker 40:185-8+ S 12 '64
Sunny Jim's lament. R. Riger. il Esquire 60: 83-6 Ag '63
Sweet revenge; Preakness. Time 81:60 My 24 '63
Taken for a Virginia reel; Northern Dancer loses to Virginia's Quadrangle in Belmont. W. Tower. il Sports Illus 20:30-1 Je 15 '64
Tax on quality; increase the harness racing season by twenty-six days. Sports Illus 18: 11-12 F 18 '63
Their hats are in the ring; owners of Kentucky Derby top contenders. W. Tower. il Sports Illus 20:26-32 My 4 '64
Thinking man's jockey. Sports Illus 18:6 Mr 4 '63
Third race; Aqueduct. New Yorker 39:32-4 My 11 '63
Third world of the turf. W. B. Furlong. il Sat Eve Post 236:74-6 S 21 '63
Three for the Derby. il Newsweek 61:84 My 6 '63
Three for the Triple crown; Northern Dancer. W. Tower. il Sports Illus 20:26-9 My 25 '64
Touch of gold in the saddle; J. Rotz. G. Holland. il Sports Illus 20:24-6+ Mr 23 '64
Triumph for nonconformists; Garden state won by Sadair. W. Tower. il Sports Illus 21:28-9 N 23 '64
Two colts go after one Derby; Candy Spots and Never Bend. W. Tower. il Sports Illus 18:18-23 Ap 8 '63
Two for the money; Northern Dancer at Preakness. il Time 83:85 My 22 '64
Two, four, six, eight, who do we depreciate? W. Tower. il Sports Illus 21:45-6 Ag 24 '64
Two ladies in search of the world; Woodward stakes. W. Tower. il Sports Illus 19:26-7 O 7 '63
Two take dead aim at Candy; Never Bend and No Robbery. W. Tower. il Sports Illus 18:18-20 My 6 '63
Tyranny of the little men; Kentucky Derby top jockeys. W. Tower. il Sports Illus 20: 28-9 Ap 27 '64
Vanderbilt vs. racing's establishment. A. Wright. il Sports Illus 19:18-20+ Ag 12 '63
Watchers of the race; photographs. J. Cooke. Sports Illus 21:26-33 N 9 '64
We was robbed! riots at Long Island's Roosevelt raceway. il Time 82:77 N 15 '63
Winner almost didn't start the race; Belmont stakes at Aqueduct. W. Tower and W. Leggett. il Sports Illus 18:26-31 Je 17 '63
Winner was the Ruler with floppy ears. W. Tower. il Sports Illus 19:16-17 S 16 '63
Yanks have landed; American-owned horses of English racing. Sports Illus 18:7 Mr 11 '63
Young blood in a lively old tradition; harness racing of N. S. Woolworth. G. Holland. il Sports Illus 19:20-2+ Jl 15 '63
See also
Book making (betting)
Harness racing
Jockeys
Race tracks

Accidents and injuries
See Sports—Accidents and injuries

Caricatures and cartoons
Steinberg at the races. S. Steinberg. il Sports Illus 19:40-7 N 11 '63

HORSE shows
Blood in the ring again; American Royal in Kansas City. A. Higgins. Sports Illus 19:58 N 4 '63
Day the jumping stopped and the revolt began; Devon, on Pennsylvania main line. A. Higgins. Sports Illus 20:69-70+ Je 15 '64
Devon beat the virus and Kelley beat the band. A. Higgins. il Sports Illus 18:58-9 Je 17 '63
From the Near East to the Far West; Arabian horses popular in U.S. A. Higgins. Sports Illus 18:55 Mr 11 '63

HORSE shows—*Continued*
It was more than your money's worth; New York National horse show. A. Higgins. Sports Illus 19:92+ N 25 '63
Of horses and fashion plates; Dublin show with photographs by Slim Aarons. Holiday 33:64-9+ Ap '63
Over seventy-three fences; National horse show. il Newsweek 62:76 N 18 '63
Southwest horse spectacular; Scottsdale's All-Arabian horse show. J. T. Stark. il Look 27:44-9 O 8 '63
U.S. horse shows. J. H. Winchester. il Travel 120:34-6 S '63
Untouchable and inaudible; National horse show. A. Higgins. Sports Illus 21:86-7 N 23 '64

HORSE training
Continental touch of Senor Horatio Luro. A. Wright. il Sports Illus 20:33-5 My 4 '64
How to coax a horse aboard; entering a trailer. il Sunset 133:104 Jl '64
It's not a sport it's a business; horse racing. P. Ryan. il Sports Illus 20:41-3 Je 8 '64
Plotting revenge for Hoot Mon; to win the Hambletonian. K. Rudeen. il Sports Illus 18:80 My 20 '63
Very irreverent horse trainer. W. Leggett. il Sports Illus 18:42+ F 4 '63
See also
Horse racing

HORSEBACK riding. See Horsemanship

HORSEMANSHIP
Charge, Sir Knight! Maryland state jousting tournament. S. James. il Pop Mech 121:120-1 Mr '64
Come on, my beauty! equitation school. il Life 54:64A-66 My 10 '63
Horseback in the classroom; Foxcroft school. P. Downey. il Sports Illus 19:24-7 N 11 '63
Rampart of pedigree. H. Horn. il Sports Illus 18:62-70 F 11 '63
You've taught me more than any teacher; unique horse program of New Hampshire university. R. Hoffmann. il Mlle 59:134-7 O '64
See also
Polo
Rodeos

HORSEPOWER (mechanics)
Bolt on eighty horsepower. L. Smith. il Hot Rod 16:78-81 O '63
Where do all the horses go? A. Robertson. il Pop Sci 185:48-9+ Jl '64

HORSES
Admiral, the great Morgan horse. il Vogue 143:130-1 Je '64
Blood in the ring again; American Royal in Kansas City. A. Higgins. Sports Illus 19:58 N 4 '63
Dancer dazzles old Kentucky. W. Tower. il Sports Illus 20:22-7 My 11 '64
Derby favorite comes through a grim trial; Candy Spots at Santa Anita. W. Tower. il Sports Illus 18:18-20 Mr 11 '63
Derby star rises; rating the leading Kentucky Derby colts. W. Tower. il Sports Illus 20:16-19 Mr 9 '64
From the Near East to the Far West; Arabian horses popular in U.S. A. Higgins. Sports Illus 18:55 Mr 11 '63
Grass, alas; Kelso. Time 82:50+ N 22 '63
Here comes Ayres. Sports Illus 21:13 Jl 6 '64
He's a freak; Gun Bow. il Time 84:80 S 4 '64
Home on the range; wild horse range in southern Nevada. il Newsweek 62:30+ S 2 '63
Horse of a different color; rare white thoroughbreds are born in France and Kentucky. il Life 55:83-4+ N 15 '63
How the Indian got the horse. F. Haines. il Am Heritage 15:16-21+ F '64
How to keep racehorses in the running; patching cracked hoofs. S. V. Jones. il Sci Digest 55:50-1 Ap '64
Hunting horse. J. O'Connor. il Outdoor Life 132:43-7+ Jl '63
It's not a sport it's a business; horse racing. P. Ryan. il Sports Illus 20:41-3 Je 8 '64
Jack's back and so is Carry. W. Tower. Sports Illus 19:56 Ag 12 '63
Kelly the great; Kelso, U.S. horse of the year. il Newsweek 64:75-6 N 23 '64
Mike and Max; Arabian stallion owned by Mike Nichols. New Yorker 40:32-3 Ap 11 '64
Misters Big; favorites for the Kentucky Derby. il Time 81:78-9 Mr 15 '63
Move over Man o' War; Kelso top U.S. thoroughbred. W. Tower. il Sports Illus 19:36-8 N 11 '63
Moving toward a day in May; Kentucky Derby candidates: Candy Spots and Never Bend. il Sports Illus 18:18-19 Mr 4 '63
Prince of trotters. K. Rudeen. il Sports Illus 18:42+ My 13 '63
Quadrangle fits nicely in a racing oval; Derby threat to Hill Rise and Northern Dancer. W. Tower. il Sports Illus 20:66-8+ Ap 27 '64
Race track. A. Minor. See issues of New Yorker
Southwest horse spectacular; Scottsdale's All-Arabian horse show. J. T. Stark. il Look 27:44-9 O 8 '63
Sporting scene; Saratoga Springs, N.Y. R. Angell. New Yorker 40:185-8+ S 12 '64
Sweet talk about Candy Spots; possible Kentucky Derby winner. W. Tower. Sports Illus 18:55+ F 11 '63
Teen-age girls love horses, and what to do about it. il Changing T 17:45-7 N '63
Triumph for nonconformists; Garden state won by Sadair. W. Tower. il Sports Illus 21:28-9 N 23 '64
Two for the money; Northern Dancer at Preakness. il Time 83:85 My 22 '64
Two, four, six, eight, who do we depreciate? W. Tower. il Sports Illus 21:45-6 Ag 24 '64
Ugly iron duckling rides again: Kelso, the unlovely but durable Horse of the year; with report by M. Smith. il Life 55:126-7+ N 22 '63
Whoop-de-doo; Kelso. il Newsweek 62:94 N 4 '63
Worried man with a frightening filly. E. Havemann. il Sports Illus 19:16-17 Jl 22 '63
See also
Colts

Names

Big risk for pipe smokers; tobacco company's contest to name a two-year-old colt. E. Havemann. il Sports Illus 20:32-4+ Ap 13 '64

Photographs

See Animals—Photographs

Training

See Horse training

Transportation

Horse trailers. il Sunset 133:54-7 Jl '64

HORSES in art
Ornamental equines; with photographs from Appaloosa, the spotted horse in art and history. Natur Hist 73:26-33 F '64

HORSESHOE crabs. See King crabs

HORSESHOE pitching
High old fling at the national ringer derby; National horseshoe pitching championships. J. O'Reilly. il Sports Illus 19:56-60 S 16 '63

HORSESHOEING
Shoein' horses; a mighty man is he; training of farriers. W. B. Norse. il Am For 70:32-4 O '64

HORSFALL, William R. and Anderson, J. F.
Thermally induced genital appendages on mosquitoes. bibliog Science 141:1183-4 S 20 '63

HORST, Louis
Louis Horst, 1884-1964; excerpt from address. W. Sorell. Dance Mag 38:39 Mr '64

HORTICULTURAL exhibitions
Come to the flower show; report from Hamburg, Germany. H. S. Hull. il Flower Grower 50:37-9 Jl '63

HORTICULTURAL societies
Hortus club. New Yorker 38:24 F 2 '63
Members' news. See issues of Horticulture
See also
American rhododendron society

HORTICULTURE
Northern pointers. H. V. Wilson. See issues of Flower grower
Weather in the garden. R. D. Roe. il Horticulture 41:412-13 Ag '63
See also
Gardening

Bibliography

Books and reviews (cont of) New books. See issues of Horticulture
Garden reference books; analysis of the best of them. G. H. M. Lawrence. Horticulture 42:40-2 Ap '64
New books. See issues of Horticulture

HORTICULTURE (periodical)
Garden club yearbook winners! il Horticulture 42:26-7+ Ja '64

HORTMAN, Norman
Flying circus. New Yorker 40:20-2 Ag 29 '64

HORTON, B. M.
Probable energy control by fluids unveiled. Sci N L 85:403 Je 27 '64

HORTON, Douglas
Harvard dean's tribute; John XXIII. America 108:859-60 Je 15 '63

HORTON, Frank J.
Hoodlums on the loose; interview. por U S News 57:39-40 Ag 10 '64
HORTON, John P.
Street-cleaning revolution. bibliog Am City 78:106-8 Mr; 104-6 Ap '63
Sweepers whisk the snow away. Am City 79: 76-7 D '64
HORTON, Philip
After the test ban. Reporter 29:14+ Ag 15 '63
Our Yemen policy: pursuit of a mirage. Reporter 29:28-35 O 24 '63
HORWITZ, Julius
Grim state of welfare. Look 27:72+ Mr 26 '63
Our middle-class ghettos. Look 28:42-3+ Ja 14 '64
HOSE, Garden. See Garden hose
HOSHIZAKI, Takashi, and Hamner, K. C.
Circadian leaf movements: persistence in bean plants grown in continuous high-intensity light. Science 144:1240-1 Je 5 '64
HOSIERY
All about hosiery. il Redbook 123:74-5+ S '64
Crazy legs; or, The biography of a fashion. G. Steinem. il N Y Times Mag p58+ N 8 '64
Lure of lacy legs. il Life 56:80-1+ F 28 '64
Merry legs; festooned Christmas stockings. il Ladies Home J 81:72-3 N '64
Motties of perfection; textured stockings. il Time 85:31 Ja 8 '65
Nylon faces challenger. Bsns W p31 O 3 '64
Stocking story. il Ebony 19:113-14+ Ag '64
Surgical stockings stride into fashion. il Bsns W p96 Je 27 '64
Vogue's eye view: the greatest legs. il Vogue 144:53-9 Ag 15 '64
What's so special about support stockings? il Good H 157:144 Ag '63

Testing

How long may nylon hose last? il Consumer Bul 46:17 Ap '63
HOSIERY supporters. See Garters
HOSKINS, Fred
Announcement. Christian Cent 81:134, 358 Ja 29, Mr 18 '64

about

Hoskins returns to parish ministry. Christian Cent 81:391 Mr 25 '64
HOSKINS, Katherine
Out of environment; Explication de texte; Now plus then; poems. Poetry 103:289-91 F '64
Wedding in the country; Byfield rabbit; In praise; Life of action; Education; poems. Yale R 53:76-84 O '63
HOSLEY, Eleanor M.
Part-time care: the day-care problem. Ann Am Acad 355:56-61 S '64
HöSLI, L. See Monnier, M. jt. auth.
HOSMER, Craig
Excerpt from address, March 10, 1964. Cong Digest 43:203+ Ag '64
Speaking out. por Sat Eve Post 236:10+ S 7 '63
HOSMER, Harriet
Harriet Hosmer. S. Van Rensselaer. il por Antiques 84:424-8 O '63
HOSPICE of St Bernard
Tunnel under the Alps. R. Gelatt. Reporter 28:38 Ap 11 '63
HOSPITAL bills. See Billing
HOSPITAL care
Why can't mothers stay in hospitals with their children? N. Wessel and N. Simon. il Redbook 121:41+ Ag '63
HOSPITAL libraries. See Libraries, Hospital
HOSPITAL nursing. See Nurses and nursing
HOSPITAL patients. See Sick, The
HOSPITAL recreation work. See Recreation therapy
HOSPITAL service, Cost of. See Medical service, Cost of
HOSPITAL service, State. See Medical service, State
HOSPITAL ships
Ship of hope. R. L. Tobin. Sat R 47:18 Mr 28 '64
Ship of hope; American hospital ship Hope. R. L. White. il Todays Health 41:62-7 Jl '63
S.S. Hope for the world. il Parents Mag 38: 86-7 O '63
HOSPITAL visiting. See Hospitals—Visitors
HOSPITAL workers. See Hospitals—Employees
HOSPITALITY
How to put the gracious gloss on hospitality. M. Gough. il House B 105:96-7+ Jl '63
Who stole the welcome mat? J. L. O'Neill. Am Home 67:9 Je '64
See also
Guests
HOSPITALITY of the house; story. See Disney, D. M.
HOSPITALIZATION insurance. See Insurance, Hospitalization
HOSPITALS
Hospitals worry patients. F. Marley. Sci N L 84:151 S 7 '63
Truth about medication errors in hospitals. W. B. Furlong. il Good H 157:76-7+ N '63

Architecture

Building types study (cont) il Arch Rec 134: 161-84 N '63; 135:192-9+ Ap; 136:177-96 O '64
Computer-aided hospital planning. il Arch Rec 135:90-1+ Mr '64
Hospitals; symposium. il Arch Rec 133:179-202 Mr '63
Hospitals: the race with change. R. A. Miller. il Arch Forum 120:80-9 Ap '64
Then the bricks came tumbling down; Boston's Veterans administration hospital. Time 83:24 F 7 '64

Childrens wards

Children's pavilion in the round. il Arch Rec 136:187 O '64
High-rise for research in pediatrics. il Arch Rec 136:194-6 O '64
New kind of hospital; Hopkins children's center. il Time 83:81 My 22 '64

Emergency rooms

Hospitals; boom in emergency rooms. Time 82:33-4 Ag 16 '63

Employees

Hospital workers. Commonweal 77:656-7 Mr 22 '63
Social structure of a general hospital. R. N. Wilson. bibliog f Ann Am Acad 346:67-76 Mr '63
See also
Hospitals—Wages and hours

Equipment and supplies

Disposable hospital; inexpensive equipment which can be burned. il Newsweek 62:57 S 2 '63
Electronics: new force in hospital design. J. Falick. il Arch Forum 120:90-1 Ap '64
ICU, newest thing in nursing; Intensive care units. W. Langewiesche. il Read Digest 85:208-10+ N '64
Lighting hospital patient rooms; excerpts from Lighting for hospital patient rooms, study by U.S. Public health service. Arch Rec 134:192-3 N '63
Planning Holy Cross for effective hospital care. J. L. Ryan. il Arch Rec 133:184-9 Mr '63

Federal aid

Congress and construction: aid to housing, hospitals and poverty. Arch Rec 136:23+ O '64
Latest target for integration: private hospitals. U S News 56:6 Mr 16 '64
Private, but public; question of federal aid to segregated institutions. Time 83:52 Mr 13 '64

Home care program

Hospital care goes home. I. J. Rossman. Parents Mag 38:135+ D '63
Two-level clinic for community service. il Arch Rec 135:204-5 Ap '64

Hygiene

Environmental control in hospital design. A. Greenberg. il Arch Rec 136:202-6 O '64
Keeping hospital clean. Sci N L 86:237 O 10 '64
New technology includes cobalt-60, and superclean surgeries. il Arch Rec 133:190-2 Mr '63
Operating room ventilation evaluated. T. W. Kethley and others. bibliog il Arch Rec 133: 204-8 Mr '63
Staphylococcus aureus UC-18: agent of nosocomial infections. R. B. Kundsin and others. Science 145:1322-3 S 18 '64

Laboratories

Danger in our medical labs. M. Pines. Harper 227:84-7+ O '63

Management and regulation

Automatic care; Atomedic hospital in Montgomery, Ala. il Newsweek 62:87 D 16 '63

HOSPITALS—Management and regulation—*Continued*
Coming scandal in nursing; ed. by N. G. Stuart. E. A. Aynes. il McCalls 91:100-1+ Mr '64
Hospital design and function; excerpts. E. T. Wheeler. il Arch Rec 136:178-80 O '64
Hospitals get a new specialist. il Bsns W p70+ O 10 '64
Meeting patients' psychosocial needs in the general hospital. E. L. Brown. Ann Am Acad 346:117-25 Mr '63
Pre-packaged hospital; Atomedic hospital, Montgomery, Ala. il Sci Digest 55:84-5 F '64
Progressive patient care, all five elements in one hospital. il Arch Rec 133:193-5 Mr '63
Social structure of a general hospital. R. N. Wilson. bibliog f Ann Am Acad 346:67-76 Mr '63

Nurses homes

See Nurses homes

Operating rooms

Helpful humidity: germs in the operating room's air. Time 82:44+ Ag 23 '63
Operating room ventilation evaluated. T. W. Kethley and others. bibliog il Arch Rec 133:204-8 Mr '63
Operating rooms in the round; Clinical center in Bethesda, Md. il Time 82:84 S 13 '63
Surgeon's dream room; new wing at the research hospital of the National institutes of health at Bethesda, Md. il Life 55:93-4+ D 6 '63
See also
High-pressure oxygenation

Psychiatric service

County hospital programed for service. il Arch Rec 134:168-9 N '63
Psychiatric clinic for a general hospital. il Arch Rec 134:182-4 N '63

Standards

Way to contribute to good medical care. Consumer Rep 29:519 N '64

Visitors

Illness in the family. L. Strong. il N Y Times Mag p67 Ag 18 '63

Volunteer workers

Where a friend counts most. M. K. Cole. Farm J 88:84 My '64

Wages and hours

Earnings in hospitals in mid-1963. G. L. Stelluto. bibliog f il Mo Labor R 87:552-5 My '64

Great Britain

Weaknesses of the National health service. J. Reckless. bibliog f Cur Hist 45:34-40 Jl '63

Hong Kong

Hong Kong doctor with 1,000 patients; Our Lady of Maryknoll hospital in Hong Kong. C. Morrison. il Look 28:24-9 Je 16 '64

India

Note about Vellore. J. K. G. Webb. Sat R 47:22 O 3 '64
Paul Brand and his mission: healing and the pursuit of pain at a hospital in India. N. Cousins. il Sat R 47:21-3+ O 3 '64; Reply. P. W. Brand. 47:25 N 21 '64

United States

Challenge to our doctors. J. R. Moskin. il Look 28:26-38+ N 3 '64; Discussion. 28:6+ D 15 '64
Church strives to keep hospitals open. Christian Cent 80:854 Jl 3 '63
Expansible regional hospital; New Hanover memorial hospital, Wilmington, N.C. il Arch Rec 136:192-3 O '64
Hospital construction: very healthy. H. C. F. Arnold. il Arch Rec 135:26 Ap '64
Hospital hospitality. il Newsweek 63:106 Mr 16 '64
Medical care in the U.S. O. L. Peterson. il Sci Am 209:19-27 bibliog(p 140) Ag '63
Segregated sickness; Catholic hospitals. J. Leo. Commonweal 81:406-7 D 18 '64
Speaking out; hospital rivalry costs you money. G. R. Metcalf. Sat Eve Post 236:12+ O 19 '63
Way to contribute to good medical care. Consumer Rep 29:519 N '64
Whadda ya mean, hospital? H. E. Klarman. il New Repub 149:9-12 N 9 '63
See also
United States—Veterans administration hospitals
also subhead Hospitals under names of cities, e.g. Los Angeles—Hospitals

HOSPITALS, Prefabricated
Prefabricated aluminum hospital flown to World's fair; Atomedic hospital. il Pop Sci 184:79 Mr '64

HOSPITALS, Psychiatric
Check list of spaces for a community mental health center; comp. by the Architectural and engineering branch, Division of hospital and medical facilities, U.S. Public health service. Arch Rec 134:196 N '63
Current trends in construction. H. C. F. Arnold. il Arch Rec 134:18 N '63
Dial a psychiatrist. R. P. Goldman. il Sat Eve Post 236:41-2 N 23 '63
Geriatrics building for a mental hospital. il Arch Rec 135:192-3 Ap '64
How we can eliminate our overcrowded state mental hospitals. A. Q. Maisel. Read Digest 83:59-63 Ag '63
Institutional peonage; our exploitation of mental patients. F. L. Bartlett. Atlan 214:116-19 Jl '64
Mental hospitals. W. B. Foxhall. Arch Rec 134:161 N '63
Out of the snake pits. il Time 81:82 Ap 5 '63
Psychiatry; a stay at the Institute of living. il Sci Digest 55:25-7 Je '64
Unlocking our mental hospitals. J. Star. il Look 27:34-6+ F 26 '63
See also
Mentally ill—Care and treatment

HOSS, Virgil L.
Get 'em while they're cold. por Outdoor Life 131:70-1+ Je '63
Gold for fishermen. pors Outdoor Life 133:54-7+ Ap '64

HOSTAGES
Agonizing choice; 1,000 white civilians held by Congo rebels. il Newsweek 64:58 N 30 '64
Another nasty stunt; kidnaping of U.S. colonel by Venezuela's F.A.L.N. il Time 84:54 O 16 '64
Captives in the hills. il Time 82:26-7 D 20 '63
Four American hostages released by Bolivian miners; Department statement, December 16, 1963. Dept State Bul 50:9 Ja 6 '64
Free at last; American hostages in Bolivia. il Time 82:29 D 27 '63
Hostages. il Time 84:36 N 27 '64
Hostages of a mob of miners; with report by M. Acoca. il Life 56:62-6 Ja 3 '64
No apologies; Congo rescue mission; excerpts from address, 1964. A. Stevenson. Sr Schol 85:18-19 Ja 7 '65
Rebellion in the Congo; with 1,000 whites as hostages. il U S News 57:11 N 30 '64
U.S. informs U.N. of withdrawal of Congo rescue mission; text of letter to the president of the Security council, December 1, 1964. A. E. Stevenson. Dept State Bul 51:891 D 21 '64
Walking out; release of American hostages in Bolivia. Newsweek 62:31 D 30 '63

HOSTAS. See Plantain lilies

HOSTELS. See Youth hostels

HOSTESSES, Air. See Airlines—Hostesses

HOSTETTER, Anita
Anita Hostetter. F. F. Morton. por ALA Bul 57:854-5 O '63

HOSTICK, King V.
Autographs. See issues of Hobbies
(ed) Autographs. See issues of Hobbies

HOT-air balloons. See Balloons

HOT chocolate, stiff collar; story. See Salsamendi, A.

HOT dogs (meat) See Frankfurters

HOT line (Washington and Moscow)
Department notes anniversary of hot line agreement; Department statement, August 29, 1964. Dept State Bul 51:369 S 14 '64
Hot line release? Sr Schol 83:20 D 13 '63
Hot line to Moscow: how it will work. il U S News 55:8 Jl 1 '63
Open wire to Kremlin. il Bsns W p36 Je 29 '63
Signals & feedback in the arms dialogue. T. C. Schelling. Bul Atomic Sci 21:5-10 Ja '65
U.S.—Russian hot line agreement. Cur Hist 45:178-9+ S '63

HOT rod (periodical)
Hot rod gets a spark plug. il Hot Rod 16:24 Jl '63

HOT rod clubs. See Automobile clubs

HOT rod racing. See Automobile racing

HOT spot; musical comedy. See Musical comedies, revues, etc.—Criticisms, plots, etc.

HOT SPRINGS, Ark.
No more alligator shoes; casinos closed down. il Newsweek 63:102 Ap 20 '64
Notes for a gazetteer. P. Hamburger. il New Yorker 40:170+ N 7 '64

HOT Springs, Ark.—*Continued*
Showdown in Arkansas: no dice in Hot Springs. J. Skow. il Sat Eve Post 237:78-9 S 19 '64
Sixty-five miles from home. Nation 198:282 Mr 23 '64

HOT springs
Little "hells" around Beppu on Japan's Inland Sea. il Sunset 131:110-11 O '63
Vandalism in Yellowstone Park. R. W. Witzke. il Nat Parks Mag 38:13-15+ F '64

HOT water supply
Does your house have enough hot water? R. Charles. il Parents Mag 39:66-7+ Ja '64
See also
Water heaters

HOT water tanks. See Water heaters

HOT weather
Beat the heat. il Suc Farm 61:55 Ag '63
Heat's off summer cooking. il Ladies Home J 80:88-90+ Jl '63
If summer poohs you out. il Changing T 17:23-4 Ag '63
Keeping cool in summer heat. il Sci N L 86:10-11 Jl 4 '64
Nine ways to beat the heat. W. R. Vath. Read Digest 83:152-3 Jl '63
Worst U.S. heat waves in 1930's and 1950's. Sci N L 84:72 Ag 3 '63

HOT weather menus. See Menus

HOTBEDS
Practical hotbed. C. O. Dean. Horticulture 42:12 F '64
See also
Cold frames

HOTCHKISS, Christine
U.S. navy conquers Holy Loch. Read Digest 83:114-18 Jl '63
(ed) See Wyszynski, S. Ask Americans to pray for us

HOTCHNER, A. E.
White House. Criticism
New Yorker 40:78+ My 30 '64
Time il 83:49 My 29 '64

HOTEL architecture. See Hotels, taverns, etc.

HOTEL decoration
Art collection commissioned for New York Hilton. il Arch Rec 133:106 F '63
Art for the New York Hilton. B. H. Friedman. il Craft Horiz 23:8-15+ Jl '63
What housekeepers can learn from hotelkeepers. P. Hyde. il House B 106:130-3 Mr '64

HÔTEL de la Côte d'or, Saulieu. See Restaurants—France

HOTEL Dixie. See New York (city)—Hotels, restaurants, etc.

HOTEL management
Running hotels with a loose rein; Western hotels chain. il Bsns W p92+ F 23 '63

Study and teaching

Food expert teaches at Cornell. il Ebony 18:73-4+ Ag '63
Short course in perfection; Professional school of the Swiss hotelkeepers' association. R. Joseph. il Esquire 60:100-2 Jl '63

HOTEL Santa Claus; drama. See Miller, H. L.

HOTELS, taverns, etc.
By golly! Hilton chain. il Time 82:66-8+ Jl 19 '63
Capsule history of American hotels. A. L. Todd. Holiday 33:54-5 F '63
Cesar Balsa: a thousand keys to his kingdom. R. Joseph. il Esquire 59:118-20 Mr '63
Check-out time; gradual shift in tastes of hotel guests. il Newsweek 64:74-5 S 21 '64
Chic U.S. resorts. J. Gaylor. il Travel 120:44-9 N '63
Culture of the non-hotel. J. Morgenstern. Horizon 5:115-17 Mr '63
Ebony's annual vacation guide. il Ebony 18:132-3 Je '63
Famous firsts: Shangri-la of the tycoon era; Yama-no-uchi in the southern Catskills. il Bsns W p 142-4 O 3 '64
Famous hotel now college dorm. W. V. Rakestraw. il Negro Hist Bul 27:140-1 Mr '64
Hosts to the new travel host. I. Wolfert. il Travel 120:50-2+ S '63; Same abr. with title Around the world with the bedroom builders. Read Digest 83:173-6+ S '63
Hotel headliners. See issues of Travel
Hotels I have known. F. Sparks. il Sat R 47:39-40+ Ja 4 '64
Hotels: time to stop and rest. S. Freedgood. il Fortune 68:162-5+ Jl '63
In nineteen lands instant America. D. J. Hamblin. il Life 55:67-8+ Ag 30 '63
Inns are out for travel dollar. il Newsweek 61:79-81 Je 17 '63
Lowdown on the high hotel business. A. Herzog. il N Y Times Mag p 18+ Je 23 '63
Miniature hotels in the sky. B. Hackett. il Recreation 56:269-70 Je '63
New good moves for travellers. Vogue 143:8 Ja 15 '64
New good moves for travellers; Florida's Lucayan Beach and Irish château hotel. Vogue 143:24 Mr 15 '64
New good moves for travellers in the U.S.A. Vogue 143:68+ F 1 '64
New Hampshire: a late-summering guide. Vogue 142:133 S 1 '63
Paradise Valley hotel. P. M. Tilden. Nat Parks Mag 38:2 Mr '64
Personal business; top-ranking summer hotels. Bsns W p91-2 Je 1 '63
Place to leave the kids; hotels for children. il Time 84:75 D 11 '64
Retirement hotels. N. D. Ford. il Travel 119:36-40 Ap '63
That old hotel in Paradise; hotel operations in Paradise Valley, Wash. L. Gallagher. il Nat Parks Mag 38:4-7 Ja '64
Where the water is safe; luxury hotels throughout the world. il Time 81:97 Ap 5 '63
Will there be tourists to keep them all full? U.S.-international hotels around the world. il Bsns W p 108+ N 2 '63
See also
Apartment hotels
Hilton hotels corporation
Hotel decoration
Motels
Restaurants
Sheraton corporation of America
Western hotels, incorporated
also subhead Hotels, restaurants, etc. under names of cities, e.g. New York (city)—Hotels, restaurants, etc.

Designs and plans

Grand hotel, new version; New York Hilton. il Arch Rec 134:153-60 N '63
Hanging gardens on the rocks in Hawaii; Sheraton Maui hotel. il Arch Rec 135:149-54 Mr '64
Hotels; symposium. il Arch Rec 136:165-76 O '64

Drive-in and curb services

See Drive-in and curb services

Employees

Brotherhood of the Golden keys; concierge, major-domo of the European hotel. G. Kent. il Read Digest 84:151-2+ Ja '64
Wages in hotels and motels, June 1963. F. W. Mohr. il Mo Labor R 87:549-51 My '64

Finance

Not enough guests to go around. il Bsns W p65-6+ S 14 '63

Inspection

Inspector. New Yorker 39:18-19 Ag 24 '63

Bahama Islands

Travel notes. R. Joseph. Esquire 62:26+ O '64

Barbados

Resort hotel forms own environment. il Arch Rec 136:168-9 O '64

Bermuda

Travel notes. R. Joseph. Esquire 61:31+ Ap '64

England

Inn for all seasons. H. Innes. il Holiday 36:60-5+ S '64
Tranquillity and warm beer. G. Thomas. il Holiday 35:80-1+ My '64

Europe, Western

Amusing logistics of a double Hilton opening: London and Athens. D. Messinesi. il Vogue 142:108+ S 1 '63
Brotherhood of the Golden keys; concierge, major-domo of the European hotel. G. Kent. il Read Digest 84:151-2+ Ja '64
Europe for people who hate tourists. R. Joseph. il Esquire 59:68-77+ F '63
Fit for a king; castles as inns. il Time 81:54 Je 28 '63
Live like a king in a castle. L. Lawrence. il Read Digest 83:158-63 Jl '63
Lovely lodgings, low-priced. N. Buxton. Mlle 56:205+ Mr '63
Quest for the best hotel in the world. J. Wechsberg. il N Y Times Mag p97+ Ap 7 '63
Velvet Europe. F. Morton. il Holiday 33:58-71+ My '63

France

Baron Edmond de Rothschild's party; Mont d'Arbois hotel above Mégève. F. de Langlade. il Vogue 141:162-5 Mr 15 '63

HOTELS, taverns, etc.—France—*Continued*
Going places, finding things in the Relais de Campagne; excerpts from France personal. N. Barry. il House & Gard 125:52+ My '64
Night at Longjumeau. C. W. Morton. il Atlan 213:116+ F '64
Plus ça change. . . Guide Michelin and Hôtel de la Côte-d'or. Newsweek 63:69 Mr 30 '64
Star boarding in the French provinces. J. Egan. Atlan 211:100+ Ap '63

Germany (Federal Republic)

In Germany's castle-hotels. il Sunset 132:41+ Mr '64

Great Britain

Let's travel to Europe. il Mlle 57:156-8 O '63

Anecdotes, facetiae, satire, etc.

Stilly night in rural Britain. C. W. Morton. il Atlan 214:165-6 N '64

Greece, Modern

Tourist hotel on an ancient coast. il Arch Rec 136:170-1 O '64
See also
Athens, Greece—Hotels, restaurants, etc.

Hawaii

Hawaiian hotel opens to landscape. il Arch Rec 136:174-5 O '64

Hong Kong

Royal debut for hotel; Hong Kong's new Mandarin. il Bsns W p 104-6 N 2 '63

Ireland

Irish hotels. R. Postgate. Holiday 33:154 Ap '63

Japan

Spectacular playground in Tokyo's backyard. il Sports Illus 21:20-5 Ag 31 '64

Korea (Republic)

$5,000,000 bingo parlor; Walker hill. il Time 81:46 Ap 19 '63

Rumania

Place to sleep in Romania. G. Bailey. Reporter 31:33-4 N 5 '64

Switzerland

Sportier tune for the yodel. il Bsns W p32-3 Ag 29 '64
Swiss incidentals: the high points. Vogue 142: 84+ O 1 '63

HOTH, William E.
What programming can do for English. Sr Schol 84:14T Mr 13 '64

HOTHEM, Larry
Boomer of the bird world. Field & S 69: 59+ My '64

HOTHOUSES. See Greenhouses

HOUCK, Carter
How to get the most from your sewing machine. por Parents Mag 40:16 Ja '65

HOUDON, Jean Antoine
Cult of personality; exhibition at Worcester, Mass. art museum. il Newsweek 63:76 F 3 '64
Honest chiseler. il Time 83:44 Ja 31 '64
Houdon's Americans reunited. il Art N 62:28 Ja '64
Living faces of our past. il por Life 57:72-8 Jl 3 '64

HOUGH, Cass Sheffield
Rifle called Daisy. J. D. Brown. il por Sports Illus 18:58-64+ Ap 29 '63

HOUGH, Jerry A.
Stalin-Trotsky split: a lesson for Kremlinologists. Reporter 29:37-9 D 5 '63

HOUGHTON, Amory, Jr
Houghton of Corning glass. por Fortune 69: 39 Je '64

HOUGHTON, Arthur Amory, 1906-
Custodian of continuity. Newsweek 64:89 S 28 '64
Metropolitan president. New Yorker 40:25-6 Ja 16 '65

HOUGHTON, Ev
Want to write? get a camera. Writer 76:26-7 Jl '63

HOUGHTON, Norris
Spotlight on the stage critic. Sat R 47:44-5 O 10 '64

HOUGHTON library. See Harvard university—Libraries

HOUK, Ralph
Man in the pin-striped suit: Ralph Houk. E. Linn. il pors Sat Eve Post 236:89-93 S 28 '63

HOULIHAN, H. Joseph
ABC's of stocking the bookstore. Pub W 186: 55-60 Jl 27 '64

HOULTON, William
Shakespeare year. NEA J 53:60-2 F '64

HOUNDS
Coon fever, our favorite epidemic. S. James. il Pop Mech 119:117-20+ F '63
Handy hounds. D. M. Duffey. il Outdoor Life 132:116-18+ N '63
See also
Basset hounds
Beagles (dogs)

HOUNDS of summer; story. See McCarthy, M.

HOUPHOUET-BOIGNY, Félix
Ivory Coast, Africa's big success story. D. Reed. il por Read Digest 86:107-12 Ja '65
Juju justice. il por Time 83:35 Ap 24 '64

HOURANI, Albert
Near Eastern nationalism yesterday and today. For Affairs 42:123-36 O '63

HOURMOUSIADES, Kriton
(tr) See Vassilikos, V. Letter from Athens

HOURS, Books of
Dutch master in New York; exhibition of the Book of hours of Catherine of Cleves at Morgan library. il Art N 63:44-5+ S '64
Golden almanac; Book of hours for Catherine of Cleves bought by Pierpont Morgan library. il Time 84:40-4 D 25 '64
Treasure of 15th century manuscript bookmaking; Hours of Catherine of Cleves. il Pub W 186:94-6 O 5 '64

HOURS of labor
Earnings and hours; tables. See issues of Monthly labor review
Four days shalt thou labor? E. T. Chase. il N Y Times Mag p28+ S 20 '64
Hours of work in the United States and abroad. il Mo Labor R 86:925-34 Ag '63
Japanese workers protest. America 109:445 O 19 '63
Labor shudders at leisure. D. Wakefield. Nation 196:325-7 Ap 20 '63; Discussion. 196:inside cover My 11; inside cover My 18 '63
Making jobs for the jobless. B. L. Masse. America 110:362-4 Mr 21 '64
Must we push up costs? H. Hazlitt. Newsweek 63:67 F 3 '64
New union drive for thirty-five hour week. U S News 54:97 Mr 11 '63
Plan for a flexible work week; thirty-five hour week at forty hours' pay. Bsns W p27 Mr 2 '63
Shorter week by year 2000? excerpts from news conference, October 9, 1963. J. F. Kennedy. U S News 55:115 O 21 '63
Shorter workweek. J. C. Rothwell. il Nation 197:382-7 D 7 '63
Spare time? what spare time? il Changing T 18:18-20 My '64
That twenty-five-hour week. Newsweek 61: 81+ My 27 '63
Thirty-five hour week. New Repub 149:5 N 30 '63; Reply with rejoinder. D. Rader. 149:31 D 28 '63
Thirty-five hour week: how soon? il U S News 55:84-5 O 28 '63
Union agenda for security. J. Seidman. Mo Labor R 86:636-44 Je '63
Why the twenty-five hour week hasn't caught on; New York electricians' special situation. il Bsns W p90+ Jl 6 '63
See also
Night work
Overtime
Rest periods
Retail workers—Wages and hours
Vacations, Employee

HOUSE, Edward Mandell
Memorandum: January 5, 1938. pors Am Heritage 14:6-9+ Ag '63

about

Colonel's folly and the President's distress; with editorial comment. G. T. Grayson. il por Am Heritage 15:4-7+ O '64
End of a friendship; with memorandum by E. M. House. C. Seymour. il pors Am Heritage 14:4-9+ Ag '63

HOUSE, Robert J.
Management development is a game. bibliog f Harvard Bsns R 41:130-43 Jl '63

HOUSE administration committee. See United States—Congress—House of representatives—Committees

HOUSE appropriations committee. See United States—Congress—House of representatives—Committees

HOUSE armed services committee. See United States—Congress—House of representative—Committees

HOUSE banking and currency committee. See United States—Congress—House of representatives—Committee
HOUSE boats
Captain Handy; cruising houseboat of rugged Maine-fisherman construction. il Yachting 116:52+ D '64
Family holiday in a rented houseboat. il Sunset 130:78+ Mr '63
Greenhouseboat; a new term in naval architecture. il Sunset 133:64-5 S '64
Honeymoon on a houseboat. il Motor B 112: 46-7 S '63
Houseboat heyday. F. M. Paulson. il Field & S 69:124-7+ My '64
Houseboat in the Everglades. M. Hunn. il Motor B 114:33-5+ N '64
Houseboats 64-65. il Motor B 113:184 Ja '64; 115:152-3 Ja '65
John's other wife; a home-built houseboat. J. Gale. il Motor B 111:45-6+ F '63
Lazy, lovely life on the Pride of Kashmir. M. Leatherbee. il Life 57:95+ Ag 14 '64
'Ousebot, a 24-foot fantasy. il Motor B 111: 86+ F '63
Suburban houseboat. il Holiday 35:88-9 F '64
HOUSE building. See Building
HOUSE building materials. See Building materials
HOUSE buying. See Home ownership
HOUSE cleaning
Better safe than sorry. Am Home 66:81 My '63
For beauty at your windows. House & Gard 123:198 Ap '63
House cleaners to the rescue. S. Schuler. Am Home 67:102+ Ja '64
Housecleaning: modern story. il McCalls 90: 122-3+ Ap '63
How to edit clutter. House & Gard 123:123 Ap '63
How to get your house clean as a whistle. House & Gard 126:35+ S '64
Redbook's guide to easier housecleaning. R. M. Burnley. il Redbook 123:81-8 My '64
Whatever happened to housecleaning? symposium. House B 106:119-53+ Mr '64
HOUSE committee on un-American activities. See United States—Congress—House of representatives—Committees
HOUSE crickets. See Crickets
HOUSE decoration
Add-on house. il Ladies Home J 80:55-61+ My '63
And inside, great decorating! N. Seney. il Bet Hom & Gard 42:44-9 Mr '64
Art of assemblage; fine furnishings collected by V. Skrebneski. G. O'Brien. il N Y Times Mag p36-7 Jl 26 '64
At home through the ages; excerpts from Les styles. P. Julian. il Horizon 5:80-3 Mr '63
At the Calders. F. Du Plessix. il House & Gard 124:154-9+ D '63
Best of two worlds. B. Reynolds. il Suc Farm 61:84-5+ F '63
Big and old and just right for us. D. Zork. il Am Home 67:38-41 Je '64
Buyable pleasures to bring summer indoors. il House & Gard 125:130-1 Je '64
Claudette Colbert's other home in the sun. il House B 106:98-101 Ja '64
Color from your garden brightens the indoors. J. J. Simpkins. il Flower Grower 50:71 Ag '63
Come into the house, into the sun, and stay cool. il House B 106:114-23+ F '64
Comfort for a man. F. Byerly. il Bet Hom & Gard 41:46-51 Mr '63
Compositions in white. G. O'Brien. il N Y Times Mag p36-7 Je 21 '64
Decorating clinic. il Bet Hom & Gard 41:66-7 F; 82 My; 66-7 Je '63; 42:22 F '64
Decorating newsletter. V. D. Hahn. Am Home 68:38 Ja '65
Decorating pep ups for fall. Am Home 66:84-5+ O '63
Decorating with unusual fabrics. Good H 157:153 S '63
Decorating wrongs made right. il Bet Hom & Gard 42:124 Mr; 38 Je '64
Decorator's diary. See issues of House beautiful
Doing it better. D. X. Manners. il House B 105:60+ My '63
Dramatic decorating: you can make it happen to any room! il Bet Hom & Gard 42:56-65 N '64
Enjoy your treasures. R. Martens. il Farm J 88:80-1+ My '64
Fill the house with lively fabric. il Am Home 67:50-3 Ja '64
Foolproof decorating for beginners. il McCalls 92:120-7 O '64
Four ways to stretch your decorating dollars. il House & Gard 125:144-55 My '64
Fourteen ways to add spring to your home. il Pop Mech 121:134-48 Ap '64
Fresh currents of change. il House & Gard 125:78-83 Ja '64
Furniture with the sweet taste of variety. F. Heard. il House B 105:158-61+ Ap '63
Garden in the house. G. O'Brien. il N Y Times Mag p 104-5+ Ap 14 '63
George Washington slept here; but you sleep here. il McCalls 91:130-7+ Ap '64
Get a decorating jump on spring. Am Home 66:22-3 Mr '63
Good decorating brings a new sparkle to an ordinary house. R. W. Houseman. il Am Home 66:38-41 Je '63
Green brick front, green woods behind. il House & Gard 123:142-7+ My '63
Hallers make a house come alive! E. Gilrain. il Bet Home & Gard 41:48-51 My '63
Harvest of ideas you can emulate wherever you live. il House & Gard 126:84-93 Jl '64
Here is more of today's great decorating. il Bet Hom & Gard 42:50-7 Mr '64
Here's a house that's practically maintenance-free! J. D. Bloodgood. il Bet Hom & Gard 42:66-71 N '64
Hold the phone! il McCalls 90:90-3 My '63
Homes are for children and parents! il Am Home 67:35-49 S '64
H&G's house of ideas for 1963-1964. il House & Gard 124:81-117 Ag '63; 126:73-107, 138-9 Ag '64
House for all seasons. il House & Gard 125: 98-109+ F '64
How a diversified harvest of antiques was united by a background. il House & Gard 123:162-5 My '63
How to design a second way of living; part-time homes. il House & Gard 123:91-9 Je '63
How to find beauty in the junkyard. il House B 106:166-9 Mr '64
How to make a little house feel big. il House & Gard 126:80-3 Jl '64
How to make an old house look as fresh as tomorrow. il House & Gard 123:134-41 My '63
If you can't build in, build out! il Am Home 66:48-53 Ap '63
Imagination plus! il Am Home 67:46-9 Ap '64
Inside story of San Francisco. C. Kellogg. il Ladies Home J 80:62-5 Je '63
Living on three levels. il Good H 157:115-24 S '63
Living with antiques: Hacienda, Florida residence of H. R. Sharp. J. A. L. Hyde. il Antiques 85:76-9 Ja '64
MacNeils tackle another house. H. Stark. il Bet Hom & Gard 41:54-7 My '63
Made to your order. il House & Gard 126: 168-79 O '64
Make your farm home suit you! J. Holmstrand. il Suc Farm 63:88-9 Ja '65
Man's home as his lab. R. Reif. il N Y Times Mag p96-7 O 20 '63
Man's idea of comfort married to a woman's idea of beauty; Gardner Cowles' New York city apartment. il House & Gard 124:70-5 Jl '63
Mrs Guest and Monsieur Boudin. il Vogue 141:148-9+ Ap 1 '63
My favorite things: excerpts. D. Rodgers. il McCalls 91:120-5 My; 60+ Je; 102-3+ Jl '64
New again kitchens; How to remodel your kitchen beautifully. il McCalls 90:148-50+ F '63
New beauty of architectural decorating. R. W. Houseman. il Am Home 66:42-7 My '63
100 ideas under $100. il Bet Hom & Gard 41: 10+ Jl '63; 42:28-59 Jl '64
Paint happy. il McCalls 90:88-95 Mr '63
Personal taste, the great blender. il House & Gard 124:218-23 N '63
Precious beauty, unprecious stones; use of rocks in decoration. il McCalls 90:92-5 Ap '63
Ready-mades rate you an A. R. W. Houseman. il Am Home 67:46-9 Mr '64
Room without a view. il Am Home 66:46-9 Ja '63
Scene changers. il House & Gard 125:92-101 Je '64
Set to music; home of E. Leinsdorf. il McCalls 91:88-93 Mr '64
Seven smart ideas for your home. il Pop Sci 185:124-5 S '64
Six big ideas for your home. il Pop Sci 183: 124-5 S '63
Speaker nobody sees. il House & Gard 125: 166-7 My '64
Speaker of the house; your personality; excerpts from Profession: housewife. P. McGinley. Ladies Home J 81:30+ My '64

HOUSE decoration—*Continued*
Spring is a good idea; freshen up your home, inside and out. il Bet Hom & Gard 42:50-77+ Ap '64
Subject is privacy. il Am Home 67:43-9 O '64
Take a small piece of fabric. il Am Home 66:12 N '63
Taste of tradition. il McCalls 90:114-21 Ap '63
Ten rooms designed to keep themselves clean. P. Doherty and A. Wiglama. il House B 106:136-44 Mr '64
They don't make décor that way any more. R. P. Smith. il McCalls 90:61 Je '63
Three French kings helped to remodel a stable-garage. il House & Gard 123:106-11 F '63
Three World's fair houses! P. Lindberg. il Bet Hom & Gard 42:48-65 S '64
Tough decorating problems solved! F. Byerly. il Bet Hom & Gard 41:32-41 Ag '63
Turn ready-mades into made-to-order with borders. F. Heard. il House B 105:80-5 Jl '63
Twenty-one week-end specials for home remodelers. il Pop Mech 120:124-37 S '63
What's new for living. il House & Gard 123:116 Ap '63
When and how to use a decorator. E. Enright. il Redbook 122:56-7+ F '64
Whole new look for $87! D. Popplestone. il Bet Hom & Gard 41:54-5 Jl '63
Who's afraid of Elsie De Wolfe? C. Amory. il Vogue 141:116-23+ Je '63
World's fair house. il Good H 158:100-13+ My '64
Wrongs made right. il Bet Hom & Gard 41: 26+ F '63
You can work wonders with problem walls. il Parents Mag 39:61+ Ja '64
You don't have to give up elegance when you give up dirt. J. Ellestad. il House B 106:122-7 Mr '64
Your second home: decorating for carefree living. il Am Home 67:22+ Ap '64
See also
Antiques
Apartments
Art in the home
Basements and cellars
Bathroom fixtures
Bathrooms
Bedrooms
Ceilings
Childrens rooms
Christmas decorations
Color in house decoration
Curtains and draperies
Decoration and ornament, Architectural
Floor coverings
Flower boxes, planters, etc.
Furniture
Furniture, Arrangement of
Furniture, Built in
Guest houses
Household furnishings
Interior decorators
Kitchens
Laundries
Living rooms
Music rooms and equipment
Painting, Industrial and practical
Plants in house decoration
Rooms
Rugs and carpets
Screens (furniture)
Slip covers
Tapestry
Textile fabrics
Wallpaper
Window shades

HOUSE decoration, American
Bucks County home of Mr and Mrs Hiram D. Rickert; excerpt from Living with antiques, ed. by A. Winchester and others. il Antiques 84:306-11 S '63
California, what a way to live! il McCalls 90:56-61 Jl '63
Colonial with a flair. G. O'Brien. il N Y Times Mag p58-9 S 22 '63
Early New England homes with 20th-century owners. R. W. Houseman. il Am Home 66: 26-31 Mr '63
Hudson River Valley portfolio. J. T. Butler. il Antiques 85:432-7 Ap '64
Interesting people have the most interesting homes. il House B 105:131-55+ Ap '63
Jan Martense Schenck house in the Brooklyn museum. M. D. Schwartz. il Antiques 85: 421-8 Ap '64

HOUSE decoration, Colonial and early American. See House decoration, American

HOUSE decoration, English
English country look revitalized for today's rooms. il House & Gard 124:218-21 O '63
On the street where you live. il Ladies Home J 81:134-6+ Ja '64

HOUSE decoration, Exterior
Color indoors and outdoors. il House & Gard 124:136-7 S '63

HOUSE decoration, Hawaiian
Your talent for living. il House & Gard 126. 51+ Jl '64

HOUSE decoration, Mediterranean
Tangy seasoning for contemporary rooms. il House & Gard 125:120-7 F '64

HOUSE decoration, Spanish
World unto itself; adaptation of Spanish colonial style. il Am Home 68:46-7 Ja '65

HOUSE dresses. See Clothing and dress

HOUSE education subcommittee. See United States—Congress—House of representatives —Committees

HOUSE expansion. See Houses, Remodeled

HOUSE for sale; story. See Maxwell, J. A.

HOUSE gift; story. See Maher, J. T.

HOUSE guests. See Guests

HOUSE heating. See Heating

HOUSE insulation. See Insulation (heat)

HOUSE judiciary committee. See United States —Congress—House of representatives—Committees

HOUSE lighting. See Electric lighting

HOUSE models
John Blauer's castle, Maynard manor. S. A. Parvin. il Hobbies 68:114 S; 114-15 O '63
Remodeling in miniature. S. A. Parvin. il Hobbies 68:118 Ja '64

HOUSE museums. See Historic house museums

HOUSE of commons. See Great Britain—Parliament—House of commons

HOUSE of Mitsubishi. See Japan—Industries

HOUSE of representatives. See United States—Congress—House of representatives

HOUSE of rest, Milan. See Old age homes

HOUSE office building. See Washington, D.C. —Public buildings

HOUSE on the corner; story. See O'Hara, J.

HOUSE paint. See Paint

HOUSE painting
Personalize your home with paint. il Am Home 66:44-7 Ap '63

HOUSE painting, Interior. See Painting, Industrial and practical

HOUSE pets. See Pets

HOUSE plans. See Architecture, Domestic—Designs and plans

HOUSE plants
All around the place. J. Milton. Pop Gard 15:61 F '64
Answers to your house plant questions. C. H. Sherwood. Suc Farm 62:100-1 Ja '64
Big, bold, decorative. R. M. Peters. il Pop Gard 15:30-1 F '64
Bring color indoors with house plants. il Pop Gard 14:20-1 S '63
Colorful Christmas plants. C. Hodgson and others. il Horticulture 41:602-3 D '63
Colorful foliage for your window sill. R. C. Hands. il Horticulture 41:102 F '63
Delight of table-top gardens. il House & Gard 123:122-5 F '63
Face the facts about gardening indoors. E. D. Ballard. il Horticulture 42:22-5 Mr '64
First aid for ailing houseplants. il Good H 156:150-1 F '63
Hanging baskets for summer color. G. Taloumis. il Horticulture 41:372-3 Jl '63
Hints on exhibiting house plants. W. H. Hull, jr. il Horticulture 41:457 S '63
House plants from A to Z. il Flower Grower 50:33-5+ O '63
House plants go outdoors. il Pop Gard 14:20 My '63
House plants, their treatment and care. Consumer Bul 47:25 O '64
How to be an indoor landscape designer. il Am Home 68:14 Ja '65
How to care for your houseplants. Am Home 68:16 Ja '65
Keeping house plants healthy. H. V. Wilson. Flower Grower 52:22 Ja '65
Lush gardens bloom indoors. C. Kellogg. il Ladies Home J 80:80-2 S '63
Make your holiday plants bloom again. il Pop Gard 15:14-15 Ja '64
Making new plants out of old plants. Mrs W. H. Hull, jr. il Horticulture 41:524 O '63
My wide world of house plants. H. V. Wilson. il Flower Grower 51:17-19 N '64
On and off the avenue (cont) New Yorker 39:174-6+ N 30 '63
Orchid for your window. J. Kramer. il Flower Grower 52:35 Ja '65
Picture your winter windows. il House & Gard 124:164-7+ D '63

HOUSE plants—*Continued*
Plant palette for winter windows. J. Fanning. House & Gard 124:192-3+ D '63
Quick and easy tips. il Pop Gard 16:36-7 Ja '65
Start gardening right now! H. Mason. il Bet Hom & Gard 43:62-5+ Ja '65
Suitable plants, whether your room is well lighted or not. Mrs. W. Hull, jr. il Horticulture 42:40-1 F '64
These arrangements grow in water. il Sunset 131:175 Ag '63
Widen your house plant horizon. R. K. Stroh. il Pop Gard 15:22-3 N '64
Window gardens are interesting. B. Brinhart. il Horticulture 42:54 Ja '64
Young house plants from old. il Pop Gard 16:32-5 F '65
See also
African violets
Begonias
Bromeliads
Episcias
Ferns
Flamingo flowers
Flower boxes, planters, etc.
Geraniums
Lantana
Norfolk Island-pine
Plants, Potted
Poinsettias
Ti plant
Window gardening

HOUSE prices. See Housing—Costs

HOUSE public works committee. See United States—Congress—House of representatives—Committees

HOUSE repairing. See Repairing

HOUSE rules committee. See United States—Congress—House of representatives—Committees

HOUSE selling. See Home ownership

HOUSE sparrows. See Sparrows

HOUSE trailers. See Automobile trailers

HOUSE ventilation. See Ventilation

HOUSE ways and means committee. See United States—Congress—House of representatives—Committees

HOUSE wiring. See Electric wire and wiring

HOUSEBOATS. See House boats

HOUSECLEANING. See House cleaning

HOUSEHOLD, Geoffrey
Battle of Mussolini; story. Atlan 214:51-7 S '64

HOUSEHOLD ammonia. See Ammonia

HOUSEHOLD appliances
Battle for the kitchen; Europe's industries. P. Siekman. il Fortune 69:108-11+ Ja '64
Before you buy kitchen equipment, know all the market offers. il House B 106:213+ My '64
Cool comforts for year 'round use. il Parents Mag 38:124 Je '63
Doing it better. D. X. Manners. See issues of House beautiful
Expanding ownership of household equipment. T. R. Tibbetts. il Mo Labor R 87:1131-7 O '64
Impact of the Negro on the furniture market. B. Van Alstine. il Ebony 18:99-104 Ap '63
It's worth mentioning. J. Polshek. See issues of House beautiful
Keeping up to date (title varies) (cont) il Farm J 87:93 F; 78-9 Ap; 51 Ag; 74 O '63; 88:42+ Ag; 78 O '64
Looking for gold in offbeat gadgets; housewares show in Chicago. il Bsns W p44-5 Jl 27 '63
Mechanical marvels of a motor manufacturer. il House B 105:140-3+ Ap '63
New again kitchens; How to remodel your kitchen beautifully. il McCalls 90:148-50+ F '63
New for your home. See issues of Popular mechanics
New products for the house. il Arch Rec 133:132+ mid-My '63; 135:129+ mid-My '64
Pint-size marvels that do a big job. il House & Gard 125:122-5+ Ap '64
What's new for living. See issues of House & garden incorporating Living for young homemakers
What's new in furnishings and housewares. R. Martens and J. Gillies. il Farm J 88:84-5 Mr '64
What's new in homemaking. See issues of Successful farming
Your home (cont) il Consumer Rep 28:88-217 D '63
Your household (cont) il Consumer Rep 28:218-39+ D '63
Your second home: planning and equipping your kitchen. il Am Home 67:29 Ap '64
See also
Electric apparatus and appliances, Domestic
Gadgets
Gas appliances
Kitchen utensils
Laundry equipment
Vacuum cleaners

Anecdotes, facetiae, satire, etc.

Appliance is something that gets attached to you. R. P. Smith. il McCalls 91:98 Ap '64
Last resort. L. E. Carlton. il Atlan 213:102-3 Ja '64; Same abr. with title When things get out of whack. Read Digest 84:183-4+ Mr '64

Care

Use and care of household appliances (cont) Consumer Rep 28:273-8 D '63

Manufacture

Houseful of helpers awake at the switch. J. Atwater. il Sat Eve Post 237:15-21 D 5 '64

Repairing

Time-saving, money-saving advice from your repairman. R. M. Burnley. il Redbook 121:58-9+ Ag '63

HOUSEHOLD budget. See Budget, Household

HOUSEHOLD cleaning preparations. See Cleaning compositions

HOUSEHOLD employees
Amah, amen! protesting maidservants of southeast Asia. il Time 82:24+ S 6 '63
Cat in the icebox. il Time 81:74 My 3 '63
Girls by rotation; au pair system. il Time 84:60+ O 30 '64
Help! excerpt from Profession: housewife. P. McGinley. il Ladies Home J 80:60+ Ap '63
How America solved the servant problem. R. Lynes. il Harper 227:46-54 Jl '63
Isabell the inscrutable. C. G. Finney. il Harper 228:51-8 Ap '64
Speaking out; more people should be servants. C. Bird. Sat Eve Post 237:6+ Je 20 '64; Same abr. with title Help wanted. Read Digest 85:235-7+ N '64
What the butler saw, by E. S. Turner. Review New Yorker 39:82+ Ag 10 '63. N. Bliven Sat R il 46:35 Mr 23 '63. I. Haverstick Time il 81:108+ Mr 15 '63
Who needs a maid? you do. J. L. O'Neill. Am Home 67:6 Ap '64
Why can't I get help? E. D. Fales, jr. Am Home 66:25 N '63

Anecdotes, facetiae, satire, etc.

Household help! A. Buchwald. McCalls 90:50 Ap '63

HOUSEHOLD furnishings
Agreeable cube. il House & Gard 125:164-7 Mr '64
American & beautiful. R. W. Houseman. il Am Home 66:30-5+ Ap '63
Bravura color coolly controlled. il House & Gard 124:160-3 D '63
Buy your vacation house completely furnished. il Am Home 67:82 Ap '64
Buying with the power to discern. il Bsns W p58-60 Ag 31 '63
Collect a Christmas wardrobe. il Am Home 67:46-7 D '64
Color that makes tradition come alive. M. Gough. il House B 105:134-47 Mr '63
Connoisseur's corner. See issues of House & garden
Decorator's diary. See issues of House beautiful
Enchanting rooms that fool the eye. il House & Gard 125:106-13 Ap '64
Expanding ownership of household equipment. T. R. Tibbetts. il Mo Labor R 87:1131-7 O '64
Harvest of ideas you can emulate wherever you live. il House & Gard 126:84-93 Jl '64
Home: 1963-1964. G. O'Brien. il N Y Times Mag pt2 p 15-23+ S 29 '63; pt2 15-23+ S 27 '64
How to benefit from the intensive use of objects. il House B 105:88-93 Jl '63
Impact of the Negro in the furniture market. B. Van Alstine. il Ebony 18:99-104 Ap '63
Is there a truly comfortable corner in your house? il House B 105:170-2 Mr '63
Keeping up to date in your home (title varies) il Farm J 87:78-9 Ap '63; 88:72 S; 90 N '64
My favorite things; excerpts. D. Rodgers. il McCalls 91:120-5 My; 60+ Je; 102-3+ Jl '64
New old art nouveau. B. Plumb. il N Y Times Mag p 116-17+ O 11 '64

HOUSEHOLD furnishings—*Continued*
New products for the house. il Arch Rec 133: 132+ mid-My '63
100 ideas under $100. il Bet Hom & Gard 41: 10+ Jl '63; 42:28-59 Jl '64
Pint-size marvels that do a big job. il House & Gard 125:122-5+ Ap '64
Sit back and relax. M. Casserly. il Bet Hom & Gard 42:29-35 Ag '64
Taste of tradition. il McCalls 90:114-21 Ap '63
There are children in your house. L. Sloane. il Am Home 67:24+ S '64
Turn ready-mades into made-to-order with borders. F. Heard. il House B 105:80-5 Jl '63
Urbanity in the lush Nuanu Valley. il House B 106:104-7 Ja '64
Use little luxuries for big results; How to afford the grand gesture. il Am Home 68: 42-5 Ja '65
Value plus versatility. E. Sverbeyeff. il N Y Times Mag p82-4 My 24 '64
What's new for living. See issues of House & garden incorporating Living for young homemakers
World's fair house. il Good H 158:100-13+ My '64
Wrongs made right. il Bet Hom & Gard 41: 26+ F '63
Your home (cont) il Consumer Rep 28:88-217 D '63
Your room is the sum of simple addition. il Seventeen 22:174-5 S '63
Your second home: decorating for carefree living. il Am Home 67:22+ Ap '64
See also
Color in house decoration
Laundry equipment
Silverware

Exhibitions

Chicago: best of show. G. O'Brien. il N Y Times Mag p40-1 F 2 '64
Smithsonian preview. C. M. Watkins. il Antiques 85:86-7 Ja '64

HOUSEHOLD inventories. See Inventories, Household
HOUSEHOLD linens. See Linen, Household
HOUSEHOLD management. See Home economics
HOUSEHOLD records. See Family records
HOUSEKEEPERS, Visiting. See Visiting housekeepers
HOUSEKEEPING. See Home economics
HOUSELEEKS
Sun & rock lovers. E. W. Finch. il Flower Grower 50:36-7+ Ag '63
HOUSEMAN, John
Charlie's Chaplin. Nation 199:222-5 O 12 '64
HOUSEMATES. See Roommates
HOUSER, George M.
Our about-face on African policy. Christian Cent 80:675-6 My 22 '63
HOUSER, Theodore V.
Government and business: the vital balance. Sat R 47:27-9 Ja 11 '64
HOUSES
Building cracks tell tales. Am Home 67:96-7 Mr '64
How to design a second way of living: part-time homes. il House & Gard 123:91-9 Je '63
Ideas in houses. il Life 58:85-91 Ja 15 '65
If you're looking for a good two-story, this is it! J. D. Bloodgood. il Bet Hom & Gard 42:62-5 Je '64
Luxury of waste space. il Time 83:75 Mr 6 '64
What people want most for their houses. House & Gard 125:140-1 Ap '64
What you should know about your new house. Am Home 67:104-5 My '64
See also
Architecture, Domestic
Architecture, Domestic—Designs and plans
Building
Concrete houses
Cottages
Home ownership
Ranch houses
Summer homes

Air conditioning

See Air conditioning

Decontamination

See Decontamination (from gases, chemicals, etc)

Equipment

Budgeting for unexpected new-home expenses. il Am Home 67:97 My '64

Location

See Building sites

Maintenance and repair

Fall maintenance. D. L. Gregg. il Bet Hom & Gard 42:135-6+ O '64
Home maintenance. il Suc Farm 62:86 Mr '64
Home maintenance clinic; questions and answers. il Am Home 67:92-3 Ap; 106-7 My; 87-8 Je; 106-7 Jl; 94 S; 109 O; 90-1 N; 92-3 D '64
What to do about a drafty house. C. Sclarenco. il Bet Hom & Gard 42:125 N '64

Orientation

See Orientation (architecture)

Prices

See Housing—Costs

Ventilation

See Ventilation

HOUSES, Air conditioned. See Air conditioning
HOUSES, Dampness in. See Dampness in buildings
HOUSES, Exchange of
Home swapping. Newsweek 63:66 F 17 '64
Hotel is not a house. H. Sutton. Sat R 46:39+ Ap 13 '63
Swap: New Yorkers with San Francisco visitors to fair. New Yorker 40:19-20 Ag 29 '64
HOUSES, Miniature. See House models
HOUSES, Portable
Booked for travel; the mysterious West. H. Sutton. il Sat R 47:36-9 F 15 '64
HOUSES, Prefabricated
Development house built of an architect-designed steel component system. il Arch Rec 133:82-5 mid-My '63
Here's an up-to-date report on factory-built houses. il Bet Hom & Gard 42:22+ Mr '64
House you'll build from four boxes. B. Smallman. il Pop Sci 183:102-4 D '63
Prefabs' uphill fight. il Bsns W p74-7 Jl 4 '64
Shell shock. il Time 81:75 Mr 1 '63
Two-story house using a system of steel components. il Arch Rec 133:126-9 mid-My '63
What makes manufactured homes so popular? R. Charles. il Parents Mag 39:83+ S '64
Where's the ceiling on new houses? J. McDonald. il Fortune 67:128-32+ Je '63
Your second home: should you consider a prefab? il Am Home 67:27+ Ap '64
HOUSES, Remodeled
Addition fits cottage for a new way of life. il Arch Rec 133:90-3 mid-My '63
Additions don't come any better. P. Lindberg. il Bet Hom & Gard 42:14 Ap '64
At home in a barn. C. Kellogg. il Ladies Home J 80:68-71 Jl '63
Before you plan, you must dare to dream; remodeled boathouse on the east coast of Florida. C. Calkins. il House B 106:68-71+ Jl '64
Best of two worlds. B. Reynolds. il Suc Farm 61:84-5+ F '63
Build modern living into an old house. J. Holmstrand. il Suc Farm 61:52-3 Jl '63
Century-old house opened to a garden. il House & Gard 125:174-7 My '64
Cinderella rooms created by transforming under-exploited space. il House & Gard 125: 184-91 My '64
Colonial barn is transformed into a country estate. il Am Home 67:98+ My '64
Daring transformation. il House & Gard 125: 132-7+ Je '64
Enter: daylight. G. O'Brien. il N Y Times Mag p50-1 Jl 19 '64
Fifty-six-year-old house begins its second life; Los Altos, Calif. il Sunset 132:102-5 Je '64
Five steps from big garage to handsome home. il Am Home 66:92 N '63
Funny what paint, shutters, and a little less porch can do. L. R. Forester. il Am Home 66:80 O '63
Hopeless house, remodeled. R. Martens. il Farm J 88:90-2 Ap '64
House grows up. G. O'Brien. il N Y Times Mag p54-5 Je 28 '64
House revised. G. O'Brien. il N Y Times Mag p52-3 Ag 4 '63
House that grew. G. O'Brien. il N Y Times Mag p32-3 S 1 '63
How to avoid pitfalls in home remodeling. il Good H 156:161-3 Ap '63
How to spot great responsibilities. P. Lindberg. il Bet Hom & Gard 41:56-9 Ag '63
How to transform your attic into an inviting room. il House & Gard 123:168-71 My '63
How to update an old square house. R. Martens. il Farm J 87:68-9 N '63

HOUSES, Remodeled—*Continued*
Imagination plus! il Am Home 67:46-9 Ap '64
It looks like a whole new house. il Am Home 66:94 N '63
Last look at Blair House. il Travel 119:45-7 Je '63
Latest ways to modernize your home. il Pop Mech 120:138-43 S '63
Magic of remodeling; a fresh new face to the street. il Sunset 132:60-1 Ja '64
Mediterranean house handsomely done over. il Sunset 133:120-1 N '64
More room, same house. il Bet Hom & Gard 43:31 Ja '65
My beautiful Greek house, handmade for $2,000. P. Glanville-Hicks. il Vogue 141:14+ Ap 1 '63
New house for old. il Am Home 67:135 Jl '64
New house in town; remodeled carriage house in Manhattan. G. O'Brien. il N Y Times Mag p28-9 D 27 '64
New light for an old house. G. O'Brien. il N Y Times Mag p74-5 Ja 12 '64
New vistas for an old house. M. White. il Ladies Home J 81:44-9 Ag '64
Nine ways to increase your living space. il Ladies Home J 80:103-4+ Mr '63
Pitch a tent ceiling in a small room to give it large-scale glamour. il Bet Hom & Gard 41:42 S '63
President cites importance of home improvement programs; with telegram. J. F. Kennedy. Am Home 66:85 Ap '63
Remodel or move? the vote was remodel. il Sunset 130:102-15 Ap '63
Remodeler's notebook (cont) il House & Gard 123:30+ Mr; 34+ Ap; 124:116+ S; 246-7 O; 22-3 N '63; 125:192-5 Mr '64
Room at the top; new second story. il Bet Hom & Gard 42:118+ Ap '64
Setting for American folk art in old remodeled barns. il House B 105:138-9 Ap '63
Smart trim tricks for home remodeling jobs; door casings, baseboards, and moldings. E. M. Love. il Pop Sci 186:148-9 Ja '65
Their new bedroom is in the trees. il Sunset 131:122-3 O '63
They outgrew open planning. il Am Home 67:92-3 N '64
They traded in the old porch! P. Lindberg. il Bet Hom & Gard 41:114 N '63
Three French kings helped to remodel a stable-garage. il House & Gard 123:106-11 F '63
To start your home improvement. il Bet Hom & Gard 41:6+ O '63
Treasure under your hand; symposium. il House B 105:135-216 S '63
Trend to major additions. N. Seney. il Bet Hom & Gard 42:42-51+ O '64
Two-story wing doubles the space. il Am Home 68:82 Ja '65
Under one roof diversity: Southport, Conn. G. O'Brien. il N Y Times Mag p76-7 My 26 '63
Urban renewal saves homes, York, Pa. il Am City 78:103 S '63
We enclosed our porch for a family room. R. Charles. il Parents Mag 38:77-80+ N '63
We inspire remodeling of fire-damaged home. B. Colvin. il Am Home 66:87 Ap '63
We think this addition is great! il Bet Hom & Gard 41:64-7+ My '63
What can you do with an old house? N. Seney and P. Lindberg. il Bet Hom & Gard 41:70-1 Ap '63
What's happened to the family heirloom. Mrs B. Tucker. il Suc Farm 61:66-9 My '63
Why live in a carbon copy? il Pop Mech 120: 118-23 S '63
Winners in our 1962 home improvement contest. il Bet Hom & Gard 41:41-2+ O '63
Wondrous house, formerly a Baptist church. V. Lawford. il Vogue 143:164-73+ F 1 '64
You and your home. House & Gard 123:18-19 Ap '63
See also
Remodeling (architecture)

HOUSES, Restored
Living with antiques: Pagoda House in Newport, Rhode Island. J. A. L. Hyde. il Antiques 84:158-61 Ag '63

HOUSES, Seashore. See Beach architecture

HOUSES, Toy. See Doll houses

HOUSES, Tree. See Tree houses

HOUSES, Two-family
House that easily converts into a duplex. il Arch Rec 133:147-50 Je '63

HOUSEWARES. See Household appliances

HOUSEWIVES
Book committee chairman reports survey on housewives' reading; excerpts from address, December 10, 1964. N. H. Strouse; with summary. Library J 90:212-13, 328 Ja 15 '65
Dilemmas of a househusband. R. Varga. Sat R 48:100-3 Ja 2 '65
Educated housewife's bill of rights. C. Seton. Redbook 123:47+ My '64
Encore for twelve high-kicking housewives; former Rockettes at Radio City music hall. L. H. Lapham. il Sat Eve Post 237:72+ O 24 '64
Fraud of femininity; excerpts from The feminine mystique. B. Friedan. McCalls 90:81+ Mr '63; Discussion. 90:38+ Ag '63
Have American housewives traded brains for brooms? B. Friedan. il Ladies Home J 80: 24+ Ja '63
Home is not obsolete. Mrs S. Udall. il Ladies Home J 81:32+ Jl '64
Island of time; condensation of Creative woman. D. Goldberg. il Redbook 121:52-3+ My '63
Long day's monotony of TV. B. Brower. il Sat Eve Post 237:76-8 S 26 '64
My husband was ashamed of me. il Good H 156:16+ Ap '63
Myth of the pampered housewife. J. Goodsell. il Read Digest 85:64-6 Jl '64
Off the cuff. A. Marple. Writer 76:5-6 Je '63
On being a woman. J. Brothers. Good H 158:48-50 Mr '64
Perfectionist or what's wrong with being right. D. B. Thompson. Am Home 68:28-9 Ja '65
Sixpence in her shoe, by P. McGinley. Review
Time il 84:90 O 9 '64
What does she do all day? record of a typical day. il Changing T 19:24-8 Ja '65
Why she really goes to market. H. H. Martin. il Sat Eve Post 236:40-3 S 28 '63; Same abr. with title When a woman goes to market. Read Digest 84:115-18 Mr '64
Wives and the moonlight adventure: excerpt from Sixpence in her shoe. P. McGinley. Ladies Home J 81:30+ Ag '64; Same abr. Read Digest 86:72-4 Ja '65

Anecdotes, facetiae, satire, etc.

Confessions of a happy homemaker. R. Hochstein. Good H 157:50+ O '63

HOUSEWORK. See Home economics

HOUSING
Conserving the old. W. Von Eckardt. New Repub 149:16-18 S 28 '63
Man's struggle for shelter in an urbanizing world, by C. Abrams. Review
Nation 199:199-201 O 5 '64. D. Gurin
Who cares for the city? America 112:10 Ja 2 '65
See also
Aged—Housing
Discrimination in housing

Costs

Architect's home is development prototype. il Arch Rec 133:102-5 mid-My '63
Cost of Record houses near you. il Arch Rec 133:131 mid-My '63
Could houses cost less? these men on the job say yes! symposium. D. Jordan. il Bet Hom & Gard 41:66-7 Mr '63
Room shortage; western Europe. il Time 84:92 Jl 10 '64
Simple, well-designed house for $15,867. il Arch Rec 133:94-7 mid-My '63
Where's the ceiling on new houses? J. McDonald. il Fortune 67:128-32+ Je '63

Federal aid

Apartment roundtable asks: what price urban living? il Arch Forum 120:84-91 Mr '64
Congress and construction: aid to housing, hospitals and poverty. Arch Rec 136:23+ O '64
Supermarket for subsidies; address, January 6, 1964. E. P. Neilan. Vital Speeches 30: 237-9 F 1 '64

Finance

See Housing finance

Slum clearance

See Slums

Statistics

Replacement demand for housing growing. G. A. Christie. il Arch Rec 137:18 Ja '65

Brazil

See also
Rio de Janeiro—Housing

California

California: going, going. C. Abrams. il Arch Forum 119:104-7 S '63
California housing and civil rights; proposed ammendment to 1963 Rumford act. E. G. Bianchi. America 111:174 Ag 22 '64

HOUSING—California—*Continued*
City-cage; Proposition fourteen, backed by National association of real estate boards. S. Alsop. Sat Eve Post 237:14 O 10 '64
Courageous pastoral; Archbishop Joseph T. McGucken of San Francisco on Proposition fourteen. America 111:541 N 7 '64
Crucial questions for November 4; proposition fourteen. Christian Cent 81:1291 O 21 '64
Experts tackle California's housing. Arch Forum 118:7+ F '63
Proposition fourteen and the liturgy. N. J. Andersen. America 11:658+ N 21 '64. Discussion. 112:49-50 Ja 9 '65
Showdown in California; Proposition fourteen on the November ballot. L. Zimpel. Commonweal 81:153-5 O 30 '64
Spotlight on California; realtor-sponsored Proposition fourteen. R. M. Brown. Christian Cent 81:1202-4 S 30 '64; Reply. G. Aki. 81:1470 N 25 '64
See also
Discrimination in housing

Colombia

See also
Bogotá, Colombia—Housing

Europe, Western

Room shortage. il Time 84:92 Jl 10 '64

Florida

FHA's winter come-on; modern Florida homes. il Newsweek 63:66 Ja 13 '64

France

Counter-revolution on the Côte; Village du Merlier. il Time 84:49 Ag 21 '64
Levitt's ville; housing projects in France. Newsweek 63:70 Je 22 '64

Germany (Federal Republic)

Price breaker; Germany's J. Neckermann. il Bsns W p 104-6 Mr 21 '64

Great Britain

See also
London—Housing

Italy

See also
Milan, Italy—Housing

Japan

Changing population patterns in Japan. A. Doi. il Cur Hist 46:219-22 Ap '64
$18 million an acre. Time 85:22 Ja 8 '65

New Jersey

Boldness in New Jersey; Horizon house. il Arch Forum 118:96-9 Ap '63

Puerto Rico

Boomerang in Puerto Rico. il Arch Forum 118:91 Ap '63

Russia

Russian housing: better, but... C. Foltz. il U S News 56:94-5 F 17 '64

Sweden

Housing as a social problem. il Arch Rec 135:162-4 Ap '64

Underdeveloped areas

Housing needs in development decade. U N Rev 11:31-4+ Mr '64

United States

Affluence, ltd. Nation 197:82-3 Ag 24 '63
Apartment roundtable asks: what price urban living? il Arch Forum 120:84-91 Mr '64
Big city Christmas. J. O'Gara. Commonweal 79:388 D 27 '63
Boom with a nervous tone. il Bsns W p30-2 Jl 13 '63
Dry rot in the long postwar housing boom. il Newsweek 64:92-4 O 12 '64
Federal housing agencies encouraging good design; symposium. il Arch Rec 136:103-9 Ag '64
Good news for house buyers. il Changing T 18:7-10 Mr '64
High-level housing. il Fortune 69:28+ Ap '64
Houses America needs. J. Brenneman. Ladies Home J 80:53+ My '63
HHFA honor awards, 1964. il Arch Rec 136:165-74 N '64
Housing and slum clearance: elusive goals. W. G. Grigsby. bibliog f il Ann Am Acad 352-107-18 Mr '64
Housing message calls for aid to suburbs. Arch Rec 135:32 Mr '64
Housing puzzle. il Fortune 70:32+ O '64
How to bring suburban joys to town. House & Gard 125:168-9 My '64
How we live; symposium. il Look 28:13-28+ Ja 14 '64
New look in public housing, too little and too late? D. B. Carlson. il Arch Forum 119:116-19 Jl '63
PHA and design: commissioner outlines aims; excerpts from address, December 5, 1963. M. C. McGuire. Arch Rec 135:23+ Ja '64
Public housing as community; with editorial comment. A. Mayer. il Arch Rec 135:9, 169-78 Ap '64
Tomorrow's suburbs: better living for less money. il Changing T 18:23-4 Ap '64
Urban renewal: a new face on the American city. D. B. Carlson. il Arch Forum 119: 80-5 Ag '63
See also
Automobile trailer camps
Building industry
Housing finance
Housing laws and legislation—United States
Housing projects, Government
Negroes in the United States—Housing
United States—Housing and home finance agency
also subhead Housing under names of cities, e.g. Chicago—Housing

HOUSING, Discrimination in. See Discrimination in housing

HOUSING and home finance agency. See United States—Housing and home finance agency

HOUSING codes. See Housing laws and legislation

HOUSING construction. See Building industry

HOUSING finance
Housing gets another transfusion. Bsns W p 117 S 12 '64
Many ways to finance home remodeling. il Good H 156:170 My '63
Truth about the cost of money for remodeling. M. Colean. il House B 105:188-91 S '63
221d3: the key to moderate-income housing? R. Schafer. Arch Forum 118:85 Ap '63
Worry amid one boom: where quick profits fade. il U S News 55:81-2 Jl 1 '63
You and your home; how to pay for your major remodeling project. House & Gard 123:18-19 Ap '63
See also
Mortgages
United States—Federal home loan bank board
United States—Federal housing administration

HOUSING for the aged. See Aged—Housing

HOUSING laws and legislation
See also
Building laws and regulations

Great Britain

See also
Rent laws

United States

California: a wild card in the deck; amendment designed to establish racial discrimination as a property owner's right. J. Lewis. Reporter 31:29+ O 22 '64
Fair housing battle: California contest. America 110:271-2 F 29 '64
Fair housing under attack; California's Rumford fair housing act. America 110:839 Je 20 '64
For LBJ's housing bill: mostly criticism; with editorial comment. il Arch Forum 120:5, 79 Ap '64
Housing bills: what LBJ will ask. il Arch Forum 120:5 F '64
How we live; symposium. il Look 28:13-28+ Ja 14 '64
Movers and voters: opposition to anti-bias housing legislation in California. il Newsweek 63:30 Mr 9 '64
New housing law: what it does. Changing T 18:6 N '64
Why new houses cost too much. A. M. Watkins. il Sat Eve Post 236:19-25 S 21 '63

HOUSING of students. See College students—Housing

HOUSING projects
Churches enter the housing business. L. E. Schaller. Christian Cent 80:1263-5 O 16 '63; Discussion. 80:1548 D 11 '63
Public housing projects receive design awards; low-rent housing projects in Marin City, Calif; Minneapolis, Minn; and Philadelphia, Pa. il Am City 79:82-3 D '64
Their first house. J. Poppy. il Look 28:24-7 Ja 14 '64
See also
Levitt and sons, incorporated

HOUSING projects—*Continued*

Site planning

Architect talks about the spaces between buildings. A. H. Keyes, jr. il Arch Rec 134:194-5 S '63
Cluster zoning: one step toward a better suburbia. G. D. Lloyd. il Am Home 67:46-7 Je '64
Clusters instead of slurbs. A. L. Huxtable. il N Y Times Mag p36-7+ F 9 '64
Community and privacy: toward a new architecture of humanism, by S. Chermayeff and C. Alexander. Review
Arch Forum il 119:106-7 D '63. D. B. Carlson
Counter-revolution on the Côte; Village du Merlier, France. il Time 84:49 Ag 21 '64
Zoning for today's needs; White Plains, N.Y. J. E. Curtis. Recreation 57:16-17 Ja '64

HOUSING projects, Government
New look in public housing, too little and too late? D. B. Carlson. il Arch Forum 119:116-19 Jl '63
Recreation in low-cost housing projects. Recreation 57:79 F '64
See also
United States—Public housing administration

HOUSTON, Jim
Rider from Omaha. il por Newsweek 64:61 D 14 '64

HOUSTON, Walter Scott
Deep-sky wonders. See issues of Sky and telescope

HOUSTON, Tex.
Air-conditioned metropolis. il Time 81:26-7 Ap 12 '63
Deadly female; encephalitis epidemic. il Newsweek 64:58 S 7 '64
Houston centralizes motor maintenance. K. E. Ping and O. J. Cole. il Am City 78:86-8 N '63

Architecture

Design against sun and glare; home office, Humble oil and refining company. il Arch Rec 134:173-8 O '63
First Cullen center units opened. il Arch Rec 134:153-6 Ag '63
In Texas the glass box goes 3-D; Tennessee building. il Arch Forum 119:124-31 S '63
Pavilion of glass and concrete trees. il Arch Rec 135:122-3 Ja '64

City planning

Keeping a city in good shape. il Bsns W p-110-14 Je 6 '64
On a Texas prairie, space city for 200,000. il U S News 54:66-9 F 18 '63
What your city needs to grow. il Nations Bsns 52:31-3+ S '64

Description

Things are looking up in Houston. H. Sutton. il Sat R 47:42+ N 14 '64

Education

IMS merger: a/v and library services together. E. Alexander. il Library J 89:4107-9 O 15 '64

Hospitals

Smell of charity. J. Adcock and C. Adcock. il Nation 200:5-8 Ja 4 '65; Reply. G. I. Sànchez. 200:75 Ja 25 '65

Housing

Arch form as a facade motif; Inwood Manor. il Arch Rec 136:118-19 Ag '64

Music

Houston progress. A. Holmes. Opera N 27:33 F 16 '63
Little John in big Texas. il Time 82:63 N 1 '63
[Musical events] il Mus Am 84:22-3 Ap; 77 D '64
Two in Houston. A. Holmes. Opera N 28:32 Mr 7 '64
See also
Houston symphony orchestra

Newspapers

One down in Houston; death of the Press. Time 83:59 Ap 3 '64
See also
Houston post

Politics and government

Tussle in Texas. S. Friedman. Nation 198: 114-17 F 3 '64

Theater

Rise of rep. il(p57) Time 83:61 F 14 '64

HOUSTON chronicle
Improving the product in Houston. Time 82: 36 Ag 23 '63

HOUSTON endowment, incorporated
Quiet man stands tall in Houston. il Bsns W p44-6+ D 26 '64

HOUSTON grand opera association
Glory that was Venice; presentation of Otello. H. Roussel. il Mus Am 84:11-12 F '64
Houston's tenth. A. Holmes. Opera N 29:32 Ja 30 '65

HOUSTON museum of fine arts
Sweeney's way. il Time 81:74 Je 14 '63

HOUSTON Oilers (football club) See Football clubs

HOUSTON post
Three for the Post. Time 81:40 Mr 1 '63

HOUSTON stadium. See Stadiums

HOUSTON symphony orchestra
Gold and silver waltz; two Texas anniversaries. E. Lewis. il Mus Am 83:14-15+ O '63
Musical events; concert at Philharmonic Hall. W. Sargeant. New Yorker 40:158 Mr 14 '64

HOUSTONIA caerulea. See Bluets

HOVDA, Robert W.
Reform without reformers. Commonweal 80: 571-3 Ag 21 '64

HOVERCRAFT. See Ground effect machines

HOVET, Thomas, jr
Role of Africa in the United Nations; address, April 11, 1964; with questions and answers. Ann Am Acad 354:122-34 Jl '64

HOVHANESS, Alan
Alan Hovhaness: pilgrimage to the Orient. J. Wade. por Mus Am 83:56 S '63
Far east of Boston; works recorded by Poseidon society. O. Daniel. Sat R 46:124 O 12 '63
Hovhaness and Giannini symphonies: a complete success. A. Cohn. Am Rec G 30:853-4 My '64

HOVING, Lucas
Lucas Hoving and company at Fashion institute auditorium. D. Hering. Dance Mag 37:55 F '63
Lucas Hoving and dance company, 92nd street Y. J. Maskey. Dance Mag 38:73 My '64

HOVIS, W. A. jr
Infrared emission spectra of organic solids from 5 to 6.6 microns. Science 143:587-8 F 7 '64

HOW the West was lost; story. See Berger, T.

HOW to forget baseball; story. See Sturgeon, T.

HOW to move a mountain; story. See Weidman, J.

HOWARD, Albert
Public relations on the playground. Recreation 56:169 Ap '63

HOWARD, Charles W.
This ho-ho-ho business. A. Levy. il por Sat Eve Post 237:20-1 D 12 '64

HOWARD, D. D. See Corsini, R. J. jt. ed.

HOWARD, Elizabeth Jane
Dangerous thing. New Yorker 39:208-10+ N 16 '63

HOWARD, Elston
New Mr Yankee. il pors Ebony 19:39+ O '64

HOWARD, Frances Minturn
Ballast: poem. New Yorker 40:27 Ja 9 '65

HOWARD, Frank
Dodgers' troubled giant. W. Leggett. il pors Sports Illus 20:66+ My 25 '64

HOWARD, Harlan L.
Decision for Susie Jones. PTA Mag 57:27-9 Je '63

HOWARD, Jack
War on poverty. NEA J 53:47-8 D '64

HOWARD, Jane
Arts in New Hampshire. Mlle 57:52+ Je '63
Belated success of Henry Roth. Life 58:75-6 Ja 8 '65
Big dig for the lost earring. Life 56:75-6+ My 1 '64
Creative capacity to astonish. Life 57:39-40+ Ag 21 '64
Doom and glory of knowing who you are. Life 54:86B+ My 24 '63
He takes a grip on life. Life 55:29-30+ Ag 2 '63
I don't want to look like a bum. Life 56: 98+ F 21 '64
Me and my XBX. Life 55:17 N 8 '63
Merry, angry mother hen. Life 57:59-60+ N 27 '64
Most hated woman in America. Life 56:91-2+ Je 19 '64
She travels the fastest. Mlle 56:70+ F '63
Wrong man behind the bars. Life 56:57-8+ My 15 '64
(ed) See Baskin, L. On pop art, Blake and Bohemianism

HOWARD, Jane—*Continued*
(ed) See Bayh, M. Imagine me here in D.C!
(ed) See De Mille, A. We take leap after leap in the dark
HOWARD, John A.
Excerpt from address, March 13, 1963. Cong Digest 42:251+ O '63
Federal aid to education; address, March 13, 1963. Vital Speeches 29:434-7 My 1 '63
HOWARD, Lisa
Fidel and Lisa: TV interview with Castro. por Newsweek 61:69 My 13 '63
No one dodges Lisa. il por Time 82:68 O 25 '63
Viewing the unseeable. Nation 198:407 Ap 27 '64
HOWARD, Mia
Dolls from nowhere. Redbook 121:32 S '63
Moon garden; story. Redbook 121:62-3 Jl '63
HOWARD, Peter
New aim for America; address, February 4, 1964. Vital Speeches 30:339-43 Mr 15 '64
HOWARD, Richard
Career in consciousness. Nation 200:63-4 Ja 18 '65
Five poets. Poetry 101:412-18 Mr '63
Full circle. Nation 198:400-2 Ap 20 '64
Innocence by association. Poetry 104:245-53 Jl '64
Passes in glass. Nation 199:469-70 D 14 '64
Poetry chronicle. Poetry 102:182-92, 250-9 Je-Jl '63
209 Canal; Difference; poems. Poetry 103: 351-2 Mr '64
Voice of a survivor. Nation 199:278-80 O 26 '64
(tr) See Beauvoir, S. de. Question of fidelity
(tr) See Le Clézio, J. M. G. Day Beaumont grew acquainted with his pain
(tr) See Mandel, A. France's Algerian Jews
(tr) See Mauriac, F. Enigmatic fascination of Charles de Gaulle

about

Five poets. T. Cassity. Poetry 103:192-5 D '63
HOWARD, Roy Wilson
He stopped a war. por Newsweek 64:64 N 30 '64
Obituary
Sat R por 47:62 D 12 '64
HOWARD, Ruby
Birds on the cruise deck. Audubon Mag 67:8-9 Ja '65
HOWARD, Seymour
Formwork. Arch Rec 136:254-6 S '64
Notes on exposed concrete surfaces. Arch Rec 136:250-3 S '64
HOWARD, Steven J.
Johnny, get your calking gun. Pop Mech 120: 156-60 N '63
There's danger in desert-dry air. Pop Mech 120:158-65+ D '63
Who says you can't lay ceramic tile? Pop Mech 121:156-60+ F '64
HOWARD, Toni
Will success spoil your marriage? McCalls 90:88-9+ Jl '63
HOWARD, Willard W.
Are we looking at the wrong budget? Reporter 28:41-2+ My 23 '63
HOWARD, William E. See Bylinsky, G. jt. auth.
HOWARD Johnson restaurants. See Restaurants—United States
HOWARD university, Washington, D.C.
Howard university to conduct Foreign affairs scholars program; statement, October 9, 1963. D. Rusk. Dept State Bul 49:684 O 28 '63
Playing their way through college; Howard university steel band. il Ebony 19:113-17 D '63
Race problem at Howard is how to win; first Negro institution to crash exclusive college rowing. H. Whall. Sports Illus 20: 72+ Ap 27 '64
Slum and gown; Communty services project at Howard university. il Newsweek 63:82 My 4 '64
HOWE, Florence
Doris Lessing's free women. Nation 200:34-7 Ja 11 '65
HOWE, George Augustus
King's cousins. il por Am Heritage 15:99 F '64
HOWE, Gordie
Elusive 545th. il pors Time 82:55 N 22 '63
Gordie speaks. Sports Illus 21:19 S 7 '64
Howe: the who, what and why of the Red Wings. M. Kram. il pors Sports Illus 20: 30-2+ Mr 16 '64
If they go in. por Newsweek 62:80 N 11 '63
They call him the greatest on ice. W. B. Furlong. il pors N Y Times Mag p36+ F 23 '64
HOWE, Harold, 2d
Schools and character development. Sat R 46:66-7 S 21 '63
HOWE, Irving
Celine: the sod beneath the skin. New Repub 149:19-22 Jl 20; 17-20 Ag 17 '63
Dreiser and the Tragedy. New Repub 151:25-8 Ag 22 '64
European as revolutionary. New Repub 150: 30-2 Mr 7 '64
Life of Trotsky. New Repub 150:20-3 Mr 21 '64
Lonely white man. New Repub 151:19-21 Jl 4 '64
Madness, vision, stupidity. New Repub 151: 22-4 N 28 '64
New Yorker & Hannah Arendt. Commentary 36:318-19 O '63
Peretz off-Broadway. Commentary 37:71-3 Ja; 27 Ap '64
Predicaments of Soviet writing. New Repub 148:19-21 My 11; 19-22 My 18 '63
Real world. Commentary 37:80+ Ap '64
Robert Frost: a momentary stay. New Repub 148:23-8 Mr 23 '63
Stature of Theodore Dreiser. New Repub 151:19-21 Jl 25 '64
Tevye on Broadway. Commentary 38:73-5 N '64

about

Assault on Whittaker Chambers. W. F. Buckley, jr. il Nat R 16:1100-2 D 15 '64
Books. R. Adler. New Yorker 40:60-8+ Jl 4 '64
Irving Howe, the socialist imagination. T. Solotaroff. Commentary 37:61-4 Je '64
HOWE, Richard
King's cousins. il por Am Heritage 15:99 F '64
HOWE, Russell Warren
China as the trump in the African pack. New Repub 151:16 S 5 '64
Congo: plugging a sieve with pinheads. Reporter 29:37-8 O 10 '63
Congo triumvirate. New Repub 151:6 O 24 '64
Everybody's problem child. New Repub 148: 10-12 Ap 27 '63
Pan-Africanism comes of age. New Repub 148:15-17 Je 15 '63
Racism in Africa. New Repub 149:18-20 O 5 '63
Rebellion in Rhodesia? New Repub 151:13-14 N 14 '64
Splintering of Africa. New Repub 152:9-10 Ja 30 '65
What's happening in the Congo? New Repub 149:10 N 30; 31 D 21 '63
HOWE, Warner
Closer control of concrete construction. Arch Rec 136:156 Ag '64
HOWE, Sir William
Case of the general's dog. il Am Heritage 15: 112 Je '64
Enigma of General Howe. T. J. Fleming. il por Am Heritage 15:6-11+ F '64
HOWEL, John
Ordeal of William Penn. F. Biddle. il Am Heritage 15:30-3+ Ap '64
HOWELL, Richard
Twenty-four hours in the life of an obstetrician. E. M. Wylie. il Read Digest 82:52-61 Ap '63
HOWELL, Ted
I had trouble with elk. pors Outdoor Life 134:50-3+ O '64
HOWELLS, William Dean
Christmas every day; dramatization. See McGowan, J.
Depicter of American democracy. M. W. Hess. Christian Cent 81:1457-8 N 25 '64
HOWES, Barbara
Dead toucan; poem. Atlan 214:91 S '64
Dressmaker's dummy as scarecrow; Town meeting Tuesday; What bird; Troy weight taken; Governess's tale; Round; Footnote; poems. Poetry 103:343-7 Mr '64
Headlong; Thinking of K.H.S; Stand of birches; poems. Poetry 102:71-3 My '63
Late November window; poem. Sat R 46:46 N 9 '63
Rune for C; poem. New Yorker 40:30 Je 20 '64
Sea school; poem. New Yorker 40:32 Ja 9 '65
HOWES, Robert G.
Religious leaders allied for civic goals. Cath World 197:114-19 My '63
Sunday sermon; poem. Cath World 198:222 Ja '64
HOWIE, Virginia
Grow lilies from seed. Pop Gard 14:34+ F '63
How to store summer bulbs. il Horticulture 42:36-7 O '64

HOWIE, Virginia—*Continued*
Lilies in the living room. Pop Gard 14:49+ N '63
Summer bulbs; drawings. Horticulture 42:34-5 Je '64
HOWLAND, T. W.
Anyone want a tow? Yachting 114:67 O '63
HOWLAND, Wallace
Steam returns to the San Juans. il Yachting 113:40-1+ Mr '63
HOWLERS. See Blunders
HOWLETT, Duncan
Minister delivers sermon calling for enactment of Wilderness bill. por Am For 69:6 My '63
HOWLEY, Frank L.
Plan to free Cuba. por Read Digest 83: 89-92 Jl '63
HOWLING succcess; drama. See Garver, J.
HOWSE, Ernest Marshall
United church of Canada: perils of ecclesiasticism. Christian Cent 80:976-9 Ag 7 '63
HOYER, Bill H. and others
Complementary RNA in nucleus and cytoplasm of mouse liver cells. bibliog Science 140:1408-12 Je 28 '63
Molecular approach in the systematics of higher organisms. bibliog Science 144:959-67 My 22 '64
HOYLE, Edmond
On the fringe. H. Frankel. Sat R 47:40 Mr 21 '64
HOYLE, Fred
Can we learn from other planets? excerpt from Of men and galaxies. por Sat R 47: 63-7 N 7 '64
Life and death of the universe. il Newsweek 63:64-7 My 25 '64
Math plus Mach equals far-out gravity. il por Time 83:63 Je 26 '64
Way of a galaxy. il por Time 81:58+ F 8 '63
HOYLE, Graham, and McAlear, J. H.
Mechanism of supercontraction in a striated muscle fiber. bibliog Science 141:712-13 Ag 23 '63
HOYT, Austin
Down the back to the Arctic. por Sports Illus 19:34-6+ Ag 26 '63
HOYT, Charles Alva
Days of rhyme and roses. Sat R 46:22 N 2 '63
HOYT, Murray. See Stevenson, N. C. jt. auth.
HOYT, Norris
Rough ride on a sea of troubles. il Sports Illus 19:16-17+ Ag 5 '63
HOYT, Robert G.
Church journalism. Commonweal 79:488-9 Ja 24 '64
Issue is greatness. Commonweal 77:534-8; 78: 136-7 F 15, Ap 26 '63
HRUBAN, Zdenek, and Swift, Hewson
Uricase: localization in hepatic microbodies. bibliog Science 146:1316-18 D 4 '64
HRUSKA, Roman L.
Excerpt from statement, January 23, 1964. Cong Digest 43:144-6 My '64
HSIA, C. T.
Love in lotus blossom time. Sat R 47:63 D 5 '64
HSIA, T. A.
Demons in paradise: the Chinese images of Russia. bibliog f Ann Am Acad 349:27-37 S '63
HSIAO, Catherine. See Fraenkel, G. jt. auth.
HSIAO, George C. C. See Bugliarello, G. jt. auth.
HSIEH, Alice Langley
Sino-Soviet nuclear dialogue: 1963. bibliog Bul Atomic Sci 21:16-21 Ja '65
HSU, Konrad C. and others
Fluorescent, electron microscopic, and immunoelectrophoretic studies of labeled antibodies. bibliog Science 142:1471-3 D 13 '63
HUANG, Jeanette Tung-hsiang. See Blackwell, R. Q. jt. auth.
HUANG, Su-shu
Jeans' criterion of gravitational instability. Sky & Tel 26:77-9 Ag '63
Recent findings about early solar ssytem history. Sky & Tel 28:13-15 Jl '64
Understanding the main-sequence stars. Sky & Tel 25:136-8 Mr '63
HUARTE, John
Two for a quarterback. H. L. Masin. por Sr Schol 85:26 N 18 '64
HUB caps. See Automobiles—Hub caps
HUBBARD, Clarence T.
Wildlife has a place on the Christmas plates of Denmark. Audubon Mag 66:368-9 N '64
HUBBARD, Deon W.
Facts and fallacies about farm corporations. Suc Farm 61:61+ Mr '63
HUBBARD, E. C. See Cohen, C. J. jt. auth.
HUBBARD, Frank W.
Millions of children and their teachers are being handicapped by overcrowded classes. NEA J 52:52-4 Mr '63
HUBBARD, Howard W. See Krettek, G. jt. auth.
HUBBARD, Lafayette Ronald
Have you ever been a boo-hoo? J. Phelan. il pors Sat Eve Post 237:81-5 Mr 21 '64
HUBBARD, Mabel
Listen, my heart; condensation of Make a joyful sound. H. E. Waite. il pors Read Digest 82:297-308+ Ap '63
HUBBARD, Orville L.
Operation eyesore stops urban decay. Am City 78:165-6 My '63
—and Archer, R. K.
Ice skaters enjoy heat breaks. Am City 78: 86-7 D '63
HUBBARD, Walter W.
Virginia's Shenandoah. Travel 121:30-6 My '64
HUBBARD, Ward N.
Calorimetry. Science 147:312-14 Ja 15 '65
HUBBARD medal
President Kennedy presents the Hubbard medal; American Mount Everest expedition. il Nat Geog Mag 124:514-15 O '63
HUBBELL, John G.
Secret mission of Lieutenant Hilsman. Read Digest 84:137-8+ F '64
Things my wife drags home! Read Digest 84:125-8 My '64
Tough Tommy Power, our deterrent-in-chief. Read Digest 84:71-6 My '64
We are a different breed of cat, sir. Read Digest 85:225-6+ N '64
—See Daniel, J. jt. auth.
HUBBERT, M. King
Are we retrogressing in science? bibliog Science 139:884-90 Mr 8 '63
HUBBS, Kenneth Douglass
Tragic rebirth of the Chicago Cubs. T. Cohane. il Look 28:60+ Je 16 '64
HÜBE, Torun Bülow-. See Bülow-Hübe, T.
HUBEL, David H.
Visual cortex of the brain; with biographical sketch. Sci Am 209:30, 54-62 bibliog(p 186) N '63
HUBER, William W.
Our loving public. Am For 69:6-7+ Ag '63
HUBERMAN, John
Discipline without punishment. Harvard Bsns R 42:62-8 Jl '64
HUBERMAN, Leo
Viewing U.S. economy with a Marxist glass. por Bsns W p67-8+ Ap 13 '63
HUBERT, Adelyn C.
Keeping yacht club juniors interested. Motor B 112:50-1+ D '63
HUCK, Susan
What's in store for Iraq. Nat R 14:193-4 Mr 12 '63
HUDES, Ted
American investment pays off. Look 27:82a-82c Jl 2 '63
HUDGINS, Florence P.
Negro beauty culturist goes eastern. F. L. Spellmon. il por Negro Hist Bul 28:15 O '64
HUDSON, Charles J. jr
This month in the South (cont of) Things to do this month in the South. See issues of Popular gardening
HUDSON, Deatt
In the attic of the Shelburne museum; poem. New Yorker 39:175 S 14 '63
HUDSON, G. F.
Soviet soft line towards the West. Cur Hist 45:230-4+ O '63
HUDSON, George E.
Frequency & time standards. Electr World 72:20-3 Ag '64
HUDSON, J. Paul
English bronze wool weights. Antiques 84:691-3 D '63
HUDSON, L. F.
X-line nite light. Pop Electr 21:57-8 Ag '64
HUDSON, Lois Phillips
Where the fields are fresh and green; story. Reporter 30:42-5 Ja 16 '64
HUDSON, Richard
As the Cubans see Castro. Sat R 47:97-9+ O 10 '64
Big problems of a small planet. Sat R 46:28-30 N 30 '63
Might no longer makes right. Sat R 48:50 Ja 9 '65
No finish line for the arms race. Sat R 46: 40 Ag 24 '63
HUDSON, Robert B.
New and future trends in the use of audio-visual materials; excerpts from address, July 14, 1963. por ALA Bul 58:39-42 Ja '64
HUDSON, Rock
Is he the next Cary Grant? K. Baskette. por Good H 156:80-1+ Ap '63

HUDSON BAY
Eskimo north. H. Innes. il Holiday 35:88-93+ Ap '64
HUDSON institute, incorporated
Report on a think factory. A. Herzog. il N Y Times Mag p30+ N 10 '63
HUDSON motor car company
Special-interest cars; Hudson-Essex- Terraplane. M. R. Marks. il Motor T 16:79 N '64
HUDSON RIVER
Dig they must? proposed hydro power plant at Storm King Mountain. il Newsweek 64: 67-8 D 21 '64
From a mountaintop to 1,000 fathoms deep. R. H. Boyle. il Sports Illus 21:74-82 Ag 17 '64
Great battle for Storm King. J. Ridgeway. New Repub 151:8-9 N 28 '64
Hudson River: Cruising gateway. F. S. Blanchard. il Yachting 113:42-5+ Mr '63
To preserve the scenic Hudson. C. W. Buchheister. il Aubudon Mag 66:358 N '64
HUDSON RIVER bridges
High-level lighting for a new lower level; George Washington Bridge. il Am City 78: 117-18 F '63
HUDSON RIVER school. See Painting, American
HUDSON RIVER VALLEY
Hudson River Valley portfolio. J. T. Butler. il Antiques 85:432-7 Ap '64
New York's great river; new holiday shunpike tour. B. Ballantine. il Holiday 36:21-8 Jl '64
North of Broadway. R. Deardorff. il Redbook 121:68-9+ O '63
HUDSPETH, William J.
Strychnine: its facilitating effect on the solution of a simple oddity problem by the rat. bibliog Science 145:1331-3 S 18 '64
HUEBNER, R. J. and others
Inhibition by 5-iododeoxyuridine of the oncogenic effects of adenovirus type 12 in hamsters. Science 142:488-90 O 25 '63
HUEBSCH, B. W.
Obituary
Pub W por 186:27 Ag 17 '64
HUEFFER, Ford Madox. See Ford, F. M.
HUEFTLE, Keene
Cougar chase. por Outdoor Life 133:74-5+ Ap '64
HUEG, W. F.
How to make good corn silage; interview, ed. by L. Zeman. Suc Farm 61:39+ S '63
HUEG, W. F. jr, and Zeman, L. E.
Harvest hay by the calendar. Suc Farm 62:44-5 Je '64
HUFF, Betty Tracy
Beat that bongo; drama. Plays 24:13-22 N '64
Professor Hobo; drama. Plays 23:1-14 N '63
Too many cooks; drama. Plays 23:1-12, 108 My '64
HUFF, Darrell
Easy way to build a skylight. Pop Sci 185:144-5 Ag '64
Happy wedding: cement mixer and barrow. Pop Sci 185:146-7 Ag '64
How to score better on tests. Bet Hom & Gard 41:106+ F '63
So I built my own fireplace. Pop Sci 183:129-31+ N '63
HUFF, Robert
Hit dirge from a flop; poem. Mlle 59:104 Jl '64
Old line for daughter; poem. Mlle 59:209 My '64
Oxbow; poem. Mlle 58:72 D '63
HUFF, Sally D. and Fuller, J. L.
Audiogenic seizures, the dilute locus, and phenylalanine hydroxylase in DBA/1 mice. bibliog Science 144:304-5 Ap 17 '64
HUFF, Sam
Sad Sam. il por Newsweek 64:104 O 5 '64
HUFFINES, Robert
Three for a pyramid. il por Time 81:108+ My 17 '63
What's in it for Eddie, Bob, and Vic? S. H. Brown. il por Fortune 70:139-43+ S '64
HUFFORD, Ruby
Bleach printing. il Design 66:8-9 N '64
HUFNAGEL, Harold
Slim twosome. Pop Electr 21:63-4 D '64
HUGGINS, Charles E.
Reversible agglomeration used to remove dimethylsulfoxide from large volumes of frozen blood. bibliog Science 139:504-5 F 8 '63
HUGGLER, Thomas E.
Crows a la carte. pors Outdoor Life 131:26-7+ Ja '63
HUGH-JONES, E. M.
Labour tries to broaden the base. il Reporter 29:26-30 N 7 '63
HUGH-JONES, Siriol
Fonteyn, the enchantress. Vogue 142:64-7 S 15 '63
Lord and the regalia. Horizon 5:92-6 My '63
HUGH-JONES, Stephen
India's new military strength. New Repub 151:11-13 D 19 '64
Pakistan flirts. New Repub 151:15-16 S 5 '64
HUGHES, Allen
Francis Poulenc 1899-1963. Mus Am 83:20 F '63
HUGHES, Catharine
Odets: the price of success. Commonweal 78:558-60 S 20 '63
Paradoxical play; The deputy. Commonweal 79:654-6 F 28 '64
HUGHES, Daniel
Poetry's larger views. Nation 196:550-2 Je 29 '63
HUGHES, Darcy W. O'Gorman, and Diamond, L. K.
Chloramphenicol in blood: simple chemical estimations in patients receiving multiple antibiotics. bibliog Science 144:296-7 Ap 17 '64
HUGHES, David
Music at Harvard today. por Mus Am 83:7-9 Je '63
HUGHES, Edward C.
Can a mother's illness harm her unborn baby? Redbook 123:22+ Jl '64
HUGHES, Emmet John
Candidate from New York. por Newsweek 64: 27 S 21 '64
Castro and candor. por Newsweek 61:21 My 6 '63
Crime and politics. por Newsweek 64:25 O 19 '64
Crucial four-letter word. por Newsweek 63:15 Je 29 '64
Echo in the silence. por Newsweek 62:52 D 2 '63
Echo of two conventions. por Newsweek 64:15 S 7 '64
French recipe for folly. por Newsweek 62:15 Jl 15 '63
Fruitful choice. por Newsweek 64:31 O 5 '64
Gaullism. por Newsweek 64:23 N 30 '64
Glance at a decade. por Newsweek 62:15 Ag 26 '63
Goldwaterism. por Newsweek 64:17 Jl 27 '64
GOP and Rockefeller. por Newsweek 61:15 Je 3 '63
GOP's Chinese wing. por Newsweek 62:13 Jl 29 '63
GOP's unmerry Christmas. por Newsweek 64:9 D 28 '64
Great debate on Asia. por Newsweek 65:13 Ja 11 '65
Is it confidential, or is it history? N Y Times Mag p24+ My 12 '63
Lesson from Vietnam. por Newsweek 62:17 S 9 '63
Letter to a governor. por Newsweek 61:19 Je 17 '63
Lively papacy. por Newsweek 61:19 Ap 22 '63
Mann for LBJ's season. por Newsweek 63:25 My 18 '64
Mildly welcomed truce. por Newsweek 62:31 O 21 '63
Mysteries of policymaking. por Newsweek 65: 17 Ja 25 '65
Native son rises. Sat R 46:40-1 Je 15 '63
Nature of the presidency; excerpts from address. Pub W 183:32-3 Je 24 '63
Neutralist. por Newsweek 63:13 Je 1 '64
New diplomatic style. por Newsweek 63:15 Ap 6 '64
Non-debate. por Newsweek 63:19 Mr 23 '64
Odds against Goldwater. por Newsweek 62:21 N 4 '63
One-man band. Newsweek 64:59 O 26 '64
Other fellow. por Newsweek 64:23 N 16 '64
Party of Ike. por Newsweek 63:15 My 4 '64
Pause before the din. por Newsweek 64:15 Jl 13 '64
Pope John XXIII: gentle shepherd of a revolution. Newsweek 61:42-4+ Je 10 '63
Rockefeller resolve. por Newsweek 62:23 S 23 '63
Salvaging of Republicanism. por Newsweek 64:21 N 2 '64
Schoolrooms and prayers. por Newsweek 62: 15 Jl 1 '63
Season of diplomacy. por Newsweek 61:23 Mr 25 '63
Shadows over Latin Europe. por Newsweek 61:23 My 20 '63
Two little words. por Newsweek 61:19 Ap 8 '63
Vatican II, scene two. por Newsweek 62:27 O 7 '63
Vatican II: striving for a new spring. por Newsweek 64:55-7 D 14 '64
Vietnam, with reason. por Newsweek 62:27 N 18 '63

HUGHES, Emmet John—*Continued*
View from defeat. por Newsweek 63:20-1 Je 15 '64
West's backlash. por Newsweek 64:13 Ag 10 '64
Zooming non-candidate. por Newsweek 63:29 Ap 20 '64

about

Author. M. K. Harvey. por Sat R 46:86 Mr 16 '63
Valet's view. il por Time 81:17-19 Mr 22 '63

HUGHES, Gail B.
Why can't Susan stay? Parents Mag 39:60-1+ O '64

HUGHES, H. Stuart
Most unstuffy man. Nation 197:408-9 D 14 '63
New Italy & its politics. Commentary 38:46-51 O '64
On being a candidate. Commentary 35:123-31 F '63
SANE marches on. Nat R 16:10-11 Ja 14 '64

HUGHES, Harold
Drought ends in Iowa. D. Mabry. Reporter 29:27 Jl 4 '63

HUGHES, Harold Everett
One man's triumph. F. Knebel. il pors Look 28:97-8+ O 6 '64

HUGHES, Helen
Eighteen; story. Redbook 122:40-1 F '64

HUGHES, Howard Robard
CAB to demand appearance by Hughes. R. H. Cook. Aviation W 80:39-40 Je 15 '64
Celebrated hermit. Time 81:91 My 10 '63
Grabbing again for TWA controls. il por Bsns W p 168+ My 16 '64
Howard Hughes; he is battling for control of a billion-dollar empire. J. R. Phelan. il pors Sat Eve Post 236:15-23 F 9 '63
Hughes battles to avoid court appearance. J. R. Ashlock. Aviation W 78:39-40 F 11 '63
Hughes breaks a date in fight for TWA. Bsns W p26 F 16 '63
Hughes' silence is major issue in merger. Aviation W 78:47 F 4 '63
Hughes takes a trick. Bsns W p27 Jl 18 '64
In devious battle. Newsweek 63:72+ My 11 '64
TWA will seek Hughes default order. J. R. Ashlock. Aviation W 78:49 F 18 '63

HUGHES, John
A monthly of Africa's daily life. Sat R 46:19-20 Ag 17 '63
Tough young man from Kenya. Sat R 46:32 N 30 '63

HUGHES, John H.
Home-rule powers for urbanizing counties and towns. Am City 78:169-70+ S '63

HUGHES, Kenneth
Christianity and Islam in West Africa. Christian Cent 81:264-7, 298-302 F 26-Mr 4 '64

HUGHES, Langston
Bread and butter side. por Sat R 46:19-20 Ap 20 '63
Profile. I. J. Wertz. por Negro Hist Bul 27:146-7 Mr '64
Tambourines to glory; dramatization of novel. Criticism
New Yorker 39:96 N 9 '63
Newsweek 62:72 N 18 '63

HUGHES, Marie M.
What teachers do and the way they do it. NEA J 53:11-13 S '64

HUGHES, Patrick E.
Watching bird flights by radar. Audubon Mag 66:182-4 My '64

HUGHES, Richard
Across the vast, silent land called Siberia. N Y Times Mag p 12-13+ My 31 '64
Ayo Gorkhali! N Y Times Mag p34-5+ O 18 '64
Borneo, Britain's South Vietnam. N Y Times Mag p9+ Jl 19 '64
Hong Kong: the new Shanghai. Sat R 48:43+ Ja 2 '65
I am Chinese! I live in the southern ocean! N Y Times Mag p9+ Ag 4 '63
Mao, at seventy, tries a big leap in the world. N Y Times Mag p 10+ F 2 '64
Mao: Nationalist first, Communist second. N Y Times Mag p 17+ Je 7 '64
Peking's indispensable front man. N Y Times Mag p 16+ O 4 '64
Warning to Mao, it's the year of the dragon. N Y Times Mag p24-5+ Mr 1 '64

HUGHES, Richard J.
Duty of professional associations; address, November 9, 1962. Vital Speeches 29:254-6 F 1 '63

HUGHES, Riley
Awards to the new tale-tellers. Sat R 46:27 Jl 20 '63

HUGHES, Robert
Golden grin. Nation 199:189-91 O 5 '64

HUGHES, Spike
Great opera houses: Sadler's Wells. Opera N 28:26-31 Ja 25 '64

HUGHES, Ted
Cadenza; poem. New Yorker 40:38 My 30 '64
Foxgloves; poem. New Yorker 39:28 Jl 27 '63
Full moon; poem. Atlan 212:72 D '63
Music on the moon; poem. New Yorker 39:24 Ag 10 '63
Poems to Robert Graves perhaps; On Westminster bridge; After Lorca; Heatwave; Era of giant lizards; Small hours; poems. Poetry 103:152-6 D '63
Stealing trout; poem. New Yorker 40:44 Mr 21 '64
Sunday evening; poem. Atlan 211:59 My '63

HUGHES, Thomas
Colony of younger sons. J. Keats. il por Holiday 35:22+ F '64

HUGHES, Thomas Lowe
Making the world safe for diversity; address, June 8, 1964. Dept State Bul 51:6-17 Jl 6 '64

HUGHES, V. E.
(ed) See Kaminsky, M. Swing band era

HUGHES aircraft company
Incentive potential of $4.8 million in Hughes-Comsat corp. contract. Aviation W 80:23 Mr 30 '64

HUGHES tool company
CAB bureau criticizes Toolco agreement. R. G. O'Lone. Aviation W 81:40 O 26 '64
Court voids CAB order on Toolco-TWA. J. W. Carter. Aviation W 81:30-1 D 14 '64
Hughes appeals TWA default judgment. Aviation W 78:45 Je 3 '63
Hughes judgment appeal denied. Aviation W 80:34 Je 8 '64
Hughes makes new pass at TWA. Bsns W p32 O 10 '64
Hughes to sell TWA debentures. il Aviation W 79:40 O 7 '63
Hughes tool co. drops Northeast support. Aviation W 79:41 Ag 12 '63
In devious battle; Hughes to repurchase TWA? Newsweek 63:72+ My 11 '64
Northeast decision seen aimed at Hughes. R. H. Cook. Aviation W 78:38-9 Ap 22 '63
Northeast, Hughes file trust agreement; step toward regaining Trans World airlines. J. W. Carter. Aviation W 81:34-5 O 12 '64
Northeast seeking cancellation of debts. J. R. Ashlock. Aviation W 79:31 Jl 29 '63
TWA to pay $16 million interest on debt. J. R. Ashlock. Aviation W 80:34-5 My 25 '64
TWA will seek Hughes default order. J. R. Ashlock. Aviation W 78:49 F 18 '63

HUGHEY, Elizabeth
Climate for progress. por(p3242) Library 89:3255-60 S 15 '64

HUGHEY, J. D.
Theological frame of religious liberty. Christian Cent 80:1365-8 N 6 '63

HUGHIE; drama. See O'Neill, E. G.

HUGO Carlos, prince of Bourbon-Parma
Exciting life; wedding of Carlos and Irene. il por Newsweek 63:40 My 11 '64
Her royal choice. por Newsweek 63:51-2 F 17 '64
Irene and Carlos in love affair of state; with report by P. Saporiti. il pors Life 56:40-40B F 21 '64
Love finds a way. il por Sr Schol 84:17 F 28 '64
Love with the proper stranger. il por Time 83:38 F 21 '64

HUGO, Richard F.
In Stafford country; Tahola; poems. Poetry 102:23-4 Ap '63
Squatter on company land; poem. Yale R 52:416 Mr '63

about

Run of three. J. M. Morrison. Poetry 101:281-2 Ja '63

HUGO, Victor
He also wrote novels. il Time 81:66 Ap 26 '63

HUIE, William Bradford
Death of an innocent. Look 28:23-5 Mr 24 '64
FBI agent as missionary. New Repub 151:10-11 N 21 '64
Untold story of the Mississippi murders. Sat Eve Post 237:11-15 S 5 '64

about

Southerner goes North. New Repub 150:8 Ap 25 '64

HUITT, Ralph K.
What's right and wrong with Congress. Nations Bsns 52:40-1+ N '64

HUIZINGA, J. H.
Disappointments of Ayub Khan. Reporter 28:30-1 Je 6 '63
Hussein of Jordan. New Repub 149:10-11 S 14 '63
HUIZINGA, Johan
Johan Huizinga and the task of cultural history. R. L. Colie. bibliog f Am Hist R 69:607-30 Ap '64
HUJER, Flower
Flower Hujer dance theatre at Town Hall. M. Marks. Dance Mag 37:30 N '63
HUKBALAHAPS
Last of the Huks. Time 83:28 Je 5 '64
HULET, Claude L.
Goal: economic freedom. Sat R 47:43-4 F 15 '64
HULL, Andrew P.
Health physics. Science 142:73-4 O 4 '63
HULL, Bobby
Go, Bobby! go, to beat the magic 50. W. Leggett. il pors Sports Illus 22:14-17 Ja 25 '65
Hockey's golden boy. G. Astor. il pors Look 29:87-90 Ja 26 '65
Hullabaloo. il por Newsweek 65:71 F 1 '65
Superman shoots up the league. il pors Life 56:84-5 Ja 31 '64
HULL, Clinton R.
Now, a jet drive for your outboard. Pop Sci 182:122-4+ Je '63
HULL, Cordell
Cordell Hull, by J. W. Pratt. Review
Time por 83:89 My 29 '64
HULL, Dale O.
How much machinery do I need? Suc Farm 62:82-3 Ja '64
Save that crop with combine know-how. Suc Farm 62:52-3 S '64
HULL, George
Waterlilies. il Pop Gard 14:38-9+ My '63
HULL, Helen S.
Come to the flower show. Flower Grower 50:37-9 Jl '63
They changed the face of this country. Flower Grower 51:56-7 Ja '64
To the queen! Flower Grower 50:12 O '63
HULL, Isaac
By heaven, that ship is ours! L. McKee. il por Am Heritage 16:4-11+ D '64
HULL, Judith
Curl up and read. Seventeen 23:64 Ag '64
HULL, Robert Marvin. See Hull, B.
HULL, Roger
Immortality through premiums? Christian Cent 81:239-40 F 19 '64
HULL, W. T.
How a diesel engine works. Motor B 114:28-30+ O '64
HULL, William Henry, Jr
Hints on exhibiting house plants. Horticulture 41:457 S '63
HULL, Mrs William Henry, Jr
Lipstick plant. Horticulture 42:46 Ja '64
Making new plants out of old plants. Horticulture 41:524 O '63
Moving plants outdoors. Horticulture 42:36-7+ Je '64
Suitable plants. Horticulture 42:40-1 F '64
HULME, Kathryn C.
Timeless Kauai swamp. Atlan 215:68-71 Ja '65
HULTIN, Johan V.
Physician's R-x for auto safety. il por Todays Health 42:38 N '64
HUMAIRA, consort of Mohammed Zahir, king of Afghanistan
People of the week. por(p 14) U S News 55:24 S 16 '63
HUMAN behavior. See Behavior (psychology)
HUMAN beings. See Man
HUMAN betterment association for voluntary sterilization, incorporated
Birth control by surgery. J. Ridgeway. New Repub 151:9-11 N 14 '64
HUMAN body. See Physiology
HUMAN development institute, incorporated, Atlanta
Programming harmony; Relationship improvement program. il Bsns W p 142+ Ap 18 '64
HUMAN ecology
Geology and trace elements: relation to nutrition; report on symposium at the annual meeting of the Geological society of America. H. L. Cannon. Science 143:704+ F 14 '64
Reviews: man and nature joined in quiet crisis. W. Vogt. Natur Hist 73:4+ Mr '64
HUMAN embryo. See Fetus
HUMAN equality. See Equality
HUMAN evolution. See Evolution
HUMAN factor; story. See Ely, D.
HUMAN fertility. See Fertility, Human
HUMAN figure in art
Fay Lansner; deliberate contraries. B. Guest. il Art N 62:36-7+ D '63
Figure paintings of A. Henry Nordhausen. L. Schmeckebier. il Am Artist 29:34-9+ F '65
Letter from Paris: nudes in Fontainebleau *maniériste* school at L'Oeil. Genêt. New Yorker 39:84+ Ja 25 '64
Picasso and the nude. J. S. Boggs. il Art N 62:29-31+ Ja '64
See also
Figure drawing
Human figure in photography
Nude in art
HUMAN figure in photography
Art-o-focus. L. Barry. il Pop Phot 55:136-7 D '64
Challenging nude figure. Gowland. il Pop Phot 55:10+ O '64
Color work-shop. F. Bond. il Mod Phot 27:23+ Mr '63
Glamor; try shooting underwater. P. Gowland. il Pop Phot 53:12 Jl '63
Lighting the nude. P. Gowland. il Pop Phot 54:14+ Ja '64
Model in the pool. P. Gowland. il Pop Phot 55:14+ S '64
More art than sex. il U S Camera 26:62-3+ Jl '63
New look in nudes. J. Morris. il U S Camera 26:58-61+ Jl '63; Discussion. 26:25 S '63
Nude, most difficult of all subjects. il U S Camera 27:64-5 Mr '64
P.S. on the topless. Gowland. il Pop Phot 55:44 D '64
Year's best glamor book. J. M. Zanutto. il Pop Phot 52:70-5 Ap '63
HUMAN heredity. See Heredity
HUMAN nature
Social nature of man; programs at AAAS Montreal meeting, 26-31 December 1964. il Science 146:801-3 N 6 '64
HUMAN race. See Anthropology; Man
HUMAN relations
Absence makes the heart grow. J. R. Gaver. Read Digest 85:100-1 Jl '64
Am I my brother's keeper? symposium. il Seventeen 23:102-5+ D '64
Chasm widens between old and young. Christian Cent 82:38 Ja 13 '65
Conflict in human values. R. N. McMurry. Harvard Bsns R 41:130-6+ My '63
Excuse we should never use. B. Mandelbaum and V. M. Ratner. Read Digest 83:79-80 D '63
Fine art of keeping one's head. W. Fitz-Gibbon. Read Digest 83:62-5 S '63
Future is ours; encyclical Pacem in terris. Life 54:4 Ap 26 '63
Pacem in terris: for all humanity; with excerpts. il Newsweek 61:21-2 Ap 22 '63
Pacem in terris; Pope John's encyclical. Commonweal 78:123-4 Ap 26 '63
Redbook dialogue. A. Quinn; H. Belafonte. il Redbook 120:54-5+ Mr '63
Sons and fathers. W. Saroyan. Reporter 31:52-3 S 24 '64
Things old and new in Pacem in terris. J. C. Murray. America 108:612-14 Ap 27 '63
What we are for: summary of new encyclical on world peace. John XXIII. il Time 81:60+ Ap 19 '63
See also
Brotherhood of man
Conversation
Courtesy
Love
Marriage
Neighbors
Popularity
Praise
Prejudice
Relatives
Sex relations
Teachers—Adjustment
Study and teaching
See also
Human development institute, incorporated, Atlanta
HUMAN rights. See Civil rights
HUMAN rights, Universal declaration of. See Universal declaration of human rights
HUMAN rights commission. See United Nations—Commission on human rights
HUMAN rights day and week
Bill of rights day, Human rights day; proclamation. L. B. Johnson. Dept State Bul 51:887 D 21 '64
Bill of rights day, Human rights day, proclamation, December 2, 1963. L. B. Johnson. Dept State Bul 50:21 Ja 6 '64
Fifteenth anniversary of Universal declaration of human rights; statement, December 9, and address, December 8, 1963. A. E. Stevenson; R. N. Gardner. bibliog f Dept State Bul 50:19-24 Ja 6 '64

HUMAN rights day and week—*Continued*
Story of progress in achieving international human rights. M. Tree. il NEA J 52:50-3 N '63
HUMAN rights fellowship. See Scholarships and fellowships
HUMAN rights year (proposed) See International human rights year (proposed)
HUMAN temperature. See Temperature, Animal and human
HUMAN voice. See Voice
HUMAN welfare. See Social welfare
HUMANISM
Hemlock and the cross: humanism, Socrates and Christ, by G. MacGregor. Review
Christian Cent 80:1107 S 11 '63. L. C. Rudolph
HUMANIST; story. See Gary, R.
HUMANISTIC studies, Aspen institute for. See Aspen institute for humanistic studies
HUMANITIES
Future of humanities in graduate school. Sch & Soc 92:119+ Mr 21 '64
Sorry state of history. J. H. Plumb. il Horizon 5:97-100 S '63
See also
Commission on the humanities
Liberal education
Science and the humanities

Bibliography

Arts and humanities; paperback books. D. Zamchick. Sr Schol 83:32T Ja 17; 85:23T D 2 '64

Study and teaching

Humanities and non-western studies. A. H. Marckwardt. Ann Am Acad 356:45-53 N '64
HUMANITIES fair. See Education—Exhibitions and museums
HUMANITY (mankind) See Man
HUMASON comet. See Comets
HUMBLE oil and refining company
For Humble: Esso or Enco? Bsns W p64 Jl 20 '63
Humble crashes the West Coast subsidiary of Jersey standard. il Bsns W p82+ F 22 '64
Humble oil lays out a new Texas town; Bayport development. il Bsns W p67-8 F 8 '64
Humble on its own in West; Tidewater deal off. Bsns W p28 My 9 '64
Phantom city; Bayway refinery. New Yorker 39:26-8 Ja 18 '64
Welding an oil giant. il Bsns W p 118-20+ Ap 27 '63
HUMBOLDT REDWOODS STATE PARK. See California—Parks and reserves
HUMBOLDT university. See Colleges and universities—Germany (Democratic Republic)
HUME, Ivor Noël
Digging up Jamestown; excerpts from Here lies Virginia. Am Heritage 14:66-77 Ap '63
Late seventeenth-century pottery kiln site near Jamestown; excerpts from Here lies Virginia. Antiques 83:550-2 My '63
Search for New Bremen and the glass of John Frederick Amelung. Antiques 85:310-13 Mr '64
Some English glass from colonial Virginia. Antiques 84:68-71 Jl '63
HUME, Michael
Connecticut votes dogs for medical research; letter. Science 142:147 O 11 '63
HUMESTON, E. J. Jr
Public library bookstore. Wilson Lib Bul 37:563-4+ Mr '63
HUMIDIFIERS
Humidifiers. il Consumer Rep 30:27-32 Ja '65
Lack of humidity, or why we crack up. il House & Gard 124:14+ D '63
There's danger in desert-day air. S. J. Howard. il Pop Mech 120:158-65+ D '63
Water-spray humidifier for a warm-air furnace. A. N. Anderson. il Pop Sci 186:156-7 Ja '65
HUMIDITY
Air too dry in your house? il Changing T 19:44 Ja '65
Even in winter, it's the humidity! il Good H 158:148+ Ja '64
Humidifiers. il Consumer Rep 30:27-32 Ja '65
Is your home too dry for comfort. R. M. Burnley. il Redbook 122:54-5+ F '64
Wintertime dryness; is humidification the answer? il Consumer Bul 47:37-40 Ja '64
See also
Hygrometers

Physiological effects

There's danger in desert-dry air. S. J. Howard. il Pop Mech 120:158-65+ D '63
HUMILITY
Ecumenical humility. America 109:339 S 28 '63
HUMLIKON, Switzerland
Village that lost its parents. C. McCarry. il Sat Eve Post 236:96+ D 7 '63
HUMMERSTONE, Robert G.
Outcast of Lebanon. Nation 199:303-5 N 2 '64; 200:inside cover Ja 11 '65
HUMMINGBIRDS
Adventures with hummingbirds; photographing the family life of ruby-throats. R. Austing. il Audubon Mag 66:252-6 Jl '64
Feathered jewels. J. Walters. il Flower Grower 51:20-1+ Ag '64
How to lure hummingbirds to your garden. O. K. Moore. il House B 105:22+ Je '63
Hummingbirds by the dozen. H. B. Alsebrook. Audubon Mag 65:246-7 Jl '63
Invitation to the hummers. R. D. Roe. il Pop Gard 15:90-1 Jl '64
HUMOR
Campaign jokes. Time 84:74+ S 18 '64
Checklist for humor writers. P. C. King. Writer 77:13-14+ N '64
Cultivate their sense of humor; humor of children. J. Wakeman. il Parents Mag 39:40-1+ Ag '64
Elephanting humor; excerpt from Elephant book. il N Y Times Mag p23 Ag 25 '63
Elephants by the trunk; elephant joke. Time 82:41 Ag 2 '63
Fine art of political wit, by L. A. Harris. Review
Newsweek 64:92+ S 14 '64
It all started with my mother and father. R. Armour. Writer 77:12-13 O '64
Joke, joke. America 110:505-6 Ap 11 '64
Jokes with the LBJ brand. A. Shuster. il N Y Times Mag p 100+ S 13 '64
Let a little nonsense in! symposium. Farm J 88:61+ Ja '64
Minstrel malice, racially oriented jokes. Christian Cent 81:1191 S 23 '64
Ruminants and factitioners. J. Ciardi. Sat R 46:20 Je 15 '63
What's red and goes boo-boo? M. A. Guitar. il N Y Times Mag p 102-3 S 15 '63
Why is everyone so helpful? excerpt from Ralph Reppert and his electric wife. R. Reppert. Read Digest 86:160D-160E Ja '65
Women have no sense of humor. R. T. Allen. il Read Digest 84:134-6 Ap '64
See also
Laughter
Limericks
Parodies
Satire
Television broadcasting—Humor
HUMOR, American
Lighter mood hits Washington; quotations. L. B. Johnson. U S News 56:47-8 My 11 '64
Party lines; election year humor. Newsweek 64:45 Ag 3 '64
What's happening to humor? J. Beatty, jr. Sat R 47:49 Ag 29 '64
Who's been grinding your valves, Mac? excerpts from Sorry I stirred it. B. Vaughan. il Read Digest 85:277-8+ N '64
HUMOR, Egyptian
Laughs from Cairo; comp. by H. Smith. N Y Times Mag p 131 D 13 '64
HUMOR, English
Noble deb ribs the nobs; with excerpts from Coronet among the weeds. il Life 54:97-8 Ap 26 '63
HUMOR, Pictorial
See also
Comics (books, strips, etc)
Moving pictures—Animated cartoons
HUMOR, Russian
Behind the smile on Krokodil. T. Shabad. il N Y Times Mag p22-3+ Je 7 '64
Jokes that seep through the iron curtain. P. Streit. il N Y Times Mag p28+ Ap 19 '64
HUMORISTS
World of Eliana Simón; humorist in Chilean El Mercurio. R. S. Castro. il Américas 15:40-1 Jl '63
See also
Comedians
HUMPBACK whales. See Whales
HUMPERDINCK, Engelbert
Hansel and Gretel. H. Glass. il Am Rec G 31:408-9 Ja '65
HUMPHREY, George Magoffin
Ike's Svengali? K. Crawford. Newsweek 63:36 Je 22 '64
HUMPHREY, Hubert Horatio, 1911-
Alliance for progress; address, January 20, 1964. Vital Speeches 30:307-11 Mr 1 '64

HUMPHREY, Hubert Horatio—*Continued*
American system; address, August 12, 1964. Vital Speeches 30:682-5 S 1 '64
Big business is it too big? reprint. pors Look 28:84-6 O 20 '64
Case for the Democratic party. por Sat R 47:21-3 O 31 '64
Debate on civil rights; March 18, 1964. por U S News 56:102-4 Mr 30 '64
Excerpt from address, April 3, 1963. Cong Digest 42:204+ Ag '63
Excerpt from address, November 26, 1963. Cong Digest 43:52+ F '64
Excerpt from testimony, February 25, 1963. Cong Digest 42:306+ D '63
Excerpt from testimony, July 24, 1963. Cong Digest 43:76+ Mr '64
G.O.P. jihad; holy war; reprint. Christian Cent 81:1172 S 23 '64
Myths about federal drug policies. New Repub 150:10-12 My 16 '64
Paperback attack on poverty: free book program for needy children; excerpts from address, April 1964. Library J 89:2128 My 15 '64
(ed) Racial integration in education: excerpts from Integration vs. segregation. Sch & Soc 92:97-100 Mr 7 '64
Spiritual quest. por Library J 89:3243-5 S 15 '64
To move Congress out of its ruts. N Y Times Mag p39+ Ap 7 '63
U.S. policy in Latin America. For Affairs 42: 585-601 Jl '64
What I expect; interview. por Nations Bsns 52:33+ D '64

about

Available for foreign service. il por Time 84: 22-3 D 4 '64
Close-up of the vice-presidential candidates. il por Sr Schol 85:12 S 23 '64
Coming ADA government? J. Burnham. Nat R 16:954-9 N 3 '64
Cracking the whip for civil rights. il pors Newsweek 63:26-8+ Ap 13 '64
Democratic team. H. Brandon. Sat R 47:18+ S 26 '64
Echo of two conventions. E. J. Hughes. Newsweek 64:15 S 7 '64
Filibuster buster. K. Crawford. Newsweek 63:38 Mr 16 '64
Firebrand Senator cools down. il por Bsns W p29-30 Je 1 '63
First ADA president? Nat R 16:801 S 22 '64
He smelleth the battle afar off. Time 84:20 S 11 '64
Hubert fills the President's Rx. il pors Life 57:29 S 4 '64
Hubert Humphrey: a close-up. il pors U S News 57:40-2 S 7 '64
Hubert Humphrey comes on strong. S. Shaffer. il pors N Y Times Mag p 11+ Ag 25 '63
HHH anonymous. K. Crawford. Newsweek 65:32 Ja 11 '65
HHH, complete statist. R. Moley. Newsweek 64:96 S 14 '64
HHH: we work together. il por Newsweek 64:30 N 9 '64
Hubert strikes oil. il por Newsweek 64:28 S 28 '64
Hubert's holiday. il por Time 84:31 N 20 '64
Humphrey: an excellent choice. Sat Eve Post 237:86 S 26 '64
Humphrey comes up strong for no. 2 spot. pors Bsns W p 17-18 Ag 8 '64
Humphrey's successor. il por Newsweek 64: 35 N 30 '64
Informal visit with Hubert Humphrey. G. Zimmermann. il pors Look 28:82-4 O 20 '64
Johnson and Humphrey: political saga. il pors U S News 57:56-8 N 16 '64
Johnson-Humphrey. New Repub 151:3-4 Ag 8 '64
Johnson-Humphrey elected. por Sr Schol 85: 8 N 11 '64
Johnson-Humphrey ticket, or —? il por U S News 57:15 Ag 10 '64
Letter from Atlantic City. R. H. Rovere. il New Yorker 40:112-17 S 5 '64
LBJ's running mate: the man he favors. il por U S News 57:32-3 Ag 3 '64
Making of HHH. il pors Newsweek 64:18-26 S 7 '64
Man who quit kicking the wall. il pors Time 84:20-2 S 4 '64
New drugs: is government supervision adequate? M. Mintz. il Reporter 28:46-9+ Mr 28 '63
On the short end. il Time 84:43 O 2 '64
One man's day. il Time 84:25 O 9 '64
Politics is my life. P. Hamill. il pors Sat Eve Post 237:82-5 O 10 '64
Poorest rich man. Newsweek 64:71 O 5 '64
President Humphrey? S. Alsop. por Sat Eve Post 237:12 My 2 '64
President's wise selection. Life 57:4 S 4 '64
Real test of Hubert Humphrey. New Repub 151:4 S 5 '64
Senate; Mr Humphrey's conquering hosts. M. Kempton. New Repub 150:6-8 Ap 4 '64
Senate test ploy. K. Crawford. Newsweek 62:28 Jl 22 '63
Sentimental journey. J. Lindsay. il Newsweek 64:31-3 S 21 '64
They want to be second. B. H. Bagdikian. il pors N Y Times Mag p30-3+ O 11 '64
Triple-H brand on the vice-presidency. D. S. Broder. il pors N Y Times Mag p30-1+ D 6 '64
Vice Presidency: how big a job. il por U S News 57:41 S 7 '64
What the new no. two man is really like. il pors U S News 58:41-3 Ja 25 '65
Why Humphrey gets taken for granted. W. V. Shannon. New Repub 151:10-12 Jl 4 '64; Correction. 151:37 Ag 8 '64
With LBJ, what a day! J. P. Sutherland. il U S News 57:43 S 7 '64
Wonderful world of Hubert. J. Chamberlain. por Nat R 16:767-9 S 8 '64

HUMPHREY, Hubert Horatio, family
Humphreys: their assets and debts. por U S News 57:28 O 5 '64
Official home for the Hubert Humphreys? il U S News 57:8-9 D 28 '64

HUMPHREY, Muriel
Girl he married. il por Newsweek 64:19 S 7 '64

HUMPHREY, William
Ballad of Jesse Neighbours; story. Esquire 60:120 S '63
Monument and the shadow; story. Sat Eve Post 237:33-5 N 7 '64
Pump; story. Esquire 60:196 D '63
Voice from the woods; story. Atlan 212: 96-101 O '63

HUMPHREYS, J. R.
Fields and fairs of Iowa. Holiday 36:20+ S '64
Minnesota wilderness. Holiday 33:22+ Je '63
Sleepy South of Illinois. Holiday 34:18+ S '63

HUMPHREYS, Richard F.
Interdependence of administration and faculty. Sch & Soc 92:48-9 F 8 '64

HUMPHRY, John A. and Wickersham, Lucille
Report on Rhode Island libraries recommends sweeping changes; summary. Library J 88: 1844 My 1 '63

HUNDERE, Al
I learned about flying from that! Flying 74: 52+ My '64

HUNDLEY, Norris, Jr
Colorado waters dispute. For Affairs 42:495-500 Ap '64

HUNDT, Alan G. and Premack, David
Running as both a positive and negative reinforcer. bibliog Science 142:1087-8 N 22 '63

HUNEEUS-COX, Francis
Electrophoretic and immunological studies of squid axoplasm proteins. bibliog Science 143:1036-7 Mr 6 '64

HUNEKER, James Gibbons
James Gibbons Huneker, by A. T. Schwab. Review
Nation 197:224-6 O 12 '63. H. Clurman
New Yorker 39:208+ O 26 '63. W. Sargeant
Newsweek 62:94 S 9 '63

HUNGARIAN cookery. See Cookery, Hungarian

HUNGARIAN short haired pointers. See Pointers (dogs)

HUNGARIAN state opera house, Budapest. See Opera houses

HUNGARIANS
Letter from Budapest. J. Wechsberg. il New Yorker 40:121-2+ Mr 14 '64

HUNGARY
New Hungary. P. Ben. New Repub 150:7 F 15 '64
See also
Architecture—Hungary
Ballet—Hungary
Budapest
Catholic church—Relations (diplomatic)—Hungary
Catholic church in Hungary
Communism—Hungary
Jews in Hungary
United Nations—Hungary

Description and travel

Halt in Hungary. L. Thompson. il Travel 120:31-3 S '63

HUNGARY—*Continued*

Economic conditions

Hungary: renaissance after revolt. D. Holden. il Sat Eve Post 237:38+ Ap 25 '64
Hungary seven years later. A. Rothberg. Christian Cent 80:1174-6 S 25 '63
A look inside Hungary; seven years after uprising. A. Kucherov. il U S News 55:50-3 D 30 '63; Correction. 56:9 Ja 6 '64

Foreign relations

Rapid change. il Newsweek 62:46-7 Jl 29 '63

Politics and government

Hungary faces the future. F. A. Váli. Cur Hist 44:288-93 My '63
Letter from Budapest. J. Wechsberg. il New Yorker 40:121-2+ Mr 14 '64
A look inside Hungary; seven years after uprising. A. Kucherov. il U S News 55:50-3 D 30 '63; Correction. 56:9 Ja 6 '64

Religious institutions and affairs

Limits of liberalization. Time 84:24 D 25 '64

Social conditions

New aristocracy. il Newsweek 64:39-40 Jl 27 '64

Social life and customs

Courting customs in the workers' paradise. J. Kosa. Reporter 30:46-7 F 13 '64
See also
Budapest—Social life and customs

HUNGER
Hunger and sacrifice; World food congress. Christian Cent 80:875-6 Jl 10 '63
Hunger round the world: 10,000 die every day. il Newsweek 61:43-4+ Je 17 '63
Man, land and food, by L. R. Brown. Review U S News il 56:28-31 Ja 6 '64
National freedom from hunger week, 1964; proclamation, August 15, 1964. L. B. Johnson. Dept State Bul 51:388 S 14 '64
Temperature changes in the rat in response to feeding. A. J. Rampone and M. E. Shirasu. bibliog il Science 144:317-19 Ap 17 '64
See also
Famines

HUNGERFORD, Mary Jane. See Thoms, H. jt. auth.

HUNN, Max
By outboard to the Marquesas. il Yachting 116:52-3+ N '64
Florida's unusual trees. il Am For 70:17-19 Ap '64
Georgia's famous trees. Am For 70:42-5 N '64
Houseboat in the Everglades. il por Motor B 114:33-5+ N '64
Through the mangrove wilderness. il Yachting 114:54-5+ N '63

HUNN, Milda H.
Lawn problem? we solved it with zoysia. il Flower Grower 51:24 My '64

HUNSAKER, Gordon D.
Career day. por Recreation 56:234 My '63

HUNT, C. Raymond
Victory by design. il por Time 82:68-9 S 27 '63
Yachting interviews: Ray Hunt. B. D. Barker, 3d. il pors Yachting 116:47-9+ Jl '64

HUNT, Donald H.
Full-time recruiting: the Pennsylvania story. pors Library J 89:2031-6 My 15 '64

HUNT, Douglas W.
Secondary education and international understanding. Sch & Soc 91:243 Sum '63

HUNT, Dudley, Jr
Corporate architectural practice. Arch Rec 133:163-6 My '63

HUNT, Fern Bowers
Fresh flowers vs. phony posies. Horticulture 41:96 F '63

HUNT, Graham R. and Salisbury, J. W.
Lunar surface features: mid-infrared spectral observations. bibliog Science 146:641-2 O 30 '64

HUNT, Haroldson Lafayette
H. L. Hunt: portrait of a super-patriot; Life line. R. G. Sherrill. por Nation 198:182-95 F 24 '64
Hunt strikes ink. por Newsweek 65:49 Ja 18 '65

HUNT, Jeannette T.
Giving baseball back to the boys. Recreation 56:235 My '63

HUNT, John Clark
Beware the Moonlight Estates. il Am For 69:12-14+ Je '63
Big mop up. Am For 70:10-13+ Ap '64
Neighborhood where I live. Am For 70:36-7+ N '64
Peaceful warpath. Am For 70:36-8+ Mr '64
Pollution; everybody's fight. Am For 70:17-20 S '64

HUNT, John H.
World understanding at Plattsburgh. NEA J 53:29-30 Ja '64

HUNT, Kenneth W.
Let's share a country common. Recreation 57:26 Ja '64

HUNT, Morton M.
Answer to some foolish theories about women. Redbook 121:66-7+ S '63
Are you the new kind of girl who fits in the new kind of world? Seventeen 22:86-7+ O '63
Limits of intimacy. Read Digest 85:69-71 S '64
Major and minor emotional problems. Redbook 121:35-46 S '63
Profiles (cont) New Yorker 40:37-40+ Ag 22; 37-8+ Ag 29; 37-40+ S 5 '64
Remarkable self-healing powers of the mind. Read Digest 84:87-90 F '64
Side effects: a new worry for doctors. Look 27:24-6+ D 31 '63
—and Corman, Rena
Tormented generation. Sat Eve Post 236:30, 33-4 O 12 '63

HUNT, Patricia
Playing cupid is a tough problem for a zoo-keeper. Life 57:54A Ag 21 '64
Rattanfungers and wunks. Life 56:63 F 7 '64
Snakes: but why are we all so afraid of them? Life 54:52+ Mr 1 '63
Editor in charge of whales, white tigers and sifakas. G. P. Hunt. por Life 56:3 F 7 '64

HUNT, Richard
Art. H. Kramer. Nation 196:255-6 Mr 23 '63

HUNT, Richard P.
Atomic question for the city. N Y Times Mag p46+ O 6 '63
Caesar or Como, the laughs are by Ace. N Y Times Mag p42+ S 15 '63
Ship of state rocks Hyannis Port. N Y Times Mag p30-1+ My 26 '63

HUNT, Rolfe Lanier
Should public funds aid parochial schools? por Parents Mag 38:70-1+ N '63
Unhidden persuader. Sat R 46:82 N 16 '63

HUNT, Ron
Mets' throwback to Cobb. M. Kram. por Sports Illus 21:48+ Jl 13 '64

HUNT, Ronald D.
Aberrant thyroid tissue in the mouse. bibliog Science 141:1054-5 S 13 '63
—See Tanzer, M. L. jt. auth.

HUNT, Vilma R. See Radford, E. P. jr. jt. auth.

HUNT foods and industries, incorporated
Hunt for the best. Time 83:92 Ap 24 '64
Tomato philosopher. il Time 82:64-5 Ag 23 '63

HUNTEN, Donald M.
Metallic emissions from the upper atmosphere. bibliog Science 145:26-31 Jl 3 '64

HUNTER, Charlayne Alberta
Image. por Time 82:27 S 13 '63
Reporter at large. C. Trillin. New Yorker 39:30-4+ Jl 13; 32-6+ Jl 20; 34-6+ Jl 27 '63
Where integration led to intermarriage. por U S News 55:10 S 16 '63

HUNTER, Edith Fisher
Bridge to the past. Parents Mag 38:64-6+ Mr '63
Give them something to hold onto. Parents Mag 39:36-7+ D '64
Grand opening. Redbook 123:49+ O '64
Peace of great books. bibliog Horn Bk 40: 651-9 D '64

HUNTER, Evan
Sure thing; story. Redbook 120:46-7 F '63

HUNTER, Jesse Coleman, Jr
Oil-rich Texan asks the whole U.S. to visit. V. Kraft. il por Sports Illus 21:73-4+ D 21 '64

HUNTER, John, d 1809
Forerunner in vascular surgery. por Todays Health 42:65 Ap '64

HUNTER, John M.
Testing ground in Colombia. bibliog Cur Hist 46:8-14+ Ja '64

HUNTER, John O.
Slowing down; reprint. Library J 89:300 Ja 15 '64

HUNTER, Kathryn
Illuminate the whole road. NEA J 53:62-3 N '64

HUNTER, Les
Tornado alley's emergency net. Pop Electr 20:37-8+ Ap '64

HUNTER, Madeline
What to measure in elementary school. NEA J 53:15-16 My '64

HUNTER, Marjorie
Public servant without pay: the First lady. N Y Times Mag p 10+ D 15 '63
When the President says: ten more for lunch. N Y Times Mag p26-7+ S 20 '64

HUNTER, William H.
War in Vietnam, Luce version. New Repub 148:15-17 Mr 23 '63

HUNTER, William W.
How to find fish with your boat. Field & S 68:50-3 Je '63
Most underfished river in the U.S. Outdoor Life 132:24-7+ Ag '63
When the kings run. pors Outdoor Life 133: 56-7+ Je '64

HUNTER college, New York
Life among the libs (Hunter college division) S. Buck. Nat R 16:275-7+ Ap 7 '64; Discussion. 16:329 Ap 21 '64

HUNTER-farmer relations. See Farmer-hunter relations

HUNTERS
Old man McGurkin. E. Allison. il Field & S 68:38-9+ Je '63
That night before. C. Dickey. il Field & S 68:58-60+ Mr '64
You can tell a hunter by what he hunts. V. Bourjaily. il N Y Times Mag p38-9+ N 29 '64
See also
Women as hunters

HUNTERS (horses) See Horses

HUNTING, Constance
Poetry chronicle. J. B. Hall. Poetry 104:49 Ap '64

HUNTING
Gist of it; digest of the outdoor news; ed. by H. Moore. See issues of Outdoor life
Hunting in the snow. T. Trueblood. il Field & S 68:16+ D '63
Quotes: hunting; comp. by E. F. Murphy. N Y Times Mag p 145 N 29 '64
Shotgunner's mystique. R. Starnes. Field & S 69:14+ D '64
Sportsman's notebook. H. G. Tapply. See issues of Field & stream
Tally-ha! basseting and beagling. il Newsweek 61:56 Ap 8 '63
Troublesome trifles. T. Trueblood. il Field & S 68:24+ Ap '64
Where to go fishing, vacationing, hunting, all over the world (title varies) P. A. Parsons. See issues of Outdoor life
Wild, free days. T. Trueblood. Field & S 69: 16+ D '64
See also
Airplanes in hunting and fishing
Falconry
Game preserves
Hunting with bow and arrow
Tracking and trailing
Whaling
also Deer hunting and similar headings

Accidents and injuries

Dark tragedy; ed. by B. East. D. Mosher. il Outdoor Life 131:20-3+ F '63

Anecdotes, facetiae, satire, etc.

Letter from Stan Delaplane. S. Delaplane. Todays Health 42:82 N '64

Ethical aspects

All out for cripples. W. Curtis. il Field & S 69:70+ O '64
Find that deer. P. Fournier. il Field & S 69:71-2+ O '64
Following wounded game. J. O'Connor. il Outdoor Life 132:20-3+ N '63
Growing antagonism to hunting. D. L. Allen. il Field & S 68:12-16 S '63
Hypo-arrow archery. C. Conley. il Field & S 68:43-5+ Je '63
Planes vs. fair chase. E. Zern. il Field & S 68:10-11+ Ag '63
Speaking out; hunting is humane. V. Bourjaily. Sat Eve Post 237:6+ F 15 '64
See also
Sportsmanship

Safety devices and measures

Little details make the difference. L. Parkinson. il Field & S 68:54-6+ Ap '64
Unexpected. J. Halliburton. il Outdoor Life 134:64-6+ O '64

Study and teaching

Primer on squirrel hunting. C. Patterson. il Outdoor Life 131:62-3+ Je '63

Africa

Born smart, and suspicious. J. O'Connor. il Outdoor Life 132:32-3+ D '63
Grancel Fitz's last trophy. G. Fitz. il Outdoor Life 132:56-9+ S '63
Three 7 mm.'s in Africa. J. O'Connor. il Outdoor Life 131:52-6 Ja '63

Africa, East

Last safari. R. Joseph. il Esquire 60:124-7 N '63
Leopard in large type. K. Roosevelt. il Outdoor Life 133:50-3+ Ap '64
Sentimental safari. M. Hemingway. il Life 54:88-92+ Ap 19 '63
Two birds bet a million on a club in the bush. R. Coughlan. il Sports Illus 18:84-8+ My 20 '63

Alabama

Cornfield gobbler. W. Page. il Field & S 68: 57-9+ Ap '64
Deer hunt country style. K. Shrout and B. Shrout. il Field & S 68:54-7+ O '63
Monarch of wolf creek. C. Elliott. il Outdoor Life 131:48-9+ Mr '63

Alaska

Big game hunting forecast for Alaska & Canada. il Field & S 69:98-9 Ag '64
Dam' bear ain't there! S. R. Harris. il Outdoor Life 134:20-3+ N '64
Dateline walrus. B. Klineburger. il Field & S 67:23-5 F '63
Everything else but. W. Page. il Field & S 67:37-9+ Mr '63
Fat duck in the fall. F. Dufresne. il Field & S 68:34-5+ N '63
Going for broke; ed. by M. K. Sloan. S. R. Sloan, 3d. il Outdoor Life 131:72-5+ My '63
Headlong bears. D. Knight. il Outdoor Life 133:36-9+ Mr '64
Hunt against odds. B. Munger. il Outdoor Life 131:20-3+ Ja '63
Moose by the yard. C. Ormond. il Outdoor Life 132:40-3+ Jl '63
Muzzle of meese. W. Page. il Field & S 69:25-7+ Ag '64
My Eskimo adventure. G. M. Daetz. il Outdoor Life 131:48-9+ F '63
New world record polar bear; ed. by W. E. Anderson. S. Longoria. il Field & S 69:56-7 O '64
No. 1 Alaska guide. F. Dufresne. il Field & S 69:32-4 D '64
One for the bears. J. O'Connor. il Outdoor Life 133:17-19+ Ja '64
Ram to begin on. J. O'Connor. il Outdoor Life 133:58-9+ Ap '64
Shot with luck. J. Van Wormer. il Outdoor Life 131:28-9 Mr '63

Angola

Big lion of Mucusso. J. O'Connor. il Outdoor Life 131:17-19+ F '63

Arizona

Javelina jackpot. E. Park. il Outdoor Life 131:24-5+ Ja '63
Lions almost anytime. I. Morden. il Outdoor Life 131:46-9+ Ja '63
$10 turkey. C. E. Gillham. il Field & S 67: 26-8+ F '63

Austria

Too good to shoot. R. Camp. il Field & S 67:56-7+ Mr '63

Bechuanaland

Africa's new big-game utopia. E. T. Gates. il Field & S 69:43-5+ My '64
Goose that carries a knife; spur-winged goose. R. B. Aitken. il Field & S 69:10-13 D '64

Brazil

Poppy was a real hunting dog. S. E. Brock. il Outdoor Life 133:36-9+ Ja '64

California

California deer camp. F. Dufresne. il Field & S 69:36-7+ Ag '64
Charged by a dove. C. Dickey. il Field & S 68:56-7+ S '63
Cottontails to spare. C. Dickey. il Outdoor Life 131:64-5+ Ap '63
Crisis in California. F. Dufresne. il Field & S 68:12-15+ Jl '63
Desert duck hunting. V. L. Oertle. il Field & S 69:84-5 D '64
I learn about quail. C. Dickey. il Outdoor Life 132:28-31+ N '63
I love a quail named Gambel. N. Riley. il Outdoor Life 132:50-1+ Ag '63
My wild Spanish goat; Catalina Island bow hunt. G. H. Gillelan. il Outdoor Life 135: 58-61+ F '65

HUNTING—California—*Continued*
Oh, I'll never go there anymore. C. E. Gillham. il Field & S 67:50-2+ Ap '63
Sport of stalking. J. O'Connor. il Outdoor Life 132:52-5+ O '63

California, Lower

Permit no. 4. M. Nash, jr. il Outdoor Life 134:44-7+ N '64

Canada

Ambush by four bears. E. I. Neighbor. il Outdoor Life 134:32-3+ Jl '64
Archer stalks the mighty grizzly. D. Moser. il Life 55:104-6+ N 8 '63
Bad beginning. P. Kollar. il Outdoor Life 134:36-9+ N '64
Ballplayer's moose hunt. R. Bressler. il Outdoor Life 135:66-9+ F '65
Big game hunting forecast for Alaska & Canada. il Field & S 69:98-9 Ag '64
Bugle call for a bull elk. E. A. Bauer. il Field & S 68:21-3+ Ag '63
Bulls of Oyster Creek. E. A. Bauer. il Outdoor Life 134:48-51+ S '64
Case of the killer grizzly. D. Robertson. il Outdoor Life 134:29-31+ S '64
Do-it-yourself bighorns. R. M. Hobbs. il Outdoor Life 132:20-3+ D '63
Extra-special moose. H. J. Samuels. il Outdoor Life 132:33-5+ O '63
Field & stream big game hunting forecast for Alaska & Canada. il Field & S 68:86-7 Ag '63
First moose at Mindedo. N. Smith. il Outdoor Life 134:60-1+ O '64
Grand slam doubled. M. K. Sloan. il Outdoor Life 131:68-71+ Ap '63
I had trouble with elk. T. Howell. il Outdoor Life 134:50-3+ O '64
I'll take those trash ducks. M. Ellis. il Field & S 68:36-7+ Ag '63
Land of the unexpected. J. Pless. il Field & S 69:46-8+ Ag '64
Legacy of a French Noah; whitetail deer to Anticosti Island. J. Olsen. il Sports Illus 19:62-4+ O 7 '63
Moose enough for two. R. Voss. il Outdoor Life 134:24-7+ Ag '64
Now you shoot! M. Ellis. il Field & S 69:46-8+ N '64
Ox hunt for moose. H. Schaefer. il Outdoor Life 134:36-9+ S '64
Pack dog hunt. W. Bever. il Outdoor Life 133:28-31+ Ja '64
Ram for the records. G. Morris. il Outdoor Life 134:46-7+ Ag '64
Ross and his rifle. D. Peck. il Outdoor Life 131:32-5+ Ja; 36-9+ F '63
Snows of Ile aux Grues. N. Karas. il Field & S 69:51-3+ O '64
Suddenly there was a bear. H. J. Samuels. il Outdoor Life 133:58-9+ Je '64
Take it easy. T. Trueblood. il Field & S 68:24+ S '63
Terror in the Cassiars. J. Ashlock. il Outdoor Life 131:52-5+ Ap '63
Too many caribou. J. Rearden. il Outdoor Life 132:33-5+ S '63
Two rams for the money. F. C. Hibben. il Field & S 68:56-7+ Je '63
Wild wolf hunt. D. Brown. il Outdoor Life 134:17-19+ D '64

Colombia

Jaguar for a gypsy. E. A. Bauer. il Outdoor Life 134:24-7+ Jl '64

Colorado

Double on deer. T. NcNally. il Outdoor Life 132:40-3+ S '63
Mountain of mule deer. B. Jourdan. il Outdoor Life 134:40-1+ D '64

Costa Rica

Budget safari. il Time 83:88 Ap 10 '64

Denmark

Day in Denmark. W. Page. il Field & S 69:36-7 D '64

Dominican Republic

In the land of Oh-by-Jingo. V. Heilner. il Field & S 69:110-13 N '64

Europe, Eastern

Marxmen all; hunting behind the iron curtain. il Time 84:29 N 6 '64

Florida

Decoys for doves. R. F. Burgess. il Outdoor Life 132:44-7+ D '63
Florida fox hunt. D. M. Duffey. il Outdoor Life 135:116-18+ Ja '65
Florida quail cruise. C. Dickey. il Field & S 68:31-3+ N '63
Upland shooting down on Florida's Gold Coast. V. Kraft. il Sports Illus 18:52+ Mr 4 '63

Idaho

Black bear posse. D. Walker. il Outdoor Life 132:40-3+ D '63
Cougar for everybody. L. Miracle. il Outdoor Life 134:44-7+ D '64
Education of ruff. T. Trueblood. il Field & S 69:53-6+ S '64
Harder the better. C. Conley. il Field & S 68:33-5+ O '63
How to hunt chukars. T. Trueblood. il Field & S 69:24+ O '64
Idaho's instant goat hunt. W. Galligan. il Outdoor Life 131:72-5+ Je '63
Where the outdoor experts go. K. N. Anderson. il Todays Health 41:44-7+ S '63

Illinois

We track pheasants. B. Cary. Outdoor Life 134:20-3+ D '64

India

My greatest trophy: tiger with an arrow; by B. East. F. Bear. il Outdoor Life 134:40-3+ O '64
Tiger, and the unexpected. R. S. Smith. il Outdoor Life 135:44-7+ F '65

Iowa

Calling all fox squirrels. H. Bradshaw. il Field & S 69:65-7+ S '64

Ireland

Shooting in Mayo and Kerry and Cork; reproductions of paintings. R. A. Parker. Sports Illus 19:38-43 O 7 '63

Kentucky

Spooking up on chucks. S. L. Simmons. il Outdoor Life 133:64-5+ Mr '64

Kenya

Lion mangled me. J. Kingsley-Heath. il Outdoor Life 131:20-3+ Mr '63
My last safari. R. Ruark. il Sat Eve Post 236:76-81 Ap 27 '63

Laos

Mekong madness. C. W. Stockwell. il Outdoor Life 132:12-13+ Jl '63

Louisiana

Deer of Thanksgiving. G. Gresham. il Outdoor Life 134:40-1+ N '64

Maine

Cross and doublecross. B. Geagan. il Outdoor Life 133:42-3+ Ja '64
Deer camp on wheels. L. Dietz. il Field & S 68:37-9+ D '63
Duck shooting on Maine's icy ledges. D. Barnes. il Sports Illus 21:74-6+ N 30 '64
Like artillery coming in. C. Bergen. il Outdoor Life 132:44-5+ N '63
Mixed bag down East. T. Janes. il Field & S 67:74-6+ Ap '63
Old Mose of Paddy Mill Creek. L. Dietz. il Field & S 68:58-60+ My '63
Place for everything; go out for bass, come back with duck. A. W. Prince. il Outdoor Life 134:52-3+ S '64

Maryland

Hunters follow where the wild goose leads. il Bsns W p26-7 D 19 '64
Tidewater quail. T. Janes. il Outdoor Life 134:28-9+ N '64
Ways and ways for ducks. E. A. Bauer. il Outdoor Life 134:32-5+ N '64

Massachusetts

Duck hunters: take to the swamps. K. Botty. il Outdoor Life 132:48-9+ O '63
Pine tree pheasants. A. Davenport. il Field & S 68:56-7+ F '64

Mexico

Border pigeon shoot. D. Barnes. il Sports Illus 18:18-21 Mr 18 '63
Chachalaca. C. E. Gillham. il Field & S 68:54-5+ S '63
Chicken feed. W. Page. il Field & S 69:66-7 My '64
Dwarf deer in Sonora. J. O'Connor. il Outdoor Life 131:42-3+ Mr '63
Ram with a corset. W. Page. il Field & S 69:34-7+ Jl '64

Michigan

Crows a la carte. T. E. Huggler. il Outdoor Life 131:26-7+ Ja '63

HUNTING—Michigan—*Continued*
Great little cat. B. East. il Outdoor Life 135: 24-7+ Ja '65
Guarantee your grouse. J. O. Cartier. il Field & S 68:62-3+ O '63
Here a bear walked. R. Vincent, jr. il Outdoor Life 132:60-1+ O '63
Hit and miss. H. F. Zeman. il Outdoor Life 133:50-1+ F '64
I eat words, and rabbits. J. B. Gleason. il Outdoor Life 132:38-9+ N '63
My hare turns white. B. East. il Outdoor Life 134:50-2+ D '64
Picture yourself. H. F. Zeman. il Outdoor Life 132:44-7+ Ag '63
Two best ways to get a deer. B. East. il Outdoor Life 132:46-7+ N '63

Minnesota

Minnesota brush bucks. H. Bradshaw. il Field & S 69:138-41+ O '64
Whitetails for all. E. A. Bauer. il Outdoor Life 132:36-9+ O '63

Mississippi

Backwoods buck. C. Elliott. il Outdoor Life 132:48-9+ D '63
How to call ducks. R. M. Russell. il Outdoor Life 133:44-7+ Ja '64

Montana

Bargain goat hunt. E. A. Bauer. il Field & S 69:31-3+ Ag '64
Dark tragedy; ed. by B. East. D. Mosher. il Outdoor Life 131:20-3+ F '63
Earthquake deer. E. A. Bauer. il Outdoor Life 131:56-9+ Je '63
Elk in the tall timber. N. H. Jensen. il Field & S 69:40-2+ S '64
Elk on the roof. W. J. McRae. il Outdoor Life 134:48-9+ N '64
How I shot the no. 1 deer. E. T. McMaster. il Outdoor Life 134:17-19+ N '64
Pop picket pins. B. W. Dalrymple. il Outdoor Life 133:48-9+ F '64
Pronghorns for profit; reproductions of paintings by B. Kuhn. J. Linduska. Field & S 68:24-9 Ag '63
Where the antelope play; paintings by B. Shields; with account by D. Barnes. Sports Illus 21:46-54 O 12 '64

Mozambique

Buffalo make me nervous. J. O'Connor. il Outdoor Life 132:20-3+ Ag '63
What a beautiful morning. W. Page. il Field & S 68:46-7+ Mr '64

Nebraska

Five-year stalk: new record whitetail. A. Dawson. il Outdoor Life 132:32-5+ Ag '63
Real deer sleeper. P. Czura. il Field & S 68:104-6+ N '63
Red carpet for pheasant hunters. H. Titus. il Field & S 68:47-9+ S '63
Turkeys plus. J. Tische. il Field & S 68:26-7+ D '63

Nepal

Night belongs to the tiger. H. Klein. il Field & S 68:38-40+ S '63

Nevada

Cougar chase. K. Hueftle. il Outdoor Life 133:74-5+ Ap '64

New England

Far-out chucks. T. Janes. il Outdoor Life 132:50-1+ O '63

New Hampshire

Double buck. A. Davenport. il Field & S 69: 30-1+ D '64

New Jersey

Clapper clapper clapper. C. Conley. il Field & S 68:35-7+ S '63
Clapper rail. G. Santillo. il Outdoor Life 132: 66-8+ S '63
Don't blow it. O. Lagelbauer. il Outdoor Life 132:38-9+ D '63
Double for the captain. A. Parsons. il Outdoor Life 133:46-7+ Mr '64

New Mexico

Coon hunter's life ain't easy. R. Rawlins. il Outdoor Life 131:80-1+ My '63
New game in New Mexico. A. Napier. il Sports Illus 18:57-60 My 27 '63

New York (state)

Biggest bear in the East; ed. by N. Drahos. R. Avery. il Outdoor Life 131:52-5+ My '63
Camouflaged bunnies. R. Camp. il Field & S 68:28-30+ N '63
Mixed bag at Spring farm; shooting preserve, Sag Harbor. A. MacBain. il Field & S 68:178+ Ap '64
Partridge are honest birds. D. Tracy. il Outdoor Life 134:56-9+ O '64
Pilgrim Mountain buck. C. V. Whitney. il Field & S 68:32-4+ F '64
State cooperation. A. MacBain. il Field & S 68:96+ Ag '63
We move for crows. T. Janes. il Outdoor Life 133:52-5+ My '64

Ohio

Christmas hasenpfeffer. E. A. Bauer. il Outdoor Life 132:28-31+ D '63
Double hat rack; ed. by B. East. P. Helser. il Outdoor Life 134:24-7+ D '64
How to hunt foxes. E. A. Bauer. il Outdoor Life 133:24-7+ F '64
Midwinter bird hunt. E. A. Bauer. il Outdoor Life 131:32-5+ F '63

Oregon

Deer in the dunes. F. H. Ames. il Outdoor Life 134:48-9+ Ag '64
Deer in your pocket. B. Cary. il Outdoor Life 132:54-5+ S '63
Dog man from Oregon. F. Dufresne. il Field & S 69:52-3+ N '64
Oregon. T. Bacon. il Flying 75:43-4+ Jl '64
Secrets of black brant. E. Park. il Field & S 69:21-3+ Ja '65
Tied up by topknots. J. Van Wormer. il Outdoor Life 132:62-3+ O '63
Very special goose: black brant. E. Park. il Outdoor Life 133:50-2+ Ja '64

Pennsylvania

Bowhunting for gunners. G. H. Gillelan. il Outdoor Life 132:12-13+ Ag '63
Deer by the dozen. T. Janes. il Outdoor Life 132:17-19+ N '63
Deer hunting with dad. R. Bressler. il Outdoor Life 133:60-3+ My '64
Hunting the Pennsylvania hearthlands. G. X. Sand. il Field & S 68:27-9+ O '63
Reunion with rabbits. G. X. Sand. il Outdoor Life 132:32-5+ Jl '63
Turkey talk. C. Conley. il Field & S 68:36-7+ N '63
Where to bowhunt for deer. G. H. Gillelan. il Outdoor Life 134:12+ Ag '64
Wisdom of whitetails. D. J. Anderson. il Field & S 69:62-4+ O '64

South Africa

See also
Hunting—Bechuanaland

South Dakota

Gobbler goes west. W. Bever. il Outdoor Life 131:60-1+ My '63
Mid-continent roosters. W. Page. il Field & S 68:130-2+ Ap '64
More pheasants than people. W. Page. il Field & S 69:37-9 S '64

Southwestern states

Horn hunters' heaven. O. A. Washburn. il Field & S 68:49-51 O '63

Sudan

Elusive Mrs Gray. F. C. Hibben. il Field & S 67:66-7+ Ap '63

Surinam

Beastly place for a hunt. J. Olsen. il Sports Illus 21:62-6+ N 9 '64

Tanganyika

Elephant. J. O'Connor. il Outdoor Life 134:56-9+ S '64

Tennessee

Boar for the Bronx; ed. by L. Miracle. J. Altieri. il Outdoor Life 131:48-51+ Je '63
Dirt on chucks. C. Vinson. il Outdoor Life 133:46-7+ Je '64
Ghost town grouse. H. L. Lawrence. il Outdoor Life 135:70-1+ F '65
Railroad bird hunt. D. D. Dickey. il Field & S 69:59-61 Je '64

Texas

Big on pigs. J. C. Rikhoff. il Outdoor Life 134:34-5+ Ag '64
Boat-float bucks. B. W. Dalrymple. il Field & S 69:54-5+ Jl '64
Coyote hounds in Texas. D. M. Duffey. il Outdoor Life 134:118-20+ N '64
My first doe. H. Stilwell. il Field & S 68:36-7+ O '63
Oil-rich Texan asks the whole U.S. to visit. V. Kraft. il Sports Illus 21:73-4+ D 21 '64

HUNTING—Texas—*Continued*
Santa Claus brought waterfowl. H. Bradshaw. il Outdoor Life 135:32-3+ Ja '65
Sounds and hounds of a Texas wolf hunt. J. Olsen. il Sports Illus 21:66-72+ S 14 '64
Story of LBJ and a hunting incident. U S News 56:8 My 18 '64
Team for squirrels. R. Tinsley. il Outdoor Life 134:54-5+ S '64
World's biggest deer camp. W. Page. il Field & S 68:25-7 N '63

Uganda

Marsh walker. W. Page. il Field & S 68:40-1+ Ja '64

United States

Are we wasting our best hunting? B. East. il Outdoor Life 131:32-5+ Mr '63
Black phantom. W. Jarvis. il Field & S 68:50-1+ Mr '64
Capricious Asian is a citizen at last; chukar partridge. V. Kraft. il Sports Illus 19:76-9 D 9 '63
Combat those bluebird blues. B. M. Blum. il Field & S 69:32-4+ N '64
Count in the weatherman. D. L. Allen. il Field & S 68:40-2+ Je '63
Field & stream big game hunting forecast for Alaska & Canada. il Field & S 68:86-7 Ag '63
Field & stream 1964 hunting forecast, small & big game. il Field & S 69:73-80 O '64
Hunter and the landowner. A. Lincoln, jr. Am For 70:40 Ag '64
Hunting (cont) il Sports Illus 18:52+ Mr 4; 57-60 My 27 '63
Hunting by air photos. L. Pringle. il Outdoor Life 131:50-1+ F '63
Hunting, with gun and wallet. C. Dickey. il Esquire 60:212-13+ D '63
I had trouble with elk. T. Howell. il Outdoor Life 134:50-3+ O '64
1963 Field & stream hunting forecast and game laws. il Field & S 68:41-8 O '63
No more free hunting? A. Grahame. il Outdoor Life 131:14-15+ F '63
Place to hunt; Dutchess County cooperative hunting area. T. Janes. il Outdoor Life 134:33-5+ O '64
Private shooting preserves; list prepared by the Sportsman's service bureau of New York city. Esquire 60:93+ D '63
Sermons and buckshot. L. Wulff. Esquire 62:109+ N '64
Surrenders continue; national recreation areas. Nat Parks Mag 38:15 Ap '64
Tips for planning a hunting trip this fall. H. Bradshaw. il Suc Farm 61:38+ S '63
Top trophy of North America? G. Fitz. il Outdoor Life 133:17-21+ F '64
Twenty best places to kill deer in the U.S; symposium. il Outdoor Life 134:44-7+ O '64
What every goose hunter should know. E. A. Bauer. il Field & S 68:23-5+ D '63
Where the deer are; symposium. il Outdoor Life 132:44-7+ O '63
You can tell a hunter by what he hunts. V. Bourjaily. il N Y Times Mag p38-9+ N 29 '64
Your fishing and hunting routes to the World's fair; symposium. il Field & S 68:41-8+ Ap '64

Utah

Lions beat them all; ed. by S. P. English, jr. G. Acosta. il Outdoor Life 131:64-7+ My '63
Secret side of Manta-La Sal. B. Behme. il Field & S 69:21-3+ D '64
Where the ducks are. F. Calkins. il Field & S 69:41-3+ N '64
Wild deer area opens; the Triangle. H. Wixom. il Outdoor Life 132:38-9+ Ag '63

Vermont

Bears were bad enough. D. C. Lawrence. il Outdoor Life 132:28-9+ Ag '63

Viet Nam

Double take on elephant. J. M. Barker. il Outdoor Life 132:32-5+ N '63

Virginia

Elk hunt in Virginia? ed. by G. H. Gillelan. T. Somerville. il Outdoor Life 135:42-3+ Ja '65

Washington (state)

Bears with a handgun. A. J. Georg. il Outdoor Life 135:28-31+ Ja '65
Beast of buckless gulch. C. Chatfield. il Outdoor Life 134:54-5+ O '64
Fastest gunning in the West. C. Chatfield. il Outdoor Life 134:40-1+ S '64
40th buck. C. Chatfield. il Outdoor Life 132:28-9+ Jl '63
Hippity hop and away we go. V. Kraft. il Sports Illus 21:40-2+ S 28 '64
Ten years better; Grand Coulee Dam transformed Grant County, Wash. F. Dufresne. il Field & S 68:124-6+ O '63
Thirteen days in a blizzard. G. J. Tucker. il Outdoor Life 133:20-3+ Ja '64

West Virginia

Blackwater paradise. G. B. Evans. il Field & S 69:29-31+ N '64

Western states

Know your grouse. T. Trueblood. il Field & S 68:44-6+ S '63
Valleys of the West. C. Conley. il Field & S 69:82-5 O '64

Wisconsin

Biggest black ever killed; ed. by B. East. D. Streubel. il Outdoor Life 133:46-8+ My '64
Wisconsin's biggest day of the year. G. Laycock. il Field & S 68:60-1+ O '63
X marks the spot. M. Ellis. il Field & S 69:50-2+ S '64

Wyoming

Antelope hunt with Ace Reid. B. Dalrymple. il Farm J 87:42-3+ O '63
Buffalo Bill was a piker; D. C. Basolo's one-day record for buffalo kills. H. Peterson. il Sports Illus 21:76+ O 19 '64
Day at Saratoga; deer and trout in one day. W. Page. il Field & S 69:35-7 N '64
Fog horns. G. Laycock. il Outdoor Life 131:38-9+ Ja '63
I killed crooked horn. A. E. Hollemon. il Outdoor Life 133:68-9+ Ap '64
Lost sheep; ed. by C. Elliott. J. F. Lane. il Outdoor Life 134:44-6+ S '64
Pronghorn crawl. C. Elliott. il Outdoor Life 132:48-9+ S '63
Rams were my bugaboo. C. Ormond. il Outdoor Life 131:28-9+ F '63
Saddlebag safari. C. Elliott. il Outdoor Life 132:40-3+ N '63

HUNTING, Photography of. See Photography of sports

HUNTING clubs
Hunting, with gun and wallet. C. Dickey. il Esquire 60:212-13+ D '63
Private shooting preserves; list prepared by the Sportsman's service bureau of New York city. Esquire 60:93+ D '63

HUNTING dogs
Dogs. D. M. Duffey. See issues of Outdoor life
Not poodle, not pointer, but both dogs in one; pudelpointer. D. Barnes. il Sports Illus 19:68-70 N 18 '63
Off-beat dogs. J. Stetson. il Field & S 68:108+ Jl '63
Outdoors. V. Bourjaily. Esquire 62:40+ O '64
Poppy was a real hunting dog. S. E. Brock. il Outdoor Life 133:36-9+ Ja '64
Should you pen your dog? J. Stetson. il Field & S 67:186-8+ Ap '63
Spoilers. J. Stetson. il Field & S 68:114+ N '63
Squirrel dogs. D. M. Duffey. il Outdoor Life 132:98-100 Jl '63
See also
Beagles (dogs)
Bird dogs
Harriers (dogs)
Hounds

HUNTING for hoot owls; story. See West, J.

HUNTING guides. See Guides

HUNTING laws. See Game laws

HUNTING knives. See Knives

HUNTING on farm lands. See Farmer-hunter relations

HUNTING outfits
All-purpose hunting tool; Skachet. C. Conley. il Field & S 69:127 O '64
Rifle strap. W. Page. il Field & S 68:96-101 F '64
Saks of safaris. il Newsweek 62:91 O 21 '63
Things I could kick myself for. T. Trueblood. il Field & S 67:16+ F '63
Your belt is a gun sling. H. G. Tapply. il Field & S 69:60 N '64
See also
Archery—Equipment
Packs
Tripods

HUNTING preserves. See Game preserves

HUNTING rifles. See Rifles

HUNTING trophies. See Trophies, Sport

HUNTING with bow and arrow
Archer stalks the mighty grizzly. D. Moser. il Life 55:104-6+ N 8 '63
Archery. G. H. Gillelan. See issues of Outdoor life
Guides for bowhunting. G. H. Gillelan. il Outdoor Life 132:80-3 Jl '63
Hit and miss. H. F. Zeman. il Outdoor Life 133:50-1+ F '64
Hypo-arrow archery. C. Conley. il Field & S 68:43-5+ Je '63
Ishi, first modern bowhunter. G. H. Gillelan. il Outdoor Life 132:68+ D '63
My greatest trophy; tiger with an arrow; ed. by B. East. F. Bear. il Outdoor Life 134:40-3+ O '64
My wild Spanish goat; Catalina Island bow hunt. G. H. Gillelan. il Outdoor Life 135: 58-61+ F '65
Too much bear. A. LaHa. il Outdoor Life 135:17-19+ Ja '65
Turkey on the wing. B. W. Dalrymple. il Outdoor Life 132:60-3+ S '63

HUNTINGTON, Judith L. See Kupke, D. W. jt. auth.

HUNTINGTON, Roger
Automobiles: 1964 model review. Consumer Bul 46:14-20 N '63
Belted tires. Motor T 15:26-9+ Jl '63
Bigger engines for compacts in '64. Motor T 15:50-3 Ag '63
Disc brakes. Hot Rod 17:28-33 D '64
Fit your car for your trailer. Consumer Bul 48:2+ F '65
Future of performance. Motor T 15:26-9 D '63
Gas mileage engineering. Motor T 15:72-3+ Mr '63
GM's new torque converter. Motor T 15:71+ D '63
Heating up the Spyder. Hot Rod 16:80-3 Mr '63
How about a heavy wheel? Hot Rod 16:46-7+ F '63
How to pick a power pack. Motor T 16:28-31+ Mr '64
If you're buying a new car. Consumer Bul 47: 10-12 F '64
MT road test; Pontiac 421 H.O. Motor T 15: 44-9 Mr '63
New V-8 for the F-85. Motor T 15:68-70 D '63
New variables: camshaft & compression. Motor T 16:50-1+ My '64
Pontiacs on a diet. Hot Rod 16:32-5 My '63
Rocket, stage two. Hot Rod 17:54-9 N '64
Roll 'me. Hot Rod 18:48-9 Ja '65
Special section; 1965 engines. Motor T 16:36-47 D '64
Speed minders. Motor T 15:40-1+ Je '63
Stock swaps for more stuff. Hot Rod 16: 90-2+ N '63; 17:78-81+ F; 76-9 Je '64
Super turbocharging the F-85. Motor T 15: 34-7+ Ap '63
365 mph with 400 hp? Hot Rod 17:30-3 Je '64
Transmission transplant. Hot Rod 17:42-5 Jl '64
Tubing and beams. Hot Rod 16:44-7+ Jl '63
Weight transfer. Hot Rod 16:76-9 Ap '63
What's coming in disc brakes. Motor T 16: 90-5 N '64
What's new on the '65 cars? Consumer Bul 47:6-12 N '64
Will camshafts be kicked upstairs? Motor T 16:56-7+ Jl '64

HUNTINGTON, Trumbull
Censorship: a bookseller's view. Pub W 185: 57 Mr 2 '64
Store windows and in-store display. Pub W 185:76-8 Ja 6 '64

HUNTINGTON Hartford collection. See Gallery of modern art, New York

HUNTLEY, Chet
Sound of beauty. por Seventeen 23:152+ F '64
about
On the news beat. il por Newsweek 63:74-5 Je 1 '64

HUNTLEY-Brinkley effect; story. See Bernstein, B.

HUNTZINGER, Robert
Water torture. il Sat Eve Post 236:30-3 Ag 24 '63

HUNZA, Pakistan
Hunza in the Himalayas. J. Clark. il Natur Hist 72:38-45 O '63

HUNZAS. See Burusho

HUNZUKUTS. See Burusho

HUONG, Tran-van-. See Tran-van-Huong

HUPP corporation
Troubled town; question of closing Gibson refrigerator Greenville plant. Newsweek 61:74+ My 20 '63

HURD, E. S.
Should we change the name of conservation? Am For 70:22-3+ Mr '64

HURD, Peter
Last frontiersman. il por Time 85:82-4 Ja 29 '65

HURDLE racing
King of the hurdlers. il Ebony 19:63-6 Ap '64

HURE, Anne
Tips. por Pub W 186:65 Jl 20 '64

HURKOS, Peter
Hunt for the strangler. il por Newsweek 63: 31 F 24 '64
Now a seer helps stalk the Boston strangler. P. Mandel. il pors Life 56:49-50 Mr 6 '64

HURLBUT, Kaatje
Giant at the window: story. Redbook 121:50-1 My '63
Self that walks like a cat; story. Redbook 122:70-1 Ap '64

HURLEY, Denis Eugene, abp
Africa and the council. Commonweal 79:10-12 S 27 '63
Report from Rome. America 109:633-4 N 16 '63

HURLEY, Laurel
Queen of hearts; interview, ed. by J. W. Freeman. por Opera N 28:26 Mr 14 '64

HURLEY, Lois J.
Happiness is a journey. Farm J 88:43+ Jl '64

HURLEY, Neil P.
Image revolution. America 110:137-9 Ja 25 '64

HURLEY, Richard J.
New revolution on the Potomac. Sr Schol 82:13T Mr 13 '63

HURLEY, Robert J. and Fink, L. K.
Ripple marks show that countercurrent exists in Florida Straits. Science 139:603-5 F 15 '63

HURLOCK, Charles J.
Lay listener. Opera N 29:16 D 5 '64

HUROK, Sol
Impresario; interview, ed. by F. Stevenson. il por Opera N 29:18-19 S 26 '64
Plisetskaya. Vogue 143:164-7 Ap 1 '64
about
Hurok: adventurer in the arts. R. Sabin. il pors Dance Mag 38:40-6+ Ja '64

HURON, LAKE
See also
North Channel

HURON NATIONAL FOREST. See National forests

HURRICANE waves. See Waves

HURRICANES
Aircraft follow hurricane from Genesis. G. Alexander. il Aviation W 81:80-1+ O 19 '64
Big mop up; Columbus day storm. J. C. Hunt. il Am For 70:10-13+ Ap '64
Bills to be paid for Cleo's damage. il U S News 57:6 S 7 '64
Calamitous Cleo. il Time 84:77 S 4 '64
Carla's computer. il Pop Electr 18:48-9 Ap '63
Clear facts about stormy weather. il Good H 157:142-3 Ag '63
Common sense about hurricanes. F. T. Moss. il Motor B 114:50-3 Ag '64
Cuba: the moment is now; aftermath of hurricane Flora. Nat R 15:379 N 5 '63
Day hurricane Hilda slammed in; with report by B. Fellows. il Life 57:48-48B+ O 16 '64
Deadliest hurricane in western hemisphere: Flora. Sci N L 84:242 O 19 '63
Experiment in hurricane modification: preliminary results. R. H. Simpson and J. S. Malkus. il Science 142:498 O 25 '63
Experiments in hurricane modification. R. H. Simpson and J. S. Malkus. il Sci Am 211: 27-37 bibliog(p 154) D '64
Eyes on hurricane eye. B. Tufty. il Sci N L 84:26-7 Jl 13 '63
First pictures: what Flora did to Cuba. il Life 55:36B-37 N 1 '63
Flora strikes, the deadliest ever. il Life 55: 34-43 O 18 '63
Florida skippers weather the storm. J. Martenhoff. Motor B 114:98 N '64
Get the streets open first; Atlantic City, N.J. W. F. Casey. il Am City 78:26 Ap '63
Huge Florida water loss blamed on fickle Flora. Sci N L 84:281 N 2 '63
Hurricane backtracking does not happen often. Sci N L 84:296 N 9 '63
Hurricane killers learn where to aim. C. P. Gilmore. il Pop Mech 119:114-18+ Mr '63
Hurricane warning system now ready. Sci N L 83:376 Je 15 '63

HURRICANES—*Continued*
Hurricanes and tropical meteorology; report of technical conference on hurricanes and tropical meteorology at Mexico city. R. H. Simpson. Science 141:935-6+ S 6 '63
Hurricanes still mystery. Sci N L 86:205 S 26 '64
Incident I'll never forget; seeing is believing: Texas tower being towed. A. W. Moffat. il Yachting 115:47+ Mr '64
Just read the emergency instructions. E. Gold. il Am City 79:22 Ag '64
Mystery of hurricane Flora. il U S News 55:60 O 21 '63
New clues to hurricanes. Sci N L 85:404 Je 27 '64
On the origin and possible modification of hurricanes. H. Riehl. bibliog il Science 141:1001-10 S 13 '63
Ordeal of Snowcloud one; flight into the eye of hurricane Cleo. E. D. Fales, jr. il Pop Sci 185:56-61+ D '64
Remember hurricane Carol. F. Kern. il Yachting 116:58-60+ Ag '64
Slow hurricane by seeding. Sci N L 84:292 N 9 '63
Storm killers; Project stormfury. il Time 82:37 Ag 16 '63
Storm with an eye for demagogues; Flora's rampage. il Time 82:32-3 O 18 '63
Terrible Flora. Newsweek 62:74 O 21 '63
Tracking the hurricane. E. R. Yarham. il UNESCO Courier 16:24-7 S '63
What hurricane Flora really did to Cuba. U S News 55:8 O 28 '63
Wild wet fury of weather gone mad; hurricane Dora. il Life 57:36-41 S 25 '64
Will '64 be a big year for hurricanes? il U S News 57:6 S 21 '64
Wind, weather and waldorf salad. A. Erxleben. il Pop Electr 21:36-7 Jl '64

HURRICANES and building. See Building, Stormproof

HURST, William D.
William D. Hurst; the generalist. por Am City 78:150-1 My '63

HURT, John
Little John. por Time 82:64 S 27 '63
Mississippi John. por Newsweek 63:87-8 F 17 '64

HURT, Lester E.
Publish-or-perish policy. NEA J 53:31-2+ D '64

HURWITZ, Al
Improvising with clay. il Design 65:66-7 N '63
Prints and drawings. Sch Arts 62:16-18 Je '63
With inner tube and linoleum block. NEA J 53:32-3 My '64

HURWITZ, H. M. B.
Method for discriminative avoidance training. Science 145:1070-1; 146:1600 S 4, D 18 '64

HURWITZ, Howard L.
Books for your professional bookshelf. Sr Schol 84:15T-16T Mr 6 '64
Cleopatra: history or bunk? Sr Schol 83:22T-23T+ O 4 '63
Current revolution in economics teaching. Sr Schol 83:7T-8T S 13 '63
Europe: on $5 an hour? Sr Schol 85:10T-11T Ja 7 '65
Jefferson's wall and the schools. Sr Schol 84:9T F 7 '64
Lincoln and the Emancipation proclamations. Sr Schol 82:8T-10T F 13 '63
New books in education. Sr Schol 85:18T-21T O 7 '64
New books on the American Negro. Sr Schol 83:8T-10T N 15 '63
New paperbacks in the social sciences. Sr Schol 85:20T-22T D 2 '64
New perspectives on the great wars. Sr Schol 85:18T-19T N 11 '64
New professional books: issues and approaches. Sr Schol 85:24T D 2 '64
Social science textbook for Soviet schools. Sr Schol 85:9T+ N 18 '64
(ed) Teaching about the great world wars. Sr Schol 85:6T-10T+ N 11 '64
What caused the great world wars? Sr Schol 85:6T-10T N 11 '64
(ed) What's happening in social studies: summaries of periodical articles and reports. Sr Schol 83:15T O 11; 10T N 1; 13T D 6 '63; 84:7T Ja 31; 7T F 28; 13T Ap 10; 85:8T O 14; 21T D 9 '64

HURWITZ, Samuel J.
Medical care before World war II. Cur Hist 45:2-5+ Jl '63
Roots of British foreign policy. Cur Hist 46:296-9+ My '64

HURWITZ, Sidney
Etchings of Sigmund Abeles. Am Artist 28:58-63+ S '64

HUSBAND and wife. See Family life; Husbands; Marriage; Marriage counseling

HUSBANDS
Does a good date make a good mate? D. Sugarman and R. Hochstein. il Seventeen 23:148-9+ Ap '64
Husband's diary of his wife's pregnancy; ed. by V. Cadden. L. Krohner. il Redbook 123:36-7+ Je '64
Man that I marry. R. Hochstein. il Good H 156:86-9 F '63
My husband was cold; ed. by D. C. Disney. Ladies Home J 80:22+ My '63
Pregnancy & the young husband. D. R. Mace. il McCalls 90:162+ Ap '63
Privacy vs. secrecy. L. Strong. Am Home 67:38-9 O '64
She sought refuge from domestic chaos in a job. D. C. Disney. il Ladies Home J 80:10+ O '63
Ten ways to keep a husband young. P. McGinley. Ladies Home J 80:97+ Ja '63
What every husband should know. J. D. Wassersug. Todays Health 42:48-9+ Ap '64
What the husbands think. A. Toffler. Ladies Home J 81:26+ Je '64
Why husbands run away. D. C. Disney. Ladies Home J 80:94 Ja '63
Why women can't talk to their husbands; Why men don't talk to their wives. M. Holmes. il Todays Health 42:28-33+ Ap '64
See also
Marriage

Anecdotes, facetiae, satire, etc.

Help! help! C. Ogburn, jr. il Harper 229:65-9 N '64
How to live with a husband. J. Agle. il Good H 156:62+ Ap '63
Problems of being the perfect husband. A. Buchwald. il McCalls 90:28 Jl '63; Same abr. Read Digest 83:231-2 O '63
Why do husbands. . .? L. Reinhard. il Ladies Home J 80:48+ O '63

HUSBAND'S tale; story. See Arkin, F.

HUSSEIN, king of Jordan
Holy Land, my country. por Nat Geog Mag 126:784-9 D '64
about
Genius for survival. il Time 81:30 My 3 '63
Hi-ho King Hussein al Hashimiyah. il pors Life 56:36-36A My 1 '64
Hussein of Jordan. J. H. Huizinga. New Repub 149:10-11 S 14 '63
Hussein; portrait of a king. J. Knowles. por Holiday 33:84-5+ Mr '63
I'm no quitter. il Newsweek 61:44 My 6 '63
King and President puting on pressure. por Newsweek 63:56-7 Ap 20 '64
Two more kings in trouble. il por U S News 54:96-7 My 6 '63

HUSSEY, Charles
And now there's the anti-Establishment. N Y Times Mag p42+ My 3 '64
Call me mister! the peers request. N Y Times Mag p 18+ Ag 25 '63
Fine art of insult. N Y Times Mag p57+ Ja 5 '64
Osborne looks forward in anger. N Y Times Mag p71-2+ O 25 '64

HUSTON, James A.
Election of 1916. Cur Hist 47:205-9+ O '64

HUSTON, John
John Cardinal Huston. il pors Life 55:61-2+ N 22 '63
John Huston, actor. por Newsweek 61:102 Mr 18 '63
John Huston's best of all worlds. N. Barry. il House & Gard 126:140-7 D '64
Problems in paradise. Newsweek 64:90+ S 14 '64

HUSTON, John L. and others
Xenon tetroxide: mass spectrum. Science 143:1161-2 Mr 13 '64

HUSTON, Perdita
Report from an Algerian village. N Y Times Mag p20-1+ O 13 '63

HUSTWITT, Arthur
Largest meeting of CBA ever held outside of Chicago. Pub W 184:38-41 S 9 '63

HUTCHENS, John K.
Broadway was their way. Sat R 47:39 D 5 '64
That's why the lady was a terror. Sat R 47:73 O 24 '64

HUTCHERSON, Ruth E.
Books that help children. bibliog por Library J 88:2083-6 My 15 '63

HUTCHES, Colonial. See Cupboards

HUTCHESON, Robert J.
Eleazar De Carvalho: orchestra builder. Mus Am 84:58-9 My '64

HUTCHINGS, F. G. B.
Profile: twice a president. Library J 88:1956-7 My 15 '63

HUTCHINGS, Hugh
Organization of the USPS. por Motor B 113: 43+ F '64
HUTCHINS, Carleen Maley
Mother of a new family of fiddles. il pors Life 55:61-2 N 29 '63
HUTCHINS, Robert Maynard
Conversation on education; questions and answers. por Library J 88:2821-8 Ag '63
Letter on reading. por ALA Bul 57:1027-33 D '63
Speaking out. por Sat Eve Post 236:6+ Je 8 '63
about
Hutchins in Chicago. J. Epstein. New Repub 151:24-6 N 28 '64
Hutchins of Chicago. R. A. Nisbet. Commentary 38:52-5 Jl '64
Hutchins swings broadax. Christian Cent 81: 542 Ap 29 '64
Our footloose correspondents. J. Bainbridge. il New Yorker 39:105-6+ N 9 '63
HUTCHINSON, Doris
Tailored to fit the child. NEA J 52:27-8 F '63
HUTCHINSON, Edmond C.
American aid to Africa; address, April 10, 1964; with questions and answers. Ann Am Acad 354:65-74 Jl '64
Role of U.S. foreign assistance in Africa; address, December 8, 1964. Dept State Bul 51: 915-18 D 28 '64; Same. Vital Speeches 31: 165-7 Ja 1 '65
HUTCHINSON, Edward
Excerpt from debate, April 7, 1964. Cong Digest 43:191 Je '64
HUTCHINSON, Eric
Politics and higher education; address, June 10, 1964. bibliog Science 146:1139-42 N 27 '64
HUTCHINSON, Fred
Analysis by an expert; ed. by R. Creamer. por Sports Illus 19:25 O 14 '63
Fred Hutchinson: angry boss of the Reds. T. Cohane. pors Look 27:66-9 Ag 27 '63
HUTCHINSON, G. E. and Cowgill, U. M.
Chemical examination of a core from Lake Zeribar, Iran. Science 140:67-9 Ap 5 '63
HUTCHINSON, Joseph C.
Language laboratory: how effective is it? por Sch Life 46:14-17+ Ja '64
HUTCHINSON, Peggyann
Thread of evidence. Am For 69:30-1+ Jl '63
HUTCHINSON, Robert
Grove street: selling the news; poem. Sat R 48:71 Ja 16 '65
HUTCHISON, Bruce
Canada's gadfly; the Winnipeg free press. Harper 226:82-6 Ap '63
Nation in the making. Holiday 35:70-1+ Ap '64
Two peoples under one flag. N Y Times Mag p29+ Ag 23 '64
HUTCHISON, Frank L.
Arab refugee today. Christian Cent 81:823-6 Je 24 '64
HUTCHISON, Lloyd S.
(ed) See Shuster, B. H. Dizziness: your body's warning light
HUTCHISON, Robert W.
Goddard's technical manpower. Electr World 71:62-3 Je '64
HUTCHISON, William
R/C model airplanes revisited. Pop Electr 20:43-7+ My '64
HUTCHISON, William J.
Youth leads. America 111:213 Ag 29 '64
HUTHMACHER, J. Joseph
1960's: the issues and the candidates. Cur Hist 47:229-35+ O '64
HUTTENLOCHER, Janellen
Children's language: word-phrase relationship. Science 143:264-5 Ja 17 '64
HUTTER, Donald
Family man; story. Sat Eve Post 237:64-6 F 22 '64
HUTTON, Clayton
Escape secrets of World war II; excerpt from Official secret. por Pop Sci 184:69-73+ Ja '64
HUTTON, Graham
Crisis in the western alliance; British view. Commentary 35:190-8 Mr '63
HUTTON, Harry K.
Compulsory professional teacher training in England. bibliog f Sch & Soc 92:358-9 N 28 '64
HUTTON, John J. and others
Hemoglobin solubility and α-chain structure in crosses between two inbred mouse strains. bibliog Science 143:252-3 Ja 17 '64
HUTTON, Sidney B.
Rose is born. Pop Gard 14:29-32 Jl '63
HUUS, Helen
Contemporary educational issues. Sch & Soc 91:45-6 Ja 26 '63
HUXLEY, Aldous
Devils of Loudun; dramatization. See Whiting, J. Devils
Only way to write a modern poem about a nightingale. Harper 227:62-6 Ag '63
Salt. House & Gard 123:116-17 Mr '63
about
Aldous Huxley in California. A. Loos. por Harper 228:51-5 My '64
Aldous Huxley in California. C. Isherwood. Atlan 214:44-7 S '64
Aldous Huxley: style was the man. R. Parmenter. por Sat R 46:12-13 D 21 '63
Aldous Huxley: the late author felt scientists tend to search for truth, ignore consequences. J. Walsh. Science 142:1445-6 D 13 '63
Obituary
Newsweek por 62:93A+ D 9 '63
Pub W 184:27 D 9 '63
HUXLEY, Andrew Fielding
Excitation and conduction in nerve: quantitative analysis; address, December 11, 1963. bibliog Science 145:1154-9 S 11 '64
Nobel medical awards. por Sci N L 84:259 O 26 '63
Nobel prize: 1963 award honors three for research on nerve functioning. M. G. F. Fuortes. por Science 142:468-70 O 25 '63
Nobels for nerves. Newsweek 62:90-1 O 28 '63
HUXLEY, Elspeth
African affairs. por Nat R 16:65-6, 351-2+, 531-2+, 651-2, 868-9, 1105-6 Ja 28, My 5, Je 30, Jl 28, O 6, D 15 '64
Bringing home the hippo. N Y Times Mag p 134-7 N 29 '64
Clues to the African personality. N Y Times Mag p 18+ My 31 '64
Dateline Africa. por Nat R 15:437+ N 19 '63
Kenya tries to put the clock ahead. N Y Times Mag p 18+ My 19 '63
Rise and fall of the Watusi. N Y Times Mag p 10+ F 23 '64
Serengeti National Park. Nat Parks Mag 38:10-14 My '64
Why Africa is in chaos; interview, ed. by J. Fromm. por U S News 56:46-9 F 17 '64
Witches' brew. Nat R 16:191-2 Mr 10 '64
HUXLEY, Sir Julian
All about love. Read Digest 85:127-9 Jl '64
about
Huxley the humanist. W. R. Smith. New Repub 150:28-30 Je 27 '64
HUXLEY, Maria
Aldous Huxley in California. A. Loos. Harper 228:51-5 My '64
HUXLEY, Susan
She prefers animals to ancestry. il pors Life 57:61-2+ D 11 '64
HUXLEY, Thomas Henry
Spokesman for Darwin, and for science. A. Ashforth. il por N Y Times Mag p64+ Ap 7 '63
HUXTABLE, Ada Louise (Landman)
Clusters instead of slurbs. N Y Times Mag p36-7+ F 9 '64
He adds elegance to modern architecture. N Y Times Mag p 18-19+ My 24 '64
New patterns for city housing. N Y Times Mag p 12-13 Ag 25 '63
World's fair preview. N Y Times Mag p38-41 O 6 '63
HUYCK, Dorothy Boyle
Exodus East; New York world's fair. Am For 70:34-7 F '64
EV and camping clubs. Am For 70:10-11+ Je
Proposed Cape Lookout National Seashore. Nat Parks Mag 38:4-8 S '64
They know their target. por Am For 71:18-21+ Ja '65
HUZAYYIN, S. A.
New university is born. UNESCO Courier 16:41-3 Jl '63
HWANG, Shuh-wei, and others
Freezing and viability of tetrahymena pyriformis in dimethylsulfoxide. bibliog Science 144:64-5 Ap 3 '64
HYACINTHS
Grow hyacinths indoors. E. S. Parcher. Horticulture 42:16+ O '64
Hyacinth in a glass. il Sunset 133:260-1 N '64
HYACINTHS, Water. See Water hyacinths
HYALINE membrane disease. See Respiratory organs—Diseases
HYALURONIDASE
Binding of an alpha globulin to hyaluronateprotein in pathological synovial fluids. J. Sandson and D. Hamerman. bibliog il Science 146:70-1 O 2 '64

HYAMS, Joe
Season of Sommer. Sat Eve Post 237:70-3 Ap 18 '64
When love goes on location. McCalls 90:88-93 Je '63
—See Wanger, W. jt. auth.
HYANNIS PORT, Mass.
Ship of state rocks Hyannis Port. R. P. Hunt. il N Y Times Mag p30-1+ My 26 '63
HYATT, Donald B.
Gary Cooper. McCalls 90:96-7+ Mr '63
HYBRID amaryllis. See Amaryllis
HYBRID rockets. See Rockets
HYBRIDIZATION
Biochemical anomaly in flower extracts of interspecific hybrids between lotus species. P. M. Harney and W. F. Grant. bibliog il Science 142:1061 N 22 '63
Crossbreeding beef cattle. C. Peterson, jr. il Suc Farm 62:48-9 My '64
Crossbreeding research. L. N. Hazel. Suc Farm 62:95 My '64
Crossing species produces strange life forms. L. Ehrman. il Sci Digest 53:70-6 Mr '63
Hybridization of rapidly labeled nuclear ribonucleic acids. R. P. Perry and others. bibliog il Science 145:504-7 Jl 31 '64
Leopard+lion=leopon. B. Reynolds. il Look 28:78-9 D 1 '64
New flowers by new methods. C. Weddle. il Horticulture 43:18-19+ Ja '65
Rose is born; Christian Dior of Meilland. S. B. Hutton. il Pop Gard 14:29-32 Jl '63
Selection of hybrids from matings of fibroblasts in vitro and their presumed recombinants. J. W. Littlefield. bibliog il Science 145:709 Ag 14 '64
Test boars in crosses? ed. by J. Bickers. W. O. Robinson. Farm J 88:44B Je '64
Why we hybridize lilies. J. De Graaff. il Pop Gard 14:28-9+ S '63
You can make more beef with crossbreds. J. Dyer. il Farm J 88:38-9+ My '64
See also
Tree breeding
also subhead Hybrids under various subjects, e.g. Sorghum—Hybrids
HYDE, Betty Vance
We can protect our children from fear. Redbook 120:53+ Ap '63
HYDE, H. Montgomery
Composite portrait of the Soviet spy. N Y Times Mag p 14+ F 16 '64
HYDE, J. A. Lloyd
Living with antiques. Antiques 84:158-61 Ag '63; 85:76-9 Ja '64
HYDE, Sister Mary Olivero. See Jensen, J. jt. auth.
HYDE, Philip
Steam means trouble in Lassen's Section thirty-six. il Nat Parks Mag 37:4-6 Je '63
HYDE, Phoebe
Embossing, the new easy way to make holiday decorations. House B 105:244-7+ N '63
HYDE, Vance
Who says you have to choose? Redbook 123:33+ Je '64
HYDE PARK, N.Y.

Roosevelt estate

I remember Hyde Park: a final reminiscence. E. Roosevelt. McCalls 90:71-3+ F '63; Same abr. il Read Digest 82:95-100 Je '63
HYDRA (island)
By hydrofoil to Hydra. il Sunset 131:45 S '63
HYDRA (zoology)
Behavior in hydra: contraction responses of hydra pirardi to mechanical and light stimuli. N. B. Rushforth and others. bibliog Science 139:760-1 F 22 '63
Behavior in hydra: inhibition of the contraction responses of hydra pirardi. N. B. Rushforth and others. bibliog il Science 145:602-4 Ag 7 '64
Dedifferentiation and redifferentiation of cells in hydra viridis. J. Haynes and A. L. Burnett. bibliog il Science 142:1481-3 D 13 '63
Symbiosis: on the role of algae symbiotic with hydra. L. Muscatine and H. M. Lenhoff. bibliog il Science 142:956-8 N 15 '63
Zinc activation a coordinated response in hydra. H. M. Lenhoff and J. R. Zwisler. bibliog il Science 142:1666-8 D 27 '63
HYDRA-CADENCE prosthesis. See Artificial limbs
HYDRANGEAS
Now's the time to plant hydrangeas. il Sunset 132:242+ Je '64
HYDRATED electrons. See Electrons
HYDRAULIC brakes, Automobile. See Brakes, Automobile
HYDRAULIC control
Fluid control devices. S. W. Angrist. il Sci Am 211:80-8 D '64
Fluid systems technology. P. J. Klass. il Aviation W 81:36-7+ N 30; 52-3+ D 7 '64
HYDRAULIC engineering
Hydraulic civilizations. P. Armillas. il UNESCO Courier 17:60-3 Jl '64
See also
Irrigation
Rivers
HYDRAULIC equipment for airplanes. See Airplanes—Hydraulic equipment
HYDRAULIC gates. See Gates, Hydraulic
HYDRAULIC jacks
Lab that jacks built; one-story structure jacked up and first floor and basement built under it. il Bsns W p 138-40 My 9 '64
HYDRAULIC models
Models map the sea's surge. il Motor B 111:154-5 Je '63
HYDRAZINE
Hydrazine-water system: the water-rich eutectic. J. A. McMillan and S. C. Los. bibliog il Science 145:1307 S 18 '64
HYDROCARBONS
Alkanes in natural and synthetic petroleums: comparison of calculated and actual compositions. R. A. Friedel and A. G. Sharkey, jr. bibliog il Science 139:1203-5 Mr 22 '63
Benzo(a)pyrene and other polynuclear hydrocarbons in charcoal-broiled meat. W. Lijinsky and P. Shubik. bibliog il Science 145:53-5 Jl 3 '64
Chemiluminescence resulting from electrochemically generated species. D. M. Hercules. bibliog il Science 145:808-9 Ag 21 '64
Diffusion coefficients of hydrocarbons in water: method for measuring. D. N. Saraf and others. bibliog il Science 142:955-6 N 15 '63
Genesis of hydrocarbons of low molecular weight in organic-rich aquatic systems. J. D. Mulik and J. G. Erdman. bibliog il Science 141:806-7 Ag 30 '63
Hexanedione from hydrocarbon polymer oxidation. E. M. Bevilacqua and P. M. Norling. bibliog il Science 147:289-90 Ja 15 '65
Hydrocarbon fuel cells may power tracking sites. W. Beller. il Miss & Roc 12:26+ Ap 29 '63
Large electron pulses in hydrocarbons. A. H. Samuel and others. bibliog Science 144:839 My 15 '64
Petroleum hydrocarbons: generation from fatty acid. J. W. Jurg and E. Eisma. bibliog il Science 144:1451 Je 19 '64
Positive-ion chemistry: high yields of heavy hydrocarbons from solid methane by ionizing radiation. D. R. Davis and W. F. Libby. bibliog Science 144:991-2 My 22 '64
Pristane in zooplankton. M. Blumer and others. bibliog il Science 140:974 My 31 '63
Pyrene and fluoranthene in manganese nodules. D. W. Thomas and M. Blumer. bibliog il Science 143:39 Ja 3 '64
HYDROCEPHALUS
Hydrocephalus; the water that kills. W. R. Vath. il Todays Health 41:52-3+ My '63
HYDROCHLORIC acid
Hydrochloric acid used to make cottage cheese. Sci N L 85:392 Je 20 '64
HYDROCORTISONE
Cortisol from human nerve. J. C. Touchstone and others. il Science 141:1275 S 27 '63
Glycogen synthetase: its response to cortisol. H. G. Sie and W. H. Fishman. bibliog il Science 143:816 F 21 '64
Intestinal invertase: precocious development of activity after injection of hydrocortisone. R. G. Doell and N. Kretchmer. bibliog il Science 143:42-4 Ja 3 '64
Wasting disease induced in young mice by administration of cortisol acetate. M. Schlesinger and R. Mark. bibliog il Science 143:865-6 F 28 '64
HYDRODYNAMICS
Groundwater: flow toward an effluent stream. J. H. Lehr. bibliog il Science 140:1318-20 Je 21 '63
Location of an aircraft impact from gravity waves. D. E. Amstutz and S. Neshyba. il Science 145:921-3 Ag 28 '64
See also
Vortex motion
HYDROELECTRIC plants
Big Soviet project gets the ax; hydroelectric aluminum complex at Bratsk. il Bsns W p62+ Ja 25 '64
Dig they must? proposed hydro power plant at Storm King Mountain. il Newsweek 64:67-8 D 21 '64

HYDROELECTRIC plants—*Continued*
Great battle for Storm King. J. Ridgeway. New Repub 151:8-9 N 28 '64
Storm King question; hydropower project in Hudson Highlands. Nat Parks Mag 39:21 Ja '65
Striking up a power partnership; U.S. and Canada. il Bsns W p 134+ F 15 '64

HYDROELECTRIC power
Con Ed switches plan; hydro power from Labrador. Bsns W p43 Ja 11 '64
Energy. S. H. Schurr. il Sci Am 209:110-14+ bibliog(p307) S '63
See also
Hydroelectric plants
Tide power

HYDROFOIL models
Water bug. R. L. Clough, jr. il Pop Mech 119:128-30 Je '63

HYDROFOILS
Commutaboat hydrofoil. J. E. Mitchell. il Motor B 111:38-9+ F '63
Dream boat; H. S. Denison. il Newsweek 62: 80 S 9 '63
Foil-borne ferry approved by Coast guard. W. H. Koelbel. il Motor B 111:72+ F '63
Forty knot sailboat; aerohydrofoil. B. P. Winawer. il Motor B 112:122-3 S '63
Just above water; Albatross's maiden voyage on the Port Washington, L.I.-Wall Street run. il Time 82:59 Jl 26 '63
On air; abroad the Albatross, hydrofoil ferry, American hydrofoil lines. New Yorker 39: 19-20 Ag 31 '63
Squirt gun on hydrofoils. il Pop Mech 119: 92-3 My '63
To toil by foil; commuter service. il Newsweek 61:84 Ap 15 '63
Ungainly waterbug; new hydrofoil craft. M. Morgan. il Sat Eve Post 236:68-9 Jl 13 '63
What's up that's out. il Motor B 111:60-1 F '63
Yo ho! to the fair by boat. W. Robberson. il Yachting 116:164 Jl '64

HYDROGEN
Artificial inspiration: our dependency of three principle key elements. il Sci Digest 57:86-9 Ja '65
Hydrogen atom thermal parameters. L. H. Jensen and M. Sundaralingam. bibliog il Science 145:1185-7 S 11 '64
Hydrogen: electrolytic technique for purifying it and removing it from a gas stream. S. H. Langer and R. G. Haldeman. il Science 142:225-6 O 11 '63
Hydrogen energy levels: perturbation caused by proton structure. W. S. Porter. il Science 143:1324-5 Mr 20 '64
Hydrogen in a tektite vesicle. J. A. O'Keefe and others. Science 143:39 Ja 3 '64
Hydrogen in galaxies. M. S. Roberts. il Sci Am 208:94-100+ Je '63
Hydrogen ion incorporation in crystals. D. McConnell. bibliog Science 141:171 Jl 12 '63
Hydrogen-water vapor mixtures: control of hydrothermal atmospheres by hydrogen osmosis. H. R. Shaw. bibliog il Science 139:1220-2 Mr 22 '63
Reaction of hydrogen with oxygen adsorbed on a platinum catalyst. H. W. Kohn and M. Boudart. bibliog il Science 145:149 Jl 10 '64

Isotopes

See also
Deuterium

Storage

Invisible bottle used to hold unearthly fire; magnetic bottle. Sci N L 84:56 Jl 27 '63

HYDROGEN, Liquid
Hoofs of hydrogen. il Time 82:97-8 D 6 '63
Hydrogen is headache for Saturn engineers. Sci N L 85:379 Je 13 '64
USAF will produce slush hydrogen soon. Aviation W 81:26 N 2 '64

Storage

Emphasis on space cryogenics advances at Linde; experimental studies of slush hydrogen. J. F. Judge. il Miss & Roc 13:22-4 S 23 '63

HYDROGEN bomb
New device to control H-bomb reactions. Sci N L 86:40 Jl 18 '64
See also
Nuclear fusion

Economic aspects

See Atomic power—Economic aspects

Ethical aspects

See Atomic warfare—Ethical aspects

HYDROGEN ion concentration
Carbonate rocks: cleaning with suspensions of hydrogen-ion exchange resin. S. F. Percival, jr. and others. il Science 142:1456 D 13 '63
Effect of traces of large molecules containing nitrogen on hydrogen overvoltage. W. Juda and others. bibliog il Science 146:521-3 O 23 '64
Ion exchange at edge and interlayer in montmorillonites differing in size. E. C. Jonas. bibliog il Science 140:75-6 Ap 5 '63
Vibrational excitation in some four-center transition states. S. H. Bauer and E. L. Resler, jr. bibliog il Science 146:1045-8 N 20 '64

HYDROKARTS
Those silly shingles. B. Grant and J. E. Boykin. il Pop Mech 121:141-3 Mr '64

HYDROLOGIC research
International hydrological decade: worldwide programme of scientific research. M. Batisse. il UNESCO Courier 17:4-9 Jl '64

HYDROLOGY. See Water

HYDROLYSIS
Intramolecular catalysis of the hydrolysis of *n*-dimethylaminomaleamic acid. G. Dahlgren and N. L. Simmerman. bibliog il Science 140:485 My 3 '63

HYDROMECHANICS
Fluid mechanics before the Society for natural philosophy; report of second meeting. C. Truesdell. Science 143:382 Ja 24 '64

HYDRONIUM. See Ions

HYDROPHOBIA. See Rabies

HYDROPHONES
Amateur scientist; two devices for listening in on underwater sound. F. Watlington. il Sci Am 210:131-6+ Mr '64
Now hear this; Artemis, electronic listening system. Newsweek 62:43 D 30 '63
Science in action; listening under water. W. A. Watkins. il Natur Hist 73:57-9 D '64

HYDROPLANE racing. See Motor boat racing

HYDROPLANES
Aerohydroski uses lift from skis, wings. M. L. Yaffee. il Aviation W 81:72-3+ O 26 '64
Pieces and quiet; inquiry into the hibernation of the hydroplane. E. Crimmin. il Motor B 111:137-9 F '63

HYDROPLANES, Jet propelled
Staudacher: man with a mission. E. Crimmin. il Motor B 115:109-11+ Ja '65

HYDROSKIMMERS. See Ground effect machines

HYDROSOME rivieri
Minnesota hydrosome. F. Knock. il Horticulture 41:407 Ag '63

HYDROSTATIC transmission. See Automobiles —Transmission

HYDROTHERAPY
See also
Baths, Moor and mud

HYDROXYBUTYRIC acid. See Butyric acid

HYDROXYCHLORPROMAZINE. See Chlorpromazine

HYDROXYL
Galactic center probed. Sci N L 86:66 Ag 1 '64
Infrared absorption of hydroxyl groups in kaolinite. V. C. Farmer. bibliog il Science 145:1189-90 S 11 '64
OH in interstellar space. Sci N L 84:323 N 23 '63
OH in interstellar space. Sky & Tel 27:71+ F '64

HYDROXYPROLINE
Alpha-ketoglutaric semialdehyde: a metabolic intermediate. R. M. M. Singh and E. Adams. bibliog il Science 144:67-8 Ap 3 '64

HYDROXYSTEROID dehydrogenase. See Dehydrogenases

HYDROXYUREA. See Urea

HYEK, James L.
Why substitute? NEA J 53:45 S '64

HYGIENE
Health quiz. G. Baker. Farm J 88:60J Mr '64
One person, one towel. Time 82:78 N 15 '63
Outwit those stay-around staph germs. L. F. Nichols. il Parents Mag 38:74-5+ O '63
See also
Woman—Health and hygiene

Study and teaching

Vital ties between health and education; adaptation of address. D. Oberteuffer. il NEA J 53:57-61 Mr '64

HYGROMETERS
Heat or humidity? how to make your own discomfort index meter. R. M. Benrey. il Pop Sci 183:96-7 Ag '63
Humidity indicators. il Consumer Bul 47:31-3 N '64
Liquid film hygrometer. R. J. Charlson. il Science 143:1031-2 Mr 6 '64

HYGROMETERS—*Continued*
Systematic error in leaf water potential measurements with a thermocouple psychrometer. S. L. Rawlins. bibliog il Science 146:644-6 O 30 '64
There's danger in desert-dry air. S. J. Howard. il Pop Mech 120:158-65+ D '63
HYKSOS
Rulers in the East. E. Anati. il Natur Hist 72:18-27 Ag '63
HYMAN, Herbert H.
Chemistry of noble gas compounds. bibliog Science 145:773-83 Ag 21 '64
Noble gas compounds. Science 141:61-3 Jl 5 '63
—and Sheatsley, P. B.
Attitudes toward desegregation; with biographical sketch. Sci Am 211:14, 16-23 bibliog(p 142) Jl '64
HYMAN, Joe
Professor. por Time 82:115A-115B D 6 '63
HYMAN, Mervin
Basketball's week. See issues of Sports illustrated published during basketball season
College football. Sports Illus 21:68+ O 19 '64
Football's week. See issues of Sports illustrated published during football season
HYMAN, Sidney
Excerpt from testimony, February 28, 1964. Cong Digest 43:151 My '64
How Mr Kennedy gets the answers. N Y Times Mag p 17+ O 20 '63
Qualities that make a president. N Y Times Mag p23+ D 1 '63
Why there's trouble on the New frontier. Look 27:30+ Jl 2 '63
HYMAN, Stanley Edgar
Canon of a critic at arms. G. Hicks. Sat R 46:19-20 N 2 '63
HYMEN, Artificial
Artificial virgins. Newsweek 61:89 Ap 22 '63
HYMENOCALLIS
Hymenocallis ovata. H. B. Fox. Horticulture 42:25 Ja '64
HYMENOPTERA
Disc electrophoresis of hymenoptera venoms and body proteins. R. O'Connor and others. bibliog il Science 145:1320-1 S 18 '64
Hymenoptera: pure venom from bees, wasps, and hornets. R. O'Connor and others. il Science 139:420 F 1 '63
HYMES, James L. Jr,
Our children in these times. Farm J 87:91-2 F '63
Parent and child. N Y Times Mag p91 O 27 '63
Quiz for parents of preschoolers. Parents Mag 39:52-4+ Ja '64
—and Taylor, Toni
One year old and rarin' to go. Parents Mag 39:68-9 Ap '64
Up-and-coming threes. Parents Mag 39:56-7 Je '64
Wonderful world of two. Parents Mag 39:52-3 My '64
HYMNALS. See Hymns
HYMNOLOGY. See Hymns
HYMNS
Challenge to hymn writers. C. J. McNaspy. America 111:674-6 N 21 '64
Glimmers of light; new hymnals. C. J. McNaspy. America 111:220 Ag 29 '64
Joyful noise. il Time 81:48+ Mr 1 '63
Savings and quality in Seabury's web-offset Prayer book, Hymnal. il Pub W 186:74-6 D 7 '64
We shall overcome. C. J. McNaspy. America 109:531-2 N 2 '63
Who's got the hymns? W. H. Du Bay. il America 109:158-9 Ag 17 '63
HYNEK, J. A.
Lindheimer astronomical research center. Sky & Tel 28:216-18 O '64
—and Dunlap, J. R.
Image orthicon astronomy. Sky & Tel 28:126-30 S '64
HYNEMAN, Charles S.
This Court now sees itself as above the Constitution; interview. por U S News 58:57-60 Ja 18 '65
HYNES, Samuel
Off to war. Commonweal 80:642-3 S 18 '64
Old Man at King's. Commonweal 79:635-8 F 21 '64
Poet and prime minister. Commonweal 81:84-5 O 16 '64
HYPERAMMONEMIA. See Ammonia in the body
HYPERBARIC oxygen chambers. See High-pressure oxygenation
HYPERSENSITIVITY. See Allergy
HYPERSONIC aerodynamics. See Aerodynamics, Supersonic
HYPERSONIC airplanes. See Airplanes, Supersonic
HYPERTENSION
Angiotensin pressor inhibition by aldosterone in the rabbit. Y. J. Katz and others. bibliog il Science 141:725 Ag 23 '63
Blood-pressure hormone. Time 81:48 Mr 15 '63
Drug promises to control high blood pressure. Sci N L 85:345 My 30 '64
High blood pressure seen from salt in baby foods. Sci N L 84:9 Jl 6 '63
Hypertensive vascular disease produced by homologous renin. G. M. C. Masson and others. bibliog il Science 145:178-80 Jl 10 '64
Neurogenic component of chronic renal hypertension. J. W. McCubbin and I. H. Page. il Science 139:210+ Ja 18 '63
New enzyme discovery. Sci N L 85:405 Je 27 '64
Stress and the Zulu. Sci Am 209:60+ O '63
HYPERTHYROIDISM. See Thyroid gland
HYPNOTISM
Athletes get help from hypnotists. D. Moser. il Life 54:71-2+ Je 7 '63
Cataleptic set; hypnoteuse Collins. il Time 82:37-8 Ag 2 '63
Experimenter bias in hypnotist performance. S. A. Troffer and C. T. Tart. bibliog il Science 145:1330-1 S 18 '64
Head-to-toe hypnosis. il Time 82:45 D 20 '63
Hilarious hypnotist. il Life 56:125-6 My 8 '64
Hoppety hypnotism. E. S. Dean. Sat R 46:46-7 S 7 '63; Discussion. 46:54 N 2 '63
Hypnosis helps hay fever. Sci N L 85:306 My 16 '64
Hypnosis: the fad and the facts. H. Rosen. il Todays Health 41:38-9+ O '63
Hypnotic effect. il Newsweek 62:79 O 21 '63
Hypnotism stops shivers in 40° temperature. Sci N L 86:72 Ag 1 '64
Nystagmus as a criterion of hypnotically induced visual hallucinations. J. P. Brady and E. E. Levitt. bibliog Science 146:85-6 O 2 '64
Voice recordings show experimenters biased. Sci N L 86:232 O 10 '64
You will go deep asleep; hypnotism nightclub act. Newsweek 63:106+ My 25 '64
HYPO-sniffer-outer. See Photography—Apparatus and supplies
HYPOCHONDRIA
Are you a hypochondriac? J. D. Ratcliff. il Read Digest 82:151-2+ Ap '63
Hypochondria. A. Lake. McCalls 92:67+ O '64
Sex and the hypochondriac. G. Ace. Sat R 47:16-17 S 12 '64
Sick, sick, sick; West German hypochondriacs. Newsweek 63:44+ Mr 23 '64

Anecdotes, facetiae, satire, etc.

Art of hypochondria. G. Ace. Sat R 47:12 Jl 11; 9 Jl 25; 8 Ag 1 '64
Typos and hypos. G. Ace. Sat R 47:9 S 5 '64
HYPOGLYCEMIA. See Blood sugar
HYPOPHYSECTOMY. See Brain—Surgery
HYPOTHALAMUS
Attack elicited by stimulation of the thalamus cats. M. F. MacDonnell and J. P. Flynn. bibliog il Science 144:1249-50 Je 5 '64
Estradiol: evidence for its direct effect on hypothalamic neurons. R. D. Lisk and M. Newlon. bibliog il Science 139:223-4 Ja 18 '63
Hypothalamic temperature in the cat during feeding and sleep. T. Adams. bibliog il Science 139:609-10 F 15 '63
Identical feeding and rewarding systems in the lateral hypothalamus of rats. D. L. Margules and J. Olds; reply with rejoinder. J. R. Brobeck. 140:218-20 Ap 12 '63
Interaction of evoked potentials of neocortical and hypothalamic origin in amygdala. R. Caruthers and others. bibliog il Science 144:422-3 Ap 24 '64
Lateral hypothalamic lesions: effects on drinking elicited by carbachol in preoptic area and posterior hypothalamus. G. Wolf and N. E. Miller. bibliog il Science 143:585-7 F 7 '64
Life-giving balancing act. R. Campbell. il Life 55:72-3 N 8 '63
Light: evidence for its direct effect on hypothalamic neurons. R. D. Lisk and L. R. Kannwischer. bibliog il Science 146:272-3 O 9 '64
Reciprocal activities of the ventromedial and lateral hypothalamic areas of cats. Y. Oomura and others. bibliog il Science 143:484-5 Ja 31 '64
Spreading depression and recovery from lateral hypothalamic damage. P. Teitelbaum and J. Cytawa. bibliog il Science 147:61-3 Ja 1 '65

HYPOTHERMIA
Hypothermia, asphyxia, and cardiac glycogen in guinea pigs. J. A. Miller, jr. and others. bibliog il Science 144:1226-7 Je 5 '64
HYSLOP, Beatrice F.
(comp) Articles and other books received; France. See issues of American historical review
HYSTERESIS loop
Hysteresis-loop plotter. J. H. Fasal. bibliog il Electr World 69:29-31+ My '63
HYSTERICAL amnesia. See Amnesia
HYYPIA, Jorma
How to poison bugs, but not yourself. Pop Sci 182:106-9+ Je '63

I

IAEA. See International atomic energy agency
IA-ECOSOC. See Inter-American economic and social council
IAF. See Industrial areas foundation; International astronautical federation
IAM. See International association of machinists
IATA. See International air transport association
IAU. See International astronomical union
IBEC. See International basic economy corporation
IBM. International business machines corporation
ICAO. See International civil aviation organization
ICBM (international ballistic missiles) See Guided missiles
ICC. See International chamber of commerce; United States—Interstate commerce commission
ICCA (International car club association) See Automobile clubs
ICL. See International Christian leadership (organization)
ICNND. See United States—Interdepartmental committee on nutrition for national defense
ICO (Interagency committee on oceanography) See United States—Federal council for science and technology
ICY. See International cooperation year (proposed)
IDA. See Institute for defense analyses; International development association
IDB. See Inter-American development bank
IDU. See Idoxuridine
IEEE. See Institute of electrical and electronics engineers
IFIF. See International federation for internal freedom
IFLA. See International federation of library associations
IFPW. See International federation of petroleum workers
IGFA. See International game fish association
IGY. See International geophysical year
I got shoes; drama. See Merlin, F.
IHD. See International hydrological decade
I had a ball; musical comedy. See Musical comedies, revues, etc.—Criticisms, plots, etc.
IIE. See Institute of international education
ILA. See International longshoremen's association
ILC. See United Nations—International law commission
ILGWU. See International ladies' garment workers' union
ILO. See International labor organization
ILS (instrument landing system) See Airplanes —Landing
ILWU. See International longshoremen's and warehousemen's union
IMC. See Instructional materials centers; International minerals and chemical corporation; International music council
IMCC (Integrated mission control center) See United States—National aeronautics and space administration
IMF. See International monetary fund
IMP (interplanetary monitoring platform) See Artificial satellites—Use in research
INA. See Insurance company of North America
INCAP. See Institute of nutrition of Central America and Panama
INRA. See International research associates, incorporated
INSEA. See International society for education through art
IOCU. See International office of consumers' unions
IOD (international one-designs) See Sailboat racing
IPA. See International publishers association
I play kings; story. See Tyler, A.
IQ. See Intelligence quotient
IQSY. See International years of the quiet sun
IRA. See International reading association
IRC. See American library association—International relations committee
IRI. See Ibec research institute, New York
IRO. See American library asociation—International relations office
IRRA. See Industrial relations research association
IRS. See United States—Internal revenue service
ISA. See United States—Defense, Department of—International security affairs division
ISIS (International satellites for ionospheric studies) See Artificial satellites, Canadian
ISO. See Institute of student opinion
ISOMATA. See Idyllwild school of music and the arts
I spend my days in longing; story. See O'Hara, J.
ITA (initial teaching alphabet) See Alphabet
IT and T. See International telephone and telegraph corporation
ITT. See International telephone and telegraph corporation
ITU. See International telecommunications union; International typographical union
IUCD (intra-uterine contraceptive devices) See Contraceptives
IUD. See American federation of labor and Congress of industrial organizations—Industrial union department
IUDR. See Idoxuridine
IUE. See International union of electrical, radio and machine workers
I was a teen-age parasite; story. See Preston, B. B.
I was dancing; drama. See O'Connor, E.
I was looking for you; story. See Randall, F. E.
I, who never kissed your head; story. See Terrien, M.
I will keep her company; story. See Davies, R.
I wisk you a Merry Christmas; story. See Brown, M. F.
I wouldn't twist with just anyone; story. See Schoen, B.
IWW. See Industrial workers of the world
IYRU. See International yacht racing union
IACOCCA, Lido Anthony
Ford's bid for a better year. il por Bsns W p47-8+ S 28 '63
Ford's young one. il pors Time 83:92-102 Ap 17 '64
Mustang, a new breed out of Detroit. il pors Newsweek 63:97-101 Ap 20 '64
Mustang twins move up. por Time 85:67-8 Ja 22 '65
IAKOVOS, abp, and others
Come, creator spirit; 1964 Pentecostal message from the presidents of the World council of churches. Christian Cent 81:627 My 13 '64
IAMS, Jack
Anyone for buried treasure? Sat Eve Post 237:64-6 Je 13 '64
Jack of all trades. Sat Eve Post 236:80-3 My 11 '63
Quiz is back in biz! Sat Eve Post 236:64-5 S 14 '63
Search for the strangler. Sat Eve Post 236: 28+ My 18 '63
Sweeps vs. the law. Sat Eve Post 237:74+ S 12 '64
IANNI, Francis A. J.
Educational research: the state of the art; summary of address. por Pub W 187:46-8 Ja 11 '65
USOE cooperative research. Sch Life 46:28-9 O; 15-16 N; 20-1 D '63; 26-7 Mr '64
—and Josephs, Lois
Needed, a way to save curiosity. bibliog f Sch Life 46:23-4 N '63
IBA, Hank
Who says you can't win 'em all? T. C. Brody. il Sports Illus 20:104-5 Ap 13 '64
IBAÑEZ, Félix Martí-. See Martí-Ibáñez, F.
IBARGOYEN ISLAS, Saúl
Six Uruguayan poets. Américas 16:16-21 S '64
IBARRA, José María Velasco. See Velasco Ibarra, J. M.

IBEC research institute, New York
Rich wasteland; Brazil's untapped campos cerrados. J. R. Camp. il Américas 15:11-14 Jl '63

IBERS, James A. and La Placa, S. J.
Molecular structure of the synthetic molecular oxygen carrier $O_2IrCl(CO)(P[C_6H_5]_3)_2$. bibliog Science 145:920-1 Ag 28 '64

IBIAM, Sir Francis Akanu
Sir Francis Ibiam condemns missionaries. Christian Cent 81:1133 S 16 '64

IBISES
See also
Wood storks

IBN Sa'ūd, king of Saudi Arabia
Desert king, by D. Howarth. Review
New Repub 151:18-19 S 12 '64. E. Monroe
Sat R por 47:29-30 Jl 18 '64. M. Khadduri

IBSEN, Henrik
On the murder of Abraham Lincoln; poem, tr. by R. Bly. Nation 196:142 F 16 '63

about

Doll's house; tr. by R. F. Sharp. Criticism
New Yorker 38:68+ F 9 '63
Newsweek 61:56 F 18 '63
Theatre Arts il 47:12-13 Ap '63
Little Eyolf. Criticism
Nation 198:355-6 Ap 6 '64
New Yorker 40:138 Mr 28 '64
Rain check on Utopia. R. Bimonte. Reporter 30:46-8 Je 4 '64

IBUKA, Masaru
Sony's purposeful dreams. il por Fortune 70: 83-4+ Jl '64

ICAZA, Jorge
Poetry of protest. J. Yglesias. Nation 198: 376-7 Ap 13 '64

ICE
Dislocations in ice. C. E. Hayes and W. W. Webb. bibliog il Science 147:44-5 Ja 1 '65
Glacial ice from Everest. Sci N L 83:379 Je 15 '63
Glacier geophysics. B. Kamb. bibliog il Science 146:353-65 O 16 '64
Glaciology. C. R. Bentley and J. C. Behrendt. Science 142:415-16 O 18 '63
Ice van cometh; Cold regions research and engineering laboratory, Hanover, N.H. il Newsweek 62:98 N 25 '63
Salt incorporation in natural ices. A. W. Cobb. il Science 141:733 Ag 23 '63
Splendor of winter. B. Tufty. il Sci N L 84: 378-9 D 14 '63
Vapor pressure of ice containing D_2O. S. Matsuo and others. bibliog il Science 145: 1454-5 S 25 '64
Water molecule in biological systems; report on conference on forms of water in biologic systems. J. F. Saunders. Science 147:179-81 Ja 8 '65

Manufacture

Ice as you like it. il House & Gard 125:160-1 Je '64
They don't make ice boxes that way any more. R. P. Smith. McCalls 90:52 Ag '63

Polar Regions

What caused the cold? il Time 83:50 Ja 24 '64

ICE age. See Glacial epochs

ICE age national scientific reserve (proposed) See National parks and reserves—United States

ICE and snow building. See Building, Ice and snow

ICE boats and ice boating
Chilly hot-rodding on the ice; with photographs by N. Leifer. Sports Illus 22:30-7 Ja 11 '65
How to ride mosquitoes. il Time 83:50+ F 21 '64
Lady of the frozen lakes; J. Pegel of Chicago and Williams Bay, Wis. H. Whall. il Sports Illus 22:39 Ja 11 '65
Now it's ice-scratchers. It beats walking. R. Sherin. il Outdoor Life 131:50-1 Ja '63
Racing a Great South Bay scooter. C. R. Meyer. il Motor B 114:50-1+ D '64
What! no rudder? story of the Great South Bay scooter (cont) A. M. Underhill, jr; H. G. Smith. il Yachting 113:54-6+ F '63

ICE breaking vessels
Antarctic drama: ship vs. iceberg. il U S News 56:12 Mr 9 '64
Busting through the Arctic aboard the atomic ship Lenin; with report by R. Brigham. il Life 57:30-34C Jl 17 '64

ICE carving. See Ice sculpture

ICE chisel. See Chisels

ICE cream, ices, etc.
August is ice cream time. il Sunset 133:102+ Ag '64
Cold, soft, luscious, spoony thick whips. il Seventeen 23:150-1+ My '64
From fruit to nuts. il McCalls 91:106-7+ Ag '64
Happy marriage: ice-cream bombe jubilee. il McCalls 91:56 S '64
Ice cream dazzler. il Bet Hom & Gard 41: 97 S '63
Ice cream desserts in delectable variety. G. Maddox. il Todays Health 42:42-7 Je '64
Ice cream plus. il Bet Hom & Gard 42:112 Je '64
It's a crystalline cream; parfait. il Sunset 132:162+ F '64
Marvelous match: ice cream and meringues. C. Claiborne. il N Y Times Mag p51 Ag 4 '63
Matter of labeling. il Consumer Bul 46:11 S '63
New sherbet-like melon dessert. R. Behnke. il Farm J 87:56-7 Jl '63
Seventeen split. il Seventeen 22:166 S '63
Successful recipes; ice cream and sauces. il Suc Farm 62:57-8 Je '64
Summer dessert cook book. J. Platt. il House & Gard 123:179+ My '63
Sundaes and shakes. il Bet Hom & Gard 41: 81-2 Ag '63
Susan makes chocolate cinnamon ice cream. il Good H 156:226 My '63
See also
Good humor corporation
Tastee-Freez corporation of America

ICE cream sauces. See Sauces

ICE crushers
Three handy appliances. Am Home 67:130 Jl '64

ICE cubes

Manufacture

See Ice—Manufacture

ICE fishing. See Fishing, Winter

ICE hazards in aviation. See Airplanes—Ice protection

ICE hockey. See Hockey

ICE manufacture. See Ice—Manufacture

ICE massage. See Massage

ICE navigation. See Ice breaking vessels

ICE on rivers, lakes, etc.

Control

All-winter wet storage; recent developments in bubbler systems. D. Lowry. il Yachting 114:68+ N '63
Ice-free wet storage. il Motor B 112:27+ O '63

ICE party; story. See Bingham, S.

ICE removal. See Snow and ice removal

ICE scooters. See Ice boats and ice boating

ICE sculpture
Ice cool; ice carving ideas. il Sunset 133:52-5 Ag '64

ICE skates. See Skates

ICE skating rinks. See Skating rinks

ICE wagon going down the street; story. See Gallant, M.

ICE yachts. See Ice boats and ice boating

ICEBERGS
See also
International ice patrol

ICEBREAKERS. See Ice breaking vessels

ICED drinks. See Beverages

ICED tea. See Tea

ICELAND
Land of fire and ice continues to rise. Sci N L 84:399 D 21 '63
See also
Airlines—Iceland

Description and travel

Iceland saga. J. H. Winchester. il Travel 120:26-31 Ag '63
Lonely beauty of Iceland. F. L. Lucas. il Holiday 34:56-61+ S '63

ICELAND and the United States
Vice President Johnson visits northern Europe; address, September 16, 1963. L. B. Johnson. Dept State Bul 49:592-4 O 14 '63

ICELAND poppies. See Poppies

ICELANDIC airlines. See Airlines—Iceland

ICELANDIC music
See also
Phonograph records—Icelandic music

ICES. See Ice cream, ices, etc.

ICHIKAWA, Kon
Outdoing Olympia. il por Newsweek 64:106 S 21 '64

ICHIKAWA, Ryushi, and others
Strontium and calcium reabsorption in renal tubules of the newt, triturus pyrrhogaster. bibliog Science 144:53-4 Ap 3 '64
ICHIMURA, Kiyoshi
Sparrow catching. il por Newsweek 62:92-3 O 7 '63
ICHINOSE, Ruby R. and Nandi, Satyabrata
Lobuloalveolar differentiation in mouse mammary tissues in vitro. bibliog Science 145:496-7 Jl 31 '64
ICINGS
Cake in bloom. il McCalls 92:90-1+ Ja '65
Cookies and dips; with recipes. il Seventeen 22:230-1+ Ag '63
Frosting favorites. il Bet Hom & Gard 42: 101-2 N '64
Frosting masterpieces-every easy step! N. Wilton. il Bet Hom & Gard 41:74-7+ F '63
Happy birthday cakes. il Redbook 123:76-9 My '64
ICKERINGILL, Nan
Food. N Y Times Mag p56 Ja 19; 111-12 S 27 '64
ICONS
Mount Sinai's holy treasures. K. Weitzmann. il Nat Geog Mag 125:107-27 Ja '64
Touch of iconomania. J. Hitrec. il Harper 229:20+ Jl '64
I'D rather die than say no; story. See White, R.
IDAHO
Idaho will mark its centennial. Sunset 131: 47 Jl '63
See also
Coeur d'Alene
Fishing—Idaho
Hunting—Idaho
Law—Idaho
Libraries—Idaho
Salmon River

Description and travel

If you like your mountains all to yourself, consider Idaho's Seven Devils. il Sunset 130: 40+ Je '63
Summer weekend in Idaho. B. Ballantine. il Holiday 36:16+ Ag '64

Religious institutions and affairs

News of the Christian world. Christian Cent 81:380 Mr 18 '64
IDE, Leta Foster
She wore a red germanium. Pop Electr 22: 58-9+ Ja '65
IDEA of a university; story. See Nemerov, H.
IDEAL cement company
Ready-mixed competition. il Bsns W p61-2+ My 23 '64
IDEAL states. See Utopias
IDEAS
Great ideas today, by M. J. Adler and R. Hutchins. Review
Nat R 14:233-5 Mr 26 '63. J. Leonard
Magnet for ideas; brainstorming in education. F. L. Redefer. Sat R 47:20 Ag 8 '64
Manner of speaking. J. Ciardi. Sat R 46:34 Je 22 '63
There's something knocking at the door. R. Bach. Writer 77:13-15+ My '64
Why do you want to write? C. R. Bittle. Writer 77:18-19 Ag '64
IDEAS in business
Big power of little ideas; excerpts from Managing for results: economic tasks and risk-taking decisions. P. F. Drucker. Harvard Bsns R 42:6-8+ My '64
Creativity is not enough. T. Levitt. bibliog f il Harvard Bsns R 41:72-83 My '63
Industry's search for ideas; presidents' panel report. il Duns R 82:39-40B+ S '63
Make the most of new ideas. C. A. Cerami. Nations Bsns 52:50-2+ Jl '64
See also
Suggestion systems
IDENTICAL bidding. See Contracts, Government
IDENTICAL quadruplets. See Quadruplets
IDENTICAL twins. See Twins
IDENTIFICATION
Box that catches criminals; Identi-Kit. F. Sondern, jr. Read Digest 84:37-8+ Ap '64
Call me 552. F. J. Taylor. il Read Digest 83:123-4 Ag '63
Eighteen year hunt to find his father's killer. H. Suydam. il Life 55:58-60+ Ag 2 '63
Rape of the lock. Time 83:49 Ap 24 '64
Somebody has a file on you! Changing T 17:33-6 S '63
Your portrait by the police; Identi-kit. A. Hamilton. il Sci Digest 55:31-4 Mr '64
See also
Fingerprints
Justice, Miscarriage of
Writing—Identification

Anecdotes, facetiae, satire, etc.

Why do I look so familiar? C. Ford. Read Digest 85:19-20+ Ag '64
IDENTIFICATION of infants. See Infants—Identification
IDENTIFICATION tags, bracelets, etc.
Alert signal for medical emergencies. il Changing T 17:4 O '63
For special care in emergency; device of American medical association. il U S News 54:16 Je 24 '63
Lifesaving bracelet. il Time 81:57 Je 7 '63
Medical I. D. tag can save your life. R. Dunlop. il Todays Health 41:8-13 Jl '63; Same abr. with title Tag that can save your life. Read Digest 83:217-19+ O '63
This jewelry means danger; Medic alert tags. il Sci Digest 54:50 N '63
IDENTI-KIT. See Identification
IDENTITY, Personal. See Personality
IDEOGRAPHY. See Chinese language—Writing
IDEOLOGY
Revolt against ideology. H. D. Aiken. Commentary 37:29-39 Ap '64; Discussion. 38:14+ S; 69-76 O '64
Teaching of ideologies; report from fifth biennial Atlantic study conference on education. Sch & Soc 92:388+ D 12 '64
IDHRA. See Hydra (island)
IDIOCY
See also
Mongolism
IDIOT savant. See Mentally handicapped
IDLEMAN, Hillis
Do-it-yourself plumbing. Consumer Bul 46: 31-4 Ap '63
IDLEMAN, Peter
Ski boots. Consumer Bul 46:9-13+ O '63
IDLENESS
Wealthy American bum. R. Kirk. Nat R 14: 198 Mr 12 '63; Reply. R. W. Blair. 14:333 Ap 23 '63
IDOXURIDINE
Bright future foreseen. A Ewing. Sci N L 85:23 Ja 11 '64
5-iodo-2′-deoxyuridine: relation of structure to its antiviral activity. N. Camerman and J. Trotter. bibliog il Science 144:1348-50 Je 12 '64
Found: drug that cures a blinding virus. il Life 55:78+ S 6 '63
Inhibition by 5-iododeoxyuridine of the oncogenic effects of adenovirus type 12 in hamsters. R. J. Huebner and others. il Science 142:488-90 O 25 '63
Therapeutic antiviral action of 5-trifluoromethyl-2′-deoxyuridine in herpes simplex keratitis. H. E. Kaufman and C. Heidelberger. bibliog il Science 145:585 Ag 7 '64
IDRIS I, king of Libya
Smell of oil. por Newsweek 63:40-1 Ap 6 '64
IDYLLWILD arts foundation
See also
Idyllwild school of music and the arts
IDYLLWILD school of music and the arts
Cultural haven in the California pines. C. Zapata. il Américas 16:22-6 Je '64
IDZERDA, Stanley J.
Scraping the top of the barrel. NEA J 52: 14-15 My '63
IF a slicker meet a slicker; story. See Perelman, S. J.
IF winter comes; story. See Kokjohn, J. E.
IF you can't lick 'em; story. See Longee, L.
IFFLAND, Donald W. and Allison, P. V.
Nematode-trapping fungi: evaluation of axenic healthy and galled roots as trap inducers. bibliog Science 146:547-8 O 23 '64
IGLAUER, Edith
Reporter at large (cont) New Yorker 39: 188+ N 23 '63; 40:54-6+ Mr 7 '64
IGLESIAS, Antonio
Music in Madrid. por Américas 17:1-5 Ja '65
IGLOI, Mihaly
According to plan; indoor two-mile record. Time 81:78 Mr 15 '63
How a man of spirit wrecked Igloi's computer. T. Maule. il Sports Illus 18:26-9+ Je 3 '63
Magic of the Great Igloi; with report by J. Beatty. il pors Life 54:54B-9 Mr 1 '63
IGNATOW, David
Figures of the human; Sky is blue; poems. Nation 199:174 S 28 '64

IGNATOW, David—*Continued*
To nowhere; If my hand; As I stumble; Beautiful and kind; poems. Poetry 103:353-4 Mr '64
Two friends; poem. Nation 196:431 My 18 '63

IGNEOUS rocks. See Rocks, Igneous

IGNITION devices. See Automobile engines—Ignition; Marine engines—Ignition

IGNITION noise. See Automobile engines—Noise; Marine engines—Noise

IGNOFFO, C. M. and others
Sex attractant of cabbage looper, trichoplusia ni (Hübner) bibliog Science 141:902-3 S 6 '63

IGUANODON. See Dinosaurs

IGUASSÚ FALLS, Argentina and Brazil
Iguassú Falls. M. Shepard. il Travel 120:34-7 D '63

IHLENFELD, Klaus
Klaus Ihlenfeld. il por Sch Arts 64:21-6 Ja '65

IKEDA, Hayato
Contented yawn. il Newsweek 62:54-6 N 25 '63
Ikeda's low-posture. New Repub 149:9-10 N 23 '63
Narrow shave. Time 84:29 Jl 17 '64
Players. il por Newsweek 64:57 N 9 '64
U.S. and Japan inaugurate transpacific telephone cable; remarks, June 18, 1964. Dept State Bul 51:26 Jl 6 '64

IKER, Sam
Satellite eavesdropper in an attic. Pop Mech 121:102-3 Ap '64

IKEYA comet. See Comets

IKONS. See Icons

ILEX. See Holly

ILFORD, Mary
(tr) See Haring, B. Responsible parenthood
(tr) See Janssens, L. Morality of the pill

ILG, Frances Lillian, and Ames, L. B.
Viewpoint on school readiness; excerpt from School readiness: behavior tests used at the Gesell institute. Sch & Soc 92:397-402 D 26 '64
—See Ames, L. B. jt. auth.

about

What parents ask most about children. J. H. Pollack. il Todays Health 41:24-7+ F '63

ILIKON corporation
New weapon for aluminum? Bsns W p 142 Ja 26 '63

I'LL walk you home; story. See Cave, H.

ILLEGAL radio broadcasting stations. See Radio stations, Illegal

ILLEGITIMACY
American children: alien by birth. P. S. Buck. Ladies Home J 81:36+ N '64
Babies without homes. W. Trombley. il Sat Eve Post 236:15-21 F 16 '63
Bombastardy: status of illegitimate children in West Germany. Newsweek 64:40+ S 7 '64
Illegitimacy and value dilemmas. C. E. Vincent. Christian Cent 80:801-4 Je 19 '63
Illegitimate family; conditions in Venezuela. Time 81:30 Mr 8 '63
Mothers without joy. J. Rinehart. Sat Eve Post 236:29-30+ Mr 23 '63; Same abr. Read Digest 83:83-7 Jl '63
Tragedy of the unwanted child. A. F. Guttmacher. Parents Mag 39:43+ Je '64
See also
Mothers, Unmarried

ILLÍA, Arturo Umberto
Argentina: struggle for recovery. A. P. Whitaker. Cur Hist 48:16-20+ Ja '65
Doctor in the casa. Newsweek 62:45 Ag 12 '63
Mocking the turtle. Time 84:32-3 Jl 31 '64
Nation again. il por Time 82:31 Ag 9 '63
New deal now in Argentina? por U S News 55:51 Jl 22 '63
President again. il por Time 82:33 O 18 '63
Puff the magic Perón. Newsweek 62:49 Jl 22 '63
We can go home. por Time 82:22 Jl 19 '63
What is Illia? New Repub 149:8 Ag 17 '63

ILLIG, Carol
Jennifer. Mlle 56:61+ F '63
(ed) See Guest, L. Their dream is not to be nervous

ILLIG, Lillian
How to grow, freeze and dry your own chives. House B 106:45-6+ Je '64

ILLINOIS
See also
Agriculture—Illinois
American literature—Illinois
Booksellers and bookselling—Illinois
Cook County
Hunting—Illinois
Law—Illinois
Prisons—Illinois
Public welfare—Illinois
Water supply—Illinois

Antiquities

See Indians of North America—Antiquities—Illinois

Description and travel

Sleepy South of Illinois. J. R. Humphreys. il Holiday 34:18+ S '63

Land tenure

See Land tenure—United States

Legislature

Confusion and chaos in Illinois balloting. il U S News 57:16 D 7 '64

Parks and reserves

Apple River Canyon State Park. E. G. Benton. il Nat Parks Mag 37:19 Je '63
First Illinois nature preserve; Illinois Beach State Park. Nat Parks Mag 38:15 D '64

Politics and government

Any other questions? Time 82:22 Jl 12 '63
Bed-sheet ballot. Newsweek 63:27 Ja 27 '64
Crowded crossroads. il Newsweek 64:39 O 19 '64
Grand old politesse. il Newsweek 62:30 S 9 '63
Illinois: bellwether state? pre-election study. R. Bendiner. il Reporter 31:23-5+ O 22 '64
Illinois: chaos at the polls. J. L. McDowell. Reporter 30:30-2 Mr 26 '64
Illinois legislature: study in corruption; ed. by A. Balk. P. Simon. Harper 229:74-8 S '64
Kerner's winning way. il Time 84:41 N 13 '64
New challenger to the Kennedy clan; C. Percy. W. Trombley. il Sat Eve Post 236:38-9 S 28 '63
Percy's pace. il Time 83:21 Ap 24 '64
Perils of Percy. il Newsweek 62:25-6 Jl 15 '63
Roulette in Illinois. Newsweek 63:18-19 F 3 '64
True to form. il Time 83:22 Ja 31 '64
Twenty-four hours in the life of Adlai E. Stevenson, 3rd. T. Meehan. McCalls 92:80+ N '64
What can happen when courts step into state elections. il U S News 57:39 S 21 '64
What upset Ev. il Time 83:19-20 Je 26 '64
What's in a name? election result. Time 84:34 D 11 '64
With the courage to purge. il Time 83:37 Je 12 '64

Race problems

Race in the land of Lincoln. J. DeMuth. il Commonweal 78:44-6 Ap 5 '63

Religious institutions and affairs

News of the Christian world (cont) Christian Cent 80:693-4; 81:349-50, 893-4, 972, 1118 My 22 '63, Mr 11, Jl 8, 29, S 9 '64

ILLINOIS BEACH STATE PARK. See Illinois—Parks and reserves

ILLINOIS institute of technology, Chicago
Future and the Illinois institute of technology. J. T. Rettaliata. Sch & Soc 92:272-4 O 3 '64

Institute of design

Home workshop tools you'll see tomorrow. il Pop Mech 119:106-9+ Ap '63
Imagination is the product. C. B. Hicks. il Pop Mech 121:116-20+ Ja '64

ILLINOIS library association
Statewide library planning in Illinois. ALA Bul 57:210 Mr '63

ILLINOIS news broadcasters association
Uses of diversity; concerning H. J. Skornia's speech on Television in the courtroom. R. L. Shayon. Sat R 47:27 Je 20 '64

ILLINOIS public aid commission. See Public welfare—Illinois

ILLINOIS state penitentiary. See Prisons—Illinois

ILLINOIS. University, Urbana
Clinic on data processing at University of Illinois. Library J 88:987 Mr 1 '63
Fresh wind in Illinois. D. Young and R. Auler. Nat R 14:495 Je 18 '63
Giant Illinois dome nears completion. il Arch Forum 118:117 Mr '63
Illinois' flying saucer; spectacular assembly hall; reprint. il Recreation 57:340-1 S '64

ILLINOIS. University, Urbana—*Continued*
Illinois vs. Oliver; academic freedom and article in American opinion on assassination of President Kennedy. Nat R 16:264 Ap 7 '64
Marxmanship at Illinois; case of R. P. Oliver Time 83:56 Mr 27 '64
Perils of big brotherhood; Dean Swift; with account by J. Poppy. il Look 27:53-6+ Mr 12 '63; Discussion. 27:20+ Ap 23 '63
Then how about Koch? Nation 198:206-7 Mr 2 '64
They go to college in wheel chairs; University of Illinois' unique Rehabilitation-education division. G. E. Maxwell. il Todays Health 42:26-9+ Jl '64
University of Illinois spectacular. il Arch Rec 134:111-16 Jl '63

Chicago campus

Big campus for Chicago. il Arch Forum 121: 148-51 Ag '64
Chicago campus for the University of Illinois. il Arch Rec 134:117-24 Ag '63

Krannert center for the performing arts

Four single purpose halls for a performing arts center with a big budget. il Arch Rec 136:122-3 D '64

ILLITERACY
African nations urge eradication of illiteracy. Sch & Soc 92:94-5 Mr 7 '64
Books as weapons. K. Molz. il Wilson Lib Bul 38:840-3+ Je '64
Campaign for world literacy; Campaign against hunger and disease; Science and technology for development. U N Rev 11: 31-4 Ja '64
Changing conditions in Guatemala; Literacy project. C. A. Hauberg. bibliog f Cur Hist 44:106-10+ F '63
Correctional institutions helping the functionally illiterate. P. Chenault. bibliog f ALA Bul 58:804-9 O '64
Cost of literacy. E. Moon. Library J 89: 1515 Ap 1 '64
Crime and illiteracy in the Nation's capital. U S News 55:8 Jl 22 '63
Dangers of adult illiteracy. Sch & Soc 92: 95+ Mr 7 '64
Eradication of illiteracy; excerpts from statement, October 18, 1963. R. Maheu. il U N Rev 10:34-5 D '63
Federal aid for the illiterate; address, April 8, 1964. R. B. Minnis. il Wilson Lib Bul 38:844+ Je '64
Fight against illiteracy: towards a world campaign; with excerpts from resolution. R. Maheu. UN Mo Chron 1:82-6 D '64
Housewife becomes literate in Communist China; testimony, tr. by D. C. Chu. L. Y. Wang. Sch & Soc 91:379-80 N 30 '63
How many of the world's people can read and write. il Sr Schol 83:44 O 4 '63; 85:48 O 7 '64
Illiteracy in the U.S. W. V. Grant. il Sch Life 45:18 Ap '63
Illiteracy; the key to poverty! B. Asbell. McCalls 91:96-7+ F '64
Librarian plays the central role; correctional institutions. C. J. Eckenrode. il ALA Bul 58:810-11 O '64
Literacy and learning in Asia. H. H. Smythe and N. Sasidhorn. il Sch & Soc 91:371-3 N 30 '63
Massive attack on illiteracy: Cook County experience; excerpts from address, July 13, 1963. R. M. Hilliard. il ALA Bul 57:1034-8 D '63
Only $2 billion to end illiteracy. Christian Cent 80:901 Jl 17 '63
Printing and the mind of man; reprint. il Wilson Lib Bul 38:392-6 Ja '64
Programming ABCs; Project literacy to help Mississippi Negro voter registration. il Bsns W p74+ Jl 18 '64
Service to inmates and staff. L. L. MacKenzie. ALA Bul 58:809 O '64
Struggle against illiteracy: the most exalting venture of our generation; address, August 26, 1964. R. Maheu. il UNESCO Courier 17: 4-8 O '64
Unemployment and the reading problem. Sat Eve Post 236:70 F 9 '63
Unesco's adult literacy program. Sch & Soc 93:4 Ja 9 '65
War on poverty: conference sponsored by American book publishers council and the American textbook publishers institute; with editorial comment. il Pub W 185:32-43, 52 My 4 '64
World fifty per cent illiterate. Sci N L 83: 150 Mr 9 '63

ILLNESS. See Sickness
ILLUMINATED manuscripts. See Hours, Books of; Illumination of books and manuscripts
ILLUMINATION. See Electric lighting
ILLUMINATION of books and manuscripts
Bad bishop's book of love songs. il Horizon 6:26-31 Wint '64
Monsieur Georges; illuminated miniatures from Wildenstein collection at Manhattan's Cloisters. il Time 81:56-9 Mr 1 '63
Pages from an international dealer's private collections. H. La Farge. il Art N 61:45+ F '63
See also
Hours, Books of
ILLUSION of reality. See Trompe-l'oeil
ILLUSIONISTS; story. See Friel, B.
ILLUSIONLESS man & the visionary maid; story. See Wheelis, A.
ILLUSIONS, Optical. See Optical illusions
ILLUSIONS and hallucinations
Nystagmus as a criterion of hypnotically induced visual hallucinations. J. P. Brady and E. E. Levitt. bibliog Science 146:85-6 O 2 '64
Visual hallucinations during sensory deprivation: a problem of criteria. P. Suedfeld and J. Vernon. bibliog il Science 145:412-13 Jl 24 '64
ILLUSTRATION of books and periodicals
Aesopian art; Five centuries of illustrated fables, at Metropolitan museum of art. il N Y Times Mag p40-1 O 11 '64
Album and the artist. N. Streatfeild. il Horn Bk 40:159-61 Ap '64
Artist at work. il Horn Bk 39:576-9; 40:34-41, 162-5, 269-72, 409-14, 520-2 D '63, F-O '64
Bernard Garbutt, animal draughtsman. J. Lovoos. il Am Artist 27:53-7+ F '63
Careless artist? or Careless editor? J. F. Davis. Pub W 183:136 F 18 '63
Colors of prophecy; reproductions of W. Blake's illuminated books. J. E. Grant. Nation 200:91-2 Ja 25 '65
Creative America, by J. F. Kennedy and others. Review
Pop Phot 55:68-9 Ag '64. D. Vestal
Fashion plates of Anaïs Toudouze. R. B. M. Askew. il Antiques 85:575-7 My '64
Frank E. Schoonover: an exemplar of the Pyle tradition. H. C. Pitz. il Am Artist 28:64-9+ N '64
George Giusti, graphic designer. F. Johnson. il Am Artist 28:46-51+ D '64
Gerald Ferguson: art director of a science magazine. C. Weiss. il Am Artist 27:42-7+ Je '63
Good words; excerpts from address. H. R. Mayes. Am Artist 28:73-4 D '64
Illustrations for books. H. C. Pitz. il Design 65:120-5+ Ja '64
Illustrators '63. il Am Artist 27:36-42+ O '63
Illustrators '63; moods and movements in book illustration. il Pub W 183:92-4 Je 3 '63
Joan Walsh Anglund and her books. il Pub W 184:104-6 Jl 8 '63
Leslie Saalburg, illustrator of mode. F. Whitaker. il Am Artist 27:20-5+ F '63
Maurice Sendak, illustrator of the child's world. J. H. Michel. il Am Artist 28:44-9+ S '64
Provensens; book artists for children. il Pub W 186:111-12 Jl 13 '64
Quiet beauty; exhibition of illustrated books at Washington's National gallery of art. il Newsweek 62:74 Ag 26 '63
Right to be real. E. J. Keats. il Sat R 46:56 N 9 '63
Rudolf Freund, scientific illustrator. H. C. Pitz. il Am Artist 28:20-5+ My '64
Whimsical illustrations of Hilary Knight. J. H. Michel. il Am Artist 27:49-53+ Mr '63
See also
Bible—Pictorial illustrations
Picture books for children
ILLUSTRATORS
Artist at work. il Horn Bk 39:576-9; 40:34-41, 162-5, 269-72, 409-14, 520-2 D '63, F-O '64
See also
Evers, C. G.
Freund, R.
Giusti, G.
Hogrogian, N.
Knight, H.
Landstrom, B.
Lovell, T.
Moodie, J.
Mozley, C.
Sendak, M.
Society of illustrators
I'M ugly; story. See Sherp, R.
IMAGE of love; story. See Combs, P.

IMAGE orthicon camera. See Television cameras
IMAGES and imagery (psychology)
Image revolution. N. P. Hurley. il America 110:137-9 Ja 25 '64; Reply. J. McLaughlin. 110:430-4+ Mr 28 '64
IMAGINATION
Dearest freshness deep down things; excerpt from address, March 14, 1964. E. Cameron. il Horn Bk 40:459-72 O '64
Emotion in non-fiction writing. E. M. Dean. Writer 77:26-7 S '64
How we discourage creative children. J. K. Lagemann. il Redbook 120:44-5+ Mr '63; Same abr. with title Your child may be more gifted than you think. Read Digest 82:245-6+ My '63
Poet and the machine, by P. Ginestier. Review
Poetry 101:292-4 Ja '63. W. Fowlie
See also
Creation (literary, artistic, etc)
Empathy
IMBAU, Fred E.
Wiretapping: yes or no? Christian Cent 82: 75-6 Ja 20 '65
IMBRIE, Andrew
Three against Christmas. Criticism
Opera N il 29:32 Ja 23 '65
IMIPRAMINE
Errorless discrimination learning in the pigeon: effects of chlorpromazine and imipramine. H. S. Terrace. bibliog il Science 140:318-19 Ap 19 '63
Fetal death from nicotinamide-deficient diet and its prevention by chlorpromazine and imipramine. I. Fratta and others. bibliog il Science 145:1429-30 S 25 '64
IMITATION antiques. See Antiques
IMITATION in music
Tristan's children. E. Downes. il Opera N 27:8-12 F 23 '63
IMMACULATE conception. See Mary, Virgin
IMMIGRANTS in Australia
Omerta in the Antipodes; Italian immigrant shootings. il Time 83:30 Ja 31 '64
IMMIGRANTS in France
Human cargo; illegal Portuguese immigrants. Newsweek 63:40-1 My 4 '64
IMMIGRANTS in the United States
Beyond the melting pot, by N. Glazer and D. P. Moynihan. Review
Time il 82:124+ O 18 '63
Do minorities tyrannize American life? address, November 15, 1963. L. R. Sussman. bibliog Vital Speeches 30:125-8 D 1 '63
See also
Irish in the United States
Naturalization
New York (city)—Foreign population

Education

Language and the dignity of youth. C. J. Calitri. il Sat R 46:46-7+ Jl 20 '63
See also
Libraries—Work with foreign born
IMMIGRATION and emigration
See also
Migration, Internal

Law

See Immigration and emigration law

Australia

Asians, keep out! Time 82:25 D 20 '63
Exodus from Britain; no room at the top. C. McWilliams. Nation 197:151-5 S 21 '63
Letter from Australia. A. Moorehead. il New Yorker 40:216+ O 10 '64
Medicare, labor, race: how Australia handles them; interview. H. Beale. il U S News 54:92-7 Mr 25 '63
Migration fever. Time 81:24 My 31 '63
White Australia. America 108:628 My 4 '63

South Africa

Go south, young (white) man. il Time 83:27 Ja 24 '64

United States

Catholics as immigrants. J. H. Smylie. Christian Cent 80:1396-9 N 13 '63
Department urges Congress to revise immigration laws; statement, July 31, 1964. D. Rusk. Dept State Bul 51:276-80 Ag 24 '64
Foreign aid & immigration bills. Time 85:17 Ja 22 '65
Foreign and domestic implications of U.S. immigration laws; address, April 3, 1964. A. P. Schwartz. Dept State Bul 50:675-82 Ap 27 '64
Hypocrisy of our immigration laws. Sat Eve Post 237:78 F 15 '64
If bars on immigration were lowered. il U S News 55:58-9 Ag 5 '63
Immigration: how wide and for whom the golden door? il Sr Schol 84:5-7+ F 28 '64
Immigration quota established for Malawi; proclamation, October 31, 1964. L. B. Johnson. Dept State Bul 51:753-4 N 23 '64
Immigration struggle. America 110:587 My 2 '64
Nation of immigrants, by J. F. Kennedy. Review
Sat R 47:51 O 31 '64. J. MacCracken
Open door policy on immigration? U S News 58:8 Ja 25 '65
Open golden door. America 109:188 Ag 24 '63
Opening the door. il Newsweek 62:24 Ag 5 '63
Place for a change. Commonweal 81:557 Ja 29 '65
President determines immigration quota for Kingdom of Tonga; proclamation, September 4, 1964. L. B. Johnson. Dept State Bul 51:443 S 28 '64
President Johnson determines certain immigration quotas; proclamations. L. B. Johnson. Dept State Bul 50:212-14 F 10 '64
President Johnson determines immigration quota for Kenya; proclamation, April 30, 1964. L. B. Johnson. Dept State Bul 50:829 My 25 '64
Puerto Rican tide begins to turn; migrants returning to their island now match the numbers moving to the island of Manhattan. A. W. Maldonado. il N Y Times Mag p84-5+ S 20 '64
Racism in immigration. America 112:158 Ja 30 '65
Should the gates be opened wider? campaign charges over immigration. il Bsns W p 114+ O 17 '64
Welcome, stranger. K. Detzer. il Read Digest 83:19-20+ S '63
With clean hands and a clear conscience; excerpt from A nation of immigrants; with editorial comment. J. F. Kennedy. Sat Eve Post 237:21-3, 92 O 3 '64
See also
Quarantine
United States—Foreign population

History

Nation of immigrants; excerpts. J. F. Kennedy. il N Y Times Mag p6-7+ Ag 4 '63
IMMIGRATION and emigration law
Department urges Congress to revise immigration laws; statement, July 31, 1964. D. Rusk. Dept State Bul 51:276-80 Ag 24 '64
End racist immigration! Christian Cent 81: 1003 Ag 12 '64
Foreign aid & immigration bills. Time 85:17 Ja 22 '65
Foreign and domestic implications of U.S. immigration laws; address, April 3, 1964. A. P. Schwartz. Dept State Bul 50:675-82 Ap 27 '64
Foreign policy aspects of U.S. immigration laws; statement, July 2, 1964. D. Rusk. Dept State Bul 51:98-101 Jl 20 '64
Immigration bill. America 109:650 N 23 '63
Immigration: how wide and for whom the golden door? il Sr Schol 84:5-7+ F 28 '64
Immigration: quotas vs. quality. P. Duke and S. Meisler. il Reporter 32:30-2 Ja 14 '65
Immigration revision. E. Lederer. Sci N L 87:51 Ja 23 '65
Jaime García Terrés and the *lista negra.* F. H. Wardlaw. Harper 230:16+ Ja '65
McCarran act. New Repub 149:6 D 28 '63
Nation of immigrants, by J. F. Kennedy. Review
Newsweek il 64:124-5 O 12 '64
Needed: a new immigration law. Christian Cent 81:1611-12 D 30 '64
President Johnson urges new immigration legislation; remarks, January 13, 1964. L. B. Johnson. Dept State Bul 50:211-12 F 10 '64
President recommends revision of immigration laws; letter, July 23, 1963. J. F. Kennedy. Dept State Bul 49:298-300 Ag 19 '63
What about the odious McCarran act? T. F. Coon. Nat R 16:726 Ag 25 '64
With clean hands and a clear conscience; excerpt from A nation of immigrants; with editorial comment. J. F. Kennedy. Sat Eve Post 237:21-3, 92 O 3 '64
IMMIGRATION and naturalization service. See United States—Immigration and naturalization service
IMMIGRATION quotas. See Immigration and emigration—United States
IMMORAL literature and pictures
April events of interest; publication of The perfumed garden. E. J. Gaines. ALA Bul 58: 453-4 Je '64
Battle against mail-order pornography. D. Wharton. Read Digest 84:147-8+ F '64

IMMORAL literature and pictures—*Continued*
Booksellers warned on smut following priest's fast. Pub W 184:28-9 N 4 '63
Cardinal Spellman calls for censorship group; summary of address. F. J. Spellman. Pub W 185:68 Je 22 '64
Censorship: strategy for defense; booksellers position. P. S. Jennison. Pub W 185:58-61 Mr 2 '64
Clearly-worded law; opinion of a three-judge criminal court in Manhattan. Time 82:61 N 22 '63
Come out of hiding. America 108:659 My 11 '63
Community standards; public opinion poll to determine contemporary community standards of decency. America 110:357 Mr 21 '64
Disgusting books upheld by New York Supreme court. Pub W 184:39 S 23 '63
Eros convicted of obscenity. Pub W 183:44 Je 24 '63
Fanny Hill found obscene in London. Pub W 185:135-6 F 24 '64
Ginzburg passes. America 108:895 Je 29 '63
Impurities in Yorkville; Father Morton Hill's campaign against pornography. M. Kempton. New Repub 148:13-15 Mr 16 '63
Is any book legally obscene any more? Life 55:8 S 27 '63
Mayor Wagner appoints antipornography commission. Pub W 186:23-4 Ag 17 '64
More dirty books. America 108:388, 482 Mr 23, Ap 13 '63; Discussion. 108:654 My 11 '63
Nation of peeping Toms; with editorial comment. America 112:34, 38 Ja 9 '65
N.Y. court dismisses carpetbaggers indictments. Pub W 183:67-8 Ap 15 '63
Obscenity: U.S. style; United States of America vs. West Coast news co. inc; reprint. R. R. Kirsch. ALA Bul 58:269-72 Ap '64
Of social importance; Ohio anti-obscenity law. America 108:430 Mr 30 '63
Poison in print and how to get rid of it. C. W. Hall. Read Digest 84:94-8 My '64
Pornography, sex and the church. R. A. Cannon. Christian Cent 80:576-9 My 1 '63
Propaganda and pornography. P. Revell. Library J 88:3562+ O 1 '63
Publisher of Eros loses obscenity appeal. Pub W 186:52 N 16 '64
Publisher of Eros sentenced to five years. Pub W 184:41 D 30 '63
Puritan revolution. America 111:224 S 5 '64
Sale of smut can be stopped. B. M. Silverman. il Parents Mag 40:48-9+ Ja '65
Second thoughts on obscenity; New Jersey ruling on Fanny Hill. il Time 84:43 D 18 '64
Sex and the Supreme court; with editorial comment. A. Lewis. Esquire 59:6, 82-3+ Je '63
Smut and the FBI; fight urged by New York academy of medicine. America 11:792 D 19 '64
Speaking out; paperback pornography. C. Amory. Sat Eve Post 236:10+ Ap 6 '63
Supreme court tackles obscenity: a constitutional definition. Christian Cent 80:637 My 15 '63
Tempest in a teapot; Rhode Island commission to encourage morality in youth. America 108:322 Mr 9 '63
Twenty-eight errors of Eros. Newsweek 61:75 Je 24 '63
Two dangers: smut and censorship. Christian Cent 81:261 F 26 '64
Two definitions of obscenity. il Time 81:44 Je 21 '63
What community's standards govern obscenity? H. F. Pilpel. Pub W 183:46 F 4 '63
What is pornography? J. Ciardi. Sat R 46:20 Jl 13 '63
See also
Censorship
Obscenity (law)

IMMORALIST; drama. See Goetz, A. and Goetz, R.

IMMORTALITY
How to rise above the fear of death. N. V. Peale. Read Digest 82:103-6 Ap '63
Immortality through premiums? R. Hull. Christian Cent 81:239-40 F 19 '64
Prospect of immortality, by R. C. W. Ettinger. Review
Christian Cent 81:1206+ S 30 '64. L. J. Putnam; Reply. E. T. Culver. 81:1469 N 25 '64

IMMUNITIES, Diplomatic. See Diplomatic privileges and immunities

IMMUNITY
Cancer immunity possible. Sci N L 86:69 Ag 1 '64
Have you kept your immunity up to date? D. A. Dukelow. Todays Health 42:8-9+ Ap '64
Heterogeneity of the immune response. J. W. Uhr. bibliog il Science 145:457-64 Jl 31 '64
Homologous disease reactivation by X-radiation. R. S. Schwartz and L. Beldotti. bibliog Science 140:171-2 Ap 12 '63
How antibody is made. il Time 85:29 Ja 8 '65
Immune reactivity in mice thymectomized soon after birth: normal response after pregnancy. D. Osoba. bibliog il Science 147:298-9 Ja 15 '65
Immune to sperm. il Newsweek 62:80 O 21 '63
Immunologic phenomena: cold-blooded vertebrates; report of meeting of the Federation of the American society for experimental microbiology. M. M. Sigel. Science 141:543+ Ag 9 '63
Immunological tolerance induced in animals previously sensitized to simple chemical compounds. J. R. Frey and others. bibliog Science 144:853-4 My 15 '64
Neuraminidases and influenza virus infection in embryonated eggs. C. A. Johnson and others. bibliog il Science 143:1051-2 Mr 6 '64
New disease weapon; adjusting to disease-causing bacteria. Sci N L 83:283 My 4 '63
Ontogeny of the immune response. A. M. Silverstein. bibliog Science 144:1423-8 Je 19 '64
Resistance of mice infected with Moloney leukemia virus to Friend virus infection. W. P. Rowe. bibliog il Science 141:40-1 Jl 5 '63
Shots that save. P. M. Stimson. il Parents Mag 39:47+ N '64
Thymectomy: effect on secondary disease in radiation chimeras. L. M. van Putten. bibliog il Science 145:935-6 Ag 28 '64
Thymus and the development of immunologic responsiveness. J. F. A. P. Miller. bibliog il Science 144:1544-51 Je 26 '64
Thymus: role in maturation of fetal lymphoid precursors. M. L. Tyan. bibliog il Science 145:934-5 Ag 28 '64
See also
Antigens and antibodies
Conglutination
Vaccination

IMMUNITY (exemption) See Privileges and immunities

IMMUNOGLOBULINS. See Serum globulins

IMMUNO-OSMOPHORESIS. See Electrophoresis

IMPACT
New instrument is heart of Ames momentum test. Miss & Roc 13:22-3 S 9 '63

IMPATIENS. See Touch-me-nots

IMPEDANCE (electricity)
Cathode-follower nomogram. A. L. Teubner. il Electr World 70:33 S '63
Simplified audio impedance matching. J. E. Pugh, jr. il Electr World 69:50-1+ Ap '63

IMPERFECT listener; story. See Stanton, W.

IMPERIAL chemical industries, limited
British giant tries for more size. il Bsns W p66-8+ Je 22 '63
Comeback at Courtaulds. il Time 82:82+ Jl 5 '63
Head start on red trade; ICI pushing for deals with Russia. il Bsns W p 100+ My 9 '64
Imperial tiger. Time 81:106 My 3 '63
Tougher Courtaulds comes out fighting. il Bsns W p97-8 D 21 '63

IMPERIALISM
Beyond imperialism. G. Lichtheim. New Repub 148:17-19 Mr 16 '63
Is communism a menace? Russell's answer. B. Russell. il N Y Times Mag p35+ Ap 7 '63; Discussion. p4+ Ap 21 '63
See also
Colonies

IMPLEMENTS, utensils, etc.
Ancient copper and copper-arsenic alloy artifacts: composition and metallurgical implications. C. A. Key. bibliog il Science 146:1578-80 D 18 '64

IMPORT quotas
Beef from abroad. America 111:208 Ag 29 '64
Major trading nations remove restrictions on U.S. exports; Department announcement. January 10, 1964; with list of import liberalizations. Dept State Bul 50:214-18 F 10 '64

IMPORT tax. See Tariff

IMPORTANCE of being earnest; drama. See Wilde, O.

IMPORTED cabbage worms
Focus on a hardy nuisance; Small white butterfly; pieris rapae. il Natur Hist 72:53-7 N '63

IMPORTS. See United States—Commerce

IMPOSTORS and imposture
Brilliant & fantastic; Thomas Novak, unlicensed physician. Time 84:62 S 18 '64
Masquerade of a counterfeit doctor; T. Novak, unlicensed physician. B. Lindeman. il Sat Eve Post 238:83-7 Ja 30 '65
This prince led Cinderella to death; case of N. Sturdza and Mrs Bird. C. McCarry. il Sat Eve Post 237:20-1 My 16 '64
See also
Fraud
Quacks and quackery
IMPRESARIOS
Hurok: adventurer in the arts. R. Sabin. il Dance Mag 38:40-6+ Ja '64
IMPRESSIONISM (art)
Birth of impressionism. J. Rewald. il Art N 62:30-1+ Mr '63
Corinth retrospective: exhibition at Gallery of modern art. M. Kozloff. Nation 199:230-2 O 12 '64
Impressionism. H. F. Collins. il Sch Arts 62:20-1 Ap '63
Impressionism as a cultural impulse. C. T. Davis. bibliog il Sch Arts 63:12-15 F '64
Q tip pointillism. J. C. Vitale. il Design 64:158-9 Mr '63
IMPRESSIONISM (literature)
Impressionism as a cultural impulse. C. T. Davis. bibliog il Sch Arts 63:12-15 F '64
IMPRESSIONISM (music)
Impressionism as a cultural impulse. C. T. Davis. bibliog il Sch Arts 63:12-15 F '64
IMPRINTING (birds) See Birds—Habits and behavior
IMPRISONMENT, False. See False imprisonment
IMPROMPTU at Versailles; drama. See Molière, J. B. P.
IMPROVISATION (acting)
See also
Comedia dell' arte
IMSANDE, John, and Ephrussi, Boris
Reevaluation of assays used to show RNA induction of glucose-6-phosphatase in ascites cells. bibliog Science 144:854-6 My 15 '64
IN a word; story. See Hale, N.
IN acknowledgment of a chief rabbi; story. See Levinson, D.
IN and out of never-never land; story. See Brennan, M.
IN case of Indians; story. See Meade, W.
IN-flight movies. See Airlines—Passenger service
IN God we trust(motto) See Mottoes
IN-laws. See Relatives
IN memory of our marriage; story. See Owen, J. Z.
IN one's own house; story. See Hazzard, S.
IN our time; story. See Kozol, J.
IN search of a kiss; story. See West, J.
IN-service librarian education. See Librarians—Education in service
IN-service teacher education. See Teachers—Education in service
IN the counting house; drama. See Weiner, L.
IN the J. Robert Oppenheimer affair; drama. See Kipphardt, H.
IN the lobby; story. See Steegmuller, F.
IN the middle of nowhere; story. See Stewart, N.
IN the sun; story. See Taylor, E.
IN the valley; story. See Nissenson, H.
IN their own good time; story. See Stolz, M.
IN vivo; story. See Savage, M.
IN white America; drama. See Duberman, M. B.
IN your own back yard; story. See Cave, H.
INAGAWA, Hiroyoshi
Way of chivalry. por Newsweek 64:42 S 14 '64
INAGUA, Bahama Islands
Wild flamingoes on parade. A. Sprunt, jr. il Audubon Mag 65:352-5 N '63
INAUDIBLE sound. See Ultrasonics
INAUGURATION day. See Inaugurations
INAUGURATIONS
For LBJ, a Texas-size inaugural. il Newsweek 65:21-2 Ja 25 '65
Inaugural parade: how it's being changed. U S News 58:10 Ja 4 '65
Inaugural, y'all come. il Newsweek 65:22+ Ja 18 '65
Inauguration of President Johnson. il Life 58:24-33 Ja 29 '65
Inauguration: 36th U.S. President. il Time 85:10-19A Ja 29 '65
Lamplight inauguration. C. M. Wilson. il Am Heritage 15:80-6 D '63
Lyndon Johnson's pledge: I will lead, and I will do the best I can; Hail to the Chief. il Newsweek 65:10-17 F 1 '65
No wonder Madison said, I'd rather be in bed. D. Oberdorfer. il N Y Times Mag p 10-11+ Ja 17 '65
Oxford gray for LBJ at the inaugural. il U S News 57:4 D 21 '64
Wood to launch a president. F. T. Gilley. il Am For 71:2-3+ Ja '65
Yale inauguration. New Yorker 40:42-3 Ap 25 '64
INBOARD motor boats. See Motor boats
INBOARD-outboard motors. See Marine engines
INBREEDING
Inbreeding & dwarfism. il Time 84:59-60 Ag 21 '64
Inheritance of avoidance conditioning in mice: a diallel study. R. L. Collins. bibliog il Science 143:1188-90 Mr 13 '64
INCANDESCENT lamps. See Electric lamps, Incandescent
INCAPARINA
Eating but still starving. R. Yoshioka. il Sci N L 83:346-7 Je 1 '63
New food for hungry children. H. Manchester. il Read Digest 83:137-41 S '63
New foods and new hopes. il Newsweek 61:51 Je 17 '63
INCARNATION
Christmas and the world. J. V. Schall. Commonweal 79:389-92 D 27 '63
INCAS
See also
Machu Picchu, Peru
Vilcabamba, Peru
INCENDIARISM. See Arson
INCENTIVE pay. See Incentives in industry
INCENTIVES in industry
Atwood calls reputation best incentive. Aviation W 79:36-7 Ag 12 '63
Employee-inventor gets his cut. il Bsns W p 133-4 Mr 23 '63
End of incentive pay? T. R. Brooks. Duns R 84:45-6 D '64
Incentives marked by profit formulas; with editorial comment. W. Beller. il Miss & Roc 14:24-5, 54 Ja 20 '64
Incentives prove useful, but no cure-all. Aviation W 81:64 Jl 13 '64
Is incentive pay headed for shelf? automation vs incentive worker. il Bsns W p51-2 Je 27 '64
Landmark in labor relations; Kaiser-United steelworkers agreement. H. Malmgren. New Repub 148:7 Mr 16 '63
Low fees may undermine incentive goal; cost plus incentive fee. B. Backe. il Aviation W 82:69+ Ja 11 '65
Neither communism nor capitalism; Russia recognizes profit motive. E. Crankshaw. il N Y Times Mag p36-7+ O 6 '63
Sales & distribution; performance incentive programs. J. B. Weiner. Duns R 82:45 Ag '63
Some indicators of incentive plan prevalence. R. B. McKersie and others. bibliog f il Mo Labor R 87:271-6 Mr '64; Reply with rejoinder. B. Gottlieb. 87:893-4 Ag '64
Who are your motivated workers? M. S. Myers. il Harvard Bsns R 42:73-88 Ja '64
See also
Profit sharing
Wage payment plans
INCH, Standard of. See Standards of length
INCH plants
For bare spaces, inch plant. L. P. Bell. il Horticulture 41:284 My '63
INCHON invasion. See Korean war, 1950-1953—Campaigns and battles
INCIDENT at Vichy; drama. See Miller, A.
INCINERATORS. See Refuse incinerators
INCLUSION bodies. See Cells—Inclusions
INCOME
Americans never had it so good: what figures show. il U S News 56:93-4 Ap 6 '64
Buying power, more gains coming; interview. E. Clague. il Nations Bsns 52:31-3+ Ap '64
Contrasts in spending by urban families; variations in 1960-61. K. R. Murphy. il Mo Labor R 87:1408-15 D '64
First findings of the 1963 survey of the aged; Income of the aged in 1962. L. A. Epstein. il Mo Labor R 87:1171-3 O '64
First findings of the 1963 survey of the aged; Work experience and earnings of the aged in 1962. E. Palmore. il Mo Labor R 87:1173-6 O '64
Guaranteeing an income; new constitutional right for the developing post-industrial age. R. Theobald. il Commonweal 80:603-6 S 4 '64

INCOME—*Continued*
Higher income for retired teachers. M. L. Ware. NEA J 53:14 F '64
How new law saves taxes for old folks. F. Bailey, jr. Suc Farm 62:72 My '64
Income and expenditures of low-income families; excerpt from address. A. E. Chase. il Mo Labor R 87:889-90 Ag '64
Income level and education. Sch & Soc 92: 300 O 31 '64
Job pickup boosts incomes. il Bsns W p70-1 Je 29 '63
Measure of personal income (title varies) tables. See issues of Business week
More cash despite the storms. Bsns W p42 Jl 4 '64
Taxpayers under the microscope. F. J. Cook. il N Y Times Mag p20+ Ap 12 '64
Trends in Soviet personal income components; excerpt of Recent trends in Soviet personal income and consumption. R. E. Golden. bibliog f il Mo Labor R 86:385-7 Ap '63
U.S. incomes: at record level, and going up. il U S News 54:57 My 13 '63
Where millionaires and others get their money. U S News 55:8 Jl 29 '63
Who's rich, who's poor? what's myth what's fact? excerpts from Rich man, poor man. H. P. Miller. il Changing T 18:19-21 F '64
Why you feel pinched; more we make, the less we seem to have. il Changing T 18: 7-12 N '64
See also
Gross national product
Salaries
Wealth, Distribution of

INCOME tax
Unbearables; income tax from boxers. Sports Illus 20:14 My 11 '64

Anecdotes, facetiae, satire, etc.

Notes and comment. il New Yorker 40:31 Ap 11 '64

Capital gains tax

Capital-gain tax reform. H. Hazlitt. Newsweek 61:86 My 27 '63
Capital gain vs. income. H. Hazlitt. Newsweek 61:82 Je 17 '63
Capital gains: the sweet; the sour. il Newsweek 61:69 F 4 '63
Don't burn the barn down, Mr Dillon. Am For 69:13+ Mr '63
Tax plan: where it will bite. il Bsns W p76-8 F 2 '63

Collection

See Withholding tax

Deductions

Ahead, a tax return as simple as a check? with summary of plan approved by Senate finance committee. il U S News 55:75-6 D 30 '63
Are you wise about taxes? Bet Hom & Gard 42:92 Ja '64
Blow at philanthropy. America 108:246 F 23 '63
Business practices under the new T&E rules. V. H. Rothschild, 2d. il Duns R 82:40-2+ N '63
Cashing in on the new tax rate. Bsns W p86 D 12 '64
Collecting on crop insurance? here's how you may save taxes. Suc Farm 62:41 N '64
Cut in tax deductions. il U S News 54:33-5 F 11 '63
Deduction of medical bills. Sci N L 85:22 Ja 11 '64
Do you really know the tax rules? il Changing T 17:37-9 S '63
Expense-account party at home. il U S News 55:46 Jl 29 '63
Family money management. Bet Hom & Gard 42:6+ F '64
Family money questions answered. il Bet Hom & Gard 41:30+ Mr '63
Here are those new rules on expense accounts. il U S News 54:50-1 Ap 8 '63
How income averaging can cut your tax bill. F. Bailey, jr. Suc Farm 62:36 N '64
How to get twenty new tax breaks. J. Carlson. Farm J 88:26-7 D '64
How to make the most from the coming tax cut. U S News 55:120 O 21 '63
How to plan now to save income tax dollars. B. Brantley and G. B. Whitman. il Suc Farm 61:27+ D '63
How to save on your '64 taxes. il U S News 57:72-5 N 23 '64
How to save tax dollars on cars and trucks. F. Bailey, jr. Suc Farm 63:72-4+ Ja '65
Income tax tips for photographers. K. Kirkpatrick. il Pop Phot 54:68-9+ Mr '64
Income taxes: stick up for your rights! il Changing T 18:7-8 Ap '64
Is flying fun deductible? C. Newlon. il Flying 74:34-5+ Je '64
Jolt in the tax cut. il U S News 56:42 Mr 30 '64
Last-minute tax checklist. J. Carlson. Farm J 89:50 Ja '65
Last-minute tax reminders on machinery. G. B. Whitman. Suc Farm 62:36 Ap '64
Librarian of Congress asks for tax break for LC. Library J 88:1636 Ap 15 '63
Machines are more important than people (yes or no?) attitude test. P. M. Stern. il N Y Times Mag p33+ D 1 '63
Making these tax mistakes? H. D. Guither. Farm J 89:38F Ja '65
Making your money count. S. Margolius. il Ladies Home J 80:22 Ap '63
Medical expenses which are tax deductible. il Good H 158:164 Mr '64
New tax form: what it's like; Tax returns: an easy plan. U S News 57:107-8 O 19 '64
Now it's official: tax guide for expense accounts. il U S News 55:98-100 Jl 8 '63
Now you can estimate your '64 tax; official rates; with chart. U S News 56:124-5 F 24 '64
Personal business. Bsns W p 106 Ja 19; p 141-2 D 7 '63
Personal business; deducting travel and entertainment expenses. Bsns W p89 Ap 6 '63
Personal business; filing your 1963 return. Bsns W p 139-40 Mr 28 '64
Personal business; medical expenses. Bsns W p97 Jl 20 '63
Professors, research, and taxes. W. W. Brickman. Sch & Soc 92:148+ Ap 4 '64
Prospects now on tax changes. U S News 56:97 F 17 '64
Save taxes by being sharp on deductions. B. Brantley. Suc Farm 63:70A+ Ja '65
School librarians would gain by pending tax legislation. Library J 89:2160+ My 15 '64
Seeks income tax aid for college students. Christian Cent 80:877 Jl 10 '63
Self-employed: it's time to act on pensions; Self-employed individuals tax retirement act. il U S News 55:118-20 N 11 '63
Should you pay your year-end bills in December or January? Bet Hom & Gard 41:6 N '63
Tax deductions homeowners can take. Good H 156:148 Mr '63
Tax deductions under the new law; with explanation by M. M. Caplin. B. Mills. il Motor B 111:50-1+ Mr '63
Tax help for single people. il Changing T 17:43-5 Mr '63
Tax incentives for campaign contributions? pro and con discussion. Sr Schol 83:8-9 N 1 '63
Tax-plan rules being eased. U S News 54: 94-6 F 18 '63
Tax provision stirs hornets' nest; 5 per cent floor on contributions to churches and charities. Christian Cent 80:230 F 20 '63
Tax returns: changing patterns. U S News 56:98 Ja 27 '64
Tax writers turn tough; goal: 1 billion new revenue. il U S News 55:86-7 Jl 1 '63
Taxpayers under the microscope. F. J. Cook. il N Y Times Mag p20+ Ap 12 '64
Ways to save on your tax bill for '62. il U S News 54:77-81 Mr 25 '63
Ways you can save on your 1963 tax. il U S News 56:93-6 Mr 23 '64
What expense-account rules are doing to conventions. il U S News 54:113-16 Ap 8 '63
What you can and cannot do on an expense account. il U S News 54:54-7 Ap 15 '63
Why penalize firms hiring handicapped workers? H. B. Burr. Harvard Bsns R 41:56-8 Jl '63
Yes, you can save on taxes. il Changing T 17:35-7 F '63
Your income tax deductions. F. S. Shapiro. NEA J 53:65 Ja '64
Your income tax; questions and answers (cont) il Changing T 17:13-14 Ap '63; 18: 30-2 F; 17-19 Mr '64
See also
Amortization deductions
Depletion allowances
Expense accounts (business)
Tax planning

Anecdotes, facetiae, satire, etc.

Fiction as strange as fact: death of another salesman; excerpts from address, March 18, 1963. T. R. Groom. il U S News 54:51-3 Ap 22 '63
Many happy returns. C. Ford. il Field & S 68:6+ Ap '64

Forms

See Tax forms

Refunds

Late claim, a refund lost. U S News 54:115 Ap 22 '63

INCOME tax—*Continued*

Returns

See Tax returns

Study and teaching

Income tax in the classroom. S. Cochell. il Sr Schol 82:5T Ap 3 '63

France

Liberté egalité mais vérité? Time 81:28 My 10 '63

United States

At last you can see your tax cut; report on bill adopted by House and approved by Senate finance committee; with charts. U S News 56:40-1 F 3 '64
Buy, lease, or hire it done? machinery tax management. J. D. Keast. Farm J 88:22+ F '64
Cold war and the income tax, by E. Wilson. Review
  Commonweal 79:434-5 Ja 10 '64. W. Sheed
  Nat R 16:71-4 Ja 28 '64. J. Dos Passos
  Reporter 29:63-4 D 5 '63. G. Weales
Fair shares. New Repub 148:4 Ap 20 '63
For 1964: tax dates to remember. U S News 56:35 Ja 6 '64
Great tax myth. S. Alsop. Sat Eve Post 236: 18 N 23 '63
How a simple income tax could work. il U S News 54:31-4 Ap 1 '63
How city men cut taxes by farming. C. E. Ball. Farm J 87:26 O '63
How much can coach Butts keep? 3-million-dollar libel award. U S News 55:6+ S 2 '63
Income tax finds a proponent; study by Brookings institution. Bsns W p 132+ D 19 '64
New retirement plan. N. E. Harl. il Suc Farm 61:39+ O '63
Should we tax incomes less? tax sales or manufacturing more; with editorial comment. il Bsns W p 150+, 156 Je 20 '64
Soak the writers! G. W. Johnson. New Repub 148:5-6 Mr 9 '63
Start saving taxes now. il Changing T 18:33-5 N '64
Still another tax overhaul urged; concerning American bar association plan. U S News 56:102 My 11 '64
Tax-cut mirage. G. T. Altman. il Nation 196: 137-8 F 16 '63; Reply with rejoinder. A. D. Tussing. 196:inside cover Mr 16 '63
Tax deviates; excerpt from The great Treasury raid. P. M. Stern. New Repub 150:11-13 F 1 '64
Tax ideas that won't stay down. il U S News 57:57-8 D 28 '64
Tax warning. New Repub 150:5 Mr 7 '64
Taxes. M. O. Shulman. Dance Mag 37:129 D '63
Taxes: the long view. H. Hazlitt. Newsweek 62:59 Jl 1 '63; Same abr. with title Progression: toward what? Read Digest 83:205+ S '63
Unbearables; income tax from boxers. Sports Illus 20:14 My 11 '64
What's wrong with today's income tax; interview. M. Caplin. il U S News 57:66-70 Ag 17 '64; Same abr. Read Digest 85:173-4+ N '64
Year-end income tax tips. B. Brantley. Suc Farm 62:27+ D '64
Your income tax, all those forms and schedules. il Changing T 18:29-33 Ja '64
  See also
Tax evasion

History

After fifty years of a rising income tax. il U S News 54:75-6 F 25 '63
Capsule history of the income tax. M. Frome. Holiday 35:66-7 My '64

INCONSISTENCY. See Consistency

L'INCORONAZIONE di Poppea; opera. See Monteverdi, C.

INCORPORATED farms. See Farms, Incorporated

INCREASE of population. See Population, Increase of

INCUBATION
Birth of a chick; photographs. Sci Digest 55:8-11 Mr '64
Testosterone-induced incubation patches of phalarope birds. J. E. Johns and E. W. Pfeiffer. bibliog Science 140:1225-6 Je 14 '63

INCUBATOR babies. See Infants, Premature

INCUBATORS, Baby. See Infants, Premature

INCURABLES
How much should a cancer victim know? il Sci Digest 54:49-50 N '63

INDELIBLE spot; story. See Bosch, J.

INDEPENDENCE, Political. See Autonomy

INDEPENDENCE day. See Fourth of July

INDEPENDENT metal workers union
NLRB cracks down on union bias; failure to process a Negro's grievance of Hughes tool co, Houston. Bsns W p50 Jl 11 '64

INDEPENDENT moving picture producers. See Moving picture production and direction

INDEPENDENT regulatory commissions

United States

Headless branch. il Time 84:57-8 Jl 31 '64
New role for regulators. Nations Bsns 53:36-7+ Ja '65
Public be damned. Nation 196:150 F 23 '63
Regulators pinpoint new targets. C. B. Seib. il Nations Bsns 51:38-9+ F '63
Who shall watch the watchman? Nation 197: 190 O 5 '63

INDEPENDENT study
Cape Kennedy's high school for sky-high learning. B. Asbell. il PTA Mag 58:14-16 Ja '64

INDEPENDENT television authority. See Television broadcasting—Great Britain

INDEX librorum prohibitorum
Life of Jesus, by J. Steinmann. Review
  America 109:597-8 N 9 '63. J. A. Fitzmyer

INDEXES
Our man in London; first presentation of Wheatley medal for an outstanding index. New Yorker 40:48-51 N 28 '64
  See also
Biological and agricultural index
Public affairs information service
Readers' guide to periodical literature
Science citation index

INDEXING
Inverted indexing on edge-notched cards. J. G. Roney, jr. bibliog Science 142:227-8 O 11 '63
Science citation index, a new dimension in indexing. E. Garfield. bibliog Science 144: 649-54 My 8 '64

INDEXING (machine work)
Precision indexer for your jigsaw. W. E. Burton. il Pop Mech 119:194-6+ Mr '63

INDIA
Big country adrift; how long can aid save India? il U S News 56:64-9 Je 1 '64
Eight clues to India; photographs. A. M. Rosenthal. N Y Times Mag p 18-19 Je 7 '64
Feeling of drift. Time 84:35 S 4 '64
India: a world in transition, by B. P. Lamb. Review
  Sat R 46.40 S 14 '63. E. C. Dimock
India in crisis. J. Scofield. il Nat Geog Mag 123:599-661 My '63
India without Nehru. V. Koilpillai. Christian Cent 81:834+ Je 24 '64
To India, with love. P. S. Buck. Ladies Home J 82:18+ Ja '65
  See also
Agriculture—India
Airlines—India
Airplanes, Military—India
Americans in India
Architecture—India
Astronomical observatories—India
Atomic power—India
Badrinath
Birth control—India
Bombay
Books and reading—India
Economic assistance in India
Education—India
Fatehpur Sikri
Festivals—India
Food supply—India
Hunting—India
Ladakh
Law—India
Liquor traffic—India
Manipal
Paleontology—India
Prices—India
Prohibition—India
Public health—India
Sikkim
Space research—India
Textbooks—India
United Nations—India
Untouchables

Antiquities

See also
Harappa culture

Armed forces

India now: if there's a new attack by Chinese reds. S. W. Sanders. il U S News 54:88-90 Ap 8 '63
India's new military strength. S. Hugh-Jones. New Repub 151:11-13 D 19 '64

INDIA—*Continued*

Army

Communique from India's mountain front. C. Armstrong. il N Y Times Mag p 10-11+ Jl 7 '63
India's front lines in the high Himalayas. P. Anderton. il Reporter 30:38-40 Ja 16 '64
Updating the Indian army. R. Knox. il Reporter 31:36-8 O 8 '64

Boundaries

Alarm rings in India. A. M. Rosenthal. Read Digest 82:84-8 F '63
China: jealous neighbor. V. P. Dutt. bibliog f Cur Hist 44:135-40+ Mr '63
India after the blow. E. von Kuehnelt-Leddihn. Nat R 14:236 Mr 26 '63
India, Pakistan, and the shadow of red China. il Sr Schol 83:8-11 O 18 '63
Mountaintop war in remote Ladakh. W. E. Garrett. il Nat Geog Mag 123:664-87 My '63
Sikkim. D. Doig. il Nat Geog Mag 123:398-429 Mr '63
Sino-Indian border war. W. Levi. Cur Hist 45:136-43 S '63
Stake: freedom for half of mankind. B. Ward. il N Y Times Mag p 19+ Ap 14 '63
Uneasy border. Newsweek 61:38+ F 4 '63
Will India be realy if red China strikes again? S. W. Sanders. il U S News 55:68-9 S 23 '63

Commercial treaties and agreements

United States and India conclude cotton textile agreement; Department announcement; with exchange of notes effecting the agreement; exchange of notes concerning category thirty-six exports. il Dept State Bul 50:914-17 Je 8 '64

Defenses

Bomb on a bullock cart; India debating whether to build A-bombs of its own. Time 84:29 N 6 '64
Growing pains of Indian democracy. N. D. Palmer. bibliog f Cur Hist 44:147-54 Mr '63
India now: if there's a new attack by Chinese reds. S. W. Sanders. il U S News 54:88-90 Ap 8 '63
India under the gun. L. Kraar. il Life 55:9+ N 1 '63
Indians to receive military aid from U.S. British, Soviet Union. L. L. Doty. Aviation W 81:20 S 28 '64
India's front lines in the high Himalayas. P. Anderton. il Reporter 30:38-40 Ja 16 '64
India's new defenses. Commonweal 77:632 Mr 15 '63
India's new military strength. S. Hugh-Jones. New Repub 151:11-13 D 19 '64
More guns; long-range military aid. New Repub 148:8 Je 8 '63
U.S. and India sign agreement to strengthen India's air defense. Dept State Bul 49:245-6 Ag 12 '63
Updating the Indian army. R. Knox. il Reporter 31:36-8 O 8 '64

Description and travel

How to see India: be young. L. Gottlieb and P. Gottlieb. il Mlle 56:136-7+ F '63
Kipling's India; photographs, with commentary. B. Brake. Horizon 6:67-71 Autumn '64
New blaze of India; with editorial notes on background and travel. R. Godden. il Vogue 144:194-5+, 284-5 D '64
Return to India. A. Menen. il Holiday 35:38-55 My '64
Southern India. M. Atwater. il Travel 123:38-40 Ja '65
Travel notes. R. Joseph. Esquire 59:35-6+ Je '63

Economic conditions

Boldest experiment. il Newsweek 63:38-40+ Je 29 '64; Same abr. with title India after Nehru, will it work? Read Digest 85:138-42 S '64
Development of India. P. Pant. il Sci Am 209:189-92+ bibliog(p308) S '63
End of the gold age; controls on India's private gold holdings. Newsweek 61:40 F 4 '63
Headway in India. Commonweal 79:244 N 22 '63
India after Nehru. Christian Cent 81:787-8 Je 17 '64
India after the Chinese attack. H. C. Hart. bibliog f Ann Am Acad 351:50-7 Ja '64
India opens wider to foreign funds. il Bsns W p79-80 Ap 11 '64
India's agricultural problems. A. Taylor and S. R. Ahsan. bibliog il Focus 14:1-6 S '63
Mahatma Gandhi was wrong. L. Hazard. il Atlan 214:45-9 Jl '64
No substitute in India. America 111:731-2 D 5 '64
Return to India: the Ambassador's view. C. Bowles. il N Y Times Mag p20-1+ N 10 '63
$69-a-year men. Newsweek 61:44+ Mr 11 '63
See also
Budget—India

Economic policy

Behind India's woes: an economic treadmill. il Bsns W p63 N 7 '64
Development of India. P. Pant. il Sci Am 209:189-92+ bibliog(p308) S '63
India's battle for food. H. Maddick. bibliog il Cur Hist 44:160-6+ Mr '63
Industrialization in India's development. W. Malenbaum. Cur Hist 44:167-73+ Mr '63
Thriving under fetters; Union carbide India, ltd. il Bsns W p58-60 N 7 '64
What's wrong with planning: the case of India. W. Letwin. il Fortune 67:118-21+ Je '63; Discussion. 68:94 Ag '63

Foreign relations

Beyond the borders. il Newsweek 63:44+ Je 29 '64; Same abr. with title India after Nehru, will it work? Read Digest 85:139-41 S '64
Challenge for Indian leadership. M. V. Pylee. Cur Hist 46:78-82+ F '64
Changing India. J. Nehru. For Affairs 41:453-65 Ap '63
Changing roles. Newsweek 62:38-9 Ag 5 '63
Nehru's India. America 110:814 Je 13 '64
With Nehru gone, can India be held together? il U S News 56:48-9 Je 8 '64

China (People's Republic)

China: jealous neighbor. V. P. Dutt. bibliog f Cur Hist 44:135-40+ Mr '63
Nehru all alone? New Repub 148:6 F 2 '63
Uneasy border. Newsweek 61:38+ F 4 '63
See also
India—Boundaries

Great Britain

India's ties to the Commonwealth. R. N. Berkes. Cur Hist 44:155-9+ Mr '63

Pakistan

Blood and borders. Newsweek 62:47 S 23 '63
Feeling is fatal; Hindu-Moslem riots. Time 83:42 Ap 3 '64
Troubled India and her neighbors. S. S. Harrison. For Affairs 43:312-30 Ja '65

Russia

India and the Soviet Union. S. Gupta. bibliog f Cur Hist 44:141-6 Mr '63
Troubled India and her neighbors. S. S. Harrison. For Affairs 43:312-30 Ja '65

United States

Indian non-alignment and United States policy. P. C. Chakravarti. il Cur Hist 41:129-34+ Mr '63
U.S. and India reaffirm agreement on basic values and objectives; joint communique, June 4. 1963. J. F. Kennedy and S. Radhakrishnan. Dept State Bul 48:969-70 Je 24 '63

Hindu-Moslem relations

Blood in the streets. Time 83:22 Ja 24 '64
Hindu-Moslem killings. New Repub 150:9 Ap 11 '64

History

Stake: freedom for half of mankind. B. Ward. il N Y Times Mag p 19+ Ap 14 '63

Industries

Ancient gods & modern methods; Kirloskar group. il Time 84:119-20 N 13 '64
Cow & the tractor. il Time 81:95 My 10 '63
Industrialization in India's development. W. Malenbaum. Cur Hist 44:167-73+ Mr '63
Remarkable house of Tata. J. E. Frazer. Read Digest 82:248-52 Ap '63
See also
Steel industry and trade—India

Languages

Battle of babel; official language. Newsweek 61:34+ Ap 29 '63
Bureaucracy by doublespeak; Hindi becomes India's official language. il Time 85:25A+ Ja 29 '65

INDIA—*Continued*

Native races

Downing the *daos*; Naga armistice. Time 84: 31-2 Jl 10 '64

Neutrality

Indian non-alignment and United States policy. P. C. Chakravarti. il Cur Hist 44: 129-34+ Mr '63
Sea lawyer. Time 82:24 D 27 '63

Politics and government

After Nehru. il Time 83:40-1 Je 12 '64
After Shastri, who? il Time 84:31 Jl 10 '64
Atlantic report. Atlan 214:24+ Ag '64
Back with the rain. Time 84:30+ Ag 7 '64
Banyan falls. C. Lacy. Christian Cent 81:883-5 Jl 8 '64
Can Krishna Menon make a comeback? U S News 57:22 N 9 '64
Case of Nehru's dog. il Time 82:21 Ag 30 '63
Challenge for Indian leadership. M. V. Pylee. Cur Hist 46:78-82+ F '64
Changing India. J. Nehru. For Affairs 41:453-65 Ap '63
Empty chair. il Time 83:21 Ja 17 '64
Growing pains of Indian democracy. N. D. Palmer. bibliog f Cur Hist 44:147-54 Mr '63
India after Nehru. Christian Cent 81:787-8 Je 17 '64
India after the blow. E. von Kuehnelt-Leddihn. Nat R 14:236 Mr 26 '63
India after the Chinese attack. H. C. Hart. bibliog f Ann Am Acad 351:50-7 Ja '64
India tomorrow. J. T. Crown. Nation 198: 599-602 Je 15 '64
India turns to a conciliator. L. I. Rudolph and S. H. Rudolph. il N Y Times Mag p 11+ Je 14 '64
India under the gun. L. Kraar. il Life 55:9+ N 1 '63
India without Nehru. il Sr Schol 85:12-14+ O 14 '64
India's crisis: a diary. J. Mander. Commentary 35:326-34 Ap '63
Jawaharlal Nehru 1889-1964. il Newsweek 63: 57-9 Je 8 '64
Leader under fire; Nehru's opposition grows. U S News 55:12 S 2 '63
Leadership crisis in India. Newsweek 63:22 Mr 30 '64
Mr Nehru's rabbit punch. New Repub 149:9 O 26 '63
Nehru's choice: Shastri; more neutralism for India. U S News 56:21 Je 15 '64
Nehru's mantle falls on middle-of-roader. il Bsns W p 131-2+ Je 6 '64
Nehru's successor? Gandhi disciple moves up. U S News 56:14 F 3 '64
New initiatives. il Newsweek 64:34-5 Ag 31 '64
Next prime minister. New Repub 150:8 F 15 '64
One million walk out. New Repub 149:8 Ag 31 '63
Party and country. Newsweek 63:49 Je 29 '64
Problems of inheritance. Newsweek 64:60+ O 26 '64
Question of confidence; murder of India's Solicitor-General. Newsweek 64:49-50 S 21 '64
Quiet man takes over. Newsweek 63:42+ Je 15 '64
Quit, Nehru, quit. il Newsweek 62:36-7 Ag 26 '63
Roses and riots. Newsweek 63:40 Ja 27 '64
Shastri at helm. Sr Schol 85:32 S 23 '64
Sleepy country. Time 84:45 S 18 '64
Thunder on left & right. il Time 82:28 Ag 23 '63
Under the banyan tree. Time 82:42 N 15 '63
Uneasy truce among Nehru's heirs. R. Knox. il Reporter 31:19-21 Jl 2 '64
Vacuum of leadership. Time 83:22 Mr 27 '64
When the body fails: annual conference of India's Congress party. il Newsweek 63: 32+ Ja 20 '64
Who'll succeed Nehru? when he's sick, India worries. U S News 56:14 Ja 20 '64
Will India falter after Nehru? il Bsns W p24-5 My 30 '64
With Nehru gone, can India be held together? il U S News 56:48-9 Je 8 '64
Without Nehru? Newsweek 62:46 S 2 '63
See also
Communist party (India)
Elections—India
Indian national congress

Population

Accepting the positive. America 108:389 Mr 23 '63
Return to India: the Ambassador's view. C. Bowles. il N Y Times Mag p20-1+ N 10 '63

Religious institutions and affairs

Crossfire; protests against Pope's proposed visit to Bombay. Newsweek 64:89 N 16 '64
Methodists and North India union; plan rejected. R. V. Marble. Christian Cent 80: 1173-4 S 25 '63
News of the Christian world (cont) Christian Cent 80:505-6, 1347-8; 81:747, 945-6, 1374, 1444 Ap 17, O 30 '63, Je 3, Jl 22, N 4, 18 '64
See also
Buddha and Buddhism
Catholic church in India

Riots

Blood in the streets. Time 83:22 Ja 24 '64

Social conditions

Afternoon with Nehru. E. M. Borgese. il Nation 198:506-8 My 18 '64
Boldest experiment. il Newsweek 63:38-40+ Je 29 '64; Same abr. with title India after Nehru, will it work? Read Digest 85: 138-42 S '64
How to save a few million lives, and save money at the same time. J. Fischer. Harper 229:14+ O '64; Discussion. 229:4+ D '64
How to see India; be young. L. Gottlieb and P. Gottlieb. il Mlle 56:136-7+ F '63
Hungry generation. il Time 84:44 N 20 '64
India in crisis. J. Scofield. il Nat Geog Mag 123:599-661 My '63
See also
Castes

Social life and customs

India in crisis. J. Scofield. il Nat Geog Mag 123:599-661 My '63
Mother doesn't do much; the ambassador's wife in India. C. A. Galbraith. il Atlan 211:47-52 My '63
Royal wedding at Jaisalmer. M. Silverstone. il Nat Geog Mag 127:66-79 Ja '65

INDIA, India; story. See Buck, P. S.
INDIA and the United States
Twisted image, by A. Goodfriend. Review
Am Heritage 14:102-3 Je '63
Sat R 46:29 My 25 '63. B. Smith
INDIA in art
India in aquatints; works of T. and W. Daniell. il Time 81:52 F 8 '63
INDIA ink. See Ink
INDIA-Pakistan dispute. See Kashmir
INDIAN affairs, Bureau of. See United States—Indian affairs, Bureau of
INDIAN arrow points. See Arrowheads
INDIAN arts and crafts. See Indians of South America—Industries
INDIAN baskets. See Baskets
INDIAN beads. See Indians of North America—Costume and adornment
INDIAN cookery (East Indian) See Cookery, Indian (East Indian)
INDIAN costumes. See Indians of North America—Costume and adornment
INDIAN dancing (East Indian) See Dancing, Indian (East Indian)
INDIAN fiction (East Indian)
Fiction in India. R. White. bibliog il Reporter 28:54+ F 14 '63; Reply with rejoinder. Z. L. Kaul. 28:12+ Mr 14 '63
INDIAN flax. See Flax
INDIAN legends (East Indian) See Legends, Indian (East Indian)
INDIAN licorice. See Crabs eye vine
INDIAN mounds. See Mounds and mound builders
INDIAN music (East Indian) See Music, Indian (East Indian)
INDIAN national congress
Nehru's new centrism; concerning Congress party. A. Kumari. Reporter 29:32-5 D 5 '63
Party and country. Newsweek 63:49 Je 29 '64
INDIAN OCEAN
Cretaceous, paleocene, and pleistocene sediments from the Indian Ocean. Y. Herman. bibliog il Science 140:1316-17 Je 21 '63
Indian Ocean has unusual wind, currents. Sci N L 83:312 My 18 '63
New current discovered under Indian Ocean. Sci N L 85:89 F 8 '64
Seismic investigations of Seychelles and Saya de Malha Banks, Northwest Indian Ocean. G. G. Shor, jr. and D. D. Pollard. bibliog il Science 142:48-9 O 4 '63
INDIAN refugees (East Indian) See Refugees, Indian (East Indian)
INDIAN relics. See Indians of North America—Antiquities
INDIAN reservations. See Indians of North America—Reservations

INDIAN sculpture (East Indian) See Sculpture, Indian (East India)
INDIAN; story. See Updike, J.
INDIAN tobacco pipes. See Tobacco pipes
INDIAN weaving. See Weaving
INDIANA, Robert
What is pop art? interview; ed. by G. R. Swenson. il Art N 62:26+ N '63
about
Commanding painter. il por Time 83:72 My 22 '64
INDIANA
See also
Education—Indiana
Industries
Indiana dunes and pressure politics. W. Peeples. Atlan 211:84-8 F '63
Parks and playgrounds
Indiana dunes and pressure politics. W. Peeples. Atlan 211:84-8 F '63
Politics and government
Who's got the budget? Newsweek 61:35 Mr 25 '63
Religious institutions and affairs
News of the Christian world (cont) Christian Cent 80:628-9, 1010; 81:58-60 My 8, Ag 14 '63, Ja 8 '64
INDIANA dunes. See Sand dunes
INDIANA DUNES NATIONAL PARK (proposed) See National parks and reserves—United States
INDIANA primary. See Primaries
INDIANA. University, Bloomington
Annals of business; Crest toothpaste. B. Bliven, jr. New Yorker 39:83-4+ Mr 23 '63
Bloomington blooper. Nation 198:338 Ap 6 '64
Formula: hurt, pain, agony; swimming team. il Time 82:42 Ag 23 '63
Hoadley's test case in Indiana. J. Neugeboren. New Repub 149:14 S 21 '63
Hoosier witch hunt. N. R. Hanson. il Nation 196:443-4 My 25 '63; Discussion. 196:inside cover. 529 Je 22 '63
Meetings to be held at Indiana university. Américas 16:38 D '64
Singing at Indiana; Opera theater's presentation of Parsifal. il Time 83:56+ Mr 27 '64
Start them young; Hilltop gardening program. F. D. Cavinder. il Pop Gard 14:72+ F '63
School of music
Great adventure; operatic productions. J. Ardoin. il Mus Am 84:15-17 Ap '64
Music at Indiana U. H. F. Gaugh. il Mus Am 84:12-14 Ap '64
INDIANAPOLIS
Shooters solve the pigeon problem! Indianapolis pigeon rid project. C. Conley. il Field & S 68:10-11+ D '63
Clowes memorial hall for the performing arts
Indianapolis arrives. D. R. Richards. il Opera N 28:34 Ja 4 '64
Education
School board fight in Indianapolis; Citizens school committee vs Non-partisans of better schools. Christian Cent 81:598 My 6 '64
Housing
Federal aid? Indianapolis says, Uncle, go home! P. Friggens. Read Digest 82:266-8+ Je '63
First units of Indianapolis renewal ready. il Arch Rec 135:144-7 Ja '64
Music
[Musical events] (cont) il Mus Am 83:15 F; 12 Je; 61 D '63
Sanitary affairs
Unkempt; unswept label touches off a storm; installation of enclosed baskets. R. G. Bredell. il Am City 79:114-15 O '64
INDIANAPOLIS automobile races. See Automobile racing
INDIANAPOLIS coliseum explosion. See Explosions
INDIANAPOLIS motor speedway. See Speedways
INDIANOLA, Ia.
Parks and playgrounds
Starting from scratch. J. Kerr. il Recreation 56:178+ Ap '63

INDIANS
Art
See also
Indians of North America—Art
Totem poles
INDIANS in literature
Indian in Latin American fiction. E. S. Urbanski. il Américas 15:20-4 My '63
INDIANS of Alaska. See Indians of North America—Alaska
INDIANS of Canada. See Indians of North America—Canada
INDIANS of Central America
Antiquities
See also
Mayas
Guatemala
Microenvironments and Mesoamerican prehistory. M. D. Coe and K. V. Flannery. bibliog il Science 143:650-4 F 14 '64
Mysterious Maya: who was he? skeleton discovered at Tikal. il Life 54:101-3+ Ap 26 '63
INDIANS of Mexico
Saint's day; Oaxaca, Mexico, and nearby Indian village. A. Marriott. New Yorker 39:111+ O 19 '63
Warihio; Indians of Sonora-Chihuahua area. Hobbies 69:114+ Je '64
See also
Aztecs
Mixtec Indians
Antiquities
Ancient Mesoamerican civilization. R. S. MacNeish. bibliog il Science 143:531-7 F 7 '64
Ancient rain god on the move; statue of Tlaloc taken to Mexico city. il Life 57:89-90+ D 11 '64
Aztec basketball court unearthed in Mexico. Sci N L 85:312 My 16 '64
Lost worlds of Don Pablo. C. Phinizy. il Sports Illus 21:80-4+ N 30 '64
Microenvironments and Mesoamerican prehistory. M. D. Coe and K. V. Flannery. bibliog il Science 143:650-4 F 14 '64
Origins of New World civilization. R. S. MacNeish. il Sci Am 211:29-37 bibliog(p 154) N '64
Rain of Tlaloc; Tlaloc the rain god moved from Coatlinchán to Mexico city. il Newsweek 64:53 Jl 27 '64
San Lorenzo head; reprint. J. J. Sweeney. il Am Artist 28:67-73 Mr '64
See also
Mayas
Teotihuacán, Mexico
Dances
Voladores! dance of the flying pole. by Totonac Indians; photographs. Travel 119:34-7 My '63
Education
Mexico and the Indian; role of National Indianist institute. A. C. Flores. il Américas 16:9-16 F '64
Food
Domestication of corn. P. C. Mangelsdorf and others. bibliog il Science 143:538-45 F 7 '64
Legends
Legends of a Mexican Plymouth Rock. W. Wille. il Américas 16:24-9 N '64
Music
See also
Phonograph records—Indian music (Mexican)
Social life and customs
Beer party is basic to Tarahumara life. Sci N L 83:376 Je 15 '63
INDIANS of North America
He caught the splendor of the first Americans; G. Catlin's paintings. L. R. Peattie. il Read Digest 85:257-62 O '64
Help the neediest first! Christian Cent 81:693 My 27 '64
Indian-head nickel: some words with himself. A. Glaser. il Esquire 61:58+ Mr '64
Peaceful warpath. J. C. Hunt. il Am For 70:36-8+ Mr '64
Prehistoric Indians. Hobbies 68:112 Ja '64
Slow recovery since Wounded Knee. J. Collier. il Sat R 46:31-2 Je 15 '63
—Vanishing race. L. T. King. Commonweal 81:385-8 D 11 '64
Why no integration for the American Indian. il U S News 55:62-6 S 2 '63
See also
Crow Indians
Dakota Indians
Hopi Indians

INDIANS of North America—See also—*Cont.*
Iroquois Indians
Karok Indians
Mohawk Indians
Navaho Indians
Papago Indians
Pueblo Indians
Seminole Indians
Seneca Indians
Totem poles

Antiquities

Functional classification. C. Miles. Hobbies 68:114-15+ My '63
Indian relics. C. Miles. See issues of Hobbies
Microenvironments and Mesoamerican prehistory. M. D. Coe and K. V. Flannery. bibliog il Science 143:650-4 F 14 '64
Museums for the traveler. C. Miles. Hobbies 68:112 S '63
Vermont Indians; summary of booklet. T. E. Daniels. il Hobbies 69:112-13+ Mr '64
See also
Cliff dwellers and cliff dwellings
Pueblo Bonito, N.Mex.

Arizona

Archeology as anthropology: a case study, Pueblos. W. A. Longacre. bibliog Science 144:1454-5 Je 19 '64
Did American Indians see the guest star? discovery of prehistoric drawings. W. C. Miller. il Sat R 47:37-9 Jl 4 '64; Reply. R. Plank. 47:58-9 O 3 '64
Three Turkey House; Navajo archeological site near Canyon de Chelly National Monument. O. F. Oldendorph. il Nat Parks Mag 38:8-9 Ag '64

California

California's legacy of Indian rock art. C. Grant. il Natur Hist 73:32-41 Je '64
Waterworks indicates West Coast Indian site. Sci N L 83:216 Ap 6 '63

Illinois

Pre-Columbian solar observatories; Cahokia, Ill. Sci Am 211:84 S '64
Prehistoric city had Indian woodhenge; excavations at Cahokia. il Sci N L 86:86 Ag 8 '64

Maine

Red paint people. B. Geagan. Hobbies 68:115-16 Ap '63

Nevada

Mystery hunters of Lovelock cave. N. Karas. il Field & S 69:42-5+ Je '64

New Mexico

Exploring New Mexico's ancient city ruins. il Sunset 133:52-9 S '64

Ohio

Hopewell cult. O. H. Prufer. il Sci Am 211: 90-4+ D '64
Ohio's Mound circuit. B. G. Loveless. il Travel 122:38-40 S '64

Art

American Indian. M. Libhart. il Craft Horiz 24:104-11 My '64
Indian art; tribes of Southwest U.S. il Look 27:43 O 8 '63
Nature of Indian and Eskimo artifacts. C. Miles. il Hobbies 69:112-14 D '64
Our Indian crafts. M. Frome. il Holiday 34: 179-84 D '63
See also
Totem poles

Costume and adornment

California shell ornaments. C. Miles. il Hobbies 68:112+ Ag '63
Indian clothing and material. C. Miles. il Hobbies 68:114+ Mr '63
Prehistoric type Indian beads. C. Miles. il Hobbies 68:113-15 Je '63

Culture

How the Indian got the horse. F. Haines. il Am Heritage 15:16-21+ F '64

Dances

Struggles of One Bull and Good Feather. D. Duncan. il Dance Mag 37:25-6 F '63

Dwellings

See also
Cliff dwellers and cliff dwellings

Economic conditions

American Indian; ghettos in the desert. S. Steiner. il Nation 198:624-7 Je 22 '64
Indian and the poverty war; with editorial comment. T. E. Connolly. America 111:245, 260-1 S 12 '64
See also
Indians of North America—Migration

Education

American Indian; ghettos in the desert. S. Steiner. il Nation 198:624-7 Je 22 '64
Educating the American Indian. S. Gifford. il Sch Life 47:10-12 N '64
Manpower training in Navajo land. V. S. Hart. il Sch Life 45:26-9 Mr '63

Fairs

Indian fair; on the Crow Indian reservation, southeastern Montana. M. Jensen. il Am For 69:20-1+ My '63

Food

Have some Navajo fry bread. il Sunset 133: 122 S '64
Indian bones tell health story. Hobbies 68:115 Je '63

Government relations

American Indian; ghettos in the desert. S. Steiner. il Nation 198:624-7 Je 22 '64
Commissioner Nash on Indian needs. Christian Cent 80:453-4 Ap 10 '63
Do these Indians really own Florida? R. Bongartz. il Sat Eve Post 237:62-3+ F 1 '64
Indian administration in the United States; address, December 6, 1962. P. Nash. Vital Speeches 29:278-83 F 15 '63
Is fair treatment a civil right? Christian Cent 81:510 Ap 22 '64
Just bad Indians; state jurisdiction over Indian affairs. New Repub 148:8 Mr 30 '63
Senecas suffer another blow. Christian Cent 81:1421 N 18 '64
See also
Dakota Indians—Treaties
Indians of North America—Treaties

Health and hygiene

Animal-borne viruses; encephalitis virus among Seminole Indians. F. Marley. Sci N L 86:69 Ag 1 '64
Apaches have high blood pressure, few coronaries. Sci N L 85:11 Ja 4 '64
Cutting Indians in; welfare and improvement programs. America 110:213 F 15 '64
Serological evidence of arbovirus infection in the Seminole Indians of southern Florida. T. H. Work. bibliog il Science 145:270-2 Jl 17 '64

Implements

Early man in the New World; report on symposium of the AAAS. G. A. Agogino and others. il Science 143:1350-2 Mr 20 '64

Legal status, laws, etc.

See Indians of North America—Government relations

Migration

Indians move to cities. Christian Cent 81:877 Jl 8 '64

Missions

Kino missions of Sonora and Arizona. G. Meek. il Américas 16:18-22 Ja '64
Location list in progress: I. McCoy's History of Baptist Indian missions. Mrs S. Hayward. Library J 88:1790+ My 1 '63

Mixed bloods

Almost white, by B. Berry. Review
Sat R 46:28 My 25 '63. O. La Farge

Religion and mythology

Even insects had souls American Indians believed. Sci Digest 53:27-8 Ap '63
Indian heavens. E. Cardenal. il Américas 16: 23-7 Ja '64
See also
Peyote
Totem poles

Relocation

See Indians of North America—Government relations

Reservations

Arizona's fish and fun spot: Apache-land. B. Minette and R. Dunlop. il Todays Health 41:22-5+ O '63
Hon dah (be my guest) J. Cook. il Am For 69:26-7+ Ap '63
Navajo country. il Sunset 131:60-71 S '63
Now you can camp at the Rosebud Indian reservation. H. Bradshaw and V. Bradshaw. il Suc Farm 62:48 Ag '64
Walpole Island; Indian reservation. W. Henning. il Travel 102:43-6 Jl '63

INDIANS of North America—*Continued*

Treaties

Propose another Lake of Perfidy; high dam on Flathead River in Montana; reply. J. E. Nolan. Christian Cent 80:833 Je 26 '63

Senecas to be flooded out; Kinzua Dam project. Sr Schol 84:17 Mr 20 '64

See also

Dakota Indians—Treaties

Wars

There are no Indians left now but me. M. Rosenberg and D. Rosenberg. il Am Heritage 15:18-23+ Je '64

See also

United States—History—French and Indian war, 1755-1763

Alaska

Biggest liar in Alaska. F. Dufresne. il Field & S 68:44-5+ Mr '64

Canada

Mohawk beauty with a mission. C. Brossard. il Look 28:91-4 Ja 28 '64

Montreal: historical note; letter. P. S. Miller. Science 145:1257-8 S 18 '64

INDIANS of Peru. See Indians of South America—Peru

INDIANS of South America

Antiquities

Ecuador

Early man in the Andes. W. J. Mayer-Oakes. il Sci Am 208:116-22+ My '63

Peru

See also

Pottery, Peruvian

Children

We have no childhood; ed. by R. Llewellyn. S. Lombardi. il Sat Eve Post 236:76-7 S 7 '63

Industries

Andean handicrafts. M. de Ortega. il Américas 15:29-32 Je '63

Missions

Lost empire; ruins in eastern Paraguay and western Argentina. D. S. Carter. il Travel 120:37-40 O '63

Religion and mythology

Indian heavens. E. Cardenal. il Américas 16:23-7 Ja '64

Argentina

We have no childhood; ed. by R. Llewellyn. S. Lombardi. il Sat Eve Post 236:76-7 S 7 '63

Brazil

Indians of the Amazon darkness. H. Schultz. il Nat Geog Mag 125:736-58 My '64

Last primitives. il Sci Digest 55:46-51 My '64

Paradise found: Xinguanos. il Newsweek 65:41 Ja 4 '65

Science in action; on ethnological tactics; among the Kuikuru of central Brazil and the Amahuaca of eastern Peru. R. L. Carneiro. Natur Hist 73:58-9+ Ag '64

Ecuador

Looms of progress; Salasacas weave a new life. H. O'Hara. il Américas 17:22-6 Ja '65

Paraguay

Pirates of Paraguay. J. Piá. il Américas 15:31-8 Mr '63

Peru

Domestic peace corps; Cooperación popular program. Newsweek 65:37-8 F 1 '65

Five worlds of Peru. K. F. Weaver. il Nat Geog Mag 125:212-66 F '64

Miracle at Vicos. L. Stowe. il Read Digest 82:222-6+ Ap '63

Modern laboratory set for ancient Inca site; study of Quechua Indians. Sci N L 85:392 Je 20 '64

Science in action; on ethnological tactics; among the Kuikuru of central Brazil and the Amahuaca of eastern Peru. R. L. Carneiro. Natur Hist 73:58-9+ Ag '64

Songs of Andean pastures. S. Q. Jara. il Américas 15:37-9 My '63

When to be is not to be; semantic approach to Quechua culture. R. Kusch. il Américas 15:19-22 O '63

Venezuela

Jungle captive. J. Liedloff and R. Massie. il Sat Eve Post 236:85-9 Ag 10 '63

Prehistory of the West Indies. I. Rouse. bibliog il Science 144:499-513 My 1 '64

Transferrins in Venezuelan Indians: high frequency of a slow-moving variant. T. Arends and M. L. Gallango. bibliog il Science 143:367-8 Ja 24 '64

Venezuela builds on oil. T. J. Abercrombie. il Nat Geog Mag 123:362-8 Mr '63

INDIANS of the West Indies

Prehistory of the West Indies. I. Rouse. bibliog il Science 144:499-513 My 1 '64

INDIC authors. See Authors, Indian (East Indian)

INDIC fiction. See Indian fiction. (East Indian)

INDICATORS for gas and oil engines

Engine temperature indicator. W. T. Davis. il Electr World 71:36+ Ap '64

INDICK, Benjamin P.

Books have wings; drama. Plays 24:63-6 N '64

INDICTMENTS

Anecdotes, facetiae satire, etc.

Who, me? C. W. Morton. Atlan 214:120+ Jl '64

INDIGESTION. See Dyspepsia

INDIK, Bernard P. See Goldstein, B. jt. auth.

INDIUM

Crystal structures at high pressures of metallic modifications of compounds of indium, gallium, and aluminum. J. C. Jamieson. bibliog il Science 139:845-7 Mr 1 '63

INDIUM antimonide

Indium antimonide: superconductivity of the metallic form. H. E. Bömmel and others. il Science 139:1301-2 Mr 29 '63

Indium antimonide: the metallic form at atmospheric pressure. A. J. Darnell and W. F. Libby. bibliog il Science 139:1301 Mr 29 '63

New synthetic metal similar to tin produced. Sci N L 83:361 Je 8 '63

Superconducting indium antimonide. S. Geller and others. bibliog Science 140:62 Ap 5 '63

INDIUM telluride

Blue metal produced at very high pressure. Sci N L 84:152 S 7 '63

High-pressure metallic indium telluride: preparation and crystal structure. C. B. Sclar and others. bibliog il Science 143:352-3 Ja 24 '64

High pressure transitions in $A^{(III)} B^{(VI)}$ compounds: indium telluride. M. D. Banus and others. bibliog il Science 142:662-3 N 8 '63

Indium telluride metal. A. J. Darnell and others. bibliog il Science 141:713-14 Ag 23 '63

Superconductivity of metallic indium telluride. H. E. Bömmel and others. il Science 141:714 Ag 23 '63

INDIVIDUAL and society

Accent on the individual. G. Hauge. Sat R 47:48 Ja 11 '64

Confidence in life. R. O. Johann. America 111:740 D 5 '64

Decline of the individual. H. G. Rickover. Sat Eve Post 236:11-13 Mr 30 '63

Good society; excerpts from address. N. Glazer. Commentary 36:226-31+ S '63; Discussion. 36:430 D '63

Lincoln and modern America: the heritage of a free choice in an organized society. il Time 81:20-5 My 10 '63

Political frustration: cause and cure. R. Rienow and L. T. Rienow. Sat R 46:25-8 S 28 '63; Discussion. 46:29 O 19 '63

Road to self-fulfillment. W. D. Bonis. Christian Cent 81:1365-6+ N 4 '64

Self-renewal, by J. W. Gardner. Review
Sat R 47:39 F 8 '64. W. S. Lynch
Science 144:164-5 Ap 10 '64. C. Kerr.

To form great individuals; address, August 24, 1963. H. C. Case. Vital Speeches 29:708-10 S 15 '63

Urbanization and human needs. L. J. Duhl. Christian Cent 81:930-3 Jl 22 '64

INDIVIDUAL and state

Friendly letter to Mr Zorin. N. Cousins. Sat R 46:22 N 30 '63

INDIVIDUAL differences

Behavior genetics and individuality understood; excerpts from discussions at symposiums. J. Hirsch. bibliog il Science 142:1436-42 D 13 '63

See also

Sex differences

INDIVIDUAL instruction

Individualizing instruction with paperbacks. D. H. Moscow. il NEA J 53:21-2 Ap '64

Textbooks and teaching aids: with study-discussion program. by D. B. Harris and E. S. Harris. N. Larrick. bibliog il PTA Mag 58:4-6, 35-6 D '63

INDIVIDUAL liberty. See Liberty

INDIVIDUALISM

Individualism and big business. by L. R. Sayles. Review
Bsns W il p 100 O 5 '63
Reporter 30:47+ Ja 16 '64. J. W. Ward
Lincoln and modern America; the heritage of a free choice in an organized society. il Time 81:20-5 My 10 '63
Middle ground of a Midwest Republican. R. Taft, jr. Sat R 47:14-16 Ag 22 '64
Pitfalls of intentional community. F. D. Hall. Christian Cent 80:1000-2 Ag 14 '63
Scientists and Jesuits, gypsies and Jews; letter. M. Amrine. Science 142:913 N 15 '63; Reply. R. B. Davis. 143:763-4 F 21 '64
Self-renewal, by J. W. Gardner. Review
Science 144:164-5 Ap 10 '64. C. Kerr
See also
Conformity
Individual and state
Personalism

INDIVIDUALITY

Person in a machine age. P. Tournier. Christian Cent 81:793-6 Je 17 '64
Who are you going to be this year? D. Klein. il Seventeen 22:200-1+ Ag '63
See also
Self

INDOCHINA, French

History

Civil war, 1946-1954

Dienbienphu: battle to remember; end of French military influence in Asia. B. B. Fall. il N Y Times Mag p21+ My 3 '64
Dienbienphu: could it happen again? Time 83:43 My 15 '64

INDOCTRINATION

Love affair of Comrade Wang; utter denial of personal freedom. J. Marcuse. il N Y Times Mag p40-1+ N 8 '64

INDOLE

Tryptophan- and indole-excreting bacterial mutants. P. G. Lim and R. I. Mateles. bibliog Science 140:388 Ap 26 '63

INDOLEACETIC acid

Auxin in coleus stems: limitation of transport at higher concentrations. T. K. Scott and W. P. Jacobs. bibliog il Science 139: 589-90 F 15 '63
Indoleacetamide as an intermediate in the synthesis of indoleacetic acid in pseudomonas savastanoi. A. R. Magie and others. bibliog il Science 141:1281-2 S 27 '63
Indoleacetic acid synthesis by polyphenols in the extraction of pinus phloem and cambial tissue. F. W. Whitmore and R. Zahner. bibliog il Science 145:166-7 Jl 10 '64

INDONESIA

Adventurer. Newsweek 62:46 O 7 '63
Bamboo bomb. Time 84:37 N 27 '64
Indonesia: a dissent. S. Lens. Commonweal 81:478-81 Ja 8 '65
Malaysia; a game of footsy in southeast Asia. D. Warner. New Repub 148:11-12 Mr 16 '63
Reporter in Indonesia. B. Krisher. il Newsweek 64:83-6 O 5 '64
See also
Bali
Chinese in Indonesia
Communism—Indonesia
Economic assistance in Indonesia
Jakarta
Petroleum industry and trade
United Nations—Indonesia

Description and travel

Going places, finding things in new fields for adventurous wayfarers. J. Sakol. il House & Gard 125:22+ Ja '64

Economic conditions

How Sukarno keeps his revolution spinning. D. Warner. il Reporter 30:33-6 Ap 23 '64
Indonesia: time bomb in the South Pacific. W. J. Lederer and E. Burdick. il Read Digest 82:129-34 Mr '63
Of rice & rats. Time 83:40 F 28 '64
Outlook brightens for U.S. trade with Indonesians. Nations Bsns 51:59 Ag '63

Economic policy

Atlantic report. Atlan 212:23+ N '63

Economic relations

Complete draw. il Fortune 68:79-80+ Ag '63
Help from a bitten hand; Dutch expropriated by Sukarno six years ago, sign a technical-aid agreement. Time 83:37 Ap 10 '64

Foreign relations

Awkward visitor; Liu Shao-chi in Indonesia. il Newsweek 61:44 Ap 29 '63
Borneo, Britain's South Vietnam; British troops and Sukarno guerrillas. R. Hughes. il N Y Times Mag p9+ Jl 19 '64
Cassava, anyone? il Time 85:24-5 Ja 15 '65
Clouds in the South Seas; with report by R. K. McCabe. il Newsweek 61:42-4 Mr 4 '63
Confrontation continued; Indonesian guerrilla raids on Borneo. Newsweek 64:34+ Jl 6 '64
Eyewitness report: Borneo: where a new war is heating up; concerning Sarawak and Sabah. S. W. Sanders. il U S News 56:58-60 Ja 27 '64
Feathers from a frog. Time 84:108 D 4 '64
Gobble, gobble? Sukarno's campaign of harassment against Malaysia. Newsweek 64:33 S 14 '64
How Australia is rearming against threats of war. il U S News 57:10 N 23 '64
I will eat you. J. Burnham. Nat R 16:60 Ja 28 '64
Indonesia, how peaceful its neutralism? il Sr Schol 82:10-13 F 27 '63
Indonesia: waiting for a letter; secession from the U.N. il Newsweek 65:27 Ja 18 '65
Malaya sees Sukarno as danger for southeast Asia; interview. A. Rahman. il U S News 54:80-1 Mr 18 '63
Malaysia feels bite of war threat; Indonesian guerrillas. il Bsns W p58+ Ja 16 '65
Meddling by Sukarno: why Filipinos turn against U.S. il U S News 58:59 Ja 11 '65
Nationalism: a matter of pride and prejudice; Indonesia vs. Malaysia. il Sr Schol 85:18 O 7 '64
New sea of trouble in southeast Asia. il U S News 54:46-8 F 11 '63
Next war. Nation 199:150 S 28 '64
No solution; collapse of peace talks between Indonesia and Malaysia. Newsweek 63:52 Mr 16 '64
Power balance in Indonesia. A. Vandenbosch. il Cur Hist 46:95-100 F '64
Punch-drunk. New Repub 150:13 Ja 18 '64
Ritual dance. Newsweek 65:40 Ja 25 '65
Sukarno: back for more Kremlin arms? il U S News 57:24 O 12 '64
Sukarno leads from weakness. J. Jacquet-Francillon. New Repub 149:11-12 N 23 '63
Sukarno: regional bully. B. Grant. il Nation 198:111-14 F 3 '64
Sukarno stirs up another Asian storm. S. S. King. il N Y Times Mag p 14-15+ Ja 19 '64
Sukarno's war; will it involve U.S? il U S News 57:63 S 21 '64
This mob for hire. il Time 82:31-2 S 27 '63
This war in Borneo: whose side are we on? H. F. Armstrong. il Reporter 30:16-20 Je 4 '64
Tunku and the pirates. Life 58:4 Ja 15 '65
We are going to change this damn world! J. A. Rose. il Sat Eve Post 236:77-81 N 2 '63
What we got for pampering Sukarno. D. Warner. il Reporter 31:30-2 O 8 '64
What's the fuss? Indonesian aggression against Malaysia. il Newsweek 64:50 S 21 '64

Politics and government

Atlantic report. Atlan 212:16+ N '63
How Sukarno keeps his revolution spinning. D. Warner. il Reporter 30:33-6 Ap 23 '64
In dreamland. il Newsweek 63:34 My 4 '64
Indonesia: another Cuba? il Bsns W p59-60+ Ap 27 '63
Indonesia, how peaceful its neutralism? il Sr Schol 82:10-13 F 27 '63
Indonesia: time bomb in the South Pacific. W. J. Lederer and E. Burdick. il Read Digest 82:129-34 Mr '63
Power balance in Indonesia. A. Vandenbosch. il Cur Hist 46:95-100 F '64
Sukarno: on the road to disaster? U S News 56:74 My 18 '64
Sukarno: regional bully. B. Grant. il Nation 198:111-14 F 3 '64
Unhealthy conflict; potential heirs to Sukarno. Newsweek 64:31 D 28 '64
Whither Sukarno? New Repub 148:9 My 18 '63

INDONESIAN art. See Art, Indonesian

INDONESIAN cookery. See Cookery, Indonesian

INDONESIAN dancing. See Dancing, Indonesian

INDONESIAN folk literature. See Folk literature, Indonesian

INDONESIAN poetry
See also
Anwar, C.

INDOOR archery. See Archery

INDOOR gardening. See Greenhouses; House plants; Window gardening

INDOOR gardens. See Gardens, Indoor

INDOOR golf. See Golf, Indoor

INDOOR plants. See House plants
INDOOR track. See Track athletics
INDUCTANCE
Experimenter's L bridge; inductance tester. C. Green. il Pop Electr 22:61-3+ Ja '65
INDUCTION (electricity)
See also
Inductance
INDUCTION coils
See also
Tesla coils
INDUSTRIAL adhesives. See Adhesives
INDUSTRIAL agreements. See Trade agreements
INDUSTRIAL arbitration. See Arbitration, Industrial
INDUSTRIAL areas foundation
This is war; attack against poverty, misery, delinquency, disease and injustice. H. Black. il Sat Eve Post 237:60-3 Ja 25 '64
INDUSTRIAL arts
Shaker form & function. W. R. Stewart. bibliog il Sch Arts 63:26-8 Ap '64
Study and teaching
Elementary school industrial arts in Los Angeles and in Kansas City; symposium. il NEA J 53:31-3 Ja '64
INDUSTRIAL buildings
Building types study. il Arch Rec 134:115-34 D '63; 136:163-78 Jl '64; 137:151-70 Ja '65
Dividends from design. il Duns R 83:pt2 116-18+ Mr '64
Industrial buildings: staging a comeback. H. C. F. Arnold. il Arch Rec 134:18 D '63
Industry scrambles to get plants built; Engineering news-record report. il Bsns W p54-5 D 26 '64
John Deere's sticks of steel. il Arch Forum 121:76-85 Jl '64
One-man magnet for industry; C. E. Daniel of Greenville, S.C. il Bsns W p50-2+ Ja 11 '64
Plowmen's palace; new headquarters of Deere and company. il Time 84:64-5 Ag 7 '64
Private spending will strengthen prosperity. R. Newcomb. il Nations Bsns 52:40-1+ S '64
Space program has infinite variety; ground facilities for NASA space flight centers. il Arch Rec 133:151-8 Je '63
See also
Warehouses
Heating and ventilation
Heat pump, radiant panels condition electronics plant. il Arch Rec 135:170-1 Ja '64
Lighting
Utilities set on the roof of Phoenix shopping center. il Arch Rec 134:136-8 D '63
INDUSTRIAL chemical research. See Chemistry, Technical—Research
INDUSTRIAL cooperation
Labor cooperation will grow; symposium. il Nations Bsns 51:34-5+ Ag '63
What you can learn from success. A. Uris. il Nations Bsns 51:76-8 Jl '63
INDUSTRIAL corporation bonds. See Bonds
INDUSTRIAL design. See Design, Industrial
INDUSTRIAL designers. See Designers
INDUSTRIAL diseases. See Diseases, Industrial
INDUSTRIAL districts
From city dump to industrial park; Columbia, S.C. C. C. Burnett. il Am City 78:95-6 Jl '63
Stanford: boom in electronics in the San Francisco Bay area was ignited down on the farm. J. Walsh. Science 143:1305-7 Mr 20 '64
Toledo's play for industry; Fort industry industrial park. il Bsns W p 106-8 Ap 4 '64
Turning one into many; plant in southwest Chicago. il Bsns W p 174-5 My 23 '64
INDUSTRIAL diversification. See Diversification in industry
INDUSTRIAL drama. See Entertaining in sales promotion
INDUSTRIAL education
See also
Apprentices
Employees—Training
Engineering education
Industrial relations—Study and teaching
Technical education
Trade schools
INDUSTRIAL efficiency. See Efficiency, Industrial
INDUSTRIAL equipment leasing. See Machinery—Leasing
INDUSTRIAL espionage. See Spies, Industrial
INDUSTRIAL expansion
Catching up with the facts. il Fortune 68:47-8 N '63
Encourage private capital to aid American industry; address, June 6, 1963. F. G. Binswanger. Vital Speeches 29:689-90 S 1 '63
Expansion as policy. il Fortune 67:39-40 Mr '63
Good times will get better; views of key men. il Nations Bsns 52:56-8 Jl '64
How to get most from growth. C. A. Cerami. il Nations Bsns 51:34-5+ Jl '63
Humble oil lays out a new Texas town; Bayport development. il Bsns W p67-8 F 8 '64
More expansion likely in 1964. Nations Bsns 51:106-7 N '63
Nation's business outlook symposium. il Nations Bsns 51:40-1+ N '63
New realities of plant investment. il Duns R 81:pt2 S92-4+ Mr '63
Peace trend will bring better business. C. T. Stewart, jr. il Nations Bsns 52:66-8+ Je '64
Prime mover begins to move. G. Burck and S. Parker. il Fortune 67:110-14+ F '63
Trend of business; banner year. J. Phillips. il Duns R 82:8-9 O '63
When the crowd goes one way Litton goes the other. C. Rieser. il Fortune 67:114-19+ My '63
See also
Capital investments
INDUSTRIAL fair and congress, Los Angeles. See Exhibitions
INDUSTRIAL films. See Moving pictures in industry
INDUSTRIAL forecasting. See Business forecasting
INDUSTRIAL forestry. See Forest management
INDUSTRIAL gaming. See Management games
INDUSTRIAL leasing and finance, limited
Leasing grows in Britain. Bsns W p61-2 Jl 20 '63
INDUSTRIAL location. See Location in business and industry
INDUSTRIAL management and organization
Backlog syndrome. E. R. Gomersaill. il Harvard Bsns R 42:105-15 S '64
Can industry harness the elusive engineer? H. E. Klein. il Duns R 83:48-9+ My '64
Case of the disputing divisions. J. Dearden. il Harvard Bsns R 42:158-9+ My '64
Cutback in middle management. J. B. Weiner. il Duns R 84:32-3+ Jl '64
Focusing farther and sharper; long-range planning. il Bsns W p54+ Je 1 '63
Hierarchy of objectives. C. H. Granger. bibliog f il Harvard Bsns R 42:63-74 My '64
Improve your profits day by day! F. O. Hoffman. Harvard Bsns R 41:59-67 Jl '63
Long-range planning and cloudy horizons. J. J. Friedman. Duns R 81:42-3+ Ja '63
Management of international production; excerpts from research report. C. W. Skinner. il Harvard Bsns R 42:125-36 S '64
New life on leasing. il Duns R 81:65-6+ Ap '63
New realities of plant investment. il Duns R 81:pt2 S92-4+ Mr '63
Optimistic world of Edgar Kaiser. W. Guzzardi, jr. il Fortune 67:90-7+ Ap '63
Profits, prices, and excess capacity. R. S. Schultz. bibliog f il Harvard Bsns R 41:68-81 Jl '63
Questions for solving the inventory problem. J. L. Morgan. il Harvard Bsns R 41:95-110 Jl '63
Russians yearn for the managerial mind. D. W. Ewing. Harper 230:67-72 Ja '65
Total managerial failure; difficulties in Britain. W. W. Allen. Fortune 69:62+ My '64
When science supplants technology; with comments by prominent businessmen. T. Levitt. il Harvard Bsns R 41:14-16+ Jl '63
When the crowd goes one way Litton goes the other. C. Rieser. il Fortune 67:114-19+ My '63
See also
Budget, Business
Business management and organization
Collective bargaining
Controllership
Grievance procedures
Industrial relations
Inventories
Linear programming
Management rights
Personnel management
Technological innovations

INDUSTRIAL management and organization—*Continued*

Study and teaching

Spreading the business gospel; industrialists and educators from developing countries at U.S. business schools. il Bsns W p99-100 S 7 '63

See also

Executives—Training

Great Britain

British analysis goes deep; Tavistock institute study of automation. il Bsns W p 122+ O 26 '63

INDUSTRIAL market

Gentle art of stitch-in-timemanship; trade relations director. il Bsns W p74 My 11 '63

Pinpointing America: analysis of industrial markets; tables. il Duns R 84:43-50 Ag '64

Systems selling: industrial marketing's new tool. T. J. Murray. il Duns R 84:51-2+ O '64

INDUSTRIAL medical service. See Medical service, Industrial

INDUSTRIAL morale. See Employee morale

INDUSTRIAL museums

See also

Museum of science and industry, Chicago

INDUSTRIAL musicals. See Entertaining in sales promotion

INDUSTRIAL parks. See Factories—Grounds; Industrial districts

INDUSTRIAL pensions. See Pensions, Industrial

INDUSTRIAL photography. See Photography in industry

INDUSTRIAL plants. See Factories; Industrial buildings

INDUSTRIAL production. See Production

INDUSTRIAL protection. See Protection systems, Industrial

INDUSTRIAL psychiatry. See Psychiatry, Industrial

INDUSTRIAL recreation

Employees at play are big business; recreation's benefits hard to measure. il Bsns W p98-100 Ap 11 '64

Sis-boom-bah! for amalgamated sponge. B. Gilbert. il Sports Illus 22:54-60+ Ja 25 '65

Using our leisure is no easy job. B. Bliven. il N Y Times Mag p 18-19+ Ap 26 '64

Where is the golf course of the workers? G. S. Brown. il Sports Illus 19:42-4 Ag 26 '63

INDUSTRIAL relations

Account of American labor in 1964. P. Groom. Mo Labor R 87:1385-92 D '64

American labor in 1962; a retrospect. P. Groom. bibliog f Mo Labor R 86:14-23 Ja '63

Automation and full employment; the problem of government, industry and labor; address, March 9, 1964. D. J. McDonald. Vital Speeches 30:409-12 Ap 15 '64

Breakthrough at Kaiser; automation and unemployment. L. T. King. Commonweal 78: 11-12 Mr 29 '63

Brighter future for collective bargaining. E. R. Livernash. Harvard Bsns R 42:66-70 S '64

Collective bargaining: shift for the sixties. T. R. Brooks. il Duns R 82:30-2 Jl '63

Conflicts in human values. R. N. McMurry. Harvard Bsns R 41:130-6+ My '63

Developments in industrial relations. See issues of Monthly labor review

Double standard builds union power; with views of six executives. W. H. Peterson. il Nations Bsns 51:69-72+ My '63

Economic dilemmas of collective bargaining. M. Rothbaum. bibliog f Ann Am Acad 350: 95-103 N '63

Employers take initiative as unions change. il Nations Bsns 51:36-7+ Je '63

GM strike: prototype for more conflict. B. J. Widick. il Nation 199:349-52 N 16 '64

Getting a jump on '64 auto talks; joint committees to study complex issues. il Bsns W p 161 Ap 20 '63

Government, labor and management; address, December 3, 1962. J. L. Block. Vital Speeches 29:250-4 F 1 '63

Heading off strikes; a new strategy spreads; study committees. il U S News 54:97-8 Je 10 '63

Human attitude in steel talks. il Newsweek 61:81-2 Je 24 '63

Individual's legal rights as an employee. B. Aaron. Mo Labor R 86:666-73 Je '63

It's good business; Eastman Kodak company's employee relations. L. L. L. Golden. Sat R 47:59 Jl 11 '64

Labor and management; excerpts from address. H. F. Dunning. Duns R 81:23-4 Ap '63

Labor in a prosperous Japan. S. B. Levine. bibliog f Cur Hist 46:212-18 Ap '64

Labor-management relations; address, February 4, 1963. W. P. Reuther. Vital Speeches 29:376-9 Ap 1 '63

Labor-management relations; role of labor; address, December 5, 1963. D. J. McDonald. Vital Speeches 30:189-92 Ja 1 '64

Labor policy controversy. T. R. Brooks. Duns R 83:60-1 Je '64

Labor unions are worth the price. M. Ways. il Fortune 67:108-13+ My '63; Discussion. 67:20 Je '63

Labor's crisis of public confidence. A. H. Raskin. il Sat R 46:21-5+ Mr 30 '63

Labor's welfare state; the New York electrical workers. A. H. Raskin. Atlan 211: 37-44 Ap '63

Latest trends in pay, fringes, bargaining. U S News 55:72-4 Ag 12 '63

Leadership factor in union growth; excerpt from address. J. Barbash. Mo Labor R 86: 133-6 F '63

Management's adjustment to change. E. L. Cushman. Mo Labor R 86:630-5 Je '63

Managerial freedom and job security, by M. Stone. Review

Duns R 83:58-9 Ap '64. T. R. Brooks

Managers have to manage. C. P. Ives. Nat R 14:157-8 F 26 '63

Managing your manpower; effects of automation. T. R. Brooks. Duns R 83:71-2+ My '64

Managing your manpower; employers' rights in union elections. T. R. Brooks. Duns R 82: 81 O '63

Managing your manpower; industry application of some behavioral science techniques. T. R. Brooks. Duns R 85:65-6+ Ja '65

Pope on industrial society. America 111:83 Jl 25 '64

Real issue in autos, as industry sees it; intrusion of union in the field of management. il U S News 56:83-5 Ap 13 '64

Security of worker institutions. G. W. Brooks. Mo Labor R 86:652-8 Je '63

Significant decisions in labor cases. See issues of Monthly labor review

Six challenges for tomorrow's manager. J. H. Healey. il Duns R 84:60-1+ O '64

Spokesmen for steel and rails see era of labor peace ahead; excerpts from statements. R. M. Blough; J. E. Wolfe. U S News 57:98 O 19 '64

Strikes and the public. H. Malmgren. New Repub 148:6 Ap 20 '63

Toward an integrated approach for industrial relations research; excerpt from address. W. F. Whyte. Mo Labor R 87:136-9 F '64

Transportation's labor crisis. E. B. Shils. bibliog f Harvard Bsns R 42:84-98 My '64

Union bargaining strength: Goliath or paper tiger? G. Strauss. bibliog f Ann Am Acad 350:86-94 N '63

Way out of our strike dilemma. M. Lerner. Look 27:84+ Ap 23 '63; Same abr. with title Our strike dilemma. Read Digest 83: 75-8 Jl '63

When to speak up. il Nations Bsns 51:88-90+ Mr '63

Worker security in a changing economy; symposium. bibliog f il Mo Labor R 86:612-702 Je '63

See also

Collective bargaining
Employees, Reporting to
Employees representation in management
Grievance procedures
Industrial management and organization
Labor disputes
Management rights
Open and closed shop
Personnel management
Strikes
United States—Labor policy
United States—National labor relations board

Study and teaching

For labor schools. America 108:847 Je 15 '63

INDUSTRIAL relations research association

Papers from the IRRA annual meeting; excerpts. il Mo Labor R 86:133-44, 268-84; 87:125-36 F-Mr '63, F '64

INDUSTRIAL research

Aerospace to oceanography. Nation 196:365 My 4 '63; Reply. R. C. Vetter. 197:inside cover Jl 6 '63

Aiming at the market instead of the moon. il Time 81:83 Je 21 '63

Alchemy of ultrahigh pressure. G. A. W. Boehm. il Fortune 70:144-8+ O '64

INDUSTRIAL research—*Continued*
By 1970, a $20-billion plateau? government R&D spending. il Bsns W p64-6 Jl 25 '64
Case of the dubious deferral; with discussion. D. F. Hawkins. il Harvard Bsns R 41:162-4+ My '63
Civilian technology: concern over pace of growth inspires program for research and development effort. D. S. Greenberg. Science 139:576-7 F 15 '63
Cultural lag in manufacturing. H. E. Klein. il Duns R 82:37-8+ Ag '63
Fundamental research can be planned; excerpts from studies. J. B. Quinn and R. M. Cavanaugh. Harvard Bsns R 42:111-24 Ja '64
Harnessing the R. and D. monster. H. Kay. il Fortune 71:160-3+ Ja '65
How Pert-cost helps the general manager. H. W. Paige. il Harvard Bsns R 41:87-95 N '63
Industrial R&D: competition from universities, non-profits, alarms independent laboratories. E. Langer. Science 144:273-4 Ap 17 '64; Discussion. 144:1293 Je 12 '64
Industry research pays student bills. il Bsns W p82+ S 19 '64
New think factories. il Duns R 81:pt2 S104-5 Mr '63
Ohio: old laissez-faire attitude on linking education, research, and industry undergoing change. J. Walsh. Science 145:468-70 Jl 31 '64
On target; concerning H. Wilson's speech at the Labour party's convention. Nation 197: 249 O 26 '63
Organizing for product innovation. J. W. Lorsch and P. R. Lawrence. il Harvard Bsns R 43:109-18+ Ja '65
Politics: Johnson and Goldwater scientist groups show differing views on civilian technology. D. S. Greenberg. Science 146: 509+ O 23 '64
Rate your company's research productivity. M. H. Hodge, jr. bibliog f il Harvard Bsns R 41:109-22 N '63
R&D, industry's maverick. S. Nicholson. il Duns R 81:63-4+ Ap '63
R&D is more efficient in small companies. A. C. Cooper. bibliog f Harvard Bsns R 42:75-83 My '64
Technology; promise and problems. il Duns R 81:pt2 S128-31+ Je '63
Transferring research results to operations. J. B. Quinn and J. A. Mueller. il Harvard Bsns R 41:49-66 Ja '63
Twelve fables of research management. P. F. Drucker. il Harvard Bsns R 41:103-8 Ja '63
When science supplants technology; with comments by prominent businessmen. T. Levitt. il Harvard Bsns R 41:14-16+ Jl '63
Where the R&D dollars go. il Bsns W p54+ S 28 '63
Wild birds find a corporate roost. T. Alexander. il Fortune 70:130-4+ Ag '64
See also
Market research
Midwest research institute
National research corporation
Operations research
Research laboratories
Wood research

Federal aid

Civilian technology: opposition in Congress and industry leads to major realignment of program. D. S. Greenberg. Science 143: 660-1 F 14 '64
Civilian technology: program to boost industrial research heavily slashed in House. D. S. Greenberg. Science 140:1380-2 Je 28 '63
Sabotaging R&D. Nation 197:83 Ag 24 '63

INDUSTRIAL research laboratories. See Research laboratories
INDUSTRIAL revenue bonds. See Municipal bonds
INDUSTRIAL revolution, Great Britain. See Great Britain—Economic history
INDUSTRIAL revolution, United States. See United States—Economic history
INDUSTRIAL secrets. See Trade secrets
INDUSTRIAL sociology. See Sociology, Industrial
INDUSTRIAL spies. See Spies, Industrial
INDUSTRIAL statistics
Where automation's pinch will be; Labor dept.'s analysis. il Bsns W p 114-16+ My 30 '64
See also
Employment—Statistics
INDUSTRIAL technicians. See Technicians in industry
INDUSTRIAL testing. See Testing
INDUSTRIAL tours
Industry tours: a different kind of travel fun. il Good H 158:166 Je '64
INDUSTRIAL towns. See Company towns
INDUSTRIAL union department. See American federation of labor and Congress of industrial organizations—Industrial union department
INDUSTRIAL waste. See Trade waste
INDUSTRIAL workers of the world
Rebel voices: an I.W.W. anthology, ed. by J. L. Kornbluh. Review
Sat R 48:30 Ja 16 '65. M. R. Konvitz
INDUSTRIALIZATION
Abundance and the future of man. G. Piel. Atlan 213:84-90 Ap '64
Can a poor nation grow on an empty stomach? not until food production is increased. il Bsns W p56-7 D 26 '64
How to make a national market; address, October 1, 1963. W. W. Rostow. Dept State Bul 49:667-73 O 28 '63
Industrial development goals. U N Rev 10:51 Je '63
Industrial development; proposed new organization within United Nations. il U N Rev 11:24-5 F '64
Industrialitis. H. Hazlitt. Newsweek 63:94 My 25 '64
Industrialization, vital key for progress in Asia and the Far East; address, March 11, 1963. P. de Seynes. U N Rev 10:19-22 Ap '63
Mahatma Gandhi was wrong. L. Hazard. il Atlan 214:45-9 Jl '64
Pressing for change in Spain; government-controlled unions. il Bsns W p94-6 Mr 7 '64
See also
Economic development
Underdeveloped areas
INDUSTRY
Special report on industrial facilities; symposium. il Duns R 83:pt2 98-110+ Mr '64
See also
Business
Cities and towns—Industries
Inventions
New business enterprises

Charitable contributions

See Corporations—Charitable contributions

Location

See Location in business and industry

Social aspects

See Sociology, Industrial

INDUSTRY and art. See Art and industry
INDUSTRY and education. See Business and education
INDUSTRY and state
Abundance, threat or promise? R. Theobald. Nation 196:387-412 My 11 '63; Discussion. 196:inside cover Je 15 '63
Aerospace firms chafe at government control. Miss & Roc 12:21 Je 10 '63
Aerospace leaders to continue in Senate. G. C. Wilson. Aviation W 81:26 S 21 '64
Argentina: inflation in the midst of a recession. il Bsns W p54 My 2 '64
As business leaders size up Lyndon Johnson. U S News 56:84-5 My 18 '64
Banish your fears; President Johnson's plea to businessmen. il Time 82:87 D 13 '63
Banker's warning to businessmen; excerpts from address, March 26, 1964. E. P. Neilan. U S News 56:20 Ap 6 '64
Barrage of verbal flak. Fortune 69:98 Mr '64
Big business; is it too big? reprint. H. H. Humphrey. il Look 28:84-6 O 20 '64
Britain: if labor wins. il Fortune 69:51-2+ Je '64
Britain's crisis in efficiency. il Bsns W p82-4 D 26 '64
Budget cuts and the AEC. Bul Atomic Sci 20:39-40 Mr '64
Business and government: cold war should end, Du Pont head says; excerpts from address, February 10, 1964. L. D. Copeland. U S News 56:16 F 24 '64
Business and government; symposium. il Nations Bsns 53:32-41+ Ja '65
Business and Johnson savor a love feast. il Bsns W p28-9 Ja 18 '64
Business pledges its support. il Bsns W p32+ N 30 '63
Business' responsibility in government relationships; address, November 10, 1964. N. H. McElroy. Vital Speeches 31:139-40 D 15 '64
Businessmen's latest worry: the Kennedy labor board. il U S News 54:96+ Ap 8 '63

INDUSTRY and state—*Continued*
California: aerospace industry has meant a second gold rush; climate and education get credit. J. Walsh. Science 143:1151-3 Mr 13 '64
Carriers may protest SST delivery policy. L. L. Doty. Aviation W 79:43 N 4 '63
Changes coming in business controls? il U S News 55:59 D 16 '63
Coming: new look at business regulation. Nations Bsns 51:102-3+ S '63
COMSAT: private satellite firm working out ties with government; basic decisions are still open. E. Langer. il Science 142:1558-60 D 20 '63
Congress considers impact of defense reductions. B. G. Lall. Bul Atomic Sci 20:31-2 F '64
Costly chaos in cotton, time to end it! R. S. Strother. Read Digest 82:149-50+ Je '63
Crisis in antitrust. R. H. Bork and W. S. Bowman, jr. Fortune 68:138-40+ D '63
DOD seeking industry comments on component supply proposal. P. J. Klass. Aviation W 81:22 D 21 '64
DOD to brief firms on long-range plans. Aviation W 80:37 Ja 27 '64
Does automation require a new economy? interview, ed. by T. R. Brooks. J. I. Snyder, jr. Duns R 83:51-2+ F '64
Dream businessmen are losing. Fortune 68: 91-2 S '63
Drug politics: industry seeks Court of appeals to challenge FDA rulings on drug safety. E. Langer. Science 145:139-41 Jl 10 '64; Reply. I. S. Ravdin. 146:12 O 2 '64
Economic planning, European-style. W. P. Blass. bibliog f il Harvard Bsns R 41:109-20 S '63
Ending another cold war. L. L. L. Golden. Sat R 48:73-4 Ja 9 '65
FCC Comsat contract role questioned. P. J. Klass. Aviation W 79:33 Ag 19 '63
FCC procurement restrictions on Comsat corp. are protested. Aviation W 79:33 S 16 '63
FDA gets tough. Bsns W p 19 Jl 4 '64
For a guaranteed income. M. D. Reagan. il N Y Times Mag p20+ Je 7 '64
From business, a contented purr. il Bsns W p23-5 Ap 4 '64
Future of non-profit groups under cloud; facing increased competition and Defense dept. restrictions. K. Johnsen. Aviation W 81: 16-17 D 21 '64
Government and business: the vital balance. T. V. Houser. il Sat R 47:27-9 Ja 11 '64
Government buying erodes management. P. F. Hannah. bibliog f Harvard Bsns R 42:53-62 My '64
Government, labor and management; address, December 3, 1962. J. L. Block. Vital Speeches 29:250-4 F 1 '63
Government puts growth policies on trial. il Nations Bsns 51:31-3+ F '63
Growing issue: high cost of justice; with case history. Nations Bsns 51:78-80+ My '63
Here's way to make more jobs; interview. H. R. Northrup. il Nations Bsns 52:36-7+ Mr '64
History lesson. W. J. Coughlin. Miss & Roc 15:46 O 26 '64
How much ground can arbitrators cover? Bsns W p52+ O 26 '63
How to play unpolitics. W. J. Coughlin. Miss & Roc 15:50 O 5 '64
Ike on government in business; excerpts from address, December 9, 1964. D. D. Eisenhower. U S News 57:61 D 21 '64
In defense of antitrust. H. M. Blake and W. K. Jones. Fortune 70:135+ Ag '64
Industry comment shows poor rapport. Miss & Roc 14:43-4 Mr 30 '64
Industry guide to DOD decision-makers. il Miss & Roc 12:73-121 Mr 25 '63
Intense interest forces defense to shift industry briefing plans. Aviation W 80:28 Ap 27 '64
Issues as business sees them; symposium. il Nations Bsns 52:84-6 Ap '64
It's a boom, but nobody has fun. il Bsns W p23-4 N 16 '63
Johnson's economics; quotations from statements on major economic issues. L. B. Johnson. il Bsns W p47-8+ O 31 '64
King Cotton loses big one in New Orleans; victim to federal policies. il Bsns W p28-9 Jl 18 '64
Lyndon Johnson's open secret. Fortune 69: 93-4 Je '64
Man to see on business issues. Bsns W p50+ Jl 13 '63
Management or mediocrity? W. J. Coughlin. Miss & Roc 12:54 Ap 15 '63; Reply. C. K. Simon. 12:7 Ap 29 '63
Merry-go-round. W. J. Coughlin. Miss & Roc 16:46 Ja 18 '65
Nation and world face sweeping changes; study of Technical military planning operation. il Nations Bsns 52:23-5+ Ja '64
NLRB's new, rough line. M. R. Lefkoe. il Fortune 68:164-6+ N '63
New actions will ease government competition. il Nations Bsns 52:108-9+ S '64
New crackdown on business? il U S News 56: 39:41 My 25 '64
New merry-go-round; excerpts from address. J. T. Ramey. Aviation W 82:11 Ja 11 '65
News lines. See issues of U.S. news & World report
Olive branch for business. Bsns W p204 My 18 '63
Paradox in government-industry relations: peace at top, strife at bottom; address, June 5, 1964. B. C. Goss. Vital Speeches 30:555-8 Jl 1 '64
Pesticides: minute quantities linked with massive fish kills; federal policy still uncertain. E. Langer. Science 144:35-7 Ap 3 '64; Discussion. 144:1294 Je 12 '64
Political test faced by aviation ministry in fall election. Aviation W 81:138-9+ S 7 '64
Politics and procurement. W. J. Coughlin. Miss & Roc 12:58 Mr 4 '63; Reply. J. E. Karth. 12:8 Mr 25 '63
Politics and technology. E. T. Chase. Yale R 52:321-39 Mr '63
President's business. America 108:633 My 4 '63
Prosperity gap. S. M. Linowitz. Sat R 48: 42 Ja 9 '65
Relationship. W. J. Coughlin. Miss & Roc 13:46 Jl 8 '63
Requirements merry-go-round; excerpts from remarks. J. T. Ramey. Aviation W 80:21 My 18 '64
Revolt against Santa Claus? Duns R 82:29 S '63
Revolution: changes in U.S. military policy and military organization. W. J. Coughlin. Miss & Roc 14:148 Mr 30; 54 Ap 6; 46 Ap 13 '64
SEC vs. Wall Street. R. A. Phalon. il Duns R 81:56-7+ Ap '63
Self-help is the answer. Duns R 83:39 My '64
Shifting winds. R. Hotz. Aviation W 79:21 S 16 '63
Showcase for U.S. exports. il Fortune 69:67-8 Mr '64
Space technology: pay-off from spin-off. J. G. Welles and R. H. Waterman, jr. bibliog f il Harvard Bsns R 42:106-18 Jl '64
State of the Union. W. J. Coughlin. Miss & Roc 13:46 Jl 22 '63; Discussion. 13:7 Ag 12 '63
Supersonic pace. R. Hotz. Aviation W 80:21 Ap 13 '64
Tax plan: business gives it a sour reception; Kennedy's tax cut proposals. il Bsns W p26-7 F 2 '63
TV commercials; the government ducks the issue. D. Smith. Nation 198:286-9 Mr 23 '64
There oughtn't to be a law; deterioration of American self-reliance; address, October 24, 1963. B. C. Goss. Vital Speeches 30: 81-4 N 15 '63
This proposal shortchanges your customers; federal credit control plan. il Nations Bsns 51:98-102 Mr '63
Tobacco: administration showing little enthusiasm for follow-up on Public health service report. D. S. Greenberg. Science 143:1417-19 Mr 27 '64
Triumph of conservatism, by G. Kolko. Review
Nation 198:398-400 Ap 20 '64. J. Weinstein
U.S. goals require new federal policy; symposium. il Nations Bsns 51:32-3+ Ag '63
War on business. R. Moley. Newsweek 64:84 Jl 20 '64
Washington desk. J. R. Slevin. See issues of Dun's review and modern industry
Washington; who's got the action? C. Levy. il Duns R 81:pt2 S137-8+ Je '63
Watch on prices; steel industry. Newsweek 62:81 N 4 '63
What business can do for America. J. F. Kennedy. Nations Bsns 51:29-31+ S '63
What government can and can't do. il Nations Bsns 51:34-5+ Je '63
What the hell do those fellows want? Fortune 67:81-2 F '63; Same abr. with title What those fellows want. Read Digest 82:86-8 Ap '63
What's needed for greater growth; views of key men. Nations Bsns 52:64-6 Jl '64

INDUSTRY and state—*Continued*
What's needed to boost sales abroad; symposium. il Nations Bsns 52:62-4+ Ja '64
Why businessmen keep a worried eye on Washington. il U S News 54:55-7 Ap 1 '63
You can't win; overdose of regulation. Newsweek 63:88+ My 18 '64
Your partner; the federal government; address, September 25, 1963. C. R. Sligh, jr. Vital Speeches 30:51-4 N 1 '63
See also
Economic planning
Free enterprise
Gas industry—Regulation
Industrial research—Federal aid
Labor laws and legislation
Price regulation by government
Public utilities—Regulation
Railroads and state
Stock exchange—Regulation
Strikes—United States—Government intervention
Trusts, Industrial
United States—Federal power commission
United States—Federal trade commission
United States—Interstate commerce commission
United States—Labor policy

INEFFICIENCY. See Efficiency, Industrial

INEQUALITY. See Equality

INERTIAL guidance systems
Airline use of inertial navigation seen. P. J. Klass. Aviation W 79:51+ N 11 '63
Apollo optical-inertial guidance detailed. P. J. Klass. il Aviation W 79:32-3 S 30 '63
Inertial system uses electrostatic gyros. P. J. Klass. il Aviation W 79:87-9 S 30 '63
Inertial systems favored as SST navaid. P. J. Klass. Aviation W 80:27-8 Je 22 '64
Litton expedites low-cost inertial aid. B. Miller. il Aviation W 81:62+ D 7 '64
Navy standardizes Polaris SINS system. Aviation W 80:16 My 4 '64
Pan Am 707s to have inertial guidance. Aviation W 81:30-1 Jl 27 '64
Perkin-Elmer theodolite system for Saturn tested at Cape Canaveral. M. Getler. il Miss & Roc 13:62+ S 30 '63
707 navaid stresses maintenance ease. P. J. Klass. il Aviation W 81:45-6+ S 28 '64
Squeeze-film technique suspends inertial gyros, accelerometers. Aviation W 81:48 N 2 '64
Suspended-particle inertial gyro appears feasible in early tests. il Aviation W 81:67 Jl 13 '64
USAF effort seeking simple inertial navaid. Aviation W 79:42 N 11 '63
Use foreseen for surplus Minutemen. Miss & Roc 16:34 Ja 25 '65
Wernher Von Braun answers your questions on inertial guidance. W. Von Braun. il Pop Sci 182:18+ Ap '63
X-20A guidance system completes flight-testing series. C. D. LaFond. il Miss & Roc 13:16-18 Ag 19 '63
See also
Guided missiles—Control

INEZ, Colette
Cold waltzes; poem. Nation 197:354 N 23 '63
Shah of the tundra; poem. Nation 198:123 F 3 '64

INFALLIBILITY. See Catholic church—Infallibility

INFALLIBILITY, Papal. See Popes—Infallibility

INFANCY of animals. See Animals, Infancy of

INFANT baptism. See Baptism

INFANT feeding. See Infants—Nutrition

INFANT mortality
Anguish of a couple whose six babies have died one after another. M. H. Cadwalader. Life 55:8+ Jl 12 '63
Infant mortality. Sci Am 209:59 O '63
Infant mortality: no change; U.S. death rate. Time 82:48 S 6 '63
Sudden death syndrome; crib deaths. il Time 82:88 O 4 '63
Sudden-death syndrome; report on conference. E. P. Benditt and R. J. Wedgwood. Science 143:156-8 Ja 10 '64
U.S. infant mortality decreasing very slowly. Sci N L 84:150 S 7 '63
We could save 40,000 babies a year. L. Engel. il N Y Times Mag p31+ N 17 '63
Why babies die; mystery of crib deaths. V. Cadden. il Redbook 122:58-9+ N '63
Why do we let these babies die? ed. by J. D. Ratcliff. D. D. Rutstein. Read Digest 85:56-60 Ag '64
See also
Obstetrics

INFANT psychology. See Child study

INFANTE, Anthony A. and others
Adenosine triphosphate: changes in muscles doing negative work. bibliog Science 144: 1577-8 Je 26 '64

INFANTILE paralysis. See Poliomyelitis

INFANTILE paralysis virus. See Poliomyelitis virus

INFANTS
And baby makes three. C. Riker and A. Riker. il Parents Mag 39:52-3+ Mr '64
See also
Adoption

Accidents

See Accidents

Breathing

See Respiration

Care and hygiene

Box-bred babies. il Time 81:72 F 15 '63
Danger in the nursery. Time 82:67 Jl 5 '63
Doctor Spock talks with mothers. B. Spock. See issues of Ladies' home journal to September 1963
Don't fight the baby. J. Winchester. il Parents Mag 38:38-9+ Jl '63
Healthy children need doctors, too. M. A. Wessel. il Parents Mag 38:70-1+ O '63
How to care for a sick baby. E. Sunley. il Parents Mag 38:76-7+ O '63
Parents forget early experiences with baby. Sci N L 83:249 Ap 20 '63
Planning nurseries for newborn in the general hospital. il Arch Rec 133:179-82 Mr '63
Plight of the brand new parent. F. Bauer. il N Y Times Mag p 152 Ap 7 '63
Raising two under two. D. Sokolow. il Parents Mag 40:50-1+ Ja '65
Report on the testing of advertised products; Mennen's baby products. E. M. McCabe. il Parents Mag 38:24+ Mr '63
Short cuts in baby care. M. A. Gillmor. il Parents Mag 39:36-7+ Ag '64
Simple ways to keep children cool. il Good H 157:128-9 Jl '63
Toilet training. B. Spock. il Ladies Home J 80:48+ My '63
Toilet training. B. Spock. Redbook 122:38+ N '63
Treating diaper area irritation. E. M. McCabe. il Parents Mag 39:12+ Je '64
Tub fun for two. B. H. Patterson. il Parents Mag 38:50-1+ My '63
When baby is ill. A. Bullock. Parents Mag 39:154-5 S '64
See also
Children—Care and hygiene

Crying

Why babies cry; ed. by W. J. Schwartz. E. J. Schwartz. il Todays Health 41:26-8 S '63
Why some babies cry so much. T. B. Brazelton. il Parents Mag 39:56-7+ Ap '64

Food

See Infants—Nutrition

Growth and development

Beginning of love. M. B. Hoover. il Redbook 120:15 Ap '63
Bottle, blanket and thumb; comfort or bad habit? B. Spock. il Redbook 122:26+ F '64
Getting to know your baby. G. Hechinger. il Parents Mag 39:36-7+ Jl '64
How speech grows; with study-discussion program, by R. Strang. M. M. Lewis. bibliog il PTA Mag 59:8-10, 35 N '64
Is your baby a sparkler? M. A. Wessel and N. Simon. il Parents Mag 38:68-9+ F '63
Life and times with a two-year-old. S. H. Fraiberg. il Parents Mag 38:54-5+ D '63
Magic of mothering. M. Smart. Parents Mag 40:35+ Ja '65
No more bedtime battles. M. Bernath. il Parents Mag 39:54-5+ Je '64
One year old and rarin' to go. J. L. Hymes, jr. and T. Taylor. il Parents Mag 39:68-9 Ap '64
Portrait of a two-year-old. D. Q. Phillips. Parents Mag 38:90 Jl '63
Safety on all fours. E. Sunley. il Parents Mag 39:46-7+ O '64
Why some babies become too attached to their bottles. B. Spock. Ladies Home J 80:21 S '63
Your baby doesn't need a clock. E. Sunley. il Parents Mag 38:52-3+ Mr '63
Your baby is a high achiever. M. Bernath. il Parents Mag 39:64-5+ F '64
Your baby's five senses and how they develop. R. N. Smith. il Parents Mag 38:64-5+ S '63

INFANTS—*Continued*

Identification

How hospitals prevent baby mix-ups. il Good H 156:153 F '63

Language

See Children—Language

Management and training

See Children—Management and training

Nutrition

Baby's new bottle; Beniflex infant-feeding system. il Time 81:52 Je 7 '63
Breast or bottle? G. Baker. Redbook 121:28 Ag '63
Difficulties in breast feeding. B. Spock. il Redbook 123:16+ Je '64
Food, the good medicine. Sci N L 83:114 F 23 '63
How to succeed as a nursing mother. M. Birchfield. il Parents Mag 39:40-1+ My '64
On being a woman. J. Brothers. Good H 158: 32-3 F '64
Packaged baby formulas could prove dangerous. Sci N L 86:296 N 7 '64
They teach the joys of breast-feeding; excerpt from Nursing your baby. K. Pryor. Read Digest 82:103-6 My '63
Why some babies become too attached to their bottles. B. Spock. Ladies Home J 80: 31 S '63
Why women may fail in breast feeding. il Good H 157:140 Ag '63
Whys and why nots of breast feeding. B. Spock. il Ladies Home J 80:22+ Jl '63
Your baby doesn't need a clock. E. Sunley. il Parents Mag 38:52-3+ Mr '63

INFANTS, Deformed. See Deformities

INFANTS, Newborn
Baby's first four days scientifically important. Sci N L 84:88 Ag 10 '63
Bilirubin: acute effects in newborn rhesus monkeys. R. E. Behrman and E. Hibbard. bibliog il Science 144:545-6 My 1 '64
Boys weaker than girls. Sci N L 84:223 O 5 '63
First breath. C. A. Smith. il Sci Am 209:27-35 O '63
Is your baby a sparkler? M. A. Wessel, and N. Simon. il Parents Mag 38:68-9+ F '63
Newborn attention as affected by medication during labor. G. Stechler. bibliog il Science 144:315-17 Ap 17 '64
Pattern vision in newborn infants. R. L. Fantz. bibliog il Science 140:296-7 Ap 19 '63

INFANTS, Photography of. See Photography of children

INFANTS, Premature
Be home soon, doctor. S. M. Spencer. il Ladies Home J 80:72-3 D '63
Help for preemies. il Newsweek 63:54 Ja 13 '64
How medical progress has hastened the passing of the side show. J. Lentz. il Todays Health 42:48-51 Mr '64
Miniature maharajahs in the Taj Mahal; new unit at Palo Alto-Stanford hospital center. il Time 82:48 Jl 19 '63
Protecting the preemie. R. Holter. il Parents Mag 38:46-7+ Ap '63
Respiratory distress: relation to prematurity and other factors in newborn monkeys. W. F. Windle. bibliog il Science 143:1345-6 Mr 20 '64
Time of tragedy for the Kennedys; Baby specialist explains the fatal illness; hyaline membrane disease. il U S News 55:8 Ag 19 '63
Tiny G suits advised for premature infants. Sci N L 85:201 Mr 28 '64
We could save 40,000 babies a year. L. Engel. il N Y Times Mag p31+ N 17 '63
Whys of caesareans; Patrick Bouvier Kennedy's death. il Newsweek 62:50+ Ag 19 '63

INFANTS, Stillborn. See Stillbirth

INFANTS, Travel with. See Travel with children

INFECTION
Bowery blood. Time 81:78 Ap 19 '63
How to reduce infection risks in your home. Good H 156:137-9 Mr '63
Preventing infection. C. J. Potthoff. Todays Health 42:52 Jl '64
Schistosoma mansoni: development of challenge infections in mice exposed to irradiated cercariae. A. P. Szumlewicz and L. J. Olivier. bibliog il Science 140:411-12 Ap 26 '63

INFECTIOUS diseases. See Communicable diseases

INFERTILITY. See Sterility

INFIELD, Glenn
Flying flip. Esquire 61:84+ Je '64

INFINITY of mirrors; story. See Condon, R.

INFLAMMATION
Citrus flavonoid complex: chemical fractionation and biological activity. L. Freedman and A. J. Merritt. bibliog il Science 139:344-5 Ja 25 '63

INFLATED structures. See Domes

INFLATION (finance)
Accounting for inflation; accounts of Latin American subsidiaries. J. Thackray. il Duns R 84:39-40+ D '64
Big rise hits down under. il Bsns W p92-3+ D 21 '63
Brazil: anti-inflation plans collapse. il Bsns W p80 Ag 3 '63
Brazil: land of massive problems. R. H. Bolton. Christian Cent 81:1235-9 O 7 '64
Choice for Chile: which way to go left? democratic left or Marxist. il Bsns W p48+ Ag 8 '64
Country where inflation is the way of life; Brazil. D. B. Richardson. U S News 55: 67-9 Ag 12 '63
Creeping inflation: how bad? what's happened since 1948. il U S News 57:96-7 S 14 '64
Danger signs appear in Europe's boom. il U S News 57:64-6 Ag 3 '64
DeGaulle's war against inflation. il Bsns W p62+ S 21 '63
Europe: inflation danger signals. il Fortune 69:59-60+ My '64
Fed's dilemma. il Fortune 69:27-8 Ap '64
France: rigid controls keep the lid on inflation. Bsns W p 124 Jl 11 '64
Germany's inflated currency following World war 1. C. French. Hobbies 68:102 F '64
Halt to cuts but no inflation; with charts. Bsns W p26-7 O 26 '63
How new is inflation? H. Hazlitt. Newsweek 64:90 O 19 '64
How to beat inflation. H. Hazlitt. Newsweek 64:82 S 28 '64
How we hope Europe foils inflation. il Bsns W p82-3 F 15 '64
If creeping inflation begins to run; ways of controlling inflation. H. C. Wallich. il N Y Times Mag p34+ S 13 '64
Inflation, danger ahead? G. L. Bach. il Harvard Bsns R 42:49-61 Jl '64
Inflation in Europe. H. Hazlitt. il Newsweek 63:98 My 18 '64
Inflation: more money, less value; negotiations between UAW and auto industry. Sr Schol 85:18 O 14 '64
Inflation spiral over the Continent; eleventh annual monetary conference. il Newsweek 63:59-61 Je 1 '64
Inflation vs. growth. H. Hazlitt. Newsweek 63:80 My 4 '64
Les inflations sud-americaines, by D. Lambert. Review
Américas 15:39-41 F '63. D. Lambert
Is inflation actually on the way back? il U S News 57:68-9 N 2 '64
Is inflation on the way? a look ahead. il U S News 55:25-8 D 23 '63
Is inflation on the way back? il U S News 54:50-4 My 6 '63
Look at the force behind Europe's boom. il U S News 54:79-80 Ap 1 '63
No tightening up, yet; with editorial comment. il Bsns W p33-4, 200 S 26 '64
Outlook report: business future for U.S. and Europe. il U S News 56:88-90 Ap 13 '64
Problems ahead. H. Hazlitt. Newsweek 64: 81 N 16 '64
Relationship of sound money to freedom; address, April 8, 1964. K. Brandt. Vital Speeches 30:623-8 Ag 1 '64
Seven forces will block inflation. J. Backman. il Nations Bsns 52:38-9+ Ap '64
Spending pressures raise inflation danger. il Nations Bsns 52:30-1+ Ja '64
There's nothing under the bed now. Bsns W p 148 My 4 '63
UAW breaches the bargaining guidelines. T. R. Brooks. Duns R 84:45 D '64
Washington desk. J. R. Selvin. Duns R 83:5-6 Ap '64
Watch on prices; wage-price inflation. Bsns W p 19-20 F 1 '64
When inflation runs wild; Brazil's problems. C. T. Stewart, jr. il Nations Bsns 53:78-82 Ja '65
When inflation sours. H. Hazlitt. Newsweek 63:84 Je 15 '64
Where inflation fails to boost stocks. il Bsns W p 150+ Ap 11 '64
With inflation talk in the air, borrowing still will be easy. U S News 57:115-17 S 28 '64

INFLATION (finance)—*Continued*
World of inflation. H. Hazlitt. Newsweek 63:67 Mr 30 '64
Worldwide inflation: what it means to U.S. il U S News 55:58-60 O 28 '63
Worry shifts to Europe; with editorial comment. il Bsns W p81-2, 156 Je 27 '64
See also
Currency question

INFLIGHT motion pictures, incorporated
Coffee, tea or Doris Day; introduction of inflight entertainment. il Time 84:103-4 O 16 '64
High see; movies in the air. il Time 84:87 Jl 10 '64

INFLUENCE of altitude. See Altitude, Influence of

INFLUENCE of literature. See Literature, Influence of

INFLUENCE of music. See Music, Influence of

INFLUENZA
Asian flu epidemic hits U.S. Sr Schol 82:15-16 F 27 '63
Complex epidemiology of respiratory virus infections. C. H. Andrewes. bibliog Science 146:1274-7 D 4 '64
Flu & paraflu. il Time 81:72 F 22 '63
Flu epidemic spreads, but end is in sight. U S News 54:6 F 25 '63
Flu spreads death. il Bsns W p29 Mr 2 '63
Flu, the underestimated enemy. D. Murray. Read Digest 86:95-8 Ja '65
Protected from Asian flu. F. Marley. Sci N L 83:94 F 9 '63
What flu in. il Newsweek 61:58 F 25 '63
What's the truth about those flu shots? W. B. Furlong. Good H 158:73+ Ap '64
Winter enemy no. 1; the flu. M. J. E. Senn. il McCalls 91:84+ N '63

Vaccines

Antiviral activity of 1-adamantanamine (amantadine) W. L. Davies and others. il Science 144:862-3 My 15 '64
Flu needle; verdict delivered at annual meeting of the American public health association. il Newsweek 62:72 N 25 '63
Flu shots still approved. Sci N L 84:366 D 7 '63
Flu vaccine kept current. Sci N L 86:244 O 17 '64
No malformation from flu. Sci N L 83:66 F 2 '63
what's the truth about those flu shots? W. B. Furlong. Good H 158:73+ Ap '64

INFLUENZA, Swine. See Swine—Diseases and pests

INFLUENZA virus
Endogenous pyrogen release from rabbit blood cells incubated in vitro with parainfluenza virus. E. Atkins and others. bibliog il Science 146:1469-70 D 11 '64
Great Asian flu mystery. B. Davidson. il Sat Eve Post 236:58 Ap 27 '63
Human influenza A viruses: rapid plaque assay in hamster kidney cells. S. E. Grossberg. bibliog il Science 144:1246-7 Je 5 '64
Inside the cell. il Newsweek 63:96 Ap 27 '64
Neuraminidases and influenza virus infection in embryonated eggs. C. A. Johnson and others. bibliog il Science 143:1051-2 Mr 6 '64
Physical interaction of a murine leukemia virus with influenza virus in vitro. T. E. O'Connor and F. J. Rauscher. bibliog il Science 146:787-90 N 6 '64

INFORMATION. See Knowledge

INFORMATION, Freedom of
Foreign policy and the people's right to know; address, May 5, 1964. R. J. Manning. Dept State Bul 50:868-77 Je 1 '64
Freedom of information; a place in the church today? É. Gabel. America 109:133-5 Ag 10 '63
See also
Free speech
Freedom of the press
Government and the press
Security classification (government documents)

INFORMATION, Technical. See Technical information

INFORMATION agency (United States) See United States—Information agency

INFORMATION leaflets. See American education week

INFORMATION service, Public affairs. See Public affairs information service

INFORMATION services
Information explosion, real or imaginary? national system of handling scientific and technical information. J. C. Green. Science 144:646-8 My 8 '64
Information, please; Parisian telephone-answering service SVP. Newsweek 64:78+ Jl 20 '64
There's a source of information about every state in the union. il Pop Phot 54:138-9 Ap '64
Where to get free help in planning a trip. Good H 156:144-5 Mr '63
See also
Documentation
Successful farming (periodical)

INFORMATION storage and retrieval systems
A.I.A. aids information retrieval quest. Arch Rec 134:10 O '63
Automatic information processing in western Europe. G. Salton. bibliog Science 144:626-32 My 8 '64
Can management information be automated? J. Dearden. Harvard Bsns R 42:128-35 Mr '64
Centralizing storage and retrieval not recommended by recent report; study for the Office of science information services by Arthur D. Little, inc. Library J 88:3816 O 15 '63
Chemist looks at information retrieval. B. Phillips. Library J 88:964-6 Mr 1 '63
Copyright implications in the new science of data storage and retrieval; conference sponsored by copyright committee of the American textbook publishers institute. Pub W 186:20-3 N 30 '64
Copyrighting writing on the wall. D. Dempsey. Sat R 47:39-40 S 19 '64
CLR annual report notes computer's cultivated language; excerpts from introduction. V. W. Clapp. Library J 89:82 Ja 1 '64
CLR finances two projects in automation and information storage. Library J 88:2860 Ag '63
Council on library resources: three grants. Wilson Lib Bul 38:31 S '63
Documentation pitt. A. Kent. Library J 89:206, 818+, 1202-3, 2046-7, Ja 15, F 15, Mr 15, My 15 '64
Ethics of scientific publication. D. J. de S. Price. bibliog Science 144:655-7 My 8 '64; Reply. G. R. Wendt. 145:110+ Jl 10 '64
False front; language of automatic data processing. J. Berry. Library J 89:2750 Jl '64
Information explosion, real or imaginary? national system of handling scientific and technical information. J. C. Green. Science 144:646-8 My 8 '64
Information retrieval. R. R. Shaw. bibliog Science 140:606-9 My 10 '63
Information retrieval at a book fair; Minneapolis public library. il Library J 88:962-3 Mr 1 '63
Information retrieval for students; with profile of Education centre library, Toronto. L. H. Freiser. il Library J 88:1121-3 Mr 15 '63; Discussion. 88:1566+, 1922+, 2372, 3251-3, 4412 Ap 15, My 15, Je 15, S 15, N 15 '63
Information retrieval in action; Center for documentation and communication research conference, school of library science, Western Reserve university. Wilson Lib Bul 37:837 Je '63
Information retrieval systems. J. A. Swets. bibliog il Science 141:245-50 Jl 19 '63
Information revolution. G. L. Haller. il Sci Digest 55:69-73 My '64
Information storage requirements for the contents of the world's libraries. J. W. Senders. bibliog il Science 141:1067-8 S 13 '63; Reply. Sci Am 209:72+ N '63
Information systems: learning, adaptation, and control; report of Computer and information science symposium. J. T. Tou. Science 141:1070+ S 13 '63
Information transfer and retrieval. P. H. Abelson. Science 141:319 Jl 26 '63
Inverted indexing on edge-notched cards. J. G. Roney, jr. bibliog Science 142:227-8 O 11 '63
Magnetic core memories. R. B. Rusch. il Electr World 71:37-9 Ap '64
Medical libraries are in trouble; address, October 1962. S. Adams. bibliog il Library J 88:2615-21 Jl '63
MEDLARS project. J. Becker. il ALA Bul 58:227-30 Mr '64
O! medium, O! media; reflections on work-study conference on the Implications of the new media for the teaching of library science. J. H. Shera. Library J 88:4149-51 N 1 '63
Preparing for IR. R. E. Steere, jr. il Duns R 82:pt2 107-9+ S '63
Science citation index, a new dimension in indexing. E. Garfield. bibliog Science 144:649-54 My 8 '64
Second Rutgers seminar presents SYNTOL: discussion. Library J 89:214 Ja 15 '64

INFORMATION storage and retrieval systems —*Continued*
Special librarian: his future; bright or bleak? address, June 1964. A. M. Rees. bibliog il Library J 89:4288-94 N 1 '64
There's money in memory. il Duns R 82:pt2 110-13+ S '63
UDC dissected and discussed at first of Rutgers' seminars: Systems for the organization of information report. T. C. Hines. Library J 88:4592-4 D 1 '63
What is MEDLARS? Medical literature analysis and retrieval system. H. Schiller. il Library J 88:949-53 Mr 1 '63
Who really started World war 1? W. S. Bacon. il Pop Electr 20:40-2+ Ap '64; Same abr. with title Computer tells who started World war 1. Sci Digest 56:44-7 Jl '64
See also
Data tapes
Electronic data processing
Libraries—Automation
Microfilms
Programmng (calculating machines)
Programming languages (calculating machines)
School libraries—Automation

Anecdotes, facetiae, satire, etc.

It's right here somewhere. R. L. Dean. America 108:404-5 Mr 23 '63
Ms. found in a bottle. G. Dui. Wilson Lib Bul 38:401-3 Ja '64

INFORMATION system sciences, Congress on the. See Congress on the information system sciences

INFORMATION systems, Management
Chart room, new style; complex briefing centers. il Bsns W p 150-2 N 2 '63
Millennium for decision makers. il Bsns W p54+ Ag 10 '63

INFORMATION tests
Air your knowledge; questions and answers. J. Daugherty and M. Daugherty. il Sci Digest 55:45-7 Ja '64
Are you a cave man? questions and answers. J. Daugherty and M. Daugherty. il Sci Digest 54:5-7 D '63
Big drip; questions and answers. J. Daugherty and M. Daugherty. il Sci Digest 55:45-7 F '64
Changing times quiz (cont) Changing T 17: 48 Ap; 48 Ag; 48 D '63; 18:48 Ap; 48 Ag; 48 D '64
Chemistry in the raw; questions and answers. J. Daugherty and M. Daugherty. il Sci Digest 56:76-8 S '64
Colorful quiz. J. Daugherty and M. Daugherty. il Sci Digest 55:43-5 My '64
Contemporary affairs test. il Sr Schol 85:25-6 S 16 '64
Do you know your NEA? M. S. Fenner. NEA J 53:84 O '64
Electromagnetic function quiz. R. P. Balin. il Pop Electr 20:65+ Je '64
Family quiz game. D. K. Whyte. See issues of Parent's magazine & better homemaking
Gem of a quiz. J. Daugherty and M. Daugherty. il Sci Digest 54:25-7 N '63
Health quiz. G. Baker. Farm J 88:60J Mr '64
Hereditary quiz. J. Daugherty and M. Daugherty. il Sci Digest 56:89-91 N '64
Holiday quiz; sing a song of cities. A. A. Brown. Holiday 34:117 S '63
Hot and cold quiz. J. Daugherty and M. Daugherty. il Sci Digest 57:83-5 Ja '65
How's your gamebird savvy? quiz. D. Du Bois. Outdoor Life 134:38-9 Jl '64
Instant deer hunt; questions and answers. D. Du Bois. il Outdoor Life 134:62-4 S '64
Keep your mind alive. il Changing T 18:15-18 F '64
Know your fibers and fabrics; questions and answers. J. Daugherty and M. Daugherty. il Sci Digest 56:27-9 O '64
Quiz for April 1. J. Klein. il Read Digest 84: 204F+ Ap '64
Restful quiz. J. Daugherty and M. Daugherty. il Sci Digest 55:5-7 Mr '64
Senior scholastic end-term review test (cont) il Sr Schol 82:25-6 My 15 '63; 83:19-20 Ja 10; 84-25-6 My 8 '64; 85:19-20 Ja 14 '65
Test your citizenship. Read Digest 82:29 F '63
Test your political beliefs. C. E. Johnson and J. S. Davis. Nations Bsns 52:34-5+ S '64
Thanks for the memory; news in 1963. il Good H 158:64-5+ Ja '64
Touching quiz. J. Daugherty and M. Daugherty. Sci Digest 55:5-7 Je '64
Way out quiz. J. Daugherty and M. Daugherty. il Sci Digest 55:66-8 Ap '64
What do those food labels mean? questions and answers. J. Daughtery and M. Daughtery. Sci Digest 56:5-7 Ag '64
What's your quake I.Q? questions and answers. J. Daughtery and M. Daughtery. il Sci Digest 56:57-9 Jl '64
Whose confessions? Harper 226:72 My '63
Wood you know? questions and answers. J. Daugherty and M. Daugherty. il Sci Digest 56:93-5 D '64
Your literary I.Q; ed. by J. T. Winterich. See issues of Saturday review
See also
Vocabulary tests

INFORMATION theory
Man-machines may talk first to Dr Shannon. B. Brower. Vogue 141:88-9+ Ap 15 '63

INFORMATIONAL media guaranty program. See United States—Information agency

INFORMATIONAL picketing. See Picketing

INFORMERS (law)
Box 100; New York's address for informers' tips. M. Abramson. il N Y Times Mag p72+ S 15 '63
Clough in the clear; newsman's right to protect his source. Newsweek 61:56 F 11 '63
Fact & fancy; reporting the Vassall case. Time 81:62 F 8 '63
Flap lips; Sidney Slater. Newsweek 61:31 Ap 15 '63
Inside peeks; British newsmen's right to protect their sources. Newsweek 61:90 F 18 '63
Journalists' privilege? Pub W 183:53 Ap 29 '63

INFRARED heating. See Heating, Infrared

INFRARED rays
Black light for brilliant color. P. Farber. il U S Camera 27:38-9+ Ag; 28-9 O '64
Infrared emissivity of the Sahara from Tiros data. K. J. K. Buettner and C. D. Kern. bibliog Science 142:671-2 N 8 '63
Infrared radiation from the atmosphere over the Arctic Ocean. W. B. Murcray. bibliog il Science 141:802-4 Ag 30 '63
Use of infrared testing technique grows. P. J. Klass. il Aviation W 80:82+ My 4 '64
See also
Photography, Infrared

Astronomical applications

Lunar surface features: mid-infrared spectral observations. G. R. Hunt and J. W. Salisbury. bibliog il Science 146:641-2 O 30 '64

Industrial applications

Infrared; quick, new home cure for cracked asphalt. J. Joseph. il Pop Sci 182:168-70+ Ap '63

INFRARED sensors. See Aeronautic instruments

INFRARED thermography. See Photography, Infrared

INFRARED viewers. See Viewers, Infrared

INFRASTRUCTURE projects. See Semi-automatic ground environment system

INGALLS, Jeremy
First came Christmas; poem. Christian Cent 81:1584 D 23 '64

INGALLS, Theodore H. and others
Acquired chromosomal anomalies induced in mice by injection of a teratogen in pregnancy. bibliog Science 141:810-12 Ag 30 '63

INGATE, Margaret Rose
History in towns: Mobile, Alabama. Antiques 85:294-309 Mr '64

INGE, William
Natural affection. Criticism
Commonweal 77:598 Mr 1 '63
Nation 196:148 F 16 '63
New Repub 148:29 F 23 '63
New Yorker 38:66+ F 9 '63
Newsweek il 61:84 F 11 '63
Reporter 28:48-9 Ap 25 '63
Sat R 46:25 F 16 '63
Theatre Arts il 47:58-9 Mr '63
Time 81:56 F 8 '63

INGERMAN, Elizabeth A.
(ed) See Hagen, E. Personal experiences of an old New York cabinetmaker

INGERSOLL, John H.
Beauty of wood paneling. Pop Sci 184:118-34 Mr '64
Big light in a little package. Pop Sci 186:151 Ja '65
Blow the snow away. Pop Gard 14:10-11 N '63
Five point plan for fall. Pop Gard 15:32-5 N '64
Garden is full of a number of things. Pop Gard 15:36-9 Jl '64
How to buy a storm door without getting stuck. Pop Sci 185:148-51+ O '64
Now, carve with power. Pop Sci 185:148-9 D '64

INGERSOLL, John H.—*Continued*
Place for everything. Pop Gard 14:49-55 S '63
Plastics: the big idea in remodeling materials. Pop Sci 183:126-9+ S '63
INGERSOLL-Rand company
Blocking a merger in advance. Bsns W p92+ My 4 '63
INGLE, Dwight J.
Chicago story: after Negroes moved in, the trials of a community; excerpts from I went to see the elephant. por U S News 55: 96-7 S 16 '63
Racial differences and the future. bibliog Science 146:375-9, 1528-30; 147:6-7 O 16, D 18 '64, Ja 1 '65
INGLE, Harold. See Seltzer, L. jt. auth.
INGLESSIS, Emilios
(ed) See Maximos IV, Patriarch Maximos IV and Vatican council II
INGLESSIS, Eva
(ed) See Maximos IV, Patriarch Maximos IV and Vatican council II
INGLIS, Brian
Acupuncture. Vogue 143:134+ Je '64
Aspirin jungle. Nation 197:83-6 Ag 24; inside cover S 14 '63
INGLIS, David R.
Disarmament after Cuba. Bul Atomic Sci 19: 18-21 Ja; 29-30 Mr '63
Rest of the test ban. Bul Atomic Sci 19:39-40 D '63
Step-by-step disarmament. Cur Hist 47:88-92+ Ag '64
INGOTS, Aluminum. See Aluminum ingots
INGRAHAM, Leonard
Exhibits (NCSS) Sr Schol 85:7T Ja 7 '65
INGRAM, Ada A.
Conference in Oklahoma. por Wilson Lib Bul 39:323-4 D '64
INGRAM, R. L. and Carver, R. K.
Malaria parasites: fluorescent antibody technique for tissue stage study. bibliog Science 139:405-6 F 1 '63
INGRAM, Vernon M. See McLaughlin, C. S. jt. auth.
INGRAM, William T.
Role of the manager in industry; address, November 2, 1964. Vital Speeches 31:94-6 N 15 '64
INGRES, Jean Auguste Dominique
Jean Auguste Dominique Ingres, portrait of Madame Simard. C. B. Johnson. il Sch Arts 62:48 Je '63
INGSTAD, Helge
Vinland ruins prove Vikings found the New World. pors Nat Geog Mag 126:708-34 N '64
INHALATION (therapeutics)
Prevent common colds; experimental inhalant, viractin. F. Marley. Sci N L 86:355 D 5 '64
INHERITANCE
Live rich without money. D. Van Ark. il Good H 158:44+ My '64
$250,000 bonanza; Bushnell Dimond leaves his entire estate to a casual acquaintance. R. Lemon. il Sat Eve Post 237:70-1+ N 14 '64
See also
Estate planning
Wills
INHERITANCE tax
Tax outlook for inheritances. U S News 55: 103 S 9 '63
See also
Gifts—Taxation
INITIAL teaching alphabet. See Alphabet
INITIALISMS. See Acronyms
INJECTIONS
Lingual vein injection in the rat. J. M. Anderson. Science 140:195 Ap 12 '63
See also
Inoculation
INJECTORS, Fuel. See Fuel pumps
INJURIES. See Accidents; First aid in illness and injury; *also* subhead Wounds and injuries under names of organs and regions of the body, e.g. Brain—Wounds and injuries
INJURIES (law) See Personal injuries
INJURIES from sports. See Sports—Accidents and injuries
INK
Ink experiments. C. H. Taylor. il Sch Arts 64:29-30 S '64
INK brushwork. See Brush drawing
INK rubbings. See Rubbings
INLAND navigation
Blue-water cruise on Green Bay. F. M. Paulson. il Field & S 68:30-2+ Ag '63
Hudson River: cruising gateway. F. S. Blanchard. il Yachting 113:42-5+ Mr '63
Our footloose correspondents; cruising inland waterway aboard Coastal queen. A. Bailey. il New Yorker 40:141-2+ O 31 '64
There's a way to ride a river; conquering the wild, white Rogue. B. Goldrath. il Pop Mech 119:104-6 My '63
There's a way to ride a river; probing the Kobuk's Arctic wilderness. S. McCutcheon. il Pop Mech 119:107-9+ My '63
See also
Inland water transportation
River trips
Waterways
INLAND shipping. See Inland water transportation
INLAND water transportation
By barge, river transportation's confluence. Y. Catlin. Ann Am Acad 345:89-94 Ja '63
Flood tide for the barges. il Bsns W p48-51 Ag 1 '64
Inland shippers thirst for water; low levels curtailing waterway operations. il Bsns W p 132+ Ja 23 '65
See also
Ferries
INLAND waterway. See Intracostal Waterway
INLAND waterways. See Waterways
INLAY
Pique: a minor metal art. G. Kaler. il Hobbies 68:42+ Mr; 42-3+ Ap; 42-3+ My '63
INNER ear. See Labyrinth (ear)
INNES, Hammond
Eskimo north. Holiday 35:88-93+ Ap '64
Inn for all seasons. Holiday 36:60-5+ S '64
INNES, Michael
Death as a game. Esquire 63:55-6 Ja '65
Few words concerning this picture. Esquire 62:132-3 N '64
INNIS, Pauline
That Kodiak bear is at the backdoor. Audubon Mag 67:16-17 Ja '65
Wild swans risk crash landings for corn. Audubon Mag 66:304-5 S '64
INNOCENT; story. See Sandburg, H.
INNOCENTS; story. See Collier, Z.
INNOVATIONS, Technological. See Technological innovations
INNSBRUCK, Austria
Arena for heroes. il Sports Illus 20:30-1 Ja 27 '64
Austria: winter Olympics. V. Creed. il Travel 120:44-6 D '63
Our underdogs at Innsbruck; Winter Olympics. F. Graham, jr. il Sat Eve Post 237: 22-7 F 1 '64
Sauerkraut and caviar. F. R. Smith. il Sports Illus 19:58-62 N 25 '63
Winter Olympics; Innsbruck 1964. F. R. Smith. Sports Illus 19:52 Ag 12 '63
INOCULATION
Shots that save. P. M. Stimson. il Parents Mag 39:47+ N '64
When should you have booster shots? il Redbook 120:28 F '63
See also
Vaccination
INÖNÜ, Ismet
Just any government at all. por Time 82:35 D 13 '63
Our far-flung correspondents. C. Frankel. il New Yorker 40:136+ Je 6 '64
INOSITOL
Radioactive myoinositol: incorporation into streptomycin. H. Heding. bibliog il Science 143:953-4 F 28 '64
INOUE, Taro
Nasal salt gland: independence of salt and water transport. bibliog Science 142:1299 D 6 '63
INOUYE, Shugen
Shugen Inouye: potter. J. S. Eagle. il Craft Horiz 23:33-5+ N '63
INPUT-output analysis. See Linear programming
INPUT-output equipment. See Calculating machines—Input-output equipment
INRO. See Costume—Japan
INSALATA, S. John
Deceptive business practices; address, February 21, 1963. Vital Speeches 29:473-5 My 15 '63
INSANE
Legal status, laws, etc.
See Mental health laws
INSANE, Criminal and dangerous
I am a second Hitler; schizophrenic attacks children and teachers in Cologne school. Newsweek 63:42+ Je 22 '64
INSANITY
See also
Mental illness
Jurisprudence
Defendant Ruby will meet the ghost of a long dead Scot; M'Naghten rules. E. Havemann. il Life 56:30-1 F 21 '64

INSANITY—Jurisprudence—*Continued*
Law, liberty and psychiatry, by T. S. Szasz. Review
Commentary 37:78-80 Mr '64. G. P. Elliott
Nat R 16:201-3 Mr 10 '64. R. M. Schuchman
New Repub 150:24+ My 9 '64. J. S. Wright; Discussion. 150:28 My 30; 36-7 Je 27 '64
Nobody is hardly ever mad enough to be a madman. Sci Digest 54:57-8 Jl '63
Redefining insanity. Time 82:54 N 29 '63
See also
Forensic psychiatry

INSCRIPTION rock. See El Morro National Monument

INSCRIPTIONS
American antiquities. J. Ciardi. Sat R 47:14 Ja 4 '64
See also
Hieroglyphics

INSCRIPTIONS, Cuneiform. See Cuneiform inscriptions

INSCRIPTIONS, Minoan
Decipherment of Minoan. C. H. Gordon. il Natur Hist 72:22-31 N '63

INSCRIPTIONS, Sumerian. See Cuneiform inscriptions

INSECT allergy. See Allergy

INSECT baits and repellants
Chemical insect attractants. M. Jacobson and M. Beroza. bibliog il Science 140:1367-73 Je 28 '63; Discussion. 142:447-8; 143:526 O 25 '63, F 7 '64
Insect repellents that are effective. il Good H 157:123 Jl '63
Let's rout patio pests. il Pop Gard 15:54 My '64

INSECT bites and stings
August's deadly stings. il Life 55:57-8+ Ag 9 '63
Death in the back yard from bees and spiders. Sci N L 84:233 O 12 '63
Extract for the allergic; whole insect extract. F. Marley. Sci N L 83:277 My 4 '63
First aid; mosquito and chigger bites. C. J. Potthoff. Todays Health 42:68 Je '64

INSECT brain. See Brain

INSECT camouflage. See Mimicry (biology)

INSECT control. See Insects, Injurious and beneficial—Control

INSECT control by airplanes. See Airplanes in insect control

INSECT eggs. See Insects—Eggs

INSECT hormones. See Hormones

INSECT nests. See Nests

INSECT repellents. See Insect baits and repellents

INSECT sex attractants
Battle of the sexes; New Jersey pest control. Nat Parks Mag 38:18 S '64
Chemical insect attractants. M. Jacobson and M. Beroza. bibliog il Science 140:1367-73 Je 28 '63; Reply. A. L. Babson. 142:447-8 O 25 '63
Insect attractants. M. Jacobson and M. Beroza. il Sci Am 211:20-7 Ag '64
Isolation and identification of the sex attraction of the American cockroach. M. Jacobson and others; reply with rejoinder. D. R. A. Wharton and others. bibliog Science 142:1257-8+ D 6 '63
Olfactory receptor response to the cockroach sexual attractant. J. Boeckh and others. bibliog il Science 141:716 Ag 23 '63
Sex attractant of cabbage looper, trichoplusia ni (Hübner) C. M. Ignoffo and others. bibliog il Science 141:902-3 S 6 '63

INSECT-spraying machines. See Spraying and dusting apparatus

INSECT traps
Lights that trap insects. il Good H 156:167 My '63

INSECTICIDES
Birth of a garden chemical. B. C. Kilvert, jr. il Flower Grower 51:18-19 Ag '64
Chlorinated insecticides; fate in aqueous suspensions containing mosquito larvae. M. C. Bowman and others. bibliog il Science 146:1480-1 D 11 '64
Consumers are reading the labels on insecticides. Consumer Bul 46:32-3 Ag '63
Daily rhythm in the susceptibility of an insect to a toxic agent. C. L. Cole and P. L. Adkisson. bibliog il Science 144:1148-9 My 29 '64
Death scent for gypsies; carbaryl. il Time 84:55 Jl 17 '64
Household insecticides. il Consumer Rep 28:321-7 Jl '63
How we saved our shade: killing elm leaf beetles with Sevin; Colusa, Calif. J. Miller. il Am City 78:24 S '63
If you didn't have poison sprays. il U S News 54:74-5 Je 3 '63
Insect control calendar (cont) P. P. Pirone. Pop Gard 14:100-1 F; 58-9 Ap '63
Insecticides; how to use them safely. il Horticulture 41:212-13+ Ap '63
New way to treat with insecticide; misting. Farm J 88:58E N '64
New ways to kill flies; SIMAX, containing Ciodrin. il Farm J 87:54+ My '63
Nonhydrolytic pathway in metabolism of n-methylcarbamate insecticides. H. W. Dorough and others. bibliog Science 140:170-1 Ap 12 '63
Pesticides: facts, not fear. H. Earle. il Todays Health 41:18-23+ F '63
Proper use of home insecticides. il Consumer Rep 28:392-7 Ag '63
Rout pests and disease early. R. L. Hering. il Pop Gard 16:46-7 Ja '65
Systemics, are they the answer to garden pest control? P. P. Pirone. Horticulture 42:20+ Ag '64
We can save our elms; inoculating Bidrin insecticide. C. B. Hicks. il Pop Mech 121:122-5+ Ap '64
You can control soil insects in the winter. H. B. Petty. il Suc Farm 61:74-5+ F '63
Your household. il Consumer Rep 28:240-4 D '63
Your 1963-1964 guide to insect-free cornfields. Suc Farm 61:39 Ap '63; 62:16 Ap '64
See also
DDT (insecticide)
Endrin
Parathion
Pesticides
Thimet

Injurious effects

And was it a silent spring? Sheldon, Ill. C. B. Hicks. il Pop Mech 119:85-8+ Je '63
Chlorinated insecticides in the body fat of people in the United States. W. E. Dale and G. E. Quinby. bibliog il Science 142:593-5 N 1 '63
DDT and dieldrin in rivers: a report of the National water quality network. A. W. Breidenbach and J. J. Lichtenberg. bibliog il Science 141:899-901 S 6 '63; Reply with rejoinder. F. J. Wolf. 142:1020-1 N 22 '63
Damned if we do, damned if we dont! controversy over R. Carson's Silent spring. E. Fritz. Am For 69:34-5 F '63; Discussion. 69:2 Ap '63
Death in parts per trillion; endrin responsible for death of fish in Mississippi River. Sci Am 210:64 My '64
Fish deaths renew insecticide inquiries. Sci N L 85:242 Ap 18 '64
Great debate over pests and pesticides. L. Galton. il N Y Times Mag p34+ Ap 14 '63
Insecticide Sevin: effect of aerial spraying on drift of stream insects. C. G. Coutant. bibliog il Science 146:420-1 O 16 '64
Insecticides: effects on cutthroat trout of repeated exposure to DDT. D. Allison and others. bibliog il Science 142:958-61 N 15 '63
Invisible death. C. C. Van Fleet. il Atlan 214:53-5 Jl '64
Nicotinic acid analogs: effects on response of chick embryos and hens to organophosphate toxicants. J. C. Roger and others. bibliog Science 144:539-40 My 1 '64
Parathion activation by livers of aquatic and terrestrial vertebrates. J. L. Potter and R. D. O'Brien. bibliog il Science 144:55-7 Ap 3 '64
Peripatetic reviewer. E. Weeks. Atlan 213:130+ Je '64
Pieces of the puzzle; chlordane dust kills ringneck snakes. S. G. Ernst. il Nat Parks Mag 37:20-1 Ap '63
Poisoning by DDT: relation between clinical signs and concentration in art brain. W. E. Dale and others. bibliog il Science 142:1474-6 D 13 '63
Rachel Carson answers her critics. R. Carson. Audubon Mag 65:262-5+ S '63
Rachel Carson vs. pest control. Am City 78:7 Mr '63
Solid evidence shows fish die of insecticide. Sci N L 85:226 Ap 11 '64
Speaking out; the myth of the pesticide menace; concerning Silent spring. E. Diamond. Sat Eve Post 236:16+ S 28 '63
Spray chemicals; are they really dangerous? concerning charges made in Rachel Carson's Silent spring. C. Westcott. Am Home 66:12+ Mr '63; Same. il Am For 69:15+ Ap '63

INSECTICIDES—Injurious effects—*Continued*
To spray or not to spray? Sci N L 83:215 Ap 6 '63
Wiesner report; summary. J. B. Wiesner. Am For 69:11 Je '63

Residues

DDT antagonism to dieldrin storage in adipose tissue of rats. J. C. Street. bibliog il Science 146:1580-1 D 18 '64
Persistence of DDT in soils of heavily sprayed forest stands. G. M. Woodwell and F. T. Martin. bibliog il Science 145:481-3 Jl 31 '64
See also
Insecticides—Injurious effects

INSECTICIDES, Resistance to. See Insects, Injurious and beneficial—Resistance to control

INSECTIVOROUS plants
Insect-trapping plants. V. N. Argo. il Natur Hist 73:28-33 Mr '64
Nematode-trapping fungi. D. Pramer. bibliog il Science 144:382-8 Ap 24 '64
See also
Pitcher plants
Venus's flytraps

INSECTS
See also
Color of insects
Metabolism (insects)
Photography of insects
Sound production by insects
also names of insects, e.g. Fireflies

Anatomy

See also
Sense organs—Insects

Control

See Insects, Injurious and beneficial—Control

Development

Control of growth and development in insects; excerpts from address, December 28, 1962. H. A. Schneidermann and L. I. Gilbert. bibliog il Science 143:325-33 Ja 24 '64
Hormonal activation of the insect brain. S. D. Beck and N. Alexander. bibliog il Science 143:478-9 Ja 31 '64
Monarch's emergence. A. B. Klots. il Natur Hist 73:50-3 My '64
Photoperiodic reversibility of diapause induction in an insect. R. A. Bell and P. L. Adkisson. bibliog il Science 144:1149-51 My 29 '64
Sclerotization in the blowfly imago. C. E. Sekeris. bibliog il Science 144:419 Ap 24 '64
Spontaneous electrical activity in the brains of diapausing insects. L. M. Schoonhoven. il Science 141:173-4 Jl 12 '63
See also
Insects—Eggs

Ear

See Ear (insects)

Eggs

Ornamental eggs of the insects. A. Peterson. il Natur Hist 74:46-51 Ja '65

Eyes

See Eye (insects)

Flight

Neuromimes: action of a reciprocally inhibitory pair. L. D. Harmon. bibliog il Science 146:1323-5 D 4 '64

Food

Chromic oxide indicator method for measuring food utilization in a plant-feeding insect. A. J. McGinnis and R. Kasting. bibliog il Science 144:1464-5 Je 19 '64

Habits and behavior

Arachnid behavior; report on symposium. C. J. Goodnight. Science 144:82 Ap 3 '64
Trail marking substance of the Texas leaf-cutting ant: source and potency. J. C. Moser and M. S. Blum. il Science 140:1228 Je 14 '63
See also
Courtship of insects
Periodicity

Migration

Aerial migration of insects. C. G. Johnson. il Sci Am 209:132-8 bibliog(p 180) D '63

Molting

See Molting

Physiology

Carbohydrate digestion in the cockroach. W. M. Banks. bibliog il Science 141:1191-2 S 20 '63
Mechanoreceptors in the cuticle of the honey bee: fine structure and stimulus mechanism. U. Thurm. bibliog il Science 145:1063-5 S 4 '64
Pheromones. E. O. Wilson. il Sci Am 208:100-6+ My '63
Stretch receptor-like organs in the fly larva: their possible role in growth regulation. J. M. Whitten. bibliog il Science 143:260-1 Ja 17 '64
Thysanuran median frontal organ: its structural resemblance to photoreceptors. R. S. Pipa and others. bibliog il Science 145:829-31 Ag 21 '64
Uric acid in the reproductive system of males of the cockroach blattella germanica. L. M. Roth and G. P. Dateo, jr. bibliog il Science 146:782-4 N 6 '64
Venom and venom apparatus of the bull ant, myrmecia gulosa, fabr. G. W. K. Cavill and others. bibliog il Science 146:79-80 O 2 '64
See also
Insect sex attractants

Resistance to control

See Insects, Injurious and beneficial—Resistance to control

INSECTS, Aquatic
Stonefly aquatic in the adult stage. S. G. Jewett, jr. bibliog Science 139:484-5 F 8 '63

INSECTS, Effect of radiation on. See Insects, Injurious and beneficial—Control; Radiation—Physiological effects

INSECTS, Fossil
Ancient scorpions found. il Sci N L 85:226 Ap 11 '64
Flowers, insects, and evolution; Ruby Range fossils. H. F. Becker. il Natur Hist 74:38-45 bibliog(p70) F '65

INSECTS, Injurious and beneficial
All bugs are not bad. G. Arnold. il Horticulture 41:406 Ag '63
Bugs about me; insect attraction. E. R. Paxton. Sci Digest 55:57-61 Je '64
Man's eternal friends and enemies; reprint. il Sci Digest 55:69-72 Ap '64
What's biting you? questions and answers. L. E. Steinmetz. il Sci Digest 54:69-71 Ag '63
See also
Gipsy moths
Grasshoppers
Red spiders
Termites

Control

Are there thieves in your grain bin? L. E. Zeman. il Suc Farm 61:56-7+ N '63
Aroused spring; concerning U.S. government's report on the use of pesticides. Time 81:81 My 24 '63
Billions of bugs: Willapa looper project. J. B. Craig. il Am For 70:42-8 F '64
Bug- and disease-proof your garden. B. Hering. il Pop Gard 15:60-3 My '64
Chickadee helps check insect invasion. A. D. Telford and S. G. Herman. il Audubon Mag 65:78-81 Mr '63
Electronic bat sounds drive insects away; bollworms. Sci N L 86:233 O 10 '64
Fishing without flies. H. G. Tapply. il Field & S 68:64 Je '63
Germ warfare on insects by biological control. Sci N L 85:377 Je 13 '64
Good-bye to bugs. R. M. Peters. il Pop Gard 14:72 My '63
How to beat bugs with other bugs. il Bsns W p50+ Je 22 '63
How to bug the bugs; anti-metabolites used to protect textiles. Newsweek 64:100+ S 21 '64
How to succeed in controlling insects without really trying. il House & Gard 126:298-9+ N '64
If bee and wasp nests are a problem. il Good H 156:167 Ap '63
Insect attractants. M. Jacobson and M. Beroza. il Sci Am 211:20-7 Ag '64
Insect control by nontoxic means; letter. R. H. Wright. bibliog Science 144:487 My 1 '64
Insect control calendar (cont) P. P. Pirone. Pop Gard 14:100-1 F; 58-9 Ap '63
Insect control in mainland China. T. H. Cheng. bibliog il Science 140:269-77 Ap 19 '63; Reply with rejoinder. R. C. Liu and others. 141:576-9 Ag 9 '63
Insect fertility: inhibition by folic acid derivatives. M. M. Crystal. bibliog il Science 144:308-9 Ap 17 '64
Insects, eat, but starve. Sci N L 87:53 Ja 23 '65
Man's friend, the wasp. Newsweek 63:93 Je 8 '64
Needed: solutions, not epitaphs! R. O. Cornelius. il Am For 70:24-7 Je '64

INSECTS, Injurious and beneficial—Control— *Continued*

Pest control symposium, 131st AAAS annual meeting, Montreal, 26-31 December, 1964. il Science 146:672-3 O 30 '64

Pest destroyers; excerpt from Beneficial insects. L. A. Swan. bibliog il Audubon Mag 67:46-51 Ja '65

Pest-eating insects; lady beetles and fireflies; excerpt from Beneficial insects. L. A. Swan. bibliog f il Audubon Mag 66:314-19 S '64

Pest-ridden spring; concerning testimony before a Senate committee. Time 82:55 Jl 5 '63

Photoflashes: a potential new tool for control of insect populations. R. J. Barker and others. bibliog il Science 145:1195-7 S 11 '64

Proper use of home insecticides. il Consumer Rep 28:392-7 Ag '63

Radiation kills weevil eggs in wheat. Farm J 87:49 O '63

Sex used as weapon to save West's pine forests. Sci N L 86:56 Jl 25 '64

Sleeping bacteria grown to kill Japanese beetles. Sci N L 84:159 S 7 '63

Spray chemicals: are they really dangerous? concerning charges made in Rachel Carson's Silent spring. C. Westcott. Am Home 66: 12+ Mr '63; Same. il Am For 69:15+ Ap '63

Suffocation used as new weapon against insects. Sci N L 85:201 Mr 28 '64

U.S. expels alien insects. E. Hall. Sci N L 84:132 Ag 31 '63

Viruses mass-produced for infecting insects. Sci N L 86:313 N 14 '64

Wanted : dead or alive; America's top twenty backyard enemies. il Pop Mech 119:150-4 My '63

War against insects. il Sci N L 86:74-5 Ag 1 '64

War on the insect felons; address. C. Westcott. Am For 70:28+ F '64

Weapons against insects. Sci N L 87:37 Ja 16 '65

What do you know about biological control? P. P. Pirone. il Horticulture 42:20-3 O '64

World's fair pests bite the dust. il Am City 79:105 O '64

Worst pet in the world. S. Schuler. il Pop Sci 184:124-6+ Ap '64

See also

Airplanes in insect control
Chemosterilants
Cockroaches—Extermination
Flies—Extermination
Insecticides
Mosquitoes—Extermination
Pesticides
Spraying and dusting

Resistance to control

Chlorinated insecticides: fate in aqueous suspensions containing mosquito larvae. M. C. Bowman and others. bibliog il Science 146: 1480-1 D 11 '64

Dieldrin susceptibility: partial restoration in anopheles selected with a carbamate. G. P. Georghiou and R. L. Metcalf. bibliog il Science 140:301-2 Ap 19 '63

How insects resist insecticides. D. B. Peakall. il Audubon Mag 66:32-4 Ja '64

Insecticide resistance: effects of WARF antiresistant on toxicity of DDT adult houseflies. D. Spiller. bibliog il Science 142:585-6 N 1 '63

INSECTS, Predatory

Animal husbandry in the animal kingdom; how and why carpenter ants protect caterpillars. il Time 82:98 D 6 '63

See also

Sciomyzids

INSECTS as carriers of infection

Bedbug's big bite. Time 82:77 Jl 12 '63

See also

Mosquitoes as carriers of infection
Ticks

INSECURITY, Feeling of. See Security and insecurity (psychology)

INSECURITY, Social and economic. See Social and economic security

INSEMINATION, Artificial. See Artificial insemination, Human

INSENSIBILITY. See Coma

INSIGNIA

See also

Emblems
United States—Armed forces—Insignia

INSIGNIA, Army. See United States—Army—Insignia

INSOLVENCY. See Bankruptcy

INSOMNIA

Can't sleep? don't blame coffee. Sci Digest 54:81-2 Jl '63

Sleep for sale? B. Seeman. il Todays Health 42:22-3+ S '64

Vestibular nuclei: activity of single neurons during natural sleep and wakefulness. E. Bizzi and others. bibliog il Science 145:414-15 Jl 24 '64

See also

Sleep

INSPECTION

See also subhead Inspection under various subjects, e.g. Hotels, taverns, etc.—Inspection

INSPECTION for disarmament. See Disarmament—Inspection

INSPECTION of sewers. See Sewer inspection

INSPIRATION

Mama and the roomer. K. Forbes. Read Digest 82:228E-228F Ap '63

There's something knocking at the door. R. Bach. Writer 77:13-15+ My '64

Why do you want to write? C. R. Bittle. Writer 77:18-19 Ag '64

INSTALMENT plan

Charge accounts & instalment plans. il Changing T 17:35-8 Mr '63

How to finance that car. il Changing T 18: 25-8 Mr '64

Lenders rub their hands. il Bsns W p93-4 Ap 6 '63

Official report: what borrowers need to know. il U S News 56:85-6 Je 29 '64

What it costs to finance appliances & cars. il Changing T 17:37-8 Mr '63

Why credit controls would hurt. P. W. McCracken and others. Nations Bsns 52:34-5+ D '64

See also

Credit

Laws and regulations

Caveat venditor; decisions by Nebraska's Supreme court. il Time 82:76+ N 8 '63

Nebraska fiasco: buy now, pay never; legislative blunder. J. Skow. il Sat Eve Post 237:66-8 F 29 '64

Time sales law upheld. Bsns W p 122 My 2 '64

INSTAMATIC cameras. See Cameras

INSTANT mashed potatoes. See Potatoes, Dried

INSTITUTE for advanced study, Princeton, N.J.

Leisure of the theory class. M. Mayer. Esquire 59:16+ Mr '63

INSTITUTE for defense analyses

Braintrust aids decision-makers. il Miss & Roc 12:115 Mr 25 '63

Game to the end. il Newsweek 62:20+ Ag 12 '63

How a think tank works. il Bsns W p82 Jl 13 '63

Ruina taking top post at IDA. J. Trainor. Miss & Roc 15:15 S 21 '64

Verification and response in disarmament agreements; excerpts from report. Bul Atomic Sci 19:44-8 Ap '63

INSTITUTE for retired professionals. See New school for social research, New York

INSTITUTE for scientific information, Philadelphia

Science literature index produced by computer. Library J 88:4182 N 1 '63

INSTITUTE of aerospace sciences

Scientists galore; annual conventions. New Yorker 38:24 F 16 '63

INSTITUTE of design, Chicago. See Illinois institute of technology—Institute of design

INSTITUTE of electrical and electronic engineers

Communication and the growth of scientific knowledge. Pub W 183:74 Ap 15 '63

Electronics executives view future. Miss & Roc 14:13 Mr 30 '64

IEEE breaks all records. W. A. Stocklin. Electr World 69:6 Je '63

Sandia development tops IEEE hardware. C. D. LaFond. Miss & Roc 14:44+ Ap 6 '64

Symposium stresses data compression. R. Pay. Miss & Roc 15:35 O 12 '64

Ultrasonics: report on symposium 14-16 October, Santa Monica, Calif. J. J. G. McCue. Science 147:309-10 Ja 15 '65

INSTITUTE of human relations

Inter-American center at Loyola. C. J. McNaspy. America 112:36 Ja 9 '65

INSTITUTE of international education

IIE to assist in aiding African students who left Bulgaria; Department statement. Dept State Bul 48:448 Mr 25 '63

International educational and cultural exchanges: a look back and a look ahead; address, October 24, 1963. D. Rusk. Dept State Bul 49:742-4 N 11 '63

Room of his own; design for conference space in new Institute of international education, Manhattan. il Time 84:84+ D 11 '64

INSTITUTE of living, Hartford, Conn. See Hospitals, Psychiatric
INSTITUTE of modern art, New York
Art barge; Summer art center at Napeague Harbor, Amagansett. New Yorker 39:33-4 S 21 '63
INSTITUTE of nutrition of Central America and Panama
What's in a meal? B. Burton. il Américas 15: 5-6 F '63
INSTITUTE of sound
Sound on file. R. C. Striker. il Sat R 46: 47-9 N 30 '63
INSTITUTE of student opinion. See Scholastic research center
INSTITUTE of traffic engineers
Traffic engineers search for balanced transportation. il Am City 78:120+ D '63
INSTITUTES, Library. See Library institutes and workshops
INSTITUTES, Religious. See Religious institutes and workshops
INSTITUTES, Teachers. See Teachers institutes
INSTITUTES for the achievement of human potential, Philadelphia
Pattern of recovery? rehabilitation therapy at the Institutes for the achievement of human potential, Philadelphia. il Newsweek 63:84-5 My 4 '64
That's our kid; excerpt from How to teach your baby to read. G. J. Doman. il PTA Mag 59:23-5+ D '64
INSTITUTIONAL investors. See Stockholders
INSTRUCTIONAL materials centers
Columbia holds work conference on the instructional materials center; school library as a center. Library J 89:4132+ O 15 '64
IMC in the continuous progress school. J. Berry. il Library J 89:4599-602 N 15 '64
IMS merger: a/v and library services together; Houston, Tex. independent school district. E. Alexander. il Library J 89:4107-9 O 15 '64
Instructional resource center. F. Simmons. il ALA Bul 57:170-4 F '63
INSTRUCTORS, Aviation. See Air pilots—Training
INSTRUCTORS, College. See College professors and instructors
INSTRUMENT boards (automobiles) See Automobiles—Dashboards
INSTRUMENT boards (space vehicles) See Space vehicles—Instrument boards
INSTRUMENT boards (yachts) See Yachts—Instrument boards
INSTRUMENT flying. See Aviation—Instrument flying
INSTRUMENT landing. See Airplanes—Landing
INSTRUMENTAL music
See also
Chamber music
Phonograph records—Instrumental music
INSTRUMENTS
See also
Musical instruments
Scientific apparatus and instruments
INSTRUMENTS, Testing. See Testing instruments
INSULATED-gate transistor. See Transistors
INSULATED jugs. See Thermos containers
INSULATING materials
Foamed plastics for flat roof insulation. R. E. Polson. il Arch Rec 133:197-8 Je '63
See also
Polyethylene
INSULATION (electric)
X-ray-induced bulk photovoltaic effect in insulators. S. I. Taimuty and others. il Science 144:173 Ap 10 '64
INSULATION (heat)
Heat conservation in the electrically-heated house. E. R. Ambrose. il Arch Rec 135:7+ mid-My '64
Insulation: the hidden money-saver. Bet Hom & Gard 42:112 O '64
What to do about a drafty house. C. Sclarenco. il Bet Hom & Gard 42:125 N '64
See also
Clothing, Cold weather
Weather stripping
INSULATION (sound) See Soundproofing
INSULIN
Antigens in insulin determinants of specificity of porcine insulin in man. S. A. Berson and R. S. Yalow. bibliog il Science 139: 844-5 Mr 1 '63
Artificial insulin made. F. Marley. Sci N L 84:261 O 26 '63
First man-made protein in history. il Life 56:47+ My 8 '64
Genetic differences in antibody production to determinant groups on insulin. E. R. Arquilla and J. Finn. bibliog il Science 142:400-1 O 18 '63
Hepatic glucokinase: a direct effect of insulin. J. W. Vester and M. L. Reino. bibliog il Science 142:590-1 N 1 '63
Insulin action in alloxan diabetes modifed by actinomycin D. A. Gellhorn and W. Benjamin. bibliog il Science 146:1166-8 N 27 '64
Please save my son! case of J. Havens. D. O. Woodbury. Read Digest 82:157-8+ F '63
Protein block-building; synthetic insulin. il Bsns W p73-4 O 26 '63
Synthetic insulin. Sci Am 209:72 D '63
Synthetic insulin close at hand. il Todays Health 42:59 Mr '64
Victory over the sugar sickness; ed. by J. D. Ratcliff. C. H. Best. Todays Health 42: 56-8+ Mr '64; Same abr. with title How we discovered insulin. Read Digest 84:43-7 Mr '64
Winning combination; race to synthesize the hormone insulin. Newsweek 63:74 Mr 2 '64
INSURANCE
Better insurance for less money. S. Margolius. Ladies Home J 80:16 Jl '63
Insurance checklist for vacationers. il Good H 158:172 Je '64
Insure savings to $25,000? U S News 54:110-11 Ap 15 '63
Negro has the same risks. Time 83:90 F 7 '64
Who needs insuring and why? Bet Hom & Gard 42:90 Ja '64
Your family's insurance needs. R. G. Engelsman. il Parents Mag 38:74-5+ S '63

Adjustment of claims

After the fire. il Newsweek 63:64 Ja 13 '64
Photographs are excellent proof; photographic record of your possessions. il Sunset 133: 116+ S '64

All risk policies

Homeowner's insurance: what does it cover. Bet Hom & Gard 41:12+ Je '63
Personal business; big-city robberies. Bsns W p 125-6 N 23 '63
Prepare for the unexpected. P. Roalman. il Field & S 68:40-2+ D '63
You and your home. House & Gard 124:166+ O '63
Your complete guide to homeowners insurance. N. Kuehnl and G. Bush. il Bet Hom & Gard 42:7-8+ O '64

Fraudulent claims

Accident fraud is highway robbery. C. Remsberg. Read Digest 84:201-4 F '64
Insurance claims racket. F. Sullivan. il Motor T 15:116-17 N '63

History

Insurance among Negroes prior to the Civil war. J. E. Gloster. bibliog Negro Hist Bul 27:42-3 N '63

Reinsurance

Insuring the insurers. il Bsns W p 125-6+ My 18 '63

Risks

Risky business. Time 83:90 My 1 '64

Self insurance

Going it alone with self-insurance. il Bsns W p94-6 Jl 6 '63

Taxation

Kennedy plan that may penalize millions. U S News 54:11 Ap 15 '63

Terminology

Insurance: better know what the words mean. il Changing T 18:17-21 D '64
INSURANCE, Accident
Traffic jam; who pays how much for auto accidents. il Time 83:40 Ja 10 '64
See also
Insurance, Disability
Insurance, Liability
INSURANCE, Agricultural
Collecting on crop insurance? here's how you may save taxes. Suc Farm 62:41 N '64
Crop insurance; bigger payments in 1963. Farm J 87:62B Mr '63
How to buy insurance on your livestock. H. D. Guither. Suc Farm 62:32 Ap '64
Tax tips that the experts use. C. W. Gifford. Farm J 88:63 N '64
INSURANCE, Automobile
Auto insurance. il Consumer Rep 28:417-26 D '63

INSURANCE, Automobile—*Continued*
Coming: major changes in auto insurance. Changing T 18:6 Jl '64
Hot rod insurance. D. Wells. il Hot Rod 17: 108-9 S '64
Insurance claims racket. F. Sullivan. il Motor T 15:116-17 N '63
Premium choice. H. E. Dark. il Travel 119: 44-5 F '63
Traffic jam; who pays how much for auto accidents. il Time 83:40 Ja 10 '64
Why car insurance costs keep rising. B. Brantley. Suc Farm 62:39 D '64
Your complete guide to automobile insurance. N. Kuehnl and G. Bush. il Bet Hom & Gard 42:7-8 D '64

INSURANCE, Aviation
U.S. carriers oppose State dept. bid to increase travelers' liability. Aviation W 81:36 Ag 24 '64
U.S. seeks to end crash liability limits. R. H. Cook. Aviation W 80:41+ F 10 '64

INSURANCE, Burglary
Fidelity and crime insurance for schools. R. N. Finchum. Sch Life 45:16-17 Je '63
What if you're robbed? il Changing T 17: 21-3 Je '63

INSURANCE, Business
$5 million man. Newsweek 61:78 Mr 25 '63
Life insurance for your business, too. il Changing T 18:37-40 Ja '64

INSURANCE, Credit
President announces determination on Exim-bank credit guarantees; letters, January 28, 1964. L. B. Johnson. Dept State Bul Bul 50:298 F 24 '64
Red insurance man; Garant insurance, Vienna. Time 82:91-2 D 13 '63

INSURANCE, Dental
Now, insurance to pay dental expenses. il Good H 157:172 N '63
What about insurance for dental care? H. Higdon. Todays Health 42:52-3+ S '64

INSURANCE, Disability
Buy insurance against disability? il Changing T 17:25-8 O '63
Personal business; long-term disability. Bsns W p 125 Ja 26 '63
Two expanded NEA insurance plans. E. Funderburk. NEA J 52:60 Mr '63
When you insure against loss of income. Good H 157:148 Ag '63

INSURANCE, Fire
We learned the hard way about fire in the house. P. Wylie. Read Digest 84:157-8+ Je '64

Rates

Bad year for fire losses. il Bsns W p87-8 My 25 '63

INSURANCE, Flood
Federal flood insurance: necessity or costly error? pro and con discussion. il Sr Schol 82:14-15 Ap 24 '63

INSURANCE, Hail
Pointers in buying hail insurance. H. Guither. Suc Farm 62:70 Ap '64

INSURANCE, Health
Considerations for policy-makers; the European experience; new US patterns. A. R. Somers; R. S. Morison. New Repub 149: 36-41 N 9 '63
Health, medical care, and education. il Sr Schol 85:25 O 28 '64
Personal business. Bsns W p 129 Ag 15 '64
Special retirement provisions in industry; excerpt from Corporate retirement policy and practices. H. Fox and M. C. Kerpen. il Mo Labor R 87:781-5 Jl '64
Your complete guide to health insurance. N. Kuehnl and G. Bush. Bet Hom & Gard 42: 7-8+ N '64
See also
Insurance, Dental
Insurance, Disability

Belgium

Do doctors have a right to strike? il U S News 56:10 Ap 20 '64
Doctors strike. il Sr Schol 84:15 Ap 24 '64
℞: peace; new agreement on health insurance plan. Time 84:25 Jl 3 '64
Why 10,000 doctors went on strike. U S News 56:8 Ap 13 '64

Canada

Canada for health plan, but worried over cost. U S News 57:10 Jl 6 '64
Canada likes medicare, but—. il U S News 57:45 S 21 '64
Canada's health programs. J. E. F. Hastings. bibliog f Cur Hist 44:326-32+ Je '63
Medicare in Canada; the costs are rising. U S News 56:10 Je 22 '64
T.R.B. from Washington; Canadian example: comprehensive national medicare plan. New Repub 151:2 Jl 4 '64
Will medical care bankrupt Canada. il U S News 57:98-9 O 5 '64

Germany (Federal Republic)

Health insurance in West Germany. A. Price. bibliog f Cur Hist 44:345-50 Je '63

New York (state)

State care; New York state's mental hygiene program. P. H. Hoch. Atlan 214:82-5 Jl '64

Sweden

Socialized medicine in Sweden. J. H. Wuorinen. bibliog f il Cur Hist 44:333-8 Je '63

United States

Age of termination. New Repub 150:5 F 15 '64
America's medical future: a Briton's view. S. J. L. Taylor. Nation 197:177-9 S 28 '63
Are you covered? F. Fielding-Jones. il Parents Mag 38:181-3 O '63
Challenge to our doctors. J. R. Moskin. il Look 28:32+ N 3 '64; Discussion. 28:6+ D 15 '64
Coverage for aged. America 109:128 Ag 10 '63
Federal health estimates, 300 per cent wrong. B. S. Sanders. il Nations Bsns 52:31-3+ N '64; Reply. R. J. Myers. 53:10 Ja '65
Federal health insurance for all? pro and con discussion. bibliog il Sr Schol 83:10-12 N 22 '63
Health and insurance benefits for salaried employees. A. H. Anderson and W. F. Hahn. Mo Labor R 86:1266-74 N '63
Health as a fringe benefit. J. Pollack. il New Repub 149:21-3 N 9 '63
Health bill. Time 85:18 Ja 15 '65
Health care for the aged: here are the two plans. il U S News 56:46-8 F 24 '64
Health insurance in the revised CPI. J. C. Daugherty. il Mo Labor R 87:1299-300 N '64
Insuring mental illness. T. R. Brooks. Duns R 81:102+ My '63
It's not the doctor's dilemma, it's the insurance plan's. D. M. MacIntyre. New Repub 149:19-21 N 9 '63
Just for the record; Senate approves social security-financed medicare plan for the aged. Time 84:22-3 S 11 '64
Medicare by Easter? Newsweek 65:52 Ja 25 '65
Medicare comes back; administration's medicare program vs Chmn. Mills of Ways & means. Bsns W p25 Je 8 '63
Medicare is coming. Nat R 16:1048-9 D 1 '64
Medicare, the cure that could cause a setback. H. B. Meyers. il Fortune 67:131-3+ My '63
Mills's terms for medicare; excerpts from address, December 2, 1964. W. Mills. U S News 57:74 D 21 '64
More for mental illness. Sci N L 85:372 Je 13 '64
National health insurance? S. E. Harris. Cur Hist 45:110-14 Ag '63
Odds on aged health care. America 110:500 Ap 11 '64
President renews insurance plan; proposes a Senior citizens act. Christian Cent 80:324 Mr 13 '63
Spouse clause. T. R. Brooks. Duns R 81:101-2 My '63
This month's feature: proposals to expand medicare for aged. Cong Digest 42:193-224 Ag '63
Time the US caught up; excerpt from address, June 13, 1963. J. F. Kennedy. New Repub 149:35 N 9 '63
Tips on buying better health insurance coverage. F. C. Wendt. Todays Health 41:44-5 N '63
Voluntary health insurance. H. J. Becker. Cur Hist 45:92-7+ Ag '63
What you should know about health insurance. S. S. Steinberg. Suc Farm 62:84 O '64
Who pays for the care of the aged? controversy over government vs. private health insurance. Bsns W p68-9 N 23 '63
Who will be helped by medicare. il U S News 57:52-5 D 14 '64
Why we need medicare. M. H. Alderman. New Repub 151:17-20 D 26 '64
Will medicare alter private plans? il Bsns W p 100+ D 5 '64
See also
Aged—Medical care

INSURANCE, Hospitalization
Family money questions answered. il Bet Hom & Gard 41:40+ Ap '63
Hospital insurance bill of 1963. Cur Hist 45: 41-6, 116+ Jl, Ag '63

INSURANCE, Hospitalization—*Continued*
It pays to be a patient. il Sci Digest 56: 55-6 N '64
Medical care for the aged, what young families should know. B. Spock. Redbook 123:34+ My '64
Personal business; hospital bills. Bsns W p 113 Ag 10 '63
This month's feature: proposals to expand medicare for aged. Cong Digest 42:193-224 Ag '63
INSURANCE, Investment guaranty
FCIA program broadened. A. O. Stanley. Duns R 81:54-5 Mr '63
Insurance for exporters. il Fortune 67:69-70+ Je '63
President Kennedy on foreign aid; message to Congress, April 2, 1963. J. F. Kennedy. Cur Hist 44:366 Je '63
INSURANCE, Liability
Better insurance for less money. S. Margolius. Ladies Home J 80:16 Jl '63
Paying guests on the farm? check your liabilities! R. A. Golden. Suc Farm 62:36 Ag '64
Prepare for the unexpected. P. Roalman. il Field & S 68:40-2+ D '63
Research indemnification: new VA insurance policy offers greater security to researchers. E. Langer. Science 145:798+ Ag 21 '64
See also
Insurance, Aviation
Sports—Insurance aspects
INSURANCE, Library
Protecting the library and its resources, ed. by E. M. Johnson. Review
Library J il 88:4152-6 N 1 '63. H. L. Roth; W. W. Curley; Discussion. 89:2+. 426+ Ja 1, F 1 '64
INSURANCE, Life
As an investment: term vs. permanent insurance; with statement by B. Graham. U S News 55:102 O 7 '63
Companies are the big customers; key man and group policies. il Bsns W p45-6+ Ag 15 '64
Expanded NEA life insurance plan. il NEA J 53:16-17 O '64
How to use life insurance in your farm business. C. W. Gifford. il Farm J 88:42B+ Ap '64
Investing in insurance. il Fortune 68:229-30+ S '63
Life insurance, with dividends or without? il Changing T 18:25-8 Ap '64
Religion of life insurance. A. Welsh. Christian Cent 80:1541-3, 1574-6 D 11-18 '63; Discussion. 81:118-19, 239-40 Ja 22, F 19 '64
What life insurance do farmers need? questions and answers, with editorial comment. C. W. Gifford. il Farm J 88:4, 36-7+ Mr '64
What you should know about buying life insurance; interview. D. W. Gregg. U S News 55:94-102 O 7 '63
Your complete guide to life insurance. N. Kuehnl and G. Bush. il Bet Hom & Gard 43:137-40 Ja '65
Your family's insurance needs. R. G. Engelsman. il Parents Mag 38:74-5+ S '63
See also
Annuities
Benefit societies
Insurance, Disability
Insurance, Soldiers and sailors

Agents

How to select a life insurance agent. il Good H 158:172 Ap '64

Policies

Insurance: new billions for new policies. il Newsweek 64:84-6+ O 19 '64
Is there a best kind of life insurance? Bet Hom & Gard 41:30-1 O '63
Is your life insurance up to date? il Changing T 18:35-7 My '64
Straight life: best all-around policy. il Changing T 17:7-11 Jl '63
Which kind of term insurance? il Changing T 18:39-41 S '64

Taxation

See Insurance—Taxation

War risks

See also
Insurance, Soldiers and sailors
INSURANCE, Marine
Insurers count ship crash toll; damage suits against Shalom and Norwegian tanker. il Bsns W p 144+ D 5 '64
Perils of the sea, who's liable? J. W. Giles. Motor B 111:44 Mr '63
See also
Lloyd's, London
INSURANCE, Medical. See Insurance Health
INSURANCE, Military. See Insurance, Soldiers and sailors
INSURANCE, Mortgage
Behind the man behind the loan; MGIC. il Bsns W p 120+ S 28 '63
INSURANCE, Self. See Insurance—Self insurance
INSURANCE, Social
How to get your money's worth out of social security. G. B. Whitman and B. Brantley. il Suc Farm 61:45-56 F '63
Is it a good idea for you? questions and answers. C. W. Gifford. Farm J 88:62+ My '64
Social security and the Alliance for progress; seventh Inter-American conference on social security, Asunción, Paraguay, May 31-June 5, 1964. I. C. Merriam. Dept State Bul 51:320-1 Ag 31 '64
Who provides welfare? H. Hazlitt. Newsweek 61:97 Je 24 '63

United States

Are you missing out on social security payments? M. Belloise. Read Digest 82:73-6 Je '63
Check up on your social security. il Changing T 17:25-9 D '63
Final call for clergy; social security coverage. America 111:766-7 D 12 '64
Grow old along with me; question of not reducing benefits of widows who remarry. Newsweek 65:29+ Ja 25 '65
Increase in your social security taxes? U S News 54:9 Je 10 '63
Social expenditures and worker welfare. I. C. Merriam. il Mo Labor R 86:687-94 Je '63
Where taxes are sure to keep on rising; social security tax. il U S News 55:67-9 N 11 '63
Your questions answered about social security. il Changing T 17:21-2 Ag '63
Your wife's income can boost social security benefits. F. Bailey, jr. Suc Farm 62:130 Mr '64
See also
Insurance, Unemployment—United States
Old age pensions—United States
Old age, survivors' and disability insurance trust fund
Workmens compensation—United States
INSURANCE, Soldiers and sailors
Your GI insurance today. il Changing T 17: 32-4 Je '63
INSURANCE, Sports. See Sports—Insurance aspects
INSURANCE, Strike
Managing your manpower; new legislative push. T. R. Brooks. Duns R 81:69-70+ Ja '63
INSURANCE, Surety and fidelity
Bonding troubles for Hoffa; underwriters refuse security. Bsns W p72 F 2 '63
Fidelity and crime insurance for schools. R. N. Finchum. Sch Life 45:16-17 Je '63
Teamster bonds. New Repub 148:4-5 F 23 '63
INSURANCE, Theft. See Insurance, Burglary
INSURANCE, Unemployment
Workers almost envy jobless. U S News 56:94 My 18 '64

Canada

Inquiry into Canada's unemployment insurance system. A. B. Ratcliff. Mo Labor R 86: 524-9 My '63

Pennsylvania

On a cross of falsehoods. Time 83:26 F 21 '64

United States

Again the issue of the welfare state. A. Hacker. il N Y Times Mag p9+ Mr 22 '64
Attraction at Club 55. il Time 82:16 Ag 9 '63
Public systems for distributing risks to security. P. Booth. bibliog f il Mo Labor R 86:622-9 Je '63
Scandal in unemployment insurance. Atlan 213:84-6 F '64; Discussion. 213:36+ My '64
Unemployment insurance legislation in 1963. G. H. Rubin. il Mo Labor R 87:168-72 F '64

Wyoming

Wyoming tightens up on happy-time money. E. Selby and A. Selby. Read Digest 86:53-7 Ja '65
INSURANCE, Weather
See also
Insurance, Hail
INSURANCE agents
Bookies of doom; insurance salesmen. D. Jenkins. il Sports Illus 19:36-8+ N 4 '63
See also
Insurance, Life—Agents
Kelly, John P. agency

INSURANCE companies
Bad year for fire losses. il Bsns W p87-8 My 25 '63
Casualties ahead. il Time 84:81 Ag 21 '64
Companies are the big customers; key man and group policies. il Bsns W p45-6+ Ag 15 '64
Insurance man's best friend; the computer. il Bsns W p 100+ N 7 '64
Shielding the flame; India's state-owned Life insurance corp. il Time 82:113 O 18 '63
Train robbery's sequel: covering the loss; $7-million holdup. il Bsns W p 108+ Ag 17 '63
See also
Government investigations—Insurance companies
also names of insurance companies, e.g. North Carolina mutual life insurance company

Finance

Mysterious $5.5-million: Manhattan casualty case. Bsns W p76-8 Ag 24 '63

Regulations

Pension fund race gets hotter. Bsns W p66 F 2 '63

Securities

Executive investor; life insurance stocks for capital appreciation, and income. il Duns R 82:75-8 S '63
Lure of stock options tempts insurance men. il Bsns W p76+ O 3 '64
Mortgages, stocks lure insurers. il Bsns W p 132 D 12 '64

INSURANCE company of North America
INA ties itself into a package; centralized setup geared to customer. il Bsns W p52+ Ja 9 '65
Stressing the package. Bsns W p64+ Je 6 '64

INSURANCE law
Lloyd's settles a Florida claim. Bsns W p74 Je 8 '63
Mysterious $5.5-million; Manhattan casualty case. Bsns W p76-8 Ag 24 '63

INSURANCE salesmen. See Insurance agents

INSURANCE tax. See Insurance—Taxation

INSURRECTIONS. See Revolutions

INTAGLIOS
Five figures, intaglio print. H. A. Altman. il Sch Arts 62:24-5 Je '63

INTEGRATED circuits. See Electronic circuits

INTEGRATED mission control center. See United States—National aeronautics and space administration

INTEGRATION of libraries. See Libraries and Negroes

INTEGRATION of public schools. See Public schools—Desegregation

INTEGRITY
Let's dare to be square. C. H. Brower. Read Digest 82:49-51 Ap '63
Stand up for what you believe in. W. S. Coffin, jr. il Parents Mag 38:49+ D '63
Thin gray line. M. Mannes. McCalls 91:53+ Ja '64; Same abr. Read Digest 84:61-3 Ap '64

INTELECTRON corporation
Paper on intellectronics highlight for 25,000 at NEC exhibition. C. D. LaFond. Miss & Roc 15:34 O 26 '64

INTELLECT
Awakening of the mind; excerpt from History of mankind. J. Hawkes. il UNESCO Courier 16:8-10 Je '63
Eureka process; excerpt from Act of creation. A. Koestler. il Horizon 6:16-25 Autumn '64
Homes that nurture intellect; with study-discussion program, by D. B. Harris and E. S. Harris. W. G. Hollister. bibliog il PTA Mag 57:8-10, 36 My '63
Need of intellect. R. O. Johann. America 111: 234 S 5 '64
Paper on intellectronics highlight for 25,000 at NEC exhibition. C. D. LaFond. Miss & Roc 15:34 O 26 '64
See also
Reason

INTELLECTUAL cooperation
See also
Educational exchanges
Exchange of persons programs
Exchanges, Literary and scientific
Inter-American institute of agricultural sciences
United Nations educational, scientific and cultural organization
United States—Cultural relations
United States—State, Department of—International scientific affairs, Office of

INTELLECTUAL freedom committees. See subhead intellectual freedom committee under names of library associations, e.g. American library association—Intellecutal freedom committee

INTELLECTUAL liberty
Aftermath and fallout; Catholic university hassle over the acceptability of four prominent theologians as speakers. America 108:387 Mr 23 '63
Artists and bureaucrats. R. Brustein. New Repub 149:36+ N 2 '63
Controversy within Catholicism; barring Catholic ecumenists from lecturing. C. D. Kean. Christian Cent 80:358-9 Mr 20 '63
Courage and cowardice; address, November 15-17, 1962. E. Castagna. Library J 88:504 F 1 '63
Freedom to read; active voice; excerpts from address, 1964. F. H. Wagman. il ALA Bul 58:473-81 Je '64
Goldfish bowl; ban on Catholic theologians. America 108:329 Mr 9 '63
I may, I might, I must; address, May 1962. D. Broderick. Library J 88:507-10 F 1 '63; Discussion. 88:1090+, 1924+ Mr 15, My 15 '63
Intellectual freedom. A. McNeal. ALA Bul 58: 537 Je '64
Intellectual freedom and the federal government; address, May 15, 1963. J. V. Lindsay. Pub W 183:18-21 My 27 '63
Law, liberty and libraries; excerpts from address, May 1, 1963. W. J. Brennan, jr. il Library J 88:2417-20 Je 15 '63
Trustee's role; freedom to read in Helen Kate Furness free library, Wallingford, Pa. H. A. Johnson. ALA Bul 57:631-3 Jl '63
Uninvited; speakers in a student-sponsored lecture series at Catholic university. Commonweal 77:608-9 Mr 8 '63
See also
Academic freedom
American civil liberties union
American library association—Intellectual freedom committee
Ontario library association—Intellectual freedom committee

INTELLECTUAL life
Geography of intellect, by N. Weyl and S. Possony. Review
Nat R 16:287-9 Ap 7 '64. A. J. Gregor
Printing and the mind of man; reprint. il Wilson Lib Bul 38:392-6 Ja '64
See also
Books and reading
also subhead Intellectual life under names of countries, states, cities, e.g. United States—Intellectual life

INTELLECTUALS
Anti-intellectualism in American life, by R. Hofstadter. Review
New Yorker 39:102+ Ja 25 '64. D. Malcolm
Reporter 29:37-40 Jl 4 '63. K. S. Lynn
Catholic intellectualism again. P. Gleason. America 112:112-19 Ja 23 '65
Doings and undoings; the fifties and after in the American writing, by N. Podhoretz. Review
Nation 198:298-300 Mr 23 '64. N. Hentoff
Historical relationship of liberals and intellectuals to organized labor in the United States. M. F. Neufeld. bibliog Ann Am Acad 350:115-28 N '63
Intellectual and the market place. G. J. Stigler. Nat R 15:473-4+ D 3 '63
Italy's intellectuals steer to the left. J. M. Cook. il N Y Times Mag p32+ My 26 '63
New debate: Catholic intellectual life. A. M. Greeley; J. D. Donovan; J. W. Trent. il Commonweal 81:33-42 O 2 '64
On crying for the moon. E. Capouya. Sat R 46:20 Ag 31 '63
President and the intellectuals. W. V. Shannon. Commonweal 79:386-7 D 27 '63
Washington insight; Kennedy and the intellectuals. J. Kraft. Harper 227:112+ N '63
You can't make a policy without breaking eggheads. Nat R 14:141+ F 26 '63

INTELLIGENCE
Genetics and intelligence: a review. L. Erlenmeyer-Kimling and L. F. Jarvik. bibliog il Science 142:1477-9 D 13 '63; Discussion. 144:80, 891 Ap 3, My 15 '64
I believe; ed. by J. Alley. I. Cuffey. Seventeen 23:54 Mr '64
Imitation of man by machine. U. Neisser. bibliog Science 139:193-7 Ja 18 '63; Discussion. 140:212-14+ Ap 12 '63
Intelligence and genetic trends; letter. H. B. Newcombe. bibliog Science 141:1104-6+ S 13 '63
Intelligence: source and early development. PTA Mag 59:18 S '64

INTELLIGENCE—*Continued*
One big reason why some people are poor: results of Armed forces qualification test. il U S News 56:98-9 F 24 '64
Your child's intelligence; reprint. il Todays Health 41:59-60 My; 11 Je; 70 Jl; 45 Ag; 74 S; 90 O '63
See also
Intellect

INTELLIGENCE, Military. See Military intelligence

INTELLIGENCE levels
Racial differences and the future. D. J. Ingle. bibliog Science 146:375-9 O 16 '64; Discussion. 146:1415-18, 1526-30; 147:6-7 D 11-18 '64, Ja 1 '65

Negroes

Chattel law and the Negro; excerpts from Crisis in black and white. C. E. Silberman. Fortune 69:142-3+ My '64
Geography of intellect, by N. Weyl and S. Possony. Review
Commentary 38:61-3 Jl '64. M. Mayer; Reply with rejoinder. M. Kotler. 39:11-12+ Ja '65
Intelligence or prejudice? questions and answers. E. Van Den Haag. Nat R 16:1059-63 D 1 '64
Race and reason, by C. Putnam. Review
New Repub 147:23-4 S 10 '62; 148:9-10 Ja 5 '63. D. S. Simmons; Discussion. 148:30 Ja 19; 29-31 F 23 '63
Science and the race problem; report of the AAAS committee on science in the promotion of human welfare. bibliog Science 142: 558-61 N 1 '63; Discussion. 142:1419; 143:306-8, 913-15; 144:365 D 13 '63, Ja 24, F 28, Ap 24 '64
Segs; symposium, ed. by R. Cleghorn. il Esquire 61:71-6+ Ja '64

INTELLIGENCE of animals. See Animal intelligence

INTELLIGENCE quotient
Big families for low IQ couples doesn't hurt intelligence level. Sci Digest 53:28-9 Ap '63
Genius explosion. Time 83:74 F 21 '64
Homes that nurture intellect; with study-discussion program, by D. B. Harris and E. S. Harris. W. G. Hollister. bibliog il PTA Mag 57:8-10, 36 My '63
Perceptual quotient devised for children. Sci N L 86:302 N 7 '64
Scandal of educational testing; excerpt from They shall not pass. H. Black. il Sat Eve Post 236:72+ N 9 '63

INTELLIGENCE service. See Secret service

INTELLIGENCE tests
How to test a baby's intelligence. il Sci Digest 55:8-11 Ja '64
How worthwhile are group IQ tests? il Good H 158:167 Je '64
Measure for crackpots. F. J. Gruenberger. il Science 145:1413-15 S 25 '64; Reply. H. Schenck, jr. 146:718 N 6 '64
Psychological testing and public responsibility; report on symposium sponsored by the Board of professional affairs of the American psychological association. L. F. Carter. Science 146:1695-7 D 25 '64
Scandal of educational testing; excerpt from They shall not pass. H. Black. il Sat Eve Post 236:72+ N 9 '63
Stretch your mental muscles; excerpt from Your key to creative thinking. S. S. Baker. il Read Digest 84:35-6+ My '64
True or false? tests tell the story; with study-discussion program by D. Harris and E. Harris. E. S. Bordin. il PTA Mag 59:4-6, 35-6 Ja '65
Useful genius; intelligence, creativity, and American values. K. Kreuter and G. Kreuter. il Sat R 47:64-7 O 17 '64
See also
Ability tests
Aptitude tests

Anecdotes, facetiae, satire, etc.

High I.Q. frat. S. Alexander. il Life 55:11+ Ag 16 '63
I don't like you, I.Q. P. Jennings. il Esquire 62:82-3+ Ag '64

INTERAGENCY committee on oceanography. See United States—Federal council for science and technology

INTER-AMERICAN center, Loyola university, New Orleans. See Institute of human relations

INTER-AMERICAN commission on human rights
Human rights and democracy. P. P. Camargo. il Américas 15:33-6 My '63
Prisoners in Cuba; summary of report. Américas 15:46 Jl '63

INTER-AMERICAN committee on the Alliance for progress. See Alliance for progress

INTER-AMERICAN conference of ethnomusicology
Music of the people; first Inter-American conference of ethnomusicology. A. Pardo-Tovar. il Américas 15:26-9 Jl '63

INTER-AMERICAN conference on social security
Social security and the Alliance for progress; seventh Inter-American conference on social security, Asunción, Paraguay, May 31-June 5, 1964. I. C. Merriam. Dept State Bul 51:320-1 Ag 31 '64

INTER-AMERICAN development bank
Achievements of the Inter-American development bank; statement, April 14, 1964. D. Dillon. Dept State Bul 50:717-22 My 4 '64
Everyone's bank. Time 81:29 Ap 26 '63
Our bank. Time 83:25 Ap 24 '64

INTER-AMERICAN economic and social council
IA-ECOSOC committees. Américas 15:45 Je '63
United States delegations to international conferences. Dept State Bul 49:800; 51:858-9 N 18 '63, D 14 '64

Meetings, 1963

IA-ECOSOC meetings. Américas 15:44-5 N '63
Progress of the Alliance. W. Velloso. il Américas 16:10-13 Ja '64

Meetings, 1964

Inter-American economic and social council reviews Alliance for progress; statement, December 8, 1964. T. C. Mann. Dept State Bul 51:898-901 D 28 '64

INTER-AMERICAN highway. See Pan American highway

INTER-AMERICAN institute of agricultural sciences
Agricultural institute. il Américas 16:44 Je '64
Agricultural training; expansion of graduate school at Tropical center for research and graduate education in Turrialba, Costa Rica. Américas 15:47 Jl '63

INTER-AMERICAN meeting of science and technology
Science, technology, and development. J. D. Perkinson. il Américas 16:1-5 Mr '64

INTER-AMERICAN peace committee
Situation in Panama; communiques, January 10 and January 15, 1964. Dept State Bul 50:152, 156 F 3 '64

INTER-AMERICAN program for advanced social science studies in the Caribbean area. See Organization of American states—Inter-American program for advanced social science studies in the Caribbean area

INTER-AMERICAN relations
For inter-American understanding: Pan American societies in the United States. G. Meek. il Américas 15:27-34 Ag '63
Interdependence and the principles of self-determination and nonintervention; address, April 16, 1963. E. M. Martin. Dept State Bul 48:710-15 My 6 '63
Our hemisphere; the long and short views; address, April 15, 1963. A. E. Stevenson. Dept State Bul 48:704-9 My 6 '63; Excerpts. Américas 15:44 Je '63
Partners in dissent; towards an inter-American dialogue; address, April 29, 1964. A. Morales-Carrión. Vital Speeches 30:522-6 Je 15 '64
Too many revolutions to the South. R. G. Mead, jr. il Sat R 48:85-6 Ja 2 '65
Torpedoes and concerts; joint maneuvers in South American waters. C. E. Erbsen. il Américas 15:35-8 Ag '63
See also
Organization of American states

INTER-AMERICAN scholarly book center
University press center opens in Mexico city. il Pub W 186:49 D 28 '64

INTER-AMERICAN treaty of reciprocal assistance
Ninth meeting of consultation: OAS foreign ministers vote measures against Cuba; concerning Rio treaty, with resolution and excerpts from governmental statements. il Américas 16:1-10 S '64

INTERCHANGE of students. See Students, Interchange of

INTERCHANGE of teachers. See Teachers, Interchange of

INTERCITY cooperation. See Intercommunity cooperation

INTERCOLLEGIATE athletics. See College athletics

INTERCOLLEGIATE debating. See Debates and debating

INTERCOLLEGIATE football. See Football

INTERCOLLEGIATE rowing association regatta. See Regattas

INTERCOMMUNICATING systems
Back talk from your house wiring. C. Tepfer. il Pop Sci 182:155-7 F '63
Build a surplus phone intercom. D. D. Darling. il Pop Mech 119:142 F '63
Communicating in a high-noise environment. R. P. Devaney. il Electr World 72:39-41+ N '64
Keep in touch. il Pop Gard 15:61 Jl '64
Simple home intercom. il Consumer Bul 47:43 Mr '64
Transistorized wireless intercom. L. M. Dezettel. il Electr World 69:76-7 F '63
Your second voice: the intercom. il McCalls 91:124-5 Mr '64

INTERCOMMUNION. See Lords Supper

INTERCOMMUNITY cooperation
Epidemic of friendship. D. D. Eisenhower. il Read Digest 83:132-8 N '63
More than the diplomats; people-to-people, programs of Wichita, Kan. and Rockville Centre, N.Y. il Am City 80:120+ Ja '65
Ship of hope. R. L. Tobin. Sat R 47:18 Mr 28 '64

INTERCONTINENTAL ballistic missiles. See Guided missiles

INTERCONTINENTAL ballistic transport. See Rockets, Military transport

INTERCULTURAL education
See also
Encampment for citizenship

INTERCULTURAL relations. See Cultural relations

INTERDENOMINATIONAL cooperation. See Religious cooperation

INTERDEPARTMENTAL committee on nutrition for national defense. See United States—Interdepartmental committee on nutrition for national defense

INTERDISCIPLINARY research, College. See Colleges and universities—Research

INTERESSENGEMEINSCHAFT farbenindustrie aktiengesellschaft
What am I bid? Newsweek 61:79 Mr 18 '63

INTEREST
Balance of payments; special message to Congress, July 18, 1963. J. F. Kennedy. Dept State Bul 49:250-9 Ag 12 '63
Bank rate: brake and throttle on credit. il Sr Schol 85:11 D 9 '64
Banks bow grudgingly; with editorial comment. il Bsns W p30, 160 D 12 '64
Banks hold breath over interest rates. il Bsns W p26-7 D 5 '64
Bond stickler: how deep the well? il Bsns W p83-4 Ap 4 '64
Brokers look to cut their own loan costs. il Bsns W p72+ D 26 '64
Cost of borrowing going up again? il U S News 55:111-12 S 23 '63
Do you know what you pay for credit? il Changing T 18:17-18 O '64
Fed cuts long-term buying; operation nudge. Bsns W p54 My 11 '63
How to find the true interest rate. il Changing T 18:16-17 My '64
How we hope Europe foils inflation. il Bsns W p82-3 F 15 '64
Interest rates level off. Bsns W p 144 My 23 '64
Know what it's costing you to borrow. B. Brantley. Suc Farm 62:39+ Je '64
Living it up; British bank rate raised. Time 83:95 Mr 6 '64
Money rates face new push. Bsns W p 142 O 26 '63
New fight over interest rates. U S News 57:88 D 14 '64
No jump in the cost of money; with charts. Bsns W p30-1 Ja 2 '65
Outlook on credit: rates will creep up. il Bsns W p42-3 D 28 '63
Raising the rate; increased bank rate in Britain. Newsweek 63:70 Mr 9 '64
Rigging interest rates. H. Hazlitt. Newsweek 64:76 Jl 13 '64
Talking of money. Fortune 71:117-18 Ja '65
What it costs to finance appliances & cars. il Changing T 17:37-8 Mr '63
When you borrow, when you buy, watch those interest rates! I. Ross. Read Digest 83:157-8+ N '63
Will interest rates rise? here's what bankers say. il U S News 56:90+ F 10 '64
See also
Instalment plan

INTEREST (psychology)
See also
Curiosity

INTERFAITH cooperation. See Religious cooperation

INTERFERENCE (light)
Amateur scientist; moiré patterns. G. Oster. il Sci Am 211:134-8+ N '64
Michelson-Morley experiment. R. S. Shankland. il Sci Am 211:107-14 N '64
Moiré patterns. G. Oster and Y. Nishijima. il Sci Am 208:54-63 bibliog(p 192+) My '63

INTERFERENCE, Radio. See Radio interference

INTERFERENCE, Television. See Television interference

INTERFEROMETERS
Accurate length measurement of meter bar with helium-neon laser. K. D. Mielenz and others. bibliog il Science 146:1672-3 D 25 '64
Amateur scientist; how to make a series interferometer. G. F. Pearce. il Sci Am 210:122-4+ Je '64
New dimensions for the stars. il Time 83:48 Ap 3 '64
Stellar interferometer at Narrabri observatory. R. H. Brown. il Sky & Tel 28:64-9 Ag '64
Unit promises laser output control. il Miss & Roc 13:38 N 4 '63

INTERFERON
Circulating interferon in mice after intravenous injection of virus. S. Baron and C. E. Buckler. bibliog il Science 141:1061-3 S 13 '63
Cytochemical assay of interferon produced by duck hepatitis virus. E. A. Sueltenfuss and M. Pollard. bibliog il Science 139:595-6 F 15 '63
Foreign nucleic acids. A. Isaacs. il Sci Am 209:46-50 bibliog(p 156) O '63
Host cell species specificity of mouse and chicken interferons. S. Baron and others. bibliog il Science 145:814 Ag 21 '64
Interferon production in chickens injected with brucella abortus. J. S. Youngner and W. R. Stinebring. bibliog il Science 144:1022-3 My 22 '64
Interferon; report on special symposium held at the sixty-fourth annual meeting of the American society for microbiology. M. M. Sigel. Science 146:956-7 N 13 '64
Interferons: selectivity and specificity of action in cell-free systems. A. J. Glasky and others. bibliog il Science 144:1581-3 Je 26 '64
New role for interferon. Sci Am 209:84+ S '63
Purified interferons: physical properties and species specificity. T. C. Merigan. bibliog il Science 145:811-13 Ag 21 '64

INTERINDUSTRY analysis. See Linear programming

INTERIOR, Department of. See United States—Interior, Department of

INTERIOR decoration
How architects practice interior design; summary of interviews. W. B. Foxhall. il Arch Rec 136:89+ N '64
Oldtime clutter is crowding back; with photographs by Milton H. Greene. Life 55:50-7 S 6 '63
See also
Hotel decoration
House decoration
Offices
School decoration
Yacht decoration

INTERIOR decorators
How to work with a decorator. Bet Hom & Gard 41:91 S '63
Interiors by Taylor. il Ebony 19:68-70+ Ap '64
When and how to use a decorator. E. Enright. il Redbook 122:56-7+ F '64

INTERLIBRARY loans
Access to information. M. M. Reynolds. Library J 89:1692-4 Ap 15 '64; Discussion. 89:1698, 2470 Ap 15, Je 15 '64
More libraries using teletype for interlibrary loan service. il Library J 89:4880 D 15 '64

INTERMARRIAGE of races
Are Americans afraid to be free? H. J. Creary. Cath World 198:115-21 N '63
Are interracial homes bad for children? il Ebony 18:131-2+ Mr '63
Bedroom issues; interracial marriage in Florida. Newsweek 64:21 D 21 '64
Breaking the rules; S. Fuller-Sandys and M. Dube. il Time 81:42 My 17 '63
Court will consider miscegenation laws; Florida ban. Christian Cent 81:693 My 27 '64; Reply. J. H. Willson. 81:935 Jl 22 '64
How the NAACP stands on intermarriage. U S News 55:9 S 2 '63
Image. il Time 82:27 S 13 '63
Integrated cohabitation; Florida miscegenation statute. A. M. Bickel. New Repub 150:4-5 My 30 '64

INTERMARRIAGE of races—*Continued*
Intermarriage and the race problem; interviews with leading authorities. il U S News 55:84-93 N 18 '63
Interracial cohabitation; case in Florida. New Repub 151:5 D 19 '64
Marriage by choice; miscegenation by cohabitation. il Time 83:61 My 8 '64
Miscegenation and the law. America 109: 619 N 16 '63
Mixed marriages: what justices said. U S News 57:7 D 21 '64
Negro-white marriages; New York city. E. C. Parker. Christian Cent 80:1383-4 N 6 '63
Race, sex and the Supreme court. A. Lewis. il N Y Times Mag p30+ N 22 '64
Should churches back mixed marriages? U S News 55:8 D 2 '63
Strange, isn't it? America 109:112 Ag 3 '63
Strict caution on miscegenation; case of McLaughlin v. Florida. Time 84:43 D 18 '64
We fell in love. il Newsweek 62:27-8 S 16 '63
When Negroes and whites intermarry; the problems. il U S News 55:63 O 7 '63
Where integration led to intermarriage. il U S News 55:10 S 16 '63
Will High court O.K. mixed marriages? il U S News 57:10 O 26 '64
Will High court rule on mixed marriages? U S News 56:14 My 11 '64
You can do something about prejudice. C. Thompson. Christian Cent 81:138-40 Ja 29 '64
See also
Indians of North America—Mixed bloods
Mulattoes
INTERMARRIAGES, Religious. See Marriages, Mixed
INTERMETALLIC compounds
Intermetallic compounds. W. W. Scanlon. bibliog il Science 142:1265-9 D 6 '63
INTERMEZZO; opera. See Strauss, R.
INTERNAL migration. See Migration, Internal
INTERNAL revenue. See Excise tax
INTERNAL revenue service. See United States —Internal revenue service
INTERNAL secretions. See Secretions
INTERNAL security
As security becomes a growing issue. U S News 57:6+ N 2 '64
Q-clearance: the development of a personnel security program. H. P. Green. il Bul Atomic Sci 20:9-15 My '64
Secretary Rusk's news conference of March 27, 1964. D. Rusk. Dept State Bul 50:570-6 Ap 13 '64
Tangled drama and private hells of two famous scientists. R. Coughlan. il Life 55:87A-94+ D 13 '63
World problems and national security: address, April 25, 1963. B. Goldwater. Vital Speeches 29:482-6 Je 1 '63
See also
Loyalty investigations
Official secrets
INTERNAL security, Senate subcommittee on. See United States—Congress—Senate—Committees
INTERNAL structure of the earth. See Earth —Internal structure
INTERNATIONAL academy of astronautics
Warsaw parley proposes joint lunar lab. W. C. Wetmore. Aviation W 81:34 S 14 '64
INTERNATIONAL academy of management
Brain trust for brass. il Bsns W p 180+ S 14 '63
INTERNATIONAL agreements. See Treaties
INTERNATIONAL AIESEC congress. See Students, Interchange of
INTERNATIONAL air cadet exchange. See United States—Civil air patrol
INTERNATIONAL air transport association
Air fares will drop. il Bsns W p 121-2+ S 7 '63
Airlines planning ticket swindle defense. J. W. Carter. Aviation W 80:26-9 Mr 23 '64
Atlantic air fares. America 108:732 My 25 '63
British say: raise air fares, or else. Bsns W p34 My 4 '63
Carrier concern mounting over rising ticket frauds and thefts. Aviation W 80:41 My 11 '64
Fare is foul, foul is fare for overseas air customers. il Newsweek 61:75 My 27 '63
Great air-fare snare. M. Elfin. Reporter 30: 36-8 Mr 12 '64
Hildred urges new lures for IATA market; Bogota meeting. J. R. Ashlock. Aviation W 81:38-9 S 14 '64
How to fix prices. Nat R 14:439 Je 4 '63
IATA delegates seek end to fare battle; with editorial comment. L. L. Doty. Aviation W 79:21, 26-8 O 7 '63
IATA fares chaos could force governments to negotiate rates. Aviation W 78:41 Ap 22 '63
IATA session delegates face reappraisal. L. L. Doty. Aviation W 79:41 O 14 '63
IATA traffic meeting recesses; early fare solution is unlikely. Aviation W 79:45 N 4 '63
Key Athens issues include credit, fares. J. W. Carter. Aviation W 81:36 S 21 '64
Knuckling under; international air fares. Time 81:94 My 24 '63
Lower-fare jet service challenges IATA. W. Wright. il Aviation W 79:40-1 D 2 '63
Major fare changes seen unlikely to follow IATA traffic session. L. L. Doty. Aviation W 81:39-40 O 19 '64
Meeting of worriers. Time 84:92+ S 25 '64
Nations agree to retain IATA fares role. L. L. Doty. Aviation W 79:28-9 Jl 29 '63
Objections expected on CAB fare rejection. Aviation W 78:43 F 25 '63
Pace of Athens meeting slowed by infighting over group fares. Aviation W 81:39 O 26 '64
Pan Am's ploy; suggested new thrift class. Newsweek 62:68 Jl 8 '63
Protests flood in as air fare dam breaks. Bsns W p34 My 18 '63
Restriction on fare veto asked at Bogota. J. R. Ashlock. Aviation W 81:35 S 21 '64
SST economics worry IATA conferees. J. R. Ashlock. il Aviation W 81:29-30 S 28 '64
SST model wind tunnel tests due Nov. 1. Aviation W 80:26 Je 1 '64
Transatlantic air fares. New Repub 148:5 My 25 '63
U.S. draws a bead on IATA; international air fares. Bsns W p30-1 My 25 '63
INTERNATIONAL arbitration. See Arbitration, International
INTERNATIONAL association of machinists
Blow to union shop. Bsns W p72 F 2 '63
Boeing holding out on union shop issue. Bsns W p54+ Ap 13 '63
Boeing strike delayed pending IAM vote. Aviation W 78:36 My 6 '63
Compromise ends tension at Boeing. Bsns W p 166 Ap 20 '63
IAM prepares for Boeing strike. Aviation W 78:37 Ap 15 '63
Sagging union shops; failure to get a union shop at Lockheed. Time 81:88 F 8 '63
Strike by IAM at Boeing averted. Aviation W 78:37 Ap 22 '63
Union's reward for not striking; ruling by National labor relations board. U S News 55:94 S 16 '63
What Boeing and union agreed on; machinists union. U S News 54:96 Ap 29 '63
Where unions have hit a roadblock. il U S News 54:88-90 F 11 '63
Why Wichita said no; rejection of new contract between the Boeing co. and the international assn. of machinists. il Bsns W p 106 Ap 27 '63
Workers reject new Boeing contract. Aviation W 78:27 Ap 29 '63
Workers vote on final Boeing proposal. Aviation W 78:29 Ap 1 '63
INTERNATIONAL astronautical congress
Meeting, 1964. S. F. Singer. Science 147:74-6 Ja 1 '65
INTERNATIONAL astronautical federation
Anti-G drug research described. W. C. Wetmore. Aviation W 81:24 S 21 '64
French underline growing IRBM/space integration; report on some principal papers presented. F. G. McGuire and others. Miss & Roc 13:18-19 O 14 '63
IAF stresses more cooperation. W. Beller. Miss & Roc 15:16-17 S 14 '64
Russians discuss space radiation findings at conference. H. David. Miss & Roc 13:34 O 21 '63
Use of drugs and servos urged to aid astronauts. W. Beller. il Miss & Roc 15:16-17 S 21 '64
INTERNATIONAL astronomical union
Astronomical news service. Sky & Tel 28:331 D '64
Astronomical notes from Hamburg. il Sky & Tel 28:341-4; 29:19-22 D '64, Ja '65
Evolution of galaxies; report on twelfth congress of the International astronomical union. T. Page. bibliog il Science 146: 804-6+ N 6 '64
Facts about the 1962 space bomb. J. Lear. il Sat R 46:45-8 Ap 6 '63
IAU at Hamburg: a first note. Sky & Tel 28:191 O '64
International discussion of Milky way research. B. J. Bok. il Sky & Tel 26:4-7 Jl '63
My trip to the IAU meeting. D. A. Hemenway. il Sky & Tel 28:260-3 N '64

INTERNATIONAL astronomical union—*Cont.*
New advances: sun, space astronomy, the galaxy; summaries of addresses at meeting. A. B. Severny; L. Goldberg; J. H. Oort. il Sky & Tel 28:264-7 N '64
Symposium on abundances of elements in stars. B. W. Sitterly. il Sky & Tel 29:11-14 Ja '65
Triennial review of astronomy; report on twelfth general assembly of the International astronomical union. V. K. McElheny. bibliog il Science 146:627-30 O 30 '64
INTERNATIONAL atomic energy agency
Atom scientists link work for new ideas; conference at Brookhaven national laboratory sponsored by IAEA. il Bsns W p 194-6 O 19 '63
Atoms-for-peace: hope deferred. H. L. Nieburg. Bul Atomic Sci 20:35-40 Ja '64
Four U.S. nuclear reactors placed under IAEA safeguards. Dept State Bul 51:27 Jl 6 '64
Global budgeting for science. J. Lear. Sat R 46:28 N 23 '63; Discussion. 47:95-6 Ja 4 '64
International atom; address, October 27, 1964. G. T. Seaborg. bibliog f Dept State Bul 51:781-4 N 30 '64
Nonproliferation of nuclear weapons. B. T. Feld. il Bul Atomic Sci 20:2-6 D '64
Nuclear energy for the benefit of man; statement, September 15, 1964. G. T. Seaborg. Dept State Bul 51:519-24 O 12 '64
On IAEA's future. A. Z. Rubinstein. Bul Atomic Sci 21:25-7 Ja '65
President Johnson reasserts U.S. support for IAEA; statement, December 8, 1963. L. B. Johnson. Dept State Bul 49:1019 D 30 '63
Radiochemical methods of analysis; report on symposium in Salzburg. W. W. Meinke. Science 147:182-3 Ja 8 '65
Rowe's reactor; open to inspection by I.A.E.A. il Time 83:27 Mr 13 '64
U-turn; cut back in production of materials for nuclear weapons. il Newsweek 63:85 My 4 '64
United States delegations to international conferences; IAEA meeting on desalting water; and general conference of IAEA. Dept State Bul 49:563-4 O 7 '63
United States favors extension of IAEA safeguards system; statement, September 27, 1963. H. D. Smyth. Dept State Bul 49:1019-21 D 30 '63
U.S. makes proposals for safeguards for peaceful nuclear activities and for bomber destruction; statements, March 5 and March 19, 1964. A. S. Fisher. bibliog f Dept State Bul 50:641-5 Ap 20 '64
World atom agency: Indian reactor accord, agreement on Japan point to more significant role for IAEA. D. S. Greenberg. Science 141:29 Jl 5 '63
World atom agency; negotiations on Indian reactor hold promise of brighter future for IAEA. D. S. Greenberg. Science 140:163 Ap 12 '63
INTERNATIONAL audio fair, London. See Audio fairs
INTERNATIONAL automobile show. See Automobiles—Exhibitions
INTERNATIONAL balance of payments. See Balance of payments
INTERNATIONAL bank for reconstruction and development
Charting new ways to settle accounts; World bank and IMF; with editorial comment. il Bsns W p94+, 152 S 28 '63
Consortium to aid India pledges $1 billion for 1964-65: communique, May 26, 1964. il Dept State Bul 50:943 Je 15 '64
Facing up to the fiscal facts of life. il Newsweek 62:100-2+ O 14 '63
Financial Olympics; meeting in Tokyo. Newsweek 64:90+ S 21 '64
International bank issues six-month financial statement. Dept State Bul 48:301 F 25 '63
Road to Huddersfield. by J. Morris. Review
Harper 227:93-4 Ag '63. P. Pickrel
Speeding up World bank's pace; Pres. Woods' goal. il Bsns W p 172+ S 12 '64
World bank and affiliates examine pressing problems of economic development. G. D. Woods. UN Mo Chron 1:59-62 N '64
World bank issues financial statement for first quarter. Dept State Bul 49:875-6 D 2 '63
World bank issues financial statement for fiscal year 1963. Dept State Bul 49:339 Ag 26 '63
World bank issues six-month financial statement. Dept State Bul 50:299 F 24 '64
World bank reports net income of $97.5 million in fiscal 1964. Dept State Bul 51:322-3 Ag 31 '64
World bank reports net income of $33 million in first quarter. Dept State Bul 51:790 N 30 '64
INTERNATIONAL bank of economic cooperation
Khrushchev as banker. New Repub 150:4 F 8 '64
INTERNATIONAL basic economy corporation
Profitable do-gooder. il Time 81:96 Ap 12 '63
INTERNATIONAL beauty congress. See Beauty contests
INTERNATIONAL biological program. See International council of scientific unions
INTERNATIONAL book fair, Frankfurt. See Book fairs
INTERNATIONAL book programs. See Books and reading—International aspects
INTERNATIONAL boundaries. See Boundaries
INTERNATIONAL boundary and water commission (United States and Mexico)
Peace on the Rio Grande. New Repub 149:7 S 21 '63
INTERNATIONAL boy scout jamboree. See Boy scouts
INTERNATIONAL brotherhood of electrical workers
How to stop strikes before they start. il Bsns W p43-4 Ag 24 '63
Labor's welfare state; the New York electrical workers. A. H. Raskin. Atlan 211:37-44 Ap '63
Story of two strikes: what unions are running up against; oil refinery in Texas, telephone company in Florida. U S News 55:97 Ag 19 '63
Why the twenty-five hour week hasn't caught on; New York electricians' special situation. il Bsns W p90+ Jl 6 '63
INTERNATIONAL brotherhood of firemen and oilers
Railroad hires new firemen, but . . . il U S News 55:75 Ag 12 '63
INTERNATIONAL brotherhood of teamsters, chauffeurs, warehousemen and helpers of America
Act II in Hoffa trial. Bsns W p 102+ Jl 18 '64
Aides quit, but Hoffa stays in driver's seat. il Bsns W p94+ D 14 '63
Big spender. Newsweek 62:33 O 14 '63
Can Hoffa hold on? il Bsns W p92+ Ja 11 '64
Can they find courage to fight? teamster leaders against Hoffa. il Bsns W p28-9 Mr 14 '64
Dream come true. Time 83:16 Ja 24 '64
For Hoffa: money problems, too; personal legal expenses out of teamsters treasury. U S News 56:97 My 11 '64
Freewheeling finances of the teamsters union. il Duns R 83:48+ Ja '64
Happy Hoffa. Newsweek 63:68 Ja 27 '64
Hoffa again; plan to achieve a common expiration date for teamster contracts. Nation 197:379 D 7 '63
Hoffa beats back dissidents; locals reject bid to rejoin AFL-CIO. il Bsns W p47 My 4 '63
Hoffa forever? J. O'Gara. Commonweal 78:240 My 24 '63; Reply. J. F. Flynn. 78:401 Jl 5 '63
Hoffa: new strong man of U.S. labor. U S News 54:46 My 13 '63
Hoffa reaches out; latest contract demands. Bsns W p47-8 N 16 '63
Hoffa wins again. T. Brooks. Reporter 28:34-5 My 23 '63
Hoffa's funds. Newsweek 63:36 My 25 '64
Hoffa's goal: nationwide contract. U S News 55:98 S 9 '63
Hoffa's throne totters. Bsns W p32 Mr 7 '64
Hoffa's voice on Capitol hill; S. Zagri. il Bsns W p45-6+ S 14 '63
If Hoffa stumbles. Reporter 30:12+ Ja 16 '64
Is Hoffa finished? A. H. Raskin. Reporter 30:22-4 Mr 26 '64
Is Hoffa washed up? U S News 56:114-15 Mr 23 '64
Life and times of Tony Pro. R. S. Gallagher and R. Semple. Reporter 29:37-40 S 12 '63
Limit of devotion. il Newsweek 62:75-6 D 16 '63
Managing your manpower: J. Hoffa's leverage technique. T. R. Brooks. Duns R 83:61-4 F '64
More trouble for teamsters. U S News 54:89 Je 17 '63
My private war with Hoffa; ruin of Coffey transfer by teamsters union. T. Coffey. il Sat Eve Post 237:68-70 Ja 4 '64
Now Hoffa has the power to call a nationwide strike. U S News 56:94-5 Ja 27 '64
Pattern for truckers; trucking industry's new contract. Bsns W p 105-6+ Ja 25 '64
Postscript on Tony Pro. Reporter 31:8 D 31 '64
Power of James R. Hoffa. A. H. Raskin. il Atlan 213:39-45 Ja '64

INTERNATIONAL brotherhood of teamsters, chauffeurs, warehousemen and helpers of America—*Continued*
Report (favorable) on a teamsters local; truck union, local 816 in New York. A. H. Raskin. il N Y Times Mag p53-4+ N 1 '64
Revolt against Hoffa? T. R. Brooks. Commonweal 79:385-6 D 27 '63
Revolt against Jimmy. Time 82:29 D 13 '63
Stakes in the struggle against Hoffa. L. Velie. Read Digest 84:92-6 Mr '64
Strike ends, cars get rolling; Operation haul-away. il Bsns W p25 Ag 1 '64
There's no revolt; Hoffa sentenced. il Newsweek 64:59-60 Ag 31 '64
Two down, one to go; Justice dept. vs teamsters chief Hoffa. il Bsns W p62-3 Ag 1 '64
Verdict on Hoffa. il Newsweek 63:30-1 Mr 16 '64
What's next for the teamsters? il U S News 57:66-8 Ag 10 '64
When Hoffa gets the power he wants; demand for a contract between trucking industry and teamsters union. il U S News 55:121 N 18 '63
Where union stands on Hoffa. U S News 57:68 Ag 31 '64
Will the law ever get Hoffa? H. Bigart. il Sat Eve Post 236:68-71 Mr 30 '63
INTERNATIONAL bureau of weights and measures
Scientists get a new way to measure time; vibration rate of cesium-133 atom. il Bsns W p84+ O 24 '64
INTERNATIONAL business machines corporation
Apostle of growth: the unorthodox Mr Watson. J. B. Weiner. Duns R 84:33-4 N '64
Aquinas on IBM tape. America 111:433-4 O 17 '64
Assault on fortress I.B.M. G. Burck. il Fortune 69:112-16+ Je '64
Can IBM keep up the pace? il Bsns W p92-8 F 2 '63
Computer system mixes science, business tasks; System/360. Sci N L 85:248 Ap 18 '64
Do-all thinkmachine; System/360. il Time 83:117 Ap 17 '64
$5-million search for answers; Harvard to begin a ten-year study, financed by IBM. il Bsns W p84+ Jl 4 '64
Flexible class scheduling by computer. Sch & Soc 92:220+ Sum '64
Going after the leader; IBM's System 360 and RCA's Spectra 70. il Bsns W p 122+ D 12 '64
Inside IBM's World's fair egg. H. B. Comstock. il Pop Sci 185:58-9+ Jl '64
IBM developing optical transistor. il Miss & Roc 12:40 Ap 1 '63
IBM goes to school. Newsweek 63:55-6 Ja 6 '64
IBM lab taps European science skills. P. J. Klass. il Aviation W 78:76-8 Ap 8 '63
I.B.M. on the Riviera. il Fortune 67:92-3 F '63
IBM unwraps its billion-dollar gamble; System/360 data equipment. il Bsns W p67-8+ Ap 11 '64
IBM v. the others. il Time 81:86+ Mr 8 '63
IBM's growth power. il Duns R 82:33-5+ Jl '63
IBM's study of employee relations and work-measurement standards. T. R. Brooks. Duns R 84:41+ Ag '64
New challenge to IBM; computers by Honeywell and GE. il Bsns W p30 D 7 '63
Now system 360. il Newsweek 63:91-3 Ap 20 '64
Science research assoc. sold to IBM for $62 million. Pub W 184:33 D 30 '63
Thinking man's exhibit; IBM pavilion at World's fair. il Esquire 60:118-23 O '63
Thought in suburbia; IBM's new world headquarters in Armonk, N.Y. Time 84:80 Ag 7 '64
INTERNATIONAL car club association. See Automobile clubs
INTERNATIONAL center for training in civil aviation, Mexico city. See Aviation schools
INTERNATIONAL chamber of commerce
Settled out of court. O. Schisgall. Read Digest 84:25-6+ Mr '64
INTERNATIONAL chemical workers union
Scripto on strike; the race-wage picket line. C. J. Levy. Nation 200:31-2 Ja 11 '65
INTERNATIONAL Christian leadership (organization)
Prayer for today; Presidential prayer breakfast. il Newsweek 61:87 F 18 '63
INTERNATIONAL church of the foursquare gospel
Foursquare with Aimee. il Time 83:62 F 28 '64
INTERNATIONAL city managers' association
Civil rights and the city manager. Am City 79:120+ Ja '64
Fiftieth City manager's convention highlights past, present, future. Am City 80:126-7 Ja '65
INTERNATIONAL civil aviation organization
Charting skies for supersonic air travel. R. M. MacDonnell. U N Rev 10:38-9 Mr '63
INTERNATIONAL club. See Washington, D.C.—Clubs
INTERNATIONAL code signals. See Signals and signaling
INTERNATIONAL coffee council
International coffee council meets. Dept State Bul 49:272-3 Ag 12 '63
INTERNATIONAL commission of jurists
Justice by publicity. il Time 85:41 Ja 15 '65
INTERNATIONAL committee of the Red cross. See Red cross—International committee, Geneva
INTERNATIONAL committee on space research. See International council of scientific unions—Committee on space research
INTERNATIONAL conference of genetics
Life sum-up. il Time 82:59 S 20 '63
INTERNATIONAL conference of women engineers and scientists
Talk of the town. New Yorker 40:22-3 Jl 4 '64
INTERNATIONAL conference on congenital malformations
Lyon & the Mouse. Time 82:64 Jl 26 '63
INTERNATIONAL conference on public education
Guidance and the lack of primary school teachers. Sch & Soc 91:338 N 2 '63
International politics and international education. W. W. Brickman. Sch & Soc 92:326 N 14 '64
INTERNATIONAL conference on the peaceful uses of atomic energy, 3d, Geneva, 1964
Age of nuclear power; excerpts from statement. G. T. Seaborg. il Sci N L 86:178 S 19 '64
Atom at work for peace; summary of views presented. UN Mo Chron 1:59-66 O '64
Building a peaceful world; excerpts from statement. Thant. il Sci N L 86:178+ S 19 '64
Conference on peaceful uses of atomic energy opens at Geneva; statements, August 29 and August 30, 1964. G. T. Seaborg; L. B. Johnson. Dept State Bul 51:408-12 S 21 '64
Electric power from atom. W. Davis. il Sci N L 86:147-8 S 5 '64
On the eve of the third Conference on the peaceful uses of atomic energy. V. S. Emelyanov. UN Mo Chron 1:84-6 Jl '64
Pricing the atom; third international Atoms-for-peace meeting. Newsweek 64:82 S 14 '64
Third atoms for peace conference. U N Rev 10:62-5 F '63
Third conference on peaceful uses of atomic energy opens in Geneva. UN Mo Chron 1:57-9 Ag; 43-5 O '64
INTERNATIONAL conference on youth
Meeting, 1964. Sch & Soc 92:365-6 N 28 '64
INTERNATIONAL conferences
Behind test ban talks. il Bsns W p26-7 Jl 13 '63
Calendar of international conferences and meetings. See issues of Department of state bulletin
Cartography in Africa; United Nations regional cartographic conference for Africa, Nairobi, Kenya, July 1-13, 1963. G. E. Pearcy. Dept State Bul 49:1014-18 D 30 '63
Foreign leaders gathered at an informal summit conference. R. A. Haeger. il U S News 55:38-41 D 9 '63
International meetings. See issues of United Nations review
Labor ministers' conference on the Alliance for progress; excerpts from address. W. W. Wirtz. Mo Labor R 86:789-93 Jl '63
More talks with the Russians; American and Soviet leaders of public opinion meet in Leningrad. N. Cousins. Sat R 47:30 S 26; 30-1 O 10 '64
New temperature; nuclear test ban treaty conference, Moscow. il Time 82:15-20 Ag 2 '63
PTA concerns are world concerns. J. Moorhead. il PTA Mag 58:26-8 Ja '64
President reports on progress of test ban talks at Moscow; statement, July 17, 1963. J. F. Kennedy. Dept State Bul 49:198 Ag 5 '63
President sends message to Bogotá conference of labor ministers; text of message, May 7, 1963. J. F. Kennedy. Dept State Bul 48:884-5 Je 3 '63
Rival missions to Moscow; Peking-Moscow talks and test ban conference. Bsns W p29 Jl 20 '63

INTERNATIONAL conferences—*Continued*
Spirit of Moscow. il Time 82:22-3 Jl 26 '63
United States delegations to international conferences. See occasional issues of Department of state bulletin
U.S. tries again to get an A-test ban; new talks set in Moscow. il Bsns W p26-7 Je 15 '63
When feuding Arabs held summit talks. il U S News 56:8 Ja 27 '64
See also names of international conferences, e.g. Conference of non-aligned nations, Cairo, 1964

INTERNATIONAL congress for scientific management
All over the world, a dilemma of purpose; 13th CIOS congress. il Bsns W p 102+ S 28 '63
Brain trust for brass. il Bsns W p 180+ S 14 '63
Business peace corps. il Newsweek 62:72 S 30 '63
Change of ideas. il Time 82:79 S 27 '63
SLA schedules participation in CIOS management congress. Library J 88:3186 S 15 '63
Summit meeting for world executives; CIOS 13th congress. il Bsns W p 114-15+ S 21 '63
Summit meeting of management. il Fortune 68:71-2+ N '63

INTERNATIONAL congress of philosophy
Athens below the border. Newsweek 62:94-5 S 23 '63
Man and the world: thirteenth International congress in Mexico. I. Quiles. il Américas 16:14-17 Ja '64

INTERNATIONAL congress of zoology
International congress of zoology. A. S. Romer. Science 140:1113-14+ Je 7 '63

INTERNATIONAL congress on education of the deaf
Meeting, 1963. Sch & Soc 92:34-5 Ja 25 '64

INTERNATIONAL congress on medical librarianship
International medical body: a congressional investigation in Washington. L. T. Morton. il Library J 88:2847-8 Ag '63

INTERNATIONAL convention for the high seas fisheries of the North Pacific Ocean
North Pacific fishery conference adjourns at Tokyo: statement, October 7, 1963; with final conference press release. B. A. Smith. Dept State Bul 49:709-10 N 4 '63
North Pacific fishery conference held at Tokyo; statement, September 10, 1963. J. F. Kennedy. Dept State Bul 49:519 S 30 '63
U.S. and Canada, and Japan resume fisheries talks at Ottawa; statement, September 4, 1964. L. B. Johnson. Dept State Bul 51: 441-2 S 28 '64
U.S. Canada, and Japan to discuss north Pacific fisheries. Dept State Bul 48:914 Je 10 '63

INTERNATIONAL convention of Christian churches. See Disciples of Christ

INTERNATIONAL cookery. See Cookery, International

INTERNATIONAL cooperation
Advancing the frontiers of human knowledge for the benefit of all mankind; remarks, January 18, 1964. L. B. Johnson. Dept State Bul 50:150-2 F 3 '64
Common problems of industrial and developing countries; statement, March 25, 1964. G. W. Ball. Dept State Bul 50:634-40 Ap 20 '64
Economic development: some lessons of a common experience; address, August 19, 1963. W. W. Rostow. Dept State Bul 49:422-30 S 16 '63; Same. Vital Speeches 29: 712-17 S 15 '63
Health for peace and vice versa; address, September 27, 1963. H. Cleveland. Dept State Bul 49:676-81 O 28 '63
Hope for reasoned agreement; remarks March 24, 1964. L. B. Johnson. Dept State Bul 50:576-7 Ap 13 '64
International aspects of development; address, April 5, 1963. U Thant. il U N Rev 10:12-14 Ap '63
International co-operation now a myth? D. Lawrence. U S News 57:120 D 7 '64
International economic cooperation; address, October 21, 1964. G. G. Johnson. Vital Speeches 31:67-71 N 15 '64
Open system in North-South relations, April 9, 1964. G. W. Ball. Dept State Bul 50:657-62 Ap 27 '64
Our common enterprise: a non-apocalyptic view. M. Todd. Bul Atomic Sci 20:27-9 F '64
Politics of population: a blueprint for international cooperation; address, May 4, 1963. R. N. Gardner. Dept State Bul 48:906-14 Je 10 '63
Promise of science and technology; address, November 12, 1964. A. E. Stevenson. Dept State Bul 51:810-15 D 7 '64
Science, a force for peace; remarks, February 6, 1964. L. B. Johnson. Dept State Bul 50:285-7 F 24 '64
Science and international cooperation; address, October 22, 1963. J. F. Kennedy. Dept State Bul 19:778-82 N 18 '63; Excerpt. Bul Atomic Sci 19:42 D '63
Security and freedom: a free-world responsibility; address, February 26, 1963. D. Rusk. Dept State Bul 48:383-8 Mr 18 '63
State of the North Atlantic alliance; address, July 12, 1963. D. Rusk. Dept State Bul 49:190-8 Ag 5 '63
Toilsome path to peace; address, March 19, 1964. D. Rusk. Dept State Bul 50:530-5 Ap 6 '64
Trading weather data; U.S-Soviet space cooperation. il Bsns W p77 Je 13 '64
U.N. adopts resolutions on cooperation in outer space; U.S. reaffirms offer to work with Soviet Union on manned lunar landing; statement, December 2, 1963; with texts of resolutions, December 13, 1963. A. E. Stevenson. bibliog f Dept State Bul 49:1005-14 D 30 '63
United States and Japan: common interests in the building of a peaceful world; address, January 28, 1964. D. Rusk. bibliog f Dept State Bul 50:230-5 F 17 '64
See also
Economic assistance
Economic planning, International
Inter-American relations
Science—International aspects
United Nations—Economic and social council
United States book exchange

INTERNATIONAL cooperation year
Building a great world society; address, June 10, 1964. L. B. Johnson. Dept State Bul 50:991-2 Je 29 '64; Excerpts. Sci N L 86:7 Jl 4 '64
Feast of reason. N. Cousins. NEA J 54:11 Ja '65
International cooperation in science; symposium. Bul Atomic Sci 21:32-9 Ja '65
International co-operation year. R. Enckell. UN Mo Chron 1:71-4 D '64
International cooperation year in 1965 called for by Assembly. U N Rev 10:65-6 F '63
Observance of International co-operation year, 1965. UN Mo Chron 2:35-6 Ja '65
Political year of the quiet sun; address, February 27, 1964. H. Cleveland. Dept State Bul 50:452-7 Mr 23 '64; Same. Vital Speeches 30:457-60 My 15 '64
President Johnson proclaims 1965 as International cooperation year; remarks at White House ceremonies, October 2, 1964; with text of proclamation. L. B. Johnson; D. Rusk. Dept State Bul 51:555-60 O 19 '64
President names Cabinet committee for International cooperation year. Dept State Bul 51:857-8 D 14 '64
Xerox, the U.N. and I.C.Y. C. Soule. il Christian Cent 81:1305-6 O 21 '64

INTERNATIONAL copyright. See Copyright

INTERNATIONAL correspondence
Ambassador by letter. J. Bartolini. il Recreation 57:64-5 F '64
Eleven-cent diplomats. il McCalls 90:56+ S '63
Letter to the Ghanaian times. E. Bayer. il Parents Mag 39:37+ My '64

INTERNATIONAL council of scientific unions
Mobilizing the world's biologists; International biological program. C. H. Waddington. Bul Atomic Sci 19:39-41 N '63

Committee on space research
Cosmonauts to fly this year. W. Beller. Miss & Roc 12:14-15 Je 10 '63
Facts about the 1962 space bomb. J. Lear. il Sat R 46:45-8 Ap 6 '63
Russians describe space tests at Cospar. W. C. Wetmore. Aviation W 80:33-4 My 18 '64
Soviet COSPAR papers cite disorders experienced by several cosmonauts. F. G. McGuire. Miss & Roc 14:44+ My 25 '64
U.S. space activities. Sci N L 83:375 Je 15 '63

Scientific committee on oceanic research
Mining the bottom of the sea; excerpts from study. R. Revelle. il Sat R 47:60-1 O 3 '64

INTERNATIONAL court of arbitration, The Hague
Secretary designates U.S. members of Permanent court of arbitration. Dept State Bul 49:32 Jl 1 '63

INTERNATIONAL court of justice, The Hague
International court of justice; election of five members. U N Rev 10:22-3 D '63
International court of justice; judgement on preliminary objections in the case of Barcelona traction, light and power company, limited. UN Mo Chron 1:66-9 Ag '64
Mankind's highest tribunal. il Time 82:50 N 1 '63
Role of international law in world affairs; remarks, November 14, 1964. D. Rusk. Dept State Bul 51:802-3 D 7 '64
Rule of law, now; address, July 3, 1963. A. Chayes. Dept State Bul 49:162-7 Jl 29 '63; Same. Vital Speeches 29:696-9 S 1 '63
Too grave a risk: the Connally amendment, by D. Kitchel. Review
Nat R 14:463 Je 4 '63. H. Alexander and H. Alexander
Tribunal of the nations. il Time 82:58+ N 22 '63

Decisions

Northern Cameroons; judgment. U N Rev 11:41-2 F '64

INTERNATIONAL criminal police commission
Pounding a beat that's worldwide. il Bsns W p68-70 N 28 '64

INTERNATIONAL date line
Daylight saving is one result of international time standard. T. D. Nicholson. il Natur Hist 73:54-6 Ap '64

INTERNATIONAL design conference
Aspen: International design conference. R. Tarschys. il Craft Horiz 24:50 S '64

INTERNATIONAL development association
New resources to be contributed for replenishment of IDA funds. il Dept State Bul 51:119-20 Jl 27 '64
Poorer nations face a debt crisis; repaying creditors. il Bsns W p 110+ D 7 '63
President signs International development association bill; remarks, May 26, 1964. L. B. Johnson. Dept State Bul 50:935 Je 15 '64
Soft approach. Time 85:85 Ja 15 '65

INTERNATIONAL documents
See also
International federation for documentation

INTERNATIONAL economic planning. See Economic planning, International

INTERNATIONAL economic policy. See Economic policy

INTERNATIONAL education
Education for world understanding. E. U. Condon. Bul Atomic Sci 20:18-19 Mr '64
Idea of a world college; experiment in global education. H. Taylor. Sat R 47:29-32+ N 14 '64; Discussion. 47:33 D 5; 33 D 12; 17 D 19 '64
International living in the universities of the past. W. W. Brickman. Sch & Soc 92:40 F 8 '64
International politics and international education. W. W. Brickman. Sch & Soc 92:326 N 14 '64
National development and international education. P. G. Purcell. Sch & Soc 92:209-10 My 2 '64
Ugly American undergraduate; adaptation of address, December 7, 1963. C. R. Wilson. Sch & Soc 92:351-4 N 28 '64
See also
Area studies
Experiment in international living (organization)
Institute of international education
International relations—Study and teaching
International schools service, incorporated
Salzburg seminar in American studies
Travel study courses
United Nations educational, scientific and cultural organization

INTERNATIONAL educational exchanges. See Educational exchanges

INTERNATIONAL eucharistic congress. See Eucharistic congresses

INTERNATIONAL exchange cadets, Civil air patrol. See United States—Civil air patrol

INTERNATIONAL executive service corps
Executive peace corps. Time 84:102 D 4 '64
Moving into action. il Bsns W p58+ N 28 '64
Paunch corps. Newsweek 63:77-8 My 4 '64

INTERNATIONAL expositions. See Exhibitions

INTERNATIONAL federation. See International organization

INTERNATIONAL federation for documentation
International federation for documentation. D. J. Foskett. Library J 89:4478-80 N 15 '64

INTERNATIONAL federation for internal freedom
Dangerous magic of LSD. J. Kobler. il Sat Eve Post 236:30-2+ N 2 '63
Hallucinogenic drug cult. N. Gordon. il Reporter 29:35-43 Ag 15 '63; Discussion. 29:6+ S 12; 8 S 26 '63
No illusions; psilocybin tests at Harvard. il Newsweek 61:92-2 Je 10 '63
Strange case of the Harvard drug scandal. A. T. Weil. Look 27:46+ N 5 '63

INTERNATIONAL federation for modern languages and literatures
Merchants of light. R. J. Clements. Sat R 46:32-3 S 21 '63

INTERNATIONAL federation of airline pilots associations
Pilots group maps SST operations policy. H. J. Coleman. Aviation W 79:47+ N 25 '63

INTERNATIONAL federation of library associations
International standardization of library statistics. F. L. Schick. ALA Bul 58:1011-13 D '64
Strong American representation at IFLA meeting in Bulgaria. Library J 88:3811-12 O 15 '63
Turning point. Library J 89:4481-2 N 15 '64

INTERNATIONAL federation of petroleum workers
Oil strikers get global support; IFPW back OCAW. il Bsns W p60+ My 25 '63

INTERNATIONAL festival of cinematographic art. See Moving picture festivals

INTERNATIONAL festival of music and drama, Edinburgh
Highland measures; 17th Edinburgh festival. M. Cooper. il Mus Am 84:17-18 O '64

INTERNATIONAL festival of Strasbourg. See Music festivals—France

INTERNATIONAL film festival, Cannes. See Cannes international film festival

INTERNATIONAL film festival of America. See Moving picture festivals

INTERNATIONAL finance. See Finance, International

INTERNATIONAL game fish association
Blue marlin blues. Sports Illus 21:6 Ag 10 '64

INTERNATIONAL geophysical year
Antarctic dilemma. R. Lewis. Bul Atomic Sci 19:37-9 F '63
First it was IGY, now it's IQSY. B. H. Frisch. il Sci Digest 53:46 My '63
Results of the IGY: aeronomy, glaciology, meteorology, and oceanography; report of National academy of sciences symposium. Science 142:414-16+ O 18 '63

INTERNATIONAL government. See International organization

INTERNATIONAL harvester company
Harvester tries for richer crop. il Bsns W p66-7+ O 3 '64
Numerical controls get a new chore; techniques of mass production. Bsns W p54 Ag 3 '63

INTERNATIONAL health organization. See World health organization

INTERNATIONAL horticultural exhibition, Hamburg. See Horticultural exhibitions

INTERNATIONAL human rights year (proposed)
International human rights year; statement, October 21, 1964. F. H. Williams. Dept State Bul 51:787-9 N 30 '64

INTERNATIONAL hydrological decade
Science in action; new wage for hydrology. R. L. Nace. Natur Hist 74:63-4+ Ja '65
U.S. supports International hydrological decade. Dept State Bul 51:321-2 Ag 31 '64

INTERNATIONAL ice patrol
International ice patrol warnings start soon. Sci N L 83:98 il(p97) F 16 '63

INTERNATIONAL institute of educational planning
Education's role in the developing nations. P. H. Coombs. il Sat R 46:29-30 Ag 17 '63

INTERNATIONAL institute of science and technology (proposed)
Plans move ahead for ole' International tech. Sci Digest 53:52-3 My '63

INTERNATIONAL joint commission (United States and Canada)
U.S. requests three IJC studies on water levels and pollution; texts of letters. W. R. Tyler; D. Rusk. Dept State Bul 51:598-600 O 26 '64

INTERNATIONAL labor office
See also
International labor organization

INTERNATIONAL labor organization
Boycott at Geneva; African walkout. America 109:4 Jl 6 '63
International labour conference. UN Mo Chron 1:99 Ag '64
International labor conference of 1963. L. R. Klein. Mo Labor R 86:914-19 Ag '63
ILO and the bishops. B. L. Masse. America 111:797-9 D 19 '64
ILO director-general's speech on the South African question; excerpt, June 18, 1963. D. A. Morse. Mo Labor R 86:920-4 Ag '63

INTERNATIONAL labor organization—*Cont.*
ILO report on forced labor accepted. U N Rev 10:33 Mr '63
NAM and ILO. America 110:132 Ja 25 '64
Partial exclusion of South Africa from ILO meetings. U N Rev 10:59-60 Jl '63
Study reports acute shortage of experienced air controllers. Aviation W 79:54+ D 16 '63
United States delegations to international conferences. Dept State Bul 51:67-8 Jl 13 '64

INTERNATIONAL ladies' garment workers' union
David Dubinsky: why his throne is wobbling. P. Jacobs; discussion. Harper 226:12+ F '63
New giant in union funds; merger of ILGWU pension funds. Bsns W p36+ Ag 8 '64
Testing labor's ultimate weapon; boycott of unfair goods. il Bsns W p50+ Jl 25 '64

INTERNATIONAL language. See Language, Universal

INTERNATIONAL latex corporation
Annals of business; trade secrets in development of space suits issue in Goodrich vs D. W. Wohlgemuth case. J. Brooks. New Yorker 39:37-8+ Ja 11 '64

INTERNATIONAL law
Case for international law; addresses, April 25, 26 and 27, 1963. S. M. Schwebel; R. N. Gardner; F. T. P. Plimpton. Dept State Bul 48:785-800 My 20 '63
Department releases first volume of Digest of international law; Department announcement, July 15, 1963; with remarks by Secretary Rusk. Dept State Bul 49:204-5 Ag 5 '63
Father Francisco de Vitoria. il Américas 15:40-1 N '63
Foreign policy and the rule of law; address, May 3, 1963. G. C. McGhee. Dept State Bul 48:867-71 Je 3 '63
Foundations of modern international law; excerpts from address, October 8, 1963. J. A. Mora. Américas 15:1 N '63
International law in a divided world. O. J. Lissitzyn. bibliog f Int Concil 542:3-69 Mr '63
International law: old and new. C. G. Fenwick. il Américas 15:26-9 S '63
One world, one law? M. R. MacGuigan. Commonweal 81:450-3 D 25 '64
President and Chancellor Erhard reaffirm commitment to U.S.-German cooperation within free-world community; joint communique, December 29,1963; with exchanges of remarks, December 28 and December 29, 1963. L. Erhard; L. B. Johnson. Dept State Bul 50:74-80 Ja 20 '64
Principles of international law concerning friendly relations and cooperation among states: international law and nonintervention; statement, December 3, 1963. F. T. P. Plimpton. bibliog f Dept State Bul 50:133-43 Ja 27 '64
Principles of international law concerning friendly relations and cooperation among states: sovereign equality of states; statement, December 3, 1963. E. F. Kelly. Dept State Bul 50:264-7 F 17 '64
Principles of international law concerning friendly relations and cooperation among states: threat or use of force; statement, November 11, 1963. F. T. P. Plimpton. Dept State Bul 49:973-83 D 23 '63
Role of law in political aspects of world affairs; address, December 29, 1962. L. C. Meeker. Dept State Bul 48:83-8 Ja 21 '63
Rule of law as a foreign policy; address, April 7, 1964. C. S. Rhyne. Vital Speeches 30:467-70 My 15 '64
See also
Blockade
Claims
Extradition
International commission of jurists
Rule of law
Territorial waters
United Nations—Legal committee

INTERNATIONAL law commission. See United Nations—International law commission

INTERNATIONAL league for the rights of man
Roger Baldwin. W. Morris. New Repub 150:8-10 Ja 25 '64

INTERNATIONAL loans. See Loans, Foreign

INTERNATIONAL London daily express offshore powerboat race. See Motor boat racing

INTERNATIONAL longshoremen's and warehousemen's union
Aloha a la sinistra. L. V. Cott. il Nat R 15:57-8 Jl 30 '63
Hawaii's unions get mainland look. il Bsns W p86+ S 7 '63
Man who made the most of automation. Time 82:19 D 27 '63
New Harry Bridges. F. Porter. New Repub 149:5-6 O 26 '63
On the waterfront. Newsweek 62:61 Jl 29 '63
Strange twilight of Harry Bridges. B. H. Wolfe. Harper 228:78-80+ Mr '64

INTERNATIONAL longshoremen's association
Another strike on the docks: why? U S News 57:92-3 O 12 '64
Clash is brewing on docks. Bsns W p66 Jl 4 '64
Crippling dock strike settled. il Sr Schol 82:22 F 6 '63
Dock dispute goes back to the umpires; walkout over size of work gangs on piers. il Bsns W p34 Ag 8 '64
Dock strike gets T-H treatment. Bsns W p48 O 10 '64
Dockers take a second look at pact. Bsns W p 124 Ja 23 '65
I don't request; squabble over wheat shipments to Russia. il Newsweek 63:62 Mr 2 '64
Jailing a whole local; longshoremen's refusal to load Canadian ship at Chicago. Bsns W p 134+ D 7 '63
Jobs and machines; reply. T. Donovan. America 108:184 F 9 '63
New dock boss barks, but will he bite? Bsns W p75+ Jl 27 '63
Political picketing by unions? U S News 56:88 Je 8 '64
Russia's grain is last straw; ILA boycott. il Bsns W p 106-7 F 22 '64
Shippers give in but blast panel. il Bsns W p34 Ja 26 '63
Taking the heat off wheat; end of ILA boycott. Bsns W p24-5 F 29 '64
They'd rather strike than work. il Time 85:66-7 Ja 22 '65
U.S. dock talks race deadline. Bsns W p52 N 14 '64
Waterfront hot potato; Labor dept. study of longshore work practices. il Bsns W p 128+ Mr 14 '64
Waterfront revisited. B. Schulberg. il Sat Eve Post 236:28-32+ S 7 '63
Why dock settlement backfired. il Bsns W p28 Ja 16 '65

INTERNATIONAL Los Angeles music festival. See Music festivals—California

INTERNATIONAL management congress. See International congress for scientific management

INTERNATIONAL marriages. See Marriages, International

INTERNATIONAL micrographic congress
Int'l micrographic congress established in Ann Arbor. Pub W 183:34 Ap 1 '63

INTERNATIONAL minerals and chemical corporation
For global gamesmen; INTOP for executives. Bsns W p70 N 30 '63

INTERNATIONAL monetary fund
After the dollar wins. Bsns W p 116+ N 23 '63
Balance of payments; special message to Congress, July 18, 1963. J. F. Kennedy. Dept State Bul 49:250-9 Ag 12 '63
Bigger role for IMF. Bsns W p30 S 21 '63
Charting new ways to settle accounts; World bank and IMF; with editorial comment. il Bsns W p94+. 152 S 28 '63
Deliberate pace for monetary reform; IMF Tokyo meeting. il Bsns W p 111-12 My 30 '64
Developing strength of the International monetary system; statement, September 8, 1964. D. Dillon. Dept State Bul 51:444-8 S 28 '64
Dollar and the international monetary system. J. W. Angell; reply with rejoinder. E. N. Adams. Science 140:1141-2+ Je 7 '63
Easier world credit; concerning Brookings institution report. il Bsns W p 17-18 Ag 3 '63
Facing up to the fiscal facts of life. il Newsweek 62:100-2+ O 14 '63
Fattening the fund. Newsweek 63:38+ Je 29 '64
Financial Olympics. il Time 84:106 S 18 '64
Financial Olympics; meeting in Tokyo. Newsweek 64:90+ S 21 '64
For world bankers caution is the word; plan to strengthen payments system. il Bsns W p24-5 Ag 15 '64
From banque to bank. Newsweek 62:55 Jl 1 '63
Future of the fund. Newsweek 64:70-1 Ag 17 '64
General practitioner. Time 81:78+ Je 28 '63
Group of ten releases report on International monetary system; statement, August 1, 1964. V. Giscard d'Estaing. Dept State Bul 51:323-5 Ag 31 '64

INTERNATIONAL monetary fund—*Continued*
How real is the drain on dollars? il Bsns W p43-4+ S 5 '64
Innovation at IMF. A. O. Stanley. Duns R 81:60-1 Je '63
IMF feels impact of stronger Europe. Bsns W p 150-2+ Je 15 '63
IMF group of ten agrees to undertake study of international monetary system; statement, October 2, 1963. C. D. Dillon. Dept State Bul 49:615 O 21 '63
International monetary fund: its work and its future. M. D. Goldstein. il Dept State Bul 49:465-76 S 23 '63
Latest idea: instant gold. U S News 54:107 Je 3 '63
Monetary fund has its own ideas; increasing world credit. Bsns W p28 S 14 '63
Monetary fund outlook: new chief, but few changes. U S News 55:18 Jl 1 '63
More credit for world trade. il Bsns W p25-7 O 5 '63
Plan or no plan or un-plan? economic planning in Canada; address, June 3, 1963. W. E. McLaughlin. Vital Speeches 29:637-9 Ag 1 '63
Powerful IMF. Time 81:96 Mr 15 '63
Protecting the dollar with francs and marks; Treasury taps IMF. Bsns W p26 F 22 '64
Reforming the international monetary system. R. V. Roosa. For Affairs 42:107-22 O '63
Rift in IMF bursts into open. il Bsns W p30-1 S 12 '64
Schweitzer approach. Fortune 68:75-6+ S '63
Search for a successor. Newsweek 61:80+ My 20 '63
Skeleton that didn't rattle; report on annual meeting. M. A. Heilperin. Fortune 68: 104 D '63
Strengthening the international monetary system; remarks and statements, September 30-October 4, 1963. J. F. Kennedy; C. D. Dillon; G. W. Ball. Dept State Bul 49:610-23 O 21 '63
Towards an expanding world economy. P. P. Schweitzer. UN Mo Chron 1:63-6 N '64
Undo the IMF system. H. Hazlitt. Newsweek 62:101 N 11 '63
United States makes first drawing from International monetary fund. Dept State Bul 50:466-7 Mr 23 '64
When dollars begin to stay home. Bsns W p24 Ag 8 '64
When the dollars come home. il Time 82:98 O 11 '63
World bankers take a cautious step. Bsns W p 144 Ag 22 '64
World monetary order. H. Hazlitt. Newsweek 63:92 Ap 27 '64
World monetary reform. H. Hazlitt. Newsweek 62:96 O 21 '63
World money reform. H. Hazlitt. Newsweek 64:74 S 7 '64
World money reform gets stronger support. Bsns W p26 O 17 '64

INTERNATIONAL music council
Opera conference in Hamburg; International congress of contemporary music theater. O. Daniel. Sat R 47:40-1 Ag 22 '64

INTERNATIONAL music fund
Koussevitzky recording awards. R. Jacobson. Mus Am 83:46 My '63

INTERNATIONAL North Pacific fisheries commission
Fishing, not for fun. il Bsns W p32-3 Je 29 '63
U.S. accepts recommendations on halibut abstention; statement, March 23, 1963. Dept State Bul 48:574 Ap 15 '63

INTERNATIONAL office of consumers' unions
Rising tide; third biennial conference of the International organization of consumers' unions. Consumer Rep 29:415 S '64

INTERNATIONAL Olympic committee. See Olympic games

INTERNATIONAL one-designs. See Sailboat racing

INTERNATIONAL organization
Arms control and behavorial science; excerpts from address, September 2, 1963. W. H. Goodenough. bibliog Science 144:821-4 My 15 '64
Atlantic community: an American view; address, May 9, 1963. W. W. Rostow. Dept State Bul 48:855-60 Je 3 '63
Case against international control of weapons. W. R. Kintner. Cur Hist 47:103-6+ Ag '64
Foreign policy and the individual: identity in diversity; address, March 12, 1964. K. Louchheim. Dept State Bul 50:591-4 Ap 13 '64
Foreign policy and the rule of law; address, May 3, 1963. G. C. McGhee. Dept State Bul 48:867-71 Je 3 '63
Great power and great diversity: the perceptions and policies of President Kennedy; address, December 1, 1963. H. Cleveland. Dept State Bul 49:964-9 D 23 '63
International force. M. Roshwald. Bul Atomic Sci 19:24-7 Ap '63
International organization and space law; address, May 1, 1963. A. Chayes. Dept State Bul 48:835-8 My 27 '63
Is it time for the second step? remaining tasks in the search for peace. J. F. Wharton. Sat R 46:8-11+ Ag 17 '63
Politics in the twentieth century, by H. J. Morgenthau. Review
Commentary 35:506-16 Je '63. G. Lichtheim
Stitching the world together; toward a global democracy. P. C. Jessup. Sat R 47:17-19+ F 1 '64
World government: last refuge of liberalism. F. S. Meyer. Nat R 14:197 Mr 12 '63

Regional organizations

Tides of change; address, February 12, 1963. J. R. Schaetzel. Dept State Bul 48:322-8 Mr 4 '63
See also
Atlantic community
Organization of American states

Study and teaching

Law and order: courses for teachers. Sr Schol 84:2T F 14 '64

INTERNATIONAL Passamaquoddy tidal power project. See Passamaquoddy tidal power project

INTERNATIONAL peace film festival. See Moving picture festivals

INTERNATIONAL petroleum company
Canceling the oil concession. il Time 82:42 N 8 '63
For young artists: series of national salons begins in Bogotá. L. J. Ahlender. il Américas 17:36-8 Ja '65

INTERNATIONAL police
International force. M. Roshwald. Bul Atomic Sci 19:24-7 Ap '63
See also
United Nations—Armed forces

INTERNATIONAL printing machinery and allied trades exhibition. See Exhibitions

INTERNATIONAL publishers association
Int'l publishers assn. names new secretary. Pub W 185:33 Ap 13 '64
17th congress of the IPA: publishing in an age of change. il Pub W 186:38-40 D 28 '64

INTERNATIONAL publishers company
Court orders hotel to allow publisher's reception; 40th anniversary of International publishers at the Statler Hilton hotel in New York. Pub W 187:275-6 Ja 25 '65

INTERNATIONAL publishers congress. See International publishers association

INTERNATIONAL publishers prize
Formentor and International publishers prizes awarded. Pub W 185:42 My 18 '64

INTERNATIONAL reading association
Meeting. Sr Schol 82:1T+ My 15 '63
Meeting, 1964. Sr Schol 84:1T-3T My 15 '64

INTERNATIONAL recreation association
World recreation congress. il Recreation 57: 66 F '64

INTERNATIONAL Red cross. See Red cross

INTERNATIONAL Red cross committee. See Red cross—International committee, Geneva

INTERNATIONAL relations
Adenauer sizes up de Gaulle; interview, ed. by K. Lachmann. K. Adenauer. U S News 54:31 F 11 '63
Adenauer talks about Johnson; interview, ed. by K. Lachmann. K. Adenauer. il U S News 55:44-7 D 16 '63
Advancing the American national interest without war. A. I. Waskow. Bul Atomic Sci 20:23-5 F '64; Reply with rejoinder. A. Forbes. 20:36-8 Je '64
After the test ban. P. Horton. Reporter 29: 14+ Ag 15 '63
After the test ban: the US must take the initiative in Europe. Z. Brzezinski. New Repub 149:18-21 Ag 31 '63; Reply; R. Steel. 149:36+ O 5 '63
Allies at the funeral. New Repub 149:4-5 D 7 '63
As a famed historian sees the world of the future; interview, ed. by J. Fromm. A. J. Toynbee. il U S News 56:78-82 Mr 30 '64
As de Gaulle sees world issues now; excerpts from news conference, July 23, 1964. C. de Gaulle. il U S News 57:10 Ag 3 '64
As Polaris ship sails with seven nation crew; destroyer U.S.S. Biddle, demonstration ship for MLF or multilateral force. il U S News 57:48-9 Ag 3 '64

INTERNATIONAL relations—*Continued*
As tensions ease, a time to look inward. il Newsweek 63:49 Ap 20 '64
Big three talks. New Repub 149:5 O 12 '63
Can a nuclear world war be avoided? N. A. Graebner. Ann Am Acad 351:132-9 Ja '64
Catholics and isolationism; Peace on earth. J. O'Gara. Commonweal 78:219 My 17 '63
CIA analysis. New Repub 151:3-4 S 12 '64
Change and contrast; governments of Soviet Union, Great Britain, United States. D. Lawrence. U S News 57:148 O 26 '64
Coalition diplomacy in a nuclear age. H. A. Kissinger. For Affairs 42:525-45 Jl '64
Comment on the world's news fronts; excerpts from the press. See issues of Senior scholastic
Communism and peaceful coexistence; address, October 1, 1963. Earl of Home. Vital Speeches 30:5-9 O 15 '63
Confused alliances. Newsweek 61:37-8 Mr 11 '63
Cracked alliance. L. J. Halle. New Repub 148:17-20 F 23 63
Cuba crisis and nuclear arms; why de Gaulle goes his own way; reprint. C. B. Luce. U S News 54:64-5 F 18 '63
Day the cold war changed. J. Lomax. Nation 197:10-12 Jl 6 '63
De Gaulle's pursuit of grandeur; excerpt from American foreign policy. D. Brandon. Cath World 199:224-9 Jl '64
Demilitarized world and how to get there. W. Millis. Sat R 47:18-22+ S 12 '64
Détente through firmness. K. U. von Hassel. For Affairs 42:184-94 Ja '64
Diplomacy of mutual example. Nation 198:41 Ja 13 '64
Disarmament after Cuba. D. R. Inglis; discussion. Bul Atomic Sci 19:28-30 Mr '63
East and West enter a new phase; strange alliance between U.S. and U.S.S.R. E. Crankshaw. il N Y Times Mag p 16+ Ag 30 '64
East-West detente. New Repub 149:6-7 Jl 20 '63
East-West, North-South. il Newsweek 63:28-9 Ja 13 '64
East-West relations; address, January 22, 1964. D. Ormsby Gore. Vital Speeches 30:286-8 F 15 '64
East-West relations and the United Nations; address December 2, 1962. U Thant. U N Rev 10:55-9 Ja '63
Facing the dictators, by A. Eden. Review
Nat R 14:120+ F 12 '63. T. Molnar
Fulbright and myths. Commonweal 80:101-2 Ap 17 '64
Future is ours; encyclical Pacem in terris. Life 54:4 Ap 26 '63
Great deflation. il Time 81:19-20 My 3 '63
Gullibility of the neutrals. O. Handlin. Atlan 211:41-7 Mr '63
Haile Selassie I, addresses General assembly; summary of address, October 4, 1963. Haile Selassie I. il U N Rev 10:4-5 N '63
Has race trouble tarnished U.S. image abroad? il U S News 55:66 Ag 19 '63
He who says no; obstacle to appeasement with the Soviet bloc. Nat R 15:88-9 Ag 13 '63
Illusion of victory. D. Brandon. Commonweal 78:473-6 Ag 9 '63
In an era of self-interest. il Time 83:21-2 Mr 13 '64
In 1963, we survived. Christian Cent 80:1599-601 D 25 '63
International relations and the psychologist. N. Jordan. Bul Atomic Sci 19:29-33 N '63; Discussion. 19:33-6+ N '63; 20:24 Mr '64
Is it peaceful? is it coexistence? J. E. Mosely. il N Y Times Mag p7+ S 1 '63
Just a minute. il Time 84:21-2 D 4 '64
Kennedy, Khrushchev and Mao. J. Burnham. Nat R 15:17 Jl 16 '63
Less danger, more trouble. W. Lippmann. Newsweek 63:11 F 17 '64
Let's make the test pact go for us. Life 55:4 Ag 9 '63
Mapping the sore spots. il Time 83:19-20 F 7 '64
Mildly welcomed truce. E. J. Hughes. Newsweek 62:31 O 21 '63
More than the diplomats; programs of Wichita, Kan. and Rockville Centre, N.Y. il Am City 80:120+ Ja '65
Morgenthau on nuclear war. P. Ramsey. Commonweal 78:554-7 S 20 '63
Nationalism; strength of France; address, April 28, 1964. M. Couve De Murville. Vital Speeches 30:487-90 Je 1 '64
New encyclical; a question of perspective; Pacem in terris. W. Herberg. il Nat R 14:364-5 My 7 '63; Reply. J. Elligett. 14:469 Je 4 '63
New frontier and Europe: moment for choice. F. W. Neal. il Nation 197:234-6 O 19 '63
New myths for old; concerning Senator Fulbright's speeches. W. V. Shannon. Commonweal 80:102-3 Ap 17 '64
New problems, little money as U.N. meets; with excerpts from address by J. F. Kennedy. il U S News 55:57-61 S 30 '63
New strategy for survival. il Newsweek 61:20-4 F 11 '63
New year's thoughts 1965. E. Rabinowitch. Bul Atomic Sci 21:2-5 Ja '65
Next step: playing it by ear. il Newsweek 62:29-30 O 7 '63
No quick thaw ahead. il Bsns W p20-1 Ag 3 '63
Normal world. D. Lawrence. U S News 55:96 Jl 15 '63
Normalcy. D. Lawrence. U S News 54:100 F 11 '63
Notes on conferencemanship. C. B. Marshall. New Repub 148:15-17 F 16 '63
On disarmament issues: peacekeeping since 1946. B. G. Lall. il Bul Atomic Sci 20:37-40 My '64
On putting detente to good use. R. Aron. New Repub 149:12-13 N 23 '63
Opening on a note of optimism; U.N. General assembly session. Sr Schol 83:17 O 11 '63
Openings for diplomacy; cracks in the blocs. F. W. Neal. Nation 196:111-13 F 9 '63
Our far-flung correspondents; journal of a pseudo-event. R. H. Rovere. New Yorker 39:76-8+ Jl 13 '63
Pacem in terris: for all humanity; with excerpts. il Newsweek 61:21-2 Ap 22 '63
Peace negotiations. Commonweal 79:447 Ja 17 '64
Politics of bedlam. F. D. Wormuth. il Bul Atomic Sci 19:28-30 D '63
Polycentrism and western policy. G. F. Kennan. For Affairs 42:171-83 Ja '64
Prayer for reason. M. Ascoli. Reporter 30:14 Ja 2 '64
Predictability gap. Time 83:21-2 F 21 '64
President Kennedy holds talks at Nassau with Prime Minister Macmillan; joint communique and statement on nuclear defense systems, December 21, 1962. J. F. Kennedy and H. Macmillan. Dept State Bul 48:43-5 Ja 14 '62
Prospects for democracy around the world; address. A. E. Stevenson. Vital Speeches 29:305-9 Mr 1 '63
Public opinion and national security; address, July 19, 1963. H. M. Jackson. Vital Speeches 29:642-4 Ag 15 '63
Realistic look at the world. D. Lawrence. U S News 56:104 Ja 13 '64
Reallocation of world responsibilities; address January 31, 1964. G. W. Ball. Vital Speeches 30:293-6 Mr 1 '64; Same. Dept State Bul 50:287-93 F 24 '64
Resolving vicious circles in international affairs. C. D. Bolton. Bul Atomic Sci 19:17-20 Ap '63
Season of diplomacy. E. J. Hughes. Newsweek 61:23 Mr 25 '63
Secretary Rusk interviewed on NBC's Today program; interview, January 21, 1963. ed. by M. Agronsky and H. Downs. D. Rusk. Dept State Bul 48:202-7 F 11 '63
Seven assumptions that beset us. H. M. Jackson. il N Y Times Mag p5+ Ag 4 '63; Same abr. with title Cold war isn't over. Read Digest 83:99-102 N '63; Discussion. N Y Times Mag p6+ Ag 18 '63
Seventeen year trend to Castro; address, January 22, 1963. C. B. Luce. Vital Speeches 29:295-9 Mr 1 '63
Solving a Chinese puzzle. N. Cousins. Sat R 46:14 S 7 '63
Some major issues before the United Nations; address, March 5, 1963. U Thant. Vital Speeches 29:360-4 Ap 1 '63; Same abr. U N Rev 10:16-19 Mr '63; Excerpts. Sat R 46:26 Mr 23 '63
State of affairs. H. Brandon. Sat R 47:14 F 22; 6 Mr 7; 6 Mr 21; 9 My 9; 16-17 Ag 15; 6+ N 28; 6 D 12 '64
Talk of peace but plenty of troubles. il U S News 55:19-20 Ag 12 '63
There is no weakening of the cold war spirit. J. Grigg. il N Y Times Mag p22+ S 27 '64
Things old and new in Pacem in terris. J. C. Murray. America 108:612-14 Ap 27 '63
Toast of democracy; address, January 22, 1963. Viscount Hailsham. Vital Speeches 29:300-3 Mr 1 '63
Tomorrow's world; questions and answers. W. Lippmann. Atlan 214:50-5 Ag '64
Towards a theology of survival. F. D. Wilhelmsen. Nat R 17:17-19 Ja 12 '65
Transition in the Middle East. E. Monroe. New Repub 150:21+ My 30 '64

INTERNATIONAL relations—*Continued*
Turn of the kaleidoscope. J. Burnham. Nat R 14:154 F 26 '63
Twain shall meet; Latin America, an East-West bridge. I. Quiles. il Américas 17:6-9 Ja '65
Two days that shook the world; Moscow, London, Washington and Peiping. il U S News 57:8 O 26 '64
Uncertainty and anxiety abroad; India, Great Britain, Italy. New Repub 149:11-12 D 7 '63
Unilateral initiatives: a cynic's view. R. A. Levine; reply. A. I. Waskow. Bul Atomic Sci 19:35 Ap '63
U.S. and world affairs annual 1963-64. il Sr Schol 83:10-42+ O 4 '63
U.S. and world affairs annual 1964-65; ed. by E. R. Floyd. il Sr Schol 85:12-39+ O 7 '64
U.S. foreign policy: problems and challenges for 1963; address, January 11, 1963. R. J. Manning. Dept State Bul 48:138-44 Ja 28 '63
U.S, New Zealand, and Australia reaffirm ties of friendship; remarks, July 17, 1964. D. Rusk; K. J. Holyoake; P. Hasluck. Dept State Bul 51:194-7 Ag 10 '64
Universal appeal of the Declaration of independence. D. Rusk. Dept State Bul 51:74-8 Jl 20 '64
Unless we lead, all will falter. S. Gruson. il N Y Times Mag p22+ D 8 '63
Vials of wrath were ready to break. E. Kern. il Life 56:46-61 Ja 3 '64
Vision of order. America 109:9 Jl 6 '63
Walter Lippmann, 1964; interview on CBS, ed. by E. Sevareid. New Repub 150:15-18 Ap 25 '64
War, violence, and human nature. J. Marmor. Bul Atomic Sci 20:19-22 Mr '64
War without killing. E. Mirel. Sci N L 83:405 Je 29 '63
We and they; Senator Fulbright calls for a reassessment of U.S. policies. New Repub 150:3-4 Ap 18 '64
Week that was will long be with us. Life 57:4 O 30 '64
We're all coexisters now. Nat R 15:556 D 31 '63
What we are for; summary of new encyclical on world peace. John XXIII. il Time 81: 60+ Ap 19 '63
What's happening to the cold war? East-West relations. il Sr Schol 85:14-18 S 16 '64
World: and now, a short pause; question of international policy after Khrushchev's overthrow and the explosion of China's nuclear device. il Newsweek 64:47 N 2 '64
World in change, meaning for U.S. il U S News 57:36-7 N 2 '64
World order in the sixties. R. Ducci. For Affairs 42:379-90 Ap '64
World perspectives, 1964. G. Kirk. For Affairs 43:1-13 O '64
World problems and national security; address, April 25, 1963. B. Goldwater. Vital Speeches 29:482-6 Je 1 '63
World today as de Gaulle sees it; news conference, July 29, 1963. C. de Gaulle. U S News 55:62-3 Ag 12 '63
Year of special importance; 1963, a crucial time; address, October 2, 1963. P. H. Spaak. Vital Speeches 30:37-41 N 1 '63
See also
Agriculture—International aspects
Alliances
Arbitration, International
Atlantic community
Balance of power
Business council for international understanding
Church and international relations
Diplomacy
Disarmament
Economic policy
Europe and the United States
Geopolitics
Imperialism
International conferences
International cooperation
International law
International organization
International police
International security
League of Nations
Militarism
Monroe doctrine
Nationalism
Neutrality
Peace
Power (political science)
Race problems
Treaties
United Nations
War
War, Prevention of
Women and international relations
World politics

Anecdotes, facetiae, satire, etc.

Le grand snow job. D. Snell. il Life 54:15 Ap 5 '63
Today, I dominate pugilism and prosody; tomorrow, perhaps, the world. L. M. Friedman. Nat R 15:305-6 O 8 '63

Bibliography

Recent books on international relations; comp. by H. L. Roberts. See issues of Foreign affairs
Source material; comp. by D. Wasson. See issues of Foreign affairs
World scene (cont) F. Canavan. America 108: 675-6+ My 11 '63
World scene. R. A. Graham. America 109: 664-5; 110:648-50; 111:698+ N 23 '63, My 9, N 28 '64

Study and teaching

And what does he know of England who only England knows? improving the teaching of world affairs. H. M. Long. il Sr Schol 83: 9T-10T S 27 '63
Great decisions program; to be conducted by Foreign policy association. R. C. Mastrude. il Sr Schol 83:12T D 6 '63
Idea of a world college; experiment in global education. H. Taylor. Sat R 47:29-32+ N 14 '64; Discussion. 47:33 D 5; 33 D 12; 17 D 19 '64
Leadership and world society; LAWS program at Emma Willard boarding school for girls. A. L. Homan. il Sr Schol 83:11T S 27 '63
Teaching the fundamentals of international understanding; address, September 8, 1964. D. Rusk. Dept State Bul 51:437-41 S 28 '64

INTERNATIONAL relations committee. See American library association—International relations committee
INTERNATIONAL relations office. See American library association—International relations office
INTERNATIONAL research associates, incorporated
Access study advisory committee has second thoughts on branches. Library J 88:4176+ N 1 '63
Access study; symposium. il Library J 88: 4685-709 D 15 '63; Discussion. 88:4710-12; 89:424, 976+ D 15 '63, F 1, Mr 1 '64
Access to education; concerning Access to public libraries survey; symposium. bibliog il Wilson Lib Bul 38:335-51+ D '63; Reply. S. L. Jackson. 38:465 F '64
Access to libraries study; statement, September 30, 1963. H. W. Tucker. ALA Bul 57:1042 D '63
Access to public libraries study. il ALA Bul 57:742-5 S '63
Reading the lessons: standing of Access study now? E. Moon. Library J 89:817 F 15 '64
Report on the study of access to public libraries. ALA Bul 58:299-304 Ap '64
Two kinds of access; concerning the report, Access to public libraries. E. Moon. Library J 88:2849 Ag '63
INTERNATIONAL rice research institute
Rice, hope, and IRRI. N. Cousins. il Sat R 47:20-1 Ap 4 '64
INTERNATIONAL school, United Nations. See United Nations international school
INTERNATIONAL schools foundation, incorporated. See International schools services, incorporated
INTERNATIONAL schools services, incorporated
American schools abroad. New Repub 150:7 Ja 25 '64
INTERNATIONAL science and technology (periodical)
Gerald Ferguson: art director of a science magazine. C. Weiss. il Am Artist 27:42-7+ Je '63
INTERNATIONAL scientific affairs, Office of. See United States—State, Department of—International scientific affairs, Office of
INTERNATIONAL scientific committee of Antarctic research. See International union of geodesy and geophysics
INTERNATIONAL scientific radio union
International discussion of Milky way research. B. J. Bok. il Sky & Tel 26:4-7 Jl '63
INTERNATIONAL security
America's efforts toward world order; address, August 12, 1964. L. B. Johnson. Dept State Bul 51:298-301 Ag 31 '64; Same with title Restraint and law. Vital Speeches 30:674-5 S 1 '64

INTERNATIONAL security—*Continued*
Big problems of a small planet. R. Hudson. Sat R 46:28-30 N 30 '63
Collective security and American foreign policy: from the League of nations to NATO, by R. N. Stromberg. Review
Reporter 30:54+ F 27 '64. R. A. Stone
Détente through firmness. K. U. von Hassel. For Affairs 42:184-94 Ja '64
Evolution of rising responsibility; address, December 13, 1964. H. Cleveland. Dept State Bul 52:7-12 Ja 4 '65
First step to what? Soviet proposal of a nonaggression pact. E. A. Gross. Reporter 29:30-2 S 12 '63
Morgenthau on nuclear war. P. Ramsey. Commonweal 78:554-7 S 20 '63
National strategy, security, and arms control; address, October 31, 1963. W. C. Foster. Dept State Bul 49:824-9 N 25 '63
1914-1939-1964: is the cycle broken? B. Ward. il N Y Times Mag p5+ D 29 '63
Order in the house. Christian Cent 81:1451 N 25 '64
Prospects for war and peace; interview. H. Kahn. Nations Bsns 52:34-5+ Jl '64
Secretary Rusk holds press and radio news briefing at Los Angeles. D. Rusk. Dept State Bul 48:361-8 Mr 11 '63
Security and freedom: a free-world responsibility; address, February 26, 1963. D. Rusk. Dept State Bul 48:383-8 Mr 18 '63
World security and developing nations. A. Salam. il Bul Atomic Sci 20:6-8 S '64
See also
Disarmament
International organization
International relations
Peace

INTERNATIONAL security affairs division. See United States—Defense, Department of—International security affairs division

INTERNATIONAL shoe company
Wage chronology: International shoe co (cont) il Mo Labor R 86:536-7 My '63

INTERNATIONAL society for education through art
INSEA 1963; report of International assembly. R. Saunders. Sch Arts 63:18 D '63

INTERNATIONAL society for stereology
Stereology congress. F. Chayes. Science 140:1247-8 Je 14 '63

INTERNATIONAL standards. See Standards, International

INTERNATIONAL students' day
Declaration for November 17th: the International students' day. R. Berka and V. Laska. Sch & Soc 92:110 Mr 7 '64

INTERNATIONAL telecommunication union
Clear channels: conference in Geneva. Newsweek 62:81 N 18 '63
Telecommunications union seeks Comsat frequencies agreements. Aviation W 79:35 O 14 '63
Worldwide Comsat frequencies allocated. C. Brownlow. Aviation W 79:35-6 N 18 '63

INTERNATIONAL telephone and telegraph corporation
Battle brewing on Comsat board control. Aviation W 81:25 Ag 24 '64
ITT gets a dead line in buzz with AT&T; attempt to get into domestic telephone business. il Bsns W p70 Ap 25 '64
One man's $1-billion company; ITT. il Bsns W p80-2+ My 4 '63

INTERNATIONAL television. See Television broadcasting—International aspects

INTERNATIONAL tin council
Another run-up in tin prices. Bsns W p30 N 2 '63
Tin council and U.S. officials consider long-range tin disposal. Dept State Bul 50:379 Mr 9 '64
U.S. and International tin council discuss surplus disposal; joint announcement, November 22, 1963. Dept State Bul 49:945-6 D 16 '63
United States extends interim tin disposal program; Department statement, January 18, 1963. Dept State Bul 48:182 F 4 '63

INTERNATIONAL trade. See Commerce

INTERNATIONAL trade fairs. See Exhibitions

INTERNATIONAL travel. See Travel

INTERNATIONAL trusteeships
See also
New Guinea, Territory of

INTERNATIONAL trusts. See Trusts, Industrial—International trusts

INTERNATIONAL typographical union
After a three-month shutdown, what striking printers got. U S News 54:98 Mr 18 '63
Automation and the news strike. R. Severo. il Reporter 28:29-30+ Mr 14 '63
Crisis for the independent daily. J. Tebbel; reply. L. F. Kent. Sat R 46:63 F 9 '63
Democracy's way at the ITU; printers' latest election campaign. Bsns W p78+ Je 6 '64
Dilemma of a guild reporter. M. Bracker; discussion. Reporter 28:10+ F 14 '63
For newspapers, new roadblocks; New York. U S News 54:124 Mr 25 '63
Hard times. il Time 81:13-17 Mr 1 '63
Negotiations deadlocked on New York ITU contract. Pub W 184:43-4 N 18 '63
New look at the New York newspaper strike. il U S News 54:50-2 Mr 4 '63
N.Y. printers contract plans to halt discrimination. Pub W 184:21-2 D 9 '63
Printers prepare for change; Colorado Springs center. il Bsns W p68-70 Ag 31 '63
Union kicks over the applecart; New York typographers reject strike settlement. il Bsns W p32-3 Mr 23 '63
Where are the reformers? W. F. Buckley, jr. Nat R 14:227 Mr 26 '63

INTERNATIONAL understanding. See Internationalism

INTERNATIONAL union for the conservation of nature and natural resources
Latin American park committee is organized. Nat Parks Mag 38:17 My '64

INTERNATIONAL union of architects
Maekawa, Prouvé, Doxiadis group wins awards for 1963. Arch Rec 133:114 My '63
Mexico city scene of U.I.A. meeting and Pacific Rim architectural conference. Arch Rec 134:10 O '63
U.I.A. sessions meet in Havana and Mexico; excerpts from report of the U.I.A. sessions. W. Perry. il Arch Rec 134:23+ D '63

INTERNATIONAL union of electrical, radio and machine workers
Can GE follow steel's path? Joint study committees. Bsns W p35 Ag 3 '63
Different way to deal with unions; GE with IUE. il U S News 55:120-1 O 7 '63
International union of electrical workers. R. T. Selby. Mo Labor R 87:1258-9 N '64
IUE chief accuses GE; charge of Boulwarism. il Bsns W p71-2+ S 28 '63
IUE raps Local 301's GE pact; conversion from incentive to hourly pay. Bsns W p56 O 17 '64
Is GE policy fair to labor? NLRB examiner says no. Bsns W p73 Ap 6 '63
Is incentive pay headed for shelf? automation vs incentive worker. il Bsns W p51-2 Je 27 '64
New fuel for IUE power struggle; battle between J. B. Carey and A. Hartnett. Bsns W p 118 O 5 '63
New speech limit on employers? U S News 54:107-8 Ap 15 '63
Union leaders face growing revolt. Bsns W p54+ O 3 '64
Westinghouse signs with IUE. Bsns W p53 N 2 '63

INTERNATIONAL union of geodesy and geophysics
Antarctica: the international laboratory. A. P. Crary. il Bul Atomic Sci 20:27-30 Ja '64
Geodesy and geophysics; report on 13th General assembly. J. Oliver. Science 142:1594+ D 20 '63
Messages from inside the earth. G. H. T. Kimble. il N Y Times Mag p 14-15+ Ap 28 '63

INTERNATIONAL union of solar system physics (proposed)
Proposal for an international union of solar system physics. H. G. Booker. il Science 141:673-4 Ag 23 '63

INTERNATIONAL voluntary workcamps
Voluntary workcamping; UNESCO fosters self-help programs in Latin America. A. L. Gillette. il Américas 15:13-18 O '63

INTERNATIONAL volunteer service. See Volunteer service, International

INTERNATIONAL wilderness; story. See Cheever, J.

INTERNATIONAL woodworkers of America
Rival unions team up on plywood's Big six. Bsns W p74+ Je 15 '63

INTERNATIONAL yacht racing union
International YRU meetings. R. N. Bavier, jr. Yachting 114:140-1 D '63
Rulings of the IYRU. P. Scott. Yachting 113:174 Je '63
Selecting the Olympic classes. R. N. Bavier, jr. Yachting 115:62-3+ Ap '64
Tricks of match racing; excerpt from Cornelius Shields on sailing. C. Shields. il Sports Illus 20:38-47 Je 29 '64

INTERNATIONAL years of the quiet sun
And quiet shines the sun. R. Lewis. Bul Atomic Sci 20:30-2 Ja '64
First it was IGY, now it's IQSY. B. H. Frisch. il Sci Digest 53:46 My '63
International years of the quiet sun, 1964-65. M. A. Pomerantz. bibliog il Science 142:1136-43 N 29 '63

INTERNATIONAL years of the quiet sun—*Cont.*
Manic-depressive sun. Time 81:74 Mr 15 '63
Noisy quiet sun. Sci Am 211:62 D '64
Quiet sun. Newsweek 62:54 D 23 '63
Solar activity during the first six months of the International years of the quiet sun. H. W. Dodson and others. il Science 145: 1050-2 S 4 '64
Solar minimum and the International years of the quiet sun. H. W. Dodson and E. R. Hedeman. bibliog il Science 143:237-40 Ja 17 '64
Soviets planning extensive IQSY effort. Aviation W 81:65+ Ag 24 '64
Unquiet IQSY? Sky & Tel 27:150 Mr '64
Years of the quiet sun. E. Hall. il(p353) Sci N L 84:362-3 D 7 '63
INTERNATIONAL young operatic singers competition, Sofia. See Singing—Competitions
INTERNATIONALE gartenbau ausstellung. See Horticultural exhibitions
INTERNATIONALISM
Challenged to reconcile. I. Travers-Ball. America 109:736-7 D 7 '63
Little man, big idea. A. Morrissett. Commonweal 78:549-50 S 20 '63
Role of law in political aspects of world affairs; address, December 29, 1962. L. C. Meeker. Dept State Bul 48:83-8 Ja 21 '63
World understanding at Plattsburgh. J. H. Hunt. NEA J 53:29-30 Ja '64
INTEROCEANIC canals. See Canals
INTERPLANETARY communication
Communicating with intelligent life on other worlds; adaptation of address, March 27, 1963. A. G. W. Cameron. il Sky & Tel 26: 258-61 N '63
Communication with other planets; excerpt from We are not alone. W. Sullivan. il Sat R 47:78-9 D 5 '64
INTERPLANETARY dust. See Matter, Interstellar
INTERPLANETARY monitoring platform. See Artificial satellites—Use in research
INTERPLANETARY navigation. See Navigation (space flight)
INTERPLANETARY shock waves. See Shock waves
INTERPOL. See International criminal police commission
INTERPRETATION (music) See Music—Analysis, interpretation, etc.
INTERPRETERS, United Nations. See United Nations—Employees
INTERPRETERS and interpretation. See Translations and translating
INTERPUBLIC group of companies, incorporated
$500 million whale. Newsweek 62:86+ O 21 '63
Mavericks on Madison avenue. P. B. Bart. Sat R 46:60+ D 14 '63
To the top at last. Time 82:102 O 18 '63
Under Marion Harper's big tent. S. H. Brown. il Fortune 69:128-32 My '64
What makes Marion Harper run. il Newsweek 63:63-6 Mr 30 '64
INTERRACIAL adoption. See Adoption
INTERRACIAL attitudes. See Attitudes
INTERRACIAL cooperation
Adopting Negro children. E. Shepherd. New Repub 150:10-12 Je 20 '64
Anti-bias coffee klatsch; interracial home visit day. il Ebony 18:67-8+ Ap '63
Are interracial homes bad for children? il Ebony 18:131-2+ Mr '63
Bringing home the world. M. H. Bacon. il Parents Mag 38:52+ N '63
Brown and Tougaloo. Commonweal 80:280 My 29 '64
Children and discrimination. B. Spock. il Redbook 123:30+ S '64
Ethnic democracy: the Brazilian example. G. Freyre. il Américas 15:1-6 D '63
Home visit day. America 110:529 Ap 18 '64
How shall we act? Christian Cent 81:1095 S 2 '64
Mommy, do white puppies like us? Project friendship. G. McMillan. il Good H 157:64+ O '63
New poll: the whites most trusted by Negroes. il U S News 56:16 Ap 20 '64
New world threats: poverty and race; with editorial comment. P. Mason. il Nation 198: 63, 68-71 Ja 20 '64
Protecting children from the harm of discrimination. B. Spock. Redbook 123:26+ O '64
Second chance. il Ebony 18:88-9 F '63
Ten most trusted whites. A. Poinsett. il Ebony 19:36-8+ Ap '64
Universities adopt-a-school plan; Northern university aid in raising Negro college standards. il Time 83:63 My 29 '64
Up from apathy, the Woodlawn experiment; excerpts from Crisis in black and white. C. E. Silberman. Commentary 37:51-8 My '64; Discussion. 38:14+ O '64
Uses of diversity; address, September 9, 1963. H. Cleveland. Dept State Bul 49:461-4 S 23 '63
INTERRACIAL council for business opportunity. See Business consultants
INTERRACIAL councils, Catholic. See Catholic interracial councils
INTERRACIAL marriages. See Intermarriage of races
INTERRACIAL relations. See Race relations
INTERREGNUM, Presidential. See Presidents—United States
INTERSECTION of roads. See Roads—Intersections
INTERSERVICE data exchange program. See Electronic apparatus industry and trade—United States
INTERSEXUALITY. See Hermaphroditism
INTERSTATE commerce
Better at moralizing than legalizing; Power & the precedent; concerning Title II of civil rights legislative package. Time 82: 19-20 Jl 12 '63
Civil rights bill: no limits on the customers. Bsns W p95 Je 29 '63
Public accommodations on trial; racial barriers. il Time 84:69 O 16 '64
Sticky questions; racial discrimination by businesses serving the public. Newsweek 62:20-1 Jl 15 '63
History
Steamboat's charter of freedom; Gibbons v. Ogden. G. Dangerfield. il Am Heritage 14: 38-43+ O '63
INTERSTATE commerce commission. See United States—Interstate commerce commission
INTERSTATE highway system. See Express highways; Roads—United States
INTERSTATE mobility. See Migration, Internal
INTERSTELLAR matter. See Matter, Interstellar
INTER-VARSITY Christian fellowship
God & man on 800 campuses. il Time 85:55 Ja 15 '65
INTERVENTION
Plan to free Cuba. F. L. Howley. Read Digest 83:89-92 Jl '63
Principles of international law concerning friendly relations and cooperation among states: international law and nonintervention; statement, December 3, 1963. F. T. P. Plimpton. bibliog f Dept State Bul 50:133-43 Ja 27 '64
INTERVIEW; story. See Friedman, B. J.
INTERVIEWING
Art director and you. Design 64:212+ Je '63
Big job of job hunting. il Sr Schol 85:23-4 N 11 '64
Exploring the exploratory sample. R. A. Bauer. Harvard Bsns R 41:128-31 Mr '63
Fidel and Lisa; TV interview with Castro. il Newsweek 61:69 My 13 '63
Job interview and the follow through. il Sr Schol 83:19+ N 8 '63
Strategies of effective interviewing. S. G. Trull. Harvard Bsns R 42:89-94 Ja '64
See also
Personnel management
INTERZONAL chess tournament. See Chess
INTESTINAL and parasitic worms. See Worms, Intestinal and parasitic
INTESTINES
Intestinal invertase: precocious development of activity after injection of hydrocortisone. R. G. Doell and N. Kretchmer. bibliog il Science 143:42-4 Ja 3 '64
Mutarotase inhibition by 1-deoxyglucose. A. S. Keston. bibliog il Science 143:698-700 F 14 '64
Strontium and calcium reabsorption in renal tubules of the newt, triturus pyrrhogaster. R. Ichikawa and others. bibliog il Science 144:53-4 Ap 3 '64
Vitamin D_3: direct action on the small intestine of the rat. D. Schachter and others. bibliog il Science 143:143-4 Ja 10 '64
Diseases
Cystinuria: in vitro demonstration of an intestinal transport defect. S. Thier and others. bibliog il Science 143:482-4 Ja 31 '64
Diverticulosis: big name for some little pockets. J. F. Montague. il Todays Health 42: 38-9 Je '64

INTESTINES—Diseases—*Continued*
Intestinal disaccharidases: absence in two species of sea lions. P. Sunshine and N. Kretchmer. bibliog il Science 144:850-1 My 15 '64
See also
Appendicitis
Colitis
INTOLERANCE. See Prejudice; Toleration
INTOURIST. See Travel agencies
INTOXICATION
See also
Alcohol—Physiological effects
INTRACOASTAL WATERWAY
Along a salty eastern seaboard. il Motor B 112:22 Ag '63
Dwellers and voyagers. I. Anthony. il Yachting 116:43+ D '64
Going South; Intracoastal Waterway. J. Emmett. il Yachting 116:64+ O '64
Our footloose correspondents; cruising inland waterway aboard Coastal Queen. A. Bailey. il New Yorker 40:141-2+ O 31 '64
INTRAMURAL athletics. See School athletics
INTRA-THORACIC pump. See Heart, Artificial
INTRA-UTERINE contraceptive devices. See Contraceptives
INTUITION of duration. See Time perception
INULIN
Inulin and albumin absorption from the proximal tubule in necturus kidney. W. N. Scott and others. bibliog il Science 146:1588-90 D 18 '64
INVALIDS. See Sick, The
INVASION, June 6, 1944. See World war, 1939-1945—Campaigns and battles—Western
INVENTIONS
Champions for radical new inventions. D. A. Schon. bibliog f Harvard Bsns R 41:77-86 Mr '63
Doctor J. H. McLean's Peace Makers. Review
Am Heritage il 14:109-12 Je '63. R. M. Ketchum
Employee-inventor gets his cut. il Bsns W p 133-4 Mr 23 '63
Fifteen myths about inventions. S. V. Jones. Sci Digest 56:63-7 Ag '64
Get set, folks, here comes tomorrow; sporting miracle of tomorrow. il Sports Illus 21:46-59 D 21 '64
How industry can adapt space inventions. il Sci Digest 56:32-3 D '64
How to cash in on your invention. N. Carlisle. il Pop Sci 183:122-4+ O '63
Inventions necessity isn't the mother of. S. V. Jones. N Y Times Mag p 16+ Ap 7 '63; p29 Ja 5 '64
Inventions, patents, processes. See issues of Science digest
Inventors' corner. J. H. Kraus. Pop Mech 121:40+ Mr '64
New ideas from the inventors. See issues of Popular science monthly
1963-1964 science review. Sci N L 84:393-4; 86:395-6 D 21 '63, D 19 '64
Now, inventing is easier than ever! N. Carlisle. il Pop Sci 182:72-4+ My '63
Patent rights under federal R&D contracts. il Harvard Bsns R 41:6-7+ S '63
Some of Edison's famous firsts. Look 28: 102 F 25 '64
U.S. patent policy and government research. R. L. Wright. il Bul Atomic Sci 19:9-13 D '63; Reply with rejoinder. M. A. Holman. 20:32-4 O '64
What is the key to progress? il Bsns W p 132+ My 16 '64
What to do with a bright idea. N. Carlisle. il Pop Sci 185:110-11+ O '64
Wild birds find a corporate roost. T. Alexander. il Fortune 70:130-4+ Ag '64
You can invent by accident. O. A. Battista. il Sci Digest 54:87-90 Ag '63
See also
Inventors
Patents
United States—Patent office

Caricatures and cartoons

François Dallegret; inventions. Arch Forum 120:109-14 My '64
INVENTORIES
Business outlook; possible impact of tax cut. Bsns W p 19-20 Ja 26 '63
Distribution dilemma. K. Schwartz. Duns R 81:98+ Ap '63
Great accumulations? Fortune 69:28+ F '64
Industry's inventory: shelves low, hope high. il Bsns W p28-9 Je 15 '63
Inventories: ready to move. il Fortune 68:32+ Ag '63
Inventories to the fore. il Fortune 68:43+ N '63
Inventory buildup. il Fortune 67:44+ My '63: 69:24+ My '64
NACS: management seminar studies how to measure, control pilferage; retail inventory method. M. Saul. il Pub W 186:30-3 S 21 '64
Questions for solving the inventory problem. J. I. Morgan. il Harvard Bsns R 41:95-110 Jl '63
Restraint in the stockroom. il Time 83:86+ Mr 20 '64
Sales and stocks. il Fortune 70:16+ Ag '64
Stripped for action. il Bsns W p25-6 Ap 11 '64
Up with inventories. il Fortune 70:28+ N '64
See also
Stores or stock-room keeping
INVENTORIES, Household
Photographs are excellent proof; photographic record of your possessions. il Sunset 133: 116+ S '64
INVENTORS
Co-inventors quiz. R. P. Balin. il Electr World 73:90 Ja '65
Electronic inventors quiz. R. P. Balin. il Pop Electr 19:67+ N '63
Inventor of the month. S. V. Jones. See issues of Science digest
Origin of the electron microscope. M. M. Freundlich. bibliog il Science 142:185-8 O 11 '63
Soviet patent policy: new incentives for the inventor; reprint. A. Kiron. Bul Atomic Sci 19:12-13 D '63
Thinking men earn big. il Ebony 19:73-4+ O '64
See also
Inventions
INVENTORY control. See Industrial management and organization
INVERTASE
Intestinal invertase: precocious development of activity after injection of hydrocortisone. R. G. Doell and N. Kretchmer. bibliog il Science 143:42-4 Ja 3 '64
INVESTIGATIONS, Government. See Government investigations
INVESTMENT. See Investments
INVESTMENT bankers association of America
Chip off the shoulder; annual meeting. Newsweek 64:78 D 14 '64
Sharp pencils and sharp tongues. Bsns W p85-6 Je 29 '63
INVESTMENT banking
Basic principle of the free world; address, November 29, 1962. A. Ames. Vital Speeches 29:248-50 F 1 '63
Cashing in on specialization; Eberstadt approach to banking. il Bsns W p90-2 Mr 30 '63
How bankers size up the outlook now. il U S News 55:50-3 D 16 '63
Sharp pencils and sharp tongues. Bsns W p85-6 Je 29 '63
Wherever you look, there's Loeb, Rhoades. T. A. Wise. il Fortune 67:128-31+ Ap '63
Young man, be a banker. E. Hobbing. il Esquire 59:150-6 My '63
See aso
Development banks
INVESTMENT clubs
How-to-get-rich-in-the-stock-market clubs. M. T. Bloom. il N Y Times Mag p72+ Ap 28 '63
Those clubs that invest in stocks. il Good H 157:132 Jl '63
To build a better nest egg. J. K. Lagemann. Read Digest 84:108-11 Je '64
See also
National association of investment clubs
INVESTMENT companies. See Investment trusts
INVESTMENT counselors. See Investments—Advisers
INVESTMENT trusts
Back in favor; comeback of the mutual funds. il Fortune 70:77-8 D '64
Balance tips to the bulls; mutual fund managers outlook. il Bsns W p 132+ Mr 16 '63
Buy fund shares in supermarkets? Sears, Roebuck & company of Chicago. U S News 55:120 D 9 '63
Fund differences fade; closed-end investment companies. il Bsns W p 122+ Je 20 '64
Funds again merging with holding groups; practice of swapping shares. Bsns W p 109-10 My 9 '64
Funds in ferment. D. Seligman and others. il Fortune 68:247-8+ N '63
Funds under fire. Bsns W p95-6 Ag 17 '63
Gains, but not up to averages. il Bsns W p82+ Ja 11 '64
Getting comfortable; mutual funds regaining popularity. il Time 84:77 D 18 '64
Hidden premium. G. S. Patchet. Atlan 212: 106-7 S '63

INVESTMENT trusts—*Continued*
How the big funds are investing their money. il U S News 55:79-80 Ag 12 '63
How the funds are faring. Time 82:93+ O 25 '63
How to rate management of investment funds. J. L. Treynor. il Harvard Bsns R 43:63-75 Ja '65
Investing in Wall Street. il Fortune 70:93+ N '64
Lehman fund tries again. il Bsns W p29 Jl 25 '64
Mutual disenchantment; SEC report. il Time 82:65 Ag 16 '63
Mutual funds answer critics. U S News 56: 99-100 Mr 16 '64
Mutual funds: balance sheet. U S News 55: 96-7 N 4 '63
Mutual funds in court battles. il Bsns W p 130+ My 25 '63
Mutual funds: mostly defensive; survey of investment companies. il Bsns W p 104+ F 29 '64
Mutual funds: pick with care; Wharton report. il Changing T 17:25-8 F '63
NEA mutual fund. T. F. Davis. NEA J 53: 29-30 N '64
Neither all bad nor all good; Cohen report on the Nation's securities markets. il Newsweek 62:64-7 Ag 19 '63
New drive by mutual funds. U S News 57:95 Ag 24 '64
New faces in the stock market. D. Seligman and T. A. Wise. il Fortune 69:92-5+ F '64
Not so eager to plunge. il Bsns W p 174 N 14 '64
Playing it safe but profitably; mutual funds vs the averages. il Bsns W p72+ Ag 8 '64
Putting the heat on fund directors. Bsns W p88 Mr 7 '64
Sears is set to enter the mutual fund race. il Bsns W p 112+ F 15 '64
Sears recants fund plan. Bsns W p 130 F 23 '63
Sizing up an unknown force. il Bsns p 164-6+ N 14 '64
Stocks the big funds are buying now. il U S News 56:93-4 Je 8 '64
Swap funds have troubles, too. il Bsns W p97 Ja 19 '63
They're confident of the market's momentum. il Newsweek 61:75 Ap 29 '63
Thirteen years of prudent investing. il Changing T 17:23 Mr '63
What investment funds are doing with their money. U S News 54:92+ F 11 '63
See also
Massachusetts investors trust
Real estate investment trusts
Small business investment companies

INVESTMENTS
Comsat; speculation in the space age. R. Burkhardt. New Repub 150:11-13 Je 27 '64; Reply. M. D. Reagan. 151:37-8 Jl 25 '64
Executive investor. See issues of Dun's review and modern industry
How new tax plan affects investors. U S News 55:32-3 S 2 '63
How people in Europe invest their money. il U S News 55:56-9 N 4 '63
How to handle your money now; as experts see it; symposium. il U S News 58:44-8 Ja 4 '65
How to handle your money now; interview. B. Graham. il U S News 55:66-70 Ag 5 '63
How to rate management of investment funds. J. L. Treynor. il Harvard Bsns R 43:63-75 Ja '65
Institutions begin to hedge. il Bsns W p 140+ Je 15 '63
Junior mortgages: high yields for the wary. J. Thackray. il Duns R 83:46-8+ F '64
New tax plan for investors. il U S News 54: 106-9 Je 10 '63
Offbeat profits on Wall Street. N. Buckley. il Duns R 82:37+ S '63
Personal investing. See issues of Fortune
Real diamonds vs. real blue chips. C. Bird. il N Y Times Mag p69+ Ap 14 '63
SEC vs. Wall Street. R. A. Phalon. il Duns R 81:56-7+ Ap '63
$7,000 dividends tax-free: how? U S News 55:104 S 16 '63
Small firms face tight financing period. W. Wright. Aviation W 78:89+ Je 3 '63
Smart money: riding the upswing hard. Bsns W p25-6 Mr 21 '64
Tax bill: not so bad for investors after all. U S News 54:105-6 Je 24 '63
Technology and the investor. N. Calder. Bul Atomic Sci 20:47-8 Ap '64
That might pump, Prudential. R. Sheehan. il Fortune 69:98-103+ Ja '64
Today's problem for investors. il U S News 57:47-9 Jl 27 '64
What's in the market for you? C. Loomis. Mlle 59:122-3+ S '64
When and where to invest off the farm. B. Brantley and others. il Suc Farm 62:52+ N '64
Why canny investors are sitting it out. il Bsns W p 164+ S 12 '64
You & your money; stocks and bonds: key differences to know. il Good H 158:132 Ja '64
Your investments; how fast are they really growing? il Changing T 17:16-17 Jl '63
See also
Annuities
Banks and banking—Investments
Bonds
Capital investments
Electric utilities—Securities
Finance, Personal
Insurance, Life
Investment banking
Investment clubs
Investment trusts
Mortgages
Public utilities—Securities
Real property
Saving and savings
Speculation
Stockholders
Stocks
Trade unions—Investments
Trusts and trustees
Women as investors

Advisers
Bullish but not boomish. Newsweek 61:85 My 27 '63
Court to rule on scalping; injunction against Capital gains research bureau, inc. U S News 54:84 F 4 '63
Courting the big stock buyers: research-oriented brokerage house. il Bsns W p96-8+ F 22 '64
Get experts to help you invest? il Changing T 18:7-11 My '64
Letter from a broker. P. Wyckoff. Sat R 46: 62-3 D 14 '63
P.S. from the SEC. Newsweek 61:76+ F 25 '63
Year for caution, but not for alarm; symposium. il Bsns W p56-8 Ja 2 '65
See also
New York society of security analysts

INVESTMENTS, Foreign
Aid, or investment? H. Hazlitt. Newsweek 62:77 D 16 '63
Big steal abroad. il U S News 55:57-9 D 2 '63
Business around the globe. See issues of Fortune
Businessman talks about doing business abroad; excerpts from address. A. C. Long. il U S News 56:96-7 My 4 '64
Dollars in the wrong place. America 109:503 N 2 '63; Discussion. 109:719-20 D 7 '63
Economic development through private enterprise. E. G. Collado. For Affairs 41:708-20 Jl '63
Financing overseas expansion. J. G. McLean. il Harvard Bsns R 41:53-65 Mr '63
Foreign investment task force reports to President. Dept State Bul 50:804 My 18 '64
Global stake of U.S. business. il Fortune 68: 129-31 D '63
How to solve the payments imbalance. il Newsweek 62:51 Ag 5 '63
Inflation is the cause. H. Hazlitt. Newsweek 62:71 Ag 12 '63
Invest in foreign stocks? il Changing T 17: 38-40 Je '63
Investment as scapegoat. H. Hazlitt. Newsweek 62:65 D 23 '63
Investment no, aid yes? concerning views of Secretary Dillon. H. Hazlitt. Newsweek 63: 84 F 17 '64
Is it over, over there? interviews, ed. by J. B. Weiner. L. C. Yaseen; L. C. Hoch. il Duns R 83:pt2 108-10+ Mr '64
Let's be realistic; exports and foreign investment; address, November 17, 1964. K. Rush. Vital Speeches 31:171-4 Ja 1 '65
Lure of many lands. il Time 84:94+ S 4 '64
Money curve. Newsweek 63:71 Je 22 '64
No help to the dollar. H. Hazlitt. Newsweek 62:62 Ag 5 '63
No. 1 dollar defender; Treasury's interest equalization tax. Bsns W p90+ Ag '63
Overseas lure Newsweek 63:59-60 F 3 '64
Overseas upturn. Newsweek 62:98 O 14 '63
Promotion of foreign investment in U.S. companies to be studied. Dept State Bul 49: 752 N 11 '63
Push overseas keeps going strong; McGraw-Hill survey. il Bsns W p27-8 S 7 '63
Rise and fall. Newsweek 61:84+ Ap 15 '63

INVESTMENTS, Foreign—*Continued*
Rushing to span the globe; McGraw-Hill survey; with editorial comment. il Bsns W p 19-21, 100 Ag 8 '64
Saints & sinners in foreign investment. R. Vernon. il Harvard Bsns R 41:146-9+ My '63
Shortsighted tariff. H. Hazlitt. Newsweek 62:84 O 28 '63
Shortsighted tax; tax on the purchase of foreign stocks and bonds by Americans. H. Hazlitt. Newsweek 63:91 Mr 23 '64
Silent market. Fortune 70:90+ Jl '64
Speculating in exchange. il Fortune 67:201-2+ F '63
Tax bill did its work while Congress mulled; interest equalization tax. il Bsns W p67 Jl 4 '64
Welcome grows cool. il Time 84:78 D 18 '64
What U.S. companies are doing abroad. See issues of U.S. news & World report
Where to put your money overseas. il Bsns W p 158 My 16 '64
Where welcome sign is coming down for U.S. dollar. il U S News 55:66-8 Jl 8 '63
See also
Banks and banking—Foreign subsidiaries
Branch factories, Foreign
Business—Foreign expansion
Insurance, Investment guaranty
Loans, Foreign

Taxation

About new taxes on foreign issues. U S News 57:82 Ag 17 '64
Canadian issues to be exempt from interest equalization tax; executive order; September 2, 1964. L. B. Johnson. Dept State Bul 51:442 S 28 '64
How foreign securities tax would work. Bsns W p34 Ag 17 '63
Longer life likely for dollar gap tax. Bsns W p 162+ O 10 '64
Tax law sparks a modern odyssey; Greek shipowners leaving U.S. il Bsns W p43-4 Ap 6 '63

INVESTMENTS, Foreign (by Europe)
Are Europe's markets a magnet? il Bsns W p28-9 Je 20 '64

INVESTMENTS, Foreign (in Africa)
New Rhodes. il Time 85:71 Ja 22 '65
Short and long term. Nation 197:122 S 14 '63

INVESTMENTS, Foreign (in Asia)
Investment opportunities in Asia; address, September 29, 1964. D. E. Bell. Vital Speeches 31:61-4 N 1 '64

INVESTMENTS, Foreign (in Australia)
American invasion of Australia. il Newsweek 64:53-6 Ag 10 '64
Those widows in San Francisco. New Repub 149:8 S 28 '63

INVESTMENTS, Foreign (in Brazil)
American capital and Brazilian nationalism. W. Baer and M. H. Simonsen. Yale R 53: 192-8 D '63
Investors beware; case of American & foreign power co. Time 82:90 Jl 12 '63
Profitable invasion; increased Japanese investment in Brazilian steel mills. il Newsweek 62:67-8 Ag 19 '63
Revolution: real winners in Brazil and what it means to U.S. D. B. Richardson. il U S News 56:31-3 Ap 13 '64

INVESTMENTS, Foreign (in Canada)
American capital in Canada and a boom in iron ore. il U S News 56:72-4 My 4 '64
Big copper rush, U.S. financed that, too. il U S News 56:74 My 4 '64
Bite, not bark. Time 81:23 Je 21 '63
Canada plans new pinch on outsiders; pressure on U. S. business. il Bsns W p27 F 15 '64
Canada's car push hits a roadblock; tariff rebate plan on auto parts challenged. Bsns W p91-2 Jl 25 '64
Is Canada taking Mexico's line toward U.S. investors? U S News 55:90 Jl 1 '63
Mr Gordon drops a shoe. Fortune 69:56+ F '64
More than neighborly; imminent tax withdrawn. Time 83:86 Mr 27 '64
Pearson loses round one. R. E. Spencer. Nation 198:43-6 Ja 13 '64
Race for Canada's riches; it's breaking out all over. il U S News 56:108-9 My 25 '64
U.S.-Canada brawl: a matter of capital. Bsns W p29-30 N 2 '63
When Canada looks to its future. il U S News 55:62-5 Ag 5 '63
Will they or won't they sell shares in Canada? il Bsns W p50+ Ja 25 '64
Yankee go home. Newsweek 61:82 Je 24 '63

INVESTMENTS, Foreign (in Chile)
Chile: an example of U.S. troubles in Latin America. il U S News 57:77-80 N 9 '64
Chile's new deal with U.S. firms. il U S News 58:69 Ja 4 '65
Choice for Chile: which way to go left? democratic left or Marxist. il Bsns W p48+ Ag 8 '64

INVESTMENTS, Foreign (in Cuba)
Contested cargo; legal battle between expropriated company, C.A.V. and Cuba's Banco nacional. Time 83:71-2 Ap 3 '64
Courts can't bar seizures; suit by Banco nacional de Cuba against U.S. firm. Sr Schol 84:20+ Ap 10 '64

INVESTMENTS, Foreign (in Europe)
Affluence abroad. Newsweek 63:60 Mr 30 '64
American investments in Europe. E. Taylor. il Reporter 31:25-9 D 3 '64; Reply. H. Knappstein. 32:10 Ja 28 '65
Behind west Europe's alarm over Yankee imperialism. il U S News 57:110-11 N 23 '64
Capital gain; French plan to curb American investment in Europe. il Newsweek 61: 68+ Ap 8 '63
Is Europe still a good business bet? il Bsns W p88-91 F 9 '63
Paris-Milan express. Time 84:60 Jl 31 '64
U.S. capital stirs fear in Europe. il Bsns W p 114+ D 5 '64
Yankee dollars in Europe. il Newsweek 61: 78 F 11 '63

INVESTMENTS, Foreign (in France)
U.S. investments in France. R. Grenier. il Reporter 28:23-4+ Je 6 '63

INVESTMENTS, Foreign (in Indonesia)
U.S. diplomatic triumph in Indonesia; U.S. oil rights. Bsns W p72 Je 22 '63

INVESTMENTS, Foreign (in Ireland)
Ireland's open door to Europe. T. O'Hanlon. il Duns R 85:47-9+ Ja '65

INVESTMENTS, Foreign (in Japan)
International markets; Japan frees the yen. A. O. Stanley. Duns R 81:67 Ap '63
Japan woos U.S. investors. il Bsns W p76+ Ap 6 '63

INVESTMENTS, Foreign (in Latin America)
Debut for ADELA. Time 83:66 Ja 24 '64
First aid for an ailing Alliance; meeting of Latin American economic & social council. il Bsns W p47-8+ N 9 '63
How to survive foreign expropriation. il Bsns W p86+ Je 1 '63
Japanese presence. il Time 81:85 Ap 26 '63
Latin America bites U.S. again; dispute over oil development rights. Bsns W p26-7 N 16 '63
Latin America; encouragement for investors; address, November 20, 1963. D. D. McConkey. Vital Speeches 30:209-14 Ja 15 '64
Latin America: help needed. A. O. Stanley. Duns R 81:58+ Je '63
New office to spur Alliance investment. Bsns W p85-6 Mr 30 '63
Pool for ventures; joint U.S.-European effort. Bsns W p93 S 28 '63
Saints & sinners in foreign investment. R. Vernon. il Harvard Bsns R 41:146-9+ My '63
This month's feature: U.S. and the Alliance for progress. Cong Digest 42:67-77+ Mr '63
Top brass tackle Latin aid. il Bsns W p 134 O 10 '64
Turmoil on Latin aid; with editorial comment. Bsns W p27, 156 F 23 '63
U.S. dollars going where they feel safe. il Bsns W p82+ N 21 '64
U.S. still a bogeyman to Latin Americans. il Bsns W p27-8 D 7 '63
Why not invest in Latin America? J. Grunwald. Harvard Bsns R 41:123-8 N '63

INVESTMENTS, Foreign (in Nigeria)
Investment opportunities in Nigeria. H. J. Massaquoi. il Ebony 19:67-8+ Mr '64
Texas on the Guinea Gulf. il Fortune 69:69-70+ Ap '64

INVESTMENTS, Foreign (in Russia)
Will the West now bail out Khrushchev? il U S News 55:36-8 D 30 '63

INVESTMENTS, Foreign (in South Africa)
Should Americans invest in South Africa? C. B. Randall. il Duns R 81:44-6 Ja '63

INVESTMENTS, Foreign (in Southeast Asia)
French violets. il Time 84:82 Ag 28 '64

INVESTMENTS, Foreign (in Spain)
Spain: headed up and aiming higher. il Bsns W p 118 D 7 '63
Spain turns charm on investors; four-year development called El plan. il Bsns W p 133-4+ O 17 '64

INVESTMENTS, Foreign (in Taiwan)
Other China builds up. il Bsns W p 120-2 Jl 13 '63

INVESTMENTS, Foreign (in underdeveloped areas)
Negotiating investment in emerging countries. S. Williams. Harvard Bsns R 43:89-99 Ja '65
INVESTMENTS, Foreign (in United States)
Are Europe's markets a magnet? il Bsns W p28-9 Je 20 '64
Going international in reverse; Libby, McNeill & Libby. Bsns W p34 Ag 10 '63
One world or many? foreign issues tax. H. Hazlitt. Newsweek 62:95 O 7 '63
Silent market. Fortune 70:90+ Jl '64
Trying to lure foreign investors to these shores; Fowler panel proposals. il Bsns W p94 My 2 '64
Welcome invaders. Time 81:89-90 My 24 '63
INVESTORS. See Stockholders
INVESTORS overseas services
Fundman of fundmen. il Newsweek 64:82-3 D 7 '64
INVISIBLE inventions, incorporated; drama. See Murray, J.
INVISIBLE man; drama. See Olfson, L.
INVITATION to the wedding; story. See Curry, P. S.
INVOCATION. See Prayer
INVOLUNTARY servitude amendment. See United States—Constitution—Amendments
INYO NATIONAL FOREST. See National forests
IOANNINA, Greece
In Greece. D. Messinesi. Vogue 144:24 Ag 1 '64
IODIDES
See also
Silver iodide
IODINE
Atmospheric iodine abates smog ozone. W. F. Hamilton and others. il Science 140:190-1 Ap 12 '63
Electron miscroscope autoradiography of bacteria labeled with iodine-125. N. O. Kuhn and C. G. Harford. bibliog il Science 141: 355-6 Jl 26 '63
Isotopes
Antibody suppression by antigen heavily labeled with iodine-131. M. M. Webber. bibliog il Science 143:132-3 Ja 10 '64
Iodine-131 fallout from underground tests. E. A. Martell. bibliog il Science 143:126-9 Ja 10 '64
Iodine-131 in the thyroids of North American deer and caribou: comparison after nuclear tests. W. C. Hanson and others. bibliog il Science 140:801-2 My 17 '63
Iodine-131 in Utah during July and August 1962. R. C. Pendleton and others. bibliog il Science 141:640-2 Ag 16 '63
Iodine-131 thyroid dose from milk in Italy during the period September 1962 to February 1963. A. A. Cigna and F. G. Giorcelli. bibliog il Science 143:379-80 Ja 24 '64
Iodine-125 distribution between follicular colloid and colloid droplets in mouse thyroid gland. W. C. Bauer and J. S. Meyer. bibliog il Science 145:1431-2 S 25 '64
Meteorological evaluation of the sources of iodine-131 in pasteurized milk. R. J. List and others. bibliog il Science 146:59-64 O 2 '64
Nevada fallout: past and present hazards. L. Mattison and R. Daly. il Bul Atomic Sci 20:41-5 Ap '64; Reply with rejoinder. G. M. Dunning. 20:29-30 S '64
Precaution in the use of iodine-125 as a radioactive tracer. Y. S. Bakhle and others. il Science 143:799-800 F 21 '64
Radioiodine: its nature and effects: report of symposium at the Hanford laboratories, Richland, Wash. L. K. Bustad. Science 142: 510+ O 25 '63
Radioiodine metabolism in children and adults after the ingestion of very small doses. M. A. Van Dilla and M. J. Fulwyler. bibliog il Science 144:178-9 Ap 10 '64
IODINE in the body
Protein-bound iodine in serum of rats breathing 99 percent oxygen. P. Felig and others. bibliog il Science 145:601 Ag 7 '64
Radioiodine metabolism in children and adults after the ingestion of very small doses. M. A. Van Dilla and M. J. Fulwyler. bibliog il Science 144:178-9 Ap 10 '64
IODODEOXYURIDINE. See Idoxuridine
ION absorption in plants. See Plants—Ion exchange
ION engines
Can ion engines conquer space? il Bsns W p 110+ Mr 30 '63
EOS research to better ion engines. J. F. Judge. il Miss & Roc 12:28-9 Ap 22 '63
Eye on ions. il Newsweek 64:71 Ag 3 '64
NASA announces no further SERT flights are necessary. Miss & Roc 15:15 O 19 '64
No further SERT-type tests needed. Miss & Roc 15:32 S 7 '64
One ion rocket could hold satellite synchronous. Miss & Roc 13:31 Ag 5 '63
Rocket engine of future? il(p49) Sci N L 86:50 Jl 25 '64
SERT-1 flight shows ion engine potential. Aviation W 81:21 Jl 27 '64
SERT I shot is key step in ion engine development effort. il Miss & Roc 15:17 Jl 13 '64
Steering with mouse burps; ion rocket. Time 84:79 O 16 '64
Surface tension is energy source; EOS ion rocket systems. R. Hawkes. il Miss & Roc 15:24-6 S 7 '64
ION exchange
Amethyst: optical properties and paramagnetic resonance. T. I. Barry and W. J. Moore. il Science 144:289-90 Ap 17 '64
Electrokinetic behavior of ion-exchange resin. D. H. Freeman and G. Scatchard. il Science 144:411 Ap 24 '64
Geometry of the perxenate ion. W. C. Hamilton and others. bibliog il Science 141:532-4 Ag 9 '63
Heat adaptation and ion exchange in bacillus megaterium spores. G. Alderton and others. il Science 143:141-3 Ja 10 '64
Ion-exchange removal of sodium chloride from water with calcium hydroxide as recoverable regenerant. K. Popper and others. bibliog il Science 141:1038-9 S 13 '63
Permselective membranes: spectroscopic and conductivity effects. G. Stein and C. Forgacs. il Science 142:953-4 N 15 '63
Phosphate glass electrode with good selectivity for alkaline-earth cations. A. H. Truesdell and A. M. Pommer. bibliog il Science 142:1292-4 D 6 '63
ION pumps. See Vacuum pumps
ION rockets. See Ion engines
IONENES
Ionene: a thermal degradation product of β-carotene. W. C. Day and J. G. Erdman. bibliog il Science 141:808 Ag 30 '63
IONESCO, Eugène
Bald soprano; tr. by D. M. Allen. Criticism
New Yorker 39:94+ S 28 '63
Newsweek 62:60 S 30 '63
Earliest Ionesco. R. Gilman. Commonweal 79:77-8 O 11 '63
Exit the king. Criticism
America 109:512-14 N 2 '63
Theatre Arts il(p29) 48:31-2 Ja '64
I am a witness. por Newsweek 63:60 My 11 '64
Lesson; tr. by D. M. Allen. Criticism
New Yorker 39:96 S 28 '63
Openings, Paris. J. P. Lenoir. il Theatre Arts 47:60-1+ F '63
Pedestrian of the air. Criticism
Newsweek il 63:96-7 Mr 16 '64
Victims of duty. Criticism
New Yorker 40:88-9 Je 6 '64
IONIAN ISLANDS
Serene isles. il Life 54:54-71+ Je 14 '63
See also
Corfu (island)
IONIZATION
Deuterated water effects on acid ionization constants. R. B. Martin. bibliog Science 139:1198+ Mr 22 '63
Positive-ion chemistry: high yields of heavy hydrocarbons from solid methane by ionizing radiation. D. R. Davis and W. F. Libby. bibliog Science 144:991-2 My 22 '64
IONIZATION, Gaseous
See also
Plasma (ionized gases)
IONOSPHERE. See Atmosphere, Upper
IONOSPHERE Explorer I satellite. See Artificial satellites—Use in research
IONOSPHERIC radio wave propagation
Ionosphere and radio propagation in the lower frequencies; report on third western national meeting of the American geophysical union. T. N. Gautier. Science 143: 1197+ Mr 13 '64
New radar telescope to map ionosphere. P. J. Klass. il Aviation W 79:84-5+ Ag 19 '63
Skip, hop, and jump. S. Leinwoll. il Pop Electr 21:73-5+ N '64
Very-low-frequency radio waves and the ionosphere; report of symposium at the Central radio propagation laboratory, National bureau of standards, Boulder, Colo. D. D. Crombie. Science 142:508+ O 25 '63
IONS
Elasticity of articular cartilage: effect of ions and viscous solutions. L. Sokoloff. bibliog il Science 141:1055-7 S 13 '63

IONS—*Continued*
Infrared spectra of hydronium ion in micaceous minerals. J. L. White and A. F. Burns. bibliog il Science 141:800-1 Ag 30 '63
Ionic intermediates and energy transfer in radiation chemistry; report of Faraday society discussion on fundamental processes in radiation chemistry. R. A. Holroyd and I. A. Taub. Science 142:1196-7 N 29 '63
Phosphate incorporation in desheathed nerves: effects of potassium and calcium ions. L. G. Abood and I. Koyama. bibliog il Science 141:1277-8 S 27 '63
Site of preference energy and selective uptake of transition-metal ions from a magma. R. G. Burns and W. S. Fyfe. bibliog il Science 144:1001-3 My 22 '64
See also
Electrons
Thermionic emission

IOWA
See also
Agriculture—Iowa
Education—Iowa
Gardens—Iowa
Hunting—Iowa
Libraries—Iowa
Prohibition—Iowa

Boundaries
Squatter squabble. il Newsweek 64:28-9 Ag 10 '64

Description and travel
Fields and fairs of Iowa. J. R. Humphreys. il Holiday 36:20+ S '64
See colorful northeast Iowa. W. R. Wilson. il Suc Farm 62:106 O '64

Politics and government
Why Democrats swept a Republican state: case study. il U S News 57:44-6 N 30 '64

Religious institutions and affairs
News of the Christian world (cont) Christian Cent 80:186, 594, 988, 1344-5; 81:246+, 1446 F 6, My 1, Ag 7, O 30 '63, F 19, N 18 '64

IOWA beef packers, incorporated
Ahead of the herd in automation. il Bsns W p 104-6 Je 27 '64

IOWA state university of science and technology, Ames, Ia.
Pure water while you wait. E. R. Baumann. il Am City 78:23 D '63

IOWA. University, Iowa City
Computer services for schools; UPDATE, Iowa program introducing automation of clerical tasks. Sch & Soc 91:274+ O 5 '63
Individuality at Iowa. il Time 84:60-1 D 11 '64
State university of Iowa. C. Kentfield. il Holiday 34:88-91+ N '63
See also
Meredith-Iowa writer's award

IPOUSTEGUY, Jean
Profound primitive. il Time 84:62-3 Ag 21 '64

IPPEN, Arthur T. See Jobin, W. R. jt. auth.

IPPOLITO, Felice
Misunderstood. il por Newsweek 64:50 N 16 '64
Who's left where? por Newsweek 62:48+ N 4 '63

IRA Haupt and company. See Haupt, Ira, and company

IRAN
Future to outshine ancient glories. Mohammed Reza Pahlevi. il Life 54:52-62+ My 31 '63
See also
Dams—Iran
Elections—Iran
France—Foreign relations—Iran
Geology—Iran
Guerrillas—Iran
Land tenure—Iran
Poor—Iran

Antiquities
Sciences meet in ancient Hasanlu. R. H. Dyson, jr. il Natur Hist 73:16-25 O '64
Sequence of 6,000 years of prehistory revealed; Hasanlu. Sci N L 87:9 Ja 2 '65

Civilization
Future to outshine ancient glories. Mohammed Reza Pahlevi. il Life 54:52-62+ My 31 '63

Description and travel
Iran. V. S. Pritchett. il Holiday 33:40-53+ Je '63
Stopping off in the middle of the Middle East. il Sunset 131:26-8 D '63

Economic conditions
Iran and a king's revolution. il Sr Schol 82:10-14+ Ap 17 '63
Middle East paradox, the beggar rich. F. M. Esfandiary. il N Y Times Mag p22+ N 3 '63

Economic policy
Grand vizier. il Time 82:40 N 1 '63
No longer for the corrupt. il Time 81:37 My 24 '63

Foreign relations
Neither protocol nor freedom. il Time 82:45 N 29 '63

Politics and government
18th Premier. il Time 83:36 Mr 20 '64
Here he is again. Nation 198:565-6 Je 8 '64
Hurrying history along. Newsweek 61:44 F 11 '63
Iran and a king's revolution. il Sr Schol 82:10-14+ Ap 17 '63
Iran's Shah leads a white revolution. J. Waltz. il N Y Times Mag p23+ O 27 '63
Legal revolution; voters support Iran's shah. U S News 54:16 F 11 '63
Rioting for Islam. New Repub 148:10 Je 29 '63
Shah of Iran congratulated on results of referendum; exchange of messages. J. F. Kennedy; Mohammed Reza Pahlavi. Dept State Bul 48:316 Mr 4 '63

Reconstruction
Future to outshine ancient glories. Mohammed Reza Pahlevi. il Life 54:52-62+ My 31 '63
Progress at a price; riots. il Time 81:34-5 Je 14 '63

Social conditions
Iran: remolding a nation nearer to the heart's desire. H. B. Bloomer. il Reporter 30:32-6 Ja 16 '64

Social life and customs
Persian courtship; excerpts from Persia revisited. A. S. Mehdevi. Harper 228:48-53 Je '64

IRANIAN art. See Art, Persian

IRAQ
See also
Guerrillas—Iraq
Paleontology—Iraq
United States—Foreign relations—Iraq

Antiquities
Prehistory in Shanidar Valley, northern Iraq. R. S. Solecki. bibliog il Science 139:179-93 Ja 18 '63

Description and travel
Marsh Arabs, by W. Thesiger. Review
Sat R 48:86-7 Ja 2 '65. H. Lehrman

Economic conditions
Iraq reroutes a revolution. il Sr Schol 82: 10-13 Mr 13 '63

Foreign relations
Another first step; Syrian-Iraqi pact. Newsweek 62:46 S 16 '63
Target of revolt: an anti-American regime. il U S News 54:8 F 18 '63
What's in store for Iraq. S. Huck. il Nat R 14:193-4 Mr 12 '63

Politics and government
Arab against Arab. P. Seale. New Repub 149:11-13 D 14 '63
Ba'ath take-over. il Newsweek 62:56 N 25 '63
Baghdad between revolutions. L. Hamalian. il Nation 199:423-5 D 7 '64
Baghdad: coup by consent. D. Holden. il Reporter 29:30-2 D 19 '63
Better than nothing; Kurdish truce with the Iraq government. il Newsweek 63:45 F 24 '64
Coupmaker of Baghdad: Abdel Salam Aref. il Newsweek 62:62 D 2 '63
Emergence of the Ba'ath. P. Seale. New Repub 148:7-8 Mr 23 '63
Friends & brothers; insurrection. il Time 81: 31-2 F 15 '63
Green armbands, red blood. il Time 81:28 F 22 '63
Iraq reroutes a revolution. il Sr Schol 82: 10-13 Mr 13 '63
Iraq: the background. Nat R 14:144 F 26 '63
Kassem is gunned down; with report by R. Morse. il Life 54:24-9 F 22 '63
Kassem's legacy. D. Stewart. Nation 196: 222-4 Mr 16 '63
My bigger brother. New Repub 148:7 F 23 '63
New turn in Mideast: anti-red. J. Law. il U S News 54:52 F 25 '63

IRAQ—Politics and government—*Continued*
Oil will continue to flow. Nation 196:149-50 F 23 '63
Once again, bloodshed in Baghdad. il Sr Schol 82:14 F 27 '63
Plot that failed; attempted Baathist coup. il Time 84:63 O 2 '64
Revolt in Baghdad. Newsweek 61:53 F 18 '63
Target of revolt: an anti-American regime. il U S News 54:8 F 18 '63
Under Secretary Ball interviewed on issues and answers; transcript of interview, February 10, 1963. G. W. Ball. Dept State Bul 48:369 Mr 11 '63
Until the next coup. il Time 82:46 N 29 '63
Vive nobody; report by J. Rigos. Newsweek 61:38+ F 25 '63
What's in store for Iraq. S. Huck. il Nat R 14:193-4 Mr 12 '63

IRAZU. See Volcanoes

IRBY, Kenneth
For Gordon Clark; Only love is holy and love's ecstasy; poems. Poetry 105:94-8 N '64

IRELAND, George
King of the hill is no patsy. J. Underwood. il Sports Illus 20:50-2 Mr 9 '64
Ramblers wreck Cincy; NCAA championship playoff. J. Underwood. il Sports Illus 18:22-5+ Ap 1 '63

IRELAND
Ireland: symposium. il Holiday 33:10+ Ap '63
Ireland: the Kennedy cult; they cried the rain down that night. J. Roddy. il Look 28:66-72+ N 17 '64
Irish winds of change. C. McWilliams. Nation 197:191-3 O 5 '63
Kennedy homestead. il Newsweek 62:31 Jl 1 '63
Lifting the green curtain. il Time 82:28-40 Jl 12 '63; Same abr. with title Why Irish eyes are smiling. Read Digest 84:207-8+ Mr '64
Sure, and it's County Kennedy now; Wexford. T. P. Coogan. il N Y Times Mag p7-9+ Je 23 '63
See also
Airports—Ireland
Athlone
Birds—Ireland
Colleges and universities—Ireland
Country estates—Ireland
Famines—Ireland
Fishing—Ireland
Forests and forestry—Ireland
Gardens—Ireland
Irish
Music festivals—Ireland
National parks and reserves—Ireland
Northern Ireland
Public health—Ireland
Television broadcasting—Ireland
Tourist trade—Ireland

Bibliography
Legends, leprechauns and a literary tour. Holiday 33:191 Ap '63
Reading I've liked. C. Fadiman. Holiday 33:20-1 Ap '63

Commercial treaties and agreements
United States concludes meat agreement with Ireland. State-Agriculture announcement; with exchange of notes, February 25, 1964. Dept State Bul 50:468-9 Mr 23 '64

Description and travel
Day of joy and sadness; Ted Kennedy's retracing of brother's trip. E. Behr. il Sat Eve Post 237:36-7 Jl 11 '64
Garland of Irelands. A. O'Neill-Barna. il N Y Times Mag p26-7 Mr 15 '64
Gloamin', where and how to roam in it. Holiday 33:188 Ap '63
Going places, finding things in Ireland. J. Wilson and A. Leaman. il House & Gard 125:142-9 Ap '64
Going places, finding things on an Irish motor tour. il House & Gard 125:170-5+ Ap '64
Medieval tour; Bunratty castle. J. Park. il Travel 119:16 F '63
Oases outside Dublin. W. Bittner. il Atlan 213:168+ Mr '64
Other island. N. Mitford. il Sat R 46:39-40+ Mr 16 '63
Personal business; trip to Emerald Isle. Bsns W p 145-6 Mr 16 '63
Voices of Ireland. L. Lee. il Mlle 59:165-6+ O '64
See also
Blarney castle

Economic conditions
Close-up of Ireland's basic problem. T. Guthrie. il N Y Times Mag p22+ Ja 19 '64
Ireland's changing face; story of a new boom. il U S News 57:84-5 Jl 6 '64

Economic relations
Ireland's open door to Europe. T. O'Hanlon. il Duns R 85:47-9+ Ja '65

Foreign relations
President de Valera of Ireland visits United States; texts of exchanges of arrival remarks and toasts and President de Valera's address to Congress, May 28, 1964. L. B. Johnson; E. De Valera. Dept State Bul 50:927-33 Je 15 '64
Prime Minister of Ireland visits the United States; exchange of greetings, October 15, 1963 and text of communique, October 17, 1963. J. F. Kennedy; S. F. Lemass. Dept State Bul 49:737-8 N 11 '63

Historic houses, etc.
Curraghmore. il Vogue 143:92-7 Je '64

History
Great hunger, by C. Woodham-Smith. Review Newsweek il 61:108+ Mr 25 '63
Troubled history. A. M. Maughan. il Holiday 33:70-1+ Ap '63
See also
Famines—Ireland

Bibliography
Articles and other books received; British Commonwealth and Ireland, comp. by L. H. Carlson. See issues of American historical review

Sinn Fein rebellion, 1916
Easter rebellion, by M. Caulfield. Review Newsweek il 62:74 Jl 29 '63

Home rule
Use of the American Civil war in the debate over Irish home rule. J. M. Hernon, jr. bibliog f Am Hist R 69:1022-6 Jl '64

Maps
Ireland. Holiday 33:54-5 Ap '63

Nobility
Aristocrats; with photographs by Slim Aarons. Holiday 33:84-93 Ap '63

Politics and government
See also
Elections—Ireland
Ireland—Home rule

Population
Irish population decline. Sci N L 83:367 Je 8 '63

Religious institutions and affairs
News of the Christian world (cont) Christian Cent 80:1114+, 1346; 81:314-16, 947 S 11, O 30 '63, Mr 4, Jl 22 '64
See also
Catholic church in Ireland

Social life and customs
Notes on Irish life. M. Bence-Jones. Holiday 33:136+ Ap '63
Of horses and fashion plates; Dublin show with photographs by Slim Aarons. Holiday 33:64-9+ Ap '63

Union (proposed)
See Irish unification question

IRELAND, NORTHERN. See Northern Ireland

IRELAND and England. See England and Ireland

IRELAND and the United States
Visit to Ireland; address, June 28, 1963. J. F. Kennedy. Dept State Bul 49:128-32 Jl 22 '63

IRENE, princess of the Netherlands
Conversions vs. ecumenism? Dutch reaction to Princess Irene's reception into the Catholic church. America 110:211 F 15 '64
Death of a princess. il por Time 83:22 F 14 '64
Exciting life; wedding of Carlos and Irene. il por Newsweek 63:40 My 11 '64
Headstrong princess. il por Time 83:44 Ap 17 '64
Her royal choice. por Newsweek 63:51-2 F 17 '64
Irene and Carlos in love affair of state; with report by P. Saporiti. il pors Life 56:40-40B F 21 '64
Irene, good-by. por Newsweek 63:53-4 Ap 20 '64
Love finds a way. il por Sr Schol 84:17 F 28 '64
Love with the proper stranger. il por Time 83:38 F 21 '64
People of the week. por U S News 56:19 F 17 '64
Royal road to romance. Nat R 16:141 F 25 '64

IRIDACEAE. See Tigerflowers
IRIDESCENT glass. See Glassware
IRION, Mary Jean
  Hammock; poem. Christian Cent 81:1108 S 9 '64
IRISES
  August blooming vesper iris. M. C. Dolton. il Horticulture 41:256 My '63
  Best dressed iris for 1963. M. Price. il Flower Grower 50:30-1+ Je '63
  Cool white iris. C. E. Quinn. il Pop Gard 15:12-13 Jl '64
  Do this dividing in August. il Sunset 133:154+ Ag '64
  Fashion your own iris. M. Price. il Flower Grower 50:20 Jl '63
  For a surprise come February; iris reticulata. il Sunset 131:307 O '63
  Fragrant little iris. K. Corbin. il Flower Grower 50:28+ Ap '63
  Iris. K. Twomey. il Pop Gard 14:38-9+ Jl '63
  Iris. M. E. O'Brien. il Pop Gard 15:26-7 My '64
  Iris are foolproof favorites. M. Price. il Flower Grower 51:34-7 Je '64
  Iris ayes are smiling. Flower Grower 50:21 Je '63
  Iris; the tall bearded; P. F. Frese. il Pop Gard 14:30-2 My '63
  Jewels for your garden. L. G. DeLeeuw. il Flower Grower 50:34-5 Ap '63
  Other iris. G. Douglas. il Horticulture 42:20-1+ My '64
  Plant new iris, divide crowded clumps. il Pop Gard 15:14-15 Jl '64
  Spurias that mimic butterflies. E. McCown. il Pop Gard 14:33+ My '63
  Try iris in your garden. M. Costigan. il Horticulture 41:329 Je '63
  Try little iris for big results. V. M. Quist. il Horticulture 41:176 Mr '63
  Year's favorite iris. Flower Grower 51:49 Je '64
    See also
  American iris society
IRISH
  Irish character. V. S. Pritchett. il Holiday 33:56-63+ Ap '63
  Irish eccentrics. M. Bence-Jones. Vogue 144:124+ O 1 '64
  Kennedy homestead. il Newsweek 62:31 Jl 1 '63
  Lifting the green curtain. il Time 82:28-40 Jl 12 '63; Same abr. with title Why Irish eyes are smiling. Read Digest 84:207-8+ Mr '64
  People of Belfast. B. Moore. il Holiday 35:58-63 F '64
  Sure, and it's County Kennedy now; Wexford. T. P. Coogan. il N Y Times Mag p7-9+ Je 23 '63
  Visit to Ireland; address, June 28, 1963. J. F. Kennedy. Dept State Bul 49:128-32 Jl 22 '63
IRISH AMERICANS
  American Irish, by W. V. Shannon. Review
    Commonweal 79:695-6 Mr 6 '64. R. D. Cross
    New Repub 150:22-4 Ja 18 '64. R. L. Strout
    Reporter 30:44 Mr 26 '64. J. P. Roche
  Irish in America. J. O'Gara. Commonweal 78:415 Jl 12 '63
  Irish of New York D. P. Moynihan. Commentary 36:93-107 Ag '63; Discussion. 37:18 Ja '64
  Sons of St. Patrick. il Newsweek 63:68 F 3 '64
  Southie is my home town; why the Irish love South Boston. J. McCarthy. Holiday 35:60-1+ Mr '64
  They never came back. O. D. Edwards. America 110:336-40 Mr 14 '64; Discussion. 110:512-13 Ap 11 '64
IRISH AMERICANS in Ireland
  Ireland in my blood. J. McCarthy. il Holiday 33:82-3+ Ap '63
IRISH bulls. See Bulls, Colloquial
IRISH Faustus; drama. See Durrell, L.
IRISH film society. See Moving picture societies
IRISH free state. See Ireland
IRISH in the United States
  Irish in America. J. O'Gara. Commonweal 78:415 Jl 12 '63
    See also
  Irish Americans
IRISH literature
  Irish comic tradition, by V. Mercier. Review
    Commonweal 78:484 Ag 9 '63. R. M. Ohmann
    See also
  Irish poetry
IRISH poetry
  Irish chronicle. A. Clarke. Poetry 103:185-7 D '63
  Party of one; themes of Irish poetry. W. Golding. Holiday 33:10+ Ap '63
  Some Irish poets. T. Kinsella. Poetry 102:324-9 Ag '63
IRISH revolt, 1916. See Ireland—History—Sinn Fein rebellion, 1916
IRISH silver. See Silverware
IRISH unification question
  How to end partition. America 108:629 My 4 '63
  Irish winds of change. C. McWilliams. Nation 197:191-3 O 5 '63
IRITA Van Doren literary award
  Irita Van Doren award established by Tribune. Pub W 183:58 Je 17 '63
  Irita Van Doren award goes to B. W. Huebsch. il Pub W 185:51-2 Je 29 '64
IRIZARRY, Carmen A.
  That certain fanaticism. America 110:771 My 30 '64
IRON

Isotopes

  Human bone marrow distribution shown in vivo by iron-52 and the positron scintillation camera. H. O. Anger and D. C. Van Dyke. bibliog il Science 144:1587-9 Je 26 '64

Metallography

  High-pressure polymorph of iron. T. Takahashi and W. A. Bassett. bibliog il Science 145:483-6 Jl 31 '64

Physiological effect

  Beware of iron. il Time 84:66 O 9 '64
IRON curtain. See Europe, Eastern
IRON deficiency anemia. See Anemia
IRON gates; story. See Freeman, J. T.
IRON hands. See Manipulators
IRON in the body
  Iron absorption: the effect of an iron-deficient diet. S. Pollack and others. bibliog il Science 144:1015-16 My 22 '64
IRON industry and trade

Wages and hours

  Wages in the basic iron and steel industry, March 1962. L. E. Lewis. il Mo Labor R 86:289-92 Mr '63
IRON metallurgy
  Iron direct from ore; Strategic-Udy process. il Bsns W p34 Jl 20 '63
IRON mines and mining

Canada

  American capital in Canada and a boom in iron ore. il U S News 56:72-4 My 4 '64

Gabon

  Jungle Mesabi; excerpts from report. P. Deutschman. il Fortune 68:81-2+ D '63

Liberia

  Mountain of riches. il Time 82:99 O 25 '63

Venezuela

  Iron direct from ore; Strategic-Udy process. il Bsns W p34 Jl 20 '63
IRON ores
  Mössbauer spectrum of iron-57 in iron metal at very high pressures. M. Nicol and G. Jura. bibliog il Science 141:1035-8 S 13 '63
    See also
  Taconite

Taxation

  Constitutional balm for an old sore; occupation taxes in Minnesota's mining industry. Bsns W p 112 S 14 '63
IRON poisoning
  Potent new Swiss drug used for iron poisoning; ferrous sulfate poisoning in anemia patients. Sci N L 84:57 Jl 27 '63
IRONCLADS. See Warships
IRONING
  Home sewing; pressing a garment as you make it. M. Carter. Redbook 120:50 Ap '63
  How to iron a shirt in 6 minutes. B. G. Wadsworth. il Parents Mag 38:144 Ap '63
  Make short work of ironing. J. Gillies. il Farm J 88:86-7 F '64
  Pressing facts about irons. Am Home 66:88-9 N '63
IRONING board covers
  Covers for ironing boards. il Consumer Rep 29:389-91 Ag '64
IRONING boards
  Ironing boards. il Consumer Rep 30:20-3 Ja '65
IRONING equipment. See Laundry equipment

IRONS, Evelyn
Evening with Virginia Woolf. New Yorker 39:115-16+ Mr 30 '63
IRONWORK
See also
Forging
IROQUOIS Indians
Grasping the drama of a culture. H. W. Hertzberg. il NEA J 52:44-6 F '63
See also
Seneca Indians
IRRADIATED food. See Food, Effect of radiation on
IRRADIATION
Design seen as interim solution to circuit irradiation. M. Getler. Miss & Roc 14:37-8 Mr 2 '64
Neutron irradiations: biological effects; report on symposium. H. H. Smith. Science 143:1466+ Mr 27 '64
IRREGULAR verb to love; drama. See Williams, H. and Williams, M.
IRRIGATION
Stones that make the desert bloom. il Sci Digest 54:67-8 Ag '63
Usually best to irrigate every row. Suc Farm 61:26 Je '63
Water. R. Revelle. il Sci Am 209:92-100+ bibliog(p307) S '63
When and how to irrigate. Suc Farm 61:91 Ag '63
See also
Drainage
Watering of gardens, lawns, etc.
Arizona
Management of water in arid lands. G. H. Davis. il Natur Hist 73:26-33 Ag '64
California
Management of water in arid lands. G. H. Davis. il Natur Hist 73:26-33 Ag '64
Israel
Plants are thriving in salty water. Sci N L 85:217 Ap 4 '64
Negev
River of hope, and danger. R. Payne. il N Y Times Mag p 10-11 Ja 19 '64
Russia
Khrushchev in Astrakhan; future of the lower Volga area; interview. N. S. Khrushchev. Bul Atomic Sci 20:12-14 Ja '64
Sahara Desert
Fresh-water gushers in the Sahara. il Pop Sci 185:98-9 O '64
United States
Irrigate crops this fall. Suc Farm 61:91 O '63
Virginia
Irrigation water from a tidal creek. B. A. Roth. il Farm J 87:54-5 D '63
IRRIGATION, Underground
Underground rain used in Russia to irrigate crops. Sci Digest 53:40-1 Ap '63
IRRIGATION pipes
New way to irrigate. O. Bay. il Farm J 87:58 My '63
IRRIGATION water
Beets and spinach thrive in salt water. Sci N L 86:73 Ag 1 '64
Plants are thriving in salty water. Sci N L 85:217 Ap 4 '64
IRVINE, George M. Jr
Fiberglass. Motor B 114:22-7 D '64
IRVINE, Joan
88,000 golden acres waiting for the dust to settle. S. Freedgood. il pors Fortune 68:142-7+ N '63
IRVINE, John
Song and its fountains. Ladies Home J 80:137 My '63
IRVINE, Keith
Angola: a non-self-governing territory. bibliog f Cur Hist 45:321-8 D '63
IRVINE ranch, Calif. See Ranches
IRVING, Don
Visual materials. Sch Arts 63:28-9 D '63
IRVING, K. C.
Midas of the maritimes. il por Time 83:67 Ja 31 '64
IRVING, R. See Harrison, J. M. jt. auth.
IRVING P. Krick associates
Your weather. See issues of Farm journal
IRWIN, Helen
Business woman collects miniatures. S. A. Parvin. il por Hobbies 69:119+ O '64
IRWIN, John B.
Astronomers visit Alaska. il por Sky & Tel 26:120-5 S '63
Serendipity in astronomy. Sky & Tel 28:192-5 O '64
IRWIN, May
Six comediennes. J. Walsh. il por Hobbies 68:35-7+ Je; 32-5 Jl '63
IRWIN, Ray
Who's afraid of Virginia Woolf, hunh? Atlan 213:122+ Ap '64
IRWIN, Theodore
About: bourbon. N Y Times Mag p75-6 Mr 8 '64
About: mailing lists. N Y Times Mag p96-7 Mr 22 '64
Don't doctor yourself! Todays Health 42:36-9+ D '64
Memo on memos (six copies, please) N Y Times Mag p46+ N 17 '63
Mom! mom! I can see! Sat Eve Post 236:71-2 My 25 '63
Ordeal of Linda Harris. Good H 158:42+ F '64
Should your parents move to a retirement village? Am Home 66:8+ Ja '63
They don't loaf in retirement. Todays Health 41:28-9+ F '63
Your life is in their hands. Todays Health 42:30-3+ Ag '64
ISAAC, Heinrich
Isaac and friends. J. W. Barker. il Am Rec G 31:110-12 O '64
ISAAC, Rael Jean
Children who need adoption: a radical view. Atlan 212:45-50 N '63; Discussion. 213:30+ Ja '64
ISAAC, Ted
New word; poem. Sat R 46:10 O 26 '63
ISAAC bound; story. See Schiff, M.
ISAACS, Alick
Foreign nucleic acids. Sci Am 209:46-50 bibliog(p 156) O '63
ISAACS, Gertrude
Receives world's first Ph.D. in nursing science. il por Todays Health 41:84 N '63
ISAACS, Harold R.
Reporter at large (cont) New Yorker 40:60-4+ D 12; 75-6+ D 19 '64
ISAACS, John D.
Atmospheric jet streams. Science 141:1045-6 S 13 '63
Night-caught and day-caught larvae of the California sardine. bibliog Science 144:1132-3 My 29 '64
ISAACS, Kenneth L.
New man for the club. por Time 85:75 Ja 29 '65
ISBELL, Harold
Crisis; poem. Cath World 197:350 S '63
For the giver of gods; poem. Commonweal 81:576 Ja 29 '65
Room 301; poem. Commonweal 79:307 D 6 '63
ISBERT, Margot Benary-. See Benary-Isbert, M.
ISBRANDT, Ralph H.
Rambler engineering. Motor T 15:40-5+ F '63
ISELIN, Columbus O'D.
What sank Thresher, the A-sub? ed. by J. Lear. Sat R 46:57-60 O 5 '63
ISELIN, Columbus O'Donnell, 2d
Pastures of the sea. Nation 198:413-14+ Ap 27 '64; Same abr. with title Five coming breakthroughs in oceanography. por Sci Digest 56:11-13 Ag '64
about
Last of the hardy sailor-scientists; reprint. J. A. Long. il Sci Digest 56:8-10 Ag '64
ISELIN, Sally
Water rats. Mlle 57:140-3+ My '63
ISENBERG, Robert M.
Rural disadvantaged. NEA J 52:27 Ap '63
ISHERWOOD Christopher
Aldous Huxley in California. Atlan 214:44-7 S '64
Christopher Isherwood on Images by Cecil Beaton. Vogue 142:208-11 S 1 '63
ISHI (Indian)
Ishi, the last of the Yanas, a primitive Indian between two worlds. A. Métraux. il pors UNESCO Courier 16:10-13 F '63; Same abr. with title Last stone age man in the U.S. Sci Digest 54:22-7 Jl '63
ISHIHARA, Yujiro
Honshu's James Dean. por Time 82:57 S 6 '63
ISICA, Carl
Dodge Palomino sport pickup. Motor T 16:78-9 Ap '64
Fine art of used car buying. Motor T 16:66-9 S '64
Hitch & go. See issues of Motor trend
Summer driving. Motor T 16:32-5 Je '64
Track-testing trailers. Motor T 16:86-7+ F '64

ISLAM
Christianity and Islam in West Africa. K. Hughes. Christian Cent 81:264-7, 298-302 F 26-Mr 4 '64
Pakistan moves toward state religion. Christian Cent 80:485 Ap 17 '63
Rebirth of Islam? America 110:472 Ap 4 '64
Why 400,000,000 follow Mohammed. R. Payne. il N Y Times Mag p 18+ Ag 4 '63; Discussion. p2+ Ag 25 '63
See also
Bahaism
Moors (people)
Ramadan
ISLAM and Christianity. See Christianity and other religions
ISLAMABAD, Pakistan
Islamabad: new capital for Pakistan. il UNESCO Courier 17:30-1 Je '64
ISLAMIC architecture. See Architecture, Islamic
ISLAMIC literature
Anthology of Islamic literature, ed. by J. Kritzeck. Review
Reporter 30:46-7 Mr 26 '64. A. Fremantle
ISLAND airlines. See Airlines—Hawaii
ISLAND of Hydra. See Hydra (island)
ISLAND teacher; story. See O'Connell, C. C.
ISLANDIA NATIONAL MONUMENT (proposed) See National monuments
ISLANDS
American islomania. K. Davis. Mlle 57:122-3+ Je '63
Lure of islands. il Motor B 112:18-25 Ag '63
Pattern of uplifted islands in the main ocean basins. J. T. Wilson. bibliog il Science 139:592-4 F 15 '62
Serene isles; Greek islands. il Life 54:54-71+ Je 14 '63
See also names of islands, and groups of islands, e.g. Scilly Islands
ISLANDS, Artificial. See Artificial islands
ISLANDS of the Adriatic Sea
Serene isles. il Life 54:54-71+ Je 14 '63
ISLANDS of the Pacific
Origin of high-alumina basalt, andesite, and dacite magmas. W. Hamilton. bibliog il Science 146:635-7 O 30 '64
Out West, Catalina and beyond. il Motor B 112:24-5 Ag '63
See also
Micronesia
Oceania
Trust Territory of the Pacific Islands
ISLAS, Saúl Ibargoyen. See Ibargoyen Islas, S.
ISLE OF PINES (Kunie) See Pines, Isle of (Kunie)
ISLE ROYALE NATIONAL PARK
Isle Royale: predator vs prey. D. L. Allen. il Field & S 68:21-3 Ja '64
Wolves versus moose on Isle Royale. D. L. Allen and L. D. Mech. il Nat Geog Mag 123:200-19 F '63
ISLES OF SHOALS, Me. and N.H.
Star Island. M. S. Neagle. il Travel 120:48-9+ S '63
ISOIMMUNE serum. See Serum
ISOLATION, Sensory. See Sensory deprivation
ISOLATION, Social
Are you still there? ECHO chamber experiments. Newsweek 61:62+ Mr 11 '63
Loneliness affects brain. Sci N L 87:38 Ja 16 '65
Long-term isolation stress in rats. A. Hatch and others. bibliog il Science 142:507 O 25 '63
Long voyage in inner space. T. Flaherty. il Life 54:119-20 My 17 '63
Mental strains of Antarctic solitude. P. Law. il UNESCO Courier 16:26-30 Je '63
Solitude: who can take it and who can't. B. H. Frisch. il Sci Digest 55:12-18 Mr '64
Stress build-up ends isolation. Sci N L 83:280 My 4 '63
ISOLATIONISM (United States) See United States—Foreign relations
ISOMERISM
Photoisomerism a colorless photoinduced intermediate of *o*-nitrobenzylpyridine. J. A. Sousa and J. D. Loconti. bibliog il Science 146:397-8 O 16 '64
ISOMERS
Lactic acids: chemistry and metabolism; report on conference, New York city, 12-14 November 1964. R. H. Dunlop. Science 147:315-17 Ja 15 '65
ISOMETRIC contraction. See Exercise
ISONIAZID
Genetics of isoniazid metabolism in Caucasian, Negro, and Japanese populations. A. P. Dufour and others. bibliog il Science 145:391 Jl 24 '64
ISOPROPYL alcohol
Azeotrope of isopropyl alcohol and isopropyl borate. W. D. English and R. L. Kidwell. bibliog il Science 139:341-2 Ja 25 '63
Polymorphism in isopropyl alcohol. G. S. Ross and others. bibliog Science 141:1043-4 S 13 '63
ISOTOPE separation
Isotopic molecules: separation by recycle gas chromatography. J. W. Root and others. bibliog il Science 143:676-8 F 14 '64
ISOTOPES
Isotopes; different yet the same. il Sci Digest 55:78-80 Ap '64
See also
Radioisotopes
also subhead Isotopes under names of chemical elements. e.g. Carbon—Isotopes
ISOZYMES. See Enzymes
ISRAEL, Lawrence J.
Basic necessities of store design. Arch Rec 135:157-65 Je '64
ISRAEL
Big small country. G. Gersh. Commonweal 80:113-16 Ap 17 '64
Israel after fifteen years. G. Gersh. Christian Cent 80:487-9 Ap 17 '63
Israel: years of challenge, by D. Ben-Gurion. Review
Sat R 46:45 N 9 '63. H. Lehrman
Non-Europeans; Ashkenazim being outnumbered by Sephardic Jews. New Repub 150:7-8 My 2 '64
Notes on Israel. D. M. Friedenberg. il Commonweal 81:381-5 D 11 '64; Reply. E. Berger. 81:554-5 Ja 29 '65
Reach of Rassco; Rural & suburban settlement co. ltd. il Time 82:63 D 27 '63
See also
Airlines—Israel
Airplane industry and trade—Israel
Airplanes, Military—Israel
Arabs in Israel
Birds—Israel
Booksellers and bookselling—Israel
Cities and towns—Israel
Colleges and universities—Israel
Elath
Finance—Israel
Irrigation—Israel
Jerusalem
Jews in Israel
Jordan River
Masada (fortress)
Music festivals—Israel
Negev
Space research—Israel
Theater—Israel
Trade unions—Israel
United Nations—Israel
Vocational education—Israel
Water supply—Israel
Zionism

Antiquities

Antiquities uncovered: a visit to four celebrated digs in Israel. il Sunset 133:36+ S '64
Masada dig. D. Gavron. Commentary 38:52-6 O '64

Boundaries

Jets over the Jordan; Israeli-Syrian border clash. Newsweek 64:48 N 23 '64
United States urges restraint on Israel and Syria; statement, December 3, 1964. A. E. Stevenson. Dept State Bul 52:27-9 Ja 4 '65
Why Israel wants peace. D. Ben-Gurion. Look 27:62-5 Ag 27 '63

Defenses

How worried are the Israelis? P. Ben. New Repub 148:13-14 Ap 20 '63

Description and travel

Conquest of the Holy City. F. Shor. il Nat Geog Mag 124:839-55 D '63
Contrasts in the Holy Land. L. Barry. il Pop Phot 54:24+ Ap '64
Going places, finding things in Israel. M. M. Hemingway. il House & Gard 126:19+ Ag '64
Holy Land; photographs. J. Bryson. Ladies Home J 81:49-55 Ap '64
Land of Jesus. il Vogue 142:93-101 D '63
Land that holds the legend of our lives. L. Hellman. il Ladies Home J 81:56-7+ Ap '64
Let's travel to Israel. il Mlle 57:175-9 S '63
Place like no other; scenes of the Holy Land. N Y Times Mag p6-7 D 22 '63

Economic conditions

German reparations and the Israeli economy. W. Mehlman. Reporter 29:43-5 S 12 '63

Foreign relations

Egypt, the Soviet Union and Israel. New Repub 150:11-12 Je 6 '64

ISRAEL—Foreign relations—*Continued*
Free-booters; German scientists hired by the Egyptians to help build weapons. New Repub 148:6 Ap 6 '63
Germany's amends to the Jews. R. Littell. Read Digest 83:215-20 Ag '63
How worried are the Israelis? P. Ben. New Repub 148:13-14 Ap 20 '63
Israel-OAS cooperation. Américas 16:44-5 Ag '64
Nasser's hired Germans; Israelis fight to stop missiles being built. S. de Gramont. il Sat Eve Post 236:60-1+ Jl 13 '63
Rockets in Egypt; German technicians in Egypt's military factory 333. Newsweek 61:50+ Ap 15 '63
Trouble for 333; Egypt's military factory. Time 81:34+ Ap 5 '63
Troubled waters. Newsweek 63:30-1 Ja 6 '64
Water war; Syrian-Israeli dispute. Time 84:40 N 27 '64
Why Israel wants peace. D. Ben-Gurion. Look 27:62-5 Ag 27 '63

United States

U.S. and Israel exchange views on matters of mutual interest; exchange of greetings, with joint communique, June 2, 1964. L. B. Johnson; L. Eshkol. Dept State Bul 50:958-60 Je 22 '64

History

Why Israel wants peace. D. Ben-Gurion. Look 27:62-5 Ag 27 '63

Industries

Israel. J. S. Haupert. bibliog il Focus 14:1-6 Mr '64

Intellectual life

Mission to Israel. H. Weiner. Commentary 36:108-18 Ag '63

Nationalism

Israel and Zionism. A. Segal. il Nation 197:293-6 N 9 '63

Politics and government

Changes are coming in Israeli politics. New Repub 151:6 N 21 '64
Judaism for all seasons. L. R. Sussman. Christian Cent 80:427-9 Ap 3 '63
King David departs. il Newsweek 62:30+ Jl 1 '63
Kosher or non-kosher? New Repub 150:11 Mr 7 '64
Trouble in Zion; revival of the Lavon affair. il Newsweek 64:29-30 D 28 '64
Vale atque ave. il Time 81:30 Je 28 '63
Why did Ben-Gurion resign? New Repub 148:9 Je 29 '63

Popular culture

Mission to Israel. H. Weiner. Commentary 36:108-18 Ag '63
Traveling with Mlle: Israel. il Mlle 57:171-4 S '63

Relations (diplomatic)

Catholic church

See Catholic church—Relations (diplomatic)—Israel

Religious institutions and affairs

Christian schools & Israeli children. H. Weiner. Commentary 38:39-45 Jl '64; Discussion. 39:14+ Ja '65
Religious conflicts in Israel. N. Levin. il Commonweal 79:344-6 D 13 '63
Wild goats of Ein Gedi: a journal of religious encounters in the Holy Land, by H. Weiner. Review
Christian Cent 80:430 Ap 3 '63. L. A. Whiston, jr
See also
Jews in Israel

Social conditions

Israel: image and reality. S. Avineri. New Repub 151:7-9 S 26 '64

ISRAEL aircraft industries, limited. See Airplane industry and trade—Israel

ISRAEL and Germany
German reparations and the Israeli economy. W. Mehlman. Reporter 29:43-5 S 12 '63

ISRAEL and the United States
Science, a force for peace; remarks, February 6, 1964. L. B. Johnson. Dept State Bul 50:285-7 F 24 '64

ISRAEL-Arab relations. See Jewish-Arab relations

ISRAELI fiction
Israeli stories, ed. by J. Blocker. Review
Nation 196:122-3 F 9 '63. R. Sanders

ISRAELI-Franco-British aggression. See Egypt—History—Invasion, 1956

ISRAELI technical assistance. See Technical assistance, Israeli

ISRAELIS
Israel after fifteen years. G. Gersh. Christian Cent 80:487-9 Ap 17 '63
What Pope Paul's visit was not. E. Berger. Christian Cent 81:524 Ap 22 '64

ISRAELS, L. G. and others
Shunt bilirubin: evidence for two components. bibliog Science 139:1054-5 Mr 15 '63

ISSAWI, Charles
Five on the desert. Nation 199:36-7 Jl 27 '64

ISSIGONIS, Alex A.
Designer who laughs at the conventional. il por Bsns W p 126 Mr 9 '63

ISTANBUL
Our far-flung correspondents. C. Frankel. il New Yorker 40:136+ Je 6 '64

Description

Emphatic Istanbul. R. Lynes. il Harper 229:22+ O '64
Travel notes. R. Joseph. Esquire 63:8+ Ja '65

Santa Sophia

Coptic and Byzantine. C. J. McNaspy. America 111:161-3 Ag 15 '64
Structure of St Sophia; with editorial comment. R. L. Van Nice. il Arch Forum 118:131-8+, 154 My '63; 121:45-9 Ag '64

ISTOMIN, Eugene
Notes from abroad; interview, ed. by R. McMullen. por Hi Fi 14:12+ Ja '64

IT seems I heard the violins; story. See McWhirter, M.

IT was different with Cinderella; story. See Shore, W.

ITALIAN cookery. See Cookery, Italian

ITALIAN line. See Steamship lines

ITALIAN literature
Riddle of Turandot; concerning Gozzi's Turandot. P. J. Smith. Opera N 29:24-5 Ja 16 '65
See also
Italian poetry

ITALIAN manuscripts. See Manuscripts, Italian

ITALIAN opera. See Opera, Italian

ITALIAN painting. See Painting, Italian

ITALIAN poetry
Between Aristotle and Plato. G. Cambon. Poetry 102:198-201 Je '63

Translations into English

After many deaths; tr. by S. Raiziss. A. de Palchi. Nation 197:244 O 19 '63
Little diary on growing old (XVIII) tr. by I. L. Salomon. C. Betocchi. Commonweal 77:664 Mr 22 '63
Summer song; tr. by I. L. Salomon. C. Betocchi. Commonweal 79:250 N 22 '63
Winter that kills; tr. by S. Raiziss. A. de Palchi. Nation 196:166 F 23 '63
Word; tr. by D. Hoffman and J. Mangione. R. Domino. Poetry 104:85 My '64

ITALIAN question, 1848-1870
See also
Carbonari

ITALIAN RIVIERA. See Riviera

ITALIAN sculpture. See Sculpture, Italian

ITALIAN society of agricultural colonization
Italian colonists in Costa Rica. D. G. Cole. il Américas 15:38-41. Je '63

ITALIAN SOMALILAND. See Somalia

ITALIAN visitors in Eastern Europe. See Foreign visitors in Eastern Europe

ITALIAN visitors in the United States. See Foreign visitors in the United States

ITALIAN wines. See Wine

ITALIANS
Italian character; excerpts from Italians. L. Barzini. il Harper 229:33-40 Ag '64
Italian man; with photographs by Paul Shutzer. Life 55:54-9 Ag 23 '63
Italians, by L. Barzini. Review
Commonweal 81:425-6 D 18 '64. R. Bimonte
Newsweek il 64:85 Ag 24 '64
Time il 84:100+ S 25 '64
Living in a nice place to visit. G. Gersh. Sat R 47:37 O 17 '64
Milan: a capital in search of a country. F. Du Plessix. il Vogue 142:152-5+ N 15 '63
See also
Neapolitans

ITALIANS in Costa Rica
Italian colonists in Costa Rica. D. G. Cole. il Américas 15:38-41 Je '63

ITALIC writing. See Penmanship

ITALY
See also
Architecture—Italy
Architecture, Domestic—Italy

ITALY—See also—*Continued*
Art—Italy
Automobile industry and trade—Italy
Booksellers and bookselling—Italy
Churches—Italy
Communism—Italy
Como, Lake
Cortina D'Ampezzo
Dams—Italy
Electric power—Italy
Electronic apparatus industry and trade—Italy
Festivals—Italy
Finance—Italy
Floods—Italy
Garda, Lake
Gardens—Italy
Genoa
Geology—Italy
Government ownership—Italy
Libraries—Italy
Montecatini Terme
Music festivals—Italy
Music—Italy
Opera—Italy
Parma
Petroleum industry and trade—Italy
Piedmont
Political parties—Italy
Publishers and publishing—Italy
Railroads—Italy
Research—Italy
Roads—Italy
San Remo
Sardinia
Science—Italy
Sirmione
Space research—Italy
Strikes—Italy
Taxation—Italy
Television broadcasting—Italy
Tourist trade—Italy
Tyrol
Valdagno

Antiquities

Ancient Cumae. R. V. Schoder. il Sci Am 209:108-21 D '63
This way to hell; archeologists discover Gates of Hades. il Newsweek 64:80 S 14 '64
See also
Herculaneum
Pompeii
Sybaris

Colonies

See also
San Vito de Java

Description and travel

Discursive tour of Verdi's Italy. R. Gelatt. il Hi Fi 13:70-8 O '63
Europe as we see it. H. De Becker. il Dance Mag 38:19+ My '64
Going places, finding things in southern Italy. P. Dallas. il House & Gard 124:24-6+ S '63
Italian Riviera, land that winter forgot. H. Walker. il Nat Geog Mag 123:743-89 Je '63
Our man on the Settebello. New Yorker 40:41-4 Ap 18 '64
Southern Italy. S. O'Faolain. il Holiday 36:38-47+ S '64
Travel notes; northern Italy. R. Joseph. Esquire 60:72+ O '63
Well traveled camera; touring Italy by car. M. A. Matzkin. il Mod Phot 27:44+ Jl '63
See also
Cities and towns—Italy

Economic conditions

Apertura a sinistra: second round. C. Sterling. il Reporter 29:28-32 N 21 '63
Atlantic report; southern Italy; La Cassa per il Mezzogiorno. Atlan 212:30+ N '63
Butterflies in the boom: Italy's credit-happy economy. il Time 82:111 O 18 '63
End of the miracle. Newsweek 63:30 Mr 30 '64
Food and revolution. J. Burnham. Nat R 14:490 Je 18 '63
Fundamental instrument; Istituto per la ricostruzione industriale. Time 83:86 Mr 27 '64
Italy: putting the brakes on inflation. il Bsns W p96 Mr 28 '64
Italy: stability and inflation fight it out. il Bsns W p 114 Ag 17 '63
Italy's postwar economic miracle. il Sr Schol 82:14-17 My 1 '63
Italy's stake in the Common market. B. Foa. Cur Hist 45:289-94+ N '63
Miracle is over: Italy's morning after. C. Sterling. Reporter 31:33-4+ S 24 '64
Mr Moro tries again. E. V. Kuehnelt-Leddihn. Nat R 16:689 Ag 11 '64
Noonday land; the Italian South. J. J. Navone. America 110:44-6 Ja 11 '64
Southern Italy. S. O'Faolain. il Holiday 36:38-47+ S '64
Will Italy shake EEC? political crisis and inflation. Bsns W p29 Jl 11 '64
Year of the *sboom*. Time 84:106+ S 18 '64
See also
Italy—Industries
Rome (city)—Economic conditions

Fascist movement

See Fascism—Italy

Foreign relations

President Kennedy holds talks with Prime Minister of Italy; joint communique, January 17, 1963. J. F. Kennedy and A. Fanfani. Dept State Bul 48:164 F 4 '63

Europe, Western

Italy's stake in the Common market. B. Foa. Cur Hist 45:289-94+ N '63

Great Britain

Macmillan at Rome. M. Painelle. America 108:265-6 F 23 '63

United States

Foreign Minister of Italy holds talks in Washington. J. F. Kennedy and A. Piccioni. Dept State Bul 49:636 O 21 '63

History

Anachronism of Verdi; tr. by W. Weaver. A. Moravia. Hi Fi 13:79-81 O '63

Bibliography

Articles and other books received; Italy, comp. by E. P. Noether. See issues of American historical review

Industries

Boom in a have-not area; southern Italy. J. Law. il U S News 55:102-4 O 21 '63
Changing the face of a land; ambitious efforts to help the South. il Time 84:109 O 16 '64
Destiny of dynasties; Fiat buys one-third of Olivetti. il Time 83:106 Ap 17 '64
New chemical hybrid; Italy's Montecatini and Royal Dutch Shell oil combine. il Bsns W p70-3 Ja 11 '64
Stormy engagement; negotiations between Royal Dutch Shell and Italy's Montecatini complex. Time 82:89 N 22 '63
Stretching spaghetti; Paolo Agnesi & sons, Italy's oldest pasta maker. il Time 83:108 My 15 '64
Using his head. Time 82:62 D 27 '63
See also
Electric apparatus industry
Olivetti

Parliament

Mr Moro tries again. E. V. Kuehnelt-Leddihn. Nat R 16:689 Ag 11 '64

Chamber of deputies

Signor Fanfani's self-made bed. A. Leone-Moats. il Nat R 14:404-5 My 21 '63

Politics and government

Adzhubei and Italy today. M. Painelle. America 108:405-6 Mr 23 '63
Anxious moment. Time 81:23 My 31 '63
Apertura a sinistra: second round. C. Sterling. il Reporter 29:28-32 N 21 '63
At odds and ends. New Repub 149:8 Jl 13 '63
Atlantic report. Atlan 212:45-6+ O '63
Buccia di banana; Moro's government toppled. Time 84:24-5 Jl 3 '64
Center moves left. F. Giannattasio and D. E. Turner. il America 108:606-8 Ap 27 '63
Communists in good faith; Italian bishops joint pastoral. America 109:621 N 16 '63
Converging parallels. Newsweek 62:60+ D 9 '63
Democratic process; eighteenth Presidential ballot. il Newsweek 65:28 Ja 4 '65
Down the river? New Repub 148:8 Ap 27 '63
Epitaph for the apertura. il Time 81:29-30 Je 28 '63
Filling the salad bowl; presidential election, Italian-style. Newsweek 64:27 D 28 '64
Gambler; Premier A. Moro resigns. Newsweek 64:40 Jl 6 '64
Italian socialism chooses the things that are possible. E. Forcella. New Repub 149:13-14 N 16 '63
Italian tightrope act. C. Sterling. Reporter 30:30-2 F 13 '64
Italy: a new village around an old fountain. E. M. Borgese. Nation 196:327-9 Ap 20 '63
Italy: problem for Pope Paul. H. W. Flannery. Cath World 197:372-9 S '63

ITALY—Politics and government—*Continued*
Italy's coalition government. E. R. Rosen. Cur Hist 47:339-44 D '64
Italy's democratic coalition. America 110:8 Ja 4 '64
Italy's new partnership. il Time 82:31 D 13 '63
Italy's postwar economic miracle. il Sr Schol 82:14-17 My 1 '63
Left and center? Newsweek 62:62-3 N 11 '63
Lurching left? il Newsweek 61:47 My 13 '63
Man in the middle. Newsweek 64:37 Jl 13 '64
Marriage of inconvenience. il Time 82:38 D 6 '63
Miracle is over: Italy's morning after. C. Sterling. Reporter 31:33-4+ S 24 '64
Moro cabinet falls. America 111:34-5 Jl 11 '64
Narrow opening. il Newsweek 62:60+ D 2 '63
New Italy & its politics. H. S. Hughes. Commentary 38:46-51 O '64
Opening to nowhere. Newsweek 62:32 Jl 1 '63
Parenthesis in Italy. C. Sterling. Reporter 30:10 Ja 2 '64
Persuader. New Repub 150:11-12 Ja 18 '64
Scramble for succession; resignation of President Segni. Newsweek 64:37 D 21 '64
Search for the feasible. il Time 81:33 My 24 '63
Second half; Moro's new government. Newsweek 64:35 Ag 3 '64
This ship is leaking. il Time 82:35 N 8 '63
Till the next crisis. Time 84:21-2 Jl 31 '64
Trouble with Italian politics. A. Mennen. il N Y Times Mag p28-9+ N 22 '64
What now for Italy? America 112:156 Ja 30 '65
Why communism hangs on: the comrades are middle class. il Time 84:38-9 N 20 '64
Will Italy shake EEC? political crisis and inflation. Bsns W p29 Jl 11 '64
See also
Communist party (Italy)
Elections—Italy
Fascism—Italy
Political parties—Italy

Relief work

Italian government provides Vaiont Dam disaster relief. Dept State Bul 50:803-4 My 18 '64

Religious institutions and affairs

See also
Catholic church in Italy

Social conditions

Fellini's La dolce italia. J. J. Navone. Commonweal 77:639-41 Mr 15 '63

Social life and customs

Age of malaise, by D. M. Grove. Review Christian Cent 80:831 Je 26 '63. J. Scott
Mediterranean mosaic. H. Mitgang. il Harper 226:26+ Ap '63

ITALY and Argentina
Italian way. il Time 82:54 N 15 '63

ITALY and the United States
Attraction of Italy for American painters. O. Wittmann. il Antiques 85:552-7 My '64
President Segni of Italy visits the United States; exchange of greetings, January 14, 1964; with text of communique. A. Segni; L. B. Johnson. Dept State Bul 50:196-8 F 10 '64

ITCHING
Fine art of scratching; interview, ed. by H. G. Earl. S. Ayres, jr. il Todays Health 43: 38-41+ Ja '65

ITEK corporation
Itek refocused. il Time 82:85-6 N 8 '63

ITHACA, N.Y.
Rental housing as architecture. il Arch Rec 136:143-8 D '64

ITHACUS. See Rockets, Military transport

ITKIN brothers, incorporated
Itkins: Manhattan's furniture kings. P. Korenvaes. il Duns R 82:pt2 125 S '63

IT'S only a game; story. See Loeser, K.

IVAN IV, the Terrible, czar of Russia
Ivan the corpse; tomb opened. por Newsweek 62:38 Ag 12 '63
Man like no other. R. Payne. il pors N Y Times Mag p79-80+ S 8 '63

IVANOV, Evgenii E.
Doctor Stephen Ward returns. R. West. Esquire 62:141+ S '64

IVERSON, Marion Day
Bed rug in colonial America. bibliog Antiques 85:107-9 Ja '64

IVERSON, R. M. See Stafford, D. W. jt. auth.

IVES, C. P.
Managers have to manage. Nat R 14:157-8 F 26 '63

IVES, Charles Edward
Ives revived. Newsweek 62:65 O 14 '63
On Cambridge, CRI, and Vox, that supremely individual creative genius, Chas. E. Ives. A. Cohn. por Am Rec G 30:760-2+ My '64

IVES, Ronald L.
Burned-out pilot-lamp indicators. Electr World 69:40 Je '63
Quieting audio switching transients. Electr World 72:51 N '64
Tone-modulated frequency calibrator. Electr World 72:56-7+ O '64
Transient evaluator. Electr World 69:45+ My '63
Tunable phase-shift audio filter. bibliog Electr World 69:48-50 My '63

IVINSKAIA, Olga
Lara's return. il por Time 84:54 N 13 '64

IVORY COAST
Africa's Ivory Coast. B. B. Carton. il Travel 122:44-6 D '64
Ivory Coast, Africa's big success story. D. Reed. il Read Digest 86:107-12 Ja '65

IVY, Andrew Conway
Curious case of krebiozen. H. Margolis. Bul Atomic Sci 20:29-31 Mr '64
Fantastic krebiozen story. R. P. Goldman. il pors Sat Eve Post 237:15-19 Ja 4 '64
Incredible story behind a cancer cure. S. Blum. il Redbook 123:40-1+ Je '64
Krebiozen in court. il por Newsweek 64:91 N 30 '64
What ever happened to Dr Ivy? W. R. Young. il pors Life 57:110-12+ O 9 '64; Same abr. with title Krebiozen, the tragic obsession of Andrew Ivy. Read Digest 83:193-4+ Ja '65

IVY
Ghost ivy grows like a tree. il Sunset 130: 264-5 Mr '63
Tricks with ivy. G. Aske. il Flower Grower 51:29 N '64

IVY-leaved geraniums. See Geraniums

IVY poisoning. See Poison ivy

IWAMOTO, David
Reactions to shared time. NEA J 53:49+ D '64

IWASA, Yoshizane
Straight-from-the-shoulder Japenese reminder; excerpts from address. Fortune 69:110 My '64

IWO JIMA, Battle of, 1945
First flag-raising on Iwo Jima. R. Wheeler. il Am Heritage 15:54-9+ Je '64

IXORA
Ixora coccinea: flame of the woods. M. C. Dolton. il Horticulture 41:202 Ap '63

IYER, V. N. and Szybalski, Waclaw
Mitomycins and porfiromycin: chemical mechanism of activation and cross-linking of DNA. bibliog Science 145:55-8 Jl 3 '64

IZARD, Anne Rebecca
Publishers' library edition seen as a monster. Pub W 185:110+ F 3 '64

IZQUIERDO, Estrellita
Ballet Granada of Estrellita and Raul. W. Como. il pors Dance Mag 38:50-1+ My '64

IZQUIERDO, Raul
Ballet Granada of Estrellita and Raul. W. Como. il pors Dance Mag 38:50-1+ My '64

J

J. C. Penney catalog. See Catalogs, Mail order

J. C. Penney company. See Penney, J. C. company

JCS. See United States—Joint chiefs of staff

J. P. Morgan and company. See Morgan guaranty trust company

JSP (Japan Socialist party) See Political parties—Japan

JABLONSKI, Edward
Unlikely corners. See issues of American record guide

JABLOW, Evelyn
Designs on your future. Sat Eve Post 237: 22-7 O 17 '64

JACK, Homer A.
Conference of the nonaligned. Christian Cent 81:1364-5 N 4 '64
Disarmament at the U.N: discussions in detente. Bul Atomic Sci 20:33-6 F '64
Disarmament at the U.N: the quiet Assembly. Bul Atomic Sci 19:39-40+ F '63
Disarmament picture, 1965. Christian Cent 82:104-6 Ja 27 '65

JACK, Homer A.—*Continued*
From Cairo: the nonaligned confer. Bul Atomic Sci 20:34-5 D '64
Geneva: progress and problems. Sat R 47: 19+ Je 27 '64
Oxford conference: organizing the non-aligned. Bul Atomic Sci 19:38-40 Je '63
Religion-state conference on civil rights legislation. Christian Cent 81:1566-7+ D 16 '64
Rocky road to a test ban. Christian Cent 80:615-16 My 8 '63
Seventeen continue. Bul Atomic Sci 20:43-5 Je '64

JACK, Mattie
Left for dead; ed. by D. French. por Outdoor Life 134:36-7+ O '64

JACK and the magic beanstalk; drama. See Thane, A.

JACK fishing. See Crevallé fishing

JACK-in-the-pulpits
Solomon's seal Jack-in-the-pulpit. E. W. Reed. il Horticulture 41:182-3 Mr '63

JACK-o'-lanterns. See Halloween

JACK pine. See Pine

JACKS
Keep those lifters quiet! hydraulic valve lifters and mechanical lifters. F. Greenwald. il Pop Sci 185:90-3 S '64

JACKS, Hydraulic. See Hydraulic jacks

JACKSNIPES. See Snipes

JACKSON, Andrew
Andrew Jackson, seventh President 1829-1837. F. Freidel. il pors Nat Geog Mag 127:82-9 Ja '65
First assassination attempt on a U.S. President. il Sr Schol 84:4 Ja 31 '64

JACKSON, Anne
Talk with the stars. por Newsweek 61:56 F 18 '63
What's with the Wallachs? at home or onstage it's Luv. il pors Life 58:79-81+ Ja 8 '65

JACKSON, Barbara (Ward) lady. See Ward, B.

JACKSON, Charles
Loving offenders; story. McCalls 90:54-5 Jl '63

JACKSON, Charles Douglas
C. D. Jackson, March 16, 1902-September 18, 1964. E. R. Belmont; A. A. Bliss; J. D. Rockefeller, 3d. por Opera N 29:16 N 14 '64
C. D. Jackson, 1902-1964. G. P. Hunt. por Life 57:3 O 2 '64
Goodby, C. D. Sports Illus 21:15 S 28 '64
Letter from the publisher. B. M. Auer. por Time 84:13 S 25 '64

JACKSON, Charlotte
Books for children. Atlan 214:160-4 D '64

JACKSON, Donald
Crack-ups on the campus. Life 58:72+ Ja 8 '65
Evolution of an assassin. Life 56:68A-72+ F 21 '64

JACKSON, Elmore
U.S. announces pledge to UNRWA for current fiscal year; statement, December 20, 1962. Dept State Bul 48:101 Ja 21 '63

JACKSON, Frederick H.
Instruction in Chinese and Japanese in secondary schools. Ann Am Acad 356:113-18 N '64

JACKSON, George
Naked in its native beauty. Dance Mag 38: 32-7 Ap '64

JACKSON, H. Nelson
Automotive milestones; first car across the U.S: Winston, 1903. il Motor T 15:60-1+ My '63

JACKSON, Henry M.
Help wanted by our ambassadors. N Y Times Mag p36+ O 11 '64
Public opinion and national security; address, July 19, 1963. Vital Speeches 29:642-4 Ag 15 '63
Seven assumptions that beset us. N Y Times Mag p5+ Ag 4; 11 Ag 18 '63; Same abr. with title Cold war isn't over. por Read Digest 83:99-102 N '63
Test ban: summing up; excerpt from address, September 13, 1963. Reporter 29:18 S 26 '63

JACKSON, James P.
Ebb of winter. Am For 70:14-15+ Mr '64
In defense of bird watching. Am For 70: 37+ My '64
Park of champions. il Am For 69:9+ My '63
Shadows of a deserted farm. Am For 69:8+ Ap '63

JACKSON, John F. and Lindahl-Kiessling, Kerstin
Polyploidy and endoreduplication in human leukocyte cultures treated with β-mercaptopyruvate. bibliog Science 141:424-6 Ag 2 '63

JACKSON, Joseph Harrison
Five million Baptists plan progress drive. il pors Ebony 20:76-80+ D '64
Jackson's way. por Newsweek 64:76 S 21 '64

JACKSON, Katherine Gauss
Books in brief. See issues of Harper's magazine
For Christmas. Harper 227:126-7 D '63

JACKSON, Larry
Player of the week; Chicago Cubs' ace right-hander. por Sports Illus 21:100 S 28 '64

JACKSON, Luther P.
First Negro U.S. president. Negro Hist Bul 28:6 O '64
Needed: the truth about Harlem. Negro Hist Bul 28:11-12 O '64
Negro father speaks. Good H 156:79+ My '63
Uncle Remus again. Negro Hist Bul 28:70 D '64

JACKSON, M. L. See Schwertmann, U. jt. auth.

JACKSON, Mahalia
In God she trusts. D. Gold. por Ladies Home J 80:66-7 N '63
Love comes to Mahalia. E. B. Thompson. il pors Ebony 20:50-2+ N '64

JACKSON, Marian
History and significance of Negro history week. Negro Hist Bul 27:72+ D '63

JACKSON, Miles M.
American librarians abroad. por Wilson Lib Bul 39:51+ S '64

JACKSON, Phyllis
Boss ladies; symposium, ed. by L. L. Tornabene. por(p 104) Esquire 63:102+ Ja '65

JACKSON, R. C.
Preferential segregation of chromosomes from a trivalent in haplopappus gracilis. bibliog Science 145:511-13 Jl 31 '64

JACKSON, Richard M.
Seaboard president attacks case for Pan American-TWA merger; summary of address. Aviation W 78:44 Ja 21 '63

JACKSON, Shirley
Speaking out. por Sat Eve Post 237:8+ Je 6 '64

about

WLB biography. P. Edge. por Wilson Lib Bul 38:352 D '63

JACKSON, Sidney L.
Teaching of research in the library schools. por Library J 88:2206-7 Je 1 '63

JACKSON, Stan
Sixty-six years, and still steaming. Motor T 15:72-3 Je '63

JACKSON, William A.
Obituary
Pub W 186:42 N 2 '64

JACKSON, Miss.
Artistic boycott. Time 83:73 Mr 20 '64

Churches

Another pilgrimage to Jackson; seven ministers barred from Capitol street Methodist church. T. Thompson. Christian Cent 81: 511-12 Ap 22 '64
Easter in Jackson; Methodist bishops barred from Galloway memorial Methodist church. J. K. Mathews. Christian Cent 81:478-80 Ap 15 '64
Racists challenge Methodists; Methodist bishops barred from Galloway Methodist church. Christian Cent 81:454 Ap 8 '64

Negroes

Battle of Jackson. il Newsweek 61:28-9 Je 10 '63
Celebrity boycott. J. De Muth. New Repub 150:8-9 Ap 25 '64; Reply. D. Bar-Illan. 150:38 My 16 '64
Demonstration defused by Methodist bishops. Christian Cent 80:1489-90 D 4 '63
Denies right to go to church; Capitol street Methodist church. Christian Cent 80:1324 O 30 '63
Divided flocks in Jackson. G. Forshey. Christian Cent 80:1469-71 N 27 '63
Five days in Mississippi. T. B. Morgan. il Look 27:86-90 Jl 16 '63
Inquiry into the Mississippi mind. C. Sitton. il N Y Times Mag p 13+ Ap 28 '63
Mississippians repudiate religious freedom; Capitol Street Methodist church. Christian Cent 80:1425-6 N 20 '63

JACKSON, Miss, coliseum. See Stadiums

JACKSON, Tenn.
Jackson II. W. A. Geier. Christian Cent 81: 24-5 Ja 1 '64

JACKSON and Perkins company
Weathervane; death of C. H. Perkins. R. G. Miner. Flower Grower 50:6 My '63

JACKSON HOLE VALLEY
In riverbottom wilds. F. A. Blackburn. il Liv Wildn 83:5-10 Spring '63

JACKSONVILLE, Fla.

Courts

Jacksonville's jury of juvenile peers. F. Sondern, jr. Parents Mag 38:47+ Ag '63; Same abr. Read Digest 83:82-5 Ag '63

Music

Design for good acoustics in a big hall. il Arch Rec 136:134-5 D '64

Riots

How it feels to be beat up by a rampaging mob. M. Durham. il Life 56:44-5 Ap 3 '64
Long day. il Newsweek 63:20-2 Ap 6 '64
Toward a long, hot summer. il Time 83:28-9 Ap 3 '64
Where violence has started the Jacksonville riots. il U S News 56:35-6 Ap 6 '64

Stores

Parking decks combined with Florida store. il Arch Rec 133:170-1 Je '63

JACKSONVILLE, Ore.
Bach before Shakespeare. il Sunset 133:28+ Ag '64

JACKSONVILLE BEACH, Fla.
Underground power distribution cuts costs, promotes city growth. H. Brantley. il Am City 80:93-4 Ja '65

JACOB, J. and Sirlin, J. L.
Synthesis of RNA in vitro stimulated in dipteran salivary glands by 1.1.3-tricyano-2-amino-1-propene. bibliog Science 144: 1011-12 My 22 '64

JACOBS, Dee V.
My children will read and write. NEA J 52:46-7 My '63

JACOBS, Florence B.
Changeling; poem. Ladies Home J 80:121 Mr '63
Happy mood; poem. McCalls 91:182 Mr '64
Tree in the plaza; poem. McCalls 92:162 D '64
Weather report in basic English; poem. McCalls 90:133 Mr '63

JACOBS, Harvey
Midnight voice; story. Ladies Home J 80:94-6 O '63

JACOBS, Harvey C.
Pioneers of 1933; address, February 11, 1963. Vital Speeches 29:347-9 Mr 15 '63

JACOBS, Hayes B.
Bell grows two billion dollars bigger. N Y Times Mag p29+ Mr 1 '64
Birth of a salesman. New Yorker 39:209-12+ D 7 '63
Far out Far Eastern exercise. Sat Eve Post 236:68-9 My 18 '63
New look at old liquor laws. N Y Times Mag p 19+ N 10 '63
Unhappy talk. Harper 226:95-7 Mr '63
Wake-up war between patient and nurse. N Y Times Mag p 19+ My 10 '64
Warning: new century ahead. New Yorker 39: 138+ Ap 27 '63
Word to the word-wise. N Y Times Mag p 18 Jl 26 '64

JACOBS, Jane
Right way to save our cities; condensation. Read Digest 84:229-34+ Ap '64

JACOBS, Jay
Hungry man. Reporter 30:54-5 F 13 '64
Living with a legend. Reporter 31:52+ D 3 '64
Simenon's mosaic. Reporter 32:38-40 Ja 14 '65
Way the world ends. Reporter 30:48+ F 27 '64

JACOBS, Leland B.
Martin Mayer, Leland B. Jacobs speak at New books preview. Library J 88:3277-8 S 15 '63

JACOBS, Lou
Lower depths. U S Camera 27:52-3+ Ag '64

JACOBS, Lou, jr
Elusive child. U S Camera 26:50-1 Je '63
Hollywood musical. U S Camera 26:70-1 Jl '63
(ed) See Baer, M. Composition: a discussion with Morley Baer

JACOBS, Louis
Heretical rabbi. por Newsweek 63:66 My 18 '64
Jacobs affair. A. Sherman. Commentary 38: 60-4 O '64
Jews of Britain. por Time 83:63 My 22 '64

JACOBS, M. E. and Brubaker, K. K.
Beta-alanine utilization of ebony and non-ebony drosophila melanogaster. bibliog Science 139:1282-3 Mr 29 '63

JACOBS, Paul
Birchers lose. New Repub 150:5 F 8 '64
David Dubinsky: why his throne is wobbling. Harper 225:75-8+ D '62; 226:14+ F '63
Man with a hoe, 1964; excerpts. Commentary 38:26-9 Jl '64
Reform for the union movement? three writers suggest ways. por U S News 54:88-9 Je 24 '63

JACOBS, Rudolph A. jr
Loudness control. Electr World 70:34-5+ D '63

JACOBS, Stanley S.
There's hope for teen-age drivers! Todays Health 41:18-21+ Mr '63

JACOBS, Walter C.
More municipal office space per building. Am City 79:113+ Je '64

JACOBS, Walter Darnell
Straight from the horse's mouth. Nat R 15: 68-70 Jl 30 '63

JACOBS, Wilbur R.
Francis Parkman's oration Romance in America. bibliog f Am Hist R 68:692-6 Ap '63

JACOBS, William P. See Scott, T. K. jt. auth.

JACOBS ladder
Two wild flowers that adapt well to the regular garden. E. W. Reed. il Horticulture 41:248 My '63

JACOB'S Pillow dance festival. See Dance festivals

JACOB'S Pillow school. See Dance schools

JACOBSEN, Arne
On from antiquity; St Catherine's college at Oxford. il Time 84:114-15 O 2 '64

JACOBSEN, Elwood
Death of the missionaries. Time 81:44 Mr 15 '63

JACOBSEN, Josephine
Arrival of rain; poem. Commonweal 80:544 Ag 7 '64
Arrivals; poem. Commonweal 77:595 Mr 1 '63
December 13th at Forty-ninth and Fifth; poem. Sat R 48:55 Ja 9 '65
Five poets. Poetry 105:201-6 D '64
Legacy of three poets. Commonweal 78:189-92 My 10 '63
Mrs Throstle; poem. New Repub 148:26 Je 15 '63
Murmurers; poem. New Yorker 39:30 F 15 '64
On the absurd. Commonweal 79:548-52 Ja 31 '64
Poet of the particular. Commonweal 81:349-52 D 4 '64
Reindeer and engine; Three children; Homage to Henri Christophe; poems. Poetry 103: 374-80 Mr '64
Starfish; poem. Nation 198:78 Ja 20 '64
Tree angel; poem. Nation 196:335 Ap 20 '63

JACOBSON, Dan
Another day; story. Atlan 213:91-4 Ap '64
Jewish writing in England. Commentary 37: 46-50 My '64
Led astray; story. New Yorker 40:34-9 Ja 23 '65
Matter of faith; memoir. Commentary 37: 38-42 Ja '64
Meeting at Dors River; story. New Yorker 40:52-9 D 5 '64
Survivor; story. Commentary 35:501-5 Je '63

JACOBSON, Gershon
Black and white; Harlem: killers, go home. New Repub 151:14-16 Ag 8 '64

JACOBSON, Harold Karan
Test-ban negotiations: implications for the future. Ann Am Acad 351:92-101 Ja '64

JACOBSON, Howard
It's not a sport it's a business. P. Ryan. il por Sports Illus 20:41-3 Je 8 '64

JACOBSON, Jerome
Role of the international coffee agreement in today's market; address, January 20, 1964. Dept State Bul 50:260-3 F 17 '64

JACOBSON, K. Bruce. See Fritz, P. J. jt. auth.

JACOBSON, Martin, and Beroza, Morton
Chemical insect attractants. bibliog Science 140:1367-73 Je 28 '63
Insect attractants; with biographical sketches. Sci Am 211:10, 20-7 Ag '64
—and others
Isolation and identification of the sex attraction of the American cockroach. bibliog Science 139:48-9; 142:1258+ Ja 4, D 6 '63

JACOBSON, N. L. and Van Horn, H. H.
Life-cycle dairy feeding. pors Suc Farm 62:50-1+ Ap; 42-3 My '64

JACOBSON, Robert
Festival preview. Mus Am 83:8-11 Mr '63
Gist of Jennie. Mus Am 83:32-3 Je '63
Koussevitzky recording awards. Mus Am 83: 46 My '63
Stopping the crack. Mus Am 83:16 My '63

JACOBSON, Sol
Student academic freedom and communist speakers on campus. Sch & Soc 92:336-7 N 14 '64

JACOBSSON, Per
Death of a father. por Time 81:114 My 17 '63
Search for a successor. por Newsweek 61:80+ My 20 '63
JACOBUS, Joan M.
Our summer house guests. Redbook 123:6+ Jl '64
JACOBUS, John
Midwestern vision. Nation 200:90 Ja 25 '65
JACOBY, Emile
Family of racing giants: the Jacobys; interview. por Motor B 112:44-5+ Jl '63
JACQMAR, Will
Big snook is disaster. Outdoor Life 131:40-1+ F '63
Casting's fun, but can you catch trout? Outdoor Life 131:17-19+ Mr '63
Picture this vacation. il Outdoor Life 133:52-5+ Je '64
JACQUELINE Grennan, Sister. See Grennan, J.
JACQUET-FRANCILLON, Jacques
Borders of China. New Repub 148:18-22 Ap 20 '63
China today. New Repub 148:19-21 Mr 16; 17-21 Mr 23 '63
Sukarno leads from weakness. New Repub 149:11-12 N 23 '63
JADA library service, Denver. See Libraries—Colorado
JADE
Kraft jade. H. D. Brown. il Hobbies 67:124+ F '63
JADE plants
It's a refeshing way to say Merry Christmas. il Sunset 133:48-51 D '64
JAENSCH, Fritz
What America means to me. Good H 156:62+ Je '63
JAFFA, Harry V.
Celebration of tradition. Nat R 15:360-2 O 22 '63
JAFFARIAN, Sara
EB school library award; Lexington, Massachusetts. por Wilson Lib Bul 39:398-400 Ja '65
JAFFE, Allan
Upbeat for old jazz. il por Bsns W p32-3 F 8 '64
JAFFE, Dan
Excursion; poem. Ladies Home J 80:135 Mr '63
To Calypso: five-week-old German shepherd; poem. Sat R 47:73 Ja 9 '65
JAFFE, George J.
Color movies find hidden cancers. Sat Eve Post 236:72+ Je 29 '63
JAFFE, Joseph, and others
Markovian model of time patterns of speech. bibliog Science 144:884-6 My 15 '64
JAFFE, Morris
Old lenses never die. U S Camera 27:24 Ja '64
JAFFE, Rona
Guess who this is: story. Esquire 59:71 My '63
Who is Rima, what is she? story. Ladies Home J 81:80-1 Je '64
JAGAN, Cheddi
Atlantic report. Atlan 214:18+ Jl '64
Calling for help. Time 81:22 Je 21 '63
Cheddi's last stand. il por Time 84:37 D 18 '64
Dentist at work. il por Newsweek 62:59 S 23 '63
Husband & wife team. por Time 81:27 My 3 '63
Jagan's future. New Repub 149:10 N 16 '63
Marxists in trouble: Jagans of British Guiana. por U S News 54:19 Je 24 '63
Picking up the pieces. Newsweek 62:49 Jl 22 '63
Red's own race war in Guiana: signs of another Congo. il por U S News 56:60-1 Je 15 '64
Shaky truce in a race war. il por U S News 55:52 Jl 22 '63
Where a Communist leader was voted out. il por U S News 57:16 D 21 '64
JAGAN, Janet (Rosenberg)
Husband & wife team. por Time 81:27 My 3 '63
Janet's challenge. il por Newsweek 63:58 Je 15 '64
Marxists in trouble: Jagans of British Guiana. por U S News 54:19 Je 24 '63
JAGENDORF, A. T. and Kok, B.
Photosynthesis. Science 143:388+ Ja 24 '64
JAGER, Otto A.
Art of Ethiopia a folk tradition centuries old. UNESCO Courier 17:18-23 O '64
JÄGERSTÄTTER, Franz
In solitary witness, by G. C. Zahn. Review
America 112:81 Ja 16 '65. A. T. Sheehan
Newsweek por 65:57 Ja 25 '65
JAGGER, Mick
People are talking about.. por Vogue 144:72-3 Jl '64
JAGIELLONIAN university, Cracow. See Colleges and universities—Poland
JAGUAR hunting
Jaguar for a gypsy. E. A. Bauer. il Outdoor Life 134:24-7+ Jl '64
JAGUARS
Top trophy of North America? G. Fitz. il Outdoor Life 133:17-21+ F '64
JAHN, Friedrich
Chicken and strudel. Newsweek 3:92 My 25 '64
JAHNKE, Jeanne
School library promotion. por Wilson Lib Bul 39:478-9 F '65
JAHODA, William J.
Folding deck for cartop boat. Pop Mech 119:167-8 Ap '63
JAI alai. See Pelota (game)
JAILS. See Prisons
JAKARTA, Indonesia
New Asian nation and new trouble for the West. il U S News 55:8 S 30 '63
Sukarno's lavish ganefo was mostly snafu. T. P. Ross. il Sports Illus 19:28-31 D 2 '63
This mob for hire. il Time 82:31-2 S 27 '63
Travel notes: Indonesia. Vogue 143:24 Je '64
Troubled start for new nation. Sr Schol 83:16-17 O 11 '63
JAKOBSON, Irving
Hull: metal. Yachting 115:43+ Ap '64
JAKOPP, Heinrich
Who's who in foreign business. por Fortune 68:118 Jl '63
JAM. See Jelly, jam, etc.
JAMAICA
Race with unrest. Time 84:50 O 30 '64
See also
Airlines—Jamaica
Fishing—Jamaica
Forests and forestry—Jamaica
Tourist trade—Jamaica
Youth—Jamaica

Description and travel

Going places, finding things in the Bahamas and Jamaica. D. Beal. il House & Gard 127:38+ Ja '65
Jamaica. A. Ross. il Mlle 59:174-5+ My '64
Personal business. Bsns W p 149 O 31 '64
Real Jamaica. P. Abrahams. il Holiday 33:96-105+ Mr '63
They're off at Jamaica. H. Sutton. il Sat R 46:42-3 Ap 6 '63
Travel notes. R. Joseph. Esquire 61:46+ My '64
Well traveled camera. P. Caulfield. il Mod Phot 27:40+ D '63

Industries

From rum and bananas to modern industry. il U S News 57:70 Ag 10 '64
See also
Mines and mineral resources—Jamaica

Politics and government

Prospects in the Caribbean. P. Sherlock. For Affairs 41:744-56 Jl '63
Year after. Time 82:49 D 6 '63
JAMAICA BAY wildlife refuge. See Bird sanctuaries
JAMAICAN cookery. See Cookery, Jamaican
JAMES, Saint
St James scallop. A. G. Melvin. il Hobbies 68:130+ Ja '64
JAMES I, king of Great Britain
Bibles once owned by King James I. P. W. Schmidtchen. il por Hobbies 69:106-7 Ap '64
JAMES, Alice
Thistledown personality. G. W. Allen. por Sat R 47:25+ S 5 '64
JAMES, Arthur Curtiss, foundation. See Arthur Curtiss James foundation
JAMES, E. S.
Changing times. por Newsweek 61:77 Mr 4 '63
JAMES, Estelle
Managing your manpower; J. Hoffa's leverage technique. T. R. Brooks. Duns R 83:61-4 F '64
JAMES, Esther
Collecting the winnings. Time 82:60 D 6 '63
JAMES, H. and Binks, Carolyn
Escape and avoidance learning in newly hatched domestic chicks. bibliog Science 139:1293-4 Mr 29 '63
JAMES, Harry
Ciribiribin. por Newsweek 63:73 Mr 23 '64
JAMES, Henry
Daisy Miller; dramatization. See Greene, B. Summer of Daisy Miller
Henry James and the Jacobites, by M. Geismar. Review
Reporter 29:52+ N 7 '63. K. S. Lynn

JAMES, Henry—*Continued*
Henry James, by L. Edel. Review
Nat R por 14:166 F 26 '63. A. Shulenberger
New Yorker 39:151-7 S 7 '63. N. Bliven
Wings of the dove: or, False gold; excerpt from Henry James and the Jacobites. M. Geismar. Atlan 212:93-8 Ag '63

JAMES, J. N.
Voyage of Mariner II; with biographical sketch. Sci Am 209:28, 70-84 bibliog(p 171) Jl '63

JAMES, Joe
Two guys named Joe jolt Ithaca. M. Kane. il por Sports Illus 20:28-9+ Ap 6 '64

JAMES, K. W.
Mid-frequency amplifier-gain nomogram. Electr World 71:31+ Je '64

JAMES, Kenneth W.
Trend has led to better-made books. Pub W 185:112+ F 3 '64

JAMES, Laylin K. jr, and Berry, D. J. O.
Evaporation enhancement by protein films. bibliog Science 140:312-14 Ap 19 '63

JAMES, Pat
Magical Mexico. U S Camera 27:22-3 Ja '64
Palm Sunday. U S Camera 27:14-15 Ap '64

JAMES, Preston
New look at Latin America: how bright the future; interview. por U S News 55:72-83 Jl 8 '63

JAMES, Ralph
Managing your manpower; J. Hoffa's leverage technique. T. R. Brooks. Duns R 83:61-4 F '64

JAMES, Rosa
Scented geraniums grow indoors and out. Flower Grower 51:40-2 F '64

JAMES, Selwyn, and Goldfarb, R. W.
Three sets of twins in three years. Redbook 121:58-9+ My '63

JAMES, Sidney L.
Letter from the publisher. Sports Illus 20:4 F 17; 6 Mr 9; 4 Mr 16 '64

JAMES, Stephen D.
Moscow mission. New Yorker 40:25-7 F 29 '64

JAMES, Stewart
Skin diving; one part fun, one part danger. Read Digest 85:152-4+ Ag '64

JAMES, Suzanne
Plan a children's art show. Am Home 67:26 N '64

JAMES, T. W. and Anderson, N. G.
Continuous recording of cell number in logarithmic and synchronized cultures. bibliog Science 142:1183-5 N 29 '63

JAMES, Walter
Expansion of British training colleges. Sch & Soc 91:309-10 O 19 '63

JAMES, William
Skirmishes with a publisher; excerpts from Owl among colophons: a survey of American book publishing. C. A. Madison. por Sat R 46:24-5 N 16 '63
Waterspouts of God. por Time 82:80 Jl 19 '63

JAMES foundation of New York, incorporated
Cornell students study abroad; semester program in New York city. Arch Rec 134:33 N '63

JAMES H. Heineman, incorporated. See Heineman, James H, incorporated

JAMESON, A. Gregory
Diffusion of gases from alveolus to precapillary arteries. bibliog Science 139:826-8 Mr 1 '63

JAMESON, David L. See Resnick, L. E. jt. auth.

JAMESTOWN, Va.
Digging up Jamestown; excerpts from Here lies Virginia. I. N. Hume. il Am Heritage 14:66-77 Ap '63

JAMEZ RIVER watershed. See Watersheds

JAMIESON, John C.
Crystal structures adopted by black phosphorus at high pressures. bibliog Science 139:1291 Mr 29 '63
Crystal structures at high pressures of metallic modifications of compounds of indium, gallium, and aluminum. bibliog Science 139: 845-7 Mr 1 '63
Crystal structures at high pressures of metallic modifications of silicon and germanium. bibliog Science 139:762-4 F 22 '63
Crystal structures of titanium, zirconium, and hafnium at high pressures. bibliog Science 140:72-3 Ap 5 '63
X-ray diffraction studies on dysprosium at high pressures. bibliog Science 145:572-4 Ag 7 '64

JAMIL, Ben
Challenger to princess. il por Bsns W p78+ Ja 26 '63

JAMISON, David
Vroman's stock control system is unwieldy but it is effective. Pub W 185:64-6 My 4 '64

JAN Martense Schenck house. See New York (city)—Historic houses, etc.

JANAČEK, Leoš
Cunning little vixen. Criticism
New Yorker 40:168 My 16 '64
Sat R 47:51 My 23 '64
Janacek; Katya Kabanova at Juilliard school of music. M. Bernheimer. Sat R 47:35 My 16 '64
Music to my ears; Slavonic mass. I. Kolodin. Sat R 46:46 F 9 '63
Whole man from Moravia. R. Silverberg. por Hi Fi 13:55-7+ Mr '63

JANE, J. A. and others
Pyramidal tract: a comparison of two prosimian primates. bibliog Science 147:153-5 Ja 8 '65

JANE Winston's ordeal; story. See Dillon, J.

JANECEK, Blanche
Orientation; centralization; cooperation. por ALA Bul 57:166-8 F '63

JANER, Albert Christ-. See Christ-Janer, A.

JANES, Kelly
Unwelcome gift; poem. Christian Cent 81:334 Mr 11 '64

JANES Ted
Allagash story. pors Outdoor Life 134:32-3+ Ag '64
Canandaigua can-can. Outdoor Life 134:40-3+ Jl '64
Deer by the dozen. pors Outdoor Life 132: 17-19+ N '63
Far-out chucks. por Outdoor Life 132:50-1+ O '63
Great new lake. Outdoor Life 131:24-7+ Mr '63
Mixed bag down East. por Field & S 67:74-6+ Ap '63
Mystery beasts. Outdoor Life 134:17-19+ Jl '64
Place to hunt. Outdoor Life 134:33-5+ O '64
Promised land of bass. por Outdoor Life 131: 76-7+ Je '63
Tidewater quail. por Outdoor Life 134:28-9+ N '64
We move for crows. Outdoor Life 133:52-5+ My '64

JANESVILLE, Wis.
More convenient than a shopping center. J. Lustig. il Am City 79:116-17 S '64

JANET, Sister Mary. See Mary Janet, Sister

JANEWAY, Elizabeth
Accident; novel. McCalls 91:104-7 My; 96-7 Je '64
First lady: a professional at getting things done. Ladies Home J 81:64-5+ Ap '64
Opinion, please. Mlle 59:190 Ag '64
Water. House & Gard 124:146-7 S '63

JANITORS
My father, the custodian; school custodian of North school, Portland, Ore. R. Reed. Sr Schol 84:13T F 7 '64

JANKOWSKI, J. Moor-. See Moor-Jankowski, J.

JANNEY, Jack R.
How structural models are used in practice. Arch Rec 133:206-9 Ap '63

JANOFF, Aaron, and Zweifach, B. W.
Adhesion and emigration of leukocytes produced by cationic proteins of lysosomes. bibliog Science 144:1456-8 Je 19 '64

JANOWITZ, Morris
Military in the political development of new nations. Bul Atomic Sci 20:6-10 O '64

JANSEN, John Frederick
Quest renewed. Christian Cent 81:1598-9 D 23 '64

JANSEN, Marius B.
American studies in Japan. bibliog f Am Hist R 70:413-17 Ja '65

JANSON, Donald
House Nebraska built. Harper 229:124+ N '64
New name on the list. Sr Schol 84:1T-2T Ap 10 '64

JANSSEN, E. A.
Steel bands stop joint leakage. Am City 78: 149 My '63

JANSSEN, Peter A.
Getting Negroes into college; some schools give them a break; reprint. U S News 56: 82-3 My 25 '64

JANSSENS, Jean Baptiste
Father and captain. America 111:434 O 17 '64

JANSSENS, Louis
Morality of the pill; excerpt from Morale conjugale et progestogènes, tr. by M. Ilford. Commonweal 80:332-5 Je 5 '64

about

Roman Catholics: a new view on birth control; Rev. L. Janssens endorses oral contraceptive pills. il por Time 83:59-60 Ap 10 '64; Discussion. America 110:563, 751 Ap 25, My 30 '64
Where is the consensus? Commonweal 79:737 Mr 20 '64; Reply. M. Novak. 80:149 Ag 24 '64

JANTZEN knitting mills
Decorating the world's beaches. il Bsns W p84-5 F 2 '63

JANUARY
In January; few of the dates, memorable and not so, coming up next month (title varies) (cont) il N Y Times Mag p30 D 29 '63; 22 Ja 3 '65
Winter's second half; period following January thaw. Sci N L 85:62 Ja 25 '64

JANUARY thaw; story. See Chute, B. J.

JAPAN
Her course is set. A. Koestler. il Life 57:63+ S 11 '64; Same abr. with title Japan; where East equals West. Read Digest 85:97-100 D '64
Japan battles off a banzai of white. il Life 54:36-7 F 8 '63
Japan in search of itself. il Newsweek 65: 42-5 Ja 25 '65
Japan; practical notes for Occidentals. D. Messinesi. Vogue 144:44 Ag 15 '64
Japan; special issue; with editorial comment. il Life 57:2-3, 10-23+ S 11 '64
Japan today; symposium. bibliog f il Cur Hist 46:193-237+ Ap '64
Penn's Japan; photographs. I. Penn. Vogue 144:86-98 Ag 15 '64
Proud new jazzy age. R. Steinberg. il Sat Eve Post 237:76-8+ O 17 '64
Regrettable destruction of peaceful corps existence. Time 84:63 O 2 '64
U.S. executive in Japan. il Bsns W p 142-4+ Je 13 '64

See also
Advertising—Japan
Aeronautics, Military—Japan
Airplane industry and trade—Japan
Americans in Japan
Architecture—Japan
Architecture, Domestic—Japan
Arts and crafts—Japan
Automobile industry and trade—Japan
Beppu
Birds—Japan
Birth control—Japan
Birth rate—Japan
Christmas—Japan
Colleges and universities—Japan
Costume—Japan
Crime and criminals—Japan
Earthquakes—Japan
Elections—Japan
Electronic apparatus industry and trade—Japan
Famines—Japan
Finance—Japan
Fisheries—Japan
Folklore—Japan
Foreign students in Japan
Hiroshima
Hotels, taverns, etc.—Japan
Housing—Japan
Japanese
Jazz music—Japan
Justice, Administration of—Japan
Kyoto
Labor and laboring classes—Japan
Libraries—Japan
Moving pictures—Japan
Music festivals—Japan
Nara
National parks and reserves—Japan
Natural resources—Japan
Newspapers—Japan
Nikko
Opera—Japan
Political parties—Japan
Railroads—Japan
Recreation—Japan
Reporters and reporting—Japan
Rites and ceremonies—Japan
Science—Japan
Space research—Japan
Sports—Japan
Steel industry and trade—Japan
Strikes—Japan
Television broadcasting—Japan
Tokyo
Tourist trade—Japan
Women—Japan
Youth—Japan

Cabinet

Covering it like a tent; cabinet shakeup. il Time 82:56 Jl 26 '63

Civilization

Japan: of dynamo and destiny. N. Cousins. il Sat R 47:32-3 My 9 '64
Tokyo and the Olympics. G. Lauria. il Atlan 213:122+ My '64

Commerce

Collision coming for Japanese cars; Toyota motor co. il Bsns W p70+ Je 27 '64
Japan: the open door with a catch. L. Banks. il Fortune 68:134-41+ Jl '63
Japan's position in world trade. V. Galbraith. bibliog f Cur Hist 46:207-11+ Ap '64
Ohara's big deal with Communist China. Newsweek 62:64 S 2 '63
Sparrow catching; Ichimura companies. il Newsweek 62:92-3 O 7 '63
Ties that bind in the Orient; Japan and red China. il Bsns W p60+ Ap 25 '64
Yen for the games. il Bsns W p40-1 S 26 '64

Commercial treaties and agreements

U.S. and Japan agree on exports of zipper chain from Japan; Department announcement, exchange of letters between Ambassador Ryuji Takeuchi and Assistant secretary of state for economic affairs G. Griffith Johnson, and attachment. Dept State Bul 49:449 S 16 '63
United States and Japan conclude arrangement for cotton textile trade, 1963-65; joint announcement, exchange of notes and letters between Ambassador Ryuji Takeuchi and Assistant secretary of state for economic affairs G. Griffith Johnson, and attachments. Dept State Bul 49:440-9 S 16 '63
United States and Japan sign compensatory trade agreements; Department announcement, December 31, 1962; with schedules. Dept State Bul 48:108-9 Ja 21 '63

Cultural relations

U.S.-Japan cultural conference to be held at Washington. Dept State Bul 49:582-3 O 14 '63

Defenses

Going along with the US. A. Axelbank. New Repub 152:7-8 Ja 9 '65
Japan early warning competition. Aviation W 78:31 Ap 15 '63
Japan may intensify early warning effort. Aviation W 78:29 Mr 4 '63
Japan's security policy in transition. J. W. Morley. Cur Hist 46:200-6 Ap '64
Notes on an incredible country. N. Cousins. il Sat R 47:24-6 My 16 '64

Description and travel

Camera guide to Japan. L. Barry. il Pop Phot 51:80-1+ D '62
Fun and merry talks along the Mitsubishi concert circuit. J. Lowenthal. il Mus Am 84:60-1 O '64
Heritage of Hiroshige. C. Mitchell. il Sports Illus 19:106-10+ D 23 '63
Japan; photographs by B. Brake. Life 57:10-23+ S 11 '64
Mystic image of Japan; photographs. A. Kane. Look 27:44-9 S 10 '63
Travel & camera. il U S Camera 26:28 D '63
Well traveled camera. il Mod Phot 27:24+ S '63

Diet

From the cow-walk to the brawl. Time 82: 31-2 Jl 5 '63

Earthquake, 1923

See Earthquakes—Japan

Economic conditions

Can Japan maintain the pace? il Bsns W p71-5+ D 19 '64
Consumer's day dawns in Land of Rising Sun. il Bsns W p 128-30+ Mr 21 '64
Japan. H. Kublin. bibliog il Focus 14:1-6 F '64
Japan. R. Okamoto. il Look 27:15-17 S 10 '63
Japan: search for a better balance. il Bsns W p69 F 22 '64
Japan tries for a second miracle. P. F. Drucker. Harper 226:72-8 Mr '63; Same abr. Read Digest 82:181-2+ Je '63
Labor in a prosperous Japan. S. B. Levine. bibliog f Cur Hist 46:212-18 Ap '64
New role of Japan in world affairs: an American policy view; address, October 6, 1964. R. W. Barnett. Dept State Bul 51:586-91 O 26 '64
Straight-from-the-shoulder Japanese reminder; excerpts from address. Y. Iwasa. Fortune 69:110 My '64

Economic policy

Japan: the open door with a catch. L. Banks. il Fortune 68:134-41+ Jl '63
Japan tries for a second miracle. P. F. Drucker. Harper 226:72-8 Mr '63; Same abr. Read Digest 82:181-2+ Je '63
Japan's position in world trade. V. Galbraith. bibliog f Cur Hist 46:207-11+ Ap '64
Notes on an incredible country. N. Cousins. il Sat R 47:24-6 My 16 '64

JAPAN—*Continued*

Economic relations

Atlantic report. Atlan 214:22+ S '64
Briefcase brigades. il Time 81:81 F 8 '63
Japan's relations with China. P. F. Langer. bibliog f il Cur Hist 46:193-9+ Ap '64
Joint U.S.-Japan committee concludes third meeting; joint communiqué, January 28, 1964. Dept State Bul 50:235-8 F 17 '64
Straight-from-the-shoulder Japanese reminder; excerpts from address. Y. Iwasa. Fortune 69:110 My '64
Tokyo talks; U.S. delegation in Tokyo. il Newsweek 63:65 F 10 '64
U.S.-Japan joint communiqué on trade. Cur Hist 46:238-40 Ap '64

Emperors and empresses

See also
Hirohito, emperor of Japan

Foreign relations

Japan, the United States, and Europe; address March 28, 1963. U. A. Johnson. Dept State Bul 48:606-12 Ap 22 '63
New role of Japan in world affairs: an American policy view; address, October 6, 1964. R. W. Barnett. Dept State Bul 51:586-91 O 26 '64

China (People's Republic)

China and Japan. P. F. Langer. bibliog f Cur Hist 45:144-50+ S '63
Going along with the US. A. Axelbank. New Repub 152:7-8 Ja 9 '65
Japanese cash register. A. Axelbank. New Repub 151:13-14 S 5 '64
Japan's relations with China. P. F. Langer. bibliog f il Cur Hist 46:193-9+ Ap '64
Reversing the dummies. New Repub 150:9 F 29 '64

Russia

About face; Mikoyan visit to Tokyo. Newsweek 63:30 Je 1 '64

United States

America encounters Japan, by W. L. Neumann. Review
Nat R il 16:871-2+ O 6 '64. G. Morgenstern
Going along with the US. A. Axelbank. New Repub 152:7-8 Ja 9 '65
Japan, the U.S, and war in South Vietnam; interview, ed. by R. P. Martin. E. Sato. U S News 58:42-3 Ja 11 '65
Japanese security and American policy. G. F. Kennan. For Affairs 43:14-28 O '64
Pilgrim on flight 800. Time 85:24 Ja 15 '65

History

As Japan changes, so does the emperor. A. M. Rosenthal. il N Y Times Mag p 13+ My 19 '63
Portuguese Sancho Panza in the Far East. A. J. Saraiva. il UNESCO Courier 16:14-19 Ap '63
Yankee Barbarian at the Shogun's court. E. Hahn. il Am Heritage 15:60-3+ Je '64
See also
Russo-Japanese war, 1904-1905

History, Naval

Ordeal of the Kanrin Maru; with editorial comment. E. V. Warinner. il Am Heritage 14:95-7 Ag '63

Imperial diet

See Japan—Diet

Industries

Biggest in a land of giants; Mitsubishi companies. il Bsns W p52+ Je 8 '63
Briefcase brigades. il Time 81:81 F 8 '63
Clocker of the games; K. Hattori & co. ltd. Japan's biggest watchmaker. Time 84:109-110 O 16 '64
Colossus of the Orient; Hitachi, ltd. il Life 55:56A-63 Ag 30 '63
Japan sews up a market; sewing machine industry. il Bsns W p76+ Ag 3 '63
Japan: the open door with a catch. L. Banks. il Fortune 68:134-41+ Jl '63
Japanese giant that wouldn't stay dead; Mitsubishi group. R. Lubar. il Fortune 70:141-9+ N '64
Japan's prime natural resource is people. il Fortune 68:142-9 Jl '63
Just like old times; reemergence of Japan's cartels. il Time 82:58 Ag 30 '63
Meet Mr Matsushita; with report by J. Mills. il Life 57:107-14 S 11 '64
Mitsubishi seeking U.S. sales penetration. il Aviation W 79:98-9+ Ag 26 '63
O, tempora! Japanese undercut by copycats. Newsweek 63:42 My 18 '64
Pass the chocolates; Japanese manufacturers turning out some 400 chocolate products. il Newsweek 63:82 My 11 '64
Pianos on the assembly line: Nippon Gakki to build modern plant. Time 83:91 F 14 '64
Pole sitters; labor disputes in Okinawa. New Repub 150:7-8 My 30 '64
Sewing up the game; Riccar sewing machine co. il Time 83:90 My 8 '64
Shipbuilder to the world. il Time 83:76-7 Ja 3 '64
Small wonder; Tokyo's Sony corp. il Time 82:91 Jl 12 '63
Sony turns small things into big profits. J. D. Ratcliff. il Read Digest 84:201-4 Je '64
Tokyo on the Hudson; Mitsubishi companies. il Bsns W p30-2 N 23 '63
Wooing the mild ones; Japan's Honda motor co. il Bsns W p26-7 Mr 30 '63
See also
Airplane industry and trade—Japan
Electronic apparatus industry and trade—Japan
Fisheries—Japan
Pearl fisheries
Pearl industry and trade
Photographic apparatus industry and trade
Steel industry and trade—Japan

Intellectual life

Japanese intellectuals: cliques, soft edges, and the dread of power. J. Fischer. Harper 229:14-15+ S '64; Discussion. 229:14+ N '64

Nationalism

Japan's new nationalism. G. R. Packard, 3d. Atlan 211:64-9 Ap '63

Navy

See also
Japan—History, Naval

Parliament

See Japan—Diet

Politics and government

Chaos at Hiroshima; break between Socialist party and Communist party. New Repub 149:9 Ag 31 '63
Factional politics in Japan. H. H. Baerwald. il Cur Hist 46:223-9+ Ap '64
Ikeda's low-posture. New Repub 149:9-10 N 23 '63
Japan, the United States, and Europe; address March 28, 1963. U. A. Johnson. Dept State Bul 48:606-12 Ap 22 '63
Narrow shave; Japan's Prime Minister elected for third term. Time 84:29 Jl 17 '64
Picking a new premier. il Time 84:27 N 6 '64
Players; picking a new premier. il Newsweek 64:57 N 9 '64
Toward leadership. il Time 84:36 N 20 '64
See also
Elections—Japan
Japan—Diet

Popular culture

Japan: the kitchen and the garden. A. W. Burks. bibliog f Cur Hist 46:230-7 Ap '64

Population

Changing population patterns in Japan. A. Doi. il Cur Hist 46:219-22 Ap '64
See also
Birth rate—Japan

Religious institutions and affairs

Japan's new religions and the Christian community. R. H. Drummond. Christian Cent 81:1521-3 D 9 '64
News of the Christian world (cont) Christian Cent 80:278-80, 629-30, 784, 1222, 1284-6; 81:345, 410, 944-5, 1380-1 F 27, My 8, Je 12, O 2, 16 '63, Mr 11, 25, Jl 22, N 4 '64
Value creators; Soka Gakkai militant new Buddhist sect. il Newsweek 64:40 Jl 13 '64
See also
Soka Gakkai (sect)

Riots

Pro-U.S. premier; anti-U.S. riots. il U S News 57:20 N 23 '64

Royal family

Happiness is not a princess. K. Beech. McCalls 91:104-5+ Mr '64

Social conditions

Japan. R. Okamoto. il Look 27:15-17 S 10 '63
See also
Geishas

JAPAN—*Continued*

Social life and customs

So sorry: Japan's fabled courtesy is in serious danger of extinction. Newsweek 62:38 Ag 12 '63
Travel notes. R Joseph. Esquire 61:14+ Ja '64
See also
Children—Japan
Geishas
Women—Japan

Travel regulations

See Travel regulations

JAPAN-America cultural center. See United States—Cultural relations
JAPAN and the United States
Famous Japanese judges the U.S. giant; tr. by D. Keene. Y. Mishima. il Life 57:81+ S 11 '64
Inevitable partners. E. O. Reischauer. Life 57:27-8 S 11 '64
New role of Japan in world affairs: an American policy view; address, October 6, 1964. R. W. Barnett. Dept State Bul 51:586-91 O 26 '64
United States and Japan: common interests in the building of a peaceful world; address, January 28, 1964. D. Rusk. bibliog f Dept State Bul 50:230-5 F 17 '64
Yankee, stay away. Newsweek 61:42+ Je 3 '63
See also
Hiroshima maidens
JAPAN student science fair. See Science fairs
JAPAN-United States committee on scientific cooperation. See Joint United States-Japan committee on scientific cooperation
JAPANESE
Exuberant finish in Tokyo; unforgettable ceremony. J. Underwood. il Sports Illus 21:24-31 N 2 '64
Letter from Sendagaya. J. M. Flagler. il New Yorker 40:58+ Jl 25; 86+ Ag 15 '64
Our far-flung correspondents; American visitors in Japan. C. Frankel. New Yorker 39:74+ My 25 '63
Proud new jazzy age. R. Steinberg. il Sat Eve Post 237:76-8+ O 17 '64
JAPANESE art. See Art, Japanese
JAPANESE attack on Hawaii. See Pearl Harbor, Attack on, 1941
JAPANESE automobiles. See Automobiles, Foreign
JAPANESE aviators. See Air pilots
JAPANESE baths. See Bathrooms
JAPANESE beetles
Prepare for Japanese beetle invasion. D. J. Ross. il Pop Gard 15:64-6 My '64
Sleeping bacteria grown to kill Japanese beetles. Sci N L 84:159 S 7 '63
JAPANESE cherry trees. See Oriental flowering cherry
JAPANESE cookery. See Cookery, Japanese
JAPANESE court music. See Music, Japanese
JAPANESE drama
Japanese masks. il Design 66:22-4 N '64
JAPANESE earthquake, 1923. See Earthquakes—Japan
JAPANESE flower arrangements. See Flowers, Arrangement of
JAPANESE flowering cherry. See Oriental flowering cherry
JAPANESE gardens. See Gardens, Japanese
JAPANESE gardens of Kildare. See Gardens—Ireland
JAPANESE honeysuckle. See Honeysuckles
JAPANESE houses. See Architecture, Domestic—Japan
JAPANESE in the United States
Fair foursome from Japan; hostesses at Japanese pavilion. il Look 28:60+ S 22 '64
Tokyo on the Hudson; Mitsubishi companies. il Bsns W p30-2 N 23 '63
JAPANESE irises. See Irises
JAPANESE language

Study and teaching

Chinese and Japanese in high school. Sch & Soc 91:288+ O 5 '63
Instruction in Chinese and Japanese in secondary schools. F. H. Jackson. Ann Am Acad 356:113-18 N '64
JAPANESE music. See Music, Japanese
JAPANESE poetry
Haiku in Detroit: contest sponsored by Japan air lines over WDTM. R. L. Shayon. il Sat R 46:32 D 28 '63
Hymns in haiku. Time 81:54+ Mr 15 '63

Translations into English

Dry sedge; Parabola. J. Nishiwaki. Poetry 103:160 D '63
On haiku. H. Behn. il Horn Bk 40:166-7 Ap '64
JAPANESE pottery. See Pottery, Japanese
JAPANESE prints. See Prints
JAPANESE quails. See Quails
JAPANESE tourists. See Travelers
JAPENGA, Ronald. See Kramer, N. jt. auth.
JAR cap removers. See Cap removers
JARA, Sergio Quijada
Songs of Andean pastures. Américas 15:37-9 My '63
JARDEN, David
Hudson Bay and back by canoe. por Outdoor Life 132:36-9+ S '63
JARDETZKY, Oleg
Magnetic resonance in biological systems. Science 146:552-3 O 23 '64
JARDIN botanique de Montréal. See Montreal botanical garden
JARDINE, Winnifred C.
Cooking up a memory. Bet Hom & Gard 42:114+ N '64
JARGON
How to unsettle a dispute; adapted from an address. W. W. Wirtz. Sat R 46:28 Mr 9 '63
JARMAN, Rufus
Clean rural comedy. Harper 226:43-7 My '63
JARMAN, Walton Maxey
Personalities. por Time 82:96 O 11 '63
JAROLIMEK, John
New orbits in social studies. PTA Mag 59:24-6 bibliog(p36) O '64
JARRELL, Randall
In galleries; poem. Atlan 213:81 Ap '64
In Montecito; poem. New Yorker 39:50 O 5 '63
It's a gloomy world, gentlemen; excerpts from introduction to Six Russian short novels. Atlan 211:76-82 Ap '63
Lost world; poem; excerpts. Poetry 103:37-47 O '63
Mockingbird; poem. New Yorker 39:48 N 2 '63
Next day; poem. New Yorker 39:58 D 14 '63
Thinking of the lost world; poem. Poetry 103:149-51 D '63
(tr) See Chekhov, A. P. Three sisters

about

Daylight. H. Carruth. Poetry 105:194-5 D '64
JARRETT, James L.
Great books in paperback. Sat R 46:66-7 Mr 23 '63
JARRETT, John H.
Traveling-wave tubes. bibliog Electr World 71:25-8 Mr '64
JARVIK, Lissy F. See Erlenmeyer-Kimling, L. jt. auth.
JARVIS, Alan
Art in Canada. Atlan 214:124-34 N '64
JARVIS, Derek, and Du Vigneaud, Vincent
Crystalline deamino-oxytocin. bibliog Science 143:545-8 F 7 '64
JARVIS, Wilbur. See Hamblin, D. J. jt. auth.
JARVIS, Woody
Black phantom. Field & S 68:50-1+ Mr '64
JASELSKIS, Bruno
Sodium perxenate and xenon (II) difluoride reduction at the dropping-mercury electrode. bibliog Science 146:263-4 O 9 '64
Xenic acid: reduction at the dropping-mercury electrode. bibliog Science 143:1324 Mr 20 '64
JASHEMSKI, Wilhelmina
Pompeii. Natur Hist 73:30-41 D '64
JASIONE perennis. See Sheep's-bit
JASKI, Tom
Constant-voltage transformer operation. Electr World 71:40-1 Ap '64
JASLOW, Robert I. and Ebling, George, jr
Disease and delinquency. PTA Mag 57:18-20 Je '63
JASTROW, Robert, and Cameron, A. G. W.
Space: highlights of recent research. bibliog Science 145:1129-39 S 11 '64
—and Newell, H. E.
Why land on the moon? Atlan 212:41-5 Ag '63
—and Panagakos, Nicholas
Planet Jupiter. Science 139:351-2+ Ja 25 '63
JAUNDICE
Infant jaundice traced. Sci N L 83:306 My 18 '63
JAVA
See also
Forests and forestry—Java

Antiquities

See also
Borobudur

JAVELINA hunting. See Peccary hunting
JAVITS, Jacob Koppel
Excerpt from address, October 3, 1963. Cong Digest 43:58+ F '64
Excerpt from testimony, July 9, 1963. Cong Digest 42:274+ N '63
Road back for the G.O.P. N Y Times Mag p28-9+ N 15 '64
Senator Javits urges expansion of USIA; summary of address. por Pub W 185:25-6 Mr 23 '64
To preserve the two-party system. N Y Times Mag p 15+ O 27 '63
about
Call to Republicans. W. Barrett. Atlan 213: 136-8 My '64
How to carry New York. A. Hacker. Commentary 38:68-70 Ag '64
How to win the cities. il por Time 83:24 My 1 '64
New libel. Nation 199:234-5 O 19 '64
Order of battle, by J. K. Javits. Review Sat R 47:41-2 My 23 '64. R. Drummond
Trimming the Democratic turkey with Republican parsley. W. A. Rusher. por Nat R 16:544 Je 30 '64
JAY, Byron
New men for A&P's top rungs. Bsns W p32 Je 20 '64
JAY, John
New speed and old in skiing abroad; interview. Mlle 60:189+ N '64
JAY, Leticia
Wonderful old-time hoofers at Newport. Dance Mag 37:18-19 Ag '63
JAYCEE awards. See United States junior chamber of commerce
JAYNE, Horace H. F.
Tyson collection: a painter's eye on masterworks. Art N 63:28-30+ S '64
JAYNES, Richard A.
Chestnuts. Horticulture 42:16-17+ S '64
JAYS
Audubon mystery; magpie or Columbia jay on new stamp. J. K. Terres. il Audubon Mag 66:91 Mr '64
JAZZ bands. See Bands (music)
JAZZ dance. See Dancing
JAZZ festivals. See Music festivals
JAZZ music
Among the neophones; Stan Kenton's neophonic orchestra. il Newsweek 65:73 Ja 18 '65
Antic arts; M. Davis, moody potentate of jazz. K. Tynan. Holiday 33:101-3+ F '63
Anything for Eddie; salute to E. Condon at Carnegie Hall. il Newsweek 64:47 Ag 3 '64
Audience is shrinking; Broadway's Birdland. il Time 83:50 My 8 '64
Beautiful persons. il Time 81:33 Je 28 '63
Bossa nova. il Ebony 18:103-6 Mr '63
Bossa nova from the source. R. F. Thompson. Sat R 47:42-3 Jl 11 '64
Bossa nova nova; San Francisco's jazz workshop. il Time 84:46 Jl 31 '64
Cecil Taylor and the new tradition. J. Goldberg. Sat R 46:42-3 F 9 '63
Clare Fischer: the Pan-American way. R. F. Thompson. Sat R 47:46-7 N 28 '64
Duke in India; interview, tr. from a tape recording by S. Dance. il Sat R 47:66-7 Ja 11 '64
Duke's ball. Newsweek 63:84 Ap 13 '64
Grand old man; salute to Eddie Condon at Carnegie Hall. il Time 84:46 Jl 31 '64
Have no fear and keep it clear; the jive is comin' and The Lion's here; excerpts from Music on my mind. W. Smith. il Esquire 61:68-71+ Je '64
Jacobins of jazz. N. Hentoff. Mlle 57:268-9+ Ag '63
Jazz. B. Boretz. Nation 196:382-4 My 4 '63
Jazz and race. N. Hentoff. Commonweal 81: 482-4 Ja 8 '65
Jazz; B. Powell's bebop style. W. Balliett. New Yorker 40:154+ S 12 '64
Jazz; B. Webster's music. W. Balliett. New Yorker 39:138-9 O 5 '63
Jazz; C. Mingus' music. W. Balliett. New Yorker 40:133-5 Je 13 '64
Jazz composer: a study in symbiosis. G. Lees. Hi Fi 13:55-7+ Ag '63
Jazz concerts. W. Balliett. See issues of New Yorker
Jazz; drummers, both swinging and unswinging. W. Balliett. New Yorker 39:75-7 Ja 18 '64
Jazz in New York. D. Morgenstern. Mus Am 84:55 Ja '64
Jazz in New York. M. W. Stearns. Mus Am 83:35 F '63
Jazz; O. Coleman's music. W. Balliett. New Yorker 40:117-18+ Ja 16 '65
Jazz; Pee Wee Russell's music. W. Balliett. New Yorker 39:123-4 S 14 '63
Jazz roots in Nigeria. R. F. Thompson. il Sat R 47:52-3 Ap 11 '64
Jazz: the happy sound is dying. R. Morgan. Esquire 59:148-50 Ap '63
Juilliard blues; classical jazz. il Time 81:83 Ap 19 '63
Last trip up the river. M. Williams. il Sat R 47:46-7 Je 13 '64
Mangelsdorff matter. W. Hobson. Sat R 47: 64 My 16 '64
Meditations with a beat. S. Dance. Sat R 46:45 F 9 '63
Mister Solal. il Time 81:66+ Je 7 '63
Monk; high priest of jazz. L. H. Lapham. il Sat Eve Post 237:70+ Ap 11 '64
Monterey, and all that jazz. L. Robinson. il Ebony 20:54-8+ D '64
Open soul; Benny Goodman quartet. Newsweek 63:79 My 18 '64
Orientation course. W. Hobson. Sat R 47:60 F 29 '64
Paying the new jazz dues. N. Hentoff. Nation 198:635+ Je 22 '64
Plenty of horn. N. Hentoff. Reporter 30:39-40 Ja 2 '64
Re: jazz; quotations; comp. by E. F. Murphy. N Y Times Mag p38 Je 28 '64
Real New Orleans sound. J. S. Wilson. il Hi Fi 13:59-61+ S '63
Reluctant art: the growth of jazz, by B. Green. Review
Reporter 28:56+ Ap 25 '63. N. Hentoff
Secular music; rock and roll music. D. Newman. Esquire 62:102+ D '64
Senior Scholastic talks to Pete Jolly; interview, ed. by R. Hemming. P. Jolly. Sr Schol 84:13 My 1 '64
Some place near Despairsville; rock 'n' roll. il Time 83:60+ Je 5 '64
Syncopated dirges, ragtime parades. K. Chase. il Américas 16:16-20 Mr '64
Talent scout; Hickory house. New Yorker 39: 24-6 F 23 '63
Upbeat Down beat. il Newsweek 63:56+ Je 29 '64
Upbeat for old jazz; New Orleans' old musicians, creators of Dixieland jazz. il Bsns W p32-3 F 8 '64
What do they get from rock 'n' roll? J. Larner. il Atlan 214:44-9 Ag '64; Same abr. Read Digest 85:181+ N '64
What is jazz? Giuffre's experiments in sound. Newsweek 62:53 S 2 '63
See also
Phonograph records—Jazz music
Anecdotes, facetiae, satire, etc.
Sing along with Bach. R. Schoenstein. Sat R 46:60 N 30 '63
History
Jazz concerts; Recent developments in jazz, concert at Carnegie recital hall. W. Balliett. New Yorker 39:99-100 Ap 27 '63
Jazz notes; the place. E. Larrabee. Harper 227:101 Ag '63
Africa
Tom-tomcats; Africa's favorite jazz band. il Time 82:32 Ag 2 '63
Great Britain
Damned good, what? Kenny Ball and his Dixieland band. il Newsweek 62:65 O 14 '63
Japan
Jazz conquers Japan. L. Feather. il Ebony 19:127-8+ O '64
Russia
At Red square, no cool sounds allowed; excerpts from interview, ed. by R. Hemming and G. Nikolaieff. B. Midney; I. Barukshtis. Sr Schol 85:23 D 2 '64
Far-out *dzhaz*. Time 84:30 Ag 28 '64
JAZZ musicians. See Musicians, American
JAZZ pianists. See Pianists
JAZZ singers. See Singers
JAZZ slang. See Slang
JAZZMEN. See Musicians, American
JAZZMEN, Negro. See Negro musicians
JEALOUSY
Brotherly love? E. J. LeShan. il N Y Times Mag p 114+ N 22 '64
Can this marriage be saved? D. C. Disney. Ladies Home J 80:10+ N '63
How one mother solved the jealousy problem. il Todays Health 42:74-7 Ja '64
Jealousy; questions and answers. A. Wood. Seventeen 23:12-7+ My '64
My problem and how I solved it: family triangle. il Good H 158:12+ My '64

JEAN, Lorena
(ed) See Sullivan, M. Sculptor & teacher

JEANMAIRE, Zizi
Fun to be me. por Newsweek 64:93 N 30 '64

JEANNE d'Arc au bûcher; opera. See Honegger, A.

JEANNERET-GRIS, Charles Édouard. See Le Corbusier

JEANS, Sir James Hopwood
Jeans' criterion of gravitational instability. S. S. Huang. il Sky & Tel 26:77-9 Ag '63

JEANS. See Clothing and dress—Children

JEDEDIAH SMITH REDWOODS STATE PARK. See California—Parks and reserves

JEDLICKA, Albert
Detective from the city room. por Time 83:44+ Mr 27 '64

JEEP racing. See Automobile racing

JEEPNEYS. See Motor buses

JEEPS. See Automobiles; Motor vehicles

JEFFERIES, K. A.
Seven steps to better municipal purchasing. Am City 79:118+ My '64

JEFFERS, Robinson
First and last things. J. Dickey. Poetry 103:320-1 F '64
Recent criticism. H. Strickhausen. Poetry 104:264-5 Jl '64

JEFFERS, Vaughan
Twelve weeks to the wedding. Suc Farm 61:90-1 Mr '63

JEFFERSON, Blanche
Colored account. Newsweek 63:98 Ap 27 '64

JEFFERSON, Nelson C. and others
Humoral factor from the brain which activates gastric motility. Science 144:58-9 Ap 3 '64
Stomach contraction upon central vagus stimulation. Science 140:810-11 My 17 '63

JEFFERSON, Thomas
Affectionately yours; excerpts from To the boys and girls, ed. by E. Boykin. por Ladies Home J 81:136-8+ N '64

about

Day Jefferson got plastered. D. B. Webster, jr. il por Am Heritage 14:24-7 Je '63
Deadlock of democracy, by J. M. Burns. Review
Reporter 28:48-9 Mr 14 '63. A. Ranney; Reply. J. M. Burns. 28:6+ Ap 11 '63
* The Fourth; Jefferson's replacement library for LC. R. Stokes. Library J 88:2648 Jl '63
Jefferson & civil liberties, by L. W. Levy. Review
Commentary 37:81-2+ My '64. E. L. McKitrick
Time por 83:101 Je 5 '64
Jefferson and the ordeal of liberty, by D. Malone. Review
Sat R il 46:32 F 16 '63. C. A. Madison
Marbury v. Madison: case of the missing commissions. J. A. Garraty. il por Am Heritage 14:6-9+ Je '63
Nature's God and the founding fathers. E. M. Halliday. il por Am Heritage 14:4-7+ O '63
Our legacy from Mr Jefferson. B. Bliven. por Read Digest 82:160-2+ Mr '63
Perspective on the founders. V. Miller. por Nat R 14:117-19 F 12 '63
They made our world. L. Rosten. por Look 27:52-3 Jl 30 '63
Thomas Jefferson, gourmet. J. H. Hazelton. il Am Heritage 15:20-1+ O '64
Thomas Jefferson, third President 1801-1809. F. Freidel. il pors Nat Geog Mag 126:664-71 N '64

JEFFERSON national expansion memorial. See St Louis—Monuments, statues, etc.

JEFFERSON PARISH, La.
New Orleans: Cosa nostra's Wall Street. B. Davidson. il Sat Eve Post 237:15-21 F 29 '64

JEFFERY, G. A.
Nobel prize in chemistry awarded to crystallographer. Science 146:748-9 N 6 '64

JEFFORD, Norman O. See Carozza, M. J. jt. auth.

JEFFRIES, Fran
Performer. G. B. Leonard. il pors Look 28:67-70+ Jl 14 '64

JEFFRIES, James Jackson
Jeff, it's up to you! excerpts from Black champion; with editorial comment. F. Farr. il por Am Heritage 15:64-77 F '64

JEHOVAH'S Witnesses
On from Yankee stadium. il Time 82:40 Ag 2 '63
On the side of life; question of blood transfusion .Time 83:76+ F 21 '64
Witnesses in town; New York convention. America 109:87 Jl 27 '63

JELLICOE, Ann
Knack. Criticism
Nation 198:612 Je 15 '64
New Yorker 40:86+ Je 6 '64
Newsweek 63:90 Je 15 '64
Sat R 47:28 Je 20 '64
Vogue 144:30 Ag 1 '64

JELLINEK, Hedy D.
Guide to European music festivals-1963. Sat R 46:98-9 Mr 16 '63

JELLY, jam, etc.
Fig jelly, and it's good. Sunset 133:160 S '64
Great new recipes for jams, jellies, and pickles. J. Figg. il Suc Farm 62:76-7 Ag '64
If you want to make preserves; pickled figs and tomato fruit relish. Sunset 131:155 S '63
It's time to make winter's spreads. Sunset 131:134 Ag '63
Jams and jellies. il Bet Hom & Gard 42:73-4 Ag '64
Pomegranate or pyracantha jelly. Sunset 131:218 N '63
Preserves fabulous flavor in fifteen minutes. M. J. Engel. il Ladies Home J 81:98-100 Ag '64

JELLY-rolls. See Cake

JELLYFISHES
See also
Portuguese man-of-war

JELMOLI (department store) See Zurich, Switzerland—Stores

JEN, C. K.
Free radicals. Science 142:261-2+ O 11 '63

JENCKS, Christopher
College entrance exams. New Repub 148:7 Ap 20 '63
Diets for tiny minds. New Repub 148:30-2 My 4; 29-30 Je 1 '63
Education: cultivating greater diversity. New Repub 151:33-6+ N 7 '64
Education stalemate. New Repub 148:6 F 9 '63
Great New York boycott; what will happen if the cry for better schools fails? New Repub 150:12-14 F 15 '64
Johnson vs poverty. New Repub 150:15-18 Mr 28 '64
Mississippi. New Repub 151:15-18 Jl 25; 17-21 Ag 22 '64
Our miseducated teachers. New Repub 149:21-5 Jl 6 '63
Paying for education. New Repub 150:13-16 F 1 '64
Professors and pedagogues. New Repub 150:28+ My 16 '64
Schoolmaster Rickover. New Repub 148:14-16 Mr 2; 17 Ap 27 '63
Segregating the gifted. New Repub 150:26-8 Ap 25 '64
Sex and the college girl. New Repub 150:18-21 Ap 4 '64
Why bail out the states? New Repub 151:8-10 D 12 '64
Will Congress pay for education? New Repub 150:11-14 Ja 11 '64

JENGHIS Khan
Chingis Khan and the Mongol conquests. O. Lattimore. il por Sci Am 209:54-60+ bibliog(p 140) Ag '63

JENKINS, Carol Heiss
One battle I had to win; ed. by R. Hochstein. por Good H 156:89 My '63

JENKINS, Clara. See Bomar, C. P. jt. auth.

JENKINS, Dan
Board, books and birdies. Sports Illus 18:43-4+ My 20 '63
Bookies of doom. Sports Illus 19:36-8+ N 4 '63
Bridge. Sports Illus 20:78+ My 25 '64
College football. Sports Illus 19:49-51 O 7; 50+ N 4; 59-60 D 16 '63; 21:64-5 S 28; 73-4 O 5; 60-1 O 26 '64
Confederate air force flies at last. Sports Illus 19:58-63 Ag 12 '63
Debatable football scandal in the Southeast. Sports Illus 18:18-21 Mr 25 '63
Football. Sports Illus 19:44-5 Jl 8 '63
Poorly packed for a Chicago trip. Sports Illus 19:16-17 Ag 12 '63
Scandalous notes. Sports Illus 18:24-5+ Ap 8 '63
Throw throw throw. Sports Illus 19:30-45 S 23 '63
Too many Chiefs made too many touchdowns. Sports Illus 19:26-8+ S 16 '63
Trial that has the South seething. Sports Illus 19:18-21 Ag 5 '63

JENKINS, Elizabeth
Other Elizabeth. Opera N 28:8-13 Mr 7 '64

JENKINS, Florence Foster
Angel of mirth. F. Stevenson. por Opera N 27:26-7 Mr 16 '63
Roses for Lady Florence. P. Moor. il Harper 226:28-31 F '63

JENKINS, George W.
George pleasures them with groceries. T. G. Harris. il pors Look 28:102+ My 5 '64
JENKINS, Gladys Gardner, and Conafay, K. R.
Home economics can be a bridge. NEA J 52: 21-3 D '63
JENKINS, Howard, Jr
Key post for Negro; Jenkins gets Labor board job. por U S News 55:24 Ag 5 '63
JENKINS, L. Howard
BMI work, outlook; summary of report. por Pub W 184:71-2+ O 14 '63
JENKINS, Margaret E.
Delegate at Stockholm. PTA Mag 57:29-31 F '63
Presidents message. See issues of PTA magzine to June 1964
JENKINS, Marie M.
Bipolar planarians in a stock culture. bibliog Science 142:1187 N 29 '63
JENKINS, Robert J. See Butler, C. P. jt. auth.
JENKINS, Walter Wilson
As the morals issue took a new turn. U S News 57:6+ N 9 '64
From Washington straight. Cato. Nat R 16:948 N 3 '64
Jenkins and the public concern. W. F. Buckley, Nat R 16:947 N 3 '64
Jenkins case. Nation 199:290-1 N 2 '64
Jenkins case. il por Newsweek 64:32-3 O 26 '64
Jenkins case. W. V. Shannon. Commonweal 81:151-2 O 30 '64
Jenkins case: unanswered questions. il por U S News 57:48 N 2 '64
Jenkins in January. il Newsweek 64:24 D 21 '64
Jenkins report. Newsweek 64:26-7 N 2 '64
Jenkins report. Time 84:33-4 O 30 '64
Johnson & the Jenkins case. Time 84:20-1 N 6 '64
Now, the Jenkins case: meaning to the campaign. il por U S News 57:54-6 O 26 '64
President Johnson's indispensable man. por U S News 55:35 D 23 '63
Senior staff man. il pors Time 84:19-23 O 23 '64
Shocker in the White House: the Jenkins mess. il pors Life 57:43-4 O 23 '64
What road back from ruin? L. Wainwright. Life 57:31 O 30 '64
What the FBI found in the Jenkins case; Aftermath: sympathy and job offers for Walter Jenkins. por U S News 57:6 N 2 '64
Will the lid stay clamped? Time 83:26 Ap 3 '64
JENKINS public library, Jenkins, Ky.
What happened after the award. C. Shaw. il ALA Bul 57:337-8 Ap '63
JENKINTOWN, Pa.
See also
Abington library society
JENNETT, Richard P.
James R. Phillips: a pen name. por Negro Hist Bul 27:85 Ja '64
JENNETTE, Robert C.
Have a creative corner in your room. Sch Arts 62:33-5 Mr '63
JENNEY, Warren
Permanence and durability: different qualities and needs. Pub W 185:121+ F 3 '64
JENNIE; musical comedy. See Musical comedies, revues, etc.—Criticisms, plots, etc.
JENNINGS, C. Robert
Bloom in love. Sat Eve Post 237:70-1 S 12 '64
Body by MacLaine, in originals by Edith Head. Sat Eve Post 236:24-9 N 30 '63
Dick Van Dyke: the star who thinks he isn't. Ladies Home J 80:78-9 O '63
Golden rule. Sat Eve Post 237:72+ Je 13 '64
Good grief, Charlie Schulz! Sat Eve Post 237:26-7 Ap 25 '64
Odd odyssey of Sandra Dee. Sat Eve Post 236:22-3 Je 22 '63
On screen. Horizon 5:34-5 Mr '63
Romy Schneider. Sat Eve Post 236:36-8 N 23 '63
Waif becomes a woman. Sat Eve Post 236:22-3 S 14 '63
JENNINGS, Dean
Ann-Margret. Sat Eve Post 236:70-3 My 4 '63
Calif. shop offers unique service to good customers. il por Pub W 185:51-3 Mr 16 '64
(ed) See Warner, J. L. My first hundred years in Hollywood
JENNINGS, Frank
Beyond the obvious. Sat R 47:70-1+ S 19 '64
Companion to Spock. Sat R 46:48-9 Ag 17 '63
Creative revolutions. Sat R 47:63-4 Je 20 '64
For such a tide is moving. Sat R 47:74-5+ My 16 '64
Franklin book program for the U.S.? Sat R 47:43 D 19 '64
Of textbooks and trapped idealists. Pub W 184:34-43 Ag 5 '63
On book-borne magic. Sat R 46:66-7 O 19 '63
Textbooks and trapped idealists; excerpt from American reading public. Sat R 47:57-9+ Ja 18 '64
JENNINGS, Gary
Pidgin: no laughing matter. Harper 227:69-73 Jl '63; Same abr. with title Pidgin: the language that can do. Read Digest 83:151-4 S '63
JENNINGS, Gertrude
Personal selling, or self-service. Pub W 187: 124-5 Ja 18 '65
Short history of the ABA book buyer's handbook. Pub W 186:57-8 N 2 '64
JENNINGS, Gordon
Bonny poppers. Hot Rod 17:70-3 Jl '64
JENNINGS, J. S.
Unrecorded landscape by J. S. Jennings. P. N. Perrot. il Antiques 84:586-8 N '63
JENNINGS, Paul
I don't like you, I.Q. Esquire 62:82-3+ Ag '64
Union leaders face growing revolt. por Bsns W p54+ O 3 '64
JENNINGS, Ralph
Drums along the highway (cont) Hot Rod 16:72-5+ F; 70-5+ Mr '63
Latest word on transistor ignitions. Motor T 16:84-9 N '64
Spark plug. Motor T 16:40-5 Je; 66-9 Jl; 64-7 Ag '64
Weekend mechanic. Motor T 17:66-8 Ja '65 (to be cont)
JENNISON, C. S.
Ballad of Gregory's leg; poem. Atlan 213:166 Mr '64
I admire men, but then again. . ; poem. Atlan 213:126 Je '64
Intrusive patient. Atlan 214:122+ Jl '64
JENNISON, Keith
Last stand: poem. Sat R 46:45 Je 8 '63
JENNISON, Peter S.
American books abroad. Bul Atomic Sci 19: 31-3 D '63
Book publishing and national development. ALA Bul 57:512-16 Je '63
Book trade organization progressing in south Asia. Pub W 183:35-7 Ap 15 '63
Censorship: strategy for defense. Pub W 185: 58-61 Mr 2 '64
Comstockery and the courts. Sat R 47:27 Ag 22 '64
Inter-American book fair and seminar in Mexico city. Pub W 186:38-41 Jl 20 '64
JENNYS, Richard
Collectors' notes. E. Gaines. Antiques 86:85 Jl '64
JENNYS, William
William Jennys in New Hampshire. E. Gaines. il Antiques 86:84 Jl '64
JENRICH, Charles H.
Cleopatra's barge. Motor B 114:116-17 D '64
JENSEN, A. H. and Hoefer, J. A.
What slotted floors will and won't do for you. Suc Farm 61:66-7 F '63
JENSEN, Albert C.
Search for super-trees. Am For 70:16-18+ Ag '64
JENSEN, Alfred
World view of Alfred Jensen. A. Kaprow. il por Art N 62:28-31+ D '63
JENSEN, Amy La Follette
President's lady. Am Heritage 15:54-61 Ag '64
JENSEN, Clyde E.
Don't panic. Field & S 68:30-2+ O '63
JENSEN, Creighton R. and Kirkham, Don
Labeled oxygen: increased diffusion rate through soil containing growing corn roots. bibliog Science 141:735-6 Ag 23 '63
—and others
Labeled oxygen: transport through growing corn roots. Science 144:550-2 My 1 '64
JENSEN, Eileen
Androcles & the librarian; story. Ladies Home J 80:110b Jl '63
Don't tell it, say it. Writer 76:14-16 F '63
I remember Androcles. Writer 77:7-10 Ap '64
Portrait of the artist; story. McCalls 91:72-3 Jl '64
Those magic one-liners. Writer 78:9-11 Ja '65
JENSEN, Joerg, and Hyde, M. O.
Apocatalase of catalase-negative staphylococci. bibliog Science 141:45-6 Jl 5 '63
JENSEN, L. H. and Sundaralingam, M.
Hydrogen atom thermal parameters. bibliog Science 145:1185-7 S 11 '64
JENSEN, Lloyd
Postwar disarmament negotiations. Cur Hist 46:336-40+ Je '64
JENSEN, Margaret
Indian fair. Am For 69:20-1+ My '63
JENSEN, Neil H.
Elk in the tall timber. Field & S 69:40-2+ S '64

JENSEN, Oliver
Depot. Horizon 6:42-51 Sum '64
Do we want to save "gentried"? Horizon 6: 120 Wint '64
See Manhattan while it lasts. Horizon 5:116-20 My '63
We are all descended from grandfathers! Am Heritage 15:4-13+ Je '64
JENSEN, Pauline L.
Fun for a young convalescent. Parents Mag 38:82-3+ O '63
JEPPESEN and company
Charting the future with Jeppesen. R. B. Weeghman. il Flying 74:42-3+ Ja '64
JEPPESEN guides. See Aeronautic charts
JEQUIRITY pea. See Crabs eye vine
JEREMY, Sister Mary. See Mary Jeremy, Sister
JERISON, Harry J. and Pickett, R. M.
Vigilance: the importance of the elicited observing rate. bibliog Science 143:970-1 F 28 '64
JERKED beef. See Meat, Dried
JERNE, Niels K. and Nordin, A. A.
Plaque formation in agar by single antibody-producing cells. Science 140:405 Ap 26 '63
JEROME, Jay
Why bands play on in Philly. il Bsns W p52-4 D 28 '63
JEROME, John. See Gendebien, O. jt. auth.
JEROME, Judson
Alchemist; poem. Ladies Home J 80:108j S '63
For summer, a wave of new verse. Sat R 46:30-2 Jl 6 '63
Meditation in a booth; poem. Harper 227:59 D '63
Twenty bookes, clad in blak or reed. Harper 228:100+ Je '64
about
Five poets. J. Engels. Poetry 102:402 S '63
JERSEY CITY, N.J.
Negroes
Rampage in New Jersey. Time 84:17-18 Ag 14 '64
Politics and government
Jersey bounce; first Italian-American mayor. Newsweek 62:32 O 7 '63
Rise and fall of Jersey City. J. J. Farmer. il Reporter 31:47-9 Ag 13 '64
JERUS, George R.
Plumbing code allows for service conditions. Arch Rec 136:179-80 D '64
JERUSALEM
Jerusalem, my home. B. S. Vester. il Nat Geog Mag 126:826-47 D '64
Y.M.C.A. for Jews. il Time 85:44 Ja 1 '65
Church of the Holy Sepulcher
Where Jesus died; restoration begun. il Newsweek 64:73 Jl 27 '64
Description
Conquest of the Holy City. F. Shor. il Nat Geog Mag 124:839-55 D '63
Israel's three cities. D. Pryce-Jones. Commentary 35:58-61 Ja '63
Jerusalem the imperishable. C. Northcott. Christian Cent 80:575 My 1 '63
Road to Jerusalem. J. Knowles. il Holiday 34:52+ D '63
Maps
Holy Land today. il Nat Geog Mag 124:856-7, sup(folded map) D '63
Music
Song of Caesarea; Stravinsky's cantata Abraham and Isaac. il Newsweek 64:79 S 7 '64
Religious institutions and affairs
Israel's three cities. D. Pryce-Jones. Commentary 35:58-61 Ja '63
JESNESS, O. B.
Across the editor's desk; summary of letter, ed. by D. Hanson. Suc Farm 61:12 F '63
JESSE, William H.
New library buildings: some strengths and weaknesses. por Library J 89:4700-4 D 1 '64
JESSUP, John Knox
He gave the world the wildest ride in the park. Life 57:40A O 23 '64
about
Handwritten letters to a favorite aunt. G. P. Hunt. por Life 56:3 Je 26 '64
JESSUP, Philip C.
Stitching the world together. Sat R 47:17-19+ F 1 '64
JESTERS. See Fools and jesters

JESUITS
Brilliancy does not suit us; Jesuit artists. C. J. McNaspy. America 108:346-8 Mr 9 '63
See also
Kino, E. F.
Martindale, C. C.
Missions
Lost empire; ruins in eastern Paraguay and western Argentina. D. S. Carter. il Travel 120:37-40 O '63
JESUS, Society of. See Jesuits
JESUS CHRIST
Gospels revised. Newsweek 61:46 F 4 '63
Man nobody knows, by B. Barton. Review
Commonweal 77:557-9 F 22 '63. W. Percy
Who was the man Jesus? R. Coughlan. il pors Life 57:86-96+ D 25 '64
Word (cont) V. P. McCorry. America 108: 239-40, 623-4, 723-4; 109:498; 110:526-7; 111: 498; 112:27-8, 149-50, 205-6 F 16, Ap 27, My 18, O 26 '63, Ap 11, O 24 '64, Ja 2, 23, F 6 '65
See also
Sacred Heart, Devotion to
Salvation
Second advent
Appearances
Word. V. P. McCorry. America 110:554-5, 582-3 Ap 18-25 '64
Art
Modern artists encounter Christ. C. Sussman and I. Sussman. il pors America 111:548-51 N 7 '64
Atonement
See Atonement
Bibliography
New perspectives. H. H. Wernecke. Christian Cent 80:1242-4 O 9 '63
Biography
Rewriting the Gospels; during Lent. Christian Cent 80:486 Ap 17 '63
Trial of Jesus. P. Winter. bibliog f Commentary 38:35-41 S '64
Birth
See Jesus Christ—Nativity
Crucifixion
Who killed Jesus of Nazareth? Christian Cent 81:262 F 26 '64
Divinity
Word. V. P. McCorry. America 108:450-1 Mr 30 '63
Drama
Hill, by H. Fast. Review
Christian Cent 81:400 Mr 25 '64. C. R. Andrews
Iconography
See also
Jesus Christ—Art
Incarnation
See Incarnation
Nativity
Christmas fact & fancy. il Time 82:57-8 D 20 '63
Exegete at the manger. J. L. McKenzie. Commonweal 81:439-42 D 25 '64
See also
Christmas
Christmas cribs
Incarnation
Parables
Teacher's words. il Life 57:102-9 D 25 '64
Word. V. P. McCorry. America 108:210 F 9 '63
Word; loaves and fishes. V. P. McCorry. America 108:422-3 Mr 23 '63
Passion
Word. V. P. McCorry. America 110:324-5, 352-3, 380-1 Mr 7-21 '64
Resurrection and ascension
Interpreting the resurrection. D. T. Rowlingson. bibliog f Christian Cent 80:459-61 Ap 10 '63
Living and the dead. Christian Cent 80:387 Mr 27 '63
Turn to religion; address, March 29, 1964. Paul VI. Vital Speeches 30:386-7 Ap 15 '64
Who will roll away the stone? Christian Cent 80:451 Ap 10 '63
Word (cont) V. P. McCorry. America 110: 466-7, 496-7 Mr 28-Ap 4 '64

JESUS CHRIST—*Continued*

Teaching

Christ's message to the disinherited; excerpts from Jesus and the disinherited. H. Thurman. Ebony 18:58+ S '63
God is no more, by W. Pelz and L. Pelz. Review
Christian Cent 81:863-4 Jl 1 '64. L. J. Averill
His familiar and welcome message. F. C. Grant. il Life 57:110-11 D 25 '64

Transfiguration

Word. V. P. McCorry. America 108:348 Mr 9 '63

Trial

Word; trial of Christ. V. P. McCorry. America 110:268 F 22 '64
See also
Easter

JET air travel. See Air travel

JET airplane engines
Engine changes proposed for X-15A-2; ramjet engines. il Aviation W 80:24 Mr 23 '64
NASA moves to develop ramjet. H. Taylor. Miss & Roc 15:17 N 23 '64
RB.178 aimed at long/short-haul uses; bypass engine. H. J. Coleman. il Aviation W 81:59+ D 21 '64

Fuel

Airlines studying jet fuel contamination. J. R. Ashlock. Aviation W 78:40-1 Ap 22 '63
Committee reviews SST fuel test data. Aviation W 82:34-5 Ja 25 '65
Pan Am, TWA choose kerosene to ease public JP-4 controversy. J. R. Ashlock. Aviation W 82:32 Ja 25 '65

Lubrication

Lubricants screend for U.S. SST engines. Aviation W 82:57 Ja 11 '65
R&D efforts seek advanced lubricants. M. L. Yaffee. Aviation W 82:55+ Ja 11 '65

Starting devices

Jet starter development effort growing. M. L. Yaffee. Aviation W 82:49+ Ja 25 '65

JET airplane fares. See Airlines—Fares
JET burners. See Burners
JET business planes. See Airplanes, Business
JET cargo planes. See Airplanes, Freight
JET engine noise. See Airplanes—Noise
JET fighter-bomber. See Airplanes, Military
JET freighters. See Airplanes, Freight
JET helicopters. See Helicopters, Jet propelled
JET hydroplanes. See Hydroplanes, Jet propelled
JET pilots. See Air pilots
JET propelled airplanes. See Airplanes, Jet propelled
JET propelled motor boats. See Motor boats, Jet propelled

JET propulsion
Air-breathing boosters gain favor. W. Beller. il Miss & Roc 12:22-3+ Mr 18 '63
Jet propulsion. J. Goldman. il Motor B 111:50-1+ F '63
Now a jet drive for your outboard. C. R. Hull. il Pop Sci 182:122-4+ Je '63
Where is science taking us? jet propulsion principles applied to the problems of land transportation. J. V. Foa. il Sat R 47:68-9 N 7 '64
X-15 use planned in ramjet evaluations. I. Stone. il Aviation W 81:57+ Ag 31 '64

JET propulsion laboratory
Changing man's view; flight of Ranger VII. il Time 84:39-42 Ag 7 '64
Controversial mutuality clause out in 2-year JPL contract extension. Aviation W 82:19 Ja 4 '65
DuBridge defends JPL; denies top-level management shakeup. Aviation W 80:32 F 24 '64
House unit will recommend NASA resident official to oversee JPL. D. E. Fink. Aviation W 80:23-4 My 11 '64
How should a space lab be organized? debate between NASA and Jet propulsion laboratory. il Bsns W p 112-13 My 2 '64
Hyprox to cut altitude chamber cost. R. Hawkes. il Miss & Roc 12:27 Ap 22 '63
JPL developing advanced liquid engine concept. R. Hawkes. il Miss & Roc 12:32-3 F 25 '63
JPL facing Mariner C avionics problems. B. Miller. Aviation W 80:16-17 Je 29 '64
JPL outlines requirements for lightweight roving lunar vehicle. Aviation W 79:36 Jl 1 '63
JPL program growth forces increased contracting to industry. il Miss & Roc 13:181-2+ N 25 '63
JPL: Ranger VI failure increases speculation on jet lab's future links with space agency, Caltech. J. Walsh. Science 143:1014-16 Mr 6 '64
JPL receives Mars radar signal echoes. Aviation W 78:39 F 25 '63
JPL using two radar techniques to prepare map of surface of Venus. R. Pay. Miss & Roc 15:35 D 21 '64
Management problems delay new contract between NASA and JPL. D. E. Fink. Aviation W 80:34 Ap 20 '64
Many a slip 'twixt earth and moon, and measles too. J. Hicks. il Life 57:36A Ag 14 '64
Men who shot the moon. Sci Digest 56:20 O '64
Most accurate measurement of Mercury. Time 81:59 Je 7 '63
100 eyes to the sky. il Pop Electr 21:56 O '64
$150-million failure; mission of Ranger VI. W. J. Coughlin. Miss & Roc 14:50 F 10 '64
Pentagon and campus; the sullen marriage. W. Marx. il Nation 198:499-501 My 18 '64
Ranger design and management criticized; reports. A. J. Kelley; E. D. Hilburn. Aviation W 80:56+ My 11 '64
Ranger management compromise sought. W. J. Normyle. Aviation W 80:25-6 Je 22 '64
Ranger: oversight subcommittee asks why NASA doesn't prevail on JPL to rigidize projectwise. J. Walsh. Science 144:824-6 My 15 '64
Shoot and hope Ranger effort charged. D. E. Fink. Aviation W 80:25-7 My 4 '64
Space agency wants JPL to reorganize. H. Taylor. Miss & Roc 14:16 F 17 '64
Tighter control over JPL urged in report of House space committee. H. M. David. Miss & Roc 14:15 Je 22 '64
Voyage to the morning star; findings of Mariner II. il Time 81:76-80 Mr 8 '63; Same abr. with title Voyage to Venus. Read Digest 82:120-5 Je '63

JET streams
Atmospheric jet streams. J. D. Isaacs. Science 141:1045-6 S 13 '63; Reply. D. O. Staley and others. 143:489 Ja 31 '64

JETS (football club) See Football clubs
JEUNESSES musicales. See Musical societies
JEWBIRD; story. See Malamud, B.

JEWELERS
Man of many facets; H. Stern's jewelry showrooms. il Time 84:104-6 S 11 '64
Some Franco-American silversmiths and jewelers. F. J. Dallett. il Antiques 84:706-9 D '63
See also
Tiffany and company

JEWELL, Malcolm E.
Reapportionment and the courts. New Repub 148:17-19 F 2 '63

JEWELRY
American jewelry, 1963. H. Halverstadt. il Craft Horiz 23:23-34+ Mr '63
Antique aura: heirloom charm in modern creations of costume jewelry. il Seventeen 23:78-9 D '64
Do-it-yourself jewelry; the hot-and-cold technique for making fried marble gems. il Design 64:154-5+ Mr '63
Egyptian paste jewelry. O. C. Waldo. il Sch Arts 62:36-7 Mr '63
For an Arabian nights lady. B. Perkins. il N Y Times Mag p92-3+ D 13 '64
From wax on ice to jewelry. H. Diemert. il Sch Arts 63:5-10 My '64
Give him (or her) electronic jewelry. B. G. Wels. il Pop Electr 21:56 D '64
Gold jewellery from the Mediterranean. il Vogue 141:128 F 15 '63
Helpful tips on wearing jewelry. Good H 158:157 Mr '64
Jewelry. il Craft Horiz 24:69-73 My '64
Jewelry and gemstones. G. V. Axon. il Consumer Bul 47:12-15 My '64
Jewelry by Torun. A. Karlikow. il Craft Horiz 23:20-1+ Jl '63
Jewelry making. J. A. Carey. il Sch Arts 63:31-2 F '64
Jewelry to build on; costume jewelry. il Redbook 124:66-9+ D '64
Jewels that crawl; megazopherus chiliensis. W. I. Fischman. il Sat Eve Post 236:68 My 11 '63
Little money but champagne taste. il Good H 157:110-11 D '63
Mlle Toussaint, her extraordinary jewels, the animal kingdom she made famous. il Vogue 143:112-13 Je '64
Precious animals. il Vogue 143:110-11 Je '64
Real thing can graduate into your life. il Seventeen 22:126-7+ My '63

JEWELRY—*Continued*
Sinhalese decorative art. G. Kaler. il Hobbies 68:42+ F '64
Stained glass jewelry. B. Ruff. il Design 65: 75 N '63
Washington: wonderful world of women and jewels. P. Mesta. il McCalls 91:16+ Ja '64
See also
Beads
Diamonds
Earrings
Jewelers
Lockets
JEWELRY, Ancient
Silver from Ur of ancient Mesopotamia. J. W. Mellichamp and M. Levey. il Science 142:44-5 O 4 '63
JEWELRY trade
See also
Tiffany and company
Zale jewelry company
JEWELS, Crown. See Crown jewels
JEWETT, John Figgis
When is it safe to induce labor? Redbook 122:44+ Ap '64
JEWETT, Stanley G. Jr
Stonefly aquatic in the adult stage. bibliog Science 139:484-5 F 8 '63
JEWFISH fishing
Battle with a heavyweight. G. Heinold il Outdoor Life 133:10-11+ Ja '64
JEWISH American authors. See American literature—Jewish authors
JEWISH-Arab relations
Arab refugee today. F. L. Hutchison. Christian Cent 81:823-6 Je 24 '64; Discussion. 81: 1016 Ag 12 '64
Blowup in Mideast? Nasser puts squeeze on Israel. il U S News 54:22 My 20 '63
In no man's land; disputed road. il Newsweek 64:52+ N 16 '64
Israel after fifteen years. G. Gersh. Christian Cent 80:487-9 Ap 17 '63
Israel's new waterline: will it bring war? O. Schisgall. il Look 27:82+ Ap 9 '63
Jordan waters; when Israel turns the tap. L. Seligson. il Nation 198:622-4 Je 22 '64
Jordan's troubled waters. W. Mehlman. il Reporter 30:29+ Ja 30 '64
Nationalism: a matter of pride and prejudice; Arabs vs. Israelis. il Sr Schol 85:19 O 7 '64
Toward Arab-Israeli coexistence. G. D. Young; discussion. Christian Cent 80:181 F 6 '63
See also
United Nations—Israel
JEWISH art. See Art, Jewish
JEWISH authors. See Authors, Jewish
JEWISH civilization. See Jews—Civilization
JEWISH community centers. See Community centers
JEWISH cookery. See Cookery, Jewish
JEWISH education. See Jews—Education
JEWISH English authors. See English literature—Jewish authors
JEWISH-gentile marriages. See Marriages, Mixed
JEWISH law
Law that bound Israel. W. F. Albright. il Life 57:55-6 D 25 '64
JEWISH literature
Jewish. M. Liben. Commentary 38:74-8 S '64
See also
Booksellers and bookselling—Jewish literature
JEWISH literature (American)
Breakthrough? D. Daiches. Commentary 38: 61-4 Ag '64; Reply. I. Stark. 38:8+ D '64
JEWISH musicians. See Musicians, Jewish
JEWISH newspapers
Jewish chronicle and others. J. Gross. Commentary 36:387-9 N '63
JEWISH parochial schools. See Jews—Education
JEWISH philosophy. See Philosophy, Jewish
JEWISH question. See Anti-Semitism
JEWISH rabbis. See Rabbis
JEWISH refugees. See Refugees, Jewish
JEWISH sects
See also
Hasidism
JEWISH theology
Ben Emunah li-Kheflrah; between faith and heresy, by E. Shemueli. Review
Commentary 36:174-6 Ag '63. M. Fox
Future needs the past. F. Heer. Christian Cent 81:635-8 My 13 '64
Jacobs affair. A. Sherman. Commentary 38: 60-4 O '64
Worship and ethics: a study in rabbinic Judaism, by M. Kadushin. Review
Commentary 38:78+ D '64. M. Fox

JEWS
Dissent on Brother Daniel. M. Galanter. Commentary 36:10-17 Jl '63; Discussion. 37: 19-20+ Ja '64
Maurice Samuel & Jewish letters. R. Alter. Commentary 37:50-4 Mr '64
Some attitudes toward Jews. M. Himmelfarb. Commentary 35:424-8 My '63; Discussion. 36:276 O '63
Wants Moslem-Jewish rapprochement. Christian Cent 81:1613; 82:38 D 30 '64, Ja 13 '65
What is a Jew? M. Adler. Harper 228:41-5 Ja '64; Discussion. 228:6 Mr '64
What Pope Paul's visit was not. E. Berger. Christian Cent 81:524 Ap 22 '64
Word. V. P. McCorry. America 111:333-4 S 19 '64
Writing about Jews. P. Roth. Commentary 36:446-52 D '63; Discussion. 37:6+ Ap '64
See also
Anti-Semitism
Catholic church—Relations—Jews
Israel
Zionism

Civilization

Age of prophets. M. D. Zeik. Commonweal 78:67-70 Ap 12 '63
Future needs the past. F. Heer. Christian Cent 81:635-8 My 13 '64
Natural and the supernatural Jew, by A. A. Cohen. Review
Commentary 35:353-6 Ap '63. M. Fox

Education

Jewish parochial schools. America 110:589 My 2 '64
Yoke of the Torah; excerpts from memoirs, tr. by J. Sloan. M. Amer. Commentary 38: 40-6 Ag '64

History

Before the Bible; the common background of Greek and Hebrew civilizations, by C. H. Gordon. Review
Commentary 36:333-6 O '63. H. L. Ginsberg; Reply with rejoinder. C. H. Gordon. 36:424+ D '63
Essenes or zealots? excavations at Massada. il Newsweek 63:72 F 10 '64
Jewish & other nationalisms. H. R. Trevor-Roper. Commentary 35:15-21 Ja '63
Jews, God, and history, by M. I. Dimont. Review
Commentary 36:256-7 S '63. A. Hertzberg
Meaning of Jewish history, by J. B. Agus. Review
Commentary 37:75-7 Ap '64. D. Daiches; Discussion. 38:15 Ag '64; 39:10-11 Ja '65 Reply with rejoinder. J. B. Agus. 38:15 Ag '64
Promised city: New York's Jews, 1870-1914, by M. Rischin. Review
Commentary 37:76-9 F '64. A. Kazin
Trial of Jesus. P. Winter. bibliog f Commentary 38:35-41 S '64
See also
David, king of Israel

Intellectual life

Entering the mainstream. A. M. Greeley. Commonweal 81:34 O 2 '64; Reply. R. Gordis. 81:102-3 O 16 '64

Law

See Jewish law

Persecutions

Dering case; surgeon at Auschwitz. M. Ellmann. Commentary 38:19-25 Jl '64
Literature of the holocaust. A. Alvarez. Commentary 38:65-9 N '64
Pius XII, the Jews, and the German Catholic church. G. Lewy. bibliog Commentary 37:23-35 F '64; Discussion. 37:6+ Je '64
Survivors, by N. Muhlen. Review
Commentary 36:401-2+ N '63. T. Frankel; Discussion. 37:8+ Mr '64

Religion

See Judaism

Rites and ceremonies

Jeffrey becomes a man; Bar mitzvah. C. Morrison. il Look 27:24-8+ Ag 13 '63
JEWS and Catholics. See Catholic church—Relations—Jews
JEWS and Christians, National conference of. See National conference of Christians and Jews
JEWS and the World war. See World war, 1939-1945—Jews
JEWS in Algeria
France's Algerian Jews; tr. by R. Howard. A. Mandel. Commentary 35:475-82 Je '63; Reply. B. M. Halpern. 36:277 O '63

JEWS in Austria
Trip into the blue. R. Berczeller. New Yorker 39:20-1 Ag 24 '63

JEWS in Denmark
Danish Jews; how their countrymen saved them from the Nazis. R. Tunley. il Sat Eve Post 236:74-5+ F 23 '63

JEWS in England
Jacobs affair. A. Sherman. Commentary 38: 60-4 O '64

JEWS in France
Du ghetto à L'Occident, by C. Roland. Review
Commentary 37:90-1 My '64. S. D. Temkin
France's Algerian Jews; tr. by R. Howard. A. Mandel. Commentary 35:475-82 Je '63; Reply. B. M. Halpern. 36:277 O '63

JEWS in Germany
Germany without Jews? il Newsweek 61:94 Ap 8 '63
Jews in Germany. A. Schalk. Commonweal 79:185-7 N 8 '63
Jews in Germany today. G. Samuels. il Harper 228:45-50 My '64; Reply. W. Iggers. 229:8 Ag '64
Pius XII, the Jews, and the German Catholic church. G. Lewy. bibliog Commentary 37:23-35 F '64; Discussion. 37:6+ Je '64

JEWS in Great Britain
Heretical rabbi; split in British Jewry. il Newsweek 63:66 My 18 '64
Jews of Britain; theological schism. Time 83: 63 My 22 '64

JEWS in Hungary
Roncalli and Jews' baptism. America 108:874 Je 22 '63

JEWS in Israel
How many Israels? M. Himmelfarb. Commentary 37:64-7 Ja '64; Reply with rejoinder. A. Antonovsky. 37:18 My '64
Most Orthodox Orthodox; Mea She'arim, Jerusalem. il Time 82:38 Ag 9 '63
Notes on Israel. D. M. Friedenberg. il Commonweal 81:381-5 D 11 '64; Reply. E. Berger. 81:554-5 Ja 29 '65
Religious conflicts in Israel. N. Levin. il Commonweal 79:344-6 D 13 '63

JEWS in Latin America
Revival below the border. Newsweek 64:44 Ag 3 '64

JEWS in literature
Jewish writing in England. D. Jacobson. Commentary 37:46-50 My '64; Reply. B. Glanville. 38:20+ S '64
Nerve of Günter Grass. G. Steiner. Commentary 37:77-80 My '4
Return of Europe's Jews. E. Roditi. Commentary 36:63-8 Jl '63
Writing about Jews. P. Roth. Commentary 36:446-52 D '63; Discussion. 37:6+ Ap '64

JEWS in Morocco
Yoke of the Torah; excerpts from memoirs tr. by J. Sloan. M. Amer. Commentary 38:40-6 Ag '64

JEWS in Palestine
See also
Jewish-Arab relations
Zionism

Resistance movement

Deed, by G. Frank. Review
Reporter 28:44-6 Je 6 '63. S. Elmerl
Sat R 46:33 My 4 '63. Q. Reynolds

JEWS in Poland
Chapter to remember; Warsaw ghetto uprising. Newsweek 61:38 Ap 22 '63
Heroes of Warsaw's ghetto; photographs. N Y Times Mag p22-3+ Ap 21 '63
Letter from Warsaw. J. Wechsberg. New Yorker 38:112-13 F 9 '63
Living ghosts of the concentration camps. L. W. Wells. il N Y Times Mag p 13+ Ja 26 '64
Our last days in the Warsaw ghetto. A. Donat. il Commentary 35:378-89 My '63; Reply. S. Dyon. 36:272 O '63
Twilight of the dove. H. Bowser. Sat R 46:20 My 18 '63

JEWS in Russia
Jews in the Soviet Union. L. S. Feuer. New Repub 149:11-12 N 30 '63
Plight of Soviet Jews. S. A Fineberg. Christian Cent 81:429-31 Ap 1 '64
Pot and kettle dialogue; anti-Semitism in Soviet Union and U.S. Christian Cent 80: 972 Ag 7 '63
Religion in the Soviet Union. G. Bailey. il Reporter 31:29 Jl 16 '64
Russia eases restrictions; matzoth for Passover. Christian Cent 81:327 Mr 11 '64
Russian anti-Semitism. Time 83:84 Ap 17 '64
Some attitudes toward Jews. M. Himmelfarb. Commentary 35:424-8 My '63; Discussion. 36:276 O '63
Soviet anti-Semitism: an exchange. B. Russell; A. Vergelis. Commentary 39:35-7 Ja '65
Soviet anti-Semitism exposed. Christian Cent 81:508 Ap 22 '64
Soviet Jewish minority. S. M. Schwarz. Cur Hist 47:299-302+ N '64
Soviet regime persecutes Russian Jews. Christian Cent 80:1358 N 6 '63
Soviet Union seeks to strangle Judaism. Christian Cent 80:485 Ap 17 '63
State of Soviet Jewry. M. Friedberg. Commentary 39:38-43 Ja '65
Status of the Jews in the Soviet Union. M. Decter. For Affairs 41:420-30 Ja '63
To be a Jew in Russia. il Newsweek 63:70 Ap 20 '64

JEWS in Spain
Christians and Jews in Spain. J. J. Oldfield. America 110:218-19 F 15 '64
Spanish anti-Semitism today. R. Alan. Commentary 38:64-6 Ag '64; Discussion. 39:6+ Ja '65

JEWS in the United States
As violence grows in a big city; radio-car patrols of Hasidic Jews in Brooklyn. il U S News 56:6 Je 8 '64
Being Jewish. Newsweek 64:38 D 28 '64
Christians and Jews: a new rapprochement; excerpt from America is different. S. E. Rosenberg. Christian Cent 81:295-8 Mr 4 '64; Reply. A. T. K. Zadig. 81:801-3 Je 17 '64
Coat upon a stick, by N. Fruchter. Review
Commentary 35:262-4 Mr '63. R. Alter
How we are. M. Himmelfarb. Commentary 39:69-74 Ja '65
In the community (cont) M Himmelfarb. Commentary 35:66-70, 424-8; 36:249-51; 37: 64-7 Ja, My, S '63, Ja '64
Interfaith dialogue and church-state issues. B. J. Coughlin. America 108:900-3 Je 29 '63
Intermarriage & the Jewish future. M. Sklare. Commentary 37:46-52 Ap '64; Discussion. 38:16 Ag; 8+ S '64
Maccabees and the Mau Mau. Nat R 16:479 Je 16 '64
Maccabees ride again; Hasidic Jews patrol Crown Heights, Brooklyn. A. G. Aronowitz. il Sat Eve Post 237:32+ Je 27 '64
Negroes & Jews: the new challenge to pluralism. N. Glazer. Commentary 38:29-34 D '64
Only in Brooklyn; Hasidic Jewish patrols in Crown Heights. il Newsweek 63:52 Je 8 '64
Pluralism & brotherhood. S. Lynd. Commentary 35:81-4 Ja '63
Promised city: New York's Jews, 1870-1914, by M. Rischin. Review
Commentary 37:76-9 F '64. A. Kazin
Taboo; Goldwater's Jewishness. M. Lerner. Time 82:93 N 22 '63
Vanishing American Jew. T. B. Morgan. il Look 28:42-3+ My 5 '64
See also
American Jewish committee
Central conference of American rabbis

JHABVALA, R. Prawer
Aliens; story. Yale R 52:385-403 Mr '63
Widow; story. New Yorker 39:22-30 Ag 10 '63

JIGS
Grinding jigs for lathe chisels. A. Youngquist. il Pop Mech 121:182-5+ Mr '64
Perfect disks every time; adjustable sanding jig. E. P. Kushner. sr. il Pop Mech 121:174 Ap '64
Tenoning jig for fine wood joints. R. Wortham. il Pop Sci 184:156-7 Mr '64
Uniform tapers cut in jig time. il Pop Mech 121:165 Ap '64

JIGSAW puzzles. See Puzzles

JIGSAWS
Jigsaw. il Pop Sci 183:172-3 N '63
Precision indexer for your jigsaw. W. E. Burton. il Pop Mech 119:194-6+ Mr '63

JILL-in-the-Box: drama. See Watts, F. B.

JIM Crow laws. See Negroes in the United States—Segregation

JIM THORPE, Pa.
Sentiment in Mauch Chunk. Sports Illus 21:6-7 Ag 3 '64

JIMENEZ, Fernando, Volio-. See Volio-Jimenez, F.

JIMÉNEZ, Juan Ramón
Diary of a newly married poet. R. Gullón. il por Américas 16:11-15 Mr '64

JIMÉNEZ, Marcos Pérez. See Pérez Jiménez, M.

JIMÉNEZ DE ARÉCHAGA, Eduardo
International law commission. por U N Rev 10:42-4 Ag '63

JIMMY Bennett doesn't work here any more; story. See Purcell, J. Q.

JINGLES. See Doggerels

JINNAH, Fatima
Lady & the field marshal. il por Time 84:40+ O 30 '64
Lesson in basic democracy. Newsweek 64:58 N 30 '64
Trouble with Mother. il por Time 84:24 D 25 '64
Votes for mother. il por Newsweek 64:54+ N 2 '64
Zindabad! for Miss Jinnah. J. Nevard. il pors N Y Times Mag p36+ N 8 '64

JIU-jitsu
Brains versus brawn; judo expert. il Ebony 19:83-4+ N '63
Indiana's top gentle way family. il Ebony 19: 102-4+ Je '64
When in doubt, yell and run. L. Strong. il N Y Times Mag p92 Mr 22 '64

JO; musical comedy. See Musical comedies, revues, etc.—Criticisms, plots, etc.

JOACHUM, Heinz
Dedication of the house. Mus Am 83:21 N '63
Montezuma and the Messiah. Mus Am 84:20 My '64

JOAD, Cyril Edwin Mitchinson
Justice for Joad. J. A. Davidson. Christian Cent 80:1238-9 O 9 '63

JOANNA & Ulysses; story. See Sarton, M.

JOB analysis
See also
Performance standards

JOB aptitude tests. See Aptitude tests

JOB corps. See United States—Job corps

JOB interviews. See Interviewing

JOB mobility. See Occupational mobility

JOB performance. See Employees—Rating

JOB performance standards. See Performance standards

JOB quitting. See Labor turnover

JOB satisfaction
Stale in your job? try this. C. A. Cerami. il Nations Bsns 51:88-90 O '63
We traded security for happiness. M. A. Facklam. il Redbook 120:6+ Mr '63
Where is the organization man? L. W. Porter. bibliog f il Harvard Bsns R 41:53-61 N '63
Your first job. il Changing T 18:31-3 My '64
See also
Employee morale

JOB security. See Employment systems—Guaranty of employment

JOB tenure. See Seniority, Employee

JOB training. See Employees—Training

JOB vacancy index
New job scoreboard: survey of job openings by Labor dept. Bsns W p29 Ag 22 '64

JOBBERS
See also
Book jobbers

JOBE, Barbara, and Longwell, Maude
How we manage good times all year long. Farm J 88:106-7 Mr '64

JOBIN, William R. and Ippen, A. T.
Ecological design of irrigation canals for snail control. bibliog Science 145:1324-6 S 18 '64

JOBS. See Employment; Occupations

JOCKEYS
Big job for little men; submarine construction work. il Sci Digest 53:74 Je '63
Men they call boys. H. Horn. il Sports Illus 20:72-4+ Je 8 '64
Shoeshine boy; B. Ussery. il Time 84:58+ Jl 24 '64
Touch of gold in the saddle; J. Rotz. G. Holland. il Sports Illus 20:24-6+ Mr 23 '64
Tyranny of the little men; Kentucky Derby top jockeys. W. Tower. il Sports Illus 20: 28-9 Ap 27 '64
See also
Baeza, B.
Hartack, B.
Horse racing
Longden, J.
McCurdy, R.
Shoemaker, W.

JODRELL bank observatory. See Radio telescope

JOEL, Lydia
(ed) See Magwood, D. Conversation with Dolores Magwood

JOELSON, Charles S.
Excerpt from address, March 6, 1963. Cong Digest 42:155+ My '63

JOFFE, Bruce
Bruce Joffe's private library; an unusual childrens library in Flushing, L.I. S. Havens. il por Library J 88:2066-8 My 15 '63

JOFFREY, Robert
Dance magazine's 1963 awards. por Dance Mag 38:34+ Mr '64

JOFFYROY, René
René Joffroy and the Vix krater. il por Horizon 7:2-3 Wint '65

JOHANN, Robert O.
Moral response. America 108:761-2 My 25 '63
Philosopher's notebook. America 108:497; 109: 14, 160, 359, 568, 795; 110:191, 370, 606, 822; 111:111, 234, 487, 740; 112:76 Ap 13, Jl 6, Ag 17, S 28, N 9, D 21 '63, F 8, Mr 21, My 2, Je 13, Ag 1, S 5, O 24, D 5 '64, Ja 16 '65

JOHANNES, R. E.
Phosphorus excretion and body size in marine animals: microzooplankton and nutrient regeneration. bibliog Science 146:923-4 N 13 '64

JOHANNESBURG

Music

Christmas in South Africa. S. R. Karnovsky. Opera N 28:32 F 1 '64

JOHANNESSEN, Carl L.
Marshes prograding in Oregon: aerial photographs. bibliog Science 146:1575-8 D 18 '64

JOHN of Cronstadt, Saint
New Russian saint. America 111:649 N 21 '64

JOHN XXIII, pope
Christmas meditation. Ladies Home J 81:68 D '64
Journal of a soul. pors Ladies Home J 81:57-61+ N; 66-7+ D '64; 82:52+ Ja '65
What we are for; summary of new encyclical on world peace. por Time 81:60+ Ap 19 '63

about

Appreciation of Pope John. E. Waugh. il Sat Eve Post 236:84-5 Jl 27 '63
Back of the changes in Vatican policy; Pacem in terris. il por U S News 54:60-1 Ap 29 '63
Catholic church: which way now? il por U S News 54:37-9 Je 17 '63
Changes in church and world, the work of Pope John. il pors U S News 54:50-1 Je 10 '63
Declaration of interdependence; encyclical Peace on earth; with excerpts. N. Cousins. il Sat R 46:18-20 My 4 '63
Diary of a pope. por Newsweek 63:71 Mr 30 '64
Divini redemptoris to Pacem in terris. F. S. Meyer. Nat R 14:406 My 21 '63
Ecumenical council; progress report. S. De Gramont. il por Sat Eve Post 236:86-91 F 23 '63
Encyclical's impact; reactions to Pacem in terris. America 108:632 My 4 '63
Fiat lux; private meeting between Pope John and Khrushchev's son-in-law. Time 82:53 S 6 '63
From Pope John: praise for Americans. por U S News 54:16 Ap 1 '63
Future is ours. Life 54:4 Ap 26 '63
Good Pope John; symposium. America 108: 854-60 Je 15 '63
Good Shepherd. America 108:852 Je 15 '63
Great priest; British press praises the deceased Pontiff. America 108:848 Je 15 '63
Greatness of Pope John. R. Etteldorf. America 108:884-6 Je 22 '63
Habitable world. P. O'Donovan. New Repub 148:9-10 Je 8 '63
Heritage of Pope John. C. Pell. por America 109:48-9 Jl 13 '63
Holy father. M. Ascoli. Reporter 28:10 Je 20 '63
Hominibus bonae voluntatis; encyclical Pacem in terris. J. Burnham. Nat R 14: 353 My 7 '63
In solemn splendor the church gives John to the ages. il pors Life 54:52-6 Je 21 '63
John XXIII. Nation 196:517 Je 22 '63
John XXIII appeals for world peace; Pacem in terris. Christian Cent 80:517 Ap 24 '63
John XXIII: surprising pontiff. Christian Cent 80:567 Ap 24 '63
John XXIII: the pope of unity. Sat Eve Post 236:94 Je 29 '63
Let the good not be interred. Life 54:4 Je 14 '63
Letter from London. M. Panter-Downes. New Yorker 39:100 Je 15 '63
Letter from Vatican City. X. Rynne. il New Yorker 39:41-2+ Je 15 '63; 88+ Ja 18; 40: 166+ S 19 '64
Letter from Vatican City: Cardinal Bea. X. Rynne. il New Yorker 39:120+ My 11 '63
Light to the nations: Pacem in terris? America 108:604 Ap 27 '63
Looking back at Pope John. L. M. Örsy. America 108:903-5 Je 29 '63
New encyclical; a question of perspective; Pacem in terris. W. Herberg. il Nat R 14: 364-5 My 7 '63; Reply. J. Elligett. 14:469 Je 4 '63

JOHN XXIII, pope—about—*Continued*
New pope. Nat R 16:711+ Ag 25 '64
Obituary
Christian Cent 80:763-4 Je 12 '63
Pacem in terris. Commonweal 78:123-4 Ap 26 '63
Pacem in terris. M. Ascoli. Reporter 28: 20-1 My 23 '63; Discussion. 28:8 Je 20 '63
Pacem in terris a year later. J. Cogley. Commonweal 80:356-7 Je 12 '64
Pacem in terris: for all humanity; with excerpts. il por Newsweek 61:21-2 Ap 22 '63
Pain and exaltation of the holy dying. D. Martin; J. Monfante; T. Green. Life 54:28 Je 14 '63
Paul VI and the bishops. O. Hastings. il Reporter 29:23-5 D 19 '63
Paul VI to continue Pope John's reforms. Sr Schol 83:11-12 S 13 '63
Peace on earth. J. Cogley. Commonweal 78: 158-9 My 3 '63
Perspectives on Paul VI. E. Duff. Christian Cent 80:1128-31 S 18 '63
Pope and atheist; visit of A. I. Adzhubei to Vatican. Newsweek 61:52 Mr 18 '63
Pope John. Commonweal 78:315-16 Je 14 '63
Pope John calls for world unity; encyclical Pacem in terris (Peace on earth) il por Sr Schol 82:16 Ap 24 '63
Pope John: new look. P. S. Land. America 108:395-6 Mr 23 '63
Pope John, pacem in coelis. Nat R 14:486 Je 18 '63; Reply. G. M. Armstrong. 14:541 Jl 2 '63
Pope John: the astonishing Catholic pontiff. J. Roddy. il pors Look 27:18-29 Jl 2 '63
Pope John XXIII. N. Cousins. Sat R 46:18 Je 15 '63
Pope John XXIII: gentle shepherd of a revolution. E. J. Hughes. il pors Newsweek 61:42-4+ Je 10 '63
Pope John XXIII, in memoriam; poem. E. L. Pierce. Christian Cent 80:823 Je 26 '63
Pope John XXIII pastor and theologian. F. X. Murphy. Cath World 197:318-23 Ag '63
Pope John XXIII; symposium. Commonweal 78:367-75 Je 28 '63
Pope John's great gift. por Read Digest 82: 141-6 Ap '63
Pope John's letter; interpretation of Pacem in terris. T. N. Davis America 108:707-10 My 18 '63
Pope John's vision. P. Pavan. il Commonweal 81:231-4 N 13 '64
Pope meets Communist. il Time 81:53 Mr 15 '63
Pope of the dialogue. B. Ward. por Atlan 212:54-7 S '63
Pope Paul follows along Pope John's path. R. Neville. il N Y Times Mag p23+ S 22 '63
Pope's bombshell; meeting with A. Adzhubei. G. D. Kumlien. Commonweal 78:71-2 Ap 12 '63
Pope's formula for world peace. il por U S News 54:25 Ap 22 '63
Pope's illness. il Newsweek 61:78 Je 3 '63
Requiem for Pope John. S. Vanocur. Read Digest 83:63 Ag '63
Restraints on American Catholic freedom. J. Victor. bibliog f Harper 227:33-9 D '63
Riddle of Pope Paul VI. A. Leone-Moats. il Nat R 15:347-9+ O 22 '63
Roncalli and Jews' baptism. America 108: 874 Je 22 '63
Servant of the servants. Commonweal 78:292 Je 7 '63
Slavic heritage; encyclical Magnifici eventus. America 108:797 Je 1 '63
Tasks of Pope Paul VI. il por U S News 55: 43-4 Jl 1 '63
That beloved rock of a man; with report by M. L. West. il pors Life 54:78-87 Je 7 '63
Things old and new in Pacem in terris. J. C. Murray. America 108:612-14 Ap 27 '63
Toward peace and justice; Pacem in terris. H. Schomer. Christian Cent 80:703-6 My 29 '63
Turning point in Kremlin-Vatican relations? il U S News 54:21 Mr 18 '63
Uncharted waters. America 108:393-4 Mr 23 '63
Under suspicion. America 108:455 Ap 6 '63
United Nations tribute to Pope of unity and peace. il por U N Rev 10:32-3 Je '63
Vatican revolutionary. il pors Time 81:41-3 Je 7 '63
Vatican II: legacy of John XXIII. il por Sr Schol 83:3+ N 1 '63
Vatican II, session 2. E. Duff. Christian Cent 81:1034-7, 1057-61 Ag 19-26 '64
Vere Papa mortuus est. por Time 81:46 Je 14 '63
Wit of Pope John XXIII; excerpts from Pope laughs. Horizon 6:112-13 Autumn '64

JOHN Big Tree, Seneca chief
Indian-head nickel: some words with himself. A. Glaser. il por(cover) Esquire 61:58+ Mr '64

JOHN, Sister Helen James. See Helen James John, Sister

JOHN Nepomucene Neumann, Blessed. See Neumann, J. N.

JOHN, E. Roy, and others
Signal analysis of evoked potentials recorded from cats during conditioning. bibliog Science 141:429-31 Ag 2 '63

JOHN, Erwin E.
Flyin-n-fishin weather in Minnesota. Flying 74:33 Je '64

JOHN, Otto
Return of the scoundrel. Newsweek 62:49 S 30 '63

JOHN, Gospel of. See Bible—New Testament—John

JOHN Barrow Rosedale, actor's actor; story. See O'Hara, J.

JOHN Birch society
Bark of the Birch. il Newsweek 62:34-5 N 4 '63
Birch policemen. Commonweal 81:404 D 18 '64
Birch society adopts new guise. Christian Cent 81:5 Ja 1 '64
Birch view of JFK. Newsweek 63:29-30 F 24 '64
Birchbark curtain; John Birch society bulletin urging protest against U.N. television specials. R. L. Shayon. Sat R 47:29 O 3 '64
Birchers denied access to Massachusetts library; Brockton public library. Library J 88:2462 Je 15 '63
Blue book on the index? America 111:246 S 12 '64
Books and banners; case of censoring Dictionary of American slang in California. J. A. King. Sat R 46:28-9+ N 9 '63
Cardinal re-endorses Birch society. Christian Cent 81:596 My 6 '64
Cell 772, or Life among the extremists. W. Morris. Commentary 38:31-9 O '64
Christmas story; UNICEF Christmas cards and the John Birch society in California. Newsweek 64:30 D 21 '64
Conspiracy on the right. New Repub 151:3-4 N 28 '64
Exploiters of grief. Newsweek 62:16-17 D 30 '63
Friends of Lee Oswald, inc. Nat R 16:183-5 Mr 10 '64
Goldwater and the John Birch society. W. F. Buckley, jr. Nat R 15:430 N 19 '63
How it might have been: a hypothetical Times editorial. Nat R 15:557 D 31 '63
John Birch society: anatomy of a protest, by J. A. Broyles. Review
Christian Cent 81:806 Je 17 '64. M. Polner
John Birch society operates fleet of bookmobiles. Library J 88:3566+ O 1 '63
Monterey fair. R. Fariña. Mlle 58:188+ Mr '64
On the far right. Commonweal 79:384 D 27 '63
Pleasantville's unpleasantness. il Time 83:44 Mr 20 '64
Police Birchites: the blue blacklash. P. Hoffman. il Nation 199:425+ D 7 '64
Rampant right invades the GOP. T. G. Harris. il Look 27:19-25 Jl 16 '63
Real poop; concerning R. Welch's editorial on Barry Goldwater's electoral defeat. Time 84:35 D 11 '64
Report to our readers; concerning letters on Children's story. Ladies Home J 81: 15+ Ap '64
Responsibles; Council for civic responsibility vs front organizations. Nat R 16:942-4 N 3 '64
Sick, sick, sick. K. Crawford. Newsweek 64: 32 Ag 31 '64
Strange tactics of extremism, by H. Overstreet and B. Overstreet. Review
Sat R 47:95-6 O 10 '64. R. L. Tobin
They're trying to tell us something. J. Cogley. Commonweal 78:270-1 My 31 '63
Turnabout; California Republican assembly. Newsweek 61:28 Mr 11 '63
Why I can't join the John Birch society; letter. R. G. Bacon. il Look 28:76+ N 3 '64; Discussion. 28:10+ D 15 '64

JOHN boats. See Boats and boating

JOHN Cotton Dana publicity awards
Seven libraries share top honors in John Cotton Dana awards. Library J 88:2262-3; 89:2972-4 Jl '63, Ag '64

JOHN F. Kennedy memorial library, Boston
Advisors named for Kennedy library; Venezuela pledges first foreign gift. Library J 89:1572 Ap 1 '64
American architect to be chosen for Kennedy memorial library. Library J 89:2301-2 Je 1 '64

JOHN F. Kennedy memorial library, Boston— *Continued*
Building a library; fund-raising. il Time 83:24 My 29 '64
Fund-raising goal of $6 million set for Kennedy memorial library, at Harvard university. Library J 89:210 Ja 15 '64
I. M. Pei chosen to design Kennedy library. Arch Rec 137:26 Ja '65
John F. Kennedy library exhibit: first display of tour. E. Cameron. il Wilson Lib Bul 39:63-5 S '64
JFK memorials move forward. il Arch Forum 120:9 My '64
JFK's last campaign; projected President John F. Kennedy library. il Newsweek 63:25+ Mr 9 '64
Kennedy legend. J. Star. il Look 28:19-21 Je 30 '64
Kennedy library, at Harvard university. E. Rudin. Library J 89:300 Ja 15 '64
Kennedy library fund established; would be open to all the people, at Harvard university. Library J 89:335 Ja 15 '64
Kennedy memorial library. M. McGrory. America 110:333 Mr 14 '64
Pei selected as architect for Kennedy memorial library. Library J 90:214-15 Ja 15 '65
Stalling on the arts; plans for John F. Kennedy library. W. Von Eckardt. New Repub 150:8 Mr 21 '64
TV and movie vignettes planned for Kennedy library; at Harvard university. Library J 89:826-7 F 15 '64
Ten thousand pennies; gift from Negro children of Prince Edward County. E. Moon. Library J 89:2297 Je 1 '64
Toward a living memorial. il Look 28:M10-16 N 17 '64

JOHN Foster Dulles international airport. See Washington, D.C.—Airports

JOHN Foster Dulles library. See Princeton university—Libraries

JOHN Hay fellows program. See John Hay Whitney foundation

JOHN Hay Whitney foundation
Year of study and reflection; the John Hay fellows program. E. Logan. il Sat R 46:73-4 N 16 '63

JOHN Henry (ballad) See Ballads, American

JOHN LaFarge institute
America house; special report. il America 111:435-42 O 17 '64
Announcing the John La Farge institute. T. N. Davis. America 110:791-3 Je 6 '64
John LaFarge institute: members of the planning committee of the institute's permanent board. il America 112:46-7 Ja 9 '65

JOHN Muir awards. See United States—Interior, Department of

JOHN MUIR NATIONAL MONUMENT (proposed) See National monuments

JOHN Muir trail. See Trails

JOHN Muir wilderness area. See Wilderness areas

JOHN PENNEKAMP CORAL REEF STATE PARK. See Florida—Parks and reserves

JOHN Secrist collection. See Phonograph records—Collectors and collecting

JOHN Sobieski runs; story. See Buechler, J.

JOHN XXIII center for eastern Christian studies
For East-West dialogue. America 108:454-5 Ap 6 '63

JOHNNY Appleseed's vision; drama. See Fisher, A. and Rabe, O.

JOHNS, Charley Eugene
Florida's sinner safari; Johns committee. E. Peter, jr. New Repub 148:13-15 Ap 27 '63

JOHNS, J. E. and Pfeiffer, E. W.
Testosterone-induced incubation patches of phalarope birds. bibliog Science 140:1225-6 Je 14 '63

JOHNS, Jasper
What is pop art? interview; ed. by G. R. Swenson. il Art N 62:43+ F '64

about

Art; exhibition at Jewish museum. M. Kozloff. Nation 198:274-6 Mr 16 '64
Artists for artists; exhibition at Allan Stone gallery. New Yorker 39:32-4 Mr 9 '63
Catcher of the eye. il por Time 84:84-7 D 4 '64
Education of Jasper Johns. F. Porter. il Art N 62:44-5+ F '64
Jasper Johns. il por Vogue 143:174-7+ F 1 '64
Jasper Johns. B. Kaufman. Commonweal 80:157-9 Ap 24 '64
Younger. il por Newsweek 63:82-3 F 24 '64

JOHN'S bargain stores corporation
Everybody's far-out bargain store. il Bsns W p 110+ My 25 '63

JOHNS Hopkins hospital. See Baltimore—Hospitals

JOHNS Hopkins press
Johns Hopkins to publish Eisenhower papers. Pub W 185:57 Ja 6 '64

JOHNS Hopkins university
Johns Hopkins digs down; Homewood library. J. H. Berthel. il Library J 89:4752-4 D 1 '64

JOHNSON, Alton C. See Miljus, R. C. jt. auth.

JOHNSON, Alvin
Alvin Johnson at 90. New Repub 151:5 D 26 '64

JOHNSON, B. B. jr
Motorized refuse collectors. Am City 79:103-4 F '64

JOHNSON, Bernard
Jazz pants age! W. Como. il pors Dance Mag 38:53-4 Mr '64

JOHNSON, Bruce, and Bowers, Blair
Transport of neurohormones from the corpora cardiaca in insects. bibliog Science 141:264-6 Jl 19 '63

JOHNSON, Budd
Jazz concerts; B. Webster and B. Johnson at Philharmonic Hall. W. Balliett. New Yorker 39:82-3 Ag 17 '63

JOHNSON, C. G.
Aerial migration of insects; with biographical sketch. Sci Am 209:30, 132-8 bibliog(p 180) D '63

JOHNSON, Carol
After Pausanias; poem. Commonweal 78:42 Ap 5 '63
Honors section; poem. Commonweal 80:292 My 29 '64
Journey through Spain; poem. Poetry 101:252 Ja '63
On ecstasy; poem. Commonweal 81:542 Ja 22 '65

JOHNSON, Cecile
Painting on a world tour. il por Am Artist 27:48-9+ Ap '63

JOHNSON, Chalmers
Again the Sorge case. N Y Times Mag p89-90+ O 11 '64
China's Manhattan project. N Y Times Mag p23+ O 25 '64

JOHNSON, Charles F.
Up from the South, and fast! por Motor B 112:78-9+ S '63

JOHNSON, Charles Van Dell
Van Johnson: back from the edge. M. Davidson and B. Davidson. por McCalls 90:86-7+ Ag '63

JOHNSON, Charles Y.
Where is science taking us? Sat R 46:59-60 Mr 2 '63

JOHNSON, Charley
Charley's job. il pors Newsweek 62:68-9 D 9 '63

JOHNSON, Charlotte Buel
Gallery for young people. See issues of School arts
Jean Dubuffet: Chemin bordé d'herbe 1901. Sch Arts 62:23 F '63
Wilhelm Lehmbruck, 1881-1919. Sch Arts 62:47 Mr '63
Yellow Christ. Sch Arts 63:22-3 D '63

JOHNSON, Cheryl
Life, death and miracles. Seventeen 22:80-1+ D '63

JOHNSON, Clarence A. and others
Neuraminidases and influenza virus infection in embryonated eggs. bibliog Science 143:1051-2 Mr 6 '64

JOHNSON, Clarence Leonard
A-11 proven in reconnaissance missions; with editorial comment. il Aviation W 80:11, 16-18 Mr '64
Collier trophy. B. Kocivar. il pors Look 28:34+ O 6 '64

JOHNSON, Claudia Alta (Taylor)
Mrs Lyndon B. Johnson's challenge to women; excerpt from address, June 24, 1964. pors Sat Eve Post 237:88-9 Je 27 '64

about

As friends tell it: LBJ talks about some campaign issues. U S News 57:59 N 16 '64
As I see our First lady. A. M. Lindbergh. por Look 28:100+ My 19 '64
At the front. Newsweek 63:14 Ja 20 '64
Down on the farm. il Newsweek 63:32 My 25 '64
First lady: a professional at getting things done. E. Janeway. il pors Ladies Home J 81:64-5+ Ap '64
First Lady Bird. il pors Time 84:20-3 Ag 28 '64
First lady on the move; schedule stirs memories of Eleanor Roosevelt. il pors U S News 56:16 Ja 27 '64
Getting over the tourist feeling. il por Time 82:15 D 27 '63
Her interest is people. K. Louchheim. il por Ladies Home J 81:56-7+ Mr '64

JOHNSON, Claudia Alta (Taylor)—about—*Cont.*
Lady Bird Johnson: the new First lady. il por U S News 55:16 D 2 '63
Lady Bird special: how many votes did it switch? il pors U S News 57:22 O 19 '64
Lady Bird's bandwagon. il por Newsweek 64:30-1 O 19 '64
Latest on the Johnson fortune. il U S News 56:38 Je 22 '64
Life on the ranch: a day at home with LBJ. J. P. Sutherland. il U S News 56:67-8 Ap 13 '64
LBJ's LBJ. First lady of the land. il pors Newsweek 64:11-14 D 28 '64
Lyndon Johnson's Lady Bird. B. Clark. por Read Digest 83:108-13 N '63
Mrs Johnson to participate in Campobello Park ceremonies. Dept State Bul 51:312 Ag 31 '64
More on the Johnson fortune: Lady Bird's pine lands and her tenants. il por U S News 56: 43-5 My 4 '64
Multimillionaire. il Time 84:15-16 Ag 21 '64
New First lady. por Time 82:33 N 29 '63
New political issue: Mrs LBJ's property. U S News 56:12 My 25 '64
Norman Rockwell paints from the life of Lady Bird Johnson. N. Rockwell. il pors McCalls 92:102-3 N '64
Our new First lady. N. Robertson. il pors Sat Eve Post 237:20-5 F 8 '64
Our very busy First lady. C. Sadler. il por McCalls 91:79-81+ Mr '64
People are talking about: the First lady. por Vogue 143:146-7 My '64
Perle Mesta's party notebook: a belated birthday luncheon for Lady Bird Johnson. P. Mesta. il por McCalls 90:134+ My '63
Powerful persuaders; Lady Bird's trip through the South. H. Fuller. New Repub 151:11-12 O 24 '64
Public servant without pay: the First lady. M. Hunter. il pors N Y Times Mag p 10+ D 15 '63
So glad, so glad; first official trip outside Washington. il por Time 83:24-5 Ap 3 '64
Story of the Johnson family fortune. il pors U S News 55:75 D 16 '63; 56:38-42 My 4 '64
Three other LBJ's. il por Newsweek 62:26+ D 9 '63
What kind of woman is our new First lady? R. Montgomery. por Good H 158:32+ Mr '64
Zest and sanity from Lady Bird; concerning address at Radcliffe. Life 57:4 Jl 10 '64

JOHNSON, Clyde Edwin, and Davis, J. S.
Test your political beliefs. Nations Bsns 52: 34-5+ S '64

JOHNSON, D. Gale
Soviet agriculture. Bul Atomic Sci 20:8-12 Ja; 35-6 Je '64

JOHNSON, David B.
Academic poker game. Sat R 46:70-1 Je 15 '63

JOHNSON, David F. and others
Cholesterol in higher plants. bibliog Science 140:198-9 Ap 12 '63

JOHNSON, Don H.
Let the computer tabulate your traffic counts. Am City 78:135 Mr '63

JOHNSON, Donald E.
Goal of the American legion; address, September 24, 1964. Vital Speeches 31:48-50 N 1 '64
Red China and Russia; their position in the U.N; address, November 18, 1964. Vital Speeches 31:141-3 D 15 '64

JOHNSON, Dorothy
Miss Universe: beauty from around world. il pors Ebony 19:102-4+ O '64

JOHNSON, Douglas William
Corrupt society. F. J. Cook. Nation 196:455 Je 1 '63

JOHNSON, E. Harper
Africa's golden past. il pors Ebony 19:28-30+ O '64
—See Hansberry, W. L. jt. auth.

JOHNSON, Ed
Mutual benefit. por Recreation 57:188-9 Ap '64

JOHNSON, Electa. See Johnson, I. jt. auth.

JOHNSON, Elle
Never too busy. R. Clark. il pors Dance Mag 37:16-17 Ap '63

JOHNSON, Eric W.
Will he be a leader? Parents Mag 38:52-3+ My '63

JOHNSON, Eugene
Way through the web. por(p3242) Library J 89:3246-8 S 15 '64

JOHNSON, Frances Kennon
School libraries. See issues of Wilson library bulletin
—and Bomar, C. P.
Planning school library quarters. ALA Bul 58:103 pors(p 104) F '64

JOHNSON, Frank Minis, 1918-
Judges; a Lincoln man. por Time 83:76 F 21 '64

JOHNSON, Fridolf
Artists' Christmas cards. Am Artist 27:44-8+ N '63
Can you read your own writing? Am Artist 27:50-5+ S '63
George Giusti, graphic designer. Am Artist 28:46-51+ D '64
Hermann Zapf's letters. Am Artist 28:42-7+ O '64
How to prepare a professional portfolio. Am Artist 28:36+ Je '64
Samuel Chamberlain. Am Artist 29:28-33+ F '65
Sir Francis Meynell and the Nonesuch press. Am Artist 28:38-43+ F '64

JOHNSON, G. Griffith
Climate of world trade and U.S.-Canadian trade relations; address, September 15, 1963. Dept State Bul 49:543-8 O 7 '63
Cotton textile agreements concluded with Greece and Turkey; with texts of U.S. notes, July 17, 1964. Dept State Bul 51:291-4 Ag 24 '64
Foreign policy and the regulation of international shipping; statement, August 11, 1964. Dept State Bul 51:314-17 Ag 31 '64
International aviation policy of the United States; address, September 10, 1963. Dept State Bul 49:508-13 S 30 '63
International economic cooperation; address, October 21, 1964. Vital Speeches 31:67-71 N 15 '64; Same with title Progress and prospects in international economic cooperation. bibliog f Dept State Bul 51:708-14 N 16 '64
Perspective on the United Nations conference on trade and development; address, February 21, 1964. Dept State Bul 50:410-15 Mr 16 '64
Western Europe and the American balance of payments; address, April 6, 1963. Ann Am Acad 348:110-20 Jl '63

JOHNSON, Geoffrey
All souls night; poem. Cath World 200:94 N '64

JOHNSON, Georgia Douglas
Nor white nor black; poem. Negro Hist Bul 28:54 D '64

JOHNSON, Gerald W.
Anatomy of quackery. New Repub 151:25-6 S 5 '64
Art of being free. Atlan 213:60-4 Ja '64
Crime and punishment. New Repub 148:26+ Je 22 '63
Enemies of radical nonsense. New Repub 151: 27-8 O 17 '64
Epidemic of gooseflesh. Atlan 212:43-6 D '63
Horror-story from Kentucky. New Repub 148:22 Jl 20 '63
Inert Senate. Atlan 214:89-91 S '64
Judgment in Mississippi. New Repub 151: 13-14 D 26 '64
King in spite of his mother: Edward VII. Atlan 213:58-61 Je '64
Let's talk about politics. New Repub 150:17-18+ Mr 14 '64
Live and let live; excerpts from Hodcarrie. Atlan 213:90-2+ F '64
Once touched by romance. New Repub 149: 15 D 7 '63
Ordeals of the President. New Repub 151:21 O 24 '64
President and his power. New Repub 151:19-20 N 28 '64
Reviving the two-party system. New Repub 152:20 Ja 2 '65
Robert Oppenheimer. New Repub 148:9-10 Ap 20 '63
Shriver the dynamo. New Repub 151:30-1 Jl 25 '64
Soak the writers! New Repub 148:5-6 Mr 9 '63
Triple revolution. New Repub 150:38-9 Ap 11 '64
Will you join the dance? New Repub 148:7 My 4 '63
William S. White's best man. New Repub 150:25 Je 13 '64

JOHNSON, Greer
Do-it-yourself program is best. Am City 78: 103-4 Mr '63

JOHNSON, Gus
Big days in the pea capital. T. C. Brody. Sports Illus 18:50-2 F 18 '63
Touch and a tooth of gold. M. Kram. il por Sports Illus 21:60-3 D 21 '64

JOHNSON, Harold Keith
Three top soldiers. por Time 84:16 Jl 3 '64

JOHNSON, Harry J.
Performance and the tired businessman. Duns R 85:45-6+ Ja '65

JOHNSON, Horton A.
Redundancy and biological aging. bibliog Science 141:910-12 S 6 '63

JOHNSON, Howard M.
Human blood group A_1 specific agglutinin of the butter clam saxidomus giganteus. bibliog Science 146:548-9 O 23 '64
JOHNSON, Hubert A.
Trustee's role. ALA Bul 57:631-3 Jl '63
JOHNSON, Hugh
Corkscrew. House & Gard 124:168+ S '63; 125: 172+ Mr; 154+ Ap; 126:120+ Ag '64
Lesser wines of Europe. House & Gard 124: 168+ S '63
Wines for snobs, friends, and young girls. Vogue 142:137+ D '63
JOHNSON, Hugh A.
(ed) See Cox, C. I survived tetanus
JOHNSON, Irving, and Johnson, Electa
Inside Europe aboard Yankee. pors Nat Geog Mag 126:157-95 Ag '64
JOHNSON, J. Richard
Precise measurement of radio frequencies. Electr World 72:47-50 Ag '64
JOHNSON, Jack
Black champion, by F. Farr. Review
Nation 198:660-1 Je 29 '64. W. Ward
Newsweek por 63:95 My 4 '64
Jeff, it's up to you! excerpts from Black champion; with editorial comment. F. Farr. il por Am Heritage 15:64-77 F '64
JOHNSON, James P.
Jazz records. W. Balliett. New Yorker 39: 154-6+ My 11 '63
JOHNSON, James T. jr. See Hayman, J. L. jr. jt. auth.
JOHNSON, James W.
Dispossessed sandhill cranes. Audubon Mag 65:212-17 Jl '63
JOHNSON, Jerry W.
Trends in municipal finance. Am City 79: 114-15 Ap '64
JOHNSON, John A. See Fleming, J. R. jt. auth.
JOHNSON, John Henry
Kiss the guy or tackle him? M. Cope. il por Sat Eve Post 236:76-7 O 26 '63
JOHNSON, John J.
Brazil in quandary. Cur Hist 48:9-15+ Ja '65
New armies take over in Latin America. N Y Times Mag p 14+ Mr 8 '64
New Latin American nationalism. Yale R 54:187-204 D '64
Potential in Brazil. Cur Hist 46:1-7 Ja '64
JOHNSON, Joseph E.
Reconciler resigns. Christian Cent 80:229 F 20 '63
JOHNSON, Jotham
Re-uses of the past. Horizon 6:4-15 Autumn '64
JOHNSON, Julian
Bel canto in brass. Opera N 29:6-7 D 12 '64
JOHNSON, Karl
Casualties in a jungle war. il por Time 82:48+ Jl 19 '63
JOHNSON, Lady Bird. See Johnson, C. A. T.
JOHNSON, Laverne C. and Corah, N. L.
Racial differences in skin resistance. bibliog Science 139:766-7 F 22 '63
JOHNSON, Leighton H.
Education of Hyman Rickover. Sch & Soc 92: 203-4 My 2 '64
JOHNSON, Leroy R.
Georgia's Negro senator. L. Bennett, jr. il pors Ebony 18:25-8+ Mr '63
JOHNSON, Lester
Lester Johnson on the Bowery. L. Campbell. il por Art N 62:46-7+ F '64
JOHNSON, Lionel
Temperature regime of deep lakes. bibliog Science 144:1336-7 Je 12 '64
JOHNSON, Louis
Louis Johnson and the Calvin White singers at 92nd street Y. D. Hering. Dance Mag 37:64 My '63
JOHNSON, Lucetta
Uncle Tom's Canadian cabin. Hobbies 68:124-5 S '63
JOHNSON, Lucy Baines
I'm blue-eyed in a brown-eyed family; ed. by B. Wise. pors Life 56:94-5 My 15 '64

about

In the spotlight, too: the Johnson daughters. il por U S News 56:20 My 11 '64
Luci B. Johnson talks about her life; ed. by H. Thomas. pors Seventeen 23:124-7+ S '64
Now it's teen-age time at the White House. por U S News 56:14 F 3 '64
She looked him in the eye and said, blood. G. P. Hunt. il por Life 56:3 My 15 '64
Suddenly it's teensville on Pennsylvania avenue; with photographs by Stan Wayman. Life 56:90-5 My 15 '64
Teen-age party in the White House. il pors Look 28:22-3 Mr 10 '64
Texas team makes its musical bow; Luci Baines Johnson and Van Cliburn. il pors Life 57:53-4+ Ag 7 '64
JOHNSON, Lynda Bird
If Lynda Bird marries a Roman Catholic. il por U S News 56:14 F 3 '64
In the spotlight, too: the Johnson daughters. il por U S News 56:20 My 11 '64
Lynda Bird shows the Johnson touch in Hawaii. il pors Life 56:42-42A Je 26 '64
Now it's teen-age time at the White House. por U S News 56:14 F 3 '64
JOHNSON, Lyndon Baines
Advancing the frontiers of human knowledge for the benefit of all mankind; remarks, January 18, 1964. Dept State Bul 50:150-2 F 3 '64; Excerpts. Nat Geog Mag 125:668-79 My '64
Alliance for progress; address, May 11, 1964 Vital Speeches 30:482-3 Je 1 '64
Alliance for progress marks second anniversary; statement, August 20, 1963. Dept State Bul 49:401-3 S 9 '63
Alsop interviews L.B.J. ed. by S. Alsop. Sat Eve Post 236:80 D 14 '63
American civilization: excerpts from address. Time 83:18 My 29 '64
American education week message from the White House. Sr Schol 85:1T N 4 '64
American way of life; as Lyndon Johnson sees it; interview. pors U S News 55:112-14 D 9 '63
America's efforts toward world order; address, August 12, 1964. Dept State Bul 51:298-301 Ag 31 '64; Same with title Restraint and law. Vital Speeches 30:674-5 S 1 '64
Atlantic community: common hopes and objectives; address, December 3, 1964. Dept State Bul 51:866-9 D 21 '64
Balance of payments, trade expansion, development assistance; excerpts from economics report. Dept State Bul 50:222-3 F 10 '64
Blueprint for the great society; excerpt from address, May 22, 1964. por Am For 70:33 Jl '64
British Prime Minister visits Washington; exchange of greetings, December 7, 1964. Dept State Bul 51:902 D 28 '64
Building a great world society; address, June 10, 1964. Dept State Bul 50:990-2 Je 29 '64; Excerpts. Sci N L 86:7 Jl 4 '64
Business pulse of the Nation; summary of Economic report. Newsweek 63:65-8 Ja 27 '64
Canadian Prime Minister visits Washington; U.S. and Canada agree on Columbia River development and establishment of Campobello Park; joint communique; with joint statements and texts of agreements, January 21-23, 1964. Dept State Bul 50:199-206 F 10 '64
Candidates spell out the issues. por N Y Times Mag p23+ N 1 '64
Century of the educated man; address, June 9, 1963. Vital Speeches 29:653-5 Ag 15 '63
Ceremony at Mexican border marks settlement of Chamizal dispute; address, September 25, 1964. Dept State Bul 51:545-9 O 19 '64
Challenge of education. Sr Schol 85:4 Ja 21 '65
Challenge of success; address, October 12, 1963. Vital Speeches 30:36-7 N 1 '63
Charter day ceremonies, UCLA; remarks, February 21, 1964. Dept State Bul 50:399-400 Mr 16 '64
Chinese Communists conduct nuclear test; statement, October 16, 1964. Dept State Bul 51:612 N 2 '64
Committee to study economic impact of defense and disarmament; White House announcement, with text of memorandum, December 21, 1963. Dept State Bul 50: 120 Ja 27 '64
Conference on peaceful uses of atomic energy opens at Geneva; remarks, August 30, 1964. Dept State Bul 51:411-12 S 21 '64
Dedication of George C. Marshall research library; remarks, May 23, 1964. Dept State Bul 50:922-4 Je 15 '64
Desire for beauty, the hunger for community: building the Great society; excerpt from address, May 22, 1964. New Repub 151:32 N 7 '64
Direction and control of nuclear power; address, September 16, 1964. Dept State Bul 51:458-60 O 5 '64
Economic goals: view from the White House; address, November 19, 1964. Sat R 48:28-30 Ja 9 '65
Eulogy to John F. Kennedy, November 23, 1963. Vital Speeches 30:98 D 1 '63

JOHNSON, Lyndon Baines—*Continued*
Exclusive interview with the President of the United States; ed. by J. P. Sutherland. por U S News 57:46-7 N 16 '64
Export expansion and balance of payments; remarks, April 7, 1964. Dept State Bul 50:663-4 Ap 27 '64
Foreign aid; message to Congress, March 19, 1964. Dept State Bul 50:518-22 Ap 6 '64
Four principles of American foreign policy; remarks, September 23, 1964. Dept State Bul 51:543-4 O 19 '64
Friendly flight to northern Europe. pors Nat Geog Mag 125:268-93 F '64
General Pulaski's memorial day, 1964; proclamation, August 15, 1964. Dept State Bul 51:354 S 7 '64
Great society. pors Sat Eve Post 237:30-1 O 31 '64
Guest editorial by the President of the United States. Parents Mag 39:54 S '64
Here are Johnson's promises for a Great society; State-of-the-Union message, January 4, 1965. por U S News 58:98-102 Ja 18 65; Same. Vital Speeches 31:194-8 Ja 15 '65; Summary. Newsweek 65:18 Ja 18 '65
Hope for reasoned agreement; remarks, March 24, 1964. Dept State Bul 50:576-7 Ap 13 '64
Hopefulness of these times; remarks, December 18, 1964. Dept State Bul 52:41 Ja 11 '65
How LBJ views the world situation now; excerpts from address, February 21, 1964. por U S News 56:13 Mr 2 '64
I do not agree; summary of address to Community action assembly. Time 84:21-2 D 18 '64
In memory of President Kennedy; address, December 22, 1963. Vital Speeches 30:162 Ja 1 '64
Is government too big? what Ike and LBJ say; excerpts from address, June 8, 1964. U S News 56:15 Je 22 '64
Johnson: I intend to submit new proposals to slow arms race; excerpts from address, October 21, 1964. U S News 57:97-8 N 2 '64
Johnson on U.S. problems abroad; excerpts from address, February 11, 1964. por U S News 56:41 F 24 '64
Johnson reply to Khrushchev message, January 18, 1964. Cur Hist 46:362-3 Je '64
Johnson: three goals prosperity, justice, peace; address, September 7, 1964. por U S News 57:115-16 S 21 '64; Same with title Wants of the people. Vital Speeches 30:742-3 O 1 '64
Johnson's economics; quotations from statements on major economic issues. por Bsns W p47-8+ O 31 '64
Keeping and strengthening the peace; address, December 17, 1963. Dept State Bul 50:2-4 Ja 6 '64
Letter to NATO Secretary General, October 1, 1964. Dept State Bul 51:673 N 9 '64
Lighter mood hits Washington; quotations. por U S News 56:47-8 My 11 '64
Lighting of the national Christmas tree; remarks, December 22, 1963. Dept State Bul 50:38-9 Ja 13 '64
Local community and world affairs; remarks, April 21, 1964. Dept State Bul 50:746-9 My 11 '64
LBJ's campaign opener: we offer a choice; address, August 27, 1964. pors U S News 57:66-9 S 7 '64; Same with title Democratic national convention. Vital Speeches 30:708-10 S 15 '64
Lyndon Johnson talks about Congress and the presidency; excerpts from interview. por U S News 56:25 Ja 6 '64
Message from the President; letter to ALA conference. ALA Bul 58:609 Jl '64
Message from the President. Seventeen 23: 110-11 S '64
Mr Johnson defines his political creed; excerpts from statements. U S News 55:114 D 9 '63
Moment of history; address. por America 111: 62-3 Jl 18 '64
National security and world responsibilities; address, June 3, 1964. Dept State Bul 50: 950-2 Je 22 '64
New NATO Secretary General assured of U.S. support; letter, August 1, 1964. Dept State Bul 51:275 Ag 24 '64
19th anniversary of United Nations; remarks, October 23, 1964. Dept State Bul 51:697 N 16 '64
North Atlantic council holds ministerial meeting; message, December 16, 1963. Dept State Bul 50:29-30 Ja 6 '64
NATO, a growing partnership; remarks, April 3, 1964. Dept State Bul 50:606-8 Ap 20 '64
Our system of government; address, November 28, 1963. Vital Speeches 30:131-2 D 15 '63
Our world policy; address, April 20, 1964. Vital Speeches 30:418-22 My 1 '64; Same with title America as a great power. Dept State Bul 50:726-32 My 11 '64; Excerpt. Cur Hist 47:47 Jl '64
Partnership in public service; excerpts from address, August 1963. Am City 79:7 Ja '64
Peaceful revolution; address, December 17, 1963. Vital Speeches 30:162-4 Ja 1 '64; Same. U N Rev 11:11-12 Ja '64; Excerpts. Nat R 15:554-5 D 31 '63
Philosophy of President Lyndon B. Johnson; excerpts from interview. por U S News 55:41 D 2 '63
Pledge to freedom renewed on 20th anniversary of D-day; remarks, June 3, 1964. Dept State Bul 50:954 Je 22 '64
Politics of the space age; excerpt from Space: its impact on man and society, ed. by L. Levy. por Sat Eve Post 237:22-3 F 29 '64
President and Chancellor Erhard reaffirm commitment to U.S.-German cooperation within free-world community; joint communique, December 29, 1963; with exchanges of remarks, December 28 and December 29, 1963 Dept State Bul 50:74-80 Ja 20 '64
President and Congress: Mr Johnson's first message; address, November 27, 1963. por U S News 55:102-3 D 9 '63; Same. Vital Speeches 30:130-1 D 15 '63; Dept State Bul 49:910-12 D 16 '63; Cong Digest 43:1-2 Ja '64; Excerpts. Newsweek 62:22 D 9 '63; Summary. Bsns W p23-4 N 30 '63
President appoints committee to review foreign aid programs; statement, December 26, 1963. Dept State Bul 50:128-9 Ja 27 '64
President approves bill for study of sea-level canal site; statement, September 24, 1964. Dept State Bul 51:554 O 19 '64
President calls for increase in Peace corps; statement, November 2, 1964. Dept State Bul 51:735-6 N 23 '64
President congratulates Malta on independence; letter, September 18, 1964. Dept State Bul 51:503 O 12 '64
President de Valera of Ireland visits United States; arrival remarks, and toast, May 27, 1964. Dept State Bul 50:927-9 Je 15 '64
President disapproves legislation on import marking requirements; memorandum of disapproval, December 31, 1963. Dept State Bul 50:129 Ja 27 '64
President-elect of Mexico visits President Johnson at LBJ ranch; remarks, November 12, 1964. Dept State Bul 51:805-6 D 7 '64
President expresses grief at death of Prime Minister Nehru; letter, May 27, 1964. Dept State Bul 50:926 Je 15 '64
President greets Public advisory committee for trade negotiations; remarks, April 21, 1964. Dept State Bul 50:749-50 My 11 '64
President hails first anniversary of nuclear test ban treaty; statement, July 30, 1964. Dept State Bul 51:228 Ag 17 '64
President Johnson calls upon Soviet Union for concrete actions to promote peace; letter, January 18, 1964. Dept State Bul 50: 157-8 F 3 '64
President Johnson commissions U.S.S. Sam Rayburn; remarks, December 2, 1964. Dept State Bul 51:877 D 21 '64
President Johnson dedicates the Society's new headquarters; with excerpts from addresses. pors Nat Geog Mag 125:668-79 My '64
President Johnson discusses the presidency; television interview, March 14, 1964. Dept State Bul 50:523-9 Ap 6 '64
President Johnson lauds conservation Congress; excerpts from address. Am For 70:13 N '64
President Johnson meets with NATO Secretary General; exchange of toasts at luncheon and remarks on departing from Offutt air force base, September 29, 1964. Dept State Bul 51:582-5 O 26 '64
President Johnson pledges redoubled efforts to Alliance for progress; remarks, May 11, 1964. Dept State Bul 50:854-7 Je 1 '64
President Johnson proclaims 1965 as International cooperation year; remarks at White House ceremonies, October 2, 1964; with text of proclamation. Dept State Bul 51:555-7 O 19 '64
President Johnson reasserts U.S. support for IAEA; statement, December 8, 1963. Dept State Bul 49:1019 D 30 '63
President Johnson receives chiefs of diplomatic missions; remarks, December 13, 1963. Dept State Bul 49:996 D 30 '63

JOHNSON, Lyndon Baines—*Continued*
President Johnson sends message to nonalined nations conference. Dept State Bul 51:581-2 O 26 '64
President Johnson signs amended, expanded NDEA; excerpts from address, October 16, 1964. Library J 89:4990 D 15 '64
President Johnson speaks out on education; special statement for the National education association. por NEA J 53:12-14 Ja '64
President Johnson to General Gursel; letter, December 26, 1963. Dept State Bul 50:90 Ja 20 '64
President Johnson to President Goulart; letter, December 18, 1963. Dept State Bul 50:47-8 Ja 13 '64
President Johnson to Prime Minister Moro; letter, December 9, 1963. Dept State Bul 50:47 Ja 13 '64
President Johnson to Soviet leaders; letter, January 1, 1964. Dept State Bul 50:121 Ja 27 '64
President Johnson urges Congress to increase U.S. aid to Viet-Nam; message to Congress, May 18, 1964. Dept State Bul 50:891-3 Je 8 '64
President Johnson urges disarmament conference to take further steps toward peace; remarks and message, January 21, 1964. bibliog f Dept State Bul 50:223-5 F 10 '64
President Johnson urges full appropriations for foreign aid; statement, December 14, 1963. Dept State Bul 49:999 D 30 '63
President Johnson urges new immigration legislation; remarks, January 13, 1964. Dept State Bul 50:211-12 F 10 '64
President Johnson welcomes NATO Parliamentarians; remarks, September 18, 1964. Dept State Bul 51:478 O 5 '64
President Macapagal of Philippines visits United States; greeting and toast. Dept State Bul 51:628-34 N 2 '64
President meets with Cabinet; reviews world situation; statement, October 20, 1964. Dept State Bul 51:653 N 9 '64
President meets with consultants on foreign affairs; statement, October 21, 1964. Dept State Bul 51:663 N 9 '64
President names new ambassador to Saigon, reiterates U.S. policy; statement, June 23, 1964. Dept State Bul 51:46-7 Jl 13 '64
President names panel of citizens as consultants on world problems; statement, September 9, 1964. Dept State Bul 51:441 S 28 '64
President of Malagasy Republic visits Washington; exchange of greetings, July 27, 1964. Dept State Bul 51:229 Ag 17 '64
President outlines basic themes of U.S. policy in southeast Asia; statement, June 2, 1964. Dept State Bul 50:953 Je 22 '64
President outlines Latin American policy in letter to Mr Mann. Dept State Bul 50:9-10 Ja 6 '64
President outlines position on balance of payments and trade; statements, October 24 and October 28, 1964. Dept State Bul 51:751-2 N 23 '64
President pledges continuing support to Republic of Viet-Nam; message, December 31, 1963. Dept State Bul 50:121-2 Ja 27 '64
President praises Immigration and naturalization service; statement, January 17, 1964. Dept State Bul 50:212 F 10 '64
President praises OAS action condemning Cuban aggression; statement, July 30, 1964. Dept State Bul 51:184 Ag 10 '64
President reaffirms pledge to Latin America; address, November 26, 1963. Dept State Bul 49:912-13 D 16 '63
President reaffirms U.S. support for Alliance for progress; statement, November 13, 1964. Dept State Bul 51:804 D 7 '64
President reports on operation of foreign assistance program; letter, October 3, 1964. Dept State Bul 51:675-7 N 9 '64
President reports on operation of trade agreements program, September 23, 1964. Dept State Bul 51:516-17 O 12 '64
President requests increased appropriation for Peace corps; letter, January 16, 1964. Dept State Bul 50:198 F 10 '64
President restates U.S. position on Panama and Canal Zone; statement, January 23, 1964. Dept State Bul 50:195-6 F 10 '64
President signs bill extending Food for peace program; statement, October 8, 1964. Dept State Bul 51:677-8 N 9 '64
President signs congressional resolution on southeast Asia; remarks, August 10, 1964. Dept State Bul 51:302-3 Ag 31 '64
President signs Cuban claims bill; asks study of vesting provision; statement, October 17, 1964. Dept State Bul 51:674-5 N 9 '64
President signs International development association bill; remarks, May 26, 1964. Dept State Bul 50:935 Je 15 '64
President signs $135 million library bill; excerpts from statement, February 11, 1964. Library J 89:1046 Mr 1 '64; Same. ALA Bul 58:172-3 Mr '64
President speaks to American field service students; remarks, July 20, 1964. Dept State Bul 51:189 Ag 10 '64
President supports bill to impose interest equalization tax; letter to Representative W. Mills, February 25, 1964. Dept State Bul 50:464 Mr 23 '64
President's message on education; excerpts. Wilson Lib Bul 39:440+ F '65
Prime Minister of Malaysia visits Washington; exchange of greetings and toasts, July 22, 1964. Dept State Bul 51:190-1 Ag 10 '64
Principles of defense management; excerpts from message to Congress, January 18, 1965. Aviation W 82:17 Ja 25 '65; Miss & Roc 16:11 Ja 25 '65
Proclamation, November 23, 1963. Dept State Bul 49:882 D 9 '63
Prosperity has continued unbroken; excerpts from address, October 16, 1964. U S News 57:98 N 2 '64
Quotable Mr President; excerpts from addresses; ed. by J. Prokop. por Am For 70:8+ Ja '64
Radio free Europe; remarks, December 2, 1964. Dept State Bul 51:876-7 D 21 '64
Ranger VII; briefing for Johnson brings out high level chit chat on various aspects of space. Science 145:563-5 Ag 7 '64
Ranger VII photographs of moon sent to leaders of 110 nations; statement, August 16, 1964. Dept State Bul 51:348 S 7 '64
Remarks at Great Falls, Vancouver, and Peace Arch ceremonies, September 16, 1964. Dept State Bul 51:504-9 O 12 '64
Remarks at Mexican fiesta, February 22, 1964. Dept State Bul 50:401-3 Mr 16 '64
Report released on program to develop desalination; statement, October 25, 1964. Dept State Bul 51:723-4 N 16 '64
Russia, China and England; our basic policy remains unchanged; address, October 18, 1964. Vital Speeches 31:34-6 N 1 '64; Same with title President reports on change in Soviet leadership, Chinese nuclear test, and new British government. Dept State Bul 51:610-14 N 2 '64
School aid: what LBJ and Goldwater believe; excerpt from statement. U S News 57:15 S 28 '64
Science, a force for peace; remarks, February 6, 1964. Dept State Bul 50:285-7 F 24 '64
Signing of communications satellite agreements hailed by the President; statement, August 20, 1964. Dept State Bul 51:348 S 7 '64
Single goal of peace; excerpts from address, June 28, 1964. Dept State Bul 51:79-81 Jl 20 '64
State of the Union; address, January 8, 1964. Dept State Bul 50:110-11 Ja 27 '64; Same. U S News 56:66-9 Ja 20 '64; Vital Speeches 30:194-7 Ja 15 '64; Cur Hist 46:176-8+ Mr '64
Statements on education by the Democratic and Republican presidential candidates. por NEA J 53:12-13 O '64
Tax-reduction bill; address. Vital Speeches 30:322-3 Mr 15 '64
Text of President's A-11 statements. Aviation W 81:17 Ag 3 '64
Third anniversary of the Alliance for progress; address, March 16, 1964. Dept State Bul 50:535-8 Ap 6 '64
U.N. Secretary-General U Thant visits Washington; greeting, August 6, 1964. Dept State Bul 51:303-4 Ag 31 '64
U.N. Security council adopts resolution on Cyprus; remarks, March 4, 1964. Dept State Bul 50:465 Mr 23 '64
U.S. and Brazil reaffirm commitment to peace; letter to President Castelo Branco, August 25, 1964. Dept State Bul 51:436 S 28 '64
U.S. and Canada, and Japan resume fisheries talks at Ottawa; statement, September 4, 1964. Dept State Bul 51:441-2 S 28 '64
U.S. and Israel exchange views on matters of mutual interest; exchange of greetings, with joint communique, June 2, 1964. Dept State Bul 50:958-60 Je 22 '64
U.S. and Japan inaugurate television link via Syncom III; statement, October 7, 1964. Dept State Bul 51:591-2 O 26 '64

JOHNSON, Lyndon Baines—*Continued*
United States and NATO members sign new agreement for cooperation in exchange of atomic information; message to Congress, June 30, 1964. Dept State Bul 51:93 Jl 20 '64
United States and Panama reestablish diplomatic relations; statement, April 3, 1964. Dept State Bul 50:655-6 Ap 27 '64
United States and Soviet Union sign consular convention; statement, May 27, 1964. Dept State Bul 50:979 Je 22 '64
United States and U.S.S.R. agree to cooperate in weather matters; White House announcement, with letter to Secretary Hodges, October 23, 1964. Dept State Bul 51:791-4 N 30 '64
U.S. economic problems; address, December 2, 1964. Vital Speeches 31:130-2 D 15 '64; Excerpts. U S News 57:92-3 D 14 '64
USIA foreign service officers to become part of FSO corps; statement, October 3, 1964. Dept State Bul 51:663 N 9 '64
United States international aviation month, 1964; proclamation, July 28, 1964. Dept State Bul 51:314 Ag 31 '64
U.S. joins in independence ceremonies in Zambia; message, October 26, 1964. Dept State Bul 51:722-3 N 16 '64
U.S. letter on Cyprus, March 4, 1964. Dept State Bul 50:446 Mr 23 '64
U.S. marks final day of mourning for President Kennedy. Dept State Bul 50:39 Ja 13 '64
U.S. participation in the U.N. during 1963; message to Congress, August 20, 1964. bibliog f Dept State Bul 51:349-50 S 7 '64
U.S. plans new sea-level canal and new treaty on existing canal; statement, December 18, 1964. Dept State Bul 52:5-6 Ja 4 '65
U.S. prepared to review differences with Panama; statement, March 21, 1964. Dept State Bul 50:538-9 Ap 6 '64
United States ratifies Chamizal convention; remarks, December 20, 1963. Dept State Bul 50:49 Ja 13 '64
U.S. reaffirms its commitment to the Atlantic community; statement, November 28, 1964. Dept State Bul 51:846-7 D 14 '64
U.S. reports on success of Alliance for progress; remarks, October 27, 1964. Dept State Bul 51:705-6 N 16 '64
U.S. sends message to conference of African leaders at Cairo; message, July 17, 1964. Dept State Bul 51:147 Ag 3 '64
United States supports economic cooperation in Africa; message, February 19, 1964. Dept State Bul 50:509 Mr 30 '64
United States takes measures to repel attack against U.S. forces in southeast Asia; statement, addresses and message to Congress, August 3-5, 1964. Dept State Bul 51:259-63 Ag 24 '64
Unity of the American people; excerpts from address, September 17, 1964. Dept State Bul 51:461-2 O 5 '64
Urban program of President Johnson; excerpts from address, January 1964. Am City 79:154+ Mr '64
Vice President Johnson visits Benelux countries; statement, November 4, and addresses, November 7 and 8, 1963. Dept State Bul 49:850-4 D 2 '63
Vice President Johnson visits northern Europe; addresses, September 4-16, 1963. Dept State Bul 49:583-94 O 14 '63
Views on the future of the U.S. in space; excerpts from addresses. por Miss & Roc 15:16-18 O 26 '64
What I believe, and why. Read Digest 84:45-8 Ja '64
What LBJ, as a senator, said about civil rights; excerpts from debate, ed. by J. L. McClellan. U S News 56:14 Ap 27 '64
What the President said about the stereo; statement, January 23, 1964. por U S News 56:59 F 3 '64
Where I stand on farming; questions and answers. por Farm J 88:32-3+ O '64
—and Douglas-Home, A. F.
British Prime Minister holds talks with President Johnson; communique, February 13, 1964. Dept State Bul 50:336-7 Mr 2 '64; Same. Cur Hist 46:304-5 My '64
—and Erhard, Ludwig
U.S. and Germany reaffirm agreement on East-West problems; joint communique, June 12, 1964. Dept State Bul 50:992-4 Je 29 '64
—and López Mateos, Adolfo
President Johnson and President López Mateos of Mexico hold talks in California; joint communique, February 22, 1964. Dept State Bul 50:396-8 Mr 16 '64
—and Orlich, F. J.
President Orlich of Costa Rica visits Washington; text of joint communique, July 1, 1964. Dept State Bul 51:81 Jl 20 '64

about

Above the battle; concerning opening campaign speech in Detroit. il por Time 84:30 S 18 '64
Across the Nation: the story of the '64 election; with charts. il U S News 57:38-44 N 16 '64
Act seven. Newsweek 63:28 Mr 16 '64
Adenauer talks about Johnson; interview, ed. by K. Lachmann. K. Adenauer. il por U S News 55:44-7 D 16 '63
Aesthetic politics. New Repub 151:4 D 12 '64
After JFK, what? W. D. Burnham. il Commonweal 79:340-3 D 13 '63
After the shots: the ordeal of Lyndon Johnson. F. Knebel. por Look 28:26-8+ Mr 10 '64
All over? or just starting? il por Time 84:19-19A S 4 '64
Alliance: time for guidelines. il por Newsweek 64:17 D 21 '64
And how about the Pentagon now? new era in Washington. M. S. Johnson. il por U S News 55:64-5 D 16 '63
And now we look abroad. M. Ascoli. Reporter 31:24 N 19 '64
Another beginning. New Repub 149:3 D 7 '63
Appraising a president; editorial reaction to first speech before Congress. Time 82:81 D 6 '63
Arnold Newman photographs the President. il pors Pop Phot 55:40-1 O '64
As business leaders size up Lyndon Johnson. U S News 56:84-5 My 18 '64
As dog lovers took pen in hand. U S News 56:6 My 11 '64
As friends tell it: LBJ talks about some campaign issues. U S News 57:59 N 16 '64
As high school students see it. il Sr Schol 85:11 O 28 '64
As Johnson really takes over. . . . il pors U S News 56:31-3 Ap 6 '64
As labor sees LBJ now. U S News 58:90-1 Ja 25 '65
As '64 campaign gets going. il por U S News 57:31-2 Jl 20 '64
As the campaign got rougher. por U S News 57:11 O 19 '64
As the race ends: who'll win? il pors U S News 57:25-31 N 2 '64
At home on the range; LBJ ranch, Tex. il pors Bsns W p 19-20 Ja 4 '64
Atlantic City without the girls. W. F. Buckley, jr. Nat R 16:763-5 S 8 '64
Atlantic report. Atlan 213:6+ F; 214:4+ S '64
Austin-Boston axis. il por Newsweek 63:19-20 Ja 13 '64
Back of the change in LBJ. por U S News 56:49 Je 15 '64
Band-aid program? war on poverty. il Newsweek 63:35-6+ F 17 '64
Banking feud: LBJ takes a hand. U S News 56:97 Mr 30 '64
Barry vs. LBJ: the fireworks start. il por U S News 57:31-2 S 14 '64
Barry's chances against LBJ. il U S News 56:31-3 Je 22 '64
Beginning. H. Brandon. Sat R 47:6 Mr 7 '64
Beyond November. il por Time 84:24 O 9 '64
Big, bold plans of Lyndon the Lucky. B. H. Bagdikian. il pors Sat Eve Post 237:17-19 D 12 '64
Big political sprint. T. Wicker. il por Sat Eve Post 237:76-7 Ap 25 '64
Big scare vs the issues. Farm J 88:114 N '64
Blandness in the White House. S. Alsop. il por Sat Eve Post 238:18 Ja 30 '65
Bloody ground of Texas politics. M. Kempton. New Repub 150:6-8 F 1 '64
Bobby Kennedy on LBJ's ticket? il pors U S News 56:42-4 Mr 23 '64
Bold gamble by the President; concerning State of the Union message. il por Newsweek 63:13-14 Ja 20 '64
Boom LBJ sees ahead. il por U S News 56:29-31 F 3 '64
Brand of LBJ. Newsweek 64:32+ Ag 17 '64
Breaking the logjam. il por Bsns W p23-4 O 10 '64
Bright lights. Reporter 30:10 My 7 '64
Business and Johnson savor a love feast. il por Bsns W p28-9 Ja 18 '64
Business, and the party platforms. T. O'Hanlon. il por Duns R 84:55-7+ O '64
Businessmen's vote: it's going to be a tough decision. il pors Bsns W p23-5 S 5 '64
Campaign and the candidates. F. Knebel. il Look 28:23-5 N 3 '64
Campaign report from the East: if the people were voting for president now. il U S News 57:37-8 S 21 '64

JOHNSON, Lyndon Baines—about—*Continued*
Campaign report: on the road with the candidates. il por U S News 57:124-5 O 12 '64
Campaign time; when Secret service worry grows. il U S News 56:63-4 Ap 13 '64
Campaign: what does it all add up to? with editorial comment. S. Alsop. por Sat Eve Post 237:71-3, 76 O 31 '64
Case for Lyndon B. Johnson. por Ebony 20:70-1 N '64
Change of pace. Newsweek 64:27+ Jl 20 '64
Civil rights, government money, and the vote in the South. il U S News 57:41-2 O 19 '64
Civil rights: the White House meeting. Newsweek 64:15 Ag 3 '64
Clean bill of health for the President. U S News 57:8 S 7 '64
Clear choice. Nation 199:81 S 7 '64
Clear choice. E. Moon. il por Library J 89: 3926-7 O 15 '64; Discussion. 89:4232+, 4448+, 4872+ N 1-15, D 15 '64
Cliff Carter: LBJ's political liaison man. U S News 56:20 Ja 13 '64
Close look at the South and LBJ's home state. il U S News 57:45-6 O 12 '64
Close-up of the Democratic presidential candidate. il pors Sr Schol 85:8-9 S 23 '64
Coming attack on Lyndon Johnson. S. Alsop. por Sat Eve Post 237:15 Mr 28 '64
Confession on the presidency. L. Wainwright. Life 58:23 Ja 22 '65
Congressmen size up LBJ and his first six months. il pors U S News 56:57-9 Je 8 '64
Countrywide report on election race. il por U S News 57:39-42 S 28 '64
Course ahead for LBJ. J. L. McCaskill. NEA J 53:15 Ja '64
Covenant: concerning inauguration speech. il por Time 85:9-10 Ja 29 '65
Crushed by the crowds, Johnsons worry their guards. il U S News 56:19 My 4 '64
Day in the life of the President; with report by I. Shelton. il pors U S News 56: 36-46+ Mr 2 '64
Defeating of LBJ. E. J. Hughes. Newsweek 63:17 F 24 '64
Demag, Tex. concerning State of the Union message. Nat R 16:54 Ja 28 '64
Democratic team. H. Brandon. Sat R 47: 18+ S 26 '64
Democratic view. il por Newsweek 64:31 Jl 27 '64
Despite frugality, the budget rises. Newsweek 62:21 D 16 '63
Different kind of President. D. Lawrence. U S News 58:84 Ja 4 '65
Diplomacy at LBJ ranch; Erhard visit. il por U S News 56:26 Ja 6 '64
Does Johnson have a foreign policy? J. Burnham. Nat R 16:190 Mr 10 '64
Down on the ranch; hospitality to Washington press corps. il por Time 83:50-1 Ja 17 '64
Dual image? reprint. H. Gemmill. U S News 56:96+ F 10 '64
Election. Nat R 16:999-1001 N 17 '64
Emotional campaign will test voters' judgment. P. Lisagor. por Nations Bsns 52:23-4 S '64
Enter: the ten-gallon era; working vacation at Texas ranch. il pors Life 56:20-7 Ja 10 '64
Everybody's president. K. Crawford. Newsweek 62:31 D 16 '63
Everything's O.K. on the LBJ. K. Fleming. il por Newsweek 64:34-5 N 23 '64
Extremism in defense of the Democratic party. C. B. Luce. Nat R 16:719-21 Ag 25 '64
Farm problem that closely concerns the new President. il U S News 55:76-7 D 16 '63
Fashion czar in the White House. il pors Bsns W p94+ Mr 21 '64
Fear & the facts. il Time 84:15-19 S 25 '64
Fight over double-time pay. U S News 56: 88 Mr 2 '64
Fine art of president-baiting. M. Greenfield. por Reporter 31:29-33 S 24 '64
First fifty days. Newsweek 63:15 Ja 27 '64
First state social by the Chief. il pors Life 56:32-32A Ja 24 '64
Five gallon. il Newsweek 63:68 F 10 '64
Flying high, and fast. il pors Bsns W p21-4 My 2 '64
Flying White House. F. Knebel. il pors Look 28:86-92+ Je 2 '64
Focus on Nov. 3. Nat R 16:943 N 3 '64
For LBJ, a Texas-size inaugural. il por Newsweek 65:21-2 Ja 25 '65
For LBJ: eighteen hours' work, six hours' sleep. por U S News 56:14 Ja 20 '64
Foreign countries, too, mourn first citizen of the world. il U S News 55:48-9 D 2 '63
Foreign policy: LBJ's test. Newsweek 63: 19-20 F 10 '64
Foreign policy: same goals, sterner style. Bsns W p31-2 N 30 '63
Four tactics in the Johnson campaign. T. Wicker. il por N Y Times Mag p 14+ O 4 '64
F.O.B. Detroit. il por Newsweek 64:23 Jl 6 '64
From Washington straight. Cato. Nat R 16: 268, 807, 948, 1006; 17:15 Ap 7, S 22, N 3-17 '64, Ja 12 '65
Full treatment; President Johnson and Congress. Time 82:25 D 13 '63
Future for President Lyndon Johnson. E. T. Folliard. America 109:726 D 7 '63
Goldwater: the home stretch. F. S. Meyer. Nat R 16:447 Je 2 '64
Goldwater vs. LBJ; '64 choice? il por U S News 56:35-7 Je 15 '64
Good beginning; concerning State of the Union message. M. Ascoli. Reporter 30:26 Ja 30 '64
Good-times issue and party prospects. E. T. Folliard. America 110:533 Ap 18 '64
Hand on the trigger. J. Burnham. Nat R 16: 1013 N 17 '64
Hard-won destiny of Lyndon Johnson. D. Cater. por Reporter 29:17-19 D 19 '63
Harsh challenge to Johnson: hotter war in Vietnam. il U S News 55:104 D 9 '63
Him, her, and LBJ. K. Crawford. Newsweek 63:34 My 11 '64
His first tests are coming soon. il pors Bsns W p 15-16 Ja 4 '64
Hope and reality; concerning President Johnson's inaugural address. K. Crawford. Newsweek 65:24 F 1 '65
Hour of decision: what LBJ faces now. il por U S News 57:29-35 D 7 '64
House & farm; concerning President Johnson's special message to Congress. Time 83:21 F 7 '64
How a president should use the intellectuals. J. R. Roche. por N Y Times Mag p 10+ Jl 26 '64
How Democrats expect to win. Nations Bsns 52:76+ Je '64
How Democrats plan victory. il por U S News 57:25-8 Ag 31 '64
How farmers will vote, and why. C. W. Gifford. il Farm J 88:29+ N '64
How LBJ got the nomination. P. Potter. il por Reporter 30:16-20 Je 18 '64
How LBJ is doing his job; interview, ed. by J. Fromm. R. E. Neustadt. il pors U S News 57:34-7 Ag 3 '64
How LBJ is wooing businessmen. U S News 56:58 My 11 '64
How LBJ works. il Newsweek 63:23 F 24 '64
How LBJ's early-warning system works for pay, prices. il U S News 56:86-8 F 10 '64
How the President keeps informed. H. Smith. il pors N Y Times Mag p 15+ Ag 30 '64
How the world sizes up LBJ now. il pors U S News 57:33-5 D 14 '64
How the world sizes up the President. il por U S News 56:54-5 My 18 '64
How to cut a budget. il Newsweek 63:15 Ja 20 '64
How to take up the slack; President and foreign policy. il Time 83:13 Mr 27 '64
How union leaders feel about Johnson now. il U S News 56:86-7 Mr 2 '64
How unions stand with Johnson now. U S News 57:101-3 N 16 '64
How White House is changing; Kennedy team adjusts to Johnson style. il pors U S News 55:34-6 D 23 '63
I paint the candidates; with portraits. N. Rockwell. Look 28:50-3 O 20 '64
If it's Goldwater v. Johnson, who will win? R. De Toledano. por Nat R 16:101-2+ F 11 '64; Reply. F. Meyers. 16:248 Mr 24 '64
If Johnson wins big. New Repub 150:3-4 F 29 '64
If Lyndon Johnson wins big; what the changes will be. il pors U S News 57:48-50+ O 12 '64
Image Johnson is trying to create. il por U S News 56:32-3 F 3 '64
Imponderables. il por Time 84:19 O 23 '64
In the dust and above it. il por Newsweek 64:69 O 5 '64
In the home stretch: can Goldwater still make it? il por U S News 57:35-8 O 19 '64
In U.S. heartland: how candidates shape up. il U S News 57:43-6 S 28 '64
Inauguration. il pors Time 85:10-19A Ja 29 '65
Inauguration of President Johnson. il pors Life 58:24-33 Ja 29 '65
Inside report: changes LBJ has brought in six months. il pors U S News 56:46-50+ My 18 '64
Interim reflections on LBJ. M. Ascoli. Reporter 30:10 Mr 12 '64

JOHNSON, Lyndon Baines—about—*Continued*
Into the '64 campaign homestretch. Sr Schol 85:8-11 O 28 '64
Is an Austin-Boston coalition possible? E. T. Folliard. America 110:402 Mr 28 '64
Is LBJ slipping? il Nat R 16:902-4 O 20 '64
Is President Johnson in labor's corner? concerning State-of-the-Union message. il por U S News 58:72-3 Ja 18 '65
Is the South to be solid again? L. H. Bean. il U S News 56:34 Ja 20 '64
Issue isn't personal. R. Moley. Newsweek 62:64 D 30 '63
It is the people who face the test; standpattism in Congress. T. Wicker. il N Y Times Mag p 19+ D 8 '63
It's called Goldwater country; but who's leading? il por U S News 57:68-9 O 5 '64
It's one year after JFK: the changes; with interview with J. M. Burns. il pors U S News 57:60-6 N 23 '64
I've got a secret. J. Deakin. New Repub 152:13-15 Ja 30 '65
Jenkins case; unanswered questions. il U S News 57:48 N 2 '64
Johnson addresses the world. Christian Cent 81:3-4 Ja 1 '64
Johnson and Humphrey: political saga. il pors U S News 57:56-8 N 16 '64
Johnson and labor: the 1964 outlook. U S News 55:94 D 2 '63
Johnson and Roosevelt. R. Moley. Newsweek 65:80 F 1 '65
Johnson & the Jenkins case. Time 84:20-1 N 6 '64
Johnson and the people; photographs. N Y Times Mag p 12-13 My 3 '64
Johnson and the polls. S. Alsop. il por Sat Eve Post 237:16 F 1 '64
Johnson as party leader. New Repub 149:7-8 D 28 '63
Johnson as tactician. Nation 198:1 Ja 4 '64
Johnson begins his presidency. M. Ascoli. Reporter 32:26 Ja 28 '65
Johnson Congress: what it will do. il por Nations Bsns 52:32-3+ D '64
Johnson dresses down; business suit at inauguration. Bsns W p30 D 19 '64
Johnson gives labor the word. il Bsns W p25-6 My 9 '64
Johnson-Humphrey elected. por Sr Schol 85:8 N 11 '64
Johnson in a Gallup. Nat R 16:802 S 22 '64
Johnson inherits cultural leadership. il por Arch Forum 120:5 Ja '64
Johnson maneuvers. W. V. Shannon. Commonweal 80:593-4 S 4 '64
Johnson or Goldwater, two scientists explain their choice. G. B. Kistiakowsky; E. Teller. Science 146:380-2 O 16 '64
Johnson prepares: in the White House; And back at the ranch. il pors N Y Times Mag p28-31 N 29 '64
Johnson program. Commonweal 79:359 D 20 '63
Johnson program; continuity and action; with photographs by G. Tames. N Y Times Mag p20-1 D 8 '63
Johnson sets his course. il pors U S News 55:35-6 D 16 '63
Johnson staff: new faces, new ways at the White House. il por U S News 55:44 D 2 '63
Johnson starts moving fast. il pors Bsns W p 19-21 D 7 '63
Johnson stress on military space seen; President's space, military background. Aviation W 79:26-8 D 2 '63
Johnson style. New Repub 149:2+ D 7 '63
Johnson sweep. il por U S News 57:33-4 N 16 '64
Johnson takes oath as nation mourns Kennedy. il por Sr Schol 83:14 D 6 '63
Johnson takes over: the untold story. S. Alsop. il pors Sat Eve Post 237:17-23 F 15 '64
Johnson, the first hundred days. P. Potter. New Repub 150:6-8 Mr 7 '64
Johnson the man: born to politics. il pors U S News 57:36-40 S 7 '64
Johnson touch. H. H. Martin. il pors Sat Eve Post 237:21-9 O 31 '64
Johnson woos press. il por Bsns W p34+ F 8 '64
Johnson? yes! Christian Cent 81:1099-1101 S 9 '64
Johnson's campaign machinery. M. Viorst. New Repub 151:9-10 S 5 '64
Johnson's faith. il por Time 83:65 Ap 3 '64
Johnson's grand design; concerning State of the Union message; with editorial comment. il Bsns W p 19-21, 108 Ja 9 '65
Johnson's health his doctor's report; questions and answers. G. G. Burkley. U S News 58:11 Ja 11 '65
Johnson's heart: all signs are good; report of Drs Cain and Hurst. il por Bsns W p 18-19 D 21 '63
Johnson's heart good. Sci N L 84:359 D 7 '63
Johnson's image abroad. Time 83:41 My 29 '64
Johnson's men: valuable hunks of humanity; T. Wicker. il por N Y Times Mag p 11+ My 3 '64
Johnson's miracle. New Repub 150:3-5 Ja 18 '64
Johnson's next four years. J. Kraft. Harper 229:44+ N '64
Johnson's program and its prospects; concerning State-of-the-Union message. il pors U S News 56:29-31 Ja 20 '64
Johnson's window on Utopia; concerning message to Congress on the State of the Union. Life 58:4 Ja 15 '65
Jokes with the LBJ brand. A. Shuster. i por N Y Times Mag p 100+ S 13 '64
K and LBJ: a time for taking stock. il Newsweek 62:33 D 16 '63
Kennedy legacy, the people's task. Commonweal 79:335-6 D 13 '63
Labor's price tag for election; it's up to LBJ. il U S News 57:85-6 D 7 '64
Lady Bird Johnson: the new First lady. il por U S News 55:16 D 2 '63
Latest on the Johnson fortune. il U S News 56:38 Je 22 '64
Let us reason together; person-to-person approach. N. B. Brown. il pors N Y Times Mag p8-9 D 15 '63
Letter from Atlantic City. R. H. Rovere. il New Yorker 40:112-17 S 5 '64
Letter from Washington. R. H. Rovere. New Yorker 39:51-3 N 30; 78-84+ D 21 '63; 133-8 F 15; 40:101-7+ Ag 22; 235-8+ N 14; 156-8+ D 19 '64; 122-7 Ja 16 '65
Letter from Washington; concerning State of the Union message. R. H. Rovere. New Yorker 39:35-6+ Ja 25 '64
Life on the ranch: a day at home with LBJ. J. P. Sutherland. il pors U S News 56:67-8 Ap 13 '64
Listening post: how the pros see the election. por Newsweek 64:20-2 Ag 31 '64
Lyndon and the South: to reapportion or not. Cato. Nat R 16:762 S 8 '64
LBJ. Reporter 29:14 D 5 '63
Lyndon Baines Johnson. il por Sr Schol 83:18 D 6 '63
L.B.J. all the way. il pors Time 84:19A-19B S 4 '64
LBJ and big strikes; is rail fight a pattern? il U S News 56:99-101 Ap 27 '64
LBJ and Congress. K. Crawford. Newsweek 65:26 Ja 18 '65
LBJ and Congress; now a test. il por U S News 56:33-4 Ja 13 '64
LBJ and Congress; the next 100 days. il pors U S News 56:31-2 Mr 30 '64
LBJ and Cuba: what comes next. U S News 55:41 D 23 '63
LBJ and his Congress: made for each other; concerning State of the Union message. Newsweek 65:17 Ja 18 '65
LBJ and KTBC; a hot potato for the FCC. il Newsweek 63:83-4 Ap 27 '64
LBJ and RFK. S. Alsop. Sat Eve Post 237:10 F 29 '64
LBJ and science: policies marked by continuity, but a few events suggest developments for future. D. S. Greenberg. Science 143:939-40 F 28 '64
LBJ and the budget: the outlook. il U S News 57:107-8 N 16 '64
LBJ and the formal news conference. E. T. Folliard. America 110:303 Mr 7 '64
LBJ and the press. K. Crawford. Newsweek 63:18 F 17 '64
LBJ and unions: what he tells them, what they want. il por U S News 55:106-7 D 16 '63
LBJ answers some New-frontier critics. U S News 55:26 O 28 '63
L.B.J. country; excerpt from The President's homeland. B. Porterfield. il por Sat Eve Post 237:28-32+ O 3 '64
LBJ down on the farm. por T. Wicker.. Esquire 62:90-3+ O '64
LBJ: I ask for a mandate to begin. il por Newsweek 64:16-18 S 7 '64
LBJ: I said let them through! Slambang. C. Roberts. il por Newsweek 64:31-3 O 12 '64
LBJ image. il Newsweek 64:27 Ag 31 '64
LBJ looks ahead. Newsweek 64:15-16 D 28 '64
LBJ: man in charge. C. W. Bailey, 2d. il pors Look 28:24-5 Mr 10 '64
LBJ maps an agenda, lines up the team. il Bsns W p34-6 N 7 '64
LBJ, Meany at odds on wages. U S News 56:89 Ap 6 '64

JOHNSON, Lyndon Baines—about—*Continued*
LBJ: my thanks to all America; Winners. il por Newsweek 64:25-7 N 9 '64
LBJ news conference, family style. il pors U S News 56:19 My 18 '64
LBJ on civil rights. Cato. Nat R 16:311 Ap 21 '64
LBJ on tour: another FDR or JFK? il por U S News 56:17 Je 29 '64
LBJ: perpetual motion. il pors Newsweek 63: 17-18 My 4 '64
LBJ takes command. il pors Newsweek 62: 20-3 D 9 '63
LBJ talked calories and profits at White House business lunch. il Newsweek 64:57-8 Ag 3 '64
Lyndon B. Johnson: the new President; what he stands for. il por U S News 55:36-7 D 2 '63
LBJ: tug, twist, and massage; Untroubled waters. Newsweek 62:13-14 D 23 '63
LBJ vs. Goldwater, a study in contrasts. por U S News 57:32-4 S 7 '64
LBJ vs. Republicans: what the polls show. U S News 56:8 F 3 '64
LBJ: who's that? K. Crawford. Newsweek 61:39 F 11 '63
LBJ's balance. K. Crawford. Newsweek 63:22 Ja 6 '64
LBJ's big health plan: cradle to grave; concerning first legislative message to the new Congress. il U S News 58:34-5 Ja 18 '65
LBJ's brand goes on the economy; with editorial comment. il por Bsns W p71-4+, 136 Ja 25 '64
LBJ's drive is no puzzle to insiders. P. Lisagor. il por Nations Bsns 52:23-4 Jl '64
LBJ's first three months: spending hits a record. il U S News 56:95-6 Ap 13 '64
LBJ's first union showdown; how wheat strike came out. il por U S News 56:89-90 Mr 9 '64
L.B.J.'s great good bear hug. Life 56:4 My 15 '64
LBJ's great society. R. Moley. Newsweek 64:102 S 28 '64
LBJ's Great society, what will it be? il por U S News 57:33-7 N 23 '64
LBJ's hunt for womanpower. P. Lisagor and M. Higgins. il pors Sat Eve Post 237: 86-7 Je 27 '64
LBJ's LBJ, First lady of the land. il pors Newsweek 64:11-14 D 28 '64
LBJ's own aid cut. Newsweek 63:17 Mr 30 '64
LBJ's pep pill for business: quick tax cuts in recessions; concerning State-of-the-Union message. il U S News 58:83-4 Ja 18 '65
L.B.J.'s romance with business. H. B. Meyers. il pors Fortune 70:130-3+ S '64
LBJ's running mate: the man he favors. il por U S News 57:32-3 Ag 3 '64
LBJ's skin growths: what they are, why they were removed. il U S News 57:22 D 14 '64
LBJ's State of the Union. il Sr Schol 84:16 Ja 31 '64
LBJ's way of operating; what makes it different; intimate portrait of Lyndon Johnson. il pors U S News 56:35-7 Ja 13 '64
Lyndon Johnson, philanthropist. il pors U S News 56:49-50 Je 29 '64
Lyndon Johnson, Rex. W. F. Buckley, jr. Nat R 16:438 Je 2 '64
Lyndon Johnson: the man and his record. il pors U S News 55:38-40 D 2 '63
Lyndon Johnson: trained for power. F. Knebel. il pors Look 27:20-3 D 31 '63
Lyndon Johnson: will he win? story the polls tell. il U S News 57:44-7 S 7 '64
Lyndon Johnson's life. il pors Life 55:72D-76 N 29 '63
Lyndon Johnson's open secret. Fortune 69: 93-4 Je '64
Lyndon Johnson's pledge: I will lead, and I will do the best I can: Hail to the Chief. il pors Newsweek 65:10-17 F 1 '65
Lyndon plays it cool. il Bsns W p27 Ag 15 '64
Lyndon's detractors. il por Newsweek 64:25-6 Ag 10 '64
Lyndon's pace. il por Newsweek 64:29-30 O 19 '64
Lyndon's ways. il pors Time 82:23-4 D 13 '63
Making of HHH. il pors Newsweek 64:18-26 S 7 '64
Man of the year. il pors Time 85:14-27 Ja 1 '65
Man who became President: Lyndon Baines Johnson, 36th President. il pors U S News 55:84-6 D 9 '63
Man who is chief. por Bsns W p25-6 N 30 '63
Man who is the President. K. Wheeler and W. Lambert. il pors Life 57:24-9+ Ag 14; 62-6+ Ag 21 '64
Mark Twain and Lyndon B. Johnson. C. Clemens. Hobbies 69:112+ Ap '64
Master of the art of the possible. R. Baker. il pors N Y Times Mag p26+ D 1 '63
Men Johnson will lean on. il por Bsns W p27-8 N 30 '63
Men Johnson will need. V. P. Rock. Nation 199:348-9 N 16 '64
Men Lyndon likes. il Time 82:27-27A D 6 '63
Message; concerning President Johnson's first message to Congress. Nation 197:406 D 14 '63
Mr Johnson flunks. Nation 198:613 Je 22 '64
Mr Johnson: larger than life. il pors Newsweek 64:16-19 Ag 31 '64
Mr Passman meets his match. E. B. Drew. Reporter 31:40-3 N 19 '64
Mixed praise for L.B.J.'s hundred days. Life 56:4 F 28 '64
Modern Utopia. il por Time 85:15-16 Ja 15 '65
Most hopeful times? K. Crawford. Newsweek 65:19 Ja4 '65
Multimillionaire. il por Time 84:15-16 Ag 21 '64
National yelp over an earlift. R. Wallace. il por Life 56:34-34A My 8 '64
Negro leaders meet LBJ; here are the results they see. por U S News 55:48-9 D 16 '63
New administration: indications are it will bring few changes for scientific, academic worlds. D. S. Greenberg. Science 142:1277-8 D 6 '63
New brand on the White House. M. McGrory. America 110:34 Ja 11 '64
New chief moves boldly to his big tasks. il pors Life 55:50-1 D 6 '63
New Congress; it may get out of hand. il U S News 58:23-4 Ja 11 '65
New diplomatic style. E. J. Hughes. Newsweek 63:15 Ap 6 '64
New era in Washington: its meaning. il pors U S News 55:35-50, 78-83 D 9 '63
New mandates; with editorial comment. por Bsns W p33-4, 188 N 7 '64
New President. Nation 197:405-6 D 14 '63
New President. S. Alsop. il pors Sat Eve Post 236:20-1+ D 14 '63; Same abr. with title LBJ: portrait of the President. Read Digest 84:59-66 F '64
New shield around the President. il U S News 55:29 D 30 '63
New times, new leaders. H. Brandon. Sat R 48:13 Ja 16 '65
News and comment; what can be expected of the Johnson administration. D. S. Greenberg. Science 142:1151-2 N 29 '63
News management (cont) Reporter 30:14+ F 27 '64
Nine months to election: what polls show. il U S News 56:37 F 10 '64
'65 budget: more for less? il Sr Schol 84:20 F 7 '64
1965: the prime task. Nation 200:21 Ja 11 '65
1964 election. E. Weeks. Atlan 214:49 O '64
1964: who's ahead? H. Brandon. Mlle 58:130-1 Mr '64
No more, no less. Newsweek 61:23 Ap 8 '63
Nobody is for poverty. R. Moley. Newsweek 63:82 Ja 27 '64
Now a Lyndon Johnson party; LBJ and RFK. il por Newsweek 64:18-19 Ag 10 '64
Now for U.S: a tougher line in the world? il por U S News 57:47-8 N 23 '64
Now, the Jenkins case: meaning to the campaign. il por U S News 57:54-6 O 26 '64
Now the real race begins. il por U S News 57:27-8 S 7 '64
Now the trumpet summons again. . . il Bsns W p21-3 N 30 '63
Old leader and the new. Life 58:4 Ja 29 '65
On a poverty trip with LBJ. il pors U S News 56:58 My 25 '64
On the side of change. New Repub 152:5-6 Ja 30 '65
On the '64 campaign trail. Sr Schol 84:16 Mr 20 '64
One weakness of L.B.J. S. Alsop. por Sat Eve Post 237:12 S 19 '64
Only Johnson can beat Johnson. S. Alsop. por Sat Eve Post 237:12 Ja 4 '64
Optimist in Washington. America 110:534 Ap 18 '64
Ordeals of the President. G. W. Johnson. New Repub 151:21 O 24 '64
Other fellow. E. J. Hughes. Newsweek 64:23 N 16 '64
Our day with President Johnson. il pors Suc Farm 62:41-3+ Mr '64
Our new President. M. Ascoli. Reporter 29: 14 D 19 '63
Overexposure as a presidential policy. E. T. Folliard. America 110:756 My 30 '64
Overtime-pay plan: ending LBJ's honeymoon with businessmen. U S News 56:113 F 24 '64

JOHNSON, Lyndon Baines—about—*Continued*
Part of the way with LBJ. Reporter 31:12+ Jl 16 '64
Party's responsibility. J. T. Crown. por Nation 197:411-13 D 14 '63
Peace issue. il por Newsweek 64:24 N 2 '64
Platform for L.B.J. Sat Eve Post 237:84 Ag 22 '64
Political campaign goes into high gear. U S News 57:21 S 21 '64
Political mood of U.S. now. il por U S News 57:54-63 Ag 24 '64
Portrait of the President as a reasonable man; inaugural day. M. Phelps. America 112:157 Ja 30 '65
Powerful persuaders; Lady Bird's trip through the South. H. Fuller. New Repub 151:11-12 O 24 '64
Presidency. See issues of Time
President. New Repub 152:3-4 Ja 16 '65
President. S. Alsop. por Sat Eve Post 237-12 N 7 '64
President. See issues of Newsweek
President: a free man first. J. M. Burns. il por Sat R 47:27-8 Ap 11 '64
President and the intellectuals. W. V. Shannon. Commonweal 79:386-7 D 27 '63
President and the press. il por U S News 55: 34-5 D 30 '63
President and the press. T. Lewis. Nation 198:207-9 Mr 2 '64
President and the press corps, what to expect. il por U S News 56:15 Ap 20 '64
President behind the candidate. J. M. Burns. Life 57:95-6+ O 9 '64
President: both advocate and candidate. J. N. Eller. America 110:591 My 2 '64
President-candidate. M. Ascoli. Reporter 31: 22 S 10 '64
President committed to war on poverty. J. N. Eller. America 110:182 F 8 '64
President Johnson. America 109:729 D 7 '63
President Johnson and public architecture: convictions on architect's role recalled. Arch Rec 135:10 Ja '64
President Johnson and the tasks ahead; with statements by L. B. Johnson. il pors Sr Schol 83:6-9 D 13 '63
President Johnson and the tides of ideology. F. S. Meyer. Nat R 16:23+ Ja 14 '64
President Johnson's book is U.S. literary first. Pub W 186:37 S 21 '64
President Johnson's health record. por U S News 55:39 D 2 '63
President Johnson's vigorous start. Christian Cent 80:1535-6 D 11 '63
President Lyndon Baines Johnson. por Vogue 143:54-5 Ja 15 '64
President must now find the answers. por Bsns W p29-30 D 5 '64
President shows his style. il por Bsns W p23-4 D 14 '63
President takes office. il por Sr Schol 85: 6-9 Ja 21 '65
President will run scared. E. T. Folliard. America 111:32 Jl 11 '64
Presidential car: it's safer now; What LBJ says about the danger from crowds. il U S News 57:14 O 19 '64
Presidential politics in LBJ style. J. Kraft. Harper 228:113-16 Mr '64
Presidential '64: rewriting the political rule-book. il por Sr Schol 85:8-11+ S 16 '64
Presidential tenure. U S News 55:38 D 2 '63
President's calculated risk. M. J. Rossant. por Reporter 30:27-9 Ja 30 '64
President's day. il Am Heritage 15:106-7 Ag '64
President's heart. Asklipios. Esquire 62:89-92+ Ag '64
President's own. il por Newsweek 62:54 D 30 '63
Private wealth in public office. Life 57:4 Ag 28 '64
Professional, by W. S. White. Review
New Repub 150:25 Je 13 '64. G. W. Johnson
Promised land; concerning State of the Union address. M. Lerner. Time 85:67 Ja 15 '65
Prospectus for the Great society. H. Brandon. Sat R 48:14-15 Ja 30 '65
Question now: Johnson vs. which Republican? il U S News 55:32-3 D 23 '63
Race riots: Goldwater boon. F. Knebel. il Look 28:34+ S 22 '64
Ready, in his own right. il pors Bsns W p 11-13 D 26 '64
Rediscovery of poverty; concerning State of the Union address. Nation 198:61 Ja 20 '64
Reporter at large. R. H. Rovere. New Yorker 40:217-22+ O 17 '64
Republican party and the conservative movement; symposium. Nat R 16:1053-6+ D 1 '64
Right down the center. il Bsns W p25-7 Ag 29 '64
Second era of good feeling? S. Alsop. Sat Eve Post 237:14 My 9 '64
Secret service worry now: how to protect President Johnson; report. il por U S News 57:59 O 12 '64
Sell it. Nation 198:385 Ap 20 '64
Shoo-in fallacy. Nation 198:158-9 F 17 '64
Six vs. LBJ: latest on the Republican scramble. il por U S News 56:57-8 Ja 13 '64
Some day you'll be sitting in that chair. il por Time 82:32-3 N 29 '63
Some facts about 'sixty-four and 'sixty-eight. E. T. Folliard. America 108:429 Mr 30 '63
Space program support to grow; with editorial comment. H. Taylor. por Miss & Roc 13: 14-15, 48 D 2 '63
Speaking out. R. M. Nixon. Sat Eve Post 237: 12+ Je 27 '64
Stand-in. il Newsweek 63:14 F 17 '64
State of LBJ; concerning State of the Union message. W. F. Buckley, jr. Nat R 17:56 Ja 26 '65
State of the President. il por Newsweek 65: 17 Ja 11 '65
State of the Union. il pors Newsweek 65:15-19 Ja 11 '65
State of the Union and of its libraries. G. Krettek. ALA Bul 58:77 F '64
State of the Union message stresses need for libraries. Library J 89:584 F 1 '64
Story of eighty-seven votes that made history. il pors U S News 56:46-50 Ap 6 '64
Story of Johnson's health. il pors U S News 56:40-2 Ja 27 '64
Story of the Johnson family fortune. il pors U S News 55:75 D 16 '63; 56:38-42 My 4 '64
Strange case of Bobby Baker. il U S News 56:40-2 F 10 '64
Strength of President Johnson. W. F. Buckley, jr. Nat R 16:143 F 25 '64
Student's choice. por Sr Schol 85:1T O 28 '64
T.R.B. from Washington; en route with Lyndon. New Repub 151:2 O 17 '64
Task ahead for the President. Bsns W p 156 D 7 '63
Teacher of the President. NEA J 53:19 My '64
Texan remembers Lyndon; with editorial comment. S. Long. por Nation 199:233, 235-9 O 19 '64
Texan sits tall in a new saddle; with report by J. L. Steele. pors Life 55:26-35 D 13 '63
36th U.S. President. il pors Newsweek 62: 28-30+ D 2 '63
This is Lyndon, and it is. il por Newsweek 62:22 D 16 '63
This is LBJ's country. il U S News 55:60-4 D 23 '63
Tick-tock of the campaign clock. il por Newsweek 64:29-30 S 21 '64
Tiptoeing forward. W. V. Shannon. Commonweal 81:470-1 Ja 8 '65
To bind up the Nation's wound. Christian Cent 81:1292 O 21 '64
To the editor; letters. Nat R 15:577 D 31 '63
Top man's tones. Time 84:27-8 O 30 '64
Touring Vice President LBJ visits Scandinavia. il por U S News 55:24 S 16 '63
Trains keep running; settlement of the 4½-year-old featherbedding dispute. por Bsns W p29 Ap 25 '64
Triumphant ticket whoops it up and saddles up way down at the LBJ. R. B. Stolley. il por Life 57:36-7 N 13 '64
Trying, and gaining. il pors Bsns W p23-5 Ja 23 '65
Two Lyndon Johnsons and the U.S. of 1964. M. Ways. il Fortune 69:80-3+ Ja '64
Uncle Lyndon. S. Alsop. por Sat Eve Post 237:16 O 24 '64
Uncommon cold. il Newsweek 65:17-18 F 1 '65
Unions rally to Johnson. Bsns W p46+ N 30 '63
U.S. and Britain: LBJ calls the tune. por U S News 57:25-6 D 21 '64
Unkown LBJ. New Repub 152:2 Ja 9 '65
Unprecedented succession. R. S. Hirschfield. Nation 197:414-15 D 14 '63
Vice President to visit Belgium, Luxembourg, and the Netherlands: Department statement, October 1, 1963. Dept State Bul 49:630 O 21 '63
Vice Presidential skirmish. por Newsweek 63:27-8 Mr 16 '64
Vice President's chances in '64. por U S News 54:14 F 25 '63
Vile campaign. W. F. Buckley, jr. Nat R 16:853-6+ O 6 '64
Vision of LBJ: something for all; concerning State-of-the-Union message. il por U S News 58:31-3 Ja 18 '65

JOHNSON, Lyndon Baines—about—*Continued*
Visit with President Johnson; White House luncheon attended by editors of six leading women's magazines. il por Redbook 123:6 Je '64
Wage law: changes LBJ wants. U S News 56:88 F 10 '64
War on want, at home; State of the Union message; with editorial comment. il pors Bsns W p 19-21, 112 Ja 11 '64
Was there a plot to assassinate LBJ? il por U S News 56:48-9 Ap 27 '64
Washington desk. J. R. Slevin. Duns R 83: 5-6 Ja; 84:5-6 S '64
What comes naturally. il pors Newsweek 62: 41-2 D 30 '63
What doctors say about LBJ's health; excerpts from interviews, ed. by F. E. Carey, J. W. Hurst; J. W. Cain. por U S News 58:14 Ja 4 '65
What farmers can expect from LBJ. C. E. Ball and C. W. Gifford. il por Farm J 88:35+ Ja '64
What happened to L.B.J. por Time 81:27-8 Ap 5 '63
What Johnson plans now. il U S News 57:34-7 N 16 '64
What kind of president will Johnson make now? interview. A. Schlesinger, jr. U S News 57:53-5 N 16 '64
What Lyndon Johnson found next door to Russia. R. W. Ruth. il por U S News 55: 73-4 S 23 '63
What Negroes can expect from President Lyndon Johnson. L. Bennett, jr. il pors Ebony 19:81-4+ Ja '64
What price Johnson? Johnson cult in Bismarck Archipelago. Time 84:30-1 O 9 '64
What the FBI found in the Jenkins case. il U S News 57:6 N 2 '64
What you can expect from the new Congress. il U S News 58:36-7 Ja 4 '65
Whatever you say, honey; first days of Christmas. il por Time 83:28-9 Ja 3 '64
What's he like? and how will he do? J. Reston. il pors N Y Times Mag p8-9+ Ja 17 '65
Wheat problem: back at White House. il por U S News 55:39 D 30 '63
When Johnson plans a speech—. U S News 56:33 F 3 '64
When LBJ tackled threat of walkout. il por U S News 56:77 Ap 20 '64
Where both candidates stand on the big issues; with editorial comment. il por Bsns W p64-6+, 192 O 10 '64
Where President Johnson goes to church. S. Lansdowne. America 111:443 O 17 '64
Where things get done; State of the Union address, as blueprint for the coming presidential campaign. Sat Eve Post 237:76 F 1 '64
Which way with LBJ? J. Chamberlain. Nat R 15:525-7 D 17 '63
White House garden: LBJ loves it. il por U S News 56:10 My 11 '64
White House week that was. il por Newsweek 63:15 F 3 '64
Who gets the billions in LBJ's school plan. il U S News 58:66-7 Ja 25 '65
Who gets the cash in the war on poverty. il U S News 56:33-5 Mr 30 '64
Who won what in the rail dispute; How a five-year-old fight was settled in thirteen days. il por U S News 56:76-7 My 4 '64
Who's really for LBJ? R. Moley. Newsweek 64:126 O 12 '64
Who's to be who in the new Johnson term. il por U S News 57:27-9 D 21 '64
Why LBJ will win. New Repub 151:3-4 O 31 '64
Why Lyndon Johnson must be elected. Sat Eve Post 237:80 S 19 '64
Why the President crossed six men off the list as possible running mates; Johnson-Humphrey ticket, or—? il pors U S News 57:14-15 Ag 10 '64
Will Congress nail together the Great society? President's State of the Union message. R. B. Stolley. il Life 58:36-7 Ja 15 '65
Will Goldwater sweep the South? il por U S News 57:41-2 Ag 10 '64
Will it be nine years for LBJ? il U S News 58:37-40 Ja 25 '65
Will success spoil LBJ's carnival of compatibility? P. Lisagor. il Nations Bsns 52: 21-2 D '64
With LBJ, what a day! J. P. Sutherland. il U S News 57:43 S 7 '64
Women's magazine editors visit President Lyndon B. Johnson at the White House. il por Parents Mag 39:28 Je '64
Wooing the West. il Newsweek 64:27-8 S 28 '64
World challenge to Mr Johnson. L. J. Halle. il pors N Y Times Mag p 17+ Ap 5 '64
World has changed; sixth week of presidential campaign. il por Newsweek 64:34-5 O 26 '64
World of Lyndon B. Johnson. S. S. Harrison. New Repub 149:13-14 D 7 '63
World trouble spots facing L.B.J. Sr Schol 85:10-11 Ja 21 '65

Anecdotes, facetiae, satire, etc.

Department of amplification: letter. E. J. Kahn, jr. New Yorker 40:159-60+ Je 6 '64
Uncle Cornpone greets the press. W. F. Gavin. Nat R 16:867 O 6 '64

Bibliography

New Horatio Alger series starring L.B.J; campaign biographies. J. Feiffer. Life 56: 10+ Je 5 '64

Caricatures and cartoons

Finding a president. Time 83:52 Ap 10 '64

JOHNSON, Lyndon Baines, family
All eyes are on Lyndon's ladies. il pors Life 55:30-1 D 13 '63
Another round on the Johnson family fortune; with chart. il U S News 57:34-5 Ag 31 '64
Another TV station for the Johnsons? KLFY-TV. U S News 57:14 D 14 '64
Fashion czar in the White House. il Bsns W p94+ Mr 21 '64
Folksy holiday season for the LBJ's. il U S News 56:12-13 Ja 6 '64
Home away from home; Johnson family in White House. il Newsweek 62:16 D 23 '63
How the Johnsons run their family. il U S News 55:20 D 9 '63
I believe: White House boarder; ed. by F. R. Schreiber. W. L. Smith. il Seventeen 23: 196-7 S '64
Johnson family: all-out campaigners. il U S News 57:20 Ag 31 '64
Johnsons: home on the ranch. il pors Newsweek 63:16-17 Ja 20 '64
LBJ white house. J. B. Young. il Am Home 67:5-6 Mr '64
LBJ's wealth grows as an issue; both candidates are millionaires. il Bsns W p32 Ag 22 '64
Man who is the President; how L.B.J.'s family amassed its fortune. K. Wheeler and W. Lambert. il Life 57:62-6+ Ag 21 '64
Modest sum; family's net worth. Time 84:19-20 Ag 28 '64
Multimillionaire. il Time 84:15-16 Ag 21 '64
New life for the Johnson girls. P. Mesta. il McCalls 91:24+ My '64
Our first ninety days in the White House. F. R. Schreiber. il Good H 158:86-9+ My '64
There's a new social style at the White House. il U S News 56:60-1+ F 17 '64
Three other LBJ's. pors Newsweek 62:26+ D 9 '63
Up from poverty. il Time 83:19-20 Je 19 '64
When LBJ outdanced the diplomats; excerpts from report. D. McCardle. il U S News 56: 14 F 24 '64
With a new family in the White House. il U S News 55:68-9 D 16 '63
Yes, my darling daughters. il Time 83:35 Ap 17 '64

JOHNSON, Lyndon B, foundation. See Johnson City foundation

JOHNSON, Marguerite
Woodcuts from color transparencies. Pop Mech 119:182-3 Mr '63

JOHNSON, Martha. See Thompson, D. jt. auth.

JOHNSON, Marvin R. A.
How the architect works. por ALA Bul 58: 109-11 F '64

JOHNSON, Mauritz, jr
Magic numbers of 7-8-9. NEA J 52:50-1 Mr '63

JOHNSON, Max S.
Russia's plans for the next war. U S News 54:52-5 Ap 8 '63

JOHNSON, P. D. and others
Apatite: origin of blue color. bibliog Science 141:1179-80 S 20 '63

JOHNSON, Pamela Hansford
Belgium. Mlle 58:111-12 Ja '64
Compulsory sex scene. Vogue 145:134-5 Ja 1 '65
(tr) See Anouilh, J. Rehearsal

JOHNSON, Paul
Ginger man. por Newsweek 65:62 Ja 25 '65

JOHNSON, Paul Burney, 1916?-
Change of command. il por Newsweek 63:26-7 F 3 '64
Election issue: who's against JFK most? por U S News 55:15 Ag 19 '63
Governor Johnson's new image. Christian Cent 81:199 F 12 '64

JOHNSON, Paul Burney—*Continued*
If you try & don't succeed; runoff for governor. Time 82:17 Ag 16 '63
Who was right? P. B. Johnson jr's gubernatorial campaign. il por Newsweek 62:25 S 9 '63
Words make news in Mississippi. Life 56:4 F 7 '64

JOHNSON, Paul C. and others
Autoregulation of blood flow. Science 140:203-5 Ap 12 '63

JOHNSON, Pauline
Approach to design. Sch Arts 62:16-20 Mr '63
Art tips for bookbinding. Design 65:68-74 N '63
Wizardry with paper. Design 64:142-5 Mr '63

JOHNSON, Philip Cortelyou
Architectural details. il Arch Rec 135:137-52 Ap '64
Bad bad world? E. Goble. Arch Rec 134:9 O '63
He adds elegance to modern architecture. A. L. Huxtable. il por N Y Times Mag p 18-19+ My 24 '64
Philip Johnson. C. Amory. il por Vogue 143:184-92+ My '64

JOHNSON, Priscilla
New men of the Soviet sixties. Reporter 28:16-21 My 9 '63
Oswald in Moscow. Harper 228:46-50 Ap '64
Russia: poetry, politics, and the unpredictable. Reporter 29:44-8 N 21 '63

JOHNSON, Pyke, jr
Censorship, critical thinking, and the paperback; excerpts from address, December 3, 1964. por Library J 90:296-301 Ja 15 '65
Distribution of paperbound books. por ALA Bul 57:534+ Je '63
Mad Tom books: a venture in roadside selling of paperbacks. Pub W 186:38-40 O 5 '64
What books can do for toy sales. Pub W 183:156-9 F 18 '63

JOHNSON, Rafer
Our Olympic chances; interview, ed. by H. L. Masin. por Sr Schol 85:54 O 7 '64

about

None but the brave. il pors Ebony 19:110-12+ O '64

JOHNSON, Richard
Daylilies today. Horticulture 42:22-3+ Jl '64

JOHNSON, Richard N.
Ministerial health and unhealth. Christian Cent 80:706-8 My 29 '63

JOHNSON, Ronald
Four orphic poems: Sentences uttered; There is an exquisite movement, like it were chaos; At night in the New Jersey woods, we were awakened; Nebula, whirlpool, mist & cloud; knotted, assymetrical branchings. Poetry 104:210-16 Jl '64
Sweet orange, sour, osage & mock-orange; poem; excerpts. Poetry 103:48-62 O '63

JOHNSON, Roy L.
People of the week. por U S News 57:12 Ag 17 '64

JOHNSON, S. C, and son
Johnson's wash-'n-wax. il Time 83:80+ Je 26 '64

JOHNSON, Samuel
Boswell; the ominous years, 1774-76; ed. by C. Ryskamp and F. A. Pottle. Review
New Yorker 39:78+ Je 29 '63. W. Balliett
Johnson's dictionary, a modern selection, comp. by E. L. McAdam, jr. and G. Milne. Review
Time por 81:M28+ Mr 29 '63

JOHNSON, Samuel Ealy, family
L.B.J. scrapbook. N. B. Brown. il N Y Times Mag p56 Mr 1 '64

JOHNSON, Thomas F.
Arrau at sixty. Mus Am 83:27 Mr '63

JOHNSON, U. Alexis
Aid, investment in the future; address, April 23, 1963. Dept State Bul 48:829-34 My 27 '63
American policy in international affairs; address, February 17, 1964. Dept State Bul 50:364-9 Mr 9 '64
American policy in the Near East; address, January 20, 1964. Dept State Bul 50:208-11 F 10 '64
Japan, the United States, and Europe; address, March 28, 1963. Dept State Bul 48:606-12 Ap 22 '63
Rising Afro-Asian nations. Dept State Bul 48:449-56 Mr 25 '63
United States and southeast Asia; address, April 8, 1963. Dept State Bul 48:635-41 Ap 29 '63
U.S. foreign policy in the Far East; address, June 20, 1963. Dept State Bul 49:78-82 Jl 15 '63
What to expect of new American leaders in Vietnam. por U S News 57:12 Jl 6 '64

JOHNSON, Wallace
Millionaire: a self-portrait; interview, ed. by C. Sopkin. por Esquire 61:92-3+ F '64

JOHNSON, Walter
Greatest pitcher of them all. L. Koppett. il por N Y Times Mag p26+ O 4 '64
Most unforgettable character I've met. V. X. Flaherty. por Read Digest 82:115-19 Je '63

JOHNSON, Walter, 1915-
Have faith in the twentieth century. Bul Atomic Sci 21:10-15 Ja '65
Late President on the podium. Sat R 47:24 Je 27 '64
Uneven road to equality. Sat R 47:53+ My 9 '64

JOHNSON, William
Movies: have they come of age? Sr Schol 83:11-15 O 25 '63

JOHNSON, William A.
Important theology. Christian Cent 81:337-9 Mr 11 '64
Of Catholic interest. Christian Cent 80:1404-7 N 13 '63

JOHNSON, William Benjamin
REA's Johnson; managing a transportation supermarket. por Duns R 81:pt2 S112 Je '63
Transportation: the political dimensions of an economic dilemma. bibliog f Ann Am Acad 345:47-57 Ja '63

JOHNSON, William R. jr
Bahamian boatbuilding. Motor B 112:30-1+ D '63
Bahamian sailing craft. il Yachting 114:49-51+ N '63

JOHNSON, William Weber
Hush-hush resort. Sat Eve Post 236:24-7 F 16 '63

JOHNSON family
Ancestors: President Johnson's relation to R. Barnett and J. A. E. W. Spencer-Churchill, tenth duke of Marlborough. New Yorker 40:25-6 Ja 23 '65

JOHNSON and Johnson
Developing a shampoo for babies. E. M. McCabe. il Parents Mag 38:24+ Jl '63

JOHNSON CITY, Tex.
Boomlet in the Johnson country. T. L. Christie. il Sat R 47:37-8 My 23 '64
L.B.J. country; excerpt from The President's homeland. B. Porterfield. il Sat Eve Post 237:28-32+ O 3 '64
This is LBJ's country. il U S News 55:60-4 D 23 '63

JOHNSON CITY foundation
Lyndon Johnson, philanthropist. il U S News 56:49-50 Je 29 '64

JOHNSTON, Denis
Sean O'Casey. Nation 199:198 O 5 '64
What's wrong with the new theatres. Theatre Arts 47:16-18+ Ag '63

JOHNSTON, Don P.
Conservation diplomat. por Am For 70:6 N '64

JOHNSTON, Elizabeth
Our world. Sch Arts 63:18-19 Je '64

JOHNSTON, Eric Allen
Robust striving. por Newsweek 62:32 S 2 '63

JOHNSTON, Logan T.
Five-letter word for progress; address, November 17, 1964. Vital Speeches 31:185-8 Ja 1 '65

JOHNSTON, Maxine
How to organize a do-it-yourself play school. Parents Mag 38:62-3+ S '63

JOHNSTON, Richard F. and Selander, R. K.
House sparrows: rapid evolution of races in North America. bibliog Science 144:548-50 My 1 '64

JOHNSTON, Robert
Lament of the reassigned foreign service officer; poem. Atlan 211:116 Je '63

JOHNSTON, W. H. and Zeman, L. E.
Five ways to cut grain losses. Suc Farm 61:30 Jl '63

JOHNSTON, W. T.
Encyclopedias. Consumer Bul 47:2+ Ja '64

JOHNSTONE, William C.
United States policy in southern Asia. Cur Hist 46:65-70+ F '64

JOINT adventures
Art gets its own mutual fund; joint purchase of art works by Houston collector-investors. il Bsns W p30-1 O 31 '64
Industry's problem children. il Bsns W p51-2+ O 24 '64

JOINT chiefs of staff. See United States—Joint chiefs of staff

JOINT committee on contemporary China of the American council of learned societies and the Social science research council
Communist China: what science wants to know about it. J. Lear. Sat R 47:43-6 Mr 7 '64; Discussion. 47:44-6 Ag 1 '64
On teaching Chinese. J. Lear. Sat R 47:61 N 7 '64

JOINT council on economic education
Upgrading economics. Sr Schol 85:1T-2T N 11 '64

JOINT economic committee. See United States—Congress—Committees

JOINT plants. See Inch plants

JOINT strategic target planning staff. See United States—Joint chiefs of staff

JOINT undertakings. See Joint adventures

JOINT United States-Canadian committee on trade and economic affairs
U.S.-Canada economic committee concludes eighth meeting; joint communique, September 21, 1963. Dept State Bul 49:548-50 O 7 '63
U.S.-Canada economic committee concludes ninth meeting; joint communique, April 30, 1964. Dept State Bul 50:774-6 My 18 '64
U.S.-Canadian economic committee to meet at Ottawa. Dept State Bul 50:670 Ap 27 '64
U.S.-Canadian economic committee to meet at Washington. Dept State Bul 49:297 Ag 19 '63

JOINT United States—Japan committee on scientific cooperation
Neurophysiology: United States-Japan joint symposium; report. T. H. Bullock. Science 144:1361-4 Je 12 '64
U.S.-Japan science committee concludes fourth meeting; announcement, remarks by Secretary Rusk, and text of joint communique. Dept State Bul 51:61-3 Jl 13 '64

JOINTERS
Jointer-planer. il Pop Sci 183:180+ N '63

JOINTS

Diseases

See also
Arthritis

JOINTS (carpentry)
ABCs of building chests and cabinets. R. J. De Cristoforo. il Pop Sci 185:116-21 N; 132-5 D '64 (to be cont)
Tenoning jig for fine wood joints. R. Wortham. il Pop Sci 184:156-7 Mr '64
Woodworking joints that lock. R. J. De Cristoforo. il Pop Sci 185:162-5 O '64

JOINTS, Pipe. See Pipe joints

JOKES. See Humor

JOKES, Egyptian. See Humor, Egyptian

JOKES, Practical. See Practical jokes

JOLAYEMI, James
Big chickens of James and Samuel. P. Conklin. Reporter 28:30-1 Je 20 '63

JOLLY, Iva D.
Atamasco lily. Horticulture 41:409 Ag '63
Bloodroot; hepatica. Horticulture 41:463 S '63
Two attractive native ground covers. Horticulture 41:68 F '63

JOLLY, Pete
Senior scholastic talks to Pete Jolly; interview, ed. by R. Hemming. por Sr Schol 84:13 My 1 '64

JOLLY, William L. See Kirschke, E. J. jt. auth.

JOMON pottery. See Pottery, Japanese

JONAS, Edward C.
Ion exchange at edge and interlayer in montmorillonites differing in size. bibliog Science 140:75-6 Ap 5 '63

JONAS, Gerald
Night thought; poem. New Yorker 40:205 O 17 '64
Sea is not the sum of its parts; poem. New Yorker 39:73 Ag 17 '63
Summer: New York; poem. New Yorker 39:52 Jl 6 '63

JONAS, Louis Paul
Getting there is half the fun. H. B. Comstock. il por Pop Sci 183:50-3 S '63

JONAS brothers
Brothers under the skin. il Bsns W p 136-8+ O 26 '63

JONATHAN, Sister Mary. See Mary Jonathan, Sister

JONATHAN, Will
Chief watchman. Sat R 47:43 Jl 4 '64
Macro-micro man. Sat R 47:46-7 Mr 7 '64
Portable astronomer. Sat R 47:36-7 S 5 '64
Scientist's scientist. Sat R 47:36-7 Ag 1 '64
Theorist in hardrock Sat R 46:36-7 Jl 6 '63
Wind's deputy. Sat R 46:48-50 F 2 '63
Year of the quiet son. Sat R 47:56 F 1 '64

JONES, A. E. and others
Mangabey *a* and *b* wave electroretinogram components: their dark-adpated luminosity functions. bibliog Science 146:1486-7 D 11 '64

JONES, Alan Pryce-. See Pryce-Jones, A.

JONES, Alice Eleanor
Little brother; story. Redbook 121:58-9 Je '63
Ordinary day; story. Redbook 123:48-9 Je '64

JONES, Antony Charles Robert Armstrong-, 1st earl of Snowdon. See Snowdon, A. C. R. A.-J.

JONES, Arthur Keppel-. See Keppel-Jones, A.

JONES, Barbara A.
Choice; poem. Ladies Home J 81:116 My '64

JONES, Barrett H. and Kane, Walter
Two new purchasing procedures. Am City 78: 117-18 Mr '63

JONES, Bill
Secrets of a supersalesman. il pors Ebony 19: 83-4+ Ag '64

JONES, Bryant L.
Medical assistance. il Motor B 111:41+ Je '63

JONES, Chris
Two models on modeling. por Mlle 60:144-7 N '64

JONES, Clarence F.
Brazil. Focus 15:1-6 N '64

JONES, Daniel W.
Ordeal at Devil's Gate. W. Stegner. Esquire 61:100-1+ Je '64

JONES, David
Epic poet. K. Raine. Poetry 101:426-30 Mr '63
Tads. New Yorker 39:27-8 F 23 '63

JONES, David A.
Davy Jones: salesman of the sea. pors Duns R 81:pt2 S 124 Je '63

JONES, David Albert Charles Armstrong-, viscount Linley. See Linley, D. A. C. A.-J.

JONES, David Lloyd-. See Lloyd-Jones, D.

JONES, David Pryce-. See Pryce-Jones, D.

JONES, David R.
Steel: the giant under fire. Sat Eve Post 237: 21-9 Je 27 '64

JONES, Dorothy
Third dimension. por Recreation 56:282-4 Je '63

JONES, Doug
Sporting scene; Clay vs. Jones fight. A. J. Liebling. New Yorker 39:122+ Mr 30 '63

JONES, E. Stanley
Keeping up with. . . por Time 83:34 Ja 24 '64
Memorable fortnight. W. W. Richardson. Christian Cent 81:216 F 12 '64

JONES, Eddie
Down river in a Mark Twain idyl. il pors Life 55:91-2 Jl 19 '63

JONES, Edith Mae (Irby)
Edith Irby revisited. il pors Ebony 18:52-4+ Jl '63

JONES, Everet C.
Tremoctopus violaceus uses physalia tentacles as weapons. bibliog f Science 139:764-6 F 22 '63

JONES, Frances
Made with macaroni. Design 64:98-9+ Ja '63

JONES, Frances Fielding-. See Fielding-Jones, F.

JONES, Grover
Search; suspect of hit-and-run death in Celina, Tenn, 1944. Newsweek 62:24+ Jl 22 '63

JONES, Gwyneth
Big eisteddfod. por Newsweek 64:93 D 7 '64
Presto chango. il por Time 84:52 D 4 '64

JONES, H. M. and others
Orbital lifetime of the West Ford dipoles. Science 140:1173 Je 14 '63

JONES, Harry
Quintuplets and other news from Aberdeen, S.D. Redbook 122:42-3+ Ja '64

JONES, Hayes
King of the hurdlers. il pors Ebony 19:63-6 Ap '64

JONES, Helen L.
Over the editor's shoulder; reprint. por Library J 89:4969-71 D 15 '64

JONES, Holly
Airplane; poem. Horn Bk 39:332 Je '63

JONES, Howard Mumford
Press and professor; excerpts from address. por(p37) Pub W 184:41-2 Jl 15 '63

JONES, J. Leslie
Ozone damage; protection for plants. bibliog Science 140:1317-18; 142:447 Je 21, O 25 '63

JONES, J. Raymond
New face at Tammany. por Newsweek 64: 27 D 14 '64

JONES, Jack
Clean-cut chip. por Newsweek 64:82 D 14 '64

JONES, James
Flippers! gin! weight belt! gin! faceplate! gin! Esquire 59:124-7+ Je '63

JONES, James—*Continued*
Letter home. Esquire 60:28+ D '63; 61:28+ Mr; 62:22+ D '64
Phony war films. por Sat Eve Post 236:64-7 Mr 30 '63
Two writers talk it over. por Esquire 60: 57-9 Jl '63
Valentine; story. Sat Eve Post 236:36-9 F 16 '63

JONES, James Allen
Scholastic teacher interviews: James Allen Jones; ed. by H. Langer. por Sr Schol 84: 10T-11T F 28 '64

JONES, James Earl
Dynamo. por Newsweek 62:68 D 2 '63

JONES, Jenkin Lloyd
Teach your child to love the storm. Read Digest 82:126-7 F '63
Time to get new schoolbooks; reprint. U S News 54:71 Mr 25 '63
What is a liberal? address, October 23, 1964. Vital Speeches 31:209-12 Ja 15 '65

JONES, Jesse
How Jesse Jones built his empire. por Bsns W p46 D 26 '64

JONES, John
Jones collection and the American club in London. W. J. Sainsbury. il por Antiques 85:185-9 F '64

JONES, John Paul
Action off Flamborough Head; excerpt from Great sea battles. O. Warner. il por Am Heritage 14:42-9+ Ag '63

JONES, John T. Jr
Quiet man stands tall in Houston. il pors Bsns W p44-6+ D 26 '64

JONES, John William
Reconstruction legislators in Alabama. C. A. Brown. bibliog Negro Hist Bul 26:198-9 Mr '63

JONES, Junetta
Fresh voices; interview, ed. by R. D. Daniels. por Opera N 28:28 Mr 7 '64

JONES, K. C.
How K.C. won an Oscar in the NBA. F. Deford. Sports Illus 20:58+ Ap 20 '64

JONES, Karl P.
Climbing and pillar roses. Horticulture 41: 334-5 Je '63

JONES, LeRoi
After the ball; poem. Nation 196:163 F 23 '63
Dark bag. Poetry 103:394-401 Mr '64
In the ring. Nation 198:661-2 Je 29 '64
Like Rousseau; History as process; poems. Poetry 105:161-2 D '64
Morning purpose; poem. Nation 198:37 Ja 6 '64
Myth of a Negro literature. por Sat R 46:20-1 Ap 20 '63
Tight rope; poem. Nation 197:40 Jl 13 '63
Valéry as dictator: Liar; Snake eyes; poems. Poetry 103:157-9 D '63

about

Dutchman. Criticism
New Yorker 40:78-9 Ap 4 '64
Newsweek por 63:60 Ap 13 '64
Vogue 144:32 Jl '64
Slave. Criticism
Nation 200:16-17 Ja 4 '65
New Repub 152:32-3 Ja 23 '65
New Yorker 40:50+ D 26 '64
Newsweek 64:56 D 28 '64
Sat R 48:46 Ja 9 '65
Time por 84:62-3 D 25 '64
Vogue 145:98 F 1 '65
Three at the Cherry Lane. H. Clurman. Nation 198:383-4 Ap 13 '64
Toilet. Criticism
Nation 200:16 Ja 4 '65
New Repub 152:32-3 Ja 23 '65
New Yorker 40:50+ D 26 '64
Newsweek 64:56 D 28 '64
Sat R 48:46 Ja 9 '65
Time il 84:62 D 25 '64
Vogue 145:98 F 1 '65

JONES, Louis C.
Leader ahead of his times. Am Heritage 14: 58-9+ Je '63

JONES, Margaret Hubbard. See Carterette, E. C. jt. auth.

JONES, Marion W.
Horseplayer wins $81,000. il pors Ebony 19: 124-6+ Jl '64

JONES, Mark Bence-. See Bence-Jones, M.

JONES, Martha W.
Orientation. NEA J 53:46-8 O '64

JONES, Mary Ellen
Carbamyl phosphate. bibliog Science 140:1373-9 Je 28 '63

JONES, Mary Lange
Pair of stockings; story. Redbook 122:42 D '63
Tree cutters; story. Redbook 121:44-5 Je '63

JONES, Meredith L.
Beauty and science. Natur Hist 72:18-21 Ap '63
Complexities in the substrate. Natur Hist 72:10-17 My '63

JONES, Mervyn
Three weeks in the Middle kingdom. Horizon 6:58-63 Sum '64

JONES, Milbrey L.
Socio-economic factors in library service to students; excerpts. ALA Bul 58:1003-6 D '64

JONES, Orlan, and Jones, Wini
Don't overlook the obvious. Writer 77:25-6+ Ap '64

JONES, Parnelli
Rhubarb at Indy. il por Time 81:82-3 Je 7 '63
Two against the clock at Indy. K. Rudeen. il por Sports Illus 18:26-8+ Je 10 '63

JONES, Patrick Pelham-. See Pelham-Jones, P.

JONES, Paul
Liberty and junior's driving license. PTA Mag 59:21-2 O '64
Stop and go signals for teen-age drivers. PTA Mag 57:4-6 Mr '63

JONES, Paul E.
Rooting cuttings with patience, sand and water. Horticulture 41:128-9 Mr '63

JONES, Paul H.
Wells replace surface supply. Am City 78: 74-5 Jl '63

JONES, Phil B. and Maddex, R. L.
Fit feed lot layout to your needs. Suc Farm 62:54-5 N '64
How to plan a beef feeding layout. Suc Farm 62:38-41 O '64
Planning guide for dairymen. Suc Farm 63: 30-1 Ja '65
They get two family incomes from 580 crop acres. Suc Farm 62:28-9 D '64

JONES, Raymond F. See Kates, J. R. jt. auth.

JONES, Richard W.
Engineer looks at physiology. Science 140: 461-4 My 3 '63

JONES, Robert
Harnessing the antenna. Electr World 71:46-7 Ap '64
How big is your volt? Electr World 71:42+ Je '64
Making special resistors. Electr World 70:96 N '63
Meter reading conversion nomograms. Electr World 72:24-5 Ag '64
Power & resistor charts. Electr World 72:33 S '64

JONES, Robert L. and others
Microfossils in Wisconsinan loess and till from western Illinois and eastern Iowa. bibliog Science 140:1222-4 Je 14 '63

JONES, Robert Trent
Bogeyman. il por Newsweek 63:62+ Je 15 '64

JONES, Russell S. See Peric-Golia, L. jt. auth.

JONES, Siriol Hugh-. See Hugh-Jones, S.

JONES, Stacy V.
Crisis in the patent office. Sci Digest 55:65-70 Mr '64
Danger: tidal wave! Sci Digest 56:83-7 Jl '64
Fifteen myths about inventions. Sci Digest 56:63-7 Ag '64
Fifty years of zip. N Y Times Mag p 108-9 Ap 28 '63
Invention lag. Sci Digest 57:65-70 Ja '65
Inventions necessity isn't the mother of. N Y Times Mag p 16+ Ap 7 '63; 29 Ja 5 '64
Inventor of the month. See issues of Science digest

JONES, Stephen Hugh-. See Hugh-Jones, S.

JONES, Thomas V.
World of the renaissance executive. il por Newsweek 62:92-4 N 18 '63

JONES, Virginia Lacy
Consultants' column (cont) Library J 88: 739+, 3178+ F 15, S 15 '63
Genuine effort to seek truth. por Library J 88:4703-5 D 15 '63

JONES, Wally
Wally's cue: Sidney! Sidney! J. Underwood. il por Sports Illus 20:26-8 F 10 '64

JONES, Wendell P.
Emerging Africa. bibliog NEA J 52:38-41 My '63

JONES, Will
He likes to cook. por Bet Hom & Gard 42:76 Mr '64

JONES, William K. See Blake, H. M. jt. auth.

JONES, Wini. See Jones, O. jt. auth.

JONES, Wyman
Foursome for Dallas. Library J 89:4733-6 D 1 '64
On the grindstone. por Library J 89:72, 580, 1044, 1516, 1924, 2298, 2752+, 2967, 3114+, 3706, 4304, 4762 Ja 1, F 1, Mr 1, Ap 1, My 1, Je 1, Jl-S 1, O 1, N 1, D 1 '64

JONES and Laughlin steel corporation
Really rolling; steel production is running ahead. il Time 83:84-5 F 21 '64

JONES enterprises. See Houston endowment, incorporated

JONSON, Ben
Alchemist. Criticism
Commonweal 81:73 O 9 '64
New Yorker 40:160+ S 26 '64
Newsweek 64:91 S 28 '64
Volpone. Criticism
Nation 199:59 Ag 10 '64

JORDAN, A. C.
Professor of Xhosa at Wisconsin. Sch & Soc 92:121 Mr 21 '64

JORDAN, C. W. E.
Painted in darkness; ed. by A. Gordon. il por Read Digest 83:140-4 N '63

JORDAN, David Starr
Can one predict success in science? R. W. Dexter. Science 139:670 F 15 '63
Three lives of David Starr Jordan. F. J. Taylor. por Read Digest 82:113-17 My '63

JORDAN, Edward D.
Inventor of the month. S. V. Jones. il por Sci Digest 56:16 D '64

JORDAN, Eileen Herbert
After thirty, what indeed? story. McCalls 92:102-3 O '64
Beautiful sloops; story. McCalls 91:80-1 F '64
Faraway places; story. McCalls 90:84-5 My '63
Legacy; story. McCalls 90:84-5 F '63
Mornings at 7:45; story. McCalls 91:58-9 Ja '64
Phantom lover; story. McCalls 91:84-5 Je '64

JORDAN, Nehemiah
International relations and the psychologist. Bul Atomic Sci 19:29-33 N '63; 20:24 Mr '64

JORDAN, Robert Paul
Gettysburg and Vicksburg: the battle towns today. Nat Geog Mag 124:4-57 Jl '63

JORDAN, Robert T.
Economics library selections. por Library J 88:1625-9 Ap 15 '63

JORDAN, Walfredo
I believe. por Seventeen 22:28 Ap '63

JORDAN
Cloudburst at Petra. il Time 81:44 Ap 19 '63
See also
Bethlehem
Dams—Jordan
Petra
Roads—Jordan

Antiquities

City of Solomon's cauldrons; Tell es-Sa'idiyeh. il Time 83:48 Mr 13 '64

Description and travel

Holy Land, my country. King Hussein. il Nat Geog Mag 126:784-9 D '64
Land of Jesus. il Vogue 142:96-7 D '63
Land that holds the legend of our lives. L. Hellman. il Ladies Home J 81:56-7+ Ap '64
Other side of Jordan. L. Marden. il Nat Geog Mag 126:790-825 D '64

Foreign relations

Another border, another war. New Repub 149:8 O 26 '63
King and President putting on pressure. Newsweek 63:56-7 Ap 20 '64
Quick change. Time 82:41 O 11 '63

United States

President Johnson holds talks with King Hussein of Jordan; joint communique, April 15, 1964. Dept State Bul 50:697 My 4 '64

Politics and government

Genius for survival. il Time 81:30 My 3 '63
Hot breath of Nasser. Time 81:38 Ap 26 '63
Hussein of Jordan. J. H. Huizinga. New Repub 149:10-11 S 14 '63
I'm no quitter. il Newsweek 61:44 My 6 '63
Monarchy at stake. Newsweek 61:42 Ap 29 '63

JORDAN RIVER
Euphoria on the Nile. il Time 83:23 Ja 24 '64
Israel's new waterline: will it bring war? O. Schisgall. il Look 27:82+ Ap 9 '63
Jordan's troubled waters. W. Mehlman. il Reporter 30:29+ Ja 30 '64
Moderation in Cairo; Arab leaders conference. il Newsweek 63:35 Ja 27 '64
Pumping out the Jordan. New Repub 150:9 Ja 11 '64
River of hope, and danger. R. Payne. il N Y Times Mag p 10-11 Ja 19 '64
Storm over Galilee; initial test tapping in Israeli Jordan waters project. il Time 83:44 My 15 '64

JORDY, William H.
Style and chaos. Art N 62:44+ O '63
—and Wright, Henry
PSFS; Philadelphia savings fund society. Arch Forum 120:124-9+ My '64

JORGENSEN, Clive D. See Wells, P. V. jt. auth.

JORGENSEN, Thorvald
Beef imports, what's happening now? Suc Farm 62:66 Jl '64

JORIS, Françoise Mallet-. See Mallet-Joris, F.

JOSEPH, Saint
Saint for ecumenism. America 108:390 Mr 23 '63

JOSEPH (Indian chief)
Memorial to an Indian Moses. P. R. Smith, jr. il por Nat Parks Mag 37:13-15 F '63; Reply. J. R. Williams. 37:23 S '63

JOSEPH, James
Close call in Silo ten. Pop Sci 185:85-8+ N '64
Cryogenics, electronics' frigid frontier. Pop Electr 21:41-4+ D '64
Infrared; quick, new home cure for cracked asphalt. Pop Sci 182:168-70+ Ap '63
New epoxy stops leaks. Pop Sci 183:107-9+ Ag '63
New jet-engined challenger. Pop Mech 120:120-2 N '63
Now they're welding with explosives. Pop Mech 121:118-20+ Ap '64
Para-kiting: dawn of the human antenna. Pop Electr 18:94 F '63
Plastic planks. Pop Mech 120:132-3+ O '63
Ranger 6, where are you? Pop Sci 182:64-8+ Je '63
Shrinkless concrete! it's crack-free. Pop Sci 184:110-11+ Je '64
(ed) See Greene, F. Tests that can cinch a better job

JOSEPH, Myron L.
Protect your freedom to subcontract. Harvard Bsns R 41:98-102 Ja '63

JOSEPH, Richard
Art for the man on foot. Esquire 60:90-3 S '63
Bahamas for fun and profit. Esquire 62:121+ O '64
Captain's table. Esquire 59:86-8 My '63
Cesar Balsa: a thousand keys to his kingdom. Esquire 59:118-20 Mr '63
Elegant life. Esquire 59:62-7 Ap '63
Europe for people who hate tourists. Esquire 59:68-77+ F '63
Europe in the fall. Esquire 62:124-7 S '64
Genial landfall. Esquire 61:68-71 Ap '64
Grand salaam. Esquire 59:84-7 Je '63
Greece: get your ambrosia here. Esquire 61:66-7+ Je '64
Last chance at Land's End. Esquire 62:88-9+ Jl '64
Last safari. Esquire 60:124-7 N '63
Lost weekend of Willielmum Shaxpere. Esquire. 61:120-3 Mr '64
Pacific/Orient '63: scrutiny of the bounty. Esquire 60:42-53 Ag '63
Short course in perfection. Esquire 60:100-2 Jl '63
Skiing among the angels. Esquire 62:194-7 D '64
Sportsman in Japan. Esquire 61:90-3+ Ja '64
Thanksgiving for Turkey. Esquire 63:76-9 Ja '65
This way to the great Pacific-Orient getaway. Esquire 62:68-78 Ag '64
Travel notes. See issues of Esquire
Various pleasures of South Africa. Esquire 62:140-1 N '64
Why they're still flying down to Rio. Esquire 60:214-17 D '63

JOSEPH P. Kennedy, Jr. foundation
Finish his fight; prizes and research grants. Newsweek 63:68 F 17 '64

JOSEPH Schlitz brewing company. See Schlitz, Joseph, brewing company

JOSEPHINE, consort of Napoleon I, emperor of the French
Empress Josephine, by E. Knapton. Review Time il 83:103-4+ F 7 '64
Napoleon and Josephine; the biography of a marriage, by F. Mossiker. Review
Sat R 48:89 Ja 2 '65. J. H. Plumb

JOSEPHS, Devereux C.
Business and the arts; address, November 11, 1963. Mus Am 83:159-60 D '63

JOSEPHS, Lois
USOE cooperative research. Sch Life 46:12-13 Je '64
—See Ianni, F. A. J. jt. auth.

JOSEPHSON, Eric
Study of blind readers. bibliog f por ALA Bul 58:543-7 Je '64

JOSEPHUS, Flavius
World of Josephus. by G. A. Williamson. Review
Time il por 85:96+ Ja 29 '65
JOSETTA, Sister Mary. See Mary Josetta, Sister
JOSEY, Elonnie J.
Dynamics are missing. por Library J 88:4705-7 D 15 '63
Libraries and Emancipation centennial. Negro Hist Bul 26:219-21 Ap '63
Mouthful of civil rights and an empty stomach. por Library J 90:202-5 Ja 15 '65
Negro college libraries and ACRL standards. bibliog por Library J 88:2989-96 S 1 '63
Reading: Negro youths' quest for certainty. Negro Hist Bul 27:158-9+ Ap '64
about
Two stars from Georgia; reflections on the ALA conference in St Louis. E. Moon. il por Library J 89:2919-28 Ag '64
JOSLYN, M. A. and Goldstein, J. L.
Conversion of leucoanthocyanins into the corresponding anthocyanidins. bibliog Science 143:954-5 F 28 '64
Les **JOUETS**; drama. See Michel, G.
JOURDAN, Bob
Mountain of mule deer. pors Outdoor Life 134:40-1+ D '64
JOURNAL of ecumenical studies
For that new guide to ecumenics: welcome. Christian Cent 81:510 Ap 22 '64
New ecumenical journal. America 110:400 Mr 28 '64
JOURNAL star. See Peoria, Ill.—Newspapers
JOURNALISM
Advice from a millionaire publisher; address. J. H. Whitney. Sat R 47:71-3 D 12 '64; Discussion. 48:66 Ja 9 '65
A.P.'s cliche hunt. Time 84:76 D 4 '64
Filling the gag bag. T. R. Burton. Sat R 46:27 Ap 20 '63
Hail to the cliche; Associated press computer assesses use of clichés. R. L. Tobin. Sat R 48:65-6 Ja 9 '65
How to spot a newsman. J. Hohenberg. Sat R 46:55 Je 8 '63
Journalism of tomorrow. M. A. Guitar. il Mlle 56:162-3+ Mr '63
Journalism's challenge and answers. J. Tebbel. Sat R 46:50-1 Je 8 '63
Real sins of the press. L. Markel; discussion. Harper 226:6 F '63
When the press shapes the news. H. Brucker. il Sat R 47:75-7+ Ja 11 '64; Discussion. 47:46-7 F 8; 123+ Mr 14 '64
See also
Freedom of the press
Libel and slander
News
Newspaper court reporting
Reporters and reporting
Anecdotes, facetiae, satire, etc.
Copyreaders. W. Bourke. il Atlan 212:130 O '63
Study and teaching
Newspapers finally face a fact. R. L. Tobin. Sat R 46:53-4 My 11 '63; Discussion. 46:48 Je 8 '63
What's happening to journalism education? J. Tebbel. Sat R 46:52-3 O 12 '63; 47:103-4+ O 10 '64; Discussion. 46:82-3 N 9; 66 D 14 '63; 47:76-7 N 14; 64 D 12 '64
France
See also
Newspapers—France
Great Britain
See also
Newspapers—Great Britain
Russia
Coexistence: the fashionable disease. Time 81:58 Je 28 '63
United States
Behold the grass-roots press, alas! B. H. Bagdikian. Harper 229:102-5+ D '64
Freedom or secrecy. by J. R. Wiggins. Review
Nation 200:60-2 Ja 18 '65. L. M. Lyons
Newspapers finally face a fact. R. L. Tobin. Sat R 46:53-4 My 11 '63; Discussion. 46:48 Je 8 '63
Raising their voices; critics of the press. Newsweek 64:48 D 21 '64
Try for the New Yorker. C. W. Morton. Atlan 211:45-9 Ap '63
Washington press establishment. K. E. Meyer. Esquire 61:73-6+ Ap '64
See also
Catholic press
Negro press
Newspapers—United States
JOURNALISTIC ethics
Business-wise editor; case of J. Purtell formerly of Time. Sat Eve Post 236:74 Je 1 '63
Right of privacy: an approach worth considering. H. F. Pilpel. Pub W 184:244-5 Ag 26 '63
School crime wave. Nation 198:310 Mr 30 '64
See also
Crime and the press
JOURNALISTIC photography. See Photography, Journalistic
JOURNALISTS
Fidel and Lisa; TV interview with Castro. il Newsweek 61:69 My 13 '63
Last of the personal journalists? (cont) H. Golden. Sat R 46:48 F 9 '63; Reply. P. McKee. 46:64 Mr 9 '63
Looking backward; memoirs of newspapermen. J. F. Fixx. Sat R 47:54 F 8 '64
Newssleuths get their man. il Time 84:54 Ag 21 '64
Not enough good men. Time 82:84+ N 29 '63
They discover America. C. W. Hall. Read Digest 82:81-6 Je '63
They never left home. J. Tebbel. Sat R 46:56+ My 11 '63; Discussion. 46:48-9 Je 8 '63
See also
Gridiron club
Women as journalists
JOURNALS. See Periodicals
JOURNALS, Personal. See Diaries
JOURNEY; story. See Stuart, N. G.
JOURNEY to the day; drama. See Hirson, R. O.
JOUSTING. See Tournaments
JOUVE, Pierre Jean
Ténèbre; A la beauté; poems, with English tr. by W. Fowlie. Poetry 104:273-7 Ag '64
JOUVENEL, Bertrand de
Letter from France. Bul Atomic Sci 20:27-9 O '64
Political consequences of the rise of science. Bul Atomic Sci 19:2-8 D '63
JOVANOVICH, William
How good are our English texts? Sr Schol 84:10T-11T F 7 '64
Sex, crime, and, to a lesser extent, sports; excerpt from Now, Barrabas. Sat R 47:14-17+ Jl 18 '64
When publishers go public. Sat R 47:19-22+ My 16 '64
JOY, E. T.
English furniture exports to America, 1697-1830. Antiques 85:92-8 Ja '64
JOY. See Happiness
JOYCE, Dwight P.
Glidden goes for less width but more depth. il pors Bsns W p60-2+ Mr 30 '63
JOYCE, James
Finnegans wake; dramatization. See Erdman, J. Coach with the six insides
Roll away the reel world; new delvings into the dream-stuff of quarter-century-old Finnegans wake. W. T. Noon. America 111:517-20 O 31 '64
Sister. New Yorker 40:34-6 Mr 14 '64
JOYCE, James Avery
Priorities in African education. Sat R 47:55-7+ Ag 15 '64
Strength of U Thant. Christian Cent 80:1047-50 Ag 28 '63
JOYE, Judy
Refit the boat for diving. Motor B 111:28-31 Mr '63
JOYNER, Conrad
Whose Republican party? New Repub 150:10-11 Je 13 '64
JOYNER, Victoria
Out of the dark. Am City 78:111 N '63
JOYOUS season; novel. See Dennis, P.
JUAN Carlos, count of Barcelona
Don Juan of Spain. J. Bryan, 3d. il por Holiday 33:96-9+ My '63
JUANA
Juana. 92nd street Y. J. Maskey. Dance Mag 38:28 Jl '64
JUBB, Annanell C.
Forty-four ways to enjoy beans. Flower Grower 51:22-4 Jl '64
Kitchen garden (title varies) See issues of Flower grower
JUCKER, Ed
Coach of every year. W. Bingham. il por Sports Illus 18:47-8+ F 11 '63
JUCKER, Edwin Lewis. See Jucker, E.

JUDA, Walter, and others
Effect of traces of large molecules containing nitrogen on hydrogen overvoltage. bibliog Science 146:521-3 O 23 '64

JUDAISM
Abraham Geiger and liberal Judaism, comp. by M. Wiener. Review
Commentary 35:172-4 F '63. A. Hertzberg
Age of prophets. M. D. Zeik. Commonweal 78: 67-70 Ap 12 '63
Changing dimensions of faith. R. B. Gittelsohn. il Sat R 47:39-40+ Mr 7 '64
Church, state, and the Jews. A. Hertzberg. Commentary 35:277-88 Ap '63; Discussion. 36:192+ S '63
Irrelevance of modernity. America 109:278 S 21 '63
Jewish-Christian argument: a history of theologies in conflict, by H. J. Schoeps. Review
Christian Cent 80:1375-6 N 6 '63. L. D. Streiker
Jewish need for theology. E. B. Borowitz; discussion. Commentary 35:165-7 F '63
Jews of Britain; theological schism. Time 83: 63 My 22 '64
Judaism for all seasons. L. R. Sussman. Christian Cent 80:427-9 Ap 3 '63
Kant and Judaism. E. L. Fackenheim. Commentary 36:460-7 D '63
Modern rabbi. J. J. Petuchowski. Commentary 35:153-8 F '63
Natural and the supernatural Jew, by A. A. Cohen. Review
Commentary 35:353-6 Ap '63. M. Fox
Time 81:98-9 F 15 '63
New elders; chief rabbis elected. il Time 83:60 Mr 27 '64
Pagan rites in Judaism, by T. Reik. Review
Sat R 47:37 Je 6 '64. S. Siegel
Prophets, by A. J. Heschel. Review
Commentary 35:537-40 Je '63. D. Daiches
Protestant renewal: a Jewish view. A. J. Heschel. Christian Cent 80:1501-4 D 4 '63
Recurrent pattern: studies in anti-Judaism in modern thought, by N. Rotenstreich. Review
Commentary 38:92-5 N '64. W. J. Dannhauser
Religious conflicts in Israel. N. Levin. il Commonweal 79:344-6 D 13 '63
Tension in reform Judaism. E. B. Borowitz. Christian Cent 81:729-32 Je 3 '64
What is a Jew? M. Adler. Harper 228:41-5 Ja '64; Discussion. 228:6 Mr '64
Zionism and Judaism. C. E. Schulman. Christian Cent 80:858-60 Jl 3 '63
See also
Jewish theology

History

Meaning of Jewish history, by J. B. Agus. Review
Commentary 37:75-7 Ap '64. D. Daiches; Discussion. 38:15 Ag '64;39:10-11 Ja '65
Rise of Reform Judaism; a sourcebook of its European origins, by W. G. Plaut. Review
Commentary 37:72-4 Je '64. M. Fox

JUDAISM and Christianity. See Christianity and other religions

JUDD, George E.
Expectant mother. Redbook 123:42+ My '64

JUDD, Walter H.
Keep red China out! condensation of address. Read Digest 85:114-18 N '64
Our greatest source of strength. Read Digest 85:61-70 N '64

JUDE, James R.
Two physicians named outstanding young men. il por Todays Health 41:5+ Mr '63

JUDGE, Joseph
Matter of style; story. Sat Eve Post 236:46-9 Jl 27 '63

JUDGES
California cleans its courts. M. T. Bloom. Read Digest 82:91-3 Mr '63
Changing U.S. effects of Supreme court decisions. il U S News 55:70-2 Jl 1 '63
Douglas vs. Black: old friends fall out. il U S News 54:20 Je 17 '63
Fascinating & frenetic Fifth; Deep South's Fifth circuit court of appeals. il Time 84: 46+ D 4 '64
Festivals and judges; two decisions. M. Himmelfarb. Commentary 35:67-70 Ja '63
Fifth circuit vacancy. New Repub 150:4 Ap 25 '64
For a better bench; campaign against the election of judges. Time 83:52 F 7 '64
Good behavior of judges: who defines it? reprint. D. Lawrence. U S News 57:92+ Jl 6 '64
High court: its growing impact; with excerpts from majority and dissenting opinions. il U S News 56:34-7 Je 29 '64
How LBJ beat deadline in naming a judge. U S News 56:8 Ja 20 '64
How Supreme court is reshaping the country. il U S News 57:31-3 Jl 6 '64
In High court: when Goldberg says yes, White says no. il U S News 54:64 My 27 '63
Inside view of the High court. W. J. Brennan, jr. il N Y Times Mag p35+ O 6 '63
Is the Supreme court reaching for too much power? il U S News 55:64-5 O 7 '63
Limits that create liberty & the liberty that creates limits; Supreme court justices. il Time 84:48-50+ O ° '64
Men beneath the robes. il Time 83:58+ Ja 17 '64
More bench experience for High-court justices? U S News 54:6 Mr 25 '63
More on Kennedy's judges. New Repub 149: 5 O 26 '63
Now, a one-vote margin for Court's liberals? pors U S News 54:19 Mr 4 '63
Other eight, libertarian vs.: conservative Supreme court justices. il Newsweek 63:27 My 11 '64
Outward signs of inward grace; life of legal London. F. Cowper. il Horizon 6:38-40 Spr '64
Picking of judges. New Repub 149:5 Jl 20 '63
Senate problem: judgeships for two ex-union men? il U S News 55:12 N 11 '63
Speaking out: too many judges are political hacks. H. Brownell. Sat Eve Post 237:10+ Ap 18 '64
Storm center of justice. E. Havemann. il Life 56:108-10+ My 22 '64; Same abr. with title Warren court. Read Digest 85:130-5 S '64
Supreme court opens new term. Sr Schol 83:19 N 15 '63
Switch for justices: Black, Clark split on sit-ins. U S News 57:13 D 28 '64
Those Kennedy judges; segregationists of the southern bench. il Time 84:44+ N 6 '64
What is the right punishment? first federal Sentencing institute. il Time 83:54 F 28 '64
See also
Contempt of court
Negro judges
Women as judges

JUDGING Keller; story. See Rogin, G.

JUDGING of photographs. See Photography—Exhibitions

JUDGING of sports. See Sports—Judging

JUDGMENT day
See also
End of the world

JUDGMENTS
Courts; decisions. Time 82:51 D 20 '63
Of booze, broth & anguish. Time 83:78+ My 15 '64
Trials; verdicts. Time 82:60 D 6 '63

JUDICIAL decisions. See Judgments

JUDICIAL review
Supreme court on trial, by C. S. Hyneman. Review
Nat R 16:29-31 Ja 14 '64. L. B. Bozell

JUDICIARY. See Judges

JUDITH, Sister
Mara's unsaid words, beneath; poem. Christian Cent 81:672 My 20 '64

JUDO. See Jiu-jitsu

JUDSON, Sheldon
Erosion and deposition of Italian stream valleys during historic time. bibliog Science 140:898-9 My 24 '63

JUDY Bond, incorporated
Testing labor's ultimate weapon; boycott of unfair goods. il Bsns W p50+ Jl 25 '64

JUGO, Miguel de Unamuno y. See Unamuno y Jugo, M. de

JUGS
English and Irish cream jugs. J. Stone. il Antiques 87:94-8 Ja '65
Singular double; Toby jugs. E. Gaines. il Antiques 83:458 Ap '63

JUHNKE, Louise
Tribute to Olaus; poem. Liv Wildn 84:10 Sum '63

JUILLIARD dance theater
Juilliard dance ensemble, Juilliard concert hall. D. Hering. Dance Mag 38:33+ Je '64

JUILLIARD string quartet. See String quartets

La **JUIVE**; opera. See Halévy, F.

JUJITSU. See Jiu-jitsu

JUJUBES
Plentiful dates. J. Milton. il Pop Gard 16:21+ F '65

JUKEBOXES
Scooby-ooby Scopitone. il Time 84:49 Ag 21 '64
Yippee! Scopitone, a cinematic jukebox in Spark's pub south, New York. New Yorker 40:21-2 Jl 11 '64

JULESZ, Bela
Binocular depth perception without familiarity cues. bibliog Science 145:356-62 Jl 24 '64

JULIA Davis fund. See Negro literature—Collections

JULIAN the Apostate, emperor of Rome
Ascetic pagan. il por Time 83:122+ Je 12 '64
Julian. A. T. Leone. Cath World 199:381-4 S '64

JULIAN, Hubert Fauntleroy
Black Eagle and other birds. il por Time 84:24 Jl 31 '64

JULIAN, Philippe
At home through the ages; excerpts from Les styles. il Horizon 5:80-3 Mr '63

JULIAN calendar. See Calendar

JULIUS, Eloise
Fun and games for parties. Parents Mag 39:40-1+ Ja '64

JULY
In July; few of the dates, memorable and not so, coming up next month (title varies) (cont) il N Y Times Mag p50 Je 30 '63; 26 Je 28 '64

JULY fourth. See Fourth of July

JULY revolution, 1830. See France—History—July revolution, 1830

JUMP the rope. See Rope jumping

JUMPING
Big jump: a Siberian champion tells his story. V. Brumel. il Sports Illus 18:38-41 F 4 '63
Sickle game. J. A. Dawson. il Recreation 57:176-7 Ap '64
See also
Animal locomotion

JUMPING ropes. See Rope jumping

JUNE
In June; list of anniversaries, events and other dates coming up next month (title varies) (cont) il N Y Times Mag p 16 My 26 '63; 15 My 31 '64

JUNEAU, Alaska
Juneau knows that machine accounting pays. H. Cargin. il Am City 78:94-5 Ap '63

JUNEBERRIES. See Serviceberries

JUNG, Carl Gustav
Books. L. Mumford. New Yorker 40:155-6+ My 23 '64
C. G. Jung: oneirologist par excellence. Christian Cent 80:319 Mr 6 '63
Dark & light of dreams. por Time 81:100 My 10 '63
Inner life in an outer-space age. E. F. Edinger. por Sat R 46:23+ Je 1 '63

JUNG, Eva Maria
Cardinal Ottaviani: the bulwark. Cath World 199:80-8 My '64
Table-talk with the Russian observers. Cath World 196:273-8 F '63
Women at the council: spectators or collaborators? Cath World 200:277-84 F '65
(ed) See Sarkissian, A. K. Interview with the Armenian observer at the council

JUNG, Louise. See Gleitman, H. jt. auth.

JUNGLE
Boat into the jungles around San Blas, Mex. il Sunset 130:81-2+ Ap '63
See also
Rain forests

JUNGLE doctors. See Physicians

JUNIOR chamber of commerce. See United States junior chamber of commerce

JUNIOR college libraries. See College libraries

JUNIOR colleges
After high school: the role of the community college. T. E. O'Connell. New Repub 152:17-20 Ja 30 '65
Burgeoning community college. F. P. Merlo; B. Schwartz. il Sat R 47:50-4+ D 19 '64
Changes in the junior college. Sch & Soc 91:187 Ap 20 '63
College, J. G. il Newsweek 63:108+ Ap 20 '64
Communities meet own needs in surge of two-year colleges. F. Morley. il Nations Bsns 52:27-8 O '64
Community college and technical education. Sch & Soc 91:54 F 9 '63
Community college growth described at ATPI meeting; summary of address. E. J. Gleazer, jr. Pub W 186:35-6 O 19 '64
Eighty brand-new colleges. il Changing T 17:13-15 N '63
Flowering of a campus hybrid; two-year community, or junior, college. F. M. Hechinger. il N Y Times Mag p36-7+ S 13 '64
Junior college in the 1960's. Sch & Soc 91:297 O 19 '63
Junior college: pros and cons: with study-discussion program by C. Smallenburg and H. Smallenburg. J. P. Cosand. il PTA Mag 59:22-4, 36 Ja '65
Social sciences in two-year colleges. S. L. Guterman. Sch & Soc 91:200 Ap 20 '63
Standards of excellence in the junior college; excerpt from address, June 17, 1963. F. Keppel. Sch & Soc 91:329-30 N 2 '63
Two-year college trend. Sch & Soc 92:199-200 My 2 '64
Two-year community colleges. R. Carson. il Parents Mag 39:66-7+ Ap '64
Where will they go after high school? H. A. Littledale. il Parents Mag 38:58-9+ Ap '63
Why junior colleges are increasing. il Good H 158:156 Mr '64
See also names of junior colleges, e.g. Stephens college, Columbia, Mo.

Attendance

Junior college enrollment boom. Sch & Soc 92:300-1 O 31 '64

Enrollment

See Junior colleges—Attendance

Finance

Financing the public junior college. H. A. Campion. NEA J 53:67-8 O '64

JUNIOR curators. See Museum workers

JUNIOR forestry and conservation conference
City boys and forestry. R. Leadbrand. il Am For 69:8-9 S '63

JUNIOR great books program
Great books program goes Junior, and the kids are reading it up. Library J 88:4448-9+ N 15 '63

JUNIOR high schools
Junior high accreditation? pro and con discussion. H. R. Douglass; H. T. Gumaer. il NEA J 53:36-7 O '64
Magic numbers of 7-8-9. A. H. Skogsberg; M. Johnson, jr. NEA J 52:50-1 Mr '63

JUNIOR league
Junior Mrs. Newsweek 63:70+ My 18 '64

JUNIOR librarians. See Librarians

JUNIOR literary guild. See Literary guild of America

JUNIOR rocketeers. See Rockets—Amateur experiments

JUNIOR rodeos. See Rodeos

JUNIOR volunteers. See Volunteer service

JUNIOR year abroad programs. See Foreign students in foreign countries

JUNIPER
Consider the lowly juniper. E. S. Colprit. il Horticulture 41:516-17 O '63
Getting to know the junipers. il Sunset 132:174+ F '64

JUNK
How to find beauty in the junkyard. il House B 106:166-9 Mr '64
See also
Scrap metal

JUNK dealers
That's where the old cars go; auto graveyards. J. Keats. il N Y Times Mag p42+ S 20 '64

JUNK sculpture. See Metal sculpture

JUNKER, Howard
Real life of the tramp. Commonweal 81:104-5 O 16 '64

JUNKINS, Donald
Processions; poem. Poetry 102:92 My '63

JUNKS
Junket on a Chinese junk. C. P. Gilmore. il Pop Mech 120:102-6+ S '63

JUNKYARDS
Treasure from the junkyard. C. Kellog. il Ladies Home J 80:156-8+ O '63

JUPITER (planet)
Amateur measurement of Jupiter's diameter. G. Solberg. il Sky & Tel 26:302 N '63
Disturbances on Jupiter. il Sky & Tel 25:160 Mr '63
DX'ing Jupiter! S. Gibson. il Pop Electr 21:41-3+ Ag '64
Faraday rotation on decametric radio emissions from Jupiter. J. W. Warwick and G. A. Dulk. bibliog il Science 145:380-3 Jl 24 '64
Jupiter rotation slowed. Sci N L 85:290 My 9 '64
Jupiter temperatures. Sci N L 85:388 Je 20 '64
Jupiter's magnetic poles found in unusual position. Sci N L 86:331 N 21 '64

JUPITER (planet)—*Continued*
Jupiter's satellites and their shadows. il Sky & Tel 28:182 S '64
Planet Jupiter; conference at NASA's Institute for space studies, New York, October 1962. R. Jastrow and N. Panagakos. il Science 139:351-2+ Ja 25 '63
Radar observations of Jupiter. R. M. Goldstein. bibliog il Science 144:842-3 My 15 '64
Radio observations of Jupiter's rotation. il Sky & Tel 28:63+ Ag '64
Radio waves from Jupiter. K. L. Franklin. il Sci Am 211:34-42 bibliog(p 142) Jl '64
Red spot mystery. il Time 83:73 My 8 '64
Repeatability of Jupiter's decametric radio emission. J. W. Warick. bibliog il Science 140:814-16 My 17 '63
Studies of Jupiter and Saturn. il Sky & Tel 28:133 S '64
Temperature study of Jupiter. il Sky & Tel 27:17 Ja '64
Tired Jupiter; slowing down. il Newsweek 63:86 My 11 '64
Widespread activity on Jupiter. L. J. Robinson. il Sky & Tel 26:364-6 D '63

Atmosphere

What makes the shadows hot. Time 83:80 My 29 '64

Satellites

See Satellites

JURA, George. See Nicol, N; Souers, P. C. jt. auths.
JURASSIC period. See Paleontology—Jurassic
JURG, J. W. and Eisma, E.
Petroleum hydrocarbons: generation from fatty acid. bibliog Science 144:1451 Je 19 '64
JURIES, Art
Art juries: is there order in the court? K. Kuh. Sat R 46:31-2 Mr 30 '63
Looking at Latin America; group of juries assembles exhibits for forthcoming exhibition in Washington. F. Getlein. New Repub 152:28-30 Ja 30 '65
Who can tell? N. Kent. Am Artist 27:3+ Je '63
JURISDICTIONAL disputes. See Trade unions—Jurisdictional disputes
JURISPRUDENCE
Justice and the death penalty. D. R. Gordon. Christian Cent 80:955 Jl 31 '63
Law and justice. H. Bedau. bibliog Nation 196:357-61 Ap 27 '63
Sources of law. W. Berns. Nat R 16:690-1 Ag 11 '64
JURJI, Edward J.
Neo-Nietzschean. Christian Cent 81:179-80 F 5 '64
JURY
Brief for the jury in civil cases. J. D. Fuchsberg. il N Y Times Mag p34+ Mr 1 '64; Discussion. p4+ Mr 22 '64
Cool on contempt; Supreme court decision to uphold summary criminal-contempt power. il Time 83:57 Ap 17 '64
Death in the family; R. M. Cohn's mistrial. il Time 83:76 My 1 '64
Death penalty and fair trial. W. E. Oberer. Nation 198:342-4 Ap 6 '64
Defendant who wants attention; fair trial for Ruby in Dallas? il Time 83:23 F 21 '64
Desegregating the jury box. Time 84:44+ Jl 24 '64
Hoffa trial. F. J. Cook. il Nation 198:415-39 Ap 27 '64
How to make lawyers wish you'd go away. R. Bingham. Reporter 29:42 S 26 '63
Jury system on trial. il Sr Schol 84:8-10 Mr 20 '64
Jury tampering in Tennessee. C. R. Mollenhoff. il Look 27:79-82 My 21 '63
Jury trial barred; Supreme court decision to uphold summary criminal contempt power. Sr Schol 84:15-16 Ap 24 '64
Like picking a wife; jurors for Ruby trial. il Time 83:53 F 28 '64
Longest trial; U.S. v. Samuel Garfield, et al. Time 81:25-6 F 22 '63
Notes and comment; two days of jury duty. New Yorker 40:47 N 21 '64
Ordeal of William Penn. F. Biddle. il Am Heritage 15:30-3+ Ap '64
Ruby jurors. il Time 83:25 Mr 13 '64
Ruby trial: a chance to redeem a tragedy. S. Bedford. il Life 56:36-36B F 28 '64
Should it take thirty-four months for a trial? C. S. Desmond. il N Y Times Mag p29+ D 8 '63
Trial by juries; experimental case in Chicago. Newsweek 62:33 N 4 '63
Trial by jury. Commonweal 80:164-5 My 1 '64
Trial without jury; case of Ross R. Barnett and Paul B. Johnson, jr. New Repub 150:5-6 Ap 18 '64
Twelve white men and true; discrimination in jury selection. M. Meltsner. New Repub 150:11-12 My 23 '64; Reply. L. S. Korns. 150:36 Je 13 '64
Two-way prejudice? Newsweek 61:22 Je 3 '63
Unfair integration. Time 84:76 N 20 '64
See also
Women as jurors
Youth jury
JUST, Ward S.
Attack and revenge: the battle of Ktima. Newsweek 63:37 Mr 23 '64
Day the news managers quit. Reporter 28:36-7 My 9 '63
Scrapping of Skybolt. Reporter 28:19-21 Ap 11 '63
JUST and lasting peace; drama. See DuBois, G.
JUST like Jessica; story. See Potts, J.
JUST wild about Harry; drama. See Miller, H.
JUSTICE, Donald
Crossing Kansas by train; poem. New Yorker 39:161 D 14 '63
Variations for two pianos; poem. New Yorker 39:69 Je 29 '63
JUSTICE, June. See Heneghan, P. J. jt. auth.
JUSTICE
Justice and love in the racial crisis. L. D. Kliever. Christian Cent 81:1055-7 Ag 26 '64
Justice and the death penalty. D. R. Gordon. Christian Cent 80:955 Jl 31 '63
On trying to be just. H. J. Morgenthau. Commentary 35:420-3 My '63
Word. V. P. McCorry. America 111:95-6 Jl 25 '64
JUSTICE, Administration of
Criminalistics. P. L. Kirk. bibliog Science 140:367-70 Ap 26 '63
How to tell the truth in court. L. Nizer. il McCalls 90:86-7+ Mr '63
See also
Criminal law
Criminal procedure
Due process of law
Judges
Judgments
Jury
Public defenders

Angola

Travel far and near; the African poison test. M. Ennis. il Natur Hist 74:67-9 F '65

Europe, Western

How courts in Europe deal with criminals. il U S News 58:48-9 Ja 18 '65

Germany (Federal Republic)

Reform in West Germany; investigative arrest curbed. il Time 84:53 Jl 3 '64

Great Britain

Deterrent sentences; twelve train robbers. Time 83:34 Ap 24 '64

Japan

Even worms can dream; murder retrial. il Newsweek 61:37 Ap 1 '63
Noose or pneumonia? il Time 81:37 F 15 '63

Russia

Comrades & their courts. il Time 84:118 O 2 '64
Crime in Moscow. G. Feifer. il Sat Eve Post 237:36-7+ My 9 '64
Justice in Moscow, by G. Feifer. Review
Nation 198:605-6 Je 15 '64. H. J. Berman
Newsweek il 64:78+ Jl 6 '64
Sat R il 47:26-7 Je 27 '64. R. D. Henson
Russia has Socialist crime, too. G. Feifer. il N Y Times Mag p20+ Ap 5 '64
Signs of a Soviet switch. Time 84:59 D 11 '64

Scandinavia

They fight city hall, and win. G. Kent. Read Digest 83:29-30+ Jl '63

United States

Better lawyers for our criminal courts. J. E. Lumbard. il Atlan 213:86-90 Je '64
Brief for the jury in civil cases. J. D. Fuchsberg. il N Y Times Mag p34+ Mr 1 '64; Discussion. p4+ Mr 22 '64
Case of trial by press. A. Lewis. il N Y Times Mag p31+ O 18 '64
Civil rights counterattack; old and new laws all over the South. il Time 82:55 N 1 '63
Clemency in Annapolis; case of the Giles brothers and Joseph Johnson. M. Kempton. New Repub 149:6-8 O 26 '63

JUSTICE, Administration of—United States —*Continued*
Commitment, by W. Uphaus. Review
New Repub 148:26+ Je 22 '63. G. W. Johnson
Cool look at the crime crisis. J. V. Bennett. Harper 228:123-7 Ap '64
Crash echoes across the Nation. il Life 55: 22-7 Jl 19 '63
Crime, wealth and justice. R. Goldfarb. New Repub 151:15-16 Ag 22 '64
Criminals, cops and the Constitution. Y. Kamisar. il Nation 199:322-6 N 9 '64
Danville on trial. S. Belfrage. New Repub 149: 11-12 N 2 '63
Day of accusation in Mississippi; Mississippians implicated in murder of civil rights workers; with report by D. Nevin. il Life 57:34-9 D 18 '64
Declaring a war on injustice. R. Goldfarb. New Repub 152:15-17 Ja 16 '65
Defendant who wants attention; fair trial for Ruby in Dallas? il Time 83:23 F 21 '64
Dignity and justice. Nation 198:205 Mr 2 '64
Double standard for murder? H. Carter. il N Y Times Mag p20+ Ja 24 '65
Due process is for all. Nation 196:82 F 2 '63
Equal justice for the poor, too. A. J. Goldberg. il N Y Times Mag p24+ Mr 15 '64
Farce in Birmingham. il Time 82:27-8 O 18 '63
Federal viewpoint on combating organized crime. H. J. Miller, jr. bibliog f Ann Am Acad 347:93-103 My '63
Focus on chapter V; Warren commission report. Nation 199:205-6 O 12 '64
Government lawyer looks at the crime problem; Fourth amendment and the administration of criminal justice. il U S News 57:74-6 S 28 '64
Growing issue; high cost of justice; with case history. Nations Bsns 51:78-80+ My '63
High cost of justice; handicaps of poverty. Newsweek 63:30 F 24 '64
Hoffa trial. F. J. Cook. il Nation 198:415-39 Ap 27 '64
Homosexuality as crime in North Carolina. A. M. Bickel. New Repub 151:5-6 D 12 '64; 152:5 Ja 9 '65
How to beat a murder rap; copping a plea in Worthington case. il Time 84:54 O 23 '64
Indictments this time; case of murdered civil rights workers near Philadelphia, Miss. Time 85:21 Ja 22 '65
Is the federal government helpless? A. M. Bickel. New Repub 151:14 D 26 '64
Jesus no! preliminary hearing of civil rights murder case in Meridian, Miss. il Newsweek 64:21-2 D 21 '64
Judge Pye and the hundred sit-ins; Atlanta, Ga. B. M. Galphin. New Repub 150:8-9 My 30 '64
Judgment in Mississippi; arraignment and release of twenty-one persons in connection with murder of civil rights workers. G. W. Johnson. New Repub 151:13-14 D 26 '64
Justice and Oswald. H. L. Cartwright. Nation 197:inside cover D 21 '63
Justice falls on three duck lovers; case in Los Angeles. R. B. Stolley. il Life 55:11 Ag 2 '63
Justice for the poor; the banner of Gideon. R. G. Sherrill. il Nation 198:367-72 Ap 13 '64
Justice in Mississippi; notes on the Beckwith trial. J. Herron. Nation 198:179-81 F 24 '64
Justice with a southern accent; do our federal courts need emancipating? L. Lusky. Harper 228:69-70+ Mr '64; Discussion. 228: 9 My '64
Local and state action against organized crime. E. H. Lumbard. Ann Am Acad 347: 82-92 My '63
New union target; the courts. il Nations Bsns 52:32-3+ Ja '64
Of ducks & men; case of Raymond Lopez and widow Hanush. il Time 82:13-14 Ag 2 '63
Other grand jury; arrests in Mississippi. Newsweek 64:44 O 12 '64
Poor man in the scales. R. B. Ribman and S. M. Ribman. il Harper 228:150-4+ Ap '64
Problem of quality; U.S. commissioners. il Time 84:55 D 25 '64
Role of the courts: conscience of a sovereign people. J. S. Wright. il Reporter 29:27-30 S 26 '63; Reply. N. Thomas. 29:12 O 24 '63
Shoofly Pye; Atlanta judge v. U.S. Court of appeals. il Time 83:58 Ap 17 '64
Should it take thirty-four months for a trial? C. S. Desmond. il N Y Times Mag p29+ D 8 '63
Should the offended try the offender? il Time 83:48 Ap 10 '64
Southern justice: lawyers walk in fear. W. M. Kunstler and A. Kinoy. il Nation 198:576-80 Je 8 '64
Space age electronics; address, June 16, 1964. H. Ellenbogen. Vital Speeches 30:662-5 Ag 15 '64
Speaking out; lawyers are failing the law. M. L. Ernst. Sat Eve Post 237:8+ Mr 7 '64
Strategic retreat; charges dropped against twenty-one men. il Time 84:23 D 18 '64
Throwing the bone. Nation 199:262 O 26 '64
Timid lawyers and neglected clients. D. H. Pollitt. Harper 229:81-6 Ag '64; Discussion. 229:8 O '64
Traffic courts; cash register justice. L. Scandur. il Nation 198:144-5 F 10 '64
Two trials; Jack Ruby and the man accused of slaying Medgar Evers. Nation 198:82 Ja 27 '64
Very good folks; eighteen indicted in murder of three civil-rights workers. il Newsweek 65:26+ Ja 25 '65
What is the right punishment? first federal Sentencing institute. il Time 83:54 F 28 '64
What the judge said to Hoffa. F. Wilson. U S News 56:114 Mr 23 '64
When a Negro is on trial in the South. B. M. Galphin. il N Y Times Mag p 17+ D 15 '63
When newsmen become newsmakers; problem of publicity before and during a trial. E. N. Griswold. Sat R 47:21-3 O 24 '64; Reply. W. O'Neil. 47:25 N 21 '64
See also
Courts—United States
Jury
Sacco-Vanzetti case
Trials
United States—Justice, Department of

JUSTICE, Department of. See United States—Justice, Department of

JUSTICE, Miscarriage of
Ordeal of an innocent man. H. M. Greenwald. il Sat Eve Post 236:82+ O 5 '63
Thank God, thank God; Gerald M. Anderson freed. Newsweek 61:34+ F 11 '63
See also
False imprisonment

JUSTICES. See Judges

JUSTIFICATION
What Luther meant by faith alone. M. W. Hess. Cath World 199:96-101 My '64

JUSTIN, K. Thannhauser, collection. See Art—Private collections

JUSTINIAN
Emperor's vices; excerpt from Secret histories, tr. by A. Atwater. Procopius. Horizon 5:10 N '63

JUTLAND, Battle of, 1916
Thunder at Jutland. il Life 56:66-73 Ap 17 '64

JUVENILE courts
Do children have rights? M. G. Paulsen. il PTA Mag 58:7-9 F '64
Judge tells how to deal with under-age hoods. R. Gardner. U S News 55:44-5 Ag 26 '63
Justice for juveniles. il Time 84:65-6 Ag 21 '64
Open house for young hoods. D. J. Giese. Read Digest 84:125-9 Ap '64
People versus Baby. G. Samuels. il N Y Times Mag p40-1+ Ja 17 '65

JUVENILE delinquency
Delinquency! national crisis. J. Viorst. il Sci N L 84:202 S 28 '63
Disease and delinquency. R. I. Jaslow and G. Ebling, jr. il PTA Mag 57:18-20 Je '63
Free crime school? TV explosion. America 108:425 Mr 30 '63
Ingredients of crime same around the world. Sci N L 83:382 Je 15 '63
Juvenile gang; a cultural reflex. H. A. Bloch. bibliog f Ann Am Acad 347:20-9 My '63
Open house for young hoods. D. J. Giese. Read Digest 84:125-9 Ap '64
Overprivileged; Darien, Conn. delinquents. il Newsweek 61:29 My 27 '63
Paradoxical case of the affluent delinquent. J. Lelyveld. il N Y Times Mag p 13+ O 4 '64
School crime wave. Nation 198:310 Mr 30 '64
Social tensions in our nation's capital. M. McGrory. America 108:603 Ap 27 '63
Speaking out; too many kids are loafing. R. Gardner. Sat Eve Post 236:10+ Je 22 '63
Tense generation. S. Grafton. il Look 27:17-23 Ag 27 '63; Same abr. Read Digest 83: 61-6 N '63; Discussion. Look 27:14+ O 8 '63
Too much and too little. America 109:33 Jl 13 '63

JUVENILE delinquency—*Continued*
What triggers violence? il Newsweek 64:94+ N 16 '64
Whiting doesn't spare the rod. K. Detzer. il Read Digest 82:167-70+ My '63
Why young people get into trouble. Farm J 87:82 Ag '63
Wild youth: a worldwide program. G. Lucy. Read Digest 85:167-9+ O '64
World side story; excerpts from Juvenile delinquency, a problem for the modern world. W. C. Kvaraceus il UNESCO Courier 17:4-11 My; 4-9 Je; 28-32 S '64
See also
Gangs
Juvenile courts
New York (city)—Youth board
Problem children

Prevention

Building better boys; Better boys foundation Archie Moore gym, Chicago, Ill. il Ebony 19:75-8+ D '63
Don't take the police for granted. R. Brecher and E. Brecher. il Parents Mag 39:56-7+ Mr '64
Helping the child who comes into conflict with the law. R. G. Farrow. Ann Am Acad 355:90-7 S '64
How to spot a pre-delinquent. Sci Digest 55:76 F '64
It's tough to be a teen-ager; ed. by R. L. Smith. J. F. Phelan, jr. Read Digest 82: 31-2+ Mr '63
Jacksonville's jury of juvenile peers. F. Sondern, jr. Parents Mag 38:47+ Ag '63; Same abr. Read Digest 83:82-5 Ag '63
Jury of peers; Terre Haute experiment. il Newsweek 63:22 Ja 20 '64
Litter clean-up out of the ordinary; Portsmouth, Va. and Pleasant Hill, Calif. Am City 79:34 Ap '64
Nature centers and delinquency. J. J. Shomon. Audubon Mag 66:14-15 Ja '64
Providence takes a hand. E. D. Baldoni. Recreation 56:364-5 O '63
Residential treatment center. J. G. Milner. bibliog f Ann Am Acad 355:98-104 S '64
Tryout in Harlem. M. Kempton. New Repub 148:11-13 F 23 '63; Reply. D. L. Hackett. 148:38 Ap 13 '63
Two new ways to curb JD. Life 54:4 Ap 5 '63
We can beat J.D; New York's Mobilization for youth. H. Page. il Parents Mag 39: 56-8+ O '64
Why tough kids go straight; Warren residential group center, New Jersey. A. Stahr. il Parents Mag 38:56-7+ D '63

Prognosis

Five signs on the highroad. N. Gordon. il Sat R 46:49-52 Ap 6 '63

Statistics

Running wild. Time 84:38 S 18 '64

Great Britain

Battle of the yobs. il Time 83:29 My 29 '64

Poland

Unhappy hooligans. il Newsweek 62:64 D 2 '63

JUVENILE delinquency, Senate subcommittee on. See United States—Congress—Senate—Committees
JUVENILE hormones. See Hormones
JUVENILE literature. See Childrens literature
JUVISY observatory. See Astronomical observatories—France

K

KGB. See Secret service—Russia
KKK. See Ku Klux klan
KLM (airline) See Airlines—Netherlands
K meson. See Mesons
KABAT, Jack
Advertising designs of Jack Kabat. il por Am Artist 28:56-60+ Ja '64
KABIR, Humayun
Outlawing of India's caste system. UNESCO Courier 16:12-14 D '63
KABOBS. See Cookery—Meat
KABUKI
Letter from Tokyo. H. Clurman. Nation 197: 118-20, 147-8 S 7-14 '63
Theatre USA; East-West center; University of Hawaii; production of Kabuki plays. A. Slagle. il Theatre Arts 48:70-1+ Ja '64
KAC, Mark
Probability; with biographical sketch. Sci Am 211:28+, 92-6+ bibliog(p269) S '64
KACHARIAN, John C.
When lightning strikes. Todays Health 42: 14-17+ Jl '64
KADÁR, János
Humanizing communism. il por Time 82:40 S 13 '63
Hungary: renaissance after revolt. D. Holden. il por Sat Eve Post 237:38+ Ap 25 '64
Letter from Budapest. J. Wechsberg. il New Yorker 40:121-2+ Mr 14 '64
A look inside Hungary; seven years after uprising. A. Kucherov. il por U S News 55:50-3 D 30 '63; Correction. 56:9 Ja 6 '64
10,000,000 Hungarians can't be wrong. D. Binder. il pors N Y Times Mag p6-7+ D 27 '64
Rapid change. il Newsweek 62:46-7 Jl 29 '63
KADEY, Maria
Planned for chartering. por Yachting 114: 56-7+ N '63
KADLEC, John E. and Atkinson, J. H.
Where should you spend money on your farm? Suc Farm 62:52+ O '64
KADOORIE, Horace
Remarkable Kadoorie brothers of Hong Kong. C. W. Hall. il por Read Digest 82:273-8 My '63
KADOORIE, Lawrence
Remarkable Kadoorie brothers of Hong Kong. C. W. Hall. il por Read Digest 82:273-8 My '63
KAEL, Pauline
Are movies going to pieces? Atlan 214:61-6 D '64
KAFALAS, James A. and Mariano, A. N.
High-pressure phase transition in tin telluride. bibliog Science 143:952 F 28 '64
KAFATOS, Fotis C. and Williams, C. M.
Enzymatic mechanism for the escape of certain moths from their cocoons. bibliog Science 146:538-40 O 23 '64
KAFIR language (Bantu)
Professor of Xhosa at Wisconsin. Sch & Soc 92:121 Mr 21 '64
KAFIR tomb figures. See Tomb figures
KAFIRS (Nuristan) See Nuristan—Native races
KAFKA, Franz
Kafka East, Kafka West. H. Cox. il Commonweal 80:596-600 S 4 '64
Kafka's nightmare comes true. G. Bailey. Reporter 30:15-20 My 7 '64
KAHN, Albert E.
Particular treasure; excerpts from Days with Ulanova. Dance Mag 37:40-8 S '63
KAHN, Ely Jacques, 1884-
Needed: oases in the asphalt desert. N Y Times Mag p54-5+ My 26 '63
KAHN, Ely Jacques, 1916-
Department of amplification; letter. New Yorker 40:159-60+ Je 6 '64
Honest ski is the best policy. Mlle 60:142-3+ D '64
Letter from Bangkok. New Yorker 40:165-6+ D 5 '64
Our far-flung correspondents (cont) New Yorker 40:155-6+ N 21 '64
Please keep your dog off my court. Sports Illus 21:40-4 Jl 13 '64
Profiles. New Yorker 40:34-6+ Ag 15 '64; 37-8+ Ja 9; 40-2+ Ja 16 '65
Sporting scene. New Yorker 40:110+ O 17; 236-8+ O 24; 195-202 O 31 '64
Thank you, Madam President. New Yorker 40:103-4+ My 2 '64
KAHN, Gordon
Capsule history of gold. Holiday 33:72-3 My '63
Capsule history of shoes. Holiday 33:54-5 Je '63
KAHN, Hannah
Green year; poem. Ladies Home J 80:96 Je '63
Make mine a la mode; poem. Good H 157:266 O '63
Wednesday club; poem. McCalls 90:151 Mr '63
KAHN, Herman
Multilateral force or farce? debate. por N Y Times Mag p25+ D 13 '64
Prospects for war and peace; interview. por Nations Bsns 52:34-5+ Jl '64
about
Report on a think factory. A. Herzog. il por N Y Times Mag p30+ N 10 '63
KAHN, Lothar
Isaac Bashevis Singer. Commonweal 81:538-40 Ja 22 '65

KAHN, Louis I.
Light, form, and power: new work of Louis Kahn. V. Scully. il Arch Forum 121:162-70 Ag '64
KAHN, Morley D. See Myers, M. R. jr, jt. auth.
KAHN, Otto H.
Kahn, Morgan, and Salome. por Sat R 47:60 My 30 '64
Many lives of Otto Kahn, by M. J. Matz. Review
Opera N 28:34 F 1 '64. M. E. Peltz
KAHN, Roger
Bill Miller: the G.O.P.'s tough, shrewd pro. Sat Eve Post 237:81-3 Ag 8 '64
Goldwater's desperate battle. Sat Eve Post 237:19-25 O 24 '64
Harlem sketchbook: white man, walk easy. Sat Eve Post 237:26-8+ Je 13 '64
Is there a Doris Day? Ladies Home J 80: 62-5 Jl '63
Our Davis cup runneth over. Sat Eve Post 237:66-9 S 26 '64
Robert Frost: a reminiscence. Nation 196:121 F 9 '63
Speaking out. por Sat Eve Post 237:8+ O 10 '64
Yankees: descent from Olympus. Sat Eve Post 237:80-3 S 12 '64
KAHUNA sorcery. See Witchcraft
KAI, Una
Meet Una Kai. S. Goodman. il por Dance Mag 37:19-21+ O '63
KAIBAB squirrels. See Squirrels
KAISER, Edgar Fosburgh
Edgar Kaiser, maverick in motion. W. Trombley. il pors Sat Eve Post 236:20-1 Je 22 '63
Optimistic world of Edgar Kaiser. W. Guzzardi, jr. il por Fortune 67:90-7+ Ap '63
Personalities. por Time 82:76 S 27 '63
KAISER, Frederick F.
Jamie, the deadrise coaster. Motor B 113: 112-13+ My '64
KAISER, Henry J.
Henry Kaiser. L. Elliott. il pors Sci Digest 53:58-65 My '63
KAISER, Robert B.
And now the search begins for the new pope. Life 54:57-8 Je 21 '63
Vatican II, act II: reportage, speculation and gossip. Commonweal 80:517-18 Jl 24 '64
KAISER, Robert G.
Whiffenpoofs are expensive. Esquire 62: 134-7+ N '64
KAISER, Walter H.
Self-shelving by children. Library J 89:2146-8+ My 15 '64
KAISER aluminum and chemical corporation
Instant money plan: blank checks to suppliers. Bsns W p90 O 12 '63
Problem in organization. S. Nicholson. il Duns R 31:43-4+ Je '63
KAISER industries corporation
Córdoba's biennial comes to Washington. J. Gómez-Sicre. il Américas 15:16-19 F '63
Kaiser: model for Latin America. D. Smyth. il Nation 197:415-17 D 14 '63
Optimistic world of Edgar Kaiser. W. Guzzardi, jr. il Fortune 67:90-7+ Ap '63
Special-interest cars; Kaiser-Frazer. D. Moore. il Motor T 16:80 N '64
Willy name gone from auto world; now Kaiser jeep corp. Bsns W p72 Mr 16 '63
KAISER savings-sharing plan. See Savings-sharing plan in industry
KAISER steel corporation
Breakthrough at Kaiser: automation and unemployment. L. T. King. Commonweal 78:11-12 Mr 29 '63
Landmark in labor relations; Kaiser-United steelworkers agreement. H. Malmgren. New Repub 148:7 Mr 16 '63
Outsiders keep peace at Kaiser. Bsns W p 105 O 24 '64
Second look at profit sharing. U.S. News 56: 78-9 Je 22 '64
KALAH. See Games
KALAMAZOO, Mich.
Employee suggestions. S. Kelley. il Am City 79:95 Ja '64
City planning
Long-term benefits of a shoppers' mall. C. H. Elliott. il Am City 79:91-2 Mr '64
Streets
Cut-rate paving assessments. D. A. Southern. il Am City 79:96 Ap '64
Instant traffic lines, inlaid, too. R. B. Carroll. il Am City 79:15 S '64
KALAMAZOO college, Kalamazoo, Mich.
Kalamazoo college's foreign study program. Sch & Soc 92:219 Sum '64
Kalamazoo coup. Newsweek 62:69 Jl 29 '63
KALANCHOES
Flowering kalanchoes. E. A. Flickinger. il Flower Grower 50:29-30 My '63
KALB, Marvin
Death by order of the dictator. Sat R 47: 135-6 Mr 14 '64
Poet-hero of the young at heart. Sat R 46: 20-1 Ag 10 '63
(ed) See Rusk, D. Secretary Rusk participates in CBS reports program
KALDOR, Nicholas
Will underdeveloped countries learn to tax? For Affairs 41:410-19 Ja '63
KALER, Grace
Old metals. See issues of Hobbies
KALIJARVI, Thorsten V.
Obstacles to European unification. Ann Am Acad 348:46-53 Jl '63
KALIN, D. A.
Rubber-asphalt paving. Am City 79:106-7 My '64
KALINE, Al
Torments of excellence. J. Olsen. il pors Sports Illus 20:32+ My 11 '64
KALISH, Harry I. See Haber, A. jt. auth.
KALITSI, E. A. K.
African metamorphosis. UNESCO Courier 16: 44-9 Jl '63
KALKSTEIN, Marvin
Paradoxes of deterrence. Bul Atomic Sci 19: 26-7 Je '63
Preventing the spread of nuclear weapons. Bul Atomic Sci 20:18-19 D '64
—See Phelps, J. jt. auth.
KALLAI, Sandor
Music critic looks at basic LP collections. por Library J 88:3802-3 O 15 '63
KALLE, Gurudutt P. and Gots, J. S.
Genetic alteration of adenylic pyrophosphorylase in salmonella. bibliog Science 142:680-1 N 8 '63
KALLIKREIN
Antibodies to bradykinin and angiotensin: a use of carbodiimides in immunology. T. L. Goodfriend and others. bibliog il Science 144:1344-6 Je 12 '64
Bradykinin: vascular relaxant, cardiac stimulant. D. Montague and others. bibliog il Science 141:907-8 S 6 '63
KALLMAN, Burton J. and Andrews, A. K.
Reductive dechlorination of DDT to DDD by yeast. Science 141:1050-1 S 13 '63
KALLMAN, Chester
Six poets. J. Woods. Poetry 104:108-9 My '64
KALMANSON, George M. See Guze, L. B. jt. auth.
KALS, W. S.
Winter weather in the palm belt. Yachting 116:42-3+ N '64
KALVAR corporation
Kalvar; from a wastebasket, dazzling suspense. S. Mahoney. il Fortune 67:110-13+ Mr '63
KALVIN, George
Topology, the art of distortion; excerpt from Mathematics. Design 66:26-7 S '64
KALVODA, Josef
Academic freedom in the age of conflict; address, May 1, 1963. Vital Speeches 29: 526-31 Je 15 '63
Freedom; its responsibilities; address, March 13, 1964. Vital Speeches 30:439-41 My 1 '64
KAMARAJ, Kumaraswami
Nehru's new centrism. A. Kumari. Reporter 29:33-5 D 5 '63
KAMARCK, Andrew M.
Recent economic growth in Africa. Ann Am Acad 354:46-53 Jl '64
KAMB, Barclay
Glacier geophysics. bibliog Science 146:353-65 O 16 '64
KAMEHAMEHA schools. See Schools—Hawaii
KAMEN, Martin D.
Early history of carbon-14. bibliog Science 140:584-90; 141:861-2 My 10, S 6 '63
KAMEN, Milt
Rich wild life of Milt Kamen. M. Kitman. il por Sat Eve Post 236:75-6 D 14 '63
KAMENTSKY, Louis A. and others
Ultraviolet absorption in epidermoid cancer cells. bibliog Science 142:1580-3 D 20 '63
KAMENY, Frank E.
Man-killer. New Repub 149:15-16 S 21 '63
KAMES, Joseph M. See Pilgrim, F. J. jt. auth.
KAMINETZKY, Dov
Preventing cracks in masonry walls. Arch Rec 136:210-14 N '64
KAMINSKY, Max
Swing band era; ed. by V. E. Hughes. Harper 226:57-64 Ap '63

KAMINSKY, Merle
Ten ways to help your substitute. Sr Schol 85:9T O 14 '64
KAMISAR, Yale
Criminals, cops and the Constitution. Nation 199:322-6 N 9 '64
KAMMERER, Gladys M. and DeGrove, J. M.
Urban leadership during change. bibliog f Ann Am Acad 353:95-106 My '64
KAMMERER, Rafael
Artur Schnabel: the complete Beethoven piano sonatas. Am Rec G 30:378-80+ Ja '64
First complete recording of Gottschalk's symphony. A night in the Tropics. Am Rec G 30:102-3 O '63
Great pianists. Am Rec G 30:591-2 Mr '64
Horowitz collection. Am Rec G 30:14-16 S '63
Legendary masters of the piano. Am Rec G 30:810-12 My '64
Liszt by Horowitz, c. 1932. Am Rec G 29:552+ Mr '63
Virgil Fox plays the Philharmonic Hall organ at Lincoln Center. Am Rec G 29:958-9 Ag '63
KAMUNDIA, Cyrus A.
Books about Africa. Horn Bk 39:79-80 F '63
KANATANI, Haruo
Spawning of starfish: action of gamete-shedding substance obtained from radial nerves. bibliog Science 146:1177-9 N 27 '64
KANDEL, I. L.
Bagley, Kandel, and the SAE. W. W. Brickman. Sch & Soc 92:258 O 3 '64
KANDINSKY, Wassily
Art; Kandinsky at the Guggenheim museum. H. Kramer. Nation 196:167-8 F 23 '63
Art on the move; exhibition at the Guggenheim. C. J. McNaspy. America 108:314-16 Mr 2 '63
Eye for the future; retrospective exhibition at the Guggenheim museum. K. Kuh. il Sat R 46:39-40 F 23 '63
Form and freedom; retrospective exhibitions at New York's Guggenheim museum and the Pasadena, Calif, art museum. il por Newsweek 61:58 F 4 '63
Kandinsky at the Guggenheim. F. Getlein. New Repub 148:25-6 Mr 16 '63
Kandinsky; last of the heresiarchs. J. Kroll. il Art N 61:38-41+ F '63
Kandinsky's craft. B. Kaufman. Commonweal 78:28-9+ Mr 29 '63
Kandinskys for sale. Newsweek 63:91 F 17 '64
Landmarks of modern art. K. Kuh. il Sat R 46:30 Je 22 '63
My association with Kandinsky. E. Harms. il Am Artist 27:36-41+ Je '63
Record price for abstracts. Time 84:70 Jl 10 '64
Retrospective in the round; show at Manhattan's Guggenheim museum. il Time 81:74-7 F 15 '63
KANE, Art
Dynamic distortions. R. T. Hammarlund. il U S Camera 26:49-55+ Ap '63
Mystic image of Japan. il Look 27:44-9 S 10 '63
Through the looking glass. il U S Camera 27:44-7 D '64
KANE, Arthur W.
Temperature method. America 110:596+ My 2 '64
KANE, Francis X.
Security is too important to be left to computers. por Fortune 69:146-7+ Ap '64
KANE, John J.
How tense are interreligious tensions? Cath World 197:351-8 S '63
KANE, Martin
Fishing (cont) Sports Illus 18:42-3 Ja 28 '63
KANE, Maury
Try northern California for fishing at its best. Todays Health 42:46-51+ My '64
KANE, Robert S.
Kenya. Travel 119:30-5 Ap '63
KANE, Walter. See Jones, B. H. jt. auth.
KANE, Will
Mexico's new rail thrill. Travel 119:34-7 F '63
KANFER, Allen
Frostbitten mourner and Beethoven; poem. Poetry 101:242-3 Ja '63
Portrait; Love and snow; Sermon; Separation; poems. Poetry 103:249-50 Ja '64
KANFER, Stefan
Yiddish theater. Atlan 212:104-6+ O '63
KANGAROO rats
Ears of dipodomys; bannertail kangaroo rat. D. B. Webster. il Natur Hist 74:26-33 F '65
Milk analysis of the kangaroo rat, dipodomys merriami. G. L. Kooyman. bibliog il Science 142:1467 D 13 '63
KANGAROOS
Kangaroo cave life. E. H. M. Ealey. il Natur Hist 72:42-9 D '63
Me white kangaroo; creation of Sir E. Hallstrom. il Life 54:49-52+ Ap 26 '63
Meet the ghost kangaroo. il Sci Digest 55:48-9 Ap '64
Palm Beach: hopped up about Joey. J. Rieker. il Life 56:25 Ap 3 '64
Tie me kangaroo, down. il Time 83:35 Mr 6 '64
KANIN, Garson
Don't forget; story. Ladies Home J 80:74-9 S '63
Echo of love; story. Sat Eve Post 236:42-5 F 16 '63
Trips to Felix. Atlan 213:55-62 Mr '64; Same abr. with title Conversations with Felix. Read Digest 84:116-20 Je '64
KANKAKEE, Ill.
Bubbles break the ice. il Am City 78:112-13 O '63
KANNO, Y. and Loewenstein, W. R.
Intercellular diffusion. bibliog Science 143:959 F 28 '64
KANNWISCHER, L. R. See Lisk, R. D. jt. auth.
KANSAS
See also
Booksellers and bookselling—Kansas
Education—Kansas
Rice County
KANSAS CITY, Kan.

Religious institutions and affairs

News of the Christian world (cont) Christian Cent 81:1506 D 2 '64
KANSAS CITY, Mo.
Birthday parties at the zoo. G. K. Clarke. il Am City 78:101-2 Mr '63
Happiness is being somewhere else; K.C. A's. F. Graham, jr. il Sat Eve Post 237:73-7 Ap 4 '64
Tell-tale powder nabs meter vandals. S. E. Cross. il Am City 79:110 Jl '64

Architecture

Powerful grid for a prairie tower; Kansas City's new BMA building. il Arch Forum 121:86-91 Jl '64

Education

Elementary school industrial arts in Kansas City. T. G. Boyd. il NEA J 53:32-3 Ja '64

Music

[Musical events] (cont) Mus Am 83:16 Mr; 268 D '63; 84:21 Jl '64
See also
Kansas City lyric theater

Politics and government

Leadership in a large manager city: the case of Kansas City. S. T. Gabis. bibliog f Ann Am Acad 353:52-63 My '64

Religious institutions and affairs

News of the Christian world (cont) Christian Cent 80:654; 81:526+ My 15 '63, Ap 22 '64

Water supply

Two-stage water-plant expansion. L. W. Bremser. il Am City 78:78-80 D '63
KANSAS CITY Athletics (baseball) See Baseball clubs
KANSAS CITY Chiefs (football club) See Football clubs
KANSAS CITY lyric theater
Kansas City lyrics. S. Kallai. il Opera N 28:31-2 D 21 '63
Kansas City progress. S. Kallai. Opera N 29:31 D 19 '64
KANT, Immanuel
Kant and Judaism. E. L. Fackenheim. Commentary 36:460-7 D '63
KANTOR, MacKinlay
Dear cousin William. McCalls 91:77+ F '64
Legend of Jones City. McCalls 91:63 D '63
KANTOR, Tim
Tim Kantor; with portfolio of images of Latin America. U S Camera 26:46-51 Mr '63
KANTROWITZ, Arthur R.
Moon landing: we might find more exciting things to do; interview. por U S News 54:64-6 Ap 15 '63
KANZLER, Hal
Back packing; family style. por Field & S 68:35-7 Je '63
Best gear for backpacking. Field & S 69:62-5 My '64
Four seconds to shoot. Field & S 68:95 Ag '63
Outdoor footwear. Field & S 68:50-1+ S '63
Partners to the end. Field & S 69:24 N '64
KAOLINITE
Infrared absorption of hydroxyl groups in kaolinite. V. C. Farmer. bibliog il Science 145:1189-90 S 11 '64

KAOLINITE—*Continued*
Infrared study of selective deuteration of kaolinite and halloysite at room temperature. R. L. Ledoux and J. L. White. bibliog il Science 145:47-9 Jl 3 '64
Infrared study of the OH groups in expanded kaolinite. R. L. Ledoux and J. L. White. bibliog il Science 143:244-6 Ja 17 '64
Transformation of montmorillonite to kaolinite during weathering. Z. S. Altschuler and others. bibliog il Science 141:148-52 Jl 12 '63

KAPITZA, Petr Leonidovich
Ball lightning. H. W. Lewis. il Sci Am 208:106-8+ bibliog(p 190+) Mr '63
Science milestone; Russian who talks back to Khrushchev. A. Parry. il pors Sci Digest 53:45-51 Je '63

KAPLAN, Donald M.
On unperfect actors. E. Capouya. Sat R 46:40-1 D 14 '63

KAPLAN, Gerald
Open shop for lawyers. Nat R 16:603-4 Jl 14 '64

KAPLAN, Henry S. and Moses, L. E.
Biological complexity and radiosensitivity. bibliog Science 145:21-5 Jl 3 '64

KAPLAN, Hymen R.
Just what is coast guard approved? Motor B 111:48-9+ Mr '63

KAPLAN, Jules, and Kaplan, Mrs Jules
Heredity vs. environment a surprising new answer. Sci Digest 56:59-62 D '64

KAPLAN, Mrs Jules. See Kaplan, J. jt. auth.

KAPLAN, Milton
For a special occasion; story. Redbook 120:58-9 Mr '63

KAPLAN, Robert A. See Davies, D. S. jt. auth.

KAPPEL, Frederick Russell
Inflation and morals; AT&T's chief voices concern; excerpts from statements. por U S News 57:24 O 12 '64
New developments in communications; address, August 11, 1964. Vital Speeches 30:759-62 O 1 '64

about

Bell is ringing. il pors Time 83:74-8 My 29 '64
For the Bell system, all phones are ringing. il por(cover) Bsns W p64-70 Ja 9 '65
You can't win. Newsweek 63:88+ My 18 '64

KAPPLER, Frank
Dealing with earthly hells. Life 57:98+ N 6 '64
Life book review. Life 56:10 My 15 '64
Life movie review. Life 56:12 My 29 '64

KAPROW, Allan
Segal's vital mummies. Art N 62:30-3+ F '64
Should the artist become a man of the world? Art N 63:34-7+ O '64
What is an environment? il Vogue 143:125 Ap 1 '64
World view of Alfred Jensen. Art N 62:28-31+ D '63

about

Eat; an unsettling experience with an Allan Kaprow environment. B. Rollin. il Vogue 143:124-5+ Ap 1 '64

KAPSTEIN, Jonathan
Vietnam: in the French footsteps. Nation 199:479-82 D 21 '64

KARABERIS, C. A.
Martell, Karaberis share management responsibility in separate offices. il por Miss & Roc 15:35-7 S 21 '64

KARACHI, Pakistan
Reader's choice. A. Carlson. Travel 121:13 My '64

KARAJAN, Herbert von
Conversation with von Karajan; ed. by H. Pendergast. por Sat R 46:57-8+ O 26 '63

about

Austrian bouts. J. Wechsberg. Opera N 29:31 D 19 '64
Halftone crisis; La Scala opera company. Time 81:60 F 8 '63
Herr musik diktator; with report by P. Dragadze. il pors Life 57:55-6+ O 2 '64
Karajan and the Nine. R. Lawrence. por Sat R 46:34-5 Ag 31 '63
Notes from our correspondents. K. Blaukopf. Hi Fi 14:28 Je '64
People are talking about. . . por Vogue 145:68-9 Ja 15 '65
Portrait of the conductor as celebrity. H. C. R. Landon. pors Hi Fi 13:52-5+ S '63
Walking conductor. por Newsweek 63:58 My 25 '64

KARAJAN, Wolfgang von
Brother Wolfgang. il por Time 81:68-9 Mr 1 '63

KARALEKAS, Peter C. and Manganaro, C. A.
Two gigantic reservoirs. Am City 79:73-5 Jl '64

KARAMANLIS, Constantine
Goodbye again. il por Time 82:25 D 20 '63
King wants to travel. por Time 81:29 Je 21 '63

KARAMU house. See Cleveland, Ohio—Theater

KARAS, Nicholas
Mystery hunters of Lovelock cave. Field & S 69:42-5+ Je '64
Snows of Ile aux Grues. Field & S 69:51-3+ O '64

KARATE. See Self defense

KARDINER, Abram
Mental health: search for a theory. Nation 198:34-5 Ja 6 '64

KARL, Jean
Books for an uncertain world; excerpts from address, October, 1964. por Library J 89:4964-6 D 15 '64
Progress towards standards based on performance. Pub W 185:110 F 3 '64

KARL, Max H.
Behind the man behind the loan; MGIC. il por Bsns W p 120+ S 28 '63

KARL Schwarzschild observatory. See Astronomical observatories—Germany (Democratic Republic)

KARLEN, Arno
Arts in Yugoslavia. Nation 199:499-502 D 21 '64
Capsule history of beards. Holiday 35:50-1 F '64
Capsule history of world's fairs. Holiday 36:68-9 Jl '64
Farewell the plumed troop. Nation 199:54-5 Ag 10 '64
Holiday handbook. bibliog Holiday 36:103-6 S '64
Mr Bloom meets the atom man. Nation 198:583-8 Je 8 '64
Wages of risk. Nation 198:331-4 Mr 30 '64

KARLIKOW, Abe
Jewelry by Torun. Craft Horiz 23:20-1+ Jl '63

KARLIN, Gene
CB range nomogram. Electr World 71:29 Ja '64

KARLOVY VARY, Czechoslovakia. See Karlsbad, Czechoslovakia

KARLSBAD, Czechoslovakia
Karlsbad. J. Wechsberg. il Sat R 48:44-5+ Ja 2 '65

KÁRMÁN, Theodore von. See Von Kármán, T.

KARMATZ, F. N.
Thresher inquiry. New Repub 148:7-8 Je 1 '63

KARMEL-WOLFE, Henia
His friend Vanka; story. Harper 226:64-8 Mr '63
Month of his birthday; story. Mlle 60:112-13 D '64

KARMEN, Arthur
Biological implications of gas chromatography. bibliog Science 142:163-72 O 11 '63

KARNICK, Irwin H.
Atop the Verrazano. il U S Camera 27:60-1 D '64

KARNOW, Stanley
Boxing. Sports Illus 18:44 Ja 28 '63
Chiang Kai-shek: the crumbling facade. Sat Eve Post 236:101-5 D 7 '63
Edge of chaos. Sat Eve Post 236:27-37 S 28 '63
Fall of the House of Ngo dinh. Sat Eve Post 236:75-9 D 21 '63
Fashions: the Asian rag race. Sat Eve Post 237:24-31 Ja 25 '64
Found: a cool million. Life 54:8 Mr 1 '63
GI who chose communism. Sat Eve Post 236:104-7 N 16 '63
How Communist economics failed in China. Fortune 68:154-7+ Jl '63
Laos: the settlement that settled nothing. Reporter 28:34-7 Ap 25 '63
Opium. Sat Eve Post 237:80-2 F 22 '64
Opium must go through. Life 55:11-12 Ag 30 '63
Quandary of Henry Cabot Lodge. Sat Eve Post 237:70-3 F 8 '64
Refugee reports on red China. Reporter 29:39-42 Jl 18 '63
Sinkiang: Soviet rustlers in China's Wild West. Reporter 30:36-9 Je 18 '64
These Americans must be gods. Sat Eve Post 237:72-3 Ap 25 '64
This is our enemy. Sat Eve Post 237:19-25 Ag 22 '64
Where did all that money come from? Sat Eve Post 237:62-3+ O 31 '64

KARNS, E. B.
Painting the city with light. Am City 79: 97-8 N '64
KAROK Indians
Indians fish the Ishi Pishi. il Sunset 131:37 O '63
KARP, Ivan C.
Anonymous art. New Yorker 40:50-1 N 14 '64
KARP, Tony
Confused about CdS vs. selenium exposure meters? Mod Phot 27:64-5+ Jl '63
How to care for cameras. Mod Phot 28:138+ D '64
Lowdown on portable electronic flash units. Mod Phot 28:82-7 Ja '64

about

Bizarre effects. il U S Camera 27:56-9 Ja '64
KARPATKIN, Marvin M.
Waydown yonder in New Orleans. New Repub 150:10-11 My 23 '64
KARR, Gary
Look at the future. por Mus Am 83:11 Jl '63
KARRAKER, Cyrus
Education for our rural slums. Sch & Soc 91:276-7 O 5 '63
Task for a Peace corps. Christian Cent 80: 237-8 F 20 '63
KARRAS, Alex
Back in bounds. Newsweek 63:54-5 Mr 30 '64
Big man who wasn't there; Green Bay Packers vs Detroit Lions. T. Maule. il por Sports Illus 19:76+ S 30 '63
Gigantic midget among giant men; photographs by M. E. Newman; with account by T. Maule. Sports Illus 21:46-52 N 30 '64
KARRE, Wilma. See Malone, D. P. jt. auth.
KARRO, Anne
Friends of Danville. America 110:633-5 My 9 '64
KARSH, Eileen B.
Changes in intensity of punishment; effect on running behavior of rats. bibliog Science 140:1084-5 Je 7 '63
KART engines. See Automobile engines
KART racing. See Karting
KARTH, Joseph E.
Representative Karth urges U.S. sell boosters; interview, ed. by W. Beller. por Miss & Roc 13:21-2 Ag 26 '63
KARTING
Double header kart Nationals. T. Medley. il Hot Rod 17:46-9 N '64
International micro midget championships; Bartlesville, Okla. M. Henderson. il Hot Rod 17:70-3 D '64
Red Bug; Hot rod kart test. T. Medley. il Hot Rod 17:100-1 Ag '64
Two stroke stuff. T. Medley. il Hot Rod 17: 102 Mr; 82 Ap; 86-7 My; 100-1 Je; 106-7 Jl; 106-7 S; 107 O '64; 18:96 Ja '65
KARTS (midget cars)
Double header kart Nationals. T. Medley. il Hot Rod 17:46-9 N '64
International micro midget championships; Bartlesville, Okla. M. Henderson. il Hot Rod 17:70-3 D '64
Red Bug; Hot rod kart test. T. Medley. il Hot Rod 17:100-1 Ag '64
Two stroke stuff. T. Medley. il Hot Rod 17: 102 Mr; 82 Ap; 86-7 My; 100-1 Je; 106-7 Jl; 106-7 S; 107 O '64; 18:96 Ja '65
KARTS, Hydro. See Hydrokarts
KASDAN, Alan Richard
Toward a new order in international trade. Bul Atomic Sci 20:40-3 D '64
KASELOW, Joseph
Frankenstein in ad alley. Sat R 47:46-7 Ag 8 '64
Madison avenue. Sat R 47:106 O 10 '64
KASER, Tom
Loyalty oath: 1964-65. Sat R 47:60+ N 21 '64
KASHMIR
As prickly as cactus; dispute between India and Pakistan. Time 81:36 F 15 '63
Beyond the borders; India's dispute with Pakistan. il Newsweek 63:44+ Je 29 '64
Cobra & the mongoose. Time 83:33 Mr 6 '64
India and Pakistan urged to make new effort on Kashmir problem; statement, February 14, 1964. A. E. Stevenson. Dept State Bul 50:425-6 Mr 16 '64
India, Pakistan, and the shadow of red China. il Sr Schol 83:8-11 O 18 '63
India-Pakistan question. il U N Rev 11:5-11+ Mr '64
Kashmir settlement may now be possible. H. R. Vohra. New Repub 150:11-12 Mr 21 '64
Lion on the loose. Newsweek 63:57 Ap 20 '64
Nationalism: a matter of pride and prejudice; India vs. Pakistan. il Sr Schol 85:18-19 O 7 '64
Recent triumph; Pakistan-India dispute and the West. Nat R 15:223 S 24 '63
Return of the lion. Time 83:34 Ap 10 '64
Signing with the red Chinese. il Time 81:44 Mr 15 '63
Touch of self-righteousness. il Time 83:34 Ap 24 '64
Vacation in a fabled vale; with report by M. Leatherbee. il Life 57:91-5+ Ag 14 '64
See also
Ladakh
United Nations—Kashmir

Riots

Hair of the prophet. Newsweek 63:32+ Ja 13 '64
KASKEL, Alfred
Stampede to the sun. il por Bsns W p 108-10+ Mr 9 '63
KASPER, Hirschel
Steel's Abel to raise Cain. New Repub 152: 11-13 Ja 16 '65
KASPER, J. S. See Bundy, F. P; Wentorf, R. H. jr, jt. auths.
KASPER, Karl
Pooling drug research. il por Bsns W p66-8+ O 26 '63
KASPERICK, Dan
On the military front; reprint. Recreation 56: 460-3 D '63
KASS, Gus. See Rostenberg, A. jr, jt. auth.
KASSAN, Roberta
On the D line; story. Seventeen 23:152-3 N '64
KASSEL, Germany (Federal Republic)
City theater. G. E. K. Smith. il Arch Rec 134:186-9 O '63
KASSEM, Abdul Karim
Green armbands, red blood. il Time 81:28 F 22 '63
Iraq reroutes a revolution. il Sr Schol 82: 10-13 Mr 13 '63
Iraq: the background. Nat R 14:144 F 26 '63
Kassem is gunned down; with report by R. Morse. il pors Life 54:24-9 F 22 '63
Kassem's legacy. D. Stewart. Nation 196: 222-4 Mr 16 '63
New turn in Mideast: anti-red. J. Law. il U S News 54:52 F 25 '63
Revolt in Baghdad. por Newsweek 61:53 F 18 '63
Target of revolt: an anti-American regime. il por U S News 54:8 F 18 '63
What's in store for Iraq. S. Huck. il Nat R 14:193-4 Mr 12 '63
KASTENDIECK, Miles
Ronald Ondrejka, assistant conductor Buffalo philharmonic, New York. Mus Am 83:12 My '63
KASTING, R. See McGinnis, A. J. jt. auth.
KASTNER, Jacob, and others
Muscle-equivalent environmental radiation meter of extreme sensitivity. bibliog Science 140:1100-1 Je 7 '63
KATANGA
How Katanga fell; with editorial comment. B. Littell. il Sat Eve Post 236:74-6+, 84 My 11 '63
Is there a historian in the House? Nat R 14:185 Mr 12 '63
President Kennedy welcomes end of Katanga secession; statement, January 21, 1963. J. F. Kennedy. Dept State Bul 48:207 F 11 '63
Report by the officer-in-charge of the United Nations operation in the Congo (cont) U N Rev 10:59-65 Ja '63
See also
Banks and banking—Katanga
KATCHEN, Julius
Notes from our correspondents. C. Reid. Hi Fi 14:17+ Ap '64
KATE Greenaway medal
Carnegie-Greenaway medals given at London dinner. Pub W 186:53-4 Jl 20 '64
KATEB, George
Basis of democracy. Commentary 39:81-4 Ja '65
Moral society. Commentary 38:88+ N '64
KATERINE Ismailova; opera. See Shostakovich, D.
KATES, George N.
Tirol: 1363-1963. Art N 62:28-30+ S '63
KATES, Joseph R. and Jones, R. F.
Fluoroacetate inhibition of amino acids during photosynthesis of chlamydomonas reinhardti. bibliog Science 143:145-6 Ja 10 '64
KATMAI NATIONAL MONUMENT
Lonely wonders of Katmai. E. Gruening. il Nat Geog Mag 123:800-31 Je '63
KATONA, George
Expert takes a critical look at the polls: interview. por U S News 57:35-6 S 21 '64

KATONA, George—*Continued*
Why consumers spend and save; excerpts from Mass consumption society. Nations Bsns 52:60-2+ O '64
KATSH, Grace F. and others
Acceptance or rejection of male skin by isologous female mice: effect of injection of sperm. bibliog Science 143:41-2 Ja 3 '64
KATSOYANNIS, Panayotis G.
Protein block-building. il por Bsns W p73-4 O 26 '63
KATSUMI, M. and others
Growth response of the d-5 and an-1 mutants of maize to some kaurene derivatives. bibliog Science 144:849-50 My 15 '64
KATZ, Alex
Rudolph Burckhardt: multiple fugitive. Art N 62:38-41 D '63
about
Katz: collage, cutout, cut-up. E. Denby. il Art N 63:42-5 Ja '65
KATZ, Bill
Cultural desert for writers? por Library J 88:2430-4 Je 15 '63
KATZ, Joseph
Wrapping it up. New Yorker 40:22 D 26 '64
KATZ, Menke
Bits of sun; poem. Atlan 212:53 Jl '63
KATZ, Sidney
Alcoholism controversy. Sci Digest 55:31-6 My '64
Marriage as it really is; reprint. Sci Digest 55:6-19 F '64
KATZ, Yale J. and others
Angiotensin pressor inhibition by aldosterone in the rabbit. bibliog Science 141:725 Ag 23 '63
KATZBAN, John M.
Togetherness solves a water problem. Am City 78:86-8 O '63
KATZENBACH, Edward L. Jr
Poker, pawns, and power; adaptation of address. Sat R 46:25 Mr 23 '63
about
You're in the classroom now. il por Time 83:72 Ja 17 '64
KATZENBACH, Nicholas deBelleville
Civil rights act of 1964; address, September 18, 1964. Vital Speeches 31:27-9 O 15 '64
about
Man on the inside. por Newsweek 64:24 S 14 '64
KATZOFF, Paul
Logs. New Yorker 40:20-1 F 22 '64
KATZUNG, B. G. See Barnes, C. D. jt. auth.
KAUAI (island)
Timeless Kauai swamp. K. C. Hulme. il Atlan 215:68-71 Ja '65
Upriver from Nawiliwili; Huleia River. il Sunset 131:61-2 O '63
KAUFERT, F. H.
Controversy in canoeland. Am For 70:24-7+ O '64
KAUFFMAN, Earl
Leaders of leisure. por Recreation 57:463-4 N '64
KAUFFMAN, George
Cruise; poem. Nation 196:363 Ap 27 '63
KAUFFMAN, Joseph Patrick
Justice for Captain Kauffman. Nation 198:3 Ja 4 '64
Ordeal of Captain Kauffman. F. J. Cook. Nation 197:123-38 S 14 '63
KAUFFMANN, Stanley
Author in search of a character. New Repub 148:21-2+ F 23 '63
Fabian abroad. New Repub 148:28-30 Je 22 '63
Films. See issues of New republic
Importance of being Frank. New Repub 149: 23-7 D 28 '63
Life movie review. Life 58:8 Ja 15 '65
Man named Chaffin. New Repub 151:19-21 O 3 '64
Mark Twain from under ground. New Repub 148:20-2 Ap 6 '63
Paris and Hemingway in the spring. New Repub 150:17-18+ My 9 '64
Through a glass brightly. New Repub 150: 17+ Ja 11 '64
KAUFMAN, Betty
Art. See occasional issues of Commonweal
KAUFMAN, Donald D. and others
Simazine: degradation by soil microorganisms. bibliog Science 142:405-6 O 18 '63
KAUFMAN, Edwin N.
Li'l TC. Pop Electr 21:33-5 Jl '64
KAUFMAN, Herbert E. and Heidelberger, Charles
Therapeutic antiviral action of 5-trifluoromethyl-2'-deoxyuridine in herpes simplex keratitis. bibliog Science 145:585 Ag 7 '64
KAUFMAN, Irving R.
Supreme court and its critics. Atlan 212:47-53 D '63
Uncertain criminal law: rights, wrongs, and doubts. Atlan 215:61-7 Ja '65
KAUFMAN, Sherwin A.
Truth about female hormones. Ladies Home J 82:22-3 Ja '65
KAUFMAN, Shirley
Aquarium; poem. Atlan 213:81 F '64
Crab catchers; poem. Atlan 214:90 N '64
Masaccio's expulsion; poem. Harper 230:73 Ja '65
KAUFMAN, Sue
First day; story. Redbook 124:32-3 Ja '65
Mary Pride; story. Atlan 211:69-74 Je '63
Pride of the morning; story. Atlan 211:74-8 F '63
KAUFMAN, William C.
Bioastronautics: fundamental and practical problems. Science 143:1199+ Mr 13 '64
KAUFMANN, Edgar, Jr
Designer for the corporate image. Sat R 46: 38 F 2 '63
How to look at architecture. Harper 230:120-4 Ja '65
KAUFMANN, Ludwig
Story of Schema seventeen. por Cath World 200:8-14 O '64
KAUFMANN'S department store. See Pittsburgh—Stores
KAULA, William M. See O'Keefe, J. A. jt. auth.
KAUNDA, Kenneth
Born to riches. il por Newsweek 64:65-6 O 26 '64
End of a dream in Southern Rhodesia. C. Sterling. il Reporter 28:30-3 My 9 '63
Kaunda of Zambia. C. Northcott. Christian Cent 81:238-9 F 19 '64
Rhodesia's rare asset. por Newsweek 63:36 F 3 '64
Roar of the Black Lion. il por Time 83:30 Je 5 '64
Warning from Africa; emphasis on material development. America 108:820 Je 8 '63
KAVADAS, Theodore M.
Student approach to recruitment; high-school students. por Recreation 57:318-19 Je '64
KAVANAGH, Aidan
Liturgical movement: phase three. America 111:183-5 Ag 22 '64
KAVANAU, J. Lee
Behavior: confinement, adaptation, and compulsory regimes in laboratory studies. bibliog Science 143:490; 145:1461-2 Je 31, S 25 '64
KAVANAUGH, Robert E.
Problems at State university. America 108: 540-4+ Ap 20 '63
KAY, Hubert
California's S.&L.'s: the boom the bankers knock. Fortune 70:118-23+ Ag '64
Harnessing the R. and D. monster. Fortune 71:160-3+ Ja '65
Strange leveling off in land. Fortune 68:124-9+ O '63
There's no stopping REA, or is there? Fortune 67:118-21+ F '63
Third force in urban renewal. Fortune 70: 130-3+ O '64
To live and die for Armstrong. Fortune 69: 124-9+ Mr '64
We're the most enterprising utility in this country. Fortune 69:138-41+ My '64
KAY, Hugh
Portuguese way in Africa. Fortune 69:112-15+ Ja '64
KAY, Jane H.
Reviews: Boston. Art N 63:17+ S '64
KAY, Kenneth
Don't start with too much. Writer 76:10-13 Ap '63
—and Rieke, W. O.
Tuberculin hypersensitivity: studies with radioactive antigen and mononuclear cells. bibliog Science 139:487-9 F 8 '63
KAYAK racing
Tippy canoe, kayaks, too; West River slalom, Jamaica, Vt. il Newsweek 63:79 Je 1 '64
KAYAKS
Craft you can tote. J. A. Emmett. il Outdoor Life 135:112-15 F '65
Folding kayak. J. E. Rathbun. il Pop Mech 119:152-5 Je '63
How you can build a kayak. il Sunset 130:40+ Mr '63
KAYE, Betty Gorman
Loop & dart with round ornaments pattern. Hobbies 68:84-5 Ag '63
KAYE, Danny
Happiest man. Read Digest 82:94-8 Mr '63
about
A-okaye. por Newsweek 61:90 Ap 22 '63
Danny Kaye. G. Casey and T. Nagle. pors Flying 74:46+ Mr '64

KAYE, Danny—about—*Continued*
Day there was no money; publicity stunt in Winsted, Conn. W. K. Zinsser. Reporter 29:46-8 S 12 '63
Fun on TV. pors Dance Mag 38:31 N '64
Innocent delight. por Time 81:68+ Ap 19 '63
Theatre; entertainment at the Ziegfeld. J. McCarten. New Yorker 39:96 Ap 20 '63
Wednesday question: want to watch Danny Kaye? il pors Newsweek 62:43-5 D 23 '63

KAYLOR, Joseph F.
Outdoor recreation policies: some differences. R. Agnew. por Am For 69:35 Je '63

KAYON, Judy
Lestrigonian; story. Mlle 59:296-7 Ag '64

KAYSEN, Carl
Alfred Sloan's success story. New Repub 150: 21-3 F 29 '64
Truants' return. il por Newsweek 62:76 O 7 '63

KAYWELL, Grace
Can we improve our Olympic chances? Dance Mag 37:52-7 N '63

KAZAKES, Jerry
I believe. M. Woodward. por Seventeen 22: 108 Ag '63

KAZAKHSTAN
Reasons why; problem-plagued virgin lands. Time 81:32 Mr 29 '63

KAZAKOV, Yuri
Autumn in the oak woods; story. Esquire 60:133 O '63
On the island; story. Esquire 60:170 D '63
Out hunting; story. Esquire 60:123 N '63
Smell of bread; story. Esquire 60:80-1 S '63

about

Meant offense. E. Pawel. Nation 198:150 F 10 '64

KAZAN, A. B.
Engineering technician. Pop Mech 119:30+ Ap '63

KAZAN, Elia
One chance in a million; story of S. Giallelis; from Greek village to stardom. E. Miller. il Seventeen 22:124-5+ S '63
Streetcar named Kazan. G. Rogoff. Reporter 31:38+ D 17 '64
Who cares what the boss thinks? J. F. Fixx. il por Sat R 46:14-15 D 28 '63

KAZANTZAKIS, Nikos
City in torment over Kazantzakis. E. T. Moore. ALA Bul 57:305-6 Ap '63
Poet armed. por Time 81:106+ Je 7 '63

KAZIMIERZ
Letter from Poland. M. Kuncewicz. Nation 197:423-4 D 14 '63

KAZIN, Alfred
Cher maitre. Reporter 29:62-4 Ag 15 '63
First and the last; New England in the novelist's imagination; address. Sat R 46: 12-15+ F 2 '63
Hemingway as his own fable. Atlan 213:54-7 Je '64
My friend Saul Bellow. Atlan 215:51-4 Ja '65
Party of one. bibliog Holiday 34:16+ O '63
Remembering Jewish history. Commentary 37:76-9 F '64
Strength of Robert Frost. Commentary 38: 49-52 D '64
Young man, old man. Reporter 29:33-40 D 19 '63

KAZMAIER, Dick
Open letter to a college president. por Sports Illus 19:57-8 O 14 '63

KEACH, Donald L.
Down to Thresher by bathyscaph. pors Nat Geog Mag 125:764-77 Je '64

KEALLY, Francis
Architect's view of library planning. por Library J 88:4521-5 D 1 '63

KEAN, Charles Duell
Controversary within Catholicism. Christian Cent 80:358-9 Mr 20 '63
Obituary
Christian Cent 80:1325 O 30 '63

KEANE, Gustave R.
Control system for architects' office costs. Arch Rec 134:125-6 Jl '63

KEANE, Johnny
Everyman's hero. Nation 199:291 N 2 '64
Speed won the world series. W. Leggett. il por Sports Illus 21:36-7 O 26 '64
That Johnny Keane is a fine manager is what he sure is. J. Olsen. por Sports Illus 20:110-14+ Ap 13 '64

KEANE, Walter
Mystery. il Newsweek 63:54 Mr 2 '64

KEARNEY, Michael
Michael of the movies. J. Hamilton. il pors Look 27:79-82 S 10 '63

KEARNEY, Paul W.
Driver education pays off. Parents Mag 39: 64+ O '64; Same with title Why driver education is a must. Read Digest 85:129-32 O '64
How to lick the hazards of foul-weather driving. Read Digest 83:58-60 D '63
If you have an accident. Read Digest 86: 201+ Ja '65
News for winter drivers: tires with built-in chains. Read Digest 85:103-5 N '64
So you don't use seat belts? Read Digest 83:121-3 Jl '63
Why doctors are bad samaritans. Read Digest 82:87-90 My '63

KEARNEY, Vincent S.
Africa's dilemma. America 110:274 F 29 '64
Gourd amid cactuses. America 110:345 Mr 14 '64
Land of the free. America 110:573 Ap 25 '64
Vietnam dilemma. America 109:237-8 S 7 '63
Year of the dragon. America 110:226 F 15 '64

KEARNEY and Trecker corporation
Putting machine shops on tape; Kearney & Trecker use numerical controls. il Bsns W p 100 Mr 7 '64

KEARNS, Francis E.
Incident at a college. Commonweal 79:215, 431 N 15 '63, Ja 10 '64
Marching for justice. Commonweal 78:551-4: 79:169-70 S 20, N 1 '63
Sit-in at Georgetown. Commonweal 78:94+, 251-2 Ap 19, My 24 '63

about

Kearns case. J. Leo. Commonweal 81:562-6 Ja 29 '65

KEARNS, Jack, and Fraley, Oscar
Days of wine and bloody noses; excerpt from Million dollar gate. por Sports Illus 20:50-4+ Ja 20 '64
He didn't know the gloves were loaded; excerpt from Million dollar gate. por Sports Illus 20:48-56 Ja 13 '64

KEARNS-Kwee comet. See Comets

KEARNY, Philip
Uncelebrated soldier. F. Vandiver. Sat R 46:37 F 9 '63

KEAST, Allen
Australia's spotted diamondbirds. Natur Hist 74:28-31 Ja '65

KEAST, J. D.
Buy, lease, or hire it done? Farm J 88:22+ F '64
Tax management tips for machinery and equipment. Farm J 87:50B D '63

KEASY, Ken
One flew over the cuckoo's nest; dramatization. See Wasserman, D.

KEATING, Bern
Fresh look at Arkansas. Holiday 34:52-5 S '63
Fresh look at Kentucky. Holiday 36:80-5+ N '64
Fresh look at New Mexico. Holiday 33:64-7 F '63
Language lessons at home. Holiday 35:133-8 My '64; Same abr. with title Teach yourself a language. Read Digest 85:161-3+ Jl '64
Rodeo goes to college. Holiday 35:134+ F '64

KEATING, Charles H. Jr
National decent literature chairman held in contempt at California trial. Library J 89: 4764 D 1 '64
Poison in print and how to get rid of it. C. W. Hall. Read Digest 84:94-8 My '64

KEATING, John
Glittering era of The merry widow. N Y Times Mag p 12-13+ Ag 16 '64
Now angels wing along the Rialto. N Y Times Mag p28+ D 8 '63
When they buy a rolling status symbol. N Y Times Mag p28+ S 27 '64

KEATING, Kenneth Barnard
Cyprus; address, July 3, 1964. Vital Speeches 30:695-6 S 1 '64
Excerpt from address, December 19, 1963. Cong Digest 43:152+ My '64
Intelligence. Reporter 29:6 S 12 '63
Latest facts on Russia's Cuban base; interview. por U S News 54:43-5 F 11 '63
My advance view of the Cuban crisis. pors Look 28:96+ N 3 '64
Senator Keating explains his stand; excerpts from news conference, August 18, 1964. por U S News 57:33 Ag 31 '64
What about Republicans? Keating takes another look; summary of interview. por U S News 57:20 D 7 '64
Why help the reds win the cold war? Read Digest 83:66-71 O '63

about

Brothers. Nation 199:366 N 23 '64
Campaigning. New Yorker 40:48-9 O 31 '64

KEATING, Kenneth Barnard—about—*Cont.*
Cinderella story. K. Crawford. Newsweek 61:31 F 18 '63
For senator from New York. W. H. von Dreele. Nat R 16:967 N 3 '64
For senator: Henry Paolucci. Nat R 16:900 O 20 '64
Hosts of unreason; Kennedy vs Keating in New York state. M. Kempton. New Repub 151:11-12 S 12 '64
How long are the coattails? il por Time 84:30-3 O 30 '64
Keating for senator. Nation 199:101 S 14 '64; Discussion. 199:inside cover S 28 '64
Keating, Kennedy, in a ripsnorter that has everything. il pors Life 57:32-7 O 9 '64
Keating vs. Kennedy: high stakes in New York. il pors Newsweek 64:35-6+ O 12 '64
Kenneth Keating, critic of our Cuban policy. J. Daniel. por Read Digest 82:190-2+ My '63
Kennedy-Keating: off to slashing start. il por U S News 57:24 S 21 '64
Kennedy or Keating; stakes are bigger than a Senate seat. il pors U S News 57:72-4 O 5 '64
Kennedy vs. Keating. Reporter 31:12+ N 5 '64
Luce vs. Keating? New York race shapes up. por U S News 57:14 Ag 17 '64
New York: the Keating record. M. Greenfield. il Reporter 31:33-6 O 22 '64
New York's Keating: from a poolside chat, a Cuba critic. por Time 81:24 Mr 8 '63
Two prophets; question of missiles in Cuba. Reporter 28:18 Mr 14 '63; Discussion. 28:8 Ap 11 '63
Why Robert Kennedy? New Repub 151:3-4 S 19 '64; Discussion. 151:36-8 O 3; 29 O 10; 37 O 17 '64

KEATING, L. Clark
American aid to education in Peru. Sch & Soc 92:206-8 My 2 '64

KEATON, Buster
Beckett; production of his first screenplay for Evergreen theatre. New Yorker 40:22-3 Ag 8 '64
Happy pro. New Yorker 39:36-7 Ap 27 '63
Watch out, Buster, you're being watched. il pors Life 57:85-6+ Ag 14 '64

KEATS, Ezra Jack
Caldecott award acceptance; address, July 15, 1963. il Horn Bk 39:361-3 Ag '63
Collage. Horn Bk 40:269-72 Je '64
Right to be real. Sat R 46:56 N 9 '63

about

Ezra Jack Keats. A. Duff. il por Library J 88:1292-4 Mr 15 '63
Ezra Jack Keats. E. Hautzig. il por Horn Bk 39:364-8 Ag '63
Newbery-Caldecott medals; Madeleine L'Engle, Ezra Jack Keats win 1963 awards. il por Pub W 183:18-20 Mr 11 '63

KEATS, John, 1795-1821
Chameleon poet. il Time 82:106+ O 25 '63
Days of rhyme and roses. C. A. Hoyt. Sat R 46:22 N 2 '63
Not writ in water. M. L. Rosenthal. Reporter 30:52-4 F 13 '64

KEATS, John, 1920-
Box car to the West; story. Sat Eve Post 236:70-3 Ag 10 '63
College majority; dropouts. Life 54:70-4+ Je 21 '63
Colony of younger sons. Holiday 35:22+ F '64
Fierce Moros. Holiday 34:124+ D '63
Old-car craze shifts into high. N Y Times Mag p50+ S 29 '63
Speaking out. por Sat Eve Post 236:8+ O 26 '63
Ten million hoping for a mistake. N Y Times Mag p60+ My 5 '63
That's where the old cars go. N Y Times Mag p42+ S 20 '64

KEAY, Colin S. L. See Ellyett, C. D. jt. auth.

KEBLE, John
John Keble, by G. Battiscombe. Review
Christian Cent 81:1218 S 30 '64. B. Winter

KECK, George E.
Personalities. por Time 82:96 O 11 '63

KECSKEMETI, Paul
Nuclear abolitionism. Commentary 36:43-8, 396-8 Jl, N '63

KEEFER, Carolyn
Instant experience. Am City 79:171 Je '64

KEEGAN, Lawrence V.
Apocalypse; poem. America 108:750 My 25 '63

KEEL, John A.
Adding sound to slides & movies. U S Camera 26:70-1+ O '63

KEEL, John S.
Sir Herbert Read on the teaching of art. bibliog Sch Arts 63:19-21 D '63

KEELER, Christine
Case of the sensitive osteopath. il por Time 81:29 Mr 29 '63
Crisis over Christine. E. Behr. il pors Sat Eve Post 236:77-85 Jl 13 '63
Dial S for squalor; Regina v. Stephen Thomas Ward. il por Time 82:22+ Ag 2 '63
Doctor Stephen Ward returns. R. West. Esquire 62:138+ S '64
Goddess of the gravel pits. por Time 81:25-6 Je 28 '63
I'm all right, Jack. il Newsweek 62:45 Jl 15 '63
Is Super Mac to be undone by sex? il Newsweek 61:45-6 Je 24 '63
John Bull & John Profumo. J. Gross. Commentary 36:144-50 Ag '63
Less than a pound; jail for perjury. Time 82:30 D 13 '63
Lost leader; concerning House of commons debate on the Profumo case. il Time 81:22-5 Je 28 '63
Missing model. Newsweek 61:33 Ap 1 '63
New pornocracy. il por Newsweek 62:35-6 Jl 8 '63
Out of circulation. por Newsweek 62:46 D 16 '63
Personal report on Britain's biggest scandal. L. Bergquist. il por Look 27:81-6 Jl 30 '63
Price of Christine. il por Time 81:32-3 Je 14 '63
Profumo affair. C. Brogan. Nat R 14:528-9+ Jl 2 '63
Temptress rocks the Empire; with report by P. Worsthorne. il pors Life 54:18-23 Je 21 '63
Time of the trollop. pors Time 81:24+ Je 21 '63
'What the hell. . .' il por Newsweek 61:38+ Je 17 '63
While the prisoner sketched. il por Time 82:25 Jl 5 '63

KEELER, Ralph
When Chicago burned. Am Heritage 14:54-61 Ag '63

KEELER polygraph. See Lie detectors

KEELEY, Edmund
Genesis: a commentary. Poetry 105:16-20 O '64
Translator's notes on proper names; Amorgós: a commentary. Poetry 105:31-5 O '64
(tr) See Elytis, O. Axion esti: The genesis
(tr) See Gatsos, N. Amorgós
(tr) See Seferis, G. Santorini; Salamis in Cyprus; Three mules
(tr) See Sinopoulos, T. Magda; Sophia etc; Sight and vision; Ioanna's invitation; One of Constantine's nights; Beheading

KEELING, Rolland O. jr. and Wick, D. A.
Magnetite: preferred orientation on the basal plane of partially reduced hematite. bibliog Science 141:1175-6 S 20 '63

KEEN, Elizabeth
Elizabeth Keen and Margaret Beals at Judson Hall. J. Maskey. Dance Mag 37:68 Je '63

KEENE, Donald
(tr) See Mishima, Y. Famous Japanese judges the U.S. giant

KEENE, George T.
Color in astrophotography. il Sky & Tel 26:74-6 Ag '63

KEENE, N. H.
Parking meters keep downtown alive. W. Bridgham. il Am City 79:129+ S '64

KEEP a place for me; story. See Alexander, R. W.

KEEPERS of the house; story. See Grau, S. A.

KEESEY, Richard E.
Intracranial reward delay and the acquisition rate of a brightness discrimination. bibliog Science 143:702-3 F 14 '64

KEEVAN, Thomas. See Cosulich, W. F. jt. auth.

KEFAUVER, Estes
Annals of legislation. R. Harris. New Yorker 40:49-50+ Mr 14; 75-6+ Mr 21; 46-8+ Mr 28 '64
Fitting memorial. Nation 199:451 D 14 '64
Kefauver and the price-makers. B. D. Nossiter. Nation 197:12-13 Jl 6 '63
Kefauver's last interview. B. H. Frisch. il pors Sci Digest 54:10-18 N '63
Kefauver's reward. Nation 198:23 Ja 6 '64
Obituary
Nat R 15:142 Ag 27 '63
Nation 197:101 S 7 '63
New Repub 149:5 Ag 31 '63
Newsweek por 62:18-19 Ag 19 '63
Time por 82:15 Ag 16 '63
Real voice, by R. Harris. Review
Nation 199:166-8 S 28 '64. E. Langer

KEFFORD, N. P.
Natural plant growth regulators. Science 142:1495-8+ D 13 '63

KEHM, George H.
Manipulation remains. Christian Cent 81:211 F 12 '64
KEIM, John
Taming a troublesome water. Am City 79: 157-8 S '64
KEISER, H. and others
Collagen-like protein in human plasma. bibliog Science 142:1678-9 D 27 '63
KEISER, Marjorie
Consumer service bureau report. pors Parents Mag 39:12+ Ag; 38+ S; 12+ O; 20+ N; 12+ D '64; 40:18+ Ja '65
Introducing the new director of PM's Consumer service bureau. G. J. Hecht. por Parents Mag 39:12+ Jl '64
KEISLER, William
What it's like to be little. Parents Mag 39: 48-9+ Mr '64
KEITH, Barbara
Death on the wind. il por Newsweek 63:20+ F 3 '64
KEITH, Joseph Joel
Pets' cemetery; poem. Nation 196:108 F 2 '63
KEITH, M. L. and Anderson, G. M.
Radiocarbon dating: fictitious results with mollusk shells. bibliog Science 141:634-7 Ag 16 '63
KEITH, Stuart
600 club: America's top-ranking birders. Audubon Mag 65:376-7 N '63
KEITH-LUCAS, Alan
Child welfare services today: an overview and some questions. bibliog f Ann Am Acad 355:1-8 S '64
(ed) Programs and problems in child welfare. bibliog f Ann Am Acad 355:1-139 S '64
KEITHLEY, George
Winter; poem. Christian Cent 81:1558 D 16 '64
KEKKONEN, Urho Kaleva
Letter from Finland. J. Bainbridge. il New Yorker 40:141-2+ O 3 '64
KELEHER, Don
Rest from racing. Yachting 115:202-4 My '64
KELEN, Emery
Odd, sad waif. P. L. Buckley. Nat R 16:199-200 Mr 10 '64
Road maps to opinion. il por Time 82:96 O 4 '63
KELKER, Norman E. See Moskowitz, M. jt. auth.
KELLAND, Clarence Budington
Obituary
Pub W 185:43 Mr 2 '64
Sat Eve Post 237:82 Mr 14 '64
KELLE, Reidi
Future question; Brave Meredith; poems. Negro Hist Bul 26:215 Ap '63
KELLEHER, P. C. and others
Serum protein synthesis by the fetal rat. bibliog Science 139:839-40 Mr 1 '63
KELLEN, Konrad
I brought Chagall to America. Esquire 62: 60+ D '64
KELLER, Barbara. See Freedman, D. G. jt. auth.
KELLER, Charles
Charles Keller: impassioned advocate. B. F. Brown. il Sat R 46:72+ N 16 '63
KELLER, E. C. jr, and Glassman, Edward
Xanthine dehydrogenase: differences in activity among drosophila strains. bibliog Science 143:40-1 Ja 3 '64
KELLER, George C. and Hawes, G. R.
Where the girls are. Esquire 61:119-23+ Je '64
KELLER, Hannes
35mm techniques; covering a 1,000-foot dive off Catalina. P. Stackpole. U S Camera 26: 15+ Mr '63
KELLER, Helen Adams
Editor's notebook. M. S. Fenner. NEA J 52:72 N '63
KELLER, Joseph. See Berson, A. jt. auth.
KELLERMAN, Annette
Where are they now? pors Newsweek 62:12 Jl 22 '63
KELLERMAN, Richard
Political impact of TV. Nation 200:24-6 Ja 11 '65
KELLEY, Albert J.
Ranger design and management criticized. Aviation W 80:56+ My 11 '64
KELLEY, Dean M.
Church and state. Christian Cent 80:1509-12 D 4 '63
How many hands has God? Christian Cent 82:19-20+ Ja 6 '65
N.A.E. on church-state. Christian Cent 80: 454-5 Ap 10 '63
Protestants and parochial schools. Commonweal 79:520-4 Ja 31 '64
KELLEY, Everett E.
Technical manuals for surplus equipment. Electr World 69:79 Je '63
KELLEY, George
Rights, not ratios. America 109:424-5 O 12 '63
KELLEY, James B.
We're bigger than they are! America 109: 628-30 N 16 '63
What's happening in our schools. America 108:547-9 Ap 20 '63
KELLEY, Marjorie L.
When are children ready to read? Sat R 46: 58 Jl 20 '63
KELLEY, Myron T. and others
Analytical chemistry in nuclear technology. Science 144:570-2 My 1 '64
KELLEY, Reeve Spencer
Bard of Albuquerque; poem. Sat R 46:37 N 2 '63
First and last day in a poetry class; poem. Sat R 47:44 Je 13 '64
I try to say something; poem. Sat R 46:38 Ap 27 '63
Spectator's spectator; poem. Sat R 47:30 Ag 22 '64
Winesburg and Willoughby; poem. Poetry 103:241 Ja '64
KELLEY, Richard E.
For SBICs, a new flexibility. por Bsns W p94 D 26 '64
KELLEY, Robert
Saratoga Springs. Travel 120:50-2 Ag '63
KELLEY, Stanley
Employee suggestions. Am City 79:95 Ja '64
KELLEY, William Melvin
Ivy league Negro. Esquire 60:54-6+ Ag '63
Saint Paul and the monkeys; story. Sat Eve Post 236:42-5 Ap 13 '63
Servant problem; story. Mlle 58:174 Mr '64
KELLMEYER, Fern Lee
Six and the single girl. por Newsweek 63: 59+ Mr 23 '64
KELLOGG, Charles E.
Soil-use planning for individual and public goals. Bul Atomic Sci 20:15-18 N '64
KELLOGG, Cynthia
At home in a barn. Ladies Home J 80:68-71 Jl '63
Lush gardens bloom indoors. Ladies Home J 80:80-2 S '63
KELLOGG, Frederick R.
Modern lateen rig. il Yachting 113:194 My '63
KELLOGG, M. W, company
Telling the world about breakfast. il Time 83:92 Mr 13 '64
KELLOGG, Ruth E.
Elkhart corners space. Library J 88:4543-4 D 1 '63
KELLOGG, Winthrop N. and Rice C. E.
Visual problem-solving in a bottlenose dolphin. bibliog Science 143:1052-5 Mr 6 '64
KELLY, Edna F.
Principles of international law concerning friendly relations and cooperation among states: peaceful settlement of disputes; address, November 19, 1963. bibliog f Dept State Bul 50:57-66 Ja 13 '64
Principles of international law concerning friendly relations and cooperation among states: sovereign equality of states; statement, December 3, 1963. Dept State Bul 50: 264-7 F 17 '64
KELLY, Ellsworth
Ellsworth Kelly: the big form. W. Rubin. il por Art N 62:32-5+ N '63
KELLY, Emmett
Celebrity register. C. Amory. por McCalls 91:166 Mr '64
KELLY, Frank
Our footloose correspondents. J. Bainbridge. il New Yorker 39:105-6+ N 9 '63
KELLY, Gene
Celebrity register. C. Amory. por McCalls 91:166 Mr '64
KELLY, Gerald. See Ford, J. C. jt. auth.
KELLY, George W.
Flowers, trees, gardens and parks in the Rocky Mountains. Horticulture 42:34-5+ Ag '64
KELLY, Hal V.
Supervised correspondence courses. NEA J 52:26-7 N '63
KELLY, John J.
Not late once in seven years. Am City 78: 84-5 F '63
KELLY, John Kenneth
New York cop studies crime of two cities: London and New York. H. Ehrlich. il pors Look 27:57-63 Jl 30 '63
KELLY, John P, agency
Cutting the cake; Connecticut's insurance with Kelly agency. Time 81:29 My 17 '63
Spoils and spoilers. Newsweek 61:37 My 13 '63

KELLY, Richard
First night; poem. Poetry 104:233 Jl '64

KELLY, Robert
Limits to deviant behavior in the gifted. Sch Life 47:4-6 O '64
New money; poem. Nation 199:146 S 21 '64
Ordering; poem. Nation 199:232 O 12 '64
Vesalius; poem. Nation 199:118 S 14 '64

KELLY, Robert Glynn
Novelist's dilemma. Writer 76:7-9+ Mr '63

KELLY, Tony
Tony Kelly's America. il Pop Phot 55:148-53+ D '64

KELLY, Walt
Ka-platz; delight in the unexpected. Atlan 211:92-6 Mr '63

about

Celebrity register. C. Amory. por McCalls 91:166 Mr '64

KELLY girl service, incorporated
Anybody here seen the boss? il Bsns W p32-3 My 18 '63

KELMAN, Ken
Anticipations of the light. Nation 198:490-4 My 11 '64

KELMSCOTT press. See Printing—Private presses

KELP
Translocation in the giant kelp macrocystis. B. C. Parker. bibliog il Science 140:891-2 My 24 '63

KELSEY, Frances Oldham
Lady cop. il por Newsweek 61:100 Je 24 '63
Reward. J. Lear. por Sat R 46:47 F 2 '63
Thalidomide heroine seeks new culprits. Sci Digest 53:32 My '63

KEM, William. See Emlen, S. T. jt. auth.

KEMAL ATATURK, Mustafa
Our far-flung correspondents. C. Frankel. il New Yorker 40:136+ Je 6 '64

KEMBLE family
Operatic Kembles; England's most distinguished theater clan. R. Rushmore. il Opera N 29:6-11 Ja 23 '65

KEMENY, John G.
Once the professor was a teacher. N Y Times Mag p 14+ Je 2 '63

KEMENY, Zoltan
Couleur-douleur. C. B. Johnson. il School Arts 63:45 Mr '64

KEMMERER, Jack B.
Los Angeles 60,000 years ago. il Sci Digest 54:48-51 S '63
Monkey business in Oregon. Pop Sci 183:60-3 S '63

KEMP, Lysander
Artillery hill, Panama, 1944; poem. Sat R 47:56 F 22 '64
(tr) See Arreola, J. J. Two sketches
(tr) See Melo, J. V. Hidden signs
(tr) See Rulfo, J. Hill of the comadres

KEMPER, Charles A.
Tower for tv; 30,000 dead birds. Audubon Mag 66:86-90 Mr '64

KEMPER, Robert G.
Reformation or defamation? Christian Cent 80:465-6 Ap 10 '63

KEMPFF, Wilhelm
Art of Wilhelm Kempff. M. Schafer. por Mus Am 84:58-9 O '64
Kempff's debut. M. Bernheimer. Sat R 47:76 O 31 '64

KEMPHER, Ruth Moon
Actually, it barely matters; poem. McCalls 91:162 Mr '64

KEMPNER, Ellis S.
Upper temperature limit of life. bibliog Science 142:1318-19 D 6 '63

KEMPNER, Mary Jean
Dogs. Sports Illus 20:72+ My 11 '64
Greatest bridge of them all. Harper 229:70-6 N '64
Ice tiger. Harper 227:36-41 Ag '63
Little churches of Ohrid, etc. Harper 228:28+ Ap '64
Traveling with young eyes. Harper 230:128-30 Ja '65

KEMPSELL, George F. Jr
Rector resigns under pressure. Christian Cent 80:165 F 6 '63; Discussion. 80:406 Mr 27 '63

KEMPTON, Murray
A. Philip Randolph. New Repub 149:15-17 Jl 6 '63
Adam Powell. New Repub 148:10-13 My 25 '63
Adult congressman. New Repub 148:11-13 Ap 6 '63
Average newspaper is not a public utility. New Repub 148:16-18 Mr 30 '63
Black and white: but whose Great society? New Repub 151:75-8+ N 7 '64
Bobby Baker's affairs. New Repub 150:6-8 F 8 '64
Bubbles, bubbles. New Repub 149:15-16 Ag 17 '63
Che cosa? means what's that? New Repub 149:6-7 O 12 '63
Clemency in Annapolis. New Repub 149:6-8 O 26 '63
Coat upon a stick. New Repub 148:12-13 Ap 27 '63
Conscience of a convention. New Repub 151:5-7 S 5 '64
Daughters. New Repub 148:6-7 My 4 '63
Dirksen delivers the souls. New Repub 150:9-11 My 2 '64
Epistles from the Eisenhower age. Commentary 35:232-8 Mr '63
Gloria, Gloria. New Repub 149:15-17 N 16 '63
GOP disestablishment. New Repub 151:5-7 Jl 11 '64
Half-way house. New Repub 148:8-10 Mr 23 '63
Heroes on the right. New Repub 149:4 N 9 '63
Hoffa the pure. New Repub 150:16-18 Ja 18 '64
Impurities in Yorkville. New Repub 148:13-15 Mr 16 '63
Jack Ruby on trial. New Repub 150:17-20 Mr 7 '64
Johnson's young helper. New Repub 149:9-11 D 21 '63
Karl Hess. New Repub 151:10-14 Ag 8 '64
Kids in Prince Edward. New Repub 149:14-15 O 5 '63
Lord of the Flies. New Repub 148:9-10 Je 22 '63
Man who hates publishers. New Repub 148:20-3 Je 8 '63
March on Washington. New Repub 149:19-20 S 14 '63
New York politics. New Repub 152:8-10 Ja 23 '65
Oh dad, poor dad. New Repub 149:6-7 S 28 '63
Orange is squeezed. New Repub 150:15-18 Ja 25 '64
Oswald; may we have some facts, please? New Repub 150:13-15 Je 13 '64
Pilgrimage to Jackson. New Repub 148:14-16 My 11 '63
Rendezvous of the federal prosecutors. New Repub 150:6-7 Ap 18 '64
Ribbons and bibbons. New Repub 149:13-16 N 30 '63
Robert F. Kennedy. New Repub 150:9-11 F 15 '64
Rockefeller: he has it if he wants it, and he does. New Repub 148:11-14 Mr 2 '63
Roy Cohn. New Repub 148:15-17 Ap 20 '63
Scranton of Pennsylvania. New Repub 148:9-12 F 16 '63
Senate; Mr Humphrey's conquering hosts. New Repub 150:6-8 Ap 4 '64
Slow-down Smith. New Repub 149:8-9 D 14 '63
Stephen E. Smith. New Repub 148:15-17 Mr 9 '63
They got him. New Repub 151:8-11 Jl 25 '64
Tryout in Harlem. New Repub 148:11-13 F 23 '63
Vender. New Repub 149:17-20 O 19 '63
Warren report; case for the prosecution. New Repub 151:13-17 O 10 '64
Washrooms of power. New Repub 149:9-13 Ag 3 '63
When you mobilize the poor. New Repub 151:11-13 D 5 '64
White elephant sale. New Repub 150:11-12 Ap 25 '64
Will to believe. New Repub 150:17-20 Ap 11 '64
Write right. Newsweek 64:64 Ag 10 '64
—and Ridgeway, James
Romans. New Repub 149:9-11 D 7 '63

about

Art of not writing novels. G. Wills. Nat R 16:31-3 Ja 14 '64
He quoted me. por Newsweek 61:62 Je 17 '63

KEMSLEY, William
Put self-doubt on your payroll. Writer 77:30-2 My '64

KEN dolls. See Dolls

KENDAL, Gloria
Madam's mark. il por Time 84:34 N 20 '64

KENDALL, Donald McIntosh
Businessmen in the news. por Fortune 68:55 O '63
Pepsi v. Coke. il Time 82:101-2 O 18 '63

KENDALL, Elaine
Art without artists. Reporter 28:45-6 My 23 '63
D. Boone would have been shocked. N Y Times Mag p43+ O 13 '63
Don't they know it's a turkey? N Y Times Mag p27+ Ap 14 '63

KENDALL, Elaine—*Continued*
Man's office is his castle. N Y Times Mag p52+ Mr 15 '64
Men's fashions, too, reflect the times. N Y Times Mag p 18-19 Ag 2 '64
Need for a sidewalk cafe society. N Y Times Mag p 12-13+ Jl 5 '64
Who killed romance? Mlle 56:125+ F '63; Same abr. Read Digest 82:103-4 Mr '63
KENDALL, Paul Murray
Young man of the sonnets. New Repub 151: 16-19 N 28 '64
KENDALL, William J.
Transponders are coming. Flying 75:49+ Ag '64
KENDALL, Willmoore
Opinion, the public, democracy. Nat R 14: 243-4 Mr 26 '63
State of our understanding. Nat R 15:491-4 D 3 '63
KENDE, H.
Preservation of chlorophyll in leaf sections by substances obtained from root exudate. bibliog Science 145:1066-7 S 4 '64
KENDREW, John C.
Myoglobin and the structure of proteins; address, December 11, 1962. bibliog Science 139:1259-66 Mr 29 '63
KENDRICK, Klaude
Pentecostal movement: home and hazards. Christian Cent 80:608-10 My 8 '63
KENEALY, William J.
Inalienable rights of all; address, July 10, 1963. Vital Speeches 29:686-9 S 1 '63
KENILWORTH ivy
Ground covers for house plants. E. S. Parcher. il Horticulture 42:38 F '64
KENNAN, George Frost
Can we deal with Moscow? por Sat Eve Post 236:38+ O 5 '63
Fresh look at our China policy. N Y Times Mag p27+ N 22 '64
Japanese security and American policy. For Affairs 43:14-28 O '64
Our foreign policy is paralyzed; summaries of statements, ed. by J. R. Moskin. pors Look 27:25-7 N 19 '63
Polycentrism and western policy. For Affairs 42:171-83 Ja '64
Price we paid for war. Atlan 214:50-4 O '64

about

Goodbye to Tito. il por Time 81:22 My 3 '63
Sadly powerless. Newsweek 62:38+ N 11 '63
KENNAN, Richard Barnes
Professional sanctions: where, when, and how. NEA J 52:37-8 D '63
Realistic view of the NEA. Sch. & Soc 91: 107 Mr 9 '63
KENNARD, Clyde
Case closed. Reporter 29:20 Jl 18 '63
Mississippi mercy. Reporter 28:19 F 14 '63
KENNEDY, Adrienne
Funnyhouse of a Negro Criticism
New Yorker 39:76+ Ja 25 '64
KENNEDY, Andrew
Peacemaker in La Paz. America 111:583 N 14 '64
KENNEDY, Arthur
Punch for portables. Pop Mech 121:196-8 Ja '64
KENNEDY, Bob
Tragic rebirth of the Chicago Cubs. T. Cohane. il por Look 28:60+ Je 16 '64
KENNEDY, Caroline
Caroline's wonderful little White House school. H. Thomas. il por Good H 157:84-5+ O '63
A look inside the White House school. il por U S News 55:70-2 O 7 '63
KENNEDY, David M.
Kangaroo jumps. por Newsweek 64:62 Ag 24 '64
KENNEDY, Donald
Inhibition in visual systems. Sci Am 209:122-4+ Jl '63
KENNEDY, E. P. and Westheimer, F. H.
Nobel laureates: Bloch and Lynen win prize in medicine and physiology. Science 146: 504-6 O 23 '64
KENNEDY, Edward Moore
Canvas cast. il Newsweek 64:56 Jl 6 '64
Day of joy and sadness. E. Behr. il pors Sat Eve Post 237:36-7 Jl 11 '64
How Senator Ted kept a promise. il pors U S News 57:13 D 28 '64
In walks Ted as the 89th gets under way; with report by R. Ajemian. il pors Life 58:28-35 Ja 15 '65
Rendezvous. il por Newsweek 63:20 Je 29 '64
Senators Kennedy. il por Newsweek 65:21 Ja 18 '65
Teddy's ordeal. il por Time 83:20 Je 26 '64
Very special patient. il Time 84:46 Jl 3 '64
KENNEDY, Edward Moore, family
New Mrs Kennedy in Washington. S. Seay. il Look 27:21-5 F 26 '63
KENNEDY, Ethel (Skakel)
Kiss me, Toots, I love you. por Newsweek 61:29 Mr 18 '63
KENNEDY, George
Whole darn capital was his beat. S. Lansdowne. America 111:650 N 21 '64
KENNEDY, Gerald Hamilton, bp
Aldersgate and 1963. Christian Cent 80:677-8 My 22 '63
Challenge of fortune. il pors Time 83:74-8 My 8 '64
Wide-awake bishop. por Newsweek 63:90-1 My 11 '64
KENNEDY, Jacqueline Lee (Bouvier)
Christmas message. Look 27:14-15 D 31 '63
Memoir. Look 28:36 N 17 '64
These are the things I hope will show how he really was. por Life 56:32-34A My 29 '64
(ed) Words JFK loved best. Look 28:84-90 N 17 '64

about

After the shots: the ordeal of Lyndon Johnson. F. Knebel. Look 28:26-8+ Mr 10 '64
Aftermath of tragedy. il pors Sr Schol 83: 18-20 D 13 '63
Another profile in courage. il pors U S News 55:58-9 D 9 '63
Arabian nights; visit to Morocco. Time 82: 24-5 O 25 '63
As time draws near for Kennedys' new baby. por U S News 55:23 Ag 5 '63
Beneficial change; move to New York. il Newsweek 64:35 Jl 20 '64
Caesar's wife. il pors Newsweek 62:20-1 O 28 '63
Change of address. il Time 82:12 D 20 '63
Chic though pregnant. il Bsns W p32 My 4 '63
Christmas paintings of Jacqueline Kennedy; fund raising for National cultural center. il McCalls 91:98-9+ D '63
Congratulations, whispered Jackie, and thanks for my birthday letter. S. Alexander. il por Life 57:30-1 S 4 '64
Dear Mrs Kennedy; personal mail. M. V. Thayer. pors Ladies Home J 80:76-7 My '63
Favored sport of Jacqueline; color photographs; with account by D. Phillips. M. Hawkins. Sat Eve Post 236:24-8+ F 23 '63
First lady has a style all her own. M. McGrory. America 108:249 F 23 '63
First lady's tour. il pors U S News 55:24 O 28 '63
For President Kennedy an epilogue. T. H. White. Life 55:158-9 D 6 '63
Future of a noble lady. W. V. Shannon. il pors Good H 158:76-81+ Ap '64
Grecian holiday. il por Time 82:27 O 11 '63
Her legend will live. K. A. Porter. por Ladies Home J 81:58-9 Mr '64
Hers was a gentle world. il pors Life 54:26-33 Ap 26 '63
Hollywood's new cover girl. il pors Time 85:44 Ja 22 '65
How Jackie restyled the White House; paintings, antiques and historic objects. por Sat Eve Post 236:42-51 O 26 '63
How Jacqueline Kennedy saved a child's life. N. M. Lobsenz. il Redbook 121:46-7+ Jl '63
In her time of trial. por Newsweek 62:29 D 9 '63
In love with night; reception at Democratic national convention. il por Newsweek 64: 28 S 7 '64
In turkey-chawed country; purchases of paintings by T. Anshutz. il Time 81:72 Mr 22 '63
Jackie Kennedy's perplexing sister. B. Walters. por Good H 156:30+ Mr '63
Jacqueline Kennedy; from memories; a new mission. il pors Newsweek 63:15-18 Ja 6 '64
Lady in black. E. F. Granton. il pors Ebony 19:81-2+ F '64
Letters of sympathy to Mrs John F. Kennedy. McCalls 91:82-3 Je '64
Lonely summer for Jacqueline. L. Bergquist. Look 28:45 N 17 '64
Looking ahead. il Newsweek 62:16-17 D 23 '63
Mrs Kennedy at the moment. G. Steinem. pors Esquire 62:125-7+ O '64
Mrs Kennedy says thank you to 800,000 friends. por Life 56:32B-32C Ja 24 '64
Mrs Kennedy to New York: a search for privacy. il pors U S News 57:74-5 Jl 20 '64
Mrs Kennedy's decisions shaped all the solemn pageantry. D. J. Hamblin. il Life 55:48-9 D 6 '63
Moving out. il por Time 82:25-6 D 13 '63
NAEA awards. Am Artist 27:8 Mr '63

KENNEDY, Jacqueline Lee (Bouvier)—about —*Continued*
New home for Jacqueline Kennedy and children. il U S News 55:18 D 9 '63
New life. il por Newsweek 62:24-5 D 16 '63
New role for Jacqueline Kennedy? M. Mead. Redbook 123:24+ Je '64
Profile in courage. America 109:722 D 7 '63
Sacre d'un deuil. S. Perse. Vogue 143:144-5 F 1 '64
Still pouring in; flood of mail for Mrs Kennedy. il U S News 56:8-9 Ja 20 '64
Toward the ideal; White House project. il por Time 82:60-7 S 6 '63
Valiant is the word for Jacqueline. L. Bergquist. il pors Look 28:72-4+ Ja 28 '64
What three Presidents say about their wives; excerpt from Woman in the White House. M. Means. il por Good H 157:60-1+ Ag '63
What women really think of the Kennedys. R. Carter. il por Good H 156:73-5+ Je '63
Work, memories, old friends. R. B. Stolley. il por Life 56:34B My 29 '64
Year of mourning set by Mrs Kennedy. il U S News 55:8 D 23 '63

KENNEDY, James Walter
Basketball's Irish czar. T. Smith. il pors Sat Eve Post 237:54-5 F 8 '64

KENNEDY, Jessie Callan
Read your paper with scissors. Writer 78: 30-1 Ja '65

KENNEDY, Joan (Bennett)
New Mrs Kennedy in Washington. S. Seay. il pors Look 27:21-5 F 26 '63

KENNEDY, John Fitzgerald, 1917-1963
Administration urges Congress to support $4.1 billion aid bill; statement, August 20, 1963. Dept State Bul 49:399 S 9 '63
Air cover: what President Kennedy says; excerpt from news conference. U S News 54: 31 F 4 '63
Alliance for progress marks second anniversary; remarks, August 17, 1963. Dept State Bul 49:401 S 9 '63
Balance of payments; special message to Congress, July 18, 1963. Dept State Bul 49:250-9 Ag 12 '63
Basic challenge; excerpt from message to Congress, May 25, 1961. Aviation W 79:25 D 2 '63
Battle for progress with freedom in the western hemisphere; address, November 18, 1963. Dept State Bul 49:900-4 D 9 '63
Delegation of authority under 1949 wheat agreement act; executive order, May 22, 1963. Dept State Bul 48:914 Je 10 '63
Dropout campaign; exchange of letters between President Kennedy and Commissioner Keppel; September 5 and September 15, 1963. Sch Life 46:3 O '63
Emancipation proclamation centennial, statement. por Ebony 18:20 S '63
Emergency preparedness functions assigned to Secretary of state; executive order, February 26, 1963. Dept State Bul 48:629-30 Ap 22 '63
Emperor of Ethiopia visits the United States; texts of an exchange of toasts between President Kennedy and the Emperor, October 1, 1963, and a joint communique October 2, 1963. Dept State Bul 49:674 O 28 '63
Exactly how Kennedy would cut and raise taxes; summary of message to Congress, January 24, 1963. por U S News 54:46-53 F 4 '63
Exchange of greetings, October 15, 1963, President Kennedy to Prime Minister Lemass; with text of communique, October 17, 1963. Dept State Bul 49:737-8 N 11 '63
Exchange of greetings, October 17, 1963; President Kennedy to President Tito; with text of communique. Dept State Bul 49: 738-40 N 11 '63
Excerpt from address, September 25, 1961. Cong Digest 43:202+ Ag '64
Fiscal responsibility; address, September 30, 1963. Vital Speeches 30:13-14 O 15 '63
Free-world defense and assistance programs; message to Congress, April 2, 1963. Dept State Bul 48:591-9 Ap 22 '63; Same with title President Kennedy on foreign aid. Cur Hist 44:366 Je '63
From the White House; letter to ALA conference. ALA Bul 57:733 S '63
Goal of the United States; text of speech to have been delivered before the Dallas citizens council, Dallas, Tex, November 22, 1963. Vital Speeches 30:105-7 D 1 '63
Heavy traffic on a two-way street; excerpts from press conference. Time 82:12 Jl 26 '63
How Kennedy sizes up Goldwater's chances; excerpts from news conference, October 9, 1963. U S News 55:6 O 21 '63
I look forward. . . . por Recreation 57:3 Ja '64
Ideas, attitudes, purposes; gleanings from writings and speeches. Sat R 46:26 D 7 '63
Jean Monnet honored as Mr Europe. Dept State Bul 48:195 F 11 '63
John F. Kennedy, 1917-1963; excerpts from addresses. Pub W 184:17+ D 2 '63
JFK urges dropouts return to school; excerpts from statement. Sr Schol 83:41 N 8 '63
JFK: what women can do now for peace; interview. por McCalls 91:102-3+ N '63
Kennedy at the U.N; excerpts from address, September 20, 1963. Bul Atomic Sci 19:45 N '63; Summary pors U N Rev 10:9-10 '63
Kennedy speaks at Frost library dedication; summary of address, October 26, 1963. Wilson Lib Bul 38:317 D '63; Excerpts. Arch Forum 119:67 D '63; por Sr Schol 83:1T D 6 '63
Kennedy tells businessmen why a tax cut is needed now; remarks, September 10, 1963. por U S News 55:98-101 S 23 '63; Same with title Tax reduction. Vital Speeches 29:740-3 O 1 '63
Late President's last reflections on the arts; excerpt from Creative America. Sat R 47:16-17 Mr 28 '64
Latin America; necessity for political democracy and stability; address, November 18, 1963. Vital Speeches 30:102-5 D 1 '63
Letter from Kennedy to Khrushchev, December 28, 1962. Bul Atomic Sci 19:34-6 Mr '63
Letter from President Kennedy to Chancellor Adenauer. Dept State Bul 49:697 N 4 '63
Limited test ban treaty ratified, enters into force; remarks, October 7, 1963, and text of proclamation, October 10, 1963. Dept State Bul 49:658-9 O 28 '63
Nation of immigrants; excerpts. N Y Times Mag p6-7+ Ag 4 '63
NAS celebrates 100th year; summary of address. por(p273) Sci N L 84:274 N 2 '63
Negro job quotas? Kennedy says no; excerpts from news conference, August 20, 1963. U S News 55:8 S 2 '63
New social order; address, June 25, 1963. Vital Speeches 29:578-81 Jl 15 '63
North Pacific fishery conference held at Tokyo; statement, September 10, 1963. Dept State Bul 49:519 S 30 '63
On history. por Am Heritage 15:2-4 F '64
Our obligation to the family of man; address, November 8, 1963. Dept State Bul 49:806-10 N 25 '63; Same with title Foreign aid. Vital Speeches 30:591-9 Ap 22 '63
Our relations with Russia; address, October 19,1963. Vital Speeches 30:34-5 N 1 '63; Excerpts. U S News 55:126-7 N 11 '63
Pan American congress of architects to meet at Washington in 1965; statement, October 12, 1963. Dept State Bul 49:801 N 18 '63
Passamaquoddy-Saint John report received by President Kennedy; remarks, July 16, 1963. Dept State Bul 49:248-9 Ag 12 '63
Physical fitness; report of progress. Look 27:82-3 Ag 13 '63
Pioneers for peace; address, September 26, 1963. Dept State Bul 49:631-6 O 21 '63
Platform Kennedy; excerpts from addresses. Sat R 46:27-9 D 7 '63
Poetry and power. por Atlan 213:53-4 F '64
President cites importance of home improvement programs. Am Home 66:85 Ap '63
President discusses Viet-Nam on CBS and NBC news programs; September 2 and September 9, 1963. Dept State Bul 49:498-500 S 30 '63
President expresses hope for success of U.N. science conference; statement, January 25, 1963. Dept State Bul 48:302 F 25 '63
President greets Conference of national organizations; letter, March 7, 1963. Dept State Bul 48:531 Ap 8 '63
President Kennedy accepts custody of flag of Cuban brigade; remarks, December 29, 1962. Dept State Bul 48:88-90 Ja 21 '63
President Kennedy and General Clay urge restoration of aid funds; interview, August 30, 1963. Dept State Bul 49:476-8 S 23 '63
President Kennedy on steel prices; statement. por U S News 54:37 Ap 22 '63
President Kennedy talks about you, your children and peace; ed. by R. Robinson. por Good H 157:73+ N '63
President Kennedy talks to women about peace; excerpts from interview. pors Redbook 122:51-3+ N '63
President Kennedy to Chairman Khrushchev, December 28, 1962; letter. Dept State Bul 48:200-1 F 11 '63

KENNEDY, John Fitzgerald—*Continued*
President Kennedy visits Europe; texts of joint communiques released at Bonn, Birch Grove house, Sussex, and Rome, with major addresses and remarks, June 23-July 2, 1963. Dept State Bul 49:114-37 Jl 22 '63
President Kennedy welcomes end of Katanga secession; statement, January 21, 1963. Dept State Bul 48:207 F 11 '63
President receives Clay report on AID program; letter, March 22, 1963. Dept State Bul 48:574 Ap 15 '63
President recommends expansion of Peace corps; letter to Lyndon B. Johnson, July 4, 1963. Dept State Bul 49:170-2 Jl 29 '63
President recommends revision of immigration laws; letter, July 23, 1963. Dept State Bul 49:298-300 Ag 19 '63
President reports on progress of test ban talks at Moscow; statement, July 17, 1963. Dept State Bul 49:198 Ag 5 '63
President sends message to Bogotá conference of labor ministers; text of message, May 7, 1963. Dept State Bul 48:884-5 Je 3 '63
President sends message to Bogota meeting of ministers of education; August 5, 1963. Dept State Bul 49:412 S 9 '63
President sends message to conference of African leaders at Addis Ababa, May 22, 1963. Dept State Bul 48:902 Je 10 '63
President transmits proposal for Academy of foreign affairs; letter to Lyndon B. Johnson, February 11, 1963. Dept State Bul 48: 427-9 Mr 25 '63
President urges Senate approval of test ban treaty; letter to Senate leaders, September 11, and news conference statement, September 12, 1963. Dept State Bul 49:496-8 S 30 '63
President's civil rights message. Ebony 18: 233-4 S '63
President's letter to Senate; transmitting the conventions on slavery, forced labor, and the political rights of women, July 22, 1963. Dept State Bul 49:322-3 Ag 26 '63
Presidents' meeting at San José; statements, addresses and remarks, March 18-21, 1963. Dept State Bul 48:511-20 Ap 8 '63
President's message on education; January 29, 1963. Sch Life 45:5-7+ F '63; Excerpts Wilson Lib Bul 37:709 Ap '63
President's message; transmitting copy of test ban treaty to the Senate, August 8, 1963. Dept State Bul 49:316-18 Ag 26 '63; Excerpts Time 82:13 Ag 16 '63
President's NLW statement stresses education. Pub W 183:30 Ap 22 '63
Principals named for negotiations on NATO multilateral force; statement, January 24, 1963. Dept State Bul 48:197 F 11 '63
Private letters of John F. Kennedy; ed. by R. G. Deindorfer. por Good H 156:74-5+ F '63
Prosperity insurance; address, September 18, 1963. Vital Speeches 29:738-40 O 1 '63
Race problem: the solution as the President sees it; address, June 11, 1963. por U S News 54:79-80 Je 24 '63; Same with title Moral imperative. Vital Speeches 29:546-7 Jl 1 '63; Excerpts. Newsweek 61:30 Je 24 '63; Sr Schol 83:18-19 S 13 '63
Realities underlying the Atlantic alliance; statement, January 24, 1963. Dept State Bul 48:197 F 11 '63
Responsibilities of the United Nations; address, September 20, 1963. Vital Speeches 30:2-5 O 15 '63; Same with title New opportunities in the search for peace. Dept State Bul 49:530-5 O 7 '63; Excerpts. U S News 55:60-1 S 30 '63
Satellite communications and international understanding; statement, November 20, 1963. Dept State Bul 49:904 D 9 '63
Science and international cooperation; address, October 22, 1963. Dept State Bul 49: 778-82 N 18 '63; Excerpts. Bul Atomic Sci 19:42 D '63; Science 142:1129 N 29 '63
Secretary assigned leadership in international aviation policy; letter to Secretary Rusk, June 22, 1963. Dept State Bul 49:160-1 Jl 29 '63
Selling wheat to Russia: Kennedy gives his reasons, statement, October 9, 1963. por U S News 55:53 O 21 '63
Shorter week by year 2000? excerpts from news conference, October 9, 1963. U S News 55:115 O 21 '63
Sir Winston Churchill becomes honorary citizen of United States; exchange of remarks, April 9, 1963; with the text of proclamation. Dept State Bul 48:715-16 My 6 '63
State of the Union; address, January 14, 1963. Vital Speeches 29:226-30 F 1 '63; Same. Cur Hist 44:174-6+ Mr '63; Excerpts. Dept State Bul 48:159-64 F 4 '63; Summary. por Sr Schol 82:15-17 Ja 30 '63
Strategy of peace; address, June 10, 1963. Vital Speeches 29:558-61 Jl 1 '63; Same. Dept State Bul 49:2-6 Jl 1 '63; Excerpts. Time 81:18-19 Je 21 '63; Summary. New Yorker 39:96-8 Je 22 '63
Strength for peace and strength for war; address, October 19, 1963. Dept State Bul 49:694-7 N 4 '63
Strength of the United States; address, November 21, 1963. Vital Speeches 30:101-2 D 1 '63
Strengthening the international monetary system; remarks, September 30, 1963. Dept State Bul 49:610-13 O 21 '63
Tariff schedule on importation of butter oil amended; proclamation, October 5, 1963. Dept State Bul 49:685 O 28 '63
Tax cut, reforms, recession; Kennedy's latest views; questions and answers. por U S News 54:86-8 Mr 11 '63
Test ban: the first concrete measure. Bul Atomic Sci 19:40+ O '63
Test ban treaty; address, July 26, 1963. Vital Speeches 29:644-7 Ag 15 '63; Same with title Nuclear test ban treaty: a step toward peace. Dept State Bul 49:234-8 Ag 12 '63; Excerpts. U S News 55:6 Ag 5 '63; Summary Time 82:9 Ag 2 '63
Thoughts on the first anniversary of November 22, 1963; quotations from his speeches and writings. por Sr Schol 85:17 N 18 '64
Time the US caught up; excerpt from address, June 13, 1963. New Repub 149:35 N 9 '63
Unclaimed property of victims of Nazi persecution; executive order, February 26, 1963. Dept State Bul 48:618 Ap 22 '63
United in spirit and in arms; Rendezvous with destiny; addresses, March 18 and March 21, 1963. Vital Speeches 29:386-9 Ap 15 '63
United Nations day, 1963; proclamation, April 20, 1963. Dept State Bul 48:806 My 20 '63
U.S. and Venezuela take firm stand against Communist threats. Dept State Bul 48:445 Mr 25 '63
United States assures Saudi Arabia of support and friendship; letter, October 25, 1962. Dept State Bul 48:144-5 Ja 28 '63
U.S. grain dealers to be allowed to sell wheat to Soviet Union and eastern Europe; statement, October 9, 1963. Dept State Bul 49: 660-1 O 28 '63
U.S. policy on East Germany not affected by test ban treaty; interview. Dept State Bul 49:354 S 2 '63
U.S. troops in Alabama. por U S News 54: 41 My 27 '63
Unspoken message; extract from undelivered speech. Vogue 143:70a Ja 1 '64
Visit to Ireland; address, June 28, 1963. Dept State Bul 49:128-32 Jl 22 '63
Visit to Italy; address, July 2, 1963. Dept State Bul 49:134-7 Jl 22 '63
What business can do for America. pors Nations Bsns 51:29-31+ S '63
White House Emancipation proclamation centennial by the President of the United States of America; a proclamation. Negro Hist Bul 26:195 Mr '63
White House holds conference on export expansion; address, September 17, 1963. Dept State Bul 49:595-9 O 14 '63
Why the U.S. crackdown on anti-Castro raids; news conference, April 3, 1963. por U S News 54:35 Ap 15 '63
Why U.S. had to test to stay ahead; excerpts from address, March 2, 1962. U S News 55:67 Ag 26 '63
With clean hands and a clear conscience; excerpt from A nation of immigrants. por Sat Eve Post 237:21-3 O 3 '64
Words of John Fitzgerald Kennedy: a man does what he must; quotations from addresses. Newsweek 62:46-7 D 2 '63
World food congress meets at Washington; welcoming remarks, June 4, 1963. Dept State Bul 49:58-60 Jl 8 '63

—and Chiari, R. F.
U.S. and Panama agree on certain procedural matters in Canal Zone; joint communique, January 10, 1963. Dept State Bul 48:171-2 F 4 '63
U.S. and Panama announce results of Canal Zone talks; joint communique, July 23, 1963. Dept State Bul 49:246-7 Ag 12 '63

—and Fanfani, Amintore
President Kennedy holds talks with Prime Minister of Italy; joint communique, January 17, 1963. Dept State Bul 48:164 F 4 '63

—and Macmillan, Harold
President Kennedy holds talks at Nassau with Prime Minister Macmillan; joint communique and statement on nuclear defence systems, December 21, 1962. Dept State Bul 48: 43-5 Ja 14 '63

KENNEDY, John Fitzgerald—*Continued*
Visit to the United Kingdom; joint communique, June 30, 1963. Dept State Bul 49:132-3 Jl 22 '63
—and Mohammed Zahir
King of Afghanistan visits United States; joint communique, September 7, 1963. Dept State Bul 49:535 O 7 '63
—and Paz Estenssoro, Victor
President Paz of Bolivia visits United States; text of communique between President Kennedy and President Paz, October 23, 1963. Dept State Bul 49:787-8 N 18 '63
—and Pearson, L. B.
President Kennedy and Prime Minister Pearson of Canada hold talks; joint communique, May 11, 1963. Dept State Bul 48:815-17 My 27 '63
—and Piccioni, Attilio
Foreign Minister of Italy holds talks in Washington. Dept State Bul 49:636 O 21 '63
—and Radhakrishnan, Sarvepalli
U.S. and India reaffirm agreement on basic values and objectives; joint communique, June 4, 1963. Dept State Bul 48:969-70 Je 24 '63

about

All the news that manages to fit. A. Krock. Nat R 14:182 Mr 12 '63
And then it was November 22 again. il pors Newsweek 64:25-8 N 30 '64
Annals of legislation. R. Harris. New Yorker 40:46-8+ Mr 28 '64
Another Cuban fiasco? il por U S News 54:33-6 Ap 29 '63
Appeal to the President. W. J. Coughlin. Miss & Roc 12:46 Mr 18 '63
Appraisal of Kennedy as world leader. L. J. Halle. il por N Y Times Mag p7+ Je 16 '63
Armies of ignorance. L. J. Halle. New Repub 149:16-17 D 7 '63
Assailing a legend. Time 85:65 Ja 29 '65
Atlantic City and a memory. L. Wainwright. Life 57:17 S 4 '64
Atlantic report; review of the Kennedy administration. Atlan 212:4+ Jl '63
Beating a path to Kennedy's door; visiting dignitaries. il pors U S News 55:46-7 N 4 '63
Beware, the mousetrap; Cuba policy. L. B. Bozell. Nat R 14:354 My 7 '63
Big hike. Nation 196:171 Mr 2 '63
Birch view of JFK. Newsweek 63:29-30 F 24 '64
Care and feeding of the Kennedy image. il pors U S News 55:92-3 S 9 '63
Change of course; President's commitment to the Negro. W. Lippmann. Newsweek 62:15 Jl 8 '63
Changing times: religious issue in American political life; Dr E. S. James and Baptist views. Newsweek 61:77 Mr 4 '63
Coat upon a stick. M. Kempton. New Repub 148:12-13 Ap 27 '63
Collapse of Kennedy's Grand design. S. Alsop. il pors Sat Eve Post 236:78-81 Ap 6 '63
Common action for the control of conflict, by V. P. Rock. Review
U S News il por 55:64-6 N 18 '63
Consumers lose a friend. C. E. Warne. Consumer Rep 29:15 Ja '64
Crisis in Birmingham; federal government's part. W. V. Shannon. Commonweal 78:238-9 My 24 '63
Criticisms of Kennedy. New Repub 148:2 My 18 '63
Cuba, Castro and John F. Kennedy. R. M. Nixon. Read Digest 85:281-4+ N '64
Cuba crisis and nuclear arms; why de Gaulle goes his own way; reprint. C. B. Luce. U S News 54:64-5 F 18 '63
Cuban crisis: how close we were to war; excerpts from Politics of policy-making: the Kennedy years. R. Hilsman. il Look 28:17-21 Ag 25 '64
Decisions, decisions; in high places from Moses to the current President. Reporter 29:16+ Ag 15 '63
Decline of Mr Kennedy? W. F. Buckley, jr. Nat R 15:95 Ag 13 '63
Design for culture in Washington. W. Von Eckardt. il Sat R 47:20-3 My 23 '64
Economic education of John F. Kennedy. M. J. Rossant. por Reporter 28:22-5 F 14 '63; Discussion. 28:10+ Mr 14 '63
Education of presidents. R. Kirk. Nat R 15:308 O 8 '63
End and a beginning; concerning President's TV-radio speech on the American dilemma of race. il Newsweek 61:29-34 Je 24 '63
Enemies he made. K. Crawford. Newsweek 62:35 D 2 '63
Epilogue. D. F. Fleming. Ann Am Acad 351:180 Ja '64
Fasten your seat belts. M. Ascoli. Reporter 29:22 N 7 '63; Reply. S. McCalmont. 29:8+ D 5 '63
First of the month; excerpt from letter in the Harvard alumni bulletin concerning resignation from Harvard's Board of overseers. C. Amory. Sat R 46:6 My 4 '63
From bully! to vigah! A. Robertson. il pors Horizon 5:68-71 N '63
Goldwater out front: will he be blocked? il U S News 55:41-3 Jl 15 '63
Hail to the O'Chief. D. Behan. il por Life 54:12 Je 21 '63
Hard, close fight; views presented at news conference. Newsweek 62:36 O 21 '63
Hard-won destiny of Lyndon Johnson. D. Cater. Reporter 29:17-19 D 19 '63
How a president should use the intellectuals. J. R. Roche. por N Y Times Mag p 10+ Jl 26 '64
How JFK and Ike compare as golfers. il pors U S News 55:24 Ag 5 '63
How JFK surpassed Abraham Lincoln. S. Booker. il pors Ebony 19:25-8+ F '64
How LBJ got the nomination. P. Potter. il Reporter 30:16-20 Je 18 '64
How Mr Kennedy gets the answers. S. Hyman. il por N Y Times Mag p 17+ O 20 '63
How President Kennedy upset Cuban invasion of April 1961. U S News 54:29-30+ F 4 '63
How the President runs the White House; excerpts from addresses, April 18 and May 9, 1963. T. C. Sorensen. il pors U S News 54:70-2 Je 3 '63
How the public rates JFK. il pors Look 27:34 Ag 13 '63
If Congress gives Kennedy his way on civil rights. il U S News 55:30-1 Jl 1 '63
If it's Rockefeller vs. Kennedy in 1964—. il por U S News 54:56-8 F 11 '63
In brief: this is Kennedy's latest plan on civil rights. U S News 55:30-1 Jl 1 '63
In remembrance; anniversary of assassination. por Time 84:32-3 N 27 '64
Indelible mark. R. Hotz. Aviation W 79:21 D 2 '63
Into the big country; "non-political" Presidential tour. il por Newsweek 62:31-2 O 7 '63
Is a U.S. deal with Russia near? il pors U S News 55:27-9 Jl 22 '63
Is JFK weaker politically? How the voting went in important areas. il por U S News 55:43-6 N 18 '63
Is Kennedy in political trouble at home? il U S News 55:38-40 Jl 8 '63
Issue isn't personal. R. Moley. Newsweek 62:64 D 30 '63
It's one year after JFK: the changes; with interview with J. M. Burns. il pors U S News 57:60-6 N 23 '64
Jack's town; impact on Washington, D.C; Foreign relations. por Time 81:19-21 Je 7 '63
J.F.K. as theologian. Christian Cent 80:631 My 8 '63
JFK: bricks and broken glass. J. P. Roche. Reporter 29:48+ N 7 '63
JFK: chipper at forty-six, pointing to '64. il por Newsweek 61:17-18 Je 3 '63
JFK in a truce with business? il U S News 54:35-6 Je 3 '63
JFK in Goldwater country; what he found out. il U S News 55:49-50 O 7 '63
JFK in the bully pulpit. por Newsweek 61:27 Je 24 '63
JFK memorial issue; symposium. il pors Look 28:33-46+ N 17 '64
John F. Kennedy, portrait of a president. J. Kraft. Harper 228:96+ Ja '64
J.F.K: reflections a year later. Life 57:4 N 20 '64
JFK termed brilliant in managing the news. U S News 54:10 Mr 11 '63
JFK, the magazines, and peace. J. Tebbel. il Sat R 46:56-7 D 14 '63
J.F.K: the man & the myth, by V. Lasky. Review
Nat R 15:309-10 O 8 '63. M. S. Evans
Newsweek 62:96 S 16 '63. R. Moley
Time 82:28 S 20 '63
JFK's last campaign. il Newsweek 63:25+ Mr 9 '64
John F. Kennedy's tribute to his older brother. V. Cadden. por Redbook 122:46-7+ F '64

about

Die jungen herren der alten erde, by W. S. Schlamm. Review
Nat R 15:400-1 N 5 '63. S. J. Tonsor
Kennedy and '64: out to grass roots. il pors U S News 54:35-6 Je 17 '63
Kennedy and the liberals. S. E. Harris. New Repub 148:15-16 Je 1 '63

KENNEDY, John Fitzgerald—about—*Continued*
Kennedy as target. New Repub 148:3-5 Je 1 '63
Kennedy comes home to trouble. il por U S News 55:29-30 Jl 15 '63
Kennedy death affects publishing; new editions of books announced. Library J 89:334 Ja 15 '64
Kennedy homestead. il Newsweek 62:31 Jl 1 '63
Kennedy pro arte, et sequitur? A. Frankfurter. pors Art N 62:23+ Ja '64
Kennedy: profile of a technician; with editorial comment. T. Lewis. Nation 196:81, 92-4 F 2 '63
Kennedy receives AIA citation for policies on architecture, art. il por Arch Rec 134:33 Ag '63
Kennedy the Catholic. J. Cogley. Commonweal 79:422-4 Ja 10 '64
Kennedy the Catholic. T. J. Fleming. Nation 198:571-2 Je 8 '64; Discussion. 199:inside cover Jl 13 '64
Kennedy without tears. T. Wicker. por Esquire 61:108-11+ Je '64
Kennedy's back injury: another flare-up. il U S News 55:22 S 9 '63
Kennedy's latest plan for aid to schools. il U.S. News 54:60 F 11 '63
Kennedy's offer stirs confusion, dismay; with editorial comment. A. P. Alibrando. Aviation W 79:21, 26-7 S 30 '63
Kennedys: scoring anew on crowd appeal. il U S News 55:11 Jl 29 '63
Kennedy's strategy for the '64 election. il por U S News 55:34-6 Ag 19 '63
Kennedy's voyage of discovery. S. Vanocur. Harper 228:41-5 Ap '64
Kennedy's worry: is the solid South lost for '64? il por U S News 55:35-7 O 28 '63
Khrushchev-Kennedy treaty. F. S. Meyer. Nat R 15:107 Ag 13 '63
Last loving remembrance of John F. Kennedy; excerpts from Day in the life of President Kennedy. J. Bishop. il pors Good H 158:71-4+ Mr '64
Late President on the podium. W. Johnson. Sat R 47:24 Je 27 '64
Late President, successor saw development of space program. il pors Aviation W 79:30-1 D 2 '63
Legacy of John F. Kennedy. J. Aslop. il pors Sat Eve Post 237:15-19 N 21 '64
Letter from Washington; determination of the Negroes for justice. R. H. Rovere. New Yorker 39:100-4+ Je 1 '63
Letter from Washington; government for complete equality for Negro. R. H. Rovere. New Yorker 39:90+ Je 22 '63
Letter from Washington; managed news. R. H. Rovere. New Yorker 39:164-9 Mr 30 '63
Libraries as important as schools, says Kennedy in NLW message. Library J 88:1962 My 15 '63
Lights, action, camera: JFK. il pors U S News 55:67 N 4 '63
Man JFK picked to play his wartime role: PT-109. il pors Look 27:48-50 Je 18 '63
Man or myth? il por Newsweek 62:27-8 S 23 '63
Meeting of two minds. M. Ascoli. Reporter 28:22-3 F 28 '63
Memo from a secretary about her boss: John Fitzgerald Kennedy. E. Lincoln. il por McCalls 91:68+ Jl '64
Memorials, yes: this one, no. J. Ciardi. Sat R 47:20 S 5 '64
Memories of a President; papers and mementoes on exhibition at I.B.M. building. il N Y Times Mag p48+ My 10 '64
Military legacy. W. V. Kennedy. America 109:790 D 21 '63
Mr Kennedy and apathy. Commonweal 78:267-8 My 31 '63
Mr Kennedy's management of the news. A. Krock. Fortune 67:82+ Mr '63; Excerpts. Nat R 14:182 Mr 12 '63
Money's not for spending; Kennedy half-dollar. il Bsns W p34 Je 13 '64
More tax cuts coming. il por Nations Bsns 52:38-41+ My '64
My advance view of the Cuban crisis. K. Keating. il Look 28:99-100+ N 3 '64
New era in Washington: its meaning. il U S News 55:35-50, 78-83 D 9 '63
New plan for aid abroad, JFK's version. U S News 54:8 Ap 15 '63
New what? W. V. Shannon. Commonweal 77:481-2 F 1 '63
Now a new worry for Kennedy: the white vote in '64. il U S News 55:36-7 S 9 '63
Now, for JFK: ten copters, four jets, two yachts, big cars. il U S News 55:60-1 Jl 22 '63
Now, Kennedy moves on civil rights. il U S News 54:52 Mr 11 '63
On Kennedy and existential politics. N. Mailer. Esquire 60:26+ N '63
One week with the President: a minute-by-minute account. il pors U S News 54:48-52 My 13 '63
Policy and legacy. J. Walsh. Science 142:1152-3 N 29 '63
Politics: JFK's lost votes. il por Newsweek 62:55-6 O 21 '63
Politics of courage. K. Crawford. Newsweek 61:41 Je 24 '63
Poll puzzler; effect of stand on civil rights. Newsweek 62:21-2 Jl 8 '63
Presidency. See issues of Time to November 29, 1963
Presidency and the peace. M. Bundy. For Affairs 42:353-65 Ap '64
President (title varies) See issues of Newsweek to November 18, 1963
President and his son. L. Bergquist. il pors Look 27:26-34+ D 3 '63
President and the arts. A. Heckscher. Sat R 46:6+ D 14 '63
President is ready now for '64. E. T. Folliard. America 108:877 Je 22 '63
President Kennedy presents the Hubbard medal. il pors Nat Geog Mag 124:514-15 O '63
President Kennedy talks about women and world peace. R. S. Cramer. il pors Parents Mag 38:57+ N '63
President Kennedy's tour. Liv Wildn 84:45 Sum '63
President renews hope for peace; concerning commencement address at American university. Christian Cent 80:822 Je 26 '63
President vs. a governor: another school showdown. il U S News 55:42-3 S 23 '63
President who loved sport. Sports Illus 19:20-1 D 2 '63
President's health: a progress report. il U S News 55:16 Jl 22 '63
Progress on the home front. W. V. Shannon. Commonweal 78:294-5 Je 7 '63
PT's ride again; excerpt from At close quarters. R. J. Bulkley, jr. il Motor B 112:28-31 Jl '63
Q's and A's about the press conference. T. Wicker. il pors N Y Times Mag p24-5+ S 8 '63
Racial crisis summons President's leadership. Christian Cent 80:766 Je 12 '63
Records and tapes. H. J. Langer. Sr Schol 84:30T Mr 20 '64
Reporter engagé; concerning report by J. Daniel. Newsweek 62:70 D 23 '63
Schlesinger at the White House; ed. by H. Brandon. A. Schlesinger, jr. Harper 229:55-60 Jl '64
Scrimshaw collector. C. Barnes, jr. and C. Bowen. il Am Heritage 15:8-13 O '64
Second-term time. il por Newsweek 62:30 N 25 '63
Secretary Rusk participates in CBS reports program; interview, ed. by M. Kalb. D. Rusk. Dept State Bul 50:4-7 Ja 6 '64
Space program support to grow; with editorial comment. H. Taylor. Miss & Roc 13:14-15, 48 D 2 '63
Strategy of peace; concerning President Kennedy's speech at the American university in Washington on June 10, 1963. Nation 196:537 Je 29 '63
Strength of President Johnson. W. F. Buckley, jr. Nat R 16:143 F 25 '64
Striking the theme; Conservation tour. il por Time 82:34+ O 4 '63
Ted Sorensen of Nebraska. W. L. Miller. Reporter 30:24-7 F 13 '64
Tensions ease under the sign of the moon; President Kennedy addresses the U.N. General assembly. il por Newsweek 62:17-18 S 30 '63
These are the things I hope will show how he really was; exhibit of mementos. J. Kennedy. il Life 56:32-34A My 29 '64
Through a brother's eyes; excerpt from foreword to Profiles in courage. R. Kennedy. Time 83:26 F 21 '64
Tragedy and a challenge. Bsns W p 124 N 30 '63
Travel fleets of two Presidents. il U S News 55:65 S 16 '63
Truman vs. Kennedy: debate over William Walker. U S News 54:20 Ap 29 '63
Turn toward peace. D. F. Fleming. bibliog f Ann Am Acad 351:157-69 Ja '64
Two genii; present and future problems. Nation 197:1-2 Jl 6 '63
U.S. failing in Europe? J. Fromm and F. C. Painton. il por U S News 54:48-52 Mr 25 '63
Vatican and U.S: closer ties? il por U S News 55:37 Jl 15 '63

KENNEDY, John Fitzgerald—about—*Continued*
Voyage, travel, change of place. il por Newsweek 61:21-2 Je 17 '63
Wait till next term; Kennedy administration. Reporter 28:16+ Mr 28 '63
Warmest way to remember him. il pors Life 55:101-4 N 29 '63
Washington insight; Kennedy and the intellectuals. J. Kraft. Harper 227:112+ N '63
What JFK is promising to Central Americans. U S News 54:55 Mr 25 '63
What three newsmen report about Kennedy news tactics; reprints. A. Krock; H. W. Baldwin; M. S. Watson. U S News 54:42 Ap 15 '63
What was killed was not only the President but the promise. J. Reston. il pors N Y Times Mag p24-5+ N 15 '64
What women really think of the Kennedys. R. Carter. il por Good H 156:73-5+ Je '63
What's fit to print? concerning Kennedy interview with J. Daniel. Reporter 30:12 Ja 2 '64; Reply with rejoinder. J. Daniel. 30:10+ F 27 '64
Where Kennedy is changing course. il U S News 55:31-2 N 4 '63
White House years. il pors Newsweek 62:45-8 D 2 '63
Why Congress doesn't give JFK what he wants. il pors U S News 54:38-42 Mr 18 '63
Why Kennedy, Goldwater are going to the voters now. il por U S News 55:43-4 S 16 '63
Will Germany now edge closer to U.S? Kennedy and the Germans. il por U S News 54:62-3 Je 24 '63
Will it be Nixon vs. Kennedy again in '64? il U S News 55:34-5 N 25 '63

Assassination

After great pain, a formal feeling. M. McGrory. America 109:764 D 14 '63
After the shots: the ordeal of Lyndon Johnson. F. Knebel. Look 28:26-8+ Mr 10 '64
And a child's yellow flowers. il Newsweek 62:36-7 D 2 '63
Apocalypse and after. Christian Cent 80:1487 D 4 '63
As Warren inquiry starts: latest on the assassination. il U S News 55:28-30 D 30 '63
Assassin. B. H. Bagdikian. il Sat Eve Post 236:22-7 D 14 '63
Assassination, as the plot unfolds: case against Oswald: How the President was shot. il U S News 55:68-71 D 9 '63
Assassination inquiry: slow, careful. il U S News 56:49 Ja 27 '64
Assassination of President Kennedy; with report by T. H. White. il por Life 55:22-32H N 29 '63
Assessing the blame in the President's death; excerpts from address, December 14, 1963. P. Daniel. U S News 55:73 D 30 '63
Author chosen for story of assassination. Pub W 185:27 Ap 6 '64
Autopsy. Time 82:18 D 27 '63
Awful interval. il Newsweek 63:19-20 Ja 6 '64
Burden of guilt. Christian Cent 81:37-8 Ja 8 '64; Discussion. 81:243 F 19 '64
Campaign time; when Secret service worry grows. il por U S News 56:63-4 Ap 13 '64
Climate of hate. America 109:758 D 14 '63
Collective guilt in the U.S? take a look at the world; with excerpts from address by T. B. Morton. il U S News 55:72-4 D 23 '63
Collective or individual guilt? U S News 55:10 D 16 '63
Commentary of an eyewitness. R. Dudman. New Repub 149:18 D 21 '63
Compendium of curious coincidences; parallels in the lives and deaths of A. Lincoln and J. F. Kennedy. il Time 84:19 Ag 21 '64
Covering the tragedy; news coverage. il Time 82:84 N 29 '63
Dallas rejoinder. Nation 198:519 My 25 '64
Day Kennedy died. il por Newsweek 62:20-6 D 2 '63
Day the President died; its meaning and impact. G. R. Krupp. il Redbook 122:49+ Mr '64
Dear cousin William. M. Kantor. McCalls 91:77+ F '64
Death in emergency room no. one; Parkland memorial hospital. J. Breslin. il Sat Eve Post 236:30-1 D 14 '63
Death of a President; told in direct testimony; excerpts. il U S News 57:68-70 D 7 '64
Did press pressure kill Oswald? reprint. L. Grove. il U S News 56:78-9 Ap 6 '64
Different look at Dallas, Texas. il U S News 56:42-6 F 3 '64
Do they really hate to hate? W. F. Buckley, jr. Nat R 15:559 D 31 '63
Does TV crime reporting jeopardize justice? pro and con discussion. il Sr Schol 84:6-7 Mr 20 '64
End, and a beginning. il Newsweek 62:19-20 D 9 '63
End to nagging rumors: the six critical seconds. P. Mandel. Life 55:52F D 6 '63
Fact of mortality. R. Gilman. Commonweal 79:337-8 D 13 '63
Foreign countries, too, mourn first citizen of the world. il por U S News 55:48-9 D 2 '63
Foreword: postscript. D. F. Fleming. Ann Am Acad 351:x Ja '64
From friend and foe in America: sense of shock and dismay at the despicable act; statements. U S News 55:49 D 2 '63
Government still lives. il por Time 82:21-7 N 29 '63; Same abr. with title Death in Dallas. Read Digest 84:39-44 Ja '64
Hatred knows no logic. Sat Eve Post 237:80 Ja 4 '64
Have we learned our lessons? Christian Cent 80:1567-8 D 18 '63
History's jury. il Newsweek 62:25-7 D 16 '63
How America felt. Newsweek 63:33 Mr 16 '64
How JFK died. Newsweek 62:55 D 30 '63
How sorrowful bad; world reactions. il Time 82:38-9 N 29 '63
Hypothetical case; letter. Nat R 15:515-16 D 17 '63; Discussion. 16:36 Ja 14 '64
If you can keep your head when all about you: television and news magazine coverage of the Kennedy assassination story. R. L. Tobin. il Sat R 46:53-4 D 14 '63; Discussion. 47:74 Ja 11 '64
In the Nation's interest; commission to investigate the assassination of President John F. Kennedy. America 109:789 D 21 '63
Incredible tragedy. D. Lawrence. U S News 55:104 D 2 '63
Interim reflections. M. Ascoli. Reporter 31:12 O 22 '64
It will be many years. . . D. Wise il Good H 158:90-1+ F '64
J.F.K: the murder & the myths. il Time 83:44+ Je 12 '64
JFK's murder: sowers of doubt. il por Newsweek 63:22-4 Ap 6 '64
Johnson takes oath as nation mourns Kennedy. il Sr Schol 83:14 D 6 '63
Johnson takes over: the untold story. S. Alsop. il Sat Eve Post 237:17-23 F 15 '64
Kennedy alive in hospital. il Sci N L 86:229 O 10 '64
Kennedy legacy, the people's task. Commonweal 79:335-6 D 13 '63
Kennedy's assassination: study organized by social scientists. E. Langer. Science 142:1446-7 D 13 '63
Killing still mystery. il Sci N L 86:230 O 10 '64
Letter from London. M. Panter-Downes. New Yorker 39:196-8 D 7 '63
Letters to the editor; with editorial comment. Sr Schol 83:18 Ja 10 '64
Lingering doubts; survey of public opinion. Newsweek 63:19 Ja 6 '64
Long vigil. M. Mannes. il Reporter 29:15-17 D 19 '63
Man who killed Kennedy. il Time 82:33A-34 D 6 '63
Manchurian candidate in Dallas. R. Condon. Nation 197:449-51 D 28 '63
Memo about a Dallas citizen. T. G. Harris. il Look 28:64+ Ag 11 '64
Memo from a Dallas citizen. J. M. Shea, jr. Look 28:88+ Mr 24 '64
Mrs Kennedy says thank you to 800,000 friends. J. L. Kennedy. Life 56:32B-32C Ja 24 '64
Moment of tragedy. il U S News 55:6 D 2 '63
More than one man. America 109:722 D 7 '63
New light on the assassination: a secret agent's story; excerpts from interview, ed. by G. Troelstrup. A. Sassa. il U S News 56:38-9 Je 8 '64
Nightmare revisited; re-enactment for Warren commission. il Newsweek 63:48 Je 8 '64
No time for collective guilt; reprint. V. Royster. U S News 55:72 D 9 '63
Note from Texas. J. W. Turnbull. Commonweal 79:337 D 13 '63
Notes and comment. New Yorker 39:45 D 7 '63
November in Dallas. W. Jones. Library J 89:72 Ja 1 '64
November 22, 1963. J. Ciardi. Sat R 46:16+ D 7 '63
Now the trumpet summons again. . . il por Bsns W p21-3 N 30 '63

KENNEDY, John Fitzgerald—Assassination —*Continued*

Of chaos and courage. J. Ciardi. Sat R 46: 25 D 28 '63
On the far right. Commonweal 79:384 D 27 '63
One thing worse than this; sermon delivered at Northaven Methodist church, Dallas, November 24, 1963. W. A. Holmes. Christian Cent 80:1555-6 D 11 '63
Oswald affair. L. Sauvage. Commentary 37: 55-65 Mr '64; Discussion. 38:16-17 Jl '64
Oswald and the weight of evidence. il Newsweek 62:36+ D 9 '63
Oswald in Dallas: a few loose ends. L. Sauvage. il Reporter 30:24-6 Ja 2 '64; Discussion. 30:6+ Ja 30 '64
Oswald killing discussed. Sci N L 84:355 D 7 '63
Plot to clear Lee Oswald. Nat R 16:265 Ap 7 '64
Questions from abroad. H. Brandon. Sat R 47:9 My 9 '64; Reply. T. Tamama. 47:21 Je 27 '64
Reaction to assassination; excerpts from reports of Christian century's news correspondents. Christian Cent 80:1618-19 D 25 '63
Reaction to killings. Sci N L 84:358 D 7 '63
Reaction to the Warren commission report. Sr Schol 85:17 O 14 '64
Reactions in the South. Newsweek 62:27 D 16 '63
Report from the FBI. il Newsweek 62:19-20 D 23 '63
Reporter must trust his instinct. T. Wicker. Sat R 47:81-2+ Ja 11 '64
Romans. M. Kempton and J. Ridgeway. New Repub 149:9-11 D 7 '63
Sad & solemn duty; commission to investigate the assassination of J. Kennedy. il Time 82:26-7 D 13 '63
Seeds of doubt; some questions about the assassination. J. Minnis and S. Lynd. il New Repub 149:14-17+ D 21 '63; Discussion. 150:28-30 Ja 11 '64
Senseless tragedy. il Sat Eve Post 236:19 D 14 '63
Seventy-two hours and what they can teach us. Life 55:4 D 6 '63
Shame of Dallas. Sat R 46:26 D 28 '63
Shock, then recovery; impact of the assassination of Pres. Kennedy, opinions of US economists. il Bsns W p92-3 N 30 '63
Since that day in Dallas; ed. by M. Drury. Mrs J. Connally. McCalls 91:78-9+ Ag '64
Speaking out; hate knows no direction. R. E. McGill. Sat Eve Post 236:8+ D 14 '63
Strange world of Lee Oswald: more light on the assassination. il U S News 55:60-2 D 16 '63
TV sees it now, for seventy hours. il Bsns W p34 N 30 '63
This nation, under God; statement by the editors. Read Digest 84:37-9 Ja '64
Thousand well-wishers, and one assassin. W. W. Hercher. il U S News 55:34-5 D 2 '63
Time between. Reporter 29:14 D 5 '63
To heal the wounds. D. Hessel. Christian Cent 81:15 Ja 1 '64
To the editor; letters. Nat R 15:577 D 31 '63
Tragedy in Dallas: letters to the editor. Christian Cent 80:1588-9 D 18 '63
Tragic end of John F. Kennedy. il pors U S News 55:31-3 D 2 '63
Untold stories: aftermath of the assassination. il U S News 57:58-62 O 12 '64
Verdict: one man alone. il Sr Schol 85:9-10 O 7 '64
Warren commission. Nation 197:445 D 28 '63
Warren commission; testimony and evidence. il Time 84:25-7 D 4 '64
What they saw that dreadful day in Dallas; testimony and evidence published. il por Newsweek 64:28-30+ D 7 '64
When Castro heard the news. J. Daniel. New Repub 149:7-9 D 7 '63
When Kennedy died: psychological impact. il Newsweek 64:61 S 14 '64
When the highest office changes hands. D. D. Eisenhower. il por Sat Eve Post 236:15 D 14 '63
Where the shots came from. New Repub 149: 7 D 28 '63
Why a plot was feared when Kennedy was shot. U S News 56:7 Ja 6 '64
World mourns in doubt, fear, hope. Newsweek 62:56-8 D 9 '63
World resounds; symposium. America 109: 767-71 D 14 '63
World weeps and waits. il Bsns W p30-1 N 30 '63

See also

United States—President's commission to investigate the assassination of President Kennedy

Bibliography

Books. A. E. Gropp. Américas 16:40-1 Ja '64
In memoriam. il pors Time 82:31-2 D 20 '63
Personal business. Bsns W p 110 N 30 '63
Remembering the President. J. Tebbel. por Sat R 47:50-1 F 8 '64; Reply. S. Ferderber. 47:70+ Ap 11 '64

Eulogies

After JFK, what? W. D. Burnham. il Commonweal 79:340-3 D 13 '63
All this will not be finished. il pors Time 82:29-32 N 29 '63
Are you forgotten? R. Rubin. Seventeen 23: 43 S '64
Between the lines. R. Stein. por Redbook 122: 4 F '64
Bulletin. G. Krettek. ALA Bul 57:1014 D '63
Death of the President. Commonweal 79:299-301 D 6 '63
Death teaches lessons. Sci N L 85:27 Ja 11 '64
Deeper reality. R. Squirru. Américas 16:1 Ja '64
Echo in the silence. E. J. Hughes. Newsweek 62:52 D 2 '63
Editorial. Bul Atomic Sci 19:1 D '63
Editorial. R. Orthwine. Dance Mag 38:29 Ja '64
Eulogies to John F. Kennedy. Vital Speeches 30:98-101 D 1 '63
Eulogy: John Fitzgerald Kennedy. A. M. Schlesinger, jr. por Sat Eve Post 236:32-32a D 14 '63
Great power and great diversity: the perceptions and policies of President Kennedy; address, December 1, 1963. H. Cleveland. Dept State Bul 49:964-9 D 23 '63
Hail to the chief. J. W. Cataldo. il Sch Arts 63:38-9 Je '64
He had that special grace. B. Bradlee. il por Newsweek 62:38 D 2 '63
Humane and sane. J. M. Cameron. Commonweal 79:338 D 13 '63
In memory of John F. Kennedy. pors Redbook 124:68-81 N '64
In memory of John F. Kennedy. W. Attwood. il por Look 27:11-13 D 31 '63
In memory of President Kennedy; address, December 22, 1963. L. B. Johnson. Vital Speeches 30:162 Ja 1 '64
In solemn tribute. D. Powills. il Hobbies 68:114-15 F '64
Intelligent, courageous presidency; editorial. Life 55:4 N 29 '63
John Fitzgerald Kennedy. Am Hist R 69: 602-3 Ja '64
John Fitzgerald Kennedy. A. N. D. Brooks. por Negro Hist Bul 27:49 D '63
John Fitzgerald Kennedy. C. W. Buchheister. por Audubon Mag 66:17 Ja '64
J.F.K; a final word. J. Cogley. Commonweal 80:190-1 My 8 '64
John Fitzgerald Kennedy: a readers' memorial; symposium. il por Ebony 20:180-8 N '64
John F. Kennedy: a remembrance. J. B. Wiesner. Science 142:1147-50 N 29 '63
John F. Kennedy and the new Catholic image. J. B. Sheerin. Cath World 198:203 Ja '64
John F. Kennedy; editorial. Nation 197:405 D 14 '63
John F. Kennedy, 1917-1963. il pors U S Camera 27:42-5 F '64
John Fitzgerald Kennedy, 1917-1963. por Vogue 143:70b-71 Ja 1 '64
John Fitzgerald Kennedy, 1917-1963. S. E. Morison. Atlan 213:47-9 F '64
Kennedy years. il por Sr Schol 83:17-19 D 6 '63
Last full measure; the world pays tribute to President Kennedy. M. B. Grosvenor. il pors Nat Geog Mag 125:307-55 Mr '64
Legacy of John F. Kennedy. N. Cousins. pors Sat R 46:21-7 D 7 '63
Legacy of the 1,000 days. J. M. Burns. il pors N Y Times Mag p27+ D 1 '63
Letter from Paris. Genêt. New Yorker 39:133-4+ D 7 '63
Letter from Vatican City. X. Rynne. New Yorker 39:91-2+ Ja 18 '64
Letter from Washington. R. H. Rovere. New Yorker 39:51-3 N 30 '63
The man and his meaning. D. S. Greenberg. Science 142:1151 N 29 '63
Man and his milestones. il pors Newsweek 62:39-42 D 2 '63
May he rest in peace. America 109:728 D 7 '63
Memoir. J. Kennedy. Look 28:36 N 17 '64
Mood in Washington. W. V. Shannon. Commonweal 79:339-40 D 13 '63
Morning after. Nat R 15:512 D 17 '63
Most unstuffy man. H. S. Hughes. il por Nation 197:408-9 D 14 '63

KENNEDY, John Fitzgerald—Eulogies—*Cont.*
Notes and comment. New Yorker 39:45 D 14 '63
Notes and comment; Kennedy in Miami. New Yorker 39:49-51 N 30 '63
November 22, 1963. K. Molz. Wilson Lib Bul 38:408 Ja '64
Once touched by romance. G. W. Johnson. New Repub 149:15 D 7 '63
Out of control? il Newsweek 62:17 D 23 '63
President and Congress: Mr Johnson's first message; address, November 27, 1963. L. B. Johnson. il U S News 55:102-3 D 9 '63; Same. Vital Speeches 30:130-1 D 15 '63; Dept State Bul 49:910-12 D 16 '63; Cong Digest 43:1-2 Ja '64; Excerpts. Newsweek 62:22 D 9 '63
President is buried. J. O'Gara. Commonweal 79:308 D 6 '63
President Kennedy and the Congo. B. Luykx. America 110:17 Ja 4 '64
President's empty chair. G. P. Hunt. Life 55:3 N 29 '63
Proclamation, November 23, 1963. L. B. Johnson. Dept State Bul 49:882 D 9 '63
R.I.P; reprint. Nat R 15:511 D 17 '63
Robert Kennedy's tribute to JFK; foreword to new edition of Profiles in courage by J. F. Kennedy; with editorial comment. R. F. Kennedy. il pors Look 28:37-8+ F 25 '64
Sorrow rings a world; tributes to President Kennedy; with report by R. Brigham. Life 55:117-26+ D 6 '63
Statements by U.S. officials on President's death; symposium. Dept State Bul 49:883 D 9 '63
To the memory of our beloved President, friend to all mankind. il pors Nat Geog Mag 125:1A-1B Ja '64
Tribute. F. H. Wagman. ALA Bul 57:994 D '63
Tribute to John F. Kennedy. por Ebony 19:90-1 Ja '64
Tributes to President John F. Kennedy. il U N Rev 10:i-iv+ D '63
22nd of November. M. Ascoli. Reporter 29:19 D 5 '63
200,000 miles in safety, and then—. J. P. Sutherland. il por U S News 55:60 D 9 '63
U.N. General assembly holds memorial meeting; statements. C. Sosa-Rodriguez; Thant; A. E. Stevenson. Dept State Bul 49:892-5 D 9 '63
U.S. marks final day of mourning for President Kennedy. L. B. Johnson. Dept State Bul 50:39 Ja 13 '64
Valiant is the word for Jacqueline. L. Bergquist. il por Look 28:72-4+ Ja 28 '64
What was Kennedy's greatest accomplishment? symposium. Américas 16:2-3 Ja '64
White House revisited. N. Cousins. Sat R 47:20 F 8 '64
World leaders pay tribute to President Kennedy; messages of condolence sent to President Johnson and Mrs Kennedy. Dept State Bul 49:884-91 D 9 '63
Year after the assassination the U.S. recalls John F Kennedy. il pors Newsweek 64:26-7 N 30 '64

Funeral rites and ceremonies

Aftermath of tragedy. il Sr Schol 83:18-20 D 13 '63
As the world wept. . . il U S News 55:51-7 D 9 '63
Family in mourning. il Time 82:27A-27B D 6 '63
Foreign dignitaries attend funeral of President Kennedy; list. Dept State Bul 49:895-9 D 9 '63
Funeral. il Time 82:28-33 D 6 '63
Last full measure; the world pays tribute to President Kennedy. M. B. Grosvenor. il pors Nat Geog Mag 125:307-55 Mr '64
Long vigil. M. Mannes. il Reporter 29:16-17 D 19 '63
May the angels, Dear Jack, lead you into paradise. il Newsweek 62:30-3 D 9 '63
President Kennedy is laid to rest; with report by D. J. Hamblin. il Life 55:38-49 D 6 '63
President's rites viewed throughout the world. Sci N L 84:355 D 7 '63

Memorial services

For John F. Kennedy: birthday tributes. il U S News 56:10 Je 8 '64
Memorial; New York city's memorial service for President Kennedy, on steps of city hall. New Yorker 39:45-6 D 14 '63
Notes from our correspondents; service in Boston's Holy Cross cathedral. W. B. Syer. il Hi Fi 14:17 Ap '64

Memorials

Aftermath of tragedy. il Sr Schol 83:18-20 D 13 '63
Cape Canaveral renamed for the late President. Sci N L 84:375 D 14 '63
Commercialization of J.F.K. tawdry souvenirs. A. Chamberlin. il Sat Eve Post 237:20-1 N 21 '64
In love with night; filmed memorial at Democratic national convention. il pors Newsweek 64:27-9 S 7 '64
JFK legacy. il por Newsweek 63:46+ Je 8 '64
Kennedy book to finance Memorial award. Pub W 184:34 D 30 '63
Kennedy family's gentle suggestion: restore original name to Md. library. Library J 89:1211 Mr 15 '64
Kennedy libraries drive collects over 4000 books. Pub W 185:57 Ja 6 '64
Kennedy memorabilia. T. M. Gannon. America 111:304-6 S 19 '64
Kennedy memorial albums. C. Brown. Redbook 123:30 Jl '64
Kennedy memorial albums. H. Kupferberg. il Atlan 213:134+ Ap '64
Land of Kennedy; renaming of plazas, bridges, parks, etc. il Time 82:27 D 13 '63
Magic of memory. il Time 84:29 S 4 '64
Memorial boom. il pors Newsweek 62:49-50 D 30 '63
More on JFK. Newsweek 63:53 Ja 13 '64
New JFK memorial playground. il Ebony 20:190-4 N '64
Out of control? il Newsweek 62:17 D 23 '63
Peace corps placing Kennedy libraries abroad. Pub W 184:22 D 16 '63
Say it with trees! J. B. Craig. Am For 70:11 Ja '64
Visiting botanists; State Memorial Park with arboretum in Dunganstown. New Yorker 40:30 Je 13 '64
When a just man dies: song by I. Stravinsky. Newsweek 63:75 Ap 20 '64
See also
John Fitzgerald Kennedy memorial library, Boston

Poetry

Death has taken away a friend; tr. by R. Connally. R. Squirru. por(cover) Américas 15:inside cover D '63
Friday, November 22, 1963. L. Coxe. Poetry 104:30 Ap '64
He sleeps; in memory of President John F. Kennedy, November 22, 1963. E. Menard. por(p 25) Negro Hist Bul 28:48 N '64
How silent the forest. C. W. Byrd. il Am For 70:6 Ap '64
In memoriam: seven poems. Redbook 124:79-80 N '64
November 26, 1963. W. Berry. Nation 197:437 D 21 '63
November 22, 1963: World stage; Monometal; Assassin; Clay figure. M. A. Carter. Christian Cent 80:1540 D 11 '63
To John F. Kennedy. E. Phelps. il Seventeen 23:43 S '64

Statues, portraits, etc.

As honors grow for John F. Kennedy. U S News 55:4 D 9 '63
Image distilled from 800 pictures; bronze head by R. Berks. il pors Life 56:28-31 Ja 3 '64
New Kennedy painting. N. Rockwell. Look 28:60-1 Jl 14 '64
Painting a portrait of the President. E. De Kooning. Art N 63:37+ Sum '64
Quest for a famous likeness. Life 56:120-2 My 8 '64

Tomb

Arlington. il Look 28:81-3 N 17 '64
J.F.K. grave. America 111:732 D 5 '64
Kennedy grave design is disclosed. il Arch Rec 137:12-13 Ja '65
Still they come to the hillside; Arlington national cemetery. J. Breslin. il Sat Eve Post 237:22-3 N 21 '64
Tomb for J.F.K. il Time 84:96 N 20 '64
Visit to the grave. L. Wainwright. Life 56:15 F 14 '64
Visitors to the Kennedy grave, an endless line. il U S News 56:79-81 My 25 '64

Visit to Europe, 1963

After the Kennedy trip. il por U S News 55:35 Jl 15 '63
American in Rome; visit of President Kennedy to Pope Paul VI. America 109:32 Jl 13 '63
Crowds hail President in European visit. Christian Cent 80:853 Jl 3 '63
Europe after Kennedy: what changes? il pors U S News 55:31-5 Jl 8 '63

KENNEDY, John Fitzgerald—Visit to Europe, 1963—*Continued*
Good staging for JFK. il Bsns W p31 Je 22 '63
Ireland: the Kennedy cult; they cried the rain down that night. J. Roddy. il Look 28:66-72+ N 17 '64
Is this trip necessary? New Repub 148:5 Je 8 '63
JFK to the Vatican. America 108:792 Je 1 '63
J.F.K.'s voice fills a hush in the cold war. Life 55:4 Jl 12 '63
'Ken-ah-dee' abroad: the common cause. il por Newsweek 62:31-2+ Jl 8 '63
Kennedy enraptures Germany, challenges de Gaulle. il Life 55:30-1 Jl 5 '63
Kennedy tries to stem the tide in Europe. il por Bsns W p28-9 Je 29 '63
Mr Kennedy's trip. Commonweal 78:411-12 Jl 12 '63
Moving experience. il por Newsweek 62:18 Jl 15 '63
Moving experience. il por Time 82:21 Jl 12 '63
Not necessary, but nice. il pors Time 82:13-15 Jl 5 '63
Notes on the grand tour. Nat R 15:9 Jl 16 '63
Off in a cloud; trip to four countries. Newsweek 62:19 Jl 1 '63
Our far-flung correspondents; journal of a pseudo-event. R. H. Rovere. New Yorker 39:76-8+ Jl 13 '63
President in Germany. Reporter 29:16+ Jl 18 '63
President Kennedy visits Europe; texts of joint communiques released at Bonn, Birch Grove house, Sussex, and Rome, with major addresses and remarks, June 23-July 2, 1963. J. F. Kennedy. Dept State Bul 49:114-37 Jl 22 '63
President Kennedy's European trip; joint communiqués issued from Germany, the United Kingdom, and Italy, June 24-July 2, 1936. Cur Hist 45:304-6+ N '63
Too many stops drain impact from Kennedy travels abroad. M. Smith. Nations Bsns 51:21-2 Ag '63
Visit to County Wexford, Ireland. J. Robbins. por Redbook 124:76-8 N '64
When Kennedy went home to Ireland. il por U S News 55:21 Jl 8 '63
Why Kennedy is going to Europe. il U S News 54:41 Je 10 '63
Why western Europe cheered Kennedy. il U S News 55:32-4 Jl 15 '63
Will Kennedy win in Europe? il por U S News 55:27-9 Jl 1 '63

KENNEDY, John Fitzgerald, 1960-
A look inside the White House school. il pors U S News 55:70-2 O 7 '63
President and his son. L. Bergquist. il pors Look 27:26-34+ D 3 '63
Two is the age of firsts. A. D. Buchmueller. il por McCalls 90:102-3 Ag '63

KENNEDY, John Fitzgerald, family
As thousands continue to pay tribute. il U S News 56:9 Ja 6 '64
Big year for the clan. il Time 81:23 Ap 26 '63
Burial plot in Arlington for the Kennedys. il U S News 55:8 D 16 '63
Caroline's wonderful little White House school. H. Thomas. il Good H 157:84-5+ O '63
Children's letters to Jacqueline Kennedy and her children. il Redbook 123:50-1+ My '64
Dream house: John F. Kennedy's new hideaway on Rattlesnake Ridge. il Newsweek 61:27 Mr 25 '63
Family in mourning. il Time 82:27A-27B D 6 '63
First family has everything but privacy. M. Smith. il Nations Bsns 51:23-4 My '63
Gathering of the clan; vacation at Aspen. il Time 85:30 Ja 8 '65
Hyannis Port revisited. L. Bergquist. il Look 28:37-44 N 17 '64
Kennedy's estate: 7.6 million, after taxes? U S News 56:4 Ja 6 '64
Last loving remembrance of John F. Kennedy; excerpts from Day in the life of President Kennedy. J. Bishop. il Good H 158:71-4+ Mr '64
New family in town; new life in New York. il pors Newsweek 64:31-2 S 28 '64
Newport notes: the Kennedys and other salts. G. Plimpton. il Harper 226:39-47 Mr '63
Pages from a family album. il Look 28:103-5+ N 17 '64
Profile in family courage. B. Davidson. il Sat Eve Post 236:32b-35 D 14 '63
Struggle of the baby boy; Patrick Bouvier Kennedy. il Time 82:14 Ag 16 '63
Tenants for the new Kennedy place; on Rattlesnake Mountain. il U S News 54:16 My 6 '63
Time of tragedy for the Kennedys; Baby specialist explains the fatal illness. il U S News 55:8 Ag 19 '63
With a new family in the White House. il U S News 55:68-9 D 16 '63
With a new kind of loneliness; birth and death of the Kennedy baby. il Newsweek 62:17-18 Ag 19 '63

KENNEDY, John L.
But what are the behavioral sciences? Science 144:683-4 My 8 '64

KENNEDY, Joseph C.
African students in Russia. Commonweal 78:161-3 My 3 '63

KENNEDY, Joseph Patrick
Father of the President. R. J. Whalen. il por Read Digest 83:150-1+ O '63
Founding father, by R. J. Whalen. Review
 Duns R 84:147-9 N '64. G. R. Rosen
 Nat R 16:1064-5 D 1 '64. J. Didion
 New Repub 151:21-2 D 26 '64. W. V. Shannon
 Sat R il por 47:20-2 D 19 '64. M. L. Coit
 Time il pors 84:117+ D 11 '64
Joseph P. Kennedy; excerpt from The founding father. R. J. Whalen. il pors Sat Eve Post 237:26-9+ O 10; 30-2+ O 17 '64
Pragmatist por Newsweek 64:105-105A+ D 7 '64

KENNEDY, Joseph Patrick, 1915-1944
John F. Kennedy's tribute to his older brother. V. Cadden. por Redbook 122:46-7+ F '64

KENNEDY, Joseph Patrick, family
Family in mourning. il Time 82:27A-27B D 6 '63
Growing Kennedy clan. il U S News 54:20-1 Ap 29 '63
Inscrutable Mr Smith. L. Bergquist. il Look 27:28-30+ S 24 '63
John F. Kennedy's tribute to his older brother. V. Cadden. il Redbook 122:46-7+ F '64
Joseph P. Kennedy: excerpt from The founding father. R. J. Whalen. il Sat Eve Post 237:26-9+ O 10; 30-2+ O 17 '64
Profile in family courage. B. Davidson. il Sat Eve Post 236:32b-35 D 14 '63

KENNEDY, Mary
Laetare Sunday; poem. Cath World 199:15 Ap '64
Venus and the polar bear; poem. McCalls 92:164 O '64

KENNEDY, Ray. See Mandel, P. jt. auth.

KENNEDY, Robert Francis
Attorney General Kennedy completes mission to Far East; interviews and remarks, January 28, 1964. Dept State Bul 50:239-43 F 17 '64
Bold proposal for American sport. pors Sports Illus 21:12-15 Jl 27 '64
Closing a debate. Reporter 31:6+ D 3 '64
Excerpt from statement, June 26, 1963. Cong Digest 42:268+ N '63
Free trade in ideas; excerpts from address. Sat R 46:43-4 F 16 '63
He restored confidence in his country's ideals; excerpts from interviews, ed. by T. G. Harris. por Look 28:61 N 17 '64
Robert Kennedy defines the menace. por N Y Times Mag p 15+ O 13 '63
Robert Kennedy's tribute to JFK. por Look 28:37-8+ F 25 '64
Sanctity of the law is in jeopardy; address, September 27, 1963. por U S News 55:120-2 O 14 '63
Setting the record straight: what U.S. news & World report said about air support at the Bay of Pigs; excerpt from interview. U S News 54:31 F 4 '63
Through a brother's eyes; excerpt from foreword to Profiles in courage. Time 83:26 F 21 '64
U.S. grain dealers to be allowed to sell wheat to Soviet Union and eastern Europe; letter, October 9, 1963. Dept State Bul 49:661-7 O 28 '63
What about a Peace corps spirit at home? Sat R 46:20-1 My 25 '63
What it means. por Sat Eve Post 236:20 Ag 10 '63

about

Ambitions of Bobby Kennedy. J. Kraft. il pors Look 28:22-8+ Ag 25 '64
As the buildup begins for Robert Kennedy. il por U S News 56:38 F 10 '64
Behind the plot to assassinate Robert Kennedy. C. R. Mollenhoff. il por Look 28:49-50+ My 19 '64
Better at moralizing than legalizing. Time 82:19-20 Jl 12 '63
Bit of a split; Democratic leaders dissatisfaction with R. Kennedy. il Time 81:23 My 3 '63
Bobby for president? W. F. Buckley, jr. Nat R 16:481 Je 16 '64

KENNEDY, Robert Francis—about—*Continued*
Bobby for veep? il por Time 83:21-2 Mr 20 '64
Bobby Kennedy: he hates to be second. F. Knebel. il pors Look 27:91-4+ My 21 '63
Bobby Kennedy in '68, the buildup has begun. G. Vidal. por U S News 54:19 Mr 4 '63
Bobby Kennedy on LBJ's ticket? il por U S News 56:42-4 Mr 23 '64
Bobby Kennedy's future. il pors U S News 57:36-8 Jl 13 '64
Bobby tests the water. Nat R 17:54 Ja 26 '65
Bobby's back. Newsweek 63:14 Ja 20 '64
Brothers. Nation 199:366 N 23 '64
Campaigning. New Yorker 40:50-1 O 24 '64
Can a Kennedy beat the Republicans in New York? il por U S News 57:31-2 Ag 31 '64
Can Kennedy take New York? P. Maas. il por Sat Eve Post 237:32-4 O 31 '64
Carpetbag as chic luggage. Life 57:4 S 4 '64
Carpetbagger. Time 84:18 Ag 21 '64
Case for Bobby. W. F. Buckley, jr. Nat R 16:1050 D 1 '64
Department of justice. T. Coffin. il Holiday 33:94-5+ Mr '63
End of road for Hoffa? what his conviction means. il por U S News 56:46-7 Mr 16 '64
For senator from New York. W. H. Von Dreele. Nat R 16:967 N 3 '64
For senator: Henry Paolucci. Nat R 16:900 O 20 '64
Goodbye Bobby; President Johnson against Kennedy as vice-presidential candidate. il por Time 84:18-19 Ag 7 '64
Heebie-jeebies. il Newsweek 64:32 Ag 17 '64
Here we go again; more investigations. W. F. Buckley, jr. Nat R 15:272 O 8 '63
Hosts of unreason; Kennedy vs Keating in New York state. M. Kempton. New Repub 151:11-12 S 12 '64
How Kennedy won New York backing. il por U S News 57:13 S 7 '64
How long are the coattails? il pors Time 84:30-3 O 30 '64
How LBJ got the nomination. P. Potter. il por Reporter 30:16-20 Je 18 '64
How President Kennedy upset Cuban invasion of April 1961. U S News 54:29-30+ F 4 '63
How Robert Kennedy sizes up his future. por U S News 55:24 D 16 '63
If the Kennedys get the power they ask. por U S News 55:49-50 Jl 8 '63
Imagine me here in D.C; ed. by J. Howard. Life 55:44 Jl 26 '63
In love with night; reception at Democratic national convention. il por Newsweek 64:27-9 S 7 '64
In the Far East: still no real peace. il por U S News 56:6 F 3 '64
Is an Austin-Boston coalition possible? E. T. Folliard. America 110:402 Mr 28 '64
Is Robert Kennedy eligible to be a Senator from New York? il por U S News 57:15 Ag 24 '64
Journey out of grief: R.F.K.'s mission to Asia. H. Sidney. il por Life 56:32-3 Ja 31 '64
Keating for senator. Nation 199:101 S 14 '64; Discussion. 199:inside cover S 28 '64
Keating vs. Kennedy: high stakes in New York. il pors Newsweek 64:35-6+ O 12 '64
Kennedy and Baldwin: the gulf. Newsweek 61:19 Je 3 '63
Kennedy family: another chapter. il por U S News 57:48 N 16 '64
Kennedy hegemony. R. Moley. Newsweek 64:88 S 7 '64
Kennedy in New York politics. M. McGrory. America 111:284 S 19 '64
Kennedy-Keating: off to slashing start. il por U S News 57:24 S 21 '64
Kennedy non-axis. il por Newsweek 64:30+ N 16 '64
Kennedy or Keating; stakes are bigger than a Senate seat. il por U S News 57:72-4 O 5 '64
Kennedy touch. Newsweek 63:36+ F 3 '64
Kennedy vs. Keating. M. Ascoli. Reporter 31:14 S 24 '64; Discussion. 31:6+ O 22; 12+ N 5; 6+ D 3 '64
Kennedy? why? Christian Cent 81:1134-5 S 16 '64
Kennedys: scoring anew on crowd appeal. il U S News 55:11 Jl 29 '63
Lights, action, camera: JFK. il pors U S News 55:67 N 4 '63
Looking ahead. il Newsweek 62:16-17 D 23 '63
LBJ and RFK. S. Alsop. por Sat Eve Post 237:10 F 29 '64
Magic of memory. il por Time 84:29 S 4 '64
Man pressing for a civil-rights law. il por U S News 55:19 Jl 15 '63
Man's week to reckon. R. Ajemian. il pors Life 57:24-31 Jl 3 '64
Marriage of necessity. il por Newsweek 64:28-9 Ag 31 '64
Memories at Kuala Lumpur. il por Newsweek 63:38 F 3 '64
Mission to Malaysia. Sr Schol 84:7 F 14 '64
Mr Kennedy's crusade. America 110:841-2 Je 20 '64
New dissent to a Robert Kennedy speech. C. Bloch. U S News 55:10 O 28 '63
New Yorker from Massachusetts. il pors Life 57:32-32A S 4 '64
Nine young men in charge of integrating America. il por U S News 55:58-61 Jl 29 '63
Now a Lyndon Johnson party. il por Newsweek 64:18-19 Ag 10 '64
Now there are two Senators Kennedy. il por Newsweek 64:35 N 9 '64
Off and running. Newsweek 64:29 S 7 '64
People of the week. U S News 54:20 Ap 15 '63
Political powerhouse in action. J. Chamberlain. Read Digest 85:189-90 N '64
Portrait of a man emerging from shadows. P. Lisagor. il pors N Y Times Mag p 15+ Jl 19 '64
Position wanted. Time 83:24 My 22 '64
Problems of being Bobby. por Time 84:18 Ag 14 '64
Riot squad for the New frontier. J. Kraft. Harper 227:69-75 Ag '63
Robert F. Kennedy. M. Kempton. New Repub 150:9-11 F 15 '64
RFK for senator? Newsweek 63:35 My 25 '64
RFK's power play. E. Moley. Newsweek 63:116 Mr 16 '64
R.F.K.'s unfinished job. Sat Eve Post 237:74 S 5 '64
Robert Kennedy and New York: decision point. il por Newsweek 64:22-4+ Ag 24 '64
Robert Kennedy's aim: prevent a Sukarno war. por U S News 56:15 Ja 27 '64
Seaweed & soothing words. il por Time 83:21 Ja 24 '64
Senator Kennedy, provincial New Yorker. M. Kempton. New Repub 152:6 Ja 2 '65
Senators Kennedy. il pors Newsweek 65:21 Ja 18 '65
Shell game; peacemaking trip through southeast Asia. Time 83:31-2 F 7 '64
Squeeze in the South; drive to speed up Negro voting in the South. il por Time 81:22-3 My 3 '63
Tour time. il por Newsweek 64:34+ Jl 13 '64
Tourist; visit to Poland. Time 84:24-5 Jl 10 '64
Trial by press release. Nation 199:83 S 7 '64
Veep. Cato. Nat R 16:682 Ag 11 '64
Vice Presidential skirmish. por Newsweek 63:27-8 Mr 16 '64
What are the magazines saying, dear? il Time 81:37 Mr 1 '63
What drives Bobby Kennedy. A. Lewis. il pors N Y Times Mag p34+ Ap 7 '63
What makes Bobby run? il pors Newsweek 61:26-30+ Mr 18 '63
What will R.F.K. do next? P. Maas. il pors Sat Eve Post 237:17-21 Mr 28 '64
What's Bobby going to do? an informal talk with RFK. il pors Newsweek 64:24-6 Jl 6 '64
When Bobby cruised, coast guard was near. il por U S News 54:24 Mr 25 '63
When Robert Kennedy invaded the South. il por U S News 54:6 My 6 '63
Why Robert Kennedy? New Repub 151:3-4 S 19 '64; Discussion. 151:36-8 O 3; 29 O 10; 37 O 17 '64
Will Bobby Kennedy run in New York? M. Kempton. New Repub 150:7-8 Je 6 '64
Willing to deal; civil rights bill, House hearing. il por Time 82:16 Jl 5 '63

KENNEDY, Robert Francis, family
Gathering of the clan; vacation at Aspen. il Time 85:30 Ja 8 '65
Hyannis Port revisited. L. Bergquist. il Look 28:37-44 N 17 '64
Kennedy children and integrated schools. il pors U S News 54:10-11 Je 17 '63
Life goes to the christening of Bobby Kennedy's son. il Life 55:37-9 Ag 9 '63
Robert Kennedy speaks his mind on living outdoors family style. J. E. Roper. il pors Pop Gard 14:26-9 My '63

KENNEDY, Rose (Fitzgerald)
My son the President. il Time 81:19 My 31 '63

KENNEDY, Ted. See Kennedy, E. M.

KENNEDY, William J. Jr
If I were young today. por Ebony 8:52 My '63

KENNEDY, William V.
Big airlift. America 109:622 N 16 '63
Cold war GI bill? America 108:822 Je 8 '63
Desert strike. America 110:866 Je 27 '64
Do we need the draft? America 111:85-6+ Jl 25 '64
Inquiry. America 112:11 Ja 2 '65

KENNEDY, William V.—*Continued*
Lesson in Vietnam. America 110:401 Mr 28 '64
McNamara vs. Goldwater. America 111:259 S 12 '64
Military legacy. America 109:790 D 21 '63
Morality of American nuclear policy. Cath World 199:363-70 S '64
Shadow world. America 110:225 F 15 '64
TFX and elements of high tragedy. America 108:522 Ap 20 '63
Then one day in Saigon. America 109:760 D 14 '63
View from the Brick chapel. America 109:184 Ag 24 '63
War in Vietnam. America 109:504 N 2 '63
KENNEDY, X. J.
Aristophanes in American. Poetry 102:56-60 Ap '63
Emblems and documents. Poetry 104:378-80 S '64
Poet in the playpen. Poetry 105:190-3 D '64
Reed Whittemore's mock epics. Poetry 101: 356-7 F '63
Underestimations. Poetry 103:330-3 F '64
KENNEDY brothers
Kennedy brothers' dream; a new chapter. il U S News 57:33-5 S 14 '64
Rockefeller vs. Kennedy. il U S News 54:36-9 Ap 1 '63
What's next for the Kennedys? pors U S News 55:18 D 9 '63
Which Senator Kennedy can do the most for his state? pors U S News 58:19 Ja 18 '65
With Bobby Kennedy out: a family dream fades. il U S News 57:63-5 Ag 17 '64
KENNEDY family
Kennedy's Irish kin. il Life 55:69-75 Jl 5 '63
Origins. New Yorker 39:25-7 Je 15 '63
Sure, and it's County Kennedy now; Wexford. T. P. Coogan. il pors N Y Times Mag p7-9+ Je 23 '63
KENNEDY, CAPE
Big plans for Canaveral. R. A. Winer. il Motor B 114:85 N '64
Birds of Cocoa Beach. B. Thielen. Holiday 35:64-5+ Je '64
Cape Canaveral renamed for the late President. Sci N L 84:375 D 14 '63
Disappearing object; Vertical assembly building. A. Drexler. il Sat R 47:14-15 My 23 '64
Moonward ho! H. Sutton. Sat R 47:50-1 Ja 11 '64
Planners ponder Canaveral space boom. il Arch Forum 118:9 Ap '63
President visits the big birds at Cape Canaveral and Merritt Island. il Bsns W p36 N 23 '63
Rail dispute delays work at Cape. Aviation W 80:37 F 17 '64
Team wins contract for Saturn V VAB. Miss & Roc 14:16 Ja 13 '64
Transforming the Cape into a spaceport. il Bsns W p56-60+ Ap 6 '63
Visit to the three Cape Kennedys. R. G. Whalen. il N Y Times Mag p34-5+ D 13 '64
See also
Proving grounds
KENNEDY, J. Fitzgerald, library. See John F. Kennedy memorial library, Boston
KENNEDY half dollar. See Money—United States
KENNEDY international airport. See New York (city)—Airports
KENNEDY memorial library. See John F. Kennedy memorial library, Boston
KENNEDY stamps. See Postage stamps
KENNELS
How to select a dog kennel. il Good H 158: 168 My '64
Kennel-run surfaces. D. M. Duffey. il Outdoor Life 132:90-2 D '63
Self-service kennel. J. Stetson. il Field & S 69:150-2+ O '64
KENNER, Hugh
Meditation and enactment. Poetry 102:109-15 My '63
On the laps of the snow gods. por Nat R 16:405+ My 19 '64
Poetry and such (cont) por Nat R 14:237; 15:238-9, 441+ Mr 26, S 24, N 19 '63
Seven-year shaman. Nat R 16:113-14 F 11 '64
Speaking out. por Sat Eve Post 237:12+ N 14 '64
T. S. Eliot, RIP. Nat R 17:63-4 Ja 26 '65
Word for the wild man. Nat R 16:654-6 Jl 28 '64
KENNERLY, Sarah Law
Catcher in the library. Library J 89:1822-4 Ap 15 '64
KENNEY, Ann D.
(ed) Family movie guide. See issues of Parents' magazine & better homemaking
KENNEY, Francis T. See Wicks, W. D. jt. auth.
KENNEY, Nathaniel T.
Chesapeake country. por Nat Geog Mag 126: 370-411 S '64
Mighty Enterprise. Nat Geog Mag 123:430-48 Mr '63
KENNINGTON, Julie
My river; poem. Horn Bk 40:419 Ag '64
KENNON, Leslie B. and Markle, Tom
Art and the student teacher. Sch Arts 63: 5-10 Ap '64
KENNY, Herbert A.
At a rest home; poem. Commonweal 78:476 Ag 9 '63
Dark glass; poem. Sat R 47:47 D 12 '64
Robert Frost, RIP. Nat R 14:100 F 12 '63
KENOSHA, Wis.

Water supply

Piecemeal water-improvement plan. O. F. Nelson. il Am City 78:88-9 Ag '63
KENSLER, C. J. See Thayer, P. S. jt. auth.
KENT, Allen
Documentation pitt. por Library J 89:206, 818+, 1202-3, 2046-7 Ja 15, F 15, Mr 15, My 15 '64
KENT, Charles
Peabody heritage. Mus Am 83:16-17 Ap '63
KENT, George
Beirut: city of money and mystery. Read Digest 85:25-6+ N '64
Brotherhood of the Golden keys. Read Digest 84:151-2+ Ja '64
Enchantress from the Louvre. Read Digest 83:176-8+ Jl '63
Europe's wildest winter. Read Digest 83: 198-201+ S '63
Exuberant genius of Peter Paul Rubens. Read Digest 85:146-51 Ag '64
Father Schönig: circus priest extraordinary. Read Digest 84:74-8 Je '64
Happily ever after with the brothers Grimm. Read Digest 86:167-9+ Ja '65
He opened the door to modern art. Read Digest 83:158-60+ D '63
Not far from God. Read Digest 82:236-8+ Je '63
Strange life of Paul Gauguin. Read Digest 83:188-93 O '63
They fight city hall, and win. Read Digest 83:29-30+ Jl '63
200,000 persecutions prevented. Read Digest 82:169-70+ Mr '63
Up goes London. Read Digest 82:213-16 Ap '63
KENT, George O.
Pope Pius XII and Germany: some aspects of German-Vatican relations, 1933-1943. bibliog f Am Hist R 70:59-78 O '64
KENT, Morris Allen, jr
Can a sane robber be an insane rapist? U S News 54:6 Ap 8 '63
KENT, Norman
Impressions of Scandinavia. Am Artist 28: 40-7+ Ap '64
Making numerous drawings of one subject. il Am Artist 28:56-61+ Je '64
Portfolio of drawings by Paul Hogarth. Am Artist 27:42-7+ Ap '63
Portfolio of woodcuts by James Grashow. Am Artist 28:26-9+ Ja '64
Portrait sketches of Norman Rockwell. por Am Artist 28:38-43+ S '64
KENTFIELD, Calvin
Llorona; story. New Yorker 40:28-36 Ag 8 '64
State university of Iowa. Holiday 34:88-91+ N '63
KENTUCKY
See also
Cumberland Plateau
Fort Knox
Geology—Kentucky
Hunting—Kentucky
Law—Kentucky
Paleontology—Kentucky
Roads—Kentucky

Description and travel

Fresh look at Kentucky. B. Keating. il Holiday 36:80-5+ N '64

Economic conditions

Appalachia: the path from disaster. H. Caudill. il Nation 198:239-41 Mr 9 '64
Night comes to the Cumberlands, by H. M. Caudill. Review
Science 141:889-92 S 6 '63. J. Walsh
Permanent poor; lesson of eastern Kentucky. H. M. Caudill. Atlan 213:49-53 Je '64; Discussion. 214:30 Ag '64

KENTUCKY—*Continued*

History

World of Daniel Boone. R. P. Warren. Holiday 34:162+ D '63

Parks and reserves

State parks recreation menu. W. H. Radke. il Recreation 57:272-4 Je '64

Politics and government

Happy ending: gubernatorial nomination. il Newsweek 61:33 Je 10 '63
Happy ending in Kentucky. J. A. Maxwell. Reporter 28:22-4 Je 20 '63
Kentucky horse race. il Time 82:28-9 O 18 '63
Old Happy. il Time 81:18 Mr 29 '63
Sad day for Happy. il Time 81:22-3 Je 7 '63

Race problems

Hunger sit-in. W. Peeples. New Repub 150: 9-10 Ap 25 '64

Religious institutions and affairs

News of the Christian world (cont) Christian Cent 80:411, 834 Mr 27, Je 26 '63

Social conditions

Warning from Appalachia: we are on our way to becoming a welfare reservation; interview. H. M. Caudill. il U S News 56: 68-71 My 11 '64

Social life and customs

I have monkeys on my roof. M. Gellhorn. Ladies Home J 81:26+ Jl '64

KENTUCKY bluegrass. See Grasses

KENTUCKY Derby. See Horse racing

KENTUCKY RIVER
In the wake of Daniel Boone. J. Gribbins. il Motor B 113:38-9+ Je '64

KENTUCKY. University

Medical center

Role for behavioral science in a university medical center. R. Straus. bibliog f Ann Am Acad 346:99-108 Mr '63

KENWOOD, Chicago. See Chicago—Housing

KENWORTHY, E. W. See Kenworthy, J. jt. auth.

KENWORTHY, John, and Kenworthy, E. W.
Under standing Neorger and his right to vote. Reporter 30:32-4 Mr 26 '64

KENWORTHY, Leonard S.
New approach to social studies. NEA J 52: 44-5 Mr '63

KENYA
Exodus, 1963; Kenya's Asians and white settlers leaving. Newsweek 62:50 N 18 '63
Harambee! Newsweek 64:32+ D 21 '64
Marchesa Sieuwke Bisleti in Kenya. S. G. Wood. il Vogue 142:64-7 Jl '63
Uhuru to jamhuri with concern; independence celebrations and leftist intrigue. Time 84:32-3 D 18 '64
Who owns what? il Time 81:28 Mr 22 '63
See also
Airlines—Kenya
East African Federation (proposed)
Economic assistance in Kenya
Education—Kenya
Fishing—Kenya
Hunting—Kenya
Magadi, Lake
Malindi
Nairobi
United Nations—Kenya

Description and travel

Kenya. R. S. Kane. il Travel 119:30-5 Ap '63

History

Kenya tries to put the clock ahead. E. Huxley. il N Y Times Mag p 18+ My 19 '63

Native races

East Africa's one-man peace corps. il Todays Health 41:20-5 Je '63
Future of Tom Mboya; Kikuyus. S. Meisler. il Reporter 28:41-4 F 14 '63
Strangest Africans; El Molo tribe. il Sci Digest 55:48-51 F '64
Tribal life in a country soon to govern itself; Masai and the Wakamba. A. J. Meyers. il U S News 54:95-7 My 20 '63

Politics and government

Atlantic report. Atlan 213:24+ F '64
Black & white *harambee*! il Time 82:24 Ag 23 '63
Do white men have a future in Africa? T. J. Mboya. il N Y Times Mag p24-5+ D 8 '63
From Mau Mau to P.M. il Newsweek 61: 59 Je 10 '63
Future of Tom Mboya. S. Meisler. il Reporter 28:41-4 F 14 '63
Harambee in Kenya. C. Legum. Cur Hist 46:142-7 Mr '64
Independence. New Repub 149:10 D 14 '63
Independence comes to Kenya. il Sr Schol 83:10-13 D 6 '63
Independence for Kenya: and now to build a nation. il Newsweek 62:36-8+ D 16 '63
Kenya discovers the perils of *uhuru*. C. Sterling. il Reporter 30:26-9 My 7 '64
Kenya tries to put the clock ahead. E. Huxley. il N Y Times Mag p 18+ My 19 '63
Kenya's achievement. P. Crane. America 111: 216-17 Ag 29 '64
Kenya's cauldron. E. Huxley. Nat R 15:437+ N 19 '63
Kenya's choice. il Newsweek 61:42 Je 3 '63
KANU, KADU, Kenya. il Newsweek 61:45-6 Ap 8 '63
Landslide for Kenyatta. New Repub 148:8 Je 8 '63
Not quite off with the old. New Repub 150:9 Ap 4 '64
One-party way. Time 84:27-8 Ag 28 '64
Party system and democracy in Africa. T. J. Mboya. For Affairs 41:650-8 Jl '63
Return of Burning Spear. il Time 81:28 Je 7 '63
Two key leaders in a new African nation. il U S News 54:22 Je 10 '63
Uhuru comes to Kenya. L. Bennett. il Ebony 19:127-8+ F '64
Uhuru is not enough. il Time 82:20-1 D 20 '63
Where whites are wanted, but. . . F. C. Painton. il U S News 55:46-8 D 23 '63

Race problems

Harambee in Kenya. C. Legum. Cur Hist 46:142-7 Mr '64
Where whites are wanted, but. . . F. C. Painton. il U S News 55:46-8 D 23 '63
See also
Mau Mau

KENYAN teachers in the United States. See Foreign teachers in the United States

KENYATTA, Edna May
New premier with three wives. il por U S News 55:14 D 23 '63

KENYATTA, Jomo
Black & white *harambee*! il por Time 82:24 Ag 23 '63
From Mau Mau to P.M. il por Newsweek 61: 59 Je 10 '63
Future of Tom Mboya. S. Meisler. il Reporter 28:41-4 F 14 '63
Harambee in Kenya. C. Legum. Cur Hist 46:142-7 Mr '64
Independence comes to Kenya. il por Sr Schol 83:10-13 D 6 '63
Independence for Kenya: and now to build a nation. il por Newsweek 62:36-8+ D 16 '63
Kenya discovers the perils of *uhuru*. C. Sterling. il Reporter 30:26-9 My 7 '64
Kenya's cauldron. E. Huxley. Nat R 15:437+ N 19 '63
Mau Mau or moderate? Kenyatta keeps changing. il por U S News 57:16 D 21 '64
New premier with three wives. il U S News 55:14 D 23 '63
Return of Burning Spear. il por Time 81: 28 Je 7 '63
Two key leaders in a new African nation. por U S News 54:22 Je 10 '63
Uhuru comes to Kenya. L. Bennett. il pors Ebony 19:127-8+ F '64
Uhuru is not enough. il pors Time 82:20-1 D 20 '63
Where whites are wanted, but. . . F. C. Painton. il pors U S News 55:46-8 D 23 '63

KENYON, Karl W.
Recovery of a fur bearer. il Natur Hist 72: 12-21 N '63

KENYON review
Culture and gallantry. il Newsweek 63:79-80 Ja 27 '64

KEOGH law. See Pensions—Laws and regulations

KEOSAUQUA, Ia.
Smalltown, U.S.A. L. Hanscom. il Newsweek 62:17-20 Jl 8 '63

KEPLER, Johann
Checking up on Kepler. Sky & Tel 28:70 Ag '64
Forgotten moon voyage of 1609. J. Lear. il por Sat R 46:39-44 My 4 '63
Life in hell's vestibule; Kepler's ingenious biography. J. Lear. por Sat R 46:45-6 My 4 '63

KEPPEL, Francis
Books and the crisis in U.S. education. il por Pub W 183:30-2 Je 3 '63

KEPPEL, Francis—*Continued*
Dropout campaign; exchange of letters between President Kennedy and Commissioner Keppel; September 5 and September 15, 1963. Sch Life 46:2-3 O '63
Excerpt from testimony, February 5, 1963. Cong Digest 42:244+ O '63
Federal aid for school libraries. por Library J 90:293-5 Ja 15 '65
Into the century of the educated man. Sat R 46:37-8 D 21 '63
Kind of public schools we want; address. Vital Speeches 29:569-72 Jl 1 '63
Libraries: future unlimited; address, June 28, 1964. por ALA Bul 58:991-4 D '64; Excerpts. Sch & Soc 92:374-6 D 12 '64
Money makes a difference. Parents Mag 39: 80+ F '64
Poverty; target for education: address, February 15, 1964. Vital Speeches 30:510-12 Je 1 '64
Right and the responsibility. por NEA J 52: 15 O '63
Scholastic teacher interviews: Francis Keppel. por Sr Schol 84:1T-2T+ Ap 24 '64
Schools without libraries: our national disgrace. McCalls 92:116+ N '64. Summary. Library J 89:4614 N 15 '64
Spanking of students, what education chief thinks; excerpts from interview. por U S News 54:20 Je 24 '63
Standards of excellence in the junior college; excerpt from address, June 17, 1963. Sch & Soc 91:329-30 N 2 '63

about

Francis Keppel of Harvard: Pied Piper of American education. F. Parker. bibliog por (p 105) Sch & Soc 91:126-8+ Mr 9 '63
Going up fast. por Time 85:50 Ja 15 '65
School aid: can Dean Keppel call the class to order? M. Elfin. il Reporter 28:32-5 Mr 14 '63

KEPPEL-JONES, Arthur
Rhodesian trap. Nation 197:111-13+ S 7 '63

KEPPLER, Herbert
Keppler on the SLR. See issues of Modern photography
Sharp crisp classic landscapes. Mod Phot 27: 86-9+ O '63
Sound advice. Mod Phot 27:34+ O '63
Use a bellows for mouse to moon. Mod Phot 27:64-9 Ap '63

KERATITIS. See Eye—Diseases and defects

KERBER, E. R.
Wheat: reconstitution of the tetraploid component (AABB) of hexaploids. bibliog Science 143:253-5 Ja 17 '64

KERCIU, G. Ray
Obscence & indescent. il por Time 81:76-7 Ap 19 '63
Them damn pictures. T. B. Hess. il Art N 62:23 My '63

KERCKHOFF, Richard K. See Gould, F. jt. auth.

KERKAM, Earl Cavis
Kerkam's mirror imagery. il Art N 62:44+ Mr '63

KERLAN, Irvin
Irvin Kerlan, fifty-one, book collector, killed by auto in Washington, D.C. Library J 89:931-2 F 15 '64
Obituary
Pub W 185:53 Ja 13 '64

KERMAN, Henry S.
Korea; land of the morning calm. por Am For 69:36-9 Ag '63

KERMAN, Joseph
Chase. Opera N 28:8-12 D 28 '63
Why bother with words? Hi Fi 13:39-41+ Jl '63

KERMAN, Sheppard
Mr Simian. Criticism
Commonweal 79:284 N 29 '63
New Yorker 39:95-6 N 2 '63

KERMODE, Frank
Reading Eliot today. Nation 197:263-4 O 26 '63

about

Sense and sensitivity. J. Gray. Sat R 46:24 Mr 2 '63

KERN, Clifford D. See Buettner, K. J. K. jt. auth.

KERN, Edward
Bush fox of Africa. Life 56:87-8+ My 8 '64
Immortal adventure that won a world. Life 54:64-5 My 3 '63
Last years of splendor. Life 55:71-88 N 22 '63
Q-ships and raiders. Life 56:74+ Ap 17 '64
Vials of wrath were ready to break. Life 56: 46-61 Ja 3 '64

about

Writer with an eye on history. G. P. Hunt. por Life 56:3 Ja 3 '64

KERN, Florence
Remember hurricane Carol. Yachting 116: 58-60+ Ag '64
Wintering in the Chesapeake. Yachting 114: 28-30+ D '63

KERN, John A.
Look right into your sewer problems. por Am City 79:84-5 Ag '64

KERNAN, Alvin B.
Wall and the jungle: the early novels of Evelyn Waugh. Yale R 53:199-220 D '63

KERNAN, Edward J.
Student-faculty work program. Sch & Soc 91:59 F 9 '63

KERNAN, Henry S.
American forestry abroad. Am For 70:38-9+ Ap '64
Forests of Viet-Nam. Am For 70:31+ Je '64

KERNER, Fred
Love: it makes the world go 'round. Todays Health 42:42-7+ Ap '64

KERNER, Otto
Chuck's luck. Time 84:39 O 16 '64
Kerner's winning way. il por Time 84:41 N 13 '64

KERNS, Grace
Grace Kerns and John Barnes Wells. J. Walsh. pors Hobbies 69:32-5+ My; 32-5+ Je; 32-5 Jl; 34 Ag '64

KERNS, Mary
Animal kingdom. Sch Arts 63:23 Je '64

KEROSENE lamps. See Lamps

KEROSENE lanterns. See Lanterns

KERPEN, Miriam C. See Fox, H. jt. auth.

KERR, Alfred
Gerhart Hauptmann and Alfred Kerr. E. Locher. UNESCO Courier 16:33 Mr '63

KERR, Alix
New wonder drug: DMSO. Life 57:37-8+ Jl 10 '64

KERR, Barbara
(tr) See. Bertil, G. What's dimming the city of lights?

KERR, Chester
World opens up for scholarly publishing. Sat R 47:28-9 My 30 '64

KERR, Clark
California's new campuses. Arch Rec 136: 175 N '64
Ideopolis for the world; summary of address. por Time 81:88+ My 3 '63
Multiversity: are its several souls worth saving? excerpts from Uses of the university. Harper 227:37-42 N '63
Society and the status quo: the individual and the innovative society. Science 144:164-5 Ap 10 '64

KERR, Deborah
Days and nights of the iguana. Esquire 61: 128-30+ My '64

KERR, Ed
Louisiana's wonderful invention. Harper 227: 94-6 O '63

KERR, George T.
Zeolite ZK-5: a new molecular sieve. Science 140:1412 Je 28 '63

KERR, Jean
Poor Richard. Criticism
New Yorker 40:152+ D 12 '64
Newsweek il 64:84 D 14 '64
Sat R 47:25 D 19 '64
Time il 84:73 D 11 '64
Vogue 145:27 Ja 15 '65
She never does the dishes. J. Davis. il pors Ladies Home J 81:64-5+ Je '64

KERR, Jerry
Starting from scratch. por Recreation 56: 178+ Ap '63

KERR, Paul F.
Quick clay; with biographical sketch. Sci Am 209:32, 132-8+ bibliog(p 188) N '63
—See Rooney, T. P. jt. auth.

KERR, Robert Samuel
Seaports for Oklahoma. il por U S News 54:66-9 F 11 '63
Senate's richest man left an outdated will. U S News 54:11 F 18 '63

KERR, Walter
Along nightmare alley. Vogue 141:119 Ap 1 '63
Love letters of a tough critic. por Life 56: 113-14 Je 19 '64

KERR-Mills act. See Aged—Medical care

KERRIGAN, Anthony
Color of seed. Poetry 101:345-9 F '63
Death of a poet. Nat R 15:306 O 8 '63
For two ladies ascending a bus; Zion of echoing sound; poems. Poetry 105:167-8 D '64
(tr) See Cela, C. J. Inventory of the dark
(tr) See Unamuno y Jugo, M. de. Cloud-music; Bull

KERRY Dan: story. See Sullivan, A. M.
KERSEY, Roy
Indoor seed sowing. Flower Grower 51:48-9+ Ja '64
Transplanting seedlings indoors. Flower Grower 51:38-9+ F '64
KERSH, Gerald
Bargain with Cashel; story. Sat Eve Post 236:54-7 Ap 27 '63
KERTÉSZ, André
Andre Kertesz, photographer. M. R. Weiss. il por Sat R 47:28-30 D 26 '64
Kertész; rebirth of an eternal amateur. J. Deschin. por Pop Phot 55:32+ D '64
KERTESZ, Z. I. and Parsons, G. F.
Ozone formation in air exposed to cobalt-60 gamma radiation. bibliog Science 142:1289-90 D 6 '63
KESEY, Ken
One flew over the cuckoo's nest; dramatization. See Wasserman, D.
KESSEL, Dmitri
Crown of Toledo; photographs. Life 55:64-75 D 13 '63
Olympic winter in the Tyrol. il Sports Illus 19:48-58 N 25 '63
KESSINGER, James B.
Take a ride through a coal mine. Am City 78:31 Ap '63
KESSLER, Alice
Carbon copy kids; Kessler song-and-dance team. pors Life 54:65-6+ F 22 '63
KESSLER, Charles C.
Vanes. New Yorker 40:39-40 S 12 '64
KESSLER, Edward
Students; poem. Sat R 47:51 My 23 '64
Voice on Third avenue; poem. Sat R 47:61 Je 13 '64
KESSLER, Ellen
Carbon copy kids; Kessler song-and-dance team. pors Life 54:65-6+ F 22 '63
KESSLER, Jane W.
How to test their readiness for school. PTA Mag 58:15-17 bibliog(p35) My '64
Moving toward maturity: the mind at 3+. PTA Mag 57:22-4 bibliog(p35) F '63
My son, the underachiever. PTA Mag 57:12-14 Je '63
KESSLER, Milton
Called home; poem. Nation 197:76 Ag 10 '63
KESSLER, Sydney
Extrapolation; poem. Sat R 47:76 O 24 '64
Then; poem. Sat R 47:77 My 30 '64
With the first cold rains of autumn; poem. New Repub 149:22 O 19 '63
KESTON, Albert S.
Mutarotase inhibition by 1-deoxyglucose. bibliog Science 143:698-700 F 14 '64
KETCHAM, Edward C.
Obituary
Pub W 185:43 My 18 '64
KETCHES. See Sailing vessels
KETCHUM, Richard M.
Doctor J. H. McLean's Peace Makers. Am Heritage 14:109-12 Je '63
Faces from the past (cont) Am Heritage 14:24-5 F; 38-9 Ap; 32-3 Ag; 52-3 O; 15:52-3 D '63; 28-9 Ap; 16:30-1 D '64
KETHLEY, T. W. and others
Operating room ventilation evaluated. bibliog Arch Rec 133:204-8 Mr '63
KETLEY, A. D. and Werber, F. X.
Stereospecific polymerization. bibliog Science 145:667-73 Ag 14 '64
KEVERN, Niles R.
Strontium and calcium uptake by the green alga, oocystis eremosphaeria. bibliog Science 145:1445-6; 146:1488 S 25, D 11 '64
KEVLES, Barbara
20th century school of dance. Dance Mag 38:20-2 My '64
KEY, C. A.
Ancient copper and copper-arsenic alloy artifacts: composition and metallurgical implications. bibliog Science 146:1578-80 D 18 '64
KEY, Ted
Map for cartoonists. il Design 66:2 N '64
KEY-man insurance. See Insurance, Business
KEY; story. See Roueché, B.
KEYES, Arthur H. Jr
Architect talks about the spaces between buildings. Arch Rec 134:194-5 S '63
KEYES, Frances Parkinson
Romantic realities. Travel 121:48-50 Ap '64
KEYLON, Don A.
Eleven small water systems unite. Am City 78:131+ Ag '63
KEYNES, John Maynard Keynes, 1st baron
Economics in a free society, by W. Roepke. Review
Bsns W p72+ Ap 13 '63
Keynes formula sweeps on. G. Schwartz. il pors N Y Times Mag p32+ S 8 '63
Keynesian system, by D. M. Wright. Review
Nat R 14:239-41 Mr 26 '63. W. Roepke
Keynesianism: retrospect and prospect, by W. H. and Hutt. Review
Nat R 16:158-60 F 25 '64. M. Palyi
Thrift vs. borrowing, which way to good times? with excerpts from book by P. A. Samuelson. il por U S News 54:38-9 Mr 4 '63
KEYS, Sandy
Special-interest cars. Motor T 16:81 N '64
KEYS, FLORIDA. See Florida Keys
KEYSERLING, Leon H.
Books. Sci Am 210:141-2+ Ja '64
Will unemployment rise? New Repub 148:39 Je 15 '63
KEYSTONE; story. See Powers, J. F.
KHABAROVSK, Siberia
Where Soviet frontier faces red China. il Bsns W p48-50+ F 15 '64
KHADDURI, Majid
From camels to Cadillacs. Sat R 47:29-30 Jl 18 '64
Military mecca. Sat R 47:48-9 F 15 '64
KHAIRALLAH, Philip A. and others
Angiotensinase with a high degree of specificity in plasma and red cells. bibliog Science 140:672-4 My 10 '63
KHALIFAH, R. A. and others
New natural growth promoting substance in young citrus fruit. bibliog Science 142:399-400 O 18 '63
KHAN, Hashim
Sporting scene. H. W. Wind. il New Yorker 39:87-90+ F 1 '64
KHAN, Mohammad Ayub. See Ayub Khan, M.
KHAN, Mohibullah
Sporting scene. H. W. Wind. il New Yorker 39:87-90+ F 1 '64
KHAN, Sir Muhammad Zafrulla. See Zafrulla Khan, M.
KHANH, Emmanuelle
Power of positive patches. il pors Life 56:61-2+ Mr 13 '64
KHANH, Nguyen. See Nguyen Khanh
KHEEL, Theodore
Informed neutrals score a triumph. por Bsns W p43-4+ My 9 '64
Theodore Kheel: master mediator. T. J. Murray. pors Duns R 83:37-8+ Je '64
KHOMAN, Thanat
Which road for southeast Asia? For Affairs 42:628-39 Jl '64
KHOVANSHCHINA; opera. See Musorgskii, M. P.
KHRUSHCHEV, Nikita Sergeevich
Behind the Russian-Chinese split; interview, ed. by M. Gordey. por Look 27:32-3+ F 12 '63
Chairman Khrushchev to President Kennedy, December 19, 1962 and January 7, 1963; letters. Dept State Bul 48:198-200, 201-2 F 11 '63
Dispensing the word, Kremlin-style, summary of address. Sr Schol 82:16-17 Mr 13 '63
If you'll pardon the expression. . : remarks at exhibition of Soviet art. Newsweek 61:34-5 Ap 1 '63
Khrushchev hits Soviet industry planning; excerpts from address, November 19, 1962. Aviation W 78:105+ Ja 21 '63
Khrushchev in Astrakhan; interview. Bul Atomic Sci 20:12-14 Ja '64
Khrushchev message on the use of arms, December 31, 1963. Cur Hist 46:357-62 Je '64
Khrushchev on overkill; excerpt from address, January 16, 1963. Bul Atomic Sci 19:7 Ap '63
Letters from Khrushchev to Kennedy, December 19, 1962; January 7, 1963. Bul Atomic Sci 19:33-4+ Mr '63
Reducing nuclear materials production; statement. Cur Hist 47:47-8 Jl '64
Russian art & anti-Semitism; debate. Commentary 36:434 D '63
Soviet letter of December 31, 1963; unofficial translation of message sent to heads of state. Dept State Bul 50:158-63 F 3 '64
Soviet letter on Cyprus, February 7, 1964. Dept State Bul 50:447-8 Mr 23 '64
This is the absolute end; excerpts from address, September 17, 1963. por Fortune 68:122 N '63
What Nikita Khrushchev told U.S. businessmen touring Europe; excerpts from addresses, November 6 and November 7, 1963. U S News 55:62 N 18 '63
—and Brezhnev, Leonid
Soviet leaders to President Johnson; letter, January 1, 1964. Dept State Bul 50:121 Ja 27 '64

KHRUSHCHEV, Nikita Sergeevich—*Continued*

about

Afro-Asian Arab; Khrushchev attends inauguration of Aswan High Dam's first stage. Time 83:40 My 15 '64
After all of Cuba's troubles, what's ahead for Castro. il U S News 55:34-5 N 4 '63
After Khrushchev: what next? H. R. Swearer. bibliog f Cur Hist 47:257-65 N '64
After Khrushchev what? with report by K. Lachmann. il pors U S News 57:39-45 O 26 '64
Another big race the Russians are losing. il U S News 57:122-4 N 9 '64
Any friend of goulash can't be all bad. Life 56:4 Ap 17 '64
As Moscow slept, a new era began. il pors Newsweek 64:45-6+ O 26 '64
B after K? por Newsweek 62:26 D 23 '63
Back of Russia's sudden soft line. il por U S News 55:25-8 S 2 '63
Back to the beginning of the tumultuous life of Nikita Khrushchev. H. H. Martin. il por Sat Eve Post 237:18-26 N 7 '64
Becoming an unperson. Time 85:25 Ja 22 '65
Best laid plans. il por Newsweek 64:35 Ag 3 '64
Billions in U.S. aid and Tito wants to bury capitalism. A. Kucherov. il U S News 55: 68-9 S 16 '63
Brinkmanship phase of Russian and Chinese diplomacy. il por Newsweek 63:41 Ap 13 '64
Cabbages and kings; tour of Denmark. il Newsweek 63:28+ Je 29 '64
Camp Nikita; seaside hideaway. il por Time 82:19 Ag 16 '63
Campaigning in Hungary. Newsweek 63:50 Ap 20 '64
Candidate with three suits; concerning stump speech to constituents from Moscow's Kalinin. il Time 81:37 Mr 8 '63
Capitalistic invasion; R. Thomson's audience with Khrushchev. por Time 81:54 F 22 '63
Castro, Khrushchev, and Mao. T. Draper. il Reporter 29:27-31 Ag 15 '63
Castro's mysterious trip to Russia. il por U S News 56:16 Ja 27 '64
Changes in Russia: U.S. size-up. U S News 57:53 O 26 '64
Cheers in Norway. U S News 57:20 Jl 13 '64
Close-up of Khrushchev: less zip, more caution. il por U S News 55:22 S 16 '63
Close view of the Kremlin boss; S. Topping. pors N Y Times Mag p20+ Ag 11 '63
Cold war will not end in our time. J. Grigg. il N Y Times Mag p7+ F 2 '64
Common action for the control of conflict, by V. P. Rock. Review
U S News il por 55:64-6 N 18 '63
Conference with Khrushchev and Helbich. F. Luepsen. Christian Cent 80:1012 Ag 14 '63
Cracks in Russia's empire. il U S News 57: 79-81 O 5 '64
Cuba crisis and nuclear arms; why de Gaulle goes his own way; reprint. C. B. Luce. U S News 54:64-5 F 18 '63
Cuban crisis: how close we were to war; excerpts from Politics of policy-making: the Kennedy years. R. Hilsman. il Look 28:17-21 Ag 25 '64
Day he dies. W. J. Coughlin. Miss & Roc 14:50 My 4 '64
Echoes of Stalinism. A. Werth. Nation 196: 308-9 Ap 13 '63
Elevator mates; list of political errors and acts of personal misconduct. il Newsweek 64:48 N 9 '64
Fall of Nikita K; with comment on the world's news fronts. il por Sr Schol 85:17-18+. 24 O 28 '64
Family problems; visit to Yugoslavia. il por Newsweek 62:38 S 2 '63
Fan of Henry Ford's; visit to Yugoslavia. il por Time 82:22 Ag 30 '63
Farmer frustrates Khrushchev. E. Crankshaw. il pors N Y Times Mag p 17+ S 20 '64
Fine Italian hand; Khrushchev under pressure. Time 81:30 Ap 12 '63
Flowers, swallows & strangers. il por Time 84:28 Ag 7 '64
Frosty North; visit to Sweden. il por Newsweek 64:40 Jl 6 '64
Grandchildren. D. Lawrence. il por U S News 56:116+ My 18 '64
Great improviser. I. Shenker. il pors Life 55:81+ S 13 '63
Growing troubles in Khrushchev's empire. il U S News 55:54-6 O 21 '63
Hard day's night: story of N. Khrushchev's fall. il Time 84:37-8 O 30 '64
Heir to Khrushchev? Brezhnev steps up. il por U S News 57:16 Jl 27 '64
Horse-trade in Moscow. por Bsns W p25-6 My 4 '63
How blows the East wind? J. Burnham. Nat R 16:230 Mr 24 '64
How Nikita & Nina came back to No. 3 Granovsky street. il Time 84:26 N 6 '64
How to slice the cake. il Time 83:42 Ap 17 '64
In the day's after Khrushchev's ouster. U S News 57:14 N 2 '64
Intelligent woman's guide to politics in the Kremlin. M. Frankel. il McCalls 92:56+ N '64
Is a U.S. deal with Russia near? il por U S News 55:27-9 Jl 22 '63
Is Khrushchev Dr Strangelove? U S News 57:51 O 5 '64
Just when Nikita seemed all smiles; halt of U.S. military convoy en route to Berlin by Soviet troops. il por U S News 55:62-3 N 18 '63
K and LBJ: a time for taking stock. il por Newsweek 62:33 D 16 '63
Khrushchev and Tito join forces to bury capitalism. il por U S News 55:22 S 9 '63
Khrushchev at home. Newsweek 65:43 Ja 18 '65
Khrushchev at seventy. Nation 198:407 Ap 27 '64
Khrushchev at seventy: the hidden dangers of success. il pors Newsweek 63:48-9 Ap 27 '64
Khrushchev at seventy; who is next? P. E. Mosely. il pors N Y Times Mag p 14+ Ap 12 '64
Khrushchev at the crossroads. il Newsweek 62:29-30+ Jl 22 '63
Khrushchev backlash. il Newsweek 64:48+ N 2 '64
Khrushchev eats his words. A. Werth. por Nation 198:64-6 Ja 20 '64
Khrushchev era. New Repub 148:7-8 My 11 '63
Khrushchev faces a Khrushchevian dilemma. M. Frankland. il por N Y Times Mag p21+ My 12 '63
Khrushchev in Africa, why he's making the trip. U S News 56:20 My 18 '64
Khrushchev mends some fences. C. Wassermann. Reporter 29:36-8 S 26 '63
Khrushchev takes a hand; Goldwater's nomination. Nat R 16:678-9 Ag 11 '64
Khrushchev, the generals and Goldwater. R. D. Senter New Repub 151:8-9 N 21 '64
Khrushchev: the red riddle. R. Harrity and R. G. Martin. il pors Look 27:34-6+ N 19 '63
Khrushchev the terrible. Nation 199:289-90 N 2 '64
K's African campaign. il por Newsweek 63: 52 My 18 '64
Khrushchev's dilemma in Cyprus and Vietnam. F. B. Stevens. por U S News 57:43 Ag 31 '64
Khrushchev's losing fight with his marshals. V. Zorza. il por Life 57:42-3+ N 6 '64
Khrushchev's paper bear. C. J. V. Murphy. por Fortune 70:114-15+ D '64
Khrushchev's sea of troubles. S. Alsop. pors Sat Eve Post 237:18 Ja 25 '64
Khrushchev's tour: no great triumph. il por U S News 56:14 Je 1 '64
Kremlin plays Russian roulette. H. E. Salisbury. il por N Y Times Mag p25+ O 25 '64
Kremlin votes no confidence. A. Werth. Nation 199:291-5 N 2 '64
More about Khrushchev. N. Cousins. Sat R 47:24+ N 21 '64
Near the breaking point? il Sr Schol 84:14 Ap 24 '64
New B & K show opens in Red square. R. Brigham. il Life 57:40-42B O 30 '64
New image: as Khrushchev passes seventy. por U S News 56:15 Ap 27 '64
New look at Russia from the inside; interview. I. D. Levine. U S News 55:92-3 Ag 26 '63
Nikita & the capitalists; American executives on a European tour. il por Time 82:38-9 N 15 '63
Nikita in Titoland. U S News 55:12 S 2 '63
Nikita Khrushchev: Maoist. J. Burnham. Nat R 16:644 Jl 28 '64
Nikita's monologue. Newsweek 62:42+ N 18 '63
Notes and comment. New Yorker 40:21 Ja 9 '65
Notes on a 1963 visit with Khrushchev. N. Cousins. il pors Sat R 47:16-21+ N 7 '64
Notes on the Khrushchev ouster. J. Burnham. Nat R 16:952 N 3 '64
Of firs, flies & fears: Khrushchev's blast against recent artistic expression. il Time 81:26 Mr 22 '63

KHRUSHCHEV, Nikita Sergeevich—about —Continued
On the other hand; question of successor. il por Time 81:32 My 3 '63
Paper bear. W. J. Coughlin. Miss & Roc 16:46 Ja 11 '65
Patching up Russia's planned economy. J. M. Montias. Reporter 28:22-4 Ap 11 '63
Postmortem. J. A. Morris, jr. il Newsweek 63:30+ Je 1 '64
President in Germany. Reporter 29:16+ Jl 18 '63
Proof of the Soviet plum pudding. Bsns W p 100 D 21 '63
Race to help Nasser. il por U S News 56:70 Je 8 '64
Reasons why. Sr Schol 85:9 N 1 '64
Red rumors; courtesy of Khrushchev. Sr Schol 82:21 My 15 '63
Report from Belgrade. New Repub 149:8 S 21 '63
Reverse response. Time 84:36 Jl 10 '64
Revolt in the Kremlin. il por Time 84:28-31 O 23 '64
Robert Frost confronts Khrushchev. F. D. Reeve. Atlan 212:33-9 S '63
Russia-China split: how real? il por U S News 54:44-7 Mr 18 '63
Russia: Khrushchev and after. O. Gass. bibliog f Commentary 36:353-63 N '63
Russian foreign aid: big headache for Khrushchev. il U S News 54:50-3 My 27 '63
Russia's greatest failure. R. Wilson. il Look 28:88+ F 25 '64
Russia's latest plan: confession of a failure. il por U S News 55:44-5 D 23 '63
Shades of Lenin. Newsweek 63:40+ F 24 '64
Shuffle in the Kremlin. il por Newsweek 64: 37 Jl 27 '64
Soviet-American relations; address, February 28, 1963. R. F. Starr. bibliog Vital Speeches 29:468-73 My 15 '63
Soviet economic developments; Khrushchev and after. O. Gass. bibliog f il Commentary 37:54-68 F '64
Spirit of Moscow. il por Time 82:22-3 Jl 26 '63
Splintered legacy of Karl Marx. il Newsweek 63:47-8+ Ap 27 '64
Step toward limbo. Newsweek 64:40 Ag 24 '64
Strange aftermath of the Cuban deal. il U S News 55:51-2 N 11 '63
Stravinsky talks with Khrushchev; excerpts from Dialogues and a diary. R. Craft. il Vogue 142:134-5+ N 1 '63
Suddenly Nikita's day was done; with report by J. K. Jessup. il pors Life 57:30-40B O 23 '64
Test ban: a rosy glow on the horizon. il por Newsweek 62:45 Jl 29 '63
Tito of Yugoslavia: new role for an old rebel? il por Sr Schol 83:12-15+ O 11 '63
Tour time. il Newsweek 64:34+ Jl 13 '64
Traveling act; journey through Scandinavia. il Time 83:34 Je 26 '64
Two steps forward, one step back. E. Griffiths. il pors Newsweek 61:37-40 Ap 8 '63
Victory of the clerks. Z. Brzezinski. New Repub 151:15-18 N 14 '64
Visit to the Land of the Sphinx J. A. Morris. jr. il pors Newsweek 63:41 My 25 '64
Weapon to kill everybody; or just cold-war bluster? por U S News 57:8 S 28 '64
What Khrushchev is thinking; as reported from private conferences in Moscow. il por U S News 55:42 D 16 '63
What really happened to Khrushchev? with editorial comment. S. Alsop and E. Stevens. il por Sat Eve Post 237:81-6 N 7 '64; Same abr. without editorial comment. Read Digest 86:90-4 Ja '65
What's bothering Khrushchev: crises at home and abroad. il por U S News 54:75-6 Ap 1 '63
When Khrushchev and Castro get together. il pors U S News 54:37-9 My 13 '63
Who runs Russia now? il U S News 57:52-4+ N 9 '64
Who shall be master? J. Burnham. Nat R 16:688 Ag 11 '64
Who would succeed Mr K? F. B. Stevens. il por U S News 56:53 Ap 27 '64
Why Khrushchev changed his mind. F. B. Stevens. U S News 55:28 S 2 '63
Why Khrushchev needs to buy wheat. il U S News 55:43 O 14 '63
Widening gulf between Mao and Khrushchev. D. S. Zagoria. il Reporter 28:38-40 Ap 25 '63
Will Khrushchev be forced out? por U S News 54:43-4 My 6 '63
Will the West now bail out Khrushchev? il U S News 55:36-8 D 30 '63
With Khrushchev on campaign. il por U S News 56:15 Ap 20 '64
With test-ban treaty, has Khrushchev changed his ways? interview. Z. Brzezinski. U S News 55:72-3 S 30 '63

KHRUSHCHEV, Sergei Nikitovich
Nikita's boy. por Time 83:40-1 My 15 '64

KHRUSHCHEVA, Nina Petrovna
Secret life of Nina Khrushchev. J. Gunther. por McCalls 90:52-3+ Jl '63

KHUMJUNG, Nepal
Highest school in the world; Sir E. Hillary's latest conquest in the Himalayas. R. J. Spector. il UNESCO Courier 17:12-17 O '64

KHUSH, Gurdev S. and others
Genetic activity in a heterochromatic chromosome segment of the tomato. bibliog Science 145:1432-4 S 25 '64

KIBALCHICH, Victor Lvovich. See Serge, V.

KIBBUTZIM. See Collective settlements—Israel

KIDDER, Alfred, 2d
Rediscovering America. Horizon 6:73-87+ Sum '64

KIDNAPING
American crime. Time 84:30-1 Jl 10 '64
Another nasty stunt: kidnaping of U.S. colonel by Venezuela's F.A.L.N. il Time 84:54 O 16 '64
Kidnaped. A. Argoud. Nat R 15:15-16 Jl 16 '63; Reply. J. Soustelle. 15:209 S 10 '63
Kidnaper who panicked; Sinatra kindnaping. Time 82:17-18 D 27 '63
My state of mind was fear; F. Sinatra jr. il Time 83:25 F 28 '64
Rule by terror; political kidnaping in East Germany. America 111:104 Ag 1 '64
Sinatra caper. il Newsweek 62:20-2 D 23 '63
There's nothing to be sorry for; Frank Sinatra's nineteen-year-old son. il Time 82:14-15 D 20 '63
Time to finish the Communist bridgehead; kidnaping of Col. Chenault in Venezuela. il Time 82:49 D 6 '63
See also
Trials (kidnaping)

KIDNEY tumors. See Tumors

KIDNEYS
Autoradiographic distribution of radioactive sodium in rat kidney. P. F. Mercer and R. H. Wasserman. bibliog il Science 143: 695-6 F 14 '64
Blood vessels of the mammalian renal medulla. R. K. Plakke and E. W. Pfeiffer. bibliog il Science 146:1683-5 D 25 '64
Estrogen-induced 16-hydroxysteroid dehydrogenase activity in rat kidney. K. J. Ryan and others. bibliog il Science 142:243-4 O 11 '63
Ethacrynic acid: diuretic property coupled to reaction with sulfhydryl groups of renal cells. R. M. Komorn and E. J. Cafruny. bibliog il Science 143:133-4 Ja 10 '64
Keeping the filters working. il Time 84:50 Jl 24 '64
Life-giving balancing act. R. Campbell. il Life 55:74-5 N 8 '63
Methlyurea and acetamide: active reabsorption by elasmobranch renal tubules. B. Schmidt-Nielsen and L. Rabinowitz. bibliog il Science 146:1587-8 D 18 '64
Renal baroceptor control of renin secretion. S. L. Skinner and others. bibliog il Science 141:814-16 Ag 30 '63
Renal tubular localization of chlormerodrin labeled with mercury-203 by autoradiography. R. P. Wedeen and M. H. Goldstein. bibliog il Science 141:438-40 Ag 2 '63
Serum factor in renal compensatory hyperplasia. L. M. Lowenstein and A. Stern. bibliog il Science 142:1479-80 D 13 '63

Diseases

Action of erythromycin on protoplasts in vivo. L. B. Guze and G. M. Kalmanson. bibliog il Science 146:1299-300 D 4 '64
Chimp supply meager. F. Marley. Sci N L 86:3 Jl 4 '64
Keeping the filters working. il Time 84:50 Jl 24 '64
Lingering infection from disguised bacteria. Sci N L 85:345 My 30 '64
Persistence of bacteria in protoplast form after apparent cure of pyelonephritis in rats. L. B. Guze and G. M. Kalmanson. bibliog il Science 143:1340-1 Mr 20 '64
See also
Uremia

KIDNEYS, Artificial
Artificial kidney for fifteen patients. il Time 83:42 Ap 24 '64
Artificial kidney machine in the home. il Life 57:55-6+ D 4 '64

KIDNEYS, Artificial—*Continued*
Cleaning up the blood; artificial kidney moving out of the hospital, into the home. il Time 84:64 N 13 '64
Help kidney function with plastic tube. il(p387) Sci N L 83:399 Je 22 '63
Welcome to Kidney Towers. S. Alexander. Life 57:31 N 20 '64
KIDNEYS, Transplantation of. See Transplantation of organs, tissues, etc.
KIDWELL, Roger L. See English, W. D. jt. auth.
KIECKER, James
Paradox; poem. Christian Cent 80:426 Ap 3 '63
KIEFER, Rick
TIMM components work throughout high-intensity radiation bombardment. Miss & Roc 15:34 Ag 24 '64
KIELY, Robert
Exercises in extremity. Nation 196:549-50 Je 29 '63
KIEN, Alvin E. Friedman-. See Friedman-Kien, A. E.
KIENZ, Ethel T.
Before you move to Florida look both ways! Consumer Bul 47:6-9 F '64
Mobile home living. Consumer Bul 46:2+ S '63
KIERAN, John
Time to stump the experts; excerpt from Not under oath. por Horizon 6:106-11 Autumn '64
about
Falcons and famous friends. R. L. Perkin. il Sat R 47:75-6 O 24 '64
KIERKEGAARD, Søren Aabye
Browning and Kierkegaard as heirs of Luther. M. W. Hess. Christian Cent 80:799-801 Je 19 '63
Letter from Paris. Genêt. New Yorker 40:170 My 16 '64
S.K: prophet with honor. Christian Cent 80:943 Jl 24 '63
What Luther meant by faith alone. M. W. Hess. Cath World 199:96-101 My '64
KIERNAN, T. J.
United States concludes meat agreement with Ireland; Irish note, February 25, 1964. Dept State Bul 50:468-9 Mr 23 '64
KIES, Marian W. and Alvord, E. C. Jr
Demyelinating diseases. Science 144:320-1 Ap 17 '64
KIES, Paul P.
Mascagni vs. America. Opera N 28:24-6 Ap 11 '64
KIESLER, Frederick
Art in orbit; excerpts from Kiesler's journals. Nation 198:486-8 My 11 '64
Environmental sculpture; excerpt from The endless search. Arch Forum 121:118 Jl '64
about
Empty altars. il por Newsweek 63:62 My 18 '64
Endless sculpture; exhibition of Environmental sculpture in the Guggenheim museum. il Time 83:86 My 15 '64
Kiesler and Mondrian, art into life. K. Levin. il Art N 63:38-41+ My '64
KIESSEL, William C.
Riding with the king's men. Sat R 47:49 F 15 '64
KIESSLING, Kerstin Lindahl-. See Lindahl-Kiessling, K.
KIESTER, Edwin, Jr
Better books for traveling. Redbook 120:32+ F '63
Traveling by book. Redbook 122:42+ Mr '64
KIGHT, Murley K.
Stitchery. Sch Arts 63:32-3 S '63
KIHLMAN, Ake
Who's who in foreign business. il por Fortune 68:80 Ag '63
KIKUTAKE, Kiyonori
1963 Pan Pacific citation awarded to Japan's Kikutake. il por Arch Rec 135:14-15 Mr '64
KIKUYUS. See Kenya—Native races
KILAUEA (crater)
Hawaii's trees of stone. D. L. Hamilton. il Nat Parks Mag 38:15-17 Ja '64
KILBRACKEN, John Raymond Godley, 3d baron
Long, deep dive. por Nat Geog Mag 123:718-31 My '63
KILBURN, Paul D.
Contamination of the environment; address, January 28, 1963. Vital Speeches 29:475-8 My 15 '63
Exponential values for the species-area relation. bibliog Science 141:1276 S 27 '63
KILDAY, G. W.
Refuse trains bring three-way savings. Am City 80:88-90 Ja '65
KILDUFF, Malcolm
Awful interval. il por Newsweek 63:19-20 Ja 6 '64
KILGALLEN, Dorothy
Yesterday's globe-trotter. por Time 82:53 O 25 '63
KILGALLEN, Eleanor
Boss ladies; symposium, ed. by L. L. Tornabene por(p 106) Esquire 63:102+ Ja '65
KILGORE, Wendell W. See Suzuki, H. jt. auth.
KILHAM, Lawrence, and Margolis, George
Cerebellar ataxia in hamsters inoculated with rat virus. bibliog Science 143:1047-8 Mr 6 '64
—See Ferm, V. H. jt. auth.
KILIMANJARO
Secretary Udall assaults Kilimanjaro. il Life 55:55-6+ O 11 '63
KILIMANJARO machine; story. See Bradbury, R.
KILIT, Mehmet Ihsan
I am but a simple murderer. il por Time 84:35 Jl 24 '64
KILIUS, Marika
Flash of fire on the ice. J. Bell. il por Sports Illus 20:52-3 Ja 27 '64
Girl of ice. por Newsweek 65:56 Ja 18 '65
KILLAM, Bob
New England heritage cruise. Motor B 111:20-7+ Ap '63
KILLEBREW, Harmon
Instant homer king! H. L. Masin. il por Sr Schol 84:30 My 15 '64
Nuclear bomber. il Time 84:44 Ag 14 '64
Out of the park on a half swing. B. Heilman. por Sports Illus 18:85+ Ap 8 '63
KILLEN, John J.
Backbone fire training has a few new wrinkles. Am City 78:89-91 Jl '63
KILLENS, John Oliver
Explanation of the black psyche. N Y Times Mag p37-8+ Je 7 '64
KILLER whales. See Whales
KILLIAN, James R. Jr
Crisis in research. Atlan 211:69-72 Mr '63
Doctor Killian's warning; excerpts from address. Aviation W 80:21 Ap 27 '64
KILLING, Mercy. See Euthanasia
KILLING of animals. See Hunting—Ethical aspects
KILMARX, Robert A.
Soviet space program. Cur Hist 45:200-4+ O '63
KILMER, Joyce
Sad goodbye; Kilmer oak at Rutgers university. R. F. West. il Am For 69:12+ N '63
KILMER oak. See Trees, Historic
KILNS
Late seventeenth-century pottery kiln site near Jamestown; excerpts from Here lies Virginia. I. N. Hume. il Antiques 83:550-2 My '63
KILPATRICK, F. P. and others
Oh, Mister President! excerpt from The image of the federal service. Sat R 47:50-1 Mr 7 '64
KILPATRICK, Harold
Dissidents confounded. Christian Cent 80:466-8 Ap 10 '63
KILPATRICK, James Jackson
Civil rights and legal wrongs. Nat R 15:231-6, 497+ S 24, D 3 '63
Crossroads in Dixie. Nat R 15:433-5 N 19 '63
Goldwater country. Nat R 14:281-2 Ap 9 '63
Ike plan cometh. Nat R 16:483-6 Je 16 '64
South goes back up for grabs. Nat R 15:523-4+ D 17 '63
To a young prince. Nat R 14:241-2 Mr 26 '63
What a southern conservative thinks. Sat R 47:15-18 Ap 25 '64
KILVERT, B. Cory, Jr
Big league lawn. il Flower Grower 50:46-7 O '63
Choose the right tool; then use it right. il Flower Grower 51:50-5 Mr '64
Hand tools still high on list of gardening aids. Flower Grower 50:43-4 Je '63
Have you heard? See issues of Flower grower
Planting makes a terrace a garden. Flower Grower 50:32-3 My '63
Pools to grace a garden. Flower Grower 50:48-51 Ag '63
Power to spare: do's & don'ts of dusting and spraying. Flower Grower 51:38-9 My '64
Propagating plants by hardwood cuttings. Flower Grower 50:21-2 O '63
Spring attack vital in defeat of crab grass. Flower Grower 51:27 F '64
Starting tomatoes from seed is easy and fun. Flower Grower 50:26-7 Ap '63
Stop! look! listen! Flower Grower 50:30+ Jl '63

KILVERT, B. Cory, jr.—*Continued*
Take your pick of power. Flower Grower 51:30-2 N; 12-13 D '64
Well-mannered honeysuckles. Horticulture 41: 136-7 Mr '63
KIM, Chong Pil
Academic exit. il por Time 83:31 Je 26 '64
Over to you, gentlemen. il por Time 81:34+ Mr 8 '63
KIM, Le-kwang-. See Le-kwang-Kim
KIM, Richard E.
Author. M. K. Harvey. por Sat R 47:58 F 22 '64
Best-selling Korean. il pors Life 56:125-6 Mr 20 '64
Big puff. I. Gold. Nation 198:462-3 My 4 '64
KIMBALL, Charles
Why the Midwest is lagging, and what can be done about it; excerpts from address, June 22, 1964. por U S News 57:80-2 Ag 10 '64
KIMBALL, Penn T.
Secret of Balliol. Sat R 46:37-8+ Ag 17 '63
KIMBLE, Constance R.
High cost of playing. por Redbook 124:10+ Ja '65
KIMBLE, Daniel P.
Learning, remembering and forgetting. Science 146:1605 D 18 '64
—and Pribram, K. H.
Hippocampectomy and behavior sequences. bibliog Science 139:824-5 Mr 1 '63
KIMBLE, George H. T.
Continents are still on the move. N Y Times Mag p 13+ Jl 21 '63
Handicap for new nations: climate. N Y Times Mag p35+ S 29 '63
Messages from inside the earth. N Y Times Mag p 14-15+ Ap 28 '63
Racialism is an African sickness, too. N Y Times Mag p38-9+ O 11 '64
That hellish and dismal cloud. N Y Times Mag p26+ Ap 21 '63
True story of black Africa and its future; interview. por U S News 54:72-9 F 11 '63
U.S. of Africa? not very likely. N Y Times Mag p 10+ Mr 29 '64
KIMBREL, M. Monroe
Our international financial position; address, January 21, 1963. Vital Speeches 29:303-5 Mr 1 '63
KIMBROUGH, Emily
I like whistlestops. Travel 122:34-5+ Jl '64
Koula; excerpt from Forever old, forever new. Ladies Home J 81:87+ N '64
KIMELDORF, D. J. See Cooper, G. P. jt. auth.
KIMLING, L. Erlenmeyer-. See Erlenmeyer-Kimling, L.
KIMMEL, Oscar A.
Plan your farm service center. Suc Farm 63:45+ Ja '65
KINARD, Epsie
Enjoy the new feast of Debussy recordings. House B 105:30+ O '63
Intrigue your mind while your hands work. House B 105:54+ S '63
Take advantage of the Gilbert and Sullivan recording boom. House B 105:30+ Mr '63
KINCAID, Mary
Gallic comic. il por Time 81:86 Ap 12 '63
KINCAID, William B.
Single-frequency receiver. Electr World 71: 44-5+ Ap '64
KIND, Joshua
Albright: humanist of decay. Art N 63:43-5+ N '64
Art news from Chicago. Art N 63:52 S '64
Reviews: Chicago. Art N 63:21-2 My '64
KINDALL, Alva F. and Gatza, James
Positive program for performance appraisal. Harvard Bsns R 41:153-4+ N '63
KINDERGARTEN
In defense of the five-year-old. R. Hillman. Sat R 46:76+ N 16 '63
Is play obsolete? D. Weisman. il Sat R 46: 77-8 N 16 '63
Montessori in the space age? E. Beyer. il NEA J 52:35-6 D '63
Show-and-tell in the kindergarten. H. Laufer. NEA J 52:63 O '63
See also
Montessori method of education
KINDERGARTEN teachers. See Teachers
KINDLER, S. H. See Galun, R. jt. auth.
KINDLEY, Bob
Backpack for better hunting. pors Outdoor Life 134:50-2+ N '64
KINDNESS
Enjoy adventures in friendliness. B. Day. il Read Digest 85:175-6+ Ag '64
Word. V. P. McCorry. America 111:144 Ag 8 '64
KINDRED heart; story. See Boles, P. D.

KINETIN
Toxic effect of pseudomonas tabaci on RNA metabolism in tobacco and its counteraction by kinetin. L. Lovrekovich and others. bibliog il Science 145:165 Jl 10 '64
KING, A. Bruce
Mass spectrometry. Science 146:90-1 O 2 '64
KING, Alan
Fit for what? por McCalls 90:46+ F '63
How I feel about banks is unbalanced. McCalls 91:42+ Ja '64
To: the finest little old sanitation men in the whole world. McCalls 91:44 D '63
about
Large, loud mouth of Alan King. M. Kitman. il pors Sat Eve Post 237:68+ N 28 '64
KING, Bruce
Nelle Fisher, Bruce King, and assisting dancers at Judson Hall. D. Hering. Dance Mag 37:22 F '63
KING, C. G.
International nutrition programs. bibliog Science 147:25-9 Ja 1 '65
KING, C. T. G.
Teratogenic effects of meclizine hydrochloride on the rat. bibliog Science 141:353-5 Jl 26 '63
KING, Calvin
Daredevil auto stunt man. il pors Ebony 19: 91-2+ D '63
KING, Charles Jeron Criswell
Boastradamus; Criswell predicts. por Newsweek 62:56 Jl 15 '63
KING, Coretta Scott
Come by here, my Lord. por Newsweek 64: 94 N 30 '64
KING, David C.
Sideroad into yesterday. Travel 122:42-3 D '64
KING, Eddie
Plugging and pitching: a great relief. il por Newsweek 62:70 O 7 '63
KING, Edwin
Insider stays to fight. C. S. Wren. il pors Look 28:26-8 S 8 '64
KING, Eleanor
Magic of masks. Dance Mag 37:34-7 Ag '63
KING, Elizabeth R. and others
Genesis of the Arctic Ocean Basin. bibliog Science 144:1551-7 Je 26 '64
KING, Fred M.
Manuscript and cursive writing. NEA J 53: 27-8 N '64
KING, Gilbert W. and Chang, H. W.
Machine translation of Chinese; with biographical sketches. Sci Am 208:30, 124-35: 209:8+ Je, O '63
KING, Harry M.
Big idea: live in the whole attic. Pop Sci 183:120-1 S '63
KING, Helen Carter
Cathedral in the forest; poem. Liv Wildn 85:24 Wint '64
KING, James H. See Anglin, E. M. jt. auth.
KING, John A. and others
Age of weaning in two subspecies of deer mice. bibliog Science 139:483-4 F 8 '63
KING, Joseph A.
Books and banners. Sat R 46:28-9+ N 9 '63
KING, Lambert N. and others
Resistance to erysiphe polygoni of red clover infected with bean yellow mosaic virus. bibliog Science 146:1054-5 N 20 '64
KING, Larry L.
Washington's second banana politicians. Harper 230:41-7 Ja '65
KING, Lawrence T.
Breakthrough at Kaiser. Commonweal 78:11-12 Mr 29 '63
Great land swindle. Commonweal 78:477-9 Ag 9 '63
Ireland: wretched, rebellious and dependent on the potato. Commonweal 78:51-2 Ap 5 '63
Tax triumph. Commonweal 80:111-13 Ap 17 '64
Union shop at Lockheed? Commonweal 77: 489-91 F 1 '63
Vanishing race. Commonweal 81:385-8 D 11 '64
Water, water. Commonweal 79:623-6 F 21 '64
KING, Marshall
How to get by as a navigator. Yachting 114: 126-7 D '63
KING, Martha Bennett
Polly Goodwin receives the Constance Lindsay Skinner award. Pub W 186:108-10 Jl 13 '64
KING, Martin Luther, 1929-
Bold design for a new South. Nation 196:259-62 Mr 30 '63
Boycotts will be used; interview. por U S News 56:59-61 F 24 '64

KING, Martin Luther—*Continued*
Dispute between Hoover and King: the FBI's answer to criticisms; FBI analysis of telegram. por U S News 57:46+ D 7 '64
Dream, I have a dream; excerpts from address to Washington marchers, August 28, 1963. por Newsweek 62:21 S 9 '63
Hammer of civil rights. Nation 198:230-4 Mr 9 '64
In a word: now. N Y Times Mag p91-2 S 29 '63
Is it all right to break the law? por U S News 55:6 Ag 12 '63
It's a difficult thing to teach a president; excerpts from interviews, ed. by T. G. Harris. por Look 28:61+ N 17 '64
Letter from Birmingham jail. Christian Cent 80:767-73 Je 12 '63; Excerpts. Ebony 18:23-6+ Ag '63; Time 83:15 Ja 3 '64; Same. Negro Hist Bul 27:156 Mr '64
Martin Luther King's reaction: a statement and a disagreement. U S News 57:58 N 30 '64
Negro is your brother. por Atlan 212:78-81+ Ag '63
Speaking out. por Sat Eve Post 237:8+ N 7 '64
Two perspectives, one goal; accepts peace prize. por Time 84:21 D 18 '64
Visit with Martin Luther King; ed. by E. Dunbar. pors Look 27:92-6 F 12 '63
Why we can't wait; excerpts. pors Life 56:98-100+ My 15 '64; Sat R 47:17-20+ My 30 '64

about

Aim: registration; promoting desegregation in Selma, Ala. il por Time 85:20-1 Ja 29 '65
Back on the home front. il por Time 82:17 D 27 '63
Big man is Martin Luther King, jr. il por Newsweek 62:30-2 Jl 29 '63
Connor and King. il Newsweek 61:28+ Ap 22 '63
Copyright case involves new use of material; unauthorized recording of speech by M. L. King. H. F. Pilpel. Pub W 185:26 Ap 6 '64
Doctor King's Nobel prize. America 111:503 O 31 '64
Dogs, kids & clubs. il Time 81:19 My 10 '63
Endorse Dr King for Nobel prize. Christian Cent 81:1006 Ag 12 '64; Discussion. 81:1308 O 21 '64
Equality is not negotiable. Christian Cent 80:1069 S 4 '63
Hoover-King meeting. il por Newsweek 64:22+ D 14 '64
Hotter fires; friction between organizations; with report by K. Fleming. il Newsweek 62:19-21 Jl 1 '63
I like the word black; increasingly militant mood. il por Newsweek 61:27-8 My 6 '63
King proposed for peace prize. Christian Cent 81:198 F 12 '64
King receives Nobel prize. Christian Cent 81:1324 O 28 '64
King wants white demonstrators. Christian Cent 81:724-5 Je 3 '64
King's targets. il por Newsweek 63:26+ Je 22 '64
Knives sharpening. Nat R 16:1094 D 15 '64
Man of conflict wins a peace prize. por U S News 57:24 O 26 '64
Man of the year. il pors Time 83:13-16+ Ja 3 '64; Reply. Nation 198:41-2 Ja 13 '64
Martin Luther King jr, apostle of crisis. R. Cleghorn. il pors Sat Eve Post 236:15-19 Je 15 '63
Martin Luther King, Jr: man of 1963. por Negro Hist Bul 27:136-7 Mr '64
No false moves for King. Christian Cent 80:919 Jl 17 '63
Nobel peace prize goes to Martin Luther King. C. W. Thomas. por Negro Hist Bul 28:35 N '64
Nobelman King. por Newsweek 64:77 O 26 '64
Odds on freedom; gambler's choice in Georgia. P. De Lissovoy. il Nation 198:618-21 Je 22 '64
Off Hoover's chest; with excerpts from press conference. por Newsweek 64:30 N 30 '64
Peace prize causes controversy; reactions in Atlanta. Christian Cent 82:39 Ja 13 '65
Peace with justice. Commonweal 78:268 My 31 '63
Peaceful kingdom. Nat R 16:1135 D 29 '64
Poorly timed protest; Birmingham Negroes. il por Time 81:30-1 Ap 19 '63
Religious right to violate the law? W. Herberg. Nat R 16:579-80 Jl 14 '64; Discussion. 16:741-2, 783-4 Ag 25-S 8 '64; Correction of S 8 issue. 16:794+ S 22 '64
Shades of Bull Connor; attacked in Selma, Ala. hotel. il Newsweek 65:21-2 F 1 '65
Top man of the Negro revolution. por U S News 54:21 Je 10 '63
Tribute to Martin Luther King, jr. por Ebony 20:126-7 D '64
Two good choices. Nation 199:319 N 9 '64
Up from Montgomery. il por Newsweek 64:40-1 D 21 '64
Youngest ever. il por Time 84:27 O 23 '64

KING, Mrs Martin Luther, jr
My dream for my children. por Good H 158:77+ Je '64

KING, Martin Luther, family
My dream for my children. Mrs M. L. King, jr. il Good H 158:77+ Je '64

KING, Michael
Where a Negro captain lives: his problem or ours? il pors Look 27:36-7 D 17 '63

KING, Mike
Automotive milestones; the Corvair's granddaddy. Motor T 16:84-5 Ag '64

KING, Nicholas
Citizen of two worlds. Sat R 46:43 F 2 '63

KING, Peggy Cameron
Checklist for humor writers. Writer 77:13-14+ N '64
If you can read, you can cook. . . Am Home 67:108 Jl '64
Lonely little old lady; drama. Plays 24:29-38 D '64
Woman, stay away from my workshop! Am Home 67:103 O '64

KING, Seth S.
Sihanouk, prince under pressure. N Y Times Mag p42+ S 13 '64
Sukarno stirs up another Asian storm. N Y Times Mag p 14-15+ Ja 19 '64

KING, Sol
Developments in industrial construction. Arch Rec 136:175-6 Jl '64

KING, Terry Johnson
Ladies Thursday afternoon; sailing and sinking society. Yachting 115:74-5+ Ja '64
Li'l orphan islands. Travel 122:61-2+ N '64

KING, Tsoo E. See Takemori, E. jt. auth.

KING, Walter
High old fling at the national ringer derby; National horseshoe pitching championships. J. O'Reilly. il por Sports Illus 19:56-60 S 16 '63
Little Snow White; drama. Plays 23:79-82 Ja '64

KING, Wayne
Last waltz at Aragon. il pors Bsns W p30-1 F 15 '64

KING, William C.
Glass-ware patents of William King. A. G. Peterson. il Hobbies 69:72 Ja '65

KING-HALL, Stephen
S.S. Lunatic. Nation 196:298 Ap 13 '63

KING and I; musical comedy. See Musical comedies, revues, etc.—Criticisms, plots, etc.

KING-Anderson bill. See Insurance, Health—United States

KING Caliban; story. See Wain, J.

KING crabs
N-Ethylmaleimide inhibition of horseshoe crab hemocyte agglutination. F. T. Bravan and others. bibliog il Science 144:1147-8 My 29 '64
Ultraviolet eye; horseshoe crab. Sci Am 210:62+ Ap '64

KING in the kitchen; drama. See Slattery, M. E.

KING Lear; drama. See Shakespeare, W.—Plays

KING radio corporation
After the revolution, a King; navcom equipment. W. J. Kendall. il Flying 74:42-3+ My '64

KING salmon fishing. See Salmon fishing

KINGDON, Robert M.
Calvinism and democracy: some political implications of debates on French reformed church government, 1562-1572. bibliog f Am Hist R 69:393-401 Ja '64

KINGETT, Robert P.
Danger, divers below. il Motor B 111:39-40+ Je '63
Three thousand bucks and a brick. Motor B 111:46-7+ My '63
Your buying guide for blue-water cruising. Motor B 114:44-5+ N '64

KINGFISH fishing
Wicked kings. H. G. Boughton. il Outdoor Life 131:60-1+ Je '63

KINGFISHERS
Home fit for a kingfisher! R. Grierson and S. Grierson. il Audubon Mag 66:300-1 S '64

KINGMAN, Dong
Dong Kingman paints Peking in Spain. il por Am Artist 27:40-1 S '63

KINGMAN, Helena Kuo
How to give a dinner party in Chinese. House & Gard 125:108-11+ Ja '64
KINGMAN, Lee
Chapters from Horn book history. Horn Bk 39:92-3 F '63
KINGMAN, Kan.
Power costs drop. il Am City 79:124+ Ap '64
KINGS, Ann Huxley
Four against the Bank of England; condensation. Read Digest 85:195-200+ Ag '64
KINGS and rulers
Fall of the dynasties, by E. Taylor. Review Am Heritage 14:108-9 Ap '63
Last years of splendor. E. Kern. il Life 55: 71-88 N 22 '63
Succession and monarchy: the controversy of 1679-1681. C. A. Edie. bibliog f Am Hist R 70:350-70 Ja '65
See also
Hapsburg, House of
KINGS CANYON NATIONAL PARK
High country in Kings Canyon Park; photographs. C. E. Peters. Nat Park Mag 38: 9-11 S '64
Our fragile wilderness. D. G. Newcomb. il Field & S 68:10-11+ F '64
See one big tree, and you want to see another. il Sunset 131:30-2 Jl '63
Tehipite Valley-Cedar Grove; to be incorporated into the park. Nat Parks Mag 38: 16 Ag '64
KINGSEED, Elizabeth
Lo, the poor parent. por ALA Bul 57:779-80 S '63
KINGSLEY, Buffy
South West Africa. Travel 119:50-4 Mr '63
KINGSLEY, J. D.
Optical masers. Science 145:839-40 Ag 21 '64
KINGSLEY-HEATH, John
Lion mangled me. pors Outdoor Life 131:20-3+ Mr '63
KINGSPORT, Tenn.

Streets

Don't compromise on quality. M. L. West and S. K. Addington. il Am City 78:87-8 Mr '63
KINGSPORT press, incorporated
Kingsport loses challenge to union representation. Pub W 186:151-2 Jl 13 '64
Kingsport press strike goes on and on. Pub W 185:37 Je 1 '64
Kingsport unions backed by AFL-CIO; firm states view. il Pub W 184:28-30 D 2 '63
NLRB authorizes union election at Kingsport. Pub W 185:31 Mr 23 '64
No settlement in sight for Kingsport press strike. Pub W 184:26-7 N 4 '63
One for the unions. Bsns W p 154+ Mr 21 '64
Unions explain their side of Kingsport strike. il Pub W 184:43-4 S 2 '63
KINGSTON, Jeremy
Distances; poem. New Yorker 40:95 Ja 23 '65
Drawing and quartering; story. New Yorker 40:177-80 S 26 '64
KINGSTON, N.Y.
Meters save water. E. T. Cloonan. il Am City 79:147-8 Mr '64
KINGSTON trio. See Choral groups and societies
KINIGSTEIN, Jonah
Perpetual motion. F. Getlein. New Repub 151:34+ O 3 '64
KINKEAD, Katharine T.
Reporter at large (cont) New Yorker 40:51-2+ My 23 '64
KINKEAD, Maeve
Curl up and read. Seventeen 22:164 S '63
KINMONT, Jill
What you can do with what you have. il pors Life 56:75-87 Je 19 '64
KINNANE, Mary
Speech as a liberal study. Sch & Soc 91:330+ N 2 '63
KINNE, Russ
Bee portrait. Pop Phot 52:54-5+ F '63
Kinne on flash. il Pop Phot 53:68-75+ O '63
Microscopes. Pop Phot 51:88-91 D '62
Pocketable speedlight. il Pop Phot 54:62-7+ Mr '64
Shooting with infrared; the light you can't see. il Pop Phot 52:68-73 Je '63
Test report: the amphibious Nikonos. il Pop Phot 54:70-3+ Mr '64
Water work. Flying 74:22 Je '64
KINNELL, Galway
Cells breathe in the emptiness; poem. Nation 197:460 D 28 '63
Lunch hour; poem. Nation 196:360 Ap 27 '63
Ruins under the stars; poem. Poetry 103:348-50 Mr '64
Spindrift; poem. New Yorker 39:36 F 15 '64
KINNEY, Cle. See Kinney, J. jt. auth.
KINNEY, Jean, and Kinney, Cle
New zip for the family album. U S Camera 26:54-5+ Je '63
Start with a sketch pad. U S Camera 26:61-3+ N '63
Three key pictures. U S Camera 26:54-7+ My '63
KINNEY, John E.
Our fictitious water famine; excerpt from address, October 22, 1962. Am City 78: 142+ Ap '63
KINNEY, Lucien B.
Certification and professional autonomy; excerpt from Certification in education. bibliog Sch & Soc 91:434-9 D 28 '63
KINNEY service corporation
Parking by computer. Time 83:94 My 22 '64
KINO, Eusebio Francisco
Cowboy and priest. E. J. McDermott. America 108:465 Ap 6 '63
Kino in the Capitol; statue to be placed in National statuary hall in Washington. America 111:245 S 12 '64; Reply. P. C. Rinaudo De Ville. 111:430 O 17 '64
Kino missions of Sonora and Arizona. G. Meek. il Américas 16:18-22 Ja '64
KINOY, Arthur. See Kunstler, W. M. jt. auth.
KINSELLA, Thomas
In the beginning; poem. Reporter 31:44 Jl 16 '64
Some Irish poets. Poetry 102:324-9 Ag '63
KINSEY, Helen
Big four speak. por Library J 88:2071-2+ My 15 '63
KINSHIP
Ties that don't bind; kinship ties have become stronger. Newsweek 64:55 S 14 '64
KINSOLVING, Lester
What about therapeutic abortion? Christian Cent 81:632-5 My 13 '64
KINTNER, William R.
Case against international control of weapons. Cur Hist 47:103-6+ Ag '64
Projected European union and American military responsibilities; address, April 6, 1963; with questions and answers. Ann Am Acad 348:121-31 Jl '63
KINTSCH, Walter
All-or-none learning and the role of repetition in paired-associate learning. bibliog Science 140:310-12 Ap 19 '63
KINZER, H. M.
Focus on Fritz Henle. Pop Phot 55:142-9+ N '64
Head-hunting. Pop Phot 53:131 N '63
Ideas in images. Pop Phot 52:68-71+ Mr '63
Kinzer on Photography '63 show. Pop Phot 54:28+ F '64
Ten-second pictures. See issues of Popular photography to July 1963
What we all see every day, instants of transfiguration. Pop Phot 54:60-1 Mr '64
KINZUA DAM. See Dams
KIOTO. See Kyoto, Japan
KIPLING, Rudyard
Lonely nationalism of Rudyard Kipling. K. W. Deutsch and N. Wiener. Yale R 52:499-517 Je '63
Rudyard Kipling: he outlives the empire. C. E. Carrington. il por Horizon 6:60-6 Autumn '64
KIPNIS, Igor
Book reviews. Am Rec G 29:477-80 F '63
Looking at the maestro from the front. Am Rec G 30:436-8 Ja '64
about
Introducing Igor Kipnis. J. W. Barker. il por Am Rec G 30:709 Ap '64
KIPPHARDT, Heinar
In the J. Robert Oppenheimer affair. Criticism
Newsweek por 64:93 N 16 '64
Time il 84:70 N 20 '64
KIR, Félix
Reverend mayor of Dijon. il por Time 83:48 Ja 31 '64
KIRBY, Allan P.
Gladder to get out than sorry to lose out. por Time 81:107 Ap 19 '63
Kirby comes home the winner. por Bsns W p 110-11 Jl 13 '63
Kirby's last laugh. Newsweek 62:63-4 Jl 15 '63
Personalities. il por Time 82:88 D 13 '63
Winner by a knockout. por Time 82:88 Jl 12 '63
KIRBY, James C, Jr
Excerpt from statement, January 22, 1964. Cong Digest 43:159 My '64
KIRBY, Minnie Frances
Wax dahlia tubers for longer life. Flower Grower 50:19 N '63

KIRCH, Patti
Return: story. Seventeen 24:38-9 Ja '65
KIRCHENTAG. See Religious conferences
KIRCHER, Donald P.
Now the transnational enterprise. Harvard Bsns R 42:6-8+ Mr '64
about
It's a spryer Singer. E. K. Faltermayer. il por Fortune 68:144-8+ D '63
Personalities. por Time 82:96 O 25 '63
KIRCHOF, R. L.
Just-right purchasing. Am City 79:136+ F '64
KIRK, Donald
How many strings on aid to India? Reporter 29:52-5 Ag 15 '63
KIRK, Grayson
Responsibilities of the educated man; address, April 9, 1964. Vital Speeches 30:471-4 My 15 '64
Toward an Atlantic community; address, February 8, 1963. Vital Speeches 29:293-5 Mr 1 '63
World perspectives, 1964. For Affairs 43:1-13 O '64
about
Columbia explosion. New Yorker 39:31-2 Ap 6 '63
KIRK, J. Earl, and McHale, Paul
Sewer construction takes a dip. Am City 78: 25 Mr '63
KIRK, Lucile D.
Good looks. See issues of Parents' magazine & better homemaking
KIRK, Paul L.
Criminalistics. bibliog Science 140:367-70 Ap 26 '63
KIRK, Philip
Modular metal lab furniture is tailored to specific jobs. Arch Rec 133:173-4+ Ja '63
KIRK, R. S. and Vaišnys, R. J.
Electrical and thermal measurements with Bridgman anvils. bibliog Science 143:1436-7 Mr 27 '64
KIRK, Roland
Finding the lost cord. por Time 82:55 Ag 9 '63
KIRK, Russell
From the academy. See issues of National review
Is Washington too powerful? N Y Times Mag p22+ Mr 1 '64
Letter from Rabat. por Nat R 15:442 N 19 '63
Mind of Barry Goldwater. Nat R 15:149-51 Ag 27 '63
Mood of conservatism. Commonweal 78:297-300 Je 7 '63
To educate the educators. Nat R 15:24-5 Jl 16 '63
about
Conservatism of reflection. J. Chamberlain. Nat R 16:198-9 Mr 10 '64; Reply. J. L. Johnson. 16:294 Ap 7 '64
KIRK, Stanley
Rising from the ashes. il por Bsns W p87+ S 26 '64
KIRKENDALL, Lester A.
He stands in the wings, waiting impatiently for a cue. PTA Mag 58:8 My '64
Sex on the campus: evaded problem. Nation 198:165-7 F 17 '64
KIRKER, James
Bulfinch's houses for Mrs Swan. Antiques 86:442-4 O '64
KIRKHAM, Don. See Jensen, C. R. jt. auth.
KIRKLAND, Douglas
Crisis in beautiful, bewildered Canada. il Look 27:49-55 Ap 9 '63
Keep it fresh! il Pop Phot 52:59+ Je '63
KIRKPATRICK, Dow
Methodists meet in Malaysia. Christian Cent 81:175-6 F 5 '64
KIRKPATRICK, Ken
Income tax tips for photographers. Pop Phot 54:68-9+ Mr '64
KIRKPATRICK, Ralph
Life and times of Ralph Kirkpatrick. E. Helm. por Mus Am 83:34+ Ja '63
KIRKWOOD, Robert C.
Old five-and-ten spreads new wings. il pors Bsns W p58-60+ N 14 '64
KIRKWOOD, Mo.
Consolidate your utility bills. W. H. Pfitzinger. il Am City 78:80-1 Ag '63
KIROV ballet
Balletic view of Distant planet. E. Palatsky. il Sat R 47:60-1 S 26 '64
Dancing that counts. il Time 84:60 S 25 '64
Friendly visit. J. Anderson. il Dance Mag 38: 18-21+ N '64
Leningrad-Kirov ballet. R. Krokover. il Mus Am 84:54+ O '64
Letter from Paris; Russian movie of Tchaikovsky's La Belle au bois dormant. Genêt. New Yorker 40:98+ My 2 '64
Missing magic; engagement at the Metropolitan. il Newsweek 64:78 S 21 '64
Music to my ears; Kirov. I. Kolodin. il Sat R 47:32 O 3 '64
Prince of a Cinderella. I. Kolodin. Sat R 47: 33+ S 26 '64
What ever happened to Prince Charming? second United States tour. D. Hering. il Dance Mag 38:44-8+ N '64
KIRSCH, Robert R.
Obscenity: U.S. style; reprint. ALA Bul 58: 269-72 Ap '64
KIRSCHENBAUM, A. D. and Grosse, A. V.
Barium xenate. bibliog Science 142:580 N 1 '63
KIRSCHKE, Ernest J. and Jolly, W. L.
Reversibility of reaction of potassium with liquid ammonia. bibliog Science 147:45-6 Ja 1 '65
KIRSH, Barbara
Graphics: experiment & discovery. Sch Arts 64:10-12 Ja '65
KIRSTEIN, George G.
Crusade in America. Nation 197:349-50 N 23 '63
Day the ads stopped. Nation 198:555-7 Je 1 '64
Death's darkest feast. Nation 199:409-11 N 30 '64
Letter from San Juan. Nation 197:400-2 D 7 '63
Manpower revolution; call for debate. Nation 198:140-4 F 10 '64
KIRSTEIN, Lincoln
Art books of 1964. Nation 199:470-2, 502-3, 519-22 D 14-28 '64
First night in Minneapolis. Nation 196:437-8 My 25 '63
Ford in its future; grants to New York city ballet and the School of American ballet. Time 82:37 D 27 '63
KIRTLAND'S warblers. See Warblers
KIRTLEY, M. B.
How to get paid for quality hogs. Suc Farm 62:40-1 Ag '64
KIRVAN, John J.
Ostergothenburg revisited. por Cath World 198:308-13 F '64
KISELEV, Evgenii
Obituary
U N Rev por 10:39-40 My '63
KISH, Frances
(ed) See Sullivan, E. Ed Sullivan screens Europe's entertainment
KISIELESKI, Walter E. See Baserga, R. jt. auth.
KISS mama; drama. See Panetta, G.
KISS; story. See Macken, W.
KISSEL, John W.
Nutating annular cage for measuring motor activity. Science 139:1224-5 Mr 22 '63
KISSING
Wayward buss. il Time 82:41 N 8 '63
Yes please, no thanks; excerpt from Boys and other beasts. B. Lang. il McCalls 91: 60+ S '64
KISSING bugs
Village beyond despair; Itacambira, Brazil. T. Armbrister. il Sat Eve Post 236:66-9 N 9 '63
KISSINGER, Henry A.
Coalition diplomacy in a nuclear age. For Affairs 42:525-45 Jl '64
Goldwater and the bomb: wrong questions, wrong answers. Reporter 31:27-8 N 5 '64
NATO's nuclear dilemma. Reporter 28:22-33+ Mr 28; 10 My 9 '63
Strains on the Alliance. For Affairs 41:261-85 Ja '63
KISTIAKOWSKY, George B.
Case for Johnson. por Science 146:380-2 O 16 '64
National academy: public policy group, headed by Kistiakowsky, seems bound for important role; Committee on science and public policy. D. S. Greenberg. Science 141:27-8 Jl 5 '63
KITAGAWA, Daisuke
Appendage in Africa. Christian Cent 80:1210 O 2 '63
Racial strife hinders mission work; excerpts from address. Christian Cent 80:876 Jl 10 '63
KITAJ, Ronald B.
Art news from London. J. Russell. il Art N 62:46+ Mr '63
KITCHEL, Denison
Men behind Goldwater. R. G. Spivack. il por Look 28:45+ N 3 '64
KITCHEN, Hyram, and others
Hemoglobin polymorphism: its relation to sickling of erythrocytes in white-tailed deer. bibliog Science 144:1237-9 Je 5 '64

KITCHEN, Robert
Competition aims to improve kitchen design. Arch Rec 136:352 S '64
KITCHEN cabinets
Best storage ideas we've seen. il Bet Hom & Gard 41:7+ Ap '63
Big idea: roll-out kitchen cabinets. il Pop Sci 183:122 S '63
For kitchen glamour add personalized shades and new cabinet faces. il Bet Hom & Gard 41:46 S '63
How to un-waste space in a kitchen. il Bet Hom & Gard 42:96 D '64
Meticulously planned storage keeps the Lesters' kitchen pleasantly uncluttered. il House & Gard 123:172-4 Mr '63
Recessed pantry for cramped kitchens. H. R. Pfister. il Pop Mech 120:136-7 Jl '63
Revolutionary new cabinet system. N. Craig. il House B 106:174-5 My '64
These cabinets are overlaid plywood. il Sunset 130:156+ Mr '63
KITCHEN clocks, Electric. See Clocks, Electric
KITCHEN desks. See Desks
KITCHEN furniture
Borrow an idea from these three mix centers. J. Gillies. il Farm J 87:74 S '63
Easy kitchen additions. il Good H 158:102-4 Ja '64
Making the most of a window view. il House B 106:124 Ap '64
Pull-out lunch counter. il Sunset 133:102 Jl '64
Serving space where you need it; cook-and-serve area. il Bet Home & Gard 42:128+ N '64
Swing-and-serve kitchen. R. Charles. il Parents Mag 39:78-9+ N '64
Top choices for kitchen counters. Bet Hom & Gard 41:94-5 Je '63
Traveling appliances for dining a la cart or cooking on the spot. Am House 66:74 My '63
You pull it out for breakfast. il Sunset 132:153 My '64
KITCHEN gadgets. See Gadgets
KITCHEN gardening. See Vegetable gardening
KITCHEN knives. See Knives
KITCHEN lighting. See Lighting
KITCHEN ranges. See Stoves
KITCHEN sinks. See Sinks
KITCHEN storage. See Storage in the home
KITCHEN thermometers. See Thermometers, Cooking
KITCHEN utensils
Baking equipment and procedures. il House & Gard 126:184-6 D '64
Barbecue cupboard. il Pop Gard 15:74 Ja '64
Best buys for your kitchen. il House & Gard 124:240-2 O '63
Buyer's guide to outdoor cooking equipment. Am Home 67:78+ My '64
Cheese slicing board has self-storing cutter. il Pop Mech 119:150 Ap '63
Cooking kits. T. Trueblood. il Field & S 68:16+ F '64
Cookware tablemates for Centura settings. il Consumer Rep 29:4 Ja '64
Easy-does-it kitchen helpers. il Good H 158:110-15 Mr '64
Fancy new cooking gadget; spoon-thermometer combination. il Consumer Rep 29:110 Mr '64
Fast and fancy with your slicer. il Bet Hom & Gard 41:107 My '63
Few pointers about griddles. il Redbook 121:74-5+ Je '63
Flame tamer. il House & Gard 124:210 N '63
Give your everyday a lift: work with color. il Farm J 87:66-7+ Je '63
How many kitchen musts do you have? McCalls 90:155 F '63
How to benefit from the intensive use of objects. il House B 105:88-93 Jl '63
Institute reports on new Duranel pots and pans. il Good H 158:6 Mr '64
Lesson on nonstick cookware. McCalls 90:185 My '63
Look what's new to cook in! B. G. Wadsworth. il Parents Mag 39:114 My '64
McCall's dandy dictionary of handy helpers. il McCalls 90:106-7 F '63
Promising presents. il Good H 157:182+ D '63
Quality aluminum cookware. E. M. McCabe. il Parents Mag 39:22+ My '64
Some of the most important things in the kitchen are very small. E. Kinard. il House B 106:172-3 My '64
Star performer; the triple grater. il House & Gard 125:73+ My '64
Take-it-easy news. il McCalls 90:132 My '63
Take stock of your kitchen tools. B. G. Wadsworth. il Parents Mag 39:29 F '64
Tools of the kitchen trade. M. Kaytor. il Look 29:58-9 Ja 26 '65
Tools of the trade; excerpts from Profession: housewife. P. McGinley. il Ladies Home J 80:82+ Mr '63
Treasury of kitchen antiques. il McCalls 91:118-23 O '63
Twenty years with the wrong pan. Am Home 66:76 Jl '63
Two homemades for your house; food slicer. P. McCafferty. il Pop Sci 183:100-1 D '63
Western kitchen. See issues of Sunset
Wife saver; Teflon coating for non-stick pots and pans. il Am Home 67:54-5+ Je '64
Wonderful world of nonstick cookware. il House & Gard 126:52+ S '64
Your second home: planning and equipping your kitchen. il Am Home 67:29 Ap '64

Care

How to season new cookware. Sunset 130:202 Ap '63
KITCHEN ventilators. See Ventilators
KITCHENS
All-electric kitchen. il Good H 158:110-13+ My '64
Another kitchen like all others, except! V. T. Habeeb. il Am Home 66:78+ Jl '63
At its best when it's busiest. il Am Home 67:76-7 D '64
California country kitchen. il McCalls 91:102-3 Je '64
Carrousel kitchen. R. Charles. il Parents Mag 39:69+ Je '64
Color's new role in the kitchen. il House & Gard 125:136-41 Mr '64
Come-sit-by-the-fire kitchen. il Good H 156:120-2+ F '63
Comfortable and convenient with a commanding view of the Pacific. il Am Home 67:76-7 Ap '64
Competition aims to improve kitchen design. Arch Rec 136:352 S '64
Considerate kitchen. il Good H 158:182-3 Ap '64
Cook-together kitchen. il House & Gard 125:114-17+ Ja '64
Designed for small and large scale entertaining. il Am Home 67:68-9 Je '64
Disappearing kitchen. il House & Gard 127:128-31 Ja '65
Eat in the kitchen. il House & Gard 125:124-7 Je '64
Everyone's in the kitchen with mother, but nobody's in her way. J. Gillies. il Farm J 87:73 My '63
Family kitchen; an old favorite with a new look. M. Davidson. il Ladies Home J 80:88-9 Ap '63
Family room into regal kitchen. il House B 105:160-5+ S '63
Fine full life; Edith Head entertains. J. Peter and M. Kaytor. il Look 27:56-9 F 26 '63
Four recipes for kitchens. G. O'Brien. il N Y Times Mag p80-1 Ap 19 '64
Functional kitchen is the hub of the house. V. T. Habeeb. il Am Home 67:74 Mr '64
Gem of compact efficiency. B. Reynolds. il Suc Farm 61:82-3 Ap '63
Handy storage ideas for your kitchen. il Farm J 87:114 F '63
Hospitable kitchen of a distinguished cook. il House & Gard 125:132-3 F '64
H&G designs a kitchen-in-the-round. il House & Gard 126:214-17 O '64
How to camouflage an open kitchen with color. il House & Gard 124:176-7 O '63
How to know a good kitchen when you see one. R. M. Schneider and G. V. Young. il Bet Hom & Gard 41:60-7+ My '63
How to update a kitchen without structural changes. N. Craig. il House B 105:165-9+ S '63
Hub-of-the-house kitchen for lots of cooking. il Farm J 88:70-1 Ja '64
It's all gas! il McCalls 90:152-3 Ag '63
Kitchen designed for easy entertaining. il Am Home 67:80 N '64
Kitchen ideas international! il Bet Hom & Gard 42:46-7 Ag '64
Kitchen in carport. M. Davidson. il Ladies Home J 80:106-7 Mr '63
Kitchen in the center of things. il Am Home 67:76-7 S '64
Kitchen of his own. il House & Gard 124:94-5+ Jl '63
Kitchen planning. G. T. Warren. il Arch Rec 135:25+ mid-My '64
Kitchen prettier than a parlor. il House B 105:77-85+ F '63

KITCHENS—*Continued*
Kitchen that swings. M. Davidson. il Ladies Home J 81:132-4 Mr '64
Kitchen to borrow from. il Am Home 67:86-8 O '64
Kitchens are for cooking; excerpt from Sixpence in her shoe. P. McGinley. Ladies Home J 81:38+ S '64
Kitchens for friend and foe. M. Davidson. il Ladies Home J 80:120-5 O '63
Kitchens then & now; reproductions of paintings. L. Corcos. Good H 157:48-9 O '63
Let your personality show in the kitchen. V. T. Habeeb. il Am Home 66:46-52+ Mr '63
Little extras are a big help; photographs. J. Gillies. Farm J 87:90-1 Mr '63
Little-jewel kitchens. il House & Gard 125: 114-15 Ap '64
More-for-the-money kitchens. il Good H 157: 113-17+ N '63
My control-tower kitchen has its own private sky. il House B 105:68-9+ Jl '63
New again kitchens; How to remodel your kitchen beautifully. il McCalls 90:148-50+ F '63
New cook's tour; World's fair dream kitchens. J. Peter. il Look 28:M10-13 S 8 '64
New ease for a kitchen. il Bet Hom & Gard 41:73 O '63
New island in the kitchen's middle. il Sunset 131:140 O '63
New kitchen in an old house so it's all in wood. il Sunset 133:100-1 O '64
New kitchen is bright, gay, efficient. il Sunset 131:110-12 Jl '63
New style and efficiency for a kitchen. il Bet Home & Gard 41:76-7 O '63
Our fair kitchen. M. Davidson. il Ladies Home J 81:98-9 Jl '64
Our pantry-shelf kitchen: a fresh look at kitchen design. V. T. Habeeb. il Am Home 67:80-2+ Ja '64
Plan for a central location. J. Holmstrand. il Suc Farm 62:82-3 S '64
Plan for a conveniently arranged kitchen. il Suc Farm 62:50-1 Jl '64
Plan for individuality in your kitchen. J. Holmstrand. il Suc Farm 62:72-3 Ag '64
Plan for plenty of work space. J. Holmstrand. il Suc Farm 62:54-5 Je '64
Plan for specialized storage. J. Holmstrand. il Suc Farm 62:76-7 My '64
Ready-made kitchens. il House & Gard 124: 258-9 O '63
Remodeled kitchens that glow with imagination. il House & Gard 123:80-5+ F '63
$700 brings a new look to a well-planned kitchen. il Am Home 67:76-7 My '64
Seven ideas that make these farm kitchens so convenient! J. Gillies. il Farm J 87:48-9 Ag '63
Seven kitchens done over. il Sunset 132:70-80+ F '64
So many fresh ways to go with kitchen color. R. M. Schneider and G. V. Young. il Bet Hom & Gard 41:66-9 Ap '63
So wise for their size. il McCalls 91:140-1 O '63
Special kitchen issue. il House B 106:147-200+ My '64
Step-saver kitchen, handy, roomy and pretty. J. Gillies. il Farm J 88:52-3 Je '64
Swing-and-serve kitchen. R. Charles. il Parents Mag 39:78-9+ N '64
They opened up their old kitchen. il Sunset 130:148 Mr '63
Thirty ways to make work easier in any kitchen. J. Gillies. il Farm J 88:72-4 My '64
This is a very good kitchen remodeling! G. V. Young. il Bet Hom & Gard 42:124+ My '64
This is a very practical kitchen! R. M. Schneider and G. V. Young. il Bet Hom & Gard 41:82-4 N '63
This kitchen was planned to a T. R. M. Schneider. il Bet Hom & Gard 41:80-1 Jl '63
Three families remodel to gain a kitchen office. il Sunset 131:84 Jl '63
Three ideal kitchens. il McCalls 91:136+ S '64
Touch of Dutch in the kitchen. V. T. Habeeb. il Am Home 66:30-1 N '63
Translated from the Chinese. il McCalls 91: 128-9 F '64
Unforgettable kitchens. M. Davidson. il Ladies Home J 80:70-3 Ja '63
Update your kitchen, 1963. J. Gillies and R. Martens. il Farm J 87:35-9+ Je '63
Vacation kitchen. il House & Gard 123:108-11 Je '63
Very enjoyable family kitchen. R. M. Schneider. il Bet Hom & Gard 41:66-7 Ag '63
Wall section simply disappears in this Hawaiian kitchen. il Sunset 132:100-1 Mr '64
Warm, friendly kitchen planned around work centers. J. Gillies. il Farm J 87:84-5 O '63
Way-out-ahead kitchen. N. Craig. il House B 105:208-11+ O '63
We need handy storage for pots and pans. J. Gillies. il Farm J 88:93 Ap '64
We planned the ideal farm kitchen. J. Holmstrand. il Suc Farm 62:99-103 Ap '64
When the cook must keep her eye on young children; kitchen between family room and outdoor play area. il Sunset 132:120-1 Je '64
Where can you go for kitchen design help? J. Holmstrand. il Suc Farm 62:87-91+ O '64
White-glove kitchens. il House & Gard 123: 130-5+ Mr '63
Why be stereotyped in your kitchen? V. T. Habeeb. il Am Home 66:64-5 S '63
Your guide to a better kitchen. R. M. Burnley. il Redbook 120:79-86 F '63
Your second home: planning and equipping your kitchen. il Am Home 67:29 Ap '64

KITCHENS, Outdoor
Build this cook-out counter for your patio. H. Sibley. il Pop Sci 183:110-12 Ag '63

KITCHENS of Sara Lee, incorporated
Programming a cake; computer as head chef. il Bsns W p 154-6+ Mr 14 '64
Saga of Sara Lee. il Newsweek 64:71 S 14 '64

KITES
Go fly a kite. W. Waltner and E. Waltner. il Pop Mech 119:160-4 Mr '63
Kitemaker; photographs. P. Turner. Sports Illus 21:28-35 Ag 3 '64
Man's world; kite fighting in Thailand. il Time 83:96 My 15 '64
Who says flying is for the birds? ski-kite. R. Gannon. il Pop Sci 183:52-3 Ag '63

KITES (birds)
Lonely gourmet of the swamps fights for his life; Everglades kite. G. Cant. il Sports Illus 21:53-5 Ag 10 '64
Protection for Everglade kite; temporary closure of Loxahatchee national wildlife refuge in Florida. Nat Parks Mag 38:18 Jl '64

KITMAN, Jamie L. and Kitman, Suzy
Speaking out. pors Sat Eve Post 237:8+ D 19 '64

KITMAN, Marvin
Be the first on your block to have a ton of steel. Sat Eve Post 237:26-7 Ap 4 '64
I'm in the fight to the last ballot. pors Sat Eve Post 237:22-3 Jl 11 '64
Large, loud mouth of Alan King. Sat Eve Post 237:68+ N 28 '64
My first political crisis. pors Sat Eve Post 237:24-5 Mr 14 '64
My secret Swiss stake. Sat Eve Post 236: 62-3 F 16 '63
One man's search for free silver. por Sat Eve Post 236:78+ O 26 '63
Rich wild life of Milt Kamen. Sat Eve Post 236:75-6 D 14 '63
Year of the bull in worthless Chinese bonds. Sat Eve Post 237:72-3 Ag 22 '64

KITMAN, Suzy. See Kitman, J. L. jt. auth.

KITSINGER, Norine
Japanese technique on pellon. Design 64:104-5 Ja '63

KITT, Olga
Making faces. Sch Arts 63:33 O '63

KITT PEAK national observatory. See Astronomical observatories

KITTEL, Dorothy A.
From the Library services branch. J. G. Lorenz and H. A. Carl. ALA Bul 58:23 Ja '64

KITTELSON, C. E.
Instant police via citizens-band radio. por Am City 78:147 D '63

KITTIKACHORN, Thanom. See Thanom Kittikachorn

KITTLESON, James F.
Denim; poem. Commonweal 78:224 My 17 '63
Rocky Mountain literature. T. R. Madden. Commonweal 78:330 Je 14 '63

KIWANIS clubs
Whitewash in Whitewater; letter to the editor. S. D. Robertson. Library J 89:2900+ Ag '64

KIWI rockets. See Rockets, Atomic powered

KIZER, Carolyn
After Tu Fu: Déjeuner sur l'herbe; Tourist park; poems. Poetry 103:63-5 O '63
Hugh MacDiarmid: hailing us all. Poetry 102:177-81 Je '63
Poets old and young. Poetry 102:393-9 S '63
Thwarted; poem. Poetry 105:163-4 D '64

KIZER, Ken
What is a computer? reprint. Sci Digest 57:75-8 Ja '65

KLABEN, Helen
Couple who wouldn't die. T. Whiteside. il pors Sat Eve Post 236:56-65 Je 22 '63
Fit survive. il por Newsweek 61:27 Ap 8 '63
Girl behind a frozen scream. D. J. Hamblin and W. Jarvis. il pors Life 54:68B-73+ Ap 12 '63
How long people can last without food. il por U S News 54:20 Ap 8 '63
—and Day, Beth
Hey, I'm alive! excerpt. pors Good H 158: 52-5+ Ja '64
KLABER, Doretta
Edging plants that are different and easy. il Pop Gard 15:34 Ap '64
Gentians for your garden. Horticulture 41:606-7; 42:16-17 D '63, Ja '64
Snowflake or snowdrop? Pop Gard 15:23 F '64
Try quick groundcovers where grass is slow. Pop Gard 15:70+ Jl '64
Waterside plants. Pop Gard 14:45+ Ap '63
KLABIN, Israel
Rothschilds of the south. por Time 81:80 Je 28 '63
Who's who in foreign business. por Fortune 67:64 Mr '63
KLAINER, Albert S. and others
Staphylococcal alpha-hemolysin: detection on the erythrocyte membrane by immunofluorescence. bibliog Science 145:714-15 Ag 14 '64
KLAMATH MOUNTAINS
Afoot or on horseback; exploring the heartland of California's Salmons. il Sunset 133: 30-2+ Jl '64
KLAMATH RIVER
Klamath offers some easy drifting. il Sunset 133:30-2+ S '64
Steelheading at Ishi Pishi. il Sunset 130:48+ F '63
KLAPPROTH, W. H.
Electronics de-irritate an intersection. por Am City 78:86-7 Jl '63
KLARMAN, Herbert E.
Whadda ya mean, hospital? New Repub 149:9-12 N 9 '63
KLASSEN, Frank
Teacher education in Ethiopia. Sch & Soc 91:96-8 F 23 '63
KLAUSLER, Alfred P.
Beecher lectures. Christian Cent 80:1206 O 2 '63
First-person poignancy. Christian Cent 81:1042 Ag 19 '64
Let us praise poets. Christian Cent 80:369-70 Mr 20 '63
Radiation and social ethics. Christian Cent 80:199-200 F 13 '63
Time bomb. Christian Cent 80:1612-13 D 25 '63
KLAW, Spencer
Englewood, New Jersey: visitors in the classroom. Reporter 29:14-17 Jl 4 '63
Field guide to government jargon. Reporter 30:52 Ja 30 '64
Harvard's Skinner. Harper 226:45-51 Ap '63
Letter from an old locomotive. Reporter 31: 18+ O 22 '64
Nationalization of U.S. science. Fortune 70: 158-60+ S '64
Old Scratchhead wakes up in Chester, Pennsylvania. Reporter 30:31-4 Je 18 '64
Soap wars: a strategic analysis. Fortune 67: 122-5+ Je '63
KLAW, Susan
Life; poem. Horn Bk 39:331 Je '63
KLEBERG, Tonnes
Cooperation in acquisitions. por Library J 88:4319-22 N 15 '63
KLEE, Manfred R. and Offenloch, Kurt
Postsynaptic potentials and spike patterns during augmenting responses in cat's motor cortex. bibliog Science 143:488-9 Ja 31 '64
KLEE, Margaret
Penelope; story. Mlle 57:238-9 Ag '63
KLEE, Paul
Escape from style; the Diaries of Paul Klee. K. Kuh. il Sat R 47:26-7 N 28 '64
Landmarks of modern art. K. Kuh. il Sat R 46:34 F 2 '63
Paul Klee, by F. Klee. Review
Sat R 46:37-8 Mr 9 '63 H. Rosenberg
Psychic penmanship. por Time 84:70 Ja 1 '65
Self-probings of a master artist. R. A. Welchans. Commonweal 81:545 Ja 22 '65
Swiss behind the colors. A. H. Mayor. Nation 199:414-15 N 30 '64
KLEEBERG, Fred
What production asks of management. Pub W 183:83-5 My 6 '63
KLEEBERG, Fred M.
Columbia's 1903 grand opera series. Am Rec G 29:772-5 Je '63
KLEIBER, Erich
Erich Kleiber dirigiert. H. Glass. por Am Rec G 29:855 Jl '63
KLEIHAUER, Aylsworth
Science does not travel alone. il Sch Arts 62:29-32 My '63
KLEIMAN, Robert
What France is out to get. Read Digest 84: 100-4 Ja '64
KLEIN, Anna Lou
Let's lower sights and raise the caliber of student writing. NEA J 53:17-18 N '64
KLEIN, B. H. and others
Report favors prototype development. Aviation W 78:135+ Je 10 '63
KLEIN, Carole. See Lazar, E. jt. auth.
KLEIN, Cornelis, Jr. See Marvin, U. B. jt. auth.
KLEIN, David
Can you predict which boy will drive you home safely? Seventeen 23:134-5+ Mr '64
Plotting your course through college. Seventeen 23:114-15 Ap '64
What do I say next? Seventeen 23:124-5+ O '64
When your teen-ager starts to drive. Ladies Home J 81:25+ My '64
Where is the ivy greenest? Seventeen 22: 142-3+ Ap '63
Who are you going to be this year. Seventeen 22:200-1+ Ag '63
KLEIN, Elaine
Moving day; drama. Plays 23:37-44, 70 My '64
KLEIN, Elinor, and Giddon, Franklin
Crashing off your diet. Mlle 59:112-13+ My '64
KLEIN, Erwin
Champ of the chop and loop. B. La Fontaine. il por Sports Illus 20:54-6+ My 11 '64
KLEIN, Eva. See Klein, G. jt. auth.
KLEIN, George, and Klein, Eva
Antigenic behavior of Moloney lymphomas: independence of virus release and immunosensitivity. bibliog Science 145:1316-17 S 18 '64
KLEIN, H. Arthur
Hold on life. Nation 196:123-4 F 9 '63
KLEIN, Herb
Night belongs to the tiger. Field & S 68: 38-40+ S '63
KLEIN, Herbert E.
Automation on the assembly line. Duns R 84:37-8+ D '64
Computer in the boardroom. Duns R 84:pt2 102-3+ S '64
Cultural lag in manufacturing. Duns R 82: 37-8+ Ag '63
Detroit: proving ground for new technology. Duns R 83:49-50+ Ap '64
Golden key to production profits. Duns R 81:50-2+ Ap '63
Inside industry. See issues of Dun's review and modern industry to April 1963
Missing links in automation. Duns R 81:38-41 F '63
More value for the office dollar. Duns R 82:pt2 116-18+ S '63
New power on the production line. Duns R 83:43-5+ F '64
Production's new brew. Duns R 82:38-40+ O '63
Quiet revolution in mixed materials. Duns R 84:32-3+ Ag '64
Test it, but don't break it. Duns R 83:50-2+ Ja '64
Wonder industrial adhesives. Duns R 84: 53-4+ O '64
KLEIN, Howard S.
Too much, too soon, a study in timing. Pub W 185:124-5 Je 8 '64
KLEIN, Irwin
Discovery. P. Caulfield. il Mod Phot 28:70-1+ Ag '64
KLEIN, Jerry
Quiz for April 1. Read Digest 84:204F+ Ap '64
KLEIN, Lawrence R.
International labor conference of 1963. Mo Labor R 86:914-19 Ag '63
KLEIN, Michael. See Gelboin, H. V. jt. auth.
KLEIN, N. W. and Pierro, L. J.
Actinomycin D: specific inhibitory effects on the explanted chick embryo. bibliog Science 142:967-9 N 15 '63
KLEIN, Ralph. See Scheer, M. D. jt. auth.
KLEIN, Stanley
Hiroshima eyewitnesses. Christian Cent 80: 1108-9 S 11 '63
KLEIN, Walter J.
Take a surprise vacation. Redbook 124:28+ D '64
KLEIN, William
William Klein. P. Caulfield. il Mod Phot 29:84-9 Ja '65

KLEIN, Woody
Crime in the streets. Nation 200:30-1 Ja 11 '65
Ghetto ignites. Nation 199:49-51 Ag 10 '64
People vs. politicians: defeat in Harlem. Nation 199:27-9 Jl 27 '64

KLEINMANN, Jack H.
Merit pay; the big question. NEA J 52:42-4 My '63
—and others
Fringe benefits for teachers. NEA J 52:17-18 N '63

KLEINMUNTZ, Benjamin
Personality test interpretation by digital computer. Science 139:416-18 F 1 '63

KLEINSCHMIDT, Albrecht K. and others
Electron microscopy of the replicative form of the DNA of the bacteriophage ØX174. bibliog Science 142:961 N 15 '63

KLEMPERER, Otto
Klemperer's Bruckner: two views. J. Diether; C. J. Luten. Am Rec G 29:446-7 F '63

KLEMPERER, Wolfgang B.
Solar eclipse from a jet. por Nat Geog Mag 124:784-96 N '63

KLEYDORFF, Ludwig V.
Thorough approach to foreign markets; address, June 18, 1963. Vital Speeches 29:631-3 Ag 1 '63

KLIEVER, Lonnie D.
Justice and love in the racial crisis. Christian Cent 81:1055-7 Ag 26 '64

KLIEWER, Warren
Art and the religious community. Christian Cent 80:1605-7 D 25 '63
Riot of the relics; poem. Christian Cent 81:171 F 5 '64
Variations on a theme by Paul Tillich; poem. Christian Cent 82:79 Ja 20 '65

KLIMESH, Cy
Try posterization. U S Camera 26:60-1 Ag '63

KLINE, Dale R.
Sir, the word is moral! Christian Cent 81:455-8 Ap 8 '64

KLINE, Franz
Art galleries; memorial exhibition at Sidney Janis gallery. R. M. Coates. New Yorker 39:70-2 D 21 '63

KLINE, George
Pair that got hooked hunts specimens in distant reefs. il por Life 57:54A Jl 10 '64

KLINE, Harry
Charting the Bahamas. Yachting 114:58-60+ N '63

KLINE, Mary
Pair that got hooked hunts specimens in distant reefs. il por Life 57:54A Jl 10 '64

KLINE, Morris
Geometry; with biographical sketch. Sci Am 211:28, 60-9 bibliog(p269) S '64

KLINE, Nathan S.
Lift from depression. il por Time 84:106 N 27 '64
Quick lift for depression; hydroxytryptophane injection. Time 82:48 S 6 '63
Second first. Newsweek 64:101 N 23 '64
What tranquilizers have done. il por Time 83:43-4 Ap 24 '64

KLINEBERG, Otto
Life is fun in a smiling, fair-skinned world. bibliog Sat R 46:75-7+ F 16 '63

KLINEBURGER, Bert
Dateline walrus. por Field & S 67:23-5 F '63

KLINGENDER, A. K.
He keeps the bacteria jumping. Sat R 47:51-2 My 2 '64

KLINGER, Paul D. See Agranoff, B. W. jt. auth.

KLINGHAMMER, Erich, and Hess, E. H.
Imprinting in an altricial bird: the blond ring dove streptopelia risoria. bibliog Science 146:265-6 O 9 '64

KLINGLER, Annemarie
Public ugliness is not necessary. House B 106:96-9+ Jl '64

KLINMAN, N. R. and others
Valence and affinity of equine nonprecipitating antibody to a haptenic group. bibliog Science 146:401-3 O 16 '64

KLOKKE, Karl
Knockdown! Yachting 117:73+ Ja '65

KLONSKY, Milton
Squash & stretch. Esquire 60:162-3+ D '63

KLONSKY, Robert
L.A. paperback store in full operation after fire; Book fair in Westwood Village, Los Angeles. Pub W 185:238 Ja 27 '64

KLOPFER, Peter H.
Imprinting: a reassessment. bibliog Science 147:302-3 Ja 15 '65
—and Hailman, J. P.
Perceptual preferences and imprinting in chicks. bibliog Science 145:1333-4 S 18 '64

KLOPSTEG, Paul E.
Justifying basic research. Science 147:11 Ja 1 '65
Potpourri and gallimaufry. Science 140:594-8 My 10 '63

KLOSE, Virginia Taylor
Mother of the groom. Ladies Home J 81:120 My '64

KLOSSOWSKI, Balthus. See Balthus

KLOSTERMAN, Earle W.
What about silage additives? Suc Farm 61:43 Ag '63

KLOTS, Alexander B.
Monarch's emergence. Natur Hist 73:50-3 My '64
On the character of color. Natur Hist 72:30-9 Je '63

KLOTSCHE, J. Martin
Promise and fulfillment of American democracy; address, September 23, 1963. Vital Speeches 30:14-17 O 15 '63

KLUGE, P. F.
Life music review. Life 57:28 O 2 '64

KLUGER, Richard
Less rural, more wistful America. Harper 230:94-7 Ja '65

KLUNDER, Bruce W.
My husband died for democracy. Mrs B. W. Klunder. il pors Ebony 19:27-30+ Je '64
Placing our bodies. . . il Newsweek 63:34 Ap 20 '64
We are dedicated. il Time 83:36 Ap 17 '64

KLUNDER, Mrs Bruce W.
My husband died for democracy. pors Ebony 19:27-30+ Je '64

KLUSMANN, Charles F.
Mysterious Pentagon. il por Newsweek 64:33 S 14 '64

KLUTNICK, Philip M.
Five challenges to our cities. Arch Forum 120:106-8 My '64

KNACK; drama. See Jellicoe, A.

KNAKE, Ellery, and Feight, J. J.
Now you can control quackgrass. Suc Farm 62:61 S '64

KNAPP, Arthur, Jr
Importance of starts. por Yachting 115:106-8+ Ja '64

KNAPP, Harold A. Jr
Planning for civil defense: five requirements. Bul Atomic Sci 19:39-41+ Ap '63

KNAPP, Patricia B.
Library as a way to excellence in education. por ALA Bul 57:1039-42 D '63

KNAPP, Pauline Park Wilson. See Osborn, D. K. jt. auth.

KNAPP, Robert P. Jr
Best-laid plans. Reporter 28:47-8 Je 20 '63
Captive commanders. Reporter 31:42+ Jl 16 '64
Marshall: who was he? Reporter 29:60+ N 21 '63
Our wandering course in the flowery kingdom. bibliog Reporter 30:48-9+ Mr 12; 6 Ap 23 '64
World turned upside down. Reporter 28:54-5 My 23 '63

KNAPP, William
Should girls go to college? Reporter 20:60+ O 10 '63

KNAPP foundation
Caught Knapping; two winners of grants. R. L. Chisolm. Library J 88:3272-3 S 15 '63
Immediate applications invited for phase two of Knapp project. Library J 88:3573 O 1 '63
Knapp project names three schools in second phase of five year program. Library J 89:2160 My 15 '64
Knapp project names two schools in first phase of 5-year goal. Library J 88:3276 S 15 '63
Knapp-sack of progress; visits to two schools selected for Knapp school libraries project. P. Sullivan. il Wilson Lib Bul 39:392-6 Ja '65
Librarian's dream come true; Knapp school libraries project, Marcus Whitman elementary school, Richland, Wash. P. Sullivan. il NEA J 53:46-7 S '64
Peggy Anne Sullivan. E. Rudin. Library J 88:1287 Mr 15 '63
Phase 1 of Knapp project under way; applicants must apply by April first. Library J 88:841 F 15 '63
Underway: the Knapp project's first year. P. Sullivan. Library J 89:2143-5 My 15 '64

KNAPP school libraries project. See American association of school librarians

KNAPPSTEIN, K. Heinrich
Investing in Europe. Reporter 32:10 Ja 28 '65
Projected European union and the question of German unity. Ann Am Acad 348:73-81 Jl '63

KNAPSACKS
Backpacking the Grand Canyon. C. Fletcher. il Field & S 68:33-7+ Mr '64
KNAUSS, John A.
Oceanography. Science 142:418+ O 18 '63
—and Taft, B. A.
Equatorial undercurrent of the Indian Ocean. bibliog Science 143:354-6 Ja 24 '64
KNAUTH, Percy
Makers of the sports page. Sports Illus 19:34-6+ S 16 '63
KNEBEL, Fletcher
After the shots: the ordeal of Lyndon Johnson. Look 28:26-8+ Mr 10 '64
Bobby Kennedy: he hates to be second. Look 27:91-4+ My 21 '63
Campaign and the candidates. Look 28:23-5 N 3 '64
Goldwater. Look 27:36-7 O 8 '63
Governor Romney: why the Republican pros distrust him. Look 28:75-7 Mr 10 '64
Lyndon Johnson: trained for power. Look 27:20-3 D 31 '63
One man's triumph. Look 28:97-8+ O 6 '64
One vote for the convention system. N Y Times Mag p21+ Ag 23 '64
Race riots: Goldwater boon. Look 28:34+ S 22 '64
Scarlett O'Hara's millions. Look 27:39-40+ D 3 '63
Seven days in May: the movie the military shunned. Look 27:90-5 N 19 '63
Story of the Presidents at Christmas. Look 27:16-19 D 31 '63
Traitor to my class. pors Look 28:32+ Ag 25 '64
Unknown JFK; work-a-day politican. Look 28:46+ N 17 '64
—and Bailey, C. W.
Fight over the A-bomb. pors Look 27:19-23 Ag 13 '63
(ed) See Goldwater, B. M. Goldwater speaks
KNEBELKAMP, Wathen Regel
Soft sell brings a million-dollar gate. il por Sports Illus 18:21 My 6 '63
KNEE
Anatomy for the ballet teacher; ed. by W. Como. R. Gelabert. il Dance Mag 37:53-5 My; 62-3 Je; 142-4 D '63
KNELLER, George F.
Analytic philosophy and educational thought; excerpt from Foundations of education. bibliog f Sch & Soc 91:61+ F 9 '63
KNESSL, Lothar
Tempest in a coffee pot. Mus Am 84:68-9 Ja '64
KNICKERBOCKER, Suzy. pseud. See Mehle, A.
KNIFE sharpeners, Electric. See Electric apparatus and appliances, Domestic
KNIFE sharpening. See Sharpening
KNIGHT, Arthur
Bloom in the cultural desert. Sat R 47:43-5 D 26 '64
Flip side. Sat R 46:20 D 28 '63
My second-fare lady. Dance Mag 38:30-2 D '64
Ripple effect. Sat R 46:60-1 O 12 '63
SR goes to the movies. See issues of Saturday review
Travels with Charlie and friends. Sat R 47:45 O 10 '64
What golden years? Sat R 47:169-71 Ag 29 '64
KNIGHT, Bob
Hunting a new movie target? U S Camera 27:72-3 Jl '64
KNIGHT, Doug
Headlong bears. pors Outdoor Life 133:36-9+ Mr '64
Warden's way. Field & S 69:46-7+ Je '64
KNIGHT, Douglas Maitland
Duke and Knight. il por Newsweek 62:61 S 9 '63
New Duke. il por Time 82:90-1 S 13 '63
KNIGHT, Hilary
Whimsical illustrations of Hilary Knight. J. H. Michel. il Am Artist 27:49-53+ Mr '63
KNIGHT, John Alden
Tarpon are sissies. Field & S 69:30-1+ Ja '65
KNIGHT, Samuel Howell
Farewell, groves of academe. por Time 82:80 Jl 12 '63
KNIGHT, Sidney E.
Gardening in South Africa. Pop Gard 14:63-4 Mr '63
KNIGHT, W. Rea, and others
Acetophenazine and fighting behavior in mice. bibliog Science 141:830-1 Ag 30 '63
KNIGHTS must fall; story. See Preston, B. B.
KNIGHTS of Columbus
Extending the dialogue. America 111:224 S 5 '64
Knights again. America 110:214 F 15 '64; Reply. R. J. Coates. 110:354 Mr 21 '64
K. of C. blackballing. America 111:26 Ag 8 '64; Discussion. 111:242, 430; 112:93-5 S 12, O 17 '64, Ja 23 '65
K. of C. integration. America 110:179 F 8 '64
K. of C.'s and race. America 109:693 N 30 '63
KNIPHOFIA. See Torch lilies
KNISELEY, Ralph M.
Radioisotope scanning. Science 145:416+ Jl 24 '64
KNISKERN, Maynard
Clues to the midwestern mind. N Y Times Mag p33+ S 15 '63
KNIT goods
Right care for knitwear. Good H 158:164 F '64
KNITTING
See also
Knit goods
KNITTING machinery. See Textile machinery
KNIVES
Care and keeping of knives. il House & Gard 124:180 S '63
Cook's guide to cutlery. R. M. Burnley. il Redbook 122:76-7+ Mr '64
Electric-powered carving knives a luxury or a real convenience for modern living? il Consumer Bul 48:27-9 Ja '65
Electric slicing knives. il Consumer Rep 29:547-9 N '64
Electrifying sales; electric slicing knife. il Bsns W p53 Mr 2 '63
From African anvils. L. Siroto. il Horizon 6:122-4 Sum '64
General electric's powerful snickersnee electric slicing knife. il Consumer Rep 28:316 Jl '63
Get a good knife. E. Gaydn. il Outdoor Life 132:54-5+ N '63
Good ways to sharpen knives. Good H 156:152 Je '63
Helpful pointers on knives for outdoorsmen. K. Warner. il Pop Sci 186:120-3+ Ja '65
Kitchen knives, points to check before you buy. il Changing T 17:37-8 My '63
Knife. M. Moore. House & Gard 123:98-9+ F '63
Now, carve with power. J. H. Ingersoll. il Pop Sci 185:148-9 D '64
Paring knives. il Consumer Bul 46:22-4 S '63
Sharp! electric slicing knife and electric sharpener. il McCalls 92:76 N '64
KNIVES, Stone. See Stone implements and weapons
KNOBCONE pine. See Pine
KNOCK, Florence
Minnesota hydrosome. Horticulture 41:407 Ag '63
KNOCKE, Fred J.
Go to the show and take your dahlias too. Flower Grower 51:34+ Ag '64
KNOEBEL, Robert M.
Plan for teaching teachers of data processing. por Sch Life 46:7-10 D '63
KNOEDLER company. See Art dealers
KNOLL, Erwin, and Stern, Laurence
Closing the books on Baker. Reporter 30:17-20 Ap 9 '64
—See Stern, L. jt. auth.
KNOOP, A. Peter
How to succeed at a dog show without really cheating. H. Horn. il por Sports Illus 18:35-7 F 11 '63
KNOPF, Alfred A. 1892-
Publishing then and now 1912-1964; excerpts from address, October 21, 1964. por Pub W 186:20-6 N 23 '64; Library J 89:4312-14 N 1 '64; Sat R 47:21-3+ N 21; 17+ N 28 '64
about
Historians honor Alfred A. Knopf. il por Pub W 187:277-8 Ja 25 '65
Publisher to an era. J. Tebbel. Sat R 47:131-3+ Ag 29 '64
KNOTS and splices
Basic monofilament knots. W. Davis. il Outdoor Life 131:74 F '63
If you can't tie it. . , nail it! A. J. McClane. il Field & S 69:42-5 Jl '64
Knots every angler should know; drawings. H. G. Tapply. Field & S 67:52 F '63
Know your ropes. J. A. Emmett. il Outdoor Life 134:96+ N '64
To seize is not to knot. G. S. Smith. il Motor B 113:266 Ja '64
KNOTT, John C.
Father O'Brien's article. America 109:225 S 7 '63
KNOTT, Walter
One man's crusade for everybody's freedom. F. J. Taylor. Read Digest 84:139-42 Je '64

KNOWLAND, William F.
Real strength of our nation; address, July 15, 1963. Vital Speeches 29:682-6 S 1 '63

KNOWLEDGE
Advancing the frontiers of human knowledge for the benefit of all mankind; remarks, January 18, 1964. L. B. Johnson. Dept State Bul 50:150-2 F 3 '64
Automation of knowledge; address, April 19, 1964. L. Mumford. Vital Speeches 30:441-6 My 1 '64
Fact and fancy; fashion for facts. E. Wesimiller. Atlan 212:93-5 O '63
Knowledge: the biggest growth industry of them all. G. Burck. il Fortune 70:128-31+ N '64
Laugh or perish! appeal for scholarly sanity. R. G. Gruenler. Christian Cent 80:204-5 F 13 '63
Production and distribution of knowledge in the United States, by F. Machlup. Review Science 140:473-4 My 3 '63. R. R. Nelson
See also
Education
Intellect
Research
Science
Truth

Anecdotes, facetiae, satire, etc.

Half-life begins at thirty. A. B. C. Atlan 214: 109 Ag '64

KNOWLEDGE; story. See Berkowitz, D.

KNOWLEDGE, Theory of
See also
Reality

KNOWLES, Everett, Jr
He takes a grip on life; boy who made medical history puts his sewed-on arm to work. J. Howard. il pors Life 55:29-30+ Ag 2 '63
Look who's on first! por Time 81:66 My 31 '63

KNOWLES, Harry
Radar vs. speeding. pors Am City 79:119 Ap '64

KNOWLES, Jocelyn W.
Lessons with Carmelita Maracci. Dance Mag 38:38-41 My '64

KNOWLES, John
Hussein; portrait of a king. Holiday 33:84-5+ Mr '63
In the light of the Aegean. Horizon 6:98-104 Spr '64
Melina the Greek. Holiday 35:101+ Ja '64
Petra: the city of stone. Holiday 34:42+ N '63
Road to Jerusalem. Holiday 34:52+ D '63

about

WLB biography. N. Morgan. por Wilson Lib Bul 39:343+ D '64

KNOWLES, John H.
Mental disease and the urban hospital. Atlan 214:107-11 Jl '64

KNOWLES, Ruth Sheldon
Communism's failure in Cuba; an on-the-ground report; reprint. pors U S News 54: 66-8 Je 17 '63

KNOWLTON, Perry
He likes to cook. Bet Hom & Gard 42:97 Je '64

KNOWLTON, Robert A.
Come home to us now; story. Good H 158: 100-1 Je '64
Counterfeit castle; story. McCalls 90:102-3 Ap '63
First gift, first love; story. Good H 157: 62-3 D '63
Man who understood women; story. Good H 157:62-3 Ag '63
Perfect match; story. Good H 158:98-9 My '64
Small hotel; story. Good H 156:78-9 Ap '63
To call my own; story. Good H 157:54-5 Jl '63
Trouble with trouble. Writer 76:15-16+ Je '63

KNOX, Bernard
Archaeological buff. New Repub 150:19-21 Ap 25 '64

KNOX, Bob, and Knox, Wilma
Pamper your camp gear. Pop Mech 120:111-13+ S '63

KNOX, Bruce E.
Science advisory staffs for House and Senate; letter. Science 141:593 Ag 16 '63

KNOX, Cameron. See Haeff, A. V. jt. auth.

KNOX, Ernie
Last fight. Newsweek 62:88 O 28 '63

KNOX, John
Great confrontations: Mary, queen of Scots and John Knox. H. R. Trevor-Roper. il por Horizon 5:28-32 Jl '63

KNOX, John, 1900-
Greatest missionary: Paul. Life 57:112-20+ D 25 '64

KNOX, Lucy
Conservation in a Girl scout camp. Nat Parks Mag 37:14-16 N '63

KNOX, R. G.
Interstate highway system. Motor T 15:118-21 N '63

KNOX, Rawle
Uneasy truce among Nehru's heirs. Reporter 31:19-21 Jl 2 '64
Updating the Indian army. Reporter 31:36-8 O 8 '64

KNOX, W. T.
Librarians and technical literature; letter. Science 142:9+ O 4 '63

KNOX, Wilma. See Knox, B. jt. auth.

KNOX, FORT. See Fort Knox

KNOX gelatin company
Unflavored gelatine and the family that made it famous. E. M. McCabe. il Parents Mag 39:16+ Ap '64

KNOXVILLE, Tenn.
Hopeful dialogue of the races. W. Dykeman and J. Stokely. il N Y Times Mag p 10+ Ag 11 '63
Mommy, do white puppies like us? Project friendship. G. McMillan. il Good H 157:64+ O '63

City planning

Award winning mall. J. J. Duncan. Am City 79:74-5 N '64

KNUDSEN, Edwin J
Midwest is dinghy country, too. Motor B 112: 39 Ag '63
Midwest watch. Motor B 112:92 O '63; 113: 173 Mr; 124+ Ap; 66+ My; 114:99+ Jl; 116+ S; 126-8 O; 122 N; 78-9 D '64; 115:234 Ja '65

KNUDSEN, Kathleen
On the magnanimity of God; poem. Sat R 47:6 Mr 7 '64

KNUDSEN, Thomas W.
Importance of drawing in high school. il Sch Arts 62:36-8 Je '63

KNUDSEN, Vern O.
Architectural acoustics; with biographical sketch. Sci Am 209:30, 78-92 bibliog(p 187) N '63

KNUDSON, James K.
Storm warnings for those who would proceed. Ann Am Acad 345:32-8 Ja '63

KNUTSON, Robert C.
To a minister, sacked and gone; poem. Christian Cent 80:804 Je 19 '63

KNUTTI, Ralph E.
Youthful science of aging. Todays Health 42:16-19+ Je '64

KO, Teck Kin
Chinese big shots branch out. il por Fortune 70:60 D '64

KOBAK, James B.
How to use accounting. Pub W 183:26-7 My 20 '63

KOBAYASHI, Hideshi, and others
Cholinergic substance in the caudal neurosecretory storage organ of fish. bibliog Science 141:714-16 Ag 23 '63

KOBLER, John
Crime town USA. Sat Eve Post 236:71-5 Mr 9 '63
Dangerous magic of LSD. Sat Eve Post 236: 30-2+ N 2 '63
First tycoon. Sat Eve Post 238:28-32+ Ja 16 '65
Priest who haunts the Catholic world. Sat Eve Post 236:42-51 O 12 '63
Who stole the formula? Sat Eve Post 236: 82+ Je 29 '63

KOBLICK, Freda
Plastics in perspective; interview. il Craft Horiz 23:38-41+ Mr '63

KOBUK RIVER, Alaska
There's a way to ride a river; probing the Kobuk's arctic wilderness. S. McCutcheon. il Pop Mech 119:107-9+ My '63

KOBULNICKY, Mike
Marshmallow becomes a man. il pors Life 57:58-65 Ag 7 '64

KOCH, Adrienne
Strange New World. New Repub 151:30+ N 28 '64

KOCH, Charles W. See Williamson, S. M. jt. auth.

KOCH, Dorothy C.
Class trip. NEA J 53:17-20 Ap '64

KOCH, John
New York at 6:30 p.m. D. Parker. il Esquire 62:96-101 N '64

KOCH, Kenneth
Verse. L. Bogan. New Yorker 39:210-11 O 12 '63

KOCH, Lauge
Land of silence, fascination and beauty; excerpt from Arctic Riviera. Natur Hist 72: 46-55 Mr '63

KOCH, Peter
Muslims, too. America 110:326 Mr 14 '64
KOCH, Robert
Doctor Koch and the boiled potato. il por Todays Health 41:77 D '63
Momentous look into the microscope; March 24, 1882. il por UNESCO Courier 17:8-10 Ap '64
KOCH, Theodora
Slavic stamp. Opera N 28:6-7 F 29 '64
KOCHER-BECKER, Ursula, and others
Exovagination of newt endoderm: cell affinities altered by the mesodermal inducing factor. bibliog Science 147:167-9 Ja '65
KOCZY, Friedrich F. See Bader, R. G. jt. auth.
KODACHROME films. See Photography—Films
KODALITH ortho film. See Photography—Films
KODIAK bears. See Bears
KOECKERT quartet. See String quartets
KOEGLER, Horst
Great opera houses: Hamburg. Opera N 28: 26-8 D 14 '63
Trials and triumphs in Stuttgart. Dance Mag 39:37-9+ Ja '65
KOELBEL, William H.
Foil-borne ferry approved by Coast guard. Motor B 111:72+ F '63
Great American sailboats: Erin. Motor B 114: 54+ Ag '64
Seagoing ketch Jonquil. Motor B 111:152+ Je '63
KOELLA, Werner P. and Ferry, A.
Cortico-subcortical homestasis in the cat's brain. bibliog Science 142:586-9 N 1 '63
KOELLE, George B. and others
Anticholinesterase agents. Science 141:63-5 Jl 5 '63
KOELREUTERIA paniculata. See Goldenrain trees
KOELSCHE, Charles L. See Brogdon, W. M. jt. auth.
KOEN, Ann L. See Shaw, C. R. jt. auth.
KOENIG, Franziskus, cardinal
Austria's Cardinal at the council; interview, ed. by W. M. Abbott. America 108:671-2 My 11 '63
KOENIG, Louis W.
American politics: the first half-century. Cur Hist 47:193-8+ O '64
Codes of ethics; all honorable men. Nation 198:551-4 Je 1 '64
Floor plans for both the Houses. Sat R 47: 29-30 Je 13 '64
If he hesitates, all may be lost. Sat R 46:50-1 S 28 '63
More power to the President (not less) N Y Times Mag p7+ Ja 3 '65
Most unpopular man in the North. Am Heritage 15:12-15+ F '64
No time left to legislate. Sat R 47:41-2 F 1 '64
KOENIGSBERGER, Guy
He likes to cook. por Bet Hom & Gard 41:80 Je '63
KOERNER, James D.
Education of teachers; address, February 14, 1963. Vital Speeches 29:412-16 Ap 15 '63
Findings and prejudices in teacher education; excerpt from The miseducation of American teachers. bibliog f Sch & Soc 92:127-34 Mr 21 '64
How not to teach teachers. Atlan 211:59-63 F '63
Speaking out. por Sat Eve Post 236:8+ Je 1 '63
about
Doctor Conant's bombshell. F. M. Hechinger. Reporter 29:44-6 S 26 '63
KOESTLER, Arthur
Aesthetics of snobbery; excerpt from Act of creation. Horizon 7:50-3 Wint '65
Eureka process; excerpt from Act of creation. Horizon 6:16-25 Autumn '64
Her course is set. Life 57:63+ S 11 '64; Same abr. with title Japan; where East equals West. Read Digest 85:97-100 D '64
KOFFAN, Károly
Ways of a parasitic bird. il Natur Hist 72:48-51 Je '63
KOFORD, Carl B.
Rank of mothers and sons in bands of rhesus monkeys. bibliog Science 141:356-7 Jl 26 '63
KOFRANEK, Anton M.
Designing and planting your atrium garden. Am Home 66:77-8 S '63
KOFYAR (native race) See Nigeria—Native races
KOGAN, Irving Smith
When you speak for the trade. Sat R 46: 52-3 F 9; 78 Ap 13 '63
KOGEN, James H.
Distortion in phono cartridges. Electr World 72:28 Ag '64
KOHLER, Elizabeth Jan
I believe; ed. by A. Armstrong. por Seventeen 23:166 Je '64
KOHLER, Foy D.
Ambassador Kohler makes Fourth of July address on Moscow TV; tr. of address. Dept State Bul 51:108-9 Jl 27 '64
U.S. and U.S.S.R. sign agreement on exchanges for 1964-65; remarks, February 22, 1964. Dept State Bul 50:451-2 Mr 23 '64
about
What Soviet broadcasts say about the U.S. now. U S News 56:6 My 18 '64
KOHLER, Mary Conway, and Fontaine, André
Are you cheating your child out of a living? Good H 157:76-7+ S '63
KOHLER company
Without due process; National labor relations board against Kohler company. Nat R 15:141 Ag 27 '63
KOHLMAN, Alan
The 1,000. Nation 198:662-3 Je 29 '64
KOHLRABI
Two-flavored vegetable. L. K. Lantz. il Flower Grower 50:32 Ap '63
KOHN, Alan J.
Mollusks. Science 145:518-19 Jl 31 '64
KOHN, Clyde F. and others
Modern geography curriculums. NEA J 54: 58-60 Ja '65
KOHN, Hans
Future of political unity in western Europe; address, April 6, 1963; with questions and answers. Ann Am Acad 348:95-101 Jl '63
Germany in world politics. bibliog f Cur Hist 44:202-7+ Ap '63
Prospects for world peace; an overview. bibliog f Cur Hist 46:321-5+ Je '64
KOHN, Harold W. and Boudart, Michel
Reaction of hydrogen with oxygen adsorbed on a platinum catalyst. bibliog Science 145: 149 Jl 10 '64
KOHN, Leonard. See Freedman, A. D. jt. auth.
KOHN, Robert R. and others
Cross-linkages in collagen. Science 145:186-8 Jl 10 '64
KOHN, Sherwood
Family at the fair. Ladies Home J 81:108 Jl '64
Flowering of fake flowers. N Y Times Mag p54+ Ag 23 '64
H_2S. N Y Times Mag p 121-2 S 13 '64
KOHS, Ellis B.
Lulu in the Provinces. Mus Am 83:270 D '63
KOK, B. See Jagendorf, A. T. jt. auth.
KOKJOHN, Joseph E.
Dearly beloved; story. Harper 227:71-8 S '63
If winter comes; story. Commonweal 80:200 My 8 '64
KOKOMO, Ind.
Remodeled pool is bigger and better. J. W. Miller. il Am City 79:94-6 F '64
KOLASA, Bernard D.
Churches feel tax squeeze. America 111:185-7 Ag 22 '64
KOLB, Charles R.
Military problems in cold regions. Science 147:71-3 Ja 1 '65
KOLB, Ken
Let us a-quarreling go; story. Redbook 123: 50-1 Jl '64
KOLBE, John W.
William McGovern, RIP; letter. Nat R 17: 14 Ja 12 '65
KOLERS, Paul A.
Illusion of movement; with biographical sketch. Sci Am 211:20, 98-106 O '64
KOLESNIK, Walter B.
Sex differences and education. America 108: 552-5 Ap 20 '63
KOLKO, Gabriel
Our quarrel with Castro. New Repub 150: 29-30+ F 15 '64
KOLLAR, Pete
Bad beginning. Outdoor Life 134:36-9+ N '64
KOLLER, D. See Whiteman, P. C. jt. auth.
KÖLLNER effect. See Color sense
KOLLWITZ, Käthe (Schmidt)
Art of Kaethe Kollwitz. A. Werner. il por Am Artist 27:24-9 N '63
KOLM, Henry H. and Dresselhaus, M. S.
High magnetic fields: production and application. Science 142:271-5 O 11 '63
KOLODIN, Irving
Bouquet for Strauss. Sat R 47:55-7 My 30 '64
Britten's War requiem. Sat R 46:45-6 My 25 '63

KOLODIN, Irving—*Continued*
City Center; success story. Theatre Arts 47: 17-19+ Mr '63
First recording of Siegfried. Sat R 46:31-2 Ag 31 '63
Fritz Reiner: in memoriam. Sat R 46:45-7 D 28 '63
Merit of Poulenc. Sat R 46:49-50+ F 23 '63
Music to my ears. See issues of Saturday review
New mood for the new Met. Sat R 47:45-7+ Ja 25 '64
New York's newest showplace. Sat R 47: 31+ F 22 '64
One for the road. Sat R 47:51-2 Ap 25 '64
Price-Corelli-Karajan Carmen. Sat R 47:43 Ag 22 '64
Recordings in review. See last issue of each month of Saturday review
Recordings reports: miscellaneous LPs & tapes. See last issue of each month of Saturday review
Recordings reports: orchestral LPs. See last issue of each month of Saturday review
World of Wanda Landowska. Sat R 47:43+ N 28 '64

KOLODZIEJ, Edward A.
Lyndon Johnson's stake in reform. New Repub 151:14-15 N 21 '64
What does the test ban mean? Bul Atomic Sci 20:22-3 Mr '64

KOLOMBATOVICH, Oscar
Excalibur, ltd; interview, ed. by F. Stevenson. por Opera N 28:12-13 Ap 11 '64

KOLOWRAT, Ernest
Boys nation: leadership for young Americans. Sr Schol 83:9+ S 7 '63

KOMAIKO, Jean R.
Grooming a future bride. Parents Mag 39: 42-3+ Ja '64
Lefties are all right. Parents Mag 38:50-1+ Jl '63
Travel abroad family style. Parents Mag 38: 56-7+ Ap '63

KOMAROV, Vladimir
See also
Space flight—Manned flights—Komarov-Yegorov-Feoktistov flight, 1964
—and others
Cosmonauts' own story of epic three-man orbit. pors Life 58:34-34C Ja 22 '65

KOMINISKI, Jacob
Happiest man. D. Kaye. por Read Digest 82: 94-8 Mr '63

KOMINSKY, Morris
Say it isn't so, Morris; letters to the editor. Nat R 15:411 N 5 '63

KOMMAGENE. See Commagene

KOMODO dragons. See Lizards

KOMORN, Robert M. and Cafruny, E. J.
Ethacrynic acid: diuretic property coupled to reaction with sulfhydryl groups of renal cells. bibliog Science 143:133-4 Ja 10 '64

KOMOSKI, P. Kenneth
Programmed instruction abroad. Sr Schol 84:13T Mr 13 '64

KONER, Pauline
Dance magazine's 1963 awards. por Dance Mag 38:35+ Mr '64
My words echo thus. D. Hering. il pors Dance Mag 38:42-5 F '64
Pauline Koner and company at 92d street Y. J. Maskey. Dance Mag 38:23 Ja '64

KONG LE
Awakening. il pors Time 83:24-8 Je 26 '64
Embattled neutralist on the Plaine des Jarres. C. J. V. Murphy. por Fortune 69:160 My '64
Evil spirits on the plain. il Time 82:32 Jl 5 '63
Man in the middle. Takashi Oka. New Repub 148:11-13 Je 15 '63

KONGELBECK, Sverre
World's first automatic guided missile launcher. S. V. Jones. il por Sci Digest 55:26-7 Mr '64

KONIGSBERG, Irwin R.
Clonal analysis of myogenesis. bibliog Science 140:1273-84 Je 21 '63
Embryological origin of muscle. Sci Am 211: 61-6 Ag '64

KONINGSBERGER, Hans
Female of our species. Holiday 34:56-67+ Jl '63
Fuehrer's not for burning. Nation 198:272-4 Mr 16 '64
(comp) Love letters; excerpts from letters of famous men and women. Ladies Home J 80:44+ Ja '63
Movies. Horizon 5:110-12 My '63
When the Russians were our allies. New Repub 152:20+ Ja 9 '65

KONORSKI, J. See Ellison, G. D. jt. auth.

KONSTAM, Patricia Smothers
Israel and the pilgrimage. Christian Cent 81:204-6 F 12 '64

KONVITZ, Milton R.
Another day, an extra dollar. Sat R 47:31 Ag 8 '64
Laborers follow the leaders. Sat R 47:40-1 F 29 '64
Meaning of religion in the First amendment: the Torcaso case. por(p287) Cath World 197:288-95 Ag '63
What the Wobblies wanted. Sat R 48:30 Ja 16 '65

KONWITSCHNY, Franz
Da capo; recordings. S. Smolian. Am Rec G 29:815-16 Je '63

KONYA, Sandor
Sandor Konya: interview, ed. by S. Fleming. por Hi Fi 13:40 F '63
about
Quote; unquote; interview, ed. by E. Helm. por Mus Am 83:17 Ag '63

KOO, F. K. S.
Synergistic effect of 5-bromodeoxyuridine and gamma rays on chromosomes. bibliog Science 141:261-2 Jl 19 '63

KOO, Vi Kyuin Wellington
Koo papers to Columbia. Wilson Lib Bul 38: 229 N '63

KOOK, Edward F.
Temporary theatre, permanent example. Sat R 47:30 F 22 '64

KOOMEN, M. J. and others
Night airglow observations from orbiting spacecraft compared with measurements from rockets. bibliog Science 140:1087-9 Je 7 '63

KOON, Helene
Pierre Patelin; dramatization of The farce of Master Pierre Patelin. Plays 24:37-48 Ja '65

KOONTZ, Elizabeth Duncan
Profile with excerpts from Charlotte, N.C. Observer. por Negro Hist Bul 28:55-6 D '64

KOOYMAN, Gerald L.
Milk analysis of the kangaroo rat, dipodomys merriami. bibliog Science 142:1467 D 13 '63

KOPAL, Zdenek, and Rackham, T. W.
Lunar luminescence and solar flares. Sky & Tel 27:140-1 Mr '64

KOPIT, Arthur
Conquest of Everest: a divertissement. Mlle 60:158-9+ N '64
about
Adventurous ones. por Vogue 142:77 Ag 1 '63

KOPKIND, Andrew D.
Round vs square in California. New Repub 150:9-11 My 30 '64

KOPPETT, Leonard
Ex-national sport looks to its image. N Y Times Mag p 18-19+ D 20 '64
Greatest pitcher of them all. N Y Times Mag p26+ O 4 '64
In first place, the Met fans. N Y Times Mag p26+ Je 14 '64
Stengel ponders. The year of the Berra. N Y Times Mag p21+ Ap 12 '64

KOPPLE, K. D. See Lupinski, J. H. jt. auth.

KOPPLE, Robert
Ho hum, come to the fair. M. Mayer. Esquire 60:117+ O '63

KOPS, Bernard
Angst in the pangst. Newsweek 62:93 S 16 '63
Dead end kids. por Time 82:62 Ag 30 '63

KORBONSKI, Andrzej
COMECON. bibliog f Int Concil 549:3-62 S '64

KORDAN, Herbert A.
Starch synthesis in excised lemon fruit tissue growing in vitro. bibliog Science 142:971 N 15 '63

KOREA
See also
United Nations—Korea

KOREA (People's Democratic Republic)
See also
Panmunjom

Army

As an old war heats up. R. P. Martin. il U S News 55:35 Ag 12 '63
Flare-up. il Time 82:20 Ag 9 '63

Foreign relations

U.S. comments on Communist inspired incidents in Korea; Department statements, July 29 and July 30, 1963. Dept State Bul 49:283 Ag 19 '63

KOREA (Republic)
Department notes anniversary of Korean armistice; statement, July 26, 1963. Dept State Bul 49:246 Ag 12 '63
Korea. J. T. Laney. Christian Cent 81:646 My 13 '64

KOREA (Republic)—*Continued*
Korea; address, November 8, 1963. K. Pak. Vital Speeches 30:220-3 Ja 15 '64
See also
Child welfare—Korea (Republic)
Elections—Korea (Republic)
Hotels, taverns, etc.—Korea (Republic)
Natural resources—Korea (Republic)
Periodicals—Korea (Republic)
Technical assistance in Korea

Economic conditions
Brightening outlook. il Fortune 70:65-6+ N '64
Rough sea. J. M. Truitt. il Newsweek 65:20+ Ja 4 '65

Economic policy
Secretary comments on Korean exchange rate system reform; statement, May 3, 1964. D. Rusk. Dept State Bul 50:830 My 25 '64

Foreign relations
Secretary Rusk holds talks with President of Korea; joint communique, January 29, 1964. D. Rusk and C. H. Park. Dept State Bul 50:238 F 17 '64
United States and Korea ratify consular convention. Dept State Bul 49:905 D 9 '63
United States and Korea reaffirm policy of cooperation; joint statement, October 3, 1964. T. W. Lee; W. P. Bundy. Dept State Bul 51:542 O 19 '64

Politics and government
Back to business; post-riot measures. Newsweek 63:42 Je 22 '64
Bone for the tiger; military rule. Newsweek 61:46-7 Ap 22 '63
Caged tiger. Newsweek 62-37 Ag 26 '63
Ex-General's problem: making democracy work. U S News 55:10 D 30 '63
Exit the junta? il Newsweek 61:44 Mr 11 '63
Fatigues to flannels. Time 82:24 D 27 '63
He didn't say yes; he didn't say no. New Repub 148:8-9 Ap 13 '63
Heat's off. Time 81:28+ Mr 22 '63
In Korea, a go-ahead for guided democracy. U S News 55:72 O 28 '63
No tears; cancellation of elections. Newsweek 61:52 Mr 25 '63
Over to you, gentlemen. Time 81:34+ Mr 8 '63
Park under pressure. Newsweek 61:46-7 Ap 8 '63
Park's law. Newsweek 62:46 O 28 '63
Silent Sam, the pressure man. Time 81:44+ Ap 19 '63
Squeeze in Seoul. il Time 81:32 Mr 29 '63
Stop Japan; students try to disrupt talks between Korea and Japan. Newsweek 63:38 Ap 6 '64
Variable Park. Newsweek 61:35-6 Ap 1 '63
Who needs democracy? New Repub 148:7 F 16 '63

Religious institutions and affairs
News of the Christian world (cont) Christian Cent 80:687-8; 81:26, 1182; 82:120 My 22 '63, Ja 1, S 23 '64, Ja 27 '65
Question for the press. America 109:472 O 26 '63

Riots
After the shadow; rioting students. il Time 83:42 Je 12 '64
As a new crisis erupted in Korea. il U S News 56:10 Je 15 '64
Asia: a violent student outburst in Korea... il Life 56:40-1 Je 19 '64
Deadly choice; student riots. il Newsweek 63:46 Je 15 '64

Social conditions
Hooch is not a home; Korean mistresses. il Time 84:48 O 16 '64

KOREA, NORTHERN. See Korea (People's Democratic Republic)
KOREA and the United States
See also
Korean war, 1950-1953—American participation
KOREAN armistice. See Korean war, 1950-1953 —Peace and mediation
KOREAN dancing. See Dancing, Korean
KOREAN war, 1950-1953
Korea: the limited war, by D. Rees. Review
New Repub 151:19-20 Jl 11 '64. C. B. Marshall
Sat R 47:31-2 My 2 '64. J. M. Allison

American participation
Crossing of the Yalu. Nat R 16:342-4 My 5 '64
MacArthur story; with interview with D. MacArthur and report by H. Handleman. il U S News 56:38-46 Ap 20 '64
MacArthur: the greatest captain of his era. R. E. Dupuy. il U S News 56:78-9 Ap 27 '64
Reminiscences; excerpts. D. MacArthur. il Life 57:36-8+ Jl 24 '64; Read Digest 85: 263-6+ O '64
See also
United States—Armed forces—Forces in Korea
United States—Army—Forces in Korea

Campaigns and battles
Reminiscences; excerpts. D. MacArthur. il Life 57:36-8+ Jl 24 '64; Read Digest 85: 263-6+ O '64

Peace and mediation
Korea ten years later: war that never ends. R. P. Martin. il U S News 55:62-5 Jl 22 '63
Panmunjom: is that still going on? J. M. Truitt. il Newsweek 65:23 Ja 4 '65
Place of 10 million words; tenth anniversary of the truce. Time 82:21 Ag 2 '63

Prisoners and prisons
See also
Prisoners of war in Korea

Strategy
Atom bombs and a cobalt belt; MacArthur's controversial plan. il Newsweek 63:37-8+ Ap 20 '64
Here is what MacArthur really meant. Life 56:4 Ap 24 '64
MacArthur interviews. C. B. Marshall. New Repub 150:7 Ap 25 '64
Threnody & thunder. il Time 83:40-1 Ap 17 '64

KORENGOLD, Robert J.
Russia revisited: contrast with a twist. por Newsweek 64:36-8 Ag 31 '64
KORENVAES, Patricia
Peter Drucker: troubleshooter at the top. Duns R 84:43+ Jl '64
KORESKO, Minnie B. See Hearst, E. jt. auth.
KOREY, Ruth Anne
Planetariums in the United States. Sky & Tel 26:147-50 S '63
KOREY, William
Embarrassed American. Sat R 47:24-5 O 31 '64
KORIAKOV, Mikhail
Denisovich: Russia's voice. America 108:338-9 Mr 9 '63
KORMOS, George
Leadership by association. por Recreation 57: 191 Ap '64
KORN, Bennet H.
Battle cries. Newsweek 61:69 My 13 '63
Closed end. Time 81:83 My 10 '63
KORN, Edward D. and Greenblatt, C. L.
Synthesis of α-linolenic acid by Leishmania enriettii. bibliog Science 142:1301-3 D 6 '63
KORN, Pearl
Kids and cameras go together. U S Camera 26:28-9+ Je '63
KORN, Richard
Mona's master. Opera N 28:6-7 Ja 11 '64
KORNACKER, Melodee S. and Lowenstein, J. M.
Citrate cleavage enzyme in livers of obese and nonobese mice. bibliog Science 144: 1027-8 My 22 '64
KORNELL, Billy
Master of the bulls; photographs. B. Ballantine. Sat Eve Post 237:60-3 S 5 '64
Sporting life. il por Newsweek 62:80 N 11 '63
KORNFEDER, Joseph Zack
Joseph Zack Kornfeder, RIP. Nat R 14:396 My 21 '63; Reply. A. G. Grant, jr. 14:509 Je 18 '63
KORNIENKO, G. M.
U.S. supports preconditions for conference on Laos; Soviet statement, July 26, 1964. Dept State Bul 51:220 Ag 17 '64
KORNITZER, Bela
(ed) See Cushing, R. J. Cardinal Cushing remembers: twice, I saw Jack Kennedy cry
KORNS, William A.
Congress against itself. New Repub 150:26+ Je 27 '64
Disestablishmentarianism. New Repub 148:6 Mr 16 '63
Target: the President. New Repub 148:25-6 Ap 27 '63
KOROBKOV, Gavriil
But the Russian coach says the smog was bad. por Life 57:25-7 Ag 7 '64
KOROLYOV, Sergei Pavlovich
Mystery duo; engineers behind the Soviet space effort. Newsweek 62:73 N 25 '63

KOROTKIN, Fred
On July 20 next the world will not come to an end. Sci Digest 54:19-21 Jl '63
Post card gold mine in your home town. Hobbies 69:120-1+ My '64
Wood for eternity. Am For 70:28-9 D '64
KORSAKOV, Nikolaĭ Andreevich Rimskiĭ-. See Rimskiĭ-Korsakov, N. A.
KORTH, Fred
Korth denies he was asked to resign; statement, October 19, 1963. Aviation W 79:23 O 28 '63

about

Anchors aweigh. il por Time 82:25 O 25 '63
Conflict-of-interest ghost walks again. por Bsns W p29 O 26 '63
Korth urges all-nuclear line fleet. Aviation W 79:34 N 4 '63
Korth's resignation: more questions. por U S News 55:15 N 4 '63
McClellan to press Korth conflict probe. G. C. Wilson. Aviation W 79:26-7 O 21 '63
Man in the middle. il por Time 81:25 Je 14 '63
Senate probers scrutinize Korth letters. G. C. Wilson. Aviation W 79:22-4 O 28 '63
Turbulent wake. Newsweek 62:27 N 4 '63
Why top-level jobs changed hands at the Pentagon. U S News 55:26 O 28 '63
With uncommon speed. il por Newsweek 62:22 O 28 '63
KORTZ, Ralph G.
Recorders and duplicating machines speed police reporting. Am City 79:81 Jl '64
KOS, Greece
Rough map of Greece. P. L. Adams. il Atlan 211:73-7 Mr '63
KOSA, John
Courting customs in the workers' paradise. Reporter 30:46-7 F 13 '64
KOSHLAND, D. E. jr
Correlation of structure and function in enzyme action; excerpts from address. bibliog Science 142:1533-41 D 20 '63
Where is science taking us? excerpt from Horizons in biochemistry. por Sat R 46:46 Je 1 '63
KOSHLAND, Marian E. and others
Differences in the amino acid composition of a third rabbit antibody. bibliog Science 143:1330-1 Mr 20 '64
KOSINSKI, Leonard V.
New look at the bilingual student. bibliog Sr Schol 83:14T O 4 '63
KOSKI, Jorman I.
Two-way radio. Am City 79:151-2 My '64
KOSLER, Zdenek
Triumphant trio. por Time 81:62 Ap 12 '63
KOSMA, Joseph
Electronic love. Criticism
Opera N il 28:27 S 28 '63
KOSOFF, Harold
Inventor of the month. S. V. Jones. il por Sci Digest 56:28-9 Jl '64
KOSOFSKY, Eve
Curl up and read. Seventeen 23:18 Ja '64
KOSSODO, Gunter
Angel's Boris Godunov. Am Rec G 29:692-3+ My '63
Glitter from the golden age of Wagner singing. Am Rec G 29:426-7 F '63
Melchior's Siegfried, the greatest then and the greatest still. Am Rec G 30:108-10 O '63
KOSTANECKI, Andrew. See Sutphen, J. jt. auth.
KOSTELANETZ, Andre
Adventure of discovering. por Seventeen 23:180+ Ap '64
KOSTELANETZ, Anne
Ruskin redivivus. Commonweal 80:64-7 Ap 3 '64
KOSTER, R. M.
New riots in Panama? New Repub 151:9-10 N 28 '64
Peru: a scenario worthy of Zanuck. New Repub 152:6-7 Ja 9 '65
KOSTKA, Dorothy
Emily's pupils; the strength of a city. Read Digest 83:123-6 S '63
KOSYGIN, Alekseĭ Nikolaevich
USSR 1965; address, December 10, 1964. Vital Speeches 31:213-24 Ja 15 '65

about

After Khrushchev what? with report by K. Lachmann. il por U S News 57:39-45 O 26 '64
Fall of Nikita K; with comment on the world's news fronts. il por Sr Schol 85:17-18+, 24 O 28 '64
Khrushchev's heirs: a look at the line-up. F. B. Stevens. U S News 54:44 My 6 '63
Kosygin and the Russian consumer; with statements by U.S. academic experts. il por Newsweek 64:73-4+ N 9 '64
Kremlin chiefs pledge business as usual. il pors Bsns W p30-3 O 24 '64
Mixture as before. il por Newsweek 64:40 D 21 '64
New B. & K. S. Bieler. il Reporter 31:25-6 N 5 '64
New men at the top in the Kremlin. por U S News 57:21 O 26 '64
Number two was a whiz kid. il por Life 57:35 O 23 '64
Revolt in the Kremlin. il pors Time 84:28-31 O 23 '64
Two for one: after K, the gray-flannel men move in. por Newsweek 64:46-7 O 26 '64
Who runs Russia now? il por U S News 57:52-4+ N 9 '64
KOTEN, Bernard
On translating Voznesensky. Nation 199:337-8 N 9 '64
KOTLOWITZ, Robert
Boadicea in Walthamstow. Hi Fi 15:52-6 F '65
KOTO
Eto & the koto. il Time 85:48 Ja 8 '65
KOTO students; story. See Harris, M.
KOTSCHNIG, Walter M.
African development; statement, February 22, 1963. Dept State Bul 48:625-8 Ap 22 '63
KOUFAX, Sandy
Good life of baseball's no. 1 hero; with comments on himself and his job, ed. by T. Thompson. pors Life 55:54-6 Ag 2 '63
I'm only human; ed. by M. Gross. pors Look 27:51-6 D 31 '63

about

Best of the better. por Time 82:50 Jl 19 '63
It's news only when he loses. J. Murphy. por N Y Times Mag p 133-4+ S 8 '63
Koo-foo the Killer; world series. W. Leggett. il por Sports Illus 19:18-25 O 14 '63
One, two, three. Newsweek 63:64 Je 15 '64
Show of hands for the no. 1 arm. W. Leggett. il por Sports Illus 19:18-19 S 16 '63
Six quitters. por Esquire 62:103 S '64
Sporting scene. R. Angell. New Yorker 39:184+ O 26 '63
Third for Sandy; no-hit game. il por Time 83:80 Je 12 '64
Urgent matter of one index finger. R. Creamer. il por Sports Illus 18:20-2+ Mr 4 '63
Very best act in town. J. Olsen. il pors Sports Illus 19:20-2+ Jl 29 '63
KOUNTZ, Samuel L.
New hope for kidney transplants. il pors Ebony 20:119-20+ N '64
KOUSSEVITZKY international recording award
Koussevitzky recording awards. R. Jacobson. Mus Am 83:46 My '63
KOVACH, Bill
Racism wasn't the issue in Tennessee. Reporter 31:37-8 S 24 '64
KOVACH, Nora
Ballet, violins and shish kebab! Bihari. E. Carroll. il por Dance Mag 37:27-8 D '63
KOVACS, B. A. and others
Isolation of an antihistaminic principle resembling tomatine from crown gall tumors. bibliog Science 144:295-6; 146:670 Ap 17, O 30 '64
KOVACS, Ernie
Year in the life of Edie Adams. R. W. Lewis. il Sat Eve Post 236:24-7 Ap 13 '63
KOVALEFF, Alex J.
Create color by solarizing. H. Keppler and P. Caulfield. il Mod Phot 28:52-4 Ap '64
KOVDA, Victor A.
S.T.P: index of prosperity. UNESCO Courier 16:18-23 Jl '63
KOVEL, Ralph, and Kovel, Terry
Waterford glass. Hobbies 68:77+ My '63
KOVEL, Terry. See Kovel, R. jt. auth.
KOVEN, Stanley
Dark corners. Criticism
New Yorker 40:165 My 16 '64
Mr Grossman. Criticism
New Yorker 40:165-6 My 16 '64
KOVNER, Milton
Sino-Soviet dialogue. bibliog f Cur Hist 45:129-35 S '63
Sino-Soviet dispute: communism at the crossroads. bibliog f Cur Hist 47:129-35+ S '64
KOWAL, Charles. See Sandage, A. jt. auth.
KOWALD, Kenneth
Nassau County attacks automotive air pollution. Am City 78:109 O '63

KOWALSKI, Frank
American plants abroad. Nation 197:197-9 O 5 '63
KOYAMA, I. See Abood, L. G. jt. auth.
KOZINN, Philip J. and others
Conjunctiva contains factor inhibiting growth of Candida albicans. bibliog Science 146:1479-80 D 11 '64
KOZLOFF, Max
Aesthetics of failure. Nation 197:202-3 O 5 '63
Art. See occasional issues of Nation
Art books of 1963. Nation 197:459-62 D 28 '63
KOZLOV, Frol Romanovich
Khrushchev's heirs: a look at the line-up. F. B. Stevens. por U S News 54:44 My 6 '63
Man to watch. por Newsweek 61:40 Ap 22 '63
KOZMETSKY, George
Infant with a giant appetite. il por Bsns W p66-8 Ja 11 '64
KOZOL, Jonathan
In our time: story. Esquire 61:116 Ap '64
KOZYREV, Nikolai A.
Atmosphere of Mercury; tr. by A. Boyko. Sky & Tel 27:339-41 Je '64
KRAAR, Louis
India under the gun. Life 55:9+ N 1 '63
KRABACH, Richard
Austerity in Ohio. R. Giles. il Reporter 29:39-42 N 7 '63
KRACHT, Avis
Little things make my life interesting; ed. by R. Martens. por Farm J 87:106-7 F '63
KRAELING, Emil G.
Prophets. Life 57:75-8+ D 25 '64
KRAFT, Eve F.
Health plan for young teens. Parents Mag 39:60-1+ N '64
KRAFT, Joseph
Ambitions of Bobby Kennedy. Look 28:22-8+ Ag 25 '64
Foreign aid: saved by the Bell? Harper 226:73-6+ F '63
Old crocodile on the New frontier. Sat Eve Post 236:66-7 S 14 '63
Riot squad for the New frontier. Harper 227:69-75 Ag '63
Treasury's Dillon. Harper 226:51-6 Je '63
Washington insight. See issues of Harper's magazine November 1963-
KRAFT, L. M. See Adams, W. R. jt. auth.
KRAFT, Virginia
Archery. Sports Illus 19:40-2 Ag 5 '63
Dogs (cont) Sports Illus 18:43 F 18; 99-100+ Ap 8; 52+ Je 10; 19:67-8 N 25 '63
Hunting (cont) Sports Illus 18:52+ Mr 4; 19:76-9 D 9 '63; 21:50-3 D 14 '64
Nature. Sports Illus 21:73-4+ D 21 '64
KRAFT foods company
Kraft lays a decholesteroled egg; Miracle egg. Consumer Rep 29:54 F '64
Pasteurized process cheese, its development and nutritive value. il Parents Mag 38:42+ S '63
KRAG, Jens Otto
Cutting back with Krag. il por Time 81:34 Mr 8 '63
KRAG-Jorgensen rifle. See Rifles
KRAHN, Fernando
Epic of man (with apologies to Life magazine) il Horizon 5:108-12 S '63
KRAININ, Bette Finley
Foreign bazaar. Holiday 35:34 My '64
Treasures from the foreign bazaars. Holiday 34:94-9 N '63
KRAKATOA (island)
Day the earth blew up. D. MacClure. il Pop Sci 183:48-51+ Ag '63
KRAL, Barbara
We rattle off to Abidjan by money bus. Life 56:94+ Ap 17 '64
KRAM, Mark
Baseball. Sports Illus 20:56-8 Je 22; 21:48+ Jl 13; 54-7 Ag 24 '64
Emperor in harness. Sports Illus 20:44+ Je 15 '64
Fame and terror at 200 MPH. Sports Illus 21:26-8+ Ag 31 '64
Howe: the who, what and why of the Red Wings. Sports Illus 20:30-2+ Mr 16 '64
Touch and a tooth of gold. Sports Illus 21:60-3 D 21 '64
KRAMER, Barry
Roll out the Barry! H. L. Masin. il por Sr Schol 84:26 Ja 31 '64
Scholarship for Barry: recruiters at work. M. Gross. il pors Sat Eve Post 236:20-3 F 23 '63
KRAMER, C. S.
Water-sewage courses become formal school. Am City 79:122-3 O '64
KRAMER, Hilton
Anything goes. Reporter 29:62+ S 12 '63
Art. See issues of Nation to June 22, 1963
Art and revolution. Nation 198:18-19 Ja 4 '64
Chagall, innocent in Paris. Commentary 38:57-60 Jl '64
Conscience & revolution. Commentary 37:85-7 Ap '64
He never left home. Reporter 28:46-7 Je 20 '63
Higher conformity. Commentary 37:84+ My '64
His heart belongs to dada. Reporter 28:43-6 My 9 '63
Light and the dark. New Repub 150:23+ F 15 '64
Masks he wore. Reporter 30:44+ Ja 2 '64
New ways in architecture. Reporter 29:58-60+ D 5 '63
Portraits of three painters. Reporter 31:35-6 D 17 '64
Skimming a life. Nation 197:283-4 N 2 '63
Threepenny artist. Reporter 29:57+ O 24 '63
KRAMER, Jack
Begonias as house plants most beauty for least care! Am Home 67:94 N '64
Bizarre brilliant bromeliads. Flower Grower 50:42-4 O '63
Orchid for your window. Flower Grower 52:35 Ja '65
Orchids lead an indoor outdoor life. Am Home 67:54-5+ My '64
Trouble with tennis. il por Esquire 61:119-23 My '64
KRAMER, James R.
Sea water; saturation with apatites and carbonates. bibliog Science 146:637-8 O 30 '64
KRAMER, Norman, and Japenga, Ronald
Self-protecting transistor hi-fi amplifier. Electr World 71:32-3+ Je '64
KRAMER, Paul J. See O'Leary, J. W. jt. auth.
KRAMER, Rita
Parent and child. N Y Times Mag p85-6 Ap 5: 47 My 31; 122+ O 18 '64; 39 Ja 3 '65
KRAMER, Sam
Obituary
Craft Horiz il 24:11 Jl '64
KRAMER, Samuel Noah
O ye daughters of Sumer! Horizon 5:108-9 Jl '63
KRAMER, William
(tr) See Heinzelmann, G. Priesthood and women
KRANEPOOL, Edward E.
Youngest Met. G. Zimmermann. il pors Look 27:83-7 Jl 2 '63
KRANNERT center for the performing arts. See Illinois. University, Urbana—Krannert center for the performing arts
KRANTZ, Judith
Lonely wife. McCalls 91:142-3+ N '63
Sybil Burton starts over. McCalls 91:108+ Ap '64
This man says he's Peter Sellers. McCalls 90:42+ Ag '63
KRASSNER, Paul
Man with a ho. por Newsweek 64:50-1 Ag 3 '64
KRASZNA-KRAUSZ, Andor
K.K. on komposition. Mod Phot 28:80-1 Je; 17+ Jl; 16+ N '64
KRAUS, Alfred P. and Neely, C. L. jr
Human erythrocyte lactate dehydrogenase: four genetically determined variants. bibliog Science 145:595-7 Ag 7 '64
KRAUS, Alfredo
Four recitals by Alfredo Kraus. Am Rec G 30:200-1 N '63
KRAUS, John D.
Large radio telescope of Ohio state university. il Sky & Tel 26:12-16 Jl '63
KRAUS, Joseph H.
Inventors' corner. Pop Mech 121:40+ Mr '64
KRAUSE, Adolph
This little pigskin went to market. il por Bsns W p48+ D 7 '63
KRAUSE, Dale C.
Guinea fracture zone in the equatorial Atlantic. bibliog Science 146:57-9 O 2 '64
KRAUSZ, Andor Kraszna-. See Kraszna-Krausz, A.
KRAUSZ, N. G. P.
Hunters on your farm? Suc Farm 62:36 O '64
What you should know about checks: questions and answers. Suc Farm 62:74 O '64
—and Hipp, D. B.
Avoid legal tangles in using credit. Suc Farm 62:54+ S '64
KRAUTHAMER, George M.
Inhibition of evoked potentials by striatal stimulation and its blockage by strychnine. bibliog Science 142:1175-6 N 29 '63
KRAWITZ, Herman E.
Man at the Center. J. Ferris. il por Opera N 29:11-13 Ja 16 '65
KREBIOZEN
AMA, the FDA and quacks. J. Ridgeway. New Repub 149:31-3 N 9 '63

KREBIOZEN—*Continued*
Another round in the krebiozen battle. il Time 82:64 Jl 26 '63
Answer on krebiozen: it's useless. il Life 55:47-8+ O 4 '63
Curious case of krebiozen. H. Margolis. Bul Atomic Sci 20:29-31 Mr '64; Reply. A. C. Ivy. 20:28 S '64
Deadline for krebiozen. il Newsweek 61:71 My 27 '63
End of krebiozen. Sci Am 209:54-6 O '63
Fantastic krebiozen story. R. P. Goldman. il Sat Eve Post 237:15-19 Ja 4 '64
Federal decision on an anticancer drug. U S News 55:14 O 28 '63
Incredible story behind a cancer cure. S. Blum. il Redbook 123:40-1+ Je '64
Indicting krebiozen. Time 84:106 N 27 '64
Krebiozen: a dozen years after introduction, controversy over cancer treatment still flares. E. Langer. Science 140:1294-6 Je 21 '63
Krebiozen analyzed. Time 82:85 S 13 '63
Krebiozen & cancer. Time 81:45 Mr 1 '63
Krebiozen application meets FDA deadline. Sci N L 83:392 Je 22 '63
Krebiozen availability after June 7 in doubt. Sci N L 83:322 My 25 '63
Krebiozen case closed. Sci N L 84:258 O 26 '63
Krebiozen: FDA deadline brings new, but not the final, episode in controversy over cancer drug. E. Langer. Science 141:31-3 Jl 5 '63
Krebiozen: FDA, NIH still on trail of anti-cancer drug; and Congress on trail of agencies. E. Langer. Science 141:1021-3 S 13 '63
Krebiozen: government indicts sponsors of alleged cancer drug; Ivy, Durovic, among those named. E. Langer. Science 146:1282 D 4 '64
Krebiozen identified. Sci N L 84:181 S 21 '63
Krebiozen in court. il Newsweek 62:76 Jl 15 '63; 64:91 N 30 '64
Krebiozen: nearly a decade of controversy spent in pursuit of fair, government-sponsored test. E. Langer. Science 140:1383-5 Je 28 '63
Krebiozen: no clinical test, says National cancer institute. E. Langer. Science 142:472 O 25 '63
Krebiozen scandal. New Repub 151:5 D 5 '64
Krebiozen: the end of the road. Nation 197:170-1 S 28 '63
Krebiozen unmasked? W. Cloud. Pop Sci 183:21-2+ N '63
Krebiozen; why it hasn't been tested. Consumer Rep 28:441-3 S '63
Medical case against krebiozen. il Consumer Rep 29:93-6 F '64
Responsibility for drug belongs to developers. Sci N L 84:232 O 12 '63
Suit dismissed by krebiozen backers. Sci N L 84:376 D 14 '63
What ever happened to Dr Ivy? W. R. Young. il Life 57:110-12+ O 9 '64; Same abr. with title Krebiozen, the tragic obsession of Andrew Ivy. Read Digest 86:193-4+ Ja '65
Woman chemist directs krebiozen analysis. Sci N L 84:196 S 28 '63

KREBS, Albert V. Jr
Anatomy of a headline. America 109:662-4 N 23 '63
Church of science. Commonweal 80:467-76 Jl 10 '64

KREBS, Charles J.
Lemming cycle at Baker Lake, Canada, during 1959-62. bibliog Science 140:674-6 My 10 '63

KREGER, William G.
Elusive newspaper market. U S Camera 26:18+ S '63

KREH, Bernard
Crazy skeet. Outdoor Life 131:74-5+ Ap '63

KREIDER, Claude M.
Magic fish trap. Outdoor Life 133:36-7+ F '64

KREIDLER, Robert N.
Scientists and national policy. Science 143:1156 Mr 13 '64

KREINHEDER, Arthur Carl
Lonely Lutheran monk. il por Time 81:53 Mr 1 '63

KREISLER, Fritz
Fritz Kreisler in immortal performances. P. L. Miller. il pors Am Rec G 29:430-1 F '63

KRELOVE, Lillian
Your state flower (cont) Flower Grower 50:27 Mr; 26 My; 46 Jl; 26 S '63; 51:66 F; 65 Ap; 46 My '64

KREMLIN. See Moscow—Kremlin

KREPS, Juanita M.
Six clichés in search of a woman; address, October 22, 1964. Vital Speeches 31:147-9 D 15 '64

KRESGE, S. S. company
Strength in variety. il Time 84:63 N 20 '64

KRESH, Paul
Words only. See issues of American record guide

KRESS, James J.
Yep, we were there. por Time 84:28-9 O 9 '64

KRETCHMER, Norman. See Doell, R. G. Sunshine, P. jt. auths.

KRETTEK, Germaine
State of the Union and of its libraries. ALA Bul 58:77 F '64
—and Cooke, E. D.
ALA Washington notes. Wilson Lib Bul 38:569, 693+, 783+, 868+; 39:85-6, 183-4, 264+, 341, 417+ Mr '64-Ja '65
Washington report: from the ALA Washington office. ALA Bul 58:181, 275-7, 460-4, 597-9, 681-2, 771-3, 985-8; 59:22-3 Mr-Ap, Je-O, D '64-Ja '65
—and Hubbard, H. W.
ALA Washington notes. See issues of Wilson library bulletin to February 1964
Washington report: from the ALA Washington office. ALA Bul 57:121, 497-9, 635-6, 717-20, 823-4, 1014-16; 58:95-7 F, Je-O, D '63, F '64

KRETZ, T.
Subjective seasons; poem. Commonweal 81:100 O 16 '64

KRETZMANN, O. P.
Student freedom. Commonweal 78:379 Je 28 '63

KREUTER, Gretchen. See Kreuter, K. jt. auth.

KREUTER, Kent, and Kreuter, Gretchen
Useful genius; intelligence, creativity, and American values. Sat R 47:64-7 O 17 '64

KREUTTNER, John D.
Kreuttner festival. il Nat R 16:645-8 Jl 28 '64
Poems to seven peacemakers. Nat R 14:346 My 7 '63

KREVITSKY, Nik
Magic world of art. Sch Arts 63:11-16 Ap '64
On stitchery. il Craft Horiz 23:18-20+ N '63

KRICK, Irving P, associates. See Irving P. Krick associates

KRIEG, John G.
Purchasing for pennies a serving. Am City 79:80 Jl '64
Testing traffic paint. Am City 79:92-3 N '64
We shopped around, and saved. Am City 78:99 Jl '63

KRIEG, Lowell E.
Old gun, new ramrod. il por Bsns W p 168-70+ Je 15 '63

KRIEGEL, Leonard
Surrender to symbols. Nation 199:339 N 9 '64

about

Difficult birth. M. Rosenthal. Nation 199:144+ S 21 '64

KRIEGER, Robert
6 A.M; Some quarrels do not stop in Reno, Nevada; Island storm; poems. Poetry 104:161-3 Je '64

KRIEGH, Ben
Village bookstore in Boulder, Colo. adds trade books to technical stock. il Pub W 184:86-8 N 11 '63

KRIESE, Gladys
Dryad; interview, ed. by R. D. Daniels. por Opera N 27:15 F 16 '63

KRILL, John
How to plant an English walnut. il Flower Grower 51:38 Mr '64
Tips on tents. Outdoor Life 132:90-1 Jl '63

KRIPALANI, Sucheta
Wife of the critic. il por Newsweek 62:46+ O 7 '63

KRIPS, Josef
Quote; unquote; interview, ed. by C. S. Susa. por Mus Am 84:23 Mr '64
Right spirit; interview, ed. by A. M. Lingg. il por Opera N 29:24-5 N 14 '64

about

Musical events; concert performed by New York philharmonic. W. Sargeant. New Yorker 40:144-5 N 7 '64
Perfect doctor. pors Time 82:64 D 13 '63
San Francisco discord. Newsweek 63:79 My 18 '64

KRISHER, Bernard
Reporter in Indonesia. Newsweek 64:83-6 O 5 '64

KRISHNAMACHARI, Tiruvallur Thattaf
India opens wider to foreign funds. il por Bsns W p79-80 Ap 11 '64

KRISHNA MENON, Vengalil Krishnan
Can Krishna Menon make a comeback? por U S News 57:22 N 9 '64

KRISTI, Grigori Vladimirovich
Stanislavsky; revolutionary of the modern theatre. UNESCO Courier 16:12-14 N '63

KRISTOL, Irving
From the land of the free to the big PX. N Y Times Mag p7+ D 20 '64
Is the welfare state obsolete? Harper 226: 39-43 Je; 227:8 S '63; Same abr. with title Why the welfare state doesn't work. Read Digest 83:86-90 N '63
KRIVENKO, Sonia
Green bells are so good! Flower Grower 50:6+ S '63
KRIVISIKY, Pamela
Choicest co-ed. por Esquire 60:76 S '63
KROCK, Arthur
All the news that manages to fit. Nat R 14: 182 Mr 12 '63
Crucial choice for the Republicans. N Y Times Mag p5+ Jl 12 '64
Mr Kennedy's management of the news. Fortune 67:82+ Mr '63; Excerpts. Nat R 14:182 Mr 12 '63
What three newsmen report about Kennedy news tactics; reprint. U S News 54:42 Ap 15 '63
about
JFK termed brilliant in managing the news. U S News 54:10 Mr 11 '63
Letter from Washington; managed news. R. H. Rovere. New Yorker 39:165-9 Mr 30 '63
What is managed news, dad? Time 81:37 Mr 1 '63
Where are the reformers? W. F. Buckley, jr. Nat R 14:227 Mr 26 '63
KROCK, Edward
Three for a pyramid. il por Time 81:108+ My 17 '63
What's in it for Eddie, Bobb, and Vic? S. H. Brown. il por Fortune 70:139-43+ S '64
KROEGER, Louis J.
Men to match our problems; excerpts from address. Recreation 57:76-8 F '64
KROEHLER manufacturing company
Putting young ideas to work on furniture; sponsored youth seminars. il Bsns W p66-8 Ja 23 '65
KROHNER, Les
Husband's diary of his wife's pregnancy; ed. by V. Cadden. Redbook 123:36-7+ Je '64
KROKER, Bruno
East-West theological dialogue. Christian Cent 80:585-6 My 1 '63
KROKODIL (periodical) See Periodicals—Russia
KROKOVER, Rosalyn
Ballet; Balanchine's Midsummer night's dream. Mus Am 84:7-8 My '64
Dance. Mus Am 84:54-5 Ja; 42-3 F '64
Leningrad-Kirov ballet. Mus Am 84:54+ O '64
North of the border. Mus Am 84:46-7 Mr '64
Records for dance. See issues of Dance magazine to December 1963
—and Schonberg, H. C.
Ballet in America: one-man show? Harper 229:92-6 S; 13 N '64
KROLL, Jack
Kandinsky: last of the heresiarchs. Art N 61:38-41+ F '63
KROLOFF, George
Operation niños. Sch Life 46:9-11 Je '64
KRONBORG castle. See Castles
KRONENBERGER, Louis
Aphorisms. Vogue 143:138 Mr 1 '64
Gambler in publishing: Horace Liveright. Atlan 215:94-104 Ja '65
Not sealed off from life. Vogue 141:136-9 F 1 '63
Opinion, please; from Boston. Mlle 58:16-17+ Ja '64
Return to civilian life. Theatre Arts 47:14-15+ F '63
Whatever became of personal ethics? Horizon 5:60-1 Mr '63
KRONICK, Paul L.
Organic solid state. Science 145:730+ Ag 14 '64
KROPOTKIN, Igor
ABA section; with editorial comment. Pub W 185:63, 75 Ja 6 '64
Canadian booksellers association holds its twelfth annual convention. Pub W 183:39-42 Je 3 '63
Canadian booksellers meeting dealt constructively with trade problems. Pub W 185: 28-31 Je 1 '64
Discounting: a growing problem in Denver: summary of address. Pub W 184:21-3 N 18 '63
Looking backward. Pub W 185:76-7 F 17 '64
KROPOTKIN, P. N.
Research frontier. Sat R 46:39-40 Jl 6 '63
KROSNEY, Herbert
Mobilization for youth: feuding over poverty; excerpts from Hard times, good times. Nation 199:455-61 D 14 '64
KRUBNER, Ralph
Try a stock agency to turn your travel pictures into cash. Pop Phot 54:140-3 Ap '64
KRUG, Edward A.
Impact of World war I on the American high school; excerpt from Shaping of the American high school. bibliog f Sch & Soc 92: 161-71 Ap 4 '64
KRÜGER, Hans
Hexed ministry. Newsweek 63:34 F 3 '64
KRUGER, Juliane
Look, luv, quick, it's Westminster! Mlle 59: 334 Ag '64
KRUGHOFF, Merrill F.
What makes a good community survey. Recreation 56:221-2, 264-6 My-Je '63
KRUIJFF, Jan de
Notes from our correspondents (cont of) Notes from abroad. Hi Fi 13:34 Mr '63; 14:26 S; 16+ D '64
KRUMLIEN, Gunnar D.
Trend to the left. Commonweal 78:244-5 My 24 '63
KRUPA, Gene
Jazz records. W. Balliett. New Yorker 40: 155-8 Je 6 '64
KRUPP, George R.
Day the President died. Redbook 122:49+ Mr '64
KRUPP family
House of Krupp. W. Manchester. il Holiday 36:84-90+ O; 76-9+ N; 84-5+ D '64; 37:78-9+ Ja '65
Krupp: father or child of history? il Newsweek 62:81+ S 23 '63
KRUPP works, Essen
Ambassador from Krupp. il Time 82:82 Jl 5 '63
House of Krupp. W. Manchester. il Holiday 36:84-90+ O; 84-5+ D '64
Krupp: father or child of history? il Newsweek 62:81+ S 23 '63
KRUSZELNICKA, Salomea
Rococo presents. A. Favia-Artsay. por Hobbies 68:30 Ja '64
KRUTCH, Joseph Wood
Brain vs. the machine. Sat R 47:17-19+ Ja 18 '64
Can we survive the fun explosion? Sat R 48:14-16 Ja 16 '65
Confessions of a square. Sat R 47:23-6 My 9 '64
Creative dilemma. Sat R 47:14-17+ F 8 '64
Men, apes, and termites. Sat R 46:22-5 S 21 '63
Miracle of grass. House & Gard 123:112-13+ Je '63
Through happiness with slide rule and calipers. Sat R 46:12-15 N 2 '63
Uses of literature in an age of science; excerpts from address. por Sat R 47:80-1 D 5 '64
What are flowers for? House & Gard 125: 150-1 Mr '64
Wilderness as a tonic. Sat R 46:15-17 Je 8 '63
KRUUSE, Elsa
Our own have-nots. Christian Cent 81:990 Ag 5 '64
KRYPTON
Acid of krypton and its barium salt. A. G. Streng and A. V. Grosse. bibliog Science 143:242-3 Ja 17 '64
Krypton difluoride: preparation and handling. D. R. MacKenzie. bibliog Science 141:1171 S 20 '63
Krypton fluoride: preparation by the matrix isolation technique. J. J. Turner and G. C. Pimentel. bibliog Science 140:974-5 My 31 '63
Krypton key. Newsweek 62:73 Ag 26 '63
Krypton tetrafluoride: preparation and some properties. A. V. Grosse and others. bibliog il Science 139:1047-8 Mr 15 '63
KRYSIAK, Frank M.
Hitch-um and pitch-um camping. por Recreation 57:130-1 Mr '64
KU KLUX klan
Anarchy in St Augustine. L. Goodwyn. il Harper 230:74-81 Ja '65
. . . But the klan. America 110:619 My 9 '64
Button-down bed sheets. il Newsweek 62:32-3 Ag 26 '63
Four klansmen; arrest for murder of L. Penn. Newsweek 64:29 Ag 17 '64
Imperial wizard explains the klan. M. Long. il N Y Times Mag p8+ Jl 5 '64
Klan scourges old St Augustine. G. McMillan. il Life 56:21 Je 26 '64
Klan still rides. B. Law. America 110:755 My 30 '64

KU KLUX klan—*Continued*
Ku Klux klan on the way back. il U S News 57:51-2 O 19 '64
Ku Klux klan: we got nothing to hide; with editorial comment. H. Martin and K. Fairly. il Sat Eve Post 238:26-33,88 Ja 30 '65
Ku Klux klan's White Knights; Mississippi brand of klansmanship. il Newsweek 64:22-4 D 21 '64
Next step: button-down robes. il Time 83:23 My 1 '64
Once more the K.K.K. C. Sitton. il N Y Times Mag p8-9 Ag 11 '63
Portrait of an extremist; C. Lynch. T. Armbrister. il Sat Eve Post 237:80-3 Ag 22 '64
Strange, tight little town, loath to admit complicity. D. Nevin. il Life 57:38-9 D 18 '64

KUBEK, Tony
Rational rebel in pinstripes. L. Shecter. il pors Sports Illus 18:76-8+ My 13 '63

KUBIC, Milan J.
Brazil's adroit new leader. Reporter 31:21-3 D 17 '64

KUBITSCHEK, Juscelino
Let us have faith in the Alliance; excerpt from report. por Américas 15:48 Ag '63
Re-evaluation; excerpt from address, December 14, 1962. por Américas 15:45 F '63

about

Crossing out the ex. Time 83:30+ Je 19 '64
Dissatisfaction down south. por Time 81:22-3 Mr 22 '63
Seeds of injustice? il por Time 83:50 Je 12 '64
Under the volcano. Nation 198:614 Je 22 '64

KUBLIN, Hyman
Japan. bibliog Focus 14:1-6 F '64

KUBLY, Herbert
Care and feeding of artists. Horizon 5:26-33 Mr '63
Vanishing novel. Sat R 47:12-15+ My 2 '64

KUBRICK, Stanley
Astonishing Stanley Kubrick. P. Lyon. por Holiday 35:101-2+ F '64
Contradicting the Hollywood image. L. Tornabene. il por Sat R 46:19-21 D 28 '63
Direct hit. il por Newsweek 63:79-80 F 3 '64

KUCH, T. D. C.
Gislebertus hoc fecit; poem. Commonweal 79:224 N 15 '63

KUCHEL, Thomas Henry
Plot!! to overthrow America!!! por N Y Times Mag p6+ Jl 21 '63

about

Fright peddlers fed on irresponsible charges. J. N. Eller. America 108:734 My 25 '63
Like a lone tree. por Time 81:24 Je 7 '63
Strange case of Thomas Kuchel. Cato. Nat R 16:716 Ag 25 '64

KUCHTA, Gladys
Kuchta's Bruennhilde. M. Bernheimer. Sat R 46:31 D 14 '63

KUCKUCK, F. D.
Incinerator can be attractive. Am City 78: 96-8 Mr '63

KUCYN, Chester J.
Check-out for your electronics. Motor B 112: 39+ S '63
Installing a marine generating plant. Motor B 112:38-9+ N '63

KUDU hunting. See Antelope hunting

KUEHNELT-LEDDIHN, Erik Maria, ritter von
America: Baroque and Gothic. Nat R 16: 736-7 Ag 25 '64
Letter from Asia (cont) por Nat R 14:236 Mr 26 '63
Letter from South America (cont) por Nat R 17:62+ Ja 26 '65
Letter from the Continent. See occasional issues of National review
Reasoned ethics. Nat R 17:25-6 Ja 12 '65
Russia, thirty years later. Nat R 15:479-81+ D 3 '63

KUEPPERS, Friedrich, and others
Hereditary deficiency of serum α_1-antitrypsin. bibliog Science 146:1678-9 D 25 '64

KUESTER, David
Time to study. Harper 226:31-4 Je '63

KUETTNER, Klaus E. and Lindenbaum, Arthur
Heparinic acids: determination of equivalent weights and sulfate to carboxyl ratios. bibliog Science 144:1228-9 Je 5 '64

KUH, Frederick
Back seat for the liberals. Nation 196:522-4 Je 22 '63
New Russo-Chinese equation. Nation 199:294 N 2 '64

KUH, Katharine
Art in the Soviet Union. Sat R 46:17-26 Ag 24 '63
Art of collecting. Sat R 47:37-52 Ja 18 '64
Artist looks at children. Sat R 46:35-8 D 14 '63
Art's voyage of discovery. Sat R 47:149-51+ Ag 29 '64
Beware of sculpture. Vogue 141:26+ Mr 1 '63
Day pop art died. Sat R 47:24-5 My 23 '64
Delacroix: prophet in paint. Sat R 46:21-3 Je 22 '63
Fine arts. See occasional issues of Saturday review
(ed) See Mies Van Der Rohe: modern classicist

KUHLMANN-WILSDORF, Doris, and Wilsdorf, H. G. F.
Dislocation movements in metals. bibliog Science 144:17-25 Ap 3 '64

KUHN, Allan
Ice-blue ending. il por Newsweek 65:24+ Ja 18 '65
Open locker 0911. il por Time 85:23 Ja 15 '65
$350,000 loot in a 25c locker. M. Acoca. il pors Life 58:30-3 Ja 22 '65

KUHN, Dave
Thrust lever. See issues of Flying

KUHN, Delia
Nine lives lived for their country. Sat R 47:33-4 Ag 8 '64

KUHN, Ferdinand
Melee in Singapore. Sat R 46:41-2 N 9 '63

KUHN, Irene Corbally
Passing scene. Nat R 14:504-5 Je 18 '63

KUHN, James W.
Prospects for organization of white-collar workers. Mo Labor R 87:129-31 F '64

KUHN, Nobuko O. and Harford, C. G.
Electron microscope autoradiography of bacteria labeled with iodine-125. bibliog Science 141:355-6 Jl 26 '63

KUHNER, W. R.
Practical preventive maintenance. Am City 79:112-13 F '64

KUIKURU Indians. See Indians of South America—Brazil

KUIPER, Gerard P.
Lunar and planetary laboratory. por Sky & Tel 27:4-7, 88-92 Ja-F '64
Portable astronomer. W. Jonathan. por Sat R 47:36-7 S 5 '64

KUIPER, Pieter J. C.
Inducing resistance to freezing and desiccation in plants by decenylsuccinic acid. bibliog Science 146:544-6 O 23 '64
Water transport across root cell membranes: effect of alkenylsuccinic acids. bibliog Science 143:690-1 F 14 '64

KULICKE and Soffa manufacturing company
When tiny parts must be moved just a bit. il Bsns W p 100-2 S 21 '63

KULKARNI, Arun B. See Eriksen, S. P. jt. auth.

KULUKUNDIS lines, incorporated
Father and son; U.S.-flag fleet. Newsweek 61:78 Mr 11 '63
New blow to Kulukundis; liens by India and Pakistan. Bsns W p78 S 14 '63
Shipwreck of an epic fleet. il Bsns W p60-1+ Ag 10 '63

KULWANT, Roy
Himalayan pilgrimage. il Travel 121:51-3 Ap '64

KUMARI, Ashwini
Nehru's new centrism. Reporter 29:32-5 D 5 '63

KUMIN, Maxine W.
January 25th; poem. Atlan 215:67 Ja '65
July fifth in the old burying ground; poem. Harper 229:67 Jl '64
Man who sits up nights; poem. Atlan 212: 120 Jl '63
May tenth; poem. New Yorker 40:46 My 9 '64
Microscope; poem. Atlan 211:129 Mr '63
Poetry workshop. See issues of Writer
Quarry, pigeon cove; poem. Harper 226:39 Ap '63
Widow; poem. Harper 228:95 Ap '64

KUMLIEN, Gunnar D.
Council, right and left. Commonweal 79:362-3 D 20 '63
Crescent and cross. Commonweal 80:364-5 Je 12 '64
Gandhi of Sicily. Commonweal 79:745-6 Mr 20 '64
Gift of holiness; Pope John. Commonweal 78: 371-2 Je 28 '63
Khrushchev and the Italian Communists. Commonweal 81:408-9 D 18 '64
Pope's bombshell. Commonweal 78:71-2 Ap 12 '63
Suffragette nuns. Commonweal 81:95-7 O 16 '64

KUMMER, Clare
Her master's voice. Criticism
New Yorker 40:84+ Ja 9 '65

KUMQUATS
Kumquats make colorful gifts. il Sunset 131:186 D '63

KUNCEWICZ, Maria
Letter from Poland. Nation 197:423-4 D 14 '63
Tips. Pub W 184:94-5 S 16 '63
KUNDSIN, Ruth B. and others
Staphylococcus aureus UC-18: agent of nosocomial infections. Science 145:1322-3 S 18 '64
KÜNG, Hans
Church and freedom. Commonweal 78:343-53 Je 21 '63
Father Kueng speaks on mixed marriages. Christian Cent 80:453 Ap 10 '63
Interview with Hans Küng; ed. by J. B. Sheerin. Cath World 197:159-63 Je '63
Latin: the church's mother tongue? excerpts from Council in action. Harper 227:60-4 O '63
Reunion and the Jews. Christian Cent 80:829 Je 26 '63
Understanding the church's teaching office; excerpt from The council in action. Cath World 198:21-7 O '63
Word of thanks. America 108:826-9 Je 8 '63
about
Church of silence. A. V. Krebs, jr. il Commonweal 80:467-76 Jl 10 '64
Clear it with the Vatican. por Time 82:72 S 20 '63
Coming of Küng. R. M. Brown. Commonweal 78:133-5 Ap 26 '63
Ecumenical voices. il por Time 81:52 Ap 5 '63
Küng in America. Newsweek 61:74 Ap 1 '63
Not as a stranger. America 108:353 Mr 16 '63
On discussing freedom. America 108:663 My 11 '63
Spirit bloweth; concerning Father Hans Kung's address at Georgetown university. A. Dun. New Repub 148:8 My 18 '63
Theologian is an unusual visitor. M. McGrory. America 108:823 Je 8 '63
KUNG, Ignatius, bp
Absent from Vatican II. America 109:652 N 23 '63
KÜNG, Kurt
Swiss view of U.S. strikes: you lose orders, and jobs. U S News 54:37 F 4 '63
KUNG, Shiu-shia, and others
Potentiation of 5-fluorouracil inhibition of Flexner-Jobling carcinoma by glucose. bibliog Science 141:627-8 Ag 16 '63
KUNHARDT, Dorothy Meserve
And his face was chalky white. Life 54:87-8 F 15 '63
Everyone told Lincoln to keep his speech short. Life 55:118+ N 15 '63
Willie was the favorite. Life 55:11 Ag 23 '63
KUNI, Masami
Contrast in climates. por Dance Mag 37:18-19 Je '63
KUNIN, Vladimir N.
Underground water: wasted treasure. UNESCO Courier 17:14-18+ Jl '64
KUNITZ, Stanley
Roethke: poet of transformations. New Repub 152:23-9 Ja 23 '65
(tr) See Voznesenskiĭ, A. Fire in the architectural institute
KUNKEL, Henry G. and others
Individual antigenic specificity of isolated antibodies. bibliog Science 140:1218-19 Je 14 '63
—See Allen, J. C. jt. auth.
KUNKEL, Marguerite P.
Charm is where thalictrums grow. Horticulture 41:250 My '63
Geum. Horticulture 42:43 My '64
Penstemons for color impact. Horticulture 41:72 F '63
Use phlox carpeting. Horticulture 41:307 Je '63
KUNKLE, Hannah Josephine
Junior book collectors. Wilson Lib Bul 38:176-7 O '63
KUNSTLER, William M.
Fair bail for all. Nation 197:52-3 Jl 27 '63
Lawyer. Nation 199:507-9 D 28 '64
—and Kinoy, Arthur
Southern justice: lawyers walk in fear. Nation 198:576-80 Je 8 '64
KUNTZ, Garland P.
SCA; background-music demultiplexer. Electr World 72:44-5 S '64
KUP, Karl
Medieval codex of Italy. Natur Hist 72:30-41 D '63
KUPCHAN, S. Morris, and others
Calotropin, a cytotoxic principle isolated from asclepias curassavica. L. bibliog Science 146:1685-6 D 25 '64
KUPERMAN, Albert S. and others
Procaine action: antagonism by adenosine triphosphate and other nucleotides. bibliog Science 144:1222-3 Je 5 '64
KUPERSTOCK, Kit
Family facts on file. Parents Mag 38:54+ Jl '63
No feeding problems at our house. Parents Mag 38:69-71+ My '63
Seven signs of readiness for school. Parents Mag 38:56-7+ Je '63
KUPFERBERG, Herbert
Record reviews. See issues of Atlantic
Record reviews. Atlan 211:124-5 F; 124 Je; 212:121 Jl; 115 Ag; 115 S; 144-5 O; 150-1 D '63; 213:111-12 Ja; 132-3 F; 178-9 Mr '64
They shall have music. See issues of Atlantic
KUPKA, Frank
Bright Orpheus. il Time 84:36-7 Jl 31 '64
KUPKE, D. W. and Huntington, J. L.
Chlorophyll *a* appearance in the dark in higher plants; analytical notes. bibliog Science 140:49-51 Ap 5 '63
KURALT, Wallace
Birth control and the poor: a solution. J. Shepherd. il por Look 28:64-7 Ap 7 '64
KURDS
Better than nothing; Kurdish truce with the Iraqi government. il Newsweek 63:45 F 24 '64
Journey among the brave men, by D. A. Schmidt. Review
Sat R 47:34 Je 20 '64. E. Wakin
Kurdish dream; autonomy. il Newsweek 61:49+ Mr 25 '63
Men of the mountains. il Time 81:25-6 My 31 '63
Turkey in crisis; jungle of interrelated nightmares. G. Gersh. Christian Cent 80:231-3 F 20 '63
Ultimatum and war; Kurdish tribesmen and Iraqi troops. Newsweek 61:56 Je 24 '63
KURFURSTENDAMM. See Berlin (West Berlin)—Streets
KURLAND, Philip B.
Court feels free to decide what is best for the Nation; interview. por U S News 58:60-2 Ja 18 '65
Protecting the right of privacy. PTA Mag 58:10-12 Mr '64
KURNITZ, Harry
Billy the Wild. Holiday 35:93-4+ Je '64
KUROSAWA, Akira
Seven bullets. Newsweek 63:84 Mr 9 '64
KURSH, Harry
Don't get trapped by a psychoquack. Todays Health 42:28-3+ Mr '64
KURTH, Marguerite. See Frey, M. K.
KURTZ, Abraham N. See Herrett, R. A. jt. auth.
KURTZ, Henry I. See Fried, J. P. jt. auth.
KURTZ, Vernon
Hop along, Oliver. Redbook 120:44 Ap '63
KURZ, Selma
Die goettliche Kurz and others. G. Breuer. por Am Rec G 30:884-5 My '64
Kurz d'Andrade, Santley, Van Rooy. A. Favia-Artsay. por Hobbies 68:30-1 My '63
KURZBAND, Toby K.
(ed) Why I want to teach art. Sch Arts 63:5-7 N '63
KURZMAN, Dan
Frustration of infiltration. Sat R 46:25 Jl 20 '63
Lament for a land in torment. Sat R 47:49 S 26 '64
One side of truth. Sat R 46:44-5 Mr 30 '63
KUSCH, Rodolfo
When to be is not to be. Américas 15:19-22 O '63
KUSH. See Cush
KUTA, Edwin J.
Polarographic investigation of conjugated fat-soluble vitamins. bibliog Science 144:1130-1 My 29 '64
KUTILA, Mary
Drawing approaches for the intermediate grades. Sch Arts 62:3-6 Je '63
KUTSCHBACH, Hans F.
Battle of the bulbs. Pop Electr 21:44-5+ Ag '64
KUTTNER, Stephen G.
Yale's Catholic professor. por Time 82:36 D 27 '63
KUWABARA, Takeo
Oriental echoes of the Social contract; summary of address, 1962. UNESCO Courier 16:24-6 Mr '63
KUWAIT
Auto age in Kuwait. il N Y Times Mag p 108-9 S 15 '63
Crisis in paradise. il Newsweek 65:37-8 Ja 11 '65
Kuwait: a super-affluent society. F. Shehab. For Affairs 42:461-74 Ap '64
Kuwait: Wall Street of the Middle East. R. Hewins. il Nation 198:234-6 Mr 9 '64

KUWAIT—*Continued*
Where the money is. il Time 81:96 My 24 '63
See also
Liquor laws and legislation—Kuwait
Petroleum industry and trade—Kuwait
United Nations—Kuwait

KUZIN, Alexander M.
Fall-out hazards now and yesterday. UNESCO Courier 17:11-13 N '64

KUZMA, Greg
Diminutive me sleeps green; poem. Atlan 214:57 Ag '64

KUZNETS, Simon S.
Is the long cycle why we don't grow? creeping pace of industrial growth. por Bsns W p78+ F 16 '63

KVARACEUS, William C.
How to spot a dropout. Sr Schol 83:10T N 8 '63
PTA: the irrelevant giant. Nation 197:200-1 O 5 '63
Speaking out. por Sat Eve Post 237:6+ My 2 '64
World side story; excerpts from Juvenile delinquency, a problem for the modern world. UNESCO Courier 17:4-11 My; 4-9 Je; 28-32 S '64

KVIETYS, Dalia
Jonathan and Milly. See issues of Seventeen to August 1964

KWASHIORKOR
Eating but still starving. R. Yoshioka. il Sci N L 83:346-7 Je 1 '63
For the child who has nothing. New Repub 151:7-9 D 26 '64

KWESKIN, Jim
But only use a 10¢ comb. il por Time 82:37 D 27 '63

KY, Nguyen-cao-. See Nguyen-cao-Ky

KYES, John F.
Autumn harvest; Worcester music festival. Mus Am 84:20 Ja '64

KYLBERG, Anna Maria
Children's library service in Sweden; short survey. por Library J 88:4417-20 N 15 '63

KYLE, Jim
Design trends in receiver frequency control. Electr World 72:52-4+ D '64
Diode curve-tracer & analyzer. Electr World 71:44-5+ Je '64
Electronic sirens. Electr World 71:32-3 Ap '64
Electronic tachometers. Electr World 71:34-5+ My '64
Measuring the sonic boom. Electr World 72:58-60+ O '64
Resistor power-rating nomogram. Electr World 71:29 Ap '64

KYLE, Keith
This strange thing called African socialism. Reporter 28:27-9 Je 6 '63

KYLLONEN, Ronald R.
Behavior: disturbed or disturbing? NEA J 53:50-2 S '64

KYOTO, Japan
Chrysanthemums are blooming now at Nijo castle. il Sunset 133:74+ N '64
New Japan. R. Blackmon. il Vogue 144:84-5+ Ag 15 '64
On a hurried tour, an unhurried look; Katsura and Shugakuin imperial villas. il Sunset 131:39-40 N '63

KYPRIANOU, Spyros
Symbol of peace. UN Mo Chron 1:9-10 O '64

KYTLE, Calvin
Testament of a transplanted white southerner. Sat R 47:20-1+ My 30 '64

L

LAD. See American library association—Library administration division

LAFTA. See Latin American free trade association

LARA (light armed reconnaissance aircraft) See Airplanes, Military—United States

LASV (low altitude supersonic vehicle) See Guided missiles

LAWS (leadership and world society) See International relations—Study and teaching

LBJ company
Johnsons' holdings put on ice; in trust for the duration. il Bsns W p23 D 7 '63

LBJ ranch. See Ranches

LC. See United States—Library of Congress

LDH (lactic dehydrogenases) See Dehydrogenases

LEERS (long-endurance experimental research submarine) See Submarine boats, Atomic powered

LEM (lunar excursion module) See Space vehicles—Landing systems

LMI. See Logistics management institute

LOP (line of position) See Radio aids to navigation

LSCA (Library services and construction act) See Library laws and legislation

LSD. See Lysergic acid diethylamide

LTP. See American library association—Library technology project

LAAS, William, and Du Bay, Theodore
Boom times for piggy-bankers. Sat Eve Post 237:66+ F 15 '64

LABANOTATION. See Dance notation

LA BARRE, Weston
Diabolic root. N Y Times Mag p96+ N 1 '64

LABBE, Robert F. See Onisawa, J. jt. auth.

LABELING of books. See Books—Labeling, marking, etc.

LABELS
Attention bird owners: a penny saved. . . ! bird charcoal. il Consumer Bul 46:22 Jl '63
Beware the snake. il Time 83:48 Mr 27 '64
Child nutrition à la advertising; Royal custard style dessert. Consumer Rep 29:158 Ap '64
Consumers are reading the labels on insecticides. Consumer Bul 46:32-3 Ag '63
Contents anonymous; Zestees. Consumer Rep 28:414-15 S '63
Deceptive packaging, deceptive claims of an antiseptic mouthwash for a sore throat. il Consumer Bul 48:43+ F '65
Food package labels always of interest; more chemicals than food materials. Consumer Bul 47:39 My '64
Gummed label art; paper labels make offbeat screen print motif. il Design 65:56 N '63
Hazardous substances. il Consumer Bul 46:39 Ag '63
Important seals of approval and what they mean to the consumer. il Consumer Bul 46:24-5+ Jl '63
Label on the pack? Newsweek 64:62 Jl 6 '64
New poison symbol irks snake expert; not all snakes are poisonous. Sci N L 86:120 Ag 22 '64
Nutrition: fad vs. fact; stricter rules for labeling. il Changing T 17:34-6 Jl '63
Packagers take a hint from the Hart bill. il Bsns W p47 N 23 '63
Quick and easy home label maker; Dymo home labelmaker. il Consumer Rep 29:317-18 Jl '64
Should medicine be labelled? il Sci Digest 55:89 My '64
Smoke & ire; FTC requirement of health warnings on all cigarette packages. Time 84:78 Jl 3 '64
So simple, so treacherous; mislabeled drugs. T. Taylor. il Sat Eve Post 237:66-7 N 28 '64
Some sublimely ridiculous labels. Consumer Rep 29:365-6 Ag '64
Warning on every pack; new FTC rule. Bsns W p36 Je 27 '64
What the labels do not say. C. Callison. Audubon Mag 65:164 My '63
What would you do? il Consumer Bul 47:43 Ap '64
When a hazard warning isn't enough; X-33 water repellent. Consumer Rep 29:4-5 Ja '64
Who goes there? bumper stickers. Newsweek 64:80+ Ag 24 '64
See also
Marks of origin

LABOR (obstetrics) See Childbirth

LABOR, Compulsory
Convention on abolition of forced labor; text. Dept State Bul 49:326-7 Ag 26 '63

LABOR, Department of. See United States—Labor, Department of

LABOR, Migrant. See Migrant labor

LABOR agreements. See Trade agreements

LABOR and laboring classes
See also
Absenteeism
Employment
Hours of labor
Migrant labor
National industrial recreation association
Right to labor
Unemployment
Work

Bibliography

Book reviews and notes. See issues of Monthly labor review

LABOR and laboring classes—*Continued*

Education

Educational attainment of workers, March 1962. D. F. Johnston. il Mo Labor R 86: 504-15 My '63
See also
Trade unions—Educational work

International aspects

See Trade unions—International aspects

Non-wage payments

See Non-wage payments

Statistics

Current labor statistics. See issues of Monthly labor review
See also
Accidents, Industrial—Statistics

Argentina

Peronism without Perón; General confederation of labor day long take over of factories and businesses. Newsweek 63:40+ Je 1 '64

Asia

See also
Trade unions—Asia

Australia

Medicare, labor, race: how Australia handles them; interview. H. Beale. il U S News 54: 92-7 Mr 25 '63
See also
Trade unions—Australia

Belgium

See also
Trade unions—Belgium

British Guiana

See also
Strikes—British Guiana

Canada

See also
Insurance, Unemployment—Canada
Trade unions—Canada

China (People's Republic)

Happiness says Mao is a hard day's work. I. Stewart. il N Y Times Mag p34+ S 27 '64

Europe, Western

In Europe: where paychecks beckon across borders. il U S News 58:75-7 Ja 18 '65

Looking for labor. il Time 84:106 O 23 '64

France

Patterns of industrial strike activity in France during the July monarchy. P. N. Stearns. bibliog f Am Hist R 70:371-94 Ja '65
See also
Labor laws and legislation—France
Strikes—France
Trade unions—France
Wages—France

Germany (Federal Republic)

Men of leisure. il Newsweek 63:46+ My 25 '64

Passing of work-obsessed Germany. T. Prittie. il N Y Times Mag p41+ Ap 21 '63

Pause in West Germany's boom. il Bsns W p60 Je 8 '63

Where business is so good that workers have to be imported. U S News 57:109-10 S 28 '64
See also
Trade unions—Germany (Federal Republic)

Great Britain

Making of the English working class, by E. P. Thompson. Review
Commentary 38:69-71 Jl '64. B. B. Seligman
Commonweal 80:521-2 Jl 24 '64. Mayhew

New training law in Great Britain. Mo Labor R 87:III-IV Ag '64
See also
Labor party (Great Britain)
Strikes—Great Britain
Trade unions—Great Britain
Trades union congress
Unemployment—Great Britain
Wages—Great Britain

History

Making of the English working class, by E. P. Thompson. Review
Nation 198:349-51 Ap 6 '64. N. Fruchter

Hawaii

See also
Trade unions—Hawaii

India

Collective bargaining contracts in India. il Mo Labor R 86:300-1 Mr '63

Japan

Japan's prime natural resource is people. il Fortune 68:142-9 Jl '63

Labor in a prosperous Japan. S. B. Levine. bibliog f Cur Hist 46:212-18 Ap '64
See also
Strikes—Japan
Trade unions—Japan

Latin America

Declaration of Cundinamarca; Inter-American conference of ministers of labor on the Alliance for progress. il Américas 15:44-5 Jl '63
See also
Trade unions—Latin America

Mexico

Revolutionary promise. Time 82:27 D 20 '63

Netherlands

See also
Wages—Netherlands

Pennsylvania

See also
Unemployment—Pennsylvania

Russia

Pressure on Khrushchev. P. Ben. New Repub 148:7-8 Mr 8 '63
See also
Labor laws and legislation—Russia

Southern states

Ethnic and economic minorities: unions' future or unrecruitable? R. Marshall. bibliog f Ann Am Acad 350:63-73 N '63

Spain

See also
Trade unions—Spain

United States

Business and labor meet the President. il Newsweek 62:65 D 16 '63

Chronology of recent labor events. See issues of Monthly labor review

Doubts amid plenty. il Time 84:97 S 11 '64

Labor at the crossroads. il Sr Schol 82:4-6+ F 27 '63

Labor force and employment, 1960-62. J. L. Meredith. il Mo Labor R 86:497-503 My '63

Labor in 1963. J. F. Strickland. bibliog f Mo Labor R 86:1398-404 D '63

Labor month in review. See issues of Monthly labor review

Marital and family characteristics of workers, March 1962. J. Schiffman. il Mo Labor R 86:24-36 Ja '63

Obsolescent unions. A. H. Raskin. Commentary 36:18-25 Jl '63

On the labor front. J. O'Gara. Commonweal 78:43 Ap 5 '63

Politics of protest; address, November 30, 1963. J. T. Conway. Vital Speeches 30:313-17 Mr 1 '64

Room above the bottom; demand for skilled and semi-skilled workers. il Time 83:87 My 1 '64

Rumbles from the rank and file. A. H. Raskin. il Reporter 32:27-30 Ja 28 '65

Special labor force report. See issues of Monthly labor review

What's ahead for labor? N. W. Chamberlain. Atlan 214:34-7 Jl '64

Worker security in a changing economy; symposium. bibliog f il Mo Labor R 86: 612-702 Je '63
See also
American federation of labor and Congress of industrial organizations
Labor laws and legislation—United States
Migrant labor
Negroes in the United States—Employment
Strikes—United States
Trade unions—United States
Unemployment—United States
United States—Labor, Department of
Wages—United States

Bibliography

Labor at the crossroads. A. A. Blum. Harvard Bsns R 42:6-8+ Jl '64

History

Organized labor in American history, by P. Taft. Review
Duns R 84:65-6 O '64. T. R. Brooks

LABOR and laboring classes—United States —*Continued*

Political activities

See Trade unions—Political activities

Yugoslavia

See also
Unemployment—Yugoslavia

LABOR and libraries. See Libraries—Work with trade unions

LABOR banks. See Banks and banking, Trade union

LABOR boards
See also
United States—National labor relations board

LABOR camps
Holiday cure for bored teen-agers. A. Gillette. il UNESCO Courier 16:24-7 '63
Summers with purpose. J. Cook. il N Y Times Mag p55 Mr 29 '64
See also
International voluntary workcamps
United States—Civilian conservation corps

LABOR conferences
See also
International labor organization

LABOR contracts
See also
Trade agreements

LABOR cost
Costs stay in line as business expands. il Bsns W p43-4+ Jl 18 '64
International comparisons of unit labor cost: concepts and methods. W. C. Shelton and J. H. Chandler. bibliog f il Mo Labor R 86:538-47 My '63
Labor costs at the World's fair. U S News 57:74 Jl 6 '64
Role of labor cost in foreign trade. W. C. Shelton and J. H. Chandler. bibliog f il Mo Labor R 86:485-90 My '63
Unit labor costs in eight countries since 1950. J. H. Chandler and P. C. Jackman. bibliog f il Mo Labor R 87:377-84 Ap '64

LABOR day
You can't get there from here: Labor day beach party. C. Ford. Field & S 68:6+ S '63

LABOR displacement. See Unemployment, Technological

LABOR disputes
Battle of Dagenham; Ford motor co. of England. Newsweek 61:76+ Mr 18 '63
Dictated settlement. H. Hazlitt. Newsweek 61:82 F 11 '63
Jailing a whole local; longshoremen's refusal to load Canadian ship at Chicago. Bsns W p 134+ D 7 '63
Labor experts urge new policies; interviews. G. D. Reilly; G. Farmer. il Nations Bsns 51:66-8+ Ap '63
Labor relations; role of government; address, August 27, 1964. C. Donahue. Vital Speeches 30:751-5 O 1 '64
Labor's crisis of public confidence. A. H. Raskin. il Sat R 46:21-5+ Mr 30 '63
New era in bargaining? T. R. Brooks. Duns R 81:91-2+ Ap '63
New look at arbitration. L. Stessin. il N Y Times Mag p26+ N 17 '63
New union target; the courts. il Nations Bsns 52:32-3+ Ja '64
Puzzle in the courts. T. R. Brooks. Duns R 81:52+ Je '63
Should the U.S. have a labor court? T. R. Brooks. Duns R 83:59-62 Mr '64
Triumph by telephone: boycott on loading ships with wheat for Russia. Newsweek 63:71 Mr 9 '64
See also
Arbitration, Industrial—United States
Grievance procedures
Strikes
United States—Federal mediation and conciliation service
United States—National labor relations board

LABOR education. See Industrial relations—Study and teaching

LABOR in politics. See Trade unions—Political activities

LABOR laws and legislation
Approaches to union security in Switzerland, Canada, and Columbia: excerpt from address. M. Dudra. Mo Labor R 86:136-8 F '63
See also
Picketing

Europe, Western

Freedom of association in eight European countries. H. Brickman. bibliog f Mo Labor R 86:1020-5 S '63

France

De Gaulle's labor policy on trial: what the French strikes are about. il U S News 54:90-1 Ap 1 '63

Great Britain

Labor law nobody wants; Contracts of employment act. Bsns W p55 Je 27 '64

Hawaii

Hawaii's unions get mainland look. il Bsns W p86+ S 7 '63

Russia

Neither communism nor capitalism. E. Crankshaw. il N Y Times Mag p36-7+ O 6 '63

United States

American labor in 1962; a retrospect. P. Groom. bibliog f Mo Labor R 86:14-23 Ja '63
Antitrust laws for labor unions? il U S News 54:13 Ap 8 '63
Canada copes with automation. Bsns W p75 Ja 26 '63
Closing the loophole; jurisdiction over right-to-work issues. Time 82:87 D 13 '63
Economics of training the unemployed: manpower development and training act of 1962. L. A. Cornelsen. il Sch Life 47:17-18 O '64
Executives who deal with unions give their views. il Nations Bsns 51:70-1 My '63
Fairer wages for the fair sex; Fair labor standards act. il Bsns W p74 Je 6 '64
For the new President: big tests ahead on labor front. il U S News 55:108-9 D 9 '63
Government, labor and management; address, December 3, 1962. J. L. Block. Vital Speeches 29:250-4 F 1 '63
Hoffa's newest enemy: a law's fine print; Landrum-Griffin act. Bsns W p47-8+ Ap 4 '64
How the law backs Benny the Bug. Bsns W p85-6 N 7 '64
Individual and the union. A. W. Blumrosen. Mo Labor R 86:659-65 Je '63
Individual's legal rights as an employee. B. Aaron. Mo Labor R 86:666-73 Je '63
Inflationary pay. Nations Bsns 51:79-80 Ag '63
Is Kennedy board rewriting labor law? including Landrum-Griffin act. il U S News 55:91-2 Jl 8 '63
Is President Johnson in labor's corner? concerning State-of-the-Union message. il U S News 58:72-3 Ja 18 '65
Johnson and labor: the 1964 outlook. U S News 55:94 D 2 '63
Labor in 1963. J. F. Strickland. bibliog f Mo Labor R 86:1398-404 D '63
Labor outlook hinges on government. il Nations Bsns 51:38-9+ D '63
Labor secretary speaks. Bsns W p48+ O 17 '64
Labor's Bill of rights. T. R. Brooks. Duns R 82:53 N '63
Labor's crisis of public confidence. A. H. Raskin. il Sat R 46:21-5+ Mr 30 '63
Last chance for bargaining. Bsns W p 160 S 7 '63
Legalized labor chaos. H. Hazlitt. Newsweek 61:82 F 25 '63
LBJ and unions: what he tells them, what they want. il U S News 55:106-7 D 16 '63
Managing your manpower; right-to-work movement. T. R. Brooks. Duns R 81:91 Ap '63
Manpower development and training act; the 1963 amendments. il Sch Life 46:12-16 Mr '64
Manpower planning and the new pariahs. E. M. Brandes. il Reporter 30:17-19 Mr 26 '64
Only the cream; Manpower development and training act. il Newsweek 62:69 D 16 '63
Power but no push; AFL-CIO convention in New York. il Bsns W p25-7 N 23 '63
Re-education; Manpower development and training act. il(p 1T) Sr Schol 82:2T+ F 13 '63
Right to work: a hard one for LBJ. L. Baker. il Reporter 32:23-5 Ja 14 '65
Right to work battles planned. U S News 54:88-9 Mr 4 '63
Right to work: the test of union strength in Congress. il U S News 57:70-1 D 21 '64
Role of government in union growth. P. Ross. Ann Am Acad 350:74-85 N '63
Significant decisions in labor cases. See issues of Monthly labor review
State labor legislation enacted in 1963. S. R. Weissbrodt. Mo Labor R 86:1297-301 N '63
State labor legislation enacted in 1964. N. M. Diamond. Mo Labor R 87:1291-4 N '64
Striking facts. J. O'Gara. Commonweal 77:556 F 22 '63
This month's feature: Administration's youth employment bill. Cong Digest 42:291-310 D '63
Train the job-hunter to fit the job. il Changing T 19:21-3 Ja '65
Training for a job under MDTA. R. W. Dugger. il Sch Life 45:17-22 F '63

LABOR laws and legislation—United States —*Continued*
Victory for right to work law: an issue in 1964 campaign? banning of agency shop and union shop. U S News 55:108 D 16 '63
Wage law: changes LBJ wants. U S News 56: 88 F 10 '64
When pickets are used to scare away customers. il U S News 54:74-5 F 4 '63
Whose equal rights? National labor relations act, right to work laws. D. Lawrence. U S News 55:104 Ag 19 '63
Will Congress toughen anti-walkout laws? il Bsns W p88-9 Ja 19 '63
You can't steal a union anymore. L. Velie. Read Digest 83:125-9 Ag '63
See also
Arbitration, Industrial—United States
Child labor laws and legislation—United States
Insurance, Unemployment—United States
Minimum wage—United States

Taft-Hartley law

Mr Johnson' quest for unanimous love; promise to repeal section 14-B of the Taft-Hartley act. E. T. Folliard. America 112: 103 Ja 23 '65
Payoff: repeal of Taft-Hartley's section on Right-to work. Nat R 16:1090 D 15 '64
Unions get a White House nod; repeal right-to-work laws. Bsns W p80 Ja 9 '65
Will Congress toughen anti-walkout laws? il Bsns W p88-9 Ja 19 '63

LABOR leaders. See Trade unions—Officials

LABOR-management cooperation. See Employees representation in management

LABOR-management relations. See Industrial relations

LABOR market. See Labor supply

LABOR mobility. See Occupational mobility

LABOR officials. See Trade unions—Officials

LABOR output. See Labor productivity

LABOR party (Great Britain)
Addendum on Holy Loch. Newsweek 63:44 Mr 23 '64
Anatomy of Britain's Labor party. S. Gruson. il N Y Times Mag p 17+ Ap 19 '64
Britain's policy if labour wins. H. Wilson. Atlan 212:61-5 O '63
Britain's Prime Minister in waiting. U S News 54:16 F 25 '63
British defense policy under Labor. A. Verrier. For Affairs 42:282-92 Ja '64
British elections. R. Williams. Nation 199: 154-7 S 28 '64
British labor accepts the challenge. H. Brandon. Sat R 47:18 N 14 '64
British labour goes suburban. New Repub 148:6-7 F 2 '63
British Labor looks at Europe. R. H. S. Crossman. For Affairs 41:732-43 Jl '63
British labour's arms plan. W. Young. New Repub 150:12-14 My 23 '64
Conservative enemy: a program for radical reform in the sixties, by C. A. R. Crosland. Review
Commentary 36:178-80 Ag '63. L. A. Coser; Discussion. 37:12 Ja '64
Could have been worse, but is it good enough? Time 84:39-40 N 20 '64
Dons & brothers; new Labor cabinet. il Time 84:35 O 23 '64
Familiar and unfamiliar: some faces of labor; the Wilson government. il Newsweek 64:51 N 2 '64
Harold Wilson's Britain. N. MacKenzie. Harper 228:73-6+ F '64
Harold Wilson's hour. C. Sterling. il Reporter 31:17-20 N 5 '64
Harold Wilson's new look. A. Lejeune. Nat R 14:320 Ap 23 '63
Honorable government. il Time 84:24-5 N 6 '64
If the Socialists take over in Britain. il U S News 55:58-9 O 21 '63
It's Harold vs. Harold as Labor picks a leader. il Newsweek 61:33 F 25 '63
Labour tries to broaden the base. E. M. Hugh-Jones. il Reporter 29:26-30 N 7 '63
Labor's big ten: if Harold Wilson wins they are ready for duty. il Newsweek 64:46-7 S 28 '64
Labour's first few weeks. A. Burnet. New Repub 151:11-12 N 14 '64
Labour's new leader. H. Massingham. New Repub 148:17 Mr 2 '63
Labor's opportunity. Commonweal 81:148-9 O 30 '64
Labour's shadow diplomacy; interview; ed. by G. Brook-Shepherd. P. G. Walker. il Reporter 30:37-40 F 13 '64
Left vs. right in Britain's Labor party. U S News 54:20 F 18 '63
Letter from London. M. Panter-Downes. New Yorker 39:145 My 25 '63
Letter from London; annual conference. M. Panter-Downes. New Yorker 39:207-8+ O 19 '63
Letter from London; death of H. Gaitskell. M. Panter-Downes. New Yorker 38:94+ F 2 '63
Leyton affair. il Time 85:23 Ja 29 '65
Looking left; Harold Wilson's ministers. il Time 84:39 O 30 '64
Mr Wilson's predicament. H. Massingham. New Repub 151:8-9 O 31 '64
Other Harold; new leader. il Time 81:29-30 F 22 '63
People matter. Newsweek 63:44+ Mr 16 '64
Politics of the possible: the British scene. N. Birnbaum. Nation 196:244-7 Mr 23 '63
Relationship of Britain and United States; address, April 1, 1963. H. Wilson. Vital Speeches 29:418-21 My 1 '63
Road to Jerusalem; annual conference. il Time 82:34-8 O 11 '63
Rough days ahead in British politics. il Bsns W p28-9 Ja 26 '63
Search for an heir. il Newsweek 61:33+ F 4 '63
State of affairs. H. Brandon. Sat R 48:14-15 Ja 2 '65
Strange death of Tory England. J. Mander. Commentary 38:41-5 D '64
Successor to Gaitskell. R. F. Charles. America 108:248 F 23 '63
Victory in the air; annual conference. Newsweek 62:44 O 14 '63
What a labor government would be like. Time 81:24 Je 28 '63
Who'll lead Labor? il Newsweek 61:42 F 18 '63
Wilson: Labor's gray mystery; will these men run Britain? il Newsweek 61:42-4+ Ap 15 '63; Same abr. with title Harold Wilson: Britain's question mark. Read Digest 83:109-13 O '63
Wilson seems shoo-in; probable results of Profumo scandal. il Bsns W p28-9 Je 22 '63
Wooing the middle class. il Time 81:35 F 15 '63

LABOR productivity
Costs stay in line as business expands. il Bsns W p43-4+ Jl 18 '64
Fallacies and facts about automation. V. R. Fuchs. il N Y Times Mag p27+ Ap 7 '63
Improving individual productivity, by J. D. Staley and I. A. Delloff. Review
Duns R 83:76+ Ja '64. T. R. Brooks
International comparisons of unit labor cost: concepts and methods. W. C. Shelton and J. H. Chandler. bibliog f il Mo Labor R 86: 538-47 My '63
Job analysis. il Fortune 67:44+ F '63
Job performance of federal mail sorters by age. J. F. Walker. bibliog f il Mo Labor R 87:296-300 Mr '64
Making cost control work. R. Likert and S. E. Seashore. bibliog f il Harvard Bsns R 41:96-108 N '63
More in less time. il Time 82:104 N 15 '63
Output per man-hour in the private economy, 1947-63. S. B. Gottlieb. il Mo Labor R 87:429-30 Ap '64
Profit from the learning curve. W. B. Hirschmann. bibliog f il Harvard Bsns R 42:125-39 Ja '64
Real promise of rising productivity. Bsns W p 128 Je 8 '63
Role of labor cost in foreign trade. W. C. Shelton and J. H. Chandler. bibliog f il Mo Labor R 86:485-90 My '63
Total managerial failure; difficulties in Britain. W. W. Allen. Fortune 69:62+ My '64
What productivity does to jobs; report by Columbia university's Bureau of applied social research. il Bsns W p 188-9 S 14 '63
Why steel foresees a feast; with tables. Bsns W p20-1 D 28 '63
See also
Work measurement

LABOR racketeering. See Racketeering

LABOR relations. See Industrial relations

LABOR relations board, National. See United States—National labor relations board

LABOR requirements (for production)
Labor and material requirements for one-family houses. H. J. Rothberg. il Mo Labor R 87:797-800 Jl '64
Labor and material requirements for public housing. S. F. Miller. il Mo Labor R 87: 1029-32 S '64
Labor and material requirements: highway construction, 1958 and 1961. J. C. Wakefield. il Mo Labor R 86:394-8 Ap '63
Labor requirements for army civil works. R. V. Murray. il Mo Labor R 87:532-5 My '64

LABOR saving devices
Take it easy! J. Polshek. See issues of House beautiful

Anecdotes, facetiae, satire, etc.

Tinker's itch. C. Fadiman. il Read Digest 82:19-20+ Mr '63

LABOR statistics, Bureau of. See United States—Labor statistics, Bureau of

LABOR supply
Plant location: where the people are. il Duns R 83:pt2 106-7 Mr '64
See also
Manpower

United States

Coming: a crisis for young workers; Labor dept. study. il Bsns W p27 F 16 '63
Comprehensive manpower and employment planning. Mo Labor R 87:III-IV Je '64
Government and manpower requirements; excerpt from report, March 9, 1964. Mo Labor R 87:407-13 Ap '64
Labor force and employment in 1963. S. S. Holland. il Mo Labor R 87:645-53 Je '64
Labor month in review; young people in the labor market. Mo Labor R 86:III-IV Mr '63
Manpower resources and use; excerpts from Manpower report. W. W. Wirtz. Mo Labor R 86:237-9 Mr '63
Unemployment and labor market policy; excerpt from address. G. P. Schultz. Mo Labor R 86:808-10 Jl '63
Unemployment paradox. il Fortune 70:20+ Ag '64
Where automation's pinch will be; Labor dept.'s analysis. il Bsns W p 114-16+ My 30 '64
Workers are scarce. Nations Bsns 51:95-6 Ap '63

LABOR turnover
Job mobility in 1961. G. Bancroft and S. Garfinkle. il Mo Labor R 86:897-906 Ag '63
Labor turnover; tables. See issues of Monthly labor review
Multi-employer pensions & labor mobility excerpts from Labor mobility from the viewpoint of the older workers. R. C. Miljus and A. C. Johnson. bibliog f Harvard Bsns R 41:147-8+ S '63
When & how to quit a job. C. R. Shelton and M. Colgrove. il Nations Bsns 52:96-8+ O '64
See also
Occupational mobility

LABOR unions. See Trade unions

LABOR vote. See Trade unions—Political activities

LABORATORIES
Lab that jacks built; one-story structure jacked up and first floor and basement built under it. il Bsns W p 138-40 My 9 '64
See also
Atomic research laboratories
Biological laboratories
Medical laboratories
Research laboratories
Testing laboratories

Air conditioning

Air-conditioning design guides for laboratory facilities. A. Greenberg. il Arch Rec 135:197-201 My '64

Architecture

Campus plan for a mountain-top research complex; Bethlehem steel company. il Arch Rec 134:121-5 D '63
Field-free laboratory in a wooded setting; Lawrence radiation laboratory, University of California, Berkeley. il Arch Rec 134: 184-7 S '63
High mountain monastery for research; National center for atmospheric research, Boulder, Colo. il Arch Forum 120:82-5 Ja '64
New laboratory at IBM. il Arch Forum 120: 86-7 F '64
Pharmaceutical castle for the Long Island plain. il Fortune 70:205-6 N '64
Precision laboratory in an industrial park. il Arch Rec 134:128-9 D '63
Word in Britain: character; Leicester university. R. Banham. il Arch Forum 121: 118-25 Ag '64

Equipment

Chassis design for labs: wired units for experimentation and circuit study. J. W. Essex. il Electr World 70:91-2 S '63
Convertible laboratory furniture. il Arch Rec 134:169-72 Ag '63

LABORATORY animals
Connecticut votes dogs for medical research: letter. M. Hume. Science 142:147 O 11 '63
Cruel kindness. America 109:3 Jl 6 '63
Cruelty in the lab? il Newsweek 62:76 Ag 12 '63
First of the month; protection of laboratory animals. C. Amory. Sat R 46:6 My 4; 6 Je 1; 6 Ag 3 '63; Discussion. 46:15 Je 1; 25-6 Je 22; 15 Jl 13; 17-18 Jl 27; 30 S 21; 42 S 28; 26 N 16 '63
Humane laws: action unlikely on variety of animal welfare laws still pending in Congress. E. Langer. Science 143:339-40 Ja 24 '64; Reply with rejoinder. F. B. Orlans. 144:367+ Ap 24 '64
Planned animal care necessary for research. Sci N L 83:130 Mr 2 '63
Speaking out; science is needlessly cruel to animals. C. Amory. Sat Eve Post 236:10+ Jl 27 '63; Discussion. 236:4+ Ag 24; 88 S 7 '63
See also
Animal experimentation
Germ free animals
Monkeys
Rats

LABORATORY schools. See Schools, Experimental

LABORATORY technicians
Danger in our medical labs. M. Pines. Harper 227:84-7+ O '63; Discussion. 227:4+ D '63

LABOREL, Jacques. See Van Andel, T. H. jt. auth.

LABRADOR
See also
Fishing—Labrador

Description and travel

Lifting the lid on Labrador. E. Buck. il Am For 70:28-31+ Ag '64

LABRADOR dogs
Fetch. D. M. Duffey. il Outdoor Life 134:98-101 D '64

LA BRANCHE, Elmer J.
Where copper is king. Travel 122:40-2 Jl '64

LA BREA, Los Angeles
Los Angeles 60,000 years ago; tar pits in Hancock park. J. B. Kemmerer. il Sci Digest 54:48-51 S '63

LABUNSKI, Stephen B.
Mr Labunski and the Camp Fire girls; concerning FCC local television hearings in Omaha. R. L. Shayon. Sat R 46:41 F 23 '63

LABYRINTH (ear)
Ayes and ears; two astronauts afflicted with inner ear troubles. il Newsweek 63:94-5 Ap 27 '64
Inside the inner ear. il Time 83:68 Ap 10 '64
What makes you dizzy. T. Berland. Redbook 121:20+ O '63

LABYRINTH; opera. See Menotti, G. C.

LAC DU FLAMBEAU
See also
Flambeau River

LACE stockings. See Hosiery

LACEBARK pine. See Pine

LACED pinks. See Pinks

LACERDA, Carlos
Brazil; address, June 23, 1964. Vital Speeches 30:717-19 S 15 '64

about

Early bird. Time 84:35 N 20 '64
Front-runner and giant-killer. por Bsns W p76 Ap 11 '64
Hammer & the anvil. il por Time 82:53-4 N 15 '63
Long campaign. il por Newsweek 64:60 N 23 '64
Milk, motherhood and the American flag. New Repub 150:10-11 Ja 4 '64
Most dangerous man in Brazil. J. Dos Passos. il Nat R 15:53-7 Jl 30 '63
Shaking down. Newsweek 64:40 Ag 3 '64

LACEY, Mother Mary Gregory
Let your light shine, sister. America 109:302-5 S 21 '63

LACHAISE, Gaston
Late Lachaise, uncensored at last; two retrospectives, at the Whitney and a New York gallery. E. C. Baker. il Art N 63:44-5+ Mr '64
Radiating sex & soul; exhibition at Los Angeles' County museum of art. il por Time 83:66 Ja 17 '64
Wobbling pivot. il Newsweek 63:54 Mr 2 '64

LACHANCE, Roland
Smooth skating. Recreation 57:356 S '64

LACHENBRUCH, David
Component id and the package ego. Hi Fi 13:64-5+ S '63
—See Sinclair, C. jt. auth.

LACHTER, Lou
HPI telescreen. U S Camera 26:93 F '63
Photographic program featured at Vermont resort. il U S Camera 26:17 F '63
LACKEY, Melvin W.
Filling in the spaces. Sat R 46:39 Ag 17 '63
LACKS, S.
Subunit structure of proteins. Science 146: 559-60+ O 23 '64
LACOSTE, Richard
Floating spacecraft tracking stations. Electr World 72:17-19+ Ag '64
LA COURSE, Guerin
Innocence of John Updike. Commonweal 77: 512-14 F 8 '63
LACQUER and lacquering
18th century art of vernis Martin. G. Kaler. il Hobbies 68:42-3+ Je '63
LACRIMAL organs
Tears and the lacrimal gland. S. Y. Botelho. il Sci Am 211:78-84+ bibliog(p 142) O '64
LACROSSE
Federal power takes over; Navy beats Army for national title. F. Deford. il Sports Illus 20:66+ Je 8 '64
What's a midfielder? il Newsweek 63:54 Je 1 '64
LA CROSSE, Wis.
Do penance; new Lenten regulations. America 110:244 F 22 '64
From farmers' market to parking ramp. M. R. Birnbaum. il Am City 78:128+ Mr '63
LACRYMAL glands. See Glands
LACTATE. See Lactic acid
LACTIC acid
Excess lactate: an index of reversibility of shock in human patients. G. Broder and M. H. Weil. bibliog il Science 143:1457-9 Mr 27 '64
Lactic acids: chemistry and metabolism; report on conference, New York city, 12-14 November 1964. R. H. Dunlop. Science 147: 315-17 Ja 15 '65
LACTIC dehydrogenases. See Dehydrogenases
LACY, Creighton
Banyan falls. Christian Cent 81:883-5 Jl 8 '64
Irenic approach. Christian Cent 80:1007 Ag 14 '63
LACY, Dan
Book distribution. por ALA Bul 57:505-6 Je '63
Copyright; excerpt from address. Pub W 184: 49-50 Jl 15 '63
Dissemination of print; address, May 1963. Wilson Lib Bul 38:54-64 S '63
LACY, Ed
Have typewriter, should travel. Writer 77: 16-17+ Ap '64
LACY, Joe M.
Shopper's park. Am City 78:73-5 D '63
LADAKH
Communique from India's mountain front. C. Armstrong. il N Y Times Mag p 10-11+ Jl 7 '63
Mountaintop war in remote Ladakh. W. E. Garrett. il Nat Geog Mag 123:664-87 My '63
LADA-MOCARSKI, Polly
Modern French book art. Craft Horiz 24:36-41 Ja '64
LADAS, Alexis
Waiting for the firing squad. Harper 229: 87-90 N '64
LADBROKE and company
Britain's no. 1 book. A. Carthew. il N Y Times Mag p85-6+ My 10 '64
LADD, David L.
Invention: is it keeping up? interview. por U S News 55:70-3 Jl 15 '63
LADD, Everett C. Jr
Agony of the Negro leader. Nation 199:88-91 S 7 '64
Negro's priorities: welfare or status. Nation 199:243-6+ O 19 '64
LADDERS
How to stay alive on a ladder. B. Gladstone. il Pop Mech 120:166-9 Ag '63
Ladder safety. il Suc Farm 61:71-2 S '63
Swimming ladder for your boat; transom ladder. G. P. Manning. il Motor B 113:31+ Mr '64
Teak ladder for the flying bridge. N. Meiners. il Motor B 112:51+ O '63
LADEJINSKY, Wolf
Agrarian reform in Asia. For Affairs 42:445-60 Ap '64
LADER, Lawrence
Landing a jet without looking. Sat Eve Post 237:64-5 F 15 '64
LADIES home journal
World we want. C. Anderson. il Ladies Home J 80:49 Ja '63
LADONIA, Tex.
Water saved this town. il Am City 78:107 S '63
LADY beetles. See Ladybirds
LADY bugs (womens organization) See Womens clubs and societies
LADY from Blue Rock; story. See Wright, B. R.
LADY in waiting; story. See Mills, H. B.
LADY of the camellias; drama. See Cooper, G. and McNally, T.
LADY-slippers. See Ladys slippers
LADYBIRDS
Pest-eating insects; lady beetles; excerpt from Beneficial insects. L. A. Swan. bibliog f il Audubon Mag 66:314-19 S '64
LADYBUGS. See Ladybirds
LADYS slippers
Cross-pollination of an orchid; Showy lady's-slipper. H. L. Gibson. il Natur Hist 73:42-3 Ap '64
Native orchid, lady's-slipper. D. E. Rose. il Horticulture 41:291+ My '63
To the queen! H. S. Hull. il Flower Grower 50:12 O '63
LAENNEC, Rene Theophile
Discoverer of the stethoscope. il Todays Health 42:68 Mr '64
LAETRILE
Laetrile and cancer. Todays Health 41:69 Je '63
LAEUCHLI, Samuel
Fence-collapser. Christian Cent 80:1273-4 O 16 '63
LAFARGE, John
Baggage of the past. Sat R 46:23-5 Mr 16 '63
Blessed Elizabeth Seton. America 108:371 Mr 16 '63
Four eyes on the Washington march. America 109:252 S 14 '63
Voices out of a wilderness of hate. Sat R 46: 42-3 D 14 '63
Washington front. America 108:897 Je 29 '63
about
Announcing the John LaFarge institute. T. N. Davis. por America 110:791-3 Je 6 '64
John Lafarge, S.J: first anniversary of his death. R. A. Graham. America 111:695-6 N 28 '64
No postponement; concerning Jesuit letter on the race question. America 109:762-3 D 14 '63
Obituary
America 109:725 D 7 '63
Pub W 184:27-8 D 9 '63
LAFARGE, John, institute. See John LaFarge institute
LA FARGE, Oliver
Ancient strength. New Yorker 39:26-34 Ag 31 '63
Caviar remembered; story. Esquire 60:114 O '63
Much pride, little hope. Sat R 46:28 My 25 '63
about
Obituary
Pub W 184:40 Ag 12 '63
LAFARGE, Phyllis
Warm-hearted guide to certain girls' schools. Harper 226:73-9 Ap '63
LAFAYETTE, Marie Joseph Paul Yves Roch Gilbert du Motier, marquis de
Lafayette papers acquired by Cornell. Wilson Lib Bul 38:510 Mr '64
LAFAYETTE, La.
Thirteen stories of parking pleasure. J. R. Bertrand. il Am City 79:113 Jl '64
LAFAYETTE college, Easton, Pa.
Lafayette college, Pa., new library. il Wilson Lib Bul 38:454 F '64
Lafayette in sequence; new library building. C. L. Haselden. il Library J 88:4577-9 D 1 '63
Tolerance and the law. K. R. Bergethon. Sch & Soc 91:60-1 F 9 '63
LAFFERTY, Boyd M.
Mosquitoes, beware! foggers go to school. Am City 79:100-1 S '64
LAFFLY, Georges
Evian treaty; Ben Bella laughing at de Gaulle? Nat R 15:392-5 N 5 '63
LA FOLLETTE, Suzanne
Frank Hanighen, R.I.P. Nat R 16:55 Ja 28 '64
LAFOND, Henri
Determined ones. il Time 81:40 Mr 15 '63
LA FONTAINE, Barbara
Busiest voice in a busy, busy clan. Sports Illus 20:38-40+ Je 22 '64
Champ of the chop and loop. Sports Illus 20: 54-6+ My 11 '64
Girl behind a Golden Door. Sports Illus 21: 68-72+ N 2 '64

LAFORE, Laurence
One campus, two cultures. Science 145:790-5 Ag 21 '64
LAGE, Alice
Report from Malaya. Library J 90:201 Ja 15 '65
LAGELBAUER, Otto
Don't blow it. Outdoor Life 132:38-9+ D '63
LAGEMANN, John Kord
Better never than late. House & Gard 125: 110-11 F '64
How we discourage creative children. Redbook 120:44-5+ Mr '63; Same abr. with title Your child may be more gifted than you think. Read Digest 82:245-6+ My '63
It's never too early to learn the economic facts of life. PTA Mag 59:4-7 N '64; Same abr. with title How children can learn the economic facts of life. Read Digest 85:65-9 D '64
New way for children to learn. Redbook 122:42-3+ F '64
Something special in vacations. Read Digest 82:222-3+ Je '63
Stop, look, and see! Read Digest 83:128-31 Jl '63
They can see again. Read Digest 84:217-18+ F '64
To build a better nest egg. Read Digest 84: 108-11 Je '64
Who says do not touch? Read Digest 84:125-8 Ja '64
LAGENARIAS. See Gourds
LAGERWALL, Gabriele
Out of the nowhere into the here. por Time 82:102 O 25 '63
LAGIN, Lazar
Glass of water; story, tr. by M. Ginsburg. Reporter 31:29 N 19 '64
LAGMANOVICH, David J.
Mental health. Américas 15:1-5 Mr '63
LAGOMARCINO, Paul D.
Car by any other name. New Repub 150:12 Ap 4 '64
If Wallace stole the dome. New Repub 150: 13 My 9 '64
Judgment day traffic jam. New Repub 150:5 F 15 '64
LAGOONS, Manure. See Manure lagoons
LAGOONS, Sewage. See Sewage lagoons
LA GRANGE, Ill.
Salt, plow and haul. R. E. Meyer. il Am City 78:90-1 O '63
LA GUARDIA airport. See New York (city)—Airports
LAGUNA NIGUEL, Calif.
Wonderful new kind of town. il House & Gard 126:106-7 Ag '64
LAHA, Art
Too much bear. por Outdoor Life 135:17-19+ Ja '65
LAHAINA, Hawaii
Lahaina. il Sunset 134:40-55 Ja '65
LA HIVE, Laurent de. See La Hyre, L. de
LAHR, Bert
Bert Lahr and the beauties. J. Anderson. il pors Dance Mag 38:24-5 S '64
LAHRge world. S. J. Perelman. pors Theatre Arts 47:20-1 F '63
Love letters of a tough critic. W. Kerr. por Life 56:113 Je 19 '64
Ungaluk, mukaluk. por Newsweek 63:56 Mr 2 '64
LA HYRE, Laurent de
Museum evaluations. A. Frankfurter. il Art N 63:26+ Ja '65
LAI, L. and others
Acid phosphatases of human red cells: predicted phenotype conforms to a genetic hypothesis. bibliog Science 145:1187-8 S 11 '64
LAICH, Katherine
Origin and development of the Library administration division. ALA Bul 57:346-50 Ap '63
LAIDLEY, Richard A. and DuBois, R. L.
Dome-shaped volcanic gas vents in Arizona. Science 145:153-4 Jl 10 '64
LAING, Alexander
Condottiere; poem. Atlan 211:93 Je '63
Poet and preceptor. Nation 197:95-6 Ag 24 '63
LAING, Dilys
Bearing gifts; poem. Reporter 28:40 Je 20 '63
Flowers out of rock; poem. Poetry 104:14 Ap '64
Hero in two metals; poem. Reporter 31:44 D 17 '64
How many days? poem. Reporter 28:45 F 28 '63
Ite, missa est; poem. Ladies Home J 80:120 Je '63
Love song for young Oedipus. Ladies Home J 81:96 My '64
Maintenant; poem. Nation 197:54 Jl 27 '63
Power; poem. Nation 197:98 Ag 24 '63
Second expulsion; poem. McCalls 90:177 Ap '63
LAIRD, Jean E. and Harris, D. B.
How strict should parents be? Parents Mag 39:35+ Ag '64
LAIRD, Melvin R.
America's strategy gap; address, December 4, 1962. Vital Speeches 29:245-8 F 1 '63
McNamara's ground rules for doing business with the Pentagon; excerpts from Congressional record. por U S News 54:43 My 13 '63

about

In the House: a new Republican image. por U S News 58:36-7 Ja 18 '65
One platform for all. il por Time 84:22-4 Jl 10 '64
LAITY
Act of interdependence. America 111:33 Jl 11 '64
Age of the layman. J. Cordeiro. America 111:347 S 26 '64
American layman. J. O'Gara. Commonweal 79:364 D 20 '63
America's Catholic community: increasing involvement. B. Cooke. Christian Cent 80:360-2 Mr 20 '63
Apostolic few. il Time 81:69 My 24 '63
Baiting the layman. J. O'Gara. Commonweal 81:32 O 2 '64; Reply. W. J. Smith. 81:240-1 N 13 '64
Bishops and the thinkers. J. Cogley. Commonweal 80:626-7 S 18 '64
Cardinal Suenens on the church; interview, ed. by W. M. Abbott. L. J. Suenens. America 108:360-1 Mr 16 '63
Charter for laymen, 1822. G. Traynor. Commonweal 81:418-21 D 18 '64; Reply. M. Novak. 81:555+ Ja 29 '65
Dilemma of the Catholic layman; excerpt from Mind of the Catholic layman. D. Callahan. Cath World 198:80-6 N '63
For the world of tomorrow. R. C. Miller. Christian Cent 81:544-6 Ap 29 '64
Good start; proposed archdiocesan dialogue conference in St Louis. Commonweal 81: 468-9 Ja 8 '65
Inverted clericalism. C. Davis. America 110: 91 Ja 18 '64
Lagging laity. America 109:339 S 28 '63
Lay co-responsibility; concerning Cardinal Cushing's pastoral letter. America 108:705 My 18 '63
Lay elite. L. M. Madigan. America 109:193-5 Ag 24 '63
Lay leadership. T. R. Paden. Christian Cent 80:1616 D 25 '63
Lay theologians in parishes. E. C. Bianchi. America 109:772-3 D 14 '63
Layman rediscovered. J. Cogley. Commonweal 79:253-5 N 22 '63
Layman's role. E. S. Stanton; discussion. America 108:294-6 Mr 2 '63
Layman's role; members of governing body in Baltimore. Commonweal 78:182 My 10 '63
Layman's role today, by F. K. Wentz. Review
Christian Cent 80:1109-10 S 11 '63. M. E. Marty
Laymen and the council; concerning chapter IV of the constitution on the church. America 111:795-6 D 19 '64
Militant ministry, by H. R. Weber. Review
Christian Cent 81:1173 S 23 '64. H. A. Schulz
Mind of the Catholic layman, by D. Callahan. Review
Commonweal 79:171-2 N 1 '63. J. T. Ellis
Reporter 29:56+ N 21 '63. A. M. Greeley
Our reluctant laity and the seminaries. J. Sellers. Christian Cent 81:551-2+ Ap 29 '64
Parish anti's. K. Quinn. America 108:748+ My 25 '63
People of God; Boston sodality for priests and laymen. E. S. Stanton. America 110: 420-2 Mr 28 '64
Pope Paul to the laity. J. O'Gara. Commonweal 79:70 O 11 '63
Public opinion in the church; excerpts from pastoral letter. R. J. Cushing. Commonweal 78:426-7 Jl 12 '63
Revisiting Brideshead. J. Cogley. Commonweal 80:103-6 Ap 17 '64
Same again please: a layman's hopes of the Vatican council. E. Waugh; discussion. Nat R 13:521; 14:37 D 31 '62-Ja 15 '63; Commonweal 77:487-9 F 1 '63; America 108:440-2 Mr 30 '63
Sharing in the council. America 109:227 S 7 '63
Speak, or be silent? America 110:563-4 Ap 25 '64

LAITY—*Continued*
Structures, not rhetoric. J O'Gara. Commonweal 81:503 Ja 15 '65
Toward a responsible laity. Commonweal 81:403-4 D 18 '64
Word. V. P. McCorry. America 110:128 Ja 18 '64
Working together; modern lay outlook. C. Davis. America 111:42 Jl 11 '64

LAJES field, Azores islands. See Air bases

LAKE, Albert
Book selection: education or communication? Wilson Lib Bul 37:672+ Ap '63

LAKE, Alice
Beautiful gamble for Johnny. McCalls 91:62+ S '64
Five came to Aberdeen. McCalls 91:106-7+ D '63
Five husbands who might have lived. McCalls 92:126-7+ N '64
Hypochondria. McCalls 92:67+ O '64
Last summer in Mississippi. Redbook 124:64-5+ N '64
Little boy who couldn't learn. Redbook 123:46-7+ Je '64
Obstetrician. McCalls 91:102-3+ Ag '64
Patients nobody wanted. Sat Eve Post 237:87-91 D 5 '64
Snack diet. McCalls 90:26+ Jl '63

LAKE, Carlton
Artist at work: Marc Chagall. Atlan 212:85-112 Jl '63
—See Gilot, F. jt. auth.

LAKE BLUFF, Ill.
Big splash for bath and tennis. F. Deford. il Sports Illus 19:36-41 S 2 '63

LAKE central airlines
Lake central purchase of French aircraft may spur U.S. industry. R. H. Cook. Aviation W 80:29 Mr 30 '64

LAKE CHAMPLAIN. See Champlain, Lake

LAKE CHELAN. See Chelan, Lake

LAKE cruises. See Cruising

LAKE DISTRICT, England
Literature and English Lakeland. G. Bott. il Sr Schol 85:12T Ja 7 '65
Touring England's Lake District. il Sunset 134:19 Ja '65

LAKE ELSINORE. See Elsinore, Lake

LAKE EMERALD. See Emerald Lake, British Columbia

LAKE ERIE. See Erie, Lake

LAKE FOREST, Ill.
Garage full of ideas. G. L. Watson and H. R. Von Huben. il Am City 78:71-3 Jl '63

LAKE FOREST academy. See Private schools

LAKE FOREST college, Lake Forest, Ill.
New science center added at Lake Forest. il Arch Rec 134:138-40 Ag '63

LAKE GEORGE, N.Y. See George, Lake, N.Y.

LAKE GEORGE opera festival. See Music festivals—New York (state)

LAKE HAVASU. See Havasu Lake

LAKE herring fishing. See Cisco fishing

LAKE MEAD. See Mead, Lake

LAKE MEAD national recreation area
Interior department supports Lake Mead protection. Nat Parks Mag 37:16 Je '63

LAKE MOOSEHEAD. See Moosehead, Lake

LAKE OF THE WOODS, Minnesota and Canada
Cruising Lake of the Woods. F. M. Paulson. il Field & S 69:42-5+ Ag '64

LAKE OKEECHOBEE. See Okeechobee, Lake

LAKE PATZCUARO. See Patzcuaro, Lake

LAKE PONTCHARTRAIN. See Pontchartrain, Lake

LAKE POWELL. See Lakes, Artificial

LAKE SHAVER. See Shaver, Lake

LAKE TAHOE. See Tahoe, Lake

LAKE trout fishing. See Trout fishing

LAKELAND, Fla.
Our good neighbor, the sewage-purification plant. G. McElhenney. il Am City 78:94-6 F '63

LAKENAN, Frances
Be an artist with nature's leftovers. por Farm J 88:48-9 Ag '64

LAKES
Depth of lakes told by photo measuring. Sci N L 83:222 Ap 6 '63
Fractionation of sulfur and carbon isotopes in a meromictic lake. E. S. Deevey, jr. and others. bibliog il Science 139:407-8 F 1 '63
Montana's valley of hush. E. Thane. il Travel 119:46-9 F '63
Propeller on a platform preserves a pond; Newton, Mass. J. B. Penney. il Am City 79:84-5 Jl '64

Clearing

Drawdown for better fishing. D. L. Allen. il Field & S 67:52-3+ Mr '63
Goodbye, lily pads; Brightwaters, N.Y. G. J. Guinta. il Am City 79:14 Mr '64
Recreational lakes spring from swamp; Woodbury, N.J. J. I. Butzner. il Am City 79:31 S '64

LAKES, Artificial
Army lakes float U.S. boatmen. J. Graham. il Motor B 112:34+ Ag '63
Boating in the Land of Lincoln. C. B. Meurer. il Motor B 111:29+ Je '63
Fill'er up: a new lake is born; Lake Powell, Glen Canyon National Recreation Area. J. R. Muench. il Motor B 113:21-3+ My '64
Lake Powell is being filled. L. Corbeau. il Motor B 112:44-6 Ag '63
Lake Roosevelt; sailor's luck. E. Crimmin. il Motor B 114:90-4 Ag '64
LCRA spells fish! R. Tinsley. il Travel 121:56-8 F '64
Reclaimed sewage becomes a community asset; Santee, Calif. J. Merrell and R. Stoyer. il Am City 79:97-101 Ap '64

LAKEWOOD, N.J.
Community for senior citizens. il Am City 79:102 Ap '64

LAKEWOOD, Ohio

Housing

Offset plan produces six corners. il Arch Rec 136:120-1 Ag '64

LAKIN, H. W. and Thompson, C. E.
Tellurium: a new sensitive test. bibliog Science 141:42-3 Jl 5 '63
—and others
Tellurium content of marine manganese oxides and other manganese oxides. bibliog Science 142:1568-9 D 20 '63

LAKING, Leslie
Garden for every child. Flower Grower 51:36+ F '64

LAKOFF, Sanford A.
Nth culture problem. Bul Atomic Sci 20:21-3 My '64

LAKONIA fire. See Ships—Fires and fire protection

LAKSHMINARAYANAIAH, Nallanna, and Shanes, A. M.
Thin membranes of parlodion. Science 141:43-4 Jl 5 '63

LALL, Arthur S.
Nonaligned in disarmament negotiations. Bul Atomic Sci 20:17-21 My '64

LALL, Betty Goetz
Congress considers impact of defense reductions. Bul Atomic Sci 20:31-2 F '64
Diminishing the danger of surprise attack in Europe. Bul Atomic Sci 20:31-4 Mr '64
Disarmament policy and the Pentagon. Bul Atomic Sci 20:37-40 S '64
Information in arms control verification. Bul Atomic Sci 20:43-5 O '64
Mainland China and U.S. security. Bul Atomic Sci 20:24-7 Ap '64
Nato-Warsaw detente? Bul Atomic Sci 20:37-9 N '64
On disarmament issues: peacekeeping since 1946. Bul Atomic Sci 20:37-40 My '64
On disarmament issues: the Polish plan. Bul Atomic Sci 20:41-3 Je '64
Questions and answers on the U.S. production freeze proposal. Bul Atomic Sci 20:30-4 D '64
Substantial reductions in strategic delivery vehicles. Bul Atomic Sci 21:45-8 Ja '65

LALLA Nouzha, princess
Royal wedding festival. il pors Vogue 145:72-7 Ja 15 '65

L'ALLEMAND, Gordon
World run on walnut. Am For 69:12-15+ Ag '63

LAM-van-Phat
Continued progress. il por Time 84:39 S 18 '64

LAMALE, Helen H.
Workers' wealth and family living standards. Mo Labor R 86:676-86 Je '63

LAMAR, Donald L. See Romig, M. F. jt. auth.

LA MARCHINA, Robert
New maestro. por Newsweek 62:59 D 30 '63

LAMB, Edward
Freedom is not enough; address, August 6, 1964. Vital Speeches 30:719-21 S 15 '64
United community of North America; address, September 30, 1964. Vital Speeches 31:46-8 N 1 '64

LAMB, Gerald A.
Negro political progress in New England. A. Morrison. il pors Ebony 18:30+ O '63

LAMB, Helen B.
Paris exiles. Nation 197:65-8 Ag 10 '63

LAMB, Hubert
Music in the age of Zak; address. Harper 226:76-8+ My '63
LAMB, Marjorie
Communist apparatus in Canada today; address, October 28, 1963. Vital Speeches 30: 141-4 D 15 '63
LAMB, Mary Wright
Late discoverer's song; poem. Ladies Home J 80:150 Ap '63
LAMB, Patricia
Peace; poem. Commonweal 78:454 Jl 26 '63
LAMB, Tom
Eavesdropping on satellites. Pop Electr 18: 52-3+ F '63
LAMB, W. Kaye
Archivist and the historian; address. Am Hist R 68:385-91 Ja '63
LAMB (meat)
Lamb: preview of springtime. G. Maddox. il Todays Health 42:68-72 Ja '64
See also
Cookery—Meat
LAMBARÉNÉ, Gabon
Albert Schweitzer: an anachronism. J. Randal. il Time 81:35 Je 21 '63
God bless all living beings. E. Anderson. il Ladies Home J 80:26-8 D '63
Jungle doctor go home. N. Cousins. Sat R 46:30 Mr 16 '63; Same with photographs. Sci Digest 54:44-52 Jl '63
LAMBERT, Darwin
Mysteries of Mount McKinley. Nat Parks Mag 37:8-10+ Ap '63
LAMBERT, Denis
Inflation. Américas 15:39-41 F '63
LAMBERT, Eric
Return to innocence; story. Good H 157:67-9 S '63
LAMBERT, Frank L. and others
Coupling of butyl bromide on hot magnesium. bibliog Science 146:1049 N 20 '64
LAMBERT, Sam M.
Angry young men in teaching. NEA J 52:17-20 F '63
LAMBERT, William. See Wheeler, K; Young, W. R. jt. auths.
LAMBING crates and pens
Labor-free lambing; environmental control. D. Hagen. Farm J 87:52L My '63
LAMBO, Adeoya
Modern magician of the soul. il pors Ebony 20:36-8+ D '64
LAMBRECHT, Arn
Folding saw table for big panels. Pop Sci 185:140-1 N '64
LAMBROSA, John
Weight training for teenagers. por Recreation 57:516 D '64
LAMBS
How to help yourself to a bigger lamb crop. J. W. Bailey. Suc Farm 62:74D Ap '64
These ideas save lambs. il Suc Farm 62:91 Mr '64
LAMBUTH, David
Golden words at Dartmouth. por Time 82:36 D 27 '63
LAMELLA trusses. See Trusses
LAMICA, Louise
Theater in the garden. Recreation 56:474-5 D '63
LAMINAR flow wings. See Airplane wings
LAMINATED plastics. See Plastics, Laminated
LAMINATED wood. See Wood, Laminated
LAMM, Michael
Editor's auto-graphs. Motor T 16:8 Ja; 8 Ap '64
LAMMERS, Joseph E.
Emphasis on the contemporary. Mus Am 83: 34-6 S '63
LAMMERS, W. T.
Density-gradient separation of organic particles by centrifugation. bibliog Science 139: 1298-9 Mr 29 '63
LAMMEY, W. Clyde
Game-bird savers. Pop Mech 121:158-61+ Ja '64
In-a-wall, home maintenance center. Pop Mech 119:122-7 Je '63
Owls I have known. Am For 71:38-40+ Ja '65
Powered rasps. Pop Mech 120:184-9 O '63
Rollaway workshops. Pop Mech 121:169-73 Ja '64
Tips for shotgunners. Pop Mech 120:154-5 O '63
LAMON, H. J.
6.4 footcandles downtown. Am City 79:118 Ag '64
LAMOTT, Kenneth
Whaling off the Golden Gate. Holiday 34:148+ D '63
LAMP shades
Decorating wrongs made right. il Bet Hom & Gard 42:26 My '64
Hooked feather pattern; blown iridescent glass shades. C. K. Bassett. Hobbies 69: 78-9 Je '64
How to clean a lamp shade. Bet Hom & Gard 42:80 Ag '64
Light way to brighten your room. il Seventeen 23:250 Ag '64
You can make these hanging lights. il Sunset 132:94+ F '64
You make it with viscose straw. il Sunset 130:106+ F '63
LAMPEDUSA, Giuseppe di
Lampedusa in Sicily; the lair of the leopard. A. Colquhoun. pors Atlan 211:91-3+ F '63
LAMPEN, J. Oliver
Fungi and yeasts: chemistry and biochemistry. Science 142:603 N 1 '63
LAMPMAN, Ben Hur
Where to bury a dog; excerpt from How could I be forgetting? Read Digest 84:26B My '64
LAMPORT, Felicia
Hellas bent; poem. New Yorker 40:81 Ag 8 '64
Mr Masoch and Count de Sade; poem. Harper 227:96 Ag '63
One critic's cherce: from bad to worse. Life 57:12+ D 18 '64
LAMPS
Beginner's pottery project: hanging lamps. il Sunset 131:161+ O '63
Donkey and elephant lamps. A. G. Peterson. il Hobbies 69:85 N '64
Lamp patents in the United States. A. G. Peterson. il Hobbies 68:82-3 Jl; 82-4 Ag '63
Lamps to adorn your outdoor world. il House & Gard 125:14+ Je '64
Light your way to A's. il Seventeen 22:168+ S '63
Lighting devices from a New Hampshire collection. H. W. Stone. il Antiques 86:82-3 Jl '64
Make this beautiful hanging lamp. il Bet Hom & Gard 41:36 S '63
See also
Electric lamps
Gas lamps
Lighting fixtures
LAMPSHADES. See Lamp shades
LAMPYRIDAE. See Fireflies
LANAHAN, Frances
Merry Christmas from the Smiths! New Yorker 39:32-3 D 21 '63
LANAIS. See Outdoor rooms
LANCASTER, Burt
Will the real Burt please stand up? S. Alexander. il pors Life 55:80-5 S 6 '63
LANCASTER, Donald
Chirp, a new radar technique. bibliog Electr World 73:42-3+ Ja '65
Four and five layer semiconductor diodes. Electr World 72:61-4+ O '64
Light dimmer & power-tool control. Electr World 72:46-7+ Jl '64
Multipurpose electronic control. Electr World 73:36-7 Ja '65
New SCR developments. Electr World 72: 25-7+ D '64
Simplified solid-state color organ. Electr World 71:50+ Ja '64
Solid-state 3-channel color organ. Electr World 69:55-8+ Ap '63
LANCASTRIAN system. See Monitorial system of education
LANCE, Don M.
What whitetails taught me. por Outdoor Life 134:30-1+ N '64
LANCEFIELD, Rebecca Craighill
Ravages of strep. il por Time 84:68 O 30 '64
LANCER books, incorporated
Lancer edition starts Candy paperback scramble. Pub W 187:103-4 Ja 18 '65
LAND, Edwin H.
Color vision: an experiment. P. Farber. il U S Camera 27:50-1+ Ja '64; Discussion. 27:16+ Ap '64
Polaroid snaps into color. il por Bsns W p80-2 Ja 19 '63
LAND, Gloria H.
Mama, you're pretty inside. por Redbook 123:12+ S '64
LAND, Philip S.
Pius XII and the Jews. America 108:730-1 My 25 '63
Pope John: new look. America 108:395-6 Mr 23 '63
Reactions to an encyclical; Mater et magistra. America 108:407-8 Mr 23 '63
LAND, Roy
Membership in ALA. por ALA Bul 57:809-10 O '63
LAND, William G.
Practical and academic orientations of liberal arts colleges. bibliog f Sch & Soc 91:113-15 Mr 9 '63

LAND
Green ex-pastures; land in Cleveland County, N.C. Time 81:26 Ap 12 '63
See also
Land grants

Prices

See Land values

Taxation

See also
Property tax

Europe, Western

Hungry for land. Time 83:89 My 8 '64

Minnesota

Minnesota sets a brisk pace. J. Morris. Am For 69:35+ N '63

United States

As the snow flies; cropland converted for winter recreation projects. H. E. Winkley. il Recreation 58:11 Ja '65
Consuming the land. N. T. Di Giovanni. Nation 198:100-1 Ja 27 '64
Federal legislation for land acquisition; excerpts from address. J. P. Anderson. il Recreation 58:22-3 Ja '65
High-density communities can preserve open spaces; Cook County, Ill. il Am City 79: 110 S '64
Land lords, by E. Rachlis and J. E. Marqusee. Review
New Repub 149:21-4 O 19 '63. D. M. Friedenberg
New paths to recreation space; symposium. il Recreation 57:12-26+ Ja '64
See also
Public lands—United States

Wisconsin

Wisconsin's beauty plan; an idea that will spread? il U S News 58:33 Ja 11 '65

LAND BETWEEN THE LAKES. See Wilderness areas
LAND cameras. See Polaroid Land cameras
LAND clearing. See Clearing of land
LAND fill. See Municipal dumps
LAND fills. See Filling (earthwork)
LAND grant colleges
Facts about state and land-grant universities. Sch & Soc 92:285+ O 17 '64
Humanities in land grant universities. J. F. A. Taylor. il Sat R 47:64-5+ Ap 18 '64; Reply. J. D. Hickerson. 47:67 My 16 '64
LAND grants
Most improveablest land; provinces of East New Jersey and West New Jersey. J. Brooks. il Am Heritage 15:62-3+ O '64
Ohio land patents. K. W. Duckett. Hobbies 68:110-11+ Ag '63
LAND management, Bureau of. See United States—Land management, Bureau of
LAND mines. See Mines, Military
LAND owning trees. See Trees, Historic
LAND patents. See Land grants
LAND pollution. See Soil pollution
LAND reform. See Land tenure
LAND Rover (automobile) See Automobiles, Foreign
LAND slides. See Landslides
LAND speculation
Still more gold in California land; speculative land investment. il Bsns W p 112-14 Ja 23 '65
LAND surveying. See Surveying
LAND tenure
See also
Forest ownership

Asia

Agrarian reform in Asia. W. Ladejinsky. For Affairs 42:445-60 Ap '64

Brazil

Lesson learned. il Newsweek 63:37 Ja 13 '64

Colombia

Land-grabbers of Cali. J. P. Powelson. Reporter 30:30-1 Ja 16 '64

Costa Rica

Land reform in Costa Rica. O. C. Esquivel. il Américas 15:11-15 F '63

Iran

Iran's Shah leads a white revolution. J. Walz. il N Y Times Mag p23+ O 27 '63
Next big blowup, Iran? J. Law. il U S News 54:82 Mr 25 '63

Latin America

Land reform. America 109:762 D 14 '63
Latin America's most explosive problem. G. W. Hill. Read Digest 85:169-70+ S '64
Take now, pay later. America 109:35 Jl 13 '63

Mexico

Land-reform lesson. il Time 82:28 Ag 30 '63
Looking for water; moving families from La Laguna to Campeche. Time 81:37 Mr 15 '63
Out of the dust bowl. il Time 82:27 D 20 '63

Peru

Dealing from strength. Time 83:30+ F 14 '64
Peru's new politics: the hit-or-miss approach. G. Delmas. il Reporter 29:35-8 O 24 '63
Return to the land; land-reform law. Newsweek 63:49 Je 22 '64
Sensible land-reform law. Time 84:22 Jl 3 '64

United States

Why tenants don't stay with farming. H. Guither. Suc Farm 61:22 Ap '63
See also
Homesteads

Venezuela

Latin America's most explosive problem. G. W. Hill. Read Digest 85:174+ S '64

LAND utilization
California going, going . . . our state's struggle to remain beautiful and productive, by S. E. Wood and A. E. Heller. Review
Liv Wildn 82:23-4 Winter '62. W. Stegner
Call to action; land for recreation and camping. D. E. Harlow. il Recreation 57:108-10 Mr '64
Crash program for parkland acquisition; New Jersey green acres program. A. Brown, jr. il Recreation 57:397-9 O '64
Found: million-acre cow pasture. G. A. Yackulic. il Sci Digest 53:79-81 My '63
Khrushchev in Astrakhan; future of the lower Volga area: interview. N. S. Khrushchev. Bul Atomic Sci 20:12-14 Ja '64
Land coming out of soil bank? W. D. Pardee. Suc Farm 62:44-5 Ja '64
Nature is murdered. B. Tufty. il Sci N L 84:90-1 Ag 10 '63
New Jersey's Green Acres program. L. Fiedler. il Am For 70:40-2 Je '64
New land rush: government stakes its claims. il U S News 57:78-90 D 7 '64
New paths to recreation space; symposium. il Recreation 57:12-26+ Ja '64
New York land acquisition program. C. W. Mattison. il Recreation 56:259-62 Je '63
Obsolete assumptions; excerpts from address, March 1963. S. L. Udall. il Recreation 56: 359-61 O '63
Urban pattern. H. Blumenfeld. Ann Am Acad 352:74-83 Mr '64
See also
Soil conservation
Suburbs
LAND values
Beware the Moonlight Estates. J. C. Hunt. il Am For 69:12-14+ Je '63
Big Bill on Broadway: too many kibitzers. il Newsweek 62:65 Jl 22 '63
Costly land for housing projects; roles of General accounting office and Federal housing administration U S News 55:82-3 D 23 '63
Hungry for land; western Europe. Time 83: 89 My 8 '64
Spiraling land. Time 83:92+ Mr 13 '64
Strange leveling off in land. H. Kay. il Fortune 68:124-9+ O '63
Why the price of land is soaring; Amazing land boom abroad. il U S News 56:72-5 F 17 '64
LAND yachts. See Campers and coaches, Truck
LANDAIS, Pierre
Action off Flamborough Head; excerpt from Great sea battles. O. Warner. il por Am Heritage 14:42-9+ Ag '63
LANDAU, Elliott D.
Of storytelling, national dilemma, and human grace. Horn Bk 39:485 O '63
LANDAU, Lev Davidovich
Whiz kid of Soviet science. A. Parry. il pors Sci Digest 54:83-9 D '63
LANDAU, Siegfried
Orchestra grows in Brooklyn. por Mus Am 84:56-7 Jl '64
LANDEGGER, Karl F.
Paper tiger. il por Newsweek 62:68+ Ag 19 '63
Paper world of Karl Landegger. E. K. Faltermayer. il por Fortune 70:168-71+ N '64

LANDEN, David
Alaska earthquake, 27 March 1964. Science 145:74-6 Jl 3 '64
LANDER, Richard
What NCATE means to the teacher. NEA J 52:30-1 F '63
LANDEROS, Oscar, and Frost, H. M.
Cell system in which rate and amount of protein synthesis are separately controlled. bibliog Science 145:1323-4 S 18 '64
LANDERS, Ann
Booze and you; excerpt from Ann Landers talks to teen-agers about sex. Read Digest 84:133-4+ Mr '64
about
Mail-order psychology. J. Stanley. il por Mlle 59:94-5+ Je '64
LANDFILLS. See Filling (earthwork); Municipal dumps
LANDING of airplanes. See Airplanes—Landing
LANDING systems for space vehicles. See Space vehicles—Landing systems
LANDIS, James E.
I can't hear, doctor; is there any help? Todays Health 41:24-5+ S '63
LANDIS, James McCauley
Busy man. Newsweek 62:28 Ag 12 '63
Careless crusader. Time 82:15 Ag 9 '63
Instant sentence. Time 82:17 S 6 '63
Nothing much to say. por Newsweek 62:31 S 9 '63
LANDIS, Jo
Adolescence; poem. por Seventeen 22:102 Ag '63
LANDLORD and tenant
Whom to complain to? Call for action. Time 84:68 S 25 '64
See also
Farm tenancy
Leases
LANDMAN, David
Article market place; excerpt from Prose by professionals, ed. by T. Morris. Writer 77:21-2 Je '64
LANDMAN, Juanita M.
Teaching library skills with an overhead projector. Library J 89:923-4 F 15 '64
LANDMAN, W. J.
Designed to work hard. Am City 79:106-7 Mr '64
LANDMARKER; story. See Auchincloss, L.
LANDMARKS, Historic. See Historic houses, etc; United States—Historic houses, etc.
LANDO, Barry M.
Our man in Paraguay. Nation 196:157-9 F 23 '63
LANDOLFI, Tommaso
Lost in a surrealist landscape. Sat R 46:62-3 D 7 '63
LANDOLINA, Ruth
Flower of the blessed night. Horticulture 41:620-1 D '63
North Carolina's enchanted garden. Horticulture 41:170-1 Mr '63
LANDON, Alf
Man once buried in a landslide watches the new one. D. Nevin. il por Life 57:44 N 13 '64
LANDON, H. C. Robbins
Gloria in excelsis Deo: the Haydn Masses. Hi Fi 14:56-9+ D '64
New integral set of the nine; to add to the best. Hi Fi 13:79-80 S '63
Notes from abroad (cont) Hi Fi 13:20 Je '63
about
Second look at Manfredini. P. H. Lang. Hi Fi 13:57-9 Ap '63
LANDOWSKA, Wanda
From the Landowska notebooks; tr. by D. Restout and R. Hawkins. pors Hi Fi 14:48-52+ D '64
about
World of Wanda Landowska. I. Kolodin. il pors Sat R 47:43+ N 28 '64
LANDRUM, Phil
Georgia story: two men, two districts. por Newsweek 63:16-17 Mr 2 '64
LANDRUM-Griffin act. See Labor laws and legislation—United States
LANDSBERG, Hans H.
Plenty of resources if we use them right; report with charts. Bsns W p84-6 Ap 6 '63
Resources for 300 million; summary of report. W. Davis. Sci N L 83:227 Ap 13 '63
LANDSBURG, Robert E.
We ran the blackwater. Outdoor Life 132:40-3+ Ag '63
LANDSCAPE
Affluent slumland; the American landscape. E. Sevareid. il Recreation 58:4 Ja '65
God's own junkyard, by P. Blake. Review Commonweal 80:296-8 My 29 '64. W. Sheed
LANDSCAPE architecture. See Landscape gardening
LANDSCAPE gardening
Cutting a big house down to size. J. T. Cox. il Suc Farm 61:92-3 Mr '63
Designs to surround a home. E. W. Finch. il Flower Grower 51:24-7 N '64
Dwarf evergreens in modern landscaping. H. Latimer. il Horticulture 41:520-1 O '63
Feel of the forest. F. B. Quigg. il Am For 69:28-31+ N '63
Front yards. J. Taylor. il Horticulture 42:16-17 Jl '64
Garden in the making. J. P. Elliott, jr. il Flower Grower 51:20-1 S '64
Garden of ideas in outdoor living. il Sunset 130:100-7 My '63
Garden remodeling (cont) J. R. Rebhan. Pop Gard 14:35-43 F; 40-1 Mr '63
Garden with a view. il Sunset 130:118-25 Ap '63
Have some fun with garden rock. il Sunset 130:184+ F '63
He paints with lakes and wooded slopes; landscape architecture. J. S. Martin. il Am Heritage 15:14-19+ O '64
Hobby gardener enjoys himself in Topanga Canyon. il Sunset 130:278-9 Ap '63
How to enhance the natural beauty of rock. E. L. Sculthorp. il House B 106:176-9+ Ap '64
How to put color in your landscape. il House & Gard 125:156-9+ My '64
How to rescue land lost on a slope. C. Calkins. il House B 105:174-7+ Ap '63
Ideas to profit by; front yard flower garden. J. B. Brimer. il Flower Grower 51:34 Jl '64
Italian accent; excerpt from European sketchbook. J. Brimer. il Flower Grower 50:28-9 Je '63
Just what is a landscape architect? M. F. Bunting. il Horticulture 41:88-9 F '63
Landscaping can add value to your home. il Good H 156:164-5 Ap '63
Landscaping good enough to eat. A. U. Smith. il Pop Gard 15:22-4 My '64
100 ideas under $100. il Bet Hom & Gard 41:10+ Jl '63; 42:28-59 Jl '64
Plan an easy-upkeep garden. il Pop Gard 15:24-28+ Ja '64
Plan your shadows to foil the heat of the sun. il House B 106:108-10 Ja '64
Plant to suit your site. il House & Gard 125:150-3 Ap '64
Planting for a turncourt. R. S. Maxwell. il Flower Grower 51:29 O '64
Planting turned this frontyard into a garden. il Pop Gard 14:70 Jl '63
Pool should be more than a body of water for swimming. il House B 105:162-71+ Ap '63
Raised plant beds for low upkeep. il Pop Gard 15:20-1 My '64
Saved trees mean so much. J. R. Rebhan. il Flower Grower 52:30-1+ Ja '65
They did not want to live as look-alikes; how to give a tract house an individual character. il Sunset 133:66-9 Jl '64
This tract house used to look like all the others. il House B 105:182-3 S '63
Translation from German gardens. J. B. Brimer. il Flower Grower 50:34-5 Mr '63
Trees: how to use them on your site. il House & Gard 125:118-21 Ja '64
Trees of Mount Auburn. D. Wyman. il Horticulture 42:38-9+ Je '64
Turn your problem slope into a landscape asset. G. Harshbarger. il Am Home 66:40-1+ My '63
Where auto meets garden. il Sunset 130:94-9 Je '63
Where man and nature conspire; urban landscape design. F. Gutheim. Nation 200:88-9 Ja 25 '65
See also
Back yards
Garden design
Gardens, Japanese
Hedges
Home grounds
Lawns
Outdoor rooms
Topiary work
LANDSCAPE leasing, incorporated. See Rental services
LANDSCAPE models
Idea from Japan; a tray landscape. il Sunset 132:133-4 Ap '64
LANDSCAPE painting
Art galleries; American scene. H. Rosenberg. New Yorker 39:147-8+ Mr 16 '63

LANDSCAPE painting—*Continued*
Benjamin Champney and the American Barbizon, 1850-1857. W. G. Hennessy and F. A. Sharf. il Antiques 84:566-9 N '63
Charles François Daubigny, forerunner of impressionism. R. N. Gregg. il Antiques 85:548-51 My '64
L.B.J.'s favorite painter. J. Langguth. il N Y Times Mag p75+ Mr 15 '64
Painting of Thomas Moran: sources and style. W. H. Gerdts. il Antiques 85:202-5 F '64
Richard Whorf: painter of Americana. J. Lovoos. il Am Artist 28:32-7+ Ap '64
Some aspects of English landscape painting; collection of Mr and Mrs Paul Mellon. J. Baskett. il Antiques 84:581-5 N '63
Uniqueness of Albert Bierstadt. F. Lewison. il Am Artist 28:28-33+ S '64
Unrecorded landscape by J. S. Jennings. P. N. Perrot. il Antiques 84:586-8 N '63
LANDSCAPE photography. See Photography—Landscapes
LANDSCAPE planning
Foundation planting. il House & Gard 125:128-31 F '64
LANDSLIDES
Quick clay; landslides in Scandinavia and Canada. P. F. Kerr. il Sci Am 209:132-8+ bibliog(p 188) N '63
LANDSTROM, Björn
Bjorn Landstrom: writer, illustrator, designer. il Pub W 185:104-6 My 4 '64
LANDVER, Rose
One-woman show; interview, ed. by F. Stevenson. por Opera N 28:26-7 Mr 7 '64
LANE, Bruce S.
Mercedes-Knight. Motor T 15:78-81+ Mr '63
LANE, Carol
Tips on touring. See issues of Travel to September 1963
LANE, Charles E.
Deadly fisher. pors Nat Geog Mag 123:388-97 Mr '63
LANE, Frederic C.
Economic meaning of the invention of the compass. bibliog f Am Hist R 68:605-17 Ap '63
LANE, Gloria
Two fine Glorias. Time 83:59 Mr 13 '64
LANE, Helen R.
Last rites for a fat cat. Nation 198:558-60 Je 1 '64
LANE, John F.
Lost sheep; ed. by C. Elliott. por Outdoor Life 134:44-6+ S '64
LANE, Lisa
Chess candidate. New Yorker 40:43-4 S 19 '64
LANE, Mills B. jr.
Wonderful world of Mills B. Lane, jr. il pors Bsns W p 124-6+ F 22 '64
LANE, Thomas A.
Art of command. Nat R 16:610+ Jl 14 '64
Craft of objectivity. Nat R 16:244+ Mr 24 '64
Staff officer. Nat R 16:33-4 Ja 14 '64
LANE, Will
Vagabond camera. See issues of Travel
When filming solar eclipse July 20 beware of your camera and eyesight! Travel 120:58-60 Jl '63
LANE publishing company
Lane starting new building in Menlo park. Pub W 184:30 N 4 '63
LANG, Barbara
And now he (she) drives. N Y Times Mag p 110+ N 8 '64
Boys and other beasts; excerpts. McCalls 91:68+ F; 74+ Mr; 78+ Ap; 66+ Jl; 58+ Ag; 60+ S; 92:64+ N '64
Parent and child. N Y Times Mag p47+ Jl 19 '64
LANG, Daniel
Reporter at large (cont) New Yorker 39:35-6+ Je 22; 34-8+ D 21 '63; 40:100+ O 10 '64
LANG, Ernst M.
Jambo, first gorilla raised by its mother in captivity. Nat Geog Mag 125:446-53 Mr '64
LANG, Frederic A.
It's a hard way to lay pipe; Colonial pipeline co. il Bsns W p37-8 D 21 '63
LANG, Marie
Every kindergarten needs a Tino. PTA Mag 58:25 O '63
LANG, Nancy
Szeryng's (and Rubinstein's) Brahms. Am Rec G 29:444-5 F '63
LANG, Paul Henry
Birth of comedy. Opera N 27:8-11 F 16 '63
Claude Monteux, conductor Hudson Valley philharmonic, New York. Mus Am 83:10 My '63
LP and the well-appointed library. por Library J 88:1809-12 My 1 '63
Paradox of opera. Theatre Arts 47:10-12 Mr '63
Second look at Manfredini. Hi Fi 13:57-9 Ap '63
(ed) See Szell, G. Mixture of instinct and intellect
LANG, Pearl
Pearl Lang and dance company, Brooklyn academy of music. J. Maskey. Dance Mag 38:31 My '64
Pearl Lang at Fashion institute. M. Marks. Dance Mag 37:64 Je '63
LANG, Reginald R.
Politics as conciliation. Nat R 15:113-14 Ag 13 '63
LANG, V. R.
Poetry chronicle. R. Howard. Poetry 102:190-2 Je '63
LANGAN, Thomas D.
Polish paradox. Commonweal 80:228-32 My 15 '64
LANGBAUM, Robert
Function of criticism once more. Yale R 54:205-18 D '64
Liberal target. Commentary 38:79-81 O '64
LANGDON, Grace, and Stout, I. W.
Conscience and character. PTA Mag 58:4-6 bibliog(p35) F '64
What parents think of homework. NEA J 52:9-11 D '63
LANGE, Phil C.
Selection and use of programed learning materials. NEA J 53:28-9 Ap '64
LANGE, Victor
How to make things. New Repub 151:20-1 N 28 '64
Monologue of an old man. New Repub 150:17-19 F 1 '64
Solitude of Jean Genet. New Repub 149:23-6 N 23 '63
To find the man in man. New Repub 149:30-2+ S 21 '63
LANGENBERG, D. N. and Peart, R. F.
Solid-state physics. Science 144:1365-6 Je 12 '64
LANGER, Elinor
Congress and science: Senate seeks review of government's program in fields of science and technology. Science 139:817-18 Mr 1 '63
Consumer motivation: handy handbook reveals discovery, mystery surrounds the cheese. Science 145:907+ Ag 28 '64
Crusade and after. Nation 199:166-8 S 28 '64
Electron microscopes; committee in House urges reinstatement of former tariff on foreign models. Science 139:892-3 Mr 8 '63
Experimental animals; proposals to regulate use bring clash of scientists and humane societies. Science 139:1275 Mr 29 '63
Patents: proposal to change NASA regulations. Science 139:1188 Mr 22 '63
LANGER, Howard J.
Melbourne: ungraded high. Sr Schol 83:18T-19T O 4 '63
Records and tapes. Sr Sch 84:30T Mr 20 '64
Team teaching at Dundee. Sr Schol 82:5T-6T+ F 27 '63
(ed) See Carr, W. G. Scholastic teacher interview
(ed) See Cogen, C. Scholastic teacher interview
(ed) See D'Amour, O. C. Scholastic teacher interview
(ed) See Davis, T. Scholastic teacher interview
(ed) See Duckworth, C. J. Scholastic teacher interview
(ed) See Fischer, J. H. Scholastic teacher interview
(ed) See Jones, J. A. Scholastic teacher interview
(ed) See Megel, C. J. Scholastic teacher interview
(ed) See Rafferty, M. Scholastic teacher interview
(ed) See Trent, W. J. jr. Scholastic teacher interview
LANGER, Paul F.
China and Japan. bibliog f Cur Hist 45:144-50+ S '63
Japan's relations with China. bibliog f Cur Hist 46:193-9+ Ap '64
LANGER, Richard B. See Condie, R. M. jt. auth.
LANGER, Stanley H. and Haldeman, R. G.
Hydrogen: electrolytic technique for purifying it and removing it from a gas stream. Science 142:225-6 O 11 '63
LANGER, William L.
Black death; with biographical sketch. Sci Am 210:32, 114-18+ bibliog(p 152) F '64
Europe's initial population explosion. bibliog f Am Hist R 69:1-17 O '63
LANGEVIN, André
Reporter at large. E. Wilson. New Yorker 40:132+ N 21 '64

LANGEVIN, R. A. and Owens, M. F.
Computer analysis of the nuclear test ban treaty. bibliog Science 146:1186-9 N 27 '64
LANGEWEISCHE, Priscilla
How to be at home abroad. House B 105:148-9+ Mr '63
LANGEWIESCHE, Wolfgang
Air fares are coming down to earth. Read Digest 85:63-7 Ag '64
How polluted is the air around us? Read Digest 83:117-22 S '63
ICU, newest thing in nursing. Read Digest 85:208-10+ N '64
Look at the new flying machines. Read Digest 84:85-9 Je '64
Public affair of the SST. Read Digest 85: 141-5 O '64
Thing that hit us from outer space. Read Digest 82:81-5 Ap '63
Tricks to speed up the breeze through your house. House B 105:80-3+ Ag '63
LANGFORD, Jerome J.
One Galileo case is enough. Cath World 200: 205-10 Ja '65
LANGGUTH, Jack
Buddhist way in Vietnam. N Y Times Mag p29+ O 11 '64
Inheritor of a wretched war. N Y Times Mag p27+ N 15 '64
L.B.J.'s favorite painter. N Y Times Mag p75+ Mr 15 '64
Smiling through with Thanom of Thailand. N Y Times Mag p 12-13+ Ja 3 '65
LANGILLE, Alan R. See Flanagan, T. R. jt. auth.
LANGLADE, Françoise de
Baron Edmond de Rothschild's party. Vogue 141:162-5 Mr 15 '63
LANGLAND, Joseph
Poems, books of poems, and character. Poetry 103:256-61 Ja '64
Wheel of summer; poem. Poetry 101:259-64 Ja '63
LANGLEY, Harold D. See Patterson, R. S. jt. auth.
LANGLEY, Thomas Huntington Wiser
Hints on rock gardening. Horticulture 41:204-5 Ap '63
LANGLEY research center. See United States—National aeronautics and space administration—Langley research center
LANGMUIR, Sally Ames
Boston girl's long voyage home. A. Zich. il pors Sports Illus 18:40-2+ Ap 1 '63
LANGNER, Lawrence
Play construction; excerpt from Play's the thing. Writer 76:17-24 F '63

about

To Lawrence Langner; tributes. K. Hepburn; E. Norton. por Theatre Arts 47:10-11+ My '63
Trade winds. J. G. Fuller. por Sat R 46:10 F 9 '63
Versatility. Theatre Arts 47:9 F '63
LANGRIDGE, Robert
Ribosomes; a common structural feature. bibliog Science 140:1000 My 31 '63
—and Gomatos, P. J.
Structure of RNA. bibliog Science 141:694-8 Ag 23 '63
—and Marmur, Julius
X-ray diffraction study of a DNA which contains uracil. bibliog Science 143:1450-1 Mr 27 '64
LANGSNER, Jules
Art news from Los Angeles (cont) Art N 62:48 My; 47 Sum; 16-17 S '63; 50+ Ja '64
Artist and the scientist; excerpt from The artist in the modern world (cont) Craft Horiz 23:37-8 Ja '63
LANGSTON, John Mercer
Know your congressmen. N. L. Milton. Negro Hist Bul 26:252 My '63
LANGUAGE, Artificial
See also
Esperanto
LANGUAGE, Psychology of. See Language and languages—Psychology
LANGUAGE, Universal
One language for the world? excerpts. M. Pei. UNESCO Courier 16:23+ N '63; Reply with rejoinder. 17:33 F '64
Pidgin: no laughing matter. G. Jennings. Harper 227:69-73 Jl '63; Same abr. with title Pidgin: the language that can do. Read Digest 83:151-4 S '63
LANGUAGE and languages
Linguistics. W. G. Moulton. bibliog il NEA J 54:49-53 Ja '65
Loom of language and the fabric of imperatives: the case of Il principe and Utopia. J. H. Hexter. bibliog f il Am Hist R 69:945-68 Jl '64
Mechanical translation and related language research. R. See. bibliog Science 144:621-6 My 8 '64; Discussion. 145:6 Jl 3 '64
Speech began with hunting. Sci Digest 54: 72 D '63
Stability and change. W. Weaver; discussion. Science 139:245-7 Ja 18 '63
See also
Bilingualism
Children—Language
Dictionaries
Jargon
Slang
Translations and translating
also subhead Languages under names of continents, countries, cities, etc, e.g. Canada—Languages
also English language; German language; etc.

Philosophy

Language and the dignity of youth. C. J. Calitri. il Sat R 46:46-7+ Jl 20 '63

Psychology

Mind and language; address, October 2, 1964. R. T. Oliver. Vital Speeches 31:22-7 O 15 '64
Redundancy in children's texts. E. C. Carterette and M. H. Jones. bibliog il Science 140:1309-11 Je 21 '63

Religious aspects

See Religion and language

Study and teaching

Foreign language teaching: casting out devils. E. Hocking. il NEA J 54:12-14 Ja '65
Language teaching, a scientific approach, by R. Lado. Review
Américas 16:34 D '64. J. Villaverde
To be able to speak; language tuition in Catholic schools. America 109:126 Ag 10 '63
See also
Summer institute of linguistics
LANGUAGE and religion. See Religion and language
LANGUAGE and thought. See Thought and language
LANGUAGE arts
Trends in the language arts; reprint. H. W. Painter. il Wilson Lib Bul 39:151-3 O '64

Study and teaching

Language arts and language learners; with study-discussion program, by D. Harris and E. Harris. A. T. Burrows. bibliog il PTA Mag 59:28-30, 36 N '64
New approach to reading; San Diego County reading study project. R. Van Allen. bibliog f il Wilson Lib Bul 39:154-9 O '64
Visuals and language arts. B. L. Gumm. il Sr Schol 85:10T Ja 21 '65
When teaching the language arts. Sister Mary Josetta. NEA J 52:43-4 D '63
LANGUAGE laboratories
Language laboratory how effective is it? J. C. Hutchinson. il Sch Life 46:14-17+ Ja '64
Three new language labs. il Arch Forum 118: 59+ Mr '63
LANGUAGE shop; drama. See Hall, M.
LANGUAGE teaching records. See Phonograph records—Language teaching records
LANGUAGES. See Language and languages
LANGUAGES, Modern

Bibliography

Foreign language paperbacks. T. G. Bruni. Sr Schol 83:33T Ja 17 '64

Study and teaching

Bull market in foreign languages. T. O. Brandt. Sch & Soc 92:225-7 Sum '64
Charting the trends. il Sat R 46:68 F 16 '63
Drinking in German dreaming in French. D. Boroff. il Mlle 56:130-1+ F '63
Early language study for slum children. Sch & Soc 92:348+ N 28 '64
Foreign accents in the grades; FLES (foreign languages in the elementary school) with study-discussion program, by D. Harris and E. Harris. E. H. Ratté. bibliog il PTA Mag 58:24-6, 35-6 S '63
Foreign languages stage a comeback. F. M. Hechinger. il Sat R 46:64-6+ F 16 '63; Reply. E. C. Knox. 46:56 Mr 23 '63
From school to college in foreign languages. T. Andersson. NEA J 53:35-6 Ap '64
Ka-platz; delight in the unexpected. W. Kelly. il Atlan 211:92-6 Mr '63
Language institutes show the way; National defense language institutes. J. M. Spillane. NEA J 53:25-6 My '64

LANGUAGES, Modern—Study and teaching —*Continued*
Language lessons at home. B. Keating. il Holiday 35:133-8 My '64; Same abr. with title Teach yourself a language. Read Digest 85:161-3+ Jl '64
Non-western world in higher education; symposium, ed. by D. N. Bigelow and L. H. Legters. bibliog f il Ann Am Acad 356:1-167 N '64
Personal business; learning another language. Bsns W p 101-2 My 11 '63
Sonny LeMatina? il Newsweek 63:79-80 Mr 9 '64
Teaching of foreign languages; current issues and the future; condensation of address. W. Starr. Sch Life 46:7-10 N '63
U.S. weakness in languages. Sch & Soc 92: 348 N 28 '64
We're breaking the language barrier. J. Ornstein. il Parents Mag 38:58-9+ D '63
What is a language laboratory? A. S. Hayes. il Sat R 46:70-1 F 16 '63
Which language for your child? il Changing T 18:13-14 Je '64
See also
Berlitz schools of languages
Language laboratories
Phonograph records—Language teaching records

LANHAM, Edwin
Front seat on the roller coaster; story. Sat Eve Post 236:36-7 Je 8 '63

LANIARIUS. See Shrikes

LANIER, R. S.
Acoustics in-the-round at the Berlin philharmonic. Arch Forum 120:98-105 My '64
Acoustics; what happened at Philharmonic Hall? Arch Forum 119:118-23 D '63

LANIER, Sidney
Off Broadway. il por Time 84:68 N 27 '64

LANIN, Lester
Bands of gold. B. Day. il por Sat Eve Post 236:20, 23-5 Ap 20 '63

LANNUIER, Charles Honoré
Distinctive character of the work of Lannuier. L. W. Pearce. il Antiques 86:712-17 D '64

LANOUE, Fred
Drownproofing. Recreation 57:132-3 Mr '64

LANPHERE, Marvin A. and others
Potassium-argon and lead-alpha ages of plutonic rocks, Bokan Mountain area, Alaska. bibliog Science 145:705-7 Ag 14 '64

LANSDALE, Bruce M.
Now see here, Mr Stuart. por Am For 70:6-7 Ja '64

LANSDALE, Edward G.
Viet Nam: do we understand revolution? For Affairs 43:75-86 O '64

LANSDALE, Nelson
Art in New York during the World's fair. Am Artist 28:42-9+ Je '64
Chase Manhattan bank, a patron of art & artists. Am Artist 29:32-7+ Ja '65
Everything here is chaos. Dance Mag 38: 22-5+ Je '64
John Singer Sargent; his private world. il por Am Artist 28:58-63+ N '64
New museum in New York. Am Artist 29: 55-7+ F '65
Preview: New York state theatre. Dance Mag 38:36-8+ Mr '64

LANSDOWNE, Stuart
Washington front (cont) America 109:185; 111:443, 650 Ag 24 '63, O 17, N 21 '64

LANSING, Robert W.
Electroencephalographic correlates of binocular rivalry in man. bibliog Science 146: 1325-7 D 4 '64

LANSING, Mich.
Libraries
Lansing builds a nerve center; Department of school libraries and Public library department. C. S. Paine. il Library J 89:4711-13 D 1 '64

Parks and playgrounds
Hand labor is dead. T. J. Haskell. il Am City 78:79-80 Ap '63

LANSING Job training center. See Employees —Training

LANSNER, Fay
Fay Lansner: deliberate contraries. B. Guest. il por Art N 62:36-7+ D '63

LANTANA
New lantanas are colorful and they thrive on neglect. il Sunset 133:178-9+ S '64
New spreading lantana, fountain of bloom. M. C. Dolton. il Horticulture 41:110 F '63

LANTERMAN, James L.
A.G.C. for receiver audio. Electr World 71: 78 Ap '64

LANTERNS
Aluminum lanterns offer beauty and dependability. B. C. Kilvert, jr. il Flower Grower 50:17 N '63
Camp lanterns. il Consumer Rep 29:344-7 Jl '64

LANTZ, Thomas W.
Tom Lantz retires! por Recreation 57:92 F '64

LANZL, Lawrence H. and Pingel, J. H.
Radiation accidents and emergencies. Science 143:1352-6 Mr 20 '64

LAO refugees. See Refugees, Lao

LAOS
Awakening. il Time 83:24-8 Je 26 '64
First aerial photos of reds in Laos. il Life 56:42-3 Je 19 '64
Importance of Laos in southeast Asia. F. N. Trager. bibliog f Cur Hist 46:107-11+ F '64
Improvement, if not joy. il Time 84:40 O 30 '64
Losing proposition; feuding forces. il Time 81:31 My 3 '63
One more try. Newsweek 63:48 My 11 '64
Recon & retaliation. Time 84:36 N 27 '64
Springtime on the plain. il Time 83:25-6 My 29 '64
U.S. supports preconditions for conference on Laos; U.S. & Soviet statements, July 26 and July 30, 1964. D. Rusk; G. M. Kornienko. Dept State Bul 51:218-20 Ag 17 '64
See also
Communism—Laos
Economic assistance in Laos
Guerrillas—Laos
Hunting—Laos
Natural resources—Laos

Defenses
Choices get grimmer in southeast Asia; with editorial comment. il Bsns W p 26-7, 180 My 23 '64
For U.S: it's war with one arm; firsthand report on red sanctuary in Laos. S. W. Sanders. il U S News 57:46-8 Jl 20 '64
Pathet Lao tip the balance. il Newsweek 63: 28-30 Je 1 '64
Reporter at large. R. Shaplen. il New Yorker 40:78+ Ja 16 '65
Time to think. Newsweek 63:32+ Je 29 '64

Economic conditions
Letter from a dusty Graustark. A. Hogg. Nat R 14:375-7 My 7 '63

Foreign relations
Around the world with Savang Vatthana. il Time 81:25 Mr 8 '63
Doublecross for the U.S. in Laos. il U S News 54:66-7 Ap 22 '63
King of Laos visits Washington, talks with President Kennedy; joint communique, February 27, 1963. Dept State Bul 48:447-8 Mr 25 '63

History
Laos. L. Unger. bibliog il Focus 14:1-6 My '64

Neutrality
And then there were three. il Time 81:29 Mr 1 '63
Atlantic report. Atlan 214:28+ N '64
Beckoning the undertaker. il Time 81:51 Ap 19 '63
Consultations held at Vientiane on situation in Laos; joint communique, June 29, 1964. Dept State Bul 51:88-91 Jl 20 '64
Divorce, Laotian style. Newsweek 61:47-8 Ap 22 '63
Laos and Viet-Nam, a prescription for peace; address, May 22, 1964. D. Rusk. Dept State Bul 50:886-91 Je 8 '64; Same with title International agreements. Vital Speeches 30: 546-9 Jl 1 '64
Laos: continuing crisis. E. Pace. For Affairs 43:64-74 O '64
Laos, Cuba, and two visitors to Moscow. il Newsweek 61:39-40 My 6 '63
Laos: more trouble for U.S. il U S News 56:37 My 4 '64
Laos peace broken by red moves. il Sr Schol 82:16-17 My 8 '63
Laos: the settlement that settled nothing. S. Karnow. il Reporter 28:34-7 Ap 25 '63
Laotian lesson: who wants to win? il Newsweek 63:31 My 4 '64
Man in the middle. Takashi Oka. New Repub 148:11-13 Je 15 '63
New civil war? il Time 81:30 Ap 26 '63
On the Laotian brink. il Newsweek 61:33 Ap 29 '63
Premier Khrushchev reaffirms support for neutral Laos; joint communique between the United States and the Soviet Union, April 26, 1963. Dept State Bul 48:775 My 20 '63

LAOS—Neutrality—*Continued*
Underground in the Northeast. D. Warner. New Repub 148:8-9 Ap 6 '63
Very fragile structure. New Repub 148:8 My 4 '63

Politics and government

Atlantic report. Atlan 211:12+ Je '63
Blood begets blood. Newsweek 61:47-8 Ap 15 '63
Catastrophic non-war in Laos. D. Warner. il Reporter 30:21-4 Je 18 '64
Challenge to freedom in Asia; address, June 14, 1963. R. W. Hilsman. Dept State Bul 49:43-50 Jl 8 '63
Conversation in Vientiane. Newsweek 63:41-2 Je 15 '64
Coup and confusion. il Sr Schol 84:21 My 8 '64
Demon beneath the pagoda. il Time 83:27-8 My 1 '64
Evil spirits on the plain. il Time 82:32 Jl 5 '63
Experiment in neutrality; Laos since the Geneva agreement. D. Warner. New Repub 148:12-14 F 2 '63
Laos: more trouble for U.S. il U S News 56:37 My 4 '64
Laotian lesson: who wants to win? il Newsweek 63:31 My 4 '64
Pathet Lao tip the balance. il Newsweek 63:28-30 Je 1 '64
Relaxed crisis. il Newsweek 63:42 My 18 '64
Reporter at large. R. Shaplen. il New Yorker 40:78+ Ja 16 '65
U.S. calls for action to insure restoration of cease-fire in Laos; statement, April 8, 1963. Dept State Bul 48:646 Ap 29 '63
Water pistols at ten paces. Time 83:33-4 Ap 24 '64

LAOTIANS
Letter from a dusty Graustark. A. Hogg. Nat R 14:375-7 My 7 '63

LAP-honing. See Honing

LAPE, Fred
Cold skies, cold day; poem. Nation 198:586 Je 8 '64
Dream for our schools. Am For 70:8-11+ Ag '64

LAPE, Jane M.
Ticonderoga, key to a continent. Antiques 84:57-9 Jl '63

LAPHAM, Lewis
America's cup: racing for glory. Sat Eve Post 237:26-33 Ag 22 '64
Can the manatee save Florida? Sat Eve Post 237:38-9 Je 27 '64
Encore for twelve high-kicking housewives. Sat Eve Post 237:72+ O 24 '64
Everyone's in the kitchen with Julia. Sat Eve Post 237:20-1 Ag 8 '64
Feely is here. Sat Eve Post 237:28-9 Ap 18 '64
Have pawn, will travel. Sat Eve Post 237:18-19 F 8 '64
Illusive, elusive Miss Tammy Grimes. Sat Eve Post 237:60-3 Ap 4 '64
Let me tell you about Mae West. Sat Eve Post 237:76-8 N 14 '64
Monk; high priest of jazz. Sat Eve Post 237:70+ Ap 11 '64
Music for machines. Sat Eve Post 237:66+ Ja 18 '64
Passion for rhinoceros. Sat Eve Post 237:66-8 F 1 '64
Secret life of Walter (Mitty) Cronkite. Sat Eve Post 236:65-7 Mr 16 '63
That so nece$$ary ingredient. Sat Eve Post 237:56-9 S 5 '64
Wacky search for gold. Sat Eve Post 236:66-71 D 14 '63
What ever happened to burlesque? Sat Eve Post 237:72-4 Mr 14 '64
(ed) See Phillips, D. She's just one of the fox hunters

LAPIERRE, Dominique. See Collins, L. jt. auth.

LA PLACA, Sam J. See Ibers, J. A. jt. auth.

LAPLAND
Norway's North. J. Lieber. il Travel 122:46-8 Jl '64
Tourist crop grows under midnight sun; Sweden, Norway, and Finland compete for tourists. il Bsns W p30-1 Jl 18 '64
See also
Lapps
Rovaniemi

LAPORTE, Raymond
M. Laporte. New Yorker 39:37-8 Ap 20 '63

LAPP, Ralph E.
Einstein letter that started it all. N Y Times Mag p 13+ Ag 2 '64
Strategy of overkill. Bul Atomic Sci 19:4-11 Ap '63

LAPP, W. S. and others
Tolerance between host and donor tissue in birds. bibliog Science 141:818-20 Ag 30 '63

LAPPS
New era for an ancient business; modern herding practices of Sweden's Laplanders. il Bsns W p34-5 Ja 2 '65

LAPWOOD, Ralph
China's living church. C. Northcott. Christian Cent 82:39-40 Ja 13 '65

LAQUEUR, Walter Z.
Gomulka compromise. New Repub 148:11-12 Je 29 '63
Poland. New Repub 149:10 Jl 13 '63

LARAMIE, Wyo.
Notes for a gazetteer. P. Hamburger. New Yorker 39:152 N 16 '63

LARCOM, Guy C. Jr
City hall sets the pace for downtown growth. Am City 79:93-4 Ja '64

LARDNER, Rex
Hockey. Sports Illus 21:81-2 N 23 '64
Rowing. Sports Illus 18:56+ My 20; 53-4 My 27 '63
Swimming. Sports Illus 18:67 Ap 1 '63; 20:48+ Mr 23 '64

LARDNER, Ring, 1885-1933
Bush-league Swift. K. S. Lynn. Reporter 28:60-2 F 14 '63
Sporting life. R. L. Tobin. Sat R 47:8+ Jl 11 '64
Writer. R. L. Tobin. Sat R 47:6 Ja 25 '64

LARDNER, Susan
Where have you been all my life? story. Seventeen 23:156-7 Ap '64

LARGE families. See Family. Size of

LARGEMOUTH bass. See Bass

LARGEMOUTH bass fishing. See Bass fishing

LARIMORE, Jon H.
Surplus stereophones. Pop Electr 20:100 My '64

LARKIN, Frank
Church secession. America 111:90-1 Jl 25 '64

LARKIN, Philip
Larkin's poetry. R. F. Deen. Commonweal 81:459 D 25 '64

LARKSPURS. See Delphiniums

LARMOYEUX, Jack. See Trimble, G. R. jr. jt. auth.

LARNER, Jeremy
What do they get from rock 'n' roll? Atlan 214:44-9 Ag '64; Same abr. Read Digest 85:181+ N '64

about

Spk, he bggd. H. Frankel. Sat R 47:40-1 S 19 '64

LA ROCHE, Betty G.
Six flavorful ways to serve pork. Farm J 89:66-8 Ja '65

LAROCHE, Emmanuel
Lost civilization emerges from the past. UNESCO Courier 16:14-20 F '63

LA ROCQUE, A. See Weber, J. N. jt. auth.

LAROUSSE (firm) See Publishers and publishing—France

LARRABEE, Eric
Books on Guerrilla warfare, fifteen years overdue. Harper 228:120-3 My '64
Jazz notes. See issues of Harper's magazine
Letter from Skopje. New Yorker 40:131-2+ O 17 '64
Saarinen's dark tower: the CBS building and how it grew. Harper 229:55-61 D '64
Scientists in collision: was Velikovsky right? Harper 227:48-50+ Ag; 87 D '63

LARRABEE, Harold A.
Trumpeter of doomsday. Am Heritage 15:34-7+ Ap '64

LARRICK, George P.
FDA: drug agency answers critics by attempting to step up science, but many critical problems remain. E. Langer. por Science 142:1280-2 D 6 '63

LARRICK, Nancy
Letter to parents. Sr Schol 84:8T F 14 '64
New channels for book distribution through the schools. por ALA Bul 57:544-8 Je '63
Textbooks and teaching aids. PTA Mag 58:4-6 bibliog(p35-6) D '63
What forty-four letters can do. Sat R 47:66-7 S 19 '64

LARSEN, Jack Lenor
Apartment where change is the rule. il House & Gard 123:146-51 Ap '63
Jack Lenor Larsen. J. McDevitt. Craft Horiz 24:49-50 Mr '64

LARSEN, Joseph R.
Fine structure of the interpseudotracheal papillae of the blowfly. bibliog Science 139:347 Ja 25 '63

LARSON, Arthur
GOP, liberal origins and the future. Nation 198:236-9 Mr 9 '64
How the Republicans can win. Sat Eve Post 237:21-3 Ja 25 '64
Republican looks at extremism. D. R. Maxey. il pors Look 29:24-7 Ja 26 '65
What every U.N. critic should know. Sat R 46:13-15+ Je 15 '63
What is liberal Republicanism? por Sat R 47:14-17 F 29 '64
What the U.N. can do, if it will. Sat R 47: 20 Je 27 '64
What to teach about the United Nations. NEA J 53:26-8 Ja '64

LARSON, B. Jeanette
NACS: can college stores cope with the paperback boom? summary of address. por Pub W 184:16-21 D 16 '63

LARSON, Carl H.
Designing rugs. Sch Arts 64:19-20 D '64

LARSON, Cedric A.
Who needs vacations? Sci Digest 54:77-80 Jl '63

LARSON, Don W.
New life-saving method. Outdoor Life 132: 48-9+ Ag '63
Why waste winter? Outdoor Life 133:24-7+ Ja '64

LARSON, Donald A. See Skvarla, J. J. jt. auth.

LARSON, Knute
Secondary school discipline. NEA J 52:12-17 S '63

LARSON, Leonard W.
We are interested in Johnny, too. Todays Health 41:82-4 O '63

LARTIGUE, Jacques Henri
People are talking about . . . il Vogue 142:199 S 1 '63
Spinning circles; beauty and speed in photography. il por Newsweek 62:60 Jl 22 '63
World leaps into an age of innovation. il pors Life 55:65-72B N 29 '63

LARTIGUE, O. Gallien-. See Gallien-Lartigue, O.

LARVAE
Night-caught and day-caught larvae of the California sardine. J. D. Isaacs. bibliog il Science 144:1132-3 My 29 '64

LASAGNA, Louis
G.P. is still needed. N Y Times Mag p 18+ Ap 19 '64
Now Dr Robot enters the scene. N Y Times Mag p 15+ Je 16 '63
Old wives' tales; true or false? N Y Times Mag p88+ My 5 '63; Same abr. with title Which old wives' tales do you believe? Read Digest 83:211-13 Ag '63
Problems of drug development. Science 145: 362-7 Jl 24 '64
Why are doctors out of step? New Repub 152:13-15 Ja 2 '65
Would Hippocrates rewrite his oath? N Y Times Mag p 11+ Je 28 '64

LA SCALA opera company. See Opera—Italy

LASCAUX murals. See Cave drawings and paintings

LASCHEVER, Barnett D.
Back roads lead to discovery. Pop Phot 52: 140-1 Ap '63
Travelers' tales. Sat R 46:62-4+ Mr 16 '63

LASCHEVER, Barney
What hath Columbus wrought? Sat R 47: 67-8+ O 10 '64

LASER diffraction velocimeter. See Velocimeters

LASER flow meters. See Flow meters

LASER modulators. See Modulators

LASERS. See Light amplifiers

LASERSON, Nina
Curl up and read. Seventeen 23:44 S '64

LASH, Henry
Rewards and hazards of book reviewing. por ALA Bul 57:860-1 O '63

LASH, Joseph P.
Tales out of Katanga. New Repub 148:23-4+ Ap 6 '63

LASHER, E. C. R.
Case for diversification. Ann Am Acad 345: 109-14 Ja '63

LASKA, Vaclav. See Berka, R. jt. auth.

LASKER, Gabriel W.
American association of physical anthropologists. Science 146:289 O 9 '64

LASKER awards. See Albert Lasker awards

LASKEY, Harold H.
Combined book exhibit program for communication between paperback book publishers and educational market. Wilson Lib Bul 38:31 S '63

LASKY, Francis Joseph
Frank with plenty of mustard! H. L. Masin. por Sr Schol 83:21 N 1 '63

LASS, Abraham
Choose your college. Sat R 47:73-4 N 21 '64
Fruits of automation. Sat R 47:69-70 S 19 '64
Nongraded high school. Sat R 47:70+ Ja 18 '64

LASSAW, Ibram
Four sculptors, four styles. il Art N 62:37+ Sum '63

LASSEN, L. J. See Delahunt, C. S. jt. auth.

LASSEN VOLCANIC NATIONAL PARK
Lively Lassen. W. F. Heald. il Travel 122: 46-7 N '64
Steam means trouble in Lassen's Section thirty-six. P. Hyde. il Nat Parks Mag 37: 4-6 Je '63

LASSER, Terese
After breast cancer: learning to live again. S. Robinson. McCalls 91:32+ Ap '64

LASSITER, Luther
You don't beat Wimpy at the game he loves. T. Fox. pors Sports Illus 20:58-61 Mr 23 '64

LAST analysis; drama. See Bellow, S.

LAST and most blessed Christmas gift; story. See Taylor, T.

LAST believer; story. See Sexton, A.

LAST bite of buttercups; story. See Ellingson, M.

LAST gasps; stories. See Newman, D.

LAST minstrel; drama. See Yerby, L.

LAST savage; opera. See Menotti, G. C.

LAST train to Zanzibar; story. See Oppenheimer, M.

LAST wish; story. See Layefsky, V.

LAS VEGAS, Nev.
Clouds over Las Vegas. il N Y Times Mag p80 D 1 '63
Las Vegas! T. K. Wolfe. il Esquire 61:97-103+ F '64

Hotels, restaurants, etc.

French dresssing; lavish Las Vegas revue. il Sat Eve Post 236:24-7 Ap 6 '63
It makes money; Las Vegas's Casino de Paris. il Newsweek 64:90 S 28 '64

LAS VEGAS, N.Mex.
Las Vegas, N.M, gets natural gas. il Am City 79:96 D '64

LATCHES
Collectors' latchstrings. il House & Gard 123: 28-9 Ap '63
It feels good in your hand. il Sunset 130: 141-2 Mr '63

LATE-blooming flowers; story. See Chekhov, A.

LATE show; story. See Hemenway, R.

LATENESS. See Tardiness

LATERITE
Lateritic soils. M. McNeil. il Sci Am 211:96-102 N '64

LATERNA magika. See Theater—Czechoslovakia

LATEX paint. See Paint

LATH houses
Lath cylinder, a practical modern shade house. J. Fanning. il Pop Gard 14:63 Jl '63

LATHAM, Earl
Mr Holmes makes his mark. Nation 197:36-8 Jl 13 '63

LATHAM, Sid
New shotshells turn misses into hits. Pop Sci 183:154-6 S '63

LATHE bits. See Lathes

LATHES
Compound slide rest for your wood lathe; accessory for metal turning. W. E. Burton. il Pop Mech 119:190-4+ F '63
Hitch a router to your lathe! for turned-wood projects. R. J. De Cristoforo. il Pop Sci 183:116-18 Ag '63
How to do lathework on your table saw. R. J. De Cristoforo. il Pop Sci 182:138-41 F '63
How to get started with a metal lathe. J. Burroughs. il Pop Sci 182:106-10+ Mr '63
I built this wood lathe for $10.67. E. R. Haan. il Pop Mech 120:170-2 Ag '63
Midget lathe that does mighty jobs. H. Walton. il Pop Sci 183:146-9+ O '63
Now, automatic turning for your lathe. R. J. De Cristoforo. il Pop Sci 182:168-9 F '63
Origins of the lathe. R. S. Woodbury. il Sci Am 208:132-40+ bibliog(p202) Ap '63
Right lathe bit for the job. J. Payne. il Pop Sci 185:150-3 D '64
Traveling lathe oiler. il Pop Mech 119:189 Mr '63
Wood lathe; Metal lathe. il Pop Sci 183:176-8 N '63

LATIMER, Helen
Dwarf evergreens in modern landscaping. Horticulture 41:520-1 O '63

LATIMER, Rebecca H.
Every town has two faces. Harper 227:26+ N '63

LATIN. See Latin language

LATIN AMERICA
Aims of Christian democracy; excerpt from Religion, revolution, and reform, ed. by F. B. Pike and W. V. D'Antonio. E. Frei. Commonweal 81:63-6 O 9 '64
Challenge in Latin America; symposium. bibliog f il Cur Hist 48:1-39+ Ja '65
Comes the revolution; Catholic attitudes. America 108:796-7 Je 1 '63
Invisible Latin America, by S. Shapiro. Review
Commentary 37:85-6 F '64. K. Botsford
Latin America, 1964; symposium. bibliog il Cur Hist 46:1-37+ Ja '64
Latin America progress report. G. J. Mangone. America 111:10-14 Jl 4 '64
Outlook in Latin America: an official size-up; interview. T. C. Mann. il U S News 57:58-62 Jl 20 '64
Region in ferment; address, August 26, 1963. D. S. Morrison. Vital Speeches 30:11-13 O 15 '63
South America: travel's sleeping beauty. T. Moscoso. il Sat R 47:53-4+ O 10 '64
Too many revolutions to the South. R. G. Mead, jr. il Sat R 48:85-6 Ja 2 '65
Twain shall meet; Latin America, an East-West bridge. I. Quiles. il Américas 17:6-9 Ja '65

See also
Agriculture—Latin America
Airlines—Latin America
Alliance for progress
Anti-Communist movements—Latin America
Art—Latin America
Automobile touring—Latin America
Aviation—Latin America
Birth control—Latin America
Book industries and trade—Latin America
Christmas—Latin America
Cities and towns—Latin America
Communism—Latin America
Cost of living—Latin America
Economic assistance in Latin America
Education—Latin America
Electric power—Latin America
Ethnology—Latin America
Food relief—Latin America
Government ownership—Latin America
Guerrillas—Latin America
Investments, Foreign (in Latin America)
Jews in Latin America
Labor and laboring classes—Latin America
Land tenure—Latin America
Libraries—Latin America
Library schools and education—Latin America
Music—Latin America
Newspapers—Latin America
Nutrition problems—Latin America
Opera—Latin America
Poor—Latin America
Prisons—Latin America
Public health—Latin America
Roads—Latin America
Science—Latin America
Taxation—Latin America
Technical assistance in Latin America
Tourist trade—Latin America
Trade unions—Latin America
Women—Latin America
Youth—Latin America

Anecdotes, facetiae, satire, etc.
Tranquilized in Latin America. M. Miller. il Harper 230:131-4 Ja '65

Antiquities
Rediscovering America. A. Kidder, 2d. il Horizon 6:73-87+ Sum '64

Armed forces
Last best hope? American training of the military in Latin America. New Repub 149:4 O 19 '63

Bibliography
SR's check list of 1963's books on Latin America; comp. by R. Brown. Sat R 46:16+ O 12 '63

Civilization
Sources of Latin American culture. P. Damaz. il Craft Horiz 23:21-3 S '63

Commerce
Brighter opportunities ahead in Latin America. B. DeSoissons. il Nations Bsns 51:80-2+ S '63
Common markets south of the border. Duns R 81:51+ Mr '63
Facts and figures of the Americas. il Américas 16.47 Ag '64
Latin America; encouragement for investors; address, November 20, 1963. D. D. McConkey. Vital Speeches 30:209-14 Ja 15 '64
Opportunities and obstacles in Latin America; address, December 5, 1962. F. Herrera. Vital Speeches 29:242-5 F 1 '63
Prosperity: a continent's aspiration. il Newsweek 63:36-7 Mr 30 '64
What French salesman de Gaulle was selling in Latin America. il U S News 56:100 Ap 6 '64

See also
Latin American free trade association

Cultural relations
Nueva York; Hispanic culture makes its mark on New York. J. V. Amaral. il Américas 16:6-11 Jl '64
Picture window on the arts. F. Alegria. il Américas 15:27-30 Mr '63

Defenses
Arming against terror. il Bsns W p68+ Ap 27 '63
Latin America and military aid. E. Lieuwen. Sat R 46:16-17 My 4 '63
On military aid; arming the Latin Americans. A. Neish. New Repub 148:12-13 My 11 '63; Reply. P. de Mesones. 148:30-1 Je 22 '63

Description and travel
Art in Latin American architecture. P. Damaz. il Craft Horiz 23:12-39+ S '63
Capricorn uncensored. T. Szulc. il Sat R 46:64+ O 12 '63

Economic conditions
After five years in South America; story of change. D. B. Richardson. il U S News 57:72-6 S 21 '64
Alliance for progress. L. Guernsey and A. Taylor. bibliog il Focus 14:1-6 Ap '64
Alliance for progress; address, May 13, 1964. T. C. Mann. Dept State Bul 50:857-63 Je 1 '64
American revolution; address, June 19, 1963. J. B. Martin. Vital Speeches 29:649-53 Ag 15 '63
Anglo-America and Latin America: can they become better neighbors? address, August 16, 1963. G. L. White. Vital Speeches 29:746-50 O 1 '63
Another view of the Latin-American problem. J. P. Davies, jr. il N Y Times Mag p 15+ Ag 25 '63
Are we ignoring Latin America? A. A. Berle. il N Y Times Mag p26+ N 24 '63
Building on quicksand. S. Lens. Commonweal 79:159-61 N 1 '63
Crisis for capitalism. R. Armstrong. il Sat Eve Post 237:17-29 Mr 21 '64
Doing business with a revolution; address, April 24, 1963. J. T. Connor. Vital Speeches 29:537-40 Je 15 '63
First aid for an ailing Alliance; meeting of Latin American economic & social council. il Bsns W p47-8+ N 9 '63
Focus on Latin America. il Sr Schol 83:38-9 O 4 '63
Les inflations sud-americaines, by D. Lambert. Review
Américas 15:39-41 F '63. D. Lambert
Latin America: a massive indictment. A. Neish. Nation 197:182-3 S 28 '63
Latin America; necessity for political democracy and stability; address, November 18, 1963. J. F. Kennedy. Vital Speeches 30:102-5 D 1 '63
Latin American problems in today's world economy; text of statement. P. de Seynes. il U N Rev 10:18-20+ Je '63
Latin America's troubled cities. C. M. Haar. For Affairs 41:536-49 Ap '63
Latin sky is brighter. Life 55:4 Ag 16 '63
New look at Latin America: how bright the future; interview. P. James. il U S News 55:72-83 Jl 8 '63
Opportunities and obstacles in Latin America; address, December 5, 1962. F. Herrera. Vital Speeches 29:242-5 F 1 '63
Progress for whom? New Repub 149:3-4 N 30 '63
Seven myths about Latin America. D. B. Richardson. il U S News 54:77-9 My 6 '63
Trends in Latin American economic development; statement, May 8, 1963. E. M. Martin. Dept State Bul 48:918-23 Je 10 '63
Why can't we save Latin America? R. Armstrong. il Sat Eve Post 236:34-6 N 30 '63
Why not invest in Latin America? J. Grunwald. Harvard Bsns R 41:123-8 N '63
Why the new upheaval in Latin America. il U S News 55:43-5 O 21 '63

LATIN AMERICA—Economic conditions—*Cont.*
See also
Inter-American economic and social council
Poor—Latin America
United Nations—Economic commission for Latin America

Economic policy

Alliance for progress; address, March 10, 1964. W. W. Rostow. Dept State Bul 50: 496-500 Mr 30 '64
Alliance for progress; August 1964; address, August 7, 1964. W. W. Rostow. Dept State Bul 51:306-11 Ag 31 '64
Journeys toward progress, by A. O. Hirschman. Review
Américas il 15:39-41 Ag '63. A. O. Hirschman
Let's stop financing socialism in Latin America. J. G. Tower. Read Digest 84:121-4 Ja '64
Strengthening the Alliance for progress; statement, November 13, 1963. W. A. Harriman. Dept State Bul 49:937-45 D 16 '63
Toward a dynamic development policy for Latin America; excerpts. R. Prebisch. il U N Rev 10:13-21 My '63

Economic relations

Bringing Latin unions into the Alliance; Declaration of Cundinamarca. il Bsns W p 174+ My 18 '63
Economic development in Latin America; address; July 29, 1963. T. G. Upton. Vital Speeches 29:693-6 S 1 '63
Inter-American economic relations; address, April 2, 1964. F. Herrera. Vital Speeches 30:427-32 My 1 '64
Prosperity: a continent's aspiration. il Newsweek 63:36-7 Mr 30 '64

United States

U.S. business image in Latin America; address, September 23, 1964. D. Rockefeller. Vital Speeches 31:7-10 O 15 '64

Foreign relations

De Gaulle's mission. New Repub 150:11 Mr 14 '64
Honest intervention. Christian Cent 80:731-2 Je 5 '63

Canada

Canada and Latin America; remarks, February 1964. J. M. Dessureault. il Américas 16:36-7 Ap '64

Communist countries

Latin America and the Communist bloc. R. J. Alexander. Cur Hist 44:73-7+ F '63

Cuba

Castro problem more serious than ever; statement. M. Ydigoras Fuentes. U S News 54: 49 Mr 18 '63
Neighbors object. Nat R 14:185+ Mr 12 '63
No time to let up on Castro. Life 57:4 Ag 7 '64
O.A.S. resolution on Cuba; text. Cur Hist 44:111+ F '63
Stop, & stop now! OAS diplomatic and economic sanctions against Communist Cuba. il Time 84:32 Jl 31 '64

France

On the long, hot road with General de Gaulle; tour of South America. il Newsweek 64:76+ O 5 '64

Israel

Israel-OAS cooperation. Américas 16:44-5 Ag '64

United States

Ali, ali, anza free-o! Tiresias. Nat R 14:113-14+ F 12 '63
Calming a Latin tempest; with editorial comment. il Bsns W p64-8, 96 F 1 '64
Choice for Latin America: Castro threat or Leoni promise. il Newsweek 63:34-6+ Mr 30 '64
Cold war drift in Latin America. P. S. Holbo. bibliog f il Cur Hist 44:65-72+ F '63
Crisis of casualness in Latin America. J. P. Davies, jr. Harper 229:12+ Ag '64; Reply. R. R. White. 229:6 O '64
U.S. still a bogeyman to Latin Americans. il Bsns W p27-8 D 7 '63
When they shout, Yanqui, no! A. A. Berle. il N Y Times Mag p9+ Ja 26 '64
Why the new upheaval in Latin America. il U S News 55:43-5 O 21 '63

History

Conquest and the cross; summary of address. L. Hanke. il Am Heritage 14:4-19+ F '63

Bibliography

Articles and other books received; comp. by K. M. Schmitt. See issues of American historical review to April 1964
Articles and other books received; comp. by W. N. Simonson. Am Hist R 69:1207-10; 70: 315-17 Jl, O '64
Recent developments in Latin-American history. R. N. Burr. bibliog f Ann Am Acad 353:122-30 My '64

Industries

Brighter opportunities ahead in Latin America. B. DeSoissons. il Nations Bsns 51:80-2+ S '63
Facts and figures of the Americas. il Américas 15:42-3 Ag '63
See also
Paper making and trade

Intellectual life

Culture comes into its own. M. I. Anderson. il Américas 15:2-6 N '63
I have faith in the new man. R. Squirru. Américas 15:1 Je '63
In defense of culture; excerpts from address, September 1963. C. V. Moog. il Américas 15:1 O '63
Latin America and the Atlantic culture. E. Squirru. il Américas 15:13-17 N '63

Maps

Map of Latin America (cont) Sr Schol 83:23 O 4 '63; 85:27 O 7 '64
Northwestern South America opens new frontiers. Nat Geog Mag 125:267, sup (folded map) F '64

Nationalism

New Latin American nationalism. J. J. Johnson. Yale R 54:187-204 D '64

Politics

Continent of upheaval. Time 84:56 N 13 '64
Crisis of casualness in Latin America. J. P. Davies, jr. Harper 229:12+ Ag '64; Reply. R. R. White. 229:6 O '64
Democratic ideal in our policy toward Latin America; address, June 7, 1964. T. C. Mann. Dept State Bul 50:995-1000 Je 29 '64
Latin America: a broad-brush appraisal. P. W. Quigg. For Affairs 42:399-412 Ap '64
Latin America: no war, but... il U S News 58:27 Ja 4 '65
Latin America's future leaders. V. Alba. New Repub 149:12-13 S 21 '63
New armies take over in Latin America. J. J. Johnson. il N Y Times Mag p 14+ Mr 8 '64
One Mann & twenty problems. il Time 83: 15-18 Ja 31 '64
Seven myths about Latin America. D. B. Richardson. il U S News 54:77-9 My 6 '63
Slogan for the unwary. America 109:346 S 28 '63
U.S. in Latin America. R. M. Schneider. bibliog f Cur Hist 48:1-8+ Ja '65
U.S. policy regarding military governments in Latin America; statement, October 6, 1963. E. M. Martin. Dept State Bul 49:698-700 N 4 '63
Why we are wrong in Latin America. Tiresias. il Nat R 16:225-6+ Mr 24 '64
Winds of revolution, by T. Szulc. Review
Reporter 30:58 Ja 30 '64. R. M. Schneider

Population

Brake on the Alianza. H. Rosenhouse. New Repub 150:19-21 Mr 28 '64
Facts and figures of the Americas. il Américas 15:40-3 My '63
Population growth and the Alliance for progress; address, November 9, 1964. T. C. Mann. Dept State Bul 51:807-10 D 7 '64
Population: planning group hears encouraging reports on efforts to start Latin American programs. D. S. Greenberg. Science 144:513-15 My 1 '64; Reply with rejoinder. W. D. Bellamy. 144:1409-10 Je 19 '64

Religious institutions and affairs

Latin America: testing ground of ecumenism; excerpt from Unity: man's tomorrow. R. Schutz. il Cath World 197:28-35 Ap '63
See also
Catholic church in Latin America
Church of England in Latin America

Social conditions

Health and social progress in Latin America; address, October 10, 1964. M. W. Williams. Dept State Bul 51:747-51 N 23 '64
Latin America: a massive indictment. A. Neish. Nation 197:182-3 S 28 '63

LATIN AMERICA—Social conditions—*Cont.*
Preventive counterrevolution. Nation 199:395 N 30 '64
Wine is bitter, by M. S. Eisenhower. Review
Sat R 46:22-3 Jl 20 '63. H. Lavine

Statistics

Facts and figures of the Americas; balance of payments, 1965. Américas 17:47 Ja '65

LATIN AMERICA and the United States
Anglo-America and Latin America: can they become better neighbors? address, August 16, 1963. G. L. White. Vital Speeches 29:746-50 O 1 '63
Another view of the Latin-American problem. J. P. Davies, jr. il N Y Times Mag p 15+ Ag 25 '63
Battle for progress with freedom in the western hemisphere; address, November 18, 1963. J. F. Kennedy. Dept State Bul 49:900-4 D 9 '63
Formula for prosperity. D. Rockefeller. Sat R 46:28 O 12 '63
Invisible Latin America, by S. Shapiro. Review
Commentary 37:85-6 F '64. K. Botsford; Reply. S. Halper. 37:16 Je '64
Money will not make them free. H. Lavine. il Sat R 47:28-9 Ja 25 '64
Policy for Latin America. T. D. White. Newsweek 61:59 Mr 25 '63
Seven presidents. Newsweek 61:54+ Mr 25 '63
Spirit of San Jose. Nation 196:258 Mr 30 '63
United States and Latin America; ed. by H. L. Matthews. Review
Américas 15:41 D '63. F. P. Hebblethwaite
See also
Americans in Latin America
Inter-American relations

LATIN AMERICA in art
Monvoisin in South America. A. R. Romera. il Américas 15:7-11 My '63

LATIN AMERICAN art. See Art, Latin American

LATIN AMERICAN artists. See Artists, Latin American

LATIN AMERICAN authors. See Authors, Latin American

LATIN AMERICAN committee on national parks. See International union for the conservation of nature and natural resources

LATIN AMERICAN fiction
Indian in Latin American fiction. E. S. Urbanski. il Américas 15:20-4 My '63
Poetry of protest. J. Yglesias. Nation 198:376-7 Ap 13 '64
Prize stories from Latin America: winners of the Life en español literary contest. Review
Sat R 46:28 Jl 20 '63. H. Frankel
See also
Ecuadorian fiction

LATIN AMERICAN free trade association
To ket bolder or give up. Time 84:103-4 O 30 '64
Toward more trade. F. Harmon. il Américas 16:31-5 Ap '64

LATIN AMERICAN literature
Spanish-American literature: a history, by E. Anderson-Imbert; tr. by J. V. Falconieri. Review
Sat R 46:40 O 12 '63. G. Rabassa
See also
Argentine literature

LATIN AMERICAN painting. See Painting, Latin American

LATIN AMERICAN philosophy. See Philosophy, Latin American

LATIN AMERICAN poetry
See also
Salvadorian poetry

LATIN AMERICAN students
Violence in the universities; pro-Castro students. R. Winet. New Repub 148:12-13 Ap 13 '63

LATIN AMERICAN students in the United States. See Foreign students in the United States

LATIN AMERICAN studies. See Area studies

LATIN AMERICANS
High cost of manliness. Time 82:30-1 S 6 '63
Our faith in tomorrow: New world man; excerpts from address, 1963. M. L. Pérez Marchand. Américas 16:2-4 Ag '64
South Americans. L. Gross. il Look 28:72-8+ Je 2 '64
See also
Brazilians

LATIN AMERICANS in the United States
Nueva York; Hispanic culture makes its mark on New York. J. V. Amaral. il Américas 16: 6-11 Jl '64

LATIN language
After hours; Auxilium Latinum. C. M. Wilson. Harper 226:28-32 My '63
Language of encyclicals. America 108:825 Je 8 '63
Latin: the church's mother tongue? excerpts from Council in action. H. Küng. Harper 227:60-4 O '63

Study and teaching

Latin and the curriculum. W. W. Brickman. Sch & Soc 92:346 N 28 '64
Majoring in resistance. H. F. Ellis. il Atlan 214:104-6 S '64

LATIN poetry

Bibliography

Latin verse: a universe apart. K. Rexroth. Nation 198:148-50 F 10 '64

Translations into English

Any author to any friend; tr. by D. Fitts. Martial. Atlan 213:90 My '64
Pange lingua; tr. by J. Moffitt. St Thomas Aquinas. America 109:314 S 21 '63
To Ligurinus, relentlessly a poet; tr. by D. Fitts. Atlan 214:44 Jl '64

LATITUDE; story. See Gerber, M. J.

LATOURETTE, Kenneth Scott
Achievement of Kenneth Scott Latourette. M. E. Marty. Christian Cent 80:336-7 Mr 13 '63

LA TRAZ, Jean de
Moumou; adaptation. See Green, M. and Feilbert, E. Pajama tops

LATTA, Delbert L.
Excerpt from debate, April 7, 1964. Cong Digest 43:187+ Je '64

LATTER-day saints. See Mormons and Mormonism

LATTIMORE, Owen
Chingis Khan and the Mongol conquests; with biographical sketch. Sci Am 209:14, 54-60+ bibliog(p 140) Ag '63

LATTIMORE, Richmond
Game resumed; poem. New Yorker 39:145 My 11 '63
Sestina of sandbars and shelters; poem. Sat R 47:36 My 9 '64
Skeleton in the closet; poem. New Yorker 40:36 Mr 28 '64
Wabash blues; poem. Poetry 102:369-70 S '63

LATVIA

Industries

Light industry; lingerie management in Latvia. il Life 55:71 S 13 '63

LAU, Glenn
Lake Erie's living legend. W. Seifert. il por Field & S 69:34-5+ Ag '64
Terror on an open lake. por Outdoor Life 134: 48-9+ Jl '64

LAU, Ted
Made with popsicle sticks. Design 65:100-1 Ja '64

LAUBER, Jean K.
Sex-linked albinism in the Japanese quail. bibliog Science 146:948-50 N 13 '64

LAUBIN, Gladys
Struggles of One Bull and Good Feather. D. Duncan. il pors Dance Mag 37:25-6 F '63

LAUBIN, Reginald
Struggles of One Bull and Good Feather. D. Duncan. il pors Dance Mag 37:25-6 F '63

LAUDON, Thomas S. See Behrendt, J. C. jt. auth.

LAUER, Rosemary
Thomism today. Commonweal 80:39-42, 262 Ap 3, My 22 '64
Women and the church. Commonweal 79:365-8; 80:151 D 20 '63, Ap 24 '64

LAUFER, Helen
Show-and-tell in the kindergarten. NEA J 52: 63 O '63

LAUFF, George H.
Estuaries. Science 146:553-4 O 23 '64

LAUGHEAD, Jim
Mad hatter in photoland. E. Shrake. il pors Sports Illus 21:78-80+ S 21 '64

LAUGHING sickness. See Diseases

LAUGHLIN, James
Natural art. C. Tomlinson. Poetry 105:125-8 N '64

LAUGHLIN, Virginia
Tell me again; story. Good H 158:94-5 My '64

LAUGHLIN, William S.
Eskimos and Aleuts: their origins and evolution. bibliog Science 142:633-45 N 8 '63
—See Black, R. F. jt. auth.

LAUGHTER
Laugh now, pay later. R. Hatch. il Horizon 5:106-9 Mr '63
See also
Humor
Smiles

LAUGHTON, D.
Special-interest cars. Motor T 16:83 N '64
LAUN, H. Charles
It's time for mutiny on the bounties. Audubon Mag 65:146-9, 232-5 My-Jl '63
LAUNCHERS, Rocket. See Rocket launchers
LAUNCHING guided missiles. See Guided missiles—Launching
LAUNCHING of boats. See Boats—Launching
LAUNCHING pads for missiles. See Guided missiles—Launching pads
LAUNCHING sites for space vehicles. See Space vehicles—Launching sites
LAUNDRIES
Any room is room for a laundry. il McCalls 90:110-11+ S '63
Create a luxury laundry. J. Holmstrand. il Suc Farm 62:90-3 Ja '64
Is your laundry in the right location? il Redbook 123:76-9+ S '64
Laundry in the round. R. Charles. il Parents Mag 39:88-91 Ap '64
Laundry room has added attractions. il Am Home 67:72 Je '64
Look where the laundry is. M. Davidson. il Ladies Home J 80:84 S '63
More convenience in the laundry. il Sunset 132:122+ Mr '64
New laundry room in a garage. il Bet Hom & Gard 41:50 O '63
Now four jobs can be done instead of one. il House B 105:210-11 S '63
Whatever happened to the laundry area? G. V. Young. il Bet Hom & Gard 42:70-5 S '64

Caricatures and cartoons

Rube Goldberg's washday wonder. McCalls 90:142-3 Mr '63
LAUNDRIES, Commercial
Coin-ops get through the wash. il Bsns W p 105-6 S 19 '64
Pay-as-you-go washers and dryers. E. Taylor. il Good H 158:189 Ap '64
Re-use by laundries poses problems. Am City 79:20 Je '64

Wages and hours

Earnings in laundries and cleaning services, June 1963. C. M. O'Connor. bibliog f il Mo Labor R 87:419-22 Ap '64
LAUNDRIES, Self service. See Laundries, Commercial
LAUNDROMATS. See Laundries, Commercial
LAUNDRY
Best approach to washday problems. il Redbook 120:74-5+ Ap '63
Doing the kids' laundry. Am Home 67:85 S '64
Easy laundry guide. M. Davidson. il Ladies Home J 81:44 N '64
Handbook to successful laundry. McCalls 90:151 Mr '63
Hold everything! il McCalls 92:132-3+ O '64
How a bleach helps in your family's laundry. E. M. McCabe. il Parents Mag 38:20+ Ag '63
Our new improved washday! il Good H 157:136+ O '63
Right way to use soaps, detergents and bleaches. B. G. Wadsworth. Parents Mag 38:48 N '63
Tips on tough wash jobs. il Bet Hom & Gard 41:93 S '63
You can make washday twice as easy! R. Charles. il Parents Mag 39:65-8+ O '64
LAUNDRY; drama. See Guerdon, D.
LAUNDRY equipment
Any room is room for a laundry. il McCalls 90:110-11+ S '63
Five-part laundry. il House & Gard 124:200-1 O '63
What's new in ironing? ease! il Good H 158:6 Ap '64
See also
Ironing board covers
Ironing boards
Washing machines

Advertising

Candor at convention time; or how cool is an iron? Consumer Rep 28:207 My '63
LAUNDRY marking pens. See Pens
LAUNDRY workers

Anecdotes, facetiae, satire, etc.

Shirt shrift. D. L. Guth. New Yorker 40:141-2 Mr 28 '64
LAUNOIS, John
Echo of western hoofbeats. il Sat Eve Post 236:20-7 My 4 '63
South Seas close to home. il Sat Eve Post 237:26-33 Mr 14 '64
LAUREL international. See Horse racing
LAURENCE, Margaret
Bird in the house; story. Atlan 214:64-71 N '64
To set our house in order; story. Ladies Home J 81:80-2 Mr '64
Very best intentions. Holiday 36:107-8+ N '64
LAURENCE, William Leonard
Laurence of Nagasaki. por Newsweek 63:74 F 3 '64
Science of reporting. por Time 82:32-3 D 27 '63
LAURENTIAN MOUNTAINS
Skiing among the angels. R. Joseph. il Esquire 62:194-7 D '64
LAURENZI, Gustave A. and others
Clearance of bacteria by the lower respiratory tract. bibliog Science 142:1572-3 D 20 '63
LAURIA, George
Tokyo and the Olympics. Atlan 213:122+ My '64
LAURIE, Gini
Aids for quads and respos. bibliog f por ALA Bul 58:785-9 O '64
LAURIE, Peter
Jim Clark, a whizz in a car. Vogue 144:289-91 D '64
Londonderrys. Vogue 144:112-119+ Ag 1 '64
So young, so cool, so misunderstood; Mods & Rockers. por Vogue 144:68-9+ Ag 1 '64
LAURIE, Victor W.
Molecular structure and spectroscopy. Science 141:654+ Ag 16 '63
LAURUS, Sister Mary. See Mary Laurus, Sister
LAURY, Jean, and Aiken, Joyce
Nature craft. Bet Hom & Gard 42:96 O; 121 N '64
LAUSCHE, Frank J.
Dangerous failings of our State department. Read Digest 84:54-60 Je '64; Excerpts. por U S News 56:22 Je 8 '64
Excerpt from debate, February 6, 1962. Cong Digest 42:51+ F '63
Excerpts from address, February 6, 1963, and from debate, August 14, 1963. Cong Digest 43:21+ Ja '64
LAUTENSCHLAGER, E. See Hofer, A. A. jt. auth.
LAUTERBURG, Lotti
Fabric batik; excerpts from Fabric printing. Sch Arts 63:33-7 N '63
LAUTREC, Mapie, countess de Toulouse-. See Toulouse-Lautrec, M. de
LAUTREC MONFA, Henri Marie Raymond de Toulouse-. See Toulouse-Lautrec Monfa, H. M. R. de
LAUX, Dean M.
Science and math. Sr Schol 85:28T D 2 '64
LAUYANS, Sherry
Curl up and read. Seventeen 23:20 Jl '64
LAVA
See also
Volcanoes
LAVAL, Pierre
Was it treason? il por Newsweek 61:117 Je 24 '63
LAVALLEE, Hugh
I thought, oh God, it's truth serum. por Life 55:50-2 S 13 '63
LAVATORIES
Lesson in how much things cost. il House B 105:172-3 S '63
LAVEE, S.
Natural kinin in peach fruitlets. bibliog Science 142:583 N 1 '63
LAVENDER
Fragrance of lavender. H. Guzelis. Horticulture 41:279 My '63
Lavender is for giving. P. L. Jensen. il Pop Gard 15:19+ My '64
LAVENDER scarf; story. See Sire, G. and Sire, J.
LAVER, James
Chic-ness crosses the channel. N Y Times Mag p86-7+ N 24 '63
LAVER, Rod
Laver's progress. Sports Illus 18:5-6 Ap 8 '63
Pro prodigy. il por Newsweek 61:85 Ap 29 '63
Sporting scene. H. W. Wind. New Yorker 39:128+ F 23 '63
LAVERY, J. J. and Foley, P. J.
Altruism or arousal in the rat? Science 140:172-3 Ap 12 '63
LAVI, Daliah
Lord Jim in a jungle paradise; ed. by E. Miller. pors Seventeen 23:220+ N '64
about
Daliah Lavi. E. O'Brien. por Vogue 144:130-1 N 15 '64

LA VIA, Mariano F. and others
Antibody formation in embryos. bibliog Science 140:1219-20 Je 14 '63

LAVIN, Leonard H.
Scalping the competition. il por Time 82:88 Jl 12 '63

LAVIN, Mary
Cuckoo spit; story. New Yorker 40:58-62 O 3 '64
Heart of gold; story. New Yorker 40:29-38 Je 27 '64

LAVINE, Arthur
Don't short-change the background. Pop Phot 54:82-3+ Je '64

LAVINE, Harold
Defeat on the beach. Sat R 47:41+ My 16 '64
How to evolve a revolution. Sat R 46:22-3 Jl 20 '63
Last chance on death row. Sat Eve Post 236:76+ Je 29 '63
Money will not make them free. Sat R 47:28-9 Ja 25 '64

LAVONGAI
What price LBJ? New Hanover island. Newsweek 63:47 Je 22 '64

LAVORANTE, Alejandro
Sad victory for a heavyweight. il pors Life 55:97-8+ S 27 '63

LAW, Bernard
Klan still rides. America 110:755 My 30 '64

LAW, Francis E.
How Bobby Baker made some more money; summary of testimony. U S News 56:8 F 17 '64

LAW, Lloyd William
Thymus: role in resistance to polyoma virus oncogenesis. bibliog Science 147:164-5 Ja 8 '65
—and others
Humoral thymic factor in mice: further evidence. bibliog Science 143:1049-51 Mr 6 '64

LAW, Philip
Mental strains of Antarctic solitude. por UNESCO Courier 16:26-30 Je '63

LAW, Robert O, company
Rand McNally to buy Robert O. Law company. Pub W 185:106 Ja 20 '64

LAW, Warren A. and Crum, M. C.
New trend in finance: the negotiable C.D. Harvard Bsns R 41:115-26 Ja '63

LAW
See also
Banking law
Confession (law)
Conflict of laws
Constitutional law
Copyright
Criminal law
Evidence (law)
Informers (law)
International law
Justice
Libel and slander

Curiosa and miscellany

Of booze, broth & anguish. Time 83:78+ My 15 '64

Language

Mislabeled bills mislead voters. V. J. Burke. il Nations Bsns 51:92-5 F '63

Philosophy

On trying to be just. H. J. Morgenthau. Commentary 35:420-3 My '63

Quotations, maxims, etc.

In brief, the law; comp. by R. Block. il N Y Times Mag p60 Ag 9 '64

Study and teaching

New approach to criminal law. B. J. George, jr. Harper 228:183-8 Ap '64
Obsolescence of casebook method in legal education. Sch & Soc 91:274 O 5 '63
See also
Law schools

Terminology

Concrete prose and the cement mind. J. Ciardi. Sat R 46:17 F 9 '63

California

Rag doll legislation; concern about the innards of stuffed toys, California. Consumer Rep 28:509-10 N '63
State pays for welfare. Time 83:76 F 14 '64
What about therapeutic abortion? L. Kinsolving. Christian Cent 81:632-5 My 13 '64

Connecticut

Encore: no birth control. H. G. Lewis. Christian Cent 81:940 Jl 22 '64; Reply. C. Chotkowski. 81:1177 S 23 '64
Test for an ancient law; banning of contraceptives. Time 84:44 D 18 '64

England

See Law—Great Britain

Europe, Western

See also
Justice, Administration of—Europe, Western

Florida

And the Court said unto Gideon. Time 82:53 O 18 '63
Annals of law; Gideon case. A. Lewis. il New Yorker 40:144+ Ap 25 '64
Court will consider miscegenation laws; Florida ban. Christian Cent 81:693 My 27 '64; Reply. J. H. Willson. 81:935 Jl 22 '64
Ex-con overturns the law; with report by M. Durham. il Life 56:83-4+ Je 12 '64
How to beat a murder rap; copping a plea in Worthington case. il Time 84:54 O 23 '64

Georgia

Justice, southern style; Ashton Jones vs Atlanta's First Baptist church. J. Gillies. Christian Cent 81:112-14 Ja 22 '64; Reply. R. O. McClain. 81:270-2 F 26 '64

Ghana

Justice, black & white. Time 82:42+ N 15 '63

Great Britain

Common law; address, May 22, 1963. A. L. Goodhart. Vital Speeches 29:589-91 Jl 15 '63
Outward signs of inward grace; life of legal London. F. Cowper. il Horizon 6:33-40 Spr '64

Idaho

Seek repeal of gambling law. W. Peabody. Christian Cent 81:1091 S 2 '64

Illinois

Illinois birth control policy in peril. Christian Cent 80:389-90 Mr 27 '63
Illinois Senate ousts a birth control champion. Christian Cent 80:637-8 My 15 '63

India

India follows the U.S. Time 84:54+ O 23 '64

Israel

Dissent on Brother Daniel. M. Galanter. Commentary 36:10-17 Jl '63; Discussion. 37:19-20+ Ja '64

Kentucky

Legal age: eighteen. Sr Schol 85:19-20 Ja 21 '65

Maryland

Clemency in Annapolis; case of the Giles brothers and Joseph Johnson. M. Kempton. New Repub 149:6-8 O 26 '63

Mississippi

FBI agent as missionary; branch office in Jackson, Miss. W. B. Huie. New Repub 151:10-11 N 21 '64
Lawyer; experience in Mississippi. W. M. Kunstler. il Nation 199:507-9 D 28 '64

Nebraska

Nebraska fiasco: buy now, pay never; legislative blunder. J. Skow. il Sat Eve Post 237:66-8 F 29 '64

New Hampshire

Commitment, by W. Uphaus. Review
New Repub 148:26+ Je 22 '63. G. W. Johnson

New York (state)

Crimes for the times; New York state's penal code reorganized. Time 83:36 Mr 27 '64
Whole new world may open for use of subsidiary rights; New York law on the right of privacy. H. F. Pilpel. Pub W 185:63-4 F 3 '64

North Carolina

North Carolina's gag law; H.B. 1395, Act to regulate visiting speakers at state-supported colleges and universities. A. W. Stewart. Christian Cent 81:1336-8 O 28 '64

Pennsylvania

Charity solicitations; under state control. Am City 79:150+ Mr '64

Poland

Control yourselves; new penal code. Newsweek 61:52+ Je 10 '63

Russia

See also
Courts—Russia

LAW—*Continued*

South Africa

Search and detention; ninety-day detention clause. Christian Cent 81:1316-17 O 21 '64

Southern states

Civil rights counterattack; old and new laws all over the South. il Time 82:55 N 1 '63

United States

Alabama goes to Court. L. B. Bozell. Nat R 14:445 Je 4 '63
Common law; address, May 22, 1963. A. L. Goodhart. Vital Speeches 29:589-91 Jl 15 '63
Courts; decisions. Time 84:118 O 2 '64
Crowd of umbrella heads; states' rights amendments. Reporter 28:10-11 Je 6 '63
Expanding pattern of American law; address, May 2, 1964. J. A. Farley. Vital Speeches 30:497-9 Je 1 '64
Law and justice; extra-legal Negro demands. New Repub 148:3-5 Je 22 '63
November 22: what did it mean? E. Roper. Sat R 47:28 My 9 '64
Only hope. D. Lawrence. U S News 54:112 Je 10 '63
See here, General Kennedy; federal government empowered to use state militia and federal troops for law enforcement in states. Time 84:45-6 Jl 10 '64
Sex vs. the law: a study in hypocrisy. H. F. Pilpel. il Harper 230:35-40 Ja '65
Speaking out; lawyers are failing the law. M. L. Ernst. Sat Eve Post 237:8+ Mr 7 '64
Trial of the future, by B. Botein and M. A. Gordon. Review
Commonweal 78:331-2 Je 14 '63. N. Hentoff
What mass protests can't do. L. Lomax. Sat R 46:11-12 Jl 6 '63
See also
American law institute
Courts—United States
Justice, Administration of—United States
Law enforcement
Legislation—United States
Marriage law—United States
United States—Constitution
United States—Constitutional law

Virginia

Justice in Virginia. New Repub 148:5 Mr 2 '63

LAW, Medical. See Medical laws and legislation

LAW, Mosaic. See Jewish law

LAW, Natural. See Natural law

LAW, Sunday. See Sunday legislation

LAW and ethics
Corrupt society; with foreword by the editors. F. J. Cook. Nation 196:453-96a Je 1 '63; Discussion. 196:inside cover Je 22; inside cover Je 29 '63
Is it ever right to break the law? C. Frankel. il N Y Times Mag p 17+ Ja 12 '64
Law or violence? J. B. Sheerin. Cath World 199:333-6 S '64; Reply. F. D. Webber. 200:70 N '64
Morality of law, by L. L. Fuller. Review
Nat R 16:690-1 Ag 11 '64. W. Berns
Overview of organized crime: mores versus morality. R. K. Woetzel. bibliog f Ann Am Acad 347:1-11 My '63
War on crime. America 108:848 Je 15 '63

LAW and mental illness. See Mental health laws

LAW and religion. See Religion and law

LAW and sex. See Sex and law

LAW and society. See Jurisprudence

LAW and society institute. See Religious institutes and workshops

LAW clerks. See Secretaries, Legal

LAW day
Law day, U.S.A. 1963; proclamation. J. F. Kennedy. Dept State Bul 48:297 F 25 '63

LAW enforcement
Answer to the rise in crime and violence; excerpts from address, September 8, 1964. G. B. McClellan. il U S News 57:89-90 N 9 '64
Bill of obligations; balance is vital to us; address, June 13, 1963. N. Topping. Vital Speeches 29:634-6 Ag 1 '63
Can integration be forced by federal law? address. C. E. Whittaker. U S News 56:99-101 Mr 23 '64; Reply. D. Lawrence. 56:108 Mr 30 '64
Civil liberties and police power. Commonweal 80:29 Ap 3 '64
Criminals, cops and the Constitution. Y. Kamisar. il Nation 199:322-6 N 9 '64
Detroit; a lesson in law enforcement. G. Edwards. Ann Am Acad 347:67-73 My '63
Enforcing the law: interview with J. Edgar Hoover. J. E. Hoover. il U S News 57:36-40 D 21 '64
Government by mob. D. Lawrence. U S News 55:92 Jl 1 '63
Interdisciplinary attack on organized crime. G. Tyler. bibliog f Ann Am Acad 347:104-12 My '63
Is it all right to break the law? M. L. King; W. E. Ringel. il U S News 55:6 Ag 12 '63
Law enforcement. R. Moley. Newsweek 64:84 D 21 '64
Lawyer's duty in civil rights; pro and con. R. F. Kennedy; J. C. Satterfield. U S News 55:120-3 O 14 '63
Local and state action against organized crime. E. H. Lumbard. Ann Am Acad 347:82-92 My '63
Mental urges of the mob. D. Lawrence. U S News 54:112 Je 17 '63
New approach to the control of organized crime. M. Ploscowe. Ann Am Acad 347:74-81 My '63
U.S. troops in Alabama; Governor, President, and the law; telegrams, text of law. G. Wallace; J. F. Kennedy. U S News 54:40-1 My 27 '63
War against crime; excerpt from address, June 3, 1964. D. Lawrence. U S News 56:112+ Je 29 '64
What's become of law and order? D. Lawrence. U S News 55:104 Ag 5 '63
Will city streets ever be safe again? interview. S. R. Schrotel. il U S News 54:80-3 Ap 8 '63
Worldwide survey: why foreign streets are safer. il U S News 56:44-5 Je 15 '64
See also
Law—United States
Police

LAW in literature
See also
Shakespeare, W.—Law

LAW librarians

Anecdotes, facetiae, satire, etc.

Mr Dooley on law librarians; excerpts from address, 1963. E. J. Bander. il Library J 89:575-7 F 1 '64

LAW libraries
See also
American association of law libraries

LAW making. See Legislation

LAW of nations. See International law

LAW of relativity. See Relativity (physics)

LAW research service, incorporated
Automating the archives; computer to take over the lawyer's plodding search through archives. Time 82:82 D 13 '63
Univac for the defense; automation can save a lawyer time. Newsweek 62:55 D 16 '63

LAW schools
Cram, cram, cram. il Time 84:62 Jl 17 '64
Dean departs from Ole Miss. R. Cleghorn. Reporter 29:42 O 24 '63
From the mouths of babes; law reviews. il Time 83:49-50 Ap 24 '64
See also
Association of American law schools
Yale university—School of law

LAWBREAKER; story. See O'Hara, J.

LAWFORD, Patricia (Kennedy)
Barred from 117 E. 72nd. il por Newsweek 63:44 Ap 20 '64

LAWFORD, Peter
Barred from 117 E. 72nd. il por Newsweek 63:44 Ap 20 '64

LAWFORD, Valentine
Consuelo Vanderbilt Balsan: portrait of a unique American. Vogue 141:124-33+ F 1 '63
Denmark. Vogue 144:194-211+ O 1 '64
Duke and Duchess of Windsor in Paris. Vogue 143:176-87+ Ap 1 '64
Gardener in her garden. Vogue 144:275-6+ D '64
Leland Haywards of Haywire house. Vogue 143:124-7 F 15 '64
Living with flowers. Vogue 141:142-5+ Ap 1 '63
Power of dreams. Vogue 142:86-97 Jl '63
Pucci the magnificent. Vogue 143:156-63 Mr 15 '64
Wait now for bombs. Atlan 212:59-69 Jl '63
Wondrous house. Vogue 143:164-73+ F 1 '64
Young joyous life of Mr and Mrs. S. Carter Burden, junior. Vogue 145:178-85+ F 1 '65
Young, lyric Irish life of the Desmond Guinesses at Leixlip castle and its folly. Vogue 144:144-55+ N 15 '64

LAWFORD, Valentine—*Continued*

about

Personal prism. por Newsweek 62:90-1 Jl 22 '63

LAWLER, Barbara B.
We found more time for each other. por Redbook 121:6+ Je '63

LAWLER, Justus George
Nuclear warfare. Commonweal 80:214-16 My 8 '64

LAWN bowling. See Bowling

LAWN furniture. See Furniture, Outdoor

LAWN games. See Games

LAWN lamps. See Lighting fixtures

LAWN mowers
Caution! heed the directions. M. H. Gage. il Horticulture 41:252 My '63
Gasoline-powered rotary mowers. il Consumer Rep 28:332-7 Jl '63
Hand lawn mowers. il Consumer Bul 46:10-12 Je '63
How to build a battery-powered lawn mower. W. T. Boyd. il Pop Sci 182:110-12+ Je '63
How to use power mowers safely. il Good H 156:166 My '63
New safety seen in mower blade. B. C. Kilvert, jr. il Flower Grower 50:34 D '63
Points to remember when mowing your lawn. P. F. Frese. il Pop Gard 15:57-8 Ap '64
Safety with power lawn mowers. il Pop Gard 14:48-51 Ap '63
Twenty-five tips on shopping for lawn mowers. J. Hand. il Pop Mech 119:74-7 My '63

LAWN mowing. See Lawns

LAWN parties
Guests serve themselves from the fruit tower. il Sunset 131:104+ Jl '63

LAWN seeds. See Grasses—Seed

LAWN sprinklers. See Sprinklers

LAWN sweepers
Do lawn sweepers earn their keep? J. Hand. il Pop Sci 184:142-4+ My '64

LAWN tennis. See Tennis

LAWN tools. See Garden tools, equipment and supplies

LAWNER, Lynne
Nightingales at Nemi; poem. Atlan 211:80 My '63
Plea; poem. Atlan 212:71 Ag '63
Recognition; poem. Atlan 212:84 O '63

about

Lady poetry. K. Rexroth. Nation 198:494-5 My 11 '64

LAWNS
Aids to a perfect lawn. Pop Gard 14:73 Ap '63
Big league lawn; Yankee stadium. B. C. Kilvert, jr. il Flower Grower 50:46-7 O '63
Color it green. Newsweek 63:70 My 18 '64
Cut lawn and garden work. il Suc Farm 61:28 Je '63
Don't pamper the lawn this spring. il Changing T 18:15-16 Mr '64
Flower grower's turf tips. R. W. Schery. Flower Grower 51:41+ Ap '64
Grass can be greener in your own backyard. R. Lawrence. il Pop Gard 14:46-7+ Ap '63
Grass-killing disease. Sci N L 86:11 Jl 4 '64
Green grass will grow wherever you live; symposium. Am Home 66:32-3+ Mr '63
Have you heard? B. C. Kilvert, jr. il Flower Grower 50:62-3 My '63
How good a lawn do you want? symposium. il Horticulture 42:26-8+ Mr '64
How to grow a better lawn. il Consumer Bul 46:43+ Mr '63
How to make your lawn better than it is. R. E. Engel. House B 105:217-19 S '63
Is a perfect lawn possible? il Sunset 131:72-5 S '63
Keep on the grass! play lawn. W. H. Daniel. Am Home 67:80-1 S '64
Lawn insects and diseases; symposium. Horticulture 42:22-4 My '64
Lawn maintenance. P. F. Frese. il Pop Gard 15:52-8 Ap '64
Lawn making made easy. P. F. Frese. il Pop Gard 15:27-9 Mr '64
Lawn problem? we solved it with zoysia. M. H. Hunn. il Flower Grower 51:24 My '64
Lawn you can use. il Pop Gard 15:86 Jl '64
Lawns for the lazy. J. Peter. il Look 28:86+ Ap 7 '64
Lawns the way you want them. Flower Grower 50:42-3 Ap '63
Live with your lawn and like it! R. W. Schery. il Flower Grower 50:34-5+ S '63
Summer lawn care made easy. il Good H 157:125 Jl '63
They built their lawn on subsoil. il Sunset 131:153 Ag '63
Three ways to start your lawn. Bet Hom & Gard 42:103 My '64
Your lawn & common sense. F. Rockwell. il Flower Grower 51:30+ S '64

See also

Grasses

Diseases and pests

H&G's 1964 guide to a durable lawn, C. Westcott. House & Gard 125:212 Ap '64
Time now to prevent snow mold on lawns. R. M. Carleton. Flower Grower 50:11 O '63

LAWNS, Watering of. See Watering of gardens, lawns, etc.

LAWRENCE, Andrea Mead
Let's not spoil their sport. pors Sports Illus 20:18-20 F 3 '64

LAWRENCE, Carol
Lawrence of Illinois. N. Poirier. il pors Sat Eve Post 237:72+ Mr 21 '64

LAWRENCE, David
Civil rights and civil wrongs. Read Digest 84:127-8 Je '64
Excerpt from New York herald tribune, inc, January 27, 1964. Cong Digest 43:149+ My '64
War against crime; excerpt from address, June 3, 1964. U S News 56:112+ Je 29 '64

about

It hardly behooves . . . Newsweek 62:52 S 30 '63

LAWRENCE, David C.
Bears were bad enough. Outdoor Life 132:28-9+ Ag '63

LAWRENCE, David Herbert
D.H.L. the second time around. G. Hicks. Sat R 47:31-2 Mr 7 '64
Our literary Tocqueville. R. Sklar. Reporter 31:50 N 5 '64
Poet in a fugitive cause. K. Rexroth. Nation 199:382-3 N 23 '64

LAWRENCE, David Leo
Man to watch at the Democratic convention. H. Fuller. Harper 229:47-52 Ag '64

LAWRENCE, Elizabeth
Southern wild flowers at their best. Pop Gard 14:37+ Mr '63

LAWRENCE, Frieda
Fleshly muse. il por Time 84:92 D 18 '64
From Black Forest to pink plaza. H. T. Moore. il por Sat R 47:37+ N 14 '64
Lost paradise. il por Newsweek 64:118 N 23 '64
Other Lawrence. M. Green. Commonweal 81:346-8 D 4 '64

LAWRENCE, George H. M.
Garden reference books. Horticulture 42:40-2 Ap '64
Linnaeus. Horticulture 42:22-3 N '64

LAWRENCE, H. C.
Auxiliaries can get more from their radios. Motor B 112:40-1+ N '63
Do you need a radiotelephone on board? Motor B 113:32-3+ Ap '64

LAWRENCE, H. Lea
Another gorge to fish. Outdoor Life 133:78-82 Ap '64
Big trout on the little T. Field & S 68:42-3+ Ja '64
Ghost town grouse. Outdoor Life 135:70-1+ F '65
Man plant's return. Natur Hist 73:34-7 My '64

LAWRENCE, Harold G.
Vanished cities of West Africa. Negro Hist Bul 27:117-19 F '64

LAWRENCE, Jacob
Jacob's dream. il por Newsweek 61:100 Ap 15 '63

LAWRENCE, Lee
Strange case of Lee Lawrence. T. Congdon. il pors Sat Eve Post 236:85-9 Ap 20 '63

LAWRENCE, Lydia
Live like a king in a castle. Read Digest 83:158-63 Jl '63
Rugged challenge for teen-agers. Read Digest 82:183-4 Ap '63

LAWRENCE, Merloyd
Barcelona. Atlan 212:108+ Ag '63
Dubrovnik. Atlan 213:126+ F '64
Traveling with Mlle: the Yucatán; daiquiris and chacmools. Mlle 60:135-6+ D '64

LAWRENCE, Paul R. See Lorsch, J. W. jt. auth.

LAWRENCE, Robert
Beatrice et Benedict. Sat R 46:70 Ap 27 '63
Case for Meyerbeer. Mus Am 84:26-7 My '64
Figures on the battlements. Opera N 28:6-7 Ja 4 '64
Furtwängler file. Sat R 47:66 O 31 '64
Karajan and the Nine. Sat R 46:34-5 Ag 31 '63
Missing record; reprint. Mus Am 84:12-13+ N '64

LAWRENCE, Robert—*Continued*
Opera in translation. Mus Am 83:11+ N '63
Quote: unquote; interview. ed. by J. Ardoin. por Mus Am 83:45 S '63
Reprieve for Massenet. Hi Fi 14:47-9+ Mr '64

LAWRENCE, Roderick
Grass can be greener in your own backyard. Pop Gard 14:46-7+ Ap '63

LAWRENCE, Steve
Steve Lawrence, a guy from Brooklyn. R. Atcheson. il pors Sat Eve Post 237:30-1 Je 27 '64

LAWRENCE, Thomas Edward
Unpublished letter of Lawrence of Arabia. Nat R 15:203-5 S 10 '63

about

Mystery of Lawrence. por Sr Schol 82:11 Ja 30 '63
Real Lawrence of Arabia. L. Thomas. il pors Read Digest 84:252-6+ Je '64
T. E. Lawrence and the riddle of S.A. R. Graves. por Sat R 46:16-17 Je 15 '63; Discussion. 46:15 Jl 6 '63

LAWRENCE, Kan.
Stretching the street dollar. G. Williams and A. T. Hodges. il Am City 78:102-3 O '63

LAWRENCE radiation laboratory, Livermore, Calif.
Meet Johnny Foster; reprint. D. M. Wilkes. il Sci Digest 54:30-7 S '63
New try at caging atom fusion; Astron program. il Bsns W p 138+ Ag 22 '64

LAWRENCEBURG, Ind.
It looks like a school; sewage-purification plant. E. R. Hamilton. il Am City 79:98-100 O '64

LAWRENSON, Helen
Difference between men and husbands. McCalls 90:81+ S '63
Man who never got to speak for National youth day. Esquire 61:82-5+ My '64
Marcello Mastroianni: Latin lover, new style. Look 28:26+ Ag 11 '64

LAWS of motion. See Motion

LAWS of nature. See Nature, Laws of

LAWSON, Christyne
Black nativity at Philharmonic Hall. M. Marks. Dance Mag 37:56 F '63

LAWSON, Herbert G.
Coming new birth control measures. Sci Digest 55:86-90 Mr '64

LAWSON, Jean
Plants for crevices. Pop Gard 15:64-5 Jl '64
Rock pile to garden wall. Pop Gard 15:24-5 Ap '64

LAWSON, Marjorie
Pinpoint portrait. J. H. Roy. Negro Hist Bul 26:252 My '63

LAWSUITS. See Actions and defenses

LAWTON, Fred E.
Small-boat radar, now and tomorrow. Motor B 112:44-7 N '63

LAWYER, John Q. pseud.
How to conspire to fix prices. Harvard Bsns R 41:95-103 Mr '63

LAWYERS
Are there too many lawyers in Congress? A. Hacker. il N Y Times Mag p 14+ Ja 5 '64
Better lawyers for our criminal courts. J. E. Lumbard. il Atlan 213:86-90 Je '64
Casus Belli; Ruby trial. il Time 83:34+ Mr 27 '64
Dearth of defenders. il Time 83:54 Je 19 '64
Factories: law firms. il Time 83:32-3 Ja 24 '64
Get Percy Foreman; trial lawyer from Houston. T. Martin and P. O'Bryan. il Sat Eve Post 237:40+ N 14 '64
Hope for bilked clients; proposed registration fee. Time 83:59 Ja 31 '64
How can the lawyer help? F. Biddle. New Repub 149:12 Jl 6 '63
How to improve the profession. Time 83:40-1 Ja 10 '64
Lawyer's unneeded veil. Life 54:4 My 31 '63
Legal help needed; cases arising out of segregation. G. W. Crockett, jr. and E. Goodman. Nation 196:inside cover Je 1 '63
Looking backward? il Time 83:52+ F 7 '64
New approach to criminal law. B. J. George, jr. Harper 228:183-8 Ap '64
Outward signs of inward grace; life of legal London. F. Cowper. il Horizon 6:36-7 Spr '64
Sensitive subject; intra-professional harassments in the South. Nation 200:43 Ja 18 '65
Southern justice: lawyers in fear. W. M. Kunstler and A. Kinoy. il Nation 198:576-80 Je 8 '64
Speaking out; lawyers are failing the law. M. L. Ernst. Sat Eve Post 237:8+ Mr 7 '64
Timid lawyers and neglected clients. D. H. Pollitt. Harper 229:81-6 Ag '64; Discussion. 229:8 O '64
Wall Street lawyer, by E. O. Smigel. Review Newsweek il por 63:92+ Ap 13 '64
Washington lawyers. J. Kraft. Harper 228: 102+ Ap '64
When newsmen become newsmakers; problem of publicity before and during a trial. E. N. Griswold. Sat R 47:21-3 O 24 '64; Reply. W. O'Neil. 47:25 N 21 '64

See also

American bar association
Judges
Justice, Administration of
Negro lawyers
Right to counsel
Women as lawyers

Salaries, fees, etc.

See Cost (law)

LAX, Benjamin
Semiconductor lasers. bibliog Science 141:1247-55 S 27 '63

LAXALT, Robert
Basque troubadour. Atlan 212:136+ O '63

LAXATIVES. See Cathartics

LAY apostolate. See Catholic action

LAYARD, Sir Austen Henry
Road to Nineveh, by N. B. Kubie. Review Sat R il 47:34 Mr 7 '64. L. Cottrell
Sci Digest 55:73 Ap '64. D. Cohen

LAYCOCK, Frank
Division and dialogue in the house of learning. Sat R 47:58-61+ S 19 '64

LAYCOCK, George
Ahead; summer week ends in the great outdoors. Todays Health 41:46-9+ My '63
Determined ant. Field & S 68:61+ My '63
Feathered bomber. Field & S 69:35+ D '64
Fiery fish. Outdoor Life 131:64-7+ Je '63
Fire! Field & S 68:30-1 Jl '63
Fog horns. Outdoor Life 131:38-9+ Ja '63
Goose hunting is getting better. il Suc Farm 62:108-9 O '64
Great turtle mystery. Field & S 68:10-12+ Mr '64
Mischief in the melon patch. Field & S 69: 10-12+ Je '64
Owl that stays at home. Field & S 69:41+ Jl '64
Pollution: it's deadlier than you think. Field & S 68:10-13 Ja '64
Potluck on the Red Cedar. por Field & S 68:112-14+ S '63
Prairie chicken and his friends. Field & S 68:52-3+ S '63
Something for a rainy day. pors Outdoor Life 135:44-7+ Ja '65
Where northerns come big. por Outdoor Life 134:44-5+ Ag '64
Wisconsin's biggest day of the year. Field & S 68:60-1+ O '63

LAYEFSKY, Virginia
Last wish; story. Ladies Home J 80:38 Ap '63

LAYING up of boats. See Boats—Storage

LAYMEN. See Laity

LAYMEN'S national committee

See also

National Bible week

LAYS, Nancy Jane
Boat is an island. por Motor B 115:94-7+ Ja '65

LAYSAN albatrosses. See Albatrosses

LAYTON, Winifred Heiskell
Forest crying; poem. Am For 70:52 My '64

LAZAR, Eve, and Klein, Carole
Parent and child. N Y Times Mag p78+ My 24 '64

LAZAREFF, Hélène Gordon
Si elle lit elle lit Elle. por Time 83:69-70 My 22 '64

LAZARETH, William H.
Church and change. Sat R 47:38-9 Jl 18 '64

LAZARUS, F. and R. company. See Columbus, Ohio—Stores

LAZARUS, George
Chicago school of advertising. Sat R 47:60+ Jl 11 '64
Chicago: second city in advertising. Sat R 47: 60-1 Je 13 '64
Madison avenue. Sat R 47:68-9 S 12; 84-6 N 14 '64; 48:71+ Ja 9 '65

LAZARUS, Ralph
Age of fulfillment; address, November 16, 1963. Vital Speeches 30:301-4 Mr 1 '64; Excerpt. Recreation 57:335-6 S '64

LAZO, Mario
Decision for disaster; condensation. por Read Digest 85:241-4+ S '64

LAZOWSKI, Yurek
Nuance makes the difference. il pors Dance Mag 38:48-51 Ap '64

LAZZARO, Charles A.
San Diego's listening and viewing centers. Sr Schol 85:20T Ja 21 '65

LE, Kong
U.S.-backed neutrals. U S News 54:21 Ap 29 '63

LE-kwang-Kim
Viet-Nam: twenty years of change and turmoil. UNESCO Courier 17:22-7 S '64

LE-thuy-Nhu
Deadeye Le Thuy goes gunning in Texas. il pors Life 55:46-7 N 8 '63

LEABO, Loi
I'm proud to be a gypsy. Dance Mag 38:42-3+ O '64

LEACH, David G.
Rhododendrons that stay low. Flower Grower 51:31+ S '64

LEACH, Richard
Fitting memorial. America 110:186-8 F 8 '64

LEACOCK, Stephen
Are the darned things mushrooms? Read Digest 85:188H O '64

LEAD, S.D.
Digging for gold over one mile deep; Homestake mine. J. Liston. Pop Sci 185:68-71 N '64

LEAD

Isotopes

Isotopic composition of lead and strontium from Ascension and Gough Islands. P. W. Gast and others. bibliog il Science 145:1181-5 S 11 '64
Lead isotope variation with growth zoning in a galena crystal. R. S. Cannon, jr and others. bibliog il Science 142:574-6 N 1 '63

LEAD-core lines. See Fishing tackle

LEAD mines and mining

United States

Built-in brakes for Ozarks boom. il Bsns W p 190-2+ N 21 '64

LEAD poisoning
Lead; killer of young children. il Consumer Bul 46:36-40 O '63
Lead paint in Chicago. Time 82:36 Ag 9 '63
Lead poisoning is still a threat. Good H 157: 145 Ag '63

LEAD soldiers. See Toy soldiers

LEADABRAND, Russ
City boys and forestry. Am For 69:8-9 S '63
Day the dam broke. Am For 70:30-3+ F '64

LEADERSHIP
Agony of the Negro leader. E. C. Ladd, jr. il Nation 199:88-91 S 7 '64
Being wise in membership; those who are called leaders. B. W. Overstreet. il PTA Mag 58:24-6 Mr '64
Challenge to leadership; address, July 14, 1964. M. A. Rapp. Vital Speeches 30:654-7 Ag 15 '64
Foreign policy and the individual: identity in diversity; address, March 12, 1964. K. Louchheim. Dept State Bul 50:591-4 Ap 13 '64
Functions of protocol in today's world; address, February 6, 1964. A. B. Duke. Dept State Bul 50:344-7 Mr 2 '64
Hour for leadership; reprint. Duns R 84:35 S '64
Human dilemmas of leadership. A. Zaleznik. Harvard Bsns R 41:49-55 Jl '63
Ideals for export; excerpts from address, September 19, 1963. C. H. Malik. Harvard Bsns R 42:51-9 Ja '64
Involvement and leadership; address, October 2, 1964. L. S. Bickmore. Vital Speeches 31: 55-7 N 1 '64
Junior leadership pays off. J. C. Carter. Recreation 57:178 Ap '64
Leadership and the sane society; address, March 24, 1963. R. F. Eubanks. Vital Speeches 29:478-80 My 15 '63
New Negro radicalism. S. Lynd. Commentary 36:252-6 S '63
New times, new leaders. H. Brandon. Sat R 48:13 Ja 16 '65
None does his job alone; adaptation of address. J. A. Smith. Recreation 57:48 F '64
Of leaders and followers; address, May 28, 1963. E. M. Clark. Vital Speeches 29:602-6 Jl 15 '63
Old age brings honor to those who serve. F. Morley. il Nations Bsns 51:27-8 Je '63
Taste for change; address, September 23, 1963. J. S. Dickey. Vital Speeches 30:24-5 O 15 '63
Today's youth, tomorrow's leaders; roundtable discussion from 1963 Williamsburg student burgesses. il Sr Schol 82:16-17 Mr 27 '63
Tomorrow's leaders. L. E. Lomax. il Ebony 18:41-4+ S '63
Will he be a leader? with program for discussion group, by E. G. Neisser. E. W. Johnson. il Parents Mag 38:38+, 52-3+ My '63

LEAF, Albert L.
Pure maple syrup: nutritive value. bibliog Science 143:963-4 F 28 '64

LEAF, Margaret
Nickle words for a golden mission. K. Molz. il Wilson Lib Bul 39:44-7 S '64

LEAF, Munro
Nickle words for a golden mission. K. Molz. il pors Wilson Lib Bul 39:44-7 S '64

LEAF cactus. See Epiphyllums

LEAF designs. See Design, Decorative—Plant forms

LEAGUE of brothers. See Broederbond (League of brothers)

LEAGUE of composers
Composers' letters; ed. by C. R. Reis. il Mus Am 83:14-17 Ja '63

LEAGUE of nations
Collective security and American foreign policy: from the League of nations to NATO, by R. N. Stromberg. Review
Reporter 30:54+ F 27 '64. R. A. Stone
Colonel's folly and the President's distress; with editorial comment. G. T. Grayson. il Am Heritage 15:4-7+ O '64
Peace in their time, by E. Kelen. Review
Nat R 16:199-200 Mr 10 '64. P. L. Buckley

Constitution

League of Nations and the United Nations; address, April 2, 1964. Thant. UN Mo Chron 1:70-5 My '64

LEAGUE school, Brooklyn. See Special classes and special schools

LEAKE, Chauncey D.
Biology future predicted; ed. by F. Marley. Sci N L 83:259 Ap 27 '63
British association for the advancement of science. Science 142:688-9 N 8 '63
Science information. Science 139:1088 Mr 15 '63

LEAKE, James D.
Denver graduates come up to PAR. NEA J 52:24-5 N '63

LEAKEY, Louis S. B.
Adventurous ones. por Vogue 142:74 Ag 1 '63
Discovery in Africa. il por Newsweek 63:48 Mr 30 '64
Earliest man on earth? F. Drake and K. Drake. il por Read Digest 84:157-61+ Ja '64
Homo habilis. il por Newsweek 63:86 Ap 13 '64
Man's new pygmy ancestor. il por Sci Digest 56:64-6 Jl '64
Pygmy progenitor? il por Time 83:68 Ap 24 '64

LEAKEY, Mary
Earliest man on earth? F. Drake and K. Drake. il Read Digest 84:157-61+ Ja '64

LEAMAN, Arthur. See Wilson, J. jt. auth.

LEANING tower of Pisa. See Pisa—Campanile (leaning tower)

LEAP year
1964: bad year for bachelors? women's special leap-year privilege. il Todays Health 42:52 Ap '64
Till leap year gives it twenty-nine. il Sr Schol 84:4 F 28 '64

Quotations, maxims, etc.

On guard, men; comp. by E. F. Murphy. N Y Times Mag p73 F 9 '64

LEAR, John
America, the navigator's error. Sat R 46:86-8 O 12 '63
Documenting the case against fluoridation. Sat R 47:85-92 Ja 4 '64; Same abr. Sci Digest 55:34-9 Ap '64
Future of God. Sat R 47:173-5+ Ag 29 '64
Global budgeting for science. Sat R 46:28 N 23 '63
Research in America. See issues of Saturday review
What the moon ranger couldn't see. Sat R 47:35-43 S 5; 63-4 O 3; 32+ O 10 '64
(ed) See Iselin, C. O. What sank Thresher, the A-sub?

LEAR, Martha Weinman
Best of teens, the worst of teens. N Y Times Mag p34+ N 1 '64
But where are the chaperons? N Y Times Mag p22+ F 23 '64
Diaper service. McCalls 91:84-5+ Ja '64
Plea to let sleeping men lie. N Y Times Mag p49+ S 27 '64
Unhappy baby doctors. McCalls 90:76-9 Jl '63

LEAR, Robert W.
No easy road to market orientation. Harvard Bsns R 41:53-60 S '63
LEAR, William P.
Lear takes the controls. il pors Bsns W p 108-11 Mr 7 '64
Memo from the publisher. E. D. Muhlfeld. por Flying 75:6 Jl '64
LEAR Siegler, incorporated
Lear Siegler pushes autoland time-lead. P. J. Klass. il Aviation W 82:59-62 Ja 18 '65
LEARD, H. H.
Heresy of Isaac Houston Bass. Am For 69: 20-1+ S '63
LEARNED journals. See Periodicals
LEARNING, Maze. See Maze tests
LEARNING, Psychology of
All-or none learning and the role of repetition in paired-associate learning. W. Kintsch. bibliog il Science 140:310-12 Ap 19 '63
Arithmetic behavior in chimpanzees. C. B. Ferster. il Sci Am 210:98-104+ My '64
Attitude statements as positive and negative reinforcements. C. Golightly and D. Byrne. il Science 146:798-9 N 6 '64
Behavior affects learning; summaries of addresses. M. Hughes; A. Keliher. Sr Schol 84:4T My 1 '64
Conditions increasing self-reflective learning in art; research report. R. C. Burkhart. il Sch Arts 64:23-30 O '64
Errorless discrimination learning in the pigeon: effects of chlorpromazine and imipramine. H. S. Terrace. bibliog il Science 140:318-19 Ap 19 '63
Forgetting. B. J. Underwood. il Sci Am 210: 91-4+ bibliog(p 152) Mr '64
Group learning of speech sequences without awareness. D. Shapiro. bibliog il Science 144:74-6 Ap 3 '64
Imitation of man by machine. U. Neisser. bibliog Science 139:193-7 Ja 18 '63; Discussion. 140:212-14+ Ap 12 '63
Is play obsolete? D. Weisman. il Sat R 46: 77-8 N 16 '63
Kids and computers; studies at Harvard univ.'s Center for cognitive studies; summary of address. J. Bruner. Sr Schol 83:3T N 22 '63
Learning, remembering and forgetting; report on New York academy of sciences conference. D. Kimble. Science 146:1605 D 18 '64
Learning; symposium. il NEA J 52:19-32 Mr '63
Methodological questions in the study of one-trial learning. I. Rock and G. Steinfeld. bibliog Science 140:822-4 My 17 '63
New look at readiness; excerpt from Democracy and excellence in American secondary education. H. S. Broudy and others. bibliog Sch & Soc 91:424-30 D 28 '63
Prediction of discrimination from generalization after variations in schedule of reinforcement. A. Haber and H. I. Kalish. bibliog il Science 142:412-13 O 18 '63
Reassuring report about children with odd study habits. F. Riessman. il Redbook 124: 59+ N '64
There's no limit to learning. J. Murphy and R. Gross. il Parents Mag 39:62-3+ F '64
Toddlers can be taught more than you think. M. K. Frey. il Parents Mag 38:56-7+ My '63; Same abr. with title Children can be taught life, early. Read Digest 83:95-6 Jl '63
Uncommitted cortex; the child's changing brain. W. Penfield. Atlan 214:77-81 Jl '64
What makes children want to learn? with study-discussion program, by D. B. Harris and E. S. Harris. P. Witty. bibliog il PTA Mag 58:21-3, 35-6 N '63
What you can do about an underachiever. M. Grant. il Parents Mag 38:56-7+ Mr '63
When a child is failing in school. S. H. Fraiberg. il Parents Mag 39:54-6+ My '64
See also
Attention
Maze tests
Memory
Problem solving
Psychology, Educational
LEARNING ability. See Ability
LEARNING and scholarship
Methodology of educational research and scholarship. C. V. Good. Sch & Soc 91:140-4 Mr 23 '63
Scholar strikes back; adaptation of address. J. Pelikan. Cath World 200:149-54 D '64
Scholar strikes back; excerpts from address, May 19, 1964. J. J. Pelikan. il Pub W 185: 52-5 Je 15 '64
Teacher-opinion poll; are they learning as much today? il NEA J 53:7 Ap '64
See also
Commission on the humanities
Humanities
Knowledge
LEARNING materials. See Teaching—Aids and devices
LEARY, Francis T.
Quarterbacking a nation's news. J. F. Fixx. por Sat R 46:48-9 Ag 10 '63
LEARY, Lewis
Appetite for imagery. Sat R 47:39-40 D 19 '64
Man who invented himself. Sat R 47:33 My 30 '64
LEARY, Lewis Sheridan
Five brave Negroes with John Brown at Harpers Ferry. por Negro Hist Bul 27:164-9 Ap '64
LEARY, Mary Ellen
As the braceros leave. Reporter 32:43-5 Ja 28 '65
LEARY, Paris
Cruger's Island; poem. Sat R 47:172 Ag 29 '64
LEARY, Robert V. See Wylie, E. M. jt. auth.
LEARY, Thomas P.
Amateur scientist. Sci Am 208:167-70+ My '63
LEARY, Timothy Francis
Dangerous magic of LSD. J. Kobler. il por Sat Eve Post 236:30-2+ N 2 '63
Getting alienated with the right crowd at Harvard. M. Mayer. Esquire 60:73+ S '63; Reply with rejoinder. R. Alpert and T. Leary. 61:42+ Je '64
Hallucinogenic drug cult. N. Gordon. il Reporter 29:35-43 Ag 15 '63
LSD and all that. il por Time 81:72+ Mr 29 '63
No illusions; psilocybin tests at Harvard. por Newsweek 61:92-3 Je 10 '63
Straight scene. por Newsweek 64:74 Jl 27 '64
Strange case of the Harvard drug scandal. A. T. Weil. il Look 27:38+ N 5 '63
LEAS, Donald S. jr
Square knot. il Newsweek 62:43-4 N 11 '63
LEASES
Case against capitalizing leases. D. C. Cook. bibliog f Harvard Bsns R 41:145-50+ Ja '63
How to update your lease. F. J. Reiss. il Suc Farm 61:104 O '63
Ins & outs of a lease. il Changing T 18:31-3 Ap '64
Personal business; ins and outs of conventional leases. Bsns W p95 Ag 31 '63
See also subhead Leasing under various subjects, e.g. Automobiles—Leasing
LEASING of equipment. See Agricultural machinery—Renting
LEASING of farm buildings. See Farm buildings—Renting
LEASOR, James
Dr Jason Love and the curious equation; story. Vogue 145:70-1 Ja 15 '65
LEATHER
Keeping the dash in leather. Vogue 142:88+ N 1 '63
Rush to leather. il Vogue 141:56-63 F 15 '63
This little pigskin went to market; Hush Puppies, shoes of pigskin. il Bsns W p48+ D 7 '63
Care
Do's and don't's for leather garments. Good H 157:138 Jl '63
Protection
Leather longevity; neat's-foot oil. R. Scharff. Field & S 68:118-19 My '63
LEATHER, Artificial. See Leather substitutes
LEATHER handbags. See Handbags
LEATHER industry and trade
Wages and hours
Earnings in leather tanning and finishing, March 1963. G. L. Stelluto. il Mo Labor R 86:944-6 Ag '63
LEATHER substitutes
Big news in shoes; Corfam poromeric material. D. Wharton. Read Digest 84:59-62 Mr '64
Corfam, leather-substitute in shoes is put to the test of use. il Consumer Bul 48:25-6 Ja '65
Corfam vs. leather for shoe uppers. Consumer Rep 29:517-18 N '64
Research: if the shoe fits, another winner for industry. il Newsweek 63:65-6 Ap 6 '64
Synthetic rival for leather; Du Pont's Corfam. il Bsns W p34 O 5 '63
Synthetic shoe-in; Corfam. il Time 83:92 Ap 3 '64
Synthetics ride hell-bent for leather. L. Lessing. il Fortune 70:172-5+ N '64

LEATHERBEE, Mary
Lazy, lovely life on the Pride of Kashmir. Life 57:95+ Ag 14 '64
Roaming, helping fishermen and eating well. Life 57:73-4+ O 23 '64
LEAVE of absence
Extended vacations at Alcoa; SUB plan. E. D. Mairs. Mo Labor R 87:404-6 Ap '64
Extended vacations at Timken. D. G. Rayl. Mo Labor R 87:406 Ap '64
Long vacations? cool reactions. U S News 55:93 Jl 8 '63
Next step for sabbaticals. Bsns W p35-6 Ag 3 '63
Now we have it, what do we do? steelworkers. il Bsns W p70-2 F 8 '64
Sabbaticals for labor. Nation 197:23 Jl 13 '63
Should management take sabbaticals? L. A. Blumenthal. Duns R 83:45-6+ Ja '64
Steel settles; industrial sabbaticals. Bsns W p23 Je 22 '63
LEAVE-taking; story. See Hazzard, S.
LEAVENS, Peter A.
Shoot the solar eclipse! il U S Camera 26:42-3 Jl '63
Space astronomy at the World's fair. il Sky & Tel 27:332-4 Je '64
LEAVES
Circadian leaf movements: persistence in bean plants grown in continuous high-intensity light. T. Hoshizaki and K. C. Hammer. il Science 144:1240-1 Je 5 '64; Reply. E. Bunning. bibliog 146:551 O 23 '64
Fall foliage focus: Maine. J. T. Boyd. il Travel 122:24-7 O '64
Foliage can be beautiful. E. S. Parcher. il Horticulture 42:36 Ja '64
Important factor in plants: texture. H. S. Ortloff. il Horticulture 41:82 F '63
Leaves are for keeping. R. L. Hering. il Pop Gard 15:28-9 S '64
Systematic error in leaf water potential measurements with a thermocouple psychrometer. S. L. Rawlins. bibliog il Science 146:644-6 O 30 '64
See also
Color of leaves
LEAVES, Color of. See Color of leaves
LEAVES, Pressed. See Flowers, Dried
LEAVES; story. See Updike, J.
LEAVIS, F. R.
Dog that didn't bark. H. Corke. New Repub 148:27-30 Ap 13 '63; Discussion. 148:36-7 My 4 '63
Pride, prejudice and wit. J. Daniel. Nation 198:170-1 F 17 '64
Snow affair. M. S. Simpson. Bul Atomic Sci 19:28-32 Ap '63
LEAVITT, Betty
New York's new night life. Look 28:32-7 Jl 28 '64
LEAVITT, Hart
Rock-n-roll prose; summary of address. Sr Schol 82:1T-2T+ My 8 '63
—and Sohn, David
Eye for writing; excerpts from Stop, look, and write! Sr Schol 85:18T-19T D 2 '64
LEAVITT, Jack
John Doe meets Super court. Nation 199:280 O 26 '64
LEAVITT, Murray
Life TV review. Life 57:17 O 23 '64
LEAVITT, Scot
I've come back, cried Tom Swiftly. Life 54:19 My 31 '63
LEAVY, Bill, family
Three sets of twins in three years. S. James and R. W. Goldfarb. il Redbook 121:58-9+ My '63
LEBANON
Sweet era. il Time 84:28-9 Ag 28 '64
See also
Airlines—Lebanon
Banks and banking—Lebanon
Beirut
Music festivals—Lebanon
Presidents—Lebanon
Real property—Lebanon

Description and travel

Sarcophagi and skyscrapers. W. Sansom. il Holiday 35:62-73+ Mr '64

Nationalism

Fear in Lebanon. America 108:732-3 My 25 '63

Social life and customs

Little white beds; Bal des petits lits blancs. il Newsweek 64:45 Jl 20 '64
LEBANON, Pa.
Outcast of Lebanon. R. G. Hummerstone. il Nation 199:303-5 N 2 '64; Reply with rejoinder. E. U. Sowers, 2d. 200:inside cover Ja 11 '65
LEBOEUF, Randall J. Jr
Staffordshire and steam. Antiques 85:666-70 Je '64
LE BRUN, Charles
Official artist; exhibition at the Château de Versailles. il Time 82:50-1 Ag 23 '63
LEBRUN, Marie Louise Elisbeth Vigée-. See Vigée-Lebrun, M. L. E.
LEBRUN, Rico
Wanting to tell the truth. il por Time 83:47 Ja 31 '64
LEC, Stanislaw
More unkempt thoughts; excerpts from Unkempt thoughts, tr. by J. M. Galazka. Holiday 34:44-5 S '63; 36:132 N '64
LE CARRÉ, John, pseud. See Cornwell, D.
LECHÍN, Juan
Captives in the hills. il por Time 82:26-7 D 20 '63
On the brink. il Newsweek 62:35-6 D 23 '63
Ruling rivalries. Newsweek 63:47 F 10 '64
LECHLER, Eckhard, and Roberts, H. R.
Hemophilias. Science 144:1043-4 My 22 '64
LECHLITNER, Ruth
Moment electric; poem. Christian Cent 81:606 My 6 '64
LECHTZIN, Stanley
Workshop: electrofabrication of metals. bibliog Craft Horiz 24:40-3 N '64
LECHWE. See Antelopes
LECLER, René
Cinderella princesses. Ladies Home J 81:52-3+ S '64
How motherhood has changed Princess Margaret. Good H 156:82-3+ My '63
When the Queen has a baby. Good H 158:86-7+ F '64
LECLERCQ, Tanaquil
Bright victory. R. Sabin. il pors Dance Mag 38:38-40 Ap '64
LE CLÉZIO, J. M. G.
Day Beaumont grew acquainted with his pain; story, tr. by R. Howard. Mlle 59:118-19 O '64
LECOMPTE, Garé
Letter from Sofia. Nation 197:304-5 N 9 '63
—and Hamalian, Leo
Syria: test of Arab unity. Nation 196:375-6+ My 4 '63
LE CORBUSIER
Architecture. W. McQuade. Nation 196:145-6 F 16 '63
Corbu show in Chicago. P. Gardner. Christian Cent 80:832 Je 26 '63
First U.S. building by Corbu completed. il Arch Rec 133:10 Mr '63
Hand & the head; Visual arts center, Harvard university. il Time 81:72-5 Mr 8 '63
Le Corbusier at Harvard. W. Von Eckardt. New Repub 149:27-9 Jl 6 '63; Reply. S. Zetterberg. 149:38-9 Ag 31 '63
Le Corbusier at Harvard: a disaster, or a bold step forward? imaginary debate. il Arch Forum 119:104-7 O '63
Le Corbusier completes his first U.S. building. il Arch Forum 118:78-81 Mr '63
Le Corbusier designs for Harvard. il Arch Rec 133:151-8 Ap '63
People are talking about. . . il por Vogue 141:115 Mr 1 '63
Too far out? award of the Gold medal of the Boston society of architects voted down. Newsweek 61:90 Je 10 '63
LECOUVREUR, Adrienne
Born for tragedy. F. Stevenson. il pors Opera N 27:8-13 F 9 '63
LECTURES and lecturing
Banning the campus speaker. W. W. Van Alstyne. Nation 196:267-8+ Mr 30 '63
Every good thing has its price; artists as lecturers and demonstrators. N. Kent. Am Artist 28:3 F '64
LED astray; story. See Jacobson, D.
LEDBETTER, Myron C. and Porter, K. R.
Morphology of microtubules of plant cells. bibliog Science 144:872-4 My 15 '64
LEDDICK, David
Everyman's African roots. Dance Mag 38:20-1 O '64
LEDDIHN, Erik Maria, ritter von Kuehnelt-. See Kuehnelt-Leddihn, E. M. von
LEDER, Philip. See Nirenberg, M. W. jt. auth.
LEDERER, Walther
He knows where the money goes. por Newsweek 62:63 S 2 '63
LEDERER, William J.
Democracy triumphs in the Philippines. Read Digest 82:289-94+ Ap '63

LEADERER, William J.—*Continued*
50th state, at five, goes mainland. N Y Times Mag p24+ Ag 16 '64
Sailor's Christmas gift. Sat Eve Post 236:40 D 21 '63
—and Burdick, Eugene
Indonesia: time bomb in the South Pacific. Read Digest 82:129-34 Mr '63
—See Burdick, E. jt. auth.
LEDERLE laboratories
Missing microbes. Newsweek 63:70 Ja 20 '64
New polio vaccine; Orimune. Consumer Rep 28:413-14 S '63
LEDERMAN, Leon M.
Two-neutrino experiment; with biographical sketch. Sci Am 208:32, 60-70 bibliog(p 188+) Mr '63
LEDGER, Robert P.
Day camping, an answer to summer needs. Recreation 57:116-17 Mr '64
LEDLEY, Robert S.
High-speed automatic analysis of biomedical pictures. bibliog Science 146:216-23 O 9 '64
LEDOUX, Robert L. and White, J. L.
Infrared study of selective deuteration of kaolinite and halloysite at room temperature. bibliog Science 145:47-9 Jl 3 '64
Infrared study of the OH groups in expanded kaolinite. bibliog Science 143:244-6 Ja 17 '64
LEDUC, Violette
Letter from Paris. Genêt. New Yorker 40:108+ Ja 23 '65
LEE, Betty Jean. See Newlon, R. jt. auth.
LEE, David B.
Speaking out. por Sat Eve Post 237:3+ D 5 '64
LEE, Douglas H. K.
Arid lands: environmental physiology and psychology. Science 140:1002-3+ My 31 '63
LEE, Elsie
Expand or contract? Writer 76:18-20+ D '63
LEE, Ettie
Little cash down. por Newsweek 63:30 Ja 27 '64
LEE, Fitzhugh
Seapower and the mid-South; address, May 21, 1963. Vital Speeches 29:690-3 S 1 '63
LEE, Frank. See Hamill, P. jt. auth.
LEE, Henry
They signed away their lives. Todays Health 41:32-5+ Jl '63
LEE, J. Oscar
Racism, effects, origins, remedies. Christian Cent 80:907-9 Jl 17 '63
LEE, Jacob J. van der
Community economic relations with associated African states and other countries. Ann Am Acad 348:15-24 Jl '63
LEE, James G.
VHF adventurer. Pop Electr 19:41-6 O; 57-63 N; 61-6+ D '63
LEE, John J. and Freudenthal, Hugo
Neglected amoebas in culture. Natur Hist 72:54-61 D '63
Tiny drifters of the sea. Natur Hist 73:44-5 O '64
LEE, Kendall H.
Multi-purpose pavilion-bandstand. Am City 78:157-8 Mr '63
LEE, Kuan Yew
Atlantic report. Atlan 213:14+ F '64
Hurray for Harry; final obstacle to independence cleared away. il por Time 82:41 S 20 '63
Our far-flung correspondents; Federation of Malaysia. R. Shaplen. il New Yorker 39:130+ Ap 6 '63
LEE, Laurie
First love; story. Vogue 143:115 Mr 15 '64
Firstborn. il Mlle 60:116-17 D '64; Same abr. with title Wonder of the firstborn. Read Digest 86:141-3 Ja '65
Journey through Mexico. Mlle 57:190-1+ My '63
San Francisco. Mlle 57:50+ Je '63
Traveling with Mlle: Holland. Mlle 58:117-22 D '63
Voices of Ireland. Mlle 59:165-6+ O '64
What I would like to give my child. il Mlle 60:100-1+ Ja '65

about

Rights and permissions. P. Nathan. Pub W 185:83 F 17 '64
LEE, Lawrence
Montgomery: an elegy. Yale R 54:236 D '64
LEE, Lawrence D
Used cars in Uruguay. Motor T 16:52-4 Mr '64
LEE, Mabel Barbee
No place for a lady; condensation of Cripple Creek days. Read Digest 84:255-60+ My '64
LEE, Marjorie
I would have sworn; poem. McCalls 90:130 Je '63
LEE, Oliver M.
Communist China and western Europe. bibliog f Cur Hist 47:143-8+ S '64
LEE, Peggy
Timeless charm of Peggy Lee. T. C. Wheeler. il pors Sat Eve Post 237:24-5 O 10 '64
LEE, Richard M.
Conditioning of a free operant response in planaria. Science 139:1048-9; 141:392 Mr 15, Ag 2 '63
—See Zeitz, L. jt. auth.
LEE, Robert
Meaning of leisure; excerpt from Religion and leisure in America. bibliog f Christian Cent 81:665-8 My 20 '64
Sharing the anomaly. Christian Cent 81:210 F 12 '64
LEE, Robert E. 1912-
Education for the new diplomacy; address, March 2, 1963. Dept State Bul 48:423-7 Mr 25 '63
LEE, Robert Edward
Lee after the war, by M. W. Fishwick. Review
Am Heritage 14:101-2 Je '63
Seven days, by C. Dowdey. Review
Am Heritage 15:111-13 Ap '64. B. Catton
Suppose Lee had won at Gettysburg. il U S News 55:60-1 Jl 8 '63
LEE, Tong Won
United States and Korea reaffirm policy of cooperation; joint statement, October 3, 1964. Dept State Bul 51:542 O 19 '64
LEE, Virginia
Virginia Lee's scrapbook of an era. W. Como. il pors Dance Mag 38:49-53+ N '64
LEE, Welby
Search; suspect of hit-and-run death in Celina, Tenn. 1944. por Newsweek 62:24+ Jl 22 '63
LEE manufacturing company
Factory grows in former dance hall; Boley, Okla. il Ebony 19:48+ Ag '64
LEE Wilson and company. See Wilson, Lee, and company
LEED, Jacob
Death; poem. Nation 198:246 Mr 9 '64
Guards; poem. Nation 198:382 Ap 13 '64
LEEDHAM, Charles
First dogs of the land. N Y Times Mag p 11 Je 21 '64
Flying the beam when the fog rolls in. N Y Times Mag p22+ My 24 '64
Toward a world weather bureau. N Y Times Mag p29+ S 22 '63
Vee-Stol: airplane of the future? N Y Times Mag p66+ O 6 '63
Vision of a crashproof car. N Y Times Mag p34+ O 25 '64
Who will win the supersonic race? N Y Times Mag p38 +Ag 23 '64
LEEDOM, Boyd
Dissenter praises Labor board; summary of address, December 4, 1963. U S News 55:108 D 16 '63
LEEDY, Paul D.
What, then, is all this teaching for? address, April 10, 1964. Vital Speeches 30:501-4 Je 1 '64
LEEMING, Bernard
Are Americans human? America 109:76-9 Jl 20 '63
Ecumenical dialogue and conversions. Cath World 198:223-9 Ja '64
Liturgy and mystery. America 109:153-5 Ag 17 '63
LEEN, Nina
Shells; photographs. Life 57:46-53+ Jl 10 '64
Top show dogs. Life 56:56-62 F 7 '64
LEES, Benjamin
Out of the fashion. por Time 81:69 Mr 1 '63
LEES, Gene
Jazz composer. Hi Fi 13:55-7+ Ag '63
LEES, Hannah
Making of a Negro middle class. Reporter 31:41-4 O 8 '64
New open door policy for wayward girls. Ladies Home J 80:26+ S '63
Philadelphia, Pennsylvania: a process of fragmentation. Reporter 29:18-20 Jl 4 '63
Self-help in Philadelphia. Reporter 31:15-17 D 17 '64
(ed) See Lober, K. When my husband lost his job
LEEUWENHOEK, Anthony van
Dutch genius of the lens. Todays Health 42:63 Ja '64
LEFEVRE, Paul G. and others
Phospholipid-sugar complexes in relation to cell membrane monosaccharide transport. bibliog Science 143:955-7 F 28 '64
LEFF, James J.
Report from the bench. Nat R 16:26 Ja 14 '64

LEFFERTS, Barney
Now the Mike Nichols touch. N Y Times Mag p34+ N 22 '64
Revolution of the Tin Lizzie. N Y Times Mag p 18-19 Jl 28 '63

LEFFLER, John E.
How to outwit forms. Atlan 213:122 F '64

LEFKOE, M. R.
NLRB's new, rough line. Fortune 68:164-6+ N '63
Strange case of Sun oil. Fortune 68:117+ Ag '63

LEFKOWITZ, Louis J.
New York; criminal infiltration of the securities industry. Ann Am Acad 347:51-7 My '63

LEFRAK, Samuel J.
Sam Lefrak; he builds them cheaper by the dozen. D. B. Carlson. il por Arch Forum 118:102-5 Ap '63

LEFRAK City. See Queens, N.Y.—Housing

LEFT and right (political science) See Right and left (political science)

LEFT- and right-handedness
Lefties are all right. J. R. Komaiko. il Parents Mag 38:50-1+ Jl '63
Right gift for the left-handed. Good H 157: 174 D '63
Sporting scene; left-handed golfer winning British Open championship. H. W. Wind. il New Yorker 39:52+ Ag 3 '63

LEFTOVERS. See Cookery—Leftovers

LEFTWICH, Lloyd
Lloyd Leftwich, Alabama state senator; reconstruction legislator and his family. C. A. Brown. bibliog por Negro Hist Bul 26: 161-2 F '63

LEG
Anatomy for the ballet teacher; interview, ed. by W. Como. R. Gelabert. il Dance Mag 37:62-3 Je; 59-62 Jl; 59-60 Ag; 60-3 S '63
Beauty: new legs to stand on. D. A. Robinson. il Ladies Home J 81:80-3 N '64
Lithe lovely legs by summer. il Good H 158: 236-8 My '64
What you should know about shaving your legs. il Good H 156:154 F '63
See also
Femur

Surgery

How to stretch a leg. il Sci Digest 56:53 N '64

Wounds and injuries

What parents ask about growing pains. M. J. E. Senn. il McCalls 90:70+ My '63

LEGACIES
See also
Wills

LEGACIES, Unclaimed
Billions of dollars unclaimed! A. Rankin. Read Digest 84:77-81 My '64

LEGACY; story. See Jordan, E. H.

LEGAL aid
Legal Blue cross? legal-aid plan set up by Brotherhood of railroad trainmen upheld. Time 83:76+ My 1 '64

LEGAL bibliography. See Legal research

LEGAL defenders. See Public defenders

LEGAL documents
See also
Receipts (acknowledgements)

LEGAL education. See Law—Study and teaching; Law schools

LEGAL ethics
Canon 35: the case for the defendant; question; should photographers be allowed in courtrooms? B. Warner. il U S Camera 26:64-5+ Jl '63; Reply. P. Stackpole. 26: 12-13 S '63

LEGAL fees. See Cost (law)

LEGAL literature
Dark science of conflict; new Triennial Coif award. il Time 85:42 Ja 8 '65

LEGAL photography. See Photography, Legal

LEGAL profession. See Lawyers

LEGAL research
From the mouths of babes; law reviews. il Time 83:49-50 Ap 24 '64
See also
Calculating machines—Legal applications

LEGAL secretaries. See Secretaries, Legal

LEGENDS
See also
Indians of Mexico—Legends
Mythology

LEGENDS, Chinese
Legend of Tchi-Niu; adaptation by P. S. Buck. il McCalls 91:114-15+ My '64

LEGENDS, Indian (East Indian)
Blindfolded traveller in New Delhi; excerpts from Encounters and celebrations. G. Fradier. il UNESCO Courier 16:4-11 S '63

LEGENDS, Irish
See also
Cuchulain

LÉGER, Fernand
Touch of Léger; Moscow exhibition. il Newsweek 61:92 F 25 '63

LEGER, Paul Emile, cardinal
Cardinal Léger; interview, ed. by W. M. Abbott. America 108:862-4 Je 15 '63
Cardinal urges prayer for W.C.C. meeting. Christian Cent 80:261 F 27 '63

LEGGE, Walter
Letter from London. M. Panter-Downes. New Yorker 40:118-19 Ap 4 '64

LEGGETT, John
Stalking the muse on publishers' row. Harper 230:64-6 Ja '65

LEGGETT, Stanton
Upgrading existing school facilities. Arch Rec 133:163-71 F '63

LEGGETT, William
Baseball (cont) Sports Illus 20:60+ Je 8; 21:98-101 S 21 '64
Basketball. Sports Illus 18:53-6 My 6; 19:84-5 N 25 '63
Horse racing (cont) Sports Illus 18:42+ F 4 '63
Hot team in the old town. Sports Illus 18: 18-21 Ap 29 '63
Pro basketball. Sports Illus 19:30-2+ O 28 '63

LEGION, American. See American Legion

LEGION of decency. See National legion of decency

LEGION of honor. See Decorations of honor

LEGISLATION
See also
Lobbying

Terminology

See Law—Language

United States

Civil rights, then the tax cut? il Newsweek 62:29 O 14 '63
Easy congressional victories are hard-won. J. N. Eller. America 110:275 F 29 '64
Giving Congress the vote. Commonweal 79:448 Ja 17 '64
How a bill becomes a law (cont) il Sr Schol 84:20-1 F 14 '64
How the rights vote was engineered. New Repub 150:17-19 F 29 '64
Libraries and the war on poverty; relevant federal legislative programs, chart, with introd. by G. T. Stevenson; comp. by P. Winnick. ALA Bul 59:43-8 Ja '65
Mislabeled bills mislead voters. V. J. Burke. il Nations Bsns 51:92-5 F '63
Referendum & initiative; states measures. Time 84:43 N 13 '64
Speaking out; doesn't Congress have ideas of its own? A. Ribicoff. Sat Eve Post 237: 6+ Mr 21 '64
Tax cut and civil rights: not mutually exclusive. J. N. Eller. America 109:448 O 19 '63
Three for four? President Johnson's messages to Congress during past week. Newsweek 65:22 Ja 25 '65
What happened to the Kennedy program. R. Wilson. Look 28:117-18+ N 17 '64
Who makes decisions in Washington. B. Hays. il Nations Bsns 53:40-1+ Ja '65
See also
Agricultural laws and legislation
Judicial review
Labor laws and legislation—United States
Library laws and legislation
School laws and legislation—United States
Social legislation—United States
United States—Congress
United States—Supreme court

LEGISLATIVE bodies

United States

See also
State legislatures
United States—Congress
also subhead Legislature under names of states, e.g. Illinois—Legislature

LEGISLATIVE reference service, Library of Congress. See United States—Library of Congress

LEGISLATORS
Moral missions of the legislature; address, April 24, 1963. W. J. Mahoney. Vital Speeches 29:655-7 Ag 15 '63
See also
Negro legislators

LEGISLATURES, State. See State legislatures

LEGITIMACY (law) See Illegitimacy

LEGLER, Philip
Death; poem. Commonweal 80:152 Ap 24 '64

LÉGLISE, Paul
Hidden face of the cinema (cont) UNESCO Courier 16:26-31 F; 28-32 Ap; 21-3+ My '63
LEGS. See Leg
LEGS, Artificial. See Artificial limbs
LEGS, Table. See Tables
LEGTERS, Lyman H. See Bigelow, D. N. jt. ed.
LEGUM, Colin
Harambee in Kenya. Cur Hist 46:142-7 Mr '64
West at bay. Nation 197:70-3 Ag 10 '63
What kind of radicalism for Africa? For Affairs 43:237-50 Ja '65
LEGUMES
Eight great legumes and how to manage them. L. E. Zeman. il Suc Farm 62:52-7 Mr '64
See also
Sainfoin
LEHAR, F.
On records; Merry widow. Opera N 28:34 D 21 '63
LEHMAN, Beverly
Sometimes I lead a double life. por Farm J 87:55+ S '63
LEHMAN, Herbert Henry
Herbert H. Lehman of New York. N. Glazer. Commentary 35:403-9 My '63
Highest form. il por Time 82:29 D 13 '63
Lehman: a legendary liberal. por Newsweek 62:60 D 16 '63
Notes and comment. New Yorker 39:23 D 28 '63
Obituary
Reporter 29:12 D 19 '63
Senator Lehman. Nation 197:447 D 28 '63
LEHMAN, Milton
How Lindbergh gave a lift to rocketry; excerpts from This high man: a biography of Dr Robert H. Goddard. Life 55:115-18+ O 4 '63
LEHMAN brothers (brokers)
Don't fence him in; Gen. L. D. Clay, a senior partner. Newsweek 61:80 F 11 '63
Lehman fund tries again. il Bsns W p29 Jl 25 '64
LEHMANN, Gary A.
Low-cost solid-state power supply. Electr World 70:92-3 O '63
LEHMANN, Helmut
Loccum, a Protestant monastery. Christian Cent 80:1167-9 S 25 '63
Reconciliation in action. Christian Cent 80: 824-6 Je 26 '63
LEHMANN, Lotte
Happy birthday to a great lady of song. G. Bowen. por Am Rec G 29:424-5 F '63
LEHMANN, Otto
Gift for borrowing. Opera N 28:24-5 F 1 '64
Sea-change. Opera N 29:24-5 Ja 30 '65
LEHMANN, Paul
Inadmissible default. Christian Cent 81:908-9 Jl 15 '64
On keeping human life human. Christian Cent 81:1297-9 O 21 '64
LEHMBRUCK, Wilhelm
Wilhelm Lehmbruck, 1881-1919. C. B. Johnson. il Sch Arts 62:47 Mr '63
LEHMKUHL, Joakim
Time bomb for watchmakers. il por Bsns W p96+ N 16 '63
LEHR, Jay H.
Groundwater: flow toward an effluent stream. bibliog Science 140:1318-20 Je 21 '63
LEHRER, Stanley
Man, automation, and dignity. Sch & Soc 92: 303 O 31 '64
LEHRMAN, Daniel S.
Reproductive behavior of ring doves. Sci Am 211:48-54 N '64
LEHRMAN, Hal
Look back on promised land. Sat R 46:45 N 9 '63
Uniform of the Fifth republic. Sat R 47:28+ Ap 4 '64
Where the grass is always wet. Sat R 48:86-7 Ja 2 '65
LEIBER, Fritz
Christmas syndrome. Sci Digest 54:16-21 D '63
Don't be ashamed of your daydreams. Sci Digest 54:14-20 Ag '63
How to live with machines. Sci Digest 53: 26-30 Je '63
LEIBER, Robert
Pius XII and the Jews. P. Land. America 108: 730-1 My 25 '63
LEIBOWITZ, Herbert
Aiken as a novelist. New Repub 150:24+ My 2 '64
LEIBOWITZ, Melvin, and Pappas, Charles
Compact 6-meter transceiver. Electr World 69:43-5 Ap '63
LEIBOWITZ, Samuel Simon
Jurist before the bar. por Time 82:70 N 15 '63
LEIBY, Paul D. and Olsen, O. W.
Cestode echinococcus multilocularis in foxes in North Dakota. bibliog Science 145:1066 S 4 '64
LEICAFLEX cameras. See Cameras
LEICESTER university. See Colleges and universities—England
LEICH, Alexander, and Leich, Roland
Automotive milestones. Motor T 16:78-81 Jl '64
LEICH, Roland. See Leich, A. jt. auth.
LEICHTLING, Alan
Make it louder! Seventeen 24:28 Ja '65
LEIDEN, Carl
Middle East misconceptions. Nat R 16:67-9 Ja 28 '64
LEIF Ericsson
Leif Erikson day, 1964; proclamation. L. B. Johnson. Dept State Bul 51:401 S 21 '64
New recognition for Leif Ericson? il U S News 56:20 Mr 16 '64
LEIFER, Neil
Candid color portraits. il U S Camera 27:50-1 Ap '64
LEIGH, Carma R.
State libraries. ALA Bul 58:532 Je '64
LEIGH, Douglas
Unspectacular Douglas Leigh. J. F. Fixx. il por Sat R 47:54-5 Jl 11 '64
LEIGH, Vivian
Muzhikal. por Time 81:46 Mr 29 '63
LEIGHTON, Delmar
Farewell, groves of academe. por Time 82:80 Jl 12 '63
LEIGHTON, Joseph, and others
Temperature-dependent histotypic changes in Walker carcinosarcoma in the chorioallantois. Science 141:1181-2 S 20 '63
LEIGHTON, Margaret
Portrait of a gazelle. A. Pumphrey. por Theatre Arts 47:16-18 F '63
LEIGHTON, Morris M. and Brophy, J. A.
Illinoian and Wisconsin (Farmdale) drifts recently exposed at Rockford, Illinois. bibliog Science 139:218-21 Ja 18 '63
LEIGHTON, Richard M.
Overlord revisited: an interpretation of American strategy in the European war, 1942-1944. bibliog f Am Hist R 68:919-37 Jl '63
LEIMAN, Herbert
Special-effects box. Pop Phot 55:110 O '64
LEIN, Russ
Unique shell collection. A. G. Melvin. por Hobbies 69:130+ Mr '64
LEINSDORF, Erich
Why the world now looks to America for concert pianists. House B 106:118+ Ag '64
about
Balancing accounts. H. Rogers. Mus Am 83: 20-1 Ap '63
Big brother watches over Tanglewood. E. Coleman. il por N Y Times Mag p20+ Je 28 '64
Erich Leinsdorf: musician of the year. M. Esterow. il pors Mus Am 83:16-19 D '63
Home at last. il por Newsweek 63:84 Ap 13 '64
Leinsdorf in Boston. J. M. Conly. il pors Hi Fi 13:44-7+ D '63
New Boston tea party. Sat R 46:73 Mr 30 '63; Discussion. 46:72-3 Ap 27; 62 My 25 '63
Set to music. il McCalls 91:88-93 Mr '64
Tree grows at Tanglewood. por Time 82:34 Ag 30 '63
LEINWOLL, Stanley
Short-wave broadcast predictions (title varies) See issues of Popular electronics
LEIPZIG, Arthur
Old Africa's people of the village. il Natur Hist 73:10-19 Ap; 38-45 My '64
LEIPZIG
New look into East Germany. il U S News 54:48 Ap 1 '63
LEIS
How you can adapt the enchanting custom of the lei. il House & Gard 126:96-9 Jl '64
LEISER, Dorothy
Cain; poem. Christian Cent 80:1199 O 2 '63
LEISTER, Mary McFarland
All clematis don't climb. Horticulture 42:42 F '64
Cold frame convert. Flower Grower 50:56-7 Mr '63
Glorious mornings with morning-glory. il Flower Grower 50:13-14 N '63
Good old chicken wire. Flower Grower 50:20 Ag '63
Know the bright stars among petunias. Flower Grower 51:32+ My '64
Secret that grows delphinium. Flower Grower 50:23+ Jl '63

LEISURE
Age of fulfillment; address, November 16, 1963. R. Lazarus. Vital Speeches 30:301-4 Mr 1 '64; Excerpt. il Recreation 57:335-6 S '64
And make it count; acquiring a new skill. il Am Home 67:26+ Jl '64
Can community recreation meet the needs of youth? J. A. Wylie. il Recreation 56:406-8 N '63
Challenge of leisure; address, February 17, 1964. D. Rockefeller. Vital Speeches 30: 379-81 Ap 1 '64
Creative use of leisure time; address, November 11, 1963. A. J. Goldberg. Mus Am 83: 161 D '63
Critical issues in recreation; report from the 46th National recreation congress. il Recreation 57:489-92+ D '64
Free men accept the challenge of free time; National purpose project. A. L. New. Recreation 56:189 Ap '63
Labor shudders at leisure. D. Wakefield. Nation 196:325-7 Ap 20 '63; Reply. H. Bugbee. 196:inside cover My 18 '63
Leisure, its meaning and implications; excerpts from addresses. R. Theobald; C. K. Brightbill. Recreation 57:9-11 Ja '64
Leisure: new national resource. D. Rockefeller. Recreation 57:390-2 O '64
Leisure, the heart of living; topic for 45th National recreation congress. S. Case. il Recreation 56:224-5 My '63
Meaning of leisure; excerpt from Religion and leisure in America. R. Lee. bibliog f Christian Cent 81:665-8 My 20 '64
Meet tomorrow's customer. P. F. Drucker. il Nations Bsns 51:102-4+ Je '63
Observations from the 45th National recreation congress. il Recreation 56:453-6 D '63
Perils of leisure. D. Gabor. il Horizon 5:102-9 N '63
Questions to ask ourselves. G. Romney. Recreation 57:7-8 Ja '64
Religion and leisure in America, by R. Lee. Review
Christian Cent 81:899 Jl 15 '64
Space for the basic urge to be ornery. B. Furst. Recreation 56:163 Ap '63
Spare time; America's wasted resource? il Sr Schol 84:11-12+ My 1 '64
Spare time? what spare time? il Changing T 18:18-20 My '64
Theology of leisure. America 111:151 Ag 15 '64
Time to reflect, time to feel. M. Mead. Redbook 123:14-16+ Ag '64
Too much leisure. E. Havemann. il Life 56: 76-80+ F 14; 84-6+ F 21 '64; Same abr. with title Leisure, the great new challenge. Read Digest 85:125-8 Ag '64
Toward understanding leisure; outline for discussion. A. New. Recreation 58:36-7 '65
Uses of leisure. R. Gross. Commonweal 78: 185-7 My 10 '63
Using our leisure is no easy job. B. Bliven. il N Y Times Mag p 18-19+ Ap 26 '64
Weekends, U.S.A: what ever happened to fun? excerpt from The weekenders. M. Gunther. McCalls 91:70-1+ Je '64
What a wonderful weekend! il Am Home 67: 19-20+ Je '64
What kind of America? excerpt from address, September 23, 1964. L. S. Rockefeller. il Audubon Mag 66:376-81 N '64
Where did you go? home; what did you do? nothing. S. S. Fader. House B 106:42+ Mr '64

See also
Hobbies
Idleness
Recreation
Time, Use of

Bibliography

On the off-beat bookshelf. H. Frankel. Sat R 47:36-7 Ap 18 '64

LEISURE VILLAGE, Lakewood, N.J. See Aged—Housing

LEISURE World, Seal Beach, Calif. See Aged—Housing

LEITE, José R. Teixeira. See Teixeira Leite, J. R.

LEITER, Saul
What we all see every day, instants of transfiguration. H. M. Kinzer. il Pop Phot 54: 60-1 Mr '64

LEITH HILL Place. See England—Historic houses, etc.

LEITNER, Irving A.
Basketball for the physically handicapped; excerpts from Book of basketball. Todays Health 42:50-1+ Ja '64

LEITNER, Nathan B.
Pre-printed covers: how to reduce casing-in problems. Pub W 185:80-2 Ap 6 '64

LEJEUNE, Anthony
Arrows of cleverdom. Nat R 15:63-4 Jl 30 '63
Letter from London (cont) Nat R 14:159, 320; 16:770, 970, 1144 F 26, Ap 23 '63, S 8, N 3, D 29 '64
Price of appeasement. Nat R 15:403-4 N 5 '63
Shallow stream. Nat R 16:1019-20+ N 17 '64
SuperMac rides out the storm. Nat R 15: 189-90 S 10 '63
UN operation smash. Nat R 14:242-3 Mr 26 '63

LEKACHMAN, Robert
Liberalism & the economy. Commentary 37: 71-2 Je '64
No, but I read the reviews; reprint. Wilson Lib Bul 39:325-30 D '64
Tax trimmers. Commentary 35:289-95 Ap '63
That slow steady progress. Commentary 38: 95-8 N '64

LEKSELL, Lars
Now, knifeless brain surgery. il Sci Digest 55:71-2 Mr '64

LELAND, Dorothy E.
(comp) Books for boys & girls. See issues of Parent's magazine & better homemaking

LELAND, Sara
Brief biography. S. Goodman. pors Dance Mag 39:50-1 Ja '65

LELASH, Marjorie
He who laughs last. Opera N 28:24-6 Mr 21 '64
Triumph of incongruity. Opera N 29:24-5 Ja 9 '65

LELYVELD, Joseph
Mr Simpson of Vassar. N Y Times Mag p30-1+ D 13 '64
Paradoxical case of the affluent delinquent. N Y Times Mag p 13+ O 4 '64
Se habla espanol? N Y Times Mag p65-6+ Je 14 '64
Stranger in Philadelphia, Mississippi. N Y Times Mag p5+ D 27 '64

LEMA, Betty
Tony Lema: touring golf pro and his wife. G. Astor. il pors Look 28:121-6 My 5 '64

LEMA, Tony
Champagne Tony has a winning look. G. S. Brown. por Sports Illus 18:26-8+ Mr 25 '63
Humbling game. il por Time 84:72-3 Jl 17 '64
No substitute for swinging. il Time 83:46+ Je 19 '64
Room for a fourth? il pors Newsweek 61:85 Ap 22 '63
Tony Lema: touring golf pro and his wife. G. Astor. il pors Look 28:121-6 My 5 '64
Victorious crusade in the valley of sin. J. Lovesey. il pors Sports Illus 21:16-19 Jl 20 '64

—and Brown, G. S.
Pro golfer's candid story; excerpts from Golfers' gold. pors Sports Illus 20:62-6+ Mr 23; 30-2+ Mr 30; 45-6+ Ap 6 '64

LEMAIRE, Etienne
Thomas Jefferson, gourmet. J. H. Hazelton. il Am Heritage 15:20-1+ O '64

LEMASS, Sean F.
Exchange of greetings, October 15, 1963, Prime Minister Lemass to President Kennedy; with text of communiqué, October 17, 1963. Dept State Bul 49:737-8 N 11 '63
Summary of address, October 17, 1963. por U N Rev 10:9 D '63

about

Lifting the green curtain. il por Time 82: 28-40 Jl 12 '63; Same abr. with title Why Irish eyes are smiling. Read Digest 84:207-8+ Mr '64

LEMAY, Curtis E.
Civic action by the air force; address, October 19, 1963. Vital Speeches 30:150-2 D 15 '63
Combat vs. computers; testimony before the House defense appropriations subcommittee. Aviation W 80:11 My 4 '64
General LeMay's case for new strategic aircraft; excerpts from statement before House defense appropriations subcommittee, February 26, 1964. Aviation W 80:21 Ap 20 '64

about

From LeMay to McConnell; a change to the new breed. T. D. White. por Newsweek 65:16-17 Ja 4 '65

LEMAY, Harding
Tantalizing look behind Chaplin's mask. Life 57:24+ O 2 '64

LEMBCKE, Paul A.
Is this operation necessary? New Repub 149: 15-17 N 9 '63

LEMELIN, Roger
Reporter at large. E. Wilson. New Yorker 40:116+ N 21 '64
LEMMINGS
Lemming cycle at Baker Lake, Canada, during 1959-62. C. J. Krebs. bibliog il Science 140:674-6 My 10 '63
Lemming madness. il Newsweek 62:55 Ag 12 '63
New theory on a fabled exodus; lemming psychosis. K. Curry-Lindahl. il Natur Hist 72:46-53 Ag '63
LEMMON, Jack
Does everybody here like Jack? P. Bunzel. il pors Life 54:103-5+ Mr 22 '63
Go find something wrong with him! R. Lemon. il pors Sat Eve Post 238:68-70+ Ja 16 '65
Under the Lemmon skin. M. Davidson. il pors Ladies Home J 80:115-19 S '63
LEMMON, Robert S.
Obituary
Flower Grower 51:44 My '64
LEMMON, William B. and Patterson, G. H.
Depth perception in sheep: effects of interrupting the mother-neonate bond. bibliog Science 145:835-6; 146:1189 Ag 21, N 27 '64
LEMNITZ, Tiana
Historical records. A. Favia-Artsay. por Hobbies 67:30-1 F '63
LEMNITZER, Lyman L.
Facing the iron curtain: how good is western defense? interview. ed. by A. J. Meyers. por U S News 55:54-9 D 30 '63
LEMON, Richard
Go find something wrong with him! Sat Eve Post 238:68-70+ Ja 16 '65
Happy birthday, dear Beverly. Sat Eve Post 237:76-81 D 5 '64
House that art built. Sat Eve Post 238:72-7 Ja 30 '65
Small-fry boom. Sat Eve Post 237:58-63 D 19 '64
$250,000 bonanza. Sat Eve Post 237:70-1+ N 14 '64
LEMON trees
Starch synthesis in excised lemon fruit tissue growing in vitro. H. A. Kordan. bibliog il Science 142:971 N 15 '63
LEMON-verbena
Herb with a lemon scent. G. Taloumis. il Flower Grower 50:39 D '63
LE MONE, Evelyn
Records for teachers. See issues of Dance magazine
LEMONS, Abe
Abe Lemons and his poor ol' hongry farm boys. F. Deford. il Sports Illus 22:46-7 Ja 4 '65
LEMONS
1-Octopamine in citrus: isolation and identification. I. Stewart and T. A. Wheaton. bibliog il Science 145:60-1 Jl 3 '64
See also
Cookery—Fruit
LE MOYNE, Jean
Reporter at large. E. Wilson. New Yorker 40:74+ N 21 '64
LEMS, Carol
Displacement; poem. Christian Cent 80:300 Mr 6 '63
Existential lullaby. Christian Cent 80:173 F 6 '63
LEMURS
Madagascar lemurs: isolated primates. J. J. Petter. il Natur Hist 72:22-7 Mr '63
See also
Pottos
LENCHEVSKY, Oleg
Regards from an outcast. por Time 83:40 My 22 '64
LENDE, Richard A.
Cerebral cortex: a sensorimotor amalgam in the marsupialia. Science 141:730-2 Ag 23 '63
L'ENGLE, Madeleine
Expanding universe; Newbery award acceptance; address, July 15, 1963. por Horn Bk 39:351-5 Ag '63
Key, the door, the road; address, March 20, 1964. Horn Bk 40:260-8 Je '64
Mystery of the first law of thermodynamics; or, Trading stamp sex; address, 1964. por Library J 89:4851-6 D 15 '64
Three songs of Mary: O simplicitas; O oriens; O sapientia. Horn Bk 39:615-21 D '63
about
Lindsay and L'Engle speak at N.Y. New books preview. il Library J 89:3280 S 15 '64
Madeleine L'Engle. H. D. Vursell. por Library J 88:1288-91 Mr 15 '63
Madeleine L'Engle. H. Franklin. il pors Horn Bk 39:356-60 Ag '63
Newbery-Caldecott medals; Madeleine L'Engle, Ezra Jack Keats win 1963 awards. il por Pub W 183:18-20 Mr 11 '63
LENGTH measurement
Accurate length measurement of meter bar with helium-neon laser. K. D. Mielenz and others. bibliog il Science 146:1672-3 D 25 '64
Lasers for length measurement. A. G. McNish. bibliog il Science 146:177-82 O 9 '64
LENGTH of life. See Longevity
LENGTH of service. See Seniority, Employee
LENGYEL, Emil
Countries in search of a character. Sat R 47:54 My 9 '64
LENHOFF, Howard M. and Zwisler, J. R.
Zinc activation of a coordinated response in hydra. bibliog Science 142:1666-8 D 27 '63
—See Muscatine, L. jt. auth.
LENIN, Vladimir Il'ich
Battle over the tomb. il pors Time 83:26-30 Ap 24 '64
Dead hand that still rules Russia. F. Barghoorn. Life 56:10+ Je 19 '64
If Lenin were alive today. H. Schwartz. il pors N Y Times Mag p 14+ Jl 14 '63
Is Lenin's face red? N. Stock. por Nat R 16:25 Ja 14 '64
Lenin on libraries; excerpts from Life and death of Lenin. Library J 89:4301+ N 1 '64
Lenin the ideologist. R. V. Allen. por Nat R 16:1024-6 N 17 '64
Was Lenin necessary? L. Schapiro. Commentary 38:57-60 D '64
Tomb
What they say as they wait to see Lenin. J. Wolfenden. il por N Y Times Mag p26-7+ D 13 '64
LENINGRAD
Wonders of Leningrad. M. Druon. il Vogue 144:224-37+ D '64
Description
Leningrad notes. A. Talmey. Vogue 144:154+ D '64
Russia shines up its window on West. il Bsns W p78-80 Jl 25 '64
LENINGRAD, Siege of, 1941-1944
Siege of Leningrad, by L. Gouré. Review Nation 196:208-10 Mr 9 '63. C. Dreher
LENINGRAD Kirov ballet. See Kirov ballet
LENK, Irene. See Lenk, J. D. jt. auth.
LENK, John D.
Sure cure for ham, CB mobile noise. Pop Electr 19:65-6 O '63
—and Lenk, Irene
Shim up your stern. Pop Mech 121:152-4 Ap '64
LENNEBERG, Eric H.
How babies learn to talk. Parents Mag 39:66-7+ S '64
LENNETTE, Edwin H. See Riggs, J. L. jt. auth.
LENNON, John
All my own work. por Time 83:E7+ My 1 '64
Beatalic graphospasms. Sat Eve Post 237:40-2 Mr 21 '64
about
About the awful. P. Schickele. Nation 198:588-9 Je 8 '64
LENNON, Peter
Book censorship in Paris. Atlan 212:73-6 N '63
LENOIR, Jean Pierre
New season, Paris. Theatre Arts 47:29+ O '63
Openings, Paris (cont) Theatre Arts 47:60-1+ F; 62+ Mr; 23-4+ Ap; 28-9+ My; 33+ Je; 36+ Jl '63
LENOX, incorporated
Lenox takes a fast boat for china; sale of fine dinnerware throughout the world. il Bsns W p68-70 Ja 2 '65
LENOX ware. See Pottery, American
LENS, Sidney
Building on quicksand. Commonweal 79:159-61 N 1 '63
Decline of labor. Commonweal 80:391-4 Je 19 '64
Indonesia: a dissent. Commonweal 81:478-81 Ja 8 '65
Turkey's internal crisis. Commonweal 80:629-31 S 18 '64
LENS distortions. See Lenses, Photographic—Distortion
LENSES
Techniques tomorrow; search for color correction of lenses. B. Sherman. il Mod Phot 27:28-9+ Ag; 42+ S '63
See also
Contact lenses

LENSES, Photographic
Are mirror telephotos practical for you? D. L. Miller and B. Sherman. il Mod Phot 28:82-5 Ag '64
Behind the scenes; Russia prepares to crack the U.S. market. il Mod Phot 28:33-4 Ja '64
Close-up lenses. il Pop Phot 52:108-9 Ap '63
Color clinic; cold telephoto lens myth. D. B. Eisendrath, jr. Pop Phot 54:12 Ap '64
Converter lenses for single-lens reflex cameras. il Consumer Bul 47:23-5 D '64
Depth-of-field myths. N. Rothschild. Pop Phot 52:90-1 My '63
Do you have telephoto vision? A. Franceke-vich. il Pop Phot 56:124-5+ Ja '65
Every lens has a personality. P. Glushanok. il Pop Phot 51:112+ D '62
Facts & fables about single-lens reflexes. N. Rothschild. Pop Phot 52:111-13 Ap '63
Fantastic needle sharp super tele for SLR's; field model Questar. il Mod Phot 28:58-61+ Mr '64
1500mm telephoto for $15. il Mod Phot 28:86-7+ Ag '64
First complete guide to the art of zooming. E. Wildi. il Pop Phot 52:118-21+ My '63
First ever: wide-screen zoom; Konica 8-mm reflex. L. Drukker. il Pop Phot 55:110-11+ Jl '64
500-mm Zeiss Mirotar f/4.5; new mirror lens. C. Wright. il Pop Phot 52:115 Ap '63
Five photographers talk color & lenses; ed. by G. Pyle. il Pop Phot 54:82-91+ Ap '64
Four afternoons with a $40,000 lens. J. Durniak. il Pop Phot 54:66-7+ F '64
Four ghastly wide-angle lens errors and how to avoid them. H. Keppler. il Mod Phot 27:66-7 Ag '63
FRF, the supreme lens test. H. J. Schneider. il U S Camera 27:34+ N '64
Get sharp pictures with tele lenses. H. Keppler and E. Meyers. il Mod Phot 27:50-3 S '63
Get the picture; normal lens for rangefinder and SLR's. P. Caulfield. il Mod Phot 27:48+ My '63
Glamor: when you need a long lens. P. Gowland. il Pop Phot 53:24+ O '63
Has the zoom lens laid an optical egg? B. Sherman and H. Keppler. il Mod Phot 28:72-3+ Mr '64
How good are lens stretchers? M. Morrison. il U S Camera 27:56-7+ D '64
How good, how sharp are tele converters? H. Keppler. il Mod Phot 28:66-9+ Ag '64
How to build your lens collection. H. Keppler. il Mod Phot 27:75-83 O '63
How to stretch a lens. M. Bernam. il Pop Phot 53:78-9+ S '63
How wide can you get? M. Adler. il U S Camera 26:58-9+ S '63
Is it true? H. N. Todd and R. D. Zakia. Pop Phot 54:11-12 My '64
It brings the close in closer. J. A. Aita. il U S Camera 26:68-9 D '63
Keppler on the SLR. H. Keppler. il Mod Phot 28:28-9+ F '64
Keppler on the SLR; close-up lenses. H. Keppler. il Mod Phot 27:23-4+ Ap '63
Keppler on the SLR; dual range attachments, TelXtenders and other gadgets. il Mod Phot 28:12-13+ Mr '64
Keppler on the SLR; lens quality, lens testing, lens charts. H. Keppler. il Mod Phot 28:20+ D '64
Keppler on the SLR; long focus lenses. H. Keppler. il Mod Phot 27:10+ S '63
Keppler on the SLR; macro-micro lenses and close-up depth of field. H. Keppler. il Mod Phot 28:12+ S '64
Keppler on the SLR; tele lens coloring. H. Keppler. il Mod Phot 27:12+ Ag '63
Large camera (cont) A. Feininger. Mod Phot 27:54+ O; 28+ D '63
Large camera; choosing lenses from seven categories. A. Feininger. Mod Phot 27:28+ N '63
Lens faults: now you see them. . . E. Meyers and B. Sherman. il Mod Phot 28:80-1 Mr '64
Lenses for meters? B. Sherman and H. Keppler. il Mod Phot 28:75 Jl '64
Make your own accessory projector lens for less than $1.50. M. T. Reiter. il Pop Phot 54:86+ Je '64
Movie maker. M. A. Matzkin. Mod Phot 28:104+ Je '64
Movie maker; zoom lens and the tripod. M. A. Matzkin. il Mod Phot 27:94 Mr '63
Mutars: Rollei's answer to interchangeability. N. Rothschild. il Pop Phot 52:102-5 My '63
New TelXtender triples SLR len's focal length. L. Barry. il Pop Phot 55:98 S '64
Nikkorex zoom 35; first SLR camera with non-interchangeable zoom lens. il Pop Phot 52:118 Mr '63
1964 interchangeable lens guide; comp. by D. L. Miller. il Mod Phot 28:99+ O '64
1964-1965 directory and buying guide. il Pop Phot 56:2C-26C Ja '65
1963 interchangeable lens guide. Mod Phot 27:59+ O '63
Old lenses never die. M. Jaffe. il U S Camera 27:24 Ja '64
1000mm & more monocular. H. Keppler. il Mod Phot 28:90-1+ My '64
Paris, prisms and Picasso; photographs. D. D. Duncan. Sat Eve Post 237:24-37 Mr 7 '64
Photography: the Rube Goldberg business; lack of standardization. W. J. Sumits. Pop Phot 55:107 S '64
Photography's toughest-to-use lens; the wide-angle. B. Pierce. il Pop Phot 52:96-101+ My '63
Plastic lenses: good enough! L. Lipton. il Pop Phot 55:44-5+ Ag '64
Reaching four times as far. F. Henle. il Pop Phot 53:18 Ag '63
Russian 500-mm mirror reflex lens. K. Heyman. il Pop Phot 54:104-5+ Ja '64
SLR finders. B. Sherman. il Mod Phot 27:52-5+ Ap '63
Special lenses issue; symposium with editorial comment. il Pop Phot 54:56, 59-71+ Ap '64
Spiratone converter plus your lens. H. Keppler. il Mod Phot 27:72-3+ Mr '63
T system. H. Shaman. il Pop Phot 53:64-7 Jl '63
Techniques tomorrow; automation in camera and lens making. B. Sherman. Mod Phot 27:48+ N '63
Techniques tomorrow; development of high-speed lenses. B. Sherman. Mod Phot 28:52+ N '64
Techniques tomorrow; lens evaluation. B. Sherman. il Mod Phot 27:8-9+ My '63
Techniques tomorrow; lens tests. B. Sherman. il Mod Phot 27:24-5 Je '63
Techniques tomorrow; lenses for aerial Photography. B. Sherman. il Mod Phot 28:16-17 Mr '64
Techniques tomorrow; low-light. B. Sherman. il Mod Phot 28:16-17+ F '64
Techniques tomorrow; sharp image with tele lens. B. Sherman. Mod Phot 28:24+ Ag '64
Techniques tomorrow; superachromat lenses for color photography. B. Sherman. il Mod Phot 28:24-5+ My '64
Techniques tomorrow; ultra-wide-angle lenses. B. Sherman. il Mod Phot 28:62+ D '64
Tele? P. Caulfield. il Mod Phot 28:58-65 Ag '64
Test your lenses. D. L. Miller. il Mod Phot 28:78-9 S '64
35mm techniques. P. Stackpole. U S Camera 26:32-3 Je '63
35mm techniques; SLR? P. Stackpole. U S Camera 26:10+ My '63
Those super-speed lenses. B. Pierce. Pop Phot 54:109-10 Ap '64
Up the zoom; two ways to get bigger movie images. M. A. Matzkin. il Mod Phot 27:84-5+ F '63
Updated view of the Kilfitt system. N. Rothschild. il Pop Phot 54:136-9 Ja '64
Use a bellows for mouse to moon. H. Keppler. il Mod Phot 27:64-9 Ap '63
What a zoom lens does for you. R. L. Hering. il Pop Sci 184:122-4+ Ja '64
What focal length is best? N. Rothschild. il Pop Phot 53:142-3+ N '63
What's in a lens name? N. Rothschild. Pop Phot 54:110-11 Ap '64
When a trick is a treat. M. Morrison. il U S Camera 28:64 Ja '65
Wide angle lenses; how, what and why. J. Foldes. il U S Camera 26:52-7+ S '63

Distortion

See Photography—Distortion

Manufacture

Midway in the optics revolution. D. B. Eisendrath, jr. Pop Phot 54:59+ Ap '64

Testing

Techniques tomorrow. B. Sherman. Mod Phot 29:30-1 Ja '65
Which lens for better close-ups? H. Keppler. il Mod Phot 27:78-81 S '63

LENSES, Plastic
See also
Lenses, Photographic

LENSHINA, Alice
Alice in Lumpaland. il por Newsweek 64:38 Ag 17 '64
Alice is at it again. por Time 84:30 Ag 7 '64
Alice's new voice. Newsweek 64:42 Ag 24 '64
Voice of God. Newsweek 63:35 Ja 13 '64
You sons of God, listen. Time 84:20 Ag 21 '64

LENSKI, Lois
Creating books; condensation of address, May 1963. por Library J 88:3987-90+ O 15 '63

LENT
Autumnal Easter. Christian Cent 80:355 Mr 20 '63
Do penance; new Lenten regulations in La Crosse, Wis. America 110:244 F 22 '64
Lent begins in ashes. Christian Cent 80:259 F 27 '63
Lenten calisthenics. America 108:284 Mr 2 '63
Lenten lesson. America 108:355 Mr 16 '63
Manna for the desert; list of spiritual reading. America 110:227-8+ F 15 '64
Repenting and rejoicing; reading list. C. R. Andrews. Christian Cent 81:209 F 12 '64
Word (cont) V. P. McCorry. America 110:176-7 F 1 '64

LENTEN menus
Four tuna ideas for Lent. Sunset 130:218 Mr '63
Mahalia Jackson's Lenten recipe. F. De Knight. il Ebony 18:120+ Mr '63
New ideas for main dishes. V. T. Habeeb. il Am Home 67:58-9+ Mr '64

LENTINE, John
Architectural paintings of John Lentine. J. Lovoos. il por Am Artist 27:18-23 N '63

LENTZ, John J.
America's first woman physician. Todays Health 42:36-7+ Ja '64
Baths are more than soap and water. Todays Health 42:16+ N '64
Get rid of those bathroom booby traps! Todays Health 42:71 N '64
How medical progress has hastened the passing of the side show. Todays Health 42:48-51 Mr '64
Messages from your heart: the electrocardiogram. Todays Health 41:26-7+ Je '63
To exercise or not to exercise? Todays Health 41:28-9+ Mr '63

LENYA, Lotte
Music to my ears; evening of Kurt Weill at Carnegie Hall. I. Kolodin. Sat R 48:38 Ja 23 '65

LENZ, Sidney
Great bridge battle! C. H. Goren. il por McCalls 91:36+ O '63

LEO I, the Great, Saint, pope
Great confrontations: Leo the Great and Attila the Hun. C. V. Wedgwood. il Horizon 5:76-80 My '63

LEO, Brother
Will & two ways. por Time 82:64 N 22 '63

LEO, John
Council confidential. Commonweal 78:461-2 Jl 26 '63
DuBay case. Commonweal 80:477-82 Jl 10 '64
Kearns case. Commonweal 81:562-6 Ja 29 '65
Managing the news. Commonweal 81:5, 102 S 25, O 16 '64
On the peace circuit. Commonweal 79:123-4 O 25 '63
Pious disaster. Commonweal 80:225-6 My 15 '64
Postscript on L.A. Commonweal 80:529 Ag 7 '64
Segregated sickness. Commonweal 81:406-7 D 18 '64

LEO, M. W. M. and Walton, A.
Rhodium-102 fallout: variations in deposition and concentrations in precipitation. bibliog Science 140:1398-400 Je 28 '63

LEO A. Daly, company. See Daly, Leo A, company

LEODEGARIO
Leo de Garius fecit, 1179. A. de Egry. il Art N 62:34-7+ Ja '64

LEON, Myron A. and Yokohari, Ryuichi
Conglutination: specific inhibition by carbohydrates. bibliog Science 143:1327-8 Mr 20 '64

LEON & Bébert; story. See Connell, E. S. jr

LEONA, Sister Marian. See Marian Leona, Sister

LEONARD, Dwight, J. and Zavala, Albert
Electroconvulsive shock, retroactive amnesia, and the single-shock method. bibliog Science 146:1073-4 N 20 '64

LEONARD, Eliot
Order out of chaos? paperbacks and the twenty six categories. Pub W 185:43-4 Mr 16 '64

LEONARD, George B.
It's practical to be intellectual. por NEA J 52:31 My '63

LEONARD, Irving A.
Odyssey over the border. Sat R 46:37 O 12 '63

LEONARD, John
102 great ideas; no more, no less. Nat R 14:233-5 Mr 26 '63

LEONARD, Natalie, and Rohrke, M. C.
Amateur astronomy at Sacramento. Sky & Tel 25:82+ F '63

LEONARD, S. L. See Schane, H. P. jt. auth.

LEONARD, William J.
First fruits of the spirit. America 109:798-801 D 21 '63

LEONARDO da Vinci
Cover; Mona Lisa. il Am Artist 27:4+ Mr '63
Enchantress from the Louvre; the Mona Lisa. G. Kent. il Read Digest 83:176-8+ Jl '63
Escorting Mona Lisa to America. E. T. Folliard. il Nat Geog Mag 123:838-47 Je '63
Other Mona Lisa; Vernon Mona Lisa. J. Neary. il Life 57:11 Jl 31 '64
Poplar portrait; Mona Lisa painted on poplar wood. K. B. Pomeroy. il Am For 69:4+ Mr '63
That lady with a smile; youngsters speak out about the Mona Lisa. il N Y Times Mag p34 S 1 '63
Why they attack the Mona Lisa. S. Dali. il Art N 62:36+ Mr '63
World of Leonardo da Vinci: man of science, engineer, and dreamer of flight, by I. B. Hart. Review
Sci Am 208:169-70+ Je '63. J. Bronowski

LEONARDO da Vinci international airport. See Rome (city)—Airports

LEONARDS, G. A. See Woods, K. B. jt. auth.

LEONCAVALLO, Ruggiero
On records; La Bohème. Opera N 29:35 N 14 '64
On records; Pagliacci. Opera N 28:32 Ap 11 '64
Pagliacci. Criticism
Opera N il 28:17-20 Ap 11 '64
That other La Bohème. J. Maclain. il Am Rec G 30:928-9+ Je '64

LEONE, Arthur T.
Julian. Cath World 199:381-4 S '64
(ed) See West, M. L. Author in search of himself

LEONE-MOATS, Alice
Can anyone free Cardinal Mindszenty? Nat R 14:491-3 Je 18 '63
Riddle of Pope Paul VI. Nat R 15:347-9+ O 22 '63
Signor Fanfani's self-made bed. Nat R 14:404-5 My 21 '63

LEONE'S restaurant. See New York (city)—Hotels, restaurants, etc.

LEONHARD, Charles
Place of music. NEA J 52:40-2 Ap '63

LEONI, Rául
After Betancourt. il por Time 82:23 Jl 19 '63
Care & feeding of generals. il por Time 82:30 D 27 '63
Choice for Latin America: Castro threat or Leoni promise. il por Newsweek 63:34-6+ Mr 30 '64
Democratic precedent. por Newsweek 63:53 Mr 23 '64
Rómulo's successor: doing well. il por Time 84:35 Ag 7 '64
Si, amigo, ballots beat bullets in Venezuela. il por Sr Schol 84:13-15 F 7 '64
Test in Caracas. Reporter 29:12 D 19 '63
Time of jubilation. Time 83:29 Mr 20 '64

LEONIAN, Phillip
Nikonos: the toughest 35. U S Camera 27:58-9+ S '64
Rapid color processor. U S Camera 27:38-9 Ap '64

LEONIDOFF, Leon
Wonderworld. New Yorker 39:36-7 S 28 '63

LEONIDS. See Meteors

LEONTIEF, Wassily
Alternatives to armament expenditures; excerpts from address, December 1962. Bul Atomic Sci 20:19-21 Je '64
Proposal for better business forecasting; adaptation of address. Harvard Bsns R 42:166-7+ N '64
Structure of development; with biographical sketch. Sci Am 209:26, 148-54+ bibliog (p307) S '63

LEOPARD hunting
Leopard in large type. K. Roosevelt. il Outdoor Life 133:50-3+ Ap '64

LEOPARDS
Leopard. J. O'Connor. il Outdoor Life 134:40-3+ Ag '64
Trusted pet turns butcher in one bound. il Life 55:28-28A Ag 23 '63
See also
Leopons

LEOPOLD, A Starker, and others
War on America's wildlife. Aubudon Mag 66:228-33, 306-11 Jl-S '64
Wildlife managment in the national parks. Audubon Mag 65:166-71+ My '63

LEOPOLD, Jules
Four-minute challenges. Read Digest 86:160B Ja '65

LEOPOLD, Luna B.
Water in the world. UNESCO Courier 17:10-13 Jl '64
—See Thomas, H. E. jt. auth.
LEOPOLD, Nathan F.
Recent Chicago decision does not really clarify; case of Meyer Levin's Compulsion. H. F. Pilpel. Pub W 185:46-7 Je 29 '64
Rehabilitation of Nathan Leopold. L. Lyons. il pors Sat Eve Post 236:66-8 Je 1 '63
LEOPONS
Leopard+lion=leopon. B. Reynolds. il Look 28:78-9 D 1 '64
LEOS, Ed
Innocent camera. Sch Arts 63:8-15 Mr '64
LEPAN, Douglas V.
Dilemma of the Canadian author. Atlan 214:160-4 N '64
LEPANTO, Battle of, 1571
Lepanto. O. Warner. il Horizon 5:49 Jl '63
LEPERS. See Leprosy and lepers
LEPIDOPTERA
See also
Butterflies
LEPORSKA, Zoya
Summer musicals. D. Duncan. il pors Dance Mag 38:25-6 Jl '64
LEPP, Ignace
Church and atheists. Commonweal 81:88-90 O 16 '64
Varieties of non-religious experience. por Time 82:60 Jl 19 '63
LEPROSY and lepers
Angel of the Lazaros; E. Weaver. V. Prewett. Read Digest 83:143-4+ D '63
Lepers' lesson. J. Penn. Sat R 47:20 N 28 '64
Leprosy least catching of infectious diseases. Sci N L 85:232 Ap 11 '64
Let's remove the stigma from leprosy. L. G. Blochman. il Todays Health 43:30-3 Ja '65
New life in a leprosarium. T. Bodman. il Recreation 57:62 F '64
Paul Brand and his mission: healing and the pursuit of pain at a hospital in India. N. Cousins. il Sat R 47:21-3+ O 3 '64; Discussion. 47:25 N 21 '64; 48:21 Ja 30 '65
LEPROSY research
Leprosy germs grown in mouse foot pads. Sci N L 83:88 F 9 '63
LERMAN, Leo
Cake with 400 candles on it. Mlle 58:76-80+ F '64
Catch up with. See issues of Mademoiselle
Christmas classified. Mlle 60:138-41 N '64
Christmas gift! Mlle 58:64-5+ D '63
English look. Mlle 56:142-5 Ap '63
Lament for Broadway. Dance Mag 37:24-5 Je '63 (to be cont)
Let's travel. por Mlle 58:126-7 F '64
Most likely to succeed. Mlle 57:154-7 S '63
On bended knee. Mlle 56:98-9+ F '63
Revivals save the day. Dance Mag 37:27-9 Jl '63
Smart money in art. Mlle 59:64-8 Je '64
Something to talk about: most likely to succeed. Mlle 59:160-3 S '64
Visit to the antique world. Dance Mag 37:24-6 Ag '63
LERNER, A. Martin, and others
Ribosomal RNA in the developing chick embryo. bibliog Science 141:1187-8 S 20 '63
—See Gelb, L. D. jt. auth.
LERNER, Alan Jay
Oh, what a beautiful musical. N Y Times Mag p30-1+ My 12 '63
LERNER, Daniel
Soviet propaganda: its techniques, doctrines, and practices. Science 144:675-7 My 8 '64
Will European union bring about merged national goals? address, April 5, 1963; with questions and answers. Ann Am Acad 348:34-45 Jl '63
LERNER, Max
Love is possible. Mlle 56:83-4+ F '63
Promised land. por Time 85:67 Ja 15 '65
Return of the femme fatale. Ladies Home J 80:80-1+ Je '63
Taboo. por Time 82:93 N 22 '63
Way out of our strike dilemma. por Look 27:84+ Ap 23 '63; Same abr. with title Our strike dilemma. Read Digest 83:75-8 Jl '63
LERNER, Melvin
Marihuana; tetrahydrocannabinol and related compounds. bibliog Science 140:175 Ap 12 '63
LERNER, S. A. and others
Evolution of a catabolic pathway in bacteria. bibliog Science 146:1313-15 D 4 '64
LEROY, George V.
Carbon-14 in clinical research: report on conference. Science 144:731-2 My 8 '64
LESAGE, Laurent
Back on the roost after Proust. Sat R 46:33 Je 29 '63
Existentialist self-analysis. Sat R 47:34-5+ S 12 '64
Sin along the Seine. Sat R 47:34 Ag 8 '64
Strait was the gate to art. Sat R 46:39-40 N 16 '63
LESCH, George
Mr Hard Sell. il por Time 84:102+ D 4 '64
LESCHER, Ruth
Painless new way to detect breast cancer. Ladies Home J 80:13+ Ap '63
LESHAN, Eda J.
Helping children cope with stress. PTA Mag 58:7-9 bibliog(p35) Ja '64
Parent and child. N Y Times Mag p32 Jl 12; 104+ S 27; 114+ N 22 '64
Talking helps. Parents Mag 38:88 Ag '63
You have to say no! Parents Mag 38:38-9+ Ag '63
LESINSKI, John
Solid waste headache. Nation 198:615 Je 22 '64
LESINSKI, Thaddeus John
Forward in a fortnight? por Time 83:26 Mr 20 '64
LESIONS, Brain. See Brain
LESLIE, Arnett W.
Treat sewage as an area problem. Am City 78:169-70+ Je '63
LESLIE, Robert Franklin
Bear that came for supper. Read Digest 85:75-9 D '64
LESLIE, Sir Shane
Degeneracy or decadence? Nat R 15:445-6 N 19 '63
Jehovah. Nat R 14:163 F 26 '63
Lloyd George at close quarters. Nat R 14:458-9 Je 4 '63
Matched with his hour. Nat R 16:776+ S 8 '64
Men and manners. Nat R 16:918-20 O 20 '64
Royal archives proved lean. Nat R 16:497-8 Je 16 '64
Shattered glory. Nat R 15:111 Ag 13 '63
LESLIE, Warren
Tips. Pub W 185:80 F 3 '64
LESLIE-MOORE, Latham
White sultan. C. Miller. il por Sat Eve Post 236:80+ Ap 20 '63
LESSER, Simon O.
L'avventura: a closer look. Yale R 54:41-50 O '64
LESSER ANTILLES. See West Indies
LESSEY, Ruth
Living with antiques. Antiques 86:188-91 Ag '64
LESSING, Doris May
All seething underneath; excerpt from In pursuit of the English. Vogue 143:80-1+ F 15 '64
Doris Lessing's free women. F. Howe. Nation 200:34-7 Ja 11 '65
Play with a tiger. Criticism
New Yorker 40:86 Ja 9 '65
LESSING, Lawrence
Breaking TV out of its box. Fortune 70:150-3+ S '64
Forty miles of information every day from space. Fortune 69:116-22+ Ja '64
Laser's dazzling future. Fortune 67:138-42+ Je '63
Laws alone can't make drugs safe. Fortune 67:122-5+ Mr '63
Science journalism: the coming age. Bul Atomic Sci 19:23 D '63
Sleep. Fortune 69:122-5+ Je '64
Synthetics ride hell-bent for leather. Fortune 70:172-5+ N '64
Transistorized M.D. Fortune 68:130-4+ S '63
LESSON; drama. See Ionesco, E.
LESTOIL products, incorporated
Lestoil: the road back. il Bsns W p 118+ Je 15 '63
LESTRIGONIAN; story. See Kayon, J.
LESURE, Thomas B.
Land of the kiwis. Travel 122:26-30 S; 45-50 O '64
Mexican weekends. Travel 123:44-7 Ja '65
Motorambling in Hawaii. Travel 122:26-9+ D '64
New York's state parks. Travel 121:50-2 Mr '64
U.S. city weekends. Travel 120:28-32+ Jl '63
LET us a-quarreling go; story. See Kolb, K.
LETCHER, John S. jr
Singlehanded to Hawaii. Yachting 115:87-9+ Ja; 58-60+ F '64
LETELLIER, Phyllis
Perils and rewards of a rancher's wife. Suc Farm 62:49+ Jl '64

LETH, Carol
What to expect from your deodorant. Todays Health 41:13+ Je '63
LETHAL genes. See Genes
LETORNEY, Joseph A.
How local associations do it. NEA J 53:56 Mr '64
LETSON, John W.
In Atlanta schools. NEA J 52:46-7 D '63
LETTER home; story. See Davis, R. P.
LETTER paper. See Stationery
LETTER sorting. See Mail handling
LETTER; story. See Brooke, D.
LETTER to Doctor Edvig; story. See Bellow, S.
LETTER writing
Default of the educated man. N. Cousins. Sat R 46:18 Je 29 '63
How a lady answers a letter; sample letters from Hill's manual of social and business forms. il Am Heritage 15:112 F '64
How to write better. il Changing T 17:39-42 Jl '63; Same abr. with title How to say it in writing. Read Digest 84:25-6+ F '64
I've been meaning to write. D. C. Peattie. Read Digest 82:228D-228E My '63
Letters are more fun to get. il Seventeen 22: 152-3 S '63
Letters to boys; excerpt from Seventeen book of etiquette and entertaining. E. A. Haupt. Seventeen 23:16 Jl '64
Postman never rings, period. J. L. O'Neill. il Am Home 68:9 Ja '65
They're writing till it hurts us; pupils' letters. R. F. Flahive. il NEA J 52:57 S '63
See also
Commercial correspondence
International correspondence
Anecdotes, facetiae, satire, etc.
Repairman bites back. N. C. Farewell. il Atlan 213:127 Je '64
LETTERHEADS
Image-building by letterhead. P. D. Eimon. il Am City 79:140+ F '64
News paper for country letters. il Vogue 141: 190-2 My '63
LETTERING
Father of letter forms; Trajan column. G. Barford. il Sch Arts 64:29-32 D '64
Lettering for the public image. M. Gray and R. Armstrong. il Design 64:120-3 Ja '63
Love and joy about letters, by B. Shahn. Review
New Repub 150:25-6 Ja 25 '64. F. Getlein
Project-a-plan instant signs; using transparencies. D. M. Swartwout. il Pop Mech 120:144-6 O '63
See also
Monograms
LETTERING on book covers. See Book covers
LETTERS
Activators needed; importance of letters. America 109:228 S 7 '63
How to collect autograph letters and manuscripts. W. A. Myers. Hobbies 68:110-12+ Je '63
Letters of sympathy to Mrs John F. Kennedy. McCalls 91:82-3 Je '64
Please write; quotations, comp. by E. S. Ringold. N Y Times Mag p38 Je 23 '63
Private words and public art. H. Carruth. Nation 197:418-19 D 14 '63
They're writing till it hurts us; pupils' letters. R. F. Flahive. il NEA J 52:57 S '63
See also
Copyright—Letters
International correspondence
Letter writing
Love letters
Anecdotes, facetiae, satire, etc.
Merry Christmas from the Smiths! F. Lanahan. New Yorker 39:32-3 D 21 '63
LETTERS by children
Children's letters to Jacqueline Kennedy and her children. il Redbook 123:50-1+ My '64
Dear Mrs Kennedy; personal mail. M. V. Thayer. il Ladies Home J 80:76-7 My '63
Please answer this. . . E. Yates. Horn Bk 39:162-4 Ap '63
LETTERS from service men
Lure of soldiers' letters. P. F. Hoag. Hobbies 68:110-12 My '63
LETTERS of application. See Applications for positions
LETTERS of reference. See Recommendations for positions
LETTERS of the alphabet. See Alphabet
LETTERS to congressmen. See Lobbying
LETTERS to the editor. See Periodicals—Letters to the editor
LETTERS to the President. See Presidents—United States—Correspondence
LETTERSET printing. See Printing, Offset
LETTON, Jeannette
Glorious sun story. Redbook 123:123-50 Jl '64
LETTOW-VORBECK, Paul von
Bush fox of Africa. E. Kern. il por Life 56: 87-8+ My 8 '64
LETTUCE
Growing your own lettuce. il Sunset 132:238+ Mr '64
Most popular salad vegetable. B. Brinhart. il Pop Gard 14:40+ Ap '63
Ship lettuce in CA rail trailers. il Farm J 88:50H Ja '64
LETTUCE harvesting machinery. See Harvesting machinery
LETWIN, William
Pick the middle road for success. Nations Bsns 52:76-7 Ag '64
What's wrong with planning: the case of India. Fortune 67:118-21+ Je '63
LEUCHTENBURG, Dennis
Testing is a big part of teaching. NEA J 53:55-6 O '64
LEUCHTENBURG, William
Baron of the Northwest. Sat R 46:87 Mr 16 '63
Chaotic heritage. Life 56:84+ Je 5 '64
LEUCOCYTES
Adhesion and emigration of leukocytes produced by cationic proteins of lysosomes. A. Janoff and B. W. Zweifach. bibliog il Science 144:1456-8 Je 19 '64
Chromosome abnormalities in vitro in human leukocytes associated with Schmidt-Ruppin Rous sarcoma virus. W. W. Nichols and others. bibliog il Science 146:248-50 O 9 '64
Genetic studies on the mixed leukocyte reaction. B. Bain and L. Lowenstein. bibliog il Science 145:1315-16 S 18 '64
Virus-containing leukocytes in polioencephalitis. E. Nelson and others. bibliog il Science 139:499-501 F 8 '63
LEUCORRHEA
For a female complaint effective trichomonacide taken by mouth. Time 81:74+ Mr 29 '63
LEUCOSIS virus. See Viruses
LEUCOTHRIX mucor. See Bacteria, Marine
LEUKEMIA
Acute leukemia control. F. Marley. Sci N L 84:309 N 16 '63
Cancer immunity possible. Sci N L 86:69 Ag 1 '64
Chromosome aberrations: their role in the etiology of murine leukemia. M. A. Rich and others. bibliog il Science 146:252-3 O 9 '64
DNA contents of chromosome Ph^1 and chromosome 21 in human chronic granulocytic leukemia. G. T. Rudkin and others. bibliog il Science 144:1229-32 Je 5 '64
Death comes to a cancer virus. L. Engel. il N Y Times Mag p25+ N 8 '64
Hope for leukemia cure seen in cancer research. Sci N L 83:217 Ap 6 '63
I'm not unlucky: great football player's statement of faith. E. Davis and B. August. Sat Eve Post 236:60-2 Mr 30 '63
Immunity and susceptibility toward cheek pouch transplants of a mouse leukemia. R. A. Adams. bibliog il Science 146:944-5 N 13 '64
Leukemia. E. Frei, 3d. and E. J. Freireich. il Sci Am 210:88-96 bibliog(p 150+) My '64
Leukemia breakthrough. M. J. O'Neill. McCalls 90:48 Jl '63
Leukemia: key to the cancer puzzle? P. McGrady. il Sci Digest 53:31-6 Je '63
Medical research: Congress adds $10 million to president's budget for special studies on leukemia. E. Langer. Science 146:236+ O 9 '64
Mongolism, leukemia link. F. Marley. Sci N L 83:151 Mr 9 '63
More evidence on leukemia. Time 82:68 O 18 '63
New hope in the fight against leukemia. Good H 158:161-3 Ap '64
One, quite small, statistics. Read Digest 82: 217-18 Ap '63
Patient to patient. Time 82:78 N 15 '63
Radiation-induced mouse leukemia: consistent occurrence of an extra and a marker chromosome. N. Wald and others. bibliog il Science 143:810-13 F 21 '64
Thymus gland blamed for causing leukemia. Sci N L 86:195 S 26 '64
Thymus, leukemia linked. Sci N L 84:50 Jl 27 '63
Tracking down leukemia. Bsns W p37 S 26 '64

LEUKEMIA—*Continued*
Tracking leukemia. il Newsweek 63:68 F 17 '64
Triumph of Janis Babson; excerpts from Little girl's gift. L. Elliott. Read Digest 82:275-86+ Je '63
Virus hunters; research drive. il Newsweek 64:103-4 S 21 '64
Virus-like particles in blood of two acute leukemia patients. J. D. Almeida and others. bibliog il Science 142:1487-9 D 13 '63
Virus-like substance causes leukemia. Sci N L 83:297 My 11 '63
Why some catch leukemia. Sci Digest 55:61-2 Ja '64
Wonderful legacy of Dr Bob McCarthy. A. Hirshberg. il Good H 156:68-9+ Mr '63

Therapy

Fifteen years of progress against leukemia. W. R. Vath. il Todays Health 41:30-3+ O '63
High hope for a leukemia cure. Bsns W p52 Je 6 '64
Hydroxyurea: mechanism of action. W. N. Fishbein and P. P. Carbone. bibliog Science 142:1069-70 N 22 '63
Leukemia cure near? Sci N L 86:215 O 3 '64
Leukemia drug helpful. W. Wingo. Sci N L 83:355 Je 8 '63
Leukemic woman lives more than seven years. Sci N L 83:393 Je 22 '63
Persistent mitosis of transfused homologous leukocytes in children receiving antileukemic therapy. R. H. Levin and others. bibliog il Science 142:1305-6+ D 6 '63
Picking the best marrow. Time 83:42+ Ja 17 '64

Vaccines

Anti-leukemia vaccine reported hope of future. Sci N L 85:306 My 16 '64

LEUKEMIA viruses
Density gradient centrifugation of a murine leukemia virus. T. E. O'Connor and others. bibliog il Science 144:1144-7 My 29 '64
Human leukemia virus. F. Marley. il Sci N L 85:173 Mr 14 '64
Leukemia virus sought. F. Marley. il(p 193) Sci N L 86:195 S 26 '64
Niles cluster. il Newsweek 61:88-9 Ap 22 '63
Physical interaction of a murine leukemia virus with influenza virus in vitro. T. E. O'Connor and F. J. Rauscher. bibliog il Science 146:787-90 N 6 '64
Resistance of mice infected with Moolney leukemia virus to Friend virus infection. W. P. Rowe. bibliog il Science 141:40-1 Jl 5 '63
Tracking leukemia. il Newsweek 63:68 F 17 '64

LEUKOCYTES. See Leucocytes

LEUKORRHEA. See Leucorrhea

LEUKOSIS in poultry. See Poultry—Diseases and pests

LEUSER, Eleanore
Magic well; drama. Plays 22:91-5 My '63

LEUTZE, Emanuel
Why Washington stood up in the boat; with reproduction of painting and memoir by W. Whittredge. G. F. Scheer. por Am Heritage 16:17-19 D '64

LEVANT, Howard
Fired; poem. Yale R 52:561-2 Je '63

LEVARIE, Siegmund
Italian province. Opera N 28:6-11 Ap 18 '64

LEVEAU, Carl Walter
Looking back at PT production. Motor B 112:30+ Jl '63

LEVEL of aspiration. See Aspiration level

LEVENSON, Sam
Out of print. Read Digest 82:24E My '63

LEVEQUE, James
Thriller in a stricken plane; Scotch and diapers went, but dolls and Bibles stayed. Life 54:38B Mr 29 '63

LEVER brothers and Unilever. See Unilever, limited

LEVER brothers company
Great soap opera. il Newsweek 61:75 F 18 '63
Will Lever bros. lose all? R. Goodman. Nation 196:138-9 F 16 '63

LEVERS
Levers; labor-saving devices. il Sci Digest 55:39-41 My '64

LEVERTOV, Denise
Arena where we fight. Nation 197:440-1 D 21 '63
Claritas; Leaving forever; In abeyance; Crack; Eros at temple stream; Cure of souls; Resolve; poems. Poetry 102:211-16 Jl '63
Disclosure; poem. Nation 196:340 Ap 27 53
Eight poems: Prayer; Losing track; In mind; About marriage; Melody Grundy; Looking-glass; Our bodies; Runes. Poetry 103:66-73 O '63
Into the interior; poem. Nation 197:164 S 21 '63
Old Adam; poem. Nation 196:101 F 2 '63
One of the lucky. Nation 196:310 Ap 13 '63
Play with words. Nation 198:126 F 3 '64
Poem; Who is at my window, who, who? Nation 197:19 Jl 6 '63
William Carlos Williams. Nation 196:230 Mr 16 '63

about

Five poets. R. Howard. Poetry 101:414-15 Mr '63

LÉVESQUE, René
Words and action. Newsweek 63:54 My 25 '64

LEVEY, Martin. See Mellichamp, J. W. jt. auth.

LEVEY, Raphael H.
Thymus hormone; with biographical sketch. Sci Am 211:14, 66-71+ bibliog(p 142) Jl '64
—and others
Lymphocytic choriomeningitis infection in neonatally thymectomized mice bearing diffusion chambers containing thymus. bibliog Science 142:483-5 O 25 '63

LEVEY, Stanley
Rhetoric of Walter Reuther. Reporter 28:26-8 Mr 14 '63

LEVI, Robert H.
Do shoppers need help from the government? Changing T 18:7-12 Ag '64

LEVI, Werner
China and the United Nations. Cur Hist 47:149-55+ S '64
Sino-Indian border war. Cur Hist 45:136-43 S '63

LEVI-MONTALCINI, Rita
Growth control of nerve cells by a protein factor and its antiserum. bibliog Science 143:105-10 Ja 10 '64

LÉVI-STRAUSS, Claude
Rousseau, father of anthropology; summary of address. UNESCO Courier 16:10-15 Mr '63

LEVIN, Bernard
Paying guest. por Time 81:64+ Mr 22 '63

LEVIN, David
Autobiography of Benjamin Franklin: the Puritan experimenter in life and art. Yale R 53:258-75 D '63

LEVIN, Herbet
Broadway beehive: Herbet's theatrical dance supplies. W. Como. il por Dance Mag 37:54-5 Mr '63

LEVIN, Jane Whitbread
Parent and child. N Y Times Mag p 106+ N 17; 105-6 D 1; 100 D 8; 22 D 29 '63; 52 F 9 '64
(ed) See Chukovsky, K. From the world of Ivan jr.

LEVIN, Jonathan
Export economies between East and West. Yale R 52:373-84 Mr '63

LEVIN, Karen
Parent and child. N Y Times Mag p41-2 Ag 2 '64

LEVIN, Kim
Anything goes at the Carnegie. Art N 63:34-6+ D '64
Kiesler and Mondrian, art into life. Art N 63:38-41+ My '64
Pharaohs and fashion. Art N 62:32-3+ Ja '64

LEVIN, Martin
(ed) Phoenix nest. See issues of Saturday review

LEVIN, Millea
Our guest editors, August, '63. Mlle 57:210-11 Ag '63

LEVIN, Morton L.
Direct mail for retail bookstores. Pub W 186:53-5 S 21 '64

LEVIN, Nora
Needed: a new GI bill; the neglected vets. Nation 196:171-3 Mr 2 '63
Religious conflicts in Israel. Commonweal 79:344-6 D 13 '63

LEVIN, Phyllis Lee
Parent and child. N Y Times Mag p89-90 D 6 '64

LEVIN, Robert H. and others
Persistent mitosis of transfused homologous leukocytes in children receiving antileukemic therapy. bibliog Science 142:1305-6+ D 6 '63

LEVINE, David
Four realists: a review. F. Whitaker. il Am Artist 28:54-61+ O '64

LEVINE, Henry
Parents' questions about music lessons; interview, ed. by H. Littledale. Parents Mag 39:48-9+ My '64

LEVINE, Isaac Don
New look at Russia from the inside; interview. por U S News 55:92-3 Ag 26 '63
LEVINE, Joseph E.
Films. D. Macdonald. Esquire 59:36+ Ap '63
Joe Levine's crash diet. il Esquire 63:99 Ja '65
Supercolossal, well, pretty good, world of Joe Levine. K. Hamill. il por Fortune 69:130-2+ Mr '64
LEVINE, Lita
Girl who refused to die. E. M. Wylie. il por Good H 158:92-3+ My '64
LEVINE, Myron, and Smith, H. O.
Sequential gene action in the establishment of lysogeny. bibliog Science 146:1581-2 D 18 '64
LEVINE, Norman D.
Zoonoses. Science 143:1464-6 Mr 27 '64
LEVINE, Philip
It's mother; poem. Poetry 104:355-6 S '64
My poets; Horse; poems. Poetry 102:163-5 Je '63
Underestimations. X. J. Kennedy. Poetry 103: 331-2 F '64
LEVINE, Philip T. and others
Collagenous layer covering the crown enamel of unerupted permanent human teeth. bibliog Science 146:1676-8 D 25 '64
LEVINE, Robert A.
Open letter from a military intellectual to a sophisticated liberal leader. Bul Atomic Sci 20:24-7 S '64
LEVINE, Rosalind
Surrealist tree; poem. Sat R 46:39 Jl 13 '63
LEVINE, Samuel A.
Exercise and heart disease. Atlan 212:42-5 Jl '63
LEVINE, Seymour
Cerebral white matter: selective spread of pneumococcal polysaccharides. bibliog Science 139:605-6 F 15 '63
—and Mullins, Richard, jr
Estrogen administered neonatally affects adult sexual behavior in male and female rats. bibliog Science 144:185-7 Ap 10 '64
—and Wenk, E. J.
Allergic encephalomyelitis: a hyperacute form. bibliog Science 146:1681-2 D 25 '64
Allergic encephalomyelitis: rapid induction without the aid of adjuvants. bibliog Science 141:529-30 Ag 9 '63
LEVINE, Solomon B.
Labor in a prosperous Japan. bibliog f Cur Hist 46:212-18 Ap '64
LE VINESS, W. Thetford
George Lopez; a carver of santos. Am Artist 27:25-9+ Ap '63
LEVINSON, Deirdre
Boris; story. Commentary 37:40-8 Je '64
In acknowledgement of a chief rabbi; story. Commentary 35:320-5 Ap '63
LEVINSON, Harry
Turn anger into an asset. Nations Bsns 52: 82-4+ My '64
What killed Bob Lyons? Harvard Bsns R 41: 127-42+ Ja '63
LEVINSON, Norma
There was a time; story. Redbook 121:58-9 Jl '63
LEVIS, Michael P.
Making of a surgeon. J. Star. il pors Look 28:58-62+ Mr 24 '64
LEVISTER, Wendell W.
High-flying soldier of fortune. A. Peters. il pors Ebony 19:37-8+ Je '64
LEVIT, Michel
Building a profit circuit out of antique tubes. il por Bsns W p 118-19 N 21 '64
LEVITAN, Sar A.
Characteristics of urban depressed areas; excerpt from federal aid to depressed areas. Mo Labor R 87:48-52 Ja '64
LEVITEN, David
I am the self-consumer of my woes; poem. Nation 198:60 Ja 13 '64
LEVITT, Eugene E. See Brady, J. P. jt. auth.
LEVITT, Jacob, and others
Cytoecology of temperature. Science 141:1199-200+ S 20 '63
LEVITT, Theodore
Creativity is not enough. bibliog f Harvard Bsns R 41:72-83 My '63
When science supplants technology. Harvard Bsns R 41:14-16+ Jl '63
LEVITT and sons, incorporated
Levitt's ville: housing projects in France. Newsweek 63:70 Je 22 '64
LEVOY, Myron
Great-uncle Gadby; poem. Ladies Home J 80:99 Je '63
LEVY, Alan
A B B of Alan Schneider. N Y Times Mag p27+ O 20 '63
Artifacts of adulation. Reporter 30:40-3 F 13 '64
Bits and pieces of J. Monk. N Y Times Mag p45+ Ja 10 '65
Drama beyond the drama: first-night vigil. N Y Times Mag p 12+ D 22 '63
Fifty-eight-second film festival. Reporter 28: 39-40+ Je 20 '63
How to fight city hall. Redbook 122:61+ Ap '64
Industry dons sock and buskin. Reporter 31: 44+ S 10 '64
Machine-made love. Mile 60:72-3+ Ja '65
Second balcony: a nostalgic ode. N Y Times Mag p20+ Je 16 '63
This ho-ho-ho business. Sat Eve Post 237:20-1 D 12 '64
Would-be writer industry. Reporter 29:48+ O 24 '63
LEVY, Carol
Washington: who's got the action? Duns R 81:pt2 S137-8+ Je '63
LEVY, Charles J.
Scripts on strike; the race-wage picket line. Nation 200:31-2 Ja 11 '65
LEVY, Ferdinand K. and others
ABC's of the critical path method; excerpts from Industrial scheduling. bibliog f Harvard Bsns R 41:98-108 S '63
LEVY, Frederick M.
Finest public photographic facilities. Am City 78:28 Jl '63
LEVY, George Morton
If it moves, said George, they'll bet on it. B. Ottum. il por Sports Illus 21:30-2+ Jl 27 '64
LEVY, Henri A. See Brown, G. M. jt. auth.
LEVY, Marvin David
Quote-unquote; interview, ed. by C. S. Susa. por Mus Am 84:20 N '64
LEVY, Matthys P. and others
Role of the computer in engineering practice. Arch Rec 134:158-61 Ag '63
LEVY, Sidney J. See Boyd, H. W. jr, jt. auth.
LEVY, Stan
Isolate nature's forms. il U S Camera 27:68-9 Jl '64
LEVY, Uriah Phillips
I yam what I yam. Newsweek 62:92 S 16 '63
LEW, Lynda
Engraving on glass. Recreation 62:11 Je '63
LEWANDOWSKI, Bohdan
Trade and other economic problems considered by General assembly. por U N Rev 10:43-5+ Ja '63
LEWENTHAL, Raymond
Berlioz of the piano. Mus Am 84:44 F '64
Through a prism. Mus Am 84:49 Mr '64
LEWIN, Frank
Creating a sound film. U S Camera 26:76-7+ Mr; 30-1 Ap; 24-5+ My '63
In praise of tape recording. U S Camera 26:73+ Mr '63
LEWINTER, Oswald
Theatre of the grotesque. Nation 199:94-6 S 7 '64
LEWIS, Anthony
Annals of law. New Yorker 40:144+ Ap 25; 108+ My 2; 150+ My 9 '64
Case of trial by press. N Y Times Mag p31+ O 18 '64
Footnote on Florida. New Repub 148:9 My 11 '63
March toward equality; excerpt from Portrait of a decade. Atlan 214:58-64 S '64
New look at the Chief Justice. N Y Times Mag p9+ Ja 19 '64
Nine very human men. N Y Times Mag p 18+ Ja 17 '65
Race, sex and the Supreme court. N Y Times Mag p30+ N 22 '64
Sex and the Supreme court. Esquire 59:82-3+ Je '63
Shriver moves into the front rank. N Y Times Mag p21+ Mr 15 '64
Since the Supreme court spoke. N Y Times Mag p9+ My 10 '64
Speaking out. por Sat Eve Post 237:12+ S 26 '64
What drives Bobby Kennedy. N Y Times Mag p34+ Ap 7 '63

about

Lewis's trumpet. por Newsweek 64:53 Ag 24 '64
Modern journalism. New Repub 148:5 My 18 '63
LEWIS, Benjamin F.
Return of the rub-out: murder of Chicago's Alderman Lewis. il Time 81:28 Mr 8 '63
LEWIS, C. Day-. See Day-Lewis, C.

LEWIS, Charles
Tulips old and new at Sterling Forest. Horticulture 42:26-7+ My '64
You can fool them into early blooming. Flower Grower 51:39-40 Je '64
LEWIS, Charles S.
Detroit high school challenges nation. H. J. Bims. il por Ebony 19:25-8+ Ag '64
LEWIS, Clive Staples
On three ways of writing for children; reprint. Horn Bk 39:459-69 O '63
Speaking out. por Sat Eve Post 236:10+ D 21 '63
about
C. S. Lewis: 1898-1963. J. Hart. Nat R 16: 240+ Mr 24 '64
Defender of the faith. por Time 82:57 D 6 '63
Dialogue with deity. N. A. Scott, jr. Sat R 47:41 Mr 7 '64
My Oxford tutor, C. S. Lewis. G. Bailey. Reporter 30:37-8+ Ap 23 '64
News from Narnia. L. H. Smith. Horn Bk 39: 470-3 O '63
Obituary
Pub W 184:28 D 9 '63
LEWIS, David
3,000 miles of solitude. por Yachting 116:48-50+ O '64
LEWIS, Donald J. and Adams, H. E.
Retrograde amnesia from conditioned competing responses. Science 141:516-17 Ag 9 '63
LEWIS, E. B.
Leukemia, multiple myeloma, and aplastic anemia in American radiologists. bibliog Science 142:1492-4 D 13 '63
LEWIS, Edward
Kennedy: profile of a technician; with editorial comment. Nation 196:81, 92-4 F 2 '63
Political problems. Nation 197:409-11 D 14 '63
President and the press. Nation 198:207-9 Mr 2 '64
LEWIS, Eugene
Gold and silver waltz; two Texas anniversaries. Mus Am 83:14-15+ O '63
LEWIS, F. Dwain. See Lindeburg, F. A. jt. auth.
LEWIS, Flora
Separate papers. por Newsweek 61:91 Ap 22 '63
Ubiquitous, multifarious Sellers. N Y Times Mag p20+ Je 23 '63
LEWIS, Frederick
Britons succumb to Beatlemania. N Y Times Mag p 124-6 D 1 '63
LEWIS, Harland G.
Honest to God reformation. Christian Cent 81:736-8 Je 3 '64
LEWIS, Harold W.
Ball lightning. Sci Am 208:106-8+ bibliog(p 190+) Mr '63
LEWIS, Hazel, and Harary, Isaac
Calcium-activated adenosine triphosphatase localization in cultured beating heart cells. bibliog Science 141:47-8 Jl 5 '63
LEWIS, Jerry
Public loves him. por Newsweek 63:92+ F 17 '64
Search for Jerry Lewis. E. Linn. il pors Sat Eve Post 236:83-7 O 12 '63
LEWIS, John Llewellyn
Familiar voice with a new warning; excerpts from address, April 3, 1963. por U S News 54:20 Ap 15 '63
about
Coal: when machines took over. il por U S News 54:69-73 Ap 29 '63
John L. Lewis and the mine workers. A. H. Raskin. Atlan 211:53-8 My '63
One pension plan where things are going from bad to worse. por U S News 54:121-3 Mr 25 '63
LEWIS, John Prior
Kennedy hires one of his critics. por Bsns W p78+ My 18 '63
LEWIS, Joseph
California: a wild card in the deck. Reporter 31:29+ O 22 '64
LEWIS, M. M.
How speech grows. PTA Mag 59:8-10 bibliog (p35) N '64
LEWIS, Martha S.
Faith tree. Horticulture 41:107 F '63
LEWIS, Mary
Foster-family care: has it fulfilled its promise? bibliog f Ann Am Acad 355:31-41 S '64
LEWIS, Meriwether
I gave him barks and saltpeter. P. R. Cutright. bibliog il por Am Heritage 15:58-61+ D '63
LEWIS, Mildred, and Lewis, Milton
Lessons in going native. Sat R 47:63-4+ O 10 '64
—See Lewis, Milton, jt. auth.
LEWIS, Milton, and Lewis, Mildred
Strange justice for the judge's son. Sat Eve Post 237:75-9 Ja 4 '64
—See Lewis, Mildred, jt. auth.
LEWIS, Nolan D.
Desert is my beat. il pors Ebony 19:134-6+ Ap '64
LEWIS, Norman
Profiles. New Yorker 39:42-4+ F 8; 39-40+ F 15; 40:35-6+ F 22 '64
LEWIS, Odell
Ruffled race across a mirror; Miami-Nassau ocean power boat race. A. Zich. il Sports Illus 18:22-5 My 6 '63
LEWIS, Oscar
After the revolution; excerpt from Pedro Martínez, a Mexican peasant and his family. Reporter 30:34-6+ Ap 9 '64
In New York you get swallowed by a horse. Commentary 38:69-73 N '64
Tender violence of Pedro Martínez, a Mexican peasant and his family. Harper 228:54-60 F '64
LEWIS, Richard
And quiet shines the sun. Bul Atomic Sci 20:30-2 Ja '64
Antarctic dilemma. Bul Atomic Sci 19:37-9 F '63
Arizona compromise. Bul Atomic Sci 20:45-7 Ap '64
At sea on the moon. Bul Atomic Sci 20:35-7 N '64
LEWIS, Richard Warren
Baby doll grows up. Sat Eve Post 236:62-5 N 2 '63
Fair young Hollywood girls. Sat Eve Post 236:22-7 S 7 '63
Flashy lawyer for Oswald's killer. Sat Eve Post 237:28-30 F 8 '64
Golden hillbillies. Sat Eve Post 236:30+ F 2 '63
Hollywood's carefree child. Sat Eve Post 237: 32-4 My 9 '64
Inger Stevens. Sat Eve Post 237:20-1 Ja 4 '64
Lessons of Project Mercury. Bul Atomic Sci 19:51-3 D '63
Syncom syndrome. Bul Atomic Sci 19:43-5 O '63
TV troubles of Judy Garland. Sat Eve Post 236:92-5 D 7 '63
Tuesday past, Tuesday present. Sat Eve Post 237:28-30+ Ap 11 '64
Unsinkable Debbie Reynolds. Sat Eve Post 237:74-5+ Ag 22 '64
Year in the life of Edie Adams. Sat Eve Post 236:24-7 Ap 13 '63
LEWIS, Roger
Rescue. il por Time 83:80 Je 5 '64
LEWIS, Sinclair
Dorothy and Red, by V. Sheean. Review
Newsweek por 62:110 N 18 '63
Sat R 46:35-6 N 16 '63. G. Hicks
Time il por 82:119+ N 15 '63
Tangled romance of Sinclair Lewis and Dorothy Thompson; excerpt from Dorothy and Red. V. Sheean. il pors Harper 227:121-72 O '63; Reply. D. Argow. 227:4 D '63
LEWIS, Ted. See Lewis, Edward
LEWIS, Ted, jr
New horizons for nursing homes. Todays Health 41:56-7+ Ap '63
LEWIS, Theophilus
Reviewer's notebook. America 109:123 Ag 3 '63
Theatre. See issues of America
LEWIS, Thomas E. family
This young family lives from lot line to lot line. H. Mason. il pors Bet Hom & Gard 41:52-3 My '63
LEWIS, Virginia E. and Chambers, Hansl
New, new guard of the GOP. Nation 199: 85-8 S 7 '64
LEWIS, Wyndham
Good artist but a bad friend. H. Read. por Sat R 47:29+ Ap 4 '64
Polished and robust. F. Clinton. Nat R 16: 362+ My 5 '64
Rebel against the senses. por Time 83:108+ Ap 3 '64
Wars of Wyndham Lewis. G. Greene. Commonweal 80:195-7 My 8 '64
LEWIS and Clark centennial exposition, 1905. See Portland, Ore.—Lewis and Clark centennial exposition
LEWIS and Clark expedition
I gave him barks and saltpeter. P. R. Cutright. bibliog il Am Heritage 15:58-61+ D '63
LEWIS research center. See United States—National aeronautics and space administration—Lewis research center

LEWIS WITH HARRIS (island)
See also
Callernish, Scotland
LEWISOHN stadium concerts. See New York (city)—Music
LEWISON, Florence
Theodore Robinson, America's first impressionist. Am Artist 27:40-5+ F '63
Uniqueness of Albert Bierstadt. Am Artist 28:28-33+ S '64
LEWISTON, Idaho
If your town smells, stop breathing. P. Hirsch. New Repub 150:7-8 Mr 14 '64
LEWITIN, Landes
Lewitin: cabalist fabulist. L. Campbell. il por Art N 63:28-30+ Ja '65
LEWTER, Rufus C. jr
Dancing doctor. il pors Ebony 18:33-7 F '63
LEWY, Guenter
Pius XII, the Jews, and the German Catholic church. bibliog Commentary 37:23-35 F '64
LEXAU, Joan M.
Story of the three bears and the man who didn't write it. Horn Bk 40:88-94 F '64
LEXINGTON, Ky.
Lighting
Colonial lighting adds beauty and safety. il Am City 78:145 Je '63
LEXINGTON, Mass.
EB school library award. S. Jaffarian. Wilson Lib Bul 39:398-400 Ja '65
LEYBURN, Ellen Douglass
Comedy and tragedy transposed. Yale R 53: 553-62 Je '64
LEYDEN jars
Lightning in your living room; Van de Graaf generator. H. Walton. il Pop Sci 185:142-5 N '64
LEYLAND motor corporation
Wheels for the world; Britain's Leyland motor corp. il Time 82:69 Ag 9 '63
LEYTE GULF, Battle of, 1944. See Philippine Sea, Battles of the, 1944
L'HEUREUX, John
Bat in the monastery; poem. Atlan 214:43 Ag '64
Death of a man; poem. Atlan 213:54 F '64
Imperfect eye; poem. Commonweal 80:371 Je 12 '64
Investigation into the nature, function, and attendant circumstances of radiators; poem. Harper 229:30 S '64
Last Madonna; poem. Cath World 199:307 Ag '64
Marginal notes in a theology text; poem. Cath World 200:311 F '65
On hearing of a former student stabbed in a rumble; poem. Atlan 214:78 D '64
Spells; poem. Commonweal 78:75 Ap 12 '63
LI, Choh Hao
ACTH molecule; with biographical sketch. Sci Am 209:28, 46-53 Jl '63
LIABILITY (law)
After holocaust, who pays? question of government compensation. il Time 83:58 Ja 17 '64
Battle lost, war won; damages awarded to William Kapell's estate. Time 83:57 F 7 '64
Cured by a verdict? claims for mental injuries. Time 83:75 F 14 '64
Hunters on your farm? know your legal rights. N. G. P. Krausz. Suc Farm 62:36 O '64
Law and the liability of the public forester. J. W. Giles. Am For 69:31+ Mr '63; Reply. L. F. Marion. 69:2 Je '63
Law, liberty, and psychiatry, by T. S. Szasz. Review
Commentary 37:78-80 Mr '64. G. P. Elliott
Liability. T. Bacon. Flying 74:41+ Mr '64
Liability for lost or damaged material. H. F. Pilpel. Pub W 184:31 N 25 '63
Personal business; sports accidents. Bsns W p 183 Ap 18 '64
Skipper: just how liable are you? J. W. Giles. Motor B 113:248+ Ja '64
Smoking and liability. Newsweek 61:86 Je 17 '63
Tobacco's bout with cancer. Time 81:89 Je 14 '63
Tort liability for public park and recreation services. Recreation 57:193 Ap '64
See also
Municipal liability
LIABILITY insurance. See Insurance, Liability
LIACOPOULOS, P. and Goode, J. H.
Transplantation tolerance induced in adult mice by protein overloading of donors. bibliog Science 146:1305-7 D 4 '64
LIARS. See Lying
LIARS; story. See Pritchett, V. S.

LIBBY, Bill
Hard, lonely life of a champion driver. Sat Eve Post 236:42-3 N 2 '63
It hurts to run. Sat Eve Post 236:54-5 F 2 '63
LIBBY, W. F.
Accuracy of radiocarbon dates. bibliog Science 140:278-80 Ap 19 '63
—See Darnell, A. J.; Davies, D. R. jt. auths.
—and others
Replacement rates for human tissue from atmospheric radiocarbon. bibliog Science 146: 1170-2 N 27 '64
LIBBY-McNeill and Libby
Bravo for Libby; new plant at Vauvert, France. il Newsweek 64:78+ O 19 '64
Going international in reverse. Bsns W p34 Ag 10 '63
LIBEL and slander
Another landmark decision. Nation 198:283 Mr 23 '64
But can you do that? (cont) H. F. Pilpel. Pub W 183:41-2 Je 24 '63
But can you do that? lawyer turned author sues his publisher. H. F. Pilpel. Pub W 185: 24-5 My 11 '64
Criticism of officials: what new ruling means; Supreme court decision on damages against The New York times. U S News 56:15 Mr 23 '64
Dering case; surgeon at Auschwitz. M. Ellmann. Commentary 38:19-25 Jl '64
Fairbanks syllogism; Washington columnist sues Alaskan newspaper. Newsweek 64:48 D 14 '64
General v. the cub; E. A. Walker v. A.P's reporter Van Savell. il Time 83:46+ Je 26 '64
Go ahead and say it! boundaries of press freedom advanced by Supreme court. il Time 83: 78 Mr 20 '64
Immunity from criticism; case of advertisement concerning racial conditions in Montgomery, Ala. New Repub 150:7-8 Mr 21 '64
Important victory for a free press, a free nation. R. H. Smith. Pub W 185:33 Mr 16 '64
Laws of libel and privacy opposite on the see-saw. H. F. Pilpel. Pub W 186:295-6 Ag 31 '64
Libel and the free press; appealing of judgement from Alabama Supreme court by New York times. N. Dorsen. il Nation 198:93-5 Ja 27 '64
Libel landmark; Supreme court decision. il Newsweek 63:74 Mr 23 '64
Libel, slander and religion. J. W. Giles. Christian Cent 80:1331-3 O 30 '63
Liebling, libel, and the press. L. M. Lyons. Atlan 213:43-8 My '64
New developments in the law of libel and slander. H. F. Pilpel. Pub W 183:40-2 Mr 25 '63
New York times's vital victory; Alabama libel case. R. L. Tobin. Sat R 47:69-70 Ap 11 '64; Discussion. 47:61 My 9; 52 Je 13 '64
Plea of self-defense in defamation actions. H. F. Pilpel. Pub W 184:30 N 25 '63
Possum-playing plaintiff; case of Margot Power v. Dan Smoot. Time 85:41 Ja 15 '65
Public officials cannot be sued for libel in N.Y; date of distribution controls in statute of limitations. H. F. Pilpel. Pub W 186: 32-3 Jl 27 '64
Restricting congressional immunity; A. C. Powell vs Mrs James. Christian Cent 80: 572 My 1 '63
Right to criticize upheld; Supreme court decision to reverse libel judgment against New York times. Sr Schol 84:30 Ap 3 '64
Speak up, everybody; decision to reverse libel judgment against the New York times. Nat R 16:222 Mr 24 '64
Supreme court decision about criminal libel. H. F. Pilpel. Pub W 186:41-2 D 28 '64
See also
Trials (libel)
LIBEN, Meyer
Change of heart; story. Commentary 39:51-4 Ja '65
Jewish. Commentary 38:74-8 S '64
LIBER, Nadine
Scary pageant in Peking. Life 57:54-61 S 4 '64
LIBERAL arts colleges. See Colleges and universities; Liberal education
LIBERAL-democratic party (Japan) See Political parties—Japan
LIBERAL education
Credo of a college president; excerpt from address, October 13, 1962. J. W. Nason. Sch & Soc 91:214-16 My 4 '63
Developing the whole man. W. T. Miller. America 110:715-17 My 23 '64

LIBERAL education—*Continued*
Future of liberal education. P. Woodring. Sat R 47:53-4 Ap 18 '64; Discussion. 47:67 My 16; 47 Je 20 '64
General education for college seniors; Bowdoin college. Sch & Soc 91:302 O 19 '63
Liberal and the manual arts in education. D. Rucker. Sch & Soc 91:350-2 N 16 '63
Liberal arts; address, January 26, 1963. R. F. Goheen. Vital Speeches 29:318-20 Mr 1 '63
New approach to liberal education. N. Sanford. il Sat R 47:62-4 Ja 18 '64
Plea to save the liberal arts. D. Boroff. il N Y Times Mag p 18+ My 10 '64
Results of a liberal education; adaptation of address, 1963. E. D. Eddy, jr. Sch & Soc 92:201-3 My 2 '64
Saving liberal arts. Time 81:71 F 15 '63
Saving the liberal arts. P. Goodman. Commonweal 80:359-61 Je 12 '64
Science and the small college: to compete with the universities, colleges decide to hang together. J. Walsh. Science 142:564-6 N 1 '63
Squeeze on the liberal university. J. D. Brown. il Atlan 213:84-7 My '64
State of liberal education. W. W. Anderson. Sch & Soc 92:208-9 My 2 '64
Threat to liberal arts. Life 56:4 Ja 31 '64
See also
Humanities

LIBERAL party (Great Britain)
Letter from Brighton; annual assembly. M. Panter-Downes. New Yorker 39:115-16+ S 28 '63
On the seesaw. Time 84:57 O 2 '64

LIBERAL party (United States)
New York politics & the liberal party. B. Rosenberg. Commentary 37:69-75 F '64; Discussion. 38:11 Jl '64

LIBERAL theology. See Modernism

LIBERALISM
Anti-intellectualism in American life, by R. Hofstadter. Review
Reporter 29:37-40 Jl 4 '63. K. S. Lynn
Attack on the Congress. F. S. Meyer. Nat R 16:109-10 F 11 '64
Back seat for the liberals. F. Kuh. Nation 196:522-4 Je 22 '63
Barry Goldwater talks about liberals and liberalism; excerpts from address, June 27, 1963. B. Goldwater. il U S News 55:44-5 Jl 8 '63
Case for democratic liberalism. J. S. Clark. Sat R 47:14-17+ Jl 11 '64
Conservative strategy now. F. S. Meyer. Nat R 16:1145 D 29 '64
Freedom's other face. C. P. Romulo. Sat R 47:16+ D 19 '64
Historical relationship of liberals and intellectuals to organized labor in the United States. M. F. Neufeld. bibliog Ann Am Acad 350:115-28 N '63
How to attack a liberal. S. Allen. Nat R 14:149-52 F 26 '63; Discussion. 14:249+ Mr 26 '63
Intellectual two-party system. W. Sheed. Commonweal 80:506-8 Jl 24 '64
Liberal: what he is and isn't. E. J. McCarthy. il N Y Times Mag p8+ S 1 '63
Liberalism and the Negro; symposium, ed. by N. Podhoretz. Commentary 37:25-42 Mr '64; Discussion. 38:8+ Ag '64
Liberals and the right. Commonweal 81:372-3 D 11 '64
Liberals do believe in devils. M. S. Evans. Nat R 14:457-8 Je 4 '63
Mallorca, anyone? R. W. Blair. Nat R 14:333 Ap 23 '63
Mythmakers, by B. Nossiter. Review
Commentary 37:71-2 Je '64. R. Lekachman
New liberals: are they really 20th-century Tories? K. E. Mundt. il U S News 54:108-10 Mr 25 '63; Reply. F. Church. 54:117-19 My 6 '63
New statesman & the English left. J. Mander. Commentary 37:47-53 F '64; Discussion. 38: 10-11 Jl '64
Open letter from a military intellectual to a sophisticated liberal leader. R. A. Levine. Bul Atomic Sci 20:24-7 S '64; Discussion. 21:31 Ja '65
Platform principles for the two parties? reprint. D. Lawrence. U S News 56:108+ Je 22 '64
Power and the intellectual. R. A. Nisbet. Yale R 53:321-41 Mr '64
Public enemy. M. S. Evans. il Nat R 17:70-1 Ja 26 '65
Radical tradition, by R. H. Tawney. Review
Commentary 38:88+ N '64. G. Kater
Reapportionment & liberal myths. A. M. Bickel. Commentary 35:483-91 Je '63; Discussion. 36:342+ N '63
Suicide of the West, by J. Burnham. Review
Nat R 16:321-3 Ap 21 '64. E. A. Mowrer
Sat R 47:36+ Ap 25 '64. F. Altschul
These are the times: on being a southern liberal; excerpts from Black, white and gray. R. Dugger. Commentary 37:40-5 Ap '64; Reply. L. T. Denison. 38:28 O '64
Uneven road to equality. W. Johnson. Sat R 47:53+ My 9 '64
What is a liberal? address, October 23, 1964. J. L. Jones. Vital Speeches 31:209-12 Ja 15 '65
What is a liberal? what is a conservative? J. Roddy. Look 28:19-21 Jl 28 '64
World government: last refuge of liberalism. F. S. Meyer. Nat R 14:197 Mr 12 '63
See also
Conservatism
Progressive movement in politics
Right and left (political science)

Anecdotes, facetiae, satire, etc.

Liberalland: advertisement in National review; letters to the editor. Nat R 15:411 N 5 '63

LIBERALISM (theology) See Modernism

LIBERATION (newspaper) See Newspapers—France

LIBERIA
Economic development in Liberia; address, December 11, 1964. W. C. Trimble. Dept State Bul 51:912-14 D 28 '64
Uncle Shad forever? il Time 83:27 Ja 17 '64
See also
Iron mines and mining—Liberia
Monrovia

Cultural relations

U.S. and Liberia sign agreements on free port and cultural program; joint announcement, May 8, 1964. Dept State Bul 50:829-30 My 25 '64

Description and travel

Visit to Dimeh. A. Astrachan. il Reporter 31:37-8+ D 3 '64

LIBERMAN, Alexander
Pictures on the wall. G. O'Brien. il N Y Times Mag p28-9 Jl 7 '63
Precise vision of Alexander Liberman. P. Blake. il Arch Forum 118:128-31 Ap '63
Stones of Venice. il Horizon 5:16-24 Mr '63

LIBERMAN, Evsei
Economic controversy in the Soviet Union. M. I. Goldman. For Affairs 41:498-512 Ap '63
Looking backward. por Time 85:25 Ja 22 '65

LIBERMAN, Y. G.
Why Russia downgrades planners. por Bsns W p98-100+ O 31 '64

LIBERTY
Almost at threshold of universal freedom; excerpt from address, December 26, 1962. M. Z. Khan. U N Rev 10:7-8 Ja '63
Battle for freedom; address, July 4, 1963. R. Menzies. Vital Speeches 29:647-9 Ag 15 '63
Bill of obligations; balance is vital to us; address, June 13, 1963. N. Topping. Vital Speeches 29:634-6 Ag 1 '63
Civil rights and civil wrongs; reprint. E. F. Cummerford. U S News 56:84-6 F 17 '64
Curbing of the militant majority. J. P. Roche. il Reporter 29:34-8 Jl 18 '63; Discussion. 29:8+ Ag 15 '63
False faces for freedom. H. Seifert. Christian Cent 81:1265-7 O 14 '64
Four other freedoms; address, April 7, 1964. G. F. Getty, 2d. Vital Speeches 30:499-501 Je 1 '64
Freedom in the postwar world; address, August 29, 1964. D. Rusk. Dept State Bul 51:362-7 S 14 '64
Freedom in the western world: from the dark ages to the rise of democracy, by H. J. Muller. Review
Sat R 46:25+ Ap 13 '63. C. N. Parkinson
Freedom; its responsibilities; address, March 13, 1964. J. Kalvoda. Vital Speeches 30:439-41 My 1 '64
Freedom or virtue? L. B. Bozell; discussion. Nat R 13:223-5, 283, 327+; 15:191-5, 319, 368 S 25-O 23 '62, S 10, O 8-22 '63
Freedoms in tension. J. I. Miller. Christian Cent 81:1332-3 O 28 '64
Freedom's past in 1963 as prologue to 1964. Life 56:4 Ja 3 '64
Friendly letter to Mr Zorin. N. Cousins. Sat R 46:22 N 30 '63
Gettysburg address and our commitment to freedom; address, November 17, 1963. D. Rusk. Dept State Bul 49:842-4 D 2 '63

LIBERTY—*Continued*
Learning about freedom the democratic way; excerpt from Teaching and learning the democratic way. G. Noar. Sch & Soc 91:37-9 Ja 26 '63
Let's be honest with ourselves. D. D. Eisenhower. Sat Eve Post 236:23-5 O 19 '63; Same abr. Read Digest 83:61-8 D '63
Loss of freedom; address, May 18, 1964. J. T. Gurney. Vital Speeches 30:566-70 Jl 1 '64
Middle ground of a Midwest Republican. R. Taft, jr. Sat R 47:14-16 Ag 22 '64
National interest, 1964; address, June 7, 1964. D. Rusk. Dept State Bul 50:955-8 Je 22 '64
New social order; address, June 25, 1963. J. F. Kennedy. Vital Speeches 29:578-81 Jl 15 '63
No wonder they get away with it. W. F. Buckley. Nat R 14:103 F 12 '63
Our most precious possession; address, January 10, 1963. L. I. Doan. Vital Speeches 29:344-7 Mr 15 '63
Our strategy for 1964; our sacred heritage of freedom; address, July 12, 1963. B. Moreell. Vital Speeches 29:671-2 Ag 15 '63
Parliamentary government and the Alliance for progress; address, February 5, 1964. D. Rusk. Dept State Bul 50:305-7 F 24 '64
Prelude to independence; address, June 1, 1963. B. Ward. Vital Speeches 29:564-6 Jl 1 '63
Present prospect; address, January 22, 1964. D. Rusk. bibliog f Dept State Bul 50:190-5 F 10 '64; Same with title Our foreign policy. Vital Speeches 30:290-3 Mr 1 '64
Security and freedom: a free-world responsibility; address, February 26, 1963. D. Rusk. Dept State Bul 48:383-8 Mr 18 '63
Security checks threaten freedom. Christian Cent 80:164 F 6 '63
Soviet freedom: a balance sheet. J. R. Azrael. New Repub 148:18-20 Mr 2 '63
Still stand the embattled farmers; address, February 22, 1963. S. J. Heywood. Vital Speeches 29:408-12 Ap 15 '63
Strengthening America's heritage; address, April 17, 1964. P. F. Osborn, 3d. Vital Speeches 30:600-3 Jl 15 '64
Symbols, traditions and liberty; address, October 24, 1962. A. G. Rudd. Vital Speeches 29:256 F 1 '63
Troubled international waters; address, March 15, 1963. J. A. Farley. Vital Speeches 29:389-91 Ap 15 '63
United Nations in the fight for freedom; address, February 22, 1963. D. Rusk. Dept State Bul 48:393-8 Mr 18 '63
Voice for personal liberty. U S News 54:21 Je 10 '63
Way to freedom. R. O. Johann. America 109:568 N 9 '63
We hold these truths. . . C. H. Percy. il PTA Mag 58:4-6 Je '64
World view of freedom's hopes and dilemma; address, August 10, 1964. A. B. Duke. Dept State Bul 51:340-7 S 7 '64; Same with title Freedom. Vital Speeches 30:696-701 S 1 '64
See also
American civil liberties union
Civil rights
Democracy
Equality
Free speech
Freedom of the press
Intellectual liberty
Liberalism

LIBERTY, Religious. See Religious liberty

LIBERTY, Statue of. See Statue of liberty

LIBERTY feed yards. See Cooperative associations—United States

LIBERTY of conscience
Politics and Catholic freedom, by G. Wills. Review
Nat R 16:730-2+ Ag 25 '64. W. Herberg. Discussion. 16:829-31+ S 22 '64
See also
Religious liberty

LIBERTY of speech. See Free speech

LIBERTY of the press. See Freedom of the press

LIBHART, Myles
American Indian. Craft Horiz 24:104-11 My '64

LIBMAN, Emanuel
My most unforgettable character. J. L. Block. por Read Digest 85:107-12 D '64

LIBRARIANS
American librarians abroad. M. M. Jackson. Wilson Lib Bul 39:51+ S '64
British librarians to visit US on two-week library tour. Library J 88:1847 My 1 '63
Changing role of the librarian. C. I. Whitenack. Wilson Lib Bul 38:397-400 Ja '64
Defensive about The defenders. E. Moon. Library J 88:2210 Je 1 '63; Discussion. 88:2580 Jl '63
Diagnosis; symposium; reply. J. D. Mack. Library J 88:366 F 1 '63
Eastern college librarians confer on need to reinvent the library. Library J 89:76-7 Ja 1 '64
Fortnightly visit: British group to visit US. Wilson Lib Bul 37:738 My '63
Future, too, is prologue. J. Shera. Wilson Lib Bul 39:253 N '64
Grimm tale. H. R. Meisels. Wilson Lib Bul 39:165-7 O '64
Information sciences; special libraries and librarians. R. S. Taylor. Library J 88:4161-3 N 1 '63
Itinerant librarians. F. J. Anderson. Library J 88:3776+ O 15 '63
JMRT plans Chicago program for young/new librarians; Junior members round table. Library J 88:1968 My 15 '63
Librarian plays the central role; correctional institutions. C. J. Eckenrode. il ALA Bul 58:810-11 O '64
Lifting the lid. L. Bradshaw. Library J 88:3806+ O 15 '63
Little girls don't play librarian. J. Shera; discussion. Library J 88:894+, 1790 Mr 1, My 1 '63
Minority pace; service for the individual. H. C. Bauer. Library J 89:3923-5 O 15 '64
Neglect of the greats. E. G. Holley. bibliog il Library J 88:3547-51 O 1 '63
New generation: talkers or doers? J. Orne. Library J 88:2852 Ag '63
Noble warm-hearted rock; excerpts from address, December 24, 1961. J. C. Beaglehole. il Library J 88:2185-8 Je 1 '63
Of librarians and other aborigines. J. Shera. Wilson Lib Bul 38:781 My '64
On the grindstone. R. Stokes. Library J 88:2212-13, 3808-9, 4168 Je 1, O 15-N 1 '63
On the road with British librarians. E. Moon. Library J 88:4332 N 15 '63
Rule, Britannia; visiting British librarians; with list of names. il Wilson Lib Bul 38:364-6 D '63
Serving the teenager. G. D. Mitchell, 3d. il Library J 89:1817-19 Ap 15 '64
Special librarian. P. Wasserman; J. Harvey; A. M. Rees. bibliog il Library J 89:4279-94 N 1 '64; Discussion. 89:4840+ D 15 '64
Wanted: documents librarians. E. P. Fishbein. il Library J 89:2037-9 My 15 '64
Wealthier by the world; foreign librarians in Enoch Pratt free library, Baltimore. E. Castagna. il Wilson Lib Bul 39:48-50 S '64
What it takes to be a librarian. il Good H 158:167 Ap '64
What the young librarian thinks of his professional associations. R. Y. Weinbrecht. il Library J 88:1417-20 Ap 1 '63; Discussion. 88:1421-3, 1920+, 2952 Ap 1, My 15, S 1 '63
See also
Catalogers
Childrens librarians
Law librarians
School librarians

Anecdotes, facetiae, satire, etc.

Book for burning. J. Shera. Wilson Lib Bul 37:790 My '63
Old librarian and his almanack. H. A. Sullivan. Library J 89:1188-92 Mr 15 '64
Unauthorized report from the committee on the stereotyped librarian. M. Bennett. Library J 89:2285-6 Je 1 '64

Education

See Library schools and education: School librarians—Education

Education in service

Programed help. W. Jones. Library J 89:4304 N 1 '64
Programmed learning and in-service training in libraries. T. C. Hines. bibliog ALA Bul 58:719-24 S '64

Fiction

Androcles & the librarian. E. Jensen. il Ladies Home J 80:110b Jl '63

Recruiting

Continuing battle. M. Ricking. ALA bul 57:293-5 Ap '63
Full-time recruiting: the Pennsylvania story. D. H. Hunt. il Library J 89:2031-6 My 15 '64
Image shaper: school librarians, recruiting. J. Bradbury. Wilson Lib Bul 39:419 Ja '65
Librarians: a vanishing breed. R. Miller. Library J 89:4597-9 N 15 '64

LIBRARIANS—Recruiting—*Continued*
LED is for librarians. V. L. Jones. Library J 88:739+ F 15 '63
Massachusetts NLW group makes recruitment film. il Library J 89:1206 Mr 15 '64
Ninety-four hour week. J. Sherman. Library J 89:1198-200 Mr 15 '64; Discussion. 89:1893, 2258+ My 1, Je 1 '64
Pitch for placement. H. M. Welch. ALA Bul 57:179-85 F '63
Professional library manpower. F. L. Schick. il ALA Bul 58:315-17 Ap '64
Recruiting adult students to library work: University of Wisconsin library school. Wilson Lib Bul 39:444+ F '65
Recruiting new graduates at library schools. R. F. Clarke. Wilson Lib Bul 38:483-4 F '64
Recruitment. M. Ricking. il ALA Bul 57:267-9, 601-3, 670-1, 867-8, 1049-50; 58:236-7, 323, 567-9, 730-2 Mr, Je-Jl, O, D '63, Mr-Ap, Je, S '64
Recruitment, a part of library development. R. Blasingame, jr. ALA Bul 57:450-2 My '63
Recruitment counterpoint. Library J 88:894+ Mr 1 '63
South Carolina's program. E. P. Walker. ALA Bul 58:143-4 F '64
Three-point program. D. Thomas. ALA Bul 58:408-10 My '64
Trustee's role in recruitment. Mrs W. J. Lynch. ALA Bul 58:60-1 Ja '64
Visitors from far out. D. E. Holt. Library J 89:566-7 F 1 '64
Work-study program; University of North Carolina. J. H. Gribbin. Library J 89:568-9+ F 1 '64

Anecdotes, facetiae, satire, etc.

Recruitment rewrite. W. Jones. Library J 89:3114+ S 1 '64

Salaries

Decatur publishes annual survey of library directors' salaries. Library J 88:977 Mr 1 '63
Malady lingers on. D. E. Strout and R. B. Strout. il Library J 89:2547-55 Je 15 '64
Word is more. D. E. Strout and R. B. Strout. il Library J 88:2451-7 Je 15 '63

Bibliography

Survey of salary surveys. A. R. Schiller. il ALA Bul 58:279-86 Ap '64

Supply and demand

Crying need for librarians. il Changing T 18:30-1 Ag '64
Young man, be a librarian. A. Gingrich. Esquire 61:8 Ap '64
See also
Librarians—Recruiting

LIBRARIANS, Negro. See Negro librarians
LIBRARIANS, Reference. See College libraries—Reference work
LIBRARIANSHIP
Age of paradox: gifted child, juvenile delinquent, merit scholar, drop-out. J. Shera. Wilson Lib Bul 39:409+ Ja '65
Aroused though retired; South Carolina program; summary of letter. E. Moon. Library J 89:71 Ja 1 '64
Beautifully organized facts; reprint. Library J 89:1200 Mr 15 '64
Compleat librarian. J. Shera. Wilson Lib Bul 38:867+ Je '64
Daedalus, Icarus, and technological revolution: tradition, innovation and progress. J. Shera. Wilson Lib Bul 39:335 D '64
Dimensions of the Master's program. J. H. Shera. bibliog f ALA Bul 58:519-22 Je '64
Documentation: a synthetic science; address, 1963. F. E. Mohrhardt. bibliog il Wilson Lib Bul 38:743-9 My '64
Education of an educator; address, September 27, 1963. L. C. Powell. il Library J 89:561-5 F 1 '64
Face to the future and the past; symposium. il Wilson Lib Bul 38:391-403, 406-7 Ja '64
Flavor of librarianship. M. Ricking. ALA Bul 57:1049-50 D '63
Forecast for 1964; reports from forty-seven states. il Library J 89:39-66 Ja 1 '64
Freedom to read; active voice; excerpts from address, 1964. F. H. Wagman. il ALA Bul 58:473-81 Je '64
Future, too, is prologue. J. Shera. Wilson Lib Bul 39:253 N '64
In search of a philosophy; symposium, with introduction by L. Carnovsky. Library J 88:1112-20 Mr 15 '63
Lenin on libraries; excerpt from Life and death of Lenin. Library J 89:4301+ N 1 '64
Libraries for an affluent society with frayed edges; address, July 3, 1964. E. Castagna. ALA Bul 58:635-8 Jl '64
Library of the future: a WLB symposium. il Wilson Bul 39:228-43 N '64
Lifting the lid. L. Bradshaw. Library J 88:3806+ O 15 '63
Meeting demands: a library imperative. M. E. Monroe. Library J 88:516-18 F 1 '63
Mysterious silence. W. Jones. Library J 89:4762 D 1 '64
Need and opportunity; concerning symposium by alumni association of Rutgers library school. E. Moon. Library J 89:1922 My 1 '64
New bottles for old wine: retrieval and librarianship. A. M. Rees. bibliog il Wilson Lib Bul 38:773-9 My '64
New generation: talkers or doers? J. Orne. Library J 88:2852 Ag '63
Noble warm-hearted rock; excerpts from address, December 24, 1961. J. C. Beaglehole. il Library J 88:2185-8 Je 1 '63
Of librarians and other aborigines. J. Shera. Wilson Lib Bul 38:781 My '64
On the grindstone. R. Stokes. Library J 88:974, 1430-1, 1842+, 2212-13, 3036 Mr 1, Ap 1, My 1, Je 1, S 1 '63
Peaceable kingdom; address, October, 1963. K. Molz. il Library J 90:183-7 Ja 15 '65
Present is not what it was; Edith M. Coulter lecture, 1963. N. Harlow. bibliog Library J 89:2527-32 Je 15 '64
Progress through change. D. R. Watts. Wilson Lib Bul 38:413 Ja '64
Some leading questions. M. Chicorel. bibliog Library J 88:1424-8 Ap 1 '63
Status, and all that. B. Thomas. Library J 89:2275-80 Je 1 '64; Reply. H. Hilb. 89:2696+ Jl '64
Think nothing of it, Mr Dana, it's only a flesh wound; quotations, ed. by C. A. Goodrum. J. C. Dana. Library J 89:3687-8 O 1 '64
Thinking of a plan; excerpts from address, November, 1961; with editorial comment. N. Harlow. il Library J 88:3161-3, 3176 S 15 '63
To begin with: New Year's resolutions. E. Moon. Library J 90:76 Ja 1 '65
Toward a new dimension for library education; statement at session of ALA commission on national plan for library education, February 1963. J. H. Shera. il(cover) ALA Bul 57:313-17 Ap '63
Year's realities: report from states on library progress in 1964 and comparisons with last year's forecast. il Library J 90:56-71 Ja 1 '65

Anecdotes, facetiae, satire, etc.

Littlest librarian. B. A. Ower. Library J 89:1514+ Ap 1 '64; Discussion. 89:2002+ My 15 '64
Old librarian and his almanack. H. A. Sullivan. Library J 89:1188-92 Mr 15 '64

International aspects

Six items for export; address, October 1962. R. C. Swank. il Library J 88:711-17 F 15 '63
Struggling masses; need for special courses related to problems of librarianship in another country. R. Stokes. Library J 88:2850 Ag '63

LIBRARIE Hachette. See Publishers and publishing—France
LIBRARIES
Evaluating the small libraries project. G. K. Schenk. Wilson Lib Bul 39:346 D '64
Face to the future and the past; symposium. il Wilson Lib Bul 38:391-403, 406-7 Ja '64
Fate of public library legislation now considered to be uncertain. Library J 88:2652 Jl '63
Great step forward; Unesco missions. E. Samarasinghe. il Library J 89:4473-5 N 15 '64
Kennedy libraries drive collects over 4000 books. Pub W 185:57 Ja 6 '64
Learning: a lifelong process; excerpts from address, May 21, 1964. M. Long. Library J 90:188-91, 195 Ja 15 '65
Libraries and learning. O. Handlin. il Atlan 213:96+ Ap '64
Library of the future: a WLB symposium. il Wilson Lib Bul 39:228-43 N '64
Library service for the teacher. S. I. Fenwick and L. L. Batchelor. ALA Bul 57:129-30 F '63
Minority pace; service for the individual. H. C. Bauer. Library J 89:3923-5 O 15 '64
Mobile libraries in the park proposed by New York businessman. il Library J 88:2856 Ag '63

LIBRARIES—*Continued*
On the grindstone. R. Stokes. Library J 88: 524-5 F 1 '63
Peace corps placing Kennedy libraries abroad. Pub W 184:22 D 16 '63
Peaceable kingdom; address, October, 1963. K. Molz. il Library J 90:183-7 Ja 15 '65
See also
Books and reading
College libraries
High school libraries
Prison libraries
Research libraries
School libraries
Story telling
United Nations—Library
also subhead Libraries under names of cities, e.g. New York (city)—Libraries

Acquisitions

Booksellers can sell to libraries. F. H. Potter. Pub W 185:125-8 Je 8 '64
Cooperation in acquisitions; from Swedish to Scandia plan. T. Kleberg. il Library J 88: 4319-22 N 15 '63
On the shelf. E. Moon. il Library J 89:205. 570-4 Ja 15-F 1 '64; Discussion. 89:784, 1640 F 15, Ap 15 '64
Should retailers sell to libraries? F. Watts. Pub W 185:120-2 Ja 20 '64
See also
Subscription books

Administration

See Library administration

Advertising

See Library publicity

Architecture

See Library architecture

Audio-visual materials

See Libraries and audio-visual materials

Automation

Advance of automation: its implications for library education; report. A. J. Goldwyn. il Library J 88:2640-3 Jl '63
Automating the school library: an advanced report; Brentwood public schools, Brentwood, L.I. C. A. Vertanes. il Wilson Lib Bul 37:864-7 Je '63
Automation & library systems; excerpts from Strengthening and coordinating reference and research library sources in New York state. T. Stein. bibliog il Library J 89:2723-34 Jl '64
Automation conference proceedings published; Libraries and automation sponsored and published by LC. E. Hamer and A. McCormick. ALA Bul 58:988 D '64
Automation may rescue library from data flood. Sci N L 85:89 F 8 '64
Automation report made to LC; concerning survey team's report, Automation and the Library of Congress. Wilson Lib Bul 38: 523+ Mr '64
Beautifully organized facts; reprint. Library J 89:1200 Mr 15 '64
Buildings for books; eight new libraries. il Arch Forum 120:80-97 My '64
Clinic on data processing at University of Illinois. Library J 88:987 Mr 1 '63
Conference on libraries and automation. F. G. Poole. ALA Bul 57:658-9 Jl '63
Copyrighting writing on the wall. D. Dempsey. Sat R 47:39-40 S 19 '64
Data processing equipment in libraries. J. Becker. il ALA Bul 58:227-30, 557-60, 714-18, 822-4, 1007-10 Mr, Je, S-O, D '64
Eastern college librarians confer on need to reinvent the library. Library J 89:76-7 Ja 1 '64
Galloping automation; library of the future. W. Wingo. il Sci N L 84:310 N 16 '63
Information science? role of traditional librarians and libraries. E. Moon. Library J 89:1042 Mr 1 '64; Discussion. 89:1888+, 2464+ My 1, Je 15 '64
[Libraries and automation] symposium; ed. by J. H. Shera. bibliog il Wilson Lib Bul 38:740-79+ My '64
LC and automation; concerning survey team's report, Automation and the Library of Congress. M. J. Voigt. il Library J 89:1022-5 Mr 1 '64
Library of Congress: automation urged for bibliographic control but not prescribed as a panacea. J. Walsh. Science 143:452-5 Ja 31 '64
Library of Congress issues automation conference text. Pub W 186:24 O 26 '64
Library of Congress report outlines automation possibilities. Library J 89:820+ F 15 '64
Library 21 goes home. Wilson Lib Bul 37:836 Je '63
O brave new (push button) world! Eastern college librarians annual conference; letter to the editor. R. Z. Sellers. Library J 89:6 Ja 1 '64; Reply. W. H. Carlson. 89:1642 Ap 15 '64
Plan automated libraries; scientific data. W. Davis. Sci N L 85:371 Je 13 '64
Staffing a computer based library; Florida Atlantic university, Boca Raton. E. Heiliger. il Library J 89:2738-9 Jl '64
Turning of the worm; acceptance of automation. J. Shera. Wilson Lib Bul 39:73+ S '64
Washington report: from the Library of Congress; automation report published. E. Hamer and A. McCormick. ALA Bul 58: 184-6 Mr '64
Writers discuss automated world at CLA. Library J 89:593 F 1 '64
See also
College libraries—Automation
School libraries—Automation
Western Reserve university, Cleveland, Ohio —Center for documentation and communication research

Anecdotes, facetiae, satire, etc.

Ms. found in a bottle. G. Dul. Wilson Lib Bul 38:401-3 Ja '64

Bibliographic services

See also
School libraries—Bibliographic services

Book discarding

Opening the chambered nautilus; evaluation of uncataloged material for Francis A. Countway library. L. Ash. il Library J 89: 2040-3 My 15 '64

Anecdotes, facetiae, satire, etc.

Keep or discard? recommended form letter for public relations use. L. S. Gribbin. Library J 89:1193 Mr 15 '64

Book drives

See Book and periodical giving campaigns

Book losses

Book thieves operate on national levels; US national archives and British museum. Library J 88:4186 N 1 '63
Cutting book losses; high school libraries. Wilson Lib Bul 37:805 My '63
Detroit pl combines forces with FBI to solve bizarre document swindle case. Library J 89:825-6 F 15 '64
War of lost books. il Wilson Lib Bul 38:120 O '63
See also
Book thefts

Book mutilation

See Books—Mutilation, defacement, etc.

Book selection

See Book selection

Branches and stations

Access study advisory committee has second thoughts on branches. Library J 88:4176+ N 1 '63
Access study; symposium; with editorial comment. il Library J 88:4685-712 D 15 '63
Access survey; from the social scientist's viewpoint. H. J. Gans. bibliog Wilson Lib Bul 38:336-41+ D '63; Reply with rejoinder. M. Bloss. 38:622-5 Ap '64
Access to libraries study; statement, September 30, 1963. H. W. Tucker. ALA Bul 57: 1042 D '63
Books for Osage: deposits in general store. I. Mothner. il Look 28:60+ Ap 21 '64
Branches: more or less? Library J 89:4761 D 1 '64
Can we afford to ignore the Negro? T. F. Parker. bibliog Library J 88:4716-17 D 15 '63
Complaints and answers; address, May 1962. A. Thomas. Library J 88:510-12 F 1 '63
Free space: can public libraries receive it? report of survey of branch libraries in shopping centers by Wichita, Kan. city library. R. Waters. ALA Bul 58:232-4 Mr '64

Censorship

Adults si, children no. J. C. Challman. Library J 89:807-9 F 15 '64; Reply. J. M. Travillian. 89:1640+ Ap 15 '64
ACLU guide combats pressures on schools and libraries; excerpts from Combatting undemocratic pressures on schools and libraries. Library J 89:2052 My 15 '64

LIBRARIES—Censorship—*Continued*

ALA go home! Catholic library association publication vs stand on censorship. Library J 89:4128+ O 15 '64
Book burning; New City, N.Y. free library. Wilson Lib Bul 37:518 Mr '63
Book burning, 1963 style. Library J 88:1305 Mr 15 '63
Books and banners; case of censoring Dictionary of American slang in California. J. A. King. Sat R 46:28-9+ N 9 '63
Budgetary censorship? Negro material denied in southern libraries; letter. M. O. Walsh. Library J 89:3054 S 1 '64
California library uses form to alleviate censorship pressure; San Bernardino County free library. Library J 88:4179 N 1 '63
California right-wing front groups attack book selection in libraries. Library J 89:4874 D 15 '64
Canada considers. E. Moon. Library J 88:523 F 1 '63
Censorship column. Library J 88:2656-8 Jl '63
Censorship, critical thinking, and the paperback; excerpts from address, December 3, 1964. P. Johnson, jr. il Library J 90:296-301 Ja 15 '65
Censorship feeds on complacency; address, August 25, 1964. J. V. Lindsay. Library J 89:3909-12 O 15 '64
Censorship flares up in New City; library board member burns book. Library J 88:745 F 15 '63
City in torment over Kazantzakis. E. T. Moore. ALA Bul 57:305-6 Ap '63
Climate of intellectual freedom; why is it always so bad in California? address, November 6, 1964. E. Castagna. il ALA Bul 59:27-33 Ja '65
Courage and cowardice; address, November 15-17, 1962. E. Castagna. il Library J 88:501-6 F 1 '63
Fairfax County library storm shifts from film to book protests. Library J 88:2462 Je 15 '63
Intellectual freedom. E. J. Gaines. ALA Bul 57:711-12, 817-18, 1009-10; 58-17-18, 87-9, 177, 345-7, 453-4, 595-6, 675-6, 767-8, 983-4; 59:17-18 S-O, D '63-Mr, My-O, D '64-Ja '65; Discussion. 57:1001+; 58:590, 752-3, 975 D '63, Jl, O, D '64
Intellectual freedom. E. T. Moore. See issues of ALA bulletin to June 1963
Intellectual freedom theme of the pre-conference of California library association. Wilson Lib Bul 39:304 D '64
Issues of freedom in American libraries, by E. T. Moore. Review
ALA Bul 58:1010 D '64. R. R. Kirsch
Justice Brennan speaks on censorship at Newark library anniversary dinner. Library J 88:2217 Je 1 '63
Librarian's syndrome; letter to the editor. G. A. Somers. Library J 89:4672+ D 1 '64
Library books under political attack. C. B. Grannis. Pub W 186:39 N 30 '64
Mr and Mrs Grundy in the library and in court; CLA pre-conference meeting on intellectual freedom; excerpts from report with editorial comment. H. M. Madden. Library J 89:4857-62 D 15 '64
Month at random; concerning obscenities in Dictionary of American slang. Wilson Lib Bul 38:22 S '63
Mystery of the first law of thermodynamics or, Trading stamp sex; address, 1964. M. L'Engle. il Library J 89:4851-6 D 15 '64
National library week brings film furor to Fairfax County, Va. Library J 88:2216-17 Je 1 '63
Objectionable literature: some false synonymies. R. M. Pierson. Library J 89:3920-3 O 15 '64
On the firing line in a bad climate; California, excerpt from report. H. Madden. ALA Bul 59:33-4 Ja '65
Paterson, N.J. mayor bans The children of Sanchez. Library J 88:1128 Mr 15 '63
Practical measures to combat censors topic of ALA invitational conference. Library J 90:217 Ja 15 '65
Problem books revisited; excerpts from report on survey of small library's book selection practices in controversial areas. R. B. Agler. il Library J 89:2019-30 My 15 '64; Reply. R. S. Bravard. 89:2470+ Je 15 '64
Record crowd at New City meeting overwhelmingly supports library board. Library J 88:1128 Mr 15 '63
Satisfied conscience; concerning attack on Standard catalog for high school libraries. E. Moon. Library J 89:2045 My 15 '64
Selection, not censorship; letter to the editor. R. M. Pearl. Library J 89:428 F 1 '64
Whitewash in Whitewater; Wisconsin state college vs Kiwanis club; letter to the editor. S. D. Robertson. Library J 89:2900+ Ag '64
Yesterday's whipping boy, today's favorite. D. R. Watts. Wilson Lib Bul 37:597 Mr '63
See also
American library association—Intellectual freedom committee
Ontario library association—Intellectual freedom committee
School libraries—Censorship

Charging systems

Circulation and the computer. J. Becker. ALA Bul 58:1007-10 D '64

Childrens rooms

See Libraries, Childrens

Circulation, loans, etc.

Circulation and the computer. J. Becker. ALA Bul 58:1007-10 D '64
Daily realities; loan periods. W. Jones. Library J 89:1516 Ap 1 '64
Two libraries clamp down on overdue book borrowers. Library J 88:3576 O 1 '63
See also
Interlibrary loans
Libraries—Fines
School libraries—Circulation, loans, etc.

Classification

See Classification

Cooperative service

See Library cooperation

Equipment and supplies

See Library furniture and equipment

Federal aid

See Libraries and state

Fiction collections

Blue chip book selection; serious fiction and poetry. E. Moon. Library J 89:2562+ Je 15 '64
Mirror, mirror on the wall. D. E. Gerard. Library J 90:192-5 Ja 15 '65
Not-so-good books fund set up at Little Rock P.L. Library J 89:828 F 15 '64
Problem books revisited; excerpts from report on survey of small public library's book selection practices in controversial areas. R. B. Agler. il Library J 89:2019-30 My 15 '64; Reply. R. S. Bravard. 89:2470+ Je 15 '64

Film programs

See Libraries and moving pictures

Finance

British debate library fees. Library J 89:2757 Jl '64
Library budget rejected twice by Long Island voters; North Bellmore, N.Y. public library. Library J 89:2756 Jl '64
Points for the budget. E. Moon. Library J 89:578-9 F 1 '64
See also
Libraries and state
School libraries—Finance

Fines

California library's experiment supports abolition of fines; San Diego city college library. Library J 88:4339 N 15 '63
Common fine; report of survey by Akron public library. J. H. Rebenack. Library J 89:4868-70 D 15 '64
Nickel-a-day addiction; Anoka County library, Spring Lake Park, Minn. J. Challman. Library J 89:4866-7 D 15 '64

Fires and fire protection

Protecting the library and its resources, ed. by E. M. Johnson. Review
Library J il 88:4152-6 N 1 '63. H. L. Roth; W. W. Curley; Discussion. 89:2+, 426+ Ja 1, F 1 '64

Furniture

See Library furniture and equipment

Gifts, legacies, etc.

See also
College libraries—Gifts, legacies, etc.

Handbooks, manuals, etc.

Library handbook standards: students and faculty; report of survey. A. B. Griffith. il Wilson Lib Bul 39:475-7 F '65

LIBRARIES—*Continued*

History

Where have we been? J. Neufeld. Library J 88:3388 O 1 '63

Hours of opening

Lost weekend. E. Moon. Library J 89:4302+ N 1 '64; Correction. 90:6 Ja 1 '65
Ninety-four hour week. J. Sherman. Library J 89:1198-200 Mr 15 '64; Discussion. 89:1893, 2258+ My 1, Je 1 '64

Information service

See Libraries—Reference work

Instruction in use

Freshman term paper. A. M. Alston and E. Wilcox. il Wilson Lib Bul 37:858-9 Je '63
How to teach library skills without really being there; use of cartridge projectors in school libraries. V. S. Gerlach and I. Farnbach. il Library J 89:921-2 F 15 '64
Library handbook standards: students and faculty; report of survey. A. B. Griffith. il Wilson Lib Bul 39:475-7 F '65
Programed materials. T. C. Hines. il Library J 88:2055-8+ My 15 '63
Self-shelving by children; Flat Rock library of Wayne County, Mich. library system. W. H. Kaiser. il Library J 89:2146-8+ My 15 '64
Stephens college library instruction program. B. Bartlett. ALA Bul 58:311-14 Ap '64
Teaching library skills with an overhead projector; school libraries. J. M. Landman. il Library J 89:923-4 F 15 '64

Intermediate departments

See also
Libraries—Work with young people

International aspects

International exchange. I. F. Fraser. Wilson Lib Bul 39:415+ Ja '65
International exchange; symposium. bibliog il Wilson Lib Bul 39:39-62+ S '64

Legislation

See Library laws and legislation

Manuscript collections

Berg acquisitions; New York public library. New Yorker 40:44-5 O 3 '64
Management of manuscript collections. R. C. Berner. Library J 88:1615-16 Ap 15 '63; Reply. L. Ash. 88:2164+ Je 1 '63
Ohio rich in manuscript repositories. W. P. Marchman. Hobbies 68:110-11+ D '63

Microfilm collections

Agreement to standardize microfiche. G. T. Piez. ALA Bul 58:648-9 Jl '64
Credo of a library conservative; adaptation of address, October 29, 1963. E. Wolf, 2d. Library J 89:1903-6 My 1 '64
From the Library of Congress: union catalog of microfilms. E. Hamer and A. McCormick. ALA Bul 57:1017-19 D '63
LC and ARL announce plans for register of microfilms. Library J 88:4599-600 D 1 '63
Library of Congress plans register of microfilms. Pub W 184:26 D 16 '63

Moving picture collections

Controversy on film; address, May 1962. G. Holloway. il Library J 88:513-15 F 1 '63
Film coatings; concerning program of LTP. G. T. Piez. ALA Bul 58:237 Mr '64
Film evaluation and criticism; excerpts from address, July 13, 1963. J. L. Limbacher. ALA Bul 58:43-7 Ja '64
Guide to collecting classics in 8-MM. C. Reynolds. il Pop Phot 52:104-7+ Mr '63

Newspaper collections

Newspaper gap; concerning survey by Boston public library. E. J. Montana, jr. il Library J 89:1194-7 Mr 15 '64; Correction. 89:2260 Je 1 '64
Newspapers: a regional resource; University of North Carolina, Chapel Hill. J. Orne. Library J 88:1612-14 Ap 15 '63

Organization

See Library administration

Paperback books

Cheap paperback is no country cousin; Fraser Valley regional library. V. Richards; discussion. Library J 88:1494, 1920 Ap 1, My 15 '63
Paperback pilot project; Columbus, Ohio, public library. G. Gordon. il Library J 89:191-2 Ja 15 '64
Paperback utopia. M. Bob. Library J 88:1941-2 My 15 '63
Paperbacks for college-bound students; project of NYLA's Adult services division; with list of binders. C. E. Hieber. bibliog il Library J 89:185-90 Ja 15 '64
Paperbacks: for sale? E. Moon. Library J 89:2044 My 15 '64
Paperbacks in libraries; children and young adults; symposium. bibliog il Library J 90:296-313 Ja 15 '65
Paperbacks in school and public libraries; symposium. il Sr Schol 82:9T-10T+ Mr 13 '63; Summary. Wilson Lib Bul 37:734 My '63
Special issue on paperbacks; symposium, ed. by M. Bogart. il Sr Schol 85:17T-26T+ D 2 '64
Special issue on paperbacks; symposium, ed. by R. Beauchamp. il Sr Schol 83:21T-35T Ja 17 '64

Periodical collections

Automating the serial record. J. Becker. ALA Bul 58:557-60 Je '64
Demand for dissent? public library practice in the selection of dissident periodicals; report. J. N. Berry, 3d. il Library J 89:3912-17 O 15 '64; Discussion. 90:6 Ja 1 '65
Student use of periodicals surveyed by Montana library. Library J 88:1132 Mr 15 '63
U.S. periodicals and serials: cost indexes for 1963. il Library J 88:3556-9 O 1 '63
See also
College libraries—Periodical collections

Periodicals

See Library science—Periodicals

Phonograph and phonograph records

Don't ignore the gifted listener. G. Stevenson. il Library J 88:519-22 F 1 '63
Parents help with audio-visual aids. M. Bise. Wilson Lib Bul 37:787-8+ My '63
Plea for an a/v library: school libraries; letter to the editor. H. S. Karten. Library J 90:284 Ja 15 '65
Record players for libraries and schools; summary of Testing and evaluation of record players for libraries. il Consumer Bul 46:12-14 Mr '63
Recordings; symposium, ed. by G. Stevenson. il Library J 88:1809-40 My 1; 3783-804+ O 15 '63; Discussion. 88:4502+ D 1 '63
Sound scholarships; Michigan state university's new National voice library. il Time 83:49 F 7 '64

Public relations

Best/worst television can do; Book for burning, on The defenders. ALA Bul 57:377-8 My '63; Reply with rejoinder. L. T. Dinnan. 57:472, 477 Je '63
Displaying our wares; symposium, ed. by A. Norton. il Wilson Lib Bul 38:533-46+ Mr '64
Planning library promotion: administrator's view; Artist's view. J. W. Byrant; R. J. Cattafesta. il Wilson Lib Bul 39:464-71 F '65
Public relations: a three-way definition; who? what? why? S. L. Wallace. il Wilson Lib Bul 37:557-61 Mr '63
Public relations awry on UC public relations library. Library J 88:747 F 15 '63
Public relations planner; offer of sampler packet of materials for small public libraries. Wilson Lib Bul 38:131 O '63
Publicity that worked. il Wilson Lib Bul 37:574-80 Mr '63
Rethinking decisions. H. C. Bauer. Library J 90:206-8 Ja 15 '65
That was the day that was; opening of Casa View branch, Dallas, public library. W. Jones. Library J 89:2752+ Jl '64
See also
Adult education—Library participation
College libraries—Public relations
School libraries—Public relations

Reference work

Metropolitan reference services: patterns, problems, solutions; Detroit public library. K. G. Harris. il Library J 88:1606-11 Ap 15 '63
Regional reference services. R. P. Stewart; G. Garrison; A. F. Reilly. bibliog il Library J 89:1676-87 Ap 15 '64
See also
College libraries—Reference work
Reference books
School libraries—Reference work

Rental collections

Book rental unfair to authors, says novelist Richard Condon. Library J 89:4492 N 15 '64

LIBRARIES—*Continued*

Reports

See Library reports

Science collections

Librarians and technical literature; letter. W. T. Knox. Science 142:9+ O 4 '63

Shelving systems

Self-shelving by children; Flat Rock library of Wayne County, Mich. library system. W. H. Kaiser. il Library J 89:2146-8+ My 15 '64

Special collections

Credo of a library conservative; adaptation of address, October 29, 1963. E. Wolf, 2d. Library J 89:1903-6 My 1 '64

For circus fans only! K. Sexton. il ALA Bul 57:251-5 Mr '63

Life guide; rare books. il Life 45:9 Mr 13 '64

Princeton plans for the Scheide library. Wilson Lib Bul 38:722+ My '64

Question of definition; adaptation of address, June 1962. L. Ash. Library J 88:1617-20 Ap 15 '63

See also

Libraries—Moving picture collections

Standards

Caught with our standards down. H. S. Smith. Library J 88:4719 D 15 '63

Library services and construction act: what will it mean? address, July 1964. L. A. Martin. ALA Bul 58:689-94 S '64

Planning for the long haul toward meeting standards; Standards committee, Public library association. R. P. Tubby. ALA Bul 58:499+ Je '64

Public library association. ALA Bul 57:351-2 Ap '63

Slow cool burning; address, April 26, 1963. J. M. Cory. il Wilson Lib Bul 38:262-4+ N '63

Standards for everything; standards for special libraries. E. Moon. Library J 90:209 Ja 15 '65

Statistics

Coordination of library statistics. Wilson Lib Bul 38:121 O '63

Indexes of American public library statistics. ALA Bul 57:435 My '63

Information storage requirements for the contents of the world's libraries. J. W. Senders. bibliog il Science 141:1067-8 S 13 '63; Reply. Sci Am 209:72+ N '63

International standardization of library statistics. F. L. Schick. ALA Bul 58:1011-13 D '64

Library situation; facts and figures from Library services. Wilson Lib Bul 37:624 Ap '63

Tape recordings

Credo of a library conservative; adaptation of address, October 29, 1963. E. Wolf, 2d. Library J 89:1903-6 My 1 '64

Recorded reviews. J. E. Frey. il Wilson Lib Bul 39:333-4 D '64

Technical processes

Behind central processing. M. L. Bundy. il Library J 88:3539-43 O 1 '63

Central processing on a do-it-yourself basis; Lj book processing kits. D. Melcher. il Library J 90:316-19 Ja 15 '65

See also

School libraries—Technical processes

Theater collections

Collectors, speak up; reprint. S. C. Gross. il Library J 89:202-4 Ja 15 '64

Trustees, boards, committees, etc.

Challenge to leadership; summary of address, March 1962. W. E. Hinchliff. Library J 88:728-31 F 15 '63

Library boards: administrative or advisory? F. M. Hartz. Library J 88:733-5 F 15 '63

Trustee's role; freedom to read in Helen Kate Furness free library, Wallingford, Pa. H. A. Johnson. ALA Bul 57:631-3 Jl '63

Trustee's role in recruitment. Mrs W. J. Lynch. ALA Bul 58:60-1 Ja '64

Trustee's role in the new era of library cooperation. R. E. Williams. ALA Bul 57:559-60 Je '63

Trusteeship: trust or bust? J. Shera. Wilson Lib Bul 38:354 D '63; Discussion. 38:465, 530 F-Mr '64

Two interpreters: trustee relationships with librarian and staff; excerpt from Library trustee: a practical guide. V. G. Young. Library J 89:1184-7 Mr 15 '64

We can't afford bashful trustees. E. Hill. Library J 88:731-2 F 15 '63

See also

American library trustee association

Vandalism

See Vandalism

Volunteer workers

Cataloging by the bootstrap method; Delphi, Ind, public library. E. C. Biddle. ALA Bul 58:49-52 Ja '64; Discussion. 58:255, 261, 431-2 Ap, Je '64

On the care and feeding of volunteers. E. M. Swanker. Library J 88:1728-9 Ap 15 '63

See also

School libraries—Volunteer workers

Work with blind

Light in a dark world. R. W. White. bibliog Library J 88:4817-20+ D 15 '63

NAVH helps the visually handicapped; school children with sight problems. L. Marchi. il Library J 88:4821-2+ D 15 '63

Serving the handicapped child; Library for the blind, New York public library. E. L. Morris. il Wilson Lib Bul 38:165-9 O '63

Study of blind readers; research by American foundation for the blind. E. Josephson. bibliog f ALA Bul 58:543-7 Je '64

See also

Blind, Books for the

Talking books

Work with children

See Libraries, Childrens

Work with deaf

Bibliography for deaf children; letter to the editor. M. G. Newton. Library J 90:284 Ja 15 '65

Work with foreign born

Bilingual story hour program; NYPL branches. P. B. White. il Library J 89:3379-81 S 15 '64

Mishandled, but a landmark; San Francisco public library. W. R. Holman. il Library J 88:4698-700 D 15 '63

Multi-lingual library; Toronto public library, proposed Parkdale branch. H. C. Campbell. il Wilson Lib Bul 38:68-9+ S '63

Work with parents

Lo, the poor parent. E. Kingseed. ALA Bul 57:779-80 S '63

Work with schools

See Libraries and schools

Work with the aged

Library services for the aging to be discussed at NCOA meeting. Library J 89:592 F 1 '64

Work with the handicapped

Ferguson library entrance ramp commended by architecture group. il Library J 88:4603 D 1 '63

Hospital and institution library service; symposium, with editorial comment. bibliog il ALA Bul 58:746, 777-89+ O '64

Legs vs. architects; excerpt from Crow's nest. C. Day. Library J 88:4526-7 D 1 '63

Serving the handicapped child; Tropical school in Miami, Fla. A. Bow. il Wilson Lib Bul 38:170-2 O '63

Work with trade unions

Labor: a target for NLW? S. L. Simon. il Library J 88:1109-11 Mr 15 '63

Work with young people

Just show the movies; never mind the books! R. B. Moses. ALA Bul 59:58-60 Ja '65

Library and the teen age (cont of) Public library and the teen age. D. R. Watts. See issues of Wilson library bulletin to November 1964

On schizophrenic service; reaching teenager as a human being, not a student. E. Geller. Library J 89:3994 O 15 '64; Reply. T. Bulman. 89:4578 N 15 '64

Public library and the teen-age. D. R. Watts. See issues of Wilson library bulletin

Special section on library service to teenagers; symposium, ed. by T. Tyer. il Library J 89:1815-35+ Ap 15 '64

Supermarket come-on: paperback experiment with young adults; Boston public library. J. Manthorne. il Library J 90:302-5 Ja 15 '65

Teenage elysium: our own delusion; reprint. K. R. Shaffer. il Library J 89:4976-8 D 15 '64

LIBRARIES—Work with young people—*Cont.*
What are we all here for? J. V. Frost. Library J 89:4979-80 D 15 '64
See also
Libraries and students

Alaska

Damage to Alaskan libraries: report from the state librarian; letter. H. Dirtadian. ALA Bul 58:371 My '64

Arizona

See also
Tuscon, Ariz, public library

Arkansas

See also
Little Rock, Ark, public library

Asia

Asian and Pacific libraries ask for increased Unesco aid. Library J 89:1926 My 1 '64

California

California right-wing front groups attack book selection in libraries. Library J 89:4874 D 15 '64
Climate of intellectual freedom; why is it always so bad in California? address, November 6, 1964. E. Castagna. il ALA Bul 59:27-33 Ja '65
Governor appoints nine members to California P.L. development board. Library J 88:4590 D 1 '63
On the firing line in bad climate; excerpt from report. H. Madden. ALA Bul 59:33-4 Ja '65
Public libraries in California. ALA Bul 57:229 Mr '63
See also
Arcadia, Calif, public library
City of Commerce public library, Los Angeles
Fresno County, Calif, free library
Pasadena, Calif.—Libraries
Pasadena public library
San Bernardino, Calif, county free library
San Francisco public library
Santa Barbara, Calif, public library

Canada

See also
Canada—National library
Canadian library association
Libraries—Ontario
Toronto public library

Colorado

Denver: rapport and Round robin; JADA library service. E. Brewster. il Wilson Lib Bul 38:275-8 N '63
See also
Denver public library

Connecticut

Connecticut libraries organize. Library J 88:2221-2 Je 1 '63
Governor's committee reports on Connecticut libraries. Library J 88:740 F 15 '63
There goes that song again; report from the Governor's committee on libraries. Wilson Lib Bul 37:750+ My '63
Twelve Connecticut libraries receive foundation boost. Library J 88:4721 D 15 '63
See also
Cheshire, Conn, public library
Greenwich, Conn, library
New Haven, Conn, free public library
Westport, Conn, public library

Cuba

Cuba: public libraries and popular adult education. H. C. Campbell; reply. L. Deyá. Library J 88:1492+ Ap 1 '63

Denmark

Library adult education activities in public libraries of Germany, Denmark, and England; report. G. T. Stevenson. il ALA Bul 57:643-54 Jl '63

England

Library adult education activities in public libraries of Germany, Denmark, and England; report. G. T. Stevenson. il ALA Bul 57:643-54 Jl '63
U.S.A.A.F. 2nd air division, memorial room; Norwich, England, Central public library. il Wilson Lib Bul 38:23 S '63
See also
British museum
London—Libraries
Luton, England, public library
Norwich, England, public library

Europe

Library scene abroad. Library J 88:984-5 Mr 1 '63

Europe, Western

Library buildings of Britain and Europe, by A. Thompson. Review
Library J il 88:4529-30 D 1 '63. R. E. Ellsworth

Far East

Asian and Pacific libraries ask for increased Unesco aid. Library J 89:1926 My 1 '64

Florida

See also
Miami, Fla, public library
St Petersburg, Fla, public library

Georgia

See also
Albany, Ga.—Libraries
W. C. Bradley memorial library, Columbus, Ga.

Germany (Federal Republic)

Library adult education activities in public libraries of Germany, Denmark, and England; report. G. T. Stevenson. il ALA Bul 57:643-54 Jl '63

Great Britain

Another battle of the books; authors and librarians in Britain, 1951-1963. J. C. Harrison. il Library J 88:1946-9 My 15 '63
Book distribution in the United Kingdom. R. Barker. ALA Bul 57:523-7 Je '63
Book in hand: subject specialization, interregional cooperation. E. Moon. Library J 89:3704+ O 1 '64
British debate library fees. Library J 89:2757 Jl '64
British public libraries in search of standards; summaries of two reports. R. Surridge. il Library J 88:1950-5 My 15 '63
Great Britain reverses US problem: not enough teenagers in public libs. Library J 88:4833-4 D 15 '63
Library buildings of Britain and Europe, by A. Thompson. Review
Library J il 88:4529-30 D 1 '63. R. E. Ellsworth
New public library legislation introduced in Great Britain. Library J 89:1700 Ap 15 '64
To fill the empty mind; excerpts from address. F. M. Gardner. il Library J 89:3681-6 O 1 '64
Who cares? E. Moon. Library J 88:1958 My 15 '63
See also
Libraries—England
Library association

Hawaii

Committee on state library resources appointed by Hawaii governor. Library J 89:81 Ja 1 '64
Hawaiian public libraries have new central system. Pub W 183:47 Je 24 '63
See also
Honolulu—Library of Hawaii

Idaho

Library service in Idaho ranks 50th among states, librarian testifies; excerpts from statement, June 13, 1963. H. M. Miller. Library J 88:2862 Ag '63

Illinois

Statewide library planning in Illinois. ALA Bul 57:210 Mr '63
See also
Oak Park, Ill, public library

Indiana

See also
Delphi, Ind, public library
Elkhardt, Ind, public library
Purdue university, Lafayette, Ind.—Libraries

Iowa

Iowa: cross-county service. E. Grafton. Wilson Lib Bul 38:283-4+ N '63
See also
Cedar Rapids, Ia, public library

Italy

Italian libraries: a progress report. O. Pinto. bibliog f il Library J 88:721-3 F 15 '63

Japan

Richer by the United States; role of American cultural center. T. Osada. bibliog il Wilson Lib Bul 39:56-8+ S '64

Kansas

See also
Wichita, Kan, city library

LIBRARIES—*Continued*

Kentucky

See also
Jenkins public library, Jenkins, Ky.
Louisville free public library

Latin America

CLR grant for subject headings list to aid Latin American librarians. Library J 89:2566 Je 15 '64
Pan American union concludes Latin American seminar series. Library J 89:1212 Mr 15 '64
State department receives report on Latin American libraries. Library J 88:2220 Je 1 '63

Louisiana

Branch libraries in Louisiana shut down to improve service. Library J 89:2566 Je 15 '64
Lock-outs and arrests: groups of Negro students. Wilson Lib Bul 38:724+ My '64
Lockouts and arrests, repeat performance: groups of Negro students. Wilson Lib Bul 39:22 S '64
Negro students arrested in attempt to use library in Louisiana. Library J 89:1702 Ap 15 '64
See also
New Orleans public library

Malagasy

Mission to Malagasy. il Library J 89:4476-7 N 15 '64

Malaysia

Report from Malaya. A. Lage. Library J 90:201 Ja 15 '65

Maryland

Maryland school and pl librarians hold CWC-style local conference; Prince George's County, Md. Library J 88:4827 D 15 '63
Plan for political action; address. R. S. Ake. il Wilson Lib Bul 39:316-19 D '64
See also
Baltimore County, Md. public library
Enoch Pratt free library, Baltimore
Prince Georges County memorial library, Hyattsville, Md.

Massachusetts

Alive and wiggling; Paul Pratt memorial library, Cohasset, Mass; small library. S. E. Heywood. Library J 88:2954+ S 1 '63
Massachusetts undertakes study of regional public library systems. Library J 88:3038+ S 1 '63
Substitution and a suggestion; censorship action. E. J. Gaines. ALA Bul 57:711-12 S '63
See also
Boston public library
Brockton, Mass. public library
Concord, Mass. free public library
Worcester free public library

Michigan

See also
Detroit public library
Escanaba, Mich. Carnegie public library
Lansing, Mich.—Libraries
Michigan state library
Wayne County, Mich. library

Minnesota

See also
Anoka County library, Spring Lake Park
Minneapolis public library
St Paul public library

Mississippi

See also
Mississippi library association

Missouri

First two posters appear in Missouri's image campaign. Library J 88:4598-9 D 1 '63
Missouri tackles the image with surrealistic posters. Library J 88:3568 O 1 '63
See also
Harry S. Truman library, Independence, Mo.
St Louis County, Mo. library

Mongolia

Library scene abroad. Library J 88:984-5 Mr 1 '63

Montana

See also
Parmly Billings memorial library, Billings, Mont.

New Hampshire

New Hampshire: one-system state. M. P. McKay and R. H. Abbott. Wilson Lib Bul 38:280-3 N '63
New Hampshire story; with editorial comment. M. P. McKay and R. H. Abbott. il Library J 88:3169-72, 3176 S 15 '63
Smallness is the big problem. E. Moon; reply. M. P. McKay. Library J 88:894 Mr 1 '63
See also
New Hampshire library association

New Jersey

Library services on three levels recommended in New Jersey report. Library J 90:88 Ja 1 '65
Small library; thinking big; Mid-Bergen federation of free public libraries. E. Locke. Wilson Lib Bul 37:780-1 My '63
Statewide planning in New Jersey. ALA Bul 57:226 Mr '63
See also
Bloomfield public library
East Orange, N.J. public library
Fair Lawn, N.J. free public library
New Jersey state library, Trenton
Newark, N.J. public library
Paterson, N.J. free public library

New Mexico

Flying library: air service to Indian reservation by the Northwestern regional library. il Wilson Lib Bul 38:33 S '63

New York (state)

N.Y. library support and expenditure booms but not circulation. Library J 88:2222 Je 1 '63
New York: Pioneer revisited; Pioneer library system; report. H. Hacker. il Wilson Lib Bul 38:271-5 N '63
Panacea or Pandora's box? a look at central processing in New York state. V. J. Aceto. Library J 89:322-4+ Ja 15 '64; Discussion. 89:1284 Mr 15 '64
Patterns of partnership; address, October 1964. L. A. Martin. il Library J 89:4593-6 N 15 '64
Research for New York state 3-R program: reference and research library resources. Wilson Lib Bul 38:135 O '63
Students, LSCA, and three R's New York's targets for 1965. Library J 90:216 Ja 15 '65
See also
Buffalo and Erie County, N.Y. public library
Nassau library system
New City, N.Y. free library
New York public library
New York state library, Albany
Nioga library system
North Bellmore, N.Y. public library
Plainview-Old Bethpage, N.Y. public library
Riverhead, N.Y. free library
Westchester library system
Yonkers, N.Y. public library

North Carolina

Climate for progress. E. Hughey. il Library J 89:3255-60 S 15 '64
N. Carolina school libs. growing. Library J 89:339 Ja 15 '64

Ohio

Ohio librarians found library foundation. Library J 88:2478-9 Je 15 '63
Ohio rich in manuscript repositories. W. P. Marchman. Hobbies 68:110-11+ D '63
See also
Akron, Ohio, public library
Cleveland public library
Columbus, Ohio, public library
Ohio state library, Columbus
Public library of Cincinnati and Hamilton County
Rodman public library, Alliance, Ohio
Toledo, Ohio, public library

Oklahoma

Conference in Oklahoma; first Governor's conference on libraries. A. A. Ingram. Wilson Lib Bul 39:323-4 D '64

Ontario

Ontario reference survey recommends regional centers. Library J 89:4766 D 1 '64
See also
Toronto public library

Oregon

Report on Oregon public libraries shocking, says state librarian. Library J 88:740-2 F 15 '63
See also
Portland, Ore.—Libraries

Pakistan

Peace corps in perspective. N. Barron. bibliog il Library J 90:196-200 Ja 15 '65

LIBRARIES—*Continued*

Pennsylvania

Changing library scene; with editorial comment. K. E. Beasley. Library J 88:3155-60, 3176 S 15 '63
Full-time recruiting: the Pennsylvania story. D. H. Hunt. il Library J 89:2031-6 My 15 '64
188 in Pa; summary. R. Blasingame, jr. Wilson Lib Bul 37:834 Je '63
Pennsylvania LA conference hears first report on Blasingame survey; excerpts from report. R. Blasingame. Library J 89:4767-8 D 1 '64
Recruitment. M. Ricking. ALA Bul 57:670-1 Jl '63
See also
Abington library society, Jenkintown
Allentown, Pa, free library
Helen Kate Furness free library, Wallingford, Pa.
Martin memorial library, York, Pa.
Pennsylvania state library, Harrisburg
Philadelphia—Free library
Scranton, Pa, public library

Rhode Island

Legislative commission reports on libraries in Rhode Island. Library J 89:1048 Mr 1 '64
Legislative commission studies library laws and services in R.I. Library J 88:3814 O 15 '63
Report on Rhode Island libraries recommends sweeping changes; summary. J. A. Humphry and L. Wickersham. Library J 88:1844 My 1 '63

Russia

Impressive power of Soviet libraries reported by U.S. delegates to Russia. Library J 88:528-9 F 1 '63
International by definition; interview, ed by J. N. Berry, 3d. L. Vladimirov. il Library J 89:4469-72 N 15 '64
Soviet libraries and librarianship, by M. J. Ruggles and R. C. Swank. Review
Library J il 88:724-7 F 15 '63. V. N. Orlov
Wilson Lib Bul 37:786 My '63. F. M. Palmer

South Carolina

Aroused though retired; summary of letter. E. Moon. Library J 89:71 Ja 1 '64
South Carolina's program. E. P. Walker. ALA Bul 58:143-4 F '64

Southern states

Strengthening and improving library resources for southern higher education, by R. B. Downs. Review
ALA Bul 57:441 My '63
This is the fabric itself. R. Burns. Library J 88:4701-3 D 15 '63

Sweden

Swedish libraries; symposium, ed. by G. Ottervik. Library J 88:4299-331+ N 15 '63

Texas

See also
Dallas public library
Fort Worth public library
San Antonio, Tex, public library
Sterling municipal library, Baytown, Tex.
Texas state library, Austin

United States

Diagnosis; symposium; reply. J. D. Mack. Library J 88:366 F 1 '63
Forecast for 1964; reports from forty-seven states. il Library J 89:39-66 Ja 1 '64
If your library needs to improve. il Good H 156:169 My '63
Information retrieval. R. R. Shaw. bibliog Science 140:606-9 My 10 '63
Libraries and learning. O. Handlin. il Atlan 213:96+ Ap '64
Libraries: future unlimited; address, June 28, 1964. F. Keppel. ALA Bul 58:991-4 D '64; Excerpts. Sch & Soc 92:374-6 D 12 '64
Libraries in the USA; official Soviet report. N. F. Gavrilov and I. IU. Bagrova. ALA Bul 57:341-4 Ap '63
Library as a way to excellence in education. P. B. Knapp. ALA Bul 57:1039-42 D '63
Metropolitan public libraries in the sixties. H. T. Drennan. bibliog il Library J 89:67-70 Ja 1 '64
Needs of libraries; and what ALA can do to help meet them; report of the midwinter meetings of the Program evaluation and budget committee. ALA Bul 58:531-8 Je '64
On the road with British librarians. E. Moon. Library J 88:4332 N 15 '63
President signs $135 million library bill; excerpts from statement, February 11, 1964. L. B. Johnson. Library J 89:1046 Mr 1 '64; Same. ALA Bul 58:172-3 Mr '64
Public libraries bill approved by House education committee. Library J 88:3033 S 1 '63
Recent trends in public library adult services. E. Phinney. ALA Bul 57:262-6 Mr '63
Richer by the United States; role of American cultural center, Japan. T. Osada. bibliog il Wilson Lib Bul 39:56-8+ S '64
Sketch maps of resources. J. Lorenz. Library J 88:4708-9 D 15 '63
Small library; symposium. il Wilson Lib Bul 37:767-81 My '63; Discussion. 37:850; 38:143+, 325 Je, O, D '63
State of the Union message stresses need for libraries. Library J 89:584 F 1 '64
Substance and shadow; visit of British librarians to United States. R. Stokes. Library J 88:3808-9 O 15 '63
To overcome the myth; role of large city libraries. E. Castagna and R. Halverson. il Library J 89:3249-51 S 15 '64
Vandals in the library. J. C. Furnas. Read Digest 84:175-6+ Ja '64
Who cares? E. Moon. Library J 88:1958 My 15 '63
Who's underdeveloped? J. Berry. Library J 89:4488+ N 15 '64
Year's realities: reports from states on library progress in 1964 and comparisons with last year's forecast. il Library J 90:56-71 Ja 1 '65
Zeal and apathy. E. Moon. Library J 88:973 Mr 1 '63; Discussion. 88:1564+ Ap 15 '63
See also
Council on library resources, incorporated
Libraries, County
Library surveys
National library week
Special libraries association
United States—Library of Congress

Utah

New legislation, new buildings make 1964 big year for Utah. Library J 89:208 Ja 15 '64
See also
Salt Lake City public library

Virginia

See also
Fairfax County public library

Washington (state)

See also
Seattle public library

Wisconsin

Design for progress. Wilson Lib Bul 37:835 Je '63
See also
Milwaukee public library
Wausau, Wis, public library

Yugoslavia

Yugoslavian library faces 20th century problems; University library of Zagreb. H. Clark. il Library J 88:718-20 F 15 '63

LIBRARIES (rooms)

Old porch is now a study. il Sunset 131:179 O '63
See also
Libraries, Private

LIBRARIES, Childrens

Books are her friends; children's room, Westport, Conn, public library. il Look 27:54a-54b+ My 7 '63
Bruce Joffe's private library; an unusual childrens library in Flushing, L.I. S. Havens. il Library J 88:2066-8 My 15 '63
Children's library service in Sweden; short survey. A. M. Kylberg. il Library J 88:4417-20 N 15 '63
Junior book collectors; book fair with a twist; Louis Pasteur junior high school, Los Angeles, Calif. H. J. Kunkle. il Wilson Lib Bul 38:176-7 O '63
New children's book center opens in Madison, Wisconsin. Library J 88:4014+ O 15 '63
Notice to librarians. M. F. Danes. il Library J 88:2059-62 My 15 '63
Pioneer in the war on poverty: NYPL. A. Baker. il Library J 89:3376-9 S 15 '64
Sea room for the impressionable years. A. Sanford. il Horn Bk 40:475-84 O '64
What if. . .? E. Rudin. Library J 88:812 F 15 '63
See also
Book week
Story telling

LIBRARIES, Childrens—*Continued*

Anecdotes, facetiae, satire, etc.

In the act; excerpt from Exhibits round table, spoof on Image of the new librarian at ALA meeting. il Library J 89:4112-14 O 15 '64

Book selection

See Book selection

Projects

No eleventh book. M. A. McMillan. Horn Bk 40:251-4 Je '64
Summer reading programs. il Wilson Lib Bul 38:669-72 Ap '64
Summer reading programs; letters. il Wilson Lib Bul 37:682-6 Ap '63
To reward or not to reward, that is the question. C. W. Field. Wilson Lib Bul 37:885 Je '63

LIBRARIES, Church
Challenge of church libraries; Bethesda, Md. R. S. Smith. bibliog il Library J 88:3000-3 S 1 '63
Church library choice. Christian Cent 80:1109-10, 1137, 1172, 1241, 1310, 1339 S 11-25, O 9, 23-30 '63

LIBRARIES, College. See College libraries

LIBRARIES, County
Climate for progress; North Carolina. E. Hughey. il Library J 89:3255-60 S 15 '64
Denver: rapport and Round robin; JADA library service. E. Brewster. il Wilson Lib Bul 38:275-8 N '63
New York: Pioneer revisited; Pioneer library system; report. H. Hacker. il Wilson Lib Bul 38:271-5 N '63
See also
San Bernardino, Calif. county free library

LIBRARIES, High school. See High school libraries

LIBRARIES, Hospital
Hospital and institution library service; symposium, with editorial comment. bibliog il ALA Bul 58:746, 777-89+ O '64
Starting library service to hospitals; Columbia Mo. public library. T. F. McArthur. ALA Bul 57:859-60 O '63
See also
Association of hospital and institution libraries

LIBRARIES, Institution
Hospital and institution library service; symposium, with editorial comment. bibliog il ALA Bul 58:746, 777-89+ O '64

LIBRARIES, Instruction in use of. See Libraries—Instruction in use

LIBRARIES, Medical. See Medical libraries

LIBRARIES, Moving of. See Moving of libraries

LIBRARIES, Prison. See Prison libraries

LIBRARIES, Private
Ask the young man who owns one . . . hundred: paperbacks in high school. W. Hinchliff. Sr Schol 85:26T D 2 '64
Bruce Joffe's private library: an unusual childrens library in Flushing, L.I. S. Havens. il Library J 88:2066-8 My 15 '63
By books possessed. R. S. Fulton. il Newsweek 62:74 Ag 12 '63
For a child's library; a paperback book list. Library J 90:312-13 Ja 15 '65
Frederic Melcher library of books about books; children's collection. A. J. Richter. il Library J 89:4118-20 O 15 '64
How two book-beset writers created a tandem library. il House & Gard 125:40-1 Ap '64
One-hundred-dollar understanding: personal library of paperback books. R. Harwell and S. W. Hilyard. bibliog Library J 88:1937-40 My 15 '63
Two Connecticut girls start backyard neighborhood library; S. Blake and K. Twining. Library J 89:1393 Mr 15 '64
See also
Book collecting

LIBRARIES, Private school. See School libraries

LIBRARIES, Regional
Massachusetts undertakes study of regional public library systems. Library J 88:3038+ S 1 '63
Regional reference services. R. P. Stewart; G. Garrison; A. F. Reilly. bibliog il Library J 89:1676-87 Ap 15 '64

LIBRARIES, Rental
Rental library: a report. C. B. Anderson. Pub W 183:146-7 Je 10 '63

LIBRARIES, School. See School libraries

LIBRARIES, Ship
Seven Seas university floats a library. Library J 88:2659 Jl '63

LIBRARIES, Special
Information sciences; special libraries and librarians. R. S. Taylor. Library J 88:4161-3 N 1 '63
Interdependence. M. Griffin. Library J 88:1126 Mr 15 '63
One of a species; special library, past, present, and future; excerpts from address, April 1963. P. Wasserman. il Library J 89:797-802 F 15 '64
Special librarian. P. Wasserman; J. Harvey; A. M. Rees. bibliog il Library J 89:4279-94 N 1 '64; Discussion. 89:4840+ D 15 '64
See also
Medical libraries
Research libraries
Special libraries association

Standards

See Libraries—Standards

LIBRARIES, State
Case of the unknown library. J. F. Fixx. il Sat R 47:45-6 Ap 11 '64
Climate for progress; North Carolina. E. Hughey. il Library J 89:3255-60 S 15 '64
State librarians examine services: ALA president proposes national plan. Library J 89:77-8 Ja 1 '64
State libraries. C. R. Leigh. ALA Bul 58:532 Je '64
See also
American association of state libraries
New Jersey state library, Trenton
Ohio state library, Columbus
Pennsylvania state library, Harrisburg
Texas state library, Austin

LIBRARIES, Thefts from. See Book thefts

LIBRARIES, Traveling
See also
Bookmobiles

LIBRARIES and adult education. See Adult education—Library participation

LIBRARIES and art
Great art in the elementary library; University of Chicago laboratory schools. M. Seckel. il Library J 88:4813-16 D 15 '63
Picasso in the nursery. O. Teller. il Library J 89:4986-8 D 15 '64

LIBRARIES and audio-visual materials
ALA preconference workshop stresses A-V importance to libs. Library J 88:3275 S 15 '63
A-V avant garde; Audio-visual workshop, ALA pre-conference meeting. G. Stevenson. Library J 88:3022-3 S 1 '63
Centralization of audio-visual and professional materials; Central school district no. 1, Lake Mohegan, N.Y. S. Mahoney. il Wilson Lib Bul 37:868-9+ Je '63
New and future trends in the use of audio-visual materials; excerpts from address, July 14, 1963. R. B. Hudson. il ALA Bul 58:39-42 Ja '64
On misplaced devotion. D. M. Broderick. il Library J 90:314-15 Ja 15 '65

LIBRARIES and authors
Another battle of the books; authors and librarians in Britain, 1951-1963. J. C. Harrison. il Library J 88:1946-9 My 15 '63
Book rental unfair to authors, says novelist Richard Condon. Library J 89:4492 N 15 '64

LIBRARIES and booksellers
Business of book buying, as special librarians see it. M. Saul. il Library J 88:2636-9 Jl '63
Public library bookstore. E. J. Humeston, jr. il Wilson Lib Bul 37:563-4+ Mr '63

LIBRARIES and filmstrips
Filmstrips; selection, evaluation, cataloging, processing. C. T. Cox. bibliog il Wilson Lib Bul 38:178-82 O '63
Parents help with audio-visual aids. M. Bise. Wilson Lib Bul 37:787-8+ My '63

LIBRARIES and labor. See Libraries—Work with trade unions

LIBRARIES and moving pictures
Just show the movies; never mind the books! R. B. Moses. ALA Bul 59:58-60 Ja '65
See also
Libraries—Moving picture collections

LIBRARIES and Negroes
Access study; symposium. il Library J 88:4685-709 D 15 '63; Discussion. 88:4710-12; 89:424, 976+ D 15 '63, F 1, Mr 1 '64
Access to public libraries study. il ALA Bul 57:742-5 S '63
Albany, Ga. public library reopens on vertical integration basis. Library J 88:1638 Ap 15 '63
Branch libraries in Louisiana shut down to improve service. Library J 89:2566 Je 15 '64
Can we afford to ignore the Negro? T. F. Parker. bibliog Library J 88:4716-17 D 15 '63

LIBRARIES and Negroes—*Continued*
Day in Bedford Stuyvesant; Macon branch, Brooklyn public library. E. Moon. il Library J 89:3689-93 O 1 '64
Eleven Negroes arrested in Georgia at horizontally integrated library; Bradley memorial library in Columbus, Ga. Library J 88:2854 Ag '63
Joiner and goer service to Bedford Stuyvesant area by Brooklyn public library. K. Molz. il Wilson Lib Bul 38:349-51 D '63
Libraries and Emancipation centennial. E. J. Josey. Negro Hist Bul 26:219-21 Ap '63
Lock-outs and arrests in three Louisiana towns. Wilson Lib Bul 38:724+ My '64
Lockouts and arrests, repeat performance: in three Louisiana townships. Wilson Lib Bul 39:22 S '64
Mississippi's silence scored; letter to the editor. Library J 88:4410+ N 15 '63
Negro awakening: what librarians can do. A. Bontemps. Library J 88:2997-9 S 1 '63
Negro college libraries and ACRL standards. E. J. Josey. bibliog il Library J 88:2989-96 S 1 '63
Negro students arrested in attempt to use library in Louisiana. Library J 89:1702 Ap 15 '64
New Orleans replies to the New republic; excerpts from letter. J. Cushman. Library J 89:2758 Jl '64
Postscript on the Albany matter. ALA Bul 57:307 Ap '63
Public libraries desegregate. Christian Cent 80:948 Jl 31 '63
Public library integration in thirteen southern states; excerpts from Integration in public library service in thirteen southern states, 1954-1962. B. L. Bell. il Library J 88:4713-15 D 15 '63; Discussion. 89:424+ F 1 '64
Questioning a question; and some of the answers; segregation in recipients of Canfield Fisher awards. E. Moon. il Library J 88:2644-7 Jl '63
Race issue clouds hearings on public library legislation. Library J 88:1962 My 15 '63
Racial integration of public libraries. Sch & Soc 91:345+ N 16 '63
Reading: Negro youths' quest for certainty. E. J. Josey. Negro Hist Bul 27:158-9+ Ap '64
School library program for children in a depressed area. H. B. Brown and E. D. Sinnette. bibliog il ALA Bul 58:643-7 Jl '64
Still no decision in Albany. E. T. Moore. ALA Bul 57:111-16 F '63

LIBRARIES and publishers
AASL urges organized and wide use of trade book examination centers. Library J 88:1308 Mr 15 '63
Book exam center study completed; Publishers library promotion group. Library J 89:4126 O 15 '64
Book examination centers listed in survey by publishers' group. Publishers' library promotion group. Library J 89:3709 O 1 '64
Book-making regressing? letter to the editor. R. H. Donahugh. Library J 88:4680+ D 15 '63
Book publishers' interests in reprographic copyright; excerpts from address, May 1963. C. G. Benjamin. Library J 88:2837-41 Ag '63
Choosing the right book today: children's books; symposium, with editorial comment. bibliog il Library J 89:4963-75 D 15 '64
Libraries and university press books; summary of addresses. W. A. Wood and J. P. Dessauer. il Pub W 184:51-2 Jl 15 '63
Martin Mayer, Leland B. Jacobs speak at New books preview. Library J 88:3277-8 S 15 '63
Melody lingers on a sour note; YASD-ASD joint program. P. Allen. Library J 89:3403 S 15 '64; Discussion. 89:4578+ N 15 '64
Publishers quiz librarians in survey on book catalogs. Library J 88:2095-7 My 15 '63
Stormy marriage. J. J. Veenstra. il Library J 88:2634-5 Jl '63
What books for the young adult? publisher asks, librarian answers. A. Craig; J. Rowell. Library J 89:4103-6 O 15 '64

LIBRARIES and readers
Accent on the individual reader; why the Reading for an age of change series? M. E. Hawes. Wilson Lib Bul 38:70+ S '63
Access study advisory committee has second thoughts on branches. Library J 88:4176+ N 1 '63
Access study; symposium. il Library J 88:4685-709 D 15 '63; Discussion. 88:4710-12; 89:424, 976+ D 15 '63, F 1, Mr 1 '64
Access to education; concerning Access to public libraries survey, conducted by International research associates; symposium. bibliog il Wilson Lib Bul 38:335-51+ D '63; Reply. S. L. Jackson. 38:465 F '64
Backward to normalcy; cultural behavior patterns of the normal American family. J. Shera. Wilson Lib Bul 38:561 Mr '64
Centerpiece of a library; excerpts from address, October 10, 1964. R. J. Neutra. il Library J 89:4695-9 D 1 '64
Changing library scene; Pennsylvania's new system, with editorial comment. K. E. Beasley. Library J 88:3155-60, 3176 S 15 '63
Everybody's library: Library of Congress. E. E. Hamer. il Library J 90:49-55 Ja 1 '65
Librarian vs. scholar-user. H. Draper. il Library J 89:1907-10 My 1 '64; Discussion. 89:2694, 3056+ Jl, S 1 '64
Man-in-the-street; test ban treaty and role of libraries. E. Moon. Library J 88:3035 S 1 '63
More fruitful use of knowledge. J. M. Chancellor. ALA Bul 57:326-9 Ap '63
Mystery of the first law of thermodynamics or, Trading stamp sex; address, 1964. M. L'Engle. il Library J 89:4851-6 D 15 '64
Queue theory for libraries. R. S. Potts. Library J 88:2956 S 1 '63
Reading the lessons; standing of Access study now? E. Moon. Library J 89:817 F 15 '64
Report on the study of access to public libraries. ALA Bul 58:299-304 Ap '64
To fill the empty mind; excerpts from address. F. M. Gardner. il Library J 89:3681-6 O 1 '64
Warm puppy, or a library card? L. M. Bradshaw. Library J 88:1634 Ap 15 '63

Anecdotes, facetiae, satire, etc.

Recruitment rewrite. W. Jones. Library J 89:3114+ S 1 '64

LIBRARIES and research
Five-year analysis published of library research activities; concerning Library research in progress (LiRiP) Library J 88:4590-1 D 1 '63
Librarian vs. scholar-user. H. Draper. il Library J 89:1907-10 My 1 '64; Reply. P. R. Lewis. 89:2694 Jl '64
Librarian vs. scholar-user. H. Draper. il Library J 89:1907-10 My 1 '64; Discussion. 89:2694, 3056+ Jl, S 1 '64
Scientific library services to be studied in Britain. Library J 89:2051 My 15 '64
Teaching of research in the library schools. S. L. Jackson. Library J 88:2206-7 Je 1 '63
Tips from teachers; report by the National council of teachers of English. E. Moon. Library J 88:4167+ N 1 '63

LIBRARIES and schools
Battle for library books. J. Wakeman. il Parents Mag 38:138-9 Ap '63
Challenge and opportunity; Enoch Pratt free library, Baltimore; excerpts from address, October 12, 1963. E. Castagna. il Library J 89:1825-7 Ap 15 '64
Cooperative venture; Joint book selection committee of Miami public library and Dade County school libraries. M. H. Edmonds. Wilson Lib Bul 38:689 Ap '64
Crisis in the public libraries; summary of report. Sch & Soc 91:82 F 23 '63
In search of answers: the libraries report; symposium. il Wilson Lib Bul 37:853-62+ Je '63
Law, liberty and libraries; excerpts from address, May 1, 1963. W. J. Brennan, jr. il Library J 88:2417-20 Je 15 '63
Let them have books. M. Rossoff. il Sat R 47:64-5+ N 21 '64; Discussion. 47:44 D 19 '64
Notes on school-library cooperation. Library J 89:4994 D 15 '64
Recent developments in library service to students; excerpts from address, March 1964. H. L. Hamill. ALA Bul 58:489-96 Je '64
Student needs: response to challenge; symposium. il Wilson Lib Bul 39:383-401+ Ja '65

See also
Libraries and students

LIBRARIES and social and economic problems
Access to education; concerning Access to public libraries survey, conducted by International research associates; symposium. bibliog il Wilson Lib Bul 38:335-51+ D '63; Reply. S. L. Jackson. 38:465 F '64
Books as weapons. K. Molz. il Wilson Lib Bul 38:840-3+ Je '64
Day in Bedford Stuyvesant; Macon branch, Brooklyn public library. E. Moon. il Library J 89:3689-93 O 1 '64

LIBRARIES and social and economic problems —*Continued*
Deprived child. S. H. Wheeler. Wilson Lib Bul 39:342 D '64
Dialogue in Dedham? a report on the symposium on library functions in the changing metropolis; with address by D. Lacy. K. Molz. il Wilson Lib Bul 38:50-64 S '63
Just show the movies; never mind the books! R. B. Moses. ALA Bul 59:58-60 Ja '65
Message to American librarians. S. Shriver. Wilson Lib Bul 38:833 Je '64
Need and opportunity: concerning symposium by alumni association of Rutgers library school. E. Moon. Library J 89:1922 My 1 '64
Paperback attack on poverty: free book program for needy children; excerpts from address, April 1964. H. H. Humphrey. Library J 89:2128 My 15 '64
Providing school library services for the culturally disadvantaged; ed. by J. Lowrie. bibliog il ALA Bul 58:523-6, 643-7, 705-11, 816-21, 1003-6; 59:49-53 Je-O, D '64-Ja '65
Underprivileged reader; report on Access to public libraries survey, conducted by International research associates. E. Geller. Wilson Lib Bul 38:65-7 S '63
War on poverty; symposium, ed. with introd. by H. T. Drennan. il Library J 89:3239-74+ S 15 '64. Discussion. 89:3274, 3354, 4674+ S 15, D 1 '64
See also
Libraries—Work with foreign born

Bibliography

Culturally disadvantaged child. R. F. Berneis. ALA Bul 59:53-7 Ja '65

LIBRARIES and state
Clear choice: for President Johnson and aid to libraries. E. Moon. il Library J 89:3926-7 O 15 '64; Discussion 89:4232+, 4448+, 4872+ N 1-15, D 15 '64
Development of library resources. P. L. Berry. bibliog f Ann Am Acad 356:126-32 N '64
Full range of weapons; federal programs provide libraries for the attack on poverty. H. T. Drennan and others. il Library J 89:3266-73 S 15 '64
Libraries for an affluent society with frayed edges; address, July 3, 1964. E. Castagna. ALA Bul 58:635-8 Jl '64
Library and the legislature. R. S. Ake; C. M. Mathias, jr; A. A. Ingram. il Wilson Lib Bul 39:315-24 D '64
National education improvement act. G. Krettek and H. W. Hubbard. ALA Bul 57:309-11 Ap '63
New Hampshire story; with editorial comment. M. P. McKay and R. H. Abbott. il Library J 88:3169-72, 3176 S 15 '63
State and federal support of libraries; excerpt from address, July 13, 1963. J. E. Fogarty. ALA Bul 57:772-3 S '63
What's happening in education? new education bills. W. D. Boutwell. PTA Mag 58:13 Ap '64

LIBRARIES and students
ALA announces program for conference within a conference. Library J 88:1844+ My 1 '63
Boy who cried books; address, April 10, 1963. L. Comstock. Library J 88:2087 My 15 '63
Conference-within-a-conference with address by L. Martin. ALA Bul 57:734-41 S '63
Crisis in the public libraries; summary of report. Sch & Soc 91:82 F 23 '63
Education: a decade of dilemmas; excerpts from address, July 18, 1963. S. B. Gould. ALA Bul 57:837+ O '63
Facts, values and libraries; excerpts from address, July 16, 1963. M. W. Gross. ALA Bul 57:829-36 O '63
Figure in the carpet; report on the ALA conference within a conference. K. Molz. il Wilson Lib Bul 38:44-9 S '63
Great Britain reverses US problem: not enough teenagers in public libs. Library J 88:4833-4 D 15 '63
In search of answers: the libraries report; symposium. il Wilson Lib Bul 37:853-62+ Je '63
Lo, the poor parent. E. Kingseed. ALA Bul 57:779-80 S '63
Maryland school and pl librarians hold CWC-style local conference; Prince George's County, Md. Library J 88:4827 D 15 '63
Metropolitan reference services: patterns, problems, solutions; Detroit public library. K. G. Harris. il Library J 88:1606-11 Ap 15 '63
Mid-Manhattan facility for students planned by New York public library. Library J 89:1048-9 Mr 1 '64
Patterns of partnership: New York state libraries; address, October 1964. L. A. Martin. il Library J 89:4593-6 N 15 '64
Plans set for first-time ALA conference within a conference. Library J 88:2091-2 My 15 '63
Positive approach; Escanaba, Mich. Carnegie public library; letter to the editor. H. R. Courtright. Library J 89:1172 Mr 15 '64
Problem, no! opportunity, yes! ALA's conference within a conference looks at library service to students. E. Rudin and E. Moon. il Library J 88:2829-36 Ag '63
Reading conclave? Sr Schol 83:1T-3T S 13 '63
Recent developments in library service to students; excerpts from address, March 1964. H. L. Hamill. ALA Bul 58:489-96 Je '64
Scanty information on student use: Enoch Pratt free library. R. Ake. Library J 88:4707-8 D 15 '63
Service to students at York now reported satisfactory. Library J 88:1964 My 15 '63
Socio-economic factors in library service to students; excerpts. M. L. Jones. il ALA Bul 58:1003-6 D '64
Student needs: response to challenge; symposium. il Wilson Lib Bul 39:383-401+ Ja '65
Student problem resolved at York, Pa. library. Library J 88:976 Mr 1 '63
Student problem strikes. E. Moon. Library J 88:736-8 F 15 '63
Students and libraries. J. E. Bryan. ALA Bul 57:213 Mr '63
Students, libraries, and the educational process; excerpt from address, June 22, 1962. J. E. Bryan. Sch & Soc 91:39-41 Ja 26 '63
Up to our ears in students, or, Something's got to give; Enoch Pratt free library, Baltimore; excerpts from address, May 2, 1963. E. Castagna. il Library J 88:2421-3 Je 15 '63
See also
Libraries—Work with young people

LIBRARIES and television
Book for burning. J. Shera. Wilson Lib Bul 37:790 My '63
Reports on library-TV cooperation; NYPL and television station, WNDT. ALA Bul 58:47-8 Ja '64

LIBRARIES and the public. See Libraries—Public relations

LIBRARIES and unemployment. See Libraries and social and economic problems

LIBRARIES, documentation and archives, Division of Unesco. See United Nations educational scientific and cultural organization—Division of libraries, documentation and archives

LIBRARY administration
California LA presents plan for public library improvement. Library J 88:742 F 15 '63
Library boards: administrative or advisory? F. M. Hartz. Library J 88:733-5 F 15 '63
Shared perspectives, exchange of administrative viewpoints and knowledge. W. Jones. Library J 89:3706 O 1 '64
See also
Libraries—Trustees, boards, committees, etc.

LIBRARY administration division of ALA. See American library association—Library administration division

LIBRARY advertising. See Library publicity

LIBRARY architecture
American architect to be chosen for Kennedy memorial library. Library J 89:2301-2 Je 1 '64
Architectural awards go to seventeen libraries. il Library J 88:1963-4 My 15 '63
Architectural issue (cont) il Library J 88:4521-87; 89:4695-761 D 1 '63, D 1 '64
Architectural winners. il Library J 89:1914-17 My 1 '64
Architecture and design; Swedish public libraries. S. Mohlenbrock. il Library J 88:4326-31 N 15 '63
Be realistic in space planning, architect advises special librarians; statement, April 25, 1963. W. J. Rooney. Library J 88:2223 Je 1 '63
Bold masses in Tokyo; library for Gakushuin university. il Arch Forum 121:156-7 Ag '64
Building briefs (cont) Library J 88:539, 1973, 2430+, 2666, 2864, 3582, 4187-8, 4346, 4726; 89:1055, 1580, 3934, 4314, 4775-6, 4880-1 F 1, My 15, Je 15-Ag, O 1, N 1-15, D 15 '63, Mr 1, Ap 1, O 15-N 1, D 1-15 '64
Buildings for books; eight new libraries. il Arch Forum 120:80-97 My '64
Buildings in brief. Library J 89:1710-11, 2579, 3125 Ap 15, Je 15, S 1 '64

LIBRARY architecture—*Continued*
Call in an expert. W. Jones. Library J 89:1924 My 1 '64; Discussion. 89:2692+ Jl '64
Campbell and Aldrich win competition for Tufts university library. il Arch Rec 134: 12-13 O '63
Daring design for a German library; University of Giessen. W. M. Ostrem. il Wilson Lib Bul 38:406-7 Ja '64
Double-decker carrels; letter to the editor. W. Radford. Library J 89:1892-3 My 1 '64
Informal but private; fifth Building and equipment institute. J. H. Wright. Library J 89:2947-9 Ag '64
Lafayette college, Pa. new library. il Wilson Lib Bul 38:454 F '64
Libraries. il Arch Forum 118:114-17 F '63
LAD pre-conference institute to study building problems. Library J 88:2223-4 Je 1 '63
Library building awards. il Wilson Lib Bul 37:844-5 Je '63
Library building consultant; address, July, 1963. K. D. Metcalf. ALA Bul 57:1043-7 D '63
Library buildings award program announces second competition; American institute of architects, the American library association and the National book committee. Library J 88:4602 D 1 '63
Marble to see through; Beinecke rare book and manuscript library. il Newsweek 62: 112 O 21 '63
New building abroad. il Arch Forum 118:104-5 Je '63
Panel to advise Boston on architect for addition. Library J 88:2659 Jl '63
Planning functional quarters for the school library. J. L. Taylor. il Sch Life 47:16-20 N '64
Planning school library quarters; symposium. bibliog f il ALA Bul 58:103-11+ F '64
Plans and consultants; Building and equipment institute. H. L. Roth. Library J 88: 3027-8 S 1 '63
Rare book library at Yale dedicated. il Arch Rec 134:12-13 N '63
School for consultants held at University of Colorado; report. M. Van Buren. Library J 89:3710+ O 1 '64
Second Library buildings award program. il Wilson Lib Bul 38:620 Ap '64
Second Library buildings awards. il ALA Bul 58:381-6 My '64
Second program of library awards cites three for top honors. il Arch Rec 135:12 Ap '64
Sixteen library buildings chosen for awards. Pub W 185:50-1 Ap 20 '64
Small libraries. il Arch Rec 133:159-68 Ap '63

Air conditioning

Library air-conditioning design. A. Greenberg. il Arch Rec 135:173-4 F '64

LIBRARY assistants
Background for a beginning. W. Brahm. Library J 90:78-9 Ja 1 '65
Low-IQ page volunteers. H. S. Consear. il Library J 89:1830-1+ Ap 15 '64
Pages on wheels; Detroit public library. il Library J 88:4528 D 1 '63
See also
Catalogers

Anecdotes, facetiae, satire, etc.

Down from Valhalla; specialization among library pages. W. Jones. Library J 89:580 F 1 '64

Education

Library training programs. il Library J 88: 2194-205 Je 1 '63

LIBRARY association
Aid for British academic libraries sought by Library association. Library J 89:1926+ My 1 '64
Library association recommends standards for college libraries. Library J 89:4492 N 15 '64
Our man in London; first presentation of Wheatley medal for an outstanding index. New Yorker 40:48-51 N 28 '64
Scientific library services to be studied in Britain. Library J 89:2051 My 15 '64

LIBRARY association of Portland, Ore. See Portland, Ore.—Libraries

LIBRARY associations
Infant Canadian school library assn. begins to walk, talk, plan standards. Library J 88:2097 My 15 '63
Keep talking; with editorial comment. W. Jones. Library J 89:2966-7 Ag '64
Membership means involvement. W. Jones. Library J 89:1044 Mr 1 '64
Memo to members; concerning statement on requirements of chapter status in ALA. E. Castagna. ALA Bul 58:670-1 S '64
State library association activities. Library J 89:4126 O 15 '64
State library associations and National library week. G. T. Stevenson. ALA Bul 58: 37-8 Ja '64
Swedish library cooperation. G. Ottervik. Library J 88:4316-18 N 15 '63
Two stars from Georgia; reflections on the ALA conference in St Louis. E. Moon. il Library J 89:2919-28 Ag '64
See also names of Library associations, e.g. American library association

LIBRARY bill of rights
Courage and cowardice; address, November 15-17, 1962. E. Castagna. il Library J 88:504-6 F 1 '63

LIBRARY boards. See Libraries—Trustees, boards, committees, etc.

LIBRARY book clubs. See Book clubs

LIBRARY book trucks. See Library furniture and equipment

LIBRARY bookbinding. See Bookbinding

LIBRARY budgets. See Libraries—Finance

LIBRARY buildings. See Library architecture

LIBRARY catalogs. See Catalogs, Library

LIBRARY censorship. See Libraries—Censorship

LIBRARY classification. See Classification

LIBRARY conferences
Calendar. See issues of Library journal
Cold meet; library association meetings. J. Orne. Library J 88:1960 My 15 '63
Columbia holds work conference on the instructional materials center; school library as a center. Library J 89:4132+ O 15 '64
Conference in Oklahoma; first Governor's conference on libraries. A. A. Ingram. Wilson Lib Bul 39:323-4 D '64
Dialogue in Dedham? a report on the symposium on library functions in the changing metropolis; with address by D. Lacy. K. Molz. il Wilson Lib Bul 38:50-64 S '63
Meetings, courses, associations, etcetera. See issues of Wilson library bulletin
O! medium, O! media; reflections on work-study conference on the Implications of the new media for the teaching of library science. J. H. Shera. Library J 88:4149-51 N 1 '63
St John's conference speakers present living goals and TV. Library J 89:1210 Mr 15 '64
Too little forward motion; letter to the editor. S. L. Jackson. Library J 89:1888 My 1 '64
See also
American library association—Meetings. 1963
Conference of eastern college librarians

Anecdotes, facetiae, satire, etc.

Mr Dooley on law librarians; excerpts from address, 1963. E. J. Bander. il Library J 89:575-7 F 1 '64

LIBRARY cooperation
Agricultural library network; role of NAL or National agricultural library. K. B. Payne. bibliog il Library J 88:4143-8 N 1 '63
Book in hand: subject specialization, interregional cooperation in Britain. E. Moon. Library J 89:3704+ O 1 '64
Challenge of change; excerpts from address, October 19, 1962; with editorial comment. W. Brahm. Library J 88:3164-5, 3176 S 15 '63
Cooperate; but not too much; Nassau, N.Y. library system. E. Moon. Library J 88:1841 My 1 '63; Discussion. 88:2366+, il 3166-8, 4104+ Je 15, S 15, N 1 '63
Cooperation in acquisitions; from Swedish to Scandia plan. T. Kleberg. il Library J 88: 4319-22 N 15 '63
Interdependence. M. Griffin. Library J 88: 1126 Mr 15 '63
Interstate compact for libraries; address, November 1963. ALA Bul 58:132-4 F '64
Inter-university library cooperation demonstrated in two separate projects; Syracuse university and the University of Toronto. Library J 88:4596 D 1 '63
Logic or lip service? address, April 1964. W. Brahm. Library J 89:3093-8 S 1 '64; Reply. W. A. Wilkinson. 89:3900+ O 15 '64
Nassau library system experiments with direct access pilot study. Library J 89:4494 N 15 '64
New children's book center opens in Madison, Wisconsin. Library J 88:4014+ O 15 '63

LIBRARY cooperatin—*Continued*
Planning for cooperation; address, October 18, 1963. R. Munn. ALA Bul 58:496-9 Je '64
Report on Rhode Island libraries recommends sweeping changes; summary. J. A. Humphry and L. Wickersham. Library J 88:1844 My 1 '63
San Diego science libraries form cooperative association; Associated science libraries of San Diego. Library J 88:4181 N 1 '63
Shared perspective, exchange of administrative viewpoints and knowledge. W. Jones. Library J 89:3706 O 1 '64
Some solutions for urgent questions. G. K. Schenk. Wilson Lib Bul 39:497+ F '65
Swedish library cooperation. G. Ottervik. Library J 88:4316-18 N 15 '63
Time is a commodity; regional library service in eastern Massachusetts. D. Nyren. il Library J 88:1943-5 My 15 '63; Reply with rejoinder. B. G. Wade. 88:2582 Jl '63
Use of system borrower's cards increases in Westchester County. Library J 89:1706-7 Ap 15 '64
Working together; symposium, ed. by J. G. Lorenz. il Wilson Lib Bul 38:260-4+ N '63
See also
Interlibrary loans
United States—Library of Congress—Union catalog

LIBRARY deposit stations. See Libraries—Branches and stations

LIBRARY education. See Library schools and education

LIBRARY education division. See American library association—Library education division

LIBRARY equipment. See Library furniture and equipment

LIBRARY exhibits
Art + math = SRO; Greenwich, Conn. library. F. G. Donald. il Wilson Lib Bul 37:574-5 Mr '63
Displays for the month. See issues of Wilson library bulletin
Good reading for youth show opens in four pilot states. Library J 89:340 Ja 15 '64
John F. Kennedy library exhibit; first display of tour. E. Cameron. il Wilson Lib Bul 39:63-5 S '64
Like diamonds from Tiffany's; Greenwich, Conn. library. J. W. Bryant. il Library J 89:199-201 Ja 15 '64
Notice to librarians; displays in children's rooms. M. F. Danes. il Library J 88:2059-62 My 15 '63
$1 million book exhibit at Dallas public library. Library J 88:3575 O 1 '63
Word about displays. il Wilson Lib Bul 39:462-3 F '65
See also
Seattle—Century 21 exposition, 1962

LIBRARY extension
Extending library service; ed. by G. K. Schenk. See issues of Wilson library bulletin
See also
Bookmobiles
Libraries, County

LIBRARY files. See Files and filing (documents, etc)

LIBRARY finance. See Libraries—Finance

LIBRARY floors. See Floors

LIBRARY furniture and equipment
Casters for book trucks, what type is best for carpeted floors? G. T. Piez. il ALA Bul 57:787-9 S '63
Double-decker carrels; letter to the editor. W. Radford. Library J 89:1892-3 My 1 '64
Goods and gadgets. See issues of ALA bulletin
Informal but private: fifth Building and equipment institute. J. H. Wright. Library J 89:2947-9 Ag '64
Library buying guide 1963-1964; ed. by T. W. McConkey. Library J 88:1432+; 89:1518+ Ap 1 '63, Ap 1 '64
Library technology. See issues of ALA bulletin
Planning functional quarters for the school library. J. L. Taylor. il Sch Life 47:16-20 N '64
Products & equipment. See issues of Library journal
Shelving manufacturers plead nolo contendere in antitrust suit. ALA Bul 58:563 Je '64

Bibliography

Resources in library technology. E. N. Salmon. Library J 89:1495-502 Ap 1 '64

LIBRARY institutes and workshops
Meetings, courses, associations, etcetera. See issues of Wilson library bulletin

LIBRARY instruction. See Libraries—Instruction in use

LIBRARY insurance. See Insurance, Library

LIBRARY journal
Be it ever so mild. B. Cossar. Library J 88:366+ F 1 '63
Canadian views on Lj. A. W. Bowron. Library J 88:2460 Je 15 '63; Discussion. 88:2804 Ag '63
Central processing on a do-it-yourself basis. D. Melcher. il Library J 90:316-19 Ja 15 '65
John Berry joins Lj staff. Library J 89:1704 Ap 15 '64
Let's keep the lights lit! letter to the editor. D. Flick. Library J 88:4108 N 1 '63
Lj consultants retire; new columnists announced. Library J 88:4722 D 15 '63

LIBRARY laws and legislation
ALA Washington notes. G. Krettek and E. D. Cooke. Wilson Lib Bul 38:569, 693+, 783+, 868+; 39:85-6, 183-4, 264+, 341, 417+ Mr '64-Ja '65
ALA Washington notes. G. Krettek and H. Hubbard. See issues of Wilson library bulletin to February 1964
Boy who cried books; address, April 10, 1963. L. Comstock. Library J 88:2087 My 15 '63
Fate of public library legislation now considered to be uncertain. Library J 88:2652 Jl '63
Full range of weapons; Library services and construction act. H. T. Drennan and others. il Library J 89:3267-70 S 15 '64
Funds for libraries; Library services act. Sr Schol 84:1T Mr 6 '64
Higher education legislation goes to rules committee. Library J 88:2653 Jl '63
House appropriations committee omits provision for LSCA funds. Library J 89:2048 My 15 '64
Legislative commission studies library laws and services in R.I. Library J 88:3814 O 15 '63
Libraries: future unlimited; address, June 28, 1964. F. Keppel. ALA Bul 58:991-4 D '64; Excerpts. Sch & Soc 92:374-6 D 12 '64
Library and the legislature. R. S. Ake; C. M. Mathias, jr; A. A. Ingram. il Wilson Lib Bul 39:315-24 D '64
Lib. services and construction act approved by Senate in 89-7 vote. Library J 89:335 Ja 15 '64
Library services and construction act; background and text. Sch Life 46:23-6 My '64
LSCA: legislation into action. il Library J 89:3099-103 S 1 '64
LSCA: the official view. P. P. Price. ALA Bul 58:694-6 S '64
Library services and construction act: what will it mean? address, July 1964. L. A. Martin. ALA Bul 58:689-94 S '64
Memo to members; cheering news. D. H. Clift. ALA Bul 58:12 Ja '64
New public library legislation introduced in Great Britain. Library J 89:1700 Ap 15 '64
188 in Pa; summary. R. Blasingame, jr. Wilson Lib Bul 37:834 Je '63
President signs $135 million library bill; excerpts from statement, February 11, 1964. L. B. Johnson. Library J 89:1046 Mr 1 '64; Same. ALA Bul 58:172-3 Mr '64
Public libraries bill approved by House education committee. Library J 88:3038 S 1 '63
Public library legislation by House subcommittee. Library J 88:2214 Je 1 '63
Race issue clouds hearings on public library legislation. Library J 88:1962 My 15 '63
Rules for successful legislation; summary of address, ed. by G. K. Schenk. Wilson Lib Bul 39:181+ O '64
Senate to introduce separate bill on public library legislation. Library J 88:4180 N 1 '63
State of the Union and of its libraries. G. Krettek. ALA Bul 58:77 F '64
Washington report. J. G. Lorenz and H. A. Carl. See issues of ALA bulletin to March 1963
Washington report: from the ALA Washington office. G. Krettek and E. D. Cooke. ALA Bul 58:181, 275-7, 460-4, 597-9, 681-2, 771-3, 985-8; 59:22-3 Mr-Ap, Je-O, D '64-Ja '65
Washington report: from the ALA Washington office. G. Krettek and H. W. Hubbard. ALA Bul 57:497-9, 635-6, 717-20, 823-4, 1014-16; 58:95-7 Je-O, D '63, F '64

LIBRARY legislation. See Library laws and legislation

LIBRARY loans. See Interlibrary loans; Libraries—Circulation, loans, etc.

LIBRARY of Congress. See United States—Library of Congress

LIBRARY of Congress catalog cards. See Catalog cards

LIBRARY of Hawaii. See Honolulu—Library of Hawaii

LIBRARY pages. See Library assistants
LIBRARY patrons. See Libraries and readers
LIBRARY periodicals. See Library science—Periodicals
LIBRARY promotion. See Libraries and publishers
LIBRARY protection systems
To catch a thief; Sentronic book detector. il Time 84:98 O 2 '64
LIBRARY publicity
First two posters appear in Missouri's image campaign. Library J 88:4598-9 D 1 '63
Missouri tackles the image with surrealistic posters. Library J 88:3568 O 1 '63
Publicity projects. il Wilson Lib Bul 39:480-6 F '65
Publicity that worked. il Wilson Lib Bul 38:552-6 Mr '64
Westchester library system analyzes newspaper coverage. Library J 88:2660-1 Jl '63
See also
Library exhibits
National library week
LIBRARY reports
Comments from Canada; Toronto public library; excerpts from report. H. C. Campbell. Library J 88:2468 Je 15 '63
Drexel library school issues five-year progress report. Library J 88:2660 Jl '63
Report on reports. E. Moon. Library J 88:1124 Mr 15 '63
LIBRARY research

Anecdotes, facetiae, satire, etc.

Molesworth institute. N. D. Stevens; discussion. ALA Bul 57:208-10 Mr '63
LIBRARY research in progress (periodical)
In progress, backwards. E. Moon. Library J 89:3112 S 1 '64
LIBRARY schools and education
Accredited library schools. ALA Bul 58:939 N '64
Accredited library schools. ALA Bul 57:963-4 N '63
ALA's library education commission holds first meeting in Chicago. Library J 88:1130 Mr 15 '63
Anita Hostetter; pioneer in accreditation of library schools. F. F. Morton. ALA Bul 57:854-5 O '63
Apogees and perigees in library education; ALA bulletin for June 1964, letter. S. R. Reed. ALA Bul 58:589-90 Jl '64
Changing attitudes. M. Griffin. Library J 88:2650+ Jl '63
Dimensions of the Master's program. J. H. Shera. bibliog f ALA Bul 58:519-22 Je '64
Education of an educator; address, September 27, 1963. L. C. Powell. il Library J 89:561-5 F 1 '64
Educational exchange; education and library science. V. L. Jones. Library J 88:3178+ S 15 '63
Guide stands first; professor of library education. J. Shera. Wilson Lib Bul 38:285+ N '63
Logsdon to head ALA commission on national plan for library education. Library J 88:744 F 15 '63
Meetings, courses, associations, etc. See issues of Wilson library bulletin
Modest proposal; accreditation of undergraduate programs. H. S. Smith. Library J 88:4334+ N 15 '63; Discussion. 89:4+, 164 Ja 1, 15 '64
National plan for library education. Wilson Lib Bul 37:522+ Mr '63
Newes of the new founde worlde; what's new in the education of librarians? address, October 1962. N. Harlow. Library J 88:2189-93 Je 1 '63
O! medium, O! media; reflections on work-study conference on the implications of the new media for the teaching of library science. J. H. Shera. Library J 88:4149-51 N 1 '63
Pity the library school teacher. H. McMullen. il Library J 89:2280-4 Je 1 '64
Recruiting new graduates at library schools. R. F. Clarke. Wilson Lib Bul 38:483-4 F '64
Reinterpretation of standards. S. R. Reed. ALA Bul 57:247 Mr '63
Restatement of the program of the commission. R. H. Logsdon. ALA Bul 57:317-18 Ap '63
Sandwich seminars; lunch hour at University of Pittsburgh graduate library school. R. Wiley and D. Helfeld. Library J 88:2952+ S 1 '63
Some leading questions. M. Chicorel. bibliog Library J 88:1424-8 Ap 1 '63
South Carolina's program. E. P. Walker. ALA Bul 58:143-4 F '64
Special librarian: his characteristics and education; address, December 13, 1963. J. Harvey. bibliog il Library J 89:4283-7 N 1 '64; Discussion. 89:4840+ D 15 '64
Status or scholarship? R. Stokes. Library J 88:1430-1 Ap 1 '63
Struggling masses; need for special courses related to problems of librarianship in another country. R. Stokes. Library J 88:2850 Ag '63
Teaching and criticism; reprint. N. E. Dain. Library J 88:3538 O 1 '63
Teaching of research in the library schools. S. L. Jackson. Library J 88:2206-7 Je 1 '63
Thoughts for the commission; ALA's commission on a national plan for library education. J. L. Wheeler. Library J 88:4170-1 N 1 '63
Toward a new dimension for library education; statement at session of ALA commission on national plan for library education, February 1963. J. H. Shera. il (cover) ALA Bul 57:313-17 Ap '63
Where is today's Brother Keppel? concerning money for library education. J. Shera. Wilson Lib Bul 38:185+ O '63
Work-study program; University of North Carolina. J. H. Gribbin. Library J 89:568-9+ F 1 '64
See also
American library association—Commission on a national plan for library education
Library assistants—Education
School librarians—Education
also names of library schools, e.g. Chicago. University—Graduate library school

Latin America

Education for librarianship to be studied in Latin America; initiated by Inter-American library school of the University of Antioquia, Medellín, Colombia. Library J 88:3572 O 1 '63
Latin America project; initiated by Inter-American library school of the University of Antioquia, Medellín, Colombia. Wilson Lib Bul 38:131 O '63

Pakistan

Passage to Pakistan. M. Boaz. il Wilson Lib Bul 38:478-9 F '64
LIBRARY science
Little girls don't play librarian. J. Shera; discussion. Library J 88:894+ Mr 1 '63
See also
Cataloging
Librarianship

Bibliography

Professional reading. See issues of Library journal

Periodicals

Demise of originality? special issues of library periodicals; letter to the editor. S. Szilassy. Library J 89:978 Mr 1 '64
See also
Library journal
Library research in progress (periodicals)
Wilson library bulletin

Scholarships and fellowships

Library scholarship set up to honor Ruth Gagliardo. Pub W 185:133 F 24 '64

Study and teaching

See Library schools and education
LIBRARY service, Rural. See Rural library service
LIBRARY services act. See Library laws and legislation
LIBRARY services and construction act. See Library laws and legislation
LIBRARY services branch. See United States—Education, Office of—Library services branch
LIBRARY shelving. See Library furniture and equipment
LIBRARY shelving systems. See Libraries—Shelving systems
LIBRARY standards. See Libraries—Standards
LIBRARY statistics. See Libraries—Statistics
LIBRARY surveys
Academic and research libraries to be studied in Pennsylvania. Library J 88:4595 D 1 '63
Access study; symposium. il Library J 88:4685-709 D 15 '63; Discussion. 88:4710-12; 89:424, 976+ D 15 '63, F 1, Mr 1 '64

LIBRARY surveys—*Continued*
Access to education; concerning Access to public libraries survey, conducted by International research associates; symposium. bibliog il Wilson Lib Bul 38:335-51+ D '63; Reply. S. L. Jackson. 38:465 F '64
Access to libraries study: statement, September 30, 1963. H. W. Tucker. ALA Bul 57:1042 D '63
Access to public libraries study. il ALA Bul 57:742-5 S '63
American adults read more fiction; ALA report. Wilson Lib Bul 38:441+ F '64
Automation & library systems; excerpts from Strengthening and coordinating reference and research library sources in New York state. T. Stein. bibliog il Library J 89:2723-34 Jl '64
Common fine; report of survey by Akron public library. J. H. Rebenack. Library J 89:4868-70 D 15 '64
Decatur publishes annual survey of library directors' salaries. Library J 88:977 Mr 1 '63
Demand for dissent? public library practice in the selection of dissident periodicals; report. J. N. Berry, 3d. il Library J 89:3912-17 O 15 '64
Dewey or LC? which best for library in college with 5000-6000 enrollment? H. R. Downey. Library J 89:2292-3 Je 1 '64
Five-year analysis published of library research activities; concerning Library research in progress (LiRiP) Library J 88:4590-1 D 1 '63
Forecast for 1964; reports from forty-seven states. il Library J 89:39-66 Ja 1 '64
Free space: can public libraries receive it? report of survey of branch libraries in shopping centers by Wichita, Kan, city library. R. Waters. ALA Bul 58:232-4 Mr '64
Library handbook standards: students and faculty; report of survey. A. B. Griffith. il Wilson Lib Bul 39:475-7 F '65
Lj surveys library progress '64. Library J 90:320+ Ja 15 '65
Magic dragon; or, Life with stereo; reports from the field. ed. by G. Stevenson. il Library J 88:3799-801 O 15 '63
Medium sized P.L.'s report circulation increase in fiction: ALA report. Library J 89:586+ F 1 '64
Method study for small libraries. Wilson Lib Bul 38:123 O '63
Nation's reading interests outlined in ALA report. Library J 88:530-1 F 1 '63
Needs of libraries and what ALA is doing about them. J. E. Bryan. ALA Bul 57:319-21 Ap '63
Newspaper gap; concerning survey by Boston public library. E. J. Montana, jr. il Library J 89:1194-7 Mr 15 '64; Correction. 89:2260 Je 1 '64
Ontario reference survey recommends regional centers. Library J 89:4766 D 1 '64
Pennsylvania LA conference hears first report on Blasingame survey; excerpts from report. R. Blasingame. Library J 89:4767-8 D 1 '64
Problem books revisited; excerpts from report on survey of small public library's book selection practices in controversial areas. R. B. Agler. il Library J 89:2019-30 My 15 '64; Reply. R. S. Bravard. 89:2470+ Je 15 '64
Public library integration in thirteen southern states; excerpts from Integration in public library service in thirteen southern states, 1954-1962. B. L. Bell. il Library J 88:4713-15 D 15 '63; Discussion. 89:424+ F 1 '64
Reading the lessons; standing of Access study now? E. Moon. Library J 89:817 F 15 '64
Recent trends in public library adult services. E. Phinney. ALA Bul 37:262-6 Mr '63
Report on the study of access to public libraries. ALA Bul 58:299-304 Ap '64
Research for New York state 3-R program: reference and research library resources. Wilson Lib Bul 38:135 O '63
Restatement of the program of the commission. R. H. Logsdon. ALA Bul 57:317-18 Ap '63
Survey of salary surveys. A. R. Schiller. il ALA Bul 58:279-86 Ap '64
Two kinds of access; concerning the report, Access to public libraries, of International research associates. E. Moon. Library J 88:2849 Ag '63
Underprivileged reader; report on Access to public libraries survey, conducted by International research associates. E. Geller. Wilson Lib Bul 38:65-7 S '63
Year's realities: reports from states on library progress in 1964 and comparisons with last year's forecast. il Library J 90:56-71 Ja 1 '65
See also
School library surveys

LIBRARY technology project. See American library association—Library technology project

LIBRARY trustees. See Libraries—Trustees, boards, committees, etc.

LIBRARY 21. See Seattle—Century 21 exposition. 1962

LIBRARY/USA. See New York (city)—Worlds fair. 1964

LIBRARY vandalism. See Vandalism

LIBRARY week. See National library week

LIBRARY workers. See Librarians

LIBRARY workshops. See Library institutes and workshops

LIBRETTISTS
Of poets and poetasters: Verdi and his librettists. W. Weaver. il Hi Fi 13:109-13+ O '63
See also
Da Ponte, L.
Piave, F. M.

LIBRETTOS
Little book; new librettos on the Metropolitan opera scene. Q. Eaton. Opera N 28:6 D 7 '63

LIBYA
See also
Earthquakes—Libya
Petroleum—Libya

Economic conditions

Oil alone can't solve Libya's economic woes. map Bsns W p 102 Ja 26 '63
When a poor country strikes it rich. il U S News 57:73-4 D 14 '64

Foreign relations

Still friendly? American and British base rights not to be renewed. il Newsweek 64:38 S 7 '64

Politics and government

Smell of oil. Newsweek 63:40-1 Ap 6 '64

LICENSE plates, Automobile. See Automobiles—License plates

LICENSED merchandise. See Merchandising

LICENSES
Medicine in Missouri; refusal of state board to grant license to Dr Lischner. New Republic 151:5 D 19 '64
One license: is it feasible? A. W. Eckert. il Field & S 67:53+ Ap '63
See also
Air pilots—Licenses
Automobile drivers—Licenses

LICENSES, Radio operator. See Radio operators—Licenses

LICH, Richard L.
Resurgence of rapid transit; excerpts from address, April 25 and April 26, 1963. Am City 79:95 Mr '64

LICHENS
Fungi of lichens. V. Ahmadjian. il Sci Am 208:122-30+ F '63
Joint occurrence of a lichen depsidone and its probable depside precursor. C. F. Culberson. bibliog il Science 143:255-6 Ja 17 '64
Lichens on Galápagos giant tortoises. J. R. Hendrickson and W. A. Weber. Science 144:1463 Je 19 '64
Nature note. Sci N L 87:63 Ja 23 '65

LICHINE, Alexis
Intelligent woman's guide to wines. Ladies Home J 81:120-1 S '64

LICHINE, Gisèle
Wine: a woman's view; with recipes. por Ladies Home J 81:118-19 S '64

LICHTEN, Joseph L.
Council declaration on the Jews. Cath World 199:272-8 Ag '64
Jewish defense; excerpts from Question of judgment: Pius XII and the Jews. Commonweal 79:660-2 F 28 '64

LICHTENBERG, James J. See Breidenbach, A. W. jt. auth.
LICHTENBERG figures
Amateur scientist; apparatus for investigating the Lichtenberg figures. E. W. Saaski. il Sci Am 211:137-8+ D '64
LICHTENBERGER, Allan R.
Educational records are useful in making decisions. Sch Life 47:20-2 N '64
Principles for a program of comparable information. bibliog f por Sch Life 45:8-10 My '63
LICHTENBERGER, Arthur, bp
Bishop Lichtenberger resigns. Christian Cent 81:477 Ap 15 '64
P.B. steps down. por Time 83:60 Ap 10 '64
LICHTENSTEIN, Abba
℞ for a sick bridge. Am City 79:104-6 S '64
LICHTENSTEIN, Eugene
Higher and higher go the bids for industry. Fortune 69:118-21+ Ap '64
LICHTENSTEIN, Roy F.
What is pop art? interview; ed. by G. R. Swenson. il Art N 62:24-5+ N '63
about
Art. M. Kozloff. il Nation 197:284-7 N 2 '63
Discredited merchandise. il por Newsweek 64:94+ N 9 '64
Explosion of pop art: exhibition at the Guggenheim museum. A. B. Saarinen. il Vogue 141:134 Ap 15 '63
Is he the worst artist in the U.S.? with report by D. Seiberling. il por Life 56:79-81+ Ja 31 '64
Pop artists or copy cats? E. Loran. il Art N 62:48-9+ S '63
Pops or robbers? the big question. il Newsweek 62:90 S 16 '63
LICHTHEIM, George
Beyond imperialism. New Repub 148:17-19 Mr 16 '63
Cold war in perspective. Commentary 37:21-6 Je; 38:16+ N '64
German diary. Commentary 38:42-9 S '64
New left Marxism. Commentary 35:239-43 Mr '63
Politics of conservative realism. Commentary 35:506-16 Je '63
Post-bourgeois Europe. Commentary 35:1-9 Ja '63
Public affairs. Commentary 39:65-8 Ja '65
Reflections on Trotsky. Commentary 37:52-60 Ja; 34-5 My '64
Settled habit of behavior. Commentary 35: 168-72 F '63
Tory succession: a London letter. Commentary 36:468-72 D '63
What we don't know might kill us. E. Capouya. Sat R 47:26-7 Mr 28 '64
Xenophon versus Hegel. Commentary 36:412-16 N '63
LICHTHEIM, Miriam
Ancient Egypt: a survey of current historiography. bibliog f Am Hist R 69:30-46 O '63
LIDSTONE, John
Cardboard printing. Sch Arts 63:16-18 O '63
Potato printing. Sch Arts 62:5-9 F '63
LIE detectors
Dangerous polygraph. Sci Am 209:66-7 Jl '63
Do lie detectors lie? R. Christie. il Pop Sci 183:64-7+ S '63
Drive on lie detectors. T. R. Brooks. Duns R 82:53-4 N '63
Electronic conscience. Reporter 28:16+ Ap 25 '63
Great lie-detector hoax. B. H. Frisch. il Sci Digest 54:23-9 Ag '63
How to lie successfully to the lie detector. R. Burkhardt. New Repub 150:6-7 My 16 '64
How true are lie detectors? il Good H 158:157 Mr '64
It's none of your lousy business. S. Alsop. il Sat Eve Post 237:12 Je 13 '64
Lie detector confirms his story. il Life 56:88-9 My 15 '64
Lie detectors don't lie, but. W. Goodman. il N Y Times Mag p 12-13+ Ja 24 '65
Lie detectors: sleuthing by polygraph increasingly popular; claims of accuracy are unproved. E. Langer. Science 144:395-7+ Ap 24 '64; Discussion. 144:1177-8 Je 5 '64
Lying machine. il Newsweek 61:82 Ap 29 '63
Polygraph-happy Pentagon. Sat Eve Post 236: 82 My 4 '63
Uproar over news leaks and lie detectors. il U S News 54:8 Ap 15 '63
What is truth? Newsweek 64:27 D 7 '64
See also
Polygraph
LIEB, Irwin C.
Sight of privacy. U S Camera 26:70-3 F '63
LIEB, Margaret
Ultraviolet sensitivity of escherichia coli containing heat-inducible λ prophages. bibliog Science 145:175-6 Jl 10 '64
LIEBER, Joel
Ein Hod, an artists' village in Israel. Am Artist 27:58-63+ Ap '63
In Arab hands. Nation 199:246-8 O 19 '64
Norway's North. Travel 122:46-8 Jl '64
Pastoral perimeter. Travel 122:32-4 Ag '64
LIEBERMAN, E. James, and Duhl, L. J.
Physical and mental health in the city. Ann Am Acad 352:13-24 Mr '64
LIEBERMAN, E. M. and Swenson, P. A.
Ultraviolet radiation effects on low molecular weight inorganic phosphates of yeast. bibliog Science 142:1315-16 D 6 '63
LIEBERMAN, Elias
I had three pennies; poem. McCalls 92:197 O '64
LIEBERMAN, Laurence
Family tree; poem. New Yorker 40:52 D 12 '64
Flat; poem. Harper 227:93 O '63
Mountain hoax; poem. Poetry 103:244-6 Ja '64
My father dreams of baseball; poem. Atlan 212:103 Ag '63
Turtle; poem. New Yorker 39:30 Je 29 '63
We don't mind; poem. Atlan 212:76 S '63
Wire forests; poem. New Yorker 40:36 Ja 2 '65
LIEBERMAN, Melvin S.
Capacitor former for electronic flash units. Electr World 70:54-6 D '63
LIEBERMAN, Michael W.
Early developmental stress and later behavior. bibliog Science 141:824-5 Ag 30 '63
LIEBERMAN, William S.
René Bouché, 1906-1963: an appreciation. Vogue 142:184-9 S 1 '63
LIEBERMANN, Rolf
Liebermann colloquy; interview. por Mus Am 83:25 Ap '63
Visiting fireman; interview, ed. by J. W. Freeman. por Opera N 27:14 Ap 13 '63
LIEBERSON, Goddard
Good old days? Am Rec G 30:752 My '64
RCA Victor introduces dynagroove and Columbia calls it a backward step. por Am Rec G 29:601+ Ap '63
LIEBERT, Herman W.
Yale's iceberg. New Yorker 40:24-5 My 30 '64
LIEBES, Dorothy
Five designers, five approaches. P. Adler. il Craft Horiz 24:45 Mr '64
LIEBLING, Abbott Joseph
Books (cont) New Yorker 38:131-2+ F 9; 39:169-74+ My 11; 216-18+ O 19 '63; 128+ F 8 '64
Reporter at large (cont) New Yorker 39:95-8+ Ja 11 '64
Sporting scene (cont) New Yorker 39:122+ Mr 30; 62+ Ag 10 '63
That was New York. New Yorker 39:143-50+ O 12 '63
Wayward press (cont) New Yorker 39:173-6+ Mr 16; 143-52 Ap 13 '63
about
A. J. Liebling. New Yorker 39:107-8 Ja 11 '64
Hungry man. J. Jacobs. Reporter 30:54-5 F 13 '64
Just a reporter, and then some. W. J. Smith. Commonweal 79:436-7 Ja 10 '64
Obituary
Newsweek il por 63:52-3 Ja 13 '64
Pub W 185:62 Ja 6 '64
LIEBMAN, Max
Can TV be saved? por Esquire 60:210+ D '63
LIEBMAN, Morris I.
Civil disobedience; address, August 11, 1964. Vital Speeches 30:766-8 O 1 '64
LIEBMANN breweries, incorporated
Will the real Miss Rheingold stand out? D. L. Goodrich. il Sat Eve Post 236:48+ N 16 '63
LIECHTENSTEIN
Happy have-not. il Time 82:30 Ag 23 '63
Description and travel
Lightning guide to Liechtenstein. J. Bryan, 3d. il Holiday 33:78-83+ Mr '63
Economic conditions
Sitz-ing ducks; taxation of foreign firms. Newsweek 61:81-3 Je 10 '63
LIECHTENSTEIN collection. See Art—Private collections

LIEDER. See Songs, German

LIEDLOFF, Jean, and Massie, Robert
Jungle captive. pors Sat Eve Post 236:85-9 Ag 10 '63

LIEF, Harold I.
What your doctor probably doesn't know about sex. Harper 229:92-6 D '64

LIEFMANN, Robert E.
Hucksters of pain. R. L. Smith. il por Sat Eve Post 236:83-7 Ag 24 '63

LIEN, Thich-quang-. See Thich-quang-Lien

LIÉNART, Achille, cardinal
Visit with Cardinal Liénart; interview, ed. by W. M. Abbott. America 108:802-3 Je 1 '63

LIENS
Mechanics' liens: just what is your hazard? Sunset 131:92-3 Jl '63

LIERS, Emil
Emil Liers wins Aurianne award for his book A black bear's story. Library J 89: 1396+ Mr 15 '64

LIES. See Lying

LIEUWEN, Edwin
Latin America and military aid. Sat R 46: 16-17 My 4 '63

LIFAR, Serge
Much ado chez Serge. R. Orthwine. il pors Dance Mag 37:25-6 S '63

LIFE
Danger beyond smoking. N. Cousins. Sat R 47:22 Ja 25 '64; Same abr. Read Digest 84:41-2 My '64; Discussion. Sat R 47:31-2 F 15 '64
Meaning in the human arena. N. Cousins. Sat R 46:22 Mr 9 '63
Most beautiful word. R. L. Tobin. Sat R 46:18 Jl 20 '63
Right to life, by N. St. John-Stevas. Review
Commonweal 80:156-7 Ap 24 '64. W. H. Dempsey, jr
See also
Conduct of life
Death

LIFE (biology)
Chemical man exhibit tells life story. il (p241) Sci N L 84:244 O 19 '63
Definition of life. W. Wingo. Sci N L 84:147 S 7 '63
Exploring the secrets of life. il Newsweek 61: 63-6 My 13 '63
Made-to-order men. Sci Digest 55:80 Je '64
Man and the living world, by K. von Frisch. Review
Sci Digest il 54:28 O '63. B. H. Frisch
New clues pry at three secrets of life. il Life 54:58-9 Mr 29 '63
Perspectives for the life sciences. H. J. Muller. Bul Atomic Sci 20:3-7 Ja '64; Reply with rejoinder. D. H. Elwyn. 20:36-7 O '64
Some mysteries of life and existence; excerpts. R. E. Snodgrass. Hobbies 69:115 D '64
Test tube life doubted. F. Marley. Sci N L 86:102 Ag 15 '64
See also
Biochemistry

Origin

Is magnetism the key to life's origin on earth? J. Lear. Sat R 46:35-8 Jl 6 '63
Life: origin and evolution; report on international meeting. R. S. Young and C. Ponnamperuma. Science 143:384-5+ Ja 24 '64
Man-made life closer. Sci N L 86:6 Jl 4 '64
Organisms and molecules in evolution; adaptation from paper. G. G. Simpson. bibliog Science 146:1535-8 D 18 '64
Origin of life on the earth. O. W. Garrigan. Cath World 198:281-7 F '64
Research frontier; where is science taking us? P. N. Kropotkin. il Sat R 46:39-40 Jl 6 '63
Thermodynamic equilibria in prebiological atmospheres. M. O. Dayhoff and others. bibliog il Science 146:1461-4 D 11 '64

LIFE (periodical)
Big sale: exclusive photos of Oswald. il Newsweek 63:80 Mr 2 '64
Old soldier's memoirs. il Time 82:37 Ag 30 '63

LIFE expectancy. See Longevity

LIFE for mother; drama. See Hark, M. and McQueen, N.

LIFE in other worlds. See Life on other planets

LIFE insurance. See Insurance, Life

LIFE insurance agents. See Insurance, Life—Agents

LIFE insurance companies. See Insurance companies

LIFE is a dream; drama. See Calderón de la Barca, P.

LIFE is better than death; story. See Malamud, B.

LIFE line (radio program) See Radio broadcasting—Propaganda

LIFE line foundation, incorporated
H. L. Hunt; portrait of a super-patriot; Life line. R. G. Sherrill. Nation 198:182-95 F 24 '64

LIFE line movement. See Telephone—Religious applications

LIFE masks. See Masks (sculpture)

LIFE on other planets
Aeronutronic studying automated bio lab; search for life on Mars. Aviation W 81: 83+ S 28 '64
Ames study supports Mars life theory. H. D. Watkins. Aviation W 79:61+ N 18 '63
Boosters pace Mars life detection. R. Pay. Miss & Roc 16:32+ Ja 18 '65
Can we learn from other planets? excerpt from Of men and galaxies. F. Hoyle. il Sat R 47:63-7 N 7 '64; Discussion. 47:84-6 D 5 '64
Communicating with intelligent life on other worlds; adaptation of address, March 27, 1963. A. G. W. Cameron. il Sky & Tel 26: 258-61 N '63
Eight planet-probe robots. B. Tufty. il (p225) Sci N L 84:227 O 12 '63
Exobiology. J. Lederberg. Science 142:1126 N 29 '63
Experimental exobiology. Sky & Tel 26:132 S '63
Hello, CTA-21, is anyone there? I. Asimov. il N Y Times Mag p52+ N 29 '64
How to find life on Mars. il Sci Digest 56:90 Ag '64
Infrared emission spectra of organic solids from 5 to 6.6 microns. W. A. Hovis, jr. il Science 143:587-8 F 7 '64
Interstellar communication, ed. by A. G. W. Cameron. Review
Sci Am 210:141-6 F '64. J. R. Newman
Life beyond earth sought; Project Ozma. Sci N L 84:166 S 14 '63
Life detector; multivator. il Time 82:52 Ag 30 '63
Life detectors; Wolf Trap and multivator. Newsweek 62:56 S 30 '63
Life in all solar systems? A. Ewing. Sci N L 86:199 S 26 '64
Life in meteorites? Sky & Tel 26:132 S '63
Life may exist on Mars, but mistranslation made the canals. S. D. Gossner. il Natur Hist 72:56-7 Ap '63
Life on Mars talk dealt a setback. Sci N L 84:185 S 21 '63
Life on other planets. V. G. Dethier. il Cath World 198:245-50 Ja '64
Life on unseen planets. H. Shapley. il Sci Digest 53:59-64 F '63
Mars; are its canals full of water? is there really life there? W. Von Braun. il Pop Sci 183:18+ Ag '63
Mars biological lab designs are sought. Aviation W 80:37 Je 15 '64
Martian environment. Sci N L 83:386 Je 22 '63
Messages from space. America 111:770 D 12 '64
Microbe survivability on Mars simulated. W. C. Wetmore. Aviation W 80:75-6+ Je 29 '64
Nonprevalence of humanoids; excerpts from This view of life. G. G. Simpson. bibliog Science 143:769-75 F 21 '64; Discussion. 144: 245-6, 613-16, 954; 145:231 Ap 17, My 8, 22, Jl 17 '64
Organic matter from space. B. Mason. il Sci Am 208:43-9 bibliog(p 188) Mr '63
Other suns, other planets, but is there other life? D. Q. Posin. il Todays Health 42:56-9 N '64
Out of this world life detectors; Gulliver, astrorobot. S. D. Pursglove. il Pop Mech 119:72-5 Je '63
Philco labs developing protein detector to probe for life on Mars. Miss & Roc 14:26-7 Mr 2 '64
Prevalence of planets and the probability of life. Time 84:49-50 S 25 '64
Search for life. N. J. Berrill. Atlan 212:35-40 Ag '63
Search for life in space. Sci N L 85:46 Ja 18 '64
Signs of life on Mars; Life on Mars hard to see. Sci N L 85:339-40 My 30 '64
Somebody up there like us. R. O'Brien. Esquire 60:185-7+ D '63
Space sciences challenge. R. D. Hibben. il Aviation W 80:91-3+ F 17 '64
This view of life: the world of an evolutionist, by G. G. Simpson. Review
Sci Digest 55:42 My '64. H. Pryor
Water vapor on Venus. A. Ewing. Sci N L 85:261 Ap 25 '64

LIFE rafts. See Rafts

LIFE saving. See Rescue work

LIFE saving equipment
See also
Rafts

LIFE span. See Longevity

LIFE support systems
All-oxygen tests reveal toxicity. il Miss & Roc 13:18 Ag 5 '63
Apollo subsystems for service module delivered by Beech. il Aviation W 80:67 My 4 '64
Astronauts may make their own air on moon. Sci N L 87:57 Ja 23 '65
Can man be modified to live in space? K. N. Anderson. il Todays Health 41:20-3+ N '63
Chemosynthetic oxygen system being tested. H. M. David. il Miss & Roc 13:27 S 16 '63
Chest-back pack test planned on Gemini mission during 1966. il Aviation W 81:67-8 S 21 '64
Extracellular polysaccharides of algae: effects on life-support systems. B. G. Moore and R. G. Tischer. bibliog il Science 145:586-7 Ag 7 '64
Fire, rapid decompression pose hazards for MOL environment. Aviation W 80:48 Mr 30 '64
How to breathe on the moon. Sci Digest 55:61 F '64
Lunar surface experiment awards near. E. J. Bulban. il Aviation W 81:53+ O 26 '64
Lunar surface exploration gear analyzed. il Aviation W 81:69-71 N 16 '64
MSC seeking Gemini life support proposals. Aviation W 79:106-7 N 11 '63
NASA, Boeing resuming life-support tests. H. M. David. il Miss & Roc 14:28-9 Ja 27 '64
NASA studies locomotion, protection. Miss & Roc 14:28 Ap 20 '64
NASA to get optimized integrated life-support system early next year. H. M. David. il Miss & Roc 14:32-3 Je 15 '64
Oxygen deemed safe for thirty-day MOL mission. Miss & Roc 14:16 My 18 '64
Oxygen-helium atmosphere appears promising for manned space flight. H. M. David. Miss & Roc 15:32 Ag 3 '64
Packed for flight; modular maneuvering unit. il Newsweek 64:111 O 5 '64
Plan advanced for landing probe on Mars in 1969 as urgent U.S. goal. H. M. David. il Miss & Roc 14:14-15 Ja 6 '64
Researcher proposes thirty-day oxygen tests. Miss & Roc 13:36-7 S 23 '63
Soviets may not have extravehicular space experimentation capability. H. M. David. Miss & Roc 15:16-17 D 14 '64
Soviets see helium use in spaceships. H. M. David. Miss & Roc 15:14-15 N 23 '64
Strange air in space. Sci N L 87:6 Ja 2 '65
What it takes to survive in space. W. Von Braun. il Pop Sci 183:12+ D '63
You can live on your waste. il Sci Digest 55:37-9 F '64

LIFT pills. See Stimulants

LIFTING
See also
Weight lifting

LIFTING and carrying
Lifting with safety. C. A. Pease. il Consumer Bul 47:32 Je '64

LIFTING jacks. See Hydraulic jacks; Jacks

LIFTON, Betty Jean
Thousand cranes. Horn Bk 39:211-16 Ap '63

LIFTS. See Elevators

LIGHT, Goddard
Bookseller serves the community, but who serves him? por ALA Bul 57:528-30 Je '63
Community role of the bookseller. por Pub W 185:47-8 My 11 '64

LIGHT, Lois
I'm for Mother's day! Parents Mag 39:26+ My '64

LIGHT
See also
Diffraction
Interference (light)
Lighting
Optical illusions
Optics
Photochemistry
Photography—Light
Photons
Phototaxis
Polarization (light)
Raman effect
Spectrum analysis

Physiological effects

Beware of summer glare. A. Nelson. il Sci Digest 54:63-6 Ag '63
Diurnal rhythm and photoperiodism in testicular recrudescence of the house finch. W. M. Hamner. bibliog il Science 142:1294-5 D 6 '63
Food versus perceptual complexity as rewards for rats previously subjected to sensory deprivation. G. P. Sackett and others. bibliog il Science 140:518-20 Ag 9 '63; Reply with rejoinder. W. A. Hillix. 142:1021-2 N 22 '63
Light adaptation kinetics: the influence of spatial factors. W. S. Battersby and I. H. Wagman. bibliog il Science 143:1029-31 Mr 6 '64
Light: evidence for its direct effect on hypothalamic neurons. R. D. Lisk and L. R. Kannwischer. bibliog il Science 146:272-3 O 9 '64
Long-day production from short-day birds; with light flashes. D. Braun. Farm J 87:34 Je '63
Mating urge of birds controlled by light. Sci N L 84:201 S 28 '63
Melatonin synthesis in the pineal gland: control by light. R. J. Wurtman and others. bibliog il Science 142:1071-3 N 22 '63
Melatonin synthesis in the pineal gland: effect of light mediated by the sympathetic nervous system. R. J. Wurtman and others. bibliog il Science 143:1328-30 Mr 20 '64
Metabolic control of timing. S. B. Hendricks. bibliog il Science 141:21-7 Jl 5 '63
Mystery of the biological clocks; photoperiodism. A. Hamilton. Sci Digest 56:21-6 O '64
Photosensitizing substance in human serum; effect on HeLa cells. W. B. Wheeler and A. C. Hollinshead. bibliog il Science 141:1279-80 S 27 '63
Primate retinal responses: slow changes during repetitive stimulation with light. P. Gouras and R. E. Carr. bibliog il Science 145:413-14 Jl 24 '64
Probing the mysteries of light. R. Dunlop. il Todays Health 41:34-9+ Mr '63
See also
Plants, Effect of light on

Velocity

Another check for Einstein. Time 85:52 Ja 8 '65
Einstein's constant. Newsweek 61:63 Ap 15 '63
He measured the speed of light; A. Michelson's great experiments. R. S. Strother. il Read Digest 85:193-4+ Jl '64
Michelson-Morley experiment. R. S. Shankland. il Sci Am 211:107-14 N '64

LIGHT, Wave theory of
Light; waves that reveal the universe; reprint. il Sci Digest 55:62-6 Je '64

LIGHT, Zodiacal. See Zodiacal light

LIGHT amplification by stimulated emission of radiation. See Light amplifiers

LIGHT amplifiers
Accurate length measurement of meter bar with helium-neon laser. K. D. Mielenz and others. bibliog il Science 146:1672-3 D 25 '64
Acoustic waves from a laser beam. Sci Am 211:40 Ag '64
Advances in optical masers. A. L. Schawlow. il Sci Am 209:34-45 bibliog(p 170) Jl '63
Aerospace, military laser uses explored. B. Miller. il Aviation W 78:54-5+ Ap 22 '63
AF studying laser navigation sensors. M. Getler. il Miss & Roc 12:24-5 F 18 '63
Amateur scientist; build a gas laser in the home. C. L. Stong. il Sci Am 211:227-8+ S '64
Astounding laser. M. Gunther. il Sat Eve Post 237:68-71 O 24 '64
Bullets of light. W. E. Boggs. New Repub 148:5 Mr 16 '63
Closed-circuit laser may rival gyro in sea, space. il Sci N L 83:197 Mr 30 '63
Death to death rays; laser light. Time 81:36 Je 28 '63
DOD funds $15 million for laser R&D. Aviation W 78:75 Ap 8 '63
Destroy tooth decay with laser light beam. Sci N L 86:105 Ag 15 '64
Fused silica reflectors in laser test. W. Beller. il Miss & Roc 13:29+ O 21 '63
GE-developed laser system offers high pulse rate. il Miss & Roc 12:33 Je 10 '63
GT-10 to carry laser voice transmitter. il Miss & Roc 15:15 Ag 17 '64
Government funded optical maser and related programs in fiscal '63; chart. Aviation W 78:58-9 Ap 22 '63
Harnessing light seen. Sci N L 83:278 My 4 '63

LIGHT amplifiers—*Continued*
Here's why those do-everything lasers don't, yet. T. Berland. il Pop Mech 121: 102-6+ Mr '64
How air transmits laser light studied. Sci N L 86:36 Jl 18 '64
How spacemen can use laser beams. W. Von Braun. il Pop Sci 185:128-9+ O '64
How the ruby laser works. A. Schawlow. il Pop Sci 185:65 N '64
Interaction of light with light. J. A. Giordmaine. il Sci Am 210:38-49 bibliog(p 156) Ap '64
ITT affiliate working on gas laser for guidance system use. il Miss & Roc 15: 34-5 N 2 '64
Laser developments reported at meeting. Aviation W 78:83 Ap 29 '63
Laser emphasis shifting from research toward application and hardware. il Miss & Roc 14:26-31 Je 1 '64
Laser flash lamps; report on conference. E. H. Weinberg. Science 144:432+ Ap 24 '64
Laser flowmeter measures gases, fluids. P. J. Klass. il Aviation W 82:75-7 Ja 11 '65
Laser goes to work. C. P. Gilmore. il Pop Sci 183:80-4+ D '63
Laser gun sparks lectures. K. H. Sherwin. il Pop Sci 185:64 N '64
Laser light focused using gas as lens. il(cover) Sci N L 86:116 Ag 22 '64
Laser modulation could spur audio space role. Miss & Roc 12:48 My 27 '63
Laser optics encountering deterioration problems. R. Pay. Miss & Roc 13:27-8 S 9 '63
Laser proves useful for long-distance measuring. Sci N L 83:133 Mr 2 '63
Laser R&D cost: $25 million a year. C. D. LaFond. il Miss & Roc 12:17 Ap 1 '63
Laser radar spots clear air disturbances. Sci N L 86:105 Ag 15 '64
Laser revolution in 3D photography. il Sci Digest 57:8-9 Ja '65
Laser that produces non-stop; Tyco's semiconductor device. Bsns W p 114 S 7 '63
Laser transmits voice in showing by IBM. Aviation W 78:78 Je 3 '63
Lasers and their future. W. A. Stocklin. Electr World 69:6 My '63
Laser's dazzling future. L. Lessing. il Fortune 67:138-42+ Je '63
Lasers for length measurement. A. G. McNish. bibliog il Science 146:177-82 O 9 '64
Lasers: 100 million messages on a beam of light. B. Friedman. il UNESCO Courier 17:15-19 F '64
Lasing along. il Newsweek 63:69 My 18 '64
Light-beam transmitter powered by human voice: Retrometer. Sci N L 85:294 My 9 '64
Light fantastic. E. Nanas. il Pop Electr 19: 33-9+ Jl '63
Light fantastic. Newsweek 62:59 S 16 '63
Light of hope, or terror? H. Manchester. Read Digest 82:97-100 F '63
Light successfully used as short-range radar. Sci N L 84:182 S 21 '63
Martin laser highlights MIL-E-CON. C. D. LaFond. Miss & Roc 13:18 S 16 '63
Masers and lasers; electronic miracles of the future. il Sci Digest 56:36-8 Ag '64
Miracle ray is coming of age. il U S News 54:80-2 F 25 '63
More coherent rays; graser. W. Cloud. Pop Sci 184:29 F '64
NASA plans laser beacon flight tests. Aviation W 80:37 Ap 13 '64
NASA plans laser rendezvous guidance. B. Miller. il Aviation W 80:100-2+ My 18 '64
New chore for the laser beam. Bsns W p64 Jl 6 '63
New laser materials demonstrated. Aviation W 78:37 My 6 '63
New module splits laser beams. il Aviation W 79:95+ O 21 '63
New weather predicting: use of a laser. Sci N L 85:100 F 15 '64
NAA demonstrates laser modulator. il Miss & Roc 12:31 Mr 18 '63
ONR sponsors laser research programs. Aviation W 79:90-1+ Jl 1 '63
Optical masers; report on Optical maser symposium of the Electrochemical society. J. D. Kingsley. Science 145:839-40 Ag 21 '64
Optical radar employs multiple lasers. B. Miller. il Aviation W 80:62-3+ Mr 9 '64
PS builds a laser. R. M. Benrey. il Pop Sci 185:62-4+ N '64
Practical laser. Time 82:63 S 13 '63
Prototype laser system combines high information rate with tracking accuracy. R. Pay. il Miss & Roc 14:24-5 My 18 '64
Quantum devices, how they work. J. R. Collins. il Electr World 70:39-41+ D '63
R&D and unemployment; lasers in treatment of cancer. W. A. Stocklin. Electr World 71:10 Ja '64
Research on maser-laser principle wins Nobel prize in physics. J. P. Gordon. il Science 146:897-9 N 13 '64
Ring laser device performs rate gyro angular sensor functions. P. J. Klass. il Aviation W 78:98-9+ F 11 '63
Ruby laser as a microsurgical instrument. N. M. Saks and C. A. Roth. bibliog il Science 141:46-7 Jl 5 '63
Ruby ray guns. America 108:454 Ap 6 '63
S-66 may be first space test of laser. il Miss & Roc 13:21 Ag 5 '63
Satellite laser test; Polar ionosphere beacon satellite. A. Ewing. Sci N L 85:3 Ja 4 '64
Semiconductor lasers. B. Lax. bibliog il Science 141:1247-55 S 27 '63
Simple photoelectric amplifier. R. P. Turner. il Electr World 72:104-5 N '64
Spectroscopic ultramicroanalysis with a laser. R. C. Rosan and others. il Science 142:236-7 O 11 '63
Stanford electronics labs pursues laser, ion-propulsion studies. R. Pay. il Miss & Roc 13:24-5 S 16 '63
Starlight amplifier used by observatory. Sci N L 84:40 Jl 20 '63
Survey moon with laser. Sci N L 83:70 F 2 '63
Unit promises laser output control. il Miss & Roc 13:38 N 4 '63
USAF studies laser space uses. Aviation W 80:104 My 18 '64
Variety of techniques holds promise. C. D. LaFond and R. Pay. il Miss & Roc 15:31-2+ O 5 '64
Velocity measured by laser diffraction. il Aviation W 81:87-9 N 16 '64
World's most powerful and hottest beam. il(p353) Sci N L 83:359 Je 8 '63

Medical applications

Laser lights up the future. M. Pines. il N Y Times Mag p27+ S 8 '63

Military applications

Laser lights up the future. M. Pines. il N Y Times Mag p27+ S 8 '63

Photographic applications

Techniques tomorrow: photography without lenses. B. Sherman. il Mod Phot 28:36+ S '64

LIGHT and sound. See Son et lumière (sound and light)

LIGHT armed reconnaissance aircraft. See Airplanes, Military—United States

LIGHT bulbs. See Electric lamps

LIGHT filters
Color from B&W. P. Gridley. il Mod Phot 27:58-9 F '63
Easy guide to figuring filter factors. il Pop Phot 52:145 Ap '63
Filtering the sun. il Pop Phot 54:58-9 My '64
Filters for color; control, correct, create. N. Rothschild. il Pop Phot 52:74-87 Je '63
Filters for negative color. N. Rothschild. il Pop Phot 54:133-4 Ja '64
From Norman Rothschild's color notebook: six must filters. N. Rothschild. Pop Phot 55:67+ Jl '64
Glamor; when a filter is a friend. P. Gowland. il Pop Phot 54:14 Mr '64
Instant color correction! C. S. McCamy. il Mod Phot 28:66-7 Ja '64
Large camera. A. Feininger. Mod Phot 28:52+ O '64
Large camera: why, how and when to use filters. A. Feininger. Mod Phot 28:30+ S '64
Light sieves of photography. P. Farber. il U S Camera 28:44-5+ Ja '65
Shedding light on the filter haze. D. B. Eisendrath, jr. Pop Phot 54:10+ Mr '64
35MM: question of a Skylight filter. J. Wolbarst. Mod Phot 27:49-50 F '63
Try filters for portraits. W. P. Banner. il U S Camera 27:14+ D '64
Which filters for tele photography? B. Sherman. il Mod Phot 28:72-3 Ag '64

LIGHT in art
Movement & light in today's art. F. Popper. il UNESCO Courier 16:12-17+ S '63

LIGHT meters. See Exposure meters; Photometers

LIGHT projection
Big light from small sources. B. Pierce. il Pop Phot 52:62-3+ Ja '63
Floodlighting a shopping center; Detroit. il Am City 78:113 N '63
Floodlighting solves a problem. J. E. Curtis. il Recreation 56:230-2 My '63

LIGHT projection—*Continued*
Guide to help you end the confusion in floodlamp sources. N. Rothschild. Pop Phot 52:134-6 Ja '63
More light on sports; Irish Hills sports park, Mich. il Recreation 57:352-3 S '64
New light: floodlighting of Pan Am building. New Yorker 40:23-5 D 26 '64
Painting the city with light. E. B. Karns. il Am City 79:97-8 N '64
Scenes that are brightest. M. Gough. il House B 105:72+ F '63

LIGHT-sensitive devices. See Photoelectric cells

LIGHTBOWN, Mary Jane
Publisher's note. por Arch Forum 119:1 O '63

LIGHTHALL, Frederick F.
Student anxiety; excerpt from Anxiety as related to thinking and forgetting. NEA J 53: 26-8 D '64

LIGHTHOUSES
Life guide. Life 55:13 Jl 26 '63
Lost world of Cape Canaveral, 1911; excerpt from a student theme. J. K. Wright. il Harper 227:67 N '63
Power of a child's book; Little red lighthouse. H. H. Swift. il Sat R 46:43 My 11 '63

LIGHTING
Benevolent light bulb. D. Moraes. House & Gard 124:248-9 N '63
High daylight indoors. il Sunset 131:102-8 N '63
How to light your way to better decorating. il Bet Hom & Gard 41:103 Ap '63
Remodel lighting in redwood and fiberglass. il Sunset 131:174+ O '63
Remodeling with daylight and night light. il Sunset 131:119 S '63
This bright and fresh kitchen has its secrets upstairs. il Sunset 131:130-1 O '63
See also
Candles
Electric lighting
Gas lamps

LIGHTING, Christmas. See Christmas decorations

LIGHTING, Fluorescent. See Electric lamps, Fluorescent

LIGHTING, Outdoor
Box entry light. il Sunset 130:116 Je '63
Enjoy the major of electricity outdoors. il Pop Gard 15:58-60 Jl '64
Entry lights you can make: high and bright or low and dim. il Sunset 131:58-9 Ag '63
Lawn party lamps. D. M. Swartwout. il Pop Mech 119:138-42 Je '63
Niagara's enchanted forest; Queenston Heights Park, Niagara Falls, Ontario; excerpts. M. T. Gray. il Recreation 57:526 D '64
Night lights, good-looking by day. il Sunset 130:120 Je '63
Outdoor lighting. See issues of American city
See also
Airports—Lighting
Bridges—Lighting
Christmas decorations, Outdoor
Gardens—Lighting
Golf courses—Lighting
Light projection
Lighting fixtures
Roads—Lighting
Street lighting

LIGHTING fixtures
Barbecue cupboard. il Pop Gard 14:60-1 S '63
Enjoy the magic of electricity outdoors. il Pop Gard 15:58-60 Jl '64
How to install outdoor lighting fixtures. A. S. Green. il Pop Gard 14:41-4 S '63
It's a garden light and an indoor light. il Sunset 130:148 Ap '63
You can make these hanging lights. il Sunset 132:94+ F '64
See also
Chandeliers

LIGHTING of cities. See Street lighting

LIGHTNING
Artificial lightning from beam of particles. Sci N L 85:88 F 8 '64
Ball lightning. H. W. Lewis. il Sci Am 208: 106-8+ bibliog(p 190+) Mr '63
Ball lightning due to leak in stroke at joint. Sci N L 85:392 Je 20 '64
If lightning struck a missile... Bsns W p60 Mr 7 '64
Lightning strikes on Bugaboo Spire. C. Fletcher. il Read Digest 82:49-54 Je '63
New theoretical model for ball lightning. il Sci N L 86:199 S 26 '64
Sky fire: how science fights it. F. B. Quigg. il Am For 69:12-15+ O '63
When lightning strikes. J. C. Kacharian. il Todays Health 42:14-17+ Jl '64
See also
Aviation—Lightning hazards
Lightning protection
Thunderstorms

LIGHTNING bugs. See Fireflies

LIGHTNING protection
Jolts, volts, bolts. il Recreation 57:309-10 Je '64
Lightning need strike only once. il Pop Gard 15:89 Jl '64

LIGULARIAS
Perennials from a mandarin's garden. M. W. Stephens. il Horticulture 41:378 Jl '63

LIJINSKY, W. and Shubik, P.
Benzo(a)pyrene and other polynuclear hydrocarbons in charcoal-broiled meat. bibliog Science 145:53-5 Jl 3 '64

LIK; story. See Nabokov, V.

LIKE mother used to make; drama. See Murray, J.

LIKERT, Rensis
Principles of effective management; excerpts from New patterns of management. Harvard Bsns R 41:103 N '63
—and Seashore, S. E.
Making cost control work. bibliog f Harvard Bsns R 41:96-108 N '63

LIKES and dislikes
Party of one; antipathies. W. Golding. il Holiday 34:12+ D '63

LILACS
Choose fragrant lilacs. B. Harkness. il Am Home 67:10+ S '64
Lilacs. J. H. Alexander. il Pop Gard 15:55+ S '64
Useful small tree you should know. E. L. Sculthorp. il House B 105:86+ My '63

LILIENTHAL, David E.
Excerpt from Change, hope, and the bomb. Cong Digest 43:207+ Ag '64
Mythology of the atom; summary of addresses. Bul Atomic Sci 19:21 O '63
Skeptical look at scientific experts. N Y Times Mag p23+ S 29; 6 O 20 '63
Untold stories about Truman and Marshall; excerpts from Journals of David E. Lilienthal. por U S News 57:22 N 9 '64
Whatever happened to the peaceful atom? excerpts from Change, hope, and the bomb. Harper 227:41-6 O '63; Reply. W. B. Cottrell. 227:14+ N '63
When the atom moves next door; excerpt from Change, hope, and the bomb. McCalls 91:52+ O '63

about
Creating the hydrogen bomb. J. W. Finney. New Repub 151:24-5+ O 17 '64
David and the Goliath. il Newsweek 64:64 O 19 '64
Mr Lilienthal's worries. J. O'Gara. Commonweal 78:296 Je 7 '63
Private record of a public servant. F. Freidel. por Sat R 47:41-2 O 17 '64

LILIES
Flower Grower's home garden notebook.. il Flower Grower 51:35-6 Ag '64
For bright color all summer. il Sunset 131: 166-7 Jl '63
Grow lilies from seed. V. Howie. il Pop Gard 14:34+ F '63
Guide to hybrid lilies. R. C. Hands. Horticulture 41:447 S '63
Lilies. il House & Gard 126:204-7 O '64
Lilies. il Pop Gard 15:56 S '64
Lilies go in in November. il Sunset 131:252 N '63
Lilies in the living room. V. Howie. il Pop Gard 14:49+ N '63
Lily hybrids. il Sunset 133:238-41 N '64
Look at the future of lilies. G. L. Slate. il Horticulture 42:26-9 Ag '64
Rugged lilies for all gardeners. R. B. Ware. il Flower Grower 50:36-8 S '63
This lily is up from Mexico; aztec lily. il Sunset 133:274 O '64
Trouble-free glory of lilies. O. K. Moore. il House B 105:96-7+ Ag '63
What wonder science and devotion have worked with lilies. J. Fanning. il House & Gard 126:252-5+ O '64
Why we hybridize lilies. J. De Graaff. il Pop Gard 14:28-9+ S '63
Wonderful world of reflexed lilies. O. K. Moore. il Flower Grower 50:38+ Ag '63
See also
Calla lilies
Day lilies
Glory lilies
Torch lilies

LILIES don't bloom at Easter; story. See McClure, J. G.

LILIES of the valley
Divide plants now for bigger and better lily-of-the-valley flowers. D. K. Sampson. il Flower Grower 50:19 Ag '63
Luck with lily-of-the-valley. il Sunset 132:135 Ja '64

LILJEDAHL, J. B.
Let's plow on the level. Suc Farm 62:49 Ap '64

LILLER, Martha, and Liller, William
Planetary nebulae; with biographical sketches. Sci Am 208:38, 60-7 bibliog(p200) Ap '63

LILLER, William
Optical effects of the 1963 Project West Ford experiment. bibliog Science 143:347-41 Ja 31 '64
—See Liller, M. jt. auth.

LILLEY, Edward. See Barrett, A. H. jt. auth.

LILLIE, Beatrice
Notes from our correspondents. S. Fleming. por Hi Fi 14:12+ Jl '64
Old friend gives the low-down on Lillie. N. Coward. il por Life 56:129-30 My 15 '64

LILLIPUTIAN stars. See Stars, Subdwarf

LILLY, Doris
How to make love in five languages; excerpts from How to marry a millionaire. McCalls 91:94-5 Je '64

LILLY, John C.
Vocal mimicry in tursiops: ability to match numbers and durations of human vocal bursts. bibliog Science 147:300-1 Ja 15 '65

LILLY, Othelia
Lost love; poem. Christian Cent 80:1046 Ag 28 '63

LILY pools. See Garden pools; Water gardens

LILY-Tulip cup corporation
Plastic cups invade coffee break market. Bsns W p57 F 29 '64

LIM, P. G. and Mateles, R. I.
Tryptophan- and indole-excreting bacterial mutants. bibliog Science 140:388 Ap 26 '63

LIMA, Alceu Amoroso. See Amoroso Lima, A.

LIMA, Ohio

Newspapers

According to Hoiles. V. G. Sauter. New Repub 150:5 F 22 '64
Farewell fellow citizens. Time 83:51 Ja 17 '64

LIMA, Peru

Churches

Sanctuary; for New World's first saint. il Travel 120:41-3 D '63

Description

Five worlds of Peru. K. F. Weaver. il Nat Geog Mag 125:212-66 F '64
Lima I love you, oddly enough. R. Bissell. il Holiday 35:46-55+ Je '64

Riots

Crashing of mountains; clash between Peru and Argentina. il Time 83:36 Je 5 '64
Sport of death; world's worst sporting disaster. il Newsweek 63:60 Je 8 '64

LIMA citizen (newspaper) See Lima, Ohio—Newspapers

LIMBACHER, James L.
Film evaluation and criticism; excerpts from address, July 13, 1963. por ALA Bul 58:43-7 Ja '64
Movies are better than ever. Library J 89:2152-5+ My 15 '64
Recorded word. See issues of Library journal
(ed) Records for children. Library J 88:1297-8+, 3999-4001 Mr 15, O 15 '63
(ed) Records for children. Library J 88:3999-4001; 89:1383-4+ O 15 '63, Mr 15 '64

LIMBAUGH, Conrad
First aqualung in the U.S. J. McMillan. il por Sci Digest 56:14-18 Jl '64

LIMBER pine. See Pine

LIMBERT, Paul M.
New look at the Y.M.C.A. Christian Cent 81:760-2 Je 10 '64

LIMBLESS lizards. See Lizards

LIMBO
Limbo: unsettled question, by G. J. Dyer. Review
America 110:739-41 My 23 '64. J. E. Bruns; Reply. J. A. Slattery. 110:808 Je 13 '64
On the hem of hell. il Time 83:84 Ap 17 '64

LIME
Lime: good or bad for your garden? K. B. Rigg. il Pop Gard 14:16+ Mr '63
Lime your soil. B. Brinhart. il Horticulture 41:554-5 N '63
Liming pays big dividends. R. B. Corey and L. E. Zeman. il Suc Farm 61:72-3+ F '63

LIMERICKS
Seizure of limericks. C. Aiken. Horizon 5:100-1 N '63
Seven lively limericks. H. I. Brock. Read Digest 84:242C Je '64
There was an old man from; comp. by L. Greenblatt. N Y Times Mag p 120 D 13 '64

LIMITATION of armaments. See Disarmament

LIMITATION of population. See Population

LIMITATIONS (law)
Statute of limitations in a libel action. H. F. Pilpel. Pub W 185:32 Mr 2 '64

LIMITED-access highways. See Express highways

LIMITED editions. See Publishers and publishing—Limited editions

LIMÓN, José
Dance debuts at Lincoln Center. D. Hering. il por Dance Mag 37:23 F '63
José Limon reports on Asia tour. D. Duncan. il pors Dance Mag 38:31-2 F '64
Stage works by Paul Hindemith at Juilliard concert hall; new treatment of The demon. M. Marks. Dance Mag 37:31+ My '63

LIMULUS. See King crabs

LIN, Yu-t'ang
Citizen of two worlds. N. King. por Sat R 46:43 F 2 '63
Computer for translating. A. Gode. il Sci N L 83:374 Je 15 '63

LINCK, Tony
Flying fotographer. Flying 74:60 Mr '64

LINCOLN, Abraham
Abraham Lincoln and the people who keep him alive; outstanding names in American literature. il por(p 1) Sr Schol 84:7 F 7 '64
Carl Sandburg: tells how he thinks Great Emancipator would have reacted to today's touchy race problems; interview, ed. by M. Quigley. C. Sandburg. Ebony 18:158-9 S '63
Eisenhower on Lincoln; excerpts from TV discussion with Bruce Catton. D. D. Eisenhower. il pors Sr Schol 82:23-4 F 6 '63
Emancipation proclamation; address, January 13, 1963. S. Reese. Vital Speeches 29:283-6 F 15 '63
Few appropriate remarks at Gettysburg. T. Mahoney. il por Read Digest 83:146-52 N '63
Gettysburg address and our commitment to freedom; address, November 17, 1963. D. Rusk. Dept State Bul 49:842-4 D 2 '63
He could take it; reprint. A. B. Reincke. Read Digest 82:140-2 F '63
Lincoln and modern America; the heritage of a free choice in an organized society. il pors Time 81:20-5 My 10 '63
Lincoln and the Emancipation proclamations. H. L. Hurwitz. por Sr Schol 82:8T-10T F 13 '63
Lincoln and the first shot, by R. N. Current. Review
Am Heritage 15:109-10 D '63. B. Catton
Lincoln in photographs, by C. Hamilton and L. Ostendorf. Review
Am Heritage 15:108-9 F '64. B. Catton
Lincoln rejects a bodyguard. C. C. Hollis. Nation 198:173-4 F 17 '64
Lincoln's doctor used closed chest massage. Sci N L 84:185 S 21 '63
Lincoln's failure at Gettysburg; with report by D. M. Kunhardt. il por Life 55:116-18+ N 15 '63
Little Giant vs. Honest Abe. il por Sr Schol 85:5 O 14 '64
Long blade, short scabbard; excerpts from Incidents and anecdotes of the Civil war. D. D. Porter. Am Heritage 14:91 F '63
Man who spoke to Lincoln. il por Ebony 18:79-82+ F '63
Ms. that would not scour; centennial of Gettysburg address. Wilson Lib Bul 38:378-9 Ja '64
Mr Lincoln also spoke. R. L. Strout. New Repub 149:14 N 23 '63
New Lincoln financial note. J. T. Hickey. il Hobbies 68:110-11+ F '64
Notes for a gazetteer; Gettysburg, Pa. P. Hamburger. New Yorker 40:84+ Ap 4 '64
On the murder of Abraham Lincoln; poem, tr. by R. Bly. H. Ibsen. Nation 196:142 F 16 '63
Rare photos of Lincoln's exhumation: strange history brought to light; with report by D. M. Kunhardt. il por Life 54:83-5+ F 15 '63
Sojourner Truth. E. J. Ritter. Negro Hist Bul 26:254 My '63
Terrible swift sword, by B. Catton. Review
Nat R 15:198+ S 10 '63. G. F. Eliot
Tribute to Abraham Lincoln; address, November 19, 1963. W. W. Scranton. Vital Speeches 30:132-3 D 15 '63

LINCOLN, Abraham—*Continued*
Assassination
Compendium of curious coincidences; parallels in the lives and deaths of A. Lincoln and J. F. Kennedy. il Time 84:19 Ag 21 '64
Autographs
Abraham Lincoln signed photographs. L. Ostendorf. pors Hobbies 67:110-12 F '63
Bibliography
Lincolniana in 1962-1963. B. E. Wheeler. il por Hobbies 67:24-5+ F '63; 68:24-5+ F '64
Drama
Just and lasting peace. G. DuBois. Plays 23:25-34, 84 F '64
Lincoln umbrella. M. Hark and N. McQueen. Plays 23:55-63 F '64
Man like Lincoln. H. L. Miller. Plays 23:1-12 F '64
Fiction
Citizen of New Salem; condensation. P. Horgan. il por Read Digest 84:234-6+ F '64
Statues, portraits, etc.
Cover. Am Artist 27:6 F '63
LINCOLN, Abraham, family
Expressions of sentiment of Abraham Lincoln; reprint. R. G. McMurty. Hobbies 68:110-11+ S '63
Willie was the favorite; Lincolns, too, lost a son. D. M. Kunhardt. Life 55:11 Ag 23 '63
LINCOLN, Alexander, Jr
Hunter and the landowner. Am For 70:40 Ag '64
LINCOLN, C. Eric
Key man of the South: the Negro minister. N Y Times Mag p20+ Jl 12 '64
Negro's middle-class dream. N Y Times Mag p35+ O 24 '64
Patterns of protest. Christian Cent 81:733-6 Je 3 '64
LINCOLN, Edith M.
Preventing TB in children. Parents Mag 39:151-2 S '64
LINCOLN, Evelyn
Memo from a secretary about her boss: John Fitzgerald Kennedy. por McCalls 91:68+ Jl '64
LINCOLN, Henry Fiennes Clinton, 9th earl of
Background of a conversation piece. E. Gaines. il por Antiques 85:578-9 My '64
LINCOLN, Ignatius Trebitsch-. See Trebitsch-Lincoln, I.
LINCOLN, Keith
Run to a title; San Diego Chargers vs Boston Patriots in AFL championship. G. Rogin. il por Sports Illus 20:8-11 Ja 13 '64
LINCOLN, Marshall
State-police microwave. Electr World 71:48-50 F '64
Tune in on air traffic. Pop Electr 21:58-9+ S '64
LINCOLN, Thomas
Thomas Lincoln's corner cupboards. R. G. McMurtry. il Antiques 85:206-8 F '64
LINCOLN, William Wallace
Willie was the favorite; Lincolns, too, lost a son. D. M. Kunhardt. por Life 55:11 Ag 23 '63
LINCOLN, Neb.
Lighting
Pay-as-you-go street lighting. L. Bitney. il Am City 79:133 O '64
LINCOLN Center for the performing arts, New York
Case for a Center; questions from Opera news answered. W. Schuman. il Opera N 29:6-11 S 26 '64
Center that set off a tempest; New York's Lincoln center. T. Prideaux. il Life 58:42-3+ Ja 22 '65
Construction show at Lincoln Center. il N Y Times Mag p22-3 Je 16 '63
Inside job; dissension and criticism of Lincoln Center's administrators. il Newsweek 64:74-5 D 21 '64
Lincoln Center and corporate support. C. Francis. Mus Am 84:10 O '64
Lincoln Center progress report. il N Y Times Mag p22 S 22 '63
Lincoln Center: progress report. J. Ardoin. il Mus Am 84:10-13 My '64
Man at the Center; H. Krawitz, technical administrator of the Metropolitan. J. Ferris. il Opera N 29:11-13 Ja 16 '65
Mixing business and art. il Bsns W p42-5 Ag 3 '63
Musical events; conflict of interest. W. Sargeant. New Yorker 40:163 D 19 '64
New and hopeful role for repertory; plans for Vivian Beaumont theater. T. Guthrie. il N Y Times Mag p32-3+ N 10 '63
New Metropolitan; photographs. Opera N 28:19-21 S 28 '63
Setting the stage for Lincoln Center; Arthur Miller's After the fall. R. D. Meyer and N. Meyer. il Theatre Arts 48:12-16+ Ja '64
Stein & Day to publish for Lincoln Center theatre. Pub W 184:46-7 N 18 '63
Tour. New Yorker 40:27-30 Je 13 '64
New York state theater
Dear dance fan. E. Denby. il Dance Mag 38:34-5 Je '64
Essence of a theater. il Newsweek 63:53 My 4 '64
House of Balanchine; Johnson's New York state theater will be formally opened by the New York city ballet. Newsweek 61:88 Ap 8 '63
Inside the New York state theater. il Sat R 47:54-5 Ap 25 '64
Jewel in its proper setting. il Time 83:58-63 My 1 '64
Lincoln Center situation. E. Palatsky. il Dance Mag 37:36-8 My '63
Music to my ears; new theater at Lincoln Center. I. Kolodin. Sat R 47:46-7 My 9 '64
Musical events; opening of spring season. W. Sargeant. New Yorker 40:146+ My 9 '64
New York state theater. J. S. Harrison; R. Krokover. il Mus Am 84:6-9 My '64
New York's newest showplace. I. Kolodin. il Sat R 47:31+ F 22 '64
Now the musical theater is enshrined. R. Rodgers. il N Y Times Mag p20-3 Je 21 '64
Parlor for New York. R. Lynes. il Harper 228:28+ My '64
Preview: New York state theatre. N. Lansdale. il Dance Mag 38:36-8+ Mr '64
Theater glamour again. il Arch Rec 135:137-44 My '64
Which way to Mecca? Balanchine's New York city ballet tug-of-war with Lincoln Center. Newsweek 64:102 O 12 '64
Philharmonic Hall
Acoustics; what happened at Philharmonic Hall? R. S. Lanier. il Arch Forum 119:118-23 D '63
Childe Harold in New York; question of acoustics. il Time 82:36+ S 6 '63
Film festival at the concert hall. R. Steel. Christian Cent 80:1150-2+ D 11 '63
First recordings from Philharmonic Hall; opening night concert, September 23, 1962. R. C. Marsh. il Hi Fi 13:73-4 F '63
Lo-fi science of acoustics. il Sci Digest 54:61 Jl '63
Music to my ears; Keilholz's Philharmonic. I. Kolodin. Sat R 47:32 O 17 '64
Musical events: New York philharmonic's promenade concerts. W. Sargeant. New Yorker 40:131-3 My 30 '64
N.Y.'s Philharmonic Hall: a setting for Japanese art. il Flower Grower 51:49 Jl '64
Profiles; R. Lippold. C. Tomkins. New Yorker 39:47-50+ Mr 30 '63
Prom night; New York philharmonic Promenades. il Newsweek 61:94 Je 10 '63
Sandburg makes history at the proms. I. Kolodin. Sat R 46:51 Je 15 '63
Sound and fury; problem of acoustics. Newsweek 63:47 Ja 6 '64
Sound of words; deficiency in the bass frequencies. il Newsweek 61:92 Ap 15 '63
Stopping the crack; adjustments to improve the acoustics. R. Jacobson. Mus Am 83:16 My '63
Tale of two cities. il Arch Forum 118:94-9 F '63
Virgil Fox plays the Philharmonic Hall organ at Lincoln Center. R. Kammerer. Am Rec G 29:958-9 Ag '63
LINCOLN Center repertory theater. See New York (city)—Theater
LINCOLN-Mercury division. See Ford motor company—Lincoln-Mercury division
LINCOLN umbrella; drama. See Hark, M. and McQueen, N.
LINCOLN'S birthday
Lincoln takeover. Time 81:24 F 22 '63
100 years after Lincoln set the slaves free; integrated White House party. il U S News 54:8 F 25 '63
LIND, Jakov
Pious brother; story. Esquire 62:157 S '64
LINDAHL, Kai Curry-. See Curry-Lindahl, K.
LINDAHL-KIESSLING, Kerstin. See Jackson, J. F. jt. auth.

LINDBECK, George A.
Impressions from Helsinki, Rome and Montreal. Cath World 198:272-80 F '64
Thrust of "progressive" Catholicism. Commonweal 79:105-7 O 18 '63

LINDBERG, John
Secret life of Dag Hammarskjöld. Look 28:66-8+ Je 30 '64

LINDBERGH, Anne Morrow
As I see our First lady. por Look 28:100+ My 19 '64

LINDBERGH, Charles Augustus
Is civilization progress? Read Digest 85:67-74 Jl '64

about

How Lindbergh gave a lift to rocketry; excerpts from This high man: a biography of Dr Robert H. Goddard. M. Lehman. il por Life 55:115-18+ O 4 '63
Where did Charles Lindbergh go? W. Ross. por Esquire 60:85-8+ O '63; Same abr. with title What became of Charles Lindbergh? Read Digest 84:91-6 F '64

LINDE, Shirley Motter
What most people don't know about epilepsy. bibliog Todays Health 42:38-41+ Jl '64

LINDE air products company
New method for recovering helium. il Miss & Roc 12:48+ Ap 29 '63

LINDEBURG, Franklin A. and Lewis, F. D.
Lifesaving with a realistic touch. Recreation 57:134-5 Mr '64

LINDECKE, Fred W.
Poverty's second generation. Nation 199:163-5 S 28 '64

LINDEMAN, Bard
Cuban prisoner exchange. Sat Eve Post 236:15-17+ F 2 '63
How a stricken state met chaos. Sat Eve Post 237:24-31 My 9 '64
Long nightmare of a police witness. Sat Eve Post 236:71-2+ N 2 '63
Masquerade of a counterfeit doctor. Sat Eve Post 238:83-7 Ja 30 '65
Ohio's mad oil boom. Sat Eve Post 237:81-5 N 14 '64
Twins who found each other. Sat Eve Post 237:76-8 Mr 21 '64; Same abr. Read Digest 85:93-7 Ag '64
Who didn't kill Barbara Kralik? Sat Eve Post 238:78-81 Ja 16 '65
(ed) See Hege, R. My clothes were blood-soaked, but I never moved
(ed) See Shamma, G. I was Castro's prisoner
—and Patureau, Alan
Television ratings on trial. Sat Eve Post 237:13-17 F 8 '64

LINDEMAN, Jack
New arrival; poem. Poetry 102:19 Ap '63

LINDENBAUM, Arthur. See Kuettner, K. E. jt. auth.

LINDER, Carl
Flowing backwards; Younger man; Accident; Glass; poems. Poetry 105:99-101 N '64

LINDER, Leslie
Beatrix Potter's code writing. Horn Bk 39:140-55 Ap '63

LINDGREN, Gerry
Fastest boy in the West challenges a champion. R. Creamer. il por Sports Illus 20:66+ Ja 27 '64
Raves for the young. J. Underwood. il por Sports Illus 21:8-10 Ag 3 '64

LINDHEIMER astronomical research center. See Astronomical observatories

LINDLEY, H. Donn
One day I was the sea; poem. McCalls 92:175 N '64

LINDMAN, Erick L.
Financial status of the public schools. 1964. NEA J 53:38-9 N '64

LINDNER, Gerald S. See Freedman, T. jt. auth.

LINDNER, Richard
Painter of the crass crowd; show at Manhattan's Cordier & Ekstrom gallery. il por Time 83:70 Mr 20 '64
Stop, caution, go. il Newsweek 63:53 Mr 9 '64

LINDOS. See Rhodes (island)

LINDQUIST, Carl G.
Four new color films. il Pop Phot 55:54-5+ S '64

LINDQUIST, Clarence B.
Entering levels and college courses in freshman mathematics. por Sch Life 45:14-17 Ap '63
Oceanography: new vistas and opportunities. Sch Life 46:11-14 Ag '64

LINDQUIST, Orville A.
What makes a tree trunk spiral? Am For 69:15 Je '63

LINDQUIST, Raymond C.
Linda A. Eastman. ALA Bul 57:783-5 S '63

LINDSAY, Barrett K.
Flying fling. pors Flying 75:47-8 S '64

LINDSAY, David T.
Histones from developing tissues of the chicken: heterogeneity. bibliog Science 144:420-2 Ap 24 '64

LINDSAY, Eric
Heyday in the park. Recreation 57:388-9+ O '64
Reaching your publics. Recreation 58:14 Ja '65

LINDSAY, Franklin A.
Costs and the choices. Atlan 212:51-4 Ag '63

LINDSAY, John Vliet
Why they still go into the mines. N Y Times Mag p37+ N 24 '63

LINDSAY, John Vliet
Censorship feeds on complacency; address, August 25, 1964. por Library J 89:3909-12 O 15 '64
Inquiry into the darkness of the cloak, the sharpness of the dagger. Esquire 61:106-7+ Mr '64
Intellectual freedom and the federal government; address, May 15, 1963. por Pub W 183:18-21 My 27 '63
New G.O.P; interview, ed. by R. Manning. Atlan 215:39-43 Ja '65
Speaking out. por Sat Eve Post 237:12+ F 1 '64
Special duty for Republicans. Harper 227:94-5+ S '63

about

Destiny's tot. R. G. Smith. il Nat R 16:861-2 O 6 '64
Elephants in Tammanyland; seventeenth congressional district, Manhattan. B. Carter. il Reporter 29:41-3 N 21 '63
Lindsay and L'Engle speak at N.Y. New books preview. il por Library J 89:3280 S 15 '64
New York's Lindsay: independent problems. il por Newsweek 64:37 O 12 '64

LINDSAY, Powell
We still need Negro theatre in America. Negro Hist Bul 27:112 F '64

LINDSAY, Ted
Bad penny shines again. D. Anderson. por Sports Illus 22:50-1 Ja 18 '65

LINDSEY, Almont
Health service: its first decade. bibliog Cur Hist 45:12-18 Jl '63
Not so golden years. Sat R 46:32 My 4 '63

LINDSEY, Robert
B-3 Polaris expected to be operational in '70. Miss & Roc 15:28+ Ag 24 '64
Home-made Oscar III Comsat awaits piggyback Agena ride. Miss & Roc 15:31 Jl 6 '64
Improved launch system for Polaris. Miss & Roc 13:27-8 D 2 '63
Lockheed boosting its NASA Agena output. Miss & Roc 13:32 Ag 19 '63
120-in. boosts argument for solids. Miss & Roc 14:27-8+ Ap 27 '64
Polaris A2 parts rejection slashed. Miss & Roc 12:33-4 Ap 8 '63
Proposed fourth-generation Polaris would use state-of-art technology. Miss & Roc 14:20-1 Ja 13 '64
Radar systems guard ICBM bases. Miss & Roc 12:33-4 Mr 11 '63
Sunnyvale center preparing for Dyna-Soar control assignment. Miss & Roc 13:15 Jl 8 '63
Super-power radar nears testing. Miss & Roc 12:28 F 25 '63
Titan III-C stage zero role revamps UTC structure. Miss & Roc 14:34+ Ja 20 '64
Titan II engine explodes during static test firing. Miss & Roc 14:16 My 11 '64
UTC to fire 120-in. Titan III motor. Miss & Roc 12:36-8 F 18 '63
Upcoming tests may determine nuclear rocket reactor design. Miss & Roc 13:38 O 14 '63

LINDSLEY, Al
Big idea: a rail hoist for heavy stuff. por Pop Sci 183:106-7 S '63

LINDSLEY, D. H. and others
Ferrosilite ($FeSiO_3$): synthesis at high pressures and temperatures. bibliog Science 144:73-4 Ap 3 '64

LINDSLEY, Donald B. See Haider, M;—Weinberger, N. M. jt. auths.

LINDSLEY, E. F.
Boat pier that goes up or down in ten minutes. Pop Sci 184:162-4 Ap '64
How to build your own gas-powered snow-trac. Pop Sci 183:122-5+ N '63
Snow tires, they aren't all the same! Pop Sci 185:92-6+ N '64
When your engine misfires. Pop Sci 185:88-91 Ag '64
Your guide to buying a snow thrower. Pop Sci 185:144-7 D '64

LINDSTROM, R. S. and Markakis, P.
Nitrogen and potassium effect on the color of red roses. bibliog Science 142:1663-4 D 27 '63
LINDUSKA, Joe
Pronghorns for profit. Field & S 68:24-9 Ag '63
LINDZEY, Gardner. See Winston, H. D. jt. auth.
LINE, Les
Bird worth a forest fire. Audubon Mag 66: 370-5 N '64
LINE-painting machines. See Motor trucks, Municipal
LINEAR accelerators. See Accelerators (electrons, etc)
LINEAR programming
Structure of development; interindustry analysis, or input-output analysis. W. Leontief. il Sci Am 209:148-54+ bibliog(p307) S '63
LINEAWEAVER, Marion
Beginning of spring; poem. Ladies Home J 80:88 Mr '63
Roundel for a shell; poem. McCalls 90:194 My '63
LINEBARGER, Paul M. A.
Two Chinas. Cur Hist 47:162-5 S '64
LINEBERRY, William. See Steel, R. jt. auth.
LINEMEN
775,000 volts with bare hands. A. Hamilton. il Sci Digest 55:35-8 Ja '64
LINEN, Household
Linens deserve planned storage. il House B 105:48+ Mr '63
Monogramming ℞ for bed and bath. il House & Gard 127:124-7 Ja '65
New color for bedroom and bath! D. Popplestone and H. Stark. il Bet Hom & Gard 42: 52-7 O '64
Whimsical trappings for a child's bed and bath. il House & Gard 126:218-19 S '64
See also
Sheets
Table linen
LINERS. See Ocean liners
LING-Temco-Vought, Incorporated
Ling-Temco-Vought changes structure. Aviation W 79:31 O 21 '63
L-T-V must attain A-7A maintenance aims. G. C. Wilson. Aviation W 80:16-17 Mr 30 '64
Pivot wing up to take off; level for full speed ahead; LTV's XC-142A. il Bsns W p34 Je 20 '64
LING-Temco-Vought simulators. See Space flight simulators
LINGENFELTER, R. E. and Flamm, E. J.
Solar neutrons and the earth's radiation belts. bibliog Science 144:292-4 Ap 17 '64
—See Flamm, E. J. jt. auth.
LINGERIE. See Underwear
LINGG, Ann M.
Come to the fair. Opera N 28:8-14 Ap 4 '64
Dutchman arrives. Opera N 27:24-6 F 2 '63
Great opera houses: Central City. Opera N 28:16-20 My 2 '64
Great opera houses: Covent Garden. Opera N 27:18-22 My 4 '63
Meet Mlle Germont. Opera N 27:25 Mr 16 '63
Meet Papageno. Opera N 28:24-5 Ja 25 '64
Men in the pit. Opera N 27:28-31 Mr 16; 29-31 Mr 30; 26-9 Ap 13 '63
Mimi arrives. Opera N 28:12-13 Mr 14 '64
Opera on four cylinders. Opera N 28:21-2 O 19 '63
Rose from the South. Opera N 29:12-14 S 26 '64
Three American tsars. Opera N 27:25-7 Ap 6 '63
When opera goes to school. Read Digest 82:281-3+ Ap '63
(ed) See Merrill, N. Seconding the motion
(ed) See Solti, G. Verdi I know
LINGUISTIC analysis. See Analysis (philosophy)
LINGUISTICS. See Language and languages
LINK, Edwin A.
Our man-in-sea project. pors Nat Geog Mag 123:712-17 My '63
Tomorrow on the deep frontier. por Nat Geog Mag 125:778-801 Je '64
—See Membery, J. H. jt. auth.
about
Race for the bottom of the sea. W. Cloud. il por Pop Sci 183:35-40+ Jl '63
LINK, Frances R.
Teacher-made tests. NEA J 52:23-5 O '63
LINK, Marilyn
Lady's day in the Comanche 400; ed. by R. Beatty. por Flying 75:49-51 S '64
LINK division. See General precision equipment corporation—Link division
LINK trainers. See Flight simulators
LINKLETTER, Art
Child's garden of misinformation; excerpts. McCalls 90:58 F; 70 Mr '63; 91:70-1 Ja; 58 F; 48+ Mr; 74+ Ap; 70 My; 66 Je; 127 Ag; 59 S '64
Star and sportsman riding a wave. J. D. Brown. il por Sports Illus 21:84-6+ O 26 '64
LINLEY, David Albert Charles Armstrong-Jones, viscount
Princess Margaret's son: little Lord Linley. il pors Look 28:96+ S 22 '64
LINN, Edward
All-American saint. Sat Eve Post 237:72-3 N 21 '64
Bob Hope in the road to golf. Sat Eve Post 236:28-30+ N 9 '63
Comic who'll never be in. Sat Eve Post 237: 28-9 S 19 '64
I owe the public nothing. Sat Eve Post 237: 60-3 Ja 18 '64
Man in the pin-striped suit: Ralph Houk. Sat Eve Post 236:89-93 S 28 '63
Runaway Colts. Sat Eve Post 237:79-83 D 12 '64
Sad end of Big Daddy Lipscomb. Sat Eve Post 236:73-4+ Jl 27 '63
Search for Jerry Lewis. Sat Eve Post 236: 83-7 O 12 '63
Trials of a Negro idol. Sat Eve Post 236:70-2 Je 22 '63
Untold story of Jack Ruby. Sat Eve Post 237: 24-6+ Jl 25 '64
(ed) See Durocher, L. Candid memoirs
(ed) See Veeck, B. How I didn't buy a ball club
(ed) See Veeck, B. Speaking out; they've wrecked the American league
—See Papanek, E. jt. auth.
LINNEAUS, Carl
Linneaus. G. H. M. Lawrence. il por Horticulture 42:22-3 N '64
LINOLENIC acid
Synthesis of α-linolenic acid by Leishmania enriettii. E. D. Korn and C. L. Greenblatt. bibliog il Science 142:1301-3 D 6 '63
LINOLEUM block printing
Cover; Ernest Watson's October day. il Am Artist 28:4 O '64
Printing experience; fifth graders. C. T. McCarthy. il Sch Arts 64:7-13 S '64
Technique of my color prints. E. W. Watson. il Am Artist 28:48-53+ O '64
LINOLEUM block prints
Graphics: experiment & discovery. B. Kirsh. il Sch Arts 64:10-12 Ja '65
LINOLEUM cuts. See Linoleum block printing
LINOWITZ, Sol M.
Prosperity gap. Sat R 48:42 Ja 9 '65
University trustee reflects on freedom; excerpt from address, October 10, 1962. Sch & Soc 91:168-9 Ap 6 '63
LINSCOTT, Robert N.
Faulkner without fanfare. Esquire 60:36+ Jl '63
LINSCOTT, William D.
Contamination of commercial rabbit albumin preparations by bovine albumin. Science 142:1170-2 N 29 '63
LINSLEY, John
Where is the fat proton from? Time 81:74+ Mr 15 '63
LINTON, David
Nature and the camera (cont) Natur Hist 72:65-8 Ap; 62-5+ O '63; 73:63-6 F; 60-2 My; 64-8 Ag '64
LINTON, Derek
Roughing it around the world; Anglo-African trans-world safari. il Bsns W p48 Ja 26 '63
LINTON, M. Albert
As an investment: term vs. permanent insurance; with statement by B. Graham. U S News 55:102 O 7 '63
LINTZ, Warren L.
Low bid, generally not the best. Am City 79:115-16 Mr '64
LION hunting
Big lion of Mucusso. J. O'Connor. il Outdoor Life 131:17-19+ F '63
Lion mangled me. J. Kingsley-Heath. il Outdoor Life 131:20-3+ Mr '63
LION in love; drama. See Delaney, S.
LION in the refrigerator; story. See Rooney, A. B.
LIONEL corporation
Cohn's costly toy. Time 81:88 Mr 22 '63
Lionel's flyer; hovering spaceship. il Newsweek 63:88 Mr 23 '64

LIONEL corporation—*Continued*
New engineer at Lionel? il Newsweek 61:84-5 Mr 25 '63
Roy Cohn. M. Kempton. New Repub 148:15-17 Ap 20 '63
Three for a pyramid. il Time 81:108+ My 17 '63

LIONNI, Leo
My books for children. por Wilson Lib Bul 39:142-5 O '64
Newbery and Caldecott runners-up. il por Library J 89:1382 Mr 15 '64

LIONS
King of beasts makes his last stand. J. D. Scott. il Read Digest 84:193-4+ F '64
Lion. J. O'Connor. il Outdoor Life 133:32-5+ F '64
Poor rickety Leo; African lion as backyard pet. J. Neary. il Life 57:69-70+ D 11 '64
There are lions loose in the park; island in the Bronx park zoo. il Look 28:128-30 D 15 '64

Photographs

See Animals—Photographs

Training

Only Negro lion tamer. il Ebony 19:49-50+ O '64

LIONS (football club) See Football clubs

LIONS are loose; story. See Freitag, G. H.

LIPCHITZ, Jacques
Lipchitz: 1911-1962. C. S. Silver. il Art N 62:28 Mr '63

LIPETZ, Jacques
Plant tissue culture. Science 141:190+ Jl 12 '63

LIPETZ, Leo E.
Bionics. Science 140:1419-20+ Je 28 '63

LIPIDES
Diglyceride release from insect fat body: a possible means of lipid transport. H. Chino and L. I. Gilbert. bibliog il Science 143:359-61 Ja 24 '64
Oxidation of carbon-14-labeled endogenous lipids by isolated perfused rat heart. J. C. Shipp and others. bibliog il Science 143:371-3 Ja 24 '64
Toxic lysolipoid: isolation from pseudomonas pseudomallei. M. S. Redfearn. bibliog il Science 146:648-9 O 30 '64

LIPIZZAN horses. See Lippizaner horses

LIPKIN, John P.
New directions for India's teacher education. Sch & Soc 92:293-4 O 17 '64

LIPOIDS. See Lipides

LIPOPHILIC compounds. See Antibiotics

LIPOPOLYSACCHARIDES. See Polysaccharides

LIPOPROTEINS
Human lipoproteins: role in transport of thyroid hormones. E. Toro-Goyco and M. Cancio. bibliog Science 139:761-2 F 22 '63
Lipoprotein movement through canine aortic wall. L. E. Duncan, jr. and others. bibliog il Science 142:972-3 N 15 '63
Structure of lipoproteins: covalently bound fatty acids. W. R. Fisher and S. Gurin. bibliog il Science 143:362-3 Ja 24 '64

LIPOTROPIC hormones. See Hormones

LIPOTROPIN. See Hormones

LIPPINCOTT, Earle, and Aannestad, Elling
Management of voluntary welfare agencies. Harvard Bsns R 42:87-98 N '64

LIPPINCOTT, Ellis R. and Duecker, H. C.
Pressure distribution measurements in fixed-anvil high-pressure cells. bibliog Science 144:1119-21 My 29 '64
—See Duecker, H. C. jt. auth.

LIPPITT, Ronald, and others
Children look at their own behavior. NEA J 53:14-16 S '64

LIPPIZANER horses
Flight of a white stallion. il Sports Illus 20:30-2+ Ap 27 '64
Wonderful white stallions of Vienna; Lipizzaner stallions. F. Sondern, jr. il Read Digest 82:160-6 Ap '63

LIPPMANN, Walter
Assault on the Union. por Newsweek 61:25 Je 10 '63
Campaign debating. por Newsweek 64:13 Ag 31 '64
Change of course. por Newsweek 62:15 Jl 8 '63
Changing of the guard. por Newsweek 61:25 My 13 '63
Congress for Asia. por Newsweek 65:9 Ja 4 '65
Critique of Congress. por Newsweek 63:18-19 Ja 20 '64
Cuba and the nuclear risk. Atlan 211:55-8 F '63
Cuba once more. por Newsweek 63:23 Ap 27 '64
Dealing with the Soviet Union. por Newsweek 62:17 Jl 22 '63
Dream come true, comments on Goldwater. Reporter 31:7-8 Jl 2 '64
Dream world of Goldwater. por Newsweek 64:13 Ag 3 '64
Europe without America. por Newsweek 61:17 F 18 '63
Foreign aid. por Newsweek 61:17 Ap 29 '63
Gaullism today. por Newsweek 61:25 Je 24 '63
Gaullist explosion. por Newsweek 61:11 F 4 '63
German question. por Newsweek 62:15 S 2 '63
Goldwater movement. por Newsweek 62:13 Ag 5 '63
Goldwater threat. por Newsweek 64:13 Jl 6 '64
Hard treaty. por Newsweek 62:15 Ag 19 '63
Intermission is over. por Newsweek 64:23 N 9 '64
Less danger, more trouble. por Newsweek 63:11 F 17 '64
Managed news. por Newsweek 61:23 Ap 15 '63
Negroes' grievances. por Newsweek 62:21 S 16 '63
New Europe. por Newsweek 63:23 Je 8 '64
New isolationism. J. Burnham. Nat R 17:60 Ja 26 '65
Old Canal and old treaty. por Newsweek 63:13 F 3 '64
One problem, two solutions. por Time 85:48 Ja 1 '65
One-step thinking. por Newsweek 63:25 Mr 16 '64
Our problem in Vietnam. por Newsweek 64:23 S 28 '64
Presidential succession. por Newsweek 63:13 Mr 2 '64
Principle of the Great society. por Newsweek 65:13 Ja 18 '65
Racial crisis. por Newsweek 61:23 My 27 '63
Realignment of parties? por Newsweek 64:15 Jl 20 '64
Republican agony. por Newsweek 63:19 Je 22 '64
Republican moderates. por Newsweek 64:29 O 12 '64
Republican success. por Newsweek 63:13 Mr 30 '64
Rockefeller and the GOP. por Newsweek 61:15 Ap 1 '63
Root of the Republican disaster. por Newsweek 64:31 N 23 '64
Senator speaks out. por Newsweek 63:19 Ap 13 '64
Story of the Congo. por Newsweek 61:15 Mr 4 '63
Tomorrow's world; questions and answers. por Atlan 214:50-5 Ag '64
Ultimate decency. por Newsweek 64:13 Ag 17 '64
Uncertain world. por Newsweek 64:29 O 26 '64
Unraveling alliances. por Newsweek 61:21 Mr 18 '63
Walter Lippmann interviewed by Charles Collingwood; excerpts from CBS program. New Repub 148:15-18 My 18 '63
Walter Lippmann, 1964; interview on CBS, ed. by E. Sevareid. New Repub 150:15-18 Ap 25 '64
What preoccupies the Europeans. por Newsweek 64:15 D 21 '64

about

Editor-in-chief of democracy. J. M. Burns. por Sat R 46:19-20 Ag 3 '63
Lippmann at seventy-five. New Repub 151:5 S 26 '64
Lippmann distilled: an apprehensive view of mass society. W. D. Burnham. Commonweal 78:459-61 Jl 26 '63
Vital mind. por Newsweek 62:81 Jl 15 '63
Walter Lippmann: the philosopher as journalist. L. J. Halle. New Repub 149:17-20 Ag 3 '63
War whoop. Time 81:67 Mr 15 '63

LIPPOLD, Richard
Profiles. C. Tompkins. por New Yorker 39:47-50+ Mr 30 '63

LIPSCHUTZ, Michael E.
Origin of diamonds in the ureilites. bibliog Science 143:1431-4 Mr 27 '64
—See Sciacca, T. P. jt. auth.

LIPSCOMB, D. Barry. See Crovitz, H. F. jt. auth.

LIPSCOMB, Eugene Alan
Requiem for Big Daddy. por Esquire 60:88-9 S '63
Sad end of Big Daddy Lipscomb. E. Linn. por Sat Eve Post 236:73-4+ Jl 27 '63
LIPSCOMB, Glenard P.
Excerpt from remarks, August 23, 1963. Cong Digest 43:61+ F '64
LIPSET, Seymour Martin
How big is the bloc vote? N Y Times Mag p32-3+ O 25 '64
How to rebuild the two-party system. Harper 230:56-63 Ja '65
Private opinion on the polls. N Y Times Mag p 14+ Ag 30 '64
—and Seabury, Paul
Lesson of Berkeley. Reporter 32:36-40 Ja 28 '65
Politics of the possible: the American scene. S. Rousseas and J. Farganis. Nation 196: 240-4 Mr 23 '63; Discussion. 197:inside cover. 93 Ag 24 '63
LIPSETT, Julius
Lipsett brothers: biggest wreckers in the building world. il por Arch Forum 120:76-7 Ja '64
LIPSETT, Morris
Lipsett brothers: biggest wreckers in the building world. il por Arch Forum 120: 76-7 Ja '64
LIPSTICK
Dressing table talk. il Seventeen 22:14+ My '63
Mouth comes back. il Vogue 143:142 Ap 1 '64
LIPSTICK plants. See Blush worts
LIPSYTE, Robert M.
Cassius Clay, Cassius X, Muhammad Ali. N Y Times Mag p29+ O 25 '64
TV goes C-C. N Y Times Mag p 157+ Ap 7 '63
Trading stamps. Esquire 59:90 Ap '63
LIPTON, James
Love letter to twenty-four gypsies; reprint. Dance Mag 37:28-9 F '63
LIPTON, Leonard
Color 3-D printing process permits mass press run, glassless viewing. Pop Phot 54:92-3 My '64
Directory of sound-slide systems. Pop Phot 55:84 O '64
Four steps into space. Pop Phot 55:64-5 O '64
Home-grown animation rig. Pop Phot 55:174 N '64
Movies; twenty-five questions, twenty-four answers. Pop Phot 55:188-9 D '64
Three master sound-slide showmen. il Pop Phot 55:74-5 O '64
LIPTON, Seymour
Metaphor in metal. K. Kuh. il Sat R 47:24-5 F 29 '64
LIQUEFIED gases. See Gases, Liquefied
LIQUID assets. See Liquidity (economics)
LIQUID chlorine. See Chlorine, Liquid
LIQUID crystals
Liquid crystals. J. L. Fergason. il Sci Am 211:76-82+ Ag '64
LIQUID fertilizers. See Fertilizers and manures
LIQUID helium. See Helium, Liquid
LIQUID metals. See Metals, Liquid
LIQUID nitrogen. See Nitrogen, Liquid
LIQUID nitrogen process. See Freezing of food
LIQUID propellant rockets
Big lift; Centaur rocket. il Newsweek 62:72 D 9 '63
Different missions altering basic S-4B. H. D. Watkins. il Aviation W 79:48-9+ D 23 '63
Flight of M-1 delayed three years. H. Taylor. il Miss & Roc 12:16-17 Ap 22 '63
H_2fluorine booster stage eyed. H. Taylor. Miss & Roc 13:14 S 2 '63
Hoofs of hydrogen. il Time 82:97-8 D 6 '63
Hottest rocket passes test; hydrogen-fueled Centaur. il Bsns W p58-60 D 7 '63
How propellants are fed to liquid-rocket engines. W. Von Braun. il Pop Sci 185:98-9+ D '64
JPL developing advanced liquid engine concept. R. Hawkes. il Miss & Roc 12:32-3 F 25 '63
Oxidizer additives may boost RL-10 power. il Miss & Roc 13:38+ Ag 26 '63
P&W building rocket research facility; West Palm Beach, Fla. il Aviation W 78:98 Ap 8 '63
P&W completes liquid test complex. il Miss & Roc 12:36 Ap 8 '63
Propellant logistics problems increasing; panel members of second annual Liquid missile propellants symposium agreed. M. L. Yaffee. Aviation W 81:71+ N 30 '64
Solid vs. liquid rockets? W. Von Braun. il Pop Sci 183:61-3 N '63
Stehling cites urgent propellant needs. J. F. Judge. il Miss & Roc 12:36 F 25 '63
Titan II expected to overcome pogostick trouble. Miss & Roc 12:15 Ap 22 '63
USAF seeks combustion instability data. C. M. Plattner. il Aviation W 81:61+ Ag 10 '64
X-12 engine series to follow X-8 tests. C. M. Plattner. il Aviation W 79:99+ N 11 '63
Testing
Can Centaur recover from its third flop? il Bsns W p 17 Jl 4 '64
Columbium thrust chamber is test-fired. M. L. Yaffee. il Aviation W 80:47-8 Mr 30 '64
First Emeraude launch by French marked by guidance malfunction. Aviation W 80:24 Je 29 '64
LIQUIDAMBARS
Admirable liquidambars. il Sunset 133:269-72 O '64
LIQUIDATION
Spreading the losses. il Time 82:109-10 D 6 '63
LIQUIDITY (economics)
Affluent America in 1965; liquid assets. il U S News 58:94 Ja 18 '65
Facing up to the fiscal facts of life. il Newsweek 62:100-2+ O 14 '63
Trillion in liquid assets; offset to Americans' debts? il U S News 57:134-5 O 26 '64
LIQUIDS
Capacitance transducer systems. S. L. Silver. il Electr World 72:38-40+ S '64
Light scattering by liquids at 6937 angstroms. J. L. Lundberg and others. bibliog il Science 145:1308-10 S 18 '64
Making products flow to the customers; shipment of solids and gases in liquid form. il Bsns W p68-70 My 2 '64
Undercooling of liquids. D. Turnbull. il Sci Am 212:38-46 bibliog(p 134) Ja '65
See also
Surface tension
Viscosity
LIQUOR habit. See Alcoholism
LIQUOR industry
Cognac on the rocks? il Bsns W p 112-13 N 21 '64
Drinkers seek the light; liquor sales patterns. il Bsns W p81-3 F 23 '63
How a new model paid off for distiller. il Bsns W p80-1 F 22 '64
New York pops cork on liquor; repealing price controls. il Bsns W p66 My 2 '64
Seeing the light. il Time 81:94 Ap 5 '63
LIQUOR laws and regulations
See also
Prohibition
Alabama
Hi neighbor. Newsweek 63:83 Mr 16 '64
Connecticut
Spinning the bottle; parents arrested for serving drinks to minors in Darien. Newsweek 64:72+ O 5 '64
Youth; drinking problem; Darien, Conn. il Time 84:103 O 2 '64
Kuwait
Oil, oil everywhere, but not a drop to drink. Time 85:29 Ja 22 '65
New York (state)
Emphasis twenty-one. T. L. Conklin. Christian Cent 81:914 Jl 15 '64
Governor and booze. Life 56:2 Ap 10 '64
New look at old liquor laws. H. B. Jacobs. il N Y Times Mag p 19+ N 10 '63
New York pops cork on liquor; repealing price controls. il Bsns W p66 My 2 '64
Stars and bars; theaters to be able to operate their own bars. Time 84:71 S 11 '64
To get the bars back on their feet. S. Blum. il N Y Times Mag p68+ S 27 '64
See also
State liquor authority, New York
United States
About: bourbon. T. Irwin. il N Y Times Mag p75-6 Mr 8 '64
Across the U.S.A. with glass and bottle. W. Olcott. Esquire 61:102-3 Ja '64
Barleycorn state. Newsweek 61:33 Ap 22 '63
No toasts to the old red, white and blue; serving of alcoholic beverages within the Senate. J. N. Eller. America 108:189 F 9 '63
LIQUOR problem
Drinking increases sensuous thoughts. Sci N L 83:265 Ap 27 '63

LIQUOR problem—*Continued*
New look at old liquor laws. H. B. Jacobs. il N Y Times Mag p 19+ N 10 '63
See also
Alcoholism
Prohibition
Temperance

United States

How teen-agers look at drinking; results of poll by Institute of student opinion; table. Sr Schol 85:19 D 2 '64
Kind word for drink; American drinking habits. J. D. Brown. il Sat Eve Post 236: 64-6 My 25 '63
Latest on over-drinking: guide for social drinkers; interview. M. A. Block. il U S News 56:50-6 Je 15 '64; Same abr. with title When does social drinking become over-drinking? Read Digest 85:107-11 S '64; Correction. U S News 56:16 Je 22 '64
More in sorrow; case in Darien, Conn. Time 84:59 O 23 '64
Night of the teen-ager; debutante's party in Darien, Conn. il Time 84:61-2 O 16 '64
Sins of the parents. R. S. Eielson. il McCalls 92:48+ Ja '65
Spinning the bottle; parents arrested for serving drinks to minors in Darien, Conn. Newsweek 64:72+ O 5 '64
Stupid questions about alcohol. R. Gannon. il Pop Sci 184:70-3+ Mr '64
Teen-age dolce vita. America 112:34 Ja 9 '65
Teen-age drinkers: a problem in morals. Sat Eve Post 237:90 O 17 '64
Teen-agers and alcohol. R. W. Daniel. il PTA Mag 57:18-20 Ap '63
Teen-agers speak out on teen-age drinking; discussion. il Sr Schol 82:12-14 Ja 30 '63
Tragedy stirs furor; Teen-age drinking; with press comments. Sr Schol 85:18-19 O 21 '64; Discussion. 85:18-19 D 2 '64
When teen-agers start to drink. B. Lang. il N Y Times Mag p47+ Jl 19 '64
Youth; drinking problem; Darien, Conn. il Time 84:103 O 2 '64

LIQUOR traffic
See also
Distilling industries
Prohibition

France

Cheers! a votre santé! Common market for drinks. J. Wechsberg. il N Y Times Mag p28+ Mr 1 '64

Great Britain

Cheers! a votre santé! Common market for drinks. J. Wechsberg. il N Y Times Mag p28+ Mr 1 '64
See also
Bars and barrooms

India

Night they raided the snake-juice still. V. H. Perera. Vogue 144:58+ D '64
See also
Bootlegging

Poland

Roll out the bottle. Time 83:34-5 Mr 6 '64

Sweden

Caught in a drought. Time 81:30 Mr 29 '63

United States

Down the hatch. il Time 82:22 S 27 '63

LIQUORS
Best buys for parties in the offing. J. A. Beard. House & Gard 124:222+ O '63
Cellar and the bar; symposium. House & Gard 124:114 Jl '63
Cold facts of summer drinks. J. A. Beard. House & Gard 123:150-1 Je '63
Delightfully different summer drinks. J. A. Beard. House & Gard 124:128+ Ag '63
Drinkers seek the light; liquor sales patterns. il Bsns W p81-3 F 23 '63
Drinks of Ireland. H. Johnson. House & Gard 125:154+ Ap '64
Drinks with the Christmas spirit. J. A. Beard. il House & Gard 126:172+ D '64
How a new model paid off for distiller il Bsns W p80-1 F 22 '64
It's a great drink; what is it? special holiday drinks. Vogue 142:44 D '63
Quaffers! health hints for hot times! il Esquire 62:80-1 Ag '64
Shortened cocktail hour. J. A. Beard. House & Gard 124:46 N '63
Tempting, colorful drinks of Hawaii. P. S. Brown. House & Gard 126:100+ Jl '64
Ten fresh coolers. il Vogue 141:138-9 Je '63
What to drink with Indian food. W. Clifford. House & Gard 126:196+ S '64
What's your pleasure, Mr President? Favorite drinks of the Presidents. il Esquire 63:52-3 Ja '65
See also
Alcohol
Champagne
Cocktails
Gin
Vodka

LIRE. See Money—Italy

LISAGOR, Peter
Challenge to political shibboleths. N Y Times Mag p39+ N 24 '63
New record for V.I.P. hosting. N Y Times Mag p30+ S 29 '63
Portrait of a man emerging from shadows. N Y Times Mag p 15+ Jl 19 '64
Trends: Washington mood. See issues of Nation's business
—and Higgins, Marguerite
L.B.J.'s hunt for womanpower. Sat Eve Post 237:86-7 Je 27 '64

LISBON, Portugal

Description

Lightning guide to Lisbon. J. Bryan, 3d. Holiday 37:52-3+ Ja '65

Music

Lisbon firsts. F. T. Direito. Opera N 27:33 Mr 23 '63
Lisbon quartet. F. T. Direito. Opera N 28:26 S 28 '63
Lisbon's style. F. Teixeira Direito. Opera N 29:26 S 26 '64
Portugal lags. F. T. Direito. Opera N 28:32 Ap 4 '64
Portuguese panache. F. T. Direito. Opera N 27:24 My 4 '63

LISBON earthquake, 1755. See Earthquakes—Portugal

LISCHNER, Harold Will
Medicine in Missouri. New Repub 151:5 D 19 '64

LISH, Gordon
Man who taught too well; case at Mills high school. D. Bess. Nation 196:507-8+ Je 15 '63

LISI, Virna
Name is Virna Lisi. il pors Life 56:94A-96+ Je 5 '64

LISK, Robert D. and Kannwischer, L. R.
Light: evidence for its direct effect on hypothalamic neurons. bibliog Science 146:272-3 O 9 '64
—and Newlon, Michael
Estradiol: evidence for its direct effect on hypothalamic neurons. bibliog Science 139: 223-4 Ja 18 '63

LISLE, Clifton
My golden spring. Flower Grower 51:24-5 S '64
Our garden house has many uses. Flower Grower 51:14+ D '64
Six planting do's and don'ts. Pop Gard 14: 42-3 Ap '63

LISNER, Margrit
Missing Michelangelo? il por Life 56:45-6+ F 21 '64

LISPECTOR, Clarice
Message; story. Américas 16:33-8 S '64

LISSAJOUS patterns. See Oscillographs

LISSITZYN, Oliver J.
International law in a divided world. bibliog f Int Concil 542:3-69 Mr '63

LISSMANN, H. W.
Electric location by fishes; with biographical sketch. Sci Am 208:32, 50-9 bibliog(p 188) Mr '63

LISSNER, Will
Paupers: one tenth of our nation. Cath World 198:357-64 Mr '64

LIST, R. J. and others
Meteorological evaluation of the sources of iodine-131 in pasteurized milk. bibliog Science 146:59-64 O 2 '64

LISTEN, I love you; story. See Cave, H.

LISTENING. See Attention

LISTENING devices, Electronic. See Electronics in criminal investigation, espionage, etc.

LISTER, Bill
File awhile! U S Camera 27:32+ Je '64

LISTER, John W. and others
Reversible cold block of the specialized cardiac tissues of the unanesthetized dog. bibliog Science 145:723-4 Ag 14 '64

LISTER, Joseph
Opening the door to safer surgery. il por Todays Health 41:71 Je '63

LISTER, Richard Percival
Closing time; poem. New Yorker 40:38 Mr 21 '64

LISTER, Richard Percival—*Continued*
ESP; poem. New Yorker 39:40 S 21 '63
In the Cabot Strait; poem. New Yorker 40:46 Mr 7 '64
Man with two eyes; story. Vogue 141:96 My '63
Mid-Atlantic; poem. Atlan 214:106 S '64
Remembrance of things past; poem. Atlan 213: 102 Ja '64
Sound of a diesel. Atlan 211:139-41 Mr '63
When islands call, don't answer. Vogue 142: 224+ O 1 '63

LISTON, Charles. See Liston, S.

LISTON, James M.
If your car goes in the water. Pop Sci 182: 45-8+ Je '63

LISTON, Robert A.
Mrs Murray's war on God. Sat Eve Post 237: 83-7 Jl 11 '64
Who can we surrender to? Sat Eve Post 236:78-80 O 5 '63

LISTON, Sonny
And I'm already the greatest! il por Newsweek 63:50-1 Mr 9 '64
Champ behind the mask. J. Murphy. il pors N Y Times Mag p 18+ Jl 21 '63
Champion nobody knows. il pors Newsweek 62:54-5 Jl 22 '63
Depends on how you look at it; foreign press reports. Sports Illus 19:9 Ag 5 '63
Devil finds work for Sonny. Sports Illus 20: 8 Mr 23 '64
Fix that wasn't. Sports Illus 20:17 Ap 13 '64
Four who baffled Liston. M. Sharnik. il por Sports Illus 20:60-2+ F 10 '64
Get the lawyers out of the ring. F. Graham, jr. pors Sat Eve Post 236:70+ Jl 13 '63
Heavyweight muddle. R. Boyle and M. Sharnik. il por Sports Illus 18:12-15 Mr 25 '63
I live with myself; Patterson-Liston fight, ed. by G. Rogin. F. Patterson. Sports Illus 19:27 Ag 5 '63
I'll chop that big monkey to pieces. . . C. Clay. il por Life 54:62A+ F 15 '63
Image recaptured. Sports Illus 19:18 S 30 '63
In the ring. L. Jones. Nation 198:661-2 Je 29 '64
Left hooks and tenterhooks; Clay-Liston title fight. Sports Illus 19:5 Ag 12 '63
Liston turned on the evil eye, Clay didn't notice; with report by J. R. McDermott. il pors Life 56:34-9 Mr 6 '64
Liston's edge: a lethal left. T. Maule. il por Sports Illus 20:18-21 F 24 '64
Liston's favorite menu. D. J. Robinson. il por Ebony 18:148+ Ap '63
Man, the rabbit & the boy. il por Time 82: 52 Ag 2 '63
My cooperation. il por Newsweek 63:60-1 Ap 6 '64
One for the 19th. por Time 81:54 Mr 29 '63
$100 misunderstanding? il por Newsweek 63: 58 F 24 '64
Playing grownups. il por Time 84:104-5 N 13 '64
Preflight moods of Sonny Liston. M. Kram. il por Sports Illus 21:34+ N 2 '64
Rueful dream come true; Clay-Liston championship fight. H. Horn. por Sports Illus 19:26-7 N 18 '63
Run, Cassius, run. New Yorker 40:43-4 Mr 7 '64
Sonny & co. Time 83:88+ Ap 10 '64
Sonny Liston: king of the beasts. G. Astor. il pors Look 28:67-8+ F 25 '64
Sonny slams ahead. R. H. Boyle. il por Sports Illus 19:12-15 Jl 29 '63
Sporting scene; Patterson vs. Liston return fight. A. J. Liebling. il New Yorker 39:62+ Ag 10 '63
Still hurt and lost. G. Rogin. il pors Sports Illus 21:22-7 N 16 '64
Superman? por Newsweek 61:87 Mr 11 '63
Taking stock of Sonny Liston. R. H. Boyle. il por Sports Illus 20:24-7 Ap 6 '64
Ten thousand words a minute. N. Mailer. Esquire 59:109-20 F '63
To fight or not to fight? R. H. Boyle. il Sports Illus 21:28-31 S 7 '64
Who can beat him? il Newsweek 62:68-9 Ag 5 '63
With mouth & magic. il por Time 83:66+ Mr 6 '64
Yes, it was good and honest. T. Maule. il por Sports Illus 20:20-5 Mr 9 '64

LISZT, Franz
Emil von Sauer's Liszt: something to marvel at. R. Kammerer. il por Am Rec G 30: 296-7 D '63
Faust symphony, the Lisztian fire aflame. A. Rich. il Hi Fi 14:49-50 Jl '64
High-voltage Mr Watts. R. Kammerer. Am Rec G 29:718 My '63
Liszt by Curzon, one of his finest discs. R. Kammerer. Am Rec G 30:1038 Jl '64
Liszt by Horowitz, c. 1932; Sonata in B minor. R. Kammerer. Am Rec G 29:552+ Mr '63
Novaes plays Liszt. R. Kammerer. Am Rec G 29:942 Ag '63

LITCHFIELD, Edward Harold
King Edward of Pitt. M. Cope. il pors Sat Eve Post 236:22-3 Ap 6 '63
Pitt wins (boss's orders) J. Underwood. il pors Sports Illus 19:22-6+ O 28 '63

LITCHFIELD COUNTY, Conn.
Pastoral perimeter. J. Lieber. il Travel 122: 32-4 Ag '64

LITERACY. See Illiteracy

LITERACY tests (election law)
How about Swahili? Time 82:15 Ag 9 '63

LITERARY ability. See Creation (literary, artistic, etc)

LITERARY agents
Off the cuff. A. Marple. Writer 76:5-6 O '63; 77:6-8 Jl '64
Should every writer have an agent? excerpt from Writing and selling of fiction. P. R. Reynolds. Sat R 48:69-70+ Ja 9 '65
What beginning writers want to know. J. Reach. Writer 76:10-12 O '63

LITERARY and scientific exchanges. See Exchanges, Literary and scientific

LITERARY censorship. See Censorship

LITERARY characters. See Characters in literature

LITERARY contests. See Literature—Competitions

LITERARY correspondence. See Letters

LITERARY criticism
Adam and Eve and the third son. J. Ciardi. il Sat R 47:140-3+ Ag 29 '64
Books; polemic and the new reviewers. R. Adler. New Yorker 40:60-8+ Jl 4 '64
Canon of a critic at arms. G. Hicks. Sat R 46:19-20 N 2 '63
Critics and creators. I. Brown. Sat R 46: 13+ Ag 10 '63
Dilemma of success. J. D. Adams. Sat R 48: 19+ Ja 30 '65
Epoch and artist, by D. M. Jones. Review
New Yorker 40:114-18+ Ag 22 '64. H. Rosenberg
French poets and novelists, by H. James. Review
Nation 198:377-9 Ap 13 '64. G. Brée
Function of criticism once more. R. Langbaum. Yale R 54:205-18 D '64
Guide to hatchet jobs. W. Sheed. Commonweal 79:691-2 Mr 6 '64
Literary bird-watching. W. Sheed. Commonweal 78:23-4 Mr 29 '63
Miscellany. C. Tomlinson. Poetry 102:341-5 Ag '63
Monologues of a philolog. R. S. Stilwell. Sat R 47:34+ Je 13 '64
Norman Mailer vs. nine writers. N. Mailer. Esquire 60:63-9+ Jl '63
Poetic mythology. H. Carruth. Poetry 104: 369-74 S '64
Poets and critics: the forgotten difference. S. Spender. Sat R 46:15-18 O 5 '63
Pride, prejudice and wit. J. Daniel. Nation 198:170-1 F 17 '64
Puzzles and epiphanies, by F. Kermode. Review
Sat R 46:24 Mr 2 '63. J. Gray
Reviling the reviewers. Newsweek 64:82 Jl 27 '64
SRL's first editorial; excerpts. H. S. Canby. Sat R 47:61-2 Ag 29 '64
Waiting for the end, by L. A. Fiedler. Review
Nat R 16:654-6 Jl 28 '64. H. Kenner
See also
Book reviews
Literature—Appreciation and interpretation

Anecdotes, facetiae, satire, etc.
Pooh perplex, by F. C. Crews. Review
Reporter 29:62 D 5 '63. R. S. Gallagher

LITERARY critics. See Critics

LITERARY forgeries and mystifications
Old librarian and his almanack. H. A. Sullivan. Library J 89:1188-92 Mr 15 '64
Shapira affair, by J. M. Allegro. Review
Sat R 48:30-1 Ja 30 '65. T. H. Gaster

LITERARY form. See Style, Literary

LITERARY guild of America
Mrs Roosevelt and children's books; Junior literary guild. H. Ferris. il Library J 89:2149-51+ My 15 '64

LITERARY inspiration. See Inspiration

LITERARY landmarks
Bridge to the past; visits to historic places. E. F. Hunter. il Parents Mag 38:64-6+ Mr '63
Guide write! N. A. Touge. il Travel 120:50-2 O '63

United States

Admirable idea; Henry Beston cottage, Great Beach, Eastham, designated a National literary landmark. C. B. Grannis. Pub W 186:44 N 2 '64
LITERARY piracy. See Copyright—Unauthorized reprints
LITERARY prizes. See Rewards, prizes, etc.
LITERARY research
Advice can be dangerous. W. Brown. Writer 78:19-21 Ja '65
Research and interviewing techniques; excerpt from Prose by professionals, ed. by T. Morris. B. Schapper. Writer 77:20-3 Ja '64

Anecdotes, facetiae, satire, etc.

Mark (ye) (the) Twain. D. J. Hamblin. Life 57:13 Jl 10 '64
New deal for the academic shuffle. S. Crites. Atlan 211:117-19 My '63
LITERARY style. See Style, Literary
LITERARY symposium, Esquire. See Esquire literary symposium
LITERARY titles. See Titles of books, stories, etc.
LITERATURE
Gresham's law of literature; simplified books. A. Loftis and R. Marshall. il Sat R 46:64-5 S 21 '63
Of order, abstraction, and language. S. Burckhardt. Yale R 53:533-50 Je '64
SRL's first editorial; excerpts. H. S. Canby. Sat R 47:61-2 Ag 29 '64
Writers at work. Review
Sat R 46:23-4 My 18 '63. G. Hicks
Your literary I.Q; ed. by J. T. Winterich. See issues of Saturday review
See also
Biography
Erotic literature
Essays
Fiction
French literature
Impressionism (literature)
International federation for modern languages and literatures
Legal literature
Letters
Literary criticism
Plagiarism
Quotations
Romanticism
Translations and translating
Travel literature

Appreciation and interpretation

Artistic transaction, and essays on theory of literature, by E. Vivas. Review
Nat R il 16:500-2 Je 16 '64. G. Wills; Reply with rejoinder. E. Vivas. 16:695-6 Ag 11 '64
Literary bird-watching. W. Sheed. Commonweal 78:23-4 Mr 29 '63
Lively and responsive weekend at Princeton; Esquire's Fifth literary symposium. A. Gingrich. Esquire 60:6+ Jl '63
Peripatetic reviewer. E. Weeks. Atlan 212: 142+ N '63
Stoic comedians: Flaubert, Joyce and Beckett, by H. Kenner. Review
Nat R 14:325-6 Ap 23 '63. V. Miller
Teacher as a critic; development of appreciation. A. Nelson. il Sr Schol 83:17T O 4 '63
See also
Poetry—Appreciation

Collections

See also
Books, Condensed

Competitions

Picking the winners; publishers cash bounties. D. Dempsey. Sat R 47:26-7 Ap 11 '64
See also
Fiction—Competitions

Moral and religious aspects

See Literature and morals

Periodicals

See also
Dial (periodical)

Psychology

Case for dirty linen. W. Sheed. Commonweal 80:448-9 Jl 3 '64

Study and teaching

Eating up the classics. F. E. Wagner. il NEA J 52:24-6 F '63
High school English textbooks: a critical examination, by J. J. Lynch and B. Evans. Review
Sat R 46:54 D 21 '63. J. F. Warner
Making the most of literature notebooks. S. Cochell. il Sr Schol 84:12T Ap 10 '64
Salinger and Golding: conflict on the campus. F. E. Kearns; discussion. America 108: 242+ F 23 '63
Sex and teaching literature in high school. W. J. O'Malley. Cath World 199:116-22 My '64
See also
Literature—Appreciation and interpretation

Technique

See also
Fiction—Technique

Textbooks

Textbooks in literature are dull dogs. R. Kirk. Nat R 16:359 My 5 '64

Themes

Death of a seamstress; Mimi of Murger's Scènes de la vie de Bohème. A. W. Zorgniotti. Opera N 28:24-5 Mr 14 '64
Dilemma of Adam, Daedalus and Faust. T. Prideaux. il Life 57:92+ N 20 '64
Don't overlook the obvious. O. Jones and W. Jones. Writer 77:25-6+ Ap '64
Don't start with too much. K. Kay. Writer 76:10-13 Ap '63
Eighteen checkpoints for your story. J. Z. Owen. Writer 77:11-15 Ap '64
Fifty self-starters for fiction writers; excerpts from Writing short stories for pleasure and profit. M. Gavin. Writer 77: 11-13+ F '64
Figaro's forebears. F. Sedwick. Opera N 27: 25-6 Mr 9 '63
Imagination of disaster; literature of World war I. R. Gill. il Sat R 47:10-13+ S 5 '64
Julio Cortázar; storytelling giant. J. Durand. il Américas 15:39-43 Mr '63
Life is the raw material. R. Standish. Writer 77:20-1+ Jl '64
Only way to write a modern poem about a nightingale. A. Huxley. Harper 227:62-6 Ag '63
Party of one; themes of Irish poetry. W. Golding. Holiday 33:10+ Ap '63
Postscript to death; writings of E. Wiesel. I. Halperin. Commonweal 79:713-15 Mr 13 '64
Reaching for the ends of being. R. L. Stilwell. Sat R 47:48-50 My 30 '64
Salinger and Golding: conflict on the campus. F. E. Kearns; discussion. America 108: 242+ F 23 '63
Sex, crime, and, to a lesser extent, sports; excerpt from Now, Barrabas. W. Jovanovich. il Sat R 47:14-17+ Jl 18 '64
Speaking out; why do they slander our military men? S. L. A. Marshall. Sat Eve Post 237:6+ S 5 '64
Tarzan on the upswing. il Newsweek 62:70 Jl 29 '63
Theology as literature. K. B. Cully. Christian Cent 81:237-8 F 19 '64
Use threefold magic; build suspense into your story. J. Z. Owen. Writer 77:18-20+ O '64
What is a secret? G. H. Freitag. Writer 77:26-7 Mr '64
Where art thou, muse? science verse. M. Sagoff. Horizon 6:121 Sum '64
See also
College professors and instructors in literature
Drama—Themes
French students in literature
Indians in literature
Jews in literature
Love in literature
Negroes in literature
New York city in literature
Politics in literature
Religion in literature
Sex in literature
LITERATURE, Ancient
See also
Sumerian literature
LITERATURE, Childrens. See Childrens literature
LITERATURE, Educational. See Educational literature

LITERATURE, Immoral. See Immoral literature and pictures
LITERATURE, Influence of
Book banning and juvenile delinquency. J. Ciardi. Sat R 46:16 Ag 10 '63
Ex libris; choices of outstanding people. See issues of Christian century to June 10, 1963
Experiment in India; value of books in diplomacy. J. K. Galbraith. il Sat R 47:20-3 Ag 15 '64
Mutations in the body politic; influential books of the past forty years; with list. R. Girson. il Sat R 47:74-86+ Ag 29 '64
Tabulating Ex libris; choices of outstanding people. M. E. Marty. Christian Cent 80: 982-3 Ag 7 '63
To the new day. R. H. Viguers. Horn Bk 40:23 F '64
LITERATURE, Islamic. See Islamic literature
LITERATURE, Italian. See Italian literature
LITERATURE, Photographic. See Photographic literature
LITERATURE, Primitive
Conservations with the stone age. J. Greenway. il Sat R 47:21-3 F 15 '64
LITERATURE, Regional. See New England in literature
LITERATURE, Sumerian. See Sumerian literature
LITERATURE and communism. See Communism and literature
LITERATURE and history
William Hazlitt, by H. Baker. Review
Reporter 28:50+ Ja 17 '63. G. Steiner; Reply with rejoinder. V. Anderson. 28: 8+ F 28 '63
LITERATURE and morals
Myth motif in modern fiction. B. H. Deal. Writer 76:12-14+ N '63
Sex and teaching literature in high school. W. J. O'Malley. Cath World 199:116-22 My '64
Writer as moralist. S. Bellow. Atlan 211: 58-62 Mr '63
LITERATURE and religion. See Religion and literature
LITERATURE and science
Literature and science, by A. Huxley. Review
Nat R 15:356+ O 22 '63. J. Hart
Sat R 46:33+ O 5 '63. H. Read
Uses of literature in an age of science; excerpts from address. J. W. Krutch. Sat R 47:80-1 D 5 '64
Where art thou, muse? science verse. M. Sagoff. Horizon 6:121 Sum '64
See also
Science fiction
LITERATURE and society
Choose something like a star. J. Ciardi. Sat R 47:16 Ja 11 '64
LITERATURE as a profession. See Authorship
LITHGOW, Arthur
Shakespeare is to hear. V. Voss. Mlle 58: 122+ F '64
LITHIUM
Lithium and star aging. Sky & Tel 26:82 Ag '63
Lithium test aimed at SNAP-50/SPUR technology. R. D. Hibben. il Aviation W 81: 58-9+ N 2 '64
New star dating method. Sci N L 83:278 My 4 '63
LITHOGRAPHERS and printers national association
Books and book jackets in the Litho show. il Pub W 183:72-4 Ap 8 '63
LITHOGRAPHIC technical foundation, incorporated. See Graphic arts technical foundation
LITHOGRAPHS
Mr Hardy Lee, his yacht: excerpts, with introd. by Alexander C. Brown. Chinks. il Am Heritage 15:24-31 Je '64
Rebirth for an old art. il Design 65:171 Mr '64
LITHOGRAPHY
Artist at work: doing a book in lithography. L. Ward. il Horn Bk 40:34-41 F '64
Because water hates grease. il Time 83:82-3+ Ap 10 '64
Lane's California: an example of uncommon printing. il Pub W 183:90-2 Je 3 '63
Technique of the color lithograph. I. Aronson. il Am Artist 27:30-5+ O '63
Three eras of playing-card printing: lithographic printing. D. Powills. il Hobbies 69: 116-17 S '64
LITHUANIA
Religious institutions and affairs
Soviets fear the dead; incorrupt body of B. Umestauskas removed from crypt. America 110:212 F 15 '64
LITTELL, Blaine
How Katanga fell. Sat Eve Post 236:74-6+ My 11 '63
LITTELL, Deanna
Individualists; Mlle's annual Merit awards. il por Mlle 58:72-3 Ja '64
LITTELL, Franklin H.
Of note: religious liberty; excerpts from address. Commonweal 81:486-8 Ja 8 '65
Protestant self-study. Christian Cent 80:617-19 My 8 '63
Toward the recovery of discipline in Methodism. Christian Cent 80:826-8 Je 26 '63
Usefulness of anti-Catholicism. Commonweal 78:422-4 Jl 12 '63
LITTELL, Robert
Germany's amends to the Jews. Read Digest 83:215-20 Ag '63
Glory of the Grecian games. Read Digest 84: 204R-204S+ Ap '64
How do we look to these foreign tourists? Read Digest 82:233-4+ Ap '63
Letter from Prague. Nation 199:171-2 S 28 '64
Our best investment in the Arab world. Read Digest 82:240-1+ F '63
Schizophrenics in the sun. Read Digest 82: 201-2+ My '63
Valencia's tribunal of waters. Read Digest 83:126-30 D '63
LITTER. See Refuse and refuse disposal
LITTER (bedding)
Cornstalk bedding, how to get it in. W. J. Fletcher. il Suc Farm 61:46 O '63
See also
Poultry houses—Litter
LITTER baskets. See Refuse receptacles
LITTLE, Arthur D, incorporated
A. D. Little study probes solid propellant ignition. J. F. Judge. Miss & Roc 13:36 Jl 15 '63
Much ado about Little. W. J. Coughlin. Miss & Roc 16:46 Ja 25 '65
New spacecraft window design proposed for Apollo. M. Getler. il Miss & Roc 13:26-7+ Ag 5 '63
Prescription for stability proposed. il Miss & Roc 16:17-18 Ja 18 '65
LITTLE, Jim
I care, you care, he cares. Harper 228:169-70 Ap '64
LITTLE, Malcolm. See Malcolm X
LITTLE, Nina Fletcher
Indigenous painting in Maine, 1825-1865; excerpts from Maine and its role in American art, 1740-1963. Antiques 83:454-7 Ap '63
Indigenous painting in New Hampshire. Antiques 86:62-5 Jl '64
Livery cupboards in New England. Antiques 84:710-13 D '63
LITTLE, Brown and company
Simplified procedures at Little, Brown's new warehouse. il Pub W 186:31-4 S 7 '64
LITTLE AMERICA. See Antarctic Regions
LITTLE BIG HORN, Battle of the, 1876
As the crow fights: re-enacting Custer's last stand. il Newsweek 64:56 Jl 13 '64
LITTLE brother; story. See Jones, A. E.
LITTLE brothers of the poor
Champagne touch. Time 83:59 Ja 3 '64
LITTLE COLORADO RIVER
See also
Grand Falls, Ariz.
LITTLE did I know; story. See Calisher, H.
LITTLE Eyolf; drama. See Ibsen, H.
LITTLE FALLS, Minn.
From June bugs to fluorescents. D. L. Norgren. il Am City 79:127 F '64
LITTLE girls. See Girls
LITTLE goddess of the woods (plant) See Dianella
LITTLE heiress; story. See Davies, R.
LITTLE leagues
Bat-off-the-tee; Parma, Ohio. R. Bergstrom. Recreation 57:231-2 My '64
Big daddies of the Little league. F. Batsby. il N Y Times Mag p22+ My 31 '64
Father's day. Nation 198:520 My 25 '64
Giving baseball back to the boys. J. T. Hunt. il Recreation 56:235 My '63
Little league and big buck. Sports Illus 19:8 Ag 19 '63
Little league on the farm; J. G. Keenan farm, North Java, N.Y. il Suc Farm 62:28 Je '64
Little leaguers have big problems, their parents. J. Brosnan. il Atlan 211:117-20 Mr '63
LITTLE magazines. See Periodicals
LITTLE Mermaid (statue) See Copenhagen—Monuments, statues, etc.

LITTLE ROCK, Ark.
Little Rock finds a better way. J. A. Morris. Read Digest 83:142-6 S '63
Progress in Little Rock. Christian Cent 80:606 My 8 '63
Purchasing manual is a must. A. M. Douthit and F. B. Peek. il Am City 78:89 N '63

Education

Flexible classroom clusters provide for future changes. il Arch Rec 136:242-3 S '64
Little Rock revisited, tokenism plus. G. Samuels. il N Y Times Mag p 13+ Je 2 '63

LITTLE ROCK, Ark, public library
Not-so-good books fund set up at Little Rock P.L. Library J 89:828 F 15 '64

LITTLE ROCKY MOUNTAINS. See Rocky Mountains

LITTLE Snow White; drama. See King, W.

LITTLE theater. See Theater—Community and little theater movement

LITTLEDALE, Harold A.
How to read a bedtime story. Parents Mag 38:69+ N '63
Where will they go after high school? Parents Mag 38:58-9+ Ap '63
Your stake in better schools for all. Parents Mag 39:57-9+ S '64
(ed) See Levine, H. Parents' questions about music lessons

LITTLEFIELD, Edward W.
Gypsy moth in New York. Am For 70:42-5+ Ja '64

LITTLEFIELD, John W.
Selection of hybrids from matings of fibroblasts in vitro and their presumed recombinants. bibliog Science 145:709 Ag 14 '64

LITTLEJOHN, David
Capote collected. Commonweal 78:187-8 My 10 '63
F. Scott Fitzgerald: the dimension of greatness. Commonweal 79:198-9 N 8 '63
Finger exercises. Reporter 29:62-4 O 24 '63
Happy birthday, whoever you are. Reporter 31:56+ S 24 '64
Intellectual's journal, in the French tradition. Commonweal 81:393 D 11 '64
Realms of life. Commonweal 79:576-8 F 7 '64
Remarkable bias in favor of man's unconscious self. Commonweal 80:92-4 Ap 10 '64
Searching for France. Commonweal 79:161-5 N 1 '63
Triumph of the technocrats? Commonweal 81:512-15 Ja 15 '65
What they wrote and what they were. Reporter 28:42+ Ap 11 '63

LITTLEJOHN, Fritz
Lost horizons. Reporter 30:46-7 Mr 12 '64

LITTLETON, Harvey
Glass by Erwin Eisch. Craft Horiz 23:14-17 My '63
Offhand glass blowing. D. Smith. il Craft Horiz 24:22-3+ Ja '64

LITTLETON family
Littleton coat-of-arms. H. K. Eilers. il Hobbies 67:126-7 F '63

LITTLEWOOD, A. B.
Gas chromatography. Science 144:1597+ Je 26 '64

LITTLEWOOD, Joan
Joan and the good guys. G. Rogoff. il Reporter 31:52-4 N 19 '64
Joan Littlewood. A. Brien. il por Vogue 144:160-1+ S 15 '64
Joan of Cockaigne. K. Tynan. il Holiday 36:113+ N '64
Littlewood's war. il por Newsweek 64:104 O 12 '64
Merry, angry mother hen. J. Howard. il pors Life 57:59-60+ N 27 '64
Opening the old kit bag. il por Time 82:64-5 Jl 5 '63
Openings, London. A. Brien. il por Theatre Arts 47:31-2+ Je '63
Would little Joan Littlewood were here! A. Bailey. por Esquire 61:113-15 Ja '64

LITTMAN, Gerard
Bright light on the alcoholic. N Y Times Mag p30+ Ap 5 '64

LITTON, George W.
How much should you pay for a beef bull? Suc Farm 61:72 Je '63

LITTON Industries, incorporated
Appetite for the future. il Time 82:104-8+ O 4 '63
Litton expedites low-cost inertial aid. B. Miller. il Aviation W 81:62+ D 7 '64
Litton's drive shifts into a quieter key. il Bsns W p27-8 S 5 '64
Lost founder. Time 84:100 O 23 '64
New thorns strewing the road to mergers; companies resist acquisition. il Bsns W p58+ N 9 '63
When the crowd goes one way Litton goes the other. C. Rieser. il Fortune 67:114-19+ My '63

LITTORINA littorea. See Mollusks

LITURGICAL language
Bishops decree mass in English; Vatican approves. Christian Cent 81:757 Je 10 '64
English in the sacraments. America 111:280+ S 19 '64
English mass: needs work; first Roman Catholic mass in the English version approved by the bishops of the U.S. il Time 84:74 S 4 '64
First full mass in English; in Australia. Christian Cent 81:1101 S 9 '64
Language and liturgy. America 110:560 Ap 25 '64
Latin: the church's mother tongue? excerpts from Council in action. H. Küng. Harper 227:60-4 O '63
Liturgy and irredentism. America 110:839 Je 20 '64
Liturgy in English; letter. A. T. Straulman. Commonweal 81:424 D 18 '64
New way of worship. il Time 84:66+ N 27 '64
Only a beginning; mass celebrated in the English language for the first time in the United States. il Newsweek 64:54+ S 7 '64
Praying it in English; liturgical constitution of the 2d Vatican council. il Time 83:66 My 29 '64
Progress report on the liturgy. G. S. Sloyan. America 111:179-83 Ag 22 '64; Reply. P. T. Weller. 111:274 S 19 '64
Scandal in the liturgy. C. J. McNaspy. America 111:586 N 14 '64
Should you buy a new missal? J. F. Dearden. America 111:180-1 Ag 22 '64
Suggestion for Mr Waugh. J. Cogley. Commonweal 81:120-2 O 23 '64; Discussion. 81:352-4 D 4 '64
25th Catholic liturgical week; vernacular used. G. W. Hoyer. Christian Cent 81:1157-8 S 16 '64
Vernacular isn't everything. T. W. Guzie. America 109:164-5 Ag 17 '63
Words to pray with? forthcoming translation of the liturgy. G. B. Harrison. America 110:508-10 Ap 11 '64; Discussion. 110:676-8; 111:2 My 16, Jl 4 '64
See also
Vatican council, 2d

LITURGICAL movement

Catholic church

Coming reforms in the liturgy. F. R. McManus. Cath World 196:335-42 Mr '63
Liturgical movement: phase three. A. Kavanagh. America 111:183-5 Ag 22 '64
Maria Laach revisited. H. A. Reinhold. Commonweal 78:497-500 Ag 23 '63
Need for reform. J. B. Mannion. Commonweal 78:495-7 Ag 23 '63
Sociology and liturgy. America 108:848-9 Je 15 '63
Spare us, O Lord! S. Vishnewski. America 111:741-2 D 5 '64

LITURGICAL music. See Church music

LITURGICAL week
Liturgy and education. America 108:483 Ap 13 '63
Liturgy and freedom. C. J. McNaspy. America 111:251 S 12 '64
Liturgy and involvement. America 111:177 Ag 22 '64
Religion and art. America 109:132 Ag 10 '63
25th Catholic liturgical week; vernacular used. G. W. Hoyer. Christian Cent 81:1157-8 S 16 '64

LITURGY, Catholic. See Catholic church—Liturgy and ritual

LITVINNE, Felia
Rococo presents. A. Favia-Artsay. por Hobbies 68:30 Ja '64

LITVINOFF, Valentina
(tr) Vaganova; excerpts. Dance Mag 38:40-3 Jl; 42-4+ Ag '64

LITWACK, Lawrence
Testing: if something exists, can it be measured? Sr Schol 83:11T N 8 '63

LITWHILER, Danny
With mirrors, flat gloves and sawed-up bats. R. Creamer. il Sports Illus 18:56-8 Je 3 '63

LITZ, Katherine
Contemporary dance, inc; 92nd street Y. J. Maskey. Dance Mag 38:71 My '64

LIVE oak. See Oak

LIVER
Breakdown of rat-liver ergosomes in vivo after actinomycin inhibition of messenger RNA synthesis. T. Staehelin and others. bibliog il Science 140:180-3 Ap 12 '63

LIVER—*Continued*
Conversion of p,p' DDT to p,p' DDD in the liver of the rat. P. R. Datta and others. bibliog il Science 145:1052-3 S 4 '64
Drug-induced changes in the liver endoplasmic reticulum: association with drug-metabolizing enzymes. H. Remmer and H. J. Merker. bibliog il Science 142:1657-8 D 27 '63
Glycogen deposition in the liver induced by cortisone: dependence on enzyme synthesis. O. Greengard and others. bibliog il Science 141:160-1 Jl 12 '63
Parathion activation by livers of aquatic and terrestrial vertebrates. J. L. Potter and R. D. O'Brien. bibliog il Science 144:55-7 Ap 3 '64
Plasma protein synthesis in the liver: method for measurement of albumin formation in vivo. E. B. Reeve and others. bibliog il Science 139:914-16 Mr 8 '63
Uricase: localization in hepatic microbodies. Z. Hruban and H. Swift. bibliog il Science 146:1316-18 D 4 '64
Your liver's chemical magic. J. D. Ratcliff. il Todays Health 41:22-3+ D '63; Same abr. with title What your liver does for you. Read Digest 84:119-22 F '64

Diseases

Hepatic glucokinase: a direct effect of insulin. J. W. Vester and M. L. Reino. bibliog il Science 142:590-1 N 1 '63
Homocystinuria: an enzymatic defect. S. H. Mudd and others. bibliog il Science 143: 1443-5 Mr 27 '64
Ma foi! mon foie! French liver trouble. il Time 82:22-3 D 27 '63
Methylmalonate excretion in vitamin B_{12} deficiency. L. A. Barness and others. bibliog il Science 140:76-7 Ap 5 '63
See also
Jaundice

LIVER as food
See also
Cookery—Meat

LIVER transplants. See Transplantation of organs, tissues, etc.

LIVERANI, Giuseppe
Five centuries of Faenza majolica; excerpts. Antiques 83:684-9 Je '63

LIVERIGHT, Addie
Nostalgic twins. New Yorker 39:24-6 Mr 2 '63

LIVERIGHT, Babette
Nostalgic twins. New Yorker 39:24-6 Mr 2 '63

LIVERIGHT, Horace
Gambler in publishing: Horace Liveright. L. Kronenberger. por Atlan 215:94-104 Ja '65

LIVERMORE, Harold
Insane in Spain fell mainly. Sat R 46:39 S 21 '63

LIVERMORE, N. B. Jr
Why not PROservation? Am For 70:3+ Je '64

LIVERNASH, E. Robert
Brighter future for collective bargaining. Harvard Bsns R 42:66-70 S '64

LIVERPOOL
Land of scouse and glory. S. Hagerty. il Newsweek 64:33 D 14 '64

LIVERPOOL ware. See Pottery

LIVERS, Ronald W.
Fertility restoration and its inheritance in cytoplasmic male-sterile wheat. bibliog Science 144:420 Ap 24 '64

LIVERY cupboards. See Cupboards

LIVESTOCK
Beef news (cont of) Livestock. See issues of Farm journal
Livestock; ed. by J. Rohlf. See issues of Farm journal
See also
Cattle
Meat industry and trade
Swine

Diseases and pests

See also
Worms, Intestinal and parasitic

Prices

See also
Swine—Prices

Transportation

Jet planes turn into cattle cars; ferrying calves to Italy. il Bsns W p 121-2 S 19 '64

LIVESTOCK, Cooling of
Cool just their heads? air conditioning of dairy barns. il Farm J 87:38 Jl '63
How to beat the summer milk slump. J. W. Bailey. Suc Farm 62:63 Jl '64
How to cool a farrowing house. J. Harvey. il Suc Farm 62:40-1 Jl '64
Ten ways to keep hot hogs cool. il Suc Farm 62:65 Jl '64

LIVESTOCK feed. See Feed and feeding stuffs

LIVESTOCK markets
Chicago gets back a barnyard. il Bsns W p 126-8 Mr 16 '63

LIVESTOCK self feeders
Big trend to farmstead feeding; with editorial comment. L. M. Palmer. il Farm J 87:4, 36-7+ My '63

LIVESTOCK shows
Set records at National barrow show. R. Black. Farm J 88:40 N '64
See also
Cattle shows

LIVING. See Conduct of life

LIVING, Cost of. See Cost of living

LIVING conditions. See Standard of living

LIVING foraminifera laboratory. See American museum of natural history, New York

LIVING premise (skit) See Skits (drama)

LIVING rooms
Create a home entertainment center. J. Holmstrand. il Suc Farm 62:74-7 N '64
Fall of the pit; conversation pits. Time 81: 47 F 22 '63
Family room addition improves looks of the whole house. B. Colvin. il Am Home 67: 95 Mr '64
Find space for a multi-purpose family room. J. Holmstand. il Suc Farm 61:66-7 N '63
Formal and informal living. il Farm J 87:93 O '63
Four-way stretch: basement. C. Kellogg. il Ladies Home J 80:108 Mr '63
How to stretch space in an 11x17 living room. il Bet Hom & Gard 42:22 F '64
Is this the family room you've been waiting for? N. Seney. il Bet Hom & Gard 41:54-5 Ag '63
Living room that invites you in. il Am Home 67:42-3 N '64
Look what's happened to family rooms! R. W. Houseman. il Am Home 66:34-9 O '63
Lovely way to live. il McCalls 92:74-9 Ja '65
Making rooms livable. G. O'Brien. il N Y Times Mag pt2 p 16-18 S 27 '64
Seasonal schemes. il N Y Times Mag pt2 p22-3 S 29 '63
They traded in the old porch! P. Lindberg. il Bet Hom & Gard 41:114 N '63
We enclosed our porch for a family room. R. Charles. il Parents Mag 38:77-80+ N '63
See also
Parlors

LIVING rooms, Outdoor. See Outdoor rooms

LIVING theatre group. See New York (city)—Theater

LIVING underground. See Underground living

LIVINGSTON, Eleanor Rodewald
One lady who gives a Continental. V. Kraft. Sports Illus 18:43 F 18 '63

LIVINGSTON, Frank
Meet the mad Livingstons. C. Phinizy. il por Sports Illus 20:70-4+ Mr 16 '64

LIVINGSTON, John A.
Day sailer to capsule cruiser. il Yachting 114:66+ Jl '63
Meet the mad Livingstons. C. Phinizy. il por Sports Illus 20:70-4+ Mr 16 '64

LIVINGSTON, Myra Cohn
Not the rose. . . Horn Bk 40:355-60 Ag '64

LIVINGSTON, Robert B.
Perception and commitment. Bul Atomic Sci 19:14-18 F '63
—See Frommer, G. P. jt. auth.

LIVINGSTON, Robert Gerald
Yugoslavian unemployment trends. bibliog f Mo Labor R 87:756-62 Jl '64

LIVINGSTON, N.J.
Swimming pools by subscription. R. D. Sisco. il Am City 78:99-101 My '63

LIVINGSTONE, F. C.
Sugar, coronaries linked. Sci N L 86:131 Ag 29 '64

LIZARD plants. See Sauromatum

LIZARDS
Little snake with hands; amphisbaenidae, limbless lizards. C. M. Bogert. il Natur Hist 73:16-25 Ag '64
Living pair of dragons at San Diego zoo. il Life 55:57-8 S 27 '63
Lizard on your Hawaiian screen; gecko. il Sunset 130:63 F '63
Lizard that looks like a worm; bipes biporus. il Sci Digest 55:19 My '64

LIZARDS—*Continued*
Worm lizards; pair of two-footed amphisbaenids, at Museum of natural history. New Yorker 40:33-4 Ap 4 '64
See also
Chameleons
Gila monsters
LIZZIE Borden case. See Murder
LJUBLJANA
Music
[Musical events] Mus Am 84:16 F '64
LLERAS CAMARGO, Alberto
Alliance for progress: aims, distortions, obstacles. For Affairs 42:25-37 O '63
Let us have faith in the Alliance; excerpt from report. por Américas 15:48 Ag '63
Re-evaluation; excerpt from address, December 14, 1962. por Américas 15:44 F '63
about
Dissatisfaction down south. por Time 81: 22-3 Mr 22 '63
LLEWELLIN setters. See Setters
LLEWELLYN, Dave
Who's teaching whom? Outdoor Life 133:66-8 Mr '64
LLEWELLYN, Richard
Santiago, bright star of Chile. Holiday 34: 76-81+ N '63
São Paulo, city of promise. Holiday 33:68-77+ F '63
(ed) See Lombardi, S. We have no childhood
LLEWELYN-DAVIES, Richard, and Cowan, Peter
Future of research; excerpts from paper. Arch Rec 136:105+ S '64
LLORONA; story. See Kentfield, C.
LLOYD, Donald
Quietmouth American. Harper 227:101-2+ S '63
LLOYD, Frank
Swinging art dealers: the Marlborough boys in New York. J. Russell. il por Vogue 143: 102-5+ Ja 1 '64
LLOYD, Gerald D.
Cluster zoning: one step toward a better suburbia. Am Home 67:46-7 Je '64
LLOYD, Harvey
Mozart's world. il Opera N 29:12-15 Ja 2 '65
LLOYD, Kate
Chef's trial. Vogue 143:114-15+ Ap 15 '64
LLOYD, R. Grann
Expectations and responsibilities in higher education. Sch & Soc 92:85 F 22 '64
LLOYD, Selwyn
Speaking out. por Sat Eve Post 236:6+ Mr 2 '63; Excerpts. U S News 54:26 Mr 11 '63
LLOYD, Trevor
New perspective on the North. For Affairs 42:293-308 Ja '64
LLOYD, William Bross, jr
Toward African unity. Nation 196:544-5 Je 29 '63
LLOYD GEORGE, David, 1st earl Lloyd George of Dwyfor. See Lloyd George of Dwyfor, D. L. G.
LLOYD GEORGE of Dwyfor, David Lloyd George, 1st earl
Decline & fall of Lloyd George, by M. Beaverbrook. Review
Nat R por 14:458-9 Je 4 '63. S. Leslie
Time por 81:82+ My 31 '63
Wily Welshman at 10 Downing st. J. H. Plumb. il por Sat R 47:28 S 5 '64
LLOYD-JONES, David
Professor Borodin's indulgence. Hi Fi 13: 28-30+ Je '63
LLOYD'S, London
Lloyd's old but changing. il Bsns W p 136-8+ My 18 '63
Lloyd's settles a Florida claim. Bsns W p74 Je 8 '63
Room full of takers for any dare. J. Wechsberg. il Sat Eve Post 237:30+ My 2 '64
Taking the big risks. il Time 82:70+ Ag 16 '63
LLOYD'S register of American yachts
Social register for yachts. M. L. Hersey. il Motor B 114:54-6+ O '64
LOADING and unloading
Self-unloaders cut lime delivery costs; Chicago. il Am City 79:109 F '64
To the rescue of the marine. J. Ridgeway. New Repub 151:12 Jl 11 '64
LOADING cameras. See Cameras—Loading
LOAFING stalls. See Barns and stables—Equipment
LOAN associations. See Savings and loan associations
LOANS
Case of the lonesome loan; symposium. il Harvard Bsns R 42:6-8+ N '64
How quickly should you repay a loan? il Suc Farm 61:6 D '63
Look who wants to lend you money! Farm J 88:60 My '64
See also
Credit
Government lending
Interest
Mortgages
Pawnbroking
Student loans
LOANS, Art. See Art loans
LOANS, Bank
Banks that build new businesses around the world. O. Schisgall. Read Digest 82:128-31 F '63
Costs of borrowing stay even. il Bsns W p 107-8 Je 22 '63
Heavy buying of stock on credit? U S News 55:100-1 Ag 26 '63
Is the rise seasonal or a good deal more? corporate borrowing. il Bsns W p54+ D 7 '63
What it costs. il Time 84:103-4 S 11 '64
What's this: loans you never pay off? R. E. Geyer. Suc Farm 62:43+ N '64
LOANS, Foreign
Borrowers from abroad see Wall Street first. il Bsns W p94+ Ap 27 '63
How Europe fills the capital void. il Bsns W p47-8+ Ap 11 '64
New York is where the money is. il Bsns W p68-70 Ag 3 '63
United States and Greece sign debt settlement; Department statement, May 28, 1964. Dept State Bul 50:934 Je 15 '64
See also
International bank for reconstruction and development
LOANS, Government. See Government lending
LOANS, Interlibrary. See Interlibrary loans
LOANS, Mortgage. See Mortgages
LOANS, Personal
Do you know when money is costing you too much? Bet Hom & Gard 41:11-12 N '63
Home finance: the terms now. U S News 54:105 My 27 '63
Home loans: costs & terms. il Changing T 17:20-2 S '63
Many ways to borrow money. il Good H 158: 170 My '64
Where to borrow money. il Changing T 17: 31-5 Mr '63
LOANS, Student. See Student loans
LOBBYING
Better fishing for a nickel; letters to legislators. W. Davis. Outdoor Life 131:86+ Ap '63
Civil rights not measurable by the pound. J. N. Eller. America 110:504 Ap 11 '64
Clerical lobbyists. America 110:624 My 9 '64
Default of the educated man. N. Cousins. Sat R 46:18 Je 29 '63
Ethics of lobbying; Philippine war claims. Commonweal 78:236-7 My 24 '63
Lincoln memorial seminary; Protestant, Jewish and Catholic seminarians continuous vigil at the Lincoln memorial. America 110: 620 My 9 '64
Lobbies, Congress' third house. il Sr Schol 82:35 F 20 '63
Paralyzing power of Washington lobbies. J. A. Morris. Read Digest 82:127-32 My '63
Pennsylvania Avenue politics. R. Evans, jr. New Repub 148:19-20 F 2 '63
Research: as the stakes go up, idea of a man in Washington considered by more universities. J. Walsh. Science 142:1043-5 N 22 '63
Scientists in politics: Council founded by Szilard brings cash and sophistication to lobbying. E. Langer. Science 145:561-3 Ag 7 '64
Slow, quiet murder of tax reform; excerpts from Great Treasury raid. P. M. Stern. Harper 227:63-8 D '63; Reply with rejoinder. H. F. Byrd. 228:8+ Ap '64
Stand and be counted; Roman Catholics, Jews and Protestants support civil rights bill. il Newsweek 63:90 My 11 '64
Sugar blues; Filipino claimants for additional war damages. Newsweek 61:23 Ap 29 '63
Their men in Washington. F. J. Cook. il Nation 198:311-30 Mr 30 '64
Wandering paths of a transit bill: Urban passenger transportation association. V. J. Burke. il Reporter 31:31-3 Jl 16 '64
Washrooms of power; those anonymous propaganda peddlers. M. Kempton. New Repub 149:9-13 Ag 3 '63

LOBBYING—*Continued*

Regulations

Investigating foreign lobbyists; Senate foreign relations committee. il Bsns W p30-1 F 23 '63

LOBBYISTS

Keeper of the keys; influencing New York state senators. Newsweek 63:21-2 Mr 2 '64

LOBELINE

Tobacco substitute fails. Sci N L 84:150 S 7 '63

LO BELLO, Nino

World's wildest photographers. U S Camera 26:50+ Jl '63

LOBER, Kate

When my husband lost his job; interview, ed. by H. Lees. McCalls 90:68+ My '63

LOBLE, Lester H

Open house for young hoods. D. J. Giese. por Read Digest 84:125-9 Ap '64

LOBO, Julio

Bet that failed; Olavarria and Galban Lobo file under Bankruptcy act. por Bsns W p70+ Ag 1 '64

LOBOS ISLAND

Lobos Island. E. C. Uriburu. il Américas 15:33-7 Je '63

LOBRANO, Dorothy

No news is bad news; poem. New Yorker 39: 47 Mr 9 '63

LOBSENZ, Norman M.

Busiest mothers in the world. Redbook 122: 64-5+ Ap '64

How Jacqueline Kennedy saved a child's life. Redbook 121:46-7+ Jl '63

"My husband died for his country, and no one cares". Redbook 121:56-7+ O '63

LOBSTER trapping

Force de flap; question of French lobster boats in Brazilian waters. il Time 81:30-1 Mr 8 '63

Lobster war; Franco-Brazilian dispute. Newsweek 61:56 Mr 11 '63

LOCAL defense. See Civil defense

LOCAL educational associations. See Educational associations

LOCAL finance

State-local debt shoots up. U S News 58:75 Ja 4 '65

U.S. aid, wanted or not: report on a well-to-do county, Rice County, Kan; with excerpts from editorial by M. Moxley. il U S News 54:40-2 Ap 1 '63

Why states and cities are crying for help. il U S News 58:108-9 Ja 25 '65

LOCAL government

See also

Metropolitan areas

United States

During the blackout; what local government without newspapers can mean. G. Britt. New Repub 148:6-7 Ap 13 '63

Partnership in public service: excerpts from address, August 1963. L. B. Johnson. Am City 79:7 Ja '64

Race, riots and city administration. Am City 79:7 S '64

LOCAL history pageants. See Pageants

LOCAL representative; story. See Cole, T.

LOCAL service airlines

Cape Cod taxi offers trunk-type service. Aviation W 79:49 Ag 12 '63

Fairchild plans to increase F-27 capacity in new sales program. Aviation W 79:49 N 11 '63

Local service airlines protest adverse report, cut in subsidies. Aviation W 79:40 O 21 '63

Pacific Southwest airlines. H. D. Watkins. il Aviation W 79:48-9 Jl 1; 37 Jl 8 '63

Take-off of the feeders. il Time 82:87A-88 D 13 '63

Third-level carrier plans service between Cape Canaveral, Orlando. Aviation W 79:43 Ag 12 '63

Third-level carrier service urged to ease use it or lose it losses. Aviation W 80:34 Je 22 '64

See also

Aspen airways

Federal aid

Airlines off course? D. Teetor. il Flying 75: 64-6 S '64

CAB urges local service subsidy cuts. R. H. Cook. Aviation W 79:38-9 Ag 19 '63

FAA seeks U.S. short-haul transport aid. Aviation W 79:49 S 16 '63

Florida route shifts due priority review. Aviation W 81:39 O 26 '64

Local service group study backs subsidy. Aviation W 78:45 Mr 18 '63

Local service subsidy cut irks Congress. R. H. Cook. Aviation W 79:41-2 S 23 '63

New battle looms over subsidy levels. R. Cook. il Aviation W 80:171+ Mr 16 '64

Subsidy cut threatens class mail gains. R. H. Cook. il Aviation W 78:174-7 Mr 11 '63

Subsidy drop is shown in CAB budget; FAA seeks $810 million. L. L. Doty. Aviation W 78:41 Ja 21 '63

LOCAL taxation

As cities and counties get frantic for cash. il U S News 57:79-80 S 14 '64

In states, cities: a cry for services, a revolt on taxes. U S News 55:102-4 O 28 '63

1963: year of big jump in state, local taxes. il U S News 54:83-4 F 4 '63

Painless taxes: new gimmicks for states, cities. il U S News 57:80+ Jl 27 '64

Real-estate taxes, sales taxes and lotteries. Am City 78:7 Jl '63

State, local taxes: up, up. U S News 56:87 Ap 20 '64

Tax leaflet is a dollar stretcher. il Am City 78:122+ N '63

Tax problems of U.S. cities. U S News 58: 85-6 Ja 18 '65

Your state & local taxes, up and up and up. il Changing T 18:25-9 Jl '64

LOCALIZATION of brain functions. See Brain —Localization of functions

LOCATION in business and industry

Big plant-site scramble. il Duns R 83:pt2 104-5+ Mr '64

Brains behind the big deals; real estate researchers. il Bsns W p50+ Ag 15 '64

Critical decision: to build or modernize. J. B. Weiner. il Duns R 83:pt2 100-2+ Mr '64

Headquarters stay in asphalt jungle. il Bsns W p74+ N 30 '63

Higher and higher go the bids for industry. E. Lichtenstein. il Fortune 69:118-21+ Ap '64

Industry's view on water and sewerage facilities; survey of Illinois industrialists. il Am City 79:102+ N '64

Labor relations aspects of plant relocation. M. S. Ryder; J. H. Weeks. Mo Labor R 86:415-18 Ap '63

Let the water manager help to bring new industry; Elmira, N.Y. J. G. Copley. il Am City 79:89-90 Je '64

Made in Canada from now on; move from South Bend, Ind, to Hamilton, Ont. il Bsns W p28-9 D 14 '63

One-man magnet for industry; C. E. Daniel of Greenville, S.C. il Bsns W p50-2+ Ja 11 '64

Plant location: where the people are. il Duns R 83:pt2 106-7 Mr '64

Rough-and-tumble of site location. il Duns R 81:pt2 S97-100+ Mr '63

Scientific complex: proceed with caution. J. F. Mahar and D. C. Coddington. il Harvard Bsns R 43:140-8+ Ja '65

Shame of the cities. T. O'Hanlon. il Duns R 84:58-9+ O '64

Site finders; Fantus co. il Time 81:84 F 22 '63

So you want new industry. N. M. Martin. Am City 78:136-8 D '63

Troubled town; question of closing Gibson refrigerator Greenville plant. Newsweek 61: 74+ My 20 '63

Using tax-exempts to build business; Macy store in Topeka, aluminum mill in Lewisport, Ky. il Bsns W p45-6+ D 14 '63

Western gateway to New York; portfolio. Fortune 67:122-30 My '63

Why factories are taking to the country. il U S News 54:72-4 Je 17 '63

LOCATION of metals. See Metals—Detection

LOCATION of pipes. See Water pipes—Detection

LOCCUM, Germany

Loccum, a Protestant monastery. H. Lehmann. Christian Cent 80:1167-9 S 25 '63

LOCH NESS monster

Showdown for Loch Ness. P. Mandel. il Life 55:17-18 S 20 '63

LOCHER, David A.

Bells at Christmas; poem. America 111:801 D 19 '64

Bread; poem. America 108:711 My 18 '63

For Sir Thomas More, saint; poem. Cath World 197:365 S '63

Kevin is his name; poem. America 111:559 N 7 '64

Wise men; poem. America 109:797 D 21 '63

LOCHNER, Louis P.
(comp) See Hoover, H. C. Herbert Hoover in his own words
LOCK joints. See Joints (carpentry)
LOCK-picking. See Locks and keys
LOCKABEY, Almon
Learning by doing. Yachting 116:62-3+ Ag '64
To Acapulco with speed. Yachting 115:56-8+ Ap '64
LOCKE, Alain
Alain Locke, philosopher of the new Negro. G. Ulansky. bibliog Negro Hist Bul 26:240-3 My '63
LOCKE, Edward
Small library: thinking big. Wilson Lib Bul 37:780-1 My '63
LOCKE, Michael
Permeability of insect cuticle to water and lipids. bibliog Science 147:295-8 Ja 15 '65
LOCKERS
New idea: decorated lockers. il Seventeen 23:156 Mr '64
LOCKETS
Silver shell: Chinese locket. A. G. Melvin. il Hobbies 68:130+ F '64
LOCKHEED aircraft corporation
Angel from the Skunk works; details of the U-2's birth. il Time 82:31 S 20 '63
Blow to union shop. Bsns W p72 F 2 '63
Carrying out a plan for job integration; Marietta, Ga. il Bsns W p90+ Ap 13 '63
Industry testifies; statement before the Senate subcommittee on unemployment and manpower, November 20, 1963. Bul Atomic Sci 20:23 Ap '64
Lockheed again top DOD contractor. il Miss & Roc 14:26 Ja 6 '64
Lockheed refines jet tab technique. R. Hawkes. Miss & Roc 12:31 Ap 1 '63
Lockheed to market rigid rotor XH-51A. G. C. Wilson. il Aviation W 81:44-5 D 28 '64
Millennium for decision makers. il Bsns W p54+ Ag 10 '63
New plane cuts the red tape; C-141 Star-Lifter. il Bsns W p52-3 D 26 '64
Perils of pushing; nustling for European defense contracts. il Time 82:88 N 22 '63
Reroofing by the acre, while production continues; Lockheed-Georgia co. il Bsns W p76-7 N 23 '63
Sagging union shops; failure to get a union shop at Lockheed. Time 81:80 F 8 '63
Seaborne scientists explore inner space. il Bsns W p58-60+ O 17 '64
Successful flights of fancy. il Time 84:79-80 Ag 21 '64
Supersonic snafu. Newsweek 63:73-4 Ja 27 '64
This issue is clear so is the strategy. Nations Bsns 51:96-7 F '63
Union shop at Lockheed? L. T. King. Commonweal 77:489-91 F 1 '63
Wage chronology: Lockheed aircraft corp, California company. il Mo Labor R 87:680-5 Je '64
Where unions have hit a roadblock. il U S News 54:88-90 F 11 '63
Lockheed missile and space division
Data system used in production control; ADA system. H. D. Watkins. il Aviation W 79:62+ Ag 26 '63
Lockheed boosting its NASA Agena output. R. Lindsey. Miss & Roc 13:32 Ag 19 '63
LOCKHEED- California company. See Lockheed aircraft corporation
LOCKHEED-Georgia company. See Lockheed aircraft corporation
LOCKHEED missile and space division. See Lockheed aircraft corporation—Lockheed missile and space division
LOCKHEED propulsion company
AF, NASA officials enthusiastic about LPC's 156-in. motor test. il Miss & Roc 14:25-6+ Je 8 '64
156-in. solid motor center segment casting completed. C. M. Plattner. il Aviation W 80:52-3+ Mr 23 '64
LOCKJAW. See Tetanus
LOCKRIDGE, Frances, and Lockridge, Richard
Four hours to fear; story. Ladies Home J 81:78-80 My '64
about
Obituary
Pub W 183:48 Mr 4 '63
LOCKRIDGE, Richard. See Lockridge, F. jt. auth.
LOCKS and keys
Insuring entrance door security. E. F. Toepfer. Arch Rec 135:221-2 Ap '64
Modern-primitive lock. il Design 64:137 Mr '63
You can foil the lock artists. il Pop Mech 121:150-1+ Ap '64
LOCKWOOD, Normand
Hanging judge. Criticism
Opera N 28:26 My 2 '64
LOCMARIAQUER, France
Oysters of Locmariaquer, by E. Clark. Review
Newsweek il 64:89 Jl 13 '64
LOCOMOBILE; story. See O'Hara, J.
LOCOMOTION
See also
Animal locomotion
LOCOMOTIVES
All aboard. il Newsweek 67:77 S 16 '63
Old shay's last haul, people. S. Churchill. il Am For 70:61 My '64
LOCONTI, Joseph D. See Sousa, J. A. jt. auth.
LOCUSTS. See Grasshoppers
LODDO, B. and others
Poliovirus: guanidine dependence and loss of neurovirulence for monkeys. bibliog Science 145:945-6 Ag 28 '64
LODEESEN, Marius
Second harvest. Writer 77:7-9+ Mr '64
TV in the cockpit: the control of landing aircraft. Atlan 212:83-6 N '63
LODEN, Barbara
Best of all worlds. il por Newsweek 63:78-9 F 10 '64
People are talking about... por Vogue 143:96-7 Mr 15 '64
LODGE, Henry Cabot, 1902-
How the world's hottest spot looks to me. pors Life 56:38D-38F Ap 17 '64
We can win in Vietnam. por N Y Times Mag p 14-15+ Ja 17 '65
about
After New Hampshire. Reporter 30:10+ Mr 26 '64
Ambassador Lodge running strong. il pors Newsweek 63:21-5 Mr 23 '64
Back to the wars. Newsweek 64:20+ Jl 6 '64
Don't overlook Henry Cabot Lodge. Sat Eve Post 237:78 Ja 18 '64
Establishment view. S. Alsop. Sat Eve Post 237:16 Ap 18 '64
Footnote on Oregon; excerpts from letter to National review. S. Shadegg. Nat R 16:434-5 Je 2 '64
Homecoming. il Time 84:25 Jl 10 '64
Hot spot; ambassador to South Vietnam. por Newsweek 62:23 Jl 8 '63
Is U.S. changing policy? por U S News 57:19 Ag 31 '64
Kennedy speaks to a Lodge. Time 82:22 Jl 5 '63
Letter from Washington. R. H. Rovere. New Yorker 40:178+ Mr 21 '64
Levitation of Lodge. Nation 198:405-6 Ap 27 '64
Lodge: a surge for the man in Saigon. il por Newsweek 63:21-2 Ap 13 '64
Lodge faces his big test in Oregon; with editorial comment. J. Skow. il pors Sat Eve Post 237:15-19, 84 My 16 '64
Lodge is Oregon's bride by mail. R. B. Frazier. New Repub 150:9-10 My 9 '64
Lodge phenomenon. il pors Time 83:33-6 My 15 '64
Lodge: the little man who wasn't there. R. De Toledano. por Nat R 16:399-401 My 19 '64
New face in the presidential derby. por U S News 56:19 Mr 23 '64
New Hampshire poll: write-in fever gains. il Newsweek 63:18-21 Mr 9 '64
New leader. il por Time 83:23B Ap 10 '64
News from New Hampshire. il pors Time 83:19-21 Mr 20 '64
Nixon-Lodge again? il por Newsweek 62:15-16 D 23 '63
Oregon favorite. Newsweek 63:34-5 Ap 20 '64
Our man in South Vietnam. Sat Eve Post 236:94 S 28 '63
Our new men in Saigon; M. Taylor, to replace H. C. Lodge. por Time 84:15-16 Jl 3 '64
Portrait of the distant candidate. P. Grose. il pors N Y Times Mag p 13+ My 10 '64
Quandary of Henry Cabot Lodge. S. Karnow. il pors Sat Eve Post 237:70-3 F 8 '64
Republicans. il por Time 82:13 D 20 '63
Republicans. Newsweek 63:33 Mr 16 '64
Straws in Iowa. Newsweek 63:20 Ap 6 '64
Tough U.S. envoy moves in on the Vietnamese mess. il por Life 55:30B-30C S 6 '63
U.S. may pull rug from under Diem. il por Bsns W p22 Ag 31 '63
Vietnam: soldier to Saigon. il por Newsweek 64:18-20 Jl 6 '64
Vote for our man in Vietnam; with editorial comment. il pors Life 56:4, 32-9 Mr 20 '64
Zooming non-candidate. E. J. Hughes. Newsweek 63:29 Ap 20 '64

LODGE, John Davis
Republican party and the conservative movement. por Nat R 16:1054-5 D 1 '64

LODGES (architecture)
Lighthearted ideas from California ski lodges. il House & Gard 126:162-5 D '64

LOEB, Carl Morris
Of men, money, and marriage. por Fortune 67:131-2 Ap '63

LOEB, Carl M, Rhoades and company
Wherever you look, there's Loeb, Rhoades. T. A. Wise. il Fortune 67:128-31+ Ap '63

LOEB, Howard
Dreamy new era for fish. R. H. Boyle. Sports Illus 20:50+ Mr 30 '64

LOEB, Martin B.
Mental health: new frontiers. Nation 196: 418-21 My 18 '63

LOEB, Robert H. Jr
Teen-age manners and make-up. PTA Mag 58:30-2 bibliog(p36) D '63

LOEB, William
Excerpt from testimony, July 31, 1963. Cong Digest 42:283+ N '63
Up in New Hampshire. il por Newsweek 63:65 F 17 '64

LOEBELSON, Robert M.
Vroom! out of this world engines; reprint. Sci Digest 55:40-4 Ap '64

LOEBL, Lili
Putting the Congo together again. New Repub 148:10-11 Mr 9 '63

LOEN, Raymond O.
Sales managers must manage. Harvard Bsns R 42:107-14 My '64

LOESER, Katinka
End of a season; story. New Yorker 39:38-41 S 21 '63
Head-raiser; story. Redbook 120:42-3 Mr '63
It's only a game; story. McCalls 91:126-7 O '63
My son; story. Redbook 123:42 Ag '64
Nocturne; story. New Yorker 39:44-6 O 5 '63
On with the dance; story. McCalls 90:108-9 S '63
Roll call: story. Redbook 122:36-7 D '63

LOESS
Microfossils in Wisconsinan loess and till from western Illinois and eastern Iowa. R. L. Jones and others. bibliog il Science 140:1222-4 Je 14 '63

LOEVINGER, Lee
People of the week. por U S News 54:23 My 27 '63

LOEWE, Ralph E.
Who makes a menace out of Johnny? Sat R 46:64-5+ Je 15 '63

LOEWENSTEIN, Werner R. and others
Separation of transducer and impulse-generating processes in sensory receptors. bibliog Science 142:1180-1 N 29 '63
—See Kanno, Y; Mendelson, M. jt. auths.

LOEWY, Raymond
Paris redesigned. Newsweek 62:75-6 S 2 '63

LOFLAND, James E.
Country slicker. il por Newsweek 62:28-9 Jl 8 '63

LOFTING, Colin
Rodeo clown. Life 55:37-8+ Jl 19 '63

LOFTIS, Anne, and Marshall, Rachelle
Gresham's law of literature. Sat R 46:64-5 S 21 '63

LOFTS, Norah
Shepherd; story. Ladies Home J 81:54-5 D '64

LOFTUS, Beverly G.
(ed) First novelists, summer 1964. Library J 89:2371-7 Je 1 '64

LOG drives. See Lumbering

LOGAN, Andy
Milk train stops at Tiffany's; poem. New Yorker 39:194 Mr 16 '63

LOGAN, C. Stumpter
On Mormonism. Christian Cent 81:14 Ja 1 '64

LOGAN, D. E. Jr
Doctor's education never ends. Todays Health 42:40-1+ S '64
Short-wave samaritans. Todays Health 42: 40-1+ Je '64

LOGAN, Edgar
Light touch. NEA J 52:23 S '63
Year of study and reflection. Sat R 46:73-4 N 16 '63

LOGAN, John
Lines for a young man who talked. Nation 196:549 Je 29 '63

LOGAN, Joshua
Soft psyche of Joshua Logan. G. Talese. por Esquire 59:82-5+ Ap '63

LOGAN, Ohio
Sprinkle brine for bare pavements. il Am City 80:30 Ja '65

LOGAN, Jonathan, incorporated
$100 million in rags. S. Freedgood. il Fortune 67:151-4+ My '63

LOGAN CANYON, Utah. See Canyons

LOGGERS. See Lumberjacks

LOGGING. See Lumbering

LOGIC
Teach logical thinking. Sci N L 83:308 My 18 '63

LOGICAL empiricism. See Logical positivism

LOGICAL positivism
Analytic philosophy and education thought; excerpt from Foundations of education. G. F. Kneller. bibliog f Sch & Soc 91:61+ F 9 '63

LOGISTICS management institute
DOD considering new profit guidelines. F. G. McGuire. Miss & Roc 12:15-16 F 25 '63
LMI has growing effect on planning. Miss & Roc 12:117 Mr 25 '63

LOGS (nautical instruments)
Speedometers and logs. E. Robberson. il Yachting 116:44-6+ D '64

LOGSDON, Eugene H.
Horrors, a parlor full of Adas! Farm J 88:22-3 Ag '64
Who ran off with my. . . .? Farm J 88:66 O '64

LOGSDON, Richard H.
Restatement of the program of the commission. ALA Bul 57:317-18 Ap '63

about

Logsdon to head ALA commission on national plan for library education. Library J 88:744 F 15 '63

LOGTOWN, Miss.
Moon race blots out a town. R. Bailey. il Life 57:21 S 25 '64

LOGUE, Edward J.
Boston: what can a sick city do? W. McQuade. il por Fortune 69:132-7+ Je '64

LOH, I-cheng
Chinese reprinters and world copyright practice. por Pub W 185:22+ Mr 30 '64

LOH, Patricia. See Furth, J. J. jt. auth.

LOHENGRIN; opera. See Wagner, R.

LO-K-TOR. See Fishing—Implements and appliances

LOLLIPOPS. See Candy

LOLLOBRIGIDA, Gina
Redbook dialogue. por Redbook 121:58-9+ S '63

LOMAX, Sir John Garnett
America's jobless and Russia's markets. Nation 196:262-4 Mr 30 '63
Day the cold war changed. Nation 197:10-12 Jl 6 '63
Trade and jobs: a world view. Nation 198: 365-7 Ap 13 '64

LOMAX, Louis
Negro view: Johnson can free the South. Look 28:34+ Mr 10 '64
Speaking out. por Sat Eve Post 236:12+ S 21 '63
Tomorrow's leaders. Ebony 18:41-4+ S '63
What mass protests can't do. Sat R 46:11-12 Jl 6 '63
Why the Negroes continue to revolt. Look 27:52-4 S 10 '63

LOMBARDI, Sincero
We have no childhood; ed. by R. Llewellyn. por Sat Eve Post 236:76-7 S 7 '63

LOMBARDI, Vince
Day of the game; excerpt from Run to daylight; ed. by W. C. Heinz. il por Sports Illus 19:94-104+ S 9 '63

LOMBARDO, Guy
Sweet music. il por Newsweek 65:34-5 Ja 4 '65

LOMER, Mary
Scholar's mother; poem. Mlle 59:34 S '64

LONDON, Fritz
Quantized magnetic flux in superconductors. R. D. Parks. bibliog il Science 146:1429-35 D 11 '64

LONDON, George
Traveling man; interview, ed. by A. M. Lingg. por Opera N 27:14 F 2 '63

about

Boris from Moscow. H. Weinstock. Sat R 47: 61+ S 26 '64
Columbia's Boris. P. L. Miller. il Am Rec G 31:20-1+ S '64
Three American tsars. A. M. Lingg. Opera N 27:25-7 Ap 6 '63

LONDON, Jack
Cytochrome in thiobacillus thiooxidans. bibliog Science 140:409-10 Ap 26 '63

LONDON, Jack, 1876-1916
Buck hears the call; story; excerpt from Call of the wild. Read Digest 85:193-4 N '64
about
Jack London, by R. O'Connor. Review Nation 200:14-15 Ja 4 '65. W. Ward
Jack London today. M. Geismar. New Repub 151:29-31 N 14 '64
LONDON, Maggie
Captivating comeback for crochet. il pors Life 57:51-2+ O 31 '64
LONDON, S. J.
Origin of psychoacoustics. Hi Fi 13:44-7+ Ap '63
LONDON
Letter from London. M. Panter-Downes. See issues of New Yorker
Paddington bows to Westminster. A. P. Herbert. il N Y Times Mag p70-1+ N 3 '63
Air raids
Blitzkrieg days. E. Wright. New Yorker 40:159-64 Ap 11 '64
Airports
Report recommends tightened noise procedures at Heathrow. Aviation W 80:41 Ja 13 '64
Architecture
Letter from London; concerning obstruction of view of the west front of St Paul's cathedral by new office building. M. Panter-Downes. New Yorker 40:113-14+ Ap 4 '64
Up goes London. G. Kent. il Read Digest 82:213-16 Ap '63
Art
Art news from London. J. Russell. See issues of Art news
Banks
Prince among princes; Hambros bank, ltd. il Time 83:65 Ja 24 '64
Russia's sterling success; Narodny bank. Time 82:90-1 Jl 12 '63
British museum
See British museum
Churches
R. J. Campbell at City temple. W. S. Smith. Christian Cent 80:1132-4 S 18 '63
See also
London—St Paul's cathedral
Covent Garden
Great opera houses. A. M. Lingg. il Opera N 27:18-22 My 4 '63
See also
Friends of Covent Garden
Crime
Jack the stripper; hunt for murderer of London prostitutes. Time 83:32+ My 8 '64
Killer; Jack the stripper murders of prostitutes in London. il Newsweek 64:38 D 21 '64
Lots of loot: underworld spectaculars. Time 81:33 Je 7 '63
New York cop studies crime of two cities: London and New York. H. Ehrlich. il Look 27:57-63 Jl 30 '63
Crystal palace
Echoes of the age of Victoria; photographs. A. L. Huxtable. N Y Times Mag p46-7 Ap 7 '63
Description
Glance at Billingsgate. J. Sayre. il Holiday 33:34+ My '63
London perceived, by V. S. Pritchett. Review
New Yorker 38:131-2+ F 9 '63. A. J. Liebling
Education
Infallible Jimmy's; centennial of James, Carlisle & Gregson, tutoring school. Newsweek 64:65 N 2 '64
To kill the terror. Newsweek 62:52 Jl 15 '63
Galleries and museums
Magpie's nest in a London mansion; Sir John Soane's museum. P. Quennell. il Horizon 5:72-83 N '63
Most expensive family album; British royal children in Queen's gallery. A. Carthew. il N Y Times Mag p40-1 D 1 '63
See also
British museum
National gallery
Tate gallery
Victoria and Albert museum, South Kensington
Historic houses, etc.
Back home at No. 10. Time 82:38 O 11 '63
House that Union Jack built; No. 10 Downing street. il Time 83:70-2 Mr 20 '64
No. 10 Downing street: a house in history, by R. J. Minney. Review
Sat R il 46:52-3 S 28 '63. M. Edelman
History
London that was Shakespeare's; excerpts from Shakespeare of London. M. Chute. il UNESCO Courier 17:14-17+ My '64
Hotels, restaurants, etc.
Bleak little inn fit for any king; Claridge's of London. J. Sherlock. il Sat Eve Post 236:39-41+ N 30 '63
Let's travel to Europe; Hilton hotel. il Mile 57:156-8 O '63
Meal at Scott's. C. W. Morton. il Atlan 212:128+ O '63
Savoy of London. L. Beebe. il Holiday 33:106-7+ Mr '63
Vogue's notebook; The garrison. il Vogue 141:46-7 Mr 1 '63
Housing
Letter from London; hole in Rent act of 1957: Rachman empire. M. Panter-Downes. New Yorker 39:67-8 Ag 3 '63
Intellectual life
Peripatetic reviewer. E. Weeks. Atlan 212:126-8 Jl '63
Libraries
Libraries in London and New York. J. Hill. Sr Schol 85:25T O 7 '64
Malicious mischief, British style; Islington public libraries; summary. A. Connell. Wilson Lib Bul 37:750 My '63
See also
British museum
Markets
Glance at Billingsgate. J. Sayre. il Holiday 33:34+ My '63
Music
Dmitri's Lady: performance of Shostakovich's Katerina Ismailove at Covent Garden. il Newsweek 62:61 D 16 '63
Embarrassment of riches; London's five symphony orchestras. Time 83:112 Ap 17 '64
Great opera houses: Covent Garden. A. M. Lingg. il Opera N 27:18-22 My 4 '63
Letter from London; performance of Puccini's Tosca. M. Panter-Downes. New Yorker 39:116 F 15 '64
London returns. D. Shawe-Taylor. il Opera N 28:30-1 Mr 21 '64
London summary. D. Shawe-Taylor. Opera N 28:30 O 19 '63
London's visitors; Frankfurt city opera. F. Aprahamian. Opera N 28:32 Ja 4 '64
[Musical events] (cont) Mus Am 83:14 Jl '63; 84:28+ Ap '64
Notes from abroad. C. Reid. See issues of High fidelity
Notes from our correspondents. E. Greenfield. Hi Fi 15:30+ Ja; 30+ F '65
Notes from our correspondents. F. Aprahamian. Hi Fi 14:14+ Jl; 24+ Ag; 12+ S; 29+ N '64
Other side; London's symphony orchestras. T. Heinitz. Sat R 47:56 Ap 11 '64
Spotlight on the Wells. D. Shawe-Taylor. Opera N 27:28-9 My 4 '63
See also
Philharmonia orchestra of London
Newspapers
See also
Daily mail, London
Observer (London)
Sun (newspaper)
Sunday mirror, London
Times, London
Parks and playgrounds
Three-mile April walk in the heart of London. il Sunset 132:54-5+ Ap '64
Politics and government
London area goes metro. R. Smith. Am City 79:124+ Ag '64
London trying out metro government. il Bsns W p 108 Ag 10 '63
Religious institutions and affairs
New ministry in inner London. C. Northcott. Christian Cent 80:1547 D 11 '63

LONDON—*Continued*

Riots

Foolish display; protesting of visit by King Paul and Queen Frederika. il Time 82:30+ Jl 19 '63
Jobless riots in Britain: wildest in years. il U S News 54:6 Ap 8 '63
No midsummer dream; mob disturbances on visit to London of King Paul and Queen Frederika of Greece. il Newsweek 62:39 Jl 22 '63
Royalty, but not reds, targets of London boos. il U S News 55:8 Jl 22 '63
We want work: sack Mac, sack Mac. il Newsweek 61:33-4+ Ap 8 '63

St Paul's cathedral

Letter from London; concerning obstruction of view of the west front of St Paul's cathedral by new office building. M. Panter-Downes. New Yorker 40:113-14+ Ap 4 '64

Social life and customs

Let's travel to London. W. Petschek. il Mlle 59:117-18 Je '64
This is London. W. Petschek. il Mlle 56:94-6 Ap '63

Stock exchange

See Stock exchange—London

Stores

Ah, those colonials; emphasis shifted away from foods at Fortnum and Mason. il Time 84:80 D 18 '64
World's most unusual camera store: Wallace Heaton ltd. B. Campbell. il Pop Phot 54: 61-3+ Je '64

Street traffic

Letter from London; concerning Buchanan report on traffic. M. Panter-Downes. New Yorker 39:65-6 Ja 25 '64
What to do about traffic? some answers from abroad. il U S News 54:86-90 F 4 '63

Streets

Bond street. il Travel 119:19-20 Ap '63
Brush up your Shakespeare. N. Braybrooke. il Sat R 47:92+ Mr 14 '64

Theater

Death of a monument: Old Vic. Newsweek 62:60 Jl 1 '63
End of an old song; Windmill theatre closes. il Newsweek 64:52 N 2 '64
Great opera houses: Sadler's Wells. S. Hughes. il Opera N 28:36-31 Ja 25 '64
Great opera houses: Savoy theatre. B. D. Carte. il Opera N 29:26-9 D 12 '64
How beastly are the British? London dirty play controversy. C. D. Champlin. Life 57:15 N 6 '64
Letter from London. M. Panter-Downes. New Yorker 39:148+ My 25 '63; 200-1 N 21 '64
Lights of London. il Time 84:42 O 9 '64
Oh what a lovely class struggle: end of one of the poorest seasons. H. Hewes. Sat R 46:33 Je 22 '63
Opening the old kit bag; Oh, what a lovely war at Wyndham's theater. il Time 82:64-5 Jl 5 '63
Openings. A. Brien. See issues of Theatre arts
Royal visit. il Theatre Arts 47:19 F '63
Theatre; seizure of satire. H. Clurman. Nation 196:450+ My 25 '63
Tongues of men; World theatre season at Aldwych theatre. il Newsweek 63:80 My 18 '64
Wingless sea gull. J. Rosselli. Reporter 30: 34-5 Je 4 '64
See also
London—Covent Garden
Royal Shakespeare theatre company

Traffic problems

See London—Street traffic

LONDON, Tower of. See Tower of London
LONDON daily mail. See Daily mail, London
LONDON Economist. See Economist (London)
LONDON metal exchange
Metals' frantic five minutes. il Bsns W p46-8 Jl 6 '63
LONDON philharmonia orchestra. See Philharmonia orchestra of London
LONDON records, incorporated
London's near perfect Siegfried. G. L. Mayer. il Am Rec G 29:686-9 My '63
LONDON stock exchange. See Stock exchange —London
LONDON symphony orchestra
From London with love; concerts in New York and Boston. il Newsweek 64:94 N 2 '64
Music to my ears; Carnegie Hall concerts. I. Kolodin. Sat R 47:28 N 7 '64
Musical events; performances at Carnegie Hall under four conductors. W. Sargeant. New Yorker 40:229-31 O 31 '64
LONDON Times. See Times, London
LONDON zoological gardens
Letter from London; Regent's park. M. Panter-Downes. New Yorker 39:100+ Je 15 '63
Zoo alters animal habits. Sci N L 85:270 Ap 25 '64
LONDON zoological society. See Zoological society of London
LONDONDERRY, Alexander Charles Robert Vane-Tempest-Stewart, 9th marquis of
Londonderrys. P. Laurie. il pors Vogue 144: 112-19+ Ag 1 '64
LONDONDERRY, Nicolette (Harrison) Vane-Tempest-Stewart, marchioness of
Londonderrys. P. Laurie. il pors Vogue 144: 112-19+ Ag 1 '64
LONDONERS
Blitzkrieg days. E. Wright. New Yorker 40: 159-64 Ap 11 '64
London perceived, by V. S. Pritchett. Review
New Yorker 38:131-2+ F 9 '63. A. J. Liebling
LONELINESS
See also
Solitude
LONELINESS of the outdistanced mouse; story. See Welch, H. L.
LONELY little old lady; drama. See King, P. C.
LONELY man; story. See Baldwin, F.
LONELY price of victory; story. See McCord, J.
LONERGAN, Bernard
Birthday to notice. F. E. Crowe. America 111: 804-5 D 19 '64
Understanding understanding. por Time 85: 60-1 Ja 22 '65
LONERS; story. See J. D. Osler
LONEY, Glenn
Electronic drama. Theatre Arts 47:27-8 Jl '63
Hofstra's mechanized stagehand. Theatre Arts 47:67-8 Je '63
Opera bookshelf. Theatre Arts 47:7 Mr '63
Sweden is a summer festival. Theatre Arts 47:62-3+ Ap '63
Wagner worship in Bavaria. Reporter 29:32+ Jl 4 '63
LONG, Augustus C.
Businessman talks about doing business abroad; excerpts from address. por U S News 56:96-7 My 4 '64
Partners in excellence. por Opera N 29:8-11 D 5 '64
LONG, Charles H.
Religion and art. Christian Cent 81:19 Ja 1 '64
LONG, Charles M.
Grouping of children. Sch Life 46:17-19 D '63
LONG, Clarence D.
Observations of a freshman in Congress. N Y Times Mag p34+ D 1 '63
LONG, Clayton
Dedicatory; poem. Commonweal 80:109 Ap 17 '64
Deer in the surf; poem. Commonweal 78:503 Ag 23 '63
LONG, E. John
Benton MacKaye: the verdant prophet. por Am For 70:16-19 Jl '64
Cross-Florida Canal. Am For 70:16-19+ Je '64
Danger down the trail! Am For 70:20-3+ O '64
New landmarks on the Washington horizon. Am For 70:16-21 Mr '64
Sand + oil = trees. Am For 70:46-8 Ja '64
Timber from Jamaican ore pits. Am For 69: 22-5 S '63
Water to order. Am For 70:25+ My '64
When you must ditch at sea; reprint. Sci Digest 56:38-42 O '64
LONG, Edward LeRoy, Jr
Display case for our culture. Christian Cent 81:968-9 Jl 29 '64
LONG, Ernest G.
Application of a one-ply roofing system. Arch Rec 136:263-4 S '64
LONG, Franklin A.
Immediate steps toward disarmament. Bul Atomic Sci 20:7-10 F '64
LONG, Harold M.
And what does he know of England who only England knows? por Sr Schol 83:9T-10T S 27 '63

LONG, Huey Pierce
All the king's men: the matrix of experience. R. P. Warren. Yale R 53:161-7 D '63
Long, long ago. B. K. Hoffer. Sat R 47:6+ O 17 '64

LONG, John Allan
Last of the hardy sailor-scientists; reprint. Sci Digest 56:8-10 Ag '64

LONG, Lorence
Incident in a rural slum. Christian Cent 81: 1088-9 S 2 '64

LONG, Marcus
Learning: a lifelong process; excerpts from address, May 21, 1964. por Library J 90: 188-91, 195 Ja 15 '65

LONG, Margaret
Imperial wizard explains the klan. N Y Times Mag p8+ Jl 5 '64
Southern teen-ager speaks his mind. N Y Times Mag p 15+ N 10 '63

LONG, Melvin E.
Corn picker tune-up. Suc Farm 61:47 O '63

LONG, Norwood
Science: the wonder ingredient in science books. Library J 89:325-7 Ja 15 '64

LONG, Russell Billiu
Critic of the High court: Louisiana senator speaks out; excerpts from statements. por U S News 56:13 F 10 '64
Fighting 89th. Newsweek 65:18-19 Ja 18 '65
Ford and Long: new leaders in the 89th. por Newsweek 65:20 Ja 18 '65
How Long won election as Senate whip. il por U S News 58:19 Ja 18 '65
Kennedy's quarterback has his own ideas. por Bsns W p26 F 9 '63
Long of Louisiana. il por Time 81:17 F 8 '63

LONG, Stuart
Texan remembers Lyndon. Nation 199:235-9 O 19 '64

LONG, Sumner Adam
Object is to win the race. A. Zich. il por Sports Illus 19:32-7 Jl 1 '63

LONG, Sumner Arthur
Million dollar headache. T. Prideaux. il por Life 55:39-40+ Ag 9 '63

LONG, William G.
First defect is among the judges themselves; interview. por U S News 56:66-9 Ap 20 '64

LONG and short of it; story. See Wood, M.

LONG BEACH, Calif.

Police

Recorders and duplicating machines speed police reporting. R. G. Kortz. il Am City 79: 81 Jl '64

LONG BEACH, Calif. arena. See Stadiums

LONG BRANCH, N.J.
Store winter water for summer use. O. A. Newquist. il Am City 78:74-5 F '63

LONG Christmas dinner; opera. See Hindemith, P.

LONG day for William; story. See Burnford, S.

LONG distance xerography. See Xerography

LONG-endurance experimental research submarine. See Submarine boats, Atomic powered

LONG-focus lenses. See Lenses, Photographic

LONG ISLAND, N.Y.
Far out on Long Island. W. K. Zinsser. il Horizon 5:4-27 My '63
Fresh look at Long Island. J. McCarthy. il Holiday 35:78-9+ My '64
Long Island is becoming long city; 118-mile-long metropolis. J. McCarthy. il N Y Times Mag p 17+ Ag 30 '64
See also
Architecture, Domestic—Long Island, N.Y.
Nassau County, N.Y.

Hotels, restaurants, etc.

Long Island: some Indian summer pleasures. Vogue 142:62 O 1 '63

LONG ISLAND festival. See Music festivals—New York (state)

LONG ISLAND historical society
Centennial on Long Island. R. Davidson. il Antiques 83:460+ Ap '63

LONG ISLAND SOUND
Day to measure by. B. Robinson. il Yachting 117:110-11+ Ja '65
Profiles; two-week cruise aboard sloop Merrywend. M. M. Hunt. il New Yorker 40:37-40+ Ag 22; 37-8+ Ag 29; 37-40+ S 5 '64
Sound cruising. C. R. Meyer. il Travel 119: 38-40 Je '63
Word on local weather. C. Shields. Yachting 115:140-2 F '64

LONG night of Shubert alley; story. See Miller, W.

LONG night; story. See Warner, S. T.

LONG pants for the last day; story. See Crabb, A. L.

LONG playing record catalog. See Phonograph records—Catalogs

LONG playing records. See Phonograph records

LONG trail, Vermont. See Trails

LONGACRE, William A.
Archeology as anthropology: a case study. bibliog Science 144:1454-5 Je 19 '64

LONGDEN, Johnny
Old moneybags. por Newsweek 64:46-7 D 21 '64

LONGEE, Lynda
If you can't lick 'em; story. Seventeen 24: 86-7 Ja '65

LONGEVITY
Charlie Smith, 121 years young. il Ebony 19: 131-2+ N '63
From government reports: your life expectancy now. il U S News 57:53 Jl 6 '64
How long you have to live. il Sci Digest 55: 19-20 Ja '64
How to grow old without aging; Soviet Georgia's centenarians. A. Parry. il Sci Digest 54:86-90 O '63
Medicine: be glad you're a woman, you'll live longer. H. B. Sprague. Ladies Home J 81:43 O '64
Men, women and health. il Sci Digest 55:83-4 Ap '64
More chemists die young; summary of address. S. Soloveichik. Sci N L 84:199 S 28 '63
You'll live longer; interview. J. A. Shannon. il Nations Bsns 52:104-6+ Mr '64
See also
Aging
Centenarians

LONGFELLOW, Henry Wadsworth
Building of the ship; excerpt. Motor B 111: 27 F '63

about

Longfellow: his life and work, by N. Arvin. Review
New Yorker 39:176+ Mr 23 '63. E. Wilson
Mark (ye) (the) Twain. D. J. Hamblin. por Life 57:13 Jl 10 '64

LONGFELLOW, Isabelle Bryans
Theft; poem. McCalls 90:144 Je '63

LONGHORN CAVERN. See Caves

LONGHORN CAVERN STATE PARK. See Texas—Parks and reserves

LONGHURST, Henry
Golf. Sports Illus 18:54 Je 3 '63
Spain sent a two-man armada. Sports Illus 19:18-20 N 4 '63

LONGINELLI, A. and Tongiorgi, E.
Oxygen isotopic composition of some right- and left-coiled foraminifera. Science 144: 1004 My 22 '64

LONGO, Luigi
Longo tries Togliatti's shoes. R. Neville. il pors N Y Times Mag p32+ N 8 '64
New boss. por Newsweek 64:42 S 7 '64

LONGORIA, Shelby
New world record polar bear; ed. by W. E. Anderson. por Field & S 69:56-7 O '64

LONGSHOREMEN
Man who made the most of automation. Time 82:19 D 27 '63
Snarl in every port; Brazil's dock hands. Time 82:27 Ag 30 '63
Two-edged blade over British docks. il Bsns W p48+ N 14 '64
Where the union is the boss; Veracruz harbor. il Bsns W p 110-11 Je 13 '64
See also
International longshoremen's and warehousemen's union
International longshoremen's association
Strikes—United States—Maritime workers

Wages and hours

On the waterfront. Sr Schol 85:4T Ja 14 '65

LONGTON Hall porcelain. See Pottery, English

LONGWELL, Maude. See Jobe, B. jt. auth.

LONICERA Japonica. See Honeysuckles

LONRHO, limited
New Rhodes. il Time 85:71 Ja 22 '65

LONSDALE, A. L.
Operation sail, 1964. Motor B 113:108-9+ Ja '64

LOOK (periodical)
Admen urge promotion curbs; free copies. Bsns W p28 Mr 28 '64
Coming 3-D revolution. J. Tebbel. Sat R 47: 127-8 Mr 14 '64
Lawana Trout: teacher of the year. G. Astor. il Look 28:33-7 My 19 '64

LOOK (periodical)—*Continued*
Look on the light side; selection of cartoons. Read Digest 82:87-90 Je '63
Look's illusion; parallax panoramagram. il Time 83:66 F 21 '64
See also
All-America cities
Collier trophy
LOOK down, look down; story .See Ford, J. H.
LOOK out for sharks; story. See Freeman, J. T.
LOOKING glasses. See Mirrors
LOOM; story. See Grosser, M.
LOOMIS, Alfred F.
Blow for freedom. Nat R 16:823 S 22 '64
Destination: Bermuda. Yachting 115:50-2+ Je '64
LOOMIS, Carol
What's in the market for you? Mlle 59:122-3+ S '64
LOOMIS, Daniel P.
Merger spooks and spitballs; address, June 22, 1963. Vital Speeches 29:622-5 Ag 1 '63
Transportation; address, January 14, 1963. Vital Speeches 29:322-5 Mr 15 '63
LOOMIS, Mahlon
Real beginning of radio. O. B. Young. il por Sat R 47:48-50 Mr 7 '64; Discussion. 47:47 Ap 4 '64
LOONEY, Joe Don
Football's marvelous misfit. R. Daley. il pors Sat Eve Post 237:82+ D 5 '64
LOOP antennas. See Radio antennas
LOORY, Stuart H.
Are we wasting billions in space? Sat Eve Post 236:13-15 S 14 '63
—See Ubell, E. jt. auth.
LOOS, Anita
Aldous Huxley in California. Harper 228:51-5 My '64
LOOSE-leaf notebooks. See Notebooks
LOOTING. See Pillage
LOPEZ, George
George Lopez; a carver of santos. W. T. Le Viness. il por Am Artist 27:25-9+ Ap '63
LOPEZ, Nicolas Lindley
Peru coup topples Perez Godoy. por Sr Schol 82:16 Mr 20 '63
LOPEZ, Trini
Surf king. por Newsweek 63:77 Je 22 '64
LÓPEZ de GÓMARA, Francisco. See Gómara, F. L. de
LÓPEZ MATEOS, Adolfo
Charter day ceremonies, UCLA; remarks, February 21, 1964. Dept State Bul 50:400-1 Mr 16 '64
Pre-election valedictory; summary of address. por Time 82:45 S 13 '63
—See Johnson, L. B. jt. auth.

about

De Gaulle's Mexican hat dance. G. Delmas. por Reporter 30:30-2 Ap 23 '64
Mexico chooses stability for 1964-70. por U S News 55:83 N 18 '63
Mexico: cool revolution and cold war. S. R. Ross. Cur Hist 44:89-94+ F '63
1964 shoo-in for Mexico? il por Sr Schol 83:10-13 D 13 '63
Sunny side up; talks with President Johnson. il por Newsweek 63:17 Mr 2 '64
U.S. betting on Mexico; but there's trouble ahead. il por U S News 54:45-7 F 25 '63
Volkswagen president. il Newsweek 64:60-1 D 7 '64
LOQUATS
Loquat is a performer. il Sunset 132:120 Ja '64
LORAN, Erle
Pop artists or copy cats? Art N 62:48-9+ S '63
LORANG, Glenn. See Hardy, B. jt. auth.
LORANT, Stefan
Tips. il Pub W 186:60 N 16 '64
LORCA, Federico García. See García Lorca, F.
LORCH, Jacob
Two fossil floras of the Negev Desert. Natur Hist 72:28-37 Mr '63
LORD, Milton
Time is a commodity; regional library service in eastern Massachusetts. D. Nyren. por Library J 88:1943-5 My 15 '63; Reply with rejoinder. B. G. Wade. 88:2582 Jl '63
LORD, Tom Forrester
Two revolutions and a war. Christian Cent 81:1334-6 O 28 '64
LORD and Taylor. See New York (city)—Stores
LORD Pengo; drama. See Behrman, S. N.
LORDS day act. See Sunday legislation
LORDS day alliance. See Sunday legislation
LORDS Supper
Amen; personal amen at the moment of Holy Communion. America 110:839 Je 20 '64
Beyond the eucharist. C. Davis. America 109:98 Jl 27 '63
Body of Christ. America 108:660 My 11 '63
First holy communion. America 108:702 My 18 '63
Grass-roots ecumenism. D. J. O'Hanlon. Cath World 199:8-15 Ap '64
Johnson at the altar rail; admission of non-Episcopalians to communion. il Time 83:60 Je 19 '64
One body, one table; unresolved differences of eucharistic theology and practice. Christian Cent 80:1159-60 S 25 '63; Discussion. 80:1446 N 20 '63
See also
Catholic church—Eucharist
First communion
Mass
LOREN, Sophia
Secrets of Sophia; ed. by F. Ghedini. por McCalls 91:98-9+ Ag '64
When stripping, look into a man's eyes. por Life 56:56 Ap 10 '64

about

Carlo and Sophia. D. J. Hamblin. il pors Life 57:80-9 S 18 '64
First, I am a woman. P. Hamill. il pors Sat Eve Post 237:60-3 F 15 '64
Sophia Loren does her Easter shopping. il por Look 27:121-4+ Ap 23 '63
Sophia Loren: the strength of love. F. Wyndham. il por Vogue 142:172-3+ O 1 '63
Three Sophias for price of one; with report by S. Loren. il pors Life 56:49-50+ Ap 10 '64
LORENZ, Denis
Book selection in New Haven. por Wilson Lib Bul 39:331-2 D '64
LORENZ, John G.
Sketch maps of resources. por Library J 88:4708-9 D 15 '63
(ed) Working together. Wilson Lib Bul 38:260-4+ N '63
—and Carl, H. A.
Washington report: from the Library services branch. ALA Bul 57:393-6, 636-8, 1016-17; 58:23-5, 182-4 My, Jl, D '63-Ja, Mr '64
LORENZEN, Fred
Money man. Sports Illus 19:14 S 9 '63
LORENZO; drama. See Richardson, J.
LORICK, Tony
Rookie and the vet. il pors Ebony 20:56-8+ Ja '65
LORNING, Ray
Quiet night in jail; story. Esquire 59:108-9 My '63
LORR, John
They made an animated film. Design 65:78-9 N '63
LORRAINE, Lilith
Who has lived with mountains; poem. Nat Parks Mag 37:9 Je '63
LORRAINE, Walter
Artist at work. Horn Bk 39:576-9 D '63
LORRINSON, Leverret
Washington front. America 111:227 S 5 '64
LORSCH, Jay W. and Lawrence, P. R.
Organizing for product innovation. Harvard Bsns R 43:109-18+ Ja '65
LORTON reformatory. See Reformatories
LORTZING, Albert
Tsar and carpenter (Zar und zimmerman)
Criticism
Opera N 27:33 Ap 6 '63
LOS, S. C. See McMillan, J. A. jt. auth.
LOS ALAMOS, N.Mex.
Los Alamos gets photographed. il Am City 78:81 F '63
New Mexico: growing up in atomland; Holm family. il Look 27:38+ O 8 '63
LOS ALAMOS scientific laboratory. See United States—Scientific laboratory, Los Alamos, N.Mex.
LOS ALERCES NATIONAL PARK. See National parks and reserves—Argentina
LOS ANGELES, Victoria de
Art of de Los Angeles; symposium. por Am Rec G 29:738-41 My '63
On records; Victoria de Los Angeles. C. J. Luten. Opera N 27:36 Mr 9 '63
LOS ANGELES
See also
La Brea

Air pollution

Auto-intoxication in Los Angeles. il Time 84:65 Jl 3 '64

LOS ANGELES—Air pollution—*Continued*
Control of air pollution. A. J Haagen-Smit. il Sci Am 210:24-31 bibliog(p 152) Ja '64
New hope for Californians. S. S. Griswold. il Sci Digest 53:8-11 My '63
Smog pinpointed by infrared device. Sci N L 85:136 F 29 '64

Airports

Los Angeles satellites offer convenience. R. H. Cook. il Aviation W 79:40-1 Jl 8 '63

Art

Art news from Los Angeles (cont) J. Langsner. il Art N 62:48 My; 47 Sum; 16-17 S '63; 50+ Ja '64
Los Angeles: the second city of art. H. Geldzahler. Vogue 144:42+ S 15 '64

Center for the performing arts

Brightness in the air; opening of Los Angeles Pavilion. il Time 84:46-58 D 18 '64
Buff's elegant pavilion opens in Los Angeles. il Life 57:40-40A D 18 '64
Los Angeles hoists flag of culture; opening of new Music center and art museum. il Bsns W p32-3 N 21 '64
Music for the angels; Los Angeles music pavilion opens. il Newsweek 64:82 D 14 '64

City planning

California: highest living, and a mess. il Arch Forum 119:7-8 O '63
Los Angeles R-3 ordinance. il Am City 78: 95 D '63

Description

Travel tips. P. P. Coleman. Sr Schol 83:11T N 15 '63

Docks

Unique terminal for ship travelers. il Arch Rec 134:163-8 S '63

Education

Elementary school industrial arts in Los Angeles. W. A. Wonacott and others. il NEA J 53:31-2 Ja '64
Science workshops. il Ebony 18:66-8+ Ag '63
Teacher learns by TV in L.A. E. Richardson. Sr Schol 85:17T Ja 21 '65

Finance

Low bid, generally not the best. W. L. Lintz. il Am City 79:115-16 Mr '64

Galleries and museums

Monday night on La Cienega. il Time 82:50 Jl 26 '63
Pleasant Sunday on Olive Hill. il Sunset 130:75-6 Mr '63
See also
Los Angeles County museum of history, science and art

Hospitals

New technology includes cobalt-60, and super-clean surgeries. il Arch Rec 133: 190-2 Mr '63

Hotels, restaurants, etc.

Eat and peek; noontime skin-show at the Phone booth on Sunset strip. il Newsweek 61:72 Mr 4 '63

Housing

Balconies organized as facade pattern. il Arch Rec 136:114-15 Ag '64
West Coast twin towers approach completion. Wilshire Comstock apartments. il Arch Rec 134:210-11 S '63

Industries

Selling a city to itself; Los Angeles' industrial fair and congress. il Bsns W p54-5 Mr 14 '64
Take a number; LA claims to be nation's second largest industrial center. Newsweek 64:92+ S 21 '64

Intellectual life

Los Angeles' cultural circus. R. Lynes. il Harper 228:28+ F '64

Libraries

See also
City of Commerce public library

Music

L.A. constellation. A. Goldberg. Opera N 28:30 O 19 '63
L.A.'s golden age. A. Goldberg. il Opera N 29:22-3 S 26 '64
Los Angeles launching. A. Goldberg. il Opera N 28:32-3 Mr 21 '64
[Musical events] (cont) il Mus Am 83:73 Ja; 20 Ap; 12 Jl; 32 S '63; 84:16 My; 20 Jl; 48-50 D '64

Newspapers

See also
Los Angeles herald-examiner

Parks and playgrounds

Is your playground surfacing safe? G. D. Butler. il Recreation 56:193-4 Ap '63
Los Angeles 60,000 years ago; tar pits in Hancock park. J. B. Kemmerer. il Sci Digest 54:48-51 S '63

Police

Ambassador of goodwill for police department. il Ebony 19:40-2+ Mr '64
Cops with guns. New Repub 150:5 Ap 4 '64
Police chief talks of police brutality; interview. W. H. Parker. il U S News 57: 33-6 Ag 10 '64

Politics and government

After Sam's scalp. Time 84:15 D 25 '64
Decentralized politics of Los Angeles. F. M. Carney. bibliog f Ann Am Acad 353:107-21 My '64
Go fight city hall. Newsweek 61:28+ F 25 '63
Trouble in happyland. J. Phelan. il Sat Eve Post 236:78-80+ My 25 '63

Recreation and parks, Department of

Blueprint for organization; Los Angeles Department of recreation and parks. W. Frederickson, Jr. il Recreation 57:410-14 O '64

Religious institutions and affairs

Exile from Los Angeles; Rev J. V. Coffield leaves Los Angeles for Chicago. Newsweek 65:57 Ja 11 '65
Priestly witness; protest against failure of the archdiocese to take leaderhip on civil rights issues. America 112:66 Ja 16 '65
Priest's protest; transfer of Rev J. Coffield from Los Angeles to Chicago. Time 85:36 Ja 8 '65

Social conditions

California plan; Integration preparation plan of Bay Gulph, suburb. V. B. Miller. Nat R 16:712 Ag 25 '64

Stores

Oriental theme for West Coast Japanese store; Seibu department store. il Arch Rec 133:180-2 Je '63

Theater

Professional theatre on campus. P. Greene. il Theatre Arts 47:62-3+ F '63
Science fiction theatre; plays by R. Bradbury. J. J. McLaughlin. Nation 200:92-4 Ja 25 '65
Taste for pandemonium; Pandemonium theater company. A. Knight. Sat R 47:31 D 5 '64

Water supply

Day the dam broke; Baldwin Hills reservoir. R. Leadabrand. il Am For 70:30-3+ F '64

LOS ANGELES Angels (baseball) See Baseball clubs
LOS ANGELES archdiocese. See Catholic church—Dioceses
LOS ANGELES Catholic interracial council. See Catholic interracial councils
LOS ANGELES COUNTY, Calif.
How Los Angeles eases racial tensions; Commission on human rights. P. Deutsch and R. M. Deutsch. Read Digest 85:86-90 O '64
See also
Water supply—Los Angeles County, Calif.
LOS ANGELES COUNTY museum of history, science and art
Museum's new exhibit features ancient gold. il(p257) Sci N L 85:262 Ap 25 '64
LOS ANGELES herald-examiner
Rewards and hazards of book reviewing. H. Lash. ALA Bul 57:860-1 O '63
LOS ANGELES international airport. See Los Angeles—Airports
LOS ANGELES music festival. See Music festivals—California
LOS ANGELES state and county arboretum
Los Angeles state and county arboretum at Arcadia. G. H. Spalding. il Horticulture 42:38-41 N '64
LOS ANGELES suicide prevention center. See Suicide prevention center, Los Angeles
LOS ANGELES times. See Times, Los Angeles
LOS ANGELES trade-technical college
Are we cheating twenty million students? G. B. Leonard. il Look 27:36-40+ Je 4 '63
Rewards and hazards of book reviewing. H. Lash. ALA Bul 57:860-1 O '63

LOSER; story. See Allen, E.

LOSEY, Joseph
Who is the master? il Newsweek 63:96 Mr 23 '64

LOSI, Paul Fortune, and Woods, J. G.
Concrete trees for the beach. Am City 78:92-4 O '63

LOSING of articles. See Lost articles

LOSINSKI, Julia M.
Something new under the sun. Sr Schol 85: 23T O 7 '64

LOSS of consciousness
Underwater blackout. il Sci Digest 56:81-2 Jl '64

LOSS of memory. See Amnesia

LOSS; story. See Sire, G. and Sire, J.

LOST articles
Keep or weep? David Morris of Ohio, finds $21,259. il Time 83:52+ Mr 13 '64

Anecdotes, facetiae, satire, etc.

Who ran off with my. . . .? E. H. Logsdon. il Farm J 88:66 O '64

LOST children. See Missing persons

LOST city of the Incas. See Machu Picchu, Peru

LOST time. See Absenteeism

LOST wax process
Lost wax sculpture for high schools. C. Heiple. il Sch Arts 63:36-7 Je '64
Workshop: casting in the ceramic shell. A. Saunders, jr. il Craft Horiz 23:50-1 Jl '63

LOTS, Building. See Building sites

LOTT, J. A. and DeMaggio, A. E.
Continuous extraction during treatment with ultrasound. bibliog Science 139:825-6 Mr 1 '63

LOTT, Leroy. See Be, A. W. H. jt. auth.

LOTTERIES
Battle lost; state-sponsored sweepstakes in New Hampshire; with editorial comment. D. Novotny. Christian Cent 80:668, 685 My 22 '63
Big draw in a little state; New Hampshire sweepstakes. R. Cantwell. il Sports Illus 21:20-1 Jl 27 '64
Bonanza machine; New Hampshire lottery. il Time 84:59 S 18 '64
Case for a national lottery. E. Silberling. il McCalls 90:68+ S '63
For the record? New Hampshire lottery results. Newsweek 63:34 My 11 '64
Gambling boxscore. Christian Cent 81:1517-18 D 9 '64
Gambling for the yankee dollar; New Hampshire state lottery. R. Cantwell. il Sports Illus 20:24-6+ Mr 30 '64
Green money state; New Hampshire. il Sports Illus 18:17 My 13 '63
Green state; New Hampshire lottery. il Newsweek 63:25 Mr 23 '64
How New Hampshire's lottery worked out. U S News 57:16 S 28 '64
Justice is popeyed in Nenana, Alaska. Sports Illus 18:9 Ap 29 '63
Legal lottery; New Hampshire. il Time 81:18 My 10 '63
Long odds and sure things on the California ballot; proposition to establish state lottery. J. Saltzman and B. Saltzman. Reporter 31: 28-30 N 5 '64
Lottery, the Puritan and the devil. J. Gould. il N Y Times Mag p 16+ My 19 '63
New Hampshire hits lottery skid row. Christian Cent 80:637 My 15 '63
New Hampshire House defeats tax dodge. Christian Cent 80:901 Jl 17 '63
New Hampshire sweeps. Newsweek 61:23 Ap 29 '63
New Hampshire's lottery. D. Novotny. Christian Cent 81:994 Ag 5 '64
New Hampshire's lottery: private vice and public virtue. D. F. Ford. il Reporter 30: 32-4 Ja 2 '64
Next: state-run sweepstakes: New Hampshire. il U S News 54:58 My 13 '63
Off and running in state lottery; New Hampshire sweepstakes. il Bsns W p34-5 S 12 '64
Off to the races; New Hampshire's twice-a-year sweepstakes. il Newsweek 61:38+ My 13 '63
$100,000 prize in sweepstakes; New Hampshire. U S News 56:99 Mr 16 '64
Pro & con: should we have state-run lotteries? Read Digest 83:102-7 Ag '63
Puritan sweepstake; New Hampshire sweepstake. D. F. Ford. New Repub 150:5-6 Ap 25 '64
Real-estate taxes, sales taxes and lotteries. Am City 78:7 Jl '63
State lotteries: useful money maker or ethical skid row? pro and con discussion. Sr Schol 83:24-5 S 13 '63
Sweeps vs. the law; New Hampshire sweepstakes. J. Iams. il Sat Eve Post 237:74+ S 12 '64
Who are the losers? California's proposed lottery. R. W. Moon. Christian Cent 81: 1104-5 S 9 '64
Why a state adopts a lottery; New Hampshire sweepstakes. il Bsns W p62-4 My 11 '63
Winners often lose. B. Surface. il N Y Times Mag p96-8+ Ap 19 '64
Without portfolio; question of national lotteries. C. B. Luce. McCalls 90:12 F '63

LOTTMAN, Herbert
Selling American literary works behind the iron curtain. Pub W 187:30-3 Ja 4 '65

LOTUS
Biochemical anomaly in flower extracts of interspecific hybrids between lotus species. P. M. Harney and W. F. Grant. bibliog il Science 142:1061 N 22 '63

LOUCH, A. R.
Idols of the lab. Commentary 38:73-4 Ag '64

LOUCHHEIM, Katie (Scofield)
Citizen and foreign policy; address, September 30, 1963. Dept State Bul 49:681-4 O 28 '63
Citizen in a changing world; address, October 12, 1963. Dept State Bul 49:704-8 N 4 '63; Same. Vital Speeches 30:93-6 N 15 '63
Contribution of women in a changing world; address, April 20, 1963. Dept State Bul 48: 801-5 My 20 '63
Foreign policy and the individual: identity in diversity; address, March 12, 1964. Dept State Bul 50:591-4 Ap 13 '64
Her interest is people. Ladies Home J 81: 56-7+ Mr '64
Role of individual women in the world community; address, June 29, 1963. Dept State Bul 49:98-9 Jl 15 '63
Total cure; poem. Ladies Home J 81:93 O '64
Transient view; poem. Harper 228:82 Ja '64
Women in the service of community and nation; address, February 3, 1964. Dept State Bul 50:347-9 Mr 2 '64

about

Mrs Louchheim keynote speaker at women's organizations seminar. Dept State Bul 48: 716-17 My 6 '63

LOUD speaking apparatus
Column loudspeaker systems. G. L. Augspurger. il Electr World 69:25-7+ Je '63
Constant-voltage sound-distribution systems. A. B. Cohen. il Electr World 70:29-32 Jl '63
Electronic sirens; mobile p.a. and siren systems on public-safety vehicles. J Kyle. il Electr World 71:32-3 Ap '64
Foolproof speaker kit. il Pop Electr 18:52 Mr '63
Hi-fi loudspeaker cones. C. L. McShane. il Electr World 69:38-40+ F '63
Hi-fi speaker system for $7.61. F. H. Frantz, sr. il Pop Electr 20:61-3 Mr '64
High fidelity. H. Fantel. Opera N 28:33 Mr 28 '64
Integrated amplifier-speaker. K. Gilmore. il Electr World 71:32-5+ Mr '64
Kits for home assembly. L. Marcus. il Hi Fi 13:44-7+ Je '63
Loudspeaker code practice. F. A. Parker. il Pop Electr 20:42 My '64
Loudspeakers for transistor amplifiers. V. Brociner. il Electr World 71:42-4+ Ja '64
Loudspeakers: the ideal and the possible. Hi Fi 13:27 Je '63
Rear-deck auto speakers. il Consumer Rep 29:16-17 Ja '64
Silencing your stereo system. P. Geraci. il Pop Sci 184:100-3 Je '64
Sound advice; external speakers with tape recorders. H. A. Manoogian. Mod Phot 28: 54+ My '64
Sound ideas; electrostatic loudspeaker system. L. Zide. il Am Rec G 30:1059-60 Jl '64
Speaker nobody sees. il House & Gard 125: 166-7 My '64
Speakers: past, present, and future. N. Eisenberg. il Hi Fi 13:37-40+ Je '63
This homemade, battery-powered loud hailer talks big. R. Benrey. il Pop Sci 184:134-8 Ap '64
Twosome; miniature speaker system for pocket transistor radio. L. A. Wortman. il Pop Electr 18:57 F '63
What to listen for, and why. A. Sterling. il Hi Fi 13:41-3+ Je '63
What you should know about buying a loudspeaker system. R. Freas. Am Home 67:18 Ja '64

LOUD speaking apparatus—*Continued*

Cabinets

And don't forget the shoe polish. D. B. Weems. il Pop Electr 18:53-6+ Mr '63
Another ceramic tile enclosure. D. Weems. il Pop Electr 18:51-5+ Ap '63
Anything but a box; variety of speaker systems. il Hi Fi 14:60-2 D '64
Build the Reflectoflex speaker enclosure. J. D. Reid. il Pop Electr 19:47-50 D '63
For better sound, build the bi-coupler. D. B. Weems. il Pop Electr 21:64-7+ N '64
Six speakers for higher fi. E. Wayland. il Pop Mech 121:192-4 Mr '64
Slim silhouette speaker systems. H. H. Fantel. il Pop Electr 19:41-6 Jl '63
Slim twosome. H. Hufnagel. il Pop Electr 21:63-4 D '64
Thin loudspeaker systems. G. L. Augspurger. il Electr World 70:30-2 S '63

Testing

High fidelity measurements, science or chaos? E. Villchur. il Electr World 72:33-5+ Ag '64

LOUDON, Dorothy
Lowdown on Loudon; Garry Moore show. G. Millstein. por Sat Eve Post 236:70+ Ap 6 '63

LOUDON, J. H.
International enterprise; address, July 3, 1963. Vital Speeches 29:677-9 S 1 '63

LOUDON, John Claudius
De Tocqueville of the trees. H. W. Dengler. il Am For 69:8-9+ Ag '63

LOUGÉE, David
Lines from the end of a play; Old man in a wheelchair; Childhood; poems. Poetry 102:239-40 Jl '63

LOUGEE, Laura Barr
Amateur scientist. Sci Am 208:159-60+ F '63

LOUIS, Father M. See Merton, T.

LOUIS, Sister Mary. See Mary Louis, Sister

LOUIS, E. G.
Handy EP pack. Pop Electr 19:64 N '63
New nomenclature. Pop Electr 19:71 S '63

LOUIS, Jennifer. See Louis, V. jt. auth.

LOUIS, Morris
Art; exhibition at Guggenheim museum. M. Kozloff. Nation 197:247-8 O 19 '63
Morris Louis: triumph of color. D. Robbins. por Art N 62:28-9+ O '63
Peacock duo. il Time 85:44-5 Ja 8 '65

LOUIS, Murray
Murray Louis dance company at Henry street playhouse. M. Marks. Dance Mag 38:23-5 Ja '64
Who knows how I appear? D. Hering. il pors Dance Mag 37:46-7 N '63

LOUIS, Victor, and Louis, Jennifer
Travel in the Soviet Union. Holiday 34:143-8 O '63

LOUIS H. Silver collection. See Newberry library, Chicago

LOUISIANA
Ancient America's geometers; Poverty Point earthworks. J. Lear. il Sat R 47:53-6 O 3 '64; Discussion. 47:71-2 N 7; 86 D 5 '64
See also
Courts—Louisiana
Festivals—Louisiana
Fishing—Louisiana
Gardens—Louisiana
Hunting—Louisiana
Libraries—Louisiana
Pontchartrain, Lake
Prisons—Louisiana

Description and travel

Leisurely journey through Bayou country. R. Arnold. il U S Camera 26:14+ S '63

Historic houses, etc.

Rosedown; the house that time remembered. il House & Gard 125:98-107+ Ja '64

History

Melting pot in the Bayous; southern Louisiana; with drawings by A. R. Waud. O. Evans. il Am Heritage 15:30-51+ D '63

Politics and government

All the king's men: the matrix of experience. R. P. Warren. Yale R 53:161-7 D '63
At stake in runoff; ten electoral votes for '64? U S News 55:8 D 23 '63
Case of the crusading DA. Newsweek 61:26 F 18 '63
Contest in Louisiana; Catholic candidate for governor. America 109:784 D 21 '63
Louisiana: clues to '64 vote. il U S News 56:64 Ja 27 '64
Louisiana's wonderful invention. E. Kerr. Harper 227:94-6 O '63
Solider South. Newsweek 62:18 D 23 '63
Trend in Louisiana. R. Moley. Newsweek 63:80 Mr 30 '64
Up from the swamp. il Newsweek 63:34 Mr 16 '64
Upset, true to form. il Newsweek 63:28 Ja 27 '64
Vice man cometh. J. Phelan. il Sat Eve Post 236:67-71 Je 8 '63

Race problems

Birth of a voter; Louisiana parish registers first Negro in sixty-one years. B. Adelman. il Ebony 19:88-90+ F '64
Civil liberties are indivisible; Louisiana joint legislative committee on un-American activities. Nation 197:289-90 N 9 '63

Social conditions

Observe, judge, act. America 109:619 N 16 '63

LOUISIANA state museum, New Orleans
Louisiana state museum. Hobbies 68:52 N '63

LOUISVILLE

Music

[Musical events] Mus Am 84:21-2 Jl '64

Negroes

Hunger sit-in. W. Peeples. New Repub 150:9-10 Ap 25 '64
Louisville, Ky: city that integrated without strife. C. Morrison. il Look 27:41-4 Ag 13 '63
Southern city with northern problems. H. S. Thompson. il Reporter 29:26-9 D 19 '63

LOUISVILLE free public library
Recorded reviews. J. E. Frey. il Wilson Lib Bul 39:333-4 D '64

LOUKOPOULOS, Dimitris. See Fessas, P. jt. auth.

LOUNGING wear. See Clothing and dress

LOURANT, Arthur
Yank movie man of Japan. il pors Ebony 18:45-6+ Jl '63

LOURDES, France
Miracle of Lourdes. S. O'Faolain. Holiday 36:66-7+ N '64

LOUTFI, Omar
Obituary
U N Rev por 10:45+ Je '63

LOUVESTRE, Mary
Woman who saved the Union navy. G. A. Foster. il pors Ebony 19:48-50+ Jl '64

LOUVRE, Paris
Great Luristan mystery; Louvre exhibition. P. Amiet. il Art N 62:24-6+ Ap '63
Louvre: halls of greatness. J. Wechsberg. il Holiday 35:70-7+ Ja '64

LOVATELLI, Lorian Gaetani, countess
Countess Lorian Gaetani Lovatelli with her six young children. il por Vogue 143:162 Mr 1 '64

LOVE, Adelaide
Barnyard miracle; poem. Christian Cent 80:775 Je 12 '63
Night of moon and clouds; poem. Christian Cent 80:393 Mr 27 '63

LOVE, Edmund G.
Waiter! por Sat Eve Post 237:42+ My 23 '64
about
WLB biography. R. S. Montgomery. por Wilson Lib Bul 39:186+ O '64

LOVE, Edwin M.
Smart trim tricks for home remodeling jobs. Pop Sci 186:148-9 Ja '65

LOVE, George Hutchinson
Some benefits of looking backward; address, November 18, 1964. Vital Speeches 31:183-5 Ja 1 '65
about
Coal, cars & Love. por Time 82:78+ Jl 5 '63
SR's businessman of the year. W. D. Patterson. por Sat R 47:45-6+ Ja 11 '64

LOVE, Jean
Joy of a pinata. Design 66:14-15 N '64

LOVE, John A.
Why local government serves best; interview. pors Nations Bsns 51:38-9+ S '63

LOVE, Juanita Elaine
Artist. il pors Ebony 18:115-16+ Mr '63

LOVE, Julian Price
Beyond the ordinary. Christian Cent 80:1274-5 O 16 '63
Trenchant treatment. Christian Cent 80:494 Ap 17 '63

LOVE, Spencer
What happened at Burlington when the king dropped dead. S. Freedgood. il Fortune 69: 104-11+ Je '64

LOVE
All about love. J. Huxley. Read Digest 85: 127-9 Jl '64
Awesome power of human love; excerpt from The humanization of man. A. Montagu. Read Digest 82:80-3 F '63
Beginning of love. M. B. Hoover. il Redbook 120:15 Ap '63
By love depressed; D. de Rougemont's investigation of the western myths of love. T. Roszak. Nation 200:33-4 Ja 11 '65
Children and love. L. Miller. il Redbook 123: 58-9+ S '64
Cupid on the couch. M. Scarbrough. Seventeen 22:156 F '63
First love, first agonized encounter. P. Mortimer. Vogue 143:173-4+ Ap 1 '64
How men fall in love. D. Newman and R. Benton. Mlle 59:12+ Je '64
Listen, my heart; condensation of Make a joyful sound. H. E. Waite. il Read Digest 82:297-308+ Ap '63
Love and how it gets that way. H. Miller. Mlle 58:49-51+ Ja '64
Love is possible. M. Lerner. Mlle 56:83-4+ F '63
Love without fear, by R. C. Buckle. Review
Nat R 16:320 Ap 21 '64. R. Kirk
Marriage is neither Heaven nor hell but what is it? F. J. Sheen. Todays Health 42: 60-1+ Ap '64
Of love and the like, teen-age division. M. Weston. il N Y Times Mag p 109-10+ O 11 '64
Other side of the valentine. Esquire 59:83 F '63
Our ability to love. A. Fromme. Redbook 121:44-5+ Ag '63
Psychology of loving, by I. Lepp. Review
Commonweal 79:489-90 Ja 24 '64. R. T. Francoeur
Speaking out; erotism, sex and love. J. B. Priestley. Sat Eve Post 236:10+ Ap 27 '63
What men have done for love. J. T. Freeman. il Ladies Home J 80:88-9+ Ja '63
You've got to listen. M. Shearer. Read Digest 85:237-8 O '64
See also
Courtship

LOVE (charity) See Charity

LOVE (theology)
Power of love. R. O. Johann. il America 110: 822 Je 13 '64

LOVE, Maternal
Awesome power of human love; excerpt from The humanization of man. A. Montagu. Read Digest 82:80-3 F '63
Depth perception in sheep: effects of interrupting the mother-neonate bond. W. B. Lemmon and G. H. Patterson. bibliog il Science 145:835-6 Ag 21 '64; Reply with rejoinder. E. Klinghammer. 146:1189 N 27 '64
Lady who likes kids. J. Coogan. Ladies Home J 80:54 Je '63
What babies need most. A. Montagu. il Parents Mag 39:38-9+ My '64

LOVE affair; story. See Rackowe, A.

LOVE and Gabriella Smith; story. See Grant, B.

LOVE in literature
Books; more love in the western world. J. Updike. New Yorker 39:90-4+ Ag 24 '63
Golden casket: Chinese novellas of two millennia, tr. by C. Levenson from W. Bauer's and H. Franke's German versions of the original Chinese. Review
Sat R 47:63 D 5 '64. C. T. Hsia
Love stories: bibliography for young adults. B. Rubenstein. Library J 88:837-9 F 15 '63

LOVE is never forgotten; story. See Cave, H.

LOVE letters
Love letters; excerpts from letters of famous men and women; comp. by H. Koningsberger. Ladies Home J 80:44+ Ja '63

LOVE nest; drama. See Wahburn, D.

LOVE of three kings; opera. See Montemezzi, I.

LOVE story; story. See Rodgers, M. A.

LOVED look; story. See Holland, B.

LOVEDAY, Lilian Foerster
Unreluctant composers. Opera N 28:8-11 Ja 25 '64
(ed) See Melchior, L. Melchior today
(ed) See Solti, G. Special sound

LOVEJOY, Clarence Earle
Half-million mark; Lovejoy's college guide. il por Newsweek 62:82 D 16 '63

LOVEJOY, Elijah
Lovejoy, martyr to freedom, by P. Simon. Review
Christian Cent 81:1623 D 30 '64. R. Root

LOVELAND, D. H. See Herrnstein, R. J. jt. auth.

LOVELESS, B. G.
Ohio's Mound circuit. Travel 122:38-40 S '64

LOVELIEST thing of all; story. See Moravia, A.

LOVELL, Sir Bernard
British brain explains the brain drain. N Y Times Mag p 13+ Mr 22 '64
Erudite shepherdess of home-made moons. Sat R 46:44-6 S 7 '63
Greatest challenge to man. N Y Times Mag p 12-13+ Ap 21 '63
Is U.S. running alone in the race to the moon? interview; ed. by J. Fromm. por U S News 55:70-1 Ag 12 '63
Radio-emitting flare stars; with biographical sketch. Sci Am 211:10, 13-19 bibliog(p 116) Ag '64
Soviet aims in astronomy and space research; reprint. Bul Atomic Sci 19:36-9 O '63
Speaking out. por Sat Eve Post 237:10+ F 22 '64
When six million suns explode. N Y Times Mag p 16+ Ja 5 '64
about
Facts about the 1962 space bomb. J. Lear. il Sat R 46:46-8 Ap 6 '63
Jodrell bank observatory. V. K. McElheny. il Science 144:520-3 My 1 '64
Push to the moon: a one-horse race? il por Bsns W p48 Jl 27 '63

LOVELL, James, jr
Moon looks smooth from here. Life 55:86A S 27 '63

LOVELL, Stanley P.
Deadly gadgets of the OSS; condensation of Of spies & stratagems. Pop Sci 183:56-9+ Jl '63

LOVELL, Tom
Tom Lovell paints a Continental soldier of 1781. il Am Artist 27:24-7 Mr '63

LOVELOCK cave, Nevada. See Caves

LOVELORN columns. See Newspapers—Advice columns

LOVELY, Walter G.
Farm chemical application. Suc Farm 61:52-3 My '63
10½ per cent-moisture corn for 51c per bushel. Suc Farm 61:24 D '63

LOVELY to look at, delightful to hold; story. See O'Brien, E.

LOVEMAN, Amy, national award. See Amy Loveman national award

LOVER; drama. See Pinter, H.

LOVERING, J. F. See Morgan, J. W. jt. auth.

LOVERS; story. See O'Brien, E.

LOVERS anonymous; story. See Vonnegut, K. jr

LOVE'S in fashion; drama. See Murray, J.

LOVE'S season; story. See Stolz, M.

LOVESEY, John
Better than fancy pants. Sports Illus 19:12-15 Jl 15 '63
Boxing (cont) Sports Illus 20:44-6 Ja 20 '64
Man who jumps with the devil Sports Illus 20:42-5 Ja 27 '64
Motor sports (cont) Sports Illus 21:70-1 Ag 17 '64
Outcasts are counted in. Sports Illus 21:22+ Jl 13 '64
Tennis (cont) Sports Illus 18:54+ Je 17 '63

LOVEWELL, Paul J.
Coming; faster business growth. por Nations Bsns 51:31-3+ My '63

LOVI, George
Star charts of former days. Sky & Tel 27: 222-5 Ap '64

LOVING offenders; story. See Jackson, C.

LOVOOS, Janice
Architectural paintings of John Lentine. Am Artist 27:18-23 N '63
Bernard Garbutt, animal draughtsman. Am Artist 27:53-7+ F '63
F. Carlton Ball, a California potter. Am Artist 28:50-5+ Je '64
Four ceramists of Hawaii. Am Artist 27: 66-73+ Je '63
Kalman Aron, draughtsman. Am Artist 28: 30-5+ Mr '64
Paintings of Richard Haines. Am Artist 27: 50-7+ Ap '63
Portrait sculpture of Joseph Portanova. Am Artist 29:38-43+ Ja '65
Richard Whorf; painter of Americana. Am Artist 28:32-7+ Ap '64

LOVOOS, Janice—*Continued*
Sculpture of Robert Ortlieb. Am Artist 27:56-61+ S '63
Ted Gilien; a vigorous painter. Am Artist 27:24-9 D '63
LOVREKOVICH, L. and others
Toxic effect of pseudomonas tabaci on RNA metabolism in tobacco and its counteraction by kinetin. bibliog Science 145:165 Jl 10 '64
LOW, Sir David
David Low album selected by Low. il por N Y Times Mag p24-5 S 29 '63
about
David Low: 1891-1963. il Nation 197:224 O 12 '63
Low. il Newsweek 62:52 S 30 '63
Obituary
Time por 82:40+ S 27 '63
LOW, George
High kind of Low Life. D. Jenkins. il pors Sports Illus 21:56-60+ Jl 6 '64
LOW, Robert A.
No place like home in the city. Sat R 47:37-8 S 12 '64
Time of tin boxes. Sat R 46:43 Mr 30 '63
LOW altitude supersonic vehicle. See Guided missiles
LOW-calorie soft drinks. See Beverages
LOW fat diet. See Diet in disease
LOW-sodium diet. See Diet in disease
LOW temperature cameras. See Cameras
LOW temperature research
Boeing steps up efforts in cryogenics research. R. Twiss. Miss & Roc 16:36-7 Ja 11 '65
Cryogenics, electronics' frigid frontier. J. Joseph. il Pop Electr 21:41-4+ D '64
Hypnotism stops shivers in 40° temperature. Sci N L 86:72 Ag 1 '64
Interest gets hotter in cold, cold science: cryogenic research. Bsns W p78+ Mr 21 '64
Two new labs to sharpen Aerojet's solid, liquid capabilities. W. E. Wilks. il Miss & Roc 14:18+ Mr 23 '64
See also
Thermomagnetism
LOW temperatures
Cryogenic system using RL10 considered for Apollo backup. Aviation W 80:36 Ja 20 '64
Deep-freezing our heritage; excerpt from Cryogenic technology, ed. by R. W. Vance. A. P. Rinfret. Sat R 46:62-3 O 5 '63
Emphasis on space cryogenics advances at Linde. J. F. Judge. il Miss & Roc 13:22-4 S 23 '63
Lactate dehydrogenase isozymes: lability at low temperature. H. A. Zondag. bibliog il Science 142:965-7 N 15 '63
Soviets use charcoal to maintain low temperatures; cryogenics. Sci Digest 53:44 Ap '63
See also
Cold
Helium, Liquid
LOWDEN, Merle S.
Fire crisis in Brazil. Am For 71:42-4+ Ja '65
LOWDER, Virgil E.
Clarification at College Park. Christian Cent 81:500-2 Ap 15 '64
LOWDER, Wayne M. See Adams, J. A. S. jt. auth.
LOWE, Ann
Ann Lowe: society's best-kept secret. T. B. Congdon, jr. il por Sat Eve Post 237:74-6 D 12 '64
LOWE, David
Little more time for violence. Atlan 212:70-2 Jl '63
LOWE, Robert
Dual-purpose range. Recreation 57:359 S '64
LOWE, Violet Richardson
Dynamics of form. Writer 77:16-19+ Mr '64
LOWELL, James Russell
Books from James R. Lowell's library. P. W. Schmidtchen. il pors Hobbies 68:106-7 N '63
LOWELL, Ralph
After new high: in for trouble; interview. por U S News 54:40-1 Ap 22 '63
LOWELL, Robert, 1917-
Four Spanish sonnets: His house; Rome; Time; Roman sonnet. Poetry 103:74-7 O '63
(tr) See Akhmatova, A. Poems
(tr) See Mandel'shtam, O. E. Moscow; Century of the wolf; Leningrad; Fragments; Verses to the unknown soldier
about
In bounds. por Newsweek 64:120+ O 12 '64
New Robert Lowell. J. Wain. New Repub 151:21-3 O 17 '64
Old Glory; dramatization of stories by N. Hawthorne and H. Melville. Criticism
Cath World il 200:323-4 F '65
Nation 199:390-1 N 23 '64
New Repub 151:28+ N 21 '64
New Yorker 40:143-4 N 14 '64
Newsweek il 64:92 N 16 '64
Vogue 145:68 Ja 1 '65
Poet of the particular. J. Jacobsen. Commonweal 81:349-52 D 4 '64
Poetry of Robert Lowell. N. Braybrooke. Cath World 198:230-7 Ja '64
Robert Lowell's memento mori. G. Weales. Reporter 32:56-7 Ja 28 '65
Voice of a survivor. R. Howard. Nation 199:278-80 O 26 '64
LOWELL, Mass.
Water supply
Back to the river after seventy years. E. J. Tierney and B. Cassidy. il Am City 78:74-6 Ag '63
LOWENFELD, Andreas F.
EEC: a federation in the making; address, August 12, 1963. Dept State Bul 49:372-7 S 2 '63
LOWENFELS, Walter
Epitaph for my ego; poem. Sat R 47:24 D 26 '64
Epitaph for somebody's typewriter; poem. Sat R 47:33 Jl 4 '64
(ed) See Eisler, H. Eisler on Schoenberg
LOWENSTEIN, J. M. See Kornacker, M. S. jt. auth.
LOWENSTEIN, Leah M. and Stern, Arnold
Serum factor in renal compensatory hyperplasia. bibliog Science 142:1479-80 D 13 '63
LOWENSTEIN, Louis. See Bain, B. jt. auth.
LOWENTHAL, Abraham F.
Limits of American power; the lesson of the Dominican Republic. Harper 228:87-9+ Je '64
LOWENTHAL, Jerome
Fun and merry talks along the Mitsubishi concert circuit. Mus Am 84:60-1 O '64
Musical events: New York début. W. Sargeant. New Yorker 39:199 N 30 '63
LOWENTHAL, Richard
Communists of the world, unite? N Y Times Mag p24+ O 25 '64
Factors of unity and factors of conflict. bibliog f Ann Am Acad 349:106-16 S '63
LOWER CALIFORNIA. See California, Lower
LOWER depths: drama. See Gorky, M.
LOWER East side. See New York (city)—Description
LOWEY, Susan
Myosin substructure: isolation of a helical subunit from heavy meromyosin. bibliog Science 145:597-9 Ag 7 '64
LOWI, Theodore
How the farmers get what they want. Reporter 30:34-7 My 21 '64
LOWRIE, Donald A.
Atheism's resort to mendacity. Christian Cent 80:1513-16 D 4 '63
Children's crusade in reverse. Christian Cent 81:1141-3 S 16 '64
Every child an atheist. Christian Cent 80:776-7 Je 12 '63
Soviet atheist's Sputnik. Christian Cent 80:177-9 F 6 '63
LOWRIE, Jean
(ed) Creative elementary school library. See issues of Wilson library bulletin to June 1963
(ed) Providing school library services for the culturally disadvantaged. bibliog por ALA Bul 58:523-6, 643-7, 705-11, 816-21, 1003-6; 59:49-53 Je-O, D '64-Ja '65
LOWRY, Don
All-winter wet storage. Yachting 114:68+ N '63
LOWRY, Elizabeth Cannon
Getting the right book to the right child at the right time. bibliog Pub W 185:91-3 F 3 '64
LOWRY, W. McNeil
Foundation and the arts; address, November 11, 1963. Mus Am 83:156-7 D '63
LOYALTY, Oaths of
Allegiance cannot be coerced. Christian Cent 81:39 Ja 8 '64
Authors league condemns loyalty oaths. Pub W 186:31 O 12 '64
Flag waving; Pledge of allegiance controversy. il Newsweek 64:90 D 7 '64
Librarian fights dismissal in Buffalo court case; loyalty oath issue at State university of New York in Buffalo. Library J 89:1050 Mr 1 '64

LOYALTY, Oaths of—*Continued*
Loyalty oath: 1964-65. T. Kaser. Sat R 47: 60+ N 21 '64; Discussion. 47:44 D 19 '64; 48:46 Ja 16 '65
Me and the Texas loyalty oath. B. Appel. Pub W 186:28-30 S 7 '64

LOYALTY investigations
Snoops; private lives and public service. J. Ridgeway. New Repub 151:13-17 D 19 '64
Why invade privacy? security interviews. Christian Cent 81:1579 D 23 '64

LOYOLA seminary, Shrub Oak, N.Y. See Theological schools

LOYOLA university, New Orleans

Inter-American center

See Institute of human relations

LOZANO, Rafael Delgado
Bullfighting. Sports Illus 18:68+ Ap 15 '63
—See Griggs, L. jt. auth.

LOZIER, Herbert
Ninety firsts in American automotive history. Pop Sci 184:80-3 Mr '64

LUARD, Evan
Growth of the world community. Ann Am Acad 351:170-9 Ja '64

LUBAR, Robert
Japanese giant that wouldn't stay dead. Fortune 70:141-9+ N '64
Old Europe's young again and fretting. Fortune 67:86-91+ F '63
Trading with the devil with a shorter spoon. Fortune 69:108-12+ Ap '64
—See Heilperin, M. A. jt. auth.

LUBELL, Samuel
Changing U.S. electorate. por Fortune 70: 132-5+ Jl '64
Negro & the Democratic coalition; excerpts from White and black: test of a nation. Commentary 38:19-27 Ag '64

LUBETZKY, Seymour
Catalog code revision, 1964; address, June 2, 1964. bibliog por Library J 89:4863-5+ D 15 '64
Quest for catalogers: today and tomorrow; address, April 18, 1963. bibliog por Library J 88:3535-8 O 1 '63

LUBIN, Charles W.
How to bake a cake by automation; Kitchens of Sara Lee. il pors Duns R 82:51 D '63
Programming a cake. il pors Bsns W p 154-6+ Mr 14 '64
Saga of Sara Lee. il por Newsweek 64:71 S 14 '64

LUBIN, M. See Ennis, H. L. jt. auth.

LUBIN, Maurice A.
Five Haitian poets. Américas 17:16-21 Ja '65

LUBOLD, Joyce
Let's stamp out sex. Read Digest 83:73-5 O '63

LUBOVE, Roy
New deal and national health. bibliog f Cur Hist 45:77-86+ Ag '63

LUBRICANTS. See Lubrication and lubricants

LUBRICATION and lubricants
Giving your house a lube job. Sunset 132: 120-1 Mr '64
Motor oils; labels and claims in a state of utter confusion. il Consumer Bul 47:34-6 F '64
Those slick work-smoothing lubricants. P. McCafferty. il Pop Sci 185:164-7 N '64
See also
Airplanes—Lubrication
Automobiles—Lubrication
Bearings (machinery)
Gas and oil engines—Lubrication
Jet airplane engines—Lubrication

Additives

Be leery of those additives & gimmicks for cars. il Changing T 17:15-18 F '63; Same abr. with title Beware of quack tonics for automobiles. Read Digest 82:272-4 Je '63

LUC Gabrielle, Sister
Nun's story. il por Time 82:72 N 15 '63
Singing sister. il por Newsweek 62:51 D 23 '63

LUCAS, Alan Keith-. See Keith-Lucas, A.

LUCAS, F. L.
Across eternal Egypt. Holiday 35:66-75+ Je '64
Lonely beauty of Iceland. Holiday 34:56-61+ S '63

LUCAS, H. F. jr, and others
Radium-226, radium-228, lead-210, and fluorine in persons with osteogenic sarcoma. bibliog Science 144:1573-5 Je 26 '64

LUCAS, Harley E.
Police reserve lends valuable aid. Am City 78:20 F '63

LUCAS, Jerry
Year of the knees in the NBA. W. Leggett. Sports Illus 19:84-5 N 25 '63

LUCAS, Jim G.
(ed) See MacArthur, D. Interview with MacArthur: the storm it provoked

LUCAS, Kay
Dead men's chests. Travel 121:54-5 F '64

LUCAS, Mildred Kay
Among those present. PTA Mag 57:17 F '63

LUCAS and Jake; story. See Boles, P. D.

LUCE, Clare (Boothe)
All for the love of a lady. McCalls 91:93+ O; 20+ N '63
But some people simply never get the message. Life 54:31-3 Je 28 '63
Crisis in Soviet-Chinese relations; address, June 14, 1964. Vital Speeches 30:591-4 Jl 15 '64
Cuba crisis and nuclear arms; why de Gaulle goes his own way; reprint. por U S News 54:64-5 F 18 '63
Extremism in defense of the Democratic party. Nat R 16:719-21 Ag 25 '64
Lady is for burning: the seven deadly sins of Madame Nhu. Nat R 15:395-9 N 5 '63
Lady who wants to be president. Sat R 47: 42-3 Ap 18 '64
Seventeen year trend to Castro; address, January 22, 1963. Vital Speeches 29:295-9 Mr 1 '63
Tears for the grand old party. Nat R 16:529-30+ Je 30 '64
Unbeatable program for a fiery moderate; excerpts from interview. por U S News 56:20 F 17 '64
What really killed Marilyn. Life 57:68-72+ Ag 7 '64; Same abr. Read Digest 85:218-20+ N '64
Without portfolio. See issues of McCall's

about

Luce vs. Keating? New York race shapes up. por U S News 57:14 Ag 17 '64
Perfect platform. Time 83:15 F 14 '64
To a gallant lady. Nat R 16:760 S 8 '64

LUCE, Henry Robinson
Great thinker's joyful vision: the spiritual perfection of mankind. Life 57:12 O 16 '64
Letter to the publisher. Sports Illus 21:4 Ag 17 '64

about

First tycoon. J. Kobler. il pors Sat Eve Post 238:28-32+ Ja 16 '65
Henry R. Luce and the dialogue. G. P. Hunt. por Life 56:3 My 1 '64
Succession. por Newsweek 63:76 Ap 27 '64
Time of Henry Luce's Life. Christian Cent 80:695 My 22 '63

LUCE, Lawrence W.
Three-dimensions on the double. Pop Mech 119:114-15+ F '63

LUCE, Willard
Arches and bridges of stone. Natur Hist 73: 42-7 Ag '64

LUCERNE festival. See Music festivals—Switzerland

LUCERNE festival strings. See String ensembles

LUCEY, Cornelius, bp
Bishop denounces council experts. Christian Cent 81:724 Je 3 '64

LUCEY, Jerold F. and Behrman, R. E.
Thalidomide: effect upon pregnancy in the rhesus monkey. bibliog Science 139:1295-6 Mr 29 '63

LUCHS, Fred E.
Batch of biographies. Christian Cent 80:1549-50 D 11 '63

LUCIA, Fernando de
Fernando de Lucia. A. Favia-Artsay. il por Hobbies 69:30-1 N '64

LUCIA, Frank J.
Golden yellow for safety. Am City 78:27 Mr '63
If it works in New York city. Am City 78: 96-8 D '63; 79:100-2 Ja '64

LUCIA di Lammermoor; opera. See Donizetti, G.

LUCIADAGEN. See Christmas—Sweden

LUCIAN
Conversation at the Styx; tr. by D. Fitts. Atlan 212:70-2 D '63

LUCID eye in silver town; story. See Updike, J.

LUCIE-SMITH, Edward
Ingres's La source; poem. New Yorker 40:46 Mr 14 '64
Poets old and young. C. Kizer. Poetry 102: 394-5 S '63

LUCIENTES, Francisco José de Goya y. See Goya y Lucientes, F. J. de

LUCIFERIN
Daily rhythm of luciferin activity on gonyaulax polyedra. V. C. Bode and others. bibliog il Science 141:913-15 S 6 '63
LUCIOLI, Clara E. and Fleak, D. H.
Shut-in; waiting for what? pors ALA Bul 58: 781-4 O '64
LUCIONI, Luigi
Il Divo. il Opera N 28:23-5 O 19 '63
LUCK
Best of luck. W. Golding. il Holiday 35:12+ My '64
I can't get away with anything. C. Ford. Read Digest 85:17+ D '64
See also
Superstition
LUCKENS, Mark M. and Davis, W. H.
Bats: sensitivity to DDT. bibliog Science 146:948 N 13 '64
LUCKETT, Hubert. See Gilmore, C. P. jt. auth.
LUCKMAN, Charles
California's new state colleges. Arch Rec 136:200 N '64
From the academy. R. Kirk. Nat R 16:650 Jl 28 '64
Raising a new Garden. il Bsns W p 142 F 23 '63
LUCKS, Roy G.
New geography of trade. Sat R 47:42+ Ja 11 '64
LUCKY one; story. See Turovlin, L.
LUCRETIUS Carus, Titus
Lucretius. G. Highet. il Horizon 6:28-32 Spr '64
LUCY, Geoffrey
Wild youth: a worldwide program. Read Digest 85:167-9+ O '64
LUCY, Sean
Lost tribe; poem. Atlan 214:57 S '64
LUDERS, A. E. jr
Other man's boat. Yachting 113:64-5+ Je '63
LUDERS, Bill
Bill Luders has them crying: beat the bird! H. Whall. il por Sports Illus 21:50+ Jl 27 '64
Yachting interviews: Bill Luders. R. W. Carrick. il por Yachting 116:61+ Ag '64
LUDLOW, Howard T.
Big mediator is watching you. America 110: 789-90 Je 6 '64
LUDLUM, David B. and others
Alkylation of synthetic polynucleotides. bibliog Science 145:397-9 Jl 24 '64
LUDWIG, Allan
Stone carving in New England graveyards. Antiques 86:87-91 Jl '64
LUDWIG, Daniel Keith
Shipping king comes ashore. il por Bsns W p88-92+ N 23 '63
This man Ludwig. por Time 82:60+ Ag 2 '63
LUDWIG, Jack
European touch: Winnipeg. Holiday 35:84-5+ Ap '64
New York press: the hard sell. Holiday 36: 104+ Jl '64
LUECK, Roger H.
Scientific advisers for Congress; letter. Science 143:525 F 7 '64
LUECKE, Richard
Platform existentialism. Christian Cent 82:111 Ja 27 '65
LUEKING, F. Dean
Nostalgia is betrayal. Christian Cent 81:461-2 Ap 8 '64
Religion in Africa. Christian Cent 80:648-9 My 15 '63
LUEPSEN, Focko
European reaction to the Vatican council. Christian Cent 80:209 F 13 '63
LUFFA cylindrica. See Gourds
LUFT, Joseph
Teacher and group processes. NEA J 52: 12-14 Ap '63
LUFTHANSA. See Airlines—Germany (Federal Republic)
LUFTMAN, Alvin S.
Recording storage tubes and their applications. Electr World 69:21-4+ My '63
LUGGAGE
Bag and baggage: for the stay away. il House & Gard 124:120-1 Jl '63
Bag and baggage: for today's young scholars. il House & Gard 124:184-5 S '63
Big packages to pack. il Seventeen 23:133 D '64
Crowd of standouts. il Seventeen 23:202-3 Ag '64
Guarding against luggage loss. il Good H 157:127 Jl '63
How to drive a suitcase. il Design 65:92 Ja '64
Luggage under the tree. il Seventeen 22:136-7 D '63
New look in luggage. J. B. Weiner. Duns R 82:46 Ag '63
Pack a piece of piggyback luggage. il House & Gard 125:46-7 My '64
Pick, pack, go! il Seventeen 22:112-13 My '63
See also
Packing of luggage
LUGGAGE handling, Airlines. See Airlines—Passenger service
LUGING. See Coasting
LUIGI
Doggerel for modern jazz dance. L. Joel. il por Dance Mag 37:36-9 D '63
Tokyo dancers dig our beat. W. Como. il por Dance Mag 38:45-7 Ag '64
LUKÁCS, Georg
End of the tunnel? por Newsweek 63:42 Ap 6 '64
Fiction, society and history. A. Welsh. New Repub 148:30-1+ Mr 2 '63
Monologues of a philolog. R. S. Stilwell. Sat R 47:34+ Je 13 '64
LUKACS, John
Poker and American character. Horizon 5: 56-62 N '63
LUKAS, J. Anthony
Congo tries to build an army. N Y Times Mag p7-9+ Jl 21 '63
Crisis in search of a country. N Y Times Mag p27+ N 24 '63
Two worlds of Jimmy Nkosi. N Y Times Mag p20-1+ Ja 3 '65
LUKE, Gospel of. See Bible—New Testament—Luke
LUKENS, Donald E.
Goldwater, Rockefeller, and the Young Republicans. M. S. Evans. por Nat R 15:97-100+ Ag 13 '63
LUKENS, Samuel
Computer logic fundamentals. Electr World 71:46-8 Je '64
LÜLING, K. H.
Archer fish. Sci Am 209:100-4+ bibliog(p 171) Jl '63
LULU; opera. See Berg, A.
LUMADRAMA. See Son et lumière (sound and light)
LUMAN, Sister Mary
Joy. il Sch Arts 62:5-6 Ap '63
LUMBAGO. See Backache
LUMBARD, Eliot H.
Local and state action against organized crime. Ann Am Acad 347:82-92 My '63
LUMBARD, J. Edward
Better lawyers for our criminal courts. Atlantic 213:86-90 Je '64
LUMBER
They may trim the 2x4 some more; proposed new size standards for softwood lumber. A. Mikesell. il Pop Mech 121:113-15 Ja '64

Prices

Lumber tries annual price. Bsns W p98 Jl 25 '64

Transportation

Breach in the dike; Jones act amendment. il Time 81:82 F 22 '63
It takes more than ships; oceangoing barge of Matson company. il Bsns W p68-70+ Jl 6 '63
Old shay's last haul. people. S. Churchill. il Am For 70:61 My '64
LUMBER and sawmill workers (trade union)
Rival unions team up on plywood's Big six. Bsns W p74+ Je 15 '63
LUMBER caddies. See Carts
LUMBER industry and trade
Lowly two-by-four stirs a major wrangle. il Bsns W p 56+ Mr 7 '64
See also
Crown Zellerbach corporation
Weyerhaeuser timber company
LUMBER workers
Log drive on the Connecticut. R. E. Pike. Atlan 212:29-34 Jl '63
See also
Strikes—United States—Lumber workers
LUMBERING
Controversy in canoeland; Boundary Waters Canoe area. F. H. Kaufert. il Am For 70: 24-7+ O '64
Here comes skyhook logging! R. H. Forbes. il Am For 71:10-13+ Ja '65
Paul Bunyan moves North. W. Stewart. il Am For 70:54-6 F '64
They won't bury Paul Bunyan. il Pop Mech 119:123-5+ Ap '63
Vertical logging; by balloon or helicopter? R. H. Forbes. il Am For 70:30-2 Ja '64
See also
Boise Cascade corporation
Helicopters in lumbering
Lumberjacks

LUMBERING—*Continued*

History

Tale of two rivers. E. Swift. il Am For 70: 32-5+ Je '64

LUMBERING machinery

Mechanical lumberjack rivals Paul Bunyan; Tree Harvester. il Bsns W p52-3 Ag 3 '63
They won't bury Paul Bunyan. il Pop Mech 119:123-5+ Ap '63
See also
Wood chipping machines

LUMBERJACKS

Summer on the dales; high northeast of England. E. Ward. New Yorker 39:78+ Je 1 '63
Tale of two rivers. E. Swift. il Am For 70: 32-5+ Je '64
Who's cutting in my woodlot? Am For 70:2+ Ap '64

LUMINAIRES. See Street lighting fixtures

LUMINESCENCE

Chemiluminescence resulting from electrochemically generated species. D. M. Hercules. bibliog il Science 145:808-9 Ag 21 '64
See also
Electroluminescence
Luciferin

LUMINESCENCE, Biological

Cell that lit its own picture; bioluminescent marine cells. il Sci Digest 55:75 Je '64
Cell visible by own light; photographs of noctiluca miliaris, with light-amplifying device. A. Ewing. il Sci N L 85:178 Mr 21 '64
Luminescent crystalline particles: an organized subcellular bioluminescent system. R. De Sa and others. bibliog il Science 141: 1269-70 S 27 '63
Microdetermination of calcium by aequorin luminescence. O. Shimomura and others. bibliog il Science 140:1339-40 Je 21 '63
Mysterious glow that never gets hot. il Bsns W p66+ Je 20 '64
See also
Fireflies

LUMINOUS ceilings. See Ceilings

LUMINOUS paint. See Paint, Luminous

LUMLEY, Benjamin

Un-sound principle? J. W. Stedman. il Opera N 28:12 Ja 25 '64

LUMPA sect (Zambia)

Alice in Lumpaland; fanatic Lumpa church. il Newsweek 64:38 Ag 17 '64
Alice is at it again. Time 84:30 Ag 7 '64
Alice's new voice. Newsweek 64:42 Ag 24 '64

LUMUMBA, Patrice Emergy

Lumumba jumbo. por Time 84:21 D 25 '64

LUNAR bases

Bendix selects four-wheeled vehicle for mobile lunar lab. D. E. Fink. il Aviation W 81:38-9+ D 7 '64
Boeing official sees reliability as chief Molab systems hurdle. Miss & Roc 15:32 Ag 31 '64
Home on the moon. il Sci Digest 56:88-91 Jl '64
Lunar housing for early arrivals. il Pop Sci 182:108-9 Ap '63
Lunar proposal. W. J. Coughlin. Miss & Roc 13:52 O 14 '63; Discussion. 13:7 O 28 '63
Moon base cost set at $2 billion. W. Beller. Miss & Roc 14:17 My 11 '64
NASA RFP calls for lunar base by 1968. Miss & Roc 13:18 Ag 19 '63
NASA studying lunar base feasibility. I. Stone. il Aviation W 79:71-3 Jl 1 '63
NASA tells Congress early plans for semi-permanent base on moon. W. Beller. il Miss & Roc 14:26-7 Mr 16 '64
NASA weighs lunar logistics proposals; Molab, combination lunar shelter-laboratory and small surface vehicle. I. Stone. il Aviation W 80:52-3+ Ap 27 '64
Potential of lunar base being studied. il Aviation W 79:87-8 Jl 22 '63
Proposals requested for first study of lunar base systems. Miss & Roc 14:13 Mr 23 '64
Soviets outline approaches to construction of bases on moon. il Miss & Roc 15:24-5 O 5 '64
Warsaw parley proposes joint lunar lab. W. C. Wetmore. Aviation W 81:34 S 14 '64

LUNAR construction engineering. See Lunar bases

LUNAR dust. See Matter, Interstellar

LUNAR eclipses. See Eclipses, Lunar

LUNAR environment chamber. See Simulators

LUNAR excursion module. See Space vehicles—Landing systems—Moon

LUNAR halo. See Halos (meteorology)

LUNAR landing systems. See Space vehicles—Landing systems

LUNAR names. See Names, Lunar

LUNAR orbit and landing approach simulator. See Space flight simulators

LUNAR orbiter photo craft. See Space vehicles

LUNAR photography. See Astronomical photography; Space photography

LUNAR probes

At sea on the moon. R. S. Lewis. Bul Atomic Sci 20:35-7 N '64
Changing man's view; flight of Ranger VII. il Time 84:39-42 Ag 7 '64
Contraption that reconnoitered the moon; Ranger VII; with report by J. Hicks. il Life 57:30-36A Ag 14 '64
Early data indicates Ranger success. Aviation W 80:35 F 3 '64
First color surveys of moon now expected in 1966. il Miss & Roc 15:27-8 Jl 6 '64
Goldwater vs. moon shot. W. Wingo. Sci N L 86:77 Ag 1 '64
Haggle develops over Ranger failure. H. M. David. Miss & Roc 14:14-15 My 4 '64
House space committee slates Ranger probe. H. M. David. Miss & Roc 14:15 Ap 13 '64
House unit will recommend NASA resident official to oversee JPL. D. E. Fink. Aviation W 80:23-4 My 11 '64
How should a space lab be organized? debate between NASA and Jet propulsion laboratory. il Bsns W p 112-13 My 2 '64
Hybrids work geared to lunar survey role. W. Burkett. Miss & Roc 14:38 Mr 9 '64
It's not green cheese; pictures Ranger VII sent back. il Bsns W p82-4+ Ag 8 '64
JPL looks for answer to Ranger VI malfunction. R. Pay. il(p 1) Miss & Roc 14: 16 F 10 '64
Log of Ranger VII. il Sat R 47:39 S 5 '64
Lucky seven. R. Hotz. Aviation W 81:13 Ag 17 '64
Lunar casualties. H. A. Roloff. Miss & Roc 13:12 S 30 '63
Lunar orbiter stresses photo mission. il Aviation W 80:69+ My 25 '64
Lunar orbiter up for design review to meet delivery date in mid-'65. M. Getler. il Miss & Roc 15:35-7 O 26 '64
Management breakdown probably responsible for Ranger problems; with editorial comment. Miss & Roc 14:15, 46 My 11 '64
Moonbound Ranger goes blind; Ranger VI. il Life 56:28-9 F 14 '64
NASA hopeful on lunar flare feasibility. C. M. Plattner. il Aviation W 81:32-3 D 28 '64
NASA, JPL seek cause of Ranger 6 failure. il Aviation W 80:22-5 F 10 '64
NASA launch schedule to the moon. il Miss & Roc 13:110-11 N 25 '63
NASA lunar orbiter competition stirs broad interest in industry. E. H. Kolcum. Aviation W 79:29 S 9 '63
NASA seeks new lunar photo craft. H. Taylor. Miss & Roc 13:17 S 9 '63
NASA turns to incentives; procurement of the lunar orbiter photo spacecraft. Miss & Roc 13:28 O 7 '63
Need for pictures; failure of Ranger 6. Time 83:70 F 14 '64
Next on moon: Surveyor. J. Eberhart. Sci N L 86:101 Ag 15 '64
Officials optimistic about Ranger VII returning first U.S. moon pictures. Miss & Roc 15:13 Ag 3 '64
On the move. H. Simmons and I. Goodwin. il Newsweek 63:72-3 F 10 '64
$150-million failure; mission of Ranger VI. W. J. Coughlin. Miss & Roc 14:50 F 10 '64
Picture capability increased for Ranger 7. R. D. Hibben. il Aviation W 81:22-3 Jl 20 '64
Postmortem on Ranger. il Newsweek 63:60 F 17 '64
Probe focuses on NASA-JPL relationship. D. E. Fink. Aviation W 80:29 Ap 27 '64
Project Moon harvest. Sky & Tel 27:212 Ap '64
Ranger and Apollo. Nation 198:157 F 17 '64
Ranger design and management criticized; reports. A. J. Kelley; E. D. Hilburn. Aviation W 80:56+ My 11 '64
Ranger fixes aimed at June launch date. D. E. Fink. Aviation W 80:26-7 Ap 13 '64
Ranger photos boost confidence in Apollo. H. D. Watkins. il Aviation W 81:19-23 Ag 10 '64
Ranger 7 cameras removed, flight slips. D. E. Fink. Aviation W 80:29 F 17 '64
Ranger 7 completes early mission tests. H. D. Watkins. il Aviation W 81:18-20 Ag 3 '64
Ranger VII proves Apollo feasibility; with editorial comment. Miss & Roc 15:16+, 54 Ag 10 '64
Ranger shows no changes needed in surveyor design. Miss & Roc 15:73-4+ S 14 '64
Ranger 6. W. S. Griswold. il Pop Sci 184:77-9+ Ja '64

LUNAR probes—*Continued*
Ranger 6 reaches moon. R. N. Watts, jr. il Sky & Tel 27:162-3 Mr '64
Ranger will carry six video cameras. Aviation W 80:40 Ja 27 '64
Robot lunar scientist; mass spectrometer. Sci N L 86:357 D 5 '64
Shoot and hope Ranger effort charged. D. E. Fink. Aviation W 80:25-7 My 4 '64
Shrinking the universe; Ranger 6. il Time 83:58 F 7 '64
Surveyor orbiter RFP's expected next month. il Miss & Roc 13:18 S 2 '63
Surveyor slippage indicated. H. Taylor. Miss & Roc 14:12 Je 8 '64
Taking the measure of the moon; success of Ranger 7. il Newsweek 64:15-18 Ag 10 '64
U.S. moon shot scheduled. A. Ewing. Sci N L 83:229 Ap 13 '63
Will Ranger's failure slow moon landings? il Bsns W p98 F 8 '64
With Ranger VII, to the moon. I. Wolfert. il Read Digest 85:75-80 N '64

LUNAR rainbow. See Rainbow, Lunar

LUNAR research. See Moon

LUNAR roving vehicle. See Lunar vehicles

LUNAR simulators. See Simulators

LUNAR support equipment. See Space vehicles—Equipment

LUNAR tides. See Tides

LUNAR vehicles
Bell aerosystems studies lunar maneuvering system for NASA. I. Stone. Aviation W 81:65 S 21 '64
Bendix selects four-wheeled vehicle for mobile lunar lab. D. E. Fink. il Aviation W 81:38-9+ D 7 '64
Boeing official sees reliability as chief Molab systems hurdle. Miss & Roc 15:32 Ag 31 '64
Goodyear Molab wheel has wire mesh tire. il Aviation W 82:50-1 Ja 4 '65
How we'll travel on the moon. W. Von Braun. il Pop Sci 184:18+ F '64
I drove a jeep on the moon; Lunar roving vehicle. E. H. Arctander. il Pop Sci 182:90-2+ My '63
JPL outlines requirements for lightweight roving lunar vehicle. Aviation W 79:36 Jl 1 '63
Lunar scooter. il Sci Digest 54:77 N '63
Lunar surface exploration gear analyzed. il Aviation W 81:69-71 N 16 '64
Moon rover gets a test run on lunar-like obstacle course; Lunar roving vehicle concept il Pop Sci 184:98-9 Ja '64
NASA studies lunar exploration concepts. il Aviation W 80:79 My 18 '64
Northrop gets in LSV battle with company-funded development. R. Hawkes. il Miss & Roc 15:28+ N 23 '64
Potential of lunar base being studied. il Aviation W 79:87-8 Jl 22 '63
Ranger photos reveal no new lunar vehicle design difficulties. R. Pay. il Miss & Roc 15:32 Ag 24 '64
Reconnaissance module proposals sought. B. Miller. Aviation W 78:36-7 My 20 '63
Six-legged moon vehicle could be wheelchair. Sci N L 87:34 Ja 16 '65
Strange shapes of things to fly; with photographs by L. Schiller. Sat Eve Post 236:16-21 S 14 '63

LUNARIA. See Honesty (plants)

LUNCH counter sit downs. See Negroes in the United States—Segregation, Resistance to

LUNCHEON at the Plaza; story. See Bellah, J. W.

LUNCHEONS
Etiquette of the executive lunch. R. F. Shepard. Esquire 60:142-3+ N '63
Expense account luncheon. C. W. Morton. il Atlan 211:134+ Mr '63
First luncheon outdoors. il Vogue 143:144 Je '64
Perle Mesta's party notebook: a belated birthday luncheon for Lady Bird Johnson. P. Mesta. il McCalls 90:134+ My '63
Please come for lunch. E. Ward-Hanna. il Ladies Home J 81:74-6+ My '64
Spring luncheon. J. Hewitt. il N Y Times Mag p75 My 24 '64
Vogue's own menu; a country luncheon for six. Vogue 141:140 Je '63
Vogue's own menu; a luncheon for twelve. Vogue 141:132 Ap 15 '63
Vogue's own menu; luncheon for four. Vogue 142:228 S 1 '63
Vogue's own menu; spring luncheon for six. Vogue 141:156 Mr 15 '63
When the ladies come for luncheon; with recipes. V. T. Habeeb. il Am Home 66:56-8+ Ap '63
See also
Brunches

LUNCHES
Conversation cooking. il Sunset 130:100-1 Mr '63
Hearty bar lunch: businessman's treats at Zum Zum, Pan American building; with recipes. M. Kaytor. il Look 28:38-9 Ag 11 '64
Lunch almanac. B. M. Stover. See issues of Parents' magazine & better homemaking
Lunch selector (cont of) Lunch almanac. See issues of Parents' magazine & better homemaking
What the men are having for lunch! famous foods from famous places; with recipes. M. Johnston. il Bet Hom & Gard 41:72-7+ Mr '63
What's for lunch? with recipes. B. M. Stover. il Parents Mag 39:61+ Ag '64
See also
Outdoor meals

LUNCHROOMS
Equipment
Vending machines work for food service. H. P. Vermilya. il Arch Rec 133:194-6 My '63

LUND, Mary Graham
Child's drawing; poem. Commonweal 80:423 Je 26 '64
Vial of nard in a window; poem. Christian Cent 80:429 Ap 3 '63

LUNDA tribe. See Congo (capital Leopoldville)—Native races

LUNDBERG, Hans
World's greatest prospector. N. Carlisle. il pors Pop Sci 184:60-3+ My '64

LUNDBERG, J. L. and others
Light scattering by liquids at 6937 angstroms. bibliog Science 145:1308-10 S 18 '64

LUNDBERGH, Holger
Louisiana. House & Gard 125:210-13 My '64

LUNDBORG, Louis B.
Rx for profits; address, November 8, 1963. Vital Speeches 30:146-50 D 15 '63

LUNDEN, Allyn O. See Osborne, T. S. jt. auth.

LUNG cancer. See Cancer

LUNGS
Diffusion of gases from alveolus to precapillary arteries. A. G. Jameson. bibliog il Science 139:826-8 Mr 1 '63
Fatty acid synthesis by subcellular fractions of lung tissue. E. G. Tombropoulos. bibliog il Science 146:1180-1 N 27 '64
Granular pneumocytes: electron microscopic evidence of their exocrinic function. K. Bensch and others. bibliog il Science 145:1318-19 S 18 '64
Lung banks possible for humans in future. Sci N L 83:151 Mr 9 '63
Pulmonary alveolar cell inclusions: their development in the rat. S. Buckingham and others. bibliog il Science 145:1192-3 S 11 '64
Diseases
Detection and quantitation of fallout particles in a human lung. A. V. Wegst and others. bibliog il Science 143:957-9 F 28 '64
Lung disease detection. Sci N L 83:230 Ap 13 '63
See also
Emphysema
Pneumonia

LUNGS, Transplantation of. See Transplantation of organs, tissues, etc.

LUNN, Sir Arnold
Mountain fortress. Nat R 14:534-5 Jl 2 '63
Two marshals. Nat R 16:487-8, 537-8 Je 16-30 '64

LUNSETH, John H.
Elastic membrane: effect of increasing tension on the absorptive capacity. bibliog Science 141:438 Ag 2 '63

LUNT, Alfred
Stage-struck: the romance of Alfred Lunt & Lynn Fontanne; excerpts. M. Zolotow. il pors Look 28:92-9+ D 15 '64
They glory in a rustic, high-style hideaway. il pors Life 55:76-8 Jl 26 '63

LUO, H. L. and others
Superconducting metastable compounds. bibliog Science 145:581-3 Ag 7 '64

LUPINO, Ida
Mother Lupino. il por Time 81:42 F 8 '63

LUPINSKI, J. H. and Kopple, K. D.
Electroconductive polymers. bibliog Science 146:1038-9 N 20 '64

LUPINUS subcarnosus. See Bluebonnets (flowers)

LUPINUS texensis. See Bluebonnets (flowers)
LUPTON, John Mather
Conservatives strike up the band. A. Brownell. por Nat R 16:231-2+ Mr 24 '64
LUQUE, Guillermo Gonzalez. See Gonzalez Luque, G.
LURAY, Howard
Chaos at dawn! Yachting 115:215-17 My '64
LURÇAT, Jean
Art from the looms of Aubusson. J. D. Ratcliff. il Read Digest 82:208-12 F '63
Nine tapestries on man in the atomic age. il UNESCO Courier 17:18-19 N '64
LURIE, Diana
(ed) See Dunn, M. I'm no cutie-midget needing a mother
LURIE, Raanan
New York. il Harper 228:94-5 F '64
LURISTAN bronzes. See Bronzes
LURO, Horatio
Continental touch of Senor Horatio Luro. A. Wright. por Sports Illus 20:33-5 My 4 '64
LUSKIN, John
Benevolent Mr Field. New Repub 151:22-3 Jl 11 '64
LUSKY, Louis
Justice with a southern accent. Harper 228:69-70+ Mr '64
LUSTIG, Joseph
More convenient than a shopping center. Am City 79:116-17 S '64
LUTEIN. See Xanthophyll
LUTEN, C. J.
Art of the prima ballerina. Am Rec G 30:30-2 S '63
In memoriam: Wilhelm Furtwängler. Am Rec G 31:14-17 S '64
Klemperer's Bruckner: two views. Am Rec G 29:447 F '63
Ludwig van Beethoven nine symphonies; Berlin philharmonic orchestra conductor Herbert von Karajan. Am Rec G 30:10-12 S '63
Simultaneously, from Mercury and Columbia, Bluebeard's castle. Am Rec G 29:690-1 My '63
Strange interlude. Am Rec G 30:578-80 Mr '64
Stravinsky conducts his choral music; short pieces, and ballet music. Am Rec G 31:310-12 D '64
Toscanini conducts overtures. Am Rec G 30:660-1 Ap '64
Verdi Requiem. Am Rec G 21:420-1 Ja '65
Walter's Mahler First: the standard by which others are to be judged. Am Rec G 29:522-3 Mr '63
LUTER, John
Don't vote in the dark. Todays Health 42:58-9+ O '64
James Craik: the first White House physician. Todays Health 42:46-9+ F '64
LUTETIUM
Lutetium fissionable, rate unexpectedly high. Sci N L 86:184 S 19 '64
LUTHER, Martin
Canonize Martin Luther? J. B. Sheerin. Cath World 197:84-7 My '63
God-intoxicated man. Time 82:63 O 4 '63
Luther and the Catholics. il por Newsweek 64:46 Ag 10 '64
Luther's meditations on the gospels, tr. by R. H. Bainton. Review
Christian Cent 80:1030 Ag 21 '63. H. J. Grimm
Martin Luther, by J. M. Todd. Review
Commonweal 81:458-9 D 25 '64
Martin Luther: the new piety. G. Thomas. il Holiday 35:62-3+ Ja '64
Shirer's re-Hitlerizing of Luther. J. W. Montgomery; reply. W. Kliewer. Christian Cent 80:179-80 F 6 '63
What Luther meant by faith alone. M. W. Hess. Cath World 199:96-101 My '64
LUTHER; drama. See Osborne, J.
LUTHERAN church
See also
Lutheran world federation
LUTHERAN church in America. See Lutheran church in the United States
LUTHERAN church in Sweden
One flock, no shepherd; Christian case for abstinence from sexual intercourse before marriage. America 110:784, 857 Je 6, 27 '64
LUTHERAN church in the United States
American Lutheranism: denomination or confession? J. Pelikan. Christian Cent 80:1608-10 D 25 '63
Catholic and reformed; study on confession. America 111:471 O 24 '64
Glass, not a chalice; key issue of convention. Time 84:56 Jl 17 '64
Initial assemblage; first convention for the Lutheran church in America. R. L. Kincheloe. Christian Cent 81:1044 Ag 19 '64
Isolated synod; Wisconsin Evangelical Lutheran synod. Time 82:49 Ag 23 '63
Life-involvement learning; Lutheran long range program. il Time 84:65 S 25 '64
Lutherans open 16th store; move Puerto Rico store. il Pub W 185:96-8 F 10 '64
$3 million religious program undertaken by Lutherans. Pub W 185:32-3 Mr 23 '64
Uniting the Lutherans; proposed Lutheran council of the U.S.A. Newsweek 64:86 N 9 '64
Wisconsin synod withdraws. Christian Cent 80:1069 S 4 '63
See also
American Lutheran church
National Lutheran council
LUTHERAN world federation
Impressions from Helsinki, Rome and Montreal. G. A. Lindbeck. Cath World 198:272-80 F '64
Justifying justification; fourth assembly. il Time 82:48 Ag 23 '63
Luther up to date; fourth assembly of Lutheran world federation. il Newsweek 62:71 Ag 19 '63
Second thoughts on Helsinki. E. T. Bachmann. Christian Cent 80:1102-4 S 11 '63
Service fosters unity; refugee service in Tanganyika; with editorial comment. G. Murray. Christian Cent 81:261, 278+ F 26 '64
Under observation. Time 82:38 Ag 9 '63
LUTHULI, Albert John
Another five years. por Time 83:30 Je 5 '64
LUTON, England, public library
Luton's literary supermarket. F. M. Gardner. il Library J 88:4545-7 D 1 '63
LUTWAK, Leo, and Shapiro J. R.
Calcium absorption in man: based on large volume liquid scintillation counter studies. bibliog Science 144:1155-7 My 29 '64
LUTYENS, Elisabeth
New music. C. Sigmon. Mus Am 83:34 Jl '63
LUV; drama. See Schisgal, M.
LUXEMBOURG
Benelux countries. F. G. Eyck. Cur Hist 47:355-61 D '64
Grandest duchy; abdication of Grand Duchess Charlotte. il Time 84:40 N 20 '64
Luxembourg fete. H. Wilson. il Travel 119:31-3 F '63
Oh! what a dizzy and dolce vita. P. E. Schneider. il N Y Times Mag p39+ N 15 '64
See also
Radio broadcasting—Luxembourg
Stock exchange—Luxembourg

Description and travel

Lightning guide to Luxembourg. J. Bryan, 3d. il Holiday 35:54-9 Mr '64

Foreign relations

United States

Grand Duchess of Luxembourg meets with President Kennedy. Dept State Bul 48:776 My 20 '63

Politics and government

Millennium in Camelot. il Time 81:40 Ap 19 '63

Treaties

U.S. and Luxembourg exchange ratifications of FEN treaty. Dep't State Bul 48:403 Mr 18 '63
LUXORO, Mario. See Tasaki, I. jt. auth.
LUXURIES
Spending more on luxuries. il Bsns W p25 My 23 '64
LUYKX, Boniface
Africa speaks to the American Negro. America 110:365 Mr 12 '64
President Kennedy and the Congo. America 110:17 Ja 4 '64
LUYT, Sir Richard
Sir Richard's coup. Newsweek 63:50 Je 29 '64
LUZHIN defense; story. See Nabokov, V.
LYCÉES. See Education—France
LYCORIS
Lycoris for something different and interesting. R. C. Hands. il Horticulture 41:452-3 S '63
LYDIA
Uncover ancient tomb; burial tomb of King Gyges. il Sci N L 86:323 N 21 '64
LYFORD, Joseph P.
Proposal for a revolution. Sat R 46:19-22 O 19; 25-8+ O 26 '63
Where are the leaders? Sat R 46:10 Jl 6 '63

LYFORD, Katharine Van Etten
Christmas in Latin America. Horn Bk 40:587-95 D '64
LYFORD CAY. See Bahama Islands
LYING
Biggest liar in Alaska. F. Dufresne. il Field & S 68:44-5+ Mr '64
LYKES brothers steamship company
Piping all hands to the pushbuttons; automation at sea. il Bsns W p92-4 Ja 25 '64
Turn-around to efficiency. il Time 83:86 My 8 '64
LYMAN, John
Federal salaries in 1959. Science 141:6+ Jl 5 '63
LYMPHATIC system
Lymphatic system. H. S. Mayerson. il Sci Am 208:80-90 bibliog(p 183) Je '63
Lymphocytic choriomeningitis infection in neonatally thymectomized mice bearing diffusion chambers containing thymus. R. H. Levey and others. bibliog il Science 142:483-5 O 25 '63
Reaction of lymphocytes with purified protein derivative conjugated with fluorescein. T. A. Witten and others. bibliog il Science 142:596-8 N 1 '63
Thymus: its role in lymphoid recovery after irradiation. R. Auerbach. bibliog Science 139:1061 Mr 15 '63
Your other circulatory system. J. D. Ratcliff. Todays Health 42:30-1 D '64; Same abr. with title Our amazing white bloodstream. Read Digest 86:175-6+ Ja '65
LYMPHOCYTES
Acid phosphatase-rich granules in human lymphocytes induced by photohemagglutinin. R. Hirschhorn and others. bibliog il Science 147:55-7 Ja 1 '65
Circulating small lymphocytes: immunologically competent cells with limited reactivities. D. L. Vredevoe and W. H. Hildemann. bibliog il Science 141:1272-4 S 27 '63
Delayed hypersensitivity in man: transfer by lymphocyte preparations of peripheral blood. R. G. Slavin and J. E. Garvin. bibliog il Science 145:52-3 Jl 3 '64
Histocompatibility and immunologic competence in renal homotransplantation. A. L. Rubin and others. bibliog il Science 143:815-16 F 21 '64
Irradiation of the blood: method for reducing lymphocytes in blood and spleen. B. A. Barnes and others. bibliog il Science 145:1188-9 S 11 '64
Lymphocyte interaction: a potential histocompatibility test in vitro. F. Bach and K. Hirschhorn. bibliog il Science 143:813-14 F 21 '64
Pluripotent stem cell function of the mouse marrow lymphocyte. G. Cudkowicz and others. bibliog il Science 144:866-8 My 15 '64
Serologic typing of human lymphocytes with immune serum obtained after homografting. R. L. Walford and others. bibliog il Science 144:868-70 My 15 '64
Thymus hormone. R. H. Levey. il Sci Am 211:66-71+ bibliog(p 142) Jl '64
Tissue culture studies of the human lymphocyte. J. H. Robbins. bibliog il Science 146:1648-54 D 25 '64
LYMPHOID cells
Cytological evidence for crossing-over in vitro in human lymphoid cells. J. German. bibliog il Science 144:298-301 Ap 17 '64
Immune response and mitosis of human peripheral blood lymphocytes in vitro. K. Hirschhorn and others. bibliog il Science 142:1185-7 N 29 '63
Inhibition of antibody plaque formation by sensitized lymphoid cells: rapid indicator of transplantation immunity. H. Friedman. bibliog il Science 145:607-9 Ag 7 '64
Lymphoid organs and normal gamma-globulin in the rat. S. B. Andersen and F. Bierring. bibliog il Science 144:1219-20 Je 5 '64
LYNCH, Charles Conley
Portrait of an extremist. T. Armbrister. il pors Sat Eve Post 237:80-3 Ag 22 '64
LYNCH, Edward T.
New strength for old asphalt. Am City 79:90-1 F '64
LYNCH, Francis X.
Adequate shelters and quick reaction to warning: a key to civil defense. Science 142:665-7 N 8 '63
LYNCH, Gerald J.
Pursuit of security; address, December 21, 1963. Vital Speeches 30:504-6 Je 1 '64
LYNCH, James M. Jr
Bus 23, where are you? NEA J 53:23 Ap '64
LYNCH, John
Ideas in metal sculpture. Design 64:167-9+ Mr '63
LYNCH, Leslie
Recreation area standards. por Recreation 58:20-1 Ja '65 (to be cont)
When is a recreation area a park? por Recreation 57:394-6 O '64
LYNCH, Nancy
Lady Chatterley goes to college. Mlle 57:224-5+ Ag '63
(ed) See Baldwin, J. Disturber of the peace
LYNCH, Russell G.
Lynch wins Stokes conservation award. il por Am For 70:27 Jl '64
LYNCH, Stewart
Speaking out. por Sat Eve Post 236:6+ Mr 30 '63
LYNCH, Mrs Weldon J.
Trustee's role in recruitment. ALA Bul 58:60-1 Ja '64
LYNCH, William S.
Inertia, the enemy within. Sat R 47:39 F 8 '64
Rage in low key. Sat R 46:43 N 16 '63
LYNCHING
Summer Sunday; excerpt from Incident in Coatsville; with editorial comment. E. F. Goldman. il Am Heritage 15:50-3+ Je '64
LYND, Staughton
Long view. Commentary 39:86-8 Ja '65
New American historians. Commentary 34:271-3, 35:74-5 S '62, Ja '63
New Negro radicalism. Commentary 36:252-6 S '63
Pluralism & brotherhood. Commentary 35:81-4 Ja '63
Roots of Negro militancy. New Repub 150:5 F 22 '64
—See Minnis, J. jt. auth.
LYNDON B. Johnson foundation. See Johnson City foundation
LYNDS, Beverly T.
Littlest astronomer: letter. Science 141:594 Ag 16 '63
LYNEN, Feodor
Friends share Nobel prize. Sci N L 86:263 O 24 '64
Nobel laureates: Bloch and Lynen win prize in medicine and physiology. E. P. Kennedy and F. H. Westheimer. il por Science 146:504-6 O 23 '64
Secrets of cholesterol. il por Time 84:94 O 23 '64
LYNES, Russell
As hard as one can. Harper 226:30-1 Mr '63
Bowling goes bourgeois. Horizon 5:89-95 Mr '63
Emphatic Istanbul. Harper 229:22+ O '64
Fly-by-night trip to Morocco. Harper 227:24-9 Ag '63
Folly forgiven, or, Christmas is for beginners. Mlle 58:58-9 D '63
Gay, gaudy history of the American bedroom and bath. McCalls 91:116-17+ O '63
How America solved the servant problem. Harper 227:46-54 Jl '63
Is kindness killing the arts? Harper 227:68-71+ N '63
Los Angeles' cultural circus. Harper 228:28+ F '64
Parlor. Am Heritage 14:54-64+ O '63
Parlor for New York. Harper 228:28+ My '64
What's to become of architecture? Harper 228:16+ Je '64
Why do women have to be so rude? McCalls 91:71+ Ag '64
LYNLEY, Carol
Fair young Hollywood girls. R. W. Lewis. il pors Sat Eve Post 236:22-5 S 7 '63
Goodby, age of innocence. il pors Life 54:41-2+ My 3 '63
LYNN, Frank. See Haase, P. jt. auth.
LYNN, John C.
Excerpt from statement, March 6, 1963. Cong Digest 42:245+ O '63
LYNN, Kenneth S.
Attack on an idol. Reporter 29:52+ N 7 '63
Bush-league Swift. Reporter 28:60-2 F 14 '63
Elitism on the left. Reporter 29:37-40 Jl 4 '63
Gravey train. Reporter 29:48-50 S 26 '63
Liberal as optimist. Reporter 30:48-50 F 13 '64
Mrs Stowe and the American imagination. New Repub 148:20-1 Je 29 '63
Posthumous Adams. Reporter 31:33-4 D 17 '64
LYNNWOOD, Wash.
New sludge-disposal method. il Am City 79:110-11 F '64
LYON, Fred
Bizarre effects. il U S Camera 27:56-9 Ja '64
LYON, Mary
Elder craftsmen shop. Craft Horiz 24:22+ N '64

LYON, Mary F.
Lyon & the Mouse. por Time 82:64 Jl 26 '63

LYON, Ninette
Second fame: good food. Vogue 144:239-40 S 1 '64; 145:152-4 Ja 1; 116-18 Ja 15; 186-8 F 1 '65

LYON, Peter
Amazing Bobby Fischer. Holiday 33:125-9+ My '63
Astonishing Stanley Kubrick. Holiday 35:101-2+ F '64
Glorious nightmare. Holiday 36:48-67 Jl '64
Mr Ambassador. Holiday 33:36-9+ Je '63
Rockefeller institute. Holiday 36:52-7+ S '64

LYONS, Charlton H. sr
Up from the swamp. por Newsweek 63:34 Mr 16 '64

LYONS, Daniel
World belongs to God: address, May 19, 1963. Vital Speeches 29:542-4 Je 15 '63

LYONS, Eugene
British Guiana: another Cuba in the making? Read Digest 82:118-23 Ap '63
Herbert Hoover, RIP. Nat R 16:946 N 3 '64
Ordeal and triumph of Herbert Hoover; excerpt from Herbert Hoover, a biography. Read Digest 85:161-2+ D '64
Specter haunts the Kremlin. Read Digest 83:55-61 S '63
—See Strohm, J. jt. auth.

LYONS, Gene Martin
Military mind. Bul Atomic Sci 19:19-22 N '63

LYONS, Jesse
Don't just stand there! Parents Mag 39:32+ D '64

LYONS, Leonard
Rehabilitation of Nathan Leopold. Sat Eve Post 236:66-8 Je 1 '63

LYONS, Louis M.
Liebling, libel, and the press. Atlan 213:43-8 My '64
Nieman fellowships. por Atlan 214:99-102 D '64
Wanted: watchmen for Fourth Estate. Nation 200:60-2 Ja 18 '65

LYONS, Richard
Sleep no more. Newsweek 63:88 Ap 6 '64

LYONS, Ruth
Nobody's ever in town on Sunday; story. McCalls 91:60-1 Ja '64

LYPIATT Park. See England—Historic houses, etc.

LYRE; story. See Nabokov, V.

LYRIC opera of Chicago
Chicago. G. McElroy. il Opera N 28:34-5 Ja 4; 29:32 D 19 '64
Chicago. J. W. Stedman. Opera N 28:32 D 7 '63; 29:29 Ja 2 '65
Chicago: all's well that. . . . C. Cassidy. il Theatre Arts 47:20-1+ Mr '63
Doomed to disappointment. R. Dettmer. il Mus Am 84:22-3+ Ja '64
Old grandeur. il Newsweek 62:100 O 21 '63

LYSENKO, Trofim Denisovich
Again, Lysenko. por Sci Digest 57:45-6 Ja '65
Lysenko: attacks on his theories renewed in U.S.S.R. in aftermath of Khrushchev's removal from power. D. S. Greenberg. Science 146:1024-5 N 20 '64
Lysenko uprooted. Newsweek 64:90 N 30 '64
Notes and comment. New Yorker 40:47 N 28 '64

LYSERGIC acid diethylamide
Beyond within: the LSD story, by S. Cohen. Review
New Repub 151:15-16 N 28 '64; A. Watts; Reply. K. Link. 151:29-30 D 12 '64
Time 84:63-4 D 18 '64
Can this drug enlarge man's mind? G. Heard. Horizon 5:28-31+ My '63
Chemical mind-changers. R. Coughlan. il Life 54:81-2+ Mr 15 '63
Danger in happy drugs. E. Mirel. Sci N L 84:138 Ag 31 '63
Dangerous magic of LSD. J. Kobler. il Sat Eve Post 236:30-2+ N 2 '63
Don't fool around with LSD. Sci Digest 54:42 S '63
Drug abuse from rat race. F. Marley. Sci N L 83:389 Je 22 '63
Instant happiness. R. P. Goldman. il Ladies Home J 80:67-71 O '63
LSD: the consciousness-expanding drug, ed. by D. Solomon. Review
Nation 199:360-2 N 16 '64. W. H. McGlothlin
Lysergic acid diethylamide: its effects on a male Asiatic elephant. L. J. West and others; reply. P. D. Harwood. Science 139:684-5 F 15 '63
Serotonin binding to nerve-ending particles of the rat brain and its inhibition by lysergic acid diethylamide. R. M. Marchbanks and others. bibliog il Science 144:1135-7 My 29 '64
They split my personality. H. Asher. il Sat R 46:39-43 Je 1 '63; Discussion. 46:43-5 Jl 6 '63
Vision drug increases religious feeling. Sci N L 84:184 S 21 '63

LYSIN
Sequential gene action in the establishment of lysogeny. M. Levine and H. O. Smith. bibliog il Science 146:1581-2 D 18 '64

LYSOSOMES
Adhesion and emigration of leukocytes produced by cationic proteins of lysosomes. A. Janoff and B. W. Zweifach. bibliog il Science 144:1456-8 Je 19 '64
Antibacterial and enzymic basic proteins from leukocyte lysosomes: separation and identification. H. I. Zeya and J. K. Spitznagel. bibliog il Science 142:1085-7 N 22 '63
Lysosome. C. de Duve. il Sci Am 208:64-72 My '63
Lysosomes in the renal papillae of rats: formation induced by potassium-deficient diet. A. B. Morrison and others. bibliog il Science 142:1066-8 N 22 '63

LYSTRUP, Schack
I think in English. pors Seventeen 22:112-13+ O '63

LYTTELTON, Oliver, 1st viscount Chandos of Aldershot. See Chandos of Aldershot, O. L.

LYTTON, Bart
Bart Lytton: a billion-dollar blue-devil. por Newsweek 62:71 S 16 '63
Unabashable Bart Lytton. por Fortune 70:122-3 Ag '64

M

MACS (medium-altitude communications satellite) See Communications satellites—Military applications

MAMOS (Marine automatic meteorological observing station) See Meteorological stations

MAPP. See Mid-continent area power planners

MATS. See United States—Military air transport service

M and W gear company
Tractors pull 'em in; Heart of America farm power show. il Bsns W p 136-7 S 28 '63

MCA. See Music corporation of America

MCA, incorporated
One man's method; problems of TV film production. R. L. Shayon. Sat R 47:26 Ap 25 '64

MCHR. See Medical committee for human rights

MEM (manned Mars excursion module) See Space vehicles—Landing systems

MGIC. See Mortgage guaranty insurance corporation

MHD generators. See Electric generators

M. H. De Young memorial museum, San Francisco
Acoustiguide tour new feature at museum. Hobbies 68:52 F '64
New masterpieces at De Young museum. Hobbies 67:51 F '63

MICR (magnetic ink character recognition) See Calculating machines—Banking applications

MIT. See Massachusetts institute of technology, Cambridge

MLA. See Modern language association of America; Music library association

MLF (multilateral force) See North Atlantic treaty organization—Multilateral force (proposed)

MMRBM (mobile medium-range ballistic missile). See Guided missiles

MODS (manned orbital development station) See Space stations

MOL (manned orbital laboratory) See Space stations

MOPTS (mobile photographic tracking station) See Space vehicles—Tracking

MORC. See Midget ocean racing club

MORL (manned orbital research laboratory) See Space stations

MP. See Members of Parliament

MPF. See Multipurpose food

MRA. See Moral rearmament

MRP (Movimiento revolucionario del pueblo) See Political parties—Cuba

MSG. See Monosodium glutamate

MSU. See Michigan state university of agriculture and applied science, East Lansing

MVPCB. See Motor vehicle pollution control board

M. W. Kellogg company. See Kellogg, M. W. company

MA, Yo-yo
Wunder-kids. il por Vogue 144:222 D '64
MAAS, Peter
Can Kennedy take New York? Sat Eve Post 237:32-4 O 31 '64
Joe Valachi: the killer who told on the mob. Sat Eve Post 236:21-3 N 23 '63
Mafia: the inside story. Sat Eve Post 236: 19-25 Ag 10 '63
What will R.F.K. do next? Sat Eve Post 237:17-21 Mr 28 '64
MAAS, Susan
Wonderful woods. Horn Bk 39:418 Ag '63
MAASS, John
Stately mansions of the imagination. Horizon 5:10-27 S '63
MAASSAB, Hunein F. and Cochran, K. W.
Rubella virus: inhibition in vitro by amantadine hydrochloride. bibliog Science 145:1443-4 S 25 '64
MAAZEL, Lorin
Notes from abroad. C. Reid Hi Fi 13:18+ Ag '63
MABAAN. See Sudan—Native races
MABEE, Carleton
Freedom schools, North and South. Reporter 31:30-2 S 10 '64
Voting in the Black Belt. Negro Hist Bul 27: 50-6 D '63
MABILEAU, Jean F.
Fight against narcotics. por U N Rev 11:29-34 F '64
MABLEY, Jack
Honest quote. Time 84:61 Ag 7 '64
MABRY, Drake
Drought ends in Iowa. Reporter 29:27 Jl 4 '63
MACADAMIAS
See also
Cookery—Nuts
MCALEAR, James H. See Hoyle, G. jt. auth.
MCALEER, Ralph E.
New York city map launches United States Atlas map series. por Nat Geog Mag 126: 108-10 Jl '64
MCALESTER, A. Lee
Transitional Ordovician bivalve with both monoplacophoran and lucinacean affinities. bibliog Science 146:1293-4 D 4 '64
MACALESTER college, St Paul, Minn.
Experiment in common sense; World press institute. R. L. Tobin. Sat R 47:73-4 Ja 11 '64
MCALISTER, Lois
Cooperative planning of a curriculum unit. ALA Bul 57:164 F '63
MACANDREW, A. R.
(tr) See Evtushenko, E. A. Precocious autobiography
MCANDREWS, John
Sculptors of light and shadow. Sat R 47:37-8 F 8 '64
MACAPAGAL, Diosdado
President Macapagal of Philippines visits United States; greeting and toast. Dept State Bul 51:628-34 N 2 '64
about
Call on the princess. il por Time 84:33-4 O 9 '64
Democracy triumphs in the Philippines. W. J. Lederer. il por Read Digest 82:289-94+ Ap '63
Letter from Manila. R. Shaplen. il New Yorker 39:136-40+ Je 8 '63
New worry for the U.S; trouble with an old ally. il por U S News 57:77-9 O 12 '64
Philippines can't be taken for granted. D. Warner. Reporter 31:30-2 D 17 '64
Stalemate in Manila. il por Bsns W p 102-3+ S 5 '64
Uncle Sam's other island. il por Time 82:34 N 22 '63
Welcome visitor; one with praise for U.S. U S News 57:24 O 19 '64
MCARDLE, Richard E.
Directors select AFA committee on elections. Am For 70:49 Jl '64
MACARONI
Greek way with macaroni. Sunset 132:241 Ap '64
He likes to cook. W. Jones. il Bet Hom & Gard 42:76 Mr '64
How to make perfect pasta. il Redbook 120: 78-9+ Ap '63
Macaroni family. B. M. Stover. il Parents Mag 39:77 O '64
Macaroni or spaghetti. il Bet Hom & Gard 43:115-16 Ja '65
New dishes to replace your regular eating habits. G. Maddox. il Todays Health 42: 40-5 F '64
Pasta perfect; with recipes. il McCalls 90: 114-15+ F '63
See also
Noodles
MACAROONS. See Cookies
MACARTHUR, Charlotte
Holiday decorations. Horticulture 41:598 D '63
MACARTHUR, Douglas, 1880-1964
Duty, honor, country; address, May 12, 1962. por Life 56:36-38A Ap 17 '64; Excerpts. U S News 56:64-5 Ap 20 '64
Interview with MacArthur: the storm it provoked; excerpts, ed. by J. G. Lucas. U S News 56:40-1 Ap 20 '64
Reminiscences; excerpts. pors Life 56:46-56A Ja 10; 54-9+ Ja 17; 66-74+ Ja 24; 57: 55-6+ Jl 3; 70-4+ Jl 10; 82-3+ Jl 17; 36-8+ Jl 24 '64; Read Digest 85:215-23+ Jl; 263-6+ O '64
about
Atom bombs and a cobalt belt; MacArthur's controversial plan. il por Newsweek 63:37-8+ Ap 20 '64
Bonus march. J. D. Weaver. il por Am Heritage 14:18-23+ Je '63
By Douglas MacArthur. il pors Newsweek 64: 97-8 S 28 '64
Crossing of the Yalu. Nat R 16:342-4 My 5 '64
Deeds of valor in a single lifetime. il pors U S News 56:58-9 Ap 13 '64
Douglas MacArthur. N. Cousins. por Sat R 47:18-19 My 2 '64
Douglas MacArthur, RIP. Nat R 16:309-10 Ap 21 '64
Egotist in uniform. L. Morton. Harper 229: 138+ N '64
From the first Mrs MacArthur: an account of rivalry between two famous generals; reprint. B. Beale. por U S News 56:20 My 4 '64
General Douglas MacArthur. R. Baldwin. Nation 198:385 Ap 20 '64
General MacArthur dies. il por Sr Schol 84:19 Ap 17 '64
Here is what MacArthur really meant. Life 56:4 Ap 24 '64
Hero's memory of a hero. il por Time 84:134+ O 2 '64
Home is the soldier. il Newsweek 63:43-4 Ap 20 '64
In remembrance of MacArthur. il pors Life 56:28-35 Ap 17 '64
Long gray line. M. Cunliffe. Commentary 38: 66-8 D '64
MacArthur. il pors Time 83:24-5 Ap 10 '64
MacArthur: an old soldier dies. il pors Newsweek 63:34-5 Ap 13 '64
MacArthur interviews. C. B. Marshall. New Repub 150:7 Ap 25 '64
MacArthur story; with interview with D. MacArthur and report by H. Handleman. il por U S News 56:38-46 Ap 20 '64
MacArthur: the greatest captain of his era. R. E. Dupuy. il por U S News 56:78-9 Ap 27 '64
MacArthur the soldier. T. R. Phillips. New Repub 150:16 Ap 18 '64
Memento of twenty-five years. C. Mydans. il por Life 56:25 Ap 17 '64
Notes and comment. New Yorker 40:39 Ap 18 '64
Obituary
Reporter 30:10 Ap 23 '64. M. Ascoli
Old soldier's memoirs. por Time 82:37 Ag 30 '63
Proud hero in war and peace. M. S. Watson. por Sat R 47:42-3 S 26 '64
Salute to courage: story of a U.N. failure; reprints. D. Lawrence. U S News 56:112 Ap 20 '64
Stomach for soldiery. C. B. Marshall. New Repub 151:27-9 O 3 '64
Threnody & thunder. il Time 83:40-1 Ap 17 '64
Truman's view: MacArthur tried for presidency; excerpts from TV series. H. S. Truman. U S News 57:22 N 30 '64
Verdict of history. J. Chamberlain. il Nat R 16:1112-13 D 15 '64
MACARTHUR, Douglas, 1909-
United States trade relations with the new Europe; the challenge and the opportunities; address, January 10, 1963. Dept State Bul 48:174-9 F 4 '63
MACARTHUR, Gloria
Five tame dragons. Writer 76:25-7 Mr '63
MACARTHUR, John D.
Young Sam wins while old Mac sues. E. Shrake. Sports Illus 20:52+ Mr 2 '64
MCARTHUR, Thelma F.
Starting library service to hospitals. ALA Bul 57:859-60 O '63

MACARTHUR family
Martial roots of a warrior's glory. D. MacArthur. il pors Life 56:48-56A+ Ja 10 '64
MACAULAY, R. W.
Canadian-American relations; address, April 22, 1963. Vital Speeches 29:503-6 Je 1 '63
MACAWS. See Parrots
MACBAIN, Alastair
Preserve shooting. See issues of Field & stream to April 1964
MCBAIN, Harold J.
Changing requirements of book publishing; address. Pub W 184:72-4 N 4 '63
MCBEE, Susanna
Deliberate speed in D.C. New Repub 150:7-8 Je 20 '64
Edging away from capital punishment. New Repub 152:11-12 Ja 30 '65
Negro riots will go on, unless. . . New Repub 151:22 S 5 '64
MACBETH, George
Lemur in the supermarket at night: a view of the afterlife; poem. New Yorker 40:154 Mr 14 '64
MACBETH; opera. See Verdi, G.
MCCABE, Bernard
Steady focus on the humane consciousness. Commonweal 81:457-8 D 25 '64
MCCABE, Charles
Word for New York is bush. Sports Illus 21:56-8+ Ag 3 '64
MCCABE, Esther M.
Consumer service bureau report (cont of) Report on the testing of advertised products. See issues of Parents' magazine and better homemaking
MCCABE, Robert K.
War and death, like eating and making love; excerpts from diary. por Newsweek 62:39 Jl 15 '63
MCCAFFERTY, Phil
Belt-disk sander: a tool to own. Pop Sci 182:122-6 F '63
Carving wood with power. Pop Sci 182:142-5 Mr '63
How to make your own plastic bearings. Pop Sci 183:155-7+ O '63
How to mold a rattle-free case for car tools. Pop Sci 183:120-3 Jl '63
Patio furniture in redwood. Pop Sci 184:147-51 My; 120-3 Je '64
Those slick work-smoothing lubricants. Pop Sci 185:164-7 N '64
MCCAFFREY, Austin J.
Treatment for minority groups in textbooks: adaptation of address, October 2, 1964. por Pub W 186:22-7 O 12 '64
What publishers need to know about adult education; summary of address. por(p39) Pub W 185:41-2 F 17 '64
MCCAFFREY, Gordon
Electronic genie speeds traffic through 1,001 lights. Pop Sci 185:76-7+ S '64
MACCAGNI, Carlo
Galileo Galilei. UNESCO Courier 17:24-5+ My '64
MACCAIG, Norman
Veterans and recruits. S. F. Morse. Poetry 102:331-2 Ag '63
MCCAIN, John S. Jr
New four ocean challenge; address, September 18, 1963. Vital Speeches 30:57-61 N 1 '63
MCCALL, John P.
A+ for illiteracy. Nation 198:242-3 Mr 9 '64
MCCALL corporation
Three years later; Saturday review and McCall corporation. N. Cousins. Sat R 47:20+ F 29 '64
MCCALLA, T. M. See Norstadt, F. A. jt. auth.
MCCALL'S (periodical)
McCall's golden mike awards. il McCalls 90:28+ My '63; 91:38+ My '64
Women's vote, how will it go? survey of political opinion. McCalls 91:70+ Mr '64
MCCAMBRIDGE, Mercedes
Campaigner. il por Time 83:56 Ja 31 '64
MCCAMMAN, E. R.
Critical path method of scheduling. Arch Rec 133:155-8 Ja '63
MCCAMY, C. S.
Instant color correction! il Mod Phot 28:66-7 Ja '64
MCCANN, Frances
American singer slain. por Mus Am 83:24 Ap '63
MCCANN, J. H.
St Lawrence Seaway after four years: success or failure? interview. por U S News 54:58 Ap 22 '63
MCCANN, Sharon Quigley
No room; story. Redbook 124:40-1 D '64
MCCANN, William
Delta launches Syncom 3. Sci N L 86:133 Ag 29 '64
Mob violence control. Sci N L 86:86 Ag 8 '64
MCCARDLE, Dorothy
When LBJ outdanced the diplomats; excerpts from report. U S News 56:14 F 24 '64
MCCARRAN act. See Immigration and emigration law
MCCARRAN-Walter immigration act. See Immigration and emigration law
MCCARROLL, Don
Too busy to grow old. H. G. Earl. il por Todays Health 42:42-5+ O '64
MCCARRY, Charles
Death of a valley. Sat Eve Post 236:76-81 N 30 '63
First came rumors, fears, then the ugly truth: typhoid! Sat Eve Post 236:84-7 My 25 '63
Pietà: masterpiece at the fair. Sat Eve Post 237:24-9 Mr 28 '64
This prince led Cinderella to death. Sat Eve Post 237:20-1 My 16 '64
Village that lost its parents. Sat Eve Post 236:96+ D 7 '63
MCCARTAN, Arthur
Numbers man. il por Newsweek 61:54 Ap 1 '63
MCCARTEN, John
Current cinema (cont) New Yorker 39:147 S 7; 118 S 14 '63; 40:90 Je 13; 123+ Je 20; 58 Jl 4 '64
Theatre. See issues of New Yorker
MCCARTER theater, Princeton. See Princeton university
MCCARTHY, Clifford T.
Printing experience. Sch Arts 64:7-13 S '64
MCCARTHY, Eugene J.
Federal government and rural book distribution. por ALA Bul 57:531-3 Je '63
Liberal: what he is and isn't. por N Y Times Mag p8+ S 1 '63
Speaking out. por Sat Eve Post 237:6+ Ja 4 '64

about

Able and willing Eugene McCarthy. D. S. Broder. New Repub 150:8-9 Je 20 '64
Senator Eugene McCarthy: how to succeed by ignoring your well-wishers. M. Smelser. por Harper 228:76-8 Je '64
MCCARTHY, Joe
Barbados without tours. Holiday 33:96+ F '63
Fresh look at Long Island. Holiday 35:78-9+ My '64
Intractable Robert Moses. Holiday 36:99-100+ Jl '64; Same abr. with title Moses (Robert) and the Promised Land. Read Digest 85:117-21 S '64
Ireland in my blood. Holiday 33:82-3+ Ap '63
Long Island is becoming long city. N Y Times Mag p 17+ Ag 30 '64
Some things about Miss America they don't show on television; story. McCalls 90:82-3 S '63
Southie is my home town. Holiday 35:60-1+ Mr '64
Walk through history with Harry Truman. Holiday 34:56-61+ N; 96-7+ D '63
MCCARTHY, Joseph Raymond
For the record: Eisenhower vs. McCarthy over Conant to Germany. W. F. Buckley, jr. Nat R 16:188 Mr 10 '64
McCarthy's last stand; film of army-McCarthy hearings. il por Time 83:49 Ja 17 '64
MCCARTHY, Mary
Gingery sample of McCarthy views; interview, ed. by J. Bonfante. Life 55:64 S 20 '63
Hounds of summer; story. New Yorker 39:47-50 S 14 '63
Mary McCarthy said; interview, ed. by P. D. Smith. por Vogue 142:98-9+ O 15 '63
Polly Andrews, class of '33; story. New Yorker 39:23-32 Je 29 '63

about

Class notes from Vassar. C. B. Ohmann and R. M. Ohmann. Commonweal 79:12-15 S 27 '63
Conservative Miss McCarthy. J. Chamberlain. Nat R 15:353-5 O 22 '63
Contrary Mary; Vassar '33. il pors Newsweek 62:80-3 S 2 '63
Lady with a switchblade. il pors Life 55:61-2+ S 20 '63
Mary McCarthy and The group. M. Darrell. il pors Look 28:106-8+ F 25 '64
Mary McCarthy: one of ours? B. Cook. il por Cath World 199:34-42 Ap '64
Should girls go to college? W. Knapp. Reporter 29:60+ O 10 '63; Discussion. 29:12 N 7 '63

MCCARTHY, Mike
Rattlin' good roadster. Hot Rod 17:74-7 Ag '64
MCCARTHY, Robert
Wonderful legacy of Dr Bob McCarthy. A. Hirshberg. il por Good H 156:68-9+ Mr '63
MCCARTHY, W. E. J.
Challenge facing British unions. bibliog f Ann Am Acad 350:129-37 N '63
MCCARTNEY, James
Senate establishment. Nation 196:219-21 Mr 16 '63
MCCASKILL, James L.
Course ahead for LBJ. NEA J 53:15 Ja '64
MCCASLIN, Walt
Athens on the prairie. Sat Eve Post 237:64-5 Mr 21 '64
What are ltitle boys made of? Read Digest 84:131-3 Je '64
MCCAULEY, Patt Kirby
Keep them safe from child molesters. Parents Mag 39:50-1+ D '64
MACCHESNEY, Catherine
From the window; poem. Good H 156:201 F '63
MCCHESNEY, Malcolm
Shock waves and high temperatures. Sci Am 208:109-19 bibliog(p 185) F '63
MACCHETTA, Blanche Roosevelt (Tucker)
Blanche Roosevelt. C. Matz. il por Opera N 27:26-8 Mr 23 '63
MACCHIAIOLI. See Painting, Italian
MCCHRISTY, Quentin L.
Four pen drawings. il por Am Artist 28:75-7+ Je '64
MCCLAIN, Christine
Alaska offers new ski thrills. Todays Health 42:18-20+ Ja '64
One man's battle against rabies. Todays Health 42:56-9+ D '64
MCCLAIN, Roy O.
Another view of justice. Christian Cent 81: 270-2 F 26 '64
MCCLAIN, William A.
Cincinnati's legal head. il pors Ebony 18: 87-8+ Je '63
MCCLANAHAN, William G.
Don't be a sucker shopper! U S Camera 27: 41+ D '64
MCCLANE, A. J.
Fisherman's guide to the Maritimes. Field & S 69:126-8+ Je '64
(ed) Fishing. See issues of Field & stream
If you can't tie it . . . , nail it! Field & S 69:42-5 Jl '64
Jamaican holiday. por Field & S 68:138-41+ Mr '64
Land of ekaluk aluk. Field & S 68:46-8+ Je '63
Panama paradise. Field & S 68:52-3+ O '63
Topside togue. por Field & S 67:29-31+ F '63
MCCLARREN, J. K.
Our man in Amsterdam; U.S. food and agriculture exhibition. New Yorker 39:24-6 D 21 '63
MCCLARREN, Robert R.
Reading skills. Library J 88:3026 S 1 '63
MCCLELLAN, George B.
Answer to the rise in crime and violence; excerpts from address, September 8, 1964. por U S News 57:89-90 N 9 '64
MCCLELLAN, George Brinton
Election of 1864. J. G. Brown. il Hobbies 69:28-30 Ag '64
Seven days, by C. Dowdey. Review
Am Heritage 15:111-13 Ap '64. B. Catton
Terrible swift sword, by B. Catton. Review
Nat R 15:198+ S 10 '63. G. F. Eliot
MCCLELLAN, John Little
Taxes & spending: why the budget must be cut; interview. por Nations Bsns 51:38-9+ Ap '63
(ed) See Johnson, L. B. What LBJ, as a senator, said about civil rights

about

Another news manager. K. Crawford. Newsweek 61:29 Ap 1 '63
End of road for Hoffa? what his conviction means. il U S News 56:46-7 Mr 16 '64
What's wrong here? K. Crawford. Newsweek 62:22 D 23 '63
MCCLELLAND, David C.
Why men & nations seek success; interview. por Nations Bsns 51:32-3+ S '63
MCCLOSKEY, Mark
Airplane; poem. Sat R 47:29 O 10 '64
God of light; poem. Commonweal 81:567 Ja 29 '65
Smell of the woods; poem. Poetry 103:168 D '63
MCCLOSKEY, Matthew Henry
Bobby Baker again. por Newsweek 64:22 S 14 '64
Parties & payments. por Time 84:32-3 D 11 '64
That lingering aroma. por Time 84:21 S 11 '64
Then the bricks came tumbling down. Time 83:24 F 7 '64
MCCLOSKEY, Robert J.
Department opposes legislation ending aid to Idonesia; statement. Dept State Bul 51:313 Ag 31 '64
Mr Ball leaves for London talks on Cyprus; U.S. restates position; statement, February 8, 1964. Dept State Bul 50:284 F 24 '64
MCCLOY, John J.
Frank talk on NATO; McCloy blames no one, but—excerpts from address. 1963. por U S News 55:12 D 23 '63
MCCLUNG, Ollie
Ollie McClung's big decision. M. Durham. por Life 57:31 O 9 '64
MCCLURE, Alan
Photographing comet Ikeya. il Sky & Tel 25: 263-6 My '63
MACCLURE, Don
Day the earth blew up. Pop Sci 183:48-51+ Ag '63
MCCLURE, Eleanor
Vegetables in your garden. Horticulture 43:34-5+ Ja '65
MCCLURE, F. J.
Cariostatic effect of phosphates. bibliog Science 144:1337-8 Je 12 '64
MCCLURE, James G.
Lilies don't bloom at Easter; story. New Yorker 40:176 O 24 '64
MCCLURE, John T.
Cheerful ghost of Eisenstadt. Hi Fi 15:56-8+ Ja '65
Education and a joy. por Hi Fi 14:40-3+ Ja '64
MCCLURE, Michael
Child; Mad sonnet; Mad sonnet; poems. Poetry 102:152-4 Je '63
MCCLURE, Sam S.
How muckraking began. il por Newsweek 62: 106 S 23 '63
Success story: the life and times of S. S. McClure, by P. Lyon. Review
Atlan 213:136 F '64. E. Weeks
Sat R il por 46:58+ O 12 '63. J. F. Fixx
Tradition of McClure. E. Moers. Commentary 37:70-4 Ap '64
MCCLURE'S magazine
How muckraking began. il Newsweek 62:106 S 23 '63
Tradition of McClure. E. Moers. Commentary 37:70-4 Ap '64
MCCLURG, A. C, and company
Court put five-year ban on McClurg-Parents merger. Pub W 183:90 F 11 '63
McClurg's new distribution center: speed and service. il Pub W 186:26-9 Ag 10 '64
MCCLUSKEY, John
Harvard's egghead quarterback. il pors Ebony 20:129-30+ D '64
MCCLUSKEY, Neil G.
Changing pattern. Commonweal 79:507-11 Ja 31 '64
MCCLUSKY, Howard Y.
New developments in adult education; summary of address. por Pub W 187:49 Ja 11 '65
MACCOBY, Michael
Love and authority. Atlan 213:121-6 Mr '64
MCCOLLUM, Leonard Franklin
Conoco's widening world. R. Sheehan. il por Fortune 69:113-17+ Ap '64
Putting Conoco up with majors. il pors Bsns W p52-3+ N 30 '63
World of the renaissance executive. il por Newsweek 62:92-4 N 18 '63
MCCOMB, Miss.
Battle of McComb. M. Boyd. Christian Cent 81:1398+ N 11 '64
Bowl of gumbo for Curtis Bryant. P. Good. il Reporter 31:19-22 D 31 '64
Civil rights; do not despair. Time 84:35 N 27 '64
Manifesto in McComb. il Newsweek 64:36+ N 30 '64
Step forward in Mississippi. America 111:732 D 5 '64
Terror on schedule. il Newsweek 64:71-2 O 5 '64
MCCONAGHA, Glenn L.
Human equation and the college; excerpts from address. Sch & Soc 91:285 O 5 '63
MCCONE, John Alex
Growing risks of bureaucratic intelligence. H. W. Baldwin. il Reporter 29:48-50+ Ag 15 '63

MCCONE, John Alex—*Continued*
McCone's successor. New Repub 151:4 D 12 '64
My advance view of the Cuban crisis. K. Keating. il Look 28:96+ N 3 '64
Reds with arms and cash spreading out from Cuba; Intelligence report. por U S News 54:69 Mr 11 '63
MCCONKEY, Dale D.
Latin America; encouragement for investors; address, November 20, 1963. Vital Speeches 30:209-14 Ja 15 '64
MCCONKEY, James
Witches of love; story. Yale R 53:563-79 Je '64
MCCONKEY, Thomas W.
(ed) Library buying guide 1964. Library J 89:1518+ Ap 1 '64
(ed) Library buying guide 1963. Library J 88: 1432+ Ap 1 '63
MCCONNAUGHEY, Janet
Cat; poem. Horn Bk 40:664 D '64
MCCONNAUGHY, Mary Jane
Take time for tissue. Sch Arts 62:33-5 My '63
MCCONNEL, Frances
Wild blackberries; poem. Atlan 213:83 F '64
MCCONNELL, D. G. and Scarpelli, D. G.
Rhodopsin: an enzyme. Science 139:848 Mr 1 '63
MCCONNELL, Duncan
Hydrogen ion incorporation in crystals. bibliog Science 141:171 Jl 12 '63
MCCONNELL, H. James
I learned about flying from that. Flying 75: 67-8 S '64
MCCONNELL, James V.
Worm learns. J. Bird. il por Sat Eve Post 237:66-7 Mr 28 '64
MCCONNELL, John Paul
From LeMay to McConnell; a change to the new breed. por Newsweek 65:16 Ja 4 '65
To the top. il por Time 85:29-30 Ja 1 '65
MCCONNELL, John W. See Slavick, F. jt. auth.
MCCONNELL, Joseph
U.S. delegate reports on space radio communication conference; statement, November 8, 1963. Dept State Bul 49:835-7 N 25 '63
MCCONNELL, Joseph H.
Spiritual values of education; address, November 20, 1964. Vital Speeches 31:181-2 Ja 1 '65
MCCONNELL, Ruth, and Postell, Frances
Books for Roosevelt Grady. Library J 89: 3384-6 S 15 '64
MCCONNELL, Will
Point Pelee in March; poem. New Yorker 39: 130 Mr 23 '63
MCCORD, Jean
Lonely price of victory; story. Seventeen 23: 130-1 Je '64
MCCORMACK, Arthur
Economics of aid. Commonweal 81:227-30 N 13 '64
Food and people. Commonweal 80:79-82 Ap 10 '64
New era for the nun in the world. Cath World 199:144-51 Je '64
Population explosion. America 110:482-5 Ap 4 '64
MCCORMACK, John William
Eulogy to John F. Kennedy, November 24, 1963. Vital Speeches 30:98-9 D 1 '63

about

Heartbeat away; presidential succession. il por Newsweek 62:23-4 D 16 '63
If something happened to the President. il por U S News 55:37 D 16 '63
Job John McCormack dreads. D. Oberdorfer. il pors Sat Eve Post 237:66+ Mr 21 '64
McCormack and Hayden: no plan to quit. por U S News 55:12 D 23 '63
Men in line for the presidency now. por U S News 55:14 D 2 '63
New presidential successor. por Sr Schol 83: 19 D 6 '63
Next in line. il por Time 82:16 D 27 '63
Size-up of new Vice President. il pors U S News 55:26-7 D 30 '63
Speaker vs. the hard-liners. M. Viorst. Reporter 29:43-4 O 24 '63
What sort of president would John W. McCormack make? por Esquire 62:90-3 Jl '64
MCCORMACK, Mark H.
Shoot for a million. por Sports Illus 20:34+ Ap 6 '64
MCCORMICK, Adoreen. See Hamer, E. E. jt. auth.
MCCORMICK, Harold W. and others
Hawk that swims; excerpt from Shadows in the sea. Sat R 46:66 O 5 '63
MCCORMICK, James
Runner through the mist. Atlan 211:63-8 Mr '63
MCCORMICK, Joan
Inquietude; poem. Negro Hist Bul 27:22 O '63
Troubled time; poem. Negro Hist Bul 27: 90 Ja '64
MCCORMICK, Patricia
Brave matadora explains the bullfight. por Sports Illus 18:38-44+ Mr 11 '63
MCCORMICK, Richard A.
Conjugal love and conjugal morality. America 110:38-42 Ja 11 '64
Family size. America 110:1-2 Ja 4 '64
Laymen and theologians; toward a dialogue. Commonweal 80:313-17 Je 5 '64
Whither the pill? Cath World 199:207-14 Jl '64
MCCORMICK Selph associates
Explosive ordnance systems approach advocated. J. F. Judge. Miss & Roc 12:41+ My 27 '63
MCCORRY, Vincent P.
Paul the pilgrim. America 110:166-7 F 1 '64
Urban in the lions' den. America 108:292-4 Mr 2 '63
Word. See issues of America
MCCOWN, Eleanor
Desert is not all sand. Horticulture 41:86-7 F '63
Spurias that mimic butterflies. Pop Gard 14:33+ My '63
MCCOY, E. M.
Role-playing in comparing communism to democracy. Sr Schol 83:15T O 18 '63
MCCOY, Harriet Ann. See Swindler, D. R. jt. auth.
MCCOY, Marie Bell
True act of charity. Good H 157:104+ Jl '63
MCCOY, R. A. Jr
This line will change duties. Am City 79: 116-17 Je '64
MCCRACKEN, James
Behold the lion; interview, ed. by A. M. Lingg. por Opera N 27:15 Mr 23 '63
In praise of all people. Sat R 47:51 O 31 '64

about

Day's work. il por Time 81:39 Mr 22 '63
James McCracken: career in three acts. M. Esterow. por Mus Am 83:18 My '63
Music to my ears; a great Otello by Solti and McCracken. I. Kolodin. il por Sat R 46: 30-1+ Mr 23 '63
Return of the native. por Newsweek 61: 95 Mr 25 '63
MCCRACKEN, Paul W. and others
Why credit controls would hurt. Nations Bsns 52:34-5+ D '64
MCCREARY, Edward A.
Those American managers don't impress Europe; excerpts from Americanization of Europe. Fortune 70:138-9+ D '64
MCCREE, Wade H. Jr
Memorial for Medgar Evers; In memoriam, JFK; poems. Negro Hist Bul 27:129-30 F '64
MCCROCKLIN, James H.
Patient will live. Am City 78:7 O '63
MCCRORY corporation
But when they voted: proxy fight. Newsweek 62:104 O 14 '63
Rapid-American trouble hinted by McCrory shift. Bsns W p 168 My 18 '63
Who's to blame for Riklis?-Riklis? S. H. Brown. il Fortune 68:136-7+ O '63
MCCUBBIN, James W. and Page, I. H.
Neurogenic component of chronic renal hypertension. Science 139:210+ Ja 18 '63
MCCUDDEN, John
Question of relevance. Cath World 198:7-13 O '63
MCCUE, J. J. G.
Ultrasonics. Science 147:309-10 Ja 15 '65
MCCULLAR, Bernice
Let's make it exciting! NEA J 52:10-12 Mr '63
MCCULLERS, Carson
Ballad of the sad cafe; dramatization. See Albee, E.
Isak Dinesen: in praise of radiance. Sat R 46:29+ Mr 16 '63
Sucker; story. Sat Eve Post 236:68-71 S 28 '63
Sweet as a pickle and clean as a pig. Redbook 124:49-56 D '64

about

Pad in Brooklyn Heights. O. Evans. Nation 199:15-16 Jl 13 '64
MCCULLOCH, E. A. and others
Spleen-colony formation in anemic mice of genotype WW. bibliog Science 144:844-6 My 15 '64

MCCULLOCH, Frank W.
Effects of NLRB action on the duty to bargain; excerpt from address, May 27, 1964. Mo Labor R 87:895-8 Ag '64

MCCULLOCH, Robert, and Beale, Alice
Silversmiths of Barnstable, Massachusetts. Antiques 84:72-4 Jl '63

MCCULLOCH, William
Excerpt from debate, August 19, 1964. Cong Digest 44:20+ Ja '65
Sandman, Cato. Nat R 16:482 Je 16 '64

MCCULLOUGH, David
Strange time: story. Redbook 123:64-5 S '64

MCCULLOUGH, Geraldine
Gold medal for talent. il pors Ebony 19:113-14+ Je '64

MCCULLOUGH, John W.
Excerpt from testimony before the Committee on agriculture of the U.S. house of representatives, June 12, 1963. Cong Digest 43:188+ Je '64

MCCULLY, Robert S.
Travel far and near; art of Ajanta and Ellora. Natur Hist 73:53-7 bibliog(p63) N '64

MCCUMBER, C. A.
How one community acquired a nature center. Audubon Mag 65:244-5 Jl '63

MCCURDY, Robert
Top Negro jockey. il pors Ebony 19:63-4+ F '64

MCCUTCHEON, A. E. See McCutcheon, F. H. jt. auth.

MCCUTCHEON, F. H. and McCutcheon, A. E.
Symbiotic behavior among fishes from temperate ocean waters. bibliog Science 145:948-9 Ag 28 '64

MCCUTCHEON, Steve
There's a way to ride a river; probing the Kobuk's arctic wilderness. Pop Mech 119:107-9+ My '63

MCCUTCHEON, W. J.
Lingering sickness. Christian Cent 81:437 Ap 1 '64

MCDADE, Joseph M.
Congress in the atomic age; interview, ed. by R. Steel. pors(p 16) Sr Schol 82:18 F 20 '63

MCDANIEL, Ed
Wahoo! Wahoo! Wahoo! E. Shrake. il por Sports Illus 21:66+ O 26 '64

MCDANIEL, Shirley
Sea horses and Apache tears. por Wilson Lib Bul 37:682 Ap '63

MACDANIELS, L. H.
Hazelnuts and filberts. Horticulture 42:44-5+ O '64

MACDERMOT, Anne
Etchcraft on celluloid. UNESCO Courier 17:20-3 Ja '64

MCDERMOTT, Edwin J.
Cowboy and priest. America 108:465 Ap 6 '63

MCDERMOTT, John
Small war in Westport. J. Skow. il por Sat Eve Post 237:18-19 N 28 '64

MCDERMOTT, John J.
Basic ambiguity. Commonweal 81:21-2 S 25 '64
Prescriptions. Commonweal 79:352-4 D 13 '63

MCDERMOTT, John R.
Author says he had plenty to yell about. Life 55:40+ Ag 16 '63
Champ twenty three: a man-child taken in by the Muslims. Life 56:38-9 Mr 6 '64
Everybody his own quarterback. Life 57:15-16 D 18 '64
Opening of the Olympics. Life 57:76B-80 O 23 '64
Sobs and moans in the locker room. Life 57:110 D 11 '64
Willie the wonder. Life 56:50-2 My 15 '64
Yanks tighten the rules for two challengers by sea. Life 56:74+ Je 12 '64

MCDERMOTT, Richard Terrance
Bashful barber and a worldly kid from Smoke Rise. H. Horn. il por Sports Illus 20:20-1 F 17 '64

MCDEVITT, Charles R.
Goldwater, Rockefeller, and the Young Republicans. M. S. Evans. il Nat R 15:97-100+ Ag 13 '63

MCDEVITT, Jan
(ed) Craftsman in production. Craft Horiz 24:21-33 Mr '64
Jack Lenor Larsen. Craft Horiz 24:49-50 Mr '64

MCDIARMID, Hugh, pseud. See Grieve, C. M.

MCDIVITT, James
Whole door full of keyholes. Life 55:86A-86B S 27 '63

MCDONAGH, Donald
Ballet master. Commonweal 79:552-5 Ja 31 '64
Olympic ogre: a quite grim tale. Dance Mag 38:35-7+ N '64

MACDONALD, Alice K.
Skyscraper impressions. Sch Arts 62:37-8 Ap '63

MACDONALD, Barbara Thurlow
Time savers & time adjusters. Parents Mag 39:87+ F '64

MACDONALD, Brian
In the news. por Dance Mag 37:46 D '63

MCDONALD, C. C. and others
Nucleic acids: a nuclear magnetic resonance study. bibliog Science 144:1234-7 Je 5 '64

MCDONALD, C. H.
Match the treatment to street conditions. Am City 80:102-4 Ja '65

MACDONALD, Dave
Roar of triumph for U.S. engines. K. Rudeen. il Sports Illus 19:20-1 O 21 '63

MACDONALD, David
Bonny pipes of Scotland. Read Digest 85:112-14 S '64
Oak Island's mysterious money pit. Read Digest 86:136-40 Ja '65

MCDONALD, David J.
Automation and full employment; address, March 9, 1964. Vital Speeches 30:409-12 Ap 15 '64
Labor-management relations; address, December 5, 1963. Vital Speeches 30:189-92 Ja 1 '64

about

Battle of Pittsburgh: who to head the USW? il por Newsweek 64:81-2 N 23 '64
But I love you. il por Time 84:33-4 N 20 '64
Fight inside union; will it affect steel prices, wages? por U S News 57:80-1 N 23 '64
In steel: no strike, longer vacations, longer contracts. il por U S News 54:86 Je 24 '63
Rebellion in steel. R. W. Gibbons. Commonweal 81:540-2 Ja 22 '65
Unions' latest goal: lifetime jobs. il por U S News 58:88+ Ja 25 '65
Union's price for peace in steel. il por U S News 57:81-3 D 14 '64
USW simmers as steel talks near. il Bsns W p47-8 N 21 '64

MCDONALD, David Lamar
Merchant marine fleet; address, November 13, 1964. Vital Speeches 31:188-90 Ja 1 '65
Mixed-manned demonstration ship visits Washington; remarks, October 20, 1964. Dept State Bul 51:662 N 9 '64
Navy's role in Cuba, Panama, southeast Asia; interview. por U S News 56:66-70 Mr 2 '64
Sea power selectivity; address, October 10, 1964. Vital Speeches 31:123-5 D 1 '64

about

Bossing the brass. por Newsweek 61:36+ My 20 '63
Hot spot jobs for two admirals. por U S News 55:9 Ag 12 '63
Stormy days for the navy. il por Time 82:37 N 15 '63

MACDONALD, Dwight
Films. See issues of Esquire
New York times, alas. Esquire 59:55-7+ Ap; 104+ My '63
Our baby. New Repub 150:30 Ja 25; 29-31 F 29 '64

about

I know about the Negroes and the poor. R. J. Dwyer. por Nat R 15:517-18+ D 17 '63
Manner of speaking. J. Ciardi. Sat R 46:10+ Mr 9 '63

MCDONALD, Elvin
Beginner's guide to fall planting. Pop Gard 14:33-6 S '63
Get the most from your orange tree. Pop Gard 15:38 Ja '64
Highlights of spring planting. Pop Gard 15:31-4 Mr '64

MCDONALD, Erwin L.
Baptist editor survives attack. Christian Cent 81:1582 D 23 '64

MCDONALD, Gerald D.
Prospecting in the West. Library J 88:3021-2 S 1 '63

MACDONALD, Gordon J. F.
Deep structure of continents. bibliog Science 143:921-9 F 28 '64
Earth and moon: past and future. bibliog Science 145:881-90 Ag 28 '64

MCDONALD, Hugh C.
Box that catches criminals. F. Sondern, jr. Read Digest 84:40+ Ap '64

MCDONALD, James Edward
Pollen wettability as a factor in washout by raindrops. bibliog Science 143:1180-1 Mr 13 '64
Research frontier. Sat R 46:40 Ag 3 '63
Stratospheric cloud over northern Arizona. bibliog Science 140:292-4 Ap '63

MACDONALD, Jeanette
Funeral of the year. il por Newsweek 65: 22-3 F 1 '65
MCDONALD, John
Big steel wants a bigger share. Fortune 71:136-9+ Ja '65
Company that never left town. Fortune 70: 114-17+ Ag '64
Diamonds for the masses. Fortune 70:134-7+ D '64
Sears makes it look easy. Fortune 69:120-7+ My '64
Where's the ceiling on new houses? Fortune 67:128-32+ Je '63
MACDONALD, John D.
Matter of trust; story. Redbook 123:131-43 Ag '64
Obvious woman; story. Sat Eve Post 236:38-9 Mr 30 '63
MACDONALD, John Dann
How to live with a hero. Writer 77:14-16+ S '64
Rights and permissions. P. Nathan. Pub W 186:51 S 14 '64
MCDONALD, Julie
Man running; story. Redbook 121:133-60 Jl '63
MCDONALD, Katherine Griffith
Dark brilliance. Opera N 28:24-5 Mr 7 '64
Gods at twilight. Opera N 28:24-5 D 14 '63
Improvviso. Opera N 27:25-6 Mr 2 '63
What makes Samson run. Opera N 29:24-5 D 26 '64
MACDONALD, N. S. and others
Gamma-emitting radionuclides in newborns, infants, and children. bibliog Science 141: 1033-5 S 13 '63
MCDONALD, R. A.
Another parson's view; poem. Christian Cent 81:1595 D 23 '64
MACDONALD, Ross
Nature. Sports Illus 20:86-9 Ap 6 '64
MCDONALD, Tommy
Monsters and me. pors Sports Illus 21:58-65 Jl 27; 39-42+ Ag 3 '64
MACDONALD, William B. jr
Many faces of Mr Mac. G. Rogin. il pors Sports Illus 20:54-6+ F 17 '64
MCDONALD, William J.
Crisis at Catholic U; ban on speakers. il por Time 81:58+ Mr 29 '63
MCDONNEL, Kilian
Calvin without myths. Commonweal 81:163-6 O 30 '64
MACDONNEL Y DE GONDÉ, Enrique
Phantom war of 1804. J. C. Fernández. il Américas 15:23-8 Je '63
MCDONNELL, Helen
Why not study abroad? Sr Schol 85:13T Ja 7 '65
MCDONNELL, Lawrence V.
Priest-hero in the modern novel. Cath World 196:306-11 F '63
MACDONNELL, Malcomn F. and Flynn, J. P.
Attack elicited by stimulation of the thalamus of cats. bibliog Science 144:1249-50 Je 5 '64
MACDONNELL, R. M.
Charting skies for supersonic air travel. por U N Rev 10:38-9 Mr '63
MCDONNELL, Thomas P.
Essays on Greene. Commonweal 79:727-9 Mr 13 '64
O'Neill's drama of the psyche. Cath World 197:120-5 My '63
Poet from the West. Commonweal 78:13-14 Mr 29 '63
MCDONNELL aircraft corporation
Banshee, demon, voodoo, phantom, and bingo! R. J. Whalen. il Fortune 70:136-9+ N '64
NAA, McDonnell repeat at NASA. il Miss & Roc 14:18 Ja 20 '64
MCDONOUGH Roger H. and Richards, K. W.
State library for New Jersey. Library J 89: 4709-10 D 1 '64
MACDONOUGH, Thomas
Victory on Lake Champlain. C. S. Forester. il por Am Heritage 15:4-11+ D '63
MACDOUGAL street. See New York (city)—Streets
MACDOUGALL, H. A.
Catholicism and freedom. America 110:486-7 Ap 4 '64
MCDOUGALL, Harry
Airborne antics. U S Camera 26:76-7 Je '63
Avian gyroplane. Flying 74:44-5+ Ap '64
MCDOWALL, R.
(ed) See Oliver, L. Great Sir Laurence
MCDOWELL, Edwin
On the beach with Morrie Ryskind. Nat R 14: 318-19 Ap 23 '63
Will we lose the Canal? Nat R 16:107-8 F 11 '64
MCDOWELL, Ephraim
Pioneer in women's surgery. il Todays Health 42:55 Je '64
MCDOWELL, James L.
Illinois: chaos at the polls. J. L. McDowell. Reporter 30:30-2 Mr 26 '64
Percy's purge. New Repub 150:8 Je 27 '64
MCDOWELL, John T.
Community approach to the home: homemaker service. bibliog f Ann Am Acad 355: 62-8 S '64
MCDOWELL, P. E.
So you want to entertain the public! Am For 70:22-5+ Ja '64
MACDOWELL memorial colony, Peterboro, N.H.
Care and feeding of artists. H. Kubly. il Horizon 5:26-33 Mr '63
Short, cool summer at the colony. S. Drexler. il Art N 63:37-9+ D '64
MACDUFFIE, Malcolm
Would you like to take a sabbatical afloat? Yachting 113:55-7+ Mr '63
Yankee cruises the Chesapeake. Yachting 116:40-2+ D '64
MACE, Charles H.
Impact of international travel on U.S. balance of payments; statement, November 20, 1964. Dept State Bul 51:888-90 D 21 '64
MACE, David R.
How men feel about sex. Read Digest 82:70-2 Je '63
If you marry a foreigner. McCalls 90:60+ F '63
Pregnancy & the young husband. McCalls 90: 162+ Ap '63
MACE, Myles L.
President and corporate planning. Harvard Bsns R 43:49-62 Ja '65
MACEDONIA
History
See also
Alexander the Great
MCELENEY, Neil J.
Christian's vocation: a call to status and mission. Cath World 197:152-8 Je '63
MCELHENNEY, G.
Our good neighbor, the sewage-purification plant. Am City 78:94-6 F '63
MCELHENY, Victor K.
Biochemical laboratory at Uppsala. Science 144:1323-5 Je 12 '64
Biological research in Czechoslovakia. Science 145:799-802 Ag 21 '64
Britain confronts its technical options. Science 146:1446-9 D 11 '64
Britain's National institute of oceanography. bibliog Science 144:160-3 Ap 10 '64
French bomb: how much technical fallout? Science 147:35-6 Ja 1 '65
Great Britain: science and labor's squeak-in. Science 146:506-8 O 23 '64
International space science symposium. Science 144:1434-7 Je 19 '64
Laboratory of molecular biology, Cambridge. Science 144:398-400; 145:36-8 Ap 24, Jl 3 '64
Particle accelerators at CERN. Science 144: 983-6 My 22 '64
Research climate in Italy. Science 145:690-3 Ag 14 '64
Research in biology: new pattern of support is developing. Science 145:908-12 Ag 28 '64
Revival of oceanography in Germany. Science 146:45-8 O 2 '64
Time of trial for European research cooperation. Science 147:280-2 Ja 15 '65
Triennial review of astronomy. bibliog Science 146:627-30 O 30 '64
MCELMAN, Martha. See Randall, R. H. jr jt. auth.
MCELRATH, Dennis C. See Mack, R. W. jt. auth.
MCELROY, George
Abbé and the image. Opera N 28:12-13 D 21 '63
Forebears of Falstaff. Opera N 29:24-5 Ja 23 '65
Vice of kings. Opera N 28:22-5 Ap 4 '64
MCELROY, Neil H.
Business' responsibility in government relationships; address, November 10, 1964. Vital Speeches 31:139-40 D 15 '64
MCELROY, W. D.
Protein structure and function during differentiation. Science 140:1427-30 Je 28 '63
MCELWEE, W. D.
Street cleaning gets assembly-line techniques. Am City 78:126-7 Je '63
MCENTEE, Howard G.
All's quiet on the TV front. Pop Sci 182:140-4 Ap '63
Build your own radio remote control. Pop Sci 185:108-11 Ag '64

MCENTEE, Howard G.—*Continued*
Light-activated switch. Pop Sci 184:128-9+ Ja '64
Packaged power packs new punch. Pop Sci 184:80-3+ Je '64
MCENTEGART, Bryan
Totality of outlook; address, January 24, 1963. Vital Speeches 29:299-300 Mr 1 '63
MACEOIN, Gary
Genocide in Sudan. Commonweal 80:539-42 Ag 7 '64
MCEVOY, J. P.
Lesson in logic. Read Digest 82:200C F '63
Wanta borrow a jack? Read Digest 83:108-9 S '63
MACEWEN, Gwendolyn
Poem improvised around a first line. Atlan 214:145 N '64
about
Canadian chronicle. P. Webb. Poetry 104: 385-6 S '64
MCEWEN, Terry
Defender of the realm. Opera N 27:30-1 Mr 9 '63
MCFADDEN, Dorothy Loa
Compatible companions. House B 106:26+ Je '64
Scotland's gardens. Pop Gard 14:32-3+ Ap '63
MACFADDEN-Bartell corporation
Macfadden publisher under World's fair pact; official publisher for the Hall of education. Pub W 185:134 F 24 '64
MCFARLAN, Ethel
Pear tree; drama. Plays 22:42, 71-3 Ap '63
Winter garden; drama. Plays 23:75-8, 96 Ja '64
MCFARLAND, Walter B.
Review of funds-flow analysis. bibliog f Harvard Bsns R 41:162-4+ S '63
MCFARLANE, Alexander Nelson
Difference in being president. T. R. Brooks. pors Duns R 84:33-4 D '64
MCFEGGAN, James
Cul-de-sacs demand special snow units. Am City 79:88-9 N '64
MCFETRIDGE, William L.
House the janitors built; Marina City, Chicago. G. Cross. il por Read Digest 82:201-4 F '63
Union support of towers toppling. il Bsns W p 108 My 16 '64
MCGAHERN, John
Summer at Strandhill; story. New Yorker 39:43-8 S 21 '63
MCGAHEY, Jeanne
Family circle; poem. Poetry 102:241 Jl '63
MCGARVEY, Ayleen
Obituary for reluctant mammals. Nat R 14: 363-4 My 7 '63
MCGAUGH, James L. and Madsen, M. C.
Amnesic and punishing effects of electroconvulsive shock. bibliog Science 144:182-3 Ap 10 '64
MCGAUGHEY, James Paul
Build yourself a man-size blind. Field & S 68:80-1 N '63
MCGAVRAN, Malcolm H.
Chromaffin cell: electron microscopic identification in the human dermis. bibliog Science 145:275-6 Jl 17 '64
MCGEE, Gale
Art of politics. NEA J 52:36-9 F '63
MCGEE, Reece
Texas: the roots of the agony. Nation 197: 427-31 D 21 '63
MCGHEE, George C.
American look at Berlin; address, October 9, 1963. bibliog f Dept State Bul 49:819-24 N 25 '63
Atlantic partnership: a vital force in motion; address, April 28, 1963. Dept State Bul 48: 771-5 My 20 '63
Current look at NATO; address, January 15, 1964. Dept State Bul 50:338-44 Mr 2 '64
Dynamics of progress in central Europe; address, November 11, 1964. Dept State Bul 51:870-6 D 21 '64
East-West relations today; address, February 18, 1964. Dept State Bul 50:488-96 Mr 30 '64
Eastern Europe: a region in ferment; address, October 13, 1964. Dept State Bul 51: 716-21 N 16 '64
Foreign policy and the rule of law; address, May 3, 1963. Dept State Bul 48:867-71 Je 3 '63
International coffee agreement, 1962; statement, March 12, 1963. Dept State Bul 48: 493-7 Ap 1 '63
Parallel roles of business and diplomacy in an era of expanding frontiers; address, May 19, 1964. Dept State Bul 51:18-25 Jl 6 '64
Some American thoughts on current issues; address, July 16, 1964. Dept State Bul 51: 138-44 Ag 3 '64
United States of America and the Atlantic partnership; address, November 21, 1963. Dept State Bul 49:954-9 D 23 '63
MCGHEE, Peter S.
Biography of a tenement; from pasture to squalor. Nation 198:293-6 Mr 23 '64
Bowery bums' rush. Nation 198:483-5 My 11 '64
Island joins the march. Nation 198:51-2 Ja 13 '64
MCGILL, Ralph Emerson
Case for the southern progressive. Sat R 47: 17-20 Je 13 '64
Decade of slow, painful progress. Sat R 47: 65-6 My 16 '64
Race: results instead of reasons. Sat R 48:52 Ja 9 '65
South has many faces; excerpts from South and the southerner. por Atlan 211:83-98 Ap '63
South looks ahead. por Ebony 18:99-100+ S '63
Speaking out. por Sat Eve Post 236:8+ D 14 '63
about
Episcopal diocese censors McGill. Christian Cent 80:1260 O 16 '63
Voice of moderation. por Newsweek 61:110 Mr 25 '63
MCGILL, Thomas E. and Tucker, G. R.
Genotype and sex drive in intact and in castrated male mice. bibliog Science 145: 514-15 Jl 31 '64
MACGILLIVRAY, Leo
Place des arts: the building. Mus Am 83: 14-15 S '63
MCGINLEY, Phyllis
Cook and the book. Sat R 47:61-3 O 24 '64
Let's stop shortchanging young readers; excerpt from Hearth has its reasons. Read Digest 84:142-4 Ap '64
Little girl's room; poem. McCalls 90:74-83 Je '63
Sixpence in her shoe (cont of) Profession: housewife; excerpts. Ladies Home J 80: 87+ Ja; 82+ Mr; 60+ Ap; 26+ My; 78-9+ Je; 43+ Jl; 34+ S; 26+ O; 20+ N '63; 81: 42+ Ap; 30+ My; 22+ Jl; 30+ Ag; 38+ S '64; Same abr. of Ag issue. Read Digest 86: 72-4 Ja '65
about
Open letter to the New Yorker. R. M. Brown. Christian Cent 80:956-7 Jl 31 '63; Reply. D. E. Faust. 80:1142-3 S 18 '63
MCGINNIS, A. J. and Kasting, R.
Chromic oxide indicator method for measuring food utilization in a plant-feeding insect. bibliog Science 144:1464-5 Je 19 '64
MCGINNIS, Patrick Benedict
Hotbox for Pat. Time 82:65 Ag 23 '63
Two counts against Pat. Newsweek 62:62-3 Ag 26 '63
MCGINNIS, Ralph Y.
How can we serve? address, July 4, 1964. Vital Speeches 30:657-9 Ag 15 '64
MCGLOTHLIN, William H.
Frontier within. Nation 199:360-2 N 16 '64
MCGOVERN, George S.
Is Castro an obsession with us? N Y Times Mag p9+ My 19 '63
MCGOVERN, John P.
How to control allergy. Parents Mag 39: 95-6+ Jl '64
MCGOVERN, Margaret
Ma: a plain song. Atlan 214:67 Jl '64
MCGOVERN, Robert
At Christmas; poem. Christian Cent 81:1583 D 23 '64
MCGOVERN, William
William McGovern, RIP; letter. J. W. Kolbe. Nat R 17:14 Ja 12 '65
MCGOWAN, J. A. See Fager, E. W. jt. auth.
MCGOWAN, Jane
Birthday pie; drama. Plays 23:79-83 F '64
Christmas every day; dramatization of story by W. D. Howells. Plays 23:87-95 D '63
Christmas umbrella; drama. Plays 24:51-60 D '64
Cupid in command; drama. Plays 23:71-4 F '64
MCGRADY, Pat
Leukemia: key to the cancer puzzle? Sci Digest 53:31-6 Je '63
—and Morgan, Murray
Cancer is yielding up its secrets: excerpt from The savage cell. Sat Eve Post 237:19-23 My 9 '64
Will chemicals cure cancer? excerpt from Savage cell. Sat Eve Post 237:68-70 My 16 '64

MCGRANE, Julia
Welcome back; poem. Christian Cent 81:514 Ap 22 '64
MCGRATH, Earl J.
Plea for the year-round college. N Y Times Mag p52+ Ap 28 '63
Special mission of the church-related college. Sch & Soc 91:165-8 Ap 6 '63
MCGRATH, Edward H.
Aid for Indian steel. America 109:108 Ag 3 '63
MCGRATH, Thomas
Buffalo coat; For Eugenia; Coal fire in winter; poems. Poetry 104:361-2 S '64
MCGRATTY, Arthur R.
That the blind may read. America 108:792-3 Je 1 '63
MCGRAW, Gerald
I get 100 lbs. pork from 331 lbs. feed. por Suc Farm 61:42 Ag '63
MCGRAW-Hill, incorporated
Flexible spaces, for paper work, in the country; Hightstown, N.J. buildings. il Arch Rec 133:189-93 Ap '63
McGraw-Hill breaks ground for $8.3 million book center. Pub W 186:35 Jl 27 '64
McGraw-Hill establishes Australian subsidiary. Pub W 186:36-7 N 2 '64
McGraw-Hill opens its new European hq in England. il Pub W 184:64 N 11 '63
McGraw-Hill starts new educational division. Pub W 184:25 D 16 '63
Spending goes up, but not so fast. il Bsns W p38-9 N 7 '64
Terms set for acquisition of Webster by McGraw-Hill. Pub W 183:90 F 11 '63
MCGRAW-Hill book company. See McGraw-Hill, incorporated
MCGRAW-Hill publishing company. See McGraw-Hill, incorporated
MCGREGOR, Bobby
Scotch and a little water. J. Lovesey. il pors Sports Illus 21:34-7 Jl 20 '64
MACGREGOR, Felipe E.
Soviet university. America 111:779-80 D 12 '64
MACGREGOR, H. C. and Uzzell, T. M. Jr
Gynogenesis in salamanders related to ambystoma jeffersonianum. bibliog Science 143:1043-5 Mr 6 '64
MCGRORY, Mary
Washington front. See issues of America
MACGUIGAN, Mark R.
Canada's crisis. Commonweal 79:747-9 Mr 20 '64
One world, one law? Commonweal 81:450-3 D 25 '64
MCGUINESS, Kenneth C.
Is Kennedy board rewriting labor law? il por U S News 55:91-2 Jl 8 '63
MCGUIRE, Frank G.
After the moon, this. Sci Digest 55:71-5 Ja '64
Air force to take over PMR. Miss & Roc 13:12 Ag 12 '63
MCGUIRE, Marie C.
Federal housing agencies encouraging good design. Arch Rec 136:104+ Ag '64
PHA and design: commissioner outlines aims; excerpts from address, December 5, 1963. Arch Rec 135:23+ Ja '64
MCGURN, Barrett
Newsman's tribute; John XXIII. America 108:857-8 Je 15 '63
MACH, B. and Tatum, E. L.
Ribonucleic acid synthesis in protoplasts of escherichia coli: inhibition by actinomycin D. bibliog Science 139:1051-2 Mr 15 '63
MACHADO, Antonio
From the apocryphal songbook: Abel Martín; poem. tr. by B. Belitt. Poetry 101:312-18 F '63
To José María Palacio; Draw-wheel; Ephemeral past; O luminous late day! Grey olives; Proverbs and canticles; Winter sun; poems. tr. by C. Tomlinson. Poetry 101:303-11 F '63
about
Poet of absences. S. Moss. Poetry 105:198-201 D '64
Poetry of Antonio Machado. H. St Martin. Poetry 101:343-5 F '63
MACHADO, Gustavo
With impunity & immunity. por Time 82:37 Jl 5 '63
MACHADO, Joseph
Fuchsias outdoors. Horticulture 42:30-2 Ag '64
MACHADO, Lourival Gomes
Rousseau's message for our world today. UNESCO Courier 16:21-3 Mr '63
MCHALE, Paul. See Kirk, J. E. jt. auth.
MCHARG, Ian L.
Place of nature in the city of man. bibliog f Ann Am Acad 352:1-12 Mr '64
MACHATTIE, Lorne A. and Thomas, C. A. jr
DNA from bacteriophage lambda: molecular length and conformation. bibliog Science 144:1142-4 My 29 '64
—and others
Fragment sizes produced from T5 bacteriophage DNA molecules by acid deoxyribonuclease. bibliog Science 141:59-60 Jl 5 '63
MACHEN, Eddie
Case of the frustrated fighter. M. Morgan. il pors Sat Eve Post 236:71-2 My 18 '63
Fight in Sweden between boxing's forgotten men. T. Maule. il por Sports Illus 21:50-2 Jl 6 '64
Second chance. Newsweek 62:63 S 30 '63
MCHENRY, Dean E.
Santa Cruz campus. Arch Rec 136:176-8 N '64
MACHIAVELLI, Niccolò
Loom of language and the fabric of imperatives: the case of Il principe and Utopia. J. H. Hexter. bibliog f Am Hist R 69:945-68 Jl '64
They made our world. L. Rosten. il por Look 27:118-19 N 19 '63
MACHINE accounting. See Accounting—Mechanical aids
MACHINE age
Poet and the machine, by P. Ginestier. Review
Poetry 101:292-4 Ja '63. W. Fowlie
See also
Technocracy
Technology and civilization
MACHINE aided cognition. See Calculating machines—Cooperative use
MACHINE billing. See Billing
MACHINE in politics. See Boss rule
MACHINE shop practice
See also
Forging
MACHINE tool industry and trade
Foreign tool builders hit bumps. il Bsns W p62+ Mr 21 '64
Getting off the cyclical swing. il Bsns W p 172+ N 21 '64
Machine tools make a comeback. il Bsns W p 187-8+ Ap 20 '63
Tooling up. Time 81:89-90 My 10 '63
Unplanned obsolescence. il Newsweek 61:83-4 My 13 '63
When bottlenecks need to be broken. il Bsns W p47-8 Ag 29 '64
MACHINE tools
Lake street clan; used-machine-tool business. Newsweek 64:59-60 Ag 3 '64
Machine tools show their age; survey of metalworking equipment. il Bsns W p65-6+ My 4 '63
Multipurpose tool gets a built-in sawdust vacuum. R. J. DeCristoforo. il Pop Mech 120:109-11 N '63
New seesaw Shopsmith speeds tool changing. J. Hand. il Pop Sci 183:114-17+ N '63
PM tests the Multi-matic. il Pop Mech 121:184-5 F '64
Popular science buyer's guide to home shop tools. il Pop Sci 183:157+ N; 155-6+ D '63
Shop talk. S. M. Gallager. See issues of Popular science monthly
Short cuts and tips for machine-shop workers. H. J. Gerber. il Pop Sci 186:158-9 Ja '65
Tools you need for pipe jobs. R. Treves. il Pop Sci 183:98-100+ Ag '63
Used tools star in new roles. il Bsns W p58+ Mr 21 '64
What's new at the hardware show. S. M. Gallager. il Pop Sci 183:31+ D '63
Workshop. il Consumer Rep 29:276-91 D '64
See also
Drilling and boring machinery
Grinding machines
Lathes
Machine tool industry and trade
Vises
Control
Another coming of age. Bsns W p73 O 24 '64
No finger guides the roving pen; numerically controlled drafting machines. il Bsns W p86 Mr 28 '64
Numerical controls get a new chore; techniques of mass production. Bsns W p54 Ag 3 '63
Putting machine shops on tape; Kearney & Trecker use numerical controls. il Bsns W p 100 Mr 7 '64
Tape can run the machine better. il Bsns W p 100-2+ Mr 30 '63

MACHINE tools—*Continued*

Numerical control

See Machine tools—Control

Renting

See also

Machinery—Leasing

MACHINE translators. See Translating machines

MACHINE work

See also

Indexing (machine work)

MACHINE works

Employees

See also

Machinery industry—Wages and hours

MACHINERY

See also

Agricultural machinery
Bookbinding machinery
Engines
Textile machinery

Exhibitions

Industrial tent show; ShowMart. il Bsns W p 130 O 5 '63

Leasing

Leasing grows in Britain. Bsns W p61-2 Jl 20 '63

Moving in on leasing's middle men; commercial banks in equipment leasing. Bsns W p80-1 Ag 10 '63

MACHINERY, Automatic

AMF expects its R&D to yield new divisions. il Bsns W p 134-6+ My 4 '63

Automation on the assembly line. H. E. Klein. il Duns R 84:37-8+ D '64

Clean, quiet foundry almost runs itself; Sloan valve company foundry, Melrose Park, Ill. il Bsns W p52-3 Ap 13 '63

How to live with machines. F. Leiber. Sci Digest 53:26-30 Je '63

Industrial plant of the future; address, January 29, 1963. F. L. Whitney. Vital Speeches 29:369-72 Ap 1 '63

John Snyder's marvelous mythmaking machine; U.S. industries' transferobot. Fortune 71:127 Ja '65

New boom in material handling. T. O'Hanlon. il Duns R 82:50-1+ D '63

New directions in production. H. E. Klein. il Duns R 81:30-2+ Je '63

What life will be like when the machines take over; interview. S. Ramo. il U S News 54:64-8 Je 24 '63

See also

Automatic control
Automation
Machine tools—Control

Anecdotes, facetiae, satire, etc.

Notes and comment. New Yorker 39:23 Mr 2 '63

MACHINERY, Used

Used tools star in new roles. il Bsns W p58+ Mr 21 '64

MACHINERY in agriculture. See Agricultural machinery

MACHINERY in industry

See also

Automation
Technocracy
Unemployment, Technological

MACHINERY industry

Domestic tool sales ride high. Bsns W p56 Mr 21 '64

Machinery, tools lead the way; capital spending. il Bsns W p39-40 Ja 11 '64

See also

Machine tool industry and trade
Tractor industry and trade

Wages and hours

Earnings in the machinery industries, March-May 1963. F. W. Mohr. il Mo Labor R 86:1439-42 D '63

MACHINES, Copying. See Copying processes

MACHINES Bull manufactures. See Electronic apparatus industry and trade—France

MACHINISTS union. See International association of machinists

MACHLER, Nancy L. See Tilden, P. M. jt. auth.

MACHLIS, Joseph

Opera in translation; pro. Mus Am 83:10+ N '63

MACHU PICCHU, Peru

City on a mountain. il Sci Digest 54:39-41 Ag '63

Machu Picchu in danger; letter to the editor. C. E. Zavaleta. il Américas 16:48 O '64

Up and up and up to Machu Picchu. il Sunset 132:47-8+ Ap '64

MCHUGH, Roger

Irish television. America 108:670 My 11 '63

MACHULKOVA, Inka

Don't ask me about classic philosophy! Unfinished event; poems. Nation 199:171 S 28 '64

MCHUTCHISON, Edward

It took a tractor to turn my gardening chores into a joy ride. il Flower Grower 51:30-1 F '64

MCILRATH, Wayne J. and others

Dehydration of seeds in intact tomato fruits. Science 142:1681-2 D 27 '63

MCILVAIN, Dorothy S.

(ed) Cardboard printmaking. Sch Arts 64:27-8 D '64 (to be cont)

MACILVAINE, C. A.

Appraisal of Kaiser's sharing plan. Mo Labor R 87:401-4 Ap '64

MCILWAIN, C. E.

Radiation belts, natural and artificial. bibliog Science 142:355-61 O 18 '63

MCINERNY, Ralph

(tr) See Aron, R. Europe & the United States

MACINNES, Helen

Penelope and the poet; excerpt from Home is the hunter. Horizon 6:118-20 Sum '64

MCINTIRE, Barbara

Champion conquers a Kansas sea breeze. A. Wright. Sports Illus 21:56-7 Ag 31 '64

MCINTIRE, Carl

McIntire's good points. Christian Cent 80:1119 S 11 '63

Reformation or defamation? 20th century reformation hour. R. G. Kemper. Christian Cent 80:465-6 Ap 10 '63

Who's afraid of McIntire? Christian Cent 82:5 Ja 6 '65

MCINTIRE, Carl Thomas

Excerpt from statement, May 7, 1964. Cong Digest 43:284+ N '64

MCINTOSH, Bruce A. and Millman, P. M.

Radar meteor counts: anomalous increase during 1963. bibliog Science 146:1457 D 11 '64

MCINTOSH, Millicent Carey

Who should go to college? por Sr Schol 83:16-17 N 8 '63

about

Books for the blind. por Newsweek 62:71 S 2 '63

MCINTOSH, Patrick S.

Sunspot and granulation photography at Sacramento Peak. por Sky & Tel 27:280-2 My '64

MCINTYRE, Alice

Depressed in California. Esquire 59:67+ My '63

MACINTYRE, Duncan M.

It's not the doctor's dilemma, it's the insurance plan's. New Repub 149:19-21 N 9 '63

MCINTYRE, Edward F.

Budget for stereo. Hi Fi 14:111-14 O '64

MCINTYRE, James Francis, cardinal

Catholicism in Los Angeles. A. V. Krebs, jr; J. Leo. il Commonweal 80:467-82 Jl 10 '64; Discussion. 80:463-4, 549-50, 581 Jl 10, Ag 7-21 '64; Christian Cent 81:926 Jl 22 '64

Los Angeles, 1964. il por Newsweek 63:82 Je 29 '64

Parish priest accuses his cardinal on civil rights. S. Alexander. il por Life 56:41 Je 26 '64

Question of leadership. por Time 83:52-3 Je 26 '64

MACINTYRE, Malcolm A.

In & out at Eastern. por Time 82:94+ N 29 '63

MacIntyre gives view on Northeast finances. Aviation W 79:32 S 2 '63

MACINTYRE, William J. and others

Electroenecephalographic data: reduction by wave-width analysis. bibliog Science 144:1357-8; 146:671 Je 12, O 30 '64

MCISAAC, William M. and others

5-methoxytryptophol: effect on estrus and ovarian weight. bibliog Science 145:63-4 Jl 3 '64

MACIVER, Robert M.

On blueprinting man's future. Science 144:278 Ap 17 '64

MCJENKIN, Virginia

Streamlining essential routines. Wilson Lib Bul 37:680-1 Ap '63

MACK, Maynard

We came crying hither: an essay on some characteristics of King Lear. Yale R 54:161-86 D '64

MACK, Raymond W. and McElrath, D. C.
Urban social differentiation and the allocation of resources. Ann Am Acad 352:25-32 Mr '64
MACK trucks, incorporated
Hard line; challenge by the Justice department to merger with Chrysler corp. Newsweek 64:60 Ag 31 '64
If you're big, grow from within; Justice dept. to Chrysler and Mack. Bsns W p26 Ag 8 '64
MCKAIG, Harold L. Jr, and Zgienicki, Charles
Ultrasonic ring welding may yield truly leak-tight metal containers. Miss & Roc 15:28+ Ag 31 '64
MACKAY, D. M.
Psychophysics of perceived intensity: a theoretical basis for Fechner's and Stevens' laws. bibliog Science 139:1213-16 Mr 22 '63
MCKAY, Gardner
How to eat a piranha before it eats you. por Sports Illus 18:48-50 Mr 11 '63
MCKAY, John
Coach has all the problems. M. Durslag. il pors Sat Eve Post 236:72-3 D 14 '63
MACKAY, John A.
Cuba revisited. Christian Cent 81:200-3 F 12 '64
Fresh look at Cuba. Christian Cent 81:983-7 Ag 5 '64
MCKAY, Mildred P. and Abbott, R. H.
New Hampshire: one-system state. Wilson Lib Bul 38:280-3 N '63
New Hampshire story. pors Library J 88: 3169-72 S 15 '63
MACKAY, R. Stuart
Deep body temperature of untethered dolphin recorded by ingested radio transmitter. bibliog Science 144:864-6 My 15 '64
MACKAYE, Benton
Benton MacKaye: the verdant prophet. E. J. Long. il pors Am For 70:16-19 Jl '64
MCKAYLE, Donald
Donald McKayle and company, Hunter college assembly hall. J. Maskey. Dance Mag 38:73 Ap '64
Subject is people. M. Marks. il pors Dance Mag 37:30-5 F '63
MCKEAN, William B.
Tale of tragedy. America 109:141-2 Ag 10 '63
MCKEE, Gladys
Postscript for a Valentine; poem. McCalls 90:144 F '63
Reminder on Mother's day; poem. McCalls 90:180 My '63
MCKEE, Guy W.
Make sure seed is tops. Suc Farm 62:58-9 F '64
MCKEE, Linda
By heaven, that ship is ours! Am Heritage 16:4-11+ D '64
MCKEE, Russell
Skiing through history. Recreation 57:33-4 Ja '64
MCKEE, William F.
Major defense challenges; address, August 8, 1963. Vital Speeches 29:702-4 S 1 '63
National security strategy; address, August 29, 1963. Vital Speeches 30:21-4 O 15 '63
MCKEEGAN, Ethel
Down-to-earth advice to the new gardener. Flower Grower 51:42-3 My '64
MCKEEN, Ona Lee
Cowhand. Am Heritage 14:16-31 O '63
MCKEITHEN, John J.
Louisiana: clues to '64 vote. por U S News 56:64 Ja 27 '64
Up from the swamp. por Newsweek 63:34 Mr 16 '64
Upset, true to form. il por Newsweek 63:28 Ja 27 '64
MCKELDIN, Theodore Roosevelt
With a little bit. . . Time 81:29 My 17 '63
MCKELWAY, St Clair
Child labor and the Presbyterians. New Yorker 39:193-6+ O 12 '63
How to be happy when your newsdealer filches your Sunday times magazine. New Yorker 39:20-1 Je 29 '63
They could have danced all night, and did. New Yorker 39:34-5 My 25 '63
Up on the flying trapeze: snow and slush; is Hopkins outmoded? $215,600 for a Monet! New Yorker 40:43 Ap 4 '64
MACKEN, Walter
Kiss; story. New Yorker 39:130-5 S 7 '63
You asked for it. Writer 76:20-1 Jl '63
MCKENDRICK, Neil
Enigmatic urn. Horizon 5:63-5 N '63
MCKENNA, David L.
Crystal ball for colleges; address, January 2, 1964. Vital Speeches 30:249-52 F 1 '64
—and others
Changing objectives in American higher education, 1842-1960. Sch & Soc 91:120-3 Mr 9 '63
MCKENNA, Malcolm C.
Undersea history of America. Sat R 47:54-7 Je 6 '64
MCKENNA, Richard
Creative energy and fiction writing. Writer 76:7-9+ Je '63
MCKENNEY, J. Wilson
Stanford university's School of education. NEA J 53:46-8 Ap '64
MCKENTY, Neil
Canadian elections. America 108:602 Ap 27 '63
Crisis in Canada. America 111:135 Ag 8 '64
Explosion on Parliament hill. America 108: 267 F 23 '63
Modern Mercedarian. America 111:101 Ag 1 '64
MACKENZIE, Compton
Intimate of every household. Horizon 6:108-15 Sum '64
MACKENZIE, D. R.
Krypton difluoride: preparation and handling. bibliog Science 141:1171 S 20 '63
MACKENZIE, Fred T.
Geometry of Bermuda calcareous dune cross-bedding. Science 144:1449-50 Je 19 '64
Strontium content and variable strontium-chlorinity relationship of Sargasso sea water. bibliog Science 146:517-18 O 23 '64
MCKENZIE, John L.
Exegete at the manger. Commonweal 81: 439-42 D 25 '64
MCKENZIE, John P. G.
Build your own 2¼x3¼ film pack adapter. U S Camera 27:28 S '64
MACKENZIE, Louise L.
Service to inmates and staff. ALA Bul 58: 809 O '64
MACKENZIE, Norman
Harold Wilson's Britain. Harper 228:73-6+ F '64
MCKENZIE, Reginald I.
Industry's growth problems; excerpts from address. Aviation W 79:13 S 2 '63
MACKENZIE, Roderick A. F.
Rector magnificus. America 108:849 Je 15 '63
MACKENZIE, Ronald
Casualties in a jungle war. il por Time 82: 48+ Jl 19 '63
MCKENZIE-POLLOCK, James S.
Planning for health. New Repub 150:15-16 My 9 '64
MCKENZIE RIVER, Ore.
McKenzie River trip. W. F. Heald. il Travel 122:31-3 Jl '64
MCKEOWN, William Taylor
Safety for family sailors. Am Home 67:42 Jl '64
'64 boats for unquiet poeple. Esquire 61:72-5 Mr '64
MACKEREL fishing
Go light for mackerel. G. Heinold. il Outdoor Life 133:12+ Ap '64
MCKERSIE, Robert B. and others
Some indicators of incentive plan prevalence. bibliog f Mo Labor R 87:271-6, 894 Mr, Ag '64
MCKESSON and Robbins
Ethical problem; low-cost drug-marketing. il Newsweek 62:78 S 23 '63
MACKESY, Piers
British strategy in the war of American independence. Yale R 52:539-57 Je '63
MACKEY, Robert J. Jr
Advanced research for communications satellites. Electr World 71:64 Je '64
MACKEY, William J. Jr
Decoys of Nathan Cobb jr. Antiques 86:192-3 Ag '64
MCKIBBEN, Mary Adeline
Community sources for art education. Sch Arts 62:17-19 My '63
MCKIE, Leola
Rightist binge in Omaha. Christian Cent 80:1270-1 O 16 '63
MACKIE, Romaine P. and others
College and university programs for the preparation of teachers of exceptional children. Sch Life 45:29-35 Mr '63
MCKIE, Roy
Cruising the aisles; cartoons. Sports Illus 22:30-5 Ja 4 '65
Welcome aboard or are you? il Sports Illus 18:34-41 My 13 '63
MCKIERNAN, Flora C.
Comb collecting. Hobbies 69:28-9 Ap '64
MCKINLAY, Sam
Sporting scene. H. W. Wind. New Yorker 40:98+ Je 6 '64
MCKINLEY, Charles. See McKinley, Chuck
MCKINLEY, Chuck
Better than fancy pants; Wimbledon tournament. J. Lovesey. il por Sports Illus 19: 12-15 Jl 15 '63
High time for a U.S. victory. W. Tower. il por Sports Illus 20:18-21 Ja 6 '64

MCKINLEY, Chuck—*Continued*
One for the Yanks. il pors Time 82:60 Jl 12 '63
Small town moves into the big time. F. Deford. il Sports Illus 20:57-8 Mr 2 '64
Trouble with tennis. il por Esquire 61:119-23 My '64
Yank at Wimbledon. il por Newsweek 62: 57-8 Jl 15 '63
MCKINLEY, Daniel
Slaughter at Swan Lake. Audubon Mag 66: 144-5 My '64
MCKINLEY, Fred
Christmastide fish. Outdoor Life 132:36-7+ D '63
Extra shotgun free. Outdoor Life 135:50-1+ F '65
Fish tough. Outdoor Life 134:28-31+ Jl '64
Savage encounter. Outdoor Life 133:52-3+ Mr '64
MCKINLEY, Georgia
Shall we gather at the river? story. Redbook 121:42-3 Ag '63
MCKINLEY, Hazel
Camp isn't just for kids. Parents Mag 38: 52-3+ Jl '63
MCKINLEY, William
Dear cousin William. M. Kantor. por McCalls 91:77+ F '64
Operation on President McKinley. S. Adler. il por Sci Am 208:118-30 Mr '63
President and his critics. W. A. Williams. Nation 196:228+ Mr 16 '63
MCKINLEY, MOUNT
Mysteries of Mount McKinley; with editorial comment. D. Lambert. il Nat Parks Mag 37:2, 8-10+ Ap '63
MCKINLEY NATIONAL PARK. See Mount McKinley National Park
MCKINNEY, Glen
Printed board repair. Electr World 71:69 My '64
Repairing miniature I.F. transformers. Electr World 71:85 Je '64
Simple transistor tests. Electr World 72:63 Ag '64
MCKINNEY, Harold
Negro music, a definitive American expression. bibliog Negro Hist Bul 27:120-1+ F '64
MCKINNEY, John Paul
Disappearance of luminous designs. bibliog Science 140:403-4 Ap 26 '63
MCKINNEY, Robert M.
U.S. balance of payments; address, December 30, 1963. Vital Speeches 30:216-20 Ja 15 '64
MACKINNON, Donald MacKenzie
Cambridge objectors. por Time 83:78 Mr 6 '64
MACKINNON, G. Ernest. See Matin, L. jt. auth.
MCKINSEY and company
Nuisance item proves a big profit-maker; McKinsey study of frozen foods. il Bsns W p 116+ Mr 14 '64
Upturn in executive compensation. A. Patton. il Harvard Bsns R 41:133-7 S '63
MACKINTOSH, A. R.
Fermi surface of metals. Sci Am 209:110-20 Jl '63
MACKINTOSH, Helen K.
Language arts. Sch Life 45:16-18 Jl '63
MCKITRICK, Eric L.
First democrat. Commentary 37:81-2+ My '64
MCKITTERICK, T. E. M.
Prelude to independence. Nation 197:179-81 S 28 '63
MCKITTRICK CANYON, Tex. See Canyons
MCKNIGHT, William L.
3M's McKnight: a winner at the races? il Duns R 82:34 Ag '63
MCKRILL, Berenice
Food for winter birds. Audubon Mag 66:394 N '64
MACLACHLAN, Elaine
(tr) See Senesi, M. Breach
(tr) See Senesi, M. Father and son
MCLAGAN, Bruce
Why mergers go wrong. Duns R 84:40-1+ N '64
MACLAGAN, Michael
Our man in London. New Yorker 40:48-51 N 28 '64
MACLAIN, Jon
G. F. Handel's Rodelinda. Am Rec G 31:404-7 Ja '65
New Marina in stereo. Am Rec G 30:572-3 Mr '64
Nuits d'été. Am Rec G 30:672-4 Ap '64
That other La Bohème. Am Rec G 30:928-9+ Je '64
MCLAIN, Pete
Duck hunter's coffin. Field & S 68:10-11 N '63
Fly rod in the surf. Field & S 69:58-61 O '64
MACLAINE, Shirley
Boy meets girl. D. Garth. il por Seventeen 23: 79+ Ja '64
In an epic new movie, one Dame beats another. D. Jenkins. il pors Sports Illus 21: 50-4+ Jl 20 '64
Shirley MacLaine sounds off. M. Davidson. il pors Sat Eve Post 236:30, 33 N 30 '63
Surprising spin for Shirley. il pors Life 54: 62A-62B Je 21 '63
MCLANDRESS, Herschel
Let us now appraise famous men. M. Epernay. il Esquire 60:28-30+ O '63
MCLAREN, A. D.
Biochemistry and soil science. bibliog Science 141:1141-7 S 20 '63
MCLAREN, Norman
Etchcraft on celluloid. A. MacDermot. il por UNESCO Courier 17:20-3 Ja '64
MCLARRY, Russell W.
Other guns. por Newsweek 62:15 D 30 '63
MCLAUGHLIN, Calvin S. and Ingram, V. M.
Aminoacyl position in aminoacyl sRNA. bibliog Science 145:942-3 Ag 28 '64
MCLAUGHLIN, Dean B.
Early spectral changes of Nova Herculis 1963. Sky & Tel 25:206-7 Ap '63
MCLAUGHLIN, James
There are no Indians left now but me. M. Rosenberg and D. Rosenberg. il por Am Heritage 15:21-3+ Je '64
MCLAUGHLIN, John
Burton's Hamlet. Cath World 199:308-12 Ag '64
I made a cursillo. America 110:94-6+ Ja 18 '64
Movie of the month. Cath World 200:195-6 D '64
Screen education. America 111:341 S 26 '64
Second look at images. America 110:430-4+ Mr 28 '64
Stratford's first decade. America 111:152 Ag 15 '64
Television in the courtroom: yes. America 112:72+ Ja 16 '65
MCLAUGHLIN, John J.
Science fiction theatre. Nation 200:92-4 Ja 25 '65
MCLAUGHLIN, John J. A.
Aquatic pollution. Science 146:281+ O 9 '64
MCLAUGHLIN, Mignon
Neurotic's notebook. Atlan 211:101 Mr; 114 Je '63; 214:119 Jl '64
No game for a woman. Atlan 212:74-6 S '63
Out goes Y.O.U; story. Seventeen 22:126-7 S '63
Vamp till ready; story. Seventeen 22:76-7 Jl '63
MCLAUGHLIN, Robert R.
Kids; group of city youngsters. U S Camera 26:44-8 Je '63
MCLAUGHLIN, W. Earle
Plan or no plan or un-plan? address, June 3, 1963. Vital Speeches 29:636-9 Ag 1 '63
MCLAUGHLIN, William
Circuit riders; poem. Liv Wildn 83:10 Spring '63
Impromptu blues for Mr Eliot; poem. Commonweal 81:576 Ja 29 '65
MCLEAN, Eric
Montreal symphony: no more Hussars. Mus Am 83:22-3 S '63
MACLEAN, Sir Fitzroy Hew
Cheerful Mongolians: a visit to a very far country. Harper 229:41-7 Jl '64
Inside red China. Sat Eve Post 236:96+ N 16 '63
MCLEAN, Herbert E.
This summer, why not Alaska? il Motor B 113:26-7+ My '64
MACLEAN, Janet R.
Challenge of leisure in old age. por Recreation 56:213 My '63
MCLEAN, John G.
Financing overseas expansion. Harvard Bsns R 41:53-65 Mr '63
MACLEAN, Paul D.
Mirror display in the squirrel monkey, saimiri sciureus. bibliog Science 146:950-2 N 13 '64
MACLEAN, William
Public library bookstore. E. J. Humeston, jr. il Wilson Lib Bul 37:563-4+ Mr '63
MACLEAN'S magazine. See Periodicals—Canada
MACLEAR, Frank
Confessions of a naval architect. por Motor B 111:26+ F '63

MACLEISH, Archibald
Gift outright. Atlan 213:50-2 F '64
Must we hate? Atlan 211:79-82 F '63
Tribute to a great American lady. N Y Times Mag p 17+ N 3 '63

MCLEMORE, Henry
He's all ears for engines. Pop Sci 184:94-7+ Ja '64

MCLENDON, Irmgard
Plant pyracantha to brighten winter drabness. Horticulture 41:130-1 Mr '63
There's nothing like a rose. Pop Gard 15: 20-2 F '64

MCLENDON, Lennox Polk
People of the week. por U S News 55:18 N 25 '63
Senate shocks a Senate prober. C. Phillips. il por N Y Times Mag p20+ Ag 9 '64

MACLENNAN, Hugh
Arts in Canada: a search for identity. Mus Am 83:12-13+ S '63
Scottish touch: Cape Breton. Holiday 35: 86-7+ Ap '64

about

Reporter at large. E. Wilson. New Yorker 40:84+ N 14 '64

MACLEOD, Colin Munro
Deputy director for OST. Science 141:702 Ag 23 '63

MACLEOD, Iain Norman
Iain's in. Newsweek 62:81 N 18 '63
Low life above stairs. C. Brogan. Nat R 16:153-5 F 25 '64
Quoodle talks. il por Newsweek 63:36 Ja 27 '64

MACLEOD, John M.
Radio map of the Andromeda galaxy. bibliog Science 145:389-91 Jl 24 '64

MACLEOD, Rex
Hockey (cont) Sports Illus 18:51-2 Ap 29 '63

MCLOONE, Eugene P. See Harrison, F. W. jt. auth.

MCLOSKEY, Robert T.
Excerpt from remarks, August 5, 1964. Cong Digest 44:28+ Ja '65
Excerpt from remarks, September 25, 1963. Cong Digest 43:87+ Mr '64

MCLUHAN, Marshall
Notes on Burroughs. Nation 199:517-19 D 28 '64

about

Cool revolution. N. Compton. Commentary 39:79-81 Ja '65

MACLURE, J. Stuart
Britain's plan for higher education. Sch & Soc 92:228-31 Sum '64

MCMAHAN, Ida, and Whitehorn, Ethel
Motion picture previews. See issues of PTA magazine

MCMAHON, Franklin
Club to suit a king's fancy. il Sports Illus 19:78-85 D 23 '63
Race can be a cruise; reproductions of paintings. Sports Illus 20:28-36 F 3 '64

MCMAHON, Matthew M.
Book reviews. America 109:243-4 S 7 '63

MCMAHON, Robert O. See Yoho, J. G. jt. auth.

MCMANUS, Frederick R.
Changes in the liturgy. Commonweal 79: 594-6+ F 14 '64
Coming reforms in the liturgy. Cath World 196:335-42 Mr '63
Second session: progress toward openness. Commonweal 80:582-4 Ag 21 '64

MCMANUS, Jason
Letter from the publisher. B. M. Auer. il por Time 81:13 F 8 '63

MCMASTER, David N.
Uganda. bibliog Focus 14:1-6 Ja '64

MCMASTER, Earl T.
How I shot the no. 1 deer. pors Outdoor Life 134:17-19+ N '64

MCMASTER, Florence R.
Law librarians at Mackinac. Library J 88: 3033-4 S 1 '63

MCMASTER, Philip R. B. and others
Genetic influence on experimental allergic thyroiditis in guinea pigs. bibliog Science 147:157 Ja 8 '65
—See Bachvaroff, R. jt. auth.

MACMILLAN, Bloedel and Powell River, limited
When managerial styles clash. il Bsns W p65-6+ N 30 '63

MACMILLAN, Bonnie
Music by mail. Parents Mag 38:76-7+ S '63

MCMILLAN, George
Birmingham church bomber. Sat Eve Post 237:15-19 Je 6 '64
Integration with dignity. Sat Eve Post 236: 15-21 Mr 16 '63
Klan scourges old St Augustine. Life 56:21 Je 26 '64
Mommy, do white puppies like us? Good H 157:64+ O '63
New bombing terrorists of the South call themselves Nacirema: American spelled backward. Life 55:39-40 O 11 '63
Silent white ministers of the South. N Y Times Mag p22+ Ap 5 '64

MACMILLAN, Harold
Common market; address, January 30, 1963. Vital Speeches 29:332-3 Mr 15 '63
—See Kennedy, J. F. jt. auth.

about

Battling Tories. Time 82:34+ O 18 '63
Exmac. Time 82:23 D 27 '63
Goodbye to all that. il por Time 83:37 F 21 '64
If Macmillan is forced out. il por U S News 55:17 Jl 1 '63
Ineffectual but innocent; Lord Denning's report. il Time 82:40-1 O 4 '63
Is Super Mac to be undone by sex? il por Newsweek 61:45-6 Je 24 '63
Letter from London; backwash of the Profumo affair. M. Panter-Downes. New Yorker 39:65-7 Ag 3 '63
Letter from London; Profumo case. M. Panter-Downes. New Yorker 39:66-9 Je 29 '63
Lost leader; concerning House of commons debate on the Profumo case. il por Time 81:22-5 Je 28 '63
Mac the Slack. il Newsweek 62:29 Jl 1 '63
Macmillan's seven years. il por Newsweek 62:60 O 21 '63
Scandal that's rocking Britain; Profumo case. il U S News 54:8 Je 17 '63
SuperMac on the ropes. New Repub 148:11-12 Je 22 '63
SuperMac rides out the storm. A. Lejeune. Nat R 15:189-90 S 10 '63
That cad, Profumo. A. Burnet. New Repub 149:6 Jl 6 '63
They're off; question of general election. Time 81:29 My 3 '63
Time of the trollop. il Time 81:24+ Je 21 '63
Trollope, not Tide; with excerpts from an interview. Time 81:23-4 My 31 '63
West loses two statesmen: editorial. Sat Eve Post 236:82 N 9 '63
Whatever became of SuperMac? A. Lejeune. Nat R 14:159 F 26 '63
Without Macmillan. New Repub 149:8-9 O 26 '63

MCMILLAN, J. A. and Los, S. C.
Hydrazine-water system: the water-rich eutectic. bibliog Science 145:1307 S 18 '64

MCMILLAN, Jim
First aqualung in the U.S. Sci Digest 56:14-18 Jl '64
Science milestone; Santiago Ramon y Cajal. Sci Digest 53:81-7 Ap '63

MACMILLAN, Kenneth
Music to my ears; MacMillan week at the Royal ballet. I. Kolodin. Sat R 46:42 My 25 '63

MCMILLAN, Mary Amos
No eleventh book. Horn Bk 40:251-4 Je '64
Wild rose, briar rose. Horn Bk 39:622-8 D '63

MCMILLEN, B. R.
AIGA; the making and marketing of dual-purpose books; summary of address. Pub W 185:70+ Je 1 '64

MCMILLEN, W. P.
Fanning out from Florida. il Yachting 116:44-5+ N '64

MCMILLIN, Betty
Stitchery & the retarded child. Sch Arts 63: 18-19 Ja '64

MACMINN, Strother
Projexions. il por Motor T 15:76-9 O '63

MCMULLAN, Mary
Key to action. Sch Arts 63:5-7 Mr '64

MCMULLEN, Haynes
Pity the library school teacher. por Library J 89:2280-4 Je 1 '64

MCMULLEN, Roy
Notes from our correspondents (cont of) Notes from abroad. See issues of High fidelity

MCMULLEN, Tom
Pedal your Model A; and steer it. il Hot Rod 18:84-7 Ja '65
Wiring made easy. por Hot Rod 16:38-41+ Je '63

MCMURRAY, Joseph P.
Man who makes S&Ls toe the mark. il por Bsns W p72-4+ Ja 18 '64

MCMURRAY, Joseph P.—*Continued*
New U.S. rules for savings and loans; what 1964 will bring. por U S News 55:94-5 N 4 '63

MCMURRAY, W. C.
Bioenergetics. Science 147:413-14 Ja 22 '65

MCMURRIN, Sterling Moss
Speaking out. por Sat Eve Post 236:6+ Mr 23 '63
U.S. office of education: an inside view. Sat R 46:78-81 F 16 '63

MCMURRY, Robert N.
Conflicts in human values. Harvard Bsns R 41:130-6+ My '63
How to pick a president. Duns R 82:57-8+ O '63

MCMURTREY, Martin
Apocalyptic gold: poem. Commonweal 81:511 Ja 15 '65

MCMURTRY, R. Gerald
Expressions of sentiment of Abraham Lincoln: reprint. Hobbies 68:110-11+ S '63
Thomas Lincoln's corner cupboards. Antiques 85:206-8 F '64

M'NAGHTEN rules. See Insanity—Jurisprudence

MCNAIR, Barbara
No strings for Barbara. il pors Ebony 19:42-4+ Ja '64

MCNAIR, Carol Denise
Death of an innocent. W. B. Huie. il pors Look 28:23-5 Mr 24 '64

MCNAIR, Malcolm P.
How to sell more now; questions and answers. por Nations Bsns 51:38-9+ Ag '63

MCNALLY, John Victor
Is that you up there, Johnny Blood? G. Holland. il por Sports Illus 19:18-20+ S 2 '63

MCNALLY, Terence. See Cooper, G. jt. auth.

MCNALLY, Tom
Double on deer. pors Outdoor Life 132:40-3+ S '63
Family and fishing? roll 'em together. Outdoor Life 131:49-51+ My '63
Sailfish on a fly. por Outdoor Life 134:34-5+ D '64

MCNAMARA, Robert C. jr
Censorship of textbooks; what can the publisher do? NEA J 52:27-8 My '63

MCNAMARA, Robert Strange
Decision making in the Defense department; address, April 20, 1963. Vital Speeches 29:508-12 Je 1 '63
Defending America; as McNamara sees it now; excerpts from news conference. U S News 57:20 N 23 '64
Defense of the free world; address, May 21, 1964. Dept State Bul 50:893-9 Je 8 '64
Excerpt from testimony, April 8, 1963. Cong Digest 42:178+ Je '63
He had a moral insight; excerpts from interviews, ed. by T. G. Harris. por Look 28:52+ N 17 '64
McNamara assesses arms developments; text of testimony before House armed services committee. Aviation W 80:77-9+ F 24 '64
McNamara claims big strategic edge. Miss & Roc 15:14 Ag 24 '64
McNamara comes under new fire. por U S News 55:10 Ag 12 '63
McNamara defines his job. por N Y Times Mag p 13+ Ap 26 '64
McNamara details defense buying, R&D; summary of testimony before House armed services committee. Aviation W 78:27-30 F 4 '63
McNamara discusses retaliatory forces; text of testimony before House armed services committee. Aviation W 80:74-5+ Mr 2 '64
McNamara explains TFX award decision. Aviation W 78:81+ Mr 25 '63
McNamara on research and development; excerpts from testimony before House armed services committee. Aviation W 78:21 F 4 '63
McNamara on strategy: a change in policy? excerpts from statement, January 30, 1963. Bul Atomic Sci 19:36-9 Ap '63
McNamara views strategic aircraft role; excerpt from testimony presented to the House armed services committee, January 30, 1963. por Aviation W 78:67+ F 11 '63
McNamara's ground rules for doing business with the Pentagon; excerpts from Congressional record. por U S News 54:43 My 13 '63
Major national security problems confronting the United States; address, November 18, 1963. Dept State Bul 49:914-21 D 16 '63
Military assistance program for 1965; statement, March 25, 1964. Dept State Bul 50:705-15 My 4 '64
Military defenses of the West; address, November 18, 1963. Vital Speeches 30:114-18 D 1 '63
Secretary McNamara reports on situation in Viet-Nam. Dept State Bul 50:46 Ja 13 '64
Secretary Mc Namara's stand; excerpts from statement, March 13, 1963. por U S News 54:55 Ap 22 '63
Test ban: the military argument; excerpts from the testimony before the Senate foreign relations committee, August 13, 1963. Bul Atomic Sci 19:42-3 O '63; Excerpts. U S News 55:54-9 Ag 26 '63
U.S. defense policy; address, August 17, 1964. Vital Speeches 30:710-13 S 15 '64; Excerpts. Aviation W 81:17 Ag 24 '64
United States policy in Viet-Nam; address, March 26, 1964. Dept State Bul 50:562-70 Ap 13 '64; Same. Vital Speeches 30:394-9 Ap 15 '64; Excerpts. Aviation W 80:11 Mr 30 '64; por U S News 56:10 Ag 6 '64
United States takes measures to repel attack against U.S. forces in southeast Asia: statement, August 6, 1964. Dept State Bul 51:265-7 Ag 24 '64
Where we stand on defense; excerpts from address, November 28, 1963. pors Duns R 83:53-4+ F '64; Same. Bul Atomic Sci 20:35-9 Mr '64
Why we are stronger than Russia. por Sat Eve Post 237:15-17 N 7 '64
—See Rusk, D; Seaborg, G. T. jt. auths.

about

Achilles heel. W. J. Coughlin. Miss & Roc 12:162 Mr 25 '63
Alice in McNamaraland. W. J. Coughlin. Miss & Roc 15:46 Ag 3 '64
And how about the Pentagon now? new era in Washington. M. S. Johnson. il por U S News 55:64-5 D 16 '63
Appraisal of the Secretary of defense. T. D. White. Newsweek 63:19 Ja 6 '64
Asian apocrypha. il por Newsweek 63:52 Mr 16 '64
Atlantic report. Atlan 211:4+ Je '63
Case of McNamara and the joint chiefs. J. Alsop. Read Digest 83:102-3 Jl '63
Chilly future; concerning R. McNamara's exposition of defense policies before the House armed services committee. il por Time 81:15-16 F 8 '63
Chips on Khanh. il por Time 83:30 Mr 20 '64
Collision in Washington: McNamara vs. the Congress. por Newsweek 61:25-6 Mr 25 '63
Counting the cost. Newsweek 61:78+ Mr 25 '63
Credibility gap. R. Hotz. Aviation W 80:21 Je 15 '64
Death of Nike-Zeus. E. Ubell and S. H. Loory. il Sat Eve Post 236:15-19 Je 1 '63
Defense; the dilemma & the design. il pors Time 81:22+ F 15 '63
Embattled McNamara; photographs. N Y Times Mag p26-7 My 26 '63
Facts about McNamara's folly; TFX. J. H. Winchester. il por Sci Digest 54:14-18 Jl '63
Fallible man. W. J. Coughlin. Miss & Roc 12:78 Ap 29 '63
Fight over TFX; McNamara's side of the case. U S News 54:18+ Ap 8 '63
Fighting Bob: investigation of contract for TFX fighter plane. il por Time 81:16 Mr 22 '63
Foreign policy: LBJ's test. Newsweek 63:19-20 F 10 '64
From Washington straight. Cato. Nat R 14:189 Mr 12 '63
Ganging up on McNamara; with editorial comment. J. Greene. Nation 196:257, 264-6 Mr 30 '63
Gilpatric explains Defense decision policy. R. L. Gilpatric. Aviation W 78:32 F 11 '63
He had better be right; chorus of criticism. Time 81:18 My 31 '63
How dependable are America's long-range missiles? Goldwater vs. McNamara. il U S News 56:6 Ja 20 '64
Improved balance; NATO's year-end ministerial conference in Paris. Time 82:22 D 27 '63
In defense of the Defense secretary. Fortune 67:81-2+ Ap '63
Incorrect, illogical, etc; R. R. McNamara vs. Joint committee on atomic energy. por Time 83:31 Ja 3 '64
Letter from Washington. R. H. Rovere. New Yorker 39:125-31 Mr 2 '63
Mac finds out what's gone wrong. il pors Life 55:23-7 O 11 '63
McNamara and his critics. New Repub 148:5-6 Mr 30 '63
McNamara assails critics of TFX award. G. C. Wilson. Aviation W 78:26-9 Mr 18 '63
McNamara bombshell: merger of reservists. il por U S News 57:3 D 21 '64
McNamara effect. Sat R 47:39 Ag 1 '64
McNamara equation. S. Alsop. por Sat Eve Post 237:12 My 16 '64

MCNAMARA, Robert Strange—about—*Cont.*
McNamara gives report on assets. il U S News 54:95-6 Ap 1 '63
McNamara makes a tour of Vietnam. il por Newsweek 62:45 O 7 '63
McNamara on the job; with photographs by G. Tames. N Y Times Mag p 14-15 Ap 26 '64
McNamara-Taylor report: a long, hard war in Vietnam. por U S News 56:21 My 25 '64
McNamara: the real story. M. S. Johnson. il pors U S News 55:56-9 Jl 22 '63
McNamara under fire. Newsweek 64:33-4 O 19 '64
McNamara's ban on defense expenditures; with report by L. Norman. Newsweek 62: 28 Jl 8 '63
McNamara's band. America 111:734-5 D 5 '64
McNamara's human problem. Life 55:4 S 20 '63
Merge national guard and reserves? McNamara's plan. il U S News 57:61-2 D 14 '64
More of the same. il por Newsweek 63:46+ Mr 23 '64
NATO's nuclear dilemma. H. A. Kissinger. il Reporter 28:22-33+ Mr 28 '63
New rules for GI demonstrators. il por U S News 55:57 Jl 29 '63
Now the whiz kids are tackling the U.S. navy. il por U S News 55:59-60 N 25 '63
One of those weeks. Newsweek 63:42+ My 25 '64
Operation bulldozer. Nat R 15:555-6 D 31 '63
Pennies pinched. Newsweek 62:69-70 Jl 22 '63
People of the week. U S News 54:20-1 Ap 29 '63
Pitfalls of publicity; TFX contract. W. V. Shannon. Commonweal 78:126-7 Ap 26 '63
Price of economy. il Newsweek 62:18-19 D 23 '63
Pulling the carriers' plug. il por Time 81:16 Mr 29 '63
Reasonable man. W. J. Coughlin. Miss & Roc 14:46 Mr 2 '64
Report from South Vietnam. il por U S News 55:21 O 14 '63
Revolution in the Pentagon. T. H. White. il pors Look 27:31-44+ Ap 23 '63
Robert who? il por Time 83:17 Mr 27 '64
Search for answers; visit to South Viet Nam. il por Time 82:48 O 4 '63
Secretary is not on the defensive. M. McGrory. America 108:458 Ap 6 '63
Secretary's authority reaches peak. por Miss & Roc 12:74-5 Mr 25 '63
Speaking out; McNamara monarchy. H. W. Baldwin. Sat Eve Post 236:8+ Mr 9 '63
Still fighting; R. McNamara before the Joint defense procurement subcommittee; McNamara's portfolio. il Time 81:26-7 Ap 5 '63
TFX; a feud boils up; with editorial comment. il Bsns W p 19-20, 116 My 11 '63
TFX and elements of high tragedy. W. V. Kennedy. America 108:522 Ap 20 '63
TFX plane: what the fight is about. il por U S News 54:61-3 Mr 25 '63
TFX troubles. Commonweal 78:5 Mr 29 '63
U.S. scrapping arms of future? il U S News 54:35 Ap 1 '63
Voyage no. three; U.S. Defense secretary in South Viet Nam. il por Time 83:28 Mr 13 '64
Whiz kids vs. military men; who is shaping defense? il U S News 54:46-7 Mr 4 '63
Why it's so hard to beat the Communists in Vietnam; McNamara-Taylor mission. R. P. Martin. il por U S News 55:56-7 O 7 '63
Why McNamara is under fire. U S News 54: 22 Mr 25 '63
Wisdom of test ban: McNamara and the joint chiefs differed. il por U S News 55:36 Ag 5 '63

MCNASPY, Clement J.
Arts. See occasional issues of America
Council and the liturgy. America 111:778 D 12 '64
Cult of culture. America 110:626-8 My 9 '64
Going home to Europe; excerpts from Guide to Christian Europe. Cath World 197:126-32 My '63
Liturgy and freedom. America 111:251 S 12 '64
Liturgy and scripture: 1964; new missals. America 111:744 D 5 '64
Liturgy: barrier or bond? America 110:278-80 F 29 '64
Music. See issues of America
New books on liturgy. America 111:187-8 Ag 22 '64
Only a brother? America 108:744-5 My 25 '63
Reading for a hot summer. America 110:851-2 Je 20 '64
Return to our beginnings. America 111:351-2 S 26 '64
Scandal in the liturgy. America 111:586 N 14 '64
World's fair preview. America 110:510-12 Ap 11 '64
(ed) See Stravinsky, I. Interview with Stravinsky

MCNEAL, Archie L.
ALA as amicus curiae. ALA Bul 58:290 Ap '64
Intellectual freedom. ALA Bul 58:537 Je '64

MCNEEL, John P.
Silent war in liquid space. Pop Mech 120: 122-7+ D '63

MACNEICE, Louis
Legacy of Louis MacNeice. R. E. Elman. New Repub 149:19-21 O 26 '63
Obituary
Pub W 184:88 S 16 '63
Songs of an unsung classicist. S. Spender. por Sat R 46:25+ S 7 '63
Underestimations. X. J. Kennedy. Poetry 103: 333 F '64
Uses of typology. H. Carruth. Poetry 101: 424-6 Mr '63

MACNEIL, Cornell
Night at the opera. il por Newsweek 65:77-8 Ja 11 '65

MCNEIL, Donald R. See Ryan, E. N. jt. auth.

MCNEIL, Elton B.
Children's war revisited. Bul Atomic Sci 19:22-4 F '63
International relations and the psychologist: the scientific gulf. Bul Atomic Sci 19:33-5 N '63

MACNEIL, George, family
MacNeils tackle another house. H. Stark. il pors Bet Hom & Gard 41:54-7 My '63

MCNEIL, Mary
Lateritic soils. Sci Am 211:96-102 N '64

MACNEIL, Neil
Chester Dale: collector. McCalls 91:120-7+ N '63
Chief who stayed on to help. Life 57:72 O 30 '64
Life book review. Life 56:6+ My 29 '64

MCNEIL, Wilfred J.
Grace line revives under its Mr Mac. il por Bsns W p 172-4+ Ap 11 '64

MCNEILL, Donald Thomas
Coffee break: Breakfast club. il por Newsweek 61:80 Je 3 '63

MCNEILL, John T.
Calvin after 400 years. Christian Cent 81:702-4 My 27 '64

MCNEILL, William H.
Democracy faces a global dilemma. N Y Times Mag p27+ N 17 '63
Dilemmas of power; excerpt from Rise of the West. Sat R 46:50-1 N 2 '63
July 1914—July 1964. For Affairs 42:559-68 Jl '64

MACNEISH, Richard S.
Ancient Mesoamerican civilization. bibliog Science 143:531-7 F 7 '64
Origins of New World civilization; with biographical sketch. Sci Am 211:22, 29-37 bibliog(p 154) N '64
—See Smith, C. E. jr. jt. auth.

MACNICHOL, Edward F. jr
Three-pigment color vision. Sci Am 211:48-56 bibliog(p 154) D '64

MCNISH, A. G.
Lasers for length measurement. bibliog Science 146:177-82 O 9 '64

MCNULTY, Faith
Collision in the city; story. New Yorker 39: 25-7 Ag 3 '63
Notes from a mousekeeper's diary. Audubon Mag 66:382-7 N '64

MCNULTY, Theodore
Improving public understanding of testing. Sch & Soc 92:51-2 F 8 '64

MACNUTT, Sylvester S.
Problem of obedience. America 112:14-16 Ja 2 '65

MACONCHY, Elizabeth
New music. C. Sigmon. Mus Am 83:34 Jl '63

MACOVEI, Pompiliu
Rumanian note April 2, 1963. Dept State Bul 48:662-3 Ap 29 '63

MCPHEE, Jack
Black bears are not always timid. por Outdoor Life 133:62-5+ Ap '64

MCPHEE, John
Basketball and beefeaters. New Yorker 39: 186-90+ Mr 16 '63
Profiles. New Yorker 40:40-2+ Ja 23 '65
Speaking out. por Sat Eve Post 237:8+ O 3 '64

MCPHERSON, Aimee Semple
Foursquare with Aimee. il por Time 83:62 F 28 '64

MCPHERSON, Bruce
Greatest rainbow trip. pors Outdoor Life 133: 40-3+ My '64

MCQUADE, Walter
Architecture (cont) Nation 196:145-6, 185-6, 448-50; 197:20, 332-3; 198:19-20, 59-60, 306-7 F 16, Mr 2, My 25, Jl 6, N 16 '63, Ja 4, 13, Mr 23 '64
Boston: what can a sick city do? Fortune 69:132-7+ Je '64
Building years of a Yale man. Arch Forum 118:88-93 Je '63
College architecture; the economics and aesthetics. Fortune 67:148-50 My '63
Industrial designer with a conspicuous conscience. Fortune 68:135-8+ Ag '63
New Saarinen office. Arch Forum 118:113-19 Ap '63
(ed) Structure & design. Fortune 70:177-8+ O; 205-6+ N '64

MCQUAID, John, abp
Distorts prayer for Christian unity. Christian Cent 81:228 F 19 '64

MCQUEEN, Mildred Hark. See Hark, M.

MCQUEEN, Noel. See Hark, M. jt. auth.

MCQUEEN, Steve
Bad boy's breakout; with account by P. Bunzel. il pors Life 55:62-8 Jl 12 '63
Mild one. il por Time 81:48 Je 28 '63
Real McQueen. por Newsweek 63:42-3 Ja 6 '64
Twenty-four hours in the life of Steve McQueen. E. Havemann. por McCalls 91:138-9+ Ap '64

MACQUOWN, Vivian J.
Teenage novel; a critique. por Library J 89:1832-5 Ap 15 '64

MACRAE, A. U.
Low-energy electron diffraction. bibliog Science 139:379-88 F 1 '63

MCRAE, William J.
Elk on the roof. il por Outdoor Life 134:48-9+ N '64

MACRIDIS, Roy C.
New French politics. Yale R 52:352-65 Mr '63

MACRO lenses. See Lenses, Photographic

MCROBBIE, Kenneth
Canadian chronicle. Poetry 103:266-60 Ja '64

MACROGLOBULIN antibody. See Antigens and Antibodies

MACROGLOBULINS. See Globulins

MACROMOLECULAR chemistry. See Molecules

MACROMOLECULES. See Molecules

MACROPHAGES
Cytoplasmic interaction between macrophages and lymphocytic cells in antibody synthesis. M. D. Schoenberg and others. bibliog il Science 143:964-5 F 28 '64

MACROPHOTOGRAPHY
Large camera. A. Feininger. Mod Phot 28:40 Ag '64
Large camera; some tips on close-up and macrophotography. A. Feininger. Mod Phot 28:16+ Jl '64

MCSHANE, Charles L.
Hi-fi loudspeaker cones. Electr World 69: 38-40+ F '63

MACURDY, Jack
Redbook's guide to early American furniture. Redbook 121:76-84 Jl '63
Redbook's guide to eighteenth century furniture. Redbook 122:82-90 N '63
Redbook's guide to French provincial furniture. Redbook 122:82-90 Mr '64
Redbook's guide to Spanish furniture. Redbook 123:82-90 O '64

MACURDY, John
On the steps; interview, ed. by F. Stevenson. por Opera N 27:15 Ap 6 '63

MACVANE, John
Soho! the beagles. Field & S 68:35-7+ Ja '64

MCVARISH, Charles E.
What makes a good PR man? L. L. L. Golden. Sat R 46:73 N 9 '63

MCVAY, Harue
Four ceramists of Hawaii. J. Lovoos. il por Am Artist 27:66-73+ Je '63

MCVEA, Warren
Warren McVea goes thisaway and thataway. M. Herskowitz. il por Sports Illus 21:48-9 N 9 '64

MCVICKAR, Polly Bowditch
Storytelling in Java. Horn Bk 40:596-601 D '64

MCVITTIE, G. C.
Oscillations of quasars. Science 146:259-60 O 9 '64

MCVITTY, Marion H.
Role of the United Nations. Cur Hist 46: 331-5 Je '64

MCWHINNIE, Harold James
Let's carve a log. Sch Arts 63:16-17 F '64

MCWHIRTER, Millie
It seems I heard the violins; story. Redbook 123:56-7 Ag '64
Old memory for a new year; story. Redbook 122:46-7 Ja '64
Roses for dinner; story. Redbook 122:58-9 F '64

MCWILLIAMS, Carey, 1905-
Ethics in an affluent society; address, October 17, 1963. por Wilson Lib Bul 38:471-7+ F '64
Exodus from Britain; no room at the top. Nation 197:151-5 S 21 '63
Franco, Congress and the Pentagon. Christian Cent 80:298-300 Mr 6 '63
Goldwaterism; the new ideology. Nation 199: 68-71 Ag 24 '64
High noon in the Cow Palace. Nation 199: 23-7 Jl 27 '64
Irish winds of change. Nation 197:191-3 O 5 '63
Morning after. Nation 199:345-7 N 16 '64

MCWILLIAMS, J. A.
Tern; poem. America 110:76 Ja 18 '64

MCWILLIAMS, Wilson C.
Non-aggression pact? Commonweal 79:191-3 N 8 '63

MACY, John W. Jr
Government service; challenges and rewards. Vital Speeches 30:446-8 My 1 '64

MACY, R. H. and company
Christmas shopping for next Christmas. il Bsns W p40-1 N 7 '64
Drawing a bead on World's fair market; Macy's credit card for out-of-towners. il Bsns W p43-4 F 29 '64
Great shopping spree. il Time 85:58-61 Ja 8 '65
In touch with Mrs Macy. il Time 84:111A O 2 '64
Macy's park-and-shop; Elmhurst, N.Y. branch. il Arch Forum 120:37 Ap '64
Shopping go-round at Macy's; Queens store. il Bsns W p34 F 15 '64
Using tax-exempts to build business; Macy store in Topeka. il Bsns W p45-6+ D 14 '63

MAD (periodical)
Best things in life are free. il Time 83:68+ Ap 3 '64
Case for Mad. C. W. Morton. il Atlan 212:100 S '63
Mad: wild oracle of the teenage underground. J. Skow. il Sat Eve Post 236:62-5 D 21 '63
Parody and satire deserve substantial freedom. H. F. Pilpel. Pub W 186:42 O 5 '64
Sing along with Mad. Newsweek 63:82 Ap 6 '64
When is a parody a plagiarism? H. Pilpel. Pub W 184:31 D 30 '63

Anecdotes, facetiae, satire, etc.

Special sophistication issue: Bad. il Esquire 62:52-6 Ag '64

MADAGASCAR. See Malagasy

MADAME Pele. See Kilauea (crater)

MADDEN, Charles F.
Person-to-person teaching. Sat R 47:50-1+ Jl 18 '64

MADDEN, Henry Miller
Mr and Mrs Grundy in the library and in court; excerpts from report. por Library J 89:4857-62 D 15 '64
On the firing line in a bad climate; excerpt from report. por ALA Bul 59:33-4 Ja '65

MADDEN, Max
Booty at the back door. Nation 199:84-5 S 7 '64

MADDEN, Thomas R.
Rocky Mountain literature. Commonweal 78: 330 Je 14 '63

MADDEX, Robert L. See Jones, P. B. jt. auth.

MADDICK, Henry
India's battle for food. bibliog Cur Hist 44: 160-6+ Mr '63

MADDISON, Jennifer Chancellor-. See Chancellor-Maddison, J.

MADDOX, Gaynor
American cooking is going international. Todays Health 41:38-41+ F '63
Breakfast recipes to start the day right. Todays Health 42:24-9 S '64
Citrus fruits: updating a Christmas favorite. Todays Health 41:38-43 D '63
Coffee-hour recipes that intrigue guests. Todays Health 42:50-5 O '64
Cook-ahead meals for hot summer days. Todays Health 41:42-5+ Jl '63

MADDOX, Gaynor—*Continued*
Cookout tips from teen-agers. Todays Health 41:34-7+ My '63
Early American Thanksgiving recipes. Todays Health 42:50-5 N '64
Easter in Italy: the reverent festival. Todays Health 41:40-3+ Ap '63
Fish dinners from your supermarket shelves. Todays Health 41:30-3+ Mr '63
Fresh vegetables bring spring tonic to the table. Todays Health 42:22-7 Mr '64
How American fruits and vegetables can be used in foreign dishes. Todays Health 42: 44-9 Ag '64
Ice cream desserts in delectable variety. Todays Health 42:42-7 Je '64
Lamb: preview of springtime. Todays Health 42:68-72 Ja '64
Men enjoy hearty dishes of foreign origin. Todays Health 42:38-43 Ja '64
New dishes to replace your regular eating habits. Todays Health 42:40-5 F '64
Pancakes are fancy fare. Todays Health 41: 40-3+ O '63
Portable meals for summer pleasure. Todays Health 42:42-7 Jl '64
Seasonal wild game offers many exotic dishes for the holidays. Todays Health 42:50-5 D '64
Signs of summer: fresh fruits and berries. Todays Health 41:42-5+ Je '63
Summer dining tips from major restaurants. Todays Health 41:34-7+ Ag '63
Summer harvest of good cooking. Todays Health 41:40-3+ S '63
Superstitious side of eating. Todays Health 41:48-51+ D '63; Same adr. with title Twenty-one diet fallacies. Sci Digest 56: 57-61 O '64
Sweet challenge of candymaking. Todays Health 41:46-51 N '63
Tasty meals for cozy twosomes. Todays Health 42:22-7 Ap '64
These recipes make chicken a new dish. Todays Health 43:50-5 Ja '65
These tasty recipes will make you an outdoor grill expert. Todays Health 42:24-9 My '64

MADDOX, John
At the brink of a test ban. Commentary 35:461-6; 36:192 Je, S '63
Is the literature worth keeping? Bul Atomic Sci 19:14-16 N '63
Science policy shapes up as issue in coming British election. Science 143:1146-8 Mr 13 '64
Scientific migration: Britain agitated anew by research team's decision to move to United States. Science 143:786-8 F 21 '64
Such were the joys. Commentary 37:88-9 F '64

MADDOX, Lester
Back in business. il por Newsweek 64:31 S 7 '64

MADEIRA, Jean
Stars at home. il pors Opera N 28:14-16 D 21 '63

MADELEINE; opera. See Herbert, V.

MADEMOISELLE (periodical)
Individualists; Mlle's annual Merit awards. il Mlle 58:72-6 Ja '64
Mlle guest editors: '64. M. Pincus. il Mlle 59:224-5 Ag '64
Mlle's annual Merit awards. il Mlle 60:68-71 Ja '65
Our guest editors. August, '63. M. Levin. il Mlle 57:210-11 Ag '63
Will the real July issue of Esquire please stand? A. Gingrich. il Esquire 60:6 Ag '63

MADER, Irmgard
Beta-carotene: thermal degradation. bibliog Science 144:533-4 My 1 '64

MADHVANI brothers
Confident kinsmen. Time 82:94 S 20 '63

MADIGAN, Francis C.
Asian population conference. America 110:188-90 F 8 '64; Correction. 111:202 Ag 29 '64

MADIGAN, Lawrence M.
Lay elite. America 109:193-5 Ag 24 '63

MADISON, Charles A.
Nine speak out for the Ten. Sat R 46:29 Je 29 '63
Repercussions from Monticello. Sat R 46:32 F 16 '63
Secretary of our early wars. Sat R 46:32-3 Je 15 '63
Skirmishes with a publisher; excerpts from Owl among colophons: a survey of American book publishing. Sat R 46:24-5 N 16 '63

MADISON, James
James Madison, fourth President 1809-1817. F. Freidel. il por Nat Geog Mag 126:672-7 N '64
Nature's God and the founding fathers. E. M. Halliday. il Am Heritage 14:100-6 O '63
This honorable Court; ed. by J. A. Garraty. il por Am Heritage 14:4-9+ Je '63

MADISON SQUARE GARDEN. See New York (city)—Madison Square Garden

MADOW, Pauline
Horse's mouth. Nation 199:444-6 D 7 '64

MADRAS rumble; story. See Faust, I.

MADRID

Description

Going places, finding things in Madrid. P. K. Brooks. il House & Gard 126:32+ D '64
Madrid: amusing incidentals. Vogue 141:63 Mr 15 '63

Galleries and museums

See also
Prado museum

Hotels, restaurants, etc.

International chef; Horcher's. il Travel 119: 62 My '63

Music

Madrid's real problem; Royal theater undergoing repairs. il Opera N 28:29-30 Mr 7 '64
Music in Madrid; first music festival of the Americas and Spain; with editorial comment. A. Iglesias. il Américas 17:1-5 Ja '65
[Musical events] Mus Am 84:94+ D '64

MADRIGALS
Music for Shakespeare. S. Popper. il Opera N 28:8-12 My 2 '64
See also
Phonograph records—Madrigals

MADRONAS
Canary Islands madrone and the handkerchief tree. il Sunset 130:283-4+ My '63
Pacific madrona, a colorful tree. M. M. Taylor. il Horticulture 41:162-3 Mr '63

MADSEN, Alfred Kenneth
Never on Thursday. por Newsweek 61:33 My 6 '63

MADSEN, Edna
Children of all ages create in a variety of media. Sch Arts 62:8-11 My '63

MADSEN, Millard C. See McGaugh, J. L. jt. auth.

MAEGERLEIN, Robert
Emerging porpoise. America 111:131-2 Ag 8 '64

MAEGHT, Aimé
Dealer's choice. il por Newsweek 64:61 Ag 10 '64

MAEGHT museum. See Art—Galleries and museums

MAFATLAL, Arvind
Cow & the tractor. il por Time 81:95 My 10 '63

MAFIA
After the TV crime hearings—. il U S News 55:8 O 14 '63
But listen to his canary. Life 55:4 O 18 '63
Che cosa? mean's what's that? M. Kempton. New Repub 149:6-7 O 12 '63
Detroit vs. the Mafia: a city fights back. J. Atwater. il Sat Eve Post 237:69-73 My 30 '64
Guilty friars. Newsweek 62:46 Jl 15 '63
Honored society, by N. Lewis. Review
America 110:774 My 30 '64. R. G. Murdy
Commonweal 81:22-3 S 25 '64. G. Wagner
How Mafia killers got their man; murder of James V. Delmont. B. Davidson. il Sat Eve Post 237:38-40 O 31 '64
How the mob controls Chicago. B. Davidson. il Sat Eve Post 236:17-27 N 9 '63
In Sicily: the real Mafia; with report by R. Toporoff. il Look 27:108-10+ O 22 '63
Joe Valachi: the killer who told on the mob. P. Maas. Sat Eve Post 236:21-3 N 23 '63
Kiss of death. Newsweek 62:34+ O 7 '63
Let them kill me. Newsweek 61:44 My 6 '63
Mafia. Newsweek 63:42+ F 24 '64
Mafia in trouble on its home grounds. J. Bonfante. il Life 56:96-103 Mr 6 '64
Mafia rubs out a rebellion. il Life 55:18-25 Ag 30 '63
Mafia: the inside story; with editorial comment. P. Maas. il Sat Eve Post 236:19-25, 90 Ag 10 '63
New Mafia is deadlier. R. Neville. il N Y Times Mag p22+ Ja 12 '64
New Orleans: Cosa nostra's Wall Street. B. Davidson. il Sat Eve Post 237:15-21 F 29 '64
Our thing; Cosa nostra. il Newsweek 62:27+ Ag 19 '63
Pick a number from 000 to 999. F. Powledge. il N Y Times Mag p35+ D 6 '64
Profiles. N. Lewis. New Yorker 39:42-4+ F 8; 39-40+ F 15; 40:35-6+ F 22 '64
Robert Kennedy defines the menace. R. F. Kennedy. il N Y Times Mag p 15+ O 13 '63

MAFIA—*Continued*
Sicilian canary; Simone Mansueto. Newsweek 62:53 O 14 '63
Smell of it; Valachi hearings. Time 82:28 O 11 '63
State of the Sicilian civilian. G. Gersh. il Sat R 47:33+ Je 6 '64
TV crime story; it's for real. il Sr Schol 83:17 O 25 '63
Their thing; Cosa nostra. il Time 82:15-16 Ag 16 '63
Way big crime operates in U.S. il U S News 55:78-9 O 7 '63
What it means; Valachi case. R. F. Kennedy. Sat Eve Post 236:20 Ag 10 '63
When the Mafia takes over a city; Detroit. U S News 55:6 O 21 '63

MAGADI, Lake
Great flamingo rescue. K. Drake. il Read Digest 84:209-11+ Je '64

MAGAZINE advertising. See Advertising mediums—Periodicals

MAGAZINE art. See Illustration of books and periodicals

MAGAZINE articles. See Periodical literature

MAGAZINE covers. See Periodical covers

MAGAZINE editors. See Editors and editing

MAGAZINE fiction. See Fiction in periodicals and newspapers

MAGAZINE publishing. See Periodicals, Publishing of

MAGAZINE stands, racks, etc.
Display racks for magazines. il Sunset 131:100 S '63

MAGAZINE writers, Society of. See Society of magazine writers

MAGAZINES. See Periodicals

MAGAZINES, Childrens. See Childrens periodicals

MAGEE, John F.
Decision trees for decision making. Harvard Bsns R 42:126-38 Jl '64
How to use decision trees in capital investment. Harvard Bsns R 42:79-96 S '64

MAGELLAN, Ferdinand
Journal from Magellan's voyage. A. Pigafetta. Wilson Lib Bul 38:714 My '64

MAGELLANIC clouds
Current studies of the Magellanic clouds. D. J. Faulkner. il Sky & Tel 26:69-73 Ag '63
Large cloud of Magellan. B. J. Bok. il Sci Am 210:32-41 Ja '64

MAGGI, Louis. See Giddis, A. jt. auth.

MAGGIO musicale fiorentino. See Music festivals—Italy

MAGIC
Fearful truth; Book of secrets. Hebrew manuscript. il Newsweek 65:75-75A+ Ja 18 '65
Sorcery and society. D. Bess. Nation 199:358-60 N 16 '64

MAGIC flute; opera. See Mozart, J. C. W. A.

MAGIC pencils; drama. See Miller, H. L.

MAGIC telephone; drama. See Miller, H. L.

MAGIC well; drama. See Leuser, E.

MAGIC wishing ring; drama. See Chaloner, G.

MAGID, Beth
Danger rides two wheels. Parents Mag 38:68-9+ S '63

MAGID, Carolyn Hope
Curl up and read. Seventeen 22:24 N '63

MAGID, Marion
Auteur! auteur! bibliog f Commentary 37:70-4 Mr '64
Innocence of Tennessee Williams. Commentary 35:34-43 Ja '63
Mocking heroics. Commentary 38:81-4 N '64

MAGIE, Allan R. and others
Indoleacetamide as an intermediate in the synthesis of indoleacetic acid in pseudomonas sacastanoi. bibliog Science 141:1281-2 S 27 '63

MAGILL, Lewis M.
Get off Johnny's back! Sat R 47:64-6 F 15 '64

MAGLOFF, Joanna
Art news from San Francisco. Art N 62:51-2 Ja '64
Reviews: San Francisco. Art N 63:20 Mr; 20+ Ap; 20+ My '64

MAGMA. See Rocks, Igneous

MAGMATIC water. See Water, Underground

MAGMER, James
News management is still a live issue. Cath World 197:180-6 Je '63

MAGNAVOX company
Magnavox goes its own golden way. S. H. Brown. il Fortune 69:112-15+ F '64

MAGNER, James A.
Felipe. America 108:584+ Ap 20 '63

MAGNESIA
New technique for strengthening ceramics; magnesium oxide. Sci N L 83:216 Ap 6 '63

MAGNESIUM
Coupling of butyl bromide on hot magnesium. F. L. Lambert and others. bibliog Science 146:1049 N 20 '64

MAGNESIUM compounds
Magnesium compounds: new dense phases. P. Cannon and E. T. Conlin. il Science 145:487-9 Jl 31 '64

MAGNESIUM oxide. See Magnesia

MAGNETIC compass. See Compass

MAGNETIC converters. See Modulators

MAGNETIC field
High-field galvanomagnetic properties of metals. W. A. Reed and E. Fawcett. bibliog il Science 146:603-10 O 30 '64
Nonlinear magnetics and superconductivity; report on 2nd International conference on nonlinear magnetics. G. C. Feth. Science 145:838 Ag 21 '64
Nuclear magnetic resonance spectroscopy in superconducting magnetic fields. F. A. Nelson and H. E. Weaver. bibliog il Science 146:223-32 O 9 '64

MAGNETIC field (cosmic physics)
Exploding galaxy M82: evidence for the existence of a large-scale magnetic field. A. R. Sandage and W. C. Miller. bibliog il Science 144:405-9 Ap 24 '64
Galactic magnetism. Sci Am 211:46 Jl '64
High magnetic fields: production and application; report of international conference. H. H. Kolm and M. S. Dresselhaus. Science 142:271-5 O 11 '63
Solar and stellar magnetism; report of symposium of the International astronomical union. J. L. Greenstein. Science 142:686 N 8 '63
Solar magnetic fields; summary of address. A. B. Severny. Sky & Tel 28:264 N '64

MAGNETIC induction
See also
Hysteresis loop

MAGNETIC materials
See also
Hysteresis loop

MAGNETIC modulators. See Modulators

MAGNETIC pole. See Magnetism, Terrestrial

MAGNETIC recorders and recording
ABC's of movie sound. E. Nanas. il Pop Phot 53:100-1+ S '63
Accessories extend the scope, add to the fun of tape recording. J. Wesson. il U S Camera 26:74-5+ F '63
Adding VU meter to tape recorder. J. W. Hogan. il Electr World 72:104 O '64
All wound up in tape. S. D. Smith. il N Y Times Mag p54+ Ap 12 '64
. . . And be sure to pack a tape recorder. R. Silverberg. il Hi Fi 13:31-4 Jl '63
Attaché case makes secret recordings. H. Luckett. il Pop Sci 183:170 O '63
Auto tape threading. M. A. Matzkin. il Mod Phot 29:92+ Ja '65
Behind the scenes. il Mod Phot 27:48+ D '63
Candid recording. M. T. Reiter. il Pop Phot 52:103+ Mr '63
Christmas ribbon and magnetic tape. I. Berger. Sat R 47:58 D 12 '64
Confessions of an illicit tape recordist. P. Moor. il Hi Fi 13:38-40+ Ag '63
Faithful sound. R. Freas. Esquire 61:24+ My '64
Family message center. H. L. Davidson. il Pop Electr 21:79-81 Ag '64
From 78 to 7.5: guide to the delights of dubbing from discs to tape. C. L. Osborne. il Hi Fi 14:50-2+ Mr '64
Gifts: equipment and recordings. M. Mayer. Esquire 60:110+ D '63
Gina Bachauer; interview, ed. by S. Fleming. G. Bachauer. Hi Fi 13:46 N '63
High fidelity. H. Fantel. Opera N 28:32 S 28; 38 N 16; 35 D 14 '63
How to buy a tape recorder; mono and stereo recorders. A. J. Zuckerman. il Pop Sci 185:98-102 Jl '64
How to buy tape recorders. L. Zide. Mod Phot 28:147+ D '64
How to keep your tape recorder in shape. H. Friedman. il Pop Phot 55:76+ O '64
In praise of tape recording. F. Lewin. il U S Camera 26:73+ Mr '63
Instant movies. R. Miller. il U S Camera 26:80 Jl '63
Magnetic stripe on film. A. A. Armour. il U S Camera 26:20 S '63
Make your hi-fi system work harder: add a tape recorder. R. Freas. il Am Home 66:12+ O '63

MAGNETIC recorders and recording—*Cont.*
Microphones make the difference. I. B. Berger. il Hi Fi 14:47-50 Ag '64
Monophonic tape recorders. il Consumer Rep 29:523-7 N '64
New in tape. I. Berger. Sat R 46:57-8 S 14 '63
New tape recorders. il Pop Phot 55:74-5+ Ag '64
1965 photography directory and buying guide; showmanship. il Pop Phot 55:69-132 D '64
1964 directory & buying guide. il Pop Phot 54:49-80 Ja '64
Norelco 150: carry-corder. A. Zuckerman. il Pop Phot 55:58+ N '64
Now hear this! Tape recorder directory. J. Wesson. il U S Camera 27:65-9 O '64
Personalizing a tape recorder. T. Schwartz. il Pop Phot 54:30 Ap '64
Photographer's guide to sound; symposium; with editorial comment. il Pop Phot 53:46, 49-65+ S '63
Points on portraits in sound. T. Schwartz. il Pop Phot 55:24 D '64
Popular photography directory & buying guide. il Pop Phot 52:102-4 Ja '63
Rave review on Sony 600; reprint. N. H. Crowhurst. il Hi Fi 14:66 O '64
Recording musical instruments. G. W. Cushman. il Pop Phot 52:40+ Ap '63
Revere tape cartridge system. il Hi Fi 14: 34-5 Jl '64
Something different in tape recorders. il Consumer Rep 29:72-3 F '64
Sound. New Yorker 40:49-50 N 21 '64
Sound advice. R. N. Angus. il Mod Phot 27: 18-19 Mr; 34+ My '63
Sound advice; accessories for home recording. Mod Phot 27:93+ S '63
Sound advice; choosing and testing a tape recorder. H. Keppler. Mod Phot 27:62+ D '63
Sound advice; future of tape. H. A. Manoogian. Mod Phot 27:38 Ap '63
Sound advice; manufacturers' specifications. R. N. Angus. Mod Phot 28:162+ D '64
Sound advice; routine maintenance of tape head. L. Zide. Mod Phot 28:42+ O '64
Sound advice; simple maintenance procedures. L. Zide. Mod Phot 28:56+ S '64
Sound advice; 3M-Revere tape cartridge. B. Angus. il Mod Phot 27:18-19 Mr '63
Sound advice; transfer 78 RPM discs; to tape. R. N. Angus. Mod Phot 28:46+ Ag '64
Sound ideas. il Am Rec G 29:572-3 Mr '63
Sound ideas; the Ampex 2070. il Am Rec G 31:263-5 N '64
Sound/slides: new recorders make it easier. M. A. Matzkin. il Mod Phot 28:92+ S '64
Sound; the modern tape recorder. J. Wesson. U S Camera 26:8+ O '63
Sound traveling companion; portable tape recorders. L. Barry. Pop Phot 55:18+ O '64
Sound; why instead of how. T. Schwartz. Pop Phot 53:12 O '63
Synchronization. J. R. Gregory. il U S Camera 26:72-3 O '63
Take it from TV. S. Moritz. il U S Camera 26:74-5 Je '63
Talented tape deck. H. Luckett. il Pop Sci 185:102 Ag '64
Tape as you go. I. B. Berger. Sat R 47:64-5 Ap 25 '64
Tape changer: it's here at last. C. S. Tepfer. il Pop Sci 182:91-4+ Je '63
Tape for the road: built-in tape recorder for cars. Time 82:49 Ag 9 '63
Tape it slow. I. Berger. Sat R 47:67 Je 27 '64
Tape recorder. il Hi Fi 14:57-8 F '64
Tape recorder breakthrough: cross field head. R. N. Angus. il Mod Phot 28:93+ S '64
Tape recorder directory. J. Wesson. U S Camera 26:74-5 Mr '63
Tape-recorder equalization curves. H. Burstein. il Electr World 72:38-40 Jl '64
Tape recorder guide. M. A. Matzkin. il Mod Phot 28:99+ N '64
Tape recorders: the new models. J. M. Conly. il Atlan 214:128-9 Jl '64
Tape transports: inside out. L. Zide. il Mod Phot 28:95+ O '64
Tape-winding nomogram. F. Blechman. il Electr World 72:38-9 O '64
Tapes: facts and fallacies. G. W. Cushman. Pop Phot 52:27-8+ Mr '63
Tapeworms: increased sales. Newsweek 64: 100+ N 16 '64
Telcan: first U.S. showing. L. Klein; L. Barry; L. Drukker. il Pop Phot 54:116-17+ Ap '64
They take snapshots in sound. P. Browne. il Read Digest 82:151-3+ My '63
Things you never thought a tape recorder could do. Bet Hom & Gard 42:34 O '64
This is hi-fi? C. P. Gilmore. il Pop Sci 182: 72-5+ Mr '63
Try on-location pickups. A. Zuckerman. il Pop Phot 53:18+ Jl '63
Uses of diversity. I. Berger. Sat R 47:47+ N 28 '64
Why's and how's of raw and pre-recorded tape. B. Francois. il U S Camera 26:78-9 Mr '63
See also
Ampex corporation
Video tape recorders and recording

Educational applications

Indispensable tape recorder. S. Solomon. il Sr Schol 85:6T N 18 '64
Learning by listening to tapes; Ohio state university listening center. Sch & Soc 92: 24 Ja 25 '64

Scientific applications

Acoustic activity recorder for burrowing animals. C. Gans and J. J. Bonin. bibliog il Science 140:398 Ap 26 '63

Space flight applications

DSIF tape recorders will reduce footage needed for future missions. R. Pay. il Miss & Roc 14:40-1 My 4 '64

Stereophonic recorders

Ampex automatic tape recorder; stereo tape recorder. R. Benrey. il Pop Sci 185:116 D '64
Completing a sound track the easy way. G. W. Cushman. il Pop Phot 52:22+ Ja '63
Sound advice; stereo tapes. R. N. Angus. Mod Phot 27:109+ N '63
Stereo tape recorders. il Consumer Rep 28: 538-45 N '63
Taping FM stereo. E. T. Canby. il Hi Fi 13: 45-7+ Ag '63
Tips on taping FM-stereo broadcasts. House & Gard 126:156+ O '64
What is this thing called stereo? questions and answers. J. R. Gregory. il U S Camera 26:30+ D '63

Testing

Check your tape heads. T. Diers. il Pop Mech 120:180-1 D '63

Visual recordings

See Video tape recorders and recording

MAGNETIC recorders and recording, Portable
Buyers' guide for portable tape recorders. F. Blechman. il Pop Electr 18:67-70+ Ap '63
How to live with low-cost portables. H. Friedman. Pop Phot 55:77 O '64
Light, portable tape recorders capture live sound. G. Gilbert. il U S Camera 26:22-3+ Ag '63
Portable transistor tape recorders. il Consumer Bul 47:19-22 N '64
Vacation with music: take console sound in a suitcase. R. Freas. il Am Home 67:21+ Jl '64

MAGNETIC resonance
Magnetic resonance at high pressure. G. B. Benedek. il Sci Am 212:102-8 bibliog(p 136) Ja '65
Magnetic resonance in biological systems; report on first International conference on magnetic resonance in biological systems. O. Jardetzky. Science 146:552-3 O 23 '64

MAGNETIC resonance, Nuclear. See Nuclear magnetic resonance

MAGNETIC storms
Solar wind. E. N. Parker. il Sci Am 210: 66-76 bibliog(p 156) Ap '64

MAGNETIC tape
All recording tapes are not alike. J. Wesson. il U S Camera 26:74-5+ O '63
Audio: pitch problems; off-pitch tape. P. Davis. Mus Am 84:57 S '64
Know your tape. T. Schwartz. Pop Phot 54:28 Ja '64
Music from the electronic universe; with discography. E. Salzman. Hi Fi 14:54-7 Ag '64
Real improvement in tape machine reels; self-threading reel. Consumer Rep 29:318 Jl '64
Recording tapes, which to buy, and why. L. A. Harlow. il Pop Sci 184:126-7+ Ja '64
Ribbons of rust. I. Berger. Sat R 47:57 Mr 28 '64
Sound advice. R. Coward. Mod Phot 27:10+ F '63
Spotlight on tape. Hi Fi 13:37 Ag '63
Tape up to date. N. Eisenberg. il Hi Fi 14: 42-4+ Ag '64

MAGNETIC tape—*Continued*
Tips on tape. il Pop Mech 119:197-9+ Mr '63
What tape to choose? S. Hegeman. il Hi Fi 13:41-4 Ag '63
Which tape to use? H. Burstein. il Electr World 70:34-5 N '63
See also
Tape recordings
MAGNETISM
Magnetic monopoles. K. W. Ford. il Sci Am 209:122-5+ bibliog(p 180) D '63
Magnetism: a decade of conferences; report on tenth annual conference on magnetism and magnetic materials, Minneapolis, November 16-19, 1964. W. F. Brown, jr. Science 147:73-4 Ja 1 '65
Magnetism; report on ninth annual conference on magnetism and magnetic materials. S. H. Charap and R. F. Elfant. Science 143:604+ F 7 '64
Quantized magnetic flux in superconductors. R. D. Parks. bibliog il Science 146:1429-35 D 11 '64
Thermochemical etching reveals domain structure in magnetic. R. E. Hanss. bibliog il Science 146:398-9 O 16 '64
See also
Electromagnetism
Hysteresis loop
Magnetostriction
Thermomagnetism
MAGNETISM, Terrestrial
Distribution of narrow-width magnetic anomalies in Antarctica. J. C. Behrendt. bibliog il Science 144:993-4+ My 22 '64
Flipped magnetic poles. Sci Am 209:62 O '63
Geomagnetic polarity epochs. A. Cox and others. bibliog Science 143:351-2 Ja 24 '64
Geomagnetic polarity epochs: Sierra Nevada II. A. Cox and others. bibliog il Science 142:382-5 O 18 '63
Gravity and magnetic anomalies of the Sierra Madera, Texas, dome. J. R. Van Lopik and R. A. Geyer. bibliog il Science 142: 45-7 O 4 '63
Is magnetism the key to life's origin on earth? J. Lear. Sat R 46:35-8 Jl 6 '63
Paleontologic technique for defining ancient pole positions. F. G. Stehli and C. E. Helsley. il Science 142:1057-9 N 22 '63
Particle accretion rates: variation with latitude. R. A. Schmidt and T. J. Cohen. bibliog il Science 145:924-6 Ag 28 '64
Reversals of the earth's magnetic field. A. Cox and others. bibliog il Science 144:1537-43 Je 26 '64
Study earth's history and magnetic personality. Sci N L 87:56 Ja 23 '65
MAGNETITE
Magnetite: preferred orientation on the basal plane of partially reduced hematite. R. O. Keeling, jr. and D. A. Wick. bibliog il Science 141:1175-6 S 20 '63
Thermochemical etching reveals domain structure in magnetite. R. E. Hanss. bibliog il Science 146:398-9 O 16 '64
MAGNETOHYDRODYNAMIC generators. See Electric generators
MAGNETOHYDRODYNAMICS
Create sun matter. W. Wingo. Sci N L 85: 359 Je 6 '64
Martin generates continuing MPD power. M. L. Yaffee. il Aviation W 80:65+ Ja 6 '64
New magnet provides more efficient way to convert heat directly into electricity. Bsns W p54 Ja 19 '63
New system announced for generating electricity; magnetoplasmadynamic generator. il Sci N L 85:22 Ja 11 '64
MAGNETOMETERS
Magnetism locates ruins; submerged Greek city of Sybaris. Sci N L 86:358 D 5 '64
Pioneer program decisions expected in next few weeks; magnetic cleanliness major design problem. M. Getler. il Miss & Roc 13:22-3+ S 9 '63
World's greatest prospector. N. Carlisle. il Pop Sci 184:60-3+ My '4
MAGNETOPLASMADYNAMIC generators. See Electric generators
MAGNETOSPHERE. See Atmosphere, Upper
MAGNETOSTRICTION
Magnetostrictive delay lines. J. R. Collins. il Electr World 71:48-9 Ja '64
MAGNETOTROPISM. See Tropism (botany)
MAGNETRONS
Four-minute cake; microwave ovens. Bsns W p94+ S 12 '64
MAGNETS
Ceramic sandwich. il Time 81:66 F 15 '63
Magnet with memory. Sci N L 83:110 F 16 '63
Magnets; metals that attract metals. il Sci Digest 56:75-8 Jl '64
RCA unveils magnet breakthrough; superconductive magnet. il Miss & Roc 14:18 My 25 '64
Superstrong magnets. Sci Am 212:50-1 Ja '65
See also
Electromagnets
MAGNIFIERS
Hobby viewer, illuminated magnifying viewer. W. Waltner and E. Waltner. il Pop Mech 121:166-7 Ap '64
MAGNITUDES of stars. See Stars—Magnitudes
MAGNOLIAS
Here are magnolias you can count on. il Sunset 130:180 F '63
Look for this tree this month; star magnolia. il Sunset 134:124 Ja '65
MAGNUSON, Warren G.
Forestry's role in youth conservation. por Am For 70:12-14 Ag '64
MAGPIE jays. See Jays
MAGRATH, C. Peter
Foot in the door. Am Heritage 15:44-8+ F '64
MAGUIRE, Bassett, jr
Crustacea: a primitive Mediterranean group also occurs in North America. bibliog Science 146:931-2 N 13 '64
MAGWOOD, Dolores
Conversation with Dolores Magwood; ed. by L. Joel. por Dance Mag 38:26-7 O '64
MAHAGONNY; opera. See Weill, K.
MAHAN, Lois
How to build an airport. Flying 75:37-8+ Ag '64
MAHAR, James F. and Coddington, D. C.
Scientific complex: proceed with caution. Harvard Bsns R 43:140-8+ Ja '65
MAHAR, Mary Helen
School library reporter. Sch Life 46:29-30 O; 19 D '63; 22-3 My; 13 Jl '64
—See Brooking, W. J. jt. auth.
MAHER, Arthur
Shopping for tools. Pop Mech 119:159 My; 120:193 N '63; 121:26 Mr '64
Spring roundup of new building materials. Pop Mech 121:128-33 Ap '64
MAHER, Edward
Ethical aftermath of profit; address, August 8, 1963. Vital Speeches 29:735-6 S 15 '63
MAHER, James T.
Good night, Mister Mulcahy, good night; story. Ladies Home J 81:112-16 My '64
Great American palaces. Ladies Home J 82: 99-103 Ja '65
House gift; story. Sat Eve Post 237:52-5 Mr 7 '64
MAHER, John F. and Wesolowski, S. A.
Artificial internal organs. Science 145:76-7 Jl 3 '64
MAHER, Joseph
Half-breeds. America 111:743-4 D 5 '64
MAHER, Richard L.
Astronaut's progress. Nation 198:131-3 F 10 '64
MAHEU, René
Eradication of illiteracy; excerpts from statement, October 18, 1963. por U N Rev 10:34-5 D '63
Fight against illiteracy; with excerpts from resolution. UN Mo Chron 1:82-6 D '64
Planning for education in Latin America. Sat R 47:52-4 Ag 15 '64
Sport is education; excerpts from address, October 28, 1963. UNESCO Courier 17:4-9 Ja '64
Struggle against illiteracy: the most exalting venture of our generation; address, August 26, 1964. UNESCO Courier 17:4-8 O '64
330 million brains for a new era. UNESCO Courier 16:24-9 Jl '63
True Unesco; address, November 15, 1962. Sch & Soc 91:70-2 F 9 '63
MAHLER, Alma Maria (Schindler)
Lady with a past; interview, ed. by A. M. Lingg. por Opera N 28:14-15 D 14 '63
MAHLER, Gustav
Another view. con; Symphony no. 1 in D. J. Diether. Am Rec G 29:523-4 Mr '63
Gustav Mahler: the sadness of horns. R. De Toledano. Nat R 17:71-2 Ja 26 '64
Gustav Mahler's Symphony of a thousand. R. Sabin. Am Rec G 30:938+ Je '64
Id in march time. F. V. Grunfeld. Reporter 31:45-6+ O 8 '64
Leinsdorf's Mahler Fifth symphony. J. Diether. Am Rec G 31:120-2+ O '64
Mahler by two conductors (Mengelberg and Klemperer) who knew him personally; Symphony no. 2 in C minor and Symphony no. 4 in G. J. Diether. Am Rec G 30:421-2+ Ja '64

MAHLER, Gustav—*Continued*
Mahler's Eighth, a stereo debut. R. C. Marsh. Hi Fi 14:50-1 Jl '64
More Mahler by Bernstein, No. 5. J. Diether. Am Rec G 30:664-5 Ap '64
Most satisfactory Mahler Second yet. J. Diether. Am Rec G 31:439+ Ja '65
Musical events; comparison of A. Bruckner and G. Mahler. W. Sargeant. New Yorker 39:136-8 O 5 '63
Musical events; Mahler's Second symphony, performed by New York philharmonic. W. Sargeant. New Yorker 39:135-6 O 5 '63
On records; Das lied von der erde. Opera N 28:35 Ap 4 '64
Such music as ne'er was made by bird, harp, or maiden. J. Diether. il Am Rec G 30:582-4 Mr '64
Walter's Mahler First: the standard by which others are to be judged; Symphony no. 1 in D. C. J. Luten. il Am Rec G 29:522-3 Mr '63

MAHLER, Jane Gaston
Buddha in situ and in New York. Art N 62:36-7+ My '63

MAHLER, Roni
Brief biography. S. Goodman. pors Dance Mag 38:50-1 Jl '64

MAHON, George H.
George Mahon talks on spending; interview. por Nations Bsns 52:32-3+ Ag '64
about
Another Texan moves up, Mahon succeeds Cannon. por U S News 56:22 My 25 '64
Cannon to Mahon. Cato. Nat R 16:439 Je 2 '64
New pilot for House money bills. Bsns W p29 My 16 '64

MAHONEY, John F.
Paradoxes of parochial schools. Cath World 199:28-33 Ap '64

MAHONEY, Sally
Centralization of audio-visual and professional materials. Wilson Lib Bul 37:868-9+ Je '63

MAHONEY, Stephen
It's Hertz itself in the driver's seat. Fortune 68:118-23+ O '63
Kalvar; from a wastebasket, dazzling suspense. Fortune 67:110-13+ Mr '63
Pro football's profit explosion. Fortune 70:153-5+ N '64
Very round profits of Square D. Fortune 70:136-9+ Ag '64

MAHONEY, Tom
Few appropriate remarks at Gettysburg. Read Digest 83:146-52 N '63

MAHONEY, Walter J.
Moral missions of the legislature; address, April 24, 1963. Vital Speeches 29:655-7 Ag 15 '63
Coming of age. Nat R 15:10 Jl 16 '63

MAHONEY viruses. See Poliomyelitis virus

MAHONY, Bertha E. See Miller, B. E. M.

MAĬAKOVSKIĬ, Vladimir Vladimirovich
Talk with a tax collector; poem, tr. by R. Herschberger and M. Prychodko. Poetry 102:100-8 My '63

MAIDENHAIR tree. See Ginkgo

MAIDS (servants) See Household employees

MAIDS; drama. See Genêt, J.

MAIER, Irwin
If a government begins to deceive; excerpts from address, April 24, 1963. U S News 54:10 My 6 '63
about
Notes and comment; managed news. New Yorker 39:33 My 4 '63

MAIL (New York) See New York evening mail

MAIL boxes
Apartment house mail receptacles. il Arch Rec 134:229-30 S '63
It's mail box and house number. il Sunset 130:167 Ap '63

MAIL carriers. See Postmen

MAIL censorship. See Postal censorship

MAIL fraud. See Fraud

MAIL handling
Automation speeds mail. Sci N L 85:198 Mr 28 '64
Push-button post office. G. Astor. il Look 28:46+ Ap 21 '64
Will machines speed the mails? il U S News 54:65-7 Mr 4 '63

MAIL lobby. See Lobbying

MAIL order advertising. See Books—Advertising

MAIL order business
Bang, bang, you're dead; mail-order weapons. J. Ridgeway. New Repub 148:6 F 16 '63
Caveat emptor; pseudo liquidating. Time 83:82-3 Ja 17 '64
Don't be gypped by mail-order firms. Consumer Bul 47:38-40 Mr '64 (to be cont)
Don't buy by mail! il Changing T 17:7-11 Mr '63
Land frauds; look before you buy. T. Armbrister. il Sat Eve Post 236:17-23 Ap 27 '63
Mail-order gyps. il Consumer Bul 47:34-7 Ap '64
Mail-order items for the gadgeteer. Consumer Bul 47:10 S '64
Mail order sales help paperback bookseller; Bookcase, inc; New York city. il Pub W 185:51-2 Mr 30 '64
One 33J3663F and a 7J4202F: the buying-by-catalogue boom. il Newsweek 63:88-90 My 25 '64; Same abr. with title Booming business of buying by catalogue. Read Digest 85:189-90+ O '64
Price breaker; Germany's J. Neckermann. il Bsns W p 104-6 Mr 21 '64
Prosperity by mail; West Germany's pioneering Die quelle. Time 81:110 Ap 19 '63
Shop by mail? il Changing T 18:37-40 Ap '64
Silent salesmen. Time 83:95 Mr 13 '64
Some practices in the antiques business; buying and selling by mail. A. G. Peterson. il Hobbies 68:82-3 S '63
Speaking out; too many people have guns. J. V. Lindsay. Sat Eve Post 237:12+ F 1 '64
Where Johnny gets his gun. J. Anderson. Read Digest 83:138-40 Jl '63
Worldwide bazaar. il Ladies Home J 80:139-40+ N '63
You can't really get it wholesale. Consumer Bul 48:24-5 F '65
See also
Catalogs, Mail order
Great universal stores, limited
Sears, Roebuck and company

MAIL order catalogs. See Catalogs, Mail order

MAIL-order record clubs. See Phonograph record clubs

MAIL robberies. See Robberies and assaults

MAIL service. See Postal service

MAILER, Norman
American dream; novel. Esquire 61:77-81 Ja; 107 F; 89-92 Mr; 97-100 Ap; 124-7 My; 114-16 Je; 62:41-2 Jl; 41-3 Ag '64
Big bite. See issues of Esquire to December 1963
In the red light: a history of the Republican convention in 1964. Esquire 62:83-9+ N '64
Last night. Esquire 60:151+ D '63
Norman Mailer vs. nine writers. por Esquire 60:63-9+ Jl '63
Responses & reactions (cont) Commentary 35:146-8, 335-7, 517-18; 36:164-5 F, Ap, Je, Ag '63
Responses & reactions; excerpts from The Presidential papers. Commentary 36:320-1 O '63
Ten thousand words a minute. Esquire 59:109-20 F '63
about
Art of not writing novels. G. Wills. Nat R 16:31-3 Ja 14 '64
Hemingway who stayed home. P. Velde. Nation 198:76-7 Ja 20 '64
Misshapen image. por Time 82:106+ N 29 '63
Small comment from a penitent novelist. J. Jones. Esquire 60:40+ D '63
Way it isn't done: notes on the distress of Norman Mailer. Esquire 60:306-8 D '63
Why Mailer wants to be president. R. Gilman. New Repub 150:17-20+ F 8 '64

MAILING lists
About: mailing lists; direct-mail industry under fire. T. Irwin. N Y Times Mag p96-7 Mr 22 '64
Direct mail for retail bookstores. M. A. Levin. Pub W 186:53-5 S 21 '64
Name industry. Time 82:79 D 20 '63

MAILING machines. See Mail handling

MAILLIARD, William S.
Fifth committee discusses U.N. budget estimates for 1964; statement, October 28, 1963. Dept State Bul 49:871-5 D 2 '63

MAILLOL, Aristide
Eye on the navel. il Newsweek 63:91 F 17 '64
Letter from Paris; exhibition at France's first al-fresco museum of great modern sculpture. Genêt. New Yorker 39:82+ Ja 25 '64
Maillol garden. il N Y Times Mag p83-4+ O 4 '64

MAIMAN, Theodore H.
Adventurous ones. por Vogue 142:77 Ag 1 '63
Astounding laser. M. Gunther. il Sat Eve Post 237:68-71 O 24 '64
Lasing along. il por Newsweek 63:69 My 18 '64

MAIN, A. R.
Affinity and phosphorylation constants for the inhibition of esterases by organophosphates. bibliog Science 144:992-3 My 22 '64

MAIN line. See Philadelphia

MAINBOCHER
Main line. il por Time 82:61 S 27 '63
Mainbocher. il por Vogue 142:102-7 N 1 '63

MAINE
See also
Allagash River
Camping—Maine
Fishing—Maine
Forests and forestry—Maine
Hunting—Maine
Mount Desert Island

Antiquities

See Indians of North America—Antiquities—Maine

Description and travel

Fall foliage focus: Maine. J. T. Boyd. il Travel 122:24-7 O '64
Maine idea. M. Goodman. il Redbook 123:64-5+ Jl '64

Economic conditions

Trouble with Maine. W. S. Ellis. Nation 196:527-9 Je 22 '63

Historic houses, etc.

Tate House in Stroudwater, Maine. M. P. Smith. il Antiques 84:172-4 Ag '63

Parks and reserves

Maine's Baxter State Park: a gift of mountain wilderness. R. D. Pardo. il Am For 69:20-2+ F '63
Woodland caribou comes home to Miane. B. Geagan. il Nat Parks Mag 38:8-9 My '64

MAINE in art
Maine & American artists, 1710-1963. J. Davidson. il Am Artist 27:32-9+ D '63

MAINER, Robert, and Slater, C. C.
Markets in motion. bibliog f Harvard Bsns R 42:75-82 Mr '64

MAINTENANCE and repair of plant. See Factories—Maintenance and repair

MAINTENANCE of prices. See Price maintenance by industry

MAIRS, E. D.
Extended vacations at Alcoa. Mo Labor R 87:404-6 Ap '64

MAISEL, Albert Q.
Fantastic hazards of landing on the moon. Read Digest 83:103-7 S '63
Hope for brain-injured children. Read Digest 85:135-40 O '64
How we can eliminate our overcrowded state mental hospitals. Read Digest 83:59-63 Ag '63
Latin America turns to family planning. Read Digest 84:189-90+ Ap '64
Mental retardation, avoidable affliction? Read Digest 85:159-60+ S '64
New battle over birth control. Read Digest 82:54-9 F '63
Quest for better teacher: a progress report on the Conant plan. Read Digest 85:241-4+ O '64
Teens work for love, not money. Parents Mag 38:68+ My '63
They help boys want to be educated. Read Digest 83:100-4 D '63
What will your teen-ager do this summer? Read Digest 82:133-4+ My '63

MAISEL, Jay
Land of the buzzard and the Coromuel: photographs. Sports Illus 22:56-68 Ja 18 '65

about

Focus on Jay Maisel. J. Durniak. il Pop Phot 54:76-85+ Mr '64

MAIZE. See Corn

MAJOLICA
Five centuries of Faenza majolica; excerpts. G. Liverani. il Antiques 83:684-9 Je '63

MAJOR, Frances M.
Batik on paper. Design 64:102-3+ Ja '63
Child's best friend. Design 64:190 Je '63
Coat hanger sculpture. Design 65:98-9 Ja '64
Greetings in macaroni. Design 64:194 Je '63
Sketching with seeds. Design 65:150-1 Mr '64
Stocking faces. Design 65:186-7 My '64
Try totem poles. Design 64:173 Mr '63
—See Turner, G. jt. auth.

MAJOR, J. Russell
Crown and the aristocracy in renaissance France. bibliog f Am Hist R 69:631-44 Ap '64

MAJORITIES
Majority opinion; right or wrong? letter. P. D. Foote. Science 142:341 O 18 '63; Reply. D. W. Riley. 143:433 Ja 31 '64

MAKARIOS III, abp
Aura of doom. Newsweek 64:41 S 14 '64
Cyprus: it there a peaceful way out? il por Sr Schol 85:10-13+ S 30 '64
Cyprus problem=Makarios problem. M. Wall. il pors N Y Times Mag p38-9+ O 18 '64
Cyprus: the archbishop can't lose. C. Sterling. il por Reporter 30:12-16 Je 4 '64
His Beatitude the President. il por Time 84:70+ S 18 '64
Island in conflict. Sr Schol 83:18-19 Ja 17 '64
Letter from Cyprus. C. Foley. il Nat R 16:724-5 Ag 25 '64
Makarios: key to peace on Cyprus. U S News 57:16 Ag 24 '64
Makarios of Cyprus. Time 83:27 F 28 '64
Makarios of Cyprus: he enjoys to gamble. il por Newsweek 63:34-8 Mr 2 '64
Peerless brinkman. il Newsweek 64:40 S 7 '64
Self-determination. il por Newsweek 63:40 Ap 27 '64
What Americans face in Cyprus. J. Law. il por U S News 56:41 F 17 '64

MAKE-up
Back and welcome; the natural look. il Good H 157:84-5+ S '63
Beauty life: shape & shade. il Mlle 60:148-9 N '64
Beauty: the new image-makers. L. Faurer. il Mlle 58:180-1 Mr '64
Change in the make-up mores. il Vogue 141:148-9 Mr 1 '63
Come as a Christmas angel. il Seventeen 23:80-1 D '64
Cosmetics of war. D. Bess. Nation 197:296-8 N 9 '63
Extravagant eyelash. il Mlle 58:116 F '64
Girl with the golden eyes. il Mlle 60:102-3 D '64
How to apply eye shadow. il Ladies Home J 81:104 S '64
How to face up to a fad; discothèque make-up. il Redbook 124:86-7+ N '64
How to line your eyelids. il Ladies Home J 81:95 Ag '64
Let's make up. L. D. Kirk. il Parents Mag 38:104 D '63
Look-again look; slightly brazen book of beauty. il McCall 91:80-95 Jl '64
Look pretty in glasses; eye make-up tricks. il Seventeen 23:160-1+ S '64
Make-up: it's marvelous! il Seventeen 23:90 Ag '64
Man talk: attitude of men to makeup. D. Newman and R. Benton. il Mlle 59:74+ O '64
Monti gilds twenty Mlles. A. Hoene. il Mlle 57:264-7 Ag '63
New and meltingly lovely: the delicate, quiet-eyed look. il McCalls 91:114-15+ F '64
New ways to minimize facial faults. R. Drake. il Redbook 122:58-63+ Ja '64
New ways to supply the touch of greatness to eyes. Vogue 143:140+ Mr 1 '64
Our fair lady. D. A. Robinson. il Ladies Home J 81:85-8+ Ja '64
Pack a beauty kit for that hospital stay. L. D. Kirk. il Parents Mag 38:44 My '63
Pretty girl, pretty girl, where have you been? il Mlle 58:176-9 Ap '64
Project: you; how to apply mascara. il Ladies Home J 81:128 O '64
Put on a happy face. il Seventeen 23:122-3 My '64
Reflected glory. D. A. Robinson. il Ladies Home J 80:110-12 N '63
Secret of the porcelain veil: a Japanese geisha's make-up. il Vogue 144:252-5 D '64
Shape a pretty face. il Seventeen 22:146-7 My '63
Subtle make-up for summer. il Redbook 121:64-5+ Je '63
Sultry sidelong look. il McCalls 90:110-11+ Ap '63
Two models on modeling. il Mlle 60:144-7 N '64
Vogue's eye view of wonders; the festive eye. il Vogue 144:187-91 D '64
What ever happened to Mary Jane? interview. ed. by B. Clerke. M. J. Russell. il Ladies Home J 80:82-3 Je '63
Work in progress; today's suntan, tonight's hairdo. il Mlle 57:136-7 My '63
See also
Beauty, Personal

MAKE-up, Theatrical
Actor with a hundred faces. il UNESCO Courier 16:16-19 N '63
Becoming Azucena; Irene Dalis applies make-up. il Opera N 28:12-13 Ja 18 '64
Funnyman changes face. il Life 55:139-41 O 18 '63

MAKE-up boxes. See Boxes, cases, etc.

MAKEBA, Miriam
Miriam Makeba; trip to Kenya. il pors Ebony 18:74-6+ Ap '63

MAKINO circuits. See Radio circuits

MAKINS, Virginia. See Sampson, A. jt. auth.

MAKOW, Henry
Ask Henry! excerpts. por Read Digest 82: 205+ Je '63
Boy's advice on coping with boys; questions and answers. por Seventeen 24:92 Ja '65

MAKUEN, Donald R. See Covert, A. M. jt. auth.

MAKULEC, Alfred
Light in the right place for stores. Arch Rec 133:187-9 Je '63

MALABRE, Alfred L. jr
War on poverty: the first skirmish. Reporter 31:27-9 D 17 '64

MALAGASY
Going places, finding things in new fields for adventurous wayfarers. J. Sakol. il House & Gard 125:22+ Ja '64
Malagasy: patterns and prospects. W. J. Foltz. bibliog f il Cur Hist 46:163-8+ Mr '64
President of Malagasy Republic visits Washington; exchange of greetings, July 27, 1964; with joint communique, July 28, 1964. L. B. Johnson; P. Tsiranana. Dept State Bul 51: 229-30 Ag 17 '64
See also
Libraries—Malagasy
Zoology—Malagasy

Politics and government

Atlantic report. Atlan 211:26+ Ap '63

MALAMUD, Bernard
Black is my favorite color; story. Reporter 29:43-4 Jl 18 '63
Choice of profession; story. Commentary 36: 235-41 S '63
Jewbird; story. Reporter 28:33-6 Ap 11 '63
Life is better than death; story. Esquire 59: 78-9 My '63
Refugee; story; excerpt from Idiots first. Sat Eve Post 236:38-9 S 14 '63

about

His hopes on the human heart. G. Hicks. por Sat R 46:31-2 O 12 '63

MALANGA, Gerard
Sonnet XLVI; Some clouds; poems. Poetry 105:108 N '64
Temperature; poem. New Yorker 40:71 Ag 1 '64

MALARIA
Dialysis studies in rats on the long-acting antimalarial CI-501. J. A. Waitz and others. il Science 141:723-5 Ag 23 '63
Malaria parasites: fluorescent antibody technique for tissue stage study. R. L. Ingram and R. K. Carver. bibliog il Science 139:405-6 F 1 '63
Quartan-type malaria parasite of New World monkeys transmissible to man. P. G. Contacos and others. bibliog Science 142:676 N 8 '63
Tree rat, thamnomys surdaster surdaster, in laboratory research. M. Yoeli and others. bibliog il Science 142:1585-6 D 20 '63

Prevention and control

Europe conquers malaria. il(p 129) Sci N L 84:130 Ag 31 '63

MALARIA parasites. See Plasmodium (parasite)

MALATESTA, Edward
French Catholicism, 1964. America 110:253-5 F 22 '64

MALAWI
Approaching independence. A. G. McAdam. Christian Cent 81:713-14 My 27 '64
Banda: beware of Communists. A. C. McAdam. Christian Cent 81:809-10 Je 17 '64
Birth of a nation. A. C. McAdam. il Christian Cent 81:996-8 Ag 5 '64
Foretaste of independence; National assembly. A. C. McAdam. Christian Cent 81:916+ Jl 15 '64
God's man. Time 84:35 O 9 '64
Gods of Africa smile on Brandeis. Nat R 16: 54-5 Ja 28 '64
Nation no. 35. Time 84:32 Jl 10 '64
One-man Banda; independent member. il Newsweek 64:39 Jl 20 '64
Rhodesias and Nyasaland. F. M. G. Wilson. Cur Hist 46:148-55+ Mr '64
Shakey podium. Newsweek 64:55 O 12 '64
Short-lived elation. A. C. McAdam. Christian Cent 81:1283-5 O 14 '64
Uneasy calm. A. C. McAdam. Christian Cent 81:1408-10 N 11 '64
U.S. presents independence gifts to Malawi; statement, July 1, 1964. R. E. Clement. Dept State Bul 51:91-2 Jl 20 '64
See also
United Nations—Malawi

Politics and government

Challenge for father. Time 84:63-4 O 2 '64
Lion of Malawi. P. Schmid. il Reporter 32:20-2 Ja 14 '65

Religious institutions and affairs

New voice from the church. Christian Cent 81:714 My 27 '64

MALAY PENINSULA
See also
Malaysia

MALAYA
United States and Malaya sign cultural exchange agreement. Dept State Bul 48:265 F 18 '63
See also
Education—Malaya
Guerrillas—Malaya

MALAYSIA
Another Munich? Newsweek 62:46 Ag 19 '63
Attorney General Kennedy completes mission to Far East; interviews and remarks, January 28, 1964. R. F. Kennedy. Dept State Bul 50:239-43 F 17 '64
Birth of a nation in Asia. C. Armstrong. il N Y Times Mag p30-1 S 15 '63
Birth pains. il Time 81:36 F 15 '63
Borneo, Britain's South Vietnam; British troops and Sukarno guerrillas. R. Hughes. il N Y Times Mag p9+ Jl 19 '64
Bully boy; Indonesian war of nerves. Newsweek 63:34-5 Ja 13 '64
Cassava, anyone? campaign against Malaysia. il Time 85:24-5 Ja 15 '65
Clouds in the South Seas; with report by R. K. McCabe. il Newsweek 61:42-4 Mr 4 '63
Confrontation continued. Newsweek 64:34+ Jl 6 '64
Containing China. il Newsweek 62:44 Jl 22 '63
Difficult and delicate. Newsweek 63:46 F 17 '64
Emergence of Malaysia. by R. McKie. Review Sat R 46:41-2 N 9 '63. F. Kuhn
Forging a prosperous nation. il Time 81:35-42 Ap 12 '63
Formation of Malaysia. C. P. Bradley. bibliog f il Cur Hist 46:89-94+ F '64
Gobble, gobble? Sukarno's campaign of harassment. Newsweek 64:33 S 14 '64
Hurray for Harry; final obstacle to independence cleared away. il Time 82:41 S 20 '63
I will eat you. J. Burnham. Nat R 16:60 Ja 28 '64
In storied lands of Malaysia. M. Shadbolt. il Nat Geog Mag 124:734-83 N '63
Malaya sees Sukarno as danger for southeast Asia; interview. A. Rahman. il U S News 54:80-1 Mr 18 '63
Malaysia; a game of footsy in southeast Asia. D. Warner. New Repub 148:11-12 Mr 16 '63
Malaysia: a nation's precarious beginning. il Life 55:44A S 27 '63
Malaysia: a tempting target. D. Warner. il Reporter 31:35-8 N 5 '64
Malaysia feels bite of war threat: Indonesian guerrillas. il Bsns W p58+ Ja 16 '65
Malaysia: stormy birth of a new nation. il Newsweek 62:34+ S 30 '63
Malaysia's baptism of fire. il Sr Schol 83:10-13 N 1 '63
Man who. il Time 81:43-5 Ap 12 '63
More panic in southeast Asia. New Repub 148:8 F 9 '63
Nationalism: a matter of pride and prejudice; Indonesia vs. Malaysia. il Sr Schol 85:18 O 7 '64
New Asian nation and new trouble for the West. il U S News 55:8 S 30 '63
No names; Tunku Abdul Rahman in Washington. il Newsweek 64:30 Ag 3 '64
No solution; collapse of peace talks between Indonesia and Malaysia. Newsweek 63:52 Mr 16 '64
Notes of a new nation. J. M. Van der Kroef. il Nat R 15:390-2 N 5 '63
On and on. Newsweek 62:37-8 Ag 12 '63
Our far-flung correspondents. R. Shaplen. il New Yorker 39:130+ Ap 6 '63

MALAYSIA—*Continued*
Posies for brickbats. il Time 81:28 Je 7 '63
Pressed but uncrushed. il Time 85:22 Ja 8 '65
Prime Minister of Malaysia visits Washington; exchange of greetings and toasts; with joint communique, July 22 and July 23, 1964. L. B. Johnson; A. Rahman. Dept State Bul 51:190-3 Ag 10 '64
Quads. Time 82:32 Jl 19 '63
Ready for action. Newsweek 61:41-2 F 11 '63
Roadblock; inclusion of North Borneo and Sarawak. Newsweek 62:45-6 S 2 '63
Same old Sukarno. Time 83:28+ Je 26 '64
Snag in Malaysia; proposed establishment of Islam as the national religion. America 108:732 My 25 '63
State of emergency. Time 84:45-6 S 18 '64
Sukarno leads from weakness. J. Jacquet-Francillon. New Repub 149:11-12 N 23 '63
Sukarno: regional bully. B. Grant. il Nation 198:111-14 F 3 '64
Sukarno stirs up another Asian storm. S. S. King. il N Y Times Mag p 14-15+ Ja 19 '64
Sukarno's war in Borneo. C. Armstrong. il N Y Times Mag p 10-11 Jl 19 '64
Surest bet. il Fortune 70:59-60+ D '64
That neo-colonial plan. New Repub 149:8 S 28 '63
Then the lights went out; Manila meeting. Time 82:29-30 Ag 9 '63
This war in Borneo; whose side are we on? H. F. Armstrong. il Reporter 30:16-20 Je 4 '64
To hell with Sukarno. J. Burnham. Nat R 16:402 My 19 '64
Triplets reunited. Time 81:32 Je 21 '63
Troubled birth of Malaysia. H. F. Armstrong. il For Affairs 41:673-93 Jl '63
Troubled start for new nation. Sr Schol 83:16-17 O 11 '63
Troubles of becoming a nation; the story of Malaysia. R. P. Martin. il U S News 54:78-83 Ap 15 '63
Tunku yes, Sukarno no. Time 82:24 S 6 '63
U.S. comments on U.N. Secretary General's findings on Malaysia; Department statement. Dept State Bul 49:542 O 7 '63
Visiting team from terror tech; Indonesian guerrilla force. il Time 84:35 S 4 '64
What's the fuss? Indonesian aggression. il Newsweek 64:50 S 21 '64
Wild actions, wilder threats. Time 82:48+ O 4 '63
Wolf! wolf! Indonesian threats. il Newsweek 65:36 Ja 11 '65
See also
Airlines—Malaysia
Christians in Malaysia
Elections—Malaysia
Libraries—Malaysia
Singapore
United Nations—Malaysia

MALCOLM X
Angry spokesman Malcolm X tells off whites. por Life 54:30 My 31 '63
I'm talking to you, white man; excerpt from Autobiography of Malcolm X, by Alex Haley and Malcolm X. pors Sat Eve Post 237:30-2+ S 12 '64
Malcolm X: charismatic demagogue; interview, ed. by A. B. Southwick. Christian Cent 80:740-1 Je 5 '63
Now it's a Negro drive for segregation; interview. pors U S News 56:38-9 Mr 30 '64
about
Brother Malcolm: his theme now is violence. por U S News 56:19 Mr 23 '64
Enter Muhammed? Nat R 14:520 Jl 2 '63
Feud within the Black Muslims. G. Samuels. il pors N Y Times Mag p 17+ Mr 22 '64
Lesson of Malcolm X. Sat Eve Post 237:84 S 12 '64
Malcolm's brand X. por Newsweek 63:32 Mr 23 '64
Miami notebook: Cassius Clay and Malcolm X. G. Plimpton. por Harper 228:54-61 Je '64
Mystery of Malcolm X. H. J. Massaquoi. il pors Ebony 19:38-40+ S '64
Ominous Malcolm X exits from the Muslims. M. Crawford. il por Life 56:40-40A Mr 20 '64
Pied Piper of Harlem. Christian Cent 81:422 Ap 1 '64
Why Black Muslims are focusing on the Nation's capital now. il por U S News 54:24 My 27 '63
X on the spot. Newsweek 62:27 D 16 '63

MALCOLM, Donald
Books (cont) New Yorker 38:114+ F 2; 39:185-90 My 4 '63; 102+ Ja 25 '64

MALCOLM, Janet
Thoughts on living in a Shaker house: poem. New Yorker 39:170 N 2 '63

MALCOLMSON, David
Writer's social security. Writer 77:30-1 Ja '64

MALDARELLI, Oronzio
Only true mission. il Time 81:68 Mr 29 '63

MALDE, Harold E.
Environment and man in arid America. bibliog Science 145:123-9 Jl 10 '64

MALDIVE ISLANDS
Another atoll heard from. il Time 83:46 Ap 17 '64

MALDONADO, A. W.
Puerto Rican tide begins to turn. N Y Times Mag p84-5+ S 20 '64
Puerto Rico; the migration reverses. Nation 198:255-7 Mr 16 '64

MALE, Raymond F.
Unemployed youth in our affluent society; address, September 3, 1964. Vital Speeches 30:734-6 S 15 '64

MALE coiffure. See Hairdressing

MALENBAUM, Wilfred
Industrialization in India's development. Cur Hist 44:167-73+ Mr '63

MALEY, Frank. See Maley, G. F. jt. auth.

MALEY, Gladys F. and Maley, Frank
Feedback control of purified deoxycytidylate deaminase. bibliog Science 141:1278-9 S 27 '63

MALFORMATIONS. See Deformities

MALHOTRA, Prabha
Public medicine in India. bibliog f Cur Hist 44:359-65+ Je '63

MALHOTRA, Ram C.
Apartheid and the United Nations. Ann Am Acad 354:135-44 Jl '64

MALI (Republic)
Back to Senegal. Newsweek 61:64 Je 24 '63
Blue men rise. il Time 83:34 Ja 10 '64

MALIC dehydrogenases. See Dehydrogenases

MALIGNANT tumors. See Cancer

MALIK, Charles H.
Ideals for export; excerpts from address, September 19, 1963. Harvard Bsns R 42:51-9 Ja '64

MALINA, Frank Joseph
Malina: artist-scientist of the space age. il UNESCO Courier 16:18-19 S '63
Movement & light in today's art. F. Popper. il UNESCO Courier 16:20-1 S '63

MALINDI, Kenya
Malindi: a place of deep water. N. Adams. il Sports Illus 18:78-84+ Je 17 '63

MALINOVSKY, Rodion Y.
Critic speaks. il por Newsweek 63:39-40 F 24 '64

MALIPIERO, Gian Francesco
Malipiero and Hindemith by the Stuyvesants: magnificent. J. Lyons. Am Rec G 30:1041 Jl '64
Rispetti e strambotti reappears. A. Frankenstein. por Hi Fi 14:64 Je '64

MALKUS, Joanne S.
Cloud patterns over tropical oceans. bibliog Science 141:767-78 Ag 30 '63
—and Simpson, R. H.
Modification experiments on tropical cumulus clouds. bibliog Science 145:541-8 Ag 7 '64
—See Simpson, R. H. jt. auth.

MALLARI, Francisco
Yankees again. America 108:630 My 4 '63

MALLARMÉ, Stephane
Four poets and two dramatists. W. Fowlie. Poetry 104:189-90 Je '64

MALLARY, Robert
Air of art is poisoned. por Art N 62:34-7+ O '63
Is sculpture a step-child? a colloquy. por Art N 63:40-2+ S '64

MALLEA, Eduardo
Letter from Buenos Aires. A. Neish. Nation 196:273 Mr 30 '63

MALLERY, David
Classroom communiqué. por Time 81:60 Mr 29 '63

MALLET-JORIS, Françoise
Corpuscles of her corpus. G. Bree. por Sat R 47:42 My 23 '64

MALLISON, Carolyn
Helping hand for Carol. Parents Mag 39:66+ Mr '64

MALLORY, Dillard A.
Man in Missouri. por Time 81:102-3 My 17 '63

MALLOY, John F.
Church, state and the wall. Cath World 197:231-7 Jl '63

MALLOY, Richard J.
Crustal uplift southwest of Montague Island, Alaska. Science 146:1048 N 20 '64

MALLS, Shopping. See Business districts

MALMGREN, Harald
Economy: a case for efficient planning. New Repub 151:41-4+ N 7 '64
Europe and American defense. New Repub 150:22-4 Ja 11 '64
Landmark in labor relations. New Repub 148:7 Mr 16 '63
Money; balancing international payments. New Repub 150:13-14 Je 20 '64
President's economic report. New Repub 148:17-18 F 9 '63
Strikes and the public. New Repub 148:6 Ap 20 '63

MALMLÖW, E. G.
Atomic power in Sweden. Bul Atomic Sci 19:44-6 F '63

MALMSTROM air force base. See Air bases

MALNUTRITION. See Diet, Deficient

MALOCCLUSION. See Teeth

MALOFF, Saul
Price of a carabao; story. Sat Eve Post 237:46-8 Ja 25 '64
Viability of Utopia. Nation 197:146-7 S 14 '63

MALONE, Donald P. and Karre, Wilma
Refill mosaics. Sch Arts 62:14 F '63

MALONE, Thomas F.
Atmospheric sciences. bibliog NEA J 53:61-4 O '64

MALONEY, Elbert S.
CBers note! the rules have changed. Motor B 114:82+ N '64
New teeth for the FCC. Motor B 111:165 My '63

MALONEY, George A. and Marshall, R. H. Jr
Toward Catholic-Orthodox dialogue. Cath World 198:295-301 F '64

MALONEY, Mary R.
General Reynolds and Dear Kate; reprint. Am Heritage 15:62-5 D '63

MALONEY, Ralph
Benny; story. Atlan 214:59-65 Ag '64

MALOOF, Louis J.
John XXIII; poem. America 108:867 Je 15 '63

MALORY, Sir Thomas
Crowning of King Arthur; dramatization. See Olfson, L.

MALOTT, Deane W.
Taming Cayuga's waters. il por Time 81:73-4 Ap 5 '63

MALPRACTICE
Doctors free to choose. Sci N L 85:258 Ap 25 '64
Malpractice and the clinical laboratory. D. H. Mills. bibliog Science 144:638-42 My 8 '64
Malpractice suits, can the patient recover? R. H. Blum. Nation 196:139-41 F 16 '63
Why doctors are bad samaritans. P. W. Kearney. Read Digest 82:87-90 My '63

MALRAUX, André
Letter from Paris; excerpts from news conference. New Yorker 40:188+ Ap 18 '64
When the French lived in darkness: adaptation of address. por N Y Times Mag p 12-13+ Ja 17 '65

about

Falling in love; excerpt, tr. by A. Foulke, from autobiography. C. Malraux. il por Vogue 143:124-5+ Mr 1 '64
On the absurd. J. Jacobsen. Commonweal 79:548-52 Ja 31 '64
Renaissance man. il pors Newsweek 64:112+ O 26 '64

MALRAUX, Clara
Falling in love; excerpt, tr. by A. Foulke, from autobiography. por Vogue 143:124-5+ Mr 1 '64

MALTA
Atlantic report. Atlan 214:30+ D '64
Maltese constitution. America 111:147 Ag 15 '64
Most reluctant nation. il Time 84:65 O 2 '64
Qualified rejoicing; independence. Newsweek 64:82-3 O 5 '64
Tight little island. D. O'Grady. Commonweal 77:510-11 F 8 '63
See also
United Nations—Malta
Valetta

MALTZ, Maxwell
Hidden stranger. Criticism
Theatre Arts 47:68 F '63

MALVA moschata. See Muskmallows

MALVERNE, N.Y.
Why a northern town fights school integration: Princeton plan. M. Gunther. il Sat Eve Post 237:66-7 S 19 '64

MALVICINI, A. and others
Yttrium-88 on high-activity zirconium-95 fall-out particles. Science 139:1287 Mr 29 '63

MAMA and the spy; story. See Manoff, E.

MAMAIA, Rumania
Balkans in brief. H. Sutton. il Sat R 46:35-6 Jl 20 '63

MAMA'S old stucco house; story. See Williams, T.

MAMIS, Robert
Children should be seen. U S Camera 28:48-9+ Ja '65

MAMMALS
Enzyme regulation in mammalian tissues, report on international symposium. G. Weber. Science 144:195-7; 146:1489-92 Ap 10, D 11 '64
Mammals of McKinley Park. Nat Parks Mag 37:22 Ap '63
Olaf, the front man; New York aquarium. B. H. Frisch. il Sci Digest 56:6-10 S '64
Redundancy and biological aging. H. A. Johnson. bibliog il Science 141:910-12 S 6 '63
Science in action; launching an expedition. R. G. Van Gelder. il Natur Hist 73:64-7 Ap '64
See also
Bats
Embryology—Mammals
Mongooses
Primates

MAMMARELLA, Raymond, and Crescimbeni, Joseph
Guidance problems: cultural or cosmic? Sat R 47:67+ N 21 '64
—See Crescimbeni, J. jt. auth.

MAMMARY glands
DNA synthesis in alveolar cells of the mammary gland: acceleration by ovarian hormones. F. Bresciani. bibliog il Science 146:653-5 O 30 '64
Lobuloalveolar differentiation in mouse mammary tissues in vitro. R. R. Ichinose and S. Nandi. bibliog il Science 145:496-7 Jl 31 '64
Timing behavior after lesions of zona incerta and mammillary body. P. Ellen and E. W. Powell. bibliog il Science 141:828-30 Ag 30 '63

MAMOULIAN, Rouben
Diverse tastes of a stage director. il House B 105:150-1+ Ap '63

MAN Ray. See Ray, M.

MAN
Future of man. H. Downs. Sci Digest 56:43-5 O '64
Future of man, by P. Teilhard de Chardin. Review
Life 57:12 O 16 '64. H. R. Luce
Nat R 16:1073-4 D 1 '64. T. Molnar
Sat R 47:32-3 D 19 '64. P. A. Schilpp
Goal. A. M. Sullivan. Duns R 83:84 Je '64
Human future. F. Osborn. Sci N L 86:54-5+ Jl 25 '64
Man's approaches to life; scientifically, artistically and religiously. Sci N L 85:214 Ap 4 '64
Rights of men. America 109:761 D 14 '63
Teen-age age; 20th century power, 19th century mentality. Christian Cent 81:259 F 26 '64
Uncompleted man. L. Eiseley. il Harper 228:51-4 Mr '64
Unfamous ones who will shape 1964. M. Frankel. il N Y Times Mag p6-7 D 29 '63
Why is man? excerpt from Animal species and evoution. E. Mayr. Sat R 46:48 My 4 '63
See also
Anthropology
Civilization
Creation
Ethnology
Evolution
Human relations
Men

Attitude and movement

Hominid bipedalism: independent evidence for the food-carrying theory. G. W. Hewes. bibliog Science 146:416-18 O 16 '64

Influence of environment

Arid lands: environmental physiology and psychology; report of a symposium sponsored by UNESCO and the Central drug research institute of India. D. H. K. Lee. Science 140:1002-3+ My 31 '63
Environment and man in arid America. H. E. Malde. bibliog il Science 145:123-9 Jl 10 '64
Environmental variables in disease; subjects of symposia to be held at AAAS annual meeting, December 26-31, 1964 at Montreal. il Science 146:954-5 N 13 '64
Making of a spaceman. Sci Digest 54:67 D '63
Man's dependence on the earthly atmosphere, ed. by K. E. Schaefer. Review
Nation 196:330-1 Ap 20 '63. C. Dreher

MAN—Influence of environment—*Continued*
Medicine moves against the environmental threats to health. R. L. White. Todays Health 42:68+ My '64
Must tomorrow's man look like this? from address. T. Freedman and G. S. Lindner. il Pop Sci 183:77-80+ N '63
Social factors in disease. J. A. Clausen. bibliog f Ann Am Acad 346:138-48 Mr '63
Why African babies are more intelligent. R. Dean and M. Geber. il Sci Digest 56: 35-40 S '64
See also
Human ecology

Migrations

Polynesian origins. E. N. Ferdon, jr. bibliog il Science 141:499-505 Ag 9 '63; Reply with rejoinder. R. C. Suggs. 142:1252+ D 6 '63

Origin and antiquity

Discovery in Africa. il Newsweek 63:48 Mr 30 '64
Fluted projectile points: their age and dispersion in the New world. C. V. Haynes, jr. bibliog il Science 145:1408-13 S 25 '64
History of mankind; excerpts. il UNESCO Courier 16:4-19 Je '63
Hominids and humans. Sci Am 211:43-4 Ag '64
Homo habilis. il Newsweek 63:86 Ap 13 '64
Is magnetism the key to life's origin on earth? J. Lear. Sat R 46:35-8 Jl 6 '63
New age for ancient man. W. Davis. il Sci N L 83:154-5 Mr 9 '63
Origin of races, by C. S. Coon. Review
Natur Hist 72:4 My '63. R. Singer
Sat R 46:41 Je 22 '63. M. Mead
Sci Am 208:169-70+ F '63. T. Dobzhansky; Reply with rejoinder. C. S. Coon. 208: 12-14 Ap '63
Polynesian origins. E. N. Ferdon, jr. bibliog il Science 141:499-505 Ag 9 '63; Reply with rejoinder. R. C. Suggs. 142:1252+ D 6 '63
Prehistory and the beginnings of civilization, by J. Hawkes and L. Woolley. Review
Nation 197:55-6 Jl 27 '63. G. Daniel
Recognizing the emergence of man. R. Ascher and M. Ascher bibliog il Science 147:243-50 Ja 15 '65
Some fallacies in the study of hominid phylogeny. E. L. Simons. bibliog il Science 141: 879-89 S 6 '63
Spokesman for Darwin, and for science. A. Ashforth. il N Y Times Mag p64+ Ap 7 '63
Three histories of man. H. L. Shapiro. Natur Hist 73:4+ O '64
See also
Evolution
Man, Prehistoric
Stone age

Survival

Conditions of survival. A. Toynbee. il Sat R 47:24-6+ Ag 29 '64
Men, apes, and termites. J. W. Krutch. Sat R 46:22-5 S 21 '63; Discussion. 46:29 O 12 '63
Moral deterrent; address, February 1, 1963. V. F. Caputo. Vital Speeches 29:381-3 Ap 1 '63
Obituary for reluctant mammals. A. McGarvey. il Nat R 14:363-4 My 7 '63
Perception and commitment. R. Livingston. il Bul Atomic Sci 19:14-18 F '63
Some major issues before the united Nations; address March 5, 1963. Thant. Vital Speeches 29:360-4 Ap 1 '63; Same abr. U N Rev 10:16-19 Mr '63; Excerpts. Sat R 46:26 Mr 23 '63
Surviving fire effects of nuclear detonations. A. Broido. Bul Atomic Sci 19:20-3 Mr '63
Toward a new politics. J. Cogley. Commonweal 78:37-8 Ap 5 '63
Towards a theology of survival. F. D. Wilhelmsen. Nat R 17:17-19 Ja 12 '65

MAN (theology)
Christmas and the world. J. V. Schall. Commonweal 79:389-92 D 27 '63
Moralism vs. Christianity. F. E. Stoeffler. Christian Cent 80:1299-302 O 23 '63; Discussion. 80:1520-1 D 4 '63
New ideal: creative responsibility. R. O. Johann. America 111:111 Ag 1 '64

MAN, Effect of altitude on. See Altitude, Influence of

MAN, Effect of submersion on. See Submersion

MAN, Prehistoric
Cave man gets a new look; Cromagnon man; reprint. W. Sullivan. il Sci Digest 57:58-60 Ja '65
Discovery in Africa. il Newsweek 63:48 Mr 30 '64
Earlier man, earlier pre-men; homo habilis. Sci Am 210:62 My '64
Earliest man on earth? F. Drake and K. Drake. il Read Digest 84:157-61+ Ja '64
Earliest man, 1,820,000 years ago, was a midget; homo habilis. W. Cloud. Pop Sci 184:19-20 Je '64
Early relatives of man. E. L. Simons. il Sci Am 211:50-62 bibliog(p 142) Jl '64
Hominids and humans; third human species, homo habilis. Sci Am 211:43-4 Ag '64
Homo habilis. il Newsweek 63:86 Ap 13 '64
Man inhabited Nevada 32,000 years ago. il Sci N L 83:92 F 9 '63
Man s new pygmy ancestor; homo habilis. il Sci Digest 56:64-6 Jl '64
New age for ancient man. W. Davis. il Sci N L 83:154-5 Mr 9 '63
New fossil man found; homo habilis; other significant discoveries in anthropology. N. Lawson. il Sci N L 85:242-4 Ap 18 '64
Older man; longer pleistocene; age of zinjanthropus. Sci Am 208:69-70 F '63
Relative dating of Arlington Springs man. K. P. Oakley. il Science 141:1172 S 20 '63
Time out of mind; excerpt from Fields of noon. S. Burnford. il Atlan 214:38-43 Jl '64
Tooling up; chimpanzees who are toolmakers. Newsweek 61:98-9 My 27 '63
See also
Man—Origin and antiquity
Neanderthal race
Paleontology
Stone implements and weapons

MAN-about-town; story. See Benchley, N.
MAN and boy; drama. See Rattigan, T.
MAN and Superman; drama. See Shaw, G. B.
MAN for all seasons; drama. See Bolt, R.
MAN-hour requirements. See Labor requirements (for production)
MAN in a corner; story. See Bonham, M.
MAN like Lincoln; drama. See Miller, H. L
MAN of passion; story. See Harrison, W.
MAN on the tractor; story. See O'Hara, J.
MAN over board; story. See Ballard, J.
MAN power. See Manpower
MAN running; story. See McDonald, J.
MAN who didn't want to go home; story. See Randall, F. E.
MAN who understood women; story. See Knowlton, R. A.
MAN with a pain; story. See Sontag, S.
MAN with only one suit; story. See Ashmead, J.
MAN with two eyes; story. See Lister, R. P.
MANAGEMENT, Business. See Business management and organization
MANAGEMENT, Industrial. See Industrial management and organization
MANAGEMENT consultants. See Business consultants
MANAGEMENT education. See Industrial management and organization—Study and teaching
MANAGEMENT games
For global gamesmen; INTOP for executives. Bsns W p70 N 30 '63
Management development is a game. R. J. House. bibliog f il Harvard Bsns R 41: 130-43 Jl '63
MANAGEMENT of children. See Children—Management and training
MANAGEMENT rights
Where do the rights of management end? Supreme court must decide. il Bsns W p 114-15 D 19 '64
MANAGER; story. See O'Hara, J.
MANAGERS. See Executives
MANAGERS, Baseball. See Baseball managers
MANATEES
Can the manatee save Florida? central and southern Florida flood control district. L. H. Lapham. il Sat Eve Post 237:38-9 Je 27 '64
MANCALL, Mark
Persistence of tradition in Chinese foreign policy. bibliog f Ann Am Acad 349:14-26 S '63
MANCHESTER, Harland
Kilowatts for tomorrow. Read Digest 83:29-30+ N '63
Light of hope, or terror? Read Digest 82: 97-100 F '63
Moon power over St Malo. Read Digest 84: 37-8+ Je '64
New food for hungry children. Read Digest 83:137-41 S '63
New light on photosynthesis. Sci N L 83: 202-3+ Mr 30 '63
Old cars never die. Read Digest 82:107-10 My '63
Rising tide of noise. Read Digest 85:173-4+ O '64

MANCHESTER, William
Department of defense. Holiday 33:76-9+ My '63
House of Krupp. Holiday 36:84-90+ O; 76-9+ N; 84-5+ D '64; 37:78-9+ Ja '65
Life along the Connecticut. Holiday 33:68-73+ Je '63
Money, bears & bulls; a look at Wall Street. Holiday 35:42-53+ Mr '64

about

Author chosen for story of assassination. Pub W 185:27 Ap 6 '64

MANCHESTER, N.H.

Newspapers

See also
Manchester union leader

MANCHESTER union leader
Nation's primary primary; New Hampshire primary. D. F. Ford. il Reporter 30:37-9 F 27 '64
Up in New Hampshire. il Newsweek 63:65 F 17 '64

MANCROFT, Stormont Mancroft Samuel Mancroft, 2d baron
Again the Arabs. Newsweek 64:37 Ag 3 '64
Arab threat forces British lord to resign. Christian Cent 80:1601 D 25 '63
Simple prudence. Newsweek 62:46 D 16 '63

MANDEL, Arnold
France's Algerian Jews; tr. by R. Howard. Commentary 35:475-82 Je '63

MANDEL, Estelle
Good-looking children's books at book fair in Bologna. Pub W 186:66+ Ag 3 '64

MANDEL, H. George. See Reich, M. jt. auth.

MANDEL, Paul
Central, give me a (hot) line. Life 54:19 Ap 26 '63
End to nagging rumors: the six critical seconds. Life 55:52F D 6 '63
Gigantic gem goof. Life 56:84-6+ F 7 '64
Green grows my kudzu. Life 54:80+ My 31 '63
How Harriman earned a dinner from Khrushchev. Life 55:28-30A Ag 9 '63
How to get took in New York city. Life 56:97-8+ Je 19 '64
Life book review. Life 56:12+ Ap 17 '64
Life movies review. Life 56:18 Mr 27; 57:20 Jl 3 '64
Mightiest fire engine. Life 56:23-4 Mr 20 '64
Now a seer helps stalk the Boston strangler. Life 56:49-50 Mr 6 '64
$150 million in oil, all gone! Life 56:90-2+ Ap 3 '64
Showdown for Loch Ness. Life 55:17-18 S 20 '63
Tarzan of the paperbacks. Life 55:11-12 N 29 '63
What must have happened under massive pressures. Life 54:40-4 Ap 19 '63
What's for launch? Life 54:20 Je 14 '63
—and Kennedy, Ray
Go! said the navy; crunch! Life 55:17+ O 4 '63

MANDELA, Nelson
Accusing the accuser. por Newsweek 63:47 Je 22 '64
Fruits of apartheid. New Repub 150:21-2 My 16 '64

MANDELBAUM, Bernard, and Ratner, V. M.
Excuse we should never use. Read Digest 83:79-80 D '63

MANDELL, Arnold J. and others
Plasma corticosteroids: changes in concentration after stimulation of hippocampus and amygdala. bibliog Science 139:1212 Mr 22 '63

MANDEL'SHTAM, Osip Émil'evich
Moscow; Century of the wolf; Leningrad; Fragments; Verses to the unknown soldier; poems. tr. by R. Lowell. Atlan 211:64-8 Je '63

about

Biographical sketch. O. A. Carlisle. Atlan 211:63 Je '63

MANDER, John
Bewitchment of Bertrand Russell. New Repub 149:20-2 Ag 17 '63
Britain's new state of mind. Harper 228:76-80 Ap '64
India's crisis: a diary. Commentary 35:326-34 Ap '63
Little England. Commentary 35:139-45 F '63
New statesman & the English left. Commentary 37:47-53 F '64
Strange death of Tory England. Commentary 38:41-5 D '64
West African diary. Commentary 36:453-9 D '63

MANDEVILLE, S. E. and others
Fully deuterated euglena gracilis. bibliog Science 146:769 N 6 '64

MANDY, William J. and others
Amino acid composition of univalent fragments of rabbit antibody. bibliog Science 140:901-3 My 24 '63

MANER, William
To steal the moment; story. Good H 156:66-7 Mr '63

MANESSIER, Alfred
Religious but anticlerical. F. Getlein. New Repub 150:25-6 Ap 4 '64

MANET, Édouard
Manet. J. Canaday. il pors Horizon 6:84-105 Wint '64

MANEUVERABILITY of automobiles. See Automobiles—Maneuverability

MANEUVERS, Air. See Air maneuvers

MANEUVERS, Military. See Military maneuvers

MANEUVERS, Naval. See Naval maneuvers

MANGANARO, Charles A. See Karalekas, P. C. jt. auth.

MANGANESE
Origin of oceanic manganese minerals. G. Arrhenius and others. bibliog il Science 144:170-3 Ap 10 '64
Pyrene and fluoranthene in manganese nodules. D. W. Thomas and M. Blumer. bibliog il Science 143:39 Ja 3 '64

MANGANESE oxides
Tellurium content of marine manganese oxides and other manganese oxides. H. W. Lakin and others. bibliog il Science 142:1568-9 D 20 '63

MANGEL, Charles
Montessori: education begins at three. Look 29:61-7 Ja 26 '65

MANGELSDORF, Paul C. and others
Domestication of corn. bibliog Science 143:538-45; 145:659 F 7, Ag 14 '64

MANGELSDORFF, Albert
Mangelsdorff matter. W. Hobson. Sat R 47:64 My 16 '64

MANGER groups. See Christmas cribs

MANGIERI, A. A.
Capacitor value checker. Electr World 72:44-5+ Jl '64
Meter protection circuit. Electr World 73:48-9 Ja '65

MANGIONE, Jerre
(tr) See Domino, R. Word

MANGONE, Gerard J.
Latin America progress report. America 111:10-14 Jl 4 '64

MANGROVE
Root growth claims soil from sea. V. N. Argo. il Natur Hist 72:52-5 Ap '63

MANHATTAN. See New York (city)

MANHATTAN bail project. See New York university—School of law

MANHATTAN casualty company
Mysterious $5.5-million; Manhattan casualty case. Bsns W p76-8 Ag 24 '63

MANHATTAN festival ballet company. See Ballet companies

MANHATTAN opera company
Manhattan opera company; first season, 1906-1907. G. R. Good. il Hobbies 69:30-1+ O '64; 32 Ja '65

MANHATTAN project. See Atomic bombs—Manufacture

MANHATTAN savings bank. See New York (city)—Banks

MANHATTAN school of music
East Side marriage. M. Lelash. il Opera N 28:27 My 2 '64
Manhattan Indians: performance of Delibes' Lakmé. R. D. Daniels. il Opera N 27:27 My 4 '63
Musical events: performance of Bruckner's Ninth symphony. W. Sargeant. New Yorker 40:192-4 Ap 25 '64
Quality of life in this technological age; symposium sponsored by the Manhattan school of music. il Mus Am 83:147-62 D '63

MANHEIM, Martha
(ed) See Wallace, I. Irving Wallace bends some rules

MANHEIM, Pa.
Look right into your sewer problems. J. A. Kern. il Am City 79:84-5 Ag '64

MANHOFF, Bill
Owl and the pussycat. Criticism
New Yorker 40:131 N 28 '64
Newsweek 64:92 N 30 '64
Time il 84:104 N 27 '64

MANIC-DEPRESSIVE psychoses. See Psychoses

MANICURING
He'll be putty in your soft, caressing hands. il McCalls 91:90-1 Jl '64

MANIKINS. See Models (persons)

MANIPAL, India
University town built by a country doctor; Academy of general education. P. Almasy. il UNESCO Courier 16:37-40 Jl '63
MANIPULATORS
Industrial manipulators. R. S. Mosher. il Sci Am 211:88-94+ O '64
MANITOBA
See also
Churchill
Winnipeg
MANITOWOC, Wis.
Use models. B. Mattson. il Am City 79:118-19 Mr '64
MANJIRO. See Nakahama, M.
MANKIEWICZ, Joseph L.
Cleopatra barges in at last. pors Life 54: 72-81 Ap 19 '63
Just one of those things. il por Time 81:90 Je 21 '63
Numb; writing and directing Cleopatra. New Yorker 39:27 Je 15 '63
MANKOWITZ, Wolf
Flying fish and sugar cane. Holiday 35:72-8+ F '64
MANKS, Dorothy S.
Books are gardening tools. Horticulture 41: 522-3 O '63
MANN, Abby
Crusader. por Time 81:56 Mr 22 '63
MANN, Gerald C.
For Diversa, a deal that walks; buying and selling of companies. por Bsns W p72+ S 14 '63
MANN, Golo
Germany's new historians. Nation 198:572-6 Je 8 '64
MANN, Herbie
Gagakunized jazz. il por Newsweek 64:89 S 28 '64
Third thing. por Time 84:67 D 18 '64
MANN, Horace
Sarmiento, the educator; U.S. visits of Argentina's teacher-president. E. Correas. il por Américas 16:28-32 Ag '64
MANN, Jesse
Trials of being a bachelor. pors Ebony 18:154-7+ Ap '63
MANN, Martin
1963's brightest promise: organ transplants. Todays Health 42:24-6 Ja '64
Stupid questions about automation. Pop Sci 184:100-3+ My '64
Stupid questions about heredity. Pop Sci 183:97-9+ O '63
Truth about fatal car crashes. Pop Sci 183: 92-7+ D '63
X-raying atoms. Pop Mech 120:112-15 D '63
MANN, Mary Peabody
Sarmiento, the educator; U.S. visits of Argentina's teacher-president. E. Correas. il por Américas 16:28-32 Ag '64
MANN, Matthew Darbyshire
Operation on President McKinley. S. Adler. il por Sci Am 208:118-30 Mr '63
MANN, Peggy
We moved to the worst block in town. Redbook 122:62-3+ N '63
MANN, Sylvia
Aluette cards of Brittany (cont) Hobbies 67:120-1 F '63
Traditional playing cards of Italy. Hobbies 68:116-17 S; 118-19+ O; 118-19 N '63
MANN, Thomas Clifton
Alliance for progress: a challenge and an opportunity; address, September 23, 1964. Dept State Bul 51:593-7 O 26 '64
Alliance for progress; address, May 13, 1964. Dept State Bul 50:857-63 Je 1 '64
Alliance for progress exhibits open at Pan American union; remarks, August 12, 1964. Dept State Bul 51:305 Ag 31 '64
Democratic ideal in our policy toward Latin America; address, June 7, 1964. Dept State Bul 50:995-1000 Je 29 '64
Inter-American economic and social council reviews Alliance for progress; statement, December 8, 1964. Dept State Bul 51:898-901 D 28 '64
New look at coups; Mann tells U.S. policy; summary of address. por U S News 56:14 Mr 30 '64
Organizing for progress in Latin America; address, September 17, 1964. Dept State Bul 51:479-82 O 5 '64
Outlook in Latin America: an official size-up; interview. por U S News 57:58-62 Jl 20 '64
Population growth and the Alliance for progress; address, November 9, 1964. Dept State Bul 51:807-10 D 7 '64
Report to the President on Latin American policy. Dept State Bul 51:706-7 N 16 '64
Social justice in the United States and in the hemisphere; address, November 4, 1964. Dept State Bul 51:775-8 N 30 '64
U.S. representative to committee chairman; letter, January 13, 1964. Dept State Bul 50:155-6 F 3 '64
Western hemisphere's fight for freedom; address, September 21, 1964. Dept State Bul 51:549-52 O 19 '64
Where America gets its strength; excerpts from World economic problems and policies. por Nations Bsns 52:116-17+ N '64
about
Calming a Latin tempest; with editorial comment. il por Bsns W p64-8, 96 F 1 '64
Can LBJ help Latin America solve its problems? il por U S News 55:32-3 D 30 '63
Choice for Latin America: Castro threat or Leoni promise. il por Newsweek 63:34-6+ Mr 30 '64
Firm hand for Latin policy. por Bsns W p 17-18 D 21 '63
Mann for LBJ's season. E. J. Hughes. Newsweek 63:25 My 18 '64
Mann for the job. por Time 82:14-15 D 27 '63
Mr Latin America. New Repub 149:5 D 28 '63
My Mr Latin America. il Newsweek 63:39 Ja 6 '64
One Mann & twenty problems. il pors Time 83:15-18 Ja 31 '64
President outlines Latin American policy in letter to Mr Mann. L. B. Johnson. Dept State Bul 50:9-10 Ja 6 '64
MANN, William
Strauss; 20th century classicist. por Mus Am 84:14-15+ Jl '64
MANNED orbiting space station. See Space stations
MANNED space flight center. See United States—National aeronautics and space administration—Manned space flight center
MANNED space flights. See Space flight—Manned flights
MANNEQUINS. See Models (persons)
MANNERS, Ande
Instant politics for the busy homemaker. McCalls 91:58+ Jl '64
MANNERS, David X.
Doing it better. See issues of House beautiful
For drama at night, dim the lights. House B 105:124-5+ F '63
How to get safer, purer, softer water. House B 106:128-9+ F '64; Same abr. Read Digest 84:121-4 Je '64
How to perform a miracle in the back yards. House B 105:164-5+ Mr '63
New ways to maintain swimming pools. House B 105:182+ Ap '63
MANNERS, Robert A.
Nations growing up overnight. Sat R 47:48 Ap 18 '64
MANNERS. See Courtesy; Etiquette
MANNERS and customs
Gentle art of tiny teapot tea. P. Mooho. Esquire 62:180+ D '64
Space-age guide for social astronauts. E. Auchincloss. Mlle 56:173+ Ap '63
What is a lady? M. Mead. Redbook 120:22+ Ap '63
White gloves and ritual curtsies; excerpts from Profession: housewife. P. McGinley. Ladies Home J 80:34+ S '63
See also
Clothing and dress
Courtesy
Dating
Drinking customs
Dueling
Funeral rites and ceremonies
Hairdressing
Kissing
Marriage customs and rites
Tipping
MANNES, Marya
Anybody out there? Esquire 62:54+ N '64
Confession. Reporter 28:37-8 Je 6 '63
Defense manual for tourists. Harper 230: 125-7 Ja '65
Fear or courage? the question that comes before politics. Vogue 144:106-7 Ag 15 '64
Feminine tragique. Sat R 47:32-3 Jl 11 '64
Forgive me, but my mind shows; excerpt from Man and civilization: the potential of woman. Vogue 141:124-7+ My '63
G.O.P. and the gap. Reporter 31:28-30 Ag 13 '64
Half-world of American drama. Reporter 28: 48-50 Ap 25 '63
Happiest day. Ladies Home J 81:30+ Je '64
Juno in limbo; the trauma of size sixteen. Harper 229:37-40 Jl '64
Long vigil. Reporter 29:15-17 D 19 '63
New bites by a girl gadfly; ed by J. Howard. pors Life 56:59-60+ Je 12 '64

MANNES, Marya—*Continued*
New upper class. the kids. Vogue 142:4 Jl '63
Northern places. Reporter 29:55-8+ Ag 15 '63
Power men have over women. Vogue 143: 144-5 Mr 15 '64; Same abr. Read Digest 84:61-3 Je '64
Redbook dialogue; Mannes and Salinger. pors Redbook 123:64-5+ O '64
TV's fascinating fourth network. Ladies Home J 80:100+ Jl '63
Thin gray line. McCalls 91:53+ Ja '64; Same abr. Read Digest 84:61-3 Ap '64
Threatening crowd. Ladies Home J 81:16+ N '64
To save the life of "I." Vogue 144:172-3 O 1 '64
Violence around us; excerpts from But will it sell? McCalls 91:74+ F '64
Winter flight, blind companion; poem. Reporter 28:41-3 Mr 14 '63

MANNEY, T. R. and Mortimer, R. K.
Allelic mapping in yeast by X-ray-induced mitotic reversion. bibliog Science 143:581-3 F 7 '64

MANNHEIM, L. A.
Fight against rangefinder parallax. Mod Phot 28:98+ My '64

MANNHEIM, Germany (Federal Republic)
National theater. G. E. K. Smith. il Arch Rec 134:183-5 O '63

MANNING, Bayless
Stanford's shiny fish. por Time 84:88 O 30 '64

MANNING, Charles A. W.
In defense of apartheid. For Affairs 43:135-49 O '64

MANNING, Gordon P.
ABCs of anchoring. Pop Mech 119:142-6 My '63
Double-purpose tool box. Motor B 113:26+ Mr '64
Personalized motor cruiser mast. Motor B 112:50+ O '63
Rx for the happy yachtsman. Motor B 112: 22-3 O '63
Small-boat refrigeration: up from the ice age! Motor B 115:76-9+ Ja '65
Swimming ladder for your boat. Motor B 113: 31+ Mr '64
Things to do this winter. Motor B 112:24-6+ O '63
What holds your boat together? Motor B 111:39-41+ Mr '63

MANNING, Robert J.
Citizen's role in foreign policy legislation; address, April 23, 1964. bibliog f Dept State Bul 50:791-7 My 18 '64
Foreign policy and the people's right to know; address, May 5, 1964. Dept State Bul 50:868-77 Je 1 '64
Foreign policy: building amid turbulence; address, August 27, 1963. Dept State Bul 49: 454-60 S 23 '63
Foreign policy in the open society; statement, March 25, 1963. Dept State Bul 48:575-9 Ap 15 '63
Journalism and foreign affairs; address, March 13, 1964. Dept State Bul 50:541-9 Ap 6 '64; Same with title Press and the government. Vital Speeches 30:453-7 My 15 '64
Malaise yellow. Atlan 212:100+ Ag '63
Mr Manning interviewed on News and comment; ed. by H. K. Smith. Dept State Bul 48:500-3 Ap 1 '63
Policy and people; address, September 26, 1963. Dept State Bul 49:639-44 O 21 '63
U.S. foreign policy: problems and challenges for 1963; address, January 11, 1963. Dept State Bul 48:138-44 Ja 28 '63
(ed) See Lindsay, J. V. New G.O.P.

MANNING, S. F.
New horizons for steel boatbuilding. Motor B 114:40-1 D '64
Piggyback propulsion. il Motor B 114:44+ O '64

MANNION, John B.
Need for reform. Commonweal 78:495-7 Ag 23 '63

MANNIX, Daniel P.
Father of the Wizard of Oz. Am Heritage 16:36-47+ D '64

MANOFF, Eva
Mama and the spy; story. Mlle 57:254-5 Ag '63

MANOFF, R. Alexander, store. See Philadelphia —Stores

MANOLESCO, George
Prince of thieves, by J. J. Lynx. Review Newsweek por 63:94B F 17 '64

MANOLETE
My most unforgettable character. G. Gonzalez Luque. il Read Digest 83:264-6+ N '63

MANON; opera. See Massenet, J.

MANOOGIAN, Haig A.
Sound advice. Mod Phot 27:38 Ap '63; 28: 54+ My '64

MANOS, Elias T.
Grow abutilon. Horticulture 41:618 D '63

MANPOWER
Fellowship expansion: presidential plan criticized at hearing before House science, space committee. D. S. Greenberg. Science 139: 392-3 F 1 '63
How many people, how many jobs? E. T. Chase. New Repub 151:32-3+ Ag 22 '64
How to forecast your manpower needs. E. W. Vetter. il Nations Bsns 52:102-5+ F '64
Jobs: our no. one economic problem; president's manpower report to Congress. il Newsweek 61:75 Mr 18 '63
Manpower: activist administration finds Congress hard to convince on bigger investment in people. J. Walsh. Science 139:815-17 Mr 1 '63
Manpower development in a changing world; address, October 13, 1964. T. F. Patton. Vital Speeches 31:88-90 N 15 '64
Manpower or mind power. P. H. Abelson. Science 139:79 Ja 11 '63; Discussion. 139: 798+; 140:211 Mr 1, Ap 12 '63
Manpower planning and the new pariahs. E. M. Brandes. il Reporter 30:17-19 Mr 26 '64
OECD manpower policy for promoting economic growth; excerpt. Mo Labor R 87: 1033-4 S '64
Proper public accounting for science. P. H. Abelson. Sat R 46:51-2 F 2 '63
Technical talent utilization shifts urged. P. J. Klass. Aviation W 81:20 Jl 20 '64
Training for a job under MDTA. R. W. Dugger. il Sch Life 45:17-22 F '63
See also
Labor supply—United States

MANPOWER development and training act. See Labor laws and legislation—United States

MANRARA, Luis V.
Cuba in Communist world strategy; address, November 15, 1962. Vital Speeches 29:236-40 F 1 '63

MAN'S a man; drama. See Brecht, B.

MANSFIELD, Bill
Florida's Lake Okeechobee. Travel 120:38-40 D '63

MANSFIELD, J. P.
Creeping treelessness. Recreation 56:254 Je '63

MANSFIELD, Margery
Marriage; poem. McCalls 90:140 My '63

MANSFIELD, Michael Joseph
Eulogy to John F. Kennedy. November 24, 1963. Vital Speeches 30:99 D 1 '63
I am what I am; Mansfield answers critics; excerpts from report. por U S News 55:20 D 9 '63

about

Change of pace. Newsweek 64:30 Jl 20 '64
Chaos in the Senate; days without end. M. McGrory. America 109:653 N 23 '63
Growing foreign-policy row: two top Democrats urge changes. por U S News 56:19 Ap 6 '64
Mansfield: new possible for LBJ ticket. por U S News 57:21 Jl 20 '64
Senate: a crisis in leadership. il por Newsweek 62:29-30 N 18 '63
When is a majority a majority? il pors Time 83:22-6 Mr 20 '64

MANSFIELD, Ohio
My father's grocery store. P. M. Angle. il Am Heritage 14:34-7+ Ag '63

MANSHOLT, Sicco L.
Common market: now, Le package deal? il por Newsweek 62:72-3 D 16 '63

MANSIONS, Governors. See Governors mansions

MANSLAUGHTER. See Murder

MANSOUR, Atallah
Double *chutzpath.* por Newsweek 61:89 F 18 '63

MANSUR, Hassan Ali
18th Premier. il por Time 83:36 Mr 20 '64
Religious impulse. Newsweek 65:36 F 1 '65

MANTEGAZZINI, P. See Pepeu, G. jt. auth.

MANTEGNA, Andrea
Mantagna of Mantua. J. Canaday. bibliog f il Horizon 6:70-89 Spr '64

MANTES, Praying. See Praying mantes

MANTHORNE, Jane
Supermarket come-on. por Library J 90:302-5 Ja 15 '65

MANTLE, Mickey
Bad break. por Newsweek 61:65 Je 17 '63
For the want of a warning a pennant was lost; with editorial comment. R. Creamer. il Sports Illus 18:22-3, 68+ Je 17 '63
Homage to Mantle. Sports Illus 18:10 Je 3 '63
How to live with pain. il por Time 81:51 Je 14 '63
If it isn't one M it's another. il pors Sports Illus 19:10-15 Jl 8 '63
Mantle's breaks, and yours. D. Duncan. il por Pop Sci 185:100-3+ O '64
On the trail of a hero. E. Graham. il pors Sports Illus 19:50-5 Ag 26 '63
One who beats them. il Time 84:43 Jl 31 '64
MANTYRANTA, Eero
Lonely quest in Lapland. D. S. Connery. il pors Sports Illus 20:46-7+ Ja 27 '64
MANUELL, Cora
My most unforgettable character. M. R. Stott. por Read Digest 82:124-8 Ap '63
MANUELLI, Ernesto
Who's who in foreign business. por Fortune 68:76 O '63
MANUFACTURED houses. See Houses, Prefabricated
MANUFACTURERS
Christmas amnesty. Consumer Rep 28:508-9 N '63
MANUFACTURERS, National association of. See National association of manufacturers
MANUFACTURERS agents
Easing the squeeze on the sales rep. Bsns W p 130-1 Jl 13 '63
MANUFACTURERS excise tax. See Excise tax
MANUFACTURES
Influences of employer bargaining associations in manufacturing. M. S. Wortman, jr. il Mo Labor R 86:272-3 Mr '63
Labor turnover; tables. See issues of Monthly labor review
See also
Diversification in industry
Prices

Statistics

Fourteen important ratios in thirty-seven manufacturing lines. il Duns R 82:50-2 O '63
Ratios of manufacturing; tables. Duns R 84: 50-3 N '64

Wages and hours

Developments in manufacturing industries. R. W. Benny. il Mo Labor R 87:11-17, 1401-7 Ja, D '64
Some indicators of incentive plan prevalence. R. B. McKersie and others. bibliog f il Mo Labor R 87:271-6 Mr '64; Reply with rejoinder. B. Gottlieb. 87:893-4 Ag '64
MANUFACTURING chemists association, incorporated
Trade associations and how they grew. L. L. L. Golden. Sat R 47:64 Je 13 '64
MANUFACTURING cost. See Cost
MANUFACTURING districts. See Industrial districts
MANUFACTURING expense. See Cost accounting
MANUFACTURING plants. See Factories
MANUPELLI, George
Drawing on film. Sch Arts 63:10-11 F '64
Films & photography. il Sch Arts 62:28-32 Mr '63
MANURE lagoons
Big fuss over lagoons. il Farm J 88:57-8 Ap '64
Lagoons, where and how to. T. L. Willrich. il Suc Farm 61:38-9+ Jl '63
Latest on poultry lagoons. B. Hardy and D. Braun. il Farm J 87:28+ Jl '63
Profit-planned hog housing. J. Harvey and A. J. Muehling. il Suc Farm 62:42-3+ Ja '64
MANURES. See Fertilizers and manures
MANUS, Frank J.
Additional notes on audio sweep generator. Electr World 72:112 N '64
MANUSCRIPT division. See United States—Library of Congress—Manuscript division
MANUSCRIPT writing (script) See Penmanship
MANUSCRIPTS
See also
Bible—Old Testament—Manuscripts

Collection and preservation

Binding and related problems; reprint. H. W. Tribolet. Hobbies 69:110-11+ Jl '64
Caring for your manuscripts and related material. D. C. Anthony. Hobbies 68:110-11+ Ja '64
See also
Libraries—Manuscript collections

Conservation and restoration

Menander & the mummy; work of Institut de papyrologie at Sorbonne university, Paris. il Time 82:63+ O 11 '63
Parchment patients; Vatican's Institute for the scientific restoration of books. il Newsweek 61:90 Ap 8 '63
Protect those documents. H. W. Tribolet. Hobbies 68:110-12+ Mr '63

Prices

Auction market; reprint. G. T. Banks. Hobbies 69:110-11 D '64

Reproduction

LC expands photocopying program of European manuscripts & archives. Library J 88:1496-8 Ap 1 '63
MANUSCRIPTS (papyri)
Menander & the mummy; work of Institut de papyrologie at Sorbonne university, Paris. il Time 82:63+ O 11 '63
Papyri; meeting of American society of papyrologists. New Yorker 40:22-4 S 5 '64
Secrets cooked from a mummy. il Life 55:65+ N 15 '63
MANUSCRIPTS, Coptic (papyri)
Another disciple is heard from; concerning The Gospel of Philip. il Time 81:57-8 Mr 8 '63
MANUSCRIPTS, French
Bad bishop's book of love songs. il Horizon 6:26-31 Wint '64
MANUSCRIPTS, Hebrew
Fearful truth; Book of secrets. il Newsweek 65:75-75A+ Ja 18 '65
MANUSCRIPTS, Illuminated. See Hours, Books of; Illumination of books and manuscripts
MANUSCRIPTS, Italian
Medieval codex of Italy; Tacuinum sanitatis. K. Kup. il Natur Hist 72:30-41 D '63
MANUSCRIPTS, Rejected. See Editors and editing
MANUSCRIPTS, Theft of. See Stealing
MANVELL, Roger, and Fraenkel, Heinrich
Men who tried to kill Hitler; excerpts, ed. by J. Naar. Look 28:50-2 D 15 '64
MANWELL, Clyde
Genetic control of hemerythrin specificity in a marine worm. bibliog Science 139:755-8 F 22 '63
MANX cats. See Cats
MANY are cold; story. See Gerber, M. J.
MANZELLA, David
Educationist's influence on the teaching of art; excerpts from Educationists and the evisceration of the visual arts. Craft Horiz 23:6-8 N '63
Strike him sharply with some hard object; excerpts from Educationists and the evisceration of the visual arts. Sch Arts 63:35 Mr '64
MANZONI, Alessandro
Day of the premiere. F. Stevenson. il por Opera N 28:13-16 Mr 28 '64
MANZÙ, Giacomo
Doors of death. il Time 84:68-70 Jl 24 '64
Doors of death. por Newsweek 63:62-3 My 18 '64
MAO, Tse-tung
At home with Mao. il por Time 83:30+ Mr 6 '64
Castro, Khrushchev, and Mao. T. Draper. il Reporter 29:27-31 Ag 15 '63
China: the East wind gains force. il por Newsweek 63:43-4 F 17 '64
Glorious military thought of comrade Mao Tse-tung. S. B. Griffith, 2d. For Affairs 42: 669-74 Jl '64
How blows the East wind? J. Burnham. Nat R 16:230 Mr 24 '64
Instant page one. Newsweek 63:38 Ja 20 '64
Lines by China's poet laureate. I. Stewart. por N Y Times Mag p 12+ Mr 29 '64
Mao, at seventy, tries a big leap in the world. R. Hughes. il por N Y Times Mag p 10+ F 2 '64
Mao: Nationalist first, Communist second. R. Hughes. il pors N Y Times Mag p 17+ Je 7 '64
Mao Tse-tung, by G. Paloczi-Horvath. Review
Newsweek por 62:72-3 Jl 29 '63
Mao's heresy. America 110:564 Ap 25 '64
Nearer my God to thee. Newsweek 64:34 Ag 31 '64
Red China; ed. by Q. Reynolds. C. P. Tung. il Look 28:21-7 D 1 '64
Russia-China split: how real? il por U S News 54:44-7 Mr 18 '63
Warning to Mao, it's the year of the dragon. R. Hughes. il por N Y Times Mag p24-5+ Mr 1 '64
Widening gulf between Mao and Khrushchev. D. S. Zagoria. il Reporter 28:38-40 Ap 25 '63

MAP making. See Cartography
MAPLE
Usually it's wise to choose a small maple. il Sunset 132:232-3 Mr '64
MAPLE Leafs (hockey team) See Hockey teams
MAPLE syrup
My sap runneth all over. B. Buyer. il Life 54:10 Ap 19 '63
Pure maple syrup; nutritive value. A. L. Leaf. bibliog il Science 143:963-4 F 28 '64
MAPLES, Mitchell
Guerrilla trainer. il pors Ebony 19:47-8+ Ap '64
MAPLES, Flowering. See Flowering maples
MAPPING, Aerial
Aerial photos reduce costs, aid planning studies; Branford, Conn. il Am City 79:96 F '64
Maps and charts; pressure from private firm may bring rise in government's prices. E. Langer. Science 140:373+ Ap 26 '63
See also
Artificial satellites—Mapping applications
MAPS
Maps of the West and the world as gifts for campers, fishermen, trip planners, and armchair geographers. il Sunset 133:52-3 D '64
Maps on stamps. M. Mulford. il Hobbies 69:99 Ja '65
These children are learning their land; world around home, in map symbols. il Sunset 131:94+ S '63
See also
Shakespeare, W.—Maps
Weather maps
World maps
Protection
Fieldproof your maps. D. L. Shaw. il Outdoor Life 134:51 Ag '64
MAPS, Biblical. See Bible—Geography
MAPS, Relief. See Relief maps
MAPS, Road. See Road maps, guides, etc.
MAPS, Soil. See Soil surveys
MARA, Michael
Why the border guards defect. Atlan 212:100-2 D '63
MARA, Thalia
Thalia Mara and the National academy of ballet. E. Palatsky. il por Dance Mag 38:26-8+ F '64
MARABOUS
Bird bath: pictures. Sci Digest 55:6-7 Ja '64
MARACCI, Carmelita
Lessons with Carmelita Maracci. J. W. Knowles. il pors Dance Mag 38:38-41 My '64
MARAGING process. See Steel metallurgy
MARAGING steel. See Nickel steel
MARAIS, Ben
White South African's dilemma. Christian Cent 80:580-1 My 1 '63
MARAJO (island)
Unsolved mystery of Marajo. A. Métraux. il UNESCO Courier 16:30-2 N '63
MARAMOROSCH, Karl. See Hirumi, H; Streissle, G. jt. auths.
MARAN, Edward
Sewer pushes through a bog. Am City 79:171-2 S '64
MARANS, Moissaye
Sculpture of Moissaye Marans. F. Whitaker. il por Am Artist 28:44-9+ F '64
MARANTZ, Kenneth
Films. Sch Arts 63:52 S '63
MARAS, Turkey
Every town has two faces. R. H. Latimer. il Harper 227:26+ N '63
MARASH. See Maras, Turkey
MARATHON, Battle of, 490 B.C.
Morning at Marathon. C. W. Griffin, jr. Sat R 47:49-50 N 14 '64
MARATHON corporation
Mechanical lumberjack rivals Paul Bunyan; Tree Harvester. il Bsns W p52-3 Ag 3 '63
MARATHON races. See Running
MARATHON '33; drama. See Havoc, J.
MARBELLA, Spain
New good move for travellers. Vogue 143:26+ Je '64
MARBERRY, M. M.
Naked lady or Don't take your sister to Astley's. Horizon 6:112-18 Wint '64
MARBLE, R. V.
Methodists and North India union. Christian Cent 80:1173-4 S 25 '63
MARBLE
Marble strips distinguish precast concrete facades. il Arch Rec 135:184 Je '64
MARBLED paper. See Paper. Decorative
MARBLEHEAD, Mass.
Marblehead celebrates the 75th anniversary of its race week. B. D. Barker, 3d and L. M. Fowle. il Yachting 116:38-9+ Ag '64
MARBLES
Do-it-yourself jewelry. il Design 64:154-5+ Mr '63
MARBLIZING. See Painting
MARBURGH, Claiborne
Keeping pace with the PTA; Operation simpático. PTA Mag 58:31-2 S '63
MARBURY, William
This honorable Court; ed. by J. A. Garraty. il por Am Heritage 14:4-9+ Je '63
MARCEAU, Marcel
Marcel Marceau at New York city center. D. Hering. Dance Mag 37:30 Mr '63
Openings, New York. A. Pryce-Jones. Theatre Arts 47:67 F '63
MARCEL, Gabriel
Existential and Christian. A. E. Mayhew. Commonweal 80:152-3 Ap 24 '64
Gabriel Marcel at Gonzaga. M. Moffitt. America 109:707-9 N 30 '63
Gabriel Marcel in Albany. R. F. Creegan. Sch & Soc 92:86 F 22 '64
MARCELLINA (literary character) See Characters in opera
MARCELLO
Pope John and Communist gains. America 108:896 Je 29 '63
MARCELLO, Carlos
New Orleans: Cosa nostra's Wall Street. B. Davidson. il por Sat Eve Post 237:15-21 F 29 '64
MARCH, Peggy
Little Peggy hits the big time. C. S. Wren. il pors Look 27:Z4+ O 22 '63
MARCH
In March; few of the dates, memorable and not so, coming up this month (title varies) (cont) il N Y Times Mag p79 Mr 1 '64
MARCH of dimes campaign. See National foundation
MARCH on Washington. See Civil rights demonstrations
MARCHAND, Monelisa Lina Pérez. See Pérez Marchand, M. L.
MARCHANT, William
Venice out of season. Holiday 35:52-7+ F '64
(ed) See Davis, B. Lesson in survival
MARCHBANKS, R. M. and others
Serotonin binding to nerve-ending particles of the rat brain and its inhibition by lysergic acid diethylamide. bibliog Science 144:1135-7 My 29 '64
MARCHI, Lorraine
NAVH helps the visually handicapped. Library J 88:4821-2+ D 15 '63
MARCHING bands. See Bands (music); Bands, College
MARCHMAN, Watt P.
Ohio rich in manuscript repositories. Hobbies 68:110-11+ D '63
MARCINIAK, Edward
Breaking the housing barrier. Commonweal 77:588-91 Mr 1 '63
MARCKWARDT, Albert H.
Humanities and non-western studies. Ann Am Acad 356:45-53 N '64
Is the curriculum our business? PTA Mag 58:7-9 bibliog(p36) Ap '64
MARCO millions; drama. See O'Neill, E. G.
MARCONI, Guglielmo
Birth of worldwide communication. Sr Schol 85:5 D 9 '64
MARCUS, Adele
Adele Marcus: the challenge of teaching. R. Sabin. Mus Am 83:53 F '63
MARCUS, Adrianne
Rider; poem. Atlan 214:58 Ag '64
MARCUS, Herbert
Summer action, circus. il U S Camera 26:52-3+ Ag '63
about
Top B&W quality. E. Meyers. il Mod Phot 28:68-71 Ap '64
MARCUS, Leonard
Demonstrator. Hi Fi 13:30-3+ My '63
FM on the threshold. Hi Fi 14:65-7+ N '64
Kits for home assembly. Hi Fi 13:44-7+ Je '63
On call with an audio doctor. Hi Fi 13:61-4 N '63
Philadelphia, a paragon of versatility. Hi Fi 14:65-6 F '64
MARCUS, Philip I. See Robbins, E. jt. auth.
MARCUS, Ruth
Small wonders. See issues of Good housekeeping

MARCUS, Steven
Hunger & ideology. Commentary 36:389-93 N '63
Politics of taste. Commentary 35:351-3 Ap '63
MARCUS, Sumner
New weapons against bigness. Harvard Bsns R 43:100-8 Ja '65
Studies of defense contracting. bibliog f Harvard Bsns R 42:20-2+ My '64
MARCUSE, Herbert
World without a logos. Bul Atomic Sci 20:25-6 Ja '64

about

What we don't know might kill us. E. Capouya. Sat R 47:26-7 Mr 28 '64
MARCUSE, Jacques
Love affair of Comrade Wang. N Y Times Mag p40-1+ N 8 '64
Myth who speaks for Mao. N Y Times Mag p30-1+ N 1 '64
Report (limited) from Communist China. N Y Times Mag p9+ My 24 '64
MARDEN, Luis
Other side of Jordan. il Nat Geog Mag 126:790-825 D '64
MARDER, Arnold R.
Beryllium: effect of ultra-high pressure on resistance. bibliog Science 142:664 N 8 '63
MARDER, Louis
Problems in Shakespearian scholarship; reprint. Wilson Lib Bul 38:660-3+ Ap '64
MARDI gras. See Carnival
MARECHAL, Leopoldo
Robot; with English tr. by R. Connally. Américas 15:23-9 D '63
MAREK, George R.
From this milestone, the future. Am Rec G 30:777 My '64
Paradox of late Strauss. Hi Fi 14:39-41+ Je '64
There's magic in music at Christmas. Am Home 67:20+ D '64
MAREK, Ladislav, and Yochelson, E. L.
Paleozoic mollusk: hyolithes. bibliog Science 146:1674-5 D 25 '64
MAREK, Richard. See Chester, M. F. jt. auth.
MAREMONT, Arnold H.
Birth control, welfare funds, and the politics of Illinois. H. Bruno. il Reporter 28:32-5 Je 20 '63
Illinois Senate ousts a birth control champion. Christian Cent 80:637-8 My 15 '63
Man of many parts. il por Time 83:86 Mr 20 '64
MAREMONT corporation
Man of many parts. il Time 83:86 Mr 20 '64
MARES, Vaclav E.
East Europe's second chance. bibliog f Cur Hist 47:272-9 N '64
French new deal. bibliog f Cur Hist 45:276-82+ N '63
MARETT, Lynn
Deck the house for the holidays. Parents Mag 38:50-1+ D '63
Fit sports for pre-teens. Parents Mag 38:54-5 Je '63
Help for a shy child. Parents Mag 39:52-3+ O '64
MARFANS syndrome. See Syndromes
MARGAI, Sir Milton
African ruler: Prime Minister Margai of Sierra Leone. G. C. Turner. por Negro Hist Bul 28:13 O '64
MARGALIOTH, Mordecai
Fearful truth. il por Newsweek 65:75-75A+ Ja 18 '65
MARGARET, princess of Great Britain
Friendly royal sisters. il pors Look 28:91-3 S 22 '64
How motherhood has changed Princess Margaret. R. Lecler. il por Good H 156:82-3+ My '63
Royal dunking. il pors Life 57:104-5 Jl 17 '64
MARGARETHA, princess of Sweden
Princess & the trucker. il por Time 84:36 Jl 10 '64
MARGARINE
Margarines. il Consumer Rep 28:234-7 My '63
MARGARITA ISLAND
Tale of two isles. H. Sutton. Sat R 46:33-4+ My 18 '63
MARGENAU, Henry, and Bergamini, David
Scientific method; excerpt from Scientist. Fortune 70:100+ D '64
MARGIN of peril; story. See Canning, V.
MARGIN requirements, Stock. See Stock exchange—Regulation
MARGINS; story. See Barthelme, D.
MARGO, Bruno
Personnel problems? write dear Margo. il Bsns W p74+ D 5 '64
MARGOLIN, Janet
Father calls me a rebel; ed. by E. Miller. pors Seventeen 23:108-9+ D '64
MARGOLIS, A. J. See Doyle, L. L. jt. auth.
MARGOLIS, Art
Can you trust a drug store tube tester? Pop Electr 20:50-2+ Ja '64
—and Benrey, Ronald
Inside the '65 TVs. Pop Sci 185:66-71 D '64
MARGOLIS, George. See Kilham, L. jt. auth.
MARGOLIS, Howard
Curious case of krebiozen. Bul Atomic Sci 20:29-31 Mr '64
From Atlantic City: notes on the Democratic convention. Bul Atomic Sci 20:39-42 O '64
From New York: diplomatic game at the U.N. Bul Atomic Sci 21:40-4 Ja '65
From San Francisco: notes on the Republican convention. Bul Atomic Sci 20:31-4 S '64
From Washington: notes on the MLF. Bul Atomic Sci 20:28-30 N '64
From Washington: R and D on Capitol hill. Bul Atomic Sci 20:33-7 My '64
From Washington: the bomb in China. Bul Atomic Sci 20:36-9 D '64
Politics of fluoridation. Bul Atomic Sci 20:38-41 Je '64
Velikovsky rides again. Bul Atomic Sci 20:38:40 Ap '64
MARGOLIS, Richard J.
Do teaching machines really teach? Redbook 121:51+ S '63
MARGOLIS, William
Signatures. R. Sward. Poetry 102:339-40 Ag '63
MARGOLIUS, Sidney
Making your money count (cont of) Family money management. Ladies Home J 80:38 Ja; 22 Ap; 31 Je; 16 Jl '63
MARIA Fidelis, Sister
Hong Kong doctor with 1,000 patients. C. Morrison. il pors Look 28:24-9 Je 16 '64
MARIA di Rohan; opera. See Donizetti, G.
MARIA Laach abbey. See Abbeys
Le MARIAGE de Figaro; drama. See Beaumarchais, P. A. C.
MARIAN Leona, Sister
Script for a beginning. America 111:256-9 S 12 '64
MARIANAS ISLANDS
See also
Guam
MARIANO, Anthony N. and Warekois, E. P.
High pressure phases of some compounds of groups II-VI. bibliog Science 142:672 N 8 '63
—See Kafalas, J. A. jt. auth.
MARICOPA COUNTY, Ariz.
Desert sanctuary. I. Smith. il Nat Parks Mag 37:15-17 S '63
MARIE, Sister Cristella. See Cristella Marie, Sister
MARIE Louis Gabriel, Sister. See Gabriel, M. L.
MARIE, Buffy Sainte-. See Sainte-Marie, B.
MARIE, Marie, hold on tight; story. See Barthelme, D.
MARIGOLDS
Annual for constant color. V. McKissack. Flower Grower 50:40 D '63
Marigolds, so bright, so satisfactory. V. M. Quist. il Horticulture 41:368-9 Jl '63
MARIHUANA
Marihuana; tetrahydrocannabinol and related compounds. M. Lerner. bibliog il Science 140:175 Ap 12 '63
MARILES, Humberto
Tough guy. il por Newsweek 64:48 S 7 '64
MARIN, Juan DeDios
Inside a Castro terror school. por Read Digest 85:119-23 D '64
MARÍN, Luis Muñoz. See Muñoz Marín, L.
MARIN, Pedro Antonio
Backlands violence is almost ended. il Time 83:35 Je 26 '64
MARINA CAY (island) See British Virgin Islands
MARINA City, Chicago. See Chicago—Housing
MARINAS
Fair sailing; Flushing Meadow Park marina. B. Gold. il Motor B 113:110+ Ja '64
Fiberglass dock float systems. B. Cobb, jr. il Yachting 113:80-2 Je '63
Florida casts its bread; marine welcome station and forty-yacht marina. il Bsns W p98-9 F 16 '63
Marinas in your future. P. M. Wilson. il Motor B 115:82-6 Ja '65
Michigan's 3,000-mile marine highway. J. Miner. il Yachting 115:51-3+ Mr '64

MARINAS—*Continued*
Modern marina, from both sides of the gas dock. P. M. Wilson. il Motor B 113:75-7+ Ja '64
More than just a marina; San Leandro, Calif. G. H. Hamlin. il Am City 79:82-4 Ja '64
Pacific Coast marinas. C. West. il Motor B 113:78-9+ Ja '64
What's new when you get there; Florida. R. F. Burnham. il Motor B 112:34-7+ S '63

Caricatures and cartoons

Marina. Stevenson. New Yorker 39:24-9 Ag 24 '63
Marina life. Motor B 115:87 Ja '65

Lighting

Marina lighting; excerpt from address, June 11, 1962. R. L. Henderson. il Am City 78: 91-2 Ag '63

MARINE, Gene
New hope of the far Right. Nation 198:89-92 Ja 27 '64
New look at the oldest difference. Nation 196:247-9 Mr 23 '63; Same abr. with title Mental differences between the sexes. Sci Digest 53:21-5 Je '63
No fair! the students strike at California. Nation 199:482-6 D 21 '64
Outrage on Bodega Head. Nation 196:524-7 Je 22 '63

MARINE aquariums. See Aquariums

MARINE architecture. See Naval architecture

MARINE biological laboratory, Woods Hole. See Woods Hole, Mass, marine biological laboratory

MARINE biology
April magic in the ocean deeps. J. George. il Read Digest 82:107-11 Ap '63
Collecting: the modern shell game. S. E. Smith. il Parents Mag 38:48-9+ Ag '63
Science in action; the biological collector. J. J. Rudloe. Natur Hist 73:59-62 N '64
Underwater guinea pigs help scientists study life. H. M. Schwalb. il Sci Digest 53:6-11 F '63
See also
Marine resources
Plankton
Spawning

Study and teaching

Floating biology class. Sci N L 83:386 Je 22 '63

MARINE borers
See also
Shipworms

MARINE cookery. See Cookery, Marine

MARINE corps. See United States—Marine corps

MARINE corrosion. See Corrosion and anticorrosives

MARINE deposits. See Deep sea deposits

MARINE diesel engines. See Diesel engines, Marine

MARINE ecology
Experimental marine ecology; report on symposium on experimental marine ecology. G. A. Riley. Science 142:1685+ D 27 '63

MARINE engineering
Profiles; W. F. Gibbs. W. Sargeant. New Yorker 40:49-50+ Je 6 '64

MARINE engineers beneficial association. See National marine engineers beneficial association

MARINE engines
Astern in '65; stern drives. il Motor B 114: 36-8+ O '64
Auxiliary power by rule of thumb. F. B. Goeller. il Motor B 115:98-9 Ja '65
Boat engine, car engine; horse of a different color. N. A. Newman. il Motor B 113:95-6 Ja '64
Building a marine engine. il Yachting 117: 101-3 Ja '65
Choosing a stern drive. F. M. Paulson. il Field & S 68:100-5 Je '63
Engines. E. H. Nabb. il Yachting 115:44-5+ Ap '64
Engines: postwar to tomorrow (cont) E. H. Nabb. il Yachting 113:58-9+ F '63
How to choose; outboard or inboard-outboard? J. A. Emmett. il Outdoor Life 133:118-21 Mr '64
Jim Roe tests all the MerCruisers. J. Roe. il Pop Sci 182:116-21+ Je '63
New stern drives are red-hot. J. Roe. il Pop Sci 186:80-3 Ja '65
Rooster tales. E. Rickman. il Hot Rod 17: 104-5 O '64
Tandem-engined boat, built for big water. il Pop Sci 182:131 Mr '63
Troublefree fun with a stern drive. J. Roe. il Pop Sci 185:94-6 S '64
What's with outdrives? E. H. Nabb. il Yachting 113:45-7+ Je '63
Yachting's boat show. il Yachting 115:127-32+ Ja '64; 117:127-32+ Ja '65
See also
Gas and oil engines
Gas and oil engines, Outboard
Tachometers

Care

T.L.C. for engines. F. T. Moss. il Motor B 111:36-7, 58+ Je '63

Ignition

Transistorized electronic ignition systems. E. Robberson. il Yachting 114:63-5+ N '63

Noise

Five steps to silence aboard. R. C. Beard. il Motor B 112:37 N '63

MARINE fauna
At home in the sea. J. Y. Cousteau. il Nat Geog Mag 125:465-507 Ap '64
Olaf, the front man; New York aquarium. B. H. Frisch. il Sci Digest 56:6-10 S '64
Phosphorus excretion and body size in marine animals: microzooplankton and nutrient regeneration. R. E. Johannes. bibliog il Science 146:923-4 N 13 '64
Photographing the night creatures of Alligator Reef. R. E. Schroeder. il Nat Geog Mag 125:128-54 Ja '64
Pleistocene marine microfauna in the Bootlegger Cove Clay, Anchorage, Alaska. R. A. M. Schmidt. bibliog il Science 141:350-1 Jl 26 '63
See also
Foraminifera

MARINE gas turbines. See Gas turbines, Marine

MARINE geology. See Ocean bottom; Submarine geology

MARINE jet propulsion. See Jet propulsion

MARINE language. See Naval art and science—Terminology

MARINE midland corporation
Shortcut to statewide banking; holding company status. il Bsns W p54+ F 9 '63

MARINE painting
Charles H. Woodbury: Yankee with a paint brush. D. O. Woodbury. il Am Artist 28:40-5+ D '64
Dynasty of marine painters: the Roux family of Marseilles. J. Meissonnier. il Antiques 86:583-7 N '64
Marine art of Charles G. Evers. E. Metzl. il Am Artist 27:28-33+ Mr '63
Marine paintings by two Buttersworths. H. Comstock. il Antiques 85:99-103 Ja '64
Nova Scotia's sailor artist. S. T. Spicer. il Motor B 113:116-17+ Ja '64
Ship painters of the Mediterranean. J. Meissonnier. il Antiques 83:304-8 Mr '63

MARINE photography. See Photography—Marines

MARINE refrigerators. See Refrigerators, Electric

MARINE resources
Oceanography a wet and wondrous journey. A. Spilhaus. Bul Atomic Sci 20:11-15 D '64
Oceans will provide more food and minerals. Sci N L 87:24 Ja 9 '65
Pastures of the sea. C. O. Iselin. il Nation 198:413-14+ Ap 27 '64; Same abr. with title Five coming breakthroughs in oceanography. Sci Digest 56:11-13 Ag '64
Sea beneath us. il Bsns W p48+ My 16 '64

MARINE rope. See Rope

MARINE sediments. See Sedimentation and deposition

MARINE superstition. See Superstition

MARINE thefts. See Boats, Theft of

MARINE trades show. See Boats—Exhibitions

MARINE transport lines, incorporated
Biggest fleet: plans to purchase Niarchos fleet. il Newsweek 65:67-8 Ja 25 '65
Is Niarchos heading for port? il Bsns W p 110+ O 24 '64

MARINE turtles. See Turtles

MARINE worms
Complexities in the substrate; marine worms. M. L. Jones. il Natur Hist 72:10-17 My '63
Genetic control of hemerythrin specificity in a marine worm. C. Manwell. bibliog il Science 139:755-8 F 22 '63
Marine sediments: effects of a tube-building polychaete. E. W. Fager. bibliog il Science 143:356-9 Ja 24 '64
Pogonophora on the New England continental slope. R. L. Wigley. bibliog il Science 141: 358-9 Jl 26 '63

MARINE zoology. See Marine fauna

MARINELAND of the Pacific. See Aquariums

MARINER C probe. See Space probes
MARINER II probe. See Space probes
MARINOTTI, Franco
Who's who in foreign business. il por Fortune 71:90 Ja '65
MARIOLOGY. See Mary, Virgin—Theology
MARION, Bruce W.
Consumer's beef dollar: fair share for feeders? Suc Farm 62:38+ Mr '64
MARIONETTES. See Puppets and puppet plays
MARIOTTI, Marcello
Theory of the coiffured lasses. il Horizon 5:118-19 Mr '63
MARIS, Roger
Gift for making a bad situation much worse. R. Creamer. por Sports Illus 18:48-9 My 27 '63
If it isn't one M it's another. il por Sports Illus 19:10-15 Jl 8 '63
Player of the week; Yankee slugger. por Sports Illus 21:127 O 5 '64
MARIS Stella, Sister
For Maria the potter of San Ildefonso; poem. Commonweal 80:570 Ag 21 '64
MARISOL (Marisol Escobar)
Marisol. il por Time 81:76+ Je 7 '63
Marisol's magic mixtures. L. Campbell. il pors Art N 63:38-41+ Mr '64
Marisol's mannequins. il pors Horizon 5:102-4 Mr '63
Pace-setters; interview. por Mlle 59:281 Ag '64
MARITAL counseling. See Marriage counseling
MARITIME administration. See United States—Maritime administration
MARITIME law
For those in peril on the sea. D. Woodward. il UNESCO Courier 16:4-9 My '63
U.S. vs. the U.S (cont) R. Moley. Newsweek 61:84 F 4 '63
See also
Boats and boating—Laws and regulations
Blockade
Salvage (ships)
Territorial waters
MARITIME museums. See Naval museums
MARITIME PROVINCES, Canada
Fisherman's guide to the Maritimes. A. J. McClane. il Field & S 69:126-8+ Je '64
Lord's day controversy. R. S. Clarke. Christian Cent 80:440-2 Ap 3 '63
MARITIME workers
Courts in conflict. T. R. Brooks. Duns R 82:74B D '63
Feud; the S.S. America's lay-up. il Newsweek 62:96 O 14 '63
U.S. unions thwarted on foreign-flag ships. Bsns W p 122 F 23 '63
When machines replace seamen; mechanized ships. il Bsns W p 100+ Ja 25 '64
See also
Strikes—United States—Maritime workers
MARITO in città; story. See Cheever, J.
MARIUS, Richard C.
Ruleville; reminiscence, reflection. Christian Cent 81:1169-71 S 23 '64
MARJOLIN, Robert
Europe juggles to keep prices down, growth up. il por Bsns W p 166+ D 5 '64
MARK, Charles C.
They also dance who only sit. Dance Mag 38:54-5 F '64
MARK, H.
Macromolecules. Science 146:1023-4 N 20 '64
MARK, Larry D.
Minute men putting curb on cholera. Suc Farm 62:43+ Ap '64
MARK, Raymond. See Schlesinger, M. jt. auth.
MARK Twain, pseud. See Clemens, S. L.
MARK Twain summer institute, Clayton, Mo. See Summer schools
MARKAKIS, P. See Lindstrom, R. S. jt. auth.
MARKANDAYA, Kamala, pseud. See Taylor, K. P.
MARKARIAN, Robert E.
Teachers' syndicate of the U.A.R. Sch & Soc 91:373-5 N 30 '63
MARKEL, Helen
Fashion pace-setter. Good H 156:38-40+ Je '63
Twenty-four hours in the life of Margaret Chase Smith. McCalls 91:116-17+ My '64
(ed) See Burnett, C. My friend Julie Andrews
(ed) See Hemingway, M. Look back, a look ahead
MARKEL, Lester
Case pro and con de Gaulle. N Y Times Mag p 19+ Ja 10 '65
Management of news. Sat R 46:50-1+ F 9 '63
MARKELIUS, Sven
Architecture in a social context. Arch Rec 135:153 Ap '64
Work of Sven Markelius. il Arch Rec 135:154-64 Ap '64
MARKER lights. See Traffic markings
MARKERT, Clement L.
Lactate dehydrogenase isozymes: dissociation and recombination of subunits. bibliog Science 140:1329-30 Je 21 '63
Where life is controlled. Newsweek 65:50 Ja 11 '65
MARKET letters. See Investments—Advisers
MARKET research
Can industrial marketing match production? L. Morse. il Duns R 83:41-2+ F '64
Changing an art into a science. il Bsns W p 164+ My 23 '64
Computer simulation of consumer behavior. W. D. Wells. Harvard Bsns R 41:93-8 My '63
Exploring the exploratory sample. R. A. Bauer. Harvard Bsns R 41:128-31 Mr '63
Find your company's hidden strength. P. Drucker. Nations Bsns 52:80-2+ Mr '64
Future challenges marketing. R. C. Garretson. il Harvard Bsns R 41:168-70+ N '63
Muddle in marketing research. T. J. Murray. il Duns R 85:50-2+ Ja '65
New dimension in consumer analysis. H. W. Boyd, jr. and S. J. Levy. bibliog f il Harvard Bsns R 41:129-40 N '63
Payoff from product management. B. C. Ames. il Harvard Bsns R 41:141-52 N '63
Restive researchers. P. B. Bart. Sat R 46:47 Jl 13 '63
Rose by another name. G. Lazarus. Sat R 47:68-9 S 12 '64; Reply. P. White. 47:77 N 14 '64
Say Olympia; Marco surveys, ltd; market research in Africa. il Newsweek 63:74 Mr 9 '64
Scouting the trail for marketers. il Bsns W p90-1+ Ap 18 '64
See also
Nielsen, A. C, company
MARKET surveys
Pinpointing America: analysis of industrial markets; tables. il Duns R 84:43-50 Ag '64
See also
Consumers preferences
Youth market
MARKETING
Behind P&G's marketing success. il Duns R 81:48-51+ My '63
Changing anatomy of industrial sales distribution. L. Morse. il Duns R 81:37-8+ Ja '63
Distribution comes of age. J. F. Olesky. il Duns R 85:36-8+ Ja '65
Dogma in marketing; address, October 6, 1964. P. G. Peterson. Vital Speeches 31:43-6 N 1 '64
Dual distribution vs. the small retailer. T. J. Murray. il Duns R 84:28-9+ Ag '64
Guerrilla war on soap giants. il Bsns W p50-2 Ag 29 '64
Hard sell abroad. L. Morse. il Duns R 81:46-9+ Ap '63
Here's where you can sell abroad. il Nations Bsns 51:76-8+ Ap '63
How to sell more abroad. A. S. Beckley. il Nations Bsns 51:106-10+ Mr '63
How to sell more now; questions and answers. M. P. McNair. il Nations Bsns 51:38-9+ Ag '63
Industrial marketing's new voice. L. Morse. il Duns R 81:31-2+ Mr '63
Industry's fight for shelf space. L. Morse. Duns R 81:45-6+ F '63
Is marketing a science? R. D. Buzzell. bibliog f Harvard Bsns R 41:32-4+ Ja '63
Markets pattern (title varies) (cont) Bsns W p66 F 2 '63
Myth of the national market. J. B. Weiner. il Duns R 83:40-3+ My '64
New criteria for market segmentation. D. Yankelovich. il Harvard Bsns R 42:83-90 Mr '64
New ways in marketing strategy. L. Morse. il Duns R 83:43-4+ Ja '64
No easy road to market orientation. R. W. Lear. il Harvard Bsns R 41:53-60 S '63
See also
Advertising
American marketing association
Canvassing
Industrial market
Market surveys
Packaging
Price cutting
Retail trade
Sales promotion

MARKETING—See also—*Continued*
Salesmen and salesmanship
Supermarkets
Wholesale trade
also subhead Marketing under various subjects, e.g. Farm produce—Marketing

Direct selling

Sales begin at home. il Bsns W p74+ S 12 '64

MARKETING, Cooperative
New middleman co-op; marketing of eggs. L. M. Palmer. Farm J 87:69-70 Ap '63

MARKETING research. See Market research

MARKETING science institute
Changing an art into a science. il Bsns W p 164 My 23 '64

MARKETS
See also
Old age market

MARKETS, New
See also
Industrial market

MARKETS, Outdoor. See Street trades

MARKEY, Gene
Sunset Boulevardier. C. Amory. por Esquire 62:116-17+ O '64

MARKFIELD, Wallace
Mocking heroics. M. Magid. Commentary 38: 81-4 N '64

MARKHAM, Jesse W.
Antitrust trends and new constraints. bibliog f Harvard Bsns R 41:84-92 My '63

MARKHAM, Margaret
Little gland that keeps you well. Parents Mag 38:90+ O '63
New hope for conquering childhood cancer. Parents Mag 39:62-3+ N '64

MARKIN, Morris
Box that tailoring made. il por Time 82:62 Ag 2 '63

MARKING (students) See Grading and marking (students)

MARKING of books. See Books—Labeling, marking, etc.

MARKINKO, Dorothy
Sky-high courage. Ladies Home J 80:62-3+ Ja '63

MARKLE, Tom. See Kennon, L. B. jt. auth.

MARKLEY, Edith
Charmer: wee willie. Flower Grower 50:27 Mr '63

MARKOVA, Dame Alicia
My life in opera. pors Opera N 28:8-11 D 21 '63

about

Ladies and gentlemen of the ballet. D. Hering. il por Dance Mag 38:46-7+ My '64
Met opera ballet thinks big. D. Hering. il por Dance Mag 37:35-9+ Jl '63
Music to my ears; "on" night at the Met. I. Kolodin. Sat R 47:34+ N 28 '64
Recreating Les sylphides; Poetry in movement; presentation by Metropolitan opera ballet. pors Opera N 29:13-17 Ja 9 '65

MARKOWITZ, Hal. See Tapp. J. T. jt. auth.

MARKS, Edwin P. and Reinecke, J. P.
Regenerating tissues from the cockroach leg: a system for studying in vitro. bibliog Science 143:961-3 F 28 '64

MARKS, Joe
Foods of the future. Suc Farm 63:85+ Ja '65

MARKS, Lillian
Saul and Lillian Marks and their Plantin press in Los Angeles. P. A. Bennett. il por Pub W 186:114-18 Jl 6 '64

MARKS, Marcia B.
Building cultural bridges. Dance Mag 37:20-1 My '63
Paper bag players. Dance Mag 38:52-5+ Je '64
Reviews. See issues of Dance magazine
Subject is people. Dance Mag 37:30-5 F '63

MARKS, Matthew J.
New dimensions for the Colombo plan. Dept State Bul 48:977-83 Je 24 '63

MARKS, Meritt R.
Special-interest cars. Motor T 16:79 N '64

MARKS, Paul A. and Burka, E. R.
Hemoglobins A and F: formation in thalassemia and other hemolytic anemias. bibliog Science 144:552-3 My 1 '64

MARKS, Saul
Saul and Lillian Marks and their Plantin press in Los Angeles. P. A. Bennett. il por Pub W 186:114-18 Jl 6 '64

MARKS, W. B. and others
Visual pigments of single primate cones. bibliog Science 143:1181-3 Mr 13 '64

MARKS, Winston
Flying library: air service to Indian reservation by the Northwestern regional library. il Wilson Lib Bul 38:33 S '63

MARKS, Potters. See Pottery—Marks

MARKS and Spencer, limited
This firm threw its files away. il U S News 55:69 Jl 29 '63

MARKS of origin
President disapproves legislation on import marking requirements; memorandum, December 31, 1963. L. B. Johnson. Dept State Bul 50:129 Ja 27 '64

MARKSMANSHIP. See Shooting

MARLBORO festival of music. See Music festivals—Vermont

MARLBOROUGH fine art, limited
Aggressive giant. il Time 82:56 Jl 19 '63
Swinging art dealers: the Marlborough boys in New York. J. Russell. il Vogue 143:102-5+ Ja 1 '64

MARLBOROUGH-Gerson gallery. See New York (city)—Galleries and museums

MARLER, Louis A.
Booby prize; poem. Christian Cent 81:143 Ja 29 '64

MARLER, Peter, and Tamura, Miwako
Culturally transmitted patterns of vocal behavior in sparrows. bibliog Science 146: 1483-6 D 11 '64

MARLEY, C. F.
Double-duty hog lagoon. Suc Farm 61:104 Ap '63
Egg handling made easy. il Suc Farm 61:100 My '63

MARLEY, Faye
Antipolio substance. Sci N L 85:405 Je 27 '64
Link tooth loss, hearing; deafness after tooth extractions. Sci N L 86:117 Ag 22 '64
Poverty causes violence. Sci N L 86:114 Ag 22 '64
Test tube life doubted. Sci N L 86:102 Ag 15 '64
Women warned on drugs. Sci N L 86:130 Ag 29 '64

MARLIN fishing
Big fish story. M. Wiley. il Yachting 115: 40-4+ My '64
Budget marlin. Time 82:51-2 Ag 16 '63
Magic fish trap. C. M. Kreider. il Outdoor Life 133:36-7+ F '64
Mob of marlin in the bays of Panama. J. Olsen. il Sports Illus 18:62-8+ Ap 22 '63
Panama paradise. A. J. McClane. il Field & S 68:52-3+ O '63

MARLOW, Foster L.
Prophet, furnace cement sculpture. Sch Arts 64:20-1 O '64

MARLOWE, Christopher
It is a Marlowe year also. A. L. Rowse. il pors N Y Times Mag p 15+ F 16 '64
Tragical historie of Dr Faustus. Criticism
Commonweal 81:167 O 30 '64
Nation 199:285-6 O 26 '64
New Yorker 40:108 O 17 '64
Time il 84:77 O 16 '64

MARLOWE, Dan J.
Background vs. setting. Writer 76:12-13+ F '63
Strike a note, and hold it! Writer 76:20-1 Ag '63

MARMALADE. See Jelly, jam, etc.

MARMALADE overture; drama. See Boiko, C.

MARMER, Jeffrey
Jeffrey becomes a man; Bar mitzvah. C. Morrison. il pors Look 27:24-8+ Ag 13 '63

MARMOR, Judd
War, violence, and human nature. Bul Atomic Sci 20:19-22 Mr '64

MARMOTS
Marmots are curious about people. il Sunset 132:35 Je '64

MARMUR, Julius, and Greenspan, C. M.
Transcription in vivo of DNA from bacteriophage SP8. bibliog Science 142:387-9 O 18 '63
—See Langridge, R. jt. auth.

MARONEY, Mary F.
Figure skating: a lifetime activity. Recreation 57:29 Ja '64

MAROON, Fred J.
Where's the point of interest? il U S Camera 27:44-5 Ja '64

MAROSSI, Ruth
What did he say? Esquire 59:14+ My '63

MAROWITZ, Charles
Letter from London. Nation 196:313-14; 199: 99-100 Ap 13 '63, S 7 '64

MARPLE, Allen
Off the cuff. See issues of Writer

MARQUESAS KEYS
By outboard to the Marquesas. M. Hunn. il Yachting 116:52-3+ N '64

MARQUET, Albert
Decorum and independence. M. Kozloff. Nation 198:561-3 Je 1 '64

MARQUIS, Don
Dog that bit the circus lion; excerpt from Personality of the dog. Read Digest 85:44-7 Ag '64

MARQUIS, Weldon
Sutherland sings Norma. Mus Am 83:20 N '63

MARQUSEE, John E. See Rachlis, E. jt. auth.

MARRAKESH
Marrakesh. K. Williams. il Atlan 215:112-13+ Ja '65

MARRIAGE
Advice to a young man. A. West. Redbook 123:45+ Jl '64; Same abr. with title When is a young man ready for marriage? Read Digest 85:19+ N '64
After the honeymoon, what? Changing T 18:6 Je '64
Avoiding the no point system; risking divorce playing bridge with your spouse. L. W. Robinson. il N Y Times Mag p 19+ Ap 19 '64
Bad year of marriage. E. Forsythe. Redbook 123:62-3+ Ag '64
Can love survive indifference? il Good H 156:14+ Je '63
Can this marriage be saved? case histories, ed. by D. C. Disney. See issues of Ladies' home journal
Closing the gap between theology and marital reality. M. Novak. Commonweal 80:342-7 Je 5 '64
Conjugal love and conjugal morality. R. A. McCormick. America 110:38-42 Ja 11 '64
Day I really felt married; letters. il Redbook 120:50-1+ F '63
Difference between men and husbands. H. Lawrenson. il McCalls 90:81+ S '63
Dilemmas of a househusband. R. Varga. Sat R 48:100-3 Ja 2 '65
Do you dare to be honest in marriage? M. Holmes. il Todays Health 42:58-9 Ap '64
First year. G. B. Browning. il McCalls 91:218 N '63
Flight from marriage. il Good H 157:12+ N '63
Frank look at marital fidelity. G. Riemer. Good H 158:49+ Ja '64
Funny business of marriage. W. Saroyan. Sat Eve Post 236:44-5 O 5 '63
GBS and the fair sex; quotations, with introduction by T. C. F. Lowry. il Ladies Home J 81:128+ Ja '64
Great symbol; sexual intercourse in marriage. C. Davis. America 111:803 D 19 '64
How to get him to marry you; excerpt from Seducer's cookbook. M. Sheraton. il Mlle 57:148-9 O '63
I married an older woman. il Good H 158:10+ Ap '64
I thought I'd married a momma's boy. il Good H 158:14+ F '64
Is it immature loving? F. M. Wessling. il America 110:594-6 My 2 '64; Discussion. 110:768-70 My 30 '64
Junior population explosion; encouraging children of tender age to marry. S. Roy; discussion. Sat R 46:24 F 16 '63
Just for two. il Am Home 67:32+ Je '64
Life of a wife. G. Buckman. il Mlle 58:96-7+ Ja '64
Life without her. J. N. Bell. il Read Digest 85:49-52 S '64
Love, O love, O careful love. J. H. Adams. il America 109:481-4 O 26 '63; Discussion. 109:658-9; 110:1, 149 N 23 '63, Ja 4, F 1 '64
Making marriage work. D. C. Disney. Ladies Home J 80:94 Ja; 18 Mr; 34 Je; 52 Jl '63
Marriage as it really is; reprint. S. Katz. il Sci Digest 55:6-19 F '64
Marriage is neither heaven nor hell but what is it? F. J. Sheen. Todays Health 42:60-1+ Ap '64
Marriage questions, by J. C. Ford and G. Kelly. Review
Commonweal 80:320-3 Je 5 '64. D. Callahan
Marriage: the lay voice. M. Novak. Commonweal 79:587-90 F 14 '64; Discussion. 79:752-3; 80:48+ Mr 20, Ap 3 '64
My husband was ashamed of me. il Good H 156:16+ Ap '63
My problem and how I solved it; my husband was unfaithful. il Good H 156:10+ Mr '63
Please stop telling me that I have to have a baby. J. Seabaugh. Redbook 121:6+ My '63
Real intimacy in marriage. M. Holmes. il Todays Health 42:18-21 Ap '64
Rethinking the sacrament of matrimony; excerpt from The Johannine council. B. Haring. Cath World 197:359-65 S '63
Sex problems after ten years of marriage. M. Davis. McCalls 90:50+ My '63
Speaking out; we have no right to happiness. C. S. Lewis. Sat Eve Post 236:10+ D 21 '63
Sweet monotony of marriage. A. Maurois. il Ladies Home J 81:43 Mr '64
Tensions; his and hers. I. Rockower. il McCalls 92:114 N '64
What wives don't know about sex; ed. by J. Younger; reprint. A. Stone. Read Digest 84:78-80 Mr '64
Why young couples feel trapped; dissatisfactions of social life after marriage. S. Blum. il Redbook 123:62-3+ S '64
Will science change marriage? J. Lear. il Sat R 47:75-7 D 5 '64; Discussion. 48:100-2 Ja 2 '65
Woman's world; report on Marriage and the American woman. Time 81:66 Je 14 '63
You do marry the family. E. M. Stern. il Parents Mag 39:70-1+ Ap '64
Young moderns' marriage dreams; with study-discussion program. E. M. Duvall. bibliog il PTA Mag 57:4-7, 36 Ap '63
Young wife's world. H. Valentine. See issues of Good housekeeping

See also

Bigamy
Courtship
Divorce
Engagements, Marriage
Family life, Education for
High school students, Married
Husbands
Illegitimacy
Intermarriage of races
Love
Physical examinations, Premarital
Sex
Sex relations
Woman

Anecdotes, facetiae, satire, etc.

Absolute truth about marriage. L. Wyse. il McCalls 91:58 Je '64
Never say no! P. Cummings. Read Digest 83:24C Ag '63
What makes a man propose? A. Buchwald. il McCalls 91:62 N '63

Annulment

Annulment; masquerade for divorce? M. A. Guitar. McCalls 92:84+ Ja '65

Handbooks, manuals, etc.

Love & marriage: by the book. Time 81:54+ Je 28 '63

India

Junior population explosion; encouraging children of tender age to marry. S. Roy; discussion. Sat R 46:24 F 16 '63

Russia

Grandpa snatchers. Newsweek 63:40+ Mr 2 '64

United States

See Marriage

MARRIAGE brokers
Lady Chatterley's helper; marriage-brokerage in Czechoslovakia. Newsweek 63:52+ F 17 '64
Machine-made love. A. Levy. Mlle 60:72-3+ Ja '65
They are the product of a broker's home; West Germany's marriage agencies. Time 81:38 Mr 8 '63

MARRIAGE by proxy. See Marriage law

MARRIAGE counseling
Can this marriage be saved? case histories, ed. by D. C. Disney. See issues of Ladies' home journal
Confessors and theologians; the pastoral crisis. G. W. Casey. Commonweal 80:317-19 Je 5 '64
Fight promoter for the battle of the sexes. S. Alexander. il Life 54:102-4+ My 17 '63
First year. McCalls 90:64+ My '63
Heading off those risky teen marriages. S. Welton. il Parents Mag 39:47+ Mr '64
Marriage counselors, helpers and hurters. P. Streit. il N Y Times Mag p26+ N 3 '63
Prescription for a marriage on the rocks. N. V. Peale. Read Digest 85:89-93 S '64
What clergymen tell young people about marriage. T. Morris. Redbook 120:50-1+ Mr '63

MARRIAGE customs and rites
Here come the couples; photographs. S. Falk. N Y Times Mag p40+ N 24 '63
Love and marriage, Soviet style. E. Stevens. il N Y Times Mag p 16-17+ Ap 26 '64
Love: it makes the world go 'round. F. Kerner. il Todays Health 42:42-7+ Ap '64

MARRIAGE customs and rites—*Continued*
Royal wedding at Jaisalmer. M. Silverstone. il Nat Geog Mag 127:66-79 Ja '65
Royal wedding festival; marriage of H.R.H Pincess Lalla Nouzha in Morocco. il Vogue 145:72-7 Ja 15 '65
Teen-age wedding in Russia; matrimonial supermarket. E. Dunbar. il Look 28:M6-7 Ag 25 '64
See also
Weddings

MARRIAGE law
See also
Adultery

France

Wedding knells; post-mortem marriages. il Time 83:54 Mr 13 '64

Russia

Love and marriage, Soviet style. E. Stevens. il N Y Times Mag p 16-17+ Ap 26 '64

United States

Annulment; masquerade for divorce? M. A. Guitar. McCalls 92:84+ Ja '65
Love laughs (and cries) at obstacles. J. Ciardi. Sat R 47:7 Jl 25 '64
Speaking out; let's abolish alimony. A. Eliot. Sat Eve Post 237:12+ Ag 22 '64
Two pleas for freedom. America 108:322 Mr 9 '63
You can do something about prejudice. C. Thompson. Christian Cent 81:138-40 Ja 29 '64

MARRIAGE manuals. See Marriage—Handbooks, manuals, etc.

MARRIAGE of Figaro; drama. See Beaumarchais, P. A. C.

MARRIAGE of Figaro; opera. See Mozart, J. C. W. A.

MARRIAGE proposals
Frankly speaking. G. Wagner. il McCalls 91: 45 F '64
1964: bad year for bachelors? women's special leap-year privilege. il Todays Health 42:52 Ap '64
On bended knee. L. Lerman. il Mlle 56:98-9+ F '63

MARRIAGES, International
If you marry a foreigner. D. R. Mace. il McCalls 90:60+ Ja '63

MARRIAGES, Interracial. See Intermarriage of races

MARRIAGES, Mixed
Assimilators; Jewish intermarriage. Newsweek 62:97 O 7 '63
Children of interfaith marriage. A. Whitman. il Redbook 121:46-7+ Je '63; Discussion. 122:26+ Ap '64
Cushing wants church laws liberalized; interview, ed. by W. M. Abbott. R. Cushing. Christian Cent 80:820 Je 26 '63
Ecumenical jaywalking; marriage performed jointly by Catholic and Episcopal priests. Christian Cent 81:1325-6 O 28 '64; Reply. C. Miller, 3d. 81:1528-9 D 9 '64
Father Kueng speaks on mixed marriages. H. Küng. Christian Cent 80:453 Ap 10 '63
If Lynda Bird marries a Roman Catholic. il por U S News 56:14 F 3 '64
Intermarriage & the Jewish future. M. Sklare. Commentary 37:46-52 Ap '64; Discussion. 38:16 Ag; 8+ S '64
Intermarriage, by A. I. Gordon. Review
Christian Cent 81:1086 S 2 '64. M. P. Strommen
Mixed marriage; conclusions of Committee on church and nation of the church of Scotland. Time 81:71 My 24 '63
Mixed-marriage obstacle; Protestant sensitivity. America 111:282 S 19 '64
Mixed-marriage question; concerning Cardinal Cushing's statement. America 109:3 Jl 6 '63
Mixed marriages; experience of the Jewish community. America 109:547 N 9 '63
Rethinking the sacrament of matrimony; excerpt from The Johannine council. B. Haring. Cath World 197:359-65 S '63
Threat to survival; Judaism and interfaith marriages. il Time 83:41 Ja 17 '64
Toward easier mixed marriage. il Time 84:56 Jl 17 '64
Vanishing Jews. M. Himmelfarb. Commentary 36:249-51 S '63; Discussion. 37:23 Mr '64
Wedding in St Louis. America 111:79 Jl 25 '64

MARRIC, J. J.
Few words concerning this picture. Esquire 62:132-3 N '64

MARRIE, Edward K.
Cathode-ray oscilloscopes. Electr World 70: 50-3+ Ag '63

MARRIED college students. See College students, Married

MARRIED teachers. See Teachers, Married

MARRIED women
Surprising facts about women, work, marriage. il Sci Digest 54:79-82 O '63
See also
Wives

Employment

Best of both worlds. J. Scobey. il Mlle 57: 171-3+ My '63
Child care created by mother. A. Eisenberg. and H. Eisenberg. il Ladies Home J 81:56-7+ Je '64
For soviet women; a thirteen-hour day; average Russian wife. E. Whiteside. il N Y Times Mag p28-9+ N 17 '63
Fraud of femininity; excerpts from The feminine mystique. B. Friedan. McCalls 90:81+ Mr '63; Discussion. 90:38+ Ag '63
Have American housewives traded brains for brooms? B. Friedan. il Ladies Home J 80:24+ Ja '63
How to succeed as a working mother. M. A. Gillmor. il Parents Mag 38:58-9+ Mr '63
I'm going to get a job! B. H. Hoffman. il Ladies Home J 80:107-8 S '63
Income a working wife actually nets. il Good H 158:163 Ap '64
Marital and family characteristics of workers, March 1962. J. Schiffman. il Mo Labor R 86:24-36 Ja '63
Marital and family characteristics of workers, March 1963. V. C. Perrella. il Mo Labor R 87:149-60 F '64
Marvin's mother. K. Byrne. Commonweal 80: 395-7 Je 19 '64
Millions of working mamas. M. G. Morrow. il Sci N L 85:250-1 Ap 18 '64
Mixing math and motherhood; computer programming project. il Bsns W p86-7 Mr 2 '63
Second wind; the fortyish college educated housewife. il Time 82:56-7 N 22 '63
She sought refuge from domestic chaos in a job. D. C. Disney. il Ladies Home J 80:10+ O '63
Should mothers work? B. Spock. il Ladies Home J 80:16+ Ja '63
Special opportunity. P. H. Abelson. Science 145:115 Jl 10 '64; Discussion. 145:1123 S 11 '64
Surprising facts about women, work, marriage. il Sci Digest 54:79-82 O '63
Two breadwinners. America 108:847 Je 15 '63
What I owe to other women. M. Mead. il Redbook 122:18+ Ap '64
What the husbands think. A. Toffler. Ladies Home J 81:26+ Je '64
When mothers work. B. Spock. il Ladies Home J 80:140+ Mr '63
Wives and the moonlight adventure; excerpt from Sixpence in her shoe. P. McGinley. Ladies Home J 81:30+ Ag '64; Same abr. Read Digest 86:72-4 Ja '65
Woman: the fourth dimension. B. Friedan. il Ladies Home J 81:48-55 Je '64; Discussion. 81:47 Je; 34+ S '64
Work rules for job-holding mothers. C. H. Myers. il Parents Mag 39:46-7+ Ja '64
World outside; excerpts from My favorite things. D. Rodgers. McCalls 92:28+ O '64
See also
Part time employment

MARRIED women as teachers. See Teachers, Married

MARRINER, E. H.
Bandspreading the ARC-5. Pop Electr 20:66+ Je '64
Converting your first command receiver. Pop Electr 18:45-8+ Je '63
High seas calling. Pop Electr 21:52-4 O '64
VHF grid-dip meter. Pop Electr 20:59-61+ Ja '64

MARRIOTT, Alice
Saint's day. New Yorker 39:111+ O 19 '63

MARRIOTT, Vincent J.
Made salesman of the sixties. Duns R 82:28 Ag '63

MARROW
Hemoglobin synthesis in marrow cell culture: the effect of rat plasma on rat cells. O. Gallien-Lartigue and E. Goldwasser. il Science 145:277-9 Jl 17 '64
Human bone marrow distribution shown in vivo by iron-52 and the positron scintillation camera. H. O. Anger and D. C. Van Dyke. bibliog il Science 144:1587-9 Je 26 '64

MARS (planet)
Amateur's observations of Mars. R. G. Northcutt. il Sky & Tel 25:96 F '63
Ames study supports Mars life theory. H. D. Watkins. Aviation W 79:61+ N 18 '63
Checking up on Kepler. Sky & Tel 28:70 Ag '64

MARS (planet)—*Continued*
Clear view of Mars; balloon-borne Stratoscope II. il Time 81:74 Mr 15 '63
Experimental exobiology. Sky & Tel 26:132 S '63
Interpretation of the 3- to 4-micron infrared spectrum of Mars. D. G. Rea and others. bibliog il Science 141:923-7 S 6 '63
Life may exist on Mars, but mistranslation made the canals. S. D. Gossner. il Natur Hist 72:56-7 Ap '63
Mars less hazardous. Sci N L 83:102 F 16 '63
Mars observed; Stratoscope. il Newsweek 61:60 Mr 18 '63
Mars pollution unlikely with sterilized probes. Sci N L 85:185 Mr 21 '64
Mars' surface appears flatter than thought. Sci N L 84:230 O 12 '63
Martian chronicles. Newsweek 61:66 Je 17 '63
Precision globes of Mars. J. A. Roth. il Sky & Tel 27:19 Ja '64
Radar observations of Mars and Mercury. Sky & Tel 25:191+ Ap '63
Recent visual observations of Mars. E. E. Both. il Sky & Tel 26:17-19 Jl '63
Signs of life on Mars; Life on Mars hard to see. Sci N L 85:339-40 My 30 '64
Size and shape of Mars. Sky & Tel 25:209 Ap '63
See also
Space flight to Mars

Atmosphere

Mars air found thinner. Sci N L 85:100 F 15 '64
Parched planet. Sci Am 209:52 Ag '63
Sinton bands: evidence for deuterated water on Mars. J. S. Shirk and others. bibliog il Science 147:48-9 Ja 1 '65

Contamination

Keep Mars clean. A. Ewing. Sci N L 83:293 My 11 '63

MARS excursion module. See Space vehicles—Landing systems—Mars
MARS globe. See Globes, Astronomical
MARS landing. See Space vehicles—Landing systems—Mars
MARS probe. See Space probes
MARSAL, Sonia
Mortality writ in stone. Américas 16:22-30 S '64
MARSAN, C. Ajmone. See Matsumoto, H. jt. auth.
MARSDEN, Halsey M. and Bonson, F. H.
Estrous synchrony in mice: alteration by exposure to male urine. Science 144:1469 Je 19 '64
MARSH, Alva D. B.
Pressed-flower art. Am Home 67:124 Jl '64
MARSH, Calvin
Singing scholar; interview, ed. by F. Stevenson. por Opera N 28:27 Ap 11 '64
MARSH, James T. and others
Poliomyelitis in monkeys: decreased susceptibility after avoidance stress. bibliog Science 140:1414-15 Je 28 '63
MARSH, John
Scarlett O'Hara's millions. F. Knebel. il Look 27:39-40+ D 3 '63
MARSH, Louis Cordell
Death down a dark street. D. Peerman. Christian Cent 80:166-7 F 6 '63
Death of a youth worker. G. Samuels. il Sat Eve Post 236:74-6 Ap 6 '63
MARSH, Muriel McIntyre
Sixty-five years afloat! M. G. Belknap. il pors Yachting 115:190 Je '64
MARSH, R. E.
Forestry: a way of life; address. Am For 70:36-8+ Ag '64
Norway hosts 10th Northern forest congress. Am For 69:24-7+ My '63
MARSH, Reginald
Art galleries; memorial exhibition: ten years after his death, of paintings and other works at the Gallery of modern art. R. M. Coates. New Yorker 40:66-9 Ja 2 '65
Coney Island Rubens. il Newsweek 64:79-80 D 21 '64
MARSH, Richard
Phase programming. Sr Schol 83:7T N 15 '63
MARSH, Robert Charles
Beethoven's cello sonatas in a partnership of peers. Hi Fi 14:65 S '64
First recordings from Philharmonic Hall. Hi Fi 13:73-4 F '63
Fresh course for Boston. Hi Fi 13:72-3 Mr '63
Haydn renascence continues. Hi Fi 13:78-9 N '63
Heritage of Bruno Walter. Hi Fi 14:44-8+ Ja '64
Mahler's Eighth, a stereo debut. Hi Fi 14:50-1 Jl '64
Notes from our correspondents. Hi Fi 14:20+ Ag '64
MARSH, Tracy H.
English heroes honored in glass. Hobbies 68:86 My '63
Glass terminology. Hobbies 69:85+ O '64
Glass-ware prices way back when. Hobbies 69:78-9+ S '64
How far that little candle throws its beam. Hobbies 69:84-5 Ja '65
Politics and the glass-maker. Hobbies 69:82-3 Jl; 74-5 Ag '64
Real Yankee Doodle. Hobbies 69:80+ Je '64
Some notes on commemorative bottles. Hobbies 67:86-7 F '63
MARSH gardens. See Water gardens
MARSHACK, Alexander
Lunar notation on upper paleolithic remains. Science 146:743-5 N 6 '64
MARSHAK, Robert E.
No winner yet in the science race. N Y Times Mag p59-60+ O 11 '64
Reexamining the Soviet scientific challenge. Bul Atomic Sci 19:12-17 Ap '63
MARSHALL, A. P.
Maybe they can tell us something. por Library J 88:1421-3 Ap 1 '63
Spur to further study. por Library J 88:4700-1 D 15 '63
MARSHALL, Burke
About a man who made his job. M. McGrory. America 112:37 Ja 9 '65
Administration's way of helping Negro. il por Bsns W p25 My 11 '63
Mission accomplished. Newsweek 64:19 D 28 '64
Non-whiz kid with the quiet gun. R. Wallace. il pors Life 55:75-6+ Ag 9 '63
Quiet fighter for civil rights. S. Booker. il pors Ebony 19:90-2+ My '64
MARSHALL, C. C. A. and others
Fossil microorganisms: possible presence in precambrian shield of western Australia. bibliog Science 144:290-2 Ap 17 '64
MARSHALL, Catherine
What did you want most at seventeen? ed. by A. Ebert. por Seventeen 22:131 S '63
MARSHALL, Charles Burton
Apprenticeship of a soldier. New Repub 149:26-7 N 2 '63
His brother's keeper; remarks, September 6, 1963. New Repub 149:6 S 21 '63
MacArthur interviews. New Repub 150:7 Ap 25 '64
Notes on conferencemanship. New Repub 148:15-17 F 16 '63
Old hand speaks out. Reporter 31:52-3 S 10 '64
Our bitter tea and how we brewed it. New Repub 150:28-9 F 15 '64
Smile of safety. New Repub 148:17-18 My 25 '63
Stomach for soldiery. New Repub 151:27-9 O 3 '64
Story of one American boy. New Repub 151:28+ O 17 '64
What happened in Korea. New Repub 151:19-20 Jl 11 '64
Worried to death. New Repub 150:26-7 F 29 '64
MARSHALL, David B.
Treasure islands of wildlife. il Audubon Mag 66:160-5 My '64
MARSHALL, E. G.
Defender. por Newsweek 62:56 D 16 '63
MARSHALL, E. M.
Fall gardening in New England. Flower Grower 50:23 O '63
MARSHALL, George Catlett
Fight over the A-bomb. F. Knebel and C. W. Bailey. Look 27:19-23 Ag 13 '63
George Catlett Marshall; address. D. D. Eisenhower. il por Atlan 214:41-3 Ag '64
George C Marshall: education of a general, by F. C. Pogue. Review
Am Heritage 15:110-11 D '63. B. Catton
Nat R 16:33-4 Ja 14 '64. T. A. Lane
New Repub 149:26-7 N 2 '63. C. B. Marshall
Newsweek il por 62:118 O 14 '63
Reporter 29:60+ N 21 '63. R. P. Knapp, jr
Sat R por 46:32 O 19 '63. W. Millis
Time il pors 82:123 D 6 '63
Making of a general; excerpts from George C. Marshall: education of a general. F. C. Pogue. il pors Look 27:45-58 S 24 '63
Toward a new dimension in the Atlantic partnership; address, October 27, 1963. D. Rusk. Dept State Bul 49:726-31 N 11 '63

MARSHALL, George Catlett—*Continued*
Untold stories about Truman and Marshall; excerpts from Journals of David E. Lilienthal. D. E. Lilienthal. por U S News 57:22 N 9 '64
MARSHALL, Jack
Convalescence in Tarrasa; poem. Poetry 102: 236-7 Jl '63
For an absence; poem. Harper 228:86 Mr '64
Hitchhiker; poem. New Yorker 39:52 O 26 '63
Passage; poem. Nation 198:57 Ja 13 '64
Song of Balaam's donkey. Harper 227:70 S '63
MARSHALL, John
This honorable Court; ed. by J. A. Garraty. il Am Heritage 14:4-9+ Je '63
MARSHALL, Joseph
Hybrid bridge power supplies. Electr World 69:82-3 Je '63
Thrust, dust and friction. Hi Fi 14:49-52+ Ja '64
Turntables for stereo. Hi Fi 13:52-4+ Mr '63
MARSHALL, Lenore
What's missing in the novel. Sat R 46:15-16 F 9 '63
MARSHALL, Rachelle. See Loftis, A. jt. auth.
MARSHALL, Ray
Ethnic and economic minorities: unions' future or unrecruitable? bibliog f Ann Am Acad 350:63-73 N '63
MARSHALL, Richard H. Jr
New dimension in scientific atheism. Cath World 199:238-44 Jl '64
—See Maloney, G. A. jt. auth.
MARSHALL, Richard W. See Brodie, D. A. jt. auth.
MARSHALL, Roy K.
University of Nevada's atmospherium-planetarium. Sky & Tel 26:318-21 D '63
MARSHALL, S. L. A.
McNamara's latest reform. New Repub 152: 13-15 Ja 23 '65
Samuel Eliot Morison: admiral and historian. Atlan 212:87-90 N '63
Speaking out. por Sat Eve Post 237:6+ S 5 '64
MARSHALL scholars. See Scholarships and fellowships
MARSHALL space flight center. See United States—National aeronautics and space administration—Marshall space flight center
MARSHALS (court officials) See United States marshals
MARSHALS, Court. See United States marshals
MARSHES
Great swamp fights for survival; Morris County, N.J. C. Peet. il Am For 69:24-6+ Mr '63; Same abr. with title They love their swamp. Sci Digest 54:83-6 Ag '63
Wildlife headquarters; New York state's small-marsh program. A. MacBain. il Field & S 67:112+ F '63
See also
Everglades
MARSHES, Salt. See Salt marshes
MARSICANO, Merle
Merle Marsicano and dance company at 92nd street Y. J. Maskey. Dance Mag 37:10 Jl '63
MARSTON, Marjorie
First grade and first worries. PTA Mag 57: 14-16 bibliog(p34) Ap '63
MARSUPIALS
Cerebral cortex: a sensorimotor amalgam in the marsupialia. R. A. Lende. il Science 141: 730-2 Ag 23 '63
See also
Opossums
MARTEENA, Constance Hill
Whetting the reading appetite. Wilson Lib Bul 37:579 Mr '63
MARTEL, Charles W.
Noiseless remote switching. Electr World 71: 60 Mr '64
Remote volume control. Electr World 72:62 Jl '64
MARTELL, Charles B.
Martell, Karaberis share management responsibility in separate offices. il por Miss & Roc 15:35-7 S 21 '64
MARTELL, E. A.
Iodine-131 fallout from underground tests. bibliog Science 143:126-9 Ja 10 '64
MARTELLI, Giuseppe Enrico Gilberto
Jolly nice chap. Time 81:27 My 10 '63
MARTELLI, Juan Carlos
Seven Argentine poets. Américas 16:19-21 O '64
MARTÉN, Alberto
He helps workers become capitalists. D. S. Stroetzel. por Read Digest 84:181-5 F '64
MARTEN, George
When the police welcome false alarms. PTA Mag 57:30-1 My '63
MARTENHOFF, Jim
Beware of copycat boats! Pop Sci 184:110-11+ Ja '64
Consolan classroom. Motor B 113:24-5+ Je '64
Florida skippers weather the storm. Motor B 114:98 N '64
Florida's new boating laws. Motor B 112: 113-14 Ag '63
Kind of race Sam would have liked. Motor B 113:138+ Ap '64
Miami's wet, windy stadium. Motor B 113: 106+ Je '64
Racing to Nassau in the GX. por Motor B 112:49-50+ Jl '63
RDF: a navigator's best friend. Motor B 112:48-51+ N '63
Salt in our talk. Motor B 113:19+ F '64
Six common boating problems. Pop Sci 184: 165-6+ Ap '64
Smart stick. Motor B 113:40-1+ Ap '64
Southward ho! Motor B 112:87 O; 79+ D '63; 113:125-6 F; 170+ Mr '64
Speedboat king: Gar Wood. Motor B 114:62+ Jl '64
Thousand miles of islands. il Motor B 112:40-3 D '63
Win or sink! Motor B 113:26+ Je '64
MARTENS, Anne Coulter
American way; drama. Plays 23:13-24 F '64
Cue for Cleopatra; drama. Plays 23:1-15 O '63
Fitness is the fashion; drama. Plays 23:1-12 Ap '64
Granny from Killarney; drama. Plays 23:1-14 Mr '64
Nor long remember; drama. Plays 22:15-28, 60 My '63
Open house; drama. Plays 24:17-28 O '64
Rosemary for remembrance; drama. Plays 23:27-36 Ap '64
Star of Bethlehem; drama. Plays 24:1-4 D '64
Turnabout in time; drama. Plays 23:1-14 Ja '64
MARTENS
Marten and I. F. A. Blackburn. il Nat Parks Mag 38:11-14 Ap '64
MARTHA'S VINEYARD
Island joins the march. P. S. McGhee. il Nation 198:51-2 Ja 13 '64
Place a famous photographer loves; with photographs by Alfred Eisenstaedt. Life 55:42-52A Ag 23 '63
Trade winds; Vineyard's book-and-author colony. J. G. Fuller. Sat R 46:14 Ag 24 '63
MARTÍ, José
Martí in Mexico; days of Hidalgo lyceum. G. de Zéndegui. il por Américas 15:12-16 Je '63
Two trailblazers of modernism. R. M. Martínez. por Américas 16:17-19 D '64
MARTÍ-IBÁÑEZ, Félix
Doctor looks at death. Read Digest 84:145-6+ Mr '64
MARTIAL (Marcus Valerius Martialis)
Any author to any friend; poem, tr. by D. Fitts. Atlan 213:90 My '64
To Ligurinus, relentlessly a poet; poem tr. by D. Fitts. Atlan 214:44 Jl '64
MARTIN, pseud.
Christmas carousel: a tree phantasy; poem. America 109:797 D 21 '63
Flight of the harbingers; poem. Commonweal 81:481 Ja 8 '65
Lute (in memory of an era) poem. America 111:44 Jl 11 '64
Magic wand; poem. America 110:439 Mr 28 '64
Tidewater; poem. America 112:43 Ja 9 '65
Whisper me past; poem. America 111:217 Ag 29 '64
MARTIN, Alexander Reid
Camping as related to leisure. Recreation 56: 112 Mr '63
MARTIN, Allie Beth
Triple for Tulsa. Library J 89:4740-2 D 1 '64
MARTIN, Betsy
Ballet for bowlers! il por Sr Schol 82:20 F 27 '63
MARTIN, Clyde
Obituary
Am For por 69:35 Mr '63
MARTIN, David
In the square a crowd kneels. Life 54:28 Je 14 '63
Legless Frank Ellis can walk, run, climb and swim; he fights for a chance to fly. Life 55:55-6+ O 25 '63
Life TV review. Life 57:21+ S 18 '64
MARTIN, Dean
Dino goes dramatic. S. Gordon. il pors Look 27:89-92 Ap 9 '63
MARTIN, Dexter
Out, out . . . ! Sat R 47:59 Ap 18 '64
MARTIN, Edmund Fible
Bessie gets a new boss. il por Bsns W p82 F 8 '64
Businessmen in the news. por Fortune 69:43 Mr '64

MARTIN, Edwin M.
Communist subversion in the western hemisphere; statement, February 18, 1963. Dept State Bul 48:347-56, 404-12 Mr 11-18 '63
Cuba, Latin America, and communism; address, September 20, 1963. Dept State Bul 49:574-82 O 14 '63
Economic revolution in Mexico; address, December 6, 1963. Dept State Bul 49:959-63 D 23 '63
Excerpt from address, December 4, 1962. Cong Digest 42:82+ Mr '63
Interdependence and the principles of self-determination and nonintervention; address, April 16, 1963. Dept State Bul 48:710-15 My 6 '63
Restless Latins offer reds more openings. por Nations Bsns 51:64-6 D '63
Trends in Latin American economic development; statement, May 8, 1963. Dept State Bul 48:918-23 Je 10 '63
U.S. outlines policy toward Cuban refugees; statement, May 22, 1963. Dept State Bul 48:983-90 Je 24 '63
U.S. policy regarding military governments in Latin America; statement, October 6, 1963. Dept State Bul 49:698-700 N 4 '63
United States ratifies Chamizal convention; statement, December 12, 1963. Dept State Bul 50:50-1 Ja 13 '64

MARTIN, Ernest
Broadway's hottest producers. il por Bsns W p90-1 F 2 '63

MARTIN, F. T. See Woodwell, G. M. jt. auth.

MARTIN, Frank
On records; Le vin herbé. C. J. Luten. Opera N 27:35 F 23 '63

MARTIN, Frank R.
They come a-running. Outdoor Life 133:32-3+ Ja '64

MARTIN, George
Lulu arrives. Opera N 28:8-12 S 28 '63
Opera glossary. Opera N 28:32-3 Ja 11; 30-1 Ja 18 '64
Santa Fe at seven. Opera N 28:28-31 Ap 11 '64

MARTIN, George H. O.
Teaching airline pilots their ABCs. il pors Ebony 19:33-4+ Jl '64

MARTIN, Glenn L.
History lesson. W. J. Coughlin. Miss & Roc 15:46 O 26 '64

MARTIN, Gordon A. jr
Southern fear and Negro voting. Commonweal 80:135-7 Ap 24 '64

MARTIN, Harold
Refresher course on film. Pop Phot 52:60-3+ Je '63
What's finer than fine grain? Pop Phot 52:64-5+ Je '63

MARTIN, Harold H.
Back to the beginning of the tumultuous life of Nikita Khrushchev. Sat Eve Post 237:18-26 N 7 '64
David Sarnoff's vision. Sat Eve Post 236:56+ F 16 '63
George Wallace shakes up the political scene. Sat Eve Post 237:85-9 My 9 '64
Happy's last hurrah. Sat Eve Post 236:32+ Ag 10 '63
Help us fight! cry the angry exiles. Sat Eve Post 236:28-30+ Je 8 '63
Johnson touch. Sat Eve Post 237:21-9 O 31 '64
Mystery quints of Argentina. Sat Eve Post 237:38-43 Ja 25 '64
They are like little bulls. Sat Eve Post 237:68-72 O 3 '64
Trial of Delay Beckwith. Sat Eve Post 237:77-81 Mr 14 '64
Vivid portrait of the famous revivalist; Billy Graham. Sat Eve Post 236:17-23 Ap 13 '63
Why she really goes to market. Sat Eve Post 236:40-3 S 28 '63; Same abr. with title When a woman goes to market. Read Digest 84:115-18 Mr '64
(ed) See Prieto, I. C. de. Other babies who broke the odds
(ed) See Prieto Nava, E. L. Other babies who broke the odds
—and Fairly, Kenneth
Ku Klux Klan: we got nothing to hide. Sat Eve Post 238:26-33 Ja 30 '65
—and Oberdorfer, Don
What made John Glenn run? Sat Eve Post 237:21-5 F 22 '64

MARTIN, Harrison P.
Night vision. Motor B 114:119 Jl '64

MARTIN, James E.
Moon shot technician. il pors Ebony 20:45-6+ D '64

MARTIN, James H.
Piece of the action. Newsweek 63:31-2 Mr 9 '64

MARTIN, Janis
Siebel's flowers; interview, ed. by R. D. Daniels. por Opera N 28:31 Ja 4 '64

MARTIN, Jean
Socialist convention; lambs with a dream. Nation 198:595-7 Je 15 '64

MARTIN, Jerome
Din, the color, the mood of indoor track. il Sports Illus 20:34-9 F 24 '64

MARTIN, Jerry
Does your boat's tail drag? Pop Sci 183:122-3+ Ag '63

MARTIN, John
Ballet folklorico. Sat R 46:55 N 30 '63
Festival season in Denmark. Sat R 47:53-5 Je 27 '64
Ford foundation's ballet grants. Sat R 47:47-8+ Mr 28 '64
Jacob's Pillow revisited. Sat R 46:38+ Jl 27 '63
Martha Graham's London season. Sat R 46:68-9 S 28 '63
Nureyev, plus and minus. Sat R 46:48-9+ My 25 '63
Royal ballet's most uncommon commoner. Sat R 46:55-6+ Ap 27 '63
Water for the village. Atlan 212:144+ D '63

MARTIN, John Bartlow
American revolution; address, June 19, 1963. Vital Speeches 29:649-53 Ag 15 '63

MARTIN, John Stuart
Fishing. Sports Illus 18:50 My 27 '63
He paints with lakes and wooded slopes. Am Heritage 15:14-19+ O '64

MARTIN, Joy Logee
Begonias for winter color. Horticulture 41:280-1 My '63

MARTIN, Laurence W.
Cold war and weapons control. Cur Hist 47:1-5+ Jl '64
Disarmament: an agency in search of a policy. Reporter 29:22-6 Jl 4 '63
Honest brokers in the nuclear muddle. Reporter 30:20-4 Ja 2 '64

MARTIN, Lawrence, and Martin, Sylvia
Barnums of old blighty. Sat R 46:49-50+ Mr 16 '63

MARTIN, Lee
Americana rail cruises. Travel 121:48-9 My '64

MARTIN, Lowell
Library services and construction act: what will it mean? address, July, 1964. ALA Bul 58:689-94 S '64
Lowell Martin's CWC summary; address, July 1963. por ALA Bul 57:734-41 S '63
Patterns of partnership; address, October 1964. Library J 89:4593-6 N 15 '64

MARTIN, M.
At my gates; poem. America 109:487 O 26 '63
My friend; poem. Commonweal 79:170 N 1 '63

MARTIN, Mary
Mary Martin: perpetual motion. V. Kelly. il pors Look 27:66-70 S 10 '63

MARTIN, Mildred C.
Homemaking help in a crisis. Parents Mag 39:52-4+ Jl '64
Teaching your daughter to sew. Parents Mag 40:44-5+ Ja '65

MARTIN, N. M.
So you want new industry. Am City 78:136-8 D '63

MARTIN, Paul
Challenge of under-development; address, September 26, 1964. Vital Speeches 31:30-2 O 15 '64
International developments; address, August 24, 1963. Vital Speeches 29:752-4 O 1 '63
Secretary Martin to Secretary Rusk; notes, January 22, 1964. Dept State Bul 50:201, 205 F 10 '64

MARTIN, Pete
I call on Joe Culligan. Esquire 59:84-6+ Mr '63

MARTIN, R. Bruce
Deuterated water effects on acid ionization constants. bibliog Science 139:1198+ Mr 22 '63

MARTIN, Ralph
Pilot charts, then and now. Motor B 114:42-3+ N '64

MARTIN, Ralph G.
Old soldier looks at the new army. N Y Times Mag p26-7+ S 22 '63
—and Harrity, Richard
GI's: their war in Europe. Look 27:72-6 F 26 '63
—See Harrity, R. jt. auth.

MARTIN, Ray B.
Urban-renewal consultants. Am City 79:124+ Ja '64

MARTIN, Raymond
Wedding night. Esquire 59:87 F '63

MARTIN, Roger
France's no. 2 is trying harder. il por Bsns W p45-6+ Ja 23 '65

MARTIN, Ruth, and Martin, Thomas
Fitting words; interviews, ed. by F. Stevenson. pors Opera N 27:28 Mr 9 '63

MARTIN, Stephen P.
Make your own night-light exposure calculator. Pop Phot 55:162-3+ D '64

MARTIN, Sue
Night the world fell down; ed. by A. Burgess. por Read Digest 83:64-9 Ag '63

MARTIN, Sylvia. See Martin, L. jt. auth.

MARTIN, T. W. and Rummel, R. E.
Mass spectral studies of surface catalysis: the production of free radicals at 40°C. bibliog Science 143:797-9 F 21 '64

MARTIN, Thomas
Country I love. Sat Eve Post 237:28-31 O 24 '64
—and O'Bryan, Patrick
Get Percy Foreman. Sat Eve Post 237:40+ N 14 '64
—See Martin, R. jt. auth.

MARTIN, William McChesney, 1906-
Next year, a slowdown; economy: jolts on two fronts; interview, ed. by H. Rowen. por Newsweek 64:93 O 5 '64

about

Easier credit? dispute is on; quality of bank credit. U S News 55:127-9 O 7 '63
Economic education of John F. Kennedy. M. J. Rossant. Reporter 28:22-5 F 14 '63; Discussion. 28:10+ Mr 14 '63
Fed chief supports a tax cut. por Bsns W p26 D 14 '63
Fed remodels itself; with editorial comment. il por Bsns W p64-5+, 180 My 16 '64
Fourth term on the FRB for Martin. por U S News 54:19 F 18 '63
Is inflation on the way? a look ahead. il por U S News 55:25-8 D 23 '63
Now it's the money managers who are under fire. il por U S News 54:94-5 Ap 1 '63
Steady course at the Fed. Bsns W p 148 F 16 '63
Tighter money ahead? il U S News 54:102-3 F 25 '63
U.S. dollar; keeping up confidence. por Newsweek 63:79 Mr 16 '64
View from the street. il por Time 82:86 N 22 '63

MARTIN company. See Martin-Marietta corporation

MARTIN-Marietta corporation
Martin cuts R&D costs through standardization. W. Beller. il Miss & Roc 13:25+ S 23 '63
Martin laser highlights MIL-E-CON. C. D. LaFond. Miss & Roc 13:18 S 16 '63
Martin-Orlando begins operation of unique armament research facility. il Miss & Roc 15:32-4 D 21 '64
Millions under Martin Marietta's mattress. C. J. V. Murphy. il Fortune 68:134-41+ N '63; 69:76+ F '64
New face in computers; computer control systems. il Bsns W p32 Ja 25 '64
Taking the sting out of de-hiring; Martin Marietta hired a consultant to help place and relocate key men. Bsns W p78 Ja 2 '65
Titan III contract highly advanced. J. Trainor. Miss & Roc 14:13 My 4 '64

MARTIN memorial library, York, Pa.
Service to students at York now reported satisfactory. Library J 88:1964 My 15 '63
Student problem resolved at York, Pa. library. Library J 88:976 Mr 1 '63
Student problem strikes. E. Moon. Library J 88:736-8 F 15 '63

MARTINDALE, Cyril Charlie
C. C. Martindale, S.J. 1879-1963. I. Evans. America 108:466-7 Ap 6 '63

MARTINEAU, Julie
Assateague Island: our next national seashore? Am For 69:16-19+ Ag '63
Let's go skiing. Am For 69:36-9+ F '63
Snow is what you make of it. Am For 70:38-41 F '64
Tinkertoy, a wonderful wooden Christmas toy. Am For 70:30-1+ D '64

MARTINELLI, Elsa
Accommodation, Italian style. G. Talese. il pors Esquire 59:88-93+ F '63

MARTINELLI, Giovanni
Singing Verdi; address. Mus Am 83:14-15+ Mr '63

about

Another for Martinelli's golden anniversary. P. L. Miller. Am Rec G 30:199 N '63
Il Divo. L. Lucioni. il pors Opera N 28:23-5 O 19 '63
Evviva il Leon di Venezia! Giovanni Martinelli; golden anniversary. J. Maclain. por Am Rec G 30:182-3+ N '63
Golden gala; photographs. Opera N 28:14-16 Ja 4 '64
Musical events; celebration at Metropolitan opera house of fiftieth anniversary of New York début. W. Sargeant. New Yorker 39:200 N 30 '63

MARTINEZ, Enrique
Summer snow. D. Hering. il pors Dance Mag 37:48-9+ Mr '63

MARTÍNEZ, Rosa M.
Two trailblazers of modernism. Américas 16:17-19 D '64

MARTINEZ-SOTOMAYOR, Carlos
Young power in diplomacy. por Vogue 143:91 Ap 15 '64

MARTINI, Sister Galen
One of the crowd; poem. America 108:883 Je 22 '63

MARTINIQUE
Pick a pair of perfect islands. E. Bedell. il Sat R 47:74-5+ O 10 '64
Vive Papa Charles; de Gaulle visit. Newsweek 63:49 Ap 6 '64

MARTINIS, Gareth
Crash echoes across the Nation. il pors Life 55:22-7 Jl 19 '63
Judge's son. il por Time 82:17-18 Ag 9 '63
My son, the defendant. il Newsweek 62:26-7 Jl 15 '63
Strange justice for the judge's son. M. Lewis and M. Lewis. il pors Sat Eve Post 237:75-9 Ja 4 '64

MARTINO, Rocco L.
Olin's Martino. P. Korenvaes. por Duns R 82:pt2 106 S '63

MARTINON, Jean
Discipline plus. il por Time 84:80 O 16 '64
Jean Martinon, new maestro in Chicago. R. Dettmer. por Mus Am 83:50-2 N '63
Musical events; two concerts in Carnegie Hall performed by Chicago symphony orchestra. W. Sargeant. New Yorker 40:191-2 Ap 25 '64

MARTINS
Purple martin, harbinger of spring. B. G. Sutterfield. il Audubon Mag 65:178-9 My '63

MARTIN'S lie; opera. See Menotti, G. C.

MARTON, Velimir
Capitalistic comrade. por Time 83:94 Ap 3 '64

MARTY, Martin Emil
Achievement of Kenneth Scott Latourette. Christian Cent 80:336-7 Mr 13 '63
Church architecture: the perils of success. Christian Cent 80:390-1 Mr 27 '63
Church library choice. Christian Cent 80:1109-10, 1137, 1172 S 11-25 '63
Conversation reopened. Christian Cent 81:1014-16 Ag 12 '64
Council politics at dead end. Christian Cent 81:1519-20 D 9 '64
Future of the denominations in an ecumenical era; excerpt from What's ahead for the churches. Cath World 200:34-41 O '64
Learning about the other faiths. Commentary 35:455-60 My '63
Movies. Christian Cent 81:1599-600 D 23 '64
Protestantism-in-pluralism. Commonweal 78:416-18 Jl 12 '63
Report on special projects. Christian Cent 80:462 Ap 10 '63
Temperature of Catholic-Protestant tensions. Cath World 197:343-50 S '63
We have a council. Christian Cent 81:1489-90 D 2 '64

about

Marty to teach, edit and write. Christian Cent 80:822 Je 26 '63
Post post-Christianity. por Newsweek 64:90-1 D 7 '64
Prolific prophet. por Time 81:48 Je 14 '63

MARTYRS
Pope confers sainthood on twenty-two African martyrs. E. B. Thompson. il Ebony 20:23-6+ Ja '65
Witnesses; the forty martyrs. America 108:324 Mr 9 '63

MARUYAMA, Magoroh
Cybernetics. bibliog NEA J 53:51-4 D '64

MARVIN, Ursula B. and Klein, Cornelis, jr
Meteoritic zircon. bibliog Science 146:919-20 N 13 '64

MARWARIS. See East Indians

MARWICK, Charles
Is any anesthetic safe? Sci Digest 54:77-81 Ag '63

MARX, Groucho
Trade winds. J. G. Fuller. il por Sat R 47:8 F 8 '64

MARX, Harpo
Harpo. por Life 57:45 O 9 '64
Quiet one. por Newsweek 64:81 O 12 '64
MARX, Ivan L.
Bear who came to dinner. il Outdoor Life 132: 52-3+ S '63
Bears in my bed. por Outdoor Life 134:48-9+ D '64
It's done with mirrors. Outdoor Life 133:48-9+ My '64
MARX, Karl
New left Marxism. G. Lichtheim. Commentary 35:239-43 Mr '63
Splintered legacy of Karl Marx. il Newsweek 63:47-8+ Ap 27 '64
MARX, Leonard
But when they voted. por Newsweek 62:104 O 14 '63
MARX, Olga
What is your name? story. Seventeen 23:214-15 Ag '64
MARX, Robert
Yes, we keep our boat in a closet. Pop Sci 184:163-6 My '64
MARX, Wesley
Dial 2122428180. Nation 197:344-6 N 23 '63
Heavenly supermarket. Nation 198:372-3 Ap 13 '64
Pentagon and campus; the sullen marriage. Nation 198:499-501 My 18 '64
Your right to a car bargain. Nation 196:195-7 Mr 9 '63
MARXHAUSEN, Rheinhold
Box full of boxes. Sch Arts 62:32 F '63
MARXISM. See Communism
MARY, Virgin
Mary and ecumenism. America 110:477 Ap 4 '64
Mary and salvation. America 110:698 My 23 '64
Our lady of wisdom. America 108:629 My 4 '63
Virgin birth, by T. Boslooper. Review
Christian Cent 80:493-4 Ap 17 '63. D. G. Bloesch
Art
Letter from Paris; exhibition at Right bank Galerie Creuze, devoted exclusively to the Virgin. Genêt. New Yorker 40:121-3 Je 13 '64
Theology
Definition of Mary. il Newsweek 62:68 N 11 '63
End of the deadlock. G. Baum. Commonweal 79:251-3 N 22 '63
Mary and ecumenism. America 108:427 Mr 30 '63
Mary and the church. America 111:5 Jl 4 '64
Not to herself, but to God. il Time 84:65-6 S 25 '64
Our true mother. America 111:60 Jl 18 '64
Place of Mary. Commonweal 79:212-13; 81: 29-30 N 15 '63, O 2 '64
St Mary and Protestants. America 110:245 F 22 '64
Starting-point of Mariology; excerpt from Theology for today. C. Davis. Cath World 197:15-20 Ap '63
What Mary means to Protestants. il Time 84: 58 S 11 '64
Word (cont) V. P. McCorry. America 108: 125-6; 111:241 Ja 19 '63, S 5 '64
MARY, Virgin, in art. See Mary, Virgin—Art
MARY, queen of Scots
Great confrontations: Mary, queen of Scots and John Knox. H. R. Trevor-Roper. il por Horizon 5:28-32 Jl '63
Last and loveliest queen of the Scots. D. C. Peattie. por Read Digest 82:252-4+ F '63
MARY Anastasia Callow, Sister. See Callow, M. A.
MARY Anon, Sister
Divided, we fall. America 110:628-30 My 9 '64
MARY Anthony, Mother
Perspective; poem. Commonweal 80:257 My 22 '64
MARY Aquin, Sister
Teilhard de Chardin; poem. Commonweal 78: 353 Je 21 '63
MARY Catherine, Sister
Manner is contemporary. America 109:214-15 Ag 31 '63
MARY Cecily, Sister
For Jeremias in Advent; poem. America 109: 794 D 21 '63
MARY Dominic, Sister
Of grace and nature. America 108:763 My 25 '63
MARY Emilie, Sister
Perpetual profession; poem. America 108:223 F 16 '63
MARY Emmanuel, Sister
Lumen Christi; poem. America 109:17 Jl 6 '63
Talisman for a teacher; poem. Commonweal 79:346 D 13 '63
MARY Faith, Sister
Restless in grammar school; poem. Commonweal 80:140 Ap 24 '64
MARY Ferdinand, Sister
How to help your hospital. Todays Health 42:74-6 F '64
MARY Gregory Lacey, Mother. See Lacey, M. G.
MARY Honora, Sister
Incident; poem. America 109:796 D 21 '63
MARY Janet, Sister
Time; poem. Commonweal 80:92 Ap 10 '64
MARY Jeremy, Sister
Sleep of Boaz; poem. Commonweal 81:488 Ja 8 '65
MARY Jonathan, Sister
Pantoum for the sloganeer. Commonweal 81: 421 D 18 '64
MARY Josetta, Sister
When teaching the language arts. NEA J 52: 43-4 D '63
MARY Laurus, Sister
Story & color on film. Sch Arts 63:17-18 N '63
MARY Louis, Sister
Remember the piggy-back squirrel. NEA J 52:32 O '63
MARY Luman, Sister. See Luman, M.
MARY Philip, Sister
Appliqué for impatient fingers. Sch Arts 62: 10 Ap '63
MARY Pius, Sister
Vanishing nun. J. Star. il pors Look 27:41-5 O 22 '63
MARY Poppins (literary character) See Characters in literature
MARY St Virginia, Sister
Jews; poem. Commonweal 79:662 F 28 '64
Question; poem. Commonweal 80:18 Mr 27 '64
MARY Simplicia, Sister
Hundredfold; poem. Commonweal 80:170 My 1 '64
Lord of the temple; poem. Commonweal 80: 397 Je 19 '64
Moment before silence; poem. Commonweal 81:449 D 25 '64
MARY Sophia, Sister
Genesis at Bethlehem; poem. America 109:796 D 21 '63
Purgatorio: Canto XVIII. America 109:487 O 26 '63
MARY Sylvia, Sister
Learning about Shakespeare in his hometown. Sr Schol 84:8T-9T F 28 '64
MARY Thérèse, Sister
Each spring the arbutus; poem. Commonweal 79:15 S 27 '63
Elegy for the wild plum. Sat R 48:32 Ja 2 '65
Firebird; poem. America 108:335 Mr 9 '63
Hunters' mass; poem. America 111:691 N 28 '64
Meeting in a snowstorm; poem. Commonweal 79:43 O 4 '63
Nun writers at Red Rocks; poem. America 108:372 Mr 16 '63
Pasqueflower; poem. America 108:538 Ap 20 '63
Salutation; poem. America 111:255 S 12 '64
Speak to me, sparrow; poem. Sat R 47:26 Jl 25 '64
Where the dogwood weeps (in memory of John Fitzgerald Kennedy) poem. America 111:663 N 21 '64
MARY Ann, I love you; story. See Grove, W.
MARY Pride; story. See Kaufman, S.
MARY; story. See Brown, M. F.
MARYAN
Bad humor men. il por Newsweek 61:89 Ap 29 '63
MARYKNOLL sisters. See Sisterhoods
MARYLAND
See also
Architecture, Domestic—Maryland
Booksellers and bookselling—Maryland
Colleges and universities—Maryland
Education—Maryland
Festivals—Maryland
Fishing—Maryland
Hunting—Maryland
Libraries—Maryland
Prisons—Maryland
Smith Island
Sugar Loaf Mountain
Boundaries
See also
Mason and Dixon's line

MARYLAND—*Continued*
Description and travel
Chesapeake country. N. T. Kenney. il Nat Geog Mag 126:370-411 S '64
Historic houses, etc.
History in houses; Hampton in Baltimore Country, Maryland. R. L. Raley. il Antiques 84:434-8 O '63
Maryland house & garden pilgrimage. S. R. Sherwood. il Hobbies 69:91-2 My '64
Maryland splendor. R. Pratt. il Ladies Home J 81:56-9 My '64
Marriage law
See Marriage law—United States
Politics and government
Many-armed bandit; bill to ban slot machines. Newsweek 61:27 Ap 1 '63
Plan for political action; address. R. S. Ake. il Wilson Lib Bul 39:316-19 O '64
Race problems
State of Maryland. M. Kempton. New Repub 150:6-8 My 23 '64
Religious institutions and affairs
News of the Christian world (cont) Christian Cent 80:250, 286 F 20-27 '63
MARYLAND academy of sciences, Baltimore
Graphic time table of the heavens, 1964-1965. Sky & Tel 27:32-5; 29:33-5 Ja '64, Ja '65
MARYLAND cup corporation
At Maryland cup, it's nepotism all the way. il Bsns W p 102-3 S 7 '63
MARYLAND. University, College Park
Clarification at College Park; low moral standards among fraternity members. V. E. Lowder. Christian Cent 81:500-2 Ap 15 '64
MARYVILLE, Tenn.
This landfill has real togetherness. H. E. Best. il Am City 78:27 F '63
MARZ, Roger H.
Republican party has no future. New Repub 151:10-11 D 19 '64
MARZ, Roy
Count and the rose; Frameless; poems. Poetry 102:374-5 S '63
MARZOTTO family
Miracolo Marzotto. por Time 81:94 Mr 8 '63
MASADA (fortress) Israel
Essenes or zealots? il Newsweek 63:72 F 10 '64
Masada dig. D. Gavron. Commentary 38:52-6 O '64
MASAI (native race) See Kenya—Native races
MASCAGNI, Pietro
Cavalleria rusticana. Criticism
Opera N il 28:17-20 Ap 11 '64
Mascagni vs. America. P. P. Kies. por Opera N 28:24-6 Ap 11 '64
On records; Cavalleria. Opera N 28:32 Ap 11 '64
On records; Cavalleria rusticana. Opera N 28:35 F 15 '64
Victoria de los Angeles on three new recordings from Angel: Barber of Seville, Cavalleria Rusticana, and Mélodies de France. il Am Rec G 30:184-7 N '63
MASCARENHAS, Joseph P. See Greene, A. F. jt. auth.
MASCOTS
Old Abe the battle eagle; Wisconsin outfit's mascot during Civil war. B. Catton. il Am Heritage 14:32-3+ O '63
Old Abe, Wisconsin's Civil war eagle, was there. F. Hallam. il Audubon Mag 65:222-5 Jl '63
MASE, Tess
Brasília builds a university. Américas 15:9-11 Je '63
MASEFIELD, John
On the finish of the sailing ship race Lisbon to Manhattan 1964; poem. pors Life 57:66 Jl 24 '64
Poets old and young. C. Kizer. Poetry 102:393-4 S '63
MASERS
Maser man; share of 1964 Nobel prize in physics for Prof. C. H. Townes of Columbia university. il Newsweek 64:89 N 9 '64
Masers and lasers; electronic miracles of the future. il Sci Digest 56:36-8 Ag '64
Split award; Nobel prize in physics. Time 84:41 N 6 '64
MASETTO, Antonio Dal
Romeo and Juliet; story. Américas 17:32-5 Ja '65
MASIN, Herman L.
Sports. See issues of Senior scholastic
MASKEY, Jacqueline
Gift to a grateful New York city. Dance Mag 37:30-1 O '63
MASKS (for the face)
Aluminum maskmaking. P. Danielson. il Design 65:195 My '64
Bad-weather masks to bewitch with. il Life 55:55-6+ N 22 '63
Halloween masks you can make. R. A. Spaith. il Farm J 88:99 O '64
Japanese masks. il Design 66:22-4 N '64
Magic of masks. E. King. il Dance Mag 37:34-7 Ag '63
Masks. M. Tressler. il Sch Arts 63:14-15 O '63
Masks & Halloween. J. W. Cataldo. il Sch Arts 63:2 O '63
Quoth the raven: trick or treat. il Sunset 133:140+ O '64
MASKS (sculpture)
Day Jefferson got plastered. D. B. Webster, jr. il Am Heritage 14:24-7 Je '63
Masks from mesh. C. Browning. il Sch Arts 63:22 Mr '64
MASLAND, Frank E. jr
Exploring the Colorado: Lee's Ferry to Lake Mead. il Nat Parks Mag 38:4-7+ My '64
MASLAND, Richard L.
Tracking down the enemies of vision. Todays Health 41:52-7 N '63
MASLOW, Sophie
Lady, you bring romance. H. Smith. il Dance Mag 38:62-3 Ap '64
Sophie Maslow dance company, 92nd street Y. M. Marks il(p33) Dance Mag 38:65 Je '64
Sophie Maslow dance company; Paul Draper at Delacorte theater. D. Hering. Dance Mag 37:14 Ag '63
MASLOW, Will
Breaking the rural strangle hold. Nation 196:282-5 Ap 6 '63
Showdown on reapportionment. Nation 197:314-16 N 16 '63
MASON, A. Hughlett, and Swindler, W. F.
Mason & Dixon: their line and its legend. Am Heritage 15:22-9+ F '64
MASON, Alpheus Thomas
Supreme court under fire again. Reporter 31:45-8 S 24 '64
MASON, Bill
(ed) See Flatow, H. Tough guy with a soft heart
MASON, Brian
Organic matter from space; with biographical sketch. Sci Am 208:32, 43-9 bibliog(p 188) Mr '63
—and others
Ferric tourmaline from Mexico. bibliog Science 144:71-3 Ap 3 '64
MASON, Charles
Mason & Dixon: their line and its legend. A. H. Mason and W. F. Swindler. il Am Heritage 15:22-9+ F '64
MASON, Edward S.
Planning of development; with biographica sketch. Sci Am 209:28, 235-6+ bibliog(p310 S '63
MASON, Edwin A.
Garden is a place for birds. Horticulture 42:18-19+ My '64
MASON, Frank
Saint Anthony paintings of Frank Mason. C. Riley. il por Am Artist 28:62-7+ Je '64
MASON, Howard F. R. jr, and Foster, E. R.
Swedish view of American forestry. Am For 70:30-1+ Mr '64
—See Foster, E. R. jt. auth.
MASON, Jackie
Masonic order. Newsweek 62:56 D 30 '63
MASON, Janet
People who pity me? that's their problem. Life 56:88 Je 19 '64
MASON, Joseph G.
Find the pivot man. Nations Bsns 52:80-2+ D '64
Let others solve your problems. Nations Bsns 51:94-6 Je '63
Make yourself a better manager. Nations Bsns 52:80-2 F '64
New way to improve your decisions. Nations Bsns 52:58-60+ Je '64
What it takes to take charge. Nations Bsns 51:76-8+ D '63
MASON, Ken
How to handle any trailer. Outdoor Life 133:66-8+ Je '64
MASON, Lowell B.
Government and business; address, October 30, 1963. Vital Speeches 30:134-8 D 15 '63
MASON, Mason Jordon
Seven poets and a playwright. D. Stuart. Poetry 104:258 Jl '64
MASON, Oda
Notes for a gazetteer. P. Hamburger. New Yorker 39:157-61 N 16 '63

MASON, Pamela
Being catty to columnists. por Time 84:68 Jl 17 '64

MASON, Philip
New world threats: poverty and race. Nation 198:68-71 Ja 20 '64
South Africa and the world: some maxims and axioms. For Affairs 43:150-64 O '64

MASON, Portland
Beauty, going on fifteen. por McCalls 91: 108-9 D '63

MASON and Dixon's line
Mason & Dixon: their line and its legend. A. H. Mason and W. F. Swindler. il Am Heritage 15:22-9+ F '64

MASONIC orders. See Freemasonry

MASONRY
Preventing cracks in masonry walls. D. Kaminetzky. il Arch Rec 136:210-14 N '64

MASOUREDIS, S. P. and others
Inhibition of specific binding of antibody to the Rh_0(D) factor red cells in antibody excess. bibliog Science 145:1197-9 S 11 '64

MASS, James W. See Sudak, H. S. jt. auth.

MASS
Better vernacular needed; poverty of most English versions of the mass. America 111: 434 O 17 '64
Concelebration in St Peter's. America 111: 339 S 26 '64
English mass: needs work; first Roman Catholic mass in the English version approved by the bishops of the U.S. il Time 84:74 S 4 '64
Evening funeral masses. America 108:188 F 9 '63
First full mass in English; in Australia. Christian Cent 81:1101 S 9 '64
It couldn't be done! lay participation in the public worship of the church. America 109:204 Ag 31 '63
Liturgy and freedom. C. J. McNaspy. America 111:251 S 12 '64
Mass. il Look 27:73-8 Ap 23 '63
Mass confusion; mass in English in the US. il Newsweek 64:38 D 28 '64
Mass in Italian. America 112:98 Ja 23 '65
Mass of the future. H. A. Reinhold. Commonweal 80:565-8 Ag 21 '64
Modernizing the mass. il Time 82:80 D 13 '63
New way of worship. il Time 84:66+ N 27 '64
Now, English mass for U.S. Catholics; 25th annual liturgical week, St Louis. il U S News 57:10 S 7 '64
On sharing the mass. Commonweal 78:157 My 3 '63; Reply. J. K. Ross-Duggan. 78:306 Je 7 '63
Only a beginning; mass celebrated in the English language for the first time in the United States. il Newsweek 64:54+ S 7 '64
Praying it in English; liturgical constitution of the 2d Vatican council. il Time 83:66 My 29 '64
Renewing the mass. America 109:722 D 7 '63
Revolution in worship. il Time 82:44 Ag 30 '63
Same again please: a layman's hopes of the Vatican council. E. Waugh; discussion. Nat R 13:521; 14:37 D 31 '62-Ja 15 '63; Commonweal 77:487-9 F 1 '63
Should you buy a new missal? J. F. Dearden. America 111:180-1 Ag 22 '64
Suggestion for Mr Waugh. J. Cogley. Commonweal 81:120-2 O 23 '64; Discussion. 81: 352-4 D 4 '64
Thanksgiving day mass. America 111:60 Jl 18 '64
Word (cont) V. P. McCorry. America 109: 124-5, 644-5 Ag 3, N 16 '63
See also
Liturgical language
Vatican council, 2d

MASS (music)
English masses and some records. C. J. McNaspy. America 112:176-7 Ja 30 '65
Gloria in excelsis Deo: the Haydn Masses; with discography. H. C. R. Landon. il Hi Fi 14:56-9+ D '64
Music; first performance of Missa divina by C. A. Peloquin. C. J. McNaspy. America 108:476-8 Ap 6 '63
Music in a time of change. C. J. McNaspy. America 110:803-4, 872-3 Je 6, 27 '64
Music to my ears; Slavonic mass of L. Janaček. I. Kolodin. Sat R 46:46 F 9 '63
See also
Phonograph records—Mass

MASS communication. See Communication (speech, writing, etc)

MASS of oyster-workers; story. See Clark, E.

MASS psychology. See Crowds

MASS spectrometry
Free radicals and unstable molecules. S. N. Foner. bibliog il Science 143:441-50 Ja 31 '64
Mass spectral studies of surface catalysis: the production of free radicals at 40°C. T. W. Martin and R. E. Rummel. bibliog il Science 143:797-9 F 21 '64
Robot lunar scientist. Sci N L 86:357 D 5 '64
Xenon tetroxide: mass spectrum. J. L. Huston and others. il Science 143:1161-2 Mr 13 '64

MASSACHUSETTS
See also
Annisquam
Architecture, Domestic—Massachusetts
Booksellers and bookselling—Massachusetts
Cape Cod
Crime and criminals—Massachusetts
Education—Massachusetts
Fishing—Massachusetts
Gardens—Massachusetts
Hunting—Massachusetts
Libraries—Massachusetts
Martha's Vineyard
Music festivals—Massachusetts
Nantucket Island

Historic houses, etc.

Bulfinch's houses for Mrs Swan. J. Kirker. il Antiques 86:442-4 O '64

Parks and reserves

Awakening in Massachusetts. J. M. O'Hare il Recreation 56:262-3 Je '63

Politics and government

Brooke of Massachusetts; a Negro governor on Beacon Hill? E. R. F. Sheehan. Harper 228:41-7 Je '64
From dazzling to fizzling. Time 84:27 O 23 '64
Keeping the faith; indictments of Massachusetts officeholders. Newsweek 63:35 My 25 '64
Mess thickens; indictment of F. Furcolo. Newsweek 64:38 O 26 '64
On being a candidate. H. S. Hughes. Commentary 35:123-31 F '63
Still more scandal; crime commission indictments of four Democrats. Newsweek 64: 40 O 19 '64
Teddy vote. Newsweek 61:16 F 4 '63
Up in Massachusetts. J. Phillips; discussion. Commentary 35:257-9 Mr '63

Public works, Department of

Highway robbery in Massachusetts; misuse of Federal aid highway program. K. O. Gilmore. Read Digest 85:83-7 D '64

Religious institutions and affairs

News of the Christian world (cont) Christian Cent 80:656-8, 1561; 82:91-4 My 15, D 11 '63, Ja 20 '65

Social life and customs

Life in Massachusetts. C. W. Morton. Atlan 211:111-12 My '63

MASSACHUSETTS horticultural society
Massachusetts horticultural society garden awards for 1962. il Horticulture 41:210-11 Ap '63
Massachusetts horticultural society honorary awards for 1962. il Horticulture 41:154 Mr '63

MASSACHUSETTS institute of technology, Cambridge
Advanced engineering center set for MIT. Aviation W 78:86 My 6 '63
At MIT, students are the boss. il Bsns W p82+ Ja 23 '65
Computers that feed many mouths; MIT's project MAC. il Bsns W p54-5 F 1 '64
Designing with deference; married students housing at M.I.T. il Arch Rec 133:140-1 Mr '63
Economists on economists; outstanding economics department. il Newsweek 65:74 Ja 11 '65
Executive training by meeting the best; MIT's Sloan program. il Bsns W p46-7 Ap 6 '63
First tower at M.I.T. il Arch Rec 136:135-8 O '64
Foundation grants M.I.T. $5 million for advanced engineering study center. Arch Rec 133:29 Je '63
Freshman research at M.I.T. Sch & Soc 91: 55+ F 9 '63
M.I.T. D. Brelis. il Holiday 33:66-75+ Mr '63
M.I.T: prime contractor contends with problems produced by solving government's problems. J. Walsh. Science 140:164-5+ Ap 12 '63
MIT's new breed of engineers. il Bsns W p54-6+ Ja 18 '64

MASSACHUSETTS institute of technology —*Continued*
Profiles; center of a new world. C. Rand. il New Yorker 40:43-8+ Ap 11; 57-8+ Ap 18; 55-6+ Ap 25 '64
Success story; $98 million in gifts, grants, and pledges. Newsweek 61:89 My 20 '63
That science center called M.I.T. D. Borkoff. il N Y Times Mag p 18-19+ Ag 18 '63
Where the brains are; girls at M.I.T. il Time 82:51 O 18 '63
Why Boston is puzzled by a federal economy move. il U S News 57:84-6 N 23 '64
See also
Mitre corporation
MASSACHUSETTS investors trust
MIT fund: a lot of people are getting pollen. il Newsweek 64:63-6 Jl 27 '64
New man for the club: M.I.T. chairman. Time 85:75 Ja 29 '65
MASSACHUSETTS library association
Massachusetts lns. want, will get more courses in children's reading; role of state Division of library extension. Library J 88: 4830 D 15 '63
MASSACRES
See also
Congo massacre, 1964
MASSAGE
Ice massage. il Time 82:62-3 S 27 '63
MASSAQUOI, Hans J.
Gus Hawkins, fifth Negro congressman. Ebony 18:38-40+ F '63
Investment opportunities in Nigeria. Ebony 19:67-8+ Mr '64
Mystery of Malcolm X. Ebony 19:38-40+ S '64
South Carolina's moment of truth. Ebony 18: 96-8+ My '63
MASSE, Benjamin Louis
Are moonlighters the villains? America 110: 631-2 My 9 '64
Changing of the guard. America 111:511 O 31 '64
Churchmen meet. America 110:16-17 Ja 4 '64
Civil rights act. America 111:6 Jl 4 '64
Ethics on the job. America 110:332 Mr 14 '64
Focus on poverty. America 110:69 Ja 18 '64
ILO and the bishops. America 111:797-9 D 19 '64
Making jobs for the jobless. America 110: 362-4 Mr 21 '64
Mind of the businessman. America 111:296-8 S 19 '64
Phenomenon of professional football. America 109:548 N 9 '63
Pope John's essay on inequality. America 108:368-71 Mr 16 '63
Poverty and parochial schools. America 112: 101 Ja 23 '65
Poverty, U.S.A. America 109:73-4+ Jl 20 '63
This problem of bigness; excerpt from Justice for all. America 111:128-30 Ag 8 '64
Trading with Communists. America 110:570-2 Ap 25 '64
War on poverty. America 110:192-3 F 8 '64
The week that was. America 111:64 Jl 18 '64
Why foreign aid? America 108:637-9 My 4 '63
MASSENA, N.Y.
Largest diatomaceous-earth filters. W. K. Neubauer. il Am City 79:76-8 N '64
MASSENET, Jules
Hérodiade; excerpts. G. L. Mayer. Am Rec G 30:669 Ap '64
Manon. Criticism
New Yorker 39:179 O 26 '63
New Yorker 40:235 N 28 '64
Opera N 28:33 D 21 '63
Opera N il 28:17-20 D 21 '63
Sat R 46:42 N 2 '63
On records; Hérodiade; excerpts. Opera N 28:37 Mr 14 '64
On records; Manon. Opera N 28:34 D 21 '63; 35 Ap 18 '64
On records; Werther excerpts. C. J. Luten. Opera N 27:35 Mr 30 '63
Portrait of Manon. M. de Schauensee. Am Rec G 30:1100-1 Ag '64
Reprieve for Massenet. R. Lawrence. pors Hi Fi 14:47-9+ Mr '64
MASSEVICH, Alla
Erudite shepherdess of home-made moons. B. Lovell. il por Sat R 46:44-6 S 7 '63
MASSEY, A. G.
Boron. Sci Am 210:88-94+ Ja '64
MASSEY-STEWART, John
Behind the curtains, bamboo and iron. il N Y Times Mag p 12+ Je 16 '63
MASSIE, Robert
Chaplain to the New frontier. Sat Eve Post 236:70-2 S 21 '63
Don't tread on Grandmother Peabody. Sat Eve Post 237:74+ My 16 '64
Fight for survival of the supercarrier. Sat Eve Post 236:17-25 N 2 '63
Grace of Kelly. Sat Eve Post 236:18-19 Je 8 '63
Happy town where hearts stay healthy. Sat Eve Post 237:76-7+ O 10 '64
Harlem goes to war against the slumlords. Sat Eve Post 237:71-5 F 29 '64
Red threat in black Africa? Sat Eve Post 237: 80-5 Ap 18 '64
Should the U.S. trade with enemies? Sat Eve Post 237:19-21 F 1 '64
They live on borrowed blood. Sat Eve Post 236:32-4 My 4 '63
—See Liedloff, J; Massie, S. jt. auths.
MASSIE, Suzanne
Lady is a diplomat. Ladies Home J 81:117-21 Je '64
—and Massie, Robert
This is the U.N. at play. Sat Eve Post 236:54-7 Mr 30 '63
MASSINGHAM, Hugh
Labour's new leader. New Repub 148:17 Mr 2 '63
Mr Wilson's predicament. New Repub 151:8-9 O 31 '64
Prime Minister meets the people. New Repub 151:9-11 S 26 '64
MASSON, Georges M. C. and others
Hypertensive vascular disease produced by homologous renin. bibliog Science 145:178-80 Jl 10 '64
MASSON, Thomas H. F.
This do; poem. Christian Cent 81:399 Mr 25 '64
MASTERS, Edgar Lee
Lake boats; poem; excerpt. il Motor B 111:19 Je '63
Spoon River anthology; dramatization. See Aidman, C. Spoon River
MASTERS, John
How to succeed at writing by trying very hard. Harper 226:54-9 Mr '63
Travels in the Cévennes. Holiday 36:88-93+ N '64
MASTERS, Marcia
Figure; poem. Poetry 102:377 S '63
MASTERS, Roger D.
Realignment on the right. Reporter 29:23-6 N 7 '63
MASTERS, incorporated
Same course, new skipper; Jack Haizen as president. Bsns W p 126 Jl 18 '64
MASTERS degrees. See Degrees, Academic
MASTERS golf tournament. See Golf—Tournaments
MASTERS theses. See Dissertations, Academic
MASTITIS
Hidden mastitis costs $100 per cow. G. Lorang. Farm J 89:38 Ja '65
It helps: treat dry cows for mastitis. O. Bay. Farm J 88:32 Jl '64
Trace of mastitis can protect cows. Farm J 87:42 S '63
MASTROIANNI, Marcello
Actor, Italian style. A. Menen. por Holiday 37:95+ Ja '65
Art of anti-acting. R. Bimonte. Reporter 31: 49-50+ O 22 '64
Ciao, Marcello. D. Newman. por Esquire 60:110-11 N '63
Marcello Mastroianni: Latin lover, new style. H. Lawrenson. il pors Look 28:26+ Ag 11 '64
Marcello Mastroianni: reluctant lover. G. Bocca. por McCalls 91:64+ My '64
Socialist Savonarola. por Time 83:95-E5 My 1 '64
What Fellini thinks Mastroianni thinks about women. F. Fellini. por Vogue 142:50-1+ Ag 15 '63
MASTRUDE, Roger C.
Great decisions program. Sr Schol 83:12T D 6 '63
MASTS and rigging
How an ocean racer is rigged. B. Robinson. il Yachting 113:40-1 Je '63
Modern lateen rig. F. R. Kellogg. il Yachting 113:194 My '63
Personalized motor cruiser mast. G. P. Manning. il Motor B 112:50+ O '63
Spars, rigging and hardware. P. H. Rhodes. il Yachting 115:46-7+ Ap '64
Tate House in Stroudwater, Maine. M. P. Smith. il Antiques 84:172-4 Ag '63
Ten sheet leads for small boats. W. H. de-Fontaine. il Yachting 115:46 F '64
See also
Sails
MATA, Ruth
Mata and Hari at 92nd street Y. M. Marks. Dance Mag 38:29-30 F '64
MATADORS. See Bullfighters

MATALON, Samuel
Choirs and cantors. Mus Am 83:23 O '63
For God and for country. Mus Am 84:58 F '64
Stravinsky premiere. Mus Am 84:18 O '64

MATALON, Zack
Off Broadway; performance of Gogol's Diary of a madman. E. Oliver. New Yorker 40:130+ Ap 25 '64

MATARAZZO, Joseph D. and others
Speech durations of astronaut and ground communicator. bibliog Science 143:148-50 Ja 10 '64

MATARAZZO SOBRINHO, Francisco
Architect of peace. R. Squirru. il pors Américas 16:2-4 Ap '64

MATCH books
See also
Advertising mediums—Match books

MATELES, R. I. See Lim, P. G. jt. auth.

MATEOS, Adolfo López. See López Mateos, A.

MATER et magistra. See Encyclicals

MATERIALISM
Can we survive the fun explosion? J. W. Krutch. Sat R 48:14-16 Ja 16 '65
Christian choice in a changing world; spiritual values vs materialist pressures. J. Voorhis. Christian Cent 81:396-9 Mr 25 '64
Not by bread alone. R. Moley. Newsweek 64:88 Ag 17 '64
See also
Mechanism (philosophy)

MATERIALS
Materials on the march. H. E. Klein. il Duns R 81:60-2+ My '63
Quiet revolution in mixed materials. H. E. Klein. il Duns R 84:32-3+ Ag '64
Schriever sees materials revolution. J. Trainor. Miss & Roc 14:17 Je 1 '64
Ten rooms designed to keep themselves clean. P. Doherty and A. Wiglama. il House B 106:136-44 Mr '64
What housekeepers can learn from hotel-keepers. P. Hyde. il House B 106:130-3 Mr '64
You don't have to give up elegance when you give up dirt. J. Ellestad. il House B 106:122-7 Mr '64
See also subhead Materials under various subjects, e.g. Automobiles—Materials

Testing

See Testing

MATERIALS, Strength of. See Strength of materials

MATERIALS centers. See Instructional materials centers

MATERIALS handling
Materials handling, from field to market. il Suc Farm 62:38-41 O; 54-5 N; 28-9 D '64; 63:30-1 Ja '65
Materials handling's new sophistication. il Duns R 81:pt2 S107-8+ Mr '63
New boom in material handling. T. O'Hanlon. il Duns R 82:50-1+ D '63

MATERIALS research
German scientists investigate materials resisting supersonic rain-erosion damage. W. C. Wetmore. il Aviation W 80:110-11+ Ap 27 '64
Materials on the march. H. E. Klein. il Duns R 81:60-2+ My '63
Materials studies stress non-metals. il Miss & Roc 14:121-2+ Mr 30 '64

MATERNAL love. See Love, Maternal

MATERNITY clothes. See Clothing and dress—Maternity clothes

MATH, Irwin
Frequency synthesizers. Electr World 73:27+ Ja '65
High-stability crystal frequency standards. Electr World 72:44-5 Ag '64
Using zener diodes. Electr World 72:88 N '64

MATHE, Lew
Big hand for Big Lew. C. Goren. il Sports Illus 21:57 Ag 10 '64

MATHEMATICAL biology. See Biomathematics

MATHEMATICAL economics. See Economics, Mathematical

MATHEMATICAL formulas. See Mathematics—Formulae

MATHEMATICAL instruments
See also
Slide rule

MATHEMATICAL models
Mathematical model of the nerve impulse; model of energy transfer in predation. E. F. Moore. il Sci Am 211:150+ S '64

MATHEMATICAL physics
Mathematics in the physical sciences. F. J. Dyson. il Sci Am 211:128-34+ S '64

MATHEMATICAL recreations
Bewitched, bothered or befuddled? excerpt from Scientific American book of mathematical puzzles & diversions. M. Gardner. il Read Digest 85:21-2+ S '64
Fool your friends with numbers tricks: excerpt from Magic house of numbers. I. Adler. il Sci Digest 53:59-60 Je '63
Mathematical games. M. Gardner. See issues of Scientific American
Want to be fuddled? excerpt from Mathematical puzzles. M. Gardner. il Read Digest 83:37-8+ O '63

MATHEMATICAL societies
Mathematicians; meeting of the Society for industrial and applied mathematics, and the Research institute for advanced studies. New Yorker 39:44-5 N 16 '63

MATHEMATICIANS
Mathematicians; meeting of the Society for industrial and applied mathematics, and the Research institute for advanced studies. New Yorker 39:44-5 N 16 '63
See also
Mathematics as a profession

MATHEMATICS
Answers in set theory. Sci Am 210:55-6 Ja '64
Foundations of mathematics. W. V. Quine. il Sci Am 211:112-16+ bibliog(p269) S '64
Mathematics. S. J. Bezuszka. il NEA J 53:48-50 My '64
Mathematics in the modern world. R. Courant. il Sci Am 211:40-9 bibliog(p269) S '64
What's new about the new math? A. F. Strehler. il Sat R 47:68-9+ Mr 21 '64
See also
Algebra
Arithmetic
Economics, Mathematical
Geometry
Mathematical physics
Mathematical recreations
Numbers, Theory of
Probabilities
Topology

Anecdotes, facetiae, satire, etc.

Spare me the rods. A. B. Heath. Nat R 15:562-6 D 31 '63; Discussion. 16:81 Ja 28 '64

Bibliography

Mathematics for practically everybody. V. Guillemin, jr. Harper 227:98-9 Ag '63
Science and math; paperbacks. D. M. Laux. Sr Schol 85:28T D 2 '64

Courses of study

Entering levels and college courses in freshman mathematics. C. B. Lindquist. il Sch Life 45:14-17 Ap '63

Formulae

Formula for difficulty. Sci N L 84:38 Jl 20 '63

History

Mathematicians in industry, the first seventy-five years. T. C. Fry. il Science 143:934-8 F 28 '64
Revolutions in physics and crises in mathematics. S. Bochner. bibliog Science 141:408-11 Ag 2 '63

Problems, exercises, etc.

How to solve math problems with a square. R. Gordon. il Pop Sci 182:132-5 Ap '63

Study and teaching

Any boy can be a computer; Trachtenberg speed system. il Life 54:53-4 My 17 '63
Art & math = SRO; Greenwich, Conn. library. F. G. Donald. il Wilson Lib Bul 37:574-5 Mr '63
Higher math for the lower grades. S. H. Strait. il Parents Mag 38:60-1+ F '63
Inside numbers. il Time 83:34-5 Ja 31 '64
International evaluation of educational achievement. Sch & Soc 91:380-1 N 30 '63
Mastering modern math; with study discussion program. I. K. Feinstein. bibliog il PTA Mag 59:19-22, 36-7 S '64
Math takes a new path; with study-discussion program. by D. B. Harris and E. S. Harris. R. B. Davis. bibliog il PTA Mag 57:8-11, 36 F '63
Mathematics. E. Deans. Sch Life 45:18-19 Jl '63
New look at the old mathematics. V. Schult. il NEA J 53:12-15 Ap '64
Trials of new math. il Time 85:38 Ja 22 '65
What ever happened to Euclid? F. L. Phelps. il Américas 16:5-11 N '64
Why father can't do Johnny's math. D. R. Maxey. il Look 27:84-91 N 5 '63

MATHEMATICS as a profession
Mathematicians in industry, the first seventy-five years. T. C. Fry. il Science 143:934-8 F 28 '64
MATHEMATICS students
Manpower problems: training of mathematicians; report of conference on Manpower problems in the training of mathematicians. L. W. Cohen. Science 140:1111-13 Je 7 '63
MATHEMATICS teachers
Inservice education of mathematics teachers; with suggestions for inservice programs in mathematics. V. Schult and T. L. Abell. Sch Life 45:29-36 Jl '63
Mathematics and science teachers in U.S. high schools; excerpt from report. K. E. Brown and E. S. Obourn. il Sch Life 45:24-5 Ja '63
Standards for science teachers. D. Wolfle. Science 141:235 Jl 19 '63
MATHER, John
Africa, images and realities. NEA J 52:33-5 Mr '63
MATHER, Melissa
Something worth publishing. Writer 76:7-10+ S '63
MATHER, P. Boyd
John Wesley and Aldersgate 1963. Christian Cent 80:1581-3 D 18 '63
Methodists and renewal. Christian Cent 81:791-2 Je 17 '64
Search for sufficiency. Christian Cent 80:1139-40 S 18 '63
MATHER, Stephen Tyng
Stephen Mather, master of the wilderness. D. Peattie and L. Peattie. il por Read Digest 85:148-53 Jl '64
MATHES, Martin C.
Antimicrobial substances from aspen tissue grown in vitro. bibliog Science 140:1101-2 Je 7 '63
MATHEWS, Donald K.
Uniform can be a death trap. R. Lardner. il Sports Illus 19:41-4+ N 25 '63
MATHEWS, James Kenneth, bp
Easter in Jackson. Christian Cent 81:478-80 Ap 15 '64
MATHEWS, M. V.
Digital computer as a musical instrument. bibliog Science 142:553-7 N 1 '63
MATHEWS, Thomas F.
Priest as patron. America 110:794-5 Je 6 '64
MATHEWS, Thomas George
Caribbean kaleidoscope. Cur Hist 48:32-9 Ja '65
MATHEWS, Virginia H.
Key concerns. ALA Bul 57:1048 D '63
MATHEWSON, Rufus W. jr
New writers and the Russian tradition. Reporter 28:49-50+ F 28 '63
MATHIAS, Charles McCurdy, 1922-
Congressman's appraisal; address, April 1964. por Wilson Lib Bul 39:320-2 D '64
MATHIEU, Amy
My aunt's career; story. Seventeen 23:80-1 Ja '64
MATHIS, Buster
At the fair with fat Buster. R. H. Boyle. il por Sports Illus 20:26-8+ Je 1 '64
Big Bus. il pors Ebony 19:142-4+ S '64
MATHIS, Charles
Animalport. Pop Mech 120:102-4 D '63
MATHISON, Lavonne
How to make fall your favorite season. Farm J 87:76 O '63
MATILIJA poppies. See Poppies
MATIN, Leonard, and MacKinnon, G. E.
Autokinetic movement: selective manipulation of directional components by image stabilization. bibliog Science 143:147-8 Ja 10 '64
MATING behavior. See Sex behavior
MATO GROSSO, Brazil
Last primitives. il Sci Digest 55:46-51 My '64
MATRIARCHY
Speaking out; women don't run the country. J. B. Priestley. Sat Eve Post 237:8+ D 12 '64
MATRIMONIAL agencies. See Marriage brokers
MATRIMONY. See Marriage
MATRIX, Dr
Presenting the one and only Dr Matrix, numerologist. M. Gardner. il Sci Am 210:120+ Ja '64
MATSAS, Alexander A.
Greece and Cyprus. Atlan 214:42 D '64
MATSON navigation company
It takes more than ships. il Bsns W p68-70+ Jl 6 '63
Matson's rescue drill. il Time 81:91-2 Ap 5 '63
MATSUMOTO, H. and Marsan, C. A.
Cellular mechanisms in experimental epileptic seizures. bibliog Science 144:193-4 Ap 10 '64
MATSUMURA, Fumio. See O'Brien, R. D. jt. auth.
MATSUO, Sadao, and others
Vapor pressure of ice containing D_2O. bibliog Science 145:1454-5 S 25 '64
MATSUSHIMA, John K. and Perry, T. W.
Report on high-concentrate rations. Suc Farm 62:46-7 F '64
MATSUSHITA, Konosuke
Meet Mr Matsushita; with report by J. Mills. il pors Life 57:107-14 S 11 '64
MATSUZAKI, M. and others
Paradoxical phase of sleep: its artificial induction in the cat by sodium butyrate. bibliog Science 146:1328-9 D 4 '64
MATTEL, incorporated
Most popular doll in town; Barbie. il Life 55:73-5 Ag 23 '63
MATTEO
Hitting the road. H. Smith. il por Dance Mag 37:29-30 D '63
MATTEO, R. S. and Nahas, G. G.
Sodium bicarbonate: increase in survival rate of rats inhaling oxygen. bibliog Science 141:719-20 Ag 23 '63
MATTER, Mercedes
What's wrong with U.S. art schools? Art N 62:40-1+ S '63
MATTER
See also
Atoms
Gravitation
Particles (nuclear physics)
MATTER, Flow of. See Rheology
MATTER, Interstellar
Blowing cold and dusty; hydroxyl or OH radical. Newsweek 62:90 D 2 '63
Chemical analysis of extraterrestrial particles. Sky & Tel 27:211-12 Ap '64
Cosmic dust; report on conference. W. A. Cassidy. Science 144:1475-7 Je 19 '64
Fluctuating zodiacal cloud. il Sky & Tel 25:144-5 Mr '63
Galactic center probed. Sci N L 86:66 Ag 1 '64
Graphite grains in interstellar space. Sky & Tel 26:10 Jl '63
Luster probe seeks lunar dust samples. B. Miller. il Aviation W 80:54-5+ Je 15 '64
New data pinpoints micrometeorite size. Aviation W 78:64 Ap 29 '63
Noctilucent clouds. R. K. Soberman. il Sci Am 208:50-9 bibliog(p 183) Je '63
OH in interstellar space. Sci N L 84:323 N 23 '63
OH in interstellar space. Sky & Tel 27:71+ F '64
Particle accretion rates: variation with latitude. R. A. Schmidt and T. J. Cohen. bibliog il Science 145:924-6 Ag 28 '64
Scientists seek origin of outer-space particles. Sci N L 84:89 Ag 10 '63
Somebody up there like us. R. O'Brien. Esquire 60:185-7+ D '63
Spalled, aerodynamically modified moldavite from Slavice, Moravia, Czechoslovakia. E. C. T. Chao. bibliog il Science 146:790-1 N 6 '64
See also
Plasma (ionized gases)
MATTER of life and death; drama. See Cromwell, J.
MATTER of perspective; story. See Meade, W.
MATTER of style; story. See Judge, J.
MATTER of trust; story. See MacDonald, J. D.
MATTERHORN
They did the impossible, and then: tragedy, conquest of Matterhorn, 1865. R. Deardorff. il N Y Times Mag p74-5+ D 6 '64
MATTESON
Pappy checks the Cherokee. A. H. Sanfelici. il pors Flying 74:48-9+ Je '64
MATTESON, Tomkins Harrison
Painter of patriotic pictures. G. S. Chamberlain. Hobbies 69:44-5 S '64
MATTHEW, Archie
Teaching materials: grow 'em at home! Sr Schol 85:16T Ja 21 '65
MATTHEWS, Jack
After the old gods; poem. Commonweal 77:543 F 15 '63
Catfish; poem. Mlle 59:38 S '64
Hunting with my father in Maine: 1941; poem. Commonweal 81:90 O 16 '64
Now on these monuments falls the rain; poem. New Repub 149:23 D 28 '63
Peace the mind turns to; poem. Commonweal 79:343 D 13 '63
Ripeness of winter; poem. New Repub 148:28 Mr 2 '63
Traveling west in winter; poem. Commonweal 80:146 Ap 24 '64

MATTHEWS, Mary
At communion; poem. Christian Cent 80:1583 D 18 '63
MATTHEWS, Myron L.
Building construction costs. See issues of Architectural record to November 1964
MATTHEWS, Ruth
How to go to church. Read Digest 82:60-2 F '63
MATTHEWS, Samuel N. See Booth, W. P. jt. auth.
MATTHEWS, Scott J.
Diamond jubilee at Port Clinton. il por Motor B 115:103-5+ Ja '65
MATTHEWS, William
William Matthews, by J. T. Durkin. Review America 110:491 Ap 4 '64. H. J. Nolan
MATTHEWS, William H. 3d
Longhorn Cavern State Park. Nat Parks Mag 37:10-13 Je '63
MATTHIAS, B. T.
Superconductivity; the facts. bibliog Science 144:378-81 Ap 24 '64
MATTHIESSEN, Peter
Midnight turning gray; story. Sat Eve Post 236:56-8 S 28 '63
Tierra del Fuego; excerpts from The cloud forest. Américas 16:35-42 F '64
WLB biography. R. Montgomery. por Wilson Lib Bul 38:573-4 Mr '64
MATTICK, Paul
Growth and stagnation. New Repub 152:24-6 Ja 16 '65
MATTINGLY, Trueblood
Gwynn Oak. America 109:136-7 Ag 10 '63
MATTISON, C. W.
New York land acquisition program. Recreation 56:259-62 Je '63
MATTISON, Lindsay, and Daly, Richard
Nevada fallout; past and present hazards. Bul Atomic Sci 20:41-5 Ap; 30 S '64
MATTOON, H. Gleason
Green manuring improves soil. Horticulture 41:450 S '63
MATTOX, Matt
Open letter from Matt Mattox: a complaint. por Dance Mag 38:145 D '64
MATTRESSES
Look before you leap into an oversize bed. Consumer Rep 28:204-5 My '63
Mattresses and bedding '64. il Good H 158: 188-90+ F '64
When products change behind their names. Consumer Rep 28:208 My '63
MATTSON, Brian
Use models. Am City 79:118-19 Mr '64
MATUNAS, Edward
How to buy a good used gun. por Pop Mech 120:130-4 N '63
MATURANA, Humberto R. and Frenk, S.
Directional movement and horizontal edge detectors in the pigeon retina. bibliog Science 142:977-9 N 15 '63
MATURITY
Are you the new kind of girl who fits in the new kind of world? M. M. Hunt. Seventeen 22:86-7+ O '63
Dear teen-age audience. L. Rivers. Seventeen 23:170+ N '64
How to measure maturity. M. R. Feinberg. Nations Bsns 51:40-1+ F '63
MATURITY, Sexual. See Puberty
MATZ, Charles
Blanche Roosevelt. Opera N 27:26-8 Mr 23 '63
MATZ, Judith Ann
First aid for childhood emergencies. Parents Mag 39:42-3+ Ag '64
MATZ, Mary Jane
Great opera houses. Florence. Opera N 27:29-31 Mr 23 '63
Great opera houses: Parma. Opera N 28:26-9 D 7 '63
Great opera houses: Trieste. Opera N 29:28-31 Ja 30 '65
Music palace. Opera N 27:30-3 F 9 '63
New day for Roncole. Opera N 28:30-1 Ap 4 '64
Perfect gentleman. Opera N 27:25-7 F 9 '63
Queen of bel canto. Opera N 27:26-8 Mr 30 '63
Swan of the Veneto. Opera N 27:28-9 Mr 2 '63
Truth about Traviata. Opera N 28:24-5 Ja 11 '64
Well-versed librettist. Opera N 27:12-13 Mr 16 '63
MATZENAUER, Margarete
Margarete Matzenauer, June 1, 1881-May 19, 1963. R. Lawrence. por Opera N 28:34 N 16 '63
MATZKIN, Myron A.
Movie maker. See issues of Modern photography
Nine ideas for tiny titlers. Mod Phot 27:92-3 Mr '63
Sound for your screen. Hi Fi 14:51-3+ Ag '64
—See Miller, D. L. jt. comp.
MAU MAU
And where were you in the war, daddy? il Time 83:34 Ja 10 '64
Love for the forest. Time 83:28 Ja 17 '64
MAUCH, Gene
Let's go, Phillies! J. Olsen. il Sports Illus 21:10-15 Ag 10 '64
Whip who put snap in the Phillies. M. Cope. il por Sat Eve Post 237:74-5+ Ag 8 '64
MAUCH, James
Education joins housing and welfare in coordinated federal effort. Sch Life 45:14-16 F '63
MAUCH CHUNK, Pa.
See also
Jim Thorpe, Pa.
MAUDLING, Reginald
British policy and the United States. Atlan 212:61-4 D '63
about
Britain gets a budget; tax cuts and higher spending. por Bsns W p27 Ap 6 '63
Britain's budget bets on expansion. por Bsns W p27-8 Ap 18 '64
Struggle for power; Tory succession. por Newsweek 62:39-40 Jl 22 '63
With an eye on tomorrow. il por Time 81:32 Ap 12 '63
MAUGHAN, A. M.
Arguments of blood. Holiday 36:56-7+ O '64
Troubled history. Holiday 33:70-1+ Ap '63
MAUI (island)
Fine day at black rock. H. Sutton. il Sat R 46:26-8 Mr 9 '63
MAUKSCH, Hans O.
Becoming a nurse; a selective view. bibliog f Ann Am Acad 346:88-98 Mr '63
MAUL, Ray C.
Changing nature of the teacher shortage. NEA J 52:41-2 N '63
MAULDIN, Bill
Anyone for a backward takeoff? Sports Illus 18:68-76+ My 6 '63
Mauldin on Barry Goldwater. il New Repub 151:13 Jl 4 '64
about
Bill Mauldin: the idea factory. J. Star. il pors Look 27:71-3 Jl 30 '63
MAULDIN, William Henry. See Mauldin, B.
MAULE, Tex
Boxing. Sports Illus 20:48+ Ap 20; 21:50-2 Jl 6 '64
Pro football. See issues of Sports illustrated published during football season
Pro football scouting reports. Sports Illus 19: 47-52+ S 9 '63
Still too tender to be a tiger. Sports Illus 21:20-1 Jl 13 '64
Track (title varies) (cont) Sports Illus 18: 59-62 My 13; 46-7 Je 24 '63
MAULL, Baldwin
Shortcut to statewide banking; holding company status. il pors Bsns W p54+ F 9 '63
MAUNA KEA
Mauna Kea hillclimb; first vehicle to reach the top. R. Brock. il Hot Rod 16:48-51+ Ap '63
MAURA, Sister
Finger; poem. America 108:837 Je 8 '63
Grandmother; poem. Commonweal 80:487 Jl 10 '64
Portrait of the artist; poem. Commonweal 81:132 O 23 '64
MAUREL, Victor
Best of braggarts; first Falstaff. V. Sheean. il pors Opera N 28:27-9 Mr 21 '64
MAURER, Paul H. and others
Antigenicity of polypeptides: immunological unresponsiveness to copolymers of α-amino acids. bibliog Science 139:1061-2 Mr 15 '63
MAURIAC, François
Enigmatic fascination of Charles de Gaulle; tr. by R. Howard. por Vogue 144:174-9 S 1 '64
about
Francois Mauriac. F. Nourissier. Vogue 144: 178 S 1 '64
MAURITANIA
Daddah knows best. Time 81:51 Ap 19 '63
MAUROIS, André
Egalité for Frenchwomen, too. N Y Times Mag p62+ Je 7 '64
France changes, but not Frenchmen. N Y Times Mag p33+ N 24 '63
King's amusement; tr. by J. W. Freeman. Opera N 29:8-13 D 12 '64
Sweet monotony of marriage. Ladies Home J 81:43 Mr '64

MAURY, M. F.
Pilot charts, then and now. R. Martin. il Motor B 114:42-3+ N '64
MAUSER, Ferdinand F.
Future challenges marketing. Harvard Bsns R 41:172 N '63
MAVERICK, Maury, jr
Hill country of Lyndon Johnson. New Repub 150:12 Mr 14 '64
MAVERICK. See Sailing vessels
MAXIMILIAN, emperor of Mexico
100 years ago. S. D. Smith. il por N Y Times Mag p50+ Je 7 '64
Operator and the emperors; with portfolio. L. Thomas. il pors Am Heritage 15:6-23+ Ap '64
MAXIMILIAN Alexander Philipp, prinz von Wied-Neuwied. See Wied-Neuwied, M. A. P. von
MAXIMOS IV, patriarch
Patriarch Maximos IV and Vatican council II; interview, ed. by E. Inglessis and E. Inglessis. por Cath World 198:372-9 Mr '64
MAXIMS
See also
Aphorisms and apothegms
MAXIM'S (restaurant) See Paris—Hotels, restaurants, etc.
MAXIM'S de Chicago. See Chicago—Hotels, restaurants, etc.
MAXSON, Wilbur B.
Grading, a serious matter. NEA J 53:56-7 O '64
MAXSON electronics corporation
Single source procurement yields further Bullpup cost savings. M. Getler. il Miss & Roc 15:18+ Ag 3 '64
Vendor control aids Maxson missile bids. M. L. Yaffee. Aviation W 81:73+ N 2 '64
MAXWELL, A. E. See Spiess, F. N. jt. auth.
MAXWELL, Elsa
Cruise director. il por Time 82:61 N 8 '63
My most unforgettable character. T. Cochran. Read Digest 85:90-4 Jl '64
MAXWELL, Emily
Books (cont) New Yorker 39:210-12+ N 30 '63; 40:207-10+ D 5 '64
MAXWELL, G. Edward
Should you wear a hearing aid? Todays Health 42:26-9+ Ag '64
They go to college in wheel chairs. Todays Health 42:26-9+ Jl '64
MAXWELL, James A.
Happy ending in Kentucky. Reporter 28:22-4 Je 20 '63
House for sale; story. Reporter 29:42 N 7 '63
Ohio: is anybody happy? Reporter 31:36-8 O 22 '64
Race before the race at Indianapolis. Reporter 30:40+ My 21 '64
MAXWELL, Joel
Dream darkroom studio workshop. por Pop Phot 53:64-5+ O '63
MAXWELL, Rhoda Specht
Mirror of the Orient. Pop Gard 15:28-31 N '64
Planting for a turncourt. Flower Grower 51: 29 O '64
MAXWELL, William
Final report; story. New Yorker 39:37-43 Mr 9 '63
Value of money; story. New Yorker 40:40-8 Je 6 '64
MAY, Catherine
Lady, you are in politics! por Suc Farm 62: 73+ N '64
MAY, Ernest R.
Alliance for progress in historical perspective. bibliog f For Affairs 41:757-74 Jl '63
MAY, Henry F.
Recovery of American religious history. bibliog f Am Hist R 70:79-92 O '64
MAY, Marjorie Merriweather (Post)
Greatest satisfaction. il por Time 81:42 My 3 '63
MAY, Morton D.
Playing the art market; African art. il pors Bsns W p28-9 Ja 11 '64
MAY, Richard A.
Poor Richard's race. Reporter 31:12+ O 22 '64
MAY, Richard H. and Heald, W. F.
Mountain of glass. il Am For 69:32-4 Ag '63
MAY, Robert L.
Rudolph was almost Rollo. il por Newsweek 64:80 D 7 '64
MAY, Sophie
Dotty Dimple and the fiction award. M. Bacon. il Atlan 211:130-3 Mr '63
MAY
In May: few of the dates, memorable and not so, coming up next month (title varies) (cont) N Y Times Mag p20 Ap 28 '63; 40 My 3 '64
MAY baskets
Bring back the May basket. D. Biddle. il Pop Gard 15:14-16 My '64
MAY day
When May day was a gay day. H. F. Brooks. il Todays Health 41:38-41+ My '63
MAY day (labor holiday)
May day focus: this year's was on Havana. U S News 56:6 My 11 '64
MAY department stores company
Outlook: warm for May. il Bsns W p83-4+ Mr 14 '64
Playing the art market; African art. il Bsns W p28-9 Ja 11 '64
MAY flies
Mayfly distribution indicates water quality on the upper Mississippi River. C. R. Fremling. bibliog il Science 146:1164-6 N 27 '64
MAY witch; drama. See Brydon, M. W. and Ziegler, E. E.
MAY your days be merry and bright; story. See Shore, W.
MAYALL, R. Newton
Making portable sundials. il Sky & Tel 28: 9-12 Jl '64
MAYAN treasure. See Treasure trove
MAYAS
Mysterious Maya: who was he? skeleton discovered at Tikal. il Life 54:101-3+ Ap 26 '63
1,600-year-old skyscraper; Tikal. il Sci Digest 55:inside cover Je '64
Palenque's explorers; excerpts. C. A. Echánove. il Américas 15:16-21 Ap '63
See also
Chichen Itzá
MAYER, A. M. See Stahl, N. jt. auth.
MAYER, Albert
Architecture as total community: the challenge ahead. bibliog f Arch Rec 135:137-44 Mr; 169-78 Ap; 145-52 My; 141-6 Je; 136: 157-62 Jl; 129-38 Ag; 197-205 S; 139-48 O '64
MAYER, Arthur
New film frontier. Sat R 46:20-1+ O 5 '63
MAYER, Christian
Double stars of Christian Mayer. J. Ashbrook. il Sky & Tel 25:75-6 F '63
MAYER, David, and Greenberg, H. M.
What makes a good salesman. Harvard Bsns R 42:119-25 Jl '64
MAYER, George Louis
Die frau ohne schatten. Am Rec G 31:96-101 O '64
Jess Thomas as Angel's Lohengrin. Am Rec G 30:494-6+ F '64
London's near perfect Siegfried. Am Rec G 29:686-9 My '63
On DGG, Henze's Elegy for young lovers. Am Rec G 31:200-1+ N '64
Regina Resnik's Carmen. Am Rec G 30:382-3+ Ja '64
MAYER, Greta, and Hoover, M. B.
How serious are your problems? Seventeen 22:116-17+ S '63
MAYER, L. A.
Mamluk playing cards. Hobbies 68:118-19 Je '63
MAYER, Louis Burt
Best angel God ever saw. W. Saroyan. il por Sat Eve Post 236:94-5 N 16 '63
MAYER, Maria (Goeppert)
Shell model; address, December 12, 1963. bibliog Science 145:999-1006 S 4 '64
about
At home with Maria Mayer. il pors Sci Digest 55:30-6 F '64
Just ask Mrs Mayer. il por Newsweek 62:78 N 18 '63
Maria Mayer: the Marie Curie of the atom. M. H. Hall. por McCalls 91:38+ Jl '64
MAYER, Martin
Action in education. Bet Hom & Gard 42: 120+ S; 16+ O; 122+ N '64
Aid with strong strings. Commonweal 79:527-30 Ja 31 '64
Air force's egghead factory. Sat Eve Post 236:91-5 N 23 '63
Behind the Hathaway shirt. New Repub 149: 27+ N 2 '63
Big play for pay TV's $1.50 splendors. Sat Eve Post 237:71-5 My 2 '64
CORE: the shock troops of the Negro revolt. Sat Eve Post 237:79-83 N 21 '64
Could you pass the third grade? Esquire 63: 60-5 Ja '65
Fair trade or foul, the battle rages again! Sat Eve Post 237:66-8 Ap 11 '64
Getting alienated with the right crowd at Harvard. Esquire 60:73+ S '63; 61:50+ Je '64
High order of talent. Opera N 28:6-15 Mr 21 '64
Ho hum, come to the fair. Esquire 60:117+ O '63

MAYER, Martin—*Continued*
How alive is your high school? Seventeen 22:120-3+ F '63
Last chance for our schools? Sat Eve Post 236:24-6+ S 14 '63
Legend behind the guitar. N Y Times Mag p36+ F 16 '64
Leisure of the theory class. Esquire 59:16+ Mr '63
Lone wolf of civil rights. Sat Eve Post 237: 76-8 Jl 11 '64
Mr Bing makes the Met go. N Y Times Mag p44-5+ O 11 '64
Music contractor. Esquire 59:157-64 My '63
New York city opera sings for Julius. N Y Times Mag p38+ S 29 '63
Prodigies. Esquire 61:106-7+ My '64
Race and ability. Commentary 38:61-3 Jl '64; 39:12+ Ja '65
Recordings. See issues of Esquire
Schools, slums & Montessori. Commentary 37:33-9 Je; 38:24+ N '64
Scientists in the classroom; excerpts from Where, when, and why. Commentary 35: 312-19; 36:196 Ap, S '63
Szell, still storming after fifty years. N Y Times Mag p 13+ F 2 '64
Tour of the battlefield. Nation 198:654-6 Je 29; 199:inside cover, 53 Ag 10 '64
Transistor. Esquire 59:123+ Je '63
Yankee dollar. Sat Eve Post 237:28-30 Ja 18 '64
(ed) See Nilsson, B. And then I had to sing like an Indian
about
Martin Mayer, Leland B. Jacobs speak at New books preview. Library J 88:3277-8 S 15 '63
MAYER, Meredith
Plan for a hazard-proof playground. Parents Mag 38:64-5+ My '63
MAYER, Milton
Man with a country; excerpt from What can a man do? Harper 228:88-90+ Mr '64
To know and to do. Sat R 47:62-3+ F 15 '64
MAYER, Parm
Cry for me, cloud; poem. McCalls 92:171 N '64
MAYER, Paul Avila
(tr) See Pirandello, L. Six characters in search of an author
MAYER, Ralph
Ralph Mayer's technical question & answer page. See issues of American artist
MAYER, Tom
Homecoming; story. Harper 227:88-92 Ag '63
Minute forty seven of the second; story. Harper 228:61-8 Mr '64
Phone call; story. New Yorker 40:84+ My 30 '64
Try fifty-three for laughs. Sports Illus 18: 74-6+ Je 10 '63
about
Six quitters. por Esquire 62:102 S '64
MAYER, William Erwin
Moral imperative; address, December 6, 1963. Vital Speeches 29:266-70 F 15 '63
MAYER-OAKES, William J.
Early man in the Andes; with biographical sketch. Sci Am 208:36+, 116-22+ My '63
MAYERLE, Judine
Journey; poem. America 109:97 Jl 27 '63
MAYERS, Albert N. Browne-. See Browne-Mayers, A. N.
MAYERSON, H. S.
Lymphatic system; with biographical sketch. Sci Am 208:28, 80-90 bibliog (p 183) Je '63
MAYES, Herbert R.
Good words; excerpts from address. Am Artist 28:73-4+ D '64
MAYFIELD, John S.
Luck of a collector. Hobbies 68:110-11+ O '63
MAYFIELD, M. R.
High-performance transistor ignition system. Electr World 69:30-1+ Je '63
MAYFLIES. See May flies
MAYFLOWER (ship)
See also
Pilgrim fathers
MAYHEW, Alice Ellen
Early Camus. Commonweal 79:173-4 N 1 '63
Existential and Christian. Commonweal 80:152-3 Ap 24 '64
Forging a class. Commonweal 80:521-2 Jl 24 '64
Glory and gore. Commonweal 78:201-3 My 10 '63
Leonard Woolf's autobiography. Commonweal 81:299-302 N 20 '64
Lesson of the normal man who helped kill millions. Commonweal 78:429-30 Jl 12 '63
MAYHEW, Edgar deN.
Isaac Sheffield, Connecticut limner. Antiques 84:589-91 N '63
MAYHEW, Leonard F. X.
Cause célèbre. Commonweal 78:113-16 Ap 19 '63
Exploring the phenomenon of art. Commonweal 78:513-14 Ag 23 '63
Flannery O'Connor: 1925-1964. Commonweal 80:562-3 Ag 21 '64
Persistance of social myths. Commonweal 80:455-6 Jl 3 '64
Two for Georgia. Commonweal 80:61-4 Ap 3 '64
MAYHUGH, Charles
He manages his farm for crops and wildlife. por Suc Farm 61:82+ N '63
MAYNARD, Fred
Twin-T oscillators. Electr World 69:40-1+ My '63
Twin-T oscillators for electronic musical instruments. Electr World 71:36-9+ Je '64
MAYNARD, Jack
Triple-threat lighting program. Am City 78: 105 Jl '63
MAYNARD, Olga
Apparitions in dance. por Dance Mag 37:32-5+ O '63
Open letter. Dance Mag 38:22-4 Jl '64
San Diego's cultural center. Dance Mag 38: 148-9 D '64
Three masks of the deer dancer. Dance Mag 38:34-6+ Ja '64
View from the big eye. Dance Mag 39:40-3 Ja '65
MAYNE, Roger
Discovery. P. Caulfield. il Mod Phot 28:78-9+ Je '64
MAYNE, William
WLB biography. T. Hines. por Wilson Lib Bul 37:713 Ap '63
MAYO clinic, Rochester, Minn.
Court of last resort. il Time 84:96 O 23 '64
Mayo at 100. il Newsweek 64:66-7 S 28 '64
MAYONNAISE
Salad shenanigans; fresh herb mayonnaise salad. il Sunset 134:58-9 Ja '65
MAYOR, A. Hyatt
Accidents are inartistic. Nation 197:370-1 N 30 '63
Matter of opinion. Sat R 46:41-54 My 18 '63
Swiss behind the colors. Nation 199:414-15 N 30 '64
Velázquez monument. Art N 62:43 O '63
MAYORS
How strong mayors administer large cities; Milwaukee, Baton Rouge, New York city. Am City 78:142+ Mr '63
See also subhead Mayors under names of cities, e.g. New York (city)—Mayors
MAYR, Ernst
New versus the classical in science. Science 141:765 Ag 30 '63
Why is man? excerpt from Animal species and evolution. Sat R 46:48 My 4 '63
MAYR, Johann Simon. See Mayr, S.
MAYR, Simon
Mayr in Germany. D. Stevens. il Opera N 28: 28 S 28 '63
MAYS, Benjamin E.
Churches will follow. Christian Cent 81:513-14 Ap 22 '64
Vice president of the Association for the study of Negro life and history named to Institute of European studies. por Negro Hist Bul 26:244 My '63
MAYS, David J.
Government has no free money; interview. por Nations Bsns 52:37+ F '64
MAYS, Willie
Happy start for a happy new Willie. F. Deford. il pors Sports Illus 20:22-7 Ap 27 '64
Mays days. il pors Newsweek 63:86 My 4 '64
Mays in May. il por Time 83:85-6 My 22 '64
Trials of a Negro idol. E. Linn. il por Sat Eve Post 236:70-2 Je 22 '63
Willie Mays' new home. L. Robinson. il pors Ebony 18:88-92+ Ag '63
Willie the wonder. J. R. McDermott. il pors Life 56:50-2 My 15 '64
MAYSLES, Al
Focus on Al Maysles. C. Reynolds. il pors Pop Phot 54:128-31 My '64
MAYTAG, Lewis, Jr
Flying to success upside down. il por Time 82:73 Jl 26 '63
MAZAMA, MOUNT, Oregon. See Crater Lake National Park
MAZATLAN, Mexico
It's time to plan for carnival in Mazatlán. il Sunset 133:26+ N '64
Ten minutes by boat from Mazatlán; Isla de Piedra. il Sunset 132:22-3 F '64

MAZE tests
Alligators less curious in maze than rats. Sci N L 85:296 My 9 '64
Alteration in learning ability caused by changes in cerebral serotonin and catechol amines. D. W. Woolley and T. van der Hoeven. bibliog il Science 139:610-11 F 15 '63; Reply with rejoinder. D. E. McMillan. 145:952 Ag 28 '64
Amnesic and punishing effects of electroconvulsive shock. J. L. McGaugh and M. C. Madsen. bibliog il Science 144:182-3 Ap 10 '64
Place-learning. H. Gleitman. il Sci Am 209: 116-22 O '63
Serotonin deficiency in infancy as one cause of a mental defect in phenylketonuria. D. W. Woolley and T. van der Hoeven. bibliog il Science 144:883-4 My 15 '64

MAZESS, Richard B. and others
Accuracy of bone mineral measurement. bibliog Science 145:388-9 Jl 24 '64
—See Baker, P. T. jt. auth.

MAZO, Earl
Intelligent woman's guide to political polls. McCalls 92:80+ O '64
What's ahead for the G.O.P? Sat Eve Post 236:36 D 14 '63

MAZOR, Julian
Baltimore; story. New Yorker 38:34-40 F 9 '63

MAZOWSZE company. See Ballet—Poland

MAZOYER, Georges
Nhu deal. il Newsweek 62:65-6 N 25 '63

MAZUREK, Fred
Quiet man. il por Newsweek 64:72+ S 21 '64
Showdown for a quarterback. M. Cope. il pors Sat Eve Post 237:28-9 O 17 '64

MAZURKIEWICZ, Albert J.
How Johnny can be taught to read, a new alphabet. il U S News 56:76-7 My 18 '64

MBA, Léon
Autocrat insurance. il por Time 83:35 Ap 24 '64
Colored rulers. G. C. Turner. Negro Hist Bul 27:177 Ap '64

MBELO. See Congo (capital Leopoldville)—Native races

MBOYA, Thomas Joseph
Do white men have a future in Africa? N Y Times Mag p24-5+ D 8 '63
Party system and democracy in Africa. For Affairs 41:650-8 Jl '63

about

Freedom and after, by T. Mboya. Review Sat R 46:32 N 30 '63. J. Hughes
Future of Tom Mboya. S. Meisler. il Reporter 28:41-4 F 14 '63
Two key leaders in a new African nation. por U S News 54:22 Je 10 '63
White and black, old and new: Uhuru for all? por Newsweek 62:42-3 D 16 '63

MDIVANI, Marina
Music to my ears; concert in Carnegie Hall. I. Kolodin. Sat R 46:27+ D 14 '63

ME technician, you engineer; story. See Burke, M. H.

MEAD, Lilian
Bibliophile's itinerary of St Louis. por Wilson Lib Bul 38:860-4 Je '64

MEAD, Margaret
Aging differently in the space age; excerpts from address. Recreation 57:219+ My '64
Apprenticeship for marriage; a startling proposal. por Redbook 121:14+ O '63
Be glad your child is different. Parents Mag 39:70-1 S '64
Clocking the timetable of man. Sat R 46:41 Je 22 '63
Do we undervalue full-time wives? por Redbook 122:22+ N '63
Must women be bored with politics? por Redbook 123:20+ O '64
New role for Jacqueline Kennedy? por Redbook 123:24+ Je '64
Planned cultural transition. Sci N L 83:143 Mr 2 '63
Questions and answers. See issues of Redbook
Recapturing the future. Sat R 46:10-13 Je 1 '63
Scientist reviewers beware; letter. Science 141:312-13 Jl 26 '63
September to June: an informal report. por Redbook 121:32+ Je '63
Sex on the campus; the real issue. por Redbook 119:6+ O '62; 120:16 Mr '63
Time to reflect, time to feel. por Redbook 123:14-16+ Ag '64
We've got a blending of races right now; interview. por U S News 55:89-90 N 18 '63
What I owe to other women. Redbook 122: 18+ Ap '64
What is a lady? por Redbook 120:22+ Ap '63
What's happening to the American family; interview. pors U S News 54:48-50 My 20 '63
Why Americans must limit their families. por Redbook 121:30+ Ag '63; 122:14+ Ja '64

about

Culture by computer: Margaret Mead's ideas. il Sci Digest 53:51 My '63

MEAD, Robert G, Jr
Too many revolutions to the South. Sat R 48:85-6 Ja 2 '65

MEAD, Shepherd
Still pricking business balloons. pors Bsns W p90+ Mr 21 '64

MEAD, Sidney E.
Whose responsibility? Christian Cent 80:1342-3 O 30 '63

MEAD, William
Ordeal of William Penn. F. Biddle. il Am Heritage 15:104-10 Ap '64

MEAD, LAKE
Last high water winter at Lake Mead? il Sunset 130:38+ F '63
Paradoxical Lake Mead. J. Pepper. il Motor B 111:36-7+ My '63

MEADE, David
Plain-English orthodoxy. Christian Cent 81: 966-8 Jl 29 '64
Through the labyrinth. Christian Cent 80:1373 N 6 '63

MEADE, Edward J. Jr
American schools overseas. Sat R 46:44-5+ Ag 17 '63

MEADE, Walter
Error of judgment; story. Sat Eve Post 238: 48-50 Ja 30 '65
In case of Indians; story. Redbook 122:54-5 Ja '64
Matter of perspective; story. Seventeen 23: 132-3 F '64
One of a kind; story. Ladies Home J 81:84 N '64
Person apart; story. Redbook 124:50-1 Ja '65

MEADER, Vaughn
Fate of the myna bird. por Time 83:78 Ja 10 '64

MEADOW rues
Charm is where thalictrums grow. M. P. Kunkel. il Horticulture 41:250 My '63

MEADOW saffrons. See Autumn crocuses

MEADOWS, Clinton E.
Are you using the right dairy bull? Suc Farm 61:42-3 O '63
Now is the time to cull your cows. Suc Farm 62:30-1 D '64

MEALS
Make every meal a party meal. il Pop Gard 15:62-3 Jl '64
Marvellous food at Messel's. V. Riis-Hansen. il Vogue 142:136+ D '63
Never a dull meal. il Good H 158:74-89 Ja '64
Patio snacks. il Bet Hom & Gard 41:89-90 Je '63
Porch impromptu; snacks with drinks. il McCalls 90:112-13+ Je '63
Portfolio of holiday entertaining; with recipes. il Am Home 67:60-4+ N '64
Snacks from the ski slopes; with recipes. il Seventeen 23:168-9+ N '64
Sounds like fun! with recipes. M. Powell. il Seventeen 24:90-1+ Ja '65
Tasty meals for cozy twosomes. G. Maddox. il Todays Health 42:22-7 Ap '64

See also
Breakfasts
Buffet meals
Dinners and dining
Lunches
Menus
Table setting
Thanksgiving dinners
Wedding meals

MEALS for millions foundation. See Food relief

MEANING of life. See Life

MEANING of words. See Semantics

MEANS, Gaston Bullock
Spectacular rogue, by E. P. Hoyt. Review Newsweek por 62:82-3 Jl 8 '63

MEANS, Marianne
Oh, to be a White House pet! McCalls 91:216 N '63

MEANS, Marianne—*Continued*
What three Presidents say about their wives; excerpt from Woman in the White House. Good H 157:57-61+ Ag '63

about

Marianne. il por Newsweek 63:87-8 My 4 '64

MEANS, Richard L.
Protestantism in American sociology. Christian Cent 81:1554-6 D 16 '64

MEANY, George
Labor union of today; address, November 14, 1963. Vital Speeches 30:176-81 Ja 1 '64
Security of the United States; address, August 18, 1964. Vital Speeches 30:685-8 S 1 '64
Test-ban treaty; address, September 2, 1963. Vital Speeches 29:710-12 S 15 '63

about

AFL-CIO showdown: Meany wins. U S News 55:116 O 21 '63
Better day for brother Randolph. T. R. Brooks. Reporter 29:23 D 5 '63
Case of Mr Henning. New Repub 152:5 Ja 9 '65
Clear it with George; influence on government appointments. Time 85:16 Ja 8 '65
Labor ducks the future. B. J. Widick. il Nation 197:389-90 D 7 '63
Labor unions are worth the price. M. Ways. il por Fortune 67:108-13+ My '63
Labor's price tag for election; it's up to LBJ. il U S News 57:85-6 D 7 '64
LBJ and unions: what he tells them, what they want. il U S News 55:106-7 D 16 '63
LBJ, Meany at odds on wages. U S News 56:89 Ap 6 '64
Meany heads bias fight. Bsns W p78+ Jl 27 '63
Meany vs. Reuther; clash on rights march. U S News 55:22 Ag 26 '63
People of the week. por U S News 55:16 N 25 '63
Rhetoric of Walter Reuther. S. Levey. Reporter 28:26-8 Mr 14 '63
Wider split in the AFL-CIO? U S News 54:91 F 11 '63

MEARS, Joe
Owens; never-fail trout river. Field & S 67:31-3+ Mr '63
What makes Hot Creek hot? pors Outdoor Life 134:32-5+ S '64

MEASLES
Measles complications found in one in fifteen cases. Sci N L 86:73 Ag 1 '64
Measles: most contagious of the infectious diseases of childhood. F. H. Richardson. il Todays Health 41:44-5+ O '63
Measles nears peak. Sci N L 87:39 Ja 16 '65

Vaccines

Goodby to measles! il Life 54:85-6+ Ap 19 '63
Mass inoculation; killed-virus vaccine and live-virus vaccine. il Newsweek 61:91 Mr 18 '63
Measles season. il Newsweek 65:54 Ja 11 '65
Measles vaccination successful in Africa. Sci N L 86:104 Ag 15 '64
Measles vaccines ready. F. Marley. Sci N L 83:195 Mr 30 '63
Measles vaccines to flow. Bsns W p34+ Mr 23 '63
New measles vaccines; what you should know. U S News 54:6 Ap 1 '63
Safety in numbers; new measles vaccines. Time 81:79 Je 14 '63
Those new measles vaccines. Consumer Rep 28:397-8 Ag '63
Two against measles. Time 81:76 Mr 29 '63
Vaccines for measles. Sci Am 208:74 My '63
What parents ask about measles vaccines. M. J. E. Senn. McCalls 90:137-8 Jl '63

MEASLES, German. See Rubella

MEASUREGRAPH company
Helping women measure up. Bsns W p58 O 24 '64

MEASUREMENT
Experts size up Russia; American metrologists's visit to Russian measuring centers. Sci N L 84:36 Jl 20 '63
Measurements and standards. W. A. Stocklin. Electr World 72:6 Jl '64
Metrology developing rapidly in face of challenges of missile/space work. il Miss & Roc 14:49-51 Je 1 '64
See also
Geodesy
Length measurement
Tolerance (engineering)
Weights and measures

MEASUREMENT, Mental. See Psychometrics

MEASUREMENT, Psychological. See Psychometrics

MEASUREMENTS, Astronomical. See Astronomical measurements

MEASURING instruments
Freezing-point depression: new method for measuring ultramicro quantities of fluids. D. J. Prager and R. L. Bowman. bibliog il Science 142:327-9 O 11 '63
See also
Gages
Seismometers

MEASURING instruments, Optical
Lasers for length measurement. A. G. McNish. bibliog il Science 146:177-82 O 9 '64
Metrology developing rapidly in face of challenges of missile/space work. il Miss & Roc 14:49-51 Je 1 '64

MEAT
Cold-meat platters styled for summer. il McCalls 91:110-12 Ag '64
How to select the best cut of meat. il Bet Hom & Gard 42:50-8 Ja '64
Money-saving guide to meat. R. Brecher and E. Brecher. il Redbook 121:84-92 O '63
Spanish America's fiesta dish; cold meats and vegetable salad. il Sunset 131:116 Jl '63
See also
Cookery—Meat
Lamb (meat)

Grading and standardization

Cattlemen rap dual grading. Farm J 87:53 Mr '63
Make it lean, Angus breeders are told. J. Russell. Farm J 87:33 Ag '63

Marketing

What changes in beef retailing mean to you. R. Rust. Suc Farm 62:93 F '64

Preservation

How to corn your own beef or pork. Sunset 130:158+ F '63
How to store meat the right way. Bet Hom & Gard 42:133 N '64

Prices

Beefs about beef. il Time 83:93-4 Ap 10 '64
Big beef. il Newsweek 63:70+ Ap 13 '64
Consumer's beef dollar: fair share for feeders? B. W. Marion. Suc Farm 62:38+ Mr '64
Guaranteed prices for your beef? R. C. Black. il Farm J 88:31+ O '64
Have beef prices turned the corner? ed. by J. A. Rohlf. il Farm J 88:30+ S '64
Meat on the bargain counter. il U S News 54:52 Ap 15 '63
On the way: lower meat prices. il U S News 54:6 F 11 '63
Study of meat prices? U S News 56:45 Ap 13 '64
Trouble on the range. il Time 83:93-4 F 28 '64
Why beef prices in stores stay high. il U S News 56:52-3 Je 29 '64

MEAT, Dried
How to dry beef jerky. il Sunset 132:174 Je '64
How to make old-fashioned jerky. W. Haussamen. il Outdoor Life 133:129 F '64
Powdered beefsteak diet. B. Tufty. Sci N L 85:242 Ap 18 '64

MEAT, Frozen
Frozen beef steaks. il Consumer Rep 29:326-8 Jl '64

MEAT, Powdered. See Meat, Dried

MEAT, Smoked. See Food, Smoked

MEAT cutters union. See Amalgamated meat cutters and butcher workmen of North America

MEAT industry and trade
Beef and sheep men pay. Farm J 88:134 Ap '64
Beef from abroad. America 111:208 Ag 29 '64
Beef imports, what's happening now? T. Jorgensen. Suc Farm 62:66 Jl '64
Beef, what the big build-up means; ed. by C. W. Gifford. il Farm J 87:35+ Ap '63
Big beef on the range. R. Fleming. New Repub 150:10 Mr 7 '64
Entree for U.S. meat; beef to European markets. il Bsns W p30 Je 13 '64
Europeans as beef eaters; what's in it for U.S. il U S News 56:96 Je 15 '64
Experts see more stable beef business. J. Russell. Farm J 88:38 N '64
How to sell more lean beef. C. Peterson. jr. il Suc Farm 61:74-5+ Mr '63

MEAT industry and trade—*Continued*
How U.S. beef is selling in Britain. il U S News 57:66 Jl 6 '64
I flew with the calves; New Jersey to Italian farms; with editorial comment. L. M. Palmer. il Farm J 88:4, 30-1+ N '64
Is Europe a market for your beef? Farm J 88:30 Jl '64
Packing it away. il Time 83:82 Ja 17 '64
Super investigation. New Repub 150:5 My 16 '64
U.S. concludes meat agreements with Australia and New Zealand; State-Agriculture announcement, with exchange of notes, February 17, 1964. Dept State Bul 50:380-2 Mr 9 '64
United States concludes meat agreement with Ireland. State-Agriculture announcement; with exchange of notes, February 25, 1964. Dept State Bul 50:468-9 Mr 23 '64
U.S. concludes meat agreement with Mexico; State-agriculture announcement, with United States note, May 14, 1964. Dept State Bul 50:944-5 Je 15 '64
Will the meat import law help? Farm J 88: 105 O '64
See also
Armour and company
Iowa beef packers, incorporated

Securities

Rout in futures; prolonged debacle in pork bellies. il Fortune 70:102+ Jl '64

Wages and hours

Unions score on job rates. Bsns W p 146 S 19 '64
Wage chronology: Armour and co, 1961-63. il Mo Labor R 86:399-408 Ap '63
Wage chronology: Swift & co, 1961-63. J. Griest. il Mo Labor R 86:1048-57 S '63
Wages in meat products plants, November 1963. L. E. Lewis. il Mo Labor R 87:801-7 Jl '64

MEAT loaf, pies, etc. See Cookery—Meat
MEAT markets
Cold; freezing temperature at warehouse of Edward Davis, inc. New Yorker 39:21-2 Je 22 '63
MEAT packing industry. See Meat industry and trade
MEAT poisoning. See Food poisoning
MEAT prices. See Meat—Prices
MEAT substitutes
Meatless meats. D. Seim. il Farm J 88:31+ S '64
MEATLESS meals. See Lenten menus
MEBAN. See Sudan—Native races
MEBANE, John
Tin cans are antiques now. Hobbies 69:28-9 Je '64
MECCA, limited
This way to Mecca. il Newsweek 62:57-8 Jl 1 '63
MECH, Dave
Biggest black bear ever caught. Sci Digest 54:5-9 N '63
Can you read the signs? Outdoor Life 135: 50-1+ Ja '65
Who dined here? Outdoor Life 131:10-11 Ja '63
Who lives here? Outdoor Life 132:14-15+ D '63
MECH, Edmund V.
Child welfare research: a review and critique. bibliog f Ann Am Acad 355:20-30 S '64
MECH, L. David. See Allen, D. L. jt. auth.
MECHANICAL aids in education. See Teaching—Aids and devices
MECHANICAL devices
See also
Automatons
Manipulators
MECHANICAL drawing
Handy devices to aid the home sketcher or draftsman. il Consumer Bul 46:14+ O '63
See also
Draftsmen
MECHANICAL exercisers. See Exercising machines
MECHANICAL handling
See also
Loading and unloading
MECHANICAL hearts. See Heart, Artificial; Heart-lung machines
MECHANICAL models
See also
Automatons
MECHANICAL musical instruments. See Musical instruments (mechanical)
MECHANICAL theory of life. See Mechanism (philosophy)
MECHANICAL toys. See Toys
MECHANICAL translating. See Translating machines
MECHANICS
See also
Force and energy
MECHANICS (persons)
He's all ears for engines. H. McLemore. il Pop Sci 184:94-7+ Ja '64
Why can't I get help? E. D. Fales, jr. Am Home 66:25 N '63
See also
Automobile mechanics (persons)
MECHANICS, Household
Doing it better. D. X. Manners. See issues of House beautiful
Good news for men! il Bet Hom & Gard 42: 14+ F; 28+ Mr '64
Home maintenance clinic. Am Home 67:92-3 Mr '64
How America solved the servant problem. R. Lynes. il Harper 227:46-54 Jl '63
Mechanical marvels of a motor manufacturer. il House B 105:140-3+ Ap '63
Read before you park. il House & Gard 124: 84-5 Jl '63
MECHANICS liens. See Liens
MECHANISM (philosophy)
Brain vs. the machine. J. W. Krutch. Sat R 47:17-19+ Ja 18 '64
See also
Cybernetics
MECHANISTIC theory of life. See Mechanism (philosophy)
MECHANIZATION in agriculture. See Agricultural machinery
MECHANORECEPTORS. See Nervous system
MECKLENBURG COUNTY, N.C.
Birth control and the poor: a solution. J. Shepherd. il Look 28:63-7 Ap 7 '64; Same abr. Read Digest 85:111-14 Ag '64
MECKLEY, Richard
Compulsory high school attendance? NEA J 53:10-12 F '64
MECKLING, William H.
Economics and space technology. Bul Atomic Sci 19:15-17 My '63
MECLIZINE. See Antihistamines
MECOM, John Whitfield
Midas touch of John Mecom. il pors Bsns W p90-2+ O 10 '64
Vade, Mecom. il por Time 84:81 Jl 24 '64
MECOM, John Whitfield, jr
Big itch they call Little John. J. Olsen. il pors Sports Illus 22:50-4+ Ja 11 '65
MEDAL of freedom
American honors list. il N Y Times Mag p 16-17 Jl 14 '63
Freedom medal awards. Sci N L 84:386 D 21 '63
Honors list; Presidential medal of freedom. Nation 197:43 Jl 27 '63
Medalurgical note of distinction. Life 54:4 Mr 8 '63
President announces Medal of freedom winners. Pub W 186:152 Jl 13 '64
President awards medal of freedom to thirty. Sci N L 86:190 S 19 '64
Three Negroes receive 1964 Presidential freedom medal; with biographical sketches. C. W. Thomas. il Negro Hist Bul 28:58-9 D '64
Transition; Presidential medal of freedom. il Newsweek 62:59 Jl 15 '63
MEDAL of honor (United States)
Beyond mere duty: a night for valor; award given to Capt. R. H. C. Donlon. il Life 57:45 D 18 '64
One who was belligerent; award to Captain R. H. C. Donlon. il Time 84:31 D 11 '64
What is courage? P. Streit. il N Y Times Mag p30-1+ N 24 '63
You honor us; gathering of winners. il Newsweek 61:30-1 My 13 '63
MEDALLIONS. See Medals
MEDALS
Alvar Aalto wins 1963 A.I.A. gold medal. Arch Rec 133:26 Mr '63
Audubon and barn owl share new Hall of fame medal. J. Vosburgh. il Audubon Mag 65:155 My '63
For eloquence and precision; award of medal to S. Steinberg. Pub W 183:71 Je 3 '63
Hall of fame issues a Thoreau medal. il Audubon Mag 65:375 N '63
Heroine; Treasury department's gold medal to D. Waugh. il Time 82:28 N 1 '63
LBJ's scholars. Newsweek 63:100 My 25 '64
President challenges youth to excellence. Sci N L 85:393 Je 20 '64
Presidential scholars, 1964. il Sch Life 46:2-4 Jl '64

MEDALS—*Continued*
Scholar honors; Presidential scholars. Sr Schol 84:14 My 15 '64
See also names of medals, e.g. Newbery medal
MEDALS, Devotional
Virgin on a shell. A. G. Melvin. il Hobbies 68:130+ D '63
MEDAWAR, P. B.
Is the scientific paper fraudulent? excerpt from Experimental method. Sat R 47:42-3 Ag 1 '64
MEDER, Albert E. jr
Absolute importance of regional accreditation. Sch & Soc 91:108 Mr 9 '63
Accrediting procedures of NCATE. Sch & Soc 91:192-3 Ap 20 '63
MEDIATION, Industrial. See Arbitration, Industrial
MEDIC-alert bracelets. See Identification tags, bracelets, etc.
MEDICAL botany. See Botany, Medical
MEDICAL buildings
Flexibility and privacy for medical offices. il Arch Rec 133:158-9 Mr '63
In Washington state: variety under one roof. il Arch Forum 120:94 F '64
Six clinics. il Arch Forum 120:90-7 F '64
MEDICAL care. See Medical service
MEDICAL care for the aged. See Aged—Medical care
MEDICAL centers
Radial wards serve a teaching hospital. il Arch Rec 135:198-9 Ap '64
Self-help plan for doctorless towns; Fox Lake, Wis. H. Earle. il Todays Health 41:34-9 S '63
See also
Kentucky. University—Medical center
New York university—Medical center
MEDICAL colleges
Note about Vellore. J. K. G. Webb. Sat R 47:22 O 3 '64
On giving oneself away. E. T. Harris. Harper 229:99-101 D '64
Physicians in five years. W. R. Vath. bibliog il Todays Health 42:52-5 My '64
MEDICAL committee for human rights
Doctor; health program for Mississippi. A. O. Wells. il Nation 199:515-16 D 28 '64
MEDICAL conferences
Students attend career conference; Fifth annual biomedical career conference. il Todays Health 42:69 Mr '64
MEDICAL cooperation
Problems of collaboration between social scientists and the practicing professions. L. S. Cottrell, jr. and E. B. Sheldon. Ann Am Acad 346:126-37 Mr '63
MEDICAL delusions
Old wives' tales; true or false? L. Lasagna. il N Y Times Mag p88+ My 5 '63; Same abr. with title Which old wives' tales do you believe? Read Digest 83:211-13 Ag '63
They won't take it; case at San Diego naval training center. Time 81:52 My 24 '63
MEDICAL education
Can women take medicine? R. Hoffmann. il Mlle 57:127-9+ S '63
Doctor's education never ends. D. E. Logan, jr. il Todays Health 42:40-1+ S '64
Hands and brains; letter. E. G. Dimond. Science 142:445+ O 25 '63; Discussion. 143:198 Ja 17 '64
Loan program that helps you become a doctor. H. Earle. il Todays Health 41:36-41 Jl '63
Medical students: source, selection, and training; letter. G. H. Whipple. Science 142:541 N 1 '63; Reply. B. I. Goldberg. 143:639 F 14 '64
Oriental renaissance in education and medicine. W. Penfield. bibliog il Science 141:1153-61 S 20 '63
Physicians in five years. W. R. Vath. bibliog il Todays Health 42:52-5 My '64
Process of becoming a physician. S. W. Bloom. bibliog f Ann Am Acad 346:77-87 Mr '63
See also
Medical colleges

Federal aid

Congress; in voting assistance to health professions education, House demonstrates its folkways. J. Walsh. Science 140:469-70 My 3 '63
Health professions assistance act. Sch Life 46:16 N '63
Presidential Rx. Newsweek 61:59 F 18 '63
MEDICAL electricity. See Electrotherapy
MEDICAL electronics
Electronic medical diagnosis system in use. il(p 113) Sci N L 85:127 F 22 '64
Electronics helps to heal the sick. il Bsns W p74-6+ S 19 '64
Getting under your skin; power from the bodies of rats. Time 82:40 Jl 26 '63
Medical electronics; report of International conference on medical electronics. R. L. Bowman. Science 141:1069-70 S 13 '63
Space tracks; bioelectronics extends its frontiers. D. W. Warner. il Natur Hist 72:8-15 F '63
Surgeons' dream room: new wing at the research hospital of the National institutes of health at Bethesda, Md. il Life 55:93-4+ D 6 '63
Transistorized M.D.; systems for monitoring patients. L. Lessing. il Fortune 68:130-4+ S '63
Wiring people for life. C. P. Gilmore. il Pop Sci 185:66-8+ Ag '64
See also
Electronic anesthesia
Telemeter (physiological apparatus)
MEDICAL ethics
Hazards of new drugs. W. Modell. bibliog Science 139:1180-5 Mr 22 '63
Human experimentation: cancer studies at Sloan-Kettering stir public debate on medical ethics. E. Langer. Science 143:551-3 F 7 '64; Discussion. 144:486; bibliog 145:768 My 1, Ag 21 '64
Medical ethics: British unit offers guidelines for research involving human subjects; excerpts from annual report of Britain's Medical research council. Science 145:1024-5+ S 4 '64
MEDICAL examination of school children. See School children—Medical inspection
MEDICAL examinations. See Physical examinations
MEDICAL fakers. See Quacks and quackery
MEDICAL fees. See Medical service, Cost of
MEDICAL history. See Medicine—History
MEDICAL hypnosis. See Hypnotism
MEDICAL instruments and apparatus
Atomic drill may prove aid in cancer research. il Todays Health 42:20 N '64
Electricity of life; electronic pacemakers. il Sci Digest 55:73-4 Mr '64
For heart, home & hospital. il Time 82:66 N 1 '63
Intestinal examinations made by flexible tube. Sci N L 86:216 O 3 '64
Off-beat hearts get back in step; with tiny pacemaking devices. Sci N L 84:232 O 12 '63
Photographs from the inside; gastro camera. Sci Digest 55:79-80 Je '64
Shock treats heart flutter; cardioverter. Sci N L 84:131 Ag 31 '63
Suction replaces forceps. Sci N L 83:71 F 2 '63
Swallowed safety pins; medical tools designed around powerful magnets. Sci N L 85:21 Ja 11 '64
Wiring people for life; pacemaker. C. P. Gilmore. il Pop Sci 185:66-8+ Ag '64
See also
Respiratory apparatus
MEDICAL insurance. See Insurance, Health; Insurance, Health—United States
MEDICAL jurisprudence
See also
Insanity—Jurisprudence
Malpractice
MEDICAL kits. See Medicine kits
MEDICAL laboratories
Danger in our medical labs. M. Pines. Harper 227:84-7+ O '63; Discussion. 227:4+ D '63
Malpractice and the clinical laboratory. D. H. Mills. bibliog Science 144:638-42 My 8 '64
Science in the suburbs: private research unit discovers flaws in dependence on the local community; Waldemar medical research foundation. E. Langer. il Science 146:39-42 O 2 '64; Reply. L. Gross. 147:9 Ja 1 '65
MEDICAL laws and legislation
Why doctors are bad samaritans. P. W. Kearney. Read Digest 82:87-90 My '63
MEDICAL libraries
Esterquest report published on N.Y.'s Medical library resources; summary. R. T. Esterquest. Library J 88:1498 Ap 1 '63
Medical libraries are in trouble; address, October 1962. S. Adams. bibliog il Library J 88:2615-21 Jl '63
See also
Francis A. Countway library of medicine, Boston
United States—National library of medicine
MEDICAL library asociation
International medical body; a congressional investigation in Washington. L. T. Morton. il Library J 88:2847-8 Ag '63
Medical library association. F. B. Rogers. Science 143:1240-1 Mr 13 '64
Three-M muddle; annual meeting. M. E. Feeney. Library J 89:2960-2 Ag '64

MEDICAL literature
N.Y. academy of medicine to study medical literature resources; Greater New York area. Library J 88:3571 O 1 '63
Opening the chambered nautilus; evaluation of uncataloged material for Francis A. Countway library. L. Ash. il Library J 89: 2040-3 My 15 '64
See also
Booksellers and bookselling—Medical literature
Medicine—Periodicals
MEDICAL literature analysis and retrieval system. See Information storage and retrieval systems
MEDICAL museums
Medical museum at a crossroads of history; Prairie du Chien, Wis. K. N. Anderson. il Todays Health 41:60-6 D '63
MEDICAL office buildings. See Medical buildings
MEDICAL periodicals. See Medicine—Periodicals
MEDICAL philosophy. See Medicine—Philosophy
MEDICAL photography. See Photography, Medical
MEDICAL practice. See Medicine—Practice
MEDICAL profession. See Medicine—Practice; Physicians
MEDICAL radiology. See Radiology, Medical
MEDICAL relief work

Underdeveloped countries

Cold war of health. F. Marley. il Sci N L 84:35 Jl 20 '63
MEDICAL research
Can man be modified to live in space? K. N. Anderson. il Todays Health 41:20-3+ N '63
Carbon-14 in clinical research; report on conference. G. V. LeRoy. Science 144:731-2 My 8 '64
Casualties in a jungle war; Bolivian hemorrhagic fever. il Time 82:48+ Jl 19 '63
Doctor Koch and the boiled potato. il Todays Health 41:77 D '63
Doctor with one foot in space. K. N. Anderson. il Todays Health 42:32-5+ D '64
Institute for experimental surgical instruments in Moscow. T. Takaro. bibliog il Science 142:195-9 O 11 '63
Instrumentation for biomedical sciences; report of National biomedical sciences instrumentation symposium. F. Alt. Science 142:249-52 O 11 '63
Medical magic. P. Nathan. Parents Mag 39: 43+ N '64
Medical museum at a crossroads of history; Prairie du Chien, Wis. K. N. Anderson. il Todays Health 41:60-6 D '63
Medical progress depends on animal research. H. E. Essex. Todays Health 42:18+ N '64
Medical science reaches for the impossible. L. Galton. il Pop Sci 186:114-18 Ja '65
Medicines of tomorrow; excerpts from Science book of modern medicines. D. G. Cooley. Todays Health 41:38-42 N; 34-6 D '63
Money for medical research. il New Repub 149:29-31 N 9 '63
New hope in fight on heart disease. il Bsns W p47-8 D 12 '64
1963-1964 science review. il Sci N L 84:392-3; 86:394-5 D 21 '63, D 19 '64
Nobel laureates: Bloch and Lynen win prize in medicine and physiology. E. P. Kennedy and F. H. Westheimer. il Science 146:504-6 O 23 '64
Of flies & fevers. il Time 81:38+ F 8 '63
Oh, doctor I need you now. L. Wainwright. Life 57:29 D 11 '64
Political good fortune of medical research. M. Viorst. il Science 144:267-70 Ap 17 '64
Public wary of research. Sci N L 83:178 Mr 23 '63
Quickening war against viruses. M. Pines. Harper 228:90-2+ My '64
Research in biology: new pattern of support is developing. V. K. McElheny. Science 145: 908-12 Ag 28 '64
Research; medicine's unfinished business. I. Davidsohn. Todays Health 41:16, 19 My '63
Separating the inseparable; Albert and Mary Lasker foundation 1963 award. il Time 82: 62+ O 18 '63
Speaking out; sick people need care, not research. L. J. Vorhaus. Sat Eve Post 236:10+ My 11 '63
There's a doctor in the house. B. C. Spicer. Ladies Home J 80:49+ Je '63
They ran the heart study. il Bsns W p50-1+ D 12 '64
Veterinary medicine advances human medicine; excerpts from address. W. H. Feldman. Todays Health 41:12+ N '63
You'll live longer; interview. J. A. Shannon. il Nations Bsns 52:104-6+ Mr '64
See also
Animal experimentation
Calculating machines—Medical applications
Cancer research
Diabetes research
Laboratory animals
Life amplifiers—Medical applications
Physiological research
Rockefeller institute for medical research
Tuberculosis research
United States—National center for environmental sciences
United States—National institutes of health
United States—Navy—Naval medical research unit

Experimentation on man

Cancer; the extent of immunity; injection of hospital patients. Time 83:52 Ja 31 '64
Convict volunteers; for scientific research. T. B. Congdon, jr. il Sat Eve Post 236: 62-4 Mr 2 '63
Experimental ethics. il Newsweek 63:48 F 3 '64
Human guinea pigs and the law. J. Lear; discussion. Sat R 45:65-6 N 3 '62; 46:58-9 F 2 '63
Medical ethics: British unit offers guidelines for research involving human subjects; excerpts from annual report of Britain's Medical research council. Science 145:1024-5+ S 4 '64
Portrait of you as a guinea pig. C. Bird. Esquire 60:64-70 O '63
Volunteers behind bars. il Time 82:72 Jl 12 '63
Window to the human stomach; strangest series of experiments in medical history. il Todays Health 43:88 Ja '65

Federal aid

Death of Dayton; recommendations by President's commission on heart disease, cancer and strokes. il Newsweek 64:70 D 21 '64
Medical research: Congress adds $10 million to president's budget for special studies on leukemia. E. Langer. Science 146:236+ O 9 '64
NIH; House reverses trend, cuts budget request as a new group starts probe into research. D. S. Greenberg. Science 140:467-9 My 3 '63
Presidential medicine: Johnson panel, lay and medical, to study heart disease, cancer, and strokes. E. Langer. Science 143:1308-9 Mr 20 '64
Proper study of mankind. Nation 199:263 O 26 '64
Stimulation of health research. J. H. Cassedy. bibliog Science 145:897-902 Ag 28 '64
War on illness, disease included in new budget. Sci N L 83:66 F 2 '63
MEDICAL research council (Great Britain)
Laboratory of molecular biology, Cambridge. V. K. McElheny. bibliog il Science 144:398-400 Ap 24 '64
Medical ethics: British unit offers guidelines for research involving human subjects; excerpts from annual report of Britain's Medical research council. Science 145:1024-5+ S 4 '64
MEDICAL schools. See Medical colleges
MEDICAL service
Advantages of the National health service. G. Dain. Cur Hist 45:32-3+ Jl '63
Ambulances in a jam; inadequate ambulance services. il Newsweek 64:92 N 2 '64
Changing patterns of health service; their dependence on a changing world. M. I. Roemer. bibliog f Ann Am Acad 346:44-56 Mr '63
Health: are we the people getting our money's worth? symposium, ed. by H. H. Miller. il New Repub 149:5-43 N 9 '63
Impediments to the acquisition and use of medical knowledge; letter. R. D. Baldwin. Science 141:1237-8 S 27 '63; Discussion. 143:8-9 Ja 3 '64
Medical care and the public; case study of a medical group. E. Freidson. Ann Am Acad 346:57-66 Mr '63
Medical care for developing countries. C. E. Taylor. Atlan 213:75-6+ Ja '64
Medical care in the U.S. O. L. Peterson. il Sci Am 209:19-27 bibliog(p 140) Ag '63
Medical health care foundation is model; Onondaga foundation for medical care. Sci N L 84:200 S 28 '63
Sickness and poverty. America 110:307 Mr 7 '64; Reply. D. A. Belknap. 110:469 Ap 4 '64

MEDICAL service—*Continued*
Speaking out; sick people need care, not research. L. J. Vorhaus. Sat Eve Post 236:10+ My 11 '63
Take a second look at those new community health proposals. S. Schuler. Am Home 67: 16+ Jl '64
Tragic inefficiency of our hospital emergency wards. R. Brecher and E. Brecher. Redbook 123:55+ S '64
See also
Airplanes in medical service
Helicopters in medical service

France

France; a comprehensive health plan. H. C. Galant. bibliog f il Cur Hist 44:351-8+ Je '63

India

Public medicine in India. P. Malhotra. bibliog f il Cur Hist 44:359-65+ Je '63

Russia

Medical care in the Soviet Union. A. Z. Rubinstein. bibliog f Cur Hist 44:339-44 Je '63

Sweden

Socialized medicine in Sweden. J. H. Wuorinen. bibliog f il Cur Hist 44:333-8 Je '63

MEDICAL service, Cost of
Are medical costs too high? interview. D. B. Allman. il Todays Health 42:8-10+ S '64
Can the doctor do better? il Bsns W p 103-4+ S 26 '64
Cost of the National health service. G. Forsyth. il Cur Hist 45:19-24+ Jl '63
Deduction of medical bills. Sci N L 85:22 Ja 11 '64
Economics of American medicine, by S. E. Harris. Review
Time 83:62 Je 12 '64
France; a comprehensive health plan. H. C. Galant. bibliog f il Cur Hist 44:351-8+ Je '63
Government health care: first the aged, then everyone. E. R. Annis. bibliog f Cur Hist 45:104-9+ Ag '63
Hedging the great gamble. I. C. Merriam. il New Repub 149:17-19 N 9 '63
Metropolitan medical economics. N. K. Piore. il Sci Am 212:19-27 bibliog(p 134) Ja '65
Nation's health. O. W. Anderson. il Cur Hist 45:65-70+ Ag '63
Problem of medical costs, what can be done about it; with interview with R. E. Brown. il U S News 56:72-5 My 25 '64
Socialized medicine in Sweden. J. H. Wuorinen. bibliog f il Cur Hist 44:333-8 Je '63
Speaking out; hospital rivalry costs you money. G. R. Metcalf. Sat Eve Post 236: 12+ O 19 '63
What doctors & dentists charge. il Changing T 17:30 S '63
What doctors can do to cut the cost of medical care. T. M. Sanders. Harper 228:16+ My '64; Discussion. 229:10 Jl; 11 Ag '64
Why it costs so much to have a baby. M. T. Bloom. il Redbook 121:62-3+ S '63
You can guard against needless surgery. Good H 156:145-7 F '63

MEDICAL service, Industrial
Keeping executives healthy; Scott paper co. program. S. W. Bryant. il Fortune 67:122-3+ Ap '63

MEDICAL service, State
Considerations for policy-makers; the European experience; new US patterns. A. R. Somers; R. S. Morison. New Repub 149:36-41 N 9 '63
Doctors go on strike; doctors vs socialized-medicine in Belgium. P. Hamill. il Sat Eve Post 237:79-83 My 16 '64
Forty-nine to forty-four for medicare; Senate vote. il Newsweek 64:22-3 S 14 '64
Government and medicine abroad; symposium. bibliog f il Cur Hist 44:321-65+ Je '63
Government and medicine in Britain; symposium. bibliog il Cur Hist 45:1-40+ Jl '63
Government and medicine in the United States; symposium. bibliog f il Cur Hist 45:65-114+ Ag '63
Is socialized medicine on the way for U.S? il U S News 57:40-4 S 21 '64
Medicare, labor, race: how Australia handles them; interview. H. Beale. il U S News 54:92-7 Mr 25 '63
Medicarelessness; medical and gastroenterological clinics. Bellevue hospital, N.Y. Nat R 15:207 S 10 '63
Mental health: House committee cuts funds proposed by Kennedy. E. Langer. Science 141:791 Ag 30 '63
Private plans cut health tax need. Nations Bsns 51:44 Ag '63
Setbacks for LBJ: congressional action. Newsweek 64:29+ S 28 '64
Socialism in the armed forces. R. Dudman. il New Repub 149:24-6 N 9 '63
Speaking out; case against federalized medicine. G. M. Fister. Sat Eve Post 236:8+ F 23 '63
State medicine catches on in Canada; how it's working out. il U S News 56:90-1 Ja 27 '64
State medicine for U.S. how close is it? il U S News 58:61-4 Ja 25 '65
Time has not come; AMA opposition to extension of medical care from public sources. New Repub 149:26-8 N 9 '63
What British doctors really think about socialized medicine. R. M. Titmuss. Harper 226:16+ F '63
What next for Medicare? il New Repub 149: 28-9 N 9 '63
Why socialized health schemes fail. H. Schoeck. Nations Bsns 51:40-1+ Mr '63
See also
Great Britain—National health service

Bibliography

Readings on government and medicine. Cur Hist 45:115+ Ag '63

MEDICAL societies
How Chicago doctors spread international goodwill; Aesculapius club. H. G. Earl. il Todays Health 42:10-11+ N '64
See also
American cancer society
California medical association

MEDICAL specialists. See Specialization in medicine

MEDICAL students
How Chicago doctors spread international goodwill; Aesculapius club. H. G. Earl. il Todays Health 42:10-11+ N '64
Loan program that helps you become a doctor. H. Earle. il Todays Health 41:36-41 Jl '63
Medical students: source, selection, and training; letter. G. H. Whipple. Science 142:541 N 1 '63; Reply. B. I. Goldberg. 143:639 F 14 '64
Sex and the doctors. Newsweek 64:101 N 23 '64
What your doctor probably doesn't know about sex. H. I. Lief. Harper 229:92-6 D '64

MEDICAL subject headings. See Subject headings

MEDICAL superstitions. See Medicine, Magic, mystic, etc.

MEDICAL supplies
Medical supplies and appliances. Consumer Rep 29:240-8 D '64

MEDICAL time capsule. See Civilization—Preservation of records

MEDICAL tribune (periodical)
Human guinea pigs and the law. J. Lear: discussion. Sat R 46:58-9 F 2 '63

MEDICAL workers
Your life is in their hands; technicians. T. Irwin. il Todays Health 42:30-3+ Ag '64
See also
Laboratory technicians

MEDICAL world news
Challenging the leader. Time 85:65 Ja 29 '65

MEDICI, Mario
Music makers. R. Gelatt. il por Hi Fi 13:123+ O '63

MEDICI family
Six red balls on a field of gold. P. W. Schmidtchen. il Hobbies 69:106-7 S '64

MEDICINAL plants. See Botany, Medical

MEDICINE
Don't doctor yourself. T. Irwin. il Todays Health 42:36-9+ D '64
Keep up with medicine. See issues of Good housekeeping
Latest advances in the field of medicine. U S 57:12+ Jl 20 '64
Medical highlights of 1963. H. S. Morgan. il Parents Mag 38:54+ O '63
Medical news of the month. M. Fishbein. See issues of McCall's
Medicine and society; symposium, ed. by J. A. Clausen and R. Straus. bibliog f il Ann Am Acad 346:1-148 Mr '63
Medicines of tomorrow; excerpts from Science book of modern medicines. D. G. Cooley. Todays Health 41:38-42 N; 34-6 D '63
Plain talk about family health (title varies) See issues of Better homes and gardens
Plain talk about health and medicine (cont) G. G. Greer. Bet Hom & Gard 41:110-11 F; 92 Mr; 88 Ap '63

MEDICINE—*Continued*
Playing doctor; home remedies. Newsweek 64:94 N 16 '64
Progress of medicine. A. J. Snider. See issues of Science digest
What freedom has meant to medicine. N. A. Welch. Todays Health 42:72 Je '64
See also
Acupuncture
Biomedical engineering
Communication in medicine
Quacks and quackery
Sick, The
Specialization in medicine

Bibliography

Scientific, technical, and medical books to come; ed. by I. E. Stokvis and J. Putnam. Library J 88:4247-75; 89:1126-60+, 2835-70, 4399-436 N 1 '63, Mr 1, Jl, N 1 '64
Scientific, technical and medical books to come; ed. by M. Cooley and I. E. Stokvis. Library J 88:1040-78 Mr 1 '63
Summer scientific, technical and medical books; ed. by I. E. Stokvis and J. Putnam. Library J 88:2739-69 Jl '63

History

American association for the history of medicine; report on 37th annual meeting. J. L. Brand. Science 145:302-3 Jl 17 '64
Daniel Drake and his medical Baedeker; excerpts from Doctors on the frontier. R. Dunlop. il Todays Health 41:42-5+ Mr '63
Doctor's-eye view of the Old West; excerpts from Doctors on the frontier. R. Dunlop. il Todays Health 42:40-3+ Ag '64
Doctors of the frontier. G. Groh. il Am Heritage 14:10-11+ Ap '63
Government and health before the New deal. W. G. Carleton. Cur Hist 45:71-6 Ag '63
I give him barks and saltpeter. P. R. Cutright. bibliog il Am Heritage 15:58-61+ D '63
John Wesley: medical missionary in the New World. R. Dunlop. il Todays Health 42: 20-3+ D '64
Lincoln's doctor used closed chest massage. Sci N L 84:185 S 21 '63
Medical care before World war II. S. J. Hurwitz. Cur Hist 45:2-5+ Jl '63
Medicine, history, and the idea of man. E. D. Pellegrino. bibliog f Ann Am Acad 346:9-20 Mr '63
Science and secrets of early medicine, by J. Thorwald. Review
Sci Digest 55:72 F '64. D. Cohen
Spanish doctors in the old Southwest. R. Dunlop. il Todays Health 41:44-7+ F '63
See also
Surgery—History

Periodicals

Catalog of medical periodicals receives grant of $34,710. Library J 88:3570-1 O 1 '63
John A. Hartford foundation grant to Union catalog of medical periodicals. Wilson Lib Bul 38:122 O '63
100 new periodicals in science, technology, medicine; comp. by staff of Ulrich's international periodicals directory. il Library J 89:1036-41 Mr 1 '64

Philosophy

Medicine, history, and the idea of man. E. D. Pellegrino. bibliog f Ann Am Acad 346:9-20 Mr '63

Practice

Brilliant & fantastic; Thomas Novak, unlicensed physician. Time 84:62 S 18 '64
Changing patterns of health service; their dependence on a changing world. M. I. Roemer. bibliog f Ann Am Acad 346:44-56 Mr '63
Dangers of modern medicine. Sci Digest 55: 85-6 My '64
Doctor's duty. Newsweek 64:35 D 28 '64
Genesis of the National health service. H. Eckstein. bibliog f Cur Hist 45:6-11+ Jl '63
Government health care: first the aged, then everyone. E. R. Annis. bibliog f Cur Hist 45:104-9+ Ag '63
Is this operation necessary? P. A. Lembcke. il New Repub 149:15-17 N 9 '63
Masquerade of a counterfeit doctor; T. Novak, unlicensed physician. B. Lindeman. il Sat Eve Post 238:83-7 Ja 30 '65
Medical care and the public; case study of a medical group. E. Freidson. Ann Am Acad 346:57-66 Mr '63
Medical care in the U.S. O. L. Peterson. il Sci Am 209:19-27 bibliog(p 140) Ag '63
Real life for the doctor's wife. A. Peters. il Todays Health 42:24-5+ Je '64
Side effects: a new worry for doctors; iatrogenic diseases. M. M. Hunt. il Look 27:24-6+ D 31 '63
Social change and medical organization in the United States; a sociological perspective. T. Parsons. bibliog f Ann Am Acad 346:21-33 Mr '63
Tom Dooley writes to a young doctor; excerpt from Promises to keep, by A. W. Dooley. T. Dooley. Read Digest 82:213-14+ F '63
Truth about medication errors in hospitals. W. B. Furlong. il Good H 157:76-7+ N '63
Weaknesses of the National health service. J. Reckless. bibliog f Cur Hist 45:34-40 Jl '63
What is an internist? S. T. Donohue. il Todays Health 41:48-53+ Ap '63
What our future doctors will do about wonder drugs, abortion, medical care for the aged and the high cost of illness. W. Goodman. il Redbook 121:54-5+ My '63
See also
Diagnosis
Malpractice
Medical service
Obstetrics
Physicians
Physicians and patients
Quacks and quackery

Scholarships and fellowships

How Chicago doctors spread international goodwill; Aesculapius club. H. G. Earl. il Todays Health 42:10-11+ N '64

Study and teaching

USSR trains more MD's. Sci N L 87:50 Ja 23 '65
See also
Medical colleges
Medical education

Terminology

Doctors may soon choke on own words. Sci N L 86:308 N 14 '64
Medical language made easy. E. Davis. il Todays Health 43:34-7 Ja '65

Africa

East Africa's one-man peace corps. il Todays Health 41:20-5 Je '63

China

Medieval hormone chemistry; Chinese compendium of pharmaceutical preparations written in 1596. Sci Am 210:68 F '64

China (People's Republic)

Oriental renaissance in education and medicine. W. Penfield. bibliog il Science 141: 1153-61 S 20 '63

Europe, Western

Biomedical science in Europe. R. P. Grant and others. bibliog Science 146:493-501 O 23 '64

Germany (Federal Republic)

Herr doktor's dilemma; need for reform of an archaic system. il Newsweek 64:47 Ag 31 '64
Sick, sick, sick; West German hypochondriacs. Newsweek 63:44+ Mr 23 '64

Great Britain

Aspirin jungle. B. Inglis. Nation 197:83-6 Ag 24 '63; Reply with rejoinder. G. S. Meister. 197:inside cover S 14 '63
Government and medicine in Britain; symposium. bibliog il Cur Hist 45:1-40+ Jl '63

Hong Kong

Project concern; somebody has to care. il Ladies Home J 80:52 Ap '63
See also
Hospitals—Hong Kong

Laos

Tom Dooley writes to a young doctor; excerpt from Promises to keep, by A. W. Dooley. T. Dooley. Read Digest 82:213-14+ F '63

Mississippi

Doctor; Medical committee for human rights program. A. O. Wells. il Nation 199:515-16 D 28 '64

Peru

Ship of hope; American hospital ship Hope. R. L. White. il Todays Health 41:62-7 Jl '63

MEDICINE—*Continued*

Russia

Research at the Moscow medical stomatological institute. T. B. Coolidge. Science 140:856+ My 24 '63

USSR trains more MD's. Sci N L 87:50 Ja 23 '65

Underdeveloped areas

Jungle doctor today; American physicians in Malaysia, Cambodia and the new countries of Africa. F. Marley. il Sci N L 86: 346-7 N 28 '64

United States

Aspirin jungle. B. Inglis. Nation 197:83-6 Ag 24 '63; Reply with rejoinder. G. S. Meister. 197:inside cover S 14 '63

Challenge to our doctors. J. R. Moskin. il Look 28:26-38+ N 3 '64; Discussion. 28:6+ D 15 '64

Fresh discoveries about your health; developments reported at A.M.A. U S News 55:10 Jl 1 '63

Government and medicine in the United States; symposium. bibliog f il Cur Hist 45:65-114+ Ag '63

Grievance committee: medicine's conscience in action. P. E. Hopkins. Todays Health 42:88 Mr '64

Hands and brains; letter. E. G. Dimond. Science 142:445+ O 25 '63; Discussion. 143: 198 Ja 17 '64

Private plans cut health tax need. Nations Bsns 51:44 Ag '63

Speaking out; sick people need care, not research. L. J. Vorhaus. Sat Eve Post 236:10+ My 11 '63

Truth treatment for critics of American medicine. G. M. Fister. Todays Health 41:6+ F '63

What our future doctors will do about wonder drugs, abortion, medical care for the aged and the high cost of illness. W. Goodman. il Redbook 121:54-5+ My '63

Where we stand as 1965 begins. M. Spencer. il Todays Health 43:20-5 Ja '65

Viet Nam (Republic)

Victims; civilian casualties. Nation 198:450 My 4 '64

MEDICINE, Magic, mystic, etc.

Magical cures for an ancient disease. il Todays Health 41:42-3 Ag '63

MEDICINE, Military

See also

United States—Armed forces—Medical and sanitary affairs

MEDICINE, Popular

Anthropological perspectives on medicine and public health. B. D. Paul. bibliog f Ann Am Acad 346:34-43 Mr '63

Granny had a cure for everything. R. Dunlop. il Todays Health 41:30-3+ My '63

Health, society, and social science. R. Straus and J. A. Clausen. bibliog f Ann Am Acad 346:1-8 Mr '63

They don't make medicines that way any more. R. P. Smith. il McCalls 90:114 Jl '63

MEDICINE, Preventive

Hazards of new drugs. W. Modell. bibliog Science 139:1180-5 Mr 22 '63

Medicine moves against the environmental threats to health. R. L. White. Todays Health 42:68+ My '64

New tips on fighting some major ills. U S News 54:6 My 6 '63

See also

Immunity

Public health

MEDICINE, Primitive

Commonwealth of medicine; excerpt from History of mankind. L. Woolley. UNESCO Courier 16:17 Je '63

See also

Medicine men

MEDICINE, Psychosomatic

Anniversary illness. Newsweek 61:94 Ap 15 '63

Family factor. Newsweek 62:81 O 21 '63

Real dangers of those imaginary illnesses. Good H 158:153-4 Mr '64

What is the patient really trying to say? Time 83:48 Ja 3 '64

See also

Mind and body

MEDICINE, State. See Medical service, State

MEDICINE, Veterinary. See Veterinary medicine

MEDICINE and religion

See also

Faith cure

Psychiatry and religion

MEDICINE cabinets

Prevent child poisoning. Consumer Bul 47: 24 Jl '64

Your medicine chest. Parents Mag 38:34 O '63

MEDICINE glasses. See Glassware

MEDICINE kits

Medical supplies for the camper. il Consumer Rep 28:243-5 My '63

MEDICINE men

Blue cross with antelope horns. il Time 85:34 Ja 1 '65

MEDICINES. See Drugs

MEDICINES, Patent, proprietary, etc.

Antibiotics barred for colds. Sci N L 84:130 Ag 31 '63

Cold and cough remedies: facts to know. Good H 157:161-2 N '63

MEDICO (organization)

Prescription for travel. il Time 81:78 Je 14 '63

MEDIEVAL drama. See Drama, Medieval

MEDITATION

Just thinking. P. Wylie. il Ladies Home J 80:48+ N '63

See also

Spiritual exercises

MEDITERRANEAN cookery. See Cookery, Mediterranean

MEDITERRANEAN house decoration. See House decoration, Mediterranean

MEDITERRANEAN REGION

See also

Middle East

Defenses

Soviet proposal of nuclear-free zone in Mediterranean rejected; U.S. note of June 24, and Soviet note of May 20, 1963. Dept State Bul 49:83-6 Jl 15 '63

Description and travel

Return to our beginnings; tour around the eastern end of the Mediterranean. C. J. McNaspy. America 111:351-2 S 26 '64

Economic relations

Western Mediterranean. E. M. v. Kuehnelt-Leddihn. Nat R 15:307 O 8 '63

Politics

Western Mediterranean. E. M. v. Kuehnelt-Leddihn. Nat R 15:307 O 8 '63

MEDITERRANEAN SEA

Dinghy cruise to Turkey; from Cyprus. G. Gaskill. il Yachting 115:48-50+ Mr '64

See also

Aegean Islands

MEDIUM-altitude communications satellite. See Communications satellites—Military applications

MEDIUM; opera. See Menotti, G. C.

MEDLARS (fruit)

Neglected fruits: medlar and persimmon. M. D. Benson. Horticulture 42:15 N '64

MEDLARS (Medical literature analysis and retrieval system) See Information storage and retrieval systems

MEDLEY, Tom

Two stroke stuff. Hot Rod 17:102 Mr; 82 Ap; 86-7 My; 100-1 Je; 106-7 Jl; 106-7 S; 107 O '64; 18:96 Ja '65

MEDWIN, Thomas

Captain Medwin: friend of Byron and Shelley, by E. J. Lovell, jr. Review

Sat R 46:36+ Je 15 '63. H. T. Moore

MEE, Charles L. jr

On stage: Woody Allen. Horizon 5:46-7 My '63

MEECH, Sanford B.

Tribute; poem. Sat R 46:8 D 14 '63

MEEHAN, S. Mendelson

Higan cherry tree. Horticulture 41:538 O '63

MEEHAN, Thomas

Add hot water; serves fourteen million. New Yorker 40:35-7 Mr 28 '64

Claus. New Yorker 40:26-7 Ja 9 '65

Forgettable centenary; Horatio Alger's. N Y Times Mag p22-3+ Je 28 '64

Friday night and Saturday night. New Yorker 39:48-9 O 19 '63

Making the summer weekend scene. Mlle 58: 191-2+ Ap '64

Stand back for Walford W. Oglethorpe, jr! New Yorker 40:37-8 Ap 11 '64

Three variations on a Shakespearean theme. Mlle 58:81-3 F '64

Twenty-four hours in the life of Adlai E. Stevenson, 3rd. McCalls 92:80+ N '64

MEEK, Richard

And all I ask is a tall ship; photographs. Sports Illus 21:22-7 Jl 20 '64

MEEK, Richard—*Continued*
Dick Meek shot Polacolor at Belmont Park and America's cup races. Pop Phot 52:117 Mr '63
MEEKER, Dean
Art; exhibition at William H. Schab galleries. F. Getlein. New Repub 149:30-1 N 30 '63
MEEKER, Leonard C.
Can the United Nations keep world peace in the 1960's? address, April 20, 1964. bibliog f Dept State Bul 50:797-802 My 18 '64
Observation in space; address, April 13, 1963. Dept State Bul 48:746-51 My 13 '63
Role of law in political aspects of world affairs; address, December 29, 1962. Dept State Bul 48:83-8 Ja 21 '63
U.N. subcommittee debates law for outer space; statement, May 3, 1963. Dept State Bul 48:923-5 Je 10 '63
MEEKS, Howard
Washington mink ranch. il pors Ebony 18: 83-4+ Mr '63
MEEKS family
Meeks family of cabinetmakers. J. N. Pearce and others. il Antiques 85:414-20 Ap '64
MEEMAN, Edward J.
Total living; address, July 11, 1963. Vital Speeches 29:662-5 Ag 15 '63
MEERMAN, Jacob P.
Rickover and our schools. New Repub 148: 15-18 Ap 27; 30-1 My 27 '63
MEETING at Dors River; story. See Jacobson, D.
MEETING place; story. See Randall, F. E.
MEETINGS
Make your meetings more worth while. H. P. Zelko. il Nations Bsns 52:92-4+ S '64
Meetings; annual spring meetings, conventions, Olympiads, and symposiums in New York. New Yorker 40:41-3 My 16 '64
See also
Conventions
Stockholders meetings
MEEUS, Jean
Galileo's first records of Jupiter's satellites; reprint. Sky & Tel 27:105-6 F '64
MEGALITHIC monuments
Megaliths and men; European megaliths. G. E. Daniel. il Natur Hist 73:46-53 Ap '64
See also
Callernish, Scotland
MEGAZOPHERUS chiliensis. See Beetles
MEGEL, Carl J.
Scholastic teacher interviews; Carl J. Megel; ed. by H. Langer. por Sr Schol 83:24T-26T O 4 '63
MÉGÈVE, France
Baron Edmond de Rothschild's party; Mont d'Arbois hotel above Mégève. F. de Langlade. il Vogue 141:162-5 Mr 15 '63
MEHDEVI, Anne Sinclair
Persian courtship; excerpts from Persia revisited. Harper 228:48-53 Je '64
MEHL, John W.
Research grants, are they worth saving? Science 142:914-16 N 15 '63
—and others
Macroglobulin from human plasma which forms an enzymatically active compound with trypsin. bibliog Science 145:821-2 Ag 21 '64
MEHLE, Aileen
Suzy says; latest international gossip. P. Coffin. il Look 28:87-90+ Ag 11 '64
MEHLER, Alan H. and others
Nicotinic acid biosynthesis: control by an enzyme that competes with a spontaneous reaction. bibliog Science 145:817-19 Ag 21 '64
MEHLING, Harold
How to win the fight for a new school. Redbook 122:48-9+ Ja '64
MEHLMAN, William
German reparations and the Israeli economy. Reporter 29:43-5 S 12 '63
Jordan's troubled waters. Reporter 30:29+ Ja 30 '64
MEHNERT, Klaus
Chinese and the Russians; excerpt from Peking and Moscow. bibliog f Ann Am Acad 349:1-13 S '63
MEHREN, George L.
Agriculture and USDA policy; address December 5, 1963. Vital Speeches 30:155-7 D 15 '63
MEHTA, Ved
Call girl; story. Harper 227:82-6 Jl '63
Delinquent Chacha, esq; story. New Yorker 38:35-9 F 16 '63
Four hundred and twenty; story. New Yorker 39:56-62 D 7 '63
Onward and upward with the arts (cont) New Yorker 39:98+ My 18 '63
Profiles; B. H. Blackwell, ltd, Oxford. New Yorker 40:63-4+ O 31 '64; 87 Ja 9 '65
about
I want to know Y. il por Time 82:98+ Jl 12 '63
MEHTA, Zubin
Music to my ears; debut of Mehta. I. Kolodin. Sat R 46:37 Mr 2 '63
Musical events; concert performed by American symphony orchestra in Carnegie Hall. W. Sargeant. New Yorker 39:137-8 F 23 '63
Next Toscanini? por Time 84:38 Ag 14 '64
MEIDINGER, Shirley Rolfs
Are you up to date with freezing? Bet Hom & Gard 42:109-11 O '64
MEIER, Gilbert W.
Behavior of infant monkeys: differences attributable to mode of birth. bibliog Science 143:968-70 F 28 '64
MEIGS field. See Chicago—Airports
MEIKLEJOHN, Alexander
Alexander Meiklejohn. Nation 199:506 D 28 '64
Innovator. Newsweek 64:52 D 28 '64
MEINECKE, Ingeborg
Klaus Schultze; tr. by A. Adams. Sch Arts 64:16-18 D '64
MEINEL, Aden B.
Astronomy. Science 141:178+ Jl 12 '63
—and Meinel, C. P.
Low-latitude noctilucent cloud of 2 November 1963. Science 143:38 Ja 3 '64
—and others
Low-latitude noctilucent cloud of 15 June 1963. il Science 141:1176-8 S 20 '63
—See Meinel, M. P. jt. auth.
MEINEL, Carolyn P. See Meinel, A. B. jt. auth.
MEINEL, Marjorie Pettit, and Meinel, A. B.
Late twilight glow of the ash stratum from the eruption of Agung volcano. Science 142: 582-3 N 1 '63
MEINERS, Norm
First-aid for foundering dinghies. Motor B 113:32-3+ Mr '64
Flying bridge in kit form. Motor B 111:32-3+ Mr '63
Flying bridge instrument panel. Motor B 112:52+ O '63
Re-upholster your helmsman's seat. Motor B 113:30+ Mr '64
Teak ladder for the flying bridge. Motor B 112:51+ O '63
MEINESZ, Felix Andries Vening-. See Vening-Meinesz, F. A.
MEINKE, W. W.
Radiochemical methods of analysis. Science 147:182-3 Ja 8 '65
MEINSCHEIN, W. G. and others
Biological remnants in a Precambrian sediment. bibliog Science 145:262-3 Jl 17 '64
MEIOSIS. See Cell division (biology)
MEIR, Golda
Golda Meir; woman with a cause, by M. Syrkin. Review
Commentary 38:63-4 Jl '64. A. Sherman; Reply with rejoinder. G. Meir. 38:26+ N '64
MEISEL, Alan
Silver by Alexandra Watkins. Craft Horiz 23:26-7+ N '63
MEISELS, Henry R.
Grimm tale. por Wilson Lib Bul 39:165-7 O '64
MEISLER, Stanley
Blowing Barry's horn. Nation 197:48-9 Jl 27 '63
Dodge City syndrome. Nation 198:460:460-1 My 4 '64
Future of Tom Mboya. Reporter 28:41-4 F 14 '63
Get your gun from the army. Nation 198:568-71 Je 8 '64
Lie detectors: trial by gadget. Nation 199: 159-62+ S 28 '64
Meddling in Latin America. Nation 198:133-8 F 10 '64
Two Goldwaters. Nation 197:256-9 O 26 '63
—See Duke, P. jt. auth.
MEISLER, Stanley. See Duke, P. jt. auth.
MEISSEN china. See Pottery, German
MEISSONNIER, Jean
Dynasty of marine painters: the Roux family of Marseilles. Antiques 86:583-7 N '64
Ship painters of the Mediterranean. Antiques 83:304-8 Mr '63
MEISTER, Barbara
First cruise. Yachting 113:204-7 My '63
MEISTERMANN, Georg
Restless glass. il Time 81:68-9 Mr 29 '63
MEITNER, Lise
Looking back. por Bul Atomic Sci 20:2-7 N '64

MEJÍA, Eladia
Colombia's extraordinary teacher-builder. S. Seegers and K. Seegers. por Read Digest 82:111-15 Mr '63

MEJÍA, Gabriel Betancur-. See Betancur-Mejía, G.

MEKAS, Jonas
Cinema underground; Film-makers' coöperative, or Underground cinema. New Yorker 39:16-17 Jl 13 '63
Explosion in the movie underground. P. Hamill. il Sat Eve Post 236:82+ S 28 '63
Private. New Yorker 40:27-8 Ja 16 '65

MEKONG RIVER
Battle of time and the river. il Newsweek 62:36-8+ Jl 15 '63
Harnessing the Mekong. il UNESCO Courier 17:46-7 Jl '64
Mekong River plan. G. F. White. il Sci Am 208:49-59 bibliog(p200) Ap '63
Revolution on the Mekong. J. Burnham. Nat R 15:436 N 19 '63
Vietnam: the fourth course; international cooperation in science. G. F. White. il Bul Atomic Sci 20:6-10 D '64

MELADY, Thomas Patrick
Sweep of nationalism in Africa; address, April 11, 1964; with questions and answers. Ann Am Acad 354:91-6 Jl '64
Violence in Africa. America 109:734-5 D 7 '63
Zambia: new nation in Africa. Cath World 200:91-4 N '64

MELAMINE dinnerware. See Tableware, Plastic

MELAMINE tableware. See Tableware, Plastic

MELAND, Bernard Eugene
Modern Protestantism: aimless or resurgent? Christian Cent 80:1494-7 D 4 '63

about

Liberal theology reconstructed. D. D. Williams. Christian Cent 81:1494-6 D 2 '64

MELANIN
Melanin may modulate visual impulses. Sci Digest 53:53 F '63

MELATONIN
Melatonin, a pineal substance: effect on the rat ovary. R. J. Wurtman and others. bibliog il Science 141:277-8 Jl 19 '63
Melatonin synthesis in the pineal gland: control by light. R. J. Wurtman and others. bibliog il Science 142:1071-3 N 22 '63
Melatonin synthesis in the pineal gland: effect of light mediated by the sympathetic nervous system. R. J. Wurtman and others. bibliog il Science 143:1328-30 Mr 20 '64
5-methoxytryptophol: effect on estrus and ovarian weight. W. M. McIsaac and others. bibliog il Science 145:63-4 Jl 3 '64

MELBA, Dame Nellie
Meanest woman in the world. D. S. Russell. por Opera N 28:26-8 Ja 11 '64
Melba. A. Favia-Artsay. pors Hobbies 68: 30-1+ Mr '63

MELBOURNE, Australia
Ghastly blank; first exploration of Australia; excerpt from Cooper's Creek. A. Morehead. il Atlan 213:100-14 F '64

Stores

Down-under Macy's; Myer emporium. il Time 84:83 Jl 17 '64

MELBOURNE, Fla.

Education

Cape Kennedy's high school for sky-high learning. B. Asbell. il PTA Mag 58:14-16 Ja '64
Melbourne: ungraded high. H. Langer. il Sr Schol 83:18T-19T O 4 '63
Nongraded high school. A. Lass; J. S. Bruner. Sat R 47:70-2+ Ja 18 '64

MELBOURNE-Voyager collision. See Collisions at sea

MELBY, Ernest O.
Advancing the cause of education. por NEA J 52:29 F '63

MELCHER, Daniel
Central processing on a do-it-yourself basis. Library J 90:316-19 Ja 15 '65
Goals in national bibliography. Library J 89: 2556-9 Je 15 '64
Plea for sanity. Library J 89:3108-11 S 1 '64
Remarkable success. Library J 89:1836 Ap 15 '64

MELCHER, Frederic Gershom
Memory of Robert Frost and his influence. Pub W 183:98 F 11 '63

about

F. G. Melcher. por Library J 88:1721-2 Ap 15 '63
Frederic G. Melcher: 1879-1963. H. Bowser. por Sat R 46:29 Mr 30 '63
Frederic G. Melcher, 1879-1963. il pors Library J 88:1392-5 Ap 1 '63
Frederic G. Melcher: 1879-1963. il pors Pub W 183:16-19+ Mr 18 '63
Frederic Melcher and children's books. R. Gagliardo. il por ALA Bul 57:549-52 Je '63
Mr Melcher. E. Rudin. Library J 88:1706 Ap 15 '63
Obituary
Wilson Lib Bul por 37:618 Ap '63. H. Haycraft
To Frederic G. Melcher, 1879-1963. R. H. Viguers. Horn Bk 39:251 Je '63

MELCHER, Frederic G, book award. See Frederic G. Melcher book award

MELCHER, Terry
Doris Day I know; ed. by G. Christy. pors Good H 157:88-91+ O '63

MELCHIOR, Lauritz
Melchior today; interview, ed. by L. F. Loveday. por Opera N 28:26-7 F 1 '64
Quote: unquote; interview, ed. by J. Ardoin. por Mus Am 83:17 Je '63

about

Documentation, mostly operatic, of Melchior's fifty years in music. P. L. Miller. Am Rec G 30:110 O '63

MELCHIOR, Marcus
Danish rabbi speaks; concerning Hochhuth's play, The deputy. America 110:30 Ja 11 '64

MELCHITES. See Catholic church—Byzantine rite

MELHADO, Ruth
Dive-in premiere makes movie history. Sr Schol 84:25+ F 21 '64

MELKITES. See Catholic church—Byzantine rite

MELLAART, James
Neolithic city in Turkey; with biographical sketch. Sci Am 210:27, 94-104 Ap '64

MELLEN, Betty
Adventure in aquilegia. Horticulture 41:331 Je '63

MELLICHAMP, J. W. and Levey, Martin
Silver from Ur of ancient Mesopotamia. Science 142:44-5 O 4 '63

MELLIN, William J.
On air. New Yorker 39:19-20 Ag 31 '63

MELLO E SOUZA, Cláudio. See Netto, A. jt. auth.

MELLON, Andrew
Andrew Mellon on tax cuts. D. F. Swanson. il New Repub 148:22 Mr 23 '63
Empire built by generations of Mellons. por Bsns W p 108 Je 1 '63

MELLON, Paul
Paul Mellon. New Yorker 39:40-1 O 5 '63
People are talking about. il por Vogue 141:130-1 My '63

MELLON, Paul, collection. See Art—Private collections

MELLON, Richard King
Empire built by generations of Mellons. por Bsns W p 108 Je 1 '63

MELLON, Thomas A.
Empire built by generations of Mellons. por Bsns W p 108 Je 1 '63

MELLON collection. See Art—Private collections

MELLON national bank and trust company. See Pittsburgh—Banks

MELMAN, Seymour
Economic alternatives to arms prosperity. bibliog f Ann Am Acad 351:121-31 Ja '64
Military power and money. Sat R 46:10-12 My 4 '63

about

Melman: Overkill critic finds a welcome reception in capital, but the reasons are complicated. D. S. Greenberg. Science 144:271-3 Ap 17 '64
Overkill of Melman. Nation 198:359 Ap 13 '64

MELNICK, Joseph L. and others
Picornaviruses: classification of nine new types. bibliog Science 141:153-4 Jl 12 '63
—See Smith, K. O. jt. auth.

MELNICK, Matilda Benyesh-. See Benyesh-Melnick, M.

MELNICK, Vijaya L. Moosad. See Moosad Melnick, V. L.

MELO, Juan Vicente
Hidden signs; story, tr. by L. Kemp. Atlan 213:146-8 Mr '64

MELODIES
Why aren't more show tunes for whistling. T. Prideaux. Life 57:12 Ag 7 '64

MELODRAMA
Curses, foiled again! E. M. Halliday. il Am Heritage 15:12-23 D '63
Melodrama on Broadway: our secret lives are showing. R. Hatch. Horizon 5:106-8 My '63

MELONS
See also
Cookery—Fruit
Muskmelons

MELOY, Guy S. Jr
U.S. troops in Korea: ready and confident; interview. por U S News 55:65 Jl 22 '63

MELTON, Arthur W.
Memory. Science 140:82-4 Ap 5 '63

MELTSNER, Michael
Twelve white men and true. New Repub 150:11-12 My 23 '64

MELTZER, Robert J.
Inventor of the month. S. V. Jones. por Sci Digest 56:44 N '64

MELVILLE, Herman
Benito Cereno; dramatization. See Lowell, R. Old Glory
Melville in the darbies. por Time 83:99-E7 My 1 '64

MELVILLE ISLAND, Australia
Qualifications for adulthood. J. C. Goodale. il Natur Hist 72:10-17 Ap '63

MELVIN, A. Gordon
Deepstar for shells? Hobbies 68:130+ Mr '63
Mystic seaport. Hobbies 68:130 Je '63
Natural history. See issues of Hobbies
Shell money. il Hobbies 68:130 Ap '63
Top shell man. Hobbies 68:130+ My '63
Unique shell collection. Hobbies 69:130+ Mr '64
West Coast rock shells. Hobbies 67:130+ F '63

MELVIN, Glen E.
Spark plug diagnosis. Suc Farm 62:47 My '64

MELZER, Esther L.
For Rosie, my sister dead at fourteen; poem. Sat R 47:33 Je 27 '64

MEMBERS of Parliament
Eighteen-hour day of a British backbencher. L. Stone. il N Y Times Mag p32-3+ Ja 10 '65
Pay raise for Parliament; but nothing like Congress gets. U S News 57:12 N 30 '64
Underprivileged M.P.s; recommended salary increases. Time 84:39-40 N 27 '64

MEMBERY, Joan H. and Link, E. A.
Hyperbaric exposure of mice to pressures of 60 to 90 atmospheres. bibliog Science 144:1241-2 Je 5 '64

MEMBRANES
Cytochrome content of mitochondria stripped of inner membrane structure. B. Chance and others. bibliog il Science 143:136-9 Ja 10 '64
Membrane permeability: monolayer relationships. A. M. Shanes. bibliog il Science 140:824-5 My 17 '63
Permselective membranes: spectroscopic and conductivity effects. G. Stein and C. Forgacs. il Science 142:953-4 N 15 '63
Thin membranes of parlodion. N. Lakshminarayanaiah and A. M. Shanes. il Science 141:43-4 Jl 5 '63

MEMBRANES (biology)
Permeability of insect cuticle to water and lipids. M. Locke. bibliog il Science 147:295-8 Ja 15 '65

MEMBRANES (technology)
Artificial gill; synthetic membrane extracting oxygen from air or seawater. Sci Am 211:59-60 N '64
Cellulose acetate membranes: electron microscopy of structure. R. Riley and others. bibliog il Science 143:801-3 F 21 '64
Gills for a hamster. il Life 57:55-6 N 6 '64
Membrane filters air; silicone membrane. il(p289) Sci N L 86:293 N 7 '64
Membrane helps purify contaminated water. Sci N L 86:293 N 7 '64
Now, human gills. il Sci Digest 56:10-11 D '64

MEMOIR of a long, long war; story. See Platnick, K. B.

MEMOIRS. See Autobiography

MEMORIAL sculpture. See Sepulchral monuments

MEMORIAL services
See also
Kennedy, J. F.—Memorial services

MEMORIAL trusts. See Trusts and trustees

MEMORIALS
Monuments and landmarks; commemorating deeds of outstanding Negroes. il Ebony 18:107-10+ S '63
See also
Kennedy, J. F.—Memorials
Monuments
Statutes

MEMORIZING
Why do we neglect the useful art of memorizing? T. J. Fleming. Read Digest 82:271+ Ap '63

MEMORY
Can you improve your memory? il Changing T 17:21-3 F '63
Chemistry of memory. Newsweek 61:109 Je 24 '63
Forgetting. B. J. Underwood. il Sci Am 210:91-4+ bibliog(p 152) Mr '64
Hippocampectomy and behavior sequences. D. P. Kimble and K. H. Pribram. bibliog Science 139:824-5 Mr 1 '63
How to teach your child to remember. H. Pollan. il Parents Mag 39:54-5+ Mr '64
How we remember, why we forget? J. E. Pfeiffer. Read Digest 83:123-5 N '63
I'm absent in mind only; excerpt from Short history of fingers and other state papers. H. A. Smith. il Read Digest 84:15-16+ Mr '64
Is memory a matter of enzyme induction? C. E. Smith; discussion. Science 139:1090-2+ Mr 15 '63
Learning, remembering and forgetting; report on New York academy of sciences conference. D. Kimble. Science 146:1605 D 18 '64
Man's mysterious memory machine. D. E. Wooldridge. il Harper 226:57-63 Je '63
Memory; AAAS Philadelphia meeting, December 1962. A. W. Melton. Science 140:82-4 Ap 5 '63
Memory in mice as affected by intracerebral puromycin. J. B. Flexner and others. bibliog il Science 141:57-9 Jl 5 '63
Molecular theories of memory. W. Dingman and M. B. Sporn. bibliog Science 144:26-9 Ap 3 '64
Puromycin effect on memory fixation in the goldfish. B. W. Agranoff and P. D. Klinger. bibliog il Science 146:952-3 N 13 '64
Retention in immediate memory estimated without retrieval. H. Buschke. bibliog il Science 140:56-7 Ap 5 '63
Twins human calendars; idiot savants. Sci N L 85:343 My 30 '64
Visual problem-solving in a bottlenose dolphin. W. N. Kellogg and C. E. Rice. bibliog il Science 143:1052-5 Mr 6 '64
Where is science taking us? P. Handler. Sat R 46:49 My 4 '63
Why do we neglect the useful art of memorizing? T. J. Fleming. Read Digest 82:271+ Ap '63
See also
Maze tests
Past, The
Reminiscence
Retention (psychology)

Anecdotes, facetiae, satire, etc.

Remember me to what's his name. W. Stanton. Sat R 46:27-8 Ag 24 '63; Same abr. Read Digest 83:121-2 O '63

MEMORY, Loss of. See Amnesia

MEMORY devices (calculating machines)
Sandia development tops IEEE hardware; memory elements for use with nuclear weapon systems. C. D. LaFond. Miss & Roc 14:44+ Ap 6 '64

MEMORY; story. See Damore, L.

MEMPHIS, Tenn.
Endrin in Memphis. New Repub 150:4-5 My 2 '64
Memphis: the quiet, please city. W. R. Vath. il Todays Health 41:42-3+ F '63

Airports

Airport for jets and pistons. R. P. Harover. il Arch Rec 134:165-72 O '63

Architecture

Banking function determines form. il Arch Rec 135:124-5 Ja '64

Education

Compact three level design achieved at moderate cost. il Arch Rec 136:238-9 S '64

Music

[Musical events] Mus Am 84:24 Ap '64
See also
Memphis symphony orchestra

Negroes

Memphis moves toward racial justice. Christian Cent 81:1102-3 S 9 '64

Politics and government

New, new guard of the GOP. V. E. Lewis and H. Chambers. Nation 199:85-8 S 7 '64

MEMPHIS, Tenn.—*Continued*

Theater

Company way; another approach to The country wife. H. Hewes. Sat R 47:28 Ag 15 '64

MEMPHIS symphony orchestra
Symphony story. B. C. Tuthill. Mus Am 83:13 Jl '63

MEN
All about men; excerpt from Profession: housewife. P. McGinley. Ladies Home J 80:87+ Ja '63
How men fall in love. D. Newman and R. Benton. Mlle 59:12+ Je '64
How to please a man. il House & Gard 124:53-110 Jl '63
Italian man; with photographs by Paul Schutzer. Life 55:54-9 Ag 23 '63
Men talk: Mr Wrong. D. Newman and R. Benton. il Mlle 60:90-1 D '64
New wild West; cowboy rides. R. L. Gilbert, jr. il Esquire 60:138-9+ O '63
Older man; questions and answers. A. Wood. il Seventeen 23:224-5+ Ag '64
Pashes. L. Lerman. il Mlle 57:86-9 Je '63
See also
Bachelors
Cookery by men
Husbands
Sex differences
Young men

Clothing

See Clothing and dress—Men

Health and hygiene

How to predict the next heart attack. Bsns W p34 O 26 '63
Keeping executives healthy; Scott paper co. program. S. W. Bryant. il Fortune 67:122-3+Ap '63
Mid-career slump, the unspoken threat. T. R. Brooks. Duns R 84:38-9+ N '64
Performance and the tired businessman; causes and effects of fatigue. H. J. Johnson. il Duns R 85:45-6+ Ja '65
Sensible ways to keep fit. bibliog il Changing T 18:44-6 N '64
Way to stay healthy; a doctor's advice to businessmen; address, April 2, 1963. D. L. Farnsworth. il U S News 55:72-4 Ag 26 '63
What killed Bob Lyons? executive's emotional problems. H. Levinson. il Harvard Bsns R 41:127-42+ Ja '63

Psychology

Masculinity: what is it? with questions and answers. B. H. Hoffman. il Ladies Home J 80:96+ Ja '63

MEN and women. See Women and men

MENAGERIES
Have zoo, will travel. W. Trombley. il Sat Eve Post 237:72-3 Ag 8 '64

MENAKER, Michael
X-rays: are there cyclic variations in radiosensitivity? bibliog Science 143:597 F 7 '64

MENARCHE. See Puberty

MENARD, Edith
He sleeps; in memory of President John F. Kennedy, November 22, 1963; poem. Negro Hist Bul 28:48 N '64
John Willis Menard: first Negro elected to the U.S. Congress. bibliog por Negro Hist Bul 28:53-4 D '64

MENARD, John Willis
John Willis Menard: first Negro elected to the U.S. Congress. E. Menard. bibliog por Negro Hist Bul 28:53-4 D '64

MENARD, Wilmon
Sea gypsies of China. Natur Hist 74:12-21 Ja '65

MENASHE, Samuel
Judgment day; poem. Commonweal 79:622 F 21 '64

MENCHIN, Robert S.
Last caprice; excerpts. McCalls 90:126-7+ S '63

MENCKEN, Henry Louis
Anti-intellectualism in American life, by R. Hofstadter. Review
Reporter 29:37-40 Jl 4 '63. K. S. Lynn
Mencken: prejudices and prophecies. C. Angoff. por Sat R 46:44-5 Ag 10 '63; Discussion. 46:48 O 12; 54 D 14 '63

MENCONI, L. A.
Combine your purchases and save. Am City 78:83 D '63

MENDE, Erich
Kingmaker? il por Newsweek 63:26+ Mr 30 '64

MENDELISM
See also
Genetics

MENDELL, Stanley
Inventor of the month. por Sci Digest 55:52-3 Je '64

MENDELS, Ora
Revolution in childbirth? Ladies Home J 80:40 Ja '63

MENDELSOHN, Michael J.
(ed) See Odets, C. Odets at center stage

MENDELSON, Herbert
Polarity indicators provide an end to shore-side shock. Motor B 112:43+ N '63

MENDELSON, Martin, and Loewenstein, W. R.
Mechanisms of receptor adaptation. bibliog Science 144:554-5 My 1 '64

MENDENHALL, Howard
Conservancy districts; useful tools for water development. Am For 69:20-2+ Ag '63

MENDENHALL, Thomas Corwin
Thomas C. Mendenhall: he keeps an eye on 2,300 girls. C. S. Wren. il pors Look 28:104-8 Je 2 '64

MENDERES, Adnan
Our far-flung correspondents. C. Frankel. il New Yorker 40:136+ Je 6 '64

MENDES, E. G. and others
Cholinergic action of homogenates of sea urchin pedicellariae. bibliog Science 139:408-9 F 1 '63

MENDÈS-FRANCE, Pierre
Pierre Mendès-France; why he disagrees with de Gaulle. J. Daniel. New Repub 150:9-11 F 29 '64

MENDES PINTO, Fernão
Voyages and adventures of Ferdinand Mendez Pinto; tr. by H. Cogan; excerpts. UNESCO Courier 16:17 Ap '63

about

Portuguese Sancho Panza in the Far East. A. J. Saraiva. il UNESCO Courier 16:14-19 Ap '63

MENDEZ PINTO, Ferdinand. See Mendes Pinto, F.

MENDING
Make a point of pretty patches. B. G. Wadsworth. il Parents Mag 39:50 S '64

MENDLOVITZ, Saul H.
Teaching war prevention. Bul Atomic Sci 20:19-22 F '64

MENDOCINO COUNTY, Calif.
Mendocino's Olympian charge. D. Messinesi. Vogue 144:90 O 15 '64

MENDOZA, Eugenio
Don Eugenio shows the way. G. W. Hill. por Read Digest 82:245-6+ Je '63
Philanthropy is not enough. il por Time 81:29 Ap 12 '63

MENDOZA GIMENO, Carlos
Who's who in foreign business. por Fortune 70:84 Jl '64

MENE, mene, tekel, upharsin; story. See Cheever, J.

MENEFEE, Allen R. See Cortazzo, A. D. jt. auth.

MENEN, Aubrey
Actor, Italian style. Holiday 37:95+ Ja '65
Coat hanger; symbol of every man's dilemma. House & Gard 124:68-9+ Jl '63
Conversation with a sacred cow; story. Holiday 36:86-7 N '64
Dazzled in Disneyland. Holiday 34:68-70+ Jl '63
Discovering basketball. Holiday 33:62-3+ F '63
Etruscan enigma. Holiday 34:46-51+ S '63
Parthenon: beauty revisited. Holiday 35:54-5+ Ja '64
Pope visits a lost tribe. N Y Times Mag p34-5+ N 29 '64
Return to India. Holiday 35:38-55 My '64
Trouble with Italian politics. N Y Times Mag p28-9+ N 22 '64
Villa with a view. House & Gard 125:112-13 Je '64

MENÉNDEZ, Pedro
Fort that went to sea! F. Decoste. Am For 70:15 Ag '64

MENEZ, Joseph F.
Dilemma of succession. Commonweal 79:475-7 Ja 24 '64

MENG, John
Inviting Communists to speak at colleges; address, 1962. W. F. Buckley, jr. il Nat R 15:343-5+ O 22 '63

MENGEL, John T.
Satellite tracking, telemetry, and communications. Electr World 71:58-60 Je '64

MENHIRS
Megaliths and men. G. E. Daniel. il Natur Hist 73:46-53 Ap '64

MENICHELLI, Vincent J.
Reliable exploding bridgewire remains to be developed. Miss & Roc 13:34+ D 16 '63

MENIER, Henri
Legacy of a French Noah; whitetail deer to Anticosti Island. J. Olsen. il Sports Illus 19:62-4+ O 7 '63
MENINGITIS
Attack & repulse; cases at San Diego naval training center. Time 81:50 Mr 22 '63
Lymphocytic choriomeningitis infection in neonatally thymectomized mice bearing diffusion chambers containing thymus. R. H. Levey and others. bibliog il Science 142: 483-5 O 25 '63
Meningitis outbreak sparks new research. Sci N L 86:264 O 24 '64
Recruits' meningitis; outbreak at California's Fort Ord. Time 84:58 Ag 14 '64
Seek meningitis vaccine. Sci N L 84:291 N 9 '63
MENINGOCOCCAL meningitis. See Meningitis
MENJOU, Adolphe
Dolph Menjou. M. Ryskind. Nat R 15:440 N 19 '63
MENKEN, Adah Isaacs
Naked lady or Don't take your sister to Astley's. M. M. Marberry. il pors Horizon 6:112-18 Wint '64
Queen of the plaza, by P. Lewis. Review
Sat R 47:73 O 24 '64. J. K. Hutchens
MENLO PARK, Calif.
Education
Ages three to fourteen in one school; Peninsula school. il Arch Rec 133:177-9 My '63
MENNEN company
Report on the testing of advertised products; Mennen's baby products. E. M. McCabe. il Parents Mag 38:24+ Mr '63
MENNIN, Peter
Music to my ears; performance of Symphony no. 7 by Cleveland orchestra. I. Kolodin. Sat R 47:25 Mr 7 '64
MENNINGER, Edward J.
Catechism comes to life. America 111:36-8 Jl 11 '64
MENNINGER, Karl Augustus
Speaking out. por Sat Eve Post 237:12+ Ap 25 '64
about
Books. E. G. Boring. Sci Am 210:145-6+ Ap '64
New classification and a greater hope. il por Time 82:53 N 29 '63
MENNINGER foundation and clinic, Topeka, Kan.
Menninger builds houses for children. il Arch Rec 134:170-3 N '63
Menninger patient center. il Recreation 57: 220-1 My '64
MENNONITES
Baugo and Zagorsk: extremes in encounter. D. W. Brown. Christian Cent 81:52+ Ja 8 '64
Fill yourself up, clean your plate; with recipes. A. Robertson. il Am Heritage 15:56-66+ Ap '64
Inbreeding & dwarfism. il Time 84:59-60 Ag 21 '64
Pennsylvania Dutch. J. Hay. Holiday 36: 40-1+ Ag '64
USC focuses on the Pennsylvania Dutch. W. E. Homan. il U S Camera 27:30-1+ Ap '64
MENON, Vengalil Krishnan Krishna. See Krishna Menon, V. K.
MENOPAUSE
Durable, unendurable women. Time 84:72 O 16 '64
No more menopause? il Newsweek 63:53 Ja 13 '64
Preventing menopause. Newsweek 63:70 Mr 30 '64
Truth about female hormones. S. A. Kaufman. Ladies Home J 82:22-3 Ja '65
MENOTTI, Gian Carlo
I am the savage. por Opera N 28:8-12 F 8 '64
Quote: unquote; interview, ed. by M. Brozen. por Mus Am 84:28 Ja '64
about
Amelia goes to the ball. Criticism
New Yorker 39:96 My 18 '63
Guilt of Gian Carlo Menotti. S. Chotzinoff. il por Holiday 33:101-2+ Je '63
Labyrinth. Criticism
Opera N 27:33 Ap 13 '63
Sat R 46:94 Mr 16 '63
Last savage (Le dernier sauvage) Criticism
Life il 56:66A-66B F 14 '64
New Yorker 39:198-200 N 2 '63
New Yorker 39:60+ F 1 '64
Newsweek il 63:77 F 3 '64
Opera N 28:24-5 F 8 '64
Opera N il 28:30 D 7 '63
Opera N il 28:13-15 F 8 '64
Opera N il 28:17-20 F 8 '64
Sat R 47:27-8 F 8 '64
Sat R 48:22 Ja 16 '65
Time il 83:33 Ja 31 '64
Martin's lie. Criticism
Newsweek il 63:93 Je 15 '64
Measure of Menotti. H. Butler. Opera N 28:27 F 8 '64
Medium. Criticism
New Yorker 39:96 My 18 '63
Menotti's hour. il Time 81:46 Mr 8 '63
De morte et conscientia. il por Time 81:40 My 31 '63
Music to my ears; presentation of Death of the Bishop of Brindisi, by Boston symphony at Philharmonic Hall. I. Kolodin. Sat R 47:28 N 7 '64
Musical events; performance of Menotti's cantata Death of the Bishop of Brindisi by the Boston symphony. W. Sargeant. New Yorker 40:231 O 31 '64
On records. Opera N 28:35 F 8 '64
Profiles. W. Sargeant. por New Yorker 39:49-50+ My 4 '63
Sad savage; world premiere of Menotti's The last savage. Time 82:63 N 1 '63
MENS clothes. See Clothing and dress—Men
MENS periodicals. See Periodicals for men
MENS shirts. See Shirts
MENSA (society)
Beard with the big brain. il Life 57:73-4+ Jl 24 '64
High I.Q. frat. S. Alexander. il Life 55:11+ Ag 16 '63
MENSTRUATION
Girl talk; questions and answers. S. Williamson. Seventeen 23:132-3+ My '64
Menstrual cycle influences grooming behavior and sexual activity in the rhesus monkey. R. P. Michael and J. Herbert. bibliog il Science 140:500-1 My 3 '63
New help for the monthly blues. B. C. Spicer. Ladies Home J 80:16 Mr '63
Disorders
Why men should know more about menstruation. G. Naismith. Todays Health 41:22-3+ S '63
MENSTRUATION, Cessation of. See Menopause
MENTAL ability. See Ability; Intelligence
MENTAL chronometry. See Time perception
MENTAL deficiency
Serotonin deficiency in infancy as one cause of a mental defect in phenylketonuria. D. W. Woolley and T. van der Hoeven. bibliog il Science 144:883-4 My 15 '64
See also
Mentally handicapped
MENTAL depression. See Depression, Mental
MENTAL development of children. See Children —Growth and development
MENTAL healing
See also
Faith cure
MENTAL health laws
Mental illness & legal remedies; commitment procedures. il Time 84:76+ N 20 '64
MENTAL health research institute. See Michigan. University. Ann Arbor—Mental health research institute
MENTAL health workers. See Health workers
MENTAL hospitals. See Hospitals, Psychiatric
MENTAL hygiene
Cats, dogs help family. E. Mirel. Sci N L 84: 167 S 14 '63
Champion for the witch. il Todays Health 41:73 Ap '63
Close-up of the normal wife. R. Corman. il N Y Times Mag p52+ S 8 '63
Far right's fight against mental health. D. Robinson. il Look 29:30-2 Ja 26 '65
Guide for parents: your child's mental health. W. W. Wattenberg. bibliog il NEA J 53:35-50 F '64
Inner peace and how to find it; reprint. H. E. Fosdick. Read Digest 83:110-13 Jl '63
Inside psychiatry today. F. R. Schreiber and M. Herman. See issues of Science digest
Mental health. D. J. Lagmanovich. il Américas 15:1-5 Mr '63
Mental health: House committee cuts funds proposed by Kennedy. E. Langer. Science 141:791 Ag 30 '63
Nature and mental health. I. L. Fishbein. Audubon Mag 66:25 Ja '64
New pattern of disease. Time 82:62-3 N 22 '63
People who fear sanity; anti-mental health movement. Sci Digest 55:75-6 F '64

MENTAL hygiene—*Continued*
Physical and mental health in the city. E. J. Lieberman and L. J. Duhl. il Ann Am Acad 352:13-24 Mr '64
Psychiatry. F. R. Schreiber and M. Herman. il Sci Digest 55:8-30 Je '64
Remarkable self-healing powers of the mind. M. M. Hunt. Read Digest 84:87-90 F '64
Symbol, status, and personality, by S. I. Hayakawa. Review
Newsweek 62:104-6 D 2 '63
What's on your mind? See issues of Science digest to May 1964
See also
Adjustment, Social
Anxiety
Psychiatry
School children—Adjustment
United States—National institute of mental health

MENTAL hygiene, Industrial
See also
Psychiatry, Industrial

MENTAL illness
Major and minor emotional problems; a special report on treatment, cost and cure. M. M. Hunt. Redbook 121:35-46 S '63
Meaning of mental illness. D. Fleming. Atlan 214:72-6 Jl '64
Mental health; President's program. Commonweal 77:552 F 22 '63
Mental illness cure in brain chemistry; taraxein. Sci N L 84:357 D 7 '63
New classification and a greater hope; K. A. Menninger. il Time 82:53 N 29 '63
Racial mental health statistics slanted. Sci N L 83:153 Mr 9 '63
Vital balance, by K. Menninger and others. Review
Nation 198:34-5 Ja 6 '64. A. Kardiner
Sat R 47:33-4 Ja 25 '64. H. L. Mosse
See also
Mental hygiene
Psychoses
Schizophrenia
Television broadcasting—Medical programs

Diagnosis

Mental disorder test. il Sci N L 83:163 Mr 16 '63

Prevention and control

Depression cure foreseen. Sci N L 87:46 Ja 16 '65
Mental health: new frontiers. M. B. Loeb. il Nation 196:418-21 My 18 '63
Toward a new frontier; presidential message. il Time 81:44 F 15 '63

Statistics

Risk of mental illness equal in city, country. Sci N L 85:104 F 15 '64

Terminology

See also
Psychiatry—Terminology

Therapy

Buck-passing parents harm disturbed child. Sci N L 85:280 My 2 '64
Dial a psychiatrist. R. P. Goldman. il Sat Eve Post 236:41-2 N 23 '63
Family therapy analyzed. Sci N L 83:180 Mr 23 '63
How we can eliminate our overcrowded state mental hospitals. A. Q. Maisel. Read Digest 83:59-63 Ag '63
Patient-planned program; South Florida state hospital. R. A. Prettyman. Recreation 57: 407 O '64
Psychiatric treatment; here and in England. W. Sargant. Atlan 214:88-95 Jl '64
Schizophrenics in the sun. R. Littell. Read Digest 82:201-2+ My '63
Therapy center for a private institution. il Arch Rec 134:166-7 N '63
Therapy for the whole family. J. Viorst. il Sci N L 84:74-5 Ag 3 '63
Ultrasonic treatment helps mental patients. Sci N L 84:20 Jl 13 '63
Unlocking our mental hospitals. J. Star. il Look 27:34-6+ F 26 '63
See also
Bibliotherapy
Group psychotherapy

Africa

Modern magician of the soul: A. Lambo, Nigerian psychiatrist. il Ebony 20:36-8+ D '64

MENTAL illness and law. See Mental health laws
MENTAL processes. See Thought and thinking
MENTAL suffering. See Suffering

MENTALLY handicapped
Finish his fight. Newsweek 63:68 F 17 '64
5,600,000 of us are mentally retarded. R. P. Goldman. il N Y Times Mag p31+ N 22 '64
Imbeciles who are geniuses; idiot savants. B. Greene. Sci Digest 56:16-21 Ag '64
Mental health: new frontiers. M. B. Loeb. il Nation 196:418-21 My 18 '63
Mental health; President's program. Commonweal 77:552 F 22 '63
Mental retardation, avoidable affliction? A. Q. Maisel. Read Digest 85:159-60+ S '64
Mental retardation could be cut in half. Sci N L 84:152 S 7 '63
President signs law against human miseries. Sci N L 84:301 N 9 '63
Retardation cases high. Sci N L 84:210 O 5 '63
Toward a new frontier; presidential message. il Time 81:44 F 15 '63
Twins human calendars; idiot savants. Sci N L 85:343 My 30 '64
See also
Mongolism

MENTALLY handicapped children
Art of the mentally retarded child. I. Rapaport. il Sch Arts 63:13-17 Ja '64
Boy who tuned out; Stanford's Institute for childhood aphasia. il Newsweek 63:90 Ap 13 '64
Defects cause guilt sense. Sci N L 86:291 N 7 '64
5,600,000 of us are mentally retarded. R. P. Goldman. il N Y Times Mag p31+ N 22 '64
Homocystinuria: an enzymatic defect. S. H. Mudd and others. bibliog il Science 143:1443-5 Mr 27 '64
Hope for brain-injuried children. A. Q. Maisel. Read Digest 85:135-40 O '64
Let's get behind the bold new program to combat mental retardation in children! M. M. Eliot. Parents Mag 38:38 Ap '63
Man must look up; personal tragedy of D. Crandall of the Milwaukee Braves, and how he mastered it. T. Cohane. il Look 27:72-4+ Ag 13 '63
My two sons. Redbook 122:8+ Ja '64
New day for the mentally retarded. M. J. E. Senn. McCalls 91:62+ Mr '64
President honors retardation study. Sci N L 84:312 N 16 '63
Reducing the hazards of birth. A. C. Barnes. Harper 228:31-7 Ja '64; Discussion. 228:8+ Mr '64
Retarded child in a home full of love; Arthur Ravenel family. C. S. Wren. il Look 28: 30-4+ D 1 '64
Return to babyhood; maverick methods give help to brain-injured children; with report by J. Delay. il Life 55:31+ Ag 23 '63
See also
Recreation for the handicapped

Education

Approach to the severely disturbed child; League school, Brooklyn. H. S. Arnstein. il N Y Times Mag p 119-20 O 6 '63
Art of the mentally retarded on exhibition. P. Vandervoort. il Sch Arts 63:10-12 Ja '64
Healing power of love; educational experiment in Elmont, N.Y. L. David and I. David. il Good H 157:50+ N '63
Opening school doors to the brain-damaged; San Mateo County, Calif. S. Welton. il Parents Mag 39:78-9+ F '64
Should teachers wield the rod? S. S. Rosenberg. il Parents Mag 39:74-5+ F '64
Training for mentally handicapped children; Children's retreat and training school, Grand Rapids, Mich. il Arch Rec 133:182-3 My '63

MENTALLY ill
Disturbed Americans; symposium. il Atlan 214:71-85+ Jl '64; Discussion. 214:90-4 O; 52+ N '64
Girl who means hope to troubled boys at Wiltwyck school. B. Leavitt. il Look 27: 97-100 Je 18 '63
Return to normality. Newsweek 61:55 F 11 '63

Care and treatment

Alaska designs for a complex community. il Arch Rec 134:166-7 N '63
Check list of spaces for a community mental health center; comp. by the Architectural and engineering branch, Division of hospital and medical facilities, U.S. Public health service. Arch Rec 134:196 N '63
Healing community. Christian Cent 80:1043-4 Ag 28 '63
Help we need. G. Williams. Atlan 214:112-14 Jl '64
I'm going to kill myself. A. Hamilton. il Sci Digest 54:57-63 S '63

MENTALLY ill—Care and treatment—*Cont.*
Menninger builds houses for children. il Arch Rec 134:170-3 N '63
Mental disease and the urban hospital. J. H. Knowles. il Atlan 214:107-11 Jl '64
Mental health: slash in funds for staffing raises problems; House begins Medicare hearings. E. Langer. Science 142:1045-6 N 22 '63
New aid for mentally ill: care close to home. il U S News 55:53 S 23 '63
Programing mental health facilities. A. G. Guttersen. Arch Rec 134:165 N '63
State care; New York state's mental hygiene program. P. H. Hoch. Atlan 214:82-5 Jl '64
Two new mental-health laws: who gets what. U S News 55:8 N 4 '63
See also
Hospitals, Psychiatric

Legal status, laws, etc.
See Mental health laws

Rehabilitation
Cottage plan for a state school-hospital. il Arch Rec 134:178-81 N '63
Curious transformation of Laurie; decided to become a dog. A. Henley. il Sat Eve Post 237:83+ O 17 '64
Halfway houses for the mentally ill; returning to community life. H. Earl. il Todays Health 43:56-9 Ja '65
Mental health: new frontiers. M. B. Loeb. il Nation 196:418-21 My 18 '63

Statistics
Facts and figures of the Americas. il Américas 15:6-7 Mr '63

MENTALLY retarded children. See Children, Backward
MENTALLY superior children. See Children, Gifted
MENTALLY superior college students. See College students, Mentally superior
MENTALLY superior high school students. See High school students, Mentally superior
MENTOR, Ohio
Fogger works better than a fly swatter. il Am City 79:110-11 Ap '64
MENUDO. See Cookery, Mexican
MENUHIN, Yehudi
Fugue; private showing of G. Gould's Anatomy of fugue. New Yorker 39:47-50 D 7 '63
Holidays for strings. por Time 84:78 S 4 '64
Warm; Russian violinists. New Yorker 38:25-6 F 2 '63
MENUS
Dinner in the great tradition, but with the work shared by four. J. Child. il House B 105:136-43+ D '63
Gourmet's diet. il Esquire 59:92-4 Je '63
How to dine well on 300 calories. M. J. Engel. il Ladies Home J 80:94 Mr '63
How to read a menu. W. Root. House B 105:179+ My '63
Hurry-up dinners for two. Good H 156:180d Mr '63
Master menu cook book. P. Harvey. il House & Gard 124:273+ N '63
Meals by the clock. il Redbook 121:80-1+ S '63
Menu for a weekend. il Redbook 123:70-1+ Ag '64
Menus for summer bachelors. il Am Home 66:50-2+ Jl '63
Mobile, noble chafing dish; ten menus, ten recipes, from ten good cooks. il Vogue 141:124-6+ F 15 '63
Modest diet that won't leave you hungry. il Redbook 124:52-5+ Ja '65
[Month] menus; with recipes. See issues of Sunset
Please come for lunch. E. Ward-Hanna. il Ladies Home J 81:74-6+ My '64
Recipes you really love. il Good H 156:114-30+ Je '63
Spend & save. il Ladies Home J 81:106-8+ Je '64
Summer meals, on the table in a hurry. J. Figg. il Suc Farm 61:58-9 Ag '63
Tailgate picnic. il Sunset 130:170+ Ap '63
Vogue's own menu: a fête champêtre for twelve. Vogue 142:102 Jl '63
When the ladies come for luncheon; with recipes. V. T. Habeeb. il Am Home 66:56-8+ Ap '63
Winter picnic. il Good H 157:88-9 D '63
You and your diet. See issues of Good housekeeping
See also
Buffet meals
Camp cookery
Dinners and dining
Luncheons
Meals
Thanksgiving dinners
MENZEL, Donald H.
Debate over Velikovsky. Harper 227:83-6 D '63
MENZEL, Ronald G. and others
Strontium-90 accumulation on plant foliage during rainfall. bibliog Science 142:576-7 N 1 '63
MENZIES, Sir Robert Gordon
Battle for freedom; address, July 4, 1963. Vital Speeches 29:647-9 Ag 15 '63
U.S. and Australia to establish educational foundation: Australian announcement, August 10, 1964. Dept State Bul 51:311-12 Ag 31 '64

about

Landslide down under. Time 82:44 D 6 '63
Old, familiar faces. por Newsweek 62:66-7 D 9 '63
MEPHENESIN
Brunettes turn blond after taking sedative. Sci N L 83:280 My 4 '63
MERAS, Phyllis
Snake in the house. N Y Times Mag p80 Mr 1 '64
MERCANTILE library association, St Louis
Missouri show; exhibition at M. Knoedler & co. New Yorker 39:26 F 23 '63
MERCAPTO group
Brucella-agglutinating antibodies: relation of mercaptoethanol stability to complement fixation. R. K. Anderson and others. bibliog il Science 143:1334-5 Mr 20 '64
MERCAPTOETHANOL. See Mercapto group
MERCE Cunningham dance company
Pop ballet. il Time 84:38 Ag 14 '64
MERCEDARIANS
Modern Mercedarian. N. McKenty. America 111:101 Ag 1 '64; Reply. V. I. Kennally. 111:221 S 5 '64
MERCENARIES (soldiers) See Mercenary troops
MERCENARY troops
White mercenaries on a rabbit hunt; 51st commando at Bumba. L. Garrison. il N Y Times Mag p30-1+ N 15 '64
MERCER, Charles
Setting your literary goals. Writer 76:10-11+ Mr '63
Until tomorrow; story. Good H 158:78-9 Je '64
MERCER, Harry E.
Australia's unknown islands. Travel 120:28-31+ N '63
Just south of Sydney. Travel 122:47-51 Ag '64
Thirty minutes to incredibility. Travel 121:36-41+ F '64
MERCER, Jinx
MSC seen favoring concentric orbit Gemini-Agena rendezvous. Miss & Roc 15:30+ O 12 '64
MERCER, Mabel
Sensible art. por Newsweek 63:78-9 Ja 27 '64
MERCER, Paul F. and Wasserman, R. H.
Autoradiographic distribution of radioactive sodium in rat kidney. bibliog Science 143:695-6 F 14 '64
MERCHANDISE, Quality of. See Quality of products
MERCHANDISE vendors. See Vending machines
MERCHANDISING
Artifacts of adulation; licensing of tie-in merchandise. A. Levy. Reporter 30:40-3 F 13 '64
Manna for marketing men. il Duns R 84:94-6 D '64
New strategy: try to beat the clock. il Bsns W p50-1 F 1 '64
Not so silent salesmen; point-of-purchase displays. il Bsns W p 130+ N 21 '64
Persuading the consumer to buy more; multi-packaging. L. Blumenthal. il Duns R 84:101+ D '64
Where experts are worlds apart; Stanford conference. il Bsns W p74+ N 7 '64
Where foreign wares test the U.S. market; World sampler. il Bsns W p 118-19 O 24 '64
See also
Kresge, S. S. company
Samples (merchandising)
MERCHANT, Charles J.
Amateur scientist. Sci Am 210:136+ Mr '64
MERCHANT, Jane
Cautious definition; poem. McCalls 90:122 Jl '63
Month for waking; poem. McCalls 90:148 My '63
On loving little objects; poem. Farm J 88:78 Ap '64
Star to guide us; poem. Farm J 88:57 D '64

MERCHANT, Larry
Losing twenty games isn't easy. Sat Eve Post 236:58-61 Je 8 '63
MERCHANT, Livingston Tallmadge, 1903-
Merchant of Nassau; with editorial comment. D. Healey. New Repub 148:9-10 Mr 16 '63
Mr Merchant to represent U.S. on U.S.-Canada working group. Dept State Bul 50:448 Mr 23 '64
NATO deterrent; multinational nuclear deterrent. por Time 81:32 Mr 8 '63
Principals named for negotiations on NATO multilateral force; statement, January 24, 1963. J. F. Kennedy. Dept State Bul 48:197 F 11 '63
MERCHANT marine
Is Niarchos heading for port? il Bsns W p 110+ O 24 '64
Merchant profiles, 1819-1962. il Nat Geog Mag 123:537 Ap '63
Russia
Red flag over the seven seas. H. W. Baldwin. Atlan 214:37-43 S '64
United States
By ship, the salt of the sea not withstanding. J. M. Will. il Ann Am Acad 345:81-8 Ja '63
Iron men and atomic ships; nuclear merchant marine. il Bsns W p 114-16 Je 8 '63
Is there a future for the U.S. merchant marine? il U S News 58:104-5 Ja 25 '65
Merchant marine fleet; address, November 13, 1964. D. L. McDonald. Vital Speeches 31: 188-90 Ja 1 '65
New oil on troubled waters. il Duns R 81:pt2 S122-4+ Je '63
Remedy for a sick industry. U S News 55:84 Jl 15 '63
SOS from the merchant marine. D. Smith. il Nation 199:406-8 N 30 '64
To the rescue of the marine. J. Ridgeway. New Repub 151:12 Jl 11 '64
United States merchant marine. G. P. Morrill. il Holiday 34:64-9+ S '63
United States merchant marine; address, November 15, 1963. H. C. Bonner. Vital Speeches 30:186-9 Ja 1 '64
Water carriers scrape the bottom. il Duns R 83:pt2 136-9+ Je '64
Wheat heat; shortage of U.S. ships to carry wheat to Russia. Newsweek 63:78+ F 17 '64
See also
National maritime union of America
Shipping—United States
United States lines
United States merchant marine academy, Kings Point, N.Y.
MERCHANTS
Tug-of-war for tax savings; savings institutions vs merchandisers; with editorial comment. Bsns W p34, 192 Mr 21 '64
MERCIER, Jean
Are you woman or wren? story. Redbook 121:50-1 Je '63
MERCIER, Paul
Urban explosion in developing nations. UNESCO Courier 16:50-5 Jl '63
MERCIER, Vivian
Defective detectives. Nation 199:362-3 N 16 '64
How sincere is art? Nation 197:222-4 O 12 '63
Salon saboteur. Nation 198:217-18 Mr 2 '64
MERCOURI, Melina
Melina the Greek. J. Knowles. por Holiday 35:101+ Ja '64
Mercurial Mercouri. R. E. Ginna. por Sat Eve Post 236:24-5 My 25 '63
MERCURY
Mercury in house paint causes neuritis trouble. Sci N L 84:296 N 9 '63
Renal tubular localization of chlormerodrin labeled with mercury-203 by autoradiography. R. P. Wedeen and M. H. Goldstein. bibliog il Science 141:438-40 Ag 2 '63
MERCURY (planet)
Atmosphere of Mercury; tr. by A. Boyko N. A. Kozyrev. il Sky & Tel 27:339-41 Je '64
Medieval astronomers erred in describing Mercury and Venus. S. D. Gossner. il Natur Hist 72:48-9 F '63
Mercury, deep freeze of the solar system. D. M. Cole. il Sat R 47:54-5 F 1 '64
Radar observations of Mars and Mercury. Sky & Tel 25:191+ Ap '63
Radar observations of Mercury. R. L. Carpenter and R. M. Goldstein. bibliog il Science 142:381 O 18 '63
See also
Space flight to Mercury

MERCURY vapor lamps. See Electric lamps, Mercury vapor
MERCY
Word. V. P. McCorry. America 109:144 Ag 10 '63
MERCY killing. See Euthanasia
MEREDITH, James Howard
I can't fight alone. pors Look 27:70-2+ Ap 9 '63
Meredith's advice to Negroes; excerpt from address, July 5, 1963. por U S News 55:89 Jl 22 '63
about
Dialogue: telephone calls between Attorney General Kennedy and Governor Barnett prior to arrival of Negro student. Newsweek 62:36 O 14 '63
Draftee's diary from the Mississippi front. C. Vanderburgh. il por Harper 228:37-45 F '64
Negro dissenters; two students speak out against leaders. U S News 55:14 Jl 22 '63
New term, new South. il por Newsweek 61:29 F 11 '63
People of the week. por U S News 54:15 F 11 '63
Pinpoint portrait. J. H. Roy. Negro Hist Bul 27:36 N '63
Quiet progress in the South. Life 54:4 F 8 '63
Reporter at large. C. Trillin. New Yorker 39: 64+ Jl 27 '63
Some good men there are. J. Ciardi. Sat R 46:17 Je 29 '63
Two students. por Newsweek 62:30+ Ag 26 '63
What it cost to keep troops at Ole Miss. U S News 55:14 Ag 5 '63
MEREDITH, William
For Guillaume Apollinaire; poem. New Yorker 39:140 Ap 13 '63
MEREDITH-Iowa writer's award
Meredith and Univ. of Iowa set awards for writing. Pub W 185:72 F 3 '64
MEREDITH publishing company
Meredith press: fewer books, better promoted. Pub W 186:34-5 S 14 '64
See also
Meredith-Iowa writer's award
MERGENHAGEN, D. See Sekeris, C. E. jt. auth.
MERGENTHALER linotype company
Mergenthaler produces three-shift chemical formula typewriter. il Pub W 185:100 Ja 6 '64
MERGERS. See Business consolidations and mergers; Trusts, Industrial
MERGNER, Fred L.
New high-quality transistor amplifier. Electr World 71:42-5+ My '64
Transistors vs tubes for hi-fi. Electr World 71:45+ Ja '64
MÉRIDIENNES. See Day beds
MERIGAN, Thomas C.
Purified interferons: physical properties and species specificity. bibliog Science 145:811-13 Ag 21 '64
MERINGUE
Custard desserts with meringue. Sunset 133: 173 S '64
Dacquoise, doubly good. C. Claiborne. il N Y Times Mag p66+ My 10 '64
If they ask, say it's a floating island. il Sunset 131:187 O '63
It's a mountain of meringue. il Sunset 133:126 D '64
Marvelous match: ice cream and meringues. C. Claiborne. il N Y Times Mag p51 Ag 4 '63
MERISTEMS. See Plant cells and tissues
MERIT certificates. See Rewards, prizes, etc.
MERIT pay. See Teachers—Salaries
MERIT scholarship program. See National merit scholarship corporation
MERKEL, R. A.
Your primer of beef carcass terms. Suc Farm 62:47 Je '64
MERKER, H. J. See Remmer, H. jt. auth.
MERKIN, T. A.
Nothing proves it like a picture. Am City 79: 107-8 F '64
MERLEN, M. Monty
System transfers azimuth from tower top to ground monitor. Miss & Roc 13:32-3 Jl 15 '63
MERLIN, Frank
I got shoes. Criticism
New Yorker 38:72+ F 2 '63
MERLO, Frank P.
Higher education for all? Sat R 47:50-2+ D 19 '64
MERMAN, Ethel
Delicious, delectable, de-lovely. pors Time 82:78 N 22 '63
Now: mermania. por Newsweek 63:48 Mr 2 '64

MERNONE, Patricia
Furious fun of Pinkie and Pat. B. H. LaFontaine. il por Sports Illus 21:20-1 Ag 24 '64
MEROLA, A. J. and Arnold, A.
Estrone inhibition of cholesterol biosynthesis at the mevalonic acid stage. bibliog Science 144:301-2 Ap 17 '64
MERRELL, John, and Stoyer, Ray
Reclaimed sewage becomes a community asset. Am City 79:97-101 Ap '64
MERRELL, William S, company
Triparanol side effects. Time 83:79 Ap 3 '64
MERRIAM, Carroll F.
Eclipse observing from eastern Maine. Sky & Tel 25:91-3 F '63
MERRIAM, Eve
Again it's the tops. N Y Times Mag p 14-15 D 22 '63
Galanos. Sat Eve Post 236:54+ O 26 '63
Monstrous Christmas to all. Nation 199:463-4 D 14 '64
We're teaching our children that violence is fun. Ladies Home J 81:44+ O '64
MERRIAM, G. and C, company
Battle of publishing giants over Merriam-Webster sale. Library J 89:4309 N 1 '64
Building word power. il Bsns W p36 S 19 '64
Encyclopaedia Britannica will buy G. & C. Merriam. il Pub W 186:36-7 S 21 '64
It's official: EB buys G. & C. Merriam. Pub W 186:23-4 O 26 '64
Meeting of minds; Encyclopaedia Britannica buys the Merriam-Webster dictionaries. il Time 84:100 S 18 '64
Meeting on Merriam sale postponed until October 20. Pub W 186:30-1 O 12 '64
Temporary injunction halts Merriam sale; McGraw bids. Pub W 186:44-5 O 5 '64
25th volume; purchase of G. & C. Merriam co. Newsweek 64:92 S 21 '64
MERRIAM, Ida C.
Hedging the great gamble. New Repub 149: 17-19 N 9 '63
Social expenditures and worker welfare. Mo Labor R 86:687-94 Je '63
Social security and the Alliance for progress: seventh Inter-American conference on social security, Asunción, Paraguay, May 31-June 5, 1964. Dept State Bul 51:320-1 Ag 31 '64
MERRIAM, Joan
I flew around the world alone. pors Sat Eve Post 237:77-83 Jl 25 '64
MERRIAM-Webster dictionaries. See English language—Dictionaries
MERRICK, David
Buccaneer on Broadway. R. Brustein. New Repub 148:26-7 F 2 '63
Great void; New York theater during newspaper strike. Theatre Arts 47:8 F '63
No tickets for Clurman. Nation 197:379 D 7 '63
MERRILL, Arthur S. and others
Ancient oyster shells on the Atlantic continental shelf. bibliog Science 147:398-400 Ja 22 '65
MERRILL, James
Thousand and second night; poem. New Yorker 40:36-8 Je 13 '64
about
Leaf by leaf. M. Van Duyn. Poetry 102:262-4 Jl '63
MERRILL, Mike
How I grow 100-bushel milo. Suc Farm 62: 50-1 My '64
MERRILL, Nathaniel
Met's new Aida. pors Mus Am 83:6-9 N '63
Seconding the motion: interview. ed. by A. M. Lingg. Opera N 28:15 D 7 '63
MERRILL, Robert
On records. Opera N 29:27 O 17 '64
MERRILL, Wisc.
Conservation education, Merrill style. J. W. Craig. il Am For 69:30-1 F '63
MERRILL Lynch, Pierce, Fenner and Smith, incorporated
Break with tradition. Time 82:56 Ag 30 '63
Merrill Lynch buys up bond house. Bsns W p24-5 My 16 '64
Sweet deal. il Time 83:93 My 22 '64
U.S. pitch at British investors stirs the city. il Bsns W p 134+ Ap 13 '63
Wall Street for sale. Newsweek 62:68-9 S 2 '63
MERRITT, A. Jay. See Freedman, L. jt. auth.
MERRITT ISLAND launch area. See Proving grounds
MERRY Christmas, Mr Longfellow; story. See Fritz, J.
MERRY Mount; opera. See Hanson, H.
MERRY widow; musical comedy. See Musical comedies, revues, etc.—Criticisms, plots, etc.
MERSAND, Joseph
How to train pupils to listen. Sr Schol 85:9T N 4 '64
In the secondary schools. Sr Schol 84:14T-15T F 21 '64
Project English: a report to the profession. Sr Schol 83:15T-16T S 20 '63
Project English: improving written composition. Sr Schol 83:13T O 11 '63
(ed) Special issue on Shakespeare. Sr Schol 84:13T-16T+ F 21; 8T-9T F 28 '64
Two project English programs: cultural riches, and cultural poverty. Sr Schol 83:7T N 1 '63
MERTENS, Andre
Obituary
Mus Am por 83:28 Ag '63
MERTENS, E. Frederick
Emerald encore. Am For 69:4-6 Jl '63
MERTON, Thomas
And the children of Birmingham; poem. Sat R 46:32 Ag 10 '63
Baroque gravure; poem. Commonweal 79:167 N 1 '63
Gloss on the sin of Ixion; poem. Sat R 46:29 S 21 '63
Honest to God debate. Commonweal 80:573-4+ Ag 21 '64
Message to poets from Thomas Merton; excerpts. Américas 16:29 Ap '64
Monk in the diaspora. Commonweal 79:741-5 Mr 20 '64
Seneca; poem. Poetry 103:381 Mr '64
Why some look up to planets and heroes; poem, with comment. America 108:433 Mr 30 '63
Zen: sense and sensibility. America 108:752-4 My 25 '63
about
Emblems and documents. X. J. Kennedy. Poetry 104:378-80 S '64
Poetry chronicle. M. Swenson. Poetry 102: 120-1 My '63
MERTZ, Edwin T. and others
Mutant gene that changes protein composition and increases lysine content of maize endosperm. bibliog Science 145:279-80 Jl 17 '64
Serum uric acid in young mongoloids. bibliog Science 141:535 Ag 9 '63
MERWIN, W. S.
Caesar; poem. Atlan 214:98 O '64
Church of sounds; story. Atlan 214:85-7 D '64
Last one; Pieces for other lives; Bread at midnight; It is March; Among the eyes; Some last questions; poems. Poetry 104: 339-45 S '64
Museum; story. Atlan 213:68-73 My '64
One way; poem. Nation 197:225 O 12 '63
Recognition; poem. New Yorker 39:46 O 26 '63
Resolution; poem. New Yorker 39:34 F 1 '64
Students of justice; For the grave of posterity; Mountain town; Island in the harbor, Spring; poems. Poetry 102:384-7 S '63
about
Merwin as translator. B. Gibbs. Poetry 101: 353-5 F '63
Some questions of precision. E. Dorn. Poetry 104:184-5 Je '64
MERYMAN, Richard
Rewards of a great teacher. Life 56:70-2+ Mr '64
MESA, Ariz.
Story of a Hilda Maehling fellow; project coordinating library services with the summer school program. J. Stocker. NEA J 53:45 O '64
MESA VERDE NATIONAL PARK
Solving the riddles of Wetherill mesa. D. Osborne. il Nat Geog Mag 125:155-95 F '64
MESCAL (cactus) See Peyote
MESCALINE
Danger in happy drugs. E. Mirel. Sci N L 84:138 Ag 31 '63
MESELSON, Matthew
Books. Bul Atomic Sci 20:35-6 O '64
MESERVE, Nat
Brother-in-the-Lord Ora Gumbs; story. Christian Cent 80:1138-9 S 18 '63
MESKE, Al
Trailer the big ones down. Motor B 112:28-9+ S '63
MESLAY, Jean
Visit to Haiti. America 109:374-5 O 5 '63
MESMERISM. See Hypnotism
MESONS
Fall of time reversal? decay of the neutral K meson. Sci Am 211:81-2 S '64
Fifth force? time-reversal invariance. Sci Am 211:62 D '64

MESONS—*Continued*
New particle glues atom; epsilon. W. MacLaurin. Sci N L 86:261 O 24 '64
New short-lived atomic particle discovered; phi meson. Sci N L 83:262 Ap 27 '63
Not as a stranger. Time 81:60 Ap 26 '63
MESOPOTAMIA
Antiquities
Assyrian trading outpost. T. Özgüç. il Sci Am 208:96-102+ bibliog(p 185) F '63
See also
Nineveh
Ur
MESPILUS germanica. See Medlars (fruit)
MESQUITA, Júlio, Jr
Best in Brazil; O Estado de Sao Paulo. il por Newsweek 63:75 F 3 '64
MESQUITE
Desert Indians used mesquite in many ways. Sci N L 85:41 Ja 18 '64
MESS; story. See Taube, M.
MESSAGE; story. See Lispector, C.
MESSEL, Oliver
Transformer; interview, ed. by F. Stevenson. por Opera N 27:30 F 16 '63
about
Marvellous food at Messel's. V. Riis-Hansen. il Vogue 142:136+ D '63
MESSERLY, Wayne
Five ideas from one hog system. Suc Farm 62:98 N '64
I pay my rent in hogs. Suc Farm 61:50 Mr '63
New farrowing ideas for old buildings. Suc Farm 61:130 F '63
—and Harvey, John
Under what conditions should you switch to SPF hogs? Suc Farm 61:40-1 O '63
MESSIN, Sam
Inside a digital voltmeter. Electr World 70: 53-6+ N '63
MESSINESI, Despina
Amusing logistics of a double Hilton opening. Vogue 142:108+ S 1 '63
In Greece. Vogue 144:24 Ag 1 '64
Mendocino's Olympian charge. Vogue 144:90 O 15 '64
Sun Valley notes. Vogue 144:116 N 1 '64
Travel. Vogue 144:44 Ag 15; 108 S 1 '64; 145: 121 Ja 15; 96 F 1 '65
MESSNER, Kathryn G.
Obituary
Pub W por 186:28 Ag 17 '64
MESTA, Perle
February: a good month to look at Washington, the man and the city. McCalls 91:18+ F '64
First ladies I have known. McCalls 90:34+ Mr '63
Mile-high social life of Denver. por McCalls 91:26+ Mr '64
Perle Mesta's party notebook. See issues of McCall's to December 1963
Washington: wonderful world of women and jewels. il McCalls 91:16+ Ja '64
(ed) See Eisenhower, M. Mamie Eisenhower's longest day, D-day
about
Musical bagels, etc. il por Newsweek 64:19 Ag 31 '64
MESTHENE, Emmanuel G.
Books. Bul Atomic Sci 20:25-7 N '64
Can only scientists make government science policy? Science 145:237-40 Jl 17 '64
MESTRAL, Claude de
Quebec's quiet revolution. Christian Cent 81: 1268-70 O 14 '64
MESTROVIC, Matthew M.
Rumania looks west. Commonweal 81:10-12 S 25 '64
Tito in the United States. Commonweal 79: 181 N 8 '63
Titos return to Moscow (cont) Commonweal 77:620-1 Mr 8 '63
Will the guideposts stick? Duns R 84:41-2+ Jl '64
METABOLIC diseases. See Diseases
METABOLISM
Aromatic biosynthesis and metabolism; report of symposium. A. J. Finlayson. Science 142:981-2 N 15 '63
Carbamyl phosphate. M. E. Jones. bibliog il Science 140:1373-9 Je 28 '63
Endogenous metabolic factor in schizophrenic behavior. H. H. Berlet and others. bibliog il Science 144:311-13 Ap 17 '64
Genetics of isoniazid metabolism in Caucasian, Negro, and Japanese populations. A. P. Dufour and others. bibliog il Science 145:391 Jl 24 '64
Hemorrhagic shock: metabolic effects; report of workshop at Rockefeller institute. F. A. Simeone. Science 141:536+ Ag 9 '63
High metabolism caused by action inside cells. Sci N L 84:327 N 23 '63
Isolated neuron preparation for studies of metabolic events at rest and during impulse activity. E. Giacobini and others. bibliog il Science 140:74 Ap 5 '63
Lactic dehydrogenases: functions of the two types. D. M. Dawson and others. bibliog il Science 143:929-33 F 28 '64
Metabolic control of timing. S. B. Hendricks. bibliog il Science 141:21-7 Jl 5 '63
Nobel winners discover how metabolism works and what can go wrong. il Life 54: 63-6+ Mr 29 '63
Nonhydrolytic pathway in metabolism of n-methylcarbamate insecticides. H. W. Dorough and others. bibliog Science 140: 170-1 Ap 12 '63
Polyploidy and endoreduplication in human leukocyte cultures treated with β-mercaptopyruvate. J. F. Jackson and K. Lindahl-Kiessling. bibliog il Science 141: 424-6 Ag 2 '63
Pyruvate metabolism and control: factors affecting pyruvic carboxylase activity. A. D. Freedman and L. Kohn. bibliog il Science 145:58-60 Jl 3 '64
What jet travel does to your metabolic clock. S. W. Bryant. il Fortune 68:160-3+ N '63
See also
Bioenergetics
Plants—Metabolism
METABOLISM (insects)
Beta-alanine utilization of ebony and non-ebony drosophila melanogaster. M. E. Jacobs and K. K. Brubaker. bibliog il Science 139:1282-3 Mr 29 '63
METAL, Scrap. See Scrap metal
METAL castings
Centrifugal casting in the high school. H. F. Schlindwein. il Sch Arts 64:36-8 S '64
See also
Steel castings
METAL cleaning
See also
Sand blast
METAL coating
New plastics coating process for metals. il Arch Rec 134:239-40 O '63
Plating with permanence; Mattox method. il Time 85:58 Ja 15 '65
METAL crystals
Crystal structures at high pressures of metallic modifications of compounds of indium, gallium, and aluminum. J. C. Jamieson. bibliog il Science 139:845-7 Mr 1 '63
Crystal structures at high pressures of metallic modifications of silicon and germanium. J. C. Jamieson. bibliog il Science 139:762-4 F 22 '63
Crystal structures of titanium, zirconium, and hafnium at high pressures. J. C. Jamieson. bibliog il Science 140:72-3 Ap 5 '63
Dislocation movements in metals. D. Kuhlmann-Wilsdorf and H. G. F. Wilsdorf. bibliog il Science 144:17-25 Ap 3 '64
METAL cutting
See also
Tube cutting
METAL cutting tools
Tool crib; Gay Blade manual metal shear. il Hot Rod 16:111 S '63
METAL exchange, London. See London metal exchange
METAL finishing
Finishes for architectural metals; new manual by NAAMM. Arch Rec 136:185-6 D '64
See also
Sand blast
Tumbling barrels
METAL flo corporation
Putting new stretch in tough metal. il Bsns W p34+ D 26 '64
METAL foils
See also
Aluminum foil
METAL furniture. See Furniture, Metal
METAL implements and weapons. See Implements, utensils, etc.
METAL inlay. See Inlay
METAL locators. See Metals—Detection
METAL plating. See Metal coating
METAL powders
1,000,000,000 metal particles on the head of a pin. il Life 54:41-2+ F 15 '63
METAL protection
See also
Corrosion and anticorrosives
METAL sculpture
Art. F. Getlein. New Repub 148:26-8 F 16 '63

METAL sculpture—*Continued*
Caged action; Ferber's iron sculptures. il Time 81:74 Ap 12 '63
Calder. B. Chernow. il Sch Arts 63:24-7 D '63
Craft of bronze casting. L. Campbell and M. Millikan. il Craft Horiz 23:26-33+ Ja '63
Creative casting. L. Campbell. il Craft Horiz 23:10-17+ N '63
Detour to sculpture. D. Burt. il Am Artist 28:30-5+ Ja '64
From scrap to sculpture. D. W. Dodge. il Sch Arts 64:36-7 Ja '65
Gold medal for talent. il Ebony 19:113-14+ Je '64
Ideas in metal sculpture. J. Lynch. il Design 64:167-9+ Mr '63
Letter home. J. Jones. Esquire 61:28+ Mr '64
Metaphor in metal; Seymour Lipton's Archangel. K. Kuh. il Sat R 47:24-5 F 29 '64
My son, the safety patrol. I. Berg. il Sch Arts 63:39-40 D '63
Plowshares into sculpture. Y. Chomicky. il Sch Arts 62:22-4 Mr '63
Plumber's sculpture; photographs. Design 66: 24-5 S '64
Precise vision of Alexander Liberman. P. Blake. il Arch Forum 118:128-31 Ap '63
Woman of steel; sculptress, B. Pepper. il Newsweek 62:104+ N 11 '63
Zogbaum makes a sculpture. M. N. Tabak. il Art N 63:42-5+ D '64
See also
Bronzes

METAL trade
See also
London metal exchange

METAL work
Benjamin Gerrish, brazier. R. H. Randall, jr. il Antiques 85:320-1 Mr '64
Magnetic metalworking: Magneform. il Time 83:73 My 8 '64
Sequential program to develop textural sensitivity. P. A. Sisk. il Sch Arts 63:21-6 Ja '64
See also
Art metal work
Embossing
Forging
Swords
Welding

Projects
Metalworking tips. H. J. Gerber. il Pop Sci 182:143 F '63

METALAW. See Space law

METALDEHYDE
Artificial rain compound tested in Australia. Sci N L 84:104 Ag 17 '63

METALIOUS, Grace
Obituary
Pub W 185:44 Mr 9 '64

METALLIC films. See Films, Metallic

METALLOGRAPHY
Measuring metal grains electronically in Britain. il Sci Digest 53:61-2 Mr '63

METALLURGY
Our heritage of the elements; address, October 19, 1964. G. T. Seaborg. Vital Speeches 31:90-4 N 15 '64
See also
Iron metallurgy
Metal powders
Steel metallurgy

History
Ancient copper and copper-arsenic alloy artifacts: composition and metallurgical implications. C. A. Key. bibliog il Science 146: 1578-80 D 18 '64
Man's first encounters with metallurgy. T. A. Wertime. bibliog il Science 146:1257-67 D 4 '64

METALS
High-temperature research. A. V. Grosse. bibliog il Science 140:781-9 My 17 '63
Metal chelates in analytical chemistry; report on 16th annual analytical symposium. Q. Fernando and others. Science 143:491-2+ Ja 31 '64
New chemical theory. Sci N L 85:403 Je 27 '64
Plasmas in solids. R. Bowers. il Sci Am 209: 46-53 bibliog (p 186) N '63
See also
Fermi surfaces
Intermetallic compounds
Metallography
Metallurgy
also names of metals, e.g. Titanium

Coating
See Metal coating

Detection
Metal detectors, can they really spot buried treasure? V. L. Oertle. il Pop Sci 182:99-101+ Ap '63

Irradiation
High pressure X-ray diffraction studies on barium. J. D. Barnett and others. bibliog il Science 141:534-5 Ag 9 '63

Prices
Business outlook. Bsns W p 11-12 Jl 6 '63
Metals pinch speeds drive to tap stockpile; price-supply bind, of copper, lead and zinc. Bsns W p34 Ja 23 '65
Worrisome zoom in nonferrous prices. il Bsns W p26-7 O 10 '64
See also
Copper—Prices

Statistics
Facts and figures of the Americas. il Américas 16:42-3 Mr '64

Stockpiling
See Stockpiling

METALS, Effect of radiation on. See Metals—Irradiation

METALS, Effect of temperature on
Metals shrink, stretch as magnetic field varies. Sci N L 84:278 N 2 '63

METALS, Heat resistant. See Heat resistant alloys

METALS, Liquid
High-temperature research. A. V. Grosse. bibliog il Science 140:781-9 My 17 '63
Viscosity and self-diffusion of liquid metals. A. V. Grosse. bibliog il Science 145:50-1 Jl 3 '64

METALS, Powdered. See Metal powders

METALS, Rare. See Earths, Rare

METALWORK. See Metal work

METAMORPHIC rocks. See Rocks

METAMORPHISM
Calcite-aragonite equilibrium. G. Simmons and P. Bell. bibliog il Science 139:1197-8 Mr 22 '63; Reply. W. A. Crawford and W. S. Fyfe. 144:1569-70 Je 26 '64

METAMORPHOSES; story. See Cheever, J.

METAMORPHOSIS
Ecdysone: five biologically active fractions from Bombyx. W. J. Burdette and M. W. Bullock. bibliog il Science 140:1311 Je 21 '63
See also
Amphibia—Development

METAMORPHOSIS (insects) See Insects—Development

METARAMINOL. See Norephedrine

METASEQUOIA
Ancient trees for modern gardens. E. S. Henderson. il Horticulture 41:448-9 S '63

METASTABILITY
Superconducting metastable compounds. H. L. Luo and others. bibliog il Science 145:581-3 Ag 7 '64

METCALF, George R.
Speaking out. por Sat Eve Post 236:12+ O 19 '63

METCALF, Keyes D.
Library building consultant; address, July, 1963. ALA Bul 57:1043-7 D '63

METCALF, Lee
Utility stock options: executive incentive v. public interest. Nation 199:151-4 S 28 '64
about
Iceberg. Nation 199:206 O 12 '64

METCALF, R. L. See Georghiou, G. P. jt. auth.

METCALF, Woodbridge
American Christmas tree; poem. Am For 70: 10 D '64

METEORA monasteries. See Monasteries

METEORITE craters
Thing that hit us from outer space. W. Langewiesche. il Read Digest 82:81-5 Ap '63
Travel far and near; the meteorite search. D. M. Barringer. il Natur Hist 73:56-9 My '64
Two more ancient Canadian meteorite craters; Clearwater Lakes, Que. il Sky & Tel 26:198 O '63
See also
Stishovite

METEORITES
Ages of the Sikhote alin from meteorite. D. E. Fisher. bibliog il Science 139:752-3 F 22 '63
Artifacts made from meteorites. Sky & Tel 27:150 Mr '64

METEORITES—*Continued*
Carbon isotope abundance in meteoritic carbonates. R. N. Clayton. bibliog il Science 140:192-3 Ap 12 '63
Chondrites and chondrules. J. A. Wood. il Sci Am 209:64-8+ O '63
Contaminated meteorite; Orgueil meteorite. E. Anders and others. bibliog il Science 146:1157-61 N 27 '64
Cosmic-ray exposure age of the Farmington meteorite from radioactive isotopes. J. DeFelice and others. bibliog il Science 142:673-4 N 8 '63
Diamonds best friend of scientists too. Sci N L 85:309 My 16 '64
Did a comet collide with the earth in 1908? Tungus meteorite expedition. K. P. Florenskii. il Sky & Tel 26:268-9 N '63
Effects of cosmic rays on meteorites. M. Honda and J. R. Arnold. bibliog il Science 143:203-12 Ja 17 '64
Faked life from other worlds. Sci Am 212:52 Ja '65
Family resemblance. Sci Am 211:46+ Jl '64
Identity of organized elements in carbonaceous chondrites; letter. P. Tasch. bibliog Science 142:156+ O 11 '63
Life in meteorites? Sky & Tel 26:132 S '63
Maskelynite: formation by explosive shock. D. J. Milton and P. S. De Carli. bibliog il Science 140:670-1 My 10 '63
Meteorite with unique features. H. H. Nininger. il Science 139:345-7 Ja 25 '63
Meteoritic mineral; *sinoite*. Sky & Tel 28:340 D '64
Meteoritic zircon. U. B. Marvin and C. Klein, jr. bibliog il Science 146:919-20 N 13 '64
Organic matter from space; carbonaceous chondrites. B. Mason. il Sci Am 208:43-9 bibliog(p 188) Mr '63
Organized element; possible identification in orgueil meteorite. F. W. Fitch and E. Anders. bibliog il Science 140:1097-100 Je 7 '63
Orgueil meteorite: organic nitrogen contents. R. Hayatsu. bibliog il Science 146:1291-3 D 4 '64
Origin of diamonds in the ureilites. M. E. Lipschutz. bibliog il Science 143:1431-4 Mr 27 '64
Rhenium and osmium abundances in stony meteorites. W. Morgan and J. F. Lovering. bibliog il Science 144:835-6 My 15 '64
Silicon oxynitride: a meteoritic mineral. C. A. Andersen and others. bibliog il Science 146:256-7 O 9 '64
Sky reporter. S. D. Gossner. il Natur Hist 72:40-1 N '63
Surface features of metallic spherules. R. A. Schmidt and others. bibliog il Science 142:581-2 N 1 '63
Thermal properties of meteoritic iron from 150° to 300° Celsius. C. P. Butler and R. J. Jenkins. il Science 139:486-7 F 8 '63
Travel far and near; the meteorite search. D. M. Barringer. il Natur Hist 73:56-9 My '64
X-ray detects diamonds in dyalpur meteorite. Sci Digest 53:63 Mr '63
Zirconium and hafnium in stone meteorites. W. D. Ehmann and J. L. Setser. bibliog il Science 139:594-5 F 15 '63
See also
Chondrules
Tektites

Temperature and radiation
Temperature of an iron meteoroid in space. C. P. Butler and R. J. Jenkins. il Science 142:1567-8 D 20 '63; Reply with rejoinder. R. H. Wilson, jr. 144:80-1 Ap 3 '64

METEORITIC dust. See Matter, Interstellar

METEORITICAL society
Meteoriticists meet in Canada. D. Hoffleit. il Sky & Tel 27:15-16 Ja '64

METEOROID detection satellites. See Artificial satellites—Use in research

METEOROIDS. See Meteors

METEOROLOGICAL balloons. See Balloons, Meteorological

METEOROLOGICAL instruments
Amateur scientist; thunderstorm detectors. T. P. Leary. il Sci Am 208:167-70+ My '63
Cloud sentinel. H. E. Sanders. il Pop Electr 19:56-8+ O '63
See also
Barometers
Hygrometers

METEOROLOGICAL optics
See also
Airglow

METEOROLOGICAL research
Cloud patterns over tropical oceans. J. S. Malkus. bibliog il Science 141:767-78 Ag 30 '63
Do-it-yourself tornado made in living room. Sci N L 84:251 O 19 '63
International atmospheric study urged. R. D. Hibben. il Aviation W 78:135+ Je 17 '63
United States and U.S.S.R. agree to cooperate in weather matters; statement, October 24, 1964, with text of agreement released at the United Nations, November 5, 1964. L. B. Johnson. Dept State Bul 51:791-4 N 30 '64
Why winters are getting colder; report. W. J. Perkinson. il Sci Digest 56:83-5 D '64
See also
Artificial satellites—Meteorological applications
National center for atmospheric research
Polar research
Rain making
Rockets—Use in research
Weather control
Weather research
World meteorological organization

METEOROLOGICAL stations
Aboard a weather ship; picture section. UN Mo Chron 1:77-84 N '64
MAMOS: weather station in a rowboat. il Pop Electr 20:48 My '64

METEOROLOGY
Agricultural meteorology; report on sixth national conference on agricultural meteorology of the American meteorological society. R. F. Dale. Science 146:1601-2 D 18 '64
Gentleman of the guard. J. Lear. il Sat R 46:36-9 Ag 3 '63
Hurricanes and tropical meteorology; report of technical conference on hurricanes and tropical meteorology at Mexico city. R. H. Simpson. Science 141:935-6+ S 6 '63
Meteorology of air pollution. D. H. Pack. bibliog il Science 146:1119-28 N 27 '64
Meteorology; report of symposium, at the University of California, Los Angeles. M. J. Rubin. Science 142:416 O 18 '63
New weather predicting; use of a laser. Sci N L 85:100 F 15 '64
Rainbow of moonbeams and a high cloud ring of mystery. il Life 54:111-12 My 17 '63
Research frontier; where is science taking us? J. E. McDonald. il Sat R 46:40 Ag 3 '63
See also
Airplanes in meteorology
Atmosphere
Clouds
Droughts
Frost
Hail
Micrometeorology
Radar meteorology
Radio in meteorology
Radio meteorology
Rain and rainfall
United States—Weather bureau
Weather
Weather forecasts
Weather maps
Winds

METEOROLOGY, Aeronautic
All-weather landing progress reported. P. J. Klass. il Aviation W 79:165+ O 7 '63
Bad-weather day. Newsweek 63:70 F 3 '64
Forecast: cloudy and clearing. R. B. Parke. Flying 75:26 Jl '64
Invisible CAT pilots dread. P. C. Geraci. il Pop Mech 121:104-7+ Ap '64
Jet turbulence problems. J. R. Ashlock. Aviation W 80:45-6 F 24 '64
Near-blizzard snarls airline schedules. J. R. Ashlock. Aviation W 80:38 Ja 20 '64
PIREPS wanted. B. Hicks. il Flying 74:44-5+ My '64
Winter flying weather in Florida. W. E. Hillig. il Flying 74:52+ F '64
World's fair weather watch; Flight advisory weather service. D. L. Coveney. il Flying 74:32+ Ap '64

METEORS
Chunks off the moon. il Time 82:61 N 29 '63
Doctor Wernher von Braun tells about comets and meteors; questions and answers. W. von Braun. il Pop Sci 184:95-7 Ap '64
Fireball train observed over Israel. E. Metzger. il(p 1) Sky & Tel 26:3 Jl '63
Getting acquainted with astronomy. il Sky & Tel 26:138-9 S '63 (to be cont)
Hourly meteor rates. R. J. Defouw. il Sky & Tel 25:97 F '63
Leonid meteors. il Sky & Tel 26:303 N '63
Many amateurs count perseid meteors. L. J. Robinson. il Sky & Tel 28:240-2 O '64
Many observers count Leonids. il Sky & Tel 27:54-5 Ja '64
Meteor bits increase. Sci N L 86:404 D 26 '64
Meteors: an unexpected increase in 1963. C. D. Ellyett and C. S. L. Keay. bibliog il Science 146:1458 D 11 '64

METEORS—*Continued*
Moon influences meteors. A. Ewing. Sci N L 83:213 Ap 6 '63
1963 Geminid meteor display. il Sky & Tel 27:127 F '64
Observers report on the August Perseids. il Sky & Tel 26:298-9 N '63
Path of the March bolide. C. P. Olivier. il Sky & Tel 26:263+ N '63
Probe for comet fluff. Time 82:62+ N 8 '63
Radar meteor counts: anomalous increase during 1963. B. A. McIntosh and P. M. Millman. bibliog il Science 146:1457 D 11 '64
Strange sounds from the sky; anomalous sounds accompanying fireballs. M. F. Romig and D. L. Lamar. il Sky & Tel 28:214-15 O '64
See also
Meteorites
Space flight—Meteor hazards

METER reading
Automatic eye to read the meter. il Bsns W p 196+ S 26 '64
Meter reading conversion nomograms. R. Jones. il Electr World 72:24-5 Ag '64

METERS
See also
Dwell meters
Electric meters
Exposure meters
Odometers
Parking meters
Taximeters
Velocimeters
Voltmeters
Water meters

METERS, Exposure. See Exposure meters

METHADONE
Withdrawal from drugs. Sci N L 84:4 Jl 6 '63

METHANE
Positive-ion chemistry: high yields of heavy hydrocarbons from solid methane by ionizing radiation. D. R. Davis and W. F. Libby. bibliog Science 144:991-2 My 22 '64

METHANOL
Gamblers; Bowery habitués. il Newsweek 61:60 My 20 '63
Methanol in normal human breath. S. P. Eriksen and A. B. Kulkarni. bibliog il Science 141:639-40 Ag 16 '63

METHODISM
Doctrine of the church, ed. by D. Kirkpatrick. Review
Christian Cent 81:864 Jl 1 '64. R. A. Raines

METHODIST church
John Wesley and Aldersgate 1963. P. B. Mather. Christian Cent 80:1581-3 D 18 '63
Methodists meet in Malaysia. D. Kirkpatrick. Christian Cent 81:175-6 F 5 '64

METHODIST church in Asia
Methodists meet in Malaysia. D. Kirkpatrick. Christian Cent 81:175-6 F 5 '64

METHODIST church in Australia
Australia's Life line movement. A. Walker. Christian Cent 81:20-1 Ja 1 '64
Methodists debate union; General conference. R. Mathias. Christian Cent 80:888 Jl 10 '63

METHODIST church in Cuba
Methodists rally in Cuba. Christian Cent 81: 327 Mr 11 '64

METHODIST church in England
Anglican-Methodist merger. America 108:354 Mr 16 '63
Anglican-Methodist report. C. Northcott. Christian Cent 80:408-9 Mr 27 '63
Anglican-Methodist union proposed in England. Christian Cent 80:325 Mr 13 '63
Church in England. il Time 81:57 Mr 8 '63
Evangelization of a nation. Christian Cent 80:971-2 Ag 7 '63
Urge to merge; Anglican and Methodist churches. Newsweek 61:46 F 4 '63

METHODIST church in India
Methodists and North India union; plan rejected. R. V. Marble. Christian Cent 80: 1173-4 S 25 '63; Reply. D. B. Bauman. 80: 1473 N 27 '63

METHODIST church in the Philippines
Methodist autonomy? C. M. Ferrer. Christian Cent 81:528 Ap 22 '64

METHODIST church in the United States
All about Methodists; findings of Boston university report on The changing face of Methodism in New England. Newsweek 62:71 Ag 19 '63
Beyond lip service; quadrennial General conference in Pittsburgh compromises on civil rights. Time 83:53 My 15 '64
Challenge of fortune. il Time 83:74-8 My 8 '64
Coming home; Methodist general conference. Newsweek 63:66 My 18 '64
Demonstration defused by Methodist bishops. Christian Cent 80:1489-90 D 4 '63
Elects woman to high office; general secretary to its Board of missions. Christian Cent 81:1198 S 30 '64
Ensley heads new Methodist group; Methodist commission for ecumenical affairs. Christian Cent 81:902 Jl 15 '64
Focus on the central jurisdiction; Methodist general conference. P. Wogaman. Christian Cent 80:1296-8 O 23 '63
How to tell a Baptist from a Methodist in the South. G. Harmon. Harper 226:58-63 F '63
Methodist ministers shatter vacuum; ministers in Mississippi condemn discrimination by race, color or creed. Christian Cent 80:229 F 20 '63
Methodist missions retooled; General conference. B. Thompson. Christian Cent 81: 1273 O 14 '64
Methodist northeastern jurisdiction; meeting, Syracuse, N.Y. T. L. Conklin. Christian Cent 81:950 Jl 22 '64
Methodist students in quadrennial session. J. C. Evans. Christian Cent 82:114-16 Ja 27 '65
Methodists and renewal; quadrennial General conference. P. B. Mather. Christian Cent 81:791-2 Je 17 '64
Methodists at Pittsburgh: quadrennial General conference. M. Frakes. Christian Cent 81:662-4 My 20 '64
Methodists: crisis of conscience. R. L. Roy. il Nation 198:262-5 Mr 16 '64
Methodists in session. M. Frakes. Christian Cent 81:694-5 My 27 '64
Methodists move toward integration; election of two Negro bishops. Christian Cent 81:982 Ag 5 '64
Methodists' stand on abstinence; General board of Christian social concerns. Christian Cent 80:1293 O 23 '63
Methodists vote four-year integration. Christian Cent 81:630 My 13 '64
Middle way; quadrennial General conference of the Methodist church. J. G. Deedy, jr. Commonweal 80:353-4 Je 12 '64
Negro bishops for white areas. il Time 84: 63 Jl 24 '64
Success or sacrifice? Methodists for church renewal. il Newsweek 64:73 Jl 20 '64
Toward the recovery of discipline in Methodism. F. H. Littell. Christian Cent 80:826-8 Je 26 '63; Discussion. 80:911-13 Jl 17 '63 Ag 14 '63

METHODIST church of South Africa
South African church elects African head; S. M. Mokitimi. Christian Cent 80:1359 N 6 '63

METHODIST college, Fayetteville, N.C.
Open-door policy. A. W. Stewart. il Wilson Lib Bul 37:860-2 Je '63

METHODIST commission for ecumenical affairs. See Methodist church in the United States

METHODIST conference on human relations
Search for sufficiency; human relations conference. P. B. Mather. Christian Cent 80: 1139-40 S 18 '63

METHODIST Episcopal church, African. See African Methodist Episcopal church

METHODIST publishing house, Nashville, Tenn.
Methodist publishing house reorganizes. Pub W 183:45 Je 24 '63
175-year partnership of press and pulpit. il Pub W 186:53-8 S 28 '64

METHODIST student movement
Methodist students in quadrennial session. J. C. Evans. Christian Cent 82:114-16 Ja 27 '65

METHODIST world conference
Vernacular for unity; concerning speech given by the president of the World Methodist council. America 109:472 O 26 '63

METHODIST youth fellowship
Methodist youth in convocation; National convocation of Methodist youth. L. J. Preston. Christian Cent 81:1155-6 S 16 '64

METHOTREXATE
Methotrexate; suppression of experimental allergic encephalomyelitis. M. W. Brandriss. il Science 140:186-7 Ap 12 '63

METHOXYTRYPTOPHOL. See Melatonin

METHVIN, Eugene H.
Crusader from Connecticut. Read Digest 85: 101-6 S '64
How the reds make a riot. Read Digest 86: 63-9 Ja '65
Let's demand this new weapon for democracy. Read Digest 82:75-81 My '63
—See Gilmore, K. O. jt. auth.

METHYL compounds
Enzymatic alteration of nucleic acid structure. P. R. Srinivasan and E. Borek. bibliog il Science 145:548-53 Ag 7 '64

METHYL lysergic acid butanolamine. See Methysergide maleate

METHYL sulfide
Reduction of dimethylsulfoxide to dimethylsulfide in the cat. V. Distefano and H. H. Borgstedt. bibliog il Science 144:1137-8 My 29 '64

METHYL sulfoxide
DMSO; fact and fancy. W. B. Morse. il Am For 70:6-7+ S '64
Great DMSO mystery. B. Davidson. il Sat Eve Post 237:72-4 Jl 25 '64
New chemical makes sprays work better. Farm J 88:54 F '64
New wonder drug: DMSO. A. Kerr. il Life 57:37-8+ Jl 10 '64
Reduction of dimethylsulfoxide to dimethylsulfide in the cat. V. Distefano and H. H. Borgstedt. bibliog il Science 144:1137-8 My 29 '64
Sweet taste of DMSO. il Newsweek 62:68 D 23 '63

METHYLMETANEPHRINE
N-methylmetanephrine: excretion by juvenile psychotics. T. L. Perry. bibliog il Science 139:587-9 F 15 '63

METHYSERGIDE maleate
Drug prevents headache. Sci N L 84:39 Jl 20 '63

MÉTRAUX, Alfred
Does life end at sixty? UNESCO Courier 16:20-3 Ap '63
Ishi, the last of the Yanas, a primitive Indian between two worlds. UNESCO Courier 16:10-13 F '63; Same abr. with title Last stone age man in the U.S. Sci Digest 54:22-7 Jl '63
Unsolved mystery of Marajo. por UNESCO Courier 16:30-2 N '63

MÉTRAUX, Guy
History of mankind. UNESCO Courier 16:4-7 Je '63

METRIC system
Legacy. Sports Illus 20:8+ Je 29 '64
Metric system of measurement; letters. N. A. Weber; D. V. Frost. Science 141:1137-8+ Je 7 '63; Discussion. bibliog 142:1123-5; 143:638-9 N 29 '63, F 14 '64
Should we abolish the inch? R. Nason. il Duns R 82:35-6 S '63
Weights and measures; report on meeting of the International committee of weights and measures. A. V. Astin. Science 143:974+ F 28 '64

METRICS division. See Singer company

MÉTRO, Paris. See Paris—Subways

METROLOGY. See Measurement

METRONIDAZOLE
For a female complaint; first effective trichomonacide taken by mouth. Time 81:74+ Mr 29 '63

METRONOME
Build the audiotimer. L. E. Garner, jr. il Pop Electr 21:57-60 N '64
On the beat electronically. J. J. Borzner. il Pop Electr 18:60 My '63
Pocketable metronome. S. Stella. il Pop Electr 21:44 Jl '64
Unijunction metronome. J. F. Cleary. il Electr World 69:78-9 F '63

METROPOLITAN areas
Big squeeze in your back yard. J. Prokop. il Am For 69:6-7+ Ap '63
California going, going. . . our state's struggle to remain beautiful and productive, by S. E. Wood and A. E. Heller. Review
Liv Wildn 82:23-4 Winter '62. W. Stegner
City areas that are growing most; with chart. U S News 56:72 Ap 27 '64
Ecological perspective on urban sprawl. L. S. Hamilton. il Am For 69:38-40+ Je '63
Episcopalians consider Megabagdad. J. M. Dabbs. Christian Cent 81:302-3 Mr 4 '64
Home-rule powers for urbanizing counties and towns. J. H. Hughes. il Am City 78:169-70+ S '63
If you scare easily. Am City 79:7+ O '64
More metropolitan government than you think. Am City 78:7 Ag '63
New creation as metropolis, by G. Winter. Review
Christian Cent 80:1007 Ag 14 '63. D. L. Benedict
Shame of the cities. T. O'Hanlon. il Duns R 84:58-9+ O '64
Supplementary wage benefits in metropolitan areas, 1961-62. D. J. Blackmore. il Mo Labor R 86:293-9 Mr '63
Supplemental wage benefits in metropolitan areas, 1962-63. D. J. Blackmore. il Mo Labor R 87:536-42 My '64
Urban complex, by R. C. Weaver. Review
Sat R 47:37-8 S 12 '64. R. A. Low
Urban pattern. H. Blumenfeld. Ann Am Acad 352:74-83 Mr '64
Urban renewal for people. D. B. Carlson. il Arch Forum 120:86-9 Ja '64
Urbanization and human needs. L. J. Duhl. Christian Cent 81:930-3 Jl 22 '64
Urbanization of America, 1860-1915, by B. McKelvey. Review
Am Heritage 14:111 O '63. B. Catton
Wage payment plans in metropolitan areas. J. H. Cox. il Mo Labor R 87:794-6 Jl '64
See also
Regional planning
Urban renewal

METROPOLITAN museum of art, New York
Auction! excerpt. J. Brough. McCalls 90:112-13+ Ap '63
Bitten with acid by Rembrandt; etchings. J. Canaday. N Y Times Mag p72-3 Ap 5 '64
Custodian of continuity; A. A. Houghton, jr. newly chosen president. Newsweek 64:89 S 28 '64
Masterpieces from Peru: Nathan Cummings collection; with editorial comment. F. L. Phelps. il Américas 16:inside cover, 7-16 D '64
Metropolitan's new marble hall. H. La Farge. il Art N 63:40-1 D '64
Mona Lisa. New Yorker 38:23-4 F 9 '63
New guide for the gettingest: Met's new president, Arthur Amory Houghton, jr. il Time 84:76 S 25 '64
Peripatetic patio; Vélez interior patio at the Metropolitan museum of art. il Time 83:76 Ap 24 '64
Recently acquired European drawings. Hobbies 68:92 Ag '63
Spanish castle on Fifth avenue; Vélez Blanco patio. J. Canaday. il N Y Times Mag p 106-7 N 22 '64

American wing
American art from American collections. J. Biddle. il Antiques 83:309-16 Mr '63
Antiques; American art from American collections. A. Winchester. il(cover) Antiques 83:299 Mr '63

Cloisters
Renewal: Easter at the Cloisters. A. Fremantle. il N Y Times Mag p20-1 Ap 14 '63

Costume institute
Reoccupied in style. R. Davidson. il Antiques 85:444-7 Ap '64

METROPOLITAN national company. See Metropolitan opera national company

METROPOLITAN opera association
Beer and sausages; pictures of a Metropolitan party. Opera N 27:14-16 F 23 '63
Metropolitan repertory and roster 1964-65. il Opera N 29:16-17 O 17 '64
Year-round employment. A. A. Bliss. il Opera N 29:8-11 O 17 '64
See also
Central opera service
National council of the Metropolitan opera association

METROPOLITAN opera auditions. See Singing—Competitions

METROPOLITAN opera ballet
Ladies and gentlemen of the ballet. D. Hering il Dance Mag 38:46-7+ My '64
Metropolitan opera ballet. R. Krokover. il Mus Am 84:263 D '64

METROPOLITAN opera company
Admiral and the opera; sponsorship of the Metropolitan's opening-night Aïda. Q. Eaton. il Opera N 28:16 D 7 '63
Back to back; first and second nights of 80th season. il Newsweek 64:100 O 26 '64
Ballet boy at the Met. A. C. Hirzel. il Dance Mag 37:36-7+ S '63
Behind the nervous curtain; opening of 80th season. Time 84:92 O 23 '64
Bing repertory 1950-63; comp. by M. Bernheimer and P. Sunde. Sat R 47:46-7 Ja 25 '64
Designed for the Met. il Theatre Arts 47:66-7 O '63
Guest editorial: fifteen years with Mr Bing. R. Sabin. Mus Am 84:4+ N '64
He gets his way; R. Bing. il Newsweek 62:67-8 O 28 '63
Herbert's day. H. T. Bailey. il Opera N 28:6-7 Ja 25 '64
High order of talent; Metropolitan's production of Bernstein-Zeffirelli Falstaff. M. Mayer. il Opera N 28:6-15 Mr 21 '64
Kahn, Morgan, and Salome; previously unpublished letter concerning banishment of Strauss's Salome from the Metropolitan opera. O. H. Kahn. Sat R 47:60 My 30 '64
Man at the Center; H. Krawitz, technical administrator of the Metropolitan. J. Ferris. il Opera N 29:11-13 Ja 16 '65

METROPOLITAN opera company—*Continued*
Manon reaches the boards. F. Stevenson. il Opera N 28:24-7 D 21 '63
Men in the pit. A. M. Lingg. il Opera N 27:28-31 Mr 16; 29-31 Mr 30; 26-9 Ap 13 '63
Met, Miss Sutherland and Lucia; opening of eightieth season. J. Ardoin. il Mus Am 84: 6-9 N '64
Met moves uptown; takeover of Lewisohn stadium. Mus Am 84:7 S '64
Met opera ballet thinks big. D. Hering. il Dance Mag 37:35-9+ Jl '63
Metropolitan calendar. See issues of Opera news published during opera season
Metropolitan forecast; glimpse of 1964-65. Opera N 28:21 My 2 '64
Metropolitan forecast; 1963-64 Metropolitan repertory. Opera N 27:13 My 4 '63
Metropolitan season; scene and costume sketches in color for 1963-64, with complete roster. Opera N 28:17-20 O 19 '63
Metropolitan spring tour, 1963. Opera N 27: inside back cover Mr 2 '63
Metropolitan spring tour, 1964. Opera N 28: 35 F 29 '64
Mr Bing makes the Met go. M. Mayer. il N Y Times Mag p44-5+ O 11 '64
Music; Met season opens. C. J. McNaspy. America 109:438-9 O 12 '63
Music to my ears; "on" night at the Met; Les sylphides staged by A. Markova. I. Kolodin. Sat R 47:34+ N 28 '64
Musical events; season just past. W. Sargeant. New Yorker 40:176-8 My 2 '64
New mood for the new Met. I. Kolodin. il Sat R 47:45-7+ Ja 25 '64
50-1 F 15; 62-4 F 29 '64
Opera on four cylinders; Metropolitan spring tour in Detroit. A. M. Lingg. Opera N 28: 21-2 O 19 '63
Planning the season. R. Herman. il Opera N 28:8-11 Mr 14 '64
Reviews: opera at the Metropolitan (title varies) il Mus Am 83:31-2 N; 250+ D '63; 84:37-40 Ja; 31-2 Mr; 42-5 Ap; 36 My; 38 Jl; 22-4 N; 108-10 D '64
Salute to the World's fair; Met stages ten operas. il Opera N 28:13-16 Ap 18 '64
Singers' opera. J. Gutman. il Opera N 27: 8-12 Mr 2 '63
Smug dowager. B. Boretz. Nation 198:563-4 Je 1 '64
Sponsor; Metropolitan's new production of Aïda. New Yorker 39:45-6 N 23 '63
Spring tour casts. Opera N 27:32-3 Mr 30 '63
Switch in time; unprecedented broadcast change. F. Stevenson. il Opera N 27:13-16 Mr 9 '63
Tentative advance schedule; World's fair season. Opera N 28:inside back cover N 16 '63
Twins; operatic Mets play softball. il Sports Illus 18:13 My 27 '63
See also
Radio broadcasting—Music
METROPOLITAN opera guild
Affiliated guilds report (cont) il Opera N 27:34-5 Mr 16 '63
Enthusiasm in the classroom. il Opera N 28:30-1 Ap 18 '64
Harlem Bohème. F. Stevenson. il Opera N 28:6 Mr 14 '64
Luncheon date. il Opera N 28:6-7 Ja 18 '64
New friends; photographs of Guild student performance: Rossini's Barber of Seville. Opera N 27:14-15 Mr 16 '63
Out of many. L. Greenway. il Opera N 28:6-7 S 28 '63
Silver stars; Guild's annual luncheon for supporting members. il Opera N 29:16 Ja 23 '65
See also
Metropolitan opera studio
METROPOLITAN opera house, New York
Architecture. W. McQuade. Nation 198:59-60 Ja 13 '64
Music; Met season opens. C. J. McNaspy. America 109:438-9 O 12 '63
METROPOLITAN opera national company
Council resolutions. A. M. Lingg. il Opera N 29:32-3 Ja 2 '65
Growing national opera; symposium. il Opera N 29:10-11 N 14 '64
Metropolitan's national company. Opera N 28: 18 N 16 '63
METROPOLITAN opera on the air. See Radio broadcasting—Music
METROPOLITAN opera orchestra. See Orchestras
METROPOLITAN opera studio
Studio progress; latest report on the junior Metropolitan. A. M. Lingg. Opera N 28:16 Ja 25 '64
When opera goes to school. A. M. Lingg. il Read Digest 82:281-3+ Ap '63

METROPOLITAN stadium, Minnesota. See Stadiums
METS (baseball) See Baseball clubs
METS (softball team) See Metropolitan opera company
METUCHEN, N.J.
As soon as the first snowflake appears; plowing and removal of snow. T. Eosso. il Am City 79:10 D '64
Presto! changeo! a stage on wheels. T. Eosso. il Am City 80:24 Ja '65
METZ, Donald L.
Sonnet for Christmas. Christian Cent 81:1584 D 23 '64
METZENBERG, Robert L. and others
Irreparable mutations and ethionine resistance in neurospora. bibliog Science 145: 1434-5 S 25 '64
METZGER, A. W.
Fiber glass fabrics modify environment. Arch Rec 136:219-20 N '64
METZGER, H. and Singer, S. J.
Binding capacity of reductively fragmented antibodies to the 2,4-dinitrophenyl group. bibliog Science 142:674-5 N 8 '63
METZL, Ervine
Eight great posters. Am Artist 27:21-6 My '63
Marine art of Charles G. Evers. Am Artist 27:28-33+ Mr '63
Stamps U.S.A. il Am Artist 28:44-9+ Mr '64
METZLER, Edgar
Peace and nonviolence. Christian Cent 81: 1597-8 D 23 '64
MEURER, Clara B.
Boating in the Land of Lincoln. Motor B 111: 29+ Je '63
MEVALONIC acid. See Dihydroxymethyl valeric acid
MEWALDT, L. Richard
California sparrows return from displacement to Maryland. bibliog Science 146:941-2 N 13 '64
MEXICAN AMERICANS
Other Texans; Mexicanos. il Look 27:68-70 O 8 '63; Discussion. 27:13+ N 19 '63
Revolt of the Mexicans; election in Crystal City, Tex. il Time 81:25 Ap 12 '63
Texas giant awakens; greater political influence for Mexicanos. T. B. Morgan. il Look 27:71-2+ O 8 '63
MEXICAN ant acacias. See Acacias
MEXICAN art. See Art, Mexican
MEXICAN children in the United States. See Mexicans in the United States
MEXICAN cookery. See Cookery, Mexican
MEXICAN daylilies. See Tigerflowers
MEXICAN fiction
Novels of a dead revolution. J. Sommers. Nation 197:114-15 S 7 '63
MEXICAN freetails. See Bats
MEXICAN language. See Spanish language in Mexico
MEXICAN literature
Variety and contrast; tr. by J. M. Alonso. R. Xirau. Atlan 213:142-5 Mr '64
See also
Mexican fiction
MEXICAN music. See Music, Mexican
MEXICAN painting. See Painting, Mexican
MEXICAN poetry
Five Mexican poets; with poems. S. Mondragón. il Américas 15:7-12 O '63
Translations into English
Hecuba's testament; tr. by J. F. Nims. R. Castellanos. Atlan 213:120 Mr '64
Month of June; tr. by J. F. Nims. H. Aridjis. Atlan 213:105 Mr '64
Pause; Here; Girl; tr. by J. F. Nims. O. Paz. Atlan 213:99 Mr '64
Smoke; tr. by J. F. Nims. R. B. Nuño. Atlan 213:148 Mr '64
MEXICAN pottery. See Pottery, Mexican
MEXICAN shellflower. See Tigerflowers
MEXICAN students
Mexico's youth speaks; excerpts from a poll, comp. by E. K. Culhane. America 109:408 O 12 '63
Yankees again; anti-American lectures at Mexico university. F. Mallari. America 108:630 My 4 '63
MEXICAN tiles. See Tiles
MEXICAN-United States boundary and water commission. See International boundary and water commission (United States and Mexico)
MEXICAN villages. See Villages
MEXICANOS. See Mexican Americans
MEXICANS
Conservation with Francisco. D. W. Bazil. Christian Cent 80:366-7 Mr 20 '63

MEXICANS—*Continued*
Love and authority; study of Mexican villagers. M. Maccoby. Atlan 213:121-6 Mr '64
Mexico's man. D. Simon. il Sat R 46:74-6+ O 12 '63

MEXICANS in the United States
Another extension; importation of Mexican workers. Commonweal 79:213 N 15 '63
As the braceros leave. M. E. Leary. il Reporter 32:43-5 Ja 28 '65
Battle over the braceros; in California. Bsns W p24 Ja 9 '65
Bracero's journey. S. W. Coombs. il Américas 15:7-11 D '63
California farm labor. A. Ogle. America 111:799+ D 19 '64
California: what help for the harvest? discredited bracero program. il Newsweek 64:77 N 2 '64
California's Spanish-speaking; religious ministration in Santa Clara County. America 111:222+ S 5 '64
Churches oppose braceros program. Christian Cent 81:1580 D 23 '64
Congress extends braceros program. Christian Cent 81:5 Ja 1 '64
Education of subcultural groups. J. P. Rice, jr. bibliog f Sch & Soc 92:360-2 N 28 '64
End of bracero program. America 108:878-9 Je 22 '63
End run on braceros into the 20th century. America 111:791 D 19 '64
Fate of P.L. 78. Commonweal 78:316 Je 14 '63
Growers face loss of braceros. il Bsns W p 120 Ag 22 '64
House rejects bracero program. Christian Cent 80:766 Je 12 '63
Minister who follows the migrants; Migrant ministry program of N.C.C. M. Cope. il Sat Eve Post 237:34-6 Ja 4 '64
Storm over braceros. Sr Schol 85:20 Ja 21 '65
Where braceros once worked; California vegetable fields. il Bsns W p32-3 Ja 16 '65
See also
Mexican Americans

MEXICO
Mexico today; symposium. il Atlan 213:89-114+ Mr '64
Quick look at Mexico. R. Condon. Holiday 35:56-7 Je '64
Record of success. Time 84:28 S 11 '64
See also
Acapulco
Airlines—Mexico
Airplane industry and trade—Mexico
Architecture—Mexico
Architecture, Domestic—Mexico
Arts and crafts—Mexico
Automobile touring—Mexico
Aviation—Mexico
Birth control—Mexico
California, Lower
Camping—Mexico
Cities and towns—Mexico
Communism—Mexico
Crime and criminals—Mexico
Divorce—Mexico
Earthquakes—Mexico
Forests and forestry—Mexico
Guadalajara
Hunting—Mexico
Labor and laboring classes—Mexico
Land tenure—Mexico
Mazatlán
Mexicans in the United States
Mexico (city)
Michoacán
Mitla
Oaxaca (city)
Opera—Mexico
Paleontology—Mexico
Patzcuaro, Lake
Petroleum industry and trade—Mexico
Political parties—Mexico
Poor—Mexico
Puerto Vallarta
Railroads—Mexico
San Miguel De Allende
Space research—Mexico
Sports—Mexico
Technical assistance in Mexico
Television broadcasting—Mexico
Teotihuacán
Textbooks—Mexico
Theater—Mexico
Tijuana
Trade unions—Mexico
United States—Foreign relations—Mexico
Urique River
Veracruz
Water supply—Mexico
Xochimilco

Antiquities
See Indians of Mexico—Antiquities

Boundaries
Bending the river. il Time 82:20 Jl 26 '63
Border dispute settled. il Sr Schol 83:8 S 20 '63
Border pact: what Mexico gains, what Texas loses. il U S News 55:6 D 30 '63
Ceremony at Mexican border marks settlement of Chamizal dispute; address, September 25, 1964. L. B. Johnson. Dept State Bul 51:545-9 O 19 '64
Peace on the Rio Grande. New Repub 149:7 S 21 '63
Remember El Chamizal. Newsweek 62:49 Jl 29 '63
Slice of Texas soon to go to Mexico. il U S News 55:12 Jl 22 '63
United States and Mexico agree to conclude convention for settlement of Chamizal boundary dispute; statement, July 18, 1963; with Department statement and joint memorandum of Department and Mexican Ministry of foreign relations, July 17, 1963. J. F. Kennedy. Dept State Bul 49:199-204 Ag 5 '63
U.S. and Mexico sign convention settling Chamizal boundary; Department statement; text of convention, August 29, 1963; and text of minute, International boundary and water commission, United States and Mexico, August 28, 1963. Dept State Bul 49:480-4 S 23 '63
United States ratifies Chamizal convention. L. B. Johnson; E. M. Martin. Dept State Bul 50:49-51 Ja 13 '64

Caricatures and cartoons
Most powerful country in the world; excerpt from Best of impossible worlds. A. Quezada. Atlan 213:100-1 Mr '64

Commerce
Mexico's show window; National home fair, at Juarez. il Bsns W p68-9 S 26 '64

Commercial treaties and agreements
U.S. concludes meat agreement with Mexico; State-agriculture announcement, with United States note, May 14, 1964. Dept State Bul 50:944-5 Je 15 '64

Description and travel
Down Mexico way. il Time 83:53 My 22 '64
Journey through Mexico. L. Lee. Mlle 57:190-1+ My '63
Lessons in going native. M. Lewis and M. Lewis. il Sat R 47:63-4+ O 10 '64
Little bird that snorted; second-class bus from San Miguel de Allende to Mexico city. C. Darlington. il Sat R 46:84-5 O 12 '63
Loop trip below Arizona's border. il Sunset 132:33+ Ap '64
Magical Mexico. P. James. il U S Camera 27:22-3 Ja '64
Mexican weekends. T. B. Lesure. il Travel 123:44-7 Ja '65
Mexico, a big photo studio. L. Barry. il Pop Phot 52:30+ Mr '63
Mexico: amusing incidentals. Vogue 141:58+ Mr 15 '63
Mexico's border towns. M. Ross. il Travel 120:32-4 N '63
Mexico's new rail thrill; Ferrocarril Chihuahua al Pacifico. W. Kane. il Travel 119:34-7 F '63
New guide to old Mexico. il Bet Hom & Gard 42:139-42 N '64
Personal business. Bsns W p93-4 Ja 9 '65
Rail adventure trip across Mexico's Sierra Madre. il Sunset 132:34-6+ Mr '64
To the Panama Canal by car; a first in tourist travel. J. F. Diggs and T. J. O'Halloran. il U S News 54:70-6 My 13 '63
Travel notes. R. Joseph. Esquire 59:39-40+ Mr '63
Viva Mexico. il U S Camera 27:24 F '64
West coast of Mexico. M. Goodman. Esquire 60:28+ S '63

Discovery and exploration
Exploring, ugh! B. Gilbert. il Sports Illus 20:72-6+ Ja 27 '64

Economic conditions
Bright spot in the hemisphere: a close look at Mexico. il U S News 56:95-7 F 24 '64
Conservation with Francisco. D. W. Bazil. Christian Cent 80:366-7 Mr 20 '63
Mexico: stability is breeding a boomlet. il Bsns W p56 Ap 18 '64
Progress through revolution. Commonweal 78:548-9 S 20 '63

MEXICO—Economic conditions—*Continued*
Viva el candidato! R. Armstrong. il Sat Eve Post 237:73-7 Je 20 '64
Volkswagen president. il Newsweek 64:60-1 D 7 '64
See also
Labor and laboring classes—Mexico

Economic policy

Economic revolution in Mexico; address, December 6, 1963. E. M. Martin. Dept State Bul 49:959-63 D 23 '63
Keeping steam in Mexico's boom. il Bsns W p90+ N 28 '64
Mexico's businessmen: changing the old order. il U S News 58:88-9 Ja 11 '65
Pre-election valedictory; summary of address. A. López Mateos. il Time 82:45 S 13 '63
South of the border. Commonweal 81:405 D 18 '64

Economic relations

United States

President Johnson and President López Mateos of Mexico hold talks in California; joint communique, February 22, 1964. L. B. Johnson and A. López Mateos. Dept State Bul 50:396-8 Mr 16 '64

Foreign relations

De Gaulle's Mexican hat dance. G. Delmas. Reporter 30:30-2 Ap 23 '64
Latins together; de Gaulle's visit to Mexico. Newsweek 63:38+ Mr 23 '64
Mexico looks to the North. I. Fabela. Atlan 213:95-8 Mr '64
Rebuff to the OAS; contacts with Cuba maintained. Time 84:29 Ag 14 '64
Tour de force: de Gaulle in Mexico. il Newsweek 63:33-4 Mr 30 '64
U.S. betting on Mexico; but there's trouble ahead. il U S News 54:45-7 F 25 '63

United States

Community of interest between the U.S. and Mexico; remarks, March 5, 1964. D. Rusk. Dept State Bul 50:449-50 Mr 23 '64

History

Important dates in Mexican history. Atlan 213:98 Mr '64
1964 shoo-in for Mexico? il Sr Schol 83:10-13 D 13 '63
Novels of a dead revolution. J. Sommers. Nation 197:114-15 S 7 '63

Conquest, 1519-1540

City of the living god; excerpts from Cortés: the life of the conqueror by his secretary, tr. by L. B. Simpson. L. L. de Gómara. il Am Heritage 15:67-79 Ap '64

European intervention, 1861-1867

Operator and the emperors; with portfolio. L. Thomas. il Am Heritage 15:4-23+ Ap '64
See also
Maximilian I, emperor of Mexico

Industries

Mexican empire builder. il Bsns W p 142-4 Je 20 '64
Mexico: diversity aids a comeback. il Bsns W p54 Je 29 '63
Modern Medici: B. Pagliai. il Time 81:93 My 10 '63

Intellectual life

Martí in Mexico; days of Hidalgo lyceum. G. de Zéndegui. il Américas 15:12-16 Je '63
Mexico's performing arts. J. Dalrymple. il Travel 122:44-6 Ag '64

Native races

See Indians of Mexico

Politics and government

Bright spot in the hemisphere: a close look at Mexico. il U S News 56:95-7 F 24 '64
Changing the guard in Mexico. M. C. Needler. il Cur Hist 48:26-31+ Ja '65
Glowing start. Time 84:53 D 11 '64
Letter from Mexico City. R. Rosen. Nation 198:200-3 F 24 '64
Mexico chooses stability for 1964-70. il U S News 55:83 N 18 '63
Mexico: cool revolution and cold war. S. R. Ross. Cur Hist 44:89-94+ F '63
Mexico follows a solo camino. K. Botsford. il N Y Times Mag p20+ Ap 26 '64
Mexico: stability is breeding a boomlet. il Bsns W p 56 Ap 18 '64
1964 shoo-in for Mexico? il Sr Schol 83:10-13 D 13 '63
Presidential march: left, right. il Time 82:53 N 15 '63
Stink bombs for Castro. New Repub 149:7 S 14 '63
U.S. betting on Mexico; but there's trouble ahead. il U S News 54:45-7 F 25 '63
See also
Presidents—Mexico

Religious institutions and affairs

News of the Christian world (cont) Christian Cent 80:282+, 685-6, 1144, 1526 F 27, My 22, S 18, D 4 '63

Social conditions

Love and authority; study of Mexican villagers. M. Maccoby. Atlan 213:121-6 Mr '64
Pedro Martinez, by O. Lewis. Review
Sat R 47:29-30 My 2 '64. M. Harris
Time il 83:100+ My 8 '64
Remarks at Mexican fiesta, February 22, 1964. L. B. Johnson. Dept State Bul 50:401-3 Mr 16 '64
See also
Poor—Mexico

Social history

After the revolution; excerpt from Pedro Martínez, a Mexican peasant and his family. O. Lewis. il Reporter 30:34-6+ Ap 9 '64

Social life and customs

Vanishing pulqueria. Newsweek 63:50+ My 11 '64

MEXICO (city)
Highest Olympics. Sports Illus 19:7 N 4 '63

Description

Mexico city. il Sunset 131:42-57 Ag '63
Palm Sunday. P. James. il U S Camera 27:14-15 Ap '64

Housing

Union-financed houses rise in Latin America; AFL-CIO's Latin American investment program. il Bsns W p 128 N 28 '64

Music

[Musical events] (cont) Mus Am 84:23 My '64
September in Mexico. H. Wilhelm. il Opera N 28:30-1 D 21 '63
South of the border. K. H. Wilhelm; E. Zubryn; R. Kovacs. Opera N 29:32-3 D 12 '64

Stores

Forward's march: pioneering Arango brothers of Mexico. il Time 81:83 F 8 '63

MEXICO and the United States
Charter day ceremonies, UCLA; remarks, February 21, 1964. L. B. Johnson. Dept State Bul 50:399-400 Mr 16 '64
Overlap land, gringo and Mexican meet in the Rio Grande country. J. Graves. Holiday 35:74-5+ Mr '64
President-elect of Mexico visits President Johnson at LBJ ranch; remarks, November 12, 1964. G. Díaz Ordaz; L. B. Johnson. Dept State Bul 51:805-7 D 7 '64
Remarks at Mexican fiesta, February 22, 1964. L. B. Johnson. Dept State Bul 50:401-3 Mr 16 '64
See also
Americans in Mexico

MEXICO, University. See Colleges and universities—Mexico

MEYER, Agnes E.
Middle-class Negroes should assume more responsibility; letter. por U S News 55:61 Jl 15 '63
Nation's worst slum: Washington, D.C. Atlan 212:89-92 Ag '63

MEYER, Anne A.
Children's books about the Middle East. Horn Bk 40:308-12 Je '64

MEYER, Carl S.
History as propagation. Christian Cent 81:912 Jl 15 '64

MEYER, Charles R.
Boat financing. Motor B 113:258+ Ja '64
Fishing your way south. por Motor B 112:30-3+ S '63
Hemingway (the boatman) il Motor B 114:21-3+ Jl '64
Racing a Great South Bay scooter. Motor B 114:50-1+ D '64
Rough water boat handling. il Motor B 113:28-9+ Je '64
Sound cruising. Travel 119:38-40 Je '63
Try Florida's St Johns. Motor B 114:32-5 S '64

MEYER, Daniel
Adjustable speech filter. Pop Electr 20:49-52 My '64

MEYER, Daniel—*Continued*
Bargain page amplifier. Pop Electr 21:69-72 O '64
Experimenting with sonar. Pop Electr 21:41-5+ S '64
Ultrasonic Sniffer. Pop Electr 18:41-4+ Mr '63
MEYER, Donald A. and Nathan, Max, Jr
Electoral college: the obsolete filter. Nation 199:396-9 N 30 '64
MEYER, Frank S.
Identity of the West. Nat R 16:975-6+ N 3 '64
Just war in the nuclear age. Nat R 14:105-6+ F 12 '63
Principles and heresies. See issues of National review
MEYER, Herbert H. and others
Split roles in performance appraisal. Harvard Bsns R 43:123-9 Ja '65
MEYER, Howard N.
Four books on race. Commonweal 80:490-1 Jl 10 '64
Historical basis of emancipation, 1963; address. Negro Hist Bul 27:4-6 O '63
How J.F.K's. grandfather fought the grandfather clause. Negro Hist Bul 27:27 N '63
Myth and reality. Commonweal 79:202-3, 406-7 N 8, D 27 '63; Same. Negro Hist Bul 27:178-9 Ap '64
Struggle for equality. Negro Hist Bul 28:71 D '64
MEYER, John S. See Bauer, W. C. jt. auth.
MEYER, Karl E.
Jewel case for pre-Columbian gems. Art N 62:36-9+ F '64
Washington press establishment. Esquire 61:73-6+ Ap '64
about
Dis-establishmentarian. Newsweek 63:46-7 Mr 30 '64
MEYER, Lee
Colorado photographic art center. Pop Phot 56:136-7+ Ja '65
MEYER, Lewis
Dex Libris, invisible bookseller. Pub W 183:64-6 Mr 25 '63
Fiction, the publisher's Cinderella-child. Pub W 184:53-4 S 23 '63
It was the year of the great don't-care. Pub W 185:80-1 Ja 6 '64
MEYER, Nancy. See Meyer, R. D. jt. auth.
MEYER, Raymond E. and Gingrich, J. R.
Osmotic stress: effects of its application to a portion of wheat root systems. Science 14:1463-4 Je 19 '64
MEYER, Richard D. and Meyer, Nancy
Setting the stage for Lincoln Center. Theatre Arts 48:12-16+ Ja '64
MEYER, Robert, Jr
Autoless adventure West. Travel 120:38-42 Jl '63
New centers for theatre-goers. Travel 119:46-8 My '63
MEYER, Robert E.
Salt, plow and haul. Am City 78:90-1 O '63
MEYER, Robert Eugene, 1911-
SR/1964 world travel calendar. Sat R 47:45-50 Ja 4 '64
Shakespeare schedule. Sat R 47:98-9 Mr 14 '64
MEYER, Robert L.
Make your own safety sideshow; reprint. il Recreation 57:200-1 Ap '64
MEYER, Roy W.
Place of the Red Pipestone. il Nat Parks Mag 37:4-7 D '63
MEYER, Stanton M.
Irish Mail and the Kaiser's war. New Yorker 39:74-7 D 21 '63
MEYER, Sylvan
Streetcar named Autoferro Ecuatoriano. Sat R 46:94+ O 12 '63
MEYER zoysia. See Grasses
MEYERBEER, Giacomo
Case for Meyerbeer. R. Lawrence. il Mus Am 84:26-7 My '64
Man Meyerbeer. R. Berges. por Opera N 29:6-7 O 17 '64
MEYERHOFF, Howard A.
Energy in the United States. bibliog Focus 13:1-6 Ap '63
MEYEROWITZ, Rainer F.
How about it, Detroit? New Repub 150:10-13 Ap 4 '64
MEYERS, Albert J.
(ed) See Aron, R. Size-up of de Gaulle
MEYERS E. and Miller, D.
Rangefinder pro hints and tips. Mod Phot 27:72-3 My '63
MEYERS, F. H. See Barnes, C. D. jt. auth.
MEYERS, Harold B.
Businessman in a political jungle. Fortune 69:132-5+ Ap '64
Great uranium glut. Fortune 69:108-11+ F '64
Hell of a different way to run a railroad. Fortune 68:100-9+ S '63
Lone-wolf guardian of federal morality. Fortune 69:126-9+ Je '64
L.B.J.'s romance with business. Fortune 70:130-3+ S '64
Medicare, the cure that could cause a setback. Fortune 67:131-3+ My '63
Root of the FTC's confusion. Fortune 68:114-16+ Ag '63
United aircraft: success with a wry twist. Fortune 68:110-15+ D '63
Urban transit's new pep pill. Fortune 70:166-7+ N '64
MEYERS, John F.
Crisis in our colleges. America 110:438-9 Mr 28 '64
MEYERS, Maurice F.
Book reviews. America 111:52 Jl 11 '64
MEYERS, Samuel P. and others
Nutritional relationships among certain filamentous fungi and a marine nematode. bibliog Science 141:520-2 Ag 9 '63
MEYERS, William J. and others
Heart rate changes after reinforcing brain stimulation in rats. bibliog Science 140:1233-5 Je 14 '63
MEYERSON, Martin
Détente at Berkeley? por Newsweek 65:52 Ja 18 '65
New man at Berkeley. por Time 85:50+ Ja 15 '65
MEYNELL, Sir Francis
Sir Francis Meynell and the Nonesuch press. F. Johnson. il Am Artist 28:38-43+ F '64
MEYNEN, Johannes
Who's who in foreign business. por Fortune 69:52 F '64
MEYNER, Robert B.
Cigarette czar. por Newsweek 63:64 Je 22 '64
Tar Czar. Newsweek 64:46 D 28 '64
MEZEY, Robert
After hours: poem. Harper 226:89 Je '63
Note she might have left; poem. Harper 230:73 Ja '65
MIAMI, Fla.
Bowl of orange for a pick-me-up. M. Glaser. il Sports Illus 21:40-7 D 14 '64
Miami's Cuban refugee crisis. A. Morrison. il Ebony 18:96-100+ Je '63
Airports
Atlanta, Miami share concepts, problems. R. H. Cook. il Aviation W 79:47+ Ag 5 '63
Churches
Elegance and economy in a simple scheme; Key Biscayne Presbyterian church. il Arch Rec 134:140-1 Jl '63
Description
New and handier Havana. H. Sutton. Sat R 46:33-4 D 7 '63
Finance
Miami taxpayers howl; property tax proposed. il Bsns W p64+ Ag 22 '64
Music
Miami medley. D. Reno. Opera N 28:28 S 28 '63
Paris comes to Miami. D. Reno. Opera N 28:34 Ap 18 '64
Parades
Big bowls of glitter. il Life 56:38-45 Ja 3 '64
Parks and playgrounds
Mushrooms for uplift. J. W. Hilton. il Am City 78:37 N '63
MIAMI, Fla, public library
Cooperative venture: Joint book selection committee with Dade County school libraries. M. H. Edmonds. Wilson Lib Bul 38:689 Ap '64
MIAMI BEACH, Fla.
Yes, Virginia, there is a Miami. H. Saal. il Sat R 47:76-9+ O 10 '64
Hotels, restaurants, etc.
Stampede to the sun. il Bsns W p 108-10+ Mr 9 '63
Parks and playgrounds
Two to one in Miami Beach. J. Woody. il Recreation 57:167+ Ap '64
Recreation
Two to one in Miami Beach. J. Woody. il Recreation 57:167+ Ap '64
MIAMI herald
Pictures under pressure. B. Stapleton. il Pop Phot 52:44-7+ F '63

MIAMI university, Coral Gables, Fla.
School with teacherless classrooms. W. Hartley and E. Hartley. il Pop Mech 120:128-30 O '63
Science center emphasizes bold structure; Science building. il Arch Rec 137:122-3 Ja '65
University organization for geophysics education; excerpts from address, April 1964. W. A. Baum. Science 146:619-21 O 30 '64
MIAMI university, Oxford, Ohio
Burgeoning university enrollments and academic quality. L. Siegel and others. il Sch & Soc 91:336-8 N 2 '63
MICA
Fission-track ages and track-annealing behavior of some micas. R. L. Fleischer and others. bibliog il Science 143:349-51 Ja 24 '64
Infrared spectra of hydronium ion in micaceous minerals. J. L. White and A. F. Burns. bibliog il Science 141:800-1 Ag 30 '63
MICCOSUKEE Indians. See Seminole Indians
MICE
Lethal alleles in mus musculus: local distribution and evidence for isolation of demes. P. K. Anderson. bibliog il Science 145:177-8 Jl 10 '64
New discoveries on radiation of mice. Sci N L 84:264 O 26 '63
MICE, White footed
Age of weaning in two subspecies of deer mice. J. A. King and others. bibliog il Science 139:483-4 F 8 '63
Mice in our forests; deer mice, or white-footed mice. L. Pringle. il Am For 70:40-1+ N '64
Notes from a mousekeeper's diary. F. McNulty. il Audubon Mag 66:382-7 N '64
Peromyscus leucopus: an interesting subject for studies of socially induced stress responses. C. H. Southwick. bibliog il Science 143:55-6 Ja 3 '64
MICE and birds and boy; story. See Taylor, E.
MICHAEL, Donald N.
Free time; address, June 18, 1963. Vital Speeches 29:616-20 Ag 1 '63
MICHAEL, Richard P. and Herbert, J.
Menstrual cycle influences grooming behavior and sexual activity in the rhesus monkey. bibliog Science 140:500-1 My 3 '63
MICHAELIS, Michael
Strategy for innovation. Bul Atomic Sci 20:19-23 Ap '64
MICHAELIS, Ronald F.
Rarity in English pewter. Antiques 85:698-9 Je '64
MICHAELS, Abraham
Snow-fighters get promise of better weather forecasts. Am City 79:106-7 Je '64
—See Smallwood, D. M. jt. auth.
MICHAELS, Sidney
Dylan. Criticism
America 110:238-9 F 15 '64
Cath World 198:391-2 Mr '64
Commonweal 79:572-3 F 7 '64
Nation 198:176 F 17 '64
New Yorker 39:72 Ja 25 '64
Newsweek 63:58 Ja 27 '64
Sat R 47:22 F 8 '64
Time il 83:54 Ja 31 '64
MICHAELSON, Marc. See Snook, P. K. jt. auth.
MICHAL, Mira
At Lake Lugano; story. New Yorker 40:28-33 Ag 15 '64
MICHEL, Georges
Les jouets. Criticism
New Yorker 40:97-8 My 2 '64
MICHEL, Joan Hess
Maurice Sendak, illustrator of the child's world. Am Artist 28:44-9+ S '64
Whimsical illustrations of Hilary Knight. Am Artist 27:49-53+ Mr '63
MICHEL, Sandy
Conservation; poem. Am For 70:45 Ag '64
MICHELANGELI, Arturo Benedetti
More imports: via Odeon, the legendary Michelangeli. R. Kammerer. por Am Rec G 30:111 O '63
MICHELANGELO Buonarroti
Doubting genius. il por Newsweek 61:107-8 Je 10 '63
From the Tuscan. S. Alexander. Reporter 31:60+ S 24 '64
Genius as snob. C. Eisler. Nation 198:75-6 Ja 20 '64
Genius of Michelangelo as seen by Moore; ed. by D. Sylvester. H. Moore. il por N Y Times Mag p 16-17+ Mr 8 '64
Glory of the Sistine. il N Y Times Mag p 10-11 Je 16 '63
Keep the Pietà in Rome! Christian Cent 81:102 Ja 22 '64
Michelangelo; with report by M. G. Hager. il Life 57:54-67+ Jl 17 '64
Michelangelo year opens in Rome. M. Gendel. il Art N 63:26-8 Ap '64
Michelangelo's magnificent mirror of man. E. O. Hauser. il por Read Digest 84:176-80+ My '64
Missing Michelangelo? il Life 56:45-6+ F 21 '64
Mystery of the missing Michelangelo; long-lost St John the Baptist. K. Kuh. il Sat R 47:47-8 Je 27 '64
Pietà: masterpiece at the fair. C. McCarry. il Sat Eve Post 237:24-9 Mr 28 '64
MICHELIA figo. See Banana shrub
MICHELIN guides. See Guidebooks
MICHELON, L. C.
Economic education; address, June 18, 1964. Vital Speeches 30:648-52 Ag 15 '64
What industry expects of youth; address, May 25, 1963. Vital Speeches 29:572-6 Jl 1 '63
MICHELOSEN, John
Pitt wins (boss's orders) J. Underwood. il por Sports Illus 19:22-6+ O 28 '63
MICHELS, Robert, and others
Thyroxine: effects on amino acid incorporation into protein in vivo. bibliog Science 140:1417-18 Je 28 '63
MICHELSON, Albert A.
He measured the speed of light. R. S. Strother. il por Read Digest 85:193-4+ Jl '64
Michelson-Morley experiment. R. S. Shankland. il por Sci Am 211:107-14 N '64
MICHELUCCI, Giovanni
Church of the Autostrada. J. M. Fitch. il Arch Forum 121:100-9 Jl '64
MICHENER, Charles D.
Division of labor among primitively social bees. bibliog Science 141:434-5 Ag 2 '63
MICHENER, James A.
Caravans; novel; condensation. Ladies Home J 80:79-86 Jl '63
MICHIGAN
See also
Birds—Michigan
Education—Michigan
Fishing—Michigan
Forests and forestry—Michigan
Hunting—Michigan
Music festivals—Michigan

Historic houses, etc.

History in houses; the Noah Webster House at Greenfield Village. G. G. Gibson. il Antiques 85:196-201 F '64

Legislature

Quiet one; false identity and fraud by Detroit representative. Newsweek 64:27+ D 21 '64
Romney's trial run. New Repub 148:6 My 11 '63

Politics and government

Businessman in a political jungle. H. B. Meyers. il Fortune 69:132-5+ Ap '64
Citizens' victory. Time 81:24 Ap 12 '63
For Romney: a win, a boost. il U S News 54:44-6 Ap 15 '63
George Romney gone bust. C. A. Ferry. New Repub 150:12-15 Ja 25 '64
Lightning strikes thrice. Time 83:25 My 8 '64
Making their records. il Time 82:29 S 13 '63
Power ploy. Newsweek 61:25 F 18 '63
State GOP slaps Romney. Bsns W p80+ N 16 '63
Still listening for the lash. il Time 84:23 S 11 '64
Voters bought Romney. Newsweek 61:32+ Ap 15 '63

Religious institutions and affairs

News of the Christian world (cont) Christian Cent 80:187, 376+, 754, 1112; 81:312+, 994+, 1628+ F 6, Mr 20, Je 5, S 11 '63, Mr 4, Ag 5, D 30 '64

State waterways commission

Michigan's 3,000-mile marine highway. J. Miner. il Yachting 115:51-3+ Mr '64
MICHIGAN, LAKE
See also
Green Bay
MICHIGAN CITY, Ind.
Students plan Project '80 for Michigan City. il Arch Rec 133:81 Mr '63
MICHIGAN state library
Michigan state library submits school library plan. Library J 90:328-9 Ja 15 '65
MICHIGAN state university of agriculture and applied science. East Lansing
How to get rid of good professor. R. Kirk. Nat R 14:321 Ap 23 '63

MICHIGAN state university of agriculture and applied science, East Lansing—*Continued*
Merits for MSU. Newsweek 63:58 My 4 '64
Problems at State university. R. E. Kavanaugh. America 108:540-4+ Ap 20 '63
What ever happened to the beat generation? Student education corps; reprint. J. Reston. il Sr Schol 84:12T Ap 24 '64

Libraries

Sound scholarships; Michigan state university's new National voice library. il Time 83:49 F 7 '64
Sounds of history; recorded voices of 8,000 celebrities in National voice library. W. B. Furlong. il N Y Times Mag p72+ Mr 22 '64

Oakland branch

Dissent, si; dissenter, no; discussion. Nation 196:inside cover F 16 '63
To the top, fork in hand; weekly dinners at Oakland university. Bsns W p78+ O 17 '64

MICHIGAN. University, Ann Arbor
High-rise and low-rise grouping for Michigan campus. il Arch Rec 135:165-8 Ap '64
In a buying mood; findings of University of Michigan survey research center. Newsweek 62:85 O 21 '63
People are still in mood to buy; report from Survey research center. il Bsns W p27-8 O 12 '63
Professional theatre at Ann Arbor. L. Cook. il Theatre Arts 47:29-31 Ag '63

Graduate school of business administration

Why new businesses succeed. Nations Bsns 52:56+ Ap '64

Mental health research institute

Worm learns. J. Bird. il Sat Eve Post 237:66-7 Mr 28 '64

MICHIKO, crown princess of Japan
Happiness is not a princess. K. Beech. por McCalls 91:104-5+ Mr '64

MICHLIN, Aleksei
Resourceful Russians; Queen Elisabeth violin competition. il por Time 81:65 Je 7 '63

MICHOACÁN, Mexico
Shopping in Mexico's Michoacán. il Sunset 133:47-8+ N '64

MICHURINISM. See Genetics

MICROBIOLOGICAL conferences. See Biological conferences

MICROBIOLOGY
Applied microbiology in developing countries; report on symposium, May 1964. M. Alexander. Science 145:613-14 Ag 7 '64
Freezing and viability of tetrahymena pyriformis in dimethylsulfoxide. S. W. Hwang and others. bibliog il Science 144:64-5 Ap 3 '64
History of microbiology; report. R. N. Doetsch. Science 146:956 N 13 '64

MICROBIOLOGY, Soil. See Soil microbiology

MICROCIRCUITS. See Electronic circuits

MICROELECTRONICS. See Miniature electronic equipment

MICROFILMS
Getting more out of the files; microfilm retrieval systems. il Bsns W p96-8 Je 22 '63
Microfilm defects discussed at National archives meeting; with National bureau of standards and the Eastman-Kodak company. Library J 88:3043 S 1 '63
See also
Libraries—Microfilm collections
Municipal records on microfilm
National microfilm association

MICROMETEOROLOGY
Formula aids agriculture. Sci N L 84:165 S 14 '63
Micrometeorology. G. Sutton. il Sci Am 211:62-70+ bibliog(p 142) O '64

MICRO midget automobiles. See Karts (midget cars)

MICRO midget racing. See Karting

MICROMINIATURIZATION. See Miniature electronic equipment

MICRONESIA
See also
Trust Territory of the Pacific Islands

History

Micronesia. R. S. Hopkins. bibliog il Focus 13:1-6 Je '63

MICRONESIANS
America's neglected colonial paradise; with editorial comment. D. Oberdorfer. il Sat Eve Post 237:24-34, 76 F 29 '64; Same abr. without editorial comment. Read Digest 84:232-4+ Je '64

MICROORGANISMS
Biochemistry and soil science. A. D. McLaren. bibliog il Science 141:1141-7 S 20 '63
Biosynthesis of unsaturated fatty acids in microorganisms. J. Erwin and K. Bloch. bibliog il Science 143:1006-12 Mr 6 '64
Most abundant living creature found in soil; Q-form. Sci N L 86:103 Ag 15 '64
Standard sampler for assay of airborne microorganisms; letter. P. S. Brachman and others. Science 144:1295 Je 12 '64
See also
Neurospora
Soil microbiology
Staphylococci
Viruses

Culture mediums

System for studying microbial morphogenesis; rapid formation of microcysts in myxococcus xanthus. M. Dworkin and S. M. Gibson. bibliog il Science 146:243-4 O 9 '64
Tuberculin reactivity of a carbohydrate component of unheated BCG culture filtrate. H. Baer and S. D. Chaparas. bibliog Science 146:245-7 O 9 '64

MICROORGANISMS, Pathogenic
Cleaner tools for the dentist; dental equipment blamed for cross-contamination. il Bsns W p80-2 O 5 '63
Doctor Koch and the boiled potato. il Todays Health 41:77 D '63
Mycoplasma pneumoniae; proposed nomenclature for atypical pneumonia organism (Eaton agent) R. M. Chanock and others. bibliog Science 140:662 My 10 '63

MICROPALEONTOLOGY
Biological remnants in a Precambrian sediment; White Pine Mine, Mich. W. G. Meinschein and others. bibliog Science 145:262-3 Jl 17 '64
Clues to life's origin; discovery of biological chemicals in Precambrian shale at White Pine Mine, Mich. A. Ewing. Sci N L 86:67 Ag 1 '64
Fossil microorganisms: possible presence in precambrian shield of western Australia. C. G. A. Marshall and others. bibliog il Science 144:290-2 Ap 17 '64
Hydrocarbons of biological origin from a one-billion-year-old sediment; White Pine Mine, Mich. G. Eglinton and others. bibliog Science 145:263-4 Jl 17 '64

MICROPHONES
Build the shotgun sound snooper; tubular microphone. J. R. Hollinger and J. E. Mulligan. il Pop Electr 20:51-4+ Je '64
How to choose the right mike. L. A. Harlow. il Pop Sci 182:152-4 F '63
Microphone sensitivity rating; with nomogram. R. C. Ramsey. il Electr World 71:31+ My '64
Microphone volume control. A. Trauffer. il Electr World 69:72 Ap '63
Microphones. il Pop Electr 21:46-8+ Ag '64
Microphones for communications; two-way radio, CB and amateur applications. R. L. Conhaim. il Electr World 71:51-4 Ap '64
Microphones make the difference. I. B. Berger. il Hi Fi 14:47-50 Ag '64
Recording musical instruments. G. W. Cushman. il Pop Phot 52:40+ Ap '63
Sound advice; little mike. R. N. Angus. Mod Phot 27:34+ My '63
Sound with your pictures. G. W. Cushman. il Pop Phot 52:22+ My '63
Tele-mike for telephoto shooting. K. Poli. il Pop Phot 55:73+ O '64

MICROPHONES in criminal investigation, espionage, etc. See Electronics in criminal investigation, espionage, etc.

MICROPHOTOGRAPHY
Micro-Bible. il Time 83:94 My 1 '64
Miniature library for saving space in space; use of photochromics by astronauts. Sci N L 86:56 Jl 25 '64
Sporangium discharge in pilobolus: a photographic study. R. M. Page. bibliog il Science 146:925-7 N 13 '64

MICRORADIOGRAPHY. See Radiography

MICROSCOPE and microscopy
Cell culture perfusion chamber: adaptation for microscopy of clonal growth. J. J. Freed. bibliog il Science 140:1334-5 Je 21 '63
Dutch genius of the lens; Antoni van Leeuwenhoek. il Todays Health 42:63 Ja '64
Nature and the microscope (cont) J. D. Corrington. il Natur Hist 72:61-4 Mr; 61-4 My; 64-8 N '63; 73:58-62 Mr; 65-70 O '64
Rugged new low-cost microscopes. il Pop Sci 183:137 N '63
Spectroscopic ultramicroanalysis with a laser. R. C. Rosan and others. il Science 142:236-7 O 11 '63

MICROSCOPE and microscopy—*Continued*
Stereo microscope. C. Metcalf. il Pop Mech 121:151 F '64
See also
Bausch and Lomb, incorporated
Electron microscope and microscopy
Metallography
Photomicrography
MICROSCOPIC slides
Nature and the microscope; preparing your own blood slides. J. D. Corrington. il Natur Hist 73:65-70 O '64
MICROSPORUM nanum. See Fungi, Pathogenic
MICROSURGERY
Ruby laser as a microsurgical instrument. N. M. Saks and C. A. Roth. bibliog il Science 141:46-7 Jl 5 '63
MICROTUBULES. See Plant cells and tissues
MICROVIBRATIONS. See Shivering
MICROVISION. See Radio in aviation
MICROWAVE amplification by stimulated emission of radiation. See Masers
MICROWAVE meteorology. See Radio meteorology
MICROWAVE ovens. See Electronic ovens
MICROWAVE radio communications. See Radio communication, Short wave
MICROWAVES
Millimeter systems seek a program; extension of microwave technology. Miss & Roc 15:38+ S 7 '64
New look in microwaves. L. G. Sands. il Electr World 72:60-2 Ag '64
See also
Masers
MICROZOOPLANKTON. See Plankton
MIDAS (satellite) See Artificial satellites—Military applications
MID-CONTINENT area power planners
MAPPing a newpower network; nation's biggest power pool. il Bsns W p30 Ag 31 '63
Striking up a power partnership; U.S. and Canada. il Bsns W p 134+ F 15 '64
MIDDLE age
Art of not being thirty-seven. J. B. Cumming, jr. Esquire 60:95+ N '63
Child from thirty to forty. S. Blum. il Esquire 60:95-7 Ag '63
Help forgotten people of middle age. Sci N L 84:50 Jl 27 '63
Living in tune with time. M. Brown. Sat Eve Post 236:26-7 Mr 30 '63
Middle age motherhood for me! E. Morris. Read Digest 82:193-4 Mr '63
MIDDLE aged workers. See Age and employment
MIDDLE ages
See also
Crusades

History

Bibliography

Articles and other books received; comp. by B. J. Holm. See issues of American historical review
MIDDLE ATLANTIC states. See Atlantic states
MIDDLE classes
Keeping the poor in their place. A. Walinsky. New Repub 151:15-18 Jl 4 '64; Reply. R. Theobald. 151:36 Ag 8 '64
Negro's middle-class dream. C. E. Lincoln. il N Y Times Mag p35+ O 25 '64
MIDDLE EAST
American policy in the Near East; address, January 20, 1964. U. A. Johnson. Dept State Bul 50:208-11 F 10 '64
See also
Americans in the Middle East
Arab states
Banks and banking—Middle East
Kurds
Petroleum—Middle East
Petroleum industry and trade—Middle East

Antiquities

Shards of history. il Time 82:50-60 D 13 '63

Bibliography

Children's books about the Middle East. A. A. Meyer. il Horn Bk 40:308-12 Je '64

Defenses

Never-ended war of the Middle East. C. Sterling. il Reporter 29:24-8+ Jl 18 '63

Description and travel

Crusader road to Jerusalem. F. Shor. il Nat Geog Mag 124:797-837 D '63

Foreign relations

Middle East misconceptions. C. Leiden. il Nat R 16:67-9 Ja 28 '64

History

Britain's moment in the Middle East. by E. Monroe. Review
New Repub 150:19-20 F 1 '64. R. H. Nolte

Bibliography

Articles and other books received; Near East. comp. by S. Glazer. See issues of American historical review

Maps

Holy Land today. il Nat Geog Mag 124:856-7. sup(folded map) D '63
Map of the Middle East (cont) Sr Schol 83:30 O 4 '63; 85:34 O 7 '64

Nationalism

Near Eastern nationalism yesterday and today. A. Hourani. For Affairs 42:123-36 O '63

Politics

Arab union: can it work? New Repub 148: 9-10 My 4 '63
Arab unity. Commonweal 77:655 Mr 22 '63
Arabs and the world: Nasser's Arab Nationalist policy. by C. D. Cremeans. Review
Sat R 46:18 Je 1 '63. W. H. Stringer
At cross-purposes in the sands of Yemen. D. Holden. il Reporter 28:37+ F 14 '63
Atlantic report. Atlan 215:6+ Ja '65
Camel driver. il Time 81:22-6 Mr 29 '63
Cold war among the Arabs. New Repub 149:7 Ag 17 '63
Countries in search of a character. E. Lengyel. Sat R 47:54 My 9 '64
Coupmaker of Baghdad; Abdel Salam Aref. il Newsweek 62:62 D 2 '63
Euphoria on the Nile. il Time 83:23 Ja 24 '64
Facts about Nasser's new empire. il U S News 54:8 Ap 22 '63
Focus on the Middle East. Sr Schol 83:42 O 4 '63
Hussein at bay. New Repub 148:9-10 My 11 '63
Middle East misconceptions. C. Leiden. il Nat R 16:67-9 Ja 28 '64
Middle East; oil strengthens general prospects. il Nations Bsns 51:85-6 F '63
Mideast struggle over Yemen. il N Y Times Mag p24-5 S 22 '63
Moderation in Cairo; Arab leaders conference. il Newsweek 63:35 Ja 27 '64
Nasser: on the march again? il Newsweek 61: 40 Mr 18 '63
Nasserism stirs up the Middle East; photographs. N Y Times Mag p 10-11 My 19 '63
Nasser's dream; Arab union. Newsweek 61: 49 Mr 25 '63
Nasser's way. Commonweal 78:181 My 10 '63
Never-ended war of the Middle East. C. Sterling. il Reporter 29:24-8+ Jl 18 '63
Once again Nasser's dream of empire. il U S News 54:74-5 Mr 18 '63
199th time. il Newsweek 62:46-7 S 2 '63
Onto the bandwagon; Nasser and Arab unity. Time 81:37 Ap 5 '63
Positive negativism; Turkey, Iran, and Pakistan form Regional cooperation for development. il Newsweek 64:34-5 Ag 3 '64
So near, yet so far. il Time 81:27 Mr 22 '63
Spreading infection. il Time 81:38-9 Mr 15 '63
Syria coup move toward Arab unity? il Sr Schol 82:21 Mr 27 '63
Three stars; goal of Arab unity. il Newsweek 61:48 Ap 22 '63
Transition in the Middle East. E. Monroe. New Repub 150:21+ My 30 '64
Union now; Egypt, Syria and Iraq federation. il Time 81:39 Ap 19 '63
Who's wooing who? il Time 81:26+ Mr 1 '63
Will Nasser's dream come true? il Newsweek 61:46-9 My 20 '63
See also
Arab states—Politics

Religious institutions and affairs

See also
Catholic Near East welfare association
MIDDLE EAST youth conference. See Youth conferences
MIDDLE EASTERN studies. See Area studies
MIDDLE FORK RIVER. See Salmon River
MIDDLE WEST
Clues to the midwestern mind. M. Kniskern. il N Y Times Mag p33+ S 15 '63
See also
Architecture—Middle western states
Colleges and universities—Middle western states
Geology—Middle western states
Great Lakes
Great Plains
Mississippi Valley

MIDDLE WEST—*Continued*

Climate

Man, whatta winter! R. D. Wennblom and G. W. Wormley. Farm J 87:44 Mr '63

Description and travel

Ozark frontier trail. C. Olten. il Travel 122: 31-4 S '64
Three-week honeymoon. J. Hamilton. il Look 28:74-9 My 5 '64

Economic conditions

What's happening to the Middle West? with interview with R. C. Turner. il U S News 55:55-61 O 14 '63
Why the Midwest is lagging, and what can be done about it; excerpts from address, June 22, 1964. C. Kimball. U S News 57:80-2 Ag 10 '64

Politics

In U.S. heartland: how candidates shape up. il U S News 57:43-6 S 28 '64
Political notes from the prairies. J. Burnham. Nat R 16:278-9 Ap 7 '64; Discussion. 16:373 My 5 '64

MIDDLEBURG, Va.
Rampart of pedigree. H. Horn. il Sports Illus 18:62-70 F 11 '63

MIDDLEBURY college, Middlebury, Vt.
Drinking in German dreaming in French. D. Boroff. il Mlle 56:130-1+ F '63

MIDDLEHURST, Barbara M.
Lunar eruption in 1783? Sky & Tel 28:83-4 Ag '64

MIDDLEMEN. See Marketing

MIDDLETON, Thomas, and Rowley, William
Changeling. Criticism
Nation 199:389-90 N 23 '64
New Repub 151:25-6+ N 21 '64
New Yorker 40:99 N 7 '64
Newsweek 64:92 N 9 '64
Sat R 47:35 N 21 '64
Time 84:52 N 6 '64

MIDDLETOWN, Conn.

Education

Wesleyan tutorials. D. Morgan. il Sat R 46:68-9 Je 15 '63

MIDDLETOWN, Ohio
Customers select method of payment. R. Chesney. Am City 79:22 N '64
Extra duties. C. Dennin and W. F. Cottrell. il Am City 78:95 S '63
Foot patrolmen radio equipped. C. W. Thompson. il Am Cty 78:89 Mr '63
No more storm-water worries. C. W. Thompson. il Am City 78:93-4 Ag '63
Tote barrels. W. F. Cottrell and K. E. Young. il Am City 78:117-18 My '63

MIDGES
Fine art of midging. W. Davis. il Outdoor Life 132:54-6 Jl '63

MIDGES, Artificial. See Fishing lures, flies, etc.

MIDGET auto racing. See Automobile racing; Karting

MIDGET automobiles. See Karts (midget cars)

MIDGET buses. See Station wagons

MIDGET ocean racing club
Knockdown! rough experience in an MORC. K. Klokke. il Yachting 117:73+ Ja '65
Toughest babies afloat; tiny sailboats. A. Fontaine. Sports Illus 18:41 Ja 28 '63

MIDGETS. See Dwarfs

MIDGLEY, A. R. jr, and others
Morphogenesis of syncytiotrophoblast in vivo: an autoradiographic demonstration. bibliog Science 141:349-50 Jl 26 '63

MIDLAND, Pa.
Good lighting spells progress. R. E. Steebner. il Am City 79:82-3 Jl '64

MIDNEY, Boris
At Red square, no cool sounds allowed; excerpts from interview, ed. by R. Hemming and G. Nikolaieff. por Sr Schol 85:23 D 2 '64

MIDNIGHT sun. See Sun

MIDNIGHT suppers. See Suppers

MIDNIGHT turning gray; story. See Matthiessen, P.

MIDNIGHT voice; story. See Jacobs, H.

MIDSUMMER night's dream; opera. See Britten, B.

MIDWAY (islands)
Albatrosses of Midway. C. W. Buchheister. il Audubon Mag 66:84-5 Mr '64
Midway islands; man and birds in conflict. O. S. Pettingill, jr. il Audubon Mag 66:154-9 My '64

MIDWAY, Battle of, 1942
Six minutes that changed the world; with editorial comment. S. E. Morison. il Am Heritage 14:50-5+ F '63

MIDWAY; story. See Newman, D.

MIDWEST. See Middle West

MIDWEST program on airborne television instruction. See Television in education

MIDWEST research institute
Why the Midwest is lagging, and what can be done about it; excerpts from address, June 22, 1964. C. Kimball. U S News 57:80-3 Ag 10 '64

MIDWESTERN Baptist theological seminary, Kansas City, Mo.
Seminary loses another teacher; no academic freedom. Christian Cent 80:326 Mr 13 '63

MIDWESTERN universities research association
High-energy physics: major fight brewing as midwestern legislators take stand on MURA accelerator. D. S. Greenberg. Science 142: 208-10 O 11 '63
MURA accelerator: compromise for the Mid-West. D. S. Greenberg. bibliog Science 143: 450-2 Ja 31 '64; Reply. D. W. Kerst. 143: 1274 Mr 20 '64
Smashing war. Newsweek 63:41 Ja 13 '64
When pure science meets pure politics. D. S. Greenberg. il Reporter 30:39-41 Mr 12 '64

MIDWINTER snipe regatta, Florida. See Regattas

MIDWIVES
Speaking out; let's use midwives; to save babies. L. Hellman. Sat Eve Post 237:8+ N 21 '64
When a midwife delivers the baby. il Good H 158:162 My '64

MIELENZ, K. D. and others
Accurate length measurement of meter bar with helium-neon laser. bibliog Science 146: 1672-3 D 25 '64

MIES VAN DER ROHE, Ludwig
Mies Van Der Rohe: modern classicist; interview, ed. by K. Kuh. por Sat R 48:22-3+ Ja 23 '65

about

Architectural details. il Arch Rec 134:150-64 O '63
Master builder. por Newsweek 62:101 N 18 '63
New work of Mies van der Rohe. il por Arch Forum 119:80-91 S '63

MIFSUD, Anthony
Orchids. Horticulture 42:34-5 Jl '64

MIGA, George P.
In the twister's path. Flying 74:44+ Ja '64

MIGDOLL, Herbert
Color blur how far should you go? J. Morris. il U S Camera 27:68-9 Ap '64

MIGHTY Matterhorn; story. See Eisenberg, L.

MIGMATITE. See Gneiss

MIGRAINE. See Headache

MIGRANT labor
Another extension; importation of Mexican workers. Commonweal 79:213 N 15 '63
As the braceros leave. M. E. Leary. il Reporter 32:43-5 Ja 28 '65
Battle over the braceros; in California. Bsns W p24 Ja 9 '65
Faces from the past; Okies, victims of the Dust Bowl. R. M. Ketchum. il Am Heritage 14:32-3 Ag '63
Farm workers on the fringe. W. C. Hartmire, jr. Christian Cent 81:959-62 Jl 29 '64
House rejects bracero program. Christian Cent 80:766 Je 12 '63
Jalopy nomads. B. Carter. Reporter 30:31-3 My 7 '64
Job problem for two countries: U.S. and Mexico. U S News 58:74 Ja 18 '65
Latter-day serfs. Commonweal 77:504 F 8 '63
Miserable migrants. America 108:386 Mr 23 '63
Roots for the rootless. Christian Cent 80: 635-6 My 15 '63; Discussion. 80:887 Jl 10 '63
Still the harvest of shame. F. Bennett. Commonweal 80:83-6 Ap 10 '64
Storm over braceros. Sr Schol 85:20 Ja 21 '65
Task for a Peace corps. C. Karraker. Christian Cent 80:237-8 F 20 '63
Vagabond kings. Reporter 28:12-14 My 9 '63
Where braceros once worked: California vegetable fields. il Bsns W p32-3 Ja 16 '65
See also
Church work with migrants

MIGRANT laborers, Children of. See Children of migrant laborers

MIGRATION, Internal
Dime was our passport. H. Golden. il Travel 122:50-2 S '64
Nation that moved West. il Sr Schol 82: 6-9+ My 8 '63

MIGRATION, Internal—*Continued*
Restless temper. G. W. Pierson. bibliog f Am Hist R 69:969-89 Jl '64
Wanna go home; hillbilly migration. il Newsweek 62:30 Ag 5 '63
When whites migrate from the South; hillbillies in Chicago. il U S News 55:70-3 O 14 '63
See also
Cities and towns—Growth
MIGRATION of birds; of fishes; etc. See Birds—Migration; Fishes—Migration; etc
MIGRATION of man. See Man—Migrations
MIGRATION of Negroes. See Negroes in the United States—Migration
MIGRATORY workers. See Migrant labor
MIHURSKY, Joseph A. See Herman, S. S. jt. auth.
MIKHAILSKI, Sigmund
Sin along with Sig. Time 81:31-2 My 3 '63
MIKITA, Stan
Hotheaded Hawk. por Newsweek 61:55 F 4 '63
MIKKELSEN, Robert S.
Boil! por Outdoor Life 134:46-7+ Jl '64
MIKOIAN, Anastas Ivanovich
About face. por Newsweek 63:30 Je 1 '64
How to survive in the Kremlin. H. Tanner. il pors N Y Times Mag p26+ N 15 '64
Khrushchev's heirs: a look at the line-up. F. B. Stevens. U S News 54:44 My 6 '63
Two old hands at surviving purges. por U S News 57:14 N 2 '64
MIKSCH, W. F.
Culinary end. Atlan 213:103-4 Ja '64
Read now, pay later. Atlan 212:118-20 Jl '63
Self-made nitwit. Atlan 214:107-8 Ag '64
What stage fright? Atlan 213:126 Je '64
MILAM, Carl Hastings
Carl Hastings Milam, 1884-1963. K. Brown. por Library J 88:3586 O 1 '63
Carl Hastings Milam, 1884-1963; with excerpts from messages. D. H. Clift. por(cover) ALA Bul 57:805, 812 O '63
Obituary
Pub W 184:47 S 9 '63
MILAN, Ill.
New booster system saves 50 per cent. W. J. Reese. il Am City 79:92-3 Jl '64
MILAN, Italy
Description
Milan: a capital in search of a country. F. Du Plessix. il Vogue 142:152-5+ N 15 '63
Opera-lover's guide to Milan. M. J. Matz. il Opera N 29:28-32 Ja 16 '65
Step by step through Milan. R. Deardorff. il Travel 119:59-61 Ap '63
Housing
Angularity in Milan. il Arch Forum 118:94 Ap '63
Music
First nights in Italy. F. Soprano. il Opera N 28:32-3 F 15 '64
Notes from abroad. W. Weaver. Hi Fi 13: 28+ F; 34 Mr '63
Opera-lover's guide to Milan. M. J. Matz. il Opera N 29:28-32 Ja 16 '65
MILAN, Ohio, historical museum
Milan, Ohio, historical museum. il Hobbies 68:51 Mr '63
MILAN triennale. See Design, Industrial—Exhibitions
MILDENBERGER, Kenneth W.
Federal government and the universities. Ann Am Acad 356:23-9 N '64
MIL-E-CON. See Military electronics conference
MILES, Bebe
Early bird bulbs. Flower Grower 50:26-7+ S '63
Put a bench in your garden. Flower Grower 51:36-7+ My '64
What to do if your daffodils no longer bloom. Flower Grower 51:25-6 My '64
MILES, Betty
How to survive a family trip. Parents Mag 38:42-3 Ag '63
MILES, Charles
Indian relics. See issues of Hobbies
MILES, Eddie
Miles of talent. H. L. Masin. il pors Sr Schol 82:46 F 20 '63
MILES, Emily Winthrop
Gift of a foresighted woman. C. W. Buchheister. Audubon Mag 65:144 My '63
MILES, H. Todd, and others
Tautomerism and protonation of guanosine. bibliog Science 142:1458+ D 13 '63
Tautomerism and site of protonation of 1-methylcytosine: proof by nuclear magnetic resonance spin-spin coupling. bibliog Science 142:1569-71 D 20 '63
MILES, Josephine
Autonomy; poem. Nation 196:314 Ap 13 '63
Investiture; poem. Nation 197:146 S 14 '63
Saving the bay; poem. Atlan 215:76-8 Ja '65
about
Leaf by leaf. M. Van Duyn. Poetry 102:260-2 Jl '63
MILES, Lizzie
Death of Lizzie Miles ends great era of blues shouters. J. B. Bush. Negro Hist Bul 27:69 D '63
MILES, Nelson A.
Captor of Crazy Horse. D. M. Potter. Sat R 46:38 F 9 '63
MILES, Paul
UCLA in three stages. Library J 89:4746-9 D 1 '64
MILES, R. J.
How to place a mile-long intake. Am City 79:90-1 Ja '64
MILES, Vernal, and Holmberg, G. V.
New look at Penn's woods. Am For 70:38-40 S '64
MILES college, Birmingham, Ala.
Miles's mileage. il Time 82:81 N 8 '63
MILES laboratories, incorporated
Two challenges of Miles laboratories. T. O'Hanlon. il Duns R 84:44-6+ N '64
MILESTON, Miss.
Dream in a bean field; community center for Mileston, Miss. A. Osheroff and J. Boebel. Nation 199:514 D 28 '64
MILFORD, Wogan Philipps, 2d baron
Communist peer. por Newsweek 61:36-7 Je 3 '63
MILGRAM, Alexandra. See Milgram, S. jt. auth.
MILGRAM, Stanley, and Hollander, Paul
Murder they heard. Nation 198:602-4 Je 15 '64
—and Milgram, Alexandra
Facts of life. Nation 199:412+ N 30 '64
MILHAUD, Darius
Ecumenical symphony; Choral symphony, based on the late Pope John's encyclical Peace on earth. il Newsweek 63:93 Je 15 '64
Fugue to fungo. por Newsweek 62:50 Jl 8 '63
Let it sing! il por Time 81:65 Je 7 '63
Milhaud's view of Sophocles; and Bernstein's view of Milhaud; Les Choéphores. J. Diether. il Am Rec G 30:232-4 N '63
More interested in new than in old. J. Anderson. il pors Dance Mag 37:44-7 Je '63
On records; Les Choéphores. Opera N 28:36 Ja 4 '64
MILI, Gjon
Greece; photographs (cont) Life 54:60-1+ F 8 '63
Tea and memories and songs at a last fond visit. Life 57:92-3 O 9 '64
MILITARISM
Argentina: a fragmented society. A. P. Whitaker. Cur Hist 46:15-18+ Ja '64
Case not proved. il Newsweek 63:86-7 Ja 20 '64
Cold war; address, April 5, 1964. J. W. Fulbright bibliog f Vital Speeches 30:422-7 My 1 '64
From democracy to dictatorship in Burma. J. Silverstein. bibliog f Cur Hist 46:83-8+ F '64
No short cut to progress. A. Etzioni. Sat R 47:18-19 Jl 18 '64
Secretary Rusk's news conference of November 8, 1963. D. Rusk. Dept State Bul 49: 810-17 N 25 '63
Speaking out; why do they slander our military men? S. L. A. Marshall. Sat Eve Post 237:6+ S 5 '64
Strangelove? Seven days? not likely: U.S. military might vs constitutional government. R. L. Gilpatric. il N Y Times Mag p 15+ My 17 '64
Then one day in Saigon. W. V. Kennedy. America 109:760 D 14 '63
U.S. policy regarding military governments in Latin America; statement, October 6, 1963. E. M. Martin. Dept State Bul 49:698-700 N 4 '63
Warfare state. F. J. Cook. bibliog f Ann Am Acad 351:102-9 Ja '64
See also
United States—Armed forces—Political activities
War
MILITARY air traffic control. See Air traffic control, Military
MILITARY air transport service. See United States—Military air transport service
MILITARY airplanes. See Airplanes, Military

MILITARY art and science
DOD weighs new war concept; non-destructive warfare. J. Trainor. Miss & Roc 15: 14 O 5 '64
Dilemma of the military. R. D. Senter. il Bul Atomic Sci 19:24-7 D '63
Heusinger of the Fourth Reich, by C. R. Allen, jr. Review
Nation 198:124-6 F 3 '64. H. Pol
Military problems in cold regions. C. R. Kolb. Science 147:71-3 Ja 1 '65
Way out of Vietnam; counter-insurgency warfare. J. Kraft. Harper 229:33-4+ D '64
See also
Guerrilla warfare
Strategy

History

Siege warfare in Pharaonic Egypt. A. R. Schulman. il Natur Hist 73:12-21 Mr '64

MILITARY assistance, American
Administration urges Congress to support $4.1 billion aid bill: statement, August 20, 1963. J. F. Kennedy. Dept State Bul 49:399 S 9 '63
Air cover: what President Kennedy says; excerpt from news conference. J. F. Kennedy. U S News 54:31 F 4 '63
Air will be ours; Cuban fighters tell why they expected air cover; with excerpts from radio messages. M. A. de Varona; G. Herrera. il U S News 54:33-6 F 4 '63
Allied aid to Cuba: growing U.S. problem. il U S News 56:4 Mr 2 '64
Arming against terror; military aid to Latin America. il Bsns W p68+ Ap 27 '63
Cover story; Bay of Pigs disaster. Reporter 28:16+ F 24 '63
Defense of the free world; address, May 21, 1964. R. S. McNamara. Dept State Bul 50: 893-9 Je 8 '64
Foreign aid; message to Congress, March 19, 1964. L. B. Johnson. Dept State Bul 50:518-22 Ap 6 '64
Foreign aid program; statement, April 5, 1963; with annex, fiscal year 1964 foreign assistance program. D. Rusk. Dept State Bul 48:664-72 Ap 29 '63
Foreign aid today; address, May 1, 1964. D. E. Bell. Dept State Bul 50:831-5 My 25 '64
Foreign assistance program; statement, March 23, 1964. D. Rusk. bibliog f Dept State Bul 50:595-601 Ap 13 '64
Free-world defense and assistance programs; message to Congress, April 2, 1963. J. F. Kennedy. Dept State Bul 48:591-9 Ap 22 '63
Grand alliance: United States and Spain. Nation 199:317-18 N 9 '64
Handwriting on the wall. Nation 197:250 O 26 '63
House approves military aid funds; Vietnam policy criticized. Aviation W 80:29 Je 15 '64
India now: if there's a new attack by Chinese reds. S. W. Sanders. il U S News 54:88-90 Ap 8 '63
Indians to receive military aid from U.S, British, Soviet Union. L. L. Doty. Aviation W 81:20 S 28 '64
Japan early warning competition. Aviation W 78:31 Ap 15 '63
Last best hope? American training of the military in Latin America. New Repub 149:4 O 19 '63
Latin America and military aid. E. Lieuwen. Sat R 46:16-17 My 4 '63
Military assistance program for 1965; statement, March 25, 1964. R. S. McNamara. il Dept State Bul 50:705-15 My 4 '64
More guns; long-range military aid. New Repub 148:8 Je 8 '63
On military aid; arming the Latin Americans. A. Naish. New Repub 148:12-13 My 11 '63; Reply. P. de Mesones. 148:30-1 Je 22 '63
OAU commission on Congo talks with department officers; Department statement, with joint press communique, September 23 and September 30, 1964. Dept State Bul 51: 553-4 O 19 '64
President Johnson urges Congress to increase U.S. aid to Viet-Nam; message to Congress, May 18, 1964. L. B. Johnson. Dept State Bul 50:891-3 Je 8 '64
President Kennedy and General Clay urge restoration of aid funds; interview, August 30, 1963. J. F. Kennedy; L. D. Clay. Dept State Bul 49:476-8 S 23 '63
Setting the record straight: what U.S. news & World report said about air support at the Bay of Pigs; excerpt from interview. R. Kennedy. U S News 54:31 F 4 '63
Soviet charge on introduction of aircraft into Laos rejected; Department statement, September 6, 1963. Dept State Bul 49:500 S 30 '63
State of the North Atlantic alliance; address, July 12, 1963. D. Rusk. Dept State Bul 49:190-8 Ag 5 '63
Success of foreign aid; it must continue; address, March 3, 1964. C. Raupe. Vital Speeches 30:406-9 Ap 15 '64
Summary of U.S. recommendations for program of aid to the Congo. Dept State Bul 48:481-4 Ap 1 '63
Unfinished business; address, September 10, 1963. D. Rusk. Dept State Bul 49:490-6 S 30 '63
USAF, army fight Caribbean Communists. L. Booda. Aviation W 78:33 My 13 '63
U.S. and India sign agreement to strengthen India's air defense. Dept State Bul 49:245-6 Ag 12 '63
United States and southeast Asia; address, April 8, 1963. U. A. Johnson. Dept State Bul 48:635-41 Ap 29 '63
U.S. calls claims of Portuguese arms diversion unfounded; statement, November 29, 1962. J. B. Bingham. Dept State Bul 48: 104-5 Ja 21 '63
U.S. to increase economic and military aid to Viet-Nam; White House statement, March 17, 1964. Dept State Bul 50:522-3 Ap 6 '64
Vinson backs DOD in aircraft probe. Aviation W 80:25 My 25 '64
See also
United States—Armed forces—Forces in Viet Nam (Republic)

MILITARY assistance, British
Indians to receive military aid from U.S, British, Soviet Union. L. L. Doty. Aviation W 81:20 S 28 '64

MILITARY assistance, German
War business; West German military aid to new nations. Newsweek 62:30 Jl 1 '63

MILITARY assistance, Russian
Artful dodging; Stennis subcommittee investigation of Cuban military buildup. Nat R 14:438 Je 4 '63
Building up again? Russia's military presence in Cuba. il Time 81:32 F 8 '63
Burr under the blanket; Shut up! Cuban situation. Nat R 14:145-6 F 26 '63
Cuba: how dangerous now; with excerpt from President Kennedy's news conference, February 7, 1963. il U S News 54:58-63 F 18 '63
Cuba under the lens: no missiles but... il Newsweek 61:19-22 F 18 '63
Extent of Cuban missile threat revealed; photo-intelligence briefing by Defense Secretary Robert S. McNamara and John Hughes. Aviation W 78:31 F 11 '63
Hardening Soviet base in Cuba. il Time 81: 23 F 15 '63
Indians to receive military aid from U.S, British, Soviet Union. L. L. Doty. Aviation W 81:20 S 28 '64
Latest facts on Russia's Cuban base; interview. K. B. Keating. il U S News 54: 43-5 F 11 '63
Loud but late; photo record of the Soviet military deployment in Cuba. R. Hotz. Aviation W 78:21 F 11 '63
Official report: the Russian arms in Cuba now. il U S News 54:8 Mr 18 '63
Oh, to punch Khrushchev; excerpts from interview. F. Castro. Time 81:19-20 Mr 29 '63
Shots & a shrimp boat; firing from Soviet-built MIGs out of Cuba. il Time 81:18 Mr 1 '63
Shots heard round the world; firing on shrimp boat, Ala. il Newsweek 61:17-18 Mr 4 '63
Sino-Soviet military relations. R. L. Garthoff. bibliog f Ann Am Acad 349:81-93 S '63
Soviet MIG's shipped to India. Sr Schol 82:17 Ja 30 '63
Soviet pullout and what stayed behind. il U S News 54:6 Mr 25 '63
Two prophets; question of missiles in Cuba. Reporter 28:18 Mr 14 '63; Discussion. 28:8 Ap 11 '63
Why Soviets are rushing a military build up in Cuba. U S News 54:42-3 F 11 '63
Will the Congo be another Vietnam? il U S News 57:34-5 D 21 '64

MILITARY aviators. See Air pilots

MILITARY bands. See Bands (music)

MILITARY bases
As U.S. bases are cut back; the meaning. il U S News 57:41 N 30 '64
Hurrah for McNamara's ax; closing or curtailing of ninety-five unneeded military installations here and abroad. Life 57:4 D 4 '64
Johnson as tactician. Nation 198:1 Ja 4 '64
Ninety-five bases to be closed. Sr Schol 85:20-1 D 2 '64
Okinawa: trigger in the Pacific. J. M. Diamond. Nation 198:547-8 Je 1 '64

MILITARY bases—*Continued*
Pentagon's big cutback of bases. il Newsweek 64:73-4 N 30 '64
Shadow world; merits of closing this or that base. W. V. Kennedy. America 110:225 F 15 '64
Spain: concealed handout. L. Fernsworth. Nation 198:138-40 F 10 '64
Why cutting the budget isn't easy. il Bsns W p32-3 N 28 '64
With courage & good sense; closing down of military installations. il Time 84:29-30 N 27 '64
See also
Air bases

MILITARY budget. See United States—Armed forces—Appropriations and expenditures

MILITARY chaplains. See Chaplains, Military

MILITARY-civilian relations. See United States—Armed forces—Relations with civilians

MILITARY communications. See Communications, Military

MILITARY contracts. See Contracts, Government

MILITARY costume. See Uniforms, Military

MILITARY decorations. See Decorations of honor

MILITARY education
You're in the classroom now. il Time 83:72 Ja 17 '64

MILITARY electronics conference
Congressional rein on R&D defended. C. D. LaFond. Miss & Roc 15:18 S 21 '64

MILITARY expenditures. See United States—Armed forces—Appropriations and expenditures

MILITARY history

Bibliography

Century's battlefields. F. C. Pogue. Sat R 46:25-7 Ap 6 '63

MILITARY insignia. See United States—Army—Insignia

MILITARY installations. See Military bases

MILITARY intelligence
Artful dodging; Stennis subcommittee investigation of Cuban military buildup. Nat R 14:438 Je 4 '62
New hardware programs should aid intelligence, reconnaissance functions. il Miss & Roc 14:87-8+ Mr 30 '64
See also
Spies

MILITARY inventions. See Inventions

MILITARY life. See Soldiers

MILITARY maneuvers
Big lift and the big letdown; second armored division flown to West Germany. il Newsweek 62:23-5 N 4 '63
Big lift; Second armored division transported to West Germany. il Time 82:28-9 N 1 '63
Big lift tests army, USAF flexibilities; with editorial comment. Aviation W 79:17, 26-7 O 28 '63
Cold siege on the tundra; Exercise polar siege. C. Mydans. il Life 56:21 F 28 '64
Desert strike. W. V. Kennedy. America 110:866 Je 27 '64
Exercise big lift: opening a 5,700-mile air bridge to Europe; with analysis by M. S. Johnson. M. L. Stone and T. J. O'Halloran. il U S News 55:36-9 N 4 '63
Games with nuclear trimmings; French army's annual fall war games. il Time 82:36 O 25 '63
Helicopter-rifleman partnership demonstrated in army exercise; Hawk star. G. C. Wilson. Aviation W 80:17-18 Je 29 '64
In the vaccination stage; SEATO maneuvers, Thailand. il Time 81:34 My 24 '63
Job of getting them there fast; Operation big lift. il Bsns W p 128-9 N 2 '63
Lesson for sunland; US forces in Iran for Exercise delawar. Time 83:39-40 Ap 17 '64
Marines study SATS development results from Steel pike. R. G. O'Lone. il Aviation W 81:88-90 N 9 '64
Non-war is hell; Exercise desert strike. il Time 83:24 Je 5 '64
Operation big lift; second armored division moved to West Germany. Sr Schol 83:5 N 8 '63
Peru: a scenario worthy of Zanuck; Operación Ayacucho, combined inter-American military exercise. R. M. Koster. New Repub 152:6-7 Ja 9 '65
Plot!! to overthrow America!!! Water moccasin fright. T. H. Kuchel. il N Y Times Mag p6+ Jl 21 '63
Steel Pike tests vertical assault, SATS; joint U.S.-Spanish amphibious operation. R. G. O'Lone. Aviation W 81:21 N 2 '64
Wings of madness; Water moccasin episode. H. Bowser. Sat R 47:26 O 24 '64
See also
Air maneuvers

MILITARY miniatures
Little war can be a lot of fun; famous battles as played by brothers B. and C. Sweet. R. Gehman. il Sports Illus 22:36-41 Ja 4 '65

MILITARY missions
Diplomats in uniform. New Repub 149:13-15 N 2 '63

MILITARY models. See Military miniatures

MILITARY morale. See United States—Army—Morale

MILITARY motor vehicles. See Motor vehicles, Military

MILITARY officers, Retired. See Retired military officers

MILITARY order of lady bugs. See Womens clubs and societies

MILITARY parades. See Parades

MILITARY pensions. See Pensions, Military

MILITARY photography. See Photography, Military

MILITARY post schools, American
American schools overseas. E. J. Meade, jr. il Sat R 46:44-5+ Ag 17 '63
Getting off the base. Time 81:77 Ap 19 '63
GI mess. Newsweek 61:88 F 18 '63
NEA cautions on service schools abroad. Sch & Soc 92:42 F 8 '64
Overseas teaching. Sr Schol 82:2T F 20 '63
Teaching in overseas schools. F. E. Stoffel. il NEA J 53:8-9 My '64

MILITARY preparedness. See Preparedness, Military

MILITARY prisons. See Prisons, Military

MILITARY purchasing. See United States—Armed forces—Procurement

MILITARY radio communication. See Radio communication, Military

MILITARY reconnaissance
New hardware programs should aid intelligence, reconnaissance functions. il Miss & Roc 14:87-8+ Mr 30 '64
See also
Aerial reconnaissance
Artificial satellites—Military applications
Photography, Military

MILITARY research
McNamara on research and development; excerpts from testimony before House armed services committee. R. S. NcNamara. Aviation W 78:21 F 4 '63
Research chiefs sophisticating their $1-billion-a-year business. Miss & Roc 14:105-6+ Mr 30 '64
See also
Hudson institute, incorporated
Ordnance research
Rand corporation

MILITARY schools
Cadet Lum, sir! Thomas Hong Lee Lum. J. Morschauser. il Look 27:123-6 My 21 '63
See also
Military education
United States military academy, West Point

MILITARY secrets. See Defense information, Classified

MILITARY service
See also
Conscientious objectors

MILITARY service, Compulsory
Volunteer army. New Repub 150:6 Ja 18 '64; Reply. J. den Boer. 150:30-1 F 22 '64

Deferments and exemptions

Draft rejectees: nipping trouble in the bud. D. P. Moynihan. Reporter 30:22-4 F 13 '64

United States

Abolish the draft? pro and con discussion. il Sr Schol 85:6-7 D 9 '64
Barry on the beam; case against the draft. Nation 199:130 S 21 '64
Can we do away with the draft? Bsns W p29 S 12 '64
Change in the draft? or is the end in sight? with interview with E. Ginsberg. il U S News 56:52-7 Ja 27 '64
Do we need the draft? J. Raymond. Look 27:17-20 Jl 30 '63; Same abr. Read Digest 84:119-20+ Mr '64
Do we need the draft? W. V. Kennedy. America 111:85-6+ Jl 25 '64
Draft becomes an issue. J. C. Esty, jr. Nation 198:109 F 3 '64
Draft change: what eighteen-year-olds face now. il U S News 56:42 Ja 20 '64
Draft: many threatened, few chosen. J. C. Esty, jr. il N Y Times Mag p 13+ O 20 '63

MILITARY service, Compulsory—United States —*Continued*
Draft marches into its 100th year: with pro and con discussion. il Sr Schol 82:12-15 Mr 6 '63
End the draft and pay the soldiers. il New Repub 151:4-5 Jl 11 '64
For bachelors only. Time 82:30-1 S 20 '63
Forgotten 30,000. New Repub 151:5 Ag 8 '64
How to get rid of the draft. Nation 197:269 N 2 '63
Military choices for June graduates. il U S News 54:72-3 My 27 '63
Should we end the draft? H. W. Baldwin. il N Y Times Mag p20-1+ S 27 '64
Up to the Senate. Nation 196:238-9 Mr 23 '63
We don't need it at all. Nation 197:190 O 5 '63
We don't need the draft. J. C. Esty, jr. Nation 196:151-4 F 23 '63
What every young man should know about the draft. Todays Health 41:58+ My '63
Who will be drafted now. il U S News 54:48 S 23 '63
Will a volunteer program replace the draft? il U S News 56:8 My 4 '64
Your son and selective service. J. Raymond. Parents Mag 38:80+ S '63
See also
Conscientious objectors
MILITARY strategy. See Strategy
MILITARY tanks. See Tanks, Military
MILITARY toys. See Toys
MILITARY training
Do we need the draft? J. Raymond. Look 27:17-20 Jl 30 '63; Same abr. Read Digest 84:119-20+ Mr '64
Memoirs of a six-months trainee. J. Berendt. il Esquire 61:62-5+ Je '64
New army; use of helicopters in ground war. il Newsweek 63:35-6 Ap 27 '64
Old soldier looks at the new army. R. G. Martin. il N Y Times Mag p26-7+ S 22 '63
Seals to the rescue. il N Y Times Mag p 127 Ap 7 '63
See also
United States—Reserve officers training corps
MILITARY training camps
Conservation and the Fort Ord complex. G. Schneider. il Am For 70:22-3+ Ag '64
Fort Hood: Sparta goes suburban. D. Boroff. il Harper 228:46-53 Ja '64
Old soldier looks at the new army. R. G. Martin. il N Y Times Mag p26-7+ S 22 '63
When gentlemen prepared for war; Plattsburg training camps. F. Russell. il Am Heritage 15:24-7+ Ap '64
MILITARY transport airplanes. See Airplanes, Military transport
MILITARY uniforms. See Uniforms, Military
MILJUS, Robert C. and Johnson, A. C.
Multi-employer pensions & labor mobility; excerpts from Labor mobility from the viewpoint of the older workers. bibliog f Harvard Bsns R 41:147-8+ S '63
MILK
Are we drinking to much milk? with opposing views. W. W. Sackett, jr. Sci Digest 53:19-25 Ap '63
Do you know all the advantages of home milk dispensers? il Bet Hom & Gard 42:84 F '64
Improve fat content of milk. Suc Farm 62:63 Mr '64
In these schools the popular drink is milk. J. Bickers. il Farm J 87:46 Jl '63
Research aims at special cow-produced milk. Sci N L 83:104 F 16 '63
See also
Buttermilk
Dairying
Analysis
Devices alter dairying: two new instruments replacing chemical laboratory analyses. Sci N L 85:229 Ap 11 '64
Contamination
See Milk contamination
Flavor and odor
This makes milk taste better. Farm J 88:50B S '64
Prices
Dairymen try for higher milk prices. Farm J 88:38 D '64
Production
Four good new ideas. il Farm J 87:34 Ag '63
How to beat the summer milk slump. J. W. Bailey. Suc Farm 62:63 Jl '64
Production helps win this show. il Farm J 87:42 S '63
Thirty-one cows over 18,000 pounds, here's how. E. Richardson. il Suc Farm 62:133 Mr '64
Solids-not-fat content
How Europe makes high-solids milk. D. Braun. Farm J 87:52G My '63
Testing
New test for DDT. Farm J 87:58B Ap '63
Which way for milk? Farm J 87:58C Ap '63
See also
Cows—Testing
MILK, Acidophilus
See also
Yogurt
MILK, Canned
Sterile milk wins new markets. B. Fowler and D. Seim. Farm J 87:55 F '63
MILK containers
Make your own fairyland; using milk cartons for gift wraps! il Seventeen 22:100-1+ D '63
MILK contamination
Congress considers pay for dumped milk. il Farm J 88:42 S '64
How to read milk radioactivity reports. Am City 78:154+ O '63
Iodine-131 thyroid dose from milk in Italy during the period September 1962 to February 1963. A. A. Cigna and F. G. Giorcelli. bibliog il Science 143:379-80 Ja 24 '64
Meteorological evaluation of the sources of iodine-131 in pasteurized milk. R. J. List and others. bibliog il Science 146:59-64 O 2 '64
Pacific A-tests blamed for hot iodine in milk. Sci N L 86:247 O 17 '64
Pay for dumped milk. Farm J 88:38 D '64
Quick method spots insecticides in milk. Sci N L 83:237 Ap 13 '63
Taking the threat out of milk; removing strontium-90 from milk. Bsns W p58 S 14 '63
They told us: dump your milk. D. Braun. il Farm J 88:24+ Jl '64
Three months' milk down the ditch! S. Churchill. Farm J 88:47 F '64
MILK cooling
Milk heats wash water. E. Welch. il Farm J 87:59 Mr '63
MILK delivery. See Milk industry and trade
MILK drinks. See Beverages
MILK industry and trade
End of road for Bessie; horse drawn wagons, Abbotts' dairies, Philadelphia. il Bsns W p28 Jl 27 '63
See also
American dairy association
MILK production. See Milk—Production
MILK RIVER
Reverse flushing keeps a river clean. il Am City 79:95-6 N '64
MILK shakes. See Beverages
MILK substitutes
Food, the good medicine. Sci N L 83:114 F 23 '63
MILK tanks
Are bulk tank gauges fair to dairymen? Farm J 87:58B Ap '63
MILK testing. See Milk—Testing
MILK thistles
White-veined milk-thistle. G. R. Robinson. il Flower Grower 58:59 Ag '63
MILK train doesn't stop here anymore; drama. See Williams, T.
MILK wagon drivers. See Milk industry and trade
MILKERS nodules. See Virus diseases
MILKING
New machine spots problem milkers; Milkograf. B. Hardy. il Farm J 88:61 F '64
What you don't know about milking cows. F. E. Breth. il Sci Digest 55:39-44 Ja '64
MILKING machine gage. See Gages
MILKING machines
Check your milking machine, it may be stealing profits. L. R. Fryman and J. L. Albright. il Suc Farm 62:94+ Mr '64
MILKING parlors
Curtain doors for milking parlor. B. Hardy. il Farm J 87:30 Je '63
Horrors, a parlor full of Adas! E. H. Logsdon. il Farm J 88:22-3 Ag '64
Skid-proof floors. J. L. Parker. Farm J 87:55 F '63
What you don't know about milking cows. F. E. Breth. il Sci Digest 55:39-44 Ja '64
What's this, a revolving parlor? G. Lorang il Farm J 88:50 My '64
Equipment
Stanchion milking with parlor comfort. B. Hardy. il Farm J 87:24+ Je '63

MILKMAN, Norman. See Schoenfeld, R. L. jt. auth.
MILKWEED
Calotropin, a cytotoxic principle isolated from asclepias curassavica L. bibliog il Science 146:1685-6 D 25 '64
MILKY way
Ancient stars discovered. A. Ewing. Sci N L 83:98 F 16 '63
Happy birthday. Newsweek 61:81 My 6 '63
International discussion of Milky way research; Mount Stromlo observatory. B. J. Bok. il Sky & Tel 26:4-7 Jl '63
Local system of stars. O. Struve. il Sky & Tel 25:78-81 F '63
Milky way galaxy age. Sci N L 87:38 Ja 16 '65
Our galaxy, the Milky way, is a flat, thin island of stars. T. D. Nicholson. il Natur Hist 74:34-6 F '65
Visual Milky way. J. Ashbrook. il Sky & Tel 26:204-6 O '63
When six million suns explode. B. Lovell. il N Y Times Mag p 16+ Ja 5 '64
MILL, John Stuart
He tried to bring France to England. W. Diebold, jr. Sat R 47:41-2+ Mr 7 '64
MILLA uniflora. See Spring star flowers
MILLAN, Peter
Super bright, super sharp, super color. P. Caulfield. il Mod Phot 27:64-7 Je '63
MILLAR, Oliver
Queen's pictures. Horizon 5:92-107 Jl '63
MILLAR, Ronald
Affair; dramatization of novel by C. P. Snow; text. Theatre Arts 47:25-56 Mr '63
MILLARD, William J.
Meterless VTVM. Pop Electr 19:45-8 N '63
MILLAY, Edna St Vincent
Exiled; poem. Motor B 111:19 Ap '63
MILLBRAE, Calif.
Report on rapport; how the PTA at Glen Oaks school cooperated. A. Daley. il NEA J 52:12-13 D '63
MILLEN, J. Eugene, and others
Circulatory adaptation to diving in the freshwater turtle. bibliog Science 145:591-3 Ag 7 '64
MILLER, Alden H. and others
Hope for the California condor; excerpts from report. Audubon Mag 67:38-41 Ja '65
MILLER, Arjay Ray
Arjay way; new Ford president. il por Newsweek 61:77-8+ Ap 22 '63
Ford shifts top men. Bsns W p36 Ap 13 '63
Friden with style. por Time 81:104+ Ap 19 '63
People of the week. por U S News 54:26 Ap 22 '63
MILLER, Arthur
After the fall; text. por Sat Eve Post 237: 32-7+ F 1 '64
Our guilt for the world's evil. N Y Times Mag p 10-11+ Ja 3 '65
With respect for her agony, but with love; concerning After the fall. Life 56:66 F 7 '64
about
After the fall. Criticism
America 110:322 Mr 7 '64
Commonweal 79:600-1 F 14 '64
Life por 56:64A F 7 '64
Nat R 16:289-90 Ap 7 '64
Nation 198:153-4 F 10 '64
New Repub 150:26-8+ F 8 '64
New Yorker 39:59 F 1 '64
Newsweek 63:49-52 F 3 '64
Reporter 30:46+ F 27 '64
Sat R 47:35 F 15 '64
Theatre Arts il por 48:12-16+ Ja '64
Time il por 83:54 Ja 31 '64
Vogue 143:66 Mr 15 '64
After the fall: Arthur Miller's return. il pors Newsweek 63:49-52 F 3 '64
Crucible. Criticism
Am Rec G il 29:508-9+ Mr '63
Death of a salesman. Criticism
Sat R 46:34 Ag 24 '63
Incident at Vichy. Criticism
America 112:147-9 Ja 23 '65
Life il 58:39-40+ Ja 22 '65
Nation 199:504 D 21 '64
New Repub 151:26-7 D 26 '64
N Y Times Mag p 10-11+ Ja 3 '65
New Yorker 40:152 D 12 '64
Newsweek il 64:86 D 14 '64
Sat R 47:24 D 19 '64
Time 84:73 D 11 '64
Vogue 145:27 Ja 15 '65
MILLER, Barry
Multi-mode helicopter radar developed. Aviation W 81:88-9+ O 26 '64
New IR space sensors add to reliability. Aviation W 81:68-71 Ag 31 '64
MILLER, Benjamin F. and Goode, Ruth
Sea within us; excerpts from Man and his body. Read Digest 82:192C-192D+ Mr '63
MILLER, Bertha E. (Mahony)
Chapters from Horn book history (cont) Horn Bk 39:327-30, 412-15 Je-Ag '63
MILLER, Bonnie Trompeter
Meet Bonnie, GH's beautiful cover-girl wife. il pors Good H 158:120-3 Je '64
MILLER, Carol
I was on the ceiling. Life 55:23 D 6 '63
MILLER, Charles
Advocate for Pan-Africanism. Sat R 46:31-2 N 30 '63
Sure march into an unsure future. Sat R 47: 32-3 Ag 8 '64
To rule after *uhuru*. Sat R 47:47 Je 6 '64
Weathering the wind of change. Sat R 47: 33-4+ Je 13 '64
White sultan. Sat Eve Post 236:80+ Ap 20 '63
MILLER, Chester
Dime novels. Hobbies 69:107 N '64
MILLER, D. See Meyers, E. jt. auth.
MILLER, D. M.
Flickering in protoplasts of bacillus megaterium. Science 139:1060 Mr 15 '63
MILLER, Daniel D.
Our changing resorts. Travel 122:48-52 N '64
MILLER, David L.
Bargains in rangefinder cameras. Mod Phot 27:62-3+ My '63
(comp) 256 new cameras & how they compare. Mod Phot 28:109-32 D '64
—and Matzkin, M. A.
(comps) More than 300 new still & movie cameras & how they compare. Mod Phot 27:99-128 D '63
MILLER, Delbert C. See Shull, F. A. jt. auth.
MILLER, Dorothy
View of her own; Americans 1963, at the Museum of modern art. por Newsweek 61:90 Je 10 '63
MILLER, E. C.
Boatbuilding tools. Motor B 111:42-4+ F; 42-3+ Mr '63
MILLER, Edgar
Edgar Miller; a versatile artist & craftsman. L. Bruner. il pors Am Artist 27:38-43+ My '63
MILLER, Edward S. and others
Transistors vs tubes for hi-fi. Electr World 70:48-9 N '63
MILLER, Edwin
At the movies. See issues of Seventeen
Hollywood scene. See issues of Seventeen
Straight from the shoulder. Seventeen 23: 140-1+ My '64
Teens are listening to. . . See issues of Seventeen
MILLER, Floyd
Ahdoolo! condensation. Read Digest 82:263-9+ F '63
Race against death. Read Digest 83:140-6 O '63
(ed) See Stewart, J. This was my father
MILLER, George A.
Books. Sci Am 209:171-2+ N '63; 211:145-9 N '64
MILLER, George Paul
NASA needs a watchdog. R. Hotz. Aviation W 78:21 F 18 '63
MILLER, Harlan
There's a man in the house. See issues of Ladies' home journal to June, 1963
MILLER, Helen Hill
AID, diagnosed to death. New Repub 150:14-16 Ja 18 '64
(ed) Health: are we the people getting our money's worth? New Repub 149:5-7 N 9 '63
New drug story in Washington. New Repub 149:33-5 N 9 '63
Over sixty-five: beyond the merely bearable. New Repub 151:65-8+ N 7 '64
MILLER, Helen Louise
Attic treasure; drama. Plays 25:1-13 Ja '65
Bar-None trading post; drama. Plays 23:77-85 Ap '64
Bread and butter shop; drama. Plays 24: 69-77 Ja '65
Christmas peppermints; drama. Plays 23:49-57 D '63
Gifts for the New Year; drama. Plays 23: 69-74 Ja '64
Girls in books; drama. Plays 24:55-62 N '64
Horn of plenty; drama. Plays 24:1-12, 22 N '64
Hotel Santa Claus; drama. Plays 23:1-13 D '63
Magic pencils; drama. Plays 22:79-84, 96 My '63
Magic telephone; drama. Plays 23:65-9 F '64
Man like Lincoln; drama. Plays 23:1-12 F '64

MILLER, Helen Louise—*Continued*
Mouse that soared; drama. Plays 23:61-6, 95 O '63
Parrot and the pirates; drama. Plays 23:51-6 N '63
So long at the fair; drama. Plays 22:85-90 My '63
Three little kittens; drama. Plays 23:69-72, 96 Ap '64
Toy scout jamboree; drama. Plays 24:67-72, 86 D '64
Travel game; drama. Plays 23:77-82 My '64
White House rabbit; drama. Plays 22:37-43 Mr '63
Who's who at the zoo; drama. Plays 23:65-70 Mr '64

MILLER, Helen M.
Library service in Idaho ranks 50th among states, librarian testifies; excerpts from statement, June 13, 1963. Library J 88:2862 Ag '63

MILLER, Henrietta
Rewards of a great teacher. R. Meryman. il pors Life 56:70-2+ Mr 13 '64

MILLER, Henry
Love and how it gets that way. Mlle 58:49-51+ Ja '64
Sense of wonder. Vogue 144:216-17 D '64

about

From the twosome, a quartet. E. Moon. por Sat R 46:28-9 F 23 '63
Is Miller really a Puritan? P. Carroll. Sat R 46:29 F 23 '63
Just wild about Harry. Criticism Newsweek 62:53 Jl 15 '63
Larry & Henry. por Time 81:80 Mr 1 '63
What they wrote and what they were. D. Littlejohn. Reporter 28:42+ Ap 11 '63

MILLER, Herbert J. Jr
Federal viewpoint on combating organized crime. bibliog f Ann Am Acad 347:93-103 My '63

MILLER, Herman P.
New definition of our poor. N Y Times Mag p 11+ Ap 21 '63
Who's rich, who's poor? what's myth, what's fact? excerpts from Rich man, poor man. Changing T 18:19-21 F '64

MILLER, Herman, incorporated
But where will I keep my movie magazines? W. K. Zinsser. il Sat Eve Post 238:74+ Ja 16 '65
Office furniture tailored to the job. il Bsns W p60-2 D 19 '64
Return of the roll-top desk. il Fortune 70:178 D '64

MILLER, Howard F.
America the musical. Sr Schol 83:37 N 8 '63

MILLER, J. and Glickstein, M.
Reaction time to cortical stimulation. bibliog Science 146:1594-6 D 18 '64

MILLER, J. F. A. P.
Thymus and the development of immunologic responsiveness. bibliog Science 144:1544-51 Je 26 '64

MILLER, J. Irwin
Freedoms in tension. Christian Cent 81:1332-3 O 28 '64
Man as servant. Christian Cent 81:233-6 F 19 '64

MILLER, Jack
Members of Congress need your help. por Suc Farm 61:78 F '63

MILLER, James A. and others
Hypothermia, asphyxia, and cardiac glycogen in guinea pigs. bibliog Science 144:1226-7 Je 5 '64

MILLER, James Hull
Foldaway theater. Recreation 56:370-2 O '63

MILLER, James Nathan
Are cars as good as they used to be? Read Digest 84:53-8 F '64
California's half-million-acre greenhouse. Read Digest 83:182-4+ Ag '63
Conservation is everybody's battle. Read Digest 85:161-6+ Ag '64
King Coal comes back. Read Digest 85:88-94 D '64
Let's put a price tag on our laws. Read Digest 85:217-18+ O '64
Seven steps toward getting a job. Read Digest 82:72-5 Mr '63
Toughest corks afloat. Read Digest 83:172-4+ D '63
What's happened to the motels? Read Digest 82:213-16 Mr '63

MILLER, James Robbins
Donovan's retreat; story. McCalls 90:84-5 Mr '63

MILLER, John N.
Idyl II: fisher to fisher; poem. Commonweal 79:48 O 4 '63

MILLER, John W.
Remodeled pool is bigger and better. Am City 79:94-6 F '64

MILLER, Jonathan
Air. New Yorker 39:115-16+ N 16; 63-4 D 28 '63
Current cinema. New Yorker 39:60-1 Ag 10; 52+ Ag 17; 64-5 Ag 24; 56+ Ag 31 '63

about

Huck Finning. pors Newsweek 62:64 S 30 '63
Morose medic turned clown; with excerpts from conversations with J. Howard. il pors Life 55:65-6+ Ag 16 '63
Please feed the lions. il por Mlle 57:96-7+ Je '63

MILLER, Josef M. See Sutton, D. jt. auth.

MILLER, Julius Sumner
Frantic physicist fires 'em up. il pors Life 56:115-16+ Mr 20 '64
Mad, mad, mad, mad physicist. A. Hamilton. il por PTA Mag 59:12-14+ Ja '65; Same abr. with title Professor Miller's mighty magic. Read Digest 86:155-8+ Ja '65

MILLER, Kenneth H.
France does what comes naturally. New Repub 151:13 S 5 '64

MILLER, Lee N. See Woodwell, G. M. jt. auth.

MILLER, Leonard M.
Dropout: schools search for clues to his problems. bibliog por Sch Life 45:5-7+ My '63
—See Smith, H. M. jt. auth.

MILLER, Llewellyn
Children and love. Redbook 123:58-9+ S '64
Congress, it's my daddy. Redbook 121:50-1+ Ag '63
New baby. Redbook 120:56-7+ Ap '63

MILLER, Lloyd
Small rebellion in Miami. P. Redford. Harper 228:96-8+ F '64

MILLER, Lloyd C.
Pharmacopeia. New Yorker 40:48-9 N 21 '64

MILLER, Lloyd Eldon, Jr
Did Lloyd Miller kill Janice May? R. Applegate. il pors Sat Eve Post 237:75-9 Ja 25 '64

MILLER, Lois Mattox
Dilemma of the problem smoker. Read Digest 84:63-8 My '64
—and Monahan, James
Cigarette controversy: a storm is brewing. Read Digest 83:91-9 Ag '63
Cigarettes; tried and found guilty. Read Digest 84:71-6 Ap '64

MILLER, Loomis C.
Now anyone can steam-bend wood. Pop Sci 183:111-13+ D '63

MILLER, Loren
Freedom now, but what then? Nation 196:539-42 Je 29 '63
Prosperity through equality. Nation 197:157-60+ S 21 '63

MILLER, Lynn
(comp) SR's check list of current books. Sat R 46:14 F 23; 14+ Mr 2; 42-4 Mr 9; 17-18 Mr 16; 21+ Mr 23; 18+ Mr 30; 37-8 Ap 6; 30 Ap 13; 14+ Ap 20; 40-1+ Ap 27; 38 My 4; 41 My 11; 14 My 18; 37 My 25 '63

MILLER, Marcella Henry
Joseph and Mary Gomer, missionaries. Negro Hist Bul 26:163-4 F '63

MILLER, Marjorie B.
Help wanted: female. Recreation 58:38+ Ja '65

MILLER, Martin H.
Amateur's ten-year success story. il por U S Camera 27:92+ O '64

MILLER, Mary Lou
Mosaic mural for your school. bibliog Sch Arts 64:10-15 D '64

MILLER, Max
Economy CB S-meter. Pop Electr 20:50-1 Ap '64

MILLER, Max J. See Abedi, Z. H. jt. auth.

MILLER, Maynard M.
Our restless earth. Nat Geog Mag 126:140-1 Jl '64

MILLER, Merle
On the road in Brazil. il Harper 227:65-70+ O '63
Tranquilized in Latin America. Harper 230:131-4 Ja '65

about

Friendly lynching. por Newsweek 64:87 N 9 '64

MILLER, Mildred
Gourmet's mezzo; interview, ed. by J. W. Freeman. por Opera N 29:12 Ja 23 '65

MILLER, Mitch
Popularity explosion. por Seventeen 22:142+ F '63

MILLER, Neal E. See Davis, J. D.; Wolf, G. jt. auths.
MILLER, Norman C.
Tino's bottomless tanks of oil. Sat Eve Post 237:19-25 Ap 25 '64
MILLER, Orlando J. and Ryan, Jack
New hope in the fight against deformed births; reprint. Sci Digest 54:69-73 O '63
MILLER, Peter
My eye on the tying of a dry fly. Life 54: 14 My 10 '63
MILLER, Philip L.
ARG and how she grew. Am Rec G 30:748-9 My '64
Buried treasures. por Library J 88:1823-5 My 1 '63
First opera in dynagroove: Madama Butterfly. Am Rec G 29:684-5 My '63
Image of MLA. por Library J 89:809-11 F 15 '64
Joan Sutherland in La sonnambula. Am Rec G 29:596-8 Ap '63
Leontyne Price as Carmen. Am Rec G 31: 10-12 S '64
Leontyne Price as Tosca. Am Rec G 30:92-4 O '63
On London, Theresa Berganza as l'Italiana in Algeri. Am Rec G 30:1012-13+ Jl '64
RCA Victor's Falstaff. Am Rec G 30:564-5+ Mr '64
(ed) Recorded music. See issues of Library journal
Sutherland in I Puritani. Am Rec G 30:656-7+ Ap '64
Il trittico. Am Rec G 29:420-1+ F '63
Two new recordings of the St. John Passion. Am Rec G 30:930-3 Je '64
MILLER, R. S.
Modern water witching. por Am City 78:105-6 N '63
MILLER, Ralph
Best compact eight? U S Camera 26:52-5 N '63
Color slides. See issues of U.S. camera
From frame to fame. U S Camera 27:62-3+ S '64
How bright your screen! U S Camera 26:58+ My '63
Instant movies. U S Camera 26:80 Jl '63
Popular gardening's cameras & gardens. See occasional issues of Popular gardening & living outdoors to November 1963
Portable power probe. U S Camera 26:62-5+ Je '63
Russians are coming! U S Camera 26:49-53+ My '63
Slides to prints and vice versa. U S Camera 26:50-1+ Ag '63
Use your camera as a garden tool. Horticulture 42:38-9 My '64
MILLER, Randolph Crump
For the world of tomorrow. Christian Cent 81:544-6 Ap 29 '64
MILLER, Richard A.
Hospitals: the race with change. Arch Forum 120:80-9 Ap '64
MILLER, Richard I.
Teaching about communism. Sat R 46:62-4+ Mr 23 '63
MILLER, Robert R.
Is our native underwater life worth saving? bibliog il Nat Parks Mag 37:4-9 My '63
MILLER, Robert W.
Concept of total activity. por Wilson Lib Bul 38:544-6 Mr '64
MILLER, Rosalind
Librarians: a vanishing breed. por Library J 89:4597-9 N 15 '64
MILLER, Ruth Schmidt
How to decorate window shades. Farm J 87:75 S '63
Storybook ideas for the nursery. por Farm J 87:98-9 Mr '63
MILLER, Samuel H.
Man the believer. Christian Cent 81:1167-8 S 23 '64
MILLER, Sanford A. and Dymsza, H. A.
Artificial feeding of neonatal rats. bibliog Science 141:517-18 Ag 9 '63
MILLER, Seymour
Money managers. P. Bart. Esquire 60:204 D '63
MILLER, Shirley
Our young people. Audubon Mag 66:152-3, 67:62 My '64, Ja '65
MILLER, Vassar
Terminations, revelations. W. Stafford. Poetry 104:107-8 My '64
MILLER, Victor B.
California plan. Nat R 16:712 Ag 25 '64
MILLER, Vincent
Perspective on the founders. Nat R 14:117-19 F 12 '63
Report on the Negro question. Nat R 16:1018-19 N 17 '64
Subtle assault on academe. Nat R 14:325-6 Ap 23 '63
Whose Hamilton? Nat R 16:407-8 My 19 '64; Correction. 16:552 Je 30 '64
MILLER, W. Russ
Fifty-six minutes to paradise. por Flying 75: 42-4 Ag '64
MILLER, W. W.
Clerical help. NEA J 52:32 N '63
MILLER, Walter J.
Galileo's visits to Rome; reprint. Sky & Tel 27:101-5 F '64
MILLER, Warren
Chaos, disorder and the late show: story. Sat Eve Post 236:74-5 O 5 '63
Last of the line. Nation 200:15-16 Ja 4 '65
Long night of Shubert alley: story. Sat Eve Post 237:62-7 My 23 '64
Mother of Chianti. Nation 198:632-3 Je 22 '64
Why not Dresden? Nation 198:243-4 Mr 9 '64
MILLER, Wayne
Keep it in the family; photographs from World is young. P. Caulfield. Mod Phot 27: 74-9 Je '63
MILLER, William
Trumpeter of doomsday. H. A. Larrabee. il por Am Heritage 15:34-7+ Ap '64
MILLER, William C.
Did American Indians see the guest star? il Sat R 47:37-9 Jl 4 '64
—and Goldberg, A. L.
Getting the most from the newer media. NEA J 53:30-1 Ap '64
—See Sandage, A. R. jt. auth.
MILLER, William Edward
Backlash and the Catholic vote. R. W. Gibbons. Christian Cent 81:1303-5 O 21 '64
Barry's choice: a fighting running mate. il por U S News 57:30-1 Jl 27 '64
Bill Miller: the G.O.P.'s tough, shrewd pro. R. Kahn. il pors Sat Eve Post 237:81-3 Ag 8 '64
Bill Millers rev up for November. C. Welles. il pors Life 57:35-6 Ag 7 '64
Candidate from New York. E. J. Hughes. Newsweek 64:27 S 21 '64
Checkers Nixon, R.I.P. Reporter 31:14+ S 24 '64
Close-up of the vice-presidential candidates. il por Sr Schol 85:13 S 23 '64
Cordial affair. il por Newsweek 64:27 Jl 20 '64
Echo of two conventions. E. J. Hughes. Newsweek 64:15 S 7 '64
Gut fighter. Nation 199:149 S 28 '64
Gut fighter. New Repub 151:4-5 S 19 '64
Just one of those weeks. Time 84:24-5 O 9 '64
Man who thought of leaving politics. M. Viorst. New Repub 151:8-9 Ag 8 '64
Nasty job. il por Newsweek 64:30-1 S 21 '64
On the receiving end. il Time 84:43 O 2 '64
Order in the streets. Christian Cent 81:1195-6 S 30 '64
Point and counterpoint. il por Newsweek 64: 29 S 28 '64
Running mate. il por Time 84:28 Jl 24 '64
Running-mate problem. il por U S News 57: 33 Jl 20 '64
They want to be second. B. H. Bagdikian. il pors N Y Times Mag p30-3+ O 11 '64
Two indispensable men. R. Moley. Newsweek 61:96 F 11 '63
Who was Bill Miller? B. Carter. il por Reporter 31:21-4 N 5 '64
William E. Miller. Newsweek 64:22+ Jl 27 '64
William Miller problem: non-distinctiveness of his name. W. L. Miller. Reporter 31:29 O 8 '64
MILLER, William Edward, family
Millers: their assets and debts. il U S News 57:16 S 21 '64
MILLER, William J.
After the battle in U.S. rubber's executive suite. Fortune 70:116-23+ D '64
MILLER, William Lee
Aid to education: a better deal. Reporter 30: 20-3 Ap 23 '64
Analysis of the white backlash. N Y Times Mag p27+ Ag 23 '64
Ted Sorensen of Nebraska. Reporter 30:24-7 F 13 '64
William Miller problem. Reporter 31:29 O 8 '64
MILLER, William Robert
Nonviolence in the racial crisis. Christian Cent 81:927-30 Jl 22 '64
Spare us: a prayer for our time. Christian Cent 80:1075 S 4 '63
MILLER, William T.
Developing the whole man. America 110:715-17 My 23 '64
MILLER, Wilmer J.
First linkage of a species antigen in the genus streptopelia. bibliog Science 143:1179-80 Mr 13 '64
MILLERITES. See Second advent

MILLET, Genevieve H.
Teen-agers and the dope hazard. Parents Mag 39:46-7+ My '64
What your skin tells about you. Parents Mag 38:40-1+ Ag '63
MILLIAMMETERS. See Ammeters
MILLIGAN, Spike
Letter from London; performance of Son of Oblomov, at Comedy theatre. M. Panter-Downes. New Yorker 40:62 Ja 2 '65
—See Antrobus, J. jt. auth.
MILLIKAN, Moria. See Campbell, L. jt. auth.
MILLIMETER wavelengths. See Microwaves
MILLINERY
Where hats are made; Manhattan's millinery industry. M. Fischer. il Sat Eve Post 236:64-7 Ap 6 '63
See also
Hats
MILLION-dollar question; story. See Davenport, G.
MILLIONAIRES
Biggest cattle baron. T. G. Harris. il Look 27:62+ O 8 '63
Mr Millionaire. Newsweek 62:59 Jl 29 '63
Our 398 millionaires: a new breed. A. Shuster. il N Y Times Mag p37 S 15 '63
That so nece$$ary ingredient; Hershbergers of Wichita. L. H. Lapham. il Sat Eve Post 237:56-9 S 5 '64
Three millionaires tell how they did it; excerpts from Money talks! ed. by C. Sopkin. P. J. Sagona; W. P. Lear, sr; W. G. Riley. il Nations Bsns 52:106-8+ Ap '64
MILLIPEDS
Cyanogenic glandular apparatus of a millipede. T. Eisner and others. bibliog il Science 139:1218-20 Mr 22 '63
MILLIPEDES
Trans-2-dodecenal and 2-methyl-1, 4-quinone produced by a millipede. J. W. Wheeler and others. bibliog Science 144:540-1 My 1 '64
MILLIS, Walter
Demilitarized world and how to get there. por Sat R 47:18-22+ S 12 '64
Through the ranks to the top. Sat R 46:32 O 19 '63
MILLMAN, Peter M. See McIntosh, B. A. jt. auth.
MILLQVIST, Rolf
Supermarket without a store; Hemkop in Stockholm, Sweden. il por Bsns W p 100-2 Ja 11 '64
MILLS, Bert
Tax deductions under the new law. Motor B 111:51+ Mr '63
MILLS, Billy
Indian orphan boy from Kansas becomes an Olympic hero. il pors Life 57:109-10 O 23 '64
Lieutenant Mill's day. il por Time 84:60-1 O 23 '64
MILLS, Charles Wright
Legend of the left. por Newsweek 63:91-2 My 11 '64
Power, politics and people: the collected essays of C. Wright Mills, ed. by I. L. Horowitz. Review
Sat R por 46:27 Je 8 '63. C. N. Parkinson
MILLS, Charlie
Prince of trotters. K. Rudeen. il por Sports Illus 18:42+ My 13 '63
MILLS, Don Harper
Malpractice and the clinical laboratory. bibliog Science 144:638-42 My 8 '64
MILLS, Ernest M.
Controlling pigeons about the home. Consumer Bul 47:25-7 Jl '64
MILLS, George
JFK could lose. Look 27:94+ D 17 '63
MILLS, H. B.
Glorious failure; story. Redbook 121:64-5 S '63
Lady in waiting; story. Redbook 120:72-3 Ap '63
MILLS, Hayley
Father and daughter talk about fame, families, love and growing up. por Redbook 123:54-5+ Ag '64
about
Chip off the old block. M. Ronan. il por Sr Schol 83:10 O 25 '63
Hayley Mills grows up. pors Good H 158:34+ Je '64
I'm growing up! ed by E. Miller. pors Seventeen 23:70-1+ Ja '64
MILLS, Herbert H.
Dedication cites education goal of Children's farm. por Audubon Mag 65:84 Mr '63
MILLS, James
Idea hit me; it was ridiculous. Life 57:112-13 S 11 '64
Tales of famous aces. Life 56:78+ Mr 20 '64
MILLS, Jane
How to freeze baseball caps and other helpful household hints. Redbook 121:64-5+ Jl '63
MILLS, John
Father and daughter talk about fame, families, love and growing up. por Redbook 123:54-5+ Ag '64
MILLS, Percy B.
Mr Dulles spills the beans. New Repub 150:20-2 F 15 '64
Russians as propagandists. New Repub 150:22-4 Je 6 '64
MILLS, Ralph J. jr
Recent prose. Poetry 102:269-73 Jl '63
Roethke's last poems. Poetry 105:122-4 N '64
MILLS, Stanley E. See Pious, D. A. jt. auth.
MILLS, Wilbur Daigh
Mills's terms for Medicare; excerpts from address, December 2, 1964. U S News 57:74 D 21 '64
Wilbur Mills talks on taxes; interview. pors Nations Bsns 52:30-1+ Ag '64
about
Is this the year for Medicare? P. Duke and S. Meisler. il Reporter 30:23-6 Ap 23 '64
Key man in the new Congress. il por U S News 57:19 N 23 '64
Next tax cut: excises. por Bsns W p36 Ap 25 '64
Taxing times. Reporter 28:16+ Mr 14 '63
MILLS college, Oakland, Calif.
Let it sing! festival honoring D. Milhaud. il Time 81:65 Je 7 '63
MILLS high school. See San Francisco—Education
MILLSTEIN, Gilbert
Go-go-go of Robert Goulet. Sat Eve Post 236:24-5 Ap 27 '63
Good-bye, Lorelei. Hello, Dolly! Sat Eve Post 237:78-9 F 22 '64
Lowdown on Loudon. Sat Eve Post 236:70+ Ap 6 '63
New York, N.Y: the golden door; excerpt from New York: true north. Sat Eve Post 237:74-8+ My 23 '64
Remarkable life of a little genius. Sat Eve Post 237:32+ D 19 '4
That brassy music man returns to Broadway as poor Richard. Sat Eve Post 237:86-9 O 17 '64
You are his target. Sat Eve Post 237:38+ O 3 '64
MILNE, A. A.
Pooh perplex, by F. C. Crews. Review
Reporter 29:62 D 5 '63. R. S. Gallagher
MILNE, Ewart
Some Irish poets. T. Kinsella. Poetry 102:324-6 Ag '63
MILNER, John G.
Residential treatment center. bibliog f Ann Am Acad 355:98-104 S '64
MILO
How I grow 100-bushel milo. M. Merrill. il Suc Farm 62:50-1 My '64
MILSOME, John R.
Art & craft in the British primary school. Sch Arts 64:16-17 Ja '65
MILTON, Brock
Case of the teen-age doll. N Y Times Mag p84+ Ap 21 '63
MILTON, Daniel J. and De Carli, P. S.
Maskelynite: formation by explosive shock. bibliog Science 140:670-1 My 10 '63
—See De Carli, P. S. jt. auth.
MILTON, John
All around the place. See issues of Popular gardening & living outdoors
Differences between greenhouse and garden roses. Horticulture 41:316-17 Je '63
Fairy, a carefree rose for all. Flower Grower 51:33 F '64
Operation budworm: Maine. Am For 69:26-7+ S '63
MILTON, John, 1608-1674
Greatest of English poets! P. W. Schmidtchen. il pors Hobbies 69:106-7 My '64
Milton and the prize; letter to the editor. J. W. Daly. Nat R 17:34-5 Ja 12 '65
Style of Milton's epic. D. R. Pearce. Yale R 52:427-44 Mr '63
MILTON, Nerissa Long
Know your congressmen (cont) Negro Hist Bul 26:252; 27:17 My, O '63
Thought for Christmas. Negro Hist Bul 27:68 D '63
MILWARD, Peter
Who was Shakespeare? America 110:566-7 Ap 25 '64

MILWAUKEE
Answer to beach pollution. il Am City 78: 84-5 Ap '63
Harbor housecleaning by boat. il Am City 78:148 D '63
Crime
How one city keeps its streets safe. il U S News 57:68-71 S 28 '64
Libraries
See also
Milwaukee public library
Police department
How one city keeps its streets safe. il U S News 57:68-71 S 28 '64
Sanitary affairs
Coded signal warns of sewer surcharge. W. L. Burmeister and C. W. Schwarz. il Am City 78:96-7 S '63
Solving street cleaning's toughest problem. W. J. Rheinfrank. il Am City 79:94-5 Ap '64
Theater
Rise of rep. il(p56) Time 83:61 F 14 '64
MILWAUKEE Braves (baseball) See Baseball clubs
MILWAUKEE public library
Double header in Milwaukee; Oklahoma and Capitol branches. R. P. Bartolini. il Library J 89:4737-9 D 1 '64
MIME
Marcel Marceau at New York city center. D. Hering. Dance Mag 37:30 Mr '63
Openings, New York. A. Pryce-Jones. Theatre Arts 47:67 F '63
See also
Pantomime
MIMI (operatic character) See Characters in opera
MIMICRY (biology)
Camouflaged still-fishing. H. Hediger. il Natur Hist 72:18-21 Je '63
Living camouflage; nature's call to the colors. D. Peattie and L. Peattie. il Read Digest 83:179-83 N '63
Lowly disguise of the giant swallowtail. M. L. Donahue and R. J. Donahue. il Audubon Mag 66:320-1 S '64
Mimicry: differential advantage of color patterns in the natural environment. L. P. Brower and others. bibliog il Science 144: 183-5 Ap 10 '64
MIMIEUX, Yvette
Fair young Hollywood girls. R. W. Lewis. por Sat Eve Post 236:25-7 S 7 '63
Follow a star. C. Cooper. il por Seventeen 24:77+ Ja '65
She sure doesn't look sick. il pors Life 55: 119-21 O 25 '63
This is Yvette Mimieux; photographs. Esquire 61:102-5 My '64
Unlikely myth. por Time 81:38+ Mr 29 '63
MIMS, Donna Mae
Look fast, think pink. K. W. Purdy. il por Sat Eve Post 237:60-1 O 31 '64
MINAR, David W. See Greer, S. jt. auth.
MINAS GERAIS, Brazil
Which is the real Brazil? G. Freyre. il Américas 16:10-15 Ap '64
MIND. See Intellect
MIND and body
Cardiovascular disease; report of conference on Psychophysiologic aspects of cardiovascular disease. G. Saslow. Science 142: 601+ N 1 '63
Illness by guilt. Sci Digest 54:53-4 O '63
It's not always in your head. Sci Digest 56:58 N '64
People who love operations. A. J. Snider. Sci Digest 54:56 O '63
See also
Faith cure
Medicine, Psychosomatic
Mental hygiene
MIND your P's and Q's; drama. See Hark, M. and McQueen, N.
MINDANAO
Fierce Moros. J. Keats. il Holiday 34:124+ D '63
MINDSZENTY, József, cardinal
Can anyone free Cardinal Mindszenty? A. Leone-Moats. por Nat R 14:491-3 Je 18 '63
Cardinal's choice. por Newsweek 61:61 Ap 29 '63
Easing out Mindszenty. il por Time 81:49 Ap 12 '63
Mindszenty tragedy. T. Weyr. Commonweal 79:454-7 Ja 17 '64; Discussion. 79:719-21 Mr 13 '64
Reluctant cardinal. Newsweek 61:47-8 My 27 '63
Two cardinals meet. America 108:627 My 4 '63
Visit. Time 81:69 Ap 26 '63
MINE accidents and explosions
Forgotten miners; concerning report on safety conditions by Secretary of the interior. Nation 198:255 Mr 16 '64
From the tomb; survivors rescued from iron mine near Lengede, Saxony. il Time 82: 48 N 15 '63
Good Lady turns bad; nine rescued from limestone mine in Champagnole, France. il Newsweek 64:39 Ag 17 '64
Rescue and death; Moab, Utah potash mine. il Newsweek 62:26 S 9 '63
See also
Coal mines and mining—Accidents and explosions
MINE fires
See also
Coal mines and mining—Fires and fire protection
MINE rescue work
André was with us; subsidence deep inside Mont Rivel. Time 84:24 Ag 14 '64
Cave-in! Sheppton, Pa. A. F. Gonzales, jr. il Pop Sci 183:43-8+ D '63
Good Lady turns bad; nine rescued from limestone mine in Champagnole, France. il Newsweek 64:39 Ag 17 '64
Industry pitches in to save trapped miners; Sheppton, Pa. coal mine disaster. il Bsns W p26-7 Ag 31 '63
Start of a legend? rescue of David Fellin and Henry Throne. il Time 82:17 S 6 '63
Two miners come up from a pit of death; rescue of David Fellin and Henry Throne. il Life 55:33-5 S 6 '63
MINE roofs
Safety devices and measures
Strata control and rock mechanics; report on fourth international conference. M. T. Wane. Science 145:1075 S 4 '64
MINE subsidences
Strata control and rock mechanics; report on fourth international conference. M. T. Wane. Science 145:1075 S 4 '64
MINEAR, Lawrence
Hattiesburg: toward reconciliation. Christian Cent 81:1115-16 S 9 '64
MINEAR, Paul S.
Interconfessional research; address, February 3, 1964. Vital Speeches 30:343-6 Mr 15 '64
MINER, Edwin H.
Going to college. por Sr Schol 85:17-18 N 11 '64
MINER, Jak
Do-it-yourself yacht club. il Motor B 111: 100-1+ Je '63
Michigan's 3,000-mile marine highway. Yachting 115:51-3+ Mr '64
MINER, Lisbeth
Gals take over. il Yachting 114:65-7+ S '63
MINER, Robert G.
Weathervane. See issues of Flower grower
MINER, Virginia Scott
Love taught by time; poem. Good H 157:172 Jl '63
MINERAL fuels. See Fuel
MINERAL resources. See Mines and mineral resources
MINERAL resources in submerged lands
Inexhaustible riches from the sea. G. A. W. Boehm. il Fortune 68:132-7+ D '63; Same abr. Read Digest 84:111-15 Ap '64
Mining the bottom of the sea; excerpts from study. R. Revelle. il Sat R 47:60-1 O 3 '64
MINERAL specimens
See also
Geological specimens
MINERALOGICAL analysis
Neutron activation analysis of fluid inclusions for copper, manganese, and zinc. G. K. Czmanske and others. bibliog il Science 140:401-3 Ap 26 '63
MINERALOGY
Fission damage in calcite and the dating of carbonates. R. F. Sippel and E. D. Glover. bibliog il Science 144:409-11 Ap 24 '64
See also
Apatite
Dendrites
Tunellite
MINERALS. See Metals; Mineralogy; Mines and mineral resources
MINERALS in sea water. See Sea water
MINERALS in soils. See Soils—Mineral content
MINERALS in the body
Measurement of bone mineral in vivo: an improved method. J. R. Cameron and J. Sorenson. bibliog il Science 142:230-2 O 11 '63

MINERS
See also
Coal miners
MINES, Robert
Your guide to mind drugs. Sci Digest 55:66-70 Ja '64
—See Smith, J. B. K. jt. auth.
MINES, Land. See Mines, Military
MINES, Military
Military plans A-mines. Sci N L 87:45 Ja 16 '65
MINES and mineral resources
Minerals. J. W. Feiss. il Sci Am 209:128-36 bibliog(p307) S '63
Minerals; wealth in the earth's crust. Sci Digest 56:89-90 O '64
New tools to map our hidden mineral wealth. J. M. Bruckshaw. il UNESCO Courier 17: 28-32 Ja '64
See also
Chromite
Metals
Mineral resources in submerged lands
Prospecting
Salt

Government ownership

Latins ease threats to U.S. mining; pressure for nationalization of foreign mining operations. Bsns W p 16-17 D 26 '64

Australia

Aluminum rush; deposits of bauxite in the Weipa region. il Fortune 70:71-2 Ag '64

Bolivia

See also
Tin mines and mining—Bolivia

California

Here they mine quicksilver; New Idria mine. il Sunset 133:18+ N '64
Rockhound notes from the Lakeview-Alturas area. H. D. Brown. il Hobbies 68:122-3 N '63

Canada

Back to the mines; new mining rush. il Time 83:90 Je 19 '64
Big strike; discovery of zinc, copper and silver in the Timmins area of Ontario. Newsweek 63:88 Ap 27 '64
Billion-dollar plunge in the bush. il Life 56: 36-41 My 15 '64
Canada is riding a homemade boom. il Bsns W p66-7 Ag 1 '64
Canada's 100-billion-dollar potash pile. L. Elliott. il Read Digest 84:144-6+ My '64
Getting used to wealth; metals discovery, Timmins, Ont. Bsns W p32 My 9 '64
Mining new markets for nickel; Falconbridge. il Bsns W p62-4+ S 5 '64
Race for Canada's riches; it's breaking out all over. il U S News 56:108-9 My 25 '64
Treasure hunt at Timmins. il Newsweek 63: 73-5 My 4 '64
See also
Iron mines and mining—Canada

Colorado

Royal Gorge of the Arkansas River in Colorado. H. D. Brown. il Hobbies 69: 116-17 Ag '64

Jamaica

Timber from Jamaican ore pits. E. J. Long. il Am For 69:22-5 S '63

Middle western states

Tri-state area; Oklahoma, the southeastern corner of Kansas, and the adjacent portion of Missouri. H. D. Brown. il Hobbies 69:126-7 Jl '64

Minnesota

Iron amendment; taconite on the Mesabi. il Newsweek 64:74+ N 16 '64

Netherlands

Going private; Dutch state mines. Time 83:66 Ja 31 '64

Nevada

Copper Canyon. H. D. Brown. il Hobbies 69:125+ D '64

Russia

See also
Gold mines and mining—Russia

South Africa

Should Americans invest in South Africa? C. B. Randall. il Duns R 81:44-6 Ja '63
See also
Diamond mines and mining
Gold mines and mining—South Africa

United States

See also
Copper
Oil shales

Washington (state)

Mining Americana. H. D. Brown. Hobbies 68: 124-5 Ap '63
On the Straits of Juan De Fuca. H. D. Brown. il Hobbies 68:124 Jl '63
Pateros to Baron. H. D. Brown. Hobbies 68:123 Ja '64
San Poil Valley traverse. H. D. Brown. il Hobbies 69:118+ O '64

Western states

Conducted western mineral collecting trip. H. D. Brown. il Hobbies 68:122 S '63
Ironwood forest. H. D. Brown. il Hobbies 68: 122 O '63

Zambia

Relic of empire; British South Africa's mineral rights. il Time 84:103 O 9 '64
MINETTE, Bill, and Dunlop, Richard
Arizona's fish and fun spot: Apacheland. il Todays Health 41:22-5+ O '63
MINGUS, Charlie
Beneath the underdog. il por Time 84:88-9 O 2 '64
Jazz. W. Balliett. New Yorker 40:133-5 Je 13 '64
MINH, Duong-van-. See Duong-van-Minh
MINH, Ho-chi-. See Ho-chi-Minh
MINH, Ho-thong-. See Ho-thong-Minh
MINH, Tran
What comes next in Vietnam? New Repub 151:7-8 S 12 '64
MINIATURE automobiles. See Automobile models
MINIATURE books. See Books—Microscopic and miniature editions
MINIATURE cameras. See Cameras
MINIATURE electronic equipment
Autonetics designs advanced radar line. B. Miller. il Aviation W 78:90-1+ Je 17 '63
British firm using low-cost method to package miniature components. F. G. McGuire. il Miss & Roc 14:32-3 Mr 2 '64
Integrated circuits. L. Solomon. il Electr World 72:27-32 S '64
Invaders; rapid erosion of privacy. il Newsweek 63:81-2 Mr 9 '64
Invasion of privacy; excerpts from Naked society. V. Packard. Atlan 213:55-61 F '64
Littler than Lilliput; microminiature electronics. L. E. Garner, jr. il Pop Electr 18: 47-51+ Mr '63
Microelectronics; special report; with editorial comment. C. D. LaFond and others. il Miss & Roc 14:22-4+, 66 F 3 '64
Science of vanishing electronics; integrated circuits. L. Stern. il Sci Digest 55:44-7 Je '64
Shrinking computers; tiny all-transistorized LGP-21 computer. Bsns W p 106 Ap 6 '63
TIMM components work throughout high-intensity radiation bombardment. R. Kiefer. Miss & Roc 15:34 Ag 24 '64
MINIATURE gardens. See Gardens, Miniature
MINIATURE greenhouses. See Greenhouses, Miniature
MINIATURE houses. See House models
MINIATURE lamps. See Electric lamps
MINIATURE objects
Business man adopts world of miniaturia: Roy J. Hancock of Chesterfield Township, Mount Clemens, Mich. S. A. Parvin. il Hobbies 69:122-3 N '64; 122-4 Ja '65
Charbneau miniature museum. S. A. Parvin. il Hobbies 69:116-17+ Jl; 122-4+ Ag '64
Dorothy Hesner's miniatures. S. A. Parvin. il Hobbies 68:118 D '63
For who hath despised the day of small things! S. A. Parvin. il Hobbies 68:122-3 Ap '63
Miniature items reveal history. S. A. Parvin. il Hobbies 68:122-3 Mr '63
Mrs Henry Ford's miniatures. S. A. Parvin. il Hobbies 67:122-3 F '63
Musician collects miniature pianos and organs. S. A. Parvin. il Hobbies 68:122 Jl '63
MINIATURE painting (portraits)
Children in miniature. E. G. Paine. il Antiques 84:570-3 N '63
MINIATURE rooms. See Rooms, Miniature
MINIATURE trees. See Trees, Dwarf
MINIATURES, Military. See Military miniatures
MINIATURIZATION (electronics) See Miniature electronic equipment
MINIBUSES. See Motor buses—Small size

MINIMUM wage
United States
City sets its own minimum wage; New York. U S News 57:78 Jl 27 '64
How wage law hit small shop. U S News 57:75 Ag 17 '64
Raise for millions next month: who will get how much. il U S News 55:95-6 Ag 19 '63
What happens when minimum wages go up. Bsns W p 124 F 23 '63
MINING accidents. See Mine accidents and explosions
MINING engineering
Push-button miner mines by remote control. il(p321) Sci N L 84:324 N 23 '63
Safety measures
See also
Geophone
MINING industry and finance
Great day in the morning for Texas gulf sulphur. R. Sheehan. il Fortune 70:136-40+ Jl '64
Canada
Pot of gold, Quebec family style; Beauchemin family's complex of companies. il Bsns W p 146+ N 28 '64
Cyprus
Beleaguered California miners. il Fortune 69:67-8 My '64
Hot spot that produces plenty of cold cash. il Bsns W p 102+ O 10 '64
Netherlands
D.S.M. goes private. il Fortune 70:64+ D '64
MINING machinery
See also
Coal mining machinery
MINING towns
See also
Central City, Colo.
MINISTERS of the gospel. See Clergy
MINK, Patsy Takemoto
First Congresswoman from overseas. il pors Life 58:49-50+ Ja 22 '65
MINKS
Minks, shrews and men in a winter swamp. B. Gilbert. il Sports Illus 18:38-42+ Mr 18 '63
Washington mink ranch. il Ebony 18:83-4+ Mr '63
Yukon mink. L. C. Holden. il Field & S 68: 35 F '64
MINNAERT, M.
Solar symposium at Sydney. Sky & Tel 27: 151-3 Mr '64
MINNEAPOLIS
Blow snow off the bridges. G. Bodien and L. C. Pratt. il Am City 79:71-2 Ja '64
Architecture
Porch for pedestrians; Northwestern national life insurance co. headquarters. il Time 85:52 Ja 22 '65
Description
Land of the sky blue water. R. Deardorff. il Redbook 123:70-1+ S '64
Libraries
See also
Minneapolis public library
Music
Grimm for grownups; Minneapolis center opera company presents Carl Orff's The wise woman and the king at the Tyrone Guthrie theater. il Time 85:46 Ja 29 '65
Minneapolis news. E. L. Bolton. il Opera N 28:25 My 2 '64
[Musical events] (cont) Mus Am 83:76 Ja; 16 My '63; 84:26+ Ap '64
Negroes
Even Minnesota has racial flare-ups now. il U S News 55:8 Jl 8 '63
Parks and playgrounds
Parks that pay for themselves. R. Brecher and E. Brecher. il Read Digest 83:258-62 N '63
Stores
Retail empire reaches across the prairie: from western Wisconsin to eastern Montana. il Bsns W p70-2+ Mr 7 '64
Streets
Transit-way unveiled for Minneapolis. O. D. Gay. il Am City 78:113 Jl '63
Theater
English gardeners and American gardens; Tyrone Guthrie theater's first season. R. Brustein. New Repub 149:29-31 O 5 '63
First night in Minneapolis. L. Kirstein. Nation 196:437-8 My 5 '63
Giant of Monaghan; Tyrone Guthrie theatre. B. Friel. Holiday 35:89+ My '64
Hit & miss in Minnesota; Tyrone Guthrie theater. il Time 83:64 My 22 '64
In the land of Hiawatha; Tyrone Guthrie theater. il Time 81:87-8 My 17 '63
Northwestward ho! opening of the Tyrone Guthrie theatre. H. Hewes. Sat R 46:24 My 25 '63
Progress in Minnesota; sophomore year of the Minnesota theatre company shows progress in several respects. H. Hewes. Sat R 47:20 Ag 22 '64
Rise of rep. il(p58) Time 83:61 F 14 '64
Second season; Tyrone Guthrie theatre. Newsweek 63:68 My 25 '64
Starting from scratch. Theatre Arts 47:9 Ag '63
Theatre; Tyrone Guthrie theatre. H. Clurman. Nation 197:78-9 Ag 10 '63
Theatrical dream come true makes a miracle in Minneapolis; Tyrone Guthrie theatre. T. Prideaux. il Life 54:41-4 My 24 '63
Triumph way off Broadway; opening of the new Tyrone Guthrie theatre. il Newsweek 61:86-7 My 20 '63
Tyrone Guthrie: the artist as man of the theatre. R. Hatch. il Horizon 5:35-41 N '63
Tyrone Guthrie theatre. H. Clurman. Nation 199:59-60 Ag 10 '64
View from the East; Tyrone Guthrie theatre opening. R. Gilman. Commonweal 78:282-3 My 31 '63
Water supply
Big step toward automation. B. Corlett. il Am City 78:104-5 O '63
MINNEAPOLIS-Honeywell regulator company
Just plain Honeywell. il Time 82:57 Ag 30 '63
New challenge to IBM; computers by Honeywell and GE. il Bsns W p30 D 7 '63
MINNEAPOLIS public library
Confusion, criticism, and dissent greet new Minneapolis librarian. Library J 89:2564 Je 15 '64
Information retrieval at a book fair. il Library J 88:962-3 Mr 1 '63
Librarian-board relationship to be defined in Minneapolis. Library J 88:2462 Je 15 '63
MINNELLI, Liza
Liza Minnelli: Judy's daughter bows in. S. Castan. il pors Look 27:51-4 My 21 '63
Momma's girl; J. Garland's daughter. N. Poirier. pors Sat Eve Post 236:30-1 O 5 '63
Second generation, Garland style. por Sr Schol 84:14 Ja 31 '64
MINNESOTA
See also
Fishing—Minnesota
Hunting—Minnesota
Land—Minnesota
Mines and mineral resources—Minnesota
Climate
Flyin-n-fishin weather in Minnesota. E. E. John. il Flying 74:33 Je '64
Description and travel
Gone flying to Minnesota. V. M. Draper. il Flying 74:28-32+ Je '64
Land of the sky blue water. R. Deardorff. il Redbook 123:70-1+ S '64
Minnesota wilderness. J. R. Humphreys. il Holiday 33:22+ Je '63
Minnesota's winter magic. K. F. Rolvaag. il Travel 122:30-4 D '64
History
Phantom cities in a promised land; with reproductions of paintings. B. L. Heilbron. il Am Heritage 14:52-7 Je '63
Industries
Constitutional balm for an old sore; occupation taxes in Minnesota's mining industry. Bsns W p 112 S 14 '63
See also
Minnesota mining and manufacturing company
Politics and government
Long recount; election of Minnesota's governor. il Newsweek 61:27-8 Mr 11 '63
Minnesota winner, recount court picks Rolvaag. U S News 54:16 Ap 1 '63
Senator Eugene McCarthy: how to succeed by ignoring your well-wishers. M. Smelser. Harper 228:76-8 Je '64

MINNESOTA—Politics and government—*Cont.*
Who after Hubert? il Time 84:42 N 13 '64
Winner by decision; Minnesota's gubernatorial election. Newsweek 61:27 Ap 1 '63

Race problems

Adopting Negro children. E. Shepherd. New Repub 150:10-12 Je 20 '64

Religious institutions and affairs

News of the Christian world (cont) Christian Cent 80:442-4, 786-8, 1010-12, 1180, 1253-4, 1592-4; 81:252-4, 444-6, 778, 834, 1249-52 Ap 3, Je 12, Ag 14, S 25, O 9, D 18 '63, F 19, Ap 1, Je 10, 24, O 7 '64

MINNESOTA mining and manufacturing company
3M's formula for new products. T. R. Brooks. il Duns R 82:32-4+ Ag '63
Up from scratch. il Time 84:90+ N 6 '64

MINNESOTA multiphasic personality inventory. See Personality tests

MINNESOTA theatre company. See Minneapolis—Theater

MINNESOTA Twins (baseball) See Baseball clubs

MINNESOTA. University, Minneapolis
Statement by Board of regents of the University of Minnesota on freedom and the university. Sch & Soc 92:108-9 Mr 7 '64

MINNEY, Doris
Devil's Tower. Travel 119:52-3 Ap '63

MINNIS, Jack, and Lynd, Staughton
Seeds of doubt. New Repub 149:14-17+ D 21 '63

MINNIS, Roy B.
Federal aid for the illiterate; address, April 8, 1964 por Wilson Lib Bul 38:844+ Je '64
What's being done: the poverty program; summary of address. Pub W 185:38-9 My 4 '64

MINNOWS
Sure-locked sewed minnow. B. Riviere. il Outdoor Life 131:86 Ap '63

MINOAN inscriptions. See Inscriptions, Minoan

MINOR, Audax, pseud.
Race track. See issues of New Yorker

MINOR, Norman S.
Cleveland's living legend in law. C. L. Sanders. il pors Ebony 19:48-50+ N '63

MINOR, W. H.
Double CB talk power. Pop Electr 20:54-7 Ap '64

MINOR league baseball. See Baseball

MINOR planets. See Asteroids

MINORITIES
Beyond the melting pot, by N. Glazer and D. P. Moynihan. Review
Reporter 29:59-60 O 10 '63. G. Paulding
Bosses, machines, and ethnic groups. E. E. Cornwell, jr. bibliog f il Ann Am Acad 353:27-39 My '64
Do minorities tyrannize American life? address, November 15, 1963. L. R. Sussman. bibliog Vital Speeches 30:125-8 D 1 '63
Ethnic and economic minorities: unions' future or unrecruitable? R. Marshall. bibliog f Ann Am Acad 350:63-73 N '63
Ethnic backlash? J. W. Carey. Commonweal 81:91-3 O 16 '64
Ethnic minorities around the world; discussion at Philadelphia AAAS meeting. M. H. Fried. Science 139:1304-5 Mr 29 '63
Not only the Negroes. Nation 197:102 S 7 '63
Politics in a pluralist democracy: studies of voting in the 1960 election, by L. S. Dawidowicz and L. J. Goldstein. Review
Commentary 38:87-9 O '64. D. P. Moynihan
Recent trends in the study of minority and race relations. M. M. Gordon. bibliog f Ann Am Acad 350:148-56 N '63
Responses & reactions; excerpts from The Presidential papers. N. Mailer. Commentary 36:320-1 O '63
Treatment of minority groups in textbooks; adaptation of address, October 2, 1964. A. J. McCaffrey. Pub W 186:22-7 O 12 '64
U.S. jobs: gains for minorities. U S News 56:96 Mr 16 '64
See also
United Nations—Subcommission on prevention of discrimination and protection of minorities

MINOW, Newton N.
Après moi. . . Newsweek 61:33 Je 17 '63
Important developments in communications; address, April 2, 1963. Vital Speeches 29:425-30 My 1 '63
Leading voice in a priceless cause. PTA Mag 57:19 F '63

about

Continuing contract: FCC chairmen. R. L. Shayon. Sat R 46:32 Je 22 '63
FCC gets tougher. por Bsns W p38+ Ap 20 '63
Minow's farewell. New Repub 149:5 Jl 13 '63
Musical chairs. Newsweek 61:29-30 My 27 '63
Partial insight of Mr Minow. W. F. Buckley, jr. Nat R 14:442 Je 4 '63
Sponsor for quality. New Repub 148:3-5 My 4 '63
TV commercials: the government ducks the issue. D. Smith. Nation 198:286-9 Mr 23 '64

MINSCH, Jos
Swiss skier surprises the Austrians. R. Terrell. il por Sports Illus 18:18-21 F 25 '63

MINSTRELS
See also
Troubadours

MINT (United States) See United States—Mint

MINTS (botany)
Add a row of mint. D. E. Stebbins. Pop Gard 14:82-3 My '63
Bed of mint. D. E. Stebbins. il Horticulture 41:254-5 My '63

MINTZ, Donald E.
Force of response during ratio reinforcement. bibliog Science 138:516-17; 139:1129 O 26 '62, Mr 15 '63

MINTZ, Morton
New drugs: is government supervision adequate? Reporter 28:46-9+ Mr 28 '63

MINUTE forty seven of the second; story. See Mayer, T.

MINUTE maid company
Can orange juice fill pause that refreshes? il Bsns W p 100+ Jl 25 '64

MINUTEMAN (guided missile) See Guided missiles

MINUTEMEN (organization)
Don't wait, buy a gun now! J. Ridgeway. New Repub 150:9-10 Je 6 '64

MIOCENE period. See Geology, Stratigraphic—Miocene

MIRA, George
Mira-cle worker. H. L. Masin. por Sr Schol 83:26 O 11 '63
One wonderful conch is this Mira. J. Underwood. il pors Sports Illus 19:96-102+ S 23 '63

MIRABEAU, Roch L.
Can Haiti be helped? Nation 196:416-18 My 18 '63

MIRACLE, Leonard
Cougar for everybody. por Outdoor Life 134:44-7+ D '64
(ed) See Altieri, J. Boar for the Bronx

MIRACLE fruit. See Berries

MIRACLE of spring; drama. See Hanna, H.

MIRAMICHI RIVER
Love letter to the Miramichi. C. T. Coiner. il Esquire 60:116-19+ S '63

MIREL, Elizabeth
Golden rule invalid in space. Sci N L 85:106-7 F 15 '64

MIRÓ, Joan
Miró, Artigas; their new ceramics. D. Ashton. il por Craft Horiz 24:24-33+ Ja '64
Two masters of modern art. H. Read. Reporter 28:38-40 Je 6 '63

MIRÓ CARDONA, José
Refugee leader blames U.S. for broken promise; excerpts from statement, April 18, 1963. por U S News 54:65-7+ Ap 29 '63

about

Another Cuban fiasco? il por U S News 54:33-6 Ap 29 '63
Cuban refugee leader quits. Christian Cent 80:573 My 1 '63
Department replies to statements by Dr Miró Cardona. statements, April 15 and April 18, 1963. Dept State Bul 48:709-10 My 6 '63
Miró and Kennedy: the bitter moment. por Newsweek 61:19-20 Ap 29 '63
That month: April's cruelty. il por Time 81:21-2 Ap 26 '63
We should help the Cuban exiles find a leader. Life 54:4 My 3 '63

MIROV, Nicholas T.
Notes of a traveling forester: Burma and Thailand. Am For 69:4-5+ F '63
Notes of a traveling forester; Java. Am For 69:39+ Jl '63

MIRRO aluminum company
Quality aluminum cookware. E. M. McCabe. il Parents Mag 39:22+ My '64

MIRROR, New York (newspaper) See New York mirror

MIRROR photography. See Photography, Trick

MIRRORS
American looking glass. H. Comstock. il Antiques 85:314-19, 438-41, 679-85 Mr-Ap, Je '64
New border for a worn mirror. il Sunset 131:120 N '63
Putting mirrors to work. il Sunset 130:142+ Je '63

MIRRORS, Automobile. See Automobiles—Equipment
MIRRORS for telescopes
Amateur scientist; how to grind, polish and test an aluminum telescope mirror. W. C. Peterson. il Sci Am 209:159-60+ N '63
Refiguring the 82-inch McDonald reflector's optics. J. Texereau. il Sky & Tel 28:345-8 D '64
MIRSKY, A. E.
Books. Sci Am 211:135-8 O '64; 212:7-9 Ja '65
MIRSKY, Arthur
Polar geology. Science 143:1196-7 Mr 13 '64
MIRT, John A.
Renaissance in botanical drugs. Todays Health 41:42-5+ My '63
MIRTO, Anthony A.
No refuse refused. Am City 79:117-18 Ap '64
MIRVISH, Robert F.
Runaways; story. Ladies Home J 80:62-3 Mr '63
MISCARRIAGE. See Abortion
MISCARRIAGE of justice. See Justice, Miscarriage of
MISCEGENATION. See Intermarriage of races
MISCHE, Lena Wyan
Your child's intelligence; reprint. Todays Health 41:74 S '63
MISCONDUCT in office
Incorruptible John Williams; the conscience of the Senate. J. Daniel. Read Digest 84:105-10 My '64
MISHELL, Robert I. and Fahey, J. L.
Molecular and submolecular localization of two isoantigens of mouse immunoglobulins. bibliog Science 143:1440-2 Mr 27 '64
MISHIMA, Yukio
Famous Japanese judges the U.S. giant; tr. by D. Keene. por Life 57:81+ S 11 '64
MISHLER, Katharine B.
Why we have two brains. Sci Digest 56:81-4 Ag '64
MISNER, Paul J.
(ed) Restoration of report cards. PTA Mag 58:10-12 bibliog(p36) F '64
MISREPRESENTATION. See Fraud
MISS America contests. See Beauty contests
MISS Forsythe is missing; drama. See Murray, J.
MISS Hattie's lawn party; story. See Durant, M.
MISS Hepplewhite takes over; drama. See Murray, J.
MISS Louisa and the outlaws; drama. See Watts, F. B.
MISS Rheingold contests. See Beauty contests
MISS Teen-age America contests. See Beauty contests
MISSALS
King's treasure; Gotha missal. il Newsweek 62:73 Ag 19 '63
Liturgy and scripture: 1964; new missals. C. J. McNaspy. America 111:744 D 5 '64
Should you buy a new missal? J. F. Dearden. America 111:180-1 Ag 22 '64
MISSILE ranges. See Proving grounds
MISSILE simulator. See Flight simulators
MISSILE tracking ships. See Ships
MISSILEMEN. See Guided missile crews
MISSILES, Antitank. See Antitank missiles
MISSILES, Guided. See Guided missiles
MISSILES and rockets (periodical)
Memo from the publisher (cont) J. W. Claar. Miss & Roc 12:6 Mr 25; 13:50 S 23 '63; 14:3 Ja 6; Mr 30 '64; 16:6 Ja 4 '65
Rocket research solid microrocket wins award. il Miss & Roc 12:34-5 Ap 29 '63
MISSING books. See Libraries—Book losses
MISSING persons
Child is lost. J. P. Blank. il Redbook 120:48-9+ F '63
Long search of Laurie Van Buren. A. Hirshberg. il Good H 157:64-5+ Jl '63
Vanishing Americans. il Newsweek 63:88 F 24 '64
When a child is missing. J. E. Hoover. il Parents Mag 38:67+ Mr '63
MISSION BAY
Spend a wonderful day at Mission Bay. il Sunset 133:44-51 Ag '64
MISSION schools
Changing church. America 108:432 Mr 30 '63
MISSION; story. See Friedman, B. J.
MISSIONARIES
Death of the missionaries; victims in South Viet Nam. Time 81:44 Mr 15 '63
Go ye therefore, and teach all nations. P. Streit. il N Y Times Mag p 12+ Mr 22 '64
Joseph and Mary Gomer, missionaries. M. H. Miller. Negro Hist Bul 26:163-4 F '63
Missionary's mission in the world today. il Newsweek 62:36-9 D 30 '63
My clothes were blood-soaked, but I never moved; American missionary among rebels in Kwilu province, Congo, ed. by B. Lindeman. R. Hege. il Sat Eve Post 237:84-5 O 3 '64
Racial strife hinders mission work; excerpts from address. D. Kitagawa. Christian Cent 80:876 Jl 10 '63
See also
Missions
MISSIONARY conferences
Church and world; meeting of Commission on world mission and evangelism in Mexico city. D. Peerman. Christian Cent 81:104-5 Ja 22 '64
Home base is everywhere; meeting of Commission on world mission and evangelism, in Mexico city. D. Peerman. Christian Cent 81:70-2 Ja 15 '64
MISSIONARY societies
Commandos in the city; Chicago city missionary society. il Time 83:56 F 21 '64
MISSIONS
Ecumenical beginnings in Protestant world mission: a history of comity, by R. P. Beaver. Review
Christian Cent 80:1007 Ag 14 '63. C. Lacy
End of an era? Commonweal 80:164 My 1 '64
Everyman's burden: international flavor of mission work. Time 82:53 D 27 '63
Go ye therefore, and teach all nations. P. Streit. il N Y Times Mag p 12+ Mr 22 '64
Methodist missions retooled; General conference. B. Thompson. Christian Cent 81:1273 O 14 '64
Mission ecumenism. America 112:155 Ja 30 '65
Missionary's mission in the world today. il Newsweek 62:36-9 D 30 '63
Two worlds or none; Christian missions in secular as well as spiritual milieu. W. J. Danker. Christian Cent 80:737-9 Je 5 '63
Two worlds or none: rediscovering missions, by W. J. Danker. Review
Christian Cent 81:1040 Ag 19 '64. J. A. Scherer
See also
Catholic church—Missions
Church of England—Missions
Evangelistic work

Africa
Sir Francis Ibiam condemns missionaries; address to 12,000 youth of the World council of churches. Christian Cent 81:1133 S 16 '64
See also
Christians in Africa

Brazil
Heart on the hill; mission in a favela, Rio de Janeiro. il Newsweek 62:80 Jl 22 '63

China
See also
Catholic church in China

Indians of North America
See Indians of North America—Missions

Sudan
Sudan expels missionaries; discussion. Christian Cent 80:276, 293-4 F 27-Mr 6 '63
Sudan tightens control of Christians. Christian Cent 80:387 Mr 27 '63
Sundown on Christianity in the Sudan. V. J. Dunigan. il Cath World 199:245-52 Jl '64

United States
See also
Indians of North America—Missions
MISSIONS, Medical
See also
Catholic medical mission board
MISSIONS, Military. See Military missions
MISSISSIPPI
Mississippi; suggested cut-off of federal funds. New Repub 148:3-4 Ap 27 '63
See also
Crime and criminals—Mississippi
Education—Mississippi
Fishing—Mississippi
Forests and forestry—Mississippi
Law—Mississippi
Medicine—Mississippi

Economic conditions
Economic pinch aids racial justice. Christian Cent 82:102 Ja 27 '65

Police
Mississippi mischief. America 108:351 Mr 16 '63

MISSISSIPPI—*Continued*

Politics and government

Aaron Henry and his friends; it takes guts to work for LBJ in Mississippi. R. A. Woodley. New Repub 151:6-7 O 10 '64
Battle of the Kennedys. Newsweek 62:24+ Ag 19 '63
Change of command. il Newsweek 63:26-7 F 3 '64
Editor's easy chair: a small band of practical heroes. J. Fischer. Harper 227:16+ O '63; Discussion. 227:4 D '63
End of the beginning; Freedom democratic party. Nation 199:82-3 S 7 '64
End to Republican party in Mississippi. U S News 56:8 Mr 30 '64
Enemies of radical nonsense. G. W. Johnson. New Repub 151:27-8 O 17 '64
God bless everyone; concerning Governor Johnson's inaugural address. Time 83:22 Ja 31 '64
GOP in Mississippi. R. Moley. Newsweek 61:112 My 13 '63
If you try & don't succeed; runoff for governor. Time 82:17 Ag 16 '63
Justice and power. Nation 200:2-3 Ja 4 '65
Mississippi politics. R. Moley. Newsweek 63: 92 Ap 6 '64
Routine for red-necks. Newsweek 62:35-6 O 14 '63
Safe for democracy. Newsweek 63:22 Ap 6 '64
Upset of upsets? Time 82:29 O 25 '63
What's in a name? Mississippi Democratic convention. Newsweek 64:34 S 21 '64
Who speaks for Mississippi? R. Gleghorn. Reporter 31:31-4 Ag 13 '64
Who was right? P. B. Johnson jr's gubernatorial campaign. il Newsweek 62:25 S 9 '63

Race problems

All you have to do is lie. J. Beecher. New Repub 151:9-10 O 24 '64
Allen's army; civil-rights demonstrations deterrent force. il Newsweek 63:30 F 24 '64
And three letters home from Mississippi. P. Cowan; G. Cowan. Esquire 62:105-6+ S '64
Angry language; interim report considers cutting off federal funds for Mississippi. Newsweek 61:25-6 Ap 29 '63
Bowl of gumbo for Curtis Bryant. P. Good. il Reporter 31:19-22 D 31 '64
Cat and mouse game. E. Sutherland. il Nation 199:105-8 S 14 '64
Church burning. Commonweal 81:28 O 2 '64
Civil rights; do not despair. Time 84:35 N 27 '64
Closed society. Time 82:37 N 15 '63
Communique from the Mississippi front; war is the word for the civil-rights struggle. J. Herbers. il N Y Times Mag p34-5+ N 8 '64
Congressional challenge; Mississippi Freedom Democratic party's efforts to remove Mississippi's five congressmen from their seats in the House. Commonweal 81:532 Ja 22 '65
Congressman from Mississippi, by F. F. Smith. Review
Sat R 47:41 O 10 '64. E. M. Yoder, jr
Crime called conspiracy; Neshoba County's law officers charged with complicity in the murder of three civil rights workers. il Time 84:29-30 D 11 '64
Cruel and unusual punishments. D. Lawrence. U S News 54:108 Ap 29 '63
Crusade in Mississippi. A. Poinsett. il Ebony 19:25-8+ S '64
Curse & the hope; W. Faulkner's vision. il Time 84:44-8 Jl 17 '64
Day of accusation in Mississippi; Mississippians implicated in murder of civil rights workers; with report by D. Nevin. il Life 57:34-9 D 18 '64
Dialogue; telephone calls between Attorney General Kennedy and Governor Barnett prior to arrival of Negro student J. Meredith. Newsweek 62:36 O 14 '63
Disgrace of Mississippi. America 111:8-9 Jl 4 '64
Editor's easy chair: a small band of practical heroes. J. Fischer. Harper 227:16+ O '63; Discussion. 227:4 D '63
Educator; Mississippi summer project. R. J. Bernstein. il Nation 199:512-15 D 28 '64
End terrorist rule! Christian Cent 81:875 Jl 8 '64
Enforce the Constitution. Nation 199:1 Jl 13 '64
Evangelists; Council of federated organizations campaign. il Newsweek 64:30-2 Ag 24 '64
FBI suspects freed. Sr Schol 85:19 Ja 7 '65
Fund for burned churches and for church burners; by N.C.C. Christian Cent 81:1054 Ag 26 '64
G.O.P. and the gap. M. Mannes. Reporter 31: 28-30 Ag 13 '64
Grim roster; disappearance of three civil rights workers. il Time 84:19-20 Jl 3 '64
He said he wouldn't mind dying if. . . M. Evers. il Life 54:34-7 Je 28 '63
If we can crack Mississippi. . . J. Atwater. il Sat Eve Post 237:15-19 Jl 25 '64
Indictments this time; case of murdered civil rights workers. Time 85:21 Ja 22 '65
Inquiry into the Mississippi mind. C. Sitton. il N Y Times Mag p 13+ Ap 28 '63
Invaders; volunteers for voter-registration drives and cultural programs. il Newsweek 63:25-6 Je 29 '64
It will be a hot summer in Mississippi; Council of federated organizations and Freedom schools projects. R. Woodley. Reporter 30: 21-4 My 21 '64
Journey to understanding; four witnesses to a Mississippi summer; symposium. il Nation 199:507-16 D 28 '64
Judgment in Mississippi; arraignment and release of twenty-one persons in connection with murder of civil rights workers. G. W. Johnson. New Repub 151:13-14 D 26 '64
Justice in Mississippi; notes on the Beckwith trial. J. Herron. Nation 198:179-81 F 24 '64
Land within a land; deaths of three civil rights workers. Commonweal 80:561-2 Ag 21 '64
Lest we forget; list of church buildings in Mississippi destroyed or damaged by fire or bomb this summer. America 111:369 O 3 '64
Letter from Jackson. C. Trillin. New Yorker 40:80+ Ag 29 '64
Life for a vote. J. Hersey. il Sat Eve Post 237:34-8+ S 26 '64
Life in Liberty. Nation 198:254 Mr 16 '64
Limpid shambles of violence; search for three missing civil rights workers. il Life 57:32-34B Jl 3 '64
Martyr to an immoral system. Life 54:4 Je 28 '63
Mass arrests in civil-rights killings. il U S News 57:11 D 14 '64
Methodist ministers shatter vacuum; ministers in Mississippi condemn discrimination by race, color or creed. Christian Cent 80:229 F 20 '63
Mississippi. C. Jencks. New Repub 151:15-18 Jl 25; 17-21 Ag 22 '64
Mississippi. Nat R 16:573-5 Jl 14 '64
Mississippi airlift; cessation of free federal surplus-food allotments. Newsweek 61:30+ Mr 11 '63
Mississippi: closed society, by J. Silver. Review
New Repub 151:19-21 Jl 4 '64. I. Howe
Mississippi dilemma. Nat R 16:1136-7 D 29 '64
Mississippi, everybody's scared. il Newsweek 64:15-16 Jl 6 '64
Mississippi; gang law. New Repub 151:5-6 Jl 4 '64
Mississippi girds for its summer of discontent. il U S News 56:46-8 Je 15 '64
Mississippi murders. America 112:153 Ja 30 '65
Mississippi murders: twenty-one arrests. il Newsweek 64:21-2 D 14 '64
Mississippi must choose. J. W. Silver. il N Y Times Mag p8+ Jl 19 '64
Mississippi now: hate and fear. H. Carter. il N Y Times Mag p 11+ Je 23 '63
Mississippi: storm signals. il U S News 57:37 Jl 6 '64
Mississippi, summer of 1964: troubled state, troubled time. il Newsweek 64:18-20 Jl 13 '64
Mississippi terror; church bombings and burnings. America 111:431 O 17 '64
Mississippi: the attack on bigotry. C. S. Wren. il Look 28:20-8 S 8 '64
Mississippi: the closed society, by J. W. Silver. Review
New Yorker 40:107-12 Ag 15 '64. C. Trillin
Mississippi; when law collides with custom. C. Jencks. New Repub 151:15-18 Jl 25 '64
Mississippians create committee of concern. Christian Cent 81:1230, 1293 O 7, 21 '64; Discussion. 81:1505 D 2 '64
Must we hate? A. MacLeish. Atlan 211:79-82 F '63
Naught for your comfort: a case history. Christian Cent 81:895 Jl 8 '64
Next step in Mississippi; boycott of Mississippi goods. Christian Cent 81:1583 D 23 '64
Night and day in Mississippi; arrest of twenty-one Mississippians by the F.B.I. Christian Cent 81:1550 D 16 '64

MISSISSIPPI—Race problems—*Continued*
Old times there are not forgiven. R. Dugger. Nation 198:659-60 Je 29 '64
Out in the open. Nation 199:478 D 21 '64
Philadelphia indictments; case of Mississippi murders. Time 84:29 O 9 '64
Problem of Mississippi. America 111:792 D 19 '64
Racists attack Tougaloo. Christian Cent 81:422 Ap 1 '64
Rebuilding burned churches: progress report. Christian Cent 82:102 Ja 27 '65
Recollection of Michael Schwerner. R. Woodley. Reporter 31:23-4 Jl 16 '64
Ruleville: reminiscence, reflection. R. C. Marius. Christian Cent 81:1169-71 S 23 '64; Discussion. 81:1468 N 25 '64
Silver of Ole Miss. Nation 197:358 N 30 '63
Some good men there are. J. Ciardi. Sat R 46:17 Je 29 '63
Southern teen-ager speaks his mind. M. Long. il N Y Times Mag p 15+ N 10 '63
Stranger in Philadelphia, Mississippi. J. Lelyveld. il N Y Times Mag p5+ D 27 '64
Strategic retreat; charges dropped against twenty-one men. il Time 84:23 D 18 '64
Summer storms. Newsweek 63:45-6 Je 8 '64
Terrible silence of the decent. Life 57:4 Jl 10 '64
Terror on schedule. il Newsweek 64:71-2 O 5 '64
Their dream is not to be nervous; a volunteer with Mississippi summer project reports on teaching in a freedom school; interview, ed. by G. Illig. L. Guest. il Mlle 60:164-5+ N '64
This is Mississippi. il U S News 57:35 Jl 13 '64
Tired of being sick and tired. J. DeMuth. Nation 198:548-51 Je 1 '64
Underground election: Negro mock campaign. J. Herron. il Nation 197:387-9 D 7 '63
Uneasy conscience at a county fair. L. Wainwright. Life 57:15 Ag 21 '64
Untold story of the Mississippi murders. W. B. Huie. il Sat Eve Post 237:11-15 S 5 '64
Very good folks; eighteen indicted in murder of three civil-rights workers. il Newsweek 65:26+ Ja 25 '65
VIPs regret. Nation 198:497 My 18 '64
Why burn Negro churches? Christian Cent 81:956 Jl 29 '64

Religious institutions and affairs

Church secession; Church partition bill. F. Larkin. America 111:90-1 Jl 25 '64
Out of the ashes; funds for rebuilding burned Negro churches. il Newsweek 64:72 O 12 '64
Ruleville: reminiscence, reflection. R. C. Marius. Christian Cent 81:1169-71 S 23 '64; Discussion. 81:1468 N 25 '64

Social conditions

Account of some conversations on U. S. 45. F. Trippett. il Newsweek 64:21-3 Jl 13 '64
Why I live in Mississippi; interview, ed. by F. H. Mitchell. il Ebony 18:143-8 S '63

MISSISSIPPI delta pipe line. See Gas, Natural—Pipe lines

MISSISSIPPI library association
Mississippi's silence scored; letter to the editor. Library J 88:4410+ N 15 '63

MISSISSIPPI recreation association
Playground leaders workshop. A. Elliott. Recreation 57:179 Ap '64

MISSISSIPPI RIVER
Bungalow barges, fish bats, and bass. D. Shaw. il Field & S 69:48-51+ My '64
Businessmen at the bar; Mississippi River pilots. il Bsns W p32-4 Ap 18 '64
Cruising the upper Mississippi. F. M. Paulson. il Field & S 69:62-5+ Je '64
Journey down the Mississippi. E. Waldron. il Holiday 33:80-93+ My '63; Same abr. Read Digest 83:142-51 Jl '63
Mayfly distribution indicates water quality on the upper Mississippi River. C. R. Fremling. bibliog il Science 146:1164-6 N 27 '64
Mississippi: down, around and upon it. Holiday 33:176 My '63
Mississippi River adventure. H. Bradshaw and V. Bradshaw. il Suc Farm 61:50-2 Ag '63
To kill a river. R. Terral. il Bul Atomic Sci 20:35-7 S '64

Regulation

Ol' Man River meets his match. E. D. Fales, jr. il Pop Sci 183:48-53+ Jl '63

MISSISSIPPI State university, State College, Miss.
Repeal of the unwritten law; MSU vs desegregated teams. Sports Illus 18:10 Mr 18 '63

MISSISSIPPI. University
Closed society; Professor Silver. Newsweek 62:66+ N 18 '63
Dean departs from Ole Miss; R. J. Farley of the law school. R. Cleghorn. Reporter 29:42 O 24 '63
Dialogue; telephone calls between Attorney General Kennedy and Governor Barnett prior to arrival of Negro student J. Meredith. Newsweek 62:36 O 14 '63
Draftee's diary from the Mississippi front. C. Vanderburgh. il Harper 228:37-45 F '64
Fast action at Ole Miss; expulsion of Negro for carrying pistol. Newsweek 62:40+ O 7 '63
I can't fight alone. J. H. Meredith. il Look 27:70-2+ Ap 9 '63
Must we hate? A. MacLeish. Atlan 211:79-82 F '63
New term, new South. il Newsweek 61:29 F 11 '63
No indictment in case against Walker. U S News 54:19 F 4 '63
Ole Miss exodus; resignations of professors. Time 81:63 My 24 '63
Quiet progress in the South. Life 54:4 F 8 '63
Revolt of the professors. R. Cleghorn. New Repub 148:5-6 F 2 '63
Some good men there are. J. Ciardi. Sat R 46:17 Je 29 '63
What it cost to keep troops at Ole Miss. U S News 55:14 Ag 5 '63
What went on at Ole Miss; excerpts from report by Mississippi legislative committee. il U S News 54:77 My 20 '63

MISSISSIPPI VALLEY
Journey down the Mississippi. E. Waldron. il Holiday 33:80-93+ My '63; Same abr. Read Digest 83:142-51 Jl '63

MISSISSIPPIANS
Account of some conversations on U. S. 45. F. Trippett. il Newsweek 64:21-3 Jl 13 '64

MISSOURI
See also
Current River
Fishing—Missouri
Libraries—Missouri
Prisons—Missouri

Economic conditions

Poverty's second generation. F. W. Lindecke. il Nation 199:163-5 S 28 '64

Parks and reserves

Park of champions; Big Oak Tree State Park. J. P. Jackson. il Am For 69:9+ My '63

Registration of the healing arts, State board of

Medicine in Missouri. New Repub 151:5 D 19 '64

MISSOURI penitentiary for men. See Prisons—Missouri

MISSOURI RIVER
Busy days on the Big Muddy; portfolio. Fortune 68:154-9 N '63
Missouri River cruise. R. J. Smith. il Yachting 116:40-3+ Jl '64
Who'll get Big Muddy campsites? Missouri's development. il Bsns W p30-1 My 4 '63

MISTAKEN identity. See Identification

MISTAKES. See Errors

MISTARAS, Evangeline
Chicago restaurants and night life. ALA Bul 57:565-70 Je '63

MR Bates goes to the polls; drama. See Reay, N. B.

MR Grossman; drama. See Koven, S.

MR Simian; drama. See Kerman, S.

MR TRAVEL award
Bob Hope wins tenth annual Travel award. il Travel 121:36-8 Je '64
Voit Gilmore wins annual Travel award. il Travel 119:38-40 My '63

MR Wharton; story. See Taylor, E.

MRS Capper's birthday party; story. See Coward, N.

MRS Merriweather's black nightgown; story. See Spigelgass, L.

MRS Schyler's plot; story. See Gordon, W. J.

MRS Warren's profession; drama. See Shaw, G. B.

MISTLETOE
Magic of mistletoe. W. H. Scheib. il Sci Digest 54:61-3 D '63

MISTRESS; story. See Berriault, G.

MITCHELL, Arthur W.
Ex-solon still active twenty years after retirement. il pors Ebony 18:40-2+ Ag '63

MITCHELL, C. Bradford
Farewell to the ferry. Am Heritage 15:38-49 Ap '64
MITCHELL, Carleton
Boating (cont) Sports Illus 20:46-8 F 17; 60-1 Mr 2; 74+ Je 15; 21:54-6 N 9 '64
East of the race and west of the Cape. Sports Illus 19:46-54 Jl 22 '63
Fad and fascination of surfing. Holiday 35: 122+ My '64
Heaping cupful of twelves. Sports Illus 20:67-8+ My 18 '64
Heritage of Hiroshige. Sports Illus 19:106-10+ D 23 '63
Less a race than a ghastly rout. Sports Illus 21:30-4+ S 28 '64
On the high end of a seesaw. Sports Illus 21:18-21+ S 14 '64
MITCHELL, Chris
Better late than later. NEA J 52:23 D '63
MITCHELL, Clarence, 3d
Nation's youngest lawmaker. il pors Ebony 19:135-6+ Je '64
MITCHELL, Donald
Operas of Britten. Mus Am 84:22-5+ D '64
MITCHELL, Francis H.
(ed) See Evers, M. Why I live in Mississippi
MITCHELL, George D. 3d
Serving the teenager. Library J 89:1817-19 Ap 15 '64
MITCHELL, Harold L.
Burlwood, royalty's wood? Am For 70:22-5 D '64
MITCHELL, J. G.
Drop thy pipe. Atlan 213:174+ Mr '64
MITCHELL, J. Murray, jr
What caused the drought and when will it end? interview. por U S News 57:54-5 N 30 '64
MITCHELL, James E.
Commutaboat hydrofoil. Motor B 111:38-9 F '63
MITCHELL, James P.
Business and civil rights; address, June 5; 1964. Vital Speeches 30:549-51 Jl 1 '64
In defense of politics; address, January 25 1963. Vital Speeches 29:340-3 Mr 15 '63

about

James P. Mitchell: 1900-1964. H. Hamilton. America 111:508 O 31 '64
MITCHELL, Jean O.
Our new school. Sch Arts 63:10-11 N '63
MITCHELL, John W. and Worley, J. F.
Intracellular transport apparatus of phloem fibers. bibliog Science 145:409-10 Jl 24 '64
MITCHELL, Johnny
He's half wildcatter, half big businessman. il pors Bsns W p 103-4+ N 14 '64
MITCHELL, Joseph
Profiles. New Yorker 40:61-2+ S 19; 53-4+ S 26 '64
MITCHELL, Joseph B.
Beginnings of victory at sea. Sat R 47: 27 Ag 1 '64
MITCHELL, Joseph McDowell
Crusade against the poor; relief chiselers in 1961, Newburgh, N.Y. F. M. Eckman. il por Redbook 120:58-9+ F '63
Jury justice. por Newsweek 61:33-4 My 6 '63
Recruit for a cause. por Newsweek 62:24 Jl 22 '63
MITCHELL, Leon
Building for church recreation Recreation 57:222-3+ My '64
MITCHELL, Lucy Sprague
In the beginning there is a key word. Sat R 46:45 O 5 '63
MITCHELL, Mabel M.
Implementing the code of ethics. NEA J 53: 41 D '64
MITCHELL, Margaret
Scarlett O'Hara's millions. F. Knebel. il Look 27:39-40+ D 3 '63
MITCHELL, Maria
Summer at Maria Mitchell observatory. D. Hoffleit. il Sky & Tel 27:274-5 My '64
MITCHELL, Mary Jean
Echo of heroes. L. Hershey. il por McCalls 91:46+ Jl '64
MITCHELL, Maurice B.
Strange world of our children; excerpts from address, May 1964. PTA Mag 59:8-10 S '64

about

Mitch's biggest pitch. J. Tebbel. por Sat R 46:69-70+ N 9 '63; Reply. W. H. Niblock. 46:66 D 14 '63
MITCHELL, Robert A.
Border-to-border lighting. por Am City 79: 138 Ap '64
MITCHELL, Robert B.
(ed) Urban revival: goals and standards. bibliog f Ann Am Acad 352:1-151 Mr '64
MITCHELL, Robert Cameron
Africa's prophet movements. Christian Cent 81:1427-9 N 18 '64
MITCHELL, Sidney C.
Filling those educational gaps by mail. Parents Mag 38:70+ Mr '63
MITCHELL, Stephens
Scarlett O'Hara's millions. F. Knebel. il por Look 27:39-40+ D 3 '63
MITCHELL, William
Soldier's work between two wars. D. MacArthur. il por Life 57:56+ Jl 3 '64
MITCHELLA repens. See Partridge berries
MITCHELTREE, Wallace A.
Is watering necessary? Horticulture 42:38-9 Ag '64
MITCHUM, Robert
Man who never got to speak for National youth day. H. Lawrenson. il pors Esquire 61:82-5+ My '64
MITELBERG, Louis. See Tim
MITES
See also
Red spiders
MITFORD, Jessica
American way of death; condensation. Good H 158:69-82 F '64
American way of success. Ladies Home J 81: 22+ Je '64
Speaking out. por Sat Eve Post 236:8+ N 23 '63
Undertakers' racket. Atlan 211:56-62 Je '63
Waugh is hell, or anyhow, he was once. Life 57:12+ N 13 '64

about

Re Mitford. Nat R 15:381-2 N 5 '63; Correction. 15:500 D 3 '63
MITFORD, Nancy
Other island. Sat R 46:39-40+ Mr 16 '63
MITGANG, Herbert
D-day plus twenty years. il Look 28:78-85 F 25 '64
Mediterranean mosaic. Harper 226:26+ Ap '63
MITLA, Mexico
Surprise at Mitla. il Sunset 131:50 S '63
MITMAN, Stewart P.
Power-packed purchasing. Am City 79:122-3 D '64
MITOCHONDRIA
Cytochrome content of mitochondria stripped of inner membrane structure. B. Chance and others. bibliog il Science 143:136-9 Ja 10 '64
Cytochrome function in relation to inner membrane structure of mitochondria. B. Chance and D. F. Parsons. bibliog il Science 142:1176-80 N 29 '63
Human myopathy with giant abnormal mitochondria. G. M. Shy and N. K. Gonatas. bibliog il Science 145:493-6 Jl 31 '64
Inside the sausage. il Newsweek 61:99 My 27 '63
Mighty mitochondrion is the powerhouse. il Life 54:54-7 Mr 29 '63
Mitochondrial structure and function, a compostium; report on discussion meeting. B. Chance and R. W. Estabrook. Science 146: 957-8+ N 13 '64
Mitochondrial structure: two types of subunits on negatively stained mitochondrial membranes. D. F. Parsons. bibliog il Science 140:985-7 My 31 '63
Mitochondrion. D. E. Green. il Sci Am 210: 63-6+ bibliog(p 152) Ja '64; Reply with rejoinder. E. Rabinowitch. 210:10+ Ap '64
Participation of an intermediate of oxidative phosphorylation in ion accumulation by mitochondria. G. P. Brierley and others. bibliog il Science 140:60-2 Ap 5 '63
Particles create energy. Sci N L 83:275 My 4 '63
Phosphohistidine. P. D. Boyer. bibliog il Science 141:1147-53 S 20 '63
Plastids and mitochondria: inheritable systems. A. Gibor and S. Granick. bibliog il Science 145:890-7 Ag 28 '64
Protein as the mitochondrial site for action of uncoupling phenols. E. C. Weinbach and J. Garbus. bibliog il Science 145:824-6 Ag 21 '64
Respiratory particle. Sci Am 208:77 Je '63
Subcellular heredity. Sci Am 211:58-9 N '64
Thymidine incorporation by mitochondria in physarum polycephalum. E. Guttes and S. Guttes. bibliog il Science 145:1057-8 S 4 '64
MITOMYCIN
Mitomycin C: chemical and biological studies on alkylation. H. S. Schwartz and others. bibliog il Science 142:1181-3 N 29 '63

MITOMYCIN—*Continued*
Mitomycin C: effect on ribosomes of escherichia coli. H. Suzuki and W. W. Kilgore. bibliog il Science 146:1585-7 D 18 '64
Mitomycins and porfiromycin: chemical mechanism of activation and cross-linking of DNA. V. N. Iyer and W. Szybalski. bibliog il Science 145:55-8 Jl 3 '64
MITOSIS. See Cell division (biology)
MITRE corporation
New AF/Mitre lab may alter concepts. M. Getler. il Miss & Roc 13:36-7 Jl 1 '63
MITROPOULOS, Dimitri, international music competition. See Music—Competitions
MITSUBISHI companies. See Japan—Industries
MITSUI, Yukihiko, and others
Trachoma and inclusion conjunctivitis agents: adaptation to hela cell cultures. bibliog Science 145:715-16 Ag 14 '64
MITTWOCH, Ursula
Sex differences in cells. Sci Am 209:54-62 bibliog(p 170) Jl '63
MITZEL, Harold E.
Can we measure good teaching objectively? NEA J 53:35-6 Ja '64
MIURA, Eduardo
Breeding the bravest of bulls. il por Bsns W p 116-17+ My 25 '63
MIX, Art
Sixty-six years, and still steaming. S. Jackson. il pors Motor T 15:72-3 Je '63
MIX, Ron
I swore I would quit football. pors Sports Illus 19:62-71 S 16 '63
Was this their freedom ride? Sports Illus 22:24-5 Ja 18 '65
about
Mix Master. il Newsweek 62:78 D 16 '63
MIX, Sheldon A.
How to live to be one hundred. Todays Health 42:21-3+ Je '64
How to make that family trip: by plane, train, bus, or car? Todays Health 41:30-5+ F '63
Why do we torture our feet? Todays Health 42:56-7+ My '64
MIXED bloods (American Indians) See Indians of North America—Mixed bloods
MIXED marriages. See Marriages, Mixed
MIXED nuts. See Nuts
MIXERS
See also
Feed mixers and mixing
MIXERS, Concrete. See Concrete mixers
MIXES, Food. See Food mixes
MIXING utensils
See also
Electric apparatus and appliances, Domestic
MIXTEC Indians
Emperors' dye of the Mixtecs. P. Gerhard. il Natur Hist 73:26-31 Ja '64
MIYADI, Denzaburo
Social life of the Japanese monkeys; excerpts from paper. Science 143:783-6 F 21 '64
MIYAKE, A.
Induction of conjugation by cell-free preparations in paramecium multimicronucleatum. bibliog Science 146:1583-5 D 18 '64
MIYOSHI, Kazuo, and others
Abnormal myoglobin in ultraviolet spectrum in Duchenne type of progressive muscular dystrophy. bibliog Science 142:490-1 O 25 '63
MIZENER, Arthur
Books. R. Adler. New Yorker 40:60-8+ Jl 4 '64
MIZER, Jean E.
Cipher in the snow. NEA J 53:8-10 N '64
MOATS, Alice Leone-. See Leone-Moats, A.
MOB violence
Government by mob. D. Lawrence. U S News 55:92 Jl 1 '63
Mental urges of the mob. D. Lawrence. U S News 54:112 Je 17 '63
Mob violence control. W. McCann. Sci N L 86:86 Ag 8 '64
What's become of law and order? D. Lawrence. U S News 55:104 Ag 5 '63
See also
Lynching
MOBIL oil company
Here come the car clinics. D. Francis. il Pop Sci 182:53-6+ Mr '63
MOBIL travel guides. See Guidebooks
MOBILE, Ala.
History in towns. M. R. Ingate. il Antiques 85:294-309 Mr '64
Music
Rose from the South. A. M. Lingg. il Opera N 29:12-14 S 26 '64
MOBILE homes. See Automobile trailers; Campers and coaches, Truck
MOBILE homes manufacturers association
Mobile homes. il Consumer Bul 47:6-12 Je '64
MOBILE libraries. See Libraries
MOBILE medium-range ballistic missile. See Guided missiles
MOBILE photographic tracking station. See Space vehicles—Tracking
MOBILE public address systems. See Loud speaking apparatus
MOBILE stores. See Traveling stores
MOBILE transmitters. See Radio transmitters, Portable
MOBILES
Design in dimension; mobile constructions by Uvaral, Morellet, and LeParc. il Craft Horiz 23:20-3 Ja '63
Letter home. J. Jones. Esquire 61:28+ Mr '64
Man who made sculpture move. J. Canaday. il N Y Times Mag p32-3 N 1 '64
Mobiles, moods in motion. il Design 66:39 S '64
Non-scientific insect mobiles; fifth grade. C. J. Alkema. il Sch Arts 64:10-13 N '64
Perpetual motion. F. Getlein. New Repub 151:33-4+ O 3 '64
They swing in the rings; Kachina dolls. il Sunset 132:140 Je '64
MOBILGAS economy run. See Automobile engines—Fuel consumption
MOBILITY, Occupational. See Occupational mobility
MOBILITY, Social. See Social mobility
MOBILIZATION for youth, incorporated
Antipoverty agency that is under fire. U S News 57:14 N 23 '64
Evening at Club 169. il N Y Times Mag p82-3 My 10 '64
Honest mistake; Communist infiltration. Nat R 16:758-60 S 8 '64
MFY. Nat R 16:1045-6 D 1 '64
Mobilization for youth: feuding over poverty; excerpts from Hard times, good times. H. Krosney. il Nation 199:455-61 D 14 '64
Money isn't everthing. Nation 199:395-6 N 30 '64
Second chance for the unemployables; training of slum youths. il Bsns W p34 Je 8 '63
Tryout in Harlem. D. L. Hackett. New Repub 148:38 Ap 13 '63
We can beat J.D; New York's Mobilization for youth. H. Page. il Parents Mag 39:56-8+ O '64
When you mobilize the poor. M. Kempton. New Repub 151:11-13 D 5 '64; Reply. G. Brager. 151:30 D 19 '64
MOBLEY, Ernest N.
No federal aid for this municipal bus line. Am City 79:173-4 Je '64
MOBS. See Crowds; Mob violence
MOBUTU, Joseph Désiré
General Mobuto hits the silk. il pors Ebony 19:92-4+ N '63
MOCARSKI, Polly Lada-. See Lada-Mocarski, P.
MOCH, Jules
Latest plan for a Channel crossing; bridge-and-tunnel combination. il U S News 55:14 Jl 8 '63
MOCHA
See also
Cookery—Mocha
MOCK, Jerrie
Jerrie Mock: winner take all. B. Vail and D. Edwards. il por Flying 75:32-3+ Jl '64
Memo from the publisher. E. D. Muhlfeld. por Flying 75:6 Jl '64
Shades of Amelia. il por Newsweek 63:20 Mr 30 '64
MOCK oranges
Mockorange for fragrance. E. S. Henderson. il Pop Gard 16:40 Ja '65
MOCK United Nations General assembly. See United Nations—Study and teaching
MOCKINGBIRDS
Forest's one-man band. C. Peet. il Am For 69:10+ Mr '63
Listen to the mockingbird. A. E. Runk. Flower Grower 50:7 Ag '63
MOCKUPS of airplanes. See Airplane models
MODAVIS, Howard
Elliott Key; unique marina park. il Yachting 116:54+ N '64
MODEL car racing. See Automobile models—Racing
MODEL T Ford. See Automobiles—Design
MODELING
Children in clay. A. Entis. il Design 64:200-1 Je '63

MODELING—*Continued*
Christmas claybake. M. White. il Ladies Home J 81:56-9+ D '64
Clay modeled birds. J. Hanback. il Sch Arts 64:33 S '64
Clay modeling. M. Tressler. il Sch Arts 64:27-8 Ja '65
David's stonewares. K. R. Beittel. il Sch Arts 63:23-7 S '63
Improvising with clay. A. Hurwitz. il Design 65:66-7 N '63
Lady bug catch-all. il Design 64:191 Je '63
See also
Snow modeling

MODELL, Walter
Hazards of new drugs. bibliog Science 139: 1180-5 Mr 22 '63

MODELS
See also specific types of models, e.g. Hydraulic models

MODELS (persons)
Addis Ababa abba-dabba; portfolio. Esquire 62:172-5 D '64
Beauty biographies of four young naturals. il Seventeen 23:100-3 O '64
Blonde peril; French mannequins protest against number of foreign models in Paris. il Newsweek 64:37 D 21 '64
Direct approach. il U S Camera 27:50-1 My '64
Family affair: the story of two little models and how they grew. il Mlle 58:76-9 D '63
Five day lover. il Esquire 60:221-3 D '63
Fraulein fad; German models in the U.S. il Life 56:95-6 Mr 20 '64
Good grief! Garbo? il Life 54:55-6+ Ap 5 '63
How beautiful can you get? Mlle 57:124-5 Je '63
Integrated ads; award to advertisers for use of Negro models. Commonweal 78:236 My 24 '63
Making of a model. il Seventeen 22:84-5+ Jl '63
March on Madison; integrated advertisements. il Newsweek 62:68 S 9 '63
New angle on curves. il U S Camera 27: 54-5 Jl '64
New look in New York's models. il Newsweek 64:83-7 N 16 '64
One photographer+one model=all women. J. Morris. il U S Camera 26:64-71 My '63
Sweater boy; resemblance to Nikita Khrushchev. il Newsweek 62:88+ N 25 '63
That certain look: partly grooming, partly make-up. il Seventeen 23:112-13 Mr '64
Two models on modeling. il Mlle 60:144-7 N '64
What Walter Winchell knows about models. W. Winchell. il McCalls 90:110 Jl '63
Who are they? il Mlle 59:49-51 Jl '64
See also
Children as models

MODELS, Architectural. See Architectural models

MODELS, Geographical. See Relief maps

MODELS, Landscape. See Landscape models

MODELS, Topographical. See Relief maps

MODERATION
Extremism and all that. J. O'Gara. Commonweal 77:587 Mr 1 '63

MODERATOR
Little magazine that could. J. F. Fixx. Sat R 47:48 Ag 8 '64

MODERN architecture. See Architecture, Modern

MODERN art museum, New York. See Museum of modern art, New York

MODERN civilization. See Civilization

MODERN design. See Design

MODERN drama. See Drama

MODERN foreign language study. See Languages, Modern—Study and teaching

MODERN furniture. See Furniture

MODERN history award
International award set up for modern history. Pub W 186:63 Jl 6 '64

MODERN language association of America
Charting the trends. il Sat R 46:68 F 16 '63
Foreign languages stage a comeback. F. M. Hechinger. il Sat R 46:64-6+ F 16 '63

MODERN languages. See Languages, Modern

MODERN literature. See Literature

MODERN music. See Music

MODERN philosophy. See Philosophy

MODERN poetry. See Poetry

MODERN sculpture. See Sculpture

MODERNISM
George Tyrrell and the modernists. W. S. Smith. Christian Cent 80:490-2 Ap 17 '63
Important theology. W. A. Johnson. Christian Cent 81:337-9 Mr 11 '64
Liberals and longevity. Christian Cent 81: 687 My 20 '64
Modernist movement and Catholic renewal today. C. D. Nelson. Christian Cent 81: 1139-41 S 16 '64
Vindication of liberal theology, by H. P. Van Dusen. Review
Sat R 47:81 Ja 4 '64. C. Walsh

MODERNISM (art)
Anything goes at the Carnegie; Pittsburgh international exhibition of contemporary painting and sculpture. K. Levin. il Art N 63:34-6+ D '64
Armory show; pictures and sculptures from Show of 1913. New Yorker 39:35-6 Mr 30 '63
Armory show: revolution reenacted. H. Rosenberg. New Yorker 39:99-100+ Ap 6 '63
Art. F. Getlein. New Repub 148:26-8 F 16 '63
Art. M. Kozloff. il Nation 197:284-7 N 2 '63
Art and subversion. America 109:620 N 16 '63
Art as axle grease: man's place in the mechanical world. K. Congdon. il Américas 16:12-15 O '64
Art; environmentalism. M. Kozloff. Nation 198:107-8 Ja 27 '64
Art galleries; exhibitions at Lefebre gallery and of American federation of arts gallery's presentation of Retrospective art show of Educational Alliance. H. Rosenberg. New Yorker 39:166-72 My 4 '63
Art galleries; exhibitions of pop art, and abstract expressionism at Janis, Pace and De Nagy galleries. R. M. Coates. New Yorker 39:107-10 Ja 18 '64
Art galleries; on art movements. H. Rosenberg. New Yorker 39:159-62+ O 5 '63
Art galleries; short life of a work of art. H. Rosenberg. New Yorker 39:76-81 Ag 10 '63
Art galleries; the new as value. H. Rosenberg. New Yorker 39:136+ S 7 '63
Art in modern architecture. P. Damaz. il Craft Horiz 23:36-9+ S '63
Art without artists; pop art. E. Kendall. Reporter 28:45-6 My 23 '63
At home with Henry; R. C. Scull's collection of pop art. il Time 83:68-71 F 21 '64
Best-loved art; with reproductions of paintings. J. J. Rorimer. Seventeen 22:154-5 My '63
Biennale: how evil is pop art? T. Zevi. New Repub 151:32-4 S 19 '64
Birth of modern art. J. Canaday. il N Y Times Mag p66-7 My 26 '63
Can this be art? pop art. E. Genauer. il Ladies Home J 81:151-5 Mr '64
Complex competition; Guggenheim international award exhibition. il Newsweek 63:53 Ja 27 '64
Dissimulated pop. M. Kozloff. Nation 199: 417-19 N 30 '64
Eat; an unsettling experience with an Allan Kaprow environment. B. Rollin. il Vogue 143:124-5+ Ap 1 '64
Explosion of pop art: exhibition at the Guggenheim museum. A. B. Saarinen. il Vogue 141:86-7+ Ap 15 '63
Glorious affair; Armory show of 1913. il Time 81:58-67 Ap 5 '63
Goodies, girls, and games; pop art takes a cool view of our vulgar world. il Horizon 6:26-31 Autumn '64
I believe. il Seventeen 22:116 Je '63
James Brooks and the abstract inscape. I. H. Sandler. il Art N 61:30-1+ F '63
Jasper Johns. R. Kaufman. Commonweal 80: 157:9 Ap 24 '64
Kandinsky: last of the heresiarchs. J. Kroll. il Art N 61:38-41+ F '63
Landmarks of modern art (cont) K. Kuh. il Sat R 46:34 F 2; 56 F 16; 37 F 23; 54 Ap 20; 51 My 11; 30 Je 1; 30 Je 22 '63; 47:34 F 8 '64
Letter from London; the Happening movement. C. Marowitz. Nation 199:99-100 S 7 '64
Letter from Paris; Tableaux rares at Galerie de L'Elysée. Genêt. New Yorker 40:88+ Je 27 '64
Letter from Paris; third Biennale at the Musée d'art moderne de la ville de Paris. Genêt. New Yorker 39:147-8 N 16 '63
Misunderstandings denying the appreciation of modern art. J. Schinneller. il Sch Arts 62:25-8 Ap; 21-3 My '63
Modern on the move. F. Getlein. New Repub 150:26+ Ja 18 '64
Motion in painting: a new art form. T. Freund. il Am Artist 28:46-50+ N '64
Mystery of Arshile Gorky: a personal account. M. Osborn. il Art N 61:42-3+ F '63
New realism. H. F. Collins. il Sch Arts 63: 25-6 Mr '64

MODERNISM (art)—*Continued*
Notes and comment; pop art at Museum of modern art. New Yorker 39:24 Je 1 '63
Old American moderns; exhibition of modern Americans before 1940 at Corcoran gallery. F. Getlein. New Repub 148:28-9 My 18 '63
Op art: pictures that attack the eye. il Time 84:78-86 O 23 '64
Op art; with report by W. R. Young. il Life 57:132-40 D 11 '64
Paintings to think about; exhibition of contemporary painting and sculpture at Wadsworth atheneum, Hartford, Conn. S. J. Wagstaff, jr. il Art N 62:38+ Ja '64
Pop and public. T. B. Hess. Art N 62:23+ N '63
Pop art, cult of the commonplace. il Time 81:69-72 My 3 '63
Pop art or the art of things. R. Squirru. il Américas 15:15-21 Jl '63
Pop art sells on and on, why? J. Canaday. il N Y Times Mag p7+ My 31 '64
Pop artists or copy cats? E. Loran. il Art N 62:48-9+ S '63
Pop goes the Biennale. il Time 84:54 Jl 3 '64
Pop goes the easel. F. Getlein. New Repub 151:34+ O 17 '64
Pop pop. il Time 82:40 Ag 30 '63
Popcorn and the uses of art. F. Getlein. New Repub 150:28-9 My 2 '64
Popular art: images, not objects. B. Kaufman. Commonweal 79:22-3 S 27 '63
Profiles; R. Rauschenberg. C. Tomkins. il New Yorker 40:39-40+ F 29 '64
Rise and dissolution of the avant-garde. W. C. Seitz. il Vogue 142:182-3+ S 1 '63
Seven U. S. painters; exhibition at Pan American union. L. Alloway. il Américas 16:39-41 Jl '64
Solitude, modernity and art education. J. A. Richardson. il Sch Arts 63:34-7 S '63
Synaesthesia; exhibitions by twenty-seven artists at New York galleries. New Yorker 39:20-2 Ja 25 '64
Talkie pop; audio-visual paintings at Amel gallery, Manhattan. il Time 84:68 Jl 24 '64
They paint; you recognize. il Time 83:74-5+ Ap 3 '64
Twentieth century Mexican painting. V. M. Reyes. il Américas 16:17-26 Ag '64
Vanity fair: the New York art scene. il Newsweek 65:54-6+ Ja 4 '65
What do you think of modern art? E. W. Watson. Am Artist 27:3+ F '63
What is an environment? A. Kaprow. il Vogue 143:125 Ap 1 '64
What is pop art? interviews with eight painters; ed. by G. R. Swenson. il Art N 62:24-7+ N '63; 40-3+ F '64
When is art modern art? R. d'Harnoncourt. il N Y Times Mag p 17+ My 24 '64
You think this is a supermarket? no, hold your hats: it's an art gallery; with report by C. Tomkins. il Life 57:138-40+ N 20 '64
See also
Cubism
Dadaism

Anecdotes, facetiae, satire, etc.

Modern art; renovations of the Museum of modern art. il New Yorker 40:31-2 Ap 11 '64
Mom art. il Esquire 60:134-5 O '63
Snap, crackle, pop. il Holiday 35:68-71 F '64
Telltale art. M. Bennett. il Atlan 211:116 F '63
Up on the flying trapeze; snow and slush; is Hopkins outmoded? $215,600 for a Monet! S. McKelway. New Yorker 40:43 Ap 4 '64

MODERNISM in music. See Music

MODERNIST design. See Design

MODERNIZATION. See Social change

MODERNIZATION of houses. See Houses, Remodeled

MODESTO ash. See Ash (tree)

MODESTY
Modesty is back in style; with program for discussion group. by M. Smart. S. Blau. Parents Mag 38:42, 51+ Mr '63

MODIGLIANI, Amedeo
Between two Castros; a questionable Modigliani sold by Knoedler company. Newsweek 62:66 Jl 1 '63
Modigliani, master draughtsman. A. Werner. il Am Artist 28:18-23+ F '64

MODINE manufacturing company
Canada's car push hits a roadblock; tariff rebate plan on auto parts challenged Bsns W p91-2 Jl 25 '64

MODISANE, Bloke
Blame me on history; excerpts. por Atlan 212:96-107+ N '63
Situation; story. Reporter 29:40 D 5 '63

MODOC NATIONAL FOREST. See National forests

MODULAR design (electronics)
Packaging concept promotes versatility. B. Miller. il Aviation W 81:85-7+ D 14 '64

MODULATORS
Grid dip modulator. C. Caringella. il Pop-Electr 18:57-60 Mr '63
Magnetic modulators. S. L. Silver. il Electr World 71:65-9 Je '64
NAA demonstrates laser modulator. il Miss & Roc 12:31 Mr 18 '63
Simple AM modulator. C. Henry. il Pop Electr 20:45 Ap '64
Transistorized FM-stereo demodulator. J. W. Englund and others. il Electr World 72:34-5+ D '64

MOE, Henry Allen
Farewell, groves of academe. por Time 82:81 Jl 12 '63

MOECKEL, W. E.
Electric propulsion. bibliog Science 142:172-8 O 11 '63

MOERS, Ellen
Angry young women. Harper 227:88-92+ D '63
Tradition of McClure. Commentary 37:70-4 Ap '64

MOFCHUM, Gerald
Magic realism of Gerald Mofchum. F. Whitaker. il por Am Artist 27:24-9+ O '63

MOFFAT, Alex W.
Incident I'll never forget; seeing is believing. Yachting 115:47+ Mr '64
Pea souper. Yachting 115:147 F '64
Ventilation and stowage. Yachting 114:46+ Ag '63

MOFFAT, Donald W.
Voltage-divider nomogram. Electr World 71: 29+ Mr '64

MOFFAT, Robert W.
Amateur scientist. Sci Am 210:135-8 Ja '64

MOFFATT, Dorothy Hilliard
By the one word spoken; poem. McCalls 90: 113 Jl '63
Difference; poem. McCalls 91:145 Je '64
No such measurement; poem. McCalls 90: 182 Mr '63
Reason; poem. McCalls 90:56 Ap '63

MOFFET, Alan T.
Component shapes in double radio sources. bibliog Science 146:764-5 N 6 '64

MOFFETT, Elwood
Talking troubles out at the plant level. por Bsns W p74+ O 19 '63

MOFFETT, Hugh
Gall of Gaston the giant-killer. Life 56:78A Ap 3 '64
In splendor he shakes up the world. Life 56: 18-27 F 14 '64
Lovely gift to the Greeks. Life 57:48-50 O 9 '64
Moffetts go a-moseying. por Life 55:100-2+ S 13 '63
Top sidewalk superintendent gets a big eyeful. Life 56:40A-40D My 22 '64
Shalom, *khatirkum* and tumult in a gentle setting. Life 56:28-9 Ja 17 '64
Watching the girls is most of the fun. Life 57:52 S 4 '64
Ways of wine and noses. Life 57:111 O 30 '64
What to do about de Gaulle? Life 58:37-8+ Ja 8 '65

about

Prairie man takes over abroad. G. P. Hunt. por Life 56:3 Ja 17 '64

MOFFITT, Billie Jean
Better than fancy pants; Wimbledon tournament. J. Lovesey. il pors Sports Illus 19: 12-15 Jl 15 '63

MOFFITT, John
Direction (late winter: high noon) poem. America 110:288 F 29 '64
Ditty; poem. America 111:255 S 12 '64
In that dawning; poem. America 109:796 D 21 '63
November twenty-three; poem. America 109: 731 D 7 '63
Of many things. T. N. Davis. America 111: inside cover Jl 25 '64
This is my body; poem. America 109:486 O 26 '63
To the author of Four quartets; poem. America 112:121 Ja 23 '65
What he saw; poem. America 111:800 D 19 '64
(tr) See Thomas Aquinas, Saint. Pange lingua

MOFFITT, Michael
Gabriel Marcel at Gonzaga. America 109:707-9 N 30 '63

MOFFO, Anna
All-American prima donna. C. Sigmon. il pors Mus Am 83:18-19 Ja '63
Shopping with Moffo. il pors Opera N 28:13-15 D 28 '63

MOGGE, Robert A.
Special-interest cars. Motor T 16:77 N '64
MOGUILEVSKY, Eugene
To Russia with ease. il por Time 83:56 Je 12 '64
MOGUL architecture. See Architecture, Mogul
MOGUL art. See Art, Mogul
MOGUL painting. See Painting, Mogul
MOHAMMED
Why 400,000,000 follow Mohammed. R. Payne. il N Y Times Mag p 18+ Ag 4 '63
MOHAMMED el Badr, king of the Yemen
Under the gun. J. A. Morris. il por Newsweek 64:42 D 21 '64
MOHAMMED Reza Pahlevi, shah of Iran
Future to outshine ancient glories. pors Life 54:52-62+ My 31 '63
Shah of Iran to President Kennedy; message, January 31, 1963. Dept State Bul 48:316 Mr 4 '63
about
Here he is again. Nation 198:565-6 Je 8 '64
Image or mirage? Nation 196:366 My 4 '63
Iran and a king's revolution. il por Sr Schol 82:10-14+ Ap 17 '63
Iran's shah leads a white revolution. J. Walz. il N Y Times Mag p23+ O 27 '63
Legal revolution; voters support Iran's shah. por U S News 54:16 F 11 '63
Next big blowup, Iran? J. Law. il por U S News 54:82 Mr 25 '63
Royal reformer: Iran's shah gets a mandate. por U S News 55:16 S 30 '63
Shah was not amused. Time 85:26 Ja 22 '65
MOHAMMED Zahir, king of Afghanistan
—See Kennedy, J. F. jt. auth.
about
People of the week. por(p 14) U S News 55:24 S 16 '63
MOHAMMEDANISM. See Islam
MOHAVE DESERT. See Mojave Desert
MOHAWK airlines
Mohawk predicts BAC 111 buy will help cut subsidy in 1966. Aviation W 78:34 Mr 4 '63
MOHAWK Indians
Mohawk beauty with a mission. C. Brossard. il Look 28:91-4 Ja 28 '64
MOHAWK ISLAND. See Erie, Lake
MOHLENBROCK, Sigurd
Architecture and design. por Library J 88:4326-31 N 15 '63
MOHLER, Don
Family photography made easy. Parents Mag 39:44-5+ Jl '64
Four keys to creative movie lighting. U S Camera 26:78-9+ F '63
MOHOLE project
Drills for digging deepest hole yet; Mohole equipment. il Bsns W p44+ D 19 '64
Great Mohole mess. W. J. Cromie. il Sci Digest 54:59-63 N '63
Mohole lives. Newsweek 65:89 Ja 25 '65
Mohole may wind up no hole; congressional appropriations stopped. Bsns W p32 N 23 '63
Mohole regress report. Fortune 69:106 Ap '64
Mohole: the project that went awry. D. S. Greenberg. il Science 143:115-19, 223-7, 334-7 Ja 10-24 '64; Discussion. 143:529, 994, 1274-6, 1393-4 F 7, Mr 6, 20-27 '64
Ocean crust composition. Sci N L 83:338 Je 1 '63
Project Mohole. il UNESCO Courier 16:18-19 O '63
Project no hole? il Newsweek 61:97-9 Je 10 '63
Purine and pyrimidines in sediments from the experimental Mohole. E. Rosenberg. bibliog il Science 146:1680-1 D 25 '64
MOHOLY-NAGY, Sibyl
Architecture and the moon age; summary of address. Arch Forum 118:90-2 F '63
Yale's School of art and architecture. Arch Forum 120:76-9 F '64
MOHR, Charles
Close look at a puzzled candidate. N Y Times Mag p 11+ My 17 '64
Goldwater: a close look at a damned cowboy. Sat Eve Post 237:16-19 Ag 8 '64
Goldwater's nine. N Y Times Mag p28-9 S 13 '64
MOHR, Charles E.
Exploring America underground. il por Nat Geog Mag 125:802-37 Je '64
MOHRHARDT, Foster E.
Documentation: a synthetic science; address, 1963. bibliog por Wilson Lib Bul 38:743-9 My '64
MOHRI, R. W.
Everybody gets into the act. por Am City 78:106-7 My '63
MOIRÉ fringes. See Interference (light)
MOISEIWITSCH, Benno
Obituary
Mus Am por 83:51 My '63
MOISTER, F. Corbin
Doctor, what's wrong with me? E. Hill. il Sat Eve Post 237:64-6 My 2 '64
MOISTURE
See also
Humidity
Soil moisture
MOISTURIZERS. See Cosmetics
MOJAVE DESERT
Trapped in the desert. G. Beeman. il Read Digest 85:100-5 Ag '64
MOKADY, R. and Gal, M.
Strontium fixation by lime contained in soils. bibliog Science 145:154-5 Jl 10 '64
MOKITIMI, Seth M.
South African church elects African head. Christian Cent 80:1359 N 6 '63
MOLASSES
Made with molasses. il Suc Farm 61:89-90 Ap '63
MOLD, James D. and others
Alloocimene: absence in cigarette smoke. bibliog Science 144:1572-3 Je 26 '64
MOLDAVITES. See Tektites
MOLDAVSKAÎA, I. A. Svet-. See Svet-Moldavskaîa, I. A.
MOLDAVSKIĬ, George J. Svet-. See Svet-Moldavskiĭ, G. J.
MOLDING, Plastics. See Plastics—Molding
MOLDS (botany)
See also
Aspergillus
Fungi
Myxomycetes
Penicillium
MOLDS (for casting)
How to make a sand casting. il Sunset 130:150+ Mr '63
Sand casting at home. M. Banister. il Pop Mech 120:166-72 Jl '63
MOLDS, Butter. See Butter molds
MOLECULAR association. See Polymerization
MOLECULAR binding energy. See Chemical bonds
MOLECULAR biochemistry. See Biochemistry
MOLECULAR electronics division. See Westinghouse electric corporation—Molecular electronics division
MOLECULAR interactions. See Molecules
MOLECULAR weights
Molecular weight: measurements with gravity cells. F. N. Weber, jr and others. bibliog il Science 139:837-8 Mr 1 '63
MOLECULES
Allosteric properties of glutamate dehydrogenases from different sources. N. Talal and G. M. Tomkins. bibliog il Science 146:1309-11 D 4 '64
Atoms and molecules; reprint. il Sci Digest 53:66-9 My '63
DNA from bacteriophage lambda: molecular length and conformation. L. A. MacHattie and C. A. Thomas, jr. bibliog il Science 144:1142-4 My 29 '64
Differential dialysis. L. C. Craig. bibliog il Science 144:1093-9 My 29 '64
Effect of traces of large molecules containing nitrogen on hydrogen overvoltage. W. Juda and others. bibliog il Science 146:521-3 O 23 '64
4.5 billion years of protein molecules: what do we know now about how they are made? AAAS annual meeting, 26-31 December, Montreal. il Science 146:1076-7 N 20 '64
Free radicals and reactive molecules in clathrate cavities. P. Goldberg. bibliog il Science 142:378-9 O 18 '63
Free radicals and unstable molecules. S. N. Foner. bibliog il Science 143:441-50 Ja 31 '64
How we're cracking the code of life; radio interview, ed. by C. Collingwood. S. Ochoa. il Sci Digest 56:79-83 S '64
Hybridization of half molecules of rabbit gamma globulin. A. Nisonoff and J. L. Palmer. bibliog il Science 143:376-9 Ja 24 '64
Intermolecular cross-linking of collagen and the indentification of a new beta-component. P. Bornstein and others. bibliog il Science 144:1220-1 Je 5 '64
Intermolecular cross-linking of collagen and the identification of a new beta-component. P. Bornstein and others. bibliog il Science 144:1220-1 Je 5 '64; Reply with rejoinder. S. Bakerman. 145:837 Ag 21 '64

MOLECULES—*Continued*
Isotopic molecules: separation by recycle gas chromatography. J. W. Root and others. bibliog il Science 143:676-8 F 14 '64
Machomolecular chemistry; address, December 12, 1963. G. Natta. bibliog il Science 147: 261-72 Ja 15 '65
Macromolecules; report of Symposium on quantitative biology. R. C. Williams. Science 141:934-5 S 6 '63
Marked molecules; report on first international conference on methods of preparing and storing marked molecules. R. F. Nystrom. Science 144:1045-6 My 22 '64
Molecular beam scattering at thermal energies. R. B. Bernstein. bibliog il Science 144:141-50 Ap 10 '64
Molecular biophysics: International summer school; report. E. A. Edelsack and others. Science 146:1193 N 27 '64
Molecular configuration of nucleic acids. M. H. F. Wilkins. bibliog il Science 140: 941-50 My 31 '63
Molecular heterogeneity of enzymes: malate dehydrogenase of euglena. J. Chancellor-Maddison and C. R. Noll, jr. bibliog il Science 142:60-1 O 4 '63
Molecular structure and spectroscopy; report of symposium. V. W. Laurie. Science 141: 654+ Ag 16 '63
Molecular structure of the synthetic molecular oxygen carrier $O_2IrCl(CO)(P[C_6H_5]_3)_2$. J. A. Obers and S. J. La Placa. bibliog il Science 145:920-1 Ag 28 '64
Molecular theories of memory. W. Dingman and M. B. Sporn. bibliog Science 144:26-9 Ap 3 '64; Reply. A. L. Goldberg. 144:1529 Je 26 '64
Myoglobin and the structure of proteins; address, December 11, 1962. J. C. Kendrew. bibliog il Science 139:1259-66 Mr 29 '63
Neutral salts: the generality of their effects on the stability of macromolecular conformations. P. H. Von Hippel and K. Y. Wong. bibliog il Science 145:577-80 Ag 7 '64
New hint to cancer cause in molecular structure. Sci N L 85:82 F 8 '64
Optical studies at high pressures. L. S. Whatley and others. bibliog il Science 144: 968-76 My 22 '64
Organic photochemistry. G. S. Hammond and N. J. Turro. bibliog il Science 142:1541-53 D 20 '63
Organisms and molecules in evolution; adaptation from paper. G. G. Simpson. bibliog Science 146:1535-8 D 18 '64
Quantitative molecular approach to the permeability changes of excitation. A. M. Shanes. bibliog il Science 140:51-3 Ap 5 '63
Quantum devices, how they work. J. R. Collins. il Electr World 70:39-41+ D '63
Separation and fractionation of macromolecules and particles. A. Tiselius and others. bibliog il Science 141:13-20 Jl 5 '63
Speculation on new molecules. J. I. Musher. bibliog Science 141:736-7 Ag 23 '63
Sucrose: precise determination of crystal and molecular structure by neutron diffraction. G. M. Brown and H. A. Levy. bibliog il Science 141:921-3 S 6 '63

MOLEY, Raymond
After thirty years. por Newsweek 62:104 O 28 '63
Perspective. See issues of Newsweek

MOLIÈRE, Jean Baptiste Poquelin
Impromptu at Versailles. Criticism
New Yorker 40:66 Mr 21 '64
Scapin. Criticism
New Yorker 40:64+ Mr 21 '64
Tartuffe. Criticism
New Repub 152:34 Ja 30 '65
Newsweek 65:86 Ja 25 '65
Time il 85:46 Ja 22 '65

MOLIMETRIC system. See Gages

MOLINA, Rafael Leonidas Trujillo. See Trujillo Molina, R. L.

MOLINARA, A. J.
Simple transistor checker. Electr World 69: 94 F '63

MOLINAS, Jack
Fix was on. J. Breslin. il pors Sat Eve Post 236:15-19 F 23 '63

MOLL, Richard
Reporter at large. K. T. Kinkead. New Yorker 40:51-2+ My 23 '64

MOLLENHOFF, Clark R.
Behind the plot to assassinate Robert Kennedy. Look 28:49-50+ My 19 '64
Jury tampering in Tennessee. Look 27:79-82 My 21 '63

MOLLER, David
Christmas and Freud. Sat Eve Post 236:38 D 7 '63

MOLLESON, John
Fifty years of ASCAP. Mus Am 84:7+ F '64
Negro in music. Mus Am 83:24-5+ D '63

MOLLET, Guy
France under de Gaulle; a former premier speaks out; interview, ed. by A. J. Meyers. por U S News 55:126-7 O 14 '63
about
New popular front? E. Taylor. il Reporter 28:14-19 Je 20 '63

MOLLOY, Edward A.
Comforter. Criticism
America 111:640-1 N 14 '64
Commonweal 81:182 N 6 '64
Sat R 47:29 N 7 '64

MOLLOY, John F.
Needed: more good parents. NEA J 52:42-6 S '63

MOLLUSKS
Bohr effect; absence in a molluscan hemocyanin. J. R. Redmond. bibliog il Science 139:1294-5 Mr 29 '63
Dopamine: its occurrence in molluscan ganglia. D. Sweeney. bibliog il Science 139:1051 Mr 15 '63
Invertebrate ferritin: occurrence in mollusca. K. M. Towe and others. bibliog il Science 142:63-4 O 4 '63
Littorina littorea: an indicator of Norse settlement in North America? N. Spjeldnaes and K. E. Henningsmoen. bibliog Science 141:275-6 Jl 19 '63; Discussion. 141:762; 142: 1022 Ag 30, N 22 '63
Miracle of the mollusk. il Horizon 7:94-105 Wint '65
Mollusks; report of symposium at the Zoological society of London. A. J. Kohn. Science 145:518-19 Jl 31 '64
Pteropod ooze from Bermuda pedestal. C. Chen. bibliog il Science 144:60-2 Ap 3 '64
See also
Chitons
Embryology—Mollusks

MOLLUSKS, Fossil
Isotope ratios in marine mollusk shells after prolonged contact with flowing fresh water. J. N. Weber and A. La Rocque. bibliog il Science 142:1666 D 27 '63
Paleozoic mollusk: hyolithes. L. Marek and E. L. Yochelson. bibliog il Science 146:1674-5 D 25 '64
Radiocarbon dating: fictitious results with mollusk shells. M. L. Keith and G. M. Anderson. bibliog il Science 141:634-7 Ag 16 '63
Transitional Ordovician bivalve with both monoplacophoran and lucinacean affinities. A. L. McAlester. bibliog il Science 146:1293-4 D 4 '64

MOLLY Maguires
Lament for the Molly Maguires. by A. H. Lewis. Review
Newsweek il 64:85A-85B S 7 '64

MOLNAR, Ferenc
Superstitions of Mr Molnar, and how he got rid of them. G. Halasz. Sat R 47:6+ O 24 '64

MOLNAR, John
Relay switching for transistor ignitions. Pop Electr 20:90 My '64

MOLNAR, Thomas
African paradox. Nat R 16:826-7 S 22 '64
Death of the Federation. Nat R 16:353 My 5 '64
Ghost of appeasement past. Nat R 14:120+ F 12 '63
Letter from Africa. Nat R 16:155-6, 280, 461 F 25, Ap 7, Je 2 '64
Men and ideas. Nat R 14:464-5 Je 4 '63
Paradox of the Marxist philosopher. bibliog f Nat R 16:1107-10 D 15 '64
Six months after the coup. Nat R 16:491, 783 Je 16, S 8 '64
To the anthill with love. Nat R 16:1073-4 D 1 '64

MOLONEY virus. See Tumor viruses

MOLONY, Gerard E.
Book burning. Wilson Lib Bul 37:518 Mr '63
Censorship flares up in New City; library board member burns book. Library J 88: 745 F 15 '63
Friends and True friends in New City. E. T. Moore. ALA Bul 57:387-8 My '63
Record crowd at New City meeting overwhelmingly supports library board. Library J 88:1128 Mr 15 '63

MOLTER, Gunther
Driving the latest NSU-Wankel. Motor T 15: 64-5 F '63

MOLTING
Monarch's emergence. A. B. Klots. il Natur Hist 73:50-3 My '64
Prevent fall pullet molt. Suc Farm 61:78 O '63

MOLTON, Warren Lane
Analogue; poem. Christian Cent 81:108 Ja 22 '64
I'll build me a silence; poem. Christian Cent 80:1368 N 6 '63
Psalm to warlords everywhere. Christian Cent 80:1169 S 25 '63
Thresher men remembered; poem. Christian Cent 81:598 My 6 '64
Thresher; poem. Christian Cent 80:581 My 1 '63

MOLYBDENUM
High-pressure synthesis of molybdates with the wolframite structure. A. P. Young and C. M. Schwartz. bibliog il Science 141:348-9 Jl 26 '63

MOLYNEAUX, Dorothy
How to give a birthday party. House B 105: 235+ N '63

MOLZ, Kathleen
Nickle words for a golden mission. Wilson Lib Bul 39:44-7 S '64
Peaceable kingdom; address, October, 1963. por Library J 90:183-7 Ja 15 '65

MOMENT, Gairdner B.
Zoology: Sixteenth international congress. Science 143:164-6 Ja 10 '64

MOMSEN, Dick, jr
Portugal's Mondego Valley. Travel 121:56-8+ Mr '64

MONA LISA (painting) See Leonardo da Vinci

MONA; opera. See Parker, H.

MONACO, Mario del
Stars at home: Mario del Monaco. il pors Opera N 28:14-16 Ja 11 '64

MONACO
Princess Grace: a new role. J. Hamilton. il Look 27:64-70 F 12 '63
See also
Taxation—Monaco

Description and travel

Miniature Monaco. G. M. Grosvenor and D. K. Grosvenor. il Nat Geog Mag 123:546-73 Ap '63

Economic conditions

Death of a haven. Time 81:92 F 15 '63

Royal family

How Princess Grace chooses children's clothes. H. Obolensky. il Redbook 121:60-5 Ag '63
Memoirs of Monaco; ed by S. Fliegers. Rainier III. il McCalls 90:81-5+ Ap '63

MONAGHAN, Eileen
Eileen Monaghan believes in an individual approach; with biographical sketch. il por Am Artist 28:40-1+ O '64

MONAGHAN, May
Sister: one of J. Joyce's three surviving sisters. New Yorker 40:34-6 Mr 14 '64

MONAHAN, G. M.
Telephones give split-second emergency response. Am City 79:111 S '64

MONAHAN, James. See Miller, L. M. jt. auth.

MONAGHAN, William J.
Doctor Dessen's can-do city. Todays Health 42:48-9+ N '64

MONARCH butterflies. See Butterflies

MONARCHIST movement (France)
See also
Action française

MONARCHS. See Kings and rulers

MONARCHY
Succession and monarchy: the controversy of 1679-1681. C. A. Edie. bibliog f Am Hist R 70:350-70 Ja '65
See also
Kings and rulers

MONASTERIES
Art and architecture: a new light on monastic design; buildings for Passionist fathers, North Palm Beach, Fla. P. Damaz. il Craft Horiz 23:24-5+ Ja '63
At a Russian monastery; Holy Trinity monastery at Zagorsk. C. Stangohr. Commonweal 78:501-3 Ag 23 '63
Holy places: early monastic sites of Ireland. F. O'Connor. il Holiday 33:94-5+ Ap '63
Island of faith in the Sinai wilderness. G. H. Forsyth. il Nat Geog Mag 125:82-106 Ja '64
Loccum, a Protestant monastery. H. Lehmann. Christian Cent 80:1167-9 S 25 '63
Monks of Chevetogne. C. Northcott. Christian Cent 81:1443 N 18 '64
Next abbot: a view of the world from 1,752 feet. J. Fischer. il Harper 226:16+ Mr '63
Rock monasteries of Cappadocia; excerpt from A time to keep silence. P. L. Fermor. il Horizon 6:66-73 Wint '64
Taizé: lever for reconciliation. C. Northcott. Christian Cent 81:1561 D 16 '64
Treasury of sacred art. F. Borghini. il Américas 15:8-12 Ap '63
See also
Abbeys
Athos, Mount
Hospice of St Bernard
Secularization

MONASTICISM
Lonely Lutheran monk. il Time 81:53 Mr 1 '63
Monk in the diaspora. T. Merton. Commonweal 79:741-5 Mr 20 '64; Reply. J. Epple. 80:148-9 Ap 24 '64
See also
Benedictines

MONDALE, Walter Frederick
Filling Hubert's shoes. il por Time 84:34 N 27 '64
Humphrey's successor. il por Newsweek 64: 35 N 30 '64
Humphrey's successor: a liberal backer of LBJ. por U S News 57:22 N 30 '64

MONDRAGÓN, Sergio
Five Mexican poets. Américas 15:7-12 O '63

MONDRIAAN, Pieter Cornelis
Kiesler and Mondrian, art into life. K. Levin. il Art N 63:38-41+ My '64

MONETARY fund. See International monetary fund

MONETARY stabilization. See Money

MONEY
In search of a monetary constitution, ed. by L. B. Yeager. Review
Nat R 14:459-60+ Je 4 '63. M. Palyi
Money flows and balance-of-payments adjustment; address, October 8, 1964. R. V. Roosa. Dept State Bul 51:669-73 N 9 '64
Money has had many nicknames. C. French. Hobbies 68:102+ Ag '63
Pounds, francs, marks, or lira; currency gift for travelers. Sunset 133:32 D '64
See also
Coins
Currency convertibility
Finance
Gold as money
Inflation (finance)
Investments
Liquidity (economics)
Shell money
Silver as money

International aspects

See Finance, International

Brazil

Memorializing the centavo. Time 84:53 D 11 '64
Sinking currency. Time 82:21 Ag 23 '63

England

See Money—Great Britain

France

Paris bucks for bullion. Newsweek 65:59-60 Ja 18 '65

Germany

Germany's inflated currency following World war 1. C. French. Hobbies 68:102 F '64

Great Britain

Bailing out the British pound. il Newsweek 64:73-4+ D 7 '64
Beleaguered pound and the threatened dollar. M. J. Rossant. il Reporter 32:30+ Ja 28 '65
British pound in trouble: what's being done to aid it. U S News 57:92 D 7 '64
Cheap-money mania. H. Hazlitt. Newsweek 64:69 D 21 '64
Heroic defense; faltering British pound. il Time 84:99-100 D 4 '64
Labor faces its first major money crisis. il Bsns W p29-30 N 28 '64
Letter from London; threatened pound. M. Panter-Downes. New Yorker 40:159-60+ D 12 '64
New touch of caution; with editorial comment. il Bsns W p27-8, 154 N 28 '64
100 cents to £1? Newsweek 62:63 O 7 '63
Sterling crisis. H. Hazlitt. Newsweek 64:80 D 14 '64
Ten days that shook the Exchequer. C. Brogan. il Nat R 17:57-8 Ja 26 '65
With pound on mend, Britain hunts cure. Bsns W p27 Ja 23 '65

Greece, Modern

Found: a cool million. S. Karnow. il Life 54: 8 Mr 1 '63

Italy

Fleeing lire. Time 82:58+ Ag 30 '63

Tonga (islands)

Tonga celebrates its unique gold pocket money with the world's only round stamps. il Life 55:44 O 11 '63

MONEY—*Continued*

United States

As U.S. moves to protect the dollar: the effect. il U S News 57:89-91 D 7 '64
As world's bankers see the dollar now. il U S News 55:101-2 Ag 5 '63
Beleaguered pound and the threatened dollar. M. J. Rossant. il Reporter 32:30+ Ja 28 '65
Billions that would solve dollar problem; war debts from European nations. il U S News 55:94 N 25 '63
Close watch on the money market. il Newsweek 64:77 O 19 '64
Critical look at U.S. from Europe. il U S News 55:43 Ag 19 '63
Danger to the dollar; what Treasury wants to do about it. il U S News 55:81-2 Jl 22 '63
Daring new moves by U.S. to ease pressure on the dollar. il U S News 54:132-4 Mr 25 '63
Dollar crisis in sight: what to do? U S News 57:33 D 7 '64
Dollar in distress? il Sr Schol 84:17-18+ Ap 10 '64
Dollar: national and international bulwark; address, April 22, 1963. A. Hayes. Vital Speeches 29:490-3 Je 1 '63
For dollar: a brighter outlook. U S News 56:73-4 Ja 6 '64
For now, it's just a gentle pull. il Bsns W p72+ N 14 '64
Germany's Erhard talks about trade, tariffs, the U.S. dollar; interview, ed. by K. Lachmann and A. Zanker. L. Erhard. U S News 56:62-4 Je 8 '64
Gold: the talk gets tough. Nat R 15:224 S 24 '63
Good as gold. Newsweek 62:59-60 Jl 29 '63
How Europeans see dollar today. U S News 55:104 S 16 '63
How sound is the dollar? il Changing T 17:19-21 D '63
Indian-head nickel: some words with himself. A. Glaser. il Esquire 61:58+ Mr '64
Inventor of the month; S-money. S. V. Jones. il Sci Digest 54:52-3 S '63
Is the dollar strong or weak? il U S News 58:34-7 Ja 11 '65
Kennedy coin, a Kennedy stamp. il U S News 55:11 D 23 '63
Kennedy formula for keeping the dollar at home. il U S News 55:93-5 Jl 29 '63
Kennedy holds the line on money policy. il U S News 55:62 N 11 '63
Maybe a march to save the dollar? D. Lawrence. U S News 55:104 S 9 '63; Correction. 55:107 S 16 '63
New look at the dollar; what world bankers say about U.S. money problems. il U S News 55:53-4 O 14 '63
New touch of caution; with editorial comment. il Bsns W p27-8, 154 N 28 '64
Now it's the money managers who are under fire. il U S News 54:94-5 Ap 1 '63
Now there's a split among men who manage the dollar; Board of governors of Federal reserve system. il U S News 55:60-1 Ag 5 '63
Plenty of it, plus some worries. il Time 83:61 Ja 31 '64
Plugging the gold drain. Sr Schol 83:8-9 S 20 '63
Rediscovery of money. M. A. Heilperin. il Fortune 71:152-3+ Ja '65
Rich world that leans on U.S. dollar problem. il U S News 56:90 Je 29 '64
Small change in gold. C. French. Hobbies 68:102 Jl '63
Suddenly, new worry about the dollar. il U S News 55:31 Jl 15 '63
Suppose the U.S. dollar were devalued. il U S News 55:32-3 Jl 29 '63
Trifling: what to buy for a nickel. New Yorker 39:40-1 O 26 '63
What Europe's bankers say about dollar's health now. il U S News 56:109-11 Ap 27 '64
Where welcome sign is coming down for U.S. dollar. il U S News 55:66-8 Jl 8 '63
Wilting dollar. Nat R 14:521-2 Jl 2 '63
Yankee dollar. M. Mayer. Sat Eve Post 237:28-30 Ja 18 '64
See also
Paper money—United States
United States—Mint

History

Dollar marks 100. il Sr Schol 82:24 My 15 '63
Why dollar bills look different. il Changing T 18:43-5 My '64

Yugoslavia

Dinar. New Yorker 39:19 Je 29 '63

MONEY, Counterfeit. See Counterfeits and counterfeiting
MONEY, Lost. See Lost articles
MONEY brokers. See Brokers
MONEY management. See Budget, Household; Budget, Personal
MONEY raising campaigns. See Fund raising
MONEY rates. See Interest
MONFA, Henri Marie Raymond de Toulouse-Lautrec. See Toulouse-Lautrec Monfa, H. M. R. de
MONGAN, Agnes
Drawings of Andrew Wyeth. Am Artist 27:28-33+ S '63
MONGKUT, king of Siam
King and us. A. Robertson. il pors Horizon 6:18-25 Wint '64
MONGOLIA
Cheerful Mongolians: a visit to a very far country. F. Maclean. il Harper 229:41-7 Jl '64
Search for lebensraum? struggle between Russia and red China. il Time 84:40-1 S 18 '64

History

Chingis Khan and the Mongol conquests. O. Lattimore. il Sci Am 209:54-60+ bibliog (p 140) Ag '63
MONGOLISM
Mongolism, leukemia link. F. Marley. Sci N L 83:151 Mr 9 '63
Serum uric acid in young mongoloids. E. T. Mertz and others. bibliog il Science 141:535 Ag 9 '63
MONGOLOIDS. See Mongolism
MONGOOSES
Duluth's most controversial citizen: Mr Magoo. H. Montgomery. il Am For 69:8+ O '63
MONITOR, Radio. See Radio instruments
MONITOR, Radio frequency. See Radio frequency—Control
MONITORIAL system of education
Historical report from Madras. R. B. Sutton. Sch & Soc 92:231-2 Sum '64
MONITORS (warships) See Warships
MONIUSZKO, Stanisłav
Halka. Criticism
Opera N 29:32 Ja 30 '65
MONK, Edwin
You and your naval architect. Yachting 114:41+ D '63
MONK, Julius
Bits and pieces of J. Monk. A. Levy. il por N Y Times Mag p45+ Ja 10 '65
MONK, Maria
Maria Monk: the prehistory of dialogue. Christian Cent 80:223 F 13 '63
MONK, Thelonious Sphere
Jazz concerts. W. Balliett. New Yorker 39:92-3 Ja 11 '64
Loneliest Monk. il pors Time 83:84-8 F 28 '64
Monk: high priest of jazz. L. H. Lapham. il pors Sat Eve Post 237:70+ Ap 11 '64
Musical events. W. Balliett. New Yorker 39:89 Jl 20 '63
Thelonious Monk: arrival without departure. M. Williams. pors Sat R 46:32-3+ Ap 13 '63
MONK seals. See Seals (animals)
MONKEYS
Caudate-induced cortical potentials: comparison between monkey and cat. S. Goldring and others. bibliog il Science 139:772 F 22 '63
Choice behavior in rhesus monkeys: effect of stimulation during the first month of life. G. P. Sackett and others. bibliog il Science 147:304-6 Ja 15 '65
Hippocampectomy and behavior sequences. D. P. Kimble and K. H. Pribram. bibliog Science 139:824-5 Mr 1 '63
Hominid bipedalism: independent evidence for the food-carrying theory. G. W. Hewes. bibliog Science 146:416-18 O 16 '64
Maternal deprivation: its influence on visual exploration in infant monkeys. P. C. Green and M. Gordon. il Science 145:292-4 Jl 17 '64
Menstrual cycle influences grooming behavior and sexual activity in the rhesus monkey. R. P. Michael and J. Herbert. bibliog il Science 140:500-1 My 3 '63
Monkey babies quiet after cesarean birth. Sci N L 85:168 Mr 14 '64
Monkey business in Oregon. J. B. Kemmerer. il Pop Sci 183:60-3 S '63
Monkey talk dictionary. Sci N L 85:6 Ja 4 '64
Monkeys stand in for humans. F. Marley. il Sci N L 84:218-19 O 5 '63
Orphan monkeys afraid. Sci N L 86:114 Ag 22 '64

MONKEYS—*Continued*
Rank of mothers and sons in bands of rhesus monkeys. C. B. Koford. bibliog il Science 141:356-7 Jl 26 '63
Rhesus and crab-eating macaques: intergradation in Thailand. J. Fooden. bibliog il Science 143:363-5 Ja 24 '64
Scotopic spectral sensitivity in the monkey. D. S. Blough and A. M. Schrier. bibliog il Science 139:493-4 F 8 '63
Self-maintained visual stimulation in monkeys after long-term visual deprivation. R. H. Wendt and others. bibliog il Science 139: 336-8 Ja 25 '63
Social life of Japanese monkeys; excerpts from paper. D. Miyadi. il Science 143:783-6 F 21 '64
Tax deductible monkey business; tractor-driving monkey classified as an authentic farm hand. il Life 56:121+ My 15 '64
See also
Baboons
Chimpanzees
Gibbons
Gorillas
Orangutans

Diseases and pests

Quartan-type malaria parasite of New World monkeys transmissible to man. P. G. Contacos and others. bibliog Science 142:676 N 8 '63

MONKEYS, Experiments on. See Animal experimentation
MONKS. See Monasticism
MONNEROT, Jules
What about the Sino-Soviet split? Nat R 14:447-9, 541 Je 4, Jl 2 '63
MONNERVILLE, Gaston
France's no. 2 man. H. Giniger. il pors N Y Times Mag p24+ Ja 5 '64
MONNET, Jean
Common market stimulus. Commonweal 78: 87-8 Ap 19 '63
Jean Monnet honored as Mr Europe; text of letter from President Kennedy and remarks by Mr Ball. J. F. Kennedy; G. W. Ball. Dept State Bul 48:195-7 F 11 '63
Tides of change; address, February 12, 1963. J. R. Schaetzel. Dept State Bul 48:322-8 Mr 4 '63
MONNIER, M. and Hösli, L.
Dialysis of sleep and waking factors in blood of the rabbit. bibliog Science 146:796-8 N 6 '64
MONO recorders. See Magnetic recorders and recording
MONOAMINE oxidase
Monoamine oxidase inhibitors: augmentation of pressor effects of peroral tyramine. D. H. Tedeschi and E. J. Fellows. bibliog il Science 144:1225-6 Je 5 '64
MONOCLE (periodical)
Satire through a cocked eye. il Time 83:47 Mr 13 '64
MONOCULAR vision. See Sight
MONODELLA. See Crustacea
MONOGRAMS
How to monogram contemporary silver. il House & Gard 126:190-1+ S '64
Monogramming R for bed and bath. il House & Gard 127:124-7 Ja '65
Protocol of monogramming. House & Gard 125:38+ Je '64
MONOKLISIA
Ladies' day; one day of gynecocratic rule. il Newsweek 61:36-7 F 4 '63
MONOLOGS
Monologues: something new for creative writing. S. Cochell. il Sr Schol 83:10T O 25 '63
MONOPOLIES
Chain squeeze; power of big food; with editorial comment. D. Smith. il Nation 198:642, 646-8 Je 29 '64
MONOPOLY (game) See Games
MONORAIL railroads. See Railroads, Single rail
MONOSODIUM glutamate
Potentiator. New Yorker 40:48 D 5 '64
MONOTERPENES. See Terpenes
MONOZYGOTIC twins. See Twins
MONRO, J.
Population control in animals by overloading resources with sterile animals. bibliog Science 140:496-7 My 3 '63
MONROE, Ann D.
Britain and the European community. Cur Hist 45:271-5+ N '63
Britain's economy looks to Europe. Cur Hist 46:263-8+ My '64
MONROE, Elizabeth
How they take their independence. New Repub 150:20+ Mr 14 '64
King Ibn Saud's saga. New Repub 151:18-19 S 12 '64
Transition in the Middle East. New Repub 150:21+ My 30 '64
MONROE, Henry
Practical zoo photography. U S Camera 26: 62-3+ Ag '63
MONROE, James
James Monroe, fifth President 1817-1825. F. Freidel. il pors Nat Geog Mag 126:678-83 N '64
MONROE, Margaret E.
Meeting demands: a library imperative. por Library J 88:516-18 F 1 '63
MONROE, Marilyn
Marilyn Monroe. D. Trilling. Redbook 120: 54-5+ F '63
Marilyn, my Marilyn. il pors Time 81:47 My 31 '63
What really killed Marilyn. C. B. Luce. il pors Life 57:68-72+ Ag 7 '64; Same abr. Read Digest 85:218-20+ N '64
MONROE, Paul
50th anniversary of Monroe's Cyclopedia of education. F. Cordasco. bibliog f Sch & Soc 91:123-4 Mr 9 '63
MONROE, Conn.
Try a teamwork association; Blue Ridge estates association. E. D. Fales, jr. il Am Home 66:22+ Ap '63
MONROE calculating machine company
Buying computers by the dozen; desk-sized Monrobot XI. Bsns W p45-6 Jl 20 '63
MONROE doctrine
Monroe doctrine: dead or alive? il U S News 54:20 My 13 '63
MONROEVILLE, Pa.
Third Sunday in May; Senior citizen Sunday. W. D. Pfost. Recreation 57:236-7 My '64
MONROVIA, Liberia
U.S. and Liberia sign agreements on free port and cultural program; joint announcement, May 8, 1964. Dept State Bul 50:829-30 My 25 '64
MONSANTO chemical company
Fertilizer makes the green grow. il Bsns W p21 Ag 1 '64
Turnaround year for Monsanto; trend toward consumer orientation. R. Sheehan. il Fortune 70:124-9+ S '64
MONSARRAT, Nicholas
Fair day's work; story. Sat Eve Post 237:46-8 F 15 '64
MONSEN, R. Joseph, jr
Can anyone explain capitalism? Sat R 46: 13-15+ D 14 '63
MONSEY, Derek
Actors are people, too. Theatre Arts 47:25-6+ N '63
MONSIEUR Beaucaire; drama. See Olfson, L.
MONSOONS
May the rains come. il UNESCO Courier 17: 42-3 Jl '64
When the rains came; floods in Macherla, India. Newsweek 64:55 O 12 '64
When the rains come to Vietnam. N. Sheehan. il N Y Times Mag p 12-13+ Je 14 '64
MONSTER; story. See Cohane, J. P.
MONSTERA. See Cerimans
MONSTERS
See also
Loch Ness monster
MONSTERS (toys) See Toys
MONT BLANC tunnel. See Tunnels and tunneling
MONT TREMBLANT PARK. See Quebec (province)—Parks and reserves
MONTAGNES, James
Ontario's aerial fire fighters. Am For 69:22-3+ My '63
MONTAGU, Ashley
Awesome power of human love; excerpt from The humanization of man. Read Digest 82: 80-3 F '63
Has chastity a chance at college? McCalls 90:107+ S '63
SR Anisfield-Wolf awards. 1963. Sat R 46: 22-3 Ap 13 '63
SR-Anisfield-Wolf awards, 1964. Sat R 47:19 Ap 25 '64
To think and to feel. por NEA J 53:15 O '64
What babies need most. Parents Mag 39:38-9+ My '64
MONTAGU, Mary Churchill, duchess of. See Churchill, M.
MONTAGUE, Drogo, and others
Bradykinin: vascular relaxant, cardiac stimulant. bibliog Science 141:907-8 S 6 '63
MONTAGUE, John
Clear the way; poem. Atlan 214:126 D '64
about
Some Irish poets. T. Kinsella. Poetry 102: 326-9 Ag '63

MONTAGUE, Joseph F.
Diverticulosis: big name for some little pockets. Todays Health 42:38-9 Je '64

MONTAIGNE, Michel Eyquem de
Gentle philosopher. P. W. Schmidtchen. il Hobbies 69:106 Ag '64
Lord Howard's Montaigne; 1613 edition. P. W. Schmidtchen. il por Hobbies 67:106 F '63
They made our world. L. Rosten. por Look 28:66-7 S 22 '64

MONTALCINI, Rita Levi-. See Levi-Montalcini, R.

MONTANA, Edward J. Jr
Newspaper gap. por Library J 89:1194-7 Mr 15 '64

MONTANA
See also
Colleges and universities—Montana
Fishing—Montana
Glacier National Park
Hunting—Montana
Rocky Mountains

Description and travel

Jewel basin; northwestern Montana. R. F. Cooney. il Liv Wildn 85:7-9 Wint '64
Montana: the big ski country. K. N. Anderson. il Todays Health 43:42-7+ Ja '65
Montana's valley of hush. E. Thane. il Travel 119:46-9 F '63
Traveling camera at a Montana ropin' & ridin'. L. Barry. il Pop Phot 54:109+ Mr '64

History

Montana centennial train brings the Wild West to the East. S. Foote. il Hobbies 69:90+ My '64
See also
Little Big Horn, Battle of the, 1876

Religious institutions and affairs

News of the Christian world (cont) Christian Cent 80:838+, 1384-5; 81:652, 1186+, 82:26-8 Je 26, N 6 '63, My 13, S 23 '64, Ja 6 '65

MONTANA flood. See Floods—United States

MONTANARI, A. J.
Curious transformation of Laurie. A. Henley. il por Sat Eve Post 237:83+ O 17 '64

MONTANA'S Territorial centennial. See Centennials

MONTCHENU, Jean de
Bad bishop's book of love songs. il Horizon 6:26-31 Wint '64

MONTCLAIR Calif.
Precasting culvert prevents traffic hold-up. S. E. Scholl. il Am City 79:89 D '64

MONTCLAIR, N.J.
Radar vs. speeding. H. Knowles. il Am City 79:119 Ap '64

MONTE ALTO, Brazil
Visions & vengeance. Time 82:37 Jl 5 '63

MONTEBELLO, Calif.
Hand-written fire communications. J. N. Hale. il Am City 79:12 Mr '64

MONTE CARLO opera house. See Opera houses

MONTE CARLO rally. See Automobile racing

MONTECATINI complex. See Italy—Industries

MONTECATINI TERME, Italy
Travel well. C. Rule. il Travel 121:56-8 Je '64

MONTEFIORE, Hugh
Cambridge objectors. por Time 83:78 Mr 6 '64

MONTEMEZZI, Italo
Love of three kings (Amore dei tre re) Criticism
Opera N il por 28:6-7 Ja 4 '64

MONTENEGRO
Balkans in brief; Crna Gora and all that. H. Sutton. il Sat R 46:42-5 Je 8 '63
Montenegro. W. Sansom. il Holiday 36:54-7+ Ag '64

MONTEREY (ship) See Ocean liners

MONTEREY COUNTY, Calif.
What are they doing to Big Sur? W. Trombley. il Sat Eve Post 237:24-9 F 15 '64

MONTEREY cypress. See Cypress

MONTEREY jazz festival. See Music festivals—California

MONTERREY institute of technology. See Colleges and universities—Mexico

MONTESSORI, Maria
Montessori: education begins at three. C. Mangel. il Look 29:61-7 Ja 26 '65
Montessori in the space age? E. Beyer. il NEA J 52:35-6 D '63
Schools, slums & Montessori. M. Mayer. Commentary 37:33-9 Je '64
Vision of mankind transformed. M. Remiddi. il por UNESCO Courier 17:16-20 Ap '64

MONTESSORI, Mario
Redbook dialogue; Mario Montessori and A. S. Neill discuss their famous schools and their radical approaches to child rearing. por Redbook 124:42-3+ D '64

MONTESSORI method of education
Intellectual leap; Montessori revival at Whitby school. il Newsweek 61:106+ Je 24 '63
Montessori: education begins at three. C. Mangel. il Look 29:61-7 Ja 26 '65
Montessori in the slums. il Time 84:53-4 Jl 10 '64
Montessori in the space age? E. Beyer. il NEA J 52:35-6 D '63
Return of Montessori. E. Wakin. il Sat R 47:61-3 N 21 '64
Schools, slums & Montessori. M. Mayer. Commentary 37:33-9 Je '64; Discussion. 38:20+ N '64
Vision of mankind transformed. M. Remiddi. il UNESCO Courier 17:16-20 Ap '64
What's so special about Montessori schools? il Good H 158:164-5 My '64

MONTEUX, Claude
Claude Monteux, conductor Hudson Valley philharmonic, New York. P. H. Lang. por Mus Am 83:10 My '63

MONTEUX, Pierre
In Debussy, a special valedictory. H. Goldsmith. por Hi Fi 14:77-8 D '64
Monteux legacy. R. Freed. por Sat R 47:48-9 Ag 22 '64
Obituary
Opera N por 29:15 S 26 '64. G. Fitzgerald
Pierre Monteux: 1875-1964. P. Davis. por Mus Am 84:58 S '64
Pierre Monteux, the absolute professional. C. Raeburn. Hi Fi 14:41 S '64
When I see Brahms... por Newsweek 64:82 Jl 13 '64

MONTEVERDI, Claudio
Coronation of Poppea (L'incoronazione di Poppea) Criticism
Opera N 27:29 My 4 '63
Time il 82:69 N 22 '63
Decca's Monteverdi: nothing but praise is in order; Martial madrigals, and Amorous madrigals. J. W. Barker. Am Rec G 29:554-5 Mr '63
Immoral? from Vox, Monteverdi's L'incoronazione di Poppea. J. Diether. il Am Rec G 29:700-4+ My '63
L'incoronazione di Poppea. J. Diether. il Am Rec G 31:410-15 Ja '65
Monteverdi release of the first magnitude. J. W. Barker. Am Rec G 31:415 Ja '65
On records; L'incoronazione di Poppea; La favola d'Orfeo. Opera N 28:35 Ja 25 '64

MONTEVIDEO, Uruguay
Used cars in Uruguay. L. D. Lee. il Motor T 16:52-4 Mr '64

MONTEZUMA II, emperor of Mexico
City of the living good; excerpts from Cortés: the life of the conqueror by his secretary, tr. by L. B. Simpson. F. L. de Gómara. il Am Heritage 15:67-79 Ap '64
Great confrontations V: Cortes and Montezuma. J. H. Elliott. il pors Horizon 5:92-6 N '63

MONTGOMERIE, Archibald William, 13th earl of Eglington. See Eglington, A. W. M.

MONTGOMERY, Bernard Law, 1st viscount Montgomery of Alamein. See Montgomery of Alamein, B. L. M.

MONTGOMERY, Charlotte
Speaker for the house. See issues of Good housekeeping

MONTGOMERY, Elizabeth
Girl with the necromantic nose. il por Time 84:82+ O 30 '64
Home-model witch. I. Mothner. il pors Look 29:75-9 Ja 26 '65

MONTGOMERY, Frank A. Jr
Inside the Outer Banks. Motor B 111:28-31+ Ap '63

MONTGOMERY, Genoa
I believe; Negro high school exchange student in Farmington, Conn. from Birmingham, Ala. B. Donahue. por Seventeen 22:46+ O '63

MONTGOMERY, Herb
Duluth's most controversial citizen: Mr Magoo. Am For 69:8+ O '63

MONTGOMERY, Marion
At a season's turning; poem. Cath World 198:20 O '63

MONTGOMERY, Paul
Hard times for alley cats. N Y Times Mag p47+ Ap 12 '64

MONTGOMERY, Robert R.
What a doctor tells his own kids about smoking. Changing T 18:13-14 S '64

MONTGOMERY, Ruth
What kind of a woman is our new First lady? Good H 158:32+ Mr '64
WLB biography. Wilson Lib Bul 37:802; 38:296, 573-4; 39:186+ My, N '63, Mr, O '64

MONTGOMERY of Alamein, Bernard Law Montgomery, 1st viscount
Brad vs. Monty: an old feud revived; summary of interview. O. N. Bradley. il por U S News 58:55 Ja 18 '65
Monty. A. Lunn. por Nat R 16:537-8 Je 30 '64

MONTGOMERY, Ala.

Banks

Boo-boo at the bank; mistake in T. Thaggard's account, Union bank and trust company. D. Nevin. il Life 54:14 Je 28 '63

Hospitals

Automatic care; Atomedic hospital. il Newsweek 62:87 D 16 '63
Pre-packaged hospital; Atomedic hospital. Sci Digest 55:34-5 F '64

Negroes

Ten cents that shook America. il Esquire 62:210-13 D '64

MONTGOMERY COUNTY, Md.

Public libraries, Department of

Davis does double duty. G. B. Moreland. il Library J 89:4727-9 D 1 '64

MONTGOMERY Ward and company
When products change behind their names. Consumer Rep 28:208 My '63

MONTH (periodical)
Month's century. America 111:59 Jl 18 '64

MONTH in the country; drama. See Turgenev, I. S.

MONTH of his birthday; story. See Karmel-Wolfe, H.

MONTHLY labor review
Worker security in a changing economy: a prefatory note. W. W. Wirtz. Mo Labor R 86:612-13 Je '63

MONTI, Eugenio
Inflexible flyer. C. Phinizy. il Sports Illus 20:54-7 Ja 27 '64

MONTIAS, John Michael
Communist rule in eastern Europe. For Affairs 43:331-48 Ja '65
Patching up Russia's planned economy. Reporter 28:22-4 Ap 11 '63

MONTINI, Giovanni Battista
Nephew's portrait of Pope Paul; ed. by S. Fliegers. pors Look 28:21-7 F 25 '64

MONTINI, Giovanni Battista (Paul VI, pope)
See Paul VI, pope

MONTINI family
Pope's distinguished family. G. B. Leonard. il pors Look 28:26-32 F 25 '64

MONTMORILLONITE
Hydrogen-aluminum clays: a third buffer range appearing in potentiometric titration. U. Schwertmann and M. L. Jackson. bibliog il Science 139:1052-4 Mr 15 '63
Transformation of montmorillonite to kaolinite during weathering. Z. S. Altschuler and others. bibliog il Science 141:148-52 Jl 12 '63

MONTOGOMERY, Kathryn
(comp) New spring children's books. Library J 89:1409-38 Mr 15 '64

MONTRALDO; story. See Cheever, J.

MONTREAL

Architecture

Place Ville Marie. il Arch Forum 118:74-89 F '63
Place Ville Marie. il Arch Rec 133:127-36 F '63

Description

Montreal: the good life. il Holiday 35:158+ Ap '64

Hotels restaurants, ec.

Montreal: the good life. il Holiday 35:158+ Ap '64

Music

Multi-purpose hall for opera, concerts, musical comedy; La grande salle, Place des arts. il Arch Rec 136:136-9 D '64
[Musical events] Mus Am 84:21+ Mr '64
Place des arts: the festival. G. Potvin. il Mus Am 83:15-16 S '63
State of the unions; opening of La grande salle. H. Davidson. il Mus Am 83:23+ O '63

Parks and playgrounds

Theory and practice. Recreation 57:179 Ap '64

Religious institutions and affairs

Ecumenism in Montreal. I. Beaubien. America 109:16-17 Jl 6 '63

Subways

In Canada, subways are for building. il Bsns W p76+ Mr 9 '63

Worlds fair, 1967

Sociological challenge at the Montreal world's fair. il Fortune 71:189-90 Ja '65

MONTREAL botanical garden
Montreal botanical garden. M. Raymond. il Horticulture 42:26-9 Jl '64

MONTREAL conference on faith and order. See World conference on faith and order

MONTREAL symphony orchestra. See Orchestras

MONTRESOR, Beni
Christmas fable. il Opera N 28:6-7 D 28 '63
Gentleman of Verona; interview, ed. by F. Stevenson. por Opera N 28:26 F 8 '64

MONTREUX, Switzerland
Music in Montreux. R. Gelatt. il Hi Fi 13:50-1 Mr '63

MONUMENT and the shadow; story. See Humphrey, W.

MONUMENT VALLEY, Utah
Mysterious Monument Valley. R. De Roos. il Read Digest 82:134-9 Je '63

MONUMENTS
Life guide; monuments that have stories to tell. il Life 55:9+ O 25 '63
Monumental failures and successes. W. Walton. il N Y Times Mag p32-3+ Mr 15 '64
Monuments and landmarks; commemorating deeds of outstanding Negroes. il Ebony 18:107-10+ S '63
See also
Statue of liberty
Statues
See also subhead Monuments, statues, etc. under names of cities, e.g. Washington, D.C.—Monuments, statues, etc.

MONUMENTS, Megalithic. See Megalithic monuments

MONUMENTS, National. See National monuments

MONUMENTS, Natural. See Natural monuments

MONUMENTS, Sepulchral. See Sepulchral monuments

MONVOISIN, Raymond Quinsac
Monvoisin in South America. A. R. Romera. il Américas 15:7-11 My '63

MOODIE, John
Illustrations of John Moodie. F. Whitaker. il por Am Artist 28:50-5+ Ja '64

MOODY, Alton B.
Guide over the pathless oceans. Motor B 111:114+ Mr '63

MOODY, Barbara S.
Children's libraries. Wilson Lib Bul 37:704 Ap '63

MOODY, Howard
American Baptists: to break the bonds of captivity. Christian Cent 80:456-8 Ap 10 '63
Is the local church obsolete? Christian Cent 80:1554 D 11 '63

MOODY, Joseph N.
Habemus Papam, Paulum VI. America 109:10-11 Jl 6 '63

MOODY, M. F.
X-ray diffraction pattern of nerve myelin: a method for determining the phases. bibliog Science 142:1173-4 N 29 '63

MOODY, Mildred T.
Reader who needs remotivation. por ALA Bul 58:795-7 O '64

MOODY, Minnie Hite
Comprehension; poem. McCalls 90:198 S '63
For a husband, retiring; poem. Farm J 87:112 Mr '63
March rabbit; poem. McCalls 90:131 Mr '63

MOODY'S investors service, incorporated
Assessing gilt; nation's three bond-rating services. il Time 84:58 D 25 '64

MOOG, C. Vianna
In defense of culture; excerpts from address, September 1963. por Américas 15:1 O '63

MOOG, Florence
Intestinal phosphatase activity: acceleration of increase by puromycin and actinomycin. bibliog Science 144:414-16 Ap 24 '64

MOOHO, Pan
Gentle art of tiny teapot tea. Esquire 62:180+ D '64

MOOMBA festival. See Festivals—Australia

MOON, Carroll
Wonderful world of lids. Pop Electr 21:69-70+ D '64

MOON, Dean
Hip roddy. il Hot Rod 17:100-1 O '64

MOON, Eric
From the twosome, a quartet. Sat R 46:28-9 F 23 '63
London's first World book fair: trade show or public fair? Pub W 186:24-9 Jl 27 '64

MOON, Rexford G. Jr
More students are studying now, paying later. Sat R 46:74-5+ Je 15 '63

MOON, Robert W.
Who are the losers? Christian Cent 81:1104-5 S 9 '64

MOON, Samuel
Early fall; poem. Atlan 212:60 S '63

MOON
Aerojet is studying lunar oxygen system. Aviation W 79:107 N 11 '63
Birth of the moon. il Newsweek 63:50 Ja 27 '64
Capture of the moon. Time 81:81 My 24 '63
Getting acquainted with astronomy (cont) il Sky & Tel 25:146-7, 267-8 Mr, My '63
Lunar notation on upper paleolithic remains. A. Marshack. il Science 146:743-5 N 6 '64
Moon captured by earth. W. Davis. Sci N L 83:291 My 11 '63
Moon fragments sought in western Iowa. Sci N L 85:196 Mr 28 '64
Moon history may be clue to ancient rocks. Sci N L 84:339 N 30 '63
Moon influences meteors. A. Ewing. Sci N L 83:213 Ap 6 '63
Our neighbor the moon; excerpts from The moon. V. Brenna. il Look 27:68-74+ N 5 '63
Sun, moon, and planets this month. See issues of Sky and telescope
Waxing or waning, the moon has always interested man. S. D. Gossner. il Natur Hist 72:56-7 Mr '63
See also
Eclipses, Lunar
Occultations
Rainbow, Lunar
Space flight to the moon
Tides

Atmosphere

Moon's magnetic teardrop; magnetosphere. Sci N L 85:195 Mr 28 '64

Influence on weather

See Moon and meteorology

Names

See Names, Lunar

Orbit

Laboratory exercises in astronomy, the moon's orbit. O. Gingerich. il Sky & Tel 27:220-1 Ap '64

Photographs, maps, etc.

Album of Ranger 7 moon pictures. il Sky & Tel 28:151-8 S '64
Atlas of the moon, by V. de Callatay. Review Sci Digest 56:34-5 N '64. B. Pryor
C. B. Watts and the marginal zone of the moon. J. Ashbrook. Sky & Tel 27:94-5 F '64
—Continued
Do the moon photos change our plans? W. Von Braun. il Pop Sci 185:110-13+ N '64
Geology of the moon. E. M. Shoemaker. il Sci Am 211:38-47 O '64
Getting acquainted with astronomy (cont) il Sky & Tel 25:146-7, 267-8 Mr, My '63
In focus. il Sky & Tel 25:131+, 270+; 26:19+, 336+; 27:146+, 285+; 28:15+, 145 Mr, My, Jl, D '63, Mr, My, Jl, S '64
Mapping the face of the moon. Fortune 68:130-3 N '63
Moon map to aid Apollo astronauts. Miss & Roc 14:18 Je 29 '64
New Ranger photos show crater slopes. Aviation W 81:23 Ag 31 '64
Ranger moon pictures: implications. T. Gold. bibliog Science 145:1046-8 S 4 '64
Ranger photos boost confidence in Apollo. H. D. Watkins. il Aviation W 81:19-23 Ag 10 '64
Ranger 7 colloquium. Sky & tel 28:342-3 D '64
Ranger VII photographs of moon sent to leaders of 110 nations; statement, August 16, 1964. L. B. Johnson. Dept State Bul 51:348 S 7 '64
Ranger VII photos. Miss & Roc 15:17-18+ Ag 10 '64
Some lunar studies by T. G. Elger. G. Fielder. il Sky & Tel 25:248-51 My '63
Trail blazers for moon explorers. J. Goodyear. il Pop Mech 119:128-31+ F '63
What we know about the moon now; Ranger 7 photographs. B. H. Frisch. Sci Digest 56:15-20 O '64
See also
Space photography

Surface

Agreement on lunar surface broadens. M. Getler. il Miss & Roc 12:27-8, 31 Je 10 '63
Another lunar color phenomenon. Sky & Tel 27:3 Ja '64
Are there changes on the moon? Sky & Tel 28:3 Jl '64
At sea on the moon. R. S. Lewis. Bul Atomic Sci 20:35-7 N '64
Bendix simulating lunar magma in laboratory tests. J. F. Judge. il Miss & Roc 14:36-7 Mr 23 '64
Boeing scientists find unexpected abundance of hot spots on the moon. Miss & Roc 16:28 Ja 18 '65
Charting by blinks; lunar color phenomena. Sci N L 85:338 My 30 '64
Data indicates crushable lunar surface. W. J. Normyle. Aviation W 80:83 My 18 '64
Dusty answer. Nation 199:178 O 5 '64
Estimate of neutron albedo on the moon's surface resulting from cosmic radiation. M. V. K. Appa Rao. bibliog il Science 141:530-1 Ag 9 '63
Geology of the moon. E. M. Shoemaker. il Sci Am 211:38-47 D '64
Interpretation of Ranger photographs. J. A. O'Keefe. bibliog il Science 146:514-15 O 23 '64
Landing men on moon dust. N. A. Weil. il Sci Digest 53:4-11 Mr '63
Lively moon; five U.S. astronomers see transient luminous red spots. Sci Am 210:67-8 F '64
Luminescent moon? Sci Am 210:56 Mr '64
Luminous; observations of moon spots. New Yorker 40:24-6 Je 20 '64
Lunar eruption in 1783? B. M. Middlehurst. il Sky & Tel 28:83-4 Ag '64
Lunar lava flow; Ranger 7 photographs suggest volcanic activity. il Time 84:85 N 13 '64
Lunar luminescence. il Sky & Tel 28:201 O '64
Lunar luminescence and solar flares. Z. Kopal and T. W. Rackham. il Sky & Tel 27:140-1 Mr '64
Lunar surface debated. Sci N L 86:191 S 19 '64
Lunar surface features: mid-infrared spectral observations. G. R. Hunt and J. W. Salisbury. bibliog il Science 146:641-2 O 30 '64
Mapping the face of the moon. il Fortune 68:130-3 N '63
Month of the moon spots. il Sci Digest 55:31-2 Je '64
Moon close up. E. M. Shoemaker. il Nat Geog Mag 126:690-707 N '64
Moon like blue cheese. F. Marley. Sci N L 85:115 F 22 '64
Moon microscopy. il Sci Am 211:80-1 S '64
Moon: rougher than you think. il Time 84:52 Jl 24 '64
Moon surface strength debate revived. W. J. Normyle. Aviation W 81:31 S 7 '64; Discussion. 81:94 S 28; 118 O 19 '64
Moonglow; Ranger 7 photos. il Newsweek 64:57 S 7 '64
Moon's face, first wonder of our sky. T. D. Nicholson. il Natur Hist 73:54-6 Ag '64
Moon's seas held water. W. Wingo. Sci N L 85:133 F 29 '64
Mortar on the moon; spacecraft to study the moon's crust. Newsweek 62:86 S 9 '63
NASA hopeful on lunar flare feasibility. C. M. Plattner. il Aviation W 81:32-3 D 28 '64
New data pinpoints micrometeorite size. Aviation W 78:64 Ap 29 '63
Observing the moon, Gambart B and C. A. K. Herring. il Sky & Tel 28:243 O '64
Observing the moon, Jansen. A. K. Herring. il Sky & Tel 26:38 Jl '63
Observing the moon, Krieger. A. K. Herring. il Sky & Tel 28:49 Jl '64
Observing the moon, Lansberg D. A. K. Herring. il Sky & Tel 27:60 Ja '64
Observing the moon, Marius. A. K. Herring. il Sky & Tel 29:59 Ja '65
Observing the moon, Plato. A. K. Herring. il Sky & Tel 27:250-2 Ap '64
Observing the moon, Prinz. A. K. Herring. il Sky & Tel 26:219 O '63
Observing the moon; Ramsden. A. K. Herring. il Sky & Tel 25:221 Ap '63
Old devil moon. il Newsweek 61:62-3 Ap 15 '63
Ranger moon pictures: implications. T. Gold. bibliog il Science 145:1046-8 S 4 '64
Ranger VII proves Apollo feasibility; with editorial comment. Miss & Roc 15:16+. 54 Ag 10 '64
Recent observation of lunar color phenomena; with supplementary note by John S. Hall. J. A. Greenacre. il Sky & Tel 26:316-17 D '63
Ruby moon. il Newsweek 62:60 D 30 '63
Simolivac and the moon; producing frozen froth of silica. Sky & Tel 28:24 Jl '64
Spots on the moon; observing crater Aristarchus. il Time 82:54-5 D 27 '63

MOON—Surface—*Continued*
Sun particles cause red spots on moon. Sci N L 85:360 Je 6 '64
Surface material of the moon. C. R. Warren. bibliog il Science 140:188-90 Ap 12 '63
Surveyor must settle doubts on lunar surface. H. Taylor. Miss & Roc 15:16 S 7 '64
Taking the measure of the moon; success of Ranger 7. il Newsweek 64:15-18 Ag 10 '64
What formed the moon's sinuous rilles? il Sky & Tel 26:21 Jl '63
What the moon Ranger couldn't see. J. Lear. il Sat R 47:35-43 S 5 '64; Discussion. 47: 63-4 O 3; 32+ O 10 '64
What we know about the moon now; Ranger 7 photographs. B. H. Frisch. Sci Digest 56:15-20 O '64

Temperature

Moon's hot spots. Newsweek 65:89 Ja 25 '65
Survivability of wire on moon tested. P. J. Klass. Aviation W 78:77+ My 27 '63

MOON, Flight to the. See Space flight to the moon

MOON, Photography of. See Astronomical photography

MOON and meteorology
Lunar tides affect rain. Sci N L 87:20 Ja 9 '65

MOON bases. See Lunar bases

MOON garden; story. See Howard, M.

MOON landing. See Space vehicles—Landing systems

MOON of the arfy darfy; story. See Algren, N.

MOON probes. See Lunar probes

MOON spots. See Moon—Surface

MOON vehicles. See Lunar vehicles

MOONEY, James David
Drawing the rules from history. por Bsns W p46+ Ag 3 '63

MOONEY, Richard E.
Economic oracles of the New frontier. N Y Times Mag p8+ Ag 4 '63

MOONEY, Ross L.
Day & night; poem. Sch Arts 64:30 N '64

MOONEY, Stephen
Piano tuner; poem. New Yorker 39:120 F 15 '64

MOONEY aircraft, incorporated
Mitsubishi seeking U.S. sales penetration. il Aviation W 79:98-9+ Ag 26 '63
Mooney sales may top $12 million in 1965 with Mark 22. E. J. Bulban. il Aviation W 81:86-7+ O 12 '64

MOONFLOWER vine; novel. See Carleton, J.

MOONLIGHTERS. See Employees

MOONLIGHTING. See Supplementary employment

MOON'S up there; drama. See Nolan, P. T.

MOONSHINE light, moonshine bright; story. See Fox, W. P.

MOONSHINING
Still life. il Newsweek 61:24 F 25 '63

MOONSPOTS. See Moon—Surface

MOOR, Paul
Confessions of an illicit tape recordist. Hi Fi 13:38-40+ Ag '63
Munich and its (sometimes) favorite son. Hi Fi 14:46-9+ Je '64
Notes from abroad. Hi Fi 13:28+ Mr '63
Notes from our correspondents (cont of) Notes from abroad. Hi Fi 13:28+ Mr '63; 14:26+ S '64
Roses for Lady Florence. Harper 226:28-31 F '63

MOOR-JANKOWSKI, J. and others
Blood groups of chimpanzees: demonstrated with isoimmune serums. bibliog Science 145:1441-3 S 25 '64
—See Wiener, A. S. jt. auth.

MOORE, Anne Carroll
Miss Moore in Brooklyn: a reminiscence. I. Parin D'Aulaire. il Horn Bk 40:473-4 O '64

MOORE, B. G. and Tischer, R. G.
Extracellular polysaccharides of algae: effects on life-support systems. bibliog Science 145: 586-7 Ag 7 '64

MOORE, Barbara
—and Moore, Peter
Also on Sunday. il Mlle 58:66-9 D '63

about

Where are they now? por Newsweek 61:16 F 25 '63

MOORE, Bessie
Arkansas schools get economics-minded. il pors Bsns W p 112-14 Jl 20 '63

MOORE, Brian
People of Belfast. Holiday 35:58-63 F '64

MOORE, Cecil
Goddam boss. il por Time 84:24-5 S 11 '64
Philadelphia, Pennsylvania: a process of fragmentation. H. Lees. il Reporter 29:18-20 Jl 4 '63

MOORE, Charles F. Jr
Want to be a real pro? Read Digest 83:56-8 Ag '63

MOORE, Clement Clarke
Faces from the past. R. M. Ketchum. il por Am Heritage 15:52-3 D '63

MOORE, D. H.
Don't knock the box. U S Camera 27:54-5 Ap '64

MOORE, Davey
Aftermath. Time 81:70 Ap 5 '63
Boxing killed my husband. G. Moore. il pors Ebony 18:131-2+ Jl '63
Death of a champion. M. Sharnik. il pors Sports Illus 18:18-21+ Ap 1 '63
End of the street; Moore-Ramos fight. Time 81:54 Mr 29 '63
He fought, talked, then died. il por Life 54: 41-2 Ap 5 '63

MOORE, David
Sport in the Orient; photographs. Sports Illus 19:38-49 D 23 '63

MOORE, David G.
Psychoanalyzing the small businessman. il Bsns W p90+ S 19 '64

MOORE, David W.
Electronics primer. Pop Electr 21:52 Ag '64

MOORE, Dean
Special-interest cars. Motor T 16:80 N '64

MOORE, Douglas Stuart
Ballad of Baby Doe. Criticism
New Yorker 39:150-2 My 11 '63
Good life; interview, ed. by M. Brozen. por Mus Am 83:26 Ag '63

MOORE, Dudley
Please feed the lions. il por Mlle 57:96-7+ Je '63

MOORE, Edward F.
Mathematics in the biological sciences; with biographical sketch. Sci Am 211:30, 148-54+ bibliog(p270) S '64

MOORE, Elizabeth
I sold a house to a Negro. pors Ebony 18: 92-4+ O '63

MOORE, Everett T.
Intellectual freedom. See issues of ALA bulletin to June 1963

MOORE, Francis D.
New problems for surgery; excerpts from address, December 30, 1963. Science 144:388-92 Ap 24 '64

about

Best hope of all; with colored photographs of seven major operations. il por Time 81: 44-60 My 3 '63

MOORE, Garry
Fame is a funny thing. por Look 28:77+ S 22 '64

MOORE, Gay Montague
Living with antiques. Antiques 85:686-9 Je '64

MOORE, George
Driving Ford's experimental OHC V-8. Motor T 16:60-1 O '64
Good year for Goodyear. Motor T 16:74-7 F '64
Indy diary. Motor T 16:55-7 Ap '64
New dawn for Duesenberg? Motor T 16:76-9 S '64
One from the North; Yankee 300. Motor T 16:70-3 Ag '64
Race car safety design. Motor T 15:68-73 Jl '63
Rubber battle at Indy; Firestone fires up! Motor T 16:55-7 Mr '64
Sears tries the big time. Motor T 16:58-9 Ap '64
Transverse T-Bird FWD concept in the works for '65. Motor T 15:58-9+ My '63
Yankee 300. Motor T 15:74-7 Jl '63

MOORE, George Eugene
Surgeon for all seasons. il por Newsweek 64:92 O 19 '64

MOORE, George S.
World economic developments; address, November 16, 1964. Vital Speeches 31:162-5 Ja 1 '65

about

Moses vs. the bankers. por Newsweek 65:61 F 1 '65

MOORE, Geraldine (Welch)
Boxing killed my husband. pors Ebony 18: 131-2+ Jl '63

MOORE, Grace
More about Grace Moore. Hobbies 68:31 Ap '63

MOORE, Harry T.
Bamming the bards. Sat R 46:36+ Je 15 '63
Brief and turbulent marriage. Sat R 46:29-30 My 11 '63
From battlefield to bazaar. Sat R 47:31-2 F 29 '64
From Black Forest to pink plaza. Sat R 47:37+ N 14 '64
From Bloomsbury to Brooklyn. Sat R 47:35 Je 20 '64
Listed in the Yellow book. Sat R 47:48 My 16 '64

MOORE, Henry
(ed) Gist of it. See issues of Outdoor life

MOORE, Henry Spencer
Genius of Michelangelo as seen by Moore; ed. by D. Sylvester. N Y Times Mag p 16-17+ Mr 8 '64
Letter from London; exhibition of H. Moore's and F. Bacon's works. M. Panter-Downes. New Yorker 39:100+ S 7 '63
On the shore with Moore. il Life 55:73-4+ S 6 '63

MOORE, Herman E.
If I were young today. por Ebony 18:88 O '63

MOORE, Isabel
Category novel. Writer 77:9-13 S '64

MOORE, J. William, and Smith, W. I.
Motivation in automated instruction. Sch Life 46:21-2 N '63

MOORE, Jacqueline
Case for an independent Quebec. Harper 229: 93-5+ O '64

MOORE, James W.
Moore on movies. See issues of U.S. camera

MOORE, Joanna
Hattiesburg and central Illinois. Christian Cent 81:340-1 Mr 11 '64

MOORE, John B.
This maintenance shop sells service. Am City 78:107-8 Ap '63

MOORE, John Eugene
Afterword in November; poem. Commonweal 81:226 N 13 '64

MOORE, John Travers
Poem for editors. Cath World 198:162 D '63
Whisper; poem. Horn Bk 39:489 O '63

MOORE, Joseph Curtis, and Clark, Eugenie
Discovery of right whales in the Gulf of Mexico. bibliog Science 141:269 Jl 19 '63

MOORE, Latham Leslie-. See Leslie-Moore, L.

MOORE, Lenny
Rookie and the vet. il pors Ebony 20:56-8+ Ja '65

MOORE, Lillian
Blasis to Bournonville. Dance Mag 38:52-3+ F '64
Buried treasure. Dance Mag 38:42-7 Ap '64

MOORE, M. Brittain, jr
V.D. menace; venereal disease is curable. por Parents Mag 39:143+ F '64

MOORE, Marianne
Charity overcoming envy; poem. New Yorker 39:44 Mr 30 '63
Expedient, Leonardo da Vinci's (and a query) poem. New Yorker 40:52 Ap 18 '64
Knife. House & Gard 123:98-9+ F '63
Marianne Moore speaks; ed. by H. F. Holland. Vogue 142:88+ Ag 15 '63
Old amusement park; poem. New Yorker 40: 34 Ag 29 '64
Profit is a dead weight. por Seventeen 22:142+ Mr '63
Ten answers: letter from an October afternoon. por Harper 229:91-2+ N '64
W. S. Landor; poem. New Yorker 40:26 F 22 '64

about

Marianne Moore's Brooklyn. P. Coffin. il pors Look 27:54f+ My 7 '63
Meditation and enactment. H. Kenner. Poetry 102:109-15 My '63
World series with Marianne Moore. G. Plimpton. il Harper 229:50-8 O '64; Reply. M. Moore. 229:91-2+ N '64

MOORE, Mary M.
Sarge. Read Digest 86:49-52 Ja '65

MOORE, Mary Tyler
America's favorite TV wife. S. Gordon. il pors Look 28:M9-M10+ Ap 21 '64

MOORE, Michal
Painting with pebbles. Design 64:100+ Ja '63

MOORE, Oscar Keeling
Baffle winter. Flower Grower 50:34-6 N '63
Family of sophisticated evergreens. House B 105:289-90+ N '63
How to lure hummingbirds to your garden. House B 105:22+ Je '63
How to select tulips. House B 105:214-15+ O '63
Nearly failure-proof nasturtium. House B 106:170+ Mr '64
Trouble-free glory of lilies. House B 105: 96-7+ Ag '63
Twofold bounty of azaleas. House B 105: 164-5+ My '63
Wonderful world of reflexed lilies. Flower Grower 50:38+ Ag '63

MOORE, Paul, jr, bp
Church and city. il por Newsweek 63:62 F 24 '64

MOORE, Peter. See Moore, B. jt. auth.

MOORE, Phil
Sparkling rose wine punch. il por Ebony 18: 188+ S '63

MOORE, Rachael
Has Christmas become too commercial? Farm J 87:63 D '63

MOORE, Richard
Abroad: poem. Atlan 213:78 Ap '64
Apparition; poem. New Yorker 40:135 My 30 '64
Drought; poem. New Yorker 40:50 O 17 '64
Gem; poem. Sat R 46:100 O 12 '63
Hawks; poem. Atlan 213:87 My '64
Makers; poem. New Yorker 40:54 O 31 '64
Psychiatric discharges; poem. Harper 226:74 My '63
Suburb hilltop; poem. New Yorker 39:34 Ja 18 '64
To a child with a top; poem. Reporter 31:39 N 5 '64
To a poet; poem. Harper 227:70 N '63
To a successful student; poem. Harper 226:50 Je '63
To one on friendly terms with many poets; poem. Harper 228:18 Je '64

MOORE, Richard O. and Villee, C. A.
Malate dehydrogenase: multiple forms in separated blastomeres of sea urchin embryos. bibliog Science 142:389-90 O 18 '63

MOORE, Richard R.
Neighbor-to-neighbor purchasing plan. Am City 79:160+ O '64

MOORE, Robert H. See Carlton, L. jt. auth.

MOORE, Robert L. jr
I fought in Vietnam; interview. il pors U S News 56:40-7 Je 8 '64
True story of war in Vietnam. por U S News 56:38-41 My 18 '64

MOORE, Roger J.
(tr) See Antonioni, M. Hollywood myth has fallen!

MOORE, Rosanna
Bas-relief mural. Sch Arts 64:23 N '64

MOORE, Sam
Life radio review. Life 57:19 N 13 '64

MOORE, Shirley
Science youths start younger. Sci N L 84:170-1+ S 14 '63

MOORE, Thomas
Gadgets & gilhickies. Yachting 115:77+ My '64

MOORE, Vincent J.
Residents asked for more. Am City 78:125 S '63

MOORE, Virginia Bennett
Fire Island: a possible national seashore. Nat Parks Mag 37:4-9 F '63
Slipperiest fish in the sea. Sports Illus 18: 38-41+ Je 3 '63

MOORE, W. J. See Barry, T. I. jt. auth.

MOORE, W. Robert
Burma: gentle neighbor of India and red China. il Nat Geog Mag 123:153-99 F '63

MOORE, Wilbert E.
Corporation at war with itself. Duns R 81: 58-60 Ap '63

MOORE, William L.
Attala and the Huns. America 108:658 My 11 '63
In Bill Moore's footsteps. por Time 81:18-19 My 10 '63
No place to walk; civil-rights crusaders tribute to W. Moore. il Newsweek 61:28-9 My 13 '63
Pilgrimage to Jackson. M. Kempton. New Repub 148:14-16 My 11 '63

MOORÉA
Footloose in Polynesia. H. Sutton. Sat R 47:32-3 Ap 18 '64

MOOREHEAD, Alan
Ghastly blank; first exploration of Australia; excerpt from Cooper's Creek. por Atlan 213: 100-14 F '64
Great old man's last trip to Commons. Life 57:30-1 Ag 7 '64
Letter from Australia. New Yorker 40:216+ O 10 '64
Reporter at large (cont) New Yorker 40:39-40+ Je 27 '64

MOORHEAD, Jennelle
PTA concerns are world concerns. PTA Mag 58:26-8 Ja '64
PTA goes abroad. pors PTA Mag 59:20-2 D '64
President's message. por PTA Mag 59:2-3 S; 2-3 O; 2-3 N; 2-3 D '64; 2-3 Ja '65

MOORHEAD, Jennelle—*Continued*
about
Fight for the PTA. il por Newsweek 65:46+ F 1 '65
MOORHEAD, William S.
National humanities foundation. America 111: 597+ N 14 '64
MOORING of boats. See Boats—Mooring
MOORISH architecture. See Architecture, Islamic
MOORS (people)
Arabian knights. F. Stevenson. Opera N 28: 24-5 F 15 '64
MOOS, Malcolm
After the fall. New Repub 151:11-14 D 12 '64
Are political conventions out of date? interview. por U S News 57:70-2 S 14 '64
Case against the Democrats. N Y Times Mag p9+ Ja 12 '64
Flogging Congress. Nation 197:226-7 O 12 '63
How 'The man who' wins the prize. N Y Times Mag p8+ Je 21 '64
Is the long campaign necessary? N Y Times Mag p 14+ My 10 '64
MOOSAD MELNICK, Vijaya L. and others
Physiological studies on fruit development by means of ovule transplantation in vivo. bibliog Science 145:609-11 Ag 7 '64
MOOSE
Wolves versus moose on Isle Royale. D. L. Allen and L. D. Mech. il Nat Geog Mag 123:200-19 F '63
MOOSE hunting
Ballplayer's moose hunt. R. Bressler. il Outdoor Life 135:66-9+ F '65
Extra-special moose. H. J. Samuels. il Outdoor Life 132:33-5+ O '63
First moose at Mindedo. N. Smith. il Outdoor Life 134:60-1+ O '64
Moose by the yard. C. Ormond. il Outdoor Life 132:40-3+ Jl '63
Moose enough for two. R. Voss. il Outdoor Life 134:24-7+ Ag '64
Muzzle of meese. W. Page. il Field & S 69: 25-7+ Ag '64
Ox hunt for moose. H. Schaefer. il Outdoor Life 134:36-9+ S '64
Shot with luck. J. Van Wormer. il Outdoor Life 131:28-9 Mr '63
MOOSEHEAD, Lake
Moosehead: Thoreau's north woods lake. J. T. Starr. il Am For 70:20-3 Je '64
MORA, José A.
Foundations of modern international law; excerpts from address, October 8, 1963. Américas 15:1 N '63
Technical assistance; summary of address, March 1963. Américas 15:44-5 My '63
What is progress? Américas 15:1 S '63
MORA, Manuel R. Garcia-. See Garcia-Mora, M. R.
MORAES, Dom
Benevolent light bulb. House & Gard 124: 248-9 N '63
MORAES, Frank
Importance of being black. For Affairs 43: 99-111 O '64
MORAGA, Calif.
Education
Laboratory to test new educational methods. il Arch Rec 134:212-13 O '63
MORAIS ANDRADE, Mário Raul de
Creative force of Mário de Andrade. J. Nist. il por Américas 17:27-9 Ja '65
MORAL adoption program. See Adoption
MORAL attitudes
Extramarital sex and the pill. P. A. Bertocci. Christian Cent 81:267-70 F 26 '64; Discussion. 81:499 Ap 15 '64
Fear of immorality. J. P. Sisk. Commonweal 81:415-18 D 18 '64
Sexplosion: disregard of moral restraints. R. E. Fitch. Christian Cent 81:136-8 Ja 29 '64; Discussion. 81:372+ Mr 18 '64
MORAL codes. See Ethics
MORAL conditions
Great morality. D. Lawrence. U S News 57: 100 D 21 '64
New morality: reprint from The Daily telegraph of London, with editorial comment. U S News 55:104 Ag 26 '63
Someday: a real Christmas. D. Lawrence. U S News 55:80 D 30 '63
See also
Moving pictures—Moral aspects
also subhead Moral conditions under names of countries, states, etc. e.g. United States—Moral conditions
MORAL education
Fine art of living; ten commandments. C. S. Winters. PTA Mag 58:11-12 O '63
Jesuit at Dartmouth; reflections on the problem of good and evil in education. T. V. Purcell. America 108:534-6+ Ap 20 '63
On men and moral values; excerpt from Self-renewal: the individual and the innovative society. J. W. Gardner. Read Digest 84:167-8 Mr '64
Psychology can't substitute for morality. B. Spock. Redbook 122:22+ Ja '64
Role of the school in developing social responsibility in a free society; excerpt from Social responsibility in a free society. NEA J 52:33-8 N '63
Schools and character development. H. Howe, 2d. Sat R 46:66-7 S 21 '63
Teach your child to love the storm. J. L. Jones. il Read Digest 82:126-7 F '63
See also
Character
MORAL obligation. See Duty
MORAL philosophy. See Ethics
MORAL rearmament
New man at M.R.A. il Time 84:74 O 30 '64
Recrudescent moral disarmament. R. Kirk. Nat R 16:824 S 22 '64; Reply. J. M. Roots and B. Entwistle. 16:969 N 3 '64
MORAL sense. See Ethics
MORAL theology. See Christian ethics
MORAL values. See Worth
MORALE
Studies of teacher morale. Sch & Soc 92: 63-4 F 22 '64
Teacher teaches better. F. L. Redefer. il NEA J 53:8-10 Ap '64
See also
Employee morale
United States—Army—Morale
MORALE, Group. See Social psychology
MORALE, Home. See Family life
MORALE, National
United States
Changing mood of America; what a nationwide survey shows. il U S News 55:36-45 Jl 29 '63
Joy in Mudville. Newsweek 62:70 Jl 29 '63
Mood now: urgent concern. il Bsns W p28-30 S 7 '63
Mood of America in election year; what a national survey shows. il U S News 56:68-73 Mr 30 '64
Spring without fever. il Bsns W p23-5 Mr 30 '63
Study of the sickness called apathy; concerning Catherine Genovese's murder. A. M. Rosenthal. il N Y Times Mag p24+ My 3 '64
Where America is weakest; interview. A. Burke. il U S News 57:66-70 Jl 13 '64
Who cares? L. Gross. il Look 28:17-19 S 8 '64; Same abr. with title Is there a Samaritan in the neighborhood? Read Digest 85: 106-10 N '64
MORALES, Villeda
Another government is missing. il por Time 82:32-3 O 11 '63
MORALES-CARRIÓN, Arturo
Achievable utopia. Américas 16:1 Ap '64
Partners in dissent: towards an inter-American dialogue: address, April 29, 1964. Vital Speeches 30:522-6 Je 15 '64
MORALS. See Ethics
MORALS and law. See Law and ethics
MORALS and literature. See Literature and morals
MORAN, Janet A.
Should boys be taught to fight back? Parents Mag 39:44-5+ Je '64
MORAN, Thomas
Painting of Thomas Moran: sources and style. W. H. Gerdts. il Antiques 85:202-5 F '64
MORATH, Max
Rag peddler. por Time 81:42 F 22 '63
MORATORIUM, Bank, 1933. See Banks and banking—United States—Crisis, 1933
MORAVEC, Ivan
Ivan Moravec: a master pianist at 45 r.p.m. R. Kammerer. il por Am Rec G 29:620-1 Ap '63
On two recital discs, debut of a new Czech pianist. H. Goldsmith. por Hi Fi 13:74-5 Ap '63
MORAVIA, Alberto
Anachronism of Verdi; tr. by W. Weaver. Hi Fi 13:79-81 O '63
Escape; story; excerpt from Fetish, tr. by A. Davidson. Atlan 215:87-9 Ja '65
Head against the wall; story. Esquire 62:132 D '64

MORAVIA, Alberto—*Continued*
Loveliest thing of all; story, tr. by A. Davidson. Sat Eve Post 236:50-1 Ap 6 '63
Tough nut; story; tr. by A. Davidson. Sat Eve Post 237:52-3 Ap 25 '64
Visconti, the leopard man. Vogue 142:50-1+ Jl '63
about
Our man in Rome. New Yorker 40:34-6 Ap 4 '64
MORAY, Ann
Christ child's lullaby; story. Mlle 60:110-11 D '64
MORDEN, Irene
Lions almost anytime. pors Outdoor Life 131: 46-9+ Ja '63
MORDHORST, Dean A.
Parson and the tree; poem. Christian Cent 81:1485 D 2 '64
MORE, Sir Thomas, Saint
Loom of language and the fabric of imperatives: the case of Il principe and Utopia. J. H. Hexter. bibliog f Am Hist R 69:945-68 Jl '64
MORE stately mansions; drama. See O'Neill, E. G.
MORE than a memory; story. See Freeman, J. T.
MOREELL, Ben
Our strategy for 1964; address, July 12, 1963. Vital Speeches 29:671-2 Ag 15 '63
Right to be wrong; address, November 22, 1963. Vital Speeches 30:158-60 D 15 '63
MOREELSE, Willem
Museum evaluations. A. Frankfurter. il Art N 63:26+ Ja '65
MOREHOUSE, Ward
Foreign area studies in New York schools and colleges. Sch & Soc 91:280-2 O 5 '63
Provincialism and constitutionalism: the role of the states in foreign area studies. bibliog f Ann Am Acad 356:119-25 N '64
MORELAND, George B.
Davis does double duty. Library J 89:4727-9 D 1 '64
MORELLI, Giovanni
Critique of connoisseurship. E. Wind. bibliog il por Art N 63:26-9+ Mr '64
MORELS. See Mushrooms
MORENO, Alvaro. See Naslund, K. C. jt. auth.
MORENO, Miguel José, jr
Anti-U.S. diplomats; two spokesmen for Panama. por U S News 56:16 F 3 '64
MOREY, William R.
(ed) See Dale, R. Memoirs of a contemporary cutpurse
MORGAN, Charles, jr
Birmingham: an Alabaman's great speech lays the blame. il Life 55:44B-44C S 27 '63
Birmingham: I saw a city die; ed. by T. B. Morgan. pors Look 27:23-5 D 3 '63
Who is guilty in Birmingham? Christian Cent 80:1195-6 O 2 '63
about
Old times there are not forgiven. R. Dugger. Nation 198:659-60 Je 29 '64
Two southern liberals. J. Epstein. Commentary 38:73-4+ D '64
MORGAN, Dale L.
When the Saints came marching in. Sat R 48:31 Ja 16 '65
MORGAN, Dan
Wesleyan tutorials. Sat R 46:68-9 Je 15 '63
MORGAN, Dawn
Girl with a hole in her heart. P. Pierce. il pors Ebony 20:27-8+ D '64
MORGAN, Harold S.
Medical highlights of 1963. Parents Mag 38: 54+ O '63
MORGAN, Harry
Informing foreign journalists about America. R. Kirk. Nat R 16:1017 N 17 '64
They discover America. C. W. Hall. Read Digest 82:81-6 Je '63
MORGAN, Henry
Roaming the fair city. Ladies Home J 81:109 Jl '64
MORGAN, Howard
Sound and fury. por Newsweek 61:68 F 11 '63
MORGAN, J. P, and company. See Morgan guaranty trust company
MORGAN, J. W. and Lovering, J. F.
Rhenium and osmium abundances in stony meteorites. bibliog Science 144:835-6 My 15 '64
MORGAN, James I.
Questions for solving the inventory problem. Harvard Bsns R 41:95-110 Jl '63
MORGAN, John Pierpont
Faces from the past. R. M. Ketchum. por Am Heritage 14:24-5 F '63
Thirty years ago; a midget sat on J. P. Morgan's lap. S. D. Smith. il por N Y Times Mag p50+ My 26 '63
MORGAN, Karl Z.
Permissible exposure to ionizing radiation. bibliog Science 139:565-71 F 15 '63
MORGAN, Lael
Sailing on the edge. Motor B 114:48-9 N '64
MORGAN, Lola S.
Behind the shapes of things; poem. Cath World 198:13 O '63
MORGAN, Margaret Knox
Women in photojournalism. Pop Phot 54: 41+ F '64
MORGAN, Murray
Case of the frustrated fighter. Sat Eve Post 236:71-2 My 18 '63
Loneliness of the missile attendant. Esquire 62:50-3+ Jl '64
Ungainly waterbug. Sat Eve Post 236:68-9 Jl 13 '63
Yankee who conquered Everest. Sat Eve Post 236:40+ Je 29 '63
—See McGrady, P. jt. auth.
MORGAN, Neil
Failure of the sexual revolution in southern California. Esquire 62:57-8+ Ag '64
WLB biography. Wilson Lib Bul 39:343+ D '64
MORGAN, Russ
Jazz; the happy sound is dying. Esquire 59: 148-50 Ap '63
MORGAN, Thomas B.
Blaze Starr in nighttown. Esquire 62:58-62+ Jl '64
Class of '68. Look 28:19-33 S 22 '64
Fight against prejudice. Look 27:66+ Je 4 '63
Five days in Mississippi. Look 27:86-90 Jl 16 '63
God and man in Hollywood. Esquire 59:74-5+ My '63
Long happy life of Bennett Cerf. Esquire 61: 112-13+ Mr '64
Seventeen states vote to destroy democracy as we know it. Look 27:76+ D 3 '63
Texas giant awakens. Look 27:71-2+ O 8 '63
Two worlds of Dick Gregory. Holiday 36:125-30+ D '64
Vanishing American Jew. Look 28:42-3+ My 5 '64
(ed) See Morgan, C. jr. Birmingham: I saw a city die
MORGAN guaranty trust company
Drama at the House of Morgan. il N Y Times Mag p 12-13 Ag 11 '63
MORGAN horses. See Horses
MORGAN library. See Pierpont Morgan library
MORGENSTERN, Dan
Jazz in New York. Mus Am 84:55 Ja '64
MORGENSTERN, George
Apt pupil. Nat R 16:871-2+ O 6 '64
Little secret history. Nat R 15:158-60 Ag 27 '63
Tribune of the people. Nat R 15:66+ Jl 30 '63
MORGENSTERN, Joseph
Culture of the non-hotel. Horizon 5:115-17 Mr '63
MORGENSTERN, Oskar
Qui numerare incipit errare incipit; excerpts from On the accuracy of economic observations. Fortune 68:142-4+ O '63
MORGENTHALER, Sascha
Grandmother and her dolls. E. Gurewitsch. il pors Look 28:71-3 D 29 '64
MORGENTHAU, Hans Joachim
America and the world revolution; ed. by N. Podhoretz. Commentary 36:278-96 O '63
Crisis in the western alliance: American view. Commentary 35:185-90 Mr '63
Four designs for tomorrow's Europe. N Y Times Mag p 18+ My 17 '64
Germany gives rise to vast uncertainties. N Y Times Mag p21+ S 8 '63
Public affairs (cont) Commentary 35:62-5, 420-3; 36:384-6 Ja, My, N '63; 37:61-3 Ja; 66-9 Mr; 68-71 My; 38:65-8 S '64
Who's running the country? Sat R 47:30-1+ Ap 25 '64
about
Morgenthau on nuclear war. P. Ramsey. Commonweal 78:554-7 S 20 '63
MORHOUSE, L. Judson
Great liquor scandal. por Time 81:24-5 Ap 12 '63
More to come? por Time 81:18 F 8 '63
MORIARTY, Margaret
Fuchsias. Horticulture 41:570 N '63
Trailing ivy-leaved geraniums. Horticulture 41:126-7 Mr '63
MORIMOTO, Toshio
Entertain with tempura. Am Home 67:60-2 Ja '64

MORIN, Edward
Innocents abroad; poem. Christian Cent 81:958 Jl 29 '64
What then ought we to do? poem. Christian Cent 80:1026 Ag 21 '63

MORISON, Elting E.
History in their household. Sat R 47:24 N 28 '64

MORISON, Robert S.
Considerations for policy-makers; new US patterns. New Repub 149:38-41 N 9 '63

MORISON, Russ
My business is selling dreams. Read Digest 83:110-12 S '63

MORISON, Samuel Eliot
John Fitzgerald Kennedy, 1917-1963. Atlan 213:47-9 F '64
Six minutes that changed the world. Am Heritage 14:50-5+ F '63

about

Samuel Eliot Morison: admiral and historian. S. L. A. Marshall. Atlan 212:87-90 N '63

MORISOT, Berthe
Great ones all painted us. Mme E. Rouart. il pors Life 54:48-55 My 10 '63

MORISSEAU, James
Some basics of campus planning; excerpts from Bricks and mortarboards. Arch Rec 134:125-8 Ag '63

MORITZ, Owen
Militants. New Repub 150:5-6 My 9 '64

MORITZ, Sidney
Shoot where you are! U S Camera 27:80-1 Je '64
Take it from TV. U S Camera 26:74-5 Je '63

MORLAND, Nigel
Solving crimes on paper; excerpt from Science in crime detection. Sci Digest 53:12-23 Mr '63

MORLEY, Charles
(comp) Articles and other books received; eastern Europe. See issues of American historical review

MORLEY, Edward W.
Michelson-Morley experiment. R. S. Shankland. il por Sci Am 211:107-14 N '64

MORLEY, Felix
American conservatism today. Nat R 16:235-6 Mr 24 '64
Deliberate pace in Congress safeguards your rights. Nations Bsns 51:27-8 Mr '63
Supreme court and the Republic. Fortune 70:102+ Ag '64
Trends: the state of the Nation. See issues of Nation's business

MORLEY, Hilda
Poem: That I might go on the hunt again. Nation 197:308 N 9 '63

MORLEY, James William
Japan's security policy in transition. Cur Hist 46:200-6 Ap '64

MORMON tabernacle choir. See Choirs

MORMONS and Mormonism
Gathering of Zion: the story of the Mormon trail, by W. Stegner. Review
Sat R il 48:31 Ja 16 '65. D. L. Morgan
Memo from a Mormon: in which a troubled young man raises the question of his church's attitude toward Negroes. J. Nye. il Look 27:74+ O 22 '63; Discussion. 27:79 O 22; 17 D 3 '63
Mormonism and the Negro, by J. J. Stewart; with supplement by W. E. Berrett. Review
Nation 196:291-2 Ap 6 '63. V. L. Bullough
Mormonism on the move. R. A. Cheville. Christian Cent 80:1328-30 O 30 '63; Reply. C. S. Logan. 81:14 Ja 1 '64
Mormonism: rich, vital, and unique. S. Freedgood. il Fortune 69:136-9+ Ap '64
Mormons bar priesthood to Negroes. Christian Cent 81:1485 D 2 '64
Mormons (cont) C. Carmer. il Am Heritage 14:26-33+ F '63
Mormons in literature. M. P. Marchant; reply. J. Fraser. Library J 88:1568+ Ap 15 '63
Negro question. il Time 82:83 O 18 '63
Notes for a gazetteer. P. Hamburger. New Yorker 40:222+ N 21 '64
Third degree; exclusion of Negroes from the priesthood. Newsweek 61:60 Je 17 '63

History

Ordeal at Devil's gate. W. Stegner. Esquire 61:100-1+ Je '64

MORNING glories
Glorious mornings with morning-glory. M. M. Leister. il Flower Grower 50:13-14 N '63

MORNING glory pool. See Hot springs

MORNING; story. See Updike, J.

MORNING sun; musical comedy. See Musical comedies, revues, etc.—Criticisms, plots, etc.

MORNINGS at 7:45; story. See Jordan, E. H.

MORNINGSIDE HEIGHTS. See New York (city)

MORO, Aldo
Prime Minister Moro to President Johnson; letter, December 11, 1963. Dept State Bul 50:47 Ja 13 '64

about

Converging parallels. por Newsweek 62:60+ D 9 '63
End of the miracle. Newsweek 63:30 Mr 30 '64
Gambler. Newsweek 64:40 Jl 6 '64
Italy's new partnership. por Time 82:31 D 13 '63
Mr Moro tries again. E. V. Kuehnelt-Leddihn. Nat R 16:689 Ag 11 '64
Persuader. New Repub 150:11-12 Ja 18 '64

MOROCCAN cookery. See Cookery, Moroccan

MOROCCAN weddings. See Marriage customs and rites

MOROCCO
Secretary-General visits three African countries. U N Rev 11:12-13+ Mr '64
See also
Americans in Morocco
Earthquakes—Morocco
Elections—Morocco
Jews in Morocco
Marrakesh
Political parties—Morocco
Rehabilitation—Morocco
Tangier

Boundaries

Another border, another war. New Repub 149:8 O 26 '63
Brief interlude. il Newsweek 62:56+ N 11 '63
Buzz saw; border war. il Newsweek 62:46 N 4 '63
Clash in the Sahara. il Sr Schol 83:6-9+ N 22 '63
Double trouble in Algeria. Sr Schol 83:16 N 1 '63
Fight now, fly later; Algerian-Moroccan border clash. il Time 82:39-40 O 25 '63
Minuscule war; Moroccan-Algerian border clash. il Newsweek 62:44 O 28 '63
More than five-minute truce? border war between Morocco and Algeria. Time 82:35-6 N 8 '63
Reflections on the Barbary Coast. R. Kirk. Nat R 15:442 N 19 '63
They war over a wasteland. il Life 55:38-9 N 8 '63
Unwelcome are the peacemakers. il Time 82:36 N 1 '63
War in Africa; MIG jets on both sides; two outposts on Sahara Desert border between Algeria and Morocco. il U S News 55:6 O 28 '63

Description and travel

Fly-by-night trip to Morocco. R. Lynes. Harper 227:24-9 Ag '63
Going places, finding things in Morocco. M. R. Henry. il House & Gard 125:26+ F '64
Journey through Morocco. P. Bowles. il Holiday 33:42-53+ F '63
Morocco from A to Z. M. R. Henry. Vogue 144:40+ S 1 '64

Foreign relations

Friend in Washington. il Time 81:37-8 Ap 5 '63
King of Morocco exchanges views with President Kennedy; joint communique, March 29, 1963. Dept State Bul 48:601 Ap 22 '63
Man who came to dinner. il Time 81:27-8 Mr 22 '63
Road from Morocco: easy lies the head; with report by A. Deming. Newsweek 61:31 Ap 1 '63

Politics and government

King's headache. il Time 81:29-30 Je 7 '63

Religious institutions and affairs

Ecumenism in Morocco; Benedictine monks at Toumliline. W. Dunphy. America 111:694 N 28 '64
Nonagon: Baha'i charged with heresy. Nation 196:130 F 16 '63

Royal family

Royal wedding festival; marriage of H.R.H. Princess Lalla Nouzha in Morocco. il Vogue 145:72-7 Ja 15 '65

Social conditions

Journey through Morocco. P. Bowles. il Holiday 33:42-53+ F '63

MOROCCO—*Continued*
Social life and customs
Far and near; Moroccan Berbers cling to feudal ways. C. Wyatt. il Natur Hist 72: 60-2 N '63
MORONI, Federico
Scuola di Severino; a new home. M. D. Campell. il por Sch Arts 62:12-16 My '63
MOROS
Fierce Moros. J. Keats. il Holiday 34:124+ D '63
MOROSS, Jerome
Gentlemen, be seated! Criticism
New Yorker 39:201-2 O 19 '63
Sat R 46:56+ O 26 '63
MOROZOV, Aleksandr Dimitrievich
Comrade Blimp. Newsweek 62:50 D 16 '63
MORPHINE
Apparent concentration quenching of morphine fluorescence. R. Brandt and others. bibliog il Science 139:1063-4 Mr 15 '63
Fear and pain: their effect on self-injection of amobarbital sodium by rats. D. Davis and N. E. Miller. il Science 141:1286-7 S 27 '63
Inhibition of bacterial growth by drugs of the morphine series. E. J. Simon. bibliog il Science 144:543-4 My 1 '64
MORPHOGENESIS. See Morphology
MORPHOLOGY
Reconstruction of tissues by dissociated cells. M. S. Steinberg. bibliog il Science 141:401-8 Ag 2 '63
System for studying microbial morphogenesis: rapid formation of microcysts in myxococcus xanthus. M. Dworkin and S. M. Gibson. bibliog il Science 146:243-4 O 9 '64
MORRELL, Ottoline
Memoirs of Lady Ottoline Morrell; ed. by R. Gathorne-Hardy. Review
New Repub 150:27-8+ Je 13 '64. W. Allen
Sat R por 47:37+ Je 20 '64. L. Edel
Most marvelous party. S. Eimerl. Reporter 31:62+ Ag 13 '64
MORRESSY, John
Hyannis Port kid rides again. Nat R 15: 483 D 3 '63
MORRILL, George P.
United States merchant marine. Holiday 34: 64-9+ S '63
MORRIS, Aldyth
East-West interchange through books. America 112:44 Ja 9 '65
MORRIS, Coral K.
Five minutes a day to keep fit. Farm J 88:72 Ja '64
MORRIS, Delyte Wesley
Big voice in Little Egypt. il por Time 83:61 My 15 '64
MORRIS, Mrs Don
Reaching students through the arts. Sr Schol 84:9T Ap 24 '64
MORRIS, Effie Lee
Serving the handicapped child. por Wilson Lib Bul 38:165-9 O '63
MORRIS, Eileen
Middle age motherhood for me! Read Digest 82:193-4 Mr '63
MORRIS, Elida
Six comediennes (cont) J. Walsh. il pors Hobbies 67:32-6 F; 68:32-6+ Mr; 32 Ap '63
MORRIS, Everett B.
Crew life in Newport. Yachting 116:46-8+ S '64
Developing a 12-meter crew. Yachting 116:44-6+ Jl '64
Doubloon wins southern title. Yachting 113: 50-1+ Ap '63
Learning the hard way. Yachting 117:104-5 Ja '65
MORRIS, G. T.
Coin-operated meters prevent water losses. Am City 78:147-8 Mr '63
MORRIS, George
Ram for the records. por Outdoor Life 134: 46-7+ Ag '64
MORRIS, Herbert
Submissions; In winter, the magician; poems. Poetry 102:221-3 Jl '63
MORRIS, Ivan
Theatre. Vogue 144:152 D '64; 145:68 Ja 1; 98 F 1 '65
MORRIS, Jack
Minnesota sets a brisk pace. Am For 69:35+ N '63
MORRIS, James
By Venice possessed. Horizon 5:14-16+ Mr '63
King John's lost treasure. Sat Eve Post 237: 64+ My 30 '64
New pulse of Australia. Sat Eve Post 236: 20-3 Mr 2 '63
about
Pointillist in words. por Newsweek 62:43 Ag 5 '63
MORRIS, Jill
Hidden picture. U S Camera 26:54-5 Jl '63
Just a click apart. U S Camera 26:62-5 D '63
New look in nudes. U S Camera 26:58-61+ Jl '63
One photographer+one model=all women. U S Camera 26:64-71 My '63
Play gypsy, dance gypsy. U S Camera 27:63-7 Ap '64
Power of emotion. U S Camera 26:76-7+ F '63
MORRIS, Joe Alex
How haste in space makes waste. Read Digest 85:82-7 Jl '64
Little Rock finds a better way. Read Digest 83:142-6 S '63
Paralyzing power of Washington lobbies. Read Digest 82:127-32 My '63
Pork barrel goes into orbit. Read Digest 85:87-92 Ag '64
MORRIS, John G.
Photographers don't think! Pop Phot 51:65+ D '62
MORRIS, John W.
Changing face of Europe. Sr Schol 85:14T-15T N 11 '64
MORRIS, M. D.
Prospecting parkland. Recreation 56:109-2 Ap '63
MORRIS, Mary Ellen. See Safferman, R. S. jt. auth.
MORRIS, Newbold
Message; meeting on remodeling Washington Square park. New Yorker 40:34-5 Je 6 '64
MORRIS, Patricia H.
Star performers in late summer garden. Horticulture 41:134-5 Mr '63
MORRIS, Peggy
℞ for beauty in a day. il pors McCalls 90: 158+ My '63
MORRIS, Richard B.
Muddled problem of the succession. N Y Times Mag p 11+ D 15 '63
MORRIS, Robert
Defenders of the right. il por Newsweek 61: 20 F 4 '63
MORRIS, Robert L.
Nickel buys a ride on the minibus. Am City 79:133-4 Jl '64
MORRIS, Terence
Pathology of affluence. Nation 197:390-2 D 7 '63
MORRIS, Terry
Ordeal of Dorothy Pulver. Redbook 122:58-9+ Mr '64
What clergymen tell young people about marriage. Redbook 120:50-1+ Mr '63
(ed) See Schapper, B. Research and interviewing techniques
(ed) See Weisinger, M. Outlines and article writing
MORRIS, Thomas D.
Morris operation key to most defense spending. por Miss & Roc 12:87 Mr 25 '63
MORRIS, William Richard, 1st viscount. See Nuffield, W. R. M.
MORRIS, Willie
Cell 772, or Life among the extremists. Commentary 38:31-9 O '64
Devil theory. Nation 198:56-8 Ja 13 '64
Legislating in Texas. Commentary 38:40-6 N '64
Memoirs of a short-wave prophet. New Yorker 39:117-18+ N 30 '63
Renaissance at the University of Texas. Harper 226:76-9+ Je; 227:14+ S '63
Roger Baldwin. New Repub 150:8-10 Ja 25 '64
20,000 words a week about the state as it is. New Repub 151:6-7 D 19 '64
What makes Dallas different? New Repub 150:20-2 Je 20 '64
Word in defense of Texas. N Y Times Mag p23+ Ap 5 '64
MORRIS, Wright
Death of the reader. Nation 198:53-4 Ja 13 '64
MORRIS chairs. See Chairs
MORRISON, Allan
Black patriots were heroes at first major battle of Revolution. Ebony 19:44-6+ F '64
Crusading press. Ebony 18:204+ S '63
Dark faces in the UN. Ebony 18:23-6+ F '63
Hope for Harlem. Ebony 19:168-70+ O '64
Man behind the horn. Ebony 19:143-4+ Je '64
Miami's Cuban refugee crisis. Ebony 18:96-100+ Je '63
Negro political progress in New England. Ebony 18:25-8+ O '63
100 years of Negro entertainment. Ebony 18: 122-4+ S '63
Selassie's message to the Negro. Ebony 19: 29-32+ D '63
Top judge. Ebony 19:111-12+ Mr '64

MORRISON, Ashton B. and others
Lysosomes in the renal papillae of rats: formation induced by potassium-deficient diet. bibliog Science 142:1066-8 N 22 '63
MORRISON, Charles Clayton
Charles Clayton Morrison at ninety; tribute by his friends. por Christian Cent 81:1486-8 D 2 '64; Reply. H. S. Leiper. 82:17 Ja 6 '65
MORRISON, deLesseps Story
Excerpt from address, April 16, 1962. Cong Digest 42:88+ Mr '63
Region in ferment; address, August 26, 1963. Vital Speeches 30:11-13 O 15 '63

about

Louisiana: clues to '64 vote. por U S News 56:64 Ja 27 '64
Once more, with moderation. Time 82:14 D 20 '63
Upset, true to form. il Newsweek 63:28 Ja 27 '64
MORRISON, Doris E.
View of two cities. Sch Arts 63:28-30 F '64
MORRISON, Eilene M.
School libraries. Wilson Lib Bul 38:85 S '63
MORRISON, Harriet
Visit your own home. Am Home 67:28 N '64
MORRISON, Julia Maria
Americans and others. Poetry 104:115-19 My '64
Prothalamion; poem. Poetry 101:244 Ja '63
Run of three. Poetry 101:279-82 Ja '63
MORRISON, Kenneth J.
Set your sights on sixty, ninety, or even 120-bushel wheat. Suc Farm 62:46-7+ S '64
MORRISON, Laura E.
Get started for only $428.35. Pop Sci 184:130 F '64
MORRISON, Morton
How good are lens stretchers? U S Camera 27:56-7+ D '64
Inexpensive CdS meters. U S Camera 27:48-9+ D '64
Inexpensive speedlight studio. U S Camera 27:56-7+ Jl '64
No time to focus. U S Camera 27:46-7+ S '64
When a trick is a treat. U S Camera 28:64 Ja '65
MORRISON, William C.
Do-it-yourself boatyard. Yachting 115:198+ My '64
MORRISON family
Morrison coat-of-arms. H. K. Eilers. il Hobbies 68:120-2 D '63
MORRISON, Ill.
When Negro child meets white. T. T. Chapin. Christian Cent 80:1333-4 O 30 '63
MORRISON-Knudsen, company
Builders of anything, anywhere. il Bsns W p58-9+ D 5 '64
MORRISSETT, Ann
Here I am; poem. Harper 226:80 F '63
Little man, big ideas. Commonweal 78:549-50 S 20 '63
Mr Dunkenheimer. Redbook 122:12+ D '63
MORRISTOWN, N.J.
Ol' swimmin' hole goes modern. G. E. Burke. il Am City 79:100-1 Mr '64
MORRO, El. See El Morro National Monument
MORRO Castle fire. See Ships—Fires and fire protection
MORROW, John
Dispensable and indispensable genes in neurospora. bibliog Science 144:307-8 Ap 17 '64
MORROW, Martha G.
Millions of working mamas. Sci N L 85:250-1 Ap 18 '64
MORROW, Michael J.
Hawaiian amateur in the Arctic. il Sky & Tel 26:88-9 Ag '63
MORROW, Susan
Double jeopardy; story. Good H 157:60-1 Jl '63
MORROW COUNTY, Ohio
Ohio's mad oil boom; drilling in fields, lawns and schoolyards. B. Lindeman. il Sat Eve Post 237:81-5 N 14 '64
Oil; boom in Ohio. il Time 83:84 F 21 '64
Oil boom, Ohio style. il Bsns W p 154-6 Mr 28 '64
MORSE, B. K. See Content, J. E. jt. auth.
MORSE, Carl A.
Building skylines is his business. il por Bsns W p33-4 Jl 11 '64
MORSE, David A.
ILO director-general's speech on the South African question; excerpt, June 18, 1963. Mo Labor R 86:920-4 Ag '63
MORSE, Harriet K.
Flowers & shade. Flower Grower 50:48-9+ Mr '63
MORSE, J. G.
Energy for remote areas. bibliog Science 139:1175-80 Mr 22 '63
MORSE, J. H.
Behind the Moscow treaty. Nat R 15:242-3 S 24 '63
MORSE, Leon
Battle of do-it-yourself. Duns R 82:pt2 163-7 N '63
Changing anatomy of industrial sales distribution. Duns R 81:37-8+ Ja '63
Closing in on the customer. Duns R 81:pt2 S100-3+ Je '63
Hard sell abroad. Duns R 81:46-9+ Ap '63
How to create a salesman. Duns R 82:46-7+ D '63
Industrial marketing's new voice. Duns R 81:31-2+ Mr '63
Industry's fight for shelf space. Duns R 81:45-6+ F '63
Purchasing; from rags to riches. Duns R 81:54-6+ My '63
MORSE, Ralph
Our role in the moon assault. G. P. Hunt. il por Life 55:7 S 27 '63
MORSE, Richard L. D.
Official report: what borrowers need to know. il por U S News 56:85-6 Je 29 '64
MORSE, Richard M.
Strange career of Latin-American studies. Ann Am Acad 356:106-12 N '64
MORSE, Robert
His gold-capped teeth gleamed no more. Life 54:26-7 F 22 '63
MORSE, Roger A.
Swarm orientation in honeybees. bibliog Science 141:357-8 Jl 26 '63
MORSE, Roy W.
Good contract collection. Am City 78:191-2+ S '63
MORSE, Samuel Finley Breese
Professor Henry and his philosophical toys; with note by Mrs C. H. Danforth. M. Blow. il por Am Heritage 15:24-9+ D '63
MORSE, Samuel French
Beginning. Poetry 104:253-7 Jl '64
Boat in a tree; poem. Horn Bk 40:485 O '64
Islands in summer; poem. Poetry 104:357-9 S '64
Soldier; poem. Poetry 102:308-9 Ag '63
Veterans and recruits. Poetry 102:330-4 Ag '63
MORSE, Wayne Lyman
As one good friend to another. . : excerpts from Congressional record. Nat R 14:348 My 7 '63
Excerpt from debate, August 21, 1964. Cong Digest 44:15+ Ja '65
Excerpt from debate, February 2 and 5, 1962. Cong Digest 42:48+ F '63
Opportunities for all; address, March 27, 1963. Vital Speeches 29:457-9 My 15 '63
United States foreign policy in Asia; address, July 17, 1964. Vital Speeches 30:678-82 S 1 '64
We must leave Vietnam. N Y Times Mag p 14-15+ Ja 17 '65
When a friend of labor turned critic; criticism of railroad brotherhoods; excerpts from address, August 27, 1963. U S News 55:96 S 9 '63

about

People of the week. por U S News 55:16 N 25 '63
MORSE, William B.
Application rejected. Am For 70:32+ Jl '64
Bill Huey's birds. por Am For 69:26-7+ D '63
DMSO; fact and fancy. Am For 70:6-7+ S '64
Little brother of the snow. Am For 69:28-9+ F '63
Needed, a who's who for shrubs. Am For 70:30-1+ My '64
Shoein' horses; a mighty man is he. Am For 70:32-4 O '64
That utilizing monster. Am For 71:30-1+ Ja '65
Winema, the memorial forest. Am For 69:24-5+ Je '63
MORTALITY
Death rates show inequality of sexes. Sci N L 83:297 My 11 '63
Outlook for world population. J. M. Stycos. Science 146:1435-40 D 11 '64
Word. V. P. McCorry. America 108:652 My 4 '63
See also
Death
Infant mortality
MORTAR
Bricks without straw bosses. J. Lear. il Sat R 47:45-9 F 1 '64

MORTAR and pestle. See Pharmaceutical apparatus

MORTGAGE banks
Mortgage middlemen try opening new doors. il Bsns W p55-6+ S 26 '64

MORTGAGE guaranty insurance corporation
Behind the man behind the loan; MGIC. il Bsns W p 120+ S 28 '63
It's magic; Bobby Baker's financial affairs. il Newsweek 62:31 N 25 '63
New twists in Baker's trail. Bsns W p25 N 16 '63

MORTGAGE insurance. See Insurance. Mortgage

MORTGAGES
As foreclosures rise; bargain counter for houses; role of FHA. il U S News 56:106-7 Mr 16 '64
Consumer saving. Fortune 68:44+ O '63
Fast-growing way to raise instant cash. il U S News 57:109-10+ O 26 '64
FHA defaults cause no alarm. U S News 54:95-6 F 11 '63
Home loans: costs & terms. il Changing T 17:20-2 S '63
Home-mortgage financing eased. U S News 57:79 Ag 31 '64
House isn't just a home, it's a piggy bank. T. G. Harris. il Look 28:28+ Ja 14 '64
Housing: risky finance. Newsweek 62:70 Ag 12 '63
How large should your home mortgage be? R. Charles. il Parents Mag 39:60+ Jl '64
If you need mortgage money. il Changing T 18:35-6 S '64
It's a good time to buy a house. il Changing T 17:7-10 Ap '63
Junior mortgages: high yields for the wary. J. Thackray. il Duns R 83:46-8+ F '64
Lenders are loaded; construction industry. il Bsns W p 101-2+ Je 20 '64
More union money for housing; government-guaranteed mortgages. Bsns W p 102 F 29 '64
Newest trend in raising cash: refinancing home. il U S News 55:99 Ag 26 '63
Personal business. Bsns W p 149 My 25 '63
Relationship of unemployment to mortgage foreclosures. il Mo Labor R 86:1421-5 D '63
Truth about the cost of money for remodeling. M. Colean. il House B 105:188-91 S '63
Turning your house into cash: refinancing a mortgage. il Changing T 17:25-8 N '63
Why should your family have an open-end mortgage? Bet Hom & Gard 41:6+ Je '63
Why the growing worry over debt people owe; with statements by C. C. Balderston and J. W. Barr. il U S News 57:89-92 O 19 '64
See also
Farm finance
Insurance. Mortgage
Investments
United States—Federal housing administration

MORTICIANS. See Undertakers and undertaking

MORTIMER, Amanda
Miss Amanda Mortimer. por Vogue 141:140-1 My '63

MORTIMER, Charles G.
Industry's stake in education: address. January 16, 1963. Vital Speeches 29:270-3 F 15 '63
Let's keep politics out of the pantry. pors Look 29:80+ Ja 26 '65
Power of free choice: address. December 3, 1963. Vital Speeches 30:214-16 Ja 15 '64

MORTIMER, Penelope
First love, first agonized encounter. Vogue 143:173-4+ Ap 1 '64

MORTIMER, R. K. See Manney, T. R. jt. auth.

MORTON, Andrew Q.
Kairopractice: concerning authorship of Romans, Corinthians, and Galatians. Time 81:56 Mr 15 '63
Saint and science. Newsweek 62:82 N 18 '63

MORTON, Charles W.
Accent on living. See issues of Atlantic
Brief interlude at the New Yorker. Atlan 211:81-4 My '63
Expense account luncheon. Atlan 211:134+ Mr '63
Lean times in Boston: depression and the drys. Atlan 211:47-54 F '63
Try for the New Yorker. por Atlan 211:45-9 Ap '63

MORTON, Florrinell F.
Anita Hostetter. ALA Bul 57:854-5 O '63

MORTON, Frederic
Velvet Europe. Holiday 33:58-71+ My '63; 35:38-53 Ja '64
Velvet New York. Holiday 36:52-65+ N '64

MORTON, H. B. See Ettlinger, G. jt. auth.

MORTON, Leslie T.
International medical body. Library J 88:2847-8 Ag '63

MORTON, Louis
Egotist in uniform. Harper 229:138+ N '64

MORTON, Thruston B.
Collective guilt? a senator's answer; excerpts from address, December 12, 1963. U S News 55:74 D 23 '63
about
If not Rockefeller or Goldwater, here are two dark horses. por U S News 54:48-9 Je 3 '63
Republicans look over another possibility for '64. il pors U S News 55:42-3 Jl 8 '63
Thruston Morton, the all-purpose Republican. R. L. Riggs. New Repub 150:8-10 Je 27 '64

MORTON, W. Ross. See Becker, B. jt. auth.

MORTON salt company
Report on the testing of advertised products. E. M. McCabe. il Parents Mag 38:34+ Ap '63

MORTUARY customs. See Undertakers and undertaking

MORTUARY sculpture. See Sepulchral monuments

MOSAIC law. See Jewish law

MOSAIC virus, Tobacco. See Tobacco mosaic virus

MOSAICS
Fun of doing mosaic-craft. D. Aller and D. L. Aller. il Design 65:84-6 N '63
How to make beachcomber mosaics. il House & Gard 123:106-7 Je '63
Mosaic mural; depicting life of Abraham Lincoln in Indiana. il Design 66:28-30 S '64
Mosaic mural for your school: History of Huntingdon, in the Huntingdon junior high school, Huntingdon, Pa. M. L. Miller. bibliog il Sch Arts 64:10-15 D '64
Mosaic wall of N.Y.C. P. Greenberg. il Sch Arts 63:5-7 S '63
Mosaics in plastic. il Design 64:175 Mr '63
Refill mosaics. D. P. Malone and W. Karre. il Sch Arts 62:14 F '63
Seed mosaics. P. Degenhart. il Design 64:146-7 Mr '63
This mosaic tells time. il Sunset 132:133-4 Mr '64
Wall: mosaic tiles. K. Sawyer. il Craft Horiz 23:20-3+ My '63

MOSBACHER, Emil, jr
America's cup racing, 1964 style. Yachting 116:36-8+ S '64

MOSCONA, A. A. See Moscona, M. H. jt. auth.

MOSCONA, M. H. and Moscona, A. A.
Inhibition of adhesiveness and aggregation of dissociated cells by inhibitors of protein and RNA synthesis. bibliog Science 142:1070-1 N 22 '63

MOSCOSO, Teodoro
Excerpt from address, December 17, 1962. Cong Digest 42:92+ Mr '63
New world of Latin America. Sat R 46:23-7+ O 12 '63
South America: travel's sleeping beauty. Sat R 47:53-4+ O 10 '64
about
Incompatibility. por Newsweek 63:59 My 18 '64
Matter of tone. Time 83:48 My 15 '64
Mr Moscoso named representative to Inter-American economic units. Dept State Bul 50:89 Ja 20 '64

MOSCOVICI, Carlo, and others
Isolation of a viral agent from pseudocowpox disease. bibliog Science 141:915-16 S 6 '63

MOSCOW, David H.
Individualizing instruction with paperbacks. NEA J 53:21-2 Ap '64

MOSCOW
Moscow revisited. H. Brandon. Sat R 47:10-11 Je 6 '64

Airports
Sheremetyevo terminal designed to handle 1,600 passengers hourly. il Aviation W 81:38-40 Ag 24 '64

Description
Our footloose correspondents. V. Perera. New Yorker 39:144+ Ap 27 '63

Hotels, restaurants, etc.
Motel for Moscow. il Bsns W p50-2 Mr 7 '64

Housing
Moscow landscape 1963: it's instant housing! il Life 55:34-41 S 13 '63

MOSCOW—*Continued*

Kremlin

Crème de la Kremlin; NBC's tour of the Kremlin. il Time 81:48 My 31 '63

Monuments, statues, etc.

Latest turn in the cold war: a battle of statues; Ukrainian poet, T. Shevchenko. il U S News 56:14 Je 29 '64

Music

Great opera houses: the Bolshoi. J. A. Boromé. il Opera N 28:26-31 F 29 '64

Rapid transit

See also
Moscow—Subways

Religious institutions and affairs

Diary of an American Jesuit. W. V. Casey. il America 109:113-17 Ag 3 '63
Mission in Moscow; first American Protestant church. Newsweek 63:55 F 10 '64

Riots

African lesson for the Russians. Life 56:4 Ja 3 '64
Anger in Red square; demonstration protesting racial discrimination by African nations. il Sr Schol 83:17 Ja 10 '64
Now, race riots in Moscow's Red square. il U S News 55:5 D 30 '63
Red and black; African students demonstration in Moscow. il Newsweek 62:23 D 30 '63
We too are people; African students vs. Soviet police. il Time 82:20-1 D 27 '63

Social conditions

Russia revisited: contrast with a twist. R. J. Korengold. il Newsweek 64:36-8 Ag 31 '64

Stores

On sale at GUM, Moscow's super shop. A. R Topping. il N Y Times Mag p 13+ Jl 28 '63

Subways

How Ivan gets home. il Bsns W p98-100 Ag 15 '64

Theater

On Pushkin street; pirated production of My fair lady in Moscow. Newsweek 65:75-6 Ja 11 '65
Reporter at large: Sovremennik (Contemporary) theatre. R. Blum. il New Yorker 39: 55-6+ N 2; 59-60+ N 9; 59-60+ N 16 '63
Theatre: Moscow. H. Clurman. Nation 197: 39-40 Jl 13 '63

MOSCOW, Idaho
Big days in the pea capital. T. C. Brody. Sports Illus 18:50-2 F 18 '63

MOSCOW chamber orchestra. See Orchestras

MOSCOW circus. See Circus

MOSCOW metro. See Moscow—Subways

MOSCOW university. See Colleges and universities—Russia

MOSELEY, Alfred L.
Truth about fatal car crashes; Harvard fatal highway collisions project. M. Mann. il por Pop Sci 183:92-7+ D '63

MOSELEY, Winston
Very special murderer. L. Wainwright. Life 57:21 Jl 3 '64

MOSELY, Philip E.
Chinese-Soviet rift: origins and portents. For Affairs 42:11-24 O '63
Is it peaceful? is it coexistence? N Y Times Mag p7+ S 1 '63
Khrushchev at seventy; who is next? N Y Times Mag p 14+ Ap 12 '64
Shavian paradise lost. Sat R 47:32 Jl 18 '64
Sibling rivalry in Marxist family. Sat R 47: 27 Ap 4 '64
Soviet policy in the developing countries. For Affairs 43:87-98 O '64
When a dragon and a bear disagree. Sat R 46:38-9+ N 23 '63

MOSER, Donald
Alaska after the big quake. Life 56:21 My 29 '64
Archer stalks the mighty grizzly. Life 55: 104-6+ N 8 '63
Athletes get help from hypnotists. Life 54: 71-2+ Je 7 '63
Bush pilot's deadly, daily game. Life 57: 112-14+ N 27 '64
Ride on, you Lip of Louisville! Life 54:66 F 15 '63
Western hero. Life 55:104-9 D 20 '63

about

At the kill a catharsis. . . G. P. Hunt. por Life 55:3 N 8 '63

MOSER, Edwa
Road is long; story. Cath World 197:252-7 Jl '63

MOSER, John C.
Inquiline roach responds to trail-marking substance of leaf-cutting ants. Science 143: 1048-9 Mr 6 '64
—and Blum, M. S.
Trail marking substance of the Texas leaf-cutting ant: source and potency. Science 140:1228 Je 14 '63

MOSES ben Maimon
Of reason & revelation; new version of Guide of the perplexed. por Time 82:86+ S 13 '63

MOSES, Morris
Update your Eico 760. Pop Electr 20:52 Ap '64

MOSES, Richard B.
Just show the movies; never mind the books! por ALA Bul 59:58-60 Ja '65

MOSES, Robert
Peace through understanding. por Sr Schol 84:9T-10T Ap 3 '64
Robert Moses warns against mob rule. por Nations Bsns 52:100-2 D '64

about

Bulldozing boss of the fair. por Sr Schol 84: 27 Ap 3 '64
Ho hum, come to the fair. M. Mayer. Esquire 60:117+ O '63
Intractable Robert Moses. J. McCarthy. por Holiday 36:99-100+ Jl '64; Same abr. with title Moses (Robert) and the Promised Land. Read Digest 85:117-21 S '64
Master builder is 75. il por N Y Times Mag p 14-15 D 15 '63
Moses: brash boss of a billion-dollar fair. por Look 28:115-18 F 11 '64
Moses builds a fair. il por Arch Forum 120: 64-75 Ja '64
Moses the art slayer wins one round. T. B. Hess. Art N 63:25 Ap '64
Moses vs. the bankers. Newsweek 65:61 F 1 '65
New York's mighty Moses. E. Harris. pors Look 27:94-5+ Mr 26 '63
Old S.O.B. does it again. B. Davidson. il por Sat Eve Post 237:36+ My 23 '64

MOSES, Sidney
CPM opens a pool ten months early. Am City 79:78-9 D '64

MOSHER, Clair K.
Sweet scents. Horticulture 41:226 Ap '63

MOSHER, Clure
In Miami nearly everybody hates Clure Mosher. J. Underwood. il pors Sports Illus 19:54-8+ Jl 15 '63

MOSHER, Dick
Dark tragedy; ed. by B. East. Outdoor Life 131:20-3+ F '63

MOSHER, Harry S. and others
Tarichatoxin tetrodotoxin: a potent neurotoxin. bibliog Science 144:1100-10 My 29 '64
—See Brown, M. S. jt. auth.

MOSHER, Ralph S.
Industrial manipulators; with biographical sketch. Sci Am 211:20, 88-94+ O '64

MOSHER, Samuel Barlow
Signal in space. por Time 82:98+ N 1 '63

MOSKOS, Charles C. Jr
Can Jagan hold on? New Repub 150:10-11 Mr 21 '64

MOSKOWITZ, Merwin, and Kelker, N. E.
Sensitivity of cultured mammalian cells to streptomycin and dihydrostreptomycin. bibliog Science 141:647-8 Ag 16 '63

MOSLEMS. See Muslims

MOSLER research products, incorporated
When walls have ears, call a debugging man; business counter-espionage experts use electronic listening devices. il Bsns W p 154+ O 31 '64

MOSLER safe company
Waiting for new deals to click; rivals in selling vaults to U.S. bankers. il Bsns W p 140-2 Je 6 '64

MOSLEY, Jean Bell
Day the cows didn't come home. Read Digest 84:112-16 Ja '64

MOSLEY, Jim
Today again; poem. Nation 197:267 O 26 '63
Trope for the tired; poem. Nation 198:79 Ja 20 '64

MOSLEY, Leonard
Mr Kisskiss Bangbang. N Y Times Mag p38+ N 22 '64

MOSQUES
Shrine renewed; Dome of the rock. il Time 84:43 Ag 14 '64

MOSQUITO fish. See Gambusia

MOSQUITOES
Feeding response in aedes aegypti: stimulation by adenosine triphosphate. R. Galun and others. bibliog il Science 142:1674-5 D 27 '63
Mosquitoes; comparative serology of four species of aedes (ochlerotatus) A. E. R. Downe. bibliog il Science 139:1286-7 Mr 29 '63
Resistance to the chemical sterilant, apholate, in aedes aegypti. E. I. Hazard and others. il Science 145:500-1 Jl 31 '64
Thermally induced genital appendages on mosquitoes. W. R. Horsfall and J. F. Anderson. bibliog il Science 141:1183-4 S 20 '63

Extermination

Everybody gets into the act; insect-control program, Ames, Ia. R. W. Mohri. il Am City 78:106-7 My '63
Fogger works better than a fly swatter; Mentor, Ohio. il Am City 79:110-11 Ap '64
Mosquito control for 4¼ cents per person; St Louis. C. M. Copley, jr. and J. L. Sadowski. il Am City 78:128-9 Je '63
Mosquitoes, beware! foggers go to school; Cape May County, N.J. B. M. Lafferty. il Am City 79:100-1 S '64
What to do about mosquitos at home. il Sunset 132:252+ Je '64

MOSQUITOES as carriers of infection
Dengue types and 4 viruses in wild-caught mosquitoes in south India. D. E. Carey and others. bibliog il Science 143:131-2 Ja 10 '64
Plasmodium berghei: cyclical transmissions by experimentally infected anopheles quadrimaculatus. M. Yoeli and others. bibliog Science 144:1580-1 Je 26 '64
Scientists track disease by stinging mosquitoes. Sci N L 86:312 N 14 '64
Swamp mosquito, culiseta melanura: occurrence in an urban habitat. A. Spielman. bibliog il Science 143:361-2 Ja 24 '64

MOSS, Allyn
Whatever happened to courtship? Mlle 56: 151+ Ap '63

MOSS, Frank T.
Common sense about hurricanes. Motor B 114: 50-3 Ag '64
Day Alfandre fought Geronimo. Outdoor Life 133:70-3+ Ap '64
Great tuna war. Field & S 68:10-12+ Je '63
How to catch big stripers. Field & S 68:54-7+ My '63
Is salt-water fishing doomed? Field & S 69:10-11+ Jl '64
Repowering with diesel. Motor B 114:31-2 O '64
Running inlets. Yachting 114:43-5+ Jl '63
Taking the curse out of fog. Yachting 116: 48-50+ Ag '64
T.L.C. for engines. il Motor B 111:36-7, 58+ Je '63
Where the fish are. Motor B 114:29-32+ N '64
White wakes in the Bahamas. il Yachting 113:49-51+ F '63

MOSS, Howard
Books (cont) New Yorker 39:138+ Mr 2 '63
Circle; poem. New Yorker 39:177 O 5 '63
Companies, poem. New Yorker 40:26 Jl 18 '64
Crossing the park; poem. New Yorker 39:32 Jl 6 '63
Eva; poem. New Yorker 40:30 Ja 2 '65
Finding them lost; poem. New Yorker 40:38 S 5 '64
In the X-ray room; poem. New Yorker 39:38 F 8 '64
Looking up; poem. New Yorker 40:48 Ap 18 '64
Miriam; poem. New Yorker 40:62 N 28 '64
On the library steps; poem. New Yorker 39: 60 N 23 '63
Painting a wave; poem. New Yorker 40:51 S 19 '64
Pruned tree; poem. New Yorker 39:38 My 11 '63
Roof garden; poem. New Yorker 40:32 Ag 8 '64
September elegy. New Yorker 40:56 O 17 '64
Wild, original spring; poem. New Yorker 40: 40 Je 20 '64

about

Leaf by leaf. M. Van Duyn. Poetry 102:264-6 Jl '63

MOSS, Margaret
School libraries. Wilson Lib Bul 38:298 N '63

MOSS, Melvin L. and others
Calcified ectodermal collagens of shark tooth enamel and teleost scale. bibliog Science 145:940-2 Ag 28 '64

MOSS, Richard
Pair of designing Finns. Horizon 5:62-7 Jl '63

about

Dickie's decision. il por Time 82:56-7 S 27 '63

MOSS, Stanley
Communique from an army deserter probably Italian; poem. New Repub 148:20 My 25 '63
Dead nun's complaint after the dance; poem. Poetry 105:179 D '64
Grave song; Song for concertina. Poetry 101: 250-1 Ja '63
Poet of absences. Poetry 105:198-201 D '64

MOSS, Stirling
How to drive and survive; ed. by K. W. Purdy. pors Bet Hom & Gard 42:6+ Ja '64
I have a hunch the U.S. will be shocked. por Life 54:93-4+ My 24 '63
Motor sports. Sports Illus 21:60-2 N 2 '64

—and Purdy, K. W.
Speed and women; excerpts from All but my life. Atlan 212:110-20+ O '63

about

Bravery is not enough. J. Skow. il pors Sat Eve Post 236:78-80 Ag 10 '63
Mr Moss builds his dream car. D. Bartley. il Esquire 61:80-1+ Mr '64

MOSS, William T.
Some human aspects of camping; report of survey. Am For 70:24-5+ Ag '64

MOSS (manned orbiting space station) See Space stations

MOSS phlox. See Phlox

MÖSSBAUER effect
Mössbauer effect for surface atoms: iron-57 at the surface of π Al_2O_3. P. A. Flinn and others. bibliog il Science 143:1434+ Mr 27 '64
Mössbauer effect in chemistry and solid-state physics. G. K. Wertheim. bibliog il Science 144:253-9 Ap 17 '64
Mössbauer effect in hemoglobin with different ligands. U. Gonser and others. bibliog il Science 143:680-1 F 14 '64

MOSSE, George L.
Splendid failure. Commentary 34:178-81 35:75 Ag '62, Ja '63

MOSSE, Hilde L.
Where thought walks a tightrope. Sat R 47: 33-4 Ja 25 '64

MOSSES
Dictyotene stage of meiosis in mosses. F. J. Dill. bibliog il Science 144:541-3 My 1 '64

MOST, Harry Rutherford
Harry Most named to Committee on international book programs. Dept State Bul 49: 933 D 16 '63

MOSTAR, Roman
Seattle goes Scandinavian. Library J 88: 4553-4 D 1 '63

MOSTEL, Zero
Big mouth+massive wit+soul of a daffodil= Zero. D. J. Hamblin. il pors Life 57:108+ D 4 '64
Hail the conquering Zero. il pors Newsweek 64:94-6+ O 19 '64
Infinite Zero. il por Newsweek 63:51 Ja 13 '64
Infinite Zero. H. G. Foster. por Holiday 33: 131-3+ Mr '63
Mostel revisited. New Yorker 40:25-7 Ja 2 '65

MOSTERT, Noel
Buffalo; story. Sat Eve Post 238:40-2 Ja 30 '65
Christmas dinner; story. Harper 229:69-74 D '64
Freeze. Reporter 28:39-40 Mr 14 '63

MOTAL, Patricia
Print spotting for submin & sub-35ers. Pop Phot 53:71 Ag '63

MOTELS
And now, the boatel. il Time 84:72 Ag 7 '64
Gaudy grand motels. il Life 55:71-5 Jl 26 '63
Motel comes to town. E. Raskin. Nation 196: 197-9 Mr 9 '63
Motel for Moscow. il Bsns W p50-2 Mr 7 '64
New rooms; motor inns and motor hotels in Manhattan. New Yorker 39:39-40 O 5 '63
Office building becomes a motel; Lincoln, Neb. il Arch Forum 118:135 Ap '63
Truck stop goes fancy; Toledo 5. il Bsns W p 108-9+ Mr 16 '63
What's happened to the motels? J. N. Miller. il Read Digest 82:213-16 Mr '63
See also
Holiday inns of America, incorporated

Employees

Wages in hotels and motels, June 1963. F. W. Mohr. il Mo Labor R 87:549-51 My '64

MOTHER-child relationship. See Parent-child relationship

MOTHER Courage and her children: drama. See Brecht, B.
MOTHER-in-law plants. See Dieffenbachias
MOTHER love. See Love, Maternal
MOTHER love: story. See Benedictus, D.
MOTHERHOOD. See Mothers
MOTHERS
Behavior of adult rats is modified by the experiences their mothers had as infants. V. H. Denenberg and A. E. Whimbey. bibliog il Science 142:1192-3 N 29 '63
Casual touch; excerpt from Sixpence in her shoe. P. McGinley. Ladies Home J 81:22+ Jl '64
Disenchantment of motherhood. il Sci Digest 53:42 Je '63
Educated housewife's bill of rights. C. Seton. Redbook 123:47+ My '64
I'm for Mother's day! L. Light. il Parents Mag 39:26+ My '64
Is baby's doctor sick of mommy? E. S. Ringold. il N Y Times Mag p47-8 Ag 11 '63
Island of time; condensation of Creative woman. D. Goldberg. il Redbook 121:52-3+ My '63
Little flag for mother. E. Buckler. Farm J 87:69-70 My '63
Maternal and child health problems. A. Yankauer. bibliog f il Ann Am Acad 355: 112-20 S '64
Middle age motherhood for me! E. Morris. Read Digest 82:193-4 Mr '63
Mother and her secret. A. Capp. il Read Digest 84:45-6 My '64
Mother's daze. D. Van Ark. il Parents Mag 38:62-3+ My '63
Mothers must keep on growing, too; with group discussion program, ed. by M. R. Sherwin. E. G. Neisser. il Parents Mag 39:20+, 52-3+ Je '64
Notes from a maternity ward. S. H. Rudolph. il Atlan 211:122-5 Mr '63
Plight of the brand new parent. F. Bauer. il N Y Times Mag p 152 Ap 7 '63
Rockabye mommy. J. L. O'Neill. il Am Home 67:26 O '64
Speaking out: vote against motherhood. G. Greene; reply. D. Kosta. Sat Eve Post 236:4 F 23 '63
When children get on your nerves; refuge for mom. A. Graham. PTA Mag 58:23 Ap '64
Young mothers' story. See issues of Redbook
See also
Pregnancy
Stepparents

Anecdotes, facetiae, satire, etc.

Every day is mother's day. M. Brophy. See issues of Good housekeeping

Employment

See Married women—Employment

Quotations, maxims, etc.

Subject: mother; comp. by E. F. Murphy. N Y Times Mag p46 My 10 '64
MOTHERS, Unmarried
Mothers without joy. J. Rinehart. Sat Eve Post 236:29-30+ Mr 23 '63; Same abr. Read Digest 83:83-7 Jl '63
Nipped in the bud; compulsory sterilization bill of Mississippi. Newsweek 63:21 Mr 30 '64
What can we do about America's unwed teen-age mothers? interview, ed. by E. Harris. M. L. Allen. il McCalls 91:40+ N '63
See also
Illegitimacy
MOTHERS and daughters. See Parent-child relationship
MOTHERS day
I'm for Mother's day! L. Light. il Parents Mag 39:26+ My '64
Mother's day thoughts. H. Felkel. Hobbies 68:55 My '63

Anecdotes, facetiae, satire, etc.

Lots of cheer, mother dear. M. Tiller. il NEA J 53:27 My '64
MOTHER'S helpers. See Household employees
MOTHERS in art
Mom art; Art museum of St Louis. il N Y Times Mag p 128-9 D 8 '63
MOTHERS-in-law
You do marry the family. E. M. Stern. il Parents Mag 39:70-1+ Ap '64
MOTHERWELL, Robert
David Smith, a major American sculptor. Vogue 145:134-9 F 1 '65
Robert Motherwells who live in a brownstone with art of many periods. il por Vogue 143:88-91+ Ja 15 '64
MOTHPROOFING
Those pesky moths (and beetles, too) Consumer Bul 46:13+ Je '63
MOTHS
Before you spray or swat, have a look. il Sunset 131:156+ Jl '63
Enzymatic mechanism for the escape of certain moths from their cocoons. F. C. Kafatos and C. M. Williams. bibliog il Science 146:538-40 O 23 '64
Motor responses of moths to low-intensity X-ray exposure. J. S. Smith and others. bibliog il Science 140:805-6 My 17 '63
Nature's counter-sonar. Time 85:35 Ja 22 '65
Night fighters in a sonic duel; moth's use of hearing to evade bats. K. D. Roeder. il Natur Hist 73:32-9 Ja '64
See also
Butterflies
Gipsy moths

Ear

See Ear (insects)
MOTHS against the screen; story. See Warren, R. P.
MOTILONE Indians. See Indians of South America—Native races
MOTION
Bowling in the classroom. C. Randall. il Sci Digest 56:24-5 S '64
MOTION in art. See Action in art
MOTION picture production code. See Moving picture censorship
MOTION pictures. See Moving pictures
MOTION sculpture. See Mobiles
MOTION sickness
Deaf personnel used in artificial-G test. R. D. Hibben. Aviation W 81:117+ S 14 '64
Malady that motion can cause. A. Balk. il Todays Health 41:28-30 Jl '63
Navy gains in effort to control canal sickness. H. M. David. il Miss & Roc 15:26 Ag 31 '64
Some comforting facts about motion sickness. G. G. Greer. Bet Hom & Gard 42:34 Je '64
See also
Seasickness
MOTIONS of the stars. See Stars—Motion
MOTIVATION (education)
Identification, motivation, and training of talented students; report. A. W. Astin. Sch & Soc 92:186-9 Ap 18 '64
Key to action. M. McMullan. il Sch Arts 63: 5-7 Mr '64
Motivation in automated instruction. J. W. Moore and W. I. Smith. Sch Life 46:21-2 N '63
Motivation; new ways of seeing. M. Pappas. il Sch Arts 63:8-11 S '63
MOTIVATION (psychology)
Executive motivation: what is the spur? J. F. Olesky. il Duns R 84:42-3+ N '64
How to spur ambition. Sci N L 86:7 Jl 4 '64
Human dilemmas of leadership. A. Zaleznik. Harvard Bsns R 41:49-55 Jl '63
Measurement of motivation. H. J. Eysenck. il Sci Am 208:130-4+ My '63
Microscopic brains; adaptation of address. V. G. Dethier. bibliog Science 143:1138-45 Mr 13 '64; Reply. W. N. Tavolga. 144:1533 Je 26 '64
New findings will improve your decisions. il Nation Bsns 51:58-60+ Mr '63
Psychoanalyzing the small businessman. il Bsns W p90+ S 19 '64
What's happening in education? Hawthorne effect. W. D. Boutwell. PTA Mag 58:14 Mr '64
Why men & nations seek success; interview. D. C. McClelland. il Nations Bsns 51: 32-3+ S '63
Will to meaning. V. E. Frankl. Christian Cent 81:515-17 Ap 22 '64
MOTIVATION in literature. See Fiction—Technique
MOTIVATION research. See Market research
MOTIVES
See also
Aspiration level
MOTLEY, Constance Baker
Constitution, key to freedom. por Ebony 18: 221-2+ S '63
MOTLEY, Mary
On the edge of oasis. D. Athill. Sat R 46:43 Mr 23 '63
MOTOR boat inspection. See Motor boats—Inspection
MOTOR boat models
See also
Hydrofoil models

MOTOR boat racing
Alcohol burns in the Northwest; National outboard championship regatta. C. D. Strang. Motor B 112:112 Ag '63
All-American racing team. M. Crook. il Yachting 115:109-11 Ja '64; 117:91-3 Ja '65
Blazing winners in the Orange bowl. il Motor B 111:54+ F '63
British lose Beaverbrook trophy; International London daily express offshore powerboat race. E. F. Haylock. il Motor B 112:53+ N '63
Camera catches a spill. M. Crook. il Yachting 113:53 F '63
Daytona does it again! il Motor B 114:96-7 Ag '64
Desert full of motorboats; U.S. powerboat racers at Salton City, Calif. H. Whall. il Sports Illus 21:70-2 N 16 '64
Draggin' the waves; World championship power boat drags. D. Naef. il Hot Rod 16:112 S '63
Drama at Detroit. C. D. Strang. il Motor B 114:48-9+ S '64
Fastest club in America; Chain-O-Lakes boat club. J. Stoltz. il Motor B 111:43-4+ Je '63
First to Nassau. M. Crook. il Yachting 113:31+ Je '63
500-miles like crazy. D. Naef and E. Rickman. il Hot Rod 16:84-7 F '63
Games for boaters; gymkhana. P. K. Snook. il Pop Mech 120:106-9 Ag '63
Gold cup for Bardahl. J. Dowdall. il Motor B 112:52-3+ S '63
Hail! the Hudson River marathon. C. D. Strang. Motor B 111:156 My '63
He's sharpening up for the speedboat record. il Pop Sci 184:59 My '64
How the dragsters do it. J. Speirs. il Pop Mech 119:128-31+ Mr '63
Hudson River marathon. il Motor B 112:47-9+ Ag '63
Hydros rolled snake eyes on a gambling man's lake; Lake Tahoe, Nev. H. Whall. il Sports Illus 19:66-8 O 14 '63
In a hull of a hurry! R. Greene. il Hot Rod 17:36-7 Jl '64
Kind of race Sam would have liked. J. Martenhoff. il Motor B 113:138+ Ap '64
Mayhem under power; Miami to Key West. L. Evans. il Yachting 114:20-1 D '63
Mercer Island marathon. E. Crimmin. il Motor B 112:62+ Ag '63
Miss Bardahl retains gold cup. M. Crook. il Yachting 116:45-7+ Ag '64
Month in yachting. See issues of Yachting
More power to you. M. Crook. See issues of Yachting
Motorboat racing records. il Motor B 113:118+ Ja '64; 115:114+ Ja '65
Musson, closeup of a champion. E. Crimmin. il Motor B 114:34+ Jl '64
NDBA fuel boat drags. E. Rickman. il Hot Rod 17:80-1+ Ap '64
1964 Salton 500. E. Rickman. il Hot Rod 18:76-9 Ja '65
Ohio takes the Hudson. il Motor B 114:62-3 Ag '64
Perris when it sizzled; NDBA's fuel and gas championship. E. Dahlquist. il Hot Rod 17:44-5 D '64
Racing and the A.P.B.A. C. D. Strang. il Motor B 115:112-13+ Ja '65
Racing to Nassau in the GX. J. Martenhoff. il Motor B 112:49-50+ Jl '63
Rails with roostertails; World boat drag championships. L. Smith. il Hot Rod 17:34-7 Ja '64
Remember '63? il Motor B 113:66-74 Ja '63
Rooster tales. L. Naef. il Hot Rod 17:102-3 Je '64
Rooster tales. E. Rickman. See issues of Hot rod
Roostertails, history and the Detroit River. J. Dowdall. il Motor B 111:42+ Je '63
Rough race for Sam's sake. H. Whall. il Sports Illus 20:22-3 F 17 '64
Ruffled race across a mirror; Miami-Nassau ocean power boat race. A. Zich. il Sports Illus 18:22-5 My 6 '63
Rugged race to Nassau. M. Crook. il Yachting 115:46-9+ Je '64
Salton City 500. D. Naef. il Hot Rod 17:34-9 F '64
Salton Sea to the big bear. B. Ruskauff. il Motor B 115:204+ Ja '65
Smooth surfride to Torquay; International London daily express offshore powerboat race. E. F. Haylock. il Motor B 114:46-7+ O '64
Snake in the water! Hydrocobra. P. Biro. il Motor T 16:74-6 O '64
Special: the large economy size in gold cups; B. Muncey. R. Lardner. il Sports Illus 19:38-40+ Jl 8 '63
Speedboat king: Gar Wood. J. Martenhoff. il Motor B 114:62+ Jl '64
Summaries of the Miami-Nassau powerboat race. Yachting 113:30 Je '63
Two rooster tails wash out a fifth Gold cup. H. Whall. il Sports Illus 19:52-3 Jl 15 '63
V for victory; Miami-to-Nassau powerboat race. il Time 83:89 Ap 17 '64
Win or sink! roughest Nassau race. J. Martenhoff. il Motor B 113:26+ Je '64
Winning ways of Wee Willie. E. Crimmin. il Motor B 111:43+ My '63
With the outboarders. C. D. Strang. il Motor B 111:98 Je '63
Year that was. il Motor B 115:62-75 Ja '65

Accidents and injuries

See Sports—Accidents and injuries

MOTOR boat shows. See Motor boats—Exhibitions

MOTOR boat speed records
Motorboat racing records. il Motor B 113:118+ Ja '64; 115:114+ Ja '65
Up from the South, and fast! Miami-New York record. C. F. Johnson. il Motor B 112:78-9+ S '63

MOTOR boating (periodical)
Meet the Seasoned skipper. il Motor B 112:21+ N '63

MOTOR boats
Allison aquanaut. E. Rickman. il Hot Rod 16:44-5+ N '63
Boating '64. J. Speirs. il Pop Mech 121:133-40+ Mr '64
How 'bout that; photographs. E. Rickman. Hot Rod 17:72-3 O '64
Hydro dynamic. A. Mikesell. il Pop Mech 119:144-52+ Mr '63
New stern drives are red-hot. J. Roe. il Pop Sci 186:80-3 Ja '65
Other end of the line; America's cup motorboats. C. F. Enlow, jr. il Motor B 114:39+ Ag '64
Other man's boat; motorsailer. il Yachting 115:72-3 Ap '64
Outdoor life boating 1963. il Outdoor Life 131:52-64+ F '63
Six common boating problems. J. Martenhoff. il Pop Sci 184:165-6+ Ap '64
Your 1964-1965 boat show. il Motor B 113:119-84 Ja '64; 115:115-29+ Ja '65
See also
Hydrofoils
Hydroplanes

Accidents

See Boats and boating—Accidents

Care

Right winter lay-up for a spry boat next spring. W. Swegle. il Pop Sci 185:116-20 O '64
Your Motor boating guide to spring fitting out; with checklist; symposium. il Motor B 111:21-43+ Mr '63

Control

Trim tabs. R. W. Hobbs. il Yachting 115:44-5+ F '64

Design

Big boom in multi-keel boat bottoms. J. Roe. il Pop Sci 185:110-15 D '64
Boating trends for 1964. J. A. Emmett. il Outdoor Life 133:56-60+ F '64
Designs. See issues of Yachting
Latest boating trends. J. A. Emmett. Outdoor Life 131:56+ F '63
New boats for 1965. J. A. Emmett. il Outdoor Life 135:56-9+ Ja '65
New look at the shapes we're in. il Motor B 111:28-37 F '63
New shapes in powerboats. G. B. Leonard. il Look 27:38-9 Jl 16 '63
Pleasure boats lower the boom on gimcracks; motor boat show; with editorial comment. il Bsns W p34. 117 Ja 25 '64
Seabell. K. L. Smith; G. E. Bell. il Yachting 115:72-3+ Je '64
Snake in the water! Hydrocobra. P. Biro. il Motor T 16:74-6 O '64
Soft ride on a gull wing. A. Mikesell. il Pop Mech 120:75 D '63
Taking stock. il Motor B 111:23-5 F '63
Two startling new boat-hull designs. il Pop Sci 185:120-1 Ag '64

Electric equipment

Short circuits and fuses. B. Francois. il Motor B 111:37-8+ Mr '63

Electronic equipment

Don't neglect the electronics department. R. C. Beard. Motor B 111:36+ Mr '63
Electronics 64-65. il Motor B 113:156-61+ Ja '64; 115:156-61+ Ja '65

MOTOR boats—*Continued*

Equipment

Accessories for boatmen. J. A. Emmett. Outdoor Life 133:62-3+ F '64
Down to the sea in style; decorator décor. il Am Home 67:14 My '64
Eleven things I wouldn't be without on Roeboat. J. Roe. il Pop Sci 184:138-41+ F '64
Modern boats and model-T boating. T. Cofield. Motor B 113:46+ Je '64
New boating accessories. Outdoor Life 131: 66 F '63; 133:68 F '64; 136:61 Ja '65
Rooster tales; V-drive. D. Naef. il Hot Rod 17:102-3 Ap '64
Yachting's boat show. il Yachting 115:127-32+ Ja '64; 117:127-32+ Ja '65
Your Motor boating guide to spring fitting out; with checklist; symposium. il Motor B 111:21-43+ Mr '63

Exhibitions

Boat makers shout sales ahoy; National motor boat show. il Bsns W p30-1 Ja 23 '65
Boat-show calendar. Outdoor Life 131:70 F '63; 133:67 F '64
Cruising the aisles; cartoons. R. McKie. Sports Illus 22:30-5 Ja 4 '65
Last obstacle; National motor boat show. New Yorker 39:22-3 Ja 25 '64
National boat show '63. il Motor B 111:54-5 Mr '63
New York boat show. W. H. Taylor. Yachting 113:188 Mr '63
Pleasure boats lower the boom on gimcracks; motor boat show; with editorial comment. il Bsns W p34, 117 Ja 25 '64
Setting up a boat show; National motor boat show in New York. il Yachting 117: 68-9 Ja '65
Show boats; 1964 National motor boat show. Newsweek 63:77 Ja 27 '64
Sighted sub, sank $3.995; 55th National motor boat show. il Newsweek 65:49 F 1 '65
Yachting's boat show. il Yachting 115:127-32+ Ja '64; 117:127-32+ Ja '65

Fuel tanks

How to build gas tanks into your boat. J. Roe. il Pop Sci 182:136-7 Ap '63
Low cost auxiliary fuel tank for your outboard. K. F. Hildebrand. il Pop Mech 119: 140-1 Mr '63
Outboard fuel tanks. B. Whittier. il Yachting 113:60-2 F '63

History

Tartar. B. Slaven. il Yachting 113:54-5+ My '63

Inspection

Surveying a boat with diesel power. J. W. Smith. Motor B 114:32-3 O '64

Safety devices and measures

Just what is coast guard approved? safety requirements. H. R. Kaplan. il Motor B 111:48-9+ Mr '63
Speak up: there's a decal in the offering; Auxiliary courtesy motorboat examination. B. Woodward. il Motor B 111:76+ Mr '63
Three prime safety ingredients. J. Glaser. il Yachting 114:54-5+ Ag '63

Speed

See also
Motor boat speed records

Testing

Agony at Lake X; Kiekhaefer corporation's test bases in Florida. il Esquire 59:4-7 Mr '63
Jim Roe tests all the MerCruisers. J. Roe. il Pop Sci 182:116-21+ Je '63
Jim Roe tests OMC's new show boats. J. Roe. il Pop Sci 183:112-16 Jl '63

MOTOR boats, Jet propelled
Big wind on the water; jet-propelled Hustler. E. Rickman. il Hot Rod 17:90-2 Je '64
Hanley, jet propelled iconoclast. il Motor B 113:86+ Mr '64
Jet propulsion. J. Goldman. il Motor B 111:50-1+ F '63
Jim Roe tests: a hot handful of go-anywhere jet. J. Roe. il Pop Sci 185:118-19+ Ag '64
New jet-engined challenger; Hustler. J. Joseph. il Pop Mech 120:120-2 N '63
Now, a jet boat that goes sideways! H. Luckett. il Pop Sci 182:114-16 Ap '63
Rooster tales. E. Rickman. il Hot Rod 17:104-5 Jl '64
Up the river on a fire hose. B. Goldrath. il Sports Illus 18:52-4 Mr 18 '63

Testing

Sliding up a damp chute. B. Goldrath. il Field & S 68:46-7 Jl '63

MOTOR boats, Outboard
Big boom in multi-keel boat bottoms. J. Roe. il Pop Sci 185:110-15 D '64
Boats for coastal waters. J. A. Emmett. il Outdoor Life 133:30-1+ My '64
Eleven things I wouldn't be without on Roeboat. J. Roe. il Pop Sci 184:138-41+ F '64
New V step lift hull irons out rough ones. J. Roe. il Pop Sci 184:134-6 Je '64
Now, a jet drive for your outboard. C. R. Hull. il Pop Sci 182:122-4+ Je '63
Outboard fuel tanks. B. Whittier. il Yachting 113:60-2 F '63
Outboard motorboats; fiber-glass. il Consumer Bul 46:20-3 My '63
Sailor takes to outboards. R. N. Bavier, jr. il Yachting 114:60-1+ Jl '63
Shim up your stern; hull with lifts. J. D. Lenk and I. Lenk. il Pop Mech 121:152-4 Ap '64
Sports sled. A. Mikesell. il Pop Mech 121: 144-50+ Mr '64
See also
Gas and oil engines, Outboard
Outboard boating club of America

Care

Outboard fitting out; ed. by Z. Hollander. il Yachting 113:88-90+ Ap '63

Repairing

Outboard fitting out; ed. by Z. Hollander. il Yachting 113:88-90+ Ap '63

Steering gear

Installing your outboard steerer. B. Whittier. il Yachting 113:60-2+ Mr '63
New systems to steer your boat. J. Roe and G. Daniels. il Pop Sci 183:106-9+ D '63
Up-front steering for small outboards. D. Mathesins. il Pop Mech 119:153 Mr '63

Testing

Double-hulled and tough as Texas. J. Roe. il Pop Sci 185:88-90 Jl '64
Jim Roe tests the Evinrude Sweet-16. J. Roe. il Pop Sci 184:136-40 Mr '64
Jim Roe tests the Glastron Futura. J. Roe. il Pop Sci 183:178-81+ O '63
Jim Roe tests the Lone Star Cruise Liner II. J. Roe. il Pop Sci 182:100-4+ My '63

MOTOR boats, Theft of. See Boats, Theft of

MOTOR bus lines
Farm boy who's going to town; K. Osano of Japan. Time 83:93-4 Ap 3 '64
No federal aid for this municipal bus line; Santa Monica, Calif. E. N. Mobley. il Am City 79:173-4 Je '64
See also
Greyhound corporation

Employees

See also
Motor bus lines—Wages and hours

Stations

Nervi's bus station opens in New York. il Arch Rec 133:14 F '63

Wages and hours

Wage chronology: Carolina coach co. 1954-63. W. Fridie. il Mo Labor R 86:1058-66 S '63
Wage chronology: Western Greyhound lines, 1954-63. W. Fridie. il Mo Labor R 87:178-86 F '64

MOTOR bus travel
Holiday handbook; United States by bus. K. Simon. il Holiday 34:99-104 Jl '63
Little bird that snorted; second-class bus from San Miguel de Allende to Mexico city. C. Darlington. il Sat R 46:84-5 O 12 '63

MOTOR buses
Deer camp on wheels. L. Dietz. il Field & S 68:37-9+ D '63
Jeepney; Philippine combination of jeep and jitney bus. New Yorker 40:49-50 O 24 '64
Touring Hilo by sampan. il Sunset 130:79-80 My '63

Seats

Fiberglass seats cut transportation costs. il Am City 78:116 Ap '63

Small size

Nickel buys a ride on the minibus; Washington, D.C. R. L. Morris. il Am City 79:133-4 Jl '64
Tiny bus spurs city shopping; minibuses bring joy to stores in Washington. il Bsns W p 196+ S 12 '64

MOTOR camping. See Automobiles—Camping equipment; Camping
MOTOR cycles. See Motorcycles
MOTOR fuels. See Automobile engines—Fuel
MOTOR lodges. See Motels
MOTOR oils. See Lubrication and lubricants
MOTOR raceways. See Speedways
MOTOR sailers. See Motor boats
MOTOR scooters
Danger rides two wheels. B. Magid. il Parents Mag 38:68-9+ S '63
Fat-tire scooter for sportsmen. il Pop Mech 119:151-4+ Ap '63
Motorizing the corner policeman; Fort Worth, Tex. C. K. Duggins. il Am City 78:24 Je '63
One-man snow scooter. H. Grey. il Field & S 67:143-4 Ap '63
Put a motor on a sled, and go! il Bsns W p42-3 Ja 2 '65
Scooter camping. C. B. Colby. il Outdoor Life 133:12-14 Ja '64
Scooter that hitches a ride. M. Banister. il Pop Mech 121:182-9 Ap '64 (to be cont)
MOTOR ships
Yachtsman's dreamboat; Coastal Queen, remodeled diesel-powered oyster buy-boat. H. Bloomfield. il Yachting 114:57-9+ O '63
MOTOR sleds
How to build your own gas-powered snow-trac. E. F. Lindsley. il Pop Sci 183:122-5+ N '63
That snow-trac: a great machine. il Pop Sci 184:128 Ap '64
MOTOR traffic. See Street traffic
MOTOR trailers. See Automobile trailers
MOTOR transportation. See Transportation, Automotive
MOTOR trend (periodical)
Editor's auto-graphs. C. Nerpel. il Motor T 16:8 Jl '64
Motor trend going on fifteen. il Motor T 15:32-3 S '63
MOTOR trend award
Car of the year; Rambler. il Motor T 15:20-45+ F '63
Car of the year; the 1964 Fords. C. Nerpel. il Motor T 16:32-62 F '64
MOTOR truck drivers
See also
International brotherhood of teamsters, chauffeurs, warehousemen and helpers of America
Wages and hours
Hoffa's goal: nationwide contract. U S News 55:98 S 9 '63
MOTOR truck engines
Swirl-chamber engine runs on what's handy. K. Warner. il Pop Mech 119:110-12 Je '63
See also
Cummins engine company
Gas turbines, Automotive
MOTOR truck industry and trade
Thundering trucks; boom in truck sales in the U.S. il Time 81:78+ F 8 '63
Truck sales still barreling ahead. il Bsns W p32 Ap 6 '63
See also
Tractor industry and trade
White motor company
MOTOR truck lines
My private war with Hoffa; ruin of Coffey transfer by teamsters union. T. Coffey. il Sat Eve Post 237:68-70 Ja 4 '64
See also
Associated transport, incorporated
MOTOR truck service stations. See Automobile service stations
MOTOR truck trailers
Transportation
Green light for piggybacking. Bsns W p95 Ag 31 '63
MOTOR trucking. See Trucking
MOTOR trucks
Chassis for the masses; the Farmobil. il Newsweek 61:76 My 6 '63
Gas turbine supertruck loves drivers and gas. Sci N L 86:361 D 5 '64
International Harvester Scout 80. il Consumer Bul 46:20-1 Ag '63
New trucks for '64. il Farm J 87:48B+ O '63
New trucks for 1965. il Farm J 88:53 O '64
Pickup gets new sides and roof. il Sunset 132:124+ Je '64
Quarter-mile hauler. E. Rickman. il Hot Rod 16:48-50+ My '63
Spotlight on the versatile Ford pickup. E. Nelson. il Pop Mech 120:20+ Ag '63
Design
Trucks blossom out. il Bsns W p92+ O 26 '63
Engines
See Motor truck engines
Laws and regulations
How big should a truck get? il Bsns W p94-5 Ag 31 '63
Loading and unloading
See Loading and unloading
Manufacture
Wheels for the world; Britain's Leyland motor corp. il Time 82:69 Ag 9 '63
Testing
Dodge Palomino sport pickup. C. Isica. il Motor T 16:78-9 Ap '64
Weight
Bigger loads get a boost, movement to standardize truck weight and size limits. Bsns W p 114 S 5 '64
MOTOR trucks, Fire. See Fire apparatus, Motor
MOTOR trucks, Municipal
Monster that moves by night. B. Stengren. il Am City 78:84-5 N '63
New trucks for old; Waukegan, Ill. E. E. Smith. il Am City 79:13 Ag '64
Ultimate in a traffic-signal tower truck; Canton, Ohio. C. L. Deerwester. il Am City 78:133 S '63
See also
Refuse collection trucks
Tractors, Municipal
MOTOR trucks, Three wheel
Profitable toy; small truck of Hiroshima's Toyo Kogyo co. Time 81:90 Mr 29 '63
MOTOR trucks in repair service
How to succeed in business without an office; rolling repair shops and sales displays. H. Walton. il Pop Sci 182:64-7 Mr '63
MOTOR vehicle pollution control board
Fight against smog: GM shows it's leading the band; exhaust control devices on '66 cars. il Bsns W p24-5 Ag 22 '64
MOTOR vehicles
Day of the duners; Pismo Beach, Calif. G. Fauman. il Motor T 15:64-7 O '63
Dune crawler switches to beach patrol. G. D. Hunsaker. il Am City 79:32 N '64
Quickie desert wagon. E. Rickman. il Hot Rod 17:70-3+ Ap '64
Roadless roamers. H. Babcock. il Travel 119:60-1 F '63
Roller-tracked car goes anywhere; Canadair Fisher. il Pop Sci 185:62-3 D '64
Those mighty Minis! B. Cummins. il Motor T 16:64 Mr '64
Trespasser; filling the gap between trail bikes and commercial tractors. C. Nerpel. il Motor T 16:62-5 O '64
V6 jeep. E. Rickman. il Hot Rod 16:76-9 D '63
See also
Automobiles
Motor buses
Renting
Scramble for the leasing dollar. il Duns R 83:pt2 140-4+ Je '64
Testing
PS test-drives the Imp; new crawl-any-where car. A. Markovich. il Pop Sci 183:58-60+ N '63
MOTOR vehicles, Military
Big wheel in the army. il Life 54:43+ Mr 29 '63
Breath of air steers 850-pound jet cart; army's PFA car. il Pop Mech 119:128-9 Ap '63
See also
Tanks, Military
MOTOR vehicles, Municipal
Houston centralizes motor maintenance; Houston, Tex. K. E. Ping and O. J. Cole. il Am City 78:86-8 N '63
Practical preventive maintenance; San Diego, Calif. W. R. Kuhner. il Am City 79:112-13 F '64
Safety is only one of the benefits; bright colors for Canadian public-works vehicles. il Am City 78:97 F '63
See also
Tractors, Municipal
MOTOR vehicles, Police
Motorizing the corner policeman; Fort Worth, Tex. C. K. Duggins. il Am City 78:24 Je '63
Ultimate weapon; armored car in Jackson, Miss. Reporter 30:10+ Ap 23 '64
MOTORCYCLE accidents. See Traffic accidents

MOTORCYCLE engines
Up on two wheels; ignition timing. B. Greene. il Hot Rod 17:106-7 Je '64
MOTORCYCLE industry and trade
Wooing the mild ones; Japan's Honda motor co. il Bsns W p26-7 Mr 30 '63
MOTORCYCLE police. See Police, Motorcycle
MOTORCYCLE racing
Harley-Davidson's salt shakers. D. Francisco. il Hot Rod 17:48-51 Ag '64
No cars allowed; All-western motorcycle championship. B. Greene. il Hot Rod 17:84-9 Mr '64
One-five-0 the hard way; Bonneville. L. Nehamkin. il Hot Rod 17:82-3 N '64
Trying for a ton; Tourist trophy week, Isle of Man. il Time 81:76+ Je 21 '63
MOTORCYCLES
Barn job. B. Greene. il Hot Rod 17:48-51+ My '64
BSA trail bronc; Birmingham small arms, of England. B. Greene. il Hot Rod 17:94-5 Ap '64
Bonny boomer; Triumph. B. Greene. il Hot Rod 16:74-7 Je '63
Bonny poppers. G. Jennings. il Hot Rod 17:70-3 Jl '64
Danger rides two wheels. B. Magid. il Parents Mag 38:68-9+ S '63
Electra-glide. B. Greene. il Hot Rod 17:90-2+ O '64
Handlebar hustler. D. Francisco. il Hot Rod 16:94-8 Ap '63
Harley-Davidson's salt shakers. D. Francisco. il Hot Rod 17:48-51 Ag '64
Honda's Grizzly Cub. L. Wineland. il Hot Rod 17:80-1 S '64
How the Thunder herd boss brought a Honda boom to U.S. il Newsweek 64:66-8 Jl 6 '64
Mail order trail bike. E. Rickman. il Hot Rod 17:74-5 Je '64
Motorcycle built for you; Harley-Davidson's Sprint. B. Greene. il Hot Rod 16:44-7+ Mr '63
Mountain Cub by Triumph. B. Greene. il Hot Rod 17:92-3 My '64
Scat for the trail, by Harley-Davidson. B. Greene. il Hot Rod 17:82-3 Jl '64
Try to stop this mechanized billy goat. T. Stimson. il Pop Mech 120:92-4+ Ag '63
Two timer. R. Stender. il Hot Rod 17:54 Ag '64
Two-wheeled chic; Honda motorcycles. il Time 84:78+ S 11 '64
Up on two wheels. B. Greene. See issues of Hot rod
Yamaha, motorcycle without precedent. B. Greene. il Hot Rod 17:76-9+ Ja '64
Yamaha's little giant, Trailmaster 80. B. Greene. il Hot Rod 17:84-5 Ag '64

Testing

PS tests H-D's spirited new Sprint. E. H. Arctander. il Pop Sci 183:142-4+ O '63
Road burner. B. Greene. il Hot Rod 18:72-5 Ja '65
MOTORING. See Automobile touring
MOTOROLA, Incorporated
Aptitude tests: under a cloud. U S News 57:83-4 D 14 '64
Boss's son, Robert W. Galvin. il Time 84:88 Jl 10 '64
Motorola proposes combining Apollo communications into single system. R. Pay. il Miss & Roc 14:42-3 Ap 6 '64
Motorola's new color TV tube. il Consumer Rep 29:235 My '64
What happens when government polices your hiring. il U S News 56:87 Mr 30 '64; Same abr. with title Fair to whom? Read Digest 84:129-30 Je '64
MOTOROLA semiconductor products, Incorporated
New Motorola plant produces semiconductor microcircuits. il Aviation W 80:57 Mr 30 '64
MOTORS. See Automobile engines; Electric motors; Motor truck engines
MOTORS, Outboard. See Gas and oil engines, Outboard
MOTORSAILERS. See Motor boats
MOTORSHIPS. See Motor ships
MOTT, Charles Stewart
Lavish skinflint. por Newsweek 62:24 Jl 1 '63
Mr Flint. por Time 81:19 Je 28 '63
MOTT, Ellis
Can Soviet scientists break through the iron curtain? Todays Health 41:29-33+ S '63
Science news & views. Sci Digest 53:12-15 F; 24-6 Mr '63
MOTT, Frank Luther
Obituary
Pub W 186:42-3 N 2 '64
MOTT, George Fox
Transportation in contemporary civilization. Ann Am Acad 345:1-5 Ja '63
Transportation in orbit. Ann Am Acad 345:130-42 Ja '63
(ed) Transportation renaissance. Ann Am Acad 345:1-142 Ja '63
MOTTOES
In God we trust. America 109:694 N 30 '63
To coin a phrase: E pluribus unum; U.S. coins. il Sr Schol 84:7 Ap 10 '64
MOUILLESSEAUX, H. R.
What and why is an Allen & Wheelock lip-fire revolver? Hobbies 69:118-19 N '64
MOULIN, Jean
King of the shadows. il Time 85:36 Ja 1 '65
Letter from Paris. Genêt. New Yorker 40:111-12 Ja 9 '65
When the French lived in darkness; adaptation of address. A. Malraux. il por N Y Times Mag p 12-13+ Ja 17 '65
MOULTON, Forest Ray
Tribute to F. R. Moulton; letter. F. L. Campbell. Science 141:311 Jl 26 '63; Reply. J. J. Schifferes. 142:448 O 25 '63
MOULTON, Priscilla L.
Reviewing children's books: a cooperative venture. Library J 88:1723-4 Ap 15 '63
MOULTON, William G.
Linguistics. bibliog NEA J 54:49-53 Ja '65
MOUMOU; drama. See Green, M. and Feilbert, E.
MOUND CITY GROUP NATIONAL MONUMENT
Ohio's Mound circuit. B. G. Loveless. il Travel 122:38-40 S '64
MOUNDS and mound builders
Hopewell cult; burial mounds unearthed in southern Ohio. O. H. Prufer. il Sci Am 211:90-4+ D '64
See also
Earthworks (archeology)
MOUNSEY, Barbara
Roses and meadows and blushes on cheeks; story. Seventeen 23:84-5 Ja '64
MOUNT Ararat seen from afar; story. See Blum, R.
MOUNT ASSINIBOINE. See Assiniboine, Mount
MOUNT ASSINIBOINE PROVINCIAL PARK. See British Columbia—Parks and reserves
MOUNT ATHOS. See Athos, Mount
MOUNT AUBURN cemetery. See Cambridge, Mass.—Cemeteries
MOUNT DESERT ISLAND, Me.
Mount Desert; where the forest meets the sea. J. T. Starr. il Am For 69:36-9 N '63
See also
Acadia National Park
MOUNT EVEREST. See Everest, Mount
MOUNT FUJI. See Fuji, Mount
MOUNT HOLYOKE college, South Hadley, Mass.
Academic, social, and spiritual program at Mount Holyoke college. R. G. Gettell. Sch & Soc 92:270-2 O 3 '64
MOUNT KENYA safari club. See Sports clubs
MOUNT MCKINLEY. See McKinley, Mount
MOUNT MCKINLEY NATIONAL PARK
Development of Mount McKinley National Park. P. M. Tilden and N. L. Machler. il Nat Parks Mag 37:10-15 My '63
Implications of McKinley. A. W. Smith. Nat Parks Mag 37:2 Je '63
Mammals of McKinley Park. Nat Parks Mag 37:22 Ap '63
Mount McKinley: wilderness park of the North country; with editorial comment. O. J. Murie. Nat Parks Mag 37:2, 4-7 Ap '63
Mysteries of Mount McKinley; with editorial comment. D. Lambert. il Nat Parks Mag 37:2, 8-10+ Ap '63
Some views concerning the development of Mount McKinley National Park. H. S. Francis, jr; W. O. Pruitt, jr; A. Van Sinderen. Nat Parks Mag 37:18-19+ S '63
MOUNT OLYMPUS NATIONAL PARK. See Olympic National Park
MOUNT RAINIER. See Rainier, Mount
MOUNT RAINIER NATIONAL PARK
Paradise Valley hotel. P. M. Tilden. Nat Parks Mag 38:2 Mr '64
That old hotel in Paradise; hotel operations in Paradise Valley, Wash. L. Gallagher. il Nat Parks Mag 38:4-7 Ja '64
MOUNT RIGA. See Taconic Mountains
MOUNT SAINT HELENS cave area. See Caves
MOUNT SHASTA. See Shasta, Mount
MOUNT STROMLO observatory. See Astronomical observatories—Australia

MOUNT VERNON, N.Y.
Sanitary affairs
Flushers fill the gap. A. Annunziata. Am City 79:8 My '64
MOUNT VERNON, Va.
New effort to protect Mount Vernon; reprint. il Am For 70:5 Je '64
MOUNT WASHINGTON. See Washington, Mount
MT ZION spiritual temples, incorporated. See Sects
MOUNTAIN cabins. See Cabins
MOUNTAIN climbing. See Mountaineering
MOUNTAIN ecology
Ecology of the heights. L. W. Swan. il Natur Hist 72:22-9 Ap '63
MOUNTAIN goat hunting. See Rocky Mountain goat hunting
MOUNTAIN goats. See Rocky Mountain goats
MOUNTAIN lakes. See Lakes
MOUNTAIN lion hunting. See Puma hunting
MOUNTAIN plants. See Alpine flora
MOUNTAIN sculpture
World's biggest one-man job; mountain memorial to Sioux chief Crazy Horse. J. M. Liston. il Pop Sci 184:68-71 Je '64
MOUNTAIN sheep
New game in New Mexico. A. Napier. il Sports Illus 18:57-60 My 27 '63
Partners to the end; accidental interlocking of horns doomed the two sheep. H. Kanzler. il Field & S 69:24 N '64
Unpredictable Nelson bighorn. R. H. Wauer. il Nat Parks Mag 38:10-11 Ag '64
See also
Argali
MOUNTAIN sheep hunting
Do-it-yourself bighorns. R. M. Hobbs. il Outdoor Life 132:20-3+ D '63
Grand slam doubled. M. K. Sloan. il Outdoor Life 131:68-71+ Ap '63
Land of the unexpected. J. Pless. il Field & S 69:46-8+ Ag '64
Lost sheep; ed. by C. Elliott. J. F. Lane. il Outdoor Life 134:44-6+ S '64
Permit no. 4. M. Nash, jr. il Outdoor Life 134:44-7+ N '64
Ram for the records. G. Morris. il Outdoor Life 134:46-7+ Ag '64
Ram to begin on. J. O'Connor. il Outdoor Life 133:58-9+ Ap '64
Ram with a corset. W. Page. il Field & S 69:34-7+ Jl '64
Rams were my bugaboo. C. Ormond. il Outdoor Life 131:28-9+ F '63
Ross and his rifle. D. Peck. il Outdoor Life 131:32-5+ Ja; 36-9+ F '63
Two rams for the money. F. C. Hibben. il Field & S 68:56-7+ Je '63
MOUNTAIN sickness. See Altitude, Influence of
MOUNTAIN silverbell trees. See Silver-bell trees
MOUNTAIN states. See West
MOUNTAINEERING
American and Geographic flags top Everest. M. M. Payne. il Nat Geog Mag 124:157-157C Ag '63
Awesome challenge of Mt Aconcagua. L. Stowe. il Read Digest 84:106-11 Mr '64
Commando raid on Everest. W. W. Sayre. il Life 54:58-66+ Mr 22 '63
Everest; the American expedition is studying itself under stress as part of its scientific mission. J. Walsh. Science 140: 620-1 My 10 '63
Expedition depression. Sci N L 83:107 F 16 '63
First traverse; West ridge of Mt Everest. T. F. Hornbein and W. F. Unsoeld. il Nat Geog Mag 124:508-13 O '63
How to arrange a high hike on Oahu. il Sunset 130:47 Mr '63
How we climbed Everest. B. C. Bishop. il Nat Geog Mag 124:474-507 O '63
Human flies; scaling Cima Grande di Lavaredo's north wall. il Time 81:68-9 F 8 '63
If you like your mountains all to yourself, consider Idaho's Seven Devils. il Sunset 130:40+ Je '63
La Verte strikes back; Col D'Iserand, worst tragedy in the history of French mountain climbing. il Newsweek 64:46 Jl 20 '64
Lightning strikes on Bugaboo Spire. C. Fletcher. il Read Digest 82:49-54 Je '63
Mass attack on the mighty peak; American Mount Everest expedition, 1963, with report by J. R. Ullman. il Life 55:68-73+ S 20 '63
Mount Rainier; testing ground for Everest. B. C. Bishop. il Nat Geog Mag 123:688-711 My '63
Mountain climbing, family style. il Pop Mech 120:86-9 Jl '63
Mountain leadership on the trail. W. L. Putnam. il Recreation 56:240-2 My '63
Mountaineers: dilettantes of suicide. D. Cort. il Nation 196:423-4+ My 18 '63
Old Glory on Everest. il Newsweek 61:52 My 13 '63
Point of no return; U.S. climbers rendezvous on Mt Everest. il Time 81:64 My 31 '63
Secretary Udall asaults Kilimanjaro. il Life 55:55-6+ O 11 '63
Six to the summit; America's first Everest expedition. N. G. Dyhrenfurth. il Nat Geog Mag 124:460-73 O '63
Ten mountains almost anyone can climb. H. Higdon. il Todays Health 42:38-41+ O '64
They did the impossible, and then: tragedy, conquest of Matterhorn, 1865. R. Deardorff. il N Y Times Mag p74-5+ D 6 '64
To the top of Rainier. il Sunset 131:26 Jl '63
Up they claw in winter's Alpine epic; Great Lavaredo's north face. R. Brigham. il Life 54:22-5 F 15 '63
Up to the gods; expedition, headed by N. Dyhrenfurth. il Time 81:85 My 10 '63
Weekend climber. il Ebony 19:125-8 N '63
Yankee who conquered Everest. M. Morgan. il Sat Eve Post 236:40+ Je 29 '63
Yes, I will; J. Whittaker's climb to summit of Mount Everest. il Time 81:96 My 17 '63
You can drive most of the way up. Orizaba, Mex. il Sunset 130:67-8 Ap '63
Young mountaineers; Great Northern Mountain, Mont. G. G. Ostrom. il Field & S 69:49-51 N '64
Anecdotes, facetiae, satire, etc.
Conquest of Everest: a divertissement. A. Kopit. il Mlle 60:158-9+ N '64
MOUNTAINEERING clubs
See also
Sierra club
MOUNTAINEERS (southern states)
Wanna go home; hillbilly migration. il Newsweek 62:30 Ag 5 '63
When whites migrate from the South; hillbillies in Chicago. il U S News 55:70-3 O 14 '63
MOUNTAINS
Continental drift and the origin of mountains. E. Orowan. bibliog il Science 146:1003-10 N 20 '64
Ten mountains almost anyone can climb. H. Higdon. il Todays Health 42:38-41+ O '64
Threatening splendor of mountains. il N Y Times Mag p26-7 My 3 '64
See also
Geology, Structural
Volcanoes
MOUNTAINS, Undersea. See Ocean bottom
MOUNTAINS of Guatemala; story. See Connell, E. S. jr
MOUNTBATTEN of Burma, Louis Mountbatten, 1st earl
Mountbatten's Irish retreat. il pors Life 55: 131-3 S 20 '63
MOUNTING of pictures. See Pictures—Mounting
MOUNTZOURES, H. L.
Buoy; story. Atlan 214:66-71 O '64
MOURNING dove shooting
Charged by a dove. C. Dickey. il Field & S 68:56-7+ S '63
Decoys for doves. R. F. Burgess. il Outdoor Life 132:44-7+ D '63
Dove days. il Time 82:55 S 13 '63
Fastest gunning in the West. C. Chatfield. il Outdoor Life 134:40-1+ S '64
MOURNING doves
Is mourning dove management really management? H. M. Weber. il Am For 69:32-3+ S '63
Migratory bird now turning into settler. Sci N L 83:201 Mr 30 '63
Poetry of birds in flight. il House B 105: 104-7+ Ag '63
MOURNING fans. See Fans
MOURSUND, Albert Wadel
How an LBJ associate got a U.S. loan. por U S News 58:12 Ja 11 '65
Story of LBJ and a hunting incident. U S News 56:8 My 18 '64
Texan's Texan. por Time 84:31-2 D 11 '64
MOUSE that soared; drama. See Miller, H. L.
MOUSSE. See Desserts
MOUSSORGSKY, Modest Petrovich. See Musorgskii, M. P.
MOUTH
See also
Salivary glands

MOUTH hygiene
Nice to be near. . .you. Seventeen 22:76-7 Ag '63
MOUTH to mouth resuscitation. See Respiration, Artificial
MOUTHBREEDERS
Cultivation of tilapia. C. F. Hickling. il Sci Am 208:143-8+ My '63
MOUTON, Jane S. See Blake, R. R. jt. auth.
MOUTON. See Castles
MOVEMENT, Notation of. See Dance notation
MOVEMENT of animals. See Animal locomotion
MOVEMENT towards Christian international. See Fellowship of reconciliation
MOVIE shorts. See Moving pictures—Short subject films
MOVIELAND wax museum. See Wax figures
MOVIMIENTO revolucionario del pueblo. See Political parties—Cuba
MOVING
Hell of a way to move. E. I. Neighbor. il Outdoor Life 133:44-7+ F; 60-3+ Mr '64
Life guide; tips to make moving days easier. il Life 55:7 Ag 30 '63
Moving house at American cyanamid. il Duns R 83:pt2 103 Mr '64
Moving man, I love you. J. L. O'Neill. Am Home 67:24-5 Mr '64
Moving? what to do about schools. il Good H 157:129 Jl '63
New town, new school, new problems. G. L. Wyatt. il Parents Mag 39:68-9+ S '64
On getting the country moving again. M. Kempton. New Repub 149:9-10 Jl 20 '63
Planning to move? Consumer Bul 47:20-1+ Je '64
Taking the mess out of moving. Good H 156: 208j Ap '63
Trials of families on the move. D. C. Disney. Ladies Home J 81:16+ My '64
When move you must. J. Cook. il N Y Times Mag p52 Ja 5 '64
MOVING and storage companies
Moving man, I love you. J. L. O'Neill. Am Home 67:24-5 Mr '64
Moving rules stymied at least for a time. Consumer Rep 29:412 S '64
Moving, the rough road to home; reports on fourteen van lines. il Consumer Rep 28: 340-6 Jl '63
On getting the country moving again. M. Kempton. New Repub 149:9-10 Jl 20 '63
Some new rules of etiquette for moving men. Consumer Rep 29:329 Jl '64
MOVING day; drama. See Klein, E.
MOVING objects, Photography from. See Photography from moving objects
MOVING objects, Photography of. See Photography of moving objects
MOVING of libraries
Library moving made easy. G. Hawthorne. il ALA Bul 57:671 Jl '63
MOVING of structures, etc.
Moving 3,500 tons of building; Woodrow Wilson Hall, Princeton university. il Arch Forum 119:108-9 Jl '63
MOVING picture acting
Fading movie star. M. Farber. Commentary 36:55-60 Jl '63
MOVING picture actors and actresses
Ah, what sights; water sprites! Hollywood's rising young actresses; photographs. D. Ornitz. Life 54:58-67 Ap 26 '63
Cast menagerie; company making The night of the iguana. il Time 82:69 N 8 '63
Cleopatra; trials and tribulations of an epic film. W. Wanger and J. Hyams. il Sat Eve Post 236:28-38+ Je 1 '63
Drama the cameras missed; on location for Night of the iguana; ed. by M. Davidson. T. Victor. il Sat Eve Post 237:24-8+ Jl 11 '64
End of the great girl drought. il Life 57: 136-9 O 2 '64
Fading movie star. M. Farber. Commentary 36:55-60 Jl '63
Fair young Hollywood girls. R. W. Lewis. il Sat Eve Post 236:22-7 S 7 '63
Go find something wrong with him! R. Lemon. il Sat Eve Post 238:68-70+ Ja 16 '65
Hollywood scene. E. Miller. See issues of Seventeen
Idols junior grade; sons and daughters of stars. pors Time 82:47 Jl 26 '63
Instant portrait of the Hollywood starlet. J. D. Weaver. Holiday 33:76-7 Mr '63
James Bond's girls. il Vogue 144:74-7 Jl '64
Les girls; new faces. il Time 84:72-3 Ag 21 '64
My technicolor senator. S. Alexander. Life 57:30 D 4 '64
Old-master monsters and the new breed. il Look 28:48-9 S 8 '64
Portraits in nostalgia. il N Y Times Mag p32-3 Ap 5 '64
Sex shortage. Time 82:66+ D 13 '63
Some very winning Europeans. M. Greene. il Life 55:132-43 D 20 '63
Sometimes the dream comes true; girls of the Hollywood studio club. J. Taylor. il Seventeen 23:66-7 Mr '64
Stars fell on Mismaloya; beginning of the film production of The night of the iguana. R. Oulahan. il Life 55:69-74+ D 20 '63
Stars in your eyes. M. Ross. il Travel 119: 38-40+ F '63
Stars, second generation. V. Scott. il McCalls 90:68-9+ Jl '63
Teen-agers win movie roles. il Ebony 18: 150-2+ My '63
They kept the old flag flying; the British colony of Hollywood. G. Bocca. il Horizon 5:74-81 S '63
Topsy-turvy flashbacks to yesteryear's films: big stars take old roles. B. Stern. il Life 55:54-67 D 20 '63
Twenty years after: PT 109. il Life 54:98+ My 17 '63
When love goes on location. J. Hyams. il McCalls 90:88-93 Je '63
With a cast of thousands. J. S. Zimmer. il McCalls 91:130-3+ N '63
Young wild pack in Lord of Flies; with report by R. Wallace. il Life 55:96-9+ O 25 '63
See also
Barrymore family
Children as actors
Make-up, Theatrical
also names of moving picture actors and actresses, e.g. E. Borgnine
MOVING picture adaptations. See Film adaptations
MOVING picture authorship
Big novel syndrome. A. Knight. Sat R 46: 18 Ag 31 '63
Catch $95; novelists are invading movies. il Newsweek 63:83-4 Mr 9 '64
Crusader: A. Mann. Time 81:56 Mr 22 '63
Hollywood myth has fallen! tr. by R. J. Moore. M. Antonioni. il Pop Phot 53:94-7+ Jl '63
MOVING picture awards
See also
Academy awards (moving pictures)
MOVING picture cameras
Battery-operated 8mm camera covers broad zoom range; Kodak Electric 8. il Pop Sci 184:170 Ap '64
Best compact eight? R. Miller. il U S Camera 26:52-5 N '63
Buying guide to movie cameras. il Good H 158:164-5 My '64
Choosing the right movie camera. L. Drukker. il Pop Phot 53:180-1+ D '63
Directory of 8mm zoom cameras. J. R. Gregory. U S Camera 27:66-73+ Mr '64
Dualmatic 50. B. Hering. il Pop Sci 183:159 S '63
Easy-loading cartridge movie cameras; Autoloads. il Pop Sci 183:128 N '63
8mm auto-exposure movie cameras. il Consumer Rep 29:558-63 N '64
8mm movies lay down? H. Keppler and M. Matzkin. il Mod Phot 27:90-1+ My '63
How to test movie cameras. M. A. Matzkin and B. Sherman. il Mod Phot 28:146+ D '64
Low-priced movie cameras. il Consumer Rep 29:288-91 Je '64
Methods & materials; battery-powered 8. L. Drukker. Pop Phot 51:111+ D '62
More than 300 new still & movie cameras & how they compare; comp. by D. L. Miller and M. A. Matzkin. il Mod Phot 27:99-128 D '63
New at the trade show. L. Drukker. il Pop Phot 52:115-17+ Je '63
1965 photography directory and buying guide; showmanship. il Pop Phot 55:69-132 D '64
Test reports. See issues of Popular photography
Vagabond camera; three new 8mm zoom cameras. W. Lane. il Travel 121:54-5 Je '64
Why the new 8mm movie cameras never miss. B. Hering. il Pop Sci 185:96-100 Ag '64

Equipment

8mm movies lay down? H. Keppler and M. Matzkin. il Mod Phot 27:90-1+ My '63
MOVING picture cartoons. See Moving pictures—Animated cartoons
MOVING picture censorship
Art in court; city of angels vs. Scorpio rising. F. Haines. Nation 199:123-5 S 14 '64

MOVING picture censorship—*Continued*
Controversy on film; address, May 1962. G. Holloway. il Library J 88:513-15 F 1 '63
Face on the cutting room floor, by M. Schumach. Review
Newsweek il 64:86 Jl 13 '64
Feast for open eyes. S. Sontag. Nation 198: 374-6 Ap 13 '64; Discussion. 198:inside cover Ap 27 '64
Film classification defied. America 111:730 D 5 '64
Hidden face of the cinema. P. Léglise. il UNESCO Courier 16:28-32 Ap '63
Wilder's dirty-joke film stirs a furor. T. Thompson. il Life 58:52+ Ja 15 '65
See also
Moving pictures—Moral aspects
MOVING picture clubs
How-to-do-it; Fordham's Communications arts department course. America 109:34 Jl 13 '63
Little films that make it big; Olde time movie club, Asheville, N.C. W. P. Banner. il U S Camera 27:60-1 Ja '64
Screen education; useful books. J. McLaughlin. America 111:341 S 26 '64
MOVING picture criticism. See Moving picture plays—Criticisms, plots, etc.
MOVING picture directors
Autumn of John Ford. P. Bogdanovich. il Esquire 61:102-4+ Ap '64
Breakthrough in Hollywood. il Ebony 19:82-4+ D '63
Directors. R. Coughlan. il Life 55:156-8+ D 20 '63
Goodnight, C.B. A. De Mille. il Esquire 61: 119-31 Ja '64
Pitfalls of pratfalls; Boulting brothers comedies. W. Sheed. Commonweal 78:402-4 Jl 5 '63
Shame and glory in the movies. A. Berson and J. Keller. il Nat R 16:17-21 Ja 14 '64
Supercolossal, well, pretty good, world of Joe Levine. K. Hamill. il Fortune 69:130-2+ Mr '64
Two on the aisle. P. V. Beckley. il Sat R 47:36-7 F 8 '64
See also
Fellini, F.
Stevens, G.
MOVING picture exchanges. See Moving pictures—International aspects
MOVING picture festivals
Accent on youth at first N.Y. film festival. R. Hemming. Sr Schol 83:25 O 25 '63
After the ball was over; New York film festival. New Repub 149:33+ O 5 '63
Art movies pack the house; New York film festival at Lincoln Center's Philharmonic Hall. il Bsns W p34-5 S 19 '64
At Lincoln Center, the art of the film. S. Peck. il N Y Times Mag p76-7 S 8 '63
Chicago's Midwest film festival grows up. G. Hitchens. il Pop Phot 53:97+ O '63
Cinema's last stand; New York film festival. W. Sheed. Commonweal 79:136+ O 25 '63
Communication and art; San Francisco's eighth annual film festival. A. Knight. Sat R 47:41 N 14 '64
Critic in from the cold; Berlin film festival. H. Alpert. Sat R 47:19 Ag 1 '64
Current cinema; second New York film festival. B. Gill. New Yorker 40:134+ O 3 '64
Festival in New York. il Time 84:52+ S 25 '64
Film festival at the concert hall. R. Steel. Christian Cent 80:1150-2+ D 11 '63
Film-makers: new festival offers money, screenings; International film festival of America. G. A. Young. Pop Phot 55:40+ S '64
Films for peace; International peace film festival at Los Alamos. A. Knight. Sat R 47:23 D 19 '64
Films; New York's first film festival. R. Hatch. Nation 197:227-8 O 12 '63
Films; second New York film festival. R. Hatch. Nation 199:175-6 S 28 '64
Films; Venice film festival. D. Macdonald. Esquire 62:68+ D '64
Fortnight of films; New York film festival at Lincoln Center. il Newsweek 64-114 O 5 '64
Johnny's so long at the fair; second New York film festival. P. T. Hartung. Commonweal 81:101 O 16 '64
Methods and materials; American film festival in New York. L. Drukker. Pop Phot 55:97+ Ag '64
New look in American films; New York film festival. A. Knight. Sat R 47:28 O 17 '64
New producer; Cool world at Venice film festival. New Yorker 39:33-5 S 14 '63
New York film festival. A. Croce. Nat R 16: 1118-19 D 15 '64
News from Karlovy Vary. S. Kauffmann. New Repub 151:33-4 Ag 8 '64
One man's festival; New York film festival. H. Alpert. il Sat R 46:18-19+ O 5 '63
Religion on film; New York film festival. il Time 82:78-82 S 20 '63
SR goes to the movies; a New York festival. H. Alpert. Sat R 46:37 My 18 '63
Second thoughts; high points of the second New York film festival at Lincoln Center. H. Alpert. Sat R 47:35+ O 10 '64
Ten best of the N.Y. film festival. il Pop Phot 56:170-1 Ja '65
Venice observed; this year's Venice film festival. R. Steel. Commonweal 81:97-9 O 16 '64
West Coast festival; San Francisco international film festival. A. Knight. Sat R 46:25 N 30 '63
World on a screen: 1964 N.Y. film festival. R. Hemming and W. Johnson. il Sr Schol 85:27+ O 14 '64
See also
Cannes international film festival
Anecdotes, facetiae, satire, etc.
More film fun. R. Angell. New Yorker 40: 42-3 S 26 '64
MOVING picture film collections
See also
Libraries—Moving picture collections
MOVING picture films. See Photography—Films
MOVING picture industry
Hidden face of the cinema (cont) P. Léglise. il UNESCO Courier 16:26-31 F; 21-3+ My '63
Moving mirror of modern times. Life 55:4-5 D 20 '63
New film frontier. A. Mayer. Sat R 46:20-1+ O 5 '63
See also
Moving picture production and direction
Advertising
Well-planned Crawford; fast-paced tour plugging Strait-jacket. R. Oulahan. il Life 56: 11-12 F 12 '64
Finance
Can Cleo pay it back? il Bsns W p48-50 Je 8 '63
Cleopatra's prospects. il Fortune 67:234 My '63
Speculating in spectaculars. Fortune 67:232+ My '63
History
Million and one nights, by T. Ramsaye. Review
Esquire 61:20+ Ap '64. D. Macdonald
France
BB or bust. il Newsweek 61:76 F 25 '63
Franglais film. B. P. Solomon. Nation 199:57-9 Ag 10 '64
Italy
Sweet and sour. America 110:300 Mr 7 '64
Sweden
How Sweden's film god brings in the kronor. il Bsns W p 128-30 F 29 '64
United States
Anti-formula film; symposium. il Sat R 46: 13-24 D 28 '63
Aspen experience; second annual Aspen film conference. A. Knight. Sat R 47:27-8 O 3 '64
Box office buzzes overseas; expansion of U.S. movie makers. il Bsns W p64+ N 7 '64
Cinema underground; Film-makers' coöperative, or Underground cinema. New Yorker 39:16-17 Jl 13 '63
Cinema's ins and outs. H. Alpert. Sat R 47: 166-9 Ag 29 '64
Explosion in the movie underground; Underground cinema. P. Hamill. il Sat Eve Post 236:82+ S 28 '63
Handwriting on the screen. R. Gessner. Sat R 47:36 O 10 '64
Hollywood nursery. P. Gilliatt. Harper 226:87-90 Je '63
Meanwhile back in Hollywood, efficiency takes over; with report by D. Zeitlin. il Life 55:46-50B D 20 '63
Movie screens get back some silver; shopping center theaters. il Bsns W p41-2+ Ag 31 '63
Moviemaker, stay home. il Bsns W p68 Ja 26 '63

MOVING picture industry—United States—*Continued*
My first hundred years in Hollywood: excerpts; ed. by D. Jennings. J. L. Warner. McCalls 91:72-3+ S; 92:128-9+ O; 100-1+ N '64
Reel money. Newsweek 64:79 D 7 '64
Ripple effect; first annual Aspen film conference. A. Knight. Sat R 46:60-1 O 12 '63
Theater chain to make films. Bsns W p22 Jl 6 '63
Trimming overhead costs; Film-makers. J. B. Weiner. Duns R 83:70+ F '64
What golden years? A. Knight. il Sat R 47: 169-71 Ag 29 '64
See also
Embassy pictures corporation
Hollywood, Calif.
Twentieth century-Fox film corporation

MOVING picture make-up. See Make-up, Theatrical

MOVING picture music. See Moving pictures—Music

MOVING picture periodicals. See Moving pictures—Periodicals

MOVING picture photography
Break the rules for exciting movie color. M. A. Matzkin. il Mod Phot 27:84-5 Ag '63
Experimenting with film. C. Reynolds. Pop Phot 55:91+ S '64
Family movies on a shoestring. M. A. Matzkin. il Mod Phot 28:96-7+ My '64
Films at the fair: dazzling range of cinematic art and techniques. H. V. Fondiller. il Pop Phot 55:88-91+ Ag '64
Films '64. C. Reynolds. Pop Phot 55:193 D '64
Five basic techniques for better zoom movies. M. A. Matzkin. il Mod Phot 27:88-9 S '63
Hollywood musical. L. Jacobs, jr. il U S Camera 26:70-1 Jl '63
How to break in. H. V. Fondiller. il Pop Phot 54:107+ F '64
How to do it! monster movies. R. L. Cramer. il U S Camera 27:68-9+ S '64
How to get more sharpness, clarity, contrast in 8-mm. L. Drukker. il Pop Phot 55:82-3+ S '64
James Bond's golfing caper. il Sports Illus 20:22-5 Je 22 '64
Methods & materials. L. Drukker. See issues of Popular photography
Moore on movies. J. W. Moore. See issues of U.S. camera
Movie maker. M. A. Matzkin. See issues of Modern photography
Movies to learn from. See issues of Popular photography
Movies; twenty-five questions, twenty-four answers. L. Lipton. Pop Phot 55:188-9 D '64
Play the angles for action movies. M. A. Matzkin. il Mod Phot 28:88-9 O '64
Pro goes the amateur way. D. Streibig. il Pop Phot 54:111+ Mr '64
Saul Bass on visual excitement; interview. S. Bass. il Pop Phot 55:108-9+ Jl '64
Sharp indoor without fuss, feathers or focusing. M. A. Matzkin. il Mod Phot 27:90-1 Je '63
Shoot for showing. C. Reynolds. il Pop Phot 52:118+ Je '63
Shooting color television. D. B. Eisendrath. Pop Phot 53:10+ N '63
Snap up your summer movie landscapes. M. A. Matzkin. il Mod Phot 27:92-3 Jl '63
Think telephoto for tighter movie scenes. il Mod Phot 28:92-3 Ag '64
Toy around with your home movies. M. A. Matzkin. il Mod Phot 28:92-3 Mr '64
Try filming TV! E. Corley. il Pop Phot 53: 183+ N '63
See also
Moving pictures in medicine

Apparatus and supplies

Ciné-cues. V. J. Plesko. il U S Camera 28: 72-3 Ja '65
Eight extras for movies. M. A. Matzkin. il Mod Phot 27:92-3 Je '63
How new movie lights stack up! M. A. Matzkin. il Mod Phot 28:94-5+ Ja '64
Methods & materials. L. Drukker. Pop Phot 52:103+ Mr '63
Movie equipment. il Pop Phot 52:102-6 Ap '63
New at the trade show. L. Drukker. il Pop Phot 52:115-17+ Je '63
Nine ideas for tiny titlers. M. A. Matzkin. il Mod Phot 27:92-3 Mr '63

Bibliography

What every film-maker should read. C. Reynolds. il Pop Phot 52:117+ My '63

Competitions

Methods & materials; Ford foundation winners. L. Drukker. Pop Phot 55:97 Ag '64

Composition

See Composition (photography)

Exposure

Nine tough movie exposure problems solved for you. M. A. Matzkin. il Mod Phot 28:80-1 Jl '64

Lighting

Four keys to creative movie lighting. D. Mohler. il U S Camera 26:78-9+ F '63
Movie maker; use of back lighting. M. A. Matzkin. Mod Phot 27:52+ Jl '63

MOVING picture photography in criminal investigation. See Photography in criminal investigation

MOVING picture plays
See also
Film adaptations

Criticisms, plots, etc.

At the movies. E. Miller. See issues of Seventeen
Auteur! auteur! opposing camps. M. Magid. bibliog f Commentary 37:70-4 Mr '64
Chase. J. Kerman. il Opera N 28:8-12 D 28 '63
Children caught in adult dramas. il Life 54: 97-100+ F 8 '63
Cinema of the absurd. H. Alpert. Sat R 46:34 Mr 30 '63
Coming: the end of the world. il Newsweek 61:84 Mr 4 '63
Current cinema. B. Gill. See issues of New Yorker
Family movie guide; ed. by A. D. Kenney. See issues of Parents' magazine & better homemaking
Film seminars; experiment in movie criticism on a college campus. L. J. O'Donovan. America 109:560-2 N 9 '63
Films. D. Macdonald. See issues of Esquire
Films. M. Walsh. See issues of America
Films. R. Hatch. See issues of Nation
Films. S. Kauffmann. See issues of New republic
Following the films. P. T. Hartung. See issues of Senior scholastic
Goings on about town. See issues of New Yorker
Hollywood myth has fallen! tr. by R. J. Moore. M. Antonioni. il Pop Phot 53:94-7+ Jl '63
Life guide. See issues of Life
Life movie review. See issues of Life, March 27, 1964-
Meaningful films. M. Walsh. America 111:197-8 Ag 22 '64
Motion picture previews. I. McMahan and E. Whitehorn. See issues of PTA magazine beginning February 1964
Motion picture previews; ed. by E. Bucklin. See issues of PTA magazine to January 1964
Movie of the month. il Cath World 196:327-8, 387-9; 197:207-8, 335-6, 395-6; 198:327-8; 199: 71-2, 395-6 F-Mr, Je, Ag-S '63, F, Ap, S '64
Movie report. R. Harbert. See issues of Good housekeeping
Movies (cont) Horizon 5:109-11 Mr; 110-12 My '63
Movies (cont) Nat R 14:123-4, 167-9; 15:114+, 536-8; 16:77-9, 165, 203-4, 367-70, 413-15, 502-3, 1026-7, 1156+; 17:31-2 F 12-26, Ag 13, D 17 '63, Ja 28, F 25-Mr 10, My 5-19, Je 16, N 17, D 29 '64-Ja 12 '65
Movies. See issues of Consumer reports
Movies. See issues of Vogue beginning January 1964
Movies and the critics; symposium. il Sat R 47:10-19+ D 26 '64
Movies in brief. il Nat R 15:72 Jl 30 '63
New films in review (cont) D. R. Slavitt. Yale R 52:627-35; 53:309-15, 616-24; 54:299-307 Je, D '63, Je, D '64
New movies (cont of) Movie reviews. P. T. Hartung. See occasional issues of Senior scholastic
New movies. F. Somers. See issues of Redbook
Oscar day East; New York critics' choices for 1964. Time 85:51 Ja 8 '65
Ratings of current motion pictures. See issues of Consumer bulletin
SR goes to the movies. H. Alpert; A. Knight. See issues of Saturday review
Screen. P. T. Hartung. See issues of Commonweal

MOVING picture plays—Criticisms, plots, etc.
—*Continued*
Screen; ten best in 1964. P. T. Hartung. Commonweal 81:484-5 Ja 8 '65
Sight & sound. L. Benjamin. See issues of McCall's beginning August 1964
Sight & sound; ed. by B. Sheridan. See issues of McCall's to December 1963
Sight & sound; ed. by L. Benjamin and B. Sheridan. il McCalls 91:8+ F; 6+ Mr; 8+ Ap; 8+ My; 8+ Je; 8+ Jl '64
So deeply obscure, so widely discussed. H. Alpert. il N Y Times Mag p68-9+ Ap 21 '63
Ten best of the N.Y. film festival. il Pop Phot 56:170-1 Ja '65
Ten best pictures of 1963. M. Walsh. America 110:171 F 1 '64
Time listings. See issues of Time
We look before and after; best ten. P. T. Hartung. Commonweal 79:432 Ja 10 '64
What reviewers have not done. M. Walsh. America 109:689 N 23 '63
Which Zulu did you see? M. Walsh. America 111:94-5 Jl 25 '64
World as a fair; three films to be seen at the New York world's fair. S. Kauffmann. New Repub 151:31-2 S 19 '64

Single works

Les abysses
Nation 199:420 N 30 '64
New Repub 151:23-4 D 12 '64
New Yorker 40:203 N 28 '64
Newsweek il 64:102A N 30 '64
Sat R 47:44 D 5 '64
Time il 84:110+ N 27 '64
Vogue 145:25 Ja 15 '65
Act one
America 110:54-5 Ja 11 '64
New Repub 150:26 Ja 18 '64
Time 82:57 D 27 '63
Advance to the rear
Time il 83:91 Je 26 '64
Affair of the skin
Sat R 46:25 N 30 '63
All these women
Commonweal 81:167 O 30 '64
Life 57:19 O 16 '64
New Repub 151:28 O 31 '64
Newsweek il 64:116+ O 12 '64
Sat R 47:34 N 21 '64
All the way home
America 109:613 N 9 '63
Commonweal 79:257 N 22 '63
New Repub 149:48-9 N 9 '63
New Yorker 39:210 N 9 '63
Sr Schol 83:24 N 1 '63
Time il 82:109 N 1 '63
America America
America 110:173 F 1 '64
Commonweal 79:484 Ja 24 '64
Esquire 61:22+ Mr '64
Life il 56:113-14 Mr 6 '64
Nat R 16:413-15 My 19 '64
New Repub 150:20-2 Ja 4 '64
Newsweek il 62:74 D 23 '63
Sat R 46:29+ D 28 '63
Sr Schol 84:28 F 7 '64
Time il 83:78 Ja 3 '64
Vogue 143:64 F 1 '64
Americanization of Emily
America 111:641-3 N 14 '64
Commonweal 81:355 D 4 '64
New Repub 151:22+ D 5 '64
Newsweek 63:83 F 10 '64
Newsweek il 64:96-7 N 2 '64
Sat R 47:29 O 24 '64
Time il 84:128+ N 13 '64
Vogue 145:66 Ja 1 '65
Le amiche
New Repub 148:35 Mr 23 '63
Newsweek 61:92 Ap 8 '63
Anatomy of a marriage
Commonweal 81:290 N 20 '64
New Repub 151:28 D 19 '64
New Yorker 40:200+ N 7 '64
Newsweek il 64:100+ N 9 '64
Sat R 47:40-1 N 14 '64
Andy
Newsweek il 63:92 My 4 '64
Newsweek 65:76 F 1 '65
Antigone
Esquire 59:32+ F '63
Any number can win
Commonweal 79:195 N 8 '63
New Yorker 39:146+ O 19 '63
Newsweek il 62:110 O 7 '63
Ape woman
America 111:426 O 10 '64
Commonweal 81:18 S 25 '64
Newsweek il 64:82+ S 7 '64
Time il 84:112+ S 18 '64
Army game
New Yorker 39:167 Ap 27 '63
Newsweek 61:91 Ap 29 '63
L'avventura
Yale R 54:41-50 O '64

Baby, the rain must fall
Commonweal 81:544 Ja 22 '65
New Yorker 40:104 Ja 23 '65
Newsweek il 65:90 Ja 25 '65
Sat R 48:40 Ja 30 '65
Bad sleep well
Commonweal 77:517 F 8 '63
Newsweek 61:78 F 4 '63
Balcony
Christian Cent 80:960-1 Jl 31 '63
Commonweal 78:74 Ap 12 '63
Nation 196:430-1 My 18 '63
New Repub 148:34 Mr 23 '63
New Yorker 39:143-4 Mr 30 '63
Newsweek il 61:81 Ap 1 '63
Sat R 46:34 Mr 30 '63
Time il 81:92+ Mr 29 '63
Ballad of a Hussar
Nation 197:80 Ag 10 '63
Banana peel
Newsweek il 65:90+ Ja 25 '65
Time il 85:85 Ja 29 '65
Bandits of Orgosolo
Commonweal 80:208 My 8 '64
Nation 198:446-7 Ap 27 '64
New Repub 150:35 My 16 '64
New Yorker 25:170-1 Ap 25 '64
Newsweek il 63:104 Ap 27 '64
Sat R 47:35 My 9 '64
Time il 83:103+ Ap 24 '64
Bay of the angels
Commonweal 81:390 D 11 '64
New Repub 151:28 D 19 '64
New Yorker 40:156+ D 5 '64
Sat R 47:42 D 12 '64
Time 84:109 N 27 '64
Beach of Falesá
Time 82:47 S 27 '63
Beach party
Time il 82:74 Ag 16 '63
Bebo's girl
Commonweal 81:199 N 6 '64
Becket
America 110:379-80 Mr 21 '64
Christian Cent 81:1112-13 S 9 '64
Commonweal 79:722 Mr 13 '64
Life il 56:81-2 Mr 13 '64
Mlle il 58:42 Ap '64
New Repub 150:26-7 Mr 14 '64
New Yorker 40:155 Mr 14 '64
Newsweek il 63:95 Mr 23 '64
Sat R il 47:24-5 Mr 7 '64
Sr Schol 84:32 Mr 6 '64
Sr Schol 84:5T Ap 10 '64
Time il 83:94-5 Mr 20 '64
Bedtime story
Commonweal 80:399 Je 19 '64
New Repub 151:29 Jl 4 '64
Newsweek il 63:84+ Je 22 '64
Sat R 47:45 Je 13 '64
Time 83:91-2 Je 26 '64
Behold a pale horse
America 111:240 S 5 '64
Cath World 200:67-8 O '64
Commonweal 80:579 Ag 21 '64
Life 57:12 Ag 21 '64
New Yorker 40:78 Ag 29 '64
Newsweek 64:79 Ag 24 '64
Sat R 47:24 Ag 8 '64
Sr Schol 85:28+ S 30 '64
Sr Schol 85:10T O 7 '64
Time 84:70 Ag 28 '64
Best man
Commonweal 80:147 Ap 24 '64
Esquire 61:18+ Je '64
Life 56:15 Ap 17 '64
New Repub 150:24+ Ap 18 '64
New Yorker 40:118+ Ap 18 '64
Sat R 47:36 Ap 4 '64
Vogue 143:52 Ap 15 '64
Il bidone
Commonweal 81:389 D 11 '64
Newsweek 64:117 N 23 '64
Billy Liar
America 110:202-3 F 8 '64
Commonweal 79:314 D 6 '63
New Repub 149:27 D 14 '63
New Yorker 39:88-9 D 21 '63
Newsweek 62:74+ D 23 '63
Birds
America 108:589 Ap 20 '63
Commonweal 78:73-4 Ap 12 '63
Esquire 60:36+ O '63
New Repub 148:34-5 Ap 13 '63
New Yorker 39:177 Ap 6 '63
Newsweek il 61:92 Ap 8 '63
Sat R 46:39 Ap 6 '63
Time il 81:103 Ap 5 '63
Black like me
Christian Cent 81:807 Je 17 '64
Commonweal 80:236 My 15 '64
Ebony il 19:37-8+ My '64
New Repub 150:24+ My 23 '64
New Yorker 40:151-2 My 23 '64
Newsweek il 63:110B+ My 25 '64
Reporter 31:40 Jl 16 '64
Sat R 47:25 Ap 25 '64
Sr Schol 84:11T My 15 '64

MOVING picture plays—Criticisms, plots, etc. —Single works—*Continued*

Black zoo
Newsweek 61:103 My 20 '63
La bonne soupe
Commonweal 80:43 Ap 3 '64
New Yorker 40:147 Mr 28 '64
Sat R 47:24 Mr 21 '64
Boy ten feet tall
Commonweal 81:573 Ja 29 '65
Brass bottle
Commonweal 80:91 Ap 10 '64
Buddha
Time il 82:95 Jl 12 '63
Bushido
New Yorker 40:128 S 19 '64
Newsweek 64:107A S 21 '64
Bye bye Birdie
America 108:590-1 Ap 20 '63
Commonweal 78:107 Ap 19 '63
Newsweek il 61:103 Ap 15 '63
Sat R 46:26 Ap 27 '63
Cairo
Commonweal 77:542 F 15 '63
Call me Bwana
Time il 82:95 Jl 12 '63
Captain Newman, M.D.
America 110:295 F 29 '64
Commonweal 79:694 Mr 6 '64
Look il 28:92-4 Ap 7 '64
New Yorker 40:122 F 29 '64
Newsweek il 63:84 Mr 2 '64
Sat R 47:33 F 15 '64
Time il 83:105 F 28 '64
Vogue 143:42 Ap 1 '64
Captain Sindbad
Newsweek 62:80 Jl 15 '63
Cardinal
America 110:27 Ja 4 '64
Cath World 198:327-8 F '64
Cath World 198:365-71 Mr '64
Commonweal 79:371-2 D 20 '63
Ebony il 19:126-8+ D '63
Esquire 61:24+ Mr '64
Nat R 16:77-9 Ja 28 '64
New Repub 149:29 D 21 '63
New Yorker 39:198 D 14 '63
Newsweek il 62:90 D 16 '63
Reporter 30:44 F 13 '64
Sat R 46:32 D 7 '63
Sr Schol 83:24, 17T D 13 '63
Time il 82:97-8 D 13 '63
Caretakers
Commonweal 79:46+ O 4 '63
Sat R 46:34 Ag 10 '63
Time il 82:84 S 6 '63
Carpetbaggers
Commonweal 80:514 Jl 24 '64
Life 56:12+ Je 26 '64
Sat R 47:29 Je 20 '64
Time il 84:86 Jl 3 '64
Cartouche
New Yorker 40:74 Ag 8 '64
Time 84:63 Jl 31 '64
Ceremony
America 110:749-50 My 23 '64
Newsweek 63:89 F 24 '64
Sat R 47:27 Ja 18 '64
Chalk garden
America 110:805 Je 6 '64
Commonweal 80:298 My 29 '64
Life 56:21 Je 12 '64
New Repub 150:25-6 My 30 '64
New Yorker 40:112+ My 30 '64
Newsweek 63:84 Je 1 '64
Sat R 47:50 Je 27 '64
Sr Schol 84:11T My 15 '64
Sr Schol 84:32 My 8 '64
Time 83:85 My 29 '64
Charade
America 109:810 D 21 '63
Commonweal 79:349 D 13 '63
New Repub 149:29 D 21 '63
New Yorker 39:196 D 14 '63
Newsweek 62:90 D 16 '63
Sat R 46:24 D 14 '63
Time 82:63 D 20 '63
Vogue 143:24 Ja 1 '64
Château in Sweden
Time il 84:109 O 23 '64
Cheyenne autumn
America 112:85 Ja 16 '65
Life 57:19 N 27 '64
New Repub 152:36-7 Ja 23 '65
New Yorker 40:65 Ja 2 '65
Newsweek 65:79 Ja 11 '65
Sat R 48:36 Ja 16 '65
Sr Schol il 85:30-1 N 4 '64
Sr Schol 85:29 Ja 14 '65
Time 85:54 Ja 8 '65
Vogue 144:150 D '64
Child is waiting
America 108:275 F 23 '63
Cath World il 196:387-9 Mr '63
Commonweal 77:494 F 1 '63
New Yorker 39:126 F 23 '63
Newsweek il 61:78 F 4 '63
Time il 81:66 F 8 '63
Children of the damned
Time il 83:101 F 7 '64
Chushingura
Newsweek 62:115 O 14 '63
Circus world
America 111:75 Jl 18 '64
Time 84:97 Jl 10 '64
Ciske, the rat
New Yorker 39:60 Ag 10 '63
City lights
New Repub 149:29 D 21 '63
Clear skies
New Yorker 39:205 D 7 '63
Newsweek il 62:92 D 9 '63
Cleopatra
America 108:910, 913-14 Je 29 '63
Bsns W p34 Je 15 '63
Commonweal 78:398 Jl 5 '63
Life il 54:30 Je 21 '63
McCalls il 91:136-7 O '63
Nat R 15:114+ Ag 13 '63
Nation 197:19 Jl 6 '63
New Repub 148:27-8 Je 29 '63
New Yorker 39:61-2+ Je 22 '63
Newsweek il 61:110-12 Je 24 '63
Newsweek 62:78+ Jl 8 '63
Sat Eve Post il 236:28-38+ Je 1 '63
Sat R 46:20 Je 29 '63
Sr Schol 83:6T S 27 '63
Sr Schol il 83:22T-23T+ O 4 '63
Time il 81:90 Je 21 '63
Collector
Look il 28:90-3 O 20 '64
Come blow your horn
America 108:872 Je 15 '63
Commonweal 78:356 Je 21 '63
New Yorker 39:54+ Je 15 '63
Newsweek 61:104 Je 10 '63
Sat R 46:45 Je 15 '63
Time 81:99 Je 14 '63
Come fly with me
Sat R 46:16 Je 1 '63
Time il 81:117 My 17 '63
Condemned of Altona
New Repub 149:28 S 28 '63
New Yorker 39:209 N 9 '63
Newsweek 62:110 O 7 '63
Sat R 46:46 O 19 '63
Time il 82:83 S 27 '63
Conjugal bed
Commonweal 79:79 O 11 '63
New Repub 149:29 O 12 '63
New Yorker 39:112 S 21 '63
Sat R 46:44 O 12 '63
Time il 82:84 S 27 '63
Constantine and the cross
Newsweek 61:89 F 11 '63
Contempt
New Repub 152:21-2 Ja 2 '65
New Yorker 40:73 D 26 '64
Time 85:54 Ja 8 '65
Cool world
Commonweal 80:236 My 15 '64
Esquire 62:111-13 Jl '64
Life 56:15 Ap 24 '64
Nation 198:447-8 Ap 27 '64
New Repub 150:24+ My 23 '64
New Yorker 40:171-2 Ap 25 '64
Newsweek 63:114+ Ap 20 '64
Reporter 31:40+ Jl 16 '64
Sat R 47:25 Ap 25 '64
Sr Schol 84:10T My 15 '64
Time il 83:123+ Ap 17 '64
Vogue 143:60 My '64
Courtship of Eddie's father
Commonweal 77:665 Mr 22 '63
Newsweek 61:93 Ap 8 '63
Time il 81:103-4 Ap 5 '63
Crazy desire
Commonweal 80:369 Je 12 '64
Time 84:86 Jl 3 '64
Critic
New Repub 148:36 Je 15 '63
Critic's choice
America 108:692 My 11 '63
Commonweal 78:106 Ap 19 '63
Newsweek 61:104 Ap 15 '63
Sat R 46:31 Mr 2 '63
Cross of the living
Newsweek 61:94 F 18 '63
Crowning experience
America 110:831 Je 13 '64
David and Lisa
Nation 196:216 Mr 9 '63
Sat Eve Post 236:56, 59-60 Mr 16 '63
Day and the hour
Time il 83:84 Mr 6 '64
Day of the triffids
Commonweal 78:283-4 My 31 '63
Newsweek 61:107 My 13 '63
Days of wine and roses
America 108:238 F 16 '63
Commonweal 77:493-4 F 1 '63
New Repub 148:31 F 2 '63
Sat R 46:19+ F 2 '63

MOVING picture plays—Criticisms, plots, etc.
—Single works—*Continued*
Dead ringer
Time il 83:101 F 7 '64
Dear heart
Vogue 145:99 F 1 '65
Deserto rosso
Esquire 62:68+ D '64
Devil and the Ten commandments
New Repub 149:27 O 19 '63
Newsweek 62:115 O 21 '63
Devil's trap
Newsweek 64:81 S 7 '64
Diamond head
Commonweal 77:599 Mr 1 '63
New Yorker 39:146-7 Mr 9 '63
Time il 81:93 F 22 '63
Diary of a madman
Newsweek 61:90 Ap 29 '63
Dimka
Commonweal 79:572 F 7 '64
Disorder
Commonweal 80:370 Je 12 '64
New Repub 150:32-3 Je 13 '64
Newsweek il 63:98+ Je 8 '64
Time 83:99 Je 5 '64
Disorderly orderly
Newsweek il 65:61 Ja 4 '65
Distant trumpet
Time 83:E5 My 1 '64
Dr Crippen
Commonweal 80:17 Mr 27 '64
Time il 83:94 F 21 '64
Doctor in distress
Time 84:87 Jl 24 '64
Dr Lao
Sat R 47:20 Mr 28 '64
Dr No
Commonweal 78:355 Je 21 '63
New Repub 148:36 Je 15 '63
New Yorker 39:65-6 Je 1 '63
Newsweek il 61:106 My 13 '63
Sat R 46:16 Je 1 '63
Time il 81:80 My 31 '63
Dr Strangelove, or How I learned to stop worrying and love the bomb
America 110:462+ Mr 28 '64
Commentary 37:75-7 My '64; Discussion. 38:8+ O '64
Commonweal 79:632 F 21 '64
Esquire 61:26+ F '64
Life 56:15 Mr 13 '64
Nat R 16:203-4 Mr 10 '64
Nation 198:127-8 F 3 '64
New Repub 150:28 Mr 21 '64
New Repub 150:26-8 F 1 '64
New Yorker 39:75-6 F 1 '64
Newsweek il 63:79 F 3 '64
Reporter 30:48+ F 27 '64; Reply. J. I. Shields. 30:6 Mr 26 '64
Sat R 47:24 Ja 25 '64
Sr Schol 84:10T F 21 '64
Time il 83:69 Ja 31 '64
Dog's life
New Repub 148:25 F 16 '63
La dolce vita
Sat R 46:22 Mr 9 '63; Discussion. 46:30 Mr 30 '63
Doll
Commonweal 79:572 F 7 '64
Nat R 16:368 My 5 '64
New Yorker 39:40+ Ja 25 '64
Newsweek 63:82 Ja 20 '64
Time 83:49 Ja 17 '64
Donovan's reef
New Yorker 39:50 Ag 3 '63
Time il 82:50 Ag 2 '63
Don't tempt the devil
Commonweal 80:258 My 22 '64
New Yorker 40:86+ My 2 '64
Doulos—the finger man
Time 83:84 Mr 6 '64
Vogue 143:42 Ap 1 '64
Dürrenmatt
Christian Cent 81:1340+ O 28 '64
Easy life
America 110:172 F 1 '64
New Yorker 39:73 Ja 4 '64
Newsweek il 63:74 Ja 13 '64
Time il 83:80 Ja 10 '64
Eclipse
Christian Cent 80:1137-8 S 18 '63
Esquire 59:20+ My '63
New Repub 148:27 My 11 '63
8½
America 109:61-2 Jl 13 '63
Cath World 197:395-6 S '63
Commonweal 78:425 Jl 12 '63
Mlle 57:62 S '63
Nation 197:59-60 Jl 27 '63
New Repub 149:28-9 Jl 13 '63
New Yorker 39:62 Je 29 '63
New Yorker 39:19-20 Jl 6 '63
Newsweek il 61:112+ Je 24 '63
Sat R 46:20 Je 29 '63
Sr Schol 83:6T S 27 '63
Time il 81:82 Je 28 '63
Electra
Esquire 59:34 F '63
Elusive corporal
Commonweal 77:620 Mr 8 '63
Esquire 59:22+ My '63
New Repub 148:26 Mr 9 '63
New Yorker 39:135 Mr 2 '63
Newsweek il 61:94+ F 25 '63
Time il 81:E5 Mr 8 '63
Emil and the detectives
Commonweal 81:454 D 25 '64
Sat R 48:31 Ja 2 '65
Sr Schol 85:26 D 9 '64
Empty canvas
New Repub 150:3 Je 13 '64
New Yorker 40:114+ My 30 '64
Newsweek 63:102 My 18 '64
Time il 83:128+ Ap 17 '64
Fall of the Roman empire
America 110:553 Ap 18 '64
Commonweal 80:91 Ap 10 '64
Life 56:18 Mr 27 '64
New Yorker 40:178 Ap 4 '64
Newsweek il 63:87 Ap 6 '64
Sat R 47:36 Ap 4 '64
Sr Schol 84:21 Ap 24 '64
Fail safe
America 111:464-5 O 17 '64
Cath World 200:195-6 D '64
Commonweal 81:72 O 9 '64
Life 57:12 O 30 '64
Nat R 16:1026-7 N 17 '64
New Repub 151:26-7 S 12 '64
New Yorker 40:200-1 O 10 '64
Newsweek 64:114+ O 12 '64
Sr Schol il 85:10T O 7 '64
Sr Schol il 85:52 O 7 '64
Vogue 144:100 O 15 '64
Family diary
New Yorker 39:235 N 23 '63
Newsweek 62:107 N 18 '63
Fate is the hunter
Commonweal 81:72 O 9 '64
Sr Schol 85:22 O 14 '64
Vogue 144:100 O 15 '64
Father Goose
America 111:788 D 12 '64
Commonweal 81:355 D 4 '64
New Repub 152:21 Ja 2 '65
Sat R 48:31 Ja 2 '65
Le feu follet
New Yorker 39:148-50 N 16 '63
Fiancés
Commonweal 79:544-5 Ja 31 '64
Esquire 61:14+ My '64
New Repub 150:34-6 F 15 '64
New Yorker 39:76-7 F 1 '64
Newsweek 63:80 F 3 '64
Sat R 47:35 My 9 '64
Time il 83:69 Ja 31 '64
Fiasco in Milan
Newsweek il 61:90 Ap 29 '63
Time il 81:89 Ap 26 '63
55 days at Peking
America 109:26 Jl 6 '63
Nat R 15:72 Jl 30 '63
New Yorker 39:68 Je 1 '63
Newsweek 61:83-4 Je 3 '63
Time il 81:80 My 31 '63
Fire within
Commonweal 79:751 Mr 20 '64
Nation 198:252 Mr 9 '64
New Repub 150:35 Mr 7 '64
New Yorker 40:112+ F 22 '64
Newsweek il 63:83-4 Mr 2 '64
Time il 83:84 Mr 6 '64
First men in the moon
America 111:757 D 5 '64
Five miles to midnight
America 108:590 Ap 20 '63
Commonweal 77:599 Mr 1 '63
Newsweek il 61:99 Mr 11 '63
Sat R 46:82 Mr 16 '63
Time 81:M29 Ap 12 '63
Flaming creatures
Nation 198:374-6 Ap 13 '64; Discussion. 198:inside cover Ap 27 '64
Flight from Ashiya
America 110:749-50 My 23 '64
Flipper's new adventure
Time 84:89 Ag 7 '64
For those who think young
Time il 84:87 Jl 24 '64
Forty-nine days
Time 83:94-5 F 14 '64
40 pounds of trouble
America 108:316 Mr 2 '63
Commonweal 77:541 F 15 '63
New Yorker 38:102 F 2 '63
Sat R 46:44 F 2 '63
Time il 81:66 F 8 '63

MOVING picture plays—Criticisms, plots, etc. —Single works—*Continued*

Four days of Naples
Commonweal 77:619-20 Mr 8 '63
Nation 196:187-8 Mr 2 '63
Nation 196:296 Ap 6 '63
New Repub 148:27 Mr 16 '63
New Yorker 39:169-70 Mr 23 '63
Newsweek 61:81 Ap 1 '63
Sat R 46:82 Mr 16 '63
Time 81:102+ Mr 15 '63

4 for Texas
Time 83:80 Ja 10 '64

French game
Newsweek 62:91 S 9 '63
Sat R 46:47 S 14 '63

Freud
Cath World 196:327-8 F '63

From Russia with love
America 110:580 Ap 25 '64
Life il 56:51-2 Ap 3 '64
New Repub 150:26 Ap 25 '64
New Yorker 40:20+ Ap 18 '64
Newsweek il 63:93-4 Ap 13 '64
Sat R 47:29 Ap 18 '64
Time il 83:103+ Ap 10 '64

Fun in Acapulco
Commonweal 79:349 D 13 '63

Gathering of eagles
America 109:124 Ag 3 '63
Newsweek il 62:86 Jl 22 '63
Sat R 46:16 Jl 6 '63
Time il 82:80 Jl 26 '63

Gidget goes to Rome
Time 82:74 Ag 16 '63

Girl hunters
Esquire 60:74-6+ Jl '63
Newsweek il 62:80 Jl 15 '63
Sat R 46:34 Jl 27 '63

Girl named Tamiko
Newsweek 61:81 Ap 1 '63
Time 81:E10 Mr 22 '63

Girl with green eyes
America 111:267 S 12 '64
Commonweal 80:610 S 4 '64
Life 57:15 Ag 28 '64
New Yorker 40:87-8 Ag 22 '64
Newsweek 64:79 Ag 24 '64
Sat R 47:24 Ag 8 '64
Time il 84:85 Ag 21 '64
Vogue 144:150 D '64

Given word
Commonweal 80:117 Ap 17 '64
Time il 83:126+ Ap 17 '64

Global affair
Commonweal 79:694 Mr 6 '64
Sat R 47:23 F 29 '64
Sr Schol 84:25 F 21 '64

Goldfinger
Commonweal 81:422 D 18 '64
Life il 57:116-19 N 6 '64
New Repub 151:27 D 19 '64
New Yorker 40:73 D 26 '64
Newsweek il 64:72-3 D 21 '64
Sat R 47:42 D 12 '64

Gone are the days
America 109:494-6 O 26 '63
New Repub 149:28+ S 28 '63
New Yorker 39:178 O 5 '63
Newsweek il 62:84+ S 30 '63
Sat R 46:44 S 28 '63

Good neighbor Sam
America 111:143 Ag 8 '64
New Yorker 40:74+ Ag 8 '64
Sat R 47:50 Je 27 '64

Good soldier Schweik
Commonweal 78:458 Jl 26 '63
New Repub 149:28 S 14 '63
Newsweek 62:79 S 2 '63

Goodbye Charlie
America 111:757 D 5 '64
Commonweal 81:421 D 18 '64
Newsweek 64:100 N 30 '64
Time il 84:109-10 N 27 '64
Vogue 144:150 D '64

Gospel according to St Matthew. See Il Vangelo secondo Matteo, below

Great dictator
New Repub 150:30+ Mr 28 '64

Great escape
America 109:178-9 Ag 17 '63
Commonweal 78:458 Jl 26 '63
New Yorker 39:64 Ag 24 '63
Newsweek 62:79 Jl 15 '63
Sat R 46:16 Jl 6 '63
Time 82:78 Jl 19 '63

Greatest story ever told
Look il 28:44-5 D 29 '64

Greenwich Village story
Nation 197:80 Ag 10 '63
New Yorker 39:96 Jl 27 '63
Time il 82:80+ Jl 26 '63

Guest
Commonweal 79:571 F 7 '64
New Repub 150:26+ Ja 25 '64
Newsweek 63:84 F 10 '64
Sat R 47:33 F 15 '64
Time 83:52 Ja 24 '64

Guns at Batasi
America 111:788 D 12 '64
New Yorker 40:202 N 28 '64
Sat R 47:28 N 28 '64
Time il 84:106 N 6 '64

Hallelujah the hills
Esquire 62:111 Jl '64
New Repub 150:25 Ja 18 '64
New Yorker 39:90 D 21 '63
Sat R 47:22 F 29 '64
Time il 82:98+ D 13 '63
Vogue 143:20 F 15 '64

Hamlet
Esquire 62:74+ D '64
Nation 199:175 S 28 '64

Hand in the trap
Commonweal 78:479 Ag 9 '63
New Repub 148:28 Je 29 '63
New Yorker 39:68 Jl 13 '63
Newsweek 61:90 Je 17 '63
Sat R 46:40 Je 8 '63
Time 81:100 Je 14 '63

Happiness of us alone
New Yorker 39:166 Ap 27 '63

Harakiri
Life 57:7 S 4 '64
New Yorker 39:161-2 S 28 '63
New Yorker 40:88 Ag 22 '64
Newsweek il 64:81 Ag 17 '64

Hard day's night
Commonweal 80:638 S 18 '64
Life 57:15 Ag 7 '64
New Repub 151:26+ O 10 '64
Newsweek il 64:79 Ag 24 '64
Reporter 31:42+ N 5 '64
Sat R 47:30 S 19 '64
Seventeen il 23:236-7+ Ag '64
Time il 84:67 Ag 14 '64
Vogue 144:76 S 15 '64

Haunted palace
Newsweek 62:86+ S 16 '63

Haunting
Commonweal 79:16 S 27 '63
Life il 55:35-6+ Ag 30 '63
New Yorker 39:108 S 28 '63
Newsweek 62:101 S 23 '63
Sat R 46:44 S 28 '63
Time il 82:122+ O 4 '63

Heavens above!
Cath World 197:335 Ag '63
Christian Cent 80:1380 N 6 '63
Commonweal 78:305 Je 7 '63
Esquire 60:44 O '63
Nation 196:515-16 Je 15 '63
New Repub 148:33+ Je 15 '63
New Yorker 39:153 My 25 '63
Newsweek il 61:103 My 27 '63
Time il 81:98 My 24 '63

High and low
New Repub 149:26-7+ N 23 '63
New Yorker 39:197 D 14 '63
Newsweek il 62:105B-106 N 25 '63

Honeymoon hotel
Commonweal 80:400 Je 19 '64

Hook
America 108:275 F 23 '63
Commonweal 77:599 Mr 1 '63
New Yorker 39:145-6 Mr 9 '63
Newsweek 61:85 Mr 4 '63
Sat R 46:26 F 16 '63
Time 81:M17 Mr 1 '63

House is not a home
America 111:268 S 12 '64
Commonweal 80:637 S 18 '64
New Yorker 40:106-8 S 5 '64
Newsweek il 64:82B S 7 '64
Sat R 47:27 S 12 '64
Time 84:101-2 S 4 '64

Householder
Commonweal 79:168 N 1 '63
New Yorker 39:206-7 O 26 '63
Newsweek 62:102 N 4 '63
Time 82:98 N 8 '63

How the West was won
America 108:448 Mr 30 '63
Commonweal 78:48 Ap 5 '63
Life il 54:87-9 Mr 29 '63
Nat R 15:72 Jl 30 '63
New Repub 148:29 Ap 20 '63
New Yorker 39:175-6 Ap 6 '63
Newsweek il 61:85 Mr 4 '63
Sat R 46:42 F 23 '63
Time 81:102+ Mr 22 '63

How to murder your wife
Life 58:13 Ja 29 '65
Time il 85:85 Ja 29 '65

Hud
America 108:871-2 Je 15 '63
Commonweal 78:328 Je 14 '63
Esquire 60:50+ S '63
New Repub 148:27-8 My 25 '63
New Yorker 39:166 Je 8 '63
Newsweek il 61:84 Je 3 '63
Sat R 46:40 My 25 '63
Time il 81:100 Je 7 '63

MOVING picture plays—Criticisms, plots, etc.
—Single works—*Continued*
Hush. . .hush, sweet Charlotte
Sat R 48:56 Ja 23 '65
I could go on singing
Commonweal 78:377 Je 28 '63
Newsweek 61:98 Ap 22 '63
Time 81:112+ Ap 19 '63
I'd rather be rich
New Yorker 40:96 S 12 '64
Idiot
Commonweal 78:198 My 10 '63
New Repub 148:27 My 11 '63
Newsweek 61:94-5 My 6 '63
In the cool of the day
Commonweal 78:377 Je 28 '63
New Repub 148:36 Je 15 '63
Sat R 46:45 Je 15 '63
Time il 81:99-100 Je 14 '63
In the French style
America 109:399 O 5 '63
Commonweal 79:46 O 4 '63
New Yorker 39:106+ S 28 '63
Newsweek 62:101-2 S 23 '63
Sat R 46:44 S 28 '63
Incredible journey
Commonweal 79:349 D 13 '63
Newsweek il 62:92 D 9 '63
Sat R 46:29 N 16 '63
Time 82:120 D 6 '63
Incredible Mr Limpet
Commonweal 80:91 Ap 10 '64
Life il 56:121-2 Mr 20 '64
Sr Schol 84:38 Ap 3 '64
Insect woman
Commonweal 80:514 Jl 24 '64
Irma la douce
America 109:124 Ag 3 '63
Commonweal 78:376 Je 28 '63
New Repub 149:29 Jl 13 '63
New Yorker 39:54 Je 15 '63
Newsweek il 61:90 Je 17 '63
Sat R 46:31 Je 22 '63
Time il 81:92 Je 21 '63
Island
UNESCO Courier il 16:8-13 Ap '63
Island of love
Sat R 46:16 Je 1 '63
Island of the blue dolphins
Life 56:14+ Je 19 '64
Time il 84:87 Jl 24 '64
It's a mad, mad, mad, mad world
Commonweal 79:284 N 29 '63
New Repub 149:26-7 N 16 '63
New Yorker 39:137-8 N 30 '63
Newsweek il 62:107 N 18 '63
Sat R 46:33 N 9 '63
Sr Schol 84:43 F 14 '64
Time il 82:97+ N 22 '63
Jason and the Argonauts
America 109:143 Ag 10 '63
New Yorker 39:65 Ag 24 '63
Newsweek 62:78B+ Jl 8 '63
Time il 82:78 Jl 19 '63
John Goldfarb, please come home!
America 112:26 Ja 2 '65
Commonweal 81:422 D 18 '64
New Repub 151:27-8 D 19 '64
Sat R 48:31 Ja 2 '65
Sports Illus il 21:50-4+ Jl 20 '64
Johnny Cool
Newsweek 62:115 O 14 '63
Le journal d'une femme de chambre
New Yorker 40:186 Ap 4 '64
Joy house
Vogue 144:110 O 1 '64
Judgment in the sun
Sat R 47:26 Ja 18 '64
Julie the redhead
Newsweek il 62:115 O 21 '63
Kapo
New Repub 150:32-3 Je 13 '64
Killers
Newsweek 64:72 Ag 3 '64
Time 83:115 Je 12 '64
King Kong vs. Godzilla
Sat R 46:34 Jl 27 '63
Kings of the sun
Sat R 47:27 Ja 18 '64
Kiss me, stupid
Commonweal 81:421-2 D 18 '64
New Repub 152:26 Ja 9 '65
Newsweek il 64:53-4 D 28 '64
Sat R 48:31 Ja 2 '65
Time il 85:69 Ja 1 '65
Kisses for my president
Commonweal 80:637 S 18 '64
Sat R 47:17 S 5 '64
Time 84:101 S 4 '64
Knife in the water
Commonweal 79:195 N 8 '63
Nation 197:373 N 30 '63
New Repub 149:30 N 2 '63
New Yorker 39:195 N 2 '63
Newsweek il 62:102 N 4 '63
Sat R 46:51 O 26 '63
L-shaped room
America 109:218-19 Ag 31 '63
Commonweal 78:304-5 Je 7 '63
Nat R 15:72 Jl 30 '63
New Repub 148:26+ Je 8 '63
New Yorker 39:66+ Je 1 '63
Newsweek il 61:83 Je 3 '63
Sat R 46:40 Je 8 '63
Ladies who do
Commonweal 79:349 D 13 '63
New Yorker 39:204 D 7 '63
Newsweek il 62:97 O 28 '63
Lady in a cage
America 110:853-4 Je 20 '64
Commonweal 80:423-4 Je 26 '64
Life 56:23 Je 5 '64
New Repub 150:25 Je 20 '64
Newsweek 63:84 Je 22 '64
Sat R 47:29 Je 20 '64
Time il 83:93+ Je 19 '64
Lady with the dog
Esquire 59:30+ F '63
Ladybug ladybug
Christian Cent 81:276 F 26 '64
Commonweal 79:463 Ja 17 '64
New Repub 150:24-5 Ja 18 '64
Newsweek 62:40 D 30 '63
Sat R 46:28 D 21 '63
Time 83:78 Ja 3 '64
Lafayette
Commonweal 78:198 My 10 '63
Newsweek 61:90 Ap 29 '63
Time 81:109 My 3 '63
Landru
Commonweal 78:170 My 3 '63
New Repub 148:28-30 Ap 27 '63
New Yorker 39:113-14 Ap 20 '63
Newsweek il 61:98 Ap 22 '63
Sat R 46:26 Ap 27 '63
Time il 81:M19 Ap 26 '63
Last clean shirt
Commonweal 81:134+ O 23 '64
Last days of Sodom and Gomorrah
America 108:316 Mr 2 '63
Lawrence of Arabia
Nat R 14:167-9 F 26 '63
Sat Eve Post il 236:22-6+ Mr 9 '63
Lazarillo
Commonweal 78:170 My 3 '63
New Yorker 39:156 Ap 13 '63
Time 81:109 My 3 '63
Leopard
America 109:369 S 28 '63
Commonweal 78:563 S 20 '63
Esquire 61:20+ My '64
New Repub 149:26+ S 14 '63
New Yorker 39:54+ Ag 17 '63
New Yorker 39:70+ Jl 13 '63
Newsweek il 62:76-7 Ag 26 '63
Reporter 29:48 S 12 '63
Sat R 46:35 Ag 24 '63
Time il 82:68 Ag 23 '63
Let's talk about women
Commonweal 81:168 O 30 '64
New Yorker 40:201-2 O 10 '64
Time il 84:115 O 16 '64
Life of Oharu
Commonweal 80:209 My 8 '64
Light from Ashiya
Newsweek 63:92 My 4 '64
Lilies of the field
America 109:439-40 O 12 '63
Commonweal 79:78 O 11 '63
Ebony il 18:55-8 O '63
Newsweek 62:117 O 14 '63
Sat R 46:32 S 7 '63
Lilith
America 111:423+ O 10 '64
Christian Cent 81:1499-500 D 2 '64
Commonweal 81:101 O 16 '64
Life 57:26 O 2 '64
New Repub 151:35-6 Ag 22 '64
New Yorker 40:202 O 10 '64
Newsweek 64:115 O 12 '64
Time il 84:130+ O 2 '64
Vogue 144:64 N 1 '64
Lion
America 108:382 Mr 16 '63
List of Adrian Messenger
America 109:123 Ag 3 '63
Commonweal 78:354 Je 21 '63
New Repub 148:33 Je 15 '63
New Yorker 39:166+ Je 8 '63
Newsweek 61:105 Je 10 '63
Time il 81:98+ Je 14 '63
Loneliness of the long distance runner
Esquire 59:28+ F '63
Long ships
Time il 83:115 Je 12 '64
Lord of the Flies
America 109:398 O 5 '63
Esquire 61:28+ F '64
New Repub 149:27 Ag 17 '63
New Yorker 39:56+ Ag 31 '63
Newsweek il 62:76 Ag 26 '63
Sat R 46:14 Ag 17 '63
Sr Schol 83:27 O 11 '63
Time il 82:68+ Ag 23 '63

MOVING picture plays—Criticisms, plots, etc.
—Single works—*Continued*
Love a la carte
New Repub 152:37 Ja 23 '65
Love and larceny
America 108:421 Mr 23 '63
New Repub 148:31 F 9 '63
New Yorker 38:82 F 9 '63
Newsweek 61:93 F 18 '63
Sat R 46:21 F 9 '63
Time il 81:95 F 15 '63
Love at twenty
America 108:421 Mr 23 '63
New Repub 148:26 Mr 9 '63
New Yorker 38:147 F 16 '63
Newsweek 61:94 F 18 '63
Sat R 46:25 Mr 9 '63
Time 81:97 Mr 8 '63
Love is a ball
Commonweal 77:665-6 Mr 22 '63
Time 81:M27+ Ap 12 '63
Love on a pillow
Newsweek 63:41 D 30 '63
Time il 83:78 Ja 3 '64
Love with the proper stranger
America 110:172 F 1 '64
Commonweal 79:405 D 27 '63
New Repub 150:24 F 8 '64
New Yorker 39:85 Ja 11 '64
Newsweek 63:42 Ja 6 '64
Sat R 47:31 Ja 4 '64
Time 82:57 D 27 '63
Vogue 143:64 F 1 '64
Luck of Ginger Coffey
Commonweal 81:18 S 25 '64
Nation 199:257-8 O 19 '64
New Repub 151:28 O 31 '64
New Yorker 40:193 S 26 '64
Newsweek 64:96D-97 S 28 '64
Sat R 47:27 O 3 '64
Time il 84:124+ O 2 '64
McLintock
America 109:750 D 7 '63
Newsweek il 62:108 N 18 '63
Time il 82:113+ N 15 '63
Madame
Commonweal 77:542 F 15 '63
New Repub 148:25-6 F 16 '63
Newsweek 61:89 F 11 '63
Time 81:102 Mr 15 '63
Mafioso
America 111:53-4 Jl 11 '64
Commonweal 80:450 Jl 3 '64
Nation 199:39 Jl 27 '64
New Yorker 40:74 Jl 11 '64
Time il 84:86 Jl 3 '64
Mail order bride
Time il 83:91 Je 26 '64
Man from the Diners' club
Commonweal 78:48 Ap 5 '63
Newsweek il 61:104 Ap 15 '63
Time 81:89 Ap 26 '63
Man in the middle
America 110:380 Mr 21 '64
Newsweek il 62:104 N 25 '63
Time il 83:105 F 28 '64
Maniac
Time 82:116 N 15 '63
Man's favorite sport
Commonweal 79:694 Mr 6 '64
Sat R 47:22 F 29 '64
Time il 83:106 F 28 '64
Marilyn
New Repub 149:29 Ag 3 '63
New Yorker 39:96 Jl 27 '63
Newsweek 61:105 Je 10 '63
Marnie
America 111:161 Ag 15 '64
Commonweal 80:545 Ag 7 '64
New Yorker 40:65 Ag 1 '64
Newsweek 64:72 Ag 3 '64
Sat R 47:17 S 5 '64
Time 84:63 Jl 31 '64
Vogue 144:38 Ag 15 '64
Marriage—Italian style
Commonweal 81:519 Ja 15 '65
Life 58:10 Ja 22 '65
Nation 200:68 Ja 18 '65
New Repub 152:25-6 Ja 9 '65
New Yorker 40:64 Ja 2 '65
Newsweek il 65:60 Ja 4 '65
Time 85:69 Ja 1 '65
Marriage of Figaro
America 108:692 My 11 '63
Commonweal 78:22 Mr 29 '63
Mary, Mary
America 109:611-12 N 9 '63
Commonweal 79:225 N 15 '63
New Repub 149:49 N 9 '63
Newsweek 62:102 N 4 '63
Sat R 46:46 S 21 '63
Time il 82:97+ N 8 '63
Mary Poppins
America 111:390 O 3 '64
Commonweal 81:239 N 13 '64
Dance Mag il 38:30-2 O '64
Life 57:28 S 25 '64
New Yorker 40:132+ O 3 '64
Newsweek il 64:112+ O 5 '64
Sat R 47:22 Ag 22 '64
Sr Schol 85:24 O 21 '64
Time il 84:114+ S 18 '64
Masque of the red death
Newsweek 63:87-8 Je 29 '64
Mind benders
Commonweal 78:283-4 My 31 '63
New Yorker 39:100-1 My 11 '63
Newsweek 61:100+ My 20 '63
Time il 81:98+ My 10 '63
Miracle of the white stallions
Time il 81:101+ Ap 12 '63
Mistress for the summer
New Yorker 40:168-9 Ap 11 '64
Model murder case
Time 84:113 D 11 '64
Moderato cantabile
Newsweek 63:82+ Ja 20 '64
Time 83:49 Ja 17 '64
Monkey in winter
Nation 196:216 Mr 9 '63
New Yorker 38:148 F 16 '63
Newsweek il 61:89 F 11 '63
Sat R 46:31 Mr 2 '63
Monsieur Verdoux
Newsweek il 64:78-9 Jl 27 '64
Moon-spinners
Time il 84:107 N 20 '64
Mother Carey's chickens
Time 82:50 Ag 2 '63
Mouse on the moon
Newsweek il 62:68 Jl 1 '63
Sat R 46:37 Jl 20 '63
Time 81:92 Je 21 '63
Move over, darling
America 109:809-10 D 21 '63
Commonweal 79:405 D 27 '63
Look il 27:138+ D 17 '63
New Yorker 39:86 Ja 11 '64
Sat R 47:31 Ja 4 '64
Time il 82:57 D 27 '63
Murder ahoy
Time 84:129+ O 2 '64
Murder at the gallop
Newsweek 62:78B Jl 8 '63
Time il 82:85 Jl 5 '63
Murder most foul
Newsweek 64:90A S 14 '64
Muriel
Commonweal 79:257 N 22 '63
New Repub 149:27 N 16 '63
New Yorker 39:160-1 S 28 '63
New Yorker 39:196 N 2 '63
Newsweek 62:102+ N 11 '63
Sat R 46:34 N 23 '63
Music room
Commonweal 78:564 S 20 '63
N Y Times Mag il p54 Ag 18 '63
New Repub 149:30 N 2 '63
New Yorker 39:148+ O 19 '63
Newsweek 62:102 S 23 '63
Sat R 46:46 O 19 '63
Time 82:105+ S 13 '63
My days with Jean-Marc. See Anatomy of a marriage, above
My fair lady
America 111:569-70 N 7 '64
Commonweal 81:238-9 N 13 '64
Dance Mag il 38:30-2 D '64
Ladies Home J il 81:56-65 Ja '64
Life 57:10 N 20 '64
Look il 28:60-2+ F 25 '64
Nat R 17:31-2 Ja 12 '65
New Repub 151:32 N 14 '64
New Yorker 40:134-5 O 31 '64
Newsweek il 64:96 N 2 '64
Sat R 47:40 N 14 '64
Sr Schol 85:36 D 2 '64
Seventeen il 23:194-5 S '64
Time il 84:106 O 30 '64
Vogue il 144:152-5+ N 1 '64
My hobo
New Yorker 39:50 Ag 3 '63
Newsweek 62:72 Ag 5 '63
Time il 82:50 Ag 2 '63
My life to live
Commonweal 79:105 O 18 '63
New Repub 149:28 O 12 '63
New Yorker 39:179 O 5 '63
Newsweek 62:84 S 30 '63
Sat R 46:31 Je 22 '63
Time 82:113+ O 11 '63
My name is Ivan
Commonweal 78:459 Jl 26 '63
Nat R 16:367 My 5 '64
Nation 197:60 Jl 27 '63
New Repub 149:27+ Ag 3 '63
New Yorker 39:42 Jl 6 '63
Newsweek 62:68 Jl 1 '63
Time il 82:85 Jl 5 '63
My nights with Françoise. See Anatomy of a marriage, above
My six loves
Commonweal 78:107 Ap 19 '63
Time 81:112 Ap 19 '63

MOVING picture plays—Criticisms, plots, etc.
Single works—*Continued*
Naked autumn
Commonweal 79:313 D 6 '63
New Yorker 39:232 N 16 '63
Never let go
Newsweek 62:68 Jl 1 '63
Never put it in writing
Commonweal 80:483 Jl 10 '64
Time 84:89 Ag 7 '64
New interns
Commonweal 80:638 S 18 '64
Time 84:70 Ag 28 '64
New kind of love
America 109:612 N 9 '63
Commonweal 79:226 N 15 '63
New Repub 149:49+ N 9 '63
Newsweek 62:115 O 21 '63
Sat R 46:46 S 21 '63
Night must fall
Commonweal 80:17 Mr 27 '64
New Repub 150:28 Ap 4 '64
New Yorker 40:144 Mr 28 '64
Newsweek 63:53 Mr 30 '64
Night of the iguana
America 111:161 Ag 15 '64
Commonweal 80:580 Ag 21 '64
Life 57:11 Jl 10 '64
New Yorker 40:84-5 Ag 15 '64
Newsweek il 64:85 Jl 13 '64
Reporter 31:49-50 O 8 '64
Sat R 47:22 Jl 18 '64
Time il 84:86+ Jl 17 '64
Vogue 144:106 S 1 '64
Night tide
Time il 82:119 D 6 '63
Night walker
Newsweek il 65:76 F 1 '65
Sat R 48:56 Ja 23 '65
Night watch
Commonweal 80:117 Ap 17 '64
Nation 198:516 My 18 '64
New Repub 150:25 Ap 25 '64
New Yorker 40:164-6 Je 6 '64
Newsweek 63:104A+ Ap 27 '64
Nine days of one year
Commonweal 81:573 Ja 29 '65
Time il 85:89 Ja 15 '65
Nine hours to Rama
America 108:504-5 Ap 13 '63
Commonweal 78:140-1 Ap 26 '63
New Repub 148:27 Mr 16 '63
New Yorker 39:157 Ap 13 '63
Newsweek 61:104-5 Ap 15 '63
Sat R 46:39 Ap 6 '63
Time 81:114 Ap 19 '63
None but the brave
Ebony il 19:110-12+ O '64
Nothing but a man
America 112:62 Ja 9 '65
Commonweal 81:544 Ja 22 '65
Nation 200:67-8 Ja 18 '65
New Repub 152:27 Ja 16 '65
New Yorker 40:104 Ja 9 '65
Newsweek il 65:79A Ja 11 '65
Sat R 48:40 Ja 30 '65
Time il 85:89 Ja 15 '65
Nothing but the best
America 111:267 S 12 '64
Commonweal 80:450 Jl 3 '64
New Repub 151:35+ Jl 25 '64
Sat R 47:22 Jl 11 '64
Time il 83:99 Je 5 '64
Nutty professor
New Yorker 39:61 Ag 10 '63
Sat R 46:16 Je 1 '63
Time 82:80 Jl 26 '63
Of human bondage
Commonweal 81:18 S 25 '64
Nat R 16:1156+ D 29 '64
Newsweek 64:96+ S 28 '64
Sat R 47:34 N 21 '64
Time 84:129 O 2 '64
Of love and desire
Commonweal 79:48 O 4 '63
Of wayward love
New Repub 150:26 Ap 25 '64
New Yorker 40:178-9 Ap 4 '64
Newsweek 63:52 Mr 30 '64
One man's way
America 110:554 Ap 18 '64
Time il 83:88 Mr 27 '64
One potato, two potato
America 111:329-31 S 19 '64
Christian Cent 81:1566 D 16 '64
Commonweal 80:609 S 4 '64
New Yorker 40:65 Ag 1 '64
Newsweek il 64:72 Ag 3 '64
Sat R 47:29 Je 6 '64
Time 83:69 My 15 '64
Time il 84:89 Ag 7 '64
Vogue 144:38 Ag 15 '64
Organizer
America 110:804-5 Je 6 '64
Commonweal 80:208-9 My 8 '64
Esquire 62:62 O '64
Life 56:12 My 15 '64
Nation 198:516 My 18 '64
New Repub 150:34 My 16 '64
New Yorker 40:191 My 9 '64
Newsweek il 63:98+ My 11 '64
Sat R 47:35 My 9 '64
Vogue 144:35 Jl '64
Outrage
America 111:533 O 31 '64
Commonweal 81:136 O 23 '64
Newsweek il 64:118+ O 26 '64
PT 109
America 109:83-4 Jl 20 '63
Commonweal 78:458 Jl 26 '63
New Yorker 39:68 Jl 13 '63
Newsweek 62:79 Jl 8 '63
Sat R 46:37 Jl 20 '63
Time il 81:82 Je 28 '63
Pair of briefs
New Yorker 39:123 F 15 '64
Palm Springs weekend
America 109:715 N 30 '63
Commonweal 79:225 N 15 '63
Papa's delicate condition
America 108:382 Mr 16 '63
New Yorker 39:143 Mr 16 '63
Time il 81:M27 Mr 15 '63
Parable
Time il 83:79 Ap 24 '64
Les parapluies de Cherbourg
New Yorker 40:141-2 Mr 7 '64
Paris when it sizzles
New Repub 150:26 Ap 25 '64
New Yorker 40:167-8 Ap 11 '64
Newsweek 63:112+ Ap 20 '64
Sat R 47:29 Ap 18 '64
Time 83:130 Ap 17 '64
Patsy
Newsweek 64:72 Ag 31 '64
Time 84:70 Ag 28 '64
Pickpocket
Commonweal 78:305 Je 7 '63
New Repub 148:28 Je 8 '63
New Yorker 39:154 My 25 '63
Newsweek 61:84 Je 3 '63
Pink panther
Commonweal 80:258 My 22 '64
Newsweek 63:52 Mr 30 '64
Sat R 47:23 F 29 '64
Time 83:130 Ap 17 '64
Playboy of the western world
America 108:692 My 11 '63
Commonweal 78:22 Mr 29 '63
New Repub 148:23+ Mr 30 '63
New Yorker 39:170 Mr 23 '63
Time 81:92 Mr 29 '63
Playtime
Commonweal 77:517 F 8 '63
Pleasure-seekers
America 112:63 Ja 9 '65
La poupée
New Yorker 39:147 S 7 '63
Newsweek il 62:86 S 16 '63
Sat R 46:47 S 14 '63
Prize
Newsweek 63:74 Ja 13 '64
Sat R 47:27 Ja 18 '64
Time il 83:52 Ja 24 '64
Psyche 59
Commonweal 80:258 My 22 '64
Time 83:94 My 8 '64
Pumpkin eater
America 111:723 N 28 '64
Commonweal 81:332 N 27 '64
Life 57:15 N 13 '64
New Repub 151:28-9 D 19 '64
New Yorker 40:148-9 N 14 '64
Newsweek il 64:102 N 16 '64
Sat R 47:34 N 21 '64
Time 84:125+ N 13 '64
Vogue 145:66 Ja 1 '65
Purlie Victorious
Reporter 31:40 Jl 16 '64
Quare fellow
New Repub 148:26 Mr 30 '63
New Yorker 39:132+ Mr 2 '63
Time il 81:97 Mr 8 '63
Queen Bee
Time il 81:54+ Je 14 '63
Rampage
Newsweek 62:97 O 28 '63
Time il 82:103+ O 25 '63
Rattle of a simple man
Commonweal 81:519 Ja 15 '65
Nation 200:68 Ja 18 '65
Time il 85:54 Ja 8 '65
Raven
Commonweal 77:542 F 15 '63
Newsweek 61:78-9 F 4 '63
Reach for glory
Commonweal 79:16 S 27 '63
Newsweek 62:86 S 16 '63
Time il 82:83 S 27 '63
Resurrection
Sat R 46:44 O 12 '63
Ride the wild surf
Commonweal 80:638 S 18 '64
Vogue 144:64 N 1 '64

MOVING picture plays—Criticisms, plots, etc.
—Single works—*Continued*
Ring of treason
Time 83:112+ Je 12 '64
Rio Conchos
Time il 84:106 N 20 '64
Rita
Commonweal 79:79 O 11 '63
Robin and the seven hoods
Commonweal 80:400 Je 19 '64
Ebony il 19:90-2+ Je '64
Life 57:11 Jl 24 '64
Newsweek 64:76 Jl 6 '64
Sat R 47:29 My 16 '64
Time il 84:88 Jl 17 '64
Robinson Crusoe on Mars
Commonweal 80:638 S 18 '64
Newsweek 64:81-2 S 7 '64
Time 84:101 S 4 '64
Roustabout
Time il 84:113 D 11 '64
Run with the devil
Newsweek 62:72 Jl 29 '63
Time 82:E4 Jl 26 '63
Running man
America 109:533 N 2 '63
Commonweal 79:104 O 18 '63
New Yorker 39:178 O 5 '63
Newsweek il 62:111 O 7 '63
Sanjuro
New Repub 148:28 My 25 '63
New Yorker 39:102 My 11 '63
Newsweek il 61:103 My 20 '63
Time il 81:98+ My 10 '63
Savage Sam
Commonweal 78:328 Je 14 '63
Scorpio rising
Sat R 47:42 Ap 11 '64
Séance on a wet afternoon
America 111:788 D 12 '64
Christian Cent 82:113-14 Ja 27 '65
Commonweal 81:331 N 27 '64
Life 57:16 D 18 '64
Nation 199:420 N 30 '64
New Repub 151:22 D 5 '64
New Yorker 40:149-50 N 14 '64
Newsweek 64:102+ N 16 '64
Vogue 145:25 Ja 15 '65
Season for love
Commonweal 78:305 Je 7 '63
New Yorker 39:170+ My 18 '63
Newsweek 61:106 My 13 '63
Sat R 46:40 My 11 '63
Secret invasion
Newsweek 64:96 S 28 '64
Time 84:131 O 2 '64
Seduced and abandoned
America 111:240 S 5 '64
Commonweal 80:514 Jl 24 '64
Life 57:14 Ag 14 '64
Nation 199:40 Jl 27 '64
Newsweek 64:79A-79B Jl 20 '64
Sat R 47:22-3 Jl 11 '64
Send me no flowers
America 111:757 D 5 '64
Newsweek 64:100 N 30 '64
Servant
America 110:685-6 My 16 '64
Commonweal 79:751 Mr 20 '64
Life 56:12 Ap 10 '64
Nation 198:354-5 Ap 6 '64
New Repub 150:27-8 Mr 21 '64
New Yorker 39:207 N 30 '63
New Yorker 40:172 Mr 21 '64
Newsweek il 63:95-6 Mr 23 '64
Sat R 47:17 Mr 14 '64
Time il 83:94a-94b Mr 20 '64
Seven capital sins
Sat R 46:21 F 9 '63
Seven days in May
America 110:323-4 Mr 7 '64
Commonweal 79:632 F 27 '64
Esquire 61:14-16+ Je '64
Look il 27:90-5 N 19 '63
Nation 198:251-2 Mr 9 '64
New Repub 150:35 Mr 7 '64
New Yorker 40:112 F 22 '64
Newsweek il 63:89 F 24 '64
Sat R 47:25 F 1 '64
Sr Schol 84:21 F 28 '64
Time il 83:94 F 21 '64
Vogue 143:20 F 15 '64
Seven faces of Dr Lao
Commonweal 80:91 Ap 10 '64
Sr Schol 84:22 Ap 17 '64
Time il 84:89 Ag 7 '64
7th dawn
New Yorker 40:79 Ag 29 '64
Time il 84:87 Jl 24 '64
Sex and the single girl
Life 58:13 Ja 8 '65
Time il 85:69 Ja 1 '65
Shock corridor
Commonweal 79:48 O 4 '63
Sat R 46:34 Ag 10 '63
Shot in the dark
Commonweal 80:638 S 18 '64
New Yorker 40:58 Jl 4 '64
Newsweek il 64:76 Jl 6 '64
Reporter 31:42 N 5 '64
Sat R 47:22 Jl 11 '64
Time 84:96 Jl 10 '64
Silence
America 110:494-5 Ap 4 '64
Christian Cent 81:888 Jl 8 '64
Christian Cent 81:1144-5 S 16 '64
Commonweal 79:664 F 28 '64
Esquire 62:17-18 Ag '64
Nat R 16:368-70 My 5 '64
Nation 198:175 F 17 '64
New Repub 150:24+ F 22 '64
New Yorker 39:106+ F 8 '64
Newsweek il 63:92 F 17 '64
Sat R 47:23 F 8 '64
Time il 83:94 F 14 '64
Time il 82:72 N 15 '63
Vogue 143:64 Mr 15 '64
Small world of Sammy Lee
Commonweal 79:104 O 18 '63
New Yorker 39:52+ Ag 17 '63
Newsweek il 62:78 Ag 19 '63
Sat R 46:16 Jl 13 '63
Time 82:74 Ag 16 '63
Sodom and Gomorrah
New Yorker 38:101 F 2 '63
Soft skin
Commonweal 81:198 N 6 '64
Life 57:15 O 23 '64
Nation 199:420 N 30 '64
New Repub 151:34 N 14 '64
New Yorker 40:149-50 O 24 '64
Newsweek il 64:118 O 26 '64
Sat R 47:34 N 21 '64
Time il 84:115+ O 16 '64
Soldier in the rain
Commonweal 79:313 D 6 '63
Newsweek il 62:102 D 2 '63
Son of Captain Blood
Time il 84:70 Ag 28 '64
Son of Flubber
America 108:316 Mr 2 '63
Commonweal 77:541 F 15 '63
Time il 81:M21 F 15 '63
Sound of music
Look il 29:38-42+ Ja 26 '65
Sound of trumpets
Commonweal 78:480 Ag 9 '63
Nation 197:373 N 30 '63
New Repub 149:27 Ag 17 '63
New Yorker 39:205-6 O 26 '63
Newsweek 62:111 O 7 '63
Sat R 46:14 Ag 17 '63
Time 82:109 N 1 '63
Sparrows can't sing
Nat R 15:72 Jl 30 '63
Nation 196:430 My 18 '63
New Repub 148:30 My 18 '63
New Yorker 39:169-70 My 18 '63
Newsweek 61:105 My 13 '63
Sat R 46:40 My 11 '63
Spencer's Mountain
America 108:784-6 My 25 '63
Commonweal 78:328 Je 14 '63
Newsweek 61:104 My 27 '63
Time 81:98 My 24 '63
Station six-Sahara
Commonweal 80:637 S 18 '64
Time il 84:85 Ag 21 '64
Steppe
Commonweal 79:168 N 1 '63
Stolen hours
America 109:533 N 2 '63
Newsweek 62:97 O 28 '63
Sat R 46:29 N 16 '63
Stop train 349
Commonweal 80:298 My 29 '64
Strait-jacket
Time il 83:101 F 7 '64
Stranger knocks
New Repub 148:26 F 16 '63
Sat R 46:82 Mr 16 '63
Time il 81:M23 F 15 '63
Stray dog
New Yorker 40:169-70 Mr 7 '64
Newsweek 63:84 Mr 9 '64
Time 83:101 Mr 13 '64
Stripper
Commonweal 78:377 Je 28 '63
Sat R 46:16 Jl 13 '63
Time il 81:109 My 3 '63
Study two
Dance Mag il 38:35 Ag '64
Suitor
New Repub 149:29 O 12 '63
New Yorker 39:112 S 21 '63
Newsweek il 62:102 S 23 '63
Sat R 46:47 S 14 '63
Time il 82:106-7 S 13 '63
Summer magic
America 109:143 Ag 10 '63

MOVING picture plays—Criticisms, plots, etc.
—Single works—*Continued*
Sunday in New York
Christian Cent 81:462-3 Ap 8 '64
Commonweal 79:694 Mr 6 '64
New Repub 150:24 F 8 '64
Newsweek 63:89 F 24 '64
Sat R 47:33 F 15 '64
Time 83:94 F 14 '64
Sundays and Cybèle
Cath World 197:207-8 Je '63
Sweet and sour
Newsweek 65:90 Ja 25 '65
Sword in the stone
New Repub 149:30 D 21 '63
Sword of Lancelot
Newsweek 62:97 O 28 '63
Take her, she's mine
America 109:715-16 N 30 '63
Commonweal 79:225 N 15 '63
Tammy and the doctor
Time 82:95 Jl 12 '63
Los Tarantos
Dance Mag il 38:32-4 Ag '64
Sat R 47:23 Jl 11 '64
Tarzan's three challenges
Newsweek 62:86+ Jl 22 '63
Term of trial
America 108:238 F 16 '63
Commonweal 77:517 F 8 '63
New Repub 148:30-1 F 9 '63
New Yorker 38:82-3 F 9 '63
Time 81:M19+ F 15 '63
Terrace
Commonweal 81:390 D 11 '64
New Yorker 40:158 D 5 '64
Newsweek il 64:91A-91B D 14 '64
Thank heaven for small favors
New Yorker 40:104+ Ja 23 '65
That man from Rio
Commonweal 80:369 Je 12 '64
Esquire 62:80-1 S '64
New Repub 151:31-2 S 19 '64
New Yorker 40:123 Je 20 '64
Newsweek 63:84A Je 22 '64
Reporter 31:44 N 5 '64
Sat R 47:22 Jl 11 '64
Sr Schol 85:36 S 16 '64
Time il 83:99 Je 5 '64
Thérèse
New Yorker 39:231-2 N 16 '63
Newsweek il 62:103A+ N 25 '63
Time 82:98+ N 22 '63
They all died laughing
Commonweal 80:17 Mr 27 '64
Newsweek 63:87 Ap 6 '64
Thin red line
Life 56:12 My 29 '64
New Repub 150:33 Je 13 '64
Time il 83:85 My 29 '64
Vogue 144:35 Jl '64
Third lover
Commonweal 78:305 Je 7 '63
Newsweek il 61:100 My 20 '63
Sat R 46:37 My 18 '63
Third secret
Commonweal 80:258 My 22 '64
Life 56:16 My 1 '64
Newsweek 63:92 My 4 '64
Third street
New Yorker 40:86 My 2 '64
36 hours
Commonweal 81:572 Ja 29 '65
Life 58:13 Ja 29 '65
Sr Schol 85:22 Ja 21 '65
Thirty years of fun
Commonweal 78:48 Ap 5 '63
New Repub 148:26 F 16 '63
This madding crowd
Commonweal 80:483 Jl 10 '64
This sporting life
America 109:219 Ag 31 '63
Commonweal 78:480 Ag 9 '63
N Y Times Mag il p 126-7 Ap 14 '63
Nation 197:80 Ag 10 '63
New Repub 149:25-6 Jl 20 '63
New Yorker 39:72 Jl 20 '63
Sat R 46:16 Jl 13 '63
Time 82:78 Jl 19 '63
Those magnificent men in their flying machines or, How I flew from London to Paris in 26 hours and 11 minutes
Look il 29:44-9 Ja 12 '64
Thrill of it all
America 109:142 Ag 10 '63
Newsweek il 62:79 Ag 12 '63
Time il 82:73 Ag 9 '63
Through a glass darkly
Christian Cent 81:1144-5 S 16 '64
Ticklish affair
Time il 82:84 S 6 '63
Tiger walks
America 110:554 Ap 18 '64
Commonweal 80:92 Ap 10 '64
Time 84:E3 S 18 '64
Time out for love
Commonweal 78:199 My 10 '63
New Yorker 39:102+ My 4 '63
Newsweek 61:95 My 6 '63
To bed . . . or not to bed
Commonweal 79:572 F 7 '64
New Yorker 39:73 Ja 4 '64
Sat R 47:31 Ja 4 '64
Time 83:49 Ja 17 '64
To kill a mockingbird
America 108:273+ F 23 '63
Commonweal 77:572 F 22 '63
Look il 27:84+ F 26 '63
New Repub 148:30-1 F 2 '63
New Yorker 39:125-6 F 23 '63
Newsweek il 61:93 F 18 '63
Time il 81:93 F 22 '63
To love
Commonweal 81:390 D 11 '64
New Repub 152:21 Ja 2 '65
New Yorker 40:204 N 28 '64
Time il 84:111+ D 4 '64
Tom Jones
America 109:532 N 2 '63
Cath World il 199:71-2 Ap '64
Commonweal 79:141+ O 25 '63
Esquire 61:32+ F '64
Life il 55:120-3 O 11 '63
Nat R 16:165 F 25 '64
Nation 197:374 N 30 '63
New Repub 149:27-8 O 19 '63
N Y Times Mag il p 104-5 S 29 '63
New Yorker 39:98+ S 7 '63
New Yorker 39:169-70 O 12 '63
Newsweek il 62:116-17 O 14 '63
Reporter 29:54 N 21 '63
Sat R il 46:52 O 5 '63
Time il 82:117+ O 18 '63
Tomorrow is my turn
Newsweek 62:78 Ag 19 '63
Topkapi
America 111:391 O 3 '64
Commonweal 81:168 O 30 '64
Life il 57:55-6+ O 9 '64
New Yorker 40:194 S 26 '64
Newsweek 64:107A S 21 '64
Sat R 47:27 S 12 '64
Time 84:111 S 18 '64
Toys in the attic
New Repub 149:28 Ag 17 '63
New Yorker 39:60 Ag 10 '63
Newsweek 62:79 Ag 12 '63
Sat R 46:37 Jl 20 '63
Time il 82:73 Ag 9 '63
Trial
America 108:420-1 Mr 23 '63
Christian Cent 81:49-50 Ja 8 '64
Commonweal 77:642 Mr 15 '63
Nation 196:215-16 Mr 9 '63
New Repub 148:34-5 Mr 2 '63
New Repub 148:28 Mr 16 '63
New Yorker 39:132 Mr 2 '63
Newsweek il 61:94 F 25 '63
Sat R 46:25 Mr 9 '63
Time il 81:79-M15+ Mr 1 '63
Troublemaker
Commonweal 80:483 Jl 10 '64
New Repub 151:28-9 Jl 4 '64
Newsweek 64:76 Jl 6 '64
Sat R 47:20 Mr 28 '64
Twice told tales
Newsweek 62:102 N 4 '63
Twilight of honor
Newsweek 62:105B N 25 '63
Two are guilty
Commonweal 79:752 Mr 20 '64
Time 83:84 Mr 6 '64
Two daughters
Commonweal 78:198 My 10 '63
Nation 196:430 My 18 '63
New Repub 148:29 My 18 '63
New Yorker 39:101 My 11 '63
Newsweek il 61:94 My 6 '63
Sat R 46:40 My 11 '63
Two on a guillotine
Commonweal 81:573 Ja 29 '65
Newsweek 65:90 Ja 25 '65
Ugly American
America 108:621-3 Ap 27 '63
Commonweal 78:140 Ap 26 '63
New Repub 148:29 Ap 20 '63
New Yorker 39:112-13 Ap 20 '63
Newsweek il 61:98-9 Ap 22 '63
Sat R 46:43 Ap 20 '63
Time il 81:111+ Ap 19 '63
Umbrellas of Cherbourg
America 112:85-6 Ja 16 '65
Commonweal 81:454 D 25 '64
Life 57:20 D 11 '64
New Repub 152:21 Ja 2 '65
New Yorker 40:151 D 19 '64
Sat R 48:40 Ja 30 '65
Time 84:89+ D 18 '64
Vogue 144:184-5+ N 1 '64

MOVING picture plays—Criticisms, plots, etc.
—Single works—*Continued*
Under the yum-yum tree
Commonweal 79:225 N 15 '63
Newsweek 62:104+ N 25 '63
Sat R 46:29 N 16 '63
Time il 82:97 N 8 '63
Unholy desire
New Yorker 40:149-50 N 21 '64
Unsinkable Molly Brown
America 111:267 S 12 '64
Commonweal 80:483 Jl 10 '64
Dance Mag il 38:30-1 Ag '64
Newsweek 63:87 Je 29 '64
Sat R 47:19 Jl 25 '64
Sr Schol 84:32 My 15 '64
Seventeen il 23:80-1+ Jl '64
Time 84:96-7 Jl 10 '64
Il Vangelo secondo Matteo
Christian Cent 81:1599-600 D 23 '64
Esquire 62:76-8+ D '64
V.I.P.s
America 109:369 S 28 '63
Commonweal 79:44+ O 4 '63
New Repub 149:30 S 28 '63
New Yorker 39:104+ S 28 '63
Newsweek 62:84 S 30 '63
Sat R 46:46 S 21 '63
Time il 82:122 O 4 '63
Victors
America 110:267 F 22 '64
Commonweal 79:462 Ja 17 '64
Esquire 61:18+ Mr '64; Discussion. 61:16 Ap '64
Nat R 15:536-8 D 17 '63
New Repub 150:22-3 Ja 4 '64
New Yorker 39:52 D 28 '63
Newsweek il 62:40 D 30 '63
Sat R 46:24 D 14 '63
Time il 82:63 D 20 '63
Vogue 143:24 Ja 1 '64
Visit
America 111:533 O 31 '64
Commonweal 81:43 O 2 '64
Life 57:19 O 9 '64
Look il 28:52-9 Je 16 '64
New Yorker 40:135-6 O 31 '64
Newsweek il 64:109A+ O 19 '64
Sat R 47:34 N 21 '64
Vogue 144:76 S 15 '64
Viva Las Vegas
Time il 83:86 My 29 '64
Voice of the hurricane
New Yorker 40:90 Je 13 '64
Wall of noise
Newsweek 62:87 S 16 '63
Walleyed Nippon
New Yorker 39:118 S 14 '63
War of the buttons
Commonweal 79:463 Ja 17 '64
New Yorker 39:89 D 21 '63
Sat R 46:28 D 21 '63
Weekend
Newsweek 63:104 Ap 27 '64
Time il 83:95 My 1 '64
What a way to go!
Commonweal 80:177-8 My 1 '64
Life 56:14 My 8 '64
New Repub 150:26 My 30 '64
New Yorker 40:191 My 16 '64
Newsweek il 63:100 My 18 '64
Time 83:104+ My 22 '64
Wheeler dealers
Commonweal 79:285 N 29 '63
New Repub 149:29 N 23 '63
Newsweek 62:102 D 2 '63
Time il 82:103 N 29 '63
Where love has gone
America 111:570 N 7 '64
Commonweal 81:198 N 6 '64
Newsweek il 64:103-103A N 16 '64
Who's been sleeping in my bed?
America 109:810 D 21 '63
Commonweal 79:406 D 27 '63
Time il 83:E3 Ja 10 '64
Who's minding the store?
America 110:55 Ja 11 '64
Commonweal 79:349 D 13 '63
Wild and wonderful
Time il 83:92 Je 26 '64
Winter light
America 108:722-3 My 18 '63
Cath World 197:335-6 Ag '63
Christian Cent 80:1436-7 N 20 '63
Christian Cent 81:1144-5 S 16 '64
Commonweal 78:225-6 My 17 '63
Nation 196:515 Je 15 '63
New Repub 148:26-7 My 11 '63
New Yorker 39:173 My 18 '63
Newsweek 61:103-4 My 27 '63
Sat R 46:37 My 18 '63
Time 81:98 My 24 '63
Wives and lovers
New Yorker 39:148 S 7 '63
Newsweek 62:91 S 9 '63
Time 82:84 S 6 '63
Woman in the dunes
Nation 199:176 S 28 '64
New Repub 151:32-4 N 14 '64
New Yorker 40:202-3 N 7 '64
Newsweek 64:117A N 23 '64
Sat R 47:30 O 31 '64
Time il 84:106+ O 30 '64
Vogue 145:25 Ja 15 '65
Woman is a woman
New Repub 151:24-5 D 5 '64
Newsweek 64:100 N 30 '64
Time il 84:105 N 6 '64
Woman of straw
Commonweal 81:168 O 30 '64
Sat R 47:27 S 12 '64
World of Henry Orient
America 110:554 Ap 18 '64
Commonweal 80:43 Ap 3 '64
New Repub 150:26+ Ap 18 '64
New Yorker 40:144+ Mr 28 '64
Newsweek il 63:52-3 Mr 30 '64
Sat R 47:36 Ap 4 '64
Sr Schol il 84:34-5 Ap 10 '64
Time il 83:69 My 15 '64
Wrong arm of the law
New Repub 148:27 Mr 16 '63
New Yorker 39:176-7 Ap 6 '63
Newsweek 61:103 Mr 18 '63
Time il 81:101 Mr 22 '63
X
Newsweek 62:115 O 21 '63
Yanco
Commonweal 80:483 Jl 10 '64
Life 57:21 Jl 17 '64
New Yorker 40:56 Jl 25 '64
Sat R 47:23 Jl 11 '64
Yellow canary
Commonweal 78:355 Je 21 '63
Newsweek il 61:104 My 27 '63
Yesterday, today and tomorrow
America 110:748-9 My 23 '64
Life il 56:49-50+ Ap 10 '64
New Repub 150:27-8 Mr 14 '64
New Yorker 40:173-4 Mr 21 '64
Newsweek il 63:52 Mr 30 '64
Sat R 47:24 Mr 21 '64
Time il 83:101+ Mr 13 '64
Young and the brave
Sat R 46:34 Jl 27 '63
Young and willing
Commonweal 80:17 Mr 27 '64
Young lovers
Commonweal 81:199 N 6 '64
Young racers
Commonweal 78:356 Je 21 '63
Youngblood Hawke
America 111:724 N 28 '64
Life 57:21 D 4 '64
New Yorker 40:158-9 D 5 '64
Sat R 47:28 N 28 '64
Time il 84:105+ N 20 '64
Vogue 144:110 O 1 '64
Zorba the Greek
America 112:176 Ja 30 '65
Commonweal 81:519-20 Ja 15 '65
Life 58:8 Ja 15 '65
New Repub 152:26 Ja 16 '65
New Yorker 40:151 D 19 '64
Newsweek 65:60 Ja 4 '65
Sat R 48:35 Ja 16 '65
Time il 84:65 D 25 '64
Zulu
America 111:94-5 Jl 25 '64
Life 57:20 Jl 3 '64
New Repub 150:26 Je 20 '64
New Yorker 40:93 Jl 18 '64
Newsweek 64:85 Jl 13 '64
Time il 84:96 Jl 10 '64

MOVING picture production and direction
Act one in action; filmed in New York. il N Y Times Mag p62+ My 19 '63
Action at Hell's Gate. il Newsweek 63:110B Mr 16 '64
AH: making of My fair lady. A. Seidenbaum. il McCalls 92:96-8+ O '64
Anti-formula film; symposium. il Sat R 46:13-24 D 28 '63
Auteur theory. A. Knight. Sat R 46:22 My 4 '63
Beckett; production of his first screenplay for Evergreen theatre. New Yorker 40:22-3 Ag 8 '64
Best angel God ever saw; L. B. Mayer. W. Saroyan. il Sat Eve Post 236:94-5 N 16 '63
Bible as living technicolor. il Time 85:70 Ja 15 '65
Big-bang bagatelle. il Newsweek 60:112 Ap 20 '64
Bond wagon. il Newsweek 63:96+ My 11 '64
Brain in Spain; S. Bronston. il Time 82:57 Jl 12 '63
Carroll cavorts in Kenya; filming of Mister Moses. il Life 57:76-8 Jl 17 '64

MOVING picture production and direction—*Continued*
Cleopatra barges in at last. J. L. Mankiewicz. il Life 54:72-81 Ap 19 '63
Cleopatra: history or bunk? H. L. Hurwitz. il Sr Schol 83:22T-23T+ O 4 '63
Cleopatra papers; excerpts. J. Brodsky; N. Weiss. il Esquire 60:33-7+ Ag '63
Cleopatra; trials and tribulations of an epic film. W. Wanger and J. Hyams. il Sat Eve Post 236:28-38+ Je 1 '63
Days and nights of the iguana; a journal. D. Kerr. Esquire 61:128-30+ My '64
Declarations of independents. A. Knight. Sat R 47:33-4 My 23 '64
Directors. R. Coughlan. il Life 55:156-8+ D 20 '63
Disturber of the peace: interview, ed. by G. Bachmann. F. Fellini. il Mlle 60:152-3+ N '64
Dizzy doings on a set; making of movie, 8½. il Life 55:95-7 Jl 19 '63
La dolce far niente. il Time 81:46 Mr 1 '63
Double Fanny; film of Fanny Hill. il Newsweek 63:83 Je 1 '64
Drama the cameras missed; on location for Night of the iguana; ed. by M. Davidson. T. Victor. il Sat Eve Post 237:24-8+ Jl 11 '64
Elizabeth Taylor talks about Cleopatra; ed. by J. Hamilton. E. Taylor. il Look 27:41-7+ My 7 '63
'Enry 'Iggins in 'Ollywood; movie of My fair lady. S. Peck. il N Y Times Mag p20-1 S 1 '63
Father calls me a rebel; filming of Greatest story ever told, ed. by E. Miller. il Seventeen 23:108-9+ D '64
Films; future of the independent American film. M. Walsh. America 109:494-6 O 26 '63
Films; Mr Levine and Mr Lawrence. D. Macdonald. Esquire 59:36+ Ap '63
Focus on Al Maysles. C. Reynolds. il Pop Phot 54:128-31 My '64
Fortunes of Cleopatra. il Newsweek 61:63-6 Mr 25 '63
Four new ways to make a movie. A. Bermel. il Harper 229:76-81 O '64
Four on location. il Time 81:78+ My 17 '63
GBS in filmland. V. Delacorte. il Esquire 62:150-1+ D '64
Greatest story ever told; filming in Utah desert. W. Trombley. il Sat Eve Post 236:34-40+ O 19 '63
Greatest story ever told; with photographs by E. Elisofon. Life 56:54-67 Mr 27 '64
Hidden face of the cinema (cont) P. Léglise. il UNESCO Courier 16:26-31 F; 28-32 Ap; 21-3+ My '63
How to make movies; Inside the movie kingdom, 1964. Time 83:56-7 Mr 20 '64
In an epic new movie, one Dame beats another. D. Jenkins. il Sports Illus 21:50-4+ Jl 20 '64
Ingmar Bergman, the listener. O. Hedlund. il Sat R 47:47-9+ F 29 '64
John Cardinal Huston. il Life 55:61-2+ N 22 '63
John Huston, actor. il Newsweek 61:102 Mr 18 '63
Julie Andrews's star rises higher with The sound of music. J. Poppy. il Look 29:38-42+ Ja 26 '65
Lord Jim. P. Hamill. il Sat Eve Post 237:24-9 N 21 '64
Lord Jim in a jungle paradise; ed. by E. Miller. P. O'Toole; D. Lavi. il Seventeen 23:132-3+ N '64
Lord Jim; the perils of Peter O'Toole in filming a classic. il Life 58:85-6 Ja 22 '65
Lord of the flies. R. Gutwillig. il Vogue 141:154-7+ My '63
Making cartoons out of people. S. P. Gerber. il Sci Digest 53:27-34 F '63
Man JFK picked to play his wartime role: PT-109; Cliff Robertson. il Look 27:48-50 Je 18 '63
Most controversial director: M. Antonioni. M. S. Davis. il N Y Times Mag p34-5+ N 15 '64
My chancy life as a moviemaker. I. Shaw. il Vogue 142:162-3+ S 1 '63
My fair lady; excerpts from Beaton's diary. C. Beaton. il Ladies Home J 81:56-65 Ja '64
New faces in a smash new move; World of Henry Orient; ed. by E. Miller. T. Walker; M. Spaeth. il Seventeen 23:132-3+ Je '64
New producer; Cool world at Venice film festival. New Yorker 39:33-5 S 14 '63
New role for Sinatra-san. il Life 57:80+ Jl 3 '64
Of horses and Greeks and directors. D. MacDonald. Esquire 59:28+ F '63
On becoming a pro. L. Williams. Pop Phot 52:117+ Ap '63
Otto Preminger looks at the Catholic church. M. Walsh. Cath World 198:365-71 Mr '64
Phenomenon of Les parapluies de Cherbourg. V. Cowles. il Vogue 144:184-5+ N 1 '64
Problems in paradise; Huston's troubles making The Bible. Newsweek 64:90+ S 14 '64
Saying something; Frank Perry directs Ladybug, ladybug. il Newsweek 62:72 Ag 5 '63
Screens and screams. R. L. Shayon. Sat R 46:44 Ap 20 '63
Seven days in May: the movie the military shunned. F. Knebel. il Look 27:90-5 N 19 '63
Sight and sound; on location of Viva Las Vegas. il McCalls 91:12+ N '63
Small-budget triumph: David and Lisa. W. Trombley. il Sat Eve Post 236:56, 59-60 Mr 16 '63
So far my film has cost me $20,000 and I'm not finished. T. Swan. il Pop Phot 55:190-2+ D '64
Son of Strangelove; production of The loved one. il Newsweek 64:72-3 Ag 31 '64
Stars fell on Mismaloya; beginning of the film production of The night of the iguana. R. Oulahan. il Life 55:69-74+ D 20 '63
Tarzan in Thailand; with report by M. Orshefsky. il Life 54:99-100+ Je 14 '63
There's action in stills. H. Fondiller. il Pop Phot 53:90-3 Ag '63
They know the wild in wildlife; making films for Walt Disney. I. Petite. il Audubon Mag 66:20-5 Ja '64
Trade winds; smuggling Gregory Peck into town for a documentary. J. G. Fuller. il Sat R 47:11-12 Jl 11 '64
Under the locusts; Lilith on location. New Yorker 39:23 Ag 17 '63
Vanitas vanitatum; The Cleopatra papers. H. Alpert. Sat R 46:34 Ag 3 '63
What are the Beatles really like? first movie, Hard day's night; symposium, ed. by E. Miller. il Seventeen 23:236-7+ Ag '64
When the 20th century got off the ground; production of Those magnificent men in their flying machines or, How I flew from London to Paris in 26 hours and 11 minutes. J. Hamilton. il Look 29:44-9 Ja 12 '65
Why they let George do it; making of My fair lady. A. Seidenbaum. McCalls 92:189-90 O '64
Young wild pack in Lord of Flies; with report by R. Wallace. il Life 55:96-9+ O 25 '63
Zinnemann pictures a modern dilemma; Behold a pale horse. W. Johnson. Sr Schol 85:28 S 30 '64
See also
Moving picture directors

Anecdotes, facetiae, satire, etc.

Through a dark, glassily. J. P. Degnan. Atlan 212:102+ S '63

MOVING picture projection
8mm projectors compared! M. A. Matzkin and M. P. Hayes. il Mod Phot 28:76-9 Ap '64
Four closeups of movie projection. J. R. Gregory. il U S Camera 26:78-9+ My '63
How to buy the right movie projector. L. Drukker. il Pop Phot 54:142-4+ Ja '64
Movie maker. M. A. Matzkin. Mod Phot 27:90+ Ag '63
This family room is a theater at home. il Sunset 131:92 S '63
See also
Projection apparatus

MOVING picture screens
How bright your screen! R. Miller. il U S Camera 26:58+ My '63
HPI telescreen. L. Lachter. il U S Camera 26:93 F '63
Screens; handy but hidden. L. Drukker. il Pop Phot 52:118-20 Ap '63
Shoot for showing. C. Reynolds. il Pop Phot 52:118+ Je '63

MOVING picture scripts. See Moving picture authorship

MOVING picture serials. See Moving pictures—Serial films

MOVING picture societies
Irish film society. J. P. Driscoll. America 108:660 My 11 '63
Private; Film-makers' cinematheque. New Yorker 40:27-8 Ja 16 '65

MOVING picture sound recording
Fairchild 8 sound system goes pro; 8mm sound-on-film camera 900. J. D. Scouller. il Pop Phot 55:92+ Ag '64
How to prepare a sound track. E. Nanas. il Pop Phot 53:76+ S '63
Instant voice; song dubbing. Time 83:81-2 F 7 '64

MOVING picture sound recording—*Continued*
Shopping guide to tape recorders for the home, for the field. H. Burstein; H. V. Fondiller. il Pop Phot 53:50-6+ S '63
Through a screen, darkly. H. Alpert. Sat R 46:35 Ag 24 '63
See also
Moving pictures, Amateur—Sound recording

MOVING picture studios
Nostalgia lifts the bids; Hal Roach studios. il Bsns W p30-1 Ag 10 '63

MOVING picture theaters
British cities try municipal movie houses. C. E. Tiffen. Am City 79:154 Ap '64
Movie screens get back some silver; shopping center theaters. il Bsns W p41-2+ Ag 31 '63
Saddle shell roof for theater; movie house north of Chicago. il Arch Rec 135:155-8 Mr '64
What time does the coffee go on? R. Schoenstein. Sat R 46:17 D 28 '63
See also
New York (city)—Radio City music hall

MOVING picture theaters, Open air
Drive-in lie-in. il Newsweek 62:78 Jl 8 '63

MOVING picture theaters, Underwater
Dive-in premiere makes movie history; premiere of Incredible Mr Limpet, at Weeki Wachee Springs, Fla. R. Melhado. il Sr Schol 84:25+ F 21 '64

MOVING pictures
Are movies going to pieces? P. Kael. Atlan 214:61-6 D '64
Cinema: the global revolution. H. Alpert; A. Mayer. il Sat R 46:18-21+ O 5 '63
Do the movies have a future? H. Alpert; A. Knight; J. G. Fuller. il Sat R 47:166-72 Ag 29 '64
Electronovision; John Gielgud's production of Hamlet on film. America 111:28+ Jl 11 '64
Everybody wants to say it in films. il Life 55:38-45 D 20 '63
Feely is here; Sensorama simulator. L. H. Lapham. il Sat Eve Post 237:28-9 Ap 18 '64
Film thoughts from abroad. S. Kauffmann. New Repub 151:22-5 O 24 '64
Films at the fair. A. Knight. Sat R 47:26 Ag 15 '64
Films '64-'65. C. Reynolds. Pop Phot 55:193 D '64; 56:168 Ja '65
Hidden face of the cinema (cont) P. Léglise. il UNESCO Courier 16:26-31 F; 28-32 Ap; 21-3+ My '63
How many titles of these Cary Grant movies can you name? il Ladies Home J 80:46 Mr '63
Movies: avant-garde films. G. Wagner. Nat R 16:502-3 Je 16 '64
Movies (non-escape) il N Y Times Mag p86+ N 17 '63
Movies; twenty-five questions, twenty-four answers. L. Lipton. Pop Phot 55:188-9 D '64
Now available in 8mm sound: cartoons, comedies, westerns, sports. J. Wesson. il U S Camera 26:56-7 Jl '63
Religion on film; new status of cinema. il Time 82:78-82 S 20 '63
Screen education: useful books. J. McLaughlin. America 111:341 S 26 '64
See also
Academy awards (moving pictures)
Moving picture theaters
Shakespeare, W.—Moving pictures
Television broadcasting—Moving pictures

Anecdotes, facetiae, satire, etc.

Friday night and Saturday night. T. Meehan. New Yorker 39:48-9 O 19 '63
Last night. N. Mailer. Esquire 60:151+ D '63
More film fun. R. Angell. New Yorker 40:42-3 S 26 '64

Animal films

Cross-eyed lion; Clarence in Hollywood. il Life 57:71-2 S 25 '64
They know the wild in wildlife; making films for Walt Disney. I. Petite. il Audubon Mag 66:20-5 Ja '64

Animated cartoons

Animated movies made by computer. Sci N L 85:287 My 2 '64
Build a movie step-by-step. J. Burroughs. il Pop Phot 52:88+ Ja '63
Colorful classroom project: animated films. R. E. Wright. il Sch Arts 64:10-13 O '64
Complete works of Ernest Pintoff. D. Macdonald. Esquire 61:16+ Ap '64
East meets West in cartoon venture; Japanese animated cartoons for Video crafts, New York. il Bsns W p 104-5 My 11 '63
Etchcraft on celluloid. A. MacDermot. il UNESCO Courier 17:20-3 Ja '64
Film-makers; D. Wise, nine-year-old cartoonist. New Yorker 39:25-7 F 15 '64
Inside story of in-betweens. S. Andrews. il Pop Phot 55:172+ N '64
Learn animation from the pros. A. J. Zuckerman. il Pop Phot 55:170-1+ N '64
Magic worlds of Walt Disney; with editorial comment by M. B. Grosvenor. R. De Roos. il Nat Geog Mag 124:157D, 158-207 Ag '63
Making cartoons out of people. S. P. Gerber. il Sci Digest 53:27-34 F '63
Movie maker; key to making a successful animated movie. M. A. Matzkin. Mod Phot 28:70-1+ D '64
They made an animated film; high school art class creates a full color-and-sound cartoon. J. Lorr. il Design 65:78-9 N '63
You can't pet a chicken. S. Peterson. il Atlan 211:126-9 Mr '63
See also
Disney, Walt, productions

Criticisms, plots, etc.

Allo! hallo!
UNESCO Courier il 16:24-5 N '63
Hey there, it's Yogi Bear
Time il 83:109 Je 12 '64
Incredible Mr Limpet
Life il 56:121-2 Mr 20 '64
Of stars and men
Time il 83:109+ Je 12 '64

Art films

Art films (cont) Am Artist 27:10-11 F; 12 Mr; 8 Ap '63
By the sea. R. Abel and P. O'Neill. il Sch Arts 63:24-7 N '63
Films. Sch Art 63:52 S '63; 64:33 Ja '65
Handwriting on the screen. R. Gessner. Sat R 47:36 O 10 '64

Ballet

See Moving pictures—Dancing

Bibliography

Book notes. D. Macdonald. Esquire 59:50+ Mr '63

Censorship

See Moving picture censorship

Comedy

Hollywood laughs it up. S. Peck. il N Y Times Mag p 16-17 F 23 '64
Slapstick renaissance. W. Stuart. Reporter 31:40+ N 5 '64

Dance films

Letter from Paris; Russian movie of Tchaikovsky's La Belle au bois dormant, danced by the Leningrad Kirov troupe. Genêt. New Yorker 40:98+ My 2 '64
Pavlova rediscovered! thirty-year-old movie. E. Palatsky. il Dance Mag 38:34-6 D '64

Dancing

Laurey makes up her mind; film version of Oklahoma. A. De Mille. Dance Mag 37:34-5 Mr '63

Detective and mystery films

Go on, frighten us to death, we love it! D. J. Hamblin. Life 55:40 Ag 30 '63

Documentary films

Decline of documentary. A. Knight. Sat R 46:35 Mr 30 '63
Films and filmstrips. V. Falconer. Sr Schol 85:30T S 23; 6T O 21; 8T-9T O 28; 14T N 18 '64; 19T Ja 21 '65
Films. Recreation 57:93 F '64
Flaherty seminar: fresh air for film-makers. H. V. Fondiller. il Pop Phot 54:112-13 F '64
Flip side: cinéma verité. A. Knight. Sat R 46:20 D 28 '63
Focus on Al Maysles. C. Reynolds. il Pop Phot 54:128-31 My '64
God's spies; program of the new documentary at Gallery of modern art, New York. G. Conover. Nation 199:283-5 O 26 '64
Heyday of the documentary. J. G. Fuller. Sat R 47:172 Ag 29 '64
Hidden face of the cinema; an audience of 12,000,000,000. P. Léglise. il UNESCO Courier 16:26-31 F '63
Magic worlds of Walt Disney; with editorial comment by M. B. Grosvenor. R. De Roos. il Nat Geog Mag 124:157D, 158-207 Ag '63
Outdoing Olympia? Japan's K. Ichikawa to make documentary of Olympic games. il Newsweek 64:106 S 21 '64
Preview: films and filmstrips 1964-65. V. M. Falconer. il Sr Schol 84:9T My 15 '64
Sponsored films for schools. L. L. L. Golden. Sat R 47:80+ Ja 11 '64

MOVING pictures—Documentary films—*Cont.*
Subjects unlimited! possibilities for advanced-amateur movie makers. L. W. Bennett. il U S Camera 27:74-5+ My '64
Sunday on the river. G. Hitchens. il Pop Phot 54:134-5+ My '64
U.S.I.A. offers new jobs for apprentice film-makers. C. Reynolds. Pop Phot 51:111+ D '62
War films: World wars I and II. V. Falconer. Sr Schol 85:20T N 11 '64
Young King David; D. Wolper. il Newsweek 64:111-12 N 23 '64

Criticisms, plots, etc.

Black Fox
Commonweal 78:248 My 24 '63
Newsweek 61:95 My 6 '63
Time 81:117+ My 17 '63
Blood on the balcony
New Yorker 40:74 Jl 11 '64
Fifth freedom
Library J 88:1632-3 Ap 15 '63
Finest hours
America 111:758 D 5 '64
Commonweal 81:291 N 20 '64
New Yorker 40:149 N 21 '64
Sr Schol il 85:4T N 4 '64
Sr Schol 85:26 N 4 '64
Time 84:109 N 27 '64
Four days in November
Newsweek il 64:109-109A O 19 '64
Grand Olympics
Commonweal 80:148 Ap 24 '64
Sr Schol 84:30 My 1 '64
Time 83:119 My 15 '64
Guns of August
New Repub 152:27 Ja 16 '65
New Yorker 40:74 Ja 16 '65
Newsweek 65:60 Ja 4 '65
Time 85:54 Ja 8 '65
Vogue 145:99 F 1 '65
Hot rod story
Hot Rod il 17:18 S '64
Key to the future
Library J il 89:1206 Mr 15 '64
Lively art of picture books
Library J il 89:4110-11 O 15 '64
Mediterranean holiday
Time 85:89 Ja 15 '65
M-G-M's big parade of comedy
Life 57:19+ S 18 '64
New Yorker 40:126+ S 19 '64
Newsweek il 64:89+ S 14 '64
Mondo cane
Commonweal 78:74 Ap 12 '63
Nation 196:334-5 Ap 20 '63
New Yorker 39:158 Ap 13 '63
Newsweek 61:102+ Mr 18 '63
Sat R 46:31 Mr 2 '63
Time 81:M21 Mr 29 '63
Most
Newsweek 62:79 S 2 '63
Only one New York
New Yorker 40:185:6 O 17 '64
Time il 84:118 O 16 '64
Point of order!
America 110:174 F 1 '64
Commonweal 79:601-3 F 14 '64
Nat R 16:325-6 Ap 21 '64
New Repub 150:29-30 Ja 25 '64
New Yorker 39:72 Ja 18 '64
Newsweek 63:83 Ja 20 '64
Sat R 47:24 Ja 25 '64
Sr Schol 84:37 Mr 20 '64
Time il 83:49 Ja 17 '64
Slave trade in the world today
New Yorker 40:198+ D 12 '64
Time il 84:114 D 11 '64
To be alive!
New Yorker 40:49-52 O 10 '64
Tribute to Dylan Thomas
Commonweal 78:248 My 24 '63
Newsweek 61:107 My 13 '63
Women of the world
New Repub 149:27 Ag 3 '63
New Yorker 39:64-5 Ag 24 '63
Newsweek 62:80 Jl 15 '63
Sat R 46:34 Ag 10 '63
Time 82:95 Jl 12 '63
World without sun
Commonweal 81:453 D 25 '64
New Repub 152:37 Ja 23 '65
New Yorker 40:64 Ja 2 '65
Sr Schol 85:14T Ja 7 '65
Sr Schol 85:25 Ja 7 '65
Time il 84:65 D 25 '64

Editing

A & B roll editing. A. Siodmak. il U S Camera 26:80-1+ Ap '63
Cut your way to movie impact! M. A. Matzkin. il Mod Phot 28:98-9 Je '64
For better movies, cut! M. A. Matzkin. il Mod Phot 29:96-7+ Ja '65
Movies to learn from: see these, edit better. H. V. Fondiller. il Pop Phot 55:84-5+ S '64
Sticky business of splicing. L. Drukker. il Pop Phot 56:164-5+ Ja '65
Think edit as you country-hop L. Barry. il Pop Phot 52:24+ Ja '63

Foreign language films

So deeply obscure, so widely discussed. H. Alpert. il N Y Times Mag p68-9+ Ap 21 '63

Historical films

Hollywood's fabulous history of the world. il Life 55:146-55 D 20 '63

History

Bad guys, by W. K. Everson. Review
Newsweek il 64:90+ D 14 '64
Chase. J. Kerman. il Opera N 28:8-12 D 28 '63
Movies: have they come of age? W. Johnson. il Sr Schol 83:11-15 O 25 '63

Horror films

Are movies going to pieces? P. Kael. Atlan 214:61-6 D '64
Monster-san; Japanese monster movies. il Newsweek 64:110+ O 19 '64
Vulgarization of American demonology. B. Brower. il Esquire 61:94-9+ Je '64
Werewolves and other dogs. il Time 83:113+ My 15 '64

Industrial applications

See Moving pictures in industry

International aspects

Hidden face of the cinema. P. Léglise. il UNESCO Courier 16:21-3+ My '63
U.S.-U.S.S.R. film committee confers on exchanges. Dept State Bul 50:877 Je 1 '64
Universal magic of the movies. il Life 55:14-27 D 20 '63

Medical films

See Moving pictures in medicine

Moral aspects

Are movies fit for our families? M. Davidson. il Good H 157:94-7+ Jl '63
Dial-a-movie: taped ratings. America 110:502 Ap 11 '64
Hidden face of the cinema. P. Léglise. il UNESCO Courier 16:28-32 Ap '63
Hollywood's teen-age gold mine. H. Ehrlich. il Look 28:60-4+ N 3 '64
Report from underground; rash of "underground movies". S. Alexander. Life 58:23 Ja 29 '65
Right conscience about films. M. Walsh. America 110:657-8, 684-6 My 9-16 '64
Wilder's dirty-joke film stirs a furor. T. Thompson. il Life 58:51-2+ Ja 15 '65
See also
Moving picture censorship
National legion of decency

Music

Guide to background music; comp. by D. Sable. il Pop Phot 53:102+ S '63
To touch a moment. il Time 83:70 Ja 17 '64
See also
Phonograph records—Moving picture music

Musical films

Celluloid imports; Die fledermaus. H. Green. Opera N 28:35 Mr 14 '64
Divas in movieland. P. V. Beckley. il Opera N 29:8-13 D 19 '64
Hollywood musical. L. Jacobs, jr. il U S Camera 26:70-1 Jl '63
Laterna magika. Commonweal 80:609 S 4 '64
Laterna magika. G. Conover. Nation 199:79-80 Ag 24 '64

Opera films

See Moving pictures—Musical films

Periodicals

Farthest-out moviegoers. A. Sarris. il Sat R 47:14-15 D 26 '64

Political films

Campaign pictures. V. H. Falconer. Sr Schol 85:12T S 30 '64
Morality issue; Republican film called Choice. il Newsweek 64:25-6 N 2 '64
That sinful movie; Republican film on moral decay. Reporter 31:15 N 5 '64

MOVING pictures—*Continued*

Propaganda films

Sell with celluloid; propaganda film. D. Streibig. Pop Phot 55:94 Ag '64

Shame and glory in the movies. A. Berson and J. Keller. il Nat R 16:17-21 Ja 14 '64

Very educational; Bonn government propaganda film. Nation 196:319 Ap 20 '63

Psychological aspects

L'avventura: a closer look. S. O. Lesser. Yale R 54:41-50 O '64

Effects of observing violence. L. Berkowitz. il Sci Am 210:35-41 bibliog(p 152) F '64; Reply with rejoinder. P. Goodman. 210:8 Je '64

Home movies of early childhood: correlative developmental data in the psychoanalysis of adults. H. M. Serota. bibliog Science 143: 1195 Mr 13 '64

Picture of violence; effect of filmed violence. il Newsweek 63:91 F 24 '64

Redbook dialogue. A. Hitchcock; F. Wertham. il Redbook 120:70-1+ Ap '63

Quotations, maxims, etc.

On film; comp. by D. S. Davis. il N Y Times Mag p60+ S 13 '64

Religious films

Another passion play. America 111:28 Jl 11 '64

Greatest story ever told; with photographs by E. Elisofon. Life 56:54-67 Mr 27 '64

Jesus as a clown: film called Parable. Newsweek 63:96 Ap 27 '64

Renting

This film for hire. il Holiday 36:145-8 D '64

Science fiction

How to do it! monster movies. R. L. Cramer. il U S Camera 27:68-9+ S '64

Serial films

Continued next week. W. K. Everson. il N Y Times Mag p 16-17 Mr 29 '64

Short subject films

Penalty short. S. Beach. Harper 226:26+ Mr '63

Silent films

Letter from Stan Delaplane. S. Delaplane. il Todays Health 42:85 My '64

Sound effects

Steichen and his sound; interview, ed. by T. Schwartz. E Steichen. il Pop Phot 55:18 S '64

Sound recording

See Moving picture sound recording

Statistics

Facts and figures of the Americas: average attendance, production of full-length films. il Américas 16:47 O '64

Study and teaching

Flaherty seminar: fresh air for film-makers. H. V. Fondiller. il Pop Phot 54:112-13 F '64

Moving art. M. Eisler. il Sch Arts 64:34-6 D '64

Themes

Film ideas and where they come from. D. Streibig. il Pop Phot 53:184-5+ N '63

Hollywood's teen-age gold mine. H. Ehrlich. il Look 28:60-4+ N 3 '64

Ideas & scripts. D. Streibig. Pop Phot 53: 203-4 D '63; 54:141 My; 121 Je; 55:115 Jl '64

Love in another country (where they order it better) H. Koningsberger. Horizon 5:110-12 My '63

See also
Moving pictures, Amateur—Themes

Titles

Rock 'em, sock 'em! West German film industry renames American films. Newsweek 61:90 Je 17 '63

What a way to start; with report by D. Zeitlin. il Life 56:99-101+ F 7 '64

Travel films

Movie preview can help you plan for your vacation. Pop Phot 54:144 Ap '64

16mm movies for travel planners. Sunset 133: 8 N '64

Travel-film career girls. il Pop Phot 54:127+ My '64

War films

Phony war films. J. Jones. Sat Eve Post 236:64-7 Mr 30 '63

Take aim, fire at the agonies of war; with report by T. Prideaux. il Life 55:115-18+ D 20 '63

Westerns

Destry rides again, and again, and again. J. D. Weaver. il Holiday 34:77-80+ Ag '63

Sixty-year saga of the horse opera. W. K. Everson. il N Y Times Mag p74-5 Ap 14 '63

Western hero. D. Moser. il Life 55:104-9 D 20 '63

China (People's Republic)

By Mao: librettos and scenarios. S. Topping. il N Y Times Mag p40-1 O 25 '64

Far East

Prodigious output of the East. B. Blake. il Life 55:166-79+ D 20 '63

France

Truffaut. New Yorker 40:45-6 O 31 '64

Italy

Ermanno Olmi: the new Italian films. G. Bachmann. Nation 198:540-3 My 25 '64

Fellini's La dolce italia. J. J. Navone. Commonweal 77:639-41 Mr 15 '63

Letter from Italy. B. Renton. Nation 196: 187-8 Mr 2 '63

Anecdotes, facetiae, satire, etc.

L'lapse. D. Barthelme New Yorker 39:29-31 Mr 2 '63

Japan

Dialogue between Orient and Occident on the film The island; excerpts from Encounters and celebrations. G. Fradier and T. Takeda. il UNESCO Courier 16:8-13 Ap '63

Family of Ozu. R. Hatch. Nation 198:638-9 Je 22 '64

Yank movie man of Japan. il Ebony 18:45-6+ Jl '63

Russia

Critic speaks; question of military theme in Soviet films. il Newsweek 63:39-40 F 24 '64

Passé parable; Moscow film hit The chairman. Newsweek 65:30-1 F 1 '65

Thaw in Soviet movies? Living and the dead and Stillness. T. Shabad. il N Y Times Mag p26-7 Mr 22 '64

United States

Anticipations of the light. K. Kelman. Nation 198:490-4 My 11 '64

In the year of our Ford; grants to encourage the art of film. il Time 83:96+ Ap 3 '64

Movies that carry the freight; Motion picture service of the United States information agency. H. Alpert. il Sat R 47:69-70+ D 12 '64

New American cinema? A. Knight. Sat R 46: 41 N 2 '63

When movies joined the jet set; choice of nontheatrical and short-subject motion pictures for international festivals. J. Tebbel. il Sat R 47:78-9 N 14 '64

See also
Moving picture industry—United States

MOVING pictures, Amateur

Airborne antics. H. McDougall. il U S Camera 26:76-7 Je '63

Film for the classroom. S. A. Selby. il Pop Phot 51:114+ D '62

Film-maker: D. Wise, nine-year-old cartoonist. New Yorker 39:25-7 F 15 '64

Four keys to creative movie lighting. D. Mohler. il U S Camera 26:78-9+ F '63

Group filming. V. J. Plesko. il U S Camera 27:80-1 O '64

Home movies without hokum. L. Drukker. il Pop Phot 53:93+ Jl '63

Instant movies. R. Miller. il U S Camera 26:80 Jl '63

Latch on to the running gag. R. L. Cramer. il U S Camera 27:78-9+ Ag '64

Let chance write the script. A. R. Dodd, jr. Pop Phot 53:95+ Ag '63

Mix children with science. L. Drukker. il Pop Phot 52:86-7 Ja '63

Movie maker. M. A. Matzkin. Mod Phot 28:88+ F '64

Movie maker; summer movies. M. A. Matzkin. Mod Phot 27:96+ Je '63

Movies. See issues of Popular photography

Saying it on film, teen movie-making. il Seventeen 23:162-3+ Ap '64

MOVING pictures, Amateur—*Continued*
Shoot where you are! S. Moritz. il U S Camera 27:80-1 Je '64
Single-lamp home movie lights. il Consumer Rep 29:78-81 F '64
Small stars spoof the boss. il Life 55:133-4 O 4 '63
Small war in Westport; amateur moviemakers are waging World war I. J. Skow. il Sat Eve Post 237:18-19 N 28 '64
Squeeze time in your home movies. M. A. Matzkin. il Mod Phot 28:90-1+ S '64
Story & color on film. Sister Mary Laurus. il Sch Arts 63:17-18 N '63
Wild and wooly western. il U S Camera 26: 68-9 Ag '63
See also
Moving picture photography

Editing

Action editor: how to buy one. L. Drukker. il Pop Phot 54:108-9+ F '64
Ciné-cues. V. J. Plesko. il U S Camera 28: 72-3 Ja '65
Cut, long, short. S. Dabbs. il U S Camera 27:78-9+ Ap '64
Cut your way to movie impact? M. A. Matzkin. il Mod Phot 28:98-9 Je '64
Edit as you shoot. V. J. Plesko. il U S Camera 26:74-5 S '63
Movie maker. M. A. Matzkin. Mod Phot 27: 58+ D '63
Originals are not for cutting. E. Wildi. Pop Phot 54:118-21 Mr '64
Paris, et cetera, in your backyard! A. R. Dodd, jr. il Pop Phot 53:100-2 O '63
Six ways to edit while you shoot. M. A. Matzkin. il Mod Phot 28:82-3+ Ap '64
Transitions with imagination. S. Paley. il Pop Phot 53:186+ N '63

Music

Sound; selecting music creatively. J. Wesson. U S Camera 26:16-17 S '63
See also Moving pictures, Amateur—Sound recording

Sound effects

On cue! procedure for standardizing film and tape shows. J. Wesson. il U S Camera 26:76-7 N '63
Sound. J. Wesson. See issues of U.S. camera
Sound; highlights of the New York high fidelity show. J. Wesson. U S Camera 26:38-9 Ja '64
Sound; mixer in amateur filming. J. Wesson. U S Camera 26:26-7 N '63
Sound; music, voice and sound effects. J. Wesson. U S Camera 26:18-19 Jl '63
Synchronization. J. R. Gregory. il U S Camera 26:72-3 O '63
Why's and how's of raw and pre-recorded tape. B. Francois. il U S Camera 26:78-9 Mr '63

Sound recording

Adding sound to slides & movies; questions and answers. J. A. Keel. il U S Camera 26: 70-1+ O '63
Converting your movie projector; duplication of silent and sound films. J. R. Oswald. il U S Camera 26:88-9+ O '63
Creating a sound film. F. Lewin. il U S Camera 26:76-7+ Mr; 30-1 Ap; 24-5+ My '63
Lip-synchronized sound with your present equipment. W. Shaw. il Pop Phot 54:150-1 Ja '64
Sound for your screen; synchronizing sight and sound. M. A.Matzkin. il Hi Fi 14:51-3+ Ag '64
Sound track your home movies. A. Zuckerman. il Pop Mech 120:196-8 O '63
Stereo for sound mixing. M. A. Matzkin. il Mod Phot 28:81 Ap '64
Twelve tips for better sound in home movies. M. A. Matzkin. il Mod Phot 27:100-1 O '63
Writing the sound for your show. E. Nanas. Pop Phot 53:57+ S '63

Themes

Ideas & scripts. D. Streibig. Pop Phot 53: 203-4 D '63; 54:141 My; 121 Je; 55:115 Jl; 94 Ag; 92 S; 109 O '64
Subjects unlimited! possibilities for advanced-amateur movie maker. L. W. Bennett. il U S Camera 27:74-5+ My '64

Titles

Life for your titles. M. A. Matzkin. il Mod Phot 27:82-3 Ap '63
Movie maker; titler. M. A. Matzkin. Mod Phot 27:108+ O '63

MOVING pictures, Children. See Moving pictures for children

MOVING pictures, Silent. See Moving pictures —Silent films

MOVING pictures and children
You can't pet a chicken. S. Peterson. il Atlan 211:126-9 Mr '63
See also
Moving pictures—Moral aspects
Moving pictures for children

MOVING pictures and libraries. See Libraries and moving pictures

MOVING pictures and morals. See Moving pictures—Moral aspects

MOVING pictures and reading
Movies, TV, and paperbacks. J. M. Culkin. Sr Schol 83:28T-29T Ja 17 '64

MOVING pictures for children
Children's hour. P. T. Hartung. Commonweal 78:539 S 6 '63
Family movie guide; ed. by A. D. Kenney. See issues of Parents' magazine & better homemaking
How to bring children and books together; Weston Woods studio, near Weston, Conn. P. Upchurch. il Sr Schol 84:17T Mr 6 '64
Movies are better than ever; with list of childrens film foundation feature films. J. L. Limbacher. il Library J 89:2152-5+ My 15 '64
Of, by, for kids; summary of statements. A. W. Hodgkinson. Sr Schol 83:4T-5T Ja 17 '64
On creating films for children. R. B. Radnitz. Horn Bk 40:415-17 Ag '64

MOVING pictures for the deaf. See Deaf, Moving pictures for the

MOVING pictures in education
Drawing on film. G. Manupelli. il Sch Arts 63:10-11 F '64
Film for the classroom. S. A. Selby. il Pop Phot 51:114+ D '62
See also
Libraries and moving pictures
Moving pictures—Documentary films
Moving pictures—Study and teaching

MOVING pictures in industry
More return from your film dollar. G. W. Gibson. Harvard Bsns R 41:162-3+ Jl '63

MOVING pictures in medicine
Color movies find hidden cancers. G. J. Jaffe. il Sat Eve Post 236:72+ Je 29 '63

MOVING pictures in public relations
Make a film that helps your community. E. Corley. il Pop Phot 52:122-3+ Ap '63

MOVING pictures on airplanes. See Airlines —Passenger service

MOWAT, Farley
Cruise to the sea. il Yachting 113:57-9+ Je: 114:54-6+ Jl '63

MOWBRAY, Anne
After 500 years, new murder clue. il Life 58:36B Ja 29 '65

MOWER, Jan
World of the Bay. Yachting 115:53-6 Je '64

MOWING machines
Tree-dodging mower. B. Hardy. il Farm J 88:68 Mr '64

MOWRER, Edgar Ansel
Brinkmanship is necessary. Nat R 14:229-31 Mr 26 '63
Fifth Europe. Horizon 5:4-9 Mr '63
Will to survive? Nat R 16:321-3 Ap 21 '64

MOWRER, O. Hobart
Promised land, from afar. Christian Cent 80:430-1 Ap 3 '63
Science, religion and student values. Christian Cent 80:1200-2 O 2 '63

MOXLEY, Max
Kansas editor vs. the planners. por U S News 54:41 Ap 1 '63

MOYA, Maria
Introducing yoga; interview, ed. by J. Anderson. pors Dance Mag 38:40-1+ O '64

MOYER, J. D. and Ochs, R. J.
Microstructure of polymers by tritium autoradiography. bibliog Science 142:1316-18 D 6 '63

MOYERS, William Don
Johnson's young helper. M. Kempton. New Repub 149:9-11 D 21 '63
New man to see at White House. il por U S News 57:57-56 O 26 '64
People of the week. por U S News 54:20 Mr 4 '63
Replacement. por Time 84:23-4 O 23 '64

MOYES, Patricia
Falling star; story. Mlle 59:65-89 Jl '64

MOYLES, Lois
Thomas in the fields; poem. New Yorker 40: 196 D 5 '64

MOYNIHAN, Daniel Patrick
Blight. Reporter 28:50-2 Ap 25 '63
Draft rejectees: nipping trouble in the bud. Reporter 30:22-4 F 13 '64
Ethnicity and power. Commentary 38:87-9 O '64

MOYNIKAN, Daniel Patrick—*Continued*
Irish of New York. Commentary 36:93-107 Ag '63
Plague of our own. Reporter 31:32+ D 31 '64

MOZAMBIQUE
Across the river. il Newsweek 64:34+ D 14 '64
Mozambique: land of the good people. V. Wentzel. il Nat Geog Mag 126:196-231 Ag '64
Portugal's last stand in Mozambique. P. Schmid. il Reporter 30:37-40 My 21 '64
Portuguese way in Africa. H. Kay. il Fortune 69:112-15+ Ja '64
Public enemy no. three. il Time 84:23 Ag 14 '64
See also
Hunting—Mozambique

MOZART, Johann Chrysostom Wolfgang Amadeus
Aspects of Jupiter. J. Diether. il Am Rec G 30:936-7 Je '64
Choice & an echo. il Time 84:74 Ag 7 '64
Complete wind music of Mozart. H. Glass. il Am Rec G 30:566-7+ Mr '64
Così comes again, with wonderful things. N. Broder. il Hi Fi 13:55-6 My '63
Così fan tutte. P. L. Miller. Am Rec G 29:694 My '63
Don Giovanni. Criticism
New Yorker 39:174-5 N 2 '63
Opera N 28:23-4 D 28 '63
Opera N il 28:17-20 D 28 '63
Magic flute. Criticism
Opera N il 28:17-20 Ja 25 '64
Sat R 46:27 D 14 '63
Marriage of Figaro (Le nozze di Figaro) Criticism
New Yorker 39:202 O 19 '63
New Yorker 40:182+ O 10 '64
New Yorker 40:202 D 12 '64
Opera N 29:24-5 Ja 2 '65
Opera N il por 29:17-20 Ja 2 '65
Mozart arias from a pair of Teresas; Teresa Stich-Randall and Teresa Berganza. C. L. Osborne. il Hi Fi 13:69-70 D '63
Mozart; five different views, and all faithful. N. Broder. por Hi Fi 14:69-70 Ap '64
Mozart of our time. Discus. Harper 229:106-7 Ag '64
Mozart on the menu. E. Smith. il Hi Fi 13:58-60 N '63
Mozart the dramatist, by B. Brophy. Review Opera N 29:35 Ja 2 '65. R. J. Croan
Mozart's horn concertos thrice recorded. N. Broder. Hi Fi 14:92 N '64
Mozart's world; pilgrimage in pictures. H. Lloyd. Opera N 29:12-15 Ja 2 '65
On records; Così fan tutte. Opera N 28:34-5 D 7 '63
On records; Don Giovanni; Così fan tutte. Opera N 28:35 D 28 '63
On records; Magic flute. Opera N 28:35 Ja 25 '64
On records; Le nozze di Figaro. Opera N 29:34 Ja 2 '65
Presidential requiem mass. J. Lyons. il Am Rec G 30:560-1 Mr '64
Three by Kurt Redel, unabashed admiration. H. Glass. il Am Rec G 30:576-7 Mr '64
Unreluctant composers; conversation with Mozart, Verdi and Wagner. L. F. Loveday. il Opera N 28:8-11 Ja 25 '64
Wolfgang Amadeus Mozart: Così fan tutte. H. Glass. il Am Rec G 30:290-1+ D '63

MOZELL, Maxwell Mark
Olfactory discrimination: electrophysiological spatiotemporal basis. bibliog Science 143:1336-7 Mr 20 '64

MOZINGO, David P.
China's relations with her Asian neighbors. bibliog f Cur Hist 47:156-61+ S '64

MOZLEY, Charles
Album and the artist. N. Streatfeild. il Horn Bk 40:159-61 Ap '64

MPANDA, the beggar; story. See Dethier, V. G.

MPHAHLELE, Ezekiel
Fabric of African cultures. For Affairs 42:614-27 Jl '64

MROZEK, Slawomir
Birthday party; story. tr. by K. Syrop. Harper 226:92-4 Je '63
Four fables from Poland; tr. by K. Syrop. Mlle 57:158-61+ My '63
Lion: a fable. N Y Times Mag p92+ Ap 7 '63

MU mesons. See Mesons

MUANDAZI, Antonio
Now Angola: study of a rebel. L. Garrison. il por N Y Times Mag p 12-13+ F 16 '64

MUCH ado about ants; drama. See Heath, A. L.

MUCHA, Alphonse
Letter from London; concurrent exhibitions at Victoria and Albert museum, Arthur Jeffress gallery, and Grosvenor gallery. M. Panter-Downes. New Yorker 39:108+ Je 15 '63
Master of the tendrilous; shows at the Grosvenor and Jeffress galleries and the Victoria and Albert museum, London. il Time 81:57 My 31 '63
Mucha's divine Sarah. il por N Y Times Mag p 17 Je 2 '63

MUCHNIC, Helen
American letters in Soviet terms. Nation 196:182-3 Mr 2 '63
Common sense on Dostoevsky. Nation 197:34-5 Jl 13 '63

MUCOSAL diseases of cattle. See Cattle—Diseases and pests

MUD baths. See Baths, Moor and mud

MUDD, Roger
Mudd into gold. por Newsweek 63:74 Je 22 '64

MUDD, S. Harvey, and others
Homocystinuria: an enzymatic defect. bibliog Science 143:1443-5 Mr 27 '64

MUDSKIPPERS. See Gobies

MUEHL, Ruth D.
Charm's wound up; poem. Christian Cent 81:7 Ja 1 '64
Scientific solution; poem. Christian Cent 80:822 Je 26 '63

MUELDER, Walter G.
Christian social ethics bookshelf. Christian Cent 80:1336-7 O 30 '63

MUELLER, Allan G. and Guither, Harold
Hog raising tips to cut costs in half. Suc Farm 62:102-3 F '64

MUELLER, George Edwin
Man for the moon. por Newsweek 62:45 Ag 5 '63
Mueller succeeds Holmes; new Deputy associate administrator for Manned space flight. por Miss & Roc 13:19-20+ Jl 29 '63
New man for the moon. Time 82:11 Ag 2 '63
People of the week. U S News 55:23 Ag 5 '63
STL's Mueller replaces Holmes. Aviation W 79:26 Jl 29 '63

MUELLER, James A. See Quinn, J. B. jt. auth.

MUELLER, Lisel
Four German poets. Poetry 101:287-92 Ja '63
Lonesome dream; poem. New Yorker 40:141 My 23 '64
Prayer for rain; Blind leading the blind; Cicadas; Poem of love; poems. Poetry 103:355-8 Mr '64

MUELLER, R. F.
Chemistry and petrology of Venus: preliminary deductions. bibliog Science 141:1046-7 S 13 '63

MUELLER, Reuben
Mueller for Miller. por Time 82:80-1 D 13 '63

MUELLER, Richard J.
Can the public school foster creativity? Sat R 47:48-9+ D 19 '64

MUELLER, William R.
Drama. Christian Cent 81:1271-2 O 14 '64
Movies. Christian Cent 80:960-1, 1380, 1436-7; 81:49-50, 888, 1112-13, 1340+, 1499-500, 1566 Jl 31, N 6, 20 '63, Ja 8, Jl 8, S 9, O 28, D 2, 16 '64
Old story well told. Christian Cent 80:1203-6 O 2 '63
Reivers: William Faulkner's valediction. Christian Cent 80:1079-81 S 4 '63

MUENCH, Joyce R.
Fill'er up: a new lake is born. Motor B 113:21-3+ My '64

MUENSCHER, Minnie Worthen
Know-how of herbs. Bet Hom & Gard 42:75 D '64

MUFFINS
How do you like your muffins? il Sunset 131:182-3 O '63
Sourdough English muffins. il Sunset 130:227 My '63

MUGGERIDGE, Malcolm
Books. Esquire 60:62-3+ D '63; 62:10+ Jl; 10+ Ag; 68+ S; 14+ O; 16+ N; 36+ D '64; 63:24+ Ja '65
Dolce vita in a colder climate. Esquire 60:96-7+ N '63
Goldwater: an English view. Commentary 38:81-4 O '64
King Jack starts a dollar monarchy; excerpts from article in London daily herald. U S News 54:59 F 25 '63
Oh no, Lord Snow. New Repub 151:27-9 N 28 '64

MUGGERIDGE, Malcolm—*Continued*
People's flag is colored rose. New Repub 149: 45-8 N 9 '63
Public look at Private eye. Esquire 61:72-85+ F '64
—and Burton, Richard
Redbook dialogue. pors Redbook 121:48-9+ Je '63
about
Assailing a legend; image of J. F. Kennedy. por Time 85:65 Ja 29 '65
MUGHAL art. See Art, Mogul
MUGHAL painting. See Painting, Mogul
MUGS. See Pottery
MUHAMMAD, Elijah
Now hear the message to the Black Muslims from their leader. Esquire 59:97-101 Ap '63
about
Black Muslims. M. Berger. il Horizon 6: 48-65 Wint '64
Enter Muhammed? Nat R 14:520 Jl 2 '63
Feud within the Black Muslims. G. Samuels. il por N Y Times Mag p 17+ Mr 22 '64
MUHLEMAN, Max
Atlanta 500. Motor T 15:66-71 Je '63; 16:74-7 Jl '64
Cars to watch in '63. Motor T 15:28-33 Mr '63
Charlotte national 400. Motor T 16:72-5 Ja '64; 17:70-3 Ja '65
Charlotte World 600. Motor T 15:80-5 Ag '63
Chevy takes a 400. Hot Rod 16:80-1 F '63
Chevy tops the trials. Motor T 16:86-9 Ap '64
Darlington Southern 500. Motor T 16:66-9 D '64
Daytona, a dream come true. Motor T 15: 40-3 Mr '63
Daytona 500. Motor T 15:28-33 My '63; 16:70-3 My '64
Daytona trials. Motor T 15:70-5 Ap '63
Dixie 400. Motor T 15:60-3 F; 74-9 S '63
Firecracker 400. Motor T 15:68-73 S '63
Firecracker 400. Motor T 16:70-5 S '64
1965 stock car predictions. Motor T 17:52-7 Ja '65
1964 stock racing preview. Motor T 16:44-7 Ja '64
Stock car foresight and hindsight. Motor T 16:70-3 Mr '64
Stock talk. See issues of Motor trend
Two from the South; Rebel 300, World 600. Motor T 16:74-9 Ag '64
(ed) See Economaki, C. Profiles in racing
MUHLEN, Norbert
Germany's Jews today. Commentary 37:8+ Mr '64
MUHLER, Joseph C.
Annals of business; Crest toothpaste. B. Bliven, jr. New Yorker 39:83-4+ Mr 23 '63
MUHLFELD, Edward D.
Memo from the publisher. See issues of Flying
MUIR, Edwin
Ancestral vision. K. Raine. Poetry 101:272-4 Ja '63
MUIR, John
Conservationist John Muir honored. il pors Am For 70:46 Je '64
MUIR, R. Dalton
National parks and natural history; excerpt from address. Nat Parks Mag 39:14-15 Ja '65
MUIR, Robert M. See Sastry, K. K. S. jt. auth.
MUIR, William H.
Driftwood by design. il por Time 83:74 Mr 13 '64
MUIRHEAD, Peter P.
Graduate education; interest of the government; address, December 27, 1963. Vital Speeches 30:280-2 F 15 '64
MULATTOES
Almost white, by B. Berry. Review
Sat R 46:28 My 25 '63. O. La Farge
MULBACH, Amelia
Scrap pile puppets. Design 64:196-7 Je '63
MULCHING
Check list of mulches. Horticulture 42:44-7 Je '64
Mechanized plasticulture; polyethylene film mulches. il Time 81:75 Ap 19 '63
More garden, less work. il Changing T 18: 23-4 Jl '64
Petroleum mulch. Sci Am 208:84 Ap '63
Plastic mulch, how's it doing? C. E. Ball. il Farm J 87:52M My '63
Pretty and practical pebble mulch. il Pop Gard 15:10 S '64
Sawdust mulch for roses. O. M. Cook. il Flower Grower 50:56 Jl '63
Sprayed-on asphalt gets go-ahead; Encap, asphalt like mulch. R. G. Fowler. il Farm J 88:45 Mr '64
Use sawdust and enjoy a weed-free garden. B. Brinhart. il Flower Grower 51:42-3 Jl '64
Who said mulching is easy? L. Budny. il Pop Gard 14:80-1 Jl '63
MULE deer. See Deer
MULE deer hunting. See Deer hunting
MULELE, Pierre
Arrow in the air. il Newsweek 63:54 F 17 '64
MULFORD, Michael
New nasty PT's. Motor B 112:31 Jl '63
MULFORD, Montgomery
Maps on stamps. il Hobbies 69:99 Ja '65
MULFORD, Ralph
Automotive milestones; Mulford's leisurely Knox-Indy, 1912. il Motor T 15:60-1+ Jl '63
MULIK, James D. and Erdman, J. G.
Genesis of hydrocarbons of low molecular weight in organic-rich aquatic systems. bibliog Science 141:806-7 Ag 30 '63
MULLER, A. C.
Can flash synchronization be added to a used camera? Mod Phot 28:108 D '64
(comp) Should you buy a used camera without flash synchronization? Mod Phot 27:98 D '63
MULLER, Adolf
Hero of the spring. A. Nicholson. il por Read Digest 82:158-64 My '63
MULLER, Blackie. See Muller, G.
MULLER, Cornelius H. and others
Volatile growth inhibitors produced by aromatic shrubs. Science 143:471-3; 144:889-90 Ja 31, My 15 '64
MULLER, Godfrey
White man who couldn't be white; interview. pors Ebony 18:68-70+ My '63
MÜLLER, Heinrich
Reporter at large: Eichmann trial. H. Arendt. New Yorker 39:40-2+ F 23 '63
MULLER, Herbert J.
Second thoughts on the religious revival; excerpt from Religion and freedom in the modern world. Harper 228:82-5+ F '64
MULLER, Hermann Joseph
Perspectives for the life sciences. Bul Atomic Sci 20:3-7 Ja; 37 O '64
MULLER, Hilgard
Official case for apartheid. N Y Times Mag p28+ Je 7 '64
MÜLLER, Robert
Frankly physical. il por Newsweek 62:112 O 14 '63
MULLER, Steven
Reawakening on the Rhine. Bul Atomic Sci 20:2-6 S '64
MÜLLER-CHRISTENSEN, Sigrid. See Schuette, M. jt. auth.
MULLET fishing
They give you the jumps. J. V. Wormer. il Outdoor Life 133:56-9 Mr '64
MULLIGAN, Gerry
Mulligan rediscovered. M. Williams. por Sat R 46:56 Je 15 '63
MULLIGAN, John E. See Hollinger, J. R. jt. auth.
MULLIGAN, Joseph F.
Catholic scholarship. America 109:288-90 S 21 '63
MULLIN, Hilda, and Potter, Vilma
Symbiosis: Pasadena art museum and dance classes. Dance Mag 37:38-41 F '63
MULLIN, Willard
He likes to cook. il por Bet Hom & Gard 42:80 My '64
MULLINS, Ann
Objectionable advertising of foods and beverages. Consumer Bul 46:35-7 N '63
MULLINS, Cecil J.
Conversation in spring; poem. Good H 158: 198 Ap '64
MULLINS, Jeff
Top banana at last! H. L. Masin. il por Sr Schol 84:26 Mr 13 '64
MULLINS, Richard, jr. See Levine, S. jt. auth.
MULLOY, Gardnar Putnam
Irrepressible Mr Mulloy. G. Rogin. il pors Sports Illus 21:56-62 Jl 13 '64
Mountain of youth. por Newsweek 61:55 Mr 4 '63
Trouble with tennis. il por Esquire 61:119-23 My '64
MULTILATERAL force. See North Atlantic treaty organization—Multilateral force (proposed)
MULTILATERAL treaties. See Treaties

MULTIMETERS. See Electric meters
MULTIPLE access computer. See Calculating machines—Cooperative use
MULTIPLE birth. See Birth, Multiple
MULTIPLE job holders. See Employees
MULTIPLE jobholding. See Supplementary employment
MULTIPLE sclerosis. See Sclerosis, Multiple
MULTIPLE stars. See Stars, Multiple
MULTIPLE use plans. See Forest management
MULTIPLEX radio broadcasting. See Radio broadcasting—Multiplex system
MULTIPLEX video receiver. See Television receiving apparatus
MULTI-PRISM lenses. See Lenses, Photographic
MULTIPURPOSE auditoriums. See Auditoriums
MULTIPURPOSE food
  Rusty bells of hope. H. Bowser. Sat R 46:24 Je 22 '63
MULTIPURPOSE power tools. See Machine tools
MULTIPURPOSE rooms. See Rooms
MULTIVIBRATORS
  Wipe out vibrator hash. R. L. Winklepleck. il Pop Electr 19:41-5 D '63
MULTNOMAH COUNTY library. See Portland, Ore.—Libraries
MUMAW, Barton
  Man in space. Dance Mag 38:44-5 Jl '64
MUMFORD, George S. 3d
  Dwarf novae (cont) il Sky & Tel 26:190-3 O '63
  News notes. Sky & Tel 29:26-7 Ja '65
MUMFORD, L. Quincy
  Librarian of Congress asks for tax break for LC. Library J 88:1636 Ap 15 '63
MUMFORD, Lewis
  Automation of knowledge; address, April 19, 1964. Vital Speeches 30:441-6 My 1 '64
  Books. New Yorker 40:155-6+ My 23 '64
  Future of the city (cont) Arch Rec 133:119-26 Ja; 119-26 F '63
  Now let man take over; excerpt from address, January 21, 1963. New Repub 148:12-15 F 16 '63; Same abr. with title Are we selling our souls for progress. Sci Digest 54:85-9 Jl '63
  Sky line (cont) New Yorker 39:143-4+ D 7 '63
  Wavy line versus the cube; reprint. Arch Rec 135:111-16 Ja '64
MUMMERS parade. See Philadelphia—Parades
MUMMERS theater, Oklahoma. See Oklahoma City—Theater
MUMPS
  Mumps. F. H. Richardson. Todays Health 41: 6+ D '63
MUMS. See Chrysanthemums
MUNAKATA, Shikō
  In Hiroshige's steps. il Newsweek 62:100-1 N 18 '63
MUNCEY, Bill
  Special: the large economy size in gold cups. R. Lardner. il pors Sports Illus 19:38-40+ Jl 8 '63
  Two rooster tails wash out a fifth Gold cup. H. Whall. il Sports Illus 19:52-3 Jl 15 '63
  Winning ways of Wee Willie. E. Crimmin. il por Motor B 111:43+ My '63
MUNCH, Charles
  New Boston tea party. Sat R 46:73 Mr 30 '63; Discussion. 46:72-3 Ap 27; 62 My 25 '63
MUNCH, Edvard
  Beauty in misery. por Newsweek 61:105 Je 24 '63
  Landmarks of modern art. K. Kuh. il Sat R 47:34 F 8 '64
MUNDELL, Wallace E.
  Single-hose regulators for scuba diving. Consumer Bul 46:6-10 Ap; 33-5 My '63
MUNDT, Karl E.
  Excerpt from testimony before Committee on banking and currency, November 20, 1963. Cong Digest 43:49+ F '64
  How nations aided by U.S. vote in the United Nations. U S News 57:12 Ag 24 '64
  New liberals: are they really 20th-century Tories? por U S News 54:108-10 Mr 25 '63
MUNEMANN, Rudolf
  Germany's financial coronaries. H. Nickel and R. Sheehan. il por Fortune 69:130-1+ Je '64
MUNGER, Bob
  Hunt against odds. pors Outdoor Life 131: 20-3+ Ja '63
MUNGO, Van Lingle
  Sanitary spitter; spitball pitcher. Sports Illus 18:14 Je 17 '63

MUNICH

Clubs

  Wild West, Germany. il Newsweek 61:96 My 20 '63

Description

  München: fun capital. M. Riedl. il U S Camera 27:82-3+ N '64
  Step by step through Munich. R. Deardorff. il Travel 119:63-7 Mr '63
  Young city. il Time 83:30-9 F 28 '64

Galleries and museums

  Wittelsbach treasure. il Time 82:72-3+ D 13 '63

Music

  Berlin and Munich; visit by Moscow's second opera company. J. H. Sutcliffe; E. D. Echols. il Opera N 29:30-1 Ja 2 '65
  Dedication of the House; opening of the rebuilt Bavarian state opera house. F. Hommel. il Mus Am 84:25-6 Ja '64
  Hans Rosbaud, 1895-1962. J. Evarts. Mus Am 83:21 F '63
  Munich renascence . D. Mackinnon. il Opera N 28:32-3 Ja 18 '64
  [Musical events] (cont) Mus Am 84:27-8 Jl '64
  Notes from our correspondents (cont of) Notes from abroad (cont) K. Blaukopf. Hi Fi 14:28 Mr '64
  Strauss in Munich; Bavarian state opera's centennial tribute. D. Stevens. Opera N 28:28-9 My 2 '64

Parks and playgrounds

  Walk in Munich's English garden. il Sunset 133:54 N '64
MUNICH festival. See Music festivals—Germany (Federal Republic)
MUNICH four power agreement, 1938
  Munich. Sr Schol 83:11 S 27 '63
MUNICIPAL accounting
  Computer that pays its way; Greensboro, N.C. C. M. Conway. il Am City 79:102-3 S '64
  Forms and machine combine to streamline city operations; Salem, Ore. D. W. Ayres. il Am City 79:108-9 Je '64
  Juneau knows that machine accounting pays. H. Cargin. il Am City 78:94-5 Ap '63
  Machine-accounting benefits; Salisbury, Md. W. M. Perkins. il Am City 78:134-5 Je '63
  Machine accounting stops deficit spending. G. C. Robinett, jr. il Am City 79:100-1 Ag '64
    See also
  Accounting—Mechanical aids
  Billing
MUNICIPAL advertising
  City tells its story; ed. by P. D. Eimon. See issues of American city
MUNICIPAL and federal relations. See Federal and municipal relations
MUNICIPAL and state relations. See State and municipal relations
MUNICIPAL auditoriums. See Auditoriums
MUNICIPAL bonds
  Bonddoggle; refunding. Newsweek 62:69 Ag 12 '63
  How to win a bond program; Tacoma, Wash. B. Bond. il Am City 79:120-1 Mr '64
  Making money on refundings. Bsns W p 116+ Ja 26 '63
  Opening tax-exempts to smaller investors; tax-exempt bond funds. il Bsns W p72-4+ D 21 '63
  Public bids on bonds vs. negotiated sale. W. D. Byrne. Am City 79:135-6+ Ag '64
  Sharp pencils and sharp tongues. Bsns W p85-6 Je 29 '63
  Topeka needs Macy's? Newsweek 62:66+ D 16 '63
  Using tax-exempts to build business; Macy store in Topeka, aluminum mill in Lewisport, Ky. il Bsns W p45-6+ D 14 '63
  Yield-seekers. il Fortune 70:99 Jl '64
MUNICIPAL budget. See Budget, Municipal
MUNICIPAL buildings
  More municipal office space per building; Los Angeles Department of water and power headquarters. W. C. Jacobs. il Am City 79:113+ Je '64
  New maintenance center brings order out of chaos; Riverside, Calif. R. W. Broffle. il Am City 79:93-5 O '64
  This maintenance shop sells service; Vernon, Calif. J. B. Moore. il Am City 78:107-8 Ap '63
    See also
  City halls
  Municipal centers

MUNICIPAL centers
Boston's stage government center approved. il Arch Rec 135:26 Ja '64
Brooklyn to get a town center. il Am City 79:78 Ja '64
City as a single structure. il Arch Forum 121: 200-9 Ag '64
Civic center plan revised in New York. il Arch Rec 136:10 D '64
Colonial town center goes modern; Tenafly, N.J. C. M. Pratt. il Am City 79:122 Mr '64
Final plan unveiled for Boston's new government center. il Arch Rec 133:14-15 My '63
Government center: symbolic showpiece of a new Boston. P. Herrera. il Arch Forum 120:88-93 Je '64
Great plaza for Boston's government center. il Arch Rec 135:192-4 Mr '64
New center for Boston. il Arch Forum 120: 88-9 F '64

MUNICIPAL cooperation. See Intercommunity cooperation

MUNICIPAL corporations
Legal notes and decisions, prepared by National institute of municipal law officers. See issues of American city

MUNICIPAL dumps
Death of a dump; Wetumpka, Ala. E. Austin. il Am City 78:29 My '63
For putrescibles only; Flagstaff, Ariz. L. D. Hueppelsheuser. il Am City 80:18 Ja '65
Operation bootstrap; Beaumont, Tex. D. H. Smith. il Am City 78:78-80 Jl '63
See also
Filling (earthwork)

MUNICIPAL elections
See also subhead Elections under names of cities, e.g. New York (city)—Elections

MUNICIPAL electric plants. See Electric plants, Municipal

MUNICIPAL employees

Pensions

Solving the municipal retirement problem. S. H. Peck. il Am City 78:141+ F '63

Uniforms

See Uniforms, Civil

MUNICIPAL equipment
Big grader is best for this small town; Chestertown, N.Y. R. Van Guilder. il Am City 79:97-8 Jl '64
Decentralization and new equipment boost work output. J. R. Holt. il Am City 79:31 Ag '64
Extra duties; specialized types used in Middletown, Ohio. C. Dennin and W. F. Cottrell. il Am City 78:95 S '63
Hand labor is dead; park maintenance. Lansing, Mich. T. J. Haskell. il Am City 78:79-80 Ap '63
Mowing responsibility; Pico Rivera, Calif. W. J. Pacifico. Recreation 57:189 Ap '64
Municipal equipment show; at regional APWA meeting. il Am City 78:109 Mr '63
New equipment cuts landfill costs; Springfield, Mo. V. Osborn. il Am City 79:27 Jl '64
Old tools learn new tasks; West Chester, Pa. E. Bayliss. il Am City 79:91-3 Ap '64
Personal touch to preventive maintenance; Glencoe, Ill. R. H. Goodin. il Am City 79:47 Ja '64
600 more miles of road in six months; Virginia Beach, Va. C. Teets. il Am City 79: 107 O '64
We corral our street vehicles; El Paso, Tex. R. Hickok. il Am City 78:112-13 Je '63
See also
Motor trucks, Municipal
Salt spreaders
Snow removal equipment, Municipal
Street cleaning apparatus
Tractors, Municipal

Repairing

Houston centralizes motor maintenance; Houston, Tex. K. E. Ping and O. J. Cole. il Am City 78:86-8 N '63

MUNICIPAL finance
Administrative and fiscal considerations in urban development. W. Z. Hirsch. bibliog f Ann Am Acad 352:48-61 Mr '64
How cities get and spend their money. Am City 80:86 Ja '65
Public bids on bonds vs. negotiated sale. W. D. Byrne. Am City 79:135-6+ Ag '64
States blunt federal grab for cities. il Nations Bsns 51:108-10+ Ap '63
Urban financing, difficult but not desperate. R. A. Freeman. Am City 79:7+ Mr '64
See also
Budget, Municipal
Local taxation
Municipal accounting
Municipal bonds
Purchasing, Municipal

MUNICIPAL garages. See Garages, Municipal

MUNICIPAL gas companies. See Gas companies, Municipal

MUNICIPAL government
Administrative and fiscal considerations in urban development. W. Z. Hirsch. bibliog f Ann Am Acad 352:48-61 Mr '64
Cities feel the squeeze. il Bsns W p26-8 Mr 9 '63
City politics, by E. C. Banfield and J. Q. Wilson. Review
Nat R 16:74 Ja 28 '64. F. G. Wilson
City tells its story; ed. by P. D. Eimon. See issues of American city
Data processing's role in city government. E. F. R. Hearle. Am City 79:140+ My '64
How to fight city hall. A. Levy. Redbook 122: 61+ Ap '64
More metropolitan government than you think. Am City 78:7 Ag '63
Open wide the council door. P. D. Eimon. il Am City 79:136+ Mr '64
Our municipal notebook. See issues of American city
Political side of urban development and redevelopment. S. Greer and D. W. Minar. Ann Am Acad 352:62-73 Mr '64
Urban conference hunts spin-off; space-research results applicable to urban problems; Oakland meeting. il Am City 78:166 S '63
Value of consultants; memorandum to Thorne Sherwood. E. A. Connell. il Am City 78:99-100 D '63
See also
Cities and towns—United States
Mayors
Purchasing, Municipal
State and municipal relations
also subhead Politics and government under names of cities, e.g. New York—Politics and government

Forms, blanks, etc.

Seven steps to better municipal purchasing; Middletown, Ohio. K. A. Jefferies. il Am City 79:118+ My '64

England

See also
London—Politics and government

United States

Big cities with big problems. il Sr Schol 84:36-7 F 14 '64
Cities attack problems with new powers. Nations Bsns 52:102+ Ap '64
City bosses and political machines; symposium, ed. by L. S. Greene. bibliog f il Ann Am Acad 353:1-121 My '64

MUNICIPAL improvement
Architecture and the urban emergency. D. Canty. il Arch Forum 121:172-9 Ag '64
Easy money. Read Digest 83:129 N '63
Exploiting urban decay. Christian Cent 81: 195-7 F 12 '64; Discussion. 81:431-3, 774 Ap 1, Je 10 '64
Fitting memorial: President Kennedy's plan to get rid of urban blight; with editorial comment. R. Leach. America 110:185, 186-8 F 8 '64
Gateway becomes symbol of renaissance. il Bsns W p 14-15 Jl 4 '64
Glitter of real estate lures industry dollars. il Bsns W p32+ Mr 2 '63
Highway and the city, by L. Mumford. Review
New Repub 148:20-2 Je 1 '63. W. Von Eckardt
How one city solved its downtown problems; Pomona, Calif. il U S News 54:76-7 Mr 11 '63
How to sell the voter. M. Nathan. Recreation 56:383-4 O '63
Instead of an abandoned factory; Cambridge, Mass. il Am City 78:89 O '63
Old seaport: planning a window on the world; Boston. il Arch Forum 120:94-7 Je '64
Operation eyesore stops urban decay; Dearborn, Mich. O. L. Hubbard. il Am City 78:165-6 My '63
Public art of city building. D. A. Crane. bibliog f Ann Am Acad 352:84-94 Mr '64
Sad little story of Wink. R. S. Strother. Read Digest 85:97-100 O '64

MUNICIPAL improvement—*Continued*
Social-welfare planning. E. Wood. Ann Am Acad 352:119-28 Mr '64
States active on urban problems. Am City 79:111 Ap '64
Supermarket for subsidies; address, January 6, 1964. E. P. Neilan. Vital Speeches 30:237-9 F 1 '64
Urban renewal; address, February 14, 1964. W. L. Slayton. Vital Speeches 30:376-8 Ap 1 '64
Use models; city planning improvements, Manitowoc, Wis. B. Mattson. il Am City 79:118-19 Mr '64
See also
Business districts
City planning
Housing
Playgrounds
Trees in cities
Urban renewal
Water fronts
also subhead City planning under names of cities, e.g. Phoenix, Ariz.—City planning

Bibliography

City planning and urban renewal; guide to available reference tools. H. B. Bentley. il Library J 88:1621-4 Ap 15 '63

MUNICIPAL incinerators. See Refuse incinerators

MUNICIPAL land. See Land

MUNICIPAL law
See also
Municipal liability

MUNICIPAL liability
Municipal liability. Am City 79:129-30 Jl '64

MUNICIPAL marinas. See Marinas

MUNICIPAL motor vehicles. See Motor vehicles, Municipal

MUNICIPAL officers
See also
Mayors
Public works officers

MUNICIPAL ordinances
Legal notes and decisions, prepared by National institute of municipal law officers. See issues of American city
Los Angeles R-3 ordinance. il Am City 78:95 D '63

MUNICIPAL ownership
See also
Gas companies, Municipal

MUNICIPAL parks. See Parks

MUNICIPAL planning commissions. See City planning

MUNICIPAL public relations. See Public relations

MUNICIPAL publications

Bibliography

Municipal and civic publications. See issues of American city

MUNICIPAL purchasing. See Purchasing, Municipal

MUNICIPAL purchasing departments. See Purchasing, Municipal

MUNICIPAL records on microfilm
Records go on a diet; Chicago. S. R. Olsen. il Am City 79:79 Ja '64
200 per cent more space with microfilm; Durham, N.C. B. S. Barker. il Am City 78:95-6 O '63

MUNICIPAL recreation. See Recreation

MUNICIPAL reports
Accessories for a sparkling city report. il Am City 78:126+ D '63
Wichita asks the experts. il Am City 79:161-2+ S '64
Wichita's miracle report. il Am City 78:117-18+ Jl '63

MUNICIPAL swimming pools. See Swimming Pools

MUNICIPAL taxation. See Local taxation

MUNICIPAL tractors. See Tractors, Municipal

MUNICIPAL transportation. See Rapid transit

MUNICIPAL uniforms. See Uniforms, Civil

MUNICIPAL universities. See Colleges and universities, Municipal

MUNICIPAL waterworks. See Waterworks

MUNITIONS
U.S. scrapping arms of future? il U S News 54:35 Ap 1 '63
Virus of debate; Congressional assistants defense and disarmament seminar. Nation 196:170 Mr 2 '63
See also
Atomic weapons
Weapons systems

MUNITIONS industries
Meat and potatoes. il Newsweek 61:27-8 F 25 '63

Statistics

Importance of defense industry to each state; table. Aviation W 81:27 S 21 '64

Europe, Western

Arsenal of its own. il Time 82:74 Jl 19 '63
Clash of arms; competitive battle for contracts. il Time 84:90 S 25 '64

United States

Battle of change. il Time 83:81-2 Ja 17 '64
Defense industry is facing trouble. C. J. V. Murphy. il Fortune 70:140-2+ Ag '64
DOD official hits marketing myths. M. Getler. Miss & Roc 14:21 Je 1 '64
DOD official urges industry to consider nondefense markets. R. Hawkes. Miss & Roc 13:16-17 D 23 '63
DDR&E opens international defense markets. Miss & Roc 14:119 Mr 30 '64
Firms must anticipate future needs. Miss & Roc 12:63 Mr 25 '63
Importance of defense industry to each state: table. Aviation W 81:27 S 21 '64
Money in old-style munitions. il Bsns W p 144+ Jl 25 '64
Space and defense, a big industry with problems. il U S News 54:48-51 Mr 11 '63
Sparta and America. N. Cousins. Sat R 46:20 Ap 6 '63
Survival of the fittest. W. J. Coughlin. Miss & Roc 14:46 Je 29 '64
Swords into plowshares. New Repub 150:3-4 Ap 25 '64
Technical talent utilization shifts urged. P. J. Klass. Aviation W 81:20 Jl 20 '64
Two economies. Nation 196:237-8 Mr 23 '63
Welcome aboard. Nation 196:217 Mr 16 '63
What will take up the slack? shrinking of defense procurement; with editorial comment. il Bsns W p50+. 128 Jl 18 '64
Where the cutback cuts deep. D. Oberdorfer. il Sat Eve Post 237:17-21 S 12 '64
Who runs America? an examination of a theory that says the answer is a military-industrial complex. D. S. Greenberg; discussion. Science 139:247-8+ Ja 18 '63
See also
McCormick Selph associates

MUÑIZ, Carlos Manuel. See Rusk, D. jt. auth.

MUNKACSI, Martin
Blemish-banishing made easy. Pop Phot 53:156-7+ N '63

MUNN, Ira Y.
Foot in the door; Munn v. Illinois. C. P. Magrath. il por Am Heritage 15:44-8+ F '64

MUNN, Ralph
New ALA headquarters a symbol of accomplishment; address, July 14, 1963. por ALA Bul 57:729-33 S '63
Planning for cooperation; address, October 18, 1963. ALA Bul 58:496-9 Je '64
Profile: Ralph Munn. E. Nesbitt. por Library J 88:2424-5 Je 15 '63

MUÑOZ MARÍN, Luis
Colonialism in Congress. Reporter 28:11 Je 20 '63
Let me go back. por Newsweek 64:29+ Ag 31 '64
Muñoz declines fifth term. Christian Cent 81:1077 S 2 '64
Permit me to leave. il por Time 84:35 Ag 28 '64
Poet in the Fortress, by T. Aitken, jr. Review
Sat R il por 47:40-1 O 17 '64. A. A. Berle
Puerto Rico: island at a crossroads. J. R. Moskin. il pors Look 28:26-34+ Mr 24 '64
Welcome to a new friend. il por Time 85:24 Ja 8 '65

MUNROE, J. Spencer, and Windle, W. F.
Tumors induced in primates by chicken sarcoma virus. bibliog Science 140:1415-16 Je 28 '63

MUNSEL, Patrice
Notes from our correspondents. S. Fleming. il por Hi Fi 14:24+ N '64
Stars at home; Patrice Munsel. il pors Opera N 28:13-15 Ja 25 '64

MUNSELL color wheel. See Color charts

MUNSON, Bill
College star with a slow fuse ignites the fireproof Rams. T. Maule. il por Sports Illus 21:97-9 O 5 '64

MUNSON, Gorham
Workshops for writers. Sat R 46:45-7+ Ap 27 '63
Writers' workshops. Sat R 47:43-5+ Ap 25 '64

MUNSON, Ida Norton
Resurrection; poem. Good H 156:73 Ap '63
MUNSTER, Joe H. jr, and Smith, J. C.
Savants, sandwiches, and space suits. Science 145:1276-81 S 18 '64
MUNTZ, W. R. A.
Vision in frogs; with biographical sketch. Sci Am 210:22, 110-15+ Mr; 10+ My '64
MUNTZ TV, incorporated
Muntz makes it; comeback from bankruptcy. il Bsns W p70+ N 9 '63
MURAKAMI, William T.
Crystallization of SE polyoma virus. bibliog Science 142:56-8 O 4 '63
MURAL painting and decoration
American artist in Norway. il Am Artist 27:12 Ap '63
Animal kingdom. M. Kerns. il Sch Arts 63:23 Je '64
China unearths its greatest wall-paintings. C. C. Chu. il Art N 62:31-3+ S '63
Edgar Miller; a versatile artist & craftsman. L. Bruner. il Am Artist 27:38-43+ My '63
Millard Sheets; the story of a giant. F. Whitaker. il Am Artist 28:32-7+ D '64
Paintings of Richard Haines. J. Lovoos. il Am Artist 27:50-7+ Ap '63
Rural mural for a tractor maker; Deere's company history. il Fortune 70:144-7 D '64
See also
Frescoes
Mosaics
MURAY, Leo
Atlantic defense; de Gaulle has ideas of his own. New Repub 152:14-15 Ja 9 '65
MURCH, Walter
Midnight portrait of silver. il por Vogue 142: 172-5 N 1 '63
Silver at hand; painting. Vogue 144:212-13 O 1 '64
MURCHISON brothers
Kirby comes home the winner. il Bsns W p 110-11 Jl 13 '63
Winner by a knockout. Time 82:88 Jl 12 '63
MURCHLAND, Bernard
Putting the self into perspective. Commonweal 81:76-9 O 9 '64
Seeds of a new era or moral creativity? Commonweal 80:123-4 Ap 17 '64
MURCRAY, W. B.
Infrared radiation from the atmosphere over the Arctic Ocean. bibliog Science 141:802-4 Ag 30 '63
MURDAUGH, H. Victor, and others
Urea: apparent carrier-mediated transport by facilitated diffusion in dogfish erythrocytes. bibliog Science 144:52-3 Ap 3 '64
MURDER
Air force murder case; Nancy Johnson and her son. J. Foisie. Nation 196:285-7 Ap 6 '63
And have not love, I am nothing; murder of J. Wylie and Emily Hoffert. M. Wylie. il Ladies Home J 81:76-7+ Mr '64
Un bonjour de l'etrangleur; murder of Jean-Luc Taron near Paris. il Time 83:24-5 Je 19 '64
Case of the sudden murderers. il Sci Digest 53:41 Je '63
Course in geography; a crime of honor in Italy. il Time 84:49 O 30 '64
Crackdown on quackery. il Life 55:72B-75 N 1 '63
Death wish; captain and first officer of Pacific air lines flight 773 shot by passenger. il Time 84:22 N 6 '64
D.A.'s wrong guess; E. Weissman's mild sentence for second-degree manslaughter. Time 84:44 N 6 '64
Dying girl that no one helped. L. Wainwright. Life 56:21 Ap 10 '64
Faces from the past. R. M. Ketchum. il Am Heritage 15:28-9 Ap '64
Fear walks home with the women; with report by M. Byers. il Life 54:16-21 F 15 '63
Girls in 3-C; Janice Wylie and Emily Hoffert. Newsweek 63:24 My 4 '64
Innocent's grim ordeal; murder of wife of airman Alec Johnson, Mountain Home air force base, Idaho. J. R. Phelan. il Sat Eve Post 236:62-7 F 2 '63
Killer; Jack the stripper murders of prostitutes in London. il Newsweek 64:38 D 21 '64
Killer of little Luc; Lucien Léger, confesses to murder. il Time 84:31 Jl 17 '64
Lady-killer; Hoch murder case. A. I. Schutzer. il Am Heritage 15:36-9+ O '64
Long voyage home; captain of Pomona murdered. il Newsweek 63:20-1 Je 1 '64
Mad strangler of Boston. E. S. Gardner. il Atlan 213:49-56 My '64
Million-dollar murder? case of Mrs Carol Thompson. Newsweek 62:23 Jl 1 '63
Minister and the choir singer; Hall-Mills murder case, by W. M. Kunstler. Review Newsweek il 63:94-5 F 24 '64
Murder in the rectory; Roman Catholic church of Christ the King, Ottawa. il Newsweek 63:40 Ja 6 '64
Murdering madams; sisters González Valenzuela. il Newsweek 64:60 N 2 '64
Mystery of the ship of fear; murder of Capt. Jacob Natvig, on the Liberty ship Pomona. J. Hicks. il Life 56:47-9 Je 5 '64
Not involved? Sr Schol 84:16 Ap 24 '64
Question of confidence; murder of India's Solicitor-General. Newsweek 64:49-50 S 21 '64
Return of the rub-out; murder of Chicago's Alderman Lewis. il Time 81:28 Mr 8 '63
Room service in Lausanne; the victim: Marjorie Winifred Bird il Time 83:42 Ap 3 '64
Sisters of shame; Mexican white slavers. il Time 84:50 O 30 '64
Sniper; Douglas Godfrey. il Newsweek 61: 26+ F 18 '63
Strange case of Edgar Smith. D. G. M. Coxe. il Nat R 15:273-8 O 8 '63
Studies in murder; NYC statistics, 1962. Christian Cent 80:389 Mr 27 '63
Very special murderer; W. Moseley. L. Wainwright. Life 57:21 Jl 3 '64
Who didn't kill Barbara Kralik? A. Mitchell and W. Mosley confess. B. Lindeman. il Sat Eve Post 238:78-81 Ja 16 '65
Why was Carol killed? case of Carol Thompson. D. J. Giese. il Sat Eve Post 236:73-7 S 14 '63
See also
Assassination
MURDER trials. See Trials (murder)
MURDERERS. See Murder
MURDICK, Olin J.
Other side of the coin. America 111:230-2 S 5 '64
MURDOCH, Iris
Idea of perfection. Yale R 53:342-80 Mr '64
Severed head; dramatization. See Murdoch, I. and Priestley, J. B.

about

Surrender to symbols. L. Kriegel. Nation 199: 339 N 9 '64
—and Priestley, J. B.
Severed head; dramatization of novel by I. Murdoch. Criticism
Commonweal 81:354 D 4 '64
New Yorker 39:96+ S 7 '63
Sat R 47:53 N 14 '64
Time il 84:52 N 6 '64
MURDOCK, David H.
Shopping center for money. il por Time 84: 111C O 2 '64
MURDOCK, J. T. and Zeman, L. E.
Corn down? find out why now. Suc Farm 62: 42-3+ O '64
MURDY, Ralph G.
Book reviews. America 110:774 My 30 '64
MURFITT, Rex
Wall plants. il Horticulture 43:32-3+ Ja '65
MURGER, Henry
Death of a seamstress. A. W. Zorgniotti. Opera N 28:24-5 Mr 14 '64
MURI, John T.
On the record. Sr Schol 84:16T F 21 '64
Preview: recordings for 1964-65. Sr Schol 84:12T My 15 '64
Records and tapes. Sr Schol 85:8T-9T O 28; 10T N 4; 20T D 9 '64
MURIE, Margaret E.
Arctic honeymoon; excerpt from Two in the Far North (cont) Audubon Mag 65:16-19+ Ja '63
On the river ice; excerpt from Two in the Far North. por Liv Wildn 82:3-8 Winter '62
MURIE, Olaus J.
Mount McKinley: wilderness park of the North country. il Nat Parks Mag 37:4-7 Ap '63
What are we doing to our land? Am For 69: 15 F '63

about

Arctic honeymoon; excerpt from Two in the Far North (cont) M. E. Murie. il Audubon Mag 65:16-19+ Ja '63
John Muir awards; conservation achievement awards. por Liv Wildn 83:31 Spring '63
Obituary
Nat Parks Mag 37:15 D '63
Olaus J. Murie, 1889-1963; with tributes from newspapers. il pors Liv Wildn 84:3-14 Sum '63
Portrait of a naturalist. P. S. Curry. il pors Liv Wildn 84:15-21 Sum '63; Same. Audubon Mag 65:358-63 N '63

MURIE, Olaus J.—about—*Continued*
Wilderness council in Wyoming; September 2 to 5, 1962. M. Nadel. il por Liv Wildn 82:38-9 Winter '62
MURILLO, Gerardo, known as Dr Atl
Volcanic volcanist. por Time 84:89 Ag 28 '64
MURINE leukemia virus. See Leukemia virus
MURMURS, Heart. See Heart—Murmurs
MURPHEY, Don
Wickiup browns. Field & S 69:49-51+ Ag '64
MURPHY, Abbie M.
Catalogs can make your gardening an adventure. Horticulture 41:610-12 D '63
Oriental poppies. Pop Gard 14:41+ Jl '63
MURPHY, Austin S.
Excerpt from statement, February 28, 1963. Cong Digest 42:307+ D '63
MURPHY, Charles J. V.
Defense industry is facing trouble. Fortune 70:140-2+ Ag '64
Desperate drive to cut defense spending. Fortune 69:94-7+ Ja '64
Foreign aid: billions in search of a good reason. Fortune 67:126-30+ Mr '63
Khrushchev's paper bear. Fortune 70:114-15+ D '64
Millions under Martin Marietta's mattress. Fortune 68:134-41+ N '63; 69:76+ F '64
New Communist patterns in Latin America. Fortune 68:102-7+ O '63
Vanishing margins in Vietnam. Fortune 70:110 S '64
Vietnam hangs on U.S. determination. Fortune 69:159+ My '64
—See Hannifin, J. jt. auth.
MURPHY, Claire
How to buy upholstered furniture. Redbook 121:80-1+ O '63
MURPHY, Cora
How a real Mrs Murphy views the rights plan; reprint. il por U S News 55:23 Jl 29 '63
MURPHY, Donald R.
How will farmers vote? New Repub 150:6 My 2 '64
MURPHY, Edward F.
(comp) As school reopens. N Y Times Mag p 145 S 13 '64
(comp) Best policy? N Y Times Mag p 116 D 1 '63
(comp) Dog days. N Y Times Mag p46 Ag 4 '63
(comp) Feline; thoughts for cat week. N Y Times Mag p 110 N 3 '63
(comp) Indian perfume, pernicious weed. N Y Times Mag p50-1 F 23 '64
(comp) Muse. N Y Times Mag p87 O 11 '64
(comp) Muse-ings. N Y Times Mag p26 O 13 '63
(comp) Of trees. N Y Times Mag p60 Je 7 '64
(comp) On guard, men. il N Y Times Mag p73 F 9 '64
(comp) On human rights. N Y Times Mag p 118-19 D 8 '63
(comp) On the fly. N Y Times Mag p77 Ap 26 '64
(comp) Oratory in season. N Y Times Mag p28 O 4 '64
(comp) Quotes: education. N Y Times Mag p 102 N 24 '63
(comp) Quotes: football. N Y Times Mag p 140 N 8 '64
(comp) Quotes: hunting. N Y Times Mag p 145 N 29 '64
(comp) Quotes: labor. N Y Times Mag p24 S 6 '64
(comp) Re: jazz. N Y Times Mag p38 Je 28 '64
(comp) Reading matter. N Y Times Mag p 128 Ap 14 '63; 66 Ap 12 '64
(comp) Realm of dreams. N Y Times Mag p50-1 Ja 5 '64
(comp) Seaside season. N Y Times Mag p92 Ag 18 '63
(comp) Sires and sons. N Y Times Mag p42 Je 9 '63
(comp) Sound of —. N Y Times Mag p48 My 5 '63
(comp) Spring! N Y Times Mag p62 Ap 7 '63
(comp) Subject: mother. N Y Times Mag p46 My 10 '64
(comp) Subject music. N Y Times Mag p56 S 27 '64
(comp) Take me out to the —. N Y Times Mag p94-5 Ap 19 '64
(comp) Topic: writing. N Y Times Mag p26 O 27 '63
(comp) Up betimes and . . ; N Y Times Mag p48 D 15 '63
(comp) Winter. N Y Times Mag p 132 D 13 '64
MURPHY, Francis X.
Historian's tribute; John XXIII. America 108:858-9 Je 15 '63
Pope John XXIII pastor and theologian. Cath World 197:318-23 Ag '63
Secrecy at the council. America 109:96-7 Jl 27 '63
Vatican II: early appraisal. America 108:330-2 Mr 9 '63
Vatican II needs a new approach. Cath World 198:302-7 F '64
MURPHY, George
Hollywood pavilion. New Yorker 39:26-7 D 28 '63
How Murphy upset Salinger. por U S News 57:19 N 16 '64
Just call him senator. il por Time 84:42 N 13 '64
My technicolor senator. S. Alexander. Life 57:30 D 4 '64
New role for legendary George. W. Trombley. il pors Sat Eve Post 237:22-3 My 30 '64
Nobody's mad at Murphy. H. Gold. il pors N Y Times Mag p42+ D 13 '64
People of the week. il por U S News 56:22 Je 15 '64
Who is the good guy? il pors Time 84:34-8 O 16 '64
MURPHY, Gerald
Seven-year itch. il por Time 84:80 O 30 '64
MURPHY, J. Carter
Alternatives to key currencies. Yale R 53:61-75 O '63
MURPHY, Jack
Champ behind the mask. N Y Times Mag p 18+ Jl 21 '63
It's news only when he loses. N Y Times Mag p 133-4+ S 8 '63
Open locker 0911. il Time 85:23 Ja 15 '65
MURPHY, James
Question of custody. il por Time 84:38+ O 9 '64
Rockefeller vs. Murphy; custody suit. il Newsweek 64:29 Ag 31 '64
MURPHY, John F. Jr
Gabon. pors Nat Geog Mag 126:324-9 S '64
MURPHY, John R. and Goldberg, I. A.
Strategies for using programed instruction. bibliog f Harvard Bsns R 42:115-32 My '64
MURPHY, Judith, and Gross, Ronald
There's no limit to learning. Parents Mag 39:62-3+ F '64
MURPHY, Ken
Catamaran to Tahiti; ed. by R. Choy. Yachting 113:36-8+ Mr '63 (to be cont)
MURPHY, Lois Barclay
Children's stresses and distresses. PTA Mag 59:14-16 bibliog(p35) O '64
Psychologist's view: children and toys. J. Star. il Look 27:107-14 D 17 '63
MURPHY, Maurice Thomas
Mossie Murphy's crusade. M. Cope. il pors Sports Illus 18:18-20+ Ja 28 '63
MURPHY, Michael J.
Deceit, corruption and scars of relief. Life 56:63 Ja 31 '64

about

Chief policeman talks about his beat. R. W. Apple, jr. il por N Y Times Mag p 10+ Je 21 '64
MURPHY, Paul L.
Time to reclaim: the current challenge of American constitutional history. bibliog f Am Hist R 69:64-79 O '63
MURPHY, Raymond
Just call me football's greatest scout. M. Cope. por Sports Illus 19:32-4+ S 30 '63
MURPHY, Raymond J.
Some recent trends in stratification theory and research. bibliog f Ann Am Acad 356:142-67 N '64
MURPHY, Richard
God who eats corn; poem. Reporter 30:34-6 My 7 '64
MURPHY, Richard W.
On stage: Carmen DeLavallade. Horizon 5:48-9 My '63
MURPHY, Robert
Diplomat among warriors; excerpt. pors Sat Eve Post 237:32-4+ F 22 '64

about

He was there. il por Newsweek 63:86 Mr 9 '64
International trouble-shooter. S. F. Bemis. Sat R 47:52-3 F 22 '64
MURPHY, Robert Cushman
Wonders of Fire Island beach. Audubon Mag 66:6-9 Ja '64
MURPHY, Roland E.
Biblical instruction. Commonweal 80:418-20 Je 26 '64

MURPHY, William
This water main can bend. Am City 78:90-1 Mr '63
MURPHY, Sir William
God who eats corn; poem. R. Murphy. Reporter 30:34-6 My 7 '64
MURPHY, William Beverly
Soups & chips. il por Time 84:97-8 D 11 '64
MURPHY beds. See Beds
MURRAY, Albert
Problem is not just black and white. Life 57:8+ Jl 3 '64
MURRAY, Bruce C. and others
Venus; a map of its brightness temperature. bibliog Science 140:391-2 Ap 26 '63
MURRAY, Carolyn S.
New stacking furniture inspired by an old culture. House B 105:166-9 Mr '63
MURRAY, Don, 1924-
Condition critical: cause unknown. Todays Health 43:48-9+ Ja '65
Danger! TB is on the rise! Read Digest 84:79-82 Je '64
Flu, the underestimated enemy. Read Digest 86:95-8 Ja '65
When you take the stand. Read Digest 82:122-5 F '63
MURRAY, Elizabeth E.
Time to enjoy; reprint. Recreation 57:142 Mr '64
MURRAY, Geoffrey
Hong Kong, and interchurch aid. Christian Cent 80:1471-2 N 27 '63
Successor to Visser't Hooft. Christian Cent 81:1030 Ag 19 '64
MURRAY, Jerome
Magnetic force in the kitchen. il por Bsns W p63 My 30 '64
MURRAY, Joan Charlat
Letter for a lover; poem. Mlle 59:309 Ag '64
MURRAY, Joan Elizabeth
New job for Joan. M. Crawford. il pors Look 27:50-1+ D 17 '63
MURRAY, John
Case of mistaken identity: drama. Plays 22:13-24 Mr '63
Hear no evil, speak no evil; drama. Plays 23:15-26 Mr '64
Invisible inventions, incorporated; drama. Plays 23:13-26 Ap '64
Like mother used to make; drama. Plays 24:23-36 N '64
Love's in fashion; drama. Plays 22:29-41 My '63
Miss Forsythe is missing; drama. Plays 23:15-26, 68 Ja '64
Miss Hepplewhite takes over; drama. Plays 23:15-28, 66 N '63
My host, the ghost; drama. Plays 24:25-36 Ja '65
Visitor from outer space; drama. Plays 24:1-16 O '64
MURRAY, John Courtney
Church and the council. America 109:451-3 O 19 '63
On religious liberty. America 109:704-6 N 30 '63
Theologian's tribute; John XXIII. America 108:854-5 Je 15 '63
Things old and new in Pacem in terris. America 108:612-14 Ap 27 '63
This matter of religious freedom. America 112:40-3 Ja 9 '65

about

Murray and Weigel: dialogizing duo. Christian Cent 80:599 My 1 '63
MURRAY, Ken
Easy mixes epoxy. Motor B 111:113 Je '63
Halloween tricks. Pop Sci 185:173 O '64
Tree-trimming tips. Pop Sci 185:123 D '64
MURRAY, Madalyn
Mrs Murray's war on God. R. Liston. il pors Sat Eve Post 237:83-7 Jl 11 '64
Most hated woman in America. J. Howard. il pors Life 56:91-2+ Je 19 '64
Nevertheless, God probably loves Mrs Murray. B. Shaw. il por Esquire 62:110-12+ O '64
We fled. il por Time 84:74 Jl 3 '64
Woman who hates churches. il por Time 83:53-4 My 15 '64
MURRAY, Milton, pseud.
Picking a pet food by reading the label. Consumer Bul 48:17-18 Ja '65
MURRAY, Patrick
Museum of childhood. Horn Bk 40:255-9 Je '64
MURRAY, Philip
Ballad of the participant observer in a deviant subculture. Atlan 213:94 Ap '64
Captive; Three blind mice at Acapulco; poems. Poetry 104:159 Je '64
Salesmen; poem. Commonweal 78:14 Mr 29 '63
Simple fountain in any Roman plazza; poem. Atlan 211:135 Ap '63
MURRAY, Robert V.
Why so much crime in the Nation's capital; interview. por U S News 55:92-7 O 21; 92-3 N 4 '63

about

Washington crime as police chief sees it. por U S News 55:20 Jl 15 '63
MURRAY, Roger F.
Urgent questions about the stock market. bibliog f Harvard Bsns R 42:53-9 S '64
MURRAY, Spencer
Cruising the Sea of Cortéz; excerpt. Motor B 114:37-9 N '64
MURRAY, Thomas J.
Dual distribution vs. the small retailer. Duns R 84:28-9+ Ag '64
Theodore Kheel: master mediator. Duns R 83:37-8+ Je '64
MURRAY, William
L'Americano; story. New Yorker 40:48-53 Mr 7 '64
Day among the immortals; story. New Yorker 40:54-9 D 12 '64
Good day for Miss Tillie; story. Sat Eve Post 237:34-5 F 8 '64
Letter from Rome (cont) New Yorker 40:92+ Je 27 '64
MURRES
Birds of the sea. A. Sprunt, 4th. il Motor B 112:29+ O '63
MURROW, Edward R.
To fill the reading gap. Sat R 46:32-3 Ap 27 '63
USIA. Reporter 28:6+ My 9 '63

about

Murrow legacy. Reporter 30:12+ Mr 12 '64
Murrow resigns from USIA; Carl T. Rowan appointed. Pub W 185:65 F 3 '64
Same wave length. por Newsweek 63:17 F 3 '64
MURTAGH, John M.
Dilemma for drug addicts. America 108:740-2 My 25 '63
Principle of privacy. Sat R 46:31-2 My 4 '63
MURVILLE, Maurice Couve de. See Couve de Murville, M.
MUSCAT, Victor
Three for a pyramid. il por Time 81:108+ My 17 '63
What's in it for Eddie, Bob, and Vic? S. H. Brown. il por Fortune 70:139-43+ S '64
MUSCATINE, Leonard, and Lenhoff, H. M.
Symbiosis: on the role of algae symbiotic with hydra. bibliog Science 142:956-8 N 15 '63
MUSCLE
Blood flow through muscle; investigators in the physiological research field. S. S. Sobin. Science 140:702 My 10 '63
Bradykinin: vascular relaxant, cardiac stimulant. D. Montague and others. bibliog il Science 141:907-8 S 6 '63
Chromatography of ribonuclease-treated myosin extracts from early embryonic chick muscle. E. F. Baril and others. bibliog il Science 146:413-14 O 16 '64
Conduction of the action potential in the frog ventricle. W. G. Van Der Kloot and B. Dane. bibliog il Science 146:74-5 O 2 '64
Electrochemical coupling in potentiation of muscular contraction. A. Sandow and others. bibliog il Science 143:577-9 F 7 '64
Embryological origin of muscle. I. R. Konigsberg. il Sci Am 211:61-6 Ag '64
Enolase: multiple molecular forms in fish muscle. H. Tsuyuki and F. Wold. bibliog il Science 146:535-7 O 23 '64
Enzyme changes in flight muscle correlated with aging and flight ability in the male housefly. M. Rockstein and K. F. Brandt. bibliog il Science 139:1049-51 Mr 15 '63
Hypothesis for a pressure-sensitive mechanism in muscle spindles. C. F. Bridgman and E. Eldred. il Science 143:481-2 Ja 31 '64
Inhibitory postsynaptic potentials in grasshopper muscle. P. N. R. Usherwood and H. Grundfest. bibliog il Science 143:817-18 F 21 '64
Localization of calcium-accumulating structures in striated muscle fibers. L. L. Costantin and others. bibliog il Science 147:158-60 Ja 8 '65
Membrane propertes of barnacle muscle fiber. S. Hagiwara and others. bibliog il Science 143:1446-8 Mr 27 '64
Muscle: volume changes in isolated single fibers. J. P. Reuben and others. bibliog il Science 142:246-8 O 11 '63

MUSCLE—*Continued*
Neuromuscular function; report of international symposium on the Effects of use and disuse on neuromuscular function, Liblice, Czechoslovakia. A. Sandow. Science 139:198-200 Ja 18 '63
Red skeletal muscle fibers: relative independence of neural control. E. Bajusz. bibliog il Science 145:938-9 Ag 28 '64
Tremorine: its peripheral action on striated muscle. B. Csillik. bibliog il Science 146:765-6 N 6 '64
Vascular smooth muscle: dual effect of calcium. D. F. Bohr. bibliog il Science 139:597-9 F 15 '63

MUSCLE relaxants
See also
Kallikrein
Mephenesin

MUSCLES
Activation heat in muscle: method for determination C. L. Gibbs and N. V. Ricchiuti. bibliog il Science 147:162-3 Ja 8 '65
Adenosine triphosphate: changes in muscles doing negative work. A. A. Infante and others. bibliog il Science 144:1577-8 Je 26 '64
Anatomy for the ballet teacher; interview. ed. by W. Como. R. Gelabert. il Dance Mag 37:60-3 S '63
Atrophy of skeletal muscle in chick embryos treated with botulinum toxin. D. B. Drachman. bibliog il Science 145:719-21 Ag 14 '64
Clonal analysis of myogenesis. I. R. Konigsberg. bibliog il Science 140:1273-84 Je 21 '63
Contraction-band formation in barnacle myofibrils. R. J. Baskin and G. M. Wiese. bibliog il Science 143:134-6 Ja 10 '64
Control and training of individual motor units. J. V. Basmajian. bibliog il Science 141:440-1 Ag 2 '63
Fused cells move muscles. Sci Digest 53:22 F '63
Mechanism of supercontraction in a striated muscle fiber. G. Hoyle and J. H. McAlear. bibliog il Science 141:712-13 Ag 23 '63
Muscular contraction as regulated by the action potential. A. Sandow and H. Preiser. bibliog il Science 146:1470-2 D 11 '64
Myosin substructure: isolation of a helical subunit from heavy meromyosin. S. Lowey. bibliog il Science 145:597-9 Ag 7 '64
Single-cell muscle control. Sci Am 210:58 Mr '64
Sweating: its rapid response to muscular work. W. Van Beaumont and R. W. Bullard. bibliog il Science 141:643-6 Ag 16 '63

Diseases

Human myopathy with giant abnormal mitochondria. G. M. Shy and N. K. Gonatas. bibliog il Science 145:493-6 Jl 31 '64
See also
Dystrophy, Muscular
Myasthenia gravis

MUSCULAR dystrophy. See Dystrophy, Muscular

MUSCULAR power
510-pound strongboy. il Ebony 19:103-8 My '64

MUSÉE de Mouton. See Museums

MUSEUM des XX Jahrhunderts. See Vienna—Galleries and museums

MUSEUM education
Smithsonian head sees museum as lively spot; summary of address. S. D. Ripley, 2d. Sci N L 85:120 F 22 '64
They dig for history; Brooklyn children's museum. il Parents Mag 39:46-7 Jl '64

MUSEUM for the arts of decoration. See Cooper union for the advancement of science and art—Museum for the arts of decoration

MUSEUM loans. See Art loans

MUSEUM of African art. See Washington, D.C.—Galleries and museums

MUSEUM of childhood. See Childrens museums

MUSEUM of early American folk arts. See New York (city)—Galleries and museums

MUSEUM of fine arts, Houston. See Houston museum of fine arts

MUSEUM of history and technology. See Smithsonian institution—Museum of history and technology

MUSEUM of modern art, New York
Critics at large; Photographer and the American landscape; four reviews, with photographs. Pop Phot 54:81-9+ Ja '64
Expansion and remodeling plans for Museum of modern art. il Arch Rec 134:29 S '63
House that art built. R. Lemon. il Sat Eve Post 238:72-7 Ja 30 '65
Modern on the move. F. Getlein. New Repub 150:26+ Ja 18 '64
More modern Modern; revamped museum. il Time 83:95 Je 5 '64
New wing for the Modern. F. Getlein. New Repub 151:32 Ag 8 '64
Significant forms at engineering scale. il Arch Rec 136:16-17 S '64
Statues in silhouette; sculpture garden. il N Y Times Mag p44-5 O 18 '64
Thinking of today, and eternal things. il Newsweek 63:48-52 Je 1 '64
View of her own; Americans 1963 at the Museum of modern art. il Newsweek 61:90 Je 10 '63
When is art modern art? R. d'Harnoncourt. il N Y Times Mag p 17+ My 24 '64
See also
Institute of modern art. New York

MUSEUM of natural history. See American museum of natural history, New York

MUSEUM of science and industry, Chicago
Touch of Aristotle, a dash of Barnum. il Time 84:62-3 S 4 '64

MUSEUM; story. See Merwin, W. S.

MUSEUM workers
Curators a-borning; junior curators. il N Y Times Mag p68 My 26 '63

MUSEUMS
Gifts from museums (cont) il Consumer Rep 28:526-8; 29:544-6 N '63, N '64
Life guide; fire museums. il Life 56:21 Mr 20 '64
Life guide; sports museums. il Life 56:15 Ja 24 '64
Museum world. J. L. Stoutenburgh, jr. See issues of Hobbies
Museums. See issues of Hobbies to March 1964
Museums for the traveler; Indian exhibits. C. Miles. Hobbies 68:112 S '63
Power of dreams: Musée de Mouton. V. Lawford. il Vogue 142:86-97 Jl '63
See also
Folk museums
Historic house museums
Medical museums
Naval museums
also names of museums, e.g. British museum

Architecture

Art gallery for a university campus. il Arch Rec 134:129-31 Ag '63
Lesson in unity. il Arch Rec 133:169-72 Ap '63
Model museum: glass at Dumbarton oaks. F. Getlein. New Repub 149:27-8+ D 28 '63
Modern art on the French Riviera; Cap d'Antibes. il Arch Forum 120:98-103 Mr '64
Museum in Rio conceived as fine arts center. il Arch Rec 133:149-52 Mr '63
Personal collection in Vermont; Bundy art gallery. il Arch Forum 120:104-5 Mr '64
Upside-down museum in Manhattan; new Whitney museum of American art. il Arch Forum 120:90-3 Ja '64

Gifts, legacies, etc.

Features. R. Davidson. il Antiques 83:218 F '63

MUSEUMS, Wax. See Wax figures

MUSGROVE, Frank
Why youth riots: the adolescent ghetto. Nation 199:137-40 S 21 '64

MUSHER, Jeremy I.
Speculation on new molecules. bibliog Science 141:736-7 Ag 23 '63

MUSHROOMS
Aller aux champignons; mushroom poisoning. il Time 82:42 O 4 '63
Are the darned things mushrooms? S. Leacock. Read Digest 85:188H O '64
Deadly mushroom poison found in human tissues. Sci N L 84:88 Ag 10 '63
Know the toadstools. H. Hinds. il Horticulture 41:460-2 S '63
Outdoors. V. Bourjaily. Esquire 61:168-70 Ap '64
See also
Cookery—Mushrooms
Mycology

MUSIAL, Stan
Man behind The Man; excerpt from Stan Musial: The Man's own story; ed. by R. Broeg. por Look 28:109-10+ Ap 21 '64

about

At twice twenty-one. Time 82:41 Ag 23 '63
Attaboy, gramps! por Time 81:98 My 17 '63
Changing days of Stan Musial. T. Cohane. il pors Look 28:68-73 Ap 7 '64
Get any hits Stan? F. Bisher. il pors Sat Eve Post 236:30+ My 25 '63

MUSIAL, Stan—about—*Continued*
Last time around with Stan. T. M. O'Leary. il por Sports Illus 19:20-5 O 7 '63
Physical fitness for everyone. por Parents Mag 39:38 N '64
Stan Musial's last day. W. C. Heinz. pors Life 55:96-8 O 11 '63
Stan the incredibly durable man. J. Reddy. por Read Digest 82:175+ Ap '63
That kind of man. por Newsweek 62:66-7 Ag 26 '63

MUSIC
Enlivening avant-garde. O. Daniel. Sat R 47:50+ Mr 28 '64
Feast of astonishments; New York festival of the avant garde. F. Bowers. Nation 199: 172-5 S 28 '64
For aleatoric ears; New York première of Larry Austin's improvisations for orchestra and jazz soloists. Newsweek 63:80 Ja 20 '64
Is it music? disciples of John Cage. il Newsweek 62:53 S 2 '63
Make it louder! contemporary classical music. A. Leichtling. il Seventeen 24:28 Ja '65
Mozart on the menu. E. Smith. il Hi Fi 13: 58-60 N '63
Music to my ears; New York philharmonic program of Cage, Brown, and Feldman compositions. I. Kolodin. Sat R 47:38 F 22 '64
Musical events; atonal music in performances of Concert opera association, Cleveland orchestra, and Philadelphia orchestra. W. Sargeant. New Yorker 40:126+ F 29 '64
Musical events; concert of anti-teleological music at Judson Hall. W. Sargeant. New Yorker 39:120-3 S 14 '63
New music (cont) il Mus Am 83:196+ Ja; 52 Mr; 51 Ap; 49 My '63
Profiles; avant-garde music of J. Cage. C. Tomkins. New Yorker 40:64-6+ N 28 '64
This historic necessity for music; address, November 11, 1963. K. Dunham. Mus Am 83:157-8 D '63
Two hours before sunset; interview, ed. by K. F. Reuling. F. Toye. il Opera N 29:26-9 Ja 23 '65
See also
Calculating machines—Musical applications
Chamber music
Church music
Concerts
Copyright—Music
Impressionism (music)
Metronome
Musical instruments
Opera
Piano music
Radio broadcasting—Music
Shakespeare, W.—Music

Acoustics and physics
Origins of psychoacoustics; with editorial comment. S. J. London. Hi Fi 13:43, 44-7+ Ap '63
Prospects for psychoacoustics. I. M. Fried. Hi Fi 13:48-50+ Ap '63
See also
Musical pitch

Analysis, interpretation, etc.
Music: your silent partner. J. Nunlist. il Dance Mag 38:48-9+ Ag '64
Sea-change; revisions turned Simon Boccanegra into something rich and strange. O. Lehmann. il Opera N 29:24-5 Ja 30 '65
Triumph of incongruity; Don Pasquale succeeds largely through its use of the unexpected. M. Lelash. il Opera N 29:24-5 Ja 9 '65
Why bother with words? J. Kerman. Hi Fi 13:39-41+ Jl '63

Anecdotes, facetiae, satire, etc.
You may be deaf, Ludwig, but I'm not! F. V. Grunfeld. il Reporter 32:51-3 Ja 28 '65

Appreciation
Adventure of discovering. A. Kostelanetz. Seventeen 23:180+ Ap '64
Component id and the package ego. D. Lachenbruch. il Hi Fi 13:64-5+ S '63
Emphasis on music. M. Dorian. il Dance Mag 38:56-7 F '64
Esthetic surfeit. C. J. McNaspy. America 111:426-7 O 10 '64
How to find your own taste in music. L. Wilcox. il House B 105:80+ Ap '63
Let's play A & R man; imaginary recordings. L. Haber. il Hi Fi 14:63-4 D '64
Music in the age of Zak; address. H. Lamb. Harper 226:76-8+ My '63
Nothing but contempt; opera-lover scrutinizes opera-haters. J. Gutman. il Opera N 28:8-11 Ap 11 '64
Singers' opera; Metropolitan repertory. J. Gutman. il Opera N 27:8-12 Mr 2 '63
Story of my ear. S. Potter. Opera N 29: 26 Ja 2 '65
There's magic in music at Christmas. G. R. Marek. il Am Home 67:20+ D '64
Why bother with words? J. Kerman. Hi Fi 13:39-41+ Jl '63

Bibliography
Book reviews. See issues of American record guide

Caricatures and cartoons
Music hath charms. M. Thaler. Mus Am 83: 112-13 Ja '63

Competitions
Battle of the strings; international music competition in Budapest. G. Kroo. Mus Am 83:163 D '63
Contests. See issues of Musical America
Mitropoulos 1963 winners. E. Heim. il Mus Am 83:17 My '63
Music to my ears; Mitropoulos competition. I. Kolodin. Sat R 46:28 Ap 20 '63
Resourceful Russians; Queen Elisabeth violin competition. il Time 81:65 Je 7 '63
To Russia with ease; Queen Elisabeth piano competition. il Time 83:56 Je 12 '64
Triumphant trio; Dimitri Mitropoulos international music competition at Carnegie Hall. il Time 81:62 Ap 12 '63
See also
Singing—Competitions

Criticism
See Music—History and criticism

History and criticism
De gustibus. Hi Fi 13:41 Mr '63
Greatest opera? P. J. Smith. Opera N 28:23-4 D 28 '63
He who laughs last; Falstaff. M. Lelash. il Opera N 28:24-6 Mr 21 '64
Interpretation of Bach's keyboard works, by E. Bodky. Review
Am Rec G 29:477-80 F '63. I. Kipnis
New music and the American mainstream. B. Boretz. Nation 198:466-8 My 4 '64
New York and the country. Mus Am 83:7 Ap '63
On being a music critic; excerpts from Music observed. B. H. Haggin. Commentary 38:50-2 Jl '64; Reply. D. H. Heintz. 38:28 O '64
Pox on Broadway; ed. by M. Schumach. R. Friml. il N Y Times Mag p54+ S 15 '63
Second look at Manfredini. P. H. Lang. Hi Fi 13:57-8 Ap '63
Song and singer; excerpt from lecture-recital. N. Rorem. Am Rec G 30:468-70+ F '64
Treasury of early music. J. W. Barker. il Am Rec G 30:96-100 O '63
Wagner in travesty. J. W. Stedman. il Opera N 27:24-7 F 23 '63
See also
Jazz music
Opera—History and criticism

Instruction and study
Adele Marcus: the challenge of teaching. R. Sabin. Mus Am 83:53 F '63
Creative music teaching in the elementary school. R. B. Fitzgerald. NEA J 53:42-3 D '64
Encore for music lessons. M. Pines. il N Y Times Mag p95-6 N 3 '63
Have a policy about music lessons. L. A. Harlow. House B 105:68+ Mr '63
Music at Harvard yesterday and today; with reports by P. Campbell and R. Wilson. H. Rogers; D. Hughes. il Mus Am 83:6-9 Je '63
Music by mail. B. MacMillan. il Parents Mag 38:76-7+ S '63
Music lessons: fun or flop? il Changing T 17:15-17 Ap '63
New Manhattan project; address, November 11, 1963. J. Brownlee. Mus Am 83:162 D '63
Parents' questions about music lessons; interview, ed. by H. Littledale. H. Levine. il Parents Mag 39:48-9+ My '64
Personal business. Bsns W p 127 Mr 23 '63
Place of music in our elementary and secondary schools. C. Leonhard. il NEA J 52:40-2 Ap '63
School trains 200; students of W. M. Goins. il Ebony 18:92+ Jl '63
U.S. calendar: on and off campus. R. D. Daniels. Opera N 29:35 D 12 '64
See also
Music camps
Violin—Instruction and study

MUSIC—*Continued*

Interpretation

See Music—Analysis, interpretation, etc.

Moving pictures

See Moving pictures—Music

Periodicals

See also
Musical America (periodical)

Philosophy and aesthetics

On winning the first Aspen award: address. B. Britten. il Sat R 47:37-9+ Ag 22 '64

Psychology

See also
Music and color

Public relations

Public relations & arts. A. H. Reiss. Mus Am 83:44-5 F '63

Quotations, maxims, etc.

Sound of—; comp. by E. F. Murphy. il N Y Times Mag p48 My 5 '63
Subject: music; comp. by E. F. Murphy. il N Y Times Mag p56 S 27 '64

Recording and reproducing

See Sound—Recording and reproducing

Study and teaching

See Music—Instruction and study

Terminology

Opera glossary. G. Martin. Opera N 28:32-3 Ja 11; 30-1 Ja 18 '64

Therapeutic aspects

See Music therapy

Argentina

See also
Buenos Aires—Music

Australia

Season down under. W. Wagner. Mus Am 83: 270-1 D '63

Austria

See also
Graz, Austria—Music
Salzburg festival
Vienna—Music

Belgium

See also
Brussels—Music

Brazil

[Musical events] (cont) Mus Am 84:19 N '64
See also
Rio de Janeiro—Music

Bulgaria

See also
Sophia, Bulgaria—Music

Canada

Look at music in Quebec. J. Vallerand. il Mus Am 83:18-19 S '63
[Musical events] (cont) Mus Am 84:58 F '64
Survey: North American cities: 1962-63. Mus Am 83:290-2+ Ja '63
See also
Montreal—Music
Opera—Canada

Chile

Dance in Chile. M. Vicuña. il Américas 15:14 D '63

China

See also
Opera, Chinese

Czechoslovakia

[Musical events] il Mus Am 83:16 Jl '63; 84:21 Mr '64
See also
Prague—Music

Denmark

See also
Copenhagen—Music
Opera—Denmark

England

Music for Shakespeare. S. Popper. il Opera N 28:8-12 My 2 '64
See also
D'Oyly Carte opera company

Europe

See also
Opera—Europe

Europe, Western

European diary. E. Helm. Mus Am 84:17-18 Mr '64
Letter from Europe. E. Helm. il Mus Am 83: 38-9 S; 22 O; 271+ D '63; 84:16 F; 27-8 Ap '64
Music: European report. B. Boretz. Nation 197:187-8, 207-8 S 28-O 5 '63

France

Musical events. il Mus Am 83:14-15 Jl '63
See also
Opera—France
Paris—Music

Germany (Democratic Republic)

See also
Berlin (East Berlin)—Music

Germany (Federal Republic)

Business of music. J. Wechsberg. Holiday 36: 64-5+ O '64
[Musical events] Mus Am 83:23 Ap '63
See also
Hamburg—Music
Hanover, Germany (Federal Republic)—Music
Munich—Music
Opera—Germany (Federal Republic)

Great Britain

[Musical events] (cont) M. Cooper. Mus Am 83:20 Mr; 41-2 O '63; 84:57+ Ja '64
See also
London—Music
Opera—Great Britain

Hawaii

See also
Honolulu—Music
Honolulu symphony orchestra

Hungary

[Musical events] Mus Am 83:20 Mr '63
See also
Budapest—Music

India

See also
Music, Indian (East Indian)

Ireland

See also
Dublin—Music

Israel

See also
Jerusalem—Music
Tel Aviv, Israel—Music

Italy

Italian province. S. Levarie. il Opera N 28: 6-11 Ap 18 '64
[Musical events] il Mus Am 83:116 D '63; 84:18-19 Mr '64
See also
Florence—Music
Milan, Italy—Music
Opera—Italy
Parma, Italy—Music
Rome (city)—Music
Trieste—Music
Venice—Music
Verona, Italy—Music

Japan

Mr Dan presents Mr Dan. Newsweek 64:75 Jl 20 '64
See also
Tokyo—Music

Latin America

See also
Opera—Latin America

Mexico

See also
Mexico (city)—Music
Music, Mexican
Opera—Mexico

Netherlands

[Musical events] (cont) Mus Am 84:17-18 F '64
See also
Amsterdam, Netherlands—Music
Hague, The—Music

Peru

See also
Opera—Peru

Philippines

Philippine songs. S. J. Cohen. il Sat R 47:61 Je 27 '64

Portugal

See also
Lisbon, Portugal—Music

MUSIC—*Continued*

Russia

Here and there. Holiday 34:158 O '63
Musical Russians. S. Chotzinoff. il Holiday 34:121-6 O '63
Musical sins of the Soviet fathers. Discus. Harper 227:138+ N '63
Warm; Russian violinists. New Yorker 38:25-6 F 2 '63
See also
Jazz music—Russia
Opera—Russia
Opera, Russian

Scotland

See also
Edinburgh—Music

South Africa

[Musical events] Mus Am 83:23-4 Ap '63
See also
Johannesburg—Music
Opera—South Africa

Spain

[Musical events] Mus Am 84:19+ F '64
See also
Madrid—Music
Music festivals—Spain

Sweden

See also
Göteborg—Music
Opera—Sweden

Switzerland

See also
Geneva, Switzerland—Music
Music festivals—Switzerland

United States

America the musical. H. F. Miller. il Sr Schol 83:37 N 8 '63
Judging the judges. Nation 198:498 My 18 '64
Life guide. See issues of Life
Lighter side. Mus Am 83:7 F '63
Look at 1963. J. Ardoin. il Mus Am 83:28-9+ D '63
New York and the country. Mus Am 83:7 Ap '63
1962 a backward look. J. Ardoin. il Mus Am 83:26-7 Ja '63
1963-1964 season: coast to coast preview. il Mus Am 83:28-9+ S '63
Place of creative arts; address, September 16, 1963. H. Hanson. Vital Speeches 30:87-90 N 15 '63
Season of 2004. I. Kolodin. il Sat R 47:157-8 Ag 29 '64
Survey: North American cities: 1962-64. Mus Am 83:290-2+ Ja; 346-93 D '63
See also
Community concerts, incorporated
Handel and Haydn society
Jazz music
Kansas City lyric theater
Music, American
Musicians, American
National music league
Opera—United States
also subhead Music under names of cities, e.g. Chicago—Music

Wales

Joyful noise. G. Thomas. il Holiday 36:10+ D '64

Yugoslavia

[Musical events] (cont) Mus Am 83:19 F '63
See also
Ljubljana—Music
Zagreb, Yugoslavia—Music

MUSIC, African
See also
Music, Nigerian

MUSIC, American
From Yankee Doodle to yeah-yeah-yeah. il Sr Schol 84:5 My 1 '64
Have no fear and keep it clear, the jive is comin' and The Lion's here; excerpts from Music on my mind. W. Smith. Esquire 61:68-71+ Je '64
See also
Composers, American
Folk songs, American
Jazz music
Music—United States
Musicians, American
Songs, American

MUSIC, Baroque
Musical events; concert in Philharmonic Hall conducted by H. Scherchen. W. Sargeant. New Yorker 40:233 N 21 '64
See also
Phonograph records—Baroque music

MUSIC, Brazilian
Jazz roots in Nigeria. R. F. Thompson. il Sat R 47:52-3 Ap 11 '64

MUSIC, Byzantine
History of Byzantine music and hymnography, by E. Wellesz. Review
Am Rec G il 29:887-90 Jl '63. J. W. Barker

MUSIC, Chamber. See Chamber music

MUSIC, Chinese
See also
Opera, Chinese
Phonograph records—Chinese music

MUSIC, Church. See Church music

MUSIC, Color. See Music and color

MUSIC, Community
Let there be music. W. Bergmann. il Recreation 56:68-9 F '63

MUSIC, Czech
See also
Opera, Czech

MUSIC, Dutch
See also
Composers, Dutch
Phonograph records—Dutch music

MUSIC, Electronic
Anarchy and order; Dockstader's Eight electronic pieces. O. Daniel. Sat R 46:73 O 26 '63
Far-out at the Philharmonic; bangs & gurgles. il Time 83:79-80 F 14 '64
Father; music without instruments or electronic music. New Yorker 39:25-6 Ja 18 '64
Music. B. Boretz. Nation 196:233-6 Mr 16 '63
Music and the Olympics; Tokyo 1964. E. Cunningham. il Mus Am 84:36-7+ D '64
Music for machines. L. H. Lapham. il Sat Eve Post 237:66+ Ja 18 '64
Music from the electronic universe; with discography. E. Salzman. Hi Fi 14:54-7 Ag '64
Musical past and the electronic future; tr. by M. Bernheimer. H. Scherchen. il Sat R 47:63-5+ O 31 '64; Reply. S. J. White. 47:66 N 28 '64
Sound of cybernetics; aleatoric music performed by New York philharmonic orchestra. Newsweek 63:88 F 17 '64
See also
Phonograph records—Electronic music

MUSIC, English
Musical events; Promenade concert program at Philharmonic Hall. W. Sargeant. New Yorker 40:131-2 Je 13 '64
See also
Phonograph records—English music

MUSIC, French
Two kinds of French; Spontini's Vestale and Massenet's Navarraise. F. Merkling. Opera N 27:34 F 16 '63

MUSIC, Gipsy. See Gipsy music

MUSIC, Hindu
See also
Phonograph records—Hindu music
Shankar, R.

MUSIC, Hungarian
See also
Gipsy music

MUSIC, Imitation in. See Imitation in music

MUSIC, Incidental
See also
Phonograph records—Incidental music

MUSIC, Indian (East Indian)
Music of India; ten records of Indian music just released by Odeon. H. Yurchenco. Mus Am 84:26+ O '64

MUSIC, Influence of
Growing corn to music. C. B. Hicks. il Pop Mech 119:118-21+ My '63
Industry and music. J. Berry. il Mus Am 84:6-7+ O '64
Miraculous phonograph record. W. Saroyan. il Sat Eve Post 236:84-5 O 19 '63
See also
Music therapy
Sound—Physiological effects

MUSIC, Italian
See also
Music—Italy
Opera, Italian

MUSIC, Japanese
Buddhist chant. W. L. Purcell. il Am Rec G 30:806-8 My '64
Gagakunized jazz. il Newsweek 64:89 S 28 '64
See also
Phonograph records—Japanese music

MUSIC, Jewish
See also
Phonograph records—Jewish music

MUSIC, Latin American
Music. il Américas 16:39 Ap; 41 My; 42-3 Je; 42 Ag; 43 S; 39 O; 42 N; 38 D '64; 17:40 Ja '65

MUSIC, Mechanical
See also
Music boxes
Musical instruments (mechanical)
MUSIC, Medieval
See also
Phonograph records—Medieval music
MUSIC, Mexican
Music in transition; tr. by J. Norman. J. G. Heras. il Atlan 213:112-14+ Mr '64
MUSIC, Modern. See Music
MUSIC, Negro. See Negro music
MUSIC, Nigerian
Jazz roots in Nigeria. R. F. Thompson. il Sat R 47:52-3 Ap 11 '64
MUSIC, Oriental
See also
Phonograph records—Oriental music
MUSIC, Peruvian
See also
Folk songs, Peruvian
MUSIC, Popular (songs, etc)
Dumb sound; weird noises teen-agers call music. A. G. Aronowitz. il Sat Eve Post 236:88, 91-5 O 5 '63
Love songs to the carburetor. S. Alexander. Life 57:33 N 6 '64
Music in the age of Zak; address. H. Lamb. Harper 226:76-8+ My '63
Popular records. D. Watt. New Yorker 39: 92-4 Je 1 '63
St Joan of the jukebox. il Time 81:50 Mr 15 '63
Secular music. D. Newman. Esquire 61:50+ Ap; 62:50-3 O; 102+ D '64
That old hack magic. J. Hollander. il Esquire 59:70-1+ Mr '63
Why the girls scream, weep, flip. D. Dempsey. il N Y Times Mag p 15+ F 23 '64
Your music is your mirror. L. Gore. Seventeen 24:24 Ja '65
See also
Phonograph records—Songs
Songs, American
MUSIC, Portuguese
See also
Phonograph records—Portuguese music
MUSIC, Recording of. See Sound—Recording and reproducing
MUSIC, Russian
Soviet music since Stalin. B. Schwarz. Sat R 46:55-6+ Mr 30 '63
See also
Opera, Russian
MUSIC, Spanish
See also
Phonograph records—Spanish music
MUSIC, Swiss
How Swiss is Swiss music? A. Cohn. Am Rec G 29:520-1 Mr '63
MUSIC and children
Dear Mr Bernstein: a look at Leonard Bernstein's Young people's concerts mail. il Sr Schol 85:6+ D 2 '64
Growing up with opera. R. A. Tuggle. il Opera N 27:32-3 Mr 9 '63
Have a policy about music lessons. L. A. Harlow. House B 105:68+ Mr '63
Hidden talent for music in every child. A. Chasins. il McCalls 91:36+ Jl '64
How to lead your child to music. M. Roche. il House & Gard 126:182-3+ S '64
Let them listen, they may love it. A. Fiedler. il Am Home 67:18+ S '64
See also
Metropolitan opera guild
MUSIC and color
Un-sound principle? J. W. Stedman. il Opera N 28:12 Ja 25 '64
See also
Color organ
Music in art
MUSIC and moving pictures. See Moving pictures—Music
MUSIC and race
Music of the people; first Inter-American conference of ethnomusicology. A. Pardo-Tovar. il Américas 15:26-9 Jl '63
MUSIC and religion. See Religion and music
MUSIC and state
Melchior today; interview, ed. by L. F. Loveday. L. Melchior. Opera N 28:26-7 F 1 '64
Return to paradise; opera in Europe. W. Ducloux. il Opera N 27:8-12 My 4 '63
Role of music in cultural exchange; address, May 22, 1963. L. D. Battle. Dept State Bul 48:915-17 Je 10 '63
Visiting fireman; interview, ed. by J. W. Freeman. R. Liebermann. il Opera N 27:14 Ap 13 '63
MUSIC as a profession
Careers and opportunities in music, by A. Rich. Review
Opera N 29:7 D 12 '64. J. Honig
Launching a career. P. Hart. Mus Am 84: 10-11 Jl '64
MUSIC as recreation
Keeping harmony in the family. J. G. Harmount. il Todays Health 42:78-9 F '64
Music fun for all. E. R. Schweitzer. il Recreation 57:302-3 Je '64
Opera is recreation. il Recreation 57:451+ N '64
MUSIC associates
Why bands play on in Philly; cooperative organization of seventeen bands. il Bsns W p52-4 D 28 '63
MUSIC at midnight; drama. See Buchman, F.
MUSIC box alarm clocks. See Clocks, Electric
MUSIC boxes
Lullaby box. H. B. Smith. il Pop Electr 21:57-8 Jl '64
Wake up to your song; music box alarm clock. T. Thomas. il Pop Mech 120:176-7 Ag '63
MUSIC camps
Musical camps combine school with vacation. il Todays Health 41:20-3+ Ag '63
MUSIC conductors. See Conductors (music)
MUSIC copyright. See Copyright—Music
MUSIC corporation of America
Meanwhile back in Hollywood, efficiency takes over; with report by D. Zeitlin. il Life 55: 46-50B D 20 '63
MCA's work is other people's play. il Bsns W p90-2+ Mr 16 '63
New king of king. il Time 85:50-1 Ja 1 '65
MUSIC council, International. See International music council
MUSIC criticism. See Music—History and criticism
MUSIC critics. See Critics
MUSIC drama. See Opera
MUSIC equipment. See Music rooms and equipment
MUSIC festivals
And all that jazz; Newport jazz festival. S. Dance. Sat R 46:39+ Jl 27 '63
Festival preview. R. Jacobson. il Mus Am 83:8-11 Mr '63
Flood of festivals. il Newsweek 62:64-5 Ag 5 '63
Jazz in Pittsburgh. S. Dance. Sat R 47: 43+ Jl 11 '64
M and M at Monterey; seventh Monterey jazz festival. il Newsweek 64:120+ O 5 '64
Summer evenings: a calendar of festivals here and abroad. il Opera N 27:30-1 Ap 13 '63
Sun never sets on summer festivals. Mus Am 83:4-9 Ag '63
Austria
Tales of Bregenz. M. W. Cushing. Opera N 29:27 N 14 '64
See also
Salzburg festival
California
Bach with style. A. Bloomfield. Mus Am 84: 25 S '64
Diverse and contrasting; Los Angeles international music festival. E. B. Kohs. Mus Am 83:35 Jl '63
Monterey, and all that jazz. L. Robinson. il Ebony 20:54-8+ D '64
This year at Monterey. R. J. Gleason. il Sat R 46:118-19 O 12 '63
See also
Bach festivals
Canada
Vancouver festival. F. Campbell. Mus Am 83:9 Ag '63
Vancouver's bard: Vancouver international festival. W. Littler. il Opera N 28:30 N 16 '63
Colorado
Central City doubles. A. M. Lingg. Opera N 28:31 O 19 '63
Central City festival. A. Young. Mus Am 83: 4-5 Ag '63
Colorado counterpoint; Aspen, Colo. festival. E. B. Rogers. Opera N 28:29-30 N 16 '63
Music in the mountains; Aspen music festival's fifteenth season. A. Young. il Mus Am 83:36-7 S '63
Rocky Mountain ladies. A. Young. il Opera N 29:21 O 17 '64
Denmark
Scandinavian diet; Copenhagen festival. S. A. Roewade. Opera N 29:22 O 17 '64

MUSIC festivals—*Continued*

England

Eccentrics in Aldeburgh. K. F. Reuling. il Opera N 29:18 O 17 '64
English festivals. M. Cooper. Mus Am 83:8 Ag '63
Glyndebourne glitter. C. Mellen. il Opera N 28:30-1 O 19 '63
Glyndebourne nobility. M. E. Peltz. il Opera N 29:27 S 26 '64
Letter from London; Glyndebourne opera. M. Panter-Downes. New Yorker 39:107-8 Je 15 '63
Letter from London; Glyndebourne's new production of Rossini's La pietra del paragone (The touchstone) M. Panter-Downes. New Yorker 40:70 Ag 1 '64
Letter from London; performance of B. Britten's Curlew river, at city of London festival. M. Panter-Downes. New Yorker 40:71 Ag 1 '64
Music festival in England; Haslemere festival. Sunset 132:59 Je '64
Music to my ears; Pelléas at Glyndebourne. I. Kolodin. Sat R 46:20+ Jl 6 '63
No for an answer; Aldeburgh festival. M. Cooper. il Mus Am 84:26 Jl '64
Notes from our correspondents. F. Aprahamian. Hi Fi 14:12+ S '64

Europe

Target for the trip: a music festival in Europe. House B 106:16+ My '64

Europe, Western

Crisis in European festivals. E. Helm. Mus Am 84:10-11 Mr '64
Europe's opera festivals. J. Wechsberg. il Theatre Arts 47:59-61+ Ap '63
Guide to European music festivals-1963; preliminary forecast. H. D. Jellinek. Sat R 46:98-9 Mr 16 '63
Life guide. il Life 54:10 Ap 5 '63
Summer evenings. Opera N 28:33-4 Ap 11 '64

France

Aix marks the spot. P. Affelder. il Opera N 28:32-3 O 19 '63
French fashions; Strasbourg international festival. D. A. Mackinnon. Opera N 28:28 O 19 '63
Full life on Lac Leman (musique compris) I. Kolodin. il Sat R 46:20 Jl 20 '63
Provencal galaxy; festival at Aix-en-Provence. M. E. Peltz. il Opera N 29:19 O 17 '64

Germany (Federal Republic)

Africa and Abraham; this year's Berlin festival. E. Helm. Mus Am 84:17-19 N '64
Avant-garde: the 1964 Donaueschingen festival of contemporary music. W. Schwinger. Mus Am 84:78 D '64
Backward look; eight years of Donaueschingen festival programs. Mus Am 83:130+ D '63
Beethoven on the left bank; Bonn international festival. E. Helm. Mus Am 83:20-1 N '63
Berlin festival. R. Antoine. il Opera N 28:31 D 14 '63
Dedication of the house; West Berlin festival. H. Joachim. Mus Am 83:21 N '63
Legendary Munich. M. W. Cushing. il Opera N 29:29 N 14 '64
Mayr in Germany. D. Stevens. il Opera N 28:28 S 28 '63
Munich sacred and profane. F. J. Warnke. il Opera N 28:29 N 16 '63
Wagner worship in Bavaria; Munich festival. G. M. Loney. Reporter 29:32+ Jl 4 '63
See also
Bayreuth festival

Hawaii

Song festival in Honolulu. il Sunset 130:35 My '63

Ireland

Irish festival. M. E. Davies. il Opera N 28:34 Ja 18 '64
Song of Ireland. M. E. Davies. Opera N 29:31 Ja 23 '65

Israel

Choirs and cantors. S. Matalon. Mus Am 83:23 O '63
Mid-East summer. A. Frankenstein. Opera N 28:31 N 16 '63
Stravinsky premiere; Israel's fourth annual Festival of music and drama. S. Matalon. Mus Am 84:18 O '64

Italy

Florence May festival. F. Chapman. il Mus Am 83:7-8 Ag '63
Florence, Rome, Milan. J. Ardoin; D. A. Mackinnon. il Opera N 29:20 O 17 '64
In the chamber at Spoleto. il Time 82:38 Jl 19 '63
It opened in Venice. il Mus Am 83:14 Je '63
Italian high spots; Florence May festival. D. A. Mackinnon. Opera N 28:29 O 19 '63
Italian high spots; Spoleto's Festival of two worlds. P. Affelder. il Opera N 28:29 O 19 '63
Not so merry month of May. F. Chapman. il Mus Am 84:28-30 S '64
Rabbits from a hat; 1964 music biennale. E. Helm. il Mus Am 84:16-17 O '64
Shostakovich in Florence. H. Weinstock. Sat R 47:65 Je 13 '64
Spoleto's Silver rose. M. E. Peltz. Opera N 29:24 O 17 '64
Tale of four cities; Perugia. Mus Am 83:116+ D '63

Japan

Osaka spring; Osaka international festival. E. Cunningham. Mus Am 83:15 Jl '63

Lebanon

Mid-East summer. T. Goth. Opera N 28:31 N 16 '63

Massachusetts

Autumn harvest; Worcester music festival. J. F. Kyes. Mus Am 84:20 Ja '64
See also
Berkshire symphonic festival

Michigan

Festival by accident. J. Ardoin. il Mus Am 83:10-11 Je '63
Lost weekend; Ann Arbor 71st annual music festival. F. Gill. Mus Am 84:20-1 Jl '64

Netherlands

Birthdays in Holland. F. J Warnke. il Opera N 29:18 O 17 '64
Holland days. F. J. Warnke. il Opera N 28:26 O 19 '63
Holland festival. E. Helm. il Mus Am 83:9 Ag '63
Music to my ears; Giulini's Falstaff, and other Dutch treats. I. Kolodin. Sat R 46:34 Jl 13 '63
Operatic troubles at the Holland festival. E. Helm. Mus Am 84:27-8 S '64

New Jersey

New Jersey tercentenary summer; Festival of music in Princeton. R. Jacobson. Mus Am 84:18 S '64

New York (state)

Lake George festival. R. Jacobson. Mus Am 83:7 Ag '63
Music at Caramoor. Mus Am 83:13 Jl '63
Music in the night; 19th annual festival at Caramoor. J. S. Harrison. il Mus Am 84:23-4 S '64
Oldest festival; Chautauqua music festival. A. M. Lingg. Opera N 29:28-9 N 14 '64
Safe and familiar; Long Island festival. R. Eyer. il Mus Am 84:22 S '64
Time of the baroqueniks; midsummer music festival at Philharmonic Hall. il Time 82:55 Ag 9 '63
Two new works by John Butler; Caramoor festival. D. Hering. Dance Mag 38:28-9 Ag '64
Way of life; Chautauqua music festival. J. Ardoin. il Mus Am 84:14-15 O '64

North Carolina

Emphasis on the contemporary; Brevard music festival. J. E. Lammers. il Mus Am 83:34-6 S '63

Ohio

Cincinnati's May festival. E. B. Radcliffe. il Theatre Arts 47:67-8 My '63

Oregon

Bach before Shakespeare; Peter Britt music festival, Jacksonville. il Sunset 133:28+ Ag '64

Pennsylvania

Blues and banjos; second annual Philadelphia folk festival. H. Yurchenco. Mus Am 83:21 O '63

Poland

Frightening the fish; C. Berberian at the Warsaw autumn festival. il Time 82:72 O 4 '63
Latest styles; Warsaw international festival of contemporary music. T. Zielinski. Mus Am 84:27+ Ja '64
Question of style; second Festival of composers of western Poland. T. Zielinski. Mus Am 84:19-21 Mr '64

MUSIC festivals—*Continued*

Rhode Island

Maid of constant sorrow; fourth annual Newport folk music festival. Time 84:74+ Ag 7 '64
Milk drinkers. il Newsweek 62:80 Ag 12 '63
Third Newport folk festival. il Am Rec G 30:1072-3 Jl '64

Spain

Music in Madrid; first music festival of the Americas and Spain; with editorial comment. A. Iglesias. il Américas 17:1-5 Ja '65

Sweden

Sweden and Denmark. E. H. Palatsky. il Opera N 28:28 O 19 '63

Switzerland

Accent on opera. W. Reich. Mus Am 84:30 S '64
Music in Montreux. R. Gelatt. il Hi Fi 13:50-1 Mr '63
New goals; 1964 Lucerne festival. W. Reich. Mus Am 84:17 O '64
Zurich song. E. V. Epstein. il Opera N 28:27 O 19 '63

Tennessee

Nashville sound; Country music festival. il Time 84:76+ N 27 '64

Texas

Texas thrills. J. Rosenfield. Opera N 28:28 My 2 '64
Three kings in three acts; Montemezzi's Love of three kings. Mus Am 84:16-17 My '64

United States

Festivals: U.S; selective list of summer festival events. Mus Am 83:329-31 D '63
Hear America first. R. Sabin. il Mus Am 84:6-9 Mr '64
Sounds of a summer night. il Time 82:34-9 Jl 26 '63
Summer evenings. Opera N 28:34 Ap 11 '64

Vermont

Festival circuit; 14th annual Marlboro music festival. H. Rogers. Mus Am 84:24-5 S '64
You get a lot to like; Marlboro festival. J. M. Conly. Reporter 30:44+ Je 18 '64

Wisconsin

Contemporary accent; this year's Peninsula music festival. J. Rudolph. Mus Am 84:15 O '64
Peninsula eleven. J. Rudolph. il Mus Am 83:21 O '63

Yugoslavia

Adriatic summer; Dubrovnik festival. T. Goth. Opera N 29:19 O 17 '64
Picture in depth. D. Cvetko. Mus Am 83:16 Jl '63
Zagreb contemporaries. E. Hartzell. Opera N 28:26 O 19 '63

MUSIC for children
Harlem Bohème. F. Stevenson. il Opera N 28:6 Mr 14 '64
Magic yo-yo; a children's opera. H. Rothgarber. il Recreation 58:29+ Ja '65
Studio progress; latest report on the junior Metropolitan. A. M. Lingg. Opera N 28:16 Ja 25 '64
When opera goes to school. A. M. Lingg. il Read Digest 82:281-3+ Ap '63
See also
Phonograph records—Childrens records

MUSIC halls (variety theaters, cabarets, etc)
German cabarets flourish. R. C. Crisler, jr. il Theatre Arts 47:25-7 Je '63
My short, happy life in the theater. M. R. Bradford. il Atlan 211:136+ Mr '63
Political cabarets; source of Berlin's satire. S. Gainham. Atlan 212:95-9 D '63
See also
New York (city)—Radio City music hall

MUSIC history. See Music—History and criticism

MUSIC in art
Man through his art: music; excerpts. R. Hinks. il UNESCO Courier 17:23-5 Je '64

MUSIC in industry. See Music, Influence of

MUSIC in religion. See Religion and music

MUSIC in the home
Electric organs, home-style. il Changing T 18:45-6 S '64
See also
Music rooms and equipment

MUSIC libraries
See also
Music library association

MUSIC library association
Dynamic inaction; MLA. G. Stevenson. Library J 88:3804 O 15 '63; Discussion. 88:4502+; 89:809-11, 1480, 2000 D 1 '63, F 15, Ap 1, My 15 '64

MUSIC pavilions
See also
Bandstands

MUSIC publishing
Portrait of a music publisher: Franco Colombo, inc. M. Brozen. Mus Am 83:36 O '63

MUSIC rooms and equipment
Designed to be heard (and seen) il Good H 156:136-42+ My '63
How to arrange for big entertainment. il Bet Hom & Gard 41:94+ S '63
How to give the sound of music, and to whom. il House & Gard 124:66+ N '63
How to make room for music. M. Casserly. il Bet Hom & Gard 42:44-5 Ja '64
Listening room is an important part of your music system. R. Freas. il Am Home 66:4+ My '63
Music corners. il Seventeen 22:108-11 Mr '63
Portfolio of stereo décor; with editorial comment. J. Anderson. il Hi Fi 14:37, 38-45 F '64
These are music walls. il Sunset 131:108 S '63
Two music systems any man would envy. il House & Gard 124:86-91 Jl '63
Working music room. il House & Gard 125:128-9 Je '64

MUSIC school; story. See Updike, J.

MUSIC schools
See also
Eastman school of music, Rochester, N.Y.
Idyllwild school of music and the arts
Indiana. University, Bloomington—School of music
Manhattan school of music

MUSIC service, Planned. See Muzak corporation

MUSIC subsidies. See Music and state

MUSIC therapy
Hospital music clinic; Veterans administration hospital, Topeka, Kan. S. V. Beavers. Recreation 56:479 D '63
Power of music; address, November 11, 1963. V. Babin. Mus Am 83:158-9 D '63
See also
Sound—Physiological effects

MUSIC typewriter. See Typewriters

MUSIC week
Sound of—; comp. by E. F. Murphy. il N Y Times Mag p48 My 5 '63

MUSICAL accompaniment. See Moving pictures—Music

MUSICAL America (periodical)
On top of the news; appointment of editor. Mus Am 83:26 S '63
Sixty-five years of Musical America. il Mus Am 83:6-11 O '63
To talk of many things; Musical America's Emergency weekly edition. M. Esterow. Mus Am 83:58 Ap '63

MUSICAL appreciation. See Music—Appreciation

MUSICAL career. See Music as a profession

MUSICAL comedies, revues, etc.
Unsinkable Molly Brown; text. il Theatre Arts 47:25-56 F '63
See also
Musical comedy, revue, etc.
Phonograph records—Musical comedies, revues, etc.

Criticisms, plots, etc.

Amorous flea
New Yorker 40:108-9 F 29 '64
Around the world in 80 days
America 109:122 Ag 3 '63
Babes in the wood
New Yorker 40:84 Ja 9 '65
Time 85:32 Ja 8 '65
Bajour
America 112:25 Ja 2 '65
Commonweal 81:422-3 D 18 '64
Dance Mag 39:19-20 Ja '65
New Yorker 40:88 D 5 '64
Newsweek 64:94 D 7 '64
Time 84:88 D 4 '64
Baker's dozen
Newsweek il 63:57 Ja 20 '64
Ballad for Bimshire
America 109:643 N 16 '63
New Yorker 39:113-14 O 26 '63
Beast in me
New Yorker 39:57 My 25 '63
Newsweek il 61:93 My 27 '63
Ben Franklin in Paris
America 111:758 D 5 '64
Commonweal 81:423 D 18 '64
Dance Mag il 38:16 D '64
Newsweek il 64:92 N 9 '64
Sat R 47:53 N 14 '64
Time il 84:52 N 6 '64

MUSICAL comedies, revues, etc.—Criticisms, plots, etc.—*Continued*
Best foot forward
America 108:594 Ap 20 '63
New Yorker 39:140 Ap 13 '63
Theatre Arts il 47:12-13+ Je '63
Beyond the fringe
Cath World 197:79-80 Ap '63
Beyond the fringe (1964)
Newsweek 63:57 Ja 20 '64
Sat R 47:25 Ja 25 '64
Boys from Syracuse
New Yorker 39:84 Ap 27 '63
Sat R 46:33 Ag 10 '63
Theatre Arts 47:13 Je '63
Theatre Arts il 47:14-15 Je '63
Brigadoon
Theatre Arts 47:64-5 Mr '63
Cabin in the sky
America 110:239 F 15 '64
Café Crown
Dance Mag il 38:26-7 My '64
New Yorker 40:130 Ap 25 '64
Cambridge circus
Dance Mag 38:16-17 D '64
Nation 199:286 O 26 '64
Time 84:77 O 16 '64
Cindy
New Yorker 40:136 Mr 28 '64
Committee
Commonweal 81:73 O 9 '64
Nation 199:202-3 O 5 '64
New Yorker 40:160 S 26 '64
Newsweek 64:92 S 28 '64
Reporter 31:46+ O 22 '64
Sat R 47:28 O 3 '64
Cradle will rock
Newsweek 64:102 N 23 '64
Reporter 30:46+ My 21 '64
Establishment
America 108:237 F 16 '63
Nation 196:186-7 Mr 2 '63
New Repub 148:28-9 F 23 '63
Newsweek 62:76 N 11 '63
Reporter 28:48+ F 14 '63
Fade out-fade in
America 111:114-15 Ag 1 '64
Dance Mag il 38:17 Ag '64
Life 57:30 S 25 '64
Nation 198:611 Je 15 '64
Newsweek il 63:69 Je 8 '64
Sat R 47:28 Je 20 '64
Time 83:75 Je 5 '64
Fantasticks
Life il 57:75-6+ O 16 '64
Fiddler on the roof
America 112:25 Ja 2 '65
Commentary 38:73-5 N '64
Commonweal 81:100 O 16 '64
Dance Mag il 38:24-5+ N '64
Life il 57:104-5+ D 4 '64
Nation 199:229-30 O 12 '64
New Repub 151:31+ O 17 '64
New Yorker 40:96 O 3 '64
Newsweek 64:106 O 5 '64
Sat R 47:33 O 10 '64
Time il 84:82 O 2 '64
Vogue 144:66 N 1 '64
5 A.M. jazz
New Yorker 40:129 O 31 '64
Foxy
America 110:465 Mr 28 '64
Commonweal 79:723 Mr 13 '64
New Yorker 40:106 F 29 '64
Newsweek 63:56 Mr 2 '64
Sat R 47:23 Mr 7 '64
Time il 83:61 F 28 '64
Funny girl
America 111:114 Ag 1 '64
Commonweal 80:147 Ap 24 '64
Life 56:10 Ap 17 '64
Nation 198:384 Ap 13 '64
New Yorker 40:76 Ap 4 '64
Newsweek 63:76-7 Ap 6 '64
Sat R 47:34 Ap 11 '64
Time il 83:54 Ap 3 '64
Girl who came to supper
America 110:26 Ja 4 '64
New Yorker 39:62 D 21 '63
Sat R 47:52 Ja 11 '64
Time 82:81 D 20 '63
Vogue 143:62 F 1 '64
Golden boy
America 111:639 N 14 '64
Commonweal 81:287-9 N 20 '64
Dance Mag il 38:16 D '64
Life il 57:84A-85+ N 13 '64
Nation 199:340-1 N 9 '64
Newsweek il 64:94-5 N 2 '64
New Yorker 40:129 O 31 '64
Sat R 47:29 N 7 '64
Time il 84:79 O 30 '64
Hello, Dolly!
America 110:552 Ap 18 '64
Life il 56:107-9 Ap 3 '64
Mlle il 59:56 My '64
New Yorker 39:72 Ja 25 '64
Newsweek 63:59 Ja 27 '64
Sat R 47:22 F 8 '64
Time il 83:44 Ja 24 '64
Here's love
America 109:642-3 N 16 '63
Newsweek 62:72 O 14 '63
Sat R 46:18 N 2 '63
Theatre Arts 48:11 Ja '64
Time il 82:72 O 11 '63
High spirits
America 111:114 Ag 1 '64
Life 56:9 My 1 '64
Life il 56:125-7 My 15 '64
Look il 28:87-91 Mr 10 '64
Nat R 16:546-7 Je 30 '64
New Yorker 40:108 Ap 18 '64
Time il 83:65 Ap 17 '64
Home movies
New Yorker 40:134 My 23 '64
Hot spot
Commonweal 78:225 My 17 '63
New Yorker 39:82 Ap 27 '63
Newsweek il 61:54 Ap 29 '63
Theatre Arts il(p 12) 47:66 Je '63
Time il 81:58 Ap 26 '63
I had a ball
New Yorker 40:50 D 26 '64
Newsweek il 64:57 D 28 '64
Sat R 48:32 Ja 2 '65
Time 84:62 D 25 '64
Jennie
America 109:644 N 16 '63
New Yorker 39:113 O 26 '63
Newsweek 62:91 O 28 '63
Sat R 46:18 N 2 '63
Theatre Arts il 48:67 Ja '64
Time il 82:75 O 25 '63
Jo
America 110:322 Mr 7 '64
New Yorker 40:92+ F 22 '64
King and I
America 111:143-4 Ag 8 '64
Sat R il 47:18 Jl 25 '64
Merry widow
America 111:266 S 12 '64
Hi Fi 14:24+ N '64
N Y Times Mag il p 12-13+ Ag 16 '64
Newsweek il 64:73 Ag 31 '64
Morning sun
Theatre Arts 48:11+ Ja '64
My fair lady
Dance Mag 38:16 Ag '64
Sr Schol 85:5 O 21 '64
Vogue il 144:152-5+ N 1 '64
My people
Sat R 46:73 S 28 '63
Nowhere to go but up
Dance Mag 37:28-9 F '63
Oh what a lovely war
America 111:497-8 O 24 '64
Cath World 200:131-2 N '64
Commonweal 81:134 O 23 '64
Dance Mag 38:56-7 N '64
Esquire 60:34+ D '63
Nation 196:450+ My 25 '63
Nation 199:256 O 19 '64
New Repub 151:26 O 24 '64
New Yorker 39:76-7 Je 29 '63
New Yorker 39:98 S 7 '63
New Yorker 40:95 O 10 '64
Newsweek il 64:104 O 12 '64
Sat R 47:29 O 17 '64
Theatre Arts il 47:31-2+ Je '63
Time il 84:92 O 9 '64
Vogue 144:64 N 15 '64
Oklahoma
Dance Mag il 37:32-4 Mr '63
N Y Times Mag il p30-1+ My 12 '63
Newsweek 61:86 Mr 11 '63
Oliver!
Commonweal 77:493 F 1 '63
Theatre Arts il 47:10-11+ F '63
110 in the shade
America 109:644 N 16 '63
New Yorker 39:93 N 2 '63
Newsweek il 62:63 N 4 '63
Sat R 46:32 N 9 '63
Theatre Arts il(p66) 48:68 Ja '64
Time il 82:74 N 1 '63
Premise
New Repub 148:28-9 My 11 '63
Put it in writing
New Yorker 39:59 My 25 '63
Theatre Arts 47:12 Jl '63
Robert and Elizabeth
New Yorker 40:62-3 Ja 2 '65
Rugantino
Nation 198:204 F 24 '64
New Yorker 39:113 F 15 '64
Newsweek 63:90-1 F 17 '64
Time il 83:69 F 14 '64
She loves me
Commonweal 78:225 My 17 '63
Life il 55:49-50+ Jl 12 '63
New Yorker 39:90 My 4 '63

MUSICAL comedies, revues, etc.—Criticisms, plots, etc.—*Continued*
Newsweek il 61:83 My 6 '63
Sat R 46:26 My 11 '63
Theatre Arts il 47:12-13 Je '63
Time il 81:76 My 3 '63
Something more!
Dance Mag 39:18-19 Ja '65
Time 84:81 N 20 '64
Sophie
Newsweek 61:54 Ap 29 '63
Theatre Arts 47:66 Je '63
Streets of New York
America 109:644 N 16 '63
New Yorker 39:95-6+ N 9 '63
Newsweek 62:72 N 18 '63
Student gypsy, or The Prince of Liederkranz
Newsweek 62:77 O 14 '63
Theatre Arts 47:13 D '63
Teen-ager love
Theatre Arts il 47:66-7 Ag '63
To Broadway with love
America 111:55-6 Jl 11 '64
Dance Mag il 38:21+ Jl '64
Life 56:17 My 22 '64
Newsweek il 63:60 My 11 '64
To the water tower
New Repub 148:28-9 My 11 '63
Tovarich
America 108:651 My 4 '63
Commonweal 78:224 My 17 '63
Nat R 14:535-7 Jl 2 '63
Nation 196:334 Ap 20 '63
New Yorker 39:108+ Mr 30 '63
Newsweek 61:78 Ap 1 '63
Sat R 46:40 Ap 6 '63
Theatre Arts il 47:14-15+ My '63
Time il 81:46 Mr 29 '63
Trumpets of the Lord
New Yorker 39:60-1 Ja 4 '64
What makes Sammy run?
America 110:465 Mr 28 '64
Life 57:30 S 25 '64
Sat R 47:34 Ap 11 '64
Time 83:50 Mr 6 '64
Wonder world
Dance Mag il 38:20 Jl '64
Zizi
Dance Mag il 39:19 Ja '65
Newsweek 64:93 N 30 '64
Sat R 48:32 Ja 2 '65
MUSICAL comedies in sales promotion. See Entertaining in sales promotion
MUSICAL comedy, revue, etc.
American musical, 1964; survey of composers and lyricists. H. Hewes. Sat R 47:46-50 F 22 '64
Birth of comedy. P. H. Lang. il Opera N 27:8-11 F 16 '63
Broadway: early spring. D. Hering. il Dance Mag 38:28-9+ Je '64
Broadway: mid-autumn. D. Hering. il Dance Mag 37:22-3 D '63; 38:16-17 D '64
Broadway: midwinter. D. Hering. il Dance Mag 38:22-3 F '64
Conversation with Richard Rodgers; interview, ed. by S. Chotzinoff. R. Rodgers. Holiday 34:137-8+ D '63
Dance guide to musicals. See issues of Dance magazine to May 1963
Goings on about town. See issues of New Yorker
How to get a job as a swing dancer in a hit Broadway show. B. Evans. il Harper 230:28-31 Ja '65
How to succeed in Paris; turning How to succeed in business without really trying into a French musical. il Time 83:78 F 28 '64
Lament for Broadway; '62-'63 season roundup. L. Lerman. il Dance Mag 37:24-5 Je '63 (to be cont)
Life entertainment review. Life 56:18 Ap 24 '64
Now the musical theater is enshrined; New York state theater. R. Rodgers. il N Y Times Mag p20-3 Je 21 '64
Off-Broadway: midwinter. D. Hering. il Dance Mag 38:48-9 Ja '64
Pox on Broadway; ed. by M. Schumach. R. Friml. il N Y Times Mag p54+ S 15 '63
Revivals save the day; '62-'63 theatre roundup. L. Lerman. il Dance Mag 37:27-9 Jl '63
Satirical revues. il Theatre Arts 47:12-13 Jl '63
Star turn. G. Weales. Reporter 31:44+ D 3 '64
Summer debuts. il Time 82:60 Ag 9 '63
Summer musicals. D. Duncan. il Dance Mag 38:25-6 Jl '64
Visit to the antique world; '62-'63 theatre round-up. L. Lerman. il Dance Mag 37:24-6 Ag '63
Why aren't more show tunes for whistling. T. Prideaux. Life 57:12 Ag 7 '64
Words and music by the top: C. Porter. il N Y Times Mag p30-1 Je 9 '63
MUSICAL comedy production. See Theatrical production
MUSICAL composition. See Composition (music)
MUSICAL criticism. See Music—History and criticism
MUSICAL education
See also
Music and children
MUSICAL festivals. See Music festivals
MUSICAL heritage society, incorporated
Heritage by mail: mail-order record company devoted to seventeenth and eighteenth-century music. R. Freed. il Sat R 47:47-8 Jl 25 '64
MUSICAL instruments
Harry isn't kidding; H. Partch's homemade orchestra. il Time 82:50 Jl 5 '63
Let your child toot his own horn. il Am Home 66:17 D '63
Man with a horn; flugelhorn. il Newsweek 61:78 Mr 4 '63
Music, men and gods. C. M. Turnbull. il Natur Hist 72:47-53 My '63
Sound; home recordings. J. Wesson. U S Camera 27:16+ Jl '64
See also
Stringed instruments
also names of musical instruments, e.g. Zither
MUSICAL instruments, Electronic
Twin-T oscillators for electronic musical instruments. F. Maynard. il Electr World 71:36-9+ Je '64
MUSICAL instruments, Mechanical
Welte heritage. J. Ardoin. il Mus Am 84:46+ F '64; Reply. G. C. Stonehill. 84:5 My '64
See also
Jukeboxes
Music boxes
Player piano
MUSICAL instruments, Primitive
Indian and Eskimo musical instruments. C. Miles. il Hobbies 69:112-14 Ja '65
MUSICAL interpretation. See Music—Analysis, interpretation, etc.
MUSICAL parody. See Parody (music)
MUSICAL pitch
Pitch memory. New Yorker 39:42-3 Mr 16 '63
Pitched battle; New York philharmonic. Newsweek 61:79 F 4 '63
MUSICAL plagiarism. See Plagiarism in music
MUSICAL prodigies. See Children as musicians
MUSICAL recitals
Reviews: recitals; concerts in New York. il Mus Am 83:37-40 N; 258+ D '63; 84:48-54 Ja; 32-9 F; 37-44 Mr; 52-7 Ap; 42-7 My; 48-50 O; 36-9 N; 182+ D '64
MUSICAL societies
Carnegie and kitchens; United States enters the Fédération internationale des jeunesses musicales. Mus Am 83:15 F '63
See also
Concert artists guild
Handel and Haydn society
League of composers
MUSICAL taste. See Music—Appreciation
MUSICAL therapy. See Music therapy
MUSICIANS
Integration and the musician; concert artists refusing to play for segregated audiences. Mus Am 84:9+ Jl '64
Men in the pit. A. M. Lingg. il Opera N 27:28-31 Mr 16; 29-31 Mr 30; 26-9 Ap 13 '63
Personalities. See issues of Musical America
Power of music; address, November 11, 1963. V. Babin. Mus Am 83:159 D '63
Two hours before sunset; interview, ed. by K. F. Reuling. F. Toye. il Opera N 29:26-9 Ja 23 '65
See also
Children as musicians
Composers
Conductors (music)
Music as a profession
National music league
Singers
Women as musicians

Anecdotes, facetiae, satire, etc.

Evening the score; drawings. P. Horgan. Horizon 6:49-51 Spr '64

Bibliography

Book reviews. See issues of American record guide

Supply and demand

Case of the disappearing strings. S. Fleming. il Hi Fi 14:42-6 S '64

MUSICIANS, Amateur
Sound of music. Time 81:65+ Mr 29 '63
MUSICIANS, American
Cecil Taylor and the new tradition. J. Goldberg. Sat R 46:42-3 F 9 '63
Goodbye to all that; American jazzmen in Europe. il Time 81:52+ My 17 '63
Jazz. W. Balliett. New Yorker 39:130+ N 16 '63
Look at the future; nine young artists; with brief biographies. il Mus Am 83:8-11 Jl '63
New music and the American mainstream. B. Boretz. Nation 198:466-8 My 4 '64
Paying the new jazz dues. N. Hentoff. Nation 198:635+ Je 22 '64
Secular music. D. Newman. Esquire 62:50-3 O '64
See also
American guild of musical artists
Armstrong, L.
Baker, C.
Basie, C.
Bernstein, L.
Coleman, O.
Composers, American
Ellington, D.
Gillespie, J. B.
Hawkins, C.
Hines, E.
Ives, C.
Mann, H.
Mingus, C.
Monk, T. S.
Powell, B.
Rogers, R.
Russell, P. W.
Silver, H.
Teagarden, J.
MUSICIANS, Australian
See also
Williams, J.
MUSICIANS, Canadian
See also
Gould, G.
MUSICIANS, Chilean
See also
Arrau, C.
MUSICIANS, French
See also
Berlioz, H.
Chausson, E.
MUSICIANS, German
See also
Furtwängler, W.
MUSICIANS, Hungarian
See also
Starker, J.
MUSICIANS, Jewish
Predicament of the Jewish musician. A. Goldman. Commentary 35:102-11 F '63; Discussion. 35:535-6; 36:69-74, 275 Je-Jl, O '63
MUSICIANS, Negro. See Negro musicians
MUSICIANS, Polish
See also
Landowska, W.
Rubinstein, A.
MUSICIANS, Rumanian
See also
Haskil, C.
MUSICIANS, Russian
See also
Ashkenazy, V.
MUSICIANS, Spanish
See also
Casals, P.
MUSICIANS contracts. See Contracts
MUSICIANS in art. See Music in art
MUSIL, Rosemary Gabbert
Peach tree kingdom; drama. Plays 23:39-48, 68 Ja '64
MUSK ox; story. See Ditlev, H.
MUSK oxen
Nature note. Sci N L 86:255 O 17 '64
MUSKEGON, Mich.
Water supply
How to place a mile-long intake. R. J. Miles. il Am City 79:90-1 Ja '64
MUSKELLUNGE fishing
Five days for muskies. E. A. Bauer. il Outdoor Life 131:76-9+ Ap '63
Muskie myths exploded. M. Ellis. il Field & S 69:50-1+ Jl '64
Muskie on his back. J. C. Chapralis. il Field & S 69:70-1+ S '64
Tiger of Lake Chautauqua. E. P. Clarkson. il Motor B 112:82+ Jl '63
MUSKETS
Committee of safety musket in the American revolution. W. R. Orbelo. il Hobbies 68: 117+ Je '63
MUSKIE, Edmund S.
Excerpt from debate, February 6, 1962. Cong Digest 42:56+ F '63
Government's hidden dimension. por Sat R 47:18-22 Ap 18 '64
MUSKMALLOWS
Plant these more often. K. Corbin. il Horticulture 41:425 Ag '63
MUSKMELONS
Amateur scientist; extraction of growth-promoting substances from cantaloupe. R. C. Caggiano. il Sci Am 211:100-3 Ag '64
MUSKRATS
Musquash of the marshes. D. L. Allen. il Field & S 68:35+ Jl '63
MUSLIMS
Sudan expels missionaries; discussion. Christian Cent 80:276, 293-4 F 27-Mr 6 '63
Wants Moslem-Jewish rapprochement. Christian Cent 81:1613; 82:38 D 30 '64, Ja 13 '65
See also
Catholic church—Relations—Muslims
Islam
MUSLIMS, Black. See Black Muslim movement
MUSLIMS in Africa
Black Muslims. M. Berger. il Horizon 6:48-65 Wint '64
Christianity and Islam in West Africa. K. Hughes. Christian Cent 81:264-7, 298-302 F 26-Mr 4 '64
MUSLIMS in Egypt
Egypt's Christian minority. E. Watkin. Christian Cent 81:332-4 Mr 11 '64
MUSLIMS in India
See also
India—Hindu-Moslem relations
MUSLIMS in the Philippines
See also
Moros
MUSMANNO, Michael Angelo
Was Sacco guilty? New Repub 148:25-30 Mr 2 '63
about
Cleaning it up. Time 83:24 My 8 '64
Notes and comment; concerning review of Eichmann in Jerusalem. New Yorker 39: 17 Jl 20 '63
MUSORGSKII, Modest Petrovich
Angel's Boris Godunov. G. Kossodo. il Am Rec G 29:692-3+ My '63
Boris from Moscow. H. Weinstock. Sat R 47: 61+ S 26 '64
Boris Godunov. Criticism
Opera N il 27:17-20 Ap 6 '63
Opera N 27:25-7 Ap 6 '63
Sat R 46:53 Mr 30 '63
Columbia's Boris; G. London in title role at the Bolshoi, Moscow. P. L. Miller. il Am Rec G 31:20-1+ S '64
Khovanshchina. Criticism
Sat R 46:38 Je 29 '63
On records; Boris Godunov. Opera N 28:35 D 21 '63
On records; Boris Godunov. Opera N 29:35 Ja 30 '65
On records; Boris Godunov. C. J. Luten. Opera N 27:35 Ap 6 '63
Project Boris. R. Gelatt. il Hi Fi 13:51-6+ Ap '63
MUSQUASH. See Muskrats
MUSSELMAN, Virginia
Factors affecting the day camp program. por Recreation 56:131-4 Mr '63
MUSSEY, Barrows
Wine drinker's tour of Germany. House B 106:116-17+ Ag '64
MUSSOLINI, Benito
Brutal friendship, by F. W. Deakin. Review
Reporter 28:50+ My 23 '63. M. Salvadori
Time il por 81:118+ Ap 19 '63
Mussolini, by I. Kirkpatrick. Review
America 110:730-1 My 23 '64. D. B. Carroll
Sat R il por 47:49 My 16 '64. N. Calmer
MUSSON, Ken
Cannons for turkeys. Field & S 68:10-11 O '63
MUSSON, Ron
Musson, closeup of a champion. E. Crimmin. il por Motor B 114:34+ Jl '64
MUSTANGS. See Horses
MUSTARD, Prepared
What did we ever do without mustard? il McCalls 92:138-9+ N '64
MUSTE, Abraham Johannes
Love and power in today's setting. Christian Cent 80:639-42 My 15 '63
Peace agitator, by N. Hentoff. Review
Commentary 37:88-90 My '64. D. Dienstfrey
Radical reconciler. H. E. Fey. Christian Cent 81:211 F 12 '64

MUSTELIDS
See also
Wolverines

MUSULIN, Boris. See Shrewsberry, R. C. jt. auth.

MUTAGENETIC substances
Mutagenic and carcinogenic agents; annual symposium; Biology division of the Oak Ridge national laboratory. R. Dulbecco. Science 145:300 Jl 17 '64

MUTAROTASE
Mutarotase inhibition by 1-deoxyglucose. A. S. Keston. bibliog il Science 143:698-700 F 14 '64

MUTATION (bacteria)
Evolution of a catabolic pathway in bacteria. S. A. Lerner and others. bibliog il Science 146:1313-15 D 4 '64
Protein structure relationships revealed by mutational analysis. C. Yanofsky and others. bibliog il Science 146:1593-4 D 18 '64

MUTATION (biology)
Bacterial mutant with impaired potassium transport and methionine biosynthesis R. Damadian and A. K. Solomon. bibliog il Science 145:1327-8 S 18 '64
Biological mechanisms underlying the aging process. H. J. Curtis. bibliog il Science 141: 686-94 Ag 23 '63; Discussion. 142:540. 1261; 144:11 N 1, D 6 '63, Ap 3 '64
Erythrocyte glucose-6-phosphate dehydrogenase in Caucasians: new inherited variant. T. B. Shows, jr. and others. bibliog il Science 145:1056-7 S 4 '64
Gene action mechanisms in the determination of color and pattern in the frog (rana pipiens) J. Davison. bibliog il Science 141: 648-9 Ag 16 '63
Genetic effects. L. Pauling. Bul Atomic Sci 19:30-2 S '63
Glucose-6-phosphate dehydrogenase in drosophila: X-linked electrophoretic variants. W. J. Young and others bibliog il Science 143:140-1 Ja 10 '64
Independent action of allele-specific suppressor mutations. S. Brody and C. Yanofsky. bibliog il Science 145:399-400 Jl 24 '64
Lethal genes and analysis of differentiation. S. Gluecksohn-Waelsch. bibliog il Science 142:1269-76 D 6 '63
Mutations: incidence in drosophila melanogaster reared on irradiated medium. M. S. Swaminathan and others. bibliog il Science 141:637-8 Ag 16 '63
New mouse produced with golden hair. Sci N L 83:355 Je 8 '63
Phenotypic repair of RNA-bacteriophage mutants by streptomycin. R. C. Valentine and N. D. Zinder. bibliog il Science 144:1458-9 Je 19 '64
Proton tunneling in radiation-induced mutation. R. Rein and F. E. Harris. bibliog il Science 146:649-50 O 30 '64
Sex-linked albinism in the Japanese quail. J. K. Lauber. bibliog il Science 146:948-50 N 13 '64
Tryptophan- and indole-excreting bacterial mutants. P. G. Lim and R. I. Mateles. bibliog Science 140:388 Ap 26 '63
See also
Genetics

MUTATION (botany)
Dispensable and indispensable genes in neurospora. J. Morrow. bibliog il Science 144:307-8 Ap 17 '64
Early seed plants. H. N. Andrews. bibliog il Science 142:925-31 N 15 '63
Growth response of the d-5 and an-1 mutants of maize to some kaurene derivatives. M. Katsumi and others. bibliog il Science 144: 849-50 My 15 '64
Irreparable mutations and ethionine resistance in neurospora. R. L. Metzenberg and others. bibliog il Science 145:1434-5 S 25 '64
Mutagenic action of ethyl methanesulfonate in maize. M. G. Neuffer and G. Ficsor. bibliog il Science 139:1296-7 Mr 29 '63
Photosynthetic mutants separate electron paramagnetic resonance signals of scenedesmus. E. C. Weaver and N. I. Bishop. bibliog il Science 140:1095-7 Je 7 '63
Somatic instability caused by a cysteine-sensitive gene in arabidopsis. G. P. Rédei. bibliog il Science 139:767-9 F 22 '63
Virus as a mutagenic agent in maize. G. F. Sprague and others. bibliog il Science 141: 1052-3 S 13 '63

MUTE singer; story. See Szukalski, S.

MUTILATION of books. See Books—Mutilation, defacement, etc.

MUTINY
Martinet or martyr. W. Goldhurst. il Horizon 5:42-8 S '63

MUTUAL aid pact, Airline. See Strikes—United States—Airlines

MUTUAL funds. See Investment trusts

MUTUAL insurance companies. See Insurance companies

MUTUAL savings banks. See Savings banks

MUTUAL trust funds. See Investment trusts

MUUL, Illar, and Alley, J. W.
Night gliders of the woodlands. Natur Hist 72: 18-25 My '63

MUUSS, Rolf E.
First aid for discipline problems. NEA J 52:8-11 S '63

MUZAK corporation
But it's good for you. Time 82:34+ Ag 30 '63

MUZIK, T. J. and Whitworth, J. W.
Growth-regulating chemicals persist in plants: qualitative bioassay. bibliog Science 140:1212-13 Je 14 '63

MY aunt's career; story. See Mathieu, A.

MY big sister's romance; story. See Albee, G. S.

MY Coney Island uncle; story. See Swados, H.

MY fair lady; musical comedy. See Musical comedies, revues, etc.—Criticisms, plots, etc.

MY fair Linda; drama. See Garver, J.

MY father's courthouse; stories. See Singer, I. B.

MY host, the ghost; drama. See Murray, J.

MY kinsman, Major Molineux; drama. See Lowell, R.

MY life in art; story. See Brown, J.

MY mother, a stranger; story. See Anderson, J. M.

MY mother, my father and me; drama. See Hellman, L.

MY people; musical comedy. See Musical comedies, revues, etc.—Criticisms, plots, etc.

MY son; story. See Loeser, K.

MY uncle's death; story. See Updike, J.

MYASTHENIA gravis
Ills due to self allergy. Sci N L 86:196 S 26 '64
Thymus abnormalities linked to muscle disease. Sci N L 85:260 Ap 25 '64

MYCOBACTERIUM tuberculosis. See Tuberculosis bacilli

MYCOLOGY
Mycophiles: annual banquet of New York mycological society. New Yorker 40:22-4 Ja 9 '65

MYCOPLASMA. See Microorganisms, Pathogenic

MYCORHIZA
Endotrophic mycorrhizae influence yellow poplar seedling growth. F. B. Clark. bibliog il Science 140:1220-1 Je 14 '63

MYCOSIS fungoides
Anti-cancer drug used. Sci N L 83:306 My 18 '63

MYCTERIA. See Wood storks

MYDANS, Carl
Cold siege on the tundra. Life 56:21 F 28 '64
Far-off exiles of Tristan. Life 55:72-4+ Jl 12 '63
Flesh freezes solid in thirty seconds. il por Life 54:26-7 Mr 1 '63
Footnote to The deputy dispute: Jews of Rome, the Nazis and the Vatican. Life 56: 21 My 1 '64
Have you declared everything? Life 57:41+ Ag 28 '64
Haven on the Danube. Atlan 214:178+ N '64
Memento of twenty-five years. Life 56:25 Ap 17 '64

MYELIN. See Nerves

MYER emporium. See Melbourne, Australia—Stores

MYERS, C. Kilmer
Episcopalians: muddling through vs. creative outreach. Christian Cent 80:1459-62 N 27 '63

MYERS, Charles A.
Exportability of the American system of industrial relations. Mo Labor R 86:268-70 Mr '63

MYERS, Cora H.
Work rules for job-holding mothers. Parents Mag 39:46-7+ Ja '64

MYERS, Jack. See Holton, R. W. jt. auth.

MYERS, Jesse W.
Clarification at College Park. V. E. Lowder. Christian Cent 81:500-2 Ap 15 '64

MYERS, Joel
Joel Myers and Blenko glass. Craft Horiz 24: 36-7 Mr '64

MYERS, Kurtz
Record review. por Library J 88:1813-17 My 1 '63

MYERS, M. Scott
Who are your motivated workers? Harvard Bsns R 42:73-88 Ja '64
MYERS, Marie S.
Why uniforms? America 109:630-2 N 16 '63
MYERS, Marshall R. jr, and Kahn, M. D.
Transistors for hi-fi: promise of progress. Electr World 71:42-3+ Ap '64
MYERS, Robert D.
Alcohol consumption in rats: effects of intracranial injections of ethanol. bibliog Science 142:240-1 O 11 '63
MYERS, Ronald E. See Black, P. jt. auth.
MYERS, Walter
F.D.R. vs. the Democratic party. Esquire 59: 115+ Mr '63
MYERS, Winifred A.
How to collect autograph letters and manuscripts. Hobbies 68:110-12+ Je '63
MYKONOS (island)
Rough map of Greece. P. L. Adams. il Atlan 211:66-71 My '63
See also
Architecture, Domestic—Mykonos (island)
MYOCARDIAL infarctions. See Heart—Diseases
MYOGLOBIN
Abnormal myoglobin ultraviolet spectrum in Duchenne type of progressive muscular dystrophy. K. Miyoshi and others. bibliog Science 142:490-1 O 25 '63
Myoglobin and the structure of proteins; address, December 11, 1962. J. C. Kendrew. bibliog il Science 139:1259-66 Mr 29 '63
Myoglobin: inherited structural variation in man. S. H. Boyer and others. bibliog il Science 140:1228-31 Je 14 '63
MYOINOSITOL. See Inositol
MYOPIA; story. See Windham, D.
MYOSIN
Chromatography of ribonuclease-treated myosin extracts from early embryonic chick muscle. E. F. Baril and others. bibliog il Science 146:413-14 O 16 '64
5-bromodeoxyuridine: effect on myogenesis in vitro. F. Stockdale and others. bibliog il Science 146:533-5 O 23 '64
Myosin substructure: isolation of a helical subunit from heavy meromyosin. S. Lowey. bibliog il Science 145:597-9 Ag 7 '64
MYRA; story. See Stanton, W.
MYRDAL, Gunnar
It's time to face the future; excerpts from Challenge to affluence. Look 27:96+ N 19 '63
Liberalism and the Negro. Commentary 37: 25-42 Mr '64
Tax less spend more? that's what Myrdal advises; summary of address, December 3, 1963. U S News 55:26 D 16 '63
War on poverty. New Repub 150:14-16 F 8 '64
You can't change social situation by laws; interview. por U S News 55:84-6 N 18 '63
about
Good friend and critic. por Bsns W p57-8+ D 14 '63
Poor become poorer. B. Tufty. Sci N L 83: 387 Je 22 '63
MYRES, J. N. L.
Bodley's librarian praises great academic libraries of US; excerpts from address, July 1963. Library J 88:3810 O 15 '63
MYRIAPODS. See Millipeds
MYRSINE africana. See African boxwood
MYSTERIES, Religious
Greek myths and Christian mystery, by H. Rahner; tr. by B. Battershaw. Review
Christian Cent 80:1307 O 23 '63. B. Cooke
MYSTERY
Liturgy and mystery. B. Leeming. America 109:153-5 Ag 17 '63
MYSTERY stories. See Detective and mystery stories
MYSTERY writers of America
Nominees for 1963 MWA Edgar awards. Pub W 185:37 Ap 13 '64
MYSTIC, Conn.
Mystic seaport. A. G. Melvin. il Hobbies 68: 130 Je '63
MYSTIC seaport museum, Mystic, Conn.
Profiles; two-week cruise aboard sloop Merrywend. M. M. Hunt. New Yorker 40:60+ S 5 '64
Short stop on a long trail. L. Barry. il Pop Phot 54:24+ Mr '64
MYSTICISM
Poets and mystics. J. Fandel. Commonweal 79:309-10 D 6 '63
Religious authority & mysticism: excerpts from On the kabbalah and its symbolism. G. Scholem. Commentary 38:31-9 N '64
MYTHICAL animals. See Animals, Mythical
MYTHOLOGY
Masks of God: occidental mythology, by J. Campbell. Review
New Repub 150:24+ Je 27 '64. A. Watts
Myth motif in modern fiction. B. H. Deal. Writer 76:12-14+ N '63
Of apples and other myths. P. Tabori. il N Y Times Mag p 182+ Ap 7 '63
To tell the truth; myth as vehicle of religious truth. J. A. Sanders. Christian Cent 81:763-6 Je 10 '64
MYTHOLOGY, Greek
Greek myths and Christian mystery, by H. Rahner; tr. by B. Battershaw. Review
Christian Cent 80:1307 O 23 '63. B. Cooke
Sanctuary of Artemis at Brauron. J. Papadimitriou. il Sci Am 208:110-16+ bibliog(p 183) Je '63
Caricatures and cartoons
Greek mythology. Steig. New Yorker 40:54-7 N 14 '64
MYTHOLOGY, Hebrew
Hebrew myths: the book of Genesis, by R. Graves and R. Patai. Review
Reporter il 30:45-6 Ap 9 '64. M. Hadas
MYTHOLOGY, Indian (American Indian) See Indians of North America—Religion and mythology; Indians of South America—Religion and mythology
MYTHOLOGY in art
Aboriginal art and mythology; bark paintings. S. Scougall and P. C. Gifford. il Natur Hist 74:46-53 bibliog(p70) F '65
MYTHS. See Mythology
MYXOMYCETES
Growth of the cellular slime mold polysphondylium pallidum in a simple nutrient medium. M. Sussman. bibliog il Science 139: 338 Ja 25 '63
How slime molds communicate; dictyostelium. J. T. Bonner. il Sci Am 209:84-6+ bibliog(p 140) Ag '63
Shuttle-streaming: synchronization with heat production in slime mold. R. D. Allen and others. bibliog il Science 142:1485-7 D 13 '63
Thymidine incorporation by mitochondria in physarum polycephalum. E. Gutes and S. Guttes. bibliog il Science 145:1057-8 S 4 '64

N

NAACP. See National association for the advancement of colored people
NAB. See National association of broadcasters
NAC. See National association of counties
NACS. See National association of college stores
NADGE (NATO air defense ground environment) See Semi-automatic ground environment system
NAE. See National academy of engineering; National association of Evangelicals
NAEA. See National art education association
NAFSA. See National association of foreign student advisers
NAIC. See National association of investment clubs
NAL (National agricultural library) See United States—Agriculture, Department of —Library
NALC. See Negro American labor council
NAM. See National association of manufacturers
NAMRU. See United States—Navy—Naval medical research unit
NARAS. See National academy of recording arts and sciences
NAREB. See National association of real estate boards
NASA. See United States—National aeronautics and space administration
NASA 136. See Radio converters
NASD. See National association of securities dealers
NASSP. See National association of secondary-school principals
NASW. See National association of science writers
NATA. See National aviation trades association
NATO. See North Atlantic treaty organization
NATWA. See National auto and truck wreckers association
NAVH. See National aid to visually handicapped, incorporated, San Francisco

NBA. See National basketball association; National book awards
NBAA. See National business aircraft association
NBC. See National book committee; National broadcasting company
NBC television opera theater. See Television broadcasting—Operas
NBER. See National bureau of economic research
NCA. See National council on alcoholism
NCAA. See National collegiate athletic association
NCARB. See National council of architectural registration boards
NCATE. See National council for accreditation of teacher education
NCC. See National council of the churches of Christ in the United States of America
NCCW. See National council of Catholic women
NCEA. See National Catholic educational association
NCFA. See North Carolina forestry association
NCGE. See National council for geographic education
NCOA. See National council on the aging
NCSS. See National council for the social studies
NCTE. See National council of teachers of English
NCWC. See National Catholic welfare conference
NDBA fuel boat drags. See Motor boat racing
NDEA (National defense education act) See School laws and legislation—United States
NEA. See National education association
NEA journal
Editor's notebook (cont) M. S. Fenner. NEA J 52:64 Ap '63
NEAR (National emergency alarm repeater) See Air raid warning systems
NEC. See National electronics conference
NERVA (nuclear engine for rocket vehicle application) See Rockets, Atomic powered
NET. See National education television and radio center
NFEAC. See National foundation for education in American citizenship
NFL. See National football league
NFO. See National farmers organization
NHL. See National hockey league
NICB. See National industrial conference board
NIH. See United States—National institutes of health
NLM. See United States—National library of medicine
NLMA. See National lumber manufacturers association
NLRB. See United States—National labor relations board
NLW. See National library week
NMB. See United States—National mediation board
NMSC. See National merit scholarship corporation
NMSS (National multipurpose space station) See Space stations
NMU. See National maritime union of America
NORAD. See North American air defense command
NPA. See National planning association
NRA. See National recreation association
NRC (National referral center for science and technology) See United States—National referral center for science and technology
NRMA. See National retail merchants association
NSA. See United States—National security agency; United States national student association
NSBA. See National school boards association
NSC. See United States—National security council
NSCTE. See National society of college teachers of education
NSF. See United States—National science foundation
NSF-I. See Science fairs
NSIA. See National security industrial association
NSM. See Northern student movement
NSSFNS. See National scholarship service and fund for Negro students
NTL. See National training laboratory in group development
NTSC. See National television systems committee
NUT (National union of teachers) See Teachers unions

N. W. Ayer and son. See Ayer, N. W. and son
NYPL. See New York public library
NYSE (New York stock exchange) See Stock exchange—New York (city)
NYSSA. See New York society of security analysts
NYU. See New York university
NAAR, Jon
Travel. Vogue 144:74 S 15 '64
NABB, Edward H.
Engines. Yachting 115:44-5+ Ap '64
Engines: postwar to tomorrow (cont) Yachting 113:58-9+ F '63
What's with outdrives? Yachting 113:45-7+ Je '63
NABOKOV, Dimitri
(tr) See Nabokov, V. Lik
(tr) See Nabokov, V. Terra incognita: Triangle within circle
NABOKOV, Vladimir
Art of the duel; essay from his translation of Pushkin's Eugene Onegin. por Esquire 60:54-5 Jl '63
Lik; story, tr. by D. Nabokov. New Yorker 40:64-8 O 10 '64
Luzhin defense; story. tr. by M. Scammell. New Yorker 40:40-50 My 9; 48-56 My 16 '64
Lyre; story, tr. by M. Scammell. New Yorker 39:44-50+ Ap 13 '63
Terra incognita; story, tr. by D. Nabokov. New Yorker 39:34-7 My 18 '63
Triangle within circle; story; tr. by D. Nabokov. New Yorker 39:37-41 Mr 23 '63
Visit to the museum; story. Esquire 59:110-11 Mr '63
What Vladimir Nabokov thinks of his work, his life; interview, ed. by P. D. Smith. por Vogue 141:152-5 Mr 1 '63

about

Art of Nabokov; excerpts. A. Pryce-Jones. Harper 226:97-101 Ap '63
Grandmaster Nabokov. J. Updike. New Repub 151:15-18 S 26 '64
Master of versatility. il pors Life 57:61-2+ N 20 '64
WLB biography. L. Ash. por Wilson Lib Bul 38:410+ Ja '64
NABRIT, James M. Jr
In the shadow of the Capitol. Sat R 46:27-8 My 25 '63
Panelists dissent on the ascent. Sat R 46:26-7 Je 29 '63
NACE, Raymond L.
Science in action; new age for hydrology. Natur Hist 74:63-4+ Ja '65
Water: a common problem. Bul Atomic Sci 21:32-4 Ja '65
Water of the world. Natur Hist 73:10-19 Ja '64
NACHMAN, Ralph L. and Engle, R. L. Jr
Gamma globulin: unmasking of hidden antigenic sites on light chains. bibliog Science 145:167-8 Jl 10 '64
NACHMANN, Fritz
Peace of mind on a fragment of wood and steel; sport is luging. il por Sports Illus 20:56-7 Ja 27 '64
NADASDY, Leonard
Goldwater, Rockefeller, and the Young Republicans. M. S. Evans. il Nat R 15:97-100+ Ag 13 '63
NADEL, Michael
Pace of wilderness classification. Liv Wildn 85:16-24 Wint '64
Wilderness council in Alaska. Liv Wildn 84:47 Sum '63
Wilderness council in Wyoming. Liv Wildn 82:38-9 Winter '62
NADER, Ralph
Fashion or safety: Detroit makes your choice. Nation 197:214-16 O 12 '63
NADLER, Gerald
Broader outlook for research; letter. Science 141:763 Ag 30 '63
NADLER, Marcus
Boom raises three challenges. Nations Bsns 52:31-3 My '64
Stock market trends to watch. Nations Bsns 52:90+ D '64
Tax cut: key to '64 growth. por Nations Bsns 51:31-3+ O '63
NADLER, Ronald D. See Whalen, R. E. jt. auth.
NAEF, Dale
Draggin' the waves. Hot Rod 16:112 S '63
Rooster tales. Hot Rod 17:102-3 Ap; 106-7 My; 102-3 Je '64
NAESS, Ragnar D.
Ahead: a period of lower prices; interview. por U S News 55:51-2 S 16 '63

NAESS, Ragnar D.—*Continued*
In stocks, a reaction will begin soon; interview. por(p55) U S News 56:57-8 Mr 2 '64
People fear inflation; interview. por U S News 54:43-4 Ap 22 '63
NAGARE, Masayuki
Stone crazy. il por Time 82:74-5+ S 20 '63
NAGAS. See India—Native races
NAGASAKI
Dangerous intersection; value of experiences of Hiroshima and Nagasaki. W. T. Ellis. Sat R 46:31 Ag 24 '63
NAGEL, E. L. and others
Anesthesia for the bottlenose dolphin, tursiops truncatus. bibliog Science 146:1591-3 D 18 '64
NAGEL, Ernest
Books. Sci Am 209:145-6+ O '63
NAGEL, Jack
Maestro tunes his teen ski stars; with photographs by M. Kauffman. Sports Illus 18:24-30 F 11 '63
NAGEL, Ronald L. and Ranney, Helen M.
Haptoglobin binding capacity of certain abnormal hemoglobins. bibliog Science 144:1014-15 My 22 '64
NAGLE, Robert E. See Pierson, R. W. jt. auth.
NAGLE, Tonia. See Casey, G. jt. auth.
NAGRIN, Daniel
Tamiris Nagrin dance company at 92nd street Y. J. Maskey. Dance Mag 38:69 F '64
NAGY, Alexander, jr
Traffic school for preschoolers. il PTA Mag 57:21 Je '63
NAGY, Bartholomew
Somebody up there like us. R. O'Brien. Esquire 60:185-7+ D '63
NAGY, Sibyl Moholy-. See Moholy-Nagy, S.
NAHAS, G. G. See Matteo, R. S. jt. auth.
NAHUNTA, Ga.
Now a great place for teens. K. Davis. il Farm J 88:88-9 O '64
NAIDU, Leela
Individualists; Mlle's annual Merit awards. por Mlle 58:74 Ja '64
NAILS (anatomy)
How fast do your nails grow? Sci Digest 54:84 Jl '63
What can be done for fingernail damage? Good H 156:163 My '63
NAIPAUL, V. S.
Night watchman's occurrence book; story. Sat Eve Post 236:72-5 S 28 '63
Trinidad. Mlle 59:187 My '64
NAIR, Kamala
Day the river spoke; story. UNESCO Courier 17:26-31 Ap '64
NAIROBI, Kenya
Clubhouse dues; abolishing racial discrimination Newsweek 62:44+ O 28 '63
NAISMITH, Grace
D and C: most common operation on women. Todays Health 42:18-19+ Jl '64
Parent and child. N Y Times Mag p 109 N 24 '63
Premarital examination: its importance to both the man and the woman. Todays Health 42:50-1+ Ap '64
Why men should know more about menstruation. Todays Health 41:22-3+ S '63
NAJAN, Nala
Great discovery of royal Chhau. F. Bowers. il pors Dance Mag 38:40-1+ Mr '64
NAKAHAMA, Manjiro
Ordeal of the Kanrin Maru; with editorial comment. E. V. Warinner. il Am Heritage 14:95-7 Ag '63
NAKAJIMA, Fusanori
Summer action, sailing. C. Steinhardt. il U S Camera 26:58-9+ Ag '63
NAKAJIMA, Shigehiro
Adaptation in stretch receptor neurons of crayfish. bibliog Science 146:1168-70 N 27 '64
NAKAMURA, Masaya
Nude, most difficult of all subjects. il U S Camera 27:64-5 Mr '64
NAKAMURA, Yutaka, and others
Eel electroplaques: spike electrogenesis without potassium activation. bibliog Science 146:266-8 O 9 '64
NAKASHIMA, George
When a cabinetmaker builds, he makes wood sing. il House B 105:154-5 Ap '63
NAKEDNESS. See Nudism
NAKIAN, Reuben
November contrasts. T. B. Hess. il Art N 63:30+ N '64
NAMATH, Joe
Mr Big of the bonus baby war. il pors Life 58:56D-57 Ja 15 '65
NAMES
See also
Corporations—Names
NAMES, Geographical
Paddington bows to Westminster. A. P. Herbert. il N Y Times Mag p70-1+ N 3 '63
Turn left at Spring Creek; Wyoming. M. Hagen. il Am For 70:30-1+ S '64
What's in a name? name-coining incidents during the exploration, conquest, and settlement of western hemisphere. W. A. Naughton. il Américas 16:27-31 D '64

Russia

Name's the shame; changes in Byelorussia. Time 84:24 Ag 21 '64
NAMES, Lunar
Lunar nomenclature. il Sky & Tel 28:342 D '64
NAMES, Personal
Ann or Anne? Newsweek 62:55 Jl 15 '63
Name-droppers; Swedish computers produce potential new names. Newsweek 62:55 Jl 8 '63
Notes and comment; spelling of proper names. New Yorker 40:39 Mr 7 '64
Of onomastics, foibles, and mercy. J. Ciardi. Sat R 47:24 S 26 '64
What's in a handle? association of personality characteristics with names. W. Cloud. Pop Sci 184:29-30 F '64
See also
Pseudonyms
NAMES, Scientific. See Botany—Nomenclature
NAMES of boats. See Boats—Names
NAMES of colors. See Color names
NAMES of horses. See Horses—Names
NAMES of plants. See Botany—Nomenclature
NAMES of products. See Trade names
NAMIAS, Jerome
Why we freeze. Bsns W p34 F 2 '63
NAMIER, Sir Lewis Bernstein
Common man's historian. por Time 81:89-91 F 8 '63
NAMING contests. See Competitions
NANAS, Edward
ABC's of movie sound. Pop Phot 53:100-1+ S '63
How to prepare a sound track. Pop Phot 53:76+ S '63
Light fantastic. Pop Electr 19:33-9+ Jl '63
Neatest trick since canning. Sat Eve Post 236:64-5 Je 1 '63
Photochromic glass: it darkens in light, clears in darkness. Pop Phot 54:38+ My '64
Slide-show sound track. Pop Phot 53:62-3+ S '63
Wanted: an electronic Paul Revere. Pop Electr 18:41-3+ F '63
Where is electronics leading photography? Pop Phot 54:78-9+ F '64
Writing the sound for your show. Pop Phot 53:57+ S '63
—See Bacon, W. S. jt. auth.
NANCE, Walter E.
Genetic control of hemoglobin synthesis. bibliog Science 141:123-30 Jl 12 '63
—and others.
Lactic dehydrogenase: genetic control in man. bibliog Science 142:1075-7 N 22 '63
NANDI, Satyabrata. See Ichinose, R. R. jt. auth.
NANES, Allan S.
Britain's strategic role. bibliog f Cur Hist 46:269-74 My '64
Weapons and men, 1964. bibliog f Cur Hist 47:12-17+ Jl '64
West German policy in West Europe. Cur Hist 44:214-18+ Ap '63
NANOPHYETUS salmincola. See Fishes—Diseases and pests
NANSEN, Fridtjof
1,000 days in frozen space. E. D. Fales, jr. il Pop Sci 182:42-4 Je '63
NANTUCKET ISLAND
Atlantic lure. R. L. Young. il Travel 121:62 My '64
Christmas on Nantucket. J. Peter and M. Kaytor. il Look 28:71-7 D 15 '64
Right little island. il Holiday 36:62-7 Ag '64
NAPERVILLE, Ill.
Find the faults first; electric distribution maintenance. J. O. Turner. il Am City 79:94 N '64
NAPIER, Arch
Hunting. Sports Illus 18:57-60 My 27 '63
NAPIER, Augustus
Aftertaste; poem. Sat R 46:62 D 28 '63
Lonely two; poem. Atlan 211:73 F '63
Old surprise; poem. Sat R 46:37 Je 8 '63
Out of time; poem. Sat R 46:23 Ag 10 '63
NAPIER, John
Signatures. R. Sward. Poetry 102:336-7 Ag '63
NAPKIN rings, holders, etc.
Trinket boxes from napkin rings. il Pop Mech 119:169 Je '63

NAPLES

Description

How they live and die in Naples; with photographs by Herbert List. V. De Sica. Horizon 5:49-59 S '63

Our far-flung correspondents. R. M. Coates. il New Yorker 39:176+ N 2 '63

Step by step through Naples. R. Deardorff. il Travel 119:55-9 My '63

NAPOLEON I, emperor of the French

Bonaparte in Egypt, by J. C. Herold. Review

Nation 197:94 Ag 24 '63. C. Sykes

Great confrontations: Napoleon and Alexander. J. C. Herold. il por Horizon 5:28-32 S '63

Napoleon and Josephine; the biography of a marriage, by F. Mossiker. Review

Sat R 48:89 Ja 2 '65. J. H. Plumb

Napoleon, by F. Markham. Review

Sat R 47:43 Ap 18 '64. J. H. Plumb

Napoleon legend, a new look. R. Payne. il pors N Y Times Mag p24-5+ Ap 5 '64

What killed Napoleon? Sci N L 84:84 Ag 10 '63

NAPOLEON III, emperor of the French

Operator and the emperors; with portfolio. L. Thomas. il por Am Heritage 15:4-23+ Ap '64

NAPOLEON street; story. See Bellow, S.

NARA, Japan

Inside the great building, the great Buddha. il Sunset 130:26-7 F '63

NARAYAN, R. K.

Horse and two goats; story. New Yorker 40:30-2 Ja 23 '65

NARCISSE, Louis H.

Kingdom of King Narcisse. L. Robinson. il pors Ebony 18:112+ Jl '63

NARCISSUS

Collectors' items: the smaller tulips and daffodils. J. Thibodeau. il Horticulture 42:28-30+ Ap '64

Daffodils are superb in containers. il Sunset 133:266 O '64

Drifts of daffodils. R. C. Hands. il Horticulture 41:314 Je '63

For narcissus gifts at Christmas. il Sunset 131:273 N '63

Gardener's month; miniature daffodils. il House & Gard 126:242-4 S '64

Grow paper white narcissus. B. Brinhart. il Pop Gard 15:18 Ja '64

How to hybridize daffodils. W. H. Wheeler. il Horticulture 42:20-1+ Ap '64

September is daffodil planting time. R. C. Allen. il Horticulture 42:34-7+ S '64

What to do if your daffodils no longer bloom. B. Miles. il Flower Grower 51:25-6 My '64

NARCOTIC habit

Attack on dope. America 108:251-2 F 23 '63

Bridge for addicts. America 110:213 F 15 '64

British way with the junkie. G. Samuels. il N Y Times Mag p37+ O 18 '64

Cold turkey inhumane. F. Marley. Sci N L 85:102 F 15 '64

Dilemma for drug addicts; current laws. J. M. Murtagh. il America 108:740-2 My 25 '63

Dope invades the suburbs. R. P. Goldman. il Sat Eve Post 237:19-25 Ap 4 '64

Drug addicts need medicine not punishment. Sci N L 84:4 Jl 6 '63

Drug addicts who cure each other. L. Robinson. il Ebony 18:116-18+ F '63

Experimental narcotic addiction. J. R. Weeks. il Sci Am 210:46-52 Mr '64

Narcotic and drug abuse: report of Advisory commission prescribes for old problems, new dangers. J. Walsh. Science 143:662-6 F 14 '64; Discussion. 144:135-6 Ap 10 '64

New approach; more humane treatment. il Newsweek 61:94 Ap 15 '63

People get hooked. R. S. Baker. Commentary 35:243-6 Mr '63; Reply with rejoinder. E. H. Kaplan. 36:171 Ag '63

People versus Baby. G. Samuels. il N Y Times Mag p40-1+ Ja 17 '65

Preaching the monkey off their backs: Teen challenge centers. il Time 84:43 Ag 14 '64

Reflections on narcotics addiction. M. Hoffman. Yale R 54:17-30 O '64

Speaking out; give drugs to addicts. N. Straus, 3d. Sat Eve Post 237:6+ Ag 8 '64

Stealing and addiction are linked problems. Sci N L 84:3 Jl 6 '63

Teen-agers and the dope hazard. G. H. Millet. il Parents Mag 39:46-7+ My '64

Treatment of narcotic addicts. D. C. Cameron. Todays Health 41:12+ O '63

Withdrawal from drugs. Sci N L 84:4 Jl 6 '63

See also

Glue sniffing

Opium trade

Synanon House, Santa Monica, Calif.

NARCOTIC laws

Addiction: beginnings of wisdom. A. R. Lindesmith; reply. J. S. Williams, jr. Nation 197:inside cover O 26 '63

British way with the junkie. G. Samuels. il N Y Times Mag p37+ O 18 '64

Narcotic and drug abuse: report of Advisory commission prescribes for old problems, new dangers. J. Walsh. Science 143:662-6 F 14 '64; Discussion. 144:135-6 Ap 10 '64

Questions and answers; concerning laws. M. Mead. Redbook 120:28 Mr '63

Reflections on narcotics addiction. M. Hoffman. Yale R 54:17-30 O '64

Speaking out; give drugs to addicts. N. Straus, 3d. Sat Eve Post 237:6+ Ag 8 '64

NARCOTIC trade

Beautiful affair; French police make largest single confiscation of illegal drugs ever brought off. Time 84:44+ O 30 '64

Seldom seen; illegal narcotics. Time 83:19 Mr 27 '64

NARCOTICS

Chemical mind-changers. R. Coughlan. il Life 54:81-2+ Mr 15 '63

See also

Heroin

Stimulants

United Nations—Commission on narcotic drugs

NARCOTICS, Bureau of. See United States—Narcotics, Bureau of

NARDI, Marcia

Femelle de l'homme; poem. Atlan 214:126 O '64

NARELLE, Marie

Marie Narelle and Berrick Von Norden. J. Walsh. pors Hobbies 68:32-6+ F; 69:32-6+ Mr '64

NARROW gage railroads. See Railroads, Narrow gage

NARROW-mindedness. See Toleration

NARROWS bridge. See New York (city)—Bridges

NARUHITO, prince of Japan

Miya-chama at school. il por Newsweek 63:98 Ap 27 '64

NASCIMENTO, Edison Arantes de. See Arantes de Nascimento, E.

NASH, Charles

King Cotton. H. L. Masin. il por Sr Schol 83:22 Ja 17 '64

NASH, Jocelyn

There's an appeal on that! Yachting 113:51+ Mr '63

NASH, John W.

Shop pantograph copies anything. Pop Mech 119:164-8 Je '63

NASH, Michaux, jr

Permit no. 4. Outdoor Life 134:44-7+ N '64

NASH, Ogden

All good Americans go to Larousse; poem. New Yorker 39:36 F 23 '63

Armchair golfer; poem. Sports Illus 20:43 Je 15 '64

Bogy for Yogi; poem. New Yorker 40:32 S 5 '64

Boy and his room; poem; excerpts. McCalls 90:120 Je '63

Halloween hoodlums; go home! poem. Ladies Home J 81:66-7 O '64

I don't understand women (and I'm glad of it) Ladies Home J 81:58-9 S '64; Same abr. with title I still don't understand women. Read Digest 85:80-2 D '64

John Peel, shake hands with thirty-seven mamas; poem. New Yorker 40:42 Mr 14 '64

Kinsey report didn't upset me, either; poem. por Sat Eve Post 237:8 Mr 14 '64

Man can complain, can't he? poem. New Yorker 39:40 Ap 27 '63

Mr Twombley's ultimate triumph; poem. Atlan 211:97 Mr '63

O tempora, oh-oh! poem. New Yorker 40:30 F 22 '64

Thanks, possibly, to whatever powers may be; poem. New Yorker 39:40 Mr 23 '63

Thoughts thought while resting comfortably in Phillips House, Massachusetts general hospital, overlooking the Charles River; poem. Atlan 214:96 D '64

Will the real St Nicholas please stand up? and indeed he did; poem. Holiday 34:94-5 D '63

Yum yum, take it away; poem. Atlan 212:66 N '63

NASH, Peter W.

Canadians find a solution. America 111:302-3 S 19 '64

NASH, Philleo
Indian administration in the United States: address, December 6, 1962. Vital Speeches 29:278-83 F 15 '63
NASH, Vernon
Case for international control of weapons. Cur Hist 47:97-102+ Ag '64
NASHVILLE, Tenn.
Education
In Nashville schools. W. A. Bass. il NEA J 52:48-50 D '63
Music
Nashville sound; Country music festival. il Time 84:76+ N 27 '64
Negroes
Nashville creates biracial committee. Christian Cent 80:700 My 29 '63
New breed; militant new revolution. il Newsweek 63:21-2 My 11 '64
Newspapers
See also
Nashville banner
Politics and government
Metropolitics and professional political leadership: the case of Nashville. D. R. Grant. Ann Am Acad 353:72-83 My '64
Riots
Why riots erupted in a show case city. il U S News 56:6 My 11 '64
NASHVILLE banner
How headlines saved Nashville. W. Geier. Christian Cent 81:356-6 Mr 11 '64
NASLUND, Kenneth C. and Moreno, Alvaro
Concrete slabs made from precast boxes. Arch Rec 134:154-6 Jl '63
NASON, John W.
Credo of a college president; excerpt from address, October 13, 1962. Sch & Soc 91: 214-16 My 4 '63
Transient loyalty. Time 84:70 O 23 '64
NASON, Richard
Borrowing and the small businessman. Duns R 82:61-2+ O '63
Harvardmen vs. big business. Duns R 83:41-2+ Ja '64
S&Ls at the $1-billion crossroads. Duns R 82:43-5+ D '63
Should we abolish the inch? Duns R 82:35-6 S '63
Venture capital: money in a hurry. Duns R 82:34-5+ N '63
NASSAU COUNTY, N.Y.
Don't wait for stoppages. E. F. Gibbons and J. H. Peters. il Am City 79:79-81 N '64
Intellectual freedom committee protests censorship in Nassau. Library J 89:2300-1 Je 1 '64
Nassau County attacks automotive air pollution. K. Kowald. il Am City 78:109 O '63
NASSAU library system
Cooperate; but not too much. E. Moon. Library J 88:1841 My 1 '63; Discussion. 88: 2366+, il 3166-8, 4104+ Je 15, S 15, N 1 '63
Nassau library system experiments with direct access pilot study. Library J 89:4494 N 15 '64
Story falls in the silence; Family evening story hours. S. G. Shaw. il Wilson Lib Bul 39:179 O '64
NASSER, Gamal Abdel
Violent and vital world of Nasser; interview, ed. by R. Sherrod. pors Sat Eve Post 236: 17-23 My 25 '63
about
Atlantic report. Atlan 213:12+ Mr '64
Base motives? Newsweek 63:38 Mr 9 '64
Blowup in Mideast? Nasser puts squeeze on Israel. por U S News 54:22 My 20 '63
Camel driver. il pors Time 81:22-6 Mr 29 '63
Colonel sends his compliments. Nat R 17:10+ Ja 12 '65
Hex? il por Time 81:39 My 17 '63
If Khrushchev tries to bail out Nasser... il por U S News 56:63-4+ My 25 '64
Lucky Gamal; probable renomination for president. Time 85:26 Ja 22 '65
Man who wasn't there. il Time 84:45 O 16 '64
Nasserism stirs up the Middle East; photographs. N Y Times Mag p 10-11 My 19 '63
Nasser's brand of socialism. G. Gersh. Christian Cent 81:962-5 Jl 29 '64
Nasser's decade. A. Sherman. Commentary 36:151-7 Ag '63
Nasser's dream comes a cropper; resistance from Socialist resurrection party. il por Bsns W p46-8+ Ag 31 '63
Never-ended war of the Middle East. C. Sterling. il Reporter 29:24-8+ Jl 18 '63
Once again Nasser's dream of empire. il por U S News 54:74-5 Mr 18 '63
Our Yemen policy: pursuit of a mirage. P. Horton. il Reporter 29:28-35 O 24 '63
Race to help Nasser. il por U S News 56:70 Je 8 '64
Sea & tympany. Time 85:34-5 Ja 1 '65
Shifting sands of Arab union. il Sr Schol 83:8-11 Ja 17 '64
So near, yet so far. il por Time 81:27 Mr 22 '63
Who's wooing who? il por Time 81:26+ Mr 1 '63
Why Nasser acts the way he does. il por U S News 58:30-1 Ja 4 '65
NAST, Thomas
Man of conscience. R. L. Reynolds. il Am Heritage 14:85-7 F '63
NASTURTIUMS
Nearly failure-proof nasturtium. O. K. Moore. il House B 106:170+ Mr '64
Sunny, peppery nasturtium. M. A. Roche. il Flower Grower 50:54-5 Je '63
NATALIA Petrovna; opera. See Hoiby, L.
NATARAJAN, S.
WCOTP builds a world community of the teaching profession. por NEA J 52:30-1 O '63
NATCHEZ, Miss.
Notes for a gazetteer. P. Hamburger. New Yorker 39:110-14 Mr 2 '63
Time bombs in the Mississippi. E. D. Fales, jr. il Pop Sci 182:124-30+ Ap '63
NATHAN, George Jean
George Jean Nathan: superlative dandy. C. Angoff. New Repub 150:17-20 Ja 4 '64
NATHAN, Leonard E.
Apologia; poem. New Repub 148:22 F 23 '63
Fathers and sons; Moods of a matchmaker; poems. Poetry 101:339-42 F '63
Remember to close the door as you go out; Signs; Winter tune; poems. Poetry 104:224-6 Jl '64
about
Six poets. J. Woods. Poetry 104:110-11 My '64
NATHAN, Max, jr. See Meyer, D. A. jt. auth.
NATHAN, Maxwell
How to sell the voter. Recreation 56:383-4 O '63
NATHAN, Otto
Economics of permanent peace. Bul Atomic Sci 19:21-4 Je '63
NATHAN, Paul
Fifty-fifty split; reprint and book club royalties. Pub W 184:19-21 D 30 '63
Medical magic. Parents Mag 39:43+ N '64
Rights and permissions. See issues of Publishers' weekly
Wonderland of subsidiary rights. Sat R 46: 58-9+ D 14 '63
NATHAN, Simon
Flashbulb or speedlight? U S Camera 26:44-7+ F '63
Polaroid back for Hasselblad. U S Camera 26:14 Je '63; 27:26+ F '64
Seven new speedlights: how do they stack up? U S Camera 27:43-5 Mr '64
70mm, fad or future? U S Camera 26:33-5 My '63
Simon sez. See issues of U.S. camera to June 1963
Swinging lady with the red hatbox from Allentown, Pa. U S Camera 26:60-1+ D '63
Wide field pictures. il U S Camera 26:54-61+ O '63
NATION (periodical)
End of an episode; the Nation restored to the approved library list for high schools. Nation 196:111 F 9 '63
NATIONAL academy of ballet
Thalia Mara and the National academy of ballet. E. Palatsky. il Dance Mag 38:26-8+ F '64
NATIONAL academy of engineering
Engineers: plans for playing broader national role include National academy of engineering. J. Walsh. Science 144:980-2 My 22 '64
NAE: search for a form produces a National academy of engineering in a partnership with NAS. J. Walsh. il Science 146:1661-2 D 25 '64
NATIONAL academy of foreign affairs. See United States—National academy of foreign affairs (proposed)
NATIONAL academy of recording arts and sciences
New record award. Hi Fi 13:29 My '63
NATIONAL academy of religion and mental health. See Academy of religion and mental health

NATIONAL academy of sciences
Abstracts of papers presented at meetings, 1963-1964. bibliog il Science 140:378-86; 144: 559-69; 146:422-35 Ap 26 '63, My 1, O 16 '64
Antarctica; the international laboratory. A. P. Crary. il Bul Atomic Sci 20:27-30 Ja '64
Birth control: National academy issues report calling for major effort in population planning. D. S. Greenberg. Science 140: 281-2 Ap 19 '63; Reply. H. Frederiksen. 143:197 Ja 17 '64
Centennial of science. Sci N L 84:243-4 O 19 '63
Committee on science and public policy Federal support of science: a formula for cooperation; excerpts from Federal support of basic research in institutions of higher learning. Science 143:1300-3 Mr 20 '64; Discussion. 144:485-6 My 1 '64
Cooperative research: biologists plan international study program. E. Langer. Science 143:455 Ja 31 '64
Decade astronomy plan. A. Ewing. Sci N L 86:357 D 5 '64
International atmospheric study urged. R. D. Hibben. il Aviation W 78:135+ Je 17 '63
Long-range planning for American astronomy. il Sky & Tel 29:3+ Ja '65
Money for science: NAS studies likely to have large influence on future of government support; with editorial comment. D. S. Greenberg. Science 146:475, 508-9 O 23 '64
NAE: search for a form produces a National academy of engineering in a partnership with NAS. J. Walsh. il Science 146:1661-2 D 25 '64
NAS celebrates 100th year; summary of address. J. F. Kennedy. il Sci N L 84:274 N 2 '63
NAS elects new members. Sci N L 85:290 My 9 '64
National academy of sciences: 100th anniversary program. L. Campbell. il Science 142:561-3 N 1 '63
National academy: public policy group, headed by Kistiakowsky, seems bound for important role; Committee on science and public policy. D. S. Greenberg. Science 141:27-8 Jl 5 '63
Next 100 years; 100th anniversary. Newsweek 62:69 N 4 '63
Population control; concerning report. New Repub 148:7 Ap 27 '63; Reply. L. H. Day. 149:31 Jl 6 '63
Science academy wants post-Apollo priority for unmanned planetary shots. H. Taylor. Miss & Roc 15:11 N 2 '64
Space: National academy panel recommends exploration of Mars as major goal in 1971-85 period. J. Walsh. Science 146:1025-7 N 20 '64
Technical talent utilization shifts urged. P. J. Klass. Aviation W 81:20 Jl 20 '64
Where is science taking us? the depths of the sea. il Sat R 46:52-3 N 2 '63

Committee on science and public policy

Federal support of science: a formula for cooperation; excerpts from Federal support of basic research in institutions of higher learning. Science 143:1300-3 Mr 20 '64
Ground-based astronomy: a ten-year program; summary of report. Science 146:1641-8 D 25 '64
NAS study: public policy group offers prescription to promote science-government cooperation. D. S. Greenberg. Science 143: 1304-5 Mr 20 '64

Committee on utilization of scientific and engineering manpower

Better use of scientists. Sci N L 86:34 Jl 18 '64

NATIONAL academy of television arts and sciences. See Academy of television arts and sciences

NATIONAL advisory board council for grazing districts. See United States—National advisory board council for grazing districts

NATIONAL advisory council on the arts. See United States—Advisory council on the arts

NATIONAL aeronautics and space administration. See United States—National aeronautics and space administration

NATIONAL aeronautics association
See also
Collier trophy

NATIONAL agricultural library. See United States—Agriculture. Department of—Library

NATIONAL aid to visually handicapped, incorporated, San Francisco
NAVH helps the visually handicapped; school children with sight problems. L. Marchi. il Library J 88:4821-2+ D 15 '63

NATIONAL air museum. See Smithsonian institution—National air and space museum

NATIONAL airlines, incorporated
Flying to success upside down; progress of National airlines. il Time 82:73 Jl 26 '63

NATIONAL airport, Washington, D.C. See Washington, D.C.—Airports

NATIONAL alliance of television and electronic service associations
Time for reappraisals. W. A. Stocklin. Electr World 70:6 D '63

NATIONAL amateur astronomers convention
National convention in Denver. il Sky & Tel 28:196-200 O '64

NATIONAL amateur golf tournament. See Golf —Tournaments

NATIONAL archives. See United States—National archives

NATIONAL art education association
NAEA awards. Am Artist 27:8 Mr '63
Student art: International school art program. il NEA J 53:31-3 Mr '64

NATIONAL association for better radio and television
Our timid watchdog: FCC. Consumer Rep 29: 110-11 Mr '64

NATIONAL association for mental health
Bridge at West Point; NAMH-NAB joint conference on mental health dramas on television. R. L. Shayon. Sat R 46:41 My 25 '63
Far right's fight against mental health. D. Robinson. il Look 29:30-2 Ja 26 '65

NATIONAL association for the advancement of colored people
Angels are white; who pays the bills for civil rights? R. Cleghorn. New Repub 149: 12-14 Ag 17 '63
Angry at everybody. il Time 82:18-19 Jl 12 '63
Awful roar. il Time 82:9-14 Ag 30 '63
Constitutional commandos; Manhattan's N.A.A.C.P. legal defense and educational fund, inc. il Time 83:66 Je 5 '64
Direction of the March. R. L. Zangrando. bibliog il Negro Hist Bul 27:60-4 D '63
From satisfaction to fury. Time 84:20 Jl 3 '64
Fund; Evers scholarship fund for Evers children. New Yorker 39:21 Ag 31 '63
GM and the Negro; Detroit NAACP prepares for demonstrations. il Bsns W p36 Ap 18 '64
Hotter fires; friction between organizations; with report by K. Fleming. il Newsweek 62:19-21 Jl 1 '63
How the NAACP stands on intermarriage. U S News 55:9 S 2 '63
NAACP Freedom spectacular; all-star TV show. il Ebony 19:57-8+ Jl '64
Negro in the Supreme court, 1954-1964; address, 1964. R. L. Gill. bibliog Negro Hist Bul 28:52+ D '64
Profile of the NAACP; America's oldest and largest civil rights organization. Negro Hist Bul 27:74-6 Ja '64
Race and radicalism: the NAACP and the Communist party in conflict, by W. Record. Review
Nation 198:658 Je 29 '64. J. Weinstein
Testing the new law: legalists, publicists, activists. P. De Lissovoy. il Nation 199:7-10 Jl 13 '64
They're not going to stop. Time 81:31 Ap 19 '63
Two ways: Black Muslim and N.A.A.C.P. G. Samuels. il N Y Times Mag p26-7+ My 12 '63
What the American Negro wants; interview. R. Wilkins. il U S News 54:46-52 Ap 29 '63

NATIONAL association for the advancement of white people
Fearmongers; with report by B. Bettelheim. il Life 56:71-8+ F 7 '64

NATIONAL association of broadcasters
Bridge at West Point; NAMH-NAB joint conference on mental health dramas on television. R. L. Shayon. Sat R 46:41 My 25 '63
Church looks at television; alleged racial discrimination on television stations in Jackson, Miss. R. L. Shayon. Sat R 47:36 My 16 '64
Ether business; annual convention. Newsweek 63:72 Ap 20 '64
Fewer commercials. New Repub 148:4-5 Ap 13 '63
Moving the spirits; whisky commercials. Time 83:80 Mr 27 '64
NAB president. America 111:84 Jl 25 '64
Twenty-two straight commercials. Newsweek 61:87 Ap 15 '63

NATIONAL association of college stores
Big retailer on campus; university co-op at the University of Wisconsin. il Bsns W p42-4 F 2 '63
Doubts that commercial wholesalers can succeed; with editorial comment. J. P. Dessauer. Pub W 185:27-8, 61 Je 15 '64
First three prize-winners in NACS merchandising contest. il Pub W 185:68-70 My 25 '64
NACS associates oppose NACSCORP paperback service. Pub W 185:26-7 My 11 '64
NACS: can college stores cope with the paperback boom? summary of addresses. B. J. Larson; M. J. Goodman. il Pub W 184:16-21 D 16 '63
NACS: college stores' convention stresses general books, education; symposium, with editorial comment. il Pub W 185:30-45, 53 My 25 '64
NACS: Doubleday-N.Y.U. merchandising seminar; symposium; with editorial comment. il Pub W 183:22-35, 42 My 20 '63
NACS: making the college store a force in education; symposium. il Pub W 183:27-33 My 27 '63
NACS to wholesale three commercial paperback lines. Pub W 183:39-40 F 25 '63
NACSCORP projects seven-fold sales increase this year. Pub W 186:25-6 Ag 17 '64
1963-64 in review. Pub W 185:93-4 Ja 20 '64; 187:92 Ja 18 '65
Wholesaler questions NACS paperback jobbing scheme. A. Rabinovitz. Pub W 183: 56-7 Je 10 '63

NATIONAL association of counties
Big squeeze in your back yard. J. Prokop. il Am For 69:6-7+ Ap '63
Policy for county parks and recreation; condensed statement. Recreation 57:270-1 Je '64

NATIONAL association of engine and boat manufacturers
Boating comes of age. J. E. Choate. il Yachting 117:94-7+ Ja '65
What made boating grow? J. E. Choate. il Motor B 112:36+ O '63

NATIONAL association of Evangelicals
Donors warned against missionary swindlers. Christian Cent 80:796 Je 19 '63
Down the middle; annual convention. Time 81:82 My 3 '63
N.A.E. on church-state. D. M. Kelley. Christian Cent 80:454-5 Ap 10 '63
N.A.E. turns constructive. Christian Cent 80:607 My 8 '63; Reply. W. S. Mooneyham. 80:782 Je 12 '63
Time was right; racial justice. P. B. Mather. Christian Cent 81:653-4 My 13 '64

NATIONAL association of foreign student advisers
Foreign student in 1970. Sch & Soc 91:232+ Sum '63
Foreign students in America: problems, progress, and prospects; address, April 24, 1963. L. D. Battle. Dept State Bul 48:752-8 My 13 '63

NATIONAL association of home builders
More house for less money; Research house, Rockville, Md. A. J. Maher. il Pop Mech 120:140-3 N '63

NATIONAL association of independent schools
Meeting, 1963. E. Osgood. Sch & Soc 91:243-4 Sum '63
Meeting, 1964. E. Osgood. Sch & Soc 92:241 Sum '64

NATIONAL association of investment clubs
Investment clubs: how they look today. il Changing T 19:29-31 Ja '65

NATIONAL association of manufacturers
Flying trade show. il Bsns W p76+ D 12 '64
NAM and ILO. America 110:132 Ja 25 '64

NATIONAL association of parents and teachers
Cited for service: our National PTA chairmen. il PTA Mag 58:18-19 My '64

NATIONAL association of real estate boards
Breaking the housing barrier; dual housing market. E. Marciniak. Commonweal 77:588-91 Mr 1 '63
No time for silence; question of integration. America 109:2 Jl 6 '63

NATIONAL association of science writers
Science writing: a growing profession. P. C. Fraley and E. Ubell. il Bul Atomic Sci 19: 19-22 D '63

NATIONAL association of secondary-school principals
Meeting, 1963. Sr Schol 82:1T-2T+ Mr 6 '63
Meeting, 1963. D. W. Hunt. Sch & Soc 91:243 Sum '63
Meeting, 1964. il Sr Schol 84:1T-3T F 28 '64

NATIONAL association of securities dealers
Neither all bad nor all good; Cohen report on the Nation's securities markets. il Newsweek 62:64-7 Ag 19 '63
New protection plan on stocks. U S News 54:107 Je 17 '63

NATIONAL association of social workers
Powerless hero; new CBS program, East side, West side. R. L. Shayon. Sat R 46:40 N 2 '63; Reply. Mrs F. Decorato. 46:30 D 7 '63

NATIONAL Audubon society
Audubon wildlife films. C. W. Buchheister. il Audubon Mag 65:145 My '63
Convention to remember; with excerpts from addresses. J. Vosburgh. il Audubon Mag 65:26-31 Ja '63
Gift of a foresighted woman. C. W. Buchheister. Audubon Mag 65:144 My '63
Meeting, 1963. C. Callison. il Audubon Mag 65:202-3 Jl '63
President reports to you; excerpt from report. C. W. Buchheister. Audubon Mag 65:24-5+ Ja '63
Rachel Carson memorial fund for research; with tributes to R. Carson. C. W. Buchheister. Audubon Mag 66:208-10 Jl '64
60th annual convention. J. Vosburgh. il Audubon Mag 67:32-7 Ja '65
Udall's address paces a lively convention; with excerpts from addresses. J. Vosburgh. il Audubon Mag 66:38-47 Ja '64
See also
Audubon medal
Audubon nature centers

NATIONAL auto and truck wreckers association
That's where the old cars go; auto graveyards. J. Keats. il N Y Times Mag p42+ S 20 '64

NATIONAL automobile show. See Automobiles—Exhibitions

NATIONAL aviation facilities experimental center. See United States—Federal aviation agency

NATIONAL aviation trades association
Airlines off course? D. Teetor. il Flying 75: 64-6 S '64

NATIONAL bagasse products corporation
Putting waste to work. il Bsns W p 137-8 Mr 23 '63

NATIONAL ballet company
First steps; debut at Lisner auditorium, Washington, D.C. A. Todd. il Mus Am 83:16 Mr '63
National ballet at Brooklyn academy of music. J. Maskey. Dance Mag 37:151+ D '63; 38: 18+ D '64
New company gets a Washington inauguration. A. Todd. il Dance Mag 37:38-9+ Mr '63

NATIONAL ballet of Canada
National ballet of Canada at Brooklyn academy of music. D. Hering. il Dance Mag 38:62-3 Mr '64
North of the border; National ballet of Canada at Brooklyn academy. R. Krokover. Mus Am 84:46-7 Mr '64

NATIONAL ballet of Holland. See Ballet—Netherlands

NATIONAL banks. See Banks and banking—United States

NATIONAL Baptist convention, USA, Incorporated. See Baptists in the United States

NATIONAL baseball hall of fame and museum
Day when all the sentiment stands still; Cooperstown on Hall of fame day. Sports Illus 19:56-7 Ag 19 '63

NATIONAL basketball association
Basketball's Irish czar; J. W. Kennedy. T. Smith. il Sat Eve Post 237:54-5 F 8 '64
Follow the bouncing ball from Honolulu to Boston; Boston Celtics win their sixth NBA championship. F. Deford. Sports Illus 20:81-2+ My 4 '64
NBA gets a new image. W. Leggett. il Sports Illus 19:30-2+ O 28 '63
Sporting scene; farewell to Cousy of Boston Celtics. H. W. Wind. New Yorker 39:146+ Mr 23 '63

NATIONAL better business bureaus. See Better business bureaus

NATIONAL Bible week
Plans set for 24th National Bible week. il Pub W 186:90 S 28 '64

NATIONAL biscuit company
Nabisco's rising dough. il Time 82:106 N 15 '63

NATIONAL board of education. See United States—National board of education (proposed)

NATIONAL book awards
Authors' Oscars. Newsweek 63:99 Mr 23 '64
Expansion approved for National book awards. Pub W 184:42 S 9 '63
15th annual National book awards. il Wilson Lib Bul 38:617+ Ap '64
Five books win National book awards. Pub W 185:28 Mr 16 '64
Gloire d'Urban. America 108:387 Mr 23 '63
How the critics voted; poll of newspaper critics. Sat R 46:33 Mr 23 '63

NATIONAL book awards—*Continued*
Judges named for National book awards. Pub W 186:45 D 28 '64
Leading contenders. Wilson Lib Bul 37:518+ Mr '63
Leading contenders for NBA announced. Pub W 183:48 F 4 '63
Leading contenders for NBA announced. Pub W 185:66 F 3 '64
National book awards. Library J 89:1226 Mr 15 '64
National book awards. Wilson Lib Bul 38: 374+ Ja '64
National book awards expanded; 1964 advisory committee named. Library J 88:3564 O 1 '63
National book awards judges announce leading contenders. Library J 89:820 F 15 '64
National book awards judges announced at NBC annual meeting. Library J 90:213-14 Ja 15 '65
National book awards to William Stafford, Leon Edel, J. F. Powers; What the winners and Oppenheimer said. il Pub W 183:28-31 Mr 25 '63
National book awards: winners, parties, discussions; authors, citations and responses. il Pub W 185:21-5 Mr 23 '64
New proposals for NBA. C. B. Grannis. Pub W 183:49 Mr 25 '63
Powers, Edel, Stafford win National book awards. Pub W 183:30-1 Mr 18 '63
PPA to handle publicity for National book awards. Pub W 184:31 O 28 '63
When in doubt, leave the safety on. D. Dempsey. Sat R 46:33-4+ Mr 22 '63
Winners. Newsweek 61:108 Mr 25 '63

NATIONAL book committee
Academic libraries featured at NBC annual meeting. Library J 89:213-14 Ja 15 '64
College libraries theme of NBC annual meeting. Pub W 184:23-4 D 16 '63
Meeting. Library J 90:210+ Ja 15 '65
New officers, new plans at Nat'l book committee. il Pub W 186:45-8 D 28 '64
Reading, the fifth freedom: NLW sixth annual report. Wilson Lib Bul 38:381 Ja '64

NATIONAL brands
National brand: anatomy of an anachronism; tables. Duns R 83:43 My '64

NATIONAL broadcasting company
CBS and NBC: Walter vs. Chet and Dave. il Newsweek 62:62-5 S 23 '63
Great opera houses: NBC-TV. Q. Eaton. il Opera N 28:28-33 F 8 '64
Long, long show: three-hour special on the American Negro's fight for equal rights. Newsweek 62:56 S 2 '63
NBC turns down a golden chance; program about teenage venereal disease. R. L. Tobin. Sat R 47:61-2 D 12 '64
NBC's Olympic hurdle; question of rights to transmission by satellite. il Bsns W p34 O 10 '64
On the news beat. il Newsweek 63:74-5 Je 1 '64
VD on TV? il Newsweek 64:62 N 20 '64

NATIONAL budget. See Budget—United States

NATIONAL bureau of economic research
How to rate the forecasters; NBER study. Bsns W p39-40 Ja 9 '65
Those static statistics. Time 84:88+ Jl 10 '64

NATIONAL bureau of standards. See United States—Standards, National bureau of

NATIONAL business aircraft association
Muffled voice. W. K. Lawton. Flying 75:80+ Jl '64
NBAA reflects business jets sales push. D. A. Brown. Aviation W 81:30 N 16 '64

NATIONAL cancer institute. See United States —National cancer institute

NATIONAL capital region planning. See Washington, D.C.—City planning

NATIONAL cash register company
EDP tells Main st. il Bsns W p66 Ag 8 '64

NATIONAL Catholic book awards
Catholic press association sponsors new book awards. Pub W 185:33 Mr 23 '64

NATIONAL Catholic conference for interracial justice
Church money for justice; struggle against discrimination in employment. America 111: 373 O 3 '64

NATIONAL Catholic educational association
Meeting, 1964. Sr Schol 84:1T+ My 1 '64
Meeting, 1963. Sr Schol 82:1T My 8 '63

Caricatures and cartoons

America goes to the convention. T. Engelhardt. America 108:550-1 Ap 20 '63

NATIONAL Catholic reporter
Finding a new voice. il Newsweek 64:72 N 23 '64
New lay newspaper; National Catholic reporter. America 111:582 N 14 '64
We were first to be bored. Christian Cent 82: 63 Ja 13 '65

NATIONAL Catholic welfare conference
Collegiality. America 108:459 Ap 6 '63
Garbled text; NCWC news service. G. W. Shea. America 109:249 S 14 '63
Labor day, 1964; Social action department statement. America 111:228 S 5 '64
Managing the news: American press panel at the Vatican council. J. Leo. Commonweal 81:5 S 25 '64
Mr NC; retirement of Frank A. Hall. America 110:273 F 29 '64
Religious view of poverty; official statement by the Department of social action. Commonweal 80:117-19 Ap 17 '64
Role of Catholic agencies; work directed toward elimination of poverty throughout the world. J. Norris. Commonweal 81:235-7 N 13 '64

NATIONAL cemeteries

United States

See also
Arlington, Va.—National cemetery

NATIONAL cemeteries, American
Not far from God. G. Kent. il Read Digest 82:236-8+ Je '63
U.S. memorial grounds abroad. J. H. Winchester. il Travel 121:50-4+ My '64

NATIONAL center for atmospheric research
Probing the weather's secrets. il Bsns W p84-6+ My 16 '64

NATIONAL center for environmental sciences. See United States—National center for environmental sciences

NATIONAL championship air races. See Airplane racing

NATIONAL characteristics, American; National characteristics, French; etc. See Americans; French; etc.

NATIONAL childrens book week. See Book week

NATIONAL coffee association
World coffee agreement and U.S. foreign economic policy; address, January 14, 1963. W. M. Blumenthal. Dept State Bul 48:218-23 F 11 '63

NATIONAL collegiate athletic association
Board, books and birdies; golfers for U.S. colleges. D. Jenkins. il Sports Illus 18:43-4+ My 20 '63
Bowlderdash; financial arrangements with athletes. Sports Illus 22:6 Ja 11 '65
Cincy goes for a third; NCAA championship. J. Underwood. il Sports Illus 18:24-6+ Mr 11 '63
Games that are a ball for all; NCAA championship playoff, with photographs by J. G. Zimmerman. Sports Illus 18:30-6 Mr 18 '63
Gunners are after Cincy; Duke and Loyola basketball teams. J. Underwood. il Sports Illus 18:22-5 Mr 25 '63
Large field of unfavorites. J. Underwood. il Sports Illus 20:20-3 Mr 16 '64
Reprieve for the Redskins; U of Utah in 1944 NCAA tournament. D. Anderson. Sports Illus 18:E3-4 Mr 18 '63
Two-minute explosion; UCLA startled Kansas state and Duke, won national basketball title. J. Underwood. il Sports Illus 20: 16-19 Mr 30 '64

NATIONAL collegiate basketball championship. See Basketball tournaments

NATIONAL commission for UNESCO. See United States national commission for UNESCO

NATIONAL commission on accrediting
While school keeps; recommended changes in structure of NCATE. J. Cass. Sat R 46:70-1 Mr 23 '63

NATIONAL committee for a sane nuclear policy
Conversing with Russians; American peace groups and members of Sane visiting the Soviet Union. S. Gottlieb. Bul Atomic Sci 21:35-6 Ja '65
SANE marches on. Nat R 16:10-11 Ja 14 '64

NATIONAL committee for support of the public schools
Lighting a fire; conference sponsored by the National committee for the support of the public schools. il Newsweek 62:71 D 23 '63
Slums and suburbs. Sr Schol 82:1T-3T My 1 '63

NATIONAL company of the Metropolitan opera. See Metropolitan opera national company

NATIONAL conference of Christians and Jews
Beyond the school question. J. O'Gara. Commonweal 78:15 Mr 29 '63

NATIONAL conference of Christians and Jews
—*Continued*
Books for brotherhood. Commonweal 77:564-5; 79:628-30 F 22 '63, F 21 '64
NCCJ programs its future. America 111:792 D 19 '64
Rearing children of good will; workshop on race prejudices. E. S. Ringold. il N Y Times Mag p61-2 S 22 '63
NATIONAL conference on air pollution
Let's clear the air. Am City 78:160+ Mr '63
NATIONAL conference on church architecture
Church architecture: the perils of success. M. E. Marty. Christian Cent 80:390-1 Mr 27 '63; Reply. G. Apel. 80:510 Ap 17 '63
NATIONAL conference on outdoor recreation research
Recreation under the microscope. J. F. Shanklin. il Am For 69:32-5 Jl '63
NATIONAL conference on religion and race
Appeal to conscience; statement. Commonweal 77:518 F 8 '63
Baggage of the past. J. LaFarge. Sat R 46:23-5 Mr 16 '63
Our segregated Catholic schools. J. B. Sheerin. Cath World 196:331-4 Mr '63
Progress in Little Rock. Christian Cent 80:606 My 8 '63
Race: challenge to religion, ed. by M. Ahmann. Review
Christian Cent 80:1135-6 S 18 '63. W. Stringfellow
Religion and race. J. O'Gara. Commonweal 77:506 F 8 '63
Religion and race: local efforts. P. B. Mather. Christian Cent 80:412-14 Mr 27 '63
Summit conference on race, religion. il Ebony 18:43-4+ Ap '63
NATIONAL conference on solid waste research
Solid-waste-disposal challenge. Am City 79:25 Ja '64
NATIONAL conference on urban passenger transportation
Salvaging mass transportation in urban areas. Am City 79:148-9 Ap '64
NATIONAL congress of mothers. See National congress of parents and teachers
NATIONAL congress of parents and teachers
Among those present; First congress of mothers. M. K. Lucas. PTA Mag 57:17 F '63
Being wise in membership; affirming a new concept of parenthood. B. W. Overstreet. il PTA Mag 58:7-9 D '63
Being wise in membership; our five-cent bargain. B. W. Overstreet. il PTA Mag 58:20-2 Ja '64
New learning, new hope, new promise. M. E. Jenkins. PTA Mag 58:2-3 My '64
PTA: the irrelevant giant. W. C. Kvaraceus. Nation 197:200-1 O 5 '63
Plan for all seasons; a Founders day feature. il PTA Mag 58:20-1 F '64
Salute to our state presidents. il PTA Mag 58:16-17 Ap '64
Sixty-six; our birthday mail; symposium. PTA Mag 57:18-21 F '63
NATIONAL conventions (political)
Again, they are readying the convention halls; excerpts from Two party system. R. Harrity. il Look 28:22-30+ Jl 14 '64
Are political conventions out of date? interview. M. C. Moos. U S News 57:70-2 S 14 '64
Convention. il Look 28:19 Jl 14 '64
Convention plans and memories. P. Mesta. il McCalls 91:18+ Ag '64
Echo of two conventions. E. J. Hughes. Newsweek 64:15 S 7 '64
How not to elect a president. D. Lawrence. U S News 57:100 S 7 '64
How 'The man who' wins the prize. M. Moos. il N Y Times Mag p8+ Je 21 '64
In '64, a political convention for each coast. il U S News 55:16 Jl 8 '63
It is a zany system, but it works. T. Wicker. il N Y Times Mag p7+ Jl 19 '64
Men behind the men who—. D. S. Broder. il N Y Times Mag p 15+ Ja 5 '64
National conventions: chess tournament disguised as a circus? il Sr Schol 84:12-15 My 8 '64
1,308; who they are, what they do; convention delegates. A. Wildavsky. il N Y Times Mag p8+ Jl 12 '64
One vote for the convention system. F. knebel. il N Y Times Mag p21+ Ag 23 '64
Political conventions; address, June 29, 1964. L. Collins. Vital Speeches 30:612-17 Ag 1 '64
When the lightning strikes; dramatic moments in twelve most recent conventions. il N Y Times Mag p6-7 Jl 12 '64
Without portfolio. C. B. Luce. il McCalls 91:16+ Jl '64
Wrong way to pick a president. D. Lawrence. U S News 57:116 Jl 27 '64
See also
Television in politics
NATIONAL conventions, Democratic
All over? or just starting? il Time 84:19-19A S 4 '64
Atlantic City. M. Greenfield. Reporter 31:12+ S 10 '64
Atlantic City and a memory. L. Wainwright. Life 57:17 S 4 '64
Atlantic City without the girls. W. F. Buckley, jr. Nat R 16:763-5 S 8 '64
Battle of credentials; Alabama and Mississippi delegations. il Newsweek 64:26-7 S 7 '64
Boardwalk goes all out. il Bsns W p28-9 Ag 15 '64
Congratulations, whispered Jackie, and thanks for my birthday letter; reception for Mrs John F. Kennedy in Atlantic City. S. Alexander. il Life 57:30-1 S 4 '64
Conscience of a convention; Atlantic City. M. Kempton. New Repub 151:5-7 S 5 '64
Democratic fiesta. K. Crawford. Newsweek 64:30 Ag 10 '64
Democrats and 389 photographers. B. Brown. il Pop Phot 55:140-1+ D '64
Democrats' bonus; apportionment of delegates to national conventions. New Repub 150:4-5 F 8 '64
Extremism in defense of the Democratic party. C. B. Luce. Nat R 16:719-21 Ag 25 '64
From Atlantic City: notes on the democratic convention. H. Margolis. Bul Atomic Sci 20:39-42 O '64
Fun and games in Atlantic City. M. Connelly. Sat R 47:33-5 S 19 '64
Gay life; Atlantic City. il Time 84:22-9 S 4 '64
It was a very organized party. E. T. Folliard. America 111:248 S 12 '64
It's LBJ week in Atlantic City. il Newsweek 64:15-16 Ag 31 '64
Letter from Atlantic City. R. H. Rovere. il New Yorker 40:112-17 S 5 '64
L.B.J. all the way. il Time 84:19A-19B S 4 '64
LBJ: I ask for a mandate to begin. il Newsweek 64:16-18 S 7 '64
Magic of memory; filmed eulogy to Kennedy. il Time 84:29 S 4 '64
Man to watch at the Democratic convention. H. Fuller. Harper 229:47-52 Ag '64
Money in the till; Democratic party's convention program. Time 84:17 Ag 21 '64
Now the real race begins. il U S News 57:27-8 S 7 '64
On full fiery throttle the fight is joined. il Life 57:20-7 S 4 '64
Parties for my party. P. Mesta. il McCalls 92:34+ N '64
T.R.B. from Atlantic City. New Repub 151:2 S 5 '64
Trying to paper it over; Mississippi and Alabama delegations. il Time 84:31-2 S 4 '64
What to expect at the Democratic convention. il U S News 57:11 Ag 10 '64
NATIONAL conventions, Republican
Battle of San Francisco. J. Dos Passos. Nat R 16:640, 652 Jl 28 '64
Big new face of the G.O.P. il Life 57:20-32B Jl 24 '64
Choice not an echo; Cow Palace climacteric; Goldwater nomination; with colored photographs. il Newsweek 64:18-26 Jl 27 '64
Cinched nomination; 1964 Republican national convention. il Time 84:19-24 Jl 17 '64
Crisis at the Cow palace. S. Alsop. il Sat Eve Post 237:17-21 Jl 11 '64
Event of enormous beauty. W. Saroyan. il Sat Eve Post 237:84-5 Ag 8 '64
From San Francisco: notes on the Republican convention. H. Margolis. Bul Atomic Sci 20:31-4 S '64
Gold rush; GOP convention in San Francisco. il Newsweek 64:30-1 Jl 13 '64
Goldwater's hour. il Bsns W p23-5 Jl 18 '64
GOP in San Francisco: Alabama casts twenty votes for . . . Delegates: a grand old party. il Newsweek 64:16-21 Jl 20 '64
He came. . ; photographs. Time 84:23-6 Jl 24 '64
High noon in the Cow Palace. C. McWilliams. Nation 199:23-7 Jl 27 '64
I'm in the fight to the last ballot; only Lincoln Republican. M. Kitman. il Sat Eve Post 237:22-3 Jl 11 '64
In the Cow Palace: toads and Brinklies; TV coverage. il Newsweek 64:50-1 Jl 27 '64
In the red light: a history of the Republican convention in 1964. N. Mailer. il Esquire 62:83-9+ N '64
Late late show; Republican moderates' death battle on the platform issues. Time 84:21-2 Jl 24 '64

NATIONAL conventions, Republican—*Cont.*
Letter from San Francisco. R. H. Rovere. il New Yorker 40:77-80+ Jl 25 '64
Lineup before the voting started; Republican delegates. il U S News 57:36 Jl 20 '64
Meaning of San Francisco. E. Roper. Sat R 47:17+ Ag 22 '64
No, no a thousand times no. il Nat R 16:635-6 Jl 28 '64
Reporter at large; New York delegate. R. Harris. New Yorker 40:101-3+ S 12 '64
Roar, Republicans, roar! L. Goldenson. il Seventeen 23:63 O '64
San Francisco is next; presidential nomination. il Bsns W p23-4 Je 6 '64
T.R.B. from San Francisco. New Repub 151:2 Jl 25 '64
TV zooms in on GOP. Bsns W p32+ F 22 '64
They got him; Goldwater's nomination. M. Kempton. New Repub 151:8-11 Jl 25 '64
Truly Republican convention? D. Lawrence. il U S News 57:96 Jl 13 '64
Ugly tone of a big affair. L. Wainwright. Life 57:15 Jl 24 '64
Victory at San Francisco: how Goldwater did it. il U S News 57:42-4 Jl 27 '64
Welcome to Daly City; 1964 Republican convention. il Time 84:24 Jl 10 '64
Who came out how. il Time 84:28A Jl 24 '64

NATIONAL council for accreditation of teacher education
Accrediting procedures of NCATE. A. E. Meder, jr. Sch & Soc 91:192-3 Ap 20 '63
Conant seeks revolution; excerpts from address. J. B. Conant. Sr Schol 84:1T-2T Mr 13 '64
What NCATE means to the teacher. R. Lander. NEA J 52:30-1 F '63
While school keeps; recommended changes in structure of NCATE. J. Cass. Sat R 46:70-1 Mr 23 '63
Who should set standards? Time 81:61-2 Mr 15 '63
Why teacher can't teach. Life 54:4 Mr 22 '63
Wisconsin vs. NCATE. Sch & Soc 91:236 Sum '63

NATIONAL council for civic responsibility
Alert to extremists. E. C. Parker. Christian Cent 81:1285-6 O 14 '64
Answering the hatemongers; radical rightist organizations. Christian Cent 81:1388-9 N 11 '64
Form council against rightist propaganda. Christian Cent 81:1229 O 7 '64
Republican looks at extremism. D. R. Maxey. il Look 29:24-7 Ja 26 '65

NATIONAL council for geographic education
Meeting, 1963. Sr Schol 83:1T-2T+, 15T D 13 '63
Meeting, 1964. Sr Schol 85:1T-2T+ D 9 '64

NATIONAL council for historic sites and buildings. See National trust for historic preservation

NATIONAL council for the social studies
Four programs; summary of report. Sr Schol 82:3T-4T Ja 30 '63
Great adventure. J. T. Aubrey, jr. il NEA J 52:33-48 O '63
Meeting, 1963. il Sr Schol 83:1T+, 16T D 13 '63; 7T-9T Ja 10 '64
Meeting, 1964. il Sr Schol 85:1T+ D 9 '64; 7T Ja 7 '65
Skills development in social studies, ed. by H. M. Carpenter. Review
Sr Schol 84:7T Ja 31 '64. H. L. Hurwitz

NATIONAL council of architectural registration boards
In restraint of architectural practice. Arch Forum 120:77 My '64

NATIONAL council of Catholic women
Equal-pay bill. America 108:700-1 My 18 '63

NATIONAL council of churches. See National council of the churches of Christ in the United States of America

NATIONAL council of dance teacher organizations
Progress report. Dance Mag 38:68-9 Ja '64

NATIONAL council of farmer cooperatives
Co-ops call for more bargaining power. Farm J 87:13 F '63

NATIONAL council of Jewish women
Sam Winter retires from old age; Senior service corps. J. Shepherd. il Look 27:49-52 Ag 13 '63

NATIONAL council of teachers of English
Meeting, 1962. J. R. Squire. Sch & Soc 91:101 F 23 '63
Meeting, 1963. J. R. Squire. Sch & Soc 92:52-3 F 8 '64
Meeting, 1963. Sr Schol 83:1T+, 15T D 13 '63; 10T Ja 10 '64
Meeting, 1964. il Sr Schol 85:1T+ D 9 '64; 7T Ja 7 '65
NCTE plans English-language study. Library J 88:846 F 15 '63
Tips from teachers; report. E. Moon. Library J 88:4167+ N 1 '63
Your school listed? survey of one hundred and ten outstanding high school English programs. Sr Schol 83:5T-7T O 4 '63

NATIONAL council of the arts. See United States—National council of the arts

NATIONAL council of the churches of Christ in the United States of America
Bishop answers N.C.C. critics. Christian Cent 81:1262 O 14 '64
Church-state conference; study conference sponsored by National council of churches. America 110:245 F 22 '64
Churches meet racial crisis; with text of statement to churches. H. E. Fey. Christian Cent 80:1572-3 D 18 '63
Churchmen meet. B. L. Masse. America 110:16-17 Ja 4 '64
Dilemma for Christians; socio-economic issues. America 110:212 F 15 '64
Endorses social security health insurance. Christian Cent 81:1076 S 2 '64
Episcopalians report findings on National council. Christian Cent 81:228 F 19 '64
Ethics on the job; experiment in discussion groups. B. L. Masse. America 110:332 Mr 14 '64
Fund for burned churches and for church burners. Christian Cent 81:1054 Ag 26 '64
Glorious opportunity; establishment of Emergency commission on religion and race. Newsweek 62:55 Jl 8 '63
Hattiesburg: toward reconciliation; Hattiesburg ministers project. L. Minear. Christian Cent 81:1115-16 S 9 '64
How headlines saved Nashville. W. Geier. Christian Cent 81:335-6 Mr 11 '64
Message to the churches; December 1-7, 1963. Christian Cent 81:12-14 Ja 1 '64
Modernizing the mass. il Time 82:80 D 13 '63
N.C.C. acts on racial crisis. H. E. Fey. Christian Cent 80:797-8 Je 19 '63
N.C.C. reorganizes. H. E. Fey. Christian Cent 80:1602-4 D 25 '63
N.C.C. visits Clarksdale. S. C. Rose. Christian Cent 80:1104-6 S 11 '63
National council reorganizes. Christian Cent 81:821 Je 24 '64
National council voices sorrow, gratitude. Christian Cent 80:1536 D 11 '63
Out of work in ten years; N.C.C.-sponsored migrant ministry program. H. E. Fey. Christian Cent 80:1230-1 O 9 '63
Protestants on church-state; National study conference on church and state. W. B. Ball. Commonweal 79:689-91 Mr 6 '64
Public funds for parochial schools? by G. La Noue. Review
Commonweal 78:184 My 10 '63. J. O'Gara
Refusal to retreat; under attacks of rightist organizations. Christian Cent 81:1580 D 23 '64
Regrouped, renewed, reforming; cooperative Protestantism. Christian Cent 80:1488-9 D 4 '63
Religion in the schools; Bible-reading cases. America 108:894 Je 29 '63
Russians visit the U.S. Russian church delegation in Denver. H. E. Fey. Christian Cent 80:326-7 Mr 13 '63
Thurmond attacks the church. Christian Cent 81:421-2 Ap 1 '64
To study church-state relations in Columbus. Christian Cent 80:1489 D 4 '63
Witness on race; sixth triennial general assembly. Newsweek 62:81 D 16 '63
See also
United church women (organization)

Commission on religion and race
Churches and Mississippi; Mississippi summer project. S. C. Rose. Christian Cent 81:909-10 Jl 15 '64
N.C.C. calls assembly on civil rights; in Washington, D.C. Christian Cent 81:509 Ap 22 '64

Division of home missions
Choosing sides; conference to develop coordinated policies on role of the churches in an urbanized society. Newsweek 64:45 D 21 '64

NATIONAL council of the Metropolitan opera association
Auditions 1963. A. M. Lingg. il Opera N 27:16-17 My 4 '63
Music to my ears: Metropolitan auditions. I. Kolodin. Sat R 46:31 Ap 13 '63
National council powwow. A. M. Lingg. Opera N 28:34 F 8 '64
See also
Singing—Competitions

NATIONAL council on alcoholism
Tomorrow's alcoholic. A. Ogle. America 108: 468-9 Ap 6 '63

NATIONAL council on the aging
Library services for the aging to be discussed at NCOA meeting. Library J 89: 592 F 1 '64

NATIONAL council on the arts in education. See Educational conferences

NATIONAL cultural center. See Washington, D.C.—National cultural center

NATIONAL custom auto fairs. See Automobiles —Exhibitions

NATIONAL debt (United States) See Debts, Public—United States

NATIONAL debts. See Debts, Public

NATIONAL defense
See also
United States—Defenses

NATIONAL defense education act. See School laws and legislation—United States

NATIONAL defense language institutes. See Languages, Modern—Study and teaching

NATIONAL education association
ATA will merge, if. Sr Schol 85:6T-7T S 23 '64
Are you on the line? il NEA J 53:35-42 S '64
Be one in a million. il NEA J 52:33-40 S '63
Building local association strength: St Louis teachers association. il NEA J 52:39-41 D '63
Crack in the ice; NEA resolutions on federal support for public education. America 109: 127 Ag 10 '63
Deliberate slowness. Newsweek 62:52-3 Jl 15 '63
Do you know your NEA? M. S. Fenner. NEA J 53:84 O '64
Duty of professional associations; address, November 9, 1962. R. J. Hughes. Vital Speeches 29:254-6 F 1 '63
Editor's notebook (cont) M. S. Fenner. NEA J 52:80 Mr '63
Education for responsible freedom. R. H. Wyatt. NEA J 52:41 S '63
Education for world responsibility. L. V. Edinger. NEA J 53:23 S '64
Financial report to members. il NEA J 53:76 O '64
Great adventure. J. T. Aubrey, jr. il NEA J 52:33-48 O '63
Implementing the code of ethics. M. M. Mitchell. NEA J 53:41 D '64
Labor trouble ahead for schools? U S News 57:75 S 7 '64
Library programs at the National education association conference. ALA Bul 57:431 My '63
Local associations move toward professional negotiation. A. M. West. il NEA J 53:26-8 F '64
Mahomet goes to the hill. W. A. Abrams. NEA J 52:49 N '63
More positive expressions. J. Ciardi. Sat R 46:14 Ap 27 '63
NEA and the hill. R. Anderson. il NEA J 52:36-9 Ap '63
NEA convention and the organizing of teachers. L. R. Klein. Mo Labor R 87:882-5 Ag '64
NEA membership lag? Georgia teachers. Sr Schol 85:1T-2T Ja 7 '65
NEA mutual fund. T. F. Davis. NEA J 53: 29-30 N '64
NEA officers, 1964-65. NEA J 53:9+ O '64
NEA strengthens its stand on question of civil rights. Library J 88:3276-7 S 15 '63
NEA's new membership requirements. H. Blanchard. NEA J 52:46-7 Ap '63
NEA's special projects. NEA J 52:43 F; 49 O '63
New militants. il Time 82:45 Ag 16 '63
Professional sanctions: where, when, and how. R. B. Kennan. NEA J 52:37-8 D '63
Proposed amendments to NEA bylaws and rules. NEA J 53:68-71 Ap '64
Realistic view of the NEA. R. B. Kennan. Sch & Soc 91:107 Mr 9 '63
Report on reports. il NEA J 52:14-15 D '63
Scholastic teacher interview; ed. by H. Langer. C. J. Duckworth. Sr Schol 85:9T-10T+ O 21 '64
Scholastic teacher interviews: Carl J. Megel; ed. by H. Langer. C. J. Megel. Sr Schol 83:24T-26T O 4 '63; Discussion. 83:6T D 6 '63
Scholastic teacher interviews: William G. Carr; ed. by H. Langer. W. G. Carr. il Sr Schol 83:9T-13T Ja 17 '64
Schools and publishing: a partnership in transition; condensation of report. F. Redding. Pub W 183:22-5 Mr 18 '63
Schools for the sixties. il NEA J 53:37-52 Ja '64
Schools for the sixties; concerning National education association's report with summary of recommendations. J. S. Gow, jr. Sat R 46:58-60+ O 19 '63
Schools for the 60's; Project on instruction, summary of report. Sr Schol 83:1T+ O 18 '63
Some NEA high lights of 1963. NEA J 53: 66+ Ja '64
Strikes, sanctions, and the schools. J. Scanlon. il Sat R 46:51-5+ O 19 '63; Discussion. 46:64 N 16 '63
Thirty-three NEA departments. NEA J 52: 55-6 N '63
Time to teach; new NEA project. M. M. Provus. il NEA J 53:17-18 My '64
Toward labor monopoly in teaching? NEA, AFT and UFT. R. Kirk. Nat R 15:241 S 24 '63
Union or guild? organizing the teachers. S. Elam. il Nation 198:651-3 Je 29 '64
U.S. office of education: an inside view. S. M. McMurrin. il Sat R 46:78-81 F 16 '63; Reply. J. J. Neumaier. 46:57 Mr 23 '63
What's happening in education? Code of ethics of the education profession and guidelines for professional sanctions. W. D. Boutwell. PTA Mag 58:21 O '63
Why belong to an NEA department? J. L. Buford. NEA J 52:47 F '63
Why belong to NEA. J. E. Russell. NEA J 53:35-7 N '64; Reply with rejoinder. M. Rubin. 54:7 Ja '65
See also
American association of school administrators
Educational policies commission
National art education association

Meeting, 1963

Meeting, 1964. Sr Schol 84:4T My 15 '64
NEA convention, 1963 style. H. A. Blanchard. il NEA J 52:23 F '63
Utah key issue at NEA. Sr Schol 83:1T S 13 '63; Discussion. 83:8T O 18 '63
Voice of the Nation's teachers. il NEA J 52:24-7 S '63
You are cordially invited to attend the NEA convention in Detroit. il NEA J 52:32-3 My '63

Meeting, 1964

Birchers and PTA. Newsweek 64:54 Jl 13 '64
Civil rights dominates NEA convention. il Sr Schol 85:2T-3T S 16 '64
NEA convention, June 28-July 3, 1964. R. H. Wyatt. il NEA J 53:42-3 My '64
Seattle convention program, June 28-July 3, 1964. il NEA J 53:58 F '64

Committee on professional ethics

Employment application forms. NEA J 53:55 My '64
Local association studies ethics cases: readiness test. NEA J 53:24-5 F '64

Department of classroom teachers

Scholastic teacher interview: ed. by H. Langer. T. Davis. Sr Schol 85:9T-14T+ D 2 '64

Division of educational travel

Background for travel. il NEA J 53:64-6 F '64

Division of travel service

NEA tours in capsule. il NEA J 52:59 F '63

Research division

Expanded NEA life insurance plan. il NEA J 53:16-17 O '64
NEA works for teachers' salaries. il NEA J 52:11-14 O '63

NATIONAL education association journal. See NEA journal

NATIONAL education improvement act of 1963. See School laws and legislation—United States

NATIONAL education program (organization)
Foundations as a tax dodge. F. J. Cook. Nation 196:323-5 Ap 20 '63
Ultras. F. J. Cook; reply. G. S. Benson. Nation 196:inside cover. 97 F 2 '63

NATIONAL educational television and radio center
Clear channels ahead; labor contract between NET and AFTRA. Sr Schol 85:7T O 7 '64
Life guide: educational TV. il Life 55:13 O 18 '63
NET results. Newsweek 64:108+ N 23 '64
New NET programming. Sr Schol 83:1T O 18 '63
Parents, teachers, and early readers; televised series Preparing your child for reading by Denver public schools. D. DuBose. il Sr Schol 83:8T-9T N 1 '63
TV's fascinating fourth network. M. Mannes. il Ladies Home J 80:100+ Jl '63

NATIONAL electrical contractors association
How to stop strikes before they start. il Bsns W p43-4 Ag 24 '63
NATIONAL electronics conference
Paper on intellectronics highlight for 25,000 at NEC exhibition. C. D. LaFond. Miss & Roc 15:34 O 26 '64
NATIONAL emblems. See Emblems, National
NATIONAL emergency alarm repeater. See Air raid warning systems
NATIONAL employment association
Job referral is a proper state function. Christian Cent 80:901 Jl 17 '63
NATIONAL enquirer
No matter how vile. . . il Newsweek 65:48 Ja 18 '65
NATIONAL export expansion coordinator. See United States—National export expansion coordinator
NATIONAL farmers' educational and cooperative union. See Farmers' educational and co-operative union of America
NATIONAL farmers organization
Death in Bonduel; ethics of farmers' boycott of livestock sales. America 111:344 S 26 '64
This little piggy; National farmers organization meat-withholding action. Newsweek 64:72-3 S 7 '64
Violence off the streets; livestock-farmers' market boycott. il Time 84:38 S 18 '64
Vow; NFO holding action. il Newsweek 64:90 S 21 '64
When farmers go on strike. J. Bird. il Sat Eve Post 237:30+ N 21 '64
Why the drive to raise cattle prices failed. R. T. Cooper. New Repub 151:7-8 O 3 '64
NATIONAL farmers' union. See Farmers' educational and co-operative union of America
NATIONAL federation of independent unions (proposed)
Independent unions choose togetherness. Bsns W p50 Je 1 '63
NATIONAL field trials. See Field trials (dogs)
NATIONAL fisheries center and aquarium. See Aquariums
NATIONAL football league
All the strings; Chicago Bears win National football league championship. il Newsweek 63:71 Ja 13 '64
Browns win big in the East; chance to meet Baltimore Colts. T. Maule. il Sports Illus 21:22-5 D 21 '64
Bush-league scandal. Time 81:45 Ap 26 '63
Greasy Neale: nothing to prove, nothing to ask. G. Holland. il Sports Illus 21:32-4+ Ag 24 '64
How the West has won; West vs. East. E. Shrake. il Sports Illus 21:35-6+ N 23 '64
Judgement day; suspension of P. Hornung and A. Karras. il Newsweek 61:84 Ap 29 '63
Pro football 1964. T. Maule. il Sports Illus 21:44-66+ S 7 '64
Pro football scouting reports. T. Maule. il Sports Illus 19:54-6+ S 9 '63
Ridiculous! the NFL by fifty points; in world series. T. Maule. Sports Illus 19:26+ D 16 '63
Shadow over pro football. T. Maule. il Sports Illus 18:10-11 Ja 28 '63
These are the men who run the fourteen clubs in the NFL; photographs. Sports Illus 20:27 Ja 6 '64
Twenty-eight-million-dollar deal; CBS wins 1964-65 television rights to the NFL's regular season games. W. Leggett. il Sports Illus 20:16-17 F 3 '64
Upset of the mighty; Cleveland Browns defeat Baltimore to win NFL title. T. Maule. il Sports Illus 22:8-13 Ja 4 '65
Vintage year for pro rookies. il Sports Illus 21:32-5 D 7 '64
Why pro football must live with sin. T. Cohane. il Look 27:64-71 Jl 2 '63
NATIONAL forest products week. See Special days, weeks, and months
NATIONAL forest service. See United States—Forest service
NATIONAL forests
Controversy in canoeland; Boundary Waters Canoe area. F. H. Kaufert. il Am For 70:24-7+ O '64
Design for multiple use. W. T. Dresser. il Am For 70:12-15 Jl '64
Ed Lake, Zeb Lake, and 133 more; Winema National Forest. il Sunset 130:66+ Je '63
Enjoying the national forests. M. Frome. il Holiday 35:131-6 Je '64
Fashioning the cradle of forestry in America; Pisgah national forest, N.C. V. Rhoades. il Am For 70:34-5+ D '64
Gallatin glissade; Gallatin National Forest. J. Clark. il Field & S 68:21-3+ Jl '63
How to camp out and enjoy it. P. Czura. il Todays Health 42:32-5+ Jl '64
King on the mountain; editorial. Am For 69:11 Ag '63
Mio, Michigan: strictly for the birds; Huron National Forest Kirtland's warbler management area. J. Calkins. il Am For 69:6+ Je '63
Mountain of glass; Glass Mountain in Modoc National Forest. R. H. May and W. F. Heald. il Am For 69:32-4 Ag '63
Our smallest national forest. N. Ashby. il Am For 69:30-1+ S '63
Pace of wilderness classification; reclassification of primitive areas. M. Nadel. il Liv Wildn 85:16-24 Wint '64
Pinchot and the foresters; excerpt from The quiet crisis. S. L. Udall. il Am For 69:24-7+ N '63
Pisgah Forest in 1912. R. C. Hall. il Am For 70:34-7+ S '64
Rags-to-riches forest: Pennsylvania's Allegheny national forest. C. E. Randall. il Am For 70:12-15+ Je '64
Run to the waterfall; Caribbean National Forest. A. Vivante. New Yorker 40:29 Ag 1 '64
Sky forest of the ancients; Ancient Bristelcone Pine Forest area of Inyo National Forest. W. F. Heald. il Am For 70:34-5+ N '64
There's a long deep trail awinding; John Muir trail in Sierra National Forest. A. P. Snyder. il Am For 69:20-1+ Je '63
Whose woods these are: the story of the national forests, by M. Frome. Review
Liv Wildn il 82:20 Winter '62. C. Davis
Winema, the memorial forest. W. B. Morse. il Am For 69:24-5+ Je '63
Wonders of a cave find; in Ozark national forest; with colored photographs by A. Y. Owen. Life 57:49-50+ D 18 '64
See also
National parks and reserves—United States
NATIONAL foundation
Of muscles & enzymes; possible prevention of muscular dystrophy. il Time 84:59 Ag 21 '64
Polio postmortem; Salk vaccine. il Newsweek 62:61 Jl 1 '63
NATIONAL foundation for education in American citizenship
Foundations as a tax dodge. F. J. Cook. Nation 196:321-5 Ap 20 '63
NATIONAL foundation for infantile paralysis. See National foundation
NATIONAL foundation for the humanities (proposed) See United States—National foundation for the humanities (proposed)
NATIONAL gallery, London
Antiques abroad; last decade's acquisitions by London's National gallery. W. De Sager. il Antiques 84:184+ Ag '63
NATIONAL gallery, Millbank. See Tate gallery, London
NATIONAL gallery of art, Washington, D.C.
Print on display. F. Getlein. New Repub 149:35-6 Ag 31 '63
Teen-agers on an art binge. B. Leavitt. il Look 27:M13-14+ S 24 '63
NATIONAL general corporation
Theater chain to make films. Bsns W p22 Jl 6 '63
NATIONAL geographic magazine
Dear Aunt Sally. il Newsweek 62:83 N 11 '63
On the Geographic's 75th birthday, our best to you. M. H. Grosvenor. il Nat Geog Mag 124:459 O '63
Reprinting brings earliest Geographics to life. M. M. Payne. il Nat Geog Mag 126:688-9 N '64
Romance of the Geographic. G. H. Grosvenor. il Nat Geog Mag 124:516-85 O '63
Two cheers for the National geographic. A. Chamberlin. il Esquire 60:206-9+ D '63
Whole world inside. W. Sullivan. il Sat R 47:124-5+ Mr 14 '64; Reply. C. A. Andrews. 47:70 Ap 11 '64
NATIONAL geographic society
Advancing the frontiers of human knowledge for the benefit of all mankind; remarks, January 18, 1964. L. B. Johnson. Dept State Bul 50:150-2 F 3 '64; Excerpts. Nat Geog Mag 125:668-79 My '64
Great adventures with National geographic. Review
Nat Geog Mag il 124:728-33 N '63. M. B. Grosvenor
National geographic atlas of the world! M. B. Grosvenor. il Nat Geog Mag 123:832-7 Je '63
Partners; exhibition marking seventy-fifth anniversary of National geographic society at Museum of natural history. New Yorker 39:22 Ag 17 '63

NATIONAL geographic society—*Continued*
President Johnson dedicates the Society's new headquarters; with excerpts from addresses. il Nat Geog Mag 125:668-79 My '64
35MM scenics; work of the National geographic's photographic staff. P. Caulfield. il Mod Phot 27:74-9 F '63
Two cheers for the National geographic. A. Chamberlin. il Esquire 60:206-9+ D '63
See also
Hubbard medal

Expeditions

By parachute into Peru's lost world; 1963 Vilcabamba expedition. G. B. Baekeland. il Nat Geog Mag 126:268-96 Ag '64

Explorer's hall

New landmarks on the Washington horizon. E. J. Long. il Am For 70:16-20 Mr '64

NATIONAL goals. See United States

NATIONAL grasslands. See Wilderness areas

NATIONAL guard (United States) See United States—National guard

NATIONAL health insurance. See Insurance, Health

NATIONAL health service (Canada) See Canada —National health service

NATIONAL health service (Great Britain) See Great Britain—National health service

NATIONAL historical publications commission. See United States—National historical publications commission

NATIONAL hockey league
Officiating mess in the National hockey league. D. Anderson and R. S. Hewlett. il Sports Illus 18:26-8+ Ap 8 '63
Sporting scene: Maple Leafs vs both Canadiens and Black Hawks. H. W. Wind. il New Yorker 40:133-4+ Ap 11 '64
Why westward ho? Sports Illus 20:17-18 My 18 '64

NATIONAL horse show. See Horse shows

NATIONAL hot rod association
National scene. See issues of Hot rod
'64 drag rules. J. Hart. il Hot Rod 17:84-5+ F '64
1963 drag racing rules. J. Hart. il Hot Rod 16:76-9 F '63
Seattle custom auto fair; 1963. L. Smith. il Hot Rod 16:70-3 O '63
Sedans, rails and gassers; Winter nationals, Pomona, Calif: photographs. L. Schiller. Sat Eve Post 237:58-61 Ja 4 '64

NATIONAL hurricane research laboratory. See United States—Weather bureau

NATIONAL income. See Income

NATIONAL independent coal operators' association
UMW faces a miner's revolt; independent mining is spreading. Bsns W p70+ Ag 15 '64

NATIONAL industrial conference board
Bullish but not boomish. Newsweek 61:85 My 27 '63
Economy: another bumper year. il Newsweek 64:71 S 28 '64
Famous firsts: Shangri-la of the tycoon era; Yama-no-uchi in the southern Catskills. il Bsns W p 142-4 O 3 '64
Leading economists size up the business outlook; symposium. il U S News 58:54-63 Ja 4 '65
Planning debate comes to the U.S. il Bsns W p 140+ My 25 '63
Rising fast: cost of fringes. U S News 56:92 Ja 20 '64
Sixth annual economic conference of the NICB. M. S. Riche. Mo Labor R 86:810-13 Jl '63
Some pinch in the plants. il Time 84:87 S 25 '64
What top economists see ahead for business; symposium. il U S News 56:64-72 Ja 13 '64

NATIONAL industrial recreation association
Employees at play are big business; recreation's benefits hard to measure. il Bsns W p98-100 Ap 11 '64

NATIONAL institute of arts and letters
1964 Brunner prize awarded to Harry Weese. Arch Rec 135:20 Je '64

NATIONAL institute of mental health. See United States—National institute of mental health

NATIONAL institute of oceanography
Britain's National institute of oceanography. V. K. McElheny. bibliog il Science 144:160-3 Ap 10 '64

NATIONAL institutes of health. See United States—National institutes of health

NATIONAL labor relations act, 1935. See Labor laws and legislation—United States

NATIONAL labor relations board. See United States—National labor relations board

NATIONAL legion of decency
Catholic film newsletter. America 112:68 Ja 16 '65
Film classification defied. America 111:730 D 5 '64
Legion of decency. America 110:624-5 My 9 '64
Moral or immoral? rating of movies. il Newsweek 64:53-4 D 28 '64
Movie moguls, unite! America 110:357 Mr 21 '64
Right conscience about films. M. Walsh. America 110:657-8, 684-6 My 9-16 '64
Wilder's dirty-joke film stirs a furor. T. Thompson. il Life 58:56A-56B Ja 15 '65

NATIONAL library of Canada. See Canada—National library

NATIONAL library of medicine. See United States—National library of medicine

NATIONAL library week
Award-winning program for NLW. G. A. Somers. il Wilson Lib Bul 39:472-4 F '65
Awards and authors on parade for National library week. Library J 88:2214+ Je 1 '63
Best-read city in the U.S.A: Pasadena. S. Grafton. il McCalls 90:48+ Ap '63
Bulletin board. ALA Bul 58:664 S '64
Five weeks to D-day; symposium. il Library J 88:1101-8 Mr 15 '63
Greater involvement, greater cooperation recorded in NLW's sixth annual report. Library J 88:4724 D 15 '63
Key concerns; report. V. H. Mathews. ALA Bul 57:1048 D '63
Labor: a target for NLW? S. L. Simon. il Library J 88:1109-11 Mr 15 '63
Letter series that works: a report from the ALTA-NLW committee. R. A. Young and J. L. Love. Wilson Lib Bul 37:577 Mr '63
Libraries as important as schools, says Kennedy in NLW message. Library J 88:1962 My 15 '63
Life guide; the library scene. il Life 54:23 Ap 19 '63
National library week. D. R. Watts. Wilson Lib Bul 38:570 Mr '64
NLW backs better school libraries. Library J 88:842 F 15 '63
NLW picks 1964 theme: Reading is the key. Library J 88:4450 N 15 '63
National library week plans near completion; with editorial comment. il Pub W 183:30-1, 36 Mr 11 '63
NLW: publicity postscript. il Wilson Lib Bul 37:832 Je '63
National library week reports and press releases. Wilson Lib Bul 38:726 My '64
NLW's dazzling array; letter to the editor. H. W. Tucker. Library J 89:4 Ja 1 '64
Onward and upward towards one-fourth of one per cent. C. B. Grannis. Pub W 186:40 Jl 27 '64
Plans for National library week near completion. il Pub W 185:45-6 Ja 13 '64
President Wagman on National library week; statement. F. H. Wagman. ALA Bul 58:211 Mr '64
President's NLW statement stresses education. J. F. Kennedy. Pub W 183:30 Ap 22 '63
Reading is the key, library week theme, 1964; with editorial comment. Pub W 184:30, 35 O 28 '63
Reading is the key. NLW theme for 1964. Library J 88:4338 N 15 '63
Reading, the fifth freedom: NLW sixth annual report issued by the National book committee. Wilson Lib Bul 38:381 Ja '64
Salt spray and sperm whales; Melville whaling room, in New Bedford, Mass. free public library. J. S. Healey. il Wilson Lib Bul 37:565-8 Mr '63
Social scientists featured as NLW workshop speakers. Library J 88:3568+ O 1 '63
State library associations and National library week. G. T. Stevenson. ALA Bul 58:37-8 Ja '64
Steering committee announced for next year's NLW program. Library J 89:2976 Ag '64
Steering committee named for 1965 NLW. Pub W 186:35 Jl 27 '64
Use of National library week. M. Ricking. ALA Bul 58:236-7 Mr '64
Whitewash in Whitewater; Wisconsin state college vs Kiwanis club; letter to the editor. S. D. Robertson. Library J 89:2900+ Ag '64

NATIONAL liturgical week. See Liturgical week

NATIONAL livestock and meat board
Ruling threatens meat promotion. J. Rohlf. Farm J 87:63 Ap '63

NATIONAL lotteries. See Lotteries

NATIONAL lumber manufacturers association
Lowly two-by-four stirs a major wrangle. il Bsns W p56+ Mr 7 '64

NATIONAL Lutheran council
Lutherans and school aid. E. C. Parker. Christian Cent 80:263 F 27 '63
NATIONAL marine engineers' beneficial association
Big liner aground on inter-union reef; SS America. il Bsns W p 114+ O 5 '63
Feud; the S.S. America's lay-up. il Newsweek 62:96 O 14 '63
Unions argue, ocean liner waits; tying up United States lines' America by dispute: NMU vs. Engineers union. U S News 55:106 O 14 '63
Why engineers tied up America's nuclear ship; Savannah and Marine engineers beneficial association. il U S News 54:74-5 My 27 '63
NATIONAL maritime union of America
Big liner aground on inter-union reef; SS America. il Bsns W p 114+ O 5 '63
Feud; the S.S. America's lay-up. il Newsweek 62:96 O 14 '63
Labor's mutinous mariners. A. H. Raskin. il Atlan 214:72-8 N '64
Our strike-strangled merchant marine. R. S. Strother. Read Digest 82:75-9 F '63
Unions argue, ocean liner waits; tying up United States lines' America by dispute: NMU vs. Engineers union. U S News 55:106 O 14 '63
When machines replace seamen; mechanized ships. il Bsns W p 100+ Ja 25 '64
NATIONAL marriage and divorce law. See Marriage law—United States
NATIONAL mass media award. See Thomas Alva Edison award
NATIONAL medal for literature
Book committee announces National literature medal. Pub W 185:28 Mr 16 '64
NATIONAL medal of science.
Eleven scientists named for 1964 national medal. Sci N L 86:371 D 12 '64
Excellent start. R. Hotz. Aviation W 78:21 F 25 '63
Recipients of National medal of science named. Sci N L 84:407 D 28 '63
Von Karman wins science medal. il Miss & Roc 12:22 F 25 '63
NATIONAL mediation board. See United States—National mediation board
NATIONAL merit scholarship corporation
Choosing a college. il New Repub 150:5 F 29 '64
Identification, motivation, and training of talented students; report. A. W. Astin. Sch & Soc 92:186-9 Ap 18 '64
Merit scholars cream of the senior class crop. il Sr Schol 82:20-1 Ap 24 '63
NATIONAL microfilm association
Int'l micrographic congress established in Ann Arbor. Pub W 183:34 Ap 1 '63
NATIONAL monuments
Agate Fossil Beds National Monument. P. M. Tilden. il Nat Parks Mag 38:4-7 Ag '64
Arches and bridges of stone; Utah. W. Luce. il Natur Hist 73:42-7 Ag '64
Fascinating U.S. forts. P. Geraci. il Travel 122:24-30 Jl '64
Proposals for a John Muir National Monument. Nat Parks Mag 38:21 Ja '64
Reporter at large; northernmost Keys, proposed as Islandia National Monument. B. Roueché. New Yorker 40:37-8+ D 26 '64
See also names of national monuments, e.g. Ocmulgee National Monument
NATIONAL morale. See Morale, National
NATIONAL motor boat show. See Motor boats—Exhibitions
NATIONAL multipurpose space station. See Space stations
NATIONAL municipal league
See also
All-America cities
NATIONAL music council
Buried treasures. P. L. Miller. il Library J 88:1823-5 My 1 '63
NATIONAL music league
Twenty-five years of non-profit. J. Ardoin. il Mus Am 83:45 O '63
NATIONAL music theatre
Musical events; Land of Smiles, Carnegie Hall. W. Sargeant. New Yorker 39:164-6 Mr 16 '63
NATIONAL music week. See Music week
NATIONAL open championship. See Golf—Tournaments
NATIONAL opera association
Colorado comedies. A. Young. Opera N 29:32 Ja 23 '65
N.O.A. convention. A. M. Lingg. Opera N 27:33-4 Mr 2 '63
NATIONAL operational meteorological satellite system. See Artificial satellites—Meteorological applications
NATIONAL opinion research center
NORC, round three: study of the effects of Catholic formal education in America. Commonweal 81:555-6 Ja 29 '65
Reaction to killings. Sci N L 84:358 D 7 '63
NATIONAL park service (United States) See United States—National park service
NATIONAL parks and reserves
National parks and natural history; excerpt from address. R. D. Muir. il Nat Parks Mag 39:14-15 Ja '65
Parks as prologue. A. W. Smith. Nat Parks Mag 38:2 Jl '64
See also
National forests

Roads

New Saguaro road proposed. H. Melts. Nat Parks Mag 37:23 S '63
Nibbling here and there. Nat Parks Mag 37:19 N '63
Park road planning and finances. A. W. Smith. Nat Parks Mag 37:2 N '63
Trail is a trail, or is it? P. M. Tilden. il Nat Parks Mag 37:2 S '63

Africa

You and your camera in places where lions climb trees; tours of game reserves in east Africa. il Sunset 133:65-6+ N '64

Argentina

Sequoia of South America. E. J. Wilhelm, jr. il Nat Parks Mag 37:8-10 D '63

Australia

National parks in Australia. W. C. Robison. il Nat Parks Mag 38:11-15 Jl '64

Canada

See also
Point Pelee National Park

France

Birth of a French park; Vanoise National Park. Nat Parks Mag 38:17 Jl '64

Ireland

Visiting botanists; State Memorial Park with arboretum in Dunganstown; memorial to President Kennedy. New Yorker 40:30 Je 13 '64

Japan

National parks of Japan. E. E. Gamer. il Nat Parks Mag 37:8-11 Jl '63
Spectacular playground in Tokyo's backyard. il Sports Illus 21:20-5 Ag 31 '64

Sweden

National parks of Sweden. B. Haglund. il Am For 70:26-9+ My '64

Tanganyika

Golden plains of Tanganyika. P. Brooks. il Horizon 7:80-9 Wint '65
Serengeti National Park; with editorial comment. E. Huxley. il Nat Parks Mag 38:2, 10-14 My '64
To protect an Africa that was; Serengeti National Park and Ngorongoro conservation area. il N Y Times Mag p42-3 Ja 10 '65

United States

All-season camping. il Recreation 56:115-18 Mr '63
Assateague Island: challenge in park planning. il Nat Parks Mag 38:4-7 N '64
Assateague Island National Seashore proposal. Nat Parks Mag 37:21 S '63
Assateague Island; our next national seashore? J. Martineau. il Am For 69:16-19+ Ag '63
Assateague seashore. Nat Parks Mag 38:16 Je '64
Assault on Assateague; land speculation in proposed Assateague Island Seashore. Nat Parks Mag 39:20 Ja '65
Attractive nuisances. P. M. Tilden. Nat Parks Mag 38:2 Ag '64
Beware of Smokey the bear. H. Bloomfield. il Sat Eve Post 237:68-9 S 12 '64
Businessmen who love the land. il Fortune 67:114-21 Mr '63
Congressman Aspinall vs. the people of the United States. P. Brooks. Harper 226:60-3 Mr '63
Conservation and progress: two inseparables. A. B. Adams. il Nat Parks Mag 37:4-8 N '63
Conservation docket. See issues of National parks magazine
Conservation or recreation: our swarming national parks. K. Wilson. il Nation 198:391-5 Ap 20 '64

NATIONAL parks and reserves—United States —*Continued*
Cross-country editor: reports on national boom in auto camping. H. Grey. il Field & S 67:36-7+ F '63
Fill'er up: a new lake is born; Lake Powell, Glen Canyon National Recreation Area. J. R. Muench. il Motor B 113:21-3+ My '64
Fire Island: a possible National seashore. V. B. Moore. il Nat Parks Mag 37:4-9 F '63
From sun-clad sea to shining mountains. R. Gray. il Nat Geog Mag 125:542-89 Ap '64
Future of the world. P. H. Oehser. il Liv Wildn 82:18-19 Winter '62
Hunting in our national parks? A. W. Smith. Audubon Mag 65:6-9 Ja '63
Ice age national scientific reserve; with editorial comment. J. L. Dyson. il Nat Parks Mag 37:2, 4-9 Ag '63
Immortality of the Dunes; Indiana Dunes National Lakeshore. A. W. Smith. Nat Parks Mag 37:2 N '63
In the national parks. P. M. Tilden. Natur Hist 72:66-7 Je '63
Indian summer for the Indiana dunes? il Am For 69:20-1+ Mr '63
Indiana dunes and pressure politics. W. Peeples. Atlan 211:84-8 F '63
Indiana Dunes National Lakeshore. F. Sicher. il Nat Parks Mag 38:4-7+ Jl '64
Lands we share; address, May 3, 1963. L. C. Binford. Am For 69:16-19+ Jl '63
Leopold report appraised. il Liv Wildn 83:20-4 Spring '63
Letting George do it won't do it. W. R. Catton, jr. il Nat Parks Mag 38:4-7 Mr '64
Maryland approves Assateague National Seashore. J. M. Tawes. il Am For 69:6+ O '63
New preservations. P. M. Tilden. Natur Hist 73:63+ D '64
North Cascades Park; remarks, October 11, 1963. il Liv Wildn 85:36 Wint '64
On the national park agenda. C. H. Callison. Audubon Mag 67:25 Ja '65
Once lost, never recaptured; scenic treasures. S. L. Udall. il N Y Times Mag p38-9 S 13 '64
Our best chance to save the Indiana dunes. P. H. Douglas. il Audubon Mag 66:112-14 Mr '64
Over 88,000,000 visit national parks in 1962. Nat Parks Mag 37:17 My '63
Park system additions recommended by board. Nat Parks Mag 37:16 Je '63
Parks advisory board meets. Nat Parks Mag 38:14 D '64
Pictured Rocks Lakeshore. Nat Parks Mag 38:18 S '64
Policy report of president to trustees of National parks association; November 19, 1963. Nat Parks Mag 38:I-IV Ja '64
Possible danger for the dunes; Indiana Dunes National Lakeshore (proposed) Nat Parks Mag 38:17 S '64
Prairie National Park. Nat Parks Mag 37:19 O '63
President Johnson backs a Redwoods Park. C. W. Buchheister. Audubon Mag 66:282 S '64
Proposed Cape Lookout National Seashore; with editorial comment. D. B. Huyck. il Nat Parks Mag 38:2, 4-8 S '64
Seashore proposal; Cape Lookout National Seashore in North Carolina. Nat Parks Mag 38:16 Je '64
Sleeping Bear Park: a project stirs a row. il U S News 54:84-6 Je 10 '63
Stephen Mather, master of the wilderness. D. Peattie and L. Peattie. il Read Digest 85:148-53 Jl '64
Study of the redwoods; Redwood National Park (proposed) Nat Parks Mag 38:16 D '64
Texas governor favors Guadalupe National Park. Nat Parks Mag 38:16 Mr '64
Try camping for summer fun. C. Allen. il Ebony 18:127-8+ Je '63
Two proposed parks; Great Basin National Park and Guadalupe Mountains National Park. Nat Parks Mag 38:16 D '64
Two roads lead to conservation; facts about the wilderness bills. Bsns W p32 Ag 15 '64
Vacation fun in national parks. Parents Mag 38:121 My '63
Visitor access to the seashores and parks. A. W. Smith. Nat Parks Mag 38:2 N '64
Voyageurs National Park? Nat Parks Mag 38:14-15 N '64
Washington newsletter. P. M. Tilden. Natur Hist 72:63-7 D '63; 73:66-9 Je '64
Wildlife management in the national parks. A. S. Leopold and others. il Audubon Mag 65:166-71+ My '63
Wildlife management in the national parks. S. A. Cain and others. il Liv Wildn 83:11-19 Spring '63
Wildlife management in the national parks; Leopold committee report. il Am For 69:32-5+ Ap '63; Same. Nat Parks Mag 37:11-16 Ap '63; Discussion. Am For 69:11 Ap '63; Nat Parks Mag 37:11 Ap '63
Wonders of Fire Island beach; Fire Island National Seashore (proposed) R. C. Murphy. Audubon Mag 66:6-9 Ja '64
See also
National monuments
United States—National park service
also names of national parks and reserves, e.g. Shenandoah National Park

NATIONAL parks association
Association opposes big dams as panaceas. Nat Parks Mag 38:19 F '64
Conservation education center fall session opens. Nat Parks Mag 37:19 N '63
Meeting, 1963. Nat Parks Mag 37:11-14 S '63
NPA's 1964 annual meeting. Nat Parks Mag 38:16 Jl '64
Policy report of president to trustees; November 19, 1963. Nat Parks Mag 38:I-IV Ja '64
Your National parks association at work. See issues of National parks magazine to February 1964

NATIONAL planning
You can shape business climate; symposium. il Nations Bsns 51:61-4 Jl '63
See also
Great Britain—Reconstruction

NATIONAL planning association
Attack on poverty. Commonweal 81:436 D 25 '64

NATIONAL poison prevention week. See Special days, weeks and months

NATIONAL police gazette
Bible of the barbershop. M. Weisbord. il Sports Illus 18:54-61 F 18 '63

NATIONAL pro-amateur golf championship. See Golf—Tournaments

NATIONAL quotation bureau, incorporated
Monopoly on Front street. Fortune 68:232+ S '63

NATIONAL radio astronomy observatory, Green Bank, W.Va.
300-foot radio telescope at Green Bank. J. W. Findlay. il Sky & Tel 25:68-75 F '63

NATIONAL railway historical society
All abroad. il Newsweek 62:77 S 16 '63

NATIONAL railway labor conference
Rails close ranks in bargaining. Bsns W p52+ F 16 '63

NATIONAL rare blood club
Medicine's most exclusive club. il Look 27:74b+ Jl 16 '63

NATIONAL recreation association
Eighth National institute for public recreation executives. W. C. Sutherland. il Recreation 56:285 Je '63
Free men accept the challenge of free time; National purpose project. A. L. New. Recreation 56:189 Ap '63
High moments from N.R.A. annual district conferences 1963. il Recreation 56:320-1 S '63
Historical background of the relationship of NRA and ARS. il Recreation 56:170-3+ Ap '63
Municipal sports programs and policies; 1962 survey. il Recreation 56:214-18 My '63
NRA adds new office in Washington, D.C. il Recreation 58:6 Ja '65
New National committee chairman. il Recreation 56:385 O '63
New NRA board members. il Recreation 56:335 S '63
New NRA projects. Recreation 57:344 S '64
Opera is recreation. il Recreation 57:451+ N '64
Progress report. Recreation 56:464+ D '63
This is your NRA. il Recreation 57:56-8, 283-98 F, Je '64
Track and field development. J. B. Sharpless. il Recreation 57:230-1 My '64

NATIONAL recreation congress
Anatomy of a congress. C.E. Hartsoe. Recreation 56:307 S '63
Congress faces. il Recreation 57:490-1 D '64
Critical issues in recreation; report from the 46th congress. il Recreation 57:489-92+ D '64
45th National recreation congress; program. il Recreation 56:310-12 S '63
45th National recreation congress; Why attend this year? Recreation 56:110-11 Mr '63
Highlights of the 46th National recreation congress. il Recreation 57:337-9 S '64
Leisure, the heart of living; topic for 45th National recreation congress. S. Case. il Recreation 56:224-5 My '63
Look ahead at Miami Beach. C. M. Christiansen. il Recreation 57:55 F '64

NATIONAL recreation congress—*Continued*
Miami spectacular. il Recreation 57:216 My '64
Observations from the 45th National recreation congress. il Recreation 56:453-6 D '63
Progress report. Recreation 56:464+ D '63

NATIONAL referral center for science and technology. See United States—National referral center for science and technology

NATIONAL registry of historic landmarks. See United States—National park service

NATIONAL research corporation
1,000,000 metal particles on the head of a pin. il Life 54:41-2+ F 15 '63
Research company moves out of the lab; production of superconductor materials, niobium-zirconium and niobium-tin. il Bsns W p80+ Jl 11 '64

NATIONAL research council of Canada
Documenting the case against fluoridation. J. Lear. il Sat R 47:85-92 Ja 4 '64; Discussion. 47:49-53 F 1; 47-9 My 2 '64

NATIONAL responsibility. See Responsibility

NATIONAL retail merchants association
Now retailers put it all on tape. il Bsns W p30-1 Ja 16 '65

NATIONAL review
Debate on the Moscow treaty. Nat R 15:136-7 Ag 27 '63
Liberalland: advertisement; letters to the editor. Nat R 15:411 N 5 '63
Lion of conservatism. il Newsweek 61:94-5 My 13 '63
NR and Goldwater. Nat R 16:9 Ja 14 '64
Notes and asides (cont) il Nat R 14:225-6, 270, 441; 16:266, 310, 346+, 393, 480, 681, Mr 26-Ap 9, Je 4 '63, Ap 7-My 19, Je 16, Ag 11 '64
November 5 issue; letters to the editor. Nat R 15:497 D 3 '63
Old inaccurate us; letters to the editor. Nat R 15:319+ O 8 '63; Discussion. 15:411 N 5 '63
On the far right. Commonweal 79:384 D 27 '63
Spokesman for conservatism. Time 84:74 Jl 10 '64
Student apostasy. Christian Cent 80:1455-7 N 27 '63; Discussion. 81:86-7 Ja 15 '64

NATIONAL rifle and pistol matches. See Shooting—Competitions

NATIONAL rifle association
Be strong, carry a gun. New Repub 149:7 D 14 '63
Cannon to the right of us. New Repub 150:5 Je 20 '64
Don't wait, buy a gun now! J. Ridgeway. New Repub 150:9-10 Je 6 '64
Get your gun from the army. S. Meisler. il Nation 198:568-71 Je 8 '64
Month of bull's-eyes and Maggie's drawers; National rifle and pistol matches. il Sports Illus 21:28-33 Ag 10 '64
Rifles: target for control? il Newsweek 64:21-3 D 28 '64
Traffic in guns: a forgotten lesson of the assassination. C. Bakal. Harper 229:62-8 D '64

NATIONAL safe boating week. See Special days, weeks, and months

NATIONAL safety council
Editor's auto-graphs. C. Nerpel. il Motor T 16:8 Jl '64
Just what is the National safety council? il Good H 158:165 Ap '64

NATIONAL scholarship service and fund for Negro students
Will to succeed. Time 82:34+ D 20 '63

NATIONAL school boards association
School boards spokesman. G. Dapper. Sat R 47:73+ Mr 21 '64
Teachers' strike issue. Sr Schol 83:1T-2T N 1 '63

NATIONAL science fair. See Science fairs

NATIONAL science fair-international. See Science fairs

NATIONAL science foundation. See United States—National science foundation

NATIONAL science talent search. See Science talent search

NATIONAL science youth month
1963 National science youth month. Sci N L 84:108-11 Ag 17 '63
October is National science youth month; with President Lyndon B. Johnson's endorsement. Sci N L 86:231 O 10 '64
October, National science youth month. Sci N L 86:108-11 Ag 15 '64
October to be National science youth month. Sci N L 84:185 S 21 '63

NATIONAL science youth program. See Science youth program

NATIONAL security. See Internal security

NATIONAL security council. See United States—National security council

NATIONAL security industrial association
Aerospace to oceanography. Nation 196:365 My 4 '63

NATIONAL service corps. See Volunteers in service to America

NATIONAL shooting dog championship. See Field trials (dogs)

NATIONAL ski fair. See Exhibitions

NATIONAL socialism
See also
Fascism—Germany

NATIONAL society for the prevention of blindness
How to watch next week's eclipse: don't burn your eyes. il Life 55:41+ Jl 12 '63

NATIONAL society of college teachers of education
Conant report; is enlightened debate possible? account of the Chicago meetings of the American association of colleges of teacher education and the National society of college teachers of education, Feb. 19-22, 1964. H. D. Gideonse. Sat R 47:56-7+ S 19 '64

NATIONAL songs

United States

See also
Yankee Doodle (song)

NATIONAL steel corporation
National: a pacesetter in steel. E. K. Faltermayer. il Fortune 69:96-103+ F '64
Steel irons out casting method; vacuum degasser. Bsns W p 104 S 21 '63

NATIONAL student association. See United States national student association

NATIONAL symphony orchestra, Washington, D.C.
Greatest satisfaction. il Time 81:42+ My 3 '63

NATIONAL television systems committee
Color-pattern generators. W. J. Cerveny. il Electr World 69:50-2+ Mr '63
Fight goes worldwide for color TV sales; competition from Japan. il Bsns W p46+ My 30 '64

NATIONAL theater, British. See Theater—Great Britain

NATIONAL theater, Munich. See Opera houses

NATIONAL training laboratory in group development
Yourself as others see you; sensitivity training program. il Bsns W p 160+ Mr 16 '63

NATIONAL trust for historic preservation
American landmarks celebration seeks to preserve nation's heritage. C. W. Thomas. il Negro Hist Bul 28:24+ O '64

NATIONAL union catalog. See United States—Library of Congress—Union catalog

NATIONAL union of teachers (Great Britain) See Teachers unions

NATIONAL university of Mexico. See Colleges and universities—Mexico

NATIONAL urban league
Sponsors of the March on Washington. Negro Hist Bul 27:3-4 O '63

NATIONAL watershed congress
Mirrors of accomplishment; eleventh congress. il Am For 70:36-9 Je '64
Partners in progress. il Am For 69:28-9+ Jl '63

NATIONAL Woodrow Wilson fellowship foundation. See Woodrow Wilson national fellowship foundation

NATIONAL youth for Christ week. See Special days, weeks and months

NATIONAL zoological park, Washington, D.C.
See also
Anteater association

NATIONALISM
Again nationalism threatens. A. J. Toynbee. il N Y Times Mag p23+ N 3 '63
Back to power politics; nationalism and looser alliances. il Bsns W p27-9 O 19 '63
Is nationalism really outmoded? letter. G. Ichheiser. Bul Atomic Sci 20:35 Je '64
Jewish & other nationalisms. H. R. Trevor-Roper. Commentary 35:15-21 Ja '63
Lonely nationalism of Rudyard Kipling. K. W. Deutsch and N. Wiener. Yale R 52:499-517 Je '63
Nationalism, a global headache for Johnson; with editorial comment. il Bsns W p22-3, 76 Ja 4 '64
1964 religious issue. Christian Cent 81:1227-8 O 7 '64

NATIONALISM—*Continued*
Speaking out; America the smug. R. Niebuhr. Sat Eve Post 236:12+ N 16 '63
See also
Americanism
Autonomy
Patriotism
Racism
also subhead Nationalism under names of continents, countries, etc. e.g. Israel—Nationalism
NATIONALITY. See Citizenship
NATIONALITY, Dual. See Citizenship
NATIONALIZATION of industry. See Government ownership
NATIONALIZATION of mines. See Mines and mineral resources—Government ownership
NATIONALIZATION of railroads. See Railroads and state
NATIONS
Nations of the world: table (cont) Sr Schol 83:16-19 O 4 '63; 85:22-5 O 7 '64
NATIONS, Law of. See International law
NATIVE American church
God & peyote. il Time 84:64 S 11 '64
NATIVITY groups. See Christmas cribs
NATIVITY of Christ. See Jesus Christ—Nativity
NATSIVAAR
Seal oil and soapstone. il Horizon 5:120 Mr '63
NATTA, Giulio
Macromolecular chemistry; address, December 12, 1963. bibliog Science 147:261-722 Ja 15 '65
NATURAL affection; drama. See Inge, W.
NATURAL arches. See Arches, Natural
NATURAL areas. See Wilderness areas
NATURAL bridges. See Bridges, Natural
NATURAL childbirth. See Childbirth
NATURAL forest areas. See Wilderness areas
NATURAL forms
Nature thought of it first. J. Sidney. il Sci Digest 54:44-7 O '63
NATURAL gas. See Gas, Natural
NATURAL gas industry. See Gas industry
NATURAL history
National parks and natural history; excerpt from address. R. D. Muir. il Nat Parks Mag 39:14-15 Ja '65
Nature note. See issues of Science news letter
See also
Nature study
Television broadcasting—Nature programs
Wildlife conservation

Bibliography

Inexpensive book gifts for naturalists. Sunset 131:40-2 D '63
NATURAL history museums
Expositions, exhibits and today's museums. G. Reekie. il Natur Hist 73:20-9 Je '64
If you wonder about dinosaurs; Field house of natural history, Vernal State Park, Utah. il Sunset 132:35 My '64
Night life on the desert. J. J. Stophlet. il Nat Parks Mag 38:12-15 Mr '64
Where animals can really get to know children; Arizona-Sonora desert museum. il Sunset 130:36-8+ My '63
See also
American museum of natural history. New York
NATURAL law
Conscience and pluralism. F. Canavan. America 110:536-9 Ap 18 '64; Discussion. 110:660 My 16 '64
Natural law and modern society, by J. Cogley and others. Review
Commonweal 79:111 O 18 '63
Pacem in terris a year later. J. Cogley. Commonweal 80:356-7 Je 12 '64
NATURAL law (science) See Nature, Laws of
NATURAL lighting. See Lighting
NATURAL monuments
It's Paul Bunyan's woodpile. il Sunset 131:50 N '63
NATURAL resources
Natural resources and international development, ed. by M. Clawson. Review
Am For 70:42+ S '64. B. F. Grossling
See also
Brooks, creeks, etc.
Conservation of resources
Fuel
Marine resources
Mines and mineral resources
Water supply
Wildlife conservation

Bibliography

Reading about resources. M. Bush. See issues of American forests

Africa, West

African metamorphosis. E. A. K. Kalitsi. il UNESCO Courier 16:44-9 Jl '63

Brazil

Brazil. C. F. Jones. il Focus 15:1-6 N '64

Canada

Man tames the wilderness. R. Haig-Brown. il Atlan 214:149-50+ N '64

Great Britain

Great Britain. J. T. Coppock. bibliog il Focus 14:1-6 Je '64

Guatemala

Guatemala. R. E. Chardon. bibliog il Focus 13:1-6 My '63

Israel

Israel. J. S. Haupert. bibliog il Focus 14:1-6 Mr '64

Japan

Japan. H. Kublin. bibliog il Focus 14:1-6 F '64

Korea (Republic)

Korea: land of the morning calm. H. S. Kernan. il Am For 69:36-9 Ag '63

Laos

Laos. L. Unger. bibliog il Focus 14:1-6 My '64

Micronesia

Micronesia. R. S. Hopkins. bibliog il Focus 13:1-6 Je '63

Netherlands

Big find in a small country; Dutch strike it rich. il U S News 54:79-81 My 20 '63

Nigeria

Federal Republic of Nigeria. B. Floyd. bibliog il Focus 15:1-6 O '64

North Borneo

Sabah (North Borneo) C. F. Preuss. bibliog il Focus 14:1-6 N '63

Russia

U.S.S.R. resources for heavy industry. C. D. Harris. bibliog il Focus 13:1-6 Mr '63

Senegal

Senegal. R. J. H. Church. bibliog il Focus 15:1-6 S '64

Uganda

Uganda. D. N. McMaster. bibliog il Focus 14:1-6 Ja '64

United States

Energy in the United States. H. A. Meyerhoff. bibliog il Focus 13:1-6 Ap '63
Environment: land, air, water. R. Revelle. il New Repub 151:25-8+ N 7 '64
Future of the world. P. H. Oehser. il Liv Wildn 82:18-19 Winter '62
Happy future days; conclusions of Ford foundation study, Resources for the future. Time 81:71-2 Ap 12 '63
Is there a cure for the common scold? R. Starnes. Field & S 68:12+ N '63
Nature is murdered. B. Tufty. il Sci N L 84:90-1 Ag 10 '63
New direction from Asilomar. M. Bush. Am For 69:27+ Jl '63
Plenty of resources if we use them right; report with charts. Bsns W p84-6 Ap 6 '63
RFF resources forecast shows qualified optimism; with charts. J. B. Craig. Am For 69:16-19+ My '63
Resources for 300 million; summary of report. W. Davis. Sci N L 83:227 Ap 13 '63
Washington lookout. A. G. Hall. See issues of American forests
See also
Water supply—United States
NATURAL rights. See Natural law
NATURAL selection
See also
Evolution
NATURAL steam. See Steam, Natural
NATURAL theology
God and the professors. J. Cogley. Commonweal 78:525-6 S 6 '63
NATURALISM in art. See Realism in art
NATURALIZATION
No more second-class citizens. R. H. Amundson. America 110:847-8 Je 20 '64
See also
Citizenship

NATURE
Beauty and science. M. L. Jones. il Natur Hist 72:18-21 Ap '63
Garden is a place to play, to learn, to grow. J. DiLeo. il Pop Gard 15:32-3 Jl '64
Key to nature; address, August 1962. R. E. Carlson. il Recreation 56:64-6+ F '63
Lake Solitude sermon; reprint. H. Zahniser. il(p 1) Liv Wildn 85:2 Wint '64
Nature and mental health. I. L. Fishbein. Audubon Mag 66:25 Ja '64
Nature thought of it first. J. Sidney. il Sci Digest 54:44-7 O '63
Our alliance with nature; excerpt from address, delivered on acceptance of John Burroughs medal, April 6, 1964. J. Hay. Audubon Mag 66:395-8 N '64
Place of nature in the city of man. I. L. McHarg. bibliog f Ann Am Acad 352:1-12 Mr '64
Rocky Mountain marvels: nature's pranks. il Holiday 34:68-73 Ag '63
Transfiguration in wilderness. C. E. Graves. il Liv Wildn 82:9-10 Winter '62
Wilderness as a tonic. J. W. Krutch. Sat R 46:15-17 Je 8 '63
See also
Animals
Nature study
Bibliography
Books. See issues of Audubon magazine
Reviews. See issues of Natural history incorporating Nature magazine

NATURE, Balance of. See Balance of nature

NATURE, Laws of
Events, laws of nature, and invariance principles; address, December 10, 1963. E. P. Wigner. bibliog Science 145:995-9 S 4 '64

NATURE centers
Guidelines for a nature center. J. J. Shomon. Audubon Mag 65:384-5 N '63
How one community acquired a nature center; Forest Park wildlife refuge and nature education center, Peoria, Ill. C. A. McCumber. il Audubon Mag 65:244-5 Jl '63
Natural heritage; program sponsored by the Huron-Clinton metropolitan authority. J. Sterling. il Recreation 57:112-14 Mr '64
Nature centers and delinquency. J. J. Shomon. Audubon Mag 66:14-15 Ja '64
Naturealm; Prince Gallitzin State Park. J. J. Shomon. il Audubon Mag 66:212-15 Jl '64
Opportunity knocks for local forest lands. R. F. Holmes. il Audubon Mag 66:278 S '64
Some emerging concepts of natural areas and nature centers. J. J. Shomon. il Audubon Mag 65:176-7 My '63
Super nature center opens; Kalamazoo nature center. H. L. Batts, jr. and J. J. Shomon. il Audubon Mag 67:13-15 Ja '65
See also
Audubon nature centers

NATURE drawing. See Drawing

NATURE in art
Niagara show. M. Grosser. Nation 198:543-4 My 25 '64
Poetry of art. C. R. Rose. il Sch Arts 62:12 Mr '63
Summer to remember. F. Green. il Sch Arts 64:14-16 S '64
See also
Birds in art
Landscape painting

NATURE literature
Grey Owl: mysterious genius of nature lore. R. Cantwell. il Sports Illus 18:112-14+ Ap 8 '63
Illustrations
See Illustration of books and periodicals

NATURE of man. See Man

NATURE outings. See Nature study

NATURE photography
American landscape. P. Caulfield. il Mod Phot 28:80-1+ Ja '64
Art of the biological photographer. il Natur Hist 74:58-61 Ja '65
Case for the slow shutter. il U S Camera 26:72-3 S '63
Eliot Porter. P. Caulfield. il Mod Phot 28: 52-7+ F '64
Flash for your garden. J. J. Simpkins. Flower Grower 50:65 My '63
Focus on Steven C. Wilson. J. Durniak. il Pop Phot 53:60-3+ O '63
Focusing on nature; ed. by B. Hering. H. F. Brevoort. il Pop Sci 183:132-4+ Ag '63
How-to-photographs. J. J. Simpkins. Flower Grower 50:68-9 Mr '63
In air and light. B. Hanson. il Sch Arts 63: 34-5 Ap '64
Isolate nature's forms. il U S Camera 27:68-9 Jl '46
Kinne on flash. R. Kinne. il Pop Phot 53: 68-75+ O '63
Nature and the camera (cont) D. Linton. il Natur Hist 72:62-5+ O '63
Nature and photography. S. Dunton. il Natur Hist 74:61-5 F '65
Nature and the camera (cont) D. Linton. il Natur Hist 72:62-5+ O '63; 73:64-8 Ag '64
New wonder camera for nature close-ups; Startech cameras. J. C. Schmid. il Audubon Mag 65:266-8 S '63
Picture the wonders in your own back yard. J. J. Simpkins. il Flower Grower 50:56 O '63
Rocks or faces? J. Durniak. il Pop Phot 52: 61-3 F '63
Weathervane. R. G. Miner. Flower Grower 50:10 Je '63
Why settle for one? P. Caulfield. il Mod Phot 28:68-73 Jl '64
See also
Photography—Landscapes
Photography of animals
Photography of birds
Photography of fishes
Photography of insects
Snakes—Photographs

NATURE sanctuaries. See Wilderness areas

NATURE study
ABC's of a field trip: attitude, behavior and clothing. L. C. Fink. Audubon Mag 66:124-5 Mr '64
Animal worlds, by M. Bates. Review
Reporter 30:52+ Ja 16 '64. S. Eimerl
Discovering the wonderful world of nature. J. E. Dwyer. il Pop Gard 15:24-7 Jl '64
Experiments in nature education. J. Sterling; E. C. Waldbauer; W. Bly. il Recreation 57:112-15 Mr '64
Exploration at the pond; photographs. A. Strong. Natur Hist 73:44-5 Ap '64
Nature (cont) J. O'Reilly. il Sports Illus 19: 81-2+ S 23 '63
Nature craft. J. Laury and J. Aiken. il Bet Hom & Gard 42:96 O; 121 N '64
Nature never fails to astound; photographs from What science knows about life. H. Woltereck. N Y Times Mag p76-7 My 19 '63
Our young people. S. Miller. il Audubon Mag 67:62 Ja '65
Outdoors in the city's shadows; Riverdale outdoor laboratories. H. Williams. il Natur Hist 72:32-41 My '63
Summer secrets. B. Tufty. il Sci N L 85:394-5 Je 20 '64
Time to enjoy; reprint. E. R. Murray. Recreation 57:142 Mr '64
Tomorrow's guardians; excerpts from address, February 15, 1964. G. B. Hartzog, jr. Recreation 57:165 Ap '64
See also
Animals
Audubon nature camps
Audubon nature centers
Bird study
Camping—Educational aspects
Childrens gardens
Nature
Nature centers
Nature literature
Television broadcasting—Nature programs

NATURE trails. See Trails

NATZLER, Otto
Natzler glazes. por Craft Horiz 24:24-7+ Jl '64

NAUGHTON, Bill
Alfie! Criticism
Commonweal 81:575 Ja 29 '65
Nation 200:17 Ja 4 '65
New Yorker 40:58 Ja 2 '65
Newsweek 65:51-2 Ja 4 '65
Time 84:62 D 25 '64

NAUGHTON, William A.
What's in a name? Américas 16:27-31 D '64

NAUM, Lionel H.
Hard look at public relations. Duns R 84: 47+ N '64

NAURU (Island)
Continuing efforts toward harmonious solution for future of Nauru islanders. il U N Rev 10:27-9+ Jl '63
Special island. Time 84:40 S 11 '64

NAUSEA
See also
Motion sickness

NAUTICAL charts
Charting the Bahamas. H. Kline. il Yachting 114:58-60+ N '63
Charting the Great Lakes for yachtsmen. F. R. Shumway. Motor B 113:98+ F '64
Cooperating on charts; U.S. power squadrons and U.S. coast & geodetic survey. M. L. Hersey. Yachting 115:142 F '64

NAUTICAL charts—*Continued*
Pilot charts, then and now. R. Martin. il Motor B 114:42-3+ N '64
Sold out! new Great Lakes small-craft charts a boon to boatmen. J. Hanna and G. Wegner. Motor B 114:124-5 Jl '64
Where to get charts and helpful cruising information (cont) Motor B 111:93-5 Ap '63; 113:83-5 Ap '64
You can make these stick charts; Marshall Islanders navigational charts. il Sunset 133: 111 S '64
NAUTICAL instruments
See also
Automatic pilot (boats)
Chronometers
Compass
NAUTICAL slang. See Slang
NAUTICAL terms. See Naval art and science—Terminology
NAVA, Efrén Lubin Prieto. See Prieto Nava, E. L.
NAVAHO Indians
Arizona: booming youngster of the West. R. De Roos. il Nat Geog Mag 123:299-343 Mr '63
Manpower training in Navajo land. V. S. Hart. il Sch Life 45:26-9 Mr '63
Navajo country. il Sunset 131:60-71 S '63
Sick Navajos. Newsweek 64:72 Jl 27 '64
NAVAJO Indian reservation. See Indians of North America—Reservations
NAVAJO NATIONAL MONUMENT
Navajo country. il Sunset 131:60-71 S '63
NAVAL air bases. See Air bases
NAVAL architecture
Confessions of a naval architect. F. MacLear. Motor B 111:26+ F '63
Profiles; W. F. Gibbs. W. Sargeant. New Yorker 40:49-50+ Je 6 '64
Yachting interviews: Ray Hunt. B. D. Barker, 3d. il Yachting 116:47-9+ Jl '64
See also
Webb institute of naval architecture
Yachts—Design
NAVAL art and science
See also
Signals and signaling
Terminology
Abaft the word (cont) W. Funk. Motor B 111:62+ Ap; 56 My; 112:58 Ag '63
Pennant or burgee? W. H. Koelbel. il Motor B 114:72+ Jl '64
Say it with care, or say it with confidence. D. Butler; B. E. Nelson. Motor B 115:100-1+ Ja '65
Why of nautical language. R. M. Clancy. il Motor B 113:368-9 Ja '64
NAVAL bases. See Navy yards and naval stations
NAVAL battles
See also
Jutland, Battle of, 1916
United States—History—Revolution—Naval operations
NAVAL history
See also
Japan—History, Naval
NAVAL maneuvers
Carrier task force shows nuclear range capabilities; Operation sea orbit. il Aviation W 81:94-5+ N 16 '64
Modern Spanish armada; Steel Pike I, old-fashioned assault by sea. Time 84:23 N 6 '64
NAVAL medical research unit. See United States—Navy—Naval medical research unit
NAVAL museums
Maritime history in Vancouver. il Sunset 132: 36+ My '64
NAVAL observatory
United States
See United States—Naval observatory
NAVAL operations office. See United States—Naval operations, Office of
NAVAL power. See Sea power
NAVAL radio stations. See Radio stations, Military
NAVAL research, Office of. See United States—Naval research, Office of
NAVAL research laboratory. See United States—Naval research laboratory
NAVAL stations. See Navy yards and naval stations
NAVE, Chet, and Nave, Lois
Begonias; new hybrid Kallaking. Horticulture 42:32 Ja '64
NAVE, Lois. See Nave, C. jt. auth.
NAVIES
See also
Russia—Navy
Sea power

NAVIGATING bridge
Flying bridge for Great Lakes tugboats. il Bsns W p90 O 17 '64
Flying bridge in kit form. N. Meiners. il Motor B 111:32-3+ Mr '63
Flying bridge instrument panel. N. Meiners. il Motor B 112:52+ O '63
NAVIGATION
Correcting a course for current. H. de-Fontaine. il Yachting 117:120 Ja '65
How to get by as a navigator. M. King. Yachting 114:126-7 D '63
Navigating the Bermuda race. M. H. Farnham. il Yachting 115:41-3+ Je '64
Rough water boat handling. C. R. Meyer. il Motor B 113:28-9+ Je '64
Taking the curse out of fog. F. T. Moss. il Yachting 116:48-50+ Ag '64
See also
Artificial satellites—Navigational applications
Azimuth
Compass
Inland navigation
Nautical charts
Pilots and pilotage
Sailing
Voyages
Competitions
Benefits of predicted logging; symposium. il Motor B 111:45-50+ Ap '63
Control points. M. L. Hersey. See issues of Yachting
861 miles: now that's a log race! 1964 Alaska predicted log contest. C. West. il Motor B 114:50-3+ N '64
Logging the Pacific. J. R. West. il Yachting 116:66+ Jl '64
Powerboat skippers show the way; predicted log contests. C. F. Enloe, jr. il Yachting 115:59-61+ Ap '64
Predicted log navigation system. M. L. Hersey. il Yachting 114:50-2+ Ag '63
Put more accuracy in your predicted logging. H. Unger. il Motor B 13:106-7 Ja '64
History
Guide over the pathless oceans. A. B. Moody. Motor B 111:114+ Mr '63
Tables
Running inlets. F. T. Moss. il Yachting 114: 43-5+ Jl '63
NAVIGATION (space flight)
Canopus star sensor will provide method to correct Surveyor course. il Miss & Roc 15:36-7 Jl 6 '64
Doppler study holds promise of improved space navigation. R. Pay. Miss & Roc 13:24-5 O 14 '63
Dwarf to guide Apollo; G&N. V. Torrey. il Pop Mech 121:116-19+ F '64
Mercury taught space pilot techniques. Aviation W 79:205 Jl 22 '63
Navigating the gravity wells of interplanetary space; a primer on the guidance of spaceships through the great unknown ocean sky. J. P. Hagen. il Sat R 47:48-51 Ap 4 '64; Discussion. 47:46 S 5; 64-5 O 3 '64
Pilot control of rendezvous stressed. R. Pay. Miss & Roc 13:56+ S 30 '63
Ready, aim, wait! H. Hellman. il Sci Digest 54:35-9 D '63
Sense of direction; mechanical navigator. il Time 81:62 Je 14 '63
Star-pattern recognition device urged. Miss & Roc 12:48+ Je 24 '63
NAVIGATION, Aerial
See also
Airplanes—Piloting
Decca navigation
Helicopters—Piloting
Inertial guidance systems
NAVIGATION, Interplanetary. See Navigation (space flight)
NAVIGATION, Primitive
By dunung and bouj. J. H. Brandt. il Natur Hist 72:26-9 F '63
NAVIGATION, Submarine
Navy standardizes Polaris SINS system. Aviation W 80:16 My 4 '64
Their own star for guidance; electrically suspended gyroscope for Polaris submarines. il Bsns W p 124+ Ap 20 '63
NAVIGATION aids
Aides to the aids to navigation. M. L. Hersey. il Motor B 114:89+ Jl '64
Approach to the finish. J. Sutphen and A. Kostanecki. il Yachting 115:70-1+ Ap '64
Approach to the leeward mark. J. Sutphen and A. Kostanecki. il Yachting 115:39-41+ Mr '64
Approach to the weather mark. J. Sutphen and A. Kostanecki. il Yachting 115:50-2+ F '64

NAVIGATION aids—*Continued*
Easy accuracy at sea; Raytheon navigator. il Time 82:75 N 22 '63
Maneuvering board and the yachtsman. H. O. Webster. il Motor B 114:38-41 Jl '64
Range-finder pilotage. D. Shawn. il Motor B 111:38+ Je '63
See also
Electronic aids to navigation

NAVIGATOR, Aerial. See Aeronautic instruments

NAVONE, John J.
Fellini's La dolce Italia. Commonweal 77:639-41 Mr 15 '63
Noonday land. America 110:44-6 Ja 11 '64

NAVY

Yards and docks, Bureau of

See United States—Navy department—Yards and docks, Bureau of

NAVY (football) See Football

NAVY doctors. See United States—Navy—Medical department

NAVY slang. See Slang

NAVY test ranges. See Proving grounds

NAVY yards and naval stations
As U.S. bases are cut back; the meaning. il U S News 57:41 N 30 '64
Atlantic undersea test center to be set up in Bahamas. Dept State Bul 48:866 Je 3 '63
Caribbean, troubled waters; Guantánamo crisis. il Newsweek 63:13-14 F 17 '64
Castro's challenge to U.S: the real reasons; squeeze on Guantánamo. il U S News 56:38-9 F 17 '64
Do we need Guantanamo? M. S. Watson. New Repub 150:14-15 F 22 '64
Easing off; Guantánamo Bay. il Newsweek 63:34 F 24 '64
End of the water war. Time 83:42 F 28 '64
Hero & the hush-up; killing of a Cuban at Guantánamo in 1961. il Time 81:17 My 10 '63
How navy will desalt water in Cuba; Action to put Guantanamo in better fighting trim. il U S News 56:13 F 24 '64
Is there a plan to give up Guantanamo? expansion of naval base at Roosevelt Roads, Puerto Rico. il U S News 56:6 Mr 30 '64
New undersea test facility to go operational in December, 1965; Atlantic undersea test and evaluation center. Miss & Roc 15:78-9 S 21 '64
Ninety-five bases to be closed. Sr Schol 85:20-1 D 2 '64
Occurrence at Guantanamo; shooting of Ruben Lopez, an alleged Castro spy. Nation 196:386 My 11 '63; Reply. M. F. Walter. 196:529 Je 22 '63
Our Spanish landlord; Polaris base. Nation 196:149 F 23 '63
Pentagon's big cutback of bases. il Newsweek 64:73-4 N 30 '64
Ready for anything; Guantánamo. il Time 83:40 F 21 '64
Report from Guantánamo: we're ready for Castro's next step. H. Handleman. il U S News 56:52-3 Mr 2 '64
Rushing a Cuban water cure; Guantanamo. il Bsns W p34-5 Jl 4 '64
Suspension of water service to Guantanamo protested; text of U.S. note to Cuban government, February 9, 1964. Dept State Bul 50:282 F 24 '64
U.S. Cuba and Guantanamo. il Sr Schol 84:9-11 Mr 13 '64
U.S.-Cuban water battle; problem of water supply at Guantanamo. il Sr Schol 84:16 F 28 '64
U.S. determined to guarantee security of Guantanamo base; White House statement, February 7, 1964. Dept State Bul 50:281 F 24 '64
U.S. navy conquers Holy Loch. C. Hotchkiss. il Read Digest 83:114-18 Jl '63
Violence and silence; case of Rubén Lopez at the U.S. naval base, Guantánamo Bay. Newsweek 61:31-2 My 13 '63
Water for Guantanamo. B. Tufty. il Sci N L 85:131 F 29 '64
Water war; Guantánamo's fresh water cut off. il Time 83:30 F 14 '64
Who gets the ax? Newsweek 64:82+ N 23 '64
Why cutting the budget isn't easy. il Bsns W p32-3 N 28 '64
With courage & good sense; closing down of military installations. il Time 84:29-30 N 27 '64
With ninety-four others, down goes Brooklyn. il Life 57:50 D 4 '64
Wondering where the navy went; gloom grows at Brooklyn's navy yard. il Bsns W p30-1 O 17 '64

Anecdotes, facetiae, satire, etc.

Praise the Lord and pass that jug of water; Guantanamo. Nat R 16:139 F 25 '64

NAWRACAJ, Edward P.
Build Simplex transistorized ignition. Pop Electr 20:45-8+ F '64
—and Forman, Fred
Self-regulating lighting controller. Pop Electr 22:67-8 Ja '65

NAYLOR, Deanne
Case of the screaming silence. NEA J 53:61 Ja '64

NAYUDU, Y. R.
Carbonate deposits and paleoclimatic implications in the northeast Pacific Ocean. bibliog Science 146:515-17 O 23 '64

NAZI war criminals. See World war, 1939-1945—War criminals

NAZISM. See Fascism—Germany; Fascism—Germany (Federal Republic)

NE WIN
Burma: drifting into an uncertain future. il por Sr Schol 84:6-8 Ap 17 '64
Way to socialism & havoc. por Time 82:20-1 Ag 30 '63

NEAGLE, Marjorie S.
Star Island. Travel 120:48-9+ S '63

NEAL, Avon
Grave rubbers: early New England grave stones. C. Willard. il Look 27:M6-M7 Ag 27 '63
—See Parker, A. jt. auth.

NEAL, Franklin M.
Choosing the right street-lighting luminaire. Am City 79:94-6 D '64

NEAL, Fred Warner
New frontier and Europe: moment for choice. Nation 197:234-6 O 19 '63
Openings for diplomacy; cracks in the blocs. Nation 196:111-13 F 9 '63
Titoism in flux. Cur Hist 44:294-8+ My '63
U.S. China policy and disarmament. Bul Atomic Sci 19:5-8 N '63
Unsolved German settlement. bibliog f Ann Am Acad 351:148-56 Ja '64

NEAL, Patricia
Kiss kiss. il pors Time 83:57 Mr 20 '64

NEALE, Alfred Earle
Greasy Neale: nothing to prove, nothing to ask. G. Holland. il por Sports Illus 21:32-4+ Ag 24 '64

NEALE, Russell F.
AIGA's Fifty books: a review of the 1963 show. bibliog Pub W 183:56+ My 6 '63

NEAME, Alan
Experiences in romance; poem. Nat R 16:70 Ja 28 '64

NEANDERTHAL race
Neanderthal no relation. Sci N L 83:350 Je 1 '63

NEAPOLITANS
Ciao Fabrizio. F. Steegmuller. New Yorker 40:205-8+ O 10 '64

NEAR EAST. See Middle East

NEARY, John
Other Mona Lisa. Life 57:11 Jl 31 '64
Poor rickety Leo. Life 57:69-70+ D 11 '64

NEARY, Patricia
Brief biography. S. Goodman. pors Dance Mag 38:48-9 My '64

NEAT'S-foot oil. See Leather—Protection

NEBRASKA
See also
Fishing—Nebraska
Hunting—Nebraska
Law—Nebraska
Taxation—Nebraska

Boundaries

Squatter squabble. il Newsweek 64:28-9 Ag 10 '64

Marriage law

See Marriage law—United States

Religious institutions and affairs

News of the Christian world (cont) Christian Cent 80:184, 869-70; 81:1376 F 6, Jl 3 '63, N 4 '64

NEBRASKA. University, Lincoln
Art gallery for a university campus. il Arch Rec 134:129-31 Ag '63
Nebraska opens conference center. il Arch Rec 134:250 Ag '63
New wave: English curriculum center. il Newsweek 61:90 My 27 '63

NEBULAE
Central part of Orion nebula. il Sky & Tel 26:22 Jl '63
Grandest firework; Crab nebula. J. Lear. il Sat R 47:35-7 Jl 4 '64
Lunar occultation of X-ray emission from the crab nebula. S. Bowyer and others. bibliog il Science 146:912-17 N 13 '64

NEBULAE—*Continued*
Monochromatic photographs of the Orion nebula. W. A. Feibelman. il Sky & Tel 27:154-5 Mr '64
Moving red nebulae. Sky & Tel 27:286 My '64
New supernova theory; search for a neutron star in the crab nebula. A. Ewing. Sci N L 86:53 Jl 25 '64
Orion has provided man with beauty and mythic inspiration. T. D. Nicholson. il Natur Hist 73:44-7 N '64
Orion nebula is astronomical baby. Sci N L 85:355 Je 6 '64
Planetary nebulae. M. Liller and W. Liller. il Sci Am 208:60-7 bibliog(p200) Ap '63
Remarkable Crab nebula evolved from an exploding star. T. D. Nicholson. il Natur Hist 73:50-2 D '64
See also
Galactic systems
NECESSARY evils; story. See Rubin, M.
NECHAEV, Sergeĭ
Unmentionable Nechaev, by M. Prawdin. Review
Time por 82:110+ S 13 '63
NECK
New American fashion valuable: the neck. il Vogue 141:140-1 F 1 '63
NECKERMANN, Josef
Price breaker. il pors Bsns W p 104-6 Mr 21 '64
NECKING. See Dating
NECKLACES
This necklace is bamboo. il Sunset 130:167 My '63
NECKTIES
Neckties, points to check before you buy. il Changing T 17:24 Je '63
NECROMANCY. See Magic
NECTARINES
Dwarf peaches and nectarines: your choice is widening. il Sunset 132:188 F '64
See also
Cookery—Fruit
NECTURUS. See Salamanders
NEE, Casper
Designer's sketchbook. il Am Home 67:28+ Mr '64
NEEDHAM, Mass.
Adaptable campus plan for a junior high. il Arch Rec 134:216-17 O '63
NEEDLEPOINT
On the needle; Magic needle exhibition, New Hope, Pa. il Newsweek 63:78 Je 1 '64
NEEDLEPOINT rugs. See Rugs and carpets
NEEDLER, Martin C.
Changing the guard in Mexico. Cur Hist 48:26-31+ Ja '65
NEEDLES, Robert J.
Population and the pill. Nat R 15:70 Jl 30 '63
NEEDLES, Phonograph. See Phonograph needles
NEEDLEWORK
Bargains make your bazaar. il Suc Farm 61:68-71 O '63
Gift rug to make ahead for Christmas: wall hanging and panel. il Sunset 133:112+ O '64
Gifts to make and sell at bazaars. R. Martens. il Farm J 87:80-2 O '63
McCall's portfolio of needle work. il McCalls 90:94-9 S '63
Make a sampler. B. Rollins. il Farm J 88:58-9 Jl '64
More than 100 bazaar best-sellers! M. Garrity. il Bet Hom & Gard 41:60-5 S '63
See also
Appliqué work
Crewel work
Needlepoint
Patchwork
Quilting
Samplers
NEEDLEWORK equipment. See Sewing equipment
NEEDLEWORK pictures. See Pictures
NEELANDS, Robert W. and Reynolds, R. R.
Farm forests are bonus crops. Am For 69:9+ Je '63
NEELY, Charles L. Jr. See Kraus, A. P. jt. auth.
NEGAS, Taki. See Sorrell, C. A. jt. auth.
NEGATIVE color films. See Photography—Films
NEGATIVE resistance. See Electric resistance
NEGATIVES, Photographic. See Photography—Negatives
NEGEV
Israel's Negev comes to life. G. Gersh. il Christian Cent 81:169-71 F 5 '64
Shards of history. il Time 82:50-60 D 13 '63
Stones that make the desert bloom. il Sci Digest 54:67-8 Ag '63
Two fossil floras of the Negev Desert; Jurassic plants. J. Lorch. il Natur Hist 72:28-37 Mr '63
See also
Irrigation—Negev
NEGLIGENCE
See also
Liability (law)
NEGOTIABLE instruments
See also
Certificates of deposit
NEGOTIATION, International. See Arbitration, International; Diplomacy; International relations
NEGRI, Pola
Reporter at large. A. J. Liebling. New Yorker 39:97-8+ Ja 11 '64
NEGRO actors and actresses
Brock Peters. il Ebony 18:106-8+ Je '63
Lena Horne speaks freely on race, marriage, stage; interview. ed. by H. Feinstein. L. Horne. il Ebony 18:61-7 My '63
Negro on Broadway. il Ebony 19:186-8+ Ap '64
100 years of Negro entertainment. A. Morrison. il Ebony 18:122-4+ S '63
See also
Johnson, R.
Poitier, S.
NEGRO air pilots
High-flying soldier of fortune. A. Peters. il Ebony 19:37-8+ Je '64
Opening the cockpit doors; first Negro commercial airline pilot. il Time 81:24 My 3 '63
NEGRO airline stewardesses. See Airlines—Hostesses
NEGRO ambassadors
Ambassador; American ambassador to Finland. New Yorker 39:45-6 D 7 '63
Our man in Finland. W. Wiskari. il N Y Times Mag p63-4+ N 17 '63
Youngest U.S. ambassador. il Ebony 19:52-4+ Ja '64
NEGRO American labor council
Organized labor and the Negro worker. M. Bain. Nat R 14:455 Je 4 '63
NEGRO Americans in Africa. See Americans in Africa
NEGRO art. See Art, Negro
NEGRO artists. See Artists, Negro
NEGRO astronauts. See Astronauts
NEGRO athletes
Baseball has done it, by J. Robinson. Review
Reporter 31:58 O 22 '64. H. Higdon
High school of champions; McClymonds of Oakland, Calif. il Ebony 18:25-8+ Ap '63
How sports helped break the color line. A. S. Young. il Ebony 18:114-16+ S '63
I owe the public nothing. E. Linn. il Sat Eve Post 237:60-3 Ja 18 '64
King of the hurdlers. il Ebony 19:63-6 Ap '64
Let's boycott the Olympics. M. Whitfield. il Ebony 19:95-6+ Mr '64
Pro football roundup il Ebony 19:70-2+ N '63
Race problems at Howard is how to win; first Negro institution to crash exclusive college rowing. H. Whall. Sports Illus 20:72+ Ap 27 '64
See also
Arantes de Nascimento, E.
Davis, E.
Scott, D.
Thompson, D.
NEGRO authors
Negro in literature today. J. A. Williams. il Ebony 18:73-6 S '63
Negro writer in the United States. H. W. Fuller. il Ebony 20:126-8+ N '64
On becoming a writer; excerpt from Shadow and act. R. Ellison. Commentary 38:57-60 O '64
Panelizing dissent; report on conference on the Negro writer in the United States. K. Rexroth. Nation 199:97-9 S 7 '64
Tell it like it is; seminar sponsored by the University of California. il Newsweek 64:84 Ag 24 '64
Visible man. Newsweek 62:81 Ag 12 '63
See also
Ellison, R.
Hughes, L.
NEGRO baseball players. See Baseball players
NEGRO basketball players. See Basketball players
NEGRO business men
Aiding Negro businessmen: Small business opportunities corp, Phila. Bsns W p141 Ap 18 '64
Banker with a mission; J. H. Wheeler. il Bsns W p56+ My 16 '64

NEGRO business men—*Continued*
Breakthroughs in business. il Ebony 20:62+ N '64
Concrete step manufacturers; Thompson unit step co. Indianapolis. il Ebony 19:146-9 D '63
Drive to set Negroes up in business. il U S News 57:82 Ag 31 '64
How to start a business. A. Poinsett. il Ebony 19:85-6+ Jl '64
Making of a Negro middle class. H. Lees. il Reporter 31:41-4 O 8 '64
Mississippi chicken processor. il Ebony 18: 45-6+ F '63
Negro businessman speaks his mind; interview. S. B. Fuller. il U S News 55:58-61 Ag 19 '63
Negro in business. il Ebony 18:211-12+ S '63
Negroes get a hand. il Bsns W p38 Je 27 '64
Tribute to a business pioneer; J. W. Wills, sr. il Ebony 19:42-4+ Jl '64

NEGRO candidates, Political. See Candidates, Political

NEGRO career girls. See Business and professional women

NEGRO chaplains. See Chaplains, Military

NEGRO children
Child waits; film produced by the Federation of Protestant welfare agencies, inc. il Ebony 18:89-90+ Mr '63
Children and discrimination. B. Spock. il Redbook 123:30+ S '64
Children of Birmingham; non-violent action. P. Goodman. Commentary 36:242-4 S '63
Child's question. R. Coles. New Repub 150: 10-12 Ap 11 '64
Desegregation, after school. R. Kramer. il N Y Times Mag p47 My 31 '64
Down-to-earth idealism; Northern student movement. Time 81:102 My 17 '63
I wonder why; condensation. S. Burden. il Read Digest 84:97-107 F '64
Negro mother speaks of her challenging role in a changing world. M. B. Young. il Parents Mag 39:50-1+ Jl '64
Racial identity in school children. R. Coles. il Sat R 46:56-7+ O 19 '63
Trials of desegregation. Sci N L 83:309 My 18 '63
What can we tell our children? views of a white southern mother and a Negro mother. il Redbook 123:6+ My '64
When Negro child meets white. T. T. Chapin. Christian Cent 80:1333-4 O 30 '63

NEGRO church. See Negroes in the United States—Religion

NEGRO clergy
Church catches up. C. W. Thomas. Negro Hist Bul 28:19-20 O '64
Five million Baptists plan progress drive; J. H. Jackson. il Ebony 20:76-80+ D '64
Key man of the South: the Negro minister. C. E. Lincoln. il N Y Times Mag p20+ Jl 12 '64
Negro bishops for white areas. il Time 84:63 Jl 24 '64
Note on Daniel A. Payne. D. C. Stange. Negro Hist Bul 28:9-10 O '64
Richard Allen. L. Bennett, jr. il Ebony 19: 142-4+ My '64

NEGRO clubs
Washington who's who; Pigskin club. E. B. Henderson. il Negro Hist Bul 26:190-5 Mr '63
See also
Association for the study of Negro life and history

NEGRO college graduates. See College graduates

NEGRO colleges. See Negroes in the United States—Education

NEGRO comedians
Raceless Bill Cosby. il Ebony 19:131-2+ My '64
See also
Cambridge, G. M.
Cosby, B.
Gregory, D.

NEGRO conductors. See Conductors (music)

NEGRO congressmen
Adam Clayton Powell, enigma on Capitol hill. L. Bennett, jr. il Ebony 18:25-8+ Je '63
Ex-solon still active twenty years after retirement. il Ebony 18:40-2+ Ag '63
Gus Hawkins, fifth Negro congressman. H. J. Massaquoi. il Ebony 18:38-40+ F '63
John Willis Menard: first Negro elected to the U.S. Congress. E. Menard. bibliog Negro Hist Bul 28:53-4 D '64
Know your congressmen (cont) N. L. Milton. Negro Hist Bul 26:252; 27:17 My, O '63
Negro congressmen. C. Diggs, jr. Negro Hist Bul 27:114+ F '64
New face in Congress: J. [Conyers, jr. S. Booker. il Ebony 20:73-4+ Ja '65
Powell answers his critics: night-clubbing and nepotism defended. U S News 54:20 Mr 4 '63

NEGRO contractors. See Contractors

NEGRO costume designers. See Costume designers

NEGRO cowboys. See Cowboys

NEGRO criminals. See Negroes in the United States—Crime

NEGRO dancers
Style, essence, allusion; interview, ed. by W. Sorell. A. Ailey. il Dance Mag 37:47+ Ag '63
See also
Ellington, M.
White, M.

NEGRO debutantes. See Debutantes

NEGRO diplomats
Diplomat with an artistic touch. il Ebony 20:88-9+ N '64
Equal employment opportunity; Negro foreign service officers; remarks, March 12, 1964. D. Rusk. Dept State Bul 50:629-31 Ap 20 '64
Fulfilling our basic commitments as a Nation; statement, July 10, 1963; with comments by nonwhite diplomats. D. Rusk. Dept State Bul 49:154-9 Jl 29 '63
Policy and people; address, September 26, 1963. R. J. Manning. Dept State Bul 49: 639-44 O 21 '63
When African envoys house-hunt in capital. U S News 55:11 Jl 1 '63

NEGRO drama
Burst of Negro drama; with report by T. Thompson. il Life 56:62A-70 My 29 '64

NEGRO education. See Negroes in the United States—Education

NEGRO engineers
Rocket test team boss; Aerojet-General's W. Sprattling, jr. il Ebony 19:46-8+ My '64

NEGRO entertainers
Bubbles bounces back. il Ebony 20:49-50+ Ja '65

NEGRO family life. See Family life

NEGRO farm women. See Farm women

NEGRO farmers
New Booker T. casts down his buckets. il Ebony 20:66-8+ Ja '65

NEGRO folklore. See Folklore, Negro

NEGRO football players. See Football players

NEGRO fraternities
J. Finley Wilson, fraternal orator. M. H. Boulware. bibliog Negro Hist Bul 27:67-8 D '63

NEGRO government employees
Big man in biggest building. il Ebony 18: 84+ Ap '63
Cincinnati's legal head. il Ebony 18:87-8+ Je '63
Government's most-integrated agency; Veterans administration. il Ebony 18:65-6+ Mr '63
Hawaii's top woman politician. il Ebony 18: 51-2+ Ap '63
How JFK surpassed Abraham Lincoln. S. Booker. il Ebony 19:25-8+ F '64
More government jobs for Negroes; how it's being done. il U S News 55:40-2 Jl 22 '63
U.S. government employs one of each eighteen Negro workers. il Ebony 18:30 My '63
U.S. patent office seeks Negro employees. il Ebony 18:111-12+ O '63

NEGRO historians
John Hope Franklin at Cambridge; interview. il Ebony 18:160-2+ S '63

NEGRO history. See Negroes in the United States—History

NEGRO history bulletin
Meet the editorial board. il Negro Hist Bul 28:45-7 N '64

NEGRO history week
Challenge of the past. il Ebony 19:100-1 F '64
History and significance of Negro history week. M. Jackson. Negro Hist Bul 27:72+ D '63
Negro history and the modern Uncle Tom. Negro Hist Bul 27:134-5 Mr '64
Negro history in the field. il Negro Hist Bul 27:37 N '63
Scribbers contest winners; why Negro history week? B. C. Dickens; L. Thomas; J. Hall. Negro Hist Bul 27:153-5 Mr '64

NEGRO intelligence. See Intelligence levels—Negroes

NEGRO inventors. See Inventors

NEGRO judges
If I were young today. H. E. Moore. Ebony 18:88 O '63

NEGRO judges—*Continued*
Negro judge for D.C? President picks Robinson. U S News 55:21 O 14 '63
See also
Hastie, W. H.
NEGRO labor. See Labor and laboring classes —United States; Negroes in the United States—Employment
NEGRO lawyers
After forty years: a kiss and a cake. il Ebony 19:73-4+ F '64
If I were young today. A. T. Walden. Ebony 18:74 Je '63
Lawyer leaves Mississippi; white lawyer handling civil-rights cases. B. Carter. il Reporter 28:33-5 My 9 '63; Discussion. 28:6 Je 6 '63
See also
Minor, N. S.
NEGRO legislators
Nation's youngest lawmaker. il Ebony 19: 135-6+ Je '64
Reconstruction legislators in Alabama. C. A. Brown. bibliog Negro Hist Bul 26:198-200 Mr '63
Will California send a Negro to the Senate? il Ebony 19:25-8+ Ja '64
NEGRO librarians
Keep talking; with editorial comment. W. Jones. Library J 89:2966-7 Ag '64
Mouthful of civil rights and an empty stomach. E. J. Josey. Library J 90:202-5 Ja 15 '65
Two stars from Georgia; reflections on the ALA conference in St Louis. E. Moon. il Library J 89:2919-28 Ag '64
NEGRO life and history, Association for the study of. See Association for the study of Negro life and history
NEGRO literature
Denial of the big dream? C. Shapiro. Sat R 46:28 Je 29 '63
Ebony book shelf. See issues of Ebony
Negro writer in the United States. H. W. Fuller. il Ebony 20:126-8+ N '64
Problems of the Negro writer. L. Hughes; L. Jones; J. A. Williams. Sat R 46:19-21+ Ap 20 '63
See also
Negro drama
Negro poetry
Collections
Cover: the Julia Davis fund; rare collection of Negro literary works. il(p 157) Negro Hist Bul 27:162-3 Ap '64
NEGRO market
Boycott road to rights. Time 81:95 Je 7 '63
Impact of the Negro on the furniture market. B. Van Alstine. il Ebony 18:99-104 Ap '63
Negro and the advertiser. R. L. Tobin. Sat R 46:67-8 N 9 '63; Discussion. 46:66 D 14 '63; 47:74+ Ja 11; 56 F 8; 123 Mr 14 '64
Negro market. P. Korenvaes. Duns R 82:61-2 N '63
NEGRO ministers. See Negro clergy
NEGRO missionaries. See Missionaries
NEGRO models. See Models (persons)
NEGRO moving picture directors. See Moving picture directors
NEGRO municipal officers
See also
Carroll, G. D.
NEGRO music
Blues becomes big business; Ray Charles enterprises. L. Robinson. il Ebony 18:34-6+ Ap '63
Blues: three of a kind. L. Cohn. Sat R 46: 97+ Mr 16 '63
Negro music, a definitive American expression. H. McKinney. bibliog Negro Hist Bul 27:120-1+ F '64
See also
Jazz music
Negro songs
NEGRO musicians
Blues becomes big business; Ray Charles enterprises. L. Robinson. il Ebony 18:34-6+ Ap '63
Miriam Makeba; trip to Kenya. il Ebony 18: 74-6+ Ap '63
Negro in music. J. Molleson. Mus Am 83: 24-5+ D '63
Real New Orleans sound. J. S. Wilson. il Hi Fi 13:59-61+ S '63
Young troupers make hit debut. il Ebony 18: 156-8+ My '63
See also
Armstrong, L.
Bassey, S.
Benton, B.
Cole, N. K.
Coleman, O.
Ellington, D.
Fitzgerald, E.
Hines, E.
McNair, B.
Miles, L.
Monk, T. S.
Negro singers
Watts, A.
Wilson, N.
NEGRO newspapers. See Negro press
NEGRO pastors. See Negro clergy
NEGRO Paul Revere of Quantrill's raid; story. See Stotts, G.
NEGRO periodicals
See also
Negro history bulletin
NEGRO physical directors. See Physical directors
NEGRO physicians
Dancing doctor. il Ebony 18:33-7 F '63
Edith Irby revisited. il Ebony 18:52-4+ Jl '63
Negro physician in Detroit. C. H. Wright. Negro Hist Bul 27:109-10 F '64
New dawn in medicine. W. M. Cobb. il Ebony 18:166-8+ S '63
See also
Bailey, J. A.
Bateman, M. M.
Chenault, J. W.
NEGRO pioneers. See Pioneers
NEGRO poetry
Dark bag. L. Jones. Poetry 103:394-401 Mr '64
New Negro poets U.S.A, ed. by L. Hughes. Review
Nation 198:665-6 Je 29 '64. M. Schleifer
NEGRO police
Ambassador of goodwill for police department; Los Angeles policewoman. il Ebony 19:40-2+ Mr '64
Cook County crime fighter. il Ebony 19:101-2+ D '63
King demands Negro policemen; Birmingham, Ala. Christian Cent 80:1294 O 23 '63
Portsmouth's police chief. il Ebony 18:144+ Ap '63
NEGRO politicians. See Negroes in the United States—Politics and suffrage
NEGRO press
Crusading press. A. Morrison. il Ebony 18: 204+ S '63
Founders of the Negro press. L. Bennett, jr. il Ebony 19:96-8+ Jl '64
Victim of Negro progress. il Newsweek 62: 50-1 Ag 26 '63
NEGRO priests
Reflections of a Negro priest. B. J. Patterson. Cath World 200:269-76 F '65
See also
Chaplains, Military
NEGRO professors. See College professors and instructors
NEGRO public officers. See Public officers
NEGRO race
Faces of the racial revolution. E. T. Chase. New Repub 152:29-30+ Ja 23 '65
NEGRO reporters. See Reporters and reporting
NEGRO saints. See Saints
NEGRO schools
Michigan
Good in a ghetto; Detroit's Central high school. il Time 84:87 O 2 '64
NEGRO scientists
See also
Banneker, B.
Martin, J. E.
Price, J. I.
NEGRO service men and women
I spied on Castro's Cuba; Capt. Hennagan. il Ebony 18:114-16+ Ap '63
Military's limited war against segregation. R. Brecher and E. Brecher. Harper 227: 79-82+ S '63
Our man in Saigon. il Ebony 18:121-2+ Je '63
Where a Negro captain lives; his problem or ours? il Look 27:36-7 D 17 '63
NEGRO shipmasters. See Shipmasters
NEGRO singers
Capital music maker; Bethesda, Md. Congregational church choir. il Ebony 18:91-2+ Jl '63
Looking for the blues. il Newsweek 64:82-3 Jl 13 '64
See also
Franklin, A.
Holloway, N.
Price, L.
Small, M.
NEGRO slang. See Slang
NEGRO social workers. See Social workers
NEGRO soldiers. See United States—Army—Negroes

NEGRO songs
Battle hymn of the integrationists; We shall overcome. il U S News 55:8 Ag 5 '63
Freedom songs. R. Shelton. Nation 197:57-8 Jl 27 '63
Gospel as gimmick; Sweet chariot night club. N. Hentoff. Reporter 29:46-7 Ag 15 '63; Reply. J. Chase. 29:8 S 26 '63
Holy war; gospel-singing in nightclubs. Newsweek 61:70 Je 24 '63
In God she trusts. D. Gold. Ladies Home J 80:66-7 N '63
Jazz concerts; deep-country blues singers at Hunter college. W. Balliett. New Yorker 40:133-5 My 30 '64
Now hear the word: Sweet chariot nite club. Newsweek 61:94 My 27 '63
Pop up, sweet chariot. il Time 81:48 My 24 '63
Sing a song of freedom. R. Sherman. il Sat R 46:65-7+ S 28 '63
Without these songs; freedom music. il Newsweek 64:74 Ag 31 '64

NEGRO spies. See Spies

NEGRO state officers
Negro political progress in New England. A. Morrison. il Ebony 18:25-8+ O '63
West Virginia's director of mental health. il Ebony 19:63-8 Ja '64
See also
Johnson, L. R.

NEGRO students
Astonishing John Wideman. G. Shalit. il Look 27:30-6 My 21 '63
Detroit high school challenges nation; Central high's stepped-up program. H. J. Bims. il Ebony 19:25-8+ Ag '64
High school diploma at seventy-two; D. D. Elmore. il Ebony 19:125-6+ Ag '64
I believe: Negro high school exchange student in Farmington, Conn. from Birmingham, Ala. B. Donahue. Seventeen 22:46+ O '63
Lonely years of Hamilton Holmes. A. Wexler. il Ebony 19:101-2+ N '63
Mississippi comes North to Harlem. J. Steele. New Repub 152:10-11 Ja 30 '65
Negro child asks: why? M. Anderson. il N Y Times Mag p32+ D 1 '63
Negro children discount own mental abilities. Sci N L 84:121 Ag 24 '63
Negroes in college: what figures show. il U S News 55:81 N 25 '63
On the fringe of a golden era: the U.S. student. il Time 85:57B Ja 29 '65
Stress affects success. Sci N L 86:23 Jl 11 '64
See also
Colleges and universities—Desegregation
National scholarship service and fund for Negro students
West, J.

NEGRO suffrage. See Negroes in the United States—Politics and suffrage

NEGRO superstitions
See also
Voodooism

NEGRO surgeons
See also
Kountz, S. L.

NEGRO teachers
Alaskan school teacher. il Ebony 18:38+ O '63
American teachers association pushes activity in two vital areas; commission for improvement of teacher competency initiated. R. W. Hatch. Negro Hist Bul 27:150-2 Mr '64
Elizabeth Duncan Koontz's-president of the Nat'l education assn's dept. of classroom teachers; reprint. E. D. Koontz. il Negro Hist Bul 28:55-6 D '64
Four against the odds. il Ebony 18:55-6+ My '63
Negro teacher. T. M. Eubanks. Negro Hist Bul 27:113 F '64
See also
Alexander, J.
College professors and instructors

NEGRO theater. See Theater, Negro

NEGRO voters, Registration of. See Voters, Registration of

NEGRO-white intermarriage. See Intermarriage of races

NEGRO-white relations. See Race relations

NEGRO women
Best dressed women of 1963. il Ebony 18:132-4+ My '63
Negro woman. L. Bennett, jr. il Ebony 18:86-90+ S '63
Woman on the go for God. L. S. Calhoun. il Ebony 18:78-81+ My '63

Employment

Changing status of Negro women workers. Mo Labor R 87:671-3 Je '64

NEGRO women as engineers. See Women as engineers

NEGRO women as physicians. See Women as physicians

NEGRO women as welders. See Women as welders

NEGRO youth
Plea to the young Negro. J. D. Rockefeller, 3d. il N Y Times Mag p 16+ Ap 19 '64
Rural Negroes need help. E. Mirel. Sci N L 84:214 O 5 '63
Talk to teachers; address. J. Baldwin. il Sat R 46:42-4+ D 21 '63
Violence sends a message. il Ebony 19:140-1 S '64
Young troupers make hit debut. il Ebony 18:156-8+ My '63
See also
Negro students

NEGROES
Race and reason, by C. Putnam. Review
New Repub 147:23-4 S 10 '62; 148:9-10 Ja 5 '63. D. C. Simmons; Discussion. 148:30 Ja 19; 29-31 F 23 '63
See also
Negro songs

History

See also
Association for the study of Negro life and history

Intelligence

See Intelligence levels—Negroes

Libraries

See Libraries and Negroes

Psychology

Explanation of the black psyche. J. O. Killens. il N Y Times Mag p37-8+ Je 7 '64

NEGROES, Discrimination against. See Race discrimination

NEGROES as decorators. See Interior decorators

NEGROES as soldiers. See United States—Army—Negroes

NEGROES in Africa
Black Muslims. M. Berger. il Horizon 6:48-65 Wint '64
Champ's African love affair. il Ebony 19:85-6+ S '64
Miriam Makeba: trip to Kenya. il Ebony 18:74-6+ Ap '63
Where Negroes have the whites on the run: interview. O. B. Bennett. il U S News 55:68-75 S 9 '63
See also
Africa—Race problems

NEGROES in Brazil
Black and white. il Newsweek 64:46+ S 7 '64

NEGROES in business. See Negro business men

NEGROES in Communist countries
How the Communists are treating Negroes. U S News 54:8 F 25 '63

NEGROES in drama. See Negroes in literature

NEGROES in Europe
Black man in Europe. W. G. Smith. Holiday 37:22+ Ja '65

NEGROES in France
Negroes in Paris. il Newsweek 64:54 S 21 '64

NEGROES in Great Britain
How white backlash struck in Britain. il U S News 57:67 O 26 '64

NEGROES in Israel
American coed in Israel; J. West at Jerusalem's Hebrew university. il Ebony 18:105-6+ My '63

NEGROES in literature
American Negro in post-war French drama. A. Cismaru. Negro Hist Bul 27:79-80 Ja '64
Ebony book shelf. See issues of Ebony
First Negro U.S. president; theme of I. Wallace's The man. L. P. Jackson, jr. Negro Hist Bul 28:6 O '64
In Uncle Tom are our guilt and hope. A. Haley. il N Y Times Mag p23+ Mr 1 '64
Light on a southern exposure. W. Spearman. Sat R 46:42-3 N 16 '63
Uncle Remus again; theme of W. Miller's Siege of Harlem. L. P. Jackson, jr. Negro Hist Bul 28:70 D '64
See also
Slavery and slaves in literature

NEGROES in South Africa
South Africa's black millionaire; K. Sethunsa. il Ebony 18:73-6 My '63
White man who couldn't be white; interview. G. Muller. il Ebony 18:68-70+ My '63
See also
South Africa—Race problems

NEGROES in television. See Television broadcasting—Performers
NEGROES in the Sudan
Genocide in Sudan; Arab repression of Negroes. G. MacEoin. Commonweal 80:539-42 Ag 7 '64
Sudan's shame. America 109:4 Jl 6 '63
NEGROES in the United States
A. Philip Randolph. M. Kempton. New Repub 149:15-17 Jl 6 '63
Abraham Lincoln: unfinished business. America 110:183 F 8 '64
American dilemma, by G. Myrdal. Review
New Yorker 40:195-6+ Ap 18 '64. N. Bliven
Sci Digest 54:16-17 O '63. H. Pryor
America's 100 most influential Negroes. il Ebony 18:228-32 S '63
As they face the future, they recall the past; concerning three recent books. S. Redding; J. M. Nabrit, jr; C. Shapiro. Sat R 46:26-8 Je 29 '63
At the root of the Negro problem. . . J. Baldwin. il Time 81:26-7 My 17 '63
Atlantic report. Atlan 212:4+ Ag '63
Backlash issue; views on Negro's drive to improve his lot. L. Harris. il Newsweek 64:24+ Jl 13 '64
Beyond civil rights; lineaments of the integrated society. J. R. Nelson. Christian Cent 81:668-72 My 20 '64
Biggest reception ever; President Kennedy entertains 1,000 Negroes at White House. il Ebony 18:89-90+ My '63
Black and white: but whose Great society? M. Kempton. il New Repub 151:75-8+ N 7 '64
Black Jews of Harlem: Negro nationalism and the dilemmas of Negro leadership, by H. Bortz. Review
Commentary 38:77-9 O '64. N. Glazer
Black man in America. J. Ciardi. Sat R 46:13 Jl 6 '63
Century later: the new commitment. C. Bowles. Sat R 46:14-17 Ap 13 '63
Child's question. R. Coles. New Repub 150: 10-12 Ap 11 '64
Class, color and prejudice. B. Bettelheim. Nation 197:231-4 O 19 '63
Coming march on the capital. E. T. Folliard. America 109:109 Ag 3 '63
Coming test of American democracy. H. J. Morgenthau. Commentary 37:61-3 Ja '64; Reply. E. C. Hughes. 37:24 Ap '64
Crisis in black and white, by C. E. Silberman. Review
Nation 198:654-6 Je 29 '64. M. Mayer; Discussion. 199:inside cover, 53 Ag 10 '64
Time 83:110 My 22 '64
Cultural ambassador. America 108:628 My 4 '63
De-regionalization of a problem. N. Cousins. Sat R 46:28 O 19 '63
Education, equality and Negro rights; summary of address. W. M. Young, jr. Pub W 185:34-5 My 4 '64
Emancipation proclamation; address, January 13, 1963. S. Reese. Vital Speeches 29: 283-6 F 15 '63
Emancipation II. America 108:790 Je 1 '63
Everybody knows his name; J. Baldwin. il Esquire 62:59-64+ Ag '64
Explanation of the black psyche. J. O. Killens. il N Y Times Mag p37-8+ Je 7 '64
F.B.I. report on racial disturbances during the past summer. America 111:404-5 O 10 '64
Fire next time, by J. Baldwin. Review
Nat R il 14:408-14+ My 21 '63. G. Wills; Discussion. 14:507; 15:31+ Je 18, Jl 16 '63
First Freedom riders: quotations. Nation 197:103 S 7 '63
For the last time. Ebony 19:186 Je '64
Getting close to home. E. Roper. il Sat R 46:14+ Ag 31 '63
Ghosts of dead stereotypes. E. Blake, jr. Negro Hist Bul 26:212-14 Ap '63
Homework to be done. il Ebony 18:90-1 O '63
How to avoid a race riot. A. I. Waskow. Sat R 46:8-10+ Jl 6 '63
How whites feel about Negroes: a painful American dilemma. il Newsweek 62:44-50+ O 21 '63
I know about the Negroes and the poor. R. J. Dwyer. Nat R 15:517-18+ D 17 '63; Discussion. 16:81-4 Ja 28 '64
I like the word black; increasingly militant mood. il Newsweek 61:27-8 My 6 '63
If you had a choice. P. Putnam. Sat R 46:29+ O 26 '63
I'm talking to you, white man; excerpt from Autobiography of Malcolm X, by Alex Haley and Malcolm X. Malcolm X. il Sat Eve Post 237:30-2+ S 12 '64
India and the Negro question; here's how Birmingham and Montgomery look to people around the world. I. Travers-Ball. America 109:44-5 Jl 13 '63
Is integration the answer? O. Handlin. Atlan 213:49-54 Mr '64; Reply with rejoinder. C. Putnam. 213:45 Je '64
Is race a problem all over the U.S? il U S News 55:68-72 O 21 '63
It's great to be a Negro! il Ebony 19:92-3 Mr '64
Ivy league Negro. W. M. Kelley. il Esquire 60:54-6+ Ag '63; Reply. M. W. Davis. 61: 161-4+ Ap '64
J. Edgar Hoover speaks out on reds in the Negro movement; excerpts from Testimony before House subcommittee; with editorial comment. J. E. Hoover. U S News 56:33, 108 My 4 '64
James Baldwin's vision. J. Finn. Commonweal 78:447-9 Jl 26 '63; Reply with rejoinder. J. McCudden. 79:75-7 O 11 '63
John junior. E. Peter, jr. New Repub 148:14 Je 29 '63
Kennedy and Baldwin: the gulf. Newsweek 61:19 Je 3 '63
Law and justice; extra-legal Negro demands. New Repub 148:3-5 Je 22 '63
Letter to a governor. E. J. Hughes. Newsweek 61:19 Je 17 '63
Liberalism and the Negro; symposium, ed. by N. Podhoretz. Commentary 37:25-42 Mr '64; Discussion. 38:8+ Ag '64
Long, relentless reign of wrong. D. L. Dumond. Sat R 47:47-8 My 9 '64
Long search for pride. G. Parks. il Life 55:80-2+ Ag 16 '63
March. Nation 197:121 S 14 '63
Mississippi comes North to Harlem. J. Steele. New Repub 152:10-11 Ja 30 '65
More than equality? J. Cass. Sat R 46:49 O 19 '63
N.A.A.C.P. lawyer answers some questions. J. Greenberg. il N Y Times Mag p 16+ Ag 18 '63
Negro in America. il Newsweek 62:15-22+ Jl 29 '63; Discussion. 62:2-4 Ag 19 '63
Negro is prejudiced against himself. E. Hoffer. il N Y Times Mag p27+ N 29 '64; Same. U S News 57:48-52 D 28 '64; Discussion. N Y Times Mag p28-9+ D 13 '64
Negro leaders join forces. il U S News 55:19 Jl 15 '63
Negro racists. Nation 196:278 Ap 6 '63
Negro stock is praised. Sci N L 86:102 Ag 15 '64
Negroes & Jews: the new challenge to pluralism. N. Glazer. Commentary 38:29-34 D '64
New equality, by N. Hentoff. Review
America 111:262+ S 12 '64. R. M. Gasnick
Newsweek 64:74-5 Ag 3 '64
New hope for rural Dixie; firms in Carolinas create jobs for Negroes. il Ebony 19:50+ Je '64
New, new, new, Negro, Esq; address, September 26, 1964. S. Booker. Vital Speeches 31:53-5 N 1 '64
Nigger, by D. Gregory with R. Lipsyte. Review
Nation 199:383-5 N 23 '64. P. De Lissovoy
No time for comfort. America 110:667 My 16 '64
North and South, more race troubles. U S News 55:8 O 7 '63
Notes from the other side of April: with Negro eyes, with white; excerpt. G. Corso. Esquire 62:86-7+ Jl '64
Peace with justice. Commonweal 78:268 My 31 '63
Pistol on the steps; events on the civil rights front. il Time 82:38 O 4 '63
Plea to the young Negro. J. D. Rockefeller, 3d. il N Y Times Mag p 16+ Ap 19 '64
Poverty causes violence. F. Marley. Sci N L 86:114 Ag 22 '64
Preferential treatment for Negroes? F. M. Hechinger. il Reporter 31:22-4 D 3 '64; Discussion. 31:6 D 31 '64
Progress report, 1963. il Ebony 19:111-16 Ja '64
Proposal for a revolution. J. P. Lyford. il Sat R 46:19-22 O 19; 25-8+ O 26 '63
Quick and the dead. Nation 197:189 O 5 '63
Race against time. J. O'Gara. Commonweal 79:248 N 22 '63
Racial collision in the big cities. T. H. White. il Life 55:100-2+ N 22 '63
Ramparts at home. America 108:819 Je 8 '63
Record of injustice. J. Anderson. Commentary 38:84-6 S '64
Rhetoric and relevance. N. Hentoff. Nation 198:663-5 Je 29 '64
Right kind of Uncle Tom; Negro leadership. L. Wainwright. Life 57:17 Ag 7 '64
Rights, not ratios. G. Kelley. America 109: 424-5 O 12 '63

NEGROES in the United States—*Continued*
Role of the middle-class Negro. W. M. Young, jr. il Ebony 18:66-71 S '63
Second hundred years. H. W. Blanchette. Negro Hist Bul 27:180 Ap '64
Senator Goldwater and the Negro. M. Greenfield. Reporter 31:27-8 O 8 '64
So you like to travel. A. N. D. Brooks. Negro Hist Bul 26:204+ Mr '63
Speaking out; don't blame the ghetto. D. B. Lee. Sat Eve Post 237:8+ D 5 '64
Split in the ranks of the organizations pushing integration. il U S News 55:40 Jl 1 '63
Successful American Negroes. il Time 83:17-24 Ja 3 '64
Talk to teachers; address. J. Baldwin. il Sat R 46:42-4+ D 21 '63
Theatre of politics: the Negro. L. Abel. Nation 196:351-4 Ap 27 '63; Reply. H. F. Winslow, sr. 196:inside cover My 11 '63
36:30-3+ Ag '64
This is my country too; record of trip by an American Negro. J. A. Williams. il Holiday 36:30-3+ Ag; 58-9+ S '64; Discussion. 36:4+ O '64
Toast to America; address, May 13, 1964. J. G. Chatham. America 110:718-19 My 23 '64
Tomorrow's leaders. L. E. Lomax. il Ebony 18:41-4+ S '63
Troublesome presence: American democracy and the Negro, by E. Ginzberg and A. S. Eichner. Review
Sat R 47:35-6 S 12 '64. D. L. Dumond
Two perspectives, one goal; M. L. King, jr. accepts peace prize; President Johnson addresses Community action assembly. M. L. King, jr; L. B. Johnson. il Time 84:21-2 D 18 '64
Ultimate decency; presidential candidates and the racial conflict. W. Lippmann. Newsweek 64:13 Ag 17 '64
U.S. population: Negroes gain on whites. U S News 57:8 N 2 '64
Uses of violence; outrageous treatment of the American Negro. Nation 197:2-3 Jl 6 '63
Vive la différence? Nat R 15:50 Jl 30 '63
Voices out of a wilderness of hate. J. LaFarge. il Sat R 46:42-3 D 14 '63
Walk in dignity; address, May 2, 1964. D. Warden. Vital Speeches 30:572-5 Jl 1 '64
Week that was; historic days that followed signing of the Civil rights act. B. L. Masse. America 111:64 Jl 18 '64
What do they want? biracial human-relations committees. America 109:71-2 Jl 20 '63
What Negroes think; interviews. Christian Cent 81:1005 Ag 12 '64
What the American Negro wants; interview. R. Wilkins. il U S News 54:46-52 Ap 29 '63
Where are the leaders? J. P. Lyford. Sat R 46:10 Jl 6 '63
Who's responsible? New Repub 149:3-4 S 28 '63
Why Negroes use pressure. America 109:699 N 30 '63
Year of decision. il Ebony 20:107-10+ Ja '65
See also
Black Muslim movement
Boley, Okla.
Congress of racial equality
Interracial cooperation
National association for the advancement of colored people
National urban league
Slavery—United States
Vernon, Okla.
also subhead Negroes under names of cities, e.g. Chicago—Negroes

Bibliography

Documents of the struggle for public decency. E. Capouya. Sat R 47:13+ Jl 25 '64
Four books on race. H. N. Meyer. Commonweal 80:490-1 Jl 10 '64
New books on the American Negro. H. L. Hurwitz. il Sr Schol 83:8T-10T N 15 '63
Problem is not just black and white. A. Murray. Life 57:8+ Jl 3 '64
Reading for a hot summer. C. J. McNaspy. America 110:851-2 Je 20 '64
Toward equality. D. Clark. Commonweal 80: 518-19 Jl 24 '64

Civil rights

After a civil rights act. A. M. Bickel. New Repub 150:11-15 My 9 '64; Discussion. 150: 29 Je 6 '64
After integration, higher horizons. M. Anderson. il N Y Times Mag p 10+ Ap 21 '63
Agony of the Negro leader. E. C. Ladd, jr. il Nation 199:88-91 S 7 '64
Alabama goes to Court. L. B. Bozell. Nat R 14:445 Je 4 '63
Analysis of the white backlash. W. L. Miller. il N Y Times Mag p27+ Ag 23 '64
And the walls came tumbling down; desegregation. il Time 84:25-6 Jl 17 '64
Angels are white; who pays the bills for civil rights? R. Cleghorn. New Repub 149: 12-14 Ag 17 '63
Armistice, not peace. America 108:738 My 25 '63
Art of the necessary. Commonweal 78:317 Je 14 '63
As race tensions rise. il U S News 54:33-6 Je 24 '63
Awful roar. il Time 82:9-14 Ag 30 '63
Backlash and Christian faith. R. R. Parsonage. Christian Cent 81:1300-2 O 21 '64
Backlash; anti-Negro feeling and the coming election. T. H. White. il Life 57:100A-100B+ O 16 '64
Banker with a mission; J. H. Wheeler. il Bsns W p56+ My 16 '64
Baseball has done it, by J. Robinson. Review
Christian Cent 81:1042 Ag 19 '64. A. P. Klausler
Beyond rights, the issue of human dignity. Life 54:4 My 24 '63
Beyond tokenism; South as seen by a returning native son. D. Cater. il Reporter 29: 23-7 O 10 '63
Big five in civil rights. il Time 81:16 Je 28 '63
Birmingham and the law. New Repub 148:3-4 My 25 '63
Birmingham: I saw a city die; ed. by T. B. Morgan. C. Morgan, jr. il Look 27:23-5 D 3 '63
Birmingham: keeping our fingers crossed. R. Evans and R. Novak. New Repub 151:17-18 Ag 8 '64
Birmingham: the fuse gets shorter. il Bsns W p32-3 S 28 '63
Birth of a nation; Birmingham Negroes. M. Ascoli. Reporter 28:12 Je 6 '63
Black backlash; the crisis in Negro leadership intensifies. N. Hentoff. Commonweal 80:443-5 Jl 3 '64
Black Belt, Alabama. J. DeMuth. Commonweal 80:536-9 Ag 7 '64
Black wind rising. N. Cousins. Sat R 47:22 My 30 '64
Bold design for a new South. M. L. King, jr. Nation 196:259-62 Mr 30 '63
Boomerang in Birmingham. America 108: 705-6 My 18 '63
Brando fights for civil rights; interview. il Ebony 18:60-2+ O '63
Brooklyn chain gang. il Newsweek 62:25 Ag 5 '63
Burke Marshall: quiet fighter for civil rights. S. Booker. il Ebony 19:90-2+ My '64
Call to color blindness. W. F. Buckley, jr. Nat R 14:488 Je 18 '63; Reply. M. Whalen. 15:120 Ag 13 '63
Change of course; President's commitment to the Negro. W. Lippmann. Newsweek 62:15 Jl 8 '63
Christian obedience in a world we don't control. P. Peachey. Christian Cent 81:458-60 Ap 8 '64
Civil rights: a movement in search of a direction? with comment on the world's news fronts. il Sr Schol 85:16-20 S 30 '64
Civil rights: a new time for lawmaking. J. N. Eller. America 108:851 Je 15 '63
Civil rights aftermath. America 110:841 Je 20 '64
Civil rights battle; northern style. il Ebony 18:96-8+ Mr '63
Civil rights boil-up. A. M. Bickel. New Repub 148:10-14 Je 8 '63
Civil rights crisis: challenge to all Americans. il Sr Schol 83:13-19 S 13 '63
Civil rights decisions; distinction between public and private activity. Commonweal 78:292-3 Je 7 '63
Civil rights; do not despair. Time 84:35 N 27 '64
Civil rights: it's a two-way street. il Newsweek 62:35 Jl 29 '63
Civil rights law goes into action. il U S News 57:44-5 Jl 20 '64
Civil-rights maze. E. B. Drew. il Reporter 31: 12-14 D 17 '64
Civil rights not science. Sci N L 84:381 D 14 '63
Civil rights: slack tide. il Newsweek 62:21 Jl 8 '63
Civil writings; letters to the editor. Nat R 15:251-3 S 24 '63
Claim air wave rights for Negroes; United church of Christ, petition to F.C.C. Christian Cent 81:725 Je 3 '64

NEGROES in the United States—Civil rights
—*Continued*
Clearly up to Congress. Christian Cent 80:878 Jl 10 '63
Coming showdown in the race crisis. H. S. Ashmore. il Look 27:62-7 Jl 16 '63
Concession to common sense. America 108:482 Ap 13 '63
Congress confronted with racial issue. Christian Cent 80:821-2 Je 26 '63
Constitutional commandos; Manhattan's N.A.A.C.P. legal defense and educational fund, inc. il Time 83:66 Je 5 '64
Crisis in Birmingham; federal government's part. M. W. Shannon. Commonweal 78:238-9 My 24 '63
Crusade in Mississippi. A. Poinsett. il Ebony 19:25-8+ S '64
Crusading press. A. Morrison. il Ebony 18:204+ S '63
Cry from the dispossessed. W. M. Young, jr. il Christian Cent 81:1524-7 D 9 '64
Decade of slow, painful progress. R. McGill. il Sat R 47:65-6 My 16 '64
Desegregation decision; Brown v. Board of education, May 17, 1954. H. S. Ashmore. il Sat R 47:68-70 My 16 '64
Discrimination charged; United church of Christ's petition to F.C.C. E. C. Parker. Christian Cent 81:1018+ Ag 12 '64
Documents of the struggle for public decency. E. Capouya. Sat R 47:13+ Jl 25 '64
Drive for civil rights. Sr Schol 83:12-13 S 27 '63
Drum roll. Newsweek 61:22 Je 17 '63
Emancipation 1963; freedom's grass roots. Negro Hist Bul 26:206-7 Ap '63
End and a beginning; concerning President's TV-radio speech on the American dilemma of race. il Newsweek 61:29-34 Je 24 '63
End of gradualism. Nation 196:497 Je 15 '63
Enforcing civil rights. New Repub 149:3-4 O 26 '63; Reply. B. Marshall. 149:29-30 N 16 '63
Equality and 1984; address, June 2, 1963. B. I. Bernhard. Vital Speeches 29:594-7 Jl 15 '63
Equality is not negotiable; R. Wilkins and M. L. King on Meet the press. Christian Cent 80:1069 S 4 '63
Everybody's civil rights. il Ebony 19:110-11 N '63
FBI and civil rights: J. Edgar Hoover speaks out; excerpts from news conference, with reply by M. L. King. J. E. Hoover. il U S News 57:56-8 N 30 '64
Federal commission urges rights action. Sr Schol 83:19-20 O 18 '63
F.C.C. should not dodge church petition; concerning equal air rights for Negroes in Jackson. Christian Cent 81:820 Je 24 '64
Federalism and civil rights, by B. Marshall. Review
New Repub 151:17-18 O 31 '64. A. M. Bickel
Fire-bell in the night, by O. Handlin. Review
Sat R 47:43-4 My 16 '64. R. Baldwin
Five angry men speak their minds; symposium, ed. by G. Samuels. il N Y Times Mag p 14+ My 17 '64
Foot in the door; new Baltimore law. L. B. Dennis. New Repub 150:5 Mr 14 '64
Freedom now, but what then? L. Miller. Nation 196:539-42 Je 29 '63
Freedom through knowledge. Negro Hist Bul 27:48+ N '63
Fund raisers for freedom. il Ebony 18:120-2+ O '63
Gloria Richardson. il Newsweek 62:26+ Ag 5 '63
Hammer of civil rights. M. L. King, jr. il Nation 198:230-4 Mr 9 '64
Harlem: some reflections. America 111:125 Ag 8 '64
High policy vs. rank and file. Bsns W p38 Ag 8 '64
History of long, hot summers. A. C. Stewart. il Sat R 47:25-6 Ag 22 '64
Hopes of progress. Commonweal 80:591 S 4 '64
How JFK surpassed Abraham Lincoln. S. Booker. il Ebony 19:25-8+ F '64
How much liberty? Commonweal 78:340 Je 21 '63
If Congress gives Kennedy his way on civil rights; with President's latest plan on civil rights. il U S News 55:30-1 Jl 1 '63
Inexorable process. il Time 81:23-4 Je 14 '63
Integration: seesaw battle. Newsweek 61:19-21 Je 3 '63
Island joins the march. P. S. McGhee. il Nation 198:51-2 Ja 13 '64
Issue at issue; no walkaway now; Kentucky horse race. il Time 82:28-9 O 18 '63
It makes people mad; complaints against Mississippi sent to the U.S. civil rights commission. Time 81:24-5 Ap 26 '63
It's a difficult thing to teach a president; excerpts from interviews, ed. by T. G. Harris. M. L. King, jr. Look 28:61+ N 17 '64
JFK all the way. New Repub 148:3-4 Je 29 '63
Justice and love in the racial crisis. L. D. Kliever. Christian Cent 81:1055-7 Ag 26 '64
Justice in Georgia. il Time 82:76 N 8 '63
Kennedy and Baldwin. New Repub 148:3-4 Je 15 '63
Law is not enough. America 108:879 Je 22 '63
Lawyer leaves Mississippi; white lawyer handling civil-rights cases. B. Carter. il Reporter 28:33-5 My 9 '63; Discussion. 28:6 Je 6 '63
Lesson of Cambridge and Salisbury: was violence necessary? L. B. Bozell. Nat R 15:145-7 Ag 27 '63
Let Booker T. Washington speak again! excerpts from address, 1895; with editorial comment. B. T. Washington. U S News 55:88 S 2 '63
Let's put Christ in Christmas. E. C. Blake. Ebony 19:64 D '63
Letter from Washington. R. H. Rovere. New Yorker 39:100-4+ Je 1 '63
Letter from Washington; government for complete equality for Negro. R. H. Rovere. New Yorker 39:90+ Je 22 '63
Light and heat. K. Crawford. Newsweek 62:26 Jl 1 '63
Long march; legal history of Negro progress. il Time 81:13-17 Je 21 '63
Long, slow road. Newsweek 61:29-30 Mr 11 '63
Louisville, Ky: city that integrated without strife. C. Morrison. il Look 27:41-4 Ag 13 '63
LBJ and the Negro. il Newsweek 62:25 D 9 '63
March on Washington. America 109:131 Ag 10 '63
Mood of the Negro; with editorial comment. L. Bennett, jr. il Ebony 18:27-30+, 60-1 Jl '63
Moral crisis. Commonweal 78:363-4 Je 28 '63
More law, plus leadership. Life 54:4 Je 14 '63
Much more than law is needed. A. M. Bickel. il N Y Times Mag p7+ Ag 9 '64
Nay-sayer of the Negro revolt. L. Bennett, jr. il Ebony 19:66-8+ S '64
Negro and the candidates. R. Wilkins. Sat R 47:27-9+ S 26 '64; Reply. C. E. Goodell. 47:25-6 O 17 '64
Negro as an American; address, June 13, 1963. R. C. Weaver. Vital Speeches 29:625-9 Ag 1 '63
Negro child asks: why? M. Anderson. il N Y Times Mag p32+ D 1 '63
Negro civil rights leaders; address, October 2, 1963. T. C. Cothran. Vital Speeches 30:84-7 N 15 '63
Negro drive for jobs; with editorial comment. il Bsns W p52-4+, 124 Ag 17 '63
Negro in the Supreme court, 1954-64; address, 1964. R. L. Gill. bibliog Negro Hist Bul 28:51-2+ D '64 (to be cont)
Negro leaders meet LBJ; here are the results they see. il U S News 55:48-9 D 16 '63
Negro leaders tell their plans for '64; symposium. il U S News 56:56-62+ F 24 '64
Negro revolution. F. S. Meyer. Nat R 14:496 Je 18 '63
Negro tactics: change coming. il U S News 58:41 Ja 4 '65
Negro view: Johnson can free the South. L. E. Lomax. il Look 28:34+ Mr 10 '64
Negroes' grievances. W. Lippmann. Newsweek 62:21 S 16 '63
Negroes walk to freedom; murder lies on a nation's conscience. il Life 55:32-3 Jl 5 '63
Negroes want in; concerning editorial in Sunday telegraph. Christian Cent 80:732 Je 5 '63
New world of Negro Americans, by H. R. Isaacs. Review
Nat R 15:243 S 24 '63. M. Bain
Nonviolence in the racial crisis. W. R. Miller. Christian Cent 81:927-30 Jl 22 '64; Discussion 81:1179 S 23 '64
Non-whiz kid with the quiet gun. R. Wallace. il Life 55:75-6+ Ag 9 '63
Not enough. New Repub 149:3-4 O 12 '63
Not token freedom, full freedom. C. Sitton. il N Y Times Mag p21+ Je 9 '63
Notes and comment. New Yorker 39:19 Je 22 '63
Now, Kennedy moves on civil rights. il U S News 54:52 Mr 11 '63
100 years later. il Newsweek 61:26-7 F 25 '63
100 years later. Time 81:24 F 22 '63
Only hope. D. Lawrence. U S News 54:112 Je 10 '63

NEGROES in the United States—Civil rights —*Continued*
Opportunities for all; address, March 27, 1963. W. Morse. Vital Speeches 29:457-9 My 15 '63
Passport to progress; drive to register Sunflower's Negroes to vote. Newsweek 61:18-19 F 4 '63
Plea to twelve Negro children; address. M. Anderson. il N Y Times Mag p7+ Je 14 '64
Politics of courage. K. Crawford. Newsweek 61:41 Je 24 '63
Portrait of a decade, by A. Lewis and The New York times. Review
New Repub 151:24-7 D 19 '64. J. Greenberg
Power structure, integration, militancy, freedom now! T. H. White. il Life 55:78-80+ N 29 '63
President supports civil rights legislation. Christian Cent 81:103 Ja 22 '64
Promise and fulfillment of American democracy; address, September 23, 1963. J. M. Klotsche. Vital Speeches 30:14-17 O 15 '63
Proper stance. il Time 84:9 Jl 31 '64
Push for civil rights; newest official size-up. il U S News 55:110-12 O 7 '63
Quartet on race. M. Boyd. Christian Cent 81:1064-5 Ag 26 '64
Quiet revolution. T. G. Harris. Look 27:56+ D 17 '63
Race crisis: Kennedy decides on action. il Bsns W p24-5 Je 8 '63
Race issue & the campaign; symposium; with editorial comment. Nat R 16:813-20 S 22 '64
Race problem: the solution as the President sees it; address, June 11, 1963; with editorial comment. J. F. Kennedy. il U S News 54:79-80, 108 Je 24 '63; Same with title Moral imperative; without editorial comment. Vital Speeches 29:546-7 Jl 1 '63; Same with title President's civil right's message. Ebony 18:233-4 S '63; Excerpts. Sr Schol 83:18-19 S 13 '63
Race riots: Goldwater boon. F. Knebel. il Look 28:34+ S 22 '64
Racial crisis. W. Lippmann. Newsweek 61:23 My 27 '63
Rally on the Common; Boston demonstration. America 108:729 My 25 '63
Religion-state conference on civil rights legislation. H. A. Jack. Christian Cent 81:1566-7+ D 16 '64
Responsible tactics will win rights sooner. Life 56:4 My 1 '64
Restraint is a quality of leadership. J. N. Eller. America 111:149 Ag 15 '64
Reverse carpetbagging. Life 56:4 Ap 17 '64
Revolution. il Time 81:17-19 Je 7 '63
Rights and policy. America 109:656 N 23 '63; Reply. R. F. Currie. 109:783 D 21 '63
Rights drive too fast? what a poll shows: New York times. il U S News 57:20-1 O 5 '64
Root of the spirit. Time 82:9-10 Ag 2 '63
Second American revolution. C. Green. bibliog Negro Hist Bul 27:103-5 F '64
Should there be compensation for Negroes? parity, not preference. K. Haselden. il N Y Times Mag p43+ O 6 '63
Silent white ministers of the South. G. McMillan. il N Y Times Mag p22+ Ap 5 '64
South looks ahead. R. McGill. il Ebony 18:99-100+ S '63
South states its case; statement, June 12, 1963. R. B. Russell. U S News 54:78 Je 24 '63
Southern prophecies. America 110:471 Ap 4 '64
Speaking out; Negroes are not moving too fast. M. L. King, jr. Sat Eve Post 237:8+ N 7 '64
Spotlights on the American dilemma; symposium. il Reporter 29:6-22 Jl 4 '63
Stop the world; challenge of the November election. E. Rabinowitch. il Bul Atomic Sci 20:2-5 O '64
Struggle for equality, by J. M. McPherson. Review
Negro Hist Bul 28:71 D '64. H. N. Meyer
Summer and civil rights; fears of violence. Commonweal 80:384 Je 19 '64
Thirty miles divide folly and reason; Cambridge and Salisbury, Md; with report by M. Durham. il Life 55:18-25 Jl 26 '63
This Negro revolution. M. Ascoli. Reporter 29:22 O 10 '63; Discussion. 29:6+ N 7 '63
Threats: Negroes' latest weapon in rights drive. il U S News 55:39-40 Jl 1 '63
Time is now. D. L. Anderson. Commonweal 79:347-8 D 13 '63
Time to consolidate? W. Gremley. America 112:12-14 Ja 2 '65
To Mr Baldwin. Reporter 28:10-11 Je 20 '63
Tom Paines and Uncle Toms. Christian Cent 80:947 Jl 31 '63
Tortoise vs. hare. K. Crawford. Newsweek 61:37 Je 10 '63
Twelve white men and true; discrimination in jury selection. M. Meltsner. New Repub 150:11-12 My 23 '64; Reply. L. S. Korns. 150:36 Je 13 '64
Unequal aid to Negroes. Commonweal 78:468 Ag 9 '63
U.S. Negroes' goal: to set Africa policy. il U S News 58:60-1 Ja 11 '65
Visit with Martin Luther King; ed. by E. Dunbar. M. King. il Look 27:92-6 F 12 '63
Washington front; church leaders stand up to be counted. J. LaFarge. America 108:897 Je 29 '63
What mass protests can't do. L. Lomax. Sat R 46:11-12 Jl 6 '63
What Negroes can expect from President Lyndon Johnson. L. Bennett, jr. il Ebony 19:81-4+ Ja '64
What new turn in Negro drive means. il U S News 54:40-7 Je 17 '63
What next? five Negro leaders reply. il N Y Times Mag p27+ S 29 '63
What northerners really think of Negroes. S. Alsop and O. Quayle. il Sat Eve Post 236:17-21 S 7 '63; Discussion. 236:4 O 5 '63
What now? one Negro leader's answer. R. Wilkins. il N Y Times Mag p 11+ Ag 16 '64
What the marchers really want; Negro leaders answer five basic questions. il N Y Times Mag p7-9+ Ag 25 '63
What the Negroes want: Powell spells it out; summaries of addresses. A. C. Powell. U S News 55:11 Ag 12 '63
Where Negroes didn't vote on integration; Cambridge, Md. il U S News 55:6 O 14 '63
White and black: test of a nation, by S. Lubell. Review
Nat R 16:1018-19 N 17 '64. V. Miller
Who can we surrender to? R. A. Liston. il Sat Eve Post 236:78-80 O 5 '63; Reply. 236:82 N 2 '63
Who is guilty in Birmingham? C. Morgan jr. Christian Cent 80:1195-6 O 2 '63
Why race troubles hit one city, spare another; a case study: Cambridge and Salisbury, Md. il U S News 55:78-80 Ag 5 '63
Why we can't wait; excerpts. M. L. King, jr. il Life 56:98-100+ My 15 '64; Sat R 47:17-20+ My 30 '64
See also
Civil rights act of 1964
Civil rights demonstrations

Crime

Crisis in race relations; symposium. il U S News 57:23-40 Ag 10 '64
Jitters; wave of terror puts police on overtime. il Newsweek 63:35-6 Je 15 '64
New York city in trouble: another chapter. il U S News 56:43-5 Je 15 '64
Question of Negro crime. R. Coles. Harper 228:134-6+ Ap '64
Terror on the trains. il Time 83:38-9 Je 12 '64

Economic conditions

Economic condition of the Negro in Atlanta. G. Sisk. bibliog Negro Hist Bul 27:87-90 Ja '64
Economic status of Negroes, by V. W. Henderson. Review
New Repub 149:23-4+ O 12 '63. E. Ginzberg; Reply. E. Kramer. 149:30-1 O 26 '63
Just how well off is the American Negro? il U S News 55:44-5 Jl 22 '63
Look at the rise of the Negro middle class; with letter by A. E. Meyer. il U S News 55:56-61 Jl 15 '63
Meredith's advice to Negroes; excerpt from address, July 5, 1963. J. H. Meredith. U S News 55:89 Jl 22 '63
Negro as an American; address, June 13, 1963. R. C. Weaver. Vital Speeches 29:625-9 Ag 1 '63
Negro businessman speaks his mind: interview. S. B. Fuller. il U S News 55:58-61 Ag 19 '63
Of dollars and sense. il Ebony 19:64-5 Jl '64
Prosperity through equality. L. Miller. Nation 197:157-60+ S 21 '63
Should there be compensation for Negroes: two views. W. M. Young, jr; K. Haselden. il N Y Times Mag p43+ O 6 '63
See also
Negroes in the United States—Migration

NEGROES in the United States—*Continued*

Education

Abigail Adams, integrator. Life 55:4 Jl 5 '63
After four years with no schooling; Prince Edward County, Va. il U S News 55:10 S 2 '63
After integration, higher horizons. M. Anderson. il N Y Times Mag p 10+ Ap 21 '63
Back to school. il Newsweek 62:70 Ag 26 '63
Boost from blue chips; millions to Negro colleges. Bsns W p25 Ag 1 '64
Brown and Tougaloo. Commonweal 80:280 My 29 '64
Canterbury tale; school for Negro girls in Connecticut, 1832-34. R. Rushmore. Reporter 28:46-7 Ap 25 '63
Catching up in Prince Edward. il Time 82:56 Ag 9 '63
Classes again soon for Prince Edward Negroes. U S News 55:11 Ag 26 '63
Closing the gap. il Newsweek 64:70 S 21 '64
Crusade in Mississippi. A. Poinsett. il Ebony 19:25-8+ S '64
Desegregation decision; Brown v. Board of education, May 17, 1954. H. S. Ashmore. il Sat R 47:68-70+ My 16 '64
Diploma-giving principal; St Louis's Charles Sumner high school. il Ebony 18:76+ Je '63
Doomed ones; school themes by sixth-graders in Chicago. S. Alsop. il Sat Eve Post 237:16 Ap '64
Dull part of desegregation; legislation to educate and train Negroes for better jobs. J. Duscha. Reporter 29:43-6 Ag 15 '63
Education and the Negro. J. G. Roundtree. bibliog Negro Hist Bul 27:106-8+ F '64
Equality in education; address, November 2, 1963. R. F. Drinan. Vital Speeches 30:223-4 Ja 15 '64
Ford foundation aids Negro colleges. Christian Cent 81:925 Jl 22 '64
Four long years; Prince Edward County, Va. il Sr Schol 85:1T N 11 '64
Freedom through knowledge. Negro Hist Bul 27:48+ N '63
Geography of intellect, by N. Weyl and S. Possony. Review
  Commentary 38:61-3 Jl '64. M. Meyer; Reply with rejoinder. M. Kotler. 39:11-12+ Ja '65
Getting Negroes into college; some schools give them a break; reprint. P. A. Janssen. il U S News 56:82-3 My 25 '64
How do the teachers feel? R. Coles. il Sat R 47:72-3 My 16 '64
Ivy-league integrationists. R. W. Apple, jr. il Reporter 38:32-4 F 14 '63
Making history in Prince Edward County; Prince Edward free school association. N. V. Sullivan. il Sat R 47:59-61+ O 17 '64
Man who wouldn't quit; G. Haley. A. Haley. il Read Digest 82:54-9 Mr '63
Negro college libraries and ACRL standards. E. J. Josey. bibliog il Library J 88:2989-96 S 1 '63
Negro colleges: long ignored, southern schools now courted by major universities and foundations. E. Langer. Science 145:371-3+ Jl 24 '64
Negro colleges: their product and promise. J. Daniel. Read Digest 85:33-4+ D '64
New approach to educating Negro children in gray area schools. W. A. Parris. bibliog Negro Hist Bul 28:61-4 D '64 (to be cont)
New hope for higher learning. il Ebony 19:144-5 O '64
New wave. il Newsweek 63:24+ F 10 '64
Parent learns with child; experimental program at Howard university, Washington, D.C. il Sci N L 86:278 O 31 '64
Plea to twelve Negro children; address. M. Anderson. il N Y Times Mag p7+ Je 14 '64
Preferential treatment for Negroes? F. M. Hechinger. il Reporter 31:22-4 D 3 '64; Discussion. 31:6 D 31 '64
Prince Edward County situation. W. V. Heuvel; N. V. Sullivan. il NEA J 53:12-15 Mr '64
Prince Edward free school system thrives; awaits Supreme ct. rule. Library J 89:930 F 15 '64
Programming ABCs; Project literacy to help Mississippi Negro voter registration. il Bsns W p74+ Jl 18 '64
Reading: Negro youth's quest for certainty. E. J. Josey. Negro Hist Bul 27:158-9+ Ap '64
Right to knowledge; excerpt from address, July 12, 1964. H. T. Heald. Sch & Soc 92:376-9 D 12 '64
Road less traveled by. J. L. Brown. bibliog f Negro Hist Bul 27:144-5 Mr '64
Sam Shepard's faith. P. Friggens. il PTA Mag 58:18-20+ Mr '64; Same abr. with title Is the Negro equal in intelligence and ability? Read Digest 84:83-7 Mr '64
Scholastic teacher interview; ed. by H. Langer. C. J. Duckworth. Sr Schol 85:9T-10T+ O 21 '64
Scholastic teacher interviews: William J. Trent, jr; ed. by H. Langer. W. J. Trent, jr. Sr Schol 83:9T-11T D 6 '63
School boycotts: your city may be next. il U S News 56:6+ F 17 '64
School integration, or else. M. Weinberg. Commonweal 80:106-9 Ap 17 '64
Separate & superior; St Augustine high school in New Orleans. il Time 85:56 Ja 1 65
Speaking out; young Negroes aren't ready. L. E. Lomax. Sat Eve Post 236:12+ S 21 '63
Still separate, unequal; Arkansas schools. New Repub 150:5 Mr 28 '64
Strengthening Negro colleges. Sch & Soc 92:94 Mr 7 '64
Their dream is not to be nervous; a volunteer with the Mississippi summer project reports on teaching in a freedom school; interview, ed. by G. Illig. L. Guest. il Mile 60:164-5+ N '64
Universities adopt-a-school plan; Northern university aid in raising Negro college standards. il Time 83:63 My 29 '64
Virginia ruling; Prince Edward County. Sr Schol 83:2T Ja 10 '64
Wesleyan tutorials. D. Morgan. il Sat R 46:68-9 Je 15 '63
When school bells ring after four years' silence; Prince Edward County, Va. il U S News 55:41-3 S 30 '63
Words to teachers. A. N. D. Brooks. Negro Hist Bul 27:196 My '64
  See also
American teachers association
Colleges and universities—Desegregation
Dillard university, New Orleans
Education—Southern states
Freedom schools
Howard university, Washington, D.C.
Miles college, Birmingham, Ala.
Private schools—Desegregation
Public schools—Desegregation
Tuskegee institute

History

Mary S. Peake, 1823-62. S. N. Fen. bibliog f Sch & Soc 91:171-2 Ap 6 '63

Employment

Bargain pay rates: a new plan for training unskilled youths. U S News 56:80 Je 22 '64
Business and civil rights; address, June 5, 1964. J. P. Mitchell. Vital Speeches 30:549-51 Jl 1 '64
Business, next target for integration? J. Perry. Harvard Bsns R 41:104-15 Mr '63
Businessman and the Negro; excerpt from Crisis in black and white. C. E. Silberman. il Fortune 68:97-9+ S '63
Carrying out a plan for job integration; Lockheed's Marietta, Ga. plant. il Bsns W p90+ Ap 13 '63
Chicago starts moving on equal job question. il Bsns W p22-3 My 30 '64
Civil rights; discrimination in labor unions; address, May 12, 1964. W. M. Young, jr. Vital Speeches 30:535-7 Je 15 '64
Civil rights yes; what about jobs? Life 55:4 N 8 '63
Crashing gates to better jobs. il Bsns W p24-5 Je 22 '63
Dull part of desegregation; legislation to educate and train Negroes for better jobs. J. Duscha. Reporter 29:43-6 Ag 15 '63; Discussion. 29:8 S 26 '63
Economic growth and employment opportunities for minorities, by D. L. Hiestand. Review
  Commentary il 38:95-8 N '64. R. Lekachman
Employment of Negroes by government contractors. J. A. Brackett. il Mo Labor R 87:789-93 Jl '64
For skilled Negroes, jobs aplenty. Bsns W p38 N 28 '64
Forced hiring of Negroes; how it would work. U S News 55:83-4 Jl 29 '63
If I were young today. W. J. Kennedy, jr. Ebony 18:52 My '63
Intermingled revolutions; the Negro and automation; address, July 20, 1964. W. M. Young, jr. Vital Speeches 30:692-4 S 1 '64

NEGROES in the United States—Employment —*Continued*
Is equality unfair? Negro's plea for preferential treatment. America 109:412-13 O 12 '63
Job outlook for youth. il Ebony 18:25-8 My '63
Jobs for Negroes: how much progress in sight? il Newsweek 62:68-70+ Jl 15 '63
Jobs for Negroes, is there a real shortage? How Negro pressure gets jobs. il U S News 55:28-32 Ag 12 '63
Jobs: key to national unrest? il U S News 54: 37-41 Je 24 '63
Labor month in review; Negro unemployment. Mo Labor R 86:III-IV S '63
Managing your manpower; how employers are preparing for the civil rights act. T. R. Brooks. Duns R 84:57+ N '64
Managing your manpower; Negro employment problem. T. R. Brooks. Duns R 82:59-60+ Ag '63
Most likely to succeed; recruiting junior executives from class of '64. il Time 83: 84+ Je 19 '64
Negro businessman speaks his mind; interview. S. B. Fuller. il U S News 55:58-61 Ag 19 '63
Negro drive for jobs; with editorial comment. il Bsns W p52-4+, 124 Ag 17 '63
Negro job quotas? Kennedy says no; excerpts from news conference, August 20, 1963. J. F. Kennedy. U S News 55:8 S 2 '63
Negroes are moving up the job ladder. I. Ross. Read Digest 83:53-7 D '63
Negroes preferred? America 110:397 Mr 28 '64
Negroes push harder for construction jobs. il Bsns W p66+ Je 15 '63
Negroes take aim at GM. il Bsns W p32+ Jl 20 '63
Negro's search for a better job. il Newsweek 63:79-83 Je 8 '64
New jobs open to Negroes. Christian Cent 80:454 Ap 10 '63
New opportunities for Negroes. il Changing T 17:18-20 Ap '63
Opportunities for all; address, March 27, 1963. W. Morse. Vital Speeches 29:457-9 My 15 '63
Preferential hiring: Pitney-Bowes, inc. Newsweek 62:69 D 16 '63
Progress or publicity? Newsweek 61:27 F 25 '63
Proposal for a revolution. J. P. Lyford. il Sat R 46:19-22 O 19; 25-8+ O 26 '63
Quotas for Negroes? E. T. Chase. il Commonweal 79:451-4 Ja 17 '64
Reservoir of hate. America 111:222 S 5 '64
Right to a job. il Newsweek 62:51-2 Ag 5 '63
Rights, not ratios. G. Kelley. America 109: 424-5 O 12 '63
Scripto on strike; the race-wage picket line. C. J. Levy. Nation 200:31-2 Ja 11 '65
Some of the problems in fighting poverty; project sponsored by Norfolk division of Virginia state college. il U S News 56:86-7 Je 8 '64
Speaking out; young Negroes aren't ready. L. E. Lomax. Sat Eve Post 236:12+ S 21 '63
There isn't any time. Fortune 70:127-8 Jl '64
Toward open hiring; anti-discrimination pledges in church contracts. Commonweal 81:500 Ja 15 '65
U.S. steps up equal job opportunity. il Ebony 19:103-4+ S '64
White-collar Negroes; Hallmark employment agency in New York city. il Newsweek 63: 86+ Mr 23 '64
See also
Discrimination in employment
Negro American labor council
Negro women—Employment
United States—President's committee on equal employment opportunity

Folklore

See Folklore, Negro

Health and hygiene

Negro health in Atlanta. G. Sisk. bibliog Negro Hist Bul 27:65-6 D '63

History

Civil rights crisis: challenge to all Americans. il Sr Schol 83:13-19 S 13 '63
Correcting the image of Negroes in textbooks; address, 1964. C. E. Stewart. Negro Hist Bul 28:29-30+ N '64
Desegregated history. il Time 83:59 Mr 27 '64
Essays in the history of the Negro, by H. Aptheker. Review
Negro Hist Bul 28:69-70 D '64. E. A. Toppin
Five brave Negroes with John Brown at Harpers Ferry. il Negro Hist Bul 27:164-9 Ap '64
Historical basis of emancipation, 1963; address. H. N. Meyer. Negro Hist Bul 27:4-6 O '63
In-service education of the teacher of African history; address, 1964. W. S. Robinson. bibliog Negro Hist Bul 28:33-4+ N '64
Leader ahead of his times. L. C. Jones. Am Heritage 14:58-9+ Je '63
March: what Negroes expected, what they want next; address, August 26, 1963. A. P. Randolph. U S News 55:82-5 S 9 '63
Needed: the truth about Harlem. L. P. Jackson, jr. Negro Hist Bul 28:11-12 O '64
Negro history and the modern Uncle Tom. Negro Hist Bul 27:134-5 Mr '64
Negro who founded Chicago. L. Bennett, jr. il Ebony 19:170-2+ D '63
Negro's problem is the white's. E. Ginzberg. il N Y Times Mag p 14+ F 9 '64
Northern Negrophobia during the Civil war as reported by the London Times. N. M. Adams. Negro Hist Bul 28:7-8 O '64
Pioneers in protest. L. Bennett, jr. See issues of Ebony beginning March, 1964
President who hurt Negroes most. C. L. Sanders. il Ebony 19:110-12+ My '64
Study of Negro blasts racial myths; comments on textbooks. R. P. Alexander. Negro Hist Bul 28:3-6 O '64
Ten most dramatic events in Negro history. il Ebony 18:28-34+ S '63
Tragic legend of reconstruction. K. M. Stampp. Commentary 39:44-50 Ja '65
Uncle Tom and predestination. D. Chaput. Negro Hist Bul 27:143 Mr '64
Visit with Dr Brooks. il Negro Hist Bul 27: 200-1 My '64
Woman who saved the Union navy. G. A. Foster. il Ebony 19:48-50+ Jl '64
See also
Association for the study of Negro life and history
United States—History—Revolution—Negroes

Housing

Are cities obsolete? B. Weissbourd. il Sat R 47:12-15+ D 19 '64
Black neck in the white noose. W. Von Eckardt. New Repub 149:14-17 O 19 '63
Brotherly love. il Newsweek 62:22 S 9 '63
California plan: Integration preparation plan of Bay Gulph, suburb of Los Angeles. V. B. Miller. Nat R 16:712 Ag 25 '64
Harlem goes to war against the slumlords. R. K. Massie. il Sat Eve Post 237:71-5 F 29 '64
I sold a house to a Negro; Sarasota, Fla. E. Moore. il Ebony 18:92-4+ O '63
I'm not against it, but—. D. Faber. il N Y Times Mag p58+ O 27 '63; Discussion. p 12 N 10 '63
Incident in a rural slum; Negro slums in Riverhead. L. Long. Christian Cent 81: 1088-9 S 2 '64
Michigan's ghetto buster. il Ebony 18:55-6+ F '63
Rent strike in Harlem. il Ebony 19:112-14+ Ap '64
See also
Discrimination in housing

Migration

Geography and the Negro problem; with charts. U S News 55:50-1 Ag 26 '63
Negroes on the move: where they settle. il U S News 56:36 Ap 27 '64
One plan to end race troubles: pay people to move; summary of address, March 16, 1964; with charts. R. B. Long. il U S News 56:36-7 Mr 30 '64

Occupations

Economic status of nonwhite workers, 1955-62. M. A. Kessler. bibliog f il Mo Labor R 86:780-8 Jl '63
If I were young today. A. P. Randolph. Ebony 18:82 Jl '63
If I were young today. H. E. Moore. Ebony 18:88 O '63
If I were young today. L. B. Granger. Ebony 18:72 Ap '63
If I were young today. P. R. Williams. Ebony 18:56 Ag '63
New hope through self-help; Opportunities industrialization center, North Philadelphia. il Ebony 19:27-30+ My '64
Quiet revolution. T. G. Harris. Look 27:56+ D 17 '63
Speaking of people. See issues of Ebony
See also
Negro business men
Negro librarians

NEGROES in the United States—*Continued*

Politics and suffrage

Arithmetic lesson; vote in the South. il Newsweek 64:36 N 23 '64
As Negroes seek to vote: Canton, Miss. J. E. Sherman. Christian Cent 81:464 Ap 8 '64
Birth of a voter; Louisiana parish registers 1st Negro in sixty-one years. B. Adelman. il Ebony 19:88-90+ F '64
Chicago close-up: political side of the race issue. il U S News 55:72-3 N 4 '63
Congressional challenge; Mississippi Freedom Democratic party's efforts to remove Mississippi's five congressmen from their seats in the House. Commonweal 81:532 Ja 22 '65
Fayette fraud. Nation 199:62 Ag 24 '64
From demonstration to politics. Nation 198: 158 F 17 '64
Hattiesburg and central Illinois. J. Moore. Christian Cent 81:340-1 Mr 11 '64
How J.F.K's. grandfather fought the grandfather clause. H. N. Meyer. Negro Hist Bul 27:27 N '63
How Republican leaders view the Negro. S. Booker. il Ebony 19:25-8+ Mr '64
How to wreck two parties. D. Lawrence. U S News 55:96 Jl 29 '63
It's nearly all white in the South. P. Watters. il New Repub 150:11-12 Je 13 '64
Justice and power; Negro vote in Mississippi. Nation 200:2-3 Ja 4 '65
Life for a vote. J. Hersey. il Sat Eve Post 237:34-8+ S 26 '64
Longer view. Nation 198:641-2 Je 29 '64
Louisiana: clues to '64 vote. il U S News 56:64 Ja 27 '64
Make-believe vote. Newsweek 62:23 O 28 '63
Mind on freedom; right to vote in Greenwood, Miss. il Newsweek 61:25-6 Ap 8 '63
Needed: more vote-ins. Nation 198:469-70 My 11 '64
Negro & the Democratic coalition; excerpts from White and black: test of a nation. S. Lubell. Commentary 38:19-27 Ag '64
Negro minority vs. a white majority? R. De Toledano. Nat R 16:814-15 S 22 '64
Negro vote. Newsweek 63:32 My 18 '64
Negro vote: what will it really mean in November? with chart. il U S News 56: 34-6 Ap 27 '64
Negro votes beat Barry. P. Watters. New Repub 151:7 N 28 '64
Negroes and politics. America 110:782 Je 6 '64
Negroes come of age politically. Christian Cent 81:1451-2 N 25 '64
Negroes tip the scales. A. Brandel. New Repub 150:6 My 30 '64
People vs. politicians: defeat in Harlem. W. Klein. Nation 199:27-9 Jl 27 '64
People vs. politicians: defeat in Harlem. W. Klein. Nation 199:27-9 Jl 27 '64; Reply. W. M. Young, jr. 199:inside cover S 7 '64
Political power of the Negro in America. C. B. Luce. McCalls 92:26+ N '64
Politics: it's Kennedy 30 to 1. il Newsweek 62:28-9 Jl 29 '63
Registration in Alabama. H. Zinn. New Repub 149:11-12 O 26 '63
South looks ahead. R. McGill. il Ebony 18: 99-100+ S '63
Southern fear and Negro voting. G. A. Martin, jr. Commonweal 80:135-7 Ap 24 '64
Southern Negro drives for the vote. C. Sitton. il N Y Times Mag p28-9 S 29 '63
Southern politician; with editorial comment. F. E. Smith. Nation 199:131, 132-4 S 21 '64
Southern politics and the Negroes. P. Duke. il Reporter 31:18-21 D 17 '64
South's war against Negro votes. J. Poppy. il Look 27:38+ My 21 '63
Speaking out; G.O.P. for white men only? J. Robinson. Sat Eve Post 236:10+ Ag 10 '63
Spring offensive; Negroes plan the future. P. Watters. il Nation 198:117-20 F 3 '64
Squeeze in the South; drive to speed up Negro voting in the South. il Time 81:22-3 My 3 '63
Students get the vote out; Fayette County, Tenn. R. V. Denenberg. il Nation 199:45-9 Ag 10 '64
Summer in Mississippi; freedom moves in to stay. J. DeMuth. il Nation 199:104-5+ S 14 '64
Two political parties and the Negro vote. R. Wilkins. McCalls 92:30+ N '64
Under standing Neorger and his right to vote. J. Kenworthy and E. W. Kenworthy. Reporter 30:32-4 Mr 26 '64
Underground election: Negro mock campaign. J. Herron. il Nation 197:387-9 D 7 '63
Vote in the South. Nat R 14:437 Je 4 '63; Reply. J. W. Daly. 15:121 Ag 13 '63
Voting in Greenwood. Commonweal 78:61 Ap 12 '63
Voting in the Black Belt. C. Mabee. il Negro Hist Bul 27:50-6 D '63
White and black: test of a nation, by S. Lubell. Review
Nat R 16:1018-19 N 17 '64. V. Miller.
Who speaks for Mississippi? R. Cleghorn. Reporter 31:31-4 Ag 13 '64

Religion

Black Jews of Harlem, by H. Brotz. Review
Nation 198:662-3 Je 29 '64. A. Kohlman
Black religion, by J. R. Washington, jr. Review
Newsweek 64:73 Jl 27 '64
Fire next time, by J. Baldwin. Review
Nat R il 14:408-14+ My 21 '63. G. Wills; Discussion. 14:507 Je 18 '63
Jackson's way; National Baptist convention's 84th annual meeting. Newsweek 64:76 S 21 '64
Key man of the South: the Negro minister. C. E. Lincoln. il N Y Times Mag p20+ Jl 12 '64
Memo from a Mormon: in which a troubled young man raises the question of his church's attitude toward Negroes. J. Nye. il Look 27:74+ O 22 '63; Discussion. 27:79 O 22; 17 D 3 '63
New Negro and the church. G. S. Wilmore, jr. Christian Cent 80:168-71 F 6 '63; Discussion. 80:404 Mr 27 '63
Shelter in storm. America 110:471 Ap 4 '64
Toward the other shore; freedom movement as seen by a church leader. V. Harding. il Reporter 29:27-31 O 10 '63
We are statesmen. il Time 84:73 S 18 '64
See also
African Methodist Episcopal church
Christian Methodist Episcopal church

Segregation

Another Kennedy judge. New Repub 149: 6-7 O 5 '63
Birmingham, Alabama: a city in fear. J. D. Brown. il Sat Eve Post 236:11-19 Mr 2 '63
Birth of Jim Crow; Plessy v. Ferguson. C. V. Woodward. il Am Heritage 15:52-5+ Ap '64
Decade of slow, painful progress. R. McGill. il Sat R 47:65-6 My 16 '64
De facto segregation; summary of varying current views. B. Fielding. NEA J 53:11-14 My '64
Desegregation, after school. R. Kramer. il N Y Times Mag p47 My 31 '64
Development problems; address, February 27, 1964. R. C. Weaver. Vital Speeches 30:460-3 My 15 '64
Do you need a dentist? J. Ridgeway. New Repub 150:6 My 16 '64
11 a.m. Sunday is our most segregated hour. K. Haselden. il N Y Times Mag p9+ Ag 2 '64
Hopeful dialogue of the races. W. Dykeman and J. Stokely. il N Y Times Mag p 10+ Ag 11 '63
In High court, a blanket rule against segregation? U S News 54:65 Je 3 '63
In the courts: action for faster integration. U. S. News 54:10 Je 10 '63
Inalienable rights of all; address, July 16, 1963. W. J. Kenealy. Vital Speeches 29: 686-9 S 1 '63
Inside a segregationist. S. P. Boyle. il Ebony 18:53-4+ Je '63
Latest target for integration: private hospitals. U S News 56:6 Mr 16 '64
Let's boycott the Olympics. M. Whitfield. il Ebony 19:95-6+ Mr '64
Man who wouldn't quit; G. Haley. A. Haley. il Read Digest 82:54-9 Mr '63
March toward equality; excerpt from Portrait of a decade. A. Lewis. Atlan 214:58-64 S '64
Most dubious achievement of all. A. Gingrich. Esquire 61:12 Mr '64
My Negro problem, and ours. N. Podhoretz. Commentary 35:93-101 F '63; Discussion. 35:338-47, 430-8, 525-31 Ap-Je '63; New Repub 148:11-12 Mr 23 '63
Negro mother speaks of her challenging role in a changing world. M. B. Young. il Parents Mag 39:50-1+ Jl '64
Negro's priorities: welfare or status. E. C. Ladd, jr. il Nation 199:243-6+ O 19 '64
No time for silence; question of integration. America 109:2 Jl 6 '63; Reply. D. N. Kelly. 109:125 Ag 10 '63
Now it's a Negro drive for segregation; interview. Malcolm X. il U S News 56:38-9 Mr 30 '64

NEGROES in the United States—Segregation —*Continued*
Patience; wearing thin. il Newsweek 61:19 F 4 '63
Post and integration; editorial. Sat Eve Post 236:70 Mr 2 '63
Private, but public; question of federal aid to segregated institutions. Time 83:52 Mr 13 '64
Racial extremists fill vacuum. Christian Cent 81:539 Ap 29 '64
Remaining walls. il Ebony 18:94-5 Je '63
School integration, or else. M. Weinberg. Commonweal 80:106-9 Ap 17 '64
Seeing the unseen. Christian Cent 81:387-8 Mr 25 '64
Segregated sickness; Catholic hospitals. J. Leo. Commonweal 81:406-7 D 18 '64
Segregation in hospitals. Newsweek 62:59 Jl 22 '63
Segregation: the tender trap. J. Cogley. Commonweal 78:318-19 Je 14 '63
Since the Supreme court spoke; decision on school segregation. A. Lewis. il N Y Times Mag p9+ My 10 '64
South has many faces; excerpts from South and the southerner. R. McGill. Atlan 211: 83-98 Ap '63
Southern teen-ager speaks his mind. M. Long. il N Y Times Mag p 15+ N 10 '63
Strategy for victory. il Ebony 19:110-11 D '63
Summit conference on race, religion. il Ebony 18:43-4+ Ap '63
Ten years later; Supreme court decision on desegregation. M. Ascoli. Reporter 30:16 My 21 '64
This month's feature: Congress and public accommodations. Cong Digest 42:259-88 N '63
VIPs regret. Nation 198:497 My 18 '64
What can we tell our children? views of a white southern mother and a Negro mother. il Redbook 123:6+ My '64
Where the color bars are quietly dropping. il U S News 54:42-3 Je 24 '63
See also
Church and race problems
Libraries and Negroes
Public schools—Desegregation
Segregation in education

Anecdotes, facetiae, satire, etc.

Integrated thought; integrated troupe, the Living premise in living color. New Yorker 39:22-3 Je 22 '63

Segregation, Resistance to

After Birmingham riots, troubles linger on. il U S News 54:40-2 My 27 '63
Artistic boycott. Time 83:73 Mr 20 '64
As militancy rises in ranks of the Negroes, hatreds erupt in the North. il Life 55:32B-32C Jl 19 '63
As race tensions rise. il U S News 54:33-6 Je 24 '63
Attala and the Huns; killing of W. L. Moore. America 108:658 My 11 '63
Battle of Jackson. il Newsweek 61:28-9 Je 10 '63
Beginning in Birmingham. V. Harding. il Reporter 28:13-19 Je 6 '63; Discussion. 29: 5 Jl 4 '63
Beyond rights, the issue of human dignity. Life 54:4 My 24 '63
Billy Graham advises the wrong man; Martin Luther King. Christian Cent 80:606 My 8 '63
Birmingham, a city. Commonweal 78:212-13 My 17 '63
Birmingham and after. W. F. Buckley, jr. Nat R 14:397 My 21 '63; Reply. B. Hamby. 14:507+ Je 18 '63
Birmingham, U.S.A: look at them run. il Newsweek 61:27-8 My 13 '63
Blake and Corrigan lead bias protest; march in Baltimore. Christian Cent 80:902 Jl 17 '63
Bonds and ball points; new economic weapons. Newsweek 64:47 D 28 '64
Broken lance; William L. Moore's walk. il Newsweek 61:29-30+ My 6 '63
Brother Malcolm: his theme now is violence. U S News 56:19 Mr 23 '64
Call to color blindness. W. F. Buckley, jr. Nat R 14:488 Je 18 '63; Reply. M. Whalen. 15:120 Ag 13 '63
Celebrity boycott; Jackson, Miss. J. De Muth. New Repub 150:8-9 Ap 25 '64
Clean conscience or Black Muslims? J. B. Sheerin. Cath World 197:212-15 Jl '63
Coming showdown in the race crisis. H. S. Ashmore. il Look 27:62-7 Jl 16 '63
Congress confronted with racial issue. Christian Cent 80:821-2 Je 26 '63
Creative disruptions; race relations lecture at Vanderbilt university. W. A. Geier. Christian Cent 80:344 Mr 13 '63
Critical test for the nonviolent way. J. Herbers. il N Y Times Mag p5+ Jl 5 '64
Day it happens to each of us; excerpt from Our faces, our words. L. Smith. McCalls 92: 124-5+ N '64
Demonstrations or threats? Christian Cent 80: 877 Jl 10 '63
Dogs, kids & clubs. il Time 81:19 My 10 '63
End of fear. New Repub 148:1+ My 18 '63
Epilogue in Albany; were the mass marches worthwhile? R. Cleghorn. New Repub 149: 15-18 Jl 20 '63
Even Minnesota has racial flare-ups now. il U S News 55:8 Jl 8 '63
Even more crucial than in the South; Negro revolution in the North. G. Samuels. il N Y Times Mag p 12-13+ Je 30 '63
Federal funds and Mississippi. Sat Eve Post 236:82 My 18 '63
Five days in Mississippi. T. B. Morgan. il Look 27:86-90 Jl 16 '63
Freedom, now. il Time 81:23-5 My 17 '63
From a European's perspective. H. M. Rubin. Reporter 28:19 Je 6 '63
From Birmingham. G. Bailey. Reporter 28: 12+ My 23 '63
From Washington straight; demonstrations threatened if filibuster against civil rights bill. Cato. Nat R 15:14 Jl 16 '63
Gwynn Oak; nine Catholic priests startled Baltimore by joining with the pickets to protest segregation at an amusement park. T. Mattingly. America 109:136-7 Ag 10 '63; Reply. F. X. Gallagher. 109:249 S 14 '63
Hotter fires; friction between organizations; with report by K. Fleming. il Newsweek 62: 19-21 Jl 1 '63
In Bill Moore's footsteps. il Time 81:18-19 My 10 '63
Integrate the integration march! freedom march in Washington. Christian Cent 80: 973 Ag 7 '63
It will be a hot summer in Mississippi; Council of federated organizations and Freedom schools projects. R. Woodley. Reporter 30: 21-4 My 21 '64
Jitters. il Newsweek 61:27-8 My 27 '63
Justice, southern style; Ashton Jones vs Atlanta's First Baptist church. J. Gillies. Christian Cent 81:112-14 Ja 22 '64; Reply. R. O. McClain. 81:270-2 F 26 '64
Last chance for white Alabama? Christian Cent 80:574 My 1 '63
Letter from Birmingham jail; reply to criticism of eight clergymen. M. L. King, jr. Christian Cent 80:767-73 Je 12 '63; Discussion. 80:986 Ag 7 '63. Same; with editorial comment il Ebony 18:23-6+, 98-9 Ag '63
Lull in the storm. il Newsweek 62:28+ N 4 '63
Malcolm X: charismatic demagogue; interview, ed. by A. B. Southwick. Malcolm X. Christian Cent 80:740-1 Je 5 '63
Malcolm's brand X. Newsweek 63:32 Mr 23 '64
Man of the year: M. L. King, jr. il Time 83: 13-16+ Ja 3 '64; Reply. Nation 198:41-2 Ja 13 '64
March on Gwynn Oak park. il Time 82:17-18 Jl 12 '63
Martin Luther King jr, apostle of crisis. R. Cleghorn. il Sat Eve Post 236:15-19 Je 15 '63
Martin Luther King, jr: man of 1963. Negro Hist Bul 27:136-7 Mr '64
Meaning of Negro strategy. D. Danzig. Commentary 37:41-6 F '64; Discussion. 38:6+ Jl '64
Mr Kennedy and the Negroes, by H. Golden. Review
Sat R il 47:48-9 My 9 '64. S. Redding
Mood of the Negro; with editorial comment. L. Bennett, jr. il Ebony 18:27-30+, 60-1 Jl '63
More racial strife? yes, warns a Negro envoy. U S News 54:20 Je 3 '63
More strife & more strides. Time 82:16-17 Jl 5 '63
My dream for my children. Mrs M. L. King, jr. il Good H 158:77+ Je '64
Negro gets the blame; nonviolent demonstrations for civil rights and rioting and looting. Christian Cent 81:1103 S 9 '64
Negro is your brother. M. L. King. Atlan 212:71-81+ Ag '63
Negro revolt brewing in North? with interviews with A. C. Powell and K. B. Clark. il U S News 54:35-40 Je 10 '63
Negro revolution. F. S. Meyer. Nat R 14:496 Je 18 '63
Negroes press for showdown in South. il Bsns W p24-6 My 11 '63
No place to walk; civil-rights crusaders tribute to W. Moore. il Newsweek 61:28-9 My 13 '63

NEGROES in the United States—Segregation, Resistance to—*Continued*

Notes and comment: Harlem. New Yorker 39: 23-4 Je 15 '63
Obliterating the effect; conflict between sit-in convictions and the command of the Civil rights act of 1964. il Time 84:14 D 25 '64
Old Scratchhead wakes up in Chester, Pennsylvania. S. Klaw. il Reporter 30:31-4 Je 18 '64
Patterns of protest. C. E. Lincoln. Christian Cent 81:733-6 Je 3 '64
Pilgrimage to Jackson; Bill Moore's walk. M. Kempton. New Repub 148:14-16 My 11 '63
Plea for a new phase in Negro leadership. D. Bell. il N Y Times Mag p 11+ My 31 '64
Price of a ticket; demonstrations at Baltimore's Northwood theatre. il Time 81:20 Mr 1 '63
Prize and the risk. J. E. Evans. U S News 54:120 My 20 '63
Quid est demonstrandum? lunch counter sit ins. Nat R 15:49-50 Jl 30 '63
Race crisis: coming to a head. Bsns W p23-4 Je 8 '63
Race in the land of Lincoln. J. DeMuth. il Commonweal 78:44-6 Ap 5 '63
Reverse reaction? il Newsweek 62:19-20 Ag 12 '63
Revolution. il Time 81:17-19 Je 7 '63
Rightists, racists and separatists: a white bloc in the making? D. Danzig. Commentary 38:28-32 Ag '64
Rights and differences: some notes for liberals; sociological and cultural differences between whites and Negroes. C. L. Crowe. Christian Cent 81:1359-60 N 4 '64
Since the Supreme court spoke; photographs. N Y Times Mag p 10-11 My 10 '64
Sit-in at Georgetown. F. E. Kearns. Commonweal 78:94+ Ap 19 '63; Discussion. 78: 250-2 My 24 '63
Sit-in decision. America 108:790 Je 1 '63
Southerner appeals to the North: don't make our mistake! G. B. Leonard. il Look 28:15-19 Ag 11 '64
Spotlights on the American dilemma; symposium. il Reporter 29:6-22 Jl 4 '63
Strife & strides. il Time 81:15+ Je 28 '63
Summer of race violence on the way? il U S News 56:34-5 Ap 6 '64
Tension growing over race issue; Birmingham pattern in other cities. il U S News 54:37-9 My 20 '63
Test for nonviolence. S. C. Rose. Christian Cent 80:714-16 My 29 '63
They fight a fire that won't go out. il Life 54:26-36 My 17 '63
Threat of violence over rights debate; Can Negro leaders hold the line? Christian Cent 80:853-4 Jl 3 '63
Threats: Negroes' latest weapon in rights drive. il U S News 55:39-40 Jl 1 '63
To march or not to march. Nation 197:41-2 Jl 27 '63
To Mr Baldwin. Reporter 28:10-11 Je 20 '63
To the sound of a different drum. il Newsweek 63:25-6 Ap 27 '64
Tom Paines and Uncle Toms. Christian Cent 80:947 Jl 31 '63
Top man of the Negro revolution. U S News 54:21 Je 10 '63
Toward peace with justice in Birmingham. Christian Cent 80:515 Ap 24 '63
Troops, marchers, full jails; race tension spreads. U S News 54:65 Je 3 '63
Violence obscures issue in Birmingham. Christian Cent 80:636 My 15 '63
Visit with Martin Luther King; ed. by E. Dunbar. M. King. il Look 27:92-6 F 12 '63
Voices of Birmingham. D. Cort. il Nation 197: 46-8 Jl 27 '63
Walks and walkers; murder of William Moore. Nation 196:385 My 11 '63
Warren again; sit-in cases and Fourteenth amendment. Nat R 14:436 Je 4 '63
What new turn in Negro drive means. il U S News 54:40-7 Je 17 '63
What next? Newsweek 64:36-7 N 23 '64
What now? one Negro leader's answer. R. Wilkins. il N Y Times Mag p 11+ Ag 16 '64
When a priest made a pilgrimage. E. N. Bouton and T. F. Pettigrew. il Christian Cent 80:363-5 Mr 20 '63
When the freedom march hits Washington August 28. il U S News 55:26-7 Ag 12 '63
White man is scared, says Harlem congressman; summary of address, May 19, 1963. A. C. Powell. il U S News 54:20 Je 3 '63
Who's blocking desegregation? R. Coles. New Repub 148:17-20 Je 22 '63
Why didn't they hit back? J. Robbins and J. Robbins. Redbook 121:52-3+ Jl '63
Why I went to jail. A. I. Waskow. il Sat R 46:32-3 Ag 24 '63
Worried leaders. il Newsweek 62:19-20 Jl 15 '63

See also
Civil rights demonstrations
Civil rights workers

Social conditions

Call her Miss; ruling on calling Negroes by their first names. Time 83:51 Ap 10 '64
Cry from the dispossessed. W. M. Young, jr. il Christian Cent 81:1524-7 D 9 '64
Lady in black. E. F. Granton. il Ebony 19:81-2+ F '64
Negro's middle-class dream. C. E. Lincoln. il N Y Times Mag p35+ O 25 '64
Rural Negroes need help. E. Mirel. Sci N L 84:214 O 5 '63
Senate to shelve rights bill for weeks; waiting action on tax cut. Bsns W p28-9 F 15 '64

See also
Negroes in the United States—Segregation

Suffrage

See Negroes in the United States—Politics and suffrage

Trade union membership

See Trade unions—Negro membership

North

As race riots spread in North. il U S News 57:34 Ag 17 '64
As race trouble erupted in the North. il U S News 56:6 Mr 9 '64
Deerfield, a Negro ghost town in Weld County, Colorado; Dearfield colony. A. Harris. Negro Hist Bul 27:38 N '63
De-regionalization of a problem. N. Cousins. Sat R 46:28 O 19 '63
Englewood and the northern dilemma. G. Walker. Nation 197:7-10 Jl 6 '63
Even more crucial than in the South; Negro revolution in the North. G. Samuels. il N Y Times Mag p 12-13+ Je 30 '63
Ghetto ignites. W. Klein. il Nation 199:49-51 Ag 10 '64
Harlem is nowhere; excerpt from Shadow and act. R. Ellison. il Harper 229:53-7 Ag '64
Liberal's advice to northern Negroes; excerpts from address, January 9, 1964. R. Dilworth. U S News 56:6 Ja 20 '64
Long journey South: commitment of D. Harris. J. Wechsler. Redbook 122:68-9+ Ap '64
Looting: the high cost of race violence. il U S News 57:36-41 S 14 '64
Negro revolt brewing in North? with interviews with A. C. Powell and K. B. Clark. il U S News 54:35-40 Je 10 '63
North and West have problems, too. G. W. Foster, jr. il Sat R 46:69-72+ Ap 20 '63
Not racism, but nepotism. il Time 82:14 Ag 9 '63
Now, Birmingham violence up North; New York and Chicago. il U S News 55:4 Ag 12 '63
Race, riots and city administration. Am City 79:7 S '64
Real problem. Nation 199:41-2 Ag 10 '64
Talk is race. il Time 84:17-18 Ag 7 '64
War in the North. il Time 81:16-17 My 31 '63
What northerners really think of Negroes. S. Alsop and O. Quayle. il Sat Eve Post 236: 17-21 S 7 '63; Discussion. 236:4 O 5 '63
When the Negro faces North; symposium. il Look 27:30-8+ D 17 '63; Discussion. 28:6+ Ja 28 '64
Where racial problems flared in North: New York and Cleveland. il U S News 56:4 F 10 '64

See also
New York (city)—Harlem
also subhead Negroes under names of cities, e.g. Detroit—Negroes

South

At summer's end; Negro progress. il Time 84:44 O 2 '64
Battle-scarred youngsters. H. Zinn. Nation 197:193-7 O 5 '63
Beyond tokenism; South as seen by a returning native son. D. Cater. il Reporter 29:23-7 O 10 '63
Black like me. il Ebony 19:37-8+ My '64
Case for the new South. T. Sanford. il Look 28:81-4+ D 15 '64
Changing attitudes in the white South. il Newsweek 61:23-5 Je 17 '63
Clean conscience or Black Muslims? J. B. Sheerin. Cath World 197:212-15 Jl '63

NEGROES in the United States—South—*Cont.*
Collision course: Negro enrollment in Alabama university. il Newsweek 61:29 My 6 '63
Curse & the hope; W. Faulkner's vision. il Time 84:44-8 Jl 17 '64
Desegregation: two ways; . . . and southern lights. America 108:186-7 F 9 '63
Economic status of Negroes, by V. W. Henderson. Review
New Repub 149:23-4+ O 12 '63. E. Ginzberg; Reply. E. Kramer. 149:30-1 O 26 '63
Economics of integration. il Newsweek 62:67-8 Jl 8 '63
End of fear. New Repub 148:1+ My 18 '63
Half-cocked. il Newsweek 62:35 O 14 '63
He stands at the door. J. M. Dabbs. Christian Cent 81:359-60 Mr 18 '64
Hotter fires; friction between organizations; with report by K. Fleming. il Newsweek 62:19-21 Jl 1 '63
How can the lawyer help? F. Biddle. New Repub 149:12 Jl 6 '63
How do the teachers feel? R. Coles. il Sat R 47:72-3+ My 16 '64
How J.F.K's grandfather fought the grandfather clause. H. N. Meyer. Negro Hist Bul 27:27 N '63
I can't fight alone. J. H. Meredith. il Look 27:70-2+ Ap 9 '63
Legal help needed; cases arising out of segregation. G. W. Crockett, jr. and E. Goodman. Nation 196:inside cover Je 1 '63
Letter to a governor. E. J. Hughes. Newsweek 61:19 Je 17 '63
Letter to a northern friend. J. Chatfield. New Repub 148:13-14 My 18 '63
Long journey South; commitment of D. Harris. J. Wechsler. Redbook 122:68-9+ Ap '64
Meeting; concerning reports to New York branch of plans of Mississippi branch; student non-violent coordinating committee. New Yorker 40:33-6 Ap 11 '64
Military's limited war against segregation. R. Brecher and E. Brecher. Harper 227:79-82+ S '63
Mississippi must choose. J. W. Silver. il N Y Times Mag p8+ Jl 19 '64
Mob behind the marchers. P. Watters. Reporter 30:34-5 Je 18 '64
Mood and revelation in the South. R. Coles. New Repub 150:17-19 Ap 18 '64
Negro's future in the South; interview. R. R. Barnett. U S News 54:60-4 Je 3 '63
Not token freedom, full freedom. C. Sitton. il N Y Times Mag p21+ Je 9 '63
Other side. Newsweek 61:29-30 Je 10 '63
Poorly timed protest; Birmingham Negroes. il Time 81:30-1 Ap 19 '63
Price of brotherhood. S. P. Boyle. il Ebony 18:79-80+ S '63
Quiet progress in the South. Life 54:4 F 8 '63
Race & realism. il Time 82:77-8 Jl 5 '63
Race: results instead of reasons. R. McGill. Sat R 48:52 Ja 9 '65
Race troubles in South: bodies found, arrests made in summer of discontent. il U S News 57:6 Ag 17 '64
Segregated sickness; Catholic hospitals. J. Leo. Commonweal 81:406-7 D 18 '64
Segs; symposium, ed. by R. Cleghorn. il Esquire 61:71-6+ Ja '64
Showdown on civil rights. W. V. Shannon. Commonweal 78:389-90 Jl 5 '63
Slavery in the cities: the South 1820-1860, by R. C. Wade. Review
Nation 200:38-9 Ja 11 '65. E. D. Genovese
Sophronia's grandson goes to Washington. L. Hellman. il Ladies Home J 80:78-80+ D '63; Reply with rejoinder. R. D. McCord 81:82 Mr '64
South and Christian ethics, by J. Sellers. Review
Christian Cent 80:302-4 Mr 6 '63. E. Tilson
South has many faces; excerpts from South and the southerner. R. McGill. Atlan 211:83-98 Ap '63
South unfair to Negro citizens. J. P. Guild. Negro Hist Bul 26:256+ My '63
Southern case for school segregation, by J. J. Kilpatrick. Review
Nat R 14:199-200 Mr 12 '63. L. B. Bozell
Southern establishment. S. Southard. Christian Cent 81:1618-21 D 30 '64
Southern justice: lawyers walk in fear. W. M. Kunstler and A. Kinoy. il Nation 198:576-80 Je 8 '64
Southern politician; with editorial comment. F. E. Smith. Nation 199:131, 132-4 S 21 '64
Southern progress. Commonweal 81:340 D 4 '64
Southerner appeals to the North: don't make our mistake! G. B. Leonard. il Look 28:15-19 Ag 11 '64
Southerner's answer to the Negro question. C. V. Woodward. il Reporter 30:39-44 F 27 '64
These are the times: on being a southern liberal; excerpts from Black, white and gray. R. Dugger. Commentary 37:40-5 Ap '64; Reply. L. T. Denison. 38:28 O '64
This little light; incidents after passage of civil rights bill. P. De Lissovoy. il Nation 199:486-90 D 21 '64
Tokenism frustrates Negro hopes. Christian Cent 80:357 Mr 20 '63
Trail of blood: a Negro dies; assassination of M. Evers. il Life 54:28-9 Je 21 '63
Trip to Virginia. P. Romero. Negro Hist Bul 27:96+ Ja '64
Two southern liberals. J. Epstein. Commentary 38:73-4+ D '64
Voting in the Black Belt. C. Mabee. il Negro Hist Bul 27:50-6 D '63
What editors in the South say now; symposium. U S News 56:40-6 Je 29 '64
When a Negro is on trial in the South. B. M. Galphin. il N Y Times Mag p 17+ D 15 '63
When Robert Kennedy invaded the South. il U S News 54:6 My 6 '63
Why I live in Mississippi; interview, ed. by F. H. Mitchell. il Ebony 18:143-8 S '63
Why the South took rights law quietly. il Bsns W p28 Jl 11 '64
See also
Negroes in the United States—Politics and suffrage
also subhead Negroes under names of cities, e.g. Atlanta—Negroes

NEGROES in the United States armed forces. See United States—Armed forces—Negroes

NEGROES in the United States navy. See United States—Navy—Negroes

NEGUS, Sidney Stevens
Public information service (cont) Science 139:629-30 F 15 '63

NEHAMKIN, Lester
Engines to the rear. il Motor T 16:64-9 Je '64
One-five-O the hard way. Hot Rod 17:32-3 N '64
Rebirth of sedan racing. Motor T 15:84-5 S '63

NEHEMKIS, Peter R. jr
Excerpt from testimony, May 11, 1962. Cong Digest 42:91+ Mr '63
Misconceptions regarding Latin America; address, February 21, 1963. bibliog Vital Speeches 29:445-8 My 1 '63

NEHMER, Stanley
Record of U.S. participation during second year of long-term cotton textile arrangement; statement, December 1, 1964. Dept State Bul 52:49-56 Ja 11 '65
U.S. participation in long-term cotton textile arrangement; statement, December 3, 1963. Dept State Bul 50:96-101 Ja 20 '64

NEHRU, Jawaharlal
Changing India. For Affairs 41:453-65 Ap '63
When I die. . ; excerpts from last will and testament. Newsweek 63:45 Je 15 '64

about

After Nehru, who? Christian Cent 81:102 Ja 22 '64
Afternoon with Nehru. E. M. Borgese. il por Nation 198:506-8 My 18 '64
Banyan falls. C. Lacy. Christian Cent 81:883-5 Jl 8 '64
Big country adrift; how long can aid save India? il por U S News 56:64-9 Je 1 '64
Close to the soil; Nehru's ashes scattered. il Time 83:29 Je 19 '64
Empty chair. il por Time 83:21 Ja 17 '64
End of an era. Reporter 30:12+ Je 18 '64
India after the blow. E. von Kuehnelt-Leddihn. Nat R 14:236 Mr 26 '63
India tomorrow. J. T. Crown. Nation 198:599-602 Je 15 '64
India without Nehru. il por Sr Schol 85:12-14+ O 14 '64
India without Nehru. V. Koilpillai. Christian Cent 81:834+ Je 24 '64
Jawaharlal Nehru 1889-1964. il pors Newsweek 63:57-9 Je 8 '64
Jawaharlal Nehru, RIP. Nat R 16:480 Je 16 '64
Leader under fire; Nehru's opposition grows. por U S News 55:12 S 2 '63
Leadership crisis in India. por Newsweek 63:22 Mr 30 '64

NEHRU, Jawaharlal—About—*Continued*
Letter from London. M. Panter-Downes. New Yorker 40:92 Je 13 '64
Man of East & West. il por Time 83:26-7 Je 5 '64
Man who, with all his mind and heart, loved India; cremation ceremony. L. Hall. il pors Life 56:32-42B Je 5 '64
Nation Nehru made joins East and West. Life 56:4 Je 5 '64
Nehru. Nation 198:565 Je 8 '64
Nehru: man and symbol. N. Cousins. il pors Sat R 47:17-21+ Je 20 '64
Nehru's gift to India. Christian Cent 81:756 Je 10 '64
Nehru's India. America 110:814 Je 13 '64
Nehru's India. Commonweal 80:352 Je 12 '64
Nehru's new centrism. A. Kumari. Reporter 29:32-5 D 5 '63
Nehru's successor? Gandhi disciple moves up. U S News 56:14 F 3 '64
Notes and comment. New Yorker 40:27 Je 13 '64
Pandit Nehru. il por New Repub 150:6 Je 6 '64
President expresses grief at death of Prime Minister Nehru; letter, May 27, 1964. L. B. Johnson. Dept State Bul 50:926 Je 15 '64
Quit, Nehru, quit. il por Newsweek 62:36-7 Ag 26 '63
Roses and riots. Newsweek 63:40 Ja 27 '64
Touch of self-righteousness. il Time 83:34 Ap 24 '64
Tributes in the United Nations. il pors UN Mo Chron 1:75-84 Je '64
Two officials under fire. por U S News 56:13 Ja 6 '64
Vacuum of leadership. por Time 83:22 Mr 27 '64
When the body fails. il por Newsweek 63:32+ Ja 20 '64
Who'll succeed Nehru? when he's sick, India worries. por U S News 56:14 Ja 20 '64
Will India be ready if red China strikes again? S. W. Sanders. il por U S News 55:68-9 S 23 '63
Will India falter after Nehru? il Bsns W p24-5 My 30 '64
With Nehru gone, can India be held together? il por U S News 56:48-9 Je 8 '64
Without Nehru? Newsweek 62:46 S 2 '63

NEIDE, Peter
Kids; group of city youngsters. R. R. McLaughlin. il U S Camera 26:44-8 Je '63

NEIDLE, Amos, and Waelsch, Heinrich
Histones: species and tissue specificity. bibliog Science 145:1059-61 S 4 '64

NEIGHBOR, Eunice I.
Ambush by four bears. Outdoor Life 134:32-3+ Jl '64
Hell of a way to move. Outdoor Life 133:44-7+ F; 60-3+ Mr '64

NEIGHBORHOOD associations. See Citizens associations

NEIGHBORHOODS
Are there really ghettos in America? interview. O. Handlin. il U S News 55:70-2 Jl 22 '63
Neighborhoods: can urban renewal make everybody happy? Boston. D. B. Carlson. il Arch Forum 120:102-4 Je '64
Try a teamwork association; Blue Ridge estates association, Monroe, Conn. E. D. Fales, jr. il Am Home 66:22+ Ap '63
What makes a good neighborhood? F. Gould and R. K. Kerckhoff. il PTA Mag 57:19-21 My '63
See also
Community life

NEIGHBORS
How would you like to live next door to you? L. R. Forester. il Am Home 67:52-3+ O '64
Suburban good neighbors identify themselves; South suburban human relations council, Chicago. Christian Cent 81:901 Jl 15 '64
We had the sense to stay poor. E. Gale. il Redbook 124:8+ N '64

NEIGHBORS; story. See Bingham, S.

NEIL, E. A.
Advanced research for meteorological satellites. Electr World 71:61 Je '64

NEILAN, Edwin Peter
Banker's warning to businessmen; excerpts from address, March 26, 1964. por U S News 56:20 Ap 6 '64
Business leader stumps for higher morality; summaries of addresses. U S News 55:11 S 16 '63
Immorality in Washington; excerpt from address, September 5, 1963. Farm J 87:134 O '63
Our own public scandal; address, August 7, 1963. Vital Speeches 29:730-2 S 15 '63; Same abr. with title Political immorality, a speech that rocked Congress. Read Digest 83:126-9 N '63; Excerpts. por U S News 55:102-3 Ag 26 '63
Speaking out. por Sat Eve Post 236:8+ N 30 '63
Supermarket for subsidies; address, January 6, 1964. Vital Speeches 30:237-9 F 1 '64; Excerpts. Cong Digest 43:117+ Ap '64
about
How to get better government; interview, ed. by P. F. Healy. pors Nations Bsns 51:40-1+ My '63
Seduction by subsidy. por Time 82:98+ S 13 '63
Spoils system: more sinister than ever before. por U S News 55:16 Ag 19 '63

NEILL, A. S.
Redbook dialogue; Mario Montessori and A. S. Neill discuss their famous schools and their radical approaches to child rearing. por Redbook 124:42-3+ D '64

NEILL, John C.
Truth about contact lenses. Ladies Home J 81:40+ D '64

NEILL greenhouses, incorporated
Say it with orchids. il Bsns W p 120-2 My 9 '64

NEILY, Joseph E.
Sticky church pew. Christian Cent 81:207-8 F 12 '64

NEIMAN, Le Roy
Art; exhibition at Hammer galleries. F. Getlein. New Repub 149:30-1 N 30 '63

NEIMAN-Marcus company. See Dallas—Stores

NEIMAN-Marcus store and shopping center, Fort Worth, Tex. See Fort Worth, Tex.—Stores

NEISH, Alex
Latin America: a massive indictment. Nation 197:182-3 S 28 '63
Leaving for Buenos Aires; poem. Nation 197:444 D 21 '63
Letter from Buenos Aires. Nation 196:272-4 Mr 30 '63
On military aid. New Repub 148:12-13 My 11 '63

NEISSER, Edith G.
Mothers must keep on growing, too. Parents Mag 39:52-3+ Je '64
Preschools are not just for play. Parents Mag 39:72-3+ F '64
Sheltering circle. Parents Mag 39:132 My '64
—See Sklansky, M. jt. auth.

NEISSER, Ulric
Imitation of man by machine. bibliog Science 139:193-7 Ja 18 '63
Visual search. Sci Am 210:94-100+ Je '64

NEKRASOV, Viktor Platonovich
Blindfold odyssey. por Newsweek 63:84 Je 1 '64
Fifty-fifty vision; impressions of V. P. Nekrasov. por Newsweek 61:37 F 4 '63
Mother of Chianti. W. Miller. Nation 198:632-3 Je 22 '64

NELLHAUS, Gerhard
(tr) See Brecht, B. Der hofmeister

NELLIGAN, Emile
Reporter at large. E. Wilson. New Yorker 40:138-40 N 14 '64

NELSON, August
Beware of summer glare. Sci Digest 54:63-6 Ag '63

NELSON, Augusta
Teacher as a critic. Sr Schol 83:17T O 4 '63

NELSON, B. E.
Say it with care, or say it with confidence. Motor B 115:101+ Ja '65

NELSON, Bryan
Bass Rock gannets. Natur Hist 73:32-41 Ap '64

NELSON, Claud D.
Modernist movement and Catholic renewal today. Christian Cent 81:1139-41 S 16 '64
Protestant's tribute; John XXIII. America 108:855-6 Je 15 '63

NELSON, Dave
Football players must be students; ed. by T. Cohane. pors Look 27:82+ N 19 '63

NELSON, Donald R. and Gruber, S. H.
Sharks: attraction by low-frequency sounds. bibliog Science 142:975-7 N 15 '63

NELSON, Donawayne
Sorcerer; story. Mlle 60:42-3 Ja '65

NELSON, Ed
Spotlight on the MG 1100. Pop Mech 119:38-40 F '63

NELSON, Edward, and others
Virus-containing leukocytes in polioencephalitis. bibliog Science 139:499-501 F 8 '63

NELSON, F. A. and Weaver, H. E.
Nuclear magnetic resonance spectroscopy in superconducting magnetic fields. bibliog Science 146:223-32 O 9 '64
NELSON, Frederic
Do platforms need all those planks? Nat R 16:533-4 Je 30 '64
NELSON, George
Collaboration in Switzerland. Arch Forum 118:118-21 Je '63
NELSON, Helen
Watchdog of the British press. Sat R 47:42-3 Ag 8 '64
NELSON, J. Robert
Beyond civil rights. Christian Cent 81:668-72 My 20 '64
Questions for the World council. Christian Cent 80:1024-6 Ag 21 '63
Seven devilish ways to block church union. Time 81:77-8 My 10 '63
Two on unity. Christian Cent 82:111-12 Ja 27 '65
Worth trying. Christian Cent 81:886 Jl 8 '64
NELSON, Jack L.
Censors and their tactics; excerpts from address, November 7, 1963. Library J 88:4809-12+ D 15 '63
Censorship of textbooks; what is the problem? NEA J 52:18-21 My '63
Writer warns school librarians against creeping censorship; summary of address. Library J 88:4445 N 15 '63
—and Robinson, G. A.
Teacher education through team teaching. Sch & Soc 91:409-10 D 14 '63
NELSON, John M.
Keeping 40,000 lights in good repair. Am City 79:147+ Je '64
NELSON, Kay
Day I had my checkup. Good H 158:52+ F '64
Okay-dokay, Rosita, I tell you about life in the U.S.A. Good H 156:40+ Mr '63
Professional attitude. Writer 76:9-11+ D '63
NELSON, Kenneth V.
Inside your engine. Hot Rod 16:76-9+ Mr '63
Precision combustion timing. Hot Rod 17:40-1 F '64
NELSON, Mark L.
Loss figures for 300-ohm twin-lead. Electr World 73:30 Ja '65
NELSON, Maxine A. See Broido, A. jt. auth.
NELSON, Norbert
David Gil's Bennington potters. Craft Horiz 24:34-5 Mr '64
Imports and the craftsman. Craft Horiz 23:27+ Jl '63
NELSON, O. Fred
Piecemeal water-improvement plan. Am City 78:88-9 Ag '63
NELSON, Oliver E. and Tsai, C. Y.
Glucose transfer from adenosine diphosphate-glucose to starch in preparations of waxy seeds. bibliog Science 145:1194-5 S 11 '64
NELSON, P. G. See Fuortes, M. G. F. jt. auth.
NELSON, Randolph J. and Rothney, J. W. M.
Television and the superior student. Sch & Soc 92:385-7 D 12 '64
NELSON, Raymond L.
World of white. il por Audubon Mag 66:92-6 Mr '64
NELSON, Richard R.
Adjusting R and D. Bul Atomic Sci 20:15-19 Ap '64
Role of knowledge in economic growth. Science 140:473-4 My 3 '63
NELSON, Roy Paul
Case of the midnight Christians. Christian Cent 82:22-3 Ja 6 '65
NELSON, T. M.
Yankee ingenuity. Am City 78:109 Je '63
NELSON, Truman
WLB biography. J. M. Hatch. por Wilson Lib Bul 37:712 Ap '63
NELSON, Walter J.
Dowser who finds oil wells. W. Trombley. il pors Sat Eve Post 236:88-9 D 7 '63
NELSON, William
I have been basely murdered. H. H. Peckham. il por Am Heritage 14:88-92 Ag '63
NELSON bighorn sheep. See Mountain sheep
NEMATODES
Microscopic plant traps and kills tiny pests; acaulopage pectospora. Sci N L 83:153 Mr 9 '63
Nematode-trapping fungi. D. Pramer. bibliog il Science 144:382-8 Ap 24 '64
Nematode-trapping fungi: evaluation of axenic healthy and galled roots as trap inducers. D. W. Iffland and P. V. Allison. bibliog il Science 146:547-8 O 23 '64
Nutritional relationships among certain filamentous fungi and a marine nematode. S. P. Meyers and others. bibliog il Science 141:520-2 Ag 9 '63
Starch formation induced by a plant parasitic nematode. M. L. Schuster and others. bibliog il Science 143:1342-3 Mr 20 '64
NEMER, Martin, and Bard, S. G.
Polypeptide synthesis in sea urchin embryogenesis: an examination with synthetic polyribonucleotides. bibliog Science 140:664-6 My 10 '63
NEMEROV, Howard
Breaking of rainbows; poem. Reporter 28:49 My 23 '63
Idea of a university; story. Reporter 29:46-8 O 10 '63
Landscape with figures; poem. Nation 196:346 Ap 27 '63
May day dancing; poem. New Yorker 40:48 My 2 '64
Mud turtle; poem. New Yorker 40:32 Jl 25 '64
Sarajevo; poem. Reporter 29:51 Jl 18 '63

about

Interim report. H. Carruth. Poetry 102:389-90 S '63
Something that might simply be. M. L. Rosenthal. Reporter 29:54+ S 12 '63
NEMRUT DAG excavations. See Turkey—Antiquities
NENANA ice break lottery. See Lotteries
NENNI, Pietro
Italian socialism chooses the things that are possible. E. Forcella. New Repub 149:13-14 N 16 '63
Italian tightrope act. C. Sterling. Reporter 30:30-2 F 13 '64
Italy's new partnership. por Time 82:31 D 13 '63
Man in the middle. Newsweek 64:37 Jl 13 '64
Off & running. il Time 81:30 F 22 '63
NEO-CLASSICISM (art)
Before romanticism; masterpieces at Cleveland museum of art. il Newsweek 64:102+ O 19 '64
NEOCORTEX. See Cerebral cortex
NEOLITHIC period. See Stone age
NEON lamps. See Electric lamps, Neon
NEON oscillator. See Oscillators
NEOPRENE. See Rubber, Artificial
NEOPRINT. See Printing
NEORICKETTSIAE helminthoeca. See Dogs—Diseases and pests
NEPAL
See also
England and Nepal
Hunting—Nepal
Khumjung

Foreign relations

Atlantic report. Atlan 211:24+ Mr '63

Politics and government

Atlantic report. Atlan 211:24+ Mr '63
Royalties for the king. il Time 83:47 My 15 '64
NEPALESE
See also
Ghurkas
NEPALESE art. See Art, Nepalese
NEPENTHES. See Pitcher plants
NEPHRONS. See Kidneys
NEPOTISM
Application rejected; nepotism regulation. W. B. Morse. Am For 70:32+ Jl '64
Is nepotism so bad? D. W. Ewing. il Harvard Bsns R 43:22-6+ Ja '65
NEPTUNE (planet)
Discovery of Neptune, by M. Grosser. Review
New Yorker 39:158+ My 25 '63. J. Bernstein
Sci Am 208:169-70+ Mr '63. J. R. Newman
Libration of Pluto-Neptune. C. J. Cohen and E. C. Hubbard. bibliog il Science 145:1302-3 S 18 '64
NERO, Peter
Peter Nero: an expression of impatience. J. S. Wilson. il pors Hi Fi 13:57-9+ F '63
NERO, Robert W.
Detergents, deadly hazard to water birds. Audubon Mag 66:26-7 Ja '64
NERPEL, Charles
Editor's auto-graphs. See issues of Motor trend

NERUDA, Pablo
Boy with a hare; poem; tr. by B. Belitt. Commonweal 81:449 D 25 '64
Four love poems; tr. by S. M. Hastie. Mlle 56:90-1 F '63
about
Agonist of the intuition. W. Carrier. Poetry 101:349-52 F '63

NERVE cells
Adaptation in stretch receptor neurons of crayfish. S. Nakajima. bibliog il Science 146:1168-70 N 27 '64
Bioelectric activity in long-term cultures of spinal cord tissues. S. M. Crain and E. R. Peterson. bibliog il Science 141:427-9 Ag 2 '63
Bionic computers; imitating the neuron. K. Gilmore. il Electr World 69:25-8+ Mr '63
Cells that communicate. D. G. Cooley. il Todays Health 41:38-41+ Je '63
Electrical transmission at an excitatory synapse in a vertebrate brain. E. J. Furshpan. bibliog il Science 144:878-80 My 15 '64
Electrochemical nerve cells under study. B. Miller. il Aviation W 78:103+ F 18 '63
Growth control of nerve cells by a protein factor and its antiserum. R. Levi-Montalcini. bibliog il Science 143:105-10 Ja 10 '64
Isolated neuron preparation for studies of metabolic events at rest and during impulse activity. E. Giacobini and others. bibliog il Science 140:74 Ap 5 '63
Midbrain reticular influences upon single neurons in lateral geniculate nucleus. T. Ogawa. bibliog il Science 139:343-4 Ja 25 '63
Molecular theories of memory. W. Dingman and M. B. Sporn. bibliog Science 144:26-9 Ap 3 '64; Reply. A. L. Goldberg. 144:1529 Je 26 '64
Nerve as a tissue; report on Lankenau conference. K. Rodahl. Science 147:414-15 Ja 22 '65
Pacemaker neurons: effects of regularly spaced synaptic input. D. H. Perkel and others. bibliog il Science 145:61-3 Jl 3 '64
Pharmacology of individual neurons. G. C. Salmoiraghi and F. E. Bloom. bibliog il Science 144:493-9 My 1 '64
Separation of transducer and impulse-generating processes in sensory receptors. W. R. Loewenstein and others. bibliog il Science 142:1180-1 N 29 '63
Strychnine: its action on spinal motoneurons of cats. M. G. F. Fuortes and P. G. Nelson. bibliog il Science 140:806-8 My 17 '63
Transport of neurohormones from the corpora cardiaca in insects. B. Johnson and B. Bowers. bibliog il Science 141:264-6 Jl 19 '63
Vestibular nuclei: activity of single neurons during natural sleep and wakefulness. E. Bizzi and others. bibliog il Science 145:414-15 Jl 24 '64
See also
Electrophysiology

NERVE transplants. See Transplantation of organs, tissues, etc.

NERVES
Acetylcholine-like activity in sciatic nerve. E. A. Carlini and J. P. Green. bibliog il Science 141:901-2 S 6 '63
Alkaline phosphatase in peripheral nerves. B. Pinner and others. bibliog il Science 145:936-8 Ag 28 '64
Beading phenomena of mammalian myelinated nerve fibers. S. Ochs. bibliog il Science 139:599-600 F 15 '63
Cortisol from human nerve. J. C. Touchstone and others. il Science 141:1275 S 27 '63
Cutaneous slowly adapting mechanoreceptors in the cat. D. N. Tapper. bibliog il Science 143:53-4 Ja 3 '64; Reply with rejoinder. H. Pinkus. 144:891 My 15 '64
Delayed appearance of labeled protein in isolated nerve endings and axoplasmic flow. S. H. Barondes. bibliog il Science 146:779-81 N 6 '64
Demyelinating diseases; report on symposium. M. W. Kies and E. C. Alvord, jr. Science 144:320-1 Ap 17 '64
Hypothesis for a pressure-sensitive mechanism in muscle spindles. C. F. Bridgman and E. Eldred. il Science 143:481-2 Ja 31 '64
Mechanisms of receptor adaptation. M. Mendelson and W. R. Loewenstein. bibliog il Science 144:554-5 My 1 '64
Mutant mice, quaking and jimpy, with deficient myelination in the central nervous system. R. L. Sidman and others. bibliog il Science 144:309-11 Ap 17 '64
Negative inotropic effect of the vagus nerves upon the canine ventricle. H. DeGeest and others. bibliog il Science 144:1223-5 Je 5 '64
Nerve action clarified. Sci N L 86:82 Ag 8 '64
Neuromuscular function; report of international symposium on the Effects of use and disuse on neuromuscular function, Liblice, Czechoslovakia. A. Sandow. Science 139:198-200 Ja 18 '63
Nucleus of the trapezoid body: dual afferent innervation. J. M. Harrison and R. Irving. bibliog il Science 143:473-4 Ja 31 '64
Phosphate incorporation in desheathed nerves: effects of potassium and calcium ions. L. G. Abood and I. Koyama. bibliog il Science 141:1277-8 S 27 '63
Possible MS vaccine; demyelinating diseases research. F. Marley. Sci N L 85:67 F 1 '64
Procaine action: antagonism by adenosine triphosphate and other nucleotides. A. S. Kuperman and others. bibliog il Science 144:1222-3 Je 5 '64
Serotonin binding to nerve-ending particles of the rat brain and its inhibition by lysergic acid diethylamide. R. M. Marchbanks and others. bibliog il Science 144:1135-7 My 29 '64
X-ray diffraction pattern of nerve myelin: a method for determining the phases. M. F. Moody. bibliog il Science 142:1173-4 N 29 '63
See also
Electrophysiology
Nerve cells
Nervous system
Synapses

NERVI, Pier Luigi
Artist in concrete. E. O. Hauser. il por Read Digest 84:208-11+ F '64
Nervi gives a factory the grace of a bridge. il Arch Forum 121:110-13 Jl '64
Nervi's bus station opens in New York. il Arch Rec 133:14 F '63
Nervi's expanding paper mill. il Fortune 70:144-6 S '64
Pier Luigi Nervi. M. Salvadori. por Arch Forum 120:78-9 My '64

NERVOUS habits
How women spoil their looks. R. Drake. il Redbook 123:56-7+ Je '64

NERVOUS indigestion. See Dyspepsia

NERVOUS system
Adipose tissue: ability to respond to nerve stimulation in vitro. J. W. Correll. bibliog il Science 140:387-8 Ap 26 '63
Arousal effects on evoked activity in a non-sensory system. G. P. Frommer and R. B. Livingston. bibliog il Science 139:502-4 F 8 '63
Botulinus toxin: effect on the central nervous system of man. H. R. Tyler. bibliog il Science 139:847-8 Mr 1 '63
Brain reflexes; report on international conference. D. P. Purpura and H. Waelsch. Science 143:598+ F 7 '64
Cholinergic substance in the caudal neurosecretory storage organ of fish. H. Kobayashi and others. bibliog il Science 141:714-16 Ag 23 '63
Circuits of the senses. R. Campbell. il Life 54:64-76B+ Je 28 '63
Dopamine: its occurrence in molluscan ganglia. D. Sweeney. bibliog il Science 139:1051 Mr 15 '63
Effects of cutaneous and muscle sensory nerve volleys in awake cats: a study in perception. J. E. Sweet and others. bibliog il Science 145:1071-3 S 4 '64
Electronic junctions between teleost spinal neurons: electrophysiology and ultrastructure. M. V. L. Bennett and others. bibliog il Science 141:262-4 Jl 19 '63
Gamma globulin affinity for normal human tissue of the central nervous system. C. D. Allerand and M. D. Yahr. bibliog il Science 144:1141-2 My 29 '64
Humoral factor from the brain which activates gastric motility. N. C. Jefferson and others. Science 144:58-9 Ap 3 '64
Interaction of positive and negative reinforcing neural systems. E. S. Valenstein and T. Valenstein. bibliog il Science 145:1456-8 S 25 '64
Live brains in the lab; Cleveland metropolitan general hospital researchers keep isolated monkey brains alive. il Time 83:72 Je 19 '64
Local anesthetic drugs: penetration from the spinal extradural space into the neuraxis. P. R. Bromage and others. bibliog il Science 140:392-4 Ap 26 '63
Mechanoreceptors in the cuticle of the honey bee: fine structure and stimulus mechanism. U. Thurm. bibliog il Science 145:1063-5 S 4 '64

NERVOUS system—*Continued*
Neurobiology: interdisciplinary discussions of the nervous system; report on international symposium. E. Eidelberg and others. Science 144:1478+ Je 19 '64
Neurogenic component of chronic renal hypertension. J. W. McCubbin and I. H. Page. il Science 139:210+ Ja 18 '63
Neurophysiology: United States-Japan joint symposium; report. T. H. Bullock. Science 144:1361-4 Je 12 '64
Reaction time to cortical stimulation. J. Miller and M. Glickstein. bibliog il Science 146:1594-6 D 18 '64
Science milestone; Santiago Ramon y Cajal; structure of the nervous system. J. McMillan. il Sci Digest 53:81-7 Ap '63
Selective sensitivity to direction of movement in ganglion cells of the rabbit retina. H. B. Barlow and R. M. Hill. bibliog il Science 139:412-14 F 1 '63
Stomach contraction upon central vagus stimulation. N. C. Jefferson and others. il Science 140:810-11 My 17 '63
Synapse arising at central node of Ranvier, and note on fixation of the central nervous system. D. Bodian and N. Taylor. bibliog il Science 139:330-2 Ja 25 '63
Synaptic learning due to electroosmosis: a theory. J. B. Ranck, jr. bibliog il Science 144:187-9 Ap 10 '64
Those things you can't help doing: autonomic nervous system. C. P. Gilmore. il Pop Sci 184:90-2+ F '64
Tremorine: its effect on amines of the central nervous system. A. H. Friedman and others. bibliog il Science 141:1188-90 S 20 '63
See also
Brain
Electrophysiology
Spinal cord
Synapses

Degeneration and regeneration

Hay fever sneezes bring muscle trouble; abnormal neuromuscular function. Sci N L 86:329 N 21 '64

Diseases

Demyelinating diseases; report on symposium. M. W. Kies and E. C. Alvord, jr. Science 144:320-1 Ap 17 '64
Mutant mice, quaking and jimpy, with deficient myelination in the central nervous system. R. L. Sidman and others. bibliog il Science 144:309-11 Ap 17 '64
See also
Amaurotic family idiocy
Mental illness

NERVOUS system, Sympathetic
Autonomic mediation of the effect of raised arterial glucose upon free fatty acids. C. J. Goodner and W. A. Tustison. bibliog il Science 146:770-2 N 6 '64
Identification of acetylcholine in sympathetic ganglia by chemical and physical methods. A. J. D. Friesen and others. bibliog il Science 145:157-9 Jl 10 '64
Ionic mechanism of postsynaptic inhibition; adapted from address, December 10, 1963. J. C. Eccles. bibliog il Science 145:1140-7 S 11 '64
Release of metaraminol (aramine) from the heart by sympathetic nerve stimulation. J. R. Crout and others. bibliog il Science 145:828-9 Ag 21 '64
Serotonin rhythm in the pineal organ: control by the sympathetic nervous system. V. M. Fiske. bibliog il Science 146:253-4 O 9 '64
Simultaneus recordings of scalp and epidural somatosensory-evoked responses in man. E. F. Domino and others. bibliog il Science 145:1199-200 S 11 '64

NERVOUS tension. See Stress (physiology)

NERVOUSNESS
See also
Stage fright

NESBITT, Elizabeth
Profile: Ralph Munn. Library J 88:2424-5 Je 15 '63

NESBITT, George
George did it! por Recreation 57:141+ Mr '64

NESBITT, H. H. J. and Hart, John
Science 100, 1963-64. Science 146:895-6 N 13 '64

NESBITT, Lowell
Art as axle grease. K. Congdon. il por Américas 16:12-15 O '64

NESHYBA, Steve. See Amstutz, D. E. jt. auth.

NESS, Evaline
Woodcut illustration. il Horn Bk 40:520-2 O '64
about
Newbery and Caldecott runners-up. il por Library J 89:1380 Mr 15 '64

NEST of hornets; story. See Heller, L.

NESTINGEN, Ivan A.
Excerpt from address, May 21, 1962. Cong Digest 42:210+ Ag '63

NESTS
Anatomy of a nest; English sparrows nest. J. K. Terres. il Audubon Mag 66:356 N '64
Home fit for a kingfisher! R. Grierson and S. Grierson. il Audubon Mag 66:300-1 S '64
Just out from under a rock. J. Terres. il Sports Illus 20:50-1+ My 4 '64

NETELAND, Edward. See Stoner, L. H. jt. auth.

NETHERLANDS
Benelux countries. F. G. Eyck. Cur Hist 47:355-61 D '64
See also
Airlines—Netherlands
Airplane industry and trade—Netherlands
Airports—Netherlands
Ameland (island)
Ballet—Netherlands
Book industries and trade—Netherlands
Booksellers and bookselling—Netherlands
Dams—Netherlands
Foreign visitors in the Netherlands
Gardens—Netherlands
Music festivals—Netherlands
Natural resources—Netherlands
Opera—Netherlands
Reclamation of land—Netherlands
Rotterdam
Space research—Netherlands
Television broadcasting—Netherlands
Transportation—Netherlands

Cabinet

Quiet crisis. il Time 82:22 Ag 2 '63

Description and travel

Holland in bloom. J. H. Winchester. il Travel 119:28-30 F '63
Traveling with Mlle: Holland. L. Lee. il Mlle 58:117-22 D '63

Economic conditions

Netherlands: a finger in the wage-price dike. il Bsns W p 120 O 26 '63
See also
Wages—Netherlands

Economic relations

Feathers from a frog; resumption of Dutch-Indonesian trade. Time 84:108 D 4 '64

Foreign relations

Indonesia

Feathers from a frog; resumption of diplomatic relations. Time 84:108 D 4 '64

History

Bibliography

Articles and other books received; Low Countries, comp. by H. H. Rowen. See issues of American historical review

Industries

Holland strikes it rich in natural gas. J. H. Winchester. il Read Digest 85:83-6 Ag '64
I did it all; Verolme shipyards. il Time 81:110 Ap 19 '63
See also
Mining industry and finance—Netherlands
Philips of Eindhoven companies

Politics and government

Holland: the deftly governed. V. S. Pritchett. il Holiday 35:64-7+ Ja '64

Religious institutions and affairs

See also
Catholic church in the Netherlands

Royal family

Her royal choice; Princess Irene's engagement to Prince Hugo de Borbón y Parma. il Newsweek 63:51-2 F 17 '64
Irene and Carlos in love affair of state; with report by P. Saporiti. il Life 56:40-40B F 21 '64
Troubled Orange family. il Time 83:28 My 8 '64

NETHERLANDS Reformed church. See Reformed church in the Netherlands

NETHERLANDS WEST INDIES
See also
Aruba (islands)

NETTESHEIM, Heinrich Cornelius Agrippa. See Agrippa von Nettesheim, H. C.

NETTO, Araújo, and Mello e Souza, Cláudio
Pelé; king of the booters. Read Digest 85:203-5+ O '64

NEUBAUER, W. K.
Largest diatomaceous-earth filters. Am City 79:76-8 N '64

NEUBERGER, Maurine B.
Hazards of teen-age smoking; excerpts from Smoke screen: tobacco and the public welfare. por Parents Mag 39:51+ Ja '64
Tobacco and the public welfare. PTA Mag 58:10-11 My '64

NEUBERGER, Richard L.
Winema, the memorial forest. W. B. Morse. il por Am For 69:24-5+ Je '63

NEUBERGER, Roy
Rise of the shorts. il por Fortune 67:205-6+ Ap '63

NEUES vom Tage; opera. See Hindemith, P.

NEUFELD, Maurice F.
Historical relationship of liberals and intellectuals to organized labor in the United States. bibliog Ann Am Acad 350:115-28 N '63

NEUFFER, M. G.
Tetrasporic embryo-sac formation in trisomic sectors of maize. bibliog Science 144:874-6 My 15 '64
—and Fiosor, Gyula
Mutagenic action of ethyl methanesulfonate in maize. bibliog il Science 139:1296-7 Mr 29 '63

NEUGEBAUER, C. A.
Thin films: nucleation, growth, and structure. Science 146:1604-5 D 18 '64

NEUGEBOREN, Jay
Hoadley's test case in Indiana. New Repub 149:14 S 21 '63
They didn't have to tell the truth. NEA J 53:21-2 N '64

NEUHAUS, Paul
How to build a hazard-free home. Todays Health 42:54-7 S '64
Tent-boating: fun for the men of the family. Todays Health 41:51 Ag '63

NEUMANN, A. L.
Six ways to start or expand your beef cow herd. Suc Farm 62:40-1+ Ja '64

NEUMANN, Alfred, and others
War and peace; dramatization of novel by L. N. Tolstoĭ. Criticism
New Repub 152:33 Ja 30 '65
New Yorker 40:92+ Ja 23 '65
Newsweek 65:75 F 1 '65
Time il 85:46 Ja 22 '65

NEUMANN, Hans
Pottery of Venezuela. Craft Horiz 23:32-3+ My '63

NEUMANN, John Nepomucene, Blessed
Blessed John Neumann. America 109:276 S 21 '63
Pilgrims at a coffin; beatification. il Newsweek 62:92-3 O 28 '63

NEURATH, Hans
Protein-digesting enzymes; with biographical sketch. Sci Am 211:20, 68-79 bibliog(p 154) D '64

NEURATH, Peter W. and Berliner, M. D.
Biological rhythms: a new type in strains of a mutant of neurospora crassa. bibliog Science 146:646-7 O 30 '64

NEUREITER, Norman P.
U.S.-Japan cooperative science program. Bul Atomic Sci 21:39 Ja '65

NEUROBIOLOGY. See Nervous system

NEURONS. See Nerve cells

NEUROPHYSIOLOGY. See Nervous system

NEUROSES
He's a whiz at work but a mess at home. Sci Digest 53:18-19 My '63
Those sick, sick, sick women. Sci Digest 53:43 Je '63

NEUROSES, Experimental
Audiogenic seizures, the dilute locus, and phenylalanine hydroxylase in DBA/1 mice. S. D. Huff and J. L. Fuller. bibliog il Science 144:304-5 Ap 17 '64

NEUROSPORA
Biological rhythms: a new type in strains of a mutant of neurospora cressa. P. W. Neurath and M. D. Berliner. bibliog il Science 146:646-7 O 30 '64
Dispensable and indispensable genes in neurospora. J. Morrow. bibliog il Science 144:307-8 Ap 17 '64
Irreparable mutations and ethionine resistance in neurospora. R. L. Metzenberg and others. bibliog il Science 145:1434-5 S 25 '64
Neurospora β-galactosidase: evidence for a second enzyme. W. K. Bates and D. O. Woodward. bibliog il Science 146:777-8 N 6 '64
Neurospora mutant lacking an arginine-specific carbamyl phosphokinase. R. H. Davis. bibliog Science 142:1652-4 D 27 '63
Neurospora; report on 2nd neurospora information conference. B. J. Bachmann. Science 145:301-2 Jl 17 '64
Ribosomes and ribonucleic acids in three morphological states of neurospora. H. R. Henney, jr. and R. Storck. bibliog il Science 142:1675-6 D 27 '63
Tryptophan synthetase from neurospora: a modification in the reaction scheme. M. D. Garrick and others. bibliog Science 145:491-2 Jl 31 '64

NEUROTICS. See Neuroses

NEUROTOXIN. See Toxins and antitoxins

NEUSTADT, Richard
Excerpt from testimony, February 28, 1964. Cong Digest 43:153+ My '64
How LBJ is doing his job; interview, ed. by J. Fromm. por U S News 57:34-7 Ag 3 '64
about
He wrote the textbook. por Time 85:38 Ja 22 '65

NEUTRA, Richard J.
Centerpiece of a library; excerpts from address, October 10, 1964. por Library J 89:4695-9 D 1 '64

NEUTRALITY
Alarm rings in India. A. M. Rosenthal. Read Digest 82:84-8 F '63
Gullibility of the neutrals. O. Handlin. Atlan 211:41-7 Mr '63
If the war in Vietnam can't be won is neutralizaton an answer? il Newsweek 63:44-5 F 17 '64
New neutralism. D. Lawrence. U S News 54:116 Ap 15 '63
Nonaligned in disarmament negotiations. A. S. Lall. Bul Atomic Sci 20:17-21 My '64
Zone of peace. J. W. Still. Bul Atomic Sci 19:29-30 S '63

NEUTRALS. See Neutrality

NEUTRINO telescope. See Telescope

NEUTRINOS
Detection of solar neutrinos. H. Reeves. il Sky & Tel 27:276-8 My '64
Foxhole for neutrinos. Time 82:61-2 N 29 '63
From the sun's heart. Newsweek 65:86+ Ja 25 '65
Gigantic neutrino shower. Sci N L 84:386 D 21 '63
Key to other worlds. A. Ewing. il Sci N L 84:99 Ag 17 '63
Learning from neutrinos. Time 83:50 Ja 3 '64
Neutrinos, old and new. F. Reines. bibliog il Science 141:778-83 Ag 30 '63
Observational neutrino astronomy. J. N. Bahcall. bibliog il Science 147:115-20 Ja 8 '65
To catch a neutrino; telescope at Catholic university. Newsweek 61:98 Mr 25 '63
Two-neutrino experiment. L. M. Lederman. il Sci Am 208:60-70 bibliog(p 188+) Mr '63
Visitors from M-82. Newsweek 62:55 D 23 '63

NEUTRON activation analysis. See Radioactivation analysis

NEUTRONS
Deadly sprays on moon. W. Wingo. Sci N L 84:115 Ag 24 '63
Estimate of neutron albedo on the moon's surface resulting from cosmic radiation. M. V. K. Appa Rao. bibliog il Science 141:530-1 Ag 9 '63
Fast-neutron spectroscopy. L. Cranberg. il Sci Am 210:79-86+ Mr '64
Neutron irradiations: biological effects; report on symposium. H. H. Smith. Science 143:1466+ Mr 27 '64
Nucleon structure; report of recent international conference at Stanford university. J. H. Fregeau. Science 141:548-9+ Ag 9 '63
Proton structure jelly-like. Sci N L 85:69 F 1 '64
Solar neutrons and the earth's radiation belts. R. E. Lingenfelter and E. J. Flamm. bibliog il Science 144:292-4 Ap 17 '64

NEUWIED, Maximilian Alexander Philipp, prinz von Wied-. See Wied-Neuwied, M. A. P. von

NEVADA
See also
Fishing—Nevada
Hunting—Nevada
Mines and mineral resources—Nevada
Prisons—Nevada
Radioactive fallout—Nevada
Spring Mountains
Zoology—Nevada

NEVADA—*Continued*

Antiquities

See Indians of North America—Antiquities—Nevada

Parks and reserves

Nevada's state parks. W. F. Heald. il Travel 120:40-2 S '63

NEVADA. University, Reno
University of Nevada's atmospherium-planetarium. R. K. Marshall. il Sky & Tel 26:318-21 D '63
World's first weather theater; Atmospherium planetarium. il Pop Sci 184:57 Je '64

NEVARD, Jacques
Zindabad! for Miss Jinnah. N Y Times Mag p36+ N 8 '64

NEVELSON, Louise
Art galleries; exhibition at the Pace gallery. R. M. Coates. New Yorker 40:160-2 D 5 '64
Wood sculpture of Louise Nevelson. il Vogue 143:148-55 F 1 '64

NEVER again; story. See Bracker, M.

NEVILLE, Emily Cheney
Out where the real people are; Newbery award acceptance; address, June 30, 1964. Horn Bk 40:400-4 Ag '64

about

Emily Cheney Neville. G. Neville. il por Horn Bk 40:405-8 Ag '64
Emily Neville. U. Nordstrom. il por Library J 89:1372-3 Mr 15 '64
Newbery and Caldecott winners: Emily Neville, Maurice Sendak. il por Pub W 185:30-2 Mr 9 '64
Newbery-Caldecott awards. por Wilson Lib Bul 38:617 Ap '64
WLB biography. P. Edge. por Wilson Lib Bul 39:269 N '64

NEVILLE, Glenn
Emily Cheney Neville. por Horn Bk 40:405-8 Ag '64

NEVILLE, Robert
Bishop, sovereign, supreme pontiff. N Y Times Mag p9+ Je 16 '63
Catholic, yet Communist, why? N Y Times Mag p 12+ Je 2 '63
Longo tries Togliatti's shoes. N Y Times Mag p32+ N 8 '64
New Mafia is deadlier. N Y Times Mag p22+ Ja 12 '64
Pope Paul follows along Pope John's path. N Y Times Mag p23+ S 22 '63

NEVIN, David
Boo-boo at the bank. Life 54:14 Je 28 '63
Man once buried in a landslide watches the new one. Life 57:44 N 13 '64
She has a fresh and girlish quality. Life 54:42 My 17 '63
Show goes on, the spoilers lose the day. Life 56:35 My 1 '64
Strange, tight little town, loath to admit complicity. Life 57:38-9 D 18 '64
Voice detectives go to work on the mystery crash. Life 56:46-46A My 22 '64

NEVINS, Allan
Historian of power and elevation can serve a nation in troubled days. Horizon 5:101 S '63
Outlook for greatness. Sat R 47:51-3+ Ag 29 '64
Set of mere money-getters? Am Heritage 14:50-1+ Je '63
Untold story of the Model T. Pop Sci 183:68-72+ Jl '63

NEW, Anne L.
Free men accept the challenge of free time. Recreation 56:189 Ap '63
Toward understanding leisure. Recreation 58:36-7 Ja '65

NEW American cinema. See Moving pictures—United States

NEW BEDFORD, Mass. free public library
Salt spray and sperm whales; Melville whaling room. J. S. Healey. il Wilson Lib Bul 37:565-8 Mr '63

NEW books preview. See Book exhibits

NEW boy in town; story. See Holland, B.

NEW BRAUNFELS, Tex.
Stetsons and sausage at home on the range. il Bsns W p30-1 N 14 '64

NEW BRITAIN (island)
Mastah Freddy's modest miracle; Airmen's memorial school. J. Reddy. il Sat Eve Post 238:68+ Ja 30 '65

NEW business enterprises
Case of the lonesome loan; symposium. il Harvard Bsns R 42:6-8+ N '64
Venture capital: money in a hurry. R. Nason. il Duns R 82:34-5+ N '63
Why new businesses succeed. Nations Bsns 52:56+ Ap '64

NEW cities. See New towns

NEW CITY, N.Y. free library
Book burning. Wilson Lib Bul 37:518 Mr '63
Censorship flares up in New City; library board member burns book. Library J 88:745 F 15 '63
Friends and True friends in New City. E. T. Moore. ALA Bul 57:387-8 My '63
If ever a library needed a friend; burning of book from public library. R. H. Smith. Pub W 183:55 F 4 '63
Record crowd at New City meeting overwhelmingly supports library board. Library J 88:1128 Mr 15 '63

NEW college, New York. See Teachers college, Columbia university—New college

NEW college, Sarasota, Fla.
Newborn schools; New college starts its first classes. il Time 84:92 S 18 '64

NEW college community, North Carolina. See Teachers college, Columbia university—New college

NEW dance group. See Dance schools

NEW deal. See United States—History—1933-1945

NEW ENGLAND
See also
Arts and crafts—New England
Connecticut Valley
Fishing—New England
Hunting—New England
Northeastern states

Description and travel

Down East isles: salt boxes and rock ribs. il Motor B 112:23-4 Ag '63
English in New England. C. Brossard. il Look 28:84-5+ My 5 '64
New England heritage cruise. B. Killam. il Motor B 111:20-7+ Ap '63
Seafaring New England. W. Brebner. il Holiday 34:18+ Jl '63
Season for seashore and seaports. M. Gough. il House B 105:46+ Jl '63

Historic houses, etc.

Fresh color schemes from historic houses. il House B 105:124-33 Mr '63

History

Sailors on wheels. E. S. Allen. Motor B 113:148-51 Mr '64

Colonial period

See also
Pilgrim fathers
Puritans

Politics

Campaign report from the East: if the people were voting for president now. il U S News 57:37-8 S 21 '64
Negro political progress in New England. A. Morrison. il Ebony 18:25-8+ O '63

Religious institutions and affairs

News of the Christian world (cont) Christian Cent 80:474, 1447-8; 81:994, 1510 Ap 10, N 20 '63, Ag 5, D 2 '64

NEW ENGLAND cookery. See Cookery, American

NEW ENGLAND forestry foundation, Boston
Foundation for the future. J. T. Hemenway. il Am For 70:19-21 N '64

NEW ENGLAND glass company. See Glass manufacture—History

NEW ENGLAND in literature
First and the last; New England in the novelist's imagination; address. A. Kazin. il Sat R 46:12-15+ F 2 '63

NEW ENGLAND town meeting. See Town meeting

NEW ENGLANDERS
Personal business. D. B. Warnick. il Travel 122:44-7 S '64
See also
Vermonters

NEW FOREST, England
Touring the villages and wildlands of the New Forest. il Sunset 130:19 F '63

NEW frontiersmen. See Public officers

NEW generation (periodical)
This New generation; symposium. America 109:383-6 O 5 '63

NEW GUINEA
See also
Elections—New Guinea
New Britain (island)
West New Guinea

Description and travel

Thirty minutes to incredibility. H. E. Mercer. il Travel 121:36-41+ F '64

NEW GUINEA—*Continued*

Native races

Australian peace corps helps shed stone age. Sci N L 87:50 Ja 23 '65

NEW GUINEA, Territory of

Council hopes for quick implementation of political reforms for New Guinea. il U N Rev 10:24-7 Jl '63

New Guinea; the land that time forgot. L. Thomas. il Read Digest 84:186-92+ Ja '64

NEW HAMPSHIRE

See also

Architecture, Domestic—New Hampshire
Booksellers and bookselling—New Hampshire
Botany—New Hampshire
Finance—New Hampshire
Fishing—New Hampshire
Law—New Hampshire
Libraries—New Hampshire
Washington, Mount

Description and travel

Arts in New Hampshire. J. Howard. Mlle 57:52+ Je '63

Historic houses, etc.

Living with antiques; the Brick House, Dover. J. C. Giffen. il Antiques 86:72-6 Jl '64

Strawbery Banke, Portsmouth. D. M. Vaughan. il Antiques 86:100-1 Jl '64

History

Lottery, the Puritan and the devil. J. Gould. il N Y Times Mag p 16+ My 19 '63

NEW HAMPSHIRE library association

Freedom to read in New Hampshire. E. J. Gaines. ALA Bul 57:1009-10 D '63

NEW HAMPSHIRE lottery. See Lotteries

NEW HAMPSHIRE painting. See Painting, American

NEW HAMPSHIRE primary. See Primaries

NEW HAMPSHIRE. University

You've taught me more than any teacher; unique horse program. R. Hoffmann. il Mlle 59:134-7 O '64

NEW HANOVER. See Lavongai

NEW HARMONY, Ind.

Utopia, limited; excerpt from Vanishing America. W. E. Wilson. il Am Heritage 15:64-72 O '64

NEW HAVEN, Conn.

Architecture

Paul Rudolph designs a place to park in downtown New Haven. il Arch Rec 133:145-50 F '63

Education

Private coeducational elementary school: Foote school. il Arch Rec 133:184-6 My '63

Stepping-stones from the slums; Winchester elementary school. L. Velie. il Read Digest 83:175-80 O '63

This is the city; school renewal with urban renewal. il Newsweek 63:58 Ap 13 '64

Industries

See also

Olin Mathieson chemical corporation—Winchester-Western division

NEW HAVEN, Conn, free public library

Book selection in New Haven. D. Lorenz. Wilson Lib Bul 39:331-2 D '64

Responding to manifest needs; neighborhood center. M. Bloss. il Library J 89:3252-4 S 15 '64

NEW HAVEN and Hartford railroad. See New York, New Haven and Hartford railroad company

NEW HOPE, Pa.

Theater

From red barn to package and tent; Bucks County playhouse. E. Coleman. il N Y Times Mag p 12-13+ Jl 19 '64

NEW IBERIA, La.

When a military base closes; what happens to a city? naval air station. il U S News 56:43-4 My 11 '64

NEW JERSEY

See also

Airports—New Jersey
Architecture, Domestic—New Jersey
Education—New Jersey
Fishing—New Jersey
Forests and forestry—New Jersey
Gardens—New Jersey
Hunting—New Jersey
Libraries—New Jersey
Music festivals—New Jersey
Port of New York authority

Economic conditions

New Jersey's search for identity. B. Bahrenburg. Harper 228:87-90+ Ap '64; Discussion. 228:6 Je '64

Education, Department of

N.J. to conduct statewide survey on school use of trade paperbacks. Library J 88:4005 O 15 '63

Historic houses, etc.

Washington's Christmastime crossing. M. Rutman. il Travel 120:49-50 D '63

History

Most improveablest land. J. Brooks. il Am Heritage 15:62-3+ O '64

New Jersey's tercentenary. E. B. Adcock. il Hobbies 69:116-17 D '64

Parks and reserves

Crash program for parkland acquisition; New Jersey green acres program. A. Brown, jr. il Recreation 57:397-9 O '64

Politics and government

New Jersey's search for identity. B. Bahrenburg. Harper 228:87-90+ Ap '64; Discussion. 228:6 Je '64

Race problems

Black rage in New Jersey. Time 84:19 Ag 21 '64

White boycott; racial violence in Paterson and Elizabeth. Newsweek 64:27+ Ag 24 '64

Religious institutions and affairs

News of the Christian world (cont) Christian Cent 80:280+, 966; 81:1069, 1317-18; 82:122-4 F 27, Jl 31 '63, Ag 26, O 21 '64, Ja 27 '65

NEW JERSEY education association

Duty of professional associations; address, November 9, 1962. R. J. Hughes. Vital Speeches 29:254-6 F 1 '63

NEW JERSEY state library, Trenton

State library for New Jersey. R. H. McDonough and K. W. Richards. il Library J 89:4709-10 D 1 '64

NEW JERUSALEM church

New Jerusalem. il Time 83:53 Je 26 '64

NEW leader (periodical)

Influence before affluence. il Time 81:38-40 Mr 1 '63

NEW life; story. See Abramov, F.

NEW MEXICAN ducks. See Ducks, Wild

NEW MEXICO

See also

Architecture, Domestic—New Mexico
Booksellers and bookselling—New Mexico
Fishing—New Mexico
Hunting—New Mexico
Sangre de Cristos Mountains

Antiquities

See Indians of North America—Antiquities—New Mexico

Description and travel

Along New Mexico's haunted highway; ghost towns, San Pedro, Golden, Madrid, and Cerrillos. il Sunset 133:58 N '64

Fresh look at New Mexico. B. Keating. il Holiday 33:64-7 F '63

Religious institutions and affairs

Ecumenical gesture; Roman Catholic archdiocese of Santa Fe applies to join New Mexico council of churches. Newsweek 65:37 Ja 4 '65

News of the Christian world (cont) Christian Cent 80:317-18, 624, 892, 1312-14; 81:1410-11; 82:126 Mr 6, My 8, Jl 10, O 23 '63, N 11 '64, Ja 27 '65

NEW MEXICO state university of agriculture, engineering and science, Las Cruces

Aggiornamento on the campus; Newman center of St Albert the Great. C. Stevens. America 112:122-3 Ja 23 '65

NEW MEXICO. University

Continuity in New Mexico: university's varied plazas. il Arch Forum 119:108-11 S '63

NEW ORLEANS

Architecture

Vaulting in Louisiana. il Arch Forum 119:96-9 O '63

Crime

New Orleans: Cosa nostra's Wall Street. B. Davidson. il Sat Eve Post 237:15-21 F 29 '64

NEW ORLEANS—*Continued*

Description

U.S. city weekends. T. B. Lesure. il Travel 120:28-32+ Jl '63

Education

Separate & superior; St Augustine high school. il Time 85:56 Ja 1 '65
See also
Dillard university
Tulane university

Foreign population

Melting pot in the Bayous; southern Louisiana; with drawings by A. R. Waud. O. Evans. il Am Heritage 15:30-51+ D '63

Galleries and museums

See also
Louisiana state museum

History

Melting pot in the Bayous; southern Louisiana; with drawings by A. R. Waud. O. Evans. il Am Heritage 15:30-51+ D '63

Libraries

See also
New Orleans public library

Music

New Orleans five. J. Belsom. il Opera N 28:33 F 1 '64
Real New Orleans sound; Preservation hall concerts. J. S. Wilson. il Hi Fi 13:59-61+ S '63
Syncopated dirges, ragtime parades; Preservation hall concerts. K. Chase. il Américas 16:16-20 Mr '64
Upbeat for old jazz. il Bsns W p32-3 F 8 '64

Negroes

Little night music; big police raid on the Quorum club. J. Beecher. il Nation 199:272-5 O 26 '64
Reporter at large; Mardi gras parade by Zulu social aid & pleasure club. C. Trillin. New Yorker 40:41-2+ Je 20 '64
Way down yonder in New Orleans. M. M. Karpatkin. New Repub 150:10-11 My 23 '64

Parades

Big bowls of glitter. il Life 56:38-45 Ja 3 '64

Police

Little night music; big police raid on the Quorum club. J. Beecher. il Nation 199:272-5 O 26 '64

Politics and government

From bossism to cosmopolitanism: changes in the relationship of urban leadership to state politics. W. C. Havard. bibliog f Ann Am Acad 353:84-94 My '64

Street traffic

Clang dies out; New Orleans street railway system. il Bsns W p84-6 D 14 '63

NEW ORLEANS, Battle of, 1815
Celebration in New Orleans: battle of '65. J. H. Winchester. il Travel 122:56-7+ D '64

NEW ORLEANS cookery. See Cookery, American

NEW ORLEANS cotton exchange. See Cotton exchange

NEW ORLEANS Mardi gras. See Carnival

NEW ORLEANS opera house association
Louisiana autumn. J. Belsom. il Opera N 29:30 Ja 23 '65

NEW ORLEANS public library
New Orleans replies to the New republic; excerpts from letter. J. Cushman. Library J 89:2758 Jl '64

NEW ORLEANS shipyards. See Shipyards

NEW party. See Progressive party

NEW Philharmonia orchestra (London)
Other side; new Philharmonia. T. Heinitz. Sat R 47:74 My 30 '64
Up from the grave. Time 85:43 Ja 22 '65

NEW products. See Products, New

NEW realism. See Modernism (art)

NEW republic (periodical)
Find the typical reader. New Repub 148:5 My 18 '63
He quoted me. Newsweek 61:62 Je 17 '63
New republic after half a century. New Repub 151:15-16 N 7 '64
Remarks on the occasion of this journal's 50th year; symposium. New Repub 150:13-18 Mr 21 '64
T.R.B. from Washington; twenty years after. New Repub 150:2 Mr 7 '64

NEW RIVER train. See Railroads—Trains

NEW ROCHELLE, N.Y.

Education

Facts of de facto. il Time 82:30-1 Ag 2 '63

Hospitals

Invader; cases of enterococcus infection. Newsweek 61:80 My 6 '63

NEW school for social research, New York
Senior scholars; Institute for retired professionals. Newsweek 63:77 Ja 20 '64

NEW sources of food supply. See Food supply—New sources

NEW stars. See Stars, New

NEW states. See States, New

NEW statesman (periodical)
Ginger man. il Newsweek 65:62 Ja 25 '65
New statesman & the English left. J. Mander. Commentary 37:47-53 F '64; Discussion. 38:10-11 Jl '64
New statesman, by E. Hyams. Review
New Repub 149:45-8 N 9 '63. M. Muggeridge
When the left was always right. N. Thomas. Sat R 46:26 N 2 '63

NEW Tokaido line. See Railroads—Japan

NEW town program. See Regional planning—Great Britain

NEW towns
Brand new city for Maryland. J. W. Anderson. Harper 229:100-2+ N '64
Community: could this be our town? W. Von Eckardt. il New Repub 151:17-24 N 7 '64; Discussion. 151:37-8 N 28 '64
New approach to new-town planning; unnamed community between Washington and Baltimore. D. Canty. il Arch Forum 121:194-9 Ag '64
New towns: shape of Utopia? il Newsweek 64:112+ N 23 '64
See also
Reston, Va.

NEW World. See America

NEW YEAR
Goodbye and hello; celebration of Chinese New Year at Lichee tree, in Greenwich Village. New Yorker 40:24 F 29 '64
Japanese New Year. il Travel 121:39-43 Ja '64
New Year customs; comp. by D. T. Harrell. Hobbies 68:28 Ja '64
Out tiger, in hare. New Yorker 38:26-7 F 2 '63
S Novym Godom; New Year in Russia. il Time 85:37 Ja 1 '65

NEW YEARS balls. See Balls (parties)

NEW YEARS day parade. See Philadelphia—Parades

NEW YORK (city)
City destroying itself. R. J. Whalen. il Fortune 70:114-23+ S '64
Insider's New York from A to Z. K. Simon. Holiday 36:111-16 Jl '64
Manhattan. J. Ciardi. Sat R 47:8 D 26 '64
New New York; symposium. il Look 27:23-36+ Mr 26 '63
New York question; Mademoiselle's own New York. L. Lerman. Mlle 58:128-32+ Ap '64
Opinion, please, New York. A. Pryce-Jones. il Mlle 57:40-1 O '63
Sunday in Manhattan. H. Ehrlich. il Look 28:40+ Jl 28 '64
That other New York. S. Alsop. Sat Eve Post 237:18 My 23 '64
What's on this season. il Vogue 142:100-5 N 15 '63
See also
Bronx
Brooklyn
Lincoln Center for the performing arts, New York
Port of New York authority

Air pollution

Garbage in the air. N. Cousins. Sat R 47:22-3 Je 6 '64; Discussion 47:21 Je 27; 20 Jl 18 '64
Is New York a mess? an open letter to the mayor of New York. L. Rosten. il Look 27:92-6 F 12 '63
Murk, smog, smoke, needed: fresh air. F. J. Cook. il N Y Times Mag p 10+ D 29 '63
Reporter at large. E. Iglauer. il New Yorker 40:54-6+ Mr 7 '64

Air pollution control, Department of

Reporter at large. E. Iglauer. il New Yorker 40:54-6+ Mr 7 '64

NEY YORK (city)—*Continued*

Airports

Animalport; animal hotel at New York international airport. C. Mathis. il Pop Mech 120:102-4 D '63
Building owners fight rooftop heliport. J. R. Ashlock. il Aviation W 78:36-7 My 27 '63
Citizens' groups quiet on 727 service approval for LaGuardia. Aviation W 80:52 Ap 20 '64
Construction will start in March on Seaboard's Kennedy terminal. J. W. Carter. Avaition W 81:26 D 28 '64
Idlewild sprawl poses transfer problems. R. H. Cook. il Aviation W 79:33-4+ Jl 29 '63
LaGuardia redevelopment features new structures; photographs. Aviation W 81:37 D 21 '64
Landing fee boost seen for NY airports. Aviation W 81:34 Ag 17 '64
New York control center burden may curtail traffic after 1968. W. Wright. Aviation W 79:45 Ag 5 '63
Pan Am to begin $7-million cargo facility; Kennedy international airport. Aviation W 81:41 O 19 '64
Port in a storm; Port of New York authority. J. Sanderson. il Flying 75:24-8 Ag '64
Special lighted traffic pattern planned to reduce Idlewild noise. Aviation W 79:29 Jl 8 '63

Anecdotes, facetiae, satire, etc.

Cashing in the New York dollar. W. S. Ross. il Esquire 61:66-7+ Ap '64
Good-bye, Broadway; hello, Mr Square. S. J. Perelman. il Sat Eve Post 237:94+ My 23 '64

Aquarium

Underwater guinea pigs help scientists study life. H. M. Schwalb. il Sci Digest 53:6-11 F '63

Architecture

America's cast iron age. il Arch Forum 120:110-13 Ap '64
Anonymous art; Anonymous arts recovery society. New Yorker 40:49-51 N 14 '64
Bell builds cellar in the sky; New York telephone's skyscraper. il Bsns W p30-1 F 9 '63
Better than mere cubage. P. Blake. il Arch Forum 119:124 D '63
Building skylines is his business; C. Morse of New York's Diesel construction co. il Bsns W p33-4 Jl 11 '64
Can New York be saved? P. Blake. il Sat R 48:16-18+ Ja 23 '65
Cosmetic architecture. il Time 81:44+ Je 7 '63
Extra Grand Central; Manhattan's Pan American building. il Time 81:71 Mr 15 '63
Ford foundation's mid-Manhattan greenhouse. il Fortune 70:177-8 O '64
Help for sidewalk superintendents. S. Blum. il N Y Times Mag p30-1+ O 4 '64
Higher and lower. New Yorker 39:46-7 D 7 '63
Ill-planned and ugly; New York chapter of the American institute of architects report. Newsweek 64:74 Jl 27 '64
Lost New York of the Pan American airways building. D. Haskell. il Arch Forum 119:106-11 N '63
New light: floodlighting of Pan Am building. New Yorker 40:22-5 D 26 '64
New look for old brownstone. E. Sverbeyeff. il N Y Times Mag p94-5 D 8 '63
New York's new buildings and historic houses. il House & Gard 125:8+ F '64
Ode to the great 5'x9' outdoors; terrace in New York. S. Blum. il N Y Times Mag p21+ Ap 26 '64
Plea to curb the bulldozer; city's landmarks. W. N. Seymour, jr. il N Y Times Mag p80-1+ O 13 '63
Problem of Pan Am. M. F. Schmertz. il Arch Rec 133:151-8 My '63
Saarinen's dark tower: the CBS building and how it grew. E. Larrabee. il Harper 229:55-61 D '64
What goes up must come down. S. Blum. il N Y Times Mag p 10-11+ D 27 '64
Will hanging tower attract exchange? il Arch Forum 118:116 Mr '63
World's largest executive suite; Pan Am building. il Bsns W p70-2 Jl 20 '63

Art

Art galleries. H. Rosenberg. See issues of New Yorker from October 22, 1962 to November 2, 1963
Art galleries. R. M. Coates. See issues of New Yorker
Portfolio of drawings by Paul Hogarth. N. Kent. il Am Artist 27:42-7+ Ap '63
Vanity fair: the New York art scene. il Newsweek 65:54-6+ Ja 4 '65

Banks

After fifty years of a rising income tax. il U S News 54:75-6 F 25 '63
Bank defies SEC on trusts; First national city bank of New York. Bsns W p 136 Ap 13 '63
Chase goes new road for growth; will form holding company. Bsns W p34 Jl 18 '64
Chase Manhattan bank, a patron of art & artists. N. Lansdale. il Am Artist 29:32-7+ Ja '65
Chase Manhattan wins friends and influences people. il Newsweek 61:74-7 Ap 8 '63
New trend in finance: the negotiable C.D. W. A. Law and M. C. Crum. il Harvard Bsns R 41:115-26 Ja '63
Profiles; D. Rockefeller, president of Chase Manhattan bank. E. J. Kahn, jr. New Yorker 40:37-8+ Ja 9; 40-2+ Ja 16 '65
Wilderness; display of New York state departments of conservation and commerce at Manhattan savings bank. New Yorker 39:34-5 Je 8 '63
See also
Morgan guaranty trust company

Bellevue hospital

Big-city complex in a flexible cube. il Arch Rec 135:194-7 Ap '64
Medicarelessness; medical and gastroenterological clinics. Nat R 15:207 S 10 '63

Bibliography

New York books for the World's fair. il Pub W 185:72-5 F 17 '64

Bookstores

See Booksellers and bookselling—New York (state)

Bridges

Across the Narrows. New Yorker 40:47-8 N 28 '64
America's newest gateway; Verrazano-Narrows bridge. il Sr Schol 84:15 My 8 '64
Beauty suspended; Verrazano-Narrows bridge. G. Talese. il N Y Times Mag p32-3 N 15 '64
Biggest bridge ever; Verrazano-Narrows bridge. J. W. Frazier. il Read Digest 85:266-70 N '64
Biggest bridge in the world; Verrazano-Narrows bridge. A. P. Armagnac. il Pop Sci 185:46-9 S '64
Biggest span; Verrazano-Narrows bridge. il Life 55:81-6 Jl 12 '63
Bridge to ease New York traffic; Verrazano-Narrows bridge. il U S News 57:14 D 7 '64
Bridges of light; photographs. N Y Times Mag p22-3 Ag 16 '64
Bridges of New York. A. Rothstein. il Look 28:86-8 F 11 '64
Furor rises with new Brooklyn bridge. R. Vaughan. il Sat Eve Post 236:80-1 Je 29 '63
Greatest bridge of them all; Verrazano Narrows bridge. M. J. Kempner. il Harper 229:70-6 N '64
Longest clear-span bridge; Verrazano-Narrows bridge. il Am City 80:26 Ja '65
Mighty bridge rises; Verrazano-Narrows bridge. il N Y Times Mag p 112 Ap 7 '63
New bridge; Verrazano-Narrows. il Newsweek 64:88-91 N 23 '64
New gateway to America; Verrazano-Narrows bridge. il Sci Digest 56:31 D '64
New York's newest landmark; Verrazano-Narrows bridge. il Sci Digest 53:92 My '63
Of soaring steel and stone. il N Y Times Mag p38-9 S 15 '63

Buildings

See New York (city)—Architecture

Caricatures and cartoons

New York. R. Lurie. Harper 228:94-5 F '64

Carnegie Hall

Carnegie and opera. Q. Eaton. il Opera N 28:27-31 Mr 14 '64

Churches

Also on Sunday; New York city's Judson memorial church. B. Moore and P. Moore. il Mlle 58:66-9 D '63
Art in church; St James' church. New Yorker 39:34-6 My 4 '63

NEW YORK (city)—Churches—*Continued*
Gardener; St Bartholomew's Episcopal church. New Yorker 39:34-6 S 21 '63
Off Broadway; St Clement's Episcopal church. il Time 84:68 N 27 '64
Profiles; Church of St Matthew and St Timothy. R. Rice. il New Yorker 40:41-2+ Ag 1; 37-8 Ag 8 '64

City hall

Information; Mayor's information center, mobile unit. New Yorker 39:41-2 N 16 '63

City planning

Architects plan civic center for New York city. il Arch Rec 133:12-13 Ja '63
City slums vs. a university; Morningside Heights vs. Columbia. il U S News 56:74-7 Ap 6 '64
Dreams of glory; Times square, crossroads of the world. il Bsns W p30-1 Je 8 '63
Friend at the Chase; financial group to renew Lower Manhattan. il Bsns W p24+ D 21 '63
Future by design discussed in New York. il Arch Rec 136:23+ D '64
Hudson River waterfront development. il Arch Rec 134:12 Ag '63
Needed: oases in the asphalt desert. E. J. Kahn. il N Y Times Mag p54-5+ My 26 '63
New urban forms. W. McQuade. Nation 199: 392 N 23 '64
Printing, planning and public relations. J. Cuffe. il Am City 78:102 N '63

City planning commission

New urban forms; City planning commission's symposium, Future of design. W. McQuade. Nation 199:392 N 23 '64
Symposium; Future by design. New Yorker 40:46-8 O 31 '64

Civic center (proposed)

Architects plan civic center for New York city. il Arch Rec 133:12-13 Ja '63
Civic center plan attacked in Manhattan. il Arch Forum 120:5+ Mr '64
N.Y. moves towards its civic center. il Arch Forum 118:8-9 Ap '63

Clubs

Harvard hootenanny; folk singers at Harvard club of New York. New Yorker 40:29-30 Mr 21 '64
There's small hotel; Princeton club. il Time 81:55 Mr 22 '63
Tiger! Princeton club. New Yorker 39:23-4 F 23 '63; Reply. B. Gill. 39:136+ Mr 9 '63
See also
Explorers club
Rehearsal club

Colleges and universities

See New York (city)—Education

Columbia-Presbyterian medical center

Reporter at large; research in specific dyslexia at Pediatric language disorder clinic, Babies hospital. C. Tomkins. New Yorker 39: 127-8+ S 14 '63

Community centers

Twice as big, Hudson guild. Recreation 57: 246 My '64

Courts

Judge's son; trial of G. Martinis. il Time 82: 17-18 Ag 9 '63

Crime

As New York city tries to curb its violence and murders. il U S News 57:4 Jl 6 '64
Box 100; New York's address for informers' tips. M. Abramson. il N Y Times Mag p72+ S 15 '63
Chief policeman talks about his beat. R. W. Apple, jr. il N Y Times Mag p 10+ Je 21 '64
Crime in the streets. W. Klein. il Nation 200:30-1 Ja 11 '65
Death in the city. Time 83:23 Ap 24 '64
Death of a youth worker; L. Marsh. G. Samuels. il Sat Eve Post 236:74-6 Ap 6 '63
Is New York a mess? an open letter to the mayor of New York. L. Rosten. il Look 27: 26-7 F 12 '63
Long nightmare of a police witness; Artie Schlitz. B. Lindeman. il Sat Eve Post 236: 71-2+ N 2 '63
Mafia rubs out a rebellion. il Life 55:18-25 Ag 30 '63
My life inside the mob; ed. by Q. Reynolds. S. Slater. il Sat Eve Post 236:38-43+ Ag 24 '63
My night as a police officer. T. Gallagher. il Read Digest 82:173-4+ Je '63
New York cop studies crime of two cities: London and New York. H. Ehrlich. il Look 27:57-63 Jl 30 '63
New York scandal. C. Morrison. il Look 27: 103-4+ Mr 26 '63
Night people. C. Brossard. il Look 27:58a-58g Mr 26 '63
Price of getting involved; Hector Mangual. T. Armbrister. il Sat Eve Post 237:81-5 S 26 '64
Reporter at large; burglary. S. Black. il New Yorker 39:63-4+ D 7; 89-91+ D 14 '63
Savage stalks at midnight; Winston Moseley. il Time 83:21-2 Je 26 '64
Scene of the crime. D. Newman and R. Benton. il Esquire 62:168-9 D '64
Waterfront revisited. B. Schulberg. il Sat Eve Post 236:28-32+ S 7 '63

Description

Around the Island; boat ride around Manhattan. il U S Camera 27:62-3 Jl '64
Blimp's-eye view of a magic city. il Life 56:60-7 My 1 '64
Diary of a newly married poet; J. R. Jiménez in New York and New England. R. Gullón. il Américas 16:11-15 Mr '64
For a three-in-one vacation this year see, the World's fair, New York city, New York state. J. R. Borcherding. il Suc Farm 62: 44-5 Jl '64
In New York. E. Flaiano. Vogue 144:30+ N 1 '64
Is New York a mess? an open letter to the mayor of New York. L. Rosten. il Look 27: 26-7 F 12 '63
Lost horizons; clear view before the building boom. F. Littlejohn. Reporter 30:46-7 Mr 12 '64
My New York. A. Heifetz. il Seventeen 23: 144-5+ F '64
New American capital of Bohemia; Lower East side. E. Waldron. il Sat Eve Post 237:98-102 My 23 '64
New New York; with photographs by P. Harrington. P. Coffin. Look 27:23-30 Mr 26 '63
New York for next to nothing. S. M. Black. il Holiday 34:108+ Jl '63
New York for the fair. G. Bush and M. Vennum. il Bet Hom & Gard 42:129-34 Ap '64
New York in fair time; evaluation of city guide books. J. Brooks. il Consumer Rep 29:199-201 Ap '64
New York is a great place to live, but it's a tough place to visit. F. Knebel. il Look 27:34-6 Mr 26 '63
New York, N.Y. M. R. Weiss. il Sat R 47:28-31 Mr 28 '64
New York, N.Y: the golden door; excerpt from New York: true north; with photographs by B. Glinn. G. Millstein. Sat Eve Post 237:74-8+ My 23 '64
Roaming the fair city. H. Morgan. il Ladies Home J 81:109 Jl '64
See Manhattan while it lasts; with drawings by John Rombola. O. Jensen. Horizon 5:116-20 My '63
Sidewalks of New York. E. Scully. il U S Camera 27:43-7+ Je '64
Stranger in New York. V. S. Pritchett. il Holiday 36:32-45+ Jl; 48-53+ Ag; 66-9+ S '64
Teen travel talk. il Seventeen 23:72 Je '64
Travel tips. P. P. Coleman. il Sr Schol 83:18T D 13 '63
Travel's picture portfolio. il Travel 122:56-60 N '64
View of the city. G. Zimmermann. il Look 28: 54-66 Jl 28 '64
What to see in New York. il Sr Schol 84:11T Ap 3 '64
Whole town is a world's fair. M. Gough. il House B 106:94+ Je '64
World in New York city. P. T. White. il Nat Geog Mag 126:52-107 Jl '64

Docks

See also
Waterfront commission of New York harbor

Economic conditions

Blight begins to spread; New York newspaper strike. il Bsns W p30-2 Ja 19 '63
New Yorkers getting richer; family incomes up 50 per cent. Bsns W p 152 D 14 '63

Education

A for effort, and for new hope; Higher horizons program. il Bsns W p44-5 F 1 '64
As showdown nears on shifting of pupils. U S News 56:12 Mr 23 '64

NEW YORK (city)—Education—*Continued*
Battle of the moms; members of Parents and taxpayers (P.A.T.) il Time 84:98 O 16 '64
Better schools are the real goal of integration. Life 56:4 F 21 '64
Boycott in New York? Newsweek 63:45 Ja 6 '64
Boycott picture. il Sr Schol 84:2T+ F 21 '64
Breakthrough; pattern of segregation. Commonweal 77:633 Mr 15 '63
British English teacher in the Bronx. W. D. E. Evans. il Sat R 47:54-5+ Jl 18 '64
Busing for racial balance is wrong; excerpts from address, October 16, 1964. B. M. Goldwater. U S News 57:97 N 2 '64
City schools, a mixed report card. F. M. Hechinger. il N Y Times Mag p24+ Je 14 '64; Reply with rejoinder. J. Landers. p2+ Jl 5 '64
Cleaning up. Newsweek 62:94 O 28 '63
Cross-busing, now it's here; Princeton plan. il Life 57:44-46C S 25 '64
Decision on zoning; New York state Supreme court. Sr Schol 84:2T+ Ap 3 '64
De facto segregation; school boycott of February 3, 1964. Commonweal 79:583-4 F 14 '64
Education combined with rehabilitation; Institute for the crippled and disabled. il Arch Rec 133:180-1 My '63
Elementary school library growth. H. R. Sattley. il ALA Bul 58:482-8 Je '64
Enthusiasm in the classroom. il Opera N 28: 30-1 Ap 18 '64
Experiment in industry-education; address, September 13, 1963. S. Shenberg. Vital Speeches 30:90-3 N 15 '63
Great New York boycott; what will happen if the cry for better schools fails? C. Jencks. New Repub 150:12-14 F 15 '64
Harlem Bohème. F. Stevenson. il Opera N 28:6 Mr 14 '64
Hooky; school boycott. il Newsweek 63:62 F 17 '64
How teenagers can combat adult delinquency; address, April 5, 1963. B. Byrne. Vital Speeches 29:540-2 Je 15 '63
Instant integration? Newsweek 62:54 D 30 '63
Integrating inferiority? Harlem schools. Newsweek 62:100+ N 25 '63
Is school integration a failure in New York? U S News 56:8 My 25 '64
Madison avenue methods: teaching ideas that work; Harlem, N.Y. junior high school. S. R. Selby. Sr Schol 85:7T O 14 '64
Manhattan principal at work; H. T. Hillson of George Washington high school. L. W. Gillenson. il Sat R 47:77-9+ My 16 '64; Discussion. 47:47 Je 20 '64
Negro & the New York schools. M. Decter. bibliog f Commentary 38:25-34 S '64; Discussion. 39:16 Ja '65
N.Y.C. school boycott; Parents and taxpayers coordinating council and Joint council for better education. il Sr Schol 85:1T S 30 '64
New York dilemma; Negro boycott against segregated schools. il Time 83:49 F 7 '64
New York school boycott. M. Kempton. New Repub 151:6-7 S 26 '64; Discussion. 151:30 O 10; 30 O 24 '64
New York's boycott: what did it prove? T. R. Brooks. il Reporter 30:32-4 F 27 '64
New York's Jim Crow schools: bleak facts and bright visions. B. Carter. il Reporter 31:23-6 Jl 2 '64
No more parades? failure of the March for Democratic schools. M. Kempton. New Repub 150:5-7 My 30 '64
No picnic in the beginning; teaching in a Harlem junior high. S. R. Selby. il Sr Schol 84:10T-11T Ap 24 '64
Now, whites protest on a racial issue. il U S News 56:8 Mr 23 '64
Personal attention; our new superintendent of schools. New Yorker 39:15-16 Je 29 '63
Prospective ruin of the city colleges. R. Kirk. Nat R 16:157 F 25 '64
P.S. 165. R. Schickel. Commentary 37:43-51 Ja '64; Reply. E. F. Bondi. 37:16 My '64
Public schools; civilizing the blackboard jungle. il Time 82:86-8+ N 15 '63
Public schools: the spreading boycott. il Time 83:40+ F 14 '64
Pupil-transfer plan that is under fire. U S News 56:12 Je 15 '64
Remaking the city schools; three-member panel report. il Newsweek 63:100 My 25 '64
Reporter at large; dancers in May: P.S. 31 in Park fête in Central park. L. Ross. il New Yorker 40:35-8+ Jl 18 '64
Says a white mother: we have rights, too, New York's school problems; with statements by three school authorities. il U S News 57:71-2+ O 26 '64
Scholastic teacher interview; ed. by H. Langer. J. H. Fischer. Sr Schol 85: 8T-13T S 23 '64
School dispute, and parents arrested; sit-in against transfer of children from neighborhood school. il U S News 57:12 O 19 '64
School library program for children in a depressed area. H. B. Brown and E. D. Sinnette. bibliog il ALA Bul 58:643-7 Jl '64
School of performing arts dance concert at High school of printing auditorium. D. Hering. Dance Mag 37:14-16 Jl '63
Schools boycotted. il Sr Schol 84:19-20 F 21 '64
Social studies revision. Sr Schol 85:2T+ O 21 '64
Standing P.A.T. Time 84:44 S 25 '64
Strikes, sanctions, and the schools. J. Scanlon. il Sat R 46:51-5+ O 19 '63; Discussion. 46:64 N 16; 39 D 21 '63
Studio progress; latest report on the junior Metropolitan. A. M. Lingg. Opera N 28: 16 Ja 25 '64
Teachers get a hand in running New York; strike threat. il Time 82:51 S 20 '63
Too many pupils; too many problems. il Newsweek 62:55-8 S 16 '63
Toughest high school in the United States; Bronx high school of science. G. White. il Ladies Home J 80:69+ Ap '63
Unmoved; New Yorkers protest plan to bus children to racially mixed schools. il Newsweek 63:31 Mr 23 '64
Urban elementary school stresses a happy environment. il Arch Rec 136:236-7 S '64
Urban schools. il Arch Forum 119:77-99 N '63
White boycott; Parents and taxpayers coordinating council and the Joint council for better education. Reporter 31:18+ O 8 '64
White walkout. il Newsweek 64:87-8 S 28 '64
Why they fight for the P.A.T; pairing schools to obtain racial balance. P. Streit. il N Y Times Mag p20-1+ S 20 '64
See also
Hunter college
New school for social research
Public education association

Education, Board of

Backlash in New York: PAT vs. Board of education. A. Croce. Nat R 16:816 S 22 '64
Brooklyn pl spurs registration with help of NYC Board of Educ. Library J 89:338 Ja 15 '64
Interfaith trio blunders. Christian Cent 80: 1359 N 6 '63
Mason-Dixon line in Queens; Junction boulevard, between Jackson Heights and Corona. F. Powledge. il N Y Times Mag p 12+ My 10 '64

Elections

Elephants in Tammanyland; seventeenth congressional district, Manhattan. B. Carter. il Reporter 29:41-3 N 21 '63

Electric power

Great battle for Storm King. J. Ridgeway. New Repub 151:8-9 N 28 '64
Storm King question; hydropower project in Hudson Highlands. Nat Parks Mag 39:21 Ja '65
See also
Consolidated Edison company of New York

Fiction

Four stories about New York. il Sat Eve Post 237:50-5+ My 23 '64

Finance

Vendor-relations office. R. J. Browne. Am City 78:153 O '63

Foreign population

Beyond the melting pot, by N. Glazer and D. P. Moynihan. Review
Commentary 37:74-6 Ja '64. D. Bell; Discussion. 37:18+ My '64
Nation 197:186-7 S 28 '63. E. S. Wilentz
New Yorker 40:198+ S 26 '64. N. Bliven
Reporter 29:59-60 O 10 '63. G. Paulding
U S News il 55:100 S 30 '63
Nueva York; Hispanic culture makes its mark on New York. J. V. Amaral. il Américas 16:6-11 Jl '64
See also
Puerto Ricans in the United States

Galleries and museums

Aggressive giant; Marlborough-Gerson gallery. il Time 82:56 Jl 19 '63
Art galleries; exhibition at Marlborough-Gerson gallery, Artist and Maecenas dedicated to C. Valentin. R. M. Coates. New Yorker 39:226-8 D 7 '63

NEW YORK (city)—Galleries and Museums —*Continued*
Art in New York during the World's fair. N. Lansdale. il Am Artist 28:42-9+ Je '64
Art rite, opening night. G. Glueck. il N Y Times Mag p44-5 D 13 '64
Braque: pre-cube to post-Zen; four New York galleries join in a benefit exhibition. J. Richardson. il Art N 63:29-31+ Ap '64
Day of the browser; opening of gallery season in Manhattan. il Time 82:86 O 18 '63
Fine art of art dealing; Marlborough-Gerson, Saidenberg, and Willard galleries. K. Kuh. Sat R 46:31 D 28 '63
Folk art for big city folk; Museum of early American folk arts. B. O'Doherty. il N Y Times Mag p36-7 S 22 '63
Going for baroque; opening of Marlborough-Gerson gallery. il Time 82:72 N 22 '63
Healthy new force; Huntington Hartford's Gallery of modern art. Newsweek 62:89 S 9 '63
Marlborough country; opening of the Marlborough-Gerson gallery, inc. in New York. il Newsweek 62:74-5 N 25 '63
Nueva York; Hispanic culture makes its mark on New York. J. V. Amaral. il Américas 16:6-11 Jl '64
Reviews and previews. See issues of Art news
State of the market; Manhattan's art galleries. il Time 81:62 Je 21 '63
See also
American museum of natural history, New York
Gallery of modern art, New York
Metropolitan museum of art, New York
Museum of modern art, New York
New York historical society
Solomon R. Guggenheim museum, New York
Whitney museum of American art, New York

Gardens

Modern roses at the United Nations. il Pop Gard 14:28-9 F '63
See also
Brooklyn botanic garden
New York botanical garden

Greenwich Village

Profiles; J. Gould. J. Mitchell. il New Yorker 40:61-2+ S 19; 53-4+ S 26 '64
Squash & stretch. M. Klonsky. il Esquire 60: 162-3+ D '63
Stranger in New York. V. S. Pritchett. il Holiday 36:48-50 Ag '64
When you come to the fair, be sure to see Greenwich Village shops and galleries. il House & Gard 125:42+ Ap '64

Caricatures and cartoons

Cartoonist at large in the Village. C. Rose. N Y Times Mag p46-7 N 24 '63

Harbor

See also
Statue of liberty

Harlem

Black and white; Harlem: killers, go home. G. Jacobson. New Repub 151:14-16 Ag 8 '64
Calculated risk; Negro leadership. il Newsweek 64:26-8 Ag 10 '64
Christianity in Harlem. P. F. Berrigan. il Commonweal 81:323-5 N 27 '64
Ghetto ignites. W. Klein. il Nation 199:49-51 Ag 10 '64
Harlem goes to war against the slumlords. R. K. Massie. il Sat Eve Post 237:71-5 F 29 '64
Harlem: hatred in the streets. il Newsweek 64:16-20 Ag 3 '64
Harlem is nowhere; excerpt from Shadow and act. R. Ellison. il Harper 229:53-7 Ag '64
Harlem sketchbook: white man, walk easy. R. Kahn. il Sat Eve Post 237:26-8+ Je 13 '64
Harlem: some reflections. America 111:125 Ag 8 '64
Harlem's long hot summer begins. il Life 57:14-23 Jl 31 '64
Hope for Harlem. A. Morrison. il Ebony 19: 168-70+ O '64
How cops behave in Harlem. M. Kempton. New Repub 151:7-8 Ag 22 '64
Human geography of Harlem. T. H. Clancy. il America 109:156-8 Ag 17 '63
Mississippi comes North to Harlem. J. Steele. New Repub 152:10-11 Ja 30 '65
Needed: the truth about Harlem. L. P. Jackson, jr. Negro Hist Bul 28:11-12 O '64
New York city in trouble: story of a rising fear. il U S News 56:72-7 Je 8 '64
No picnic in the beginning; teaching. S. R. Selby. il Sr Schol 84:10T-11T Ap 24 '64
No place like home. il Time 84:11-18 Jl 31 '64
Notes and comment. New Yorker 39:23-4 Je 15 '63
Peace corps in Harlem. il Ebony 18:49-50+ Ag '63
People vs. politicians: defeat in Harlem. W. Klein. Nation 199:27-9 Jl 27 '64; Reply. W. M. Young, jr. 199:inside cover S 7 '64
Rent strike in Harlem. il Ebony 19:112-14+ Ap '64
Report from a Spanish Harlem fortress. R. Hammer. il N Y Times Mag p22+ Ja 5 '64
School library program for children in a depressed area; Negro and Puerto Rican. H. B. Brown and E. D. Sinnette. bibliog il ALA Bul 58:643-7 Jl '64
Speaking out; don't blame the ghetto. D. B. Lee. Sat Eve Post 237:8+ D 5 '64
Stranger in New York. V. S. Pritchett. il Holiday 36:50-3+ Ag '64
Subject: Spanish Harlem; photographs. H. Maristany. N Y Times Mag p82+ O 20 '63
Tryout in Harlem. M. Kempton. New Repub 148:11-13 F 23 '63; Reply. D. L. Hackett. 148:38 Ap 13 '63
Two faces of Harlem. il Look 28:22-6 Jl 28 '64
White man in Harlem. G. Talese. Esquire 62: 123 S '64
Why Harlem is angry. il N Y Times Mag p6-7 Jl 14 '63

Higher education, Board of

Prospective ruin of the city colleges. R. Kirk. Nat R 16:157 F 25 '64

Historic houses, etc.

Jan Martense Schenck house in the Brooklyn museum. M. D. Schwartz. il Antiques 85: 421-8 Ap '64
New York's new buildings and historic houses. il House & Gard 125:8+ F '64
Plea to curb the bulldozer; city's landmarks. W. N. Seymour, jr. il N Y Times Mag p80-1+ O 13 '63
Saving historic structures. Nat Parks Mag 38:15 N '64

History

Making of a city. V. S. Pritchett. il Holiday 36:66-9+ S '64
New York world's fair; celebrating a 300th birthday. il Sr Schol 84:5 Ap 3 '64
New York's great fire that wasn't. N. Brandt. N Y Times Mag p 109-10+ N 22 '64
See also
Draft riots, 1863

Hospitals

Code 99! calls a hospital to battle against death; St Vincent's hospital team; with editorial comment. il Life 56:3, 52B-61 F 28 '64
One long night in a baby hospital; Babies hospital in New York city. E. M. Wylie. il Good H 158:84-9+ Je '64
See also
New York (city)—Bellevue hospital

Hotels, restaurants, etc.

Architecture; New York Hilton. W. McQuade. Nation 197:20 Jl 6 '63
Art collection commissioned for New York Hilton. il Arch Rec 133:106 F '63
Art for the New York Hilton. B. H. Friedman. il Craft Horiz 23:8-15+ Jl '63
At Leone's they wait in line, and love it. il Bsns W p40-3 D 26 '64
Court orders hotel to allow publisher's reception; 40th anniversary of International publishers at the Statler Hilton hotel in New York. Pub W 187:275-6 Ja 25 '65
Crane, masters, Wolfe, etc. slept here; Chelsea hotel. E. Dundy. il Esquire 62:100-3+ O '64
Critic along the escoffier circuit. C. Claiborne. il N Y Times Mag p 12-13+ S 1 '63
Dial D for dinner. M. Kaytor. il Look 27:48-9 Mr 26 '63
Dining in/out with Esquire; Chez Vito. il Esquire 59:52A-52B F '63
Fun places. Vogue 143:80-1+ F 1 '64
Gain for Rayne; Manhattan's Savoy Plaza hotel to be replaced by G.M. office building. il Time 84:82 Ag 28 '64
Goings on about town. See issues of New Yorker
Grand hotel, new version; New York Hilton. il Arch Rec 134:153-60 N '63
Les hangouts; an insider's tour of the nouveau celebrity haunts. L. Smith. il Esquire 60:140-1 N '63
Hilton opening. New Yorker 39:20-2 Jl 6 '63
Inns and outs. il Newsweek 64:72 Jl 6 '64

NEW YORK (city)—Hotels, restaurants, etc. —*Continued*
International chef; Room III at Fusco's. il Travel 119:4 F '63
Kismet in New York; new Hilton. il Newsweek 62:54-5 Jl 8 '63
Leopard. C. H. McBride. il Esquire 62:130-1 S '64
Music palace; Ansonia hotel. M. J. Matz. il Opera N 27:30-3 F 9 '63
New rooms; motor inns and motor hotels. New Yorker 39:39-40 O 5 '63
New York's Spanish restaurants. P. S. Feibleman. il Holiday 34:104-5+ D '63
Old-fashioned Roman Christmas; Forum of the twelve Caesars restaurant. il Esquire 60:228-31 D '63
Personal business; dining in Manhattan. Bsns W p85-6 D 28 '63
Place downstairs; Artist & writers' club. il Time 81:65-6 My 3 '63
Profiles; Restaurant associates, inc. G. T. Hellman. il New Yorker 40:59-60+ O 17 '6.
Quest for the best hotel in the world. J. Wechsberg. il N Y Times Mag p97+ Ap 7 '63
Record cabinet; lady disc jockey for L'interdit, at Hotel Gotham. New Yorker 39:42-3 O 5 '63
Reporter at large; concerning Hotel Dixie and Times square. A. J. Liebling. New Yorker 39:95-8+ Ja 11 '64
Room with ghost $4 and up; madcap Chelsea. M. Smith. il Life 57:134-6+ S 18 '64
Self-help; Tad's steaks, inc. New Yorker 39:24-6 F 23 '63
Sí, it's Trader Vic. il Newsweek 64:83 N 30 '64
Sidewalk cafés. New Yorker 40:30-2 Je 13 '64
Special list of New York restaurants for visitors to the World's fair. Holiday 36:74+ Jl '64
Talent scout; Hickory house. New Yorker 39:34 Mr 9 '63
Velvet New York. F. Morton. il Holiday 36:52-65+ N '64
Waiter! the story of a man who is eating his way through 5,000 New York restaurants in alphabetical order. E. G. Love. il Sat Eve Post 237:42+ My 23 '64
When you come to the fair, be sure to eat in New York's inimitable restaurants. House & Gard 125:35-6+ My '64
Where the boys are not; Barbizon hotel. N. Robertson. il Sat Eve Post 236:28-33 O 19 '63
Where the king of the world goes; Jilly's. D. Newman. il Esquire 61:120-1+ Ap '64
Word for New York is bush. C. McCabe. il Sports Illus 21:56-8+ Ag 3 '64
See also
Night clubs

Housing

Biography of a tenement; from pasture to squalor. P. S. McGhee. il Nation 198:293-6 Mr 23 '64
Book focuses Republican attention on the slums; Let in the sun, by W. Klein. Pub W 186:45 N 9 '64
High life on upper Fifth. il Newsweek 61:77 My 20 '63
Instant neighborhoods. L. Mothner. il Look 27:41-3 Mr 26 '63
Let in the sun, by W. Klein. Review
Reporter 31:54+ O 22 '64. C. W. Griffin, jr
New patterns for city housing; competition for scheme in East Harlem. A. L. Huxtable. il N Y Times Mag p 12-13 Ag 25 '63
Notes and comment; fifteen-story-and-penthouse building on site of Myron C. Taylor mansion. New Yorker 39:15 Ag 24 '63
Quality co-op in Manhattan; Butterfield house. il Arch Forum 118:86-9 Ap '63
Rent strike; concerning Community council on housing. New Yorker 39:19-20 Ja 25 '64
Rent strike; in Harlem. il Newsweek 62:17-18 D 30 '63
Right not to pay; Harlem's growing rent-strike. Newsweek 63:24-5 Ja 13 '64
Ruberoid competition gives New York ideas for urban renewal. il Arch Rec 134:14-15 O '63
Single-loaded corridor for good outlook. il Arch Rec 136:124-5 Ag '64
$25,000 Ruberoid competition uses Manhattan urban renewal project. Arch Rec 133:23 F '63
Vest-pocket renewal holds new hope for the elderly. il Am City 79:105 My '64
War against the rats. Nation 198:63 Ja 20 '64
We moved to the worst block in town; West Side urban renewal plan. P. Mann. il Redbook 122:62-3+ N '63

Immigrants

See New York (city)—Foreign population

Industries

Buying for a boom; buyers on spree in New York's garment center. il Bsns W p30-1 Je 20 '64
Headquarters stay in asphalt jungle. il Bsns W p74+ N 30 '63
New York tops out its building boom. il Bsns W p34+ Ag 29 '64
Piracy on 7th ave. J. Poling. il Sat Eve Post 236:28-34 S 21 '63
Where hats are made. M. Fischer. il Sat Eve Post 236:64-7 Ap 6 '63

Intellectual life

92nd street's 90th. il Time 83:76 Ap 10 '64

Labor and laboring classes

City sets its own minimum wage. U S News 57:78 Jl 27 '64

Libraries

Libraries in London and New York. J. Hill. Sr Schol 85:25T O 7 '64
Library information resources and needs, subject of study in New York city. Library J 88:4178 N 1 '63
New hope for mobbed libraries. Wilson Lib Bul 38:521 Mr '64; Correction. 38:736 My '64
New York city library study initiated. Pub W 184:29-30 O 21 '63
Survey of reference resources recommends NYC library authority. Library J 89:823-4 F 15 '64
See also
Brooklyn public library
New York public library
Pierpont Morgan library
Queens Borough public library
Walter Hampden memorial library

Lincoln Center for the performing arts

See Lincoln Center for the performing arts, New York

Madison Square Garden

Garden loses on points. Sports Illus 19:5 Ag 26 '63
Raising a new Garden; air space over Penn station. il Bsns W p 142 F 23 '63

Maps

Mademoiselle's own New York. Mlle 58:129-32 Ap '64
New York city map launches United States Atlas map series; with fairgoers' guide to New York. R. E. McAleer. il Nat Geog Mag 126:108-11, sup(folded map) Jl '64

Markets

Fulton fish market; with photographs by L. Bernstein. Natur Hist 73:26-9 D '64
Next mayor of New York? M. K. Sanders. Harper 226:33-41 F '63

Medical and health centers

See also
New York university—Medical center

Metropolitan district

Western gateway to New York; portfolio. Fortune 67:122-30 My '63

Metropolitan museum of art

See Metropolitan museum of art

Missions

See also
East Harlem Protestant parish

Moral conditions

Mayor Wagner appoints antipornograhy commission. Pub W 186:23-4 Ag 17 '64
See also
New York (city)—Crime

Music

Athaliah and Semiramide. F. Merkling. Opera N 28:33 Ap 4 '64
Chamber music in New York (cont) il Mus Am 83:191+ Ja; 32-4 F; 37-40 Mr; 38-43 Ap; 37-40 My; 30-1 Je '63
Come to the fair. A. M. Lingg. il Opera N 28:8-14 Ap 4 '64
Compact model; T. Dunn and his Festival orchestra. il Newsweek 64:102 O 12 '64
Doing the noble thing badly; opening of New York philharmonic Promenades series. il Time 83:44 My 29 '64
Don Pablo; Casals conducts Haydn's Creation. il Newsweek 63:85 Je 29 '64

NEW YORK (city)—Music—*Continued*
Dvorak revived; Musica aeterna's Requiem. C. J. McNaspy. America 110:351-2 Mr 14 '64
Editor's choice. il Mus Am 83:22-3 F; 28-9 Mr; 26-30 Ap; 20-2 My; 18-19 Je; 24 Jl '63
Far-out at the Philharmonic. il Time 83:79-80 F 14 '64
Feast of astonishments; New York festival of the avant garde. F. Bowers. Nation 199:172-5 S 28 '64
Herod and Herodiade. F. Merkling. il Opera N 28:34 F 1 '64
Jewess and empress. F. Merkling. Opera N 28:28 My 2 '64
Land of schmaltz; Franz Lehár's Land of smiles and Emmerich Kálmán's Countess Maritza. J. W. Freeman. il Opera N 27:27-8 My 4 '63
Lewisohn stadium; 1963 Stadium season. J. Ardoin and R. Jacobson. Mus Am 83:5-7 Ag '63
Met moves uptown; future of summer concerts given at Lewisohn stadium. Mus Am 84:7 S '64
Music; new-music performance in New York by young virtuosos. B. Boretz. Nation 198: 279-80 Mr 16 '64
Music to my ears. I. Kolodin. See issues of Saturday review
Musical events. W. Sargeant. See issues of New Yorker
New mood for the new Met. I. Kolodin. il Sat R 47:45-7+ Ja 25 '64; Discussion. 47: 50-1 F 15; 62-4 F 29 '64
New works and new performances. B. Boretz. Nation 198:279-80, 380-1+ Mr 16, Ap 13 '64
New York midsummer. B. Hastings; E. Del Gaudio; R. D. Daniels. Opera N 28:28-9 N 16 '63
New York music scene. J. S. Harrison. il Mus Am 83:24-9 N; 178+ D '63; 84:30-6 Ja; 22-6 F; 24-30 Mr; 34-41 Ap; 28-35 My; 32-7 Jl '64
New York novelties. il Opera N 29:24-5 S 26 '64
New York scene. M. Lelash. Opera N 29:30 N 14 '64
Notes from our correspondents. S. Fleming. il Hi Fi 14:22+ My; 12+ Jl; 51+ O; 24+ N '64; 15:22+ Ja '65
Opera in New York. See issues of Musical America
Orchestral variations. B. Boretz. Nation 199: 342-4 N 9 '64
Orchestras in New York. See issues of Musical America
Post-season New York. O. Eaton. il Opera N 28:24-5 S 28 '63
Promenade concerts. R. Jacobson. Mus Am 83:28-9 Jl '63
Recitals in New York. See issues of Musical America
Reviews. il Mus Am 84:27-32 F; 34-45 S '64
Reviews: chamber music. il Mus Am 83:41 N; 264-6 D '63; 84:54 Ja; 39-42 F; 44-6 Mr; 57-9 Ap; 47-9 My; 46-8 Jl; 50-2 O; 39-40 N; 258 D '64
Reviews: opera at the Metropolitan (title varies) il Mus Am 83:31-2 N; 250+ D '63; 84:37-40 Ja; 31-2 Mr; 42-5 Ap; 36 My; 38 Jl; 22-4 N; 108-10 D '64
Reviews: orchestras. il Mus Am 83:32-3 N; 252+ D '63; 84:40-8 Ja; 32-7 Mr; 46-52 Ap; 38-42 My; 41-6 Jl; 48 O; 28-36 N; 119-20+ D '64
Reviews: recitals. il Mus Am 83:37-40 N; 258+ D '63; 84:48-54 Ja; 32-9 F; 37-44 Mr; 52-7 Ap; 42-7 My; 48-50 O; 36-9 N; 182+ D '64
Two kinds of French; Spontini's Vestale and Massenet's Navarraise. F. Merkling. Opera N 27:34 F 16 '63
Winter in New York. A. M. Lingg; M. Lelash; F. Merkling. il Opera N 29:33-4 Ja 30 '65
World's fair musical events. il Mus Am 84: 30-1 Ap '64
See also
Lincoln Center for the performing arts, New York
Manhattan opera company
Metropolitan opera company
New York city center of music and drama
New York city opera company
New York pro musica antiqua (organization)
Philharmonic-symphony society of New York

Negroes

Beyond the melting pot, by N. Glazer and D. P. Moynihan. Review
U S News il 55:100 S 30 '63
Black Jews of Harlem, by H. Brotz. Review
Nation 198:662-3 Je 29 '64. A. Kohlman
Blood brotherhood in Harlem? T. R. Brooks. Commonweal 80:282-3 My 29 '64
Harlem sketchbook: white man, walk easy. R. Kahn. il Sat Eve Post 237:26-8+ Je 13 '64
Is it Communist-backed guerrilla warfare in New York? il U S News 57:25 Ag 3 '64
Jitters; wave of terror puts police on overtime. il Newsweek 63:35-6 Je 15 '64
Negro leader talks tough, target: Harlem hoodlums. R. Wilkins. U S News 57:14 Jl 6 '64
New tactic in racial picketing: the chain-in. il U S News 55:6 Ag 5 '63
New York city in trouble. il U S News 56: 72-7 Je 8; 43-5 Je 15 '64
Now: a court ruling in defense of the neighborhood school. U S News 55:43 S 23 '63
Pickets; Downstate medical center hospital, in Brooklyn. New Yorker 39:18-19 Ag 10 '63
Racial crisis ahead for neighborhood schools. il U S News 55:46-8 Jl 8 '63
Report of a Harlem gang that preys on whites. U S News 56:10 My 18 '64
Terror on the trains. il Time 83:38-9 Je 12 '64
This little light; incidents after passage of civil rights bill. P. De Lissovoy. il Nation 199:486-90 D 21 '64
Who shall judge a policeman? G. Samuels. il N Y Times Mag p8+ Ag 2 '64
See also
Queens, N.Y.—Negroes

Newspapers

After a three-month shutdown, what striking printers got. U S News 54:98 Mr 18 '63
After the strike; time for reflection; with editorial comment. il Bsns W p72, 108 Ap 6 '63
And the presses roll. Nat R 14:221+ Mr 26 '63
Automation and the news strike. R. Severo. il Reporter 28:29-30+ Mr 14 '63
Dilemma of a guild reporter. M. Bracker; discussion. Reporter 28:10+ F 14 '63
Glad to be back. il Time 81:58+ Ap 12 '63
Living with the scars. Time 81:57 My 24 '63
New look at New York newspaper strike. il U S News 54:50-2 Mr 4 '63
New York finds it can live without papers. Bsns W p34 Mr 2 '63
New York press: the hard sell. J. Ludwig. il Holiday 36:104+ Jl '64
Notes and comment. New Yorker 38:23 F 9 '63
Road back; effects of strike. Time 82:58 S 13 '63
Still no news in New York. Bsns W p24-5 F 16 '63
TV is no substitute. il Time 82:70 D 13 '63
Wayward press. A. J. Liebling. New Yorker 39:143-52 Ap 13 '63
See also
National enquirer
New York herald tribune
New York mirror
New York post
New York times

Parks and playgrounds

Fourteen laps; bicycle path in Central park. New Yorker 40:46-7 S 19 '64
Friend of Central park. New Yorker 39:34-5 Mr 9 '63
He paints with lakes and wooded slopes; landscape architecture of Central park. J. S. Martin. il Am Heritage 15:14-19+ O '64
Needed: oases in the asphalt desert. E. J. Kahn. il N Y Times Mag p54-5+ My 26 '63
Out of the sandbox. il Newsweek 63:66 F 17 '64
Parks and recreation showcase at the World's fair. S. Constable. il Recreation 57:267-9 Je '64
Park cafe dispute reaches N.Y. court. il Arch Forum 119:7-8 Jl '63
Portrait of a place; Central park. E. Bubley. il U S Camera 26:58-61 Mr '63
Reporter at large; dancers in May: P.S. 31 in Park fête in Central park. L. Ross. il New Yorker 40:35-8+ Jl 18 '64
See also
New York (city)—Washington square
New York zoological park
Park association of New York city, incorporated

Police

Car 54 where are you? problem of slow police service. il Time 83:61 My 8 '64
Chief policeman talks about his beat. R. W. Apple, jr. il N Y Times Mag p 10+ Je 21 '64

NEW YORK (city)—Police—*Continued*
Cops with guns; stop or I'll shoot. L. Patterson. New Repub 150:8-9 Mr 14 '64; Discussion. 150:37-8 Mr 28; 30 Ap 25 '64
How cops behave in Harlem. M. Kempton. New Repub 151:7-8 Ag 22 '64
I don't think the cop is my friend. G. Samuels. il N Y Times Mag p28+ Mr 29 '64
Kids and cops. B. W. Wyden. il N Y Times Mag p56-7+ F 23 '64
My night as a police officer. T. Gallagher. il Read Digest 82:173-4+ Je '63
Police rules in New York city. il U S News 57:25 Ag 10 '64
Postmortem; grand jury report on killing of James Powell. Newsweek 64:26+ S 14 '64
Reporter at large; burglary. S. Black. il New Yorker 39:63-4+ D 7; 89-91+ D 14 '63
Tito and the cops. il Newsweek 62:25-6 N 4 '63
Unanimous decision; police lieut. T. Gilligan not criminally liable for James Powell's death. il Time 84:25-6 S 11 '64
Who shall judge a policeman? G. Samuels. il N Y Times Mag p8+ Ag 2 '64
See also
Helicopters in police work

Politics and government

And the big name is Wagner; Democratic primary. il Time 83:36-7 Je 12 '64
Bad night for bosses. il Newsweek 63:29-30 Je 15 '64
Destiny's tot; seventeenth congressional district, Manhattan. R. G. Smith. il Nat R 16: 861-2 O 6 '64
Jew in sheik's clothing? il Time 83:23 My 22 '64
Man who rode the tiger: the life and times of Judge Samuel Seabury, by H. Mitgang. Review
Am Heritage 14:100-1 Je '63
Sat R 46:43 Mr 30 '63. R. A. Low
New York city, can it be governed? B. Carter. il Reporter 30:42-5 Ja 30 '64; Discussion. 30:8+ F 27 '64
New York politics. M. Kempton. New Repub 152:8-10 Ja 23 '65
New York politics & the liberal party. B. Rosenberg. Commentary 37:69-75 F '64; Discussion. 38:11 Jl '64
New York preliminaries. M. Kempton. New Repub 148:5-6 Je 8 '63; Reply. L. W. Levine. 149:30-1 Jl 13 '63
New York scandal. C. Morrison. il Look 27: 103-4+ Mr 26 '63
New York: who won? il Newsweek 62:32 S 16 '63
Newly emerging peoples; Democratic politics in New York. Reporter 29:20+ O 24 '63
Road back. il Newsweek 62:27 S 2 '63
Tempest in a glass tea; Democratic congressional nomination. il Newsweek 63:31 My 25 '64
See also
New York (city)—Elections
Tammany Hall

Public buildings

Manhattan malady. il Time 81:64 My 24 '63

Public health

Metropolitan medical economics. N. K. Piore. il Sci Am 212:19-27 bibliog(p 134) Ja '65

Radio City music hall

Backstage: Christmas show. New Yorker 40: 22-3 D 26 '64
Unchangeable: thirtieth anniversary. New Yorker 39:19-20 Ag 3 '63
Unsinkable Molly green; alltime Music hall record for box-office gross. Time 84:76 S 18 '64

Rapid transit

Air-conditioned transit fleet; replacing antiquated fleet of the old Hudson and Manhattan railroad. il Am City 79:138 O '64
See also
New York (city)—Subways

Recreation

Behind the times; concerning report by the Community council of Greater New York. Recreation 56:324 S '63
Dateline New York. M. Davis. il Travel 120:12-13 S '63
See also
New York (city)—Parks and playgrounds

Religious institutions and affairs

News of the Christian world (cont) Christian Cent 80:308, 380+, 438, 810-12, 834-6, 1220, 1344, 1562; 81:154, 246, 312, 382, 467-8, 714-16, 892, 1070, 1445-6, 1541-2; 82:124-6 Mr 6, 20, Ap 3, Je 19-26, O 2, 30, D 11 '63, Ja 29, F 19, Mr 4, 18, Ap 8, My 27, Jl 8, Ag 26, N 18, D 9 '64, Ja 27 '65
See also
New York (city)—Churches

Restaurants

See New York (city)—Hotels, restaurants, etc.

Riots

Bedford-Stuyvesant. F. C. Shapiro. New Yorker 40:23-6 Ag 1 '64
Black and white; Harlem: killers, go home. G. Jacobson. New Repub 151:14-16 Ag 8 '64
Harlem: hatred in the streets. il Newsweek 64:16-20 Ag 3 '64
Harlem's long hot summer begins. il Life 57:14-23 Jl 31 '64
New York city deep in trouble; Harlem and Brooklyn's Bedford-Stuyvesant district. il U S News 57:22-6 Ag 3 '64
Racial cauldron boils over. Christian Cent 81:980 Ag 5 '64
Racial violence. Commonweal 80:528 Ag 7 '64
Short fuse; shooting of James Powell. Newsweek 64:34 Jl 27 '64
When night falls. il Time 84:10-11 Jl 31 '64
Who pays for riots? il Time 84:55 Ag 7 '64
Worse than Mississippi? riot after killing of Negro youth by off-duty policeman. il Time 84:29 Jl 24 '64

Sanitary affairs

If it works in New York city. F. J. Lucia. il Am City 78:96-8 D '63; 79:100-2 Ja '64
Little gates built big; sluice gates at New York city's Jamaica pollution-control project. il Am City 79:118 Ap '64

Sanitation, Department of

Golden yellow for safety; refuse-collection trucks. F. J. Lucia. il Am City 78:27 Mr '63

School board

See New York (city)—Education, Board of

Schools

See New York (city)—Education

Shops

See New York (city)—Stores

Social conditions

Bowery bums' rush. P. S. McGhee. il Nation 198:483-5 My 11 '64
City side; homosexuality in New York. Newsweek 62:42 D 30 '63
Information; Mayor's information center, mobile unit. New Yorker 39:41-2 N 16 '63
Report from a Spanish Harlem fortress. R. Hammer. il N Y Times Mag p22+ Ja 5 '64
Success game; concerning the report, Life stress and mental health, by Thomas S. Langner and others. Newsweek 62:88 D 2 '63
Vested interest in poverty. Nation 199:449 D 14 '64
Victims of welfare. S. Castan. il Look 27: 68-71 Mr 26 '63
See also
New York (city)—Harlem

Social life and customs

Cocktail party. J. T. Stark. il Look 27:45-6 Mr 26 '63
Elbowing in; Entrée unlimited, service agency. Newsweek 65:54 Ja 18 '65
Irish of New York. D. P. Moynihan. Commentary 36:93-107 Ag '63; Discussion. 37: 18 Ja '64
Lower East Side story. il Newsweek 65:36-7 Ja 4 '65
Party roundup. New Yorker 39:44-7 O 12 '63
Velvet New York. F. Morton. il Holiday 36: 52-65+ N '64
See also
Night clubs

Social work

See also
East Side house settlement, incorporated
Mobilization for youth, incorporated
New York (city)—Welfare, Department of

Stations

Notes and comment; transforming of Pennsylvania station. New Yorker 39:45 N 23 '63

NEW YORK (city)—Stations—*Continued*
Pennsylvania station's last stand. il Arch Forum 118:11 F '63
Raising a new Garden; air space over Penn station. il Bsns W p 142 F 23 '63
Ringer; New Year's eve: First annual bell ringer ball for mental health in Grand Central station. New Yorker 39:24-5 Ja 11 '64

Statistics

Gee whiz. Newsweek 63:90 Mr 16 '64
Statistics, N.Y. G. H. Glueck. il N Y Times Mag p29+ Je 23 '63

Stock exchange

See Stock exchange—New York (city)

Stores

Bergdorf way. il Newsweek 61:73 F 11 '63
Bloomingdale's Bloomingdale. New Yorker 40: 47-8 N 7 '64
Bonwit's lady boss. Time 85:68 Ja 22 '65
Elder craftsmen shop. M. Lyon. il Craft Horiz 24:22+ N '64
Emigrating to America; Irish merchandise at Lord & Taylor. il Time 82:108 O 11 '63
Female bearcat named Stutz; of Henri Bendel. S. J. Daly. il Sat Eve Post 236: 60-2 Ap 13 '63
Girl's best friend; diamond-switching theft at Winston's and Tiffany's. Newsweek 65: 32 Ja 25 '65
Les hangouts; an insider's tour of the nouveau celebrity haunts. L. Smith. il Esquire 60:140-1 N '63
How to spend your excess money in New York; stroll along Fifth avenue. A. Chamberlin. il Sat Eve Post 237:88+ My 23 '64
Lady in charge; new president of Bonwit Teller. Newsweek 65:71 Ja 25 '65
New store; D/R international. New Yorker 39:26 D 28 '63
New York's incomparable shops. House & Gard 125:58+ Mr '64
Parents' magazine buys F. A. O. Schwarz toy store. Pub W 184:38 S 23 '63
Split-level showcase in Manhattan; Design research, inc. il Arch Forum 120:118-21 Ap '64
Toyland dresses up its lures; F.A.O. Schwarz. Bsns W p78 Mr 7 '64
See also
Abercrombie and Fitch company
Macy, R. H. and company
Ohrbach's, incorporated

Street traffic

Barnes stops, looks, and tells. H. A. Barnes. il N Y Times Mag p21+ Ag 18 '63
Facts and fallacies of traffic engineering; interview. H. A. Barnes. il Am City 78: 114-17 Je '63
Keep 'em rolling to the final jam. P. O'Neil. il Life 57:98-100+ N 13 '64
Steel strapping cuts sign-mounting costs. H. A. Barnes. il Am City 79:137 Ap '64

Streets

Bowery bums' rush. P. S. McGhee. il Nation 198:483-5 My 11 '64
Dig they must, find they what? subterranean jungle of tubes, pipes, wires and cables. F. J. Cook. il N Y Times Mag p 19+ My 19 '63
How to spend your excess money in New York; stroll along Fifth avenue. A. Chamberlin. il Sat Eve Post 237:88+ My 23 '64
Mess; Macdougal street. New Yorker 39:22-3 Ag 31 '63
Notes and comment; buckling of Forty-second street. New Yorker 40:39 My 16 '64
Time on Fifth avenue. New Yorker 39:44-5 Mr 16 '63

Subways

Budd pulls a switch; bid on stainless steel subway cars. il Bsns W p26 Jl 26 '63
New York city in trouble: another chapter. il U S News 56:43-5 Je 15 '64
Subway in the balance; proposed 64th street route. Newsweek 63:57 Mr 9 '64
Subway saga; re: New York's sixty-year underground struggle. S. D. Smith. il N Y Times Mag p48+ N 8 '64
Subway stations of the cross. C. B. Egan. America 110:367-9 Mr 21 '64
Subways and science; two N.Y. institutions consider meaning of coexistence in crowded Manhattan. E. Langer. il Science 143:789-90 F 21 '64
Underground outing; last run of antique IRT cars at annual trip of Electric railroaders association. il New Yorker 40:48-50 N 7 '64

Maps

Baghdad on the subway. Sr Schol 84:15T Ap 3 '64

Taxation

Everything's up, up, up to date; opposition to sales tax. il Time 81:25 Ap 26 '63
Fighting the tax; city sales tax. New Yorker 39:34-5 Ap 27 '63
Passed; city sales tax. New Yorker 39:31-2 My 11 '63

Theater

A B B of Alan Schneider; Albee, Beckett and Brecht. A. Levy. il N Y Times Mag p27+ O 20 '63
Actor's friend; new rage for repertory. il Newsweek 63:70 Mr 23 '64
After the fall; Manhattan's Lincoln Center repertory theater. il Time 84:36 D 25 '64
Artists and bureaucrats; closing of the Living theater. R. Brustein. New Repub 149: 36+ N 2 '63
Best and brightest season in a decade. T. Prideaux. il Life 55:30-9 N 22 '63
Birds, beasts, and Bach; Originale by Karlheinz Stockhausen. il Newsweek 64:80 S 21 '64
Blood knot, the Habimah, But for whom Charlie. H. Clurman and R. Hatch. Nation 198:334-6 Mr 30 '64
Broadway as a crazy quilt. R. A. Duprey. Cath World 197:271-2 Jl '63
Broadway disaster; reasons why. U S News 54:8 Je 3 '63
Broadway: early autumn. D. Hering. il Dance Mag 37:26 N '63
Broadway: early spring. D. Hering. il Dance Mag 38:28-9+ Je '64
Broadway fights the doldrums. il Bsns W p30-1 O 3 '64
Broadway: late winter. D. Hering. il Dance Mag 38:22-4 Mr '64
Broadway: mid-autumn. D. Hering. il Dance Mag 37:22-3 D '63
Broadway: midsummer. D. Hering. Dance Mag 38:20-1 S '64
Broadway: midwinter. D. Hering. il Dance Mag 38:22-3 F '64
Broadway on ice; the obsolete industry. R. Hector. il Nation 198:267-9 Mr 16 '64
Broadway: pre-spring. D. Hering. il Dance Mag 38:26-7+ Ap '64
Broadway': summer's end. D. Hering; M. Marks. il Dance Mag 38:22+ O '64
Broadway's hottest producers. il Bsns W p90-1 F 2 '63
Center that set off a tempest; New York's Lincoln center. T. Prideaux. il Life 58:42-3+ Ja 22 '65
Dateline New York. M. Davis. il Travel 120:12-13 S '63
Dear me, the sky is falling; losses on Broadway. Time 81:50 Je 7 '63
Don't they know it's a turkey? E. Kendall. il N Y Times Mag p27+ Ap 14 '63
Drama beyond the drama: first-night vigil. A. Levy. il N Y Times Mag p 12+ D 22 '63
Epitaph for Lincoln Center. R. Gilman. Commonweal 80:89-91 Ap 10 '64
Fall in the theater; Broadway season. H. Hewes. Sat R 47:26 S 12 '64
From Anouilh to Zenda. il Newsweek 62:61 S 30 '63
Going through the motions. T. F. Driver. Reporter 29:53 N 21 '63
Great void; New York theater during newspaper strike. Theatre Arts 47:8 F '63
Hard life of an angel. il Fortune 70:96+ N '64
How to treat the Broadway malady of 1963. A. Bermel. bibliog f Harper 227:56-62 D '63
Instant critics; TV drama critics. il Newsweek 65:61 Ja 25 '65
Integrated thought; integrated troupe, the Living premise in living color. New Yorker 39:22-3 Je 22 '63
Ironic justice; action of the Internal revenue service against off-Broadway's Living theatre. Nation 197:290 N 9 '63
Line-up; coming Broadway season. il Time 84:51+ Ag 28 '64
Melodrama on Broadway; our secret lives are showing. R. Hatch. Horizon 5:106-8 My '63
More than 1,001 first nights. J. M. Brown. il Sat R 47:46-8 Ag 29 '64
Muddy track at Lincoln Center; Repertory theater. R. Brustein. New Repub 151:26-7 D 26 '64
New and hopeful role for repertory; plans for Vivian Beaumont theater at Lincoln Center. T. Guthrie. il N Y Times Mag p32-3+ N 10 '63
New deal for the arts; Living theater. P. Goodman. Commentary 37:68-71 Ja '64

NEW YORK (city)—Theater—*Continued*
New producer; off Broadway revival, Boys from Syracuse. New Yorker 39:16-18 Ag 10 '63
New season. H. Hewes. Sat R 46:46 S 14 '63
New season. il Time 82:50-1 Ag 30 '63
New season, New York. L. Harris. il Theatre Arts 47:11-15+ O '63
Now angels wing along the Rialto; investors in Broadway productions. J. Keating. il N Y Times Mag p28+ D 8 '63
Off-Broadway, by halves. il Time 83:70-1 Ja 3 '64
Off-Broadway girls. G. Buckman. il Mlle 58:132-3+ N '63
Off-Broadway: midwinter. D. Hering. il Dance Mag 38:48-9 Ja '64
Off-Broadway reckoning. il Time 81:63-4 F 15 '63
Off Broadway sings an old refrain. il N Y Times Mag p 104+ My 5 '63
Old Glory. H. Clurman. Nation 199:390-1 N 23 '64
Padlock on the Living theatre. R. Gilman. Commonweal 79:182 N 8 '63
Personal business. Bsns W p 105 Ja 19 '63
Personal business; Broadway theatrical season. Bsns W p 185 S 14 '63
Polling the critics; top achievements of the 1962-63 Broadway season. Sat R 46:17 Jl 13 '63
Rep trap. Newsweek 63:81 Ap 20 '64
Reviewer's notebook; the recent season. T. Lewis. America 109:123 Ag 3 '63
Rise of rep. il Time 83:54-61 F 14 '64
Scalpers scalped. il Newsweek 62:46 D 23 '63
Season's reasons. L. Lerman. il Mlle 58:128-31 N '63
Stuffed bird at forty-eight sharp; Stockhausen's Originale at Manhattan's second annual Avant-garde festival. il Time 84:81 S 18 '64
Subsidized rubbish; Lincoln Center repertory company. R. Brustein. New Repub 150:34+ Ap 11 '64
TV's first-nighters: tape recording of The advocate. il Bsns W p 146+ O 19 '63
Temporary theatre, permanent example; new ANTA-Washington square theatre. E. F. Kook. il Sat R 47:30 F 22 '64
Theater of the undiscussable. W. Sheed. Commonweal 81:454-5 D 25 '64
Trouble with Broadway is; symposium. il N Y Times Mag p30+ Ja 19 '64
Two at the mark; ten running strong. il Newsweek 61:53 F 4 '63
Walk to that exit. B. Friel. Holiday 34:48+ N '63
Weep not for Broadway. A. Cantor. Theatre Arts 47:19-20 Jl '63
What keeps us going. R. Gilman. Commonweal 78:376 Je 28 '63
What's on this season. il Vogue 142:100-5 N 15 '63
See also
Lincoln Center for the performing arts, New York
Lincoln Center for the performing arts, New York—New York state theater
New York city center of music and drama
Theatre guild, incorporated

Anecdotes, facetiae, satire, etc.

Night they all saw, at last, what was happening. J. Wulp. Esquire 60:134+ N '63

Times square

Dreams of glory. il Bsns W p30-1 Je 8 '63
Old stage, new stars. il Bsns W p 132+ O 24 '64
Reporter at large; Hotel Dixie and Times square. A. J. Liebling. New Yorker 39:95-8+ Ja 11 '64

Traffic problem

See New York (city)—Street traffic

Transportation

See also
New York (city)—Subways

Views

See New York (city)—Description

Washington square

Message; meeting on remodelling Washington Square park. New Yorker 40:34-5 Je 6 '64
Notes and comment; plan for Square's rehabilitation. New Yorker 40:21 S 5 '64

Water supply

Fluoridation fight in N.Y; why the city decided to act; reprint. H. A. Rusk. Sci Digest 55:30-3 Ap '64
New York city may get water meters. Am City 79:17 F '64
New York drowns another valley. N. Perrin. il Harper 227:76-83 Ag '63

Welfare, Department of

Grim state of welfare. J. Horwitz. il Look 27:72+ Mr 26 '63

World trade center (proposed)

Architecture; tax abatement. W. McQuade. Nation 198:306-7 Mr 23 '64
Great port city planned for New York's Lower West side. il Arch Rec 135:188-9 Mr '64
New World trade center for Manhattan. il Arch Forum 120:5+ F '64
Onward & upward. il Time 83:46 Ja 24 '64
Skyscrapers. New Yorker 39:21-2 F 1 '64
Sorry, Empire state; World trade center, tallest building in the world. B. H. Frisch. il Sci Digest 55:85-9 Ap '64
Tallest steel bearing walls. il Arch Rec 135:194-6 My '64
Towers rise, records fall; World trade center. il Newsweek 63:59 F 3 '64
Towers that top them all. il Bsns W p29 Ja 25 '64
World's biggest skyscrapers have New York up in the air. il Arch Forum 120:118-21 Mr '64
Yama designs 110-story world trade center. il Arch Rec 135:14-15 F '64

Worlds fair, 1939-1940

Fair that was. F. Zachary. New Yorker 40:122+ Ap 11 '64
1939: now that was a World's fair! B. Brower. il Esquire 61:61-5+ Ap '64
What's new and what isn't. B. H. Frisch. il Sci Digest 55:20-4 Ap '64

Time capsule

See Civilization—Preservation of records

Worlds fair, 1964

ABC of World's fair wonders. Vogue 143:99+ Ja 15 '64
All's fair in Flushing Meadow; photographs by S. Falk. N Y Times Mag p54-5 Ap 28 '63
All's fair; rash of pranks by youthful fair employes. Newsweek 64:55-6 S 14 '64
Another; preview at Time & Life building. New Yorker 39:15 Ag 10 '63
As the Hucksters see us. W. Von Eckardt. New Repub 150:14-16 My 30 '64; Reply. W. B. Richland. 150:29-30 Je 20 '64
Atomic playground; Atomsville U.S.A. il Sci N L 85:386 Je 20 '64
Automated caveman gets a rear-end drive; Ford pavillion Magic skyway. il Pop Sci 184:91-2 Ja '64
Baby-sitter at the fair: Tivoli playground at the Danish pavilion; with report on the fair. G. Zimmermann. il Look 28:78-82+ Jl 28 '64
Billion-dollar fair takes shape. il U S News 55:47-9 D 30 '63
Books at the World's fair. il Pub W 185:50-6 Ja 6 '64
Camera guide to the New York world's fair. il Pop Phot 54:119-21 My '64
Can the World's fair make a '65 comeback? U S News 57:15 O 26 '64
Chamber of educational horrors? Hall of education. F. L. Redefer. Sat R 47:53 S 19 '64
City succumbs to fair fever. il Bsns W p 120+ Mr 21 '64
Cocoon for learning; Studysphere, on display in the Hall of education. il Sci Digest 56:48 N '64
Come to the fair. il Ladies Home J 81:105-7 Jl '64
Come to the fair. A. M. Lingg. il Opera N 28:8-14 Ap 4 '64
Come to the fair, and bring the kids. D. Siegel and L. D. Kirk. il Parents Mag 39:72-3+ Ap '64
Come to the fair; in N.Y. il Newsweek 61:82-3 Mr 11 '63
Coming: the most marvelous fair ever! I. Wolfert. il Read Digest 84:91-5 Ja '64
Coventry cross visits World's fair. Christian Cent 81:326 Mr 11 '64
Day at the fair; Library/USA. S. Havens and E. Moon. il Library J 89:3694-7 O 1 '64; Discussion. 89:4240+, 4452 N 1-15 '64
Demonstrating remote retrieval by computer at Library/USA. J. Becker. il ALA Bul 58:822-4 O '64
Display case for our culture. E. L. Long, jr. Christian Cent. 81:968-9 Jl 29 '64
Doing the fair with fourteen kids; the Rocks and their family. il Life 57:81-3 Jl 24 '64

NEW YORK (city)—Worlds fair, 1964—*Cont.*
Domes and hexagons; films at the fair. il Newsweek 63:97 Je 15 '64
Don't miss these great buildings. Pop Phot 54:126 My '64
Drop anchor at the fair. il Recreation 57:59 F '64
Eating at the fair, N.Y. G. Bradshaw. il Vogue 144:114-15 Jl '64
Eighteen-minute history of man; Travelers pavilion. il Sci Digest 55:22-3 My '64
Everything here is chaos; preliminary report on dance at the 1964 New York world's fair. N. Lansdale. il Dance Mag 38:22-5+ Je '64
Exodus East: New York world's fair, tips for campers and owners. D. B. Huyck. il Am For 70:34-7 F '64
Fair. New Yorker 40:35-9 My 2 '64
Fair. H. Sutton. il Sat R 47:41-2 Je 13; 24+ Je 20 '64
Fair enough; end of first season. il Newsweek 64:108+ O 26 '64
Fair: for $2 fee, a billion-dollar spectacle. il U S News 56:12 Ap 27 '64
Fair foursome from Japan; hostesses at Japanese pavilion. il Look 28:60+ S 22 '64
Fair hits and misses. Newsweek 63:79 Je 1 '64
Fair outlook. il Newsweek 63:68 Ap 20 '64
Fair sailing. B. Gold. il Motor B 113:110+ Ja '64
Fair share of trouble; fair's finances. il Time 85:73-4 Ja 29 '65
Fair takes shape. il Look 27:52-4 N 19 '63
Fair view of future. B. Tufty. il Sci N L 85: 234-5+ Ap 11 '64
Fair's till begins to jingle; $35-million advance sale tickets. Bsns W p34 Mr 7 '64
Family at the fair. S. Kohn. il Ladies Home J 81:108 Jl '64
Films at the fair. A. Knight. Sat R 47:26 Ag 15 '64
Films at the fair: dazzling range of cinematic art and techniques. H. V. Fondiller. il Pop Phot 55:88-91+ Ag '64
Final push for New York fair. Bsns W p31 Ap 27 '63
Five-year-old at the fair; Caroline Hadley. H. Ehrlich. il Look 28:64-8 S 8 '64
Flushing frolic. D. Powills. il Hobbies 69: 118-19 Ap '64
For a quick visit to the fair. il Sunset 133:8 O '64
For a three-in-one vacation this year see, the World's fair, New York city, New York state. J. R. Borcherding. il Suc Farm 62: 44-5 Jl '64
For everybody from everywhere. il Newsweek 63:60-5 Ap 27 '64
Free for all at the fair. M. Cohen. il Redbook 123:58-9+ Je '64
Froslid's protest; concerning NY world's fair 64 on license plates. New Yorker 39:28 F 8 '64
Fun in New York. il Time 83:40-1 My 1 '64
Gardener's guide to the New York world's fair. B. Black. il Horticulture 42:12+ My '64
Getting there is half the fun; dinosaur models for Sinclair's New York world's fair exhibit. H. B. Comstock. il Pop Sci 183:50-3 S '63
Glorious nightmare. P. Lyon. il Holiday 36: 48-67 Jl '64
Golden grin. R. Hughes. il Nation 199:189-91 O 5 '64
Great fair; photographs. J. Zimmerman. Sat Eve Post 237:26-35 My 23 '64
Great French recipe, for the Folies, P. E. Schneider. il N Y Times Mag p 18+ Ap 28 '63
Hard-sell fair. C. G. Hayden. il Nation 197: 275-8 N 2 '63
He thumps the tub for the fair. il Bsns W p 120-2+ Ja 25 '64
Heliport quandary. W. J. Kendall. il Flying 74:26-9+ F '64
Hell drivers; dedication of Auto thrill stadium and sample performance. New Yorker 39: 43 N 9 '63
Ho hum, come to the fair. M. Mayer. Esquire 60:117+ O '63
Hollywood pavilion. New Yorker 39:26-7 D 28 '63
How the Fair did: more plus than minus. il Bsns W p39 S 26 '64
How to photograph the fair. il Seventeen 23:28 F '64
Impassioned Middle East feud breaks out at the fair. il Life 56:41 My 8 '64
Inside IBM's World's fair egg. H. B. Comstock. il Pop Sci 185:58-9+ Jl '64
Inside 1964's biggest show on earth. J. P. McNeel. il Pop Mech 121:137-45+ F '64
Into stride. il Time 83:42 My 8 '64
Intractable Robert Moses. J. McCarthy. Holiday 36:99-100+ Jl '64; Same abr. with title Moses (Robert) and the Promised Land. Read Digest 85:117-21 S '64
Is the World's fair worth seeing? Farm J 88:34H Jl '64
Isn't life that way here? dancers and musicians. il Newsweek 64:74-5 Jl 20 '64
It's a woman's world's fair. H. Sutton. il McCalls 91:40+ Ap '64
Jewel of the fair: the Spanish pavilion; with photographs by Mark Kauffman. Life 57: 80-3+ Ag 7 '64
Labor costs at the World's fair. U S News 57:74 Jl 6 '64
Laissez-fair. H. Backlin. il Craft Horiz 23: 40-1 S '63
Liberalism vs. the Spanish pavilion. R. Kirk. Nat R 16:774 S 8 '64
Library/USA. il Wilson Lib Bul 38:380-1 Ja '64
Library/USA. H. W. Tucker and J. Becker. il(cover) ALA Bul 58:29-31 Ja '64
Life World's fair review. Life 56:17 My 22; 57:12 Jl 10; 18 Jl 17 '64
Little girl, big bang; nuclear fusion demonstration at General electric's pavilion. il Sci Digest 55:42-3 Je '64
Macfadden publisher under World's fair pact: official publisher for the Hall of education. Pub W 185:134 F 24 '64
Man who will grow 363,800 flowers for the fair. J. J. Simpkins. il Flower Grower 51:36 Ja '64
Matinée day; Ice-travaganza. New Yorker 39:28 Ja 18 '64
Meager fair; lack of musical activity. Mus Am 84:9 Jl '64
Meeting; fair's board of directors. New Yorker 40:24-5 Jl 4 '64
Monsters arrive for the World's fair: the dinosaurs invade. il Life 55:87-8+ D 6 '63
Moses vs. the bankers; financial woes. Newsweek 65:61 F 1 '65
Movie man; maker of documentary To be alive! showing in Johnson's wax pavilion. New Yorker 40:49-52 O 10 '64
New cook's tour; World's fair dream kitchens. J. Peter. il Look 28:M10-13 S 8 '64
New copter at the fair. il Sci Digest 56:53-6 Jl '64
New York celebrates its 300th birthday with a World's fair. K. N. Anderson. il Todays Health 42:18-21+ Mr '64
New York for the fair. G. Bush and M. Vennum. il Bet Hom & Gard 42:129-34 Ap '64
New York is a picture fair. E. Scully. il U S Camera 27:38-42+ Je '64
New York world's fair. il Ebony 19:166-8+ Je '64
New York world's fair. R. C. Davids. il Farm J 88:44-5+ F '64
New York world's fair; a gardener's paradise. B. Black. Pop Gard 15:12+ Mr '64
New York world's fair 1964-1965; diagram. Holiday 36:46-7 Jl '64
N.Y. world's fair preview; symposium. il Look 28:17-32+ F 11 '64
New York world's fair; proclamation, April 3, 1964. L. B. Johnson. Dept State Bul 50:822 My 25 '64
New York's billion dollar dream fair: with report by D. J. Hamblin. il Life 56:38-50+ Ja 17 '64
New York's fair: progress and problems; foreign exhibitors. il Arch Forum 118:10-11 Je '63
News about the fair. C. W. Morton. Atlan 211:108+ Je '63
Notes and comment. New Yorker 39:21 Ja 11 '64
Notes and comment; domestic public-relations men. New Yorker 39:19 Ja 25 '64
Notes and comment; Underground world home. New Yorker 40:19 Jl 18 '64
Nuance makes the difference. il Dance Mag 38:48-51 Ap '64
Onward and upward with the arts. J. Brooks. New Yorker 39:41-2+ Je 1 '63
Out of the bull rushes. il Time 83:52-7 Ja 17 '64
Paperback exhibit signed for Worlds fair. Pub W 184:70 N 11 '63
Parks and recreation showcase at the World's fair. S. Constable. il Recreation 57:267-9 Je '64
Personal business strategy for World's fair visitors. Bsns W p 173-4 Mr 21 '64
Pickets marched in rain, but fair opened anyway. il Bsns W p32 Ap 25 '64
Pious disaster; Vatican pavilion. J. Leo. Commonweal 80:225-6 My 15 '64; Discussion. 80:370-1 Je 12 '64

NEW YORK (city)—Worlds fair, 1964—*Cont.*
Plush, and private; industry and corporate pavilions. il Bsns W p28-9 My 2 '64
Pop on the Meadow. M. Kozloff. Nation 199: 16-18 Jl 13 '64
Prefabricated aluminum hospital flown to World's fair; Atomedic hospital. il Pop Sci 184:79 Mr '64
Preliminaries. New Yorker 40:33-4 Mr 28 '64
Preview. New Yorker 39:34 My 4 '63
Preview of Disney's World's fair shows; past, present and future in twelve minutes; 1,500-seat carousel; around-the-world cruise; the living Lincoln. D. Cohen. il Sci Digest 54: 8-15 D '63
Preview of the 1964-65 New York world's fair. il Sr Schol 84:5-19+ Ap 3 '64
Preview of the World's fair. Changing T 18:5-6 Ja '64
Progress report. New Yorker 39:41-2 O 5 '63
Progress report. il Time 81:36 F 8 '63
Protestant pavilion dedicated; Protestant and Orthodox center. E. C. Parker. Christian Cent 81:714-16 My 27 '64
PS reader's guide to the fair. il Pop Sci 184:56+ Je '64
Ready to swing open the gates. il Bsns W p30-1 Ap 18 '64
Religious cafeteria; religion fare at the fair. M. E. Marty. Christian Cent 81:758-9 Je 10 '64
Rose on our cover, you will see it at the New York world's fair. il Flower Grower 51:23 Je '64
Salute to the World's fair; Met stages ten operas. il Opera N 28:13-16 Ap 18 '64
Save the Spanish paviliion. C. J. McNaspy. America 111:31 Jl 11 '64
Science exhibits; at Seattle fair, federal funds, scientists helped. New Yorkers try a different tack. J. Walsh. il Science 140: 960-2 My 31 '63
Sea shells at the New York world's fair. A. G. Melvin. il Hobbies 69:130+ S '64
Second world of the fair. il N Y Times Mag p 18-19 My 3 '64
Shakespeare views the fair; quotations, comp. by D. Curtis. il Travel 122:42-3 Ag '64
Small world; plan to turn World's fair pavilion into a tribute to UNICEF by Pepsi-Cola company. New Yorker 39:20-1 Ag 31 '63
Smasheroo of a World's fair. il Life 56:26-35 My 1 '64
Space astronomy at the World's fair. P. A. Leavens. il Sky & Tel 27:332-4 Je '64
Spanish pavilion: triumph for Franco? Christian Cent 81:1228-9 O 7 '64
Speaking out; who needs the World's fair? J. Skow. il Sat Eve Post 237:12+ My 23 '64
Take-home ideas by the gardenful; Julimar farm exhibit. il House & Gard 126:246-9 N '64
Take me out to the fairgrounds. P. K. Brooks. il Sat R 47:86+ Mr 14 '64
Teen travel talk. il Seventeen 23:44 Ap '64
Triumph for the fair. il Bsns W p 111-20+ Mr 21 '64
U.S. unveils design for New York fair. il Arch Rec 133:10 F '63
U.S. unveils new design for '64 fair. il Arch Forum 118:5 F '63
Vagabond camera. W. Lane. il Travel 122: 64-5 S '64
Well traveled camera. M. A. Matzkin. il Mod Phot 28:26+ Jl '64
What can the matter be? il Time 84:48 Ag 21 '64
What H&G found at the World's fair. il House & Gard 126:116-17 Ag '64
What's free at the fair. Seventeen 23:30 F '64
Where do you begin? photogenic spots. E. Scully. il U S Camera 27:58-61 Jl '64
Wonderworld; plans for show to be given in amphitheatre. New Yorker 39:36-7 S 28 '63
Word from Moses; hostile New York press. Time 84:42 S 25 '64
World of already. il Time 83:40-52 Je 5 '64
World's fair. See issues of New Yorker, April 18, 1964-October 17, 1964
World's fair. il Sci Digest 55:8-24 Ap '64
World's fair airports. A. Dawydoff. il Flying 74:28-30+ Ap '64
World's fair dinosaurs; life-size for the Sinclair oil corp. exhibit. il Sci Digest 54:48-9 Ag '63
World's fair fare; Terrace club and Top of the fair restaurant. New Yorker 40:36-7 Ap 4 '64
World's fair in New York. G. Meek. il Américas 16:9-16 Ag '64
World's fair musical events. il Mus Am 84: 30-1 Ap '64
World's fair news. il Arch Forum 120:12-15 My; 16-17 Je '64
World's fair of a sort. C. J. McNaspy. America 110:323 Mr 7 '64
World's fair pests bite the dust. il Am City 79:105 O '64
World's fair preview. C. J. McNaspy. America 110:510-12 Ap 11 '64
World's fair preview. il Seventeen 23:98-117+ F '64
World's fair ride proved on test track; Ford's Magic skyway. il Pop Sci 183:69 N '63
World's fair sightseeing service delayed. Aviation W 80:41 Ap 27 '64
World's fair '64; a preview. il Newsweek 63: 43-7 Ja 13 '64
World's fairest: New York. il Travel 121:31-44 Ap '64

Amusement area

Gold-tinged trouble. il Bsns W p32 Je 6 '64

Architecture

Architecture at the New York world's fair. M. F. Schmertz. il Arch Rec 136:143-50 Jl '64
Day pop art died. K. Kuh. il Sat R 47:24-5 My 23 '64
Exhibition architecture: sixteen designs for the New York world's fair. il Arch Forum 119:33+ Ag '63
If this is architecture, God help us. V. J. Scully, jr. Life 57:9 Jl 31 '64
Moses builds a fair. il Arch Forum 120:64-75 Ja '64
Preview: New York world's fair 1964-1965. il Arch Rec 135:137-44 F '64
Structural design of a free-form shell; Eastman Kodak pavilion for the 1964-1965 New York world's fair. il Arch Rec 134:222-4 S '63
They built the roof on the ground; Tent of tomorrow for the New York state pavilion. H. B. Comstock. il Pop Sci 184: 98-101 Mr '64
Thinking man's exhibit; IBM pavilion at World's fair. il Esquire 60:118-23 O '63
Where gimcrack mixes with the elegant. il Bsns W p 113-17 Mr 21 '64
World's fair preview; photographs. A. L. Huxtable. N Y Times Mag p38-41 O 6 '63

Art

Art at the fair. F. Getlein. New Repub 151:26-7 S 26 '64
Art galleries. R. M. Coates. New Yorker 40: 78-81 Ag 8 '64
Art hunting in darkest World's fair. il Art N 63:34-6+ Sum '64
Art safari: collecting in Central America and Panama. J. Gómez-Sicre. il Américas 16:12-17 N '64
Arts at the fair. il Sr Schol 84:14-15 Ap 3 '64
At the fair. Commonweal 80:434-5 Je 26 '64
Blue grotto; Michelangelo's Pietà. il Time 83:72 My 1 '64
Historic journey of the Pieta. il Life 56:83-5+ Ap 17 '64
History in portraits: World's fair exhibit called Four centuries of American masterpieces. il Time 83:66-7 Je 26 '64
Moses-Orpheus returns the fair Eurydice to Flushing. A. Frankfurter. Art N 63:27 Sum '64
Moses the art slayer wins one round. T. B. Hess. Art N 63:25 Ap '64
Outcry over Pietà. il Life 56:55-6 Je 5 '64
Pieta gets ready for the fair. il Bsns W p32-3 Ap 11 '64
Pietà: masterpiece at the fair. C. McCarry. il Sat Eve Post 237:24-9 Mr 28 '64
Sun-colored metal; new collection of pre-Columbian art at World's fair. il Time 83:76-7 Je 12 '64

Caricatures and cartoons

Fair. Kraus. New Yorker 40:26-30 Ag 29 '64
Fair. Stevenson. New Yorker 40:30-5 My 30 '64

Hall of science

Ceremonies; dedication of the Hall of science. New Yorker 40:37-8 S 26 '64
Home at last. il Newsweek 64:100 S 21 '64
Science in New York; Hall of science. il Sci Digest 56:62-3 N '64

Labor conditions

Unisphere begins to show a bit of a strain; high maintenance bills, poor service. il Bsns W p 100+ Je 27 '64

NEW YORK (city)—Worlds fair, 1964—*Cont.*

Music

Arts at the fair. il Sr Schol 84:14-15 Ap 3 '64

Public relations

Entrée: tour of World's fair by Entrée Unlimited. New Yorker 40:22-4 Je 27 '64
Reporting the World's fair. J. Tebbel. Sat R 47:83-4 Ap 11 '64

Religious exhibits

God and man at Flushing Meadow. R. S. Feuerlicht. Reporter 31:54+ Ag 13 '64

Time capsule

See Civilization—Preservation of records

Youth board

Reporter at large; girls' gang in Brownsville section of east Brooklyn. R. Rice. il New Yorker 39:153-4+ O 19 '63

Zoological park

See New York zoological park

NEW YORK (state)

See also
Adirondack Mountains
Airports—New York (state)
Architecture, Domestic—New York (state)
Art—New York (state)
Birds—New York (state)
Booksellers and bookselling—New York (state)
Camping—New York (state)
Education—New York (state)
Fishing—New York (state)
Hudson River
Hudson River Valley
Hunting—New York (state)
Insurance, Health—New York (state)
Law—New York (state)
Libraries—New York (state)
Liquor laws and regulations—New York (state)
Long Island, N. Y.
Nassau County, N.Y.
Prisons—New York (state)
Roads—New York (state)
Water supply—New York (state)

Council on the arts

Cultural empire in the Empire state. J. Anderson. il Dance Mag 38:52-4 D '64
New York state council on the arts in its 2nd year. J. Abouchar. il Dance Mag 37:22-3+ Ap '63

Description and travel

For a three-in-one vacation this year see, the World's fair, New York city, New York state. J. R. Borcherding. il Suc Farm 62:44-5 Jl '64
Going places, finding things in New York state. M. Roche. il House & Gard 124:44+ O '63
Sideroad into yesterday. D. C. King. il Travel 122:42-3 D '64

Division for youth

Salvager of New York teens. il Ebony 19:80-2+ Je '64

Economic conditions

Great society: Rockefeller style. il U S News 58:20 Ja 18 '65

Forests

See New York (state)—Parks and reserves

Historic houses, etc.

Going places, finding things in New York state. M. Roche. il House & Gard 124:44+ O '63
Hudson River Valley portfolio. J. T. Butler. il Antiques 85:432-7 Ap '64
Living with antiques; the Pavilion, Fort Ticonderoga. A. Winchester. il Antiques 84:52-6 Jl '63
Sunnyside at Tarrytown, New York. J. T. Butler. il Antiques 84:175-8 Ag '63
Toy: Boscobel. New Yorker 40:43-4 O 17 '64

History

Grasping the drama of a culture. H. W. Hertzberg. il NEA J 52:44-6 F '63

Housing and community renewal, Division of

New York gives fifteen citations. Arch Rec 136:340 N '64

Legislature

Case of New York; question of apportionment. A. M. Bickel. New Repub 151:11 D 26 '64

Liquor authority

See State liquor authority. New York

Parks and reserves

New York land acquisition program. C. W. Mattison. il Recreation 56:259-62 Je '63
New York's state parks. T. B. Lesure. il Travel 121:50-2 Mr '64

Politics and government

Can a Kennedy beat the Republicans in New York? il U S News 57:31-2 Ag 31 '64
Can Kennedy take New York? Keating's Senate seat. P. Maas. il Sat Eve Post 237:32-4 O 31 '64
Focus on Nov. 3. Nat R 16:711 Ag 25 '64
Goldwater's triumph in the Empire state. M. Kempton. New Repub 151:6-7 N 14 '64
Headless in Albany; split in Democratic ranks. il Newsweek 65:26 Ja 25 '65
Home-rule powers for urbanizing counties and towns. J. H Hughes. il Am City 78:169-70+ S '63
Hosts of unreason; Kennedy vs Keating in New York state. M. Kempton. New Repub 151:11-12 S 12 '64
Is Robert Kennedy eligible to be a Senator from New York? il U S News 57:15 Ag 24 '64
Keating vs. Kennedy: high stakes in New York. il Newsweek 64:35-6+ O 12 '64
Kennedy or Keating; stakes are bigger than a Senate seat. il U S News 57:72-4 O 5 '64
Kennedy vs. Keating. Reporter 31:12+ N 5 '64. Discussion. 31:6+ D 3 '64
Kicking the rock around. Newsweek 63:20 Ap 6 '64
Look, no hands; Democrats' new order. il Newsweek 65:14 Ja 4 '65
Luce vs. Keating? New York race shapes up. il U S News 57:14 Ag 17 '64
Lulu of a fight; bribery charges brought by mayor. il Time 85:21-2 Ja 29 '65
Marriage of necessity; Kennedy nomination for Senate. il Newsweek 64:28-9 Ag 31 '64
Mornings after; Republican election defeat. Reporter 31:20+ N 19 '64
Robert Kennedy and New York: decision point. il Newsweek 64:22-4+ Ag 24 '64
Someone will pick up the pieces. il Time 85:17 Ja 8 '65
Stephen E. Smith. M. Kempton. New Repub 148:15-17 Mr 9 '63
Three-way race? Kennedy-Keating and Clare Boothe Luce. Time 84:19 Ag 28 '64
Unity, of sorts; candidates for the U.S. Senate. il Time 84:22 S 11 '64
Why Robert Kennedy? New Repub 151:3-4 S 19 '64; Discussion. 151:36-8 O 3; 29 O 10; 37 O 17 '64
Will Bobby Kennedy run in New York? M. Kempton. New Repub 150:7-8 Je 6 '64

Religious institutions and affairs

News of the Christian world (cont) Christian Cent 80:408, 718, 962-3, 1180+; 81:1474 Mr 27, My 29, Jl 31, S 25 '63, N 25 '64

Social welfare, Board of

Birth control and welfare; concerning policy statement. Commonweal 79:560-1 F 7 '64

Youth, Division for

See New York (state)—Division for youth

NEW YORK academy of medicine

New approach; more humane treatment. il Newsweek 61:94 Ap 15 '63
Smut and the FBI; fight urged by New York academy of medicine. America 111:792 D 19 '64

NEW YORK academy of sciences

Science in New York; World science center (proposed) il Sci Digest 56:62-3 N '64

NEW YORK airways, incorporated

New York airways fights survival battle. J. R. Ashlock. Aviation W 78:38-9 My 13 '63
N.Y. airways revenues linked to World's fair, heavier schedules. Aviation W 80:39 F 24 '64
New York airways seeking IFR approval. il Aviation W 78:41+ Je 17 '63
New York airways, Sikorsky sign conditional pact for S-61N sale. Aviation W 80:37 F 10 '64
Pan Am heliport foes plan court battle. J. W. Carter. Aviation W 82:39 Ja 25 '65

NEW YORK aquarium. See Aquariums

NEW YORK automobile show. See Automobiles —Exhibitions

NEW YORK blood center

6,000,000 pints of blood is not enough. L. Galton. il N Y Times Mag p38+ Mr 29 '64

NEW YORK botanical garden

Thailand royalty visits the New York botanical garden. P. Clark. il Horticulture 42:32+ Jl '64

Yum yum; Easter show. New Yorker 39:36-7 Ap 20 '63

Expeditions

Onward and upward with the sciences. G. T. Hellman. il New Yorker 40:41-2+ My 30 '64

NEW YORK Christmas tree growers' association

Accent in quality. A. Dickson. il Am For 70:8-9 D '64

NEW YORK city ballet

Balanchine: demigod of the dance. il Newsweek 63:51-2+ My 4 '64

Balanchine prepares. il Dance Mag 37:26 Ap '63

Balanchine's return to Russia; excerpts from Balanchine. B. Taper. Harper 227:47-50+ N '63

Ballet; Balanchine's Midsummer night's dream. R. Krokover. il Mus Am 84:6-9 My '64

Comers; wealth of gifted young girls. il Time 84:73 O 30 '64

Dance. C. Barnes. Nation 196:427-8 My 18 '63

Dance; second season at the New York state theater. R. Krokover. il Mus Am 84:41-2 N '64

Dance; winter season. R. Krokover. Mus Am 84:54-5 Ja; 42-3 F '64

Dear dance fan; opening weeks at Lincoln Center's New York state theatre. E. Denby. il Dance Mag 38:34-5 Je '64

House of Balanchine; Johnson's New York state theater will be formally opened by the New York city ballet. Newsweek 61:88 Ap 8 '63

Jewel in its proper setting. il Time 83:58-63 My 1 '64

Land of long-legged butterflies. D. Hering. il Dance Mag 37:46-7+ My '63

Music to my ears; Arcade. I. Kolodin. Sat R 46:31 Ap 13 '63

Music to my ears; Balanchine's Bugaku. I. Kolodin. Sat R 46:44 Ap 6 '63

Music to my ears; notable Nutcracker. I. Kolodin. Sat R 47:31 D 26 '64

Musical events; development of stars. W. Sargeant. New Yorker 39:149-50 S 7 '63

Musical events; George Balanchine's Bugaku. W. Sargeant. New Yorker 39:148 Mr 30 '63

Musical events; George Balanchine's La valse. W. Sargeant. New Yorker 39:155 S 21 '63

Musical events; opening of spring season at City Center. W. Sargeant. New Yorker 39:78+ Mr 23 '63

Musical events; opening of spring season at New York state theater. W. Sargeant. New Yorker 40:146+ My 9 '64

Musical events; opening of winter season at the City Center. W. Sargeant. New Yorker 39:226 D 14 '63

Musical events; performance of Dim lustre. W. Sargeant. New Yorker 40:167-8 My 16 '64

New York city ballet at New York city center. S. J. Cohen. il Dance Mag 38:18-21 Mr '64

NYC ballet in The nutcracker at New York city center. D. Hering. Dance Mag 37:23+ F '63

Paradox of the New York city ballet. W. Terry. il Theatre Arts 47:14-17 N '63

Reviews; second half of spring season; New York state theater. D. Hering. Dance Mag 38:27-8 Jl '64

Under the sign of Salamu aleikum. D. Hering. il Dance Mag 37:43-5+ N '63

Which way to Mecca? Balanchine's New York city ballet tug-of-war with Lincoln Center. Newsweek 64:102 O 12 '64

Yes, but... sampling of autumn season. D. Hering. Dance Mag 38:22-4+ D '64

NEW YORK city center light opera company

Revivals save the day; '62-'63 theatre round-up. L. Lerman. il Dance Mag 37:27-9 Jl '63

NEW YORK city center of music and drama

City Center Savoyards. M. Bernheimer. Sat R 47:61-2 Ap 11 '64

French and English. F. Merkling. Opera N 28:25 My 2 '64

New York news. R. D. Daniels. Opera N 28:33 D 7 '63

On 55th street, the longest run of all. J. Dalrymple. il N Y Times Mag p84-5 D 8 '63

NEW YORK city in art

Rudolph Burckhardt: multiple fugitive. A. Katz. il Art N 62:38-41 D '63

NEW YORK city in literature

That was New York; story in Evening mail. A. J. Liebling. il New Yorker 39:143-50+ O 12 '63

NEW YORK city opera company

City Center firsts. il Opera N 29:16-17 S 26 '64

City Center; success story. I. Kolodin. il Theatre Arts 47:17-19+ Mr '63

Julius imperator; interview, ed. by Q. Eaton. J. Rudel. il Opera N 28:14-16 F 29 '64

Music to my ears; Treigle's Boris. I. Kolodin. Sat R 47:32 O 17 '64

Musical events; performance of B. Britten's Midsummer night's dream. W. Sargeant. New Yorker 39:99-100 My 4 '63

Musical events; revival of D. Moore's Ballad of Baby Doe and C. Floyd's Susannah. W. Sargeant. New Yorker 39:150-2 My 11 '63

Musical events; revival of Menotti's Amelia goes to the ball, and Medium. W. Sargeant. New Yorker 39:96 My 18 '63

New York city opera sings for Julius M. Mayer. il N Y Times Mag p38+ S 29 '63

Reviews: opera at City Center. il Mus Am 83:29-31 N '63; 84:45 Ap; 37-8 My; 40-1 Jl; 24-8 N; 110+ D '64

Rudel's Russians. F. Merkling. il Opera N 29:28 N 14 '64

Saints and singers; thirty-four debuts listed. F. Merkling. il Opera N 28:33 N 16 '63

Spring comes to City Center. il Mus Am 83:19-22 Je '63

U.S. calendar; New York city opera tour. Opera N 29:32 N 14 '64

U.S. calendar: tour program. Opera N 29:31 D 5 '64

Where meaningful meets meaningless; highlights of fall season. D. Hering. il Dance Mag 38:16-17 Ja '64

NEW YORK city transit authority

Subways and science: two N.Y. institutions consider meaning of coexistence in crowded Manhattan. E. Langer. il Science 143:789-90 F 21 '64

NEW YORK dance theatre (organization)

New York dance theatre at 92nd street Y. J. Maskey. Dance Mag 37:65-6 Je '63

NEW YORK evening mail

That was New York; story in Evening mail. A. J. Liebling. il New Yorker 39:143-50+ O 12 '63

NEW YORK federal reserve bank. See Federal reserve banks

NEW YORK film festival. See Moving picture festivals

NEW YORK flower show. See Flower exhibits

NEW YORK Giants (football club) See Football clubs

NEW YORK herald tribune

Books on the women's pages of Times and Tribune; summary of address. H. Stix. Pub W 184:32-3 D 2 '63

Crisis on New York's newspaper row. T. A. Wise. il Fortune 70:110-13+ O '64

New Trib in town; Sunday edition. il Newsweek 62:70-1 O 14 '63

Sic transit ingloria; White House ban lifted. Newsweek 62:51 Ag 26 '63

Trib's Sunday punch; new format. il Bsns W p34+ S 21 '63

Walk, walk, talk, talk; People, places and things in the Paris edition. il Newsweek 61:52-3 Ap 1 '63

See also

Book week (publication)

NEW YORK herald tribune forum for high schools

Blurred images: what misconceptions do foreign students have about the U.S. and vice versa? E. R. Floyd. il Sr Schol 84:8-9 F 28 '64

Foreign teens view the U.S. il Sr Schol 82:14-15 My 8 '63

Which way to the U.N? il Sr Schol 82:12-13 My 1 '63

NEW YORK hi-fi show. See Audio fairs

NEW YORK Hilton at Rockefeller Center. See New York (city)—Hotels, restaurants, etc.

NEW YORK historical society

Audubons; exhibition of original drawings of Birds of America at John James Audubon gallery. New Yorker 40:21-2 Ag 8 '64

New president. New Yorker 39:17-18 Jl 13 '63

NEW YORK international airport. See New York—Airports

NEW YORK Jets (football club) See Football clubs

NEW YORK Journal American
50,000-word leak; testimony of J. Ruby to the Warren commission. Time 84:40 Ag 28 '64
What's your source? premature publication of Ruby's testimony before Warren. il Newsweek 64:68-9 Ag 31 '64

NEW YORK library association
Paperbacks for college-bound students. C. E. Hieber. bibliog il Library J 89:185-90 Ja 15 '64

NEW YORK Mets (baseball) See Baseball clubs

NEW YORK military academy, Cornwall-on-Hudson, N.Y. See Military schools

NEW YORK mirror
Death in the family. il Newsweek 62:55 O 28 '63
Death of the Mirror. Commonweal 79:156 N 1 '63
Future techniques; memories of years on staff of the New York mirror. J. Reidy. U S Camera 27:16-18 Mr '64
New York mirror folds up. Bsns W p36 O 19 '63
No tears. Reporter 29:20 N 7 '63
Prudence: concerning Prudence Penny cooking column. New Yorker 39:36-7 S 14 '63
Shattered Mirror. il Time 82:50+ O 25 '63
Vanishing act. Time 82:71 N 1 '63
What killed The mirror. D. Paneth. il Nation 197:291-3 N 9 '63
Why a big city newspaper died. il U S News 55:8 O 28 '63

NEW YORK mycological society
Mycophiles: annual banquet. New Yorker 40:22-4 Ja 9 '65

NEW YORK, New Haven and Hartford railroad company
Help for commuters. il U S News 54:88-9 Mr 18 '63
It's a club on wheels. M. Gunther. il N Y Times Mag p68+ N 1 '64
Shade worse than bankrupt; plight of the New Haven. il Bsns W p 130+ My 9 '64
Study no. 22. il Newsweek 63:66-8 Ja 13 '64

NEW YORK newspaper guild
Solidarity; forever? Newsweek 61:57 F 4 '63

NEW YORK newspaper strike. See Strikes—United States—Newspapers

NEW YORK philharmonic. See Philharmonic-symphony society of New York

NEW YORK port authority. See Port of New York authority

NEW YORK post
New York gets back a paper. il Bsns W p28 Mr 9 '63
Post time; publication resumed. il Newsweek 61:60-1 Mr 11 '63
Wayward press. A. J. Liebling. New Yorker 39:173-6+ Mr 16 '63

NEW YORK pro musica antiqua (organization)
Ancient's mariner. il Time 84:48 Jl 10 '64
Carillons and vielles; New York pro musica presentation of Play of Herod. Newsweek 62:51 D 23 '63

NEW YORK public library
Berg acquisitions. New Yorker 40:44-5 O 3 '64
Expanded program and new format for NYPL's New technical books. Library J 88:534 F 1 '63
Mark Twain detective story published by NYPL. Library J 89:1210 Mr 15 '64
Mid-Manhattan facility for students planned by New York public library. Library J 89:1048-9 Mr 1 '64
Once-over; opening of shop in main building. New Yorker 40:45 D 12 '64
Pioneer in the war on poverty. A. Baker. il Library J 89:3376-9 S 15 '64
Reports on library-TV cooperation; NYPL and television station, WNDT. ALA Bul 58:47-8 Ja '64
Sea room for the impressionable years. A. Sanford. il Horn Bk 40:475-84 O '64
Wanted: new adult materials; Adult services. K. L. O'Brien. Sr Schol 85:24T O 7 '64

Branches

Bilingual story hour program. P. B. White. il Library J 89:3379-81 S 15 '64
Old Jeff to be NYPL's newest branch; Jefferson market branch. il Library J 88:2658-9 Jl '63

Dance collection

Buried treasure. L. Moore. il Dance Mag 38:42-7 Ap '64
Prints of dancers; portfolio of twelve prints published. J. Anderson. il Dance Mag 38:42-3+ N '64

Music library

New York public library announces major service; Rodgers and Hammerstein record archives to be at Lincoln Center. Hobbies 68:36 Ja '64

Science and technology division

Science-technology periodicals. G. S. Bonn. il Library J 88:954-8 Mr 1 '63

Theater collection

New York public library's Theatre collection. G. Freedley. il Wilson Lib Bul 38:636-9 Ap '64

NEW YORK Rangers. See Hockey teams

NEW YORK regional plan association. See Regional plan association, New York

NEW YORK review of books (periodical)
Civilization as a process; culture as banal repetition; address, May 27-29, 1963. J. Epstein. ALA Bul 57:665-7 Jl '63
Good bet for a Baltic baron. Time 81:51 My 31 '63
Literary newcomer. Time 81:37-8 Mr 1 '63
Outspoken newcomer. E. Moon. Library J 88:2458 Je 15 '63
Shot in the dark; tabloid-size paper. Newsweek 61:98 F 25 '63

NEW YORK securities company
Cashing in on specialization; Eberstadt approach to banking. il Bsns W p90-2 Mr 30 '63

NEW YORK Shakespeare festival
Divorce, Moorish style; presentation of Othello. H. Hewes. Sat R 47:20 Ag 1 '64
New Dane in town. il Newsweek 63:80 Je 29 '64
Off Broadway; production of Othello indoors at Martinique. E. Oliver. New Yorker 40:93-5 O 24 '64
Ordinary Othello. il Newsweek 64:49 Jl 27 '64
People's choice; production of Hamlet. H. Hewes. Sat R 47:18 Jl 4 '64
Stage seen on small screen; Central park production of Antony and Cleopatra televised. H. Hewes; R. L. Shayon. Sat R 46:17 Jl 6 '63
Up in Central park. il Newsweek 62:60-1 Jl 1 '63

NEW YORK shipping association
Clash is brewing on docks. Bsns W p66 Jl 4 '64

NEW YORK society for the experimental study of education
Panel urges schools to incorporate paperbacks; striking cases cited. H. Schiller. Library J 88:844-5 F 15 '63

NEW YORK society of security analysts
Analysts worry about splintering. Bsns W p96 Jl 18 '64

NEW YORK state council on the arts. See New York (state)—Council on the arts

NEW YORK state library, Albany
New York: the system framework. R. P. Stewart. bibliog il Library J 89:1676-9 Ap 15 '64

NEW YORK state small-marsh production program. See Marshes

NEW YORK state theater. See Lincoln Center for the performing arts. New York—New York state theater

NEW YORK state thruway. See Roads—New York (state)

NEW YORK state university
Campus planning for the State university of New York. il Arch Rec 135:171-3 My '64
New York state reaches for architecture. Arch Rec 133:48 Mr '63
N.Y's big college program progresses. il Arch Forum 119:11 S '63
Welding fifty-eight schools into one big university. il Bsns W p92-100+ O 17 '64

Agricultural and technical institute at Farmingdale, Long Island

Visit to Planting fields. il Flower Grower 51:26-7, 38 Je '64

Center of science and technology (proposed)

Building a science center overnight. Bsns W p32 Ja 26 '63

College at Fredonia

I. M. Pei's master plan for the college at Fredonia, N.Y. il Arch Rec 135:176-7 My '64

College at Plattsburgh

World understanding at Plattsburgh. J. H. Hunt. NEA J 53:29-30 Ja '64

NEW YORK state university—*Continued*

College at Potsdam

Comprehensive plan for the college at Potsdam, New York. il Arch Rec 135:174-5 My '64

Teachers college at Cortland

Libraries

Students at New York college boost library book budget. Library J 89:1706 Ap 15 '64

University at Buffalo

Librarian fights dismissal in Buffalo court case; loyalty oath issue at State university of New York in Buffalo. Library J 89:1050 Mr 1 '64

NEW YORK state youth division. See New York (state)—Division for youth

NEW YORK stock exchange. See Stock exchange—New York (city)

NEW YORK, Susquehanna and western railroad

Buying off the commuters. Time 81:91 My 10 '63

NEW YORK telephone building. See New York (city)—Architecture

NEW YORK times

Average newspaper is not a public utility. M. Kempton. New Repub 148:16-18 Mr 30 '63

Birth control series. America 109:146 Ag 17 '63

Books on the women's pages of Times and Tribune; summary of address. J. Cook. Pub W 184:32-3 D 2 '63

Dynasty's end; Rome bureau chief. Time 82: 93 N 8 '63

Family enterprise. il Time 81:58 Je 28 '63

Gone west. Newsweek 63:51 Ja 27 '64

How it might have been: a hypothetical Times editorial vs. John Birch society. Nat R 15:557 D 31 '63

If you can keep your head when all about you: television and news magazine coverage of the Kennedy assassination story. R. L. Tobin. il Sat R 46:53-4 D 14 '63; Discussion. 47:74 Ja 11 '64

Immunity from criticism; case of advertisement concerning racial conditions in Montgomery, Ala. New Repub 150:7-8 Mr 21 '64

Important victory for a free press, a free nation. R. H. Smith. Pub W 185:33 Mr 16 '64

Legwork in megalopolis. il Time 83:59-60 Ap 24 '64

Lesson: be local; publication of western edition suspended. Time 83:42+ Ja 24 '64

Libel and the free press; appealing of judgement from Alabama supreme court. N. Dorsen. il Nation 198:93-5 Ja 27 '64

Libel landmark; Supreme court decision. il Newsweek 63:74 Mr 23 '64

Life without the Times. M. Ascoli. Reporter 28:22 Mr 14 '63

Line of succession. Newsweek 61:64 Je 10 '63

Lose one, win one; libel actions. il Time 84: 74+ O 2 '64

New York times, alas. D. Macdonald. Esquire 59:55-7+ Ap; 104+ My '63

New York times changes daily book review policy. Pub W 183:43 Je 3 '63

New York times's vital victory: Alabama libel case. R. L. Tobin. Sat R 47:69-70 Ap 11 '64; Discussion. 47:61 My 9; 52 Je 13 '64

Notes and comment. New Yorker 39:33-8 Ap 13 '63

On the far right. Commonweal 79:384 D 27 '63

Pleased Punch; new publisher. Newsweek 62:41 Jl 1 '63

Putting the Times to bed. J. Tebbel. il Sat R 47:67-8+ D 12 '64

Right to criticize upheld; Supreme court decision to reverse libel judgment. Sr Schol 84:30 Ap 3 '64

Room at the top; editorial shake-up. il Newsweek 64:86 S 14 '64

Speak up; everybody; Supreme court decision to reverse libel judgment. Nat R 16:222 Mr 24 '64

Striking it poor. Time 81:65 My 3 '63

Tour of the Times book review. B. Daniels. Nat R 14:202-3, 253-4 Mr 12-26 '63

Troubled Times; western edition of New York times. il Bsns W p26 Ja 11 '64

Victory for a free press. Sat Eve Post 237: 78 Ap 4 '64

View from the heights; T. Catledge becomes executive editor of Sunday and daily Times. il Time 84:55-6 S 11 '64

What profit prestige? Newsweek 62:81 N 18 '63

NEW YORK times book review

Band together for quality reviewing. H. F. Silverman. Library J 88:2368+ Ja 15 '63

Civilization as a process; culture as banal repetition; address, May 27-29, 1963. J. Epstein. ALA Bul 57:665-7 Jl '63

Literary criticism or news of books? R. H. Smith. Pub W 183:30 Ap 22 '63

New York times, alas. D. Macdonald. Esquire 59:55-7+ Ap; 104+ My '63; Discussion. 60:64-7 S '63

NEW YORK times magazine

Girdle gazette. il Time 81:45 Je 21 '63

Anecdotes, facetiae, satire, etc.

How to be happy when your newsdealer filches your Sunday times magazine. S. McKelway. New Yorker 39:20-1 Je 29 '63

NEW YORK times national book fair. See Book fairs

NEW YORK university

Fording ahead; Ford foundation grant. Newsweek 64:73 Jl 6 '64

One-page catalogue; facsimile of original curriculum. Sat R 47:83 My 16 '64

Hall of fame for great Americans

Audubon and barn owl share new Hall of fame medal. J. Vosburgh. il Audubon Mag 65:155 My '63

Libraries

Frost books donated to N.Y.U. library. Pub W 185:105-6 Ja 20 '64

Frost's personal library goes to NYU, not to library named in his honor. Library J 89:594 F 1 '64

Rare books and automation: NYU's catalog-ing experiment. Library J 88:4723 D 15 '63

Medical center

Hospital in the city: N.Y.U.'s giant Medical center. il Arch Forum 120:92-5 Ap '64

School of law

Fair bail for all; Manhattan bail project. W. M. Kunstler. Nation 197:52-3 Jl 27 '63

Something mother would like; first National conference on bail and criminal justice. il Time 83:67-8 Je 12 '64

NEW YORK Yankees (baseball) See Baseball clubs

NEW YORK zoological park

Another Noah's ark for New York; wildlife survival centers. F. Osborn. il N Y Times Mag p24-5+ O 27 '63

Down on the farm up in the Bronx. il Life 54:NY14-15 Ap 19 '63

Good life in the zoo. F. Osborn. il Read Digest 82:147-8+ F '63

Inside the Bronx zoo. B. H. Frisch. il Sci Digest 55:43-51 Mr '64

Party; society's annual garden party and visit to Bronx zoo's new aquatic birds house. New Yorker 40:52-3 O 10 '64

Snow leopard likes it; photographs. S. Falk. N Y Times Mag p22-3 F 16 '64

There are lions loose in the park; island in the Bronx park zoo. il Look 28:128-30 D 15 '64

Zoo structure turns day into night; Bronx zoo. il Am City 78:24 D '63

NEW YORK zoological society

By parachute into Peru's lost world; 1963 Vilcabamba expedition. G. B. Baekeland. il Nat Geog Mag 126:268-96 Ag '64

Zoo party; annual members' meeting. New Yorker 40:28-9 Ja 23 '65

Zoo to rescue wild animals. Sci Digest 56:70 O '64

NEW YORKER (periodical)

Brief interlude at the New Yorker. C. W. Morton. il Atlan 211:81-4 My '63

Fundamental issue: limitation of advertising. Nation 196:518 Je 22 '63

Most of A. J. Leibling. Review

Commonweal 79:436-7 Ja 10 '64. W. J. Smith

New Yorker & Hannah Arendt. I. Howe. Commentary 36:318-19 O '63; Discussion. 38: 12+ S '64

Try for the New Yorker. C. W. Morton. Atlan 211:45-9 Ap '63 (to be cont)

NEW YORKERS

Fairest of the fair; New York girls. il Look 28:106-11 F 11 '64

Gansevoort pier; poetry readings. New Yorker 40:40-1 S 26 '64

Long-winded lady. New Yorker 40:40-2 Ap 25; 24-5 S 5 '64

New York is a great place to live, but it's a tough place to visit. F. Knebel. il Look 27:34-6 Mr 26 '63

NEW YORKERS—*Continued*
Notes and comment. New Yorker 39:33 S 14 '63
Notes and comment; little street running by midtown pedestrians. New Yorker 39:17 Jl 27 '63
Off-track betting, from the horse's mouth; voting by New Yorkers. J. M. Willig. il N Y Times Mag p55+ N 3 '63
125,000 New Yorkers work the whole night through. R. W. Apple, jr. il N Y Times Mag p53+ Ap 5 '64

NEW ZEALAND
See also
Botany—New Zealand
Censorship—New Zealand
Education—New Zealand
Elections—New Zealand
Forests and forestry—New Zealand
Space research—New Zealand
Zoology—New Zealand

Commercial treaties and agreements

U.S. concludes meat agreement with New Zealand; announcement, with New Zealand note, February 17, 1964, and United States reply. Dept State Bul 50:382 Mr 9 '64

Description and travel

Land of the kiwis. T. B. Lesure. il Travel 122:26-30 S; 45-50 O '64

Foreign relations

Australia

Tasman Sea: a moat between allies. New Repub 149:12 Jl 20 '63

Religious institutions and affairs

News of the Christian world (cont) Christian Cent 80:410-11, 1058, 1447; 81:381, 1602 Mr 27, Ag 28, N 20 '63, Mr 18, D 23 '64

Social conditions

See also
Social and economic security—New Zealand

NEW ZEALAND and the United States
Marines landed too; sentimental journey to New Zealand. R. Sherrod. il Sat Eve Post 236:30+ Ap 27 '63

NEWARK, N.J.
Resourceful street maintenance. R. G. Caprio and F. Crann. il Am City 78:96-7 Ap '63

Airports

Flying into the big-city airport. A. H. Sanfelici. il Flying 74:26-9+ Mr '64
10-million capacity planned for Newark. Aviation W 81:37 N 16 '64

Anecdotes, facetiae, satire, etc.

Newarker speaks up for Noork. D. Steinberg. il N Y Times Mag p99-100 O 20 '63

Education

Our own space project; art-science activity, Cleveland school. B. I. Forman. il Recreation 56:286 Je '63

Lighting

Stretching the recreation day. H. O. Splethoff. il Am City 78:163-4 S '63

Stores

Renaissance at Bamberger's. il Pub W 184: 24 D 2 '63

NEWARK, N.J. public library
Justice Brennan speaks on censorship at Newark library anniversary dinner. Library J 88:2217 Je 1 '63

NEWARK museum
Empire period in Newark museum. Hobbies 68:51+ S '63

NEWBERRY library, Chicago
Library, asylum, platform for uninhibited leaps; address, February 15, 1963. K. Shapiro. il Wilson Lib Bul 37:661-9 Ap '63
Rare book collection purchased by Newberry library for $2.75 million; Louis H. Silver collection. Library J 89:2570 Je 15 '64
Rare book dealer sues Silver estate. Pub W 186:24-5 Ag 17 '64
$2.75 million rare book sale sets record; Louis H. Silver collection. Pub W 185:47 My 25 '64

NEWBERY, John
Little pretty pocket book. V. Edwards. PTA Mag 57:17 Ap '63

NEWBERY medal
Book award jury hails big boy, little boy, Cat and wild things. Library J 89:1391 Mr 15 '64
Critics approved! reviews before announcement. Library J 88:1294-6 Mr 15 '63
Distinguished contribution. J. Dougherty. Pub W 183:36 Mr 11 '63
Emily Neville. U. Nordstrom. il Library J 89:1372-3 Mr 15 '64
It's like this, Cat, to appear soon in braille and talking-book editions. il Library J 89: 1839-40 Ap 15 '64
Little pretty pocket book. V. Edwards. PTA Mag 57:17 Ap '63
Loud silence. E. Rudin. Library J 89:900 F 15 '64; Discussion. 89:1800+, 3356 Ap 15, S 15 '64
Madeleine L'Engle. H. D. Vursell. Library J 88:1288-91 Mr 15 '63
Newbery and Caldecott awards. il ALA Bul 57:335 Ap '63
Newbery and Caldecott runners-up; symposium. il Library J 89:1377-82 Mr 15 '64
Newbery and Caldecott winners: Emily Neville, Maurice Sendak. il Pub W 185: 30-2 Mr 9 '64
Newbery-Caldecott awards. il Wilson Lib Bul 38:617 Ap '64
Newbery-Caldecott medals; Madeleine L'Engle, Ezra Jack Keats win 1963 awards. il Pub W 183:18-20 Mr 11 '63

NEWBORN infants. See Infants, Newborn

NEWBURGH, N.Y.
Crusade against the poor. F. M. Eckman. il Redbook 120:58-9+ F '63

Music

Nuns on the Hudson; Hudson Valley international cultural center. J. W. Freeman. Opera N 28:26 S 28 '63

NEWBY, Dangerfield
Five brave Negroes with John Brown at Harpers Ferry. por Negro Hist Bul 27:164-9 Ap '64

NEWCOMB, Alan H.
Free enterprise; address, April 28, 1964. Vital Speeches 30:730-4 S 15 '64

NEWCOMB, Duane G.
Our fragile wilderness. Field & S 68:10-11+ F '64

NEWCOMB, Robinson
Budget cuts would boost economy. Nations Bsns 51:38-9+ My '63
Five ways to cut unemployment. Nations Bsns 52:31-3+ Jl '64
Private spending will strengthen prosperity. Nations Bsns 52:40-1+ S '64
What's needed after tax cuts. Nations Bsns 52:32-3+ Mr '64

NEWCOMBE, Alan G.
Fields for edge-punched filing cards. Science 140:1312-13 Je 21 '63

NEWCOMBE, Howard B.
Intelligence and genetic trends; letter. bibliog Science 141:1104-6+; 142:1621 S 13, D 27 '63

NEWCOMEN, Thomas
Origins of the steam engine. E. S. Ferguson. il Sci Am 210:98-107 bibliog(p 152) Ja '64

NEWCOMER; story. See Randall, F. E.

NEWELL, David M.
Trail of the tarpon. Field & S 68:56-7+ Mr '64

NEWELL, Homer E.
Ranger VII; briefing for Johnson brings out high level chit chat on various aspects of space. Science 145:563-5 Ag 7 '64
Space science; address, December 26, 1962. bibliog Science 139:464-71 F 8 '63
Survival in the space age; address. Aviation W 79:21 Ag 19 '63
—See Jastrow, R. jt. auth.

NEWELL, Norman D.
Crises in the history of life; with biographical sketch. Sci Am 208:32, 76-92 bibliog (p 185) F '63
Four men who helped to win the West. Natur Hist 72:4+ Mr '63

NEWELL, Reginald E.
Circulation of the upper atmosphere; with biographical sketch. Sci Am 210:21, 62-72+ bibliog(p152) Mr '64

NEWETT, George A.
Was T.R. a drunk? J. G. Hayden. il Am Heritage 15:82-3 O '64

NEWFOUNDLAND
See also
Fishing—Newfoundland

Antiquities

Columbus wasn't first; Viking ruins L'Anse aux Meadows. il Sci Digest 55:77-80 F '64
Tiny object, big find; soapstone wheel found at L'Anse aux Meadows. il Sci Digest 56:36 N '64
Viking ruins found. il Sci N L 84:306 N 16 '63
Vinland ruins prove Vikings found the New World. H. Ingstad. il Nat Geog Mag 126:708-34 N '64

NEWHALL, Beaumont
Eloquent light. Pop Phot 54:74-5+ Mr '64
How Ansel Adams makes an exposure. Pop Phot 52:40-3 F '63
How they made daguerreotypes. Pop Phot 53:58+ Jl '63
Landmark cameras. Pop Phot 55:142-7 D '64
More living than the memory of the man. Pop Phot 55:152-3+ N '64
NEWHOFF, Harry R.
Inexpensive scope and VOM calibrator. Pop Electr 21:57-9 O '64
NEWHOUSE, John
Multilateral force: an appraisal. Bul Atomic Sci 20:13-18 S '64
NEWHOUSE, Samuel I.
Little Sam's big gift. il por Time 84:52 Ag 14 '64
Nachas for Sam. il por Newsweek 64:56 Ag 17 '64
NEWHOUSE communications center. See Syracuse university—Newhouse communications center
NEWKIRK, Gordon, Jr, and Bohlin, J. D.
First flight of Coronascope II. Sky & Tel 28:16-19 Jl '64
NEWLEY, Anthony
All-purpose Cockney; with report by R. Oulahan. il pors Life 55:55+ N 29 '63
NEWLON, Clarke
Ag-flying in Russia. Flying 74:33+ My '64
Capitol treatment. Flying 74:18+ Ap '64
Congressional flying club. Flying 74:22+ Mr '64
Is flying fun deductible? Flying 74:34-5+ Je '64
NEWLON, Michael. See Lisk, R. D. jt. auth.
NEWLON, Richard, and Lee, B. J.
Denver achieves professional negotiations. por NEA J 52:14-16 F '63
NEWMAN, Arnold
Arnold Newman photographs the President. il pors Pop Phot 55:40-1 O '64
NEWMAN, Barnett
Barnett Newman. H. Rosenberg. por Vogue 141:134-5+ F 1 '63
NEWMAN, Charles
Reflections on protection. Yale R 52:404-11 Mr '63
NEWMAN, David
Ciao, Marcello. Esquire 60:110-11 N '63
Last gasps; stories. Esquire 61:94 Ja '64
Midway; story. Esquire 59:118-21 Je '63
Secular music. Esquire 61:50+ Ap; 62:50-3 O; 102+ D '64
Where the king of the world goes. Esquire 61:120+ Ap '64
(ed) See Collins, C. C. Chemistry
—and Benton, Robert
Man talk. See issues of Mademoiselle
New date book. Mlle 57:82-5 Je '63
New sentimentality. Esquire 62:25-31 Jl '64
Pressure: buckle under, Winsocki. Esquire 62:97-100 S '64
Scene of the crime. Esquire 62:168-9 D '64
NEWMAN, Deborah
All-American tour; drama. Plays 23:71-6 My '64
Christmas tree surprise; drama. Plays 24:38, 77-80 D '64
Compass for Christopher; drama. Plays 24:73-6, 82 O '64
Something new for Halloween; drama. Plays 23:73-7 O '63
Yankee Doodle kitten; drama. Plays 23:67-71 N '63
NEWMAN, James Roy
Books (cont) Sci Am 208:169-70+ Mr; 209:161-2+ D '63; 210:141-8+ F; 211:143-9 D '64
NEWMAN, John Henry, cardinal
Light on Newman. M. J. Svaglic. Commonweal 78:204-6 My 10 '63
NEWMAN, L. Hugh
Ocean hopping monarch. Audubon Mag 66:106-9 Mr '64
NEWMAN, Louis E.
Fit your fiscal year to your business. Harvard Bsns R 42:106-9 N '64
NEWMAN, Marvin E.
Gigantic midget among giant men; photography. Sports Illus 21:46-50 N 30 '64
NEWMAN, Millard W.
Automotive milestones. Motor T 16:84-7 Je '64
NEWMAN, Neil A.
Boat engine, car engine; horse of a different color. Motor B 113:95-6 Ja '64
NEWMAN, Paul
Western non-hero named Hud; with report by P. Bunzel. il pors Life 55:45-7+ Jl 5 '63
NEWMAN, Robert B.
Where is science taking us? reprint from Sound. por Sat R 46:48-9 S 7 '63
NEWMAN, Robert E.
Book is to buy. Sat R 48:58-9 Ja 16 '65
NEWMAN clubs
Aggiornamento on the campus; Newman center of St Albert the Great, New Mexico state university. C. Stevens. America 112:122-3 Ja 23 '65
Newman apostolate. J. O'Gara. Commonweal 79:32 O 4 '63; Reply. J. S. Duryea. 79:227 N 15 '63
NEWMAR, Julie
Electronic tomato. por Time 84:81-2 D 4 '64
NEWMARK, Esther
Lady with a sextant. M. Wiley. por Yachting 116:51+ D '64
NEWPORT, R.I.
New Newport. il Newsweek 64:80 Ag 24 '64
Newport notes: the Kennedys and other salts. G. Plimpton. il Harper 226:39-47 Mr '63
There will always be a Newport. P. Mesta. McCalls 90:30+ S '63

Historic houses, etc.

Living with antiques; Pagoda House in Newport, Rhode Island. J. A. L. Hyde. il Antiques 84:158-61 Ag '63
NEWPORT, R.I. folk festival. See Music festivals—Rhode Island
NEWPORT BEACH, Calif.
Learning by doing; Ardell's sailing school, Newport Beach, Calif. A. Lockabey. il Yachting 116:62-3+ Ag '64
NEWPORT NEWS, Va.

Water supply

Water, water, everywhere. il Am City 79:73-4 Ja '64
NEWQUIST, O. A.
Store winter water for summer use. Am City 78:74-5 F '63
NEWS
Management of news. L. Markel. il Sat R 46:50-1+ F 9 '63; Discussion. 46:51+ Mr 9 '63
Managers versus manufacturers of news. J. N. Eller. America 108:286 Mr 2 '63
Rebirth of news. Nat R 16:636 Jl 28 '64
Self-management of the news. Nation 198:309 Mr 30 '64
Straws of an ill wind; bias in news presentation. R. L. Tobin. Sat R 46:41-2 Jl 13 '63
Well hello there! Nat R 16:680 Ag 11 '64
See also
Current events
Government and the press
Journalism
Reporters and reporting
Television broadcasting—News
NEWS agencies
Apprenticeship for legend; City news bureau of Chicago. il Time 85:45 Ja 22 '65
Shoe-leather school; City news bureau of Chicago. il Newsweek 65:50 Ja 4 '65
Two faces of Tass, by T. E. Kruglak. Review Bul Atomic Sci 19:33-4 F '63. H. E. Salisbury
See also
Associated press
Newspapers—Syndicate service
United press international
NEWS broadcasts. See Television broadcasting—News
NEWS commentators. See Television broadcasting—News
NEWS conferences. See Press conferences
NEWS front (periodical)
Exclusive giveaway. Time 83:67 F 21 '64
NEWS magazines. See Periodicals
NEWS of the day; opera. See Hindemith, P.
NEWS photographers. See Photographers
NEWS photography. See Photography, Journalistic
NEWS stands. See Newsstands
NEWSBOYS
Newsboys' revolt. Time 83:51 Je 26 '64
NEWSDAY (newspaper)
Boss lady. Newsweek 62:56 Jl 15 '63
Dynasty's end? Time 82:69-70 Jl 12 '63
Friendly arrangement. Time 82:36 Ag 23 '63
NEWSPAPER advertising. See Advertising mediums—Newspapers
NEWSPAPER and periodical wholesalers
Lima, Peru, distributor reports expansion plans. Pub W 185:102 Je 8 '64
NEWSPAPER collections in libraries. See Libraries—Newspaper collections
NEWSPAPER columns. See Newspapers—Sections, columns, etc.
NEWSPAPER correspondents. See Reporters and reporting
NEWSPAPER court reporting
Press & the courts. Time 84:50-1 Ag 14 '64
Trial by newspaper. Time 84:52 N 27 '64

NEWSPAPER editors. See Editors and editing
NEWSPAPER ethics. See Journalistic ethics
NEWSPAPER guild. See American newspaper guild
NEWSPAPER men. See Journalists
NEWSPAPER publishing
All the news that's fit to automate. il Time 82:52 Jl 5 '63
How to fold a newspaper: demise of some American newspapers. J. G. Colangelo, jr. il Reporter 30:45-7 Ja 16 '64
Making money by making enemies. il Time 81:94+ Ap 19 '63
New worry in government: not enough newspapers? il U S News 56:111-12 Je 15 '64
Plans for industrial peace in newspaper publishing. Mo Labor R 87:III-IV Ap '64
Signs of the future? use of computers to set type. il Newsweek 64:88 N 9 '64
Something to hoot about. Time 81:62 F 8 '63
NEWSPAPER strikes. See Strikes—United States—Newspapers
NEWSPAPERS
Journalism's challenge and answers. J. Tebbel. Sat R 46:50-1 Je 8 '63
Man with the pencil of light; newspapers of tomorrow. R. L. Tobin. il Sat R 47:138-9+ Ag 29 '64
Newspaper's role; remarks. J. H. Whitney. Time 84:49 N 20 '64
Party of one. C. Fadiman. il Holiday 34:12+ N '63
Read your paper with scissors. J. C. Kennedy. Writer 78:30-1 Ja '65
See also
Audit bureau of circulations
Editors and editing
Freedom of the press
Journalism
News
Newsboys
Religious newspapers and periodicals
Reporters and reporting

Advertising

Story of an ad: protest from kin of Americans killed in Vietnam in Washington star. Nat R 16:435-7 Je 2 '64

Advertising, Personal

See Newspapers—Personal advertisements

Advice columns

Mlle Lonelyhearts; Michele Thibault of The San Fernando Valley times today. Newsweek 62:106+ O 21 '63
Mail-order psychology; advice to the lovelorn. J. Stanley. il Mlle 59:94-5+ Je '64
Tell me, Josephine, ed. by B. Hall. Review Nat R il 16:498+ Je 16 '64. P. L. Buckley

Anecdotes, facetiae, satire, etc.

Out of print. S. Levenson. Read Digest 82:24E My '63

Book reviews

See Book reviews

Color printing

Preprinted insert. P. W. Stone. Sat R 47:38 Ag 8 '64; Reply. R. L. Eastline. 47:54+ S 12 '64

Columns

See Newspapers—Sections, columns, etc.

Crime reporting

Curbing crime news; Philadelphia bar association's guidelines. Time 85:43 Ja 8 '65
Free press & fair trial. il Time 84:72 D 18 '64
Twilight zone; Philadelphia bar association guidelines for covering crime news. Newsweek 65:50 Ja 4 '65
See also
Crime and the press

Employees

Plans for industrial peace in newspaper publishing. Mo Labor R 87:III-IV Ap '64
See also
Journalists

Financial news

How to read the financial pages without going broke. P. Bart. Harper 227:31-5 Ag '63; Discussion. 227:6+; 230:14 O '63, Ja '65

History

History above the headlines. il Sr Schol 82:17 F 6 '63
Publick occurrences both forreign and domestick. Sr Schol 85:9 S 30 '64

Personal advertisements

Personal touch; column in Saturday review. J. F. Fixx. Sat R 47:146-7 Ag 29 '64

Political activities

See Newspapers and politics

Political news

Flank attacks; foreign press reaction to Goldwater. Newsweek 63:58 Je 22 '64
See also
Government and the press

Prices

Economics and the press. il Sr Schol 82:12-15 Mr 27 '63

Religious news

Submerging the story; Pope's death. il Time 81:68 Je 14 '63
See also
Church and the press

Science news

See Science news

Sections, columns, etc.

Ask Henry! excerpts. H. Makow. Read Digest 82:205+ Je '63
Being catty to columnists. il Time 84:68 Jl 17 '64
Buchwald's Washington. il Time 82:62+ S 20 '63
Column right; Barry Goldwater column. Newsweek 65:55-6 Ja 11 '65
Columnists. il Time 84:42 S 25 '64
My son the cook; Prudence Penny, the New York mirror's cooking columnist. il Time 82:96+ O 4 '63
Navel-gazing in wasteland; advertising columns. il Time 83:67 Ap 17 '64
Off the cuff. A. Marple. Writer 76:6-8 N '63
On the beach with Morrie Ryskind. E. McDowell. il Nat R 14:318-19 Ap 23 '63
Permissiveness in Saigon. Time 82:70 D 13 '63
Personnel problems? write dear Margo; Toronto daily star. il Bsns W p74+ D 5 '64
Plastered peer; Earl of Arran's column in London evening news. Time 81:62+ F 8 '63
Practicing medicine in print; Dr William Brady's syndicated column Personal health service. il Time 84:62 D 11 '64
Prose from the pros; nation's leading golf pros turned syndicated columnists. il Time 83:58-9 Je 5 '64
Prudence; concerning Prudence Penny cooking column in the Mirror. New Yorker 39:36-7 S 14 '63
Prudence Penny; the lady columnist who really isn't. H. Goldberg. il Sat Eve Post 236:40+ D 7 '63
Small town in the big town; On the move, column in the Los Angeles times. il Time 81:55-6 My 10 '63
Walk, walk, talk, talk; People, places and things in the Paris edition of the New York herald tribune. il Newsweek 61:52-3 Ap 1 '63

Anecdotes, facetiae, satire, etc.

Aïda meets the press. C. Osborne. il Opera N 28:24-5 D 7 '63

Society page

Suzy says; latest international gossip. P. Coffin. il Look 28:87-90+ Ag 11 '64

Sports news

See Sports journalism

Sunday editions

Sagging supplements. il Newsweek 62:58 S 9 '63
Sunday paper is here to stay. R. L. Tobin. il Sat R 47:45-6 F 8 '64
Trib's Sunday punch; new format. il Bsns W p34+ S 21 '63

Syndicate service

Two hits and a strikeout. R. L. Tobin. Sat R 47:59-60 My 9 '64

Tabloid papers

See also
National enquirer

Travel news

Freewheelers; world of the travel writer. il Newsweek 63:72 Je 1 '64

Womens pages

Books on the women's pages of Times and Tribune; summary of addresses. J. Cook; H. Stix. Pub W 184:32-3 D 2 '63

NEWSPAPERS—*Continued*

Brazil

Best in Brazil; O Estado de São Paulo. il Newsweek 63:75 F 3 '64

Canada

Making headlines; North Renfrew times, Deep River. J. A. Cropley. il Recreation 57:393+ O '64

See also

Winnepeg free press

France

Letter from Paris; closing of left-wing daily newspaper Libération. Genêt. New Yorker 40:109-11 Ja 9 '65

See also

Paris—Newspapers

Germany

Hitler's paper yoke. il Time 83:68 Ap 17 '64

Germany (Federal Republic)

How free is the German press? F. E. Hirsch. Cur Hist 44:226-30+ Ap '63

Outspoken Gräfin. il Time 82:58 S 13 '63

Great Britain

Beaverbrook: Britain's rambunctious press lord. I. Ross. Read Digest 84:155-6+ Mr '64

Clashing colors; Sunday papers' color supplement. il Newsweek 64:68 S 21 '64

Imitating the imitator. il Time 84:71 Jl 24 '64

Jewish chronicle and others. J. Gross. Commentary 36:387-9 N '63

This is our business. R. Moley. Newsweek 64:72 Ag 10 '64

Thunder on the Thames; the British press and the Profumo case. J. Tebbel. il Sat R 46:44-6 Jl 13 '63

Watchdog of the British press. H. Nelson. Sat R 47:42-3 Ag 8 '64

See also

Daily mail. London

Sun (newspaper)

Sunday mirror, London

Times. London

Hawaii

See also

Honolulu—Newspapers

Israel

Double *chutzpah*. il Newsweek 61:89 F 18 '63

Japan

Bigger & better than anyone; Japan's biggest newspaper publisher. il Time 81:57-8 My 24 '63

Latin America

News and Latin America: a balance sheet. B. L. Collier. il Sat R 46:50-1 O 12 '63

South Africa

It's very hard to do, even in South Africa; press investigation. Time 83:69 My 22 '64

South Africa's voice of opposition: Rand daily mail. Time 85:37-8 Ja 8 '65

Switzerland

Lesson in Swiss; Blick's popularity. il Time 82:91 O 18 '63

United States

Advice from a millionaire publisher: address. J. H. Whitney. Sat R 47:71-3 D 12 '64; Discussion. 48:66 Ja 9 '65

All the news that's fit to automate. il Time 82:52 Jl 5 '63

Behold the grass-roots press, alas! B. H. Baglikian. Harper 229:102-5+ D '64

Biggest story in the world; excerpts from address. J. Reston. New Repub 148:15-17 My 4 '63

Celler and the first; concentration of news media ownership. Newsweek 61:72 Mr 25 '63

Crisis for the independent daily. J. Tebbel; reply. L. F. Kent. Sat R 46:63 F 9 '63

Giveaways; giveaway shopping guides. il Time 82:93-4 N 22 '63

History above the headlines. il Sr Schol 82:17 F 6 '63

Integrating the news; Dixie newspapers. Time 81:45 Je 21 '63

Liebling, libel, and the press. L. M. Lyons. Atlan 213:43-8 My '64

Midwest's nice monopolists, John and Mike Cowles. W. B. Furlong. Harper 226:64-8+ Je '63

New worry in government: not enough newspapers? il U S News 56:111-12 Je 15 '64

Newspapers and the culture beat. J. Tebbel. il Sat R 46:61+ Ap 13 '63; Discussion. 46:54-5 My 11 '63

Newspapers finally face a fact. R. L. Tobin. Sat R 46:53-4 My 11 '63; Discussion. 46:48 Je 8 '63

Presidents and the press. J. Tebbel. Sat R 46:68-70+ S 14 '63

Publick occurrences both forreign and domestick. Sr Schol 85:9 S 30 '64

Real sins of the press. L. Markel; discussion. Harper 226:6 F '63

Reporting the report; release of the Warren commission report. il Newsweek 64:100-1 O 12 '64

Sale in suburbia; nine Macy papers sold to Gannett newspapers. Time 83:52 Ap 10 '64

South's new voice; press opinion of Governor Wallace. Time 82:65 S 20 '63

Time of change for the Nation's newspapers. il U S News 55:44-5 N 4 '63

Top U.S. dailies. Time 83:58-60 Ja 10 '64

Trends in typography; newspapers compete in Ayer cup typographical competition. R. L. Tobin. il Sat R 47:51-2 Je 13 '64

Week the dam broke; handling torrents of major news events. il Time 84:75 O 23 '64

Weekly newspaper: commitment in suburbia. W. Sullivan. il Sat R 46:74-5 N 9 '63; Discussion. 46:55+ D 14 '63

Who's the oldest what? Time 83:69 My 1 '64

See also

American newspaper guild

Catholic press

Scripps-Howard newspapers

also names of newspapers, e g. Baltimore sun

also subhead Newspapers under names of cities, e.g. Chicago—Newspapers

Viet Nam (Republic)

Gregorys of Saigon. Newsweek 62:40+ S 23 '63

NEWSPAPERS, Communist. See Communist newspapers

NEWSPAPERS, Publishing of. See Newspaper publishing

NEWSPAPERS and politics

After New Hampshire. Time 83:79 Mr 20 '64

Big bite. N. Mailer. Esquire 59:98+ Mr '63

Breaking precedents. Time 84:86 O 16 '64

Campaign issue: biased reporting? il U S News 57:40 Ag 3 '64

Changing patterns. Time 84:92 O 30 '64

Covering the campaign. Time 84:74 O 2 '64

Covering the candidate; Goldwater and the press. il Newsweek 64:71-2 Jl 20 '64

Curious detachment; final weeks of presidential campaign. Time 84:35 N 6 '64

How editors stand on the candidates. U S News 57:8 S 21 '64

More early picks; early newspaper endorsements in presidential campaign. Time 84:82 S 18 '64

Out of the doldrums; press reaction to Goldwater competitor. il Time 84:60 Jl 3 '64

Sampling the winds. Time 83:55 Ja 3 '64

Six-to-one party press; presidential endorsements. Time 84:43 S 25 '64

Sizing it up; presidential election. Time 84:69 N 13 '64

This is our business. R. Moley. Newsweek 64:72 Ag 10 '64

Those outside our family; press reaction to Barry Goldwater. Time 84:28A-29 Jl 24 '64

To the LBJ corral. Newsweek 64:68+ S 21 '64

Too good to miss; 1964 presidential campaign. Time 84:71 S 4 '64

Two party press? B. H. Bagdikian. New Repub 151:11-12 O 10 '64; Correction. 151:37 O 17 '64; Discussion. 151:29-30 O 31; 36 N 14 '64

View from the Tower; Chicago tribune for Goldwater. Christian Cent 81:1262-3 O 14 '64

Who backed whom; presidential candidate endorsements. Newsweek 64:64 N 2 '64

Winds of change. il Time 84:40 Ag 28 '64

NEWSPRINT industry. See Paper making and trade

NEWSSTANDS

Improvement. New Yorker 40:21-2 Jl 25 '64

NEWTON, Douglas

Funerary figures of the Kafirs. Natur Hist 72:40-7 Je '63

NEWTON, Sir Isaac

Gravitational forces and effects. K. L. Franklin. il Natur Hist 72:12-19 O; 44-51 N '63

They made our world. L. Rosten. por Look 27:38-9 S 24 '63

NEWTON, Janet

Individualists; Mlle's annual Merit awards. il por Mlle 58:72-3 Ja '64

NEWTON, Joseph Fort
Minister's mail. Read Digest 85:119-21 O '64

NEWTON, Quigg
Counterattack at Colorado. W. H. Carroll. Nat R 14:494-5 Je 18 '63

NEWTON, Robert R.
Geodesy by satellite. bibliog Science 144:803-8 My 15 '64; Correction. 145:659-60 Ag 14 '64

NEWTON, Mass.
Eliminate the contract plowing. W. S. Pratt. il Am City 78:112-13 S '63
Propeller on a platform preserves a pond. J. B. Penney. il Am City 79:84-5 Jl '64

Education

Does Sodom love Gomorrah? reading course based on Bible at Newton high. Time 83:44 Mr 20 '64
Island of change. il Time 83:40 Ja 24 '64
Newton: pipeline from Harvard. P. Shrag. il Sat R 48:49-50+ Ja 16 '65
Schools in Newton; experiment in flexibility. C. E. Brown. Atlan 214:74-8 O '64

NEWTS
Tarichatoxin tetrodotoxin: a potent neurotoxin. H. S. Mosher and others. bibliog il Science 144:1100-10 My 29 '64

NEXT time I'll sing to you; drama. See Saunders, J.

NEY, Edward P.
Balloon observations during the July eclipse. Sky & Tel 26:251-4 N '63

NEYHART, Amos E.
Need for driver education. pors Motor T 16:102-5 N '64

NEZ Percé Indians
See also
Joseph (Indian chief)

NGO-dinh-Can
Dynasty's end; execution of Ngo dinh Can. il Time 83:42 My 15 '64
Off to court. il por Time 83:29 F 14 '64
Third brother. il por Time 83:27 My 1 '64

NGO-dinh-Diem
Diem from the grave; interview, ed. by C. W. Wiley. Nat R 15:426 N 19 '63
How to beat the reds in southeast Asia; interview, ed. by S. W. Sanders. por U S News 54:70-3 F 18 '63

about

Agony in Saigon: the lady & the cadaver. D. Warner. Reporter 29:39-42 O 10 '63
Back of the revolt in South Vietnam. il U S News 55:41 N 11 '63
Bodies. il Time 82:42 D 6 '63
Changeover in Viet Nam. il Sr Schol 83:20-1 D 6 '63
Coping with Capricorn. il por Time 82:19-20 S 6 '63
Coup in South Viet Nam. il por Sr Schol 83:18 N 15 '63
Diem and Nhu: how they died. il por U S News 55:47 N 18 '63
Diem, the mandarin. America 109:111-12 Ag 3 '63
Diem under pressure. il Newsweek 62:48 Jl 29 '63
Edge of chaos. S. Karnow. il por Sat Eve Post 236:28-37 S 28 '63
Facing hard facts in Vietnam. H. G. Fairbanks. il Cath World 199:89-95 My '64
Fall of the House of Ngo dinh. S. Karnow. il por Sat Eve Post 236:75-9 D 21 '63
Growing troubles for the Diem regime. il por U S News 55:22 Jl 29 '63
Hard choice for the U.S; get tough or get out. R. P. Martin. il por U S News 55:54-7 S 9 '63
His brother's keeper; remarks, September 6, 1963. C. B. Marshall. New Repub 149:6 S 21 '63
In Asia's hot war; more trouble for U.S. il U S News 55:58 S 2 '63
Last of the Mandarins. por Time 82:31 N 8 '63
Letter from Saigon. R. Shaplen. il New Yorker 39:201-4+ D 14 '63; 40:37-8+ Jl 11 '64
Nhu deal. K. Crawford. Newsweek 62:34 S 16 '63
On playing God. Reporter 29:14+ N 21 '63
Once again: no-win. Nat R 15:467-9 D 3 '63
Queen bee. il Time 82:21-5 Ag 9 '63
Reunifying Vietnam. New Repub 149:3-5 S 14 '63
Road to freedom for South Vietnam. Nat R 15:177-9 S 10 '63
Saigon coup. America 109:624-5 N 16 '63
Symbolic suicide; Nguyen Tuong Tam. Newsweek 62:43-4 Jl 22 '63
Time for Diem to mend ways. Life 55:4 Jl 26 '63
Truth about a war Americans aren't winning. S. W. Sanders. il por U S News 55:46-9 Ag 5 '63
Uncertain prospect for Vietnam. Commonweal 79:212 N 15 '63
U.S. may pull rug from under Diem. il Bsns W p22 Ag 31 '63
Viet Nam: in double jeopardy? il por Sr Schol 85:13-17 D 2 '64
Vietnam: getting to know the Nhus. il por Newsweek 62:33-4+ S 9 '63
Vietnam's two wars; with Gen. Dinh. S. Castan. il Look 28:32+ Ja 28 '64
What Diem thinks about the war in Vietnam. il por U S News 55:46-7 Ag 19 '63
Who killed Diem and why? V. L. Borin. il por Nat R 16:441-6 Je 2 '64
Who really runs South Vietnam? por U S News 55:13 S 2 '63
Why U.S. is losing in Vietnam, an inside story; interview. S. T. Williams. il por U S News 57:62-4+ N 9 '64

NGO-dinh-Nhu
Agony in Saigon: the lady & the cadaver. D. Warner. Reporter 29:39-42 O 10 '63
Back of the revolt in South Vietnam. il U S News 55:41 N 11 '63
Changeover in Viet Nam. il Sr Schol 83:20-1 D 6 '63
Diem and Nhu: how they died. il U S News 55:47 N 18 '63
Fall of the House of Ngo dinh. S. Karnow. il por Sat Eve Post 236:75-9 D 21 '63
Letter from Saigon. R. Shaplen. il New Yorker 39:201-4+ D 14 '63; 40:37-8+ Jl 11 '64
Nhus of Vietnam snap back at the U.S. il por Life 55:38-38A S 20 '63

NGO-dinh-Nhu, Mme
Diem's Dragon Lady breathes fire at us; interview, ed. by M. Orshefsky. por Life 55:31 Ag 16 '63
Matter of re-education. por Time 82:28+ S 27 '63
Mike Wallace interviews Madame Nhu. pors McCalls 91:192+ N '63
Noblesse oblige. Time 82:18 S 13 '63
Vietnam's Madame Nhu: I have proof people are with us; excerpts from interview. por U S News 55:36-7 S 16 '63

about

Agony in Saigon: the lady & the cadaver. D. Warner. Reporter 29:39-42 O 10 '63
Beat them; Buddhist campaign no longer a dispute over religious toleration. il Newsweek 62:46 Ag 19 '63
Bitter mother's reunion; her children in Rome. il pors Sat Eve Post 236:80-1 D 21 '63
Claws out. Newsweek 63:40 Ja 27 '64
Dialogue at the door. Time 84:21 Jl 3 '64
Dragon Lady, dragonfly. il pors Time 82:33 S 20 '63
Dragon Lady woos U. S. il por Bsns W p36 O 12 '63
Dragonfly: Mme Nhu in America. il por U S News 55:24 O 21 '63
Edge of chaos. S. Karnow. il por Sat Eve Post 236:28-37 S 28 '63
Hairy caterpillars. por Time 82:41 O 11 '63
Hard choice for the U.S.; get tough or get out. R. P. Martin. il por U S News 55:54-7 S 9 '63
I do not want my name mentioned ever, with hers. M. V. Thayer. McCalls 91:237 N '63
In the lion's cage; visit to the U.S. il por Time 82:26-7 O 18 '63
Lady is for burning; the seven deadly sins of Madame Nhu. C. B. Luce. Nat R 15:395-9 N 5 '63
Lady known as Nhu. Nation 197:269 N 2 '63
Lady's not for burning. Reporter 29:17 S 26 '63
Madame Firebrand. por Sr Schol 83:12-13 S 20 '63
Mme Nhu and the press. America 109:449-50 O 19 '63
Mme Nhu comes to town. Nat R 15:338+ O 22 '63
Madame Nhu's mission. K. Crawford. Newsweek 62:26 O 28 '63
Mme Nhu's visit. America 109:476-7 O 26 '63
Much ado and Mme Nhu. pors Newsweek 62:35-6 O 21 '63
Next: the bewitching Nhu girls give us the big eye. il pors Life 55:28-9 O 11 '63
Nhus of Vietnam snap back at the U.S. il por Life 55:38-38A S 20 '63
Nobody home; visit to US. il por Time 82:27 O 25 '63
One world; people in current news as television stars. Reporter 29:24+ O 24 '63
Queen bee. il pors Time 82:21-5 Ag 9 '63

NGO-dinh-Nhu, Mme—about—*Continued*
Recognizing Mme Nhu. il Newsweek 62:35 N 18 '63
Sad week for Mme Nhu. por Newsweek 62:30 N 11 '63
Some new volleys from Madame Nhu. por U S News 55:24 O 28 '63
U.S. rebuke for Vietnam's Mme Nhu. por U S News 55:28 O 7 '63
Vietnam: getting to know the Nhus. il pors Newsweek 62:33-4+ S 9 '63
What next for Madame Nhu and family? il por U S News 55:28 N 18 '63
Whew! visit to the US. Time 82:84 N 1 '63
Who really runs South Vietnam? por U S News 55:13 S 2 '63
Widow's retreat. Time 82:27 N 22 '63
You're in America now. il Time 82:32 N 15 '63

NGO-dinh-Thuc, abp
What's really going on in Vietnam. il Nat R 15:388-90 N 5 '63

NGORONGORO conservation area. See National parks and reserves—Tanganyika

NGUYEN-cao-Ky
To the north. il Time 84:20-1 Jl 31 '64

NGUYEN Khanh
America's new program for Vietnam war; the way it will work. por U S News 56:6 Mr 30 '64
But in South Vietnam a tough little general has other plans. H. Moffett. pors Life 56: 22-3 F 14 '64
Can Khanh? New Repub 150:3-4 Mr 28 '64
Chips on Khanh. il por Time 83:30 Mr 20 '64
First-half report. il por Newsweek 64:37 Ag 10 '64
Fresh stir of hope in Vietnam. il Bsns W p36 Mr 21 '64
General Khanh's ailment. Nation 199:101-2 S 14 '64
Hopes fade for South Vietnam. por Bsns W p29 Ag 29 '64
In Vietnam it's more than guns. il pors Bsns W p82-3+ Ag 1 '64
Intrigue in Saigon. il por Newsweek 63:42 Je 15 '64
Left hand, right hand. il Newsweek 63:30 Mr 30 '64
Letter from Saigon. R. Shaplen. New Yorker 40:37-8+ Jl 11; 179-86+ S 19 '64
National unity and stepped-up war. il por Time 83:29 F 14 '64
New title, new troubles. President Khanh of Vietnam. il por U S News 57:19 Ag 31 '64
New turn in a fifteen-year war: the real story of Vietnam. il por U S News 56:50-2 Mr 23 '64
Power play. il por Newsweek 64:34 Ag 31 '64
Quiet coup: and now General Khanh. il por Newsweek 63:33-4 F 10 '64
Remaking a revolution. Time 84:28 S 25 '64
Saigon: crucial hour? il por Newsweek 64: 22+ Ag 17 '64
Second coup. Sr Schol 84:6 F 14 '64
Taylor tries a new start in Vietnam. P. Grose. il por N Y Times Mag p 12-13+ Ag 9 '64
To the north. il Time 84:20-1 Jl 31 '64
Top man in Vietnam: General Khanh grabs power. por U S News 56:12 F 10 '64
Toward the showdown? il por Time 84:23-7 Ag 7 '64
Vietnam: descent into desperation. F. Sully. il Newsweek 64:33-4 S 7 '64
Vietnam: odds lengthen. il Newsweek 64:81 O 5 '64
Vietnam: wary eye on General Khanh. il Newsweek 64:29 Ag 3 '64

NGUYEN Thai
Vietnamese speaks out. New Repub 148:14-17 Je 8 '63

NGUYEN tuong Tam
Suicide in many forms. por Time 82:32+ Jl 19 '63
Symbolic suicide. por Newsweek 62:43-4 Jl 22 '63

NHU, Le-thuy-. See Le-thuy-Nhu

NHU, Ngo-dinh-. See Ngo-dinh-Nhu

NHU, Ngo-dinh-, Mme. See Ngo-dinh-Nhu Mme

NIACIN
Nicotinic acid analogs: effects on response of chick embryos and hens to organophosphate toxicants. J. C. Roger and others. bibliog Science 144:539-40 My 1 '64

NIAGARA FALLS
Thundering water; with portfolio. B. Catton. Am Heritage 15:32-49+ Je '64

NIAGARA FALLS, N.Y.
Honeymoon revisited, this time with the kids; tourist attractions and accommodations. il Bsns W p 144-5+ O 17 '64
Niagara Falls: servant of good neighbors. il Nat Geog Mag 123:574-87 Ap '63

NIAGARA RIVER
New York state asks permission to remove Niagara shoal. Dept State Bul 48:717 My 6 '63

Power utilization

Niagara Falls; servant of good neighbors. il Nat Geog Mag 123:580-1 Ap '63

NIARCHOS, Stavros Spyros
Biggest fleet. il por Newsweek 65:67-8 Ja 25 '65
Is Niarchos heading for port? il por Bsns W p 110+ O 24 '64

NICARAGUA

Politics and government

Evolutionary election. Time 81:29 F 15 '63
New name, same regime in Nicaragua? il Sr Schol 82:5 F 20 '63

NICCACCI, Rufino
Friar who saved 5,000 Jews. W. I. Fischman. il pors Look 28:66+ D 1 '64

NICE family; story. See Corson, M.

NICE girl for Christmas; story. See Fritz, J.

NICETIES of life; story. See O'Donovan, J.

NICHOLAS, H. G.
Financing the U.N: pressures and principles. Reporter 31:17-18 D 31 '64
Signs of things to come. Reporter 31:20-1 N 5 '64

NICHOLLS, William
Anglican view. Christian Cent 81:3331-2 Mr 11 '64

NICHOLS, Beverley
Breakfast with Oscar. Horizon 6:46-7 Autumn '64

NICHOLS, Bobby
Strokes of fortune. Newsweek 64:52-3 Ag 3 '64
Winning a barrel of beer money. A. Wright. il por Sports Illus 21:32-5 S 7 '64
With the help of St Jude. por Time 84:42-3 Jl 31 '64

NICHOLS, Clarence W.
Policy problems in international trade of agricultural products; address, February 6, 1964. Dept State Bul 50:416-23 Mr 16 '64

NICHOLS, George, Jr
Landfall on a single radio beacon. Yachting 115:148-9 F '64
—See Woods, J. F. jt. auth.

NICHOLS, Jeannette
Artist as rhinoceros; poem. Sat R 46:50 Je 1 '63
Kneeling by the window; poem. Sat R 47:56 O 31 '64
Much too sane; poem. Sat R 47:68 Ag 15 '64
My half of the apple; poem. Atlan 214:87 D '64
No one here but us; poem. Sat R 47:19 Jl 11 '64
Once we ate roses; poem. Sat R 46:39 N 2 '63
One day; poem. Atlan 212:69 D '63
One thing leads to another and; poem. Atlan 214:110 S '64
What got away; poem. Sat R 48:47 Ja 23 '65

NICHOLS, Leola F.
Outwit those stay-around staph germs. Parents Mag 38:74-5+ O '63

NICHOLS, Mike
Comic catapults to higher stage. D. J. Hamblin. il pors Life 56:100-2+ Mr 20 '64
Mike and Max. New Yorker 40:32-3 Ap 11 '64
Nichols touch. il por Time 84:86 N 27 '64
Now the Mike Nichols touch. B. Lefferts. il pors N Y Times Mag p34+ N 22 '64
People are talking about. por Vogue 144:142-3 O 15 '64

NICHOLS, Nell
Freezing & canning cookbook; excerpts. por Farm J 87:101-5+ Mr; 94-7+ Ap '63

NICHOLS, Paul, pseud. See Dallis, N. P.

NICHOLS, Rachel
Honeymoon present; story. Redbook 120:68-9 Ap '63

NICHOLS, Robert C.
Career decisions of very able students. Science 144:1315-19 Je 12 '64

NICHOLS, Robert Herman
You aren't going to believe this, but. . . A. Wright. il por Sports Illus 21:48-9 Jl 27 '64

NICHOLS, W. W. and others
Chromosome abnormalities in vitro in human leukocytes associated with Schmidt-Ruppin Rous sarcoma virus. bibliog Science 146:248-50 O 9 '64

NICHOLS, Wade H.
Fine romance, with no kisses; excerpt from address, April 14, 1964. Writer 77:18-19 Jl '64

NICHOLS, William
(ed) See Hoover, H. President Hoover and his friends
NICHOLS, William I.
Morals revolution; address, May 4, 1964. Vital Speeches 30:539-42 Je 15 '64
NICHOLSON, Anthony N.
Gravitational stress: changes in cortical excitability. Science 145:1458-9 S 25 '64
NICHOLSON, Arnold
Hero of the spring. Read Digest 82:158-64 My '63
NICHOLSON, C. A.
Texas dog days. Field & S 69:44-6 D '64
NICHOLSON, Dave
Out or out-of-the-park. il Newsweek 63:64 My 18 '64
NICHOLSON, Mary Ann
Princess too little; drama. Plays 22:79-82 Ap '63
NICHOLSON, Scott
Bright young men of information. Duns R 82:pt2 96-7+ S '63
Fast track for the rails. Duns R 81:pt2 S113-15+ Je '63
R&D. industry's maverick. Duns R 81:63-4+ Ap '63
NICHOLSON, Seth Barnes
Obituary
Sky & Tel por 26:63 Ag '63
NICHOLSON, Thomas D.
Lunar shadow on Alaska. Natur Hist 72:10-17 Je '63
Reviews. Natur Hist 72:4-6 Ag '63
Sky reporter. See issues of Natural history incorporating Nature magazine
NICHOLSON, Tom
Detroit's surprising mayor. Harper 227:76-8+ D '63
NICKEL, Herman, and Sheehan, Robert
Germany's financial coronaries. Fortune 69:130-1+ Je '64
NICKEL
Low-energy electron diffraction: improved experimental methods provide new information on the structure of surfaces of solids. A. U. MacRae. bibliog il Science 139:379-88 F 1 '63
NICKEL (coin) See Money—United States
NICKEL cadmium batteries. See Storage batteries
NICKEL mines and mining
See also
Falconbridge nickel mines, limited
NICKEL steel
New alloy for some tough jobs; maraging steel. il Bsns W p87-8 Ap 18 '64
NICKLAUS, Frederick
Old woman setting silver; Hands are first to believe; poems. Poetry 103:370-1 Mr '64
NICKLAUS, Jack
Golf. See issues of Sports illustrated
Good time to obey a mother-in-law; ed. by G. Brown. por Sports Illus 19:44-5 Ag 5 '63
I changed my game to win the masters; ed. by G. S. Brown. Sports Illus 18:18-23 Ap 22 '63
I got all keyed up and I thought I was going to win. por Sports Illus 19:20-1 Jl 1 '63
I won $100,000 and a pair of moldy salmon. por Sports Illus 19:26-7+ D 9 '63
Key to the Masters. por Sports Illus 20:30-3 Ap 6 '64
Life I lead. por Sports Illus 20:80-6+ My 11; 44-6+ My 18; 52-4+ My 25; 46-8+ Je 1 '64
Old club offers a new challenge; ed. by G. S. Brown. por Sports Illus 18:46-53 Je 17 '63
Three big ones talk about golf; interview. ed. by C. Price. pors Sat Eve Post 236:66+ Ap 13 '63

about

Children's hour; P.G.A. championship. il por Time 82:53 Ag 2 '63
He's a great pair of golfers. W. B. Furlong. il pors N Y Times Mag p 14+ S 1 '63
Hitting man's golfer. Time 83:55 F 21 '64
Hold that trap: world series of golf. por Time 82:66 S 20 '63
Master. il por Time 81:92-3 Ap 19 '63
Matter of pride at endsville. G. S. Brown. il pors Sports Illus 21:22-7 N 30 '64
More jack for Jack. por Time 81:96+ My 17 '63
Pair of pained plutocrats gave TV a show; world series of golf. G. S. Brown. il por Sports Illus 19:20-1 S 16 '63
Spain sent a two-man armada; Canada cup tournament in France. H. Longhurst. il por Sports Illus 19:18-20 N 4 '63
Triumph against all odds in Las Vegas. A. Wright. il Sports Illus 18:30-3 My 13 '63
Triumph for two swingers. A. Wright. il por Sports Illus 21:24-6 D 14 '64
Young Jack, the mighty master. A. Wright. il por Sports Illus 18:26-31 Ap 15 '63
NICKS, F. William
Innovator at the till. il por Bsns W p56-8+ Je 6 '64
NICKS, Oran W. and Reynolds, O. E.
Decontamination and sterilization of lunar and planetary spacecraft; letter. Science 142:539-40 N 1 '63
NICOL, M. and Jura, G.
Mössbauer spectrum of iron-57 in iron metal at very high pressures. bibliog Science 141:1035-8 S 13 '63
NICOLAI, Otto
Merry wives of Windsor. P. L. Miller. Am Rec G 30:941 Je 30 '64
On records; Merry wives of Windsor. Opera N 29:35 D 19 '64
NICOLAYSEN, Mary
Art for the pre-schooler. Design 65:142-5 Mr '64
NICOLIN, Curt René
Biggest employer; the Wallenbergs. il por Time 82:98 N 29 '63
NICOLL, Allardyce
Company of masks. Opera N 29:6-10 Ja 16 '65
NICOLSON, Sir Harold
Kings and queens. New Yorker 38:24-6 F 9 '63
NICOTINAMIDE
Fetal death from nicotinamide-deficient diet and its prevention by chlorpromazine and imipramine. I. Fratta and others. bibliog il Science 145:1429-30 S 25 '64
Nicotinamide adenine dinucleotidase activity in cells of tuberculous animals. A. Bekierkunst and others. bibliog il Science 145:280-1 Jl 17 '64
NICOTINIC acid. See Niacin
NIEBERDING, C. B.
How many rectangles in a square? U S Camera 27:89 F '64
NIEBUHR, Reinhold
Crisis in American Protestantism. Christian Cent 80:1498-501 D 4 '63
Panama crisis. New Repub 150:5-6 F 1 '64
Speaking out. por Sat Eve Post 236:12+ N 16 '63
NIEBURG, H. L.
Atoms-for-peace: hope deferred. Bul Atomic Sci 20:35-40 Ja '64
NIECE, Ronald L. and others
Erythroid homeostasis in normal and genetically anemic mice: reaction to induced polycythemia. bibliog Science 142:1468-9 D 13 '63
NIEDECKER, Lorine
Three poems: River-marsh-drowse; Prosperity is poverty; Now in one year. Poetry 102:302-3 Ag '63
NIEDER, Philip C. and Randall, Walter
Sound-evoked potentials in neocortex of unanesthetized opossum. bibliog Science 144:429-30 Ap 24 '64
NIEDERGERKE, R. See Orkand, R. K. jt. auth.
NIEHAUS, Margaret Stewart
Answer lady of space. M. Clapp. il pors Todays Health 41:20-1+ O '63
NIELSEN, A. C. company
Broadcast ratings lose spell; testimony before Rep. Oren Harris' Permanent investigations subcommittee. il Bsns W p30-1 Ap 13 '63
Gadget; radio and TV rating services. il Newsweek 61:80 Ap 8 '63
Great sampler. Nation 196:366-7 My 4 '63
Nielsen vs. Quixote. America 109:657 N 23 '63
Peace on earth, good will to networks. G. Ace. Sat R 47:9 D 26 '65
Scandal! TV payola uncovered. G. Ace. Sat R 48:6+ Ja 2 '65
Selling confusion. il Time 81:79-80 Ap 12 '63
Shadow strikes again. R. L. Shayon. Sat R 46:51 Jl 13 '63
Television ratings on trial. B. Lindeman and A. Patureau. il Sat Eve Post 237:13-17 F 8 '64
NIELSEN, Alice
Neglected diva. G. Pluck. pors Hobbies 69:30-1 Je '64
NIELSEN, Bodil Schmidt-. See Schmidt-Nielsen, B.
NIELSEN, Carl
Bernstein's Nielsen: an overwhelming realization. J. W. Barker. Am Rec G 29:726 My '63
NIELSEN, Jon
Sketching tour of France. il por Am Artist 28:20-5+ Ap '64

NIELSEN, Knut Schmidt-. See Schmidt-Nielsen, K.
NIELSEN, Niels C. Jr.
Religion and public education. America 108: 830-1 Je 8 '63
NIELSEN, Sivert A.
Education; address, June 7, 1964. Vital Speeches 30:603-5 Jl 15 '64
NIELSEN, Waldemar A.
Africa is poised on the razor's edge. N Y Times Mag p 11+ F 9 '64
NIEMAN, R. H. See Gardner, W. R. jt. auth.
NIEMAN fellowships
Nieman fellowships. L. M. Lyons. Atlan 214: 99-102 D '64
NIEMANN, Carl
Alpha-chymotrypsin and the nature of enzyme catalysis. bibliog Science 143:1287-96 Mr 20 '64
NIEMEYER, Gerhart
Collapsing UN. Nat R 16:313-16+ Ap 21 '64
NIEMÖLLER, Martin
Pastor Niemöller's torpedoes; blasts against warmongering. Time 85:55 Ja 15 '65
NIERING, W. A. and others
Saguaro: a population in relation to environment. bibliog Science 142:15-23 O 4 '63
NIGERIA
Land and people of Nigeria, by B. Forman and H. Forman. Review
Negro Hist Bul 28:69 D '64. M. J. Whitehead
See also
Agriculture—Nigeria
Arts and crafts—Nigeria
Education—Nigeria
Elections—Nigeria
Investments, Foreign (in Nigeria)
Natural resources—Nigeria
Public opinion—Nigeria

Description and travel

Nigeria: the waking land. T. Sterling. il Holiday 34:32+ D '63

Economic conditions

Development of Nigeria. W. F. Stolper. il Sci Am 209:168-72+ bibliog(p308) S '63
Investment opportunities in Nigeria. H. J. Massaquoi. il Ebony 19:67-8+ Mr '64
Nigeria; black Africa's brightest hope. D. Reed. il Read Digest 82:186-92 Mr '63
Up with the poor. New Repub 150:10 Je 27 '64

Economic policy

Development of Nigeria. W. F. Stolper. il Sci Am 209:168-72+ bibliog(p308) S '63

Industries

Federal Republic of Nigeria. B. Floyd. bibliog il Focus 15:1-6 O '64

Native races

Ancient beverage center of cultural focus; of the Kofyar people. Sci Digest 53:54-5 F '63

Politics and government

As Nigeria goes. E. Huxley. Nat R 16:1105-6 D 15 '64
Just in time; political crisis averted. Time 85:30 Ja 15 '65
Nation on trial. il Time 81:29-30 Mr 1 '63
Next hurdle; threat of split averted. Newsweek 65:43 Ja 18 '65
Nigeria: a unique nation; excerpts from African presence in world affairs. A. Rivkin. Cur Hist 45:329-34 D '63
Nigeria; black Africa's brightest hope. D. Reed. il Read Digest 82:186-92 Mr '63
Peace or pieces. il Sr Schol 85:21-2 Ja 14 '65
Statesmen's triumph. Sr Schol 85:20 Ja 21 '65
Verdict in Lagos. il Time 82:39 S 20 '63

Social life and customs

I believe. Seventeen 22:90-1 My '63
NIGERIAN art. See Art, Nigerian
NIGERIAN literature
Africa's market literature. J. O. Reed. Nation 196:509-10 Je 15 '63
NIGERIAN music. See Music, Nigerian
NIGERIAN students in the United States. See Foreign students in the United States
NIGERIANS
Land and people of Nigeria, by B. Forman and H. Forman. Review
Negro Hist Bul 28:69 D '64. M. J. Whitehead
NIGHT airglow. See Airglow
NIGHT clubs
Bright acts to fill the tables. il Life 57:68+ Jl 24 '64
Corruption uncorked in New York. P. Welch and others. il Life 54:22-31+ Ap 5 '63
Fun places. Vogue 143:80-1+ F 1 '64
Gospel as gimmick; Sweet chariot night club. N. Hentoff. Reporter 29:46-7 Ag 15 '63; Reply. J. Chase. 29:8 S 26 '63
Have no fear and keep it clear, the jive is comin' and The Lion's here; excerpts from Music on my mind. W. Smith. il Esquire 61:68-71+ Je '64
How to succeed; Shepheard's. il Newsweek 63:68 Mr 23 '64
I know a place in Paris. R. Gary. il Holiday 37:54-7+ Ja '65
In old Morocco; opening of Manhattan's new El Morocco. il Time 84:35 D 25 '64
Mr Fisher is open. J. Richardson. Esquire 60:158+ D '63
New York's new night life. B. Leavitt. il Look 28:32-7 Jl 28 '64
Nice kids' night places, uptown New York. il Vogue 143:78-9 F 15 '64
Night people. C. Brossard. il Look 27:58a-58g Mr 26 '63
Now hear the word; Sweet chariot nite club. Newsweek 61:94 My 27 '63
On the town. il Newsweek 62:109-10 N 25 '63
Rooms with views. il Newsweek 61:81 Je 3 '63
Le sidewalk; Le club. il Newsweek 61:52 Mr 4 '63
Sioux in Paris; Le Crazy horse saloon. il Time 85:56 Ja 22 '65
Slipping the disque; *discothèques*. il Time 83: 62 Mr 20 '64
Tables for two (cont) New Yorker 38:142-4 F 16 '63
That happy feeling; beer-and-banjo fun. il Time 84:60 S 25 '64
Tough time for puritans behind the iron curtain. C. Grenier. il N Y Times Mag p 14-15+ My 24 '64
Urbunnity; Playboy club. il Newsweek 63:48-9 Ja 6 '64
Vogue's notebook; New Jimmy's in Paris. il Vogue 141:44-5 Mr 1 '63
Way out on the town; Chicago. il Library J 88:2446-50 Je 15 '63
What goes on in those teen nightclubs. L. Dickert and A. Seidenbaum. il McCalls 90: 38+ Je '63
What's on this season; clubs in New York. il Vogue 142:100-5 N 15 '63
Where the ins go out. R. Alden. il N Y Times Mag p 12-13 D 27 '64

Employees

Funny side of the Bunny business; Playboy clubs. J. Skow. il Sat Eve Post 236:56-7 Mr 2 '63
NIGHT in Lisbon; novel. See Remarque, E. M.
NIGHT life; story. See Randall, F. E.
NIGHT lights. See Electric lamps
NIGHT out; story. See Gerber, M. J.
NIGHT photography. See Photography, Night
NIGHT talk; story. See Rogin, G.
NIGHT vision
Night vision. H. P. Martin. Motor B 114:119 Jl '64
NIGHT watchman's occurrence book; story. See Naipaul, V. S.
NIGHT work
How to live with a swing-shift husband. R. Worthington. il Parents Mag 39:50-1+ O '64
125,000 New Yorkers work the whole night through. R. W. Apple, jr. il N Y Times Mag p53+ Ap 5 '64
NIGHTCLUBS. See Night clubs
NIGHTGOWNS, pajamas, etc.
Selecting summer sleepwear. il Good H 158: 134 Je '64
NIGHTHAWKS
Boomer of the bird world. L. Hothem. il Field & S 69:59+ My '64
NIGHTINGALE; opera. See Stravinsky, I. F.
NIGHTINGALE; story. See Vivante, A.
NIGHTS before Christmas; story. See Cavanaugh, A.
NIGHTSHADE, Black
Deadly nightshade. Sci N L 86:204 S 26 '64
NIGRELLI, Ross Franco
Underwater guinea pigs help scientists study life. H. M. Schwalb. il por Sci Digest 53: 6-11 F '63
NIHILISM, Ethical. See Ethical nihilism
NIIHAU (island)
Niihau: a shoal of time. G. Daws and T. Head. il Am Heritage 14:48-51+ O '63
NIJINSKA, Bronislava
Fabulous career of Bronislava Nijinska. J. Anderson. il pors Dance Mag 37:40-6 Ag '63
NIKE-X. See Guided missiles—Defenses

NIKI-KAI opera company. See Opera—Japan
NIKKO, Japan
Day in Nikko. il Sunset 132:94-7 Ap '64
NIKODIM, abp
Russian calls on Pope but Greek snubs him. Christian Cent 80:1193 O 2 '63
NIKOLAIS, Alwin
Sanctum, by Alwin Nikolais; Henry street playhouse. D. Hering. Dance Mag 38:29 Ap '64
NIKONOS cameras. See Cameras
NIKULA, Pentti
Jump up, twist around, set another record. G. S. Brown. il por Sports Illus 18:38-9+ F 25 '63
NILE perch fishing. See Perch fishing
NILE RIVER
Bettina's Nile diary; tr. by A. Foulke. S. Bodin. il Vogue 143:132-7+ Ja 1 '64
Gods, men & the river. il Time 83:30-40 My 22 '64
Last flood. il Newsweek 62:78 S 2 '63
New Nile. il UNESCO Courier 17:34-5 Jl '64
Nile. U S Camera 27:40-7 My '64
Nile cruise. il Travel 120:45-9 O '63
Nile: problem and promise. il Nat Geog Mag 124:622-3, sup(folded map) O '63
See also
Aswan High Dam
NILSEN, Aileen Pace
College may cost less than you think. Suc Farm 62:92 My '64
NILSSON, Birgit
And then I had to sing like an Indian; ed. by M. Mayer. pors Sat Eve Post 236:86+ O 19 '63
Die Nilsson & la Nilsson; interview, ed. by W. Weaver. pors Hi Fi 15:48-51+ F '65
about
Free choice. M. Mayer. por Opera N 28:26-7 Ap 4 '64
Music to my ears; Nilsson's Leonore. I. Kolodin. Sat R 46:41 F 9 '63
Scaling the high C's with Birgit Nilsson. E. Coleman. il pors N Y Times Mag p22-3+ O 13 '63
Stars at home: photographs. Opera N 29:14-16 Ja 16 '65
NIMBUS (satellite) See Artificial satellites—Meteorological applications
NIMITZ, Chester William
Six minutes that changed the world; with editorial comment. S. E. Morison. il Am Heritage 14:50-5+ F '63
NIMROD, Jean Ann
But I'm so shy! Farm J 87:97 Mr '63
If your teen wants to marry. . ; ed. by M. Longwell. Farm J 88:54-5 Je '64
NIMS, John Frederick
Catullus, LXX; poem. Sat R 46:8 O 5 '63
Classicism of Robert Frost. Sat R 46:22-3+ F 23 '63
Curse; poem. Sat R 46:37 O 12 '63
Greatness in moderation. Sat R 46:25-7 O 19 '63
(tr) See Aridjis, H. H. Month of June
(tr) See Bonifaz Nuño, R. Smoke
(tr) See Castellanos, R. Hecuba's testament
(tr) See Paz, O. Pause; Here; Girl
NIMURA, Yeichi
Ballet arts associates at Arts and design auditorium. J. Maskey. Dance Mag 37:65+ My '63
NIÑA II. See Sailing vessels
NINA upstairs; story. See Gasner, B.
NINETEEN hundred and eighties
Future that young people will face in America. il U S News 57:50-2+ Ag 17 '64
NINETEEN hundred and eighty-four
Equality and 1984; address, June 2, 1963. B. I. Bernhard. Vital Speeches 29:594-7 Jl 15 '63
NINETEEN hundred and five
Glittering era of The merry widow. J. Keating. il N Y Times Mag p 12-13+ Ag 16 '64
NINETEEN hundred and seventies
Nation and world face sweeping changes; study of Technical military planning operation. il Nations Bsns 52:23-5+ Ja '64
NINETEEN hundred and seventy
Just seven years from now: coming changes in America. il U S News 55:62-5 D 2 '63
NINETEEN hundred and sixties
Fifth estate in the seventh decade; excerpts from address, December 28, 1963. P. M. Gross. Science 143:13-20 Ja 3 '64; Discussion. 143:917; 144:1086-7 F 28, My 29 '64
Measuring U.S. growth: report on the soaring sixties; with charts. U S News 55:42-5 N 11 '63
Perspective on the tasks of the 1960's; address, May 11, 1964. W. W. Rostow. Dept State Bul 50:864-7 Je 1 '64
NINETEEN hundred and sixty-five
1965: another good year? il U S News 58:21-4, 54-63 Ja 4 '65
Opinion, please from New York: predictions on affairs of state for 1965. H. Salisbury. il Mlle 60:13-14 Ja '65
NINETEEN hundred and sixty-four
Christmas list; some institutions and people who made worthwhile contributions. J. Fischer. Harper 229:14+ D '64
Esquire's fourth annual dubious achievement awards 1964. il Esquire 63:91-7 Ja '65
Have faith in the twentieth century. W. Johnson. Bul Atomic Sci 21:10-15 Ja '65
Letter from the editor. W. J. Coughlin. Miss & Roc 15:46 D 21 '64
1964 so far. R.I.P. Christian Cent 81:815 Je 17 '64
1964: the affluent year? il U S News 56: 38-47, 64-72, 98-9 Ja 13 '64
1964: the year that was. Sr Schol 85:1T Ja 7 '65
1964, won't you please come in? G. Steinem. il Ladies Home J 81:41-2+ Ja '64
1964's eventful non-event. Christian Cent 82: 37 Ja 13 '65
Spring 1964: bloom and boom. il Newsweek 63:15-16 Mr 30 '64
Year of decision. il Ebony 20:107-10+ Ja '65
NINETEEN hundred and sixty-three
Business in 1963. il Time 82:58-61 D 27 '63
Christmas list; some institutions, and people who made worthwhile contributions. J. Fischer. Harper 227:14+ D '63
Esquire's third annual dubious achievements awards for 1963. il Esquire 61:61-7 Ja '64; Reply. A. Gingrich. 61:12 Mr '64
Freedom's past in 1963 as prologue to 1964. Life 56:4 Ja 3 '64
In 1963, we survived. Christian Cent 80:1599-601 D 25 '63
Letter from the editor. W. J. Coughlin. Miss & Roc 13:52 D 23 '63
1963: this was the year that was. il Sr Schol 83:3T Ja 10 '64
Notes and comment. New Yorker 39:29 My 18 '63
Pax atomica: looking to '64. il Newsweek 63: 10-12 Ja 6 '64
That was the year that was. Christian Cent 81:63 Ja 8 '64
Time of hope, Christmas, 1963. il Newsweek 62:11-12 D 30 '63
Time to build. Sat Eve Post 236:82 D 21 '63
Year of special importance; address, October 2, 1963. P. H. Spaak. Vital Speeches 30:37-41 N 1 '63
Year of tragedy and progress: now— il U S News 56:21-2 Ja 6 '64
Year you won't forget. Bsns W p96 D 28 '63
NINETEEN hundred and sixty-two
1962 a backward look. J. Ardoin. il Mus Am 83:26-7 Ja '63
Pope John's great gift. Read Digest 82:141-6 Ap '63
NINETEEN hundred and thirteen
Crossroads: 1913, by P. M. Angle. Review Am Heritage 14:108-9 O '63. B. Catton
NINETEEN hundred and thirties
Literary horizons; The thirties: a reappraisal. G. Hicks. Sat R 46:27-8 My 4 '63
NINETEEN hundred and thirty-six
Notes and comment. New Yorker 39:29 My 18 '63
NINETEEN hundred and twenties
Politics of the 1920's. W. G. Carleton. Cur Hist 74:210-15+ O '64
NINETEEN hundred and twenty-four
Trade winds; special anniversary column. B. Cerf. il Sat R 47:10+ Ag 29 '64
NINEVEH
Road to Ninevah, by N. B. Kubie. Review Sci Digest 55:73 Ap '64. D. Cohen
NININGER, H. H.
Meteorite with unique features. Science 139: 345-7 Ja 25 '63
NINJA warriors. See Folklore—Japan
NIOGA library system
Library and the teen age; concerning College preparatory reading list. D. R. Watts. Wilson Lib Bul 38:795 My '64
NIPPON Gakki. See Japan—Industries
NIPSON, Herb
How good is Cassius Clay? Ebony 19:77-80+ Ap '64
Plan to save boxing. Ebony 19:59-60+ My '64

NIRENBERG, Marshall W.
Genetic code; with biographical sketch. Sci Am 208:33, 80-6+ bibliog(p 190) Mr '63
—and Leder, Philip
RNA codewords and protein synthesis. bibliog Science 145:1399-407 S 25 '64
about
Adventurous ones. por Vogue 142:76 Ag 1 '63
NIRENBERG, P. Zaltzman-. See Zaltzman-Nirenberg, P.
NISBET, George A.
Straining the complaints away. Am City 78: 98-9 Ap '63
NISBET, Robert A.
Hutchins of Chicago. Commentary 38:52-5 Jl '64
Power and the intellectual. Yale R 53:321-41 Mr '64
NISHIJIMA, Yasunori. See Oster, G. jt. auth.
NISHIMURA, Masamori
Super-wide & close-ups, too! T. Baba. il Mod Phot 27:68-9 Je '63
NISHIWAKI, Junzaburo
Dry sedge; Parabola; poems. Poetry 103:160 D '63
NISONOFF, A. and Palmer, J. L.
Hybridization of half molecules of rabbit gamma globulin. bibliog Science 143:376-9 Ja 24 '64
NISSAN motor company. See Automobile industry and trade—Japan
NISSENSON, Hugh
In the valley; story. Harper 227:78-83 O '63
Pile of stones; story. Esquire 61:92 My '64
NIST, John
Creative force of Mário de Andrade. Américas 17:27-9 Ja '65
NITRATES
Nitrate build-up in grasses. Suc Farm 62: 134 Mr '64
NITRO compounds
Photoisomerism: a colorless photoinduced intermediate of *o*-nitrobenzylpyridine. J. A. Sousa and J. D. Loconti. bibliog il Science 146:397-8 O 16 '64
NITROBENZENE
Electric fields across water-nitrobenzene interfaces. M. Blank and S. Feig. bibliog il Science 141:1173-4 S 20 '63
NITROBENZYLPYRIDINES. See Nitro compounds
NITROGEN
Biological nitrogen fixation; report on colloquium. W. A. Bulen. Science 147:310-12 Ja 15 '65
Effect of traces of large molecules containing nitrogen on hydrogen overvoltage. W. Juda and others. bibliog il Science 146:521-3 O 23 '64
Nitrogen: industrial Cinderella. J. D. Ratcliff. il Sci N L 86:90-1 Ag 8 '64; Same abr. with title Nitrogen: the marvelous stuff that does nothing. Read Digest 85:122-4 O '64
Orgueil meteorite: organic nitrogen contents. R. Hayatsu. bibliog il Science 146:1291-3 D 4 '64
Phosphorescence of rat kidneys cooled in liquid nitrogen. J. Wisotsky and others. il Science 140:671-2 My 10 '63
Radiation chemistry of the fixation of nitrogen. P. Harteck and S. Dondes. bibliog il Science 146:30-5 O 2 '64
Fixation
Algae: nitrogen fixation by Antarctic species. O. Holm-Hansen. il Science 139:1059-60 Mr 15 '63
Isotopes
Variations of nitrogen-15 abundance in soils. H. H. Cheng and others. bibliog il Science 146:1574-5 D 18 '64
NITROGEN, Liquid
Cold knife; surgery by freezing: cryosurgery. Newsweek 64:58 S 7 '64
NITROGEN in the body
Ureotelism of echidna and platypus. D. A. Denton and others. bibliog il Science 139: 1225 Mr 22 '63
NITROGEN mustards
Nitrogen mustard: diminution of toxicity in axenic mice. L. P. White and E. F. Claflin. bibliog il Science 140:1400-1 Je 28 '63
NITROGEN oxides
Nitrous oxide produced by the catalytic oxidation of organic nitrogen compounds. J. G. Christian. bibliog il Science 143:573-4 F 7 '64
NITZE, Paul H.
Future of the navy; address, January 9, 1964. Vital Speeches 30:239-43 F 1 '64
Harnessing the ocean depths; address, September 2, 1964. Vital Speeches 30:749-51 O 1 '64
Mixed-manned demonstration ship visits Washington; remarks, October 20, 1964. Dept State Bul 51:660-1 N 9 '64
Why top-level jobs changed hands at the Pentagon. por U S News 55:26 O 28 '63
NIX, James T.
Less risk with nuns. D. R. Campion. America 110:665 My 16 '64
NIXON, John H. and Gerhardt, P. H.
Urban economic development. bibliog f Ann Am Acad 352:39-47 Mr '64
NIXON, Marni
Instant voice. por Time 83:81-2 F 7 '64
NIXON, Richard Milhous
American policy abroad; address, April 20, 1963. Vital Speeches 29:486-90 Je 1 '63; Excerpts. por U S News 54:20 My 6 '63
Cuba, Castro and John F. Kennedy. Read Digest 85:281-4+ N '64
Excerpt from testimony, March 5, 1964. Cong Digest 43:153+ My '64
From party leaders: Republican future; excerpts from news conference. por U S News 57:69-70 N 16 '64
Khrushchev's hidden weakness. pors Sat Eve Post 236:23-9 O 12 '63; Same abr. Read Digest 84:59-64 Ja '64
Needed in Vietnam: the will to win. Read Digest 85:37-43 Ag '64
Speaking out. por Sat Eve Post 237:6+ Ja 18; 12+ Je 27 '64
What Nixon says about Nixon; interview, ed. by N. Thimmesch. Time 82:18 N 22 '63
Where Nixon stands; interview. pors U S News 55:84-91 O 14 '63
about
Back to life. Time 81:23 Mr 15 '63
Beware, the mousetrap; Cuba policy. L. B. Bozell. Nat R 14:354 My 7 '63
Compromise candidate? U S News 55:10 Ag 12 '63
Let's suppose. il Newsweek 63:18 F 3 '64
Mark the glove boy, by M. Harris. Review Commentary 37:86-8 My '64. J. Feiffer
Middleman. Reporter 29:24 O 24 '63
Nixon at the Gridiron; reprint. B. Beale. U S News 56:48 My 11 '64
Nixon's new role: what will it be? por U S News 54:24 Mr 25 '63
Nixon's role in 1964. R. Moley. Newsweek 64: 124 O 26 '64
Non-candidate Nixon. il por Newsweek 63: 20-1 F 24 '64
One-step thinking. W. Lippmann. Newsweek 63:25 Mr 16 '64
Re-enter Nixon. pors Newsweek 61:24 Mr 18 '63
Return to the wars. por Time 84:25-6 O 9 '64
Richard Nixon's return. Commonweal 79:87 O 18 '63
Something on the move? por Time 82:17 N 22 '63
Spoor of the demagogue. Nation 198:226 Mr 9 '64
That bug, that presidential bug. il Newsweek 62:17-18 O 28 '63
Ticket for the GOP. Nation 197:249 O 26 '63
Unmaking of a president. R. Evans and R. Novak. il por Esquire 62:90-2+ N '64
Will he or won't he? J. Bird. il pors Sat Eve Post 237:21-3 Mr 7 '64
Will it be Nixon vs. Kennedy again in '64? il U S News 55:34-5 N 25 '63
NIXON, Scott W.
Common stuff; poem. Christian Cent 81:543 Ap 29 '64
NIZER, Louis
How to tell the truth in court. McCalls 90:86-7+ Mr '63
My life in court; dramatization. See Denker. H. Case of libel
When silence is a crime. McCalls 92:95+ O '64
NKOMO, Joshua
Looking to London. il Newsweek 63:51-2 Mr 16 '64
NKRUMAH, Kwame
Atlantic report. Atlan 213:28+ My '64
Christmas message. Newsweek 63:37 Ja 6 '64
Dealing with enemies. il Time 81:38 Ap 26 '63
Ghana: a charismatic nation. L. Tiger. bibliog f Cur Hist 45:335-40 D '63
Ghana: communism's new foothold in Africa. D. Reed. il por Read Digest 85:202-7+ J '64
Jujitsu at the palace; attempts at assassination. Time 83:31 Ja 10 '64
Loyalties in the emerging nations. G. W. Shepherd, jr. Christian Cent 80:206-7 F 13 '63
Nkrumah tightens the reins. pors Sr Schol 84:11-13+ Mr 20 '64
Nyerere cuts loose. por Newsweek 64:34 Ag 3 '64

NKRUMAH, Kwame—*Continued*
Osagyefo thinks deep. T. Sterling. il Reporter 31:30-2 N 5 '46
Outrage at law. Time 82:21 D 20 '63
Portrait of Nkrumah as dictator. L. Garrison. il pors N Y Times Mag p 15+ My 3 '64
Target of assassin: strong man Nkrumah. por U S News 56:19 Ja 13 '64
True for false? attempted assassination. il por Newsweek 63:35 Ja 13 '64
Verdict overruled. Newsweek 62:34 D 23 '63

NO beginning, no end; story. See Randall, F. E.

NO drama. See Japanese drama

NO-load mutual funds. See Investment trusts

NO more bargains; story. See Rule, J.

NO room; story. See McCann, S. Q.

NO-show problem. See Airlines—Passenger service

NO visitors till noon; story. See Baker, D.

NOAH, Robert
Advocate; text. Theatre Arts 47:33-64 N '64

about

Advocate. Criticism
New Yorker 39:113 O 26 '63
Sat R 46:18 N 2 '63

NOAR, Gertrude
Learning about freedom the democratic way; excerpt from Teaching and learning the democratic way. Sch & Soc 91:37-9 Ja 26 '63

NOBEL, Alfred
Nobel's old company: still dynamite. il por Bsns W p60+ D 12 '64

NOBEL foundation
Secrecy behind the Nobel prizes. F. H. Garner. il Sci Digest 56:30-7 O '64

NOBEL prize winners; story. See Gordon, W. J. J.

NOBEL prizes
Ban the bomb winner peace prize for Dr Pauling. U S News 55:24 O 21 '63
Chemistry-minded mother. Time 84:41 N 6 '64
Controversy over peace award. Sr Schol 83:14-16 N 1 '63
For peace on earth, from a man of goodwill. A. Gingrich. Esquire 60:6+ D '63
Giorgos Seferiades wins 1963 Nobel prize. Pub W 184:27-8 N 4 '63
Harsh and tender greatness; G. S. Seferiades. Newsweek 62:52 N 4 '63
Jean-Paul Sartre rejects Nobel literature prize. Pub W 186:37-8 N 2 '64
John Steinbeck's acceptance speech. J. Steinbeck. Vogue 141:16 Mr 1 '63
Just ask Mrs Mayer. il Newsweek 62:78+ N 18 '63
King receives Nobel prize. Christian Cent 81:1324 O 28 '64
Man of conflict wins a peace prize. il U S News 57:24 O 26 '64
Maser man; share of 1964 Nobel prize in physics for Prof. C. H. Townes of Columbia university. il Newsweek 64:89 N 9 '64
Nobel award winners announced. H. A. Bethe; C. G. Overberger. il Science 142:937-9 N 15 '63
Nobel committee and Sartre. W. F. Buckley, jr. Nat R 16:1004 N 17 '64; Reply. J. W. Daly. 17:34-5 Ja 12 '65
Nobel laureates: Bloch and Lynen win prize in medicine and physiology. E. P. Kennedy and F. H. Westheimer. il Science 146:504-6 O 23 '64
Nobel medical awards. il Sci N L 84:259 O 26 '63
Nobel peace prize goes to Martin Luther King. C. W. Thomas. Negro Hist Bul 28:35 N '64
Nobel prize; ceremonies at Stockholm. J. Star. il Look 28:72-3+ Mr 24 '64
Nobel prize in chemistry awarded to crystallographer. G. A. Jeffery. Science 146:748-9 N 6 '64
Nobel prize in physics. America 111:648 N 21 '64
Nobel prize: 1963 award honors three for research on nerve functioning. M. G. F. Fuortes. Science 142:468-70 O 25 '63
Nobel prize winners; prizes in chemistry and physics. il Sci N L 86:295 N 7 '64
Nobel prize winner's triumph in Europe; M. L. King's visit to Berlin. il Ebony 20:40-2+ N '64
Nobel prizes. Sci Am 209:64 D '63; 211:60 D '64
Nobelman & Nobelwoman. il Time 82:61 N 15 '63
Nobelman King. Newsweek 64:77 O 26 '64
Nobels for nerves. Newsweek 62:90-1 O 28 '63
Our man in Helsinki; J. Steinbeck. New Yorker 39:43-5 N 9 '63
Park-bench scientist, but. Sci Digest 57:42-3 Ja '65
Pauling wins peace prize, his second Nobel award. il Sci N L 84:261 O 26 '63
Research on maser-laser principle wins Nobel prize in physics. J. P. Gordon. il Science 146:897-9 N 13 '64
Second Nobel. il Newsweek 62:38 O 21 '63
Secrecy behind the Nobel prizes. F. H. Garner. il Sci Digest 56:30-7 O '64
Secrets of cholesterol; two biochemists share 1964 Nobel prize in physiology and medicine. il Time 84:94 O 23 '64
Split award; Nobel prize in physics. Time 84:41 N 6 '64
Three Americans honored. il Sr Schol 85:10 N 11 '64
Three share physics prize; Nobel chemistry prize. W. Davis. il Sci N L 84:306-7 N 16 '63
Two good choices. Nation 199:319 N 9 '64
Two perspectives, one goal; M. L. King, jr. accepts peace prize. M. L. King, jr. il Time 84:21 D 18 '64
Two wets & a dry: 1963 prize for physiology and medicine. Time 82:64 O 25 '63
Up from Montgomery; M. L. King, jr. receives Nobel peace prize. il Newsweek 64:40-1 D 21 '64
Weird insult from Norway. Life 55:4 O 25 '63
Whiz kid of Soviet science. A. Parry. il Sci Digest 54:83-9 D '63
Youngest ever; Rev Dr M. L. King, jr. awarded the Nobel peace prize for 1964. il Time 84:27 O 23 '64
See also
Bloch, K. E.
Lynen, F.
Mayer, M. G.
Pauling, L. C.
Seferiades, G. S.

NOBLE, Horace
Cook County crime fighter. il pors Ebony 19:101-2+ D '63

NOBLE, Jeanne
Chicken noodle casserole. D. J. Robinson. il por Ebony 18:142+ Je '63

NOBLE, Mary
Southern pointers. See issues of Flower grower

NOBLE gases. See Gases, Rare

NOBLECOURT, Christiane Desroches
Tutankhamun's golden trove. Nat Geog Mag 124:624-46 O '63

NOBLES and Knights charities, incorporated
Knights and Nobles unite in Pittsburgh; corporation for benefit of youth charities. Christian Cent 81:1294 O 21 '64

NOBODY loves an albatross; drama. See Alexander, R.

NOBODY'S ever in town on Sunday; story. See Lyons, R.

NOBS, Claude
Notes from abroad. Hi Fi 13:26 S '63

NOCK, Albert Jay
Catalyst of liberty. E. A. Opitz. por Nat R 17:26+ Ja 12 '65

NOCTILUCA
Cell visible by own light; photographs of noctiluca miliaris, with light-amplifying device. A. Ewing. il Sci N L 85:178 Mr 21 '64

NOCTILUCENT clouds. See Clouds

NOCTURNE; story. See Loeser, K.

NOEL, Edgar E.
Dirt road; poem. Am For 70:63 Mr '64

NOETHER, Emiliana P.
(comp) Articles and other books received: Italy. See issues of American historical review

NOGUCHI, Isamu
Gallery for young people. C. B. Johnson. Sch Arts 64:44 Ja '65

NOISE
Battling bedlam; war on noise in Rome. Newsweek 64:40 Ag 17 '64
Communicating in a high-noise environment. R. P. Devaney. il Electr World 72:39-41+ N '64
How to stop noise. B. Fader. Am City 79 103-5 Je '64
Is noise driving you crazy? J. H. Winchester. Sci Digest 56:27-31 Ag '64
Lip service for noise control. E. Goble. Arch Rec 136:9 N '64
Memphis: the quiet, please city. W. R. Vath. il Todays Health 41:42-3+ F '63
Noise; letter. P. D. Foote. Science 143:101 Ja 10 '64; Same. Consumer Bul 47:17-18 Jl '64; Discussion. Science 143:992; 144:487 Mr 6, My 1 '64

NOISE—*Continued*
Noise: something more to worry about. il U S News 55:64-6 S 23 '63
Notes and comment; escaping from the city to Long Island. New Yorker 39:15 Jl 13 '63
Rising tide of noise. H. Manchester. il Read Digest 85:173-4+ O '64
Sounding off; noise level inside the average home. il Newsweek 64:106+ O 26 '64
What is a noise? Sci Digest 56:28-9 Ag '64
See also
Airplanes—Noise
Apartment houses—Noise
Electronic apparatus and appliances—Noise
Soundproofing
Transistors—Noise

Physiological effects

Altruism or arousal in the rat? J. J. Lavery and P. J. Foley. il Science 140:172-3 Ap 12 '63
Dangerous decibels. H. E. Klein. il Duns R 81:45-6+ Je '63
Hempstead versus jets; Idlewild airport. il Bsns W p93-4 D 7 '63
Is noise driving you crazy? J. H. Winchester. Sci Digest 56:27-31 Ag '64
NOISE, Radio. See Radio interference
NOISE filters, Radio. See Radio filters
NOISE production by fishes. See Sound production by fishes
NOISE suppressors. See Sound suppressors
NOLAN, David F.
Astronomy. Sci N L 85:74-5 F 1 '64
Finger sight for blind. Sci N L 86:119 Ag 22 '64
Growth pattern changing. Sci N L 86:166 S 12 '64
War of the computers: Nov. 3. Sci N L 86: 250-1 O 17 '64
NOLAN, Hugh J.
Book review. America 110:23 Ja 4 '64
NOLAN, James F.
Survey, plan, expedite and review. Am City 78:85-7 Ag '63
NOLAN, Paul T.
America is a song; drama. Plays 22:61-8 Mr '63
Double nine of Chih Yuan; drama. Plays 23: 78-84, 96 O '63
Going steady; drama. Plays 23:37-34, 95 Mr '64
Moon's up there; drama. Plays 22:1-10 Ap '63
NOLAN, Sidney
Art galleries; exhibition at the Marlborough-Gerson. R. M. Coates. New Yorker 40:103 Ja 23 '65
Extreme environment. il por Time 81:66-7 Ap 26 '63
NOLAND, Kenneth
Peacock duo. il por Time 85:44-5 Ja 8 '65
NOLDE, Emil
Art; survey of the works of E. Nolde at the Museum of modern art. H. Kramer. Nation 196:316 Ap 13 '63
Expressionist man; retrospective exhibition at New York's Museum of modern art. il Newsweek 61:71 Mr 18 '63
Flowers and faith in Emil Nolde. F. Getlein. New Repub 149:29-30 Jl 6 '63
Nolde's achievement. B. Kaufman. Commonweal 78:116-19 Ap 19 '63
Superart and superman; exhibition at the Museum of modern art. D. Robbins. il por Art N 62:35-7+ Ap '63
NOLDE, O. Frederick
Thinking the unthinkable; concerning address at W.C.C. conference, Buck Hill Falls. Christian Cent 81:627-8 My 13 '64
NOLE, Jack D.
I bailed out ten miles up! Read Digest 85: 73-6 S '64
NOLL, Clifford R. Jr. See Chancellor-Maddison. J. jt. auth.
NOLLER, Edward C.
Recreation harvest; farm at Cream Ridge, N.J. L. Fox. il por Recreation 57:21-4 Ja '64
NOLTE, Richard H.
Britain and the Arab East. New Repub 150: 19-20 F 1 '64
NOMA, Seiroku
Primitives of Japan, a legacy in clay. Natur Hist 72:38-45 Mr '63
NOMADS
One tribe of Africa's 700; Bororo, the nomads of Africa; photographs. N Y Times Mag p24-5 S 27 '64
NOMENCLATURE. See subhead Nomenclature under various subjects, e.g. Electronics—Nomenclature
NOMINATION expenditures. See Campaign funds
NOMINATIONS for office
So long, Chub; gubernatorial nominations. il Time 84:37 S 18 '64
NOMOGRAMS. See Charts, Calculating
NONAGGRESSION pacts. See Treaties
NON-ALIGNED nations, Conference of. See Conference of heads of state or government of non-aligned countries, Cairo, 1964
NONCONFORMITY. See Conformity; Individualism
NONDA
Beware of Greeks. il Newsweek 61:105 Je 24 '63
NON-DESTRUCTIVE warfare. See Military art and science
NONESUCH press
Sir Francis Meynell and the Nonesuch press. F. Johnson. il Am Artist 28:38-43+ F '64
NONGRADED classes. See Ungraded classes
NON-MUSICAL phonograph records. See Phonograph records—Spoken records
NON-OBJECTIVE art. See Art, Abstract
NONPUBLIC schools. See Private schools
NON-SELF-governing territories committee. See United Nations—Committee on information from non-self-governing territories
NONSTICK cookware. See Kitchen utensils
NON-STOP piano player; story. See Phelan, R. C.
NON-VIOLENT non-cooperation. See Passive resistance to government
NONVOTING. See Voting
NON-WAGE payments
Fringe benefit costs head higher. il Nations Bsns 52:104-6 S '64
Fringe benefits. M. Reagan. New Repub 148: 7-8 Je 15 '63
Health as a fringe benefit. J. Pollack. il New Repub 149:21-3 N 9 '63
How fringes are boosting labor costs. il U S News 57:81-3 S 14 '64
150,000 at GE share $110-million payout. Bsns W p80+ Mr 16 '63
Pay supplements in finance, insurance, and real estate. V. J. Sheifer. il Mo Labor R 87:305-12 Mr '64
Rising fast: cost of fringes; concerning report by National industrial conference board. U S News 56:92 Ja 20 '64
Supplemental wage benefits in metropolitan areas, 1962-63. D. J. Blackmore. il Mo Labor R 87:536-42 My '64
Supplementary pay practices in manufacturing, 1962 and 1959. A. Strasser. il Mo Labor R 87:1273-7 N '64
Supplementary wage benefits in metropolitan areas, 1961-62. D. J. Blackmore. il Mo Labor R 86:293-9 Mr '63
That extra something. Time 81:92 Ap 12 '63
Unions make these new demands. il Nations Bsns 52:36-7+ Je '64
Wages or fringes? UAW weighs the odds. il Bsns W p60+ F 15 '64
What happens to retirees when a plant shuts down? Bsns W p50 N 21 '64
What's preferred to pay raises; fringe benefits for miners. U S News 56:86 Ap 13 '64
Who gains from the fringes? D. Allen. il Nation 199:379-81 N 23 '64
Why union eyes are on fringes. il Bsns W p59-60 S 12 '64
NOODLES
Fettuccine e vino; noodles and wine the Roman way; with recipes. M. Kaytor. il Look 27:63-4 N 5 '63
It's time you used your noodles. J. M. Towne. il Am Home 66:52-3+ Ja '63
NOOE, Roger
Seal sewer leaks from the inside. Am City 79:91-2 Je '64
NOON, William T.
Roll away the reel world. America 111:517-20 O 31 '64
NOONAN, Roberta
Meal planning for children allergic to wheat, milk and eggs. Parents Mag 39:59+ My '64
NOR long remember; drama. See Martens, A. C.
NORAD. See North American air defense command
NORAIR division. See Northrop corporation
NORD, Melvin
Is your vote equal? PTA Mag 58:16-18 D '63
NORDEN, Berrick von
Marie Narelle and Berrick Von Norden. J. Walsh. por Hobbies 69:32-6+ Mr '64
NORDEN, Roger L.
Conservation workshop in Maryland. Nat Parks Mag 37:9-13 N '63
NORDFORS, Margaret
Shape in water; poem. Poetry 103:301 F '64

NORDHAUSEN, A. Henry
Figure paintings of A. Henry Nordhausen. L. Schmeckebier. il por Am Artist 29:34-9+ F '65
NORDICA, Lillian
Long voyage. D. Warren. por Opera N 28:6-7 My 2 '64
Yankee diva: Lillian Nordica and the golden days of opera, by I. Glackens. Review
Hobbies 68:31+ F '64. A. Favia-Artsay
Opera N 29:34 D 26 '64. J. Browning
NORDIN, Albert A. See Jerne, N. K. jt. auth.
NORDLAND, Gerald
Slow emergence of star sculpture. Art N 63: 30-2+ O '64
NORDSIEK, Frederic W.
My friends, the rats. por sci Digest 53:79-83 Je '63
NORDSTROM, Ursula
Emily Neville. Library J 89:1372-3 Mr 15 '64
Maurice Sendak. Library J 89:1374-6 Mr 15 '64
NORELL, Norman
He's a fashion purist with the golden touch. il pors Bsns W p64-6+ S 12 '64
Norman the conqueror. il Time 84:63 Jl 10 '64
Socko American pair. il Life 54:75-7+ Mr 1 '63
Talk, the clothes, the glitter at the New York openings; backstage notes. il pors Vogue 141:136-41+ Mr 1 '63
NORENA, Eidé
Three neglected sopranos. J. M. Alfonte. por Opera N 28:39 N 16 '63
NOREPHEDRINE
Release of metaraminol (aramine) from the heart by sympathetic nerve stimulation. J. R. Crout and others. bibliog il Science 145: 828-9 Ag 21 '64
NOREPINEPHRINE. See Arterenol
NORFOLK, Va.
Galleries and museums
Khouri memorial collection; Norfolk museum of arts & sciences. W. Caxton, jr. il Am Artist 28:24-9 F '64
NORFOLK azalea garden. See Botanical gardens
NORFOLK botanical garden. See Botanical gardens
NORFOLK ISLAND pine
Norfolk Island-pine. K. S. Phillips. il Flower Grower 51:28 N '64
NORGE division, Borg-Warner corporation. See Borg-Warner corporation
NORGREN, Donald L.
From June bugs to fluorescents. Am City 79:127 F '64
NORINYL. See Contraceptives
NORLING, P. M. See Bevilacqua, E. M. jt. auth.
NORMA; opera. See Bellini, V.
NORMAL persons. See Normality
NORMALITY
Close-up of the normal wife. R. Corman. il N Y Times Mag p52+ S 8 '63
Novelist advises teenagers that novels are bad for you. P. Roth. Library J 88:1738 Ap 15 '63
Philip Roth talks to teens. P. Roth. Seventeen 22:170+ Ap '63; Excerpts. Library J 88:1738 Ap 15 '63
NORMAN, Albert E.
Homing penguin. Sci Digest 54:42-3 Jl '63
NORMAN, Elva Kuykendall
Libraries of St Louis. por ALA Bul 58:512-18 Je '64
Stained glass for St Louis. Library J 88:4551-2 D 1 '63
NORMAN, James
(tr) See Heras, J. G. Music in transition
NORMAN, Webbs
Oak Park ice rink. Recreation 57:472-3 N '64
NORMAN-WILCOX, Gregor
Hugo Reid adobe near Los Angeles, California. Antiques 84:168-71 Ag '63
NORMANDY invasion. See World war, 1939-1945—Campaigns and battles—Western
NORMARK, Donald
Hella Skowronski. Craft Horiz 24:18-21+ Ja '64
NORODOM Sihanouk, king of Cambodia (abdicated 1955)
Balance of menaces. por Time 82:40+ N 29 '63
Cambodia cuts off U.S. aid. Sr Schol 83:18 Ja 17 '64
Cambodian puzzle, and prize. il pors N Y Times Mag p8-9 Mr 29 '64
Cambodia's high-wire act. il por Sr Schol 84:8-10 My 1 '64
Country that's neutral in favor of Communists. R. P. Martin. il por U S News 56: 80-2 Ap 27 '64
End of US aid. New Repub 149:7 N 30 '63
High scorer with either hand. A. Wright. il por Sports Illus 19:60-5 D 23 '63
In a glass house. F. Sully. Newsweek 64:57-8 N 30 '64
Man of sensitivity. Newsweek 62:28 D 23 '63
Man who wouldn't be king. il pors Time 81:28+ F 8 '63
Off again. Newsweek 63:48+ Mr 23 '64
Our far-flung correspondents. R. Shaplen. New Yorker 40:150+ Ap 18 '64
Prince & the dragon. il pors Time 83:32-6 Ap 3 '64
Problem for the U.S: handling Prince Sihanouk. por U S News 56:13 Ja 6 '64
Sihanouk, prince under pressure. S. S. King. il pors N Y Times Mag p42+ S 13 '64
Strange case of Cambodia: a trouble area for the U.S. S. W. Sanders. il por U S News 55:42-3 D 30 '63
There goes Cambodia. D. Warner. il Reporter 30:27-30 Mr 26 '64
Whose hour? il por Newsweek 62:58 D 2 '63
Why Cambodia is threatening to reject U.S. aid. il U S News 55:6 N 25 '63
Will Cambodia go Communist? J. A. Rose. il por Sat Eve Post 237:68+ Mr 28 '64
NORPAC race. See Yacht racing
NORRELL, Catherine D.
Roads to international understanding: address, January 15, 1963. Dept State Bul 48: 214-17 F 11 '63
NORRIS, Bill
Quarter starts the meter. Am City 79:116 O '64
NORRIS, Carolyn G.
Attack on poverty. bibliog Horn Bk 40:364-9 Ag '64
NORRIS, Charlotte B.
Everlastings, flowers for dry arrangements to sow in your garden now. Pop Gard 14: 90-1 My '63
NORRIS, J. C.
Delcotronic transistor ignition system. Electr World 70:39-41 Jl '63
NORRIS, James
Role of Catholic agencies. Commonweal 81: 235-7 N 13 '64
NORRIS, Louis William
Culture at college. Sch & Soc 92:263-4 O 3 '64
NORRIS, R. C.
Texas educational microwave project. Sch Life 45:11-13 Ja '63
NORRIS, T. G.
Canadian judge drops bomb on sea unions. Bsns W p85 Jl 20 '63
NORRIS William G.
Small, smart, sharp. il por Bsns W p 154+ My 25 '63
NORRISH, M.
Progress of an historic movement. por U N Rev 10:41-3 Je '63
NORSTAD, Lauris
Authority over nuclear weapons; address, January 17, 1963. Vital Speeches 29:258-60 F 15 '63
Who should control nuclear weapons; interview. por U S News 57:47-8 O 5 '64
Plan to share the weapons. Time 84:18 S 25 '64
NORSTADT, Fred A. and McCalla, T. M.
Phytotoxic substance from a species of penicillium. bibliog Science 140:410-11 Ap 26 '63
NORSTOG, Knut, and Smith, J. E.
Culture of small barley embryos on defined media. bibliog Science 142:1655-6 D 27 '63
NORTH, Arthur
Inventor of the month. S. V. Jones. por Sci Digest 54:74-5 O '63
NORTH, Henry Ringling
And now, in the center ring, profits. il por Bsns W p28-9 Mr 28 '64
NORTH, Lowell
Importance of sail trimming. Yachting 113: 74-5+ Ap '63
NORTH, Robert C.
Race between destruction and adaptability. Bul Atomic Sci 20:26-8 Mr '64
NORTH, Simeon
Simeon North pistol maker. C. Worman. il Hobbies 69:124-5 O '64
NORTH, Sterling
Rascal; condensation. Read Digest 83:229-31+ S '63
about
Newbery and Caldecott runners-up. il por Library J 89:1378 Mr 15 '64
NORTH AMERICA
See also
Birds—North America
Geology—North America
Paleontology—North America

NORTH AMERICA—*Continued*

Antiquities

First Americans. il Newsweek 61:56-7 F 11 '63

Description and travel

From sun-clad sea to shining mountains. R. Gray. il Nat Geog Mag 125:542-89 Ap '64

Discovery and exploration

See America—Discovery and exploration

Maps

New portrait of North America. il Nat Geog Mag 125:590-1, sup(folded map) Ap '64

NORTH AMERICAN air defense command
Air force presses to meet 1965 date for operation at NORAD hard site; Combat operations center. M. Getler. il Miss & Roc 14:40+ F 24 '64
Bomarc for Canada. M. Halperin. New Repub 148:6-7 Mr 2 '63
Command post for a continent: a hollowed-out mountain; NORAD combat operations center at Cheyenne Mountain, Colo. il U S News 55:49-52 S 23 '63
Mass air attack seen unlikely: defenses shifted, radars closed. Aviation W 79:24 Jl 8 '63
Mountain fortress for air defense; NORAD's Combat operations center, Colo. il Bsns W p 130-1 Ap 18 '64
New bomb alarm caps a vast network. il Life 54:28-9 Mr 1 '63
U.S. and Canadian negotiations regarding nuclear weapons; Department statement, January 30, 1963. Dept State Bul 48:243-4 F 18 '63
Vast cave shelters space-age sentries; NORAD's combat operations center. il Life 55:57+ O 18 '63

NORTH AMERICAN aviation, incorporated
Apollo funding stresses fabrication. H. Taylor. il Miss & Roc 12:16-17 F 4 '63
Apollo takes shape. il Bsns W p32-3 Ap 13 '63
Critical Apollo test modules produced. il Aviation W 79:124-31+ Jl 22 '63
First unmanned Apollo nears completion. C. M. Plattner. il Aviation W 81:40-1+ O 5 '64
Heat posing major SST design problems. J. R. Ashlock. il Aviation W 79:74-5 Jl 8 '63
How 300,000 work for three moon men. il Newsweek 64:61-5 D 21 '64
NAA demonstrates laser modulator. il Miss & Roc 12:31 Mr 18 '63
NAA, McDonnell repeat at NASA. il Miss & Roc 14:18 Ja 20 '64
NAC-100 design altered to ease loading. C. Brownlow. il Aviation W 81:43+ O 19 '64
NASARR problems hampering F-104G. C. Brownlow. il Aviation W 78:63-4 Mr 4 '63
North American sales set industry record. Aviation W 81:29 N 16 '64
North American tops defense R&D primes. Aviation W 81:27 D 7 '64
TV teachers: leading a company into space. il Bsns W p60-1+ Ag 29 '64
Wage chronology: North American aviation, inc. il Mo Labor R 87:556-60 My '64

Autonetics division

Autonetics ready for some new work. W. E. Wilks. il Miss & Roc 12:31-2 Ap 22 '63

Rocketdyne division

McGregor plant boosts its capacity. J. F. Judge. il Miss & Roc 12:26-7 Ap 1 '63
Rocketdyne developing rugged grains. Miss & Roc 13:16 N 18 '63

Space and information systems division

NAA building largest centrifuge; Rotational research facility. Miss & Roc 15:34-5 N 23 '64
Pure gold in space work. il Bsns W p 129-30+ S 12 '64

NORTH AMERICAN conservation hall of fame and museum
Another Hall of fame. S. T. Dana. il Am For 70:16+ O '64

NORTH AMERICAN Indians. See Indians of North America

NORTH AMERICAN library of world literature incorporated
Design in paperbacks: a report from NAL. il Pub W 183:76-8 Ap 8 '63

NORTH AMERICAN water shrew. See Shrews

NORTH AMERICAN wildlife and natural resources conference
Meeting, 1963. J. B. Craig. il Am For 69:4-5+ Ap '63

NORTH AMERICAN wildlife conference
See also
North American wildlife and natural resources conference

NORTH AMERICAN yacht racing union
Olympic preview. J. K. Roosevelt. il Yachting 115:41-3 F '64
There's an appeal on that! J. Nash. il Yachting 113:51+ Mr '63

NORTH ATLANTIC community. See Atlantic community

NORTH ATLANTIC treaty organization
Air attacks on Cyprus impose new strains on NATO alliance. L. L. Doty. Aviation W 81:20 Ag 17 '64
And where is France? il Newsweek 62:58 O 7 '63
Antic semantics; Anglo-American plan for an interallied nuclear force. Newsweek 61:42+ My 20 '63
Arms and stability in Europe, by A. Buchan and P. Windsor. Review
New Repub 150:22-4 Ja 11 '64. H. Malmgren
Atlantic alliance; address, April 7, 1964. D. Rusk. bibliog f Dept State Bul 50:650-5 Ap 27 '64
Atlantic defense. A. Buchan; L. Muray. New Repub 152:11-15 Ja 9 '65
Atlantic disunity and de Gaulle. Sat Eve Post 236:74 F 16 '63
Atlantic future: Europe's choice. F. Church. Harper 227:18+ N '63
Atlantic partnership: a vital force in motion; address, April 28, 1963. G. C. McGhee. Dept State Bul 48:771-5 My 20 '63
Atlantic policy advisory group of NATO meets in United States. Dept State Bul 48:721 My 6 '63
Atlantic surmounts nationalism barriers. il Aviation W 78:72-3+ Je 10 '63
Authority over nuclear weapons; address, January 17, 1963. L. Norstad. Vital Speeches 29:258-60 F 15 '63
Balance of world power at the start of a new year. il U S News 58:32-3 Ja 4 '65
Basis of partnership. F. Erler. For Affairs 42:84-95 O '63
Battlefield A-bomb: should generals control it M. S. Johnson. il U S News 57:44-5 Ag 24 '64
Boost for NATO. Commonweal 78:124 Ap 26 '63
Britain and the US. New Repub 151:3-4 D 19 '64
Coalition diplomacy in a nuclear age. H. A. Kissinger. For Affairs 42:525-45 Jl '64
Cold war, a look ahead; address, March 28, 1963. W. W. Rostow. Dept State Bul 48:551-7 Ap 15 '63
Collapse of Kennedy's Grand design; with editorial comment. S. Alsop. il Sat Eve Post 236:78-82 Ap 6 '63
Common market crisis. C. Emmet. America 108:333-5 Mr 9 '63
Crazy but sensible; plan for a NATO multilateral Polaris fleet. Time 82:39-40 O 4 '63
Current look at NATO; address, January 15, 1964. G. C. McGhee. Dept State Bul 50:338-44 Mr 2 '64
Defense; the dilemma & the design. il Time 81:22+ F 15 '63
DeGaulle and the future of the western alliance. Sr Schol 82:6-9+ Mr 27 '63
De Gaulle keeps the pot bubbling; French naval officers withdrawn from NATO military commands. il Newsweek 63:37 My 11 '64
De Gaulle vs. America: who's going to run NATO? U S News 56:20 My 11 '64
De Gaulle vs. NATO. Newsweek 62:32 Jl 1 '63
Demise of NATO. R. Steel. Commentary 35:397-402 My '63
Disintegrating alliance. R. Steel. Commonweal 78:127-9 Ap 26 '63
Dodging the issues; annual spring meeting. Newsweek 63:44+ My 25 '64
Effect of the projected European union on NATO; address, April 5, 1963. W. R. Tyler. Dept State Bul 48:648-52 Ap 29 '63; Same with questions and answers. Ann Am Acad 348:65-72 Jl '63
European integration and American foreign policy; address, February 9, 1963. A. Chayes. Dept State Bul 48:318-22 Mr 4 '63
Facing the iron curtain: how good is western defense? interview, ed. by A. J. Meyers. L. L. Lemnitzer. il U S News 55:54-9 D 30 '63

NORTH ATLANTIC treaty organization—*Cont.*

Facts without flowers; NATO's 15th spring meeting. il Time 83:41 My 15 '64

First-hand report: new look at how U.S. rates in today's world. M. S. Johnson. il U S News 57:83-4 N 9 '64

First, the shell; NATO council meeting. il Time 81:22 My 31 '63

For an Atlantic future. T. Sommer. For Affairs 43:112-25 O '64

For U.S. allies a Polaris fleet in disguise? il U S News 54:8 Mr 18 '63

Force that guards western Europe. il Bsns W p31 My 18 '63

Foreign policy: building amid turbulence; address, August 27, 1963. R. J. Manning. Dept State Bul 49:454-60 S 23 '63

Fortress America. R. Steel. Commentary 36: 119-24 Ag '63

Fortress America; latest in defense ideas. il U S News 54:56-60 Mr 25 '63

France puts new strain on NATO but is expected to aid arms output. C. Brownlow. Aviation W 78:41 F 18 '63

France's bow to China; recognition of Communist China. il Bsns W p27-8 Ja 25 '64

Frustrated NATO? D. Lawrence. U S News 57:104 S 14 '64

How can Canada make her most effective contribution to collective security? address, January 12, 1963. L. B. Pearson. Vital Speeches 29:290-3 Mr 1 '63

How to get the message. Newsweek 64:24 D 28 '64

How to lose a war. D. Lawrence. U S News 57:92 Ag 31 '64

Impact of Eisenhower. S. Alsop. Sat Eve Post 236:14 N 9 '63

Improved balance. Time 82:22 D 27 '63

Into the pool; British nuclear deterrent. il Time 84:22 D 18 '64

Is this NATO crisis necessary? A. Buchan. New Repub 151:19-21 Ag 8 '64

It's April in Paris; chestnuts in blossom; SEATO and NATO consultations. Newsweek 61:37 Ap 22 '63

Letter from Washington. R. H. Rovere. New Yorker 40:150-55 Ap 11 '64

Limited war and America defense policy, by J. Deitchman. Review
U S News 57:128 O 5 '64

Literature; foreign ministers' conference in The Hague. Time 83:29 My 22 '64

McNamara sees boost for NATO despite U.S. spending cutback. Aviation W 79:29 D 23 '63

Man who . .; election of a NATO Secretary-General. il Newsweek 63:44 My 18 '64

Merchant mission: mending defenses. il Newsweek 61:33 Mr 4 '63

More light on who does control the bomb; with report by the Republican national committee. il U S News 57:46-9 O 19 '64

Nassau reconsidered: what can America and Britain do now? A. Buchan. New Repub 148:21-3 Mr 2 '63

New frontier and Europe: moment for choice. F. W. Neal. il Nation 197:234-6 O 19 '63

New look at NATO: its strength, its weaknesses. il U S News 54:60-2 My 27 '63

New military dimension for NATO. il Bsns W p54-5+ Jl 4 '64

New NATO Secretary General assured of U.S. support; letters, August 1, 1964. L. B. Johnson; D. Rusk. Dept State Bul 51:275 Ag 24 '64

New strategy for survival. il Newsweek 61: 20-4 F 11 '63

Nonnuclear defense of Europe. H. A. Crosby. Bul Atomic Sci 20:30-1 Ap '64

North Atlantic council holds ministerial meeting at Paris; statement with text of communique and list of members of the U.S. delegation. D. Rusk. Dept State Bul 52:2-4 Ja 4 '65

North Atlantic council meets at The Hague; statement, May 12, 1964, with communique and list of members of U.S. delegation. D. Rusk. Dept State Bul 50:850-3 Je 1 '64

NATO, a growing partnership; remarks, April 3, 1964. L. B. Johnson. Dept State Bul 50:606-8 Ap 20 '64

NATO alliance is in danger! how to save it. Life 55:4 N 15 '63

NATO and Nukes: keeping up appearances; NATO ministerial council meeting in Ottawa. il Newsweek 61:33-4 Je 3 '63

NATO and world responsibilities; address, May 7, 1964. G. W. Ball. Dept State Bul 50:823-8 My 25 '64

NATO announces 1964-65 research fellowships. Dept State Bul 49:998 D 30 '63

NATO council holds 1963 spring meeting at Ottawa; text of communique, May 24, 1963; with list of members of the U.S. delegation. Dept State Bul 48:895-6 Je 10 '63

NATO disputes stall follow-on projects. C. Brownlow. il Aviation W 80:98-9+ Mr 16 '64

NATO intercept control decision nears. C. Brownlow. Aviation W 78:32 Ap 29 '63

NATO meets; divided and disordered. Newsweek 62:25-6 D 23 '63

NATO moves toward coordinated targeting. Aviation W 78:34 Ap 22 '63

NATO muddle. D. Healey. New Repub 149: 8-9 N 23 '63

NATO nagging. Time 82:16 D 20 '63

NATO plans SAGE-type system. W. Beller. Miss & Roc 15:14-15 O 12 '64

NATO shaping inter-allied force with air, sea nuclear capability. D. E. Fink. Aviation W 78:27 My 27 '63

NATO to share in SAC nuclear planning. Aviation W 78:25-7 Je 3 '63

Nato-Warsaw detente? B. G. Lall. Bul Atomic Sci 20:37-9 N '64

NATO with an atomic punch? Sr Schol 82: 16+ F 13 '63

NATO working group supports U.S. plan for mixed nuclear fleet. L. L. Doty. Aviation W 81:25 S 21 '64

NATO's gimmick. Nation 200:70 Ja 25 '65

NATO's nuclear dilemma. H. A. Kissinger. il Reporter 28:22-33+ Mr 28 '63; Discussion. 28:6+ Ap 25; 8+ My 9 '63

Nuclear deterrent and the Atlantic alliance; address, April 26, 1963. G. W. Ball. Dept State Bul 48:736-9 My 13 '63

Nuclear policy and French intransigence. M. W. Hoag. For Affairs 41:286-98 Ja '63

Off collision course; NATO ministerial meeting. il Time 84:18-19 D 25 '64

Organizing western defense. K. U. von Hassel. For Affairs 43:209-16 Ja '65

Other people's problems, annual ministerial meeting in Paris. Newsweek 62:21-3 D 30 '63

Polaris power: the new strategy for defending Europe. il U S News 54:8 F 4 '63

Practice of partnership. D. Acheson. For Affairs 41:247-60 Ja '63

President exchanges greetings with Prime Minister of Italy; letters, December 9 and December 11, 1963. L. B. Johnson; A. Moro. Dept State Bul 50:47 Ja 13 '64

President Johnson exchanges letters with NATO Secretary General Brosio; letters, October 1 and October 6, 1964. L. B. Johnson; M. Brosio. Dept State Bul 51:673 N 9 '64

President Johnson meets with NATO Secretary General; exchange of toasts at luncheon and remarks on departing from Offutt air force base, September 29, 1964. L. B. Johnson; M. Brosio. Dept State Bul 51: 582-5 O 26 '64

President Johnson welcomes NATO Parliamentarians; remarks, September 18, 1964. L. B. Johnson. Dept State Bul 51:478 O 5 '64

Principals named for negotiations on NATO multilateral force; statement, January 24, 1963. J. F. Kennedy. Dept State Bul 48: 197 F 11 '63

Probing and patching. Newsweek 62:40 S 2 '63

Projected European union and American military responsibilities; address, April 6, 1963; with questions and answers. W. R. Kintner. Ann Am Acad 348:121-31 Jl '63

Rift in West: how serious. il U S News 54:29-30 F 11 '63

Road ahead; address, February 13, 1963. D. Rusk. Dept State Bul 48:311-16 Mr 4 '63

Secretary appears on Washington reports to the people; interview, ed. by H. W. Flannery. D. Rusk. Dept State Bul 48:440-3 Mr 25 '63

Secretary Rusk addresses Advertising council; remarks, March 12, 1963; with questions and answers. D. Rusk. Dept State Bul 48: 467-75 Ap 1 '63

Secretary Rusk appears on Meet the press; transcript of interview, January 27, 1963. D. Rusk. Dept State Bul 48:244-50 F 18 '63

Secretary Rusk holds press and radio news briefing at Houston. D. Rusk. Dept State Bul 48:388-93 Mr 18 '63

Severe internal crisis threatens NATO. C. Brownlow. Aviation W 78:97+ Mr 11 '63

Short fuse on a long crisis; NATO meeting at Ottawa. il Bsns W p30-2 My 18 '63

Some current issues in U.S. foreign policy; remarks, April 18, 1963; with questions and answers. D. Rusk; G. W. Ball; W. A. Harriman. Dept State Bul 48:679-98 My 6 '63

Speaking out; excerpt from End of alliance; with editorial comment. R. Steel. Sat Eve Post 237:10+, 80 Mr 28 '64; Same abr. with title Is NATO obsolete? without editorial comment. Read Digest 85:152-4 S '64

NORTH ATLANTIC treaty organization—*Cont.*
State of the North Atlantic alliance; address, July 12, 1963. D. Rusk. Dept State Bul 49:190-8 Ag 5 '63
Tensions within the Alliance. R. R. Bowie. For Affairs 42:49-69 O '63
Tides of change; address, February 12, 1963. J. R. Schaetzel. Dept State Bul 48:322-8 Mr 4 '63
Tory bind; Washington's campaign for a mixed-crew surface force. D. Healey. New Repub 148:14-15 Je 22 '63
Trap offered de Gaulle; with reply, by T. W. Stanley. P. M. Gallois. Bul Atomic Sci 19:24-30 O '63
U.S. and Europe: the argument over defense. M. S. Johnson. il U S News 54:43 Je 3 '63
United States and NATO members sign new agreement for cooperation in exchange of atomic information; message to Congress, June 30, 1964; with accompanying documents and text of agreement. L. B. Johnson. Dept State Bul 51:93-8 Jl 20 '64
U.S. demands return on NATO funding. C. Brownlow. Aviation W 80:28-30 F 3 '64
U.S. failing in Europe? J. Fromm and F. C. Painton. il U S News 54:48-52 Mr 25 '63
U.S.-French thaw stirs fears for NATO. L. L. Doty. Aviation W 81:20 D 28 '64
United States of America and the Atlantic partnership; address, November 21, 1963. G. C. McGhee. Dept State Bul 49:954-9 D 23 '63
U.S. pressure delays NATO target buy. L. L. Doty. Aviation W 81:23 N 2 '64
Visit to Italy; address, July 2, 1963. J. F. Kennedy. Dept State Bul 49:134-7 Jl 22 '63
Visit to the United Kingdom; joint communique, June 30, 1963. J. F. Kennedy and H. Macmillan. Dept State Bul 49:132-3 Jl 22 '63
Western powers reject Soviet charges on NATO nuclear defense; exchange of notes between the United States and the Soviet Union, May 18 and April 8, 1963. Dept State Bul 48:860-6 Je 3 '63
What NATO needs to stay alive. T. D. White. Newsweek 62:34 D 16 '63
Who should control nuclear weapons; interview. L. Norstad. U S News 57:47-8 O 5 '64
See also
Atlantic community

Meetings, 1963

North Atlantic council holds ministerial meeting; message, with communique and list of the members of the U.S. delegation. L. B. Johnson. Dept State Bul 50:29-31 Ja 6 '64

Multilateral force (proposed)

ABC of MLF. A. Fontaine. il Reporter 31:10-14 D 31 '64
Allied A-fleet: dilemma for U.S; question of the multilateral nuclear force. U S News 57:32 D 7 '64
As Polaris ship sails with seven nation crew; destroyer U.S.S. Biddle, demonstration ship for MLF or multilateral force. il U S News 57:48-9 Ag 3 '64
Atlantic defense; keeping the door open for France: British plan for allied nuclear force. A. Buchan. New Repub 152:11-14 Ja 9 '65
Bomb now; bomb has become a political factor. New Repub 151:3-5 N 21 '64
Britain 1965; address, December 16, 1964. H. Wilson. Vital Speeches 31:201-8 Ja 15 '65
British seek broad NATO reorganization. Aviation W 81:16-17 N 2 '64
Change in U.S. approach fails to heal NATO rift over MLF. L. L. Doty. Aviation W 81:17-18 D 21 '64
Combined nuclear force for NATO? il Sr Schol 85:8-11+ Ja 14 '65
Compounding confusion; press reports on MLF. Reporter 31:9 D 31 '64
Crisis is a crisis. . . Newsweek 64:29-30 D 14 '64
De Gaulle's deadline. R. Steel. Commonweal 81:412-14 D 18 '64
Europe: storm signals; defiant de Gaulle threatens western unity; with reports by E. Weintal, L. Norman and A. de Borchgrave. il Newsweek 64:40-2+ N 30 '64
Fleet that could sink an alliance. il U S News 57:50-1 N 23 '64
France, U.S. at impasse on NATO policy. L. L. Doty. Aviation W 81:25 N 16 '64
From Washington: notes on the MLF. H. Margolis. Bul Atomic Sci 20:28-30 N '64
In place of NATO: Multilateral nuclear force. R. Steel. New Repub 151:19-22 N 14 '64
Khrushchev, the generals and Goldwater. R. D. Senter. New Repub 151:8-9 N 21 '64
Let's cool off on the M.L.F. Life 57:4 D 4 '64
Let's relax about Europe. S. Alsop. Sat Eve Post 238:16 Ja 16 '65
Living with the MLF; multilateral NATO nuclear force of Polaris—armed surface ships. New Repub 149:4-5 N 2 '63
Meeting de Gaulle's nuclear moves; multilateral deterrent under NATO. Bsns W p34 F 16 '63
Mixed-manned force: whom to believe? Newsweek 61:37-8 Je 17 '63
Multilateral farce? Sat Eve Post 237:92 D 5 '64
Multi-lateral force. Commonweal 81:316-17 N 27 '64
MLF, a West European view. W. Young. Bul Atomic Sci 20:19-21 N '64
Multilateral force: an appraisal. J. Newhouse. Bul Atomic Sci 20:13-18 S '64
MLF & other problems. G. Lichtheim. Commentary 39:65-8 Ja '65
MLF demonstration ship picked; USS Biddle. J. Trainor. Miss & Roc 14:14 Mr 2 '64
Multilateral force: Germany's finger on the atom. A. Etzioni. il Nation 199:208-11 O 12 '64
Multilateral force or farce? debate. A. Etzioni; H. Kahn. il N Y Times Mag p25+ D 13 '64
MLF: modified or out. New Repub 151:8 N 14 '64
Multilateral force: will it pay its way? Newsweek 62:52 N 11 '63
Multilateral muddle. Nation 199:319-20 N 9 '64
Multi-multi-multi. Nation 196:337 Ap 27 '63
New Atlantic crisis. America 111:653 N 21 '64
New signal: go slow. New Repub 152:5 Ja 2 '65
No sale; multilateral nuclear force. Newsweek 62:34+ D 16 '63
NATO deterrent; multinational nuclear deterrent. Time 81:32 Mr 8 '63
NATO today: the great poker game. A. Werth. Nation 199:399-401 N 30 '64
NATO's dilemma. il Time 84:29 N 20 '64
NATO's nuclear dilemma. H. A. Kissinger. il Reporter 28:22-33+ Mr 28 '63; Discussion. 28:6+ Ap 25; 8+ My 9 '63; Bul Atomic Sci 20:18-20 S '64
Nuclear defense of NATO; address, April 22, 1964. G. C. Smith. bibliog f Dept State Bul 50:783-90 My 18 '64; Same with title Problems of foreign policy. Vital Speeches 30:526-30 Je 15 '64
Polyglot navy; Multilateral force (MLF) Nation 199:21-2 Jl 27 '64
Senators oppose M.L.F. Christian Cent 81:1516-17 D 9 '64
Showdown for the West: story of MLF; what it is and what's at stake. M. S. Johnson. U S News 57:44-5 D 14 '64
Slow steps toward the atomic fleet; role of MLF in the Atlantic alliance. Bsns W p26-7 D 12 '64
Thinking ahead; British stand on MLF. Newsweek 64:51-2 D 7 '64
Thorniest issue; crisis over the control of nuclear weapons. il Newsweek 64:48-50 N 9 '64
To NATO's brink; French position. Time 84:54 N 13 '64
Trading off; British strategy on multilateral force. il Newsweek 64:48 Jl 20 '64
Trial run for MLF. il U S News 57:32-3 D 21 '64
U.S. & Europe: the waiting game; MLF reconsidered. Time 84:28-9 D 18 '64
U.S. reaffirms position on MLF as irrevocable in NATO planning. C. Brownlow. Aviation W 81:17-18 D 14 '64
U.S. reaffirms position on NATO multilateral nuclear force; U.S. note to the Soviet Ministry of foreign affairs, August 28, 1964. Dept State Bul 51:367-8 S 14 '64
What kind of NATO nuclear force? R. H. Dawson. bibliog f Ann Am Acad 351:30-9 Ja '64
What price MLF? E. Taylor. Reporter 31:12+ D 3 '64
What price treaty? Finger on the ANF nuclear trigger. il Newsweek 64:38-9 D 21 '64

NORTH BELLMORE, N.Y, public library
Library budget rejected twice by Long Island voters. Library J 89:2756 Jl '64

NORTH BORNEO
Borneo, Britain's South Vietnam; British troops and Sukarno guerrillas. R. Hughes il N Y Times Mag p9+ Jl 19 '64
Eyewitness report: Borneo: where a new war is heating up; concerning Sarawak and Sabah. S. W. Sanders. il U S News 56:58-60 Ja 27 '64

NORTH BORNEO—*Continued*
Our far-flung correspondents: Federation of Malaysia. R. Shaplen. New Yorker 39:163-4+ Ap 6 '63
Roadblock; inclusion of North Borneo and Sarawak Newsweek 62:45-6 S 2 '63
Sabah (North Borneo) C. F. Preuss. bibliog il Focus 14:1-6 N '63
This war in Borneo: whose side are we on? H. F. Armstrong. il Reporter 30:16-20 Je 4 '64
Troubles of becoming a nation; the story of Malaysia. R. P. Martin. il U S News 54:82-3 Ap 15 '63
See also
Sarawak
NORTH BROOKFIELD, Mass.
Children still pray in school. il Life 55:53+ N 8 '63
NORTH CAPE yacht club. See Yacht clubs
NORTH CAROLINA
See also
Education—North Carolina
Fishing—North Carolina
Forests and forestry—North Carolina
Gardens—North Carolina
Law—North Carolina
Libraries—North Carolina
Music festivals—North Carolina
Outer Banks (islands)

Boundaries

Short time between drinks. Am Heritage 15:94 F '64

Capitol

New statehouse for North Carolina. il Arch Forum 119:86-93 D '63

Economic conditions

Advance guard in war on poverty; pilot program set up with aid of Ford foundation in N.C. il Bsns W p26-7 My 30 '64

Politics and government

Where the race issue took a new turn. U S News 57:16 Jl 13 '64

Race problems

News of the Christian world. W. M. Wells, jr. Christian Cent 80:837-8 Je 26 '63

Religious institutions and affairs

News of the Christian world (cont) Christian Cent 80:312+, 965, 1449; 81:529-30, 1538-9 Mr 6, Jl 31, N 20 '63, Ap 22, D 9 '64
NORTH CAROLINA education association
Mahomet goes to the hill. W. A. Abrams. NEA J 52:49 N '63
NORTH CAROLINA forestry association
89th and 54th; joint annual meetings of North Carolina and American forestry associations. il Am For 70:15 O '64
NORTH CAROLINA mutual life insurance company
Negro has the same risks. il Time 83:90 F 7 '64
NORTH CAROLINA. University, Chapel Hill
Newspapers: a regional resource. J. Orne. Library J 88:1612-14 Ap 15 '63
Work-study program. J. H. Gribbin. Library J 89:568-9+ F 1 '64
NORTH CASCADES NATIONAL PARK (proposed) See National parks and reserves—United States
NORTH CASCADES primitive area. See Wilderness areas
NORTH CHANNEL
Cruising the North Channel. F. M. Paulson. il Field & S 68:37-9+ My '63
North Channel. K. Collins. il Yachting 115:36-8+ Mr '64
NORTH DAKOTA
We are beating water pollution. W. V. Heuvelen. il Am City 78:34 Jl '63
See also
Birds—North Dakota
Turtle Mountains

Politics and government

More sound than steam. il Time 82:26 N 1 '63
NORTH EAST, Pa.
Man-made aquifer taps a stream. J. K. Hallenburg. il Am City 79:161-2+ Je '64
NORTH Hills golf club. See Golf courses
NORTH KOREA. See Korea (People's Democratic Republic)
NORTH PACIFIC fisheries commission. See International North Pacific fisheries commission
NORTH PACIFIC fishers conference. See International convention for the high seas fisheries of the North Pacific Ocean
NORTH PACIFIC fishery conference. See International convention for the high seas fisheries of the North Pacific Ocean
NORTH PACIFIC fur seal commission
Protocol amending North Pacific fur seals convention signed. Dept State Bul 49:688 O 28 '63
NORTH PACIFIC race. See Yacht racing
NORTH VIET NAM. See Viet Nam (Democratic Republic)
NORTHAMPTON (command ship) See Warships—United States
NORTHBROOK, Ill.
Our own plant proved better. R. Weidaw and K. Bielert. il Am City 79:102-4 Ag '64
NORTHCOTT, Cecil
China's living church. Christian Cent 82:39-40 Ja 13 '65
Galilee is still Galilee. Christian Cent 80:645 My 15 '63
Jerusalem the imperishable. Christian Cent 80:575 My 1 '63
Mission to South Africa. Christian Cent 81:1550 D 16 '64
Monks of Chevetogne. Christian Cent 81:1443 N 18 '64
New ministry in inner London. Christian Cent 80:1547 D 11 '63
Prescription for survival. Christian Cent 81:168 F 5 '64
Prophet of the Kirchentag. Christian Cent 80:933-4 Jl 24 '63
Radical Rome. Christian Cent 81:1423 N 18 '64
Roman radical in London. Christian Cent 81:907-8 Jl 15 '64
Slow march to unity. Christian Cent 81:1231-2 O 7 '64
Taizé: lever for reconciliation. Christian Cent 81:1561 D 16 '64
NORTHEAST airlines, incorporated
Bid to reverse Northeast ruling seen. Aviation W 79:42 Ag 5 '63
CAB feels wind from Northeast; refusal to renew Northeast airlines' Florida certificate. il Bsns W p45-6+ O 5 '63
CAB ponders Northeast's fate. Bsns W p97 Je 29 '63
CAB reaffirms Northeast decision, court holds key to Florida route. Aviation W 81:29 D 7 '64
CAB rejects Northeast renewal in 3-2 decision on Florida route. J. R. Ashlock. Aviation W 79:43 O 14 '63
CAB reversal of Northeast ruling unlikely despite merger proposal. Aviation W 79:43 S 30 '63
Court may clarify status of NE directors. R. G. O'Lone. Aviation W 81:25 D 28 '65
Decision against Northeast. Time 82:64 Ag 23 '63
Down. New Yorker 40:30-2 Mr 21 '64
Down or out? Newsweek 62:67-8 Ag 12 '63
Further financial aid depends on Florida rights, Northeast says. Aviation W 78:37 Je 3 '63
Grabbing again for TWA controls. il Bsns W p 168+ My 16 '64
Hughes makes new pass at TWA. Bsns W p32 O 10 '64
Hughes takes a trick; wins control of TWA. Bsns W p27 Jl 18 '64
Hughes tool co. drops Northeast support. Aviation W 79:41 Ag 12 '63
MacIntyre gives view on Northeast finances. Aviation W 79:32 S 2 '63
Northeast assured planes until Sept. 11, 1963. J. R. Ashlock. Aviation W 79:30 Jl 8 '63
Northeast case pressure seen as threat. L. L. Doty. Aviation W 79:40-1 S 9 '63
Northeast decision seen aimed at Hughes. R. H. Cook. Aviation W 78:38-9 Ap 22 '63
Northeast decision sets no precedents. L. L. Doty. Aviation W 79:38 Ag 26 '63
Northeast, Hughes file trust agreement. J. W. Carter. Aviation W 81:34-5 O 12 '64
Northeast leases jet equipment, plans eighteen daily flights to Florida. Aviation W 79:40 N 18 '63
Northeast retention of aircraft proposed. J. R. Ashlock. Aviation W 79:37-8 Jl 1 '63
Northeast seeking cancellation of debts. J. R. Ashlock. Aviation W 79:31 Jl 29 '63
Northeast struggles to fend off CAB ax. Bsns W p 18 Ag 3 '63
Pressures mount on CAB over Northeast. L. L. Doty. Aviation W 79:42-3 S 23 '63
Ruling that may kill an airline. U S News 55:8 Ag 26 '63
Why Northeast faces its worst crisis yet; half local service feeder line, half long-haul trunk carrier. il Bsns W p48-51 Ja 9 '65
NORTHEASTERN states
Trailer cruising northeast. E. R. Thornton. il Motor B 111:32-4+ Ap '63

NORTHERN corn rootworms. See Corn rootworms
NORTHERN forest congress. See Forests and forestry—Scandinavia
NORTHERN ILLINOIS university, DeKalb
FTA summer experience. E. M. Anglin and J. H. King. NEA J 53:31 My '64
NORTHERN IRELAND
See also
Belfast
Irish unification question
Tourist trade—Northern Ireland

Description and travel

Northern Ireland: from Derry to Down. R. L. Conly. il Nat Geog Mag 126:232-67 Ag '64

Industries

Northern Ireland: industry hasn't destroyed its natural beauty. il Esquire 59:151-3 Ap '63

Religious institutions and affairs

Catholics may apply. America 108:389 Mr 23 '63
NORTHERN lights. See Auroras
NORTHERN RHODESIA
Roar of the Black Lion. il Time 83:30 Je 5 '64
See also
Education—Northern Rhodesia
Elections—Northern Rhodesia
United Nations—Northern Rhodesia

Politics and government

First prime minister. Time 83:24 Ja 31 '64
Rhodesia's rare asset. Newsweek 63:36 F 3 '64
Sir Roy's last gasp. New Repub 148:6-7 Mr 23 '63
Voice of God. Newsweek 63:35 Ja 13 '64
See also
Zambia
NORTHERN states power company
St Croix: who owns a river? A. D. Stedman. il Nation 199:490-3 D 21 '64
That nine-foot channel; proposal to build power plant on St Croix River. J. Ridgeway. New Repub 151:12 D 26 '64
NORTHERN student movement
Down-to-earth idealism. Time 81:102 My 17 '63
Ivy-league integrationists. R. W. Apple, jr. il Reporter 28:32-4 F 14 '63
Quiet revolution; white college students tutor Negro high school youngsters at After school programs. J. F. Warner. il Sat R 47:80-1+ My 16 '64
NORTHERN white cedar. See Arborvitae
NORTHMEN. See Vikings
NORTHROP corporation
F-5B capability span wide speed range. H. J. Coleman. il Aviation W 81:48-9+ O 12 '64
Northrop gets in LSV battle with company-funded development. R. Hawkes. il Miss & Roc 15:28+ N 23 '64
NORTHROP space laboratories. See Northrop corporation
NORTHRUP, Herbert R.
Case for Boulwarism. bibliog f Harvard Bsns R 41:86-97 S '63
Here's way to make more jobs; interview. por Nations Bsns 52:36-7+ Mr '64
NORTHWEST
High time on a low tide; geoduc hunters at Pacific Northwest. V. Kraft. il Sports Illus 21:50-3 D 14 '64
Pollution; everybody's fight. J. C. Hunt. il Am For 70:17-20 S '64
West to northwest; from Los Angeles, Cal. to Cape Flattery, Wash. C. West. il Yachting 115:58-60+ My '64

Description and travel

Better homes and gardens family-planned vacation. il Bet Hom & Gard 41:111-14 My '63
Pacific Northwest. R. Atkeson. il U S Camera 27:70-1+ My '64
Seattle to Seattle in 3,600 miles. B. Kocivar. il Look 28:80-3 My 5 '64
NORTHWEST, CANADIAN
Found: million-acre cow pasture. G. A. Yackulic. il Sci Digest 53:79-81 My '63
NORTHWEST airlines
American, Northwest granted new routes. J. R. Ashlock. Aviation W 81:29 Ag 10 '64
Northwest president sees twelve per cent gain in 1965 operating revenue. Aviation W 81:48 S 21 '64
NORTHWEST Orient airlines
Northwest orders three 727Cs. J. R. Ashlock. il Aviation W 81:27 Jl 27 '64
NORTHWESTERN Pacific railroad
Battle for a mighty good road; Union Pacific and North Western covet Rock Island line. il Bsns W p 119-20+ N 2 '63
NORTHWESTERN regional library, Aztec. See New Mexico state library—Branches
NORTHWESTERN university, Evanston, Ill.
New NU. il Newsweek 63:64 Je 8 '64

Libraries

University library employs radial plan. il Arch Rec 136:15 Jl '64

Observatory

See Astronomical observatories
NORTHWOOD institute, Midland, Mich. See Business education
NORTON, Alden
New look in Adventure. Writer 77:26-7 F '64
NORTON, Alice
(ed) Displaying our wares. Wilson Lib Bul 38:533-46+ Mr '64
NORTON, Elliot
To Lawrence Langner. Theatre Arts 47:11+ My '63
NORTON, Mike
Our dairy surplus, we import a chunk of it. Farm J 87:34 My '63
NORTON-TAYLOR, Duncan
Sword at the belly of red China. Fortune 68:150-3+ Jl '63; Same abr. Read Digest 83:127-31 S '63
NORTON company
It's no longer just grind, grind at Norton. il Fortune 68:118-23+ Ag '63
NORTON Simon foundation
Exit Lord Pengo. il Newsweek 63:61 My 4 '64
NORWALK, Ohio
Cut water-planning guesswork. J. C. Bumstead. il Am City 78:102-4 My '63
NORWAY
See also
Fishing—Norway
Forests and forestry—Norway
Lapland
Schools—Norway
Svalbard

Description and travel

Going places, finding things in north Norway. N. S. Hazelton. il House & Gard 125:23+ Je '64

Politics and government

End of an institution. Time 82:25 Ag 30 '63
NORWAY and the United States
Vice President Johnson visits northern Europe; address, September 11, 1963. L. B. Johnson. Dept State Bul 49:588-9 O 14 '63
NORWAY rats. See Rats
NORWEGIAN cookery. See Cookery, Norwegian
NORWEGIAN poetry

Translations into English

On the murder of Abraham Lincoln; tr. by R. Bly. H. Ibsen. Nation 196:142 F 16 '63
NORWEGIAN students in the United States. See Foreign students in the United States
NORWICH, Conn.
One of those things; burst dam. il Newsweek 61:25 Mr 18 '63
NORWICH, England, public library
Norwich on the square. P. Hepworth. il Library J 88:4548-50 D 1 '63
NORWOOD, Malcolm J.
New horizons for the deaf. por Sch Life 45:6-7 Ja '63
NOSE
See also
Smell
NOSE; opera. See Shostakovich, D.
NOSE drops
Hidden menace in nose drops. J. Orr. il Todays Health 42:24-5 D '64
NOSENKO, Ûriĭ Ivanovich
De-briefing process for the U.S.S.R.'s defectors. il Newsweek 63:40-1 F 24 '64
Key defector. Sr Schol 84:18 Mr 13 '64
Mystery of a Russian who fled to the west. il por U S News 56:8 F 24 '64
NOSKE-FRIEDLAENDER, Leny
Notes from our correspondents. Hi Fi 14:26+ Mr '64
NOSSAL, Frederick
China's second experiment. Nation 196:503-5 Je 15 '63
Making of Mao. Sat R 46:24-5 Jl 13 '63
NOSSAL, G. J. V.
How cells make antibodies; with biographical sketch. Sci Am 211:20+, 106-15 D '64

NOSSITER, Bernard D.
It will be a long war. Reporter 30:20-1 Mr 26 '64
Kefauver and the price-makers. Nation 197: 12-13 Jl 6 '63
Troubled conscience of American business; excerpts from Myths and mythmakers in the modern economy. Harper 227:37-43 S '63

NOSTALGIA
Camper's allergy. E. S. Ringold. il N Y Times Mag p32 Je 30 '63

NOSTRI, Robert
Boy on fire. H. Gold. il pors Sat Eve Post 237:28-9 S 12 '64

NOT because you are good; story. See Hintze, N. A.

NOT fit for man or beast; drama. See Hark, M. and McQueen, N.

NOTABLE books council. See American library association—Adult services division

NOTABLES. See Great men

NOTASULGA, Ala.
Trouble in Notasulga; Vernon Merritt free-lance photographer attacked by officers of the law. il Time 83:51 F 14 '64

NOTE paper. See Stationery

NOTEBOOKS
What's the news around school? new look in school bags and loose-leaf binders. il Seventeen 22:150-1 S '63

NOTHOMB, Charles Ferdinand
Communist China's opening to the west. Reporter 30:36-7 F 13 '64

NOTIONS (merchandise)
Exciting; National notion and novelty show. New Yorker 40:40 S 12 '64
Trade; National notion & novelty show. New Yorker 39:15-16 Ag 24 '63

NOTRE DAME, Ind. University
Goldfarb case fought by anti-censorship forces. Pub W 187:105-6 Ja 18 '65
Goldfarb vs. Notre Dame. Newsweek 64:53 D 28 '64
Importance of an image; Notre Dame injunction against Twentieth century-Fox movie. il Time 84:69 D 18 '64
Notre Dame's Irish dander rises over a movie; case against Twentieth century-Fox. il Life 57:68+ D 18 '64
Notre Dame's mosaic tower; new memorial library. V. A. Schaefer. il Library J 89: 4743-5 D 1 '64
Student freedom; censorship of articles in the Scholastic. Commonweal 78:269-70 My 31 '63; Reply. O. P. Kretzmann. 78:379 Je 28 '63
This side of the vision. T. M. Hesburgh. Time 81:88 My 3 '63
Vicious circles of Father Hesburgh. Christian Cent 80:1015 Ag 14 '63

NOTRE DAME cathedral, Paris
Cathedral centennial. C. J. McNaspy. America 109:82-3 Jl 20 '63
800 years old; with report by D. Seiberling. il Life 55:34-6 Ag 9 '63
Notre Dame: a pageant of 800 years. B. Ehrlich. il N Y Times Mag p26-7+ My 5 '63

NOTT, Kathleen
Future-mindedness. Commentary 36:49-54 Jl '63
Mortal statistics. Commentary 38:64-8 O '64

NOURISSIER, François
Bettina: a woman of change. Vogue 143:138-45+ Ja 1 '64
Bonjour ennui. Vogue 142:71 Ag 1 '63
Countess Ferdinand von Bismarck. Vogue 142:180-5+ S 15 '63
François Mauriac. Vogue 144:178 S 1 '64
Influence of the Swiss. Vogue 142:174-81+ O 1 '63

NOURRIT, Adolphe
Defender of the realm. T. McEwen. por Opera N 27:30-1 Mr 9 '63

NOURSE, Edwin G.
Not so dismal science of economics. bibliog NEA J 52:38-41 Mr '63

NOUZHA, Lalla. See Lalla Nouzha

NOVA SCOTIA
See also
Cape Breton Island
Halifax
Nova Scotians
Oak Island
Peggy's Cove

Description and travel

Circumnavigating Nova Scotia. Mrs A. E. Phillips, jr. il Yachting 115:38-40+ Je '64

Historic houses, etc.

McGinney's tavern in Nova Scotia. N. M. Hill. il Antiques 84:179-81 Ag '63

NOVA SCOTIANS
Banker to his own flesh and blood. C. Aucoin. New Yorker 40:125-6+ Ap 18 '64

NOVACULITE
Nature in rock & mineral. P. M. Tilden. il Natur Hist 73:58-61 Ap '64

NOVAE. See Stars, New

NOVAES, Guiomar
Two great women pianists. Discus. Harper 228:109-10 Ja '64

NOVAK, Gertrude
Bobby Baker story: Senate unfolds chapter one. il por U S News 55:31 D 30 '63
Cash-and-carry; Mrs Novak before Senate rules committee. por Newsweek 62:13 D 30 '63
First Baker witness. por Time 82:18 D 27 '63

NOVAK, Kim
Kim Novak in her hideaway by the sea. il pors Life 56:108-11 Ap 17 '64
Kim Novak vs. the code. V. Scott. il pors Sat Eve Post 237:16-17 S 5 '64

NOVAK, Michael
Break with the past. Commonweal 78:372-5 Je 28 '63
Catholic vote is confused. New Repub 151: 14-15 Ag 22 '64
Catholics in college. Commonweal 77:451-4; 78:19-20 Ja 25, Mr 29 '63
Closing the gap between theology and marital reality. Commonweal 80:342-7 Je 5 '64
Don't knock Dr Rock. America 108:728 My 25 '63
Ecumenical sadness and hope. Christian Cent 81:1518 D 9 '64
Intrigue in the council. New Repub 150:10-11 Ja 11 '64
Life of reason. Commonweal 78:76-8 Ap 12 '63
Marriage: the lay voice. Commonweal 79: 587-90 F 14 '64
Nuns in the world. Commonweal 79:274-8 N 29 '63
Pope Paul on the church. Commonweal 80: 631-4 S 18 '64
Pope Paul's address to the curia. Commonweal 79:89-90 O 18 '63
Prophecy and the novel. Commonweal 77: 563+ F 22 '63
Religion in the public schools. New Repub 148:16-18 Ap 13 '63
Updike's quest for liturgy. Commonweal 78: 192-5 My 10 '63
Vatican II, act III. New Repub 151:7-8 O 17 '64
When is doctrine pure? excerpt from Open church. Commonweal 80:233-5, 453-4 My 15, Jl 3 '64
Winds of change in Rome: the Vatican council moves toward renewal and reform. New Repub 149:11-13 N 16 '63

NOVAK, Robert D.
In defense of the House. New Repub 148:22-4 My 18 '63
Insiders. il por Newsweek 64:71 Jl 27 '64
Uncuttable budget. Reporter 28:41-2+ Ap 25 '63
—See Evans, R. jr. jt. auth.

NOVAK, Thomas M.
Masquerade of a counterfeit doctor. B. Lindeman. il pors Sat Eve Post 238:83-7 Ja 30 '65

NOVEL award program. See Fiction—Competitions

NOVELISTS
Catch $95; novelists are invading movies. il Newsweek 63:83-4 Mr 9 '64
First novelists, fall 1964; statements by the writers, ed. by B. G. Pearlman. il Library J 89:3779-87+ O 1 '64
First novelists, spring 1964; statements by the writers. ed. by J. Serebnick. pors Library J 89:661-9 F 1 '64
First novelists, spring-summer, fall 1963; statements by the writers, ed. by J. Serebnick. pors Library J 88:580-93, 2277-83, 3651-7 F 1, Je 1, O 1 '63
First novelists, summer 1964; statements by the writers, ed. by B. G. Loftus. il Library J 89:2371-7 Je 1 '64
See also
Women as authors

NOVELISTS, American
American first novelist, a study of commitment and the literary career. by H. A. Enzer. Review
Sat R 46:34 O 12 '63. D. Dempsey

NOVELISTS, American—*Continued*
Onward and upward with the arts; can the rich write? G. T. Hellman. New Yorker 39: 46-8+ Je 8 '63
See also
Alger, H. jr
Bellow, S.
Cheever, J.
Eastlake, W.
Ellison, R.
Faulkner, W.
Hemingway, E.
James, H.
Kim, R.
Lewis, S.
McCarthy, M.
Selby, H.
Southern, T.

NOVELISTS, Canadian
See also
MacLennan, H.

NOVELISTS, Catholic. See Catholic authors

NOVELISTS, Colombian
Industrial prize for Colombian novelists. E. Sanchez O. il Américas 16:31-2 S '64

NOVELISTS, Ecuadorian
Ecuador's novels and novelists. E. Uzcátegui. il Américas 16:29-34 My '64

NOVELISTS, English
See also
Murdoch, I.
Waugh, E.

NOVELISTS, French
Defective detectives. V. Mercier. Nation 199: 362-3 N 16 '64
See also
Céline, L. F.
Duras, M
Gascar, P.
Giono, J.
Sarraute, N.

NOVELISTS, Italian
See also
Moravia, A.

NOVELISTS, Latin American
See also
Novelists, Colombian
Novelists, Ecuadorian

NOVELISTS, Mexican
See also
Fuentes, C.
Rulfo, J.

NOVELISTS, Peruvian
See also
Alegría, C.

NOVELISTS, Russian
It's a gloomy world, gentlemen; excerpts from Six Russian short novels. R. Jarrell. Atlan 211:76-82 Ap '63

NOVELISTS, Spanish
Color of seed. A. Kerrigan. Poetry 101:345-9 F '63
Spain between the lines. P. West. Nation 199:307-8+ N 2 '64
See also
Asturias, M. A.

NOVELISTS, Venezuelan
See also
Gallegos, R.

NOVELS. See Fiction

NOVELS, American. See American fiction

NOVELS, Dime. See Dime novels

NOVEMBER
In November; list of the dates, memorable and not so, coming up this month (title varies) (cont) il N Y Times Mag p53 N 3 '63; 36 N 1 '64

NOVICK, Joe
Reverse fly. Field & S 68:90-1 S '63

NOVICK, Julius
Letter from England. Nation 196:553-5 Je 29 '63
Much ado about Shakespeare: three summer festivals. Harper 228:64-71 My '64
Theatre. Nation 199:504 D 21 '64

NOVILLE, Virginia
Reporter at large. R. Rice. il New Yorker 39: 153-4+ O 19 '63

NOVOA, Alberto Ruiz. See Ruiz Novoa, A.

NOVOSIBIRSK, Siberia
Russia's hidden science city. A. Parry. il Sci Digest 53:22-8 My '63

NOVOTNY, Antonin
Disappointment in Prague. il por Time 84: 38 N 20 '64
Gymnast. K. Ames. Newsweek 64:52+ D 7 '64

NOWAK, Edward, jr
We fought a fresh-water monster. Outdoor Life 133:48-9+ Ja '64

NOWELL, Peter C. and Cole, L. J.
Reduced incidence of persistent chromosome aberrations in mice irradiated at low dose rates. bibliog Science 141:524-6 Ag 9 '63

NOWHERE to go but up; musical comedy. See Musical comedies, revues, etc.—Criticisms, plots, etc.

NOWOSIELSKI, Józef W. and Patton, R. L.
Daily fluctuation in the blood sugar concentration of the house cricket, gryllus domesticus L. bibliog Science 144:180-1 Ap 10 '64

NOWOTNY, Otto H.
American vs. European management philosophy. bibliog f Harvard Bsns R 42:101-8 Mr '64

NOYCE, Dorothy
Ten-month terror; poem. Redbook 121:12 O '63

NOYES, Alfred
Luck of a collector; original manuscript of A seventieth birthday. J. S. Mayfield. il Hobbies 68:110-11+ O '63

NOYES, Crosby S.
Catch a falling star. il por Time 81:94 Ap 19 '63

NOYES, Eliot
Moods are not accidents. il Life 54:60 F 15 '63
about
Industrial designer with a conspicuous conscience. W. McQuade. il pors Fortune 68:135-8+ Ag '63

Le NOZZE di Figaro; opera. See Mozart, J. C. W. A.

NOZZLES, Rocket engine. See Rocket engines

NU, 1907-
Burma: drifting into an uncertain future. il por Sr Schol 84:6-8 Ap 17 '64
His nation went to prison with him. L. J. Walinsky. por Sat R 46:44 D 7 '63

NUBIA
Gods, men & the river. Time 83:40 My 22 '64
Antiquities
Threatened treasures of the Nile. G. Gerster. il Nat Geog Mag 124:586-621 O '63

NUBIANS
Exodus from Nubia. il Time 82:22+ D 20 '63

NUCLEAR detection and reporting system. See Atomic warfare—Defenses

NUCLEAR energy. See Atomic power

NUCLEAR fission
Fission damage in calcite and the dating of carbonates. R. F. Sippel and E. D. Glover. bibliog il Science 144:409-11 Ap 24 '64

NUCLEAR fuels
First nuclear reactor fuel in Smithsonian; one-inch cube of uranium. Sci N L 83:181 Mr 23 '63
See also
Plutonium
Transportation
First radioactive cargo comes into a U.S. port; Swedish shipment of nuclear fuel. il Bsns W p24-5 Jl 27 '63

NUCLEAR fusion
Fusion control closer; burnout achieved in experiments. A. Ewing. Sci N L 86:115 Ag 22 '64
Fusion control near. Sci N L 86:311 N 14 '64
New theory found for future fusion reactors. Sci N L 84:248 O 19 '63
New try at caging atom fusion; Astron program. il Bsns W p 138+ Ag 22 '64

NUCLEAR gages. See Gages

NUCLEAR magnetic resonance
Fluid flow in porous media studied by a nuclear magnetic resonance technique. A. Timur and I. Fatt. bibliog il Science 146: 1162-3 N 27 '64
Nuclear magnetic resonance spectroscopy in superconducting magnetic fields. F. A. Nelson and H. E. Weaver. bibliog il Science 146:223-32 O 9 '64
Tautomerism and site of protonation of 1-methylcytosine: proof by nuclear magnetic resonance spin-spin coupling. H. T. Miles and others. bibliog il Science 142:1569-71 D 20 '63

NUCLEAR pacifism. See Pacifism

NUCLEAR particles. See Particles (nuclear physics)

NUCLEAR physics
At home with Maria Mayer. il Sci Digest 55:30-6 F '64
High-energy physics: panel proposes construction, operation program to run through 1981. D. S. Greenberg. Science 140:958-9 My 31 '63

NUCLEAR physics—*Continued*
Nuclear theory verified. C. S. Wu. Sci N L 83:85 F 9 '63
See also
Atomic nuclei
Mössbauer effect
Particles (nuclear physics)
Time reversal

NUCLEAR power plants. See Atomic power plants

NUCLEAR pulse rockets. See Space vehicles—Propulsion systems

NUCLEAR reactions
Correlations of particles emitted in nuclear reactions; report on conference at Gatlinburg, Tenn. H. G. Pugh. Science 147:177-9 Ja 8 '65
Helium difluoride: possible preparative techniques based on nuclear transmutations. G. C. Pimentel and others. bibliog Science 143:674 F 14 '64

NUCLEAR reactors
Boil up for superheaters; GE-AEG joint research plan. Bsns W p 134 My 23 '64
Breeder reactor II produces electricity. il(p 145) Sci N L 86:150 S 5 '64
Budget reacts on plutonium. Bsns W p26-7 Ja 18 '64
Destruction on Jackass Flats: nuclear reactor Kiwi blown up. il Time 85:35 Ja 22 '65
Four U.S. nuclear reactors placed under IAEA safeguards. Dept State Bul 51:27 Jl 6 '64
New theory found for future fusion reactors. Sci N L 84:248 O 19 '63
Outrage on Bodega Head. G. Marine. il Nation 196:524-7 Je 22 '63; Discussion. 197: 62 Ag 10 '63
Perils of Pluto. W. J. Coughlin. Miss & Roc 14:46 Je 22 '64
Pluto cancellation or cutback threatened. K. Johnsen. Aviation W 80:28-9 Ja 13 '64
Reactor keeps itself going. Bsns W p76 N 16 '63
Reactor to desalt water: breeder reactors. Sci N L 84:82 Ag 10 '63
Rowe's reactor; open to inspection by I.A.E.A. il Time 83:27 Mr 13 '64
Teaching reactor in a glass pavilion, University of Washington, Seattle. il Arch Rec 134:182-3 S '63
U.S. and Euratom to cooperate on fast neutron reactors; Department announcement, May 27, 1964. Dept State Bul 50:941-3 Je 15 '64
See also
Guided missiles—Atomic power plants
Rockets, Atomic powered

Fuel

See Nuclear fuels

NUCLEAR rockets. See Rockets, Atomic powered

NUCLEAR scattering. See Scattering (physics)

NUCLEAR test ban. See Atomic bombs—Testing, Suspension of

NUCLEAR test ban treaty, 1963
Africa and the world: problems of today and tomorrow; address, August 24, 1963. G. M. Williams. Dept State Bul 49:432-6 S 16 '63
After test ban: what is next. F. B. Stevens. il U S News 55:58-9 O 7 '63
After the test ban. P. Horton. Reporter 29: 14+ Ag 15 '63
Agreeing again with Russians; plan for keeping nuclear arms out of orbits in space. Bsns W p28 O 12 '63
All about the voting. Newsweek 62:18-19 S 30 '63
Allies and the test ban. Newsweek 62:19 Ag 5 '63
Another round in the test-ban debate. il U S News 55:52-7 S 2 '63
Appraisal of Khrushchev by Harriman; political and economic pressures behind agreement with the West. W. A. Harriman. il N Y Times Mag p 10+ Ag 25 '63
A-test pact: what JFK told the Nation; excerpts from address, July 26, 1963. J. F. Kennedy. il U S News 55:6 Ag 5 '63
Beyond the test ban. Commonweal 78:491 Ag 23 '63
Big guns speak on the test ban; questions and answers. il Newsweek 62:17-18 Ag 26 '63
Both sides of test ban: debate in the Senate. U S News 55:74-5 S 30 '63
Bumps on the ratification road. il Time 82: 13-14 Ag 9 '63
Bumpy road in the Senate for test-ban treaty. U S News 55:8 S 16 '63
Case for the test-ban treaty. Bsns W p 160 S 7 '63
Clearing the air; three-power agreement initialed in Moscow. New Repub 149:3-4 Ag 3 '63
Dangers of hairsplitting; France as a non-signatory of the test-ban treaty. Nation 199:506 D 28 '64
Day in the Kremlin. America 109:146 Ag 17 '63
Debate on the Moscow treaty. Nat R 15:136-7 Ag 27 '63
Defense, AEC report to President on test ban treaty safeguards. R. S. McNamara and G. T. Seaborg. Dept State Bul 50:744-6 My 11 '64
De Gaulle speaks: the answer is no; with report by E. Weintal. Newsweek 62:29-30 Ag 12 '63
Despite the doubts. Time 82:24 S 13 '63
Detailed test and detection plans readied to back nuclear treaty. K. Johnsen. Aviation W 79:28-9 Ag 26 '63
Dirksen's way. K. Crawford. Newsweek 62: 28 Ag 12 '63
Euphoria. D. Lawrence. U S News 55:132 O 7 '63
Eyeful in Gagra, smiles in Moscow. il Newsweek 62:35-6 Ag 19 '63
Finding new ways to test A-weapons; scientists improve test techniques. il Bsns W p86+ O 5 '63
First juridical step toward peace. Christian Cent 80:1227 O 9 '63
First step, to where? Bul Atomic Sci 19:2-3 O '63
Foreign policy: building amid turbulence; address, August 27, 1963. R. J. Manning. Dept State Bul 49:454-60 S 23 '63
Foreign relations; the mellowing mood. il Time 82:11-12 Ag 16 '63
From former President Eisenhower: an O.K. for test-ban treaty, if—. U S News 55:24 S 9 '63
From Washington straight; Senate ratification. Cato. Nat R 15:144, 228 Ag 27, S 24 '63
Genie in the Senate. il Newsweek 62:19-20 Ag 19 '63
Hard treaty. W. Lippmann. Newsweek 62:15 Ag 19 '63
Just the beginning. N. Cousins. Sat R 46: 28-9 S 21 '63
Khrushchev-Kennedy treaty. F. S. Meyer. Nat R 15:107 Ag 13 '63
Khrushchev's reason. K. Crawford. Newsweek 62:32 S 2 '63
Letter from Washington; Senate ratification. R. H. Rovere. New Yorker 39:149-56 O 5 '63
Limited test ban treaty ratified, enters into force; with remarks by President Kennedy, October 7, 1963; joint communique and text of proclamation, October 10, 1963. J. F. Kennedy. Dept State Bul 49:658 O 28 '63
Man-in-the-street; test ban treaty and role of libraries. E. Moon. Library J 88:3035 S 1 '63
Man who challenges the President; chief opponent of test-ban treaty. U S News 55:12 S 2 '63
Memo from the publisher. J. W. Claar. Miss & Roc 13:50 S 23 '63
Military chiefs give views on treaty. Aviation W 79:29 Ag 26 '63
Mission to Moscow: 1963. il Newsweek 62: 15-17 Ag 12 '63
Mr Rusk and Mr Harriman discuss nuclear test ban treaty; interview on television, July 28, 1963; ed. by M. Agronsky. D. Rusk; W. A. Harriman. Dept State Bul 49:240-5 Ag 12 '63
Negotiating a limited treaty for banning nuclear tests; address, July 31, 1963. W. A. Harriman. Dept State Bul 49:278-82 Ag 19 '63
No quick thaw ahead; No pain for business. il Bsns W p20-2 Ag 3 '63
Nobelists support treaty. Sci N L 84:118 Ag 24 '63
Nonsigners. il Time 82:22 Ag 23 '63
Now, or never? Nat R 15:220-1 S 24 '63
Nuclear test ban treaty. R. S. Preston. Cur Hist 46:341-5+ Je '64
Nuclear test-ban treaty. il U N Rev 10:4-5+ Ag '63
Nuclear test ban treaty endorsed by Science advisory committee. Dept State Bul 49:430-1 S 16 '63
Nuclear test ban treaty signed at Moscow, transmitted to Senate for advice and consent to ratification; texts of remarks by Secretary Rusk, August 5, joint communique with a message from President Kennedy, August 8, 1963; and a memorandum from the acting Secretary of state. D. Rusk; J. F. Kennedy; G. W. Ball. Dept State Bul 49:314-19 Ag 26 '63

NUCLEAR test ban treaty, 1963—*Continued*
Nuclear test ban treaty: symbol of a new course; statement, August 12, 1963. D. Rusk. Dept State Bul 49:350-6 S 2 '63; Same with title Test ban treaty. Vital Speeches 29:674-7 S 1 '63
Nuclear test ban treaty; texts of communiqué issued by the three delegates and the treaty. Cur Hist 45:235-6+ O '63
Nuclear treaty nears Senate vote. il Bsns W p26-7 Ag 17 '63
Of treaties & togas; concerning testimony before Senate preparedness investigating subcommittee. Time 82:15 Ag 30 '63
On to the Senate. Nat R 15:176 S 10 '63
Peace games. M. Ascoli. Reporter 29:26 S 12 '63
Ping-pong on the Potomac. M. Greenfield. il Reporter 29:27-30 S 12 '63
Power, Senate unit voice test ban fears. K. Johnsen. Aviation W 79:30-1 S 16 '63
President hails first anniversary of nuclear test ban treaty; statement, July 30 1964. L. B. Johnson. Dept State Bul 51:228 Ag 17 '64
President urges Senate approval of test ban treaty; letter to Senate leaders, September 11, and news conference statement, September 12, 1963. J. F. Kennedy. Dept State Bul 49:496-8 S 30 '63
Pro and con of test-ban treaty: symposium. il U S News 55:54-67 Ag 26 '63
Project plowshare: AEC program for peaceful nuclear explosives slowed down by test ban treaty. E. Langer. Science 143:1153-5 Mr 13 '64
Questions begging; ratification by Senate. J. Burnham. Nat R 15:148 Ag 27 '63
Race politics enters pact ratification issues. Christian Cent 80:1124 S 18 '63
Ratify the test ban pact! Christian Cent 80:995 Ag 14 '63
Ready for debate. il Time 82:16 S 6 '63
Real meaning of the test ban. S. Alsop. il Sat Eve Post 236:20 S 28 '63
Realities of the test ban. Nation 197:101 S 7 '63
Rest of the test ban. D. R. Inglis. Bul Atomic Sci 19:39-40 D '63
Ring-around-the-rockets: France and the test ban treaty. il Time 82:19-20 Ag 9 '63
Second step. New Repub 149:3-4 Ag 31 '63
Secretary Rusk's news conference of August 16, 1963. D. Rusk. Dept State Bul 49:356-64 S 2 '63
Senate and the test ban. il Newsweek 62:17-18 Ag 5 '63
Senate committee calls test ban small, firm step to arms control. K. Johnsen. Aviation W 79:93+ S 16 '63
Senate consents. Time 82:32 O 4 '63
Senate gives advice and consent. il Sr Schol 83:17 O 11 '63
Senate roll call on test-ban treaty. U S News 55:12 O 7 '63
Senator Dirksen: Vandenberg of the '60s? role in test-ban-treaty debate. U S News 55:24 S 23 '63
Sixteen to one: hearings by the Senate foreign relations committee. Newsweek 62:23 S 9 '63
Solving a Chinese puzzle. N. Cousins. Sat R 46:14 S 7 '63
Some thoughts on destiny; excerpts from Senate debate. E. M. Dirksen. Time 82:25-6 S 20 '63
Speaking out; beware the test ban! with editorial comment. C. Hosmer. Sat Eve Post 236:10+. 88 S 7 '63
Symington cites weapons control in backing ban on nuclear tests. K. Johnsen. Aviation W 79:29 S 23 '63
Teller broadens attack on test ban agreement. D. C. Breasted. Miss & Roc 13:18 Ag 26 '63
Test ban. Bul Atomic Sci 19:2 S '63
Test ban. Sci Am 209:82 S '63
Test-ban debate. Nation 197:169 S 28 '63
Test ban: eighty to nineteen. il Newsweek 62:30 O 7 '63
Test ban reinforces French aim. Aviation W 79:27 Ag 5 '63
Test ban, so far, so good. Bsns W p96 Ag 3 '63
Test ban: summing up; excerpt from address, September 13, 1963. H. M. Jackson. Reporter 29:18 S 26 '63
Test ban: testimony on technical aspects to help senators decide if treaty is a boon or a bane. J. Walsh. Science 141:618-20 Ag 16 '63
Test ban: the first concrete measure; submitted to the Senate of the United States on August 9, 1963. J. F. Kennedy. Bul Atomic Sci 19:40+ O '63
Test ban: the military argument; excerpts from the testimony before the Senate foreign relations committee, August 13, 1963. R. S. McNamara. Bul Atomic Sci 19:42-3 O '63
Test ban: the next round. il Bul Atomic Sci 19:42-8 N '63
Test-ban treaty. Commonweal 78:467 Ag 9 '63
Test ban treaty; address, July 12, 1963. J. S. Cooper. Vital Speeches 30:201-3 Ja 15 '64
Test ban treaty; address, July 26, 1963. J. F. Kennedy. Vital Speeches 29:644-7 Ag 15 '63; Same with title Nuclear test ban treaty: a step toward peace; with texts of agreed communique and the treaty. Dept State Bul 49:234-40 Ag 12 '63; Excerpts. il U S News 55:6 Ag 5 '63
Test-ban treaty; address, September 2, 1963. G. Meany. Vital Speeches 29:710-12 S 15 '63
Test ban treaty: after signing, a Senate fight. il Bsns W p 17-18 Jl 27 '63
Test-ban treaty; first committee's recommendations. U N Rev 10:15-17+ D '63
Test ban treaty; only an illusion of peace; address, September 1963. B. Goldwater. Vital Speeches 29:767-8 O 1 '63
Test-ban treaty: some further considerations. B. G. Bechhoefer. Bul Atomic Sci 20:25-7 My '64
Test ban treaty; the military considerations; address, September 9, 1963. L. Saltonstall. Vital Speeches 29:750-2 O 1 '63
Test ban would not cut defense budget. G. C. Wilson. Aviation W 79:26-7 Ag 19 '63
Thinking about destiny; E. Dirksen and J. W. Fulbright. Newsweek 62:26-7 S 23 '63
To govern is to choose; excerpts from message to the Senate, August 8, 1963. J. F. Kennedy. Time 82:13 Ag 16 '63
Touches a nerve; West Germany's signature. Newsweek 62:36+ Ag 19 '63
Toward cautious hope. Sr Schol 83:9 S 13 '63
Toward peace; away from war; test ban treaty initialed in Moscow. il Newsweek 62:15-16 Ag 5 '63
Trading blows on the test ban. il Bsns W p27-8 Ag 24 '63
Two dissenters. Time 82:22 S 27 '63
Two nations expected to join test ban club. Sci N L 84:83 Ag 10 '63
Under the sign of the umbrella. W. F. Buckley, jr; J. Burnham. Nat R 15:180-1 S 10 '63
Unexpected opposition. Newsweek 62:28 S 16 '63
United Nations: space committee sees test ban, U.S.-Soviet accord as new footing for negotiation. J. Walsh. Science 141:1164-5+ S 20 '63
U.S, U.K, U.S.S.R. mark signing of nuclear test ban treaty; joint statement, August 5, 1964. Dept State Bul 51:270-1 Ag 24 '64
Very well, then. Nat R 15:265 O 8 '63
Weapon effects data called ban soft spot. Aviation W 81:33 S 21 '64
What does the test ban mean? E. A. Kolodziej. Bul Atomic Sci 20:22-3 Mr '64
What is best for the United States. Christian Cent 80:1093 S 11 '63
What will the Senate do? Christian Cent 80:973 Ag 7 '63
Who gains in a test-ban treaty. il U S News 55:35-6 Ag 5 '63
Who is conning whom? J. Burnham. Nat R 15:101 Ag 13 '63
Why Khrushchev changed his mind. F. B. Stevens. U S News 55:28 S 2 '63
Why the fears over a nuclear-test ban. il U S News 55:39-41 S 23 '63
Will the Senate ratify a test-ban treaty? Redbook 121:55 Ag '63
Wisdom of test ban: McNamara and the joint chiefs differed. il U S News 55:36 Ag 5 '63
With a test ban, who's ahead. U S News 55:21 Ag 12 '63
With test-ban treaty, has Khrushchev changed his ways? interview. Z. Brzezinski. U S News 55:72-3 S 30 '63
Yalta strategy; revival: Soviet-American deal. J. Burnham. Nat R 15:237 S 24 '63
York, Kistiakowsky back test ban treaty. K. Johnsen. Aviation W 79:22-3 S 2 '63
Zuckert attacks AFA on test ban stand. Aviation W 79:31 S 16 '63
NUCLEAR warfare. See Atomic warfare
NUCLEAR weapons. See Atomic weapons
NUCLEI, Atomic. See Atomic nuclei
NUCLEIC acids
Actinomycin D as a probe for nucleic acid secondary structure. R. Haselkorn. bibliog il Science 143:682-4 F 14 '64
Actinomycin D: effect on the immune response. C. J. Wust and others. bibliog il Science 143:1041-3 Mr 6 '64

NUCLEIC acids—*Continued*
Actinomycin D effects in frog embryos: evidence for sequential synthesis of DNA-dependent RNA. R. A. Flickinger. bibliog il Science 141:1063-4 S 13 '63
Biological complexity and radiosensitivity. H. S. Kaplan and L. E. Moses. bibliog il Science 145:21-5 Jl 3 '64
Complementary strand association between nucleic acids and nucleic acid gels. R. J. Britten. bibliog il Science 142:963-5 N 15 '63
Enzymatic alteration of nucleic acid structure. P. R. Srinivasan and E. Borek. bibliog il Science 145:548-53 Ag 7 '64
Exploring the secrets of life. il Newsweek 61:63-6 My 13 '63
Foreign nucleic acids. A. Isaacs. il Sci Am 209:46-50 bibliog(p 156) O '63
Histone biology and chemistry; report on first World conference on histone biology and chemistry. J. Bonner and P. O. P. Tso. Science 141:651+ Ag 16 '63
Hybrid nucleic acids. S. Spiegelman. il Sci Am 210:48-56 bibliog(p 150) My '64
Macromolecules; report of Symposium on quantitative biology. R. C. Williams. Science 141:934-5 S 6 '63
Molecular configuration of nucleic acids. M. H. F. Wilkins. bibliog il Science 140:941-50 My 31 '63
Nucleic acid metabolism in L cells infected with a member of the psittacosis group. E. M. Schechter and others. bibliog il Science 145:819-21 Ag 21 '64
Nucleic acids: a nuclear magnetic resonance study. C. C. McDonald. bibliog il Science 144:1234-7 Je 5 '64
On biochemical variability and innovation: text of paper presented at symposium on the general physiology of specialized cells. S. S. Cohen. bibliog il Science 139:1017-26 Mr 15 '63
Process of infection with øX174: effect of exonucleases on the replicative form. A. Burton and R. L. Sinsheimer. bibliog il Science 142:962-3 N 15 '63
See also
Deoxyribonucleic acid
Nucleoproteins
Ribonucleic acid

NUCLEOPROTEINS
Actinomycin D: an effect on rat liver homogenates unrelated to its action on RNA synthesis. M. Revel and others. bibliog il Science 146:1311-13 D 4 '64
Carbon tetrachloride poisoning in rats: alteration in ribosomes of the liver. E. A. Smuckler and E. P. Benditt. bibliog il Science 140:308-10 Ap 19 '63
Histone and DNA in isolated nuclei from chicken brain, liver, and erythrocytes. M. B. Sporn and C. W. Dingman. bibliog il Science 140:316-18 Ap 19 '63
Mitomycin C: effect on ribosomes of escherichia coli. H. Suzuki and W. W. Kilgore. bibliog il Science 146:1585-7 D 18 '64
Polyribosomes. A. Rich. il Sci Am 209:44-53 bibliog(p 178) D '63
Polyribosomes: size in normal and polio-infected HeLa cells. A. Rich and others. bibliog il Science 142:1658-63 D 27 '63
Reticulocyte protein synthesis: response of ribosome fractions to polyuridylic acid. I. B. Weinstein and others. bibliog il Science 140:314-16 Ap 19 '63
Ribosomal RNA on the surface of ribosomes. M. Santer. bibliog il Science 141:1049-50 S 13 '63
Ribosomes: a common structural feature. R. Langridge. bibliog il Science 140:1000 My 31 '63
Ribosomes and ribonucleic acids in three morphological states of neurospora. H. R. Henney, jr. and R. Storck. bibliog il Science 142:1675-6 D 27 '63
Ribosomes at work. il Sci Am 208:66+ F '63
Spontaneous autoimmunity in mice: antibodies to nucleoprotein in strain A/J. G. J. Friou and P. O. Teague. bibliog il Science 143:1333-4 Mr 20 '64

NUCLEOSIDES
Tautomerism and site of protonation of 1-methylcytosine: proof by nuclear magnetic resonance spin-spin coupling. H. T. Miles and others. bibliog il Science 142:1569-71 D 20 '63

NUCLEOTIDES
Alkylation of synthetic polynucleotides. D. B. Ludlum and others. bibliog il Science 145:397-9 Jl 24 '64
Hypotheses confirmed. Sci Am 210:54-6 Mr '64
Molecular approach in the systematics of higher organisms. B. H. Hoyer and others. bibliog il Science 144:959-67 My 22 '64
Nucleotides: separation from an alkaline hydrolysate of RNA by thin-layer electrophoresis. F. M. DeFilippes. bibliog il Science 144:1350-1 Je 12 '64
Oxidation of extramitochondrial diphosphopyridine nucleotide by various tissues of the mouse. B. Sacktor and A. R. Dick. bibliog il Science 145:606-7 Ag 7 '64
Procaine action: antagonism by adenosine triphosphate and other nucleotides. A. S. Kuperman and others. bibliog il Science 144:1222-3 Je 5 '64
See also
Adenosine triphosphate

NUCLEUS, Cellular. See Cells

NUDE in art
Back to the nude. J. Canaday. il Horizon 5:90-6 S '63
Weston's picture is about freedom, yours and mine. R. Hattersley. il Pop Phot 55:70-1+ S '64
See also
Human figure in art

NUDETS (nuclear detection and reporting system) See Atomic warfare—Defenses

NUDISM
On being naked. T. Sterling. il Holiday 36:8+ Ag '64

NUFFIELD, William Richard Morris, 1st viscount
Noble mechanic. il por Time 82:59 Ag 30 '63

NUFFIELD foundation
Course content improvement, British style. D. Wolfle. Science 142:1263 D 6 '63

NUGENT, John
Please don't judge us too harshly. por Newsweek 63:34 Ja 27 '64

NUMBER of love is always odd; story. See Bliven, N.

NUMBERING systems
By the numbers. Sat Eve Post 236:96 N 23 '63
If you're worried about your tax number; requirement of social security numbers. il U S News 55:85-7 S 2 '63
Now it's Tom, Dick and 002-26-8404. il Sr Schol 83:26-7 S 13 '63
Numbers game in American business. H. J. Topjian. il Duns R 82:pt2 114-15 S '63
Tax service's numbers game: it's not going so well. U S News 57:79-82 N 2 '64

NUMBERS, Symbolism of. See Symbolism of numbers

NUMBERS, Theory of
Number. P. J. Davis. il Sci Am 211:50-9 bibliog(p269) S '64

NUMBERS game. See Gambling

NUMERALS in religion, folklore, etc.
Take any number. G. Vincent. il N Y Times Mag p44+ O 13 '63

NUMERATION
Binary numbers & Boolean algebra. W. S. Andariese. il Electr World 69:72-3 Mr '63

NUMERIC identification. See Identification

NUMERICALLY controlled machine tools. See Machine tools—Control

NUMEROLOGY. See Symbolism of numbers

NUMISMATICS. See Coins

NUNES, Melvin E. and Stange, K. N.
Slo break basketball. pors Recreation 57:358-9 S '64

NUNAMIUTS. See Eskimos

NUÑEZ PORTUONDO, Emilio
If flag of surrender is waved before Castro. por U S News 56:6 Ap 13 '64

NUNLIST, Juli
Music: your silent partner. Dance Mag 38:48-9+ Ag '64

NUNNALLY, Jum C. and Flaugher, R. L.
Psychological implications of word usage. bibliog Science 140:775-81 My 17 '63

NUÑO, Rubén Bonifaz. See Bonifaz Nuño, R.

NUNS. See Sisterhoods

NUNS, Singing. See Choral groups and societies

NUNS as musicians. See Women as musicians

NUNS habit. See Religious orders—Habit

NUR, Uzi. See Brown, S. W. jt. auth.

NUREEV, Rudolf
Nureyev; an autobiography; excerpts. pors Dance Mag 37:39-43+ My; 38-41+ Je; 17+ Jl '63
about
Hottest little team in show biz. il pors Life 54:107-8 My 24 '63
New Nijinsky? il por Newsweek 61:61 My 6 '63
Not quite it: Royal ballet at Metropolitan opera house. il por Time 81:43-4 My 10 '63
Nureyev. I. Kolodin. por Sat R 46:56 Ap 27 '63

NUREEV, Rudolf—about—*Continued*
Nureyev, plus and minus. J. Martin. il por Sat R 46:48-9+ My 25 '63
Nureyev: surely this is genius. pors Vogue 143:126-7 Mr 1 '64
Nureyev: top male dancer who quit the Soviets dazzles the West. R. Schickel. il pors Look 27:26-8+ Jl 16 '63
Nureyev; with photographs by Lord Snowdon. Life 57:92-102+ N 27 '64
People are talking about... por Vogue 141:84-5 Ap 15 '63
Russian's triumph. il por Newsweek 61:95 Mr 25 '63
Vienna swoons over Nureyev and swans. L. Zamponi. Dance Mag 38:28+ D '64
Whirlwind Wednesday in Brooklyn. il pors Dance Mag 37:40-5 O '63

NUREMBERG

Markets

Non-profit style for Christmas. il Bsns W p22-3 D 21 '63

NUREMBERG trials
Reporter at large; Eichmann trial. H. Arendt. New Yorker 39:75-6+ Mr 16 '63

NURISTAN

Native races

Funerary figures of the Kafirs. D. Newton. il Natur Hist 72:40-7 Je '63

NURSE midwives. See Midwives

NURSERIES
Spanking-clean nursery. Good H 156:180e Mr '63
Storybook ideas for the nursery. R. S. Miller. il Farm J 87:98-9 Mr '63

NURSERIES (horticulture)
Christmas at the Kern's. il Am For 70:2-4 D '64
46 million Christmas trees. Am For 70:13 D '64
Weathervane. R. G. Miner. Flower Grower 50:6 Mr '63
See also
Nursery stock

NURSERY catalogs. See Catalogs, Seed and plant—Bibliography

NURSERY schools
Before selecting a nursery school: stop, look & listen. S. Schuler. il Ladies Home J 80:60+ O '63
First days of nursery school. T. D. Topping. il Redbook 121:16 S '63
Julie wants to learn. I. Mothner. il Look 28:52+ Mr 10 '64
Kids play while parents work. T. Taylor. il Parents Mag 38:65-7 F '63
Montessori in the space age? E. Beyer. il NEA J 52:35-6 D '63
Nursery for teaching, research, testing. il Arch Rec 133:174-6 My '63
Physical fitness for the sandbox set. il N Y Times Mag p48 Ja 19 '64
Preschools are not just for play. E. G. Neisser. il Parents Mag 39:72-3+ F '64
What is a good nursery school? L. L. Gore. bibliog il Sch Life 45:18-22 Je '63
What nursery schools can and cannot do; with study-discussion program, by R. Strang. I. J. Gordon. bibliog il PTA Mag 58:10-12, 35 S '63
Who's for nursery school? G. Hechinger. il N Y Times Mag p61+ Mr 1 '64
Will a neighborhood nursery school work? il Bet Hom & Gard 41:88 S '63

NURSERY stock
Guide to wise plant protection. J. Bush-Brown. il Horticulture 41:514 O '63
How big will it grow? R. C. Hands. Horticulture 41:247 My '63
Small plants pay big dividends in a home nursery. il Flower Grower 59:58-9 Mr '63

NURSES and nursing
Coming scandal in nursing; ed. by N. G. Stuart. E. A. Aynes. il McCalls 91:100-1+ Mr '64
ICU, newest thing in nursing; Intensive care units. W. Langewiesche. il Read Digest 85:208-10+ N '64
Trends in nursing as they affect library services. J. M. Geister. ALA Bul 58:812-14 O '64
Wake-up war between patient and nurse. H. B. Jacobs. il N Y Times Mag p 19+ My 10 '64
What it's like to be a nurse. il Changing T 18:39-41 D '64
You can make home nursing easier. Good H 158:165 Ap '64

Salaries, pensions, etc.

Earnings in hospitals in mid-1963. G. L. Stelluto. bibliog f il Mo Labor R 87:552-5 My '64

Training

Becoming a nurse; a selective view. H. O. Mauksch. bibliog f il Ann Am Acad 346:88-98 Mr '63
Coming scandal in nursing; ed. by N. G. Stuart. E. A. Aynes. il McCalls 91:100-1+ Mr '64
Life, death and miracles; student nurse in her first year. C. Johnson. il Seventeen 22:80-1+ D '63
Mrs Bing Crosby; student nurse. S. Gordon. il Look 27:98-100 Mr 12 '63
Modern medicine requires qualified nurses; excerpt from address. T. S. Hamilton. Todays Health 41:76 Ag '63

NURSES and nursing, Public health
How a visiting nurse can help you. il Good H 158:123 Ja '64

NURSES homes
Unusual high-rise attracts nurses to cancer center; Sloan house, Memorial Sloan-Kettering cancer center, New York. il Arch Rec 133:138-41 Ja '63

NURSING bottles. See Baby bottles

NURSING education. See Nurses and nursing—Training

NURSING homes
Neglected people in today's nursing home. A. Balk. il McCalls 91:84-7 S '64; Same abr. with title Shame of our nursing homes. Read Digest 86:161-2+ Ja '65
New horizons for nursing homes. T. Lewis, jr. il Todays Health 41:56-7+ Ap '63
Nursing home criteria based on patients' needs. il Arch Rec 135:183-8 Ap '64
Nursing homes. R. Brecher and E. Brecher. il Consumer Rep 29:30-6, 87-92, 139-42, 194-8 Ja-Ap '64
Nursing homes, bad & good. il Changing T 17:17-20 Mr '63
Old folks at home, and out of it; letter. D. Ewing. Ladies Home J 80:8 My '63
People to burn; fire hazards in nursing homes. Christian Cent 82:67 Ja 20 '65
Personal business. Bsns W p 105-6 Mr 7 '64

NUSBAUM, W. E. See Van Dyke, R. P. jt. auth.

NUSSBAUM, Albert
Good-by to Bobby One-Eye Wilcoxson. B. Clark. pors Read Digest 82:63-8 F '63

NUT trees
Shop now for these fruit, nut trees. Sunset 130:172 F '63
These trees give you shade and also give you a crop. Sunset 133:176 Jl '64

NUTCRACKER (ballet) See Ballets

NUTRITION
Battle against hunger. Commonweal 78:364 Je 28 '63
Can you tell food fact from fiction? V. R. Schulte. Parents Mag 38:92+ O '63
Everyday guide to good eating. B. M. Stover. il Parents Mag 39:69-71+ bibliog(p 143) N '64
Food fanatic's four myths of nutrition. P. L. White. Todays Health 41:72 Je '63
Just what are daily nutritional needs? Good H 156:151 F '63
Let the sea nourish your health. E. Ubell. il House B 105:122-3 Je '63
Let's talk about food; ed. by P. L. White. See issues of Today's health
Myths about nutrition. E. Weston. McCalls 92:28 Ja '64
New foods and new hopes. il Newsweek 61:51 Je 17 '63
Rusty bells of hope. H. Bowser. Sat R 46:24 Je 22 '63
Sense and nonsense about nutrition. F. J. Stare. Harper 229:66-70 O '64; Same abr. with title Sense and nonsense about the food we eat. il Read Digest 86:58-62 Ja '65
Travel well. C. Rule; E. N. Dye. See issues of Travel
See also
Aged—Nutrition
Children—Nutrition
Diet
Fasting
Food values
Starvation

NUTRITION education
Nutrition. M. C. Egan. NEA J 53:62-4 Mr '64

NUTRITION problems
International nutrition programs. C. G. King. bibliog il Science 147:25-9 Ja 1 '65
See also
Food and agriculture organization of the United Nations

Central America

New food for hungry children. H. Manchester. il Read Digest 83:137-41 S '63

NUTRITION problems—*Continued*

Latin America

What's in a meal? B. Burton. il Américas 15:1-6 F '63

NUTRITION research

Diet that might wipe out malnutrition. il Time 82:62 N 22 '63

International nutrition programs. C. G. King. bibliog il Science 147:25-9 Ja 1 '65

NUTS

Mixed nuts. il Consumer Rep 29:541-3 N '64

Neuroses in nut eating. L. Morse. Duns R 83:66+ My '64

See also

Cookery—Nuts

NUTS (machinery) See Bolts and nuts

NUTT, Mary E.

Passer-by; story. Redbook 121:54-5 S '63

NUTT, Patrick

Waterlilies. Horticulture 42:18-21 Je '64

NUTTER, G. Warren

Russia in deep trouble; will U.S. give help? interview. por U S News 56:50-7 Ap 13 '64

NUVEEN, John

Foreign aid is like an elephant. Christian Cent 80:1463-5 N 27 '63

NYANGOMA, Gervais

From Burundi. Reporter 30:8 Ap 9 '64

NYASALAND. See Malawi

NYE, Jeff

Memo from a Mormon. por Look 27:74+ O 22 '63

NYE, Joseph S. Jr

Civil rights for whites. New Repub 151:5-6 O 24 '64

NYE, Robert

Dedications; poem. Atlan 212:53 S '63

Kingfisher; poem. Atlan 212:86 N '63

Shadows; poem. Atlan 212:80 Jl '63

Trout; poem. Atlan 214:52 Jl '64

NYERERE, Julius Kambarage

African's warning: colonialism must disappear. U S News 55:22 Jl 29 '63

Colored rulers. G. C. Turner. Negro Hist Bul 26:249 My '63

Nyerere cuts loose. por Newsweek 64:34 Ag 3 '64

People of the week. U S News 54:20 F 18 '63

Tanganyika: the tribulations of a good man. C. Sterling. il Reporter 30:21-5 Ap 9 '64

Tanganyika's two years of independence. L. Cliffe. bibliog f il Cur Hist 46:136-41+ Mr '64

Tangibar. Time 83:30 My 1 '64

Who is safe? il pors Time 83:30-4+ Mr 13 '64

NYLANDER, Carl

Fall of Homer; Troy may not have fallen. Newsweek 61:95 Ap 22 '63

NYLON

Nylon chemical made by new process. Sci N L 84:242 O 19 '63

NYLON hosiery. See Hosiery

NYLON sails. See Sails

NYMPHS, Artificial. See Fishing lures, flies, etc.

NYREN, Dorothy

Small library: close-up on Concord. Wilson Lib Bul 37:778-80 My '63

Time is a commodity. por Library J 88:1943-5. 2582 My 15, Jl '63

NYSTAGMUS

Nystagmus as a criterion of hypnotically induced visual hallucinations. J. P. Brady and E. E. Levitt. bibliog Science 146:85-6 O 2 '64

O

OAR. See United States—Air force—Aerospace research, Office of

OARP plan. See Townsend old age pension plan

OAS. See Organization of American states

OAS (Organisation de l'armée secrète) See Secret army organization

OASDI. See Old age, survivors' and disability insurance trust fund

OAU. See Organization of African unity

OCAW. See Oil, chemical and atomic workers international union

ODECA (Organización de estados centro-americanos) See Organization of Central American states

OECD. See Organization for economic cooperation and development

OGO (orbiting geophysical observatory) See Artificial satellites—Astronomical applications

OH radicals. See Hydroxyl

OPC. See Overseas press club of America

ORC. See Opinion research corporation

ORRRC. See United States—Outdoor recreation resources review commission

ORT. See Organization for rehabilitation through training

OSE (Organisation de sécurité de l'état) See Secret service—France

OSI. See United States—Air force—Special investigations, Office of

OSRD. See United States—Scientific research and development, Office of

OSS (orbiting space station) See Space stations; United States—Strategic services, Office of

O the days of the Kerry dancing; story. See Brown, M. F.

OAHU (island)

How to arrange a high hike on Oahu. il Sunset 130:47 Mr '63

OAK

Oak roots search for good soil. il Sunset 130: 243 Je '63

Park of champions; Big Oak Tree State Park. J. P. Jackson. il Am For 69:9+ My '63

Trees against the winds; coastal Texas. M. Whitney. il Natur Hist 72:56-9 Je '63

OAK BROOK, Ill.

Stores

Unified variety on a fountained mall. il Arch Rec 135:166-9 Je '64

OAK HARBOR, Wash.

Fallout filters. J. Buckner. il Am City 78:107-8 Je '63

OAK ISLAND, Nova Scotia

Oak Island's mysterious money pit. D. MacDonald. il Read Digest 86:136-40 Ja '65

OAK PARK, Ill, public library

Scenic showcase for Oak Park. L. L. Stoffel. il Library J 89:4717-19 D 1 '64

OAK RIDGE, Tenn.

Oak Ridge searches for its future. Bsns W p77-8 Ja 23 '65

OAK RIDGE national laboratory

Oak Ridge searches for its future. Bsns W p77-8 Ja 23 '65

OAKES, William J. Mayer-. See Mayer-Oakes, W. J.

OAKLAND, Calif.

Airports

Oakland pushes for more airline service. R. H. Cook. il Aviation W 79:43-4 Jl 1 '63

Bridges

Award-winning bridge with a job ahead. J. E. McCarty. il Am City 79:8 N '64

City planning

Beauty in the business district. il Am City 79: 113 O '64

East Bay municipal utility district

Extra-feature two-way radio; use in routine water-service operations. L. B. Hertzberg. il Am City 78:144+ O '63

Education

High school of champions; McClymonds of Oakland, Calif. il Ebony 18:25-8+ Ap '63

Galleries and museums

New Saarinen office. W. McQuade. il Arch Forum 118:116-18 Ap '63

Lighting

Fog-proof system. J. E. Austin. il Am City 79:113-14 Mr '64

Stores

West Coast downtown store on one level. il Arch Rec 133:164-5 Je '63

OAKLAND corporation

Pittsburgh bids high for research industry; R&D center in Panther Hollow. il Bsns W p51 Je 8 '63

OAKLAND Raiders (football club) See Football clubs

OAKLEY, Kenneth P.

Dating skeletal material. Science 140:488 My 3 '63

Relative dating of Arlington Springs man. Science 141:1172 S 20 '63

OAKS, Robert Q. Jr, and Coch, N. K.

Pleistocene sea levels, southeastern Virginia. bibliog Science 140:979-83 My 31 '63

OARSMANSHIP. See Rowing

OASES

Oases in the Atacama Desert. S. Reyes. il Américas 15:10-16 S '63

OATES, James F. jr
Public policy and unemployment; address, June 6, 1964. Vital Speeches 30:594-8 Jl 15 '64
OATES, Wayne E.
Pastoral theology bookshelf. Christian Cent 80:1055-6 Ag 28 '63
OATHS
Would Hippocrates rewrite his oath? L. Lasagna. il N Y Times Mag p 11+ Je 28 '64
OATHS of loyalty. See Loyalty, Oaths of
OATS
Don't discount oats for growing pigs. R. C. Wahlstrom. il Suc Farm 61:69 Ag '63
How to make oats pay. Suc Farm 62:66 Mr '64
Oats make me as much money as corn. J. C. Everly. il Suc Farm 61:40-1 Jl '63
Two new oats average more than one hundred bu. J. Russell. il Farm J 87:52 D '63
OAXACA (city), Mexico
Saint's day. A. Marriott. New Yorker 39:111+ O 19 '63
OBECK, Victor
Slim half dozen lazy, lying-down exercises. McCalls 92:118-19 O '64
OBEDIENCE
Could we be Nazi followers? Sci Digest 55: 81-2 Ja '64
Myth of disobedience. America 109:472 O 26 '63
OBEDIENCE (canon law)
Catholic obedience. C. Davis. America 111:558 N 7 '64
Problem of obedience. S. S. MacNutt. America 112:14-16 Ja 2 '65; Discussion. 112:92-3 Ja 23 '65
OBERDORFER, Don
America's neglected colonial paradise. Sat Eve Post 237:24-34 F 29 '64; Same abr. Read Digest 84:232-4+ Je '64
Bail-bond scandal. Sat Eve Post 237:66-7 Je 20 '64
CAP and TVA: Barry's fine distinction. Reporter 31:36-8 S 10 '64
Job John McCormack dreads. Sat Eve Post 237:66+ Mr 21 '64
Judge Smith moves with deliberate drag. N Y Times Mag p 13+ Ja 12 '64
No wonder Madison said, I'd rather be in bed. N Y Times Mag p 10-11+ Ja 17 '65
Playboy sergeant who spied for Russia. Sat Eve Post 237:40+ Mr 7 '64
Survival of the fewest. Sat Eve Post 236:17-21 Mr 23 '63
Vast ghostland of Washington. N Y Times Mag p24+ Ap 26 '64
Where the cutback cuts deep. Sat Eve Post 237:17-21 S 12 '64
—See Bagdikian, B. H.; Martin, H. H. jt. auths.
OBERER, Walter E.
Death penalty and fair trial. Nation 198:342-4 Ap 6 '64
OBERGURGL, Austria
Up and up to Obergurgl. il Sunset 133:37 N '64
OBERLIN college, Oberlin, Ohio
Mock four; Oberlin's campus convention. il Newsweek 63:82 My 18 '64
Pure hall for music; Warner concert hall. il Arch Rec 136:128-9 D '64
OBERMAN, Heiko
Interview with Dr Heiko Oberman; ed. by J. B. Sheerin. Cath World 197:100-6 My '63
OBERMILLER, William
Whiting doesn't spare the rod. K. Detzer. il Read Digest 82:167-70+ My '63
OBERNDORFF, Elizabeth
How does Countess Elizabeth Oberndorff do it? il por Vogue 141:176-7+ My '63
OBERON, Merle
Children are to enjoy. il Vogue 142:94-5+ Ag 15 '63
OBERTA, Andy
Raven; poem. Miss & Roc 14:6 Ja 27 '64
OBERTEUFFER, Delbert
Vital ties between health and education; adaptation of address. NEA J 53:57-61 Mr '64
OBESITY. See Corpulence
OBIE drama awards. See Village voice (newspaper)
OBIKA, Masataka, and Bagnara, J. T.
Pteridines as pigments in amphibians. bibliog Science 143:485-7 Ja 31 '64
OBITUARIES
Anticipating death: press obituaries. Time 85:65+ Ja 29 '65
They die for the New York times. T. N. Davis. il America 109:280 S 21 '63
OBJECTIVES in education. See Education—Aims and objectives
OBJECTS, Miniature. See Miniature objects
OBLIGADO, George
Most unforgettable character I've met. Read Digest 82:115-20 F '63
OBLIGATE anaerobes. See Bacteria, Anaerobic
OBLIGATION, Moral. See Duty
OBOLENSKY, Helene
How Princess Grace chooses children's clothes. Redbook 121:60-5 Ag '63
OBOURN, Ellsworth S. See Brown, K. E. jt. auth.
OBRAZTSOV, Sergei Vladimirovich
Puppet theatre from Moscow. F. Bowers. il Theatre Arts 47:24-5 O '63
Will it go on B'way? Obraztsov puppet show. T. Prideaux. il pors Life 55:9+ S 13 '63
OBRAZTSOV puppets. See Puppets and puppet plays
O'BRIAN, Barry
Picasso comes home. Reporter 30:52-3 My 21 '64
O'BRIAN, Jack
Man with the popular mind. il por Time 84: 50 N 20 '64
O'BRIEN, Brian J.
Radiation belts; with biographical sketch. Sci Am 208:36, 84-96 My; 209:10 Jl '63
O'BRIEN, Conor Cruise
Assault on Whittaker Chambers. W. F. Buckley, jr. il Nat R 16:1098-100 D 15 '64
How to end partition. America 108:629 My 4 '63
UN operation smash. A. Lejeune. Nat R 14: 242-3 Mr 26 '63
O'BRIEN, Denis
Canada and the O.A.S. Commonweal 79:71-2 O 11 '63
O'BRIEN, Donald K.
It pays us to lease machinery. Farm J 87:50 D '63
New machines for richer silage. il Farm J 87:24+ Ag '63
O'BRIEN, Edna
Daliah Lavi. Vogue 144:130-1 N 15 '64
Four eligible bachelors in London. por Vogue 144:140-3 S 15 '64
Lovely to look at, delightful to hold; story. New Yorker 40:38-44 Mr 28 '64
Lovers; story. New Yorker 38:28-34 F 16 '63
Rug; story. New Yorker 39:55-7 Mr 16 '63
Wedding dress; a play for television. Mlle 58: 134-5+ N '63
Which of those two ladies is he married to? story. New Yorker 40:49-54 Ap 25 '64
O'BRIEN, George
Design for sport. Sports Illus 18:48-9 Je 3 '63
Home. See issues of New York times magazine
O'BRIEN, Harry R.
Pop Gardener says. See issues of Popular gardening & living outdoors
O'BRIEN, John A.
Convert decline. America 109:382, 646 O 5, N 23 '63
Family planning in an exploding population. Christian Cent 80:1050-2 Ag 28 '63
Let's end the war over birth control. Christian Cent 80:1361-4 N 6 '63
New warmth between Protestants and Catholics; excerpts from Steps to Christian unity. Read Digest 85:101-5 O '64
On family planning. America 109:333 S 28 '63
Population explosion demands worldwide action. Christian Cent 81:43-6 Ja 8 '64
about
Birth regulation; concerning an article by the Rev J. A. O'Brien. il por Newsweek 62:82 S 9 '63; Reply. America 109:345-6 S 28 '63
Father O'Brien's article. J. C. Knott. America 109:225 S 7 '63
O'BRIEN, Justin
Gide's Hamlet. Reporter 31:38-9 Jl 16 '64
Sartre resartus. Reporter 31:47-8 N 5 '64
Thrill of recognition. Reporter 28:42+ Je 20 '63
O'BRIEN, Katherine L.
Wanted: new adult materials. Sr Schol 85: 24T O 7 '64
O'BRIEN, Lawrence Francis
Bit of a split. por Time 81:23 My 3 '63
Pennsylvania avenue politics. R. Evans, jr. New Repub 148:19-20 F 2 '63
O'BRIEN, Marian
Catfish and champagne. por Library J 89: 2533-8 Je 15 '64
O'BRIEN, Mary E.
Iris. Pop Gard 15:26-7 My '64
O'BRIEN, R. A.
Pictures in time. Nation 198:36-7 Ja 6 '64
O'BRIEN, R. D. and Matsumura, Fumio
DDT: a new hypothesis of its mode of action. bibliog Science 146:657-8 O 30 '64
—See Potter, J. L. jt. auth.

O'BRIEN, Robert
Bobby Fischer; best in chess? Sat R 46:22-3 Ap 27 '63; Same abr. with title America's wizard of chess. Read Digest 82:221-2+ My '63
Challenge of confident living; condensation. Read Digest 84:211-13+ Ap '64
Magic world of dolls. Read Digest 85:146-53 D '64
Somebody up there like us. Esquire 60:185-7+ D '63
Why children have accidents. Ladies Home J 81:46+ Mr '64
O'BRIEN, William V.
American-Soviet convergence: fact or fiction? Commonweal 81:46-8 O 2 '64
Fate of counterforce. Commonweal 78:216-18 My 17 '63
OBRIG, Robert S.
Amateurs build a racing fleet. Yachting 115: 193-4+ My '64
OBRIST, Paul A.
Skin resistance levels and galvanic skin response: unilateral differences. bibliog Science 139:227-8 Ja 18 '63
O'BRYAN, Patrick. See Martin, T. jt. auth.
OBSCENE literature. See Immoral literature and pictures
OBSCENITY (law)
Chaos in the Court; ruling on Tropic of cancer. America 111:83-4 Jl 25 '64
Confusion on obscenity. America 111:30 Jl 11 '64
Is nothing obscene any more? local diversities in obscenity laws. il Time 84:45 Jl 10 '64
Law and morals. America 111:735 D 5 '64; Discussion. 112:2 Ja 2 '65
Mr and Mrs Grundy in the library and in court; CLA pre-conference meeting on Intellectual freedom; excerpts from report with editorial comment. H. M. Madden. Library J 89:4857-62 D 15 '64
More chaos in court. America 111:126-7 Ag 8 '64
Profane comedy; case of L. Bruce in Manhattan criminal court. Time 84:88 N 13 '64
Second thoughts on obscenity; New Jersey ruling on Fanny Hill. il Time 84:43 D 18 '64
Supreme court, obscenity and censorship. J. J. Regan. Cath World 200:142-8 D '64
What nine clergymen said about the Supreme court. U S News 57:15 S 21 '64
OBSERVATION (psychology)
Scaling of apparent viscosity. S. S. Stevens and M. Guirao. bibliog il Science 144:1157-8 My 29 '64
Vigilance: the importance of the elicited observing rate. H. J. Jerison and R. M. Pickett. bibliog Science 143:970-1 F 28 '64
OBSERVATORIES
See also
National radio astronomy observatory, Green Bank, W.Va.
OBSERVER (London)
Philby. D. Astor. Sat Eve Post 237:4-5 Mr 21 '64
OBSERVER, Texas. See Texas observer
OBSIDIAN
Mountain of glass; Glass Mountain in Modoc National Forest. R. H. May and W. F. Heald. il Am For 69:32-4 Ag '63
Mysterious glass bubbles found on small Island; volcanic glass. Sci N L 85:249 Ap 18 '64
OBSIDIAN tools. See Stone implements and weapons
OBSTETRICS
After the baby is born. G. E. Judd. Redbook 123:42+ My '64
Cutting the cord too soon. il Time 81:78 Ap 19 '63
Obstetrician. A. Lake. il McCalls 91:102-3+ Ag '64
Twenty-four hours in the life of an obstetrician. E. M. Wylie. il Read Digest 82:52-61 Ap '63
See also
Cesarean section
Childbirth
Midwives
OBVIOUS woman; story. See MacDonald, J. D.
O'BYRNE, Eleanor M.
This New generation. America 109:385-6 O 5 '63
OCAMPO, Victoria
Letter from Buenos Aires. A. Neish. Nation 196:273 Mr 30 '63
O'CASEY, Sean
Ode to an impudent upstart. N Y Times Mag p20+ Ap 19 '64
about
Great love for Ireland. por Newsweek 64: 91 S 28 '64
Obituary
New Repub 151:6 O 3 '64
Pub W 186:96 S 28 '64
Off Broadway; Paul Shyre's oral adaptation of I knock at the door. E. Oliver. New Yorker 40:88+ D 5 '64
Off Broadway; Paul Shyre's oral adaptation of Pictures in the hallway. E. Oliver. New Yorker 40:52-3 D 26 '64
Sean O'Casey. D. Johnston. por Nation 199: 198 O 5 '64
Sean O'Casey: genius of the theater. G. Roy. Cath World 200:259-60 Ja '65
Sean O'Casey RIP. Nat R 16:859 O 6 '64
Sean O'Casey's legacy. G. Rogoff. Commonweal 81:128-9 O 23 '64
Tea and memories and songs at a last fond visit. G. Mili. il pors Life 57:92-3 O 9 '64
OCCIDENT and Orient. See East and West
OCCIDENTAL civilization. See Civilization
OCCIDENTAL petroleum corporation
Venture capital from inside the stock family. Bsns W p66+ Mr 23 '63
OCCULT sciences
See also
Theosophy
OCCULTATIONS
California observations of a grazing occultation. il Sky & Tel 28:46-7 Jl '64
Lunar occultation of X-ray emission from the crab nebula. S. Bowyer and others. bibliog il Science 146:912-17 N 13 '64
Occupation supplement (cont) il Sky & Tel 26:275-82; 28:289-96 N '63, N '64
Photoelectric observations of occulations. il Sky & Tel 28:202 O '64
OCCUPATION tax. See Business tax
OCCUPATIONAL aptitude tests. See Aptitude tests
OCCUPATIONAL diseases. See Diseases, Industrial
OCCUPATIONAL education. See Vocational education
OCCUPATIONAL guidance. See Vocational guidance
OCCUPATIONAL literature. See Vocational literature
OCCUPATIONAL mobility
Effects of private pension plans on labor mobility. il Mo Labor R 86:285-8 Mr '63
Geographic mobility and employment status, March 1962-March 1963. S. Saben. il Mo Labor R 87:873-81 Ag '64
Increase in job mobility. T. R. Brooks. Duns R 84:51E-52 S '64
Problem of mobility. T. R. Brooks. Duns R 82:54+ N '63
Vesting provisions in private pension plans. W. W. Kolodrubetz. il Mo Labor R 87: 1014-21 S '64
What makes workers migrate; Labor dept. study. il Bsns W p61 O 3 '64
See also
Labor turnover
OCCUPATIONAL surveys
New job scoreboard; survey of job openings by Labor dept. Bsns W p29 Ag 22 '64
OCCUPATIONAL therapy
Menninger patient center. il Recreation 57: 220-1 My '64
OCCUPATIONS
Best job offers for '64 college grads. U S News 56:11 Ja 13 '64
BLS occupational trend projections: an appraisal; excerpt from address, June 27, 1963. H. Goldstein. Mo Labor R 86:1135-8 O '63
Careers in the great outdoors. il Changing T 17:21-2 Jl '63
Changing careers in a changing world; with charts (cont) il Sr Schol 83:8-21+ N 8 '63; Reply. J. H. Bivins. 84:32 F 7 '64
Don't let crowd determine career. D. Hanson. Suc Farm 62:2B Mr '64
Finding a future in future clubs. P. W. Goldman. il N Y Times Mag p83-4 Mr 8 '64
From the capital to the Catskills; interview. E. Clague. il Sr Schol 84:8T-10T Ja 31 '64
Getting ahead; questions and answers. L. R. Fibel. See issues of Popular science monthly
Is there a job for you in aerospace? J. M. Liston. il Pop Sci 184:53-7+ Mr '64
Job outlook for youth. il Ebony 18:25-8 My '63
Jobs for the future; symposium. il Nations Bsns 51:31-41+ Je '63
Jobs in the future; where biggest gains will be. il U S News 55:67-70 D 30 '63
Jobs of the future; reprint. P. Haase and F. Lynn. il Sci Digest 56:20-4 N '64
Life plans. il Sr Schol 82:1T My 1 '63
More jobs coming twice as fast. il Nations Bsns 52:31-3+ Je '64

OCCUPATIONS—*Continued*
Occupational plans of student borrowers under NDEA. R. C. Hall. il Sch Life 45:26-9 Ja '63
Occupational wage relationships in metropolitan areas, 1961-62. D. J. Blackmore. il Mo Labor R 86:1426-31 D '63
Planning your career in a changing world; ed. by G. Nikolaieff. il Sr Schol 85:13-24+ N 11 '64
Should you try for a better job? H. Yahraes. Pop Sci 182:110-11+ Ap '63
Teaching career? Sr Schol 83:1T N 8 '63
Training talent in the arts. D. Boroff. il Parents Mag 39:76-7+ F '64
U.S. job outlook for year 1970. U S News 56:102 Ap 27 '64
What will your kids do for a living? B. Rollins. il Farm J 87:58S-58T Ap '63
What's their line? sixth grade interviewing adults presently employed. R. Cohen. il Sr Schol 85:10T O 28 '64
When will your husband be obsolete? interview, ed. by P. L. Cahn. J. Diebold. il McCalls 90:64-5+ Jl '63
Where the jobs are. L. Velie. Read Digest 86:102-6 Ja '65
Your job and career: where are you headed? il Changing T 18:24-9 N '64
See also
Agriculture as a profession
Negroes in the United States—Occupations
Night work
Woman—Occupations
OCCUPATIONS, Choice of. See Occupations; Vocational guidance
OCCUPATIONS for children
Ask Henry! excerpts. H. Makow. Read Digest 82:205+ Je '63
Chores that children like. S. H. Fraiberg. il Parents Mag 39:58-9+ Ap '64
Chores; what can you expect of a child? M. B. Hoover. Redbook 121:40 Je '63
Handyboy how-to. il Bet Hom & Gard 41:115 Ap '63
My kids won't lift a finger. D. Van Ark. il Parents Mag 38:50-1+ Ag '63
Summer forecast; family fun. M. F. Gamache. il Parents Mag 38:60-1+ Je '63
Workshop of the children. K. Van Deurs. il Parents Mag 38:52-4 Ag '63
OCEAN
Pattern of uplifted islands in the main ocean basins. J. T. Wilson. bibliog il Science 139:592-4 F 15 '63
Seaside season; quotations, comp. by E. F. Murphy. il N Y Times Mag p92 Ag 18 '63
Where is science taking us? the depths of the sea. il Sat R 46:52-3 N 2 '63
See also
Diving, Submarine
Indian Ocean
Marine biology
Oceanographic research
Pacific Ocean
Sea level changes
Seashore
Tides
Waves

Economic aspects

See Marine resources

OCEAN bottom
Genesis of the Arctic Ocean Basin. E. R. King and others. bibliog il Science 144:1551-7 Je 26 '64
Ingneous rocks of the East Pacific rise. A. E. J. Engel and C. G. Engel. bibliog il Science 146:477-85 O 23 '64; Correction. 146:1637 D 25 '64
Ocean's maps and earth theories revolutionized by latest findings; mid-ocean ridge, ed. by B. H. Frisch. B. Heezen. il Sci Digest 53:4-12 Ap '63
Pile of ocean dregs under Argentine basin. Sci N L 85:104 F 15 '64
Rocks under the oceans. P. H. Abelson. Science 141:399 Ag 2 '63
Scraping the bottom; new deposits of metals on the ocean floor. Newsweek 61:66 Ap 15 '63
Sea pressure forms slopes. B. Tufty. Sci N L 85:215 Ap 4 '64
Search for Thresher; bathyscaphe Trieste. il Time 81:36 Je 28 '63
Seismic measurements on the ocean bottom. H. Bradner. bibliog il Science 146:208-16 O 9 '64
Through the glass you see an underwater coral world; Hawaii's offshore waters. il Sunset 132:28+ F '64
Trieste stalks a trail 1½ miles below the sea in its hunt for the Thresher. il Newsweek 62:27 Jl 8 '63
See also
Deep sea deposits
Faults (geology)
Submarine geology
OCEAN currents
Equatorial undercurrent and related currents off Brazil in March and April 1963. J. D. Cochrane. bibliog il Science 142:669-71 N 8 '63
Equatorial undercurrent of the Indian Ocean. J. A. Knauss and B. A. Taft. bibliog il Science 143:354-6 Ja 24 '64
New current discovered under Indian Ocean. Sci N L 85:89 F 8 '64
Ocean currents, how the world's bloodstream flows. I. Wolfert. il Pop Sci 183:76-8+ Ag '63
Ripple marks show that countercurrent exists in Florida Straits. R. J. Hurley and L. K. Fink. il Science 139:603-5 F 15 '63
See also
Gulf Stream
OCEAN fishing. See Salt water fishing
OCEAN life. See Marine biology
OCEAN liners
Annals of medicine; inspection of the France by New York quarantine station. B. Roueché. New Yorker 39:174+ O 12 '63
Big liner aground on inter-union reef; SS America. il Bsns W p 114+ O 5 '63
Captain's table. R. Joseph. il Esquire 59:86-8 My '63
Commodore leaves the sea; S.S. United States. I. Taves. il Look 28:38-40+ Ap 21 '64
Dining adventures in the South Seas; luxury cruise on S. S. Monterey. S. Spitzer. il Holiday 35:82-3+ Je '64
Dream of domination; state-owned Italian line. il Time 81:88+ Mr 29 '63
Feud; the S.S. America's lay-up. il Newsweek 62:96 O 14 '63
Italy bids to rule the waves; North Atlantic passenger service. il Bsns W p 148-50+ F 23 '63
Lightweight liner; Canberra. G. Soule. il Pop Sci 182:94-5 Ap '63
New Queen. Time 82:103 N 1 '63
Travel notes. R. Joseph. Esquire 59:28-30+ My '63
Tugs are a convenience; docking of S.S. United States without tugs. il Newsweek 63:77-8 F 17 '64
Unions argue, ocean liner waits; tying up United States lines' America by dispute: NMU vs. Engineers union. U S News 55:106 O 14 '63
Why U.S. isn't building superliners. il U S News 55:10 N 4 '63
See also
Ocean travel
Steamship lines

Food service

See Steamships and steamboats—Food service

OCEAN sounds
Carbon monoxide production by a bathypelagic siphonophore. G. V. Pickwell and others. bibliog il Science 144:860-2 My 15 '64
Science in action; listening under water. W. A. Watkins. il Natur Hist 73:57-9 D '64
Strange sounds of the skin divers' world. L. J. Milne and M. Milne. Pop Mech 120:102-3 Jl '63
Underwater sound: deep-ocean propagation. R. A. Frosch. bibliog il Science 146:889-94 N 13 '64
Whale of a heart reverberates underseas. Sci N L 84:405 D 28 '63
See also
Sound production by fishes
OCEAN; story. See Cheever, J.
OCEAN temperature
Thermometer takes sea's temperature. il Sci N L 83:343 Je 1 '63
OCEAN traffic. See Shipping
OCEAN travel
Atlantic swell; new prosperity of ship lines. il Time 81:78 Je 28 '63
Biggest trek to Europe yet. il Bsns W p34 Mr 23 '63
Dining adventures in the South Seas; luxury cruise on S.S. Monterey. S. Spitzer. il Holiday 35:82-3+ Je '64
Magical moments on shipboard. W. Sansom. il N Y Times Mag p36+ My 10 '64
Travel notes; flying down to Rio. R. Joseph. Esquire 60:91-2 D '63

OCEAN travel—*Continued*
Wings of the future. E. Hall. il Sci N L 85:298-9 My 9 '64
See also
Ocean liners
Voyages

OCEAN waves
Underwater waves make underwater weather. il Time 84:53 Jl 24 '64

OCEAN yacht racing. See Yacht racing

OCEANIA
Reflections in the Pacific community; address March 28, 1963. H. Cleveland. Dept State Bul 48:613-16 Ap 22 '63
This way to the great Pacific-Orient getaway. R. Joseph. il Esquire 62:68-78 Ag '64
See also
Islands of the Pacific
Micronesia
South Sea Islands

OCEANOGRAPHIC institution, Woods Hole. See Woods Hole, Mass. oceanographic institution

OCEANOGRAPHIC office. See United States—Oceanographic office

OCEANOGRAPHIC research
Age of the ice age. il Time 81:51-2 F 22 '63
Aluminum sub launched for deep-sea exploration: Aluminaut. il Sci N L 86:166 S 12 '64
Gigantic channels found in Indian Ocean floor. Sci N L 86:88 Ag 8 '64
Harnessing the ocean depths; address, September 2, 1964. P. H. Nitze. Vital Speeches 30:749-51 O 1 '64
Inexhaustible riches from the sea. G. A. W. Boehm. il Fortune 68:132-7+ D '63; Same abr. Read Digest 84:111-15 Ap '64
Interest grows in oceanography uses; Interagency committee on oceanography. Miss & Roc 15:71-3 S 21 '64
Man in the sea. A. F. Spilhaus. Science 145: 993 S 4 '64; Discussion. 146:471, 1113 O 23, N 27 '64
Man's future beneath the sea. W. Johnson. il Sr Schol 85:6-9+ Ja 7 '65
Men beneath the sea. il Newsweek 64:56-7 Jl 20 '64
Mining the bottom of the sea; excerpts from study. R. Revelle. il Sat R 47:60-1 O 3 '64
Modern tools probe deep water. D. F. Squires. il Natur Hist 72:22-9 Je '63
Navy deep in sea studies. Sci N L 84:94 Ag 10 '63
New look into the sea. R. H. Boyle. il Sports Illus 20:58-62+ Mr 9 '64
New old worlds to conquer; women in marine science. H. Ellsberg. il Mlle 59:106-8+ Je '64
Ocean waters studied for sound transmission. Sci N L 83:173 Mr 16 '63
Oceanography. J. A. Knauss. Science 142: 418+ O 18 '63
Oceanography: after a prosperous decade, agency planners agree on a grand design for next ten years. J. Walsh. il Science 141: 506-7 Ag 9 '63
Oceanography: cost-effectiveness technique employed to support case for basic research program. D. S. Greenberg. Science 146:1659-60 D 25 '64
Oceanography: new vistas and opportunities. C. B. Lindquist. il Sch Life 46:11-14 Ag '64
Ocean's maps and earth theories revolutionized by latest findings; ed. by B. H. Frisch. B. Heezen. il Sci Digest 53:4-12 Ap '63
Pastures of the sea. C. O. Iselin. il Nation 198:413-14+ Ap 27 '64; Same abr. with title Five coming breakthroughs in oceanography. Sci Digest 56:11-13 Ag '64
Physical oceanography: plans for U.S.-Japan cooperation; report on planning meeting on physical oceanography. M. K. Robinson. Science 146:1371-2 D 4 '64
Revival of oceanography in Germany. V. K. McElheny. il Science 146:45-8 O 2 '64
Seaborne scientists explore inner space il Bsns W p58-60+ O 17 '64
Speaking out; oceans of ignorance. M. B. Schaefer. Sat Eve Post 236:8+ F 16 '63
Time's traces in sediment. D. B. Ericson and G. Wollin. il Natur Hist 72:52-61 F '63
$2.3 billion should go into the ocean. Life 55:4 Ag 30 '63
Varieties of oceanographic experience. H. Stommel. bibliog il Science 139:572-6 F 15 '63
Without portfolio; Project Neptune. C. B. Luce. McCalls 91:18 Ap '64
See also
Bathyscaphe
National institute of oceanography

Equipment

Aid undersea exploration. il Sci N L 87:23 Ja 9 '65
Russian ships call at Boston; Soviet oceanographic vessels. il Bsns W p 120+ Ap 11 '64
Sea beneath us. il Bsns W p48+ My 16 '64
Tomorrow on the deep frontier. E. A. Link. il Nat Geog Mag 125:778-801 Je '64

OCEANOGRAPHY
Inner space: the oceans. B. Tufty. il Sci N L 87:42-3 Ja 16 '65
Oceanography: a wet and wondrous journey. A. Spilhaus. il Bul Atomic Sci 20:11-15 D '64
Oceanography of the western South Atlantic: report on symposium, Rio de Janiero, 14-18 September 1964. H. L. Sanders. Science 147: 183-4 Ja 8 '65
Productive oceanography. Nation 200:71 Ja 25 '65
See also
Ocean waves

OCEANOGRAPHY, Committee on. See National academy of sciences

OCHOA, Severo
How we're cracking the code of life: radio interview, ed. by C. Collingwood. por Sci Digest 56:79-83 S '64

OCHS, Anna L.
Reprints by rubbing. Design 66:16-18 N '64

OCHS, R. J. See Moyer, J. D. jt. auth.

OCHS, Sidney
Beading phenomena of mammalian myelinated nerve fibers. bibliog Science 139:599-600 F 15 '63

OCKEGHEM, Johannes
Johannes Ockeghem, religious mysticism and architectural subtlety, individually compounded. J. W. Barker. il Am Rec G 31:145-6 O '64

OCMULGEE NATIONAL MONUMENT
Surrender at Ocmulgee. A. W. Smith. Nat Parks Mag 37:2 Jl '63

OCONEE bells
Shortia galacifolia. G. A. Arrington. il Horticulture 42:48-9 Ja '64

O'CONNELL, Adelyn
Encounter; poem. America 111:384 O 3 '64
Fishermen; poem. Commonweal 79:135 O 25 '63

O'CONNELL, Charles C.
Island teacher; story. Atlan 211:85-90 My '63

O'CONNELL, Daniel C.
Lavanttal (on the way to early mass) poem. Commonweal 78:563 S 20 '63

O'CONNELL, Dennis J. and Benson, J. J.
Sourcing abroad for domestic profit. Harvard Bsns R 41:87-94 Mr '63

O'CONNELL, F. A.
Warning on employer rights; excerpts from address, 1964. U S News 57:87 D 7 '64
about
Managing your manpower. T. R. Brooks. Duns R 81:65-6+ F '63

O'CONNELL, Michael
Censorship on campus. America 111:611-13 N 14 '64

O'CONNELL, Robert
Patterns from the annunciation; poem. America 108:373 Mr 16 '63

O'CONNELL, Thomas E.
After high school. New Repub 152:17-20 Ja 30 '65

O'CONNOR, Chadwell
Rubber-tired loader reduces noise. Am City 78:100-1 Ag '63

O'CONNOR, Edwin
One spring morning; story. Atlan 214:103-6 D '64
about
I was dancing; dramatization of novel. Criticism
Newsweek 64:102 N 23 '64
Time 84:81 N 20 '64
Womanless world of Edwin O'Connor. R. B. Dooley. por Sat R 47:34-6 Mr 21 '64

O'CONNOR, Flannery
Why do the heathens rage? excerpt from novel. por Esquire 60:60-1 Jl '63
about
Flannery O'Connor. R. H. Rupp. Commonweal 79:304-7 D 6 '63
Flannery O'Connor: 1925-1964. L. F. X. Mayhew. Commonweal 80:562-3 Ag 21 '64
Harrowing evangel of Flannery O'Connor. R. Drake. Christian Cent 81:1200-2 S 30 '64
Obituary
Pub W 186:28 Ag 17 '64

O'CONNOR, Frank
Holy places. Holiday 33:94-5+ Ap '63
Quarreling with Yeats: a friendly recollection. Esquire 62:157+ D '64
about
Masters of instant truth. W. Bower. por Sat R 46:26 Jl 20 '63

O'CONNOR, Jack
Big lion of Mucusso. pors Outdoor Life 131:17-19+ F '63
Born smart, and suspicious. por Outdoor Life 132:32-3+ D '63
Buffalo make me nervous. Outdoor Life 132:20-3+ Ag '63
Cape buffalo. Outdoor Life 135:36-9+ D '64
Dwarf deer in Sonora. Outdoor Life 131:42-3+ Mr '63
Elephant. Outdoor Life 134:56-9+ S '64
Following wounded game. Outdoor Life 132:20-3+ N '63
Getting the range. See issues of Outdoor life
Hunting horse. Outdoor Life 132:46-7+ Jl '63
Leopard. Outdoor Life 134:40-3+ Ag '64
Lion. Outdoor Life 133:32-5+ F '64
One for the bears. Outdoor Life 133:17-19+ Ja '64
Ram to begin on. Outdoor Life 133:58-9+ Ap '64
Rhinoceros. Outdoor Life 135:36-9+ Ja '65
(ed) Shooters' problems. See issues of Outdoor life
Shooting. See issues of Outdoor life
Sport of stalking. Outdoor Life 132:52-5+ O '63
Tiger. Outdoor Life 133:36-9+ My '64

O'CONNOR, James
Cuba: invitation to reason. Nation 198:198-9 F 24 '64
Cuba: salvation through sugar. Nation 197:212-14+ O 12 '63

O'CONNOR, John
Modest proposal of Mary Perkins Ryan. Cath World 199:216-23 Jl '64
Question of purpose. Commonweal 77:538-41 F 15 '63

O'CONNOR, John Joseph, 1904-
Books to be noted; history. America 108:686-7; 109:670+; 110:645+; 111:714+ My 11, N 23 '63, My 9, N 28 '64

O'CONNOR, Mary
Encounter in a parish. Commonweal 80:568-70 Ag 21 '64

O'CONNOR, Norman J.
Play of the month. Cath World 199:135-6 My '64

O'CONNOR, Patrick
Vietnam controversy. Commonweal 78:537-8 S 6 '63

O'CONNOR, Rod, and others
Disc electrophoresis of hymenoptera venoms and body proteins. bibliog Science 145:1320-1 S 18 '64
Hymenoptera: pure venom from bees, wasps, and hornets. Science 139:420 F 1 '63

O'CONNOR, T. E. and Rauscher, F. J.
Physical interaction of a murine leukemia virus with influenza virus in vitro. bibliog Science 146:787-90 N 6 '64
—and others
Density gradient centrifugation of a murine leukemia virus. bibliog Science 144:1144-7 My 29 '64

O'CONNOR, William Van
Publish-or-perish policy. NEA J 53:30+ D '64

OCTANE
Coupling of butyl bromide on hot magnesium. F. L. Lambert and others. bibliog Science 146:1049 N 20 '64

OCTANE gasoline. See Gasoline—Anti-knock and anti-knock mixtures

OCTOBER
In October; few of the dates, memorable and not so, coming up next month (title varies) (cont) il N Y Times Mag p 16 S 29 '63; 39 S 27 '64
October, National science youth month. Sci N L 86:108-11 Ag 15 '64

OCTOBER and June: story. See Porter, W. S.

OCTOPAMINE. See Benzyl alcohol

OCTOPUS
Tremoctopus violaceus uses physalia tentacles as weapons. E. C. Jones. bibliog il Science 139:764-6 F 22 '63

OCULISTS. See Ophthalmologists

ODAKE, Senmatsu
For peace on earth, from a man of goodwill. A. Gingrich. Esquire 60:6+ D '63

O'DAY, George
Our Olympic chances. por Yachting 115:54-6+ Mr '64
about
Bathtub navy; Day Sailer and other O'Day models. il por Time 82:66-7 Ag 9 '63

ODD lot sales. See Stocks—Odd lots

ODEGARD, Peter H.
Social sciences and society; excerpts. Science 145:1127 S 11 '64

ODESSA, Russia
Grain opens up Odessa again; U.S. wheat shipments. il Bsns W p32-4 Mr 21 '64

ODESSA, Tex.
Coin-operated meters prevent water losses. G. T. Morris. il Am City 78:147-8 Mr '63

ODETS, Clifford
Odets at center stage; interview. ed. by M. J. Mendelsohn. pors Theatre Arts 47:16-19+ My; 28-30+ Je '63
about
Clifford Odets. H. Clurman. Sat R 46:10 S 14 '63
Obituary
Pub W 184:250 Ag 26 '63
Odets: the price of success. C. Hughes. Commonweal 78:558-60 S 20 '63

ODIO, Eunice
Four Salvadorian poets. Américas 16:27-31 Je '64

ODIORNE, George S.
Conflict: the vital corporate ingredient. Duns R 83:51-2+ Mr '64
Double talk cuts egghead's value to business. Nations Bsns 51:92-4 Ap '63
How to get men you want. Nations Bsns 52:70-2+ Ja '64
Management of corporate conflict. Duns R 83:47-8+ Ap '64
Poisons of corporate infighting. Duns R 83:39-40+ F '64

ODISHAW, Hugh
Laurence McKinley Gould, president-elect. Science 139:612-14 F 15 '63

O'DOHERTY, Brian
Millionaire art buff takes on the bad guys. Life 57:12+ N 27 '64

ODOMETERS
Great odometer mystery. J. Ridgeway. New Repub 152:10-11 Ja 23 '65

O'DONNELL, Edward
Stalagmites and stalactites. Natur Hist 73:22-5 My '64

O'DONNELL, James
Brave buddelers of Berlin. N Y Times Mag p32-3+ Ap 7 '63
Ludwig Erhard: a new ruler for Germany. Sat Eve Post 236:93-5 O 19 '63

O'DONNELL, John
Big (?) inches for a BMW. il Hot Rod 16:86-8 Mr '63

O'DONNELL, John A.
Sugar blues; Filipino claimants for additional war damages. por Newsweek 61:23 Ap 29 '63

O'DONNELL, Walter E.
Good physician. America 110:796-9 Je 6 '64

O'DONOGHUE, Joseph
Reforming the seminaries. Commonweal 81:194-6 N 6 '64

O'DONOVAN, Joan
Niceties of life; story. Seventeen 22:130-1 O '63

O'DONOVAN, Leo J.
Film seminars. America 109:560-2 N 9 '63

O'DONOVAN, Patrick
Habitable world. New Repub 148:9-10 Je 8 '63

ODORS
Dissociation of olfactory neural response and mucosal potential. T. Shibuya. bibliog il Science 143:1338-40 Mr 20 '64
Olfactory discrimination: electrophysiological spatiotemporal basis. M. M. Mozell. bibliog il Science 143:1336-7 Mr 20 '64
Stereochemical theory of odor. J. E. Amoore and others. il Sci Am 210:42-9 bibliog(p 152) F '64
Winter fragrance. H. V. Wilson and L. Bell. il Flower Grower 51:39+ Ja '64
See also
Deodorization
Gardens, Fragrant
Smell

ODUM, Eugene P. and others
Homeostasis of the nonfat components of migrating birds. bibliog Science 143:1037-9 Mr 6 '64

ODUM, Howard T. See Armstrong, N. E. jt. auth.

O'DWYER, William
Paper progress of the Alliance. Sat R 46:23-4 Jl 20 '63

ODYSSEY. See Homer

OEHLERT, Benjamin H. Jr
Can orange juice fill pause that refreshes? il Bsns W p 100+ Jl 25 '64

OEHSER, Paul H.
Future of the world. Liv Wildn 82:18-19 Winter '62

OERTER, Al
Big, shy man who likes to think. B. Heilman. por Sports Illus 18:60+ Je 17 '63
They came out in gale force. J. Underwood. il por Sports Illus 20:36+ My 4 '64
OERTLE, V. Lee
Better ways to trail your boat. Yachting 117:116-17+ Ja '65
Buy it, build it: ride on air! Pop Sci 183:54-5+ Jl '63
Campers. Motor T 15:62-5 Je '63
Coat it with neoprene. Pop Mech 120:154-5 D '63
Colorado River cruise. il Yachting 113:52-3 Mr '63
Desert duck hunting. por Field & S 69:84-5 D '64
Dodge's new little wagon, how does it compare? Pop Sci 185:62-4+ Jl '64
Foam boat flotation. Suc Farm 61:101 S '63
How to keep your engine cool. Pop Sci 183:156-8 Jl '63
Metal detectors, can they really spot buried treasure? Pop Sci 182:99-101+ Ap '63
1964 truck campers. Pop Sci 184:106-10+ My '64
Now: cars made to order for trailer towing. Pop Sci 182:98-100+ Je '63
Rough it right. Motor T 15:52-7 My '63
OESTERREICHER, John M.
As we await The deputy; questions and answers. America 109:570-3+ N 9 '63
OETTINGER, Katherine Brownell
Heartening bond of interest. PTA Mag 57:18 F '63
Parent and child. N Y Times Mag p68-9 My 12 '63
Protecting children from abuse. por Parents Mag 39:12 N '64
O'FAOLAIN, Julia
Give her back; story. Vogue 143:108-12 F 1 '64
O'FAOLAIN, Seán
Fair Dublin. Holiday 33:72-81+ Ap '63
Irish famines. Nation 196:269-71 Mr 30 '63
Miracle of Lourdes. Holiday 36:66-7+ N '64
On writing: interview; ed. by R. Diers. Mlle 56:151+ Mr '63
One man, one boat, one girl; story. Sat Eve Post 236:48-9 O 19 '63
Southern Italy. Holiday 36:38-47+ S '64
Too beautiful, too good; story. Ladies Home J 80:84-7 O '63
Vive moi! excerpt. por Atlan 213:81+ Ja '64
Writer in search of himself; excerpt from Vive moi! por Atlan 214:104-8+ O '64

about

Farewell, John Whelan. por Newsweek 64:111A+ S 21 '64
When the dawn came up in Erin. R. B. Dooley. Sat R 47:44 S 26 '64
OFF-board dealers. See Stocks—Marketing
OFF-Broadway theater. See New York (city)—Theater
OFF-street parking. See Automobile parking
OFF-the-floor toilets. See Water closets
OFF-track betting. See Gambling
OFFEN, Ron
Unknown, so unnamed; Elliott Carter; Donn; poems. Poetry 102:85-6 My '63
OFFENBACH, Jacques
Tales of Hoffmann (Les contes d'Hoffmann)
Criticism
Opera N 29:30 D 26 '64
To save a mockingbird; Darmstadt, Germany. il por Time 83:63 Mr 6 '64
OFFENLOCH, Kurt. See Klee, M. R. jt. auth.
OFFERING; story. See Dempsey, D.
OFFICE appliances
Designer Bergson. il Arch Forum 120:108-11 F '64
More value for the office dollar. H. E. Klein. il Duns R 82:pt2 116-18+ S '63
Office technology: the big leap forward. K. August. il Duns R 84:pt2 118-19+ S '64
See also
Adding machines
OFFICE buildings
Better than mere cubage. P. Blake. il Arch Forum 119:124 D '63
Bold office tower of cellular brick piers: Benjamin Franklin office building, Houston, Tex. il Arch Rec 137:118-19 Ja '65
Building in the cityscape. il Arch Rec 135:156-8 Ap '64
Design against sun and glare; home office, Humble oil and refining company, Houston, Tex. il Arch Rec 134:173-8 O '63
Extra Grand Central; Manhattan's Pan American building. il Time 81:71 Mr 15 '63
Free-form office building opens to views: Colorado education association headquarters building, Denver, Colo. il Arch Rec 137:116-17 Ja '65
Future of the office-building boom. D. Seligman. il Fortune 67:84-8+ Mr '63
Office building at new peak. M. B. Ayre. il Arch Rec 133:18 Ap '63
Office building boom is going nationwide. il Arch Forum 118:114-19 My '63
Old offices made new. il Arch Forum 118:126-9 Mr '63
PSFS: Philadelphia savings fund society. W. H. Jordy and H. Wright. il Arch Forum 120:124-9+ My '64
Place Ville Marie. il Arch Forum 118:74-89 F '63
Powerful grid for a prairie tower; Kansas City's new BMA building. il Arch Forum 121:86-91 Jl '64
Precast concrete wall frames delivered to building preglazed. il Arch Rec 134:152-3 Jl '63
Problem of Pan Am. M. F. Schmertz. il Arch Rec 133:151-8 My '63
Realism in corporate real estate. A. Rabinowitz. bibliog f il Harvard Bsns R 41:62-9 N '63
Recent work of William Wilson Wurster; U.S. consulate office building, Hong Kong. il Arch Rec 133:116-18 Ja '63
Small office buildings. il Arch Rec 133:153-62 Mr '63
Three office buildings. il Arch Forum 119:96-103 O '63
Vanishing glory in business buildings; portfolio of drawings by Nicholas Solovioff. Fortune 68:119-26 S '63
See also
Medical buildings
Municipal buildings
New York (city)—Architecture
Pentagon building, Arlington, Va.
Telephone company buildings

Air conditioning

Dual-duct approach for office buildings. il Arch Rec 133:216 Ap '63

Condominium plan ownership

Condominiums go commercial. Bsns W p72 Mr 23 '63

Cooperative ownership

See also
Office buildings—Condominium plan ownership

Designs and plans

Bearing walls in Iowa. il Arch Forum 118:126-30 My '63
Bold and direct, using metal in a strong, basic way. il Arch Rec 136:135-42 Jl '64
Building types study. il Arch Rec 133:181-204 Ap '63
Computer center: new building type? Westinghouse center near Pittsburgh. il Arch Rec 136:153-8 N '64
Emhart: a bold, pragmatic structure of concrete and steel. il Arch Forum 119:88-95 Jl '63
Functional grid in Japan. il Arch Forum 121:130-5 Ag '64
In Texas the glass box goes 3-D; Tennessee building. il Arch Forum 119:124-31 S '63
Innovation in Chicago; United States Gypsum's headquarters. il Arch Rec 135:133-8 Ja '64
Large spans in Chicago. il Arch Forum 118:120-5 My '63
New office building by SOM has unusual site plan, and a well integrated structural and mechanical system; American college of surgeons. il Arch Rec 136:139-43 Ag '64
Offices. il Arch Forum 118:120-3 Ap '63
Pan Am ticket office: an airy sweep of sculptured space. il Arch Forum 119:98-101 Ag '63
Payoff in design. N. Buckley. il Duns R 84:pt2 115-17+ S '64
Planning the downtown center; symposium, with introd. by M. F. Schmertz. il Arch Rec 135:177-200 Mr '64
Procession of metallic T's; headquarters of Hunt foods and industries inc, Fullerton, Calif. il Arch Forum 118:128-31 Je '63
Small office buildings; symposium. il Arch Rec 136:157-66 D '64
Small office with a large view; C. E. Silling and associates, Charleston, W. Va. il Arch Rec 134:217-20 S '63
Solid taste in Virginia; Philip Morris administration building in Richmond. il Arch Forum 121:142-3 Ag '64

OFFICE buildings—Designs and plans—*Cont.*
Stack of concrete barrels. il Arch Forum 118: 132-7 Je '63
Typhoon-proof louvers screen tropical sun; Philippine American life insurance office building, Manila. il Arch Rec 134:139-41 D '63
Yamasaki's first tower. D. B. Carlson. il Arch Forum 118:98-113 My '63

Heating and ventilation

Bootstrap heating works in chilly Toronto. R. T. Tamblyn. il Arch Rec 133:184-6 Je '63
Dual-duct approach for office buildings. il Arch Rec 133:216 Ap '63

Lighting

Design for controlled lighting; Public service company of Colorado, in Denver. il Arch Rec 136:144-6 Ag '64

Parking

Two motor club offices, two traffic solutions. il Arch Rec 133:160-1 Mr '63

Renting

Actors stage rent blitz; hard-sells office space. il Bsns W p200+ My 18 '63
Complete bank plus rental space. il Arch Rec 135:130-1 Ja '64
For rent signs go up on executive suites. il Bsns W p30-2 Ag 24 '63

OFFICE for recruitment. See American library association—Library administration division

OFFICE furniture
Action office: new concept in office furniture. il Arch Rec 137:187 Ja '65
But where will I keep my movie magazines? W. K. Zinsser. il Sat Eve Post 238:74+ Ja 16 '65
Designer Bergson. il Arch Forum 120:108-11 F '64
Furnishings. See issues of Architectural forum to July 1964
Man's office is his castle. E. Kendall. il N Y Times Mag p52+ Mr 15 '64
Modular office furniture. il Am City 78:125 Je '63
Office furniture tailored to the job. il Bsns W p60-2 D 19 '64

OFFICE holders. See Public officers

OFFICE management
Bright young men of information. S. Nicholson. il Duns R 82:pt2 96-7+ S '63
Executive trends; your paperwork burden. Nations Bsns 52:21+ My '64
House prober charges federal paperwork wastes your money; interview. A. Olsen. Nations Bsns 52:84-6+ S '64
Memo on memos (six copies, please) T. Irwin. il N Y Times Mag p46+ N 17 '63
Office: management's billion-dollar system; symposium. il Duns R 84:pt2 101-12+ S '64
Where you can cut costs next. S. Schuler. il Nations Bsns 51:58-60+ O '63
You can cut your upkeep costs. S. Schuler. il Nations Bsns 52:94-6 My '64

OFFICE manuals
Instant experience for secretaries and others in city administrative offices. C. Keefer. il Am City 79:171 Je '64

OFFICE of aerospace research. See United States—Air force—Aerospace research, Office of

OFFICE of economic opportunity. See United States—Economic opportunity, Office of

OFFICE of education. See United States—Education, Office of

OFFICE of special investigations. See United States—Air force—Special investigations, Office of

OFFICE of strategic services. See United States—Strategic services, Office of

OFFICE parties. See Business entertaining

OFFICE workers
Anybody here seen the boss? il Bsns W p32-3 My 18 '63
Idle fifth man in the office; office work measurement systems. N. Buckley. il Duns R 82:47-8+ N '63
Is there a crisis in the labor movement? no. P. Taft. Ann Am Acad 350:10-15 N '63
Managing your manpower; white collar employees. T. R. Brooks. Duns R 82:74A D '63
New fit to the white collar. T. R. Brooks. il Duns R 82:pt2 98-100+ S '63
Prospects for organization of white-collar workers; excerpt from address. A. A. Blum. bibliog f Mo Labor R 87:125-9 F '64
Revolution in office work; meaning for jobs, business. il U S News 54:84-6+ My 13 '63
Rise in white collar organizing. Duns R 81:45 Mr '63
White-collar automation. T O'Toole. il Reporter 29:24-7 D 5 '63
White-collar unionism in western Europe. E. M. Kassalow. bibliog f Mo Labor R 86: 765-71, 889-96 Jl-Ag '63
White collar unions abroad. T. R. Brooks. Duns R 83:64+ F '64
See also
Strikes—United States—Office workers

Salaries

Job pay levels and trends in metropolitan areas, 1962. K. J. Hoffmann. bibliog f il Mo Labor R 86:145-51 F '63
Job pay levels and trends in metropolitan areas, 1963. A. N. Jarrell. il Mo Labor R 87:173-8 F '64
1963 survey of white-collar salaries. H. F. Zeman. il Mo Labor R 86:1283-9 N '63
Salary adjustments in white-collar occupations. L. E. Badenhoop. Mo Labor R 87: 1281-2 N '64
White-collar pay may go up. U S News 55: 94 Jl 22 '63
White-collar raises: how big. il U S News 55:110 N 11 '63
White-collar salaries in Hawaii, Puerto Rico, and Alaska. B. B. O'Neal. bibliog f il Mo Labor R 87:301-4 Mr '64
White-collar salary study, 1964. G. Engen. il Mo Labor R 87:1425-9 D '64

OFFICERS, Retired. See Retired military officers

OFFICES
Airline showcase from an old store; Pakistan international airlines, New York. il Arch Forum 118:134 Ap '63
Architect's office from an old studio; London. il Arch Forum 119:120-1 Jl '63
Designer Bergson. il Arch Forum 120:108-11 F '64
Forum roundtable takes a look at tomorrow's office; symposium. il Arch Forum 120:110-17 Ja '64
How to fit an office into any room; your home office. E. T. Lawyer and M. Casserly. il Bet Hom & Gard 43:54-7 Ja '65
Man's office is his castle. E. Kendall. il N Y Times Mag p52+ Mr 15 '64
New design offices from an old store; Eliot Noyes and associates, New Canaan, Conn. il Arch Forum 119:122-5 Jl '63
Quiet corner for your desk work. J. Walker. il Bet Hom & Gard 41:114H Mr '63
Shocking situation; shock problem in offices with wall-to-wall carpeting. Time 83:46 Ja 3 '64
Six offices from New York's Pan Am building. il Arch Forum 120:102-9 Ja '64
This home office disappears. il Sunset 130:140 Ap '63
Walls come tumbling down. il Duns R 82:pt2 123-4 S '63
Why do some executives chill wine in a rhinoceros leg? il Newsweek 61:88-9 My 27 '63
See also
Airlines—Ticket offices

OFFICES, Display. See Showrooms

OFFICIAL entertaining. See Government entertaining

OFFICIAL secrets
AEC; energetic bargaining brings agreement on university contract clauses on security information. J. Walsh. Science 140:38-9 Ap 5 '63
Secrecy boomerang; managing the news. R. Hotz. Aviation W 78:21 Mr 18 '63
Spain: concealed handout. L. Fernsworth. Nation 198:138-40 F 10 '64
Spies for peace; British civil defense plans. Newsweek 61:39 Ap 29 '63
See also
Government and the press
Security classification (government documents)

OFFSET printing. See Printing, Offset

OFFSHORE boundaries. See Territorial waters

OFFSHORE oil fields. See Petroleum in submerged lands

OFFSHORE oil well drilling. See Oil well drilling, Submarine

O'FLAHERTY, Hugh
Rescue in wartime Rome. America 109:620 N 16 '63

O'FLYNN, Criostoir
'Tis always the same; story. Cath World 200: 178-84 D '64

O'GARA, James
All things considered. See issues of Commonweal

OGAWA, Tetsuro
Midbrain reticular influences upon single neurons in lateral geniculate nucleus. bibliog Science 139:343-4 Ja 25 '63
OGBURN, Charlton, jr
Help! help! Harper 229:65-9 N '64
OGDEN, Aaron
Steamboat's charter of freedom; Gibbons v. Ogden. G. Dangerfield. il por Am Heritage 14:38-43+ O '63
OGDEN, Utah
They all want to see the vacuum filters. il Am City 79:93-5 S '64
OGDEN corporation
Lipsett brothers: biggest wreckers in the building world. il Arch Forum 120:76-7 Ja '64
Scrappy market. il Time 81:98+ My 3 '63
OGDON, John
Music to my ears: American debut. I. Kolodin. Sat R 47:24 F 1 '64
OGILVY, Angus James Bruce
Bra, bonny bride and a fortune fair. il por Time 81:28 My 3 '63
OGILVY, David
How to get to the top of the creative tree; excerpt from Confessions of an advertising man. por Vogue 142:82-5+ O 15 '63
Should advertising be abolished? excerpts from Confessions of an advertising man. Read Digest 84:67-70 F '64

about

Behind the Hathaway shirt. M. Mayer. New Repub 149:27+ N 2 '63
Completing the circle. Newsweek 64:74+ N 30 '64
Free and new. por Newsweek 62:80-2 O 28 '63
Gentle ticking noise. R. Bingham. Reporter 29:54+ N 7 '63
How to succeed, trying. il por Time 82:98 N 1 '63
Mavericks on Madison avenue. P. B. Bart. Sat R 46:60+ D 14 '63
OGILVY and Mather, incorporated
Atlantic alliance on Madison ave. Bsns W p 142 N 28 '64
Completing the circle. Newsweek 64:74+ N 30 '64
OGILVY, Benson and Mather, incorporated
Mavericks on Madison avenue. P. B. Bart. Sat R 46:60+ D 14 '63
OGLE, Alice
California farm labor. America 111:799+ D 19 '64
Genie escapes the bottle. America 110:314 Mr 7 '64
San Francisco's peacemakers. America 111: 232-3 S 5 '64
Tomorrow's alcoholic. America 108:468-9 Ap 6 '63
OGLE, Charles
Speech that toppled a president; excerpts from address, April 14, 1840, ed. with introd. by G. Carson. por Am Heritage 15:108-11 Ag '64
OGLE, Jim
Why the Yankees fired Berra. Look 28:30+ D 29 '64
O'GORMAN, Ned
Five poets. J. Jacobsen. Poetry 105:201-3 D '64
O'GRADY, Desmond
Homecoming; poem. Atlan 213:51 Ja '64
Tight little island. Commonweal 77:510-11 F 8 '63
Why communism in Catholic Italy? Cath World 199:102-8 My '64
OGURI, Mikio
Rectal glands of marine and fresh-water sharks: comparative histology. bibliog Science 144:1151-2 My 29 '64
OH les beaux jours; drama. See Beckett, S.
OH what a lovely war; revue. See Musical comedies, revues, etc.—Criticisms, plots, etc.
O'HANLON, Daniel J.
Church structures. Commonweal 80:554-5 Ag 7 '64
Dialogue at the top. America 109:231-4 S 7 '63
Door opens wider. America 109:88 Jl 27 '63
Faith and order conference. America 109: 138-41 Ag 10 '63
Grass-roots ecumenism. Cath World 199:8-15 Ap '64
Karl Barth's theological quest. Commonweal 77:520-1 F 8 '63
Pentecostals and Pope John's new Pentecost. America 108:634-6 My 4 '63
Season of renewal. Commonweal 77:643-5 Mr 15 '63
Vatican II: a look ahead. America 109:347-9+ S 28 '63
—See Campion, D. R. jt. auth.
O'HANLON, Thomas J.
Air cargo's new flight pattern. Duns R 82: 45-6+ N '63
Bonanza in bulk shipping. Duns R 82:41-3+ O '63
New boom in material handling. Duns R 82: 50-1+ D '63
O'HARA, Francis N.
Blowers boost loading, drop costs. Am City 79:109-10 S '64
O'HARA, Frank
Introducing the sculpture of George Spaventa. Art N 63:44-7 Ap '64
Present; poem. Nation 199:518 D 28 '64
Riopelle: international speedscapes. Art N 62: 32-4+ Ap '63
O'HARA, Gerald P. abp
Cardinal Bea: an appreciation. America 108: 442-4+ Mr 30 '63
O'HARA, Hazel
Looms of progress. Américas 17:22-6 Ja '65
O'HARA, James M.
Disadvantaged newcomers to the city. NEA J 52:25-7 Ap '63
O'HARA, John
Agatha: story. New Yorker 39:33-9 F 23 '63
All tied up; story. New Yorker 40:48-55 O 3 '64
Answer depends; story. Sat Eve Post 237:46-7 Ap 18 '64
Arnold Stone; story. Sat Eve Post 237:52-9 Mr 28 '64
At the window; story. New Yorker 40:28-32 F 22 '64
Aunt Anna; story. Sat Eve Post 236:50-2 Mr 23 '63
Aunt Fran; story. Sat Eve Post 237:56-7 S 19 '64
Bonfire; story. Sat Eve Post 237:46-9 O 10 '64
Can I stay here? story. Sat Eve Post 237:44-5 My 16 '64
Christmas poem; story. New Yorker 40:34-9 D 19 '64
Clear track; story. Sat Eve Post 237:58-60 O 24 '64
Exterior: with figure; story. Sat Eve Post 236:54-61 Je 1 '63
Flatted saxophone; story. New Yorker 39: 28-9 Je 1 '63
Glendale people; story. Sat Eve Post 236: 34-6 Mr 2 '63
Hardware man; story. Sat Eve Post 237:46-50 F 29 '64
His excellency; story. Sat Eve Post 237:56-8 Jl 11 '64
House on the corner; story. Sat Eve Post 237:64-6 Ag 22 '64
I spend my days in longing; story. New Yorker 40:40-6 My 23 '64
John Barrow Rosedale, actor's actor; story. New Yorker 39:46-53 Mr 16 '63
Lawbreaker; story. Sat Eve Post 236:52-4 N 16 '63
Locomobile; story. New Yorker 39:22-7 Jl 20 '63
Man on the tractor; story. New Yorker 39: 25-30 Je 22 '63
Manager; story. New Yorker 39:42-8 My 4 '63
Our friend the sea; story. Sat Eve Post 236:60-5 Ag 24 '63
Ride from Mauch Chunk; story. Sat Eve Post 236:38-41 Ap 13 '63
School; story. Sat Eve Post 237:56-61 S 26 '64
Tackle; story. Sports Illus 21:108-13 S 21 '64
Victim; story. Sat Eve Post 237:46-51 Mr 14 '64
Wayward reader. Holiday 36:31-4 D '64
Whole cherry pie; story. Sat Eve Post 237: 32-3 F 8 '64
Zero; story. New Yorker 39:28-32 D 28 '63

about

Appointment on Long Island; byline to appear in weekend edition of Newsday. il por Time 84:42 S 25 '64
John O'Hara at fifty-eight: a rage to write. il pors Newsweek 61:53-7 Je 3 '63
Life goes on in Gibbsville. G. Hicks. Sat R 46:27-8 N 30 '63
O'Hara's turn. Newsweek 64:101 O 12 '64
Realism and fantasy. J. Ciardi. Sat R 47:6 Ag 15 '64
So long to the short for a while. G. Hicks. Sat R 47:21-2 N 28 '64
O'HARA, Tom
America's go boy! H. L. Masin. il por Sr Schol 84:24 Ap 24 '64
And now there are two. W. Bingham. il por Sports Illus 18:14-17 Mr 18 '63

O'HARA, Tom—*Continued*
Eat and run. il por Newsweek 63:58+ F 24 '64
From humdrum to well-done in one easy mile. R. Creamer. il por Sports Illus 20: 46+ F 24 '64
Joyful theme at the AAU: younger, higher and faster. G. S. Brown. il por Sports Illus 21:22-5 Jl 6 '64
Now if O'Hara really tries. T. C. Brody. il Sports Illus 20:68-9 Mr 16 '64
O'Hara burns up the mile. il pors Life 56:78-9 Mr 27 '64
Running is such sweet torture. J. Underwood. il por Sports Illus 20:26+ Je 22 '64
With Oyol on the front. por Time 83:50 F 21 '64

O'HARE, J. M.
Awakening in Massachusetts. Recreation 56: 262-3 Je '63

O'HARE international airport. See Chicago—Airports

O'HARRA, Russell
Off-street parking. Bet Hom & Gard 42:72-5 N '64

OHIO
See also
Booksellers and bookselling—Ohio
Education—Ohio
Fishing—Ohio
Geology—Ohio
Hunting—Ohio
Libraries—Ohio
Petroleum—Ohio

Antiquities
See Indians of North America—Antiquities —Ohio

Economic conditions
Austerity in Ohio. R. Giles. il Reporter 29:39-42 N 7 '63

History
Ohio land patents. K. W. Duckett. Hobbies 68:110-11+ Ag '63

Industries
Ohio: old laissez-faire attitude on linking education, research, and industry undergoing change. J. Walsh. Science 145:468-70 Jl 31 '64

Parks and reserves
Let's share a country common; Bryan park-Glen Helen region. K. W. Hunt. Recreation 57:26 Ja '64

Politics and government
In orbit. il Time 83:13-14 Ja 24 '64
Industry's brains help a state; Ohio's Little Hoover commission. il Bsns W p 131 N 23 '63
Into orbit. il Newsweek 63:18 Ja 27 '64
Ohio and Governor Rhodes. W. F. Rickenbacker. il Nat R 16:61-4 Ja 28 '64
Ohio: is anybody happy? J. A. Maxwell. il Reporter 31:36-8 O 22 '64
Ohio's Ray Bliss: the GOP picks a chairman. Newsweek 65:25 Ja 25 '65
Rough ride for a hero; senatorial contest. S. Alsop. il Sat Eve Post 237:14 Mr 14 '64
Scrubbed; J. Glenn quits primary race for U.S. senator. Newsweek 63:25-6 Ap 13 '64
Shooting for the moon. Reporter 30:16+ Ja 30 '64
Son of Mr Republican; R. Taft, jr. il Time 84:43B O 2 '64
Taft vs. Young. il Newsweek 64:36-8 O 26 '64
What beat Taft. Time 84:40 N 13 '64
What made John Glenn run? with editorial comment. H. H. Martin and D. Oberdorfer. il Sat Eve Post 237:21-5, 90 F 22 '64
Young Bob. il Time 83:37 My 15 '64

Religious institutions and affairs
News of the Christian world (cont) Christian Cent 80:502+, 597-8, 917-18, 940, 1144+, 1281+, 1311-12, 1479; 81:26-7, 185-6, 412-13, 889, 972-4, 1069-70, 1122+, 1348-50, 1627-8; 82:24-6 Ap 17, My 1, Jl 17-24, S 18, O 16-23, N 27 '63, Ja 1, F 5, Mr 25, Jl 8, 29, Ag 26, S 9, O 28, D 30 '64, Ja 6 '65

OHIO RIVER VALLEY. See Ohio Valley

OHIO state library, Columbus
Abolishment of the Ohio state library. Wilson Lib Bul 38:316 D '63
Ohio's Little Hoover commission recommends elimination of state library. Library J 88: 4174+ N 1 '63
Time table for destruction; with editorial comment Library J 88:3173-6 S 15 '63

OHIO state university, Columbus
Learning by listening to tapes. Sch & Soc 92: 24 Jan 25 '64
Minuteman U; branch campus at Ellsworth air force base. il Time 85:47 Ja 8 '65

Libraries
Professional internship: a program and a proposal; Ohio state university libraries. C. I. Wilson. bibliog il Library J 88:2201-5 Je 1 '63

OHIO. University, Athens
Famous hotel now college dorm. V. Rakestraw. il Negro Hist Bul 27:140-1 Mr '64
Peace corps training at Ohio university. R. P. Fairfield. Sch & Soc 92:339-41 N 14 '64

OHIO VALLEY
G. Washington meets a test. T. J. Fleming. il Am Heritage 14:56-9+ F '63
Ohio Valley, America's newest industrial empire. D. Reed. il Read Digest 83:193-4+ D '63

OHKUMA, K. and others
Abscisin II, an abscission-accelerating substance from young cotton fruit. Science 142:1592-3 D 20 '63

OHLES, John F.
Extended schooling versus higher education. Sch & Soc 92:156-7 Ap 4 '64

OHMANN, Carol B. and Ohmann, R. M.
Class notes from Vassar. Commonweal 79:12-15 S 27 '63

OHMANN, Richard M.
Auden's sacred awe. Commonweal 78:279-81 My 31 '63
GBS on the USSR. Commonweal 80:519 Jl 24 '64
Ireland's blend of the comic and the serious. Commonweal 78:484 Ag 9 '63
Various Audens. Commonweal 79:437-8 Ja 10 '64
—See Ohmann, C. B. jt. auth.

OHMMETERS
See also
Voltohmmeters

OHRBACH'S, incorporated
Suited for expansion; C. & A. Brenninkmeyer co. il Time 82:74 Jl 19 '63

OHTAKA, Y. and Spiegelman, S.
Translational control of proteins synthesis in a cell-free system directed by a polycistronic viral RNA. bibliog Science 142: 493-7 O 25 '63

OIL, chemical and atomic workers international union
Compromise ends Shell deadlock. Bsns W p46 Ag 10 '63
Oil strikers get global support; IFPW back OCAW. il Bsns W p60+ My 25 '63
Story of two strikes: what unions are running up against; oil refinery in Texas, telephone company in Florida; Oil workers union. U S News 55:97 Ag 19 '63

OIL burners
Oil burner tune-up. E. R. Haan. il Pop Mech 120:186-90 N '63

OIL changes, Automobile. See Automobiles—Lubrication

OIL cloth. See Oilcloth

OIL engines. See Gas and oil engines

OIL fields, Offshore. See Petroleum in submerged lands

OIL gages. See Gages

OIL industries
See also
Petroleum industry and trade
Standard oil company of New Jersey

Insurance selling
Socony trying insurance field. Bsns W p70 Mr 23 '63

OIL lamps. See Lamps

OIL lands
Louisiana splash. Time 83:64 Ja 24 '64

Royalties
Fine print; increased royalty payments. Newsweek 65:65 Ja 11 '65

OIL painting. See Painting

OIL pollution of rivers, harbors, etc.
Operation duck rescue; oil flooding of the Mississippi. E. Peller. il Audubon Mag 65: 364-7 N '63

OIL refineries
Phantom city; Bayway refinery of Humble oil & refining co. New Yorker 39:26-8 Ja 18 '64

OIL royalties. See Oil lands—Royalties

OIL shales
Copper supply can meet future needs. Sci N L 86:248 O 17 '64

OIL shales—*Continued*
Oil fever stirs Rockies. il Bsns W p 176+ My 23 '64
Shale oil gets a fresh push; shale rocks of northwestern Colorado. Bsns W p 114 S 7 '63
OIL tanks
Fuel-oil tank failures. il Consumer Bul 47:39-40 F '64
Repair, then forget, those fuel tanks. il Am City 78:159 O '63
OIL well drilling, Submarine
North Sea oil rush. il Newsweek 64:57-8 Jl 27 '64
Risking piles of money in the great gas race; beneath the North Sea. il Bsns W p 118-20+ Jl 11 '64
OIL well drilling rigs
Oil patch; roughnecks and operators on a forgotten frontier. C. Davidson. il Harper 229:41-6 Ag '64
OIL wells
School gusher; three wells on former baseball diamond of Edison, Ohio junior high school. I. H. Wenning. Sr Schol 84:3T My 8 '64
OIL workers. See Petroleum workers
OIL workers union. See Oil, chemical and atomic workers international union
OILCLOTH
Making an oil-cloth floor-covering for Pres. Andrew Johnson's home. H. Wandrus. il Hobbies 68:54+ Jl '63
OILS and fats, Edible
Facts about fats, polyunsaturated and otherwise. McCalls 92:82 N '64
Polyunsaturates studied. Sci N L 86:38 Jl 18 '64
Salad and cooking oils. il Consumer Rep 29: 341-3 Jl '64
Should you or shouldn't you show preference for polyunsaturated fats? Consumer Bul 47: 19-20 S '64
See also
Allied crude vegetable oil refining corporation
OILSTONE. See Sharpening
OIMYAKON, Russia
Coldest place on earth: Oymyakon in Siberia. B. Vandano. il Life 58:80-3 Ja 22 '65
OJELABI, Mari
Jazz roots in Nigeria. R. F. Thompson. il Sat R 47:52-3 Ap 11 '64
OKA, Takashi
China's new kinsman. New Repub 149:13-15 Jl 20 '63
General Park's victory. New Repub 149:10-11 O 26 '63
Man in the middle. New Repub 148:11-13 Je 15 '63
Saigon's mood is a mixture of euphoria and disquiet. New Repub 149:4 N 16 '63
OKAMOTO, Richard
Japan. Look 27:15-17 S 10 '63
OKAMOTO, Yoichi R.
Case of the elegant eye. J. Balish. il Mod Phot 27:66-71+ Mr '63
Days of decision. Newsweek 63:65 F 17 '64
LBJ's shadow. il por Newsweek 63:51 Ja 27 '64
OKAMURA, Akihiko
In the steps of Robert Capa. G. P. Hunt. por Life 56:3 Je 12 '64
OKANOGAN COUNTY, Wash.
Ordeal in Okanogan. G. Bassett. Nation 197: 454-6 D 28 '63
OKAZAKI, Katsuo
Economic progress in Asia; address, December 5, 1962. Vital Speeches 29:240-2 F 1 '63
OKEECHOBEE, LAKE
Florida's Lake Okeechobee. B. Mansfield. il Travel 120:38-40 D '63
Okeechobee waterway. J. Emmett. il Yachting 114:132-3 D '63
O'KEEFE, John A.
Interpretation of Ranger photographs. bibliog Science 146:514-15 O 23 '64
Tektites and impact fragments from the moon; with biographical sketch. Sci Am 210:28, 50-7 bibliog(p 152) F '64
—and Kaula, W. M.
Stress differences and the reference ellipsoid. bibliog Science 142:382 O 18 '63
—and Shute, B. E.
Origin of tektites. bibliog Science 139:1288-90 Mr 29 '63
—and others
Hydrogen in a tektite vesicle. Science 143: 39 Ja 3 '64
O'KEEFE, Patricia
Traveling with the pet set. Am Home 67:76 Je '64
O'KEEFFE, Georgia
Austerity of the desert pervades her home and her work. L. Gilpin. il House B 105: 144-5+ Ap '63
O'KEEFFE, John
Confessions of a racetrack flack. Esquire 61: 112-13+ Ap '64
OKEFENOKEE national wildlife refuge
Land of the trembling earth. J. J. Stophlet. il Nat Parks Mag 37:10-15 O '63
OKEFENOKEE swamp
Massive marsh. il Natur Hist 72:58-9 My '63
See also
Okefenokee national wildlife refuge
OKELLO, John
Latest recruit for communism. map U S News 56:6+ Ja 27 '64
O'KEY, Clifford W.
How zoning can bring beauty. Am City 78: 100-1 Ap '63
OKIES (transient labor) See Migrant labor
OKINAWA
Okinawa: trigger in the Pacific. J. M. Diamond. Nation 198:547-8 Je 1 '64
OKINAWA plywood corporation of Seattle
Pole sitters: labor disputes in Okinawa. New Repub 150:7-8 My 30 '64
OKLAHOMA
See also
Architecture, Domestic—Oklahoma
Booksellers and bookselling—Oklahoma
Fishing—Oklahoma
Libraries—Oklahoma
Transportation—Oklahoma
Industries
Seaports for Oklahoma. il U S News 54:66-9 F 11 '63
Politics and government
Basic Bud; Senate candidates. il Time 84:27-8 O 9 '64
Off the sideline. Time 83:38 My 15 '64
Religious institutions and affairs
News of the Christian world (cont) Christian Cent 80:813-14; 81:998; 82:122 Je 19 '63, Ag 5 '64, Ja 27 '65
OKLAHOMA CITY
Sonic boom town. R. Burkhardt. New Repub 151:5-6 Ag 22 '64
Airports
Era of supersonic morality; BONGO experiment to obtain public reaction to sonic boom. J. Lear. Sat R 47:49-50 Je 6 '64; Discussion. 47:46-7 Jl 4 '64
Description
Two giants rising in the Southwest. il U S News 54:69 F 11 '63
Education
It happened in Oklahoma City. B. V. Wadkins. NEA J 53:39-40 N '63
Music
Oklahoma City/a glorious discontent. R. A. Boggess. Mus Am 84:64+ Ja '64
Theater
Mummers theatre of Oklahoma City. A. J. Treanor. il Theatre Arts 47:55-9 D '63
Rise of rep. il(p58-9) Time 83:61 F 14 '64
Water supply
Simple control for a complex system. D. B. Benham. il Am City 78:81-3 Ap '63
OKLAHOMA! musical comedy. See Musical comedies, revues, etc.—Criticisms, plots, etc.
OKLAHOMA. University, Norman, Okla.
Oklahoma's college of continuing education. J. Vornholt. Sch & Soc 91:172-3 Ap 6 '63
OKOTIE-EBOH, F. S.
On self-help and foreign aid; address, April 2, 1963. Vital Speeches 29:502-3 Je 1 '63
OKUN, Arthur M.
Old reliable team. por Newsweek 64:84 N 30 '64
OLANDER, Gösta
Septuagenarian's formula for fitness: learn to relax. J. Stewart-Gordon. il Todays Health 42:22-5 Ag '64; Same abr. with title Relax and get fit! Read Digest 85:75-8 Ag '64
OLBERS, Heinrich
Some thoughts on Olbers' paradox. O. Struve. il por Sky & Tel 25:140-2 Mr '63
OLCOTT, Harold S. See Read, M. S. jt. auth.

OLCOTT, Joseph S.
Chemical strengthening of glass. bibliog Science 140:1189-93 Je 14 '63

OLCOTT, William
Across the U.S.A. with glass and bottle. Esquire 61:102-3 Ja '64

OLD, Bruce S. See Gallagher, L. V. jt. auth.

OLD age
How to live to be one hundred. S. Mix. il Todays Health 42:21-3+ Je '64
Letter to a useless friend. Christian Cent 80: 323-4 Mr 13 '63
Reflections on growing old, by J. LaFarge. Review
Cath World 198:259-60 Ja '64. C. L. Palms
These enduring truths become clear at age seventy. F. Morley. Nations Bsns 52:19-20 Ja '64
See also
Aged
Aging
Centenarians

OLD age homes
Good partnership; architect-builder partnership at Walnut Creek in the San Francisco Bay area. il Time 83:52-3 Je 19 '64
House of rest; photographs by F. Nuzzo. Opera N 28:27-9 Mr 28 '64
Why I'm glad I'm in a home. G. Gage. il Farm J 88:69 F '64
See also
Nursing homes

OLD age market
Never too old to buy. Bsns W p 170-1 My 23 '64
Old folks: an overlooked market? L. Morse. il Duns R 83:45-6+ Ap '64

OLD age pensions
See also
Pensions, Industrial

Russia

Russia joins the war on poverty; pensions to collective farmers, pay increases to teachers and doctors. Bsns W p32 Jl 25 '64

United States

Are you missing out on social security payments? M. Belloise. Read Digest 82:73-6 Je '63
Avoid these mistakes on your social security. il Changing T 18:13-15 N '64
Do you really know where you stand with social security? N. Kuehnl and G. Bush. Bet Hom & Gard 42:6+ Ag '64
First findings of the 1963 survey of the aged; Income of the aged in 1962. L. A. Epstein. il Mo Labor R 87:1171-3 O '64
High-flying cost of pensions. il Bsns W p94+ Mr 14 '64
How up-to-date is your pension plan? il U S News 56:70-3 Ja 20 '64
In the works: another boost in social security pensions. il U S News 57:79-80 Jl 6 '64
Pensions for the self-employed; Keogh act. il Changing T 17:7-12 My '63
The plan now: bigger pensions in '64. il U S News 56:85-6 Ap 20 '64
President renews insurance plan; proposes a Senior citizens act. Christian Cent 80:324 Mr 13 '63
Self-employed: it's time to act on pensions; Self-employed individuals tax retirement act. il U S News 55:118-20 N 11 '63
What future for social security? M. C. Bernstein. New Repub 152:9-11 Ja 9 '65
Writer's social security. D. Malcolmson. Writer 77:30-1 Ja '64
See also
Civil service pensions
Social security act amendments
Townsend old age pension plan

OLD age, survivors' and disability insurance trust fund
What future for social security? M. C. Bernstein. New Repub 152:9-11 Ja 9 '65

OLD airplanes

Collectors and collecting

See Airplanes—Collectors and collecting

OLD and country tale; story. See Schoonover, S. W.

OLD automobiles. See Automobiles—Collectors and collecting

OLD Believers. See Raskolniks

OLD dancers; story. See Williams, T.

OLD FAITHFUL (geyser) See Geysers

OLD folks at home; story. See Dorman, S.

OLD Glory; drama. See Lowell, R.

OLD Ironsides (ship) See Constitution (frigate)

OLD memory for a new year; story. See McWhirter, M.

OLD Order Amish. See Mennonites

OLD people. See Aged

OLD Pipes and the Dryad; drama. See Thane, A.

OLD PROVIDENCE ISLAND
Coconuts, tourists, and pirate gold; San Andrés and Providencia. B. De Holguín. il Américas 15:39-41 Ap '63

OLD Vic theatre company
Death of a monument. Newsweek 62:60 Jl 1 '63

OLDENBURG, Claes
So they say; interview. por Mlle 57:234-5 Ag '63
about
New works by Oldenburg. M. Kozloff. Nation 198:445-6 Ap 27 '64

OLDENDORPH, O. F.
Pueblo Bonito: the place of the braced-up cliff. il Nat Parks Mag 37:4-7 S '63
Three Turkey House. il Nat Parks Mag 38: 8-9 Ag '64

OLDER, Fremont
My most unforgettable character. B. Bliven. por Read Digest 85:129-33 Ag '64

OLDEST man; story. See Fisher, M. F. K.

OLDEST story ever told; story. See Gary, R.

OLDEST story; story. See Saroyan, W.

OLDFIELD, John J.
Christians and Jews in Spain. America 110: 218-19 F 15 '64

OLDHAM, Esther
Fans of sorrow. Hobbies 68:28-9 Je; 26-8 Jl '63

OLDHAM, J.
Ford transistor ignition system. Electr World 69:46-7+ Ap '63

OLDS, Glenn
Glenn Olds, innovator at Springfield. M. K. Harvey. por Sat R 47:67 F 15 '64

OLEANDERS
Oleander. N. C. Bezona. il Horticulture 41:485 S '63

O'LEARY, James W. and Kramer, P. J.
Root pressure in conifers. bibliog Science 145: 284-5 Jl 17 '64

O'LEARY, Theodore M.
Last time around with Stan. Sports Illus 19: 20-5 O 7 '63

O'LEARY, Tom
Track. Sports Illus 21:46-50+ S 14 '64

O'LEARY, W. A. and Greiff, Victor
How to estimate kilowatts in sewage-digester gas. Am City 78:92-4 Jl '63

OLEFINS
Oxygen atom reactions with condensed olefins. M. D. Scheer and R. Klein. bibliog Science 144:1214 Je 5 '64

OLESKY, Joel F.
Critical one-fifth of a second. Duns R 84:102-4+ D '64

OLFACTORY nerves
Dissociation of olfactory neural response and mucosal potential. T. Shibuya. bibliog il Science 143:1338-40 Mr 20 '64
Olfactory discrimination: electrophysiological spatiotemporal basis. M. M. Mozell. bibliog il Science 143:1336-7 Mr 20 '64
Olfactory epithelium: unitary responses in the tortoise. T. Shibuya and S. Shibuya. bibliog il Science 140:495-6 My 3 '63

OLFACTORY sense. See Smell

OLFSON, Lewy
Canterbury tales; dramatization of poem by G. Chaucer. Plays 22:97-107 My '63
Crowning of King Arthur; dramatization of Morte d'Arthur by T. Malory. Plays 24: 87-96 D '64
Five weeks in a balloon; dramatization of story by J. Verne. Plays 23:87-95 Ap '64
Invisible man; dramatization of story by H. G. Wells. Plays 24:83-93 N '64
Monsieur Beaucaire; dramatization of novel by B. Tarkington. Plays 23:83-94 N '63
Sherlock Holmes and the stockbroker's clerk; dramatization of story by A. C. Doyle. Plays 23:85-95 O '63
Swiss family Robinson; dramatization of story by J. Wyss. Plays 23:85-96 F '64
Wuthering Heights; dramatization of novel by E. Brontë. Plays 24:83-96 O '64
(ed) See Shakespeare, W. Romeo and Juliet
(ed) See Sheridan, R. B. Rivals

OLGYAY, Victor
Climate-balanced house design. Arch Rec 133:7+ mid-My '63

OLIGOCENE period. See Paleontology—Oligocene

OLIN Mathieson chemical corporation
Winchester-Western division
Old gun, new ramrod. il Bsns W p 168-70+ Je 15 '63
OLINDO, Perez Malande
Preparing for tomorrow. Natur Hist 73:60-4 Je '64
OLIPHANT, Patrick Bruce
Down under to Denver. il por Time 84:82-3 S 18 '64
OLIVA, Tony
Man nobody wanted. por Time 83:80 Je 12 '64
Terrific Tony. il pors Ebony 19:36-8+ Ag '64
OLIVE, Lindsay S.
Spore discharge mechanism in basidiomycetes. bibliog Science 146:542-3 O 23 '64
OLIVE oil
Olive oil, for those who prefer its distinctive taste. Consumer Rep 29:342 Jl '64
OLIVE warblers. See Warblers
OLIVER, Edith
Current cinema. New Yorker 39:42 Jl 6; 68 Jl 13; 72 Jl 20 '63; 40:65 Ag 1; 74+ Ag 8; 84-5 Ag 15 '64
Off Broadway. See issues of New Yorker
Theatre (cont) New Yorker 39:90+ My 4 '63
OLIVER, Jack
Earthquake prediction. Science 144:1364-5 Je 12 '64
Geodesy and geophysics. Science 142:1594+ D 20 '63
OLIVER, James A.
Behind New York's window on nature; American museum of natural history. Nat Geog Mag 123:220-59 F '63
OLIVER, Mary
Letter from home; poem. Mlle 59:34 S '64
OLIVER, Revilo Pendleton
Birch view of JFK. Newsweek 63:29-30 F 24 '64
Illinois vs. Oliver. Nat R 16:264 Ap 7 '64
Marxmanship at Illinois. por Time 83:56 Mr 27 '64
Then how about Koch? Nation 198:206-7 Mr 2 '64
OLIVER, Robert T.
Culture and communication; address, August 15, 1963. Vital Speeches 29:721-4 S 15 '63
Education in the year 2,000 A.D; a uniworld university, with local campuses; address, April 10, 1964. Vital Speeches 30:399-401 Ap 15 '64
Mind and language; adddess, October 2, 1964. Vital Speeches 31:22-7 O 15 '64
Speech and the community; address, April 5, 1963. Vital Speeches 29:459-62 My 15 '63
OLIVER! musical comedy. See Musical comedies, revues, etc.—Criticisms, plots, etc.
OLIVER'S snapweed. See Touch-me-nots
OLIVES
Oh is for olives! il McCalls 91:100-2 Ja '64
OLIVETTI
Destiny of dynasties: Fiat buys one-third of Olivetti. il Time 83:106 Ap 17 '64
Don Camillo's heritage. Newsweek 63:66 Ap 6 '64
GE tries for two feet in the door; dickering with Italy's Olivetti for Europe's computer market. Bsns W p 112+ Ag 15 '64
Riding with Fiat; deal with Olivetti. Fortune 70:60+ S '64
Why GE is joining Olivetti; hopes to get European computer market. il Bsns W p 140+ S 12 '64
OLIVETTI Underwood corporation
Switching to a black ribbon; Olivetti Underwood corp. il Bsns W p 178+ O 24 '64
OLIVIER, Charles P.
Path of the March bolide. Sky & Tel 26:263+ N '63
OLIVIER, Georges
Forests of France and the wildlife. il Audubon Mag 66:28-31 Ja '64
OLIVIER, Sir Laurence
Great Sir Laurence; interview, ed. by R. McDowall. pors Life 56:80A-88+ My 1 '64
about
Definitive Moor. por Time 83:80 My 1 '64
In his talent, Shakespeare summoned up . . . K. Tynan. il pors Life 56:101-3 My 1 '64
Letter from London; National theatre production of Othello at Old Vic. M. Panter-Downes. New Yorker 40:98 Je 13 '64
Olivier's Othello, coiling power and wounded majesty. G. Rogoff. por Hi Fi 14:34+ D '64
OLIVIER, Louis J. See Szumlewicz, A. P. jt. auth.
OLIVOS, Sergio Gutierrez-. See Gutierrez-Olivos, S.
OLLAMALITZLI. See Sports—Mexico
OLMI, Ermanno
Interview with Olmi; ed. by G. Bachmann. Nation 198:542-3 My 25 '64
about
Ermanno Olmi: the new Italian films. G. Bachmann. Nation 198:540-2 My 25 '64
Fine Italian hand. S. Kauffmann. New Repub 150:34-6 F 15 '64
OLMSTED, Fred
How to keep the value of your car high! Bet Hom & Gard 41:58-9 S '63
OLMSTED, Frederick Law
He paints with lakes and wooded slopes. J. S. Martin. il por Am Heritage 15:14-19+ O '64
OLNEY, Ross R.
Portrait of an antiquer. Flying 74:32+ Ja '64
World's longest aerial tramway. Pop Sci 183:40-3 Ag '63
OLSEN, Arnold
House prober charges federal paperwork wastes your money; interview. por Nations Bsns 52:84-6+ S '64
OLSEN, Arthur J.
Breaching the wall: the odds grow. N Y Times Mag p 11+ Ag 9 '64
Erhard finally moves toward the summit. N Y Times Mag p20+ My 5 '63
Gaullist Adenauer challenges Erhard. N Y Times Mag p 11+ Jl 26 '64
Herr Bundeskanzler comes to see us. N Y Times Mag p24+ Je 7 '64
Khrushchev's impossible man in Berlin. N Y Times Mag p37+ O 11 '64
Trackdown of the German scientist. N Y Times Mag p30+ S 22 '63
Uneventful day at the Berlin wall. N Y Times Mag p 14-15+ O 20 '63
OLSEN, Charles Oluf
Sonnet to the wilderness. Liv Wildn 85:15 Wint '64
OLSEN, Jack
Very best act in town. Sports Illus 19:20-2+ Jl 29 '63
OLSEN, Jeanne
Variety meats cookbook. Parents Mag 38:81+ F '63
OLSEN, O. Wilford. See Leiby, P. D. jt. auth.
OLSEN, Oscar A.
Keep ahead of the water demand. Am City 79:167-8 S '64
OLSEN, Sidney R.
Records go on a diet. Am City 79:79 Ja '64
OLSON, Bernhard
How prejudice is taught. por Time 81:52 Mr 29 '63
OLSON, Bobo
Fast hands and purple lights. E. Shrake. il Sports Illus 21:30-1 D 7 '64
OLSON, Charles
Poem; After the storm was over. Nation 197:396 D 7 '63
Poem: Gravelly hill. Poetry 103:78-81 O '63
OLSON, Charles J.
Electronics field engineers around the world. Electr World 70:42-3+ S '63
OLSON, Elder
Exposition of the quarrel of the birds; Old story, new hero; Taxco; poems. Poetry 102:317-22 Ag '63
Intelligence and care. R. Hecht. Poetry 104:181-3 Je '64
OLSON, F. C. W. See Dowling, G. B. jt. auth.
OLSON, Freeda
Conservation activities in the elementary school. NEA J 53:37-8 D '64
OLSON, J. Olaf
J. Olaf Olson favors painting from nature; with biographical sketch. il por Am Artist 28:32-3 My '64
OLSON, Robert E.
Vitamin K induced prothrombin formation: antagonism by actinomycin D. bibliog Science 145:926-8 Ag 28 '64; Correction. 147:66 Ja 1 '65
OLSON, Sigurd F.
North to the dwindling caribou; excerpts from Runes of the North. Audubon Mag 65:346-51 N '63
Relics from the rapids. Nat Geog Mag 124:412-35 S '63
Runes of the Far North; excerpts. Am For 69:26-7+ Je '63
OLSON, Ted
Starlings; poem. Atlan 211:130 Ap '63
OLSON, Warren E.
Responsibility: an escape and an approach. Bul Atomic Sci 19:2-6 Mr; 30 Je '63

OLSSON, Karl A.
Outside the camp; excerpt from Passion. Christian Cent 80:264-7 F 27 '63
Sprightly spoofery. Christian Cent 80:1469 N 27 '63

OLTEN, Carol
Ozark frontier trail. Travel 122:31-4 S '64

OLTON, Richard C.
Inexpensive overlay replaces seal coat. Am City 80:76-7 Ja '65

OLYMPIA, Wash.
On a side street in Olympia; Washington's State capitol museum. il Sunset 131:22+ O '63

OLYMPIA press
Stein and Day to publish Olympia press series. Pub W 186:39-40 S 21 '64

OLYMPIC airways. See Airlines—Greece, Modern

OLYMPIC games
Again, the Olympic challenge. A. J. Gould. il Nat Geog Mag 126:488-513 O '64
Baron de Coubertin, indeed! Dr Brookes's proposed revival of Olympic games. Sports Illus 21:16 N 9 '64
Capsule history of the Olympic games. B. Hersh. il Holiday 36:68-75 N '64
Carrying the torch. il Todays Health 42:26-7+ O '64
Girls in the Olympics. L. Smith. il Todays Health 42:28-31+ O '64
Giving the Olympics an anthropological once-over. M. Smith. il Life 57:81-2+ O 23 '64
Glory of the Grecian games. R. Littell. il Read Digest 84:204R-204S+ Ap '64
Manslaughter born of a fixed race. A. Eliot. il Sports Illus 21:104-8+ O 5 '64
Oldest show on earth. J. V. Grombach. il Todays Health 42:20-1+ O '64
Olympic games. il Sports Illus 19:64-5+ O 28; 47-9 N 4 '63
Olympic records, where will they end? B. H. Frisch. il Sci Digest 56:6-14 O '64
Olympic training in southern California. R. Fenton. il Yachting 115:44-5+ Je '64
Olympics: victories vs. values? il Sr Schol 85: 6-7 O 14 '64; Discussion. 85:20 D 9 '64
Our Olympic chances; interview, ed. by H. L. Masin. R. Johnson. Sr Schol 85:54 O 7 '64
Recollections of an Olympic torchbearer. F. Sparks. il Sat R 47:100-3 Mr 14 '64
Speaking out; let's pull out of the Olympics. R. Kahn. Sat Eve Post 237:8+ O 10 '64
Sport is education; excerpts from address, October 28, 1963. R. Maheu. il UNESCO Courier 17:4-9 Ja '64; Reply. D. R. Wills. 17:64-5 Jl '64
Who says you can't win 'em all? U. S. basketball players at Olympics. T. C. Brody. il Sports Illus 20:104-5 Ap 13 '64
Winter warm-up. Sports Illus 19:13 O 28 '63
See also
Pan American games

OLYMPIC games, 1964
Agony and ecstasy. il Newsweek 64:71 N 2 '64
Ah, those Hungarians; 1964 Olympics in Tokyo. Sports Illus 19:10 O 21 '63
Austria: winter Olympics. V. Creed. il Travel 120:44-6 D '63
Avalanche at Innsbruck. il Time 83:62-3 F 14 '64
Bashful barber and a worldly kid from Smoke Rise. H. Horn. il Sports Illus 20: 20-1 F 17 '64
Big spending, mad building; Japan prepares for Olympics. R. P. Martin. il U S News 55: 69-71 D 2 '63
Bob Beattie U.S. Olympic ski coach; Winter Olympics, Innsbruck, Austria. C. S. Wren. il Look 28:80-1 Ja 28 '64
Can we improve our Olympic chances? G. Kaywell. il Dance Mag 37:52-7 N '63
Death on the slopes. il Time 83:50 Ja 31 '64
Dominant swimmer for a dominant country; American swimming team at Olympics. G. S. Brown. il Sports Illus 21:30-3 O 26 '64
Don't sell the U.S. ski team short. Life 56:4 F 21 '64
Doves and gongs of Tokyo. J. Olsen. il Sports Illus 21:34-8+ O 19 '64
Easy row on the road to Japan; Harvard crew. T. C. Brody. il Sports Illus 20:30-1 My 25 '64
Exuberant finish in Tokyo; unforgettable ceremony. J. Underwood. il Sports Illus 21:24-31 N 2 '64
Fast finish; US Winter Olympic team. il Newsweek 63:86-7 F 17 '64
Favorites in Tokyo 1964. Sports Illus 21:64-9 O 5 '64
Flag flies high in Tokyo. il Life 57:74B-84+ O 30 '64
For gold, silver & bronze. il Time 84:94 O 16 '64
For the record; chart of the gold, silver and bronze medal winners of Winter Olympic games in Innsbruck. Sports Illus 20:65 F 17 '64
.4 of a second; micro-measuring the difference between victory and defeat in next month's Olympic Alpine. R. Riger. il Esquire 61:82-7 Ja '64
Fresh start; Japan prepares for the XVIII Olympiad. il Time 84:30 Jl 10 '64
Games at Innsbruck; Tough Americans: winners? U.S. Olympic skiers. il Newsweek 63:72-4 F 3 '64
Gold rush. il Newsweek 64:70+ O 26 '64
Hello! wonderful! the world is one. R. Steinberg. il Reporter 31:26-8 D 31 '64
How they chose the best team of all time; Olympic trials. H. Weiskopf. il Sports Illus 21:58-9 S 14 '64
In and out of a jam; U.S. ski coach B. Beattie. D. Jenkins. il Sports Illus 20:14-19 F 17 '64
Innsbruck's ins and outs. il Newsweek 63:56-7 F 10 '64
International ski scandal; with editorial comment. J. Lovesey. il Sports Illus 19:9, 16-7+ D 16 '63
Kansas boy with a man-size task; 135 athletes compete for 60 positions on the U.S. Olympic track and field team. T. O'Leary. il Sports Illus 21:46-50+ S 14 '64
Kind of special immortality. il Time 84:57-8 O 30 '64
King from the kitchen. il Time 83:84 F 7 '64
Let's boycott the Olympics. M. Whitfield. il Ebony 19:95-6+ Mr '64
Letter from Sendagaya. J. M. Flagler. il New Yorker 40:86+ Ag 15 '64
Lieutenant Pinkerton's week; success of U.S. Olympic team. il Time 84:60 O 23 '64
Lonely champions quest for Olympic gold; America's Olympic torchbearers. R. Daley. il Sat Eve Post 237:66-73 O 10 '64
Medal winners at the Olympics 1964. Sports Illus 21:84-6+ N 2 '64
Music and the Olympics; Tokyo 1964. E. Cunningham. il Mus Am 84:36-7+ D '64
New records set; 1964 Winter Olympics. il Sr Schol 84:19 F 21 '64
News of the Olympics. il Yachting 116:25+ Ag; 23+ S; 30-1+ O; 28-30+ D '64
No snow. Newsweek 63:76 Ja 27 '64
Olympic preview. J. K. Roosevelt. il Yachting 115:41-3 F '64
Olympic report. il Travel 122:66 S '64
Olympic winter in the Tyrol; photographs by D. Kessel with report by R. Terrell. Sports Illus 19:48-57 N 25 '63
Olympics: a comeback for U.S. il U S News 57:53 N 2 '64
Olympics: five for Pheidippides. il Motor B 114:108-9 D '64
Olympics: lots of triumphs, few troubles. il U S News 57:10 O 26 '64
Olympics: myth of the amateur. D. Cort. il Nation 199:157-9 S 28 '64
Opening of the Olympics. J. R. McDermott. il Life 57:76B-80 O 23 '64
Our Olympic chances. G. D. O'Day. il Yachting 115:54-6+ Mr '64; Discussion. 115: 35+ Je '64
Our Olympic chances; interview, ed. by H. L. Masin. R. Johnson. Sr Schol 85:54 O 7 '64
Our underdogs at Innsbruck; Winter Olympics. F. Graham, jr. il Sat Eve Post 237:22-7 F 1 '64
Proud new jazzy age. R. Steinberg. il Sat Eve Post 237:76-8+ O 17 '64
Record wreckers. il Sr Schol 85:18-19 N 4 '64
Russian blades and fast French skis. D. Jenkins. il Sports Illus 20:14-21 F 10 '64
Selecting the Olympic classes. R. N. Bavier, jr. Yachting 115:62-3+ Ap '64
Silver and bronze medals for a golden team triumph; Olympic races. C. Mitchell. Sports Illus 21:54-6 N 9 '64
Snow show goes off in big style. il Life 56: 30-4+ F 14 '64
Somebody's gonna break a record; in Tokyo. il Time 84:61-2 O 23 '64
Sport conquers all; joint North-South Korean team. Newsweek 61:49 My 27 '63
Sporting scene. E. J. Kahn, jr. il New Yorker 40:110+ O 17; 236-8+ O 24; 195-202 O 31 '64
To Tokyo by inches; U.S. Olympic track and field team. J. Underwood. il Sports Illus 21:18-21 S 21 '64
Tokyo games; Orient's first Olympiad. J. Underwood. il Sports Illus 21:34-6+ O 5 '64
Tokyo recessional. Sports Illus 21:13 N 2 '64
Tokyo takes on the Olympics. J. M. Flagler. il Read Digest 85:185-8 Jl '64

OLYMPIC games, 1964—*Continued*
Tokyo, Tokyo, Tokyo; American Olympic team. il Newsweek 64:80 Jl 13 '64
Tokyo's case of Olympic fever. il Newsweek 64:66-8 O 19 '64
Tokyo's Olympian remodeling. il Newsweek 61:42-4 Ap 29 '63
Tribulation in Tokyo. Sports Illus 18:12 F 11 '63
Two proper Britishers in a bob; Antony Nash and T. Robin Dixon. il Sports Illus 20:22-3 F 10 '64
Union of two worlds. E. O. Reischauer. il Sports Illus 19:50-4 D 23 '63
We win the five and ten. J. Underwood. il Sports Illus 21:20-31 O 26 '64
Who lost what Olympics? Time 83:66 F 21 '64
Winter Olympics; Innsbruck 1964. F. R. Smith. Sports Illus 19:52 Ag 12 '63
Winter Olympics; symposium. il Sports Illus 20:30-47+ Ja 27 '64
Yen for the games. il Bsns W p40-1 S 26 '64

OLYMPIC games, 1968
Altitude will slow runners in 1968 Olympics. Sci N L 86:377 D 12 '64
Battle in Baden-Baden; IOC meeting. Sports Illus 19:6 S 16 '63
Carrying the torch in '68. Time 82:42 O 25 '63
Highest Olympics. Sports Illus 19:7 N 4 '63
Light (torch division) that failed; Olympic torch from Los Angeles to Detroit by relay of runners. H. Higdon. il Sports Illus 19:47-9 N 4 '63
Two cities battle to host Olympics; Los Angeles and Detroit. il Bsns W p36 F 23 '63

OLYMPIC games, 1972
Portland eyes '72 Olympics. Bsns W p 132 Ap 13 '63

OLYMPIC NATIONAL PARK
Quiet day in the cathedral forest. il Sunset 131:18 Jl '63
Since you last saw Olympic Park. il Sunset 133:25-6 Jl '64
Slightly damp and a little clammy. H. Sutton. il Sat R 46:38-9 N 2 '63

OLYMPIC records. See Sports records

OLYMPIO, Sylvanus E.
President of Togo assassinated. il por Sr Schol 82:17 Ja 30 '63

OMACHI, Akira
Sulfate transport in human red cells: inhibition by some uncouplers of oxidative phosphorylation. bibliog Science 145:1449-50 S 25 '64

OMAHA, Neb.
Rightist binge in Omaha. L. McKie. Christian Cent 80:1270-1 O 16 '63

Negroes

Omaha, Nebraska: the new mood shocks the city. S. Castan. il Look 27:38+ D 17 '63

OMAHA BEACH, Battle of. See World war, 1939-1945—Campaigns and battles—Western

O'MALLEY, Walter
Walter hunts in earnest. il pors Sports Illus 21:20-1 Jl 20 '64

O'MALLEY, William J.
Sex and teaching literature in high school. Cath World 199:116-22 My '64

OMAN, Charles
England, Russia, and Virginia; seventeenth-century ties in wood and silver. Antiques 83:317-19 Mr '63

OMAN
See also
United Nations—Oman

OMBUDSMAN. See Administrative remedies

O'MEARA, Andrew P.
Inside story of Panama riots. il U S News 56:50-2 Mr 30 '64

OMEGA aircraft corporation
Production of Omega BS-12-D3S awaits court merger approval. Aviation W 79:108 N 11 '63

OMEGA-minus particles. See Particles (nuclear physics)

OMEGA navigation system. See Electronic aids to navigation

OMELETS
Late-morning breakfast well-done. Vogue 141:64 Mr 15 '63
Look and cook. il Bet Hom & Gard 41:122 Ap '63
Most perfect omelet. il Am Home 66:50-2+ O '63
Ole! omelet; with recipes. il McCalls 91:104-5+ Ag '64
Omelet's infinite variety. C. Claiborne. il N Y Times Mag p53 Je 16 '63

OMELETTES. See Omelets

ON Second avenue; story. See Charyn, J.

ON the D line; story. See Kassan, R.

ON the island; story. See Kazakov, Y.

ON-the-job training. See Employees—Training

ON the night train to Moscow; story. See Blum, R.

ON with the dance; story. See Loeser, K.

ONCE over lightly, and please hush your bazoo; story. See Perelman, S. J.

ONCE upon a weekend; story. See Shyer, M. F.

ONDREJKA, Ronald
Ronald Ondrejka, assistant conductor Buffalo philharmonic, New York. M. Kastendieck. por Mus Am 83:12 My '63

ONE day in the life of Ivan Denisovich; novel. See Solzhenitsyn, A.

ONE day it's different; story. See Stern, R. M.

ONE-day vacations. See Vacations

ONE flew over the cuckoo's nest; drama. See Wasserman, D.

ONE hundred ladies; story. See Cozzens, J. G.

ONE man, one boat, one girl; story. See O'Faolain, S.

ONE month, during the summer; story. See Grove, W.

ONE of a kind; story. Ladies Home J 81:84 N '64

ONE of the dead; story. See Wood, W.

ONE rich friend; story. See Potter, N. A. J.

ONE room apartments. See Apartments

ONE spring morning; story. See O'Connor, E.

110 in the shade; musical comedy. See Musical comedies, revues, etc.—Criticisms, plots, etc.

ONE, two, three, O'Leary; story. See Hamer, M. J.

ONE world government. See International organization

O'NEAL, Denny. See Woods, F. W.

O'NEAL, F. Hodge
Minority owners can avoid squeeze-outs. Harvard Bsns R 41:150-2+ Mr '63

O'NEAL, Frederick Douglas
Actors' new boss. il pors Ebony 19:58-60+ Je '64

O'NEAL, John
Theatre of the meaningful. E. Sutherland. Nation 199:254-6 O 19 '64

O'NEIL, D. Frank
It's up to the undecideds. Nat R 16:193-4 Mr 10 '64

O'NEIL, Paul
Barnum of the space age. Life 55:62-4+ Jl 26 '63
Box; will it revolutionize TV? Life 57:43-4+ Jl 17 '64
Green and fertile field for the Goldwater rush. Life 55:32-3 N 1 '63
In praise of trout and also me. pors Life 56:102-4+ My 8 '64
Keep 'em rolling to the final jam. Life 57:98-100+ N 13 '64
Professor who breaks the bank. Life 56:80-2 Mr 27 '64

about

Attila the Hun in a tattered sweater. G. P. Hunt. por Life 57:3 N 13 '64

O'NEILL, Barbara
I went back to college. por Redbook 122:6+ N '63

O'NEILL, David P.
New Zealand Ombudsman. America 112:166-8 Ja 30 '65
Welfare state in New Zealand. America 110:286-8 F 29 '64

O'NEILL, Elizabeth Stone
Ming jars; poem. Ladies Home J 82:75 Ja '65

O'NEILL, Eugene Gladstone
Desire under the elms. Criticism
America 108:275 F 23 '63
Commonweal 77:543 F 15 '63
Nation 196:106-7 F 2 '63
New Repub 148:26 F 2 '63
Theatre Arts il 47:10-11 F '63
Eugene O'Neill: the tragic in exile. R. Hayes. por Theatre Arts 47:16-17+ O '63
Fledgling O'Neill, tail feathers and all. T. Prideaux. Life 57:8 S 4 '64
Hughie. Criticism
Commonweal 81:518 Ja 15 '65
Nation 200:65 Ja 18 '65
New Yorker 40:58 Ja 2 '65
Newsweek 65:52 Ja 4 '65
Sat R 48:40 Ja 16 '65
Time il 85:53 Ja 1 '65

O'NEILL, Eugene Gladstone—*Continued*
Marco millions. Criticism
America 110:656 My 9 '64
Commonweal 80:89 Ap 10 '64
Nation 198:249-50 Mr 9 '64
New Yorker 40:106+ F 29 '64
Newsweek 63:56 Mr 2 '64
Sat R 47:23 Mr 7 '64
Time 83:61 F 28 '64
Vogue 143:40 Ap 1 '64
More stately mansions. Criticism
Sat R il 47:46 My 30 '64
O'Neill's drama of the psyche. T. P. McDonnell. Cath World 197:120-5 My '63
Strange interlude. Criticism
America 108:594 Ap 20 '63
Commonweal 78:72-3 Ap 12 '63
Nation 196:274-5 Mr 30 '63
New Repub 148:28-9 Mr 30 '63
New Yorker 39:73 Mr 23 '63
Newsweek il 61:97 Mr 25 '63
Sat R 46:36 Mr 30 '63
Theatre Arts il 47:12-13 My '63
Time il 81:74 Mr 22 '63
Strange interlude. C. J. Luten. il Am Rec G 30:578-80 Mr '64

O'NEILL, Gerard K.
Storage rings. bibliog Science 141:679-86 Ag 23 '63

O'NEILL, Hugh Daniel, 3d
Odd man in. il por Newsweek 63:61 Mr 16 '64

O'NEILL, Jeanne Lamb
All that mulch and no petunias. Am Home 67:10 My '64
And one to groan on. Am Home 67:17 S '64
Girl on a gravy train. Am Home 67:12 N '64
Give me ants, lots of ants. Am Home 67:6 Jl '64
Good-bye dolly. Am Home 67:23 D '64
How not to get Santa claustrophobia. Am Home 66:21+ N '63
Live pretty, please. Am Home 66:77-8 D '63
Moving man, I love you. Am Home 67:24-5 Mr '64
Postman never rings, period. Am Home 68:9 Ja '65
Rockabye mommy. Am Home 67:26 O '64
Selling a house female-style. Am Home 67:16+ Ja '64
Start your own Christmas custom. Am Home 66:12 D '63
Wedding presents; what's in and what's out? Am Home 66:17 S '63
Who needs a maid? you do. Am Home 67:6 Ap '64
Who stole the welcome mat? Am Home 67:9 Je '64

O'NEILL, Joseph P.
De Gaulle's visit to Latin America. America 111:507 O 31 '64
Elections in Chile. America 111:226 S 5 '64

O'NEILL, Mary
Mother, child's-eye view; poem. McCalls 91:157 Mr '64

O'NEILL, Michael J.
Debate on birth control. New Repub 151:9 Jl 4 '64
Leukemia breakthrough. McCalls 90:48 Jl '63
What you can do about your aching head. McCalls 90:40 Ap '63

O'NEILL, Patrick. See Abel, R. jt. auth.

O'NEILL-BARNA, Anne
Garland of Irelands. N Y Times Mag p26-7 Mr 15 '64

ONIONS
No tears for South Texas onion. il Bsns W p 108 Mr 30 '63
See also
Cookery—Vegetables

ONISAWA, Jinichi, and Labbe, R. F.
Terminal oxidation in the regulation of heme biosynthesis. bibliog Science 140:1326-7 Je 21 '63

ONLY child. See Children—Only child problem

ONODI, Lajos
Old paprika. Newsweek 65:31-2 F 1 '65

ONONDAGA foundation for medical care. See Medical service

ONOUE, Kaoru, and others
Antigen-binding activity of 6S subunits of β_2-macroglobulin antibody. bibliog Science 146:404-5 O 16 '64

ONTARIO
See also
Bruce Peninsula
Deep River
Lake of the Woods, Minnesota and Canada
Libraries—Ontario
North Channel
Point Pelee National Park
Timmins

Description and travel

Canada's dynamic heartland Ontario. M. W. Campbell. il Nat Geog Mag 124:58-97 Jl '63

Parks and reserves

On the trail of the voyageurs. M. S. Edsall. il Travel 120:42-4 Ag '63
Paul Bunyan moves North. W. Stewart. il Am For 70:54-6 F '64
Walpole Island; Indian reservation. W. Henning. il Travel 120:43-6 Jl '63

Religious institutions and affairs

News of the Christian world (cont) Christian Cent 80:348-50, 1060+; 81:745-6, 946, 1604-5 Mr 13, Ag 28 '63, Je 3, Jl 22, D 23 '64

ONTARIO air service. See Forest fire patrol, Aerial

ONTARIO library association

Intellectual freedom committee

Propaganda and pornography. P. Revell. Library J 88:3562+ O 1 '63

ONTARIO pension plan. See Pensions, Industrial

ONTARIO plan. See Pensions, Industrial

ONTOLOGY
Being and time, by M. Heidegger; tr. by J. Macquarrie and E. Robinson. Review
Christian Cent 79:1482-4 D 5 '62. W. Hordern; Discussion. 80:182-3 F 6 '63

OOCYSTIS. See Algae

OOMURA, Yutaka, and others
Reciprocal activities of the ventromedial and lateral hypothalamic areas of cats. bibliog Science 143:484-5 Ja 31 '64

OORT, Jan H.
Our galaxy: its structure and evolution; summary of address. por Sky & Tel 28:266-7 N '64

OPARIN, Aleksandr Ivanovich
Is magnetism the key to life's origin on earth? J. Lear. Sat R 46:35-8 Jl 6 '63

OPEM, John D.
Reflection of society. por Library J 88:1117-18 Mr 15 '63

OPEN air concerts. See Concerts

OPEN air moving picture theaters. See Moving picture theaters, Open air

OPEN air theater. See Theater, Open air

OPEN and closed shop
Approaches to union security in Switzerland, Canada, and Colombia; excerpt from address. M. Dudra. Mo Labor R 86:136-8 F '63
Blow to union shop. Bsns W p72 F 2 '63
Boeing holding out on union shop issue. Bsns W p54+ Ap 13 '63
Closing the loophole; jurisdiction over right-to-work issues. Time 82:87 D 13 '63
Freedom of association in eight European countries. H. Brickman. bibliog f Mo Labor R 86:1020-5 S '63
From the High court: a boost and a setback for unions. il U S News 54:87-8 Je 17 '63
Impasse at Boeing. America 108:190-1 F 9 '63
Right to work: the test of union strength in Congress; union shop and the closed shop. il U S News 57:70-1 D 21 '64
Sagging union shops; failure to get a union shop at Lockheed. Time 81:80 F 8 '63
Strikers oppose a union shop; Cleveland newspapers. U S News 54:86 F 18 '63
Trouble with the agency. Time 81:91 Je 14 '63
Union setback; legality of agency shop. Newsweek 61:73-4 Je 17 '63
Union shop at Lockheed? L. T. King. Commonweal 77:489-91 F 1 '63
Victory for right to work law: an issue in 1964 campaign? banning of agency shop and union shop. U S News 55:108 D 16 '63
What Boeing and union agreed on; machinists union. U S News 54:96 Ap 29 '63
Where pressure is rising against the union shop. il U S News 54:105-6 Ap 22 '63
Where unions have hit a roadblock. il U S News 54:88-90 F 11 '63

OPEN fires. See Fireplaces

OPEN house; drama. See Martens, A. C.

OPEN market committee. See Federal reserve banks

OPEN-mindedness. See Toleration

OPEN sandwiches. See Cookery

OPEN shop. See Open and closed shop

OPENING night; drama. See Cromwell, J.

OPERA
As if it were a play. S. Wanamaker. il Opera N 28:8-11 Ja 18 '64

OPERA—*Continued*

Fun for the Philistines; theatrical orgies. F. Stevenson. Opera N 29:14-15 D 26 '64

Graziose the grateful; interview, ed. by F. Stevenson. L. Graziose. il Opera N 29:6-7 D 5 '64

I am the savage. G. C. Menotti. il Opera N 28:8-12 F 8 '64

Idyllic retreat. J. W. Freeman. Opera N 28: 24-5 F 8 '64

Most ingenious paradox; Strauss and Hofmannsthal; composer and librettist of Ariadne. J. W. Stedman. il Opera N 27:24-7 F 16 '63

My life in opera. D. A. Markova. il Opera N 28:8-11 D 21 '63

Opera conference in Hamburg; International congress of contemporary music theater. O. Daniel. Sat R 47:40-1 Ag 22 '64

Opera: foreign; principal companies. Mus Am 83:326-9 D '63

Paradox of opera. P. H. Lang. il Theatre Arts 47:10-12 Mr '63

Scrap of paper. J. Ferris. il Opera N 29:6-7 Ja 9 '65

See also

Moving pictures—Musical films

Singers

Television broadcasting—Operas

Anecdotes, facetiae, satire, etc.

Ten nights club. S. Spaeth. il Opera N 28: 6-7 Ap 11 '64

Bibliography

Opera bookshelf. G. Loney. Theatre Arts 47: 7 Mr '63

History and criticism

Bellini and the Sleepwalker. J. A. Boromé. Opera N 27:24-5 Mr 30 '63

Birth of comedy. P. H. Lang. il Opera N 27: 8-11 F 16 '63

Capsule history of opera. W. C. Wright. Holiday 34:82-3 D '63

Chase. J. Kerman. il Opera N 28:8-12 D 28 '63

Englishman looks at opera. M. Tippett. il Opera N 29:6-9 Ja 2 '65

Figaro's forebears. F. Sedwick. Opera N 27: 25-6 Mr 9 '63

Gift for borrowing. O. Lehmann. il Opera N 28:24-5 F 1 '64

His hand on his heart. E. Downes. il Opera N 28:24-6 F 22 '64

Long, twisting road. H. Weinstock. il Opera N 28:8-13 F 29 '64

Measure for measure. J. W. Freeman. il Opera N 27:24-5 Mr 23 '63

Mixed bouquet; Cilèa's Adriana Lecouvreur. J. W. Freeman. il Opera N 27:28-9 F 9 '63

Nothing but contempt; opera-lover scrutinizes opera-haters. J. Gutman. il Opera N 28:8-11 Ap 11 '64

Pastoral tradition. H. Weinstock. il Opera N 27:8-13 Mr 30 '63

Tender irony; Mozart's Figaro. E. Downes. il Opera N 29:24-5 Ja 2 '65

This week at the Metropolitan. Opera N 27:2 F 23 '63

Tristan's children. E. Downes. il Opera N 27:8-12 F 23 '63

Verdi is heard over Wagner's thunder. H. C. Schonberg. il N Y Times Mag p 14-15+ My 19 '63

What makes Samson run. K. McDonald. il Opera N 29:24-5 D 26 '64

Instruction and study

Growing up with opera. R. A. Tuggle. il Opera N 27:32-3 Mr 9 '63

Language

Fitting words; interviews, ed by F. Stevenson. R. Martin and T. Martin. Opera N 27:28 Mr 9 '63

Fledermaus today. H. Dietz. Opera N 27:25 Ap 13 '63

O ciel! J. Ferris. il Opera N 28:6-7 Mr 7 '64

Opera in translation; pro and con discussion. J. Machlis; R. Lawrence. il Mus Am 83:10-11+ N '63

Variations on a Russian verse; three new translations of Eugene Onegin. N. Rosen. il Sat R 47:25-6 N 28 '64; Discussion. 47:17 D 19 '64; 48:37 Ja 23 '65

Where is Russian opera? V. Seroff. il Opera N 27:8-11 Ap 6 '63

Stage scenery

Designed by Eugene Berman. il Theatre Arts 47:13 Mr '63

Franco Zeffirelli: interview, ed. by W. Weaver. F. Zeffirelli. Hi Fi 14:30+ Mr '64

Gentleman of Verona; interview, ed. by F. Stevenson. B. Montresor. il Opera N 28:26 F 8 '64

Man from Milan; interview, ed. by F. Stevenson. A. Colonnello. Opera N 29:14-15 O 17 '64

Metropolitan season; scene and costume sketches in color for 1963-64, with complete roster. Opera N 28:17-20 O 19 '63

Prodigal return; interview, ed. by F. Merkling. E. Berman. Opera N 27:12-13 Mr 23 '63

Sounding the depths; interview, ed. by A. M. Lingg. H. Horner. il Opera N 28:33 Ja 25 '64

Staging Otello. H. Graf. il Opera N 27:8-11 Mr 23 '63

Transformer; interview, ed. by F. Stevenson. O. Messel. Opera N 27:30 F 16 '63

Argentina

Ginastera premiere. E. V. Ferro. il Mus Am 84:30-1 S '64

Austria

Austrian antics. C. N. Welsh. Opera N 28:33 D 28 '63

Tempest in a coffee pot. L. Knessl. Mus Am 84:68-9 Ja '64

Walking conductor; Karajan resigns from Vienna state opera. il Newsweek 63:58 My 25 '64

Belgium

Holland and Belgium. J. Mindszenthy; L. Mueller. il Opera N 27:26 My 4 '63

Canada

Canadian classics. R. Ubriaco. Opera N 29:26 S 28 '63

See also

Canadian opera company

China

See also

Opera, Chinese

Denmark

State of Denmark. S. A. K. Roewade. Opera N 28:31 D 21 '63

Europe

Sight of music. H. C. Schonberg. il Harper 230:110-14 Ja '65

Europe, Eastern

Iron curtains. J. A. Borome. Opera N 28: 30 D 14 '63

Europe, Western

Ahead of spring; ninth opera tour by Mayfair and Swissair. F. Stevenson. Opera N 27:24 My 4 '63

Europe's opera festivals. J. Wechsberg. il Theatre Arts 47:59-61+ Ap '63

France, Germany, Switzerland. D. A. Mackinnon. il Opera N 28:31-2 Mr 7 '64

Opera abroad. J. Ardoin. il Mus Am 84:12-15 S '64

Return to paradise. W. Ducloux. il Opera N 27:8-12 My 4 '63

France

Auric's Wozzeck. Newsweek 62:61 D 16 '63

Coup de disgrâce; Berlioz's Damnation of Faust as choreographed by M. Béjart. il Newsweek 63:51 Mr 30 '64

Defender of the realm. T. McEwen. Opera N 27:30-1 Mr 9 '63

Faustian scandal in Paris; M. Béjart's new production of Berlioz' The damnation of Faust. il Time 83:41 Mr 27 '64

Lulu in the Provinces: premiere at Marseille. E. B. Kohs. il Mus Am 83:270 D '63

Night at the opera. C. Rostand. il Mus Am 84:26-7 Ja '64

Right in the heart of Paris; Maria Callas in Bellini's Norma ends exciting season. il Time 83:69+ Je 26 '64

Spring in Gaul. il Opera N 29:20 S 26 '64

Two premieres. C. Rostand. Mus Am 84:27 S '64

Germany

Germany East and West. J. H. Sutcliffe. il Opera N 29:23-4 S 26 '64

Germany (Democratic Republic)

German diet. D. E. Stevens. Opera N 27:30 F 2 '63

Last week, East Berlin. il Time 81:54 My 17 '63

Midas across the wall; Komische oper. Time 82:70+ O 18 '63

Germany (Federal Republic)

Dedication of the House; opening of the rebuilt Bavarian state opera house. F. Hommel. il Mus Am 84:24-6 Ja '64

OPERA—Germany (Federal Republic)—*Cont.*
Duisburg Foscari. J. H. Sutcliffe. Opera N 28:35 Ja 4 '64
Frankfurt and Munich. D. E. Stevens. il Opera N 27:32 F 16 '63
German caprices. R. Uebel. il Opera N 29: 24 O 17 '64
German mastery. D. A. Mackinnon. il Opera N 28:28 N 16 '63
Modern mothballs; Nestroy's Der zerrissene at Hamburg. H. Joachim. il Mus Am 84:16-17 N '64
To save a mockingbird; Darmstadt, Germany's new discovery. il Time 83:63 Mr 6 '64
View from Germany; symposium. il Opera N 29:30-2 D 12 '64
Yanks in Deutschland. Newsweek 64:118+ O 5 '64
See also
Bayreuth festival

Great Britain
British Isles. F. Aprahamian. il Opera N 29:26 N 14 '64
Callas Tosca. T. Heinitz. Sat R 47:57+ F 29 '64
Covent Garden Ring. M. Cooper. il Mus Am 84:16-17 N '64
Englishman looks at opera. M. Tippett. il Opera N 29:6-9 Ja 2 '65
To the rescue: Maria Callas as Tosca in the Covent Garden revival. M. Cooper. il Mus Am 84:16-17 F '64
See also
Friends of Covent Garden

Italy
Aïda all' americana; La Scala's new production. il Time 81:41 My 3 '63
Blat and Bardolino; La Scala opera in Moscow. Newsweek 64:78+ S 21 '64
La capanna dello Zio Tom. il Time 81:39-40 Mr 22 '63
Halftone crisis; La Scala opera company. Time 81:60 F 8 '63
Italian spring. G. Fitzgerald. il Opera N 28:22-3 S 28 '63
Italian temper. F. Soprano. Opera N 28:33-4 Mr 21 '64
Italian treasures. F. Soprano. Opera N 27:25 My 4 '63
Italy high and low. F. Soprano. il Opera N 27:34 Mr 9 '63
Pair for Pietro. M. Mila. Mus Am 84:18 F '64

Japan
Italians in Nippon; Lirica italiana. B. E. Martin. Opera N 28:33 Ja 4 '64
Nipponese notes. B. E. Martin. il Opera N 27: 33 Ap 13 '63

Latin America
Premiere on the plata. G. Knepler. il Opera N 29:29 D 26 '64

Mexico
International opera season. L. Erick. Mus Am 84:19 N '64

Netherlands
Holland and Belgium. J. Mindszenthy; L. Mueller. il Opera N 27:26 My 4 '63

Peru
First new-world opera; La púrpura de la rosa. R. Stevenson. il Américas 16:33-5 Ja '64

Russia
Berlin and Munich; visit by Moscow's second opera company. J. H. Sutcliffe; E. D. Echols. il Opera N 29:30-1 Ja 2 '65
Bolshoi in Milan. il Time 84:93 N 13 '64
Great opera houses: the Bolshoi. J. A. Boromé. il Opera N 28:26-31 F 29 '64
Ivan in Milan; Bolshoi opera company at La Scala. Newsweek 64:91 N 9 '64
Moscow in Milan; Bolshoi opera co. W. Weaver. il Opera N 29:28 Ja 2 '65
See also
Opera, Russian

South Africa
Transvaal tunes. S. R. Karnovsky. il Opera N 28:23 S 28 '63

Sweden
Northern exposure; interview, ed. by A. M. Lingg. G. Gentele. Opera N 29:13 Ja 30 '65

United States
Cinderella of the opera. W. Terry. il Opera N 27:8-13 Ap 13 '63
Curtain up for fall's travel tempo. J. H. Winchester. il Travel 120:41-4 O '63
Dutchman arrives. A. M. Lingg. il Opera N 27:24-6 F 2 '63
Great adventure; opera at Indiana university. J. Ardoin. il Mus Am 84:15-17 Ap '64
Growing up with opera. R. A. Tuggle. il Opera N 27:32-3 Mr 9 '63
Mascagni vs. America. P. P. Kies. il Opera N 28:24-6 Ap 11 '64
Meanwhile, back at the ranch. D. Gillis. il Opera N 28:8-11 F 22 '64
Metropolitan spring tour, 1964. Opera N 28: 35 F 29 '64
Metropolitan spring tour, 1963. Opera N 27: inside back cover Mr 2 '63
Noisy bantling in old New York: early Verdi productions in the New World. S. Fleming. il Hi Fi 13:82-9 O '63
Opera for the ears alone; concert performances. A. Rich. il Mus Am 84:10-11+ N '64
Opera in New York. See issues of Musical America
Opera is recreation. il Recreation 57:451+ N '64
Opera: U.S; list of opera producing groups. Mus Am 83:325-6 D '63
Reviews: opera at the Metropolitan (title varies) il Mus Am 83:31-2 N; 250+ D '63; 84:37-40 Ja; 31-2 Mr; 42-5 Ap; 38 Jl '64
Singers' opera; Metropolitan repertory. J. Gutman. il Opera N 27:8-12 Mr 2 '63
Smug dowager. B. Boretz. Nation 198:563-4 Je 1 '64
Spring tour casts. Opera N 27:32-3 Mr 30 '63; 28:32 Mr 28 '64
Stars over Texas. R. L. Davis. il Opera N 29:12-15 N 14 '64
Texas roundup. J. Rosenfield. il Theatre Arts 47:23+ Mr '63
U.S. calendar (cont) Opera N 28:30-1 S 28; 34 O 19; 36 N 16 '63; 29:30-1 S 26; 28 O 17 '64
U.S. calendar: on and off campus. R. D. Daniels. Opera N 29:35 D 12 '64
U.S. opera survey: a matter of distribution. F. Merkling. il Opera N 29:21-3 N 14 '64
U.S. opera survey: second circuit. F. Merkling. il Opera N 28:23-5 N 16 '63
See also
American opera society
Baltimore civic opera
Boston opera group, incorporated
Central City opera association, Colorado
Chicago opera company
Cincinnati summer opera association
Community opera, incorporated, New York
Dallas civic opera company
Goldovsky grand opera theater
Lyric opera of Chicago
Metropolitan opera company
Metropolitan opera guild
Metropolitan opera national company
New York city opera company
Opera guilds
Philadelphia lyric opera
San Francisco opera company
Santa Fe opera association
Television broadcasting—Operas

History
Mimi arrives. A. M. Lingg. il Opera N 28: 12-13 Mr 14 '64
Yankee diva: Lillian Nordica and the golden days of opera, by I. Glackens. Review Hobbies 68:31+ F '64. A. Favia-Artsay

OPERA, American
C major chord: a dialogue with H. Hanson; interview, ed. by J. W. Freeman. il Opera N 28:8-12 N 16 '63
Crucible. W. Sargeant. il Am Rec G 29:508-9+ Mr '63
Mona's master. R. Korn. il Opera N 28:6-7 Ja 11 '64

OPERA, Chinese
Behind the mask; Festival of modern Peking opera. il Newsweek 64:47 Ag 10 '64
Letter from Paris; Opéra de Pékin, or L'ensemble artistique de la république de Chine at Théâtre Alhambra. Genêt. New Yorker 40:158-9 Mr 21 '64

OPERA, Czech
Whole man from Moravia; with discography. R. Silverberg. Hi Fi 13:55-7+ Mr '63

OPERA, French
Reprieve for Massenet. R. Lawrence. il Hi Fi 14:47-9+ Mr '64

OPERA, German
Class of 1813: reflections on Verdi vs. Wagner. P. J. Pirie. il Hi Fi 13:90-2+ O '63
Weaver of German opera. R. Eyer. il Opera N 27:8-13 F 2 '63

OPERA, Italian
Serious Rossini. F. Toye. il Opera N 27:8-12 Mr 9 '63
Verdi anniversary issue; symposium. il Hi Fi 13:10+ O '63
Verdi I know; ed. by A. M. Lingg. G. Solti. il Opera N 28:8-11 D 7 '63
Well-versed librettist. M. J. Matz. il Opera N 27:12-13 Mr 16 '63

OPÉRA, Paris. See Opera houses

OPERA, Russian
Long, twisting road. H. Weinstock. il Opera N 28:8-13 F 29 '64
Professor Borodin's indulgence; Prince Igor, with discography. D. Lloyd-Jones. il Hi Fi 13:28-31+ Je '63
Where is Russian opera? V. Seroff. il Opera N 27:8-11 Ap 6 '63

OPERA, Spanish
New Marina in stereo. J. Maclain. il Am Rec G 30:572-3 Mr '64

OPERA and state. See Music and state

OPERA audiences. See Audiences

OPERA ballet. See Ballet

OPERA broadcasts. See Radio broadcasting—Music

OPERA conducting. See Conducting (music)

OPERA films. See Moving pictures—Musical films

OPERA for children. See Music for children

OPERA guilds
Affiliated guilds report. il Opera N 28:6-7 Mr 28 '64
Circus in San Francisco; with photographs by C. M. Jones. Opera N 28:12-13 D 7 '63
Rose from the South; opera in Mobile. A. M. Lingg. il Opera N 29:12-14 S 26 '64
See also
Metropolitan opera guild

OPERA houses
Canopy of color; new ceiling for the Paris Opéra. il Time 84:78-9 N 6 '64
Chagall at the Paris Opéra; unveils a new ceiling. F. Merkling. il Opera N 29:8-12 D 26 '64
Charming folly restored; Goodspeed opera house, East Haddam, Conn. il Arch Forum 119:102-7 Ag '63
Dedication of the House: opening of the re-built Bavarian state opera house. F. Hommel. il Mus Am 84:24-6 Ja '64
Great opera houses (cont) il Opera N 27:28-31 F 23; 29-31 Mr 23; 28-31 Ap 6; 18-22 My 4; 28:26-9 D 7; 26-8 D 14; 25-9 D 28 '63; 26-31 Ja 25; 28-31 F 1; 26-31 F 29; 16-20 My 2; 29:26-9 D 12 '64; 28-33 Ja 9; 28-32 Ja 30 '65
Joys of intermission; Munich's reconstructed National theater. il Time 82:102 D 6 '63
Madrid's real problem; Royal theater undergoing repairs. il Opera N 28:29-30 Mr 7 '64
Marc Chagall's big year; stained-glass window in the United Nations Secretariat building and ceiling for the Paris Opéra. il Life 57:70-7 D 4 '64
Monte-Carlo opéra; photographs. H. Wild. Hi Fi 14:72-3 N '64
Munich renascence. D. A. Mackinnon. il Opera N 28:32-3 Ja 18 '64
Rebirth of a relic; Goodspeed opera house. il Newsweek 62:60 Jl 1 '63
Sight of music. H. C. Schonberg. il Harper 230:110-114 Ja '65
See also
Bayreuth festspielhaus
Metropolitan opera house, New York

OPERA singers. See Singers

OPERA society of Washington
Capital Abduction. F. C. Smith. Opera N 28:32 Mr 7 '64
Much ado in D.C. F. C. Smith. il Opera N 29:21 O 17 '64

OPERA tours
Ahead of spring; ninth opera tour by Mayfair and Swissair. F. Stevenson. Opera N 27:24 My 4 '63

OPERA translation. See Opera—Language

OPERACIÓN Ayacucho. See Military maneuvers

OPERAS
Lost inquiry. C. G. Burke. il Hi Fi 13:54-6+ F '63
Miscellaneous mayhem. M. E. Geib. il Opera N 28:24-6 Ja 18 '64
Opera as theater. Q. Eaton. Opera N 28:7 Ja 4 '64
See also
Gilbert and Sullivan operas
Phonograph records—Operas

Criticisms, plots, etc.
See name of composer for full entry
Adriana Lecouvreur. F. Cilèa
Aïda. G. Verdi
Amelia goes to the ball. G. C. Menotti
Amore dei tre re. See Love of three kings, below
Andrea Chénier. U. Giordano
L'ange de feu. See Angel of fire, below
Angel of fire. S. S. Prokof'ev
Ariadne auf Naxos. R. Strauss
Ballad of Baby Doe. D. S. Moore
Barber of Seville. G. Rossini
Il barbiere di Siviglia. See Barber of Seville, above
Benvenuto Cellini. H. Berlioz
La Bohème. G. Puccini
Boris Godunov. M. P. Musorgskii
Capana dello zio Tom. See Uncle Tom's hut, below
Carmen. G. Bizet
Cavalleria rusticana. P. Mascagni
Les contes d'Hoffmann. See Tales of Hoffmann, below
Coronation of Poppea. C. Monteverdi
Crucible. R. Ward
Cunning little vixen. L. Janáček
Damnation of Faust. H. Berlioz
Daphne. R. Strauss
Le dernier sauvage. See Last savage, below
Dialogues of the Carmelites. F. Poulenc
Don Carlo. G. Verdi
Don Giovanni. J. C. W. A. Mozart
Don Pasquale. G. Donizetti
Don Rodrigo. A. Ginastera
I due Foscari. G. Verdi
Electronic love. J. Kosma
Elektra. R. Strauss
Eugene Onegin. P. I. Tchaikovsky
Falstaff. G. Verdi
Faust. C. F. Gounod
Fidelio. L. van Beethoven
Die fledermaus. J. Strauss
Der fliegende Holländer. See Flying Dutchman, below
Flying Dutchman. R. Wagner
La forza del destino. G. Verdi
Die frau ohne schatten. R. Strauss
Gentlemen, be seated! J. Moross
Gianni Schicchi. G. Puccini
Götterdämmerung. R. Wagner
Guglielmo Tell. G. A. Rossini
Halka. S. Moniuszko
Hanging judge. N. Lockwood
L'incoronazione di Poppea. See Coronation of Poppea, above
Intermezzo. R. Strauss
Jeanne d'Arc au bûcher. A. Honegger
La Juive. F. Halévy
Katerine Ismailova. D. Shostakovich
Khovanshchina. M. P. Musorgskii
Labyrinth. G. C. Menotti
Last savage. G. C. Menotti
Lohengrin. R. Wagner
Long Christmas dinner. P. Hindemith
Love of three kings. I. Montemezzi
Lucia di Lammermoor. G. Donizetti
Lulu. A. Berg
Macbeth. G. Verdi
Madeleine. V. Herbert
Magic flute. J. C. W. A. Mozart
Mahagonny. K. Weill
Manon. J. E. F. Massenet
Maria di Rohan. G. Donizetti
Marriage of Figaro. J. C. W. A. Mozart
Martin's lie. G. C. Menotti
Medium. G. C. Menotti
Merry Mount. H. Hanson
Midsummer night's dream. B. Britten
Mona. H. Parker
Natalia Petrovna. L. Hoiby
Neues vom Tage. See News of the day, below
News of the day. P. Hindemith
Nightingale. I. F. Stravinsky
Norma. V. Bellini
Nose. D. Shostakovich
Le nozze di Figaro. See Marriage of Figaro, above
Otello. G. Verdi
Otello. G. Rossini
Our man in Havana. G. Greene
Pagliacci. R. Leoncavallo
Palestrina. H. Pfitzner
Parsifal. R. Wagner
Pelléas and Mélisande. C. Debussy
I Puritani. V. Bellini
Rake's progress. I. Stravinsky
Rienzi. R. Wagner
Rigoletto. G. Verdi
Der Rosenkavalier. R. Strauss
Sacco and Vanzetti. M. Blitzstein
Samson and Delilah. C. Saint-Saëns
Siegfried. R. Wagner
Simon Boccanegra. G. Verdi
La sonnambula. V. Bellini
Suor Angelica. G. Puccini

OPERAS—Criticisms, plots, etc.—*Continued*
Susannah. C. Floyd
Il tabarro. G. Puccini
Tales of Hoffmann. J. Offenbach
Tannhäuser. R. Wagner
Three against Christmas. A. Imbrie
Tosca. G. Puccini
La Traviata. G. Verdi
Tristan und Isolde. R. Wagner
Il Trovatore. G. Verdi
Tsar and carpenter. A. Lortzing
Turandot. G. Puccini
Uncle Tom. See Uncle Tom's hut, below
Uncle Tom's hut. L. F. Trecate
Vanessa. S. Barber
Die Walküre. R. Wagner
Wise woman and the king. C. Orff
Wozzeck. A. Berg
Zar und zimmerman. See Tsar and carpenter, above
Zio Tom. See Uncle Tom's hut, above

OPERATIC acting. See Acting

OPERATIC composition. See Composition (music)

OPERATIC costume. See Costume, Theatrical

OPERATIC festivals. See Music festivals

OPERATIC production
Abraham and Rigoletto; opera extras. L. Shulman. Opera N 28:6 F 22 '64
Adversaries of the Don; photographs. Opera N 28:21-3 D 28 '63
As if it were a play. S. Wanamaker. il Opera N 28:8-11 Ja 18 '64
Biblical drama; photographs of Samson and Delilah. Opera N 29:21-3 D 26 '64
Bride & groom; photographs of Marriage of Figaro. Opera N 29:21-3 Ja 2 '65
Bride of Lammermoor; photographs of Metropolitan production. Opera N 29:21-2 D 5 '64
Bringing him back alive; photographs of Last savage. Opera N 28:21-3 F 8 '64
City Center; success story. I. Kolodin. il Theatre Arts 47:17-19+ Mr '63
Day of the crisis; switch from Der fliegende Holländer to Ariadne auf Naxos. il Theatre Arts 47:24+ Mr '63
Determined lady; interview, ed. by A. M. Lingg. M. Wallmann. il Opera N 29:14-15 O 17 '64
Doge of Genoa: photographs of Simon Boccanegra. Opera N 29:21-3 Ja 30 '65
Ever free; photographs of La Traviata. Opera N 28:21-3 Ja 11 '64
Falstaff takes shape; photographs. Opera N 28:32-3 F 22 '64
Fat knight; photographs of Metropolitan Falstaff. Opera N 28:21-3 Mr 21 '64
Father's love; photographs of Rigoletto. Opera N 29:21-3 D 12 '64
Fun for all; Last savage. New Yorker 39:24-5 F 1 '64
Golden light; photographs of Metropolitan's Tristan und Isolde. Opera N 27:22-3 F 23 '63
Happy days; photographs of Fledermaus. Opera N 27:22-4 Ap 13 '63
High order of talent; Metropolitan's production of Bernstein-Zeffirelli Falstaff. M. Mayer. il Opera N 28:6-15 Mr 21 '64
Highest power; photographs of Boris Godunov. Opera N 27:22-4 Ap 6 '63
Imaginary Cyprus; photographs of Otello. Opera N 27:22-3 Mr 23 '63
In shining armor; photographs of Lohengrin. Opera N 28:21-3 F 1 '64
Jester; photographs of Rigoletto. Opera N 28:21-3 F 22 '64
Labyrinth on NBC-TV; photographs. Opera N 27:32 Ap 13 '63
Lady of the camellias; photographs. Opera N 27:22-4 Mr 16 '63
Leopard; interview, ed. by W. Hanson. L. Visconti. Opera N 28:16-18 S 28 '63
Life of pleasure; photographs of Manon. Opera N 28:21-3 D 21 '63
Living figures. P. Hall. il Opera N 29:6-9 N 14 '64
Lonely monarch; photographs of Don Carlo. Opera N 28:21-3 Mr 7 '64
Love or duty; photographs of Aïda. Opera N 28:21-3 D 7 '63
Manon reaches the boards; Metropolitan's new production. F. Stevenson. il Opera N 28:24-7 D 21 '63
Marguerite saved; photographs of Metropolitan Faust. Opera N 28:21-3 Ja 4 '64
Merry wives; photographs of Metropolitan Falstaff. Opera N 29:21-3 Ja 23 '65
Met's new Aida. N. Merrill. il Mus Am 83:6-9 N '63
Moor of Venice; photographs of Metropolitan production. Opera N 28:21-3 F 15 '64
New kind of event; world premiere of Falstaff, 1892; tr. by M. J. Matz. C. Gatti. Opera N 29:14-15 Ja 23 '65
New look in Valhalla. J. Wechsberg. il Horizon 5:40-5 My '63
Night and day; photographs of the Magic flute. Opera N 28:21-3 Ja 25 '64
Noisy bantling in old New York: early Verdi productions in the New World. S. Fleming. il Hi Fi 13:82-9 O '63
One-woman show; interview, ed. by F. Stevenson. R. Landver. il Opera N 28:26-7 Mr 7 '64
Parallel fury; photographs of Cavalleria rusticana and Pagliacci. Opera N 28:21-3 Ap 11 '64
Princess of Peking; photographs of Metropolitan production of Turandot. Opera N 29:21-3 Ja 16 '65
Rage of Paris; photographs of Cilèa's opera Adriana Lecouvreur. Opera N 27:22-4 F 9 '63
Reign of terror; photographs of Andrea Chénier. Opera N 27:22-4 Mr 2 '63
Return to paradise; opera in Europe. W. Ducloux. il Opera N 27:8-12 My 4 '63
Rhine journey; photographs of Götterdämmerung. Opera N 28:21-3 D 14 '63
Rose Knight; photographs. Opera N 29:21-3 D 19 '64
Rustic wedding; photographs of La sonnambula. Opera N 27:22-3 Mr 30 '63
Seconding the motion; interview, ed. by A. M. Lingg. N. Merrill. Opera N 28:15 D 7 '63
Skies of Paris; photographs of La Bohème. Opera N 28:21-3 Mr 14 '64
Staging Otello. H. Graf. il Opera N 27:8-11 Mr 23 '63
Stars of May; scenes from World's fair season. il Opera N 28:13-15 My 2 '64
Time is up; photographs of Flying Dutchman. Opera N 27:22-3 F 2 '63
Tolstoy goes to a rehearsal; excerpt from What is art? L. N. Tolstoĭ. Opera N 29:6-7 D 26 '64
Troubadour; photographs of Met's Il Trovatore. Opera N 28:21-3 Ja 18 '64
Truth about Traviata. M. J. Matz. Opera N 28:24-5 Ja 11 '64
Two worlds; photographs of Ariadne auf Naxos. Opera N 27:22-3 F 16 '63
Unequal match; photographs of Don Pasquale. Opera N 29:21-3 Ja 9 '65
Unrequited love; photographs of Metropolitan's Eugene Onegin. Opera N 28:21-3 F 29 '64
Useless precaution; photographs of Barber of Seville. Opera N 27:22-4 Mr 9 '63
Violent dawn; photographs of Tosca. Opera N 28:21-3 Ap 18 '64

OPERATIC societies
U.S. opera survey: second circuit. F. Merkling. il Opera N 28:23-5 N 16 '63

OPERATIC stage directors. See Theatrical directors

OPERATING rooms. See Hospitals—Operating rooms

OPERATION big lift. See Military maneuvers

OPERATION crossroads Africa. See Volunteer service, International

OPERATION niños. See Food relief—Latin America

OPERATION sea orbit. See Naval maneuvers

OPERATIONAL analysis. See Operations research

OPERATIONS, Surgical. See Surgery

OPERATIONS research
ABC's of operations research. il Duns R 82: pt2 104-6+ S '63
British analysis goes deep; Tavistock institute study of automation. il Bsns W p 122+ O 26 '63
'Pattern' planning procedure; Planning assistance through technical evaluation of relevance numbers. P. J. Klass. il Aviation W 81:56-9 D 28 '64; 82-54-5+ Ja 4 '65
Practical slants on operations research. H. M. Wagner. bibliog Harvard Bsns R 41:61-71 My '63
See also
Critical path analysis

OPERON. See Genes

OPHTHALMOLOGISTS
Eye trouble; difference between an ophthalmologist and an optometrist. il Newsweek 64:82 Ag 17 '64

OPHTHALMOLOGY
See also
Ophthalmologists

OPINION, Public. See Public opinion

OPINION, Student. See Student opinion

OPINION research. See Public opinion polls

OPINION research corporation
How the public rates JFK. il Look 27:34 Ag 13 '63
OPINIONS, Personal. See Attitudes
OPITZ, Edmund A.
Catalyst of liberty. Nat R 17:26+ Ja 12 '65
OPIUM trade
Asia
Opium. S. Karnow. il Sat Eve Post 237:80-2 F 22 '64
OPOSSUMS
Nature note. Sci N L 86:302 N 7 '64
Opossum as a player; feigning death. Sci Am 211:64 D '64
Playing possums; excerpt from Gentle people. E. Zistel. il Audubon Mag 66:290-3 S '64
Success story of the opossum. W. J. Hamilton, jr. il Natur Hist 72:16-25 F '63
What good is opossum? W. S. Boardman. Nat Parks Mag 38:19 Je '64
OPPEN, George
Bahamas; poem. New Yorker 39:228 N 16 '63
Building of the skyscraper; poem. Nation 199: 468 D 14 '64
Forms of love; Street; Primitive; Giovanni's Rape of the Sabine women at Wildenstein's; poems. Poetry 104:73-7 My '64
Philai te kou philai; Psalm; poems. Poetry 102:224-7 Jl '63
about
Two poets of New York. G. Cambon. Poetry 102:266-8 Jl '63
OPPENHEIMER, Frank
Mathematics of destruction. Sat R 48:20 Ja 16 '65
OPPENHEIMER, George
Caught between two furies. Sat R 47:46 My 30 '64
Most beautiful girl in the world. Sat R 47:30 My 2 '64
OPPENHEIMER, Harry Frederick
King of diamonds. il por Time 81:76 Mr 1 '63
South Africa's king of diamonds. G. Gaskill. por Read Digest 84:197-8+ My '64
OPPENHEIMER, Jane
Books in review. Natur Hist 74:6+ F '65
OPPENHEIMER, Joan L.
Way the world runs; story. Seventeen 23: 130-1 S '64
OPPENHEIMER, Joel
Mythology; poem. Nation 199:122 S 14 '64
OPPENHEIMER, Julius Robert
Communication and comprehension of scientific knowledge; address, October 23, 1963. Science 142:1143-6 N 29 '63
Inside story on the A-bomb; excerpt from article. por U S News 57:8 D 21 '64
Talk in Chicago; address, June 13, 1963. Bul Atomic Sci 19:4-6 O '63
about
Atomic energy award to Oppenheimer. por Sr Schol 82:19 My 1 '63
Brotherly spirit. il por Newsweek 62:54 D 16 '63
Character speaks out. il por Time 84:70 N 20 '64
Did Stalin understand? Newsweek 64:58 D 14 '64
Doctor Oppenheimer honored. Sci N L 83:243 Ap 20 '63
Fermi prize: J. Robert Oppenheimer named to receive annual AEC award. H. Bethe. por Science 140:161-3 Ap 12 '63
Honors for Oppenheimer; but security cloud remains. il por U S News 55:26 D 16 '63
Notes and comment: Fermi award. New Yorker 39:35 Ap 20 '63
Oppenheimer gets award; Enrico Fermi award. Christian Cent 80:486 Ap 17 '63
Oppenheimer play. Nat R 14:307+ Ap 23 '63
Oppie's comeback. por Newsweek 61:28-9 Ap 15 '63
Provocative pair. Nat R 15:514 D 17 '63
Rehabilitation? Nation 196:317 Ap 20 '63
Robert Oppenheimer. G. W. Johnson. New Repub 148:9-10 Ap 20 '63
Since ten years. Bul Atomic Sci 19:2 My '63
Tangled drama and private hells of two famous scientists. R. Coughlan. il pors Life 55:87A-94+ D 13 '63
Warless world? Sci N L 84:375 D 14 '63
OPPENHEIMER, Monroe
Last train to Zanzibar; story. Redbook 121: 54-5 Jl '63
Period of silence; story. Redbook 123:56-7 S '64
Subject to approval; story. Redbook 120:62-3 F '63
What could anybody say? story. Redbook 122: 64-5 Mr '64
OPPORTUNITY classes. See Special classes and special schools
OPTIC nystagmus. See Nystagmus
OPTICAL art. See Modernism (art)
OPTICAL diffraction velocimeter. See Velocimeters
OPTICAL glass. See Glass, Optical
OPTICAL glass fibers. See Fiber optics
OPTICAL illusions
Aftereffect of seen motion with a stabilized retinal image. R. W. Sekuler and L. Ganz. bibliog il Science 139:419-20 F 1 '63
Cultural differences in the perception of geometric illusions. M. H. Segall and others. bibliog il Science 139:769-71 F 22 '63; Reply with rejoinder. H. H. Spitz. 140:422+ Ap 26 '63
Distance perception in darkness. L. G. Bilderback and others. il Science 145:294-5 Jl 17 '64
Illusion of movement. P. A. Kolers. il Sci Am 211:98-106 O '64
Illusions you can use. il Sci Digest 55:14 My '64
It isn't the heat; it's midsummer science; excerpts from Penguin science survey A 1963. S. Tolansky. il Sat R 46:41-3 Ag 3 '63
Luminous figures: factors affecting the reporting of disappearances. J. R. Schuck and others. bibliog il Science 146:1598-9 D 18 '64
Luminous figures: influence of point of fixation on their disappearance. J. T. Hart. bibliog il Science 143:1193-4 Mr 13 '64
Optical illusions fool some, sometimes. Sci N L 83:162 Mr 16 '63
White is bigger to whites. E. Mirel. Sci N L 84:229 O 12 '63
OPTICAL instruments
Spiders out of business in today's rocket age. Sci N L 83:296 My 11 '63
See also
Astronomical instruments
Bausch and Lomb, incorporated
Measuring instruments, Optical
Schlieren apparatus
Telescope
OPTICAL masers. See Light amplifiers
OPTICAL modulators. See Modulators
OPTICAL reading machines. See Reading machines
OPTICAL scanners. See Reading machines
OPTICAL stimulus. See Stimulus and response
OPTICAL transistor. See Transistors
OPTICS
Optics, an action program; report on symposium held at 49th annual meeting of the Optical society of America. V. Williams. Science 146:1606+ D 18 '64
Optics; the science of sight and light. il Sci Digest 56:90-1 O '64
Rheo-optics of polymers; report on conference. R. S. Stein. Science 144:1252-3 Je 5 '64
Variety of techniques holds promise. C. D. LaFond and R. Pay. il Miss & Roc 15:31-2+ O 5 '64
See also
Diffraction
Fiber optics
Interference (light)
Photographic optics
Spectrum analysis
OPTICS, Physiological
See also
Optical illusions
OPTIMISM
Word. V. P. McCorry. America 109:468-9 O 19 '63
OPTIONS, Stock purchase. See Stock purchase options
OPTOMETRISTS
Eye trouble; difference between an opthalmologist and an optometrist. il Newsweek 64:82 Ag 17 '64
OPUS Dei
Spain: the big change is yet to come. New Repub 149:8-10 O 19 '63
ORABILEX
Another drug inquiry. Newsweek 63:57 F 24 '64
ORACION, Levi V.
Best of all worlds. por Library J 88:1118-20 Mr 15 '63
ORAL cancer. See Cancer
ORAL history recordings. See Tape recordings
ORAL hygiene. See Mouth hygiene
ORAL vaccines. See Poliomyelitis—Vaccines
ORANGE, A.
Communications in unusual media. Science 147:181-2 Ja 8 '65

ORANGE, N.J.

Negroes

Where a state is breaking up the neighborhood schools. il U S News 55:64-5 Ag 19 '63

ORANGE bowl parade. See Miami, Fla.—Parades

ORANGE trees

Get the most from your orange tree. E. McDonald. il Pop Gard 15:38 Ja '64

ORANGES

Orange squeeze; damage caused by cold. il Time 81:73 Mr 1 '63

Squeeze play; Hale Indian River orange groves. H. Sutton. Sat R 47:25-6 F 8 '64

ORANGUTANS

Borneo baby ring busted. Sci Digest 54:35 O '63

Notes and comment; mother ape and baby at Central park zoo. New Yorker 39:33 Ap 27 '63

Orang-utan, by B. Harrison. Review

Sci Digest il 54:38 S '63. D. Cohen

Wild men of Borneo; efforts to save orangutans from extinction. Newsweek 63:47 Je 1 '64

ORANS, Muriel

Fill your house with geraniums. Pop Gard 15:21+ N '64

ORANS, Tung

Modeled children. Commentary 36:330-1; 37:18 O '63, Mr '64

ORATORIOS

Four Messiahs. M. Bernheimer. Sat R 47: 71 Ja 11 '64

Meaning of the rats; R. Gerhard's The plague. Time 83:80 Ap 10 '64

See also

Phonograph records—Oratorios

ORATORY

See also

Public speaking

Anecdotes, facetiae, satire, etc.

I am a vegetarian! (cheers) C. W. Morton il Atlan 214:118+ D '64

ORATORY, Campaign. See Campaign oratory

ORBELO, William R.

Colt conversion revolvers. Hobbies 68:125 D '63

Colt new model police pistol. Hobbies 69:127 My '64

Colt Peacemaker. Hobbies 68:115 Ag '63

Committee of safety musket in the American revolution. Hobbies 68:117+ Je '63

Hints for the proper care and cleaning of antique firearms. Hobbies 69:125+ S '64

Remington double derringer. Hobbies 68:113 Mr '63

Remington zigzag derringer. Hobbies 68:123 O '63

Samuel Colt and his revolver. Hobbies 68:113 Ap '63

Sharps pepperbox pistol. Hobbies 68:113 My '63

Smith and Wesson model 1½ new issue revolver. Hobbies 69:125 Jl '64

Spencer repeater. Hobbies 68:123 S '63

U.S. percussion pistol, model 1842. Hobbies 69:121 D '64

ORBITAL flight. See Space flight

ORBITAL rendezvous (space flight)

And she didn't say, "my heavens!" J. Lear. Sat R 46:45 Jl 6 '63; Reply with rejoinder. J. Williamson. 46:44 Ag 3 '63

Apollo-type, six-man spacecraft designed to support twenty-four man orbital space station. I. Stone. il Aviation W 79:72-3+ Ag 19 '63

Gemini to be rendezvous proving ground. Aviation W 79:195-6 Jl 22 '63

House unit to probe rendezvous choice. A. P. Alibrando. Aviation W 78:30-1 Ja 28 '63

How Gemini will dock with Agena. Aviation W 78:54 My 13 '63

MSC seen favoring concentric orbit Gemini-Agena rendezvous. J. Mercer. Miss & Roc 15:30+ O 12 '64

New Soviet rendezvous attempt, eight-day flight expected in 1963. A. P. Alibrando. Aviation W 78:33-4 Je 24 '63

Pilot control of rendezvous stressed. R. Pay. Miss & Roc 13:56+ S 30 '63

Single contractor choice planned for integration of Gemini, MOL. Aviation W 80:39 Ap 20 '64

Six rendezvous missions on schedule. il Miss & Roc 14:22-3 Ap 13 '64

Spaceborne radar aimed at rendezvous guidance. M. Getler. il Miss & Roc 12:27-8 F 4 '63

Third manned Gemini will have rendezvous capability. R. Pay. Miss & Roc 15:21 Jl 6 '64

ORBITING astronomical observatory. See Artificial satellites—Astronomical applications

ORBITING geophysical observatory. See Artificial satellites—Astronomical applications

ORBITING solar observatory. See Artificial satellites—Astronomical applications

ORBITING X-ray observatory (proposed) See Artificial satellites—Astronomical applications

ORBITS

See also

Moon—Orbit

ORBITS of artificial satellites. See Artificial satellites—Orbits

ORBITS of communications satellites. See Communications satellites—Orbits

ORCHARD heating. See Frost protection

ORCHARDS. See Fruit trees

ORCHESTRA musicians. See Musicians

ORCHESTRAL conductors. See Conductors (music)

ORCHESTRAL music

See also

Phonograph records—Orchestral music

ORCHESTRAS

Bands of gold; society orchestras of M. Davis and L. Lanin. B. Day. il Sat Eve Post 236: 20, 23-5 Ap 20 '63

Embarrassment of riches; London's five symphony orchestras. Time 83:112 Ap 17 '64

Lists: international reference guide. Mus Am 83:242-62 Ja; 306-25 D '63

Men in the pit. A. M. Lingg. il Opera N 27: 28-31 Mr 16; 29-30 Mr 30; 26-9 Ap 13 '63

Montreal symphony: no more Hussars. E. McLean. il Mus Am 83:22-3 S '63

Moscow music; Moscow chamber orchestra. il Newsweek 62:77 N 11 '63

Orchestral variations. B. Boretz. Nation 199: 342-4 N 9 '64

Orchestras (cont of) Orchestral world. See issues of Musical America

Other side; London's symphony orchestras. T. Heinitz. Sat R 47:56 Ap 11 '64

Reviews: orchestras; concerts in New York. il Mus Am 83:32-6 N; 252+ D '63; 84:40-8 Ja; 32-7 Mr; 46-52 Ap; 38-42 My; 41-6 Jl; 48 O; 28-36 N; 119-20+ D '64

Revolt of the brasses. F. Grunfeld. il Reporter 29:48+ Jl 18 '63

Top U.S. orchestras. il Time 81:65 F 22 '63

Well-tempered muzykanty; Moscow chamber orchestra. il Time 82:69 N 22 '63

See also names of orchestras, e.g. Honolulu symphony orchestra

ORCHID cactus. See Epiphyllums

ORCHID houses. See Greenhouses

ORCHIDS

Grow orchids at home, it's easy. Good H 157:169 N '63

Orchid for your window. J. Kramer. il Flower Grower 52:35 Ja '65

Orchid gift in bud or bloom. il Sunset 133: 154+ D '64

Orchids. A. Mifsud. il Horticulture 42:34-5 Jl '64

Orchids lead an indoor outdoor life. J. Kramer il Am Home 67:54-5+ My '64

Orchids under artificial lights. M. A. Reinikka. il Horticulture 42:12-13 Ja '64

Start an orchid collection. H. R. Sweet. il Horticulture 42:36-7+ N '64

Top collector's best blooms. il Life 54:102-6 Ap 19 '63

See also

Ladys slippers

Neill greenhouses, incorporated

ORCHIDS in literature. See Flowers in literature

ORDAZ, Gustavo Díaz. See Díaz Ordaz, G.

ORDEAL of Conrad Pardee; story. See Stafford, J.

ORDER of DeMolay. See DeMolay, Order of

ORDINARY day; story. See Jones, A. E.

ORDMAN, Arnold

New man at NLRB. Newsweek 61:67 My 6 '63

ORDNANCE

Cannon of sterling; miniature guns of British artillery regiment. W. B. Edwards. il Hobbies 68:116-17+ Jl '63

ORDNANCE research

Martin-Orlando begins operation of unique armament research facility. il Miss & Roc 15:32-4 D 21 '64

ORDOVICIAN formation. See Geology, Stratigraphic—Ordovician

ORDWAY, Fred

Condensation model producing crystalline or amorphous tetrahedral networks. bibliog Science 143:800-1 F 21 '64

ORE carriers

New life in old ore boats; conversion to barges. Bsns W p 114 Mr 16 '63

ORE deposits
Geothermal brine well: mile-deep drill hole may tap ore-bearing magnetic water and rocks undergoing metamorphism. D. E. White and others. bibliog il Science 139: 919-22 Mr 8 '63
See also
Mines and mineral resources

OREAR, Jay
Safeguarded zonal disarmament. Bul Atomic Sci 19:18-21 F '63

OREGANO
Oregano, a herb that has two roles. G. Iobst. Flower Grower 51:20 Je '64

OREGON
See also
Architecture, Domestic—Oregon
Crater Lake National Park
Fishing—Oregon
Hunting—Oregon
Libraries—Oregon
Music festivals—Oregon
Rogue River
Wallowa Mountains

Description and travel

Loop trip out of Eugene. il Sunset 132:48+ Mr '64
Oregon's Bohemia Mountain mining district. B. Reynolds. il Travel 119:41-5 My '63

Parks and reserves

Champooick then, Champoeg today. il Sunset 131:81 O '63
Ocean camping near Tillamook. il Sunset 130: 51 My '63
View from Battle Rock. il Sunset 131:30 Ag '63
With sails, an outboard, or a paddle. il Sunset 130:72 My '63

Race problems

Race and education. M. A. Talney. Christian Cent 81:1568-70 D 16 '64

Religious institutions and affairs

News of the Christian world (cont) Christian Cent 80:690-2, 987; 81:744 My 22, Ag 7 '63, Je 3 '64

OREGON primary. See Primaries

OREGON primate research center, Beaverton, Ore.
Monkey business in Oregon. J. B. Kemmerer. il Pop Sci 183:60-3 S '63

OREGON state university, Corvallis

Libraries

Oregon plans for expansion; William Jasper Kerr library. W. H. Carlson. il Library J 89:4755-7 D 1 '64

O'REILLY, Jane
Grantsmanship. Mlle 58:90-1+ D '63

O'REILLY, John
Horseshoe pitching. Sports Illus 19:56-60 S 16 '63
Hunting. Sports Illus 20:95-6+ Ap 13 '64
Nature (cont) Sports Illus 19:81-2+ S 23 '63

O'REILLY, Mary Ellen
Lady on a river of rock; ed. by J. O'Reilly. por Sports Illus 19:26+ O 21 '63

O'REILLY, Maureen Buckley
Notes and asides. W. F. Buckley, jr. Nat R 16:681 Ag 11 '64

ORELLANA, R. G. See Thomas, C. A. jt. auth.

ORFF, Carl
On records; Antigonae. J. W. Freeman. Opera N 27:35 F 2 '63
Wise woman and the king. Criticism Time il 85:46 Ja 29 '65

ORGAN
Build-it-yourself organ. il Changing T 18:31 O '64
Considering a home organ? Bet Hom & Gard 42:84 Je '64
Electric organs, home-style. il Changing T 18:45-6 S '64
How to buy an organ. il House & Gard 124: 58+ O '63
How to give pianos and organs the place they deserve. il House & Gard 123:164-7 Ap '63
New voice for Chartres. Time 85:46 Ja 29 '65
Organ kit uses diode switching; electronic organ. il Electr World 72:75 D '64
Organs without pipes; with list of American electric and electronic organs. R. D. Darrell. il Hi Fi 14:27-30+ Jl '64
Theatre organ comes home. il House & Gard 126:20+ D '64
Twin-T oscillators for electronic musical instruments; electronic organs. F. Maynard. il Electr World 71:36-9+ Je '64

ORGAN, Color. See Color organ

ORGAN music
Virgil Fox; interview. ed. by S. Fleming. V. Fox. il Hi Fi 13:30 Ag '63
See also
Phonograph records—Organ music

ORGANELLES
See also
Lysosomes

ORGANIC evolution. See Evolution

ORGANIC solids. See Solids

ORGANISATION de l'armée secrète. See Secret army organization

ORGANISATION de sécurité de l'état. See Secret service—France

ORGANISTS
Musicians and janitors. C. J. McNaspy. America 111:74 Jl 18 '64
See also
Biggs, E. P.

ORGANIZATION for economic cooperation and development
Fifteen nations to exchange shipping information; text of a joint Department of state-Federal maritime commission statement, December 15, 1964. Dept State Bul 52:13 Ja 4 '65
Flexible formula for economic growth; Sweden's decade of progress. il Bsns W p88-9 Jl 6 '63
OECD manpower policy for promoting economic growth; excerpt. Mo Labor R 87: 1033-4 S '64
OECD ministerial council meets at Paris; communique, November 20, 1963. Dept State Bul 49:948-9 D 16 '63
Science and government: OECD ministers for science compare experiences on national policies. E. Langer. Science 142:372-3 O 18 '63
Tourism: it's more than just fun. il U S News 57:92 N 2 '64
Trade negotiations and the OECD; statement, January 31, 1963. C. A. Herter. Dept State Bul 48:298-301 F 25 '63
U.S. welcomes Japanese membership in OECD; message. D. Rusk. Dept State Bul 50:853 Je 1 '64

ORGANIZATION for rehabilitation through training
Developing Africa's human and material resources; address, January 20, 1963. G. M. Williams. Dept State Bul 48:208-11 F 11 '63

ORGANIZATION in industry. See Industrial management and organization

ORGANIZATION of African unity
Addis Ababa charter; with text of charter of the OAU. B. Boutros-Ghali. bibliog f il Int Concil 546:5-62 Ja '64
Devil's advocates. il Time 84:22+ Jl 31 '64
Fixing Humpty Dumpty; OAU meeting in Dar es Salaam. Newsweek 63:46+ F 24 '64
How to keep going; second annual meeting. Time 84:33 Jl 24 '64
Mission to Addis; Tshombe's request for African troops rejected. Time 84:46 S 18 '64
Nyerere cuts loose. il Newsweek 64:34 Ag 3 '64
One of those weeks: emergency gathering to discuss the Congo. Newsweek 64:54+ S 21 '64
OAU commission on Congo talks with department officers; Department statement, with joint press communique, September 23 and September 30, 1964. Dept State Bul 51:553-4 O 19 '64
Our policy toward Africa; address, July 18, 1963. J. W. Fredericks. Dept State Bul 49:284-90 Ag 19 '63; Same. Vital Speeches 29:699-702 S 1 '63
Pan-Africanism comes of age. R. Howe. New Repub 148:15-17 Je 15 '63

ORGANIZATION of American states
Approaching the bridge; Venezuela asks for sanctions against Castro. Newsweek 64:46 Jl 27 '64
Canada and the O.A.S. D. O'Brien. Commonweal 79:71-2 O 11 '63
Case against Castro; excerpts from report of five-nation committee. il U S News 56:59 Mr 9 '64
Castro must go! G. J. Facio. Read Digest 84:109-13 F '64
Communist subversion in the western hemisphere; statement, February 18, 1963. E. M. Martin. Dept State Bul 48:404-12 Mr 18 '63
Coping with Fidel. il Newsweek 64:39 Ag 3 '64
Cuba branded aggressor. Sr Schol 84:16 Mr 13 '64
Culture comes into its own. M. I. Anderson. il Américas 15:2-6 N '63

ORLANS, Harold
Federal expenditures and the quality of education; excerpts from address, March 21, 1963. bibliog Science 142:1625-9 D 27 '63
ORLICH, Francisco J. See Johnson, L. B. jt. auth.
ORLICK, E. M.
Fit to kill. Outdoor Life 134:46-7+ S '64
ORLOV, Vladimir N.
Report on Soviet libraries: a review. Library J 88:724-7 F 15 '63
ORLOVITZ, Gil
Impoverishment; poem. New Repub 148:19 Je 8 '63
about
Homer and the dragon: U.S. poetry before and after the beats. L. Holland. por Américas 16:28-32 Ja '64
ORLOVSKY, Peter
Back on the open road for boys. A. Glaser. il Esquire 60:48-9+ Jl '63
ORMANDY, Eugene
Eugene Ormandy talks to teens. por Seventeen 22:98+ Jl '63
ORMOND, Clyde
Heavy devils of Hell's Canyon. Outdoor Life 133:58-9+ My '64
Moose by the yard. pors Outdoor Life 132:40-3+ Jl '63
Rams were my bugaboo. por Outdoor Life 131:28-9+ F '63
ORMSBEE, Ann
Quandary in the children's room; poem. Wilson Lib Bul 39:167 O '64
ORMSBEE, Richard A. and Weiss, E.
Trachoma agent: glucose utilization by purified suspensions. bibliog Science 142:1077-8 N 22 '63
ORMSBEE, Thomas H.
Antiques; questions & answers. See issues of House & garden
ORMSBY GORE, David, 5th baron Harlech. See Harlech, D. O. G.
ORNAMENTAL cookery. See Cookery, Ornamental
ORNAMENTAL design. See Design, Decorative
ORNAMENTAL gardening. See Topiary work
ORNAMENTAL glass. See Glass, Ornamental
ORNAMENTAL plants. See Plants, Ornamental
ORNAMENTS, Christmas tree. See Christmas decorations
ORNAUER, Richard L.
Along the Trans-Canada highway with boys and station wagon. Redbook 122:60-1+ F '64
ORNE, Jerrold
Consultants' column (cont) Library J 88:1960, 2852 My 15, Ag '63
Newspapers: a regional resource. por Library J 88:1612-14 Ap 15 '63
Transliteration of modern Russian. por Library J 88:4157-60 N 1 '63
USBE story. por Library J 89:803-6 F 15 '64
ORNITHOGALUM umbellatum. See Star of Bethlehem (flower)
ORNITHOLOGY
Institutions of higher learning in the United States offering graduate degrees in ornithology. S. Miller. Audubon Mag 65:62 Ja '63
ORNITZ, Don
Ah, what sights; water sprites! il Life 54:58-67 Ap 26 '63
Color action at noon. il U S Camera 26:44-7+ Ag '63
ORNITZ, Marguerite
Restless eye of Todd Walker. U S Camera 27:46-9+ Ap '64
ORNSTEIN, Jacob
We're breaking the language barrier. Parents Mag 38:58-9+ D '63
OROSZLAN, Stephen, and Rich, M. A.
Human wart virus: in vitro cultivation. bibliog Science 146:531-3 O 23 '64
OROVAN, Mary
Travel & camera. U S Camera 27:26-7 Mr '64
OROVILLE, Calif.
Oroville's Chinese wall. il Sunset 130:44+ F '63
OROWAN, E.
Continental drift and the origin of mountains. bibliog Science 146:1003-10 N 20 '64
ORPHAN for Christmas; story. See Boyd, C.
ORPHANS and orphan asylums
Child-caring institution on the move. H. H. Hollingsworth. bibliog f Ann Am Acad 355:42-8 S '64
Hong Kong heartbeat. R. Emerson. il Travel 122:43-4 O '64
Orphans and the maidens; report from Hiroshima. N. Cousins. il Sat R 47:20-2 Ap 25 '64

ORR, Jack
Bad boys who gave the game a good name. Esquire 59:56+ My '63
ORR, Jocelyn
Hidden menace in nose drops. Todays Health 42:24-5 D '64
ORR, John Boyd, 1st baron Boyd-Orr. See Boyd-Orr, J. B. O.
ORR, Phil C.
Pleistocene chipped stone tool on Santa Rosa Island, California. bibliog Science 143:243-4 Ja 17 '64
ORR, William I.
Exterminate TV sync-bug interference! Pop Electr 19:52-3 Jl '63
Radio marathon broadcasts truth to Cuba! Pop Electr 19:58-9+ Ag '63
Secret tube that changed the war. Pop Electr 20:57-9+ Mr '64
ORRICK, William H. jr
Department supports bill to establish National academy of foreign affairs; statement, April 4, 1963. Dept State Bul 48:623-4 Ap 22 '63
New antitrust chief's goal: more power to police your business; interview. por Nations Bsns 51:38-9+ O '63
What's next in antitrust? interview, ed. by G. R. Rosen. Duns R 83:35-6+ Je '64
about
More power for trustbusters. por Time 82:75 S 6 '63
New trust-buster. por Newsweek 61:80-1 My 27 '63
People of the week. por U S News 54:23 My 27 '63
ORSHEFSKY, Milton
Gone are the pals of yesteryear. Life 54:102 Je 14 '63
Shastri takes over. Life 56:44F Je 12 '64
ÖRSY, Ladislas M.
Collegiality. America 110:760-3 My 30 '64
Looking back at Pope John. America 108:903-5 Je 29 '63
Reform of canon law. America 109:514-17 N 2 '63
ORTEGA, Aristides Martínez
Avant-garde poetry in Panama. Américas 16:12-19 Jl '64
ORTEGA, Matilde de
Andean handicrafts. Américas 15:29-32 Je '63
ORTEGA Y GASSET, José
Truth behind the veil of facts: excerpt from Man and crisis. UNESCO Courier 17:28 My '64
ORTHICON image camera. See Television cameras
ORTHICON pickup tube. See Television cameras
ORTHODONTICS
Better bite for father. il Time 82:45 D 20 '63
ORTHODOX Eastern church
Between Constantinople and Rome. W. A. Visser 't Hooft. Christian Cent 81:1106-8 S 9 '64
Descendant of St Andrew. il Time 83:39 Ja 10 '64
Eastern orthodoxy seen through Protestant eyes. C. S. Calian. Cath World 200:300-6 F '65
Greeks reject another Vatican invitation. Christian Cent 81:956 Jl 29 '64
His Beatitude the President; head of Cyprus' Orthodox church. il Time 84:70+ S 18 '64
Kiss of peace; relations between Rome and Constantinople. il Newsweek 63:76 Ja 20 '64
Orthodox at Rhodes: third Pan-Orthodox conference. M. Rinvolucri. Commonweal 81:502 Ja 15 '65
Orthodoxy; state of the faith. il Time 82:40-9 Jl 5 '63
Patriarch Maximos IV and Vatican council II; interview, ed. by E. Inglessis and E. Inglessis. Maximos IV. Cath World 198:372-9 Mr '64
Rhodes to Rome; conference of the world's fourteen Orthodox churches. il Time 84:100+ N 13 '64
See also
Catholic church—Relations—Orthodox Eastern church
ORTHODOX Eastern church, Russian
At a Russian monastery; Holy Trinity monastery at Zagorsk. C. Stangohr. Commonweal 78:501-3 Ag 23 '63
Baugo and Zagorsk: extremes in encounter. D. W. Brown. Christian Cent 81:52+ Ja 8 '64
Diary of an American Jesuit. W. V. Casey. il America 109:113-17 Ag 3 '63
Fresh persecution in USSR. America 110:212 F 15 '64

ORTHODOX Eastern Church, Russian—*Cont.*
Religion in the Soviet Union. G. Bailey. il Reporter 31:25-8 Jl 16 '64
Russian Christians visit Church of the Brethren. Christian Cent 80:1125 S 18 '63
Toward an American Orthodox church, by A. A. Bogolepov. Review
Christian Cent 81:993 Ag 5 '64. J. S. Romanides
ORTHODOX Eastern church in the United States
Eastern but Western; Church of the Divine Wisdom, Mount Vernon, N.Y. il Time 83:64 My 1 '64
Fourth faith. il Newsweek 64:52 Jl 13 '64
Orthodox: arrival and dialogue. J. S. Romanides. Christian Cent 80:1399-403 N 13 '63
Toward an American Orthodox church, by A. A. Bogolepov. Review
Christian Cent 81:993 Ag 5 '64. J. S. Romanides
ORTHODOX Eastern church in Turkey
Report Turkish pressure on orthodoxy. Christian Cent 81:540-1 Ap 29 '64; Reply. H. Yarrow. 81:911 Jl 15 '64
ORTHOPEDIA
Building a new kind of bone bank; calf cartilage for surgical use, called Boplant. Bsns W p22 Ja 2 '65
Calf bone material used in human grafts; Boplant. il Sci N L 87:39 Ja 16 '65
Calf to man; use of bone from calves. Newsweek 65:55 Ja 11 '65
Help for thalidomide victims; Abteilung 10, West Germany. il Time 81:63-4 Ap 26 '63
Thalidomide babies' care. Sci N L 83:382 Je 15 '63
ORTHWINE, Rudolf
Golden years. por Dance Mag 39:30-1 Ja '65
Much ado chez Serge. Dance Mag 37:25-6 S '63
ORTIZ-PATINO, Jimmy
Double deal for Jimmy. C. Goren. il Sports Illus 21:54 Jl 13 '64
ORTLIEB, Robert
Sculpture of Robert Ortlieb. J. Lovoos. il por Am Artist 27:56-61+ S '63
ORTLOFF, H. Stuart
Important factor in plants: texture. Horticulture 41:82 F '63
ORTMAN, George
Making cheerful symmetry. il por Time 83:76-7 Ap 24 '64
ORTMAN, Wally
Only game in Panguitch, Utah. J. Underwood. il pors Sports Illus 18:56-60+ Mr 4 '63
ORTON, Joe
Entertaining Mr Sloane. Criticism
Vogue 144:112 O 1 '64
ORTON, Samuel Torrey
Reporter at large. C. Tomkins. New Yorker 39:140+ S 14 '63
ORTUÑO, René Barrientos. See Barrientos Ortuño, R.
ORVIETO dominos, Bolsena eels; story. See Stern, R. G.
ORVIK, Nils
Isolating our allies. Reporter 29:32-3 S 12 '63
ORVIS, Charles F, company
Americana of angling; America's oldest maker of fine fishing tackle. H. Blaisdell. il Field & S 69:46-7+ My '64
ORYXES. See Antelopes
OSADA, Toshiko
Richer by the United States. bibliog por Wilson Lib Bul 39:56-8+ S '64
OSAGE, Ark.
Books for Osage: deposits in general store. I. Mothner. il Look 28:60+ Ap 21 '64
OSAKA international festival. See Music festivals—Japan
OSANO, Kenji
Farm boy who's going to town. por Time 83:93-4 Ap 3 '64
OSARA, Nils A.
Visit to FAO. H. Clepper. il pors Am For 70:12-15 Ja '64
OSBORN, Mrs Chase S.
Excerpt from Atlantic union; crucially needed next step toward disarmament. Cong Digest 43:215+ Ag '64
OSBORN, D. Keith
Ring up the curtain on Christmas. Parents Mag 38:65 D '63
—and Knapp, P. P. W.
Touch of reassurance. PTA Mag 58:10-12 bibliog(p35) D '63
OSBORN, Fairfield
Another Noah's ark for New York. N Y Times Mag p24-5+ O 27 '63
Good life in the zoo. Read Digest 82:147-8+ F '63
Long live the wild land. Sat R 46:39+ N 23 '63
OSBORN, Frederick
Human future. por Sci N L 86:54-5+ Jl 25 '64
OSBORN, M. J. and others
Lipopolysaccharide of the gram-negative cell wall. bibliog Science 145:783-9 Ag 21 '64
OSBORN, Margaret
Mystery of Arshile Gorky: a personal account. Art N 61:42-3+ F '63
OSBORN, Mary. See Person, S. jt. auth.
OSBORN, Prime F. 3d
Strengthening America's heritage; address, April 17, 1964. Vital Speeches 30:600-3 Jl 15 '64
OSBORN, Robert
When a golf course turns on you; reproductions of paintings. Sports Illus 21:36-45 Ag 31 '64
about
Time of the assassins. il Time 84:82-5 N 27 '64
OSBORN, Ronald E.
Formula in flux: reformation for the Disciples of Christ? Christian Cent 80:1163-6 S 25 '63
OSBORNE, Charles
Life radio review. Life 57:16 Ag 14 '64
OSBORNE, Conrad L.
Aïda meets the press. Opera N 28:24-5 D 7 '63
. . . And a Samson from Saint-Saëns. Hi Fi 14:66-7 Ja '64
Ariadne auf Naxos, as Strauss heard it just before the bombs fell. Hi Fi 13:72-3 Ag '63
Best grand-opera Carmen on records. Hi Fi 14:63-4 S '64
Collector's Verdi. Hi Fi 13:37-8+ O; 90+ D '63
Excerpts from Die Meistersinger, Schnorr's Hans Sachs. Hi Fi 14:63-4 Je '64
Fidelio pitched for excitement. Hi Fi 14:123-4 O '64
For the first time on records, Siegfried in its entirety. Hi Fi 13:71-2 Ap '63
From 78 to 7.5. Hi Fi 14:50-2+ Mr '64
High fidelity (title varies) (cont) Opera N 27:34 F 2; 35 F 16; 35 Mr 2; 37 Mr 16; 37 Mr 30; 35 Ap 13 '63
Madama Butterfly, a new sound from Rome. Hi Fi 13:69-70 Mr '63
Rake's progress, an opera that insists upon analysis. Hi Fi 15:69-70+ Ja '65
Two new Sir Johns help make a Falstaff year. Hi Fi 14:65-6 Mr '64
Two Rigolettos, with a surprise from Fischer-Dieskau. Hi Fi 14:75-7 D '64
OSBORNE, Douglas
Solving the riddles of Wetherill mesa. pors Nat Geog Mag 125:155-95 F '64
OSBORNE, Ernest G.
Camp for your child. PTA Mag 58:28-30 bibliog(p36) My '64
OSBORNE, John
John Osborne. P. Delvin. por Vogue 143:98-9+ Je '64
Luther. Criticism
America 109:496-7 O 26 '63
Cath World 198:135-6 N '63
Christian Cent 80:1351 O 30 '63
Commonweal 79:103-4 O 18 '63
Nat R 15:446-8+ N 19 '63
Nation 197:245-6 O 19 '63
New Repub 149:28+ O 19 '63
New Yorker 39:133 O 5 '63
Newsweek il 62:96 O 7 '63
Reporter 29:54+ O 24 '63
Sat R 46:30 O 12 '63
Theatre Arts il 47:12-13 D '63
Time 82:63 O 4 '63
Vogue 143:20 Ja 1 '64
Osborne looks forward in anger. C. Hussey. il por N Y Times Mag p71-2+ O 25 '64
OSBORNE, Karl
Bomb range bass. pors Field & S 69:43-5+ S '64
OSBORNE, Lewis D.
Westprint '64; items of book industry interest. Pub W 186:102-4+ Jl 6 '64
OSBORNE, T. Z.
Every detail. Am City 79:110-12 My '64
OSBORNE, Thomas S.
Amateur scientist. Sci Am 209:151-2+ D '63
—and Lunden, A. O.
Seed radiosensitivity: a new constant? bibliog Science 145:710-11 Ag 14 '64
OSCAR III (artificial satellite) See Communications satellites
OSCARS (prizes) See Academy awards (moving pictures)
OSCILLATORS
Accurate audio frequency measurement. A. W. Edwards. il Electr World 70:46-7+ Ag '63

OSCILLATORS—*Continued*
All's quiet on the TV front; phono oscillator. H. G. McEntee. il Pop Sci 182:140-4 Ap '63
Build the Blipper. N. Smith. il Pop Electr 21:51-2 S '64
Build the lamp lighter CPO. R. E. Pafenberg. il Pop Electr 21:55-6 Ag '64
Design of simple Q meter. D. H. Sandrock. il Electr World 72:84-6 S '64
Four-way oscillator. L. E. Byfield. il Pop Electr 20:59 F '64
Light-powered oscillator. C. Henry. il Pop Electr 20:43 Ap '64
Monitor your code. I. C. Chapel. il Pop Electr 18:56-7+ Ap '63
Mysterious walking box. R. L. Clough, jr. il Pop Mech 119:167-8 Mr '63
Report on new V.F.O. il Electr World 69:70-1 Mr '63
Squealer. F. A. Parker. il Pop Electr 19:61-3 O '63
Tone-modulated frequency calibrator; calibration oscillators. R. L. Ives. il Electr World 72:56-7+ O '64
Tune away rock-bound CB receiver. R. L. Winklepleck. il Pop Electr 20:47-50 Ap '64
Twin-T oscillators; design & application. F. Maynard. il Electr World 69:40-1+ My '63
Twin-T oscillators for electronic musical instruments. F. Maynard. il Electr World 71:36-9+ Je '64
OSCILLATORS, Crystal
High-stability crystal frequency standards. I. Math. il Electr World 72:44-5 Ag '64
OSCILLOGRAPHS
Cathode-ray oscilloscopes. E. K. Marrie. il Electr World 70:50-3+ Ag '63
Electronic switch for your oscilloscope. S. E. Bammel. il Electr World 71:38-9+ F '64
Forms of sounds as shown on oscilloscope by roulette figures. G. W. Barton, jr. and S. H. Barton. il Science 142:1455-6 D 13 '63; Reply. B. O. Pyron and F. R. Williamson, jr. 145:72-3 Jl 3 '64
Phase-shift nomogram; measuring Lissajous pattern on oscilloscope. L. W. Brindley. il Electr World 72:31 N '64
Pictures of human sounds aid to deaf children. Sci N L 85:9 Ja 4 '64
Triggered sweep for improving scopes. M. W. Barth. il Electr World 73:71-4 Ja '65
OSCILLOSCOPE cameras. See Cameras
OSCILLOSCOPES. See Oscillographs
OSCODA, Mich.
New campus of three schools to serve grades K-12. il Arch Rec 136:228-9 S '64
OSGOOD, Charles Egerton
Unilateral initiatives: a cynic's view. R. A. Levine; reply. A. I. Waskow. Bul Atomic Sci 19:35 Ap '63
OSGOOD, Esther
Importance of teachers. Sch & Soc 92:241 Sum '64
Independent school in U.S. education. Sch & Soc 91:243-4 Sum '63
OSGOOD, Robert E.
Everybody's A-bomb? New Repub 148:22-3+ F 16 '63
O'SHAY, J. Gallagher
How J. Gallagher O'Shay got the U.S. space program off the ground. J. Beatty, jr. il por Esquire 62:96-8+ O '64
O'SHEA, David
Finding jobs for foreign students. America 108:558-62 Ap 20 '63
O'SHEA, Paul
Ford's wildest Mustang. pors Hot Rod 17:26-9 Je '64
O'SHEA, Tessie
Divine whiff. por Time 83:76-7 Ja 17 '64
Tessie's show. il por Newsweek 62:46-7 D 23 '63
Two ton Tessie; with report by T. Prideaux. pors Life 56:85-6 Ja 24 '64
OSHEROFF, Abe, and Boebel, Jim
Dream in a bean field. Nation 199:514 D 28 '64
OSIER, John
Loners; story. Liv Wildn 85:10-15 Wint '64
Twelve days under Montana's big sky. il por Liv Wildn 84:22-7 Sum '63
OSK, Richard
How to live with animals. Am Home 66:90 N '63
OSKI, Frank A. and others
Erythrocyte acid phosphomonoesterase and glucose-6-phosphate dehydrogenase deficiency in Caucasians. bibliog Science 139:409-11 F 1 '63
OSMAN, Osman Ahmed
Hero of Aswan. il por Fortune 70:61+ Ag '64
OSMAN, Sülün
Greatest con man of all. J. Bryan, 3d. il por Holiday 36:46+ D '64
OSMANTHUS
Tamed holly. G. Taloumis. il Pop Gard 16:8 F '65
OSMIUM
Osmiophilic reagents: new cytochemical principle for light and electron microscopy. J. S. Hanker and others. bibliog il Science 146:1039-43 N 20 '64
Rhenium and osmium abundances in stony meteorites. J. W. Morgan and J. F. Lovering. bibliog il Science 144:835-6 My 15 '64
OSMOSIS
See also
Electroosmosis
OSMOTIC pressure
Turgor pressures in phloem: measurements on hevea latex. B. R. Buttery and S. G. Boatman. bibliog il Science 145:285-6 Jl 17 '64
OSMUNDSEN, John A.
Science looks at Beatlemania. Sci Digest 55:24-6 My '64
OSOBA, David
Immune reactivity in mice thymectomized soon after birth: normal response after pregnancy. bibliog Science 147:298-9 Ja 15 '65
OSPREYS
Senators hear Peterson on osprey decline; summary of address, April 22, 1964. R. T. Peterson. Audubon Mag 66:276-7 S '64
OSSEO, Minn.
Out of the dark. V. Joyner. il Am City 78:111 N '63
OSSERMAN, Elliott F. See Takatsuki, K. jt. auth.
OSSEWARD, John
North Cascades Park; remarks, October 11, 1963. Liv Wildn 85:36 Wint '64
OSSO buco. See Cookery, Italian
OSTAIJEN, Paul van
Autobiography; tr. by H. Van Ameyden Van Duym. Poetry 104:176 Je '64
Gedicht: een schoon gezicht heeft de dagblad-postiche; Avondgeluiden; Berceuse for grown-ups; Gedicht: zon brandt de rozelaar; Oude man; poems with English tr. by H. Van Ameyden Van Duym. Poetry 104:170-5 Je '64
about
Paul Van Ostaijen: an introduction. H. Van Ameyden Van Duym. Poetry 104:177-9 Je '64
OSTBERG, Janet
Driving for skiing. Yachting 115:115-17+ Ja '64
OSTENDORF, Lloyd
Abraham Lincoln signed photographs. Hobbies 67:110-12 F '63
OSTEOCLASTS. See Cells
OSTEOGENIC sarcoma. See Sarcoma
OSTEOMYELITIS
Condition critical: cause unknown. D. Murray. il Todays Health 43:48-9+ Ja '65
OSTER, Gerald
Amateur scientist. Sci Am 211:134-8+ N '64
—and Nishijima, Yasunori
Moiré patterns; with biographical sketches. Sci Am 208:36, 54-63 bibliog(p 192+) My '63
OSTERBERG, Charles, and others
Gamma emitters in marine sediments near the Columbia River. bibliog Science 139:916-17 Mr 8 '63
—See Cutshall, N. jt. auth.
OSTERMAN, Melvin H.
Stiff shot; grand jury investigation. Newsweek 62:35-6 N 18 '63
OSTI, Gian Lupo
Steel company in the world of culture; Italy's Italsider. il por Fortune 68:138-41 O '63
OSTLING, Gosta
Bibliotekstjänst (Library service inc) por Library J 88:4323-5 N 15 '63
OSTRACITOXIN. See Toxins and antitoxins
OSTRACODERMS
Armor-plated and jawless Devonian fish; pteraspid. D. L. Dineley. il Natur Hist 73:48-53 Ag '64
OSTREM, Walter M.
Daring design for a German library. Wilson Lib Bul 38:406-7 Ja '64
OSTROFF, Anthony
Think what's got away. . . R. Creeley. Poetry 102:46-8 Ap '63
OSTROM, G. George
Young mountaineers. Field & S 69:49-51 N '64
O'SULLIVAN, Thomas C. Jr
Disadvantages of reliable inspection. Bul Atomic Sci 19:18-19 Mr '63
Weapons and technology, 1964. bibliog f Cur Hist 47:6-11+ Jl '64

OSUMI, Tamezo
Printed cottons of Java; excerpts from Printed cottons of Asia. Craft Horiz 23:28-32 N '63

OSUNA, Rafael
It was anybody's championship, until a Mexican with a deft touch made it his. W. Bingham. il por Sports Illus 19:22-5 S 16 '63

OSWALD, James R.
Converting your movie projector. U S Camera 26:88-9+ O '63
Do you have compositional horse sense? U S Camera 27:80-1+ N '64

OSWALD, Lee Harvey
Dear Ma; excerpts from letters. por Time 82:13-14 D 20 '63
Lee Oswald's letters to his mother; with footnotes by Mrs Oswald. Esquire 61:67-73+ My '64
Oswald called it my historic diary, and it is. pors Life 57:26-31 Jl 10 '64
Oswald's own story as revealed by his diary; ed. by H. Aynesworth. il por U S News 57:54-60 Jl 13 '64

about

Accused. il por Time 82:27-8 N 29 '63
American condition. Nation 197:425 D 21 '63
Another assassination attempt by Lee Oswald? U S News 55:8 D 16 '63
As Warren inquiry starts: latest on the assassination. il U S News 55:28-30 D 30 '63
Assassin. B. H. Bagdikian. il pors Sat Eve Post 236:22-7 D 14 '63
Assassin: the man held, and killed, for murder. T. Thompson. il pors Life 55:37-9 N 29 '63
Assassination. il pors Newsweek 64:32-40+ O 5 '64
Assassination, as the plot unfolds: case against Oswald; How the President was shot. il pors U S News 55:68-71 D 9 '63
Assassination inquiry: slow, careful. il U S News 56:49 Ja 27 '64
Assassination: the trail to a verdict; with report by G. R. Ford. il Life 57:40-50B O 2 '64
Assessing the blame in the President's death; excerpts from address, December 14, 1963. P. Daniel. U S News 55:73 D 30 '63
Back of the secrecy in the assassination probe. il por U S News 56:52+ F 24 '64
Between two fires. il pors Time 83:16-20 F 14 '64
Big sale; exclusive photos for Life. por Newsweek 63:80 Mr 2 '64
Capture of a killer. il por U S News 55:10 D 2 '63
Did press pressure kill Oswald? reprint. L. Grove. il U S News 56:78-9 Ap 6 '64
Evolution of an assassin. D. Jackson. il pors Life 56:68A-72+ F 21 '64
Friends of Lee Oswald, inc. Nat R 16:183-5 Mr 10 '64
History's jury. il Newsweek 62:25-7 D 16 '63
How could it happen. New Repub 149:6 D 7 '63
Hypothetical case; letter. Nat R 15:515-16 D 17 '63; Discussion. 16:36 Ja 14 '64
In Texas a policeman and an assassin are laid to rest too. T. Thompson. Life 55:52B-52E D 6 '63
JFK's murder: sowers of doubt. il Newsweek 63:22-4 Ap 6 '64
Jumping the gun. il Newsweek 64:50 Jl 13 '64
Justice and Oswald. H. L. Cartwright. Nation 197:inside cover D 21 '63
Killing still mystery. il por Sci N L 86:230 O 10 '64
Lee Oswald's widow tells her story; summary of testimony. M. Oswald. U S News 56:19 F 17 '64
Long vigil. M. Mannes. il Reporter 29:16-17 D 19 '63
Man who killed Kennedy. il Time 82:33A-34 D 6 '63
Man who killed Oswald. il Time 82:34-5 D 6 '63
Man who wanted to kill Nixon. Time 83:21 Je 19 '64
Manchurian candidate in Dallas. R. Condon. Nation 197:449-51 D 28 '63
Marxist marine. il por Newsweek 62:27 D 2 '63
Mother who wants to write. il Time 83:23-4 F 21 '64
New clue in attempt to shoot General Walker. U S News 56:10 Ja 13 '64
Notes and comment. New Yorker 39:45 D 7 '63
Oswald affair. L. Sauvage. Commentary 37:55-65 Mr '64; Discussion. 38:16-17 Jl '64
Oswald and the FBI. H. Fellman. il por Nation 198:86-9 Ja 27 '64
Oswald and the weight of evidence. il Newsweek 62:36+ D 9 '63
Oswald case; Mark Lane's testimony to the Warren commission and letters from Russia on records. J. Diether. Am Rec G 30:1144-5 Ag '64
Oswald in Dallas: a few loose ends. L. Sauvage. il Reporter 30:24-6 Ja 2 '64; Discussion. 30:6+ Ja 30 '64
Oswald in Moscow. P. Johnson. Harper 228:46-50 Ap '64
Oswald killing discussed. Sci N L 84:355 D 7 '63
Oswald; may we have some facts, please? M. Kempton. New Repub 150:13-15 Je 13 '64
Oswald mystery grows deeper and deeper. por U S News 56:45 Mr 30 '64
Our baby. D. Macdonald. New Repub 150:30 Ja 25 '64; Discussion. 150:30 F 8; 29-31 F 29 '64
Plot to clear Lee Oswald. Nat R 16:265 Ap 7 '64
Police in Dallas. New Repub 150:8 Ja 18 '64
Portrait of a psychopath. il pors Newsweek 62:83-4 D 16 '63
Reaction to the Warren commission report. Sr Schol 85:17 O 14 '64
Report from the FBI. il Newsweek 62:19-20 D 23 '63
Sad & solemn duty; commission to investigate the assassination of J. Kennedy. il Time 82:26-7 D 13 '63
Strange world of Lee Oswald: more light on the assassination. il por U S News 55:60-2 D 16 '63
TV sees it now, for seventy hours. il Bsns W p34 N 30 '63
Unraveling the mystery of the assassination of John F. Kennedy; the official story. il pors U S News 57:35-42+ O 5 '64
Untold stories: aftermath of the assassination. il pors U S News 57:58-62 O 12 '64
Verdict: one man alone. il Sr Schol 85:9-10 O 7 '64
Warren commission report. il pors Time 84:45-50 O 2 '64
Warren report; case for the prosecution. M. Kempton. New Repub 151:13-17 O 10 '64; Reply. S. Rifkin. 151:29 O 24 '64
Warren's secret. Nat R 16:265-6 Ap 7 '64
Week in the sun. il Newsweek 63:29 F 24 '64

OSWALD, Lee Harvey, family
Prelude to tragedy; the woman who sheltered Lee Oswald's family tells her story. J. West. Redbook 123:52-3+ Jl '64

OSWALD, Marguerite
Lee Oswald's letters to his mother; with footnotes by Mrs Oswald. por Esquire 61:67-73+ My '64
Mother who wants to write. il por Time 83:23-4 F 21 '64
Others; year after the assassination of President Kennedy. il Time 84:33 N 27 '64
Week in the sun. il por Newsweek 63:29 F 24 '64

OSWALD, Marina
Lee Oswald's widow tells her story; summary of testimony. por U S News 56:19 F 17 '64

about

Between two fires. il pors Time 83:16-20 F 14 '64
Brave little woman. il por Newsweek 63:17 F 17 '64
Others; year after the assassination of President Kennedy. il Time 84:33 N 27 '64
Piece of the action. Newsweek 63:31-2 Mr 9 '64

OSYPOWSKI, Thomas. See Pope, T. jt. auth.

OTELLO; opera. See Rossini, G.

OTELLO; opera. See Verdi, G.

OTEPKA, Otto F.
Big brother is listening. B. H. Bagdikian. il il Sat Eve Post 237:68-70 Je 6 '64
From Washington straight. Cato. Nat R 15:342 O 22 '63
In the bag. por Newsweek 62:36+ N 18 '63
New turmoil over security. il por U S News 55:48 N 25 '63
Security at state. New Repub 149:5 N 23 '63

OTHELLO; drama. See Shakespeare, W.—Plays

OTIS, Alton B. Jr
Build the MPX. Pop Electr 18:63-5 Ap; 69-73+ My '63
Stereo s'lector. Pop Electr 21:73-5 S '64

OTIS, Leon S.
Dissociation and recovery of a response learned under the influence of chlorpromazine or saline. bibliog Science 143:1347-8 Mr 20 '64

OTIS, Mary
Seize the day; dramatization of novel by S. Bellow. Criticism
Commonweal 78:21 Mr 29 '63
OTIS elevator company
Elevating influence. il Time 81:74 Je 28 '63
O'TOOLE, Christopher J.
Do we have Catholic colleges? America 109: 296-8 S 21 '63
O'TOOLE, Peter
Lord Jim in a jungle paradise; ed. by E. Miller. pors Seventeen 23:132-3+ N '64
Redbook dialogue: Peter O'Toole & Rebecca West. por Redbook 122:56-7+ Mr '64
about
Lord Jim. il pors Life 58:85-6 Ja 22 '65
O'Toole of Arabia. T. Armbrister. il pors Sat Eve Post 236:22-6+ Mr 9 '63
O'Toole on the Ould Sod. G. Talese. por Esquire 60:76-8+ Ag '63
O'TOOLE, Thomas
White-collar automation. Reporter 29:24-7 D 5 '63
OTT, Gilbert R.
Underpinnings of the economy are strong; interview. por(p55) U S News 56:58-60 Mr 2 '64
OTT, John Nash
Probing the mysteries of light. R. Dunlop. il pors Todays Health 41:34-9+ Mr '63
OTTAVIANI, Alfredo, cardinal
Cardinal Ottaviani: the bulwark. E.-M. Jung. por(cover) Cath World 199:80-8 My '64
Excess of zeal. America 108:251 F 23 '63; Discussion. 108:400-1 Mr 23 '63
OTTAWA
Canadian center for the performing arts
Performing arts center for an urban redevelopment area. il Arch Rec 136:130-1 D '64
OTTAWA, Ill.
City relights its core area. P. J. Bailey. il Am City 79:113 Ja '64
OTTEN, Alan L. and Seib, C. B.
Kennedy clansman nobody knows. Sat Eve Post 236:69-70 S 7 '63
No-strings aid for the states? Reporter 32: 33-5 Ja 28 '65
Rockefeller's triple-threat brain trust. Harper 227:74-9 Jl '63
OTTERS
Otter frustration. il Read Digest 84:146-7 Je '64
Otter-torium shows otters as eaters. il Pop Mech 120:66 Ag '63
See also
Sea otters
OTTERVIK, Gosta
Big four: university librarianship in Sweden. por Library J 88:4300-5 N 15 '63
Swedish library cooperation. Library J 88:4316-18 N 15 '63
(ed) Swedish libraries. Library J 88:4299-331+ N 15 '63
OTTINGER, Richard L.
Disadvantage of being earnest. Reporter 32: 14 Ja 14 '65
OTTO, archduke of Austria
Archduke replies. Nat R 14:424; 15:33-4 My 21, Jl 16 '63
Czech crucible. Nat R 16:542+ Je 30 '64
Earthbound Messiah. Nat R 16:657-8 Jl 28 '64
about
Hapsburg returns? por Newsweek 61:52 Je 17 '63
Herr doktor. il pors Time 81:34 Je 14 '63
Otto ante portas. E. von Kuehnelt-Leddihn. Nat R 15:184 S 10 '63
OTTO, Celia Jackson
Méridienne. Antiques 83:675-9 Je '63
OTTO, Jim
OO boy! H. L. Masin. por Sr Schol 83:24 O 25 '63
OTTOMANS. See Stools
OTTUM, Bob
Driver in a tight corner. Sports Illus 20:78-80+ Je 1 '64
Fast Fords and a great Scot. Sports Illus 20: 32-5 My 25 '64
Five tall strangers shoot 'em up. Sports Illus 20:12-13 Ja 13 '64
Motor sports (title varies) Sports Illus 20: 52+ F 24; 106-7 Ap 13; 21:88+ S 7; 96-7 S 21; 91+ O 5; 68-9 D 14 '64
OTTUMWA, Ia.
Don't forget the meter shop. J. H. Turner. il Am City 80:82-3 Ja '65
Treating troublesome waters. H. C. Boeke. il Am City 79:100-2 F '64
OTUE, Adaeze
I believe. por Seventeen 22:90-1 My '63

OUCHY, Switzerland
Hotels, restaurants, etc.
My favorite hotel: Beau-Rivage-Palace. J. Wechsberg. il Esquire 60:168-9+ D '63
OUEI, Mimie
Holiday handbook of Chinese cooking. Holiday 33:125-9 F '63
OUELLETTE, Cecil M.
Grand Coulee: monument to an ancient river. Nat Parks Mag 38:12-15 S '64
OUIMET, Francis
Old man brings back a great day. M. Smith. il pors Life 54:35+ Je 21 '63
OULAHAN, Richard
Buzz bombs gave him his break. Life 55:57 N 29 '63
Cleo finally gets here, is she worth $40 million? Life 54:30 Je 21 '63
Cult grew around a many-sided writer. Life 55:69-70+ N 1 '63
Life movie review. Life 56:10 Ap 3; 15 Ap 17; 15 Ap 24; 16 My 1; 12 My 15; 23 Je 5; 14+ Je 19; 57:11 Jl 10; 11 Jl 24; 9 Jl 31; 14 Ag 14; 26 O 2; 19 O 16; 12 O 30; 15 N 13; 10 N 20; 19 N 27; 20 D 11 '64; 58:13 Ja 29 '65
Life TV review. Life 57:13 Ag 28 '64; 58:8+ Ja 22 '65
100 loops 100; thirty-two feet up, no net! Life 54:50-50B Ap 19 '63
Stars fell on Mismaloya. Life 55:69-74+ D 20 '63
Success with 30c to spare. Life 56:115-16 Mr 6 '64
Well-planned Crawford. Life 56:11-12 F 21 '64
—and Thompson, Thomas
And Sinatra tangles with the law. Life 55:93-5 S 27 '63
OUR 49th state; drama. See Fisher, A.
OUR friend the sea; story. See O'Hara, J.
OUR man in Havana; opera. See Greene, G.
OUR revels now are ended; story. See De Vries, P.
OUR working world. See Elkhart, Ind.—Education
OURSLER, Fulton
Law of unselfishness. Read Digest 84:24C F '64
Undelivered letter. Read Digest 84:73-4 Ja '64
OUSLEY, Elmon
Elmon Ousley: teacher of the year. G. Zimmermann. il pors Look 27:98-100 My 7 '63
OUT goes Y.O.U; story. See McLaughlin, M.
OUT hunting; story. See Kazakov, Y.
OUT of darkness; story. See Enright, E.
OUT of the dark; story. See Curtiss, U.
OUTBOARD boating club of America
'62 club of the year: San Leandro. C. Darlington. il Motor B 111:51+ My '63
OBC grows with boating. il Motor B 112:90-1 Ag '63
OUTBOARD marine corporation
Put a motor on a sled, and go! il Bsns W p42-3 Ja 2 '65
OUTBOARD motor boats. See Motor boats, Outboard
OUTBOARD motors. See Gas and oil engines, Outboard
OUTDOOR advertising. See Advertising, Outdoor
OUTDOOR Christmas decorations. See Christmas decorations, Outdoor
OUTDOOR concerts. See Concerts
OUTDOOR cookery. See Cookery, Outdoor
OUTDOOR education
Classrooms as big as all outdoors. A. Brinley. il NEA J 53:44-5+ Ap '64
See also
Camping—Educational aspects
Outward bound schools
OUTDOOR entertaining. See Entertaining
OUTDOOR furniture. See Furniture, Outdoor
OUTDOOR games. See Games
OUTDOOR gymnasiums. See Gymnasiums
OUTDOOR life
Call to action: land for recreation and camping. D. E. Harlow. il Recreation 57: 108-10 Mr '64
Greatest of all outdoors: Canadian wilderness. F. Bodsworth. il Holiday 35:175-82 Ap '64
Robert Kennedy speaks his mind on living outdoors family style. J. E. Roper. il Pop Gard 14:26-9 My '63
Vacation clothes. T. Trueblood. il Field & S 68:24+ Je '63
Vacation fun in national parks. Parents Mag 38:121 My '63
When a man's thoughts are pure. H. Babcock. il Field & S 69:24-6+ D '64

OUTDOOR life—*Continued*
Wonder as you wander. R. E. Carlson. il Recreation 56:272-4 Je '63
See also
Camping
Camps
Hunting
Nature
Sierra club
Tents
Walking
Woodcraft
OUTDOOR lighting. See Lighting, Outdoor
OUTDOOR markets. See Street trades
OUTDOOR meals
Dining chuck wagon style; with recipes. il Pop Gard 14:48 N '63
Family dinner on the patio; menus and recipes. McCalls 90:44+ Je '63
First luncheon outdoors. il Vogue 143:144 Je '64
Food ideas for family travel. Bet Hom & Gard 42:96-7 S '64
From car to picnic site. il Sunset 131:64-8 Ag '63
Lunch in the garden. il McCalls 90:114-15+ Je '63
Make one trip do the work of six. il House B 105:108-11 Je '63
See also
Barbecue cookery
Cookery, Outdoor
Picnics
OUTDOOR moving picture theaters. See Moving picture theaters, Open air
OUTDOOR photography. See Photography
OUTDOOR recreation. See Recreation
OUTDOOR recreation resources review commission. See United States—Outdoor recreation resources review commission
OUTDOOR restaurants. See Restaurants
OUTDOOR rooms
Add a sun deck. il Pop Sci 182:113 Je '63
Add a wood deck to catch the sun. il Pop Gard 15:35-7 My '64
Add the outdoors to an old house. il House B 105:152-3 S '63
Added outdoor living. il Bet Hom & Gard 41:66-7 O '63
Air condition your terrace. il Pop Gard 15:47 My '64
Atrium adds an indoor garden to a northern house. il Arch Rec 133:118-21 mid-My '63
Atrium house. il House B 105:57-79 Ag '63
Back yard magic. D. D. Lonie, jr. il Pop Gard 16:32-3 Ja '65
Bath-and-garden for lounging. il Sunset 133:92+ Jl '64
Beautiful ways to extend your living space. il Am Home 67:42-7 My '64
Big ideas for small patios. il Pop Gard 15: 35-7 Ap '64
Bring it down to a useful level. il House B 105:180-1+ S '63
Build a brick terrace on sand. il Flower Grower 50:36 My '63
Cast your own patio slabs. W. Radcliffe. il Pop Mech 119:164-5 My '63
Deck can change the way you live. il Sunset 130:110-11 Mr '63
Design makes the difference. P. J. Peart. il Pop Gard 15:39-41 Ja '64
Elegant small house doubles its apparent space by a semi-enclosed court. il Arch Rec 133:122-5 mid-My '63
Expansive ranch house forms its own oasis. il Arch Rec 135:76-9 mid-My '64
Five ways to control climate. il Sunset 131: 96 Jl '63
For barbecue fun; build yourself a patio. R. M. Peters. il Pop Gard 14:43-5 Jl '63
From deck to deck to deck, stepping down the hillside. il Sunset 132:66-7 F '64
Garden of ideas in outdoor living. il Sunset 130:100-7 My '63
Garden with a view. il Sunset 130:118-25 Ap '63
Good ideas for your outdoor living room. J. Hand. il Pop Sci 185:110-14 Jl '64
House in the homescape; city gardens; excerpts from Ladies' home journal book of landscaping and outdoor living. R. Pratt. il Ladies Home J 80:103-4 Mr '63
House with a built-in landscape. il House & Gard 125:170-3 My '64
How to expand a too-small patio. J. R. Rebhan. il Pop Gard 14:36-7 F '63
How to perform a miracle in the back yard. D. X. Manners. il House B 105:164-5+ Mr '63
How to rescue land lost on a slope. C. Calkins. il House B 105:174-7+ Ap '63
Indoors and out-of-doors come together in Hawaii. il Sunset 130:108-13 My '63
Island home takes full advantage of the outdoors. il Am Home 67:38-41 Ap '64
Keep cool with landscaping. M. M. Taylor. il Horticulture 41:459 S '63
Live outdoors all year in an indoor-out-door room. il Pop Gard 14:38-48 N '63
Living out-of-doors but under roof. il Sunset 131:121 O '63
On a roof top; deck garden that's completely demountable. il Sunset 130:148-9 Je '63
On deck for wonderful outdoor living; with deck construction sheet. A. C. Borg. il Am Home 66:27-33 Jl '63
Outdoor living at its best, on a level with the house. il House B 106:60+ Ap '64
Outdoor living is definitely in. il Am Home 67:30+ My '64
Patio becomes family room. il Pop Mech 121:144-5 Ap '64
Patio porch. il Pop Mech 121:142 Ap '64
Patios and pavilions are combined for a walled-in city house for a large family. il Arch Rec 135:116-19 mid-My '64
Plan your back-yard garden with your family's needs in mind. T. A. Weston. il Am Home 66:38-43+ Ap '63
Plan your shadows to foil the heat of the sun. il House B 106:108-10 Ja '64
Plant with a view in mind. J. R. Rebhan. il Pop Gard 14:34-5 Ap '63
Planting makes a terrace a garden. B. C. Kilvert, jr. Flower Grower 50:32-3 My '63
Problem: privacy in the home for owners and guests. il Am Home 66:34-5 My '63
Projects you can build and enjoy this summer. il Bet Hom & Gard 42:56-9 Je '64
Really live at home this summer! il Bet Hom & Gard 41:48-61 Je '63
Sophisticated rusticity for country house. il Arch Rec 135:88-91 mid-My '64
Terrace for all seasons. il House & Gard 124:210-15 O '63
They built a perfect patio. il Pop Gard 16: 28-30 F '65
They call it their tea garden terrace. il Sunset 133:160 Jl '64
Think of your garden as an outdoor room. il House B 105:90-5 Je '63
Two outdoor projects to make your summer more successful. D. Jordan. il Bet Hom & Gard 42:48-9 Ag '64
Two-story court forms hub of house for a large family. il Arch Rec 133:74-7 mid-My '63
Use wood rounds to build a terrace. il Bet Hom & Gard 41:51 S '63
Very best in patio privacy. J. Hedrich. il Bet Hom & Gard 42:28 Ap '64
What gravel can do for a terrace. il Bet Hom & Gard 42:102 S '64
When floor level isn't ground level, the cure is a deck. D. X. Manners. il House B 105: 176-7+ S '63
See also
Balconies
Courtyards
Screens (sun)
OUTDOOR stairways. See Stairways
OUTDOOR theater. See Theater, Open air
OUTDRIVES. See Marine engines
OUTER BANKS (Islands)
Booked for travel. T. L. Christie. Sat R 47: 28-9 S 12 '64
Inside the Outer Banks. F. A. Montgomery, jr. il Motor B 111:28-31+ Ap '63
World by the sea. B. Thielen. il Holiday 35: 72-7+ My '64
OUTER MONGOLIA. See Mongolia
OUTER seven (trade area) See European free trade association
OUTLETS, Electric. See Electric wire and wiring
OUTPUT of workers. See Labor productivity
OUTRAM, George, and company, limited
Man who snatched away a meal. Time 84: 36-7 N 6 '64
OUTRAM, Richard
Starlight has entered the giant's eye. . ; poem. Poetry 101:255 Ja '63
OUTSIDER: story. See Wright, B. R.
OUTWARD bound schools
Education: acceptance of responsibility; address, July 16, 1964. C. Pell. Vital Speeches 30:725-7 S 15 '64
Marshmallow becomes a man. il Life 57:58-65 Ag 7 '64
Rugged challenge for teen-agers; Colorado's Outward bound school. L. Lawrence. il Read Digest 82:183-4+ Ap '63
OUYANG, Tsai-wei
Bronze-age treasures discovered in China. Art N 63:40-1 Ja '65

OUZELS. See Dippers (birds)
OVARIES
Enzymatic dissection of the mammalian ovary. H. S. Grob. bibliog il Science 146:73-4 O 2 '64
5-methoxytryptophol: effect on estrus and ovarian weight. W. M. McIsaac and others. bibliog il Science 145:63-4 Je 3 '64
Melatonin, a pineal substance: effect on the rat ovary. R. J. Wurtman and others. bibliog il Science 141:277-8 Jl 19 '63
OVARY, Zoltan, and Taranta, Angelo
Passive cutaneous anaphylaxis with antibody fragments. bibliog Science 140:193-5 Ap 12 '63
OVEN cleaners. See Cleaning compositions
OVEN dinners. See Dinners and dining
OVEN liners. See Protective coatings
OVENS
Bonus benefits of broiler and oven. B. G. Wadsworth. il Parents Mag 39:34 Mr '64
See also
Electronic ovens
OVER-the-counter market. See Stocks—Marketing
OVER-the-horizon radar. See Radar defense network
OVERACHIEVEMENT, Student. See Student achievements
OVERBECK, Pat R.
Three fabulous eaters and how they grew. Parents Mag 39:80+ S '64
OVERBERGER, Charles G.
Nobel award winners announced: chemistry. Science 142:938-9 N 15 '63
—See Vandenberg, E. J. jt. auth.
OVERDUE books. See Libraries—Circulation, loans, etc; Libraries—Fines
OVEREATING. See Eating, Psychology of
OVERHANGS. See Screens (sun)
OVERHEAD projectors. See Projection apparatus
OVERHEAD screens. See Screens (sun)
OVERHOLSER, Winfred
Homosexuality: sin or disease? Christian Cent 80:1099-101 S 11 '63
OVERLAND limited. See Southern Pacific railroad company
OVERMYER, Barbara
Mortgaged wife; poem. Sat R 47:17 D 26 '64
Next to the godly; poem. Harper 227:78 S '63
Piranha: inner city; poem. Christian Cent 80:1234 O 6 '63
OVERNITE transportation company
Not too big, not too small. Bsns W p73-4 Jl 6 '63
OVERPOPULATION. See Population—Overpopulation
OVERSEAS dependents schools. See American schools abroad; Military post schools, American
OVERSEAS press club of America
Mme Nhu comes to town; visit to OPC. Nat R 15:338+ O 22 '63
OVERSTREET, Bonaro W.
Being wise in membership. PTA Mag 58:7-9 S; 18-20 O; 7-9 N; 7-9 D '63; 20-2 Ja; 14-16 F; 24-6 Mr; 24-6 Ap; 24-5 My; 10-11 Je '64
Words that are ours. PTA Mag 59:10-11 Ja '65
—See Overstreet, H. jt. auth.
OVERSTREET, Harry, and Overstreet, B. W.
How to talk about communism (cont) PTA Mag 57:12-14 F; 10-12 Mr; 8-10 Ap; 16-18 My; 8-10 Je '63
Youth is the target. Sr Schol 84:18-20 My 8 '64
OVERTIME
Business is cool to overtime pay plan. Bsns W p76 F 8 '64
Debate about overtime. Time 83:61-2 Ja 24 '64
Fight over double-time pay. U S News 56:88 Mr 2 '64
Jobs and overtime. America 110:135 Ja 25 '64
New push for double overtime pay. U S News 57:62 Ag 3 '64
Overtime crackdown: Rx for unemployment? il Bsns W p99-100 Ja 18 '64
Overtime in midst of job famine. Bsns W p54+ N 2 '63
Overtime-pay plan: ending LBJ's honeymoon with businessmen. U S News 56:113 F 24 '64
Unions mount attack on overtime. Bsns W p64+ Ja 26 '63
Where workers complain about too much pay. il U S News 56:92-3 Ja 27 '64
Why the new worry about overtime. il U S News 56:89-91 Ja 20 '64
OVERTON, Hall
Hall Overton, an important creative voice. A. Cohn. por Am Rec G 30:59 S '63

OVERTURES
See also
Phonograph records—Overtures
OVERWEIGHT. See Corpulence
OVESON, Keith E.
Trapped in Devil's Hole. por Outdoor Life 132:50-1+ S '63
OVIS ammon. See Argali
OWATONNA, Minn.
Concentric-circle design. R. Smith and others. il Am City 78:92-4 Mr '63
How to obtain quality seal coats. R. Pecore. il Am City 79:89-90 Ag '64
Late, late show. R. Pecore. il Am City 78:34 Ap '63
OWEN, Anne G.
North woods ground covers. Horticulture 41:423 Ag '63
OWEN, D. F.
Polymorphism and population density in the African land snail, limicolaria martensiana. Science 140:666-7 My 10 '63
OWEN, David
Fifteen years, anniversary of a resolution. UN Mo Chron 1:78-84 Jl '64
OWEN, Jean Z.
Eighteen checkpoints for your story. Writer 77:11-15 Ap '64
In memory of our marriage; story. Redbook 123:153-80 My '64
Use threefold magic. Writer 77:18-20+ O '64
OWEN, Pat
A. Michelsen Christmas spoons. Hobbies 68:45 D '63
OWEN, Robert
Utopia, limited; excerpt from Vanishing America. W. E. Wilson. il por Am Heritage 15:64-72 O '64
OWEN, Roger
New nations. Commentary 38:71-3 Ag '64
OWEN, Sam
Let's trail'er right. Yachting 115:112-14+ Ja '64
OWEN, W. Boyd
Equal pay for women, one view; summary of statement. U S News 54:100 Ap 8 '63
OWEN, Wilfred
Wilfred Owen. C. Tomlinson. Poetry 104:41-3 Ap '64
OWENS, Cotton
How to build a Grand national stock car racer; ed. by J. Foster. por Hot Rod 16:36-41+ F '63
OWENS, M. F. See Langevin, R. A. jt. auth.
OWENS, Marion
Treasure hunting up North; Aberfoyle flea market. il por Bsns W p 126-7 S 7 '63
OWENS, Patrick J.
Gregory came to town. New Repub 150:10-11 Mr 28 '64
Winthrop Rockefeller against Orval Faubus. New Repub 150:6-7 Ap 25 '64
OWENS VALLEY, Calif.
Alchemy in a wasteland. il Fortune 69:116-17 F '64
Giant playground. C. Phinizy. il Sports Illus 19:28-39 Ag 12 '63
Struggle in Owens Valley; conservation of tule elk. A. A. Amaral. il Am For 70:26-7+ Ag '64
OWER, Bernard A.
Littlest librarian. Library J 89:1514+ Ap 1 '64
OWINGS, Nathaniel
What are they doing to Big Sur? W. Trombley. il Sat Eve Post 237:24-9 F 15 '64
OWL, Grey. See Grey Owl
OWL and the pussycat; drama. See Manhoff, B.
OWLS
Nature note; elf owl. Sci N L 86:399 D 19 '64
Owl exhibit on conservation; great horned owl. C. Stapleton. il Audubon Mag 66:152-3 My '64
Owl in the playpen. B. Gilbert. il Sat Eve Post 237:72+ Jl 11 '64
Owl that stays at home. G. Laycock. il Field & S 69:41+ Jl '64
Owls I have known. W. C. Lammey. il Am For 71:38-40+ Ja '65
OXALIC acid
Growth of oxalic acid single crystals from solution: solvent effects on crystal habit. J. L. Torgesen and J. Strassburger. bibliog il Science 146:53-5 O 2 '64
OXENBURG, Allen Sven
Live wire; interview, ed. by F. Stevenson. Opera N 28:30-1 F 22 '64
about
Faustian firsts. Newsweek 64:82+ D 14 '64

OXFORD, England
Profiles; B. H. Blackwell, ltd. V. Mehta. il New Yorker 40:63-4+ O 31 '64; 87 Ja 9 '65
OXFORD group. See Moral rearmament
OXFORD university
Boola, boola Balliol. Time 82:80-1 Jl 12 '63
Secret of Balliol. P. T. Kimball. il Sat R 46: 37-8+ Ag 17 '63
Why not study abroad? international summer school program. H. McDonnell. il Sr Schol 85:13T Ja 7 '65
Yank returns to Oxford. B. Smith, jr. il Sat Eve Post 236:70+ Mr 23 '63
OXFORD university press
Offices and warehouse for a publisher. il Arch Rec 136:160-1 D '64
Oxford to publish new religious series. Pub W 185:78 F 10 '64
Oxford univ. press (N.Y) establishes export dept. Pub W 186:77 Ag 24 '64
Oxford university press keepsakes designed by John Begg. P. A. Bennett. il Pub W 185:92-5 Ja 6 '64
OXIDASES
Photochemical action spectrum of the terminal oxidase of mixed function oxidase systems. D. Y. Cooper and others. bibliog il Science 147:400-2 Ja 22 '65
OXIDATION, Physiological
Oxidation of extramitochondrial diphosphopyridine nucleotide by various tissues of the mouse. B. Sacktor and A. R. Dick. bibliog il Science 145:606-7 Ag 7 '64
Oxygen uptake from a reservoir of limited volume by the human cornea in vivo. R. M. Hill and I. Fatt. bibliog il Science 142:1295-7 D 6 '63
Participation of an intermediate of oxidative phosphorylation in ion accumulation by mitochondria. G. P. Brierley and others. bibliog il Science 140:60-2 Ap 5 '63
Protein-bound iodine in serum of rats breathing 99 percent oxygen. P. Felig and others. bibliog il Science 145:601 Ag 7 '64
Reduction of dimethylsulfoxide to dimethylsulfide in the cat. V. Distefano and H. H. Borgstedt. bibliog il Science 144:1137-8 My 29 '64
Stoichiometry of hemoglobin reactions. A. Schejter and others. bibliog il Science 141: 784-8 Ag 30 '63
Thyroid hormones: control of terminal oxidation. J. R. Bronk. bibliog il Science 141: 816-18 Ag 30 '63
OXIDATION ponds. See Sewage lagoons
OXIDATION reduction reaction
Anaerobic formate oxidation: a ferredoxin-dependent reaction. W. J. Brill and others. bibliog il Science 144:297-8 Ap 17 '64
Flavin sensitized photoreactions: effects of 3-(p-chlorophenyl)-1,1-dimethylurea. P. Homann and H. Graffron. bibliog il Science 141:905-7 S 6 '63
Magnetite: preferred orientation on the basal plane of partially reduced hematite. R. O. Keeling, jr. and D. A. Wick. bibliog il Science 141:1175-6 S 20 '63
Nitrous oxide produced by the catalytic oxidation of organic nitrogen compounds. J. G. Christian. bibliog il Science 143: 573-4 F 7 '64
Oxygen atom reactions with condensed olefins. M. D. Scheer and R. Klein. bibliog Science 144:1214 Je 5 '64
Radiation-chemical oxidation of peptides in the solid state. W. M. Garrison and others. bibliog il Science 146:250-2 O 9 '64
Reaction of hydrogen with oxygen adsorbed on a platinum catalyst. H. W. Kohn and M. Boudart. bibliog il Science 145:149 Jl 10 '64
Spectra of deoxyenated hemoglobin in the Soret Region. R. Benesch and others. bibliog il Science 144:68-9 Ap 3 '64
Xenic acid: reduction at the dropping-mercury electrode. B. Jaselskis. bibliog il Science 143:1324 Mr 20 '64
Xenon tetroxide: preparation and some properties. H. Selig and others. bibliog il Science 143:1322-3 Mr 20 '64
OXIDATIVE phosphorylation. See Phosphorylation
OXIDES
High-pressure B-type polymorphs of some rare-earth sesquioxides. H. R. Hoekstra and K. A. Gingerich. bibliog il Science 146: 1163-4 N 27 '64
1,4-benzoquinone tetracarboxylic acid dianhydride, $C_{10}O_8$; a strong acceptor. P. R. Hammond. bibliog il Science 142:502 O 25 '63
Plutonium dioxide: preparation of single crystals. K. D. Phipps and D. B. Sullenger. bibliog il Science 145:1048-9 S 4 '64
OXNAM, Garfield Bromley, bp
Bishop Oxnam is gone. Christian Cent 80:388 Mr 27 '63
Methodist whirlwind. por Time 81:82-3 Mr 22 '63
OXYGEN
Artificial inspiration; our dependency of three principle key elements. il Sci Digest 57:86-9 Ja '65
Molecular structure of the synthetic molecular oxygen carrier $O_2IrCl(CO)(P[C_6H_5]_3)_2$. J. A. Ibers and S. J. La Placa. bibliog il Science 145:920-1 Ag 28 '64
Oxygen-carrying properties of a simple synthetic system. L. Vaska. bibliog il Science 140:809-10 My 17 '63
Radiation action on DNA in bacteria: effect of oxygen. E. C. Pollard and P. M. Achey. bibliog il Science 146:71-3 O 2 '64
See also
Ozone
Isotopes
Oxygen isotope fractionation between coexisting calcite and dolomite. J. N. Weber. bibliog il Science 145:1303-5 S 18 '64
Oxygen isotopic composition of some right- and left-coiled foraminifera. A. Longinelli and E. Tongiorgi. il Science 144:1004 My 22 '64
Physiological effects
All-oxygen tests reveal toxicity. il Miss & Roc 13:18 Ag 5 '63
Sodium bicarbonate: increase in survival rate of rats inhaling oxygen. R. S. Matteo and G. G. Nahas. bibliog il Science 141:719-20 Ag 23 '63
Therapeutic applications
See also
High-pressure oxygenation
OXYGEN chambers, High pressure. See High pressure oxygenation
OXYGEN deficiency. See Anoxemia
OXYGEN in the body
Respiration of heart muscle as affected by oxygen tension. W. J. Whalen and J. Fangman. bibliog il Science 141:274-5 Jl 19 '63
OXYGEN process. See Steel metallurgy
OXYTOCIC hormones. See Hormones
OXYTOCIN
Slow labor speeded. F. Marley. Sci N L 86:82 Ag 8 '64
OYMYAKON. See Oimyakon, Russia
OYSTER BAY, N.Y.
Sanitary affairs
We borrowed from the steel industry; incinerator maintenance. V. J. Cerniglia and H. J. Campbell, jr. il Am City 79:89-91 My '64
OYSTER culture
Oysters of Locmariaquer, by E. Clark. Review
New Repub 151:23-4 Ag 8 '64. J. Wain
Newsweek il 64:89 Jl 13 '64
OYSTERS
Aragonite and calcite as constituents of adult oyster shells. H. B. Stenzel. bibliog il Science 142:232-3 O 11 '63
How to shuck an oyster. il Sunset 132:65 Mr '64
If you are timid about oysters raw. Sunset 131:224 N '63
Oysters: composition of the larval shell. H. B. Stenzel. bibliog il Science 145:155-6 Jl 10 '64
See also
Pearls
OYSTERS, Fossil
Ancient oyster shells on the Atlantic continental shelf. A. S. Merrill and others. bibliog il Science 147:398-400 Ja 22 '65
OYSTERS, Pearl. See Pearl fisheries
OZARK chinkapin. See Chestnut trees
OZARK MOUNTAINS
Autumn in the Ozarks. E. Allen. il Holiday 36:30+ N '64
OZARK national forest. See National forests
OZARK NATIONAL SCENIC RIVERWAYS
Ozark National Scenic Riverways in southern Missouri is authorized. il Nat Parks Mag 38:15 O '64
OZAWA, Seiji
Anguish of being young & thin & Japanese. por Time 82:38 Jl 19 '63
ÖZGÜÇ, Tahsin
Assyrian trading outpost. Sci Am 208:96-102+ bibliog(p 185) F '63
OZICK, Cynthia
America aglow. Commentary 38:66-7 Jl '64

OZONE
Ozone damage; protection for plants. J. L. Jones. bibliog il Science 140:1317-18 Je 21 '63; Reply with rejoinder. L. G. Wayne. 142:447 O 25 '63
Ozone: decomposition by ionizing radiation. P. Harteck and others. bibliog il Science 147:393-4 Ja 22 '65
Ozone formation in air exposed to cobalt-60 gamma radiation. Z. I. Kertesz and G. F. Parsons. bibliog il Science 142:1289-90 D 6 '63

OZU, Yasujiro
Family of Ozu. R. Hatch. Nation 198:638-9 Je 22 '64

P

PAA. See Pan American world airways
PAHO. See Pan American health organization
PAIS. See Public affairs information service
PAR (precision approach radar) See Radar (in aviation)
PARC (predator and rodent control) See United States—Fish and wildlife service
PASB. See Pan American sanitary bureau
PATA. See Pacific area travel association
PAU. See Pan American union
PBA. See Professional bowlers association
PERT (program evaluation review technique) See Critical path analysis
PFA IV. See Photography in the fine arts (organization)
PHA. See United States—Public housing administration
PHS. See United States—Public health service
PKU. See Phenylketonuria
PLA (People's liberation army) See China (People's Republic)—Armed forces
POAU. See Protestants and other Americans united for separation of church and state
PPO (polyphene oxide) See Plastics
PRI (Party of the institutional revolution). See Political parties—Mexico
PRSA. See Public relations society of America
P.S. I love you; drama. See Roman, L.
PT boats. See Torpedo boats
PTA. See Parents and teachers associations
PVOR (precision visual omnirange) See Radio aids to aviation
PWP. See Parents without partners, incorporated

PAAR, Jack
Jack of all trades. J. Iams. il pors Sat Eve Post 236:80-3 My 11 '63

PAARLBERG, Don
Problem of surplus; address, October 14, 1963. Vital Speeches 30:152-5 D 15 '63
We may have passed the high tide of government control of the production and pricing of farm products. Suc Farm 61:31 Je '63
Will we return to the free market? Suc Farm 61:45 Je '63

PACE, Eric
Laos: continuing crisis. For Affairs 43:64-74 O '64

PACE, Frank
Moving into action. il por Bsns W p58+ N 28 '64

PACE, Judy
Teen-agers win movie roles. il pors Ebony 18:150-2+ My '63

PACE, Stephen
Change of Pace. H. Crehan. il por Art N 63: 39-41+ Ap '64

PACEM in terris. See Encyclicals
PACEMAKER, Heart. See Medical instruments and apparatus

PACHTER, Henry M.
Popes and Communists. New Repub 148:15-17 Je 22 '63

PACIFARINS
New disease weapon: adjusting to disease-causing bacteria. Sci N L 83:283 My 4 '63

PACIFIC airmotive corporation
PAC receives certification for Tradewind. C. M. Plattner. il Aviation W 78:95+ Ap 29 '63

PACIFIC area travel association
Travel notes. R. Joseph. Esquire 60:25-9 Ag '63

PACIFIC cables. See Cables, Submarine

PACIFIC coast
North from the San Juans. W. Bagley. il Yachting 115:69-71 Je '64
PACIFIC Coast flood. See Floods—United States
PACIFIC Coast shells. See Shells (conchology)
PACIFIC Coast states. See Northwest

PACIFIC countries
Incidentals for Pacific adventures; hotels, restaurants, transportation. Vogue 142:48+ O 15 '63
Pacific adventures; a dictionary from Australia to Zamboanga. S. Rama Rau. il Vogue 142:106-11+ O 15 '63
Pacific/Orient '63: scrutiny of the bounty. R. Joseph. il Esquire 60:42-53 Ag '63
Travel notes. R. Joseph. Esquire 60:25-9 Ag '63
See also
ANZUS council

PACIFIC Crest Trail system
High road to a wild paradise: from Monument 78 to Campo. R. Cantwell. il Sports Illus 19:48-52+ Ag 5 '63
PACIFIC fisheries commission. See International North Pacific fisheries commission

PACIFIC gas and electric company
Bodega: symbol of a national crisis. K. S. Roe. il Am For 69:22-5 D '63
Expand or expire. Time 83:63-4 Ja 10 '64
Gerdes for the battle. Newsweek 62:54-5 Jl 1 '63
Outrage on Bodega Head. G. Marine. il Nation 196:524-7 Je 22 '63; Discussion. 197: 62 Ag 10 '63
PACIFIC ISLANDS. See Islands of the Pacific
PACIFIC ISLANDS, TRUST TERRITORY OF. See Trust Territory of the Pacific Islands
PACIFIC missile range. See Proving grounds
PACIFIC NORTHWEST. See Northwest

PACIFIC NORTHWEST power company
One worth waiting for; proposed dam at Mountain Sheep on the Snake River. il Time 83:88 F 14 '64

PACIFIC OCEAN
Basalts dredged from the northeastern Pacific Ocean. C. G. Engel and A. E. J. Engel. bibliog il Science 140:1321-4 Je 21 '63
Carbonate deposits and paleoclimatic implications in the northeast Pacific Ocean. Y. R. Nayudu. bibliog il Science 146:515-17 O 23 '64
From a peak in Darién: Balboa's discovery 450 years ago. E. B. Roberts. il Américas 15:40-3 S '63
See also
Islands of the Pacific
Oceania
South Sea Islands

PACIFIC school of religion, Berkeley, Calif.
Earl lectures; interdenominational pastoral conference. E. T. Culver. Christian Cent 81:316-18 Mr 4 '64
PACIFIC science center. See Seattle—Pacific science center

PACIFIC Southwest airlines
Pacific Southwest airlines. H. D. Watkins. il Aviation W 79:48-9 Jl 1; 37 Jl 8 '63
PSA slashes fares in West Coast battle. Aviation W 82:34 Ja 11 '65
PACIFIC SOUTHWEST water plan. See Colorado River

PACIFIC telephone and telegraph company
Dial 2122428180. W. Marx. il Nation 197:344-6 N 23 '63
PACIFIC tropical botanical garden. See Botanical gardens
PACIFIC TRUST TERRITORY. See Trust Territory of the Pacific Islands

PACIFICA foundation
Against the bland; licenses of the various Pacifica stations granted. Time 83:56 Ja 31 '64
Artists and bureaucrats. R. Brustein. New Repub 149:36+ N 2 '63
FCC on guard. New Repub 150:5 F 8 '64
Good decision. Nation 198:110 F 3 '64
Goose chase. New Repub 148:4 F 16 '63
Oaths and silence; investigation by Federal communications commission. il Newsweek 62:80 N 25 '63
Open channels. Newsweek 63:75 F 3 '64
Pacifica and the FCC: dangerous precedent; with editorial comment. L. B. Frantz. Nation 197:357, 359-61 N 30 '63

PACIFICI, Sergio
Penalties of Italy's prosperity. Sat R 46: 20-1 Jl 27 '63

PACIFICO, William J.
Mowing responsiblity. por Recreation 57:189 Ap '64

PACIFISM
Christian and nuclear pacifism. J. E. Dougherty. il Cath World 198:336-46 Mr '64

PACIFISM—*Continued*
Conversing with Russians; American peace groups and members of Sane visiting the Soviet Union. S. Gottlieb. Bul Atomic Sci 21:35-6 Ja '65
Cuba & the peace movement. N. Glazer; discussion. Commentary 35:438-43 My '63
Down and down he goes; B. Russell. Nat R 14:310 Ap 23 '63
Inquiry into the peace movement. A. Herzog. il N Y Times Mag p 17+ My 19 '63
Moscow mission; peace-hostage program. New Yorker 40:25-7 F 29 '64
Peace at the polls. R. Hagan. Nation 196:83-91 F 2 '63
Peace ladies. M. Decter. Harper 226:48-53 Mr '63
Peace marchers, help or hindrance to peace? pro and con discussion. il Sr Schol 82:10-11 F 13 '63
Peace movement; a program for the future. C. Bolton. il Nation 197:278-81 N 2 '63
Peace research, peace action. J. D. Singer; reply with rejoinder. J. Cohen. Bul Atomic Sci 19:35-6 My '63
See also
Committee for non-violent action

PACIFISTS. See Pacifism

PACK, Donald H.
Meteorology of air pollution. bibliog Science 146:1119-28 N 27 '64

PACK, Elizabeth
Blonde bond. por Time 82:17 D 20 '63

PACK, Jo
How wage law hit small shop. U S News 57:75 Ag 17 '64

PACK, Robert
Burning the laboratory; poem. Harper 229:98 O '64
Mist; poem. Sat R 46:34 N 2 '63
Muse is always gay. Sat R 47:60-3 N 14 '64
Welcoming poem for the birth of my son. Yale R 53:415 Mr '64
about
Five poets. J. Engels. Poetry 102:403-4 S '63

PACK dogs. See Dogs

PACK transportation
Back packing: family style. H. Kanzler. il Field & S 68:35-7 Je '63
Hell of a way to move. E. I. Neighbor. il Outdoor Life 133:44-7+ F; 60-3+ Mr '64
Package pack trips. il Sunset 130:30+ Mr '63
Pleasures of pack trips. M. A. Rodgers. il Redbook 123:35-6+ O '64
See also
Packs

PACKAGE foods
Adventures in home cooking. S. Spitzer. il Holiday 34:99-104 S '63
Manna for marketing men. il Duns R 84:94-6 D '64

PACKAGE insurance policies. See Insurance—All risk policies

PACKAGE tours. See Travel

PACKAGED buildings. See Buildings, Prefabricated

PACKAGES, Wrapping of. See Wrapping of packages

PACKAGING
Battle of do-it-yourself; or contract packaging. L. Morse. il Duns R 82:pt2 163-7 N '63
Corrupt society. F. J. Cook. Nation 196:465-6 Je 1 '63
Deceptive packaging, deceptive claims of an antiseptic mouthwash for a sore throat. il Consumer Bul 48:43+ F '65
Deceptive packaging; packaging bill. Consumer Rep 28:460 O '63
Do you know all the advantages of home milk dispensers? il Bet Hom & Gard 42:84 F '64
FTC acts on deceptive packaging. Consumer Rep 29:157 Ap '64
Hollow-wall packaging of cosmetics. il Consumer Bul 46:43+ My '63
How to ship money. C. French. Hobbies 69:102+ Je '64
New package ends need for fragile stamp; double container with shock absorbers. Sci N L 86:169 S 12 '64
Package shall not bear false witness; Truth-in-packaging bill. il Consumer Rep 28:246-9 My '63
Packaging war. il Time 81:96 My 3 '63
Potent packaging. Duns R 83:68+ My '64
Special report on packaging; symposium. Duns R 82:pt2 133-8+ N '63
Special report on packaging; symposium. il Duns R 84:89-96+ D '64
Truth in packaging. P. A. Hart. il Nation 196:542-3 Je 29 '63
What's in the package? lessons in practical detective work for supermarket shoppers. W. D. Zabel. Harper 227:12+ Ag '63
See also
Advertising mediums—Packaging
Government investigations—Packaging
Wrapping of packages

Materials
Technology powers ahead. J. B. Weiner. il Duns R 82:pt2 155-6+ N '63
War for the packaging dollar. il Duns R 84:90-1+ D '64

PACKAGING machinery
Technology powers ahead. J. B. Weiner. il Duns R 82:pt2 155-6+ N '63

PACKARD, George R. 3d
Japan's new nationalism. Atlan 211:64-9 Ap '63

PACKARD, Vance
Building the Beatle image. Sat Eve Post 237:36 Mr 21 '64
Chance for everyone to grow. Read Digest 83:114-18 N '63
Invasion of privacy; excerpts from Naked society. Atlan 213:55-61 F '64
New kinds of television; where do we go from here? Atlan 212:68-74 O '63
Right to privacy; excerpt from Naked society. Atlan 213:71-5 Mr '64
This is the new Japan. Sat Eve Post 236:28-34+ Ap 20 '63
Tips. Pub W 185:66 Ja 6 '64
Walls do have ears. N Y Times Mag p23+ S 20 '64

PACKER, Herbert L.
Gideon case. New Repub 151:21+ Jl 4 '64
Warren report: a measure of the achievement. Nation 199:295-9 N 2 '64

PACKER, Nancy Huddleston
Giving, getting. Reporter 31:28-30+ D 31 '64

PACKER, R. E.
Tomorrow: automated schools. Sci Digest 53:34-8 My '63

PACKHAM, Bruce E.
DSB and the citizens bander. Electr World 72:38-40 Ag '64

PACKING for shipment
Brand-new industrial package. L. Blumenthal. il Duns R 82:pt2 136-8+ N '63
Search for the perfect package. il Duns R 82:pt2 145-6+ N '63
Technology; promise and problems. il Duns R 81:pt2 S128-31+ Je '63

PACKING industry. See Meat industry and trade

PACKING of luggage
How to pack up and go. il Seventeen 22:94 My '63
Pack a happy vacation sack. il Am Home 67:38 Jl '64
Packing tips. il Sr Schol 82:23 Ap 3 '63
Thirty gift suggestions for the compleat traveler. il House & Gard 124:58+ N '63

PACKS
Backpack for better hunting. B. Kindley. il Outdoor Life 134:50-2+ N '64
Backpacks and frames. P. K. Snook. il Pop Mech 119:106-9 Je '63
Best gear for backpacking. H. Kanzler. il Field & S 69:62-5 My '64
Everything on your back. C. B. Colby. il Outdoor Life 133:126-30 Mr '64
Lightweight backpack. C. Conley. il Field & S 68:103-4 S '63

PACTS. See Treaties

PADDLE tennis
It's wintertime, so let's play tennis; platform tennis. R. Lardner. il Sports Illus 19:46-51 N 18 '63

PADILLA, George M. and others
Cell synchrony. Science 147:175-7 Ja 8 '65

PADOVER, Saul K.
Cultural pluralism in the United States and in the projected European union: address, April 5, 1963; with questions and answers. Ann Am Acad 348:25-33 Jl '63

PADRE ISLAND NATIONAL SEASHORE
Padre Island: Texas-size beach. B. Kocivar. il Look 27:95-7 O 8 '63

PADS, Rug. See Rug pads

PAELLA. See Cookery, Spanish

PAETZEL, Margaret Mary
For a spring show grow foxtail-lily. Flower Grower 50:60-1 N '63

PAFENBERG, Roy E.
Build panic alarm. Pop Electr 20:37-9+ My '64
Build the lamp lighter CPO. Pop Electr 21:55-6 Ag '64
Experiment in fiber optics. Pop Electr 19:41-4+ Ag '63
Freeze motion with sound. Pop Electr 22:43-6+ Ja '65

PAFENBERG, Roy E.—*Continued*
Hula Hoop: new ham or CB antenna. Pop Electr 19:25-30+ Jl '63
Hybrid circuit for transistor power. Pop Electr 20:66-7 Ap '64
Photoflood like extenders. Pop Electr 20:68-9 Ap '64
Watch those watts. Pop Electr 18:71 Mr '63

PAGAN, Burma
Letter from Pagan. D. Richie. Nation 197:166-8 S 21 '63

PAGE, Geraldine
Letter to a star. por Newsweek 64:92 N 30 '64
Out of the mold. pors Time 82:64 Jl 5 '63

PAGE, Homer
We can beat J.D. il Parents Mag 39:56-8+ O '64
Young rebels with a cause. il Parents Mag 39:42-5+ D '64

PAGE, Irvine H.
Some perils of authorship. Science 144:139 Ap 10 '64
Technicians, equipment, and originality. Science 140:451 My 3 '63
—See Corcoran, A. C; McCubbin, J. W. jt. auths.

PAGE, Patti
What did you want most at seventeen? ed. by A. Ebert. por Seventeen 22:132-3 S '63

PAGE, Robert M.
Sporangium discharge in pilobolus: a photographic study. bibliog Science 146:925-7 N 13 '64

PAGE, Ruth
Devil at the keyhole. Dance Mag 38:33 O '64

PAGE, Thornton
Evolution of galaxies. bibliog Science 146:804-6+ N 6 '64
Evolution of galaxies. bibliog il Sky & Tel 29:4-10 Ja '65 (to be cont)

PAGE, Warren
Chicken feed. Field & S 69:66-7 My '64
Cornfield gobbler. Field & S 68:57-9+ Ap '64
Day at Saratoga. por Field & S 69:35-7 N '64
Day in Denmark. Field & S 69:36-7 D '64
Everything else but. por Field & S 67:37-9+ Mr '63
Grand sportin' bird. Field & S 68:64-7 My '63
Hunters' holiday. Field & S 68:38-40 Ag '63
Marsh walker. por Field & S 68:40-1+ Ja '64
More pheasants than people. Field & S 69:37-9 S '64
Muzzle of meese. Field & S 69:25-7+ Ag '64
Ram with a corset. por Field & S 69:34-7+ Jl '64
(ed) Shooting. See issues of Field & stream
Shotgun shooter's manual. Field & S 69:56-64 S'64
Trolling for tramcars. Field & S 68:43-5 D '63
What a beautiful morning. Field & S 68:46-7+ Mr '64
World's biggest deer camp. Field & S 68:25-7 N '63

PAGE airways, incorporated. See Washington, D.C.—Airports

PAGE airways international. See Washington, D.C.—Airports

PAGEANTS
Making history on the playgrounds; Janesville, Wis. reprint. D. N. Anderson. il Recreation 57:172-4 Ap '64
Ring up the curtain on Christmas. D. K. Osborn. Parents Mag 38:65 D '63
See also
Aquatic shows
Festivals
Son et lumière (sound and light)

PAGES, Congressional. See United States—Congress—Pages

PAGES, Library. See Library assistants

PAGING systems. See Loud speaking apparatus

PAGLIACCI; opera. See Leoncavallo, R.

PAGLIAI, Bruno
Modern Medici. il por Time 81:93 My 10 '63

PAHLEVI, Mohammed Reza, shah of Iran. See Mohammed Reza Pahlevi

PAHLMANN, William
Eclectic look. G. O'Brien. il por N Y Times Mag p58-9 Mr 1 '64

PAI, T. M. A.
University town built by a country doctor. P. Almasy. il pors UNESCO Courier 16:37-40 Jl '63

PAID hunting. See Farmer-hunter relations

PAIGE, Hilliard W.
How Pert-cost helps the general manager. Harvard Bsns R 41:87-95 N '63

PAIGE, Janis
Jubilant Janis is back on Broadway. N. Poirier. pors Sat Eve Post 236:35-6 N 9 '63

PAIGE, Le Roy. See Paige, S.

PAIGE, Nancy
Breaking the permissions barrier. Library J 89:3404-5+ S 15 '64
Is it habit or law? cutting the red tape of library book buying. Library J 89:909-13 F 15 '64
New look at the N.Y times national book fairs, 1936-37. Pub W 184:28-30 D 30 '63

PAIGE, Satchel
Lift the latch for Satch. Sports Illus 18:7 Mr 11 '63
Philosopher's consolation. Sports Illus 20:17 Ja 27 '64

PAIN
Feeling no pain; studies of the mechanisms of pain at the Massachusetts mental health center. il Newsweek 62:61 Jl 8 '63
How much pain can you stand? measuring pain with dolorimeter. il Sci Digest 55:46 Ap '64
Relief of pain; University of Washington's pain clinic. il Time 81:93 My 17 '63
See also
Suffering

PAINE, Barbara B.
Challenge: Garden in the woods. il Horticulture 42:32-5 O '64
How to keep algae out of your pool. il Flower Grower 50:42-4 S '63

PAINE, Clarence S.
Lansing builds a nerve center. Library J 89:4711-13 D 1 '64

PAINE, Edward Grosvenor
Children in miniature. Antiques 84:570-3 N '63

PAINE, Philbrook
Gentlemen: about that cocktail shaker. Read Digest 85:127-9 S '64

PAINE, Ruth
Prelude to tragedy. J. West. por Redbook 123:52-3+ Jl '64

PAINE, Thomas
Best seller that helped to begin the world over again. il Sr Schol 83:5 Ja 10 '64

PAINELLE, Martin
Adzhubei and Italy today. America 108:405-6 Mr 23 '63
Elections in Italy. America 108:712-13 My 18 '63
Macmillan at Rome. America 108:265-6 F 23 '63

PAINT
Cheaper spray paint? BernzOmatic quick drying spray enamel. Consumer Rep 29:159 Ap '64
Concrete floor paints; latex and solvent for indoor use. il Consumer Rep 28:427-30 S '63
Fresh color schemes from historic houses. il House B 105:122-3 Mr '63
High temperature paint; enamel. L. Smith. il Hot Rod 17:86 F '64
House paints; two kinds of water-thinned paints; latex paint and emulsion paint. J. Hand. il Pop Sci 185:126-9 S '64
Interior paints. J. Hand. Pop Sci 186:160-2 Ja '65
Latex exterior paints. il Consumer Rep 29:238-41 My '64
Latex flat interior paints. il Consumer Rep 29:379-84 Ag '64
Multicolor paints. il Consumer Rep 28:494-5 O '63
Natural exterior finishes. J. Hand. il Pop Sci 185:158-9+ O '64
New editors' choice house paint colors! il Bet Hom & Gard 42:50-5 Je '64
New paint takes 1,000° heat. il Pop Sci 185:140 D '64
Outdoor paints; newest marvels. il House & Gard 124:156-7 S '63
PM tests the new propane spray paint. il Pop Mech 119:136 Je '63
Painting galvanized roofing. Consumer Bul 46:7 S '63
Paints. Consumer Rep 29:294-303 D '64
Plastic on the palette. Time 84:88 O 16 '64
Prescriptions for paint problems. il Am Home 67:84-5+ My '64
Towards a plastic revolution: new synthetic materials manufactured specifically for artists. B. Taylor. il Art N 63:46-9+ Mr '64
Use the right paint for your house. il Consumer Bul 47:2+ Je '64
What to know about interior paint. Bet Hom & Gard 41:26 Ag '63

Testing

Mary Carter's paints. Consumer Rep 28:113 Mr '63

PAINT, Luminous
High-visibility colors; fluorescent color safety program. il Am City 78:96-8 My '63

PAINT, Protective
New paints that last. L. M. Palmer. Farm J 87:44P S '63

PAINT brushes
Brush and watercolor; excerpts from Watercolor landscape. R. Brandt. il Design 65: 114-19+ Ja '64

PAINT industry and trade
Paint finds a new base. il Bsns W p 110-12+ F 8 '64
See also
Glidden company

PAINT rolling. See Painting. Industrial and practical

PAINT spraying
Big idea: a spray booth. G. Daniels. il Pop Sci 183:100-1 S '63

PAINTED tin. See Tôle

PAINTER, Charlotte
Sisters; story. Redbook 121:74-5 O '63
Who made the lamb; excerpts. Ladies Home J 81:49+ D '64

PAINTER, Helen W.
Trends in the language arts: reprint. Wilson Lib Bul 39:151-3 O '64

PAINTING
Discovery of painting, by R. Berger. Review Design il 66:7 S '64
Drawing & painting after dark. J. S. Walsh. il Am Artist 27:36-41+ Mr '63
Master of texture; excerpts from Painter and his techniques, by Alan B. Gruskin. W. Thon. il Design 65:215-19 My '64
Painting in polymer & mixed media. E. Betts. il Am Artist 28:34-9 O '64
Painting toward intuition. R. Henkes. il Sch Arts 62:11-13 F '63
See also
Action in art
Art
Artists
Circus in art
Color
Cubism
Encaustic painting
Finger painting
Flowers in art
Frescoes
Impressionism (art)
Light in art
Portrait painting
Realism in art
Still life painting
Water color painting

Anecdotes, facetiae, satire, etc.
See Art—Anecdotes, facetiae, satire, etc.

Competitions
See Art—Competitions

Exhibitions
See Art—Exhibitions

Philosophy
See Art—Philosophy

Study and teaching
Capture winter in oils. H. Gasser. il Design 64:124-5+ Ja '63
Floating designs; fifth grade projects. G. Turner and F. Major. il Design 65:104-7 Ja '64
Ink experiments. C. H. Taylor. il Sch Arts 64:29-30 S '64
Mirror for painting demonstrations. E. A. Whitney. il Am Artist 28:33-5+ N '64
New horizon for classroom painting. H. Horn and M. Slater. il Sch Arts 64:39-41 O '64
Oil painting. P. Albenda. il Sch Arts 62:18-19 Ap '63
Oils in one hour; demonstration methods of A. Allen. il Design 64:129-31 Ja '63

Technique
Al Held paints a picture. I. Sandler. il Art N 63:42-5+ My '64
Mixed technique of the old masters. C. Waugh. il Am Artist 28:26-31+ Ap '64
Motion in painting: a new art form. T. Freund. il Am Artist 28:46-50+ N '64
My art is compulsive. H. Rath. il Am Artist 27:34-9+ S '63
Painting became my life. H. Rubin. il Am Artist 29:46-51+ Ja '65
Painting in oil on paper. H. Sawyer. il Am Artist 28:44-9 Ja '64
Spin-a-painting. M. E. Yukich. il Design 65: 30-1+ S '63
Washout technique. M. D. Burbank. il Sch Arts 63:16-17 Je '64

Themes
See Art—Themes

PAINTING, American
America, America; Fleischman collection at the University of Arizona art gallery, Tucson. F. Getlein. New Repub 150:25-6 Mr 14 '64
American painter as a blue chip. M. Elkoff. il Esquire 63:36-42+ Ja '65
American painting collection of Henry Melville Fuller. W. H. Gerdts. il Antiques 86:66-71 Jl '64
American painting in the collection of James H. Ricau. W. H. Gerdts. il Antiques 86: 578-82 N '64
Armory influence on American art. F. Getlein. New Repub 149:24-6 Ag 3 '63
Art galleries. H. Rosenberg. New Yorker 39: 147-8+ Mr 16 '63
Art galleries; abstract expressionism at the Museum of modern art and at the Jewish museum. H. Rosenberg. il New Yorker 39: 84+ Je 15 '63
Art galleries; annual exhibition of contemporary American painting (cont) R. M. Coates. New Yorker 39:63-5 Ja 4 '64
Art galleries; on art movements. H. Rosenberg. New Yorker 39:159-62+ O 5 '63
Art USA now, ed. by L. Nordess. Review Reporter 29:62+ S 12 '63. H. Kramer
Attraction of Italy for American painters. O. Wittmann. il Antiques 85:552-7 My '64
Benjamin Champney and the American Barbizon, 1850-1857. W. G. Hennessy and F. A. Sharf. il Antiques 84:566-9 N '63
Explosion of pop art: exhibition at the Guggenheim museum. A. B. Saarinen. il Vogue 141:86-7+ Ap 15 '63
Five Americans face reality; second generation of New York school. L. Campbell. il Art N 62:25-7+ S '63
Four realists: a review. F. Whitaker. il Am Artist 28:54-61+ O '64
Hard edge and hard times at the Corcoran; Twenty-eighth biennial exhibition at the Corcoran gallery. F. Getlein. New Repub 148:27-8+ F 2 '63
Indigenous painting in Maine, 1825-1865; excerpts from Maine and its role in American art, 1740-1963. N. F. Little. il Antiques 83: 454-7 Ap '63
Indigenous painting in New Hampshire. N. F. Little. il Antiques 86:62-5 Jl '64
Maine & American artists, 1710-1963. J. Davidson. il Am Artist 27:32-9+ D '63
Museum accessions in American painting. R. Davidson. il Antiques 86:612+ N '64
New York state: the Hudson heritage. K. Kuh. il Sat R 46:29-30 Ap 27 '63
Old American moderns; exhibition of modern Americans before 1940 at Corcoran gallery. F. Getlein. New Repub 148:28-9 My 18 '63
Portrait of Maine; exhibition at the Colby college art museum. il Newsweek 61:97 My 27 '63
Primitive painters of the United States. S. Baraldi. il Américas 15:21-7 N '63
Saint Anthony paintings of Frank Mason. C. Riley. il Am Artist 28:62-7+ Je '64
Seven U.S. painters; exhibition at Pan American union. L. Alloway. il Américas 16:39-41 Jl '64
Sold out art. il Life 55:125-9 S 20 '63
Steel mistletoe. T. B. Hess. il Art N 61:46-7+ F '63
Success story of American art; Sixty years of American painting, at Whitney museum. B. O'Doherty. il N Y Times Mag p66-7 S 15 '63
Tradition of the primitive imagination denied. S. P. Feld; discussion. Antiques 83:324-5 Mr '63
Turning wheel. H. C. Pitz. il Am Artist 28: 22-8+ Mr '64
U.S. art today; exhibition of Contemporary American painting at the Whitney museum in New York city. B. Kaufman. Commonweal 79:490-1 Ja 24 '64
Weather vane; annual show at Manhattan's Whitney museum of American art. il Time 83:62-6 Ja 3 '64
See also
Albright, I.
Artists, American
Bailey, R.
Banks, R.
Biddle, G.
Biederman, C.
Bierstadt, A.
Bingham, G. C.
Blaine, N.
Bluhm, N.
Blume, P.
Bouché, L.
Brandt, H.
Brustlein, D.

PAINTING, American—See also—*Continued*
Bundy, H.
Cajori, C.
Catlin, G.
Curtis, P. C.
Daggett, N. J.
Davis, S.
De Kooning, E.
De Kooning, W.
Diebenkorn, R.
Drexler, R.
Eakins, T.
Eilshemius, L. M.
Ernst, J.
Federal art project
Ferren, J.
Field, E. S.
Fiene, E.
Frankenthaler, H.
Gilien, T.
Goldberg, M.
Gorky, A.
Gottlieb, A.
Grabach, J. R.
Greene, S.
Haines, R.
Hatofsky, J.
Held, A.
Henri, R.
Hicks, E.
Hoeflich, S.
Hofmann, H.
Hopper, E.
Hurd P.
Indiana, R.
Jennys, R.
Jennys, W.
Jensen, A.
Johns, J.
Johnson, L.
Katz, A.
Keane, W.
Kelly, E.
Kerciu, G. R.
Kerkam, E. C.
Kingman, D.
Kitaj, R. B.
Kline, F.
Koch, J.
Lansner, F.
Lawrence, J.
Lebrun, R.
Lentine, J.
Leutze, E.
Lichtenstein, R.
Lindner, R.
Louis, M.
Malina, F. J.
Manet, E.
Marsh, R.
Mofchum, G.
Moran, T.
Murphy, G.
Nesbitt, L.
Newman, B.
Nordhausen, A. H.
Ortman, G.
Pace, S.
Parker, R.
Parrish, M.
Pollet, J.
Pollock, J.
Porter, F.
Pousette-Dart, R.
Pyle, H.
Rattner, A.
Rauschenberg, R.
Ray, M.
Reinhardt, A.
Rivers, L.
Robinson, T.
Rockwell, N.
Rosenquist, J.
Salinas, P.
Sargent, J. S.
Satz, J. M.
Schoonover, F. E.
Sheeler, C.
Sheets, M.
Simpson, M. S.
Sivard, R.
Stella, J.
Still, C.
Tchelitchew, P.
Teall, E.
Thon, W.
Treiman, J.
Tworkov, J.
Walton, W.
Warhol, A.
Weber, M.
Wesselman, T.
Whistler, J. A. M.
Whitney museum of American art, New York
Whorf, R.
Wilson, J.
Woodbury, C. H.
Wyeth, A.
Wyeth, J.

PAINTING, Australian
See also
Nolan, S.

PAINTING, Australian (aboriginal) See Art, Australian (aboriginal)

PAINTING, Austrian
German and Austrian conversation pieces of the nineteenth century. A. Von Saldern. il Antiques 86:604-9 N '64

PAINTING, Baroque
Italian Baroque painting, by E. Waterhouse. Review
Art N 63:51+ O '64. J. Russell

PAINTING, Belgian
See also
Delvaux, P.
Ensor, J.

PAINTING, Brazilian
Introduction to Brazilian painting. J. R. Teixeira Leite. il Américas 16:21-8 My '64

PAINTING, British
Britannia's new wave. il Time 84:74-9 O 9 '64
British in Buffalo; Albright Knox art gallery. M. Kozloff. Nation 199:474-5 D 14 '64
English conquest in the Old Dominion; English paintings, 1700-1850, collection of Mr and Mrs Paul Mellon. C. Connolly. il Art N 62:30-3+ Sum '63
English conversation pieces from the Mellon collection. A. Winchester. il Antiques 83: 444-8 Ap '63
Genius defined; Paul Mellon collection. il Time 82:58-63 Jl 5 '63
Revival of the throb and sob; theme of trysts and troubled hearts. il Life 54:33-6 F 15 '63
Tudor, Stuart and Early Georgian pictures in the collection of H.M. the Queen, by O. Millar. Review
Art N il 62:44-5+ D '63. J. Russell
See also
Bacon, F.
Blake, W.
Grant, D.
Portrait painting
Preraphaelitism
Romney, G.
Salmon, R.
Sutherland, G.
Turner, J. M. W.

PAINTING, Byzantine. See Art, Byzantine

PAINTING, Canadian
See also
Riopelle, J. P.
Thomson, T.

PAINTING, Childrens. See Childrens art

PAINTING, Chinese
Mongol rugs in Chinese paintings: excerpts. M. S. Dimand. il Antiques 84:714-17 D '63
Treasures of T'ang. il Newsweek 62:88 S 9 '63

PAINTING, Czech
See also
Mucha, A.

PAINTING, Dutch
Back in *Stijl*; exhibition at Manhattan's Marlborough-Gerson gallery. il Time 83: 70-1 My 8 '64
Dutch focus on Italy; University of Michigan's exhibition. il Art N 63:38+ Sum '64
See also
Gogh, V. van
Mondriaan, P. C.
Moreelse, W.
Rembrandt Hermanszoon van Rijn
Van Dongen, K.

PAINTING, English. See Painting, British

PAINTING, European
Plumed serpents; COBRA, group of European artists. il Time 84:82-3 D 18 '64

PAINTING, Flemish
See also
Rubens, P. P.

PAINTING, French
Chester Dale: collector. N. MacNeil. il McCalls 91:120-7+ N '63
Dynasty of marine painters: the Roux family of Marseilles. J. Meissonnier. il Antiques 86:583-7 N '64
Great ones all painted us. J. M. Rouart. il Life 54:48-55 My 10 '63
Letter from Paris; Tableaux rares at Galerie de L'Elysee. Genêt. New Yorker 40:88+ Je 27 '64

PAINTING, French—*Continued*
Paintings and antiques; New York apartment of E. A. Bragaline. R. Davidson. il Antiques 84:556-61 N '63
See also
Barbizon school
Bonnard, P.
Braque, G.
Cézanne, P.
Cocteau, J.
Daubigny, C. F.
Degas, E.
Delacroix, E.
Derain, A.
Dufy, R.
Forain, J. L.
Fragonard, J. H.
Gauguin, P.
Gleizes, A.
Gris, J.
Gromaire, M.
Hélion, J.
La Hyre, L. de
Le Brun, C.
Léger, F.
Manessier, A.
Marquet, A.
Monvoisin, R. Q.
Rouault, G.
Rousseau, H.
Seurat, G. P.
Signac, P.
Soutine, C.
Toulouse-Lautrec Monfa, H. M. R. de
Ungerer, T.
Vigée-Lebrun, M. L. E.
Vuillard, E.

PAINTING, German
German and Austrian conversation pieces of the nineteenth century. A. Von Saldern. il Antiques 86:604-9 N '64
See also
Beckmann, M.
Bergen, C.
Bissier, J.
Corinth, L.
Dix, O.
Dürer, A.
Ernst, M.
Grosz, G.
Kollwitz, K.
Nolde, E.
Schwitters, K.

PAINTING, Greek
See also
Vases, Greek

PAINTING, Greek (modern)
See also
Nonda

PAINTING, Hungarian
See also
Vasarely, V.

PAINTING, Indian (East Indian)
See also
Painting, Mogul
Samant, M.

PAINTING, Industrial and practical
Better homes & gardens guide to painting anything! D. L. Gregg. Bet Hom & Gard 42: 18+ S '64
Decorators's notebook. il Seventeen 22:192-3 Ap '63
Latex flat interior paints. il Consumer Rep 29:379-84 Ag '64
Paint a room in one day! il Bet Hom & Gard 41:114J+ Mr '63
Paint happy. il McCalls 90:88-95 Mr '63
See also
Boats—Painting
Concrete—Painting

PAINTING, Irish
See also
Yeats, A.
Yeats, J. B.

PAINTING, Islamic
See also
Painting, Mogul

PAINTING, Italian
Italian Baroque painting, by E. Waterhouse. Review
Art N 63:51+ O '64. J. Russell
Neoclassicism in Italian pictures. H. Hawley. il Antiques 86:316-19 S '64
New-found island; macchiaioli. il Time 82:66-7 S 13 '63
Our Italian cousins; exhibition of late nineteenth-century painters from Tuscany. il Art N 62:46-7+ S '63
Paintings of the life of St Francis in Assisi, by L. Tintori and M. Meiss. Review
Art N 63:52+ O '64. J. H. Beck
Spot makers. C. J. McNaspy. America 109: 368 S 28 '63
See also
Botticelli, S.
Canal, A.
Caravaggio, M. M. da
Carpaccio, V.
Chirico, G. de
Dorazio, P.
Leonardo da Vinci
Mantegna, A.
Michelangelo Buonarroti
Modigliani, A.
Pannini, G. P.
Preti, M.
Primaticcio, F.
Ricci, M.
Tancredi
Tiepolo, G. B.

PAINTING, Landscape. See Landscape painting

PAINTING, Latin American
Art safari: collecting in Central America and Panama; exhibit in pavilion at New York world's fair. J. Gómez-Sicre. il Américas 16:12-17 N '64
Cordoba's biennial comes to Washington. J. Gómez-Sicre. il Américas 15:16-19 F '63

PAINTING, Marine. See Marine painting

PAINTING, Medieval
Lost treasures are seen again; wall paintings in remote churches, Yugoslavia. il Life 54:52-61 Ap 12 '63

PAINTING, Mexican
New direction in Mexico. il Time 81:68+ Mr 29 '63
Twentieth century Mexican painting. V. M. Reyes. il Américas 16:17-26 Ag '64
See also
Cuevas, J. L.
Murillo, G.
Rivera, D.
Siqueiros, D. A.
Tamayo, R.

PAINTING, Modern. See Modernism (art)

PAINTING, Mogul
Art galleries; exhibition: Art of Mughal India at Asia house. R. Coates. New Yorker 39: 127-8 F 15 '64
Prophet in India; loan show at Asia House, New York. H. A. La Farge. il Art N 62: 28-9+ F '64

PAINTING, Non-objective. See Art, Abstract

PAINTING, Norwegian
See also
Munch, E.

PAINTING, Oriental
See also
Painting, Mogul

PAINTING, Polish
See also
Balthus
Burstein, P.

PAINTING, Russian
All Moscow sounds off after K chews out modern art. . . il Life 54:41-2+ F 22 '63
Art in the Soviet Union. K. Kuh. il Sat R 46:17-26 Ag 24 '63
If you'll pardon the expression . .; remarks at exhibition of Soviet art. N. S. Khrushchev. Newsweek 61:34-5 Ap 1 '63
Soviet art in London; first major commercial exhibit of Soviet art in the West since 1922. il Time 83:71 Je 19 '64
Tempest in a gallery; Khrushchev's denunciation of abstract art. A. Brumberg. New Repub 148:17-20 F 16 '63
See also
Art, Russian
Chagall, M.
Kandinsky, W.

PAINTING, Spanish
Delectable foothills of Spanish painting; exhibition, El Greco to Goya. C. G. Coley. il Art N 62:22-5+ Mr '63
From El Greco to Goya. il Time 81:66-8 F 22 '63
Idiom of Spanish art; Spanish pavilion at the World's fair. J. Canaday. il N Y Times Mag p74-5 Ap 26 '64
Lucid Spanish interspace; exhibition of Spanish still-life painting at the Newark museum. il Art N 63:37+ Ja '65
Pride of Spain. C. J. McNaspy. America 108:505-7 Ap 13 '63
Spanish genius: contradiction and tradition; Spanish treasures from French provincial museums in the Louvre. P. Schneider. il Art N 62:26-7 Mr '63
See also
Goya y Lucientes, F. J. de
Miró, J.
Picasso, P.
Velázquez, D. R. de S. y
Zurbarán, F. de

PAINTING, Swiss
See also
Bodmer, C.
Klee, P.
Seligmann, K. L.

PAINTING, Turkish
Life of court & people in ancient Turkish art. il UNESCO Courier 16:18-19 D '63
PAINTING, Ukrainian
See also
Shevchenko, T. G.
PAINTING, Yugoslav
Peasant painters of Yugoslavia. il Life 56: 79-83 Ja 10 '64
PAINTING books. See Coloring books
PAINTING materials. See Artists materials
PAINTINGS
Gallery for young people. C. B. Johnson. il Sch Arts 62:49 Ap; 40 My; 48 Je; 63:31 S; 36 O '63
Paintings for collectors. R. Davidson. il Antiques 86:536+ N '64
See also
Art—Expertising
Conversation pieces (pictures)
Expressionism (art)
Triptychs

Cleaning

Antiques abroad; last decade's acquisitions by London's National gallery. W. De Sager. il Antiques 84:184+ Ag '63

Collections

See Art—Private collections

Prices

See Art—Prices

Purchasing

See Pictures—Purchasing

Renting

See Pictures—Renting

Taxation

See Taxation of works of art

PAINTINGS, Lending of. See Art loans
PAINTINGS, Theft of. See Art thefts
PAINTINGS in the home. See Art in the home
PAINTS. See Paint
PAIR of stockings; story. See Jones, M. L.
PAJAMA tops; drama. See Green, M. and Feilbert, E.
PAJAMAS. See Nightgowns, pajamas, etc.
PAK, Chong M.
Do not bring foreign students, unless... Sat R 47:62-3+ Ag 15 '64
PAK, Chung Hi. See Park, C. H.
PAK, Kun
Korea; address, November 8, 1963. Vital Speeches 30:220-3 Ja 15 '64
PAKISTAN
See also
Airlines—Pakistan
Booksellers and bookselling—Pakistan
Education—Pakistan
Elections—Pakistan
Hunza
Islamabad
Karachi
Kashmir
Library schools and education—Pakistan
Paleontology—Pakistan
Political campaigns—Pakistan
Space research—Pakistan
United Nations—Pakistan

Economic conditions

Diseases of the rich and diseases of the poor. A. Salam. Bul Atomic Sci 19:3+ Ap '63
Pakistan: the case for technological development. A. Salam. il Bul Atomic Sci 20:2-5 Mr '64

Foreign relations

Courtship in the air; Sino-Pakistan air agreement. Time 82:23 S 6 '63
Dragon's share; Pakistani-Chinese agreement. Newsweek 61:50 Mr 18 '63
Feeling is fatal; Hindu-Moslem riots. Time 83:42 Ap 3 '64
How to be friendly without getting seduced; Chou En-lai's visit. il Time 83:28 F 28 '64
New directions for Pakistan. N. D. Palmer. bibliog f Cur Hist 46:71-7+ F '64
Ominous treaty: Pakistan and Communist China. Commonweal 77:505 F 8 '63
Pakistan-American alliance. M. Ayub Khan. For Affairs 42:195-203 Ja '64
Pakistan at bay. W. Hangen. New Repub 148: 13-15 Mr 30 '63
Pakistan flirts; with China. S. Hugh-Jones. New Repub 151:15-16 S 5 '64
Pakistan: friend of our enemies. W. Unna Atlan 213:79-80+ Mr '64
Pakistan looks to Peking. il Newsweek 63: 38-40 Mr 9 '64
Whose ally? il Time 82:42 S 13 '63
Why another ally questions value of its links to U.S; with interview with M. Ayub Khan. il U S News 54:80-3 My 13 '63

Industries

Jute King. il Time 84:108 D 4 '64

Native races

See also
Burusho

Politics and government

Disappointments of Ayub Khan. J. H. Huizinga. il Reporter 28:30-1 Je 6 '63
Lady & the field marshal. il Time 84:40+ O 30 '64
New directions for Pakistan. N. D. Palmer. bibliog f Cur Hist 46:71-7+ F '64
Pakistan looks to Peking. il Newsweek 63:38-40 Mr 9 '64
Trouble with Mother. il Time 84:24 D 25 '64
Zindabad! for Miss Jinnah; long life! cry her supporters as she runs for president of Pakistan. J. Nevard. il N Y Times Mag p36+ N 8 '64

Population

Pakistan's population. America 109:545 N 9 '63

Religious institutions and affairs

Genocide in Pakistan. America 110:330 Mr 14 '64
Pakistan moves toward state religion. Christian Cent 80:485 Ap 17 '63
PAKISTAN and the United States
Pakistan-American alliance. M. Ayub Khan. For Affairs 42:195-203 Ja '64
PAKISTAN international airlines corporation. See Airlines—Pakistan
PAKISTAN-Sino air agreement. See Aviation—International aspects
PAKISTANI refugees. See Refugees, Pakistani
PALACES
Assorted pleasures and palaces for people who are going places. M. Gough. il House B 105:84+ Je '63
See also
Versailles, Palace of
PALAEOGRAPHY. See Paleography
PALATE, Cleft
Cleft palate in the mouse: a teratogenic index of glucocorticoid potency. L. Pinsky and A. M. DiGeorge. bibliog il Science 147: 402-3 Ja 22 '65
One in 1,000 babies has cleft palate or lip. Sci N L 83:350 Je 1 '63
PALATSKY, Eugene
Balletic view of Distant planet. Sat R 47: 60-1 S 26 '64
Ernie Flatt in action. Dance Mag 38:42-5 D '64
Glamorous paradox. Dance Mag 37:30-3 Ag '63
Great opera houses: Copenhagen. Opera N 28:28-31 F 1 '64
Lincoln Center situation. Dance Mag 37:36-8 My '63
Meet Ricki Starr. Dance Mag 37:27 My '63
Meet Simon Sadoff. Dance Mag 37:19-20 D '63
Pavlova rediscovered! Dance Mag 38:34-6 D '64
She dances with marvelous joy. Dance Mag 39:32-5 Ja '65
Thalia Mara and the National academy of ballet. Dance Mag 38:26-8+ F '64
PALCHI, Alfredo de
After many deaths; poem. tr. by S. Raiziss. Nation 197:244 O 19 '63
Winter that kills; poem. tr. by S. Raiziss. Nation 196:166 F 23 '63
PALDEN Thondup, maharajkumar of Sikkim
In the high Himalayas an American becomes a royal princess. N. W. Ross. il pors Sat Eve Post 236:20-5 My 11 '63
Royalty. New Yorker 40:45-7 O 3 '64
Sikkim. D. Doig. il por Nat Geog Mag 123: 398-429 Mr '63
PALENQUE. See Mayas
PALEOBIOCHEMISTRY
Purine and pyrimidines in sediments from the experimental Mohole. E. Rosenberg. bibliog il Science 146:1680-1 D 25 '64
PALEOBOTANY
Antiquity of American polyploid cotton. C. E. Smith, jr. and R. S. MacNeish. bibliog il Science 143:675-6 F 14 '64
Domestication of corn. P. C. Mangelsdorf and others. bibliog il Science 143:538-45 F 7 '64; Reply with rejoinder. M. D. W. Jeffreys. 145:659 Ag 14 '64

PALEOBOTANY—*Continued*
Early seed plants. H. N. Andrews. bibliog il Science 142:925-31 N 15 '63
Flowers, insects, and evolution; Ruby Range fossils. H. F. Becker. il Natur Hist 74:38-45 bibliog(p70) F '65
Ginkgophyton (psygmophyllum) with a stem of gymnospermic structure. C. B. Beck. bibliog il Science 141:431-2 Ag 2 '63
See also
Trees, Fossil

Jurassic

Two fossil floras of the Negev Desert: Jurassic plants. J. Lorch. il Natur Hist 72:28-37 Mr '63

Pleistocene

Pleistocene wood rat middens and climatic change in Mohave Desert: a record of juniper woodlands. P. V. Wells and C. D. Jorgensen. bibliog il Science 143:1171-4 Mr 13 '64

Tertiary

Fossil forests of Ocú, Panama. W. L. Stern and R. H. Eyde. il Science 140:1214 Je 14 '63

PALEOCLIMATOLOGY
Origin of ice ages: pollen evidence from Arctic Alaska. P. A. Colinvaux. bibliog il Science 145:707-8 Ag 14 '64
Palynological investigation of a core from the Biscay abyssal plain. J. J. Groot. bibliog Science 141:522-3 Ag 9 '63
Pleistocene wood rat middens and climatic change in Mohave Desert: a record of juniper woodlands. P. V. Wells and C. D. Jorgensen. bibliog il Science 143:1171-4 Mr 13 '64
Preliminary pollen studies at Lake Zeribar, Zagros mountains, southwestern Iran. W. van Zeist and H. E. Wright, jr. bibliog il Science 140:65-7 Ap 5 '63

PALEOGRAPHY
Old hands at it. R. Bennett. Hobbies 69:110 Mr '64
See also
Hieroglyphics

PALEOLITHIC period. See Stone age

PALEOMAGNETIC rocks. See Magnetism, Terrestrial

PALEONTOLOGY
Crises in the history of life: mass extinctions of animals by natural catastrophe. N. D. Newell. il Sci Am 208:76-92 bibliog(p 185) F '63
Fossils; life that turns to stone. il Sci Digest 54:69-71 N '63
Go dig up a fossil. il Changing T 17:11-12 Ap '63
Paleontologic technique for defining ancient pole positions. F. G. Stehli and C. E. Helsley. il Science 142:1057-9 N 22 '63
Paleontology; report on meeting of the Paleontological research institution. D. B. Sass. Science 143:166+ Ja 10 '64
True tale of two turtles; fossils. H. D. Brown. il Hobbies 68:123 D '63
See also
Foraminifera, Fossil
Insects, Fossil
Man—Origin and antiquity
Micropaleontology
Scorpions, Fossil

Cretaceous

Unmineralized fossil bacteria. W. H. Bradley. bibliog il Science 141:919-21 S 6 '63

Devonian

Armor-plated and jawless Devonian fish. D. L. Dineley. il Natur Hist 73:48-53 Ag '64

Eocene

Late eocene multituberculates and other mammals from Wyoming. P. Robinson and others. bibliog il Science 145:809-11 Ag 21 '64

Jurassic

Fossilized stomach contents of a sauropod dinosaur. W. L. Stokes. il Science 143:576-7 F 7 '64

Miocene

Aquitanian planktonic foraminifera from Erben Guyot. O. L. Bandy. bibliog il Science 140:1402-3 Je 28 '63

Oligocene

Planktonic foraminifera from the American oligocene. T. Saito and A. W. H. Be. bibliog il Science 145:702-5 Ag 14 '64

Pleistocene

Early man in the New World; report on symposium of the AAAS. G. A. Agogino and others. il Science 143:1350-2 Mr 20 '64
Pleistocene chipped stone tool on Santa Rosa Island, California. P. C. Orr. bibliog il Science 143:243-4 Ja 17 '64

Pre-Cambrian

Great infra-Cambrian ice age. W. B. Harland and M. J. S. Rudwick. il Sci Am 211:28-36 bibliog(p116) Ag '64

Africa

Ancient Africa was evolution laboratory. il Sci N L 83:211 Ap 6 '63

Alabama

Alabama boneyard sheds new light on whales. W. D. Wallace. il Sci Digest 53:77-80 Ap '63

Brazil

Recent high relative sea level stand near Recife, Brazil. T. H. Van Andel and J. Laborel. bibliog il Science 145:580-1 Ag 7 '64

California

Fossil hunting in Palos Verdes. il Sunset 134: 28+ Ja '65
Fourteen-million-year-old mammal being prepared; paleoparadoxia. il Sci N L 87:53 Ja 23 '65
Helicoplacoidea: a new class of echinoderms. J. W. Durham and K. E. Caster. bibliog il Science 140:820-2 My 17 '63
Los Angeles 60,000 years ago; tar pits in Hancock park. J. B. Kemmerer. il Sci Digest 54:48-51 S '63
Monster in the accelerator; fossilized bones of paleoparadoxia found in Palo Alto. il Time 84:38 N 6 '64
Pleistocene chipped stone tool on Santa Rosa Island, California. P. C. Orr. bibliog il Science 143:243-4 Ja 17 '64

Egypt

Radiocarbon dating of a late paleolithic culture from Egypt. P. E. L. Smith. bibliog il Science 145:811 Ag 21 '64

Great Britain

Dating skeletal material. K. P. Oakley. Science 140:488 My 3 '63

India

Middle stone age culture in India and Pakistan. H. D. Sankalia. bibliog il Science 146: 365-75 O 16 '64

Iraq

Prehistoric fauna from Shanidar, Iraq. D. Perkins, jr. bibliog il Science 144:1565-6 Je 26 '64

Kentucky

Paleontologic investigations at Big Bone Lick State Park, Kentucky: a preliminary report. C. B. Schultz and others. bibliog il Science 142:1167-9 N 29 '63

Mexico

Conchostracans: living and fossil from Chihuahua and Sonora, Mexico. P. Tasch and B. L. Shaffer. bibliog Science 143:806-7 F 21 '64

Nevada

Pleistocene wood rat middens and climatic change in Mohave Desert: a record of juniper woodlands. P. V. Wells and C. D. Jorgensen. bibliog il Science 143:1171-4 Mr 13 '64

North America

See Indians of North America—Antiquities

Pakistan

Middle stone age culture in India and Pakistan. H. D. Sankalia. bibliog il Science 146: 365-75 O 16 '64

Southwestern states

Environment and man in arid America. H. E. Malde. bibliog il Science 145:123-9 Jl 10 '64

Utah

Fossilized stomach contents of a sauropod dinosaur. W. L. Stokes. il Science 143:576-7 F 7 '64

Wyoming

Late eocene multituberculates and other mammals from Wyoming. P. Robinson and others. bibliog il Science 145:809-11 Ag 21 '64

PALERMO, Blinky
End of a long, dirty road. Sports Illus 20:5 Ja 20 '64

PALESTINE
Return to our beginnings: tour around the eastern end of the Mediterranean. C. J. McNaspy. America 111:351-2 S 26 '64
See also
Americans in Palestine
Galilee
Israel
Jordan
Zionism

Antiquities
Shards of history. il Time 82:50-60 D 13 '63

History
Palestine before the Hebrews, by E. Anati. Review
Sci Digest il 54:90 Jl '63. D. Cohon
See also
Hyksos

Jewish-Arab problem
See Jewish-Arab relations

Jewish resistance movement
See Jews in Palestine—Resistance movement

Relief work
See also
United Nations relief and works agency for Palestine refugees in the Near East

PALESTINE refugees. See Refugees, Arab

PALESTRINA; opera. See Pfitzner, H.

PALEY, Stanley
Movies to learn from. Pop Phot 52:90+ Ja; 122+ My; 98-9 Jl; 53:186+ D '63
Photographers guide to television. Pop Phot 55:186-9 N '64
Transitions with imagination. Pop Phot 53: 186+ N '63

PALEY, Mrs William S.
Sorcery of green: Mrs William S. Paley and her American garden. il pors Vogue 144: 258-9 D '64

PALEY, William Samuel
Education is a national responsibility. por NEA J 53:10 My '64
Mr CBS. il por Time 83:56-7 Ja 31 '64

PALIO (Siena horse race) See Horse racing

PALISADE, Colo.
Straining the complaints away. G. A. Nisbet. il Am City 78:98-9 Ap '63

PALL guard pumpster water purifier. See Water purifiers, Domestic

PALL MALL press, limited
Praeger buys control of Pall Mall press, London. Pub W 184:33 Jl 29 '63

PALLADIAN architecture. See Architecture, Italian

PALLAS, J. E. Jr
Transpiration and stomatal opening with changes in carbon dioxide content of the air. bibliog Science 147:171-3 Ja 8 '65

PALM BEACH, Fla.
Palm Beach: hopped up about Joey. J. Rieker. il Life 56:25 Ap 3 '64

Description
Palm Beach colours. D. Messinesi. Vogue 145:96 F 1 '65

PALM BEACH preserve. See Game preserves

PALM SPRINGS, Calif.
Palm Springs; photographs; with account by H. Gold. J. Bryson. Sat Eve Post 236:16-23 Mr 30 '63
Palm Springs: the new Karlsbad. H. Sutton. il Sat R 48:45+ Ja 2 '65
Sandy trap for a million golfers; photographs; with report by G. S. Brown. Sports Illus 20:26-37 Ja 13 '64
Sonata for a sherpa; aerial tramway. H. Sutton. il Sat R 47:26-7 F 1 '64
Springs. il Newsweek 63:78-9 Ap 6 '64
We flush and sweep for better results. T. W. Essen. il Am City 78:36 Ag '63

PALM Sunday. See Holy week

PALM trees. See Palms

PALMA DE MALLORCA, Spain
Modernization and ruination. R. Kirk. Nat R 15:352 O 22 '63

PALMAI-TENSER, Rose
Rose from the South. A. M. Lingg. il por Opera N 29:12-14 S 26 '64

PALMEDO, Philip F.
Debate on the force de frappe takes shape. Bul Atomic Sci 20:29-30 Je '64

PALMER, Arnold
Golf. Esquire 62:18-19+ Jl; 56-7 S; 54+ D '64
My game and yours. pors Sports Illus 19:28-42 Jl 15; 18-30 Jl 22; 24-30 Jl 29; 28-33 Ag 5; 40-5 Ag 12 '63
Three big ones talk about golf; interview, ed. by C. Price. por Sat Eve Post 236:66+ Ap 13 '63

about
Arnie's earnings. il Time 82:63 Jl 12 '63
Arnold Palmer gets stumped right out of the tournament. il por Life 55:34B-34C Jl 5 '63
Arnold Palmer: tycoon on the tee. T. O'Hanlon. il por Duns R 83:39-40+ Mr '64
Chief. il por Newsweek 63:72 Ap 27 '64
Hold that trap; world series of golf. por Time 82:66 S 20 '63
Master. il por Time 81:92-3 Ap 19 '63
Master to top them all. A. Wright. il por Sports Illus 20:18-27 Ap 20 '64
Matter of pride at endsville. G. S. Brown. il pors Sports Illus 21:22-7 N 30 '64
Money for the meek. Time 83:63 F 14 '64
Palmer gets fit to fight again. E. Havemann. il pors Sports Illus 18:22-5 Je 3 '63
Palmer speaks out. Sports Illus 20:7 F 24 '64
Plight of the bumblebee; U.S.G.A. rules. il Time 81:50 F 22 '63
Somebody up there loves you, Mr Palmer. il pors Life 56:42-42A Ap 24 '64
Something to go home about. por Time 81: 60+ My 24 '63
Spain sent a two-man armada; Canada cup tournament in France. H. Longhurst. il por Sports Illus 19:18-20 N 4 '63
Sporting scene. H. W. Wind. il New Yorker 40:178+ My 16 '64
Take that, you people's choice. il por Time 83:65 Ap 24 '64
Triumph for two swingers. A. Wright. il pors Sports Illus 21:24-6 D 14 '64
What's ailing Arnie? Newsweek 61:58 My 27 '63

PALMER, C. B.
Dark doings of suburban skippers. N Y Times Mag p28+ Ag 4 '63

PALMER, Earl
Next national park? Travel 120:32-5 Ag '63

PALMER, Foster M.
WLB book review. Wilson Lib Bul 37:786 My '63

PALMER, H. Mason
Boston opera company. Hobbies 69:30-1+ Ap '64

PALMER, H. R. Jr
Hull; wood. Yachting 115:43+ Ap '64

PALMER, H. V. R.
Dream boat. Yachting 113:46-7+ Mr '63

PALMER, Harvey E. and Perkins, R. W.
Cesium-134 in Alaskan Eskimos and in fallout. bibliog Science 142:66-7 O 4 '63
—and others
Cesium-137 in Alaskan Eskimos. bibliog Science 142:64-6 O 4 '63
Radioactivity measurements in Alaskan Eskimos in 1963. bibliog Science 144:859-60 My 15 '64

PALMER, J. L. See Nisonoff, A. jt. auth.

PALMER, John C.
How do you rate as a dean of admissions? Sat R 47:74-5 Mr 21 '64

PALMER, Marguerite B.
Cameo; poem. McCalls 90:118 F '63
Order of things; poem. McCalls 91:48 Ag '64

PALMER, Norman D.
Growing pains of Indian democracy. bibliog f Cur Hist 44:147-54 Mr '63
New directions for Pakistan. bibliog f Cur Hist 46:71-7+ F '64

PALMER, Orville
What report cards don't tell. Parents Mag 39: 50-1+ Je '64

PALMER, Phil
Magic change for a small narrow lot. Pop Gard 15:20-1 Mr '64

PALMER, Ralph S.
Lake Erie niche for gulls. Natur Hist 73: 48-51 N '64

PALMER, Robert T.
One place to call. Am City 79:101 O '64

PALMER method writing. See Penmanship

PALMISTRY
Is the future really in your hands? il Good H 157:167 O '63
Planets, palms, and numbers. H. Stackpole. il Mlle 60:50-1+ Ja '65

PALMS, Charles L.
Apologetics and the biblical Christ. Cath World 198:122-3 N '63
Book of the month. Cath World 199:188-9; 200:116-17 Je, N '64

PALMS
Date palm. N. C. Bezona. il Horticulture 41: 390-1 Jl '63

PALO ALTO, Calif.
Find that line for sure. J. W. Still. il Am City 79:99-100 Jl '64

Street traffic

Underground traffic detectors. J. Taylor. il Am City 79:140+ S '64

PALO DURO STATE PARK. See Texas—Parks and reserves

PALSY, Cerebral. See Paralysis

PALYI, Melchior
Keynes at Bay. Nat R 16:158-60 F 25 '64
Money puzzle. Nat R 14:459-60+ Je 4 '63

PAMPAS grass
Pampas the great defender. il Sunset 133:160 Ag '64

PAMPHLETS
Best in booklets. See issues of House & garden
Booklets. Am Home 67:32 Ap '64
Booklets worth writing for. See issues of Good housekeeping
Booklets you can use! McCalls 90:62 F '63; 91:54 F '64
Books & booklets (cont of) Helpful booklets you can send for. See issues of American home
Free or inexpensive. See issues of NEA journal
Helpful booklets you can send for. See issues of American home
Information plus. U S Camera 26:34-5 My '63
New literature for home-planning. Arch Rec 135:155+ mid-My '64
Things to write for. See issues of Changing times
Useful booklets (cont) Farm J 87:42 Ag '63; 88:47 Ag '64
Write for these. See issues of Wilson library bulletin

PAMPHLETS, Political. See Political literature

PAMPLONA, Spain
Fiesta of Pamplona. R. Trout. il Atlan 211: 142+ Mr '63

PAN-AFRICAN conference, Addis Ababa, 1963
Addis Ababa charter; with text of charter of the OAU. B. Boutros-Ghali. bibliog f il Int Concil 546:5-62 Ja '64
African conference; African unity; address, May 24, 1963. A. T. Balewa. Vital Speeches 29:620-2 Ag 1 '63
Atlantic report. Atlan 212:14+ Ag '63
Birds of a feather (?) get together. il Newsweek 61:39-40 My 27 '63
Cheers for a charter. Newsweek 61:40 Je 3 '63
Pan-Africanism comes of age. R. Howe. New Repub 148:15-17 Je 15 '63
Small taste of unity. il Time 81:22-3 My 31 '63
Together at the Summit. il Time 81:38 My 24 '63
Toward African unity. W. B. Lloyd, jr. Nation 196:544-5 Je 29 '63
Toward unity in Africa. C. Sanger. For Affairs 42:269-81 Ja '64

PAN-AFRICANISM
Africa must unite, by K. Nkrumah. Review Sat R 46:31-2 N 30 '63. C. Miller
African unity urged; fifth session of ECA. U N Rev 10:6-9+ Mr '63
Emperor tries to unite Africa. J. Walz. il N Y Times Mag p 18+ Mr 8 '64
Portrait of Nkrumah as dictator. L. Garrison. il N Y Times Mag p 15+ My 3 '64
Sahara; bridge or barrier? I. W. Zartman. bibliog il Int Concil 541:3-62 Ja '63
What kind of radicalism for Africa? C. Legum. For Affairs 43:237-50 Ja '65
See also
Pan-African conference, Addis Ababa, 1963

PANAGAKOS, Nicholas. See Jastrow, R. jt. auth.

PAN AM building. See New York (city)—Architecture

PANAMA
Ambassador in motion. il Time 82:31 S 6 '63
See also
Americans in Panama
Communism—Panama
Elections—Panama
Fishing—Panama
Guerrillas—Panama
Panama canal
Panama Canal Zone
Political campaigns—Panama
Presidents—Panama
Taboga Island
Tourist trade—Panama
United Nations—Panama

Description and travel

Personal business. Bsns W p 129 My 4 '63
Surprise stopover: Panama. J. H. Winchester. il Travel 119:34-7+ Je '63

Economic conditions

Morning after for Panama. il U S News 56: 36-8 F 3 '64
Squeeze is on in Panama. il U S News 56:40 F 17 '64
Who really owns Panama: a source of U.S. trouble. il U S News 56:64-5 Ap 6 '64

Foreign relations

Another chance; charges against United States. il Newsweek 63:47 F 10 '64
Anti-U.S. diplomats; two spokesmen for Panama. il U S News 56:16 F 3 '64
Campaigning on the Canal. Time 83:38+ F 7 '64
More than a question of flags. il Newsweek 63:42-3 Ja 20 '64
Panama: bluffs, pressures, impasse. il Newsweek 63:45 Ja 27 '64
Panama: distrust and delay. D. A. Allan and G. Sherman. Reporter 30:28-9 F 27 '64
Panama impasse. K. Crawford. Newsweek 63: 21 Mr 30 '64
Panama is first big test; with editorial comment. il Bsns W p23-5, 124 Ja 18 '64
Panama: no U.S. backdown. il U S News 56: 29-31 Ja 27 '64
Panama: the crisis we could have avoided. C. W. Hall. il Read Digest 84:34-9 Ap '64
Panama: the third force. Nation 198:225-6 Mr 9 '64
Panama: why they hate us; more than one torn flag. T. Armbrister. il Sat Eve Post 237:75-9 Mr 7 '64
President restates U.S. position on Panama and Canal Zone; statement, January 23, 1964. L. B. Johnson. Dept State Bul 50: 195-6 F 10 '64
Search for a settlement. Newsweek 63:45-6 F 3 '64
Secretary Rusk interviewed on Voice of America; ed. by R. L. Redeen. D. Rusk. Dept State Bul 50:330-6 Mr 2 '64
United States and Panama reestablish diplomatic relations; statement by President Johnson, with OAS announcement, April 3, 1964. L. B. Johnson. Dept State Bul 50:655-6 Ap 27 '64
What the squabble in Panama is all about; interview. A. I. Selden, jr. il U S News 56: 34-7 Ja 27 '64
Why Panama erupted. il U S News 56:32-3 Ja 20 '64

History

From a peak in Darién; Balboa's discovery 450 years ago. E. B. Roberts. il Américas 15:40-3 S '63

Industries

See also
Syntex corporation

Politics and government

New riots in Panama? R. M. Koster. New Repub 151:9-10 N 28 '64
Passing a test; Robles' internal reforms. il Time 85:30 Ja 22 '65
Rule of the whitetails. il Time 83:32 F 14 '64
Time to get rolling. il Time 84:36+ O 9 '64
View from the Canal. P. Poor. New Repub 150:13-14 F 22 '64

Riots

Inside story of Panama riots. il U S News 56:48-52 Mr 30 '64

Social conditions

Record of U.S. in Panama as a new era begins. il U S News 56:42-4 My 18 '64
Who really owns Panama: a source of U.S. trouble. il U S News 56:64-5 Ap 6 '64

Treaties

Should the Panama Canal treaty be renegotiated at this time? pro and con discussion. il Sr Schol 84:14-16 Ap 10 '64

PANAMA (city)
Booked for travel. H. Sutton. il Sat R 46: 25-6+ My 4 '63

PANAMA and the United States
Hungry mistress. New Repub 149:11-12 O 5 '63
OAS council moves to assist in solving U.S.-Panama dispute; statements, January 31 and February 4, 1964; with resolutions. E. Bunker. bibliog f Dept State Bul 50:300-4 F 24 '64

PANAMA and the United States—*Continued*
Panama Canal controversy; a sixty-year unresolved problem; address, March 16, 1964. M. R. Garcia-Mora. Vital Speeches 30:412-16 Ap 15 '64
Record of U.S. in Panama as a new era begins. il U S News 56:42-4 My 18 '64
Semantics, politics & passion. il Time 83:17 Ja 24 '64
Time bomb explodes. M. B. Travis and J. T. Watkins. il Nation 198:83-5 Ja 27 '64

PANAMA CANAL
After agreement, what? il Time 83:36+ Mr 6 '64
Another Panama Canal: A-blasts may do the job. il U S News 54:74-5 Je 10 '63
Biggest building job of all time. J. W. Finney. il Sci Digest 56:33-7 Jl '64
Booked for travel. H. Sutton. il Sat R 46:25-6+ My 4 '63
Canal route problems; second canal connecting the Atlantic and Pacific Oceans. B. Tufty. Sci N L 85:75 F 1 '64
Canal Zone motorboating. N. Robinson and D. Robinson. il Motor B 111:44-5+ My '63
Canal's too small anyway; problem is to find a better one. il U S News 56:32-3 Ja 27 '64
Crisis with Panama. R. Moley. Newsweek 63:84 F 3 '64
Dig we must; plans for a sea-level canal and new treaty with Panama. il Time 84:16 D 25 '64
Dig with nuclear energy; proposal for a new sea-level canal. A. Ewing. il (p 1) Sci N L 87:3 Ja 2 '65
Do we need another Panama Canal? A. P. Armagnac. il Pop Sci 185:54-7+ Ag '64
Hungry mistress. New Repub 149:11-12 O 5 '63
Internationalize the new canal! owned and controlled by O.A.S. Christian Cent 82:3-4 Ja 6 '65
Last days of the Panama Canal. N. Stanford. il Sci Digest 54:29-31 Jl '63
Man who invented Panama. E. Sevareid. Am Heritage 14:106-10 Ag '63
New canal, dug by atom bombs. L. Galton. il N Y Times Mag p24-5+ S 20 '64
New canal treaty proposed. il Sr Schol 85:17 Ja 7 '65
Notes and comment; question of Plowshare project for Panama Canal. New Yorker 39:15 Jl 13 '63
Old Canal and old treaty. W. Lippman. Newsweek 63:13 F 3 '64
On the level; new sea-level canal proposed. Newsweek 64:32 D 28 '64
Panama Canal controversy; a sixty-year unresolved problem; address, March 16, 1964. M. R. Garcia-Mora. Vital Speeches 30:412-16 Ap 15 '64
Panama Canal lobby of Philippe Bunau-Varilla and William Nelson Cromwell. C. D. Ameringer. Am Hist R 68:346-63 Ja '63
Panama is first big test; with editorial comment. il Bsns W p23-5, 124 Ja 18 '64
Record of U.S. in Panama as a new era begins. il U S News 56:42-4 My 18 '64
Second canal? J. W. Finney. il New Repub 150:21-4 Mr 28 '64; Same abr. with title Biggest building job of all time. Sci Digest 56:33-7 Jl '64; Discussion. New Repub 150:30 Ap 18 '64
Second thoughts; reactions to proposed new canal. il Newsweek 65:29 Ja 4 '65
Showdown near on future of the Panama Canal. il U S News 57:44-5 D 21 '64
Time bomb explodes. M. B. Travis and J. T. Watkins. il Nation 198:83-5 Ja 27 '64
U.S. plans new sea-level canal and new treaty on existing canal; statement, December 18, 1964. L. B. Johnson. Dept State Bul 52:5-6 Ja 4 '65
U.S. pushes plan for new canal; sea-level canal. Bsns W p32 D 26 '64
Will a new Big ditch be built? alternate sea-level waterway through Central American isthmus. il Bsns W p45-7 F 15 '64
Will we lose the Canal? E. McDowell. il Nat R 16:107-8 F 11 '64; Discussion. 16:205+ Mr 10 '64

PANAMA CANAL ZONE
Canal Zone motorboating. N. Robinson and D. Robinson. il Motor B 111:44-5+ My '63
Crisis over the Canal. il Time 83:30+ Ja 17 '64
Hardship zone. il Newsweek 63:45-6 Ja 27 '64
I guess I started this whole thing; resentments beneath the flag fight. M. Acoca and others. il Life 56:30-1 Ja 24 '64
Inside an ugly fight; with report by T. Flaherty. il Life 56:22-9 Ja 24 '64
Let's act our age in Panama. Life 56:4 Ja 24 '64
More American than America; Americans in the Canal Zone. il Time 83:18 Ja 24 '64
Outbreak in Panama. Commonweal 79:472-3 Ja 24 '64
Panama: backdrop for bloodshed. il Newsweek 63:43 Ja 20 '64
Panama crisis. R. Niebuhr. New Repub 150:5-6 F 1 '64
Panama: no U.S. backdown. il U S News 56:29-31 Ja 27 '64
Pique in Darien. Reporter 30:18+ Ja 30 '64
U.S. and Panama agree on certain procedural matters in Canal Zone; joint communique with U.S. aide memoire, January 10, 1963. J. F. Kennedy and R. F. Chiari. Dept State Bul 48:171-3 F 4 '63
U.S. and Panama announce results of Canal Zone talks; joint communique, July 23, 1963. J. F. Kennedy and R. F. Chiari. Dept State Bul 49:246-7 Ag 12 '63
What the squabble in Panama is all about; interview. A. I. Selden, jr. il U S News 56:34-7 Ja 27 '64
Why Panama erupted. il U S News 56:32-3 Ja 20 '64

PANAMA crisis, 1964
Children who caused a crisis. J. Robbins. il Redbook 123:50-1+ Ag '64
Deadlock in Panama. America 110:178 F 8 '64
Great day; new U.S.-Panamanian agreement. Newsweek 63:38 Ap 13 '64
Impartial verdict; International commission of jurists report. Newsweek 63:48 Je 22 '64
Inside story of Panama riots. il U S News 56:48-52 Mr 30 '64
Irksome Panama wrangle. P. Geyelin. il Reporter 30:14-17 Ap 9 '64
Justice and the Canal. W. Sparks. Commonweal 79:564-6 F 7 '64
Morning after for Panama. il U S News 56:36-8 F 3 '64
No end to rigidity. Time 83:42 F 28 '64
OAS in action; Panama-U.S. dispute. il Américas 16:44 Mr '64
Panama crisis; it started at the high school. il Sr Schol 84:5-7+ Ja 31 '64
Panama: why they hate us; more than one torn flag. T. Armbrister. il Sat Eve Post 237:75-9 Mr 7 '64
Should the Panama Canal treaty be renegotiated at this time? pro and con discussion. il Sr Schol 84:14-16 Ap 10 '64
Situation in Panama; White House statements, communiques, Security council debate, and exchange of letters, January 10-16, 1964. Dept State Bul 50:152-6 F 3 '64
Squeeze is on in Panama. il U S News 56:40 F 17 '64
Toward an accord? joint declaration by Panama and U.S. Sr Schol 84:19 Ap 17 '64
Verdict: the U.S. not guilty; International commission of jurists report. Time 83:30 Je 19 '64
View from the Canal. P. Poor. New Repub 150:13-14 F 22 '64
What the squabble in Panama is all about; interview. A. I. Selden, jr. il U S News 56:34-7 Ja 27 '64
What went wrong? New Repub 150:4-5 Mr 28 '64
Who incited riot in Panama; findings of official body. il U S News 56:37 Je 22 '64
Will we lose the Canal? E. McDowell. il Nat R 16:107-8 F 11 '64; Discussion. 16:205+ Mr 10 '64

PANAMANIAN poetry
Avant-garde poetry in Panama: seven poets; with poems. A. M. Ortega. il Américas 16:12-19 Jl '64

PAN-AMERICAN airways. See Pan American world airwways

PAN AMERICAN conferences
See also
Inter-American conference of ethnomusicology
Inter-American conference on social security
Inter-American meeting of science and technology

PAN AMERICAN congress of architects
Pan American congress of architects to meet at Washington in 1965; statement, October 12, 1963. J. F. Kennedy. Dept State Bul 49:801 N 18 '63

PAN AMERICAN day and week
Day for rededication. G. de Zéndegui. Américas 15:1 Ap '63
On Pan American day, 1963; proclamation. J. F. Kennedy. Américas 15:inside cover Ap '63
Our hemisphere; the long and short views; address, April 15, 1963. A. E. Stevenson. Dept State Bul 48:704-9 My 6 '63
Pan American day and Pan American week, 1964; proclamation, March 2, 1964. L. B. Johnson. Dept State Bul 50:450 Mr 23 '64

PAN AMERICAN day and week—*Continued*
Pan American day and Pan American week, 1963; proclamation. J. F. Kennedy. Dept State Bul 48:317 Mr 4 '63
PAN AMERICAN games
Flying lady of the Flying Dutchman. A. Zich. il Sports Illus 18:43-4+ Ap 22 '63
Hurrah for homebodies. il Time 81:84 My 10 '63
Lithe envoys to our Latin neighbors; women's U.S. gymnastic team. il Sports Illus 18:28-32 My 6 '63
Once again to nowhere; US basketball team. Sports Illus 18:8 Ap 22 '63
PAN AMERICAN-Grace airways
CAB must rule on Panagra ownership. Aviation W 78:42 Ja 21 '63
PAN AMERICAN health organization
PAHO executive committee; meeting. Américas 15:45 Jl '63
PAN AMERICAN highway
First pleasure drive to Panama. T. Stimson. il Pop Mech 119:86-91 My '63
Highway to progress. F. J. Hernández. il Américas 15:22-7 Ap '63
Inter-American highway: this is the route. il U S News 54:16 Ap 22 '63
Pan-American highway almost there. Sr Schol 82:18 Ap 3 '63
To the Panama Canal by car; a first in tourist travel. J. F. Diggs and T. J. O'Halloran. il U S News 54:70-6 My 13 '63
PAN AMERICAN sanitary bureau
Mental health. D. J. Lagmanovich. il Américas 15:1-5 Mr '63
PAN AMERICAN union
Alliance for progress exhibits open at Pan American union; remarks, August 12, 1964. T. C. Mann. Dept State Bul 51:305 Ag 31 '64
Art. il Américas 16:38 Ap; 40 My; 40-1 Je; 42 S; 42 O; 41 N; 37 D '64; 17:39 Ja '65
Music. il Américas 16:39 Ap; 41 My; 42-3 Je; 42 Ag; 43 S; 39 O; 42 N; 38 D '64; 17:40 Ja '65
See also
Organization of American states
PAN AMERICAN world airways
Airlines oppose new Atlantic area plan. R. G. O'Lone. Aviation W 81:31 S 28 '64
Hot route in the cold war; New York-Berlin service. Time 84:85 Jl 3 '64
Hughes' silence is major issue in merger. Aviation W 78:47 F 4 '63
London and back for $320? Bsns W p31 Je 29 '63
Making overseas friends. L. L. L. Golden. Sat R 47:84-6 Ap 11 '64
Merger seen as competitive tool. Aviation W 79:39 Ag 12 '63
New U.S. air policy threatens merger. L. L. Doty. Aviation W 78:38 F 11 '63
New York-Moscow route decision due. L. L. Doty. il Aviation W 80:34+ Ja 6 '64
N. Atlantic area concept urged. Aviation W 79:32 S 2 '63
PAA sees profit in Mystere 20 service. J. R. Ashlock. Aviation W 79:41+ Ag 12 '63
Pan Am acts to cut fares to Caribbean. Bsns W p89 D 5 '64
Pan Am adopts films; rate cut remote. J. W. Carter. Aviation W 82:36 Ja 18 '65
Pan Am attacks plan to divide transatlantic routes with TWA. J. R. Ashlock. Aviation W 79:41 Ag 5 '63
Pan Am board votes debenture issue, split. Aviation W 79:39 D 9 '63
Pan American is awarded Tahiti route. L. L. Doty. Aviation W 79:38-9 N 18 '63
Pan Am sees 1965 traffic gain. Aviation W 81:35 O 5 '64
Pan Am 707s to have inertial guidance. Aviation W 81:30-1 Jl 27 '64
Pan Am shows $15-million 1962 income. Aviation W 78:37 Ap 29 '63
Pan Am to begin $7-million cargo facility. Aviation W 81:41 O 19 '64
Pan Am to seek IATA freight rate trials for all-jet service. Aviation W 79:42 Jl 1 '63
Pan Am, TWA choose kerosene to ease public JP-4 controversy. J. R. Ashlock. Aviation W 82:32 Ja 25 '65
Pan Am, TWA differ over Atlantic policy. Aviation W 81:38 S 21 '64
Pan Am-TWU pact ends one-day strike. Aviation W 81:29 Ag 31 '64
Pan Am-TWU pact to cost airline $11.5 million during next two years. Aviation W 81:50 S 7 '64
Pan Am, TWA seek early merger action. Aviation W 78:45 Mr 18 '63
Pan American's bid for chosen instrument status. L. L. Doty. Aviation W 78:38-9+ Mr 25; 41+ Ap 1; 42-3 Ap 8 '63
Profit teams of management. J. B. Weiner. il Duns R 84:36-7+ S '64
Seaboard president attacks case for Pan American-TWA merger; summary of address. R. M. Jackson. Aviation W 78:44 Ja 21 '63
707 navaid stresses maintenance ease. P. J. Klass. il Aviation W 81:45-6+ S 28 '64
Transatlantic case delay creates dilemma on foreign competition. Aviation W 79:39 Ag 26 '63
TWA enthusiasm for merger is wavering. L. L. Doty. Aviation W 78:33 Mr 4 '63
PANATELA, pseud.
Castro and Khrushchev: the ties that bind. Reporter 28:38-9 Mr 14 '63
PANCAKES. See Griddle cakes
PANDAS
World's rarest baby. il Life 56:60+ My 8 '64
PANDIT, Vijaya Lakshmi
A Nehru back in politics. por Time 84:38 D 4 '64
PANEL construction
Building basics every man should know. il Pop Mech 120:148-53 S '63
From cultural traditions come new ways of building, and living. C. Besinger. il House B 106:92-7+ Ja '64
PANEL doors. See Doors
PANEL walls. See Walls
PANELING
Beauty of wood paneling: solid wood; plywood; wood-grained finish; plastic-surfaced, wood-grained finish; gypsum board; plastic laminate. J. H. Ingersoll. il Pop Sci 184:118-34 Mr '64
How to buy paneling. Bet Hom & Gard 41:25 O '63
Tired of the same four walls? see what paneling can do! il Am Home 66:80-4+ Ja '63
PANELS, Decorative
Bedroom boardroom; old Pullman car panels. il Duns R 82:3 O '63
Pebbles make up these panels. il Sunset 131: 86+ Ag '63
PANETH, Donald
What killed The mirror. Nation 197:291-3 N 9 '63
PANETTA, George
Kiss mama. Criticism
New Yorker 40:95-6 O 10 '64
PANICS
1929
See also
Stock exchange—Crisis, October 1929
PANKRATZ, H. Stuart. See Drum, R. W. jt. auth.
PANMUNJOM, Korea
Panmunjom: is that still going on? J. M. Truitt. il Newsweek 65:23 Ja 4 '65
PANNING (photography) See Photography of moving objects
PANNINI, Giovanni Paolo
Museum evaluations: Toledo. A. Frankfurter. il Art N 63:24+ Ja '65
PANOFSKY, W. K. H.
Blackett on strategy. Bul Atomic Sci 19:24-5 Mr '63
PANOPHIC cameras. See Cameras
PANORAS art gallery. See Art dealers
PAN-ORTHODOX conference. See Religious conferences
PANOWSKI, Josef
Religion in the Soviet Union. Nat R 16:865-7 O 6 '64
PANSIES
How to grow pansies from seed. Sunset 133: 156 Jl '64
PANT, Pitambar
Development of India. Sci Am 209:189-92+ bibliog(p308) S '63
PANTER-DOWNES, Mollie
Books (cont) New Yorker 40:233-8+ O 10 '64
Letter from Brighton. New Yorker 39:115-16+ S 28 '63
Letter from London. See issues of New Yorker
Letter from Stratford. New Yorker 40:145-50 My 23 '64
Our far-flung correspondents. New Yorker 39:66+ Ag 24 '63
PANTOGRAPH
Shop pantograph copies anything. J. W. Nash. il Pop Mech 119:164-8 Je '63
PANTOMIME
Angst merchants in BVDs; Polish mime theater. Time 85:49 Ja 15 '65
Juki Arkin in An evening in pantomime at Judson Hall. D. Hering. il Dance Mag 37: 12-13 Ag '63

PANTOMIME—*Continued*
Prague pantomime theatre, Philharmonic Hall. J. Maskey. Dance Mag 38:28-9 O '64
Sound of panto; English pantomime. il Newsweek 65:52-3 Ja 4 '65
PANTRIES
Pantry that makes the party. il House & Gard 124:152-3 D '63
Well-stocked pantry; the cans roll in by gravity. il Sunset 130:128 Je '63
PANTRY. See Pantries
PANTS. See Trousers
PAOLA, princess of Liège
Image of a princess, the hint of a queen. il pors Vogue 144:100-5 Ag 15 '64
PAOLIS, Alessio de
Alessio de Paolis. R. Shelton. pors Mus Am 83:12-13+ N '63
Roguish gallery; photographs. Opera N 28: 14-16 Mr 14 '64
PAOLOZZI, Eduardo
Assembled line. il Time 84:114+ O 2 '64
PAOLOZZI, Maria Christina Orfea
Lost little rich girl. G. Talese. il pors Sat Eve Post 236:40-2 Ag 10 '63
That audacious contessa; with report by R. Chelminski. il pors Life 55:66A-68+ S 6 '63
PAOLUCCI, Henry
For senator from New York. W. H. Von Dreele. Nat R 16:967 N 3 '64
For senator: Henry Paolucci. Nat R 16:900 O 20 '64
PAP, Michael S.
On peace and war in the atomic age; address, April 5, 1963. Vital Speeches 29:531-5 Je 15 '63
PAPACOTSIS, Chrysothemi
How Jacqueline Kennedy saved a child's life. N. M. Lobsenz. il por Redbook 121:46-7+ Jl '63
PAPACY
Bishop, sovereign, supreme pontiff; scope of the job. R. Neville. il N Y Times Mag p9+ Je 16 '63
History marches on. America 110:152 F 1 '64
Montini becomes Pope Paul VI. Christian Cent 80:852 Jl 3 '63
Tasks of Pope Paul VI. il U S News 55:43-4 Jl 1 '63
See also
Popes
Vatican
Vatican City
PAPADIMITRIOU, John
Sanctuary of Artemis at Brauron; with biographical sketch. Sci Am 208:28, 110-16+ bibliog(p 183) Je '63
PAPADOPOULOS, Epaminondas. See Nonda
PAPAGENO (operatic character) See Characters in opera
PAPAGO Indians
Isabell the inscrutable. C. G. Finney. il Harper 228:51-8 Ap '64
PAPAIN
Diphtheria antitoxin: antigen-combining and toxin-neutralizing properties of papain fragments. J. J. Cohen and others. bibliog il Science 144:1585-6 Je 26 '64
Poliovirus type I: neutralization by papain-digested antibodies. A. Vogt and others. bibliog il Science 145:1447-8 S 25 '64
PAPAL audiences
Wednesday in St Peter's. il Time 82:50 S 27 '63
PAPAL bulls. See Bulls, Papal
PAPAL encyclicals. See Encyclicals
PAPAL infallibility. See Popes—Infallibility
PAPAL volunteers. See Volunteer service, International
PAPANDREOU, Andreas
Return & fall of the native. il por Time 84:43 N 27 '64
PAPANDREOU, George
Goodbye again. il Time 82:25 D 20 '63
Old man in a hurry. Newsweek 62:49-50 N 18 '63
PAPANEK, Ernst, and Linn, Edward
Boy who survived Auschwitz. Sat Eve Post 237:34-41 Ap 11 '64
PAPASHVILY, Helen
Redwood country. Holiday 35:20+ Mr '64
PAPAYAS
New fruit treat is papaya. il Sunset 132:58-63 F '64
PAPEN, Franz von
Scales of justice. Newsweek 63:44 Je 22 '64
PAPENDICK, David E.
Loan program that helps you become a doctor. H. Earle. il pors Todays Health 41:36-41 Jl '63
PAPER
New ways to permanent files; long-lasting papers. V. Dabney. Sat R 47:67-8 My 9 '64; Reply. P. F. Della Luna. 47:55 S 12 '64; Rejoinder. 47:77 N 14 '64
Paper can be made to last 400,000 years. Pub W 187:89-90 Ja 4 '65
Paper specifications in the book. ALA Bul 58:701 S '64
Permanence and durability: different qualities and needs. W. Jenney. Pub W 185:121+ F 3 '64
Permanence/durability in books: research makes progress. Pub W 184:66+ D 2 '63
Permanent/durable book papers. V. W. Clapp. bibliog f ALA Bul 57:847-52 O '63
U. S. is paper world. B. West. il Sci N L 85:90 F 8 '64
Wood pulp paper decay threatens record of past. Sci N L 85:168 Mr 14 '64
See also
Photographic paper
Testing
Papermakers launch study of permanence, durability. Pub W 183:96 My 6 '63
PAPER, Decorative
Art tips for bookbinding. P. Johnson. il Design 65:68-74 N '63
New transformer: tortoise-shell paper. il House & Gard 124:196-7 S '63
PAPER, Waxed
Food wraps. il Consumer Rep 28:423-6 S '63
New hope for wax? Mobil-Kote. Duns R 83: 63-4 Ap '64
PAPER animals
How to make a paper menagerie. il House & Gard 125:152-3+ Mr '64
PAPER bag players. See Theater, Childrens
PAPER books. See Paperback books
PAPER collars. See Collars
PAPER cups, plates, etc.
See also
Maryland cup corporation
PAPER cutting. See Paper work
PAPER decoration. See Paper work
PAPER dolls
Doll's-eye view of history. il McCalls 90:72-5+ Jl '63
How to make a cardboard pal. il Design 65:60 N '63
Sailor, soldier, Indian chiefess; four dolls, made of paper tubing. il Design 65:57 N '63
PAPER fabrics. See Paper textiles
PAPER flowers. See Flowers, Artificial
PAPER folding. See Paper work
PAPER making and trade
Clouds in West dim paper's future. il Bsns W p 130+ D 12 '64
First rebels on the labor front. W. S. Ellis. il Nation 200:8-10 Ja 4 '65; Reply with rejoinder. G. Derrickson. 200:inside cover+ Ja 25 '65
Latin America's newsprint needs; summary of United Nations report. U N Rev 10:28 Ap '63
New paper trade organization formed. Pub W 185:113 My 4 '64
Paper leads the expansion parade. il Bsns W p70+ S 5 '64
Paper sales and tariffs. C. B. Grannis. Pub W 185:81 Mr 2 '64
Paper tiger. il Fortune 70:76 S '64
Paper unions split ranks. Bsns W p76 Je 6 '64
Paper world of Karl Landegger. E. K. Faltermayer. il Fortune 70:168-71+ N '64
U. S. is paper world. B. West. il Sci N L 85:90 F 8 '64
See also
Boise Cascade corporation
PAPER making machinery
Computer to make paper. Sci N L 83:174 Mr 16 '63
PAPER mills
Nervi's expanding paper mill; for Cartiere Burgo in Mantua, Italy. il Fortune 70:144-6 S '64
Employees
Paper unions split ranks. Bsns W p76 Je 6 '64
PAPER money
Great Britain
Rule, Phillitannia; newly designed £5 note. il Time 81:26 Mr 1 '63
United States
Now, a new type of dollar bill. il U S News 55:8 D 9 '63

PAPER money—United States—*Continued*
Obsolete notes are valuable. C. French. Hobbies 68:102 My '63
Why dollar bills look different. il Changing T 18:43-5 My '64

PAPER products
See also
Gibson Lee, incorporated

PAPER sculpture
Paper sculpture for all ages. S. Hanson. il Design 66:10-12 N '64
Totem pole art. il Design 66:36-7 S '64

PAPER textiles
Paper yarn catching on. il Bsns W p66+ F 16 '63

PAPER work
Cardboard structures. il Design 66:13 S '64
Child's best friend. F. M. Major. il Design 64:190 Je '63
Deck the party scene with paper. il Good H 157:112-14+ D '63
Festive frosting of paper; Christmas decorations. il House & Gard 126:124-31 D '64
Fold paper to learn geometry. R. Yoshioka. il Sci N L 83:138-9 Mr 2 '63
Made of gummed paper tape; excerpts from Ways with art. H. Stevens. il Design 65: 26-9 S '63
Paper mosaics. M. S. Shaw. il Sch Arts 63: 33 F '64
Scissors magic. il Design 64:148-9 Mr '63
Shoe box decorations. il Design 66:40-1 N '64
Solids from paper. J. C. Vitale. il Sch Arts 64:23-4 S '64
Take time for tissue. M. J. McConnaughy. il Sch Arts 62:33-5 My '63
Thanksgiving cutouts. J. Eisner. il Pop Mech 120:152-4 N '63
With scissors and stapler little hands can create magnificent baubles of paper; Christmas decorations. il House & Gard 126:150-4 D '64
Wizardry with paper. P. Johnson. il Design 64:142-5 Mr '63
You can create lasting delight with découpage. il House & Gard 123:118-21 F '63
See also
Paper dolls
Paper sculpture
Papier-mâché

PAPER work, Office. See Office management

PAPER yarn. See Paper textiles

PAPERBACK book covers. See Book covers

PAPERBACK book fairs. See Book fairs

PAPERBACK book jobbers. See Book jobbers

PAPERBACK book wholesalers
NACSCORP projects seven-fold sales increase this year. Pub W 186:25-6 Ag 17 '64

PAPERBACK books
Avon launches rounded corner paperbacks. il(p 19-22) Pub W 185:42 Mr 9 '64
Books USA names officers at incorporation meeting; organization formed to send paperbacks abroad. Library J 88:3564 O 1 '63
Books USA; packages of paperbacks to be sent abroad by American donors. Library J 88:532 F 1 '63
Case for bookburning; political pamphlets. Christian Cent 81:1415 N 11 '64
Category novel. I. Moore. Writer 77:9-13 S '64
Christmas in the paperback department. K. Ray. Pub W 184:39 Ag 19 '63
Current children's paperbacks. P. H. Allen. bibliog il Library J 89:2156-8 My 15 '64
Design in paperbacks: a report from NAL. il Pub W 183:76-8 Ap 8 '63
Durability isn't everything, paperback study group reports. Pub W 186:96-7 O 5 '64
Gross and Rosset speak on paperbacks at Adclub. Pub W 183:50 F 4 '63
Hall of defamers; paperbacks a major weapon of political warfare. T. Clancy. America 111:520-2 O 31 '64
Individualizing instruction with paperbacks. D. H. Moscow. il NEA J 53:21-2 Ap '64
Juvenile paperback originals. bibliog Library J 88:2081-2 My 15 '63
Languages in paperback: tool for education. M. Pei. Pub W 184:22-5 S 30 '63; Reply with rejoinder. G. Hubel. 184:18-19 O 28 '63
Mostly about paperbacks: a little light, a little heat; excerpt from American reading public. D. J. Fine. Pub W 184:26-7 O 14 '63
NACS: can college stores cope with the paperback boom? summary of addresses. B. J. Larson; M. J. Goodman. il Pub W 184:16-21 D 16 '63
New Jersey to survey school use of paperbacks. Pub W 184:44 S 2 '63
No, but I read the book twice; renaming a book or putting suggestive cover on its dust jacket. Christian Cent 82:31 Ja 6 '65
Paperback attack on poverty: free book program for needy children; excerpts from address, April 1964. H. H. Humphrey. Library J 89:2128 My 15 '64
Paperback books. NEA J 52:61+ F '63
Paperback exhibit signed for Worlds fair. Pub W 184:70 N 11 '63
Paperback pedagogy. V. Clear. Sat R 47:73 F 15 '64
Paperbacks. See issues of Publishers' weekly
Paperbacks as textbooks in Texas: a tentative no. Pub W 183:84+ F 4 '63
Paperbacks in school. D. L. Flaherty. America 111:523+ O 31 '64
Paperbacks in the schools, ed. by A. Butman and others. Review
Pub W 184:42 S 23 '63. C. B. Grannis
Paperbacks: revolution or evolution? J. Tebbel. Sat R 47:62-3 Je 13 '64
RPG elects Wolfe, discusses paperback problems; symposium. il Pub W 185:49-52 Je 15 '64
Scientific paperback revolution. H. Cirker. Science 140:591-4 My 10 '63; Discussion. 141:483-4+; 142:148+, 1619-20 Ag 9, O 11, D 27 '63
Selected list of paperbacks on Shakespeare. Christian Cent 81:497-8 Ap 15 '64
Space race in paperbacks. D. Dempsey. il Sat R 46:33+ F 16 '63
Speaking out; paperback pornography. C. Amory. Sat Eve Post 236:10+ Ap 6 '63
When someone complains; threats of book banning, Pontiac, Mich. schools. D. P. Whitmer. Sr Schol 83:27T Ja 17 '64
Worldwide hunger for books uncovered by Books USA. Library J 89:4306 N 1 '64
See also
Advertising mediums—Paperback books
Booksellers and bookselling—Paperback books
Libraries—Paperback books
Libraries, Private
Publishers and publishing—Paperback books

Bibliography

At our corner: six million boys and girls can't be wrong; new paperbacks. il Sr Schol 83:14T O 11 '63
Bard in paper. R. L. Hillier. il Library J 89: 193-8 Ja 15 '64
Forecast of paperbacks. B. A. Bannon. See issues of Publishers' weekly
Gift items in soft covers; paperbacks for Christmas. il Pub W 184:55-8 Ag 19 '63
Great books in paperback. J. L. Jarrett. il Sat R 46:66-7 Mr 23 '63
In paperback; by and about Shakespeare. C. Wonnberger. il Sr Schol 84:18T-19T F 21 '64
Look at the paperbacks. J. Brooks. Consumer Rep 28:306-7 Je '63; Excerpts. Library J 89:315-17 Ja 15 '64
Paperback books. Writer 76:38 F '63
Paperback books to come; ed. by I. Stokvis and others. Library J 88:2105-32 My 15 '63
Paperback bookshelf. See issues of Changing times
Paperback roundup (cont) America 109:521-2+; 111:525-30 N 2 '63, O 31 '64
Paperbacks to come; ed. by I. Stokvis and J. Putnam. Library J 88:3295-337; 89:346-81+, 2175-207, 3422-57; 90:336+ S 15 '63, Ja 15, My 15, S 15 '64, Ja 15 '65
Pick of the paperbacks. R. W. Saal. See issues of Saturday review
Report on special projects. M. E. Marty. Christian Cent 80:462 Ap 10 '63
Second impressions; review of paperbacks. R. M. Wallace. See issues of Nation
What you can't find in paperback. J. Brooks. Consumer Rep 29:258-9 My '64

Statistics

1963-64 paperback best sellers in the bookstores. il Pub W 185:70-7 Ja 20 '64; 187: 72-8 Ja 18 '65

PAPERBACK classics. See Capitol records, incorporated

PAPERS of presidents. See Archives—United States

PAPERWEIGHTS
Old glass paperweights. J. P. Boore. il Hobbies 69:82-5+ Mr; 82-4 Ag '64

PAPIER-MACHÉ
How to make a monster. F. De Wys. il Design 65:19-21 S '63
Our world; fifth grade project. E. Johnston. il Sch Arts 63:18-19 Je '64
Papier-mâché animals; fifth grade class. C. J. Alkema. il Sch Arts 63:16-17 Mr '64

PAPILLARY growths. See Tumors

PAPILLOMA virus. See Viruses

PAPOL, John, family
Child is lost. J. P. Blank. il Redbook 120:48-9+ F '63
PAPOL, Stephen
Child is lost. J. P. Blank. il pors Redbook 120:49-9+ F '63
PAPPAS, Charles. See Leibowitz, M. jt. auth.
PAPPAS, G. D. See Boswell, F. W. C. jt. auth.
PAPPAS, George
Art & the new environment. Sch Arts 62:17 F '63
Art. design: search for a new image. Sch Arts 63:19-20 O '63
Contemporary drawing. Sch Arts 62:44 Je '63
George Pappas, artist & teacher; interview. il por Sch Arts 63:12-15 Je '64
PAPPAS, Marilyn
Cloth assemblage, new dimensions in fabric. Sch Arts 64:14-16 O '64
Motivation; new ways of seeing. Sch Arts 63:8-11 S '63
Woven form. Sch Arts 64:34-5 S '64
PAPPAS, Milt
I'm the worst that's ever been. G. Rogin. il pors Sports Illus 20:54-6+ Ap 27 '64
PAPUA. See New Guinea, Territory of
PAPYRI. See Manuscripts (papyri)
PAPYRUS
Papyrus is graceful in its own stiff way. il Sunset 131:160-1 Ag '63
PÂQUES, Georges
Man with the cosmic view. por Time 82:42 O 4 '63
With all due modesty. Newsweek 62:58+ O 7 '63
PARABLES
Cadillac full of diamonds. J. Ciardi. Sat R 47:19 Mr 7 '64
Parables of conflict in Luke. by J. S. Glen. Review
Christian Cent 80:1274-5 O 16 '63. J. P. Love
See also
Fables
Jesus Christ—Parables
PARACELSUS
Father of rational therapy. por Todays Health 41:73 O '63
PARACHUTE jumping. See Parachuting
PARACHUTE troops
General Mobuto hits the silk. il Ebony 19:92-4+ N '63
PARACHUTES
High-wind cargo hook developed. Aviation W 78:86 F 4 '63
Parachutes that are full of holes; for better performance. il Bsns W p 119+ Ag 10 '63
See also
Parachuting
Testing
Ballute device tested as Gemini mission recovery aid. M. L. Yaffee. il Aviation W 80:40-1+ Ap 6 '64
PARACHUTES, Cargo
See also
Airdrop
PARACHUTING
Dive for the bull's-eye. il Time 84:55 Ag 28 '64
Down he goes without a chute. il Life 58:38-40A Ja 15 '65
I bailed out ten miles up! J. D. Nole. il Read Digest 85:73-6 S '64
I was the world's most scared skydiver. G. Emerson. il Read Digest 82:86-90 Mr '63
Jumping for joy. il Time 82:78 Jl 12 '63
Once I was a tiger. E. Chaze. il Life 54:17-18 F 8 '63
Parachuting for pleasure. B. Hersh. il Holiday 34:115+ D '63
Skydiver; Gloria Durham. il Ebony 18:47-8+ O '63
So long for now; with photographs by C. Bonnay. Esquire 59:86 Ap '63
They jump for joy. A. Whitman. il N Y Times Mag p93-4+ Ap 5 '64
PARADE wagons, Circus. See Circus—Equipment
PARADES
Russia shows off its missiles; with report by R. Brigham. il Life 57:42-42B+ N 20 '64
See also
Dallas—Parades
Miami, Fla.—Parades
New Orleans—Parades
Philadelphia—Parades
PARADIS, Marjorie B.
She laughs last; drama. Plays 22:25-36 Mr '63
PARADISE (Island) See Hog Island, Bahama Islands
PARADISE, Calif.
Hell breaks loose in Paradise. il Life 54:73-82+ Ap 26 '63
Intellectual freedom; raising hell with the Legionnaires. E. T. Moore. ALA Bul 57:224-6 Mr '63
PARADISE Inn. See Hotels, taverns, etc.
PARAGLIDER. See Gliders (aeronautics)
PARAGUAY
We will show them. il Time 83:36 My 8 '64
Commercial treaties and agreements
Trade with Paraguay and the United Arab Republic; proclamation. L. B. Johnson. Dept State Bul 51:120-1 Jl 27 '64
Languages
Guaraní: proud mark of the Paraguayan. R. B. Saguier. il Américas 16:6-10 Mr '64
Politics and government
Our man in Paraguay. B. M. Lando. Nation 196:157-9 F 23 '63
See also
Elections—Paraguay
PARAINFLUENZA virus. See Influenza virus
PARAKEETS. See Parrots
PARAKITES
Like a ride in the sky? try para-kiting. J. Joseph. il Pop Sci 182:86-7 Je '63
Para-kiting: dawn of the human antenna. J. Joseph. il Pop Electr 18:94 F '63
PARALLAX, Stellar
Determination of stellar distances; navy's new telescope at Flagstaff, Ariz. K. A. Strand. bibliog il Science 144:1299-309 Je 12 '64
New 61-inch astrometric reflector; U.S. naval observatory, Flagstaff, Ariz. K. A. Strand. il Sky & Tel 27:204-9+ Ap '64
See also
Stars—Distance
PARALYSIS
Aids for quads and respos. G. Laurie. bibliog f il ALA Bul 58:785-9 O '64
Cerebral palsy research. Sci N L 85:341 My 30 '64
Lessons of a CP camp. K. Hargrove. America 109:738-40 D 7 '63
Mass Moroccan rehabilitation. J. Viorst. il Sci N L 83:218-19 Ap 6 '63
Parkinson's disease from 1918 flu epidemic. Sci N L 84:360 D 7 '63
Spinal experiment gives new hope for paralytics. Sci N L 85:200 Mr 28 '64
Statistically defined displays and pattern detection of cerebral palsied children. C. F. Reed and A. Pollack. bibliog il Science 140:1331-3 Je 21 '63
Tremorine: its effect on amines of the central nervous system. A. H. Friedman and others. bibliog il Science 141:1188-90 S 20 '63
What you can do with what you have; rehabilitation of a quadriplegic, with report by J. Mason. il Life 56:75-88 Je 19 '64
PARAMECIA
Induction of conjugation by cell-free preparations in paramecium multimicronucleatum. A. Miyake. bibliog Science 146:1583-5 D 18 '64
PARAMECIUM multimicronucleatum. See Paramecia
PARAMETERS
NASA space station parameters. Aviation W 81:67 D 21 '64
PARANÁ, Brazil
Fire crisis in Brazil. M. S. Lowden. il Am For 71:42-4+ Ja '65
Great Paraná fire. G. Meek. il Américas 15:38-40 D '63
PARAPET walls. See Walls
PARASITES
Tetracycline fluorescence in permeability studies of membranes around intracellular parasites. H. G. Du Buy and others. bibliog il Science 145:163-5 Jl 10 '64
See also
Botflies
Cestoda
Symbiosis
Trichina and trichinosis
Worms, Intestinal and parasitic
PARASITIC diseases
See also
Schistosomiasis
PARASITIC plants
See also
Air plants
PARASITICIDES. See Anthelmintics

PARATHION
Parathion activation by livers of aquatic and terrestrial vertebrates. J. L. Potter and R. D. O'Brien. bibliog il Science 144:55-7 Ap 3 '64

PARATHYROID hormones. See Hormones

PARAVULCOON. See Balloons

PARC DU MONT TREMBLANT. See Quebec (province)—Parks and reserves

PARCEL post
If you will send gift packages. Sunset 131:136+ N '63
Weathervane. R. G. Miner. Flower Grower 50:6 Ap '63

PARCEL post rates. See Postal rates—United States

PARCHER, Emily Seabor
Coral bells. Horticulture 41:218 Ap '63
Foliage can be beautiful. Horticulture 42:36 Ja '64
Ground covers for house plants. Horticulture 42:38 F '64
Grow hyacinths indoors. Horticulture 42:16+ O '64

PARCO. See Producers and retailers cooperative, incorporated

PARDALOTES. See Diamondbirds

PARDÉ, Maurice
Floods! floods!! floods!!! UNESCO Courier 17:54-9 Jl '64

PARDEE, W. D.
Land coming out of soil bank? Suc Farm 62:44-5 Ja '64

PARDO, Richard D.
Maine's Baxter State Park: a gift of mountain wilderness. Am For 69:20-2+ F '63

PARDO-TOVAR, Andrés
Music of the people. Américas 15:26-9 Jl '63
Root-carver from Cali. Américas 16:35-8 N '64

PARDOE, David A.
Pebbles from a workshop. Sr Schol 84:14T My 1 '64

PARÉ, Ambroise
Barber of the battlefield. il Todays Health 41:88 N '63

PAREGORIC
Paregoric kick; cases of addiction reported. Newsweek 63:76 Je 1 '64

PARENT and child (law)
Custody by committee? Time 84:67-8 S 18 '64
Guardianship: every child's right. I. Weissman. bibliog f Ann Am Acad 355:134-9 S '64

PARENT-child relationship
Accidents don't just happen. H. H. Gibney. il Parents Mag 38:88-9+ O '63
And now a word from the youngsters. M. A. Guitar. il N Y Times Mag p79-80 My 3 '64
Are you cheating your child out of a living? M. C. Kohler and A. Fontaine. il Good H 157:76-7+ S '63
Big daddies of the Little league. F. Batsby. il N Y Times Mag p22+ My 31 '64
Case for intelligent neglect. L. Strong. il N Y Times Mag p97-8 Je 7 '64
Child worshipers, by M. W. Lear. Review
Newsweek 62:98 N 4 '63
Childhood's baffling middle years. M. Bernath. il Parents Mag 38:52-3+ Ap '63
Children are people too! W. Abraham. il Todays Health 43:28-9+ Ja '65
Children of divorce. G. B. Blaine. il Atlan 211:98-101 Mr '63
Children of interfaith marriage. A. Whitman. il Redbook. 121:46-7+ Je '63; Discussion. 122:26+ Ap '64
Delinquent parents. America 111:207-8 Ag 29 '64
Don't be an over-indulgent father. N. Hentoff. il Parents Mag 39:60-2+ Je '64
Father and son. E. Waugh. Atlan 211:48-51 Mr '63
Fathers to sons: advice without consent, ed. by A. Valentine. Review
Newsweek il 62:93-4 D 16 '63
Firstborn. L. Lee. il Mlle 60:116-17 D '64; Same abr. with title Wonder of the firstborn. Read Digest 86:141-3 Ja '65
Get off Johnny's back! L. M. Magill. il Sat R 47:64-6 F 15 '64; Discussion. 47:62-3 Mr 21 '64
Have a good time, daughter. E. L. Stokes. il Read Digest 83:202-4 Ag '63
How to get along with children. M. Eisman. il Parents Mag 39:116 N '64
How to win arguments with your parents. J. Hawkes. Seventeen 22:120-1+ N '63
Huzzle-coos with our children; with study-discussion program, by R. Strang. A. Graham. bibliog il PTA Mag 59:26-8, 34 D '64
If I were a parent. Polly. il Farm J 87:78B O '63
Is disrespect inevitable? with study-discussion program, by E. M. Duvall. R. M. Butler. bibliog il PTA Mag 57:24-6, 36 Mr '63
Lady who likes kids. J. Coogan. Ladies Home J 80:54 Je '63
Life and times with a two-year-old. S. H. Fraiberg. il Parents Mag 38:54-5+ D '63
Little boy who couldn't learn. A. Lake. il Redbook 123:46-7+ Je '64
Making memories together; with study-discussion program, by R. Strang. W. Abraham. bibliog il PTA Mag 57:27-9, 35 My '63
Mother shouldn't smother. F. C. Bauer. il N Y Times Mag p44 Jl 28 '63
My problem and how I solved it: family triangle. il Good H 158:12+ My '64
My problem is my parents! questions and answers. A. Wood. il Seventeen 23:168-9+ Ap '64
My running fight with the Easter bunny. J. Coogan. il Ladies Home J 80:55-6 Ap '63
My son came late. C. Bonner. il Harper 229:71-3 S '64
Night the stars fell; art of adding dimensions to a child's world. A. Gordon. il Read Digest 85:93-6 O '64
Our ability to love. A. Fromme. Redbook 121:44-5+ Ag '63
Parents and adolescents. Sch & Soc 91:110 Mr 9 '63
Parents who care, more or less. K. Erickson. il PTA Mag 58:25-7 Je '64
Private life of a child. D. B. Thompson. il Am Home 67:30+ O '64
Return of the prodigal. R. Hoffmann. Mlle 58:116+ D '63
School dropout and the family; adaptation of address, November 8, 1963. R. D. Strom. Sch & Soc 92:191-2 Ap 18 '64
Sheltering circle. E. G. Neisser. Parents Mag 39:132 My '64
Should newlyweds live with their parents? excerpts from Grandparents and their families. F. H. Richardson. il Todays Health 42:54-5+ Ap '64
Sins of the parents. R. S. Eielson. il McCalls 92:48+ Ja '65
Sires and sons; quotations, comp. by E. F. Murphy. il N Y Times Mag p42 Je 9 '63
So you're Kate's girl! J. Coogan. Read Digest 83:219-20+ Jl '63
Some guide rules for divorced fathers. S. Withers. il N Y Times Mag p 103 S 29 '63
Son's delinquency helps rebuild a marriage. D. C. Disney. Ladies Home J 80:52 Jl '63
Speaking out; little girls are too sexy too soon. C. Shupp. Sat Eve Post 236:12+ Je 29 '63
Stop and go signals for teen-age drivers. P. Jones. il PTA Mag 57:4-6 Mr '63
Taming the neighborhood bully; with program for discussion group, by M. Smart. S. H. Strait. il Parents Mag 38:44-5+, 140 Ap '63
Teen-age code of conduct for parents; with study discussion program, ed. by C. Smallenburg and H. Smallenburg. A. D. Buchmueller. bibliog il PTA Mag 59:4-7, 36-7 O '64
This was my father; interview, ed. by F. Miller. J. Stewart. il McCalls 91:130-1+ My '64
To my children, in gratitude. R. W. Wells. Ladies Home J 81:58+ Ag '64
Touch of reassurance; with study-discussion program, by R. Strong. D. K. Osborn and P. P. W. Knapp. bibliog il PTA Mag 58:10-12, 35 D '63
Uneasy days before college. P. Chizcott. il Parents Mag 38:40-1+ Jl '63
Vulnerable child. Newsweek 64:48 Ag 3 '64
Wanted: strong parents. J. B. Scofield. Parents Mag 38:53+ Je '63
What I would like to give my child. L. Lee. il Mlle 60:100-1+ Ja '65
What parents ask about children's fears. M. J. E. Senn. il McCalls 90:74+ Ap '63
When children get on your nerves; with study-discussion program, by R. Strang. M. Piers; E. N. Plank; A. Graham. bibliog il PTA Mag 58:21-3, 35 Ap '64; Reply. R. Goldstein. 58:35 Je '64
When is it time to come home? S. Withers. il N Y Times Mag p45 Je 23 '63
Why can't I talk to my mother? questions and answers. A. Wood. il Seventeen 22:100-1+ Je '63
Why kids rebel. J. B. Scofield. Read Digest 82:130-3 Je '63
You do marry the family. E. M. Stern. il Parents Mag 39:70-1+ Ap '64
You have to let your kids go! with study discussion program, by M. Smart. H. H. Work. il Parents Mag 39:16+, 60-1+ Mr '64

PARENT child relationship—*Continued*
You should disregard the experts. K. Belanger. il Redbook 121:45+ Jl '63; Same abr. with title When parents should disregard the experts. Read Digest 84:87-90 Ja '64
See also
Family life
Fathers
Love, Maternal
PARENT education
And baby makes three. C. Riker and A. Riker. il Parents Mag 39:52-3+ Mr '64
PARENT-teacher associations. See Parents and teachers associations
PARENT-teacher cooperation. See School and the home
PARENTI, Michael
Old neighborhood. Commentary 35:544-7 Je '63
PARENTS
America's spoiled parents. B. Spock. il Ladies Home J 80:40+ Je '63
Being wise in membership; affirming a new concept of parenthood. B. W. Overstreet. il PTA Mag 58:7-9 D '63
Birth traumas? A. P. Eliasberg. N Y Times Mag p94 O 13 '63
Book banning and junvenile delinquency. J. Ciardi. Sat R 46:16 Ag 10 '63
Helping neglectful parents. J. A. Bishop. bibliog f Ann Am Acad 355:82-9 S '64
Needed: more good parents. J. F. Molloy. il NEA J 52:42-6 S '63
Problem children or problem parents. il Sci Digest 54:75-6 N '63
Problems of teen-age parents. L. W. Sauer. PTA Mag 59:27-8 O '64
Speaking out; parents will never amount to much! J. L. Kitman and S. Kitman. Sat Eve Post 237:8+ D 19 '64
We're bigger than they are! J. B. Kelley. America 109:628-30 N 16 '63
What it's like to be little. W. Keisler. il Parents Mag 39:48-9+ Mr '64
When parents convict themselves. E. J. LeShan. il N Y Times Mag p32 Jl 12 '64
See also
Block parents
Family life
Fathers
Foster parents
Libraries—Work with parents
PARENTS and teachers associations
Action in education. M. Mayer. Bet Hom & Gard 42:120+ S; 16+ O; 122+ N '64
Adventure of an idea. M. E. Jenkins. il PTA Mag 57:2-3 F '63
Being wise in membership. B. W. Overstreet. il PTA Mag 58:7-9 S; 18-20 O; 7-9 N; 7-9 D '63; 20-2 Ja; 14-16 F; 24-6 Mr; 24-5 My; 10-11 Je '64
Double your dividends. J. Moorhead. PTA Mag 59:2-3 N '64
Fight for the PTA; right-wing attempts at infiltration. il Newsweek 65:46+ F 1 '65
For new leaders: tradition and opportunity; address. M. E. Jenkins. PTA Mag 58:2-3 Je '64
Founders of the future. M. E. Jenkins. PTA Mag 58:2-3 F '64
It's all in a summer's day. M. E. Jenkins. il PTA Mag 57:2-3 Je '63
Keeping pace with the PTA. See issues of PTA magazine
Leadership in the local PTA. B. W. Overstreet. il PTA Mag 58:24-6 Ap '64
Making of a National PTA program. J. Moorhead. PTA Mag 59:2-3 S '64
Membership proclamation. J. Moorhead. il PTA Mag 59:2-3 O '64
Membership proclamation; children and schools need you in the PTA. M. E. Jenkins. PTA Mag 58:3 O '63
New mythology. M. E. Jenkins. PTA Mag 57:2-3 Mr '63
Now it's how as well as what. M. E. Jenkins. PTA Mag 57:2-3 My '63
PTA program. R. Thielke. America 108:556-7 Ap 20 '63
PTA standards and stand on public education. M. E. Jenkins. il PTA Mag 58:2-3 N '63
PTA targets, techniques, timing. M. E. Jenkins. il PTA Mag 58:2-3 S '63
PTA: the irrelevant giant. W. C. Kvaraceus. Nation 197:200-1 O 5 '63
Report on rapport; how the PTA at Glen Oaks school cooperated. A. Daley. il NEA J 52:12-13 D '63
Speaking out: the P.T.A. is a waste of time. W. C. Kvaraceus. Sat Eve Post 237:6+ My 2 '64; Reply. PTA Mag 59:14-16 S '64
With new resolution. J. Moorhead. PTA Mag 59:2-3 Ja '65
See also
National congress of parents and teachers
PARENTS and teachers conferences. See School and the home
PARENTS attitudes. See Attitudes
PARENTS' magazine
Parents' magazine buys F. A. O. Schwarz toy store. Pub W 184:38 S 23 '63
Parents' magazine honors Dr James Bryant Conant. il Parents Mag 39:56 F '64
Parents' magazine's special award home for families with children. il Parents Mag 38:87+ S '63
Portfolio of seven award winning homes. R. Charles. il Parents Mag 38:77+ Mr '63
See also
Youth group achievement awards
PARENTS school visiting. See School and the home
PARENTS to adopt minority youngsters (PAMY) See Minnesota—Race problems
PARENTS without partners, incorporated
Parents without partners. il Changing T 18:41-2 My '64
PARETZKIN, B. and Peiser, H. S.
High-voltage Laue X-ray photography of large single crystals. bibliog Science 146:260-1 O 9 '64
PARFAITS. See Ice cream, ices, etc.
PARI-MUTUEL betting. See Book making (betting)
PARIN D'AULAIRE, Ingri. See Aulaire, Ingri Parind
PARING knives. See Knives
PARIS, Enrique Tejera-. See Tejera-Paris, E.
PARIS
City the world loves: Paris. A. Buchwald. McCalls 91:66 F '64
Letter from Paris. Genêt. See issues of New Yorker
No more dreams; Saint-Germain-des-Prés. il Newsweek 64:57-8 D 7 '64
See also
Eiffel tower

American colony
See Americans in France

Anecdotes, facetiae, satire, etc.
I was wrong about Paris. J. Crosby. il Ladies Home J 81:42+ My '64

Architecture
Man who destroyed Paris. W. Von Eckhardt. il Horizon 5:50-75 My '63
New look in Paris; five-year cleaning campaign. A. Rothberg. Commonweal 77:514-15 F 8 '63
Paris takes an epic bath. J. Daniel. il Read Digest 83:174-80 Ag '63
See also
United Nations educational, scientific and cultural organization—Headquarters

Art
Art news from Paris. P. Schneider. See issues of Art news
Letter from Paris; exhibition at the Musée national d'art moderne of Ecole de Paris paintings. New Yorker 40:182+ Ap 4 '64
Natural order; regulation of art in the Place du tertre. il Newsweek 63:36 Je 1 '64

Churches
Reach for young rebels; Protestant American church. il Time 85:61 Ja 22 '65

City planning
Letter from Paris; proposed elimination of elms over Seine for double motor highway. Genêt. New Yorker 40:100+ My 2 '64
Man who destroyed Paris. W. Von Eckhardt. il Horizon 5:50-75 My '63

Description
Bateaux Mouches; under the bridges of Paris. il Sunset 130:76 My '63
First time she saw Paris. P. Coffin. il Look 27:88-92 Jl 2 '63
I know a place in Paris. R. Gary. il Holiday 37:54-7+ Ja '65
Paris, in photographs. D. D. Duncan. il McCalls 91:84-95 F '64
Paris of Mr Clean. H. Sutton. il Sat R 47:16-17 Jl 4 '64
Paris, past perfect; photographs. E. Atget. N Y Times Mag p54-5 N 29 '64
Sunlight in stone; cleaning of buildings. il Time 84:54-9 Jl 3 '64
Vision of Paris: the photographs of Eugène Atget, the words of Marcel Proust, ed. by A. D. Trottenberg. Review
Nation 198:36-7 Ja 6 '64. R. A. O'Brien

PARIS—Description—*Continued*
Visit to Saint-Denis. il Sunset 132:20 F '64
Walk and a picnic in Paris. il Sunset 132:87-8 My '64
Weekend in Paris. H. Sutton. il Sat R 47:23-4 Jl 18 '64

Education

Elite of the elite; Lycée Louis-le-grand. il Time 81:103 My 17 '63
School for wives; L'académie Maxim's. il Time 81:65 Mr 29 '63
See also
Ecole polytechnique

Galleries and museums

Bonanza spilt; France's decision to build Museum of the 20th century in Paris. il Time 82:52 Ag 9 '63
Indian and Eskimo artifacts in Paris; Musée de l'homme. C. Miles. Hobbies 68:112+ O '63
Letter from Paris; closing of Rue de Miromesnil gallery. Genêt. New Yorker 40: 84+ Je 27 '64
See also
Louvre

History

Day Paris was liberated; August 25, 1944. L. Collins and D. Lapierre. il N Y Times Mag p23-5+ Ag 23 '64

Hotels, restaurants, etc.

Franc opinions. H. Sutton. il Sat R 47:23-5 Jl 11 '64
Going to Maxim's. S. Robinson. il McCalls 91:116-17+ Mr '64
Maxim's gets a twin; Maxim's de Chicago. il Bsns W p30-1 D 14 '63
Where to see practically everybody; Café de la paix. H. C. Wolfe. Sat R 47:104-6 Mr 14 '64
See also
Night clubs

Intellectual life

Paris; excerpts from Moveable feast; with photographs by G. Parks. E. Hemingway. Life 56:60-79 Ap 10 '64

Music

Coup de disgrâce; Berlioz's Damnation of Faust as choreographed by M. Béjart. il Newsweek 63:51 Mr 30 '64
Ecumenical symphony; Milhaud's Choral symphony performed in Notre Dame. il Newsweek 63:93 Je 15 '64
Faustian scandal in Paris; M. Béjart's new production of Berlioz' The damnation of Faust. il Time 83:41 Mr 27 '64
French fashions. M. E. Davies. Opera N 28: 27-8 O 19 '63
Letter from Paris; monthly Monday concerts at the Salle Gaveau. Genêt. New Yorker 40:175 My 16 '64
[Musical events] (cont) Mus Am 84:19 Mr; 21-2 My '64
Night at the opera. C. Rostand. il Mus Am 84:26-7 Ja '64
Notes from abroad. R. McMullen. See issues of High fidelity
Notes from our correspondents (cont of) Notes from abroad. R. McMullen. See issues of High fidelity
Paris international. M. E. Davies. Opera N 28:24 S 28 '63
Paris opera: conditions critical. J. P. Lenoir. il Theatre Arts 47:63 Mr '63
Paris pastiche. M. E. Davies. il Opera N 27: 33 Mr 2 '63
Wozzeck comes to Paris. M. E. Davies. il Opera N 28:30 Mr 7 '64

Newspapers

Le big change; L'Express in new format. il Newsweek 64:64 S 28 '64
Down & out in Paris. il Time 81:53-4 Ap 26 '63
Letter from Paris; L'Express. Genêt. New Yorker 40:82+ Je 27 '64

Opera

See Opera—France

Police

Warning to *les flics*. Time 81:33 Je 7 '63

Riots

Letter from Paris; interruptions of R. Hochhuth's play Le vicaire, or Der stellvertreter by riots. Genêt. New Yorker 39:88+ Ja 25 '64
Yé, yé, yé! 150,000 exuberant teenagers. il Newsweek 62:38 Jl 8 '63

Social life and customs

Paris problem. S. Gervis. il Esquire 61:86-8+ F '64
Snobs of Paris. P. Daninos. il Vogue 141: 124-7+ Ap 1 '63
What's dimming the city of lights? G. Dickerson. Mlle 59:104+ O '64

Stores

Poor man's style show; Galeries Lafayette, Paris department store. il Bsns W p 162-3 O 26 '63

Street traffic

Letter from Paris. Genêt. New Yorker 39: 192-4 N 30 '63
What to do about traffic? some answers from abroad. il U S News 54:86-90 F 4 '63

Streets

Champs-Elysees. Travel 119:20-1 Ap '63

Subways

Riding on air; rubber-tired subway cars for the Métro. Time 81:80 Je 28 '63

Theater

Great French recipe, for the Folies. P. E. Schneider. il N Y Times Mag p 18+ Ap 28 '63
Letter from Paris. Genêt. New Yorker 39: 75-7 Je 29; 85-6 Jl 27 '63; 40:171-2+ My 16 '64
Life force. il Newsweek 63:96-7 Mr 16 '64
New season, Paris. J. P. Lenoir. Theatre Arts 47:29+ O '63
Openings (cont) J. P. Lenoir. il Theatre Arts 47:60-1+ F; 62+ Mr; 23-4+ Ap; 28-9+ My; 33+ Je; 36+ Jl '63
Roger Planchon's plays. H. Popkin. Vogue 144:40 Ag 15 '64

Views

See Paris—Description

PARIS air and space show. See Aviation—Exhibitions
PARIS-match (periodical) See Periodicals—France
PARIS Opéra. See Opera houses
PARIS opera ballet. See Ballet—France
PARIS peace conference, 1919. See Peace conference, 1919, Versailles
PARISH, Peggy
Parent and child. N Y Times Mag p 102 S 8 '63
PARISHES
Changing city, changing parish? H. J. Browne. il Cath World 198:170-6 D '63
Churches and the campus, by J. G. Chamberlin. Review
America 110:104-5 Ja 18 '64. J. E. Rea
Encounter in a parish; parish congress pioneered by Church of St Sulpice, Paris. M. O'Connor. il Commonweal 80:568-70 Ag 21 '64
PARK, Chung Hee
As a new crisis erupted in Korea. il U S News 56:10 Je 15 '64
Back to business. Newsweek 63:42 Je 22 '64
Ex-General's problem: making democracy work. por U S News 55:10 D 30 '63
Fatigues to flannels. Time 82:24 D 27 '63
Heat's off. Time 81:28+ Mr 22 '63
In Korea, a go-ahead for guided democracy. por U S News 55:72 O 28 '63
Over to you, gentlemen. Time 81:34+ Mr 8 '63
People of the week. U S News 54:16 Ap 1 '63
Slim mandate. il por Time 82:40 O 25 '63
South Korea elects Park as president. Sr Schol 83:16 N 1 '63
Variable Park. Newsweek 61:35-6 Ap 1 '63
—See Rusk, D. jt. auth.
PARK, Clara Claiborne
What's so wonderful about English schools? Ladies Home J 82:24+ Ja '65
PARK, Ed
Javelina jackpot. Outdoor Life 131:24-5+ Ja '63
Secrets of black brant. Field & S 69:21-3+ Ja '65
Very special goose. por Outdoor Life 133:50-2+ Ja '64
PARK, J. Philip
Academic freedom at Grove City. Christian Cent 80:928-9 Jl 24 '63
PARK, Jean
Medieval tour. Travel 119:16 F '63
PARK, Kilho
Electrolytic conductance of sea water: effect of calcium carbonate dissolution. bibliog Science 146:56-7 O 2 '64

PARK, Roderic B. and Biggins, John
Quantasome: size and composition. bibliog Science 144:1009-11 My 22 '64

PARK, Rosemary
Accounting for taste. por Seventeen 23:114+ D '64
Rosemary Park: new president of Barnard. T. Ferrer. il por Sat R 46:66-8 Ap 20 '63; Reply. Mrs J. W. Cyrus. 46:62 My 18 '63
There's nothing like a dame. por Time 81:48 Ap 26 '63

PARK and shop plan. See Automobile parking

PARK association of New York city, incorporated
Wanted: new ideas for city playgrounds. V. Musselman. Recreation 57:180+ Ap '64

PARK maintenance equipment. See Municipal equipment

PARK roads. See National parks and reserves—Roads

PARK vandalism. See Vandalism

PARKE-Bernet galleries, incorporated
Artful takeover; control by London's Sotheby & co. il Time 84:82 Jl 24 '64
Auction notes. R. Davidson. il Antiques 84: 266+ S '63; 86:324+ S '64
Parke-Bernet has record year. K. V. Hostick. Hobbies 69:110-11 O '64
Parke-Bernet season's total. Hobbies 68:126+ S '63
Rule Sotheby's; purchase of Parke-Bernet galleries. Newsweek 64:53 Jl 27 '64
Sotheby's buys controlling interest in Parke-Bernet. Pub W 186:34 Jl 27 '64
Takeover bid shakes art market; Sotheby's of London to win New York's Parke-Bernet. il Bsns W p 110+ Jl 11 '64

PARKER, Al
22° Grand prix automobile. il Sports Illus 20: 44-53 My 11 '64

PARKER, Alfred
Government expenditures; address, September 15, 1964. Vital Speeches 31:15-19 O 15 '64

PARKER, Alfred Browning
Build right and prevent decay and termites. House B 106:112-13+ F '64
How architecture can affect the way we live at home; excerpts from You and architecture. il House B 105:178-81+ Ap; 182-5+ My '63
Proportion, the role it plays in architecture. House B 105:154-6+ Mr '63
Unity in architecture and how it is achieved. il House B 105:108-13 F '63
What you need to know before you build in the tropics. House B 106:102-3+ Ja '64

PARKER, Ann
Grave rubbers; early New England gravestones. C. Willard. il Look 27:M6-M7 Ag 27 '63
—and Neal, Avon
New England gravestone rubbings. Craft Horiz 23:16-19+ Jl '63

PARKER, B. F.
World you live in; your share in the future; address, June 4, 1963. Vital Speeches 29:754-6 O 1 '63

PARKER, Bonnie Elizabeth
Small allegory; poem. McCalls 90:154 Je '63

PARKER, Bruce C.
Translocation in the giant kelp marcrocystis. bibliog Science 140:891-2 My 24 '63

PARKER, Dan
Drebby and Dan. por Newsweek 63:54 Ap 13 '64

PARKER, Dixie
Cave for a child. Sch Arts 63:14-18 My '64

PARKER, Dorothy (Rothschild)
New York at 6:30 p.m. Esquire 62:96-101 N '64

about

Celebrity register. C. Amory. por McCalls 90:144 Jl '63

PARKER, E. N.
Solar wind. Sci Am 210:66-76 bibliog(p 156) Ap '64

PARKER, Everett C.
All-Africa Christianity. Christian Cent 80: 670-2 My 22 '63
Catholic position on birth control hardens. Christian Cent 82:71-2 Ja 20 '65
Lutherans and school aid. Christian Cent 80: 263 F 27 '63
—and Thompson, Betty
To Roswell P. Barnes on his retirement. Christian Cent 81:1551 D 16 '64

PARKER, Fess
Celebrity register. C. Amory. por McCalls 90:144 Jl '63

PARKER, Frank A.
C bridge. Pop Electr 19:65-6+ N '63
High wattage reducer. Pop Electr 20:57-8 F '64
Squealer. Pop Electr 19:61-3 O '63

PARKER, Franklin
Founding the Department of African education in Northern Rhodesia; address, February 1962. Negro Hist Bul 27:29-34 N '63
Francis Keppel of Harvard: Pied Piper of American education. bibliog Sch & Soc 91: 126-8+ Mr 9 '63
1964 as a centennial year in the history of education. Sch & Soc 92:31-2 Ja 25 '64
Public school desegregation. Negro Hist Bul 26:228+ Ap '63
Study of creativity. Sat R 46:49 Ag 17 '63

PARKER, Garland G.
Statistics of attendance in American universities and colleges, 1963-65. bibliog f Sch & Soc 92:5-18 Ja 11 '64; 93:5-18+ Ja 9 '65

PARKER, George E.
Battle against blue. Pop Phot 55:68-9 Jl '64

PARKER, Georgia
How Joey caught the Christmas spirit; ed. by M. Longwell. Farm J 87:64-5 D '63; 88: 89 F '64

PARKER, Herbert G.
Intermunicipal cooperation means assured water suppy. Am City 79:120-1 Ap '64

PARKER, Horatio
Mona. Criticism
Opera N il por 28:6-7 Ja 11 '64

PARKER, Jerry
Four-hour string chair. Pop Mech 119:166-7 F '63

PARKER, John C. and others
Enzootic Sendai virus infections in mouse breeder colonies within the United States. bibliog Science 146:936-8 N 13 '64

PARKER, Larry S.
Composition in sand. il Sch Arts 63:11-12 D '63

PARKER, Lucy
Be your own art director. U S Camera 27: 8 S '64

PARKER, Maynard
New Hampshire: first test for the big divorce issue. Life 56:32-3 F 7 '64

PARKER, Patrick N. See Risinger, G. E. jt. auth.

PARKER, Ralph H.
What every librarian should know about automation. por Wilson Lib Bul 38:752-4 My '64

PARKER, Raymond
November contrasts. K. Levin. il Art N 63: 30-1+ N '64

PARKER, Robert Andrew
Shooting in Mayo and Kerry and Cork. il Sports Illus 19:38-43 O 7 '63

PARKER, Sanford S. See Burck, G. H. jt. auth.

PARKER, Suzy
Celebrity register. C. Amory. por McCalls 90:144 Jl '63

PARKER, Thomas F.
Book selection for the culturally deprived. bibliog por(p3242) Library J 89:3260-5 S 15 '64
Can we afford to ignore the Negro? por bibliog Library J 88:4716-17 D 15 '63

PARKER, William H.
Police chief talks of police brutality; interview. por U S News 57:33-6 Ag 10 '64
There is a tendency to tolerate crime; interview. por U S News 56:69-72 Ap 20 '64

PARKER brothers, incorporated
Pass go and retire; Monopoly. R. Bongartz. il Sat Eve Post 237:26-7 Ap 11 '64
Play-money game that made millions; Monopoly. J. F. Wilkinson. il Sports Illus 19:52-4+ D 2 '63

PARKER DAM
See also
Havasu Lake

PARKER pen company
Penmaker to the world. il Time 81:91 Je 14 '63

PARKES, Henry Bamford
Professors and plowmen. Commentary 36: 257-8 S '63

PARKES, Katherine
Everyone needs to get mad sometimes. Parents Mag 38:72-3+ S '63

PARKHURST, Don A.
Ice rinks: construction and operation. Recreation 56:377-8 O '63

PARKHURST, John D.
Reclaiming used water. Am City 78:83-5 O '63

PARKING, Automobile. See Automobile parking

PARKING garages. See Garages

PARKING lights. See Automobiles—Lighting
PARKING lots. See Automobile parking
PARKING machines, Automatic. See Automobile parking
PARKING meters
How Fresno upgraded parking-meter service. M. J. Carozza and N. O. Jefford. il Am City 78:117+ N '63
How Syracuse selected its parking meters. W. F. Walsh. il Am City 78:86-8 Ap '63
Parking meters keep downtown alive; Keene, N.H. W. Bridgham. il Am City 79:129+ S '64
Pleasant backtracking; St Petersburg, Fla. removes its curbside parking meters. Time 84:70+ Ag 7 '64
Tell-tale powder nabs meter vandals; Kansas City, Mo. S. E. Cross. il Am City 79:110 Jl '64
PARKING ramps. See Automobile parking
PARKINSON, Allen
How to wax eloquently in California. H. Sutton. il Sat R 48:37-8 Ja 16 '65
PARKINSON, C. Northcote
Long road to liberty. Sat R 46:25+ Ap 13 '63
Now Parkinson's telephone law. N Y Times Mag p39-40 Ap 12 '64
Parkinson cautions: there's danger in growth; interview. por Nations Bsns 52:36-7+ My '64
Samplings of a master sampler. Sat R 46:27 Je 8 '63
PARKINSON, John, Jr
Sail aboard Gipsy Moth III. Yachting 113:45+ My '63
PARKINSON, Lee
Little details make the difference. Field & S 68:54-6+ Ap '64
PARKINSONS disease. See Paralysis
PARKISON, Jim
This house invites the outdoors in. Bet Hom & Gard 43:23 Ja '65
PARKMAN, Francis
Francis Parkman's oration Romance in America; with text. W. R. Jacobs. bibliog f Am Hist R 68:692-7 Ap '63
Reporter at large. E. Wilson. New Yorker 40:71-2+ N 14 '64
PARKS, Betty
Return to paradise. Recreation 57:363-4 S '64
PARKS, F. Newton
Executive trouble abroad. Duns R 82:35-6+ Ag '63
PARKS, Gordon
Flight over Africa. Vogue 144:8 Jl '64
How it feels to be black; with excerpts from The learning tree. il Life 55:72-9 Ag 16 '63
Long search for pride. Life 55:80-2+ Ag 16 '63
Paris. il Life 56:62-79 Ap 10 '64
Subdued light for color beauty. il U S Camera 26:66-9 Je '63
What their cry means to me; a Negro's own evaluation. il Life 54:31-3+ My 31 '63
PARKS, James J. See Cohen, E. P. jt. auth.
PARKS, Merritt
I'm glad I married that gal. por Farm J 88:85+ F '64
PARKS, Michael
Man who plays Adam. il pors Life 57:69-70+ N 27 '64
PARKS, R. D.
Quantized magnetic flux in superconductors. bibliog Science 146:1429-35 D 11 '64
PARKS, Rosa
Ten cents that shook America. il por Esquire 62:210-13 D '64
PARKS, Sperry Knox
We stopped living on a treadmill. por Redbook 121:6+ Ag '63
PARKS, W. George
Gordon research conferences. Science 139:1066-76+ Mr 15 '63
Gordon research conferences: program for 1964. Science 143:1203+ Mr 13 '64
Winter Gordon research conferences. Science 124:1195-6 D '64
PARKS, Winfield
Down east to Nova Scotia. il por Nat Geog Mag 125:852-79 Je '64
PARKS
None does his job alone; adaptation of address. J. A. Smith. Recreation 57:48 F '64
Parks and playgrounds. See issues of American city
Policy for county parks and recreation; condensed statement. Recreation 57:270-1 Je '64
What is a park? Mrs J. Durbin. il Recreation 57:387 O '64
When is a recreation area a park? L. Lynch. il Recreation 57:394-6 O '64
See also
Amusement parks
National parks and reserves
Playgrounds

Canada

See also
British Columbia—Parks and reserves
Roosevelt Campobello International Park

Europe, Western

Park is for people. E. M. Avedon. il Recreation 57:400-1+ O '64

United States

Against almost impossible odds; swampy slum into attractive park, near Silver Lake, Bucks County, Pa. R. W. Pierson and R. E. Nagle. il Am City 79:112-13 S '64
Battle for green acres. J. J. Shomon. il Audubon Mag 66:81 Mr '64
Fear takes over our city parks. S. Grafton. il McCalls 91:108-11+ O '63; Same abr. with title Danger stalks our parks. Read Digest 85:114-17 Jl '64
Hobbies à la carte; hobby parks. J. Reck. il Pop Mech 119:118-19 Ap '63
It's a gift! il Recreation 57:20+ Ja '64
Park development plans approved by Secretary; Piscataway park. Nat Parks Mag 38:16 Mr '64
Public gifts. J. E. Curtis. Recreation 56:61 F '63
Urban-oriented outdoor recreation: excerpts from address. L. F. Twardzik. il Recreation 56:470-3 D '63
Why not your own swim club? Or your own private park? J. Fithian; O. Bay. il Farm J 88:26-7 Ag '64
See also
National parks and reserves—United States
Roosevelt Campobello International Park
also subhead Parks and reserves under names of states and cities, e.g. Virginia—Parks and reserves
PARLIAMENT, Members of. See Members of Parliament
PARLIAMENTARY elections. See Elections—Great Britain
PARLIAMENTARY governments
See also
Democracy
PARLIAMENTARY practice
Parliamentary government and the Alliance for progress; address, February 5, 1964. D. Rusk. Dept State Bul 50:305-7 F 24 '64
PARLIAMENTS
See also
Great Britain—Parliament
PARLODION. See Pyroxylin
PARLORS
Parlor. R. Lynes. il Am Heritage 14:54-64+ O '63
PARMA, Italy
Great opera houses. M. J. Matz. il Opera N 28:26-9 D 7 '63
Music makers. R. Gelatt. il Hi Fi 13:123+ O '63
Night at the opera; caustic opera audience at Parma's Royal theater. il Newsweek 65:77-8 Ja 11 '65
PARMENTEL, Noel E. Jr
Folk songs for conservatives. Esquire 60:160-1 D '63
PARMENTER, Ross
Aldous Huxley: style was the man. Sat R 46:12-13 D 21 '63
PARMLY Billings memorial library, Billings, Mont.
Student use of periodicals surveyed by Montana library. Library J 88:1132 Mr 15 '63
PARNASSUS press
On publishing books for children. H. Schein. Horn Bk 39:629-31 D '63
PAROCHIAL schools
Church and state; textbooks for 50,000 parochial and private-school pupils. Newsweek 61:106+ Mr 25 '63
Church-related schools. New Repub 148:4-5 Mr 2 '63; Discussion. 148:30-1 Mr 16 '63
Federal aid for parochial and private schools. W. S. Vincent. Sch & Soc 92:355-7 N 28 '64
Protestants and parochial schools. D. M. Kelley. il Commonweal 79:520-4 Ja 31 '64

Federal aid

See Federal aid to education

PAROCHIAL schools, Catholic
Administration offers another school bill: Controversy renewed on parochial aid. Christian Cent 80:196 F 13 '63
Are parochial schools the answer? by M. P. Ryan. Review
America 110:444 Mr 28 '64. F. Canavan; Discussion. 111:153-6, 299-301 Ag 15, S 19 '64
Christian Cent 81:595-6 My 6 '64
Commonweal 80:8 Mr 27 '64. J. O'Gara
Commonweal 80:99-100 Ap 17 '64; Reply. F. C. Arricale. 80:258-9 My 22 '64
Sat R 47:77 Mr 21 '64. J. Scanlon
Are the schools worth it? America 111:286 S 19 '64
Catholic asks: Are parochial schools the answer? excerpt from Are parochial schools the answer? with excerpts from foreword by E. J. Primeau. M. P. Ryan. il U S News 56:75-6 Ap 13 '64
Catholic baiting? J. O'Gara. Commonweal 79: 500 Ja 31 '64
Catholic school growth. America 112:34 Ja 9 '65
Catholicism in Ohio. New Repub 149:5 N 2 '63
Catholics close first grades; Cincinnati archdiocese. F. Stauffer. Christian Cent 81:413-14 Mr 25 '64
Closing of Catholic schools in Australia. A. Foster. bibliog f Sch & Soc 91:375-7 N 30 '63
Control of schools. America 110:360-1 Mr 21 '64
Federal aid? J. M. Hanlon. America 110:418-19 Mr 28 '64
Financing parochial schools. America 108:819 Je 8 '63
Forward look in Louisville; first Catholic educational conference. America 110:302 Mr 7 '64
Jewish sentiment. M. Himmelfarb. il Commonweal 79:524-7 Ja 31 '64
Modest proposal of Mary Perkins Ryan. J. A. O'Connor. Cath World 199:216-23 Jl '64
No first grade. Newsweek 63:98 Mr 16 '64
Other side of the coin. O. J. Murdick. il America 111:230-2 S 5 '64; Reply. F. D. Rabaut. 111:365 O 3 '64
Paradoxes of parochial schools. J. F. Mahoney. Cath World 199:28-33 Ap '64
Parochial school. L. J. Shehan. America 110: 478-81 Ap 4 '64; Discussion. 110:585, 661, 693-4 My 2, 16-23 '64
Phase out the schools? America 109:506 N 2 '63; Reply. T. J. Fleming. 109:648 N 23 '63
Poverty and parochial schools; federal grants to Catholic schools. B. L. Masse. America 112:101 Ja 23 '65
Price we pay. R. T. Francoeur. il Commonweal 79:538-42 Ja 31 '64
Protestants and parochial schools. D. M. Kelley. il Commonweal 79:520-4 Ja 31 '64
Question of relevance; control by the laity. J. McCudden. Cath World 198:7-13 O '63
Running Catholic schools. America 108:483 Ap 13 '63
Scholastic teacher interviews: Msgr. O'Neil C. D'Amour; ed. by H. Langer. O. C. D'Amour. il Sr Schol 84:5T-11T Ap 10 '64
School: whose is it? F. Canavan. America 111:153-6 Ag 15 '64; Reply with rejoinder. J. J. Ryan. 111:299-301 S 19 '64
Schools. D. Callahan. Commonweal 81:473-6 Ja 8 '65
Schools and churches. New Repub 148:3-5 Mr 23 '63; Discussion. 148:28-31 Ap 6 '63
Schools under strain. il Time 83:74+ Mr 20 '64
Shadows cast before. America 111:582 N 14 '64
Should Catholic pupils get free bus rides? U S News 54:10 My 20 '63
Should public funds aid parochial schools? pro and con discussion. R. F. Drinan; R. L. Hunt. Parents Mag 38:70-1+ N '63
Speaking out; don't junk the parochial schools. W. Sheed. Sat Eve Post 237:6+ Je 13 '64
T.R.B. from Washington; Catholics and schools. New Repub 148:2 F 16 '63; Discussion. 148:4-5 Mr 2; 31 Mr 9; 39 Mr 23 '63

Desegregation

Integration in Alabama. America 110:619 My 9 '64
Public parochial schools. America 108:282 Mr 2 '63

Finance

Crisis in Catholic schools. T. J. Fleming. il Sat Eve Post 236:19-25 O 26 '63
How big is the crisis for Catholic schools? il U S News 56:60-4 F 3 '64
Trouble ahead for the Catholic schools. J. Star. il Look 27:37-40 O 22 '63
PAROCHIAL schools, Jewish. See Jews—Education
PARODIES
Best things in life are free. il Time 83:68+ Ap 3 '64
Red dawn. G. Highet. Vogue 141:131+ Ap 1 '63
Sing along with Mad. Newsweek 63:82 Ap 6 '64
Special sophistication issue: Bad. il Esquire 62:52-6 Ag '64
Spoofmaster. M. Zolotow. il Sat Eve Post 236: 26-7 Ap 20 '63
Will the real July issue of Esquire please stand? A. Gingrich. il Esquire 60:6 Ag '63
See also
Parody
PARODIZ, José J.
When the land was young. Américas 15:22-5 Jl '63
PARODY, Ovid F.
Quality secondary schools of the future. Sch Life 47:23-7 N '64
PARODY
Parody and satire deserve substantial freedom. H. F. Pilpel. Pub W 186:42 O 5 '64
See also
Parodies
PARODY (music)
Birth of comedy. P. H. Lang. il Opera N 27:8-11 F 16 '63
PAROLE
Killer had been paroled. R. P. Crossley. Read Digest 83:105-8 O '63
Waiting time. R. A. Trask. Harper 228:168-9 Ap '64
PAROS (island)
Two islands. E. Taylor. il Mlle 59:176-8+ S '64
PAROUSIA (religion) See Second advent
PARQUET flooring. See Flooring
PARR, J. Gordon
Concerning the engineers. Sat R 46:42-3 S 7 '63
PARR, Peter J.
Capital of the Nabataeans; with biographical sketch. Sci Am 209:20+, 94-102 bibliog (p 156) O '63
PARRA, Mariano
Mariano Parra and company, 92nd street Y. J. Maskey. Dance Mag 38:140 D '64
PARRIS, Wendell A.
New approach to educating Negro children in gray area schools. bibliog por Negro Hist Bul 28:61-4 D '64 (to be cont)
PARRISH, Maxfield
Grand-pop; at Manhattan's gallery of modern art. il por Time 83:76 Je 12 '64
Maxfield Parrish at ninety-three. G. E. Gillett. il Sat R 47:129-30 Mr 14 '64; Discussion. 47:70 Ap 11 '64
PARRISH, Thomas
Rope to jump, a well to dig. Reporter 31:37+ N 19 '64
PARROT and the pirates; drama. See Miller, H. L.
PARROT fever. See Psittacosis
PARROTS
Old bird won't sell; 100-year-old macaw. R. Sackett. il Life 55:13 Ag 9 '63
Sky blue. New Yorker 40:43 My 16 '64
PARRY, Albert
Destroying enemy satellites. Sci Digest 53: 35-41 Mr '63
How to grow old without aging. Sci Digest 54:86-90 O '63
Russia's hidden science city. Sci Digest 53:22-8 My '63
Science milestone; Russian who talks back to Khrushchev. Sci Digest 53:45-51 Je '63
Soviet affairs. Miss & Roc 12:40 F 4; 46 Mr 11 '63
Whiz kid of Soviet science. Sci Digest 54: 83-9 D '63
PARRY, Shelley
I believe. por Seventeen 23:231 My '64
PARRY, Stanley
Humanitarian majority. Nat R 16:1115-18 D 15 '64
Stakes in politics. Nat R 16:410+ My 19 '64
PARSEGHIAN, Ara
Ara fires up the Irish. il pors Life 57:112A-112B O 16 '64
Ara go bragh. il por Newsweek 64:72 N 2 '64
Ara the beautiful. il pors Time 84:84-6+ N 20 '64
Ara's new era. W. B. Furlong. il pors Sat Eve Post 237:72-5 N 28 '64
Century cover boon; Time cover jinx and Notre Dame's defeat. Christian Cent 81: 1575 D 16 '64

PARSEGHIAN, Ara—*Continued*
College football. il por Time 84:58 O 30 '64
Just one more game to go; with report by J. R. McDermott. il pors Life 57:101-8+ D 11 '64
Razzle-dazzle; new coach for Notre Dame. Newsweek 62:56 D 30 '63
PARSIFAL; opera. See Wagner, R.
PARSIPPANY, N.J.
Hobbies à la carte. J. Reck. il Pop Mech 119:118-19 Ap '63
PARSON, Harry L.
Flight to success. por Negro Hist Bul 26:236-7 My '63
PARSONAGE, Robert R.
Backlash and Christian faith. Christian Cent 81:1300-2 O 21 '64
PARSONS, A. Chapman
Alliance stays loose. Library J 88:4540-2 D 1 '63
PARSONS, Betty
Betty Parsons, diary of an art dealer; excerpts from An American gallery, with editoral comment. L. Alloway. il por Vogue 142:156-7+ O 1 '63
PARSONS, Donald
Detroit bank restyles its lines. il por Bsns W p76+ N 14 '64
PARSONS, Donald F.
Mitochondrial structure: two types of subunits on negatively stained mitochondrial membranes bibliog Science 140:985-7 My 31 '63
—See Chance, B. jt. auth.
PARSONS, Grace F. See Kertesz, Z. I. jt. auth.
PARSONS, Lindsey N.
Status of U.S. aerobatics. por Flying 74:43-4+ F '64
PARSONS, Louella (Oettinger)
Through a keyhole darkly. il por Time 81:52+ F 15 '63
PARSONS, M. H. C. See Sassoon, H. F. jt. auth.
PARSONS, P. A.
Genetic regulatory mechanisms at the population level in man. bibliog Science 146:924-5 N 13 '64
PARSONS, P. Allen
Double for the captain. por Outdoor Life 133:46-7+ Mr '64
Where to go fishing, vacationing, hunting (title varies) See issues of Outdoor life
PARSONS, Talcott
Social change and medical organization in the United States; a sociological perspective. bibliog f Ann Am Acad 346:21-33 Mr '63
PARSONS college, Fairfield, Ia.
Actors can be teachers. L. Sutton. il Theatre Arts 47:64-5 Ag '63
PART of growing up; story. See Bryan, C. D. B.
PART time employment
Art, creativity and the home fires. M. White. il Ladies Home J 81:66-8 Je '64
Part-time jobs for women. il Changing T 17:17-19 S '63
Part-time jobs: where and how to find them. il Good H 158:162-3 F '64
Unemployment among full-time and part-time workers. R. L. Stein and J. L. Meredith. il Mo Labor R 87:1009-13 S '64
See also
Student employment
Supplementary employment
PARTCH, Harry
Genesis of a music. P. Yates. il pors Hi Fi 13:35-8+ Jl '63
Harry isn't kidding. il por Time 82:50 Jl 5 '63
PARTHENON
Parthenon: beauty revisited. A. Menen. il Holiday 35:54-5+ Ja '64
PARTIALLY seeing children. See Blind
PARTICLE accelerators. See Accelerators (electron, etc)
PARTICLES
Virus-like particles in blood of two acute leukemia patients. J. D. Almeida and others. bibliog il Science 142:1487-9 D 13 '63
See also
Dust
PARTICLES (nuclear physics)
All atomic particles equal; summary of address. G. Chew. Sci N L 84:275 N 2 '63
Anti-matter particle, last in nuclear family. Sci N L 84:115 Ag 24 '63
Atom aristocracy backed: Dr Veksler s objection to Dr Chew's theory. Sci N L 84:295 N 9 '63
Biography of an atom and the universe; anti-Xi-zero. J. Bronowski. il N Y Times Mag p 19+ O 13 '63; Same abr. with title Amazing biography of an atom. Read Digest 84:133-6 Ja '64
Buddha's way; omega minus. il Newsweek 63:81 Mr 2 '64
Can the direction of flow of time be determined? R. G. Sachs. bibliog il Science 140:1284-90 Je 21 '63
Conservation laws of physics. G. Feinberg and M. Goldhaber. il Sci Am 209:36-45 bibliog(p 153) O '63
Eightfold way; new elementary particle, named omega minus. il Time 83:56 F 28 '64
Entirely new kind of nuclear particle found; W particle. Sci N L 84:259 O 26 '63
Game of hide and seek; anti-Xi-zero. W. Cloud. Pop Sci 183:29-30 O '63
High-energy physics; report on twelfth International conference on high-energy physics. G. Snow. Science 146:809-10+ N 6 '64
Hunting of the quark. Sci Am 210:54-6 Je '64
In a restless universe constants can vary; Westinghouse physicists prove rate of radioactive decay can be altered. Time 83:74 Je 19 '64
Lost particle: W particle. Sci Am 211:59 O '64
Magnetic monopoles. K. W. Ford. il Sci Am 209:122-5+ bibliog(p 180) D '63
New nuclear particle; b-star. Sci N L 85:84 F 8 '64
New strange particle; omega minus. il Sci N L 85:147 Mr 7 '64
Nine more particles; subnuclear particles. Sci Am 211:44 Jl '64
Nuclear zoo minus quarks. Sci N L 85:261 Ap 25 '64
Omega-minus experiment. W. B. Fowler and N. P. Samios. il Sci Am 211:36-45 O '64
Omega minus; press conference at American institute of physics. New Yorker 40:39-40 Mr 7 '64
Particle schemes. Sci Am 210:54 Ja '64
Prediction confirmed; omega-minus particle. il Sci Am 210:60-2 Ap '64
Resonant particles in high-energy physics; report of meeting at Ohio university, April 1963. L. C. L. Yuan. Science 140:1430 Je 28 '63
Search for anti-Xi-zero particle. Time 82:54 Ag 23 '63
Simple structure for nuclear particles? Sky & Tel 25:252 My '63
Strange atomic particle; baryon. Sci N L 85:179 Mr 21 '64
Strongly interacting particles. G. F. Chew and others. il Sci Am 210:74-93 bibliog(p 152) F '64
Table for thirty-two; anti Xi-zero particle. il Newsweek 62:73 Ag 26 '63
Theory of nuclear particles developed. Sci N L 84:2 Jl 6 '63
34th particle. Sci Am 209:54 O '63
Tracks of charged particles in high polymers. R. L. Fleischer and P. B. Price. bibliog il Science 140:1221-2 Je 14 '63
Weak quantum; w particle. Sci Am 210:54 Mr '64
See also
Electrons
Mesons
Neutrinos
Positrons
Van Allen radiation belts
Physiological effects
Atomic scientists link work for new ideas; conference at Brookhaven national laboratory sponsored by IAEA. il Bsns W p 194-6 O 19 '63
Size determination
Fibrous filters as particle-size analyzers. M. D. Silverman and W. E. Browning, jr. bibliog il Science 143:572-3 F 7 '64
PARTICLES, Elementary. See Particles (nuclear physics)
PARTICLES, Interplanetary. See Matter, Interstellar
PARTIES. See Balls (parties); Childrens parties; Entertaining
PARTIES, Political. See Political parties
PARTIN, Edward Grady
Scheme to kill Bob Kennedy and Kennedy's kids. pors Life 56:44-6+ My 15 '64
about
Behind the plot to assassinate Robert Kennedy. C. R. Mollenhoff. il por Look 28:49-50+ My 19 '64
Hoffa trial. F. J. Cook. il Nation 198:415-39 Ap 27 '64
Lie detector confirms his story. il por Life 56:88-9 My 15 '64
PARTISANSHIP
Bipartisanship. Commonweal 78:3 Mr 29 '63
Two little words. E. J. Hughes. Newsweek 61:19 Ap 8 '63

PARTITIONS
Decorative dividers. P. Clapp. il Am Home 67:24+ Ja '64
Dining room wall that opens, shuts. il Sunset 132:122 Ap '64
Going to pot; flower pot room divider. il Pop Mech 120:32 Jl '63
House divided. G. O'Brien. il N Y Times Mag p40-1 Je 23 '63
Interior partitions: near-total flexibility. B. P. Spring. il Arch Forum 120:117 F '64
It's a hi-fi room divider. il Sunset 133:136 O '64
Lightweight partitions cut school costs. il Arch Rec 133:212 Mr '63
Sound isolation between teaching spaces. W. R. Farrell. il Arch Rec 134:229-32 O '63

PARTNERSHIP
See also
Joint adventures

PARTNERSHIPS, Farm family. See Father-son farm operating agreements

PARTON, Margaret
When old folks become a problem. Ladies Home J 80:57+ Mr '63

PARTRIDGE berries
Two attractive native ground covers. I. D. Jolly. il Horticulture 41:68 F '63

PARTRIDGE shooting
Harder the better. C. Conley. il Field & S 68:33-5+ O '63
How to hunt chukars. T. Trueblood. Field & S 69:24+ O '64
Partridge are honest birds. D. Tracy. il Outdoor Life 134:56-9+ O '64
See also
Grouse shooting

PARTRIDGES
Capricious Asian is a citizen at last; chukar partridge. V. Kraft. il Sports Illus 19:76-9 D 9 '63

PARTY cards. See Place cards

PARTY conventions. See National conventions (political)

PARTY favors
Hard-boiled egg art. il Design 64:160-1 Mr '63
Who's who in holiday hats; make-believe millinery. il McCalls 92:126-7+ D '64

PARTY funds. See Campaign funds

PARTY games. See Games

PARTY government
Deadlock of democracy, by J. M. Burns. Review
Nat R 14:241-2 Mr '63. J. J. Kilpatrick
Reporter 28:48-50+ Mr 14 '63. A. Ranney; Reply. J. M. Burns. 28:6+ Ap 11 '63
See also
Partisanship

PARTY of the institutional revolution. See Political parties—Mexico

PARTY platforms. See Platforms, Political

PARTY whips. See United States—Congress—Voting

PARVIN, Edna M.
Christmas in miniature. Hobbies 69:122-4 D '64

PARVIN, Stuart A.
Miniaturia. See issues of Hobbies

PASADENA, Calif.

Libraries

Best-read city in the U.S.A: Pasadena. S. Grafton. il McCalls 90:48+ Ap '63

Parades

Big bowls of glitter. il Life 56:38-45 Ja 3 '64
Coming up roses. H. Sutton. il Sat R 46:30-1 D 21 '63
Smokey comes up roses. D. K. Porter. il Am For 70:4+ Mr '64

Recreation

Pooled facilities and services pay off. E. E. Bignell. il Recreation 57:346-7 S '64

PASADENA art museum
Symbiosis: Pasadena art museum and dance classes. H. Mullin and V. Potter. il Dance Mag 37:38-41 F '63

PASADENA public library
Out of the golden haze. W. Jones. il Library J 89:2298 Je 1 '64

PASARELL, Charles, Jr
Nineteen-year-old Puerto Rican brings U.S. tennis new hope. J. R. Moskin. il pors Look 27:104a-104c+ Je 18 '63

PASCAGOULA chronicle-star and advertiser
In a madhouse's din. il Newsweek 62:48 Jl 8 '63

PASCAL, Gabriel
GBS in filmland. V. Delacorte. il Esquire 62:150-1+ D '64

PASCHAL, Justin
First things; poem. Commonweal 79:310 D 6 '63
Mozart; poem. America 108:800 Je 1 '63
Song to the Virgin. America 111:189 Ag 22 '64

PASK, Henry
Cook's tour. Travel 119:51+ Ap '63

PASS-throughs
Pass-through closes on both sides. il Sunset 133:149 O '64
Pass-through to outdoors; outside shelf takes the place of a window sill. il Sunset 133:122 N '64
Pass-throughs are step savers. il Sunset 133:108 O '64
These pass-throughs serve well. il Bet Hom & Gard 43:81 Ja '65
This is a telephone pass-through. il Sunset 133:139 O '64

PASSACAGLIAS (violin)
Scordatura; and the Mysteries of the rosary. E. Salzman. Hi Fi 13:73-4 Ap '63

PASSAGE through the clouds; drama. See Billetdoux, F.

PASSAMAQUODDY project. See Passamaquoddy tidal power project

PASSAMAQUODDY tidal power project
New deal project that is being revived. il U S News 55:10 Jl 29 '63
Passamaquoddy revived. Sci Am 209:83-4 S '63
Passamaquoddy-Saint John report received by President Kennedy; remarks, July 16, 1963. J. F. Kennedy. Dept State Bul 49:248-9 Ag 12 '63
Reviving Passamaquoddy. W. S. Ellis. il Nation 199:10-12 Jl 13 '64
Taming 'Quoddy's tides. il Newsweek 62:64 Jl 29 '63
To harness the Quoddy. il Time 82:21 Jl 26 '63

PASSENGER fares. See Airlines—Fares

PASSENGER service on airlines. See Airlines—Passenger service

PASSENGER traffic (railroads) See Railroads—Passenger traffic

PASSER-by; story. See Nutt, M. E.

PASSIFLORA. See Passionflowers

PASSION music
See also
Phonograph records—Passion music

PASSION of Christ. See Jesus Christ—Passion

PASSION of Josef D; drama. See Chayefsky, P.

PASSION plays
Rock passion play; A man dies, musical drama at London's Royal Albert Hall. il Newsweek 63:83 Ap 6 '64
U.S. Oberammergau; 27th season for the Black Hills passion play of Spearfish, S.D. America 111:28 Jl 11 '64

PASSIONFLOWERS
Passion flower. E. Frederick. il Horticulture 42:41 Ja '64

PASSIVE resistance to government
Cases of conscience. J. Ciardi. Sat R 46:10-11 F 2 '63
Civil disobedience; address, August 11, 1964. M. I. Liebman. Vital Speeches 30:766-8 O 1 '64
Essence and ethics of civil disobedience. C. Cohen. il Nation 198:257-62 Mr 16 '64
Is it ever right to break the law? C. Frankel. il N Y Times Mag p 17+ Ja 12 '64
Is it ever right to break the law? pro and con discussion. il Sr Schol 84:12-13+ Mr 6 '64
Nonviolence in the racial crisis. W. R. Miller. Christian Cent 81:927-30 Jl 22 '64; Discussion. 81:1179 S 23 '64
Obeying unjust laws, the Methodist view. U S News 56:12 My 18 '64
See also
Negroes in the United States—Segregation, Resistance to

PASSLOFF, Aileen
Aileen Passloff and dance company at Brooklyn academy of music. J. Maskey. Dance Mag 37:16+ Jl '63
Aileen Passloff and dance company, Judson memorial church. D. Hering. Dance Mag 38:65 Jl '64

PASSMAN, Otto E.
Foreign aid: success or failure? Nat R 14:401-4 My 21 '63

PASSMAN, Otto E.—*Continued*
Why I am opposed to foreign aid. por N Y Times Mag p 16-17 Jl 7 '63

about

Blunting the ax. Newsweek 64:23-4 Jl 6 '64
Foreign aid forever. Nat R 16:577 Jl 14 '64
Mr Passman meets his match. E. B. Drew. Reporter 31:40-3 N 19 '64
Vanities of Otto Passman. M. Kempton. New Repub 149:14-15 D 28 '63

PASSMORE, John
Books. Sci Am 208:177-8+ My '63

PASSPORTS
Certain foreign passports valid beyond expiration date. A. P. Schwartz. il Dept State Bul 51:890 D 21 '64
How to get a passport. Bet Hom & Gard 42: 131 O '64
Jaime García Terrēs and the *lista negra*. F. H. Wardlaw. Harper 230:16+ Ja '65
Man with a country; defense of the basic American right to travel; excerpt from What can a man do? M. Mayer. Harper 228:88-90+ Mr '64; Discussion. 228:6 My '64
Passports for Communists; section 6 of the Subversive activities control act of 1950 declared unconstitutional. Time 84:51 Jl 3 '64

PAST, The
It is one world or no world. A. J. Toynbee. il N Y Times Mag p28+ Ap 5 '64
New generation in charge; old mistakes forgotten? il U S News 55:98-100 Ag 19 '63
Robert Paul Smith's attic. R. P. Smith. il McCalls 92:90+ O '64
Speaking out; who's that tampering with my clock? H. A. Smith. il Sat Eve Post 236: 10+ Ag 24 '63

PASTA, Giuditta
Queen of bel canto. M. J. Matz. il por Opera N 27:26-8 Mr 30 '63

PASTA. See Cookery, Italian; Macaroni

PASTE
Pens for pasting papers; Exec paste pen. il Consumer Bul 46:31 Ag '63
See also
Adhesives

PASTED pictures. See Collage

PASTEL drawing
Pastels for dry painting. il Design 64:210-11 Je '63
Working with oil pastel. il Design 65:188-9 My '64

PASTEL painting. See Pastel drawing

PASTORAL conferences. See Clergy conferences

PASTORAL counseling. See Counseling

PASTORAL drama
Pastoral tradition. H. Weinstock. il Opera N 27:8-13 Mr 30 '63

PASTORE, Arthur R. Jr
Beneath Toronto's skyscrapers. Travel 122:35-8 Ag '64

PASTORE, John O.
Democratic record; address, August 24, 1964. Vital Speeches 30:706-8 S 15 '64

about

Big chairman up yonder. por Time 84:19-20 Ag 7 '64
Incorrect, illogical, etc; R. McNamara vs. Joint committee on atomic energy. por Time 83:31 Ja 3 '64

PASTORS. See Clergy

PASTRANO, Willie
Champ's fist was on the sparrow's eye. T. Maule. il por Sports Illus 20:48+ Ap 20 '64

PASTRY
Cream puff's secret; chou paste. il Sunset 131:176-8+ N '63
Cream supreme. C. Claiborne. il N Y Times Mag p92+ Ap 28 '63
Fried pastry idea. il Sunset 130:178+ Mr '63
Here's how to bake Danish. il Sunset 130: 166-8+ Mr '63
Honoring the pastry cook's patron saint; St Honore cake. C. Claiborne. il N Y Times Mag p47 Ja 26 '64
Invite friends to a strudel stretch. il Sunset 132:116+ F '64
It's easier than you think. il Good H 158: 106-21+ Mr '64
More ways to use fila dough. Sunset 131:227-8 N '63
Name is *pirog*; Russian turnovers. J. Hewitt. il N Y Times Mag p 147 N 15 '64
Quiche Lorraine: French main-dish pie; with recipes. M. Kaytor. il Look 28:46-7 S 22 '64
Step by step to the stars: cream puffs & eclairs. il McCalls 90:132-3+ Ap '63
Susan our teenage cook makes chocolate eclairs. il Good H 158:156 F '64
See also
Pie
Tarts

PASTURES
Fertilize pastures! six reasons why. L. E. Zeman. il Suc Farm 61:46-7 Ag '63
Help pastures this summer. Suc Farm 62:31 Jl '64
How range fertilization pays off. Suc Farm 61:82 Je '63
Pasture management, seven tips for you. Suc Farm 62:66 Ap '64
See also
Stock ranges

PATAGONIA
Sequoia of South America. E. J. Wilhelm, jr. il Nat Parks Mag 37:8-10 D '63

PATCH, Margaret
Traveler's acknowledgments. Craft Horiz 23: 4 Ja '63

PATCHET, G. S.
Hidden premium. Atlan 212:106-7 S '63

PATCHING. See Mending

PATCHWORK
Aprons Americana made to appeal. il Good H 158:132 Ap '64

PATEE, Doris S.
Odyssey book shop opens in South Hadley, Mass. Pub W 185:71-3 My 25 '64

PATEK, John M.
What do you know about peatmoss? Horticulture 42:50-1+ Mr '64

PATENT office (United States) See United States—Patent office

PATENT rights. See Patents

PATENT searching
Automation of patents. E. Hall. Sci N L 84:213 O 5 '63

PATENTS
Creativity penalized. B. F. Miessner. Miss & Roc 14:4 My 11 '64; Reply. T. M. Morse. 14: 6 Je 8 '64
Design protection. L. Epstein. Craft Horiz 24:9-10 Mr '64
GAO urges stricter invention report rule. K. Johnsen. il Aviation W 82:101+ Ja 25 '65
How to cash in on your invention. N. Carlisle. il Pop Sci 183:122-4+ O '63
Invention lag. S. V. Jones. il Sci Digest 57: 65-70 Ja '65
Knocking down the pole; Supreme court's ruling on conflict between Sears, Roebuck and Chicago's Stiffel co. over pole lamps. Time 83:86 Mr 20 '64
New NASA patent policy to aid industry. W. J. Normyle. Aviation W 81:26-7 O 5 '64
Patent giveaway. Nation 196:259 Mr 30 '63
Patents: industry, universities renew debate on who gets rights to U.S.-sponsored medical research. E. Langer. Science 147: 134-5 Ja 8 '65
Patents of the week. See issues of Science news letter
Patents; proposal to change NASA regulations. E. Langer. Science 139:118 Mr 22 '63
Reform pending. Time 83:94+ F 28 '64
Savants, sandwiches, and space suits. J. H. Munster, jr. and J. C. Smith. Science 145: 1276-81 S 18 '64; Discussion. 146:865, 1636-7 N 13, D 25 '64
Soviet patent policy: new incentives for the inventor; reprint. A. Kiron. Bul Atomic Sci 19:12-13 D '63
U.S. pat. pend; patents for americium and curium. Newsweek 63:81 Ap 6 '64
U.S. patent policy and government research. R. L. Wright. il Bul Atomic Sci 19:9-13 D '63; Reply with rejoinder. M. A. Holman. 20:32-4 O '64
What is the key to progress? il Bsns W p 132+ My 16 '64
What's public property? A. Brynes. New Repub 148:6 Ap 6 '63
Xerox marks the spot. Time 83:86 F 21 '64
See also
Inventions
United States—Patent office

International aspects

Patents and pirates; Italy. il Fortune 67:94+ My '63
Russians are pressing foreign sale of patents. Nations Bsns 51:58 Ag '63

Searching

See Patent searching

PATENTS, Government owned
DOD may toughen patent policies. Miss & Roc 15:11 D 7 '64
DOD patent policy tightening. H. Taylor. Miss & Roc 13:14 O 21 '63

PATENTS, Government owned—*Continued*
First patent issued U.S. Sci N L 84:102 Ag 17 '63
New NASA patent policy to aid industry. W. J. Normyle. Aviation W 81:26-7 O 5 '64
Patent giveaway. Nation 196:259 Mr 30 '63
Patent rights under federal R&D contracts. il Harvard Bsns R 41:6-7+ S '63
Patent rules designed to eliminate variations in government policies. Aviation W 79:32 O 21 '63
Senate may scrutinize NASA patent waiving. Miss & Roc 16:14 Ja 4 '65

PATERSON, N.J.

Riots

Black rage in New Jersey. Time 84:19 Ag 21 '64
White boycott; racial violence in Paterson and Elizabeth, N.J. Newsweek 64:27+ Ag 24 '64

PATERSON, N.J. free public library
Paterson, N.J. mayor bans The children of Sanchez. Library J 88:1128 Mr 15 '63

PATÉS. See Cookery—Meat

PATHOGENIC bacteria. See Bacteria, Pathogenic

PATHOLOGY
Electron microscopy: proteins in experimental pathology; report of symposium at annual meeting of the Federation of American societies for experimental biology. G. W. Richter. Science 141:834-5 Ag 30 '63
Last word. il Time 82:83 O 11 '63
See also
Inflammation

PATHOLOGY, Plant. See Plants—Diseases and pests

PATHS. See Garden walks; Trails

PATIENT care. See Hospitals

PATIENTS, Hospital. See Sick, The

PATIENTS and physicians. See Physicians and patients

PATINO, Jimmy Ortiz-. See Ortiz-Patino, J.

PATIO furniture. See Furniture, Outdoor

PATIOS. See Outdoor rooms

PATMAN, Wright
Patman hits funds; excerpts from report. Sr Schol 82:1T-2T Ja 30 '63
Wright Patman: champion of cheap money; interview, ed. by G. R. Rosen. por Duns R 83:59-60+ My '64

about

Fed remodels itself; with editorial comment. il pors Bsns W p64-5+. 180 My 16 '64
Foundations as a tax dodge; Patman's probe of the activities of tax-exempt foundations. F. J. Cook. Nation 196:321-5 Ap 20 '63
Foundations: Patman maintains pressure for tighter regulation of tax-exempt organizations. J. Walsh. por Science 145:559-61 Ag 7 '64
Foundations: Patman plugs away at theme that growth, operations of tax exempts call for scrutiny. J. Walsh. Science 142:370-2 O 18 '63
Heat on foundations. Bsns W p38 S 19 '64
I'm amazed; foundation's finances. Newsweek 64:61-2 Ag 24 '64
New look at money management. Bsns W p 148 Jl 11 '64
Now it's the money managers who are under fire. il por U S News 54:94-5 Ap 1 '63
Oddball crusade of Congressman Patman. P. Duke. il pors Sat Eve Post 237:62-3 Mr 7 '64
Patman hits a raw nerve. Bsns W p68 F 8 '64
Patman shoots again. Bsns W p 146+ O 26 '63
Tighter reins on the Fed? por Bsns W p68 Jl 4 '64

PATNICK, Joe
(comp) Extremism. N Y Times Mag p35 S 20 '64

PATON, Alan, and Shah, Krishna
Sponono. Criticism
Cath World 199:199-200 Je '64
Nation 198:404 Ap 20 '64
New Yorker 40:95 Ap 11 '64
Newsweek 63:60 Ap 13 '64
Sat R 47:31 Ap 18 '64

PATON, William B.
Profile: twice a president. F. G. B. Hutchings. por Library J 88:1956-7 My 15 '63

PATRIARCHS (Bible)
God chooses a family; with article by E. A. Speiser, adapted from introductory chapter to Genesis in the Anchor Bible. il Life 57:24-35+ D 25 '64

PATRICK, J. Max
Relish of David. Sat R 46:46+ Mr 23 '63

PATRICK, Johnstone G.
Unamuno's Christ; poem. Christian Cent 81:1166 S 23 '64

PATRICK, Ted
Holiday life. por Newsweek 62:40-1 Jl 1 '63
Ted Patrick. Holiday 35:37 My '64

PATRIOTISM
Hard kind of patriotism. A. E. Stevenson. Harper 227:31-4 Jl '63
Reluctant patriot. R. Postgate. il Holiday 36:12+ N '64
Risks of patriotism. America 109:9 Jl 6 '63
See also
Americanism
Citizenship

PATRIOTS (football club) See Football clubs

PATROL boats. See Police boats

PATROL torpedo boats. See Torpedo boats

PATRON saints. See Saints

PATRONAGE (theater) See Theater—Finance

PATRONAGE, Art. See Art patronage

PATRONAGE, Political
New kind of national election; excerpts from Congress: the sapless branch. J. S. Clark. Harper 228:72-4+ My '64
Our own public scandal; address, August 7, 1963. E. P. Neilan. Vital Speeches 29:730-2 S 15 '63; Same abr. with title Political immorality, a speech that rocked Congress. Read Digest 83:126-9 N '63; Excerpts. U S News 55:102-3 Ag 26 '63
See also
Nepotism

PATTEN, Bernard C.
Plankton: optimum diversity structure of a summer community. bibliog Science 140:894-8; 144:557-8 My 24 '63, My 1 '64

PATTERNS (dress)
Pattern for profit. L. Morse. Duns R 83:74 F '64

PATTERNS (for home workshops)
Make your yard a Christmas card; Project-a-plan transparencies. D. Swartwout. il Pop Mech 120:138-43 D '63

PATTERSON, Alicia
Boss lady. por Newsweek 62:56 Jl 15 '63
Dynasty's end? por Time 82:69-70 Jl 12 '63

PATTERSON, Barbara H.
Tub fun for two. Parents Mag 38:50-1+ My '63

PATTERSON, Bernardin J.
Reflections of a Negro priest. por Cath World 200:269-76 F '65

PATTERSON, Charles
Primer on squirrel hunting. Outdoor Life 131:62-3+ Je '63

PATTERSON, Clara E.
Exercises for a younger, prettier, face; excerpt from Facial isometrics. McCalls 92:112 Ja '65

PATTERSON, E. L. and others
Ethylation: biological formation of an S-ethyl homolog of lincomycin. bibliog Science 146:1691-2 D 25 '64

PATTERSON, Elizabeth Gregg
If it's shocking, will it sell? Writer 76:17-19 Jl '63

PATTERSON, Floyd
I live with myself; ed. by G. Rogin. Sports Illus 19:27 Ag 5 '63
I want to destroy Clay; ed. by M. Gross. por Sports Illus 21:42-4+ O 19 '64

about

Continental comeback. J. Lovesey. il por Sports Illus 20:44-6 Ja 20 '64
Fight in Sweden between boxing's forgotten men. T. Maule. il Sports Illus 21:50-2 Jl 6 '64
Floyd's fight to save his pride. P. Hamill. il por Sat Eve Post 237:76-8 Je 27 '64
Goodby, Gus. Sports Illus 20:14 Je 1 '64
Heavyweight muddle. R. Boyle and M. Sharnik. il por Sports Illus 18:12-15 Mr 25 '63
Loser. G. Talese. por Esquire 61:65-8+ Mr '64
Pros and cons. Newsweek 63:58 Ja 20 '64
Sporting scene; Patterson vs. Liston return fight. A. J. Liebling. il New Yorker 39:62+ Ag 10 '63
Still too tender to be a tiger. T. Maule. por Sports Illus 21:20-1 Jl 13 '64
Ten thousand words a minute. N. Mailer. Esquire 59:109-20 F '63

PATTERSON, Frances Taylor
Madeira and Columbus; poem. Commonweal 79:667 F 28 '64

PATTERSON, Franklin, and Donovan, Gail
Citizens now, voters soon. PTA Mag 59:28-30 bibliog(p37) S '64

PATTERSON, George H. See Lemmon, W. B. jt. auth
PATTERSON, Jack E.
Challenge from Birmingham. New Repub 150:20+ My 23 '64
PATTERSON, James M.
School referenda. Vital Speeches 29:463-5 My 15 '63
PATTERSON, James T.
F.D.R. and the Democratic triumph. Cur Hist 47:216-20+ O '64
PATTERSON, John H.
Original schoolmaster. por Duns R 82:3 D '63
PATTERSON, Lew
Cops with guns; stop or I'll shoot. New Repub 150:8-9 Mr 14 '64
PATTERSON, N. A. See Pickett, A. D. jt. auth.
PATTERSON, Nancy-Lou
Climbing Mt Carmel; poem. America 108:674 My 11 '63
PATTERSON, Richard S. and Langley, H. D.
How the Department of state got its name. Dept State Bul 51:370-6 S 14 '64
PATTERSON, Robert
Count and countess; interview, ed. by P. Moed. por Opera N 28:16 F 22 '64
PATTERSON, Webster T.
College theology: career for laymen. America 110:412-16 Mr 28 '64
PATTERSON, William D.
In praise of travel. Sat R 47:28-9 Ja 4 '64
New freedom. Sat R 46:30 Ag 24 '63
SR's businessman of the year. Sat R 47:45-6+ Ja 11 '64; 48:39-40+ Ja 9 '65
SR's eleventh-twelfth annual advertising awards. Sat R 46:62-7 Ap 13 '63; 47:73-6+ Ap 11 '64
Six feet, six hours, one world. Sat R 48:22 Ja 2 '65
Tourists, pawns, and pigeons. Sat R 47:24+ Ag 15 '64
Ugly American in dark Africa. Sat R 46:18-20+ Je 22 '63
PATTI, Adelina
Romance a hundred years ago. M. E. Peltz. il pors Opera N 28:12-15 F 22 '64
PATTON, Arch
Executive compensation by 1970. Harvard Bsns R 42:137-46 S '64
Upturn in executive compensation. Harvard Bsns R 41:133-7 S '63
PATTON, Frances Gray
Two nice girls; story. Seventeen 23:164-5 Ap '64
PATTON, George Smith, 1885-1945
Before the colors fade, by F. Ayer, jr. Review
Sat R il por 47:36 Jl 11 '64. M. S. Watson
Patton family sues to stop Farago biography. Pub W 185:58-9 Je 15 '64
Patton heirs withdraw objection to Farago book. Pub W 186:51 Jl 6 '64
Patton: ordeal and triumph, by L. Farago. Review
Time por 84:112+ O 30 '64
PATTON, James George
Which is better for wheat growers? por Farm J 87:32+ Mr '63
—and others
Inspection of Cuba. New Repub 148:38-9 Mr 23 '63
PATTON, John A.
Six enemies of executive output. Duns R 81:33-4+ Mr '63
Speaking out. por Sat Eve Post 237:6+ F 29 '64
PATTON, Levi R.
Gracious living in Tennessee. il pors Ebony 18:98-100+ F '63
PATTON, Robert L. See Nowosielski, J. W. jt. auth.
PATTON, T. F.
Manpower development in a changing world; address, October 13, 1964. Vital Speeches 31:88-90 N 15 '64
PATUREAU, Alan. See Lindeman, B. jt. auth.
PATUXENT wildlife research center. See Wildlife sanctuaries
PATZCUARO, LAKE
Lake in the clouds. H. Sutton. Sat R 47:30+ Ap 4 '64
PAUKER, John
Commuter poem. New Repub 149:20 Jl 20 '63
PAUL, Saint
Greatest missionary: Paul. J. Knox. il pors Life 57:112-20+ D 25 '64
Kairopractice; concerning authorship of Romans, Corinthians, and Galatians. Time 81:56 Mr 15 '63
Saint and science; computer analysis of Pauline Epistles. Newsweek 62:82 N 18 '63
St Paul and the computer. Sci Am 210:56 Ja '64
They made our world. L. Rosten. il Look 27:34-5 D 31 '63
Word. V. P. McCorry. America 111:116 Ag 1 '64

Teaching

Greatest missionary: Paul. J. Knox. il pors Life 57:120+ D 25 '64
PAUL VI, pope
Birth control: Catholics take a new look; excerpts from address, June 23, 1964. por U S News 57:14 Jl 6 '64
Ecumenical council; address, September 14, 1964. Vital Speeches 30:738-41 O 1 '64
Letter from Pope Paul VI; concerning Pius XII and the Jews. Commonweal 79:651-2 F 28 '64
Mutual understanding and friendship; address, December 3, 1964. Vital Speeches 31:132 D 15 '64
Needs of the world; address, December 23, 1963. Vital Speeches 30:198-200 Ja 15 '64
Turn to religion; address, March 29, 1964. Vital Speeches 30:386-7 Ap 15 '64

about

After a year as pope; how Paul is changing things. por U S News 56:14 Je 1 '64
Atlantic report. Atlan 212:45-6+ O '63
Auspicious beginning. il por Newsweek 62:55-6 Jl 8 '63
Book of the month; Mind of Paul VI. C. L. Palms. Cath World 200:116-17 N '64
Breaking the walls; curia and the council. il por Newsweek 62:80 D 16 '63
Christian summit? Newsweek 62:47 D 23 '63
Conflict of interest; proposed theological study center in Jerusalem. Newsweek 64:80 S 14 '64
Conversational letter; Pope Paul's first encyclical. J. Cogley. Commonweal 81:12-14 S 25 '64
Council politics at dead end. M. E. Marty. Christian Cent 81:1519-20 D 9 '64
Development and awareness. R. W. Hanning. il Commonweal 80:634-7 S 18 '64
Dialogue in Pope Paul's encyclical. J. B. Sheerin. Cath World 200:4-7 O '64
Dialogue of salvation. America 111:176 Ag 22 '64
Easter message. Commonweal 80:77 Ap 10 '64
Ecclesiam Suam. Commonweal 80:561 Ag 21 '64
Ecumenical sadness and hope. M. Novak. Christian Cent 81:1518 D 9 '64
Franco and Pope Paul. Christian Cent 80:995-6 Ag 14 '63; Discussion. 80:1276 O 16 '63
Habemus Papam! Paulum VI. J. N. Moody. America 109:10-11 Jl 6 '63
His church. por Newsweek 64:76 Ag 24 '64
His church; first encyclical. il por Time 84:35 Ag 21 '64
History marches on. America 110:152 F 1 '64
How new Pope plans to modernize church. il por U S News 55:46-8 O 14 '63
John's spirit, Paul's task. Life 55:4 Jl 5 '63
Kiss of peace. il por Newsweek 63:76 Ja 20 '64
Language of Rome. America 111:652 N 21 '64; Reply. F. Valsasnini. 112:91-2 Ja 23 '65
Letter from Vatican City. X. Rynne. New Yorker 39:74+ Jl 20; 179-86+ S 28; 123-4+ O 26; 149-50+ N 30 '63; 88+ Ja 18; 40:166+ S 19 '64; 90-103 Ja 9 '65
Montini and photogenicity. Christian Cent 80:895 Jl 10 '63
Montini becomes Pope Paul VI. Christian Cent 80:852 Jl 3 '63
Nephew's portrait of Pope Paul; ed. by S. Fliegers. G. B. Montini. il por Look 28:21-7 F 25 '64
New encyclical; Ecclesiam Suam. R. M. Brown. Commonweal 81:14-16 S 25 '64
New era in the Catholic church. il por U S News 55:100 D 16 '63
New pope. Nat R 16:711+ Ag 25 '64
New Pope, a precedent breaker. il por U S News 55:19 Jl 8 '63
Path to follow. il pors Time 81:40-2+ Je 28 '63; Same abr. with title Pope Paul VI. Read Digest 83:88-92 S '63
Paul and the curia. il por Newsweek 62:62 S 30 '63
Paul VI and the bishops. O. Hastings. il Reporter 29:23-5 D 19 '63
Paul VI: first year. America 111:8 Jl 4 '64
Paul VI on Vietnam. America 109:337 S 28 '63
Paul VI to continue Pope John's reforms. Sr Schol 83:11-12 S 13 '63
Pauline style. America 110:35 Ja 11 '64
Paul's holy reign begins; with report by R. T. Elson. il pors Life 55:22-9 Jl 5 '63

PAUL VI, pope—about—*Continued*
Paul's way and. . . il por Newsweek 63:83 Ap 6 '64
Peace message; Pope Paul's Christmas message. Commonweal 81:467-8 Ja 8 '65
Perspectives on Paul VI. E. Duff. Christian Cent 80:1128-31 S 18 '63
Pope and observers. America 111:434 O 17 '64
Pope increases powers of Catholic bishops. Christian Cent 80:1193 O 2 '63
Pope on industrial society. America 111:83 Jl 25 '64
Pope opens second council session. Christian Cent 80:1228 O 9 '63
Pope orders liturgy changes. Christian Cent 81:199 F 12 '64
Pope Paul and a neighbor's testimony. Christian Cent 80:1021 Ag 21 '63
Pope Paul and U Thant topic: religious persecution. il por U S News 55:16 Jl 22 '63
Pope Paul, firm and realistic. J. B. Sheerin. Cath World 198:75-9 N '63
Pope Paul follows along Pope John's path. R. Neville. il pors N Y Times Mag p23+ S 22 '63
Pope Paul on the church. M. Novak. il Commonweal 80:631-4 S 18 '64
Pope Paul VI. Commonweal 78:387 Jl 5 '63
Pope Paul VI. E. Forcella. New Repub 149: 7-9 Jl 6 '63
Pope Paul VI issues first encyclical; Ecclesiam Suam (His church) Christian Cent 81:1029 Ag 19 '64
Pope Paul's address to the curia. M. Novak. Commonweal 79:89-90 O 18 '63
Pope Paul's ecumenical perspective; address. A. Dulles. Cath World 200:15-21 O '64
Pope Paul's other dialogue. J. Gremillion. il por(cover) Cath World 198:208-14 Ja '64
Pope Paul's progressive speech; concerning opening address at third session of ecumenical council. J. B. Sheerin. Cath World 200:73-7 N '64
Pope reasserts his primacy. Christian Cent 80:1227-8 O 7 '63
Pope runs the church. Time 84:66 N 27 '64
Pope sobers talks of Christian unity. Christian Cent 81:1421 N 18 '64
Pope, the bishops, and Edward Gibbon. O. Hastings. il Reporter 31:22-5 D 31 '64
Pope's words; with statement. America 111:33 Jl 11 '64
Reactions to Ecclesiam Suam. America 111: 204 Ag 29 '64
Report from Vatican City. J. Cogley. Commonweal 78:413-14 Jl 12 '63
Riddle of Pope Paul VI. A. Leone-Moats. il por Nat R 15:347-9+ O 22 '63
Rome and Saigon. Christian Cent 80:1067 S 4 '63
Russian calls on Pope but Greek snubs him. Christian Cent 80:1193 O 2 '63
Style of a Pope; Archbishop Montini's lenten pastoral. America 109:7 Jl 6 '63
Tasks of Pope Paul VI. il por U S News 55: 43-4 Jl 1 '63
To the council fathers; concerning Pope Paul VI's discourse to open second session of Vatican II. America 109:412 O 12 '63
Toward brotherhood, concerning Paul VI's second Christmas message. America 112:39 Ja 9 '65
Triumph of Paul VI. S. De Gramont. il pors Sat Eve Post 236:79-83 Jl 27 '63
Vatican and U.S: closer ties? il U S News 55:37 Jl 15 '63
Vatican II & the Jews. F. E. Cartus. Commentary 39:19-29 Ja '65
Vatican II: legacy of John XXIII. il por Sr Schol 83:3+ N 1 '63
Vatican II, session 2. E. Duff. Christian Cent 81:1034-7, 1057-61 Ag 19-26 '64
Venture in ambivalence; Ecclesiam Suam. Christian Cent 81:1051-2 Ag 26 '64
Vision of a modern church. E. M. Borgese. il Nation 198:46-9 Ja 13 '64
We have a Pope; Paul VI: baffling, brilliant. il pors Newsweek 62:42-5 Jl 1 '63
What happened to curia reform? Christian Cent 81:1101 S 9 '64
What the Pope said. R. M. Brown. Commonweal 79:165-7 N 1 '63
Where Pope Paul is leading his church. il

Visit to India, 1964

Bombay's spiritual spectacular. il Time 84: 92 D 4 '64
Catholic congress in Bombay. P. G. Altbach. Christian Cent 82:116+ Ja 27 '65
Crossfire. Newsweek 64:89 N 16 '64
Missionary Pope: passage to India. il Newsweek 64:52-4 D 14 '64
Paul in India. America 111:795 D 19 '64
Pilgrim. J. O'Gara. Commonweal 81:438 D 25 '64
Pope as pilgrim. il por Time 84:90 D 11 '64
Pope's historic passage to India. il pors Life 57:28-33 D 18 '64
Subject of controversy: the Pope's trip to India. por U S News 57:20 D 7 '64
Why the Pope made his historic trip. il por U S News 57:20 D 14 '64

Visit to the Holy Land, 1964

Ahead: a new era in religious unity? il por U S News 56:16 Ja 20 '64
Artist's reverent portrait of Pope Paul's pilgrimage; with reproductions of painting by J. Duhème. McCalls 91:113-17 Ap '64
Christ's peace and the world's. Life 56:4 Ja 17 '64
Covering a pilgrimage. il Time 83:50 Ja 17 '64
Did the world watch in vain? Christian Cent 81:131-2 Ja 29 '64
First fruits in Rome; Pope to visit Holy Land. America 109:757 D 14 '63
For the Pope: a pilgrimage to the Holy Land. por U S News 55:24 D 16 '63
Gestures and symbols. Commonweal 79:449 Ja 17 '64
Good news from Bethlehem. Christian Cent 81:99-100 Ja 22 '64
History-making trip: Pope's visit to Holy Land. il U S News 56:36-7 Ja 6 '64
Holy Land trip: pilgrims and jets. il por Newsweek 63:62-3 Ja 6 '64
Impact of a trip. America 110:156 F 1 '64
In his footsteps; announcement of visit to the Holy Land. America 109:788-9 D 21 '63
Israel and the pilgrimage. P. S. Konstam. Christian Cent 81:204-6 F 12 '64; Reply. E. Berger. 81:524 Ap 22 '64
Journey to a place like no other. R. Payne. il N Y Times Mag p5-7+ D 22 '63
Land that holds the legend of our lives. L. Hellman. il Ladies Home J 81:56-7+ Ap '64
New miracles. Nation 198:61 Ja 20 '64
Ordeal of a pilgrim. il pors Time 83:38-9 Ja 10 '64
Paul the pilgrim. V. P. McCorry. por America 110:166-7 F 1 '64
Pilgrim in the Holy Land. T. E. Bird. Commonweal 79:479-81 Ja 24 '64
Pilgrimage. il Newsweek 63:48 Ja 13 '64
Pilgrimage of faith. America 110:273 F 29 '64
Pilgrimage of Pope Paul the Sixth; with report by H. Moffett. il pors Life 56:18-30A Ja 17 '64
Pope meets Patriarch. il por Time 83:58 Ja 3 '64
Pope Paul in the Holy Land. America 110: 71 Ja 18 '64
Pope Paul in the land of Jesus. F. Topolski. il pors Vogue 143:120-3+ Mr 1 '64
Pope Paul to visit the Holy Land. Christian Cent 81:7 Ja 1 '64
Pope visits Holy Land. Christian Cent 81: 35-7 Ja 8 '64
Pope's trip. Commonweal 79:360-1 D 20 '63
Second coronation. J. Cogley. Commonweal 79:498-9 Ja 31 '64
Seed planted. il pors Time 83:36-41 Ja 17 '64
Those who follow presidents and popes. E. T. Folliard. America 110:134 Ja 25 '64
To the Holy Land. Time 82:80 D 13 '63

PAUL I, king of the Hellenes
Foolish display. il por Time 82:30+ Jl 19 '63
Greece mourns, a new king inherits a crisis. R. Chelminski. il Life 56:26-9 Mr 27 '64
King wants to travel. Time 81:29 Je 21 '63
Long live the king. Newsweek 63:42 Mr 16 '64
Long live the King! il por Time 83:29 Mr 13 '64
Sorrow in Athens; funeral. il Time 83:31-2 Mr 20 '64
She dresses the lady pioneers of the New frontier. A. Chamberlin. il por Ladies Home J 80:134+ N '63

PAUL, Benjamin D.
Anthropological perspectives on medicine and public health. bibliog f Ann Am Acad 346: 34-43 Mr '63

PAUL, Doris A.
Three-cornered achievement. Sch Arts 63:18-19 F '64

PAUL, Jan S.
Test your shutter's accuracy. U S Camera 27: 36+ D '64

PAUL, Louis
Wicked ladies. McCalls 90:94-5+ My '63

PAUL, Mme

PAUL, Mimi
Brief biography. S. Goodman. pors Dance Mag 37:62-3 D '63

PAUL Bunyan's woodpile. See Natural monuments
PAUL Taylor dance company. See Ballet companies
PAULDING, Gouverneur
Limit to rapture. Reporter 28:62-3 F 14 '63
Monument to failure. Reporter 30:52-4 Mr 12 '64
Postcards from Paris. Reporter 30:40+ Je 4 '64
Tribes of the city. Reporter 29:59-60 O 10 '63
PAULING, Linus Carl
Genetic effects. Bul Atomic Sci 19:30-2 S '63
Nuclear weapons and world sanity; excerpts from address. UNESCO Courier 17:6-10 N '64
Pauling's position. Harper 226:6 My '63

about

Ban the bomb winner Peace prize for Dr Pauling. por U S News 55:24 O 21 '63
Controversy over peace award. Sr Schol 83: 14-16 N 1 '63
It depends on which scientist. Nation 197: 269 N 2 '63
Pauling prize: a welcome honor from Norway. por Bul Atomic Sci 19:18 D '63
Pauling wins peace prize, his second Nobel award. il por Sci N L 84:261 O 26 '63
Second Nobel. il por Newsweek 62:38 O 21 '63
Weird insult from Norway. Life 55:4 O 25 '63
PAULL, Lyle
Boosters end pressure problems. Am City 78:133-4 D '63
PAULOWNIA
Tree of unusual merit. M. M. Taylor il Horticulture 41:199 Ap '63
PAULSEN, James A.
College students in trouble. Atlan 214:96-101 Jl '64
PAULSEN, Lois
I go; poem. McCalls 92:31 O '64
Sonnet to my son. McCalls 91:116 Ag '64
PAULSEN, Monrad G.
Do children have rights? PTA Mag 58:7-9 F '64
PAULSON, F. M.
Blue-water cruise on Green Bay. Field & S 68:30-2+ Ag '63
(ed) Boating. See issues of Field & stream
Cruising Lake of the Woods. por Field & S 69:42-5+ Ag '64
Cruising the North Channel. Field & S 68:37-9+ My '63
Cruising the upper Mississippi. Field & S 69: 62-5+ Je '64
Desert boating. Field & S 69:57-9+ N '64
1965 bountiful year for boatmen. Field & S 69:36-40 Ja '65
1964 lineup of new boats and motors. Field & S 68:27-34 Ja '64
Trailer trek to Timagami. Field & S 68:64+ Ap '64
PAULSON, Joan
Top dog on campus. Read Digest 83:167-8 D '63
PAULTON, Edgar
Eclipse shadow band motions, an illusion? il Sky & Tel 25:328-9 Je '63
PAULUS, Friedrich von
Battle that turned the Nazi tide. H. W. Baldwin. il N Y Times Mag p23-5+ Ap 14 '63
Paulus and Stalingrad, by W. Goerlitz. Review
Newsweek il 63:77 Ja 13 '64
PAUSTOVSKY, Konstantin
Books. N. Bliven. New Yorker 40:70-2 Ja 2 '65
Spirit of valerian. J. Yglesias. Nation 198: 488-90 My 11 '64
PAVAN, Pietro
Pope John's vision. Commonweal 81:231-4 N 13 '64
PAVEMENT markings. Traffic markings
PAVEMENT openings. See Street openings
PAVEMENTS
Where auto meets garden. il Sunset 130:94-9 Je '63
See also
Bridges—Floors
Curbs
Playgrounds—Surface treatment

Maintenance and repair

See also
Streets—Maintenance and repair

Surface treatment

Cut-rate paving assessments; Kalamazoo, Mich. D. A. Southern. il Am City 79:96 Ap '64
How to obtain quality seal coats. R. Pecore. il Am City 79:89-90 Ag '64
It costs less, accomplishes more; resurfacing with asbestos fiber, East Hills, N.Y. E. Johannemann. il Am City 79:15 Ap '64
Match the treatment to street conditions. C. H. McDonald. il Am City 80:102-4 Ja '65
New strength for old asphalt; Chino, Calif. E. T. Lynch. il Am City 79:90-1 F '64
Recipe for a nickel-a-yard slurry seal; Dunn, N.C. A. B. Uzzle. il Am City 79:33 F '64
St Louis' slurry-seal experiment. A. H. Beck. il Am City 78:78-80 F '63
Stop surface spalling; Waterloo, Ont. D. B. G. Dutton and C. W. Wood. il Am City 79:71-3 N '64
Switch to slurry seal; Waco, Tex. C. Hoge. il Am City 79:104-5 Mr '64
Tests tougher sealants at signalized intersections; Phoenix, Ariz. F. Glendening. il Am City 79:109 Ap '64
You stop better on rubber; Rocky River, Ohio. D. R. Patton. il Am City 78:8 S '63

Testing

Tests tougher sealants at signalized intersections; Phoenix, Ariz. F. Glendening. il Am City 79:109 Ap '64

Traffic lines

See Traffic markings
PAVEMENTS, Asphalt
Better paving procedure; Greenville, S.C. R. H. Cureton. il Am City 79:93 Je '64
Infrared; quick, new home cure for cracked asphalt. J. Joseph. Pop Sci 182:168-70+ Ap '63
More asphalt streets use asbestos. il Am City 78:9 My '63
New strength for old asphalt; Chino, Calif. E. T. Lynch. il Am City 79:90-1 F '64
PAVEMENTS, Bituminous
Economy street paving fills the gap; Detroit. G. C. Richards and D. Behm. il Am City 78:89-91 S '63
PAVEMENTS, Concrete
Asphalt promenade; Cape May, N.J. J. P. Sweitzer. il Am City 78:95-6 N '63
Interstate highway system. R. G. Knox. il Motor T 15:118-21 N '63
PAVEMENTS, Rubber asphalt
Rubber-asphalt paving. D. A. Kalin. il Am City 79:106-7 My '64
Rubber road erases accidents; Fostoria, Ohio. H. R. Bradner. il Am City 78:19 Je '63
PAVEMENTS, Soil cement
Soil cement streets for six cents a day; Chickasha, Okla. B. Sullivan. il Am City 78:88-9 D '63
PAVESE, Cesare
Letter from Piemonte. N. T. di Giovanni. New Repub 151:15-18 S 12 '64
PAVILION, Los Angeles. See Concert halls
PAVILIONS
Beach pavilion on Florida coast. il Arch Rec 134:148-9 Ag '63
Play pavilion for at-home recreation. il Arch Rec 134:152 Ag '63
Summer pavilion on a mountain lake. il Arch Rec 134:150-1 Ag '63
PAVING machines
Self-propelled spreaders speed seal-coat work; aggregate spreaders. il Am City 79:30 Jl '64
PAVLOVA, Anna
Pavlova rediscovered! E. Palatsky. il por Dance Mag 38:34-6 D '64
PAVLYCHKO, Dmitro
Rebel with a cause. UNESCO Courier 17:10-12 Je '64
PAVONE, Rita
Rita Pavone: her singing starts riots. il pors Look 28:M8+ Je 2 '64
PAWEL, Ernst
Ideology and the private vision. Nation 197: 301-3 N 9 '63
Meant offense. Nation 198:150 F 10 '64
(tr) See Aron, R. Why Europe fears us
PAWN shops. See Pawnbroking
PAWNBROKING
Bank of pity. R. Condon. Holiday 33:58+ Mr '63
High style for the hock shop. il Bsns W p30-1 Ag 22 '64
In hock to Aunt Dora; Vienna's state-controlled pawnshop. il Bsns W p30-1 O 26 '63

Anecdotes, facetiae, satire, etc.

Topcoat. R. Caplan. New Yorker 39:170-2+ O 5 '63
PAWSEY, Joseph Lade
Obituary
Sky & Tel 25:77 F '63

PAX. See Piasecki, B.
PAXMAN, Carolyn
Prize safari party. Seventeen 22:180 My '63
PAXTON, Edna Rehm
Bugs about me. Sci Digest 55:57-61 Je '64
PAY, Rex
Accuracy of Canoga radar tracking system is six feet in 30,000 miles. Miss & Roc 14:31+ F 17 '64
JPL looks for answer to Ranger VI malfunction. Miss & Roc 14:16 F 10 '64
Laser optics encountering deterioration problems. Miss & Roc 13:27-8 S 9 '63
PAY-as-you-see television. See Television broadcasting—Subscription programs
PAY days
All for lolly; British workers to be paid by check. Time 81:92+ Mr 22 '63
PAYMENTS, Balance of. See Balance of payments
PAYNE, Daniel A.
Note on Daniel A. Payne. D. C. Stange. por Negro Hist Bul 28:9-10 O '64
PAYNE, Howard C. and Grosshans, Henry
Exiled revolutionaries and the French political police in the 1850's. bibliog f Am Hist R 68:954-73 Jl '63
PAYNE, Jack
How to build a fold-up hinged boat. Pop Sci 184:116-19 My '64
Right lathe bit for the job. Pop Sci 185:150-3 D '64
PAYNE, Kirby B.
Agricultural library network. bibliog por Library J 88:4143-8 N 1 '63
PAYNE, Lee
Automotive milestones; the passing of Clinton Reynolds' strange car collection. Motor T 16:80-3 Ja '64
PAYNE, Melvin M.
American and Geographic flags top Everest. Nat Geog Mag 124:157-157C Ag '63
Reprinting brings earliest Geographics to life. por Nat Geog Mag 126:688-9 N '64
PAYNE, Robert
Distillation of the Sino-soul. Sat R 46:33 S 7 '63
Gentle women and the tough. N Y Times Mag p32-3 S 29 '63
In defense of R. Hood. N Y Times Mag p48+ N 17 '63
Journey to a place like no other. N Y Times Mag p5-7+ D 22 '63
Man like no other. N Y Times Mag p79-80+ S 8 '63
Mayerling remains a mystery. N Y Times Mag p34-5+ Ja 26 '64
Napoleon legend, a new look. N Y Times Mag p24-5+ Ap 5 '64
On the Orient excess. Sat R 46:24-5 Jl 6 '63
Open door, closed heart. Sat R 46:37 Je 15 '63
Shandy's Sterne. N Y Times Mag p 118-20 N 24 '63
Then Antony met Cleopatra. N Y Times Mag p26-7+ Je 2 '63
What's in a flag? everything. N Y Times Mag p20+ Ag 30 '64
Why 400,000,000 follow Mohammed. N Y Times Mag p 18+ Ag 4; 2+ Ag 25 '63
PAYNE, W. J.
Synthetic detergents in water and sewage systems. Science 139:197-8 Ja 18 '63
PAYNE-GAPOSCHKIN, Cecilia
Otto Struve as an astrophysicist. Sky & Tel 25:308-10 Je '63
PAYROLLS

Statistics

Revision of establishment employment statistics, 1963. D. Hinton. il Mo Labor R 86: 1194-5 O '63
PAYSON, Mrs Charles Shipman
Adventurous ones. por Vogue 142:75 Ag 1 '63
Mrs Payson's ball park. C. Amory. il por Vogue 144:144-5+ S 15 '64
PAYTON, Boyd
Governor Sanford pardons Boyd Payton. Christian Cent 82:69 Ja 20 '65
PAZ, Octavio
Pause; Here; Girl; poems, tr. by J. F. Nims. Atlan 213:99 Mr '64

about

Octavio Paz: Mexican poet-diplomat. J. Durand. il pors Américas 15:30-3 Jl '63
Paz in English. D. Finkel. Poetry 104:382-5 S '64
Tree of images. J. M. Cohen. Nation 198: 199-200 F 24 '64
PAZ ESTENSSORO, Victor
Summary of address, October 25, 1963. por U N Rev 10:10 D '63
—See Kennedy, J. F. jt. auth.

about

Blowup in Bolivia: why, what to expect. il U S News 57:6 N 9 '64
Durable master. Newsweek 63:52+ My 25 '64
High, hard land. il por Time 82:41 N 1 '63
Last musketeer. por Newsweek 63:57 Je 15 '64
New success story in Latin America. il por U S News 56:62-3 Je 15 '64
People of the week. U S News 55:15 N 4 '63
Progress toward a third term. il por Time 83:34 My 29 '64
Up from veep. Newsweek 64:58 N 16 '64
PEABODY, Endicott
So long, Chub. il Time 84:37 S 18 '64
This thing about Frank. J. Potter. New Yorker 39:70-4 Ag 10 '63
PEABODY, Mary Parkman
Don't tread on Grandmother Peabody; with editorial comment. R. K. Massie. il por Sat Eve Post 237:74+, 84 My 16 '64
Mother goes to jail. il por Newsweek 63:25 Ap 13 '64
PEABODY college. See George Peabody college for teachers, Nashville, Tenn.
PEABODY conservatory of music. See Peabody institute, Baltimore
PEABODY institute, Baltimore
Peabody heritage. C. Kent. il Mus Am 83:16-17 Ap '63
PEACE
Architect of peace. R. Squirru. il Américas 16:2-4 Ap '64
Armers and the disarmers; report of International symposium on arms control at University of Michigan. J. D. Singer; A. Rapoport. Nation 196:174-7+ Mr 2 '63
Can the United Nations keep world peace in the 1960's? address, April 20, 1964. L. C. Meeker. bibliog f Dept State Bul 50:797-802 My 18 '64
Chances for peace now; how U.S. and world leaders see the outlook. il U S News 55: 38-41 D 16 '63
Christmas 1964: peace on earth? il U S News 57:19 D 28 '64
Conditions of peace; concerning John XXIII's recent encyclical. America 109:38 Jl 13 '63
Development of the peacekeeping capacity of the United Nations; address, April 26, 1963. R. N. Gardner. Dept State Bul 48:789-96 My 20 '63
First twenty-five years of the United Nations from San Francisco to the 1970's; address, January 10, 1964. D. Rusk. Dept State Bul 50:112-19 Ja 27 '64
For peace on earth, from a man of goodwill. A. Gingrich. Esquire 60:6+ D '63
Freedom to hope. W. E. Hocking. Sat R 46: 12-15+ Je 22 '63
Hail automation, hail peace. N. Cousins. Sat R 47:20 Ja 18 '64
Hard way to peace, by A. Etzioni. Review Nation 196:271-2 Mr 30 '63. A. Rapoport
Hostages to fortune. H. Bowser; reply. S. D. James. Sat R 46:19 Ap 13 '63
If Christmas were only Christmas; reprint. D. Lawrence. U S News 57:76 D 28 '64
Indian Christians hold peace talks. Christian Cent 80:701-2 My 29 '63
Is peace our big danger? D. Lawrence. U S News 57:100 Ag 24 '64
Keeping and strengthening the peace; address, December 17, 1963. L. B. Johnson. Dept State Bul 50:2-4 Ja 6 '64
Last flower; parable in pictures. J. Thurber. il UNESCO Courier 17:27-8 N '64
Next steps toward peace: some notes on the two-legged process; address September 30, 1963. M. Bundy. Dept State Bul 49:625-30 O 21 '63
Pacem in terris: for all humanity; with excerpts. il Newsweek 61:21-2 Ap 22 '63
Peace and human rights; address, June 15, 1963. H. Cleveland. Dept State Bul 49:38-43 Jl 8 '63
Peace and nonviolence. E. Metzler. Christian Cent 81:1597-8 D 23 '64
Peace crowd. J. Grossman. Nation 198:66-8 Ja 20 '64; Reply. P. Lauter. 198:inside cover Mr 2 '64
Peace in our time. F. L. Greaves. il N Y Times Mag p 16+ Ap 14 '63
Peace on earth; Pope and President refuse deterministic view of contemporary history. F. Canavan. America 108:876 Je 22 '63
Peace research neglected. Sci N L 83:117 F 23 '63
Peace research, peace action. J. D. Singer; reply with rejoinder. J. Cohen. Bul Atomic Sci 19:35-6 My '63
Pope's formula for world peace. il U S News 54:25 Ap 22 '63

PEACE—*Continued*
Presidency and the peace. M. Bundy. For Affairs 42:353-65 Ap '64
President Johnson calls upon Soviet Union for concrete actions to promote peace; exchange of letters. L. B. Johnson; N. Khrushchev. Dept State Bul 50:157-63 F 3 '64
President renews hope for peace; concerning commencement address at American university. Christian Cent 80:822 Je 26 '63
Proposal to a foundation; a model World constitutional convention. N. Cousins. Sat R 46:16 Jl 27 '63
Prospects for world peace: an overview. H. Kohn. bibliog f Cur Hist 46:321-5+ Je '64
Pursuit of peace; address, August 2, 1964. D. Rusk. Dept State Bul 51:214-18 Ag 17 '64
Quest for peace. L. Hanna. il Sr Schol 85: 16T+ N 11 '64
Recapturing the future; moral and psychological changes that would result in a world freed from the threat of war. M. Mead. Sat R 46:10-13 Je 1 '63
Science talks about peace. C. Dreher. Nation 197:31-3 Jl 13 '63
Scientists organize for peace. E. Mirel. Sci N L 84:117-18 Ag 24 '63
Secretary Rusk discusses the outlook for 1964 over Japanese television; interview, December 24, 1963. D. Rusk. Dept State Bul 50:40-6 Ja 13 '64
Secretary Rusk's news conference of January 2, 1964. D. Rusk. bibliog f Dept State Bul 50:81-9 Ja 20 '64
Single goal of peace; excerpts from address, June 28, 1964. L. B. Johnson. Dept State Bul 51:79-81 Jl 20 '64
Someday: a real Christmas. D. Lawrence. U S News 55:80 D 30 '63
Speculations during a white night. J. F. Wharton. Sat R 46:14-17 Ap 6 '63
Strategy of peace; address, June 10, 1963. J. F. Kennedy. Vital Speeches 29:558-61 Jl 1 '63; Same. Dept State Bul 49:2-6 Jl 1 '63
Strengthening the machinery for peace; address, June 2, 1964. A. E. Stevenson. Dept State Bul 50:966-71 Je 22 '64
Teaching about peace and war; symposium. ed. by H. Taylor. il Sr Schol 83:9T+ N 22 '63; Discussion. 84:6T F 7 '64
Teaching war prevention. S. H. Mendlovitz. Bul Atomic Sci 20:19-22 F '64; Reply. P. Lauter. 20:28 My '64
Toilsome path to peace; address, March 19, 1964. D. Rusk. Dept State Bul 50:530-5 Ap 6 '64
Toward peace and justice; Pacem in terris. H. Schomer. Christian Cent 80:703-6 My 29 '63
Turn toward peace. D. F. Fleming. bibliog f Ann Am Acad 351:157-69 Ja '64
U.S. and Brazil reaffirm commitment to peace; exchange of letters. H. Castelo Branco; L. B. Johnson. Dept State Bul 51: 435-6 S 28 '64
Waging peace in the sixties. W. G. Carr. il PTA Mag 59:8-10 O '64
What can we do to keep peace on earth? answers of five Nobel peace prize winners; ed. by C. Bakal. il Redbook 124:46-7+ Ja '65
What price peace? W. H. Ferry. Bul Atomic Sci 19:19-23 S '63
What to teach about the United Nations. A. Larson. il NEA J 53:26-8 Ja '64
What we are for; summary of new encyclical on world peace. John XXIII. il Time 81: 60+ Ap 19 '63
See also
Disarmament
International relations
Pacifism
War
Women and peace
PEACE (theology)
Word. America 111:789 D 12 '64
PEACE conference, 1919, Versailles
Colonel's folly and the President's distress; with editorial comment. C. T. Grayson. il Am Heritage 15:4-7+ O '64
End of a friendship; with memorandum by E. M. House. C. Seymour. il Am Heritage 14:4-9+ Ag '63
PEACE conferences
Churchmen hold a peace conference; Geneva. Christian Cent 81:957 Jl 29 '64
Oxford conference: organizing the nonaligned. H. A. Jack. Bul Atomic Sci 19:38-40 Je '63
Shaping future policy; Christian peace conference. P. Peachey. Christian Cent 82: 28 Ja 6 '65
Toward a warless world. P. A. Schilpp. Christian Cent 81:212-14 F 12 '64
PEACE corps. See United States—Peace corps
PEACE corps, Domestic. See Volunteers in service to America
PEACE games. See Strategy
PEACE movement. See Pacifism
PEACE pacts. See Treaties
PEACE research institute
Virus of debate; Congressional assistants defense and disarmament seminar. Nation 196:170 Mr 2 '63
PEACE societies
Peace crowd. J. Grossman. Nation 198:66-8 Ja 20 '64; Reply. P. Lauter. 198:inside cover Mr 2 '64
Waging peace in the sixties. W. G. Carr. il PTA Mag 59:8-10 O '64
See also
Catholic association for international peace
PEACEFUL uses of atomic power. See Atomic power—Economic aspects
PEACH tree kingdom; drama. See Musil, R. G.
PEACH trees
Dwarf peaches and nectarines: your choice is widening. il Sunset 132:188 F '64
PEACHES
Natural kinin in peach fruitlets. S. Lavee. bibliog Science 142:583 N 1 '63
U.S. begins shipping peaches to Europe. Farm J 87:52J My '63
PEACHEY, Paul
Christian obedience in a world we don't control. Christian Cent 81:458-60 Ap 8 '64
Peacemaking a church calling. Christian Cent 80:952-4 Jl 31 '63
PEACOCK, Heber F.
Seminary loses another teacher; no academic freedom. Christian Cent 80:326 Mr 13 '63
PEACOCK, L. J. and Watson, J. A.
Radiation-induced aversion to alcohol. bibliog Science 143:1462-3 Mr 27 '64
PEACOCK, M. E. See Potthoff, E. H. jr, jt. auth.
PEACOCK; story. See Arpino, G.
PEAK, Bob
Pro football 1963. il Sports Illus 19:35-45 S 9 '63
PEAK; story. See Dikeman, M.
PEAKALL, David B.
How insects resist insecticides. Audubon Mag 66:32-4 Ja '64
PEAKE, Cyrus H.
Road back to mainland China. New Repub 149:10-11 Ag 17 '63
PEAKE, Mary S.
Mary S. Peake, 1823-62. S. N. Fen. bibliog f Sch & Soc 91:171-2 Ap 6 '63
PEALE, Mundy I.
Republic seeking diversification to backstop phaseout of F-105; summary of address. Aviation W 78:113 Ja 21 '63
PEALE, Norman Vincent
How to cope with criticism. Read Digest 84: 117-20 My '64
How to rise above the fear of death. Read Digest 82:103-6 Ap '63
Mightiest force in the universe. Read Digest 83:66-9 S '63
Power of the positive no! Read Digest 84:49-52 F '64
Prescription for a marriage on the rocks. Read Digest 85:89-93 S '64
Why I didn't quit the ministry. por Sat Eve Post 236:52, 55 Mr 2 '63
about
Peale pulls out all the stops. Christian Cent 81:692 My 27 '64
Reappraising Peale. Christian Cent 80:447 Ap 3 '63
PEANUT butter
Peanut butter, peanut butter, peanut best! with recipes. J. Westcott. il Seventeen 22: 140-1+ Mr '63
PEANUTS
In 110 to 120 days you'll be digging up peanuts. il Sunset 132:307 My '64
Nut which isn't a nut. R. L. Hawk. il Horticulture 41:528 O '63
Peanuts. D. Webb. Pop Gard 14:100 My '63
Toxin-producing aspergillus isolated from domestic peanuts. U. L. Diener and others. bibliog il Science 142:1491-2 D 13 '63
PEAR, Chinese. See Chinese pear
PEAR tree; drama. See McFarlan, E.
PEARCE, Ann Philippa
WLB biography. P. Edge. Wilson Lib Bul 38:697 Ap '64
PEARCE, Donald R.
Style of Milton's epic. Yale R 52:427-44 Mr '63

PEARCE, G. F.
Amateur scientist. Sci Am 210:122-4+ Je '64
PEARCE, John N.
Louisiana state museum. Hobbies 68:52 N '63
—and others
Meeks family of cabinetmakers. Antiques 85: 414-20 Ap '64
PEARCE, Lorraine W.
Distinctive character of the work of Lannuier. Antiques 86:712-17 D '64
PEARCY, G. Etzel
Cartography in Africa. Dept State Bul 49: 1014-18 D 30 '63
Geographic terminology of Europe. Dept State Bul 48:330-8 Mr 4 '63
Geopolitics and foreign relations. Dept State Bul 50:318-30 Mr 2 '64
Newly independent states. Focus 15:1-6 D '64
PEARDON, Thomas P.
Politics in Britain. Cur Hist 46:282-6+ My '64
PEARL fisheries
Gems that grow on command. R. Steinberg. il Sat Eve Post 237:70-3 Je 27 '64
PEARL HARBOR, Attack on, 1941
Tora, tora, tora! condensation. G. W. Prange. il Read Digest 83:251-8+ O; 273-8+ N '63
PEARL industry and trade
Closing the pearly gates; rising demand, higher costs. il Bsns W p84+ Ap 4 '64
PEARLMAN, Beverly G.
(ed) First novelists, fall 1964. Library J 89:3779-87+ O 1 '64
PEARLS
Cultured pearl market. J. B. Weiner. Duns R 83:69 F '64
How to buy cultured pearls. il Good H 156: 148-9 Je '63
Romance of pearls. W. Stephens and P. Stephens. il Read Digest 83:45-6+ O '63
Shoppers pick pearls on the half shell; T. Eaton co. ltd, Toronto. il Bsns W p 138-40 N 28 '64
PEARMAN, Bob
Wonderful world of mail carriers. Farm J 88:67 My '64
PEARS
All about pears. il Redbook 121:82-4+ S '63
Pears may make comeback in East. Farm J 87:50D Je '63
See also
Cookery—Fruit
PEARSON, Albert Gregory
Albie Pearson: the littlest Angel. G. Rogin. il pors Sports Illus 18:62-4+ My 27 '63
PEARSON, Bill
Very personal taste of a jockey turned art dealer. il House B 105:146 Ap '63
PEARSON, David
Peace corps volunteer returns. Sat R 47:54-6+ O 17 '64
PEARSON, Drew
Can TV be saved? por Esquire 60:210+ D '63
Fairbanks syllogism. por Newsweek 64:48 D 14 '64
—and Ritter, Norman
Dark enigma of Congress. Sat Eve Post 237: 75-9 Mr 28 '64
PEARSON, Edmund Lester
Old librarian and his almanack. H. A. Sullivan. Library J 89:1188-92 Mr 15 '64
PEARSON, Ethelyn
Empathy unlimited. Writer 76:25-6 F '63
How to cope with company. Farm J 87:29+ Jl '63
Why we take a dozen vacations a year. Farm J 87:36B Ag '63
PEARSON, Hesketh
Master confessor. Sat R 46:26 Ap 13 '63
PEARSON, Leonard B.
Cape basket. Flower Grower 51:65-6 Ja '64
PEARSON, Lester Bowles
Canadian Prime Minister visits Washington; U.S. and Canada agree on Columbia River development and establishment of Campobello Park; joint communique; with joint statements and texts of agreements, January 21-23, 1964. Dept State Bul 50:199-206 F 10 '64
Good neighborhood. For Affairs 43:251-61 Ja '65
How can Canada make her most effective contribution to collective security? address, January 12, 1963. Vital Speeches 29:290-3 Mr 1 '63
Remarks at Vancouver, and Peace Arch ceremonies, September 16, 1964. Dept State Bul 51:505-7 O 12 '64
—See Kennedy, J. F. jt. auth.

about

Ahead: a friendlier Canada. il por U S News 54:46 Ap 22 '63
As Canada heads for showdown at the polls. il por U S News 54:48 Ap 8 '63
Canada, Britain, U.S: can Pearson tie them closer? il por U S News 54:21 Ap 29 '63
Canada goes to the polls. H. Bigart. il Reporter 28:29-32 Ap 11 '63
Canada: victory for the Liberals. por Newsweek 61:50+ Ap 22 '63
Changing the guard. Time 81:28 Ap 26 '63
Honest broker. Newsweek 63:47 Ja 27 '64
Liberals gain in Canadian elections. por Sr Schol 82:16 Ap 24 '63
New leader. il pors Time 81:33-7 Ap 19 '63; Same abr. with title Lester Pearson: Canada's new leader. Read Digest 83:130-4 Ag '63
Now U.S. is the issue in Canada. il por U S News 54:32 F 18 '63
Pearson heads new Canadian regime. Christian Cent 80:516 Ap 24 '63
Pearson's campaign heats up in Canada. il pors Bsns W p28-9 Mr 30 '63
Pearson's frontier. il pors Fortune 68:113-14+ Jl '63
Pearson's progress. W. H. Hessler. il Reporter 30:24-9 Mr 12 '64
Unfinished election in Canada. il por Bsns W p27 Ap 13 '63
Washington gives Canada an election and an issue; with statement by U.S. Department of state. W. H. Hessler. Reporter 28: 29-31 F 28 '63
Weekend at Jack's. il por Time 81:32 My 17 '63
Wheat-sale dividend: new strength for Pearson. por U S News 55:16 S 30 '63
With a confident air. Time 81:39 My 10 '63
PEARSON, Nan Wade
New bridge game. Vogue 141:100+ My '63
PEARSON, Sir Richard
Action off Flamborough Head; excerpt from Great sea battles. O. Warner. il por Am Heritage 14:42-9+ Ag '63
PEARSON, Roy
Prayer for a seminary. Christian Cent 80:520 Ap 24 '63
Yank's-eye view of British logic. Read Digest 82:117-19 Mr '63
PEART, Paul J.
Design makes the difference. Pop Gard 15: 39-41 Ja '64
Do-it-yourself projects. Pop Gard 15:42 Ja '64
PEART, R. F. See Langenberg, D. N. jt. auth.
PEARY, Josephine
My most unforgettable character. E. P. Stafford. il por Read Digest 84:64-9 Ap '64
PEARY, Robert Edwin
Ahdoolo! condensation. F. Miller. il Read Digest 82:263-9+ F '63
My most unforgettable character. E. P. Stafford. il Read Digest 84:64-9 Ap '64
PEASANT art. See Folk art
PEASANTRY
See also
Land tenure

France

French paysan is angry. E. Higbee. il N Y Times Mag p20+ O 27 '63

Russia

Farmer frustrates Khrushchev; would rather work for himself than the state. E. Crankshaw. il N Y Times Mag p 17+ S 20 '64
Peasant, half of Russia; photographs. N Y Times Mag p 18-19 S 20 '64
PEASE, Charles Allen
Lifting with safety. Consumer Bul 47:32 Je '64
PEASE, William A.
Words, words, words! por Library J 88:3795-8 O 15 '63
PEAT
Ontogeny of a salt marsh estuary. A. C. Redfield. bibliog il Science 147:50-5 Ja 1 '65
Peats and other soil conditioners. il Consumer Rep 29:442-4 S '64
PEAT moss
What do you know about peatmoss? J. M. Patek. Horticulture 42:50-1+ Mr '64
See also
Peat
PEATTIE, Donald Culross
I've been meaning to write. Read Digest 82: 228D-228E My '63
Last and loveliest queen of the Scots. Read Digest 82:252-4+ F '63
Naturalist's path to faith. Read Digest 83: 61-5 O '63
Window gardens. Read Digest 83:252C-252D+ N '63
—and Peattie, L. R.
Greatest African explorer of all time. Read Digest 82:258-60+ Je '63

PEATTIE, Donald Culross—*Continued*
Living camouflage; nature's call to the colors. Read Digest 83:179-83 N '63
Royalty of the bird kingdom. Read Digest 82:252C-252D+ Ap '63
Stephen Mather, master of the wilderness. Read Digest 85:148-53 Jl '64
about
Obituary
Pub W 186:37-8 N 30 '64
PEATTIE, Louise (Redfield)
Aren't we the lucky little bozos? Read Digest 82:72-4 F '63
He caught the splendor of the first Americans. Read Digest 85:257-62 O '64
—See Peattie, D. C. jt. auth.
PEAVY, Art
Gulf streamed recreation. Recreation 57:275+ Je '64
PEBBLE mosaics. See Mosaics
PEBBLE mulch. See Mulching
PECAN trees
Heresy of Isaac Houston Bass. H. H. Leard. il Am For 69:20-1+ S '63
PECCARY hunting
Big on pigs. J. C. Rikhoff. il Outdoor Life 134: 34-5+ Ag '64
Javelina jackpot. E. Park. il Outdoor Life 131:24-5+ Ja '63
PECHMAN, Joseph A.
Case for tax reform. Reporter 28:20-3 Je 6 '63
PECILE, Jordon
Barrel lifter; story. Atlan 212:79-84 O '63
PECK, Don
Ross and his rifle. por Outdoor Life 131:32-5+ Ja; 36-9+ F '63
PECK, Gregory
Gregory. V. Scott. por McCalls 90:104-5+ S '63
PECK, Louise D.
Course, poem. Harper 229:26 Jl '64
PECK, Paula
Hors d'oeuvres ideas. House B 105:86-7+ Jl '63
Rare case of the parts being greater than the whole. House B 106:180-1+ Ap '64
This summer, explore new ways to cook vegetables. House B 105:118-19+ Je '63
PECK, Samuel H.
Solving the municipal retirement problem. por Am City 78:141+ F '63
PECK, Seymour
'Enry 'Iggins in 'Ollywood. N Y Times Mag p20-1 S 1 '63
PECK, W. M.
Pacific love song. Harper 229:90-1 D '64
PECK, William A. and others
Bone cells: biochemical and biological studies after enzymatic isolation. bibliog Science 146:1476-7 D 11 '64
PECKHAM, Howard H.
I have been basely murdered. Am Heritage 14:88-92 Ag '63
PECKHAM, Morse
Man of enlightenment. Sat R 47:44-5 Mr 28 '64
Recruiting for the saving remnant. Sat R 46:27+ N 2 '63
Who inspired her imagery? Sat R 46:41 D 28 '63
PECORE, Robert
How to obtain quality seal coats. Am City 79:89-90 Ag '64
Late, late show. Am City 78:34 Ap '63
PECTINS
Artery hardening cure? Sci N L 86:358 D 5 '64
Avian atherosclerosis: retardation by pectin. H. Fisher and others. bibliog il Science 146: 1063-4 N 20 '64
PEDDLERS and peddling
Pedlar dolls. C. H. Fawcett. il Hobbies 68: 37+ D '63
See also
Street trades
PEDERSON, John H. and Roth, F. W.
Plan a machinery service center. Suc Farm 62:64-5 Ja '64
PEDESTRIAN; drama. See Bradbury, R.
PEDESTRIAN of the air; drama. See Ionesco, E.
PEDESTRIANS
Pedestrian. New Yorker 39:19-21 Je 22 '63
Anecdotes, facetiae, satire, etc.
Pedestrian drift. S. Beach. il Atlan 211:114-16 My '63
PEDIATRIC language disorder clinic, Babies hospital, New York. See New York (city)—Columbia-Presbyterian medical center
PEDIATRICIANS
Day in the life of a pediatrician; Laurence Gesner Pray of Fargo, N.D. P. Hamill. il Sat Eve Post 237:69-73 D 19 '64
Is baby's doctor sick of mommy? E. S. Ringold. il N Y Times Mag p47-8 Ag 11 '63
Pediatrician; Dr R. Shugart. il Life 57:48A-55 Jl 31 '64
Unhappy baby doctors. M. Lear. il McCalls 90:76-9 Jl '63
When should you see your pediatrician? M. A. Wessel. il Todays Health 42:60-1+ N '64
PEDIATRICS wards. See Hospitals—Childrens wards
PEDLAR dolls. See Dolls
PEDLARS. See Peddlers and peddling
PEDODONTISTS. See Dentists
PEDRARIAS
From a peak in Darién; Balboa's discovery 450 years ago. E. B. Roberts. il Américas 15:40-3 S '63
PEEK, Floyd B. See Douthit, A. M. jt. auth.
PEEKSKILL, N.Y.
Clubs
Senior citizens in suburbia. M. G. Hickerson. Recreation 56:220 My '63
PEEL, Bruce
Alberta builds three. Library J 88:4582-5 D 1 '63
PEEPLES, William
Hunger sit-in. New Repub 150:9-10 Ap 25 '64
Indiana dunes and pressure politics. Atlan 211:84-8 F '63
PEERAGE
See also
Great Britain—Peerage
PEERMAN, Dean
Church and world; meeting of Commission on world mission and evangelism in Mexico City. Christian Cent 81:104-5 Ja 22 '64
Death down a dark street. Christian Cent 80: 166-7 F 6 '63
Genocide by bureaucracy. Christian Cent 80: 680 My 22 '63
Happy science. Christian Cent 80:936 Jl 24 '63
Home base is everywhere. Christian Cent 81:70-2 Ja 15 '64
Philanthropic philistine. Christian Cent 81: 706-7 My 27 '64
PEET, Creighton
Fending off doomsday. Am For 70:20-3 Ap '64
Forests by jet. Am For 70:48-50 O '64
Forest's one-man band. Am For 69:10+ Mr '63
Great swamp fights for survival. Am For 69:24-6+ Mr '63; Same abr. with title They love their swamp. Sci Digest 54:83-6 Ag '63
Yes, tall oaks from little acorns grow. Am For 69:24-7 O '63
PEETERS, Georges
How Cocteau managed a champion. Sports Illus 20:66-72 Mr 2 '64
PEGASUS (artificial satellite) See Artificial satellites—Use in research
PEGEL, Jane
Lady of the frozen lakes. H. Whall. il por Sports Illus 22:39 Ja 11 '65
PEGGY Guggenheim collection. See Art—Private collections
PEGGY'S COVE, Nova Scotia
Reader's choice. J. Schumer. Travel 121:15 Ap '64
PEGLER, Westbrook
For the throat; unauthorized biography. Newsweek 61:67 My 20 '63
Liberals do believe in devils. M. S. Evans. Nat R 14:457-8 Je 4 '63
Man who hates publishers. M. Kempton. New Repub 148:20-3 Je 8 '63
Party for Peg. Time 81:50+ My 31 '63
PEHRSSON, Hjalmar
Int'l publishers assn. names new secretary. Pub W 185:33 Ap 13 '64
PEI, Ieoh Ming
Pei tackles the city school problem. il Arch Forum 118:7 Mr '63
Pilgrim's prize: designing the John F. Kennedy memorial library at Harvard. il por Time 84:40 D 25 '64
PEI, Mario
Languages in paperback; tool for education. Pub W 184:22-5 S 30; 19 O 28 '63
Loss for words. Sat R 47:82-4 N 14 '64; 48: 76 Ja 9 '65
One language for the world? excerpts. UNESCO Courier 16:23+ N '63; 17:33 F '64
Parallel proverbs. Sat R 47:16-17+ My 2 '64
PEIRCE, Charles Sanders
Charles Sanders Peirce: 1839-1914. R. J. Roth. America 111:108-10 Ag 1 '64

PEIRCE, J. Trevor. See Griffard, C. D. jt. auth.
PEISER, H. Steffen. See Paretzkin, B. jt. auth.
PEJOVICH, Ted
I believe. por Seventeen 22:215 N '63
PEKING, China
Trip to China. R. Terrill. New Repub 152:9-11 Ja 2; 13-15 Ja 16; 15-16 Ja 23 '65 (to be cont)
PEKING acrobatic troupe. See Acrobats and acrobatism
PEKRUHN, John
Portable school program for Pittsburgh. Arch Rec 133:176-8 F '63
PELANDER, Carl
Kitchen fly for campers. Pop Mech 119:132-3 Je '63
PELARGONIUMS. See Geraniums
PELÉ. See Arantes de Nascimento, E.
PELEE, POINT, NATIONAL PARK. See Point Pelee, National Park
PELETTA, Pete
Ambush of a Don patrol; best USF squad. F. Deford. Sports Illus 19:100 D 23 '63
PELHAM-JONES, Patrick
Prince Charles: a schoolmate's view of a lonely boy. Redbook 122:72-3+ Ap '64
PELICANS
Birds of the sea. A. Sprunt, 4th. il Motor B 112:54+ N '63
Pelican; Jamaica Bay wildlife refuge. New Yorker 40:48-9 N 14 '64
PELIKAN, Jaroslav
American Lutheranism: denomination or confession? Christian Cent 80:1608-10 D 25 '63
Christianity's search for a new role. Harper 229:144-6 D '64
Clergy looks at bigotry. Sat R 46:32 My 11 '63
History of Christian thought bookshelf. Christian Cent 80:711-13 My 29 '63
Scholar strikes back; adaptation of address. por Cath World 200:149-54 D '64
Scholar strikes back; excerpts from address, May 19, 1964. por Pub W 185:52-5 Je 15 '64
That the church may be more fully Catholic; excerpts from address, May 5, 1963. Cath World 198:151-6 D '63
Tradition, reformation and development. Christian Cent 82:8-10 Ja 6 '65
PELISSIER, Jean
(ed) See Guitton, J. Interview with Jean Guitton, the only Catholic layman at the council
PELL, Claiborne
Berlin: a new approach. Nation 196:520-2 Je 22 '63
Come on in, politics is fine! por Seventeen 23:154+ O '64
Education; acceptance of responsibility; address, July 16, 1964. Vital Speeches 30:725-7 S 15 '64
Heritage of Pope John. America 109:48-9 Jl 13 '63
Needed: a national youth policy. por NEA J 53:17 D '64
Our run-down railroads. New Repub 150:11-14 My 2 '64
Saving the railroads. Commonweal 79:249-50 N 22 '63
Speaking out. por Sat Eve Post 237:8-9 F 8 '64
about
Senator Pell's intervention. Nation 196:338 Ap 27 '63
PELLATT, Apsley
Glasswares by Apsley Pellatt. H. Wakefield. il Antiques 87:85-8 Ja '65
PELLÉAS et Mélisande; opera. See Debussy, C.
PELLECER, Carlos Manuel
Another ex-Communist. E. K. Culhane. America 108:196-8 F 9 '63
PELLEGRINO, Edmund D.
Medicine, history, and the idea of man. bibliog f Ann Am Acad 346:9-20 Mr '63
PELLER, Edith
Operation duck rescue. Audubon Mag 65:364-7 N '63
PELLETED feed. See Feeding and feeding stuffs—Pelleted feed
PELLETIER, Gérard
Trouble with Quebec. Atlan 214:115-18 N '64
PELOPONNESIAN war, 431-404 B.C. See Greece, Ancient—History—Peloponnesian war, 431-404 B.C.
PELOQUIN, C. Alexander
Music: first performance of Missa divina by C. A. Peloquin. C. J. McNaspy. America 108:476-8 Ap 6 '63
PELOTA (game)
Handball with daiquiris; jai alai in Florida. il Time 83:47 Ja 3 '64
Jai alai goes west. il Bsns W p30-1 S 5 '64

PELTZ, Mary Ellis
Glyndebourne nobility. Opera N 29:27 S 26 '64
Many lives of Otto Kahn. Opera N 28:34 F 1 '64
Romance a hundred years ago. Opera N 28:12-15 F 22 '64
PELVIS
Anatomy for the ballet teacher; interview, ed. by W. Como. R. Gelabert. il Dance Mag 37:60-2 Mr; 67-9 Ap '63
Fractures
See Fractures
PEMBROKE, Mary (Sidney) Herbert, countess of
Psalms of Sir Philip Sidney and the Countess of Pembroke, ed. by J. C. A. Rathmell. Review
Sat R por 46:46+ Mr 23 '63. J. M. Patrick
PEMEX. See Petroleum industry and trade—Mexico
PEN and ink drawing. See Pen drawing
PEN drawing
Four pen drawings; with commentary. Q. L. McChristy. il Am Artist 28:75-7+ Je '64
He also wrote novels; drawings of V. Hugo. il Time 81:66 Ap 26 '63
New technique with a familiar medium. A. Grissett. il Sch Arts 62:15 Je '63
PEN pals. See International correspondence
PEN portraits. See Character sketches
PENAL colonies
See also
Devil's Island
PENAL law. See Criminal law
PENAL press. See Prison publications
PENANCE
Do penance; new Lenten regulations in La Crosse, Wis. America 110:244 F 22 '64
PENANCE, Sacrament of. See Confession
PENCE, Audra May
Local associations take responsibility for professional behavior. NEA J 53:22-3 F '64
PENCHENIER, Georges
Close-up of the Vietcong in their jungle. N Y Times Mag p27+ S 13 '64
PENCIL sharpeners
Important point in pencil sharpeners. il Consumer Bul 47:39-40 O '64
Pencil sharpeners. Consumer Bul 48:25 F '65
PENDERGAST, Herbert
(ed) See Karajan, H. von. Conversation with Von Karajan
PENDLETON, Robert C. and others
Iodine-131 in Utah during July and August 1962. bibliog Science 141:640-2 Ag 16 '63
PENDLETON, Ore.
Recreation
Mutual benefit. E. Johnson. Recreation 57:188-9 Ap '64
PENDULUM
See also
Foucault's pendulum
PENEDO, Brazil
Festival in Penedo. M. Ramos. il Américas 15:32-4 N '63
PENELOPE; story. See Klee, M.
PENFIELD, Wilder
Doctor in red China. Atlan 214:67-71 D '64
Oriental renaissance in education and medicine. bibliog pors Science 141:1153-61 S 20 '63
Uncommitted cortex; the child's changing brain. por Atlan 214:77-81 Jl '64
PENGUINS
Bird man of Antarctica; studies of the emperor penguin. il Sci Digest 56:48-9 D '64
Helicopters are blamed for penguin decrease. Nat Parks Mag 37:16 Mr '63
Homing penguin; Adélie penguin. A. E. Norman. il Sci Digest 54:42-3 Jl '63
Navy issues orders: save that penguin! Sci N L 85:150 Mr 7 '64
Scientists to follow penguins by plane. Sci N L 86:255 O 17 '64
PENICILLIN
Allergy test for penicillin. Bsns W p 146 Ap 25 '64
6-aminopenicillanic acid: inhibition of destruction of cephalosporin C by bacteria. R. B. Walton. bibliog il Science 143:1438-9 Mr 27 '64
Concurrent morphological and chemical events in staphylococcus aureus exposed to penicillin. J. Ciak and F. E. Hahn; reply. R. Pratt. Science 139:682+ F 15 '63
Germ killer discovered twice. A. Fleming. il Todays Health 42:10 D '64
Large penicillin G dose fights infections. Sci N L 86:185 S 19 '64

PENICILLIN—*Continued*
Persistence of bacteria in protoplast form after apparent cure of pyelonephritis in rats. L. B. Guze and G. M. Kalmanson. bibliog il Science 143:1340-1 Mr 20 '64
Tooth decay reduced by penicillin pills. Sci N L 85:248 Ap 18 '64
PENICILLIUM
Mycotoxins: aflatoxin isolated from penicillium puberulum. F. A. Hodges and others. bibliog Science 145:1439 S 25 '64
Phytotoxic substance from a species of penicillium. F. A. Norstadt and T. M. McCalla. bibliog il Science 140:410-11 Ap 26 '63
PENINGTON, Sue
Coast to coast cruising, and then some. Motor B 114:22-3+ N '64
PENINSULA music festival. See Music festivals—Wisconsin
PENITENTIARY, Alcatraz island. See Alcatraz (island)
PENKOVSKII, Oleg V.
Fear at the top. Newsweek 61:60-1 Je 10 '63
Leaks at the top? Newsweek 61:44 My 13 '63
Spies in Moscow: more than meets the eye. pors Newsweek 61:41 My 20 '63
PENMANSHIP
Can you read your own writing? F. Johnson. il Am Artist 27:50-5+ S '63
Fine italic hand. il Newsweek 64:117-117A O 5 '64
Manuscript and cursive writing; opinions differ. E. M. Templin and F. M. King. NEA J 53:26-8 N '64
PENN, Irving
Crete: a photographic essay. Vogue 145:98-113 Ja 15 '65
Penn's Japan; photographs. Vogue 144:86-98 Ag 15 '64
Scotland: the dour and the beautiful. R. Douglas-Home. il Vogue 143:132-45+ Ap 15 '64
about
Irving Penn's love letter to a farm. il Vogue 142:120-9 Ag 15 '63
PENN, Jack
Lepers' lesson. Sat R 47:20 N 28 '64
PENN, Lemuel A.
Four klansmen. Newsweek 64:29 Ag 17 '64
Random slaughter. Newsweek 64:35 Jl 20 '64
PENN, T. C.
Simple dwell meter. il Electr World 71:43+ Je '64
PENN, William
Ordeal of William Penn. F. Biddle. il Am Heritage 15:30-3+ Ap '64
PENN center, Philadelphia. See Philadelphia—City planning
PENNAME, A. pseud.
Secret system: how boys grade girls. Seventeen 23:142-3+ N '64
PENNANTS. See Flags
PENNARIO, Leonard
Quote: unquote; interview, ed. by C. S. Susa. por Mus Am 84:24 My '64
PENNEKAMP, John, Coral Reef State Park. See Florida—Parks and reserves
PENNEL, John
Alone at the top of the mark. il Sports Illus 19:16-17 S 2 '63
Borrowed pole. il por Time 82:52 Ag 16 '63
Pole bends, the great Pennel breaks 17-foot barrier. il Life 55:30D-30E S 6 '63
PENNEMAN, R. A. See Asprey, L. B. jt. auth.
PENNEY, J. C, company
Memo that moved a mountain. il Bsns W p68-9+ D 12 '64
Penney goes for completeness. Bsns W p44 F 2 '63
PENNEY, John B.
Propeller on a platform preserves a pond. Am City 79:84-5 Jl '64
PENNSYLVANIA
Pennsylvania; reproduction of paintings. D. Schwartz. Fortune 69:84-91 F '64
See also
Allegheny River
Booksellers and bookselling—Pennsylvania
Education—Pennsylvania
Fishing—Pennsylvania
Forests and forestry—Pennsylvania
Hunting—Pennsylvania
Insurance, Unemployment—Pennsylvania
Law—Pennsylvania
Libraries—Pennsylvania
Music festivals—Pennsylvania
Roads—Pennsylvania
Soils—Pennsylvania
Unemployment—Pennsylvania
Boundaries
See also
Mason and Dixon's line
Charities
Charity solicitations; under state control. Am City 79:150+ Mr '64
Description and travel
USC focuses on the Pennsylvania Dutch. W. E. Homan. il U S Camera 27:30-1+ Ap '64
Economic conditions
Scranton of Pennsylvania. R. A. Smith. il Fortune 69:80-4+ F '64
Historic houses, etc.
Living with antiques; Pennsylvania home of Mr and Mrs Andrew Wyeth. A. Winchester. il Antiques 86:592-7 N '64
Living with antiques; the Bradford-Cadwalader house, Buckingham, Pa. R. Lessey. il Antiques 86:188-91 Ag '64
Living with antiques: Walnut Hill. G. Z. Thomas. il Antiques 86:707-11 D '64
Nicholas Biddle's Andalusia, a nineteenth-century country seat today. J. Biddle. il Antiques 86:286-90 S '64
President Kennedy salutes Grey Towers. il Am For 69:22-3+ N '63
History
Tax on whiskey? never! G. Carson. il Am Heritage 14:62-4+ Ag '63
Parks and reserves
Naturealm; Prince Gallitzin State Park. J. J. Shomon. il Audubon Mag 66:212-15 Jl '64
Project 70. R. R. Widner. il Am For 70:26-9+ Ja '64
Politics and government
Bill Scranton: champion of states' rights and states' responsibilities. B. Hibbs. Read Digest 84:103-8 Ap '64
Cleaning it up; candidates for U.S. Senate nomination. Time 83:24-5 My 8 '64
Evergreen; student-congressman. Newsweek 63:23 My 11 '64
Making their records. il Time 82:29 S 13 '63
Pennsylvania politics. New Repub 150:6 Ja 18 '64
Scranton of Pennsylvania. M. Kempton. New Repub 148:9-12 F 16 '63
Scranton of Pennsylvania. R. A. Smith. il Fortune 69:80-4+ F '64
Waiting game of William W. Scranton. P. Duke. Reporter 30:30-2 F 27 '64
Religious institutions and affairs
News of the Christian world (cont) Christian Cent 80:246, 836-7, 1117-18, 1480 F 20, Je 26, S 11, N 27 '63
Social life and customs
Main line; Philadelphia's seventeen miles of countrified suburbs. S. Birmingham. il Holiday 36:86-95+ D '64
PENNSYLVANIA academy of the fine arts
Painting contests; Guggenheim international award and Pennsylvania academy awards. il Time 83:74-5 F 7 '64
PENNSYLVANIA avenue. See Washington, D.C.—Streets
PENNSYLVANIA ballet company
Pennsylvania ballet company at Paoli. D. Hering. il(p66) Dance Mag 37:28 S '63
PENNSYLVANIA Dutch. See Pennsylvania Germans
PENNSYLVANIA German cookery. See Cookery, American
PENNSYLVANIA Germans
Fill yourself up, clean your plate; with recipes. A. Robertson. il Am Heritage 15:56-66+ Ap '64
Pennsylvania Dutch. J. Hay. Holiday 36:40-1+ Ag '64
PENNSYLVANIA railroad
No. one railroad job; it goes to a merger expert. U S News 55:21 Jl 8 '63
Outlook: brighter. il Time 82:81 Jl 5 '63
Pennsy takes a gamble; sells holdings in the Norfolk & Western and the Wabash. Bsns W p31 S 19 '64
Pennsy's road ahead. T. O'Hanlon. il Duns R 83:36-8+ F '64
Switch of tracks; new chairman. Newsweek 62:72-4 Jl 8 '63
PENNSYLVANIA state library, Harrisburg
State library and library school cooperation. M. Filderman. ALA Bul 57:93-4 F '63
PENNSYLVANIA station. See New York (city)—Stations
PENNSYLVANIA turnpike. See Roads—Pennsylvania

PENNSYLVANIA. University
Dream dorm or nightmare? controversial women's residence designed by E. Saarinen. L. Baron. il Mlle 60:109+ Ja '65
Old Ben's new Penn. il Time 82:58+ Ag 23 '63
Hospital
Hospital of the University of Pennsylvania in Philadelphia. il Antiques 85:386 Ap '64
Wharton school of finance and commerce
Famous firsts: how business schools began. il Bsns W p 114+ O 19 '63
PENNY wise; drama. See Boiko, C.
PENNYPACKER, H. S.
Measurement of the conditioned eyelid reflex. bibliog Science 144:1248-9 Je 5 '64
PENONZEK, Edward M.
Catholics and sexuality. Christian Cent 81: 1624 D 30 '64
PENROSE annual
Penrose annual: new trends in design, mapmaking, automation; with editorial comment. C. B. Grannis. Pub W 186:57, 59-61 Ag 3 '64
PENS
New look in longhand: fiber-tipped pens. il Time 84:34 D 25 '64
Nib does it; Japanese fiber-tip pen Pentel. il Newsweek 64:65 Ag 3 '64
Pens to mark laundry. Consumer Bul 47:21 S '64
See also
Fountain pens
PENSION funds. See Pensions—Finance
PENSION trusts
New giant in union funds; merger of ILGWU pension funds. Bsns W p36+ Ag 8 '64
PENSIONS
See also
Civil service pensions
Income
Old age pensions—United States
Trade unions—Benefit funds
Finance
Look who's selling; corporate pension funds. Fortune 70:77 Ag '64
Looking hard at pension funds; Cabinet-level committee report. Bsns W p32 Jl 18 '64
122 billion pension dollars. il U S News 54: 106-7 Je 24 '63
Pension fund race gets hotter. Bsns W p66 F 2 '63
Pension funds pass 135 billions. U S News 56:104 Je 15 '64
Pension plans for salaried employees. H. E. Davis. bibliog f Mo Labor R 87:44-7 Ja '64
Unfunded private pension plans. H. L. Levin. il Mo Labor R 86:1414-20 D '63
Why government is looking at private pension funds. il U S News 57:86-8 Ag 31 '64
See also
Pension trusts
Laws and regulations
Federal control threatens pension plan growth: interview. C. H. Fischer. Nations Bsns 52:56-8+ N '64
Flurry in private pension plans; Keogh law. Bsns W p 167-8 N 16 '63
Now pensions go on the escalator. U S News 54:106 Je 17 '63
Personal business: HR-10 plan for the self employed. Bsns W p 133 S 28 '63
PENSIONS, Industrial
Carrying pension to new job; portable pension in Ontario. Bsns W p58+ Ap 13 '63
Characteristics of the private pension structure. W. W. Kolodrubetz. il Mo Labor R 87:774-80 Jl '64
Early retirement provisions in private pension plans. W. W. Kolodrubetz. il Mo Labor R 87:1165-70 O '64
Federal control threatens pension plan growth: interview. C. H. Fischer. Nations Bsns 52:56-8+ N '64
High-flying cost of pensions. il Bsns W p94+ Mr 14 '64
Is your pension safe? M. T. Bloom. New Repub 151:13-15 O 31 '64
Looking hard at pension funds; Cabinet-level committee report. Bsns W p32 Jl 18 '64
Multi-employer pensions & labor mobility: excerpts from Labor mobility from the viewpoint of the older workers. R. C. Miljus and A. C. Johnson. bibliog f Harvard Bsns R 41:147-8+ S '63
New type of pension plan; United auto workers union plan. U S News 56:81-2 Je 1 '64
Penchant for pensions; move toward higher pensions and earlier retirements. il Time 84:99 S 18 '64
Pension mirage. M. C. Bernstein. Nation 198: 597-9+ Je 15 '64
Pension plans for salaried employees. H. E. Davis. bibliog f Mo Labor R 87:44-7 Ja '64
Prospects of benefits under private pension plans. W. W. Kolodrubetz. il Mo Labor R 87:1283-6 N '64
Rail-pension tax: headed higher. U S News 55:122 O 7 '63
Tomorrow's pension is today's hot issue. il Bsns W p80-1 S 5 '64
Unfunded private pension plans. H. L. Levin. il Mo Labor R 86:1414-20 D '63
Vesting provisions in private pension plans. W. W. Kolodrubetz. il Mo Labor R 87: 1014-21 S '64
See also
United mine workers of America welfare and retirement fund
PENSIONS, Military
See also
Insurance, Soldiers and sailors
Germany (Federal Republic)
Scales of justice. Newsweek 63:44 Je 22 '64
United States
For veterans: higher pensions and new insurance. Changing T 19:6 Ja '65
Speaking out; let's say no to the veterans. E. P. Neilan. Sat Eve Post 236:8+ N 30 '63
PENSKE, Roger
What makes Roger race. G. Rogin. il pors Sports Illus 18:58-62+ Mr 25 '63
PENSTEMONS
Fashionable penstemons. S. Newman. il Pop Gard 15:20-1 Ap '64
Penstemons for color impact. M. P. Kunkel. il Horticulture 41:72 F '63
PENTAGON building, Arlington, Va
Biggest office building in the world. il Sr Schol 85:7 Ja 14 '65
PENTATEUCH. See Bible—Old Testament—Pentateuch
PENTECOST
Come, creator spirit; 1964 Pentecostal message from the presidents of the World council of churches. Iakovos and others. Christian Cent 81:627 My 13 '64
Tremble no more; Pentecostal message to Protestant and Orthodox churches from World council. Christian Cent 80:699 My 29 '63
PENTECOSTAL churches
Pentecostal movement: hopes and hazards. K. Kendrick. Christian Cent 80:608-10 My 8 '63
Pentecostals and Pope John's new Pentecost. D. J. O'Hanlon. America 108:634-6 My 4 '63
PENTHOUSES. See Apartments
PEONIES
How to divide and transplant peonies. il Bet Hom & Gard 41:116-17 O '63
Peonies. il Flower Grower 51:26 S '64
Peonies. il Pop Gard 15:57 S '64
Peonies. B. Black. il Pop Gard 14:30-2+ S '63
Peonies are forever. H. W. Copeland. il Flower Grower 50:20-1+ S '63
Peonies; cut them and use indoors. B. Black. il Pop Gard 15:29 My '64
Peonies; for minimum care in the garden. N. Simmons. il Pop Gard 15:28-9 My '64
This marvel is a tree peony. il Sunset 131: 277 O '63
Try the tree peonies. A. J. De Blasi. il Horticulture 42:24-5 F '64
PEOPLE to people health foundation
S.S. Hope for the world. il Parents Mag 38:86-7 O '63
PEOPLE-to-people letter exchange. See International correspondence
PEOPLE-to-people programs. See intercommunity cooperation
PEOPLE'S liberation army. See China (People's Republic)—Armed forces
PEORIA, Ill.
Newspapers
On top of the news; Peoria's Journal star helicopter in news-gathering. il Flying 74: 77 F '64
PEP pills. See Amphetamines
PEPEU, G. and Mantegazzini, P.
Midbrain hemisection: effect on cortical acetylcholine in the cat. bibliog Science 145:1069-70 S 4 '64
PEPIS, Betty
Going places, finding things in Scandinavia. House & Gard 123:36+ Mr '63
Worth thinking about. House & Gard 123:154-5 My '63
PEPITONE, Joe
Freshest rookie. il por Newsweek 62:77 S 2 '63

PEPPARD, George
George Peppard: a personality in spite of himself. E. Miller. il pors Seventeen 22:128-9+ N '63
PEPPER, Beverly
Woman of steel. il por Newsweek 62:104+ N 11 '63
PEPPER, George M.
More reflections on Gaullist France. Nat R 15:239-40 S 24 '63
PEPPER, Jack
Paradoxical Lake Mead. Motor B 111:36-7+ My '63
PEPPER, Stephen C.
Issue of evolution. Art N 62:42+ O '63
PEPPER
Big dash of pepper; with recipes. C. Claiborne. il N Y Times Mag p89-90 My 19 '63
PEPPER grinders. See Pepper mills
PEPPER mills
Pepper mill. M. Kaytor. il Look 27:44-5 Ap 9 '63
PEPPERBOXES (small arms) See Pistols
PEPPERIDGE farm, incorporated
Mrs Rudkin revisited. New Yorker 39:42-4 N 16 '63
PEPPERMINT Easter egg; drama. See Slattery, M. E.
PEPPERS
Peppers: good payoff crop. C. O. Wisham. il Farm J 88:42C S '64
See also
Cookery—Vegetables
PEPSI-COLA company
Other life of Joan Crawford. il Bsns W p90-2+ S 21 '63
Pepsi v. Coke. il Time 82:101-2 O 18 '63
Small world: plan to turn World's fair pavilion into a tribute to UNICEF. New Yorker 39:20-1 Ag 31 '63
Well-planned Crawford; promoting Pepsi-Cola. R. Oulahan. il Life 56:11-12 F 21 '64
PEPSI-COLA exhibition gallery. See Photography—Exhibitions
PEPSIN
Complement-fixing properties of pepsin-treated rabbit and sheep antibodies. P. H. Schur and E. L. Becker. bibliog il Science 141:360-2 Jl 26 '63
PEPTIC ulcers
How much of the stomach should be cut out? il Time 83:48-9 Ja 3 '64
Incidence of gastric ulcers in swine. T. W. Perry and others. il Science 139:349-50 Ja 25 '63
Month of the ulcer. W. R. Vath. il Todays Health 42:58-7+ O '64
Overfreezing a danger in new ulcer treatment. Sci N L 85:265 Ap 25 '64
Ulcers in older people caused by stagnant food; stomach ulcers. Sci N L 85:313 My 16 '64
What to do about an ulcer. L. A. Rosenblum. Parents Mag 38:139-42 N '63
You & your diet. A. A. Schaal. il Good H 156:183-6 F '63
PEPTIDES
Antibody combining site: the B polypeptide chain. O. A. Roholt and others. bibliog il Science 141:726-7 Ag 23 '63
Crystal and molecular structure of ferrichrome A. A. Zalkin and others. bibliog il Science 146:261-3 O 9 '64
Natural kinin in peach fruitlets. S. Lavee. bibliog Science 142:583 N 1 '63
Polypeptide chains of human gamma-globulin: cellular localization by fluorescent antibody. G. M. Bernier and J. J. Cebra. bibliog il Science 144:1590-1 Je 26 '64
Polypeptide chains of rabbit gamma globulin. P. A. Small, jr. and others. bibliog il Science 142:393-4 O 18 '63
Radiation-chemical oxidation of peptides in the solid state. W. M. Garrison and others. bibliog il Science 146:250-2 O 9 '64
Sialic acid-containing glycopeptide from chlorella. D. L. Correll. bibliog Science 145:588-9 Ag 7 '64
Steric factors in the chemistry of polypeptides, poly-α-amino acids and proteins. R. E. Whitfield. bibliog il Science 142:577-9 N 1 '63
Subclasses of human $\gamma_2$globulin based on differences in the heavy polypeptide chains. W. D. Terry and J. L. Fahey. bibliog il Science 146:400-1 O 16 '64
PERALTA, Gregorio
Champ's fist was on the sparrow's eye. T. Maule. il por Sports Illus 20:48+ Ap 20 '64
PERALTA AZURIDA, Enrique
First step back. Newsweek 63:60 Je 8 '64
Pingpong game is over. por Time 81:28-9 Ap 12 '63
PERCEPTION
Cortical evoked potentials and perception of paired flashes. E. Donchin and others. bibliog il Science 141:1285-6 S 27 '63
Counteracting effects of physical exercises performed during prolonged perceptual deprivation. J. P. Zubek. bibliog il Science 142:504-6 O 25 '63
Elementary art to develop visual sensitivity. G. S. Wright, jr. il Sch Arts 63:19-20 N '63
Gap between the ears; new concepts of perception. il Newsweek 63:89 My 11 '64
Illusion of movement. P. A. Kolers. il Sci Am 211:98-106 O '64
Interference in visual recognition. J. S. Bruner and M. C. Potter. bibliog il Science 144:424-5 Ap 24 '64
Letter from Cleveland. R. Plank. il Sat R 47:58-9 O 3 '64; Reply with rejoinder. C. V. B. Wilkin. 47:70 N 7 '64
Perception and commitment. R. Livingston. il Bul Atomic Sci 19:14-18 F '63
Sceptron; a sound-operated fiber-optic brain cell. L. S. Balandis. il Electr World 69:36-7+ Mr '63
Stop, look, and see! J. K. Lagemann. il Read Digest 83:128-31 Jl '63
Tell it to Sceptron! A. P. Armagnac. il Pop Sci 182:120-1 Ap '63
Visual search. U. Neisser. il Sci Am 210:94-100+ Je '64
See also
Extrasensory perception
Figural aftereffects
Space perception
Time perception
Word perception
PERCH fishing
Fishing was wild. A. W. Prince. il Outdoor Life 131:45-7+ Je '63
Hide-and-seek perch. A. J. McClane. il Field & S 68:106-9 O '63
Perch are running. J. B. Gleason. il Outdoor Life 133:66-8+ My '64
Trolling for tramcars. W. Page. il Field & S 68:43-5 D '63
Who's teaching whom? D. Llewellyn. il Outdoor Life 133:66-8 Mr '64
Wing dam walleyes. H. Bradshaw. il Field & S 68:10-11 My '63
PERCIVAL, Stephen F. jr, and others
Carbonate rocks: cleaning with suspensions of hydrogen-ion exchange resin. Science 142:1456 D 13 '63
PERCOLATORS, Coffee. See Coffee pots, percolators, etc.
PERCY, Charles Harting
We hold these truths . . . PTA Mag 58:4-6 Je '64
about
Any other questions? por Time 82:22 Jl 12 '63
Boy wonder. il por Newsweek 63:30 Ap 27 '64
Boy wonder of Illinois politics. H. Higdon. por Reporter 30:29-31 My 7 '64
Chuck Percy of Illinois: man in the middle. J. Star. il pors Look 28:101-3 O 20 '64
Chuck's luck. Time 84:39 O 16 '64
New challenger to the Kennedy clan. W. Trombley. il pors Sat Eve Post 236:38-9 S 28 '63
Percy's purge. J. L. McDowell. New Repub 150:8 Je 27 '64
Perils of Percy. il por Newsweek 62:25-6 Jl 15 '63
Through a lens brightly. il pors Time 84:33-7 S 18 '64
True to form. il por Time 83:22 Ja 31 '64
PERCY, Walker
How to succeed in business without thinking about money. Commonweal 77:557-9 F 22 '63
PERDONCINI, Guy
Not so deaf, not so dumb. il por Time 85:55 Ja 29 '65
PEREIRA, William Leonard
Man with the plan; Irvine ranch, Calif. il pors Time 82:68-72 S 6 '63
Planning for a hundred tomorrows. il por Bsns W p14-5+ O 24 '64
PERELMAN, Sidney Joseph
Do anything else, but lay off the quill. por Seventeen 23:148+ Je '64
Eat, drink, and be wary; story. New Yorker 40:53-5 N 21 '64
Good-bye, Broadway; hello, Mr Square. Sat Eve Post 237:94+ My 23 '64
Great oafs from little monsters grow. New Yorker 40:44-6 My 16 '64
Hello, central, give me that jolly old pelf. New Yorker 39:27-9 D 21 '63

PERELMAN, Sidney Joseph—*Continued*
I was a slave of love. Sat Eve Post 237:76-7 F 22 '64
If a slicker meet a slicker; story. New Yorker 39:24-7 Ja 25 '64
LAHRge world. Theatre Arts 47:20-1 F '63
Once over lightly, and please hush your bazoo: story. New Yorker 39:50-2 D 14 '63
Pastiche of the author in Sweet disarray. New Yorker 40:26-8 D 26 '64
Reunion in Gehenna; story. New Yorker 40: 24-6 F 22 '64

about

Beauty part. Criticism
Theatre Arts il 47:12-13 F '63
People are talking about. . . por Vogue 141: 112-13 F 1 '63

PERENNIALS
Annuals, perennials, summer bulbs for 1964. H. Mason. il Bet Hom & Gard 42:58-63 Mr '64
Big, bold exuberant perennials. C. Holway. il Horticulture 41:164 Mr '63
Color me! il Flower Grower 50:24-7 Jl '63
Combinations that click. J. D. Walters. il Flower Grower 50:42-3+ Ag '63
For best results with perennials. Pop Gard 15:68 Ap '64
Grace and lightness of fine-foliage perennials. E. L. Sculthorp. il House B 106:154-5+ Mr '64
If September disappointed you. il Sunset 131: 184 S '63
New for '63. il Pop Gard 14:44-6+ F '63
Now's the very best time to plant perennials. il Sunset 133:262-3 O '64
Perennials. M. Costigan. il Pop Gard 15: 30-1+ Ap '64
Perennials for color through August. D. E. Stebbins. il Horticulture 41:224-5 Ap '63
Perennials in California: plant now, or plant soon. il Sunset 131:102-5 O '63
Rare but desirable perennials for color in 1965. il Sunset 133:192+ S '64
Some late perennials. Horticulture 41:476 S '63
Summer perennials. M. L. Garra. il Horticulture 42:30-3 Je '64
Take a new look at old favorites. il Bet Hom & Gard 42:136-7 Ap '64
Use stately spires for the distant places. E. L. Sculthorp. il House B 106:134-5+ Je '64
Wake up your garden. il Flower Grower 51: 50-2 Ap '64
When and how to divide perennials. il Sunset 131:258 N '63
See also
Bulbs
also names of perennials, e.g. Phlox

PERÉNYI, Eleanor
American resistance. Esquire 59:90-1+ Mr '63
Case of the extravagant traveler. Harper 230: 105-9 Ja '65
What ever happened to American cooking? Sat Eve Post 236:68-70 Je 15 '63

PERERA, Padma
Dr Salaam; story. New Yorker 40:54-63 N 28 '64
Too late for anger; story. New Yorker 39: 28-34 Ja 25 '64
Visit from the Mahatma; story. Sat Eve Post 236:56-61 My 25 '63

PERERA, Thomas B. See Hefferline, R. F. jt. auth.

PERERA, Victor
Night they raided the snake-juice still. Vogue 144:58+ D '64
Our footloose correspondents. New Yorker 39: 144+ Ap 27 '63

PERETZ, Don
Arab refugees: a changing problem. For Affairs 41:558-70 Ap '63

PERETZ, Isaac Loeb
Theatre of Peretz; dramatization. See Sheffer, I.

PERETZ, Martin
Complicity with Spengler. Nation 197:203-5 O 5 '63

PÉREZ, Galo René
Six Ecuadorian poets. Américas 16:30-4 N '64

PEREZ, Israel
Men who make Castro's factories run. por Bsns W p 128 S 14 '63

PÉREZ, Javier Heraud
Biography of a lost poet. Time 81:21 My 31 '63

PEREZ, Leander H. sr
Perils of Plaquemines. R. Cleghorn. New Repub 149:8-10 S 21 '63
Prison Perez style; ready for race demonstrators; Fort St Phillip, Plaguemines Parish. il por U S News 55:16 N 4 '63

PEREZ-CRUET, Jorge, and others
Heart rate: differential effects of hypothalamic and septal self-stimulation. bibliog Science 140:1235-6 Je 14 '63

PÉREZ GODOY, Ricardo
Peru coup topples Perez Godoy. por Sr Schol 82:16 Mr 20 '63
When the brass fall out. il por Time 81:37 Mr 15 '63

PÉREZ JIMÉNEZ, Marcos
Asylum, too, is a human right. Nat R 15:93 Ag 13 '63
Breaking a tradition in favor of democracy. il Time 82:20-1 Ag 23 '63
Deported first. por Sr Schol 83:7 S 20 '63
Due process is for all. Nation 196:82 F 2 '63
Ex-dictator is forced to leave U.S. por U S News 55:21 Ag 26 '63
Facing the music. por Newsweek 62:47 Ag 26 '63
Legion-of-Merit dictator. Nation 196:190 Mr 9 '63
U.S. agrees to extradition of ex-President of Venezuela; Department statement, August 12, 1963; with texts of notes of Secretary Rusk and Ambassador Tejera-Paris. Dept State Bul 49:364-7 S 2 '63

PÉREZ MARCHAND, Monelisa Lina
Our faith in tomorrow; New world man; excerpts from address, 1963. Américas 16:2-4 Ag '64

PERFECT match; story. See Knowlton, R. A.

PERFECT wedding; story. See Davenport, G.

PERFECTION
Idea of perfection. I. Murdoch. Yale R 53:342-80 Mr '64

PERFORMANCE incentives corporation
Sales & distribution; performance incentive programs. J. B. Weiner. Duns R 82:45 Ag '63

PERFORMANCE standards
Yardstick for red tape. Bsns W p38 S 12 '64

PERFORMING animals. See Animals—Training

PERFUME currant. See Ribes viburnifolium

PERFUMERY
D. Boone would have been shocked; grooming aids. E. Kendall. il N Y Times Mag p43+ O 13 '63
Fragrance for your bath. il McCalls 91:136-7 My '64
Fragrance news. il Seventeen 23:216 N '64
Fragrance: the essence of giving. il Mlle 58: 148-51 N '63
Fragrant life, men's division. il Vogue 143: 150-1 Je '64
Frankly sentimental, a perfume valentine. L. D. Kirk. il Parents Mag 39:54 F '64
Greetings, friends! il Mlle 60:142-3 N '64
Invest in beauty; scents and sensibility. il Mlle 57:130 Je '63
It's a man's world; fragrance for men. il Mlle 60:108-9 D '64
Memo: to a puzzled male. Am Home 67:11 D '64
Men from A to Z; toiletries. il Vogue 141:18+ Je '63
Perfume to dream on. il Seventeen 23:140-1 F '64
Perfumed life. il Vogue 143:116-19 Ap 15 '64
Perfume's many splendors. D. A. Robinson. il Ladies Home J 80:21-2 D '63
Project: you; holiday fragrances. il Ladies Home J 81:113 D '64
Scented life. il Vogue 144:34-5 Jl '64
Sense of scent. il Ladies Home J 81:71-3 D '64
Setting in search of a character. il Vogue 142:134-5+ N 15 '63
Sex, education, and perfume. il Vogue 142:158-9 O 1 '63
V.I.P. for a V.I.P. il Mlle 58:112-15 D '63
Which fragrance is yours? il Seventeen 23: 148-9 N '64

PERGOLAS
See also
Arbors

PERGOLESI, G. B.
La serva padrona. P. L. Miller. Am Rec G 29:706 My '63

PERIC-GOLIA, Ludvik, and Jones, R. S.
Ornithocholanic acids and cholelithiasis in man. bibliog Science 142:245-6 O 11 '63

PERIGORD
Picturesque Perigord. M. Gardner. il Travel 122:28-31+ Ag '64

PERINE, W. A.
Shift the point of interest. U S Camera 27: 62-3 O '64

PERIOD furniture. See Furniture

PERIOD of silence; story. See Oppenheimer, M.

PERIODICAL advertising. See Advertising mediums—Periodicals

PERIODICAL covers
How much can you tell a magazine about its cover? A. Gingrich. Esquire 61:6 Je '64

PERIODICAL distributors. See Newspaper and periodical wholesalers

PERIODICAL literature
Article ideas: from manuscript to magazine. J. P. Fried and H. I. Kurtz. Writer 77:16-19+ D '64
Article market place; excerpt from Prose by professionals, ed. by T. Morris. D. Landman. Writer 77:21-2 Je '64
Editor's advice on article sales. C. Peterson, jr. Writer 77:14-17 O '64
Fine romance, with no kisses; excerpt from address, April 14, 1964. W. H. Nichols. Writer 77:18-19 Jl '64
Freewheelers; world of the travel writer. il Newsweek 63:72 Je 1 '64
Fresh fresh fresh eye. M. Williams. Writer 76:13-14+ Ag '63
Helping hand for a literary upstart. J. Fischer. Harper 227:20+ S '63; Discussion. 227:10+ N '63
High cost of writing; Stern and Beinecke funds. J. F. Fixx. Sat R 47:53+ Je 13 '64
Key to article sales. M. Gunther. Writer 77:12-14 Ag '64
Letter to a young article writer. R. Gehman. Writer 76:15-17 N '63
Off the cuff; questions and answers. A. Marple. Writer 77:6-8 N '64
Outlines and article writing; excerpt from Prose by professionals, ed. by T. Morris. M. Weisinger. Writer 76:12-15+ Mr '63
Put yourself in the editor's chair; rejected articles. C. Darlington. Writer 77:26-7 O '64
Research and interviewing techniques; excerpt from Prose by professionals, ed. by T. Morris. B. Schapper. Writer 77:20-3 Ja '64
Selling your poetry. P. J. Henniker-Heaton. Writer 77:18-20 Ap '64
Successful query letters. C. W. Casewit. Writer 76:15-17 D '63
Techniques and style in article writing; excerpt from Prose by professionals, ed. by T. Morris. O. Schisgall. Writer 76:14-16 S '63
Time of Henry Luce's Life. Christian Cent 80:695 My 22 '63
Variety is the spice of writing. R. Armour. Writer 76:18-19 N '63
Want to write? get a camera. E. Houghton. Writer 76:26-7 Jl '63
Writing the nonfiction narrative. R. White. Writer 76:10-12 Ag '63
See also
Fiction in periodicals and newspapers

PERIODICALS
Letter from Paris; new English-language international quarterly, Art and literature, ed. in Paris. Genêt. New Yorker 40:193-4 Ap 18 '64
Little magazines, by R. Whittemore. Review
Nation 198:98-100 Ja 27 '64. W. Wasserstrom
300 years of storing words: scientific communication; excerpt from address. J. R. Porter. il Sat R 48:92-5 Ja 2 '65
Two book review magazines appear, by teenagers for teenagers; On the book beat, Scrutinize. Library J 88:1742 Ap 15 '63
See also
Audit bureau of circulations
Libraries—Periodical collections
Religious newspapers and periodicals
Serial publications
Trade journals
also subhead Periodicals under various subjects, e.g. Business—Periodicals

Advertising
One-upmanship. il Time 83:40 Ja 31 '64
Stein song; policy of Redbook magazine. il Time 84:73 D 4 '64

Bibliography
New periodicals. See issues of Library journal

Columns
See Newspapers—Sections, columns, etc.

Indexes
Committee on Wilson indexes: how it works. E. B. Colburn. il ALA Bul 59:35-6+ Ja '65
Indexes to our journal; letter. F. Henritz. Science 144:1178 Je 5 '64
See also
Public affairs information service
Readers' guide to periodical literature

Letters to the editor
Letters to the editor. P. H. Abelson. Science 143:201 Ja 17 '64
Letters to the editor. P. Woodring. Sat R 47:61 Mr 21 '64
Letters to the editor; reprinted from the early years of SRL. Sat R 47:63+ Ag 29 '64
Of many things; hints to prospective letter writers. T. N. Davis. America 111:23 Jl 11 '64

Personal advertisements
See Newspapers—Personal advertisements

Prices
Economics and the press. Sr Schol 82:14-15 Mr 27 '63

Readers
Find the typical reader. New Repub 148:5 My 18 '63

Australia
Ecumenical in Australia. Christian Cent 81:878 Jl 8 '64

Canada
Canada's own; Maclean. il Newsweek 64:51+ Ag 24 '64

England
See Periodicals—Great Britain

France
Hi pals; Salut les copains. Newsweek 62:65 Jl 29 '63
Match game; Paris-match. il Newsweek 63:78-9 Ja 20 '64
Peking in Paris; Marxist monthly Révolution. il Newsweek 63:54 Mr 9 '64
Si elle lit elle lit Elle. Time 83:69-70 My 22 '64
They always get the picture. C. Schwalberg. il U S Camera 26:46-9+ Jl '63

Germany (Federal Republic)
Atlantic report; Spiegel affair. Atlan 211:14+ F '63
DM vs. VW; West Germany's product-testing magazine sued by Volkswagen. Newsweek 63:83 Mr 23 '64

Great Britain
British physics journals. A. C. Strickland. Science 144:986 My 22 '64
See also
Economist (London)
Encounter (periodical)
New statesman (periodical)
Penrose annual
Private eye (periodical)
Scrutiny (periodical)
Spectator (periodical)

Italy
Enough for one man; Rizzoli enterprises. il Newsweek 65:46-8 Ja 4 '65

Korea (Republic)
Fifty-seven varieties; phony Western publications circulated by North Korean propagandists. Newsweek 64:86+ S 14 '64

Russia
Atheism's resort to mendacity; falsehoods in Science and religion. D. A. Lowrie. Christian Cent 80:1513-16 D 4 '63
Behind the smile on Krokodil. T. Shabad. il N Y Times Mag p22-3+ Je 7 '64

South Africa
In the fiery continent, by T. Hopkinson Review
Sat R il 46:19-20 Ag 17 '63. J. Hughes
See also
Contact (periodical)

United States
Agonies of infancy. il Time 83:59 Ap 3 '64
Article market place; excerpt from Prose by professionals, ed. by T. Morris. D. Landman. Writer 77:21-2 Je '64
Billion-dollar year? Time 84:75 O 23 '64
For & by teen-agers: Tempo. il Time 84:61 Jl 3 '64
Hopefully, schmopefully. W. Sheed. Commonweal 81:16-17 S 25 '64
If you can keep your head when all about you: television and news magazine coverage of the Kennedy assassination story. R. L. Tobin. il Sat R 46:53-4 D 14 '63; Discussion. 47:74 Ja 11 '64
If you really want to sell. D. Hill. Writer 76:23-4 Je '63
Importance of being persistent. N. J. Stoyenoff. Writer 76:25+ My '63

PERIODICALS—United States—*Continued*
JFK, the magazines, and peace. J. Tebbel. il Sat R 46:56-7 D 14 '63
Know your markets. E. M. Dean. Writer 77:28-30 F '64
Marketing of poetry. Writer 76:19-21+ Mr '63
Newcomers. J. F. Fixx. Sat R 47:73 My 9 '64
Peripatetic reviewer. E. Weeks. Atlan 213: 134+ F '64
There are 00 trees in Russia; the function of facts in newsmagazines. O. Friedrich. Harper 229:59-65 O '64
Where to sell manuscripts. See issues of Writer
See also
Catholic press
See also names of periodicals, e.g. National review

PERIODICALS, Immoral. See Immoral literature and pictures

PERIODICALS, Prison. See Prison publications

PERIODICALS, Publishing of
In the shadow of the unforeseen. A. Gingrich. Esquire 61:6 F '64
Publishing paper & ink. Time 82:32 D 27 '63
When magazines fight together. T. Peterson. Sat R 47:74 D 12 '64

PERIODICALS, Trade. See Trade journals

PERIODICALS for men
Notes and comment. New Yorker 40:31 Je 6 '64

PERIODICALS for women
See also
Good housekeeping (periodical)

PERIODICITY
Biological rhythms: a new type in strains of a mutant of neurospora crassa. P. W. Neurath and M. D. Berliner. bibliog il Science 146:646-7 O 30 '64
Circadian leaf movements: persistance in bean plants grown in continuous high-intensity light. T. Hoshizaki and K. C. Hamner. il Science 144:1240-1 Je 5 '64; Reply. E. Bunning. bibliog 146:551 O 23 '64
Circadian periodicity in the concentration of prolactin in the rat hypophysis. R. H. Clark and B. L. Baker. bibliog il Science 143:375-6 Ja 24 '64; Reply with rejoinder. J. D. Palmer. 145:296 Jl 17 '64
Circadian rhythmicity in the sensitivity of two strains of mice to whole-body radiation. D. J. Pizzarello and others. bibliog il Science 145:286-91 Jl 17 '64
Daily fluctuation in the blood sugar concentration of the house cricket, gryllus domesticus L. J. W. Nowosielski and R. L. Patton. bibliog il Science 144:180-1 Ap 10 '64
Daily rhythm in the susceptibility of an insect to a toxic agent. C. L. Cole and P. L. Adkisson. bibliog il Science 144:1148-9 My 29 '64
Daily rhythmicity of corpus allatum and neurosecretory cells in drosophila melanogaster (meig) L. Rensing. bibliog il Science 144:1586-7 Je 26 '64
Daily sensitivity rhythm of the two-spotted spider mite, tetranychus urticae, to DDVP. B. Polcik and others. bibliog il Science 145:405-6 Jl 24 '64
Diurnal rhythm and photoperiodism in testicular recrudescence of the house finch. W. M. Hammer. bibliog il Science 142:1294-5 D 6 '63
Endogenous circadian rhythm in cytoplasm of acetabularia: influence of the nucleus. E. Schweiger and others. bibliog il Science 146:658-9 O 30 '64
Gastric erosions in the rat: effects of immobilization at different points in the activity cycle. R. Ader. bibliog il Science 145:406-7 Jl 24 '64
Life-giving balancing act. R. Campbell. il Life 55:80-1 N 8 '63
Living clocks. N. J. Berrill. il Atlan 212: 65-9 D '63
Metabolic control of timing. S. B. Hendricks. bibliog il Science 141:21-7 Jl 5 '63
Mystery of the biological clocks; circadian rhythm. A. Hamilton. Sci Digest 56:21-6 O '64
Nocturnal changes in oxidative activities of rat liver mitochondria. J. L. Glick and W. D. Cohen. bibliog il Science 143:1184-5 Mr 13 '64
Photoperiodic reversibility of diapause induction in an insect. R. A. Bell and P. L. Adkisson. bibliog il Science 144:1149-51 My 29 '64
Reinforcement as input: cyclic variable-interval schedule. J. E. R. Staddon. bibliog il Science 145:410-12 Jl 24 '64
Subtle tides of life. R. Platt. Read Digest 82:264-7 Ap '63
World's largest spectrograph probes secrets of life. H. G. Earl. il Todays Health 42: 74-6 S '64
X-rays: are there cyclic variations in radiosensitivity? M. Menaker. bibliog Science 143:597 F 7 '64

PERIODONTAL disease. See Gums (anatomy) —Diseases

PERIPHERY cameras. See Cameras

PERJURY
See also
Trials (perjury)

PERKEL, Donald H. and others
Pacemaker neurons: effects of regularly spaced synaptic input. bibliog Science 145: 61-3 Jl 3 '64

PERKIN, Robert L.
Falcons and famous friends. at R 47:75-6 O 24 '64

PERKIN-Elmer corporation
Perkin-Elmer theodolite system for Saturn tested at Cape Canaveral. M. Getler. il Miss & Roc 13:62+ S 30 '63

PERKINS, Betty
For an Arabian nights lady. N Y Times Mag p92-3+ D 13 '64

PERKINS, Charles H.
Modern roses belong in every garden. Pop Gard 14:34-5+ Mr '63
about
Obituary
Flower Grower 50:6 My '63. R. G. Miner
Tribute to Charles H. Perkins, rose king. por Pop Gard 14:6 Jl '63

PERKINS, Courtland Davis
Perkins elected AIAA president. Aviation W 80:41 Ja 27 '64

PERKINS, Dexter
Better to give than give way. Sat R 47:25 Jl 4 '64

PERKINS, Dexter, Jr
Prehistoric fauna from Shanidar, Iraq. bibliog Science 144:1565-6 Je 26 '64

PERKINS, Dwight H.
Centralization versus decentralization in mainland China and the Soviet Union. bibliog f Ann Am Acad 349:70-80 S '63

PERKINS, Eddie
He's champ of the world, but a stranger at home. il pors Ebony 20:72-4+ N '64

PERKINS, Harold J. and Strachan, G.
Decontamination of potato tubers containing cesium-137. bibliog Science 144:59-60 Ap 3 '64

PERKINS, Harold O.
Espaliers; excerpts from Espaliers and vines for the home gardener. Horticulture 42:30-1 O '64

PERKINS, J. P.
Seventeen flyways over the Great Lakes. il pors Audubon Mag 66:294-9; 67:42-5 S '64, Mr 7 '64

PERKINS, James Alfred
Ja '65
Dimensions of the modern university; address, October 4, 1963. Sch & Soc 92:100-4
about
Well endowed. Newsweek 64:96 O 26 '64

PERKINS, John A.
Challenge to teachers; address, October 25, 1963. Vital Speeches 30:172-6 Ja 1 '64

PERKINS, Joseph A. Jr. See Adams, B. K. auth.

PERKINS, Richard W. and others
Air concentrations of twelve radionuclides from 1962 through mid-1964. bibliog Science 146:762-4 N 6 '64
—See Palmer, H. E. jt. auth.

PERKINS, William M.
Machine-accounting benefits. Am City 78: 134-5 Je '63

PERKINSON, Jesse D.
Science, technology, and development. pors Américas 16:1-5 Mr '64

PERKINSON, William J.
Preview of tomorrow's nuclear terror. Sci Digest 54:50-3 Ag '63
Why winters are getting colder; reprint. Sci Digest 56:83-5 D '64

PERLEA, Jonel
Musical events; performance of Bruckner's ninth symphony by Manhattan school of music. W. Sargeant. New Yorker 40:192-4 Ap 25 '64

PERLES, Paul
Medical books in the world market. Pub W 183:41-2 Ap 15 '63

PERLMAN, Bennard B.
Story behind a great art event. Am Artist 27:26-9+ F '63

PERLMAN, D.
Antimicrobial agents and chemotherapy. Science 144:322-3 Ap 17 '64
PERLMAN, Itznak
Return of the prodigy. il por Time 85:49 Ja 15 '65
PERMAFROST. See Frozen ground
PERMANENT court of arbitration. See International court of arbitration, The Hague
PERMANENT waves. See Hairdressing
PERMEABILITY
Membrane permeability: monolayer relationships. A. M. Shanes. bibliog il Science 140: 824-5 My 17 '63
Quantitative molecular approach to the permeability changes of excitation. A. M. Shanes. bibliog il Science 140:51-3 Ap 5 '63
Tetracycline fluorescence in permeability studies of membranes around intracellular parasites. H. G. Du Buy and others. bibliog il Science 145:163-5 Jl 10 '64
PERNAMBUCO (state)
Joe nobody; Miguel Arraes, governor. Newsweek 63:34+ F 24 '64
PERODICTICUS potto. See Pottos
PEROMYSCUS. See Mice, White footed
PERÓN, Juan Domingo
All for show. il por Newsweek 64:43 D 14 '64
Morals rap. Newsweek 62:36 D 23 '63
Perón: this is the year. Time 84:30 N 6 '64
Perón's try for comeback: a bluff? U S News 57:20 D 14 '64
Powder keg politics in the land of the Pampa. il por Sr Schol 82:10-13+ Ap 24 '63
Promise from Madrid. il por Newsweek 64:44 Ag 31 '64
Puff the magic Perón. Newsweek 62:49 Jl 22 '63
Return that wasn't. il por Time 84:48 D 11 '64
Shadowy anniversary. il Newsweek 64:58 S 28 '64
Unwelcome mat. Time 84:37 D 18 '64
PERONISMO. See Argentina—Politics and government
PERRANOSKI, Ron
Earned-Ron. Newsweek 62:70 O 7 '63
PERRAULT, Charles
Puss in boots; dramatization. See Thane, A.
PERRIN, Henri
Fallen bridge. por Newsweek 64:82 Jl 20 '64
Laborer for the harvest. T. M. Switz. Christian Cent 81:1369 N 4 '64
Testing the conscience of the church. P. Steinfels. Commonweal 81:244-6 N 13 '64
PERRIN, Noel
Department of amplification; letter. New Yorker 39:63-5 Jl 6 '63
Magic word game. Vogue 142:124+ S 1 '63
New York drowns another valley. Harper 227:76-83 Ag '63
Sinus viridis Packers and the neo-eboraci Giants. New Yorker 39:213-15+ N 9 '63
PERROT, Nicholas
Medical museum at a crossroads of history; Prairie du Chien, Wis. K. N. Anderson. il Todays Health 41:60-6 D '63
PERROT, Paul N.
New York: glass of Czechoslovakia and Italy. Craft Horiz 24:42-7+ S '64
Unrecorded landscape by J. S. Jennings. Antiques 84:586-8 N '63
PERRY, Antoinette, awards. See American theatre wing
PERRY, Bernard
Progress at the ivy-clad press. Sat R 46:21-2 Je 15 '63
PERRY, Charlotte
Reminiscences and plans. por Dance Mag 37:48-51+ Ap '63
PERRY, Dick
Do not talk to the motorman while the streetcar is in motion. Read Digest 83:247-8+ O '63
Raymond & me that summer; story. McCalls 91:74-5 S '64
PERRY, Doyt
He'll never leave Ohio. J. Underwood. il pors Sports Illus 21:80-2+ S 28 '64
PERRY, Frank
New face, old pro. R. Boeth. il por Sat R 46:21-3 D 28 '63
Small stars spoof the boss. il por Life 55: 133-4 O 4 '63
PERRY, Hart
Follow a star. pors Seventeen 24:79+ Ja '65
PERRY, John
Business, next target for integration? Harvard Bsns R 41:104-15 Mr '63
PERRY, Malcolm
Death in emergency room no. one. J. Breslin. il por Sat Eve Post 236:30-1 D 14 '63
PERRY, Margaret
Christmas magic; excerpts. Flower Grower 51:18-19 D '64
PERRY, Matthew Calbraith
Yankee Barbarian at the Shogun's court. E. Hahn. il Am Heritage 15:60-3+ Je '64
PERRY, R. P. and others
Hybridization of rapidly labeled nuclear ribonucleic acids. bibliog Science 145:504-7 Jl 31 '64
PERRY, Ronald
Aria & variations; poem. Poetry 105:170-3 D '64
Warning to the reader; poem. Poetry 102: 238 Jl '63
PERRY, T. W.
Low-moisture silage for beef cattle. Suc Farm 61:98 My '63
—and others
Incidence of gastric ulcers in swine. Science 139:349-50 Ja 25 '63
—See Matsushima, J. K. jt. auth.
PERRY, Thomas L.
N-methylmetanephrine: excretion by juvenile psychotics. bibliog Science 139:587-9 F 15 '63
—and others
7-Hydroxychlorpromazine: potential toxic drug metabolite in psychiatric patients. bibliog Science 146:81-3 O 2 '64
PERRY, Wes
U.I.A. sessions meet in Havana and Mexico. Arch Rec 134:23+ D '63
PERSE, Saint John
Sacre d'un deuil. Vogue 143:144-5 F 1 '64
PERSECUTION
See also
Genocide
PERSECUTION and assassination of Marat as performed by the inmates of the asylum of Charenton under the direction of the Marquis de Sade; drama. See Weiss, P.
PERSEIDS. See Meteors
PERSHING, John Joseph
From the first Mrs MacArthur: an account of rivalry between two famous generals; reprint. B. Beale. por U S News 56:20 My 4 '64
General Pershing and I. J. T. Schneider. il por Sat Eve Post 236:70+ Ap 27 '63
PERSIA. See Iran
PERSIAN art. See Art, Persian
PERSIAN cyclamens. See Cyclamens
PERSIAN language

Study and teaching

Language study and the Middle East. C. A. Ferguson. Ann Am Acad 356:76-85 N '64
PERSIAN pottery. See Pottery, Persian
PERSIMMONS
Fruit of Jove. W. E. Broedling. il Horticulture 41:69 F '63
Neglected fruits: medlar and persimmon. M. D. Benson. Horticulture 42:15 N '64
PERSON, Harlow Stafford
Famous firsts: organizing a profession. por Bsns W p87-8 Mr 21 '64
PERSON, Stanley, and Osborn, Mary
DNA segregation in escherichia coli: observations by means of tritiated thymidine decay. bibliog Science 143:44-6 Ja 3 '64
PERSON apart; story. See Meade, W.
PERSONAL advertisements. See Newspapers—Personal advertisements
PERSONAL beauty. See Beauty, Personal
PERSONAL credit. See Credit
PERSONAL finance. See Finance, Personal
PERSONAL injuries
Outguessing the jury; Jury verdict research, incorporated's prediction tables based on amount that juries award for injuries. il Time 83:78 My 15 '64
PERSONAL liberty. See Liberty
PERSONAL loans. See Loans, Personal
PERSONAL names. See Names, Personal
PERSONAL opinions. See Attitudes
PERSONAL property. See Property
PERSONAL property insurance, All risk. See Insurance—All risk policies
PERSONAL records
Somebody has a file on you! Changing T 17: 33-6 S '63
What's on your credit record? personnel & insurance reports. il Changing T 19:33-5 Ja '65
PERSONAL responsibility. See Responsibility
PERSONAL rights. See Civil rights
PERSONALISM
Search for self. R. O. Johann. America 109: 14 Jl 6 '63

PERSONALITY
Recent developments in culture and personality. J. J. Honigmann and R. J. Preston. bibliog f Ann Am Acad 354:153-62 Jl '64
Redbook dialogue. A. Quinn; H. Belafonte. il Redbook 120:54-5+ Mr '63
Three Christs of Ypsilanti, by M. Rokeach. Review
Commonweal 80:125 Ap 14 '64. J. Holzhauer
Three types of executive personality. R. W. Wallen. Duns R 81:54-6+ F '63
Traps of identity. E. S. Dean. Nation 196: 349-51 Ap 27 '63
What daydreaming reveals about your personality. J. E. Gibson. il Todays Health 41:43+ N '63
What makes southern girls different? J. Anderson. il Ladies Home J 80:12+ My '63
Who will run your nervous system? A. Watts. New Repub 151:15-16 N 28 '64
Woman of thirty; with editorial comment. F. Sagan. il Vogue 142:30-5 Jl '63
See also
Individuality
Leadership
Psychology
Self

PERSONALITY tests
Are you normal? test yourself; Minnesota multiphasic personality inventory. il Sci Digest 54:15-18 S '63
Personality test interpretation by digital computer. B. Kleinmutz. il Science 139:416-18 F 1 '63
Those personality tests. il Changing T 18: 20-2 Ap '64
View from the couch. il Mlle 57:94-5+ Je '63

PERSONALITY training and development
Success of women's success schools. J. Robbins and J. Robbins. Read Digest 83:115-18 D '63

PERSONNEL management
Blue collar elite. T. R. Brooks. il Duns R 83:pt2 121-2+ Mr '64
Breakthrough in organization development; symposium. bibliog f il Harvard Bsns R 42: 133-55 N '64
Case for Boulwarism. H. R. Northrup. bibliog f il Harvard Bsns R 41:86-97 S '63
Conflict: the vital corporate ingredient. G. S. Odiorne. il Duns R 83:51-2+ Mr '64
Desk-pounding useless. W. Wingo. Sci N L 85:36 Ja 18 '64
Diagnosing interdepartmental conflict. J. A. Seiler. bibliog f il Harvard Bsns R 41:121-32 S '63
Discipline without punishment. J. Huberman. il Harvard Bsns R 42:62-8 Jl '64
Ergonomics and the worker. T. R. Brooks. Duns R 82:55-6 Jl '63
Family business. R. G. Donnelley. bibliog f il Harvard Bsns R 42:93-105 Jl '64
Famous firsts: sibyl of a modern science. il Bsns W p 196+ N 21 '64
Famous firsts: workers can be a team, too; Hawthorne workers. il Bsns W p49-50 My 25 '63
Find the pivot man. J. G. Mason. il Nations Bsns 52:80-2+ D '64
Free the man who's boxed in. N. Stewart. Nations Bsns 52:82-4+ Jl '64
Help the man in the middle. F. A. Shull and D. C. Miller. il Nations Bsns 51:36-7 F '63
Helping women measure up. Bsns W p58 O 24 '64
How bosses really feel. il Bsns W p58 Mr 2 '63
How to break in the college graduate. E. H. Schein. Harvard Bsns R 42:68-76 N '64
How to forecast your manpower needs. E. W. Vetter. il Nations Bsns 52:102-5+ F '64
How to head off trouble. N. Stewart. il Nations Bsns 52:68-70+ Ag '64
Integrated approach to technical staffing. E. D. Phelps and W. Gallagher. il Harvard Bsns R 41:122-9 Jl '63
Lie detectors: sleuthing by polygraph increasingly popular; claims of accuracy are unproved. E. Langer. Science 144:395-7+ Ap 24 '64; Discussion. 144:1177-8 Je 5 '64
Management of corporate conflict. G. S. Odiorne. il Duns R 83:47-8+ Ap '64
Manager vs. the self image. M. R. Feinberg. il Duns R 83:55-6+ F '64
Managing your manpower. T. R. Brooks. See issues of Dun's review and modern industry
Men to match our problems; excerpts from address. L. J. Kroeger. il Recreation 57: 76-8 F '64
Middle management enigma. Duns R 82:29 Jl '63
Personnel problems? write dear Margo; Toronto daily star. il Bsns W p74+ D 5 '64
Poisons of corporate infighting. G. S. Odiorne. Duns R 83:39-40+ F '64
Positive program for performance appraisal. A. F. Kindall and J. Gatza. Harvard Bsns R 41:153-4+ N '63
Social scientists in the plant. L. L. Ferguson. il Harvard Bsns R 42:133-43 My '64
Split roles in performance appraisal. H. H. Meyer and others. Harvard Bsns R 43:123-9 Ja '65
Tension can be an asset; if management deals with it constructively. D. W. Ewing. bibliog f Harvard Bsns R 42:71-8 S '64
What makes a best-managed company? J. B. Weiner. il Duns R 82:40-2+ D '63
When it's right to be wrong. C. Bailey. il Nations Bsns 52:98-9+ Je '64
Who are your motivated workers? M. S. Myers. il Harvard Bsns R 42:73-88 Ja '64
You can keep morale high. N. Stewart. Nations Bsns 51:70-2+ Mr '63
See also
Absenteeism
Employees—Promotion
Employment systems
Grievance procedures
Seniority, Employee

PERSONNEL selection. See Employment systems

PERSONNEL service (education)
Librarian and the counselor. M. Ricking. il ALA Bul 57:601-3 Je '63
Progress in counseling and guidance. Sch Life 45:5 Ja '63
See also
School counselors
School social work

PERSPECTIVE drafting machine. See Drawing instruments

PERSPECTIVES of new music (periodical)
Heavier side. Mus Am 83:7 F '63

PERSPIRATION
Perspiration odors and stains. E. Taylor. il Good H 157:173 Jl '63
Sweating: its rapid response to muscular work. W. Van Beaumont and R. W. Bullard. bibliog il Science 141:643-6 Ag 16 '63
What to expect from your deodorant. C. Leth. Todays Health 41:13+ Je '63

PERT. See Critical path analysis

PERTH, Scotland
Modernization and ruination. R. Kirk. Nat R 15:352 O 22 '63

PERTILE, Aureliano
Swan of the Veneto. M. J. Matz. il por Opera N 27:28-9 Mr 2 '63

PERTUSSIS. See Whooping cough

PERU
Ecological paradox of coastal Peru. E. Y. Dawson. il Natur Hist 72:32-7 O '63
Five worlds of Peru. K. F. Weaver. il Nat Geog Mag 125:212-66 F '64
Peru in serious trouble. H. Herring. Cur Hist 44:95-9+ F '63
See also
Amazon River
Birds—Peru
Communism—Peru
Education—Peru
Elections—Peru
Land tenure—Peru
Machu Picchu
Medicine—Peru
Opera—Peru
Vicos
Vilcabamba
Vilcabamba, Cordillera

Commercial treaties and agreements
Canceling the oil concession. il Time 82:42 N 8 '63

Description and travel
Going places, finding things in Brazil, Chile and Peru. D. Beal. il House & Gard 124: 270+ N '63

Economic conditions
Letter from Peru. N. Gall. Commentary 37: 64-9 Je '64
Society of colonial dames. New Repub 148:11 Je 22 '63

Economic policy
Reforms & credit. Time 82:27-8 Ag 30 '63

Industries
Industry overboard; fish meal. Time 83:38 My 8 '64

Native races
See Indians of South America—Peru

PERU—*Continued*

Politics and government

Big winner. il Newsweek 62:30 D 30 '63
Dealing from strength. Time 83:30+ F 14 '64
Forcing the issue. Newsweek 63:36-7 Ja 13 '64
Letter from Peru. N. Gall. Commentary 37: 64-9 Je '64
Now there are three. il Newsweek 61:57 Mr 18 '63
Peru coup topples Perez Godoy. Sr Schol 82: 16 Mr 20 '63
President at last. il Time 81:22 Je 21 '63
President in office. Time 82:31 Ag 9 '63
Revolution within the law. il Time 84:71 O 2 '64
Society of colonial dames. New Repub 148: 11 Je 22 '63
When the brass fall out. il Time 81:37 Mr 15 '63
See also
Political parties—Peru

Religious institutions and affairs

News of the Christian world (cont) Christian Cent 80:964; 81:780-2 Jl 31 '63, Je 10 '64

Riots

See also
Lima, Peru—Riots

Treaties

See also
Peru—Commercial treaties and agreements

PERUCHROME. See Photography—Films

PERUTZ, M. F.
Hemoglobin molecule; with biographical sketch. Sci Am 211:22, 64-76 N '64
X-ray analysis of hemoglobin. bibliog Science 140:863-9 My 24 '63

PERUVIAN art. See Art, Peruvian

PERUVIAN cormorants. See Cormorants

PERUVIAN folk songs. See Folk songs, Peruvian

PERUVIAN Indians. See Indians of South America—Peru

PERUVIAN lilies. See Lilies

PERUVIAN pottery. See Pottery, Peruvian

PERUVIAN tapestry. See Tapestry

PERVENTSEV, Arkadii Alekseevich
Bourgeois manner for the Bolshevik masses; excerpts from Continuing our discussion about the cultured man. tr. by L. Gottlieb. Horizon 6:106-11 Wint '64

PERVENTZEV, Arkady. See Perventsev, A. A.

PESIC, N. and others
Erythropoietin production following gamma irradiation and hemorrhage in dogs. bibliog Science 143:49-50 Ja 3 '64

PESONEN, David E.
Politics of fresh water. Nation 200:49-51 Ja 18 '65

PESSOA, O. Frota-. See Frota-Pessoa, O.

PESTICIDE industry. See Chemical industries

PESTICIDES
Better understanding of pesticides urged. Sci N L 86:313 N 14 '64
Case for pesticides. M. I. Anderson. il Field & S 69:12-14+ S '64
Esterase inhibitors as pesticides. J. E. Casida. bibliog il Science 146:1011-17 N 20 '64
Good signs on the pesticides front. C. H. Callison. Audubon Mag 66:243 Jl '64
Great pesticide controversy. J. Strohm and C. Ganschow. Read Digest 83:123-8 O '63
If you didn't have poison sprays. il U S News 54:74-5 Je 3 '63
Ill-advised secrecy. Consumer Rep 28:365-6 Ag '63
Indophenol blue as a chromogenic agent for identification of halogenated aromatic hydrocarbons. S. O. Graham. bibliog il Science 139:835-6 Mr 1 '63
Interior tightens pesticide controls. Nat Parks Mag 38:14 O '64
Introduction to pesticides; excerpts from Pesticides and the living landscape. R. L. Rudd. il Audubon Mag 66:222-6 Jl '64
Judgment on pesticides; concerning Science advisory committee's report. il Newsweek 61:69 My 27 '63
Life-giving spray; contrary to Rachel Carson's Silent spring. V. Kraft. il Sports Illus 19:22-5+ N 18 '63
Long-range damage of pesticides; excerpts from Pesticides and the living landscape. R. L. Rudd. il Audubon Mag 66:361-6 N '64
More pesticide research. Sci N L 83:341-2 Je 1 '63
Pesticide report. Sci Am 209:64 Jl '63
Pesticide research; report on International pesticide congress. A. E. Dimond and others. Science 143:151-2+ Ja 10 '64
Pesticides, a tough problem. Audubon Mag 66:19 Ja '64
Pesticides: facts, not fear. H. Earle. il Todays Health 41:18-23+ F '63
Pesticides not dangerous if handled carefully. Sci N L 84:199 S 28 '63
Pesticides, safety tips for all users. Consumer Bul 46:8 Ag '63
Poison sprays and health: the facts show this. il U S News 56:50-2 My 4 '64
Regulations at state level. C. Callison. Audubon Mag 65:165 My '63
Senator Ribicoff would end protest registration of insecticides. J. Prokop. il Am For 69:7+ O '63
Toxic residues in soil nine years after treatment with aldrin and heptachlor. A. T. S. Wilkinson and others. il Science 143:681-2 F 14 '64
What the labels do not say. C. Callison. Audubon Mag 65:164 My '63

Injurious effects

After Wiesner report: feeling little pain; pesticide manufacturers. Bsns W p36 My 25 '63
And was it a silent spring? Sheldon, Ill. C. B. Hicks. il Pop Mech 119:85-8+ '63
Another silent spring. Consumer Rep 29:271 Je '64
Arsenates; effect on fecundity in some diptera. A. D. Pickett and N. A. Patterson. bibliog il Science 140:493-4 My 3 '63
Biggest pesticides disaster to date; Mississippi; with editorial comment. C. H. Callison. Audubon Mag 66:146, 179 My '64
Chemical controversy; search for cause of dead fish in Mississippi and Missouri Rivers. Time 83:72+ Je 19 '64
Damned if we do, damned if we don't! controversy over R. Carson's Silent spring. E. Fritz. Am For 69:34-5 F '63; Discussion. 69:2 Ap '63
Dangers in pesticides; excerpt from interview. D. G. Campbell. il Consumer Bul 47: 33-6 Jl '64
Few pesticide poisonings. Sci N L 85:308 My 16 '64
GHQ for pollution fighters; controversy over fish killed by pesticides. il Bsns W p 136+ Ap 25 '64
Great debate over pests and pesticides. L. Galton. il N Y Times Mag p34+ Ap 14 '63
How much danger from pesticides? U S News 54:8 My 27 '63
Introduction to pesticides; excerpts from Pesticides and the living landscape. R. L. Rudd. il Audubon Mag 66:222-6 Jl '64
Long-range damage of pesticides; excerpts from Pesticides and the living landscape. R. L. Rudd. il Audubon Mag 66:361-6 N '64
Miss Carson could write another book. C. W. Buchheister. Audubon Mag 65:145 My '63
Miss Carson goes to Congress. R. Carson. il Am For 69:20-3+ Jl '63; Reply with rejoinder, E. W. Littlefield. 69:2 O '63
More dead fish. New Repub 151:7 Jl 25 '64
New pesticide antidote; protopam chloride. Sci N L 85:302 My 9 '64
New warning on pesticide dangers. Good H 157:141 Ag '63
Pesticide dangers you really face. Good H 156: 147-9 Je '63
Pesticide poisoning; fruit pickers in California. Newsweek 62:25 S 9 '63
Pesticides: minute quantities linked with massive fish kills; federal policy still uncertain. E. Langer. Science 144:35-7 Ap 3 '64; Discussion. 144:1294 Je 12 '64
Pesticides; report on first American medical association congress on environmental health problems. R. L. White. Science 145:729-30 Ag 14 '64
Pesticides washed into seas around Britain. Sci N L 87:41 Ja 16 '65
Pesticides; White House advisory body issues report recommending steps to reduce hazard to public. D. S. Greenberg. Science 140:878-9 My 24 '63
Pests and poisons: R. Carson before Senate investigative subcommittee. Newsweek 61: 86 Je 17 '63
Pieces of the puzzle; chlordane dust kills ringneck snakes. S. G. Ernst. il Nat Parks Mag 37:20-1 Ap '63
Rachel Carson's war. Sr Schol 84:18-19 My 1 '64
Silent spring on the Pacific slope; postscript to R. Carson effect on wildlife of use of pesticides. C. C. Van Fleet. Atlan 212:81-4 Jl '63

PESTICIDES—Injurious effects—*Continued*
Speaking out; the myth of the pesticide menace; concerning Silent spring. E. Diamond. Sat Eve Post 236:16+ S 28 '63
Spray chemicals; are they really dangerous? concerning charges made in Rachel Carson's Silent spring. C. Westcott. Am Home 66:12+ Mr '63; Same. il Am For 69:15+ Ap '63
States vs. pesticides. H. Titus. Field & S 68:53 Ja '64
Those pesticides; investigation by a Senate subcommittee. P. Hirsch. New Repub 149:6 Ag 17 '63
Tobacco pesticides safe? F. Marley. Sci N L 85:134 F 29 '64
Unpalatable food for thought. P. M. Tilden. Nat Parks Mag 38:2 My '64
Use of pesticides; report of the President's science advisory committee. H. G. Mattoon. Horticulture 41:384 Jl '63
Verdict on pesticides: guilty; tighter federal control. il Bsns W p26-7 My 18 '63
Was Rachel Carson right? B. H. Frisch. il Sci Digest 56:39-45 Ag '64
White House report on pesticides. C. W. Buchheister. Audubon Mag 65:210 Jl '63
Wiesner report; summary. J. B. Wiesner. Am For 69:11 Je '63
You're the guinea pig. New Repub 150:3-4 My 23 '64
See also
Feeding and feeding stuffs—Contamination by drugs and pesticides

Residues

Follow directions or fail. D. Hanson. Suc Farm 62:8 S '64

Testing

Needed: solutions, not epitaphs! R. O. Cornelius. il Am For 70:24-7 Je '64

PET foods. See Animals—Food

PET shops
Help is a warm puppy; Chicago pet shop of Bob Terese and Corinne Owen. J. Graham and J. Poling. il Ladies Home J 80:28+ N '63

PÉTAIN, Henri Philippe Benoni Omer
Dare call it treason, by R. M. Watt. Review
Am Heritage 14:111 Ap '63
Pétain of Verdun, of Vichy, of history. H. Giniger. il pors N Y Times Mag p94-5+ N 15 '64

PETER, Saint
Word. V. P. McCorry. America 110:296-7 F 29 '64

PETER (the Venerable)
Peter the Venerable and Islam, by J. Kritzeck. Review
Commonweal 81:142-3 O 23 '64. G. Roy

PETER, Emmett, jr
Florida's sinner safari. New Repub 148:13-15 Ap 27 '63
John junior. New Repub 148:14 Je 29 '63

PETER, Robert
Letter from Latin America. Nat R 16:274, 358 Ap 7, My 5 '64
Letter from South America. Nat R 15:482 D 3 '63
One day in the life of an Uruguayan. Nat R 15:222 S 24 '63
So it goes. Nat R 15:566 D 31 '63
Terrorists at work. Nat R 16:638 Jl 28 '64

PETER, Wendy
My adventures in Africa. il Seventeen 24:70-1+ Ja '65

PETER Bent Brigham hospital. See Boston—Hospitals

PETER, Paul and Mary (folk singers) See Singers

PETER, Peter Peter! drama. See Boiko, C.

PETER Warlock society
For Warlock, or Heseltine; letter. R. L. Beckhard. Sat R 47:55 D 26 '64

PETERBORO, N.H.
See also
MacDowell memorial colony

PETERDI, Gabor
Nature revisited; exhibition of paintings, drawings and prints. F. Getlein. New Repub 150:27-9 My 9 '64

PETERPAT; drama. See Rudd, E.

PETERS, Andrew J.
Strike that made a president. F. Russell. il por Am Heritage 14:44-7+ O '63

PETERS, Ann
Real life for the doctor's wife. Todays Health 42:24-5+ Je '64

PETERS, Art
High-flying soldier of fortune. il Ebony 19:37-8+ Je '64

PETERS, Brock
Brock Peters. il pors Ebony 18:106-8+ Je '63

PETERS, C. M. D.
Education of the new humanist. Sch & Soc 92:304-5 O 31 '64

PETERS, Charley
Champion on a phantom course. W. P. Fox. Sports Illus 18:E5+ Ap 8 '63

PETERS, Clay E.
High country in Kings Canyon Park; photographs. Nat Parks Mag 38:9-11 S '64

PETERS, Ewald
Suicide of an ex-Nazi. E. Behr. il pors Sat Eve Post 237:76-9 Je 13 '64

PETERS, Gary
For Peters' sake! H. L. Masin. por Sr Schol 84:30 Ap 10 '64
Player of the week; Chicago's White Sox's left-hander. por Sports Illus 21:68 Ag 10 '64

PETERS, Gloria
Inspector. New Yorker 39:18-19 Ag 24 '63

PETERS, John H. See Gibbons, E. F. jt. auth.

PETERS, Roberta
Coloratura. M. De Schauensee. por Opera N 29:26-7 Ja 9 '65

PETERS, Ruth Marie
In your greenhouse this month. See issues of Popular gardening & living outdoors to July 1963

PETERS, William
How many of these things are true about teenagers? Good H 157:92-3+ N '63
(ed) See Cooper, G. Astronaut's family problems

PETERSEN, Aage
Philosophy of Niels Bohr. Bul Atomic Sci 19:8-14 S '63

PETERSEN, Dorothy G.
Teachers' professional reading. Library J 88:1730-3 Ap 15 '63

PETERSEN, Marjorie Betts
Long way west. por Motor B 111:35-7+ Ap; 38+ My '63
Red tape and blue water. Motor B 112:26+ Ag '63

PETERSEN, Robert E.
Driving down a new road. il pors Bsns W p 143-4+ O 10 '64

PETERSON, Alvah
Ornamental eggs of the insects. Natur Hist 74:46-51 Ja '65

PETERSON, Arthur G.
Atterbury's basket weave pattern. Hobbies 68:80-1 Mr '63
Atterbury's fern, lily and mirror patterns. Hobbies 67:78-9 F '63
Atterbury's prism and reeded patterns. il Hobbies 68:80-1 Ap '63
Donkey and elephant lamps. Hobbies 69:85 N '64
Empress pattern glass. Hobbies 69:87 D '64
Glass reproductions. Hobbies 68:84 My '63
Glassware patents of Daniel Bennett. Hobbies 68:82-3 Je '63
Glass-ware patents of David Barker. Hobbies 69:66-7 Ag '64
Glass-ware patents of John Bryce. il Hobbies 69:74-5 S '64
Glass-ware patents of Washington Beck. Hobbies 69:82-3 O '64
Glass-ware patents of William King. Hobbies 69:72 Ja '65
Lamp patents in the United States. Hobbies 68:82-3 Jl; 82-4 Ag '63

PETERSON, Carolyn Sue
Intellectual laboratory for children. por Wilson Lib Bul 39:403-5 Ja '65

PETERSON, Chester, jr
Editor's advice on article sales. Writer 77:14-17 O '64

PETERSON, D. L. See Helfferich, F. jt. auth.

PETERSON, Edith R. See Crain, S. M. jt. auth.

PETERSON, Elly M.
Two open letters to teen-age girls. por Seventeen 23:233-4 S '64

PETERSON, Esther
Do shoppers need help from the government? Changing T 18:7-12 Ag '64
How to make your dollars go further. por Suc Farm 62:79+ S '64
Mrs Roosevelt's legacy. McCalls 91:84+ O '63

about

Consumer's voice in Washington. Consumer Rep 30:8 Ja '65
Lady watchdog; President's new committee on consumer interests. il por Newsweek 63:64 Ja 20 '64
Mrs Consumer. por Newsweek 64:78+ N 2 '64
New era in consumer affairs. il por Consumer Rep 29:143-4 Mr '64
So far, just a sympathetic ear. por Bsns W p32 F 15 '64

PETERSON, Gösta
Long stretch. Mile 59:314-15 Ag '64

PETERSON, Harold
Fishing. Sports Illus 20:58-60+ Je 15 '64
Happy ways of trailering. Sports Illus 18:68-74 My 13 '63
Hunting. Sports Illus 21:76+ O 19 '64
I ski 106 mph; ed. by J. Speirs. Pop Mech 119:126-7+ Mr '63

PETERSON, Harry N.
Fallacious formula. por Library J 88:4696-8 D 15 '63

PETERSON, James A.
Are you a sport shirt professional? Recreation 57:197-8 Ap '64

PETERSON, Osler L.
Medical care in the U.S; with biographical sketch. Sci Am 209:14, 19-27 bibliog(p 140) Ag '63

PETERSON, Owen
Special; story. Seventeen 24:80-1 Ja '65

PETERSON, Patricia
Christmas gifts $25 and under. N Y Times Mag p 104-5+ D 8 '63

PETERSON, Peter G.
Dogma in marketing; address, October 6, 1964. Vital Speeches 31:43-6 N 1 '64

PETERSON, Roger Tory
Bird's-eye view. See occasional issues of Audubon magazine to January 1963
Senators hear Peterson on osprey decline; summary of address, April 22, 1964. Audubon Mag 66:276-7 S '64

PETERSON, Rudolph Arvid
Debt in a new environment; address, November 5, 1964. Vital Speeches 31:149-53 D 15 '64

about

Bank of America eyes a foreign shore. il por Bsns W p 123-4+ N 16 '63
BOA's Peterson: no. one man at no. one bank. il pors Newsweek 62:83-6+ N 4 '63
New chief takes over nation's biggest bank. por U S News 55:26 N 11 '63

PETERSON, Sidney
To rob a museum. Atlan 213:81-5 Je '64
You can't pet a chicken. Atlan 211:126-9 Mr '63

PETERSON, Theodore
Madison avenue. Sat R 47:74 D 12 '64

PETERSON, Virgil W.
Chicago; shades of Capone. Ann Am Acad 347:30-9 My '63

PETERSON, Virgilia
Men, women, and others. Reporter 28:46-8 My 9 '63

PETERSON, W. C.
Amateur scientist. Sci Am 209:159-60+ N '63

PETERSON, Wilfred A.
Art of changing yourself; excerpt from Art of living. Read Digest 82:24B F '63
Art of relaxation. Read Digest 83:70 Ag '63

PETERSON, William H.
Divergent views on pricing policy. bibliog f Harvard Bsns R 41:20-2+ Mr '63
Double standard builds union power. Nations Bsns 51:69-70+ My '63
Farmstead wiring. Suc Farm 61:36-7+ S '63
Giving the consumer the what-for. Nat R 14:453-4 Je 4 '63

PETH, Wick
Rodeo clown. C. Lofting. il pors Life 55:37-8+ Jl 19 '63

PETIOT, Fernand
Barman. New Yorker 40:19-20 Jl 18 '64

PETITE, Irving
They know the wild in wildlife. Audubon Mag 66:20-5 Ja '64

PETR Lebedev (ship) See Ships, Research

PETRA, Jordan
Capital of the Nabataeans. P. J. Parr. il Sci Am 209:94-102 bibliog(p 156) O '63
Petra: the city of stone. J. Knowles. il Holiday 34:42+ N '63
Rose-red city of Petra. P. C. Hammond. il Natur Hist 73:14-25 F '64
Teen with a trowel; expedition sponsored by Princeton theological seminary. C. Sayre. il Seventeen 22:118-19+ N '63

PETRAKIS, Peter L.
Pioneering; letter. Science 142:1019 N 22 '63

PETRARCH
Laurels in lieu of the lady. R. J. Clements. por Sat R 46:59-60 D 7 '63

PETRELS
Birds of the sea. A. Sprunt, 4th. il Motor B 112:41+ Ag '63

PETRI, Egon
Petri in retrospect. J. Holcman. por Sat R 46:55-6 My 25 '63

PETRIE, Paul
Pictures of departure: Diana the huntress; poems. Poetry 104:15-17 Ap '64
Poetry chronicle. Poetry 102:49-53 Ap '63
Trip down; poem. New Yorker 39:155 S 28 '63

about

Americans and others. J. M. Morrison. Poetry 104:119 My '64

PETRIE, R. M.
B stars and galactic exploration. Sky & Tel 26:330-4 D '63

PETRIFIED forests
Petrified forests of Yellowstone Park. E. Dorf. il Sci Am 210:106-12+ Ap '64

PETROGLYPHS
Bronze age seen in granite. H. Arbman. il Natur Hist 73:36-43 N '64
California's legacy of Indian rock art. C. Grant. il Natur Hist 73:32-41 Je '64
Petroglyphs. C. Miles. il Hobbies 69:112-13+ N '64

PETROGRAD. See Leningrad

PETROLEOS mexicanos. See Petroleum industry and trade—Mexico

PETROLEUM
Marx X's the spot; formation of petroleum. Newsweek 63:87 Ap 20 '64
Research frontier; where is science taking us? P. N. Kropotkin. il Sat R 46:39-40 Jl 6 '63; Reply. J. D. Haun. 46:44-5 Ag 3 '63

See also
Hydrocarbons
Oil lands
Oil shales
Standard oil companies

Chemistry

Alkanes in natural and synthetic petroleums; comparison of calculated and actual compositions. R. A. Friedel and A. G. Sharkey, jr. bibliog il Science 139:1203-5 Mr 22 '63

International aspects

Argentine oil seizure. Commonweal 79:269 N 29 '63
Desert oil & political quicksands. il Time 84:106 D 4 '64
Eight nations, eight firms: the battle over oil profits. il Newsweek 63:61-3 Ja 13 '64
Gain & pain at E.N.I; Italy's state oil monopoly. il Time 82:91 N 8 '63
Go home Yankee trader; threat to annul Argentina's oil contracts. New Repub 149:9 N 23 '63
Italy turns now to West for oil; ENI signs with Jersey Standard. Bsns W p47-8 Mr 30 '63
Man in the business suit; Argentina's cancellation of contracts with United States oil companies. Nation 197:357 N 30 '63
More vinegar in Italy's oil; ENI. Bsns W p34 N 23 '63
Oil in the cold war. America 108:527 Ap 20 '63
Oil's world gets bigger, tougher. il Bsns W p 107-8+ N 21 '64
Paying more to pump; agreement of Organization of petroleum exporting countries. Time 85:64 Ja 8 '65
Putting Conoco up with majors. il Bsns W p52-3+ N 30 '63

Production methods

See Petroleum engineering

Prospecting

North Sea oil rush. il Newsweek 64:57-8 Jl 27 '64
Seeking a gusher under the ice. il Bsns W p86-8+ Ag 24 '63
Vade, Mecom. il Time 84:81 Jl 24 '64
Venture capital from inside the stock family; Occidental petroleum lines up investors. Bsns W p66+ Mr 23 '63
See also
Divining rod

Geophysical methods

Electronic instrumentation for oil exploration. L. E. Frenzel, jr. il Electr World 70:27-30+ D '63

Securities

Executive investor; a look at the international oils. il Duns R 82:137-8+ O '63

Transportation

See also
Petroleum pipelines

Alberta

See Petroleum—Canada

Arabia

See Petroleum—Middle East

Arctic Regions

Seeking a gusher under the ice. il Bsns W p86-8+ Ag 24 '63

PETROLEUM—*Continued*

Argentina

Slippery oil. Time 82:68 Ag 9 '63

Australia

Oil in the bush. il Time 83:99 Ap 10 '64

Canada

Boiling the oil out of stubborn sands; Athabasca oil sands. il Bsns W p66 F 9 '63

Libya

Conoco's widening world. R. Sheehan. il Fortune 69:113-17+ Ap '64
Oil alone can't solve Libya's economic woes. map Bsns W p 102 Ja 26 '63
When a poor country strikes it rich. il U S News 57:73-4 D 14 '64

Middle East

Sheik of Abu Dhabi; world's richest man? il U S News 57:54-6 Jl 6 '64

Ohio

Boom town; Mount Gilead, Ohio. il Newsweek 63:56-7 Ja 6 '64
Ohio's mad oil boom; drilling in fields, lawns and schoolyards in Morrow County. B. Lindeman. il Sat Eve Post 237:81-5 N 4 '64
Oil: boom in Ohio. il Time 83:84 F 21 '64
Oil boom, Ohio style. il Bsns W p 154-6 Mr 28 '64

Venezuela

U.S. and Venezuela take firm stand against Communist threats; exchange of greetings; with joint communique. J. F. Kennedy; R. Betancourt. Dept State Bul 48:445-7 Mr 25 '63

PETROLEUM engineering
Shooting new life into old oil fields; thermal recovery. il Bsns W p84-5 D 19 '64

PETROLEUM in submerged lands
Piping oil and gas from the deep; Red Snapper gathering system. il Bsns W p 132+ N 2 '63
Sterols in recent aquatic sediments. R. B. Schwendinger and J. G. Erdman. bibliog il Science 144:1575-6 Je 26 '64

PETROLEUM industry and trade
See also
Royal Dutch-Shell group

Finance

Angling for a cash gusher in oil; promoters looking for well-heeled investors. il Bsns W p 104-5 D 19 '64
Venture capital from inside the stock family; Occidental petroleum lines up investors. Bsns W p66+ Mr 23 '63

International aspects

See Petroleum—International aspects

Securities

Oil after the tax cut. Fortune 70:78+ D '64

Taxation

Depletion; what's at stake for thirty companies. il Fortune 67:206 Ap '63
Three-way oil deal waits on tax ruling: ABC deal. Bsns W p94+ F 9 '63

Wages and hours

Wage chronology: Sinclair oil companies, 1963. il Mo Labor R 86:1442-3 D '63

Algeria

Desert oil & political quicksands. il Time 84:106 D 4 '64

Argentina

Argentine take-over; government expropriation of foreign companies. Newsweek 64:68 Jl 6 '64
How tough? il Newsweek 62:96 N 18 '63
Neither justice nor oil. Time 84:40 D 4 '64
Triumph for nationalism. Time 82:36 N 22 '63

Brazil

Mess at Petrobrás. il Time 83:43 F 21 '64

Ceylon

U.S. protests Ceylon's decision on oil legislation; Department statement, July 24, 1963. Dept State Bul 49:245 Ag 12 '63

Cuba

Communism's failure in Cuba; an on-the-ground report; reprint. R. S. Knowles. il U S News 54:66-8 Je 17 '63

France

France roils the oilmen; state-owned, Union general des petroles. Bsns W p30 Je 29 '63

Great Britain

Oilmen in new battle of Britain. il Bsns W p66-9 Mr 2 '63

Indonesia

Complete draw. il Fortune 68:79-80+ Ag '63
President hails agreement between Indonesia and foreign oil companies; statement by President Kennedy, June 1, 1963; text of letter to Wilson Wyatt, with White House announcement. J. F. Kennedy. Dept State Bul 49:17 Jl 1 '63
U.S. diplomatic triumph in Indonesia. Bsns W p72 Je 22 '63

Italy

ENI without Mattei. il Fortune 69:56+ Je '64
Gain & pain at E.N.I.; Italy's state oil monopoly. il Time 82:91 N 8 '63
Italy turns now to West for oil; ENI signs with Jersey Standard. Bsns W p47-8 Mr 30 '63
More vinegar in Italy's oil; ENI. Bsns W p34 N 23 '63
Two-timing the seven sisters. Time 81:92+ Je 14 '63

Kuwait

Kuwait; Wall Street of the Middle East. R. Hewins. il Nation 198:234-6 Mr 9 '64

Latin America

Latin America bites U.S. again; dispute over oil development rights. Bsns W p26-7 N 16 '63

Libya

Desert oil & political quicksands. il Time 84:106 D 4 '64

Mexico

From politics to profit; Pemex. il Time 82:28 Ag 2 '63
Pemex at twenty-five. Fortune 68:87-8 Ag '63
Running without gas. il Bsns W p96+ S 19 '64

Middle East

Healing the rift on Mideast oil. Bsns W p 100 S 5 '64
Oil squeeze. Time 82:91 D 13 '63

Russia

Soviet oil exports. A. R. Plotnick. il Nation 196:302-6 Ap 13 '63
Soviets push on western markets; Comecon pipeline. il Bsns W p94-5+ Mr 2 '63

United States

He's half wildcatter, half big businessman. il Bsns W p 103-4+ N 14 '64
Midas touch of John Mecom. il Bsns W p90-2+ O 10 '64
New kind of gusher; oil company diversification. il Time 82:59-60 Ag 2 '63
Oil's new play: fertilizers; mergers of oil companies with fertilizer companies. Bsns W p28 Ag 17 '63
One stop for gas, food, lodging. il Bsns W p 118+ Je 29 '63
Petroleum reserves. J. Bivins. Science 139:798 Mr 1 '63
See also names of oil companies, e.g. Arabian American oil company

Venezuela

Corporate citizen no. 1. il Time 83:96 My 22 '64
Creole's alliances for progress. il Fortune 70:64+ S '64
Venezuela builds on oil. T. J. Abercrombie. il Nat Geog Mag 123:354-62 Mr '63
Venezuela: doing a little better. il Bsns W p86 F 2 '63

PETROLEUM pipe lines
All steel and a yard wide; Colonial pipeline. H. B. Comstock. il Pop Sci 183:130-4+ O '63
Biggest pipeline snakes to the north; Colonial pipeline. il Newsweek 62:59-62 Ag 26 '63
It's a hard way to lay pipe; Colonial pipeline co. il Bsns W p37-8 D 21 '63
Piping oil and gas from the deep; Red Snapper gathering system. il Bsns W 132+ N 2 '63
Temptation of trade; Bonn's cancellation of Soviet pipe order. Time 81:33 Ap 5 '63
Vital new artery; oil refinery, southern Germany. il Time 81:106+ My 3 '63

PETROLEUM research
Protein from petroleum. Sci Am 212:49-50 Ja '65

PETROLEUM workers
Oil patch; roughnecks and operators on a forgotten frontier. C. Davidson. il Harper 229:41-6 Ag '64
See also
Petroleum industry and trade—Wages and hours

PETROLOGY. See Rocks
PETROPULOS, Stephen F.
Automatic sampling device for study of synchronized cultures of microorganisms. bibliog Science 145:268-70 Jl 17 '64
Ultraviolet inactivation of chloroplast formation in synchronously dividing euglena gracilis. bibliog Science 145:392-3 Jl 24 '64
PETROSYAN, Tigran
Newest idol. il por Time 81:65 My 31 '63
PETROW, Henry G. See Eisenbud, M. jt. auth.
PETROW, Richard
Coast guard's worst week. Pop Sci 182:78-83+ Mr '63
PETS
Bizarre house pets are hazard to owners. Sci N L 86:39 Ag 8 '64
Cats, dogs help family. E. Mirel. Sci N L 84:167 S 14 '63
Dogged devotion to pets. il Newsweek 63:84-6 Mr 23 '64
Grand opening; family pets. E. Hunter. il Redbook 123:49+ O '64
If it cuddles, they'll keep it. il Life 54:39-94 My 31 '63
Pets on loan. W. Cross. il Parents Mag 38:60-1 Ap '63
Pets: their Christmas pampering. il House & Gard 124:57 N '63
Poor rickety Leo; African lion as backyard pet. J. Neary. il Life 57:69-70+ D 11 '64
Snake in the house; serpents as urban pets. P. Meras. il N Y Times Mag p80 Mr 1 '64
Tender regard and a seat belt for Trudy. il Life 54:103-4 My 24 '63
Trusted pet turns butcher in one bound. il Life 55:28-28A Ag 23 '63
Victoria: a pig in a pram. M. E. Chase. il McCalls 91:114-15+ O '63
What to serve under the table; food for animals, suggestions by famous people. il Redbook 121:48-9 Jl '63
Wolf can be a girl's best friend; Faye Ginsburg of Chicago. J. Star. il Look 27:M8+ D 3 '63
Wolf in the family. J. Hellmuth. il Sat Eve Post 236:38-9 O 12 '63
See also
Christmas gifts for pets
Pet shops
Travel with pets
also names of pets, e.g. Cats
PETSCHEK, Willa
Let's travel to London. Mlle 59:117-18 Je '64
One gilded night with the Duke. Ladies Home J 81:143-4 O '64
This is London. Mlle 56:94-6 Ap '63
PETSINGER, R. E.
New steels save water-works dollars. Am City 79:96-7 O '64
PETT, Larry
Group travel. Pop Phot 52:134-5 Ap '63
PETTER, J. J.
Madagascar lemurs: isolated primates. Natur Hist 72:22-7 Mr '63
PETTERSON, Gary
Two 4-H'ers you'd like to know. por Farm J 87:64 F '63
PETTIGREW, D. W.
Guide to stainless steel finishes. Arch Rec 133:217-18 Mr '63
How to use stainless steel for flashing. il Arch Rec 134:201-2 N '63
PETTIGREW, Thomas F. See Bouton, E. N. jt. auth.
PETTINELLA, D. M.
(tr) See Andrade, J. C. Official poster of green
PETTINGILL, Olin Sewall, 1907-
Bird finding. See issues of Audubon magazine
PETTY, H. B.
You can control soil insects in the winter. Suc Farm 61:74-5+ F '63
PETTY, Richard
Barracuda vs. Mustang. por Pop Sci 185:76-9 N '64
PETUCHOWSKI, Jakob J.
Modern rabbi. Commentary 35:153-8 F '63
PETUNIAS
Know the bright stars among petunias. M. M. Leister. il Flower Grower 51:32+ My '64
Petunias, color in the sun. E. McDonald. il Pop Gard 14:34-6 My '63
Pressed petunias. J. L. Russell, jr. Pop Gard 14:21 Jl '63
PETWORTH House. See England—Historic houses, etc.
PEVIANI, Sally
Our fair lady. D. A. Robinson. il pors Ladies Home J 81:85-8+ Ja '64
PEVLER, Herman H.
Move no. twenty-four. por Newsweek 62:63 Ag 26 '63
PEVSNER, Antoine
Fresh breezes in the windy city. K. Kuh. il Sat R 47:20 Jl 25 '64
PEWTER
Interchangeable parts in early American pewter. C. V. Swain. il Antiques 83:212-13 F '63
Pewter collector's progress. R. M. Vetter. il Antiques 86:179-83 Ag '64
Rarity in English pewter. R. F. Michaelis. il Antiques 85:698-9 Je '64
Ruhmann collection of decorative pewter. R. M. Vetter. il Antiques 83:690-3 Je '63
PEYOTE
Diabolic root. W. La Barre. il N Y Times Mag p96+ N 1 '64
God & peyote. il Time 84:64 S 11 '64
PEYRE, Henri
Quest for Gide. Nation 197:395+ D 7 '63
PEYSER, Joan
World's most glorious Christmas music. House & Gard 126:160-1 D '64
PFAFF, William
Our outdated vision. Commonweal 81:411-12 D 18 '64
Vietnam: the roots of the chaos. Commonweal 81:183-90 N 6 '64
PFALTZGRAFF, Robert L. jr
Biological and chemical weapons. bibliog f Cur Hist 47:18-24+ Jl '64
PFATTEICHER, Philip H.
Episcopacy for our time. Christian Cent 81:1361-4 N 4 '64
PFAU, Hugo
My days with LeBaron. por Motor T 16:80-3 Ag '64
PFEFFER, Leo
1963 First amendment conference; statement. Cath World 197:312-15 Ag '63
PFEIFFER, E. W. See Johns, J. E.; Plakke, R. K. jt. auths.
PFEIFFER, Eric
Clearing; For a pregnant lady; For N; Drowning in September; poems. Poetry 103:163-5 D '63
I'd like to throw you out; poem. Atlan 213:104 Ja '64
Moving; poem. Atlan 212:137 N '63
Real property; poem. Atlan 212:139 D '63
PFEIFFER, H. G. See Barthold, L. O. jt. auth.
PFEIFFER, John Edward
Apish origins of human tension. Harper 227:55-60 Jl '63
Boundless age of the computer. Fortune 69:153-6+ My '64
How we remember, why we forget? Read Digest 83:123-5 N '63
PFEIFFER, John F.
Dynagroove story. por Am Rec G 29:602-6+ Ap '63
PFISTER, Anne Marie
Solitary wanderer; excerpts from address, November 29, 1962 UNESCO Courier 16:16-17+ Mr '63
PFISTER, Herbert R.
Kid-powered jet swing. Pop Sci 184:146-7 Mr '64
Recessed pantry for cramped kitchens. Pop Mech 120:136-7 Jl '63
Spring car care. Pop Sci 182:158-62 Ap '63
PFISTER, Richard G.
Teach your son tractor safety. Suc Farm 62:92 Mr '64
PFITZINGER, William H.
Consolidate your utility bills. Am City 78:80-1 Ag '63
PFITZNER, Hans
Palestrina. Criticism
Opera N 29:33 Ja 30 '65
PFIZER, Charles, and company
Little company that got well. il Time 84:82 Ag 7 '64
PFOST, Warren D.
Third Sunday in May. por Recreation 57:236-7 My '64
PFUNKE, Peter C. and others
Stereotape reviews. See issues of American record guide
PHAGE. See Bacteriophage
PHALON, Richard A.
Scandal in personal bankruptcy. Duns R 81:35-6+ Mr '63
SEC vs. Wall street. Duns R 81:56-7+ Ap '63
PHANTOM lover; story. See Jordan, E. H.
PHARMACEUTICAL apparatus
Mortars as bells. L. E. Springer. il Hobbies 68:53 N '63
PHARMACEUTICAL research
Drug is born. D. G. Cooley. il Todays Health 41:18-21+ S '63
Drug safety: industry-sponsored study commission recommends expansion of research activities. E. Langer. il Science 145:1284-7 S 18 '64

PHARMACEUTICAL research—*Continued*
Pooling drug research; Interpharm GmbH & co. il Bsns W p66-8+ O 26 '63
Problems of drug development. L. Lasagna. Science 145:362-7 Jl 24 '64; Discussion. 145: 1258; 146:717 S 18, N 6 '64
World's most bountiful store of drugs; Basel. J. D. Ratcliff. il Read Digest 83:97-101 Jl '63

PHARMACOLOGY
Research
See Pharmaceutical research

PHARMACOPOEIAS
Pharmacopeia: seventeenth revision of United States pharmacopeia. New Yorker 40:48-9 N 21 '64

PHARMACY
Profession of pharmacy in the United States; address, February 8, 1963. G. F. Archambault. Vital Speeches 29:349-52 Mr 15 '63

PHASE meter. See Phasemeter

PHASEMETER
Checking stereo separation and phase. R. Glassgal. il Electr World 70:37+ O '63
Phasemeter for audio frequencies. T. E. Reamer. il Electr World 70:43-6+ N '63

PHASES (chemistry)
Phase transformation at high temperatures in hafnia and zirconia. W. L. Baun. bibliog il Science 140:1330-1 Je 21 '63

PHAT, Lam-van-. See Lam-van-Phat

PHEASANT shooting
Hit and miss. H. F. Zeman. il Outdoor Life 133:50-1+ F '64
Mid-continent roosters. W. Page. il Field & S 68:130-2+ Ap '64
More pheasants than people. W. Page. il Field & S 69:37-9 S '64
Outdoors. V. Bourjaily. Esquire 62:96-8 D '64
Pine tree pheasants. A. Davenport. il Field & S 68:56-7+ F '64
Two doubles a world apart. W. Chapman. il Sports Illus 19:100-2+ N 25 '63
We track pheasants. B. Cary. Outdoor Life 134:20-3+ D '64

PHEASANTS
One-woman shooting preserve; Rockview game farm, Clinton Corners, N.Y. A. MacBain. il Field & S 68:110+ N '63

PHELAN, James R.
American in a Mexican death cell. Sat Eve Post 236:81-5 S 21 '63
Have you ever been a boo-hoo? Sat Eve Post 237:81-5 Mr 21 '64
Howard Hughes; he is battling for control of a billion-dollar empire. Sat Eve Post 236: 15-23 F 9 '63
Innocent's grim ordeal. Sat Eve Post 236: 62-7 F 2 '63
Plucky Pierre crashes the party. Sat Eve Post 237:20-1 My 30 '64
Trouble in happyland. Sat Eve Post 236:78-80+ My 25 '63
Vice man cometh. Sat Eve Post 236:67-71 Je 8 '63

PHELAN, Joseph F. jr
It's tough to be a teen-ager; ed. by R. L. Smith. Read Digest 82:31-2+ Mr '63

PHELAN, R. C.
Good-bye possums; story. Sat Eve Post 236: 58-62 N 30 '63
Non-stop piano player; story. Sat Eve Post 236:54-9 O 12 '63

PHELPS, Donald
Land of grace and isolation. Nation 199:225-7 O 12 '64

PHELPS, Edith M.
Wilson bulletin: November 1914. Wilson Lib Bul 39:244 N '64

PHELPS, Emily
To John F. Kennedy; poem. Seventeen 23:43 S '64

PHELPS, Ernest D. and Gallagher, William
Integrated approach to technical staffing. Harvard Bsns R 41:122-9 Jl '63

PHELPS, Flora L.
Caribbean: a living laboratory. Américas 15: 17-22 Je '63
Tomorrow's pioneers. Américas 15:20-8 F '63

PHELPS, John, and Kalkstein, Marvin
Nth country problem. Bul Atomic Sci 19:50-1 D '63

PHELPS, Lyon
Elegy in Big Sur. New Yorker 39:56 N 23 '63
From In praise of Pilgrims; Song from a play; November at Bridgehampton Beach; poems. Poetry 104:82-4 My '64

PHELPS, McAndrew
Dirty business. America 110:155 F 1 '64
Washington front. America 110:155, 215, 786; 111:543; 112:157 F 1, 15, Je 6, N 7 '64, Ja 30 '65
Way they feel. America 111:205 Ag 29 '64

PHELPS, Reginald H.,
Hitler and the Deutsche arbeiterpartei. bibliog f Am Hist R 68:974-86 Jl '63

PHENETHYL alcohol
Phenethyl alcohol synergism with mitomycin C, porfiromycin, and streptonigrin. J. R. White and H. L. White. bibliog il Science 145:1312-13 S 18 '64

PHENETHYLAMINE
Norepinephrine and 3,4-dihydroxyphenethylamine turnover in guinea pig brain in vivo. S. Udenfriend and P. Zaltzman-Nirenberg. bibliog il Science 142:394-6 O 18 '63

PHENOBARBITAL
Phenobarbital increases liver enzyme action. Sci N L 85:162 Mr 14 '64

PHENOL
Phenol in quackgrass associated with dalapon. T. R. Flanagan and A. R. Langille. bibliog il Science 140:179-80 Ap 12 '63

PHENOLOXIDASE. See Enzymes

PHENOLS
Indoleacetic acid synthesis by polyphenols in the extraction of pinus phloem and cambial tissue. F. W. Whitmore and R. Zahner. bibliog il Science 145:166-7 Jl 10 '64
Phenolics of higher plants; report of symposium sponsored by the Plant phenolics group of North America. S. A. Brown. Science 142:1197-8+ N 29 '63
Protein as the mitochondrial site for action of uncoupling phenols. E. C. Weinbach and J. Garbus. bibliog il Science 145:824-6 Ag 21 '64

PHENYLALANINE
Audiogenic seizures, the dilute locus, and phenylalanine hydroxylase in DBA/1 mice. S. D. Huff and J. L. Fuller. bibliog il Science 144:304-5 Ap 17 '64
Inhibition of antibody synthesis by l-phenylalanine. W. L. Ryan and M. J. Carver. bibliog il Science 143:479-80 Ja 31 '64
Preventing mental retardation. Sci Am 211: 46 Jl '64

PHENYLKETONURIA
Detecting poisons at birth. Time 82:47 Ag 23 '63
Preventing mental retardation. Sci Am 211: 46 Jl '64
Prevention of a mental defect of phenylketonuria with serotonin congeners such as melatonin or hydroxytryptophan. D. W. Woolley and T. van der Hoeven. bibliog il Science 144:1593-4 Je 26 '64
We are not created equal; PKU due to enzyme lack. F. Marley. il Sci N L 84: 55+ Jl 27 '63

PHEROMONES
Pheromones. E. O. Wilson. il Sci Am 208:100-6+ My '63

PHI beta kappa
See also
Commission on the humanities

PHI meson. See Mesons

PHILADELPHIA
Little purchases cost lots. O. R. Winter. Am City 79:150+ Ap '64
Personal business; businessman's guide. Bsns W p 157 Je 15 '63
Philadelphia plain & fancy. N. Burt. il Horizon 5:4-27 Jl '63

Architecture
PSFS; Philadelphia savings fund society. W. H. Jordy and H. Wright. il Arch Forum 120:124-9+ My '64
See also
Philadelphia—Public buildings

City planning
Downtown's dramatic comeback. D. B. Carlson. il Arch Forum 120:102 F '64
Is this the big industry that can keep U.S. going? il U S News 54:74 F 25 '63
Midtown weed control of redevelopment areas. il Am City 79:96 Jl '64
Philadelphia: how far can renewal go? P. Herrera. il Arch Forum 121:180-93 Ag '64
Philadelphia reclaims a slum. il Am City 80:87 Ja '65
Preservation notes; urban renewal; wolf in sheep's clothing? B. Snow; discussion. Antiques 83:344 Mr '63
Race and renaissance in Philadelphia. N. Burt. il Harper 229:64-70 S '64
Under the knife, or all for their own good. il Time 84:60-3+ N 6 '64

Crime
They call me Tiger Lil. A. G. Aronowitz. il Sat Eve Post 236:28+ O 26 '63

Description
Main line: Philadelphia's seventeen miles of countrified suburbs. S. Birmingham. il Holiday 36:86-95+ D '64
U.S. city weekends. T. B. Lesure. il Travel 120:28-32+ Jl '63

PHILADELPHIA—*Continued*

Finance

Purchasing forum attracts new bidders. O. R. Winter. il Am City 79:97 Ag '64

Free library

Artist's view; library promotion. R. J. Cattafesta. il Wilson Lib Bul 39:468-71 F '65
Cory to study library needs of mid-city Philadelphia. Library J 90:89 Ja 1 '65
Newspaper and public library tangle over secret records; Philadelphia evening bulletin vs. Free library of Philadelphia. Library J 88:3042 S 1 '63

Galleries and museums

See also
Philadelphia museum of art

Gardens

Bartram's garden. C. B. Lees. il Horticulture 42:46-9+ Mr '64

Historic houses, etc.

Historic Philadelphia. B. Finnegan. Hobbies 68:121 Jl '63

History

Electronic drama; Independence Hall. G. Loney. il Theatre Arts 47:27-8 Jl '63

Hospitals

Hospital of the University of Pennsylvania. il Antiques 83:408 Ap '63

Housing

Orianna block. il Arch Rec 134:205-7 S '63
Philadelphia landmark; Hopkinson house. il Arch Forum 118:92-3 Ap '63
Philadelphia town houses. il Arch Forum 118:90 Ap '63
Tower and town houses in Philadelphia. il Arch Rec 136:110-13 Ag '64

Industries

Anti-discrimination pact signed in Philadelphia; action of Printing industries. Pub W 184:35 O 14 '63

Libraries

See also
Philadelphia—Free library

Lighting

Philadelphia cuts the lighting bill. D. M. Smallwood. Am City 78:141 Je '63

Music

Baltimore and Philadelphia. M. de Schauensee. Opera N 27:26-7 My 4 '63
Dutchman arrives. A. M. Lingg. il Opera N 27:24-6 F 2 '63
Evenings on the Schuylkill; Robin Hood Dell concerts. R. Jacobson. Mus Am 83:35 Jl '63
[Musical events] (cont) il Mus Am 83:73-4 Ja; 19 Ap; 13 Je; 61+ D '63; 84:15-16 Mr; 23 Jl; 21 S; 50+ D '64
Notes from our correspondents. S. Fleming. il Hi Fi 14:20+ Je '64
Philadelphia Fra; Auber's Fra Diavolo. D. H. Rothermel. Opera N 27:33 F 16 '63
Traditional Philadelphians. M. De Schauensee. Opera N 28:32 Ap 4 '64

Negroes

Brotherly love. il Newsweek 62:22 S 9 '63
Doing no good; all-Negro riot. il Time 84:32 S 4 '64
How Negro pressure gets jobs. il U S News 55:30-2 Ag 12 '63
New hope through self-help. il Ebony 19:27-30+ My '64
Philadelphia, Pennsylvania: a process of fragmentation. H. Lees. il Reporter 29:18-20 Jl 4 '63
Philadelphia, still closed; Catholic attitudes toward racial changes. D. Clark. Commonweal 80:167-70 My 1 '64; Discussion. 80:259-60, 366-9, 451 My 22, Je 12, Jl 3 '64
Race and renaissance in Philadelphia. N. Burt. il Harper 229:64-70 S '64
Self-help in Philadelphia; Rev. L. Sullivan's Opportunities industrialization center. H. Lees. il Reporter 31:15-17 D 17 '64; Discussion. 32:12 Ja 28 '65

Newspapers

See also
Bulletin, Philadelphia

Parades

Good-by, Mr Bones; annual Mummers parade. il Newsweek 63:24 Ja 13 '64
Mummers in Philadelphia. J. O'Gara. Commonweal 79:450 Ja 17 '64; Reply. E. Klein and D. Klein. 80:122 Ap 17 '64

Parks and playgrounds

Tapping fresh sources; excerpts from address. R. W. Crawford. Recreation 57:12-14 Ja '64
Zoo puts on a mammoth match-up; elephants carved from a solid block of granite. il Life 54:40B+ Je 7 '63

Police

Our hands are tied, cries police sergeant; reprint. U S News 57:39 S 14 '64

Politics and government

Democrats in a key city tell why they shifted votes. il U S News 55:56-7 N 25 '63

Public buildings

Circling in the square. il Arch Forum 118:120-5 F '63

Rapid transit

Non-profit mass transportation. J. A. Bailey. il Am City 78:148+ S '63

Religious institutions and affairs

Philadelphia, still closed; Catholic attitudes toward racial changes. D. Clark. Commonweal 80:167-70 My 1 '64; Discussion. 80:259-60, 366-9, 451 My 22, Je 12, Jl 3 '64

Riots

Doing no good; all-Negro riot. il Time 84:32 S 4 '64
Other Philadelphia. Newsweek 64:30 S 7 '64

Sanitary affairs

Clean-street bug is catching. D. M. Smallwood and A. Michaels. il Am City 78:98-100 S '63
For longer incinerator life. R. A. Cotton. il Am City 78:92-4 N '63

Social life and customs

Perennial Philadelphians, by N. Burt. Review
Reporter 29:64-5 O 24 '63. G. Weales

Stores

Long shop with a wide look; store for R. Alexander Manoff. il Arch Rec 135:173 Je '64
Young artists exhibit: third annual Young artists exhibition at Gimbels, Philadelphia. B. Segal. il Sch Arts 64:38-9 Ja '65

Street traffic

Parking program that benefits all. T. J. Coyle. il Am City 79:112 Ag '64

Water supply

Old filters provide new storage. il Am City 79:116-17 My '64
What 100 per cent metering did to Philadelphia's water demand. il Am City 79:130+ Ag '64

PHILADELPHIA, Miss.
Strange, tight little town, loath to admit complicity. D. Nevin. il Life 57:38-9 D 18 '64
Stranger in Philadelphia, Mississippi. J. Lelyveld. il N Y Times Mag p5+ D 27 '64

PHILADELPHIA book show. See Book exhibits

PHILADELPHIA bulletin. See Bulletin, Philadelphia

PHILADELPHIA dance academy. See Dance schools

PHILADELPHIA evening bulletin. See Bulletin, Philadelphia

PHILADELPHIA folk festival. See Music festivals—Pennsylvania

PHILADELPHIA furniture. See Furniture, American

PHILADELPHIA lyric opera company
In this corner: Aurelio Fabiani; interview, ed. by F. Stevenson. Opera N 28:16-17 N 16 '63
Philadelphia partnership; Suderland in Traviata. G. Fitzgerald. il Opera N 28:30 D 21 '63

PHILADELPHIA mint. See United States—Mint

PHILADELPHIA museum of art
Tyson collection: a painter's eye on masterworks. H. H. F. Jayne. il Art N 63:28-30+ S '64

PHILADELPHIA orchestra
Musical events; Berlioz's Requiem. W. Sargeant. New Yorker 40:98-100 Ap 11 '64
Musical events; concert at Carnegie Hall. W. Sargeant. New Yorker 40:187 Ap 18 '64
Musical events; concert in Philharmonic Hall. W. Sargeant. New Yorker 40:200-1 D 5 '64
Musical events; concert in Philharmonic Hall, conducted by H. Scherchen. New Yorker 40:231-3 N 14 '64

PHILADELPHIA orchestra—*Continued*
Musical events; performance of Harris' Ninth symphony. W. Sargeant. New Yorker 38:77-8 F 9 '63
Musical events; series of concerts in Philharmonic Hall in honor of World's fair. W. Sargeant. New Yorker 40:137-9 My 23 '64
Musical events; Shostakovich's Fourth symphony. W. Sargeant. New Yorker 39:94+ Mr 2 '63
Philadelphia, a paragon of versatility. L. Marcus. il Hi Fi 14:65-6 F '64

PHILADEPHIA Phillies (baseball) See Baseball clubs

PHILADELPHIANS
Perennial Philadelphians, by N. Burt. Review
Reporter 29:64-5 O 24 '63. G. Weales

PHILANTHROPIC foundations. See Foundations, Charitable and educational

PHILANTHROPY. See Giving

PHILATELY. See Postage stamps

PHILBY, Harold Adrian Russell
And then there were three. il Time 82:27 Jl 12 '63
Class reunion; Philby joins Guy Burgess and Donald Maclean in Russia. Newsweek 62:33 Ag 12 '63
Kim. il por Time 81:39 Mr 15 '63
Love, Kim. por Newsweek 61:40+ Mr 18 '63
Rise and fall of a Soviet agent. E. R. F. Sheehan. il pors Sat Eve Post 237:30-2+ F 15 '64; Same abr. Read Digest 84:82-91 My '64; Reply. D. Astor. Sat Eve Post 237:4-5 Mr 21 '64
Third man in the Burgess-Maclean case. U S News 55:10 Jl 15 '63

PHILBY, Kim. See Philby, H. A. R.

PHILCO corporation
Aeronutronic weighs ABL experiments. Miss & Roc 15:87 N 30 '64
Ford in its future. il Time 81:74 Mr 1 '63
New line bows, old rumor spiked; Ford and Philco festivities in New York for dealers. il Bsns W p54-6+ My 30 '64
Philco gets the T-Bird look; success of the Ford-Philco merger. il Bsns W p45-6+ Ag 17 '63

Western development laboratories

Philco division completes reorientation. R. Lindsey. il Miss & Roc 14:28+ Je 15 '64

PHILHARMONIA orchestra of London
Letter from London; indefinite suspension. M. Panter-Downes. New Yorker 40:118-19 Ap 4 '64
Strife and self-government; threatened demise. M. Cooper. Mus Am 84:21 My '64
See also
New philharmonia orchestra (London)

PHILHARMONIC Hall. See Lincoln Center for the performing arts, New York—Philharmonic Hall

PHILHARMONIC-symphony society of New York
Dear Mr Bernstein: a look at Leonard Bernstein's Young people's concerts mail. il Sr Schol 85:6+ D 2 '64
Elektra revisited. G. Fitzgerald. Opera N 29:31 Ja 23 '65
Music; New York philharmonic and public attitudes toward music. B. Boretz. Nation 197:265-7 O 26 '63
Music to my ears: Bruckner cycle III, played by New York philharmonic. I. Kolodin. Sat R 48:63 Ja 9 '65
Music to my ears: New York philharmonic program of Cage, Brown, and Feldman compositions. I. Kolodin. Sat R 47:38 F 22 '64
Musical events. W. Sargeant. New Yorker 38:112-13 F 2; 39:95 Ap 27; 156 My 25 '63
Musical events; Barber's Andromache's farewell. W. Sargeant. New Yorker 39:154 Ap 13 '63
Musical events; concert of avent-garde music performed by New York philharmonic. W. Sargeant. New Yorker 39:124-6 F 15 '64
Musical events; concert of New York philharmonic conducted by C. Abbado. W. Sargeant. New Yorker 39:110+ F 8 '64
Musical events; concert performed by New York philharmonic conducted by J. Krips. W. Sargeant. New Yorker 40:144-5 N 7 '64
Musical events; concert performed by New York philharmonic, conducted by L. Bernstein. W. Sargeant. New Yorker 40:139 My 23 '64
Musical events; first performance of Bruckner cycle. W. Sargeant. New Yorker 40:222-3 O 24 '64
Musical events; Mahler's Second symphony. W. Sargeant. New Yorker 39:135-6 O 5 '63
Musical events: New York philharmonic's promenade concerts at Philharmonic Hall. W. Sargeant. New Yorker 40:131-3 My 30 '64
Musical events; performance of Bernstein's Symphony no. 3, title Kaddish. W. Sargeant. New Yorker 40:185 Ap 18 '64
Musical events; performance of Bruckner's Seventh symphony. W. Sargeant. New Yorker 40:191 Ap 4 '64
Musical events; performance of Bruckner's Sixth symphony. W. Sargeant. New Yorker 40:55 D 26 '64
Musical events; performance of Hindemith's Symphonic metamorphoses of themes by Carl Maria von Weber and Bruckner's Fourth, or Romantic symphony. W. Sargeant. New Yorker 40:159 Mr 14 '64
Musical events; performance of Mozart's Requiem. W. Sargeant. New Yorker 40:173 Mr 7 '64
Musical events; performance of Symphony no. 6, by C. Chavez. W. Sargeant. New Yorker 40:169 My 16 '64
Radio and the Philharmonic; hitting a hip 1,000. il Sr Schol 82:12-13 Mr 20 '63
Sound of cybernetics; aleatoric music. Newsweek 63:88 F 17 '64

PHILIP, consort of Elizabeth II, queen of Great Britain
Prince Philip: England's most misunderstood man. K. W. Purdy. il pors Look 28:30+ Ap 7 '64
What is Prince Philip really like? B. H. Hoffman. il pors Ladies Home J 80:60-1+ Je '63

PHILIP, Sister Mary. See Mary Philip, Sister

PHILIP M. Stern family fund
High cost of writing; Stern and Beinecke funds. J. F. Fixx. Sat R 47:53+ Je 13 '64

PHILIPE, Anne
No longer than a sigh; excerpt from English translation of Le temps d'un soupir. pors Ladies Home J 81:64-6+ S '64

about

Grieving, going on. M. Chapsal. Reporter 31:54 O 8 '64
Letter from Paris. Genêt. New Yorker 39:144+ N 16 '63

PHILIPE, Gérard
No longer than a sigh, by A. Philipe. Review
Reporter 31:54 O 8 '64. M. Chapsal
No longer than a sigh; excerpt from English translation of Le temps d'un soupir. A. Philipe. il pors Ladies Home J 81:64-6+ S '64
Le temps de soupir (Brief as a sigh) by A. Philipe. Review
New Yorker 39:144+ N 16 '63. Genêt

PHILIPPINE air lines. See Airlines—Philippines

PHILIPPINE cookery. See Cookery, Philippine

PHILIPPINE dancing. See Dancing, Philippine

PHILIPPINE SEA, Battles of the, 1944
I'm a little late, but we came. D. MacArthur. il Life 57:82-3+ Jl 17 '64

PHILIPPINES
Eight hundred Americans; Peace corps in the Philippines. J. C. Cort. Commonweal 81:7-10 S 25 '64
Philippines can't be taken for granted. D. Warner. Reporter 31:30-2 D 17 '64
See also
Airlines—Philippines
Americans in the Philippines
Education—Philippines
Geology—Philippines
Guerrillas—Philippines
Mindanao
Moros
World war, 1939-1945—Philippines

Commercial treaties and agreements

U.S. and Philippines conclude cotton textile agreement; announcement of initialing, with U.S. note and square yard equivalent conversion factors. il Dept State Bul 50:383-5 Mr 9 '64

Defenses

Soldier's work between two wars. D. MacArthur. il Life 57:64+ Jl 3 '64

Economic conditions

Letter from Manila. R. Shaplen. il New Yorker 39:136-40+ Je 8 '63

Economic policy

Philippines, a new era; address, May 23, 1963. R. Hilsman. Dept State Bul 48:897-900 Je 10 '63
Stalemate in Manila. il Bsns W p 102-3+ S 5 '64

PHILIPPINES—*Continued*

Foreign relations

Dry tinder; question of U.S. military bases. Newsweek 65:35 F 1 '65
Meddling by Sukarno: why Filipinos turn against U.S. il U S News 58:59 Ja 11 '65
New worry for the U.S; trouble with an old ally. il U S News 57:77-9 O 12 '64
Philippines, a new era; address, May 23, 1963. R. Hilsman. Dept State Bul 48:897-900 Je 10 '63
President Macapagal of Philippines visits United States; exchange of greetings, October 5, with exchange of toasts at the White House and text of a joint communique, October 6, 1964. L. B. Johnson; D. Macapagal. Dept State Bul 51:628-34 N 2 '64

Politics and government

Call on the princess. il Time 84:33-4 O 9 '64
Democracy triumphs in the Philippines. W. J. Lederer. il Read Digest 82:289-94+ Ap '63
Legacy of scandal. Newsweek 62:39 Ag 5 '63
Letter from Manila. R. Shaplen. il New Yorker 39:136-40+ Je 8 '63
Stalemate in Manila. il Bsns W p 102-3+ S 5 '64
See also
Elections—Philippines

Religious institutions and affairs

News of the Christian world (cont) Christian Cent 80:1013, 1558; 81:712, 1186, 1602+ Ag 14, D 11 '63, My 27, S 23, D 23 '64
See also
Methodist church in the Philippines

PHILIPPINES, University. See Colleges and universities—Philippines

PHILIPPS, Wogan, 2d baron Milford. See Milford, W. P.

PHILIPS of Eindhoven companies
Philips has its eye on tomorrow. il Bsns W p 110+ D 12 '64

PHILIPSBORN, Herbert F.
Facts about the Rh factor. por Parents Mag 38:135-7 D '63

PHILIPSBURG, Pa.
$4,000 borough hall. Mrs R. B. Rickard. il Am City 78:127-8 N '63

PHILIPSON, Morris
Source book for Jungians. New Repub 152:22-4 Ja 16 '65

PHILISTINES
Original Philistines. il Horizon 6:40-1 Autumn '64

PHILLIPPE, Gerald L.
In defense of corporations. Duns R 81:52-3+ F '63
GE's Gerald Phillippe. por Duns R 81:52-3 F '63

PHILLIPS, Mrs Asa E. jr
Circumnavigating Nova Scotia. Yachting 115:38-40+ Je '64

PHILLIPS, Benjamin
Chemist looks at information retrieval. por Library J 88:964-6 Mr 1 '63

PHILLIPS, Cabell
At seventy-five, Henry Wallace cultivates his garden. N Y Times Mag p47+ O 6 '63
Senate shocks a Senate prober. N Y Times Mag p20+ Ag 9 '64
Top Kremlinologist at work. N Y Times Mag p9+ Jl 14 '63

PHILLIPS, Carleton A.
Amazing apparatus of the gay nineties. Pop Electr 22:39-42+ Ja '65

PHILLIPS, Carrie
Letters from Constant. il Time 84:27 Jl 17 '64

PHILLIPS, Charles E.
Facts and figures. Pub W 183:72+ Je 3 '63

PHILLIPS, Charles F.
Three wars; poverty, civil rights & the cold war; address, September 24, 1964. Vital Speeches 30:757-9 O 1 '64

PHILLIPS, Dale
Virgin cruising. il por Motor B 114:24-8 N '64

PHILLIPS, Delores
She's just one of the fox hunters; ed. by L. H. Lapham. Sat Eve Post 236:28+ F 23 '63

PHILLIPS, Doris Q.
Portrait of a two-year-old. Parents Mag 38:90 Jl '63

PHILLIPS, E. A.
Flying dinosaur. Flying 74:44-5+ Mr '64

PHILLIPS, Ernestine
Aesop, man of fables; drama. Plays 22:43-52 Ap '63

PHILLIPS, H. M.
Investment in people. UNESCO Courier 17:8-11+ O '64

PHILLIPS, Helen Paige
Heaven too! poem. Ladies Home J 80:111 Ja '63

PHILLIPS, Irna
Queen of the soaps. il por Newsweek 63:66-7 My 11 '64

PHILLIPS, J. H.
Crystal controlled time standard. il Electr World 69:34-6 Je '63

PHILLIPS, Jackson
Trend of business. See issues of Dun's review and modern industry

PHILLIPS, James R.
Escape of valuable slave. Negro Hist Bul 26:215 Ap '63
Little-known Negro Rough riders. Negro Hist Bul 27:59 D '63
Philips Brooks: spokesman for freedom. Negro Hist Bul 27:10 O '63

PHILLIPS, John
Up in Massachusetts. Commentary 34:431-41; 35:258-9 N '62, Mr '63

PHILLIPS, John Bertram
Prophets paraphrased. por Time 82:86 N 1 '63

PHILLIPS, Keith S.
Let's use dumbcane. Pop Gard 15:16-17 Ja '64
Norfolk Island-pine. Flower Grower 51:28 N '64

PHILLIPS, McCandlish
And there appeared to them tongues of fire. Sat Eve Post 237:30-2+ My 16 '64

PHILLIPS, Marvin
Crackdown on quackery. il pors Life 55:72B-75 N 1 '63

PHILLIPS, Mary E.
Report on Oregon public libraries shocking, says state librarian. Library J 88:740-2 F 15 '63

PHILLIPS, Michael J.
After the first kiss; poem. Nation 199:413 N 30 '64

PHILLIPS, Pauline Esther (Friedman) See Van Buren, A. pseud.

PHILLIPS, Porter William, sr family
Family of Porter William Phillips, sr. pors Negro Hist Bul 27:81-4 Ja '64

PHILLIPS, Richard I.
United States ends grant aid to Republic of China; statement, May 28, 1964. Dept State Bul 50:934 Je 15 '64

PHILLIPS, Robert Allan
These Americans must be gods. S. Karnow. il por Sat Eve Post 237-72-3 Ap 25 '64

PHILLIPS, Sidney
Exam; for Peace corps volunteers conducted by the Civil service commission, New York office. New Yorker 39:22-3 D 21 '63

PHILLIPS, Thomas R.
MacArthur the soldier. New Repub 150:16 Ap 18 '64

PHILLIPS, Wendell
Leaders of the first freedom movement. L. Bennett, jr. il por Ebony 19:68-70+ Ag '64

PHILLIPS Exeter academy. See Private schools

PHILMUS, Lois C.
Taming southern Cal's airport jungle. Flying 75:30-3+ Ag '64

PHILOLOGY, Spanish
See also
Colombia—Instituto Caro y Cuervo

PHILOSOPHERS
Philosophy in Hispano-America. A. Salgado. il Américas 15:17-22 Mr '63

PHILOSOPHY
Existential and Christian. A. E. Mayhew. Commonweal 80:152-3 Ap 24 '64
Free will, again. H. D. Aiken. Commentary 37:79-82 F '64
Idea of perfection. I. Murdoch. Yale R 53:342-80 Mr '64
Laugh or perish! appeal for scholarly sanity. R. G. Gruenler. Christian Cent 80:204-5 F 13 '63
Philosophers choose sides. R. Abel. Sat R 46:28 Je 15 '63
Rational man, by H. B. Veatch. Review
Commonweal 78:76-8 Ap 12 '63. M. Novak
Uses of thinking. J. K. Feibleman. Sat R 46:18-19+ Mr 2 '63
See also
Art—Philosophy
Atheism
Change
Civilization
Existentialism
Humanism
Individuality
International congress of philosophy
Life
Logical positivism
Man
Mysticism
Optimism

PHILOSOPHY—*See also—Continued*
Personalism
Political philosophy
Pragmatism
Rationalism
Reality
Reason
Religion
Worth
See also subhead Philosophy under various subjects, e.g. Education—Philosophy

Bibliography

Philosophical foursome. W. A. Sadler, jr. Christian Cent 80:1435-6 N 20 '63

History

Career of philosophy: from the middle ages to the enlightenment, by J. H. Randall, jr. Review
Sci Am 208:177-8+ My '63. J. Passmore

Study and teaching

Thomism today. R. Lauer. Commonweal 80: 39-42 Ap 3 '64; Reply with rejoinder. R. J. Miller. 80:261-2 My 22 '64

PHILOSOPHY, American
Spirit of American philosophy, by J. E. Smith. Review
Reporter 28:55-7 My 23 '63. V. Held

PHILOSOPHY, English
Fly and the fly-bottle: encounters with British intellectuals, by V. Mehta. Review
Sat R 46:37-8 Je 22 '63. J. K. Feibleman

PHILOSOPHY, French
See also
Bergson, H.

PHILOSOPHY, Greek
Birth of reason. G. De Santillana. il Life 54: 62+ F 8 '63
See also
Socrates

PHILOSOPHY, International congress of. See International congress of philosophy

PHILOSOPHY, Jewish
Exploring the Jewish mind. M. Fox. Commentary 35:86-9 Ja '63

PHILOSOPHY, Latin American
Philosophy in Hispano-America. A. Salgado. il Américas 15:17-22 Mr '63

PHILOSOPHY, Medieval
See also
Thomism

PHILOSOPHY, Moral. See Ethics

PHILOSOPHY, Oriental
Oriental echoes of the Social contract; summary of address, 1962. T. Kuwabara. il UNESCO Courier 16:24-6 Mr '63

PHILOSOPHY, Political. See Political philosophy

PHILOSOPHY and religion
Natural and ultimate religion; with comment by R. Kirk. G. Santayana. Nat R 15:561-2 D 31 '63
World of Wilhelm Reich. P. Rieff. Commentary 38:50-8 S '64
See also
Existentialism

Bibliography

Comparative religion, philosophy of religion bookshelf. H. Smith. Christian Cent 80: 830-1 Je 26 '63

PHILOSOPHY and science
Bearing of philosophy on the history of science; address, December 29, 1963. A. Grünbaum. bibliog Science 143:1406-12 Mr 27 '64
Field, philosophy, & esthetics. E. R. Fagan. il Sch Arts 63:24-8 My '64
Santayana and the task ahead. A. Danto. Nation 197:437-40 D 21 '63
Sartre: French philosopher is model of literary intellectual by two cultures definition. J. Walsh. Science 146:900-2 N 13 '64

PHILOSOPHY of education. See Education—Philosophy

PHILOSOPHY of history. See History—Philosophy

PHILOSOPHY of medicine. See Medicine—Philosophy

PHILOSOPHY of nature. See Nature—Philosophy

PHINIZY, Coles
Boating. Sports Illus 19:48-50 Jl 29 '63
Diving. Sports Illus 19:62-4 D 16 '63
Fire watch in a dry, dry woodland. Sports Illus 19:22-4 N 4 '63
Sporting look. il Sports Illus 18:62-3 Ap 15 '63
Swimming. Sports Illus 18:43-4+ Mr 25 '63
Two worlds in one picture. il U S Camera 26:38-9+ Jl '63

PHINNEY, Eleanor
Recent trends in public library adult services. ALA Bul 57:262-6 Mr '63

PHIPPS, Joe, and Robinson, Robert
Growing menace of nice drugs. Good H 157: 70-1+ S '63; Same abr. with title Sleeping pills and pep pills; handle with extreme caution! Read Digest 83:103-7 N '63

PHIPPS, K. D. and Sullenger, D. B.
Plutonium dioxide: preparation of single crystals. bibliog Science 145:1048-9 S 4 '64

PHLOEM. See Plant cells and tissues

PHLOX
For flowers. M. Haislip. il Flower Grower 51:32+ Ag '64
Like a drift of snow in spring; moss phlox. il Sunset 133:260 O '64
Phlox. V. Quist. il Pop Gard 15:26+ Mr '64
Two wild flowers that adapt well to the regular garden. E. W. Reed. il Horticulture 41:248 My '63
Use phlox carpeting. M. P. Kunkel. il Horticulture 41:307 Je '63
What's new about phlox? R. C. Hands. il Horticulture 42:40-1 Mr '64

PHNOM PENH
Our far-flung correspondents. R. Shaplen. New Yorker 40:150+ Ap 18 '64

PHOENICIAN language

Alphabet

How Europe began to write: Phoenician alphabet. il UNESCO Courier 17:20-1 Mr '64

PHOENIX, Ariz.
Phoenix; an escape-to-the-sun holiday in the Arizona desert. il Sunset 132:42-57 Ja '64

Airports

No-glare lighting for Phoenix airport. W. Ralston. il Am City 79:111 Ja '64

City planning

Phoenix unreborn; federal aid and urban-renewal. R. L. Gilbert, jr. Reporter 29: 48-9 N 21 '63

Housing

Ah, wilderness! Carefree project. il Time 83: 77 F 7 '64

Lighting

Streamlined street lights and power lines; Arizona public service co. il Am City 79: 138+ Je '64

Music

[Musical events] Mus Am 84:16 My '64

Newspapers

Blooming desert. il Time 82:45 S 6 '63
Death throes in Phoenix; Arizona journal. Time 81:51 F 15 '63

Recreation

Fun of retirement, by W. Peterson. Review
Recreation 57:301 Je '64

Sanitary affairs

Coming struggle to breathe. T. O. Thackrey. Sat R 47:23-5+ O 10 '64
No special district for these cities. L. E. Goodall. il Am City 79:27 Ap '64
Sweepers are part of the parade. J. A. Stokely. il Am City 78:36 S '63

Streets

Tests tougher sealants at signalized intersections. F. Glendening. il Am City 79:109 Ap '64

Water supply

New alloys produce savings in standpipes. il Am City 79:24 My '64

PHOENIX dactylifera. See Palms

PHOENIX mutual life insurance company
City life is best says Hartford firm. E. C. Freedman. il Am City 79:106 Ag '64
Payoff in design. N. Buckley. il Duns R 84:pt2 115-17+ S '64

PHOENIX steel corporation
Rising from the ashes. il Bsns W p87+ S 26 '64

PHOENIX trust, England. See Charitable uses, trusts, foundations

PHOLSENA, Quinim
After the party. Time 81:34 Ap 12 '63

PHONE call; story. See Mayer, T.

PHONETIC alphabet. See Alphabet

PHONETICS

Anecdotes, facetiae, satire, etc.

Rule of O. R. Bingham. Reporter 30:40+ Mr 26 '64

PHONIC method. See Reading—Study and teaching

PHONO amplifiers. See Amplifiers
PHONO oscillators. See Oscillators
PHONOGRAPH
Compleat virtuosi; *discothèques* of Paris. Time 82:50-1 Jl 5 '63
Easy to play but hard to listen to; Playskool magic phono. il Consumer Rep 28: 102 Mr '63
Faithful sound. R. Freas. Esquire 61:46+ Mr '64
Musical modules, a new breed of equipment. Hi Fi 14:105 O '64
Radios and phonographs. Consumer Rep 29: 90-106 D '64
Shopping the home entertainment circuit. R. Freas. il Am Home 67:85-7 D '64
Sound ideas. L. Zide. See issues of American record guide
Transistorized record player. il House & Gard 125:182-3 Ap '64
Updating your old phono. G. F. Stillwell. il Pop Mech 119:177-9 My '63
What the consumer should know about record players. E. Villchur. il Am Rec G 30:4-8+ S '63
Your leisure (cont) il Consumer Rep 28:279-300 D '63
See also
Jukeboxes

High fidelity sound systems

Criteria for hi-fi and costs. Discus. Harper 229:154+ N '64
High fidelity. H. Fantel. Opera N 29:29 S 26 '64
High fidelity (title varies) C. L. Osborne. Opera N 27:37 Mr 30 '63
Split personality spells success; H. H. Scott, inc. il Bsns W p 156+ Mr 16 '63

History

Secrist collection given to Library of Congress. Hobbies 68:124-5 My '63

Pickup

Case of the tilted stylus. R. D. Darrell. il Hi Fi 13:34-6+ My '63
Da capo. S. Smolian. il Am Rec G 30:348-9 D '63
Distortion in phono cartridges. J. H. Kogen. il Electr World 72:28 Ag '64
High fidelity newsfronts. N. Eisenberg. Hi Fi 14:31 My '64
High fidelity; the cartridge. H. Fantel. Opera N 28:35 F 22 '64
Sound ideas; A cartridge for Garrard changers. L. Zide. il Am Rec G 29:658-9 Ap '63
Turntables with arms. il Consumer Rep 29: 435-9 S '64

Record changers

Listen here; what you need to know when buying a record changer. R. Freas. Am Home 67:12 My '64

Repairing

Phono fillips. A. Trauffer. il Pop Electr 20: 56-7 Ja '64

Stereophonic equipment

A's to your Q's about stereo. H. Fantel. il Pop Sci 186:102-5 Ja '65
Audio: low-cost stereo. H. Fantel. Opera N 29:33 N 14 '64
Audio: medium-priced stereo. H. Fantel. Opera N 29:33 D 12 '64
Budget for stereo; how much should go for each component? E. F. McIntyre. il Hi Fi 14:111-14 O '64
High fidelity newsfronts. N. Eisenberg. il Hi Fi 13:41 Ap '63
High-fidelity stereo sound, with separate components. il Consumer Bul 46:21-6 N '63
Low-down on hi-fi stereo. C. P. Gilmore and H. Luckett. il Pop Sci 183:82-9+ S '63
New trends in stereo kits. I. B. Berger. il Hi Fi 15:57-9+ F '65
Portable stereo phonographs. il Consumer Rep 28:116-20 Mr '63
Professional tool, a source of enjoyment. il Hi Fi 13:66-7 S '63
Stereo in a suitcase. il Hi Fi 14:46-8 My '64
Stereo in a suitcase. E. C. Carlson. il Pop Mech 119:116-20 Je '63
Stereo record players; portables, consoles. il Consumer Bul 46:2+ D '63
What to know about stereo. M. Casserly. il Bet Hom & Gard 41:104 F '63

Stereophonic pickup

Stereo cartridges; status report. A. Sterling. il Hi Fi 15:52-5+ Ja '65
Stereo pickups. il Consumer Rep 29:67-71 F '64
Which one is the real F-7? Consumer Rep 29:108 Mr '64

Testing

Record players for libraries and schools; summary of Testing and evaluation of record players for libraries. il Consumer Bul 46:12-14 Mr '63
Short guide to test records; with discography. R. D. Darrell. il Hi Fi 13:48-51+ D '63

Tone arm

Worden articulated tone arm. il Hi Fi 13:73-4 S '63

Turntables

Automated turntable. H. Luckett. il Pop Sci 185:103 Ag '64
High fidelity. H. Fantel. Opera N 28:35 Ja 11 '64
How to use the double turntable. G. W. Cushman. il Pop Phot 51:18+ D '62
New dual 1009; auto/professional turntable. H. Luckett. il Pop Sci 184:147 F '64
Turntable testing at home. E. Villchur. il Electr World 69:29-32+ Mr '63
Turntables for stereo. J. Marshall. il Hi Fi 13:52-4+ Mr '63
Turntables with arms. il Consumer Rep 29: 435-9 S '64
Word on rumble; test program by hi fi and USTC. Hi Fi 13:51 My '63
PHONOGRAPH, Automobile
Record player for your car. H. Luckett. il Pop Sci 183:169 O '63
PHONOGRAPH, Portable
How to buy a phonograph. il Seventeen 22:174 Mr '63
Points on portables. I. Berger. il Sat R 46:42-3 Je 29 '63
Portable stereo phonographs. il Consumer Rep 28:116-20 Mr '63
Vacation with music; take console sound in a suitcase. R. Freas. il Am Home 67:21+ Jl '64
PHONOGRAPH amplifiers. See Amplifiers
PHONOGRAPH cabinets
Cabinet for connoisseurs. N. Eisenberg. il Hi Fi 13:42-3 My '63
Faithful sound. R. Freas. Esquire 62:58+ S '64
PHONOGRAPH in education
Masters; correspondence courses by phonograph records. New Yorker 39:35-6 S 14 '63
See also
Phonograph records—Language teaching records
PHONOGRAPH industry and trade
See also
Phonograph record industry
PHONOGRAPH needles
Case of the tilted stylus. R. D. Darrell. il Hi Fi 13:34-6+ My '63
High fidelity newsfronts. N. Eisenberg. Hi Fi 14:31 My '64
PHONOGRAPH radio combination. See Radio receiving apparatus—Phonograph combination
PHONOGRAPH record albums
Albums for Christmas. H. Kupferberg. il Atlan 212:148+ D '63
PHONOGRAPH record clubs
Can you satisfy a specialized music interest with a record club? Bet Hom & Gard 42:14 S '64
Music by mail. J. Tebbel. il Hi Fi 13:42-5+ Mr '63
PHONOGRAPH record covers
Record covers: hard sell, soft sell, no sell. S. Walker il Mus Am 83:20-1 Jl '63
PHONOGRAPH record industry
Artist as businessman. R. Grevatt. il Hi Fi 13:32-4+ Je '63
Da capo. S. Smolian. Am Rec G 29:663 Ap '63
Masters, matrices, & mass production. S. Fleming. il Hi Fi 15:46-51 Ja '65
Music by mail. J. Tebbel. il Hi Fi 13:42-5+ Mr '63
Music makers. R. Gelatt. Hi Fi 13:69 Ap '63
See also
Composers recordings, incorporated

Germany (Federal Republic)

Furtwängler radio performances on DGG, Strauss, Beethoven, Bruckner, and Hindemith compositions. Am Rec G 30:570-1+ Mr '64
Hi-fi from the Germans. H. Kupferberg. il Atlan 211:147-8+ Mr '63
Major label debut: Eurodisc. J. Ardoin. il Mus Am 84:48 S '64
Notes from abroad. K. Blaukopf. Hi Fi 13: 26+ Ap '63

Great Britain

See also
London records, incorporated
PHONOGRAPH record reviews
Record review; Index of record reviews. K. Myers. il Library J 88:1813-17 My 1 '63

PHONOGRAPH records
Americans all (North and South) works of American composers. R. Kammerer; A. Cohn. il Am Rec G 31:392-6 Ja '65
Bach in jazz? two views of the Jacques Loussier trio. R. Sabin; D. Heckman. Am Rec G 30:1065 Jl '64
Bach, major and minor. M. Steinberg. Sat R 46:36 Ap 13 '63
Bach's greatest hits revisited. Am Rec G 30:506-7+ F '64
Bartók on stage; Duke Bluebeard's castle, Wooden prince, Miraculous mandarin, with discography. E. Helm. il Hi Fi 14:74-7+ N '64
Building your own record library. R. Hemming. il Sr Schol 83:25 D 13 '63; 84:48 F 14 '64
Buried treasures; National music council's plan for reissuing deleted recordings. P. L. Miller. il Library J 88:1823-5 My 1 '63
Concert records (cont) D. Watt. il New Yorker 39:163-5 Je 8 '65
Critics choose the top recordings of 1963-1964. I. Kolodin. il Sat R 46:28-9+ D 14 '63; 47:30-1 D 19 '64
Cult of the best recordings. Hi Fi 13:51 S '63
Da capo; complete numerical listing of RCA Victor Red seal albums. S. Smolian. Am Rec G 30:892-5, 1002-4, 1056-8; 31:82-4, 165-7, 271-3 My-Jl, S-N '64
Discoveries from the past: curious names and obscure works. H. Kupferberg. il Atlan 214:139-40 D '64
DISCussions. R. Hemming. See issues of Senior scholastic
Enjoy the new feast of Debussy recordings. E. Kinard. House B 105:30+ O '63
Enter Eurodisc. M. Bernheimer. Sat R 47:58+ Je 27 '64
Facade; entertainment with poems. J. Diether. il Am Rec G 31:304-7 D '64
Faithful sound. R. Freas. Esquire 61:46+ Mr '64
Favorite pioneer recording artists. J. Walsh. See issues of Hobbies
Final release of recordings by the late Bruno Walter. R. Sabin. il Am Rec G 30:488-91 F '64
First recordings from Philharmonic Hall; opening night concert, September 23, 1962. R. C. Marsh. il Hi Fi 13:73-4 F '63
First recordings of Debussy and Hindemith works for narrator and ensemble. R. Sabin. il Am Rec G 30:926-7 Je '64
Fritz Kreisler in immortal performances. P. L. Miller. il Am Rec G 29:430-1 F '63
From 78 to 7.5: guide to the delights of dubbing from discs to tape. C. L. Osborne. il Hi Fi 14:50-2+ Mr '64
Gift DISCussions. R. Hemming. Sr Schol 83:36-7 N 22 '63
Heritage by mail; mail-order record company devoted to seventeenth and eighteenth-century music. R. Freed. il Sat R 47:47-8 Jl 25 '64
Heritage of Bruno Walter; discography. R. C. Marsh. il Hi Fi 14:44-8+ Ja '64
Historical records. A. Favia-Artsay. See issues of Hobbies
Holiday gift DISCussions. R. Hemming. il Sr Schol 85:32+ D 2 '64
Imports. G. Bruck. See issues of High fidelity to April 1964
In memoriam, 1899-1963: three by Poulenc. Am Rec G 29:510-11 Mr '63
Intimate music. il Am Home 67:24 O '64
Is tape really better than records? J. Wesson. U S Camera 27:24 S '64
It may scratch, but the music is not for boring; Berio: Circles; Bussotti: Frammento; Cage: Aria with Fontana mix. A. Cohn. Am Rec G 30:195 N '63
Kennedy memorial albums. H. Kupferberg. il Atlan 213:134+ Ap '64
Koussevitzky recording awards. R. Jacobson. Mus Am 83:46 My '63
Latest on the low-price record racks. il Changing T 18:41-2 Je '64
Let's play A & R man; imaginary recordings. L. Haber. il Hi Fi 14:63-4 D '64
Life guide. See issues of Life
Life music review. Life 56:15 Ap 10; 18 My 22; 10 My 29; 57:19 Jl 3; 12 Ag 7; 28 O 2 '64
Lighter side. See issues of High fidelity
Listen to the perfectionist touch. Am Home 68:31 Ja '65
Listen to these lovely sounds of summer. Am Home 67:40 Jl '64
Looking and listening; words and music to recall your travels. il House & Gard 123:24+ My '63
Major phases of the latest Ellington; Symphonic Ellington and My people. J. S. Wilson. Hi Fi 14:114 Ap '64
Mid-month recordings. See issues of Saturday review
Miscellany from all over. Am Rec G 29:812-13 Je '63
Monteux legacy; with list of recordings. R. Freed. Sat R 47:48-9 Ag 22 '64
More vintage Toscanini. P. H. Reed. il Am Rec G 30:24-5 S '63
Music. C. J. McNaspy. See issues of America
Music in the round. Discus. See issues of Harper's magazine
Music of Arnold Schoenberg: now, volume II. A. Cohn. Am Rec G 30:394-5 Ja '64
Music of Arthur Schoenberg: from Columbia, the first complete recorded edition. A. Cohn. il Am Rec G 30:192-4 N '63
Music since the LP. J. Diether. Mus Am 84:8-9 Ja '64
Musical record. B. Walter. Am Rec G 30:374-5 Ja '64
Musical world's tour. C. Brown. Redbook 121:38-9 Jl '63
National archives of sound recordings? role of Library of Congress. H. Spivacke. il Library J 88:3783-8 O 15 '63
New fall recordings: preview (cont) il Hi Fi 13:67+ Ag '63
New records in review. B. H. Haggin. See issues of Yale review
Nine Dutch composers. A. Cohn. il Am Rec G 29:610-12+ Ap '63
Nonesuch; welcome to a new label. J. W. Barker. il Am Rec G 30:1022-3 Jl '64
Notes from our correspondents; recording of memorial service for J. F. Kennedy; Holy Cross cathedral, Boston. W. B. Syer. il Hi Fi 14:17 Ap '64
Of things to come; new items. Mus Am 83:44 My '63
Of things to come: new releases. Mus Am 83:31 O '63
On Cambridge, CRI, and Vox, that supremely individual creative genius, Chas. E. Ives. A. Cohn. Am Rec G 30:760-2+ My '64
Other reviews, including stereo. See issues of American record guide
Other side. T. Heinitz. See last issue of each month of Saturday review
Outstanding recordings of 1962-3. Mus Am 83:116 Ja; 275 D '63
Outstanding records of 1964. Mus Am 84:264 D '64
Outstanding records of 1964. B. H. Haggin. New Repub 151:26-7 D 12 '64
Phonograph records. W. F. Grueninger. See issues of Consumer bulletin
Picture music. il Am Home 67:22 Je '64
Popular records. D. Watt. New Yorker 39:92-4 Je 1 '63
Preview of new fall recordings. il Hi Fi 14:58-9+ Ag '64
Pros and cons of dynagroove. I. Kolodin. Sat R 46:68 Mr 30 '63
RCA Victor introduces dynagroove and Columbia calls it a backward step. G. Lieberson. il Am Rec G 29:600-1+ Ap '63
Rarities from overseas. H. Kupferberg. il Atlan 213:110-11 Ja '64
Rarities from Rococo. J. Ardoin. il Mus Am 84:50-1 My '64
Recommended recordings. Sat R 46:75-6+ D 7 '63; 47:71-3 D 5 '64
Record forecast. Mus Am 84:48 F; 26 O '64
Record notes. R. Gelatt; N. Hentoff. See occasional issues of The reporter to August 15, 1963
Record reviews. H. Kupferberg. See issues of Atlantic
Recorded music; ed. by P. L. Miller. See issues of Library journal
Recordings. See issues of Musical America
Recordings. M. Mayer. See issues of Esquire
Recordings in review. I. Kolodin. See last issue of each month of Saturday review
Recordings in review. M. Bernheimer. il Sat R 46:40-1 Jl 27 '63
Recordings reports: miscellaneous LPs & tapes. I. Kolodin. See last issue of each month of Saturday review
Records. B. H. Haggin. See issues of New republic
Records. D. Peerman. Christian Cent 80:936 Jl 24 '63
Records (cont) B. Boretz. Nation 196:107-8, 535-6; 197:308, 374-6, 441-2; 198:155-6, 514-15, 639-40; 199:127-8, 364; 200:95-6 F 2, Je 22, N 9, 30, D 21 '63, F 10, My 18, Je 22, S 14, N 16 '64, Ja 25 '65
Records (cont of) Recordings. See issues of Musical America
Records and tapes. J. Muri. Sr Schol 85:8T-9T O 28; 10T N 4; 20T D 9 '64

PHONOGRAPH records—*Continued*
Records and tapes. R. Hemming. Sr Schol 82:10T Ap 17; 11T My 8 '63
Records are priceless treasures. il Seventeen 22:175 Mr '63
Records for your children & you; comp. by E. D. Sheehy. See issues of Parents' magazine
Records in review. See issues of High fidelity
Records of the year. B. Boretz. Nation 199: 472-4 D 14 '64
Reels, wheels, and economics. I. Berger. Sat R 47:73 My 30 '64
Reiner in Chicago; with discography. P. Hart. Hi Fi 14:42-6 Ap '64
Reissues. See issues of High fidelity
Reissues for the Delius centenary. H. Glass. il Am Rec G 30:294-5 D '63
Reissues: limited and unlimited. R. Freed. Sat R 46:49+ My 25 '63
Requiem by, and for, Paul Hindemith. R. Sabin. Am Rec G 30:756-8 My '64
Reviews of recent recordings. See issues of Consumer reports
Richard Strauss: a centennial discography. Sat R 47:62-3+ My 30 '64
SR recordings. See issues of Saturday review to August 31, 1963
Scherchen on discs. R. Freed. Sat R 47:65 O 31 '64
Sight & sound; ed. by B. Sheridan. See issues of McCall's to December 1963
Sight & sound; ed. by L. Benjamin and B. Sheridan. il McCalls 91:8+ F; 6+ Mr; 8+ Ap; 8+ My; 8+ Je; 8+ Jl '64
Sight & sound. L. Benjamin. See issues of McCall's beginning August 1964
Sound ideas; dynagroove process. L. Zide. Am Rec G 29:891-3 Jl '63
Sounds of history; supplement to the Life history of the United States. R. L. Tobin. Sat R 47:49+ S 12 '64
Special report: imports and reissues. J. Ardoin. Mus Am 83:33 O '63
Special report: new records from Germany. H. O. Springel. Mus Am 83:37 F '63
Stravinsky conducts his choral music; short pieces, and ballet music. C. J. Luten. Am Rec G 31:310-12 D '64
Sure cures for the hush that depresses; or how to keep a party lively. Am Home 67:34 N '64
Teens are listening to... E. Miller. See issues of Seventeen
Ten from Cleveland. O. Daniel. Sat R 47:58 N 28 '64
Treasury of early music. J. W. Barker. il Am Rec G 30:96-100 O '63
What's new in records. C. Brown. See issues of Redbook to September 1964
Year's best. Time 82:40 D 20 '63
See also
Libraries—Phonograph and phonograph records
Tape recordings

Animal records

Record boom in bird songs. J. Boswall. il Audubon Mag 66:48-50 Ja '64
Unique album makes this a singing bird book. il Nat Geog Mag 126:557 O '64

Ballet music

See Phonograph records—Dance music

Band music

Strike up the bands for culture; U.S. military bands. F. Reynolds. il Am Rec G 29:920-3+ Ag '63
Sweet and swinging. F. Reynolds. See issues of American record guide

Baroque music

Baroque, and earlier: introducing Telefunken's new series: Das alte werk. Am Rec G 31:356-9 D '64
Going for baroque. J. M. Conly. Reporter 31: 44-5 N 5 '64

Bird records

See Phonograph records—Animal records

Books

See Phonograph records—Spoken records

Cantatas

Bach and son. M. Bernheimer. Sat R 46:59+ Mr 30 '63
Fresh Bachian delights; Cantate's continuing cantatas. H. Glass. il Am Rec G 30: 400-1+ Ja '64
Maria Stader's latest: do not miss this record! H. Glass. Am Rec G 29:463 F '63
[Nine Bach cantatas] Am Rec G 30:933-4+ Je '64

Care

Thrust, dust and friction; record wear. J. Marshall. il Hi Fi 14:49-52+ Ja '64
Watts way. J. Crabbe. il Am Rec G 31:92-4+ O '64

Catalogs

From the editor: Schwann catalog. J. Lyons. Am Rec G 29:784 Je '63
Music critic looks at basic LP collections. S. Kallai. il Library J 88:3802-3 O 15 '63; Discussion. 88:3802, 4504+ O 15, D 1 '63
O lieber Schwann. il Hi Fi 14:95 O '64
Spinning statistics; Schwann artist listing. il Time 81:33-4 Je 28 '63

Cello music

See Phonograph records—Violoncello music

Chamber music

Art and the Offering. M. Bernheimer. Sat R 47:58 F 29 '64
Boettcher's Bach, unqualifiedly recommended; Das musikalische opfer. H. Glass. Am Rec G 30:944 Je '64
Jubilee fare; works of E. Toch and H. Cowell. O. Daniel. Sat R 46:71 Mr 30 '63
RCA Victor's million-dollar trio; Archduke trio. R. Jones. il Am Rec G 30:389+ Ja '64

Chants (Gregorian, plain, etc)

Buddhist chant. W. L. Purcell. il Am Rec G 30:806-8 My '64

Childrens records

Choosing records for children. D. Gold. Ladies Home J 81:45-6 D '64
Christmas records for the young, 1963. Sat R 46:72-4 D 7 '63
Christmas records for the young, 1964. A. Franklin. Sat R 47:68-70 D 5 '64
Classics children love. C. Brown. Redbook 120:20 Ap '63
Especially for Christmas; H. C. Andersen fairy tales. Am Rec G 31:373 D '64
On and off the avenue (cont) New Yorker 39:187-90 N 30 '63
Records for children; ed. by J. L. Limbacher. il(cover) Library J 88:3999-4001; 89:1383-4+ O 15 '63, Mr 15 '64
Some recommended records for children. E. W. Thomson. il Pub W 184:19-20 D 9 '63
Unique recordings for children. C. Brown. Redbook 121:28+ O '63

Chinese music

From Lui Tsun-yuen, a record to cherish. W. L. Purcell. il Am Rec G 30:808-9 My '64

Choral music

Art of Francis Poulenc. A. Cohn. Am Rec G 30:622-3 Mr '64
Choral music of George Frideric Handel. J. W. Barker. Am Rec G 31:24-5+ S '64
On records; Stabat mater. Opera N 28:35 Ja 18 '64
On records; Stabat mater; motets. Opera N 29:35 D 26 '64
Reflections on Gustav Holst's The hymn of Jesus. M. Serbin. il Am Rec G 29:512-14 Mr '63
Sing unto the Ford a new song; awards to stimulate the choral medium. Sat R 48:50+ Ja 30 '65
Spanish renaissance music by the Montreal Bach choir. J. W. Barker. Am Rec G 29: 779 Je '63

Christmas music

Christmas music to hear year-round. Good H 157:178 D '63
Christmas records. W. F. Grueninger. Consumer Bul 46:43 D '63
Christmas sing out with a joyful, lovely sound. R. Freas. il Am Home 66:15+ N '63
Especially for Christmas. il Am Rec G 31: 292-300 D '64
Glade jul! and other gude tydings. I. Kolodin. Sat R 47:55+ D 12 '64
Maligayang Pasko to you and yours. I. Kolodin. Sat R 46:34 D 14 '63
More records: especially for Christmas. il Am Rec G 30:283-7 D '63
Music. C. J. McNaspy. America 109:780-2; 111:532-3 D 14 '63, O 31 '64
Music can help make Christmas magic for children. L. Wilcox. il House B 105:166-7+ D '63
Portfolio of Christmas music not always heard. il House B 105:150-1+ D '63
Sing, boys, in joyful chorus. il House & Gard 124:150-1 D '63
What sweeter music? S. Fleming. Hi Fi 13:52-3 D '63
World's most glorious Christmas music. J. Peyser. il House & Gard 126:160-1 D '64

PHONOGRAPH records—*Continued*

Church music

For Giulini, a triumph; Verdi's Four sacred pieces. J. Diether. Am Rec G 30:676+ Ap '64
From Angel, DGG, and Amadeo, a feast of Bruckner's church music. J. Diether. il Am Rec G 29:850-2 Jl '63
Gloria & Credo. Opera N 29:35 D 5 '64
Johannes Ockeghem, religious mysticism and architectural subtlety, individually compounded. J. W. Barker. il Am Rec G 31:145-6 O '64
Music; sublime and exciting new releases. C. J. McNaspy. America 108:273 F 23 '63
On records; Quattro pezzi sacri. Opera N 39:27 O 17 '64

Circulation, loans, etc.

Life guide; more and more ways to rent art. il Life 55:7 O 4 '63

Clavichord music

Well-tempered clavichord. R. Sabin. Am Rec G 30:574-5 Mr '64

Collectors and collecting

Collector's Verdi. C. L. Osborne. Hi Fi 13:37-8+ O; 90+ D '63
Da capo (cont) S. Smolian. Am Rec G 29:962-4 Ag '63
Everyman's guide to discmanship. P. J. Smith. il Hi Fi 14:17-18 O '64
John Secrist collection at the Library of Congress. A. Favia-Artsay. il Hobbies 68:30-2 Je; 30-1+ Jl '63
On records; historical records. Opera N 28:34 Ja 11 '64
Secrist collection given to Library of Congress. Hobbies 68:124-5 My '63

Concertos

Beethoven concertos. B. H. Haggin. New Repub 149:24-6 S 14 '63
Brahms of Francescatti and Heifetz. B. Schwarz. Sat R 46:57 D 28 '63
Brahms piano concertos in fruitful collaborations. H. Goldsmith. il Hi Fi 13:70-1 Mr '63
Brandenburgs by Klemperer. M. Steinberg. Sat R 46:72 O 26 '63
Building your own record library. R. Hemming. il Sr Schol 84:48 F 14 '64
Corelli, Torelli, Locatelli. B. Schwarz. Sat R 47:66 Je 27 '64
Counterpoint esoteric: a superb product but. . . H. Glass. Am Rec G 30:974 Je '64
Finally, all twelve of Bach's keyboard concerti. J. W. Barker. Am Rec G 29:534 Mr '63
From the Argentine; concerto for piano and orchestra. A. Cohn. il Am Rec G 31:397 Ja '65
Inspired Hindemith; Oistrakh at his greatest. H. Glass. Am Rec G 29:874 Jl '63
Introducing John Ogdon. R. Kammerer. Am Rec G 30:384 Ja '64
Living concert, a new Cantate series. J. W. Barker. il Am Rec G 30:215 N '63
Mozart's horn concertos thrice recorded. N. Broder. Hi Fi 14:92 N '64
New wheel for the old hub. J. Lyons. il Am Rec G 29:516-17 Mr '63
Pioneer service to two young composers. R. Sabin. Am Rec G 30:971 Je '64
Rachmaninoff by Graffman and Bernstein. J. Diether. il Am Rec G 31:451 Ja '65
Ricci, a man (with strads) for all seasons. J. Diether. il Am Rec G 31:400-2 Ja '65
Simultaneously, no less than nine different Haydn concerti. J. W. Barker. Am Rec G 30:850-1 My '64
Three by Kurt Redel, unabashed admiration. H. Glass. il Am Rec G 30:576-7 Mr '64
Tippett: a genuinely stereophonic thrill; Concerto for double string orchestra. J. Diether. Am Rec G 29:810-11 Je '63

Czech music

Behind the Pilsener curtain. O. Daniel. Sat R 46:55 D 28 '63

Dance music

Art of the prima ballerina. C. J. Luten. il Am Rec G 30:30-2 S '63
Dancing into shape. L. Lerman. Mlle 58:20 N '63
From Angel, a first-class Jeux; with André Cluytens. C. J. Luten. il Am Rec G 31:313 D '64
From DGG, the first complete recording of The miraculous mandarin. J. Diether. il Am Rec G 30:826-7 My '64
From the Bolshoi: the first complete Raymonda. R. Sabin. il Am Rec G 30:1034 Jl '64
Records for dance. R. Krokover. See issues of Dance magazine to December 1963
Records for teachers. E. LeMone. See issues of Dance magazine
Rubinstein's Chopin waltzes: peerless. C. J. Luten. Am Rec G 31:328 D '64
Sweet and swinging. F. Reynolds. See issues of American record guide

Documentary records

Intrigue your mind while your hands work. E. Kinard. il House B 105:54+ S '63
That was the year that was; news recordings. R. L. Tobin. Sat R 47:56-7 F 15 '64

Dutch music

Dutch treat from Donemus. O. Daniel. il Sat R 47:40-1 Jl 25 '64

Educational applications

See Phonograph in education

Electronic music

Barzun's gambit declined. I. Kolodin. Sat R 47:59 Je 27 '64
Electronic music. A. Cohn. il Am Rec G 30:924-5+ Je '64
Music. B. Boretz. Nation 196:233-6 Mr 16 '63
New musical conceptions realized by electronic means. E. Salzman. Hi Fi 13:91 Ag '63
Stockhausen's Kontakte on DGG; a telling experience. A. Cohn. Am Rec G 29:952+ Ag '63

English music

Coates, V. W. and Morton Gould on his mettle. J. Diether. Am Rec G 30:1032 Jl '64

Flute music

Time has issued a remarkable flute record. A. Cohn. Am Rec G 30:46-8 S '63

Folk music

Badmen; fable bows to fact. O. B. Brummell. il Hi Fi 13:127-8 O '63
Basic library of U.S. folk music; with discography. I. Silber. il Library J 88:1835-8 My 1 '63
Folk (cont) H. Yurchenco. Mus Am 83:131+ Ja; 41 F; 25 Mr; 45 My; 34 O; 49 N; 281 D '63; 84:63 Ja; 52 F; 54 Mr; 56-7 My; 53-4 Jl; 56-7 S; 26+ O; 50-1 N; 270 D '64
Folk music. H. Yurchenco. See issues of American record guide
Folk music. O. B. Brummell. il Hi Fi 14:103-5 Mr; 89 My; 79-80 Jl; 123 S; 131 N '64; 15:97-8+ Ja '65
Folk music around the world a basic library collection; with discography. H. Yurchenco. il Library J 88:1838-40 My 1 '63
Folk music in the library. J. Cushman. il Library J 88:1833-4 My 1 '63
I'm a yard man; recordings of G. Cannon. Time 81:46+ Ap 5 '63
Jazz and folk recordings. N. Hentoff. Atlan 213:138+ Ap '64
Mark Twain, obscenity, folk songs. R. De Toledano. Nat R 15:160-1 Ag 27 '63
New faces in folk music. L. Cohn. il Sat R 46:56-7 N 16 '63
Newport folk festival 1963: the recordings. L. Cohn. il Sat R 48:70-1 Ja 16 '65
On and off the avenue. New Yorker 39:190 N 30 '63
Recordings reports: folk and blues LP's (cont) L. Cohn. Sat R 46:44 F 9; 50 Je 29; 42 Ag 31 '63; 47:58 Mr 28; 81 O 17 '64
Recordings reports: folk music (cont) R. Sherman. Sat R 46:68 Ap 27; 56 D 28 '63; 47:60 N 28 '64
Sad day in Texas and other folk matter. L. Cohn. il Sat R 47:66-7 N 14 '64
Third Newport folk festival. il Am Rec G 30:1072-3 Jl '64
Young folks. N. Hentoff. Reporter 31:58-9 Ag 13 '64

Gospel songs

See Phonograph records—Negro songs

Guitar music

On RCA Victor, Britten (and others) by Bream: deeply satisfying. J. Diether. il Am Rec G 31:216-18 N '64
This record is important: the innate musicality of Sandy Bull. W. Rhodes. Am Rec G 29:899 Jl '63

Harpsichord music

Finally, all twelve of Bach's keyboard concerti. J. W. Barker. Am Rec G 29:534 Mr '63

PHONOGRAPH records—Harpsichord music—*Continued*

French Baroque music for harpsichord; Igor Kipnis. J. W. Barker. Am Rec G 31:360 D '64
Introducing Igor Kipnis. J. W. Barker. il Am Rec G 30:709 Ap '64
Keyboard miscellany. R. Sabin. Am Rec G 29: 566-9 Mr '63
Recordings. M. Mayer. Esquire 61:38+ Je '64

Hindu music

Music of India. M. Pitt. il Am Rec G 30:802-5 My '64

History

Music makers. R. Gelatt. Hi Fi 13:69 Ap '63

Horn music

See also
Phonograph records—Concertos

Icelandic music

Feast of fascinations by Henry Cowell. A. Cohn. il Am Rec G 30:481 F '64

Incidental music

Milhaud's view of Sophocles; and Bernstein's view of Milhaud; Les Choéphores. J. Diether. il Am Rec G 30:232-4 N '63

Indian music (East Indian)

Music of India; ten records of Indian music just released by Odeon. H. Yurchenco. Mus Am 84:26+ O '64

Indian music (Mexican)

Artistic ferment of Mexico today. O. B. Brummell. Hi Fi 15:69-70 F '65

Instrumental music

Exciting and impressive on Everest. Gunter Wand. H. Glass. il Am Rec G 30:510-11 F '64
Julian Bream consort in an evening of Elizabethan music. J. W. Barker. il Am Rec G 30:26-9 S '63

Irish music

Sounds of Ireland. Holiday 33:189 Ap '63

Japanese music

Imperial court music of Japan; gagaku. W. L. Purcell. il Am Rec G 31:118-19 O '64

Jazz music

Amen corner. W. Hobson. See issues of Saturday review to May 16, 1964
Anthology of anthologies. M. Williams. Sat R 47:54 D 26 '64
Armstrong before Dolly. M. Williams. Sat R 47:77+ O 17 '64
Basic LP jazz library. M. Williams. Am Rec G 30:890-1 My '64
Bigger Monk and bigger Duke. M. Williams. il Sat R 47:63-4 My 16 '64
Billie Holiday: triumphant decline. M. Williams. Sat R 47:68+ O 31 '64
Bossa from both sides of the border. M. Williams. Sat R 46:57 F 23 '63
Check list. W. Balliett. New Yorker 40: 148-50+ N 7 '64
Chicago, Chicago. S. Dance. il Sat R 47:45 Jl 25 '64
Clare Fischer: the Pan-American way. R. F. Thompson. Sat R 47:46-7 N 28 '64
Coltrane triumphant. M. Williams. Sat R 48:73-4 Ja 16 '65
Critic as composer; group of compositions by A. Hodeir. M. Williams. Sat R 47:59 Mr 28 '64
Critics' choice indeed. M. Williams. Sat R 47: 64 Je 27 '64
Duke. R. De Toledano. Nat R 16:658-9+ Jl 28 '64
Ella and others. M. Williams. Sat R 47:51 N 28 '64
Ellington era; with discography. M. Williams. il Sat R 46:59-60 N 16 '63
For Bach, a bacchanal in swing. J. S. Wilson. Hi Fi 14:67-8 Ja '64
Harlem sounds. N. Hento. Reporter 31:41-2 D 3 '64
Harlem yesterdays. S. Dance. Sat R 47:74-5 S 26 '64
How to start a jazz collection. C. Brown. il Redbook 121:28 S '63
In the wake of Parker; Sonny Stitt. M. Williams. Sat R 46:71 My 11 '63
Jazz. J. S. Wilson. See issues of High fidelity
Jazz (cont) M. W. Stearns. Mus Am 83:134 Ja; 41-2 F; 25-6 Mr; 45 My; 34 O; 49 N; 281-2 D '63; 84:53-4 F; 55 Mr; 63 Ap; 57 My; 54 Jl; 57 S; 46-7 O; 270 D '64
Jazz notes. E. Larrabee. See issues of Harper's magazine
Jazz recordings. N. Hentoff. Atlan 211:137 Ap; 212:138+ N '63; 213:138 Ap '64
Jazz records. W. Balliett. See occasional issues of New Yorker
Jazz; with discography. R. Wedgeworth. il Library J 88:1830-2 My 1 '63
Krupa collected. M. Williams. il Sat R 47: 70 Ja 11 '64
L.P. recordings of Miles Davis. Holiday 33: 109 F '63
Month's jazz. M. Williams and others. See issues of American record guide
Mostly modernists. M. Williams. Sat R 46: 56 Je 15; 78 S 28; 32 D 14 '63; 47:54 F 15; 66-7 Ap 25; 72-3 S 26 '64
Night they killed the bossa nova. G. Holder. il Sat R 46:77-9+ O 12 '63
Players and popularizers. M. Williams. il Sat R 47:45 Ag 22 '64
Recordings reports: jazz LPs. S. Dance. See issues of Saturday review
Rewarding workouts by Monk and Mingus. C. Welles. Life 56:15 Ap 10 '64
Sad story of Mildred Bailey. R. De Toledano. Nat R 14:204-6 Mr 12 '63
Some real bossa nova, better late than never; Getz/Gilberto. C. Welles. Life 56:10 My 29 '64
Tenacious craft of Horace Silver. M. Williams. Sat R 46:52-3 S 14 '63

Jewish music

Gentile influence in Jewish music. M. Serbin. il Am Rec G 30:770-2+ My '64

Language teaching records

How to learn French in twenty-four easy lessons; microgroove language courses. C. L. Osborne. il Hi Fi 13:38-41+ My '63
Speak to me, comrade. Holiday 34:158-9 O '63

Lute music

On RCA Victor, Britten (and others) by Bream: deeply satisfying. J. Diether. il Am Rec G 31:216-18 N '64

Madrigals

Monteverdi release of the first magnitude. J. W. Barker. Am Rec G 31:415 Ja '65

Mass

DGG's Paukenmesse, the perfect compromise. H. Glass. il Am Rec G 30:1036 Jl '64
Flawless performance of a Haydn masterpiece; Missa Solemnis. H. Glass. Am Rec G 29:873 Jl '63
Gloria in excelsis Deo: the Haydn Masses; with discography. H. C. R. Landon. Hi Fi 14:105-6 D '64
Liturgy and opera alive; Demonstration English mass, by D. Fitzpatrick. C. J. McNaspy. America 109:143-4 Ag 10 '63
Maria Stader's latest: do not miss this record! H. Glass. Am Rec G 29:463 F '63
Music: sublime and exciting new releases. C. J. McNaspy. America 108:273 F 23 '63
New strains in worship music. C. J. McNaspy. America 110:682+ My 16 '64
On DGG and London, the genius of William Byrd. J. W. Barker. Am Rec G 31:228-9 N '64
On records; B minor mass. Opera N 28:35 F 15 '64
On records; Mass in time of war. Opera N 29:34 Ja 2 '65
On records; Mass no. 3. C. J. Luten. Opera N 28:34 O 19 '63
On records; Requiem mass. Opera N 29:34 Ja 23 '65

Medieval music

From Capitol, the notable EMI series: Musik in alten städten und residenzen; with discography. J. W. Barker. il Am Rec G 30:202-6+ N '63
From Decca, the Play of Herod. J. W. Barker. il Am Rec G 31:18-19+ S '64
From Odeon, more Musik in alten städten und residenzen. J. W. Barker. Am Rec G 31:214-15 N '64
Herod of Fleury. M. Bernheimer. Sat R 47: 59 D 12 '64
Isaac and friends. J. W. Barker. il Am Rec G 31:110-12 O '64
Spanish medieval music. J. W. Barker. il Am Rec G 29:776-7 Je '63

Moving picture music

Recordings reports: stage and screen. R. Sherman. Sat R 46:76 S 28 '63
Shakespeare film scores. J. Diether. il Am Rec G 30:881-3 My '64

PHONOGRAPH records—*Continued*

Musical comedies, revues, etc.

An entirely new musical. H. Kupferberg. il Atlan 215:119-20 Ja '65
My fair lady revisited. J. S. Wilson. Hi Fi 14:112 D '64
New musicals. A. Falleder. Sat R 48:61-2 Ja 30 '65
Recordings reports: stage and screen. R. Sherman. Sat R 46:76 S 28; 58 N 30 '63; 47:56 Ja 25; 44 Jl 11; 72 N 14 '64
Theatre on discs. J. S. Wilson. See issues of Theatre arts
Wonderful musicals. R. De Toledano. Nat R 16:920-2 O 20 '64

Negro music

Brook Benton. il Ebony 18:44-6+ My '63
Recordings reports: folk and blues LP's (cont) L. Cohn. Sat R 46:44 F 9; 50 Je 29; 42 Ag 31 '63; 47:58 Mr 28; 81 O 17 '64

Negro songs

Gospel at the box office. M. Williams. Sat R 46:41 Ag 31 '63
True gospel singing. C. Brown. Redbook 121:15 Je '63

Operas

Alkas' Katerina. V. Seroff. Sat R 47:64 Mr 28 '64
... And a Samson from Saint-Saëns. C. L. Osborne. Hi Fi 14:66-7 Ja '64
Angel's Boris Godunov. G. Kossodo. il Am Rec G 29:692-3+ My '63
Another for Straussians: the Richmond Salome. G. Kossodo. Am Rec G 30:191 N '63
Arabella. R. Sabin. il Am Rec G 30:1084-7 Ag '64
Ariadne auf Naxos; as Strauss heard it just before the bombs fell. C. L. Osborne. Hi Fi 13:72-3 Ag '63
Ariadne auf Naxos; June 11, 1944, Vienna festival performance. R. Sabin. il Am Rec G 30:188-91 N '63
Bartered bride; Angel's German recording. il Am Rec G 30:662-3 Ap '64
Bartok's Bluebeard. I. Kolodin. il Sat R 46:61 Ap 27 '63
Béatrice & Bénédict. J. W. Barker. il Am Rec G 29:696-8 My '63
Beatrice et Benedict. R. Lawrence. Sat R 46:70 Ap 27 '63
Bel canto revival. Discus. Harper 228:124-5 My '64
Berlioz first Cléopâtre. P. L. Miller. Am Rec G 29:792 Je '63
Berlioz's Béatrice et Bénédict, now the music is recorded in full. C. L. Osborne. il Hi Fi 13:59-60 Je '63
Best grand-opera Carmen on records; conductor Von Karajan with L. Price. C. L. Osborne. il Hi Fi 14:63-4 S '64
Boris from Moscow; first non-Russian to sing the role of Boris Godunov at the Bolshoi. H. Weinstock. Sat R 47:61+ S 26 '64
Callas Carmen. P. L. Miller. il Am Rec G 31:403 Ja '65
Callas's Carmen. il Newsweek 65:73 F 1 '65
La Cenerentola. H. Glass. il Am Rec G 31:196-8 N '64
Changing of the guard; Gilbert and Sullivan on records. M. Bernheimer. Sat R 47:51 D 26 '64
Collector's Verdi. C. L. Osborne. Hi Fi 13:37-8+ O; 90+ D '63
Columbia's Boris; G. London in title role at the Bolshoi, Moscow. P. L. Miller. il Am Rec G 31:20-1+ S '64
Columbia's 1903 grand opera series. A. Favia-Artsay. il Hobbies 68:30-1 O '63
Columbia's 1903 grand opera series; first recordings of opera in America. F. M. Kleeberg. il Am Rec G 29:772-5 Je '63
Così comes again, with wonderful things. N. Broder. il Hi Fi 13:55-6 My '63
Così fan tutte. P. L. Miller. Am Rec G 29:694 My '63
Cultured Così from Ringstrasse. M. Bernheimer. Sat R 46:45 Je 29 '63
Daphne. R. Sabin. Am Rec G 30:658-9 Ap '64
Dargomyzhsky: first recordings of two operas; Russalka and Stone guest. P. L. Miller. Am Rec G 30:838+ My '64
Delibes highlights from Lakmé. M. de Schauensee. il Am Rec G 30:1099 Ag '64
Don Giovanni from Aix. M. Bernheimer. Sat R 47:62 Ja 25 '64
Double Dargomyzhsky. V. Seroff. il Sat R 47:50+ F 29 '64
Echoes of the golden age. J. Ardoin. il Mus Am 83:14-15+ N '63
Erwartung by Pilarczyk. I. Kolodin. Sat R 46:55 F 23 '63
Excerpts from Die Meistersinger, Schorr's Hans Sachs. C. L. Osborne. Hi Fi 14:63-4 Je '64
Fall opera recordings. R. Lawrence; I. Kolodin; M. Bernheimer. il Sat R 46:50-1+ N 30 '63
Falstaff from Victor and London. J. Ardoin. il Mus Am 84:60 Ap '64
Fidelo. G. L. Mayer. Am Rec G 31:192-3 N '64
Fidelio pitched for excitement; with B. Nilsson and J. McCracken. C. L. Osborne. il Hi Fi 14:123-4 O '64
First opera in dynagroove: Madama Butterfly. P. L. Miller. il Am Rec G 29:684-5 My '63
First recording of Siegfried. I. Kolodin. il Sat R 46:31-2 Ag 31 '63
First recording of Tchaikovsky's Iolantha. P. L. Miller. Am Rec G 30:972 Je '64
First stereo recording of Samson et Dalila. M. de Schauensee. Am Rec G 30:497+ F '64
Die fiedermaus. H. Glass. il Am Rec G 31:208-10 N '64
For the first time on records, Siegfried in its entirety. C. L. Osborne. il Hi Fi 13:71-2 Ap '63
Four saints; humanity is the key word. A. Rich. il Hi Fi 15:70-1 F '65
Die frau from Munich. M. Bernheimer. il Sat R 47:65 S 26 '64
Die frau ohne schatten. G. L. Mayer. il Am Rec G 31:96-101 O '64
Friedrich Schorr's Hans Sachs. P. L. Miller. Am Rec G 30:976 Je '64
From Angel, a remarkably successful new recording of La Bohème. P. L. Miller. il Am Rec G 30:1020-1 Jl '64
From ultraphone, Rimsky-Korsakov's last opera; Golden cockerel. Am Rec G 31:452-4 Ja '65
G. F. Handel's Rodelinda. J. Maclain. il Am Rec G 31:404-7 Ja '65
Glitter from the golden age of Wagner singing; Die walküre. G. Kossodo. Am Rec G 29:426-7 F '63
Guglielmo restored; Così fan tutte highlights. M. Bernheimer. Sat R 47:67 My 30 '64
Handel's Rodelinda. H. Weinstock. Sat R 47:46 D 26 '64
Handel's Rodelinda, Giulio Cesare, and some arias too. C. L. Osborne. il Hi Fi 14:90-2+ N '64
Hansel and Gretel. H. Glass. il Am Rec G 31:408-9 Ja '65
Henze's Elegy for young lovers. P. Davis. il Mus Am 84:45 N '64
Hérodiade; excerpts. G. L. Mayer. Am Rec G 30:669 Ap '64
Hour of Henze; excerpts from Elegy for young lovers. I. Kolodin. il Sat R 47:63 S 26 '64
Immoral? from Vox, Monteverdi's L'incoronazione di Poppea. J. Diether. il Am Rec G 29:700-4+ My '63
L'incoronazione di Poppea: abridged Glyndebourne production. J. Diether. il Am Rec G 31:410-15 Ja '65
Jess Thomas as Angel's Lohengrin. G. L. Mayer. Am Rec G 30:494-6+ F '64
Joan Sutherland in La sonnambula. P. L. Miller. il Am Rec G 29:596-8 Ap '63
Kempe's flavorsome Smetana; Bartered bride. I. Kolodin. il Sat R 47:53 Mr 28 '64
Latest on the low-price record racks; with discography. il Changing T 17:15-16 Mr '63
Leontyne Price as Carmen. P. L. Miller. il Am Rec G 31:10-12 S '64
Leontyne Price as Tosca. P. L. Miller. il Am Rec G 30:92-4 O '63
London's near perfect Siegfried. G. L. Mayer. il Am Rec G 29:686-9 My '63
Lost inquiry. C. G. Burke. il Hi Fi 13:54-6+ F '63
Madama Butterfly, a new sound from Rome. C. L. Osborne. il Hi Fi 13:69-70 Mr '63
Die Meistersinger; Eurodisc recording. H. Glass. il Am Rec G 31:26-8+ S '64
Melchior's Siegfried, the greatest then and the greatest still. G. Kossodo. il Am Rec G 30:108-10 O '63
Merry wives of Windsor. P. L. Miller. Am Rec G 30:941 Je 30 '64
Most mellifluous Così. I. Kolodin. Sat R 46:71 S 28 '63
Moussorgsky's Boris, Berlioz' Beatrice. R. De Toledano. Nat R 15:317-18 O 8 '63
Music in the round; day and nightful of opera. Discus. Harper 226:117-18+ My '63
Music in the round; Siegfried, Beatrice and Benedict, Bluebeard. Discus. Harper 227:100-1 Ag '63

PHONOGRAPH records—Operas—*Continued*
New Boris by Christoff. B. Schwarz. Sat R 46:68-9 My 11 '63
New Marina in stereo. J. Maclain. il Am Rec G 30:572-3 Mr '64
New Oedipus Rex brings more of Stravinsky's Stravinsky. E. Salzman. Hi Fi 13:126-7 O '63
New sound for The rake's progress. I. Kolodin. Sat R 48:53 Ja 30 '65
New voices in famous roles. Discus. Harper 229:148+ D '64
Non-Scala Scala di seta. H. Weinstock. Sat R 46:65-6 Mr 30 '63
Notes from abroad; stereo recording of Lohengrin. K. Blaukopf. Hi Fi 13:18 Jl '63
Of operas (rare) and wallets (open) Hi Fi 14:59 N '64
On DGG, Henze's Elegy for young lovers. G. L. Mayer. il Am Rec G 31:200-1+ N '64
On DGG's Trovatore, and especially Bergonzi. P. L. Miller. Am Rec G 30:147-8 O '63
On London, Theresa Berganza as l'Italiana in Algeri. P. L. Miller. il Am Rec G 30:1012-13+ Jl '64
On records. See issues of Opera news
On the excerpting of operas. Hi Fi 13:43 D '63
Opera by default. B. H. Haggin. New Repub 151:30+ O 3 '64
Opera comes into its own, Bluebeard's castle twice more on discs. E. Salzman. Hi Fi 13:60-1 Je '63
Opera for Christmas; Tchaikovsky's Cherevichki. V. Seroff. Sat R 47:57 D 12 '64
Opera from the stage, a declaration and a plea. Hi Fi 14:41 Mr '64
Ormandy's Don Quixote, romantic intensity and satirical thrust. J. Diether. il Am Rec G 30:1088-9 Ag '64
Phyllis Curtin in Wozzeck excerpts. J. Diether. Am Rec G 31:120-2+ O '64
Poppea semi-vitalized. M. Bernheimer. Sat R 46:61-2 F 23 '63
Portrait of Manon; Massenet and Puccini. M. de Schauensee. Am Rec G 30:1100-1 Ag '64
Posthumous Tchaikovsky. V. Seroff. Sat R 47:48 Jl 25 '64
Price-Corelli-Karajan Carmen. I. Kolodin. il Sat R 47:43 Ag 22 '64
Project Boris. R. Gelatt. il Hi Fi 13:51-6+ Ap '63
Purcell's Dido and Aeneas freshly achieved. C. L. Osborne. il Hi Fi 13:71 F '63
Question of majesty; recordings of I Puritani. W. Cecil. Sat R 47:56-7+ Ap 25 '64
RCA Victor Porgy and Bess. R. Ellsworth. il Am Rec G 30:196-8 N '63
RCA Victor's Falstaff. P. L. Miller. il Am Rec G 30:564-5+ Mr '64
Rake's progress, an opera that insists upon analysis. C. L. Osborne. Hi Fi 15:69-70+ Ja '65
Real Ariadne? M. Bernheimer. Sat R 46:37 Ag 31 '63
Records. B. Boretz. Nation 199:127-8 S 14 '64
Records; Wagner's late works. B. Boretz. Nation 198:37-9 Ja 6 '64
Regina Resnik's Carmen. G. L. Mayer. il Am Rec G 30:382-3+ Ja '64
Rigolettos nos. 14 and 15. M. Bernheimer. Sat R 47:67 O 31 '64
Rubinstein's Demon. H. Weinstock. Sat R 47:69 O 31 '64
Simultaneously, from Mercury and Columbia, Bluebeard's castle. C. J. Luten. il Am Rec G 29:690-1 My '63
Some new opera recordings. H. Kupferberg. il Atlan 213:130+ F '64
Stars of the Polish opera 1900-1939. A. Favia-Artsay. il Hobbies 68:30-1 N '63
Strauss then and now. M. Bernheimer. Sat R 47:65 Je 27 '64
Strauss's Arabella as sung on the Munich stage. P. J. Smith. il Hi Fi 14:68-9 Ag '64
Sutherland in I Puritani. P. L. Miller. il Am Rec G 30:656-7+ Ap '64
Take advantage of the Gilbert and Sullivan recording boom. E. Kinard. House B 105:30+ Mr '63
Tebaldi and others at bargain prices. H. Glass. Am Rec G 29:466 F '63
Television Tiefland; recorded soundtrack. M. Bernheimer. Sat R 47:41 Ag 22 '64
That other La Bohème. J. Maclain. il Am Rec G 30:928-9+ Je '64
La Traviata. P. L. Miller. Am Rec G 30:95 O '63
Trial and Utopia. M. Bernheimer. Sat R 47:41 Jl 25 '64
Il trittico; three one act operas. P. L. Miller. il Am Rec G 29:420-1+ F '63
Two by Lortzing; recorded excerpts. I. Kolodin. Sat R 47:51 Ag 22 '64
Two from Italian television via RCA Victor: La serva padrona, and La scala di seta. P. L. Miller. Am Rec G 29:706-7 My '63
Two great comic operas. Discus. Harper 228:124-6 Je '64
Two new Sir Johns help make a Falstaff year. C. L. Osborne. il Hi Fi 14:65-6 Mr '64
Two operas; Mozart's Cosi fan tutte and Puccini's Madama Butterfly. R. Gelatt. Reporter 28:47-8 Je 6 '63
Two Rigolettos, with a surprise from Fischer-Dieskau; Deutsche grammophons and RCA Victor. C. L. Osborne. il Hi Fi 14:75-7 D '64
Verdi-Shakespeare discography. M. de Schauensee. il Mus Am 84:14-15+ Ja '64
Victoria de los Angeles on three new recordings from Angel: Barber of Seville, Cavalleria rusticana, and Mélodies de France. il Am Rec G 30:184-7 N '63
Vocal slaves or supremacists. Discus. Harper 227:128-9 D '63
Vox reissues its justly famous Orphée. M. de Schauensee. Am Rec G 29:872 Jl '63
Wagner in stereo. H. Kupferberg. il Atlan 212:112+ S '63
What not to do as the Romans do; RCA Victor's Falstaff. I. Kolodin. Sat R 46:31 Jl 27 '63
Why not give an opera in the garden? L. Wilcox. il House B 105:112-13+ Je '63
Wolfgang Amadeus Mozart: Cosi fan tutte. H. Glass. il Am Rec G 30:290-1+ D '63
Year of the four Falstaffs. I. Kolodin. Sat R 47:51 Mr 28 '64

Oratorios

Beethoven's Christus am Oelberg. H. Glass. Am Rec G 29:860-2 Jl '63
Handel down to size; Israel in Egypt. M. Bernheimer. Sat R 47:57 Ap 25 '64
Maurice Abravanel conducts the first recording of Handel's oratorio: Samson. J. W. Barker. il Am Rec G 30:396-9 Ja '64
On records; Christus am Oelberg. Opera N 28:35 F 15 '64
On records; Crucifixion. Opera N 28:35 D 28 '63
On records: Le vin herbé. C. J. Luten. Opera N 27:35 F 23 '63
On records; Samson. Opera N 29:35 D 26 '64
Samson from Handel. E. Salzman. il Hi Fi 14:65-6 Ja '64
Saul J. W. Barker. il Am Rec G 29:844-6+ Jl '63
Vintage Handel from Woldike: Saul. M. Bernheimer. Sat R 46:49 Je 29 '63

Orchestral music

Berger, Layton, Imbrie. B. Boretz. Nation 199:446-7 D 7 '64
Bruno Walter: two views. J. Ardoin; R. Lewenthal. Mus Am 84:48-9 Mr '64
Far east of Boston; A. Hovhaness's works, recorded by Poseidon society. O. Daniel. Sat R 46:124 O 12 '63
Fresh course for Boston. R. C. Marsh. il Hi Fi 13:72-3 Mr '63
Handel's Water music, newly, and handsomely, afloat. A. Rich. il Hi Fi 14:67-8 Ag '64
In Debussy, a special valedictory; Images conducted by Monteux. H. Goldsmith. Hi Fi 14:77-8 D '64
In memoriam: Wilhelm Furtwängler. C. J. Luten. il Am Rec G 31:14-17 S '64
Klemperer in ¾ time. R. Freed. Sat R 46:46 F 9 '63
LP overview of Debussy's seascape; La Mer. A. Chipman. il Am Rec G 30:390-3 Ja '64
Moderns from Louisville. O. Daniel. Sat R 46:77+ S 28 '63
Mozart; five different views, and all faithful. N. Broder. Hi Fi 14:69-70 Ap '64
New Artia debuts with a very valuable pair of records. J. W. Barker. il Am Rec G 30:126-8 O '63
1947-48 Copland, and Previn's conducting debut. J. Diether. il Am Rec G 30:1096-8 Ag '64
Recordings reports: orchestral LPs. I. Kolodin. See last issue of each month of Saturday review

Organ music

Art and the Offering. M. Bernheimer. Sat R 47:58 F 29 '64
Cheerful ghost of Eisenstadt; recording Haydn in Austria. J. T. McClure. il Hi Fi 15:56-8+ Ja '65
More in Aeolian-Skinner's King of instruments series. R. Kammerer. Am Rec G 30:816-17 My '64
Virgil Fox plays the Philharmonic Hall organ at Lincoln Center. R. Kammerer. Am Rec G 29:958-9 Ag '63

PHONOGRAPH records—*Continued*

Oriental music

Sense of subdued ecstasy, the music of Afghanistan and Iran. W. K. Archer. il Am Rec G 30:790-7+ My '64

Overtures

Happy news on a tenth anniversary; Brahms Tragic overture played by A. Toscanini. Hi Fi 14:41 Ap '64
On records; overtures. C. J. Luten. Opera N 29:28 S 26 '64
Toscanini conducts overtures. C. J. Luten. il Am Rec G 30:660-1 Ap '64

Passion music

For the first time, Bach's St Luke Passion. P. L. Miller. Am Rec G 29:438 F '63
Lovely bits, but not by Bach; St Luke Passion. N. Broder. il Hi Fi 13:72 F '63
On records; St John Passion. Opera N 29:27 O 17 '64
On records; St Matthew passion. Opera N 28:30 My 2 '64
Passion of Our Lord according to St Matthew. J. W. Barker. il Am Rec G 30:280-3 D '63
St John according to Richter. M. Bernheimer. Sat R 48:51 Ja 30 '65
St John Passion. H. Glass. il Am Rec G 31:418-19 Ja '65
Two new recordings of the St John Passion. P. L. Miller. il Am Rec G 30:930-3 Je '64

Periodicals

See also
American record guide (periodical)

Piano music

Again, Kempff, with Brahms, the secret is understatement. R. Sabin. Am Rec G 31:134 O '64
Anthology of pianism from a more poetic age. H. Goldsmith. Hi Fi 14:66-7 F '64
Art of Francis Poulenc. A. Cohn. Am Rec G 30:622-3 Mr '64
Artur Schnabel, a legend reëmergent; Beethoven recordings. P. Hart. Hi Fi 13:65-8+ N '63
Bach by Gould: incomparably the most fascinating. R. Sabin. Am Rec G 31:211-12 N '64
Beethoven and Brahms with a master's stamp; W. Kempff. H. Goldsmith. Hi Fi 14:124-6 O '64
Brahms by Fleisher and the Juilliard quartet. R. Sabin. Am Rec G 30:219 N '63
Emil von Sauer's Liszt: something to marvel at. R. Kammerer. il Am Rec G 30:296-7 D '63
Feast of fascinations by Henry Cowell. A. Cohn. il Am Rec G 30:480-1 F '64
For Schubert, dissimilar excellences; Wanderer fantasy. H. Goldsmith. il Hi Fi 14:70-1 Ap '64
For Schumann, a sonic replacement; for Rubinstein, artistic vindication. H. Goldsmith. Hi Fi 13:71-2 Ag '63
From Leschetizky to Gabrilowitsch; twenty pianists on piano rolls. H. C. Schonberg. il Hi Fi 14:67-8 Mr '64
From the legacy of Clara Haskil, Chopin and Falla. H. Goldsmith. Hi Fi 13:77-8 N '63
From Vox, volume II of Brendel's Beethoven; eight sonatas. R. Jones. Am Rec G 30:41 S '63
Gina Bachauer: an orchestra of one. R. Jones. Am Rec G 30:432 Ja '64
Glenn Gould: a poet and a seeker. R. Sabin. il Am Rec G 30:292-3 D '63
High-voltage Mr Watts. R. Kammerer. il Am Rec G 29:718 My '63
Horowitz collection. R. Kammerer. Am Rec G 30:14-16 S '63
Ivan Moravec: a master pianist at 45 r.p.m. R. Kammerer. il Am Rec G 29:620-1 Ap '63
Kempff on Beethoven, magnificently refurbished. J. Lyons. Am Rec G 31:130 O '64
Legendary masters of the piano. R. Kammerer. Am Rec G 30:810-12 My '64
Liszt by Curzon, one of his finest discs. R. Kammerer. Am Rec G 30:1038 Jl '64
More imports: via Odeon, the legendary Michelangeli. R. Kammerer. Am Rec G 30:111 O '63
New revelations of the Choral Fantasia. H. Goldsmith. il Hi Fi 14:67-8 S '64
Novaes plays Liszt. R. Kammerer. Am Rec G 29:942 Ag '63
On two recital discs, debut of a new Czech pianist. H. Goldsmith. Hi Fi 13:74-5 Ap '63
Pianists by the pair. Am Rec G 30:814-15 My '64
Piano that sings. H. Kupferberg. il Atlan 213:128+ My '64
Schnabel & Beethoven. J. S. Harrison. il Mus Am 83:274+ D '63
Thirty-two by Kempff. J. S. Harrison. Sat R 47:70-1 N 14 '64
Two Wanderers, one of them colossal. R. Kammerer. Am Rec G 30:682 Ap '64
Unhomogenized Smetana. J. Holcman. Sat R 46:63 Mr 30 '63
Unique George Copeland. R. Kammerer. il Am Rec G 30:812-13 My '64

Poetry

See Phonograph records—Spoken records

Portuguese music

Sound of saudade: Portugal's melancholy fado; with discography. O. B. Brummell. il Hi Fi 14:106-10 O '64

Preservation and storage

Fidelity begins in the groove. I. Berger. il Sat R 46:57 N 30 '63
High fidelity (title varies) C. L. Osborne. Opera N 27:37 Mr 16 '63
On the tender care of records. G. Dale. Mus Am 84:60 Ja '64
Proper care for phonograph records. Good H 156:147 Mr '63

Prices

Cut-rate classics. il Time 84:61 Jl 17 '64
High quality classics at half price; paperback classics and victrola records. P. Hart. Hi Fi 13:96 S '63
Latest on the low-price record racks; classical music. il Changing T 17:33-4 Ag '63
New on the low-price record racks: twentieth-century music. il Changing T 18:22-3 D '64
New on the low-price record racks; with discography. il Changing T 17:31-3 D '63
Notes from our correspondents: British record industry. E. Greenfield. Hi Fi 15:30+ F '65

Recorder music

From Columbia, Vanguard, and Angel: sweet pipes, dulcet pipes, and glad sounds; three recorded programs. J. W. Barker. il Am Rec G 30:106-7 O '63

Recording

Boadicea in Walthamstow; Sutherland recording Bellini's Norma; with editorial comment. R. Kotlowitz. il Hi Fi 15:41, 52-6 F '65
Cheerful ghost of Eisenstadt: recording Haydn in Austria. J. T. McClure. il Hi Fi 15:56-8+ Ja '65
Debut of dynagroove and some repercussions. R. D. Darrell. Hi Fi 13:37 My '63
Dumb sound; weird noises teen-agers call music. A. G. Aronowitz. il Sat Eve Post 236:88, 91-5 O 5 '63
Dynagroove in London. T. Heinitz. Sat R 46:69+ O 26 '63
Dynagroove story. J. F. Pfeiffer. il Am Rec G 29:602-6+ Ap '63
Education and a joy; B. Walter at work. J. T. McClure. il Hi Fi 14:40-3+ Ja '64
Hardy independent; Vanguard records. il J. Tebbel. Hi Fi 14:46-8 F '64
High fidelity newsfronts; direct recording process using transducer element. N. Eisenberg. il Hi Fi 14:37 S '64
Homage; recording session of Homage to Shakespeare with J. Gielgud, E. Evans and M. Leighton. New Yorker 40:35-7 My 9 '64
Madama Butterfly, a new sound from Rome. C. L. Osborne. il Hi Fi 13:69-70 Mr '63
Maria Callas; interview, ed. by E. Gelatt; with editorial comment. M. Callas. il Hi Fi 15:41, 42-7 F '65
Music makers. R. Gelatt. Hi Fi 13:67 Mr '63
Die Nilsson & la Nilsson; interview, ed. by W. Weaver; with editorial comment. B. Nilsson. il Hi Fi 15:41, 48-51+ F '65
Notes from abroad. C. Reid. Hi Fi 13:14+ O '63
Notes from abroad. W. Weaver. Hi Fi 13:10+ O '63
Notes from our correspondents. C. Reid. Hi Fi 14:22+ F '64
Notes from our correspondents. E. Greenfield. Hi Fi 15:30+ Ja '65
Notes from our correspondents. S. Fleming. Hi Fi 14:12+ Ap '64
Notes from our correspondents; recording Berlioz Requiem. S. Fleming. il Hi Fi 14:20+ Je '64
Project Boris. R. Gelatt. il Hi Fi 13:51-6+ Ap '63
Second look at dynagroove. R. D. Darrell. Hi Fi 13:92 Ag '63

PHONOGRAPH records—Recording—*Cont.*
Some matters of degree; basic facets of disc recording. I. Berger. Sat R 47:51 F 29 '64
Sonic showcase. R. D. Darrell. Hi Fi 14:90 Ja; 102 F; 95 Je; 101 Ag; 115 D '64; 15:107 F '65
Sour notes in the records; RCA Victor's dynagroove system. Bsns W p106 Mr 16 '63
Struggle for perfection: conductors' rehearsals on record. D. Stevens. il Hi Fi 14:80+ O '64
What not to do as the Romans do; RCA Victor's new studios. I. Kolodin. Sat R 46:31 Jl 27 '63

Religious records

Gospel according to Claudia; Claudia's letter. Time 81:52 Ap 12 '63
Happy science; lectures by Karl Barth. D. Peerman. Christian Cent 80:936 Jl 24 '63
On records; Maria Stader. C. J. Luten. Opera N 27:35 Ap 6 '63
Twelfth-century miracle marvelously rekindled; Play of Herod, introduced by New York pro musica. A. Rich. il Hi Fi 14:66 S '64

Requiems

Benjamin Britten's War requiem. B. H. Haggin. New Repub 149:28-9 Ag 17 '63
Benjamin Britten's War requiem. E. Salzman. il Hi Fi 13:51-2 Jl '63
Britten's War requiem. I. Kolodin. Sat R 46:45-6 My 25 '63
Britten's War requiem. T. Heinitz. Sat R 46:63 F 23 '63
From London, Britten's overpowering War requiem. J. Diether. il Am Rec G 29:916-19+ Ag '63
Notes from abroad; Britten's Requiem. C. Reid. Hi Fi 13:18+ Ap '63
On records; German Requiem. Opera N 28:35 Mr 7 '64
On records; War requiem. Opera N 28:34 D 7 '63
Presidential requiem mass. J. Lyons. il Am Rec G 30:560-1 Mr '64
Protestant requiem for a Roman Catholic President. J. W. Barker. il Am Rec G 30:598-9 Mr '64
Two views of Verdi. I. Kolodin. Sat R 47:49 N 28 '64
Verdi Requiem: two new versions, by E. Ormandy and C. M. Giulini. C. J. Luten. il Am Rec G 31:420-1 Ja '65

Sonatas

Again Biber from Cambridge, and now Vox too. J. W. Barker. Am Rec G 31:320+ D '64
Arthur Schnabel: the complete Beethoven piano sonatas. R. Kammerer. il Am Rec G 30:378-80+ Ja '64
Beethoven by Elly Ney. R. Kammerer. Am Rec G 30:680 Ap '64
Beethoven's cello sonatas in a partnership of peers; Richter and Rostropovich. R. C. Marsh. il Hi Fi 14:65 S '64
Celebration at seventy; Szigeti's Prokofiev; sonatas for violin and piano. A. Frankenstein. Hi Fi 13:56-7 My '63
Hall Overton, an important creative voice. A. Cohn. Am Rec G 30:59 S '63
Happy birthday, Herr Backhaus. R. Kammerer. Am Rec G 30:596 Mr '64
Heinrich Biber; fifteen Mystery sonatas for violin and continuo. J. W. Barker. Am Rec G 29:782-3 Je '63
Liszt by Horowitz, c. 1932; Sonata in B minor. R. Kammerer. Am Rec G 29:552+ Mr '63
Mis-tuned violin: Biber's fifteen sonatas for scordatura violin. B. Schwarz. Sat R 46:39 Ag 31 '63
Notes from our correspondents. R. Gelatt. Hi Fi 14:24+ F '64
Prokofievan revelations by Richter. C. J. Luten. Am Rec G 29:880 Jl '63
Scordatura; and the Mysteries of the rosary. E. Salzman. Hi Fi 13:73-4 Ap '63
Three by Copland from CRI. R. Kammerer. Am Rec G 30:43 S '63

Songs

And another Schwanengesang: Fischer-Dieskau. P. L. Miller. il Am Rec G 30:487 F '64
Another for Martinelli's golden anniversary. P. L. Miller. Am Rec G 30:199 N '63
Art of de los Angeles; symposium. il Am Rec G 29:738-41 My '63
Art of Elisabeth Schumann. G. Breuer. Am Rec G 29:780-1 Je '63
Art of Kirsten Flagstad. B. H. Haggin. New Repub 148:27 Mr 9 '63
Art song and song art. W. Cecil. il Sat R 46:47+ Je 29 '63
Beecham's Delius: love and understanding could do no more. R. Sabin. Am Rec G 31:136 O '64
Benjamin Britten's Sechs Hölderlin-fragmente. J. Diether. il Am Rec G 30:386-8 Ja '64
Best in American song: Ned Rorem. P. L. Miller. Am Rec G 30:864-5 My '64
Callas: two new lps. J. Ardoin. il Mus Am 84:22 O '64
Cole mine; eleven Porter songs that have been hitherto unrecorded. il Time 84:71 S 11 '64
Collector's series. Opera N 29:27 O 17 '64
Conchita Supervia, a souvenir. M de Schauensee. il Am Rec G 30:866 My '64
Confirmation and exploration: three Schubert song recitals by Prey and Souzay. H. Glass. il Am Rec G 30:482-3+ F '64
Decca's Monteverdi: nothing but praise is in order; Martial madrigals, and Amorous madrigals. J. W. Barker. Am Rec G 29:554-5 Mr '63
Documentation, mostly operatic, of Melchior's fifty years in music. P. L. Miller. Am Rec G 30:110 O '63
Evviva il Leon di Venezia! Giovanni Martinelli: golden anniversary. J. Maclain. Am Rec G 30:182-3+ N '63
Four recitals by Alfredo Kraus. Am Rec G 30:200-1 N '63
From Rococo, Strauss by Schlusnus, Lehmann, Destinn, Jeritza, Paulty, et al. P. L. Miller. Am Rec G 30:1090 Ag '64
Die goettliche Kurz and others. G. Breuer. Am Rec G 30:884-5 My '64
Handel's Rodelinda, Giulio Cesare, and some arias too. C. L. Osborne. il Hi Fi 14:90-2+ N '64
Happy birthday to a great lady of song; L. Lehmann's 75th birthday. G. Bowen. Am Rec G 29:424-5 F '63
Hermann Prey's first recital for London; superb. H. Glass. Am Rec G 29:950 Ag '63
Hotter's third and best Winterreise. H. Glass. Am Rec G 29:561-3 Mr '63
Important documentation of a great artist. P. L. Miller. Am Rec G 31:455 Ja '65
In memoriam 1895-1963; Kirsten Flagstad's farewell performance. P. L. Miller. Am Rec G 29:613 Ap '63
Joan Sutherland: Command performance. P. L. Miller Am Rec G 29:849 Jl '63
Label comes back: Griffes on EMS. P. L. Miller. Am Rec G 29:451 F '63
Lehmann's Müllerin. M. Bernheimer. Sat R 47:51 Jl 25 '64
Ludwig Senfl. J. W. Barker. il Am Rec G 30:666-7 Ap '64
Maria Callas in Paris; great arias from French opera. J. Maclain. Am Rec G 30:492-3 F '64
More taste than torment; Ernst Haefliger. M. Bernheimer. Sat R 46:57 My 25 '63
Mozart arias from a pair of Teresas; Teresa Stich-Randall and Teresa Berganza. C. L. Osborne. il Hi Fi 13:69-70 D '63
Multi-talented Ezio Flagello. M. de Schauensee. Am Rec G 29:870 Jl '63
Music of Shakespeare's time; and also Shakespeare music of more recent times. Am Rec G 30:1026-7 Jl '64
Music of the people. H. Kupferberg. il Atlan 214:182+ N '64
1903 grand opera series; arias and songs. C. J. Luten. Opera N 28:32 S 28 '63
Not one but three new versions of Pierrot Lunaire. J. Diether. Am Rec G 29:643-4+ Ap '63
Nuits d'été; completely dissimilar, Price and Crespin sing. J. Mcclain. Am Rec G 30:672-4 Ap '64
Nun's story. il Time 82:72 N 15 '63
On Angel, the latest from Maria Callas: two recitals, one of them recommended unreservedly. G. L. Mayer. Am Rec G 31:205 N '64
On Eurodisc, three for Straussians. P. L. Miller. Am Rec G 31:101-2 O '64
On records. Opera N 29:27 O 17 '64
On records; Alto rhapsody, Schicksalslied. Opera N 28:35 F 22 '64
On records; Antonio Cortis. Opera N 29:35 Ja 9 '65
On records; Birgit Nilsson. Opera N 29:35 N 14 '64
On records; Birgit Nilsson sings Verdi. J. W. Freeman. Opera N 27:35 F 2 '63
On records; La Bohème: highlights only. Opera N 28:37 Mr 14 '64
On records; Boris Christoff; Jon Vickers; Marian Anderson. Opera N 29:35 Ja 30 '65
On records; Callas; French arias. Opera N 28:34 D 21 '63
On records; Dimitri Smirnoff. J. W. Freeman. Opera N 27:32 My 4 '63

PHONOGRAPH records—Songs—*Continued*
On records; Eileen Farrell; Christa Ludwig. C. J. Luten. Opera N 27:35 F 23 '63
On records; Elena Gerhardt. Opera N 28:35 Ja 25 '64
On records; Enrico-Caruso. Opera N 28:35 Ap 4 '64
On records; Ernst Häfliger; Lotte Lehmann. C. J. Luten. Opera N 27:36 F 16 '63
On records; French song recitals. Opera N 28:36 Ja 4 '64
On records; Gedda sings French arias. Opera N 28:35 D 21 '63
On records; Geraldine Farrar. M. De Schauensee. Opera N 27:37 Mr 16 '63
On records; Hopkinson: eight songs; Burns: twelve songs. Opera N 28:35 F 8 '64
On records; Irmgard Seefried. Opera N 29:35 N 14 '64
On records; Jess Thomas. Opera N 28:32 Ap 11 '64
On records; Karin Branzell. Opera N 29:35 D 26 '64
On records; Liebeslieder. Opera N 28:35 F 22 '64
On records; Das lied von der erde. Opera N 28:35 Ap 4 '64
On records; Maria Callas. Opera N 29:33 Ja 16 '65
On records; Mario Ancona. Opera N 29:35 Ja 9 '65
On records; Netania Davrath; Giuseppe Di Stefano. Opera N 28:37 Mr 14 '64
On records; opera excerpts. Opera N 28:34-5 D 14 '63
On records; Peerce sings Handel arias. Opera N 28:35 D 21 '63
On records; Puccini arias. C. J. Luten. Opera N 27:35 Mr 2 '63
On records; Puccini & Verdi favorites. Opera N 29:33 Ja 16 '65
On records; recital discs: Joan Sutherland; Antonietta Stella; Franco Corelli. C. J. Luten. Opera N 28:35 D 7 '63
On records; recital records. Opera N 28:34-5 F 29 '64
On records; Schubert songs. C. J. Luten. Opera N 27:32 My 4 '63
On records; Sigrid Arnoldson; Jussi Bjoerling; Tiana Lemnitz; Mario Chamlee. Opera N 28:30 My 2 '64
On records; Six songs. Opera N 29:34 Ja 23 '65
On records; songs and arias. il Opera N 28:35 D 28 '63
On records; Teresa Berganza: Mozart arias; Spanish & Italian songs. Opera N 28:34 Ja 11 '64
On records; Teresa Stich-Randall. Opera N 28:35 Mr 28 '64
On records; Theodor Uppman; Ezio Flagello. J. W. Freeman. Opera N 27:35 F 9 '63
On records, three tenors: Beniamino Gigli; Enrico Caruso, Giovanni Martinelli. Opera N 28:35 Mr 7 '64
On records; La Traviata. J. W. Freeman. Opera N 27:37 Mr 16 '63
On records; two sopranos: Regine Crespin; Leontyne Price. Opera N 28:35 Mr 21 '64
On records; two tenors: Enrico Caruso and Beniamino Gigli. C. J. Luten. Opera N 27:35 Mr 23 '63
On records; Victoria de los Angeles. C. J. Luten. Opera N 27:36 Mr 9 '63
On records; Wagner excerpts. C. J. Luten. Opera N 27:35 Mr 30 '63
On records; Die winterreise; Schwanengesang. Opera N 28:35 F 1 '64
Patriot and a poet: Hopkinson and Burns songs. P. L. Miller. Am Rec G 29:632-3 Ap '63
Philippine songs. S. J. Cohen. il Sat R 47:61 Je 27 '64
Prey on Schubert. M. Bernheimer. Sat R 47:61 Mr 28 '64
Recital discs: Florence Easton. M. De Schauensee. Opera N 28:35 D 7 '63
Record and a book: Mikhail Ivanovich Glinka. J. W. Barker. il Am Rec G 30:298-9+ D '63
Recordings; Lieder singing, Gerard Souzay, some indispensable vocal releases. M. Mayer. Esquire 59:32+ Mr '63
Régine Crespin. G. L. Mayer. il Am Rec G 30:668-9 Ap '64
Russian songs and singers. W. Cecil. il Sat R 46:48-9 D 28 '63
Schorr as Sachs. I. Kolodin. Sat R 47:59 Ap 25 '64
Schubert's last songs. M. Bernheimer. Sat R 46:75 S 28 '63
Singing sister. il Newsweek 62:51 D 23 '63
Songs of life and love in ancient Nuremberg. D. Stevens. il Hi Fi 15:71 Ja '65
Spoofmaster. M. Zolotow. il Sat Eve Post 236:26-7 Ap 20 '63
Strauss then and now. M. Bernheimer. Sat R 47:65 Je 27 '64
Such music as ne'er was made by bird, harp, or maiden; Wunderhorn songs. J. Diether. il Am Rec G 30:582-4 Mr '64
Sutherland's Command performance. I. Kolodin. Sat R 46:51 My 25 '63
Treasured trash; Surfin bird record. Newsweek 63:77 F 10 '64
Two interpretations of the Duparc dozen. P. L. Miller. Am Rec G 30:840+ My '64
Unlikely corners. E. Jablonski. See issues of American record guide
Up among the Beatles; L. Armstrong's treatment of Hello, Dolly. Newsweek 63:103-4 Ap 27 '64
Up to standard. W. Cecil. Sat R 46:58-9+ Ap 27 '63
Verdi collaboration. R. Jones. il Am Rec G 30:376-7 Ja '64
Vocal miscellany, including reissues (cont) Am Rec G 29:473-4 F '63
Work of a very great artist; E. Gerhardt, mezzo-soprano. P. L. Miller. Am Rec G 31:107 O '64

Sounds

Sound advice; sound effects. H. A. Manoogian. Mod Phot 27:11+ Jl '63

Spanish music

From a great Spanish cancionero. R. de Toledano. Nat R 16:737-8 Ag 25 '64
Spanish medieval music. J. W. Barker. il Am Rec G 29:776-7 Je '63

Spoken records

Alec Guinness as Dylan. Am Rec G 30:1143-4 Ag '64
Authors, reading. J. Ciardi. Sat R 46:123 O 12 '63
Brush up your Shakespeare! recordings; with discography, comp. by F. Burnette. Wilson Lib Bul 38:655+ Ap '64
Burton Hamlet. J. Diether. il Am Rec G 30:1092-5 Ag '64
Churchill in his own voice. R. L. Tobin. Sat R 46:74 O 26 '63
Come, woo me; Shakespearean entertainment. J. Diether. Am Rec G 30:990-1 Je '64
Cornelia and the Loves of Charles; dramatic monologues. J. Ciardi. Sat R 46:35 Ap 13 '63
Do not go gentle into that good night. O. B. Brummell. il Hi Fi 14:65 Je '64
English literature on record. J. Ciardi. Sat R 46:39 Jl 13 '63
Enjoy the recorded riches of complete Shakespeare plays. E. Kinard. House B 106:38+ Mr '64
Especially for Christmas. S. Potter. Am Rec G 30:339-40+ D '63
Fine recordings commemorate 400th birthday of Shakespeare. R. Freas. il Am Home 67:15 Ap '64
First family. W. Tenn. il Am Rec G 29:428-9 F '63
For the quadricentennial; the tragedie of Hamlet, prince of Denmarke. J. Diether. il Am Rec G 30:778-81+ My '64
From Command. Sheridan's The school for scandal. J. W. Barker. il Am Rec G 29:422-3+ F '63
Hamlet by Burton and Scofield. J. Ciardi. il Sat R 47:56-7 Je 27 '64
Hamlet of brain and passion. G. Rogoff. Hi Fi 14:51-2 Jl '64
Happy science; lectures by Karl Barth. D. Peerman. Christian Cent 80:936 Jl 24 '63
Hollow crown that rounds the mortal temples; Hollow crown. J. Diether. Am Rec G 30:452-3 Ja '64
Homage; recording session of Homage to Shakespeare with J. Gielgud, E. Evans and M. Leighton. New Yorker 40:35-7 My 9 '64
Homages to Shakespeare delights, and a few dangers. G. Rogoff. Hi Fi 14:91 S '64
Intrigue your mind while your hands work. E. Kinard. il House B 105:54+ S '63
Jests and japes from the Nation's capital. il Hi Fi 13:81-2 Je '63
Kennedy memorial albums. C. Brown. Redbook 123:30 Jl '64
Life record review. Life 56:16 Je 5 '64
Mark Twain, obscenity, folk songs. R. De Toledano. Nat R 15:160-1 Ag 27 '63
Mind's ear; recorded textbooks. il Time 84:36 Ag 14 '64
Monument and magic; Bertrand Russell, Charles Laughton. J. Ciardi. il Sat R 46:72 My 11 '63
New talking records. il Changing T 17:21-2 O '63

PHONOGRAPH records—Spoken records—*Continued*

No chorus girls, but plenty of wit; Beyond the fringe. J. F. Indcox. il Hi Fi 13:101-2 F '63

Notes from abroad. W. Weaver. Hi Fi 13:28+ F '63

Olivier's Othello, coiling power and wounded majesty. G. Rogoff. Hi Fi 14:34+ D '64

On and off the avenue (cont) New Yorker 39:189-90 N 30 '63

On the record: Shakespeare, with discography. J. T. Muri. il Sr Schol 84:16T F 21 '64

Oswald case; Mark Lane's testimony to the Warren commission and letters from Russia. J. Diether. Am Rec G 30:1144-5 Ag '64

Othello: Olivier triumphant. J. Ciardi. Sat R 47:54 D 12 '64

Poets speak for themselves. G. Hicks. Sat R 47:35-6 D 5 '64

Politics on discs. J. Muri. Sr Schol 85:13T S 30 '64

Preview: recordings for 1964-65. J. Muri. il Sr Schol 84:12T My 15 '64

Recorded word. J. L. Limbacher. See issues of Library journal

Recordings of the spoken word; drama and prose. H. Kupferberg. il Atlan 212:140+ O '63

Records and tapes; J. F. Kennedy: a self portrait. H. J. Langer. Sr Schol 84:30T Mr 20 '64

Records in a bookstore: a new look. D. Ross. il Pub W 184:41-3 Ag 19 '63

Shakespeare on LP. R. Freed. Sat R 47:60-1+ My 16 '64

Shakespeare on record. J. Ciardi. Sat R 46:53+ S 14 '63

Sound scholarships; Michigan state university's new National voice library. il Time 83:49 F 7 '64

Sounds of history; recorded voices of 8,000 celebrities in National voice library. W. B. Furlong. il N Y Times Mag p72+ Mr 22 '64

Spoken records. Pub W 184:79-80 Ag 19 '63

Spoken word. E. Wagenknecht. Hi Fi 14: 87-8 F; 84 Je; 72-3 Jl; 90+ Ag; 158+ O '64

Strange interlude. C. J. Luten. il Am Rec G 30:578-80 Mr '64

Tales and tellers. J. Ciardi. Sat R 46:61 N 16 '63

Taming of the shrew. J. Diether. Am Rec G 30:36-8 S '63

They all must fall in the round I call: Cassius Clay. J. Ciardi. Sat R 46:16-17 N 16 '63

Tragedy of Coriolanus. J. Diether. Am Rec G 30:345-6 D '63

Two for Shakespeareans: Homage to Shakespeare; Shakespeare at Stratford. J. Diether. Am Rec G 31:374-5 D '64

Voice, the poet, and the poem. D. Geiger. Poetry 101:275-8 Ja '63

War records: World wars I and II. J. Muri. Sr Schol 85:21T N 11 '64

Who's afraid of Virginia Woolf? not Columbia. S. Potter. il Am Rec G 29:924-7 Ag '63

Who's afraid of Virginia Woolf? on LP. J. Gassner. Sat R 46:39-40+ Je 29 '63

With malice for all; School for scandal. J. Ciardi. il Sat R 46:52 F 23 '63

Words only. P. Kresh. See issues of American record guide

Words only. S. Potter. See issues of American record guide

Words, words, words! with discography. W. A. Pease. il Library J 88:3795-8 O 15 '63

see also
Talking books

Statistics

Spinning statistics; Schwann artist listing. il Time 81:33-4 Je 28 '63

Stereophonic records

Civil war in stereo. R. L. Tobin. Sat R 47: 120 Mr 14 '64

Dick Schory; interview, ed. by S. Fleming. D. Schory. Hi Fi 13:20 Jl '63

Magic dragon; or, Life with stereo; reports from the field, ed. by G. Stevenson. il Library J 88:3799-801 O 15 '63

More taste than torment; Ernst Haefliger. M. Bernheimer. Sat R 46:57 My 25 '63

Must stereo discs sound bad? D. H. Cooper. il Electr World 70:42-3 Jl '63

Other reviews, including stereo. See issues of American record guide

Phonograph records. W. F. Grueninger. See issues of Consumer bulletin

Reviews of recent recordings. See issues of Consumer reports

String quartet music

Feast of fascinations by Henry Cowell. A. Cohn. il Am Rec G 30:480-1 F '64

Keeping up with Kohons. J. W. Barker. il Am Rec G 30:609 Mr '64

Malipiero and Hindemith by the Stuyvesants: magnificent. J. Lyons. Am Rec G 30:1041 Jl '64

Rispetti e strambotti reappears. A. Frankenstein. il Hi Fi 14:64 Je '64

Sheer power; late Beethovens by the Amadeus. H. Glass. il Am Rec G 30:512+ F '64

Two recordings of Shostakovich's Quartet no. 8. A. Cohn. Am Rec G 30:585 Mr '64

Vox is doing us all a vast service. J. W. Barker. Am Rec G 29:543-5 Mr '63

Swiss music

How Swiss is Swiss music? A. Cohn. Am Rec G 29:520-1 Mr '63

Symphonic poems

Schoenberg, from Pelléas to Genesis. A. Frankenstein. Hi Fi 13:68-9 D '63

Symphonies

Another view, con; Symphony no. 1 in D. J. Diether. Am Rec G 29:523-4 Mr '63

Aspects of Jupiter. J. Diether. il Am Rec G 30:936-7 Je '64

At last, Prokofieff's Second symphony. J. Diether. Am Rec G 30:1016-18 Jl '64

Barbirolli's vintage fifths. R. Freed. Sat R 47:62 N 28 '64

Bernstein's Nielsen: an overwhelming realization. J. W. Barker. Am Rec G 29:726 My '63

Bruckner symphonies on records. il Hi Fi 13:49 F '63

Building your own record library. R. Hemming. Sr Schol 83:25 D 13 '63

Dorati in tandem, the conductor as composer. A. Cohn. Am Rec G 30:124 O '63

En garde, Vanguard! recording of Gottschalk's A night in the tropics. H. Shanet. Sat R 47:118 Mr 14 '64; Discussion. 47:58 Ap 11; 69 Je 27 '64

Erich Kleiber dirigiert. H. Glass. Am Rec G 29:855 Jl '63

Faust symphony, the Lisztian fire aflame. A. Rich. il Hi Fi 14:49-50 Jl '64

First complete recording of Gottschalk's symphony, A night in the Tropics. R. Kammerer. Am Rec G 30:102-3 O '63

First recordings of two Shostakovich symphonies. J. Diether. Am Rec G 30:1124-5 Ag '64

From among the symphonic treatise of Anton Bruckner. H. Goldsmith. il Hi Fi 13:67-8 D '63

From CRI, Elie Siegmeister's Symphony no. 3; truly worth attention. A. Cohn. Am Rec G 31:255 N '64

Furtwaengler: of immense historical interest; Mozart symphony no. 39; Beethoven symphony no. 5. J. Diether. Am Rec G 29:464 F '63

Gustav Mahler: the sadness of horns. R. De Toledano. Nat R 17:71-2 Ja 26 '65

Gustav Mahler's Symphony of a thousand. R. Sabin. Am Rec G 30:938+ Je '64

Haydn quake, second tremor. R. Freed. il Sat R 47:49+ Ja 25 '64

Haydn renascence continues. R. C. Marsh. il Hi Fi 13:78-9 N '63

Haydn's Bear and Haydn's Hen, the right scores make all the difference. H. C. R. Landon. il Hi Fi 14:89-90 N '64

Hovhaness and Giannini symphonies: a complete success. A. Cohn. Am Rec G 30: 853-4 My '64

In memoriam: Fritz Reiner's last recording. J. Diether. Am Rec G 31:141 O '64

Janigro: Haydn's Sturm und drang symphonies. J. W. Barker. Am Rec G 30:610+ Mr '64

Karajan and the Nine. J. S. Harrison. il Mus Am 83:44+ N '63

Karajan and the Nine. R. Lawrence. Sat R 46:34-5 Ag 31 '63

Klemperer's Bruckner: two views. J. Diether; C. J. Luten. Am Rec G 29:446-7 F '63

Last recordings of Bruno Walter. M. Bernheimer. Sat R 46:58-9 D 28 '63

Leinsdorf's Mahler Fifth symphony. J. Diether. Am Rec G 31:120-2+ O '64

Liturgy and Billingsgate. B. Boretz. Nation 199:258-60 O 19 '64

Ludwig van Beethoven nine symphonies; Berlin philharmonic orchestra conductor Herbert von Karajan. C. J. Luten. il Am Rec G 30:10-12 S '63

PHONOGRAPH records—Symphonies—*Cont.*
Mahler by two conductors (Mengelberg and Klemperer) who knew him personally; Symphony no. 2 in C minor and Symphony no. 4 in G. J. Diether. Am Rec G 30:421-2+ Ja '64
Mahler's Eighth, a stereo debut. R. C. Marsh. Hi Fi 14:50-1 Jl '64
Meanwhile, back at Symphony Hall... J. Lyons. il Am Rec G 30:1019 Jl '64
Monteux's Ninth: an exalted kind of humanity. P. L. Miller. Am Rec G 29:622 Ap '63
More Mahler by Bernstein. No. 5. J. Diether. Am Rec G 30:664-5 Ap '64
Most satisfactory Mahler Second yet. J. Diether. Am Rec G 31:439+ Ja '65
New integral set of the Nine; to add to the best. H. C. R. Landon. Hi Fi 13:79-80 S '63
Prokoviev from Boston, a new series launched. A. Rich. il Hi Fi 14:59-60 My '64
Protest to Victor; Schubert's Symphony no. 9. B. H. Haggin. New Repub 149:24+ S 28 '63
Recordings. M. Mayer. Esquire 62:26+ D '64
Records; Herbert van Karajan's recording of all nine Beethoven symphonies with the Berlin philharmonic. B. Boretz. Nation 197: 308 N 9 '63
Rehearsed but not revealed; Karajan's special disc of extracts from a rehearsal of the finale of Beethoven's Ninth. M. Bernheimer. Sat R 46:35 Ag 31 '63
Sibelius from an old hand and a new one; Ormandy and Schippers. J. Diether. il Am Rec G 30:586-7 Mr '64
Strange case of Bruckner's Eighth: five recorded performances of three different editions. J. Diether. Am Rec G 30:498-500 F '64
Symphony no. 3 Kaddish; to the beloved memory of John F. Kennedy. A. Cohn. il Am Rec G 30:1014-15 Jl '64
Szell's Strauss, stunning, supreme; Symphonia domestica. R. Sabin. Am Rec G 31:109 O '64
Three by Kurt Redel, unabashed admiration. H. Glass. il Am Rec G 576-7 Mr '64
Toscanini and Schubert: Philadelphia, November 1941; Symphony no. 9. il Am Rec G 30:18-21 S '63
Two views of the Sibelius First. J. Diether. Am Rec G 30:1126-7 Ag '64
V.W. at his most lovable. J. Diether. Am Rec G 30:876 My '64
Walter's Mahler First: the standard by which others are to be judged; Symphony no. 1 in D. C. J. Luten. il Am Rec G 29: 522-3 Mr '63
Westminster's Somogyi: a most auspicious debut. J. W. Barker. il Am Rec G 30:318 D '63
With the Philadelphians in 1941, Toscanini's Schubert Ninth. H. Goldsmith. Hi Fi 13: 125-6 O '63

Test records

Short guide to test records; with discography. R. D. Darrell. il Hi Fi 13:48-51+ D '63

Violin music

Baroque for bow and strings; Locatelli and Vivaldi. B. Schwarz. Sat R 46:65+ O 26 '63
Fifteen old violins. Discus. Harper 228:120-1 F '64
Glory of cremona. A. Cohn. il Am Rec G 30: 501 F '64
Heifetz's Beethoven again. B. Schwarz. Sat R 46:43 Jl 27 '63
Szeryng's (and Rubinstein's) Brahms. N. Lang. Am Rec G 29:444-5 F '63
This one is not for the vaults: Heifetz playing concerti written for him, by W. Walton and M. Castelnuovo-Tedesco. J. Diether. Am Rec G 31:464 Ja '65
Three violinists, three internal perspectives. R. Sabin. il Am Rec G 31:114-16 O '64
See also
Phonograph records—Concertos

Violoncello music

In memoriam: Emanuel Feuermann (1902-1942) J. Lyons. Am Rec G 30:228 N '63
Pablo Casals. R. De Toledano. Nat R 14:417-19 My 21 '63

Wind ensembles

Complete wind music of Mozart. H. Glass. il Am Rec G 30:566-7+ Mr '64
Mozart for winds. Sat R 46:53+ N 30 '63

PHONOGRAPH records, Classification of. See Classification

PHOSFON. See Growth inhibiting substances (plants)

PHOSPHATASES
Acid phosphatases of human red cells: predicted phenotype conforms to a genetic hypothesis. L. Lai and others. bibliog il Science 145:1187-8 S 11 '64
Alkaline phosphatase in peripheral nerves. B. Pinner and others. bibliog il Science 145: 936-8 Ag 28 '64
Intestinal phosphatase activity: acceleration of increase by puromycin and actinomycin. F. Moog. bibliog il Science 144:414-16 Ap 24 '64
Reevaluation of assays used to show RNA induction of glucose-6-phosphatase in ascites cells. J. Imsande and B. Ephrussi. bibliog il Science 144:854-6 My 15 '64

PHOSPHATES
Affinity and phosphorylation constants for the inhibition of esterases by organophosphates. A. R. Main. bibliog il Science 144:992-3 My 22 '64
Cadmium: uptake by vegetables from superphosphate in soil. H. A. Schroeder and J. J. Balassa. bibliog il Science 140:819-20 My 17 '63
Cariostatic effect of phosphates. F. J. McClure. bibliog il Science 144:1337-8 Je 12 '64
Cholinesterase inhibition in spider mites susceptible and resitant to organophosphate. H. R. Smissaert. bibliog il Science 143: 129-31 Ja 10 '64
Feedback control of purified deoxycytidylate deaminase. G. F. Maley and F. Maley. bibliog il Science 141:1278-9 S 27 '63
Phosphate incorporation in desheathed nerves: effects of potassium and calcium ions. L. G. Abood and I. Koyama. bibliog il Science 141:1277-8 S 27 '63
Ultraviolet radiation effects on low molecular weight inorganic phosphates of yeast. E. M. Lieberman and P. A. Swenson. bibliog il Science 142:1315-16 D 6 '63
See also
Adenosine phosphates
Apatite
Carbamyl phosphate

PHOSPHATES in the body
Participation of an intermediate of oxidative phosphorylation in ion accumulation by mitochondria. G. P. Brierley and others. bibliog il Science 140:60-2 Ap 5 '63

PHOSPHENES
Seeing without light. Sci Digest 54:52 Jl '63

PHOSPHORESCENCE
Lights that save. il Time 82:52 Jl 12 '63
Phosphorescence of rat kidneys cooled in liquid nitrogen. J. Wisotzky and others. il Science 140:671-2 My 10 '63

PHOSPHORESCENT organs in fishes. See Phosphorescence

PHOSPHORUS
Crystal structures adopted by black phosphorus at high pressures. J. C. Jamieson. bibliog il Science 139:1291 Mr 29 '63
Phosphorus excretion and body size in marine animals: microzooplankton and nutrient regeneration. R. E. Johannes. bibliog il Science 146:923-4 N 13 '64
See also
Feeding and feeding stuffs—Phosphorus content

PHOSPHORYLASES
Phosphorylase α activity in uterine muscle: stimulation by ethylenediaminetetraacetic acid. H. P. Schane and S. L. Leonard. bibliog il Science 140:811-12 My 17 '63
Specificity of potassium-activated phosphodiesterase of escherichia coli. M. F. Singer and G. Tolbert. bibliog il Science 145:593-5 Ag 7 '64

PHOSPHORYLATION
Affinity and phosphorylation constants for the inhibition of esterases of organophosphates. A. R. Main. bibliog il Science 144:992-3 My 22 '64
Phosphohistidine. P. D. Boyer. bibliog il Science 141:1147-53 S 20 '63
Protein as the mitochondrial site for action of uncoupling phenols. E. C. Weinbach and J. Garbus. bibliog il Science 145:824-6 Ag 21 '64
Sulfate transport in human red cells: inhibition by some uncouplers of oxidative phosphorylation. A. Omachi. bibliog il Science 145:1449-50 S 25 '64
2,4-dinitrophenol: lack of interaction with high-energy intermediates of oxidative phosphorylation. R. H. Eisenhardt and O. Rosenthal. bibliog il Science 143:476 Ja 31 '64

PHOTO aerial reconnaissance. See Aerial reconnaissance

PHOTO centers. See Recreation centers
PHOTO-etching. See Photography—Retouching
PHOTO finish; drama. See Ustinov, P.
PHOTO finishing. See Photographic finishing, Commercial
PHOTO-plastic recording. See Photography—Photo-plastic
PHOTO-reconnaissance. See Photography, Military
PHOTO reconnaissance rockets. See Rockets—Military applications
PHOTO timers. See Timing devices
PHOTOCELLS. See Photoelectric cells
PHOTOCHEMISTRY
Dye solutions may provide flash protection, shutters for lasers. Aviation W 81:70-1 N 9 '64
Organic photochemistry. G. S. Hammond and N. J. Turro. bibliog il Science 142:1541-53 D 20 '63
Organic photochemistry; report on International symposium on organic photochemistry. G. S. Hammond. Science 145:1469-71 S 25 '64
PHOTOCHROMIC glass. See Glass
PHOTOCHROMICS. See Microphotography
PHOTOCOMPOSING machines
ATF announces high-speed computer-slave phototypesetter. il Pub W 185:86+ Je 1 '64
ATF's new desk-top photo headlining units. il Pub W 186:87-9 S 7 '64
Debut in computing room. il Bsns W p 133-4 Ap 25 '64
Medlars data system is subject of briefing; Photon Zip model 900. Pub W 187:105 Ja 4 '65
New lino contract with GPO: ultra-fast phototypesetters; Linotron system; Harris-Intertype's electronic photosetting system announced. il Pub W 185:92-5 My 4 '64
Photon ships first Zip model for highspeed computer setting. il Pub W 185:88 Je 1 '64
Photon Zip quality setting, computer speed. Pub W 184:82 N 4 '63
Phototypesetting picks up the pace. il Bsns W p 156+ D 14 '63
PHOTOCOPYING. See Photography—Copying; Photomechanical processes
PHOTOELECTRIC cells
Advances in photosensitive devices. J. R. Collins. il Electr World 72:49-51 D '64
Photocell circuits for experiments. C. L. Henry. il Pop Electr 19:47-9 S '63
Photoelectric ecosystem. N. E. Armstrong and H. T. Odum. bibliog il Science 143:256-8 Ja 17 '64
Simple photoelectric amplifier. R. P. Turner. il Electr World 72:104-5 N '64
X-ray-induced bulk photovoltaic effect in insulators. S. I. Taimuty and others. il Science 144:173 Ap 10 '64
Control applications
High-power photocell. J. E. Cain. il Electr World 71:44-5 Mr '64
New light-operated switch; Raysistor, photocell with self-contained light source. D. E. Whateley. il Electr World 70:47+ N '63
Remote volume control; Raysistor, a photocell with self-contained light. C. W. Martel. il Electr World 72:62 Jl '64
PHOTOELECTRIC devices. See Photoelectric cells
PHOTOELECTRIC typesetting machines. See Photocomposing machines
PHOTOELECTRICITY
Photoelectric recording of astronomical seeing. Il Sky & Tel 26:83 Ag '63
PHOTOENGRAVERS' union of New York city
Mayor again is frustrated. Bsns W p34 Mr 30 '63
PHOTOENGRAVING
Architectural drawing for printing by halftone. M. F. Schmertz. il Arch Rec 133: 133-40 Je '63
Let's understand photo-engraving. il Design 64:214-15 Je '63
Three eras of playing-card printing; photoengraving. D. Powills. il Hobbies 69:114-15 O '64
PHOTOFLASH lamps. See Electric lamps, Flashlight
PHOTOGRAMMETRY
Depth of lakes told by photo measuring. Sci N L 83:222 Ap 6 '63
PHOTOGRAMS. See Shadowgrams
PHOTOGRAPH frames. See Picture frames
PHOTOGRAPHERS
Achievement awards. il U S Camera 27:52-3 Mr '64
Do you need a grant? J. Deschin. Pop Phot 55:10+ Jl '64
Feature pictures and how they were made. il U S Camera 27:46-9 Mr '64
Five photographers talk color & lenses; ed. by G. Pyle. il Pop Phot 54:82-91+ Ap '64
Flying fotographer. il Flying 74:60 Mr; 64 Ap; 56 My; 22 Je; 75:24 Jl; 75 S '64
Ken Heyman. il U S Camera 26:60-5 F '63
Merry Christmas, Judy Depp. J. Durniak. Pop Phot 55:66 D '64
Top prize winners; USC's annual contest. il U S Camera 26:78 S '63
Tough guy with a soft heart; interview. ed. by B. Mason, H. Flatow. il U S Camera 27:62-5+ Ja '64
Trouble in Notasulga; Vernon Merritt freelance photographer attacked by officers of the law. il Time 83:51 F 14 '64
World through my eyes, by A. Feininger. Review
Pop Phot il 54:68-77+ F '64
See also
Adams, A.
Atget, E.
Bachrach family
Feininger, A.
Halsman, P.
Haskins, S.
Kertesz, A.
Lartigue, J.
Okamura, A.
Steichen, E.
Wallowitch, E.
Warman, M.
PHOTOGRAPHIC albums
Be your own art director. L. Parker. il U S Camera 27:8 S '64
New zip for the family album. J. Kinney and C. Kinney. il U S Camera 26:54-5+ Je '63
Primer for old hands. P. R. Farber. il U S Camera 26:59-61+ My '63
Show your prints. J. C. Hart. il U S Camera 26:91 F '63
PHOTOGRAPHIC apparatus industry and trade
Cameras by committee won't work, Russians discover. Mod Phot 28:96+ N '64
Cameras focus on U.S. buffs; Japan and West Germany. il Bsns W p56-8+ Mr 23 '63
It started with Steinheil; vast photographic complex of the German camera industries. W. Wehran. il U S Camera 27:66-7+ N '64
World's most unusual camera store: Wallace Heaton ltd. B. Campbell. il Pop Phot 54:61-3+ Je '64
See also
Eastman Kodak company
PHOTOGRAPHIC chemistry
Mixing and storing chemicals. A. Francekevich. il Pop Phot 51:12+ D '62
Polacolor's chemistry. il Pop Phot 52:114 Mr '63
PHOTOGRAPHIC equipment. See Photography—Apparatus and supplies
PHOTOGRAPHIC exhibitions. See Photography—Exhibitions
PHOTOGRAPHIC films. See Photography—Films
PHOTOGRAPHIC finishing
See also
Photography—Retouching
PHOTOGRAPHIC finishing, Commercial
On quality standards. B. Downes. Pop Phot 54:58 Je '64
PHOTOGRAPHIC illustration. See Illustration of books and periodicals
PHOTOGRAPHIC industry. See Photographic apparatus industry and trade
PHOTOGRAPHIC laboratories
Case for custom processing. H. Amdur. il U S Camera 26:58-9+ D '63
Hata time in Honolulu. L. Barry. il Pop Phot 55:36 D '64
Truth about color print labs. E. Meyers. il Mod Phot 28:72-3 F '64
Visit with Axel Grosser. A. Francekevich. Pop Phot 55:28 D '64
PHOTOGRAPHIC lenses. See Lenses, Photographic
PHOTOGRAPHIC literature
How to non-review a photo book. J. Deschin. Pop Phot 53:16 Jl '63
PHOTOGRAPHIC measurements. See Photogrammetry
PHOTOGRAPHIC optics
Pictures without a lens; Fresnel zone plates. il(p 17) Sci N L 87:23 Ja 9 '65
PHOTOGRAPHIC paper
How black is black? A. Francekevich. Pop Phot 55:16 Jl '64
Is matte paper good for anything? N. Rothschild. Pop Phot 53:76-7 Ag '63
New FR paper makes color prints in seventeen minutes, P. Farber. il U S Camera 27:38-9+ Mr '64

PHOTOGRAPHIC paper—*Continued*
New product report; Agfa contrast no. 6. G. Gilbert. il U S Camera 27:61-3+ Mr '64
No-developer printing. C. Wright. il Pop Phot 53:154-6 D '63
Printing papers: a personal view. A. Francekevich. Pop Phot 52:14 My; 53:14+ S '63
Proof paper; darkroom in the sun. B. C. Black. il Sch Arts 63:11-13 My '64
Test reports; Kodak professional proof paper. C. Wright. il Pop Phot 53:157 D '63
Viewpoints; into the printing paper fray. J. Deschin. Pop Phot 53:22 N '63
What film, what paper, what developer for portraits? M. Bernam. il Pop Phot 53:140-1+ N '63

Testing

Printing papers; personal report on 106. D. Vestal. il Pop Phot 56:138-49+ Ja '65

PHOTOGRAPHIC research
Future techniques; electrically-charged picture-taking system. J. Reidy. U S Camera 26:12+ D '63

PHOTOGRAPHIC silk screen printing. See Silk screen printing

PHOTOGRAPHIC slides. See Transparencies

PHOTOGRAPHS
Bargains in great photographs. A. Goldsmith. il Pop Phot 55:158-61+ D '64
Best of the year. il U S Camera 26:57-60 N '63
Decorate problem wall with family photo tree. il Parents Mag 38:140 Mr '63
Important uses for your camera. il Good H 156:165 My '63
Love's warm instant: the embrace. T. Frissell. Life 55:150-6 D 6 '63
New Polaroid Land camera: pictures it takes. il Pop Phot 53:48-9+ O '63
New talent: pictures by winners in Jacob Deschin's contest. il Pop Phot 53:76-81 O '63
Photographs to live with. E. Braun. il U S Camera 27:22-3+ S '64
Pictures. il Pop Phot 51:82-7 D '62; 53:66-75 S '63
Polacolor album. il Pop Phot 52:56-8 Mr '63
Portraits. il Pop Phot 53:146-55 N '63
U.S. camera international pictures, 1965; preview. il U S Camera 27:62-5 D '64
See also
Daguerreotypes

Collections

Your prints on other people's walls. C. Schwalberg. il U S Camera 26:40+ Mr '63
See also
Photographic albums

Collectors and collecting

Down memory lane; curios, relics, novelties and photographic memorabilia. G. Gilbert. il U S Camera 27:36-7+ Ja '64

Marketing

Try a stock agency to turn your travel pictures into cash. R. Krubner. il Pop Phot 54:140-3 Ap '64

Reproducing

See Photography—Copying

Retouching

See Photography—Retouching

Trimming, mounting, etc.

Crop your way to better pictures. R. Troiano. il U S Camera 27:36-7 Ja '64
Hidden picture. J. Morris. il U S Camera 26:54-5 Jl '63
In the darkroom; versatile dry-mounting press. A. Francekevich. Pop Phot 53:14 Jl '63
Make your pictures shape up! A. Asnis. U S Camera 26:16+ N '63
Pictures under glass. S. Ross. il Pop Phot 52:64-5+ Ap '63
Right crop. il U S Camera 27:78+ My '64
Shoot it close! crop it tight! il U S Camera 26:41-7 D '63

PHOTOGRAPHS in books and periodicals. See Illustration of books and periodicals

PHOTOGRAPHY
Are slow films sharper than fast films? B. Pierce. il Pop Phot 55:46-9+ S '64
Are you as good as the old-timers? N. Rothschild. Pop Phot 54:104-5 Mr '64
Are you losing quality as you shoot? B. Pierce. Pop Phot 55:110-12 S '64
Bits & pieces. W. J. Sumits. Pop Phot 54:101 Mr '64
Book for sneaks. S. Greenberg. il U S Camera 27:66-7 Je '64
Camera angles (cont) il Sr Schol 82:24 F 13; 4 Mr 20; 83:4 O 18; 38 D 6 '63; 4 Ja 10; 84:24 F 21; 39 Ap 3; 85:28 O 10; 25 D 9 '64; 28 Ja 14 '65
Case for carrying a camera. M. Edelson. il U S Camera 27:58-9+ Ag '64
Color vs. black-and-white. C. Wright. Pop Phot 55:82-3 Jl '64
Creative color; large or small format? A. Rothstein. U S Camera 27:8+ My '64
Creative controls; with editorial comment. il Pop Phot 54:46, 49-65, 70-79 My '64
Dangerous necessity to dramatize. R. Steiner. il Pop Phot 54:48-9+ F '64
Different way of seeing things; excerpt from World through my eyes. A. Feininger. il N Y Times Mag p24-5 N 10 '63
Don't knock the box. D. H. Moore. il U S Camera 27:54-5 Ap '64
Eighteen most-asked questions about lenses. N. Rothschild. il Pop Phot 54:68-71 Ap '64
Equipment; the means to the end. il U S Camera 26:47-9 O '63
Fifteen tips from the pros. il U S Camera 27:54-5+ Mr '64
Form & content in color. R. Hattersley. il Pop Phot 55:84-91 Jl '64
Foto facts. P. Farber. See issues of U.S. camera & travel
Get the picture; how to photograph crowds. P. Caulfield. il Mod Phot 28:12-13 Je '64
Have standards declined? B. Downes. Pop Phot 53:44 O '63
Hawaii. E. Scully. il U S Camera 27:74-5+ Mr '64
How fast, how many. il Mod Phot 28:68-75 Je '64
How pictures are made; symposium. il Pop Phot 52:39-74+ F '63
How to be goof-proof. C. Wright. Pop Phot 53:75-6 Ag '63
How to photograph the fair. il Seventeen 23:28 F '64
Improvising on location, in darkroom. B. Pierce. Pop Phot 55:46+ D '64
In/out? out-of-focus foregrounds. P. Caulfield. il Mod Phot 28:66-7 O '64
Informal newsletter. W. J. Sumits. Pop Phot 53:187 D '63
Is there an off-season? D. B. Eisendrath, jr. Pop Phot 51:8+ D '62
Keppler on the SLR; stumbling blocks to sharpness. H. Keppler. il Mod Phot 29:16+ Ja '65
Methods & materials. P. Farber. il U S Camera 27:16+ Ja '64
Modern techniques with 2¼. E. Meyers. il Mod Phot 28:82-3 N '64
On the go. L. Barry. See issues of Popular photography
One man's predictions; automation. D. B. Eisendrath, jr. Pop Phot 52:66+ Ap '63
Photo tips. See issues of Popular photography
Photographically speaking. B. Hering. See issues of Popular science monthly to April 1964
Photography behind Cuba's iron curtain. B. Eccles. il Mod Phot 27:99 Ag '63
Photography: its materials and processes, by C. B. Neblette. Review
Pop Phot il 54:69 My '64. W. Clark
Picture this vacation. W. Jacqmar. il Outdoor Life 133:52-5+ Je '64
Pictures in a moment; guide to better polacolor pictures with model 100 Polaroid Land cameras. J. Wolbarst. Mod Phot 28:10+ Mr '64
Problems automatic cameras can't solve. E. Bennett. il U S Camera 27:56-9+ Je '64
Psychology of people-pictures. R. Hattersley. il Pop Phot 53:167-82 N '63
RF or SLR, which is the real you? M. Edelson and J. Ward. il U S Camera 27:40-5 S '64
Recipe for seeing. D. Vestal. U S Camera 27:41+ F '64
Resembling the after-images of memory; ballet action. B. Downes. il Pop Phot 55:64-5 Ag '64
Roll film; vacation pictures. J. Foldes. U S Camera 26:16+ Jl '63
Say it with your camera. J. Deschin. See issues of Popular photography
SLR impact! photographs by Herbert T. Marcus, amateur from Cincinnati, Ohio. P. Caulfield. il Mod Phot 28:62-71+ Mr '64
Shoot 2¼ sq. P. Caulfield and H. Keppler il Mod Phot 28:64-73 N '64
Simon sez. S. Nathan. il U S Camera 26:42 F; 38 My '63
Sixth-seventh annual travel photo handbook. il Pop Phot 52:131-46 Ap '63; 54:131-46 Ap '64
Special 35-mm issue; symposium, with editorial comment. il Pop Phot 55:30, 33-63+ Ag '64

PHOTOGRAPHY—*Continued*
Steichen, Atget. il Newsweek 62:100-1 N 4 '63
Stieglitz's experiments in life. D. Norman. il N Y Times Mag p 12-13 D 29 '63
Tahiti in July, a photographic wonderland. P. Stackpole. U S Camera 26:10+ N '63
Taking pictures that do a job. J. Burroughs. il Pop Sci 184:128-9 Je '64
Tech section. il Pop Phot 52:75-83 F '63
35mm; case for technique. J. Wolbarst. Mod Phot 28:28+ S '64
35mm techniques; built-in bugaboos. P. Stackpole. U S Camera 27:10-11 D '64
35mm techniques; review. P. Stackpole. U S Camera 27:12-13 Ap '64
Time and picture savers. C. Wright. il Pop Phot 54:99-100 F '64
Toward rising standards. J. Deschin. Pop Phot 52:44 My '63
Travel & camera: the 50th state. L. Lachter. il U S Camera 26:28 N '63
Trends in transition. M. R. Weiss. il Sat R 47:134-7 Ag 29 '64
Twin lens. F. Henle. See issues of Popular photography
Vagabond camera. W. Lane. See issues of Travel
Versatile normal lens. H. M. Kinzer. il Pop Phot 54:60-3 Ap '64
Viewpoints (cont of) Say it with your camera. J. Deschin. See issues of Popular photography
Well traveled camera. See issues of Modern photography
Well traveled camera; what to take on a trip. H. Keppler. Mod Phot 28:52+ Ag '64
What do numbers really mean? N. Rothschild. Pop Phot 53:75-6 Jl '63
What's your average. R. Halford. il U S Camera 27:56-7+ Ap '64
When filming solar eclipse July 20 beware of your camera and eyesight! W. Lane. il Travel 120:58-60 Jl '63
Where do you begin? photogenic spots of the New York world's fair. E. Scully. il U S Camera 27:58-61 Jl '64
World-wide survey of photography '63; symposium. Pop Phot 53:60-3+ Jl '63
See also
Astronomical photography
Color photography
Daguerreotypes
Electronics in photography
Macrophotography
Microphotography
Nature photography
Shadowgrams
Space photography
Stereophotography
Telephotography
Television—Photographic aspects
Tintype
also subhead Photographs under various subjects e.g. Snakes—Photographs

Advertising

Visual persuasion, by S. Baker. Review
Pop Phot il 52:72-3+ My '63. J. Durniak

Anecdotes, facetiae, satire, etc.

Are you serendipitacious? G. Haist. il U S Camera 26:18+ Ap '63
Pinhole camera. P. R. Farber. il U S Camera 26:58-9+ Ap '63
Shoot first! excerpts. R. Barter-Croissant. il Sat R 46:42-3 Mr 16 '63

Apparatus and supplies

About photography. M. M. Graff. il Pop Gard 15:60-2 Ap '64
Accent on accessories. C. W. Kennedy. Pop Phot 55:156-7 N '64
Accessories: key to the different fair. N. Rothschild. Pop Phot 54:122-3 My '64
Accessories you need for color. il Pop Phot 52:61 Mr '63
At last: Modern's '64 product preview reaches last roundup. Mod Phot 27:44+ Ag '63
Automation will dominate Chicago MPDFA show. B. C. Brown. il Pop Phot 54:74-7+ Ap '64
Bargains from the dime store. H. Harrison and W. Forbes. il Pop Phot 52:64-7 Mr '63
Basic lighting rigs. H. Shaman. il Pop Phot 53:136-7 N '63
Behind the scenes. See issues of Modern photography
Build your own 2¼x3¼ film pack adapter. J. P. G. McKenzie. il U S Camera 27:28 S '64
Camera attachment to give shadowless lighting. W. Burton. il Pop Sci 185:136-7 N '64
Case for carrying a camera. M. Edelson. il U S Camera 27:58-9+ Ag '64
CIBA enters color field. Pop Phot 52:26+ Ap '63
Color clinic; equipment. D. B. Eisendrath, jr. il Pop Phot 54:8+ My '64
Color slide products galore at convention in Atlantic City. R. Miller. U S Camera 26:34+ Je '63
Color slides; diffraction grating! R. Miller. U S Camera 26:22-3 D '63
Color workshop; Munsell color wheel. F. Bond. il Mod Phot 27:12-13 N; 10-11 D '63
Creative color; polarizing materials. A. Rothstein. U S Camera 26:8+ D '63
Dateline: Chicago. il U S Camera 27:56-60 My '64
Don't be a sucker shopper! W. G. McClanahan. U S Camera 27:41+ D '64
Electronic flash studio in a 19-inch case. H. Shaman. il Pop Phot 51:76-9+ D '62
Equipment preview '65; Master photo dealers' and finishers' association, Chicago. il Mod Phot 28:82-3 My '64
For travel picture insurance, pre-check your equipment. C. Wright. il Pop Phot 52:136-7 Ap '63
For your Christmas list. R. Miller. Pop Gard 14:8+ N '63
Forty stocking stuffers. N. Rothschild. il Pop Phot 51:68-71 D '62
Future techniques; photographic miracles of the space age. J. Reidy. il U S Camera 26:38-9 F '63
Get the picture; equipment when on vacation. P. Caulfield. il Mod Phot 27:12-13 Jl '63
Heatproof floodlight diffusers. il Pop Sci 185:134-5 N '64
Here's what's new! il Pop Phot 52:43-58 Je '63
Home-grown animation rig. L. Lipton. il Pop Phot 55:174 N '64
How to choose and test cameras, lenses, meters, electronic flash units. Mod Phot 27:14-16+ D '63
How to use small-camera bellows & extension tubes. N. Rothschild. il Pop Phot 54:42-7+ F '64
Hypo-sniffer-outer. P. Farber. il U S Camera 27:54-5+ D '64
In the darkroom; fresh air in a can. A. Francekevich. il Pop Phot 53:22 D '63
Inside those tiny new speedlights. R. M. Benrey. il Pop Sci 184:130-2+ Je '64
It wasn't here! B. Schwalberg. il U S Camera 26:59+ Je '63
Keep your safelight safe! N. Rothschild. il Pop Phot 54:111 My '64
Keppler on the SLR; bellows extensions. il Mod Phot 27:46+ Mr '63
Keppler on the SLR; gadget bag. H. Keppler. il Mod Phot 27:32+ N '63
Keppler on the SLR; valuable picture making trifles. H. Keppler. il Mod Phot 27:20+ D '63
Kodak introduces instant loading. il Pop Phot 52:45-6 My '63
MPDFA and photokina previews. il Pop Phot 52:67-9+ Ap '63
Make your own night-light exposure calculator. S. P. Martin. il Pop Phot 55:162-3+ D '64
Make your pictures bounce; handy lighting accessories. il U S Camera 28:55+ Ja '65
Making lab life easier. A. Francekevich. il Pop Phot 54:42+ Je '64
Methods & materials. P. Farber. il U S Camera 27:16+ Ja '64
Modern tests. See issues of Modern photography
Movie maker. M. A. Matzkin. il Mod Phot 29:58-9+ Ja '65
Nature and the camera; use of blinds. D. Linton. il Natur Hist 73:63-6 F '64
New at the show; report on 40th Master photo dealers' and finishers' association national convention and trade show. il Pop Phot 54:87-97 Je '64
New enlarging meter. B. Pierce. il Pop Phot 54:102-4 Mr '64
New product report. See issues of U.S. camera
New products. See issues of Modern photography to November 1963
1965 preview. il Mod Phot 28:90-7 Je '64
1964-1965 directory & buying guide. il Pop Phot 53:66-130 N; 70-135 D '63; 54:49-80 Ja; 55:1A-64A N '64; 56:1C-64C Ja '65
1964 preview of photo products. il Mod Phot 27:51-63+ Je; 84-7+ Jl '63
Omega darkroom outfit. il U S Camera 27:32 Ap '64
On learning electronics. W. J. Sumits. Pop Phot 52:107 Ap '63
Packable presents. L. Barry. il Pop Phot 53:162-5+ D '63

PHOTOGRAPHY—Apparatus and supplies—*Continued*
Photo show roundup; Chicago trade show. il U S Camera 27:90-1 Je '64
Photo tips. See issues of Popular photography
Photography. il Consumer Rep 29:352-75 D '64
Pipe-fitting light stand. J. Ramsey. il Pop Mech 120:146-7 Jl '63
Pocket studio. J. Foldes. il U S Camera 26:56+ N '63
Politics and photography: technical innovations. Pop Phot 55:131+ N '64
Popular photography directory & buying guide. il Pop Phot 52:110-32 Ja '63
Portable power probe. R. Miller. il U S Camera 26:62-5+ Je '63
Preview of photo show equipment. il U S Camera 27:37-44 Ap '64
Repronar; new pictures from old. N. Rothschild. il Pop Phot 54:96-103+ Ja '64
Rover's conversion; equipment for explorer-cameraman. H. Zipkin. il Field & S 68:156-8 Ap '64
SLR finders. B. Sherman. il Mod Phot 27:52-5+ Ap '63
Some tips on things to take along. il Pop Phot 54:146 Ap '64
Special-effects box. H. Leiman. il Pop Phot 55:110 O '64
Spiratone converter plus your lens. H. Keppler. il Mod Phot 27:72-3+ Mr '63
Studio in a suitcase. H. Shaman. il Pop Phot 55:60-3+ O '64
Super telephoto outfit for $30? yup, it's true. H. Keppler and D. L. Miller. il Mod Phot 28:13+ Ag '64
T system. H. Shaman. il Pop Phot 53:64-7 Jl '63
Tankmanship; tips on choosing and using dark loading reels. J. Wolbarst. il Mod Phot 27:76-7+ Mr '63
Tech section. il Pop Phot 52:75-83 F '63
Ten tips on taking your camera traveling. J. R. Gregg. U S Camera 27:64 O '64
That Duplex Super safelight. A. Francekevich. il Pop Phot 56:128-9+ Ja '65
35mm techniques. P. Stackpole. U S Camera 27:14-15 Jl '64
35mm techniques; equipment advances. P. Stackpole. U S Camera 26:12-13 Ap '63
35mm techniques; necessary equipment. P. Stackpole. U S Camera 26:14-15 F '63
35mm techniques; travel light or heavy? P. Stackpole. U S Camera 26:32 O '63
Travel darkroom? C. Steiner. il Pop Phot 54:134-7 Ap '64
U.S. camera test reports (cont of) New product report. il U S Camera 27:60-3+ Ag; 60-1+ S; 88+ N '64; 28:80-1+ Ja '65
Updated view of the Kilfitt system. N. Rothschild. il Pop Phot 54:136-9 Ja '64
Vagabond camera. W. Lane. il Travel 122:54-5 Jl; 56-7 Ag '64
Well traveled camera; preparing for a photo trip. H. Keppler. il Mod Phot 28:58+ N '64
What you'll see in '63. il U S Camera 26:74-7+ My '63
When you travel with camera. L. Barry. il Pop Phot 52:132-3 Ap '63
Your darkroom: what to get, where to put it. E. Meyers. il Mod Phot 28:66-9 F' 64
See also
Camera cases
Camera tripods
Cameras
Eastman Kodak company
Electric lamps, Flashlight
Exposure meters
Lenses, Photographic
Reflectors
Timing devices
View finders

Bibliography

Art books of 1964. L. Kirstein. Nation 199:470-2 D 14 '64
Bargains from Uncle Sam's bookstore. D. B. Eisendrath, jr. Pop Phot 52:84-6+ My '63
Books. See issues of Popular photography
Books (title varies) See issues of U.S. camera
Books, booklets & pamphlets, $1 & under. il Pop Phot 52:74-5+ My '63
Books in review. See issues of Modern photography
Photo books are good sellers: are booksellers in the picture? P. Andrews. il Pub W 183:21-5 Mr 11 '63
Yesterday's classics: Today's best picture books. H. M. Kinzer. il Pop Phot 52:58-61 My '63

Caricatures and cartoons

Photogoplane. J. Fuller. U S Camera 26:42 Ap '63

Cold weather conditions

And stay out! P. Caulfield. il Mod Phot 28:68-77 Ja '64
Got cold feet and cameras? try this. D. L. Miller. Mod Phot 28:94+ N '64
Pictures in a moment. J. Wolbarst. il Mod Phot 28:32 Ja '64
Simon sez; zero temperature. S. Nathan. U S Camera 26:44 Ap '63
Some tips for snow dudes. L. Barry. il Pop Phot 54:20+ Ja '64
Well traveled camera. Mod Phot 28:38+ F '64

Competitions

Amateur's ten-year success story. il U S Camera 27:92+ O '64
Baffling black-and-white; cover contest for tenth-anniversary edition of Ripley's Believe it or not. M. R. Weiss. il Sat R 47:66 S 12 '64
Color slides: new contest ideas. R. Miller. U S Camera 27:26+ Ap '64
Confessions of a color slide judge. H. Flatow. U S Camera 27:30+ D '64
Contest for talent in hiding. J. Deschin. Pop Phot 52:14 Mr '63
Feature pictures: year to remember; 21st annual White House news photographers photo contest. il U S Camera 27:68-73 Je '64
First impressions of New York through some visitors' viewfinders. il Pop Phot 51:56 D '62
How would you make pictures like these? il Pop Phot 54:56-65 F '64
Methods & materials: movie contest. L. Drukker. Pop Phot 52:117+ My '63
Monthly contest. See issues of Modern photography
New talent: pictures by winners in Jacob Deschin's contest. il Pop Phot 53:76-81 O '63
1964 photo prize winners, a gallery; with report by M. R. Weiss and note on first prizewinners. il Sat R 48:58-64 Ja 2 '65
1964 Scholastic photography awards. il Sr Schol 84:17, 36-7 My 15 '64
1963 contest winners. il U S Camera 26:39-51 S '63
1963 photo prize winners; a gallery. Sat R 47:54-9 Ja 4 '64
1963 Scholastic photography awards. il Sr Schol 82:12 My 15 '63
Pictures of the year make news. M. R. Weiss. il Sat R 46:62-3 My 11 '63
Portrait of a child; prize-winners in first 1963 contest. il Pop Phot 52:88-93 Je '63
They tried to match Weegee. il Pop Phot 53:68-9+ Jl '63
Top prize winners: USC's annual contest. il U S Camera 26:78-5 S '63
Travel in focus: Saturday review's 1963 world travel photo contest. M. R. Weiss. Sat R 47:60-1 Ja 4 '64
Travel-picture contest. L. Barry. il Pop Phot 52:16+ My '63
Travel's amateur photo contest winners; photographs. See issues of Travel
Viewpoints; are contest rewards fair? J. Deschin. Pop Phot 53:20+ O '63; Discussion. 54:18+ Ja '64

Composition

See Composition (photography)

Copying

B&W from color, here's how. H. Keppler and E. Meyers. il Mod Phot 27:68-9 F '63
Big negatives from little films. B. Pierce. Pop Phot 53:94 S '63
Cambridge copy-cats. H. M. Kinzer. Pop Phot 53:30+ Jl '63
Color from B&W. P. Gridley. il Mod Phot 27:58-9 F '63
Converting your movie projector; duplication of silent and sound films. J. R. Oswald. il U S Camera 26:88-9+ O '63
Copy machine you can build. R. M. Benrey. il Pop Sci 186:128-30+ Ja '65
Negative positive; get perfect copy exposures every time! A. Asnis. U S Camera 26:30-1 S '63
Photocopying equipment. il Consumer Bul 46:28-32 N '63
Repronar; new pictures from old. N. Rothschild. il Pop Phot 54:96-103+ Ja '64

Criticism

Critical new year. B. Downes. il Pop Phot 54:46 Ja '64
Criticism criticized. D. Vestal. Pop Phot 55:135+ D '64
Critics at large. See issues of Popular photography
Critic's choice. See issues of Popular photography

PHOTOGRAPHY—*Continued*

Darkrooms

See Photography—Studios and darkrooms

Developing and developers

Ad libs. P. R. Farber. il U S Camera 26: 34-5 F; 40-1 My '63
Ad libs; divided development. P. Farber. U S Camera 26:32+ D '63
Ad libs; new and exceptional developer. P. Farber. il U S Camera 26:28-9 Ap '63
Anscochrome processing at 80 F. D. B. Eisendrath, jr. il Pop Phot 52:8+ Ja '63
Color printing; time & effort compared! E. Meyers. il Mod Phot 27:70-1+ F '63
Developing and printing; subminiature film. Pop Phot 53:48 Ag '63
Development by inspection, the right way! A. Asnis. U S Camera 26:34-5+ Mr '63
Diafine revisited. B. Pierce. Pop Phot 53:74-5 Ag '63
Eliminating stains. A. Francekevich. Pop Phot 52:50+ Mr '63
Exclusive report on Diafine. B. Pierce. il Pop Phot 52:76-9+ Ap '63
Filtering water, developer, and wine; Micronyl filter. A. Francekevich. il Pop Phot 54:18+ My '64
Filters for negative color. N. Rothschild. il Pop Phot 54:133-4 Ja '64
Foto facts; Edwal T.S.T. P. Farber. il U S Camera 27:24+ Ag '64
Foto facts; new strain of that old stain developer PPD. P. Farber. il U S Camera 27:26+ D '64
How super are the super speed developers? J. Wolbarst. il Mod Phot 28:80-5+ S '64
How to louse up your color lab. N. Rothschild and L. Zoref. il Pop Phot 55:60-1+ S '64
I got a good straight fire-engine red; amateur uses CP-5 chemicals. G. Reid. il Pop Phot 55:58-9+ S '64
In the darkroom; Acufine revisited. A. Francekevich. il Pop Phot 52:18+ Ja '63
In the darkroom; color processing. A. Francekevich. Pop Phot 55:8+ O '64
Light develops film. Sci N L 87:46 Ja 16 '65
Methods & materials; monobath developers. P. Farber. il U S Camera 27:16+ Ja '64
Mixing and storing chemicals. A. Francekevich. il Pop Phot 51:12+ D '62
Negative positive. A. Asnis. See issues of U.S. camera & travel to December 1963
1964 film-developer roundup. J. Wolbarst. il Mod Phot 28:72-7+ O '64
1963 film-developer roundup. J. Wolbarst. il Mod Phot 27:78-83 My '63
Popular photography directory & buying guide. il Pop Phot 52:105-10 Ja '63
Processing: the inside story! (cont) W. F. Berg. Mod Phot 27:86-7 F '63
Rapid color processor. P. Leonian. il U S Camera 27:38-9 Ap '64
Reach for the shadows with underwater development. W. P. Banner. il U S Camera 27:50-1+ Ag '64
Sales & distribution; amateur photography market. J. B. Weiner. Duns R 83:59 Ja '64
Split D-12. B. Pierce. il Pop Phot 52:78-9 F '63
Split development. P. R. Farber. il U S Camera 26:72-3+ Je '63
Test report: Acutol-S; fine-grain developer from England. P. Farber. il U S Camera 27:62-3+ Je '64
Testing with Diafine. A. Francekevich. Pop Phot 54:26 F '64
35mm. J. Wolbarst. Mod Phot 28:14-15 Ja '64 (to be cont)
35mm; developing tanks. J. Wolbarst. Mod Phot 28:25+ N '64
35mm; films and developers of twenty-five years ago. J. Wolbarst. Mod Phot 27:12 My '63
35mm; new processing system for color negative prints in Great Britain. J. Wolbarst. Mod Phot 28:26-7 Mr '64
35mm: quest for film speed. J. Wolbarst. Mod Phot 28:14-15 Ja; 26+ F '64
35mm: selections from film developer charts. J. Wolbarst. Mod Phot 27:38-9+ Ag; 19-20 S '63
Today's monobaths: multi-versatile. M. Bernam. il Pop Phot 52:78-80 F '63
What film, what paper, what developer for portraits? M. Bernam. il Pop Phot 53:140-1+ N '63

Distortion

Bizarre effects. il U S Camera 27:56-9 Ja '64
Distortion for drama. il Pop Phot 54:62-3 My '64
Distortion for dramatic effect. F. Henle. il Pop Phot 54:30 Ja '64
Dynamic distortions by Kane. R. T. Hammarlund. il U S Camera 26:49-55+ Ap '63
How to control distortion without a view camera. B. Pierce. il Pop Phot 54:50-3+ F '64
Illusion of perspective distortion. C. Younger. il U S Camera 26:42-9+ N '63
Keppler on the SLR; lens distortions. il Mod Phot 27:14-16+ Jl '63
They tried to match Weegee. il Pop Phot 53:68-9+ Jl '63
Variations with Kodalith. il U S Camera 27: 50-3 D '64
What did Weegee do? il Pop Phot 52:56-7 F '63

Enlarging

B&W from color. il Mod Phot 27:60-7 F '63
Big negatives from little films. B. Pierce. Pop Phot 53:94 S '63
Correcting distortion; enlarger trick. J. Marshall. il Pop Mech 119:171 F '63
Enlarge upon your problems. L. H. Bogen. il U S Camera 26:66-7+ S '63
How to make jumbo contacts. M. M. Herron. il U S Camera 26:44-5 Jl '63
In the darkroom; rangefinder for your enlarger. A. Francekevich. il Pop Phot 53: 16+ N '63
In the darkroom; variable-contrast or graded papers? A. Francekevich. Pop Phot 52:10 Ap '63
New enlarging meter. B. Pierce. il Pop Phot 54:102-4 Mr '64
Roll film; grainless enlargements. J. Foldes. U S Camera 26:28-9 My '63
Theater and 35-mm. B. Pierce. Pop Phot 53: 76-7 Jl '63
35mm techniques; SLR? P. Stackpole. U S Camera 26:10+ My '63
Top B&W quality. E. Meyers. il Mod Phot 28:68-71 Ap '64
Up the zoom; two ways to get bigger movie images. M. A. Matzkin. il Mod Phot 27: 84-5+ F '63

Equipment

See Photography—Apparatus and supplies

Exhibitions

Adventure in seeing. il U S Camera 27:48-9 Ja '64
American landscape; exhibition at the Museum of modern art, New York. M. R. Weiss. il Sat R 46:29-35 S 28 '63
American landscape; Museum of modern art. P. Caulfield. il Mod Phot 28:80-1+ Ja '64
Are winners really winners? Kodak 1963 international color picture competition. il Mod Phot 28:38-9+ Ag '64
Automation will dominate Chicago MPDFA show. B. C. Brown. il Pop Phot 54:74-7+ Ap '64
Bent light koans; M. White one-man show. D. Vestal. Pop Phot 55:46+ N '64
Callahan shows, East & West, mark his book's publication. G. A. Young and H. M. Kinzer. il Pop Phot 54:28+ Je '64
Critics at large; Photographer and the American landscape at Museum of modern art, New York; four reviews, with photographs. Pop Phot 54:81-9+ Ja '64
Dateline: Chicago. il U S Camera 27:56-60 My '64
Dateline: Germany; photokina. W. Clark. il U S Camera 26:56-61+ Je '63
Double exposure; H. Callahan exhibition at New York's Hallmark gallery. M. R. Weiss. il Sat R 47:36-8 S 26 '64
Eloquent light: Ansel Adams' giant West Coast exhibit. P. Caulfield. il Mod Phot 28:12-13 F '64
Eloquent light; exhibition of photographs by A. Adams at M. H. de Young museum, San Francisco. B. Newhall; G. A. Young. il Pop Phot 54:74-5+ Mr '64
Exhibition; a selection of medal-winning color from the Eastman Kodak World's fair competition & show. il Pop Phot 55:78-81 Jl '64
Get the picture. P. Caulfield. il Mod Phot 28:16 My '64
Heliographers; new photographic movement. J. N. Uelsmann. il U S Camera 27:61-5 My '64
Here's what's new! il Pop Phot 52:43-58 Je '63
Ideas in images. H. M. Kinzer. il Pop Phot 52:68-71+ Mr '63
Images of endless moments; one display in Washington, the other traveling the western states. il N Y Times Mag p 134-6 N 8 '64
Kinzer on Photography '63 show: Brackett Clark gallery, Rochester, N.Y. H. M. Kinzer. il Pop Phot 54:28+ F '64
Kodak's photo wonderland. Pop Phot 54:124-5 My '64

PHOTOGRAPHY—Exhibitions—*Continued*
Matter of opinion; judging entries for photography in the fine arts exhibits. A. H. Mayor. il Sat R 46:41-54 My 18 '63
More than surface pictures; 124 photographs at the Eastman Kodak pavilion at the World's fair. il N Y Times Mag p32-3 S 20 '64
Movie maker; International amateur film festival, Cannes. M. A. Matzkin. Mod Phot 28:88+ F '64
New at the show; report on 40th Master photo dealers' and finishers' association national convention and trade show. il Pop Phot 54:87-97 Je '64
New at the trade show. L. Drukker. il Pop Phot 52:115-17+ Je '63
On gallery hanging fees. J. Deschin. Pop Phot 54:22+ Mr '64
One photographer's New York; exhibition at the Pepsi-Cola exhibition gallery. S. Falk. il N Y Times Mag p36-7 Mr 1 '64
Photo bubble surrounds you at the Swiss national exposition in Lausanne. L. Barry. il Pop Phot 54:68 My '64
Photo show roundup; Chicago trade show. il U S Camera 27:90-1 Je '64
Photographer's eye at modern museum. D. Vestal. il Pop Phot 55:42+ N '64
Photographer's eye; exhibition at New York's Museum of modern art. P. Caulfield. il Mod Phot 28:66-77 S '64
Photographs selected from The world and its people exhibit at the Kodak pavilion, New York world's fair. M. R. Weiss. il Sat R 47:34-42 Je 27 '64
Photography at the Modern; Museum of modern art. M. Kozloff. Nation 198:609-10 Je 15 '64
Photography in the fine arts IV. M. R. Weiss. il Sat R 46:39-40 My 18 '63
Photography in the fine arts, IV; exhibition at the Metropolitan museum of art, New York. R. Starrett. il Am Artist 27:44-9+ S '63
Photokina postscript. il Pop Phot 53:70-2+ Jl '63
Photokina story; fair of photography and cinematography in Cologne. N. Hall. il U S Camera 27:16-17+ N '64
Pictures under glass. S. Ross. il Pop Phot 52:64-5+ Ap '63
Popular photography's international exhibits. Pop Phot 54:123 Ja; 98 Ap; 94 My '64
Preview of photo show equipment. il U S Camera 27:37-44 Ap '64
Product parade of marvels at photokina. R. Miller. U S Camera 26:14-15 Ag '63
Russians are coming! R. Miller. il U S Camera 26:49-53+ My '63
Salon calendar. See issues of Modern photography
Show places and showcases. U S Camera 27:81 Ap; 82 My '64
Their subject was all outdoors; Photographer and the landscape exhibit at the Museum of modern art. il N Y Times Mag p80 S 22 '63
35mm techniques; Ansel Adams' one-man show. P. Stackpole. U S Camera 27:12 Mr '64
World's largest color prints; Kodak's pavilion, New York world's fair. B. Hering. il Pop Sci 184:158-61 My '64

Exposure

Bounce flash for color. C. Wright. il Pop Phot 52:46-9+ Ja '63
Camera gives pictures without using lenses; light from a mercury arc lamp or a laser. il Sci N L 84:395 D 21 '63
Color clinic; one-shot photography. D. B. Eisendrath, jr. il Pop Phot 53:8+ Jl '63
Color clinic; reciprocity failure. D. B. Eisendrath, jr. il Pop Phot 56:10+ Ja '65
Color workshop; wet street reflections. F. Bond. il Mod Phot 27:14+ Ap '63
Cora Wright's guide through the maze of exposure automation; with editorial comment. C. Wright. il Pop Phot 54:46, 49-59+ Mr '64
Crash course in color A. Francekevich. il Pop Phot 53:45-57+ Jl '63
Creative color; polarizing materials. A. Rothstein. U S Camera 26:8+ D '63
Creative color; ten common color problems. A. Rothstein. U S Camera 26:8-9 N '63
Creative exposure. P. Caulfield. il Mod Phot 28:58-65 Jl '64
Crop as you see. J. Balish. il Mod Phot 27:70-1 Je '63
Earthbound experimenter's adventures with a space-age film. K. Poli. il Pop Phot 55:50-1+ S '64
Expose Ektachrome-X at exposure index 500. E. Meyers. il Mod Phot 28:84-7+ My '64
Exposure methods & meters. P. Farber. il U S Camera 27:50-3+ Je '64
Eye as a meter. C. Wright. il Pop Phot 53:74-5 Jl '63
Eye as a meter indoors. C. Wright. Pop Phot 54:140 Ja '64
Film-speed trap. R. D. Zakia. il Pop Phot 55:68-9 S '64
Five exposure problems. U S Camera 26:40 Ag '63
Flash calculator. F. R. Shoemaker. il U S Camera 26:30+ Ag '63
For color: what is correct exposure? N. Rothschild. Pop Phot 55:79-80 Ag '64
How Ansel Adams makes an exposure. B. Newhall. il Pop Phot 52:40-3 F '63
How to live with automation. D. B. Eisendrath, jr. Pop Phot 55:12+ N '64
How to move a moon. il Pop Phot 52:50-1+ F '63
Is it true? right exposure. H. N. Todd and R. D. Zakia. Pop Phot 52:22 Ap '63
Keppler on the SLR; guide to automatic exposure control. H. Keppler. il Mod Phot 28:18+ Jl '64
Large camera; shutter-speed, aperture combinations. A. Feininger. Mod Phot 28:36 N; 44-5+ D '64
Lensless laser photography. il Pop Electr 20:60 Mr '64
Major exposure problem: backlight. il U S Camera 26:62-3 S '63
Make your own night-light exposure calculator. S. P. Martin. il Pop Phot 55:162-3+ D '64
Natural light snapshots. B. Pierce. Pop Phot 53:55-6 O '63
Negative positive; fog is a Dr Jekyll and a Mr Hyde. A. Asnis. U S Camera 26:38-9 O '63
Pictures in a moment; basic techniques for Polaroid prints. J. Wolbarst. Mod Phot 28:40+ Jl '64
RFDR cameras: real sharpness. W. Benser. il Mod Phot 27:58-61+ My '63
Simple flash exposures. C. Brandt. il U S Camera 26:52 F '63
Slow/fast how sharp? W. Benser. Mod Phot 28:88-9 S '64
Some aids for beating the international numbers game. il Pop Phot 52:144-5 Ap '63
Strictly for strobe-o-philes. P. R. Farber. il U S Camera 26:48-51 F '63
Subdued light for color beauty. il U S Camera 26:66-9 Je '63
Techniques tomorrow; film with a very wide light-level range. B. Sherman. il Mod Phot 27:16-17 Mr '63
Techniques tomorrow; low-light. B. Sherman. il Mod Phot 28:16-17+ F '64
Test report: new master photoguide. N. Rothschild. il Pop Phot 51:66-7+ D '62
35mm; basic exposure rules. J. Wolbarst. il Mod Phot 28:32+ Jl '64
Two simple shooting techniques for 35mm special effects. P. Caulfield. il Mod Phot 27:64-5 Ag '63
Under, over. P. Caulfield il Mod Phot 27:68-77 Jl '63
When & how to expose for perfect color. W. Benser. il Mod Phot 27:56-9+ Jl '63
When & how to shoot 35mm RFDR. P. Caulfield. il Mod Phot 27:64-9 My '63
Wrong exposures for the right reasons. M. Edelson. il U S Camera 28:58-9 Ja '65
See also
Exposure meters
Moving picture photography—Exposure

Films

Additive color: will it lead to better, cheaper films? N. Rothschild. il Pop Phot 54:112+ My '64
Agfacolor films; prognosis, processing, printing. Mod Phot 27:30 Je '63
Are black-and-white films too good? C. Wright. Pop Phot 52:81 F '63
As I see it: Kodak Instamatic system. E. Hannigan. il U S Camera 26:40 Je '63
As I see it; Polacolor. E. Hannigan. il U S Camera 26:42 My '63
Astronomical photography with the new XR film. W. P. Boquist. il Sky & Tel 27:12-14 Ja '64
At last! twenty-four 2¼ pictures on 120 roll film. H. Keppler and others. il Mod Phot 28:78-9+ N '64
Behind the scenes; new Agfa rapid system. il Mod Phot 28:12 Ag '64
Color clinic; films, faster and faster. D. B. Eisendrath, jr. Pop Phot 53:10+ D '63
Color clinic; reciprocity failure. D. B. Eisendrath, jr. il Pop Phot 56:10+ Ja '65

PHOTOGRAPHY—Films—*Continued*

Color films compared. il U S Camera 26:41-3+ Ag '63
Color films compared!! complete list of all available 35mm and roll films. il Mod Phot 28:84-5 O '64
Color films for transparencies. il Consumer Bul 46:6-8 O '63
Color gremlins. D. B. Eisendrath, jr. il Pop Phot 55:60-3 Jl '64
Color photos in sixty seconds. B. Hering. il Pop Sci 182:61-4+ F '63
Color workshop; faster color films. F. Bond. il Mod Phot 27:16-17+ S '63
Compare! compare! E. Meyers. il Mod Phot 28:74-5+ Ap '64
Compare 'em. H. Keppler. il Mod Phot 27: 90-5 O '63
Creative color; how to control high-speed color film to best advantage. A. Rothstein. U S Camera 26:8-9 S '63
Creative color; new 35 format. A. Rothstein. U S Camera 26:9-10 Je '63
Creative color; perfection of Polacolor. A. Rothstein. U S Camera 26:9-10 Mr '63
Daylight color films only? W. J. Sumits. Pop Phot 53:73 Jl '63
Directory of color films. U S Camera 27:52-3+ Jl '64
Earthbound experimenter's adventures with a space-age film. K. Poli. il Pop Phot 55:50-1+ S '64
8mm color movie film. Consumer Rep 28:352-3 Jl '63
Ektachrome-2, Ektachrome-3, Ektachrome-X. H. Keppler. il Mod Phot 27:66-7 Jl '63
Ektachrome-X: Modern's test shows it may even surpass Kodachrome. H. Keppler. il Mod Phot 27:74-5 Ag '63
Ektacolor S 120 film: more speed & latitude. H. Keppler and E. Meyers. Mod Phot 27:10 Mr '63
Expose Ektachrome-X at exposure index 500. E. Meyers. il Mod Phot 28:84-7+ My '64
Exposure index from .01 to 1000; multilatitude 35mm black-and-white film. E. Meyers and H. Keppler. il Mod Phot 27:78-9 Jl '63
Fast pictures taken with plastic film. Sci N L 83:233 Ap 13 '63
Film process may speed reconnaissance. B. Miller. il Aviation W 81:48-50 D 28 '64
Films for sub-35. il Pop Phot 53:63 Ag '63
Films your store may not carry. M. Bernam. il Pop Phot 52:66-7+ Je '63
Four new color films. J. Foldes. il U S Camera 26:64-5 S '63
Four new color films; Dynachrome 25; Ektacolor L; Kodacolor-X; Ektacolor S. N. Rothschild; C. G. Lindquist. il Pop Phot 55:52-5+ S '64
From Norman Rothschild's color notebook: which film? N. Rothschild. Pop Phot 55:66+ Jl '64
Heat films? B. Pierce. il Pop Phot 56:123+ Ja '65
How crucial is film choice? Pop Phot 55:45+ S '64
How to get the most out of Tri-X. R. W. Vesey. il Pop Phot 56:126-7+ Ja '65
How to sketch with a camera; contrast photography with Kodalith ortho film type 3. R. C. Wiseman. il U S Camera 27:66-7 S '64
Increasing the sensitivity of commercial films. E. A. Harlan. il Sky & Tel 27:187-8 Mr '64
Instant color photography. W. Siegrist. il Sci N L 83:250-1 Ap 20 '63
Instant color photos! K. Brown. il Pop Mech 119:100-5+ F '63
Instant 35mm. H. Keppler. il Mod Phot 27: 72-3+ Je '63
It's here! Polacolor; symposium with portfolio by famous pros. Pop Phot 52:49-63+ Mr '63
Kalvar; from a wastebasket, dazzling suspense. S. Mahoney. il Fortune 67:110-13+ Mr '63
Keep it fresh; tips about storage. D. Kirkland. il Pop Phot 52:59+ Je '63
Kodachrome II? Kodachrome-X? H/S Ektachrome? Ektachrome-X? H. Keppler. il Mod Phot 28:78-83 O '64
Kodachrome-X, Ektachrome-X; with test photos by Phillip Leonian. U S Camera 26:70-1 Je '63
Kodachrome-X: is it an improvement? S. Nathan. il U S Camera 26:56-7+ Ap '63
Kodak 'fesses up to 8mm film experiment. M. A. Matzkin. Mod Phot 28:18 S '64
Long load for 2¼ cameras. il U S Camera 27:58-9+ D '64
Modern tests four new Anscochrome films. E. Meyers. il Mod Phot 27:74-7 S '63
Movie maker; Kodak's experimental 8mm film. M. A. Matzkin. Mod Phot 28:44 N '64
Movie maker; preventing film damage and salvaging scratched film. M. A. Matzkin. Mod Phot 28:36+ Ap '64
New color films and how to tackle them. D. B. Eisendrath, jr. Pop Phot 52:10+ Je '63
New method for taking pictures developed; photo-plastic recording. il(p257) Sci N L 83:258 Ap 27 '63
9.5; a living corpse. I. Watson. il Pop Phot 56:166-7+ Ja '65
1964-1965 directory and buying guide. il Pop Phot 56:39C-51C Ja '65
Norman Rothschild's guide to daylight color slide films. N. Rothschild. il Pop Phot 53: 166-75 D '63
Peruchrome. il U S Camera 26:64-5 Ag '63
Pictures in a moment: holder conversions. J. Wolbarst. il Mod Phot 27:14+ N '63
Pictures in a moment; Kodak Tri-X Pan in a model 100 Polaroid camera. J. Wolbarst. Mod Phot 29:29+ Ja '65
Pictures in a moment; Polacolor. J. Wolbarst. il Mod Phot 27:14-15 Mr '63
Pictures in a moment; Polaroid Land film pack. J. Wolbarst. Mod Phot 28:40+ F '64
Pictures in a moment; Polaroid's new type color negative. J. Wolbarst. il Mod Phot 27:32 Jl '63
Plastic pictures; G.E.'s new picture-making process. Time 81:86 Ap 5 '63
Polacolor. il U S Camera 26:52-7 Mr '63
Polacolor six months later. D. B. Eisendrath. jr. Pop Phot 53:10+ S '63
Polaroid color. J. Wolbarst. il Mod Phot 27: 60-5+ Mr '63
Polaroid color pack camera. E. Hannigan. il U S Camera 26:50-3 O '63
Polaroid film pack, how it works. N. Rothschild. il Pop Phot 53:57-8 O '63
Polaroid Land color film. il Consumer Bul 46:9-10 Ag '63
Polaroid snaps into color. il Bsns W p80-2 Ja 19 '63
Polaroid's new color film. il Consumer Rep 28:376-7 Ag '63
Quick guide to B&W film. L. Lipton. il Pop Phot 55:64-7 S '64
Rapid cartridge system now, but... H. Keppler. il Mod Phot 29:98+ Ja '65
Refresher course on film. H. Martin. il Pop Phot 52:60-3+ Je '63
Sales & distribution; amateur photography market. J. B. Weiner. Duns R 83:59 Ja '64
70mm, fad or future? S. Nathan. U S Camera 26:33-5 My '63
Shooting with infrared; the light you can't see. R. Kinne. il Pop Phot 52:68-73 Je '63
Skin tones, sun & shade, nine films tested. H. Keppler. il Mod Phot 27:72-5 Ap '63
Special 35-mm issue; symposium, with editorial comment. il Pop Phot 55:30, 33-63+ Ag '64
Speedy film to explore fine details on moon. Sci N L 84:72 Ag 3 '63
Stop wasting your time with Kodachrome? top quality prints with Kodacolor-X. E. Meyers. il Mod Phot 28:78-9 Mr '64
Stupid questions about film. Pop Sci 184: 158-9 F '64
Super-8 film format up & coming? J. D. Scouller. il Pop Phot 55:92+ Ag '64
Technical report; XR film. R. T. Hammarlund. il U S Camera 26:45-8 My '63
Techniques tomorrow; film with a very wide light-level range. B. Sherman. il Mod Phot 27:16-17 Mr '63
Ten-second pictures; Polacolor. H. M. Kinzer. Pop Phot 52:12 My '63
35mm. J. Wolbarst. Mod Phot 28:14-15 Ja '64 (to be cont)
35mm daylight Kodachrome-X. H. Keppler. il Mod Phot 27:80-5+ Mr '63
35mm; films and developers of twenty-five years ago. J. Wolbarst. Mod Phot 27:12 My '63
35mm; Kodak's new X series color films. J. Wolbarst. Mod Phot 27:18+ O '63
35mm; on keeping unexposed color films. J. Wolbarst. Mod Phot 27:27 Mr '63
35mm; 126 film format. J. Wolbarst. il Mod Phot 27:33 Je '63
35mm; quest for film speed. J. Wolbarst. Mod Phot 28:14-15 Ja; 26+ F '64
35mm techniques; need for slower films. P. Stackpole. U S Camera 28:18 Ja '65
Those Japanese films. L. Barry. il Pop Phot 55:62-3+ S '64
Today's 8mm cartridges are versatile, tomorrow's may be instamatic. M. A. Matzkin. il Mod Phot 28:86-7+ F '64
Two different Ektachromes? N. Rothschild. Pop Phot 55:82-3 Jl '64

PHOTOGRAPHY—Films—*Continued*

Two new color films: Kodachrome-X and Ektacolor S. N. Rothschild; A. Francekevich; B. Pierce. il Pop Phot 52:18-19+ Mr '63

Two new color slide films. il Consumer Bul 47:43 Ja '64

Vagabond camera. W. Lane. il Travel 120: 62-3 O '63

Vagabond camera; Polaroid Land color film. W. Lane. Travel 119:70-1 Ap '63

Vagabond camera; Ultra speed Anscochrome used by astronaut Cooper. W. Lane. il Travel 120:60-1 Ag '63

Well traveled camera; battle against temperature and humidity when traveling. H. Keppler. Mod Phot 28:60+ O '64

Well traveled camera; color or black-and-white? H. Keppler. Mod Phot 27:111 O '63

What film, what paper, what developer for portraits? M. Bernam. il Pop Phot 53:140-1+ N '63

What'll you have in 35? il U S Camera 26:40-1 Jl '63

What's twice as long as 120 film? new Kodak 220. il Pop Phot 55:60 N '64

When rationing spurs demand; Polaroid's color film in Florida. il Bsns W p48 F 9 '63

Which film? H. Keppler. il Mod Phot 27:52-7+ F '63

Why I chose negative color. H. Power. il Pop Phot 55:92-3+ Jl '64

Why Kodachrome-X? D. B. Eisendrath, jr. Pop Phot 52:8+ My '63

Wrong film at the right time. M. Edelson. il U S Camera 27:48-9+ Jl '64

See also

Cameras—Loading

Fixing

Hypo-sniffer-outer. P. Farber. il U S Camera 27:54-5+ D '64

Is it true? on overfixation. H. N. Todd and R. D. Zakia. Pop Phot 52:24 Mr '63

Photography; fixing the world on paper. il Sci Digest 56:49-51 N '64

Processing: the inside story! W. F. Berg. Mod Phot 27:86-7 F '63

35mm; film washing. J. Wolbarst. Mod Phot 28:36 Ag '64

Toning, gimmick or valuable tool? N. Rothschild. Pop Phot 52:93-4 Mr '63

Focusing

Are RFDR viewfinders accurate? B. Sherman. il Mod Phot 27:70-1+ My '63

Big aperture and small aperture. il Pop Phot 54:50-3 My '64

Color workshop; three contrasts. F. Bond. il Mod Phot 27:20+ Je '63

Depth-of-field myths. N. Rotschild. Pop Phot 52:90-1 My '63

Do you really know how to focus? C. W. Kennedy. Pop Phot 55:66-7 O '64

Dynamic distortions by A. Kane. R. T. Hammarlund. il U S Camera 26:49-55+ Ap '63

Every lens has a personality. P. Glushanok. il Pop Phot 51:112+ D '62

Fast meter reading. C. Wright. Pop Phot 52:92-3 Mr '63

Fight against rangefinder parallax. L. A. Mannheim. il Mod Phot 28:98+ My '64

First complete guide to the art of zooming. E. Wildi. il Pop Phot 52:118-21+ My '63

Focusing for the next picture. F. Henle. il Pop Phot 55:36 S '64

Focusing systems for SLRs. G. Gilbert. il U S Camera 27:42-3+ D '64

Get the picture; normal lens for rangefinder and SLR's. P. Caulfield. il Mod Phot 27:48+ My '63

How to shoot soft-focus. N. Rothschild. il Pop Phot 54:80-1+ Ap '64

It brings the close in closer. J. A. Aita. il U S Camera 26:68-9 D '63

Keppler on the SLR; depth of field. H. Keppler. il Mod Phot 28:18+ Ja '64

Keppler on the SLR; hand-hold SLRs. H. Keppler. il Mod Phot 27:12+ Je '63

Keppler on the SLR; what you see and what you get. H. Keppler. il Mod Phot 27:10+ My '63

Key is M.O.P; mount, optics, and price. B. Pierce. il Pop Phot 54:64-7+ Ap '64

Large camera. A. Feininger. il Mod Phot 28: 18+ F; 23+ My '64

Logetronic's Focatron, an image-sharpness meter. C. Wright. il Pop Phot 52:88-9 My '63

Mutars; Rollei's answer to interchangeability. N. Rothschild. il Pop Phot 52:102-5 My '63

No time to focus. M. Morrison. il U S Camera 27:46-7+ S '64

Photography's toughest-to-use lens: the wide-angle. B. Pierce. il Pop Phot 52:96-101+ My '63

RFDR cameras: real sharpness. W. Benser. il Mod Phot 27:58-61+ My '63

Rangefinder pro hints and tips. E. Meyers and D. Miller. il Mod Phot 27:72-3 My '63

Selective focus. il U S Camera 26:66-7 Ag '63

Sharp indoor movies without fuss, feathers or focusing. M. A. Matzkin. il Mod Phot 27:90-1 Je '63

SLR finders. B. Sherman. il Mod Phot 27: 52-5+ Ap '63

Soft focus cat. il U S Camera 27:56-7 Mr '64

Test yourself for steadiness. C. Wright. Pop Phot 53:190 D '63

35mm; vision defects and the single-lens reflex user. J. Wolbarst. Mod Phot 27:42+ N; 34+ D '63

Through the looking glass; SLR. il U S Camera 27:44-7 D '64

Tonal trap. B. Pierce. Pop Phot 52:94 Mr '63

Twin lens; several maneuvers. F. Henle. il Pop Phot 52:24 Je '63

Twin lens; when to depart from the square. F. Henle. il Pop Phot 52:20 Ap '63

Use a bellows for mouse to moon. H. Keppler. il Mod Phot 27:64-9 Ap '63

With an SLR? shooting techniques. P. Caulfield. il Mod Phot 27:56-63 Ap '63

Working with subjects in depth. F. Henle. il Pop Phot 51:16 D '62

Galleries and museums

Colorado photographic art center. L. Meyer. il Pop Phot 56:136-7+ Ja '65

Questions about a photo arts center; Denver, Colo. J. Deschin. Pop Phot 54:38 Je '64

Grain

All about grain. D. Zwick. il Pop Phot 52: 56-63+ Ap '63

Are slow films sharper than fast films? B. Pierce. il Pop Phot 55:46-9+ S '64

Change of pace. il U S Camera 27:48-9 Je '64

Creative grain. A. Francekevich. il Pop Phot 55:14+ Ag '64

Grain, when it helps the picture. il Pop Phot 54:60-1 My '64

Light and the dark side of grain. A. Asnis. U S Camera 26:30-1 Je '63

Test report: Acutol-S; fine-grain developer from England. P. Farber. il U S Camera 27:62-3+ Je '64

Ultra-fine-grain processing. il Pop Phot 53:66+ Ag 63

What's finer than fine grain? H. Martin. il Pop Phot 52:64-5+ Je '63

History

Down memory lane; curios, relics, novelties and photographic memorabilia. G. Gilbert. il U S Camera 27:36-7+ Ja '64

From out of the past; photography in Germany. E. Bennett. il U S Camera 27:60-5+ N '64

Growth of photography. E. D. Collins. Hobbies 68:58+ Mr '63

Photography; fixing the world on paper. il Sci Digest 56:49-51 N '64

World leaps into an age of innovation. il Life 55:65-72B N 29 '63

Industrial applications

See Photography in industry

Judging

See Photography—Exhibitions

Landscapes

Adventure in seeing. il U S Camera 27:48-9 Ja '64

American landscape; exhibition at the Museum of modern art, New York. M. R. Weiss. il Sat R 46:29-35 S 28 '63

Ansel Adams. P. Caulfield. il Mod Phot 28: 55-65+ Ap '64

Camera guide to Japan. L. Barry. il Pop Phot 51:80-1+ D '62

Critics at large; Photographer and the American landscape at Museum of modern art, New York; four reviews, with photographs. Pop Phot 54:81-9+ Ja '64

Find the right angle for scenics. M. A. Matzkin. il Mod Phot 27:82-3 N '63

Get the picture; better scenics in less time. P. Caulfield. il Mod Phot 27:10+ Ag '63

Get the picture: critical eye on your surroundings. P. Caulfield. il Mod Phot 27:9+ Je '63

Get the picture; make more than portraits. P. Caulfield. il Mod Phot 27:23 O '63

Landscapes. il U S Camera 26:54-5 F '63

Landscapes; make your camera see what your eyes see. C. Allen. il U S Camera 27:46-7+ Ja '64

PHOTOGRAPHY—Landscapes—*Continued*
Magic eye of Dan Budnik. il U S Camera 26:64-9 Ap '63
Mexico, a big photo studio. L. Barry. il Pop Phot 52:30+ Mr '63
Nature and the camera; landscape photography. D. Linton. il Natur Hist 73:64-8 Ag '64
Operation mirage; Utah Desert. J. B. Wight. il U S Camera 26:66-7+ Jl '63
Portrait of a place; Central park, N.Y. E. Bubley. il U S Camera 26:58-61 Mr '63
Sharp crisp classic landscapes. H. Keppler. il Mod Phot 27:86-9+ O '63
35MM scenics; work of the National geographic's photographic staff. P. Caulfield. il Mod Phot 27:74-9 F '63
Well traveled camera; fall in southern Vermont. M. A. Matzkin. il Mod Phot 27:18+ N '63
Where's the point of interest? il U S Camera 27:44-5 Ja '64
Winter, an invitation to picture taking. R. L. Hering. il Pop Gard 16:14 Ja '65
Winter landscapes. E. Bush. il Horticulture 43:28-9+ Ja '65

Law

Decision which blazes a new trail: case involving photographs of public buildings. H. F. Pilpel. Pub W 187:271 Ja 25 '65
Restrictions on photography. il Pop Phot 52:146 Ap '63

Light

Color workshop; daylight. F. Bond. il Mod Phot 28:28-9+ My '64
Color workshop; three contrasts. F. Bond. il Mod Phot 27:20+ Je '63
Francekevich on portraiture: indoors and outdoors. A. Francekevich. il Pop Phot 53:132-5+ N '63
Light for color. il U S Camera 28:50-4 Ja '65
Major exposure problem: backlight. il U S Camera 26:62-3 S '63
Pictures in a moment; shooting Polacolor pictures in the shade. J. Wolbarst. il Mod Phot 28:14-15 Ap '64
Shoot into the sun. D. L. Miller. il Mod Phot 27:62-3 Jl '63
Skin tones, sun & shade, nine films tested. H. Keppler. il Mod Phot 27:72-5 Ap '63
Techniques tomorrow; possibilities of electronic light intensifiers. B. Sherman. Mod Phot 28:32-3 O '64
Ten ways to lighten shadows. il Pop Phot 54:94-5 Ja '64
Those super-speed lenses. B. Pierce. Pop Phot 54:109-10 Ap '64
Use the light you've got. H. Keppler. il Mod Phot 29:80-3 Ja '65
With an SLR? shooting techniques. P. Caulfield. il Mod Phot 27:56-63 Ap '63

Lighting

Basic lighting rigs. H. Shaman. il Pop Phot 53:136-7 N '63
Camera attachment to give shadowless lighting. W. Burton. il Pop Sci 185:136-7 N '64
Color on stage, available light or flash. il Pop Phot 52:50-1 Ja '63
Color on stage; technique. L. Barry. il Pop Phot 52:96-8 Ja '63
Color workshop. F. Bond. il Mod Phot 28:16+ Ap '64
Color workshop; combining indoor illumination with sunlit outdoor areas. F. Bond. il Mod Phot 28:20+ Jl '64
Color workshop; unusual light angles. F. Bond. il Mod Phot 28:30-1 N '64
Electronic flash studio in a 19-inch case. H. Shaman. il Pop Phot 51:76-9+ D '62
Glamor; flatter with a reflector. P. Gowland. il Pop Phot 53:20 Ag '63
Heatproof floodlight diffusers. il Pop Sci 185:134-5 N '64
How new movie lights stack up! M. A. Matzkin. il Mod Phot 28:94-5+ Ja '64
Light from behind. F. Henle. il Pop Phot 53:16 O '63
Lighting for duffers. R. Shorr. il Pop Phot 52:40-2+ Ja '63
Lighting the nude. P. Gowland. il Pop Phot 54:14+ Ja '64
Make a fan-fold umbrella light. F. L. Greenwald. il Pop Sci 185:132-4 N '64
Make your pictures bounce. il U S Camera 28:55+ Ja '65
Meters for available darkness. R. T. Hammarlund. il U S Camera 26:66-9 F '63
Movie lights better for stills? M. A. Matzkin. il Mod Phot 29:78-9+ Ja '65
Movie maker. M. A. Matzkin. il Mod Phot 29:58-9+ Ja '65
Movie maker; portable self-powered movie lights. M. A. Matzkin. il Mod Phot 28:96+ Ja '64
Movie maker; reflector floods. M. A. Matzkin. il Mod Phot 27:56+ N '63
Now! shoot color with fluorescent lighting. D. L. Miller. il Mod Phot 27:88+ F '63
One-light setups. A. Francekevich. il Pop Phot 52:43-5+ Ja '63
One-lightmanship. B. Pierce. Pop Phot 54:96-7 My '64
Photoflood life extenders. R. E. Pafenberg. il Pop Electr 20:68-9 Ap '64
Portable lights for color. B. Pierce. Pop Phot 53:188-9 D '63
Portraits like the pros. J. Burroughs. il Pop Mech 121:166-70 F '64
Problems, solutions. H. Shaman. il Pop Phot 54:106-9 Ja '64
Project your light; slide projector as a light source. J. Foldes. il U S Camera 26:48-9 D '63
Roundup: new lights. A. Francekevich. il Pop Phot 52:58-61+ Ja '63
Sane guide to indoor lighting. H. Keppler. il Mod Phot 28:58-65 Ja '64
Shooting with available light. A. Rothstein. il Pop Sci 182:102-5+ Mr '63
Shooting with infrared; the light you can't see. R. Kinne. il Pop Phot 52:68-73 Je '63
Studio in a suitcase. H. Shaman. il Pop Phot 55:60-3+ O '64
Techniques tomorrow. B. Sherman. il Mod Phot 28:16-17+ Ja '64
Why I prefer backlighting. R. Horne. il Pop Phot 52:52-5 Ja '63
See also
Moving picture photography—Lighting
Photography, Flashlight

Marines

Camera's eye; shooting a regatta. B. Robinson. il Yachting 113:36-7 My '63
Challenge of marine photography. il Motor B 112:36-9+ Jl '63
Summer action, sailing. C. Steinhardt. il U S Camera 26:58-9+ Ag '63
Water work. R. Kinne. il Flying 74:22 Je '64
Well traveled camera; traveling by ship? J. Balish. il Mod Phot 27:52+ My '63
See also
Photography of water

Negatives

Blast of fresh air (compressed); dusting negatives. A. Francekevich. Pop Phot 53:16 Ag '63
Born in a darkroom; unusual designs are india ink on a folded sheet of photo paper. E. Richmond. il Design 65:80-1 N '63
Compare! compare! E. Meyers. il Mod Phot 28:74-5+ Ap '64
Darkroom designer; excerpt from Design by photography. O. R. Croy. il Design 65:202-6 My '64
Foto facts. P. Farber. il U S Camera 28:28+ Ja '65
How not to lose pictures. A. Francekevich. il Pop Phot 52:12+ F '63
If your negatives aren't sharp. H. N. Todd and R. D. Zakia. Pop Phot 55:8 S '64
Make high contrast negatives. P. D. Borrelli. il U S Camera 27:68-9 My '64
Negatives for color. A. Francekevich. Pop Phot 54:28+ Ap '64
Paper negative. P. Farber. il U S Camera 27:60-1+ O '64
Repairing spots and scratches on the small negative. R. Hattersley. il Pop Phot 55:140-1+ N '64
Solving half-frame problems. N. Rothschild. il Pop Phot 55:54-5 Ag '64
Variations with Kodalith. il U S Camera 27:50-3 D '64
Why I chose negative color. H. Power. il Pop Phot 55:92-3+ Jl '64

Periodicals

Get the picture; Aperture and Contemporary photographer. P. Caulfield. Mod Phot 28:15 F '64

Portraits

Ah, what sights; water sprites! Hollywood's rising young actresses. D. Ornitz. Life 54:58-67 Ap 26 '63
Arnold Newman photographs the President. Pop Phot 55:40-1 O '64
Available light, by flash. il Pop Phot 52:56 Ja '63
Candid color portraits. il U S Camera 27:50-1 Ap '64
Character sketch. D. Streibig. Pop Phot 55:109 O '64
Christopher Isherwood on Images by Cecil Beaton. C. Isherwood. il Vogue 142:208-11 S 1 '63
Color workshop. F. Bond. il Mod Phot 27:23+ Mr '63; 28:11+ Ja '64

PHOTOGRAPHY—Portraits—*Continued*

Composite girl; multiple views. il U S Camera 27:60-1 Je '64
Extra-close portraits. F. Henle. Pop Phot 54:34 My '64
Feature pictures and how they were made. il U S Camera 27:40-3 Jl '64
Feininger; photographs from The world through my eyes. H. Keppler. Mod Phot 28:70-1 F '64
Get close for girl stoppers. P. Caulfield. Mod Phot 27:88-9 Je '63
Get the picture; approach for posed and candid portraits. P. Caulfield. il Mod Phot 27:14-15 S '63
Glamor. P. Gowland. See issues of Popular photography
Have fun with textures; screens from fabrics. H. Plemmons. il U S Camera 27:66-7 My '64
Home portraits. F. L. Greenwald. il U S Camera 26:74-5 N '63
Human document. M. R. Weiss. Sat R 47:100-2 O 10 '64
Informal portraits in your livingroom. J. Foldes. il U S Camera 27:82-3 Mr '64
Instant SLR for people. P. Caulfield. il Mod Phot 27:72-3 S '63
International beauty. E. Scully. U S Camera 27:14-15 O '64
Just a click apart. J. Morris. il U S Camera 26:62-5 D '63
Keppler on the SLR; shooting pictures of strangers. H. Keppler. Mod Phot 28:20+ N '64
Life in photography; excerpts. E. Steichen. il Look 27:28-37 N 5 '63
Light for color. U S Camera 28:50-4 Ja '65
Lighting. P. Caulfield. il Mod Phot 29:66-73 Ja '65
Little girl grows up. Esquire 62:208-9 D '64
Mirror, mirror on the wall. D. Duggan. il U S Camera 26:50-1 D '63
New angle on curves. il U S Camera 27:54-5 Jl '64
On being photographed by Philippe Halsman. B. Downes. Pop Phot 56:22+ Ja '65
People off-guard. J. Morris. il U S Camera 27:50-7 S '64
Perfect portraits, 35mm style. P. Stackpole. U S Camera 27:14 F '64
Pictures in a moment; snapshots of people. J. Wolbarst. Mod Phot 27:10-11 Je '63
Portrait flattery. C. Wright. Pop Phot 54:105-6 Mr '64
Portraits by press camera. M. R. Weiss. Sat R 47:52-3 Jl 11 '64
Portraits like the pros. J. Burroughs. il Pop Mech 121:166-70 F '64
Portraits: the casual way. L. Barry. il Pop Phot 54:114-18 My '64
Power of emotion. J. Morris. il U S Camera 26:76-7+ F '63
Prop it with a window. P. Caulfield. Mod Phot 27:74-5 My '63
Psychology of people-pictures. R. Hattersley. il Pop Phot 53:167-82 N '63
Rare new view at the top; Russian leaders. Life 55:72-9 S 13 '63
Screen test in Polacolor. J. Morris. il U S Camera 27:40-1 Mr '64
Sight of privacy. I. C. Lieb. il U S Camera 26:70-3 F '63
Skin tones, sun & shade, nine films tested. H. Keppler. il Mod Phot 27:72-5 Ap '63
Special portraiture issue; symposium. il Pop Phot 53:131-57+ N '63
Special techniques used in the Steinbeck portrait. P. Farber. U S Camera 27:28+ F '64
There's more than a smile. P. Gowland. Pop Phot 51:38+ D '62
Think outside-in for candid portraits. M. A. Matzken. il Mod Phot 28:62-3 F '64
Try filters for portraits. W. P. Banner. U S Camera 27:14+ D '64
TLR: today's portrait and press camera? F. Henle. il Pop Phot 53:40 D '63
2¼ SLR color way in. P. Caulfield. il Mod Phot 27:54-6 S '63
Use roller blinds as backgrounds. J. R. Coburn. il U S Camera 26:36 My '63
Von Sternberg principle; true nature of glamor. J. Von Sternberg. il Esquire 60:90-7+ O '63
We two. il U S Camera 27:58-9 N '64
What is style? excerpts from World in Vogue, with comments by P. Caulfield. il Mod Phot 27:68-77 N '63
With SLR only: control! Mod Phot 28:56-7 Mr '64
World's best people-peeper. U S Camera 28:46-7 Ja '65

See also

Daguerreotypes

Printing processes

B&W from color, here's how. H. Keppler and E. Meyers. il Mod Phot 27:68-9 F '63
Color printing; time & effort compared! E. Meyers. il Mod Phot 27:70-1+ F '63
Color 3-D printing process permits mass press run, glassless viewing. L. Lipton. Pop Phot 54:92-3 My '64
Create color by solarizing. H. Keppler and P. Caulfield. il Mod Phot 28:52-4 Ap '64
Darkroom delirium; creative printing. P. Farber. il U S Camera 27:72-5 N '64
Eliminating stains. A. Francekevich. Pop Phot 52:20+ Mr '63
Elcquence of gloss. J. Deschin. il Pop Phot 51:14+ D '62
Even the kitchen sink; convert your bath tub and kitchen sink into economical print washers. C. S. Douglas. il U S Camera 27:82 Ag '64
Far-out print techniques. B. Pierce. Pop Phot 54:98-9 F '64
Fast color printing. B. Pierce. il Pop Phot 52:89-90 My '63
Foto facts; bas-reliefs. P. Farber. il U S Camera 27:26 Je '64
Foto facts; photo-linen. P. Farber. il U S Camera 27:22+ N '64
From slide to B&W print without a negative. M. Adler. il U S Camera 26:26+ O '63
Gitzo: an amateurs optical printer. M. A. Matzkin. il Mod Phot 28:80 Ap '64
Hidden faces; magic from a bottle of india ink and a darkroom. J. Bakke and others. il Design 65:164-5+ Mr '64
How bad is B&W printing? M. A. Matzkin. il Mod Phot 28:66-7+ Je '64
How to louse up your color lab. N. Rothschild and L. Zoref. il Pop Phot 55:60-1+ S '64
How to print your slides. B. Pierce. Pop Phot 54:134-5 Ja '64
It works! Kodak rapid color processor model 11. E. Meyers. il Mod Phot 28:84-9+ Je '64
Just what is print quality? A. Francekevich. Pop Phot 55:16+ N '64
Make color prints. W. Lane. il Travel 120:56-7 S '63
Make mine toneline! H. Stenberg. il U S Camera 26:64-5 Mr '63
Make your prints shine! P. Gridley. il U S Camera 26:97 Ap '63
Master printer tells how. E. Meyers. il Mod Phot 27:86-91 N '63
Negative positive; test printing. A. Asnis. U S Camera 26:20-1 Jl '63
New FR paper makes color prints in seventeen minutes. P. Farber. il U S Camera 27:38-9+ Mr '64
New product report; Fotoval. P. Farber. il U S Camera 27:60+ Mr '64
New ways to look at slides. B. Pierce. Pop Phot 55:47 Jl '64
No-developer printing. C. Wright. il Pop Phot 53:154-6 D '63
Now: color processing in eight minutes. B. Hering. il Pop Sci 184:168-9 Ap '64
Now! use Kodak drum processor for fast color prints from slides. B. Pierce. Pop Phot 55:52+ N '64
Personalize your film development. B. Pierce. Pop Phot 55:67-9 O '64
Photography's elite of the future? J. Deschin. il Pop Phot 52:16+ Je '63
Pictures in a moment; color copies from Polaroid Land color prints. J. Wolbarst. Mod Phot 27:12+ S '63
Print spotting for submin & sub-35ers. P. Motal. il Pop Phot 53:71 Ag '63
Proof paper; darkroom in the sun. B. C. Black. il Sch Arts 63:11-13 My '64
Rapid color processor. P. Leonian. il U S Camera 27:38-9 Ap '64
Seven-min. color print process by Kodak. A. Francekevich. il Pop Phot 54:78-9+ Ap '64
Seven minute color prints in trays with machine chemicals. L. D. Smith, jr. il Pop Phot 55:56-7+ S '64
Simple color printing. A. Francekevich. Pop Phot 54:16+ Mr '64
Slides to prints and vice versa. R. Miller. U S Camera 26:50-1+ Ag '63
System for personal prints. B. Pierce. Pop Phot 55:157-9+ N '64
35mm; new processing system for color negative prints in Great Britain. J. Wolbarst. Mod Phot 28:26-7 Mr '64
Toning, gimmick or valuable tool? N. Rothschild. Pop Phot 52:93-4 Mr '63
Try posterization. C. Klimesh. il U S Camera 26:60-1 Ag '63
Unsharp positive. P. R. Farber. il U S Camera 26:56-7+ D '63
Variations with Kodalith. il U S Camera 27:50-3 D '64

PHOTOGRAPHY—Printing processes—*Cont.*
Viewpoints; into the printing paper fray. J. Deschin. Pop Phot 53:22 N '63
Visit with Axel Grosser. A. Francekevich. Pop Phot 55:28 D '64
What the instruction book doesn't say about Model 11. A. Francekevich. il Pop Phot 55:72-5+ Jl '64
Why prints differ from slides. D. B. Eisendrath, jr. Pop Phot 54:8+ Je '64
See also
Photographic finishing, Commercial

Retouching
Blemish-banishing made easy. M. Munkacsi. il Pop Phot 53:156-7+ N '63
Glamor; you can retouch on 2¼. P. Gowland. il Pop Phot 52:15+ Je '63
Make a photograph an etching with a brush. il Pop Phot 52:52-3 F '63
Paper negative. P. Farber. il U S Camera 27:60-1+ O '64

Scientific applications
Art of the biological photographer. il Natur Hist 74:58-61 Ja '65
Astronaut in orbit: shooting way out landscapes from far out space. M. A. Matzkin. Mod Phot 27:50+ Ag '63
Cell that lit its own picture; bioluminescent marine cells. il Sci Digest 55:75 Je '64
Cell visible by own light; photographs of noctiluca miliaris, with light-amplifying device. A. Ewing. il Sci N L 85:178 Mr 21 '64
High-speed automatic analysis of biomedical pictures. R. S. Ledley. bibliog il Science 146:216-23 O 9 '64
Microscopes. R Kinne. il Pop Phot 51:88-91 D '62
New in pathology: a giant jigsaw puzzle. il Todays Health 41:74 Ag '63
Probing the mysteries of light. R. Dunlop. il Todays Health 41:34-9+ Mr '63
Sedentary safari in 3-D. P. R. Farber. il U S Camera 26:62-3+ Mr '63
35mm scenics; work of the National geographic's photographic staff. P. Caulfield. il Mod Phot 27:74-9 F '63
See also
Photography, Legal
Photomicrography

Societies
See also
Camera clubs

Still life
Critic's choice. J. Deschin. il Pop Phot 54:114-15+ Ja '64
Still lifes that move. il U S Camera 27:52-5 My '64

Studios and darkrooms
Building a color-printing darkroom. B. Pierce. Pop Phot 55:80-1 Ag '64
Careers in the lab. A. Francekevich. Pop Phot 54:16 Ja '64
Coexistence in the lab. A. Francekevich. Pop Phot 52:30 Je '63
Darkroom dilemmas. C. W. Kennedy. Pop Phot 55:50+ D '64
Darkroom stumbling blocks. N. Rothschild. Pop Phot 55:66 O '64
Darkrooms of the future. W. J. Sumits. Pop Phot 54:107 Ap '64
Dream darkroom studio workshop. J. Maxwell. il Pop Phot 53:64-5+ O '63
Electronic flash studio in a 19-inch case. H. Shaman. il Pop Phot 51:76-9+ D '62
Finally, in the darkroom. il Pop Phot 54:54-5 My '64
How our cover pictures were made. il Pop Phot 52:78 Ja '63
How to make a light-tight window shield. C. E. Arnaud. il Pop Phot 54:82-3 My '64
Invisible darkroom. J. Hand. il Pop Sci 184:152-3+ F '64
Making lab life easier. A. Francekevich. il Pop Phot 54:42+ Je '64
Mister, are you clean? T. Runge. il Pop Phot 55:138-9+ D '64
Negative positive; exposé of dirty darkrooms. A. Asnis. U S Camera 26:40-1 Ap '63
Rollaway darkroom. F. C. Clark, jr. il Pop Mech 119:148-9 Je '63
Travel darkroom? C. Steiner. il Pop Phot 54:134-7 Ap '64
Your darkroom: what to get where to put it. E. Meyers. il Mod Phot 28:66-9 F '64

Study and teaching
Creative color. A. Rothstein. U S Camera 27:8+ Mr '64
Do you respect color? P. Gowland. il Pop Phot 52:16+ Ja '63
Famous photographers school: a new concept. il Pop Phot 54:90-3 Ja '64
Get the picture; workshops. P. Caulfield. Mod Phot 28:28-9 N '64
How good are the home study schools? D. L. Miller. il Mod Phot 28:78-9 F '64
Importance of composition; excerpt from a Famous photographers school lesson. il U S Camera 27:48-53 F '64
Kodak's new teaching tool. D. Vestal. il Pop Phot 54:16+ Ap '64
Photographic program featured at Vermont resort: The Silos. L. Lachter. il U S Camera 26:17 F '63
Photography at Tucson high. il U S Camera 27:50-1+ Mr '64
Photography in the schools. B. Downes. Pop Phot 52:54 Ap '63
Photography in your school. R. A. Yoder. il Sch Arts 64:19-22 N '64
Photography is possible. B. Reed. il Sch Arts 62:11-13 Ap '63
Teaching too much too soon. J. Deschin. Pop Phot 54:28 My '64
Teenage photographers; young German photographers. il U S Camera 27:70-1+ N '64
Where to study film-making. H. V. Fondiller. il Pop Phot 53:98-9+ O '63
See also
Famous photographers school

Terminology
What means what in SLR. H. Keppler. Mod Phot 28:99 Jl '64

Themes
Airports. il U S Camera 27:16-17 My '64
Amateur speaks. il U S Camera 26:70-1 Ap '63
Before and after. il U S Camera 27:70-3 F '64
Creative color; fifteen uses for Polacolor. A. Rothstein. il U S Camera 26:9-10 Ap '63
Do you see faces? I do! G. Haist. il U S Camera 27:36 F '64
Eye for writing; excerpts from Stop, look, and write! H. Leavitt and D. Sohn. il Sr Schol 85:18T-19T D 2 '64
Get the picture; documentary or experimental projects. P. Caulfield. il Mod Phot 28:12-13 O '64
Get the picture; potpourri of subjects. P. Caulfield. Mod Phot 27:54 N '63
Go shopping for pictures. D. Graham. il U S Camera 26:10-11+ S '63
Kids; group of city youngsters. R. R. McLaughlin. il U S Camera 26:44-8 Je '63
Life on the farm (U.S.A) il U S Camera 26:36 O '63
Love on the light side. il U S Camera 26:40 O '63
Photo bargains; Edmund Scientific's catalog. il Pop Phot 55:150-1+ N '64
Photographer is a rabbi. C. Schwalberg. il U S Camera 26:66-9+ O '63
Photographer on campus. J. R. Holland. il U S Camera 27:66-7+ D '64
Put comedy into your slide shows. R. Miller. U S Camera 27:16-17 F '64
Weekend amateur. il U S Camera 27:64-5 Je '64

PHOTOGRAPHY, Aerial
Europe; an aerial close-up, by C. E. Rotkin. Review
Pop Phot il 52:16+ Ap '63. D. B. Eisendrath, jr
Flying fotographer. il Flying 74:60 Mr; 64 Ap; 56 My; 22 Je; 75:24 Jl; 75 S '64
Get the picture. P. Caulfield. il Mod Phot 28:12-13 Ja '64
He looks down on Europe. il U S Camera 26:24 Ap '63
Hunting by air photos. L. Pringle. il Outdoor Life 131:50-1+ F '63
Los Alamos gets photographed. il Am City 78:81 F '63
Marshes prograding in Oregon: aerial photographs. C. L. Johannessen. bibliog il Science 146:1575-8 D 18 '64
Mobile photo interpretation cells designed for use in tactical areas. il Aviation W 81:95 Ag 10 '64
New perspective on New York. il N Y Times Mag p40-1 Mr 8 '64
Rotating prism panoramic camera adds new dimension to photo-recon technique. W. Wright. il Aviation W 78:112-13+ F 25 '63
Sky cameras; America's cold-war sentinels. C. P. Gilmore. il Pop Sci 183:116-21+ O '63
So long for now; with photographs by C. Bonnay. Esquire 59:86 Ap '63
Techniques tomorrow. B. Sherman. il Mod Phot 28:16-17 Mr '64
Techniques tomorrow; razor-sharp spy photos at 40,000 ft? B. Sherman. il Mod Phot 27:40+ F '63
2¼ SLR color way out. P. Caulfield. il Mod Phot 27:57-9 S '63

PHOTOGRAPHY, Aerial—*Continued*
View from eighty feet up. F. Henle. il Pop Phot 54:40 Je '64
See also
Aerial reconnaissance
Mapping, Aerial
Photography in agriculture
Space photography

PHOTOGRAPHY, Architectural. See Photography of buildings and structures

PHOTOGRAPHY, Artistic
Films & photography. G. Manupelli. il Sch Arts 62:28-32 Mr '63
Focus on Pete Turner. J. Durniak. il Pop Phot 52:62-71+ My '63
Heliographers; new photographic movement. J. N. Uelsmann. il U S Camera 27:61-5 My '64
Ideas in images. H. M. Kinzer. il Pop Phot 52:68-71+ Mr '63
Magic eye of Dan Budnik. il U S Camera 26:64-9 Ap '63
Nile. il U S Camera 27:40-7 My '64
Painters without brushes. il Pop Phot 55:42-9 O '64
Photographs to live with. E. Braun. il U S Camera 27:22-3+ S '64
Pictures. il Pop Phot 51:82-7 D '62
Planned SLR for design. P. Caulfield. il Mod Phot 27:70-1 S 63
Play gypsy, dance gypsy. J. Morris. il U S Camera 27:63-7 Ap '64
Rudolph Burckhardt; multiple fugitive. A. Katz. il Art N 62:38-41 D '63
Sight of privacy. I. C. Lieb. il U S Camera 26:70-3 F '63
Subjective rangefinder. P. Caulfield. il Mod Phot 28:64-71+ My '64
World through my eyes, by A. Feininger. Review
Pop Phot il 54:68-77+ F '64
Wrong film at the right time. M. Edelson. il U S Camera 27:48-9+ Jl '64
Your prints on other people's walls. C. Schwalberg. il U S Camera 26:40+ Mr '63

PHOTOGRAPHY, Astronomical. See Astronomical photography

PHOTOGRAPHY, Close-up
Cat's-eye view; photographs. J. L. Swiners. U S Camera 26:56-7 F '63
Close-up lenses. il Pop Phot 52:108-9 Ap '63
Color work-shop. F. Bond. il Mod Phot 27:14-15+ O '63
Don't short-change the background. A. Lavine. il Pop Phot 54:82-3+ Je '64
Extra-close portraits. F. Henle. Pop Phot 54:34 My '64
How easy is a close-up? H. M. Kinzer. il Pop Phot 52:99 Ja '63
How to use small-camera bellows & extension tubes. N. Rothschild. il Pop Phot 54:42-7+ F '64
Just a click apart. J. Morris. il U S Camera 26:62-5 D '63
Large camera; some tips on close-up and macrophotography. A. Feininger. Mod Phot 28:16+ Jl '64
Move in close. B. Hering. il Pop Sci 182:146-50+ Ap '63
New close-up technique. N. Rothschild. il Pop Phot 55:156+ N '64
No-fuss close-ups. C. W. Kennedy. il Pop Phot 55:52-7+ O '64
Shoot it close! crop it tight! il U S Camera 26:41-7 D '63
Super-wide & close-ups, too! T. Baba. il Mod Phot 27:68-9 Je '63
Vagabond camera. W. Lane. il Travel 120:56-7 S '63
What's in an eye? il U S Camera 26:18 D '63
Which lens for better close-ups? H. Keppler. il Mod Phot 27:78-81 S '63

PHOTOGRAPHY, Color. See Color photography

PHOTOGRAPHY, Commercial
Careers in color photography. A. Rothstein. U S Camera 27:22+ Jl '64
Focus on Fritz Henle. H. M. Kinzer. il Pop Phot 55:142-9+ N '64
Kertész: rebirth of an eternal amateur. J. Deschin. Pop Phot 55:32+ D '64
Myth of versatility. J. Deschin. il Pop Phot 54:22+ Ap '64
Picture within. J. Morris. il U S Camera 27:70-3+ O '64
Polaroid camera means business. B. Goldrath. il U S Camera 27:22+ Je '64
Tony Kelly's America; a fresh look at the good life. T. Kelly. il Pop Phot 55:148-53+ D '64
See also
Photography, Journalistic
Photography in advertising

PHOTOGRAPHY, Composite. See Photomontage

PHOTOGRAPHY, Documentary
Amateur speaks. il U S Camera 26:70-1 Ap '63
Indian-head nickel: some words with himself. A. Glaser. il Esquire 61:58+ Mr '64
Objective rangefinder. H. Keppler. il Mod Phot 28:72-9 My '64
Tony Kelly's America; a fresh look at the good life. T. Kelly. il Pop Phot 55:148-53+ D '64
William Klein. P. Caulfield. il Mod Phot 29:84-9 Ja '65

PHOTOGRAPHY, Fashion
On location in Red square. il N Y Times Mag p70 Mr 15 '64

PHOTOGRAPHY, Flashlight
AG-1 flash. D. L. Miller. il Mod Phot 29:74-5+ Ja '65
Available light, by flash. il Pop Phot 52:56 Ja '63
Big little flash. J. Wolbarst. il Mod Phot 28:78-9+ Ja '64
Color clinic; simple solutions to flash problems. D. B. Eisendrath, jr. Pop Phot 55:14+ O '64
Common sense and guide numbers; using color film. D. B. Eisendrath, jr. il Pop Phot 55:30+ Jl '64
Electronic flash: is it the perfect portable light source? R. M. Benrey. il Pop Phot 55:154-5+ N '64
Flash with color. il U S Camera 26:52-3 D '63
Flash, with forethought. F. Henle. il Pop Phot 52:28 Ja '63
Flashbulb or speedlight? S. Nathan. il U S Camera 26:44-7+ F '63
Focal plane flash problems with SLRs. D. L. Miller. il Mod Phot 28:82-3+ Mr '64
Inexpensive speedlight studio. M. Morrison. il U S Camera 27:56-7+ Jl '64
Instant guide numbers for electronic flash; with guide number nomograph. C. Wright. Pop Phot 53:92-3 S '63
Kinne on flash. R. Kinne. il Pop Phot 53:68-75+ O '63
Lighting. P. Caulfield. il Mod Phot 29:66-73 Ja '65
Lowdown on portable electronic flash units. T. Karp. il Mod Phot 28:82-7 Ja '64
Peek into the flash world of tomorrow. P. Stackpole. U S Camera 27:14 S '64
Pictures in a moment. J. Wolbarst. Mod Phot 27:43 O '63
Should you buy a used camera without flash synchronization? comp. by A. C. Muller. Mod Phot 27:98 D '63
Simple flash exposures. C. Brandt. il U S Camera 26:52 F '63
Single-lamp home movie lights. il Consumer Rep 29:78-81 F '64
35mm techniques; small flash units. P. Stackpole. U S Camera 27:18+ Je '64
When the sun needs help; fill-in flash. il U S Camera 27:54-5 Je '64
Your electronic flash exposure made easy. W. Hanson and B. T. Wolfe. il Mod Phot 28:52-3 Jl '64
See also
Electric lamps, Flashlight
Photography, High speed

PHOTOGRAPHY, Forensic. See Photography, Legal

PHOTOGRAPHY, High speed
Amateur scientist; on constructing high-speed cameras for photographing fleeting events. W. Gannaway. il Sci Am 211:118-24+ Jl '64
Bounce flash for color. C. Wright. il Pop Phot 52:46-9+ Ja '63
Creative color; how to control high-speed color film to best advantage. A. Rothstein. U S Camera 26:8-9 S '63
Flashbulb or speedlight? S. Nathan. il U S Camera 26:44-7+ F '63
Freeze motion with sound. R. E. Pafenberg. il Pop Electr 22:43-6+ Ja '65
Go slow for high speed. B. Pierce. Pop Phot 52:110-11 Ap '63
How to use Polacolor with speedlight & flashbulbs. A. Francekevich. Pop Phot 52:61 Mr '63
Keppler on the SLR. H. Keppler. il Mod Phot 27:12-13 O '63
Strictly for strobe-o-philes. P. R. Farber. il U S Camera 26:48-51 F '63
35mm daylight Kodachrome-X. H. Keppler. il Mod Phot 27:80-5+ Mr '63

PHOTOGRAPHY, Infrared
Cameras see in the dark. F. Davis. il Sci N L 83:135+ Mr 2 '63
Navy sees promise in infrared thermography for solid case checking. W. S. Beller. il Miss & Roc 16:22-3 Ja 4 '65
See also
Photography, Medical

PHOTOGRAPHY, Journalistic
As I see it. E. Hannigan. il U S Camera 27:38 F '64
As I see it; New York city news photography and live TV news. E. Hannigan. il U S Camera 26:32+ Jl '63
Bar's side of Canon 35. J. H. Yauch. Sat R 46:61-2 Mr 9 '63
Call me Daddy; story of one of Rome's most notorious peeping toms of photography. J. Morris. il U S Camera 28:82-5 Ja '65
Canon 35: the case for the defendant; question; should photographers be allowed in courtrooms? B. Warner. il U S Camera 26: 64-5+ Jl '63; Reply. P. Stackpole. 26:12-13 S '63
Creative color; impact of Polacolor on newspaper photography. A. Rothstein. U S Camera 26:14+ O '63
Crisis in photojournalism. H. Sochurek. Pop Phot 52:57+ Ap '63; Reply. G. Lockwood. 53:38 S '63
Democrats and 389 photographers. B. Brown. il Pop Phot 55:140-1+ D '64
Elusive newspaper market. W. G. Kreger. il U S Camera 26:18+ S '63
Feature pictures and how they were made. il U S Camera 27:46-9 Mr; 40-3 Jl '64
Feature pictures: year to remember; 21st annual White House news photographers photo contest. il U S Camera 27:68-73 Je '64
Focus on Marilyn Silverstone. L. Barry. il Pop Phot 56:130-5+ Ja '65
Focus on Robert Freson. C. Reynolds. il Pop Phot 54:74-81+ Je '64
Focus on Zimmerman. J. Durniak. il Pop Phot 52:82-91+ Ap '63
Future techniques; memories of years on staff of the New York mirror. J. Reidy. U S Camera 27:16-18 Mr '64
Germany looks at the world; photojournalism is the leading trend among Germany's young photographers. il U S Camera 27:44-51 N '64
Gettysburg 1963. B. Roberts. il U S Camera 26:74-7+ Ag '63
Great lady with a camera; excerpts from Portrait of myself. M. Bourke-White. il Life 54:85-8+ Je 28 '63
Hidden power of pictures. B. Whitmore. U S Camera 26:72+ Ap '63
How did photographers, TV, and the press meet the challenge of the topless swimsuit? L. Barry. il Pop Phot 55:135-9+ N '64
John F. Kennedy, 1917-1963. il U S Camera 27:42-5 F '64
Methods & materials. L. Drukker. Pop Phot 53:183+ N '63; 54:115+ Ap '64
One photographer+one model=all women. J. Morris. il U S Camera 26:64-71 My '63
Photographers don't think! J. G. Morris. Pop Phot 51:65+ D '62
Photographic team witnesses the end of Alcatraz. P. Stackpole. U S Camera 26:12-13 Jl '63
Photography in the White House; interview, ed. by O. Atkins. P. Salinger. il U S Camera 26:12+ Mr '63
Pictures under pressure. B. Stapleton. il Pop Phot 52:44-7 F '63
Politics and photography; San Francisco's news-making breakthroughs. G. A. Young. il Pop Phot 55:130-1+ N '64
Problems, solutions. H. Shaman. il Pop Phot 54:106-9 Ja '64
PR photography and some letters. J. Deschin. il Pop Phot 53:16+ S '63
Return of Eugene Smith! P. Stackpole. U S Camera 27:8 Ja '64
Screen test in Polacolor. J. Morris. il U S Camera 27:40-1 Mr '64
They always get the picture. C. Schwalberg. il U S Camera 26:46-9+ Jl '63
35mm techniques; camera reporting on TV. P. Stackpole. U S Camera 26:32+ O '63
35mm techniques; ups and downs of magazine photography. P. Stackpole. U S Camera 27:16+ O '64
Tim Kantor; with portfolio of images of Latin America. U S Camera 26:46-51 Mr '63
TLR: today's portrait and press camera? F. Henle. il Pop Phot 53:40 D '63
Unforgettable. A. Brodovitch. il Pop Phot 54: 84-5 Je '64
Want to write? get a camera. E. Houghton. Writer 76:26-7 Jl '63
Women in photojournalism. M. K. Morgan. il Pop Phot 54:41+ F '64
World's wildest photograpers. N. Lo Bello. U S Camera 26:50+ Jl '63

PHOTOGRAPHY, Legal
Say it with your camera; photography takes the stand. J. Deschin. il Pop Phot 52:14 Ap '63
See also
Photography in criminal investigation
PHOTOGRAPHY, Marine. See Photography—Marines
PHOTOGRAPHY, Medical
Camera spots tumors; positron scintillation camera. Sci N L 84:2 Jl 6 '63
Instant stroke diagnosis; thermographic test. il Sci Digest 57:16-17 Ja '65
New medical device spots hidden diseases; thermograph camera. R. P. Goldman. il Sat Eve Post 236:44-6+ S 28 '63
Safe X-ray substitute shows placenta location; thermography. Sci N L 86:345 N 28 '64
Thermography of the human body. R. B. Barnes. bibliog il Science 140:870-7 My 24 '63
Trouble with hot spots. il Time 81:78-9 Je 14 '63
PHOTOGRAPHY, Military
Chase aircraft modified for GT-2 photos. G. Alexander. il Aviation W 81:52-3+ D 14 '64
Cuba: how dangerous now; with excerpt from President Kennedy's news conference, February 7, 1963. il U S News 54:58-63 F 18 '63
Extent of Cuban missile threat revealed; photo-intelligence briefing by Defense Secretary Robert S. McNamara and John Hughes. Aviation W 78:31 F 11 '63
Loud but late; photo record of the Soviet military deployment in Cuba. R. Hotz. Aviation W 78:21 F 11 '63
Ninety dangerous days for U.S; with summary of Strike in the West. by J. Daniel and J. G. Hubbell. il U S News 54:70-2 Mr 11 '63
Recon photos reveal Soviet anti-aircraft buildup in Cuba. il Aviation W 78:28-31 F 18 '63
War preventers; photo-reconnaissance planes. S. D Pursglove. il Pop Mech 119:106-11+ F '63
See also
Aerial reconnaissance
World war, 1939-1945—Photography
PHOTOGRAPHY, Moving picture. See Moving picture photography
PHOTOGRAPHY, Night
Color action at night. G. Hoffman. il U S Camera 26:48-9+ Ag '63
Color workshop. F. Bond. il Mod Phot 28:42+ Mr '64
Eight tips for better night color. S. B. Stone. il Pop Phot 55:76-7 Jl '64
Here's your chance for colorful night pictures. Pop Phot 54:123 My '64
Long exposures for night color. il U S Camera 26:70-2 Mr '63
Make your own night-light exposure calculator. S. P. Martin. il Pop Phot 55:162-3+ D '64
Negative positive; fire at night. A. Asnis. U S Camera 26:30-1 My '63
Night exposures. M. M. Herron. il U S Camera 26:60-1 S '63
Rainy night in old London town. W. Benser. il U S Camera 26:80-1 O '63
PHOTOGRAPHY, Panoramic
Panoramic camera for under $40; Russian-made Spaceview 2. P. Schroeder. il Pop Phot 54:54-5+ F '64
PHOTOGRAPHY, Photo-plastic
PPR: entirely new system of photography! J. Reidy. il U S Camera 26:24+ Ag '63
PHOTOGRAPHY, Pictorial. See Photography, Artistic
PHOTOGRAPHY, Space. See Space photography
PHOTOGRAPHY, Stereoscopic. See Stereo-photography
PHOTOGRAPHY, Submarine
At home in the sea. J. Y. Cousteau. il Nat Geog Mag 125:465-507 Ap '64
Coming up with underwater pictures. D. B. Eisendrath, jr. il Pop Phot 55:10+ S '64
Fluorescent gems from Davy Jones's locker. P. A. Zahl. il Nat Geog Mag 124:260-71 Ag '63
Glamor; try shooting underwater. P. Gowland. il Pop Phot 53:12 Jl '63
Lower depths; photography in underwater darkness. L. Jacobs. il U S Camera 27:52-3+ Ag '64
Nikonos: the toughest 35. P. Leonian. il U S Camera 27:58-9+ S '64
Photographing the night creatures of Alligator Reef. R. E. Schroeder. il Nat Geog Mag 125:128-54 Ja '64
Search for the Thresher. F. N. Spiess and A. E. Maxwell. bibliog il Science 145:349-55 Jl 24 '64

PHOTOGRAPHY, Submarine—*Continued*
Snap in the deep. L. Barry. il Pop Phot 54:20+ F '64
35mm techniques; covering a 1,000-foot dive off Catalina. P. Stackpole. U S Camera 26: 15+ Mr '63
Thresher found? metal fragments photographed on ocean floor. il Bsns W p34 My 25 '63
Two worlds in one picture. C. Phinizy. il U S Camera 26:38-9+ Jl '63; Reply. P. Stackpole. 26:12 S '63
PHOTOGRAPHY, Table top
Color workshop. F. Bond. il Mod Phot 28: 32-3+ D '64
Sedentary safari in 3-D. P. R. Farber. il U S Camera 26:62-3+ Mr '63
Space films by people who can't go. H. V. Fondiller. il Pop Phot 52:96+ F '63
PHOTOGRAPHY, Theatrical
Color blur how far should you go? J. Morris. il U S Camera 27:68-9 Ap '64
Color on stage, available light or flash. il Pop Phot 52:50-1 Ja '63
Color on stage; technique. L. Barry. il Pop Phot 52:96-8 Ja '63
Get the picture at spectator events. P. Caulfield. il Mod Phot 27:12-13 Ap '63
Lights, action, camera! E. Rooney. il U S Camera 26:64-7+ N '63
PHOTOGRAPHY, Three dimensional. See Stereophotography
PHOTOGRAPHY, Trick
Camera tricks the amateur can use. il Good H 157:170 N '63
Color slides; repetitive image technique. R. S. Miller. il U S Camera 26:26-7 Ap '63
Color slides; techniques. R. Miller. il U S Camera 26:24+ Jl '63
Cork-screw camera. H. Keppler. il Mod Phot 27:74-5 Mr '63
Foolish fisheyes. U S Camera 27:76-7 My '64
Foto facts. P. Farber. il U S Camera 27:28-9 Jl '64
Heads or tails. il U S Camera 27:20 O '64
How to get contrast and grain. P. Gowland. il Pop Phot 52:38 My '63
More photo fun. J. Eisner. il Pop Mech 121: 138-9 Ja '64
People from paradise. J. Morris. il U S Camera 27:34-7 Jl '64
Roll film. J. Foldes. il U S Camera 26:30-1 Mr '63
Spill pix. P. Farber. il U S Camera 27:60-1+ Ap '64
Start with a sketch pad. J. Kinney and C. Kinney. il U S Camera 26:61-3+ N '63
Try these new cross-polarization techniques. P. Farber. U S Camera 27:30+ S '64
When a trick is a treat. M. Morrison. il U S Camera 28:64 Ja '65
See also
Photography—Distortion
PHOTOGRAPHY, Wide field
Wide field pictures. il U S Camera 26:54-61+ O '63
PHOTOGRAPHY and art. See Art and photography
PHOTOGRAPHY as a profession
Careers in the lab. A. Francekevich. Pop Phot 54:16 Ja '64
How to break in. H. V. Fondiller. il Pop Phot 54:107+ F '64
PHOTOGRAPHY by children. See Children as photographers
PHOTOGRAPHY centers. See Recreation centers
PHOTOGRAPHY clubs. See Camera clubs; Moving picture clubs
PHOTOGRAPHY from moving objects
Get the picture; shooting stills and movies from amusement park rides. P. Caulfield. il Mod Phot 27:22-3 F '63
PHOTOGRAPHY in advertising
Hidden power of pictures. B. Whitmore. U S Camera 26:72+ Ap '63
One way to break into photography. H. Smith. il U S Camera 27:58-9+ Ap '64
Potpourri of kids. il U S Camera 27:58-9 Mr '64
Problems, solution. H. Shaman. il Pop Phot 54:106-9 Ja '64
Restless eye of Todd Walker. M. Ornitz. il U S Camera 27:46-9+ Ap '64
What do these pictures have in common? pharmaceutical advertising. C. Schwalberg. il U S Camera 28:60-3+ Ja '65
PHOTOGRAPHY in agriculture
Infrared photos from air detect salt-damaged soil. Sci N L 84:98 Ag 17 '63
New aid for crops. Sci N L 84:379 D 14 '63
PHOTOGRAPHY in criminal investigation
Movies aid police work, reassure public; Rochester, N.Y. W. M. Lombard. Am City 79:52 Ap '64

PHOTOGRAPHY in industry
Feininger; photographs from The world through my eyes. H. Keppler. Mod Phot 28:70-1 F '64
How to split a second. C. Smith. il Pop Phot 52:58-60+ F '63
Oscilloscope photography in industry. R. A. Shiver. il Electr World 69:53-6+ Mr '63
Shooting the works. il Time 83:83 Ja 17 '64
PHOTOGRAPHY in medicine. See Photography. Medical
PHOTOGRAPHY in public works
Nothing proves it like a picture; Greenburgh. N.Y. T. A. Merkin. il Am City 79:107-8 F '64
PHOTOGRAPHY in publicity
Just looking. M. R. Weiss. il Sat R 47:144-5 Ag 29 '64
PHOTOGRAPHY in science. See Photography—Scientific applications
PHOTOGRAPHY in social work
Communicating a community service; D. J. Ransohoff's photographs of social conditions. M. R. Weiss. Sat R 46:72-3 S 14 '63
PHOTOGRAPHY in the fine arts (organization)
Photography in the fine arts IV. M. R. Weiss. il Sat R 46:39-40 My 18 '63
PHOTOGRAPHY models. See Models (persons)
PHOTOGRAPHY of animal tracks and trails. See Animal tracks and trails
PHOTOGRAPHY of animals
Animals around you. F. Henle. il Pop Phot 53:28 Jl '63
Bear who came to dinner. I. L. Marx. il Outdoor Life 132:52-3+ S '63
Close-ups; too close. J. S. Crawford. il Outdoor Life 133:28-9+ F '64
Four seconds to shoot. H. Kanzler. il Field & S 68:95 Ag '63
Get close for zoo stoppers! P. Caulfield. il Mod Phot 27:82-7 Je '63
Hard life. J. Holroyd. il Outdoor Life 133:64-5+ My '64
Head-on hits. il U S Camera 27:78 Jl '64
It's done with mirrors. I. L. Marx. il Outdoor Life 133:48-9+ My '64
Jambo gasbag safari in Africa. A. Smith. il Sat Eve Post 236:40-7 N 9 '63
My four years with grizzly bears. N. D. Weis. il Outdoor Life 135:52-7+ F '65
New outlook on spilt milk. il Pop Mech 121: 40 Ja '64
Night life on the desert; Arizona's Tucson Mountain Park. J. J. Stophlet. il Nat Parks Mag 38:12-15 Mr '64
Practical zoo photography. H. Monroe. il U S Camera 26:62-3+ Ag '63
Savage encounter. F. McKinley. il Outdoor Life 133:52-3+ Mr '64
Shot in the dark. D. Holland. il Field & S 69:38-41+ D '64
Tails out of school. T. A. Gill. il U S Camera 26:50-1+ N '63
That most curious of subjects; the cat. il U S Camera 27:75 S '64
Traveling camera at a Montana ropin' & ridin'. L. Barry. il Pop Phot 54:109+ Mr '64
Well traveled camera; fall in southern Vermont. M. A. Matzkin. il Mod Phot 27:18+ N '63
PHOTOGRAPHY of birds
Adventures with hummingbirds; photographing the family life of ruby-throats. R. Austing. il Audubon Mag 66:252-6 Jl '64
Ambassador of birdlife. R. B. Fischer. il Audubon Mag 67:26-31 Ja '65
Hunting a new movie target? B. Knight. il U S Camera 27:72-3 Jl '64
White egrets of Sagiyama. T. Tanaka. il Audubon Mag 65:298-305 S '63
PHOTOGRAPHY of buildings and structures
Architect's photographer. C. Schwalberg. il U S Camera 26:66-9+ Mr '63
Atop the Verrazano. il U S Camera 27:60-1 D '64
Back-tracking four centuries. L. Barry. il Pop Phot 53:24+ N '63
Easy does it, as the Romans do. L. Barry. il Pop Phot 51:46+ D '62
On the go; shoot history in Virginia. L. Barry. il Pop Phot 52:12+ Ap '63
Rudolph Burckhardt: multiple fugitive. A. Katz. il Art N 62:38-41 D '63
Shooting on site. M. R. Weiss. il Sat R 48: 28-30 Ja 23 '65
PHOTOGRAPHY of children
Capture the look that goes too soon. J. Schneider. il Am Home 67:104 S '64
Children should be seen. R. Mamis. il U S Camera 28:48-9+ Ja '65
Children's game. D. Streibig. il Pop Phot 54: 141+ Ja '64
Children's pictures, for a cause. S. Szasz. il Pop Phot 52:72-5+ Mr '63

PHOTOGRAPHY of children—*Continued*
Cure for single-shotitis. G. Haist. il U S Camera 27:38-9+ My '64
Family photography made easy. D. Mohler. il Parents Mag 39:44-5+ Jl '64
If baby could talk when you take his picture. P. O. Steinberg. il Farm J 88:62-3 Ja '64
Keep it in the family; photographs from World is young. P. Caulfield. Mod Phot 27:74-9 Je '63
Kids, your best subject; symposium. il U S Camera 26:43-55+ Je '63
Mix children with science. L. Drukker. il Pop Phot 52:86-7 Ja '63
Phoebe Dunn used backlighting with children. il Pop Phot 52:54-5 Mr '63
Portrait of a child; prize-winners in first 1963 contest. il Pop Phot 52:88-93 Je '63
Potpourri of kids. il U S Camera 27:58-9 Mr '64
Round face in the square frame. I. Shirley. il U S Camera 26:18+ My '63
Shoot candid kids. D. L. Miller. il Mod Phot 27:68-73 Ag '63
Summer action, kids. il U S Camera 26:54-7 Ag '63
Swinging lady with the red hatbox from Allentown, Pa. S. Nathan. il U S Camera 26:60-1+ D '63
Twin lens; other people's babies. F. Henle. il Pop Phot 52:30 My '63
Which is best? D. L. Miller. il Mod Phot 27:96-7 O '63
See also
Children—Photographs

PHOTOGRAPHY of clouds
Cloud patterns over tropical oceans. J. S. Malkus. bibliog il Science 141:767-78 Ag 30 '63

PHOTOGRAPHY of dancing
Materials of publicity: dance photographs. D. Duncan. il Dance Mag 38:37-9 D '64 (to be cont)

PHOTOGRAPHY of eclipses. See Astronomical photography

PHOTOGRAPHY of executives
Capturing the executive look. il Bsns W p 108+ Ja 18 '64

PHOTOGRAPHY of fires
Negative positive; fire at night. A. Asnis. U S Camera 26:30-1 My '63

PHOTOGRAPHY of fishes
Hot colors of cold fish. D. Faulkner. il U S Camera 26:76-9+ O '63

PHOTOGRAPHY of flowers, plants, trees, etc.
Beauty lurks in little things. E. Bennett. U S Camera 27:36-7+ S '64
Cameras & gardens. R. L. Hering. il Pop Gard 15:84-5 Jl; 79 S '64; 16:14 Ja '65
Color workshop. F. Bond. il Mod Phot 27:16+ My '63
Color work-shop; flowers and gardens. F. Bond. il Mod Phot 28:16+ Ag '64
Do you shoot in the shade? J. J. Simpkins. Flower Grower 50:63 Je '63
Focus on the flower show. M. R. Weiss. il Pop Gard 15:60-1 Mr '64
Photography season starts at the flower show. J. J. Simpkins. il Flower Grower 51:59 Mr '64
Popular gardening's cameras & gardens. R. Miller. See occasional issues of Popular gardening & living outdoors to November 1963
Practice your shooting! J. J. Simpkins. Flower Grower 50:13 Jl '63
Use your camera as a garden tool. R. Miller. Horticulture 42:38-9 My '64
What's in a flower? il U S Camera 26:14-15 My '63
Your camera keeps flowers in bloom forever. M. R. Weiss. Pop Gard 14:18+ Mr '63

PHOTOGRAPHY of insects
Assassins in your garden. il Sci Digest 54:11-13 Jl '63
Bee portrait. R. Kinne. il Pop Phot 52:54-5+ F '63
Fly's tongue in 3-D. il Life 56:69-70+ My 1 '64
Insects. J. Wexler. il U S Camera 26:62-3+ My '63
Sedentary safari in 3-D. P. R. Farber. il U S Camera 26:62-3+ Mr '63

PHOTOGRAPHY of machinery
Busy craftsmen are ideal subjects. L. Barry. il Pop Phot 53:30+ S '63

PHOTOGRAPHY of moving objects
Camera action! F. Henle. il Pop Phot 53:28 S '63
Change of pace. il U S Camera 27:48-9 Je '64
Dick Meek shot Polacolor at Belmont Park and America's cup races. D. Meek. Pop Phot 52:117 Mr '63
John Cowan; specialist in action. il U S Camera 27:40-5+ Ag '64
Motorized action. il U S Camera 26:86-7 O '63
Must dimension: motion. E. Wildi. il Pop Phot 54:110-13+ Je '64
No time to focus. M. Morrison. il U S Camera 27:46-7+ S '64
People off-guard. J. Morris. il U S Camera 27:50-7 S '64
Planned action sequence. E. Fitzgerald. il U S Camera 27:66-7 Jl '64
Slow look and the wink. il Pop Phot 54:54-7 My '64
Summer action, circus. il U S Camera 26:52-3+ Ag '63
Summer action, sailing. C. Steinhardt. il U S Camera 26:58-9+ Ag '63
When & how to shoot 35mm RFDR. P. Caulfield. il Mod Phot 27:64-9 My '63
With an SLR? shooting techniques. P. Caulfield. il Mod Phot 27:56-63 Ap '63
World leaps into an age of innovation. il Life 55:65-72B N 29 '63

PHOTOGRAPHY of nature. See Nature photography

PHOTOGRAPHY of plants. See Photography of flowers, plants, trees, etc.

PHOTOGRAPHY of shadows. See Shades and shadows

PHOTOGRAPHY of snow, ice, etc.
And stay out! P. Caulfield. il Mod Phot 28:68-77 Ja '64
Color slides. R. Miller. il U S Camera 28:20+ Ja '65
Some tips for snow dudes. L. Barry. il Pop Phot 54:20+ Ja '64

PHOTOGRAPHY of space flights
Chase aircraft modified for GT-2 photos. G. Alexander. il Aviation W 81:52-3+ D 14 '64

PHOTOGRAPHY of sports
Blur for realism. il U S Camera 28:40-3 Ja '65
Focus on your boat. F. M. Paulson. il Field & S 69:100-4 S '64
Focus on Zimmerman. J. Durniak. il Pop Phot 52:82-91+ Ap '63
Get the picture at spectator events. P. Caulfield. il Mod Phot 27:12-13 Ap '63
Innocent abroad on the baseball diamonds. E. Graham. il Sports Illus 18:64-70 Mr 18 '63
Mad hatter in photoland; sports photographer J. Laughead. E. Shrake. il Sports Illus 21:78-80+ S 21 '64
Picture yourself. H. F. Zeman. il Outdoor Life 132:44-7+ Ag '63
View from the bridge. il U S Camera 27:52-3 Ap '64
See also
Sports—Photographs

PHOTOGRAPHY of sunsets. See Nature photography

PHOTOGRAPHY of the human figure. See Human figure in photography

PHOTOGRAPHY of the nude. See Nude in art

PHOTOGRAPHY of traffic accidents
Say it with your camera; photography takes the stand. J. Deschin. il Pop Phot 52:14 Ap '63

PHOTOGRAPHY of water
Shoot cool water color. P. Caulfield. il Mod Phot 27:52-5 Ag '63

PHOTOGRAPHY of weddings
Assignment wedding; with photographs by Charles Léon. U S Camera 27:34-5 Mr '64

PHOTOGRAPHY schools. See Photography—Study and teaching

PHOTOISOMERISM. See Isomerism

PHOTOKINA. See Photography—Exhibitions

PHOTOMACROGRAPHY. See Macrophotography

PHOTOMECHANICAL processes
Architectural drawing for printing processes. M. F. Schmertz. il Arch Rec 133:137-44 F '63
Book publishers' interests in reprographic copyright; excerpts from address, May 1963. C. G. Benjamin. Library J 88:2837-41 Ag '63
Future techniques; producing low-cost photo-offset publications. J. Reidy. U S Camera 26:18+ O '63
Impact of photocopying on scholarly publishing; summary of thesis, March 1963. R. F. Clarke. il Library J 88:2625-9 Jl '63
Library photocopying: the stalemate deepens. R. H. Smith. Pub W 184:41 Ag 12 '63
Photocopying equipment. il Consumer Bul 46:28-32 N '63
Reader-printers found wanting. Wilson Lib Bul 37:830 Je '63

PHOTOMETERS
In low light, meters lie. P. Farber. U S Camera 27:30+ F '64

PHOTOMETRY
BSD chief sees present photometric techniques at limit of development. C. D. LaFond. Miss & Roc 15:13 Ag 31 '64

PHOTOMETRY, Astronomical
Photometry yields clues to temperature and distance of stars. T. D. Nicholson. il Natur Hist 73:44-7 F '64
See also
Stars—Magnitudes

PHOTOMICROGRAPHY
Brownian movement in color photomicrography. H. F. Sassoon and M. H. C. Parsons. Science 139:1285-6 Mr 29 '63
Fly's tongue in 3-D. il Life 56:69-70+ My 1 '64
How to take pictures through a microscope. B. Hering. il Pop Sci 185:104-7 Jl '64
Microscopes. R. Kinne. il Pop Phot 51:88-91 D '62
Nature and the camera. D. Linton. il Natur Hist 73:60-2 My '64
Think small, it's bigger than you think! A. Zuckerman. il Pop Phot 55:107+ O '64

PHOTOMONTAGE
You take four you make one. M. A. Matzkin. il Mod Phot 28:84-5 N '64

PHOTON, incorporated
Phototypesetting picks up the pace. il Bsns W p 156+ D 14 '63

PHOTON machine. See Photocomposing machines

PHOTONS
Measurement of bone mineral in vivo: an improved method. J. R. Cameron and J. Sorenson. bibliog il Science 142:230-2 O 11 '63
See also
Mössbauer effect

PHOTOPERIODISM. See Light—Physiological effects; Plants, Effect of light on

PHOTO-RECONNAISSANCE. See Photography, Military

PHOTOSENSITIVITY reaction. See Allergy

PHOTOSYNTHESIS
Chemical go-between. Sci N L 83:275 My 4 '63
Fluoroacetate inhibition of amino acids during photosynthesis of chlamydomonas reinhardti. J. R. Kates and R. F. Jones. bibliog il Science 143:145-6 Ja 10 '64
How sap moves in trees. M. H. Zimmermann. il Sci Am 208:132-8+ bibliog(p 192) Mr '63
New light on photosynthesis. H. Manchester. Sci N L 83:202-3+ Mr 30 '63
Photosynthesis puzzle. T. Neville. Sci N L 84:2 Jl 6 '63
Photosynthesis; report on symposium. A. T. Jagendorf and B. Kok. Science 143:388+ Ja 24 '64
Photosynthesis; why green plants are green. il Sci Digest 56:51-2 N '64
Photosynthetic mutants separate electron paramagnetic resonance signals of Scenedesmus. E. C. Weaver and N. I. Bishop. bibliog il Science 140:1095-7 Je 7 '63
Why the grass is green. Pop Sci 182:15 F '63

PHOTOTAXIS
Amateur scientist; experiments in phototaxis. W. C. Baum. il Sci Am 211:128-32 O '64

PHOTOTELEGRAPHY
M/R first U.S. journal with cover via Comsat. il Miss & Roc 12:26 My 6 '63

PHOTOTYPESETTING machines. See Photocomposing machines

PHOTOVOLTAIC cells. See Photoelectric cells

PHRASES. See English language—Terms and phrases

PHYCOCYANIN
C-Phycocyanin: minimum molecular weight. D. S. Berns and others. bibliog il Science 145:1054-6 S 4 '64

PHYLLOCACTUS. See Epiphyllums

PHYLOGENY
Phylogenetic riddle; olive warbler. W. G. George. il Natur Hist 72:44-7 F '63
Phylogeny: principles and methods; meeting sponsored by the American society of naturalists. E. Caspari. Science 139:773-4 F 22 '63
Some fallacies in the study of hominid phylogeny. E. L. Simons. bibliog il Science 141:879-89 S 6 '63

PHYSALIA. See Portuguese man-of-war

PHYSARUM. See Myxomycetes

PHYSICAL constants
In a restless universe constants can vary; Westinghouse physicists prove rate of radioactive decay can be altered. Time 83:74 Je 19 '64

PHYSICAL directors
All the marbles? baseball's first athletic director Bob Whitlow. Newsweek 61:93-4 Mr 18 '63
Coach cracks color barrier. il Ebony 19:77+ Mr '64
Coach even the faculty likes; J. Bridges of Baylor. M. Sharnik. il Sports Illus 19:52+ N 18 '63
Coach has all the problems; John McKay of U.S.C. M. Durslag. il Sat Eve Post 236:72-3 D 14 '63
Coach of every year. W. Bingham. il Sports Illus 18:47-8+ F 11 '63
Cry havoc from the bench; basketball coaches. il Sports Illus 21:48-52 D 7 '64
Enigma of the interim coach; H. Devore of Notre Dame. il Sports Illus 19:59 O 28 '63
Four against the odds. il Ebony 18:55-6+ My '63
Go get 'em, coaches! college basketball coaches recruiting techniques. J. Underwood. il Sports Illus 19:82-4+ D 9 '63
He'll never leave Ohio; D. Perry, football coach of Bowling Green university. J. Underwood. il Sports Illus 21:80-2+ S 28 '64
New man in New Haven; John Pont, head football coach at Yale. Newsweek 61:94 Mr 18 '63
No fast break for the Cooz; coach at Boston college. W. Leggett. il Sports Illus 19:20-1 D 16 '63
Positively Sain; coach for Yankees. H. L. Masin. il Sr Schol 83:48-9 O 4 '63
Razzle-dazzle; new coach for Notre Dame. Newsweek 62:56 D 30 '63
Settled out of court; Alabama vs Georgia. J. Underwood. il Sports Illus 19:20-5 S 30 '63
Throw throw throw; leading football coaches. D. Jenkins. il Sports Illus 19:30-45 S 23 '63
When in doubt, punt; coach Royal of the University of Texas. il Time 82:50 N 22 '63
Yale finds a coach; J. Pont. W. N. Wallace. il Sat Eve Post 236:74-7 O 12 '63
See also names of physical directors, e.g. B. Wilkinson

PHYSICAL education and training
Bold proposal for American sport. R. F. Kennedy. il Sports Illus 21:12-15 Jl 27 '64
Exercise program helps youngsters' schoolwork. Sci N L 84:9 Jl 6 '63
Nation-wide testing program. B. York. il Recreation 56:268+ Je '63
Physical fitness for the sandbox set. il N Y Times Mag p48 Ja 19 '64
Physical fitness pilot project. J. G. Anderson. il Recreation 56:276-7+ Je '63
Rugged challenge for teen-agers; Colorado's Outward bound school. L. Lawrence. il Read Digest 82:183-4+ Ap '63
School where fitness counts; La Sierra high school, Carmichael, Calif. B. Clark. il Read Digest 85:94-8 S '64
Spirit, mind, body. R. H. Boyle. il Sports Illus 19:76-8+ D 2 '63
Tailored to fit the child. D. Hutchinson. il NEA J 52:27-8 F '63
Teacher-opinion poll; physical exercise. il NEA J 53:60 Ja '64
To keep children fit and hardy; with study-discussion program, by D. B. Harris and E. S. Harris. W. W. Bauer. bibliog il PTA Mag 58:14-16, 36 O '63
Warning against a physical fitness mania. F. P. Foster. il N Y Times Mag p 15+ F 9 '64
Why Jean can't run; de Gaulle's physical fitness program. Newsweek 61:108 Mr 25 '63
Youth and fitness, where do we stand? il Sr Schol 82:8-9+ F 13 '63
See also
Exercise
Sports

PHYSICAL examinations
Get a medical checkup, it may save your life. S. S. Steinberg. Suc Farm 62:63 O '64
Health checkups for longer life. R. L. White. Parents Mag 38:163+ S '63
My checkup at Mayo's. J. Star. il Look 28:66+ Mr 24 '64
Otto Gerisch maneuver; method for ticklish patients. il Time 82:36 Ag 9 '63
Personal business; gadgets to diagnose ills. Bsns W p 131 N 9 '63
Should schools give physical checkups? il Good H 158:165 F '64
USAF astronauts given ten-part physical. Aviation W 81:80 N 23 '64
When the doctor examines you. W. R. Young. Read Digest 82:89-94 F '63
Why special medical tests are important. P. Deutsch and R. Deutsch. Redbook 121:26 Je '63
See also
Air pilots—Physical examinations
Medical service, Industrial

Anecdotes, facetiae, satire, etc.

Day I had my checkup. K. Nelson. il Good H 158:52+ F '64

PHYSICAL examinations, Premarital
Premarital examination: its importance to both the man and the woman. G. Naismith. Todays Health 42:50-1+ Ap '64
PHYSICAL exercise. See Exercise
PHYSICAL fitness. See Health; Men—Health and hygiene
PHYSICAL geography
Geonomists, unite; study of the earth. Newsweek 62:78 S 2 '63
See also
Continents
Deltas

United States

See also
Geology—United States
PHYSICAL research
1963-1964 science review. Sci N L 84:390-1; 86:391-2 D 21 '63, D 19 '64
PHYSICAL science. See Science
PHYSICAL theory. See Physics—Philosophy
PHYSICAL training. See Physical education and training
PHYSICALLY handicapped. See Handicapped
PHYSICIANS
American doctor: death of a legend in an era of miracles. E. Hill. il Sat Eve Post 236:30+ Je 15 '63
Blue Ridge Samaritan. S. Castan. il Look 27:82-4+ Ag 27 '63
British doctor. F. J. Spencer. Cur Hist 45:25-31+ Jl '63
Challenge to our doctors. J. R. Moskin. il Look 28:26-38+ N 3 '64; Discussion. 28:6+ D 15 '64
Check-up on M.D.'s. Newsweek 64:48 Ag 3 '64
Doctors free to choose. Sci N L 85:258 Ap 25 '64
G.P. is still needed. L. Lasagna. il N Y Times Mag p 18+ Ap 19 '64
Imperturbable man; Doc Berbos. S. M. Spencer. Sat Eve Post 236:36 N 16 '63
Jungle doctor today; American physicians in Malaysia, Cambodia and the new countries of Africa. F. Marley. il Sci N L 86:346-7 N 28 '64
What is an internist? S. T. Donohue. il Todays Health 41:48-53+ Ap '63
When should you call the doctor? P. Deutsch and R. Deutsch. il Redbook 120:26 Ap '63
Why are doctors out of step? L. Lasagna. New Repub 152:13-15 Ja 2 '65
See also
American medical association
Chiropractors
Malpractice
Medical laws and legislation
Medicine—Practice
Negro physicians
Pediatricians
Women as physicians

Anecdotes, facetiae, satire, etc.

Intrusive patient. C. S. Jennison. il Atlan 214:122+ Jl '64

Fees

See Medical service, Cost of

Recruiting

Recruiting tomorrow's doctors today. H. Earle. il Todays Health 41:34-6+ N '63
See also
Future physicians clubs

Salaries, fees, etc.

How much do doctors charge today? il Bet Hom & Gard 41:6 Je '63

Supply and demand

AMA statistics. Commonweal 79:448 Ja 17 '64
Can the doctor do better? il Bsns W p 103-4+ S 26 '64
Medic! (did someone cry wolf?) W. L. Hansen. il New Repub 149:13-14 N 9 '63
Shortage of doctors; what's causing it. il U S News 54:72-5 Mr 25 '63
PHYSICIANS and patients
Good physician. W. E. O'Donnell. il America 110:796-9 Je 6 '64
Is there too much secrecy in medicine? B. Gebhard. Ladies Home J 80:38 Jl '63
Process of becoming a physician. S. W. Bloom. bibliog f Ann Am Acad 346:77-87 Mr '63
When should you have another doctor's opinion? G. G. Greer. Bet Hom & Gard 42:52 N '64
PHYSICIANS licenses. See Licenses
PHYSICIANS strike (Belgium) See Strikes—Belgium
PHYSICIANS wives
Real life for the doctor's wife. A. Peters. il Todays Health 42:24-5+ Je '64
PHYSICISTS
Evolution of the physicist's picture of nature. P. A. M. Dirac. il Sci Am 208:45-53 bibliog(p 192) My '63
PHYSICISTS; drama. See Dürrenmatt, F.
PHYSICS
Physics. L. A. DuBridge. bibliog il NEA J 52:24-8 D '63
See also
Biological physics
Force and energy
Gravitation
Mathematical physics
Music—Acoustics and physics
Nuclear physics
Quantum theory
Solids

Experiments

Amateur scientist; on a paradoxical pump, reversing cubes, vortex rings and various other matters. il Sci Am 212:118-22 Ja '65
Amateur scientist; simulating gravitational fields with droplets of water on a soap bubble. G. Yob. il Sci Am 211:134-7 D '64
Amateur scientist; stream table to simulate geological processes. M. Schwartz. il Sci Am 208:168-70+ Ap '63
Amateur scientist; tests with rolling balls. R. Hayward. il Sci Am 211:102-6 Ag '64
Bowling in the classroom. C. Randall. il Sci Digest 56:24-5 S '64
Up and over; effect of spin inertia; excerpt from Fun with scientific experiments. M. Freeman and I. Freeman. il Sci Digest 54:42 D '63

Periodicals

British physics journals. A. C. Strickland. Science 144:986 My 22 '64

Philosophy

Evolution of the physicist's picture of nature. P. A. M. Dirac. il Sci Am 208:45-53 bibliog(p 192) My '63
Revolutions in physics and crises in mathematics. S. Bochner. bibliog Science 141:408-11 Ag 2 '63

Research

High-energy physics: budget cuts by House committees contrast with easing of funds for other fields. D. S. Greenberg. Science 144:1432-3 Je 19 '64

Study and teaching

Frantic physicist fires 'em up; J. S. Miller. il Life 56:115-16+ Mr 20 '64
Mad, mad, mad, mad physicist. A. Hamilton. il PTA Mag 59:12-14+ Ja '65; Same abr. with title Professor Miller's mighty magic. Read Digest 86:155-8+ Ja '65
Physics education crisis. Sch & Soc 92:301-2 O 31 '64
PHYSICS, Mathematical. See Mathematical physics
PHYSIOGNOMY
See also
Face
PHYSIOLOGICAL apparatus
See also
Heart, Artificial
PHYSIOLOGICAL chemistry. See Biochemistry; Homeostasis
PHYSIOLOGICAL data transmission. See Telemeter (physiological apparatus)
PHYSIOLOGICAL effect of light. See Light—Physiological effects
PHYSIOLOGICAL effects of noise. See Noise—Physiological effects
PHYSIOLOGICAL effects of radioactivity. See Radioactivity—Physiological effects
PHYSIOLOGICAL effects of tobacco. See Tobacco—Physiological effects
PHYSIOLOGICAL oxidation. See Oxidation, Physiological
PHYSIOLOGICAL research
Man's dependence on the earthly atmosphere. ed. by K. E. Schaefer. Review
Nation 196:330-1 Ap 20 '63. C. Dreher
Master switch of life. P. F. Scholander. il Sci Am 209:92-6+ bibliog(p 178) D '63
System theory and physiological processes; excerpts from addresses. R. W. Jones; J. S. Gray. Science 140:461-6 My 3 '63
See also
Electromagnetism in medicine
Space flight—Physiological aspects
PHYSIOLOGY
Body's internal balances: what can go wrong. M. Grant. il Life 55:85-6+ N 8 '63
Comforting truth about exercise. il Ladies Home J 80:134+ Ap '63
Human body (cont) il Life 54:48-59+ Mr 29; 64-76B+ Je 28; 55:68-81 N 8 '63
Muscles are his business: R. Stonewall. il Ebony 20:147-50 D '64

PHYSIOLOGY—*Continued*
Wisdom of the body; excerpts from Art of ministering to the sick. R. C. Cabot and R. L. Dicks. Read Digest 84:24B Ja '64
See also
Bones
Brain
Electrophysiology
Homeostasis
Lymphatic system
Respiration
Starvation
Weight (physiology)

History

Early concepts of the senses and the mind. A. C. Crombie. il Sci Am 210:108-16 My '64

PHYTOFLAGELLATES. See Flagellates

PHYTOPHTHORA
Sterol induction of reproduction and stimulation of growth of phythium and phytophthora. J. W. Hendrix. bibliog il Science 144:1028-9 My 22 '64

PHYTOPLANKTON
Food-producing bubbles; zooplankton. Sci Am 211:60 N '64

PI meson. See Mesons

PIA, Josefina
Pirates of Paraguay. Américas 15:31-8 Mr '63

PIAF, Edith
Adieu and adieu. por Newsweek 62:81 O 21 '63
Letter from Paris. Genêt. New Yorker 39: 200-2+ N 2 '63
Sparrow & the dilettante. por Time 82:38+ O 18 '63

PIANISTS
Cecil Taylor and the new tradition. J. Goldberg. Sat R 46:42-3 F 9 '63
Great pianists from Mozart to the present, by H. C. Schonberg. Review
Am Rec G 30:591-2 Mr '64. R. Kammerer
New Yorker 40:122+ F 22 '64. W. Sargeant
Newsweek 62:104 N 18 '63
I wear my hair short; concert pianist. L. Hollander. il Seventeen 22:330-2+ Ag '63
Jazz; B. Powell's bebop style. W. Balliett. New Yorker 40:154+ S 12 '64
Jazz; Bill Evans' music. W. Balliett. New Yorker 39:157-61 S 21 '63
Jazz records; J. P. Johnson. W. Balliett. New Yorker 39:153-6+ My 11 '63
Why the world now looks to America for concert pianists. E. Leinsdorf. il House B 106:118+ Ag '64
See also
Alkan, C. H. V.
Anda, G.
Arrau, C.
Ashkenazy, V.
Block, M.
Ellington, D.
Gilels, E.
Hines, E.
Kempff, W.
Lowenthal, J.
Mdivani, M.
Rubinstein, A.
Schnabel, A.
Smith, W.
Watts, A.
Williams, M. L.

PIANO
Buy a piano you'll keep on enjoying. J. J. Earl. il Pop Mech 121:124-7 F '64
Buying a piano. il Consumer Bul 46:15-18 My '63
How to buy a good used piano. P. Gordon. il Bet Hom & Gard 42:104-6 Mr '64
How to give pianos and organs the place they deserve. il House & Gard 123:164-7 Ap '63
No space for a grand piano? then consider a vertical instrument. il Consumer Bul 46: 6-9 Je '63
Piano care; the ABC's. House & Gard 123: 192+ Ap '63
Piano, Julie, lasts a long time. L. A. Harlow. House B 105:164-5+ D '63
See also
Player piano

Instruction and study

What music means to me; piano practice. A. Watts. il Seventeen 23:22 Ja '64

Study and teaching

Adele Marcus: the challenge of teaching. R. Sabin. Mus Am 83:53 F '63

PIANO industry and trade

Japan

Pianos on the assembly line: Nippon Gakki to build modern plant. Time 83:91 F 14 '64

PIANO music
Shoot the piano player; Satie's Vexations played 840 times in succession. Time 82:54 S 20 '63
See also
Phonograph records—Piano music

PIANO player; story. See Barthelme, D.

PIANO playing
See also
Piano—Instruction and study

PIANO tuning. See Tuning

PIANOS, Miniature. See Miniature objects

PIASECKI, Boleslaw
PAX; Poland's Proteus. J. Dohnalik. Atlan 212:79-81 D '63

PIATIER, Jacqueline
(ed) See Sartre, J. P. Jean-Paul Sartre speaks

PIATIGORSKY, Gregor
Cellist's view of conducting; excerpt from Cellist. por Sat R 48:47-8+ Ja 30 '65
about
Big two; Heifetz and Piatigorsky. il por Time 84:88 O 2 '64

PIAVE, Francesco Maria
Well-versed librettist. M. J. Matz. por Opera N 27:12-13 Mr 16 '63

PIAZZA, Ben
Exact & very strange truth; excerpt from novel. McCalls 91:96-7 Jl '64

PIAZZA, Luis G.
Gentle executioner; story. Américas 15:35-7 D '63

PICA
Pica; prevalent, peculiar, poisonous. W. D. Boaz. il PTA Mag 58:22-4 D '63
Strange hunger. Newsweek 62:68 Jl 29 '63

PICASSO, Pablo
Letter from Paris. Genêt. New Yorker 39: 185-6+ S 14 '63
Life with Picasso, by F. Gilot and C. Lake. Review
Reporter 31:52+ D 3 '64. J. Jacobs
Sat R il 47:54+ N 14 '64. S. Rodman
Time il 84:110 N 20 '64
Pablo Picasso's love: la femme-fleur; excerpt from Life with Picasso. F. Gilot and C. Lake. Atlan 214:79-84+ Ag '64
Painting is stronger than Picasso? P. Schneider. il Art N 63:35+ Mr '64
Palace for Picasso. E. V. Ronan. il pors Américas 16:32-7 Jl '64
Picasso. J. Canaday. il por Horizon 7:65-79 Wint '65
Picasso and the nude. J. S. Boggs. il Art N 62:29-31+ Ja '64
Picasso comes home. B. O'Brien. Reporter 30: 52-3 My 21 '64
Picasso vs. Franco. por Newsweek 61:57 Ap 8 '63
Picassos for New York; Justin K. Thannhauser gift to Guggenheim museum. il N Y Times Mag p72-3 N 10 '63
Power of the king . . Picasso; adventures illustrating the book, The Carmen of Carmens, tr. by A. Foulke. L. Aragon. il Vogue 145:78-9+ Ja 15 '65

PICCIONI, Attilio. See Kennedy, J. F. jt. auth.

PICEA breweriana. See Spruce

PICK, Vernon James
What became of Pick and Steen? Fortune 69:164 F '64

PICKEREL fishing
Last of the skitterers. B. Geagan. il Field & S 69:38-40+ Jl '64

PICKERING, James S.
Books in review. Natur Hist 74:6+ Ja '65

PICKERING, William Hayward
Voyage to the morning star; findings of Mariner II. il por Time 81:76-80 Mr 8 '63; Same abr. with title Voyage to Venus. Read Digest 82:120-5 Je '63

PICKERING, William Henry
W. H. Pickering and the satellites of Jupiter. J. Ashbrook. il por Sky & Tel 26:335-6 D '63

PICKETING
Is Labor board rewriting law? U S News 54: 107 Ap 22 '63
More freedom to picket; latest from Supreme court; consumer picketing. U S News 56:78 My 4 '64
Spreading tactic: a different kind of picketing; informational picketing. il U S News 57:16 O 26 '64
Unions get new picketing rights. U S News 55:97 S 30 '63

PICKETING—*Continued*
When pickets are used to scare away customers. il U S News 54:74-5 F 4 '63
When rail strike hit at moon shot; informational pickets sent to Cape Canaveral, Fla. moon-shot project, by Telegraphers union. U S News 55:98 S 30 '63

PICKETT, A. D. and Patterson, N. A.
Arsenates; effect on fecundity in some diptera. bibliog Science 140:493-4 My 3 '63

PICKETT, Deets
Another noble experiment? reprint. U S News 56:120 My 11 '64

PICKETT, Ronald M. See Jerison, H. J. jt. auth.

PICKING of fruit. See Fruit—Picking

PICKLE, J. J.
Hard one to lose. Time 82:17 D 27 '63

PICKLES and relishes
Country-kitchen relishes. N. Nichols. il Farm J 87:50+ Ag '63
Glamorous go withs. McCalls 91:88 My '64
Great new recipes for jams, jellies, and pickles. J. Figg. il Suc Farm 62:76-7 Ag '64
How to make a fruit chutney. il Sunset 133:222+ O '64
Instant pickles. il Bet Hom & Gard 42:85-6 S '64
It's time to pickle little artichokes. Sunset 133:117 D '64
Pack a peck of pickles & pickled products. il McCalls 91:106-7+ Je '64
Pickle secrets revealed! with recipes. C. G. Dubois. il Flower Grower 50:32 O '63
Way out with relishes. il Bet Hom & Gard 42:78 My '64

PICKPOCKETS. See Thieves

PICKREL, Paul
Backward glance: art books, books on art, and picture books. Harper 228:101-6 Ja '64
Love, irony, and a bit of vitriol. Harper 227:93-4 Ag '63
New books. See issues of Harper's magazine

PICKUP campers. See Campers and coaches, Truck

PICKUP trucks. See Motor trucks

PICKWELL, George V. and others
Carbon monoxide production by a bathypelagic siphonophore. bibliog Science 144:860-2 My 15 '64

PICNIC baskets, boxes, etc.
Everything you need for family picnics. il Parents Mag 39:55-8+ Jl '64

PICNIC cookery. See Cookery, Outdoor

PICNIC furniture. See Furniture, Outdoor

PICNIC shelters. See Shelters

PICNIC tables. See Tables

PICNICS
Come-and-get-it family picnics. B. M. Stover. il Parents Mag 39:61+ Jl '64
Feasting afloat. E. Ward-Hanna. il Ladies Home J 80:74-6 Jl '63
Food to leave home with. il Ladies Home J 81:93-5+ Jl '64
From car to picnic site. il Sunset 131:64-8 Ag '63
Gourmet picnic; with recipes. E. Solomon. il Sat Eve Post 236:74-5 S 7 '63
Have picnic, will travel; with recipes. il Am Home 67:70-1+ Jl '64
Let's have a picnic. il Ebony 19:166+ My '64
Luncheon buffet or a picnic with wines. il Sunset 131:128-30+ S '63
Old-fashioned picnic; with recipes for box lunches. il Look 28:87-8 Jl 28 '64
Picnic at the beach for six. il Vogue 144:124 Jl '64
Picnic to remember. N. Nichols. il Farm J 88:52-3 Jl '64
Send them on knapsack picnic. il Sunset 131:161-2 S '63
Sushi picnic with three kinds of sushi. il Sunset 133:198+ O '64
Tailgate picnic. il Sunset 130:170+ Ap '63
Three spring fever picnics; with recipes. il Seventeen 23:176-9+ Ap '64
Winter picnic. il Good H 157:88-9 D '63
See also
Cookery, Outdoor

Anecdotes, facetiae, satire, etc.

Give me ants, lots of ants. J. L. O'Neill. il Am Home 67:6 Jl '64

PICÓ, Rafael
Commonwealth of Puerto Rico. bibliog Focus 14:1-6 O '63

PICOT, Jacques Georges-. See Georges-Picot, J.

PICOTT, J. Rupert
Dedicated to an editor. Negro Hist Bul 27:185 My '64

PICSES (Inter-American program for advanced social science studies in the Caribbean area) See Organization of American states—Inter-American program for advanced social science studies in the Caribbean area

PICTOGRAPHS. See Petroglyphs; Picture writing

PICTORIAL photography. See Photography, Artistic

PICTURE board dummies. See Dummy board figures

PICTURE books
Gift books; some of the picture books are readable too. il Time 84:114+ D 4 '64
Publish your own, they did! C. Reynolds. il Pop Phot 52:76-83+ My '63
Yesterday's classics; Today's best picture books. H. M. Kinzer. il Pop Phot 52:58-61 My '63

Bibliography

For the eye's delight. G. Davenport. il Nat R 16:1113-14 D 15 '64
In striped paper and red ribbon. G. Davenport. Nat R 15:532+ D 17 '63

PICTURE books for children
Anniversary. R. H. Viguers. Horn Bk 40:457 O '64
Beauties, beasts, and band-aids. A. Dalgliesh. il Sat R 46:53 N 9 '63
Lively art of picture books. V. Haviland. il Library J 89:4110-11 O 15 '64
Meet Ed Emberley; ed. by I. Stokvis and others. il Library J 88:3991-5 O 15 '63
Picture books. A. Dalgliesh. il Sat R 46:58-65 N 9 '63; 47:48-56 N 7 '64
Pictures help books come alive. C. Blount. il Parents Mag 38:48-9+ Ap '63
Some thoughts about picture books. M. J. Durham. il Horn Bk 39:476-84 O '63
Wild rose, briar rose. M. A. McMillan. il Horn Bk 39:622-8 D '63
Wonderful silence; illustrated poems and ballads. A. Dalgliesh. il Sat R 48:51-2 Ja 23 '65
Words for the future. R. H. Viguers. Horn Bk 39:19 F '63
See also
Caldecott medal

PICTURE books for the blind. See Blind, Books, etc. for the

PICTURE cards
Bubble-gum trust. il Time 84:64 S 4 '64
Getting the picture, bubble-gum enclosures. G. Eskenazi. il N Y Times Mag p 101 Ap 19 '64

PICTURE collections
See also
Photographs—Collections

PICTURE dictionaries
See also
Dictionaries, Childrens

PICTURE frames
All about framing. H. Gasser. il Design 64:204-9+ Je '63
How to display a group of pictures. il Farm J 87:74 My '63
Not-so-easy art of framing. J. Durniak. il Pop Phot 55:166-7+ D '64
Picture frames to make in minutes. D. Jordan. il Bet Hom & Gard 43:44-5+ Ja '65
Profiles; H. Heydenryk. J. Brooks. New Yorker 39:49-50+ Ap 27 '63
Quick change picture frame. il Sunset 133:163 N '64

PICTURE history of the war; story. See Barthelme, D.

PICTURE post cards. See Post cards

PICTURE tubes. See Television receiving apparatus—Picture tubes

PICTURE writing
Pictographs along the Columbia. il Sunset 132:24+ Mr '64
See also
Hieroglyphics

PICTURED ROCKS NATIONAL LAKESHORE (proposed) See National parks and reserves—United States

PICTUREPHONE. See Telephone—Television combination

PICTURES
Be an artist with nature's leftovers; combine weeds, flowers and twigs. F. Lakenan. il Farm J 88:48-9 Ag '64
Dressed pictures. J. I. Smith. il Antiques 84:694-7 D '63
Jean Dubuffet: Chemin bordé d'herbe 1901. C. B. Johnson. il Sch Arts 62:23 F '63
Needleworks of art. V. P. Guild. il Good H 156:120-1+ Ap '63
Painting with pebbles. M. Moore. il Design 64:100+ Ja '63

Framing

See Picture frames

PICTURES—*Continued*

Mounting

All about framing. H. Gasser. il Design 64:204-9+ Je '63
Mounting a favorite chart. il Sunset 133:93+ Ag '64

Prices

See Art—Prices

Purchasing

Antiques abroad; last decade's acquisitions by London's National gallery. W. De Sager. il Antiques 84:184+ Ag '63

Renting

Life guide; more and more ways to rent art. il Life 55:7 O 4 '63

PICTURES, Framing of. See Picture frames

PICTURES, Hanging of
All about framing. H. Gasser. il Design 64:204-9+ Je '63
How to display a group of pictures. il Farm J 87:74 My '63
How to hang pictures. il Seventeen 23:185 Ap '64
If picture hanging is a problem. il Good H 156:149 F '63
Picture display on pin-up boards. il Sunset 130:165 Ap '63

PICTURES, Immoral. See Immoral literature and pictures

PIDGIN English
Pidgin: no laughing matter. G. Jennings. Harper 227:69-73 Jl '63; Same abr. with title Pidgin: the language that can do. Read Digest 83:151-4 S '63
When East meets West they speak Pidgin. Sci Digest 56:13 Jl '64

PIE
After dinner, chess pie or chess tarts. il Sunset 132:150 Mr '64
Apple pie. il Look 28:80-1 O 6 '64
Berry-cherry pie. il Sunset 130:192 Je '63
Crème de la crème pies. il McCalls 91:110-12 Je '64
Custard pies plus. C. Claiborne. il N Y Times Mag p32 S 6 '64
Fabulous fruit pies. J. Figg. il Suc Farm 61: 68-9+ N '63
Festive pie for the holidays. C. Claiborne. il N Y Times Mag p 112 N 24 '63
Fresh fruit pie should show its face. il Sunset 131:106-7 Ag '63
Fruit pies. il Bet Hom & Gard 41:89-90 Mr '63
Happy together, 'cots, strawberries. il Sunset 130:186 Je '63
Lemon chiffon, the fabulous fluff! il Bet Hom & Gard 41:86 Ag '63
Lemon meringue pie. il Bet Hom & Gard 41: 102 F '63
Mince pie from scratch. il Sunset 133:184+ N '64
My wife bakes the best pies; with recipes. N. Nichols. il Farm J 88:41+ Ag '64
New approach to peach pie. Sunset 133:129 Ag '64
Our teenage cook, makes frozen chocolate velvet pie. il Good H 158:134-5 Ja '64
Perfect pumpkin pie. il Bet Hom & Gard 41:78 D '63
Pies. B. M. Stover. il Parents Mag 39:72 N '64
Pies that go fast. il Redbook 123:82-3+ S '64
Pies to fit any festive occasion. il Am Home 66:44-5+ N '63
Pizza peach pie. V. Heffington. il Bet Hom & Gard 41:74 Ag '63
Pudding and a pie using whey. Sunset 131: 169 S '63
Pudding and pie cook book. J. A. Beard. il House & Gard 124:169+ D '63
Putting summer in the pie; with recipes. C. Claiborne. il N Y Times Mag p48 Jl 19 '64
Quiche Lorraine: Swiss-cheese pie. il McCalls 92-72 O '64
Seasonal fruit pies. il Ebony 19:128+ S '64
Select circle of prize pies. M. E. Hoehener. Good H 157:220 N '63
Serve it with fresh berries; cheese pie. il Sunset 132:168 Je '64
Spring pies and tarts. il Bet Hom & Gard 42:87-8 Ap '64
Step by step to perfectly heavenly lemon meringue pie. il McCalls 90:122-3+ Mr '63
Step-by-step to the pie on our cover. il Bet Hom & Gard 42:72 Mr '64
Successful recipes; apple pie. il Suc Farm 62: 95-6 O '64
Superb chocolate cheese pie. R. Behnke. il Farm J 87:78-9 N '63
Susan makes a cool, quick lemon pretzel pie. il Good H 157:152 Ag '63
Susan makes a perfect pie shell. il Good H 158:156 My '64
Sweet potato pie: a goblin's delight. D. J. Robinson. il Ebony 18:134+ O '63
That special ingredient, pastry! il Am Home 66:50+ N '63
Why not a tasty and beautiful pie? il Sunset 130:188-90 My '63
Yankee pumpkin pie. C. Claiborne. il N Y Times Mag p 120 N 22 '64
See also
Pastry

PIECE work
End of incentive pay? T. R. Brooks. Duns R 84:45-6 D '64

PIEDMONT, Italy
Letter from Piemonte. N. T. di Giovanni. New Repub 151:15-18 S 12 '64

PIÈGE de lumière (ballet) See Ballets

PIEL, Gerard
Abundance and the future of man. Atlan 213: 84-90 Ap '64
Advent of abundance. Bul Atomic Sci 19:2-6 Je '63

PIEMONTE. See Piedmont, Italy

PIENING, Peter
Trade marks of M. Peter Piening. L. Schmeckebier. il por Am Artist 29:52-7 Ja '65

PIERCE, Bill
BSR's, not so new, but good! Pop Phot 54: 64+ Je '64
Big light from small sources. Pop Phot 52: 62-3+ Ja '63
Diafine revisited. por Pop Phot 53:74-5 Ag '63
Exclusive report on Diafine. il Pop Phot 52: 76-9+ Ap '63
Fast color printing. por Pop Phot 52:89-90 My '63
Go slow for high speed. por Pop Phot 52: 110-11 Ap '63
Key is M.O.P. il Pop Phot 54:64-7+ Ap '64
New ways to look at slides. por Pop Phot 55:47 Jl '64
Photography's toughest-to-use lens; the wide-angle. il Pop Phot 52:96-101+ My '63
Primer on exposure meters. il Pop Phot 54: 68-73+ Je '64
Split D-23. por Pop Phot 52:78-9 F '63
Theater and 35-mm. por Pop Phot 53:76-7 Jl '63
Tonal trap. por Pop Phot 52:94 Mr '63
Two new color films: Kodachrome-X and Ektacolor S. Pop Phot 52:18-19+ Mr '63

PIERCE, Edith G.
Climbing roses. Pop Gard 14:36+ Mr '63

PIERCE, Edith Lovejoy
Black slaves; poem. Christian Cent 80:1127 S 18 '63
Civil wrongs; poem. Christian Cent 81:732 Je 3 '64
Fair housing; poem. Christian Cent 80:710 My 29 '63
Forgive us all that is past; poem. Christian Cent 81:1199 S 30 '64
Go north; poem. Christian Cent 80:929 Jl 24 '63
May Peter's choice be ours; poem. Christian Cent 80:489 Ap 17 '63
On the death of Robert Frost; poem. Christian Cent 80:205 F 13 '63
Pope John XXIII, in memoriam; poem. Christian Cent 80:823 Je 26 '63
U.S.A. 1964; poem. Christian Cent 81:1331 O 28 '64
Warren report; poem. Christian Cent 81:1264 O 14 '64

PIERCE, Franklin
Franklin Pierce, fourteenth President 1853-1857. F. Freidel. il pors Nat Geog Mag 127:114-17 Ja '65

PIERCE, John Robinson
Satellite science and technology. biblog Science 141:237-44 Jl 19 '63

about

Profiles. C. Tomkins. por New Yorker 39:49-50+ S 21 '63

PIERCE, Lawrence
Salvager of New York teens. il pors Ebony 19:80-2+ Je '64

PIERCE, Noel. See Wadsworth, B. G. jt. auth.

PIERCE, Ponchitta
Girl with a hole in her heart. Ebony 20: 27-8+ D '64

PIERCE, William H.
Redunancy in computers; with biographical sketch. Sci Am 210:32, 103-6+ bibliog (p 1052) F '64

PIERIS rapae. See Imported cabbage worms

PIERMAN, Dorothy
Case of the missing bishop. Wilson Lib Bul 37:580 Mr '63

PIERMARINI, G. J. and Weir, C. E.
Allotropy in some rare-earth metals at high pressures. bibliog Science 144:69-71 Ap 3 '64

PIERPONT Morgan library
Dutch master in New York; exhibition of the Book of hours of Catherine of Cleves. il Art N 63:44-5+ S '64
PIERRE Patelin; drama. See Koon, H.
PIERRO, Louis J. See Klein, N. W. jt. auth.
PIERS, Maria
Clearing the atmosphere. PTA Mag 58:21-2 Ap '64
Social graces and disgraces. PTA Mag 59:7-9 bibliog(p36) D '64
PIERS
Boat pier that goes up or down in ten minutes. E. F. Lindsley. il Pop Sci 184:162-4 Ap '64
Buying or building docks, piers and floats. G. Daniels. il Pop Mech 120:152-7 Ag '63
400-foot pier fabricated on shore; Bois Blanc Township, Mich. G. Gibbons. il Am City 78:185 S '63
PIERSALL, Jimmy
Individualist. il por Newsweek 61:91-2 Je 10 '63
PIERSON, David W.
Equal opportunity; letter. Science 142:154 O 11 '63
PIERSON, Frank C.
Wage-price policy approaches; excerpt from address. Mo Labor R 86:140 F '63
PIERSON, George W.
Restless temper. bibliog f Am Hist R 69:969-89 Jl '64
PIERSON, Howard
Redefining insanity. por Time 82:54 N 29 '63
PIERSON, Robert M.
Objectionable literature: some false synonymies. por Library J 89:3920-3 O 15 '64
PIERSON, Robert W. and Nagle, R. E.
Against almost impossible odds. Am City 79:112-13 S '64
PIERSON, William
Korean waifs and Yankee volunteers. il por Todays Health 42:38-9 S '64
PIES. See Pie
PIES, Meat. See Cookery—Meat
PIETA, Transportation of. See Transportation of works of art
PIETRO da Cortona. See Cortona, P. da
PIEZ, Glady T.
Adhesives for book labels. ALA Bul 57:1051-2 D '63
Casters for book trucks, what type is best for carpeted floors? ALA Bul 57:787-9 S '63
Library technology. See issues of ALA bulletin beginning December 1963
LTP book labeling system goes to market. ALA Bul 58:554-6 Je '64
PIGAFETTA, Antonio
Journal from Magellan's voyage. Wilson Lib Bul 38:714 My '64
PIGEON racing
High flying hobby! il Ebony 20:111-12+ D '64
PIGEON shooting
Border pigeon shoot. D. Barnes. il Sports Illus 18:18-21 Mr 18 '63
New wild West; Colombaire-style live-pigeon shooting, with Manauta brothers. G. Schendel. il Esquire 60:140-1+ O '63
PIGEONS
Chicken feed. W. Page. il Field & S 69:66-7 My '64
Complex visual concept in the pigeon. R. J. Herrnstein and D. H. Loveland. il Science 146:549-51 O 23 '64
Directional movement and horizontal edge detectors in the pigeon retina. H. R. Maturana and S. Frenk. bibliog il Science 142:977-9 N 15 '63
Errorless discrimination learning in the pigeon: effects of chlorpromazine and imipramine. H. S. Terrace. bibliog il Science 140:318-19 Ap 19 '63
First linkage of a species antigen in the genus streptopelia. W. J. Miller. bibliog il Science 143:1179-80 Mr 13 '64
No sayonara for Hato-san; Japanese newspapers' flocks of carrier pigeons. Time 83:41 Ja 31 '64
People vs. pigeons. D. Cort. il Nation 197:368-9 N 30 '63
Pigeons and cryptococcosis; letter. J. D. Schneidau, jr. Science 143:525 F 7 '64
Potency of conditioned reinforcers based on food and on food and punishment. G. S. Reynolds. il Science 139:838-9 Mr 1 '63
Reproductive behavior of ring doves. D. S. Lehrman. il Sci Am 211:48-54 N '64
Wavelength generalization after discrimination learning with and without errors. H. S. Terrace. bibliog il Science 144:78-80 Ap 3 '64
See also
Dove-cotes
Mourning doves
PIGEONS as carriers of infection
Controlling pigeons about the home. E. M. Mills. il Consumer Bul 47:25-7 Jl '64
Kill those pigeons? il Time 82:62 O 18 '63
Perils of pigeons. il Newsweek 62:80 O 14 '63
Please don't feed the pigeons! pigeon control programs. J. C. Devlin. Read Digest 85:12E-12F+ Ag '64
Shooters solve the pigeon problem! Indianapolis pigeon rid project. C. Conley. il Field & S 68:10-11+ D '63
PIGMENTS
See also
Carotenoids
PIGMENTS (biology)
Amino acid composition of hemerythrin in relation to subunit structure. W. R. Groskopf and others. bibliog il Science 141:166-7 Jl 12 '63
Astaxanthin in the cedar waxwing. A. H. Brush and K. Allen. bibliog il Science 142:47-8 O 4 '63
Flower pigments. S. Clevenger. il Sci Am 210:84-8+ Je '64
Genetic control of hemerythrin specificity in a marine worm. C. Manwell. bibliog il Science 139:755-8 F 22 '63
Production of oosporein and its leuco form by basidiomycete species. H. Takeshita and M. Anchel. bibliog il Science 147:152-3 Ja 8 '65
PIGMENTS, Visual. See Retina
PIGMIES. See Pygmies
PIGOTT-BROWN, Sir William Brian, 3d bart
Four eligible bachelors in London. E. O'Brien. por Vogue 144:140-1 S 15 '64
PIGS. See Swine
PIGS, Wild. See Woods hogs
PIGSKIN. See Leather
PIGSKIN club of Washington. See Negro clubs
PIKAS
Piper of the peaks. B. W. Dalrymple. il Field & S 69:49+ S '64
PIKE, Herbert
How to rent a better farm. por Suc Farm 61:36+ O '63
I should put my wife on the payroll. por Suc Farm 62:105+ Mr '64
PIKE, James Albert, bp
How should we pray? excerpt from The next day. Read Digest 85:81-4 S '64
about
Against glossolalia. Time 81:84 My 17 '63
Ecumenical setback. America 111:246 S 12 '64
Pike and prejudice. il por Newsweek 64:75+ O 26 '64
PIKE, Robert E.
Log drive on the Connecticut. Atlan 212:29-34 Jl '63
PIKE, Ruth E.
How good is your board? Recreation 58:33-5 Ja '65
PIKE fishing
Autumn jackpot. H. Bradshaw. il Outdoor Life 132:44-7+ S '63
Big bugs bug big pike. H. F. Blaisdell. il Outdoor Life 134:42-3+ S '64
Ghost pike of Manitoba. M. Ellis. il Field & S 67:120-2 Mr '63
Pike fishing by bell. R. Russell. il Atlan 214:75-8 Ag '64
Technique for northerns. J. O. Cartier. il Field & S 67:62-5+ Ap '63
Where northerns come big. G. Laycock. il Outdoor Life 134:44-5+ Ag '64
PIKES PEAK
Flowers that bloom above the clouds. E. S. Clements. il Audubon Mag 66:180-1 My '64
Pikes Peak and all that. B. Ballantine. il Holiday 34:18+ Ag '63
PIKES PEAK race. See Automobile racing
PILARCZYK, Helga
Erwartung by Pilarczyk. I. Kolodin. Sat R 46:55 F 23 '63
Music to my ears; Pilarczyk. I. Kolodin. Sat R 46:46 F 9 '63
PILARSKI, Laura
Theatre: Poland. Theatre Arts 47:71-4 Jl '63
PILATE, Pontius
Word. V. P. McCorry. America 110:352-3, 380-1 Mr 14-21 '64
PILE of stones; story. See Nissenson, H.
PILEGGI, Nicholas
Quality of rudeness. Esquire 61:98 Ja '64
PILES (disease) See Hemorrhoids
PILES and pile driving
Help for sidewalk superintendents. S. Blum. il N Y Times Mag p30-1+ O 4 '64
PILFERING. See Stealing

PILGRIM, Francis J. and Kamen, J. M.
Predictors of human food consumption. bibliog Science 139:501-2 F 8 '63
PILGRIM fathers
One small candle; condensation. T. J. Fleming. il Read Digest 83:207-12+ D '63
PILGRIM project: story. See Searls, H.
PILKINGTON, Betty
Chinese puzzle in the U.N. Christian Cent 82:50-1 Ja 13 '65
Trade is people, too. Christian Cent 81:610+ My 6 '64
Vietnam: the UN peeks in. Nation 197:273-5 N 2 '63
PILKINGTON brothers, limited
Glass revolution. il Newsweek 64:87 N 23 '64
New window on the world; float glass process. il Time 84:86 Ag 7 '64
PILLAGE
Looting: the high cost of race violence. il U S News 57:36-41 S 14 '64
PILLOW cases
Sheets and pillowcases; shop by price not by brand. il Consumer Rep 29:11-15 Ja '64
PILLOWS
Pockets full of Christmas. il House & Gard 124:268-9+ N '63
See also
Cushions
PILLS
Miraculous world of pills that cure. L. R. Chevalier. il McCalls 90:80-1+ F '63
PILLSBURY grand national bake-off. See Cookery—Competitions
PILLSBURY mills, incorporated
Never overdone; Pillsbury grand national bake-off. il Bsns W p32-3 S 21 '63
PILLTOWN, La.
Businessmen at the bar; Mississippi River pilots. il Bsns W p32-4 Ap 18 '64
PILOBOLUS. See Fungi
PILOT charts. See Nautical charts
PILOT ejection seats, capsules, etc. See Airplanes—Escape devices
PILOT lights, Electric. See Electric lamps
PILOT training. See Air pilots —Training
PILOTING, Airplane. See Airplanes—Piloting
PILOTING, Helicopter. See Helicopters—Piloting
PILOTS, Aviation. See Air pilots
PILOTS and pilotage
Businessmen at the bar; Mississippi River pilots. il Bsns W p32-4 Ap 18 '64
Proper powerboat piloting. il Yachting 115: 68 Je '64
PILPEL, Harriet F.
But can you do that? See last issue of each month of Publishers' weekly
Sex vs. the law: a study in hypocrisy. Harper 230:35-40 Ja '65
PIMA COUNTY, Ariz.
Desert is my beat. il Ebony 19:134-6+ Ap '64
PIMENTEL, George C. and others
Helium difluoride: possible preparative techniques based on nuclear transmutations. bibliog Science 143:674 F 14 '64
—See Turner, J. J. jt. auth.
PINAL pioneer parkway. See Roads—Arizona
El PINAR, Bogota, Colombia. See Botanical gardens
PINATAS
Joy of a pinata. J. Love. il Design 66:14-15 N '64
PINBALL machines
How to beat the bandits; Aussie syndicate in Las Vegas. Time 85:37 Ja 22 '65
Many-armed bandit; bill to ban slot machines in Maryland. Newsweek 61:27 Ap 1 '63
Now the no-armed bandit. Sports Illus 21:7-8 Ag 17 '64
PINCHOT, Gifford
Pinchot and the foresters; excerpt from The quiet crisis. S. L. Udall. il pors Am For 69: 24-7+ N '63
PINCHOT institute for conservation studies. See Conservation of resources—Study and teaching
PINCUS, Gregory
Tell me, doctor. Ladies Home J 80:50+ Je '63
PINCUS, John A.
What policy for commodities? For Affairs 42:227-41 Ja '64
PINCUS, Monica
Mlle guest editors: '64. Mlle 59:224-5 Ag '64
PINCUS, Walter
Fat cats are hard to find. Reporter 31:34-6 Ag 13 '64
PINDYCK, Bruce
Follow a star. por Seventeen 24:78+ Ja '65
PINE, Gerald J.
Guidance in our changing world. Sr Schol 83:9T+ N 8 '63
PINE
California's methuselah trees. W. F. Heald. il Am For 70:34-5 Mr '64
Chronic gamma radiation affects the distribution of radial increment in pinus rigida stems. G. M. Woodwell and L. N. Miller. bibliog il Science 139:222-3 Ja 18 '63
Different way to train your pine. il Sunset 130:252 Mr '63
For something different in trees. G. Taloumis. il Pop Gard 15:76-7 Ja '64
It's easy to become infatuated with pines. il Sunset 131:88-93 N '63
Methuselah of trees: the bristlecone pine. W. F. Heald. il Audubon Mag 66:50-1 Ja '64
Mio, Michigan: strictly for the birds; Huron National Forest Kirtland's warbler management area. J. Calkins. il Am For 69:6+ Je '63
Our outdoor bonsai; Scotch pine. G. Harshbarger. il Flower Grower 51:20-1 Mr '64
Pines for winter protection and beauty all year. D. Reay. il Flower Grower 50:33 N '63
Sky forest of the ancients; Ancient Bristlecone Pine Forest area of Inyo National Forest. W. F. Heald. il Am For 70:34-5+ N '64
Two unique western conifers. I. Reed. il Horticulture 41:98 F '63
Umbrella pine, sciadopitys verticillata: past and present distribution in Japan. M. Tsukada. bibliog il Science 142:1680-1 D 27 '63
Variation in the monoterpenes of pinus ponderosa laws. R. H. Smith. bibliog il Science 143:1337-8 Mr 20 '64
White pine trees made history. C. E. Randall. il Am For 69:12-14+ Ap '63
See also
Araucaria
Diseases and pests
Beetle explosion in Honduras; southern pine beetle. J. A. Beal and others. il Am For 70:31-3 N '64
Gooseberry, innocent outlaw; carrier of white pine blister rust. R. L. Hawk. il Horticulture 41:366-7 Jl '63
Seed
Forests by jet; Mexican seed-collecting program. C. Peet. il Am For 70:48-50 O '64
Seed pines direct after forest fires. D. P. Simpson. il Farm J 88:48 D '64
PINE beetles, Southern. See Pine—Diseases and pests
PINE blister rust. See Pine—Diseases and pests
PINE BLUFF, Ark.
Seven-year relighting program. O. Lites. il Am City 78:219 My '63
PINE CITY, Minn.
Dusk-to-dawn lighting. W. W. Challeen, sr. il Am City 79:134 S '64
PINE cones
Cones for Christmas. H. W. Dengler. il Am For 69:8-11+ D '63
PINE siskins. See Finches
PINEAL body
Serotonin rhythm in the pineal organ: control by the sympathetic nervous system. V. M. Fiske. bibliog il Science 146:253-4 O 9 '64
PINEAL gland. See Glands
PINES, Christine
Twenty-four short cuts to summer meals. Parents Mag 38:55-8 Ag '63
PINES, Maya
Danger in our medical labs. Harper 227:84-7+ O '63
How three-year-olds teach themselves to read, and love it. Harper 226:58-64 My '63
Laser lights up the future. N Y Times Mag p27+ S 8 '63
New ways to prevent miscarriage. Redbook 120:66-7+ Ap '63
Parent and child. N Y Times Mag p95-6 N 3 '63
Quickening war against viruses. Harper 228: 90-2+ My '64
Terra incognita. Reporter 28:37-9 My 9 '63
PINES, ISLE OF (Kunie)
After Tahiti, what? D. Warner. il Atlan 214: 130+ O '64
PINES. See Pine
PING, Keith E. and Cole, O. J.
Houston centralizes motor maintenance. Am City 78:86-8 N '63
PING pong. See Table tennis
PING-pong rockets. See Rockets—Military applications
PING pong tables. See Tables

PINGEL, John H. See Lanzl, L. H. jt. auth.

PINGUINAIN. See Enzymes

PINILLA, Gustavo Rojas. See Rojas Pinilla, G.

PINK-headed warblers. See Warblers

PINKETT, Harold T.
Archival product of a century of federal assistance to agriculture. bibliog f Am Hist R 69:689-706 Ap '64

PINKNEY, David H.
Crowd in the French revolution of 1830. bibliog f Am Hist R 70:1-17 O '64

PINKNEY, James F.
Motor carriage: the long and short of it. Ann Am Acad 345:66-72 Ja '63

PINKS
Grow this reddest pink once and you'll never be without it. bravo! il Flower Grower 50:37 Je '63
Laced pinks are for every garden. A. T. Robinson. il Horticulture 41:124-5 Mr '63
See also
Sweet williams

PINNER, Betty, and others
Alkaline phosphatase in peripheral nerves. bibliog Science 145:936-8 Ag 28 '64

PINNIPEDIA
Underwater sounds of pinnipeds. W. E. Schevill and others. bibliog il Science 141:50-3 Jl 5 '63
See also
Walruses

PINSKY, Leonard, and DiGeorge, A. M.
Cleft palate in the mouse: a teratogenic index of glucocorticoid potency. bibliog Science 147:402-3 Ja 22 '65

PINSON, Penelope
(comp) Books for parents. See issues of Parents' magazine & better homemaking

PINTER, Harold
Lover. Criticism
Commonweal 79:484-5 Ja 24 '64
Nation 198:106 Ja 27 '64
New Repub 150:28+ F 1 '64
New Yorker 39:69-70 Ja 11 '64
Sat R 47:25 Ja 25 '64
Time il 83:64 Ja 17 '64
Vogue 143:22 F 15 '64
Room. Criticism
Nation 199:523 D 28 '64
New Yorker 40:68+ D 19 '64
Newsweek 64:75-6 D 21 '64
Sat R 47:33 D 26 '64
Time il 84:86 D 18 '64
Vogue 145:98 F 1 '65
Slight ache. Criticism
Nation 199:523 D 28 '64
New Yorker 40:68+ D 19 '64
Newsweek 64:75-6 D 21 '64
Sat R 47:33 D 26 '64
Time il 84:86 D 18 '64
Vogue 145:98 F 1 '65

PINTO, Carlos Alberto de Carvalho
On the edge of the abyss. il Time 83:32 Ja 3 '64

PINTO, Edward H.
Some eighteenth-century laminated woodwork. Antiques 86:197-9 Ag '64
Tamper, rasp, and mull: wooden accessories for tobacco. Antiques 85:690-4 Je '64

PINTO, Fernão Mendes. See Mendes Pinto, F.

PINTO, Olga
Italian libraries: a progress report. bibliog f Library J 88:721-3 F 15 '63

PINTOFF, Ernest
Complete works of Ernest Pintoff. D. Macdonald. Esquire 61:16+ Ap '64
Innocent fireman. il por Newsweek 63:110+ My 25 '64
Who da hell is dot? il por Newsweek 62:79 S 2 '63

PINUS attenuata. See Pine

PINZUTI, Dom Mario
New R for old books offered by Vatican institute. Library J 88:2475 Je 15 '63

PIO da Pietreicina, Father
Padre's patience. il por Time 83:79-80+ Ap 24 '64

PIONEER library system. See Libraries—New York (state)

PIONEER life. See Frontier and pioneer life

PIONEER parachute company
Parachutes that are full of holes; for better performance. il Bsns W p 119+ Ag 10 '63

PIONEER probe. See Space probes

PIONEER village, Minden, Neb. See Villages, Restored

PIONEERS
George Washington of Centralia Washington. W. S. Savage. bibliog Negro Hist Bul 27:44-7 N '63
Ordeal at Devil's Gate. W. Stegner. Esquire 61:100-1+ Je '64

PIORE, Nora K.
Metropolitan medical economics; with biographical sketch. Sci Am 212:16, 19-27 bibliog(p 134) Ja '65

PIOUS, Donald A. and Mills, S. E.
Killing of cultured rabbit fibroblasts with isoimmune serum. bibliog Science 142:52-3 O 4 '63

PIOUS brother; story. See Lind, J.

PIPA, Rudolph S. and others
Thysanuran median frontal organ: its structural resemblance to photoreceptors. bibliog Science 145:829-31 Ag 21 '64

PIPART, Gérard
Paris: a designer's debut. M. Cantwell. il pors Mlle 58:147-9+ Mr '64

PIPE finders. See Water pipes—Detection

PIPE joints
This water main can bend; Sioux City, Ia. W. Murphy. il Am City 78:90-1 Mr '63

PIPE laying
Do-it-yourself program is best; Asheville, N.C. G. Johnson. il Am City 78:103-4 Mr '63
500 feet per day; water line for Wisconsin Rapids, Wis. il Am City 78:88 Jl '63
How to place a mile-long intake: Muskegon, Mich. R. J. Miles. il Am City 79:90-1 Ja '64
Hydraulic mining at home. il Sunset 132:178 My '64
Pipelines through the swamp; Mississippi delta. il Bsns W p 116-18 Jl 18 '64
Relocation of big mains; Staten Island, N.Y. B. J. Feitelson. il Am City 79:108-10 Mr '64
Sewer pushes through a bog; St Louis, Mo. E. Maran. il Am City 79:171-2 S '64
See also
Pipe joints

PIPE lines
Atlantic report; capsule pipelines. Atlan 212:34+ O '63
Invisible network. il Time 84:63 Ag 14 '64
Making products flow to the customers; shipment of solids and gases in liquid form. il Bsns W p68-70 My 2 '64
Paying the piper; thriving pipeline industry. il Time 84:58-63 N 20 '64
See also
Gas, Natural—Pipe lines
Petroleum pipe lines
Water pipes

Detection

Find that line for sure; Palo Alto, Calif. J. W. Still. il Am City 79:99-100 Jl '64

PIPE locators. See Pipe lines—Detection; Water pipes—Detection

PIPELESS organ. See Organ

PIPER, Nora
Sixth diamond. Read Digest 85:171-2+ D '64

PIPER aircraft corporation
Piper studying standardized parts plan. il Aviation W 79:99 O 28 '63

PIPES
See also
Water pipes

Location

See Pipe lines—Detection

PIPES, Irrigation. See Irrigation pipes

PIPES, Plastic
New super-smooth metal substitute. D. Brigham. il Sci Digest 53:27-30 Mr '63

PIPES, Tobacco. See Tobacco pipes

PIPES, Water. See Water pipes

PIPESTONE NATIONAL MONUMENT
Place of the Red Pipestone. R. W. Meyer. il Nat Parks Mag 37:4-7 D '63

PIPPEN, David L.
Gate turnoff controlled rectifier. Electr World 72:46+ Ag '64
Unijunction transistor. Electr World 71:46-7+ Ja '64

PIPPETT, Aileen
Book between trains. Sat R 46:41-2 N 16 '63

PIQUA, Ohio
Nuclear power for Piquads. J. P. Gallagher. il Am City 79:71-2 Jl '64

PIQUET, Howard S.
More tariff cuts coming. Nations Bsns 52:110+ O '64

PIRANDELLO, Luigi
Call it virtue: tr. by E. Eager. Criticism
Newsweek 61:85 Ap 8 '63
Right you are if you think you are. Criticism
New Yorker 40:109 Mr 14 '64
Six characters in search of an author; tr. by P. A. Mayer. Criticism
Commonweal 78:105-6 Ap 19 '63
Nation 196:334 Ap 20 '63
New Repub 148:30 Mr 30 '63
New Yorker 39:74-5 Mr 23 '63
Sat R 46:28 Mr 23 '63
Theatre Arts il 47:13-14 My '63

PIRANHA fishing
How to eat a piranha before it eats you. G. McKay. il Sports Illus 18:48-50 Mr 11 '63
PIRANHAS
Fish who came for dinner; South American intruder. Sports Illus 20:14 Je 15 '64
PIRATED editions. See Copyright—Unauthorized reprints
PIRATES
Pirates of Paraguay. J. Piá. il Américas 15:31-8 Mr '63
See also
Treasure trove
PIRATES (baseball) See Baseball clubs
PIRE, Dominique Georges Henri
Père Pire's peace corps. America 109:373 O 5 '63
PIRIE, Peter J.
Class of 1813: reflections on Verdi vs. Wagner. Hi Fi 13:90-2+ O '63
Fie upon Freud! Hi Fi 14:31-3+ Jl '64
PIROLO, Charles A.
See better, look better with contact lenses. Pop Sci 184:62-4+ Je '64
PIRONE, P. P.
Fruit tree spraying. Horticulture 43:38-9 Ja '65
Insect control calendar (cont) Pop Gard 14: 100-1 F; 58-9 Ap '63
Systemics, are they the answer to garden pest control? Horticulture 42:20+ Ag '64
What do you know about biological control? Horticulture 42:20-3 O '64
PIROSHKI. See Cookery, Russian
PISA
Campanile (leaning tower)
No time to lose; plans to halt the slow descent. il Newsweek 63:63 Mr 23 '64
PISANI, Bernard
How to tell when labor begins. Redbook 123: 28+ Je '64
PISANO, Giovanni
Prophetic prophet from Gothic Italy. H. A. La Farge. il Art N 62:42-3+ D '63
PISCIOTTA, Gaspare
Profiles; the Mafia. N. Lewis. New Yorker 39:53-4+ F 15 '64
PISGAH NATIONAL FOREST, N.C. See National forests
PISSALADIERE. See Cookery, Mediterranean
PISTOL ranges. See Shooting ranges
PISTOLS
Air and gas pistols. il Consumer Rep 29:134-8 Mr '64
American pepperboxes. C. Worman. il Hobbies 69:122-3+ Je '64
Fire ball; varminting handgun. W. Page. il Field & S 68:106-10 Je '63
Henry Deringer, jr. C. G. Worman. il Hobbies 68:124-5 Ja '64
I-factor. P. B. Weston. il Field & S 69:54-8 Ja '65
Remington double derringer. W. R. Orbelo. il Hobbies 68:113 Mr '63
Remington Zigzag derringer. W. R. Orbelo. il Hobbies 68:123 O '63
Remington's latest: new handgun and two new cartridges. J. O'Connor. il Outdoor Life 131:120-2 My '63
Sharps pepperbox pistol. W. R. Orbelo. il Hobbies 68:113 My '63
U.S. percussion pistol, model 1842. W. R. Orbelo. il Hobbies 69:121 D '64
World's hottest handgun. il Pop Sci 182:138-9 Je '63
PISTOLS, Air. See Air guns
PISTOLS, Toy
Children with toy guns potentially dangerous. Sci N L 85:24 Ja 11 '64
PISTON, Walter
Walter Piston at seventy. L. Chapin. por Mus Am 83:34 D '63
PISTON engines. See Automobile engines
PISZCZEK, Edward A.
White plague is still a menace. Todays Health 41:52-5 D '63
PITCH, Musical. See Musical pitch
PITCHER, Evelyn Goodenough
Male and female; excerpts from Children tell stories: an analysis of fantasy. Atlan 211: 87-91 Mr '63
PITCHER plants
Cobra lily. M. M. Taylor. il Horticulture 42:38-9 Ja '64
Malaysia's giant flowers and insect-trapping plants. P. A. Zahl. il Nat Geog Mag 125: 680-710 My '64
PITCHERS, Baseball. See Baseball players
PITCHING. See Baseball
PITMAN, Sir James
Teaching with i/t/a spreads through U.S. il Pub W 186:74-6 Ag 24 '64
PITNEY-Bowes, incorporated
Preferential hiring. Newsweek 62:69 D 16 '63
PITT, Malcolm
Music of India. Am Rec G 30:802-5 My '64
PITT, W. Page
Many commencements of Callie Trent. Read Digest 84:49-53 Je '64
PITTMAN, Claude F. jr
One-sided lighting story. Am City 79:104 Jl '64
PITTMAN, J. A. and others
Cysteine stimulation of glucose oxidation in thyroid tissue. bibliog Science 140:389 Ap 26 '63
PITTMAN, Steuart L.
Civil defense in a balanced national security. Bul Atomic Sci 20:24-6 Je '64
Rice university conference develops five factory projects. Arch Rec 134:115-20 D '63
PITTOSPORUM
Why so high and why so lush? il Sunset 131: 186 S '63
PITTS, Grover C. and Hollifield, Guy
Fatness of the total body as estimated from measurements on the eviscerated carcass. bibliog Science 141:718-19 Ag 23 '63
PITTSBURGH
Pittsburgh expands its parking program. M. A. Neale. il Am City 80:109 Ja '65
Air pollution
How Pittsburgh licked the problem. H. R. Domke. il Sci Digest 53:7-8 My '63
Art
Community sources for art education. M. A. McKibben. il Sch Arts 62:17-19 My '63
Pittsburgh grab bag; Carnegie international. M. Kozloff. Nation 199:341-2 N 9 '64
Banks
Mellon bank steps down from its pedestal. il Bsns W p 106-8+ Je 1 '63
City planning
Huge research park to bridge mile-long ravine; Pittsburgh's Panther Hollow. il Pop Sci 183:90-1 D '63
New research park; Pittsburgh's Panther Hollow. il Sci N L 83:391 Je 22 '63
Pittsburgh bids high for research industry; R&D center in Panther Hollow. il Bsns W p51 Je 8 '63
Renaissance, phase two; plans to convert Panther Hollow into a research center. il Time 81:52 Je 21 '63
Education
Case studies teach high school history; case study method. il Bsns W p94 F 1 '64
Dollars for scholars; grants for secondary schools. Sr Schol 84:4T F 7 '64
Pittsburgh polls its graduates. S. R. March. NEA J 53:27 Mr '64
Portable school program for Pittsburgh. J. Pekruhn. il Arch Rec 133:176-8 F '63
See also
Pittsburgh. University
Lighting
Pittsburgh pushes for more mercuries. F. C. Poorman. il Am City 79:131 O '64
Music
[Musical events] (cont) Mus Am 83:17 Mr '63; 84:12 F; 22-3 Jl '64
Pittsburgh midwinter. R. J. Croan. Opera N 28:32 Ap 18 '64
Pittsburgh potion. R. J. Croan. Opera N 27:33 Ap 6 '63
Pittsburgh stealers. R. J. Croan. Opera N 28:33 F 1 '64
Pittsburgh's Peking. R. J. Croan. Opera N 27:31-2 F 2 '63
Stores
New curiosity shop; Pittsburgh's Shadyside. il Bsns W p 118-20+ Ja 18 '64
Wood and stone lend warmth to Pittsburgh store; Kaufmann's. il Arch Rec 133:174-5 Je '63
PITTSBURGH. University
Economics library selections revived by U. of Pittsburgh. Library J 89:1208+ Mr 15 '64
King Edward of Pitt. M. Cope. il Sat Eve Post 236:22-3 Ap 6 '63
Undeserving; awarding of an honorary degree to Dr E. Teller. E. A. Cahill. Nation 196: inside cover Ap 27 '63
Graduate school of librarianship
Sandwich seminars; lunch hour. R. Wiley and D. Helfeld. Library J 88:2952+ S 1 '63

PITTSBURGH. University—*Continued*

Graduate school of library and information sciences

Dean's dream. C. W. Stone. il Library J 89:2740-5 Jl '64

PITTSBURGH committee for a sane nuclear policy

Undeserving; awarding of an honorary degree to Dr E. Teller. E. A. Cahill. Nation 196: inside cover Ap 27 '63

PITTSBURGH international exhibition. See Art—Exhibitions

PITTSBURGH Pirates (baseball) See Baseball clubs

PITTSBURGH plate glass company

Auto change no one will notice; float glass windows in GM cars. il Bsns W p52+ S 5 '64

PITTSBURGH steel company

Steel company's date with a data machine; total systems concept. Bsns W p 142+ My 4 '63

PITTSBURGH Steelers (football club) See Football clubs

PITTSBURGH symphony orchestra

Leader of equals. il Time 84:48 S 11 '64

PITUITARY body

ACTH molecule. C. H. Li. il Sci Am 209: 46-53 Jl '63

Freezing can destroy tumorous pituitary. Sci N L 84:366 D 7 '63

PITUITARY hormones. See Hormones

PITZ, Henry C.

Drawings of Ben Solowey. Am Artist 27: 26-31 My '63

Frank E. Schoonover: an exemplar of the Pyle tradition. Am Artist 28:64-9+ N '64

Illustrations for books. il Design 65:120-5+ Ja '64

Rudolf Freund, scientific illustrator. Am Artist 28:20-5+ My '64

Sherman Hoeflich. Am Artist 28:32-7+ F '64

Traveling in Europe with a sketchbook. il Am Artist 27:30-5+ Ap '63

Turning wheel. Am Artist 28:22-8+ Mr '64

PITZER, Kenneth S.

Bonding in xenon fluorides and halogen fluorides. bibliog Science 139:414-15 F 1 '63

PITZER college, Claremont, Calif.

Claremont's sixth. il Time 84:57 N 6 '64

PIUS IX, pope

Beatify Pio Nono? America 109:131-2 Ag 10 '63

No to Pio Nono? proposed beatification. por Newsweek 62:74 S 2 '63

PIUS XI, pope

Divini redemptoris to Pacem in terris. F. S. Meyer. Nat R 14:406 My 21 '63

PIUS XII, pope

Against Pius XII; the play Der stellvertreter. America 108:389 Mr 23 '63

As The deputy opened. E. C. Parker. Christian Cent 81:349 Mr 11 '64

As we await The deputy; questions and answers. J. M. Oesterreicher. il America 109: 570-3+ N 9 '63

Billy Rose's message. America 109:187 Ag 24 '63

Character assassination. America 110:304-5 Mr 7 '64; Discussion. 110:499 Ap 11 '64

Cry against a decision of silence; The deputy, by R. Hochhuth. E. Capouya. il Sat R 47:41-2 Mr 21 '64

Deputy controversy. Christian Cent 81:507-8 Ap 22 '64; Discussion. 81:861-2 Jl 1 '64

Footnote to The deputy dispute: Jews of Rome, the Nazis and the Vatican. C. Mydans. por Life 56:21 My 1 '64

History and a pontificate. America 110:359 Mr 21 '64

Hochhuth's Representative. C. Barnes. Nation 197:287-8 N 2 '63

New debate over a pope's views on Nazis. por U S News 57:12 N 30 '64

No letup for Der stellvertreter. E. E. Turner. Christian Cent 80:1269-70 O 16 '63

Nothing more unjust; Pope Paul's allusion to the attacks upon Pope Pius XII in The deputy. America 110:68 Ja 18 '64

Pius and the Jews. America 109:70 Jl 20 '63

Pius and the Jews. Commonweal 80:440 Jl 3 '64

Pius defended: English version of Der stellvertreter. Newsweek 62:97 O 7 '63

Pius, Hitler, and the Jews. il por Newsweek 63:78-9 Mr 2 '64

Pius XII and history; Brooklyn Jewish community council's tribute. America 110:211 F 15 '64

Pius XII & the Jews. il Time 82:85-6 N 1 '63

Pius XII and the Jews. P. Land. America 108:730-1 My 25 '63

Pius XII and the Nazis. R. A. Graham. America 111:742-3 D 5 '64; Reply with rejoinder. F. W. Wentz. 112:2 Ja 2 '65

Pius XII, criminal. America 109:785 D 21 '63

Pius XII, the Jews, and the German Catholic church. G. Lewy. bibliog Commentary 37: 23-35 F '64; Discussion. 37:6+ Je '64

Play of the month. N. J. O'Connor. Cath World 199:135-6 My '64

Play that indicts Pope Pius XII. H. Graef. por(cover) Cath World 197:380-5 S '63

Play that rocked Europe. A. G. Aronowitz. il Sat Eve Post 237:36, 39+ F 29 '64

Pope and the Jews. il por Newsweek 61:65 Mr 11 '63

Postscript on The deputy. R. M. Brown. Commonweal 80:174-6 My 1 '64

P.O.A.U. on trial; tempest over Der stellvertreter. Christian Cent 80:1124 S 18 '63

Recollections of Pius XII. G. A. Gripenberg. America 110:539+ Ap 18 '64

Rolf Hochhuth's The deputy; symposium. Commonweal 79:647-62 F 28 '64; Discussion. 80:46+, 119-21 Ap 3, 17 '64

See or read it first! Christian Cent 81:294 Mr 4 '64

Der stellvertreter: the play that caused a storm. F. V. Grunfeld. Reporter 30:46+ Ja 30 '64; Discussion. 30:6+ Mr 26 '64

Tempest over Der stellvertreter. B. Stoop. Christian Cent 80:980-1 Ag 7 '63

Vatican and Auschwitz. America 110:668 My 16 '64

Wartime view of Pius XII. America 110:534-5 Ap 18 '64

PIUS, Sister Mary. See Mary Pius, Sister

PIZZA. See Cookery, Italian

PIZZARELLO, Donald J. and others

Circadian rhythmicity in the sensitivity of two strains of mice to whole-body radiation. bibliog Science 145:286-91 Jl 17 '64

Variations in survival time after whole body radiation at two times of day. Science 139: 349 Ja 25 '63

PIZZETTI, Ildebrando

Ascetic in Rome; interview, ed. by M. J. Matz. por Opera N 28:14-16 Ja 18 '64

PLACE cards

Novel Noel place cards. il Good H 157:154 D '63

What's so special about February? holidays, that's what! C. Brock. il Good H 156:132 F '63

PLACE for chance (dramatic reading) See Dramatic readings

PLACE in the country; story. See Hazzard, S.

PLACE mats. See Table mats, tiles, etc.

PLACE names. See Names, Geographical

PLACEMENT of college professors and instructors. See College professors and instructors—Selection and appointment

PLACENTA

Cineradioangiographic visualization of the venous drainage of the primate placenta in vivo. E. M. Ramsey and others. bibliog il Science 141:909 S 6 '63

Placenta of the Indian elephant, elephas indicus. R. A. Cooper and others. bibliog il Science 146:410-12 O 16 '64

PLAGEMANN, Bentz

Fickle goddess; story. McCalls 92:98-9 N '64

PLAGIARISM

Plagiarism and the use of factual material; legal angles. Pub W 183:52-3 Ap 29 '63

When is a parody a plagiarism? H. Pilpel. Pub W 184:31 D 30 '63

PLAGIARISM in art

Critic in court; R. Hopkins' Transcending and J. Fitzgerald's Rock totem. il Newsweek 65:74 F 1 '65

PLAGIARISM in music

Dolly's my sunflower; question of copyright infringement by composer of Hello, Dolly. Time 84:81 S 18 '64

PLAGIOCLASE. See Feldspar

PLAGUE

Medieval black death exists throughout world; bubonic-pneumonic-septicemic plague. Sci N L 84:198 S 28 '63

Plague fighters. il Newsweek 61:94 Mr 25 '63

See also

Black death

PLAGUE toxin. See Toxins and antitoxins

PLAINFIELD machine company

GI guns that aren't. il Bsns W p 139-40 F 23 '63

PLAINS

See also

Great Plains

PLAINVIEW, N.Y.
Plainview welcomes paperbacks: high school library's experience. D. Cohen. bibliog il Library J 90:306-8 Ja 15 '65

PLAINVIEW-Old Bethpage, N.Y, public library
Plainview emphasizes site. J. Eisner. il Library J 89:4724-6 D 1 '64

PLAKKE, R. K. and Pfeiffer, E. W.
Blood vessels of the mammalian renal medulla. bibliog Science 146:1683-5 D 25 '64

PLANALOG. See Calculating machines—Analog computers

PLANAR graphs. See Topology

PLANARIANS
Bipolar planarians in a stock culture. M. M. Jenkins. bibliog il Science 142:1187 N 29 '63
Conditioning of a free operant response in planaria. R. M. Lee. il Science 139:1048-9 Mr 15 '63; Reply with rejoinder. E. S. Halas. 141:390+ Ag 2 '63
Planaria: memory transfer through cannibalism reexamined. A. L. Hartry and others. bibliog il Science 146:274-5 O 9 '64
Protopsychology; behavior in primitive worm. J. B. Best. il Sci Am 208:54-62 bibliog(p 184) F '63
Stimulus polarity and conditioning in planaria. C. D. Barnes and B. G. Katzung. bibliog il Science 141:728-30 Ag 23 '63
Thinking worm's molecule. W. Cloud. Pop Sci 182:32+ My '63

PLANCK'S law. See Quantum theory

PLANER, Ed
Fixing the score in '64. Reporter 29:35-6 S 12 '63

PLANERS. See Planing machines

PLANETARIUMS
Abrams planetarium in Michigan. V. H. Hogg. il Sky & Tel 27:336-8 Je '64
Coming soon is the Christmas star; Los Angeles' Griffith park. il Sunset 133:29 D '64
Galileo gala; sky show and exhibit at Hayden planetarium. New Yorker 39:28-30 F 8 '64
Johannesburg planetarium. P. Holz. il Sky & Tel 27:20-1 Ja '64
Lunar and planetary laboratory. G. P. Kuiper. il Sky & Tel 27:4-7, 88-92 Ja-F '64
New skies for St Louis; St Louis planetarium. C. A. Schweighauser. il Sky & Tel 25:316-20 Je '63
Planetarium notes. Sky & Tel 28:147-8 S '64
Planetariums in the United States; with listing of institutions. R. A. Korey. il Sky & Tel 26:147-50 S '63
Space education and the Foothill planetarium. P. E. Trejo. il Sky & Tel 28:124-5 S '64
Spool-shaped planetarium for St Louis. il Arch Forum 119:94-7 Ag '63
University of Nevada's atmospherium-planetarium. R. K. Marshall. il Sky & Tel 26: 318-21 D '63

PLANETARY nebulae. See Nebulae

PLANETS
Astronomy. See issues of Science news letter
New neighbor; companion planet to Barnard's star. Newsweek 61:58 Ap 29 '63
New planet discovered; Barnard's Star B. A. Ewing. Sci N L 83:261 Ap 27 '63
Planetary systems associated with main-sequence stars. H. Brown. bibliog il Science 145:1177-81 S 11 '64
Planets and comets: role of crystal growth in their formation. B. Donn and G. W. Sears. bibliog il Science 140:1208-11 Je 14 '63
Prevalence of planets and the probability of life. Time 84:49-50 S 25 '64
Sun, moon, and planets this month. See issues of Sky and telescope
Uranus, Neptune, and Pluto are relatively recent finds. S. D. Gossner. il Natur Hist 72:36-7 Ag '63
Way out quiz. J. Daugherty and M. Daugherty. il Sci Digest 55:66-8 Ap '64
See also
Interplanetary communication
Life on other planets
also names of planets, e.g. Mars (planet)

Atmosphere

Airglow and the physics of upper atmospheres. J. W. Chamberlain. bibliog il Science 142:91-4 N 15 '63

Contamination

Rangers may be launched unsterilized. H. Taylor. Miss & Roc 12:16 My 13 '63

Observations

Clear view of Mars; balloon-borne Stratoscope II. il Time 81:74 Mr 15 '63
Mars observed; Stratoscope. il Newsweek 61: 60 Mr 18 '63

Rotation

Jupiter rotation slowed. Sci N L 85:290 My 9 '64

Temperature and radiation

Jupiter temperatures. Sci N L 85:388 Je 20 '64
Mariner reveals 800F Venus temperature. E. H. Kolcum. il Aviation W 78:30-1 Mr 4 '63
On the recent discoveries concerning Jupiter and Venus. V. Bargmann and L. Motz; reply. P. Anderson. Science 139:670+ F 15 '63

PLANETS, Minor. See Asteroids

PLANING hulls. See Hydrofoils

PLANING machines
New twists on rotary planers. R. J. De Cristoforo. il Pop Sci 183:106-9 Jl '63
See also
Jointers

PLANING mills

Wages and hours

Wages in southern sawmills and planing mills. June 1962. G. L. Stelluto. il Mo Labor R 86:151-3 F '63

PLANK, Emma N.
With fun and fairness. PTA Mag 58:22 Ap '64

PLANK, Robert
Letter from Cleveland. Sat R 47:58-9 O 3; 71 N 7 '64

PLANKTON
Food-producing bubbles; zooplankton. Sci Am 211:60 N '64
Infestation of the copepod acartia tonsa with the stalked ciliate zoothamnium. S. S. Herman and J. A. Mihursky. bibliog il Science 146:543-4 O 23 '64
Marine life food source. B. Tufty. Sci N L 86:245 O 17 '64
Phosphorus excretion and body size in marine animals: microzooplankton and nutrient regeneration. R. E. Johannes. bibliog il Science 146:923-4 N 13 '64
Plankton: optimum diversity structure of a summer community. B. C. Patten. bibliog il Science 140:894-8 My 24 '63; Reply with rejoinder. R. W. Bachmann. 144:556-8 My 1 '64
Pristane in zooplankton. M. Blumer and others. bibliog il Science 140:974 My 31 '63
Zooplankton species groups in the North Pacific. E. W. Fager and J. A. McGowan. bibliog il Science 140:453-60 My 3 '63

PLANKTONIC foraminifera. See Foraminifera

PLANNED music service. See Muzak corporation

PLANNED parenthood. See Birth control

PLANNED parenthood federation of America
Catholics support planned parenthood. Christian Cent 80:1021 Ag 21 '63
Public policy on birth control; possible attitudes of the Catholic community on state involvement. J. E. Dunsford. America 111: 132-4 Ag 8 '64

PLANNERS, City. See City planners

PLANNING
See also
Economic planning
Regional planning

PLANNING, Business. See Business management and organization

PLANNING, Educational. See Educational planning

PLANNING, Industrial. See Industrial management and organization

PLANNING as a profession. See City planners

PLANNING of cities. See City planning

PLANS (architecture) See Architecture, Domestic—Designs and plans

PLANT, Richard
Giggle of Juan Ramirez. New Yorker 39:162+ N 2 '63
Schools at the crossroads. Sat R 46:49-51+ Jl 20 '63
Torments of a super-talent. Sat R 46:29-30 Jl 20 '63

PLANT boxes. See Flower boxes, planters, etc.

PLANT breeding
See also
Alfalfa—Hybrids
Hybridization
Tree breeding

PLANT catalogs. See Catalogs, Seed and plant

PLANT cells and tissues
Asynchronous synthesis of RNA in nucleoli of root meristem. A. K. Bal and P. R. Gross. bibliog il Science 143:808-10 F 21 '64
Control of growth in plant cells. F. C. Steward. il Sci Am 209:104-13 O '63

PLANT cells and tissues—*Continued*
Electrical resistance of cell membranes of avena coleoptiles. N. Higinbotham and others. bibliog il Science 143:1448-9 Mr 27 '64
Growth and development of cultured plant cells. F. C. Steward and others. bibliog il Science 143:20-7 Ja 3 '64
Growth of single plant cells. J. L. Gibbs and D. K. Dougall. bibliog il Science 141:1059 S 13 '63
Indoleacetic acid synthesis by polyphenols in the extraction of pinus phloem and cambial tissue. F. W. Whitmore and R. Zahner. bibliog il Science 145:166-7 Jl 10 '64
Intracellular transport apparatus of phloem fibers. J. W. Mitchell and J. F. Worley. bibliog Science 145:409-10 Jl 25 '64
Morphogenetic studies with partially synchronized cultures of carrot embryos. W. Halperin. bibliog il Science 146:408-10 O 16 '64
Morphology of microtubules of plant cells. M. C. Ledbetter and K. R. Porter. bibliog il Science 144:872-4 My 15 '64
Partial synchronization of nuclear divisions in root meristems with 5-aminouracil. H. H. Smith and others. il Science 142:595-6 N 1 '63
Plant tissue culture; meeting of experts at University Park, Pa. J. Lipetz. Science 141:190+ Jl 12 '63
Starch formation induced by a plant parasitic nematode. M. L. Schuster and others. bibliog il Science 143:1342-3 Mr 20 '64
Tobacco mosaic virus: cytological evidence of the synthesis in the nucleus. T. Hirai and A. Hirai. bibliog il Science 145:589-91 Ag 7 '64
Turgor pressures in phloem: measurements on hevea latex. B. R. Buttery and S. G. Boatman. bibliog il Science 145:285-6 Jl 17 '64
See also
Callus (botany)
Plastids
PLANT communities
Dominance and diversity in land plant communities. R. H. Whittaker. bibliog il Science 147:250-60 Ja 15 '65
PLANT cuttings. See Plant propagation
PLANT diseases. See Plants—Diseases and pests
PLANT distribution. See Geographical distribution of animals and plants
PLANT ecology. See Botany—Ecology
PLANT evolution. See Plants—Evolution
PLANT foods. See Fertilizers and manures
PLANT growth. See Growth (plants)
PLANT growth regulators. See Growth inhibiting substances (plants); Growth promoting substances (plants)
PLANT holders. See Flower boxes, planters, etc.
PLANT inspection
Plant inspection change. Sci N L 83:349 Je 1 '63
PLANT lice
Aphids spread that new corn stunt disease; compact maize disease. Farm J 88:41 N '64
Fatty acids: in vivo synthesis by the green peach aphid, myzus persicae (Sulzer) F. E. Strong. bibliog il Science 140:983-4 My 31 '63
It helps to know about aphids. il Sunset 130:274-5 Ap '63
Pea aphid: rearing on a chemically defined diet. J. L. Auclair and J. J. Cartier. bibliog Science 142:1068-9 N 22 '63
PLANT location. See Location in business and industry
PLANT pathology. See Plants—Diseases and pests
PLANT photography. See Photography of flowers, plants, trees, etc.
PLANT poisoning. See Poisonous plants
PLANT propagation
Best in show. J. Simpkins. il Flower Grower 50:38-42 Je '63
Cuttings. E. McDonald. il Pop Gard 14:69+ Jl '63
Divide plants now for bigger and better lily-of-the-valley flowers. D. K. Sampson. il Flower Grower 50:19 Ag '63
Dividends from a home nursery. F. F. Rockwell. Flower Grower 52:65 Ja '65
Flowering kalanchoes. E. A. Flickinger. il Flower Grower 50:29-30 My '63
Germinating very fine seeds. R. J. Favretti. il Horticulture 42:52-5+ Mr '64
Give old plants a new lease on life. il Pop Gard 14:42 F '63
Growth of single plant cells. J. L. Gibbs and D. K. Dougall. bibliog il Science 141:1059 S 13 '63
How I grow tuberous begonias. A. J. De Blasi. il Flower Grower 51:46+ Mr '64
How to grow & propagate Christmas begonia. E. Javorsky. il Flower Grower 52:36-7 Ja '65
How to increase azaleas & other shrubs. M. J. Dietz. il Flower Grower 51:28 Jl '64
How to make root cuttings. il Sunset 131:274 N '63
How to root cuttings the modern way. il Changing T 17:44 Ag '63
Making new plants out of old plants. Mrs W. H. Hull, jr. il Horticulture 41:524 O '63
New flowers by new methods. C. Weddle. il Horticulture 43:18-19+ Ja '65
Plant new iris, divide crowded clumps. il Pop Gard 15:14-15 Jl '64
Plant propagation, by runners and offsets. D. Henry. il Horticulture 41:411 Ag '63
Propagating plants by hardwood cuttings. B. C. Kilvert, jr. il Flower Grower 50:21-2 O '63
Rooting cuttings with patience, sand and water. P. E. Jones. il Horticulture 41:128-9 Mr '63
Roses from seed. E. W. Ferris. il Horticulture 41:276-7 My '63
Summer propagation; flowering trees and shrubs. R. G. Coggeshall. il Horticulture 42:40-1 Je '64
TVA at work; better hardwoods for the future. K. A. Taft, jr. il Am For 71:26-9+ Ja '65
Young house plants from old. il Pop Gard 16:32-5 F '65
See also
Grafting
Seedlings
PLANT proteins
Lipid-protein particles: isolation from seeds of gossypium hirsutum. L. Yatsu and A. M. Altschul. il Science 142:1062-4 N 22 '63
PLANT quarantine
See also
Plant inspection
PLANT relocation. See Location in business and industry
PLANT renting. See Rental services
PLANT shelves. See Shelves
PLANT societies. See Horticultural societies
PLANT stands. See Flower stands
PLANT supports. See Garden stakes and staking
PLANT tissues. See Plant cells and tissues
PLANT tumors. See Tumors, Plant
PLANT viruses. See Viruses, Plants
PLANTAGENET, Edward, 2d duke of York. See Edward of Norwich
PLANTAIN lilies
Handsome, shade-loving hostas. il Sunset 130:232 Mr '63
Hosta for foliage. E. Schroeder. il Flower Grower 51:33+ Ag '64
PLANTERS. See Flower boxes, planters, etc.
PLANTERS (farm machines)
Faster planting! il Farm J 88:34-5 My '64
New planter hook-ups, for corn, for soybeans; photographs. Farm J 87:32-3 My '63
PLANTIN, Christopher
King of typography. il Time 81:57 My 31 '63
PLANTIN press. See Printing—Private presses
PLANTING. See Floriculture; Gardening; Landscape gardening; Plants, Space arrangement of; Seeding; Shrubs—Planting; Tree planting
PLANTING fields arboretum. See New York state university—Agricultural and technical institute at Farmingdale, Long Island
PLANTING of corn. See Corn—Seeding
PLANTING plans and tables. See Gardening—Planting plans and tables
PLANTS
Best plants; symposium. See issues of Flower grower to July 1964
Foliage and texture in the garden. P. Shedesky. il Horticulture 41:376-7 Jl '63
Four-color flora. Time 85:42+ Ja 29 '65
Green and white accents. D. E. Stebbins. il Horticulture 41:380 Jl '63
Hard choices among new and easy plants. il House & Gard 123:195 Ap '63
If you plan to grow natives; Californian plants. il Sunset 131:266+ O '63
[Month] in your garden. See issues of Sunset
New and novelty plants; 1964. Horticulture 42:20-3+ F '64
New plants for 1964. M. C. Ohlander. il Flower Grower 51:34-5+ Ja '64
New plants for 1965. M. C. Ohlander. il Flower Grower 52:24-6+ Ja '65

PLANTS—*Continued*
New plants to brighten your 1965 garden; comp. by P. F. Frese. Pop Gard 16:26-7+ F '65
New plants to set out this fall. il Flower Grower 50:8 O '63
New shrubs, bulbs, fruits and perennials for 1963. il Horticulture 41:76-8 F '63
New this year. il Horticulture 43:20-3 Ja '65
Newcomers for 1964. P. F. Frese. il Pop Gard 15:43-5+ F '64
Plant physiology; report on sixth annual meeting of the Canadian society of plant physiologists. R. G. S. Bidwell. Science 146:91-2 O 2 '64
Some good plants for hanging baskets. il House B 105:224-5 My '63
Start gardening right now! H. Mason. il Bet Hom & Gard 43:62-5+ Ja '65
These treats are in nurseries now. Sunset 130:292+ My '63
This is my favorite. See issues of Popular gardening & living outdoors
See also
Air plants
Annuals (plants)
Ferns
Flowers
Forcing (plants)
Nursery stock
Succulent plants
Weeds

All America selections

All-America rose selections. J. A. Dwyer. il Pop Gard 16:6+ F '65
All-America winners for 1965, annuals. P. F. Frese. il Pop Gard 16:41-3 Ja '65
All-America winners for 1965; Mister Lincoln and Camelot. il Pop Gard 15:20 Jl '64
All-America winners, vegetables. il Pop Gard 16:52 Ja '65
Best flowers and plants for 1965. il Am Home 68:6+ Ja '65
Best roses, trees, and shrubs for 1964. H. Mason. il Bet Hom & Gard 42:64-9 F '64
Camelot and Mister Lincoln; 25th anniversary All-America selections. R. C. Hands. il Horticulture 42:36-7 Jl '64
New annuals for 1964. P. F. Frese. il Pop Gard 15:52-4 Ja '64
New flowers, 1964. T. A. Weston. il Am Home 67:11+ Ja '64
New roses for everybody. H. R. O'Brien. il Pop Gard 15:32-4+ F '64
1964 All-America rose selections. il Pop Gard 14:33 Jl '63
Roses for All America; Camelot and Mister Lincoln. il Flower Grower 51:20 Jl '64
Vegetables new for 1964. il Pop Gard 15:63 Ja '64

Anecdotes, facetiae, satire, etc.

Not the laurel. E. W. Thomas. Atlan 214:108 Ag '64

Cerium content

Cerium-144 and cesium-137 measurements in the 1963 United States wheat crop and milling products. D. C. Sutton and K. R. Dwyer. bibliog il Science 145:486-7 Jl 31 '64

Cesium content

Cesium in liriodendron and other woody species: organic bonding sites. G. N. Brown. bibliog il Science 143:368-9 Ja 24 '64
Cerium-144 and cesium-137 measurements in the 1963 United States wheat crop and milling products. D. C. Sutton and K. R. Dwyer. bibliog il Science 145:486-7 Jl 31 '64

Disease and pest resistance

Biochemical tests indicative of reaction of castor bean to botrytis. C. A. Thomas and R. G. Orellana. bibliog Science 139:334-5 Ja 25 '63

Diseases and pests

Ceratocystis infection in sweet potato: its effect on proteins, isozymes, and acquired immunity. D. J. Weber and M. A. Stahmann. bibliog il Science 146:929-31 N 13 '64
Dynamics of epidemics of plant disease. J. E. Van Der Plank. bibliog il Science 147:120-4 Ja 8 '65
Fight plant disease. Sci N L 83:114 F 23 '63
Garden clinic; questions and answers. Flower Grower 50:45+ My '63
H&G's 1964 guide to plant protection. C. Westcott. House & Gard 125:207-11 Ap '64
House & garden's 1963 guide to plant protection. C. Westcott. il House & Gard 123:222-7 Ap '63
How to protect your plants from bird marauders. il Sunset 130:210+ Je '63
Root diseases biologically controlled; report of international symposium on factors determining the behavior of plant pathogens in soils. W. C. Snyder. Science 141:835-7 Ag 30 '63
See also
Rusts (botany)
Tumors, Plant
See also subhead Diseases and pests under names of plants, e.g. Corn—Diseases and pests

Evolution

Evolutionary mechanisms in pollination biology. H. G. Baker. bibliog il Science 139:877-83 Mr 8 '63

Fertilization

See Fertilization of plants

Hardiness

Plant hardiness. J. H. Clarke. Horticulture 42:28-9 D '64
There's more to plant hardiness. J. Fanning. il Pop Gard 16:48 Ja '65

Ion exchange

Polar transport of calcium in the primary root of zea mays. E. C. Evans, 3d. bibliog il Science 144:174-7 Ap 10 '64

Iron content

Chlorophyll content and growth of soybean plants: possible interaction of iron availability and day length. H. M. Benedict and others. il Science 144:1134-5 My 29 '64

Metabolism

Association of rapidly metabolized DNA and RNA. J. H. Cherry. bibliog il Science 146:1066-9 N 20 '64
Growth, maturation, and senescence in fruits. J. B. Biale. bibliog il Science 146:880-8 N 13 '64
Osmotic stress: effects of its application to a portion of wheat root systems. R. E. Meyer and J. R. Gingrich. Science 144:1463-4 Je 19 '64

Nutrition

See also
Photosynthesis

Odors

See Odors

Oil and fat content

Cholesterol in higher plants. D. F. Johnson and others. bibliog Science 140:198-9 Ap 12 '63

Protection

See Plants, Protection of

Reproduction

Remarkably reduced vascular plant in the United States. W. H. Wagner, jr. and A. J. Sharp. bibliog Science 142:1483-4 D 13 '63
Saguaro: a population in relation to environment. W. A. Niering and others. bibliog il Science 142:15-23 O 4 '63
See also
Gametophytes

Resistance to disease

See Plants—Disease and pest resistance

Respiration

N^6-benzyladenine: inhibitor of respiratory kinases. V. Tuli and others. bibliog il Science 146:1477-9 D 11 '64
Great influences on plant growth. il House & Gard 123:100-5 F '63
Labeled oxygen: transport through growing corn roots. C. R. Jensen and others. il Science 144:550-2 My 1 '64
Plants need air, in quantity and in motion. il House & Gard 123:148-9+ F '63

Soilless culture

Ring culture whips tomato diseases. B. Hardy. il Farm J 88:32F Ag '64

Strontium content

Strontium-90 accumulation on plant foliage during rainfall. R. G. Menzel and others. bibliog il Science 142:576-7 N 1 '63

Translocation

Amitrole translocation in agropyron repens increased by the addition of ammonium thiocyanate. W. F. Donnalley and S. K. Ries. bibliog il Science 145:497-8 Jl 31 '64
Auxin in coleus stems: limitation of transport at higher concentrations. T. K. Scott and W. P. Jacobs. bibliog il Science 139:589-90 F 15 '63
Translocation in the giant kelp macrocystis. B. C. Parker. bibliog il Science 140:891-2 My 24 '63

PLANTS—*Continued*

Transpiration

Inducing resistance to freezing and desiccation in plants by decenylsuccinic acid. P. J. C. Kuiper. bibliog il Science 146:544-6 O 23 '64
Moisture release from cut alfalfa. G. L. Byers and others. bibliog il Science 143:1183 Mr 13 '64
Reduction of transpiration of leaves through stomatal closure induced by alkenylsuccinic acids. I. Zelitch. bibliog il Science 143:692-3 F 14 '64
Saturation deficit of the mesophyll evaporating surfaces in a desert halophyte. P. C. Whiteman and D. Koller. bibliog il Science 146:1320-1 D 4 '64
Systematic error in leaf water potential measurements with a thermocouple psychrometer. S. L. Rawlins. bibliog il Science 146:644-6 O 30 '64
Transpiration and stomatal opening with changes in carbon dioxide content of the air. J. E. Pallas, jr. bibliog il Science 147:171-3 Ja 8 '65
Transpiration by sudangrass as an externally controlled process. C. H. M. Van Bavel and others. il Science 141:269-70 Jl 19 '63
Transpiration: its effects on plant leaf temperature. G. D. Cook and others. bibliog il Science 144:546-7 My 1 '64

Water requirements

Great influences on plant growth. il House & Gard 123:154-9 Ap '63
Is watering necessary? W. A. Mitcheltree. Horticulture 42:38-9 Ag '64
Lower limit of water availability to plants. W. R. Gardner and R. H. Nieman. bibliog il Science 143:1460-2 Mr 27 '64
Osmotic stress: effects of its application to a portion of wheat root systems. R. E. Meyer and J. R. Gingrich. Science 144:1463-4 Je 19 '64
Waterside plants. D. Klaber. il Pop Gard 14:45+ Ap '63

PLANTS, Artificial
Notes and comment. New Yorker 39:41 N 9 '63
See also
Flowers, Artificial

PLANTS, Climbing. See Climbing plants

PLANTS, Cover. See Cover plants

PLANTS, Effect of chemicals on
Nitrogen and potassium effect on the color of red roses. R. S. Lindstrom and P. Markakis. bibliog il Science 142:1663-4 D 27 '63

PLANTS, Effect of climate on
Across the editor's desk. D. Hanson. Suc Farm 61:8 Je '63
Weather in the garden. R. D. Roe. il Horticulture 41:412-13 Ag '63

PLANTS, Effect of electricity on
High electrical fields damage plant growth. Sci N L 84:377 D 14 '63

PLANTS, Effect of light on
Chlorophyll *a* appearance in the dark in higher plants; analytical notes. D. W. Kupke and J. L. Huntington. bibliog il Science 140:49-51 Ap 5 '63
Floral induction and the stimulation of cell division in xanthium. R. G. Thomas. bibliog il Science 140:54-6 Ap 5 '63
Fluorescence and absorption changes in chlorella exposed to strong light: the red band. D. Rubinstein and E. Rabinowitch. bibliog il Science 142:681-2 N 8 '63
Inhibition of flowering by light in the short-day plant salvia occidentalis. S. C. Bhargava. bibliog il Science 147:60-1 Ja 1 '65
Marsilea vestita; conversion of the water form to the land form by darkness and by far-red light. J. J. Gaudet. bibliog il Science 140:975-6 My 31 '63
Metabolic control of timing. S. B. Hendricks. bibliog il Science 141:21-7 Jl 5 '63
Photoperiodism: an effect of darkness during the light period on critical night length. W. S. Hillman. bibliog il Science 140:1397-8 Je 28 '63
Plant morphology: its control in proserpinaca by photoperiod, temperature, and gibberellic acid. A. Wallenstein and L. S. Albert. bibliog il Science 140:998-1000 My 31 '63
Spring blooms all year; by adding light and chemicals. Sci N L 85:283 My 2 '64
Stomatal penetration of wheat seedlings by stem and leaf rust: effect of light and carbon dioxide. D. Yirgou and R. M. Caldwell. bibliog il Science 141:272-3 Jl 19 '63
World's largest spectrograph probes secrets of life. H. G. Earl. il Todays Health 42:74-6 S '64

PLANTS, Effect of radiation on
Amateur scientist; ionizing radiation on plants. T. S. Osborne. il Sci Am 209:151-2+ D '63
Chronic gamma radiation affects the distribution of radial increment in pinus rigida stems. G. M. Woodwell and L. N. Miller. bibliog il Science 139:222-3 Ja 18 '63
Ecological effects of radiation. G. M. Woodwell. il Sci Am 208:40-9 Je '63
Plant damage caused by irradiation of aldehydes. I. J. Hindawi and A. P. Altshuller. bibliog il Science 146:540-2 O 23 '64

PLANTS, Effect of radioactivity on
Seed radiosensitivity: a new constant? T. S. Osborne and A. O. Lunden. bibliog il Science 145:710-11 Ag 14 '64
Six years after H-bomb blasts; survey of Bikini and Eniwetok atolls. il U S News 57:64-5 N 2 '64
Yttrium-88 on high activity zirconium-95 fallout particles. A. Malvicini and others. il Science 139:1287 Mr 29 '63

PLANTS, Effect of smog on
Atmospheric aldehydes related to petunia leaf damage. E. G. Brennan and others. bibliog il Science 143:818-20 F 21 '64

PLANTS, Effect of temperature on
Cytoecology of temperature; report of international symposium. J. Levitt and others. Science 141:1199-200+ S 20 '63
Formula aids agriculture. Sci N L 84:165 S 14 '63
Inducing resistance to freezing and desiccation in plants by decenylsuccinic acid. P. J. C. Kuiper. bibliog il Science 146:544-6 O 23 '64
Plant morphology: its control in proserpinaca by photoperiod, temperature, and gibberellic acid. A. Wallenstein and L. S. Albert. bibliog il Science 140:998-1000 My 31 '63
Proper plant choice; home greenhouse. F. F. Rockwell and E. C. Grayson. il Flower Grower 50:46 N '63
Transpiration: its effects on plant leaf temperature. G. D. Cook and others. bibliog il Science 144:546-7 My 1 '64
See also
Plants—Hardiness

PLANTS, Effect of ultraviolet rays on
Ultraviolet inactivation of chloroplast formation in synchronously dividing euglena gracilis. S. F. Petropulos. Science 145:392-3 Jl 24 '64

PLANTS, Flowering of
Spring blooms all year; by adding light and chemicals. Sci N L 85:283 My 2 '64

PLANTS, Food
See also
Greens, Edible

PLANTS, Fossil. See Paleobotany

PLANTS, Geographical distribution of. See Geographical distribution of animals and plants

PLANTS, Indoor. See House plants

PLANTS, Industrial. See Factories

PLANTS, Insectivorous. See Insectivorous plants

PLANTS, Medicinal. See Botany, Medical

PLANTS, Ornamental
Colorful foliage for your window sill. R. C. Hands. il Horticulture 41:102 F '63
I grow foliages to sell. O. M. Cook. Farm J 88:103 Ap '64
Their leaves are plush. R. M. Peters. il Pop Gard 15:72-3+ Jl '64
See also
Coleus

PLANTS, Poisonous. See Poisonous plants

PLANTS, Potted
Are you short of gardening space? E. L. Sculthorp. il House B 105:180-1+ My '63
Growing roses in containers. il Sunset 130:228+ Je '63
How to plant and swing a hanging basket. il House & Gard 124:140-1 Ag '63
How to plant beauty in a basket. il House & Gard 124:120-5 Ag '63
Indoor garden tips; hanging basket gardens. Suc Farm 63:97 Ja '65
Outdoor plants make indoor surprises. il Sunset 130:80-5 F '63
Potting pointers; techniques for repotting of house plants. K. Berggrav. il Flower Grower 52:13-15 Ja '65
Pots for plants. G. Taloumis. il Flower Grower 50:32-5 Jl '63
Prepare your hanging baskets step by step. H. S. Witty. il Flower Grower 51:28-9 Ap '64
Save space in the greenhouse with hanging baskets. J. A. Eaton. il Flower Grower 51:46-8 F '64
Servicing the year-round window. J. Fanning. il House & Gard 126:194-5+ D '64

PLANTS, Potted—*Continued*
Summer plants for year-round windows. il House & Gard 126:156-9 D '64
Tubbed tomato. H. G. Matoon. il Horticulture 41:91 F '63
See also
Flower boxes, planters, etc.
House plants
PLANTS, Protection of
Avoid late winter plant damage. il Horticulture 42:34-5 F '64
Baffle winter; winterize your garden. O. K. Moore. il Flower Grower 50:34-6 N '63
Be wise: winterize. F. F. Rockwell. il Flower Grower 51:28+ O '64
Before winter comes. B. Black. il Pop Gard 14:18-21+ N '63
Getting your garden ready for a freeze. Sunset 131 190 D '63
Have you heard? use of Crylde in controlling bird damage in orchards. il Flower Grower 51:19 O '64
Plant display is also plant shelter. il Sunset 131:292 O '63
Put your garden to bed. V. H. Ries. il Horticulture 41:608-9 D '63
Success with rhododendrons. B. B. Brown. il Flower Grower 51:37+ F '64
Used Christmas trees; good garden covering material. Mrs W. Doble. il Horticulture 41:630 D '63
Well dressed for winter. J. B. Brimer. il Flower Grower 51:34 N '64
Wintering roses. A. C. Burrage. il Horticulture 42:40-2 O '64
PLANTS, Rare
Plant collector's corner. See issues of Sunset
Plants out-of the-ordinary. C. W. Wood. See issues of Flower grower
PLANTS, Renting of. See Rental services
PLANTS, Rock garden
Plants for crevices. J. Lawson. il Pop Gard 15:64-5 Jl '64
Wall plants. R. Murfitt. il Horticulture 43:32-3+ Ja '65
See also
Gardens, Rock
PLANTS, Sex in
Ameiotic alternation of generations: a new life cycle in the ferns. A. M. Evans. bibliog il Science 143:261-3 Ja 17 '64
Fertility restoration and its inheritance in cytoplasmic male-sterile wheat. R. W. Livers. bibliog il Science 144:420 Ap 24 '64
PLANTS, Shade
Flowers & shade. H. K. Morse. il Flower Grower 50:48-9+ Mr '63
For a cool look on your terrace. il Sunset 130:234-5 Je '63
Plant life under a sugar maple. Horticulture 41:152-3 Mr '63
Something for the shady side. il Bet Hom & Gard 42:111-12 My '64
These natives love the shade of summer. R. D. Roe. il Flower Grower 51:51-2 My '64
PLANTS, Shading of
Shade chrysanthemums for early bloom. K. Clapp. il Horticulture 41:508-9 O '63
See also
Shelters (agriculture)
PLANTS, Space arrangement of
Basic principles of planting. Pop Gard 14:33 Mr '63
Best time of year: spring planting. B. Black. il Pop Gard 14:28-32 Mr '63
Double rows make more silage. B. Hardy. il Farm J 88:37+ My '64
Late report on narrow-row crops. L. E. Zeman. il Suc Farm 61:54-5+ My '63
Narrow rows; the coming thing? J. Russell. il Farm J 87:36-7+ Mr '63
Thick corn in dry weather? Suc Farm 62:83 F '64
Timely planting boosts yields. L. E. Zeman. il Suc Farm 62:96 F '64
PLANTS, Staking of. See Garden stakes and staking
PLANTS, Training of
Art of growing plants as standards. il Sunset 132:86-93 Mr '64
Espaliers; excerpts from Espaliers and vines for the home gardener. H. O. Perkins. il Horticulture 42:30-1 O '64
Garden in a basket. M. W. Stephens. il Flower Grower 50:15-16 Je '63
Tricks with ivy. G. Aske. il Flower Grower 51:29 N '64
PLANTS, Water requirements of. See Plants—Water requirements
PLANTS, Watering of. See Watering of plants
PLANTS as gifts
Gift plants from $1 to $10. il Sunset 131:72-3 D '63
Give something growing for Christmas. il Am Home 67:16 D '64
House plant gifts decorated for Christmas. il Sunset 133:152-3 D '64
It's a refreshing way to say Merry Christmas. il Sunset 133:48-51 D '64
PLANTS for shady places. See Plants, Shade
PLANTS in house decoration
Living with flowers; house of Mrs Thomas Jefferson Coolidge. V. Lawford. il Vogue 141:142-5+ Ap 1 '63
PLANZ, Allen
Drought; poem. Nation 199:126 S 14 '64
Pan-American; poem. Poetry 103:302 F '64
Wetland dawn; poem. Nation 199:413 N 30 '64
PLAPINGER, Sylvia
Angels. Ladies Home J 81:47-51 My '64
I think about him all the time. Ladies Home J 81:55-7+ O '64
PLAQUEMINES PARISH, La.
Perils of Plaquemines. R. Cleghorn. New Repub 149:8-10 S 21 '63
PLAQUES, plaquettes
Wall plaque uses natural bamboo. il Sunset 132:128 Mr '64
PLASMA (ionized gases)
Photographs taken of sun-like reactions; Project Sherwood. il Sci N L 86:66 Ag 1 '64
Plasmas in solids. R. Bowers. il Sci Am 209:46-53 bibliog(p 186) N '63
Plasmas: wave interaction and dynamic nonlinear phenomena; report of conference at Pennsylvania state university. O. E. H. Rydbeck. Science 141:181-2+ Jl 12 '63
Science's exciting new frontier. S. C. Brown. il Sci Digest 56:83-8 O '64
Tapping nature's storehouse of violent energy. G. A. W. Boehm. il Fortune 68:130-4+ Ag '63
Vacuum: sputtering, desorption, and surface physics; report on annual Sherwood vacuum conference. S. O. Dean. Science 144:1251-2 Je 5 '64
PLASMA cells. See Cells
PLASMA jet
Miniature sun machine. Sci N L 86:38 Jl 18 '64
PLASMODIUM (parasite)
Plasmodium berghei: cyclical transmissions by experimentally infected anopheles quadrimaculatus. M. Yoeli and others. bibliog Science 144:1580-1 Je 26 '64
PLASTER casts
Modern plaster master. il Life 56:103-4+ Je 19 '64
Segal's vital mummies. A. Kaprow. il Art N 62:30-3+ F '64
PLASTER masks. See Masks (sculpture)
PLASTER sculpture
Riding the whirlwind. il Newsweek 61:96 Ap 22 '63
PLASTER work (craft)
Composition in sand. L. S. Parker. il Sch Arts 63:11-12 D '63
PLASTIC bearings. See Bearing (machinery)
PLASTIC bottles. See Bottles
PLASTIC bullets. See Bullets
PLASTIC cars. See Automobiles—Materials
PLASTIC cement. See Cements, Adhesive
PLASTIC coating
New plastics coating process for metals. il Arch Rec 134:239-40 O '63
PLASTIC containers. See Containers
PLASTIC cups. See Cups
PLASTIC dinnerware. See Tableware, Plastic
PLASTIC domes. See Domes
PLASTIC fabrics
Can you talk the language of man-made fabrics? M. Gough. il House B 106:148-9 Mr '64
PLASTIC floor coverings. See Floor coverings
PLASTIC flowers. See Flowers, Artificial
PLASTIC footwear. See Shoes, Rubber, plastic, etc.
PLASTIC lenses, Photographic. See Lenses, Photographic
PLASTIC molding. See Plastics—Molding
PLASTIC money. See Money—United States
PLASTIC mosaics. See Mosaics
PLASTIC mulch. See Mulching
PLASTIC paint. See Paint
PLASTIC panels. See Paneling
PLASTIC pipes. See Pipes, Plastic
PLASTIC shells. See Cartridges
PLASTIC surgery. See Surgery, Plastic
PLASTIC tableware. See Tableware, Plastic

PLASTIC trays. See Trays
PLASTIC upholstery. See Upholstery, Plastic
PLASTIC wrapping materials. See Wrapping materials
PLASTICS
Atlantic report; new kind of plastic. Atlan 212:42 O '63
Battle of the plastics; plastic shotshells. W. Page. il Field & S 69:128-30 My '64
Expanding world of plastics. R. Yoshioka. Sci N L 86:42-3 Jl 18 '64
Laboratory designed in fiber glass and plastics. il(p209) Sci N L 83:210 Ap 6 '63
More plastics per car. il Fortune 70:201 O '64
New family of plastics; polyphene oxide. il Sci N L 86:378 D 12 '64
Photoisomerism: a colorless photoinduced intermediate of o-nitrobenzylpyridine. J. A. Souse and J. D. Loconti. bibliog il Science 146:397-8 O 16 '64
Picnic jugs. il Consumer Bul 46:2+ Ag '63
Plastic planks. J. Joseph. il Pop Mech 120: 132-3+ O '63
Plastics for the patio. il Good H 157:156 Jl '63
Plastics: the big idea in remodeling materials. J. H. Ingersoll. il Pop Sci 183:126-9+ S '63
Superconducting plastics. Sci Am 211:39-40 Ag '64
Talented new plastics. il House & Gard 126: 210-13+ O '64
What's new for your home in '64. J. Ingersoll. il Pop Sci 184:102-5 Mr '64
World's fair house. il Good H 158:100-13+ My '64
See also
Delrin
Plastic coating
Polyethylene
Exhibitions
Minister to Bulgaria opens Plastics-USA exhibit in Sofia; address, July 6, 1963. E. Anderson. Dept State Bul 49:142 Jl 22 '63
Molding
How to mold a rattle-free case for car tools. P. McCafferty. il Pop Sci 183:120-3 Jl '63
Plastics in perspective; interview. F. Koblick. il Craft Horiz 23:38-41+ Mr '63
Repairing
New plastic-mending cements. J. Hand. il Pop Sci 182:169-71 My '63
PLASTICS, Laminated
Royalite on a regal line; laminated plastic body of new Cord. W. P. Bowlin. il Motor T 16:70-1 D '64
PLASTICS industry and trade
Plastics industry paradox. Bsns W p24 Ag 3 '63
PLASTIDS
Plastids and mitochondria: inheritable systems. A. Gibor and S. Granick. bibliog il Science 145:890-7 Ag 28 '64
Subcellular heredity. Sci Am 211:58-9 N '64
PLATE glass
Float glass process gets another buyer; Libbey-Owens-Ford co. Bsns W p 198 My 18 '63
PLATES (dishes) See Tableware
PLATES, Glass. See Glassware
PLATFORM paddle tennis. See Paddle tennis
PLATFORM tennis. See Paddle tennis
PLATFORMS
Presto! changeo! a stage on wheels; Metuchen, N.J. T. Eosso. il Am City 80:24 Ja '65
PLATFORMS, Political
Again the platform builders hammer away. M. R. Weisbord. il N Y Times Mag p 10+ Jl 5 '64
Battle page. il Sr Schol 85:16 S 23; 22 S 30; 11 O 7; 4 O 14; 4 O 21; 25 O 28 '64
Campaign about fundamentals. Fortune 70: 99-100 Ag '64
Case for the Democratic party. H. H. Humphrey. Sat R 47:21-3 O 31 '64
Democratic platform: principal planks, and their G.O.P. counterparts. Time 84:30 S 4 '64
Democratic platform: science section stresses work in space, oceanography, and atomic energy. D. S. Greenberg. Science 145:1161-2 S 11 '64
Do platforms need all those planks? F. Nelson. il Nat R 16:533-4 Je 30 '64
Education in the party platforms; Republican and Democratic statements. P. Woodring. Sat R 47:51-2 O 17 '64
Goldwaterism; the new ideology. C. McWilliams. Nation 199:68-71 Ag 24 '64
G.O.P. jihad; holy war; reprint. H. H. Humphrey. Christian Cent 81:1172 S 23 '64
GOP platform. New Repub 151:5-7 Jl 25 '64
How to succeed in politics without really trying. D. Lawrence. U S News 57:120 N 30 '64
Johnson vs Goldwater; Democratic party's 1964 platform. New Repub 151:3-4 S 5 '64
Johnson vs. Goldwater: the conflict on big issues. U S News 57:40 Jl 20 '64
Late late show. Time 84:21-2 Jl 24 '64
Letter from San Francisco. R. H. Rovere. il New Yorker 40:77-80+ Jl 25 '64
Make it short. R. Moley. Newsweek 62:116 N 18 '63
New voice of the GOP; 1964 contrasted with 1960 platform. Newsweek 64:30-1 Jl 27 '64
One platform for all; writing a Republican platform. il Time 84:22-4 Jl 10 '64
One team, one theme; Democrats 1964 platform. Time 84:18 Ag 28 '64
Platform built for Barry. il Newsweek 64:22+ Jl 20 '64
Platform problem. K. Crawford. Newsweek 64:26 Jl 6 '64
Platform; Republican platform. il Nat R 16: 633 Jl 28 '64
Platforms differ on defense and space. Aviation W 81:20-1 Ag 31 '64
Prosperity theme and problems; Democratic platform. il U S News 57:28 Ag 31 '64
Quantitative liberalism. W. V. Shannon. Commonweal 80:497-8 Jl 24 '64
Republican platform. F. S. Meyer. Nat R 16: 535 Je 30 '64
What Democrats offer: the party's 1964 platform; official text. il U S News 57:34-5, 94-9 S 7 '64; Excerpts. Sr Schol 85:14-15 S 23 '64; Cur Hist 47:236-8+ O '64
What Republicans offer; the party's 1964 platform; official text. il U S News 57:34-5, 106-15 Jl 27 '64; Excerpts. Time 84:21 Jl 24 '64; Sr Schol 85:14-15 S 23 '64; Cur Hist 47:236-8+ O '64
When Republicans tackled their platform. il U S News 57:35 Jl 20 '64
Where the Democrats and the Republicans stand on school aid. G. J. Hecht. Parents Mag 39:42+ O '64
Where they stand; party platforms, 1964. K. Crawford. Newsweek 64:31 S 7 '64
PLATH, Sylvia
Bees; poem. Atlan 211:70-1 Ap '63
Fever 103°; Purdah; Eavesdropper; poems. Poetry 102:292-8 Ag '63
Two campers in cloud country; Elm speaks; Mystic; Amnesiac; Mirror; Among the narcissi; Moon and the yew tree; poems. New Yorker 39:28-9 Ag 3 '63
Wishing box; story. Atlan 214:86-9 O '64
about
Five poets. R. Howard. Poetry 101:412-13 Mr '63
PLATINUM
Reaction of hydrogen with oxygen adsorbed on a platinum catalyst. H. W. Kohn and M. Boudart. bibliog il Science 145:149 Jl 10 '64
PLATNICK, Kenneth B.
Memoir of a long, long war; story. Sat Eve Post 237:54-8 F 29 '64
PLATT, Dorothy Falcon
Clematis. Horticulture 42:14-15+ Jl '64
PLATT, John R.
Physicist reviews an anthropologist's analysis of change. Bul Atomic Sci 20:25-6 D '64
Research and development for social problems. Bul Atomic Sci 20:27-9 Je '64
Strong inference; address, September 1963. bibliog Science 146:347-53 O 16 '64
—See Cone, R. A. jt. auth.
PLATT, June
Summer dessert cook book. House & Gard 123:179+ My '63
PLATT, Rutherford
Come into my garden; excerpt from The river of life. Read Digest 83:204C-204D+ S '63
Mystery of our sixth senses. Read Digest 83:75-8 S '63
Subtle tides of life. Read Digest 82:264-7 Ap '63
Wondrous inner space of living cells. Read Digest 84:195+ Je '64
PLATTNER, C. M.
Army receives Hughes OH-6A for testing. Aviation W 80:72-3+ F 3 '64
First Hiller OH-5A delivered for army LOH evaluation. Aviation W 80:64-5+ Ja 20 '64
Variable-sweep wing keynotes Boeing 733 SST proposal. Aviation W 80:36-9+ My 4 '64
PLATTSBURG citizens military training camps. See Military training camps

PLATYCODON. See Balloonflowers

PLAY
Guide to play and playthings. R. M. Goldenson. il Parents Mag 39:62-3+ O '64
Is play obsolete? D. Weisman. il Sat R 46:77-8 N 16 '63
Play is child's work. A. Schwartz. il Parents Mag 38:74-5+ N '63
Playing with toy guns; effect of warlike toys and games on children. B. Spock. Redbook 124:24+ N '64
They have to be taught to play; with study-discussion program. R. Strang. bibliog il PTA Mag 58:32-5 N '63
What children learn from play. B. Bettelheim. il Parents Mag 39:48-9+ Jl '64
World of play. S. Brown. il Sat Eve Post 237:17-21 D 19 '64

PLAY accidents. See Accidents
PLAY apparatus. See Playgrounds—Equipment
PLAY; drama. See Beckett, S.
PLAY houses. See Playhouses
PLAY of Daniel. See Drama, Medieval
PLAY of Herod. See Drama, Medieval
PLAY pens. See Playgrounds, Home—Equipment
PLAY production. See Theatrical production
PLAY with a tiger; drama. See Lessing, D.
PLAY writing. See Drama—Technique
PLAY yards. See Playgrounds, Home

PLAYBILL (periodical)
Walk to that exit. B. Friel. Holiday 34:48+ N '63

PLAYBILLS. See Theater programs

PLAYBOY (periodical)
Anatomy of Playboy. B. De Mott; discussion. Commentary 35:71-4 Ja '63
Empires of toothpicks; Playboy club's liquor license. Nation 196:366 My 4 '63
Infinite number of monkeys; researchers for Playboy philosophy series. Christian Cent 80:1063 Ag 28 '63
Playboy philosophy. J. C. Evans. Cath World 200:42-8 O '64
Two definitions of obscenity. il Time 81:44 Je 21 '63
Urbunnity. il Newsweek 63:48-9 Ja 6 '64

PLAYBOY clubs. See Night clubs

PLAYER, A. Emerson
Reluctant hero speaks his mind; with letter. il pors Ebony 19:164 Ap '64

PLAYER, Gary
Three big ones talk about golf; interview, ed. by C. Price. pors Sat Eve Post 236:66+ Ap 13 '63

about

Fatalist with finesse: Gary Player. G. Zimmermann. il pors Look 27:105-6+ Je 18 '63
Player in paradise. A. Wright. il por Sports Illus 18:22-4+ Mr 18 '63
Plight of bumblebee; U.S.G.A. rules. il Time 81:50 F 22 '63

PLAYER piano
Comeback of the player piano. il House B 106:148+ Je '64
How to restore the life of the party. H. Walton. il Pop Sci 184:102-5+ Ja; 148-50+ F '64
Player piano treasury. R. Kammerer. il Am Rec G 30:588-60 Mr '64

PLAYERS club, New York
Clubby; television program from the club. Newsweek 63:82 Mr 2 '64
See also
Walter Hampden memorial library

PLAYFAIR, Giles
Without bars: some bold and some timorous experiments. Harper 228:171-5 Ap '64
Word of Christine. New Repub 149:11-13 D 21 '63

PLAYGROUND activities
Starting from scratch; program at Indianola, Ia. J. Kerr. il Recreation 56:178+ Ap '63
Summer of surprises; playground program in Anchorage, Alaska. L. S. Wulf. il Recreation 57:168-71 Ap '64
When school's out. il Recreation 56:164-7 Ap '63

PLAYGROUND apparatus. See Playgrounds—Equipment

PLAYGROUND directors. See Recreation workers

PLAYGROUNDS
Can we save our play space? S. Schuler. il Am Home 67:48-9 Ja '64
From public nuisance to playground; Washington Court House, Ohio. J. M. Whitmer, jr. il Am City 79:117-18 O '64
Parks and playgrounds. See issues of American city
Public gifts. J. E. Curtis. Recreation 56:61 F '63
Wanted: new ideas for city playgrounds; competition sponsored by Park association of New York city. V. Musselman. Recreation 57:180+ Ap '64
Way out to play. il Time 83:73 Je 12 '64
See also
Football fields
Parks

Activities

See Playground activities

Equipment

Abstract play sculpture designed to reveal images. il Arch Rec 133:26 F '63
Bruise-proofing your playground. M. J. Golding. il Pop Mech 120:88-90+ S '63
Plan for a hazard-proof playground. M. Mayer. il Parents Mag 38:64-5+ My '63
Playgrounds take a space-age spin. il Life 54:97-9+ Mr 15 '63
Space age comes to the playground. il Pop Sci 182:88-9 Je '63
See also
Swings

Safety devices and measures

Bruise-proofing your playground. M. J. Golding. il Pop Mech 120:88-90+ S '63

Surface treatment

Is your playground surfacing safe? G. D. Butler. il Recreation 56:193-4 Ap '63

PLAYGROUNDS, Home
Garden of ideas in outdoor living. il Sunset 130:100-7 My '63

Equipment

All you need for shoot-the-chute. il Sunset 133:112+ S '64
Basketball high or low. il Sunset 131:145-6+ N '63
Garden is full of a number of things. J. H. Ingersoll. il Pop Gard 15:36-9 Jl '64
Hilary's play pen is simply big. il Sunset 133:98+ S '64
Ship ahoy, matey! back-yard sloop. F. N. Stephany. Pop Mech 120:136 Ag '63
What's a gym set's future? il Sunset 131:153 N '63
See also
Playhouses

PLAYHOUSES
Exciting playhouse that's easy to build. il Am Home 67:90 Je '64
Four small children play here. il Sunset 130:128+ Ap '63
Play center for young imaginations. J. A. Dever. il Pop Sci 183:114 Ag '63
Play's the thing. M. White. il Ladies Home J 81:137-41 Ap '64
See also
Tree houses

PLAYING off Keefe; story. See Elkoff, M. W.

PLAYMATES
Child's friends. S. Blum. il Redbook 121:49+ My '63
How important are your child's friends? W. Abraham. il Todays Health 42:6-7+ Mr '64
Ways and whys of friendship. L. Strong. il N Y Times Mag p48 Ja 26 '64

PLAYROOMS
Grand prize winner third-floor attic finished as a remarkable playroom. il Bet Hom & Gard 41:60-1 O '63

PLAYS. See Childrens plays; Dramas
PLAYS on records. See Phonograph records—Spoken records
PLAYTHINGS. See Toys
PLAYWRITING. See Drama—Technique
PLAYWRIGHTS. See Dramatists

PLAZA, Galo
Education for change; address, 1964. Américas 16:11-15 S '64

PLAZAS
Dallas develops its downtown; Main place. il Am City 79:145+ O '64
Miniature Rockefeller plaza in a midwest city; Canton, Ohio. il Arch Forum 120:98-101 Ja '64

PLEASANTS, Julian R.
Science and religion. Commonweal 78:91-3 Ap 19 '63

PLEASANTVILLE, Ia.
New name on the list; unsatisfactory educational conditions. D. Janson. il Sr Schol 84:1T-2T Ap 10 '64
Pleasantville's unpleasantness. il Time 83:44 Mr 20 '64

PLEASANTVILLE, N.Y.
I'm not against it, but—. D. Faber. il N Y Times Mag p58+ O 27 '63
PLEASE call the office; story. See Randall, F. E.
PLEASE get serious! story. See Boles, P. D.
PLEASURE
Can we survive the fun explosion? J. W. Krutch. Sat R 48:14-16 Ja 16 '65
See also
Happiness
PLEDGE of allegiance. See Loyalty, Oaths of
PLEISTOCENE period. See Geology, Stratigraphic—Pleistocene; Glacial epochs; Paleobotany—Pleistocene; Paleontology—Pleistocene
PLEMMONS, Hannell
Have fun with textures. U S Camera 27:66-7 My '64
PLESCIA, O. J. See Reiss, A. M. jt. auth.
PLESHETTE, Suzanne
Fair young Hollywood girls. R. W. Lewis. por(p24) Sat Eve Post 236:26 S 7 '63
Straight from the shoulder. E. Miller. il pors Seventeen 23:140-1+ My '64
PLESKO, Vincent J.
Ciné-cues. U S Camera 28:72-3 Ja '65
Edit as you shoot. U S Camera 26:74-5 S '63
Group filming. U S Camera 27:80-1 O '64
PLESS, John
Land of the unexpected. Field & S 69:46-8+ Ag '64
PLESSY, Homer Adolph
Birth of Jim Crow; Plessy v. Ferguson. C. V. Woodward. il Am Heritage 15:52-5+ Ap '64
PLEUROPNEUMONIALIKE organisms. See Microorganisms, Pathogenic
PLIERS
Things to know about plier-type tools. il Pop Sci 185:80-2 Jl '64
Things you never knew about pliers. il Pop Sci 184:168+ Ja '64
PLIMMER, Charlotte, and Plimmer, Denis
Perfect plan to kill de Gaulle. Read Digest 82:101-6 Je '63
Princess Anne grows older. Redbook 120:58-9+ Ap '63
Storm over a royal love affair. Redbook 121:60-1+ O '63
PLIMMER, Denis. See Plimmer, C. jt. auth.
PLIMPTON, Francis T. P.
International cooperation in outer space; statement, October 27, 1964. bibliog f Dept State Bul 51:755-9 N 23 '64
Principles of international law concerning friendly relations and cooperation among states: international law and nonintervention; statement, December 3, 1963. bibliog f Dept State Bul 50:133-43 Ja 27 '64
Principles of international law concerning friendly relations and cooperation among states: threat or use of force; statement, November 11, 1963. Dept State Bul 49:973-83 D 23 '63
Statement, May 22, 1963. Dept State Bul 49:178-81 Jl 29 '63
U.N. condemns repression of opponents to apartheid; statement, October 11, 1963. Dept State Bul 49:758-9 N 11 '63
United Nations, voting patterns and financing; address, April 27, 1963. Dept State Bul 48:796-800 My 20 '63
U.S. makes proposal on financing peacekeeping operations of U.N; statement, September 14, 1964. Dept State Bul 51:486-8 O 5 '64
PLIMPTON, George
Miami notebook: Cassius Clay and Malcolm X. Harper 228:54-61 Je '64
Newport notes: the Kennedys and other salts. Harper 226:39-47 Mr '63
Out of his league. il por Newsweek 62:92 S 9 '63
World series with Marianne Moore. Harper 229:50-8 O '64
Zero of the Lions; excerpt from Paper Lion. pors Sports Illus 21:96-102+ S 7; 26-8+ S 14 '64
(ed) See Balsan, C. V. Voices of two venerable Vanderbilts
(ed) See Vanderbilt, H. S. Voices of two venerable Vanderbilts
PLIMPTON, Susan W.
Build a cold frame for year-round use. Horticulture 41:468 S '63
Double duty from shrubs and trees. Horticulture 41:518-19 O '63
PLIOCENE period. See Geology, Stratigraphic—Pliocene
PLISETSKAYA, Maya
Plisetskaya. S. Hurok. pors Vogue 143:164-7 Ap 1 '64
Two-headed calf. T. Capote. pors Vogue 143:168-71 Ap 1 '64

PLISKOFF, Stanley S. and Hawkins, T. D.
Test of Deutsch's drive-decay theory of rewarding self-stimulation of the brain. bibliog Science 141:823-4; 142:1126 Ag 30, N 29 '63
PLOSCOWE, Morris
New approach to the control of organized crime. Ann Am Acad 347:74-81 My '63
PLOSS, Richard S.
Sodium chloride: modification of crystal habit by chemical agents. bibliog Science 144:169-70 Ap 10 '64
PLOTNICK, Alan R.
Soviet oil exports. Nation 196:302-6 Ap 13 '63
PLOTS (drama, novel, etc)
Ashtrays in vacuum. L. Conger. Writer 76:15-17 My '63
Dynamics of form. V. R. Lowe. Writer 77:16-19+ Mr '64
Goals. F. A. Rockwell. Writer 77:19-21 S '64
Have typewriter, should travel. E. Lacy. Writer 77:16-17+ Ap '64
How to plot your story. E. S. Fox. Writer 76:21-4+ D '63
I remember Androcles. E. Jensen. Writer 77:7-10 Ap '64
Plausibility. V. Thiessen. Writer 76:21-3+ O '63
Plot blueprints. F. A. Rockwell. Writer 77:16-21 My '64
Setting and background in the novel. M. Stewart. Writer 77:7-9 D '64
Twists, angles, and gimmicks. M. Corson. Writer 76:18-20+ My '63
PLOUFFE, Leo
French Canada's strange revolt; role of FLQ (Quebec liberation front) L. Bergquist. il pors Look 27:90-4+ D 3 '63
PLOWING. See Tillage
PLOWMAN, E. Grosvenor
For good or ill, users influence transportation. Ann Am Acad 345:6-13 Ja '63
PLOWMAN, Marilyn
Belief; poem. Christian Cent 80:1610 D 25 '63
Faithful; poem. Christian Cent 81:1520 D 9 '64
Ultimate concern; poem. Christian Cent 80:1403 N 13 '63
We beat him up; poem. Christian Cent 81:334 Mr 11 '64
PLOWS
Pick the right plow. il Suc Farm 63:50+ Ja '65
PLOWSHARE project. See Atomic blasting
PLUCK, Georg
Kirsten Flagstad: an appreciation. Hobbies 68:30-1 F '64
Neglected diva. Hobbies 69:30-1 Je '64
PLUG planting. See Lawns
PLUMADORE, Hayward H.
How to keep fit at Toots Shor's. Nation 197:290 N 9 '63
PLUMAS COUNTY, Calif.
Four-mile hike for trout; Jamison Lakes. il Sunset 133:17 Ag '64
PLUMB, Barbara
Home. N Y Times Mag p28-9 D 29 '63; 36-7 Ag 2; 116-17+ O 11; 144-5+ N 15 '64
PLUMB, J. H.
Best of Bonaparte. Sat R 47:43 Ap 18 '64
Dining, dancing, and dallying. Sat R 47:47-8 My 16 '64
Empire faded at her touch. Sat R 48:89 Ja 2 '65
Henry Fielding. Horizon 6:74-83 Wint '64
Sorry state of history. Horizon 5:97-100 S '63
To England, with love and candor. Sat R 46:44 N 9 '63
Wily Welshman at 10 Downing st. Sat R 47:28 S 5 '64
PLUMB, James W.
Wood. Motor B 114:34-9 D '64
PLUMB, Jim
Outboard club of the year. Yachting 117:118-19+ Ja '65
PLUMB, Robert K.
Woman who tells color by touch; reprint. Sci Digest 55:5-7 Ap '64
PLUMBER who stayed for dinner; story. See Ellingson, M.
PLUMBERS
Plumbers dispute opens long, hot summer. il Arch Forum 120:5+ Je '64
See also
United association of journeymen and apprentices of the plumbing and pipe fitting industry of the United States and Canada
PLUMBING
Automation comes to plumbing. il Pop Mech 120:154-5 S '63
Do-it-yourself plumbing. H. Idleman. il Consumer Bul 46:31-4 Ap '63

PLUMBING—*Continued*
Faucets aren't what they used to be. il House B 106:218-21 My '64
How good is the plumbing? il Changing T 18: 29-30 D '64
Stop toilet-tank sweat. E. R. Haan. il Pop Mech 120:142-3 Jl '63
What you need to know about plumbing. House & Gard 124:208+ N '63

Repairing
Stop that costly drip! M. Schultz. il Am Home 67:88-9+ Ap '64
When a single-lever faucet drips. J. Hand. il Pop Mech 119:136-8 My '63

PLUMBING codes. See Plumbing laws and regulations

PLUMBING laws and regulations
Plumbing code allows for service conditions. G. R. Jerus. il Arch Rec 136:179-80 D '64

PLUMLEY, Ladd
Excerpt from address, December 19, 1962. Cong Digest 42:217+ Ag '63

PLUMMER, Beverly J.
Get fit for a trip to the woods. Parents Mag 38:60-1+ My '63

PLUMS
Plum: widely distributed tree fruit. G. L. Slate. il Horticulture 41:90 F '63
Plums: the outsides and insides. il Sunset 133:58-63 Jl '64

PLURALISM (political science)
Conscience and pluralism. F. Canavan. America 110:536-9 Ap 18 '64
New pluralism: from nostalgia to reality. D. Callahan. Commonweal 78:527-31 S 6 '63; Discussion. 79:258-9 N 22 '63; America 109: 556-8+, 733-4; 110:308-12 N 9, D 7 '63, Mr 7 '64
New pluralism or old monism. F. Canavan. America 109:556-8+ N 9 '63

PLUTARCH
Master biographer. P. W. Schmidtchen. il Hobbies 69:107+ Je '64

PLUTCHIK, Robert, and Hirsch, H. R.
Skin impedance and phase angle as a function of frequency and current. bibliog Science 141:927-8 S 6 '63

PLUTO (planet)
Libration of Pluto-Neptune. C. J. Cohen and E. C. Hubbard. bibliog il Science 145:1302-3 S 18 '64
Pluto theories crumble. A. Ewing. Sci N L 86:213 O 3 '64

PLUTO is the furthest planet; story. See Rothberg, A.

PLUTONIUM
Accumulation of error. Nation 198:567 Je 8 '64
As plutonium fades, AEC calls industry in; private contractors lease Hanford works. il Bsns W p58-60+ D 26 '64
Atomic bombs for everyone; Egypt, Indonesia, the Congo. B. H. Bagdikian. il Sat Eve Post 236:66-9 Mr 2 '63
Plutonium dioxide: preparation of single crystals. K. D. Phipps and D. B. Sullenger. bibliog il Science 145:1048-9 S 4 '64
Plutonium fuel does the job. Bsns W p22 Jl 6 '63
Reducing nuclear materials production. L. B. Johnson; N. S. Khrushchev. Cur Hist 47: 47-8 Jl '64
Transplutonium; report of symposium at Argonne national laboratory. H. Diamond and D. C. Stewart. Science 141:184+ Jl 12 '63

PLUTONIUM reactors. See Nuclear reactors

PLYMOUTH, Mass.
See also
Pilgrim fathers

PLYMOUTH brethren
Uncontaminated; Exclusive brethren forbidden to mix with outsiders. il Time 83:52 Je 26 '64

PLYMOUTH division. See Chrysler corporation

PLYWOOD
Bumper jack does the trick in bending plywood. C. L. Hastings. il Pop Mech 119:189 F '63
Experimental plywood roof in Seattle. il Arch Forum 118:122 Ap '63
New faces of plywood. il House & Gard 125: 168-71 Mr '64
Plywood: new shapes yield new strength. il Arch Forum 120:126-31 Ap '64

PLYWOOD, Laminated. See Wood, Laminated

PLYWOOD industry
Big plywood from little logs. il Bsns W p92+ S 14 '63
Fast-growing sandwich. Time 85:75 Ja 29 '65
See also
St Maries plywood company

PLYWOOD paneling. See Paneling

PNEUMOCOCCI
Cerebral white matter: selective spread of pneumococcal polysaccharides. S. Levine. bibliog il Science 139:605-6 F 15 '63

PNEUMONIA
How not to die of pneumonia. Time 81:54 My 10 '63
Mycoplasma pneumoniae; proposed nomenclature for atypical pneumonia organism (Eaton agent) R. M. Chanock and others. bibliog Science 140:662 My 10 '63
Still a killer. Newsweek 61:91 My 13 '63

PNEUMONIC plague. See Plague

POCAHONTAS
John's royal wife. D. Garnett. il pors N Y Times Mag p 104-6 Ap 5 '64
Was Pocahontas Virginia Dare? P. W. Schmidtchen. il por Hobbies 68:106-8 S '63

POCKET billiards. See Billiards

POCKET books, incorporated
Curtis is expected to get pocket books' distribution. Pub W 185:28-9 Mr 16 '64

POCKET gophers. See Gophers

POCKETBOOKS. See Purses

POCKRISS, Judith White
How to choose and trim a Christmas tree. McCalls 92:34 D '64

POCOCK, Philip F. abp
Research into Christian wisdom. America 111: 38-41 Jl 11 '64

POCONO PINES, Pa.
Auto racing on ice; photographs. Travel 120: 41-3 N '63

PODGORNYI, Nikolaĭ Viktorovich
Bid for independence. il por Newsweek 65:39 Ja 25 '65
Two Russians who are moving to the top. por U S News 57:20 N 30 '64

PODHORETZ, Norman
Few words concerning this picture. Esquire 59:68-9 Mr '63
Hannah Arendt on Eichmann. Commentary 36:201-8 S '63; 37:11-12 F '64
My Negro problem, and ours. Commentary 35:93-101 F '63

about
Books. R. Adler. New Yorker 40:60-8+ Jl 4 '64
Cool, like blocked. N. Hentoff. Nation 198: 298-300 Mr 23 '64
Double role. por Newsweek 63:61-2 Mr 16 '64

POE, Edgar Allan
Edgar Allan Poe: the man behind the legend, by E. Wagenknecht. Review
Sat R por 46:50-1 N 9 '63. R. E. Spiller

POE, Edgar Allan, awards. See Mystery writers of America

POE, Robert H. and others
Effect of cold on the presence of staphylococcus aureus in the external nares of the rat. bibliog Science 143:487 Ja 31 '64

POETIC imagination. See Imagination

POETICAL criticism. See Literary criticism

POETICS
And the frame around it. J. Ciardi. Sat R 47:22+ D 5 '64
Did I mean that? J. Ciardi. Sat R 48:19 Ja 16 '65
Emily Dickinson: poetry and punctuation. E. P. Stamm. il Sat R 46:26-7+ Mr 30 '63; Reply. T. Ward. 46:25 Ap 27 '63; Rejoinder. 46:23 My 25 '63
Five tame dragons. G. MacArthur. Writer 76:25-7 Mr '63
Light verse in depth. E. K. Rose. Writer 77: 20-2 Ag '64
On form as a language. J. Ciardi. Sat R 47: 16+ O 31 '64
Poems, books of poems, and character. J. Langland. Poetry 103:256-61 Ja '64
Poet in a valley of dry bones. R. Graves. Horizon 5:84-8 Mr '63
Poetic mythology. H. Carruth. Poetry 104: 369-74 S '64
Poetry workshop. M. W. Kumin. See issues of Writer
Poetry's false face. R. Graves. il Horizon 5:42-7 N '63
Poet's right to invention. R. Wallace. Writer 76:16-18 Mr '63
Pointers for poets. D. D. Guyer. Writer 77: 27+ D '64
What if a much of a which of a wind. J. Ciardi. Sat R 47:18+ O 24 '64
Widgeonry; how a poem came into being. J. Ciardi. Sat R 47:15-16 S 12 '64
See also
Versification

POETRY
Adam and Eve and the third son. J. Ciardi. il Sat R 47:140-3+ Ag 29 '64
Between the sirens and the muse. D. Fitts. Sat R 47:34-6 My 2 '64
Canadian chronicle. K. McRobbie. Poetry 103: 266-70 Ja '64
Dialogue with an audience: the first seven years. J. Ciardi. Sat R 46:27-9+ S 14 '63
Innocence by association. R. Howard. Poetry 104:245-53 Jl '64
Listening for the different voice. W. T. Scott. Sat R 46:36-8 O 26 '63
Madness in the new poetry. P. Davison. Atlan 215:90-3 Ja '65
Modern poetry. M. L. Rosenthal. bibliog il NEA J 53:54-7 Ja '64
Poet as anti-specialist; adaptation of address. M. Swenson. Sat R 48:16-18+ Ja 30 '65
Poetry and power. J. F. Kennedy. Atlan 213: 53-4 F '64
Poetry's larger views. D. Hughes. Nation 196:550-2 Je 29 '63
Poets and critics: the forgotten difference. S. Spender. Sat R 46:15-18 O 5 '63
Poet's cult. S. Hazo. Commonweal 79:130-2 O 25 '63
Sense and being. J. Ciardi. Sat R 47:18+ S 19 '64
Some new poetry: from last August to this. W. J. Smith. Harper 229:99-103 Ag '64
Truth & poetry; ed. by H. V. Wilson. Flower Grower 51:79 Ja '64
Way of knowing; excerpts from address. J. Burden. bibliog Mlle 58:73+ D '63
Why read poetry? R. Graves. il Holiday 35: 10+ F '64
See also
American poetry
Childrens poetry
Christmas poetry
Easter—Poetry
English poetry
Free verse
Italian poetry
Japanese poetry
Limericks
Poetics
Poets
Sestinas
Spring—Poetry

Appreciation

Dead geraniums. J. Ciardi. Sat R 46:16+ O 26 '63
Do you dig all jive? G. Weinstein. il Sr Schol 85:13T-14T Ja 14 '65
Let's join the poets; place of poetry in the children's book collection. L. E. Cathon. Wilson Lib Bul 38:879 Je '64
Manner of speaking. J. Ciardi. Sat R 47:13+ Ap 4 '64
Mascot. Nation 197:311 N 16 '63
Not the rose. . . M. C. Livingston. Horn Bk 40:355-60 Ag '64

Authorship

Selling your poetry. P. J. Henniker-Heaton. Writer 77:18-20 Ap '64

Bibliography

New poetry. P. Davison. Atlan 212:82-5 D '63
New poetry. W. J. Smith. Harper 227:106+ S '63
Octet. S. J. Rowland, jr. Christian Cent 81: 939 Jl 22 '64
Poets ascend the technical trend. J. Schevill. il Sat R 47:30-3 Jl 4 '64
Poet's other voices, other rooms. R. D. Spector. Sat R 47:36-8 F 1 '64
Verse (cont) New Yorker 39:173-5 Ap 27; 210-12 O 12 '63; 40:178+ Ap 11; 238+ N 7 '64

Collections

See Anthologies

Quotations, maxims, etc.

Muse; comp. by E. F. Murphy. N Y Times Mag p87 O 11 '64
Muse-ings; comp. by E. F. Murphy. N Y Times Mag p26 O 13 '63

Study and teaching

Poetry: a closer look, by J. M. Reid and others. Review
Commentary 37:76-7 Ja '64. I. Feldman
See also
Poetry—Appreciation

Technique

See Poetics

Themes

See Literature—Themes

Translating

Alcools, uncut; poems, by G. Apollinaire, tr. by W. Meredith. G. Dillon. Poetry 105: 136-7 N '64
Four German poets. L. Mueller. Poetry 101: 287-92 Ja '63
Merwin as translator. B. Gibbs. Poetry 101: 353-5 F '63

POETRY (periodical)
Announcement of prize awards for 1964. Poetry 105:138-40 N '64
Announcement of prize awards for 1963. Poetry 103:202-3 D '63
Foreword. H. Rago. Poetry 103:xi O '63

POETRY, Canadian
See also
Canadian poetry

POETRY and religion. See Religion and literature

POETRY and science. See Literature and science

POETRY as recreation
Poetry, a lively art indeed! Hollywood, Fla. annual poetry night. P. J. Heneghan and J. Justice. il Recreation 57:504-5 D '64
Poetry is recreation. bibliog il Recreation 57: 67-74 F '64

POETRY for periodicals. See Periodical literature

POETRY phonograph records. See Phonograph records—Spoken records

POETRY readings. See Dramatic readings

POETS
How to identify a poet. S. Spender. il Sat R 47:14-17 Ag 8 '64
Poets and mystics. J. Fandel. Commonweal 79:309-10 D 6 '63
Poet's cult. S. Hazo. Commonweal 79:130-2 O 25 '63
See also
Women as poets

POETS, American
Answering voice. L. Untermeyer. il Ladies Home J 81:66+ My '64
Closest permissible approximation. H. Carruth. Poetry 101:358-60 F '63
Gansevoort pier; poetry readings. New Yorker 40:40-1 S 26 '64
New Negro poets U.S.A., ed. by L. Hughes. Review
Nation 198:665-6 Je 29 '64. M. Schleifer
Off the cuff. A. Marple. Writer 76:5-6+ My '63
Opinion, please: from Bread Loaf, Vt. D. Wakefield. il Mlle 60:70+ N '64
Poets in search of a public. C. Simmons. il Sat R 46:46-8 Mr 30 '63
Recent prose. R. J. Mills, jr. Poetry 102:269-73 Jl '63
Reed Whittemore's mock epics. X. J. Kennedy. Poetry 101:356-7 F '63
Some new poetry: from last August to this. W. J. Smith. Harper 229:99-103 Ag '64
See also
American poetry
Ammons, A. R.
Antoninus, Brother
Beatniks
Berg, S.
Berryman, J.
Bukowski, C.
Carruth, H.
Ciardi, J.
Creeley, R.
Cummings, E. E.
Duncan, R.
Eberhart, R.
Ferrini, V.
Field, E.
Frost, R.
Frumkin, G.
Ginsberg, A.
Goodman, P.
Hard, W.
Jeffers, R.
Kallman, C.
Lawner, L.
Longfellow, H. W.
Lowell, R. T. S. jr
Merwin, W. S.
Moore, M.
Olson, E.
Rexroth, K.
Roethke, T.
Sandburg, C.
Stephens, A.
Stuart, J.
Williams, W. C.

POETS, Argentine
Seven Argentine poets; with poems. M. Grinberg; J. C. Martelli. il Américas 16:16-21 O '64

POETS, Brazilian
See also
Brazilian poetry

POETS, Canadian
See also
Birney, E.
Canadian poetry
Pratt, E. J.
POETS, Chilean
Five Chilean poets; with poems. J. Donoso. il Américas 16:15-20 My '64
See also
Neruda, P.
POETS, Colombian
See also
Caro, J. E.
POETS, Cuban
See also
Martí, J.
POETS, Dutch
Down there on a visit: poetry in the Netherlands. T. Cassity. Poetry 102:38-42 Ap '63
See also
Ostaijen, P. van
POETS, Ecuadorian
Six Ecuadorian poets; with poems. G. R. Pérez; U. Estrella. il Américas 16:30-4 N '64
POETS, English
Verse. L. Bogan. New Yorker 40:178+ Ap 11 '64
See also
Auden, W. H.
Brooke, R.
Browne, T.
Coleridge, S. T.
Day-Lewis, C.
Eliot, T. S.
English poetry
Fuller, R.
Larkin, P.
MacNeice, L.
Mary Herbert, countess of Pembroke
Milton, J.
Muir, E.
Owen, W.
Raine, K.
Smith, S.
Tomlinson, C.
Turner, W. P.
POETS, French
See also
French poetry
Villon, F.
POETS, German
See also
Hölderlin, F.
POETS, Greek
See also
Cavafy, C. P.
Ritsos, Y.
Seferis, G.
POETS, Haitian
Five Haitian poets; with poems. M. A. Lubin. il Américas 17:16-21 Ja '65
POETS, Indonesian
See also
Anwar, C.
POETS, Irish
See also
Clarke, A.
Devlin, D.
Yeats, W. B.
POETS, Italian
See also
Belli, G. G.
Dante Alighieri
POETS, Mexican
Five Mexican poets; with poems. S. Mondragón. il Américas 15:7-12 O '63
See also
Paz, O.
POETS, Panamanian
Avant-garde poetry in Panama: seven poets; with poems. A. M. Ortega. il Américas 16:12-19 Jl '64
POETS, Russian
See also
Evtushenko, E. A.
Tyutchev, F.
Voznesensky, A.
POETS, Salvadorian
Four Salvadorian poets; with poems. E. Odio. il Américas 16:27-31 Je '64
POETS, Senegalese
See also
Senghor, L. S.
POETS, Spanish
See also
Jiménez, J. R.
Machado, A.
Vallejo, C.
POETS, Swedish
See also
Dagerman, S.
POETS, Ukrainian
See also
Shevchenko, T. G.

POETS, Uruguayan
Six Uruguayan poets; with poems. S. Ibargoyen Islas. il Américas 16:16-21 S '64
POETS, Welsh
See also
Jones, D.
Thomas, D.
POETS conferences. See Authors conferences
POGONOPHORA. See Marine worms
POGUE, Doris E.
Surprise! Farm J 88:43 Ag '64
POGUE, Forrest C.
Century's battlefields. Sat R 46:25-7 Ap 6 '63
Making of a general; excerpts from George C. Marshall: education of a general. Look 27:45-58 S 24 '63
Never a farewell to arms. Sat R 47:48 N 21 '64
POGUE, Ivan
Sculptured glass. il por Design 66:34-5 S '64
POINDEXTER, Thomas L.
Excerpt from testimony, August 1, 1963. Cong Digest 42:279+ N '63
POINSETT, Alex
Controversial Jim Brown. Ebony 20:65-6+ D '64
Crusade in Mississippi. Ebony 19:25-8+ S '64
How to get a job. Ebony 19:79-80+ My '64
How to start a business. Ebony 19:85-6+ Jl '64
Look at Cassius Clay; biggest mouth in boxing. Ebony 18:35-6+ Mr '63
Pro football's mightiest player. Ebony 19:32-4+ Ja '64
Ten most trusted whites. Ebony 19:36-8+ Ap '64
POINSETTIAS
Compact poinsettias. il Sunset 133:150-1 D '64
Flower of the blessed night. R. Landolina. il Horticulture 41:620-1 D '63
Now's the time to drive and see the great sheets of poinsettia color. il Sunset 133:20-2+ D '64
POINT, Fernand
Profiles: Mme M. L. Point. J. Wechsberg. New Yorker 39:58+ O 5 '63
POINT, Marie Louise
Profiles. J. Wechsberg. por New Yorker 39:57-8+ O 5 '63
POINT four program. See Technical assistance, American
POINT of departure; story. See Webb, L.
POINT PELEE NATIONAL PARK
Spring migration at Point Pelee. O. S. Pettingill, jr. il Audubon Mag 66:78-80 Mr '64
POINTE DE SABLE, Jean Baptiste
Negro who founded Chicago. L. Bennett, jr. il por Ebony 19:170-2+ D '63
POINTERS (dogs)
Friends in the field. il Time 82:90-2 N 1 '63
King and I. Mrs J. Keiser. Field & S 69:134 S '64
Our newest pointer: Hungarian vizsla. J. Stetson. il Field & S 69:146-8 Je '64
See also
German shorthaired pointers
POINTILLISM. See Impressionism (art)
POIRIER, Bernard
First Blue Streak arrives in Australia for ELDO use. Miss & Roc 13:35 Ag 19 '63
IRBM work aids French space hopes. Miss & Roc 12:55 Ap 29 '63
POIRIER, Normand
Extraordinary Amidon school. Sat Eve Post 237:22-3 D 19 '64
Jubilant Janis is back on Broadway. Sat Eve Post 236:35-6 N 9 '63
Lawrence of Illinois. Sat Eve Post 237:72+ Mr 21 '64
Miracle on Broadway. Sat Eve Post 237:83-4 Ap 25 '64
Momma's girl. Sat Eve Post 236:30-1 O 5 '63
Sidney Poitier's long journey. Sat Eve Post 237:26+ Je 20 '64
POISON. See Poisons
POISON arrow frogs. See Frogs
POISON gas. See Gases, Asphyxiating and poisonous
POISON ivy
Annals of medicine. B. Roueché. New Yorker 40:158+ S 12 '64
Nature note. Sci N L 86:157 S 5 '64
POISON ivy; drama. See DuBois, G.
POISONED arrows. See Arrows, Poisoned
POISONING. See Poisons
POISONOUS fishes
Formula of fugu: Japanese puffer fish. il Time 85:44 Ja 29 '65
POISONOUS gases. See Gases, Asphyxiating and poisonous
POISONOUS mushrooms. See Mushrooms

POISONOUS plants
Death in the garden. il Changing T 18:23-4 My '64
Look out for those plants & spices. Time 82:49 Jl 19 '63
Watch out for these poisonous plants. il Good H 156:156-7 Je '63
See also
Mushrooms
Poison ivy

POISONOUS snakes. See Snakes

POISONS
Air of art is poisoned; with comment by L. J. Goldwater. R. Mallary. il Art N 62:34-7+ O '63
Antidotes for poisoning and drug overdoses. Good H 156:146 Mr '63
Carbon tetrachloride poisoning in rats: alteration in ribosomes of the liver. E. A. Smuckler and E. P. Benditt. bibliog il Science 140:308-10 Ap 19 '63
Cyanide poisoning. Sci N L 86:37 Jl 18 '64
Deadly point; poisoned darts. G. Vincent. il N Y Times Mag p62+ Mr 15 '64
First aid. C. J. Potthoff. Todays Health 42:88 My '64
How to protect children against accidental poisoning. Good H 158:161-3 Je '64
One man's battle against poison. H. E. Dark. il Todays Health 42:43+ Mr '64
Season's warning; Christmas hazards. Time 84:53 D 25 '64
See also
Botulism
Insecticides
Lead poisoning
Rat poisons
Thallium poisoning

POISONS, Labeling of. See Labels

POITIER, Sidney
Lilies of the field. il pors Ebony 18:55-8 O '63
Oscar-bound pace-setter. G. Berg. por Sr Schol 84:20 Mr 20 '64
Sidney Poitier's long journey. N. Poirier. il pors Sat Eve Post 237:26+ Je 20 '64
Top actor of the year. il pors Ebony 19:123-6+ Mr '64
Wailing for them all. il por Time 83:52+ Ap 24 '64

POKE poles, Fishing. See Fishing tackle

POKER
Game, gentlemen, a game. B. W. Tuchman. il Esquire 59:114-16+ My '63
No game for a woman. M. McLaughlin. Atlan 212:74-6 S '63
Poker and American character. J. Lukacs. il Horizon 5:56-62 N '63
Poker in the smoker. R. H. Boyle. il Sports Illus 18:24+ Ap 22 '63
Poker, pawns, and power; adaptation of address. E. L. Katzenbach, jr. Sat R 46:25 Mr 23 '63
Tale of fish and chips. J. Skow. il Sat Eve Post 237:60-1 F 8 '64

Anecdotes, facetiae, satire, etc.
How to play poker. E. Zern. Field & S 68:152+ O '63

POL, Heinz
Pride of the Pentagon. Nation 198:124-6 F 3 '64

POLACOLOR. See Photography—Films

POLAND
Walk through Warsaw. L. J. Halle. New Repub 151:15-18 O 3 '64; Reply. J. Jedruch. 151:38 N 14 '64
See also
Airlines—Poland
Censorship—Poland
Colleges and universities—Poland
Communism—Poland
Concentration camps—Poland
Jews in Poland
Juvenile delinquency—Poland
Kazimierz
Law—Poland
Liquor traffic—Poland
Music festivals—Poland
Poles
Theater—Poland

Commercial treaties and agreements
Agricultural commodities agreement signed with Poland; Department announcement; text of agreement. il Dept State Bul 48:303-5 F 25 '63
U.S. and Poland sign agricultural commodities agreements; Department announcement, with texts of agreements, February 3 and February 4, 1964. il Dept State Bul 50:308-12 F 24 '64

Economic conditions
Letter from Warsaw. J. Wechsberg. New Yorker 38:115-21 F 9 '63
Slumping between two worlds. il Bsns W p 190-2+ N 16 '63

Economic policy
Polish miracle. R. H. S. Crossman. Commentary 35:210-19 Mr '63

Foreign relations
Russia
Profile of Poland. R. Staar. bibliog f il Cur Hist 44:257-64 My '63

History
Futile compromise reconsidered: Wielopolski and Russian policy in the Congress Kingdom, 1861-1863. S. J. Zyzniewski. bibliog f Am Hist R 70:395-412 Ja '65

Intellectual life
Fading freedoms; limited publication of intellectual reviews and new books challenged by intellectuals. Newsweek 63:45 My 11 '64
It happened in Poland; restrictions on allocation of paper for printing of books and periodicals. Reporter 30:9-10 My 7 '64
Poland. W. Z. Laqueur. New Repub 149:10 Jl 13 '63
Symptom; trial of Melchior Wankowicz for protest. il Time 84:38 N 20 '64

Politics and government
Gomulka compromise. W. Z. Laqueur. New Repub 148:11-12 Je 29 '63
Profile of Poland. R. Staar. bibliog f il Cur Hist 44:257-64 My '63

Religious institutions and affairs
Education in Poland. America 108:325 Mr 9 '63
PAX; Poland's Proteus. J. Dohnalik. Atlan 212:79-81 D '63
See also
Catholic church in Poland
Catholics in Poland

POLAND and the United States
From Poland with love; welcome to Robert F. Kennedy and his family. America 111:35 Jl 11 '64

POLANYI, Michael
Potential theory of adsorption. bibliog Science 141:1010-13 S 13 '63

POLAR bear hunting. See Bear hunting

POLAR bears. See Bears

POLAR exploration
See also
Arctic exploration

POLAR ice. See Ice—Polar Regions

POLAR REGIONS
Cold no longer problem in frozen Polar Regions. Sci N L 85:105 F 15 '64
See also
Antarctic Regions

POLAR REGIONS. See Antarctic Regions

POLAR research
Antarctic dilemma. R. Lewis. Bul Atomic Sci 19:37-9 F '63
Antarctica: colonization ends era of exploration, emphasis shifts to organized polar science program. J. Walsh. Science 139:578+ F 15 '63
Antarctica: the international laboratory. A. P. Crary. il Bul Atomic Sci 20:27-30 Ja '64
Bird man of Antarctica; studies of the emperor penguin. il Sci Digest 56:48-9 D '64
Scientists to follow penguins by plane. Sci N L 86:255 O 17 '64
Secrets from cold storage. W. J. Cromie. il Natur Hist 72:20-7 O '63
United States policy and international cooperation in Antarctica; excerpts from President's report to Congress; with letters of transmittal. L. B. Johnson; D. Rusk. bibliog f Dept State Bul 51:402-7 S 21 '64

POLARIMETERS. See Polariscope

POLARIS missiles. See Guided missiles—Launching from submarine boats

POLARIS submarines. See Submarine boats, Atomic powered

POLARISCOPE
Cross-polarized color. P. Farber. il U S Camera 27:38-9+ Jl '64
Measurement of optical activity: new approaches. B. Carroll and I. Blei. bibliog il Science 142:200-8 O 11 '63

POLARITY indicators. See Electric instruments

POLARIZATION (light)
Cross-polarized color. P. Farber. il U S Camera 27:38-9+ Jl '64
Optical pumping. T. R. Carver. bibliog il Science 141:599-608 Ag 16 '63
Polarized light used to study cell structure. Sci N L 86:168 S 12 '64

POLARIZATION of protons. See Protons—Polarization

POLARIZED light. See Polarization (light)

POLAROGRAPH and polarography
Polarographic investigation of conjugated fat-soluble vitamins. E. J. Kuta. bibliog il Science 144:1130-1 My 29 '64

POLAROID color film. See Photography—Films

POLAROID corporation
Automated cameras catch the customers. il Bsns W p82 Ag 3 '63
Instant color photography. W. Siegrist. il Sci N L 83:250-1 Ap 20 '63
Polaroid snaps into color. il Bsns W p80-2 Ja 19 '63

POLAROID Land cameras
Comparing the new quick loaders. K. Brown. il Pop Mech 120:112-15+ O '63
Creative color; fifteen uses for Polacolor. A. Rothstein. il U S Camera 26:9-10 Ap '63
Creative color; perfection of Polacolor. A. Rothstein. U S Camera 26:9-10 Mr '63
Featherweight contender; Automatic 100 Land camera. il Time 82:65-6 Ag 9 '63
How to be a Polaroid expert. J. Wolbarst. il Pop Sci 185:118-22 D '64
Instant color photos! K. Brown. il Pop Mech 119:100-5+ F '63
It's here! Polacolor; symposium with portfolio by famous pros. Pop Phot 52:49-63+ Mr '63
New Automatic 100 Polaroid Land camera; symposium. il Pop Phot 53:46-59+ O '63
New Polaroid camera; Polaroid Automatic 100. il Consumer Rep 28:530-1 N '63
Pictures in a moment. J. Wolbarst. See issues of Modern photography
Polacolor. il U S Camera 26:52-7 Mr '63
Polaroid camera means business. B. Goldrath. il U S Camera 27:22+ Je '64
Polaroid color. J. Wolbarst. il Mod Phot 27:60-5+ Mr '63
Polaroid color pack camera. E. Hannigan. il U S Camera 26:50-3 O '63
Polaroid Land Automatic 100; something really new in camera automation. il Consumer Bul 46:11-13 N '63
Polaroid Land automatic 101. il Consumer Bul 48:10 F '65
Polaroid Land color film. il Consumer Bul 46:9-10 Ag '63
Polaroid snaps into color. il Bsns W p80-2 Ja 19 '63
Polaroid's can't-miss electronic camera; Automatic 100. B. Hering. il Pop Sci 183:136-9 O '63
Polaroid's new color film. il Consumer Rep 28:376-7 Ag '63
Polaroid's new pack camera!! J. Wolbarst. il Mod Phot 27:84-5+ O '63
Ten-second pictures. H. M. Kinzer. See issues of Popular photography to July, 1963
Twin lens; ten-second Rollei pictures. F. Henle. il Pop Phot 54:32 Mr '64
Vagabond camera; Automatic 100. W. Lane. il Travel 120:54-5 D '63
What's newest; Automatic 100 Land camera. Newsweek 62:54 Ag 5 '63

Care

Pictures in a moment; spring checkup. J. Wolbarst. il Mod Phot 27:28+ My '63

POLAROID photography. See Photography

POLATIN, E. C.
Have a fun garden. House B 105:130-1 S '63
We're in clover. House B 105:156-7 Je '63

POLCIK, Bronislaw, and others
Daily sensitivity rhythm of the two-spotted spider mite, tetranychus urticae, to DDVP. bibliog Science 145:405-6 Jl 24 '64

POLE beans. See Beans

POLE dances. See Indians of Mexico—Dances

POLE vaulting. See Vaulting (sport)

POLEMONIACEAE. See Phlox

POLEMONIUM reptans. See Jacobs ladder

POLES
Letter from Warsaw. J. Wechsberg. New Yorker 38:106+ F 9 '63
Paul in Poland; ed. by E. Miller. P. Anka. il Seventeen 23:160-1+ Ap '64

POLES in the United States
My old ladies. M. Zavada. Reporter 29:35-6 D 5 '63

POLETTI, Charles
Onward and upward with the arts. J. Brooks. New Yorker 39:41-2+ Je 1 '63

POLI, Kenneth
Earthbound experimenter's adventures with a space-age film. il Pop Phot 55:50-1+ S '64
Tele-mike for telephoto shooting. Pop Phot 55:73+ O '64

POLICE
Police reserve lends valuable aid; Hays, Kan. H. E. Lucas. il Am City 78:20 F '63
Worldwide survey: why foreign streets are safer. il U S News 56:44-5 Je 15 '64
See also
Crime and criminals
Police patrol

Photographs

Police line-up; identify the locale of various police. Travel 122:35-7+ S '64

Political activities

Conspiracy on the right; John Birch society members. New Repub 151:3-4 N 28 '64

Training

San Francisco's peacemakers; special training for police pays off in smooth handling of civil rights disorders. A. Ogle. America 111:232-3 S 5 '64

Canada

See also
Canada—Royal Canadian mounted police

France

See also
Paris—Police

Great Britain

Bobbies in trouble. il Time 82:26 Ag 30 '63
Kicking the coppers. Newsweek 62:25 D 30 '63

United States

Birch policemen. Commonweal 81:404 D 18 '64
Car 54 where are you? problem of slow police service. il Time 83:61 My 8 '64
Case for the cop. R. Dougherty. Harper 228:129-33 Ap '64
Civil liberties and police power. Commonweal 80:29 Ap 3 '64
Cops v. the courts; standards of police search and seizure. Time 84:59-60 Ag 28 '64
Corrupt society. F. J. Cook. Nation 196:472-4 Je 1 '63
Crackdown coming on future rioters. il U S News 57:80-1 O 12 '64
Don't take the police for granted. R. Brecher and E. Brecher. il Parents Mag 39:56-7+ Mr '64
How much crime can America take? interviews. W. G. Long; W. H. Parker. il U S News 56:66-72 Ap 20 '64
Mob violence control. W. McCann. Sci N L 86:86 Ag 8 '64
Police are for protection. il Ebony 19:56-7 My '64
Police Birchites: the blue backlash. P. Hoffman. il Nation 199:425+ D 7 '64
Search & seizure; be sure it's legal. Time 83:80 My 15 '64
Storm aroud U.S. policemen; with pro and con discussion. il Sr Schol 85:12-17+ Ja 14 '65
Take the handcuffs off our police! F. Sondern, jr. Read Digest 85:64-8 S '64
Thin blue line. Nat R 16:679 Ag 11 '64
When newsmen become newsmakers; problem of publicity before and during a trial. E. N. Griswold. Sat R 47:21-3 O 24 '64
See also subhead Police under names of states, cities, etc. e.g. New York (city)—Police

Venezuela

See also
Caracas, Venezuela—Police

POLICE, International. See International police

POLICE, Motorcycle
How to train a motorcycle squad; Gainesville, Fla. C. A. Roberts. il Am City 79:99 F '64

POLICE, Negro. See Negro police

POLICE automobiles. See Automobiles, Police

POLICE bands. See Bands (music)

POLICE boats
Lake George patrol. M. Crook. il Yachting 115:96-7+ Ja '64
Marblehead's bustling boatcops. Motor B 113:80+ My '64
Patrol boat to fight river pollution; Dade County, Fla. il Am City 79:92 Mr '64
Tall in the cockpit; Seattle harbor police. E. Crimmin. il Motor B 113:24-5+ My '64

POLICE chases
Cops with guns; accidental shooting of Mrs. Schultz in California. New Repub 150:5 Ap 4 '64
Cops with guns; stop or I'll shoot. L. Patterson. New Repub 150:8-9 Mr 14 '64; Discussion. 150:37-8 Mr 28; 30 Ap 25 '64
POLICE communication systems
Recorders and duplicating machines speed police reporting; Long Beach, Calif. R. G. Kortz. il Am City 79:81 Jl '64
See also
Police radio
POLICE dogs
His master's voice by radio: Alexandria, Va. P. B. Floyd. il Am City 79:28 F '64
POLICE gazette. See National police gazette
POLICE helicopters. See Helicopters in police work
POLICE patrol
Roulette at the police station; Edina, Minn. H. M. Wrobleski. il Am City 78:90 Ag '63
POLICE radio
Foot patrolmen radio equipped; Middletown, Ohio. C. W. Thompson. il Am City 78:89 Mr '63
Instant police via citizens-band radio; Canby, Minn. C. E. Kittelson. il Am City 78:147 D '63
No more communications failures; Port Washington, N.Y. J. L. Salerno. il Am City 79:115 F '64
Radio system that thinks; Boston. E. L. McNamara. il Am City 79:22 D '64
State-police microwave. M. Lincoln. il Electr World 71:48-50 F '64
Tuning up on the new 460-Mc. police frequencies; with list of police stations on 450-460 Mc. K. Greenberg. il Pop Electr 20:56-8+ My '64
POLICE records
Constabulary style. C. Williams. il Esquire 62:106-7+ N '64
POLICE sirens. See Whistles
POLICE state. See Totalitarianism
POLICE strike, Boston, 1919. See Boston—Police
POLICEMEN. See Police
POLICEWOMEN
Ambassador of goodwill for police department. il Ebony 19:40-2+ Mr '64
POLING, Daniel A.
Christianity in search of unity. Sat R 47:32 My 30 '64
Gentle fundamentalist. por Time 84:90+ D 11 '64
POLING, James
Creature of air and darkness. Read Digest 82:39-40+ Mr '63
How science aids our overworked bees. Audubon Mag 65:280-3 S '63
World's most exotic nuisance. Read Digest 85:253-6 O '64
—See Graham, J. jt. auth.
POLIO-ENCEPHALITIS. See Encephalitis
POLIOMYELITIS
Difficult birth. M. Rosenthal. Nation 199:144+ S 21 '64
Laying low a crippler. il Todays Health 42:12 O '64
Poliomyelitis in monkeys: decreased susceptibility after avoidance stress. J. T. Marsh and others. bibliog il Science 140:1414-15 Je 28 '63
Prevention and control
No pockets of polio. Sci N L 85:374 Je 13 '64
Polio outbreaks possible. Sci N L 84:366 D 7 '63
Vaccines
Near disaster with the Salk vaccine. A. J. Snider. Sci Digest 54:40-1 D '63
New polio vaccine; Orimune. Consumer Rep 28:413-14 S '63
Oral polio vaccine safe. Sci N L 84:370 D 14 '63
Polio postmortem; Salk vaccine. il Newsweek 62:61 Jl 1 '63
Poliovirus: guanidine dependence and loss of neurovirulence for monkeys. B. Loddo and others. bibliog il Science 145:945-6 Ag 28 '64
Sabin polio vaccine. Consumer Rep 28:137 Mr '63
Three-in-one; new oral vaccine. Newsweek 62:61 Jl 8 '63
Three polio doses needed; Sabin vaccine. Sci N L 84:19 Jl 13 '63
Why there's worry over polio vaccine. il U S News 57:12 O 19 '64
POLIOMYELITIS virus
Poliovirus: growth in non-nucleate cytoplasm. T. T. Crocker and others. bibliog il Science 145:401-3 Jl 24 '64
Poliovirus: guanidine dependence and loss of neurovirulence for monkeys. B. Loddo and others. bibliog il Science 145:945-6 Ag 28 '64
Poliovirus type I: neutralization by papain-digested antibodies. A. Vogt and others. bibliog il Science 145:1447-8 S 25 '64
Polyribosomes: size in normal and polio-infected HeLa cells. A. Rich and others. bibliog il Science 142:1658-63 D 27 '63
Virus-specific double-stranded RNA in polio-virus-infected cells. D. Baltimore and others. bibliog il Science 143:1034-6 Mr 6 '64
POLIOVIRUS. See Poliomyelitis virus
POLISH art. See Art, Polish
POLISH fables. See Fables
POLISH literature
Introduction to modern Polish literature: an anthology of fiction and poetry, ed. by A. Gillon and L. Krzyzanowski. Review
Sat R 47:64 D 5 '64. R. L. Stilwell
POLISH mime theater. See Pantomime
POLISH refugees. See Refugees, Polish
POLISH reporters. See Reporters and reporting
POLISH theatre. See Theater—Poland
POLISHING
What! polish with a belt sander? H. B. Comstock. il Pop Sci 185:166-7 O '64
See also
Honing
Sand blast
Tumbling barrels
POLISHING materials
Automobile polishes and waxes. il Consumer Bul 46:8-10 S '63
POLITENESS. See Courtesy; Etiquette
POLITICAL advertising. See Advertising, Political
POLITICAL asylum. See Asylum, Right of
POLITICAL attitudes
Rationalism in politics, by M. Oakeshott. Review
Commentary 35:168-72 '63. G. Lichtheim
Scholars see trend to more security, less freedom. F. Morley. Nations Bsns 51:27-8 O '63
T.R.B. from Washington; preachers of fear: radio and television programs of COPE, and Life lines. New Repub 150:2 Ja 4 '64; Discussion. 150:30 Ja 25; 30 F 8; 29-31 F 29 '64
Texas: the roots of the agony. R. McGee. Nation 197:427-31 D 21 '63
See also
Public opinion
POLITICAL autobiography. See Autobiography
POLITICAL bosses. See Boss rule
POLITICAL boundaries. See Boundaries
POLITICAL campaigns
California's primary explosion. K. Hendrick; D. Bess. il Nation 198:472-7 My 11 '64
Children can learn from politics. E. Simonds. Parents Mag 39:45+ O '64
Coming up; Daddy Warbucks for president; use of comic strips in election campaign. il New Repub 150:10 Ap 25 '64
Echoes; California senatorial race. il Newsweek 64:34+ O 19 '64
Far-out West; humor of Richard Tuck. Reporter 31:12+ N 19 '64
How to win an election, by S. C. Shadegg. Review
Newsweek il 64:20+ Ag 10 '64
Is it wise for entertainers to take part in political campaigns? pro and con discussion. il Sr Schol 84:6-7 My 1 '64
Keating, Kennedy, in a ripsnorter that has everything; Senate race in New York. il Life 57:32-7 O 9 '64
Keating vs. Kennedy: high stakes in New York. il Newsweek 64:35-6+ O 12 '64
Key races. il Newsweek 64:20-2 S 14 '64
Lyndon's detractors. il Newsweek 64:25-6 Ag 10 '64
Name is Smith. T. Wicker. il N Y Times Mag p 11+ Jl 28 '63
1964: a chance to look at ourselves. M. Ways. il Fortune 70:102-50+ O '64
Odds on freedom; gambler's choice in Georgia. P. De Lissovoy. il Nation 198:618-21 Je 22 '64
Political pros give the ams a nod. T. Wicker. il N Y Times Mag p28+ Je 9 '63
Splits within parties produce more moderate candidates. F. Morley. il Nations Bsns 52:27-8 Je '64
Starting gun in New Hampshire. J. Desmond. Nation 198:168-9 F 17 '64

POLITICAL campaigns—*Continued*
Tuck and nip; political prankster. R. Tuck. il Newsweek 64:34 O 12 '64
Vice Presidential derby. Nation 198:130 F 10 '64
What election issues mean. il Nations Bsns 52:88-9+ Jl '64
Winthrop Rockefeller against Orval Faubus. P. J. Owens. New Repub 150:6-7 Ap 25 '64
See also
Airplanes in political campaigns
Campaign funds
Campaign literature
Campaign oratory
Candidates, Political
Fair campaign practices committee
Presidential campaigns
Television in politics

Anecdotes, facetiae, satire, etc.

Campaign jokes. Time 84:74+ S 18 '64
I'm in the fight to the last ballot; only Lincoln Republican. M. Kitman. il Sat Eve Post 237:22-3 Jl 11 '64
Matter of conscience. J. Feiffer. Commentary 38:52-4 D '64
My first political crisis. M. Kitman. il Sat Eve Post 237:24-5 Mr 14 '64

Australia

Old, familiar faces. Newsweek 62:66-7 D 9 '63

Brazil

Early bird. Time 84:35 N 20 '64
Long campaign. il Newsweek 64:60 N 23 '64

Canada

Adlai revisited? il Newsweek 61:41 Ap 1 '63
As Canada heads for showdown at the polls. il U S News 54:48 Ap 8 '63
Cabbages and premiers. Newsweek 61:48+ Ap 8 '63
Gift from Washington. Time 81:31 Ap 5 '63
Pearson's campaign heats up in Canada. il Bsns W p28-9 Mr 30 '63
Washington gives Canada an election and an issue; with statement by U.S. Department of state. W. H. Hessler. Reporter 28:29-31 F 28 '63; Discussion. 82:6+ Mr 28 '63

France

Beginning a dialogue; presidential campaign. il Time 83:24 F 14 '64

Great Britain

Anybody's race. il Time 84:31 O 9 '64
Best man in Smethwick; photographs. N Y Times Mag p 18-19 O 4 '64
Britain: a rousing election hush. L. Hall. il Life 57:40-40B O 9 '64
Britain ambles toward election. il Bsns W p32-4 O 3 '64
British election: can Labor win? il Newsweek 64:44+ S 28 '64
British elections: gentlemen vs. experts. R. Presthus. Nation 198:480-3 My 11 '64
Campaigning the British way. il U S News 57:56 O 12 '64
Choice Britain is making. il U S News 57:45 O 19 '64
Four weeks of campaigning, or a whole year; British and American elections. P. Worsthorne. il N Y Times Mag p29+ S 27 '64
Home free? Newsweek 62:52+ N 11 '63
Hotting up. il Newsweek 64:54+ O 19 '64
In Britain, an election is due, too. Bsns W p33 S 19 '64
Irreversible state. H. Hazlitt. Newsweek 64:98 O 12 '64
One of the critical sixty-five. il Newsweek 64:60+ O 12 '64
Sparking the voters; general election campaign. il Newsweek 64:52 S 21 '64
They're off! opening of campaign. Time 84:24 S 25 '64
12,000,000 who vote Tory. S. Gruson. il N Y Times Mag p 17+ O 4 '64
Who is fit to govern? windup of Britain's election campaign. il Time 84:40 O 16 '64

Hawaii

Hawaii's top woman politician. il Ebony 18:51-2+ Ap '63

Italy

Test for the apertura. il Time 81:31 Ap 26 '63

Pakistan

Votes for mother; woman in Pakistan's presidential race. il Newsweek 64:54+ N 2 '64

Panama

Before the storm. Newsweek 63:54+ My 18 '64

POLITICAL candidates. See Candidates, Political

POLITICAL cartoons. See Caricatures and cartoons

POLITICAL catchwords. See Slogans

POLITICAL clubs and associations
American conservative union. Nat R 17:13-14 Ja 12 '65
Boss and faction. J. A. Riedel. bibliog f il Ann Am Acad 353:14-26 My '64
Bosses, machines, and ethnic groups. E. E. Cornwell, jr. bibliog f il Ann Am Acad 353:27-39 My '64
Go West, young man; biennial convention of Young Republican national federation. Nat R 15:10+ Jl 16 '63
Goldwater, Rockefeller, and the Young Republicans. M. S. Evans. il Nat R 15:97-100+ Ag 13 '63
Happy scandalmonger; San Francisco convention of the Young Republicans. Nat R 15:89-90 Ag 13 '63
Names, addresses & numbers; annual convention of Young Republicans. il Time 82:17 Jl 5 '63
Rampant right invades the GOP. T. G. Harris. il Look 27:19-25 Jl 16 '63
Right dress; Young Republican national federation biennial convention. il Newsweek 62:23-4 Jl 8 '63
Son of the Birch; Robert A. Gaston, elected president of California's Young Republicans. il Newsweek 61:27-8 Mr 4 '63
Speaking of extremists, who's playing right field? W. K. Wyant, jr. New Repub 151:12-16 S 19 '64; Reply. K. Friedberg. 151:29-30 O 10 '64
White elephant sale. M. Kempton. New Repub 150:11-12 Ap 25 '64
Young Republicans. R. Moley. Newsweek 62:84 Ag 12 '63

POLITICAL conventions
Beneath the convention razzle-dazzle; what's the role of political parties today? il Sr Schol 84:8-10 Mr 6 '64
Political convention: caucus & carnival. J. D. Weaver. il Holiday 35:42-5+ Je '64
Socialist convention; lambs with a dream. J. Martin. Nation 198:595-7 Je 15 '64
Spawning season for G.O.P. delegates. Life 56:4 My 8 '64
See also
National conventions (political)
National conventions, Democratic
National conventions, Republican

POLITICAL corruption. See Politics, Corruption in

POLITICAL economy. See Economics

POLITICAL education. See Political science—Study and teaching

POLITICAL ethics
Anti-gratuity order spreading to NASA. Aviation W 81:18-19 O 5 '64
Bit of a squashy subject; DOD standards of conduct. W. J. Coughlin. Miss & Roc 15:50 O 12 '64
Call this a code? Nation 199:2 Jl 13 '64
Codes of ethics; all honorable men. L. W. Koenig. Nation 198:551-4 Je 1 '64
DOD tightens rules on employees accepting favors from contractors. Miss & Roc 15:16 O 5 '64
Ethics in government: a poisonous atmosphere. V. M. Burns. Cath World 200:78-83 N '64
Government and business; address, October 30, 1963. L. B. Mason. Vital Speeches 30:134-8 D 15 '63
Heart of the matter: B. Baker case. Nation 198:131 F 10 '64
High price of silence. W. J. Coughlin. Miss & Roc 15:46 N 23 '64
McNamara firm on conduct code; with editorial comment. Miss & Roc 15:13, 46 N 2 '64
Making senators lift lid, a little, on wealth. Bsns W p 18 Jl 4 '64
Moral missions of the legislature; address, April 24, 1963. W. J. Mahoney. Vital Speeches 29:655-7 Ag 15 '63
Peace and morality. Commonweal 81:435 D 25 '64
Shades of blackmail. K. Crawford. Newsweek 64:32 Ag 24 '64
Sins they commit; business and political ethics. America 109:72 Jl 20 '63
Speaking out; we want our politicians to be hypocrites. W. F. Buckley, jr. Sat Eve Post 237:8+ O 17 '64
See also
Politics, Corruption in

POLITICAL executions. See Executions and executioners

POLITICAL films. See Moving pictures—Political films

POLITICAL forecasts
As the race ends: who'll win? Size-up: state by state; final look at the polls. il U S News 57:25-31 N 2 '64
Bad news from the oracles. il Time 81:23 Je 7 '63
Election key: how will big cities go? il U S News 57:80-3 O 26 '64
Harris calls the election, by sex, place, race, religion. L. Harris. Newsweek 64:28-9 N 2 '64
How big is the backlash? B. Roper and E. Roper. il Sat R 47:24 O 3 '64
How the polls made out. U S News 57:14 N 16 '64
How the states will go. Time 84:28-9 O 30 '64
Intelligent woman's guide to political polls. E. Mazo. McCalls 92:80+ O '64
Newsweek's listening post: the electoral vote. il Newsweek 64:30+ N 2 '64
What to look for on November 4. M. S. Evans. Nat R 16:965-7 N 3 '64
Yer pays yer money, yer tykes yer choice; polls in Great Britain. Time 81:36+ My 17 '63
See also
Public opinion polls
POLITICAL fundamentalism. See Conservatism
POLITICAL informers. See Informers (law)
POLITICAL liberty. See Liberty
POLITICAL literature
Pamphleteers return. M. S. Evans. Nat R 16: 981 N 3 '64
POLITICAL news. See Newspapers—Political news
POLITICAL novels. See Politics in literature
POLITICAL parties
Party system and democracy in Africa. T. J. Mboya. For Affairs 41:650-8 Jl '63
See also
Communist parties
Partisanship
Platforms, Political
Political conventions
Socialist parties

Publicity

See also
Advertising, Political

Arab states

Al Baath challenges Nasser; political party that rules Syria and Iraq. D. A. Schmidt. il N Y Times Mag p42+ O 6 '63
Baghdad: coup by consent; roles of Ba'ath parties in Syria and Iraq. D. Holden. il Reporter 29:30-2 D 19 '63
Danger: professor at work; Baath party. il Time 82:28-9 N 22 '63
Shifting sands of Arab union; Ba'athists and Nasser are vying to lead the Arab peoples. il Sr Schol 83:8-11 Ja 17 '64
Tremors in the Near East. D. Stewart. il Nation 198:23-5 Ja 6 '64

Austria

Two on the seesaw. Time 81:33 Ap 5 '63

Brazil

See also
Communist party (Brazil)

Canada

French leave; fifth political party. Time 82:46 S 13 '63
Rhinos. Newsweek 63:36 F 24 '64
See also
Social credit party

Chile

Chile enters a new era. D. W. Bray. Cur Hist 48:21-5+ Ja '65
Gain for Christian democrats. Commonweal 78:125 Ap 26 '63

Cuba

After the Cuban crisis. D. H. Wrong. Commentary 35:32-3 Ja '63

France

See also
Action française
Communist party (France)
Socialist party (France)

French West Africa

French-speaking West Africa. A. R. Zolberg. bibliog f Cur Hist 45:347-54 D '63

Germany (Federal Republic)

Born to lose? Social democratic party. Newsweek 62:24 D 30 '63
Exclusive Senior scholastic interview. W. Brandt. Sr Schol 83:16+ N 15 '63
Last heil? nationalist parties. Newsweek 63: 44+ Ap 13 '64
Price of silence. Time 81:33 Ap 12 '63
Swan song on the right; new National democratic party. Newsweek 64:34 D 14 '64
See also
Socialist party (Germany [Federal Republic])

Great Britain

Atlantic report. Atlan 214:34+ O '64
Britain veers left. Nat R 14:267-8 Ap 9 '63
Conservative comeback? J. M. Cameron. Commonweal 79:562-4 F 7 '64
Letter from London. M. Panter-Downes. New Yorker 40:92+ Je 13 '64
Taxicab majority. il Time 84:32+ O 23 '64
See also
Conservative party (Great Britain)
Labor party (Great Britain)
Liberal party (Great Britain)

India

See also
Indian national congress

Italy

Elections in Italy. M. Painelle. America 108: 712-13 My 18 '63
Italian elections: even worse than before. C. Sterling. il Reporter 28:22-5 My 23 '63
Italy tries an opening to the left; Christian democrats and Nenni socialist party. il Sr Schol 83:6-8+ Ja 10 '64
Italy's coalition government. E. R. Rosen. Cur Hist 47:339-44 D '64
Leftists gain in Italy. il Bsns W p 122-3 My 4 '63
Moro and Togliatti. Newsweek 61:37+ Je 3 '63
Narrow opening. il Newsweek 62:60+ D 2 '63
Nenni at bay. America 108:895 Je 29 '63
New Italy & its politics. H. S. Hughes. Commentary 38:46-51 O '64
Party struggle in Italy. R. Kirk. Nat R 14: 160 F 26 '63
Pope John and Communist gains. Marcello. America 108:896 Je 29 '63
Signor Fanfani's self-made bed. A. Leone-Moats. Nat R 14:404-5 My 21 '63
Then there were nine; Italian socialist party of proletarian unity (PSIUP) Newsweek 63:36-8 Ja 27 '64
Trend to the left. G. D. Kumlien. Commonweal 78:244-5 My 24 '63
Will Italian democracy survive? Christian democratic party. D. Futch. Nat R 15:152-3 Ag 27 '63

Japan

Factional politics in Japan. H. H. Baerwald. il Cur Hist 46:223-9+ Ap '64

Latin America

Aims of Christian democracy; excerpt from Religion, revolution, and reform, ed. by F. B. Pike and W. V. D'Antonio. E. Frei. Commonweal 81:63-6 O 9 '64
Rising force; Christian democrats. il Time 84:48+ S 18 '64

Mexico

Changing the guard in Mexico. M. C. Needler. il Cur Hist 48:26-31+ Ja '65
Mexico follows a solo camino. K. Botsford. il N Y Times Mag p20+ Ap 26 '64
President-elect. Newsweek 64:44 Jl 13 '64
Viva el candidato! R. Armstrong. il Sat Eve Post 237:73-7 Je 20 '64

Morocco

Atlantic report. Atlan 212:28+ D '63

Peru

APRA's show of weakness. Time 82:45 S 13 '63
Peru's new politics: the hit-or-miss approach; role of APRA (American popular revolutionary alliance) G. Delmas. il Reporter 29:35-8 O 24 '63

Puerto Rico

Puerto Rican Evangelicals oppose religious parties. Christian Cent 80:1490 D 4 '63

Russia

See also
Communist party (Russia)

United States

After the election. America 111:589 N 14 '64
After the elections; both parties take stock. il Sr Schol 85:8-11 D 2 '64
Anatomy of a new politics. C. D. Bolton. il Nation 198:529-33 My 25 '64
Changing U.S. electorate. S. Lubell. il Fortune 70:132-5+ Jl '64
Crossroads in Dixie. J. J. Kilpatrick. Nat R 15:433-5 N 19 '63

POLITICAL parties—United States—*Continued*
Crucial questions for November 4. Christian Cent 81:1291 O 21 '64
Deadlock of democracy: four-party politics in America, by J. M. Burns. Review
Commentary 35:540-2 Je '63. C. V. Woodward
New Repub 148:24-6 F 2 '63. R. L. Strout
Democratic, Republican party is a mess. M. Moos; H. S. Commager. il N Y Times Mag p9+ Ja 12 '64
Do we really have a two-party system? Sr Schol 82:38-9 F 20 '63
Goldwater challenges the four-party system; liberal vs. conservative. J. M. Burns. il N Y Times Mag p7+ Je 28 '64
Goldwater seeks a new coalition. A. K. Campbell and S. Sacks. il N Y Times Mag p22+ Ag 23 '64
How the parties differ. R. Moley. Newsweek 62:84 Jl 15; 92 Jl 22 '63
How the voting went in important areas. il U S News 55:44-6 N 18 '63
How to rebuild the two-party system. S. M. Lipset. Harper 230:56-63 Ja '65
How to wreck two parties. D. Lawrence. U S News 55:96 Jl 29 '63
How will farmers vote? D. R. Murphy. New Repub 150:6 My 2 '64
Minor party candidates. il Sr Schol 85:17 S 23 '64
Morning after. C. McWilliams. Nation 199: 345-7 N 16 '64
National committees: time to modernize? J. Kraft. Harper 228:107-8+ Je '64
On the '64 campaign trail. il Sr Schol 84:15 Ja 31; 19 F 7; 17 F 21; 11 Mr 6; 26 Ap 10 '64
Parties by any other name would solve no more. F. Morley. il Nations Bsns 53:27-8 Ja '65
Political parties need more than your money. M. Smith. il Nations Bsns 51:21-2 S '63
Position papers, 1964. Sat R 47:14-17 F 29; 15-18 Ap 25; 17-20 Je 13; 14-17+ Jl 11; 14-16 Ag 22:27-9+ S 26; 21-3+ O 17; 21-3 O 31 '64
President-candidate. M. Ascoli. Reporter 31: 22 S 10 '64
Realignment on the right. R. D. Masters. Reporter 29:23-6 N 7 '63; Discussion. 29:8 D 5 '63
Republicans and Democrats: do they exist? M. Phelps. America 110:215 F 15 '64
Schizophrenia in the G.O.P. W. D. Burnham. il Commonweal 79:5-10 S 27 '63
Splits within parties produce more moderate candidates. F. Morley. il Nations Bsns 52: 27-8 Je '64
To preserve the two-party system. J. K. Javits. il N Y Times Mag p 15+ O 27 '63
Two open letters to teen-age girls. M. Price; E. M. Peterson. Seventeen 23:232-4 S '64
Two-party system: how to help it survive. Life 57:4 O 16 '64
Two political parties and the Negro vote. R. Wilkins. McCalls 92:30+ N '64
Weighing the campaign. E. Roper. Sat R 47: 28 O 31 '64
See also
Communist party (United States)
Democratic party
Liberal party (United States)
National conventions (political)
Party government
Progressive party
Republican party
Socialist party (United States)

History

American politics: the first half-century. L. W. Koenig. Cur Hist 47:193-8+ O '64
Crucial choice for the Republicans. A. Krock. il N Y Times Mag p5+ Jl 12 '64
Two parties & how they came about; excerpts from Two party system. R. Harrity. il Look 28:48-59 Jl 14 '64

Venezuela

After Betancourt. il Time 82:23 Jl 19 '63
Betancourt goes double or nothing. Bsns W p 114+ N 30 '63

POLITICAL patronage. See Patronage, Political

POLITICAL philosophy
Goldwater, the romantic regression. H. J. Morgenthau. Commentary 38:65-8 S '64
He may be right about China but wrong about Europe. L. J. Halle. New Repub 150: 16-18 F 22 '64
Lippmann distilled; an apprehensive view of mass society. W. D. Burnham. Commonweal 78:459-61 Jl 26 '63
Loom of language and the fabric of imperatives: the case of Il principe and Utopia. J. H. Hexter. bibliog f il Am Hist R 69: 945-68 Jl '64
New left Marxism. G. Lichtheim. Commentary 35:239-43 Mr '63
1964: a chance to look at ourselves. M. Ways. il Fortune 70:102-5+ O '64
Revolt against ideology. H. D. Aiken. Commentary 37:29-39 Ap '64; Discussion. 38: 14+ S; 69-76 O '64
Test your political beliefs. C. E. Johnson and J. S. Davis. Nations Bsns 52:34-5+ S '64
Utopia and its enemies, by G. Kateb. Review
Nation 197:146-7 S 14 '63. S. Maloff
Walter Lippmann; the philosopher as journalist. L. J. Halle. New Repub 149:17-20 Ag 3 '63
See also
Communism and democracy
Conservatism
Democracy
Liberalism
Natural law
Political thought
Racism

Anecdotes, facetiae, satire, etc.

Seminar in modern journalistic thought: final examination: modern social and political theory. W. F. Gavin. Nat R 16:959 N 3 '64

POLITICAL platforms. See Platforms, Political

POLITICAL poetry
Campaign trail hootenanny. W. Carroll. il Reporter 31:26-7 O 22 '64
Sing along with the liberal Republicans. Nat R 16:151 F 25 '64

POLITICAL posters. See Posters

POLITICAL power. See Power (political science)

POLITICAL pressure. See Pressure groups

POLITICAL prisoners
Request aid for South Africans. Christian Cent 81:6 Ja 1 '64
Rescuing the forgotten prisoners. I. Ross. Sat R 48:17-18+ Ja 16 '65

POLITICAL prisoners, Exchange of
Biggest fish; Cuban-American exchange. il Newsweek 16:24-5 My 6 '63
Swap; American and Cuban prisoners. il Time 81:21 My 3 '63

POLITICAL psychology
Psychopathology of politicking. F. R. Schreiber and M. Herman. il Sci Digest 56:76-81 O '64
Shock of political defeat. F. R. Schreiber and M. Herman. il Sci Digest 56:83-6 N '64
See also
Nationalism
Political attitudes

POLITICAL public speaking. See Public speaking

POLITICAL publicity. See Advertising, Political; Television in politics

POLITICAL refugees. See Refugees

POLITICAL reporting. See Reporters and reporting

POLITICAL responsibility. See Responsibility

POLITICAL rights. See Civil rights

POLITICAL satire. See Communism—Anecdotes, facetiae, satire, etc; Politics—Anecdotes, facetiae, satire, etc.

POLITICAL science
Fences against power. S. W. Rousseas. Nation 196:343-6+ Ap 27 '63
Pure theory of politics, by B. de Jouvenel. Review
Nat R 16:410+ My 19 '64. S. Parry
See also
Bureaucracy
Elections
Equality
Federal government
Liberty
Pluralism (political science)
Political parties
Political philosophy
Political thought
Politics
Power (political science)
Property
Republics
Revolutions

History

Shadow and substance: essays on the theory and structure of politics, by J. P. Roche. Review
Nat R 16:1115-18 D 15 '64. S. Parry

POLITICAL science—*Continued*

Study and teaching

Teachers, politics, and politicians; seminar at Univ. of Rochester. B. Williams. il Sr Schol 84:26T Mr 20 '64

See also

Citizenship, Education for

Anecdotes, facetiae, satire, etc.

Politics and mortal sin; how to raise ten children as God-fearing, parent-honoring Goldwater Republicans. A. B. Heath. il Nat R 16:1147-50 D 29 '64

POLITICAL science literature

Hacking away. Newsweek 61:90+ Mr 11 '63

POLITICAL shibboleths. See Slogans

POLITICAL theory. See Political philosophy; Political science

POLITICAL thought

Challenge to political shibboleths. P. Lisagor. il N Y Times Mag p39+ N 24 '63

Editor-in-chief of democracy. J. M. Burns. Sat R 46:19-20 Ag 3 '63

Fear of passion. J. H. Grainger. Nation 196: 339-42 Ap 27 '63

Freedom or virtue? L. B. Bozell; discussion. Nat R 13:223-5, 283, 327+; 15:191-5, 319 S 25-O 23 '62, S 10, O 8 '63

Goldwater's bombshell. Nation 199:393 N 30 '64

Japan: the kitchen and the garden. A. W. Burks. bibliog f Cur Hist 46:230-7 Ap '64

Paranoid style in American politics; adaptation of address, November 1963. R. Hofstadter. Harper 229:77-82+ N '64

Politics of the possible: the American scene. S. Rousseas and J. Farganis. Nation 196: 240-4 Mr 23 '63; Discussion. 197:inside cover, 93 Ag 24 '63

Rationalism in politics, by M. Oakeshott. Review

Nat R 15:360-2 O 22 '63. H. V. Jaffa

New Repub 148:21-6 F 9 '63. O. Gass

Utopia and its enemies, by G. Kateb. Review

Commentary 37:77-8+ Ap '64. D. H. Wrong

POLITICIANS

Bleed, but bleed inwardly; reactions to outrageous criticism. B. H. Bagdikian. il N Y Times Mag p 10+ Ag 9 '64

Great speeches aren't necessarily good politics. D. S. Broder. il N Y Times Mag p7+ Mr 29 '64

Political pros give the ams a nod. T. Wicker. il N Y Times Mag p28+ Je 9 '63

Shock of political defeat. F. R. Schreiber and M. Herman. il Sci Digest 56:83-6 N '64

See also

Boss rule

Statesmen

POLITICS

Dirty business. M. Phelps. America 110: F 1 '64

Divorce in politics; its meaning in U.S. and abroad. il U S News 54:44-7 Je 3 '63

In defense of politics, by B. Crick. Review

Nat R 15:113-14 Ag 13 '63

Nobody is for poverty. R. Moley. Newsweek 63:82 Ja 27 '64

Politics of hope, by A. Schlesinger, jr. Review

Commentary 36:76-8 Jl '63. L. A. Coser

Politics of textbooks. B. Crick. Commentary 38:67-9 Jl '64

Too much moralizing. America 111:245 S 12 '64

See also

Business—Political aspects

College professors and instructors—Political activities

Conservatism

Economics and politics

Geopolitics

Liberalism

Political campaigns

Political ethics

Political parties—United States

Political science

Presidential campaigns

Television in politics

Women and politics

World politics

Anecdotes, facetiae, satire etc.

And we point with pride... C. Ford. il Field & S 69:6-7+ Ag '64

Blow for freedom; consequences of banning cigarette smoking in 1974. A. F. Loomis. Nat R 16:823 S 22 '64

Political cabarets; source of Berlin's satire. S. Gainham. Atlan 212:95-9 D '63

Political virus smoked out; address. L. L. Terry. Sci N L 85:277 My 2 '64

Scrambled egos. G. Ace. Sat R 47:20 S 19 '64

Bibliography

Politics and ethics. C. C. West. Christian Cent 80:983-4 Ag 7 '63

Quotations, maxims, etc.

Extremism; in view of current campaign, comp. by J. Patnick. N Y Times Mag p35 S 20 '64

Terminology

Anatomy of a new politics. C. D. Bolton. il Nation 198:529-33 My 25 '64

Glossary: ABC's of government. Sr Schol 84:40 F 14 '64

Key words in the worlds news. Sr Schol 83: 42+ O 4 '63

Political lexicon. Sr Schol 85:9 O 21 '64

Words in the news. Sr Schol 85:50+ O 7 '64

POLITICS, Corruption in

Brooke of Massachusetts; a Negro governor on Beacon Hill? E. R. F. Sheehan. Harper 228:41-7 Je '64

Case of the crusading DA. Newsweek 61:26 F 18 '63

Dear citizen or whomever this concerns. J. N. Eller. America 111:794 D 19 '64

Ethics in government: a poisonous atmosphere. V. M. Burns. Cath World 200:78-83 N '64

Highway robbery. J. Wright. il Sat Eve Post 236:19-23 N 30 '63

Highway robbery in Massachusetts; misuse of Federal aid highway program. K. O. Gilmore. Read Digest 85:83-7 D '64

How business sometimes is done in Washington. il U S News 57:30-1 D 21 '64

Illinois legislature: study in corruption; ed. by A. Balk. P. Simon. Harper 229:74-8 S '64

Juggling that hot potato, the political gift. B. H. Bagdikian. il N Y Times Mag p 14-15+ Mr 22 '64

Keeping the faith; indictments of Massachusetts officeholders. Newsweek 63:35 My 25 '64

Korth and Baker. Commonweal 79:213-14 N 15 '63

Last dinosaur wins again. A. Balk. il Sat Eve Post 236:72-3 My 11 '63

Legacy of scandal; Filipino administration. Newsweek 62:39 Ag 5 '63

Lone-wolf guardian of federal morality. H. B. Meyers. il Fortune 69:126-9+ Je '64

Louisiana's wonderful invention. E. Kerr. Harper 227:94-6 O '63

Massachusetts; corruption is commonplace. Time 83:39 My 15 '64

Mess thickens; indictment of F. Furcolo. Newsweek 64:38 O 26 '64

137 indictments; Massachusetts crime commission. il Newsweek 63:38-9 My 18 '64

Part of what was wrong; political corruption in Brazil. il Time 84:22-3 Jl 3 '64

Power game: George Smathers, the golden senator from Florida. R. G. Sherrill. il Nation 199:426-37 D 7 '64

Safari into Washington's netherworld. B. H. Bagdikian. il N Y Times Mag p 12+ Ja 19 '64

Senate shocks a Senate prober. C. Phillips. il N Y Times Mag p20+ Ag 9 '64

Signal corps escutcheon. Nation 198:207 Mr 2 '64

Still more scandal; Massachusetts crime commission indictments of four Democrats. Newsweek 64:40 O 19 '64

Where did all that money come from? S. Karnow. il Sat Eve Post 237:62-3+ O 31 '64

See also

Boss rule

Bribery

Campaign funds

Conflict of interests (public office)

Elections—Corrupt practices

Lobbying

Patronage, Political

POLITICS and art. See Art and politics

POLITICS and business. See Business—Political aspects

POLITICS and Christianity. See Church and politics

POLITICS and education

See also

College students—Political activities

Teachers—Political activities

POLITICS and food. See Food supply—Political aspects

POLITICS and industry. See Industry and state

POLITICS and newspapers. See Newspapers and politics

POLITICS and religion. See Church and politics

POLITICS and science. See Science and state

POLITICS and war
Toward a new politics. J. Cogley. Commonweal 78:37-8 Ap 5 '63

POLITICS in literature
All the king's men: the matrix of experience. R. P. Warren. Yale R 53:161-7 D '63
Computerized convention? concerning Eugene Burdick's novel, The 480. M. S. Evans. Nat R 16:608-9 Jl 14 '64

POLITZ, Alfred
Reader total in doubt? free magazines distort figures. Bsns W p 151 D 14 '63

POLK, Benjamin
Shape of the year 2000. Sat R 48:31+ Ja 23 '65
Tropical climate control techniques. Arch Rec 135:208-10 Ap '64

POLK, James Knox
James K. Polk, eleventh President 1845-1849. F. Freidel. il por Nat Geog Mag 127:102-5 Ja '65

POLK, Sol
King of the discounters. R. Tunley. il por Sat Eve Post 236:28-9 Ap 13 '63

POLL, Bernard
Freedom to browse. Library J 88:1734 Ap 15 '63

POLL tax
Amending the amendment. Reporter 30:12+ F 13 '64
Off with the head tax. K. Crawford. Newsweek 61:34 My 6 '63
Poll tax banned. Sr Schol 84:21 F 7 '64
Twenty-fourth amendment. Cur Hist 46:240 Ap '64
Twenty-fourth amendment. Newsweek 63:27 F 3 '64
Twenty-fourth amendment ratified. Christian Cent 81:165 F 5 '64

POLLACK, Alan. See Reed, C. F. jt. auth.

POLLACK, Jack Harrison
What parents ask most about children. Todays Health 41:24-7+ F '63

POLLACK, Jerome
Health as a fringe benefit. New Repub 149:21-3 N 9 '63

POLLACK, Merrill
Holiday handbook of precious stones. Holiday 33:153-8 Mr '63

POLLACK, Peter
Positive and negative forms in and around the figure. Pop Phot 54:66-7+ My '64

POLLACK, Simeon, and others
Iron absorption: the effect of an iron-deficient diet. bibliog Science 144:1015-16 My 22 '64

POLLACK fishing
Pollock are powderkegs. G. Heinold. il Outdoor Life 131:78-9+ My '63

POLLAIUOLO, Antonio del
Purloined Pollaiuolo panels. il Time 81:85 Mr 15 '63

POLLAK, Louis H.
Anecdote of the young lieutenant. PTA Mag 58:10-12 Ap '64

POLLAK, O. J.
Atherosclerosis. Science 145:1075-6 S 4 '64

POLLAN, Herbert
How to teach your child to remember. Parents Mag 39:54-5+ Mr '64

POLLARD, Dwight D. See Shor, G. G. jr, jt. auth.

POLLARD, Ernest C.
How to remain in the laboratory though head of a department. Science 145:1018-21 S 4 '64
Ionizing radiation: effect on genetic transcription. bibliog Science 146:927-9 N 13 '64
—and Achey, P. M.
Radiation action on DNA in bacteria: effect of oxygen. bibliog Science 146:71-3 O 2 '64

POLLARD, Morris
Germfree animals and biological research. bibliog Science 145:247-51 Jl 17 '64
—See Sueltenfuss, E. A. jt. auth.

POLLARD, Richard A.
Earth problems for space men. N Y Times Mag p28+ N 3 '63

POLLEN
Freeze-dried pollen speeds tree-breeding. Farm J 87:64 Mr '63
Nature of cohesion within pollen tetrads of typha latifolia. J. J. Skvarla and D. A. Larson. bibliog il Science 140:173-5 Ap 12 '63
Organized element; possible identification in orgueil meteorite. F. W. Fitch and E. Anders. bibliog il Science 140:1097-100 Je 7 '63
Pollen wettability as a factor in washout by raindrops. J. E. McDonald. bibliog il Science 143:1180-1 Mr 13 '64

POLLEN, Fossil
Origin of ice ages: pollen evidence from Arctic Alaska. P. A. Colinvaux. bibliog il Science 145:707-8 Ag 14 '64
Palynological investigation of a core from the Biscay abyssal plain. J. J. Groot. bibliog Science 141:522-3 Ag 9 '63
Pollen accumulation rates: estimates from late-glacial sediment of Rogers Lake. M. B. Davis and E. S. Deevey, jr. bibliog il Science 145:1293-5 S 18 '64
Preliminary pollen studies at Lake Zeribar, Zagros mountains, southwestern Iran. W. van Zeist and H. E. Wright, jr. bibliog il Science 140:65-7 Ap 5 '63
Vegetation, climate, and coastal submergence in Connecticut. P. B. Sears. bibliog il Science 140:59-60 Ap 5 '63

POLLET, Joseph
Three more faces of Eve: exhibition at Schoelkopf gallery, New York. L. Campbell. il Art N 63:30+ Mr '64

POLLINATION. See Fertilization of plants

POLLINI, Maurizio
Notes from abroad. C. Reid. Hi Fi 13:12+ Jl '63

POLLITT, Daniel H.
Timid lawyers and neglected clients. Harper 229:81-6 Ag '64

POLLOCK, Jackson
Art. M. Kozloff. Nation 198:151-2 F 10 '64
Art galleries; at the Marlborough-Gerson gallery. R. M. Coates. New Yorker 39:80-4 F 1 '64
Beyond the pasteboard mask; 150 Pollocks at Manhattan's Marlborough-Gerson gallery. il por Time 83:66-9 Ja 17 '64
Flight to freedom. il por Newsweek 63:81 Ja 20 '64
Pollock: the art of a myth. T. B. Hess. il Art N 62:39-41+ Ja '64

POLLOCK, James K.
Public higher education and the needs of government; excerpt from address, April 29, 1963. Sch & Soc 92:45-7 F 8 '64

POLLOCK, James S. McKenzie-. See McKenzie-Pollock, J. S.

POLLOCK fishing. See Pollack fishing

POLLS, Public opinion. See Public opinion polls

POLLUTION, Air. See Air pollution

POLLUTION, Water. See Water pollution

POLLUTION of streams. See Water pollution

POLLY Andrews, class of '33; story. See McCarthy, M.

POLMAR, Stephen H. and Steinberg, A. G.
Dependence of a Gm(b) antigen on the quaternary structure of human gamma globulin. bibliog Science 145:928-9 Ag 28 '64

POLNER, Murray
At best a beginning. Christian Cent 81:806 Je 17 '64
Down on the farm. Commonweal 78:164-5 My 3 '63
Integrated pastime. New Repub 151:25-6 Jl 11 '64

POLO
Every Sunday in Honolulu. il Sunset 132:74 My '64
Polo's new aristocracy moves in; with photographs by J. G. Zimmerman. Sports Illus 18:26-9 F 4 '63
Too busy to grow old. H. G. Earl. il Todays Health 42:42-5+ O '64

POLO Grounds, New York. See Stadiums

POLONIUM
Cigarette radioactivity linked to cancer; effect of polonium. Sci N L 86:105 Ag 15 '64
Polonium-210; a volatile radioelement in cigarettes. E. P. Radford, jr. and V. R. Hunt. bibliog il Science 143:247-9 Ja 17 '64; Discussion. 143:917; 144:366-7, 952-3; 146:86-7 F 28, Ap 24, My 22, O 2 '64
Radioactivity in tobacco. Sci N L 85:70 F 1 '64
Radium-226 and polonium-210 in leaf tobacco and tobacco soil. T. C. Tso and others. bibliog il Science 146:1043-5 N 20 '64
Smoking; is polonium the villain? Time 83:31 Ja 24 '64

POLSHEK, Julie
It's worth mentioning. See issues of House beautiful
Take it easy! See issues of House beautiful

POLSON, Robert E.
Foamed plastics for flat roof insulation. Arch Rec 133:197-8 Je '63

POLT, James M. and Hess, E. H.
Following and imprinting: effects of light and social experience. bibliog Science 143: 1185-7 Mr 13 '64
—See Hess, E. H. jt. auth.
POLYARTHRITIS. See Arthritis
POLYCHAETA. See Marine worms
POLYCYTHEMIA
Red face can mean disease, blood too rich. Sci N L 86:264 O 24 '64
POLYDACTYLISM
Polydactylism in the offspring of mice injected with 5-bromodeoxyuridine. J. A. DiPaolo. bibliog il Science 145:501-3 Jl 31 '64
POLYETHYLENE
Mechanized plasticulture; polyethylene film mulches. il Time 81:75 Ap 19 '63
One bad apple can't spoil this pack. il Farm J 88:44F Je '64
Solid state of polyethylene. B. Wunderlich. il Sci Am 211:80-4+ bibliog(p 154) N '64
POLYGAMY
Christian polygamy? America 112:155 Ja 30 '65
POLYGONATUM. See Solomon's seal
POLYGRAPH
Lie detectors: sleuthing by polygraph increasingly popular; claims of accuracy are unproved. E. Langer. Science 144:395-7+ Ap 24 '64; Discussion. 144:1177-8 Je 5 '64
Lie detectors: trial by gadget. S. Meisler. il Nation 199:159-62+ S 28 '64
See also
Lie detectors
POLYMERIZATION
Guanine: formation during the thermal polymerization of amino acids. C. Ponnamperuma and others. bibliog il Science 143:1449-50 Mr 27 '64
Houses will soon stick together without nails. Sci N L 87:9 Ja 2 '65
Linear polymerization of a gastropod hemocyanin. R. M. Condie and R. B. Langer. bibliog il Science 144:1138-40 My 29 '64
Macromolecular chemistry; address, December 12, 1963. G. Natta. bibliog il Science 147:261-72 Ja 15 '65
Macromolecules. H. Mark. Science 146:1023-4 N 20 '64
POLYMERS
Antigens and enzymes made insoluble by entrapping them into lattices of synthetic polymers. P. Bernfeld and J. Wan. bibliog il Science 142:678-9 N 8 '63
Aromaticity; a key to polymers stable at high temperatures; report of symposium at the Polytechnic institute of Brooklyn. E. J. Vandenberg and C. G. Overberger. il Science 141:176-7 Jl 12 '63
Cross-linking of polymers by radiation; with glossary. G. Adler. bibliog il Science 141: 321-9 Jl 26 '63
Electroconductive polymers. J. H. Lupinski and K. D. Kopple. bibliog il Science 146: 1038-9 N 20 '64
Hampered vinyl polymerization by embedding biological objects. A. A. Hofer and E. Lautenschlager. Science 146:69 O 2 '64
Inorganic polymers; adapted from two lectures presented in a panel discussion on the Properties of materials. G. Barth-Wehrenalp and B. P. Block. bibliog il Science 142: 627-32 N 8 '63
Microstructure of polymers by tritium autoradiography. J. D. Moyer and R. J. Ochs. bibliog il Science 142:1316-18 D 6 '63
Polymer similar to polydeoxyadenylate-thymidylate in various tissues of a marine crab. T. Y. Cheng and N. Sueoka. bibliog il Science 143:1442-3 Mr 27 '64
Polymer structure: cross-linking of a polybenzimidazole. J. K. Gillham. bibliog il Science 139:494-5 F 8 '63
Polymers: thermal stability; report on symposium. P. B. Stickney. Science 143:704 F 14 '64
Stereospecific polymerization. A. D. Ketley and F. X. Werber. bibliog il Science 145: 667-73 Ag 14 '64
Tracks of charged particles in high polymers. R. L. Fleischer and P. B. Price. bibliog il Science 140:1221-2 Je 14 '63
See also
Silicones
POLYMORPHISM
High-pressure B-type polymorphs of some rare-earth sesquioxides. H. R. Hoekstra and K. A. Gingerich. bibliog il Science 146:1163-4 N 27 '64
High pressure polymorphism in cesium. H. T. Hall and others. bibliog il Science 146: 1297-9 D 4 '64
Polymorphism in isopropyl alcohol. G. S. Ross and others. bibliog Science 141:1043-4 S 13 '63
POLYMORPHISM (biology)
Color polymorphism in Pacific tree frogs. L. E. Resnick and D. L. Jameson. bibliog il Science 142:1081-3 N 22 '63
Hemoglobin polymorphism: its relation to sickling of erythrocytes in white-tailed deer. H. Kitchen and others. bibliog il Science 144:1237-9 Je 5 '64
Molar size sequences and fossil taxonomy. S. M. Garn and others. bibliog il Science 142:1060 N 22 '63
Serum albumin: polymorphism in man. G. Efremov and M. Braend. bibliog il Science 146:1679-80 D 25 '64
POLYNESIA
Footloose in Polynesia. H. Sutton. Sat R 47:32-3 Ap 18 '64
POLYNESIAN cookery. See Cookery, Polynesian
POLYNESIANS
Polynesian origins. E. N. Ferdon, jr. bibliog il Science 141:499-505 Ag 9 '63; Reply with rejoinder. R. C. Suggs. 142:1252+ D 6 '63
POLYNUCLEOTIDES. See Nucleotides
POLYOMA virus. See Tumor viruses
POLYPEPTIDES. See Peptides
POLYPHENE oxide. See Plastics
POLYPHENOLS. See Phenols
POLYPS
See also
Portuguese man-of-war
POLYRIBOSOMES. See Nucleoproteins
POLYSACCHARIDES
Biosynthesis of streptococcal cell walls; a rhamnose polysaccharide. L. D. Zeleznick and others. bibliog il Science 140:400-1 Ap 26 '63
Cerebral white matter: selective spread of pneumococcal polysaccharides. S. Levine. bibliog il Science 139:605-6 F 15 '63
Extracellular polysaccharides of algae: effects on life-support systems. B. G. Moore and R. G. Tischer. bibliog il Science 145:586-7 Ag 7 '64
Lipopolysaccharide of the gram-negative cell wall. M. J. Osborn and others. bibliog il Science 145:783-9 Ag 21 '64
Presipitins in the rabbit produced by protein polysaccharide from bovine nasal cartilage. N. Di Ferrante. bibliog il Science 143:250-2 Ja 17 '64
Proteinpolysaccharide in connective tissue: inhibition of phase separation. H. Weinstein and others. bibliog il Science 142: 1073-5 N 22 '63
See also
Cellulose
POLYTENE chromosomes. See Chromosomes
POLYTETRAFLUOROETHYLENE. See Teflon
POLYUNSATURATED fats. See Oils and fats, Edible
POLYURETHANE. See Urethans
POLYURIDYLIC acid
Coding ambiguity in cell-free extracts of chlamydomonas. R. Sager and others. bibliog il Science 140:304-6 Ap 19 '63
Reticulocyte protein synthesis: response of ribosome fractions to polyuridylic acid. I. B. Weinstein and others. bibliog il Science 140: 314-16 Ap 19 '63
POLYVINYL fluoride. See Vinyl fluoride
POLYVISION. See Projection apparatus
POMANDERS
How to make a pomander. J. B. Brimer. il Flower Grower 50:56 D '63
POMEGRANATES
Pomegranates like it in California. il Sunset 131:272 O '63
See also
Cookery—Fruit
POMERANTZ, Edward
Billiards with a beauty treatment. Holiday 36:110+ S '64
POMERANTZ, Martin A.
International years of the quiet sun, 1964-65. bibliog Science 142:1136-43 N 29 '63
POMEROY, Kenneth B.
AFA's third landownership study; Tarheel territory. Am For 69:16-19+ O '63
Forester's notebook. Am For 69:3+ F; 68 My '63; 70:35 Ap; 42 Jl '64
Lake states research inspected. Am For 70:33 Ja '64
Poplar portrait. pors Am For 69:4+ Mr '63
What AFA members think! Am For 70:6+ My '64
POMEROY, Ralph
Confession; To words; poems. Poetry 103: 161 D '63

POMMER, A. M. See Truesdell, A. H. jt. auth.
POMMERENING, Otto
Street maintenance, then and now. Am City 78:8 F '63
POMONA, Calif.
How one city solved its downtown problems. il U S News 54:76-7 Mr 11 '63
Pomona sets a pattern; downtown pedestrian mall. H. A. Faull. il Am City 79:77-8 Ja '64
Pomona's city hall will use precast concrete, glass. il Am City 79:114 Mr '64
POMPADOUR, Jeanne Antoinette (Poisson) marquise de
Pompadour, by J. Levron. Review
Time por 82:100 D 13 '63
POMPANO fishing
Sport with pompano. G. Heinold. il Outdoor Life 132:22+ O '63
POMPEII
Pompeii. W. Jashemski. il Natur Hist 73:30-41 D '64
They are still digging up Pompeii. il Sunset 132:79+ Ap '64
POMPIDOU, Georges
Letter from Paris: summary of address. New Yorker 40:143-4 Mr 7 '64
about
Desire under the helm. il por Time 83:34 My 1 '64
POND lilies. See Water lilies
PONDEROSA pine. See Pine
PONDS
Better fishing in your farm pond. Suc Farm 61:64-5 Jl '63
Invitation to a fish fry. R. Starnes. Field & S 69:21-2+ O '64
Is your trouble too many fish? R. K. Davis. Farm J 88:34J Jl '64
New kind of pond. B. A. Roth. Farm J 87: 64D O '63
Planning a farm pond. K. Beauchamp and L. E. Zeman. il Suc Farm 61:36-7 Je '63
Ponds that hold water; waterproof pond's bottom. G. Smith. il Farm J 87:A2 Ap '63
See also
Lakes
Water gardens
Clearing
Black plastic sheets control pond weeds. S. T. Runkel. il Suc Farm 62:98 S '64
Home ponds create a problem for public water supplies; algae infestations. Am City 79:172 O '64
PONIES
One of our children is a pony. J. Robbins and J. Robbins. il Good H 156:66+ My '63
PONNAMPERUMA, Cyril
Re-creating the pre-life earth. il por Time 81:59 Je 7 '63
—and others
Guanine: formation during the thermal polymerization of amino acids. bibliog Science 143:1449-50 Mr 27 '64
—See Young, R. S. jt. auth.
PONSELLE, Rosa
Rosa Ponselle: a grand tradition. F. Robinson. il pors Mus Am 83:14-15 Ap '63
PONSOT, Marie
Paeonia souvenir de Maxime cornu, incidentally; poem. Poetry 104:149-53 Je '64
PONS-Winnecke comet. See Comets
PONT, John
New man in New Haven. por Newsweek 61: 94 Mr 18 '63
Yale finds a coach. W. N. Wallace. il pors Sat Eve Post 236:74-7 O 12 '63
PONT-a-Mousson (industrial company) See Steel industry and trade—France
PONTCHARTRAIN, LAKE
Trailer down to New Orleans. K. Ferguson. il Motor B 113:84-5+ Ja '64
PONTE, Maurice
Who's who in foreign business. por Fortune 68:76 S '63
PONTÉ, Pierre Viansson-. See Viansson-Ponté, P.
PONTECORVO, Bruno
Key to other worlds; using a neutrino telescope. A. Ewing. il Sci N L 84:99 Ag 17 '63
PONTIAC, Mich.
Water supply
Intermunicipal cooperation means assured water supply. H. G. Parker. il Am City 79: 120-1 Ap '64
PONTIFICAL biblical institute, Rome
Rector magnificus. America 108:849 Je 15 '63
PONTIFICAL institute of medieval studies, Toronto
Research into Christian wisdom. P. F. Pocock. il America 111:38-41 Jl 11 '64
PONTIUS Pilate. See Pilate, P.
PONTOON bridges. See Bridges, Pontoon
PONY. See Ponies
PONY-tail plants. See Beaucarnea
POODLE rocket project. See Rockets, Atomic powered
POOL (game) See Billiards
POOL hustlers. See Gamblers
POOL rooms
Family pool parlor; photographs. N Y Times Mag p56 Je 9 '63
POOLE, Frazer G.
Conference on libraries and automation. ALA Bul 57:658-9 Jl '63
POOLE, Stafford
Tomorrow's seminaries. America 110:86-8+ Ja 18 '64
POOLEY, Max E.
Not cricket, Caroline! Pop Electr 21:38 Jl '64
POOLS. See Garden pools; Swimming pools
POOLS (gambling) See Gambling—Great Britain
POOR, Peggy
View from the Canal. New Repub 150:13-14 F 22 '64
POOR
New definition of our poor. H. P. Miller. il N Y Times Mag p 11+ Ap 21 '63
See also
Poverty
Tramps
Iran
Middle East paradox, the beggar rich. F. M. Esfandiary. il N Y Times Mag p22+ N 3 '63
Latin America
As the slum goes, so goes the Alliance; shantytowns of Latin America. J. Gross. il N Y Times Mag p 12-13+ Je 23 '63
Migrating masses. il Time 83:41 F 7 '64
Mexico
Pedro Martinez, by O. Lewis. Review
Commentary 38:46-50 Jl '64. K. Botsford
Tender violence of Pedro Martínez; excerpts from Pedro Martínez, a Mexican peasant and his family. O. Lewis. il Harper 228:54-60 F '64
Sicily
State of the Sicilian civilian. G. Gersh. il Sat R 47:33+ Je 6 '64
United States
Attack on poverty. Commonweal 79:415 Ja 10 '64
Birth control and the poor: a solution; Mecklenburg County, N.C. J. Shepherd. il Look 28:63-7 Ap 7 '64; Same abr. Read Digest 85:111-14 Ag '64
Can we abolish poverty? Sat Eve Post 237:74 S 5 '64
Focus on poverty. B. L. Masse. America 110:69 Ja 18 '64
Frontier of service; address, June 8, 1964. R. S. Shriver. America 111:14-16 Jl 4 '64
Grass-roots war on poverty; Southern consumers' co-operative chartered as a holding company. America 111:280 S 19 '64
High cost of ending poverty in U.S. il U S News 56:97-8 Ja 27 '64
How to help the poor; war on poverty. Farm J 88:94 Je '64
I know about the Negroes and the poor. R. J. Dwyer. Nat R 15:517-18+ D 17 '63; Discussion. 16:81-4 Ja 28 '64
Illiteracy; the key to poverty! B. Asbell. McCalls 91:96-7+ F '64
In the midst of plenty, by H. Bagdikian. Review
Christian Cent 81:990 Ag 5 '64. E. Kruuse
Commonweal 80:615-16 S 4 '64. J. Stanley
Invisible Americans. B. H. Bagdikian. il Sat Eve Post 236:28-33+ D 21 '63
It will be a long war. B. D. Nossiter. Reporter 30:20-1 Mr 26 '64
Johnson vs poverty. C. Jencks. New Repub 150:15-18 Mr 28 '64
Journey into the mind of the lower depths. R. Coles. New Repub 150:11-12 F 15 '64
Latest plan: full pay for no work. il U S News 56:84 Ap 6 '64
Let us begin: an invitation to action on poverty. J. K. Galbraith. Harper 228:16+ Mr '64
Let's not have a war against poverty. Fortune 69:75 F '64
Marketing the poverty programs. M. Harper, jr. Sat R 47:65-6 My 9 '64
Mountains of poverty; photographs. M. Hunter. N Y Times Mag p 12-13 My 17 '64

POOR—United States—*Continued*
Night comes to the Cumberlands, by H. M. Caudill. Review
Science 141:889-92 S 6 '63. J. Walsh
One big reason why some people are poor; results of Armed forces qualification test. il U S News 56:98-9 F 24 '64
One-fifth of a nation; photographs. N Y Times Mag p 10-11 Mr 22 '64
Other Washington. W. V. Shannon. Commonweal 79:738-9 Mr 20 '64
Paupers: one tenth of our nation. W. Lissner. Cath World 198:357-64 Mr '64
Permanent poor; lesson of eastern Kentucky. H. M. Caudill. Atlan 213:49-53 Je '64; Discussion. 214:30 Ag '64
Perplexing problem of poverty. Am City 79:7 Ap '64
Politics of poverty. D. Cater. il Reporter 30: 16-20 F 13 '64
Poverty & passion. Time. 83:25 F 7 '64
Poverty in America; excerpt from annual report of Council of economic advisers. il Mo Labor R 87:285-91 Mr '64
Poverty in suburbia. Nation 200:1 Ja 4 '65
Poverty is also a human issue. Christian Cent 81:981-2 Ag 5 '64
Poverty, pyramids and eggs. J. O'Gara. Commonweal 79:740 Mr 20 '64
Poverty: skeleton in the national closet. il Sr Schol 84:6-8+ Mr 13 '64
Poverty U.S.A. il Newsweek 63:19-20+ F 17 '64; Same abr. with title Poor amid prosperity. Read Digest 84:90-7 Je '64
Poverty, U.S.A. B. L. Masse. il America 109:73-4+ Jl 20 '63
Psychiatrists and the poor. R. Coles. Atlan 214:102-6 Jl '64
Reflections on poverty in America. H. M. Caudill. il PTA Mag 58:20-2 Je '64
Republican plan for fighting poverty. U S News 56:10 Mr 9 '64
Seeing the unseen. Christian Cent 81:387-8 Mr 25 '64
Shriver moves into the front rank; drive on poverty. A. Lewis. il N Y Times Mag p21+ Mr 15 '64
Sickness and poverty. America 110:307 Mr 7 '64
Statistical gaps in the war on poverty; improved statistics for Appalachia; excerpt from address. H. P. Miller. Mo Labor R 87:887-8 Ag '64
Sudden drive on poverty, why? il U S News 56:36-9 Ja 20 '64
There's already a war on poverty. il U S News 56:46 Ap 13 '64
Three wars; poverty, civil rights & the cold war; address, September 24, 1964. C. F. Phillips. Vital Speeches 30:757-9 O 1 '64
T.R.B. from Washington; the war on poverty. New Repub 150:2 Mr 14 '64
Vicious circle of poverty; with editorial comment. il Bsns W p 38-40+, 96 F 1 '64
War against the poor. Christian Cent 80:291-2 Mr 6 '63; Discussion. 80:620+ My 8 '63
War on poverty. America 111:771 D 12 '64
War on poverty. New Repub 149:3-4 D 28 '63
War on poverty. B. L. Masse. America 110: 192-3 F 8 '64; Discussion. 110:556 Ap 25 '64
War on poverty. G. Myrdal. New Repub 150:14-16 F 8 '64
War on poverty. H. Hazlitt. Newsweek 63: 74 Ap 6 '64
War on poverty, by H. H. Humphrey. Review
Sat R 47:33-4 Ag 15 '64. H. David
War on poverty: challenge to publishing. R. H. Smith. Pub W 185:38 Mr 30 '64
War on poverty; symposium. il Wilson Lib Bul 38: 38:832-44+ Je '64
Wasted Americans, by E. May. Review
Commentary 38:64-6 Jl '64. H. J. Gans; Reply with rejoinder. H. S. Falck. 38: 12+ D '64
Commonweal 80:522-3 Jl 24 '64. N. Hentoff
What happened to a family LBJ visited: W. D. Marlow of Rocky Mount, N.C. U S News 57:10 S 7 '64
What's being done: the poverty program; legislative developments; summary of address. R. B. Minnis. Pub W 185:38-9 My 4 '64
Where are the poor? New Repub 151:4 D 19 '64
Where $1-billion will go; LBJ's anti-poverty program. Bsns W p29-30 Mr 21 '64
Who are the American poor? E. K. Faltemayer. il Fortune 69:118-19+ Mr '64
Who gets the cash in the war on poverty. il U S News 56:33-5 Mr 30 '64
Who the poor are. New Repub 150:4-5 F 15 '64
Who the poor are and ways to help them. Life 57:4 Jl 31 '64
See also
Church and social problems
Economic assistance, Domestic

POOR Bitos; drama. See Anouilh, J.

POOR connection; story. See Giardina, T.

POOR relief. See Charities; Public welfare

POOR Richard; drama. See Kerr, J.

POORMAN, Fred C.
Pittsburgh pushes for more mercuries. Am City 79:131 O '64

POP art. See Modernism (art)

POPCORN
Maybe you can plant popcorn for silage; loop-hole in feed grain program. Farm J 87:31 Je '63
Popcorn explosion; with recipes. M. Kaytor. il Look 27:66 S 24 '63

POPCORN poppers. See Corn poppers

POPE, Dick
Babes in a swampland. W. B. Furlong. il por Sports Illus 19:66-70+ O 21 '63
Superswamp; Cypress gardens. R. Bongartz. il pors Sat Eve Post 236:78-81 N 23 '63

POPE, George Andrew, 1901-
Their hats are in the ring. W. Tower. il por Sports Illus 20:26-32 My 4 '64

POPE, James S.
Urbanization and higher education. NEA J 52:16-18 Mr '63

POPE, L. S.
Cow herd and replacements. Suc Farm 61: 31 D '63

POPE, Thomas, and Osypowski, Thomas
High-resolution photography. il Sky & Tel 29:52-6 Ja '65

POPE, W. Kenneth
Bishop answers N.C.C. critics. Christian Cent 81:1262 O 14 '64

POPE-HENNESSY, James
Daisy Fellowes. Vogue 143:148-9+ My '64

POPE John XXIII national seminary. See Theological schools

POPENOE, John
Fairchild tropical garden. Horticulture 42: 32-3+ D '64

POPES
Fateful conclave. America 108:874 Je 22 '63
Journalists report the council. G. Wills. Nat R 15:572-4 D 31 '63; Correction. 16: 124 F 11 '64
Next pope. America 108:878 Je 22 '63
Path to follow. il Time 81:40-2+ Je 28 '63; Same abr. with title Pope Paul VI. Read Digest 83:88-92 S '63
See also
Papacy
Papal audiences
also names of popes, e.g. Paul VI, pope

Coronation

Pope is crowned. America 109:32 Jl 13 '63
Pope is crowned with the ancient reminder: thus passes the glory of the world. il Life 55:55-8 Jl 12 '63

Election

After John XXIII? E. V. Kuehnelt-Leddihn. Nat R 14:531 Jl 2 '63
And now the search begins for the new pope. R. B. Kaiser. Life 54:57-8 Je 21 '63
Cardinals convene. Christian Cent 80:795 Je 19 '63
Election trends. Time 81:46+ Je 14 '63
Letter from Vatican City. X. Rynne. New Yorker 39:42+ Je 15; 74+ Jl 20 '63
Vatican: from eighty-two, a choice to make. il Newsweek 61:58-60 Je 17 '63
We have a pope? America 108:894 Je 29 '63

Infallibility

Infallible but uninformed. C. Davis. America 109:457 O 19 '63

Primacy

Papal primacy at Vatican II. America 111: 343 S 26 '64
Primacy and collegiality. America 110:476 Ap 4 '64
Word. V. P. McCorry. America 110:614-15 My 2 '64

Supremacy

See Popes—Primacy

POPILLIA japonica. See Japanese beetles

POPKIN, Henry
Theatre. Vogue 143:28 Ja 15; 22 F 15; 66 Mr 15; 54 Ap 15; 40 Je; 144:32 Jl; 40 Ag 15; 102 S 1; 80 S 15; 112 O 1; 94 O 15; 64 N 15 '64; 145:27 Ja 15 '65

POPKIN, John
Talent scout; Hickory house. New Yorker 39: 24-6 F 23 '63

POPKIN, Roy
Castro's crash program in education. Sat R 47:64-5+ Mr 21 '64

POPOVERS. See Bread

POPOVIĆ, Cvjetko
Murder that started World war I. R. S. Feuerlicht. il por Sat Eve Post 237:80-1+ Je 27 '64

POPP, Raymond A.
Hemoglobin loci: mice classified for their HB and SOL alleles. bibliog Science 140:893-4 My 24 '63

POPPER, Frank
Movement & light in today's art. UNESCO Courier 16:12-17+ S '63

POPPER, Karel, and others
Ion-exchange removal of sodium chloride from water with calcium hydroxide as recoverable regenerant. bibliog Science 141: 1038-9 S 13 '63

POPPER, Susanne
Music for Shakespeare. Opera N 28:8-12 My 2 '64

POPPIES
Do this dividing in August. il Sunset 133: 154+ Ag '64
Matilija, the poppy giant. il Sunset 133:201 S '64
Oriental poppies. A. M. Murphy. il Pop Gard 14:41+ Jl '63
Poppies for color. M. M. Taylor. il Pop Gard 15:16-17 S '64
They'll start to bloom in November; iceland poppies. il Sunset 131:282+ O '63

POPPINO, Rollie E.
Imbalance in Brazil. Cur Hist 44:100-5+ F '63

POPPLESTONE, Don
Decorating clinic. Bet Hom & Gard 41:66-7 F; 82 My '63
Inspiring new colors, lively but livable. Bet Hom & Gard 41:42-7 Ag '63

POPPY, John
Author. Sat R 46:46 Ap 20 '63
(ed) See Sternberg, B. Search for faith

POPPY mallow
Poppy mallow. R. Donahue and M. Donahue. il Horticulture 41:416 Ag '63

POPULAR culture
Culture change and the planner. A. N. B. Garvan. Ann Am Acad 352:33-8 Mr '64
See also subhead Popular culture under names of countries, e.g. Great Britain—Popular culture

POPULAR gardening (periodical) See Popular gardening and living outdoors (periodical)

POPULAR gardening and living outdoors (periodical)
Garden potpourri. M. E. O'Brien. Pop Gard 14:4 Ap '63; 15:6 Jl '64
Living outdoors; health, relaxation, family fun. M. E. O'Brien. il Pop Gard 14:49 My '63

POPULAR government. See Democracy

POPULAR medicine. See Medicine, Popular

POPULAR music. See Music, Popular (songs, etc)

POPULAR photography (periodical)
Critical new year. B. Downes. il Pop Phot 54:46 Ja '64
1965 photography directory and buying guide; showmanship. il Pop Phot 55:69-132 D '64
Popular photography's international exhibits. Pop Phot 54:94 My '64
Sixth-seventh annual travel photo handbook. il Pop Phot 52:131-46 Ap '63; 54:131-46 Ap '64

POPULAR songs. See Music, Popular (songs, etc)

POPULARITY
Brilliant student can be popular, if . . . A. J. Tannenbaum. il PTA Mag 57:4-6 Je '63
I believe. L. Felber. Seventeen 23:177 N '64
I don't want to be left out; questions and answers. A. Wood. Seventeen 22:170-1 F '63
Popularity explosion. M. Miller. Seventeen 22: 142+ F '63

POPULATION
Asian population conference. F. C. Madigan. America 110:188-90 F 8 '64; Correction. 111:202 Ag 29 '64
Genetic regulatory mechanisms at the population level in man. P. A. Parsons. bibliog Science 146:924-5 N 13 '64
Intensification of demographic studies, research, and training; statement, April 3, 1963; with text of resolution. J. B. Bingham. bibliog f Dept State Bul 49:28-32 Jl 1 '63
Patterns and populations; basic problems of population biology. P. R. Ehrlich and R. W. Holm; discussion. Science 138:733-4; bibliog 139:236+ N 9 '62, Ja 18 '63
Politics of population; blueprint of program advocated by the United States. R. N. Gardner. il Sat R 46:10-12+ S 7 '63
Population control; concerning report by the National academy of sciences. New Repub 148:7 Ap 27 '63; Reply. L. H. Day. 149:31 Jl 6 '63
Where the world's people live. il Sr Schol 83: 44 O 4 '63; 85:48 O 7 '64
See also
Birth control
also subhead Population under names of countries, states, cities, e.g. Latin America—Population

Overpopulation

Are smaller families coming back in style? W. Best. il Parents Mag 39:64-5+ N '64
Can science offset the population explosion? excerpt from address. A. M. Weinberg. il Sci Digest 53:17-22 F '63
Cybernetics of population control. H. Hoagland. Bul Atomic Sci 20:2-6 F '64
Food and people. A. McCormack. Commonweal 80:79-82 Ap 10 '64; Reply. R. J. Allen. 80:237 My 15 '64
For population control. C. R. Ross. Am For 69:63 Je '63
If you scare easily. Am City 79:7+ O '64
Live and let live; excerpts from Hod-carrier. G. W. Johnson. il Atlan 213:90-2+ F '64
Looking to the future. Nat Parks Mag 38:14-15 O '64
Obsolete assumptions; excerpts from address, March 1963. S. L. Udall. il Recreation 56:359-61 O '63
Population explosion demands worldwide action. J. A. O'Brien. il Christian Cent 81: 43-6 Ja 8 '64
Population planning. Commonweal 81:531-2 Ja 22 '65
Priority for population. Sci N L 84:381 D 14 '63
Question of morality. Christian Cent 80:571-2 My 1 '63; Discussion. 80:833 Je 26 '63
Self-corrective for the population explosion? Time 83:56 F 28 '64
Solving the inhuman equation; can arms control end the population crisis? G. Clark. Sat R 46:15-16+ F 16 '63
Threatening crowd. M. Mannes. Ladies Home J 81:16+ N '64
Tomorrow's world, population: too many? il Sr Schol 83:18-20 S 27 '63
Too many people in the world? il U S News 55:60-4 S 16 '63
Use of population as weapon. W. Davis. il Sci N L 83:115 F 23 '63
What women can do for peace. J. Fischer. il Harper 226:14+ Ap '63; Same abr. Read Digest 82:55-9 Je '63; Discussion. Harper 226:12+ Je '63
Why Americans must limit their families. M. Mead. Redbook 121:30+ Ag '63; 122:14+ Ja '64
See also
Population, Increase of

Statistics

Facts and figures of the Americas. il Américas 16:42-3 Ap; 46-7 Jl '64
Population. K. Davis. il Sci Am 209:62-71 bibliog(p306) S '63

POPULATION, Increase of
Atlantic report. Atlan 214:4+ D '64
By 1966 half of us will be under twenty-five. B. Bliven. il N Y Times Mag p47-8+ D 8 '63
Catholics and population. J. O'Gara. Commonweal 78:534 S 6 '63
Double by 1986; population explosion is strongest in tropical South America. il Time 84:35 Jl 17 '64
Europe's initial population explosion. W. L. Langer. bibliog f Am Hist R 69:1-17 O '63
Fertility and economic growth; India. Sci Am 210:56 Je '64
Food and people. A. McCormack. Commonweal 80:79-82 Ap 10 '64; Reply. R. J. Allen. 80:237 My 15 '64
Heat limit. Time 84:85 N 13 '64
How population explosion is changing the U.S; interview. P. M. Hauser. il U S News 57:58-63 Ag 31 '64
Largest population gain. Sci N L 83:190 Mr 23 '63
Man and more men: the population prospects; reprint. P. M. Hauser. Bul Atomic Sci 20: 4-8 Je '64
Man, land and food, by L. R. Brown. Review U S News il 56:28-31 Ja 6 '64
No more room; U.N.'s Food and agriculture organization report. Newsweek 61:36 F 4 '63

POPULATION, Increase of—*Continued*
Outlook for world population. J. M. Stycos. Science 146:1435-40 D 11 '64
Politics of population: a blueprint for international cooperation; address, May 4, 1963. R. N. Gardner. Dept State Bul 48:906-14 Je 10 '63
Politics of population; concerning United Nations resolution on population growth and economic development. R. N. Gardner. il Sat R 46:10-12+ S 7 '63
Population. K. Davis. il Sci Am 209:62-71 bibliog(p306) S '63
Population and parenthood. T. K. Burch. Commonweal 80:328-31 Je 5 '64
Population boom called world's biggest problem. Sci N L 86:142 Ag 29 '64
Population dilemma; address, June 27, 1963. K. Brandt. Vital Speeches 29:629-31 Ag 1 '63
Population explosion. A. McCormack. il America 110:482-5 Ap 4 '64
Population growth. Am City 78:7 F '63
Population growth and the Alliance for progress; address, November 9, 1964. T. C. Mann. Dept State Bul 51:807-10 D 7 '64
Population growth rate highest in history. Sci N L 86:377 D 12 '64
Population myths. D. H. Wrong. Commentary 38:61-4 N '64
Population: new U.S. interest in offering assistance reveals lags in underdeveloped nations. D. S. Greenberg. Science 143:1016-17 Mr 6 '64
Population: planning group hears encouraging reports on efforts to start Latin American programs. D. S. Greenberg. Science 144:513-15 My 1 '64; Reply with rejoinder. W. D. Bellamy. 144:1409-10 Je 19 '64
Population planning: 1963 marked by reduction of controversy and shift in government attitude. D. S. Greenberg. Science 142: 1554-6 D 20 '63; Reply. L. C Pearson. 143: 1124 Mr 13 '64
Population time-bomb. Nat Parks Mag 38:17 D '64
Race against hunger. J. O'Gara. Commonweal 81:62 O 9 '64
U.S. population rising 7,400 persons per day. Sci N L 84:31 Jl 13 '63
What the population explosion means to you. P. Appleman. Ladies Home J 80:59+ Je '63
What's ahead in the population boom; interview. R. M. Scammon. il U S News 54:68-71 My 6 '63
See also
Population—Overpopulation
POPULATION, Limitation of. See Population
POPULATION commission. See United Nations —Population commission
POPULATION pressure. See Population—Overpopulation
POPULATION reference bureau, incorporated
Double by 1986; population explosion is strongest in tropical South America. il Time 84:35 Jl 17 '64
POPULATIONS, Animal. See Animal populations
PORADA, Edith
Reviews. Natur Hist 72:4-11 N '63
PORATH, Jerker
Biochemical laboratory at Uppsala. V. K. McElheny. il por Science 144:1323-5 Je 12 '64
PORCELAIN. See Pottery
PORCELAIN figurines. See Figurines
PORCH furniture. See Furniture, Outdoor
PORCHES
Closing in porch opens up opportunities. il Am Home 67:88+ My '64
Increase your living space. il Ladies Home J 80:112 Mr '63
More Japanese ideas cross the Pacific: engawa hallway. il Sunset 130:76 F '63
Two more ways to gain living space by pushing out the rear walls. il Sunset 130:114 Ap '63
Two new versions of the old-fashioned porch. il House B 105:76-9 Jl '63
PORFIROMYCIN. See Antibiotics
PORGY fishing
Obliging porgy. G. Heinold. il Outdoor Life 132:10-11+ Ag '63
PORK
See also
Bacon
Cookery—Meat
Trichina and trichinosis
PORK barrel legislation. See United States—Appropriations and expenditures
PORK industry. See Meat industry and trade
PORNOGRAPHY. See Immoral literature and pictures; Obscenity (law)
PORPHYRIA cutanea tarda. See Hematoporphyria
PORPOISES. See Dolphins (mammals)
PORT ARTHUR, Manchuria
Coal for the fleet that had to die. L. J. R. Cecil. bibliog f Am Hist R 69:990-1005 Jl '64
PORT authority of New York. See Port of New York authority
PORT authority of Toledo-Lucas County. See Toledo-Lucas County port authority
PORT CANAVERAL, Fla.
Big plans for Canaveral. R. A. Winer. il Motor B 114:85 N '64
PORT EVERGLADES, Fla. See Fort Lauderdale, Fla.—Harbor
PORT of New York authority
Port in a storm. J. Sanderson. il Flying 75:24-8 Ag '64
Towers that top them all; World trade center. il Bsns W p29 Ja 25 '64
PORT-OF-SPAIN, Trinidad
Trinidad pleasure. D. Messinesi. Vogue 145: 121 Ja 15 '65
PORT TOWNSEND, Wash.
Little old New York in the West. H. Sutton. il Sat R 46:44-5 O 19 '63
PORT WASHINGTON, N.Y.
Built to fit the site. G. Gewecke. il Am City 78:120-1 Je '63
PORTABLE electric tools; Portable phonographs; etc. See Electric tools, Portable; Phonographs, Portable; etc.
PORTABLE pension plans. See Pensions, Industrial
PORTABLE vises. See Vises
PORTALING; story. See Hay, J.
PORTANOVA, Joseph
Portrait sculpture of Joseph Portanova. J. Lovoos. il por Am Artist 29:38-43+ Ja '65
PORTEOUS, Alvin C.
Seminary and the racial crisis. Christian Cent 81:147-8 Ja 29 '64
PORTER, Cole
Celebrity register. C. Amory. por McCalls 90:152 Ap '63
Cole mine. il por Time 84:71 S 11 '64
Cole Porter. T. Prideaux. por Life 57:46-46A O 30 '64
Fall of a meteor. por Newsweek 64:100 O 26 '64
Man of two worlds. il por Time 84:90 O 23 '64
Obituary
Mus Am por 84:60 N '64
Words and music by the top. il N Y Times Mag p30-1 Je 9 '63
PORTER, David Dixon
Long blade, short scabbard; excerpts from Incidents and anecdotes of the Civil war. Am Heritage 14:91 F '63
PORTER, Don K.
Smokey comes up roses. Am For 70:4+ Mr '64
PORTER, Eliot
Eliot Porter. P. Caulfield. il por Mod Phot 28:52-7+ F '64
PORTER, Fairfield
Education of Jasper Johns. Art N 62:44-5+ F '64
about
Fairfield Porter: minimum of melodrama. M. Benedikt. il Art N 63:36-7+ Mr '64
Point of departure. il por Newsweek 61:62-3 F 11 '63
They paint; you recognize. il por Time 83: 74-5+ Ap 3 '64
PORTER, Frank C.
New Harry Bridges. New Repub 149:5-6 O 26 '63
Retraining's brave promise. New Repub 148: 14-16 Ap 13 '63
So you want to work for the government. Sat R 47:21-3+ Ap 11 '64
PORTER, Gary
Then how about Koch? Nation 198:206-7 Mr 2 '64
PORTER, J. R.
Challenges to editors of scientific journals; address, March 19, 1963. bibliog Science 141: 1014-17 S 13 '63
300 years of storing words; excerpt from address. Sat R 48:92-5 Ja 2 '65
PORTER, Katherine Anne
Her legend will live. Ladies Home J 81:58-9 Mr '64
Paris; a little incident in the rue de l'Odéon. Ladies Home J 81:54-5 Ag '64
Violeta; story. Redbook 124:36-7 D '64

PORTER, Katherine Anne—*Continued*
about
Celebrity register. C. Amory. por McCalls 90: 184 Ap '63
Katherine Anne Porter and the art of rejection, by W. L. Nance. Review
Harper 229:146-8 N '64. C. Gordon
Ship of fools & the critics. T. Solotaroff; discussion. Commentary 35:247-50 Mr '63
PORTER, Keith R. See Ledbetter, M. C. jt. auth.
PORTER, LuLu
LuLu II. por Newsweek 62:54 Ag 19 '63
PORTER, Lyman W.
Where is the organization man? bibliog f Harvard Bsns R 41:53-61 N '63
PORTER, Norman
How many bones! how many; poem. Nation 197:328 N 16 '63
PORTER, Sylvia (Field)
Sylvia Porter's advice to young wives about money; questions and answers. Redbook 124:62-3+ N '64
about
Celebrity register. C. Amory. por McCalls 90:187 Ap '63
PORTER, Trudy Ann
Teen travel talk. Seventeen 24:20+ Ja '65
PORTER, William Samuel
Hydrogen energy levels: perturbation caused by proton structure. Science 143:1324-5 Mr 20 '64
PORTER, William Sydney
October and June; story; excerpt from The complete works of O. Henry. Read Digest 82:237-8 F '63
PORTER, Willis P.
America's first Peace corps. Sat R 46:45 Jl 20 '63
PORTERFIELD, Bill
L.B.J. country; excerpt from The President's homeland. Sat Eve Post 237:28-32+ O 3 '64
PORTERFIELD, Jeanne
Travel-film career girls. il por Pop Phot 54: 127+ My '64
PORTERFIELD, Ralph, and Borcherding, J. R.
At 17,387 now, aiming for 18,000. Suc Farm 61:66+ Mr '63
PORTERS
A. Philip Randolph. M. Kempton. New Repub 149:15-17 Jl 6 '63
PORTIS, Bernard. See Rich, S. U. jt. auth.
PORTLAND, Ore.
Dialogue in Portland. W. N. Cate. Christian Cent 80:745 Je 5 '63
June is a fine month to visit Portland, the river city. il Sunset 132:74-91 Je '64
Portland eyes '72 Olympics. Bsns W p 132 Ap 13 '63
Architecture
New girl moves into downtown Portland; Standard insurance co. building. il Fortune 71:194 Ja '65
Description
Neighborhood where I live. J. C. Hunt. il Am For 70:36-7+ N '64
Education
Good-by to homework; new plan to finish out-of-class work during school day at Marshall high school. il Newsweek 65:39 Ja 4 '65
Galleries and museums
Death of a cathedral; Forestry building. S. Churchill. il Am For 70:28-30 O '64
Hotels, restaurants, etc.
Hotel planned as urban focal point. il Arch Rec 136:172-3 O '64
Lewis and Clark centennial exposition, 1905
Neighborhood where I live. J. C. Hunt. il Am For 70:36-7+ N '64
Libraries
Books for Roosevelt Grady; a volunteer library effort of Multnomah County library. R. McConnell and F. Postell. il Library J 89:3384-6 S 15 '64
Newspapers
Odds in Portland; demise of the Reporter. Time 83:58 Mr 6 '64
Out in Oregon; Portland reporter. Newsweek 63:54 Mr 9 '64
Portland: how good is a strike? il Time 81: 44 Mr 8 '63
Reader relations. Newsweek 63:61 Mr 16 '64
Resurrection in Portland; Reporter struggles back to life. Time 83:46 Mr 13 '64

PORTLAND cement. See Cement
PORTLAND cement industry. See Cement industry and trade
PORTLAND vase
Enigmatic urn. N. McKendrick. il Horizon 5:63-5 N '63
PORTRAIT drawing
Drawing the head & face. S. L. Dieffenbach. il Sch Arts 63:39 Mr '64
Kalman Aron, draughtsman. J. Lovoos. il Am Artist 28:30-5+ Mr '64
PORTRAIT of an American; drama. See Hark, M. and McQueen, N.
PORTRAIT of the artist; story. See Jensen, E.
PORTRAIT painting
Artist looks at children; eight canvases from the Chester Dale collection. K. Kuh. il Sat R 46:35-8 O 14 '63
Figure paintings of A. Henry Nordhausen. L. Schmeckebier. il Am Artist 29:34-9+ F '65
George Chinnery in India; excerpts from George Chinnery, 1774-1852. H. Berry-Hill and S. Berry-Hill. il Antiques 83:449-51 Ap '63
Oldest art. il Newsweek 61:105 My 13 '63
Painting a portrait of the President. E. De Kooning. il Art N 63:37+ Sum '64
Pilgrim's progress: Horace Bundy and his paintings. H. O. Shepard. il Antiques 86: 445-9 O '64
Portrait sketches of Norman Rockwell. N. Kent. il Am Artist 28:38-43+ S '64
Portraits of Leonard Bahr. L. L. Winslow. il Am Artist 28:26-31+ D '64
Some greats look themselves over; excerpts from Self-portraits, by M. Gasser. il Life 55:94-9 N 29 '63
Talent comes in a bottle; glass-encased portraits. il Ebony 19:44+ Ag '64
See also
Miniature painting (portraits)
PORTRAIT sculpture
Image distilled from 800 pictures; bronze head by R. Berks. il Life 56:28-31 Ja 3 '64
Living faces of our past. il Life 57:72-8 Jl 3 '64
Portrait sculpture of Joseph Portanova. J. Lovoos. il Am Artist 29:38-43+ Ja '65
PORTRAITS
Personal business; family portrait, how much and how to pick artists. Bsns W p 125-6 My 9 '64
Portrait-illustrations. il Design 64:118-19 Ja '63
Reprints by rubbing; relief rubbed portraits. A. L. Ochs. il Design 66:16-18 N '64
See also
Conversation pieces (pictures)
Photography—Portraits
Portrait painting
Silhouettes
Exhibitions
Age of portraits; exhibition at Cleveland museum of art. il Newsweek 62:105-6 O 7 '63
History in portraits; World's fair exhibit called Four centuries of American masterpieces. il Time 83:66-7 Je 26 '64
PORTRAITS, American
Impressions in paint and words. R. Banks. il Dance Mag 37:40-1 Mr '63
Isaac Sheffield, Connecticut limner. E. deN. Mayhew. il Antiques 84:589-91 N '63
PORTRAITS, British
Duchess and William Byrd. T. Thorne. il Antiques 84:562-5 N '63
Leith Hill Place, home of Wedgwoods and Darwins. C. V. Wedgwood. pors Antiques 83:442-3 Ap '63
PORTRAITS, Pen. See Character sketches
PORTRAITS of children. See Children as models
PORTRAITURE. See Photography—Portraits; Portrait painting
PORTS
Season for seashore and seaports. M. Gough. il House B 105:46+ Jl '63
Today's port, a trade and transport hub. H. C. Brockel. Ann Am Acad 345:95-102 Ja '63
See also subhead Harbor under names of cities, e.g. Boston—Harbor
PORTSMOUTH, N.H.
Portsmouth loses its mainstay. il Bsns W p33 N 28 '64
PORTSMOUTH, Ohio
Police
Portsmouth's police chief. il Ebony 18:144+ Ap '63

PORTUGAL
See also
Algarve
Earthquakes—Portugal
Prisons—Portugal
United Nations—Portugal

Colonies

Against the last white strongholds. il Time 82:30 Ag 9 '63
Arms ban; embargo on arms shipments to Portugal for use in her African territories. il Newsweek 62:36 Ag 12 '63
Assembly urges independence for Portuguese territories. il U N Rev 10:16-28 Ja '63
Dead or alive. Newsweek 62:40+ S 30 '63
Defying the U.N; Salazar of Portugal. U S News 55:24 S 9 '63
Dictator's lament. Newsweek 62:44 Ag 26 '63
Gathering storm; African independent states against Portuguese colonialism and South Africa's racial apartheid. Newsweek 62:47-8 Jl 29 '63
Lone crusader. Nation 197:446-7 D 28 '63
Portugal: little country with big troubles. il U S News 55:46-8 Ag 26 '63
Portuguese territories. U N Rev 11:16-19 Ja '64
Portuguese territories and the United Nations. P. Wohlgemuth. bibliog f Int Concil 545:3-68 N '63
Record of the month; Portuguese territories. UN Mo Chron 1:53-4 Je '64
Security council's attention drawn to situation in Portuguese territories: with resolution on Portuguese territories. U N Rev 10:9-11+ Ap '63
Too late in the day; summary of address. A. de O. Salazar. Time 82:24 Ag 23 '63
Topsy-turvy land. Nat R 15:90+ Ag 13 '63
U.S. restates views on colonialism and Portuguese African territories; statement, March 12, 1963. S. R. Yates. Dept State Bul 48:581-3 Ap 15 '63
U.S. withdraws proposal on Angola opposed by Afro-Asian group; statements, December 18 and December 20, 1962. A. Gore; J. B. Bingham. Dept State Bul 48:105-7 Ja 21 '63
See also
Angola

Description and travel

Fabulous, feudal Portugal. P. Coffin. il Look 28:72-85+ My 19 '64
Let's travel to Portugal. S. Barry. il Mlle 59:335-7 Ag '64
Portugal's Mondego Valley. D. Momsen, jr. il Travel 121:56-8+ Mr '64
Visit to Portugal. E. Goble. Arch Rec 133:9 My '63

Foreign relations

United States

Our about-face on African policy; bases on the Azores. G. M. Houser. Christian Cent 80:675-6 My 22 '63
Portugal: little country with big troubles. il U S News 55:46-8 Ag 26 '63

History

Bibliography

Articles and other books received; Spain and Portugal, comp. by C. J. Bishko. See issues of American historical review

Politics and government

Price of the Azores; tr. from the Portuguese by G. Rabassa. H. Galvao. Nation 197: 432-3 D 21 '63

PORTUGUESE
Fabulous, feudal Portugal. P. Coffin. il Look 28:72-85+ My 19 '64

PORTUGUESE cookery. See Cookery, Portuguese

PORTUGUESE EAST AFRICA. See Mozambique

PORTUGUESE furniture. See Furniture. Portuguese

PORTUGUESE GUINEA
Another Goa? Newsweek 61:54 My 6 '63

PORTUGUESE in Africa
Portuguese way in Africa. H. Kay. il Fortune 69:112-15+ Ja '64

PORTUGUESE language in Brazil
Snafu; use of initials for words. Time 83: 27 Ja 10 '64

PORTUGUESE man-of-war
Beware the man-of-war. il Time 83:48 Mr 27 '64
Danger, don't tread on us! il Life 57:87-8 Jl 3 '64
Deadly fisher. C. E. Lane. il Nat Geog Mag 123:388-97 Mr '63
Nature note. Sci N L 86:284 O 31 '64
Tremoctopus violaceus uses physalia tentacles as weapons. E. C. Jones. bibliog il Science 139:764-6 F 22 '63

PORTUGUESE WEST AFRICA. See Angola

PORTUONDO, Emilio Nuñez. See Nuñez Portuondo, E.

PORTZ, Philip
Elderly and medical care. America 110:256-8 F 22 '64

POSA, Joseph, family
Poignant tissue of white lies. R. Stolley. il Life 54:19 F 22 '63

POSIN, Dan Q.
Other suns, other planets, but is there other life? Todays Health 42:56-9 N '64

POSITIONS, Applications for. See Applications for positions

POSITRON scintillation camera. See Cameras; Photography, Medical

POSITRONS
Spot positrons from space. Sci N L 85:39 Ja 18 '64

POSNER, David
Colloquy; poem. Nation 198:636 Je 22 '64
High school in Buffalo; poem. Sat R 46:67 O 26 '63
Jamaican ministry; poem. Sat R 47:27 D 26 '64
Mount Athos; poem. Poetry 104:23-4 Ap '64
On a recent protest against social conditions; poem. New Yorker 40:56 N 28 '64

POSSONY, Stefan T.
Peace that can be. America 112:124-7 Ja 23 '65
Pentagon courts disaster; excerpts. U S News 55:42-3 Ag 5 '63

POSSUMS. See Opossums

POST, Emily Price
On the fringe. H. Frankel. Sat R 47:40 Mr 21 '64

POST, Troy Victor
Golden castles of Troy V. Post. S. H. Brown. il pors Fortune 71:154-9+ Ja '65

POST (Denver) See Denver post

POST, New York. See New York post

POST, Washington. See Washington post and Times herald

POST cards
Classification of authors' cards. R. H. Woodward. il Hobbies 69:116-17+ N '64
Comics are collectible. B. Rutledge. il Hobbies 68:120-1 Je '63
$ in color post cards. J. Foldes. il Pop Phot 55:70-1 Jl '64
Picture post card. B. Finnegan. See issues of Hobbies
Post card album. Mrs G. Adcock. il Hobbies 68:118-19 Ap '63
Post card gold mine in your home town. F. Korotkin. il Hobbies 69:120-1+ My '64

POST office department (United States) See United States—Post office department

POST office inspection service. See United States—Post office department

POSTAGE stamps
Artists for stamps; design for special stamp to commemorate the founding of the National academy of science. A. Frankfurter. il Art N 62:23+ Sum '63
Audubon mystery. J. K. Terres. il Audubon Mag 66:91 Mr '64
Commemorative stamp for John Muir. il Nat Parks Mag 38:15 Ap '64
Design of new duck stamp; Federal migratory bird hunting stamp. il Outdoor Life 134:51 Ag '64
Fishy issue; fishermen pushing for a stamp. il Sports Illus 21:8+ Jl 6 '64
Frasconi work is exhibited; he designs new U.S. stamp. P. A. Bennett. il Pub W 184: 86+ Jl 1 '63
Kennedy coin, a Kennedy stamp. il U S News 55:11 D 23 '63
Letter from Paris; annual philatelic exhibition and market. Genêt. New Yorker 39:162 S 28 '63
Mr Barnard's slip; high price for post office Mauritius stamp. Time 82:78 O 11 '63
New JFK stamp. J. Klein. il Look 28:32 Je 16 '64
Philately of Baden-Powell. H. D. Thorsen, jr. il Hobbies 69:99+ N '64
Postage stamp blow-ups. il Sunset 131:85+ D '63
Renaissance in botanical drugs. J. A. Mirt. il Todays Health 41:42-5+ My '63
Shells on postage stamps. A. G. Melvin. il Hobbies 69:130+ My '64
Should Christmas stamp be more Christian? il U S News 57:8 D 21 '64
Slavic stamp. T. Koch. il Opera N 28:6-7 F 29 '64

POSTAGE stamps—*Continued*
Stamp act; prize for stamp to commemorate anniversary of National academy of sciences. il Time 81:90 My 17 '63
Stamps. H. Herst, jr. See issues of Hobbies
Stamps. S. L. Burns. See issues of Senior scholastic
Stamps against hunger. il UNESCO Courier 16:30-1 My '63
Stamps for art's sake. A. Shuster. il N Y Times Mag p30+ S 20 '64
Stamps U.S.A. E. Metzl. il Am Artist 28: 44-9+ Mr '64
Stories in stamps. il UNESCO Courier 17:32 Ap '64
Tonga celebrates its unique gold pocket money with the world's only round stamps. il Life 55:44 O 11 '63
See also
Covers (philately)

Anecdotes, facetiae, satire, etc.
Constitution for the New order of druids. Christian Cent 81:1543 D 9 '64

Collectors and collecting
Basic guide to stamp collecting. Good H 156: 140 Mr '63
Dealer's record price for stamp error; threepenny bonanza. il Life 55:46+ N 29 '63
More than child's play; worldwide market. il Time 81:96 Je 7 '63
Postage due; Ward collection. Time 83:46 Ja 3 '64
Stamps: fine hobby, no gold mine. il Changing T 17:19-20 F '63
Stamps from space. il Life 54:65-6+ My 17 '63
Ten million hoping for a mistake. J. Keats. il N Y Times Mag p60+ My 5 '63

POSTAL censorship
ABPC opposes new postal screening bill. Pub W 184:149 Jl 8 '63
Battle against mail-order pornography. D. Wharton. Read Digest 84:147-8+ F '64
Conviction for obscenity in private letter. H. F. Pilpel. Pub W 184:31 Jl 29 '63
Eyes on your mail. America 110:272, 329 F 29, Mr 14 '64
House passes bill to stop morally offensive mail. Pub W 186:25-6 Ag 3 '64
Low blow. Nation 198:255 Mr 16 '64
Mail industry fights back; legitimate mail advertisers try to halt the flow of obscenity through the mail. J. B. Halper. America 108:260-1 F 23 '63; Reply. G. Cunningham. 108:697 My 18 '63
Red letter days; measures for avoidance of Communist propaganda. Reporter 29:20+ Jl 18 '63
Their appointed rounds; detention of mail. New Repub 150:6 Mr 14 '64

POSTAL employees
Big step in unionizing the government. il U S News 54:6 Ap 1 '63
Job performance of federal mail sorters by age. J. F. Walker. bibliog f il Mo Labor R 87:296-300 Mr '64

POSTAL laws and regulations. See Postal service—Laws and regulations

POSTAL rates
United States
Cargo carriers seek slash in mail rates. L. L. Doty. Aviation W 80:43 Ap 13 '64
How to use the mails right. il Changing T 17:23-4 N '63
Post office stops use of educational materials; more specific identifications. Pub W 186: 150 Jl 13 '64
Weathervane (cont) R. G. Miner. Flower Grower 50:6 Ap '63

POSTAL savings banks
Postal savings: America's poorest buy. R. L. Smith. il Nation 199:140-1 S 21 '64

POSTAL scales. See Scales (weighing instruments)

POSTAL service
How other countries get the mail on time. il U S News 54:78-82 Je 17 '63
See also
Mail handling
Postal censorship
Postal savings banks

Laws and regulations
Can the post office read your mail? U S News 56:7 Mr 2 '64
Clean out your mailbox! Christian Cent 81:6 Ja 1 '64
Mail industry fights back; legitimate mail advertisers try to halt the flow of obscenity through the mail. J. B. Halper. America 108:260-1 F 23 '63; Reply. G. Cunningham. 108:697 My 18 '63
Post office refuses to modify new rules; publishers complaints. Pub W 186:23 Ag 17 '64
Red letter days; measures for avoidance of Communist propaganda. Reporter 29:20+ Jl 18 '63

Great Britain
Letter from London; postmen and post-office staffs. M. Panter-Downes. New Yorker 40:69-70 Ag 1 '64
Unlettered multitude; slowdown of nation's postmen. il Newsweek 64:36 Ag 3 '64

United States
First zip, now vim for mail. Bsns W p 188+ N 14 '64
How many numbers can you memorize? ZIP numbers of your regular correspondents? il U S News 55:16 Jl 15 '63
How to use the mails right. il Changing T 17:23-4 N '63
Mail service; address, September 10, 1964. J. A. Gronouski. Vital Speeches 30:755-7 O 1 '64
Mail-service cutback: is it blackmail? U S News 54:8 My 6 '63
New digit system to speed mail deliveries. Pub W 183:56-7 Je 17 '63
Notes and comment; Zip code. New Yorker 39:15 Ag 24 '63
Now, self-service at the post office. il U S News 58:16 Ja 18 '65
Numbers and more numbers; ZIP, Zone improvement plan. il U S News 54:10 My 13 '63
Post office extends zip code to parcels. Pub W 186:25 Ag 3 '64
What ails the post office? S. E. Cohen. Nation 197:364-7 N 30 '63
ZIP: timesaver or numerical neurosis? Newsweek 62:26 Jl 15 '63
See also
Air mail service
Parcel post
Postal employees

POSTCARDS. See Post cards

POSTELL, Frances. See McConnell, R. jt. auth.

POSTERIZATION. See Photography—Printing processes

POSTERS
Ads & posters. il Design 64:202-3 Je '63
Britain edges out of the ice age; advertising campaign for central-heating systems. A. Carthew. il N Y Times Mag p60+ D 13 '64
Britain's politics, and Britain's future. il N Y Times Mag p 10-11 O 20 '63
Eight great posters. E. Metzl. il Am Artist 27:21-6 My '63
England warns its youth: Britain's anti-smoking ads; with editorial comment. R. L. Dean. il America 108:245, 253-5 F 23 '63
Greetings in macaroni. F. M. Major. il Design 64:194 Je '63
Mucha's divine Sarah. il N Y Times Mag p 17 Je 2 '63
Project-a-plan instant signs. D. M. Swartwout. il Pop Mech 120:144-6 O '63
Public muse; exhibition of 400 posters from Pavillon Marsan of the Louvre. P. Schneider. il Art N 63:46-8+ O '64

Exhibitions
La belle epoque; Paris exhibit covering 1870-1914. il Time 84:70-1 Jl 10 '64
Gaiety was the word for them; French poster-advertisements at the Gallery of modern art. J. Canaday. il N Y Times Mag p20-1 Ag 2 '64
Posters as weapons; German posters at New school for social research. N Y Times Mag p 19 Ap 28 '63

POSTGATE, Raymond
About Scotch whisky. Holiday 33:100-1+ My '63
English drinking habits. Holiday 33:87-8+ F '63
Reluctant patriot. Holiday 36:12+ N '64
Travel in Germany. Holiday 36:131-8 O '64

POSTMARKS
See also
Covers (philately)

POSTMEN
Wonderful world of mail carriers. B. Pearman Farm J 88:67 My '64

POSTURE
Comforting truth about exercise. il Ladies Home J 80:134+ Ap '63
Do we sit? no, we collapse; new designs for sitting. S. Wright. il N Y Times Mag p26+ Ap 19 '64
Girls, be a concertina. il Newsweek 61:69-70 Je 10 '63

POSTURE—*Continued*
Poor posture; how to improve it. L. W. Sauer. il PTA Mag 59:17-18 S '64
Someone is watching you. il Seventeen 23: 146-7 F '64
What you can do about your pupils' posture. W. A. Wesley and others. il NEA J 52:12-14 N '63

POSTURE, Yoga. See Yoga

POT-au-feu. See Stew

POTASH
Canada's 100-billion-dollar potash pile. L. Elliott. il Read Digest 84:144-6+ My '64

POTASSIUM
Potassium vs. sodium; new heart disease treatment. Sci N L 86:309 N 14 '64

POTASSIUM amide
Reversibility of reaction of potassium with liquid ammonia. E. J. Kirschke and W. L. Jolly. bibliog il Science 146:45-6 Ja 1 '65

POTASSIUM bromide
Pulse radiolysis of potassium bromide solutions. B. Cercek and others. bibliog il Science 145:919-20 Ag 28 '64

POTASSIUM content of soils. See Soils—Potassium content

POTASSIUM in the body
Body composition: relative in vivo determinations from potassium-40 measurements. J. E. Christian and others. bibliog il Science 140:489-90 My 3 '63
Lysosomes in the renal papillae of rats: formation induced by potassium-deficient diet. A. B. Morrison and others. bibliog il Science 142:1066-8 N 22 '63
Potassium and sodium content of tissues of hamsters and ground squirrels during hibernation. J. S. Willis. bibliog il Science 146: 546-7 O 23 '64
Specificity of potassium-activated phosphodiesterase of escherichia coli. M. F. Singer and G. Tolbert. bibliog il Science 145:593-5 Ag 7 '64

POTATO chips
How to be in the chips. il Bet Hom & Gard 42:105 My '64

POTATO throwers; story. See Stone, A.

POTATOES
Light-induced inhibition of potato tuber sprouting. D. H. Dinkel. bibliog il Science 141:1047-8 S 13 '63
See also
Cookery—Vegetables

History

Europe's initial population explosion. W. L. Langer. bibliog f Am Hist R 69:1-17 O '63
Potatoes from the Incas. W. A. Buck. il Horticulture 43:40-3 Ja '65

Marketing

He sells spuds in a count pack. J. Russell. il Farm J 87:50D D '63
Now, ship potatoes in bulk cars. G. Lorang. il Farm J 87:54 Ap '63

POTATOES, Dried
Here are some unusual ways to use instant potatoes. Sunset 130:137-8 F '63
How good are dehydrated potatoes? Consumer Rep 28:384-5 Ag '63
Packaged potatoes cheat family of vitamin C. Sci N L 83:248 Ap 20 '63

POTATOES, Sweet. See Sweet potatoes

POTEET, Rena
My miniature rooms. por Hobbies 68:116-17+ N '63

POTENTIOMETERS
Exalted pot. F. H. Frantz, sr. il Pop Electr 21:71-2+ D '64
Gemini potentiometer calibration test ended. Aviation W 80:51 Je 29 '64

POTICNY, J. V.
All about alternators. Motor B 111:34-5+ Mr '63

POTOMAC RIVER
Board of engineers holds Potomac Basin hearings. Nat Parks Mag 37:19 O '63
Eastern River basins. A. W. Smith. Nat Parks Mag 37:2 Jl '63
Exaltation at the smokehole. B. Gilbert. il Sports Illus 20:76-82+ Ap 27 '64
Next national park? E. Palmer. il Travel 120: 32-5 Ag '63
People's river; remarks, May 15, 1964. J. A. Carver, jr. il Am For 70:22-5+ N '64
President and the Potomac. A. W. Smith. Nat Parks Mag 38:2 Je '64
Time for a change. Nat Parks Mag 38:2+ Ja '64

POTOMAC VALLEY
One site saved; Merrywood. New Repub 149:6 N 30 '63

POTPOURRI
Dried flowers and potpourri. il House & Gard 125:102-3+ Je '64

POTTED plants. See Plants, Potted

POTTER, Beatrix
Beatrix Potter's code writing. L. Linder. il Horn Bk 39:140-55 Ap '63
Imaginary correspondence; B. Potter and a present day children's book editor. R. Godden. Horn Bk 39:369-75 Ag '63

POTTER, Charles Francis
Moncure Daniel Conway at South place chapel. W. S. Smith; reply. S. D. Wakefield. Christian Cent 80:468 Ap 10 '63

POTTER, Daniel
Tomorrow; story. Redbook 121:56-7 My '63

POTTER, David M.
Captor of Crazy Horse. Sat R 46:38 F 9 '63

POTTER, Fred H.
Booksellers can sell to libraries. Pub W 185:125-8 Je 8 '64

POTTER, J. L. and O'Brien, R. D.
Parathion activation by livers of aquatic and terrestrial vertebrates. bibliog Science 144: 55-7 Ap 3 '64

POTTER, Jeffrey
Finding by the referee; story. New Yorker 40:204+ N 7 '64
This thing about Frank. New Yorker 39:70-4 Ag 10 '63

POTTER, Mary C. See Bruner, J. S. jt. auth.

POTTER, Nancy A. J.
One rich friend; story. Yale R 53:237-47 D '63

POTTER, Philip
How LBJ got the nomination. Reporter 30:16-20 Je 18 '64
Johnson; the first hundred days. New Repub 150:6-8 Mr 7 '64

POTTER, Rye
Four bookstores in the Southwest and the West. Pub W 185:39-44 Ja 13 '64

POTTER, Stephen
Story of my ear. Opera N 29:26 Ja 2 '65
Who's afraid of Virginia Woolf? Am Rec G 29:924-7 Ag '63
Words only. See issues of American record guide

POTTER, Van Rensselaer
Society and science; adaptation of address. bibliog Science 146:1018-22 N 20 '64

POTTER, Vilma. See Mullin, H. jt. auth.

POTTERS marks. See Pottery—Marks

POTTERY
Centering as dialogue; excerpt from Centering: in pottery, poetry, and the person. M. C. Richards. il Craft Horiz 24:31-3+ Jl '64
Ceramics. il Craft Horiz 24:34-60 My '64
Ceramics and enameling art. il Design 65: 38-40 S '63
Cup that cheers. il House & Gard 124:28-9 O '63
Eighteenth-century porcelain in Seattle. il Antiques 85:80-5 Ja '64
Four ceramists of Hawaii. J. Lovoos. il Am Artist 27:66-73+ Je '63
Identification of Liverpool porcelain of the early period, 1756-1765. K. Boney. il Antiques 86:728-31 D '64
Rarities in ceramics. R. Davidson. il Antiques 83:258+ Mr '63
Where to look for hard-to-find China; matching services. il Good H 157:165 N '63
See also
Ceramic sculpture
Glazes and glazing

Collectors and collecting

Rewards of collecting. J. T. Chorley. il Antiques 86:432-6 O '64

Decoration

Relief-decorated ceramics. R. E. Taggart. il Antiques 83:430-3 Ap '63

Exhibitions

22nd ceramic national. il Craft Horiz 23:12-19+ Ja '63

Marks

Marks on German porcelain. G. W. Ware. il Hobbies 69:90-1 Mr '64

Technique

Beginner's pottery project: hanging lamps. il Sunset 131:161+ O '63
Craftsman & teacher. W. Farrell. il Sch Arts 63:28-30 N '63
German salt glazing. A. Garzio. il Craft Horiz 23:20-2 Mr '63
Hamada, a Japanese folk potter. il Am Artist 28:50-1 F '64
Making pottery on the beach. il Sunset 130: 100-1 Ap '63

POTTERY—Technique—*Continued*
Miró, Artigas; their new ceramics. D. Ashton. il Craft Horiz 24:24-33+ Ja '64
Shugen Inouye: potter. J. S. Eagle. il Craft Horiz 23:33-5+ N '63
This is ceramics; excerpts from Art today. R. Faulkner and others. il Design 65:22-5+ S '63
Workshop, four-hand throwing. R. Burkhart. il Craft Horiz 23:54-5 My '63

POTTERY, American
Artistic marriage? William Wyman's homage to Robert Frost. D. P. Shultz. il Sch Arts 62:27 F '63
David Gil's Bennington potters. N. Nelson. il Craft Horiz 24:34-5 Mr '64
F. Carlton Ball, a California potter. J. Lovoos. il Am Artist 28:50-5+ Je '64
Haiku & Frost. W. Wyman. il Sch Arts 62: 25-6 F '63
Lenox takes a fast boat for china; sale of fine dinnerware throughout the world. il Bsns W p68-70 Ja 2 '65

Exhibitions

See Pottery—Exhibitions

POTTERY, Chancay. See Pottery, Peruvian

POTTERY, Danish
Wildlife has a place on the Christmas plates of Denmark. C. T. Hubbard. il Audubon Mag 66:368-9 N '64

POTTERY, English
English porcelain collection at Williamsburg; M. G. Kaufman collection of eighteenth-century porcelain. J. M. Graham, 2d. il Antiques 87:73-7 Ja '65
Rewards of collecting. J. T. Chorley. il Antiques 86:432-6 O '64
Staffordshire on American tables; the Collamore evidence. C. Fennelly. il Antiques 84:75-9 Jl '63
Wares of Thomas Whieldon. R. E. Taggart. il Antiques 83:207-11 F '63
See also
Staffordshire ware
Wedgwood ware

POTTERY, French
See also
Sèvres porcelain

POTTERY, Garden. See Garden ornaments

POTTERY, German
Colossal for the medium: Meissen porcelain sculptures. C. C. Dauterman. il Antiques 85:214-17 F '64
German salt glazing. A. Garzio. il Craft Horiz 23:20-2 Mr '63
J. G. Herold and the hidden pleasures of Meissen chinoiserie; excerpts. J. M. Dennis. il Antiques 85:558-64 My '64
Marks on German porcelain. G. W. Ware. il Hobbies 69:90-1 Mr '64
Rococo retrospective; exhibition of Bustelli figurines at Bavarian national museum, Munich. il Time 82:40-1 Ag 30 '63
Rosenthal's new look. il Time 81:90 Mr 29 '63

POTTERY, Greek
See also
Vases, Greek

POTTERY, Italian
See also
Majolica

POTTERY, Japanese
Primitives of Japan, a legacy in clay; Jomon pottery. S. Noma. il Natur Hist 72:38-45 Mr '63
Shugen Inouye: potter. J. S. Eagle. il Craft Horiz 23:33-5+ N '63

POTTERY, Mexican
Pottery snails of Tonala. A. G. Melvin. il Hobbies 69:130+ Jl '64
Shopping for Puebla pottery; Talaveran ware. Sunset 132:46 Mr '64

POTTERY, Mycenaean
Site of Mycenean civilization discovered in Turkey. Sci Digest 53:59 Mr '63

POTTERY, Persian
Village pottery in Iran. R. M. Carless. il Craft Horiz 23:34-5 Jl '63

POTTERY, Peruvian
Forgotten potters of Chancay. il Américas 16: 40-1 Je '64
Masterpieces from Peru; Nathan Cummings collection at Metropolitan museum; with editorial comment. F. L. Phelps. il Américas 16:inside cover, 7-16 D '64

POTTERY, Venezuelan
Pottery of Venezuela. H. Neumann. il Craft Horiz 23:32-3+ My '63

POTTERY industry
David Gil's Bennington potters. N. Nelson. il Craft Horiz 24:34-5 Mr '64
Design for a worldwide market. il Bsns W p47-8+ My 18 '63
See also
Lenox, incorporated

POTTERY kilns. See Kilns

POTTHOFF, Carl J.
First aid. See issues of Today's health
Suddenly you're involved! Todays Health 42:26-9+ Je '64

POTTHOFF, E. H. Jr, and Peacock, M. E.
Fluorescents instead of ornaments. Am City 79:126+ O '64

POTTING soils. See Soils, Potting

POTTOS
Potto born in captivity; letter. T. Grand and others. Science 145:663 Ag 14 '64
Visiting in perodicticus. U. M. Cowgill. il Science 146:1183 N 27 '64

POTTS, Jean
Just like Jessica; story. Redbook 120:150-74 F '63

POTTS, Willis J.
We gave Diane back her life. Read Digest 85:97-100 N '64

POTVIN, Gilles
Place des arts: the festival. Mus Am 83:15-16 S '63

POULENC, Francis
Art of Francis Poulenc. A. Cohn. por Am Rec G 30:622-3 Mr '64
Francis Poulenc 1899-1963. A. Hughes. por Mus Am 83:20 F '63
In memoriam, 1899-1963: three by Poulenc. por Am Rec G 29:510-11 Mr '63
Last French composer? with selective discography. R. Gelatt. il por Reporter 28: 52-4+ Mr 28 '63
Merit of Poulenc. I. Kolodin. il por Sat R 46: 49-50+ F 23 '63
Music to my ears; American opera society's production of Dialogues of the Carmelites. Sat R 47:24 F 1 '64
Music to my ears; Poulenc premieres. I. Kolodin. Sat R 46:53 Ap 27 '63
Musical events. W. Sargeant. New Yorker 39:107-8+ Ap 20 '63
Musical events; concert performance of Poulenc's Dialogue des Carmélites, in Carnegie Hall. W. Sargeant. New Yorker 39:94-6 Ja 25 '64
Nuns on the Hudson; Hudson Valley international cultural center. J. W. Freeman. Opera N 28:26 S 28 '63
On records; Stabat mater; motets. Opera N 29:35 D 26 '64
Poulenc puzzle. il por Time 81:83-4 Ap 19 '63
Vespers and dialogues; American opera society's performance of Dialogues des Carmélites. J. W. Freeman. Opera N 28: 33 F 15 '64

POULIN, A. Jr
October poem. Commonweal 81:45 O 2 '64
Peter; poem. Commonweal 81:222 N 13 '64
To: EP (K) poem. Commonweal 79:107 O 18 '63

POULSON, Evelyn, and others
Teratogenic effect of 5-hydroxytryptamine in mice. bibliog Science 141:717 Ag 23 '63

POULTER, Thomas C.
Sonar signals of the sea lion. Science 139: 753-5 F 22 '63

POULTRY
Birth of a chick; photographs. Sci Digest 55:8-11 Mr '64
Layers can compete on diversified farms. Farm J 87:44E S '63
Poultry; ed. by D. Braun. See issues of Farm journal
Poultry news (cont of) Poultry. See issues of Farm journal
We chart your choice in holiday birds. Sunset 131:168 N '63
What's new and outlook for. See issues of Successful farming
See also
Cookery—Poultry

Diseases and pests

Breakthrough in CRD control? Farm J 87: 50 O '63
Doctor to Long Island ducks. il Ebony 19:76-8+ S '64
Knock-out punch for CRD. Farm J 88:50H My '64
TB-like germ from fowl. Sci N L 83:171 Mr 16 '63
They're out to whip CRD. D. Braun. Farm J 87:58P-58Q Ap '63
We're closing in on a killer; leukosis. B. Hardy. Farm J 87:41 Jl '63

POULTRY—*Continued*

Egg production

Even hens are dieting now; One-to-one balanced egg. Consumer Rep 29:215 My '64
For ten years, 260 eggs per bird. J. Bickers. il Farm J 88:36B Je '64
Georgia guns for first in eggs. Farm J 88:67-8 O '64
Long-day production from short-day birds; with light flashes. D. Braun. Farm J 87:34 Je '63
When to replace layers. Suc Farm 61:84 O '63
Will the egg giants push you out? D. Braun. il Farm J 87:38-9+ O '63

Feeding

How to cut feed costs 7¢ a dozen. Farm J 88:62 F '64
How to keep pesticides out of eggs. J. Russell and D. Seim. Farm J 88:51 S '64
Toxin-producing aspergillus isolated from domestic peanuts. U. L. Diener and others. bibliog il Science 142:1491-2 D 13 '63
You can prevent cracks. Farm J 87:52 My '63

Molting

See Molting

Watering

Now, a self-cleaning waterer. il Farm J 88:50B My '64

POULTRY, Effect of light on. See Light—Physiological effects

POULTRY, Experiments on. See Animal experimentation

POULTRY, Frozen

Court decision on stuffed turkeys. Consumer Rep 29:516-17 N '64
Freezy turkey in quarters. B. G. LaRoche. il Farm J 88:65 Ja '64
Stuffed turkeys and stuffed pounds; frozen ready-stuffed turkey. Consumer Rep 29:53 F '64

POULTRY breeding

Science takes over the henhouse; Heisdorf & Nelson farms. il Bsns W p70-2 Mr 16 '63

POULTRY brooders and brooding

Four new ideas for brooding chicks. T. Wood and A. Phelps. il Farm J 88:55 Ap '64

POULTRY cages. See Poultry houses—Equipment

POULTRY farm management

Six profit stretchers for layers. C. L. Stratton. Farm J 88:64L F '64

POULTRY farms

Big chickens of James and Samuel; farm in Nigeria's western region. P. Conklin. Reporter 28:30-1 Je 20 '63
Good living from a small flock. B. Hardy. il Farm J 87:35+ My '63

POULTRY houses

Balcony for hens. J. Russell. il Farm J 87:A8 Ap '63
If you should get a duck for Easter. il Sunset 130:116-17 Ap '63
Poultry: swing to cage systems. Suc Farm 62:72 S '64
White cools birds; whitewashing roof. W. B. Rogers. Farm J 87:37 Ag '63
Windowless poultry houses. il Suc Farm 61:99 O '63

Cleaning

Cage cleaners. il Farm J 88:58D N '64
Easier cleaning for cages. B. Hardy and G. Lorang. il Farm J 87:22-3+ Je '63
Hire your chicken house cleaned. J. Russell. il Farm J 87:83 S '63
Latest on poultry lagoons. B. Hardy and D. Braun. il Farm J 87:28+ Jl '63

Equipment

Chick-raising ideas you can use. il Suc Farm 61:108 Mr '63
Don't cram your cage layers. il Farm J 88:67 O '64

See also
Poultry brooders and brooding

Heating and ventilation

New ventilation system that thinks. J. T. Clayton. il Suc Farm 62:97 F '64
New ways to ventilate your poultry house. B. Hardy. il Farm J 88:50F S '64
Solar heat without windows. B. Hardy. il Farm J 87:71 Mr '63

Lighting

Now: dim lights for pullets. O. Bay. Farm J 87:45 S '63

Litter

Cost cutters for broiler litter. Farm J 87:37 Ag '63
Wood chips for poultry litter. il Suc Farm 61:60 D '63

POULTRY industry and trade

Chicken fat. il Time 82:76+ S 6 '63
Chicken war. America 109:380-1 O 5 '63
Chicken war puts new strains on unity; EEC curbs on poultry; with editorial comment. Bsns W p25-6, 132 Ag 10 '63
Chicken-war stew; United States and the Common market. P. Hendry. Reporter 29:30+ N 7 '63
Chickens and votes. A. Byrnes. New Repub 149:14-15 O 26 '63
Eight profit pointers for today's poultrymen. J. Harvey. Suc Farm 62:73 S '64
End of the chicken war. Time 82:98 N 29 '63
Feathering; retaliatory tariffs. il Newsweek 62:61-2 Ag 19 '63
GATT asked for advisory opinion on U.S.-EEC poultry dispute; letter to Eric Wyndham White, October 16, 1963. C. A. Herter. Dept State Bul 49:751-2 N 11 '63
Gentlemen's agreement; chicken-tariff issue between US and EEC. Newsweek 62:79 O 28 '63
International poultry traffic. C. W. Morton. il Atlan 212:130 N '63; 213:101 Ja '64
Mississippi chicken processor. il Ebony 18:45-6+ F '63
Playing chicken; agreement between the United States and the European economic community. New Repub 149:5 D 21 '63
Ruffled feathers; retaliatory tariffs against the Common market chicken-tariff hike. Time 82:70 Ag 16 '63
Too many hens. il Newsweek 62:60 Ag 5 '63
Tough times ahead for poultrymen. Suc Farm 62:96 S '64
U.S. and EEC hold talks on poultry import fees; statement, May 31, 1963, and announcement, June 7, 1963. C. A. Herter. Dept State Bul 48:996-7 Je 24 '63
U.S. raises duty on four articles imported from EEC countries; proclamation, December 4, 1963. L. B. Johnson. Dept State Bul 49:969-70 D 23 '63
Ups and downs of tariffs. Sr Schol 83:10-11 S 27 '63
What the chicken war means. Farm J 87:110 S '63
What's ahead for poultry? Farm J 87:52H My '63
Why I go-it-alone with broilers; ed. by J. Dyer. M. Putnam. il Farm J 87:75 Jl '63
Yankee birds can't go to Common market. il Life 55:24-5 Ag 23 '63

See also
Turkeys

POULTRY manure. See Fertilizers and manures

POULTRY research

Chicken talk. il Time 83:50-1 Ja 24 '64

POUND, Charles E.

Our landfill plays favorites. Am City 79:85-6 Ja '64

POUND, Ezra

Mindscapes; poems. Nat R 15:197 S 10 '63

about

Aging genius in exile; with report by J. Bonfante. il pors Life 56:45-6+ Mr 27 '64
Ezra Pound: poet as sculptor, by D. Davie. Review
Sat R 47:39-40 D 19 '64. L. Leary

POUND, Roscoe

Paragon of principle. por Time 84:46 Jl 10 '64

POUND cake. See Cake

POUND sterling. See Money—Great Britain

POUSETTE-DART, Richard

Art; paintings of R. Pousette-Dart at the Whitney museum. H. Kramer. Nation 196:428-9 My 18 '63
Pousette-Dart: circles and cycles. L. Campbell. il Art N 62:42-5+ My '63
Science with love; retrospective exhibition. il por Newsweek 61:98 My 20 '63

POVERTY

Affluence in principle and practice; excerpt from address. D. P. Moynihan. Mo Labor R 87:886 Ag '64
Diseases of the rich and diseases of the poor. A. Salam. Bul Atomic Sci 19:3+ Ap '63
Facts are in. M. Harrington. Nation 198:582-3 Je 8 '64
Greatest of these. . . M. Ascoli. Reporter 30:16 Mr 26 '64
How to cure poverty. H. Hazlitt. Newsweek 63:75 Ja 27 '64

POVERTY—*Continued*
Let us begin: an invitation to action on poverty. J. K. Galbraith. Harper 228:16+ Mr '64
Local community and world affairs; remarks, April 21, 1964. L. B. Johnson. Dept State Bul 50:746-9 My 11 '64
One big reason why some people are poor; results of Armed forces qualification test. il U S News 56:98-9 F 24 '64
Other side of affluence. Bsns W p 190+ Ap 18 '64
Pius XII on poverty. America 110:505 Ap 11 '64
Politics of poverty. D. Cater. il Reporter 30: 16-20 F 13 '64
Poverty and profit; symposium; with editorial comment. bibliog f Harvard Bsns R 42:6-8+ S '64
Poverty: skeleton in the national closet. il Sr Schol 84:6-8+ Mr 13 '64
Poverty; split-level and ghetto. Duns R 84:27 Ag '64
Religious view of poverty; official statement by the Department of social action of the National Catholic welfare conference. Commonweal 80:117-19 Ap 17 '64
Sure cure for poverty. Read Digest 85:75-6 Jl '64
Uses of prosperity. B. Ward. Sat R 47:191-2 Ag 29 '64
What it's like to be underdeveloped; excerpt from The great ascent. R. L. Heilbroner. Read Digest 82:21+ F '63
World poverty and the Christian; symposium. il Commonweal 81:219-37 N 13 '64
World security and developing nations. A. Salan. il Bul Atomic Sci 20:6-8 S '64
See also
Poor
Slums

POVICH, Shirley
My son the sportswriter. il por Time 81:54+ F 22 '63

POWDER, Smokeless. See Gunpowder, Smokeless

POWDER horns
Powder horns and history. J. S. Du Mont. il Antiques 84:60-2 Jl '63

POWDER puff derby. See Airplane racing

POWDERED meat. See Meat, Dried

POWDERED metals. See Metal powders

POWELL, Adam Clayton, 1908-
Duties and responsibilities of a congressman to the United States. Esquire 60:109-12+ S '63
Excerpt from debate, January 30, 1962. Cong Digest 42:58+ F '63
What Negroes in the North are really after; interview. por U S News 54:37-8 Je 10 '63
What the Negroes want: Powell spells it out; summaries of addresses. por U S News 55:11 Ag 12 '63
White man is scared, says Harlem congressman; summary of address, May 19, 1963. por U S News 54:20 Je 3 '63
Worst race riots in history? excerpts from address, May 5, 1963. por U S News 54:8 My 13 '63
about
Adam Clayton Powell, enigma on Capitol hill. L. Bennett, jr. il pors Ebony 18:25-8+ Je '63
Adam Clayton Powell's leadership. J. Yardley. New Repub 148:30 Ap 20 '63
Adam Powell. M. Kempton. New Repub 148: 10-13 My 25 '63
After Adam. il por Time 81:23 F 22 '63
All about Adam. il por Newsweek 61:24 F 18 '63
As one good friend to another. .; excerpts from Congressional record. W. Morse; J. J. Williams. Nat R 14:348 My 7 '63
Audacious world of Adam Powell. E. Dunbar. il pors Look 27:30-4+ My 7 '63
Civil-rights message: what was Powell's role? por U S News 55:19 Jl 8 '63
Collecting the winnings. por Time 82:60 D 6 '63
Dark enigma of Congress. D. Pearson and N. Ritter. il pors Sat Eve Post 237:75-9 Mr 28 '64
Elusive Adam. il por Time 85:38 Ja 15 '65
He shouldn't be there, and he wasn't. il por Time 81:21 Mr 15 '63
Irritant and needle. il por Newsweek 61:21 Ap 1 '63
It started with Adam. il por Newsweek 61:24+ Mr 4 '63
More on the case of Adam Clayton Powell; statement. J. J. Williams. por U S News 54:50 F 18 '63
Not one word; Education and labor committee. Time 81:26-7 Mr 8 '63
Pastor-politician from Harlem. por Sr Schol 82:22-3 My 15 '63
Powell answers his critics: night-clubbing and nepotism defended. por U S News 54: 20 Mr 4 '63
Shutting Powell's mouth. il por Time 81: 25-6 Ap 12 '63
T.R.B. from Washington; that's the way it works. New Repub 148:2 F 23 '63; Discussion. 148:30 Mr 9; 31 Mr 30 '63
To the woodshed. Newsweek 61:25-6 Mr 18 '63

POWELL, Anthony Dymoke
WLB biography. R. Shor. por Wilson Lib Bul 38:411+ Ja '64

POWELL, Bud
Bud's O.K. por Time 84:78 S 4 '64
Jazz. W. Balliett. New Yorker 40:154+ S 12 '64
Sound and furies. por Newsweek 64:79-80 S 7 '64

POWELL, Dawn
Elopers; story. Sat Eve Post 236:56-7 Ag 24 '63
Weekend in town; story. Sat Eve Post 237: 58-60 Jl 25 '64
What are you doing in my dreams? story. Vogue 142:153 O 1 '63

POWELL, Donnie A. See Scott, T. R. jt. auth.

POWELL, E. W. See Ellen, P. jt. auth.

POWELL, Gordon
Doctor Wednesday; preacher at St Stephen's Presbyterian church in downtown Sydney, Australia. il por Time 84:100 N 13 '64

POWELL, James
Closed and/or open. America 109:484-6 O 26 '63

POWELL, John Wesley
Beginning of action: Carl Schurz and John Wesley Powell; excerpt from The quiet crisis. S. L. Udall. il por Am For 69:20-3+ O '63

POWELL, Lawrence Clark
Education of an educator; address, September 27, 1963. por Library J 89:561-5 F 1 '64

POWELL, Lewis F.
Excerpt from statement, February 24, 1964. Cong Digest 43:146-7 My '64

POWELL, Loleta Kenan
Dwarf cannas. Pop Gard 14:44 Ap '63

POWELL, Mary
Sounds like fun! pors Seventeen 24:90-1 Ja '65

POWELL, Ralph L.
Communist China's military potential. bibliog f Cur Hist 47:136-42 S '64

POWELL, Reed M.
How men get ahead. Nations Bsns 52:56-8+ Mr '64

POWELL, Sir Robert Baden-. See Baden-Powell, R.

POWELL, Stanley, jr
Matson's rescue drill. il por Time 81:91-2 Ap 5 '63

POWELL, Theodore
Conscience and the Constitution. PTA Mag 58:10-12 N '63
Is it legal? Sat R 47:69+ F 15 '64
School prayer battle. Sat R 46:62-4+ Ap 20 '63
Shared time. NEA J 53:29-30 Mr '64

POWELL, William
How not to die of cancer. il por Time 81:54 My 10 '63

POWELL, LAKE. See Lakes, Artificial

POWELSON, John P.
Land-grabbers of Cali. Reporter 30:30-1 Ja 16 '64

POWER, Hal
Why I chose negative color. il pors Pop Phot 55:92-3+ Jl '64

POWER, Thomas Sarsfield
Mixed strategic force; address. Aviation W 81:17 N 16 '64
Nuclear delivery: theory vs. practice; excerpts from address. Aviation W 79:21 S 23 '63
Sure way to prevent nuclear war? interview. por U S News 58:72-6 Ja 25 '65
U.S. 90 per cent confident of capability to destroy vital enemy targets; excerpt from address. Aviation W 79:39 S 23 '63
U.S. nuclear team; address, May 14, 1964. Vital Speeches 30:552-5 Jl 1 '64
about
Air-command change: Ryan succeeds Power as chief. por U S News 57:19 D 7 '64
Man who differed, and the reasons why. por Time 82:16 Ag 30 '63

POWER, Thomas Sarsfield—about—*Continued*
Of treaties & togas. Time 82:15 Ag 30 '63
Power, Senate unit voice test ban fears. K. Johnsen. Aviation W 79:30-1 S 16 '63
Sacking SAC's boss. por Time 83:22 Ap 24 '64
Tough Tommy Power, our deterrent-in-chief. J. G. Hubbell. il por Read Digest 84:71-6 My '64
POWER (mechanics)
New power on the production line. H. E. Klein. il Duns R 83:43-5+ F '64
See also
Engines
Horsepower (mechanics)
POWER (political science)
Dilemmas of power; excerpt from Rise of the West. W. H. McNeill. Sat R 46:50-1 N 2 '63
Power and the intellectual. R. A. Nisbet. Yale R 53:321-41 Mr '64
Power transformed, by R. M. MacIver. Review
Sat R 48:50 Ja 9 '65. R. Hudson
Scientific revolution: the end of history; adaptation of address, 1963. E. Rabinowitch. Bul Atomic Sci 19:9-12 N '63
Speaking out; America the smug. R. Niebuhr. Sat Eve Post 236:12+ N 16 '63
Use of power. America 111:229 S 5 '64
What's all this about a power structure in U.S? interview. A. Heard. U S News 55: 58-60 Jl 1 '63
POWER (psychology)
Crowds and power, by E. Canetti. Review
Commonweal 77:544 F 15 '63. J. P. Sisk
POWER boat racing. See Motor boat racing
POWER brakes. See Brakes, Automobile
POWER commission, Federal. See United States —Federal power commission
POWER conversion. See Force and energy
POWER drills. See Drilling and boring machinery
POWER garden tools. See Garden tools, equipment and supplies
POWER houses. See Power plants
POWER in trust; story. See Auchincloss, L.
POWER lawn mowers. See Lawn mowers
POWER lines. See Electric lines
POWER mowers. See Mowing machines
POWER of appointment; story. See Auchincloss, L.
POWER plants
Power company's new rival; waste heat. il Bsns W p80+ Je 13 '64
Radioactivity in the atmospheric effluents of power plants that use fossil fuels. M. Eisenbud and H. G. Petrow. bibliog il Science 144:288-9 Ap 17 '64
World's new temples. il Time 83:89-90+ Mr 20 '64
See also
Atomic power plants
Hydroelectric plants
POWER plants, Municipal. See Electric plants, Municipal
POWER politics. See Power (political science)
POWER resources
Energy for remote areas. Sci N L 83:115 F 23 '63
Europe; power struggle. il Time 81:90 F 15 '63
POWER saws. See Saws
POWER steering. See Automobiles—Steering gear
POWER supply. See Electric power
POWER tools. See Electric tools, Portable
POWER transmission
See also
Tractors—Transmission
POWERED hand tools. See Electric tools, Portable; Machine tools
POWERS, Bertram Anthony
Automation and the news strike. R. Severo. il Reporter 28:29-30+ Mr 14 '63
Hard times. il por Time 81:13-17 Mr 1 '63
Life without the Times. M. Ascoli. Reporter 28:22 Mr 14 '63
New look at the New York newspaper strike. il por U S News 54:50-2 Mr 4 '63
Something to hoot about. Time 81:62 F 8 '63
POWERS, Eddie
Officiating mess in the National hockey league. D. Anderson and R. S. Hewlett. il por Sports Illus 18:26-8+ Ap 8 '63
POWERS, Edward J.
New Hampshire's lottery: private vice and public virtue. D. F. Ford. il Reporter 30: 34 Ja 2 '64
POWERS, Francis Gary
Strangers on a bridge, by J. B. Donovan. Review
America 110:772 My 30 '64. D. L. Flaherty
POWERS, Gudrun
Thistle in my bed. Criticism
New Yorker 39:110+ N 30 '63
POWERS, Honora
To Emily Dickinson; poem. America 109:359 S 28 '63
POWERS, Howard A. and Wilcox, R. E.
Volcanic ash from Mount Mazama (Crater Lake) and from Glacier Peak. bibliog Science 144:1334-6 Je 12 '64
POWERS, James Farl
Keystone; story. New Yorker 39:42-6 My 18 '63
about
Morte d'Urban: concerning J. F. Powers' first novel. M. J. Henault; V. P. McCorry. America 180:290-4 Mr 2 '63
Ostergothenburg revisited. J. J. Kirvan. Cath World 198:308-13 F '64
Powers, Edel, Stafford win National book awards. Pub W 183:30-1 Mr 18 '63
WLB biography. M. L. Holton. por Wilson Lib Bul 38:80 S '63
POWERS, Jessica
Hidden Christ; poem. Commonweal 79:259 N 22 '63
POWERS, Joseph M.
Book review. America 110:50+ Ja 11 '64
POWERS, Ormund
Dash of poly sorbate-60 & zein; reprint. Consumer Bul 46:14 My '63
POWERS (political science) See Nations
POWERS, Separation of. See Separation of powers
POWILLS, Dorothy
Playing cards. See issues of Hobbies
POWLEDGE, Fred
Mason-Dixon line in Queens. N Y Times Mag p 12+ My 10 '64
One hundred million rats against us. N Y Times Mag p36+ O 18 '64
Pick a number from 000 to 999. N Y Times Mag p35+ D 6 '64
PRACHT, Mary Ellen
Bright gifts; interview, ed. by R. D. Daniels. por Opera N 27:32 Mr 16 '63
PRACTICAL jokes
Flying flip. G. Infield. Esquire 61:84+ Je '64
PRACTICE (music) See Piano—Instruction and study
PRACTICE of an art; story. See Robinson, L. W.
PRADO, Arthur
Is automation really necessary? U S Camera 27:42 Mr '64
PRADO museum, Madrid
Hay de todo in the Prado; excerpt from Spanish leaves. H. Tracy. il Horizon 6:42-5 Autumn '64
PRAEGER, Frederick A, incorporated
Praeger buys control of Pall Mall press, London. Pub W 184:33 Jl 29 '63
Rival versions of Russian novel go down to the wire; reply. F. A. Praeger. Pub W 183: 36 F 4 '63
PRAGER, Denis J. and Bowman, R. L.
Freezing-point depression: new method for measuring ultramicro quantities of fluids. bibliog Science 142:237-9 O 11 '63
PRAGMATISM
American pragmatism reconsidered. H. D. Aiken; reply with rejoinder. R. W. Hall. Commentary 35:163-4 F '63
New breed of cat. J. Cogley. Commonweal 77:609-11 Mr 8 '63
Spirit of American philosophy, by J. E. Smith. Review
Reporter 28:55-7 My 23 '63. V. Held
PRAGUE
Music
Great opera houses: Prague. D. Stevens. il Opera N 28:25-9 D 28 '63
[Musical events] (cont) il Mus Am 83:80 Ja '63; 84:19 F; 27 Jl '64
Notes from abroad. D. Stevens. Hi Fi 13:30+ O '63
Riots
Way down south in Wenceslas square; race riots. Time 81:33 My 24 '63
PRAIRIE chickens
Prairie chicken and his friends; Buena Vista marsh, Wis. G. Laycock. il Field & S 68: 52-3+ S '63
To save the Attwater's chicken. C. W. Buchheister. Audubon Mag 66:85 Mr '64
Your guide to prairie chicken dance grounds. S. Pettingill. il Audubon Mag 65:114-15+ Mr '63
PRAIRIE CREEK REDWOODS STATE PARK. See California—Parks and reserves

PRAIRIE dogs
Sod poodle enjoys his supper. il Sunset 130: 45+ Ap '63
PRAIRIE Dunes country club. See Golf courses
PRAIRIE falcons. See Falcons
PRAIRIE NATIONAL PARK (proposed) See National parks and reserves—United States
PRAISE
In praise of praise. P. B. Diederich. il NEA J 52:58-9 S '63
Praise reappraised. R. E. Farson and others. Harvard Bsns R 41:61-6 S '63
PRAMER, David
Ancient art of alchemy. Natur Hist 72:40-5 Ag '63
Nematode-trapping fungi. bibliog Science 144: 382-8 Ap 24 '64
PRANGE, Gordon W.
Tora, tora, tora! condensation. Read Digest 83:251-8+ O; 273-8+ N '63
PRATT, Clyde M.
Colonial town center goes modern. Am City 79:122 Mr '64
PRATT, E. J.
Reporter at large. E. Wilson. New Yorker 40:134+ N 14 '64
PRATT, Harriett
So much in common; story. Redbook 120:52-3 Mr '63
PRATT, L. C. See Bodien, G. jt. auth.
PRATT, Richard
Great coin shortage; interview. Read Digest 86:31-2+ Ja '65
PRATT, Truxton B. jr
Auction. Flying 74:24-5+ Mr '64
PRATT, Willard S.
Eliminate the contract plowing. Am City 78: 112-13 S '63
PRATT and Whitney company
P&W building rocket research facility; West Palm Beach, Fla. il Aviation W 78:98 Ap 8 '63
PRATT graphic art center. See Pratt institute, Brooklyn
PRATT institute, Brooklyn
Pratt graphic art center. E. M. Ettenberg. il Am Artist 28:34-8+ My '64
PRAWNS. See Shrimps
PRAYER
Gabbling in the name of the church. C. Davis. America 109:236 S 7 '63
How should we pray? excerpt from The next day. J. A. Pike. Read Digest 85:81-4 S '64
Letters to Malcolm, by C. S. Lewis. Review
Nat R 16:240+ Mr 24 '64. J. Hart
Sat R 47:41 Mr 7 '64. N. A. Scott, jr
Time 83:63 F 28 '64
Naturalist's path to faith. D. C. Peattie. Read Digest 83:61-5 O '63
Pelagians at prayer. C. Davis. America 110: 281 F 29 '64
Word. V. P. McCorry. America 109:64 Jl 13 '63
Your private devotions. America 111:686 N 28 '64
See also
Prayers
PRAYER books
See also
Church of England—Book of common prayer
PRAYER in the schools. See Public schools and religion
PRAYER meetings
Apostolic few. il Time 81:69 My 24 '63
PRAYER; story. See Sawako, A.
PRAYERS
Christmas prayer by an unknown author. Good H 157:57 D '63
Ecumenical in Lent; prayer for unity. Christian Cent 80:291 Mr 6 '63
Prayer for a seminary. R. Pearson. Christian Cent 80:520 Ap 24 '63
Prayer for Ash Wednesday. S. J. Rowland, jr. Christian Cent 81:199 F 12 '64
Prayers for our times; excerpts from Seventeen book of prayer. Seventeen 23:84-5 D '64
Prayers to remember. Read Digest 84:111 Ja '64
Spare us: a prayer for our time. W. R. Miller. Christian Cent 80:1075 S 4 '63
That they may all be one; prayer for Consultation on church union. Christian Cent 81:451 Ap 8 '64
See also
Christmas poetry
PRAYING mantes
Beneficent cannibalism. E. W. Teale. il Natur Hist 72:30-7 Ap '63
Portrait of a predator. M. F. Boss. il Flower Grower 50:53-4 Ag '63
PRAZ, Mario
Remembrances from Ricci palace. R. J. Clements. il Sat R 47:64-5 O 24 '64
PREACHING
For Catholic pulpit renewal. W. D. Thompson. Christian Cent 81:644 My 13 '64
Pastors and preaching. W. A. Sadler, jr. Christian Cent 81:582+ Ap 29 '64
PREAKNESS race. See Horse racing
PREAMBLE to the Constitution. See United States—Constitution
PREAMPLIFIERS. See Amplifiers
PREBISCH, Raúl
Evaluation of the conference on trade and development; summary of report to the United Nations Secretary-General. UN Mo Chron 1:55-7 Ag '64
Spirit of conciliation. UN Mo Chron 1:71-7 Jl '64
Toward a dynamic development policy for Latin America; excerpts, with biographical sketch. U N Rev 10:13-21 My '63
Toward a new trade policy for development; condensation of report. U N Rev 11:21-3 Ap '64
about
Tough spokesman for the world's poor. por Newsweek 63:32 Ap 6 '64
Underdeveloped get together. il por Time 83: 89 F 21 '64
PRECAMBRIAN period. See Geology, Stratigraphic—Precambrian; Paleontology—Precambrian
PRECAST concrete See Concrete, Precast
PRECEDENCE
Pass the salt; Social list of Washington, D.C. Time 82:31 O 11 '63
PRECIOUS herbs of Christmas; story. See Sawyer, R.
PRECIOUS stones
Infinite riches in a little room. il Esquire 62: 125-31 D '64
See also
Crown jewels
Gems
also names of precious stones, e.g. Jade
PRECIPITATION (meteorology)
See also
Cloud physics
Hail
Snow
PRECISION approach radar. See Radar in aviation
PRECISION casting. See Lost wax process
PRECISION measurement. See Measurement
PRECISION visual omnirange. See Radio in aviation
PRE-COLUMBIAN art. See Art, Pre-Columbian
PRECOOKED food, Frozen. See Food, Frozen
PREDATOR and rodent control. See United States—Fish and wildlife service
PREDATORY animals. See Animals, Predatory
PREDATORY insects. See Insects, Predatory
PREDESTINATION. Free will and determination
PREDICTED log competitions. See Navigation—Competitions
PREDICTION. See Prognosis
PREDICTIONS. See Forecasts
PREFABRICATED hospitals; Prefabricated houses; etc. See Hospitals, Prefabricated; Houses, Prefabricated; etc.
PREFABRICATION
Prefabricated flashing for parapet walls. H. Edwards. il Arch Rec 135:209-10 My '64
PREFERRED stocks. See Stocks
PREGNANCY
Can a mother's illness harm her unborn baby? E. C. Hughes. Redbook 123:22+ Jl '64
Cineradioangiographic visalization of the venous drainage of the primate placenta in vivo. E. M. Ramsey and others. bibliog il Science 141:909 S 6 '63
Day Elizabeth was born. C. Burch. McCalls 90:46 Je '63
Dental care before the baby is born. il Todays Health 42:61 Mr '64
Dental care during pregnancy. A. N. Cranin. Redbook 123:46+ S '64
Family way; sympathetic pregnancy among husbands. Newsweek 65:35 Ja 4 '65
Generalized Schwartzman reaction in the pregnant golden hamster. M. Galton. bibliog il Science 139:923-4 Mr 8 '63
Having a baby your own way; a guide to a healthy pregnancy. R. Brecher and E. Brecher. il Redbook 122:69-80 F '64
High level of sodium necessary in pregnancy. Sci N L 84:265 O 26 '63
Husband's diary of his wife's pregnancy; ed. by V. Cadden. L. Krohner. il Redbook 123: 36-7+ Je '64

PREGNANCY—*Continued*
Man's world reversed by pregnancy cravings; Laggala, Ceylon. Sci N L 83:265 Ap 27 '63
My life, my children; ed. by D. C. Disney. M. A. Fischer. il Ladies Home J 80:56-8+ D '63
Old maternity myths that should fade away. Good H 156:150 Je '63
Pregnancy & the young husband. D. R. Mace. il McCalls 90:162+ Ap '63
Pregnant women warned; live-virus vaccine hazards. Sci N L 85:308 My 16 '64
Unborn baby's movements. C. L. Buxton. Redbook 123:32+ Ag '64
Vitamin D warning; danger of excessive amounts taken during pregnancy. Newsweek 64:93 D 7 '64
We could save 40,000 babies a year. L. Engel. il N Y Times Mag p31+ N 17 '63
What to do about morning sickness. H. Halsey. Redbook 124:24+ D '64
When should you see your pediatrician? M. A. Wessel. il Todays Health 42:60-1+ N '64
Will my baby cost me my figure? G. C. Schauffler. Ladies Home J 80:40+ My '63
Woman's special happy time. G. Sereny. Good H 156:72+ Mr '63
See also
Abortion
Childbirth
Fetus
Obstetrics
Prenatal influences
Sex determination and control

Signs and diagnosis
Facts about pregnancy tests. Good H 157:121-2 Jl '63
Frequent pregnancy tests: measure against disasters. F. Marley. Sci N L 83:403 Je 29 '63
How can I tell I'm pregnant. J. P. Donnelly. Redbook 122:38+ Mr '64
Two-hour pregnancy test. Sci N L 83:260 Ap 27 '63
We can't afford not to pregnancy test; testing of cows. O. Bay. Farm J 87:40 D '63
PREGNANCY, Complications of
How, when, and why is a baby threatened by Rh trouble? G. G. Greer. Bet Hom & Gard 41:110-11 F '63
Pregnancy discomfort: much can be done. Good H 157:168-9 O '63
Teen-age pregnancy. Sci N L 86:2 Jl 4 '64
See also
Abortion
PREGNANCY tests. See Pregnancy—Signs and diagnosis
PREHISTORIC art. See Art, Primitive
PREHISTORIC man. See Man, Prehistoric
PREHISTORIC monuments. See Megalithic monuments
PREISER, Hanna. See Sandow, A. jt. auth.
PREJUDICE
Bias against man. H. M. Schulweis. Christian Cent 81:361-4 Mr 18 '64
Deep roots of prejudice; excerpt from Modern psychiatry: a handbook for believers. F. J. Braceland and M. Stock. Cath World 198:109-14 N '63
Faith and prejudice, by B. Olson. Review Time 81:52 Mr 29 '63
How Protestants see others. D. R. Campion. America 108:428 Mr 30 '63
Panel of American women; with excerpts from a panel. S. S. Baker. il Ladies Home J 82:33-5+ Ja '65
Protesting Catholics; attack by some New York city Catholics on the Hunter college literary magazine. Commonweal 78:388 Jl 5 '63
They, the jury; test designed to reveal prejudices. Time 82:18 Ag 9 '63
Usefulness of anti-Catholicism. F. H. Littell. il Commonweal 78:422-4 Jl 12 '63
You can do something about prejudice. C. Thompson. Christian Cent 81:138-40 Ja 29 '64
See also
Race prejudice
Toleration
PREMACK, David. See Hundt, A. G. jt. auth.
PREMARITAL physical examinations. See Physical examinations, Premarital
PREMATURE infants. See Infants, Premature
PREMINGER, Otto
How to rate a critic. por Sat R 47:16-17 D 26 '64
Otto Preminger looks at the Catholic church. M. Walsh. Cath World 198:365-71 Mr '64
PREMISE; musical comedy. See Musical comedies, revues, etc.—Criticisms, plots, etc.
PREMIUM pay. See Overtime
PREMIUMS
Premiums; show of prizes at New York Coliseum. New Yorker 39:36-7 S 21 '63
Premiums; twenty-sixth annual New York premium show, at Coliseum. New Yorker 40:51 N 7 '64
See also
Coupons
Trading stamps
PRENATAL influences
Behavior of adult rats is modified by the experiences their mothers had as infants. V. H. Denenberg and A. E. Whimbey. bibliog il Science 142:1192-3 N 29 '63
Early developmental stress and later behavior. M. W. Lieberman. bibliog il Science 141:824-5 Ag 30 '63
Handling of pregnant rats: effects on emotionality of their offspring. R. Ader and P. M. Conklin. il Science 142:411-12 O 18 '63
Newborn attention as affected by medication during labor. G. Stechler. bibliog il Science 144:315-17 Ap 17 '64
Prenatal irradiation: effects on the development of the central nervous system and postnatal behavior; report on workshop conference. J. Werboff. Science 144:84-6 Ap 3 '64
Reducing the hazards of birth. A. C. Barnes. Harper 228:31-7 Ja '64; Discussion. 228:8+ Mr '64
PRENDERGAST, Joseph
Cultural growth in capital letters! por Recreation 57:440-1 N '64
PRENTICE, T. Merrill, jr
Minstrel. New Yorker 40:22-3 Jl 25 '64
PRENTICE-Hall, incorporated
Attraction of opposites; Radio corporation of America offers to absorb Prentice-Hall inc. Time 84:58 D 25 '64
Prentice-Hall celebrates its first half-century. il Pub W 184:20-5 O 28 '63
Prentice-Hall consents to FTC order. Pub W 185:70 F 3 '64
Prentice-Hall sells Hawthorn books. Pub W 187:66 Ja 11 '65
RCA talking merger with Prentice-Hall. Pub W 186:44-5 D 28 '64
PRENTISE, Tina
Our neighborhood as inspiration. Sch Arts 63:21 Mr '64
PRENTISS, Paula
Paula Prentiss. G. Grove. pors Sat Eve Post 237:68-9 F 8 '64
PREPARATION for college. See Colleges and universities—Entrance requirements
PREPARATORY schools. See Private schools
PREPAREDNESS, Military
Sparta and America. N. Cousins. Sat R 46:20 Ap 6 '63
See also
Armaments
also subhead Defenses under names of countries, e.g. United States—Defenses
PREPAYMENT dental plans. See Insurance, Dental
PRERAPHAELITISM
Art galleries. R. M. Coates. New Yorker 40:102+ Je 13 '64
Radical romantics; Pre-Raphaelite exhibition at Huntington Hartford's Gallery of modern art, New York. A. F. Staley. il Art N 63:32-4+ My '64
Raphael rejected. il Time 83:72-4 F 14 '64
PREROGATIVES, Management. See Management rights
PRESBYTERIAN church in Canada
Cool to idea of union. D. H. Rayner. Christian Cent 81:914-16 Jl 15 '64
Presbyterian church in Canada. D. H. Rayner. Christian Cent 80:916-17 Jl 17 '63
PRESBYTERIAN church in the United States
No private domain; racism at home viewed from the church's mission posts abroad; statements of the Presbyterian board of world missions. Christian Cent 81:184 F 5 '64
Presbyterians hold line on school prayers; racial justice. Christian Cent 80:1538 D 11 '63
Presbyterians, U.S: enroute to broader concerns. A. N. Brown, jr. Christian Cent 80:1577-80 D 18 '63
See also
United Presbyterian church in the United States of America

PRESBYTERIAN church in the United States (South)
Gentle demurrers. Time 81:77 My 10 '63
Move toward union. Christian Cent 81:228 F 19 '64
Presbyterian, U.S. general assembly. J. A. Womeldorf. Christian Cent 81:680+ My 20 '64
PRESBYTERIAN church in the United States of America
Presbyterians speed integration. Christian Cent 81:630 My 13 '64
See also
United Presbyterian church in the United States of America
PRESBYTERIAN general assembly. See Presbyterian church in the United States of America
PRESBYTERIANISM
See also
Calvinism
PRESCHOOL children
Art for the pre-schooler. M. Nicolaysen. il Design 65:142-5 Mr '64
Big break for poverty's children; New York city's program of educating preschool children; with account by P. Blake. il Life 56:78B-89 Ap 3 '64
Child and the society; excerpt from Development in early childhood: the preschool years. D. B. Gardner. Sch & Soc 92:157-61 Ap 4 '64
Family business in brief. A. P. Eliasberg. il N Y Times Mag p87-8 D 13 '64
How preschoolers learn to cope with problems. M. R. Sherwin. il Parents Mag 39:48-9+ Ag '64
How to organize a do-it-yourself play school. M. Johnston. il Parents Mag 38:62-3+ S '63
Making memories together; with study-discussion program, by R. Strang. W. Abraham. bibliog il PTA Mag 57:27-9, 35 My '63
Quiz for parents of preschoolers. J. L. Hymes. il Parents Mag 39:52-4+ Ja '64
Should parents teach reading? with study-discussion program. R. Strang. bibliog il PTA Mag 57:7-9, 34 Mr '63
Should preschool children be taught the three R's? with study-discussion program. I. S. Black and J. W. Blos. bibliog il PTA Mag 59:24-6, 36 S '64
They have to be taught to play; with study-discussion program. R. Strang. bibliog il PTA Mag 58:33-5 N '63
To be continued: story of Baltimore early school admissions project. A. C. Harding. il NEA J 53:30-2 S '64
Touch of reassurance; with study-discussion program, by R. Strong. D. K. Osborn and P. P. W. Knapp. bibliog il PTA Mag 58: 10-12, 35 D '63
Try praise for preschoolers. M. R. Sherwin. il Parents Mag 38:44-5+ Jl '63
What Johnny should learn before school; adaptation of address. G. W. Beadle. Sci Digest 56:28-33 N '64
What nursery schools can and cannot do; with study-discussion program, by R. Strang. I. J. Gordon. bibliog il PTA Mag 58:10-12, 35 S '63
See also
Kindergarten
Nursery schools
Readiness for school
PRESCHOOL education. See Education of children; Nursery schools
PRESCHOOL literature. See Childrens literature
PRESCOTT, D. M.
Cell life cycle: macromolecular aspects. Science 141:547-8 Ag 9 '63
PRESCRIPTIONS
By its own name; labeling of drugs. Time 82:42-3 Ag 2 '63
PRESENT, The
See also
Past, The
PRESENTS. See Gifts
PRESERVATION hall concerts. See New Orleans—Music
PRESERVATION of food. See Canning and preserving; Food preservation and preservatives
PRESERVATION of landmarks, scenery, etc.

United States

South goes scenic. J. K. Vessey. il Am For 70:20-3 Jl '64
PRESERVATION of paper. See Paper—Preservation
PRESERVATION of vegetables. See Food preservation and preservatives
PRESERVES. See Jelly, jam, etc.
PRESERVES, Game. See Game preserves
PRESERVING. See Canning and preserving
PRESIDENT glacier area. See Glaciers
PRESIDENT; story. See Barthelme, D.
PRESIDENTIAL advisers. See Public officers
PRESIDENTIAL airplanes. See Airplanes, Government
PRESIDENTIAL automobiles. See Automobiles, Government
PRESIDENTIAL campaigns
Action is needed to preserve election stability. F. Morley. Nations Bsns 51:29-30 D '63
Art of getting elected. L. L. L. Golden. Sat R 47:105 O 10 '64
Catholic vote is confused. M. Novak. New Repub 151:14-15 Ag 22 '64
PRESIDENTIAL campaigns
Four weeks of campaigning, or a whole year; British and American elections. P. Worsthorne. il N Y Times Mag p29+ S 27 '64
How to get elected. B. A. Weisberger. il Am Heritage 15:62-77 Ag '64
How to help your candidate. il Changing T 18:31-4 S '64
Is the long campaign necessary? M. Moos. il N Y Times Mag p 14+ My 10 '64
Objective: the White House. il Nations Bsns 52:75-8+ Je '64
Political convention: caucus & carnival. J. D. Weaver. il Holiday 35:42-5+ Je '64
Why the candidates are targets for mudslingers. D. S. Broder. il N Y Times Mag p 19+ S 27 '64
World isn't waiting; international problems and coming campaign. Bsns W p23-5 F 22 '64
See also
Airplanes in political campaigns
Campaign buttons, etc.
Campaign funds
Campaign literature
National conventions (political)
National conventions, Democratic
National conventions, Republican
Platforms, Political
Presidential candidates
Presidents—United States—Election
Television in politics

1864

Election of 1864. J. G. Brown. il Hobbies 69: 28-30 Ag '64

1916

Election of 1916. J. A. Huston. Cur Hist 47: 205-9+ O '64

1948

Truman and Eisenhower: their administrations and campaigns. V. Albjerg. il Cur Hist 47:221-8 O '64

1952

Truman and Eisenhower: their administrations and campaigns. V. Albjerg. il Cur Hist 47:221-8 O '64

1960

Case for political debates on TV. F. Stanton. il N Y Times Mag p 16+ Ja 19 '64
How LBJ got the nomination. P. Potter. il Reporter 30:16-20 Je 18 '64

1964

Amoral climate. R. Moley. Newsweek 64:112 N 2 '64
As Democrats see it. il U S News 57:29-31 S 7 '64
As others see us; the Democratic team; The Republican challenge. Sat R 47:31-3+ O 24 '64
Backlash on November 3. America 111:651 N 21 '64
Barry's economic crusade. J. Tobin. New Repub 151:13-16 O 24 '64
Booing the candidates. Christian Cent 81:1324 O 28 '64
Campaign. il Time 84:30+ S 18; 19-22 S 25; 41-43A O 2; 31-3 O 16; 24-5 O 23; 19-20 N 6 '64
Campaign and candidates: letters to the editor. Christian Cent 81:1276-7+ O 14 '64
Campaign blur. Time 84:71 O 9 '64
Campaign debating. W. Lippmann. Newsweek 64:13 Ag 31 '64
Campaign ethics. Duns R 84:29 N '64
Campaign '64. C. E. Hawley. bibliog il Sr Schol 84:8T-10T Mr 6 '64
Campaign time; when Secret service worry grows. il U S News 56:63-4 Ap 13 '64
Campaigner Goldwater. S. Alsop. Sat Eve Post 237:16 O 3 '64

PRESIDENTIAL campaigns—1964—*Continued*
Can we do away with the draft? Bsns W p29 S 12 '64
Chance for confrontation. Commonweal 80: 527 Ag 7 '64
Churches' mandate. Christian Cent 81:1419-20 N 18 '64
Conservative revolution. M. Ascoli. Reporter 31:28 S 24 '64
Counting chickens; Democrats warn themselves against overconfidence. K. Crawford. Newsweek 64:74 O 5 '64
Curious campaign; point by point. il Newsweek 64:27-9 O 19 '64
Defense issue. R. Hotz. Aviation W 81:13 S 28 '64
Democratic record; address, August 24, 1964. J. O. Pastore. Vital Speeches 30:706-8 S 15 '64
Democrats to try a run on the record. J. N. Eller. America 111:342 S 26 '64
Democrats: well on the way. il Time 82:23 O 25 '63
Different campaign. K. Crawford. Newsweek 64:36 Jl 20 '64
Dignity and integrity. D. Lawrence. U S News 57:100 N 2 '64
Down to the wire; Peace issue; Morality issue. il Newsweek 64:23-6 N 2 '64
Election: partisan activity of scientists unlikely to sow discord in scientific community. D. S. Greenberg. Science 146:232-4 O 9 '64
Emotional campaign will test voters' judgment. P. Lisagor. il Nations Bsns 52:23-4 S '64
Europe nervously watches our election. D. W. Brogan. il N Y Times Mag p 15+ O 4 '64
Exclusive interview: Goldwater speaks his mind. B. M. Goldwater. il U S News 57:46-9+ D 21 '64; Reply. New Yorker 40:23 Ja 2 '65
Extremism: letters to the editor. Christian Cent 81:1306-7 O 21 '64
Fascinating angles of a dull campaign. E. T. Folliard. America 111:472 O 24 '64
Fasten your seat belts. M. Ascoli. Reporter 29:22 N 7 '63; Reply. S. McCalmont. 29: 8+ D 5 '63
Fear & the facts; control of nuclear weaponry; attitudes of presidential candidates. il Time 84:15-19 S 25 '64
Foreign policy issue of this year. Life 57:4 O 2 '64
Four tactics in the Johnson campaign. T. Wicker. il N Y Times Mag p 14+ O 4 '64
FDR's 1932 platform suits Goldwater for '64. U S News 55:6 S 23 '63
Fruitful choice. E. J. Hughes. Newsweek 64: 31 O 5 '64
Getting across to the voters. il Bsns W p32-3 S 19 '64
Goldwater for therapy. W. V. Shannon. Commonweal 81:30-1 O 2 '64
Goldwater in the old confederacy. il Newsweek 64:25-6 S 28 '64
Goldwater, Pentagon clash on defense; with editorial comment. J. Trainor. Miss & Roc 15:12, 46 Ag 17 '64
Goldwater resorts to military moderates. G. C. Wilson. Aviation W 81:21 S 28 '64
Goldwater's staff. R. Moley. Newsweek 64:88 Ag 24 '64
G.O.P. campaign preview; symposium. il Sat Eve Post 237:13-19+ Ag 8 '64
Great European frustration; world-wide interest in American presidential election. N. Cousins. Sat R 47:14 S 5 '64
His own kind of campaign. il Bsns W p 122-4+ Jl 25 '64
Horns, halos and issues. Christian Cent 81:1075 S 2 '64
How Democrats plan victory. il U S News 57:25-8 Ag 31 '64
How Republicans plan to win in November. il U S News 57:37-40 Jl 20 '64
How strong is the hate vote? white backlash. B. H. Bagdikian. il Sat Eve Post 237: 19-21 O 17 '64
Imponderables; international and national events. il Time 84:19 O 23 '64
Intermission is over. W. Lippmann. Newsweek 64:23 N 9 '64
Into the heartland; Goldwater whistle-stop tour of Mid-West. il Newsweek 64:33-4 O 12 '64
Issue for 1964. Nation 197:229 O 19 '63
It's too early to bind wounds. L. Wainwright. Life 57:31 N 13 '64
JFK in Goldwater country; what he found out. il U S News 55:49-50 O 7 '63
Johnson maneuvers. W. V. Shannon. Commonweal 80:593-4 S 4 '64
Johnson's campaign machinery. M. Viorst. New Repub 151:9-10 S 5 '64
Kennedy and '64: out to grass roots. il U S News 54:35-6 Je 17 '63
Kennedy's strategy for the '64 election. il U S News 55:34-6 Ag 19 '63
Key men on the Goldwater team. il U S News 56:20 Je 22 '64
Kickoff; presidential campaign speech in Prescott, Ariz. il Time 84:20-1 S 11 '64
Labor drive for LBJ hits own backlash. il Bsns W p49-50+ S 12 '64
Leaders and their mandates; presidential campaign and changes in Britain and the Soviet Union. M. Ascoli. Reporter 31:16 N 5 '64
Lessons of the nomination drive. W. A. Rusher. Nat R 16:641-3 Jl 28 '64
Loud silence. K. Crawford. Newsweek 64:42 N 2 '64
LBJ: I said let them through! Slam-bang. C. Roberts. il Newsweek 64:31-3 O 12 '64
Men behind the men who—. D. S. Broder. il N Y Times Mag p 15+ Ja 5 '64
Mid-campaign. Commonweal 81:60 O 9 '64
Morality issue in the campaign. M. Phelps. America 111:543 N 7 '64
Most disappointing. Time 84:27 O 30 '64
Newthink. K. Crawford. Newsweek 64:26 Ag 3 '64
1964 campaign; who's running where? il Sr Schol 83:4-7 N 1 '63
Non-debate. E. J. Hughes. Newsweek 63:19 Mr 23 '64
Notes and comment; Kennedy in Miami. New Yorker 39:49-51 N 30 '63
Now it's wives on the campaign trail. il U S News 57:23 O 12 '64
Now the 1964 race begins. il Bsns W p26-7 S 5 '64
Ohio: is anybody happy? J. A. Maxwell. il Reporter 31:36-8 O 22 '64
On presenting both sides. Christian Cent 81: 1163-4 S 23 '64
One-step thinking. W. Lippmann. Newsweek 63:25 Mr 16 '64
Order in the streets; Goldwater-Miller promise to restore order if elected in November. Christian Cent 81:1195-6 S 30 '64
Other fellow; presidential performance. E. J. Hughes. Newsweek 64:23 N 16 '64
Personal business; volunteers to help in coming campaign. Bsns W p 121-2 F 15 '64
Powerful persuaders; Lady Bird's trip through the South. H. Fuller. New Repub 151:11-12 O 24 '64
Real issues. America 111:476 O 24 '64
Republican campaign strategy. W. D. Burnham. Commonweal 80:287-90 My 29 '64; Reply. J. Russell. 80:452 Jl 3 '64
Republican campaigner; the Eisenhower role for '64. U S News 55:26 O 21 '63
Republicans looking for a break. il Time 84: 43A O 2 '64
Riddle of the labor vote. H. Harris. Harper 229:43-9 O '64
Right down the center. il Bsns W p25-7 Ag 29 '64
Rocky in Miami Beach. New Yorker 39:48-9 N 23 '63
Senator Goldwater and the Negro. M. Greenfield. Reporter 31:27-8 O 8 '64
Should the gates be opened wider? campaign charges over immigration. il Bsns W p 114+ O 17 '64
'64: the GOP could win, if. L. Harris. il Newsweek 62:25-7 Ag 26 '63
Social security argument; issue in presidential campaign. il Time 84:25 O 23 '64
Some of the issues are missing. il Time 84: 19-20 S 11 '64
Sorry campaign. Commonweal 81:179 N 6 '64
Sparkless campaign. K. Crawford. Newsweek 64:41 S 21 '64
Spymanship; Republican and Democratic skulduggery. Newsweek 64:35 O 26 '64
Tennis shoes or combat boots? E. T. Folliard. America 111:102 Ag 1 '64
That sinful movie; Republican film on moral decay. Reporter 31:15 N 5 '64
They're off: the long, hot campaign. il Newsweek 64:19-20 S 14 '64
This electoral trauma. M. Ascoli. Reporter 31:22 O 22 '64
Those politicking departments of Defense and State. Sat Eve Post 237:86 O 10 '64
Three democratic worries. W. V. Shannon. Commonweal 80:624-6 S 18 '64
Tick-tock of the campaign clock. il Newsweek 64:29-30 S 21 '64
Toward Nov. 3. il Time 84:13 Ag 21 '64
U.S. Constitution and the '64 campaign. il Sr Schol 85:6-7 S 23 '64

PRESIDENTIAL campaigns—1964—*Continued*
Venture into politics: scientists and engineers in the election campaign. D. S. Greenberg. Science 146:1440-4, 1561-3 D 11-18 '64
Washington desk. J. R. Slevin. Duns R 84:5-6 S '64
Weighing the campaign. E. Roper. Sat R 47:28 O 31 '64
What happened to the dream? Nation 199: 317 N 9 '64
What's the mainstream? who is in it? A. Hacker. il N Y Times Mag p5+ S 6 '64
When politics rip apart old loyalties. il Bsns W p38+ O 24 '64
Where both candidates stand on the big issues; with editorial comment. il Bsns W p64-6+, 192 O 10 '64
White House gears up for campaign year. C. B. Seib. il Nations Bsns 51:40-1+ O '63
Who's ahead in the sixth arrondissement? Democratic and Republican campaigns among U.S. citizens abroad. il Time 84:30 O 9 '64
Who's for whom; advertising agencies for Johnson and Goldwater. Time 84:97-8 S 11 '64
Who's really for LBJ? R. Moley. Newsweek 64:126 O 12 '64
Why he is losing; Goldwater's position. H. Hazlitt. Newsweek 64:94 O 26 '64
Why Kennedy, Goldwater are going to the voters now. il U S News 55:43-4 S 16 '63
Why LBJ will win. New Repub 151:3-4 O 31 '64
Winning the West. New Repub 149:4-5 O 12 '63
See also names of presidential candidates, e.g. L. B. Johnson

PRESIDENTIAL campaigns in literature
Convention year, 1964. P. H. Des Marais. America 111:45-7 Jl 11 '64

PRESIDENTIAL candidates
Choosing a president. D. Lawrence. U S News 55:84 D 23 '63
Decease of the log cabin legend. H. F. Graff. il N Y Times Mag p8+ Je 30 '63
Decline of the East. R. Moley. Newsweek 63:68 Ja 6 '64
For golf, money and love. New Repub 148: 8-9 My 25 '63
Forty-two campaigns ago. S. D. Smith. il N Y Times Mag p82+ O 25 '64
How 'The man who' wins the prize. M. Moos. il N Y Times Mag p8+ Je 21 '64
Man who loses. H. F. Graff. il N Y Times Mag p36+ N 15 '64
Presidential race is never a sure thing. P. Lisagor. il Nations Bsns 52:21-2 Ag '64
Presidents and president-makers. W. S. White. NEA J 53:27 O '64
Running for president. R. Moley. Newsweek 62:116 N 11 '63
What's the best road to the White House? senator or a governor. D. S. Broder. il N Y Times Mag p28+ S 22 '63
Why the candidates are targets for mud-slingers. D. S. Broder. il N Y Times Mag p 19+ S 27 '64
See also
Campaign funds

Anecdotes, facetiae, satire, etc.

Rule of O. R. Bingham. Reporter 30:40+ Mr 26 '64
Stand back for Walford W. Oglethorpe, jr! T. Meehan. New Yorker 40:37-8 Ap 11 '64

Caricatures and cartoons

On the '64 campaign trail. Sr Schol 84:20 Ap 17 '64

1960

Lyndon Johnson and the presidency. il U S News 54:18 Ap 8 '63
1960's: the issues and the candidates. J. J. Huthmacher. Cur Hist 47:229-35+ O '64

1964

After JFK, what? W. D. Burnham. il Commonweal 79:340-3 D 13 '63
After New Hampshire. Newsweek 63:33 Mr 16 '64
After New Hampshire. Reporter 30:10+ Mr 26 '64
After Oregon, what? R. Moley. Newsweek 63:88 Je 1 '64
After the attack. Commonweal 80:408 Je 26 '64
After Wisconsin: new turn in politics. il U S News 56:31-3 Ap 20 '64
Ambassador Lodge running strong; New Hampshire primary. il Newsweek 63:21-5 Mr 23 '64
Anatomy of the Goldwater boom. T. Wicker. il N Y Times Mag p7+ Ag 11 '63
As Ike sees the candidates now; summary of interview, ed. by C. Brown. D. D. Eisenhower. U S News 56:14 Ap 20 '64
As New Hampshire goes, so goes who? W. S. Ellis. il N Y Times Mag p 12+ F 2 '64
As others see us; the Democratic team; The Republican challenge. Sat R 47:31-3+ O 24 '64
As political truce ends: who's ahead for '64? il U S News 55:22-5 D 30 '63
As Republican choice narrows for '64. U S News 54:43 Mr 18 '63
As Republicans look over the field for '64. il U S News 55:64 Jl 1 '63
As shown by Gallup poll: latest on the way candidates stand. il U S News 56:33 Ap 20 '64
As '64 campaign gets going. il U S News 57:31-2 Jl 20 '64
At 8:25 p.m: I'm going to run. il Newsweek 63:21-5 Je 22 '64
Atlantic report. Atlan 214:4+ Jl '64
Big GOP test in the West; Oregon primary. L. Harris. il Newsweek 63:23 Mr 23 '64
Bleating of sheep. M. Kempton. New Repub 150:15-18 Je 20 '64
Block Goldwater movement in the GOP. il Newsweek 62:19-20 Jl 22 '63
Blowing Barry's horn. S. Meisler. il Nation 197:48-9 Jl 27 '63
Boomlet for Bill Scranton: how to succeed without trying. il Newsweek 63:19-20+ Ja 27 '64
Box score for '64; state-by-state survey. il Time 82:34-5 O 4 '63
Calling the roll of delegates. Time 83:33 Je 12 '64
Campaign and candidates: letters to the editor. Christian Cent 81:1276-7+ O 14 '64
Can Barry Goldwater be stopped? il Newsweek 63:27-31 My 18 '64
Can Rockefeller stop Goldwater? il U S News 55:34 Jl 29 '63
Candidate Smith? Newsweek 62:34 N 18 '63
Candidates polish up their images. E. T. Folliard. America 111:371 O 3 '64
Candidates' records on defense and space bills. il Miss & Roc 15:16 O 19 '64
Changing lineup for Republicans; New Hampshire primary vote; with statement by L. H. Bean. il U S News 56:39-41 Mr 23 '64
Charm treatment. il Newsweek 61:18 Je 3 '63
Choice for '64. il Newsweek 63:68-70 Mr 2 '64
Cinched nomination; 1964 Republican national convention. il Time 84:19-24 Jl 17 '64
Circumstances are not ordinary; choice of Publishers' weekly. C. B. Grannis. Pub W 186:36 O 12 '64
Clear choice. Nation 199:81 S 7 '64
Compromise candidate? Nixon's name arises again. U S News 55:10 Ag 12 '63
Contest, not a walkaway; drive for Republican nomination for president. il Bsns W p25-6 Je 20 '64
Contradictions of the 1964 campaign. E. T. Folliard. America 111:175 Ag 22 '64
Crossroads for the GOP. W. A. Rusher. il Nat R 14:109-12 F 12 '63; Reply. F. Barron. 14:331 Ap 23 '63
Crucial four-letter word: duty. E. J. Hughes. Newsweek 63:15 Je 29 '64
Cutting bait? il Newsweek 62:28+ S 30 '63
Democrats. il Time 83:14-15 Ja 17; 21-2 Ja 31; 16-17 Mr 27; 22 Ap 24; 24 My 22; 84:17 Ag 28; 19A-19B S 4 '64
Dignified loser drops one more. L. Wainwright. Life 56:27 Mr 20 '64
Don't overlook Henry Cabot Lodge. Sat Eve Post 237:78 Ja 18 '64
Draft-Goldwater drive: a progress report. W. A. Rusher. Nat R 15:185-7 S 10 '63
Draft Goldwater move starts, its meaning. il U S News 54:42-5 Ap 29 '63
Duel to the death in California; with report by T. H. White. il Life 56:24-31 My 29 '64
Edging closer: N. Rockefeller and B. Goldwater. il Newsweek 62:33 N 4 '63
Election decided in mid-July. E. T. Folliard. America 111:587 N 14 '64
Election winner will face historic problems. F. Morley. il Nations Bsns 52:27-8 Mr '64
Enter Scranton. il Newsweek 62:16 D 30 '63
Establishment view. S. Alsop. Sat Eve Post 237:16 Ap 18 '64
Faces that faded out. il U S News 57:34-5 Jl 20 '64
Fight for New Hampshire: what is really at stake. il U S News 56:44-5 Mr 9 '64
Finger of fate? Senator Goldwater's foray into New Hampshire. Newsweek 62:37-8 N 11 '63

PRESIDENTIAL candidates—1964—*Continued*
Focus on Nov. 3. See issues of National review during presidential campaign
Focus on '64. Nat R 15:92, 138, 182, 225, 336, 382, 428, 470, 515, 556 Ag 13-S 24, O 22-D 31 '63
For Romney: a win, a boost. il U S News 54:44-6 Ap 15 '63
From behind the stretch; California's Republican presidential primary. il Time 83: 19-20 My 29 '64
From grass roots of Midwest; what Illinois primary showed. il U S News 56:33 Ap 27 '64
From Washington straight. Cato. Nat R 14: 228 Mr 26 '63
Fruitful choice. E. J. Hughes. Newsweek 64: 31 O 5 '64
Gold for Goldwater. Newsweek 62:23 Ag 5 '63
Goldwater. Nat R 14:519 Jl 2 '63
Goldwater and Rockefeller. J. O'Gara. Commonweal 78:472 Ag 9 '63
Goldwater and the state. Commonweal 80:495 Jl 24 '64
Goldwater blitz described by a fellow senator. U S News 57:22 Jl 20 '64
Goldwater country. J. J. Kilpatrick. Nat R 14:281-2 Ap 9 '63
Goldwater for president? a drive is launched. U S News 54:25 Ap 22 '63
Goldwater for president: is it conceivable? is it feasible? W. F. Buckley, jr; L. B. Bozell. Nat R 14:312-13+ Ap 23 '63
Goldwater movement. W. Lippmann. Newsweek 62:13 Ag 5 '63
S 24 '63
Goldwater on extremists. R. Moley. Newsweek 62:76 Jl 29 '63
Goldwater out front: will he be blocked? il U S News 55:41-3 Jl 15 '63
Goldwater vs. Rockefeller on the big issues. il U S News 55:33 N 4 '63
Goldwater's chances. New Repub 150:5-6 Ja 11 '64
Goldwater's decision. R. Moley. Newsweek 63:78 Ja 13 '64
Goldwater's managers. R. Moley. Newsweek 63:100 Ap 13 '64
Good-times issue and party prospects. E. T. Folliard. America 110:533 Ap 18 '64
Governor Rockefeller's divorce. Commonweal 79:179 N 8 '63; Reply. T. Bourne. 79:350 D 13 '63
Governor Scranton to the rescue. M. McGrory. America 110:860 Je 27 '64
Governor Scranton's delicate situation. M. McGrory. America 110:562 Ap 25 '64
Governors size up '64 race. il U S News 55:50 Ag 5 '63
Grand old game; Republican possibilities. Time 81:17-18 My 31 '63
G.O.P. against itself. P. Duke. Reporter 31: 12-15 Jl 2 '64
G.O.P. has its convention prematurely. il Life 56:47-48A Je 19 '64
G.O.P. in '64. W. V. Shannon. Commonweal 79:417-18 Ja 10 '64
GOP race: who's up, down, and out. il Newsweek 63:19-20 My 11 '64
GOP's Goldwater: busting out all over; Listening post: a head for Rockefeller but a heart for Goldwater. il Newsweek 61:28-32 My 20 '63
Great G.O.P. logjam of presidential timber. il Life 56:28-31 F 7 '64
He cared enough, and so did Oregon; with report by L. Harris. il Newsweek 63:27-8 My 25 '64
Head honcho and Barry's loyal amateurs. il Newsweek 63:24-5 Je 15 '64
Heads off. New Repub 150:2+ Je 20 '64
Hi-ho New Hampshire! Barry goes galloping in; with reports by P. O'Neil and M. Gart. il Life 55:28-35 N 1 '63
Honest injun, it's finally time to vote: New Hampshire Republicans; with report by R. Ajemian. il Life 56:28-33 Mr 6 '64
How not to stop Barry. Cato. Nat R 14:489 Je 18 '63
How problems are piling up for Rockefeller. il U S News 54:48 My 6 '63
How Republican leaders view the Negro. S. Booker. il Ebony 19:25-8+ Mr '64
How Republican race lines up. pors U S News 56:33-5 Mr 16 '64
How the Republicans can win. A. Larson. Sat Eve Post 237:21-3 Ja 25 '64
I shall go to New Hampshire. Time 82:35 N 15 '63
If it's Rockefeller vs. Kennedy in 1964—. il U S News 54:56-8 F 11 '63
If not Rockefeller or Goldwater, here are two dark horses. il U S News 54:48-9 Je 3 '63
Ifs and buts. il Newsweek 63:21-2 Ja 20 '64
In the Republican presidential race. U S News 56:19 My 11 '64
Is it to be Goldwater? here are latest trends. il U S News 56:36-7 My 18 '64
Jet bandwagon; Goldwater's scorecard. il Newsweek 62:33-4 O 7 '63
JFK could lose. G. Mills. il Look 27:94+ D 17 '63
Johnson vs. Goldwater: the conflict on big issues. U S News 57:40 Jl 20 '64
Kennedy's worry: is the solid South lost for '64? il U S News 55:35-7 O 28 '63
Lady in the New England snow. M. McGrory. America 110:246 F 22 '64
Lady of Maine. K. Crawford. Newsweek 63: 30 F 10 '64
Let's suppose. il Newsweek 63:18 F 3 '64
Letter from Washington. R. H. Rovere. New Yorker 39:113-20 N 2; 78:84+ D 21 '63; 40: 193-8 My 16 '64
Lodge: a surge for the man in Saigon. il Newsweek 63:21-2 Ap 13 '64
Lodge is Oregon's bride by mail. R. B. Frazier. New Repub 150:9-10 My 9 '64
Lodge, Kennedy top ISO poll. il Sr Schol 84: 1T My 8 '64
Logical candidate. S. Alsop. Sat Eve Post 237:15 Ja 18 '64
LBJ down on the farm. T. Wicker. Esquire 62:90-3+ O '64
LBJ vs. —? il U S News 56:35-6 Je 8 '64
LBJ's political pulling power: what the Newsweek poll shows. L. Harris. il Newsweek 62:14-15 D 23 '63
Man to beat. il Time 83:21-2 My 8 '64
Margaret Chase Smith: woman of courage, by F. Graham, jr. Review
Sat R 47:42-3 Ap 18 '64. C. B. Luce.
Mark the man. il Newsweek 63:15-16 F 17 '64
Men behind the men who—. D. S. Broder. il N Y Times Mag p 15+ Ja 5 '64
Mind of Barry Goldwater. R. Kirk. Nat R 15:149-51 Ag 27 '63
Minor party candidates. il Sr Schol 85:17 S 23 '64
Moratorium ends. Newsweek 63:20+ Ja 6 '64
More clues to what voters are thinking. il U S News 56:33-5 My 18 '64
Name is Smith. T. Wicker. il N Y Times Mag p35 Jl 28 '63
New Hampshire. Commonweal 80:4 Mr 27 '64
New Hampshire poll: write-in fever gains. il Newsweek 63:18-21 Mr 9 '64
New presidential race. E. J. Hughes. Newsweek 62:19 D 16 '63
Next president? il Newsweek 63:23 F 10 '64
Next: the showdown primary: California. U S News 56:58 Je 1 '64
1960's: the issues and the candidates. J. J. Huthmacher. Cur Hist 47:229-35+ O '64
1964: who's ahead? H. Brandon. Mlle 58:130-1 Mr '64
1964's changing political line-ups. il Sr Schol 83:15-17+ Ja 17 '64
Nixon and Goldwater in '64? Sat Eve Post 236:82 N 30 '63
Nixon-Lodge again? il Newsweek 62:15-16 D 23 '63
Nixon's new role: what will it be? U S News 54:24 Mr 25 '63
No enter, no win; Republicans. Time 82:18 Ag 23 '63
Non-candidate. Nation 198:517 My 25 '64
Non-candidates. Time 83:13 Ja 24 '64
Notes on the American election. N. Cousins. Sat R 47:24 O 17 '64
Now they dance the nomination minuet. R. Baker. il N Y Times Mag p 10-11+ Jl 21 '63
Odds against Goldwater. E. J. Hughes. Newsweek 62:21 N 4 '63
On the '64 campaign trail. il Sr Schol 84:15 Ja 31; 19 F 7; 17 F 21; 11 Mr 6; 19 Mr 13; 33 Ap 3; 26 Ap 10; 17 My 1 '64
Only the senator can stop it now; Goldwater boom. M. McGrory. America 109:69 Jl 20 '63
Opening the big campaign; Republican primary in New Hampshire. il Bsns W p28-9 F 29 '64
Opinion, please: from Iowa City. P. Engle. il Mlle 59:34+ O '64
Oregon roundup; two weeks before presidential primary il Time 83:22 My 8 '64
Our choice: Johnson and Humphrey. Life 57:4 O 9 '64
Out of the doldrums; press reaction to Goldwater competitor. Time 84:60 Jl 3 '64
Party of Ike. E. J. Hughes. Newsweek 63:15 My 4 '64

PRESIDENTIAL candidates—1964—*Continued*
Pat Brown: LBJ's '64 running mate? il U S News 55:9 D 30 '63
Peek but don't peak. Newsweek 62:33-4 N 25 '63
Picking Barry. K. Crawford. Newsweek 62:37 S 23 '63
Planned deadlock?. R. Moley. Newsweek 62:90 S 30 '63
Political hot stove league. Time 82:28-9 O 11 '63
Political notes from the prairies. J. Burnham. Nat R 16:278-9 Ap 7 '64
373 My 5 '64
Political problems. T. Lewis. Nation 197:409-11 D 14 '63
Political punditry. Nation 197:445 D 28 '63
Politically unhappy marriage. Nat R 14:392-3 My 21 '63
Politics becoming a millionaires' game? il U S News 54:58-61 F 25 '63
Polling popularity. Newsweek 62:32 O 14 '63
Polls. Time 82:25 N 8 '63; 83:23 My 1 '64
President will run scared. E. T. Folliard. America 111:32 Jl 11 '64
Quandary of Henry Cabot Lodge. S. Karnow. il Sat Eve Post 237:70-3 F 8 '64
Question now: Johnson vs. which Republican? il U S News 55:32-3 D 23 '63
Reading entrails. M. Kempton. New Repub 150:4-5 My 23 '64
Realignment on the right. R. D. Masters. Reporter 29:23-6 N 7 '63; Discussion. 29:8 D 5 '63
Republican search. E. J. Hughes. Newsweek 63:13 Ja 27 '64
Republicans. See issues of Newsweek during presidential campaign
Republicans. See issues of Time during presidential campaign
Republicans: convention preview? il Newsweek 62:25 Jl 15 '63
Republicans: how they're running. il Time 82:24 O 25 '63
Republicans look over another possibility for '64. il U S News 55:42-3 Jl 8 '63
Republicans: one who is; one who isn't? Time 81:30 Ap 19 '63
Republicans take a brand-new look at the candidates. il pors U S News 55:65-7 D 9 '63
Republicans take another look at Governor Scranton. U S News 55:82 D 16 '63
Republicans: with an eye on July. il Newsweek 63:19 F 24 '64
Revised conclusion of James Reston. P. R. Bushnell. il Nat R 14:449-50+ Je 4 '63
Revving up for the campaign trail. E. T. Folliard. America 109:623 N 16 '63
Rockefeller and the GOP. W. Lippmann. Newsweek 61:15 Ap 1 '63
Rockefeller: into an uphill race. il U S News 55:26 N 18 '63
Rockefeller resolve. E. J. Hughes. Newsweek 62:23 S 23 '63
Rockefeller vs Goldwater. J. Duscha. New Repub 149:13-14 O 26 '63
Rockefeller's candidacy. R. Moley. Newsweek 62:124 O 14 '63
Rockefeller's cool campaign. J. Desmond. Nation 197:23-5 Jl 13 '63
Rockefeller's triple-threat brain trust. A. L. Otten and C. B. Seib. Harper 227:74-9 Jl '63
Rocky's running again. il Newsweek 62:20-2+ Ag 26 '63
Scent of gold water. Newsweek 62:36-7 S 23 '63
Scranton. New Repub 150:3-4 Je 27 '64
Scranton and Kuchel. K. Crawford. Newsweek 63:27 Ja 13 '64
Scranton: now a favorite son for '64. U S News 55:17 Jl 1 '63
Second-term time. il Newsweek 62:30 N 25 '63
Sharpening the spikes; W. W. Scranton. Newsweek 62:23-4 Jl 1 '63
Shoo-in fallacy. Nation 198:158-9 F 17 '64
Signs that point to '64. il U S News 55:48 N 4 '63
Six-to-one party press; presidential endorsements. Time 84:43 S 25 '64
Six vs. LBJ; latest on the Republican scramble. il U S News 56:57-8 Ja 13 '64
'64 election; without JFK it's wide-open race. il U S News 55:46-7 D 2 '63
Slugfest in California. W. F. Buckley, jr. Nat R 16:394 My 19 '64
Some blows for next year. il Time 81:21 Ap 12 '63
South goes back up for grabs. J. J. Kilpatrick. il Nat R 15:523-4+ D 17 '63
Speculations on the 1964 campaign. E. T. Folliard. America 110:7 Ja 4 '64
Spoor of the demagogue. Nation 198:226 Mr 9 '64
Starting gun in New Hampshire. J. Desmond. il Nation 198:168-9 F 17 '64
Still fishing. Newsweek 62:30 S 30 '63
Straws in Iowa. Newsweek 63:20 Ap 6 '64
Student opinions. Sr Schol 84:23 My 8 '64
Sweepstakes in the snow; New Hampshire primary. J. Skow. il Sat Eve Post 237:17-23 Mr 14 '64
T.R.B. from Washington; why not Goldwater? New Repub 149:2 S 21 '63
Talk with Governor Scranton. H. Brandon. il Sat R 47:12-13 Ap 4 '64
Tamper with an image? R. Moley. Newsweek 62:116 N 25 '63
Tees, tigers, titmice & a president too? G.O.P. presidential potentials. il Time 82:22-6 Mr 6 '64
Tender moment on the short steep uphill trail: with just three weeks to go Scranton makes the sparks fly; with report by R. Ajemian. il Life 56:28-37 Je 26 '64
That bug, that presidential bug. il Newsweek 62:17-18 O 28 '63
They're all in the running; photographs. N Y Times Mag p 10-11 Mr 8 '64
This president thing. il Time 81:26-31 Je 14 '63
Toward a dynamic conservatism. Fortune 69:106 Ap '64
Toward the day of reckoning. il Time 83:21-2 Ja 10 '64
Toward the target. il Newsweek 62:36+ O 21 '63
Twenty-four hours in the life of Margaret Chase Smith. H. Markel. il McCalls 91:116-17+ My '64
Two big fights start shaping up. J. Ajemian. Life 56:22 Mr 27 '64
Two Lyndon Johnsons and the U.S. of 1964. M. Ways. il Fortune 69:80-3+ Ja '64
Ultimate decency; presidential candidates and the racial conflict. W. Lippmann. Newsweek 64:13 Ag 17 '64
Vice President's chances in '64. U S News 54:14 F 25 '63
View from defeat. E. J. Hughes. Newsweek 63:20-1 Je 15 '64
Visit to Gettysburg. N. Cousins. Sat R 47:18-19 Jl 11 '64
Vote for our man in Vietnam; with editorial comment. il Life 56:4, 32-9 Mr 20 '64
Wallace in Indiana; with editorial comment. G. Englehart. Nation 198:449, 451-3 My 4 '64
Wallace in Wisconsin. Nation 198:386 Ap 20 '64
Warning from Wisconsin. Nat R 16:306-7 Ap 21 '64
Washington desk. J. R. Slevin. Duns R 83:5-6 Ja '64
We are all descended from grandfathers! grandfathers of the candidates. O. Jensen. il Am Heritage 15:4-13+ Je '64
What New Hampshire said. Nat R 16:218-21 Mr 24 '64
What now for 1964? il Newsweek 62:50 D 2 '63
What the recent polls show: Johnson, Goldwater, undecided; table. il U S News 57:37 O 19 '64
What will decide presidential race. il Nations Bsns 51:32-3+ N '63
What's ahead for the G.O.P? E. Mazo. il Sat Eve Post 236:36 D 14 '63
What's that Barry? New Repub 150:8-9 Ja 18 '64
When leaders meet: Republicans size up their candidates. il U S News 56:76 Ja 20 '64
Where Nixon stands: interview. R. M. Nixon. il U S News 55:84-91 O 14 '63
Where Romney stands; interview. G. Romney. U S News 56:70-5 Mr 9 '64
Who stands how with whom. il Time 83:28 Ap 3 '64
Who would run best against LBJ? Newsweek 63:15 Ja 13 '64
Who'll run against Kennedy in '64: survey of Republicans: governors, national committee, state chairmen. il U S News 54:53-8 My 20 '63
Who's ahead now in Republican race. il U S News 56:38-43 Ap 6 '64
Who's for Barry? What's he for? il New Repub 149:3-5 Jl 20 '63
Who's for whom; endorsement of candidates. Reporter 31:16+ O 8 '64
Who's running? Newsweek 61:28 Ap 8 '63
Why Goldwater is gaining ground. il U S News 56:31-3 Ap 27 '64
Why G.O.P. should choose Scranton. Life 57:4 Jl 3 '64

PRESIDENTIAL candidates—1964—*Continued*
Will history be a guide to the '64 race? E. T. Folliard. America 109:253 S 14 '63
Will it be Goldwater, Rockefeller, or—? poll of Republican leaders in fifty states. il U S News 55:46-8 O 7 '63
Will it be Nixon vs. Kennedy again in '64? il U S News 55:34-5 N 25 '63
Will '64 election be a surprise? il U S News 54:42-4 Mr 11 '63
Will the South bolt Kennedy in 1964? il U S News 54:76-7 My 27 '63
Woman's right; candidacy of M. C. Smith. Newsweek 63:22-3 F 10 '64
Wraps are off; Rockefeller vs Goldwater. il Newsweek 62:41 Jl 29 '63
See also names of presidential candidates, e.g. B. M. Goldwater

Anecdotes, facetiae, satire, etc.

Mom and pop; Goldwater-Smith ticket. Reporter 29:24 N 21 '63

1968

Best man 1968. G. Vidal. il Esquire 59:59-62+ Mr '63; Excerpts. U S News 54:19 Mr 4 '63
Some facts about 'sixty-four and 'sixty-eight. E. T. Folliard. America 108:429 Mr 30 '63

Protection

What's being done to protect nominees. il U S News 57:8 Ag 31 '64

PRESIDENTIAL conventions. See National conventions (political)
PRESIDENTIAL duties. See Presidents—United States—Powers and duties
PRESIDENTIAL elections. See Presidents—United States—Election
PRESIDENTIAL entertaining. See Government entertaining
PRESIDENTIAL government. See Presidents—United States
PRESIDENTIAL inaugurations. See Inaugurations
PRESIDENTIAL medal of freedom. See Medal of freedom
PRESIDENTIAL papers. See Archives—United States
PRESIDENTIAL planes. See Airplanes, Government
PRESIDENTIAL polls. See Public opinion polls
PRESIDENTIAL primaries. See Primaries
PRESIDENTIAL scholars medallion. See Medals
PRESIDENTIAL succession. See Presidents—United States—Succession
PRESIDENTS

France

Count of Paris. E. v. Kuehnelt-Leddihn. Nat R 15:102 Ag 13 '63

Lebanon

Charles the Sweet; C. Helou elected president. Newsweek 64:44 Ag 31 '64

Mexico

Meet the president. il Time 84:22 Jl 3 '64
Presidential ritual. Newsweek 62:56 N 18 '63

Nigeria

See also
Diori, H.

Panama

Panama winner Robles can he control the reds? il U S News 56:21 My 25 '64

Sierra Leone

African ruler: Prime Minister Margai of Sierra Leone. G. C. Turner. Negro Hist Bul 28:13 O '64

United States

All for the love of a lady. C. B. Luce. il McCalls 91:93+ O; 20+ N '63
Bleed, but bleed inwardly; reactions to outrageous criticism. B. H. Bagdikian. il N Y Times Mag p 10+ Ag 9 '64
Can public men have private lives? E. F. Goldman. il N Y Times Mag p 13+ Je 16 '63
Cold crusade; the Eisenhower presidency. A. Rosenthal. Nation 196:361-4 Ap 27 '63
Epilogue. D. F. Fleming. Ann Am Acad 351:180 Ja '64
Every president since Lincoln sat for the Bachrachs. il Life 55:30B-30C Ag 9 '63
Fine art of president-baiting. M. Greenfield. Reporter 31:29-33 S 24 '64
First family has everything but privacy. M. Smith. il Nations Bsns 51:23-4 My '63
How to pick a president. S. Warren. Sat R 47:10-13 Jl 4 '64
Issue of morality. R. Moley. Newsweek 64:116 O 19 '64
Limits of continuity. New Repub 149:4-6 D 14 '63
Man on Pennsylvania avenue. R. L. Tobin. Sat R 47:22 Je 13 '64
Mark Twain and Lyndon B. Johnson. C. Clemens. Hobbies 69:112+ Ap '64
Millionaire as president. C. Amory. Vogue 144:96-7+ Ag 1 '64
100 years of history in the White House; photographs. N Y Times Mag p24-5 D 1 '63
Presidency; by the presidents; excerpts from writings and addresses; comp. by H. F. Graff. il N Y Times Mag p 18-19+ Ap 12 '64
Presidency; symposium. bibliog il Am Heritage 15:1-112 Ag '64
President and his critics. W. A. Williams. Nation 196:226-8+ Mr 16 '63
President as world leader, by S. Warren. Review
Sat R 47:40-1 O 10 '64. F. Altschul
Presidential firsts, mosts and almosts; collection of facts and figures. H. Faber. il N Y Times Mag p 16+ My 24 '64
Presidential government. R. Moley. Newsweek 62:98 D 9 '63
Presidential parade; unbroken line; drawings by O. Berger. Sat Eve Post 237:74-5 O 31 '64
Presidential succession. America 109:722 D 7 '63
Presidents & politics; quiz on men & campaigns of the past. Changing T 18:24 N '64
Presidents on the presidency, by A. B. Tourtellot. Review
Newsweek 63:88+ Ap 6 '64
Profiles of the Presidents. F. Freidel. il Nat Geog Mag 126:642-87; 127:80-121 N '64, Ja '65 (to be cont)
Qualities that make a president. S. Hyman. il N Y Times Mag p23+ D 1 '63
Six qualities that make a president. D. Eisenhower. Time 81:28 Je 14 '63
Two Lyndon Johnsons and the U.S. of 1964. M. Ways. il Fortune 69:80-3+ Ja '64
We got rhythm. K. Crawford. Newsweek 61:37 Ap 15 '63
What's your pleasure, Mr President? favorite drinks of the Presidents. il Esquire 63:52-3 Ja '65
World resounds: Milwaukee; personalistic aspect of the presidency. Q. L. Quade. America 109:770 D 14 '63
See also
Inaugurations
Vice-Presidents—United States
White House

Anecdotes, facetiae, satire, etc.

From bully! to vigah! A. Robertson. il Horizon 5:68-71 N '63
Was lifted by ears as boy, no harm done. E. B. White. New Yorker 40:38 My 9 '64
When Martha goes to Washington. A. Buchwald. McCalls 91:34 Ap '64

Assassination

Assassins' toll: four U.S. presidents. il U S News 55:35 D 2 '63
Earlier assasins; killers of Presidents Lincoln, Garfield and McKinley. Time 82:28 N 29 '63
Murder most foul. A. Robertson. il Am Heritage 15:90-104 Ag '64
Presidential victims. Sr Schol 83:14-15 D 6 '63
Protecting the President: a job for Superman? Sr Schol 85:9 N 4 '64
See also
Kennedy, J.F.—Assassination

Correspondence

Default of the educated man. N. Cousins. Sat R 46:18 Je 29 '63
Ohio court enjoins use of Harding letters. Pub W 186:32 Ag 10 '64

Election

Across the Nation: the story of the '64 election; with charts. il U S News 57:38-44 N 16 '64
Alien reviews the election. E. v. Kuehnelt-Leddihn. Nat R 16:1058 D 1 '64
America votes: 1964. il Sr Schol 85:4-17+ bibliog(p43) S 23 '64
American presidential elections; symposium. bibliog f il Cur Hist 47:193-235+ O '64
Arithmetic lesson; vote in the South. il Newsweek 64:36 N 23 '64
Back to work. New Repub 151:3-5 N 14 '64

PRESIDENTS—United States—Election—*Cont.*
Better way to choose a president. D. Lawrence. U S News 54:120 Ap 8 '63
Crucial questions for November 4. Christian Cent 81:1291 O 21 '64
Despite the hoopla, it's the best system; method of choosing a president. J. M. Burns. il N Y Times Mag p 11+ Ap 26 '64
Election. Nat R 16:999-1001 N 17 '64
Election key: how will big cities go? il U S News 57:80-3 O 26 '64
Election year forecast. Nations Bsns 51:31-7+ N '63
Elections are no fun anymore. D. Brinkley. il Look 28:35+ Jl 14 '64
Electoral reform would make your vote more important. F. Morley. il Nations Bsns 51:25-6 S '63
Figures; 1964 statistics. Time 84:39 N 13 '64
Fixing the score in '64. E. Planer. Reporter 29:35-6 S 12 '63
Foreigners on U.S. elections. America 111:150 Ag 15 '64
From Washington straight. Cato. Nat R 16:1006 N 17 '64
Great presidents are lucky accidents. M. L. Coit. il Look 28:43-4+ Jl 14 '64
Hard, close fight; prediction of President Kennedy. Newsweek 62:36 O 21 '63
Have faith in the twentieth century. W. Johnson. Bul Atomic Sci 21:10-15 Ja '65
How not to elect a president. D. Lawrence. U S News 57:100 S 7 '64
How to get elected. B. A. Weisberger. il Am Heritage 15:62-77 Ag '64
How to watch the election. il Newsweek 64:27-9 N 2 '64
If good men do nothing. R. L. Tobin. Sat R 47:16 Ag 1 '64
Is Kennedy in political trouble at home? il U S News 55:38-40 Jl 8 '63
It could happen here. K. Crawford. Newsweek 61:33 Je 17 '63
Johnson sweep. il U S News 57:33-4 N 16 '64
Letter from Washington. R. H. Rovere. New Yorker 40:235-8+ N 14 '64
LBJ: my thanks to all America; Winners. il Newsweek 64:25-7 N 9 '64
LBJ's record majority; with comment on the world's news fronts. il Sr Schol 85:18-19 N 18 '64
Meaning of the margin; in election victory. S. Alsop. il Sat Eve Post 237:14 S 12 '64
Morning after. C. McWilliams. Nation 199:345-7 N 16 '64
Negro votes beat Barry. P. Watters. New Repub 151:7 N 28 '64
New mandate; with editorial comment. Bsns W p33-4, 188 N 7 '64
Newsweek poll: the women's vote. L. Harris. il Newsweek 64:32 S 21 '64
1964 election: official returns. il Time 84:25 D 18 '64
Now a new worry for Kennedy: the white vote in '64. il U S News 55:36-7 S 9 '63
On election night: you be the expert. il Changing T 18:12-14 O '64
Presidents don't lose. S. Alsop. il Sat Eve Post 236:14 N 2 '63
Real poop; concerning R. Welch's editorial on Barry Goldwater's electoral defeat. Time 84:35 D 11 '64
Recovering from Barry. W. D. Burnham. il Commonweal 81:319-22 N 27 '64
Selection of a president. J. D. Weaver. Holiday 36:40+ N '64
Silent vote. Nation 199:261 O 26 '64
'64 election; how we shall view it. America 111:103-4 Ag 1 '64
TV braces for the big count; networks pool resources for reporting the vote. il Bsns W p26-7 O 31 '64
Time for cool heads and steady hands. Christian Cent 81:1323-4 O 28 '64
Time for election reform is now. F. Morley. il Nations Bsns 52:25-6 D '64
Triumphant ticket whoops it up and saddles up way down at the LBJ. R. B. Stolley. il Life 57:36-7 N 13 '64
Uncertain world; events of past week in relation to presidential election. W. Lippmann. Newsweek 64:29 O 26 '64
VPA: the making of an avalanche, 1964. il Newsweek 64:28-9 N 9 '64
War of the computers; Nov. 3. D. F. Nolan. il Sci N L 86:250-1 O 17 '64
We support Goldwater. Nation 196:386 My 11 '63; Reply. C. Bloomer, jr. 196:inside cover Je 29 '63
What now? Johnson-Humphrey victory. Christian Cent 81:1387 N 11 '64
What's this about a landslide? with chart. U S News 57:45 Jl 27 '64
When defeat can beget victory. D. Lawrence. U S News 56:116 Je 15 '64
Who will elect the next president. il Nations Bsns 52:76-8+ Ap '64
Wrong way to pick a president. D. Lawrence. U S News 57:116 Jl 27 '64
Year of the Democrat; Johnson's landslide. il Newsweek 64:35-6 N 16 '64

See also
Electoral college
Presidential campaigns
Presidential candidates
Primaries
Television broadcasting—Election results

Families

Life with father, the President. H. F. Graff. il N Y Times Mag p 10-11+ Jl 14 '63
Story of the Presidents at Christmas. F. Knebel. il Look 27:16-19 D 31 '63

Health and hygiene

Grappling with succession & disability. il Time 83:21 Je 5 '64
He ought to try to slow up. Sat Eve Post 236:79 D 14 '63
James Craik: the first White House physician. J. Luter. il Todays Health 42:46-9+ F '64
Johnson's heart: all signs are good; report of Drs Cain and Hurst. il Bsns W p 18-19 D 21 '63
Kennedy's back injury: another flare-up. il U S News 55:22 S 9 '63
President Johnson's health record. U S News 55:39 D 2 '63
President's health: a progress report. il U S News 55:16 Jl 22 '63
Speaking out; let's stop gambling with the presidency. J. M. Burns. Sat Eve Post 237:12+ Ja 25 '64
Story of Johnson's health. il U S News 56:40-2 Ja 27 '64

History

Presidency and how it grew. F. Freidel. il Nat Geog Mag 126:642-87 N '64

Homes

See United States—Historic houses, etc.

Powers and duties

Blandness in the White House. S. Alsop. il Sat Eve Post 238:18 Ja 30 '65
Chief Executive, by L. W. Koenig. Review
New Repub 151:19-20 N 28 '64. G. W. Johnson
Criticisms of Kennedy. New Repub 148:2 My 18 '63
Decision-making in the White House, by T. C. Sorenson. Review
Sat R il 46:50-1 S 28 '63. L. W. Koenig
How Mr Kennedy gets the answers; fact-finders and reporters. S. Hyman. il N Y Times Mag p 17+ O 20 '63
How the President makes a decision; excerpts from Decision-making in the White House. T. C. Sorensen. Sat R 46:12-15+ Jl 27: 8-12+ Ag 3 '63
How to watch the White House. L. L. Henry. il Nations Bsns 52:34-5+ N '64
Is the government ready for the future? R. Drummond. Sat R 47:58+ Ag 29 '64
Johnson's next four years. J. Kraft. Harper 229:44+ N '64
Kennedy and the liberals. S. E. Harris. New Repub 148:15-16 Je 1 '63
Letter from Washington. R. H. Rovere. New Yorker 39:78-84+ D 21 '63
Limited war and American defense policy, by J. Deitchman. Review
U S News 57:128 O 5 '64. D. Lawrence
LBJ maps an agenda, lines up the team. il Bsns W p34-6 N 7 '64
Man in the White House. Sr Schol 84:10-11 F 14 '64
Men Johnson will need. V. P. Rock. Nation 199:348-9 N 16 '64
Moment of decision. B. Catton. Am Heritage 15:49-53 Ag '64
More power to the President (not less) L. W. Koenig. il N Y Times Mag p7+ Ja 3 '65
New mandate; with editorial comment. Bsns W p33-4, 188 N 7 '64
Ordeal of power, by E. J. Hughes. Review
New Repub 148:25-6 Ap 27 '63. W. A. Korns
Presidency and the peace. M. Bundy. For Affairs 42:353-65 Ap '64
President Johnson discusses the presidency; television interview, March 14, 1964. L. B. Johnson. Dept State Bul 50:523-9 Ap 6 '64
President's most powerful tool: leadership of public opinion. E. E. Cornwell, jr. il Sat R 48:16-19 Ja 2 '65
Reorganizing the presidency. D. Lawrence. U S News 55:112 D 16 '63

PRESIDENTS—United States—Powers and duties—*Continued*
Speaking out; doesn't Congress have ideas of its own? A. Ribicoff. Sat Eve Post 237: 6+ Mr 21 '64
Task ahead for the President. Bsns W p 156 D 7 '63
Twelve great problems for a new president; photographs. N Y Times Mag p28-9 D 1 '63
What Negroes can expect from President Lyndon Johnson. L. Bennett, jr. il Ebony 19:81-4+ Ja '64
Who makes decisions in Washington. B. Hays. il Nations Bsns 53:40-1+ Ja '65
Who really is the president? D. Lawrence. U S News 57:120 S 21 '64
Will success spoil LBJ's carnival of compatibility? P. Lisagor. il Nations Bsns 52: 21-2 D '64

Protection

Campaign time; when Secret service worry grows. il U S News 56:63-4 Ap 13 '64
Can you really protect the President? interview. U. E. Baughman. U S News 55:38-40 D 23 '63
Commission has concluded... major recommendations of the Warren commission. il Newsweek 64:63-4 O 5 '64
Crushed by the crowds. Johnsons worry their guards. il U S News 56:19 My 4 '64
Inaugural protection for the President: glass and armor plate. il U S News 58:10 Ja 11 '65
Lessons to be learned; Warren commission's findings. il Time 84:50+ O 2 '64
Lincoln rejects a bodyguard. C. C. Hollis. Nation 198:173-4 F 17 '64
Most worried men; Secret service. il Newsweek 62:34 D 9 '63
New shield around the President. il U S News 55:29 D 30 '63
Presidential car: it's safer now; What LBJ says about the danger from crowds. il U S News 57:14 O 19 '64
Presidential safety. Sr Schol 85:15-16 O 14 '64
President's safety. R. Moley. Newsweek 63: 112 My 18 '64
Protecting the President: a job for Superman? il Sr Schol 85:6-9 N 4 '64
Protectors of the President; spotlight on the Secret service. il Sr Schol 84:8-9+ Ja 31 '64
Safeguarding the President so it can't occur again. il Bsns W p34+ O 3 '64
Secret service worry now: how to protect President Johnson; report. il U S News 57: 59 O 12 '64
To protect the President in the future: the Warren commission recommends this. U S News 57:41 O 5 '64
Trying to protect the unprotectable; Secret service. Time 84:28 O 9 '64
Was there a plot to assassinate LBJ? il U S News 56:48-9 Ap 27 '64
We can prevent presidenial assassinations. J. H. Walker. il Look 28:124-6 F 11 '64
When the highest office changes hands. D. D. Eisenhower. il Sat Eve Post 236:15 D 14 '63
See also
Secret service—United States

Public relations

And a time for ecclesiastes; President and the press. Reporter 32:12 Ja 14 '65
As dog lovers took pen in hand. U S News 56:6 My 11 '64
Back of the change in LBJ. U S News 56:49 Je 15 '64
Care and feeding of the Kennedy image. il U S News 55:92-3 S 9 '63
Case against the fireside chat. I. J. Schulman. il N Y Times Mag p 10+ Je 14 '64
Cracks in image mirror irritate Kennedy fans. M. Smith. il Nations Bsns 51:23-4 Ap '63
Decline of Mr Kennedy? W. F. Buckley, jr. Nat R 15:95 Ag 13 '63
Drama outdraws issues on political swings. M. Smith. Nations Bsns 51:23 N '63
How a president should use the intellectuals; two men, two styles. J. P. Roche. il N Y Times Mag p 10+ Jl 26 '64
How the public rates JFK. il Look 27:34 Ag 13 '63
Inside report: changes LBJ has brought in six months. il U S News 56:46-50+ My 18 '64
Is Kennedy in political trouble at home? il U S News 55:38-40 Jl 8 '63
Kennedy's voyage of discovery. S. Vanocur. Harper 228:41-5 Ap '64
Lighter mood hits Washington: quotations. L. B. Johnson. U S News 56:47-8 My 11 '64
Lights, action, camera: JFK. il U S News 55:67 N 4 '63
LBJ and the press. K. Crawford. Newsweek 63:18 F 17 '64
LBJ's drive is no puzzle to insiders. P. Lisagor. il Nations Bsns 52:23-4 Jl '64
Midterm tone: softer at home, tougher abroad. M. Smith. il Nations Bsns 51:23-4 F '63
News management (cont) Reporter 30:14+ F 27 '64
Now a new worry for Kennedy: the white vote in '64. il U S News 55:36-7 S 9 '63
On a poverty trip with LBJ. il U S News 56:58 My 25 '64
Pawns of the President. Nation 197:211 O 12 '63
President and the press. T. Lewis. Nation 198:207-9 Mr 2 '64
Protecting the President: a job for Superman? il Sr Schol 85:6-9 N 4 '64
Will success spoil LBJ's carnival of compatibility? P. Lisagor. il Nations Bsns 52: 21-2 D '64

Reading

Education of presidents. R. Kirk. Nat R 15: 308 O 8 '63
Presidents as readers. R. L. Tobin. Sat R 47:18 Ag 22 '64

Relations with Congress

After six months: how JFK is making out with Congress. il U S News 55:32-3 Jl 22 '63
Atlantic report. Atlan 212:6+ N '63
Can Johnson get Congress moving? R. Evans and R. Novak. il Sat Eve Post 237:34+ Ap 4 '64
Case against the fireside chat. I. J. Schulman. il N Y Times Mag p 10+ Je 14 '64
Congress and Kennedy, what's coming. V. J. Burke. il Nations Bsns 51:38-9+ Jl '63
Congress is ready to admit to a stalemate. J. N. Eller. America 109:89 Jl 27 '63
Congress, the President, and the swinging pendulum. Sr Schol 83:9-11+ Ja 10 '64
Congress vs. the President. Sr Schol 82:8-9 F 20 '63
Congressmen size up LBJ and his first six months. il U S News 56:57-9 Je 8 '64
Could Kennedy budge the Congress? A. Rosenthal. New Repub 148:13-15 My 4 '63
Course ahead for LBJ. J. L. McCaskill. NEA J 53:15 Ja '64
First crisis. il Newsweek 63:13-14 Ja 6 '64
Full treatment; President Johnson and Congress. Time 82:25 D 13 '63
Giving Congress the vote. Commonweal 79: 448 Ja 17 '64
Home town voices ring louder than LBJ's. P. Lisagor. il Nations Bsns 53:23-4 Ja '65
How congressmen rate the new President. U S News 55:78-83 D 9 '63
How the President persuades Congress. il N Y Times Mag p 16-17 O 27 '63
Interregnum on the Hill. M. Greenfield. Reporter 29:19-20 D 19 '63
It is the people who face the test; standpattism in Congress. T. Wicker. il N Y Times Mag p 19+ D 8 '63; Reply with rejoinder. E. G. Janosik. p20 Ja 5 '64
JFK and Congress: counterattack. Newsweek 62:29-30 N 25 '63
Johnson and the new Congress. il U S News 57:31-2 N 23 '64
Johnson as tactician. Nation 198:1 Ja 4 '64
Johnson Congress: what it will do. il Nations Bsns 52:32-3+ D '64
Johnson way with Congress. T. Wicker. il N Y Times Mag p9+ Mr 8 '64
Kennedy and Congress; with twenty-five days to go. il U S News 55:31-3 N 25 '63
Kennedy's problem: could he get more from Congress? H. Fuller. New Repub 148:12-14 Mr 9 '63
Lethargic 88th vs. L.B.J. Life 55:4 D 13 '63
Letter from Washington. R. H. Rovere. New Yorker 39:133-8 F 15 '64
LBJ and Congress. K. Crawford. Newsweek 65:26 Ja 18 '65
LBJ and Congress; now a test. il U S News 56:33-4 Ja 13 '64
LBJ and Congress; the next 100 days. il U S News 56:31-2 Mr 30 '64
LBJ and his Congress: made for each other; concerning State of the Union message. Newsweek 65:17 Ja 18 '65
LBJ: tug, twist, and massage: Untroubled waters. Newsweek 62:13-14 D 23 '63
LBJ wants Congress to do these things. il U S News 55:46-7 D 9 '63
Lyndon Johnson talks about Congress and the presidency; excerpts from interview, 1955. L. B. Johnson. U S News 56:25 Ja 6 '64
Must legislation. C. B. Luce. McCalls 91:20+ My '64
New Congress; it may get out of hand. il U S News 58:23-4 Ja 11 '65
New frontier's thrust bogs down in political muddle. M. Smith. Nations Bsns 51:23-4 Mr '63

PRESIDENTS—United States—Relations with Congress—*Continued*
Other war. K. Crawford. Newsweek 63:25 Ja 20 '64
Pennsylvania Avenue politics. R. Evans, jr. New Repub 148:19-20 F 2 '63
President and Congress; Mr Johnson's first message; address, November 27, 1963. L. B. Johnson. il U S News 55:102-3 D 9 '63; Same. Vital Speeches 30:130-1 D 15 '63; Dept State Bul 49:910-12 D 16 '63; Cong Digest 43:1-2 Ja '64
President considers timing vital to success. M. Smith. Nations Bsns 51:23-4 Je '63
President may help elect Congress he won't like. J. Craft. il Nations Bsns 52:23-4 Ap '64
President shows his style. il Bsns W p23-4 D 14 '63
Progress robs President of traditional weapon. M. Smith. il Nations Bsns 51:23-4 Jl '63
Refusal to act is often in public interest. J. Craft. il Nations Bsns 52:25-6 F '64
Sometimes everything seems to go wrong. M. Smith. il Nations Bsns 51:25 D '63
T.R.B. from Washington; Wilson versus Kennedy. New Repub 148:2 Mr 16 '63
Tax cut that is in trouble. U S News 54:92+ F 18 '63
Tension in U.S. politics. Q. L. Quade. America 110:312-13 Mr 7 '64
Washington desk. J. R. Slevin. Duns R 82:5 N '63
What you can expect from the new Congress. il U S News 58:36-7 Ja 4 '65
Where Kennedy is changing course. il U S News 55:31-2 N 4 '63
White House vs. Congress; is power balance shifting? excerpts from address, April 3, 1963. G. Allott. U S News 54:95-6 Ap 15 '63
Who runs Congress? Reporter 28:14+ Ap 25 '63
Why Congress doesn't give JFK what he wants. il U S News 54:38-42 Mr 18 '63
Why Congress is balking. il U S News 56:23-4 Ja 6 '64

Relations with the press

See Government and the press

Religion

Johnson's faith. il Time 83:65 Ap 3 '64

Salaries, allowances, etc.

Story of the Johnson family fortune. il U S News 55:75 D 16 '63; 56:38-42 My 4 '64

Succession

After the Vice President? R. S. Hirschfield. il Nation 198:25-8 Ja 6 '64
Atlantic report. Atlan 213:8+ Mr '64
Blessings on Bayh; proposed constitutional amendment. K. Crawford. Newsweek 64:43 O 26 '64
Bobby for president? W. F. Buckley, jr. Nat R 16:481 Je 16 '64
Calling all worriers. K. Crawford. Newsweek 63:36 Ap 27 '64
Dilemma of succession. J. F. Menez. il Commonweal 79:475-7 Ja 24 '64
Heartbeat away. H. F. Graff. Am Heritage 15:81-7 Ag '64
Heartbeat away; presidential succession. il Newsweek 62:23-4 D 16 '63
How to succeed? Newsweek 62:18 D 23 '63; 63:28 Mr 16 '64
If president-elect should die—. il U S News 57:44 N 9 '64
If something happened to the President. il U S News 55:37 D 16 '63
Ike plan cometh: vice president on the Republican ticket. J. J. Kilpatrick. il Nat R 16:483-6 Je 16 '64; Reply. 16:521+ Je 30 '64
Line of succession. Commonweal 79:360 D 20 '63
Line of succession. L. Rogers. il Reporter 29:20-2 D 19 '63
McCormack and Hayden: no plan to quit. il U S News 55:12 D 23 '63
Men in line for the presidency now. il U S News 55:14 D 2 '63
Muddled problem of the succession. R. B. Morris. il N Y Times Mag p 11+ D 15 '63
Naming a successor. New Repub 150:5 Ja 25 '64
Next in line. il Time 82:16 D 27 '63
Our greatest national danger. B. Bayh, jr. Look 28:74+ Ap 7 '64
Presidential incapacity; letter to the editor. E. D. Toland. Nat R 16:125+ F 11 '64
Presidential succession. America 109:722 D 7 '63
Presidential succession. New Repub 149:3-4 D 21 '63; 150:4-5 Mr 7 '64
Presidential succession. E. J. Hughes. Newsweek 62:9 D 30 '63
Presidential succession. W. Lippmann. Newsweek 63:13 Mr 2 '64
Second most important post in the U.S. Sat Eve Post 237:80 Ja 4 '64
Should the presidential succession law be changed? pro and con discussion. Sr Schol 84:12-13+ Ja 10 '64. Discussion. 84:12-13 Ap 17 '64
Speaking out; let's stop gambling with the presidency. J. M. Burns. Sat Eve Post 237:12+ Ja 25 '64
Speaking out; we need a vice president now. R. M. Nixon. Sat Eve Post 237:6+ Ja 18 '64
Spotlight on succession. Sr Schol 84:12 F 14 '64
Succession. Nation 197:406 D 14 '63
Succession. New Repub 150:6 F 15 '64
Succession and business. H. Hazlitt. Newsweek 63:59 Ja 6 '64
Succession law. New Repub 149:3-4 D 14 '63; 150:4-5 Ja 4 '64; Reply to Ja 4 issue. B. Bayh. 150:30-1 Ja 25 '64
This month's feature: moves to change presidential succession. Cong Digest 43:130-60 My '64
To reduce uncertainty; death or disability of a president in office. H. Hazlitt. Newsweek 62:86 D 9 '63
Urgent: law on succession. Life 56:4 Ap 3 '64
Vice Presidency. H. Hazlitt. Newsweek 62:86 D 2 '63
What if the President is disabled? il Sr Schol 84:11-13 Ap 10 '64
What sort of president would John W. McCormack make? answers. il Esquire 62:90-3 Jl '64
When a president dies. Sr Schol 83:15 D 6 '63

Term

Ike plan cometh: vice president on the Republican ticket. J. J. Kilpatrick. il Nat R 16:483-6 Je 16 '64; Reply. 16:521+ Je 30 '64
Presidential tenure. U S News 55:38 D 2 '63

Wives

All for the love of a lady. C. B. Luce. il McCalls 91:93+ O; 20+ N '63
First ladies I have known. P. Mesta. il McCalls 90:34+ Mr '63
First lady: a professional at getting things done. E. Janeway. il Ladies Home J 81:64-5+ Ap '64
New political issue: Mrs LBJ's property. U S News 56:12 My 25 '64
Our very busy First lady. C. Sadler. il McCalls 91:79-81+ Mr '64
President's lady; with reproductions of paintings. A. L. Jensen. Am Heritage 15:54-61 Ag '64
Public servant without pay: the First lady. M. Hunter. il N Y Times Mag p 10+ D 15 '63
Tribute to First ladies. McCalls 91:4 F '64
What kind of a woman is our new First lady? R. Montgomery. Good H 158:32+ Mr '64
What three Presidents say about their wives; excerpt from Woman in the White House. M. Means. il Good H 157:57-61+ Ag '63

Upper Volta

See also

Yameogo, M.

Venezuela

Democratic precedent; legitimate transfer of power. il Newsweek 63:53 Mr 23 '64

PRESIDENTS addresses. See Speeches, addresses, etc.

PRESIDENT'S advisory committee to strengthen the security of the free world. See United States—President's advisory committee to strengthen the security of the free world

PRESIDENTS automobiles. See Automobiles, Government

PRESIDENTS, College. See College presidents

PRESIDENT'S commission on the status of women; President's science advisory committee; etc. See United States—President's commission on the status of women; United States—President's science advisory committee; etc.

PRESIDENTS, Company. See Executives

PRESIDENTS inaugural addresses. See Speeches, addresses, etc.

PRESIDENT'S press conferences. See Press conferences

PRESIDENTS representatives. See Public officers

PRESIDENTS wives. See Presidents—United States—Wives

PRESIDIUM. See Communist party (Russia)

PRESLEY, Elvis
Elvis: ten million dollars later. V. Scott. por McCalls 90:90-1+ F '63

PRESS, John
Song at forest retreat. New Yorker 39:69 Ag 10 '63

PRESS. See Journalism; Newspapers; Periodicals

PRESS, Catholic. See Catholic press

PRESS and crime. See Crime and the press

PRESS and government. See Government and the press

PRESS-Argus. See Van Buren, Ark.—Newspapers

PRESS conferences
Act seven; Presidential press conference. Newsweek 63:28 Mr 16 '64
Back to the Oval room; presidential press conferences. Reporter 30:10+ Ja 2 '64
Candidates on air: new ruling from FCC. U S News 57:13 O 12 '64
Family plan; newsmen's families at presidential press conference. il Newsweek 63: 34+ My 18 '64
Homespun assurance; President Johnson's first conference. il Time 82:32 D 27 '63
In splendor he shakes up the world; de Gaulle's conference announcing new neutralist cause. H. Moffett. il Life 56:18-21 F 14 '64
I've got a secret: President Johnson and the press. J. Deakin. New Repub 152:13-15 Ja 30 '65
LBJ and the formal news conference. E. T. Folliard. America 110:303 Mr 7 '64
LBJ news conference, family style. il U S News 56:19 My 18 '64
Mr Kennedy's management of the news. A. Krock. Fortune 67:82+ Mr '63
Photography in the White House; interview, ed. by O. Atkins. P. Salinger. il U S Camera 26:12+ Mr '63
President and the press. il U S News 55: 34-5 D 30 '63
Q's and A's about the press conference. T. Wicker. il N Y Times Mag p24-5+ S 8 '63
What comes naturally: President Johnson's news conferences. il Newsweek 62:41-2 D 30 '63

PRESS council. See Newspapers—Great Britain

PRESS photographers. See Photographers

PRESS photography. See Photography, Journalistic

PRESS releases
See also
Church and the press
Government and the press

PRESS telegraphers. See Telegraphers

PRESSED flowers and leaves. See Flowers, Dried

PRESSED glass. See Glassware

PRESSES
Wyman-Gordon set to build world's second biggest forging press. J. F. Judge. il Miss & Roc 16:15-17 Ja 4 '65

PRESSLER, Joan
Storytelling project for slow learners. ALA Bul 57:168-9 F '63

PRESSMAN, Gabe
Reporter. New Yorker 39:19-21 Ag 17 '63

PRESSURE
Alchemy of ultrahigh pressure. G. A. W. Boehm. il Fortune 70:144-8+ O '64
Allotropy in some rare-earth metals at high pressures. G. J. Piermarini and C. E. Weir. bibliog il Science 144:69-71 Ap 3 '64
Beryllium: effect of ultra-high pressure on resistance. A. R. Marder. bibliog il Science 142:664 N 8 '63
Crystal structures at high pressures of metallic modifications of compounds of indium, gallium, and aluminum. J. C. Jamieson. bibliog il Science 139:845-7 Mr 1 '63
Crystal structures at high pressures of metallic modifications of silicon and germanium. J. C. Jamieson. bibliog il Science 139:762-4 F 22 '63
Ferrosilite ($FeSiO_3$): synthesis at high pressures and temperatures. D. H. Lindsley and others. bibliog il Science 144:73-4 Ap 3 '64
Geological aspects of high-pressure research. F. R. Boyd. bibliog il Science 145:13-20 Jl 3 '64
High pressure: effect on dysprosium. P. C. Souers and G. Jura. bibliog il Science 145:575-7 Ag 7 '64
High-pressure phase transition in tin telluride. J. A. Kafalas and A. N. Mariano. bibliog il Science 143:952 F 28 '64
High pressure phases of some compounds of group II-VI. A. N. Mariano and E. P. Warekois. bibliog il Science 142:672-3 N 8 '63
High-pressure polymorph of iron. T. Takahashi and W. A. Bassett. bibliog il Science 145:483-6 Jl 31 '64
High pressure transitions in $A^{(III)}$ $B^{(VI)}$ compounds: indium telluride. M. D. Banus and others. bibliog il Science 142:662-3 N 8 '63
Magnetic resonance at high pressure. G. B. Benedek. il Sci Am 212:102-8 bibliog(p 136) Ja '65
Mössbauer spectrum of iron-57 in iron metal at very high pressure. M. Nicol and G. Jura. bibliog il Science 141:1035-8 S 13 '63
Optical studies at high pressures. L. S. Whatley and others. bibliog il Science 144: 968-76 My 22 '64
Pressure and electronic structure. H. G. Drickamer. bibliog il Science 142:1429-35 D 13 '63
Pressure distribution measurements in fixed-anvil high-pressure cells. E. R. Lippincott and H. C. Duecker. bibliog il Science 144: 1119-21 My 29 '64
Pressure-induced trapping phenomenon in silver iodide. H. C. Duecker and E. R. Lippincott. bibliog il Science 146:1295-7 D 4 '64
Tetragonal zirconium oxide prepared under high pressure. F. W. Vahldiek and others. bibliog il Science 142:1059-60 N 22 '63
X-ray diffraction studies on dysprosium at high pressures. J. C. Jamieson. bibliog il Science 145:572-4 Ag 7 '64
X-ray diffraction studies on tin at high pressure and high temperature. J. D. Barnett and others. bibliog il Science 141:1041-2 S 13 '63
See also
Vapor pressure

PRESSURE, Osmotic. See Osmotic pressure

PRESSURE, Political. See Pressure groups

PRESSURE, Root. See Roots

PRESSURE casting. See Steel castings

PRESSURE chambers, Surgical. See High-pressure oxygenation

PRESSURE groups
What J. Edgar Hoover says about pressure groups; excerpts from address, November 24, 1964. J. E. Hoover. U S News 57:45 D 7 '64
See also
Lobbying

PRESSURE of population. See Population—Overpopulation

PRESSURE-sensitive tape. See Tape

PRESSURE suits
Housewife in a space suit. Sci Digest 56:72-3 O '64
Manual X-20A boost control simulated. E. J. Bulban. Aviation W 78:59+ F 18 '63
See also
Astronauts—Clothing

PRESSURE transducers. See Transducers

PRESTHUS, Robert
British elections. Nation 198:480-3 My 11 '64

PRESTIGE
Let us now appraise famous men. M. Epernay. il Esquire 60:128-30+ O '63

PRESTOLITE international corporation
Prestolite builds a new world. Bsns W p63-4+ D 14 '63

PRESTON, Betty Brown
Big man on Beech street; story. Seventeen 22:102-3 D '63
Dial Emmy for murder; story. Seventeen 22: 98-9 Je '63
I was a teen-age parasite; story. Seventeen 22:130-1 Ap '63
Knights must fall; story. Seventeen 22:132-3 F '63
Sing low, sweet Harriet; story. Seventeen 23:118-19 Mr '64

PRESTON, John Hyde
Hamlet's castle. Holiday 35:24+ Ja '64

PRESTON, Ralph C.
Education graduates view education and academic courses. bibliog f Sch & Soc 92: 233-7 Sum '64

PRESTON, Richard
Nuclear test ban treaty. Cur Hist 46:341-5+ Je '64
Test ban: optimism on Project Vela. Bul Atomic Sci 19:33-7 Je '63

PRESTON, Richard J. See Honigmann, J. J. jt. auth.

PRESTON, Richard Joseph
Growth of American forestry research and education. Am For 70:36-7+ D '64

PRESTON, Robert
That brassy music man returns to Broadway as poor Richard. G. Millstein. il pors Sat Eve Post 237:86-9 O 17 '64
PRESTRESSED concrete institute
P.C.I. honors eleven structures in awards program. il Arch Rec 136:12-13 S '64
Two municipal structures win design awards. il Am City 80:92 Ja '65
PRETI, Mattia
Cover: Il Calabrese. A. Frankfurter. il Art N 63:24+ Ja '65
PRÊTRE, Georges
In fine style: interview, ed. by J. W. Freeman. por Opera N 92:13 D 26 '64
PRETTY Polly; story. See Coward, N.
PRETTYMAN, Robert A.
Patient-planned program. Recreation 57:407 O '64
PREUSS, Charles F.
Sabah (North Borneo) bibliog Focus 14:1-6 N '63
PREVENTION of accidents. See Accidents—Prevention
PREVENTION of crime. See Crime prevention
PREVENTION of war. See War, Prevention of
PREVENTIVE inoculation. See Inoculation
PREVENTIVE medicine. See Medicine, Preventive
PREVENTIVE psychiatry. See Mental hygiene
PRÉVERT, Jacques
Home life: poem. Harper 229:99 N '64
PREVIN, André
1947-48 Copland, and Previn's conducting debut. J. Diether. il por Am Rec G 30:1096-8 Ag '64
PREVOCATIONAL education. See Vocational education
PRÉVOST, Antoine-François
Abbé and the image. G. McElroy. por Opera N 28:12-13 D 21 '63
PREVOST, Sir George
Victory on Lake Champlain. C. S. Forester. il por Am Heritage 15:6-11+ D '63
PREWETT, Virginia
Angel of the Lazaros. Read Digest 83:143-4+ D '63
PREWITT, T. A.
AM-FM car radio. Electr World 69:44-5 Mr '63
PREY, Hermann
Prize count; interview, ed. by Q. Eaton. por Opera N 29:16 Ja 2 '65

about

Hermann Prey's first recital for London; superb. H. Glass. Am Rec G 29:950 Ag '63
PRIBILOF ISLANDS
Seals are about gone. J. Van Nostrand. il Am Heritage 14:10-17+ Je '63
PRIBRAM, Karl H. See Kimble, D. P. jt. auth.
PRICE, Arnold H.
(comp) Articles and other books received; Germany, Austria and Switzerland. See issues of American historical review
Health insurance in West Germany. bibliog f Cur Hist 44:345-50 Je '63
PRICE, Charles
Golf ball: a panegyric. Esquire 62:171+ D '64
(ed) See Nicklaus, J. Three big ones talk about golf
(ed) See Palmer, A. Three big ones talk about golf
(ed) See Player, G. Three big ones talk about golf
PRICE, Derek John de Solla
Astronomy's past preserved at Jaipur. Natur Hist 73:48-53 Je '64
Ethics of scientific publication. bibliog Science 144:655-7 My 8 '64
Great encyclopedia doesn't have to be good? Science 144:665-6 My 8 '64
PRICE, Don K.
Role of science and scientists in government. Science 140:622-3 My 10 '63
PRICE, Donald Lisle
Norton's Price: a prophet vindicated. por Duns R 81:46 F '63
PRICE, Edwin C. Jr
Sarawak. pors Nat Geog Mag 126:334-7 S '64
PRICE, Jack
Jack's back and so is Carry. W. Tower. por Sports Illus 19:56 Ag 12 '63
PRICE, Jessie Isabelle
Doctor to Long Island ducks. il pors Ebony 19:76-8+ S '64
PRICE, Joe
They flip for Joe Price. D. Duncan. il pors Dance Mag 38:10-12 Ag '64
PRICE, Katherine
Two ladies in search of the world. W. Tower. il por Sports Illus 19:26-7 O 7 '63
PRICE, Leontyne
Conversation with Leontyne Price; ed. by S. Chotzinoff. por Holiday 35:103-4+ Mr '64

about

Leontyne Price as Tosca. P. L. Miller. il pors Am Rec G 30:92-4 O '63
Spiritual ground. V. Sheean. por Opera N 28:22-3 Mr 28 '64
Three Negroes receive 1964 Presidential freedom medal. C. W. Thomas. por Negro Hist Bul 28:58-9 D '64
PRICE, Margaret
Two open letters to teen-age girls. por Seventeen 23:232+ S '64
PRICE, Maxwell
Year 'round fun from a sled. Pop Mech 119:146-7 Ap '63
PRICE, Melvin
Honeymoon is over; excerpts from address, November 5, 1963. por U S News 55:74 N 25 '63
PRICE, Molly
Best dressed iris for 1963. Flower Grower 50:30-1+ Je '63
Fashion your own iris. Flower Grower 50:20 Jl '63
Iris are foolproof favorites. Flower Grower 51:34-7 Je '64
PRICE, Nancy
Aerialists; poem. Reporter 28:56 Mr 28 '63
Cassandra and the double-decked doom; poem. Atlan 211:116 My '63
Churchgoers; poem. Commonweal 79:631 F 21 '64
Sarah; poem. Commonweal 81:348 D 4 '64
Stained glass; poem. Sat R 47:63 O 24 '64
Sum of Christmas; poem. McCalls 91:152 D '63
PRICE, Nathan
Wiltshire boulevard to Broadway in sixty minutes. W. Boyne. il por Sci Digest 53: 66-8 Je '63
PRICE, P. B. See Fleischer, R. L. jt. auth.
PRICE, Paxton P.
LSCA: the official view. ALA Bul 58:694-6 S '64
—and Carl, H. A.
Washington report: from the Library services branch. ALA Bul 58:352-6, 599-602, 986-8 My, Jl, D '64
PRICE, R. G. G.
Asphalt jungle. Atlan 213:116+ My '64
Burning questions. Atlan 214:122+ O '64
Here be Broadway. Atlan 212:110-11 S '63
PRICE, Reynolds
Summer games; story. Vogue 142:89 Ag 15 '63
PRICE, Robert
For Selma Lagerlöf; poem. Horn Bk 40:272 Je '64
PRICE, Robert E.
Fish the midnight eel. Outdoor Life 132:36-7+ Ag '63
October bass explosion. por Outdoor Life 132:56-9+ O '63
PRICE, Stanley
Mrs Guggenheim collection. N Y Times Mag p 16-17+ Ja 17 '65
PRICE, Vincent
Comfortable clutter of an actor in love with the arts. il House B 105:153 Ap '63
Vincent Price: king of the horror movies. C. Brossard. il pors Look 27:66a-66d+ Ap 23 '63
PRICE control. See Price regulation by government
PRICE cutting
ABA disputes cut-price deal by wholesaler, insurance co. Pub W 183:31 Mr 18 '63
Bill that can help meet the price-cutting problem: Quality stabilization bill. C. B. Grannis. Pub W 183:126 Je 10 '63
Why businessmen wage price wars. il Bsns W p 154+ N 2 '63
See also
Discount houses (retail trade)
Price discrimination
PRICE discrimination
Fair trade or foul, the battle rages again! Quality stabilization bill. M. Mayer. il Sat Eve Post 237:66-8 Ap 11 '64
Nightmare for oil marketers; Sun oil case. Bsns W p66 Ja 19 '63
PRICE fixing, Resale. See Price maintenance by industry
PRICE indexes
Announcement of the 1964 revision of the CPI. D. P. Rothwell. il Mo Labor R 86: 794-5 Jl '63
Catching up with our new habits; revision of the CPI. il Bsns W p 112-13+ Mr 7 '64

PRICE indexes—*Continued*
Consumer and wholesale prices; table. See issues of Monthly labor review
Consumer price index: barometer of living costs. il Sr Schol 85:20 N 4 '64
Contrasts in spending by urban families; trends since 1950. K. R. Murphy. il Mo Labor R 87:1249-53 N '64
Discounts that don't show; with editorial comment. il Bsns W p23-5, 100 Mr 2 '63
Food distribution changes and the CPI. E. D. Hoover and M. S. Stotz. il Mo Labor R 87: 58-64 Ja '64
Health insurance in the revised CPI. J. C. Daugherty. il Mo Labor R 87:1299-300 N '64
Indexes of hourly earnings. A. A. Belman. Mo Labor R 87:561 My '64
It all depends on what you buy; with charts and tables. Bsns W p30-1 Jl 25 '64
New features of the revised CPI. P. Groom. il Mo Labor R 87:385-90 Ap '64
New index; Bureau of labor statistics' cost of living index. Time 83:90+ Mr 6 '64
Price trends and the postwar market for appliances. J. C. Daugherty. il Mo Labor R 86:1259-65 N '63
Statistical structure of the revised CPI. S. A. Jaffe. Mo Labor R 87:916-24 Ag '64
Use of price indexes in escalator contracts. F. S. Cunningham. il Mo Labor R 86:948-52 Ag '63

PRICE maintenance by industry
Antitrust lunges again at fair trade. Bsns W p20+ Jl 4 '64
At the belt; price-fixing charges against the twelve millers. Time 83:86+ My 8 '64
Big money question; six suppliers overcharged; Philadelphia electric and UGI. il Bsns W p 176+ Ap 18 '64
Britain; politics & prices. il Time 83:95 F 7 '64
Climbing toll for the price-fixers. il Bsns W p96-8+ Ag 29 '64
Corrupt society; price-rigging by GE. F. J. Cook. Nation 196:456-65 Je 1 '63
Fair trade or foul, the battle rages again! Quality stabilization bill. M. Mayer. il Sat Eve Post 237:66-8 Ap 11 '64
FTC's new threat is compulsory licensing; makers of tetracycline guilty of price-fixing. Bsns W p27 Ag 17 '63
GE tries new tack on prices; one price for turbines. Bsns W p30 My 25 '63
Great cartel scheme; Quality stabilization act. W. Schulz. Nat R 16:196 Mr 10 '64
High cost of fair trade. J. Duscha. Reporter 30:29-30 Mr 12 '64
How to conspire to fix prices. J. Q. Lawyer. il Harvard Bsns R 41:95-103 Mr '63
Indictment; charges of conspiracy by Federal grand jury. il Newsweek 63:93-4 Ap 20 '64
Kefauver and the price-makers. B. D. Nossiter. Nation 197:12-13 Jl 6 '63
No more price-fixing; British Parliament abolishes retail price maintenance system. Bsns W p86 Jl 25 '64
Now it's quality stabilization. Nation 197:407 D 14 '63
Of cars and steel and tottering guideposts. T. R. Brooks. il Reporter 31:23-5 D 17 '64
One win, one defeat in the campaign against price-fixing; Quality stabilization bill. Consumer Rep 29:366 Ag '64
Price-fix charged; indictment by Federal grand jury. Sr Schol 84:20 My 1 '64
Price-fix in brass. America 108:388 Mr 23 '63
Price-fixing by stealth and guile; quality stabilization bill. Consumer Rep 28:462-3 O '63
Price maintenance bill encounters opposition. Pub W 184:43 N 18 '63
Price stabilization hearings to be held in April. Pub W 183:28 Ap 8 '63
Six fastener companies indicted in federal price-fixing charges. Aviation W 79:37 S 9 '63
Steel; the price-fixing charges. Time 83:102+ Ap 17 '64
Supreme court sanctions fair trade in Ohio. Pub W 185:58 Je 15 '64
Trying to untangle a price snarl. Bsns W p81-2 D 7 '63
Victory that turned sour; quality stabilization bill. Bsns W p 114 Je 20 '64
Windfall for conspiracy. R. J. Barber. il Nation 199:332-3 N 9 '64

PRICE of carabao; story. See Maloff, S.

PRICE policies
Case of the disputing divisions. J. Dearden. il Harvard Bsns R 42:158-9+ My '64
Divergent views on pricing policy; discussion of Means's thesis. W. H. Peterson. bibliog f Harvard Bsns R 41:20-2+ Mr '63
No big breaks for big buyers; pool buying arrangements. Bsns W p34 D 5 '64
Sense and sensitivity in pricing. R. T. Sampson. il Harvard Bsns R 42:99-105 N '64
Wage-price policy approaches; excerpt from address. F. C. Pierson. Mo Labor R 86: 140 F '63
What policy for commodities? J. A. Pincus. il For Affairs 42:227-41 Ja '64

PRICE regulation by government
How free shall the free market be? A. A. Berle, jr. il N Y Times Mag p 10+ Je 23 '63

Europe, Western

Untranquilized drug makers. W. Guzzardi, jr. il Fortune 68:124-8+ D '63

France

Higher & higher cuisine. il Time 84:100 N 27 '64

Latin America

Price stabilization. il Américas 15:44 My '63

United States

Can we make more jobs without inflation? symposium on employment; with editorial comment. il Bsns W p26-7, 132 F 29 '64
Comeback for inflation? W. V. Shannon. Commonweal 80:354-6 Je 12 '64
Detroit, higher wages, cheaper cars? H. Rowen. New Repub 150:17-18 Je 6 '64
FTC guide to pricing; deceptive price advertising. Bsns W p27 Ja 11 '64
How LBJ's early-warning system works for pay, prices. il U S News 56:86-8 F 10 '64
Lesson of the wage-price record. Bsns W p 120 My 30 '64
Managers have to manage. C. P. Ives. Nat R 14:157-8 F 26 '63
New wage-price spiral ahead? U S News 56: 82 Ap 20 '64
Price control by warning. H. Hazlitt. Newsweek 61:81 Ap 29 '63
Steel talks begin: new round in the wage-price spiral? il U S News 58:70-1 Ja 11 '65
Strange case of Sun oil, which is damned if it does and damned if it doesn't. M. R. Lefkoe. il Fortune 68:117+ Ag '63
Watch on prices; wage-price inflation. Bsns W p 19-20 F 1 '64
Web of prices. H. Hazlitt. Newsweek 61:78 My 6 '63
When is a discount a bargain? F.T.C. guides against deceptive pricing. Consumer Bul 47: 12+ Ja '64
White House stand on wages and prices. il U S News 56:84-5 F 3 '64

PRICE supports, Agricultural. See Agricultural administration—United States; Farm produce—Prices

PRICES
Firmer prices for producers everywhere. il Bsns W p22-3 My 11 '63
Toward more controls; worldwide commodity prices. il Time 81:108 Ap 19 '63
What policy for commodities? J. A. Pincus. il For Affairs 42:227-41 Ja '64
You can't really get it wholesale. Consumer Bul 48:24-5 F '65

See also
Inflation (finance)
Price cutting
Profit
Supply and demand
also subhead Prices under various subjects, e.g. Sugar—Prices

Stabilization

See Price regulation by government

France

Letter from Paris; Gaullist price-stabilization project. Genêt. New Yorker 39:156+ S 28 '63
See also
Price regulation by government—France

Great Britain

No more price-fixing; British Parliament abolishes retail price maintenance system. Bsns W p86 Jl 25 '64

India

Last cup. il Time 84:46+ O 16 '64

United States

After World war II, why no price drop. il U S News 54:54-5 My 13 '63
Another round of price increases. il U S News 55:39-41 O 14 '63
Are prices on the way up? what industry sees ahead. il U S News 57:86-7 Ag 24 '64
Balance of prices. il Fortune 67:48+ My '63

PRICES—United States—*Continued*
Choosing the objectives of national wage-price policy. L. Ulman. Mo Labor R 86:274-5 Mr '63
Consumer and wholesale prices; tables. See issues of Monthly labor review
Discounts that don't show; with editorial comment. il Bsns W p23-5, 100 Mr 2 '63
Greater wage-price stability ahead. il Nations Bsns 52:36-7+ S '64
Halt to cuts but no inflation; with charts. Bsns W p26-7 O 26 '63
More price rises coming. il Bsns W p23-4 Ag 24 '63
Mystery over commodity tangle. U S News 55:99 D 2 '63
Outlook for prices in '64. il Nations Bsns 51:36-7 S '63
Pace of prices. il Fortune 69:32+ F '64
Price vigilance. Time 84:61 Ag 14 '64
Trifling; what to buy for a nickel. New Yorker 39:40-1 O 26 '63
Why prices stay up. H. Wolozin. il Nations Bsns 51:64-6 F '63
See also
Cost of living—United States
Price discrimination
Price indexes
Price regulation by government—United States

PRICKETT, Kay
Last summer in Mississippi. A. Lake. por Redbook 124:64-5+ N '64

PRIDAY, Win, and others
Most complete waste-water treatment plant in the world. Am City 79:123+ S '64

PRIDE of the morning; story. See Kaufman, S.

PRIDE; story. See Deal, B. H.

PRIDEAUX, Tom
Anti-mom pile-up has become just plain dull. Life 54:96+ My 10 '63
Best and brightest season in a decade. Life 55:30-9 N 22 '63
Blue skies to you, Irving Berlin. Life 54:12+ My 3 '63
Center that set off a tempest. Life 58:42-3+ Ja 22 '65
Cole Porter. Life 57:46-46A O 30 '64
Desperate search by a troubled hero. Life 56:64B-65 F 7 '64
Dilemma of Adam, Daedalus and Faust. Life 57:92+ N 20 '64
Do they hit the target? Life 55:124+ D 20 '63
Dumpling mystery and other gastronomical fakes. Life 56:111-12 Ap 3 '64
Everything's up to date in Elsinore. Life 56:91-2+ Ap 24 '64
Girls. por Life 57:98+ S 11 '64
Life entertainment review. Life 57:12 Jl 24 '64
Life movie review. Life 57:19 O 9 '64
Life TV review. Life 56:14 Mr 27 '64
Life theater review. Life 56:16 Ap 3; 10 Ap 17; 9 My 1; 17 Je 19; 17 Je 26; 57:8 S 4; 30 S 25; 24 O 16; 17 O 30; 23 D 11 '64; 58:10 Ja 15 '65
Menotti opera runs riot with a flood of tricks. Life 54:46 Mr 8 '63
Million dollar headache. Life 55:39-40+ Ag 9 63
Poet who loved to hate. Life 57:122 S 18 '64
She plays for queens, princes and Aunt Nora. Life 56:86 Ja 24 '64
Theatrical dream come true makes a miracle in Minneapolis. Life 54:41-4 My 24 '63
Thirst for greatness. Life 55:125-6 O 11 '63
Too busy to moon over good old days. Life 55:118-19 D 13 '63
Why aren't more show tunes for whistling? Life 57:12 Ag 7 '64
Will it go on B'way? por Life 55:9+ S 13 '63

PRIEST, Jean H. See Priest, R. E. jt. auth.

PRIEST, Robert E. and Priest, J. H.
Redifferentiation of connective tissue cells in serial culture. bibliog Science 145:1053-4 S 4 '64

PRIEST workers. See Worker priests

PRIESTLEY, John Boynton
Carry on, carry on; excerpts from Margin released. por Atlan 211:64-70 F '63
Ruptured peace movement. Nation 197:251-3 O 26 '63
Speaking out. por Sat Eve Post 236:10+ Ap 27 '63; 237:8+ D 12 '64
—See Murdoch, I. jt. auth.

about

Direct approach. S. Eimerl. Reporter 28:56-7 F 28 '63

PRIESTLEY, Michael
Triumph's Spitfire 4. Pop Mech 119:122 Ap '63

PRIESTS
Left to mind the store. R. E. Auman. America 109:618 N 16 '63
Machismo and the priestly vocation. A. Weigert. il Cath World 199:152-8 Je '64
Married priest. il Time 84:66 Jl 10 '64
Married priests? Commonweal 80:223-4 My 15 '64; Reply. G. M. Dalpiaz. 80:301 My 29 '64
Married Roman Catholic priests. J. Roddy. il Look 28:103+ Mr 24 '64; Reply. America 110:405 Mr 28 '64
Noncelibate priest; first Roman Catholic married priest. il Newsweek 64:52 Jl 13 '64
See also
Negro priests
Women as priests
Worker priests

PRIESTS in literature
Morte d'Urban: concerning J. F. Powers' first novel. M. J. Henault; V. P. McCorry. America 108:290-4 Mr 2 '63
Priest-hero in the modern novel. L. V. McDonnell. Cath World 196:306-11 F '63

PRIETO, Inés Cuervo de
Other babies who broke the odds; I gave my husband five sons, ed. by H. H. Martin. pors Sat Eve Post 237:20-3 Ja 18 '64
They are like little bulls. H. H. Martin. il pors Sat Eve Post 237:68-72 O 3 '64

PRIETO NAVA, Efrén Lubin
Other babies who broke the odds; I do not feel like a famous man, ed. by H. H. Martin. pors Sat Eve Post 237:24-7 Ja 18 '64
They are like little bulls. H. H. Martin. il pors Sat Eve Post 237:68-72 O 3 '64

PRIETO quintuplets. See Quintuplets

PRIMACY of the pope. See Popes—Primacy

PRIMARIES
After New Hampshire. Reporter 30:10+ Mr 26 '64
After Wisconsin: new turn in politics. il U S News 56:31-3 Ap 20 '64
Ambassador Lodge running strong; New Hampshire primary. il Newsweek 63:21-5 Mr 23 '64
As New Hampshire goes, so goes who? W. S. Ellis. il N Y Times Mag p 12+ F 2 '64
Atlantic report. Atlan 214:4+ Jl '64
Battle to call the winner; networks lean on pollsters and computers. il Bsns W p24-6 Je 6 '64
Big GOP test in the West; Oregon primary. L. Harris. il Newsweek 63:23 Mr 23 '64
Big one; California primary. Nation 198:281-2 Mr 23 '64
California primary. Nation 198:593 Je 15 '64
Can anyone stop Goldwater now? il Newsweek 63:23-4+ Je 15 '64
Changing lineup for Republicans; New Hampshire primary vote; with statement by L. H. Bean. il U S News 56:39-41 Mr 23 '64
Despite the hoopla, it's the best system; method of choosing a president. J. M. Burns. il N Y Times Mag p 11+ Ap 26 '64
Downfall and debut; gubernatorial contest, Massachusetts and Arizona. il Newsweek 64:35 S 21 '64
Duel to the death in California; with report by T. H. White. il Life 56:24-31 My 29 '64
Fight for New Hampshire: what is really at stake. il U S News 56:44-5 Mr 9 '64
Fingers crossed; California primary campaign. il Newsweek 63:40+ Je 8 '64
Five primaries and what they showed. il U S News 56:34-5 My 18 '64
From behind the stretch; California's Republican presidential primary. il Time 83:19-20 My 29 '64
From grass roots of Midwest; what Illinois primary showed. il U S News 56:33 Ap 27 '64
Gary's rank-and-file reaction; white backlash. V. Hoffman and J. Strietelmeier. il Reporter 31:28-9 S 10 '64; Reply. D. Radler. 31:6+ O 8 '64
George Wallace shakes up the political scene. H. H. Martin. il Sat Eve Post 237:85-9 My 9 '64
Giving it & catching it; campaigning for New Hampshire primary. il Time 83:13-14 Ja 17 '64
Goofiness of American politics. S. Alsop. il Sat Eve Post 236:16 N 30 '63
Governor Wallace's victories without winning. M. Phelps. America 110:786 Je 6 '64
He cared enough, and so did Oregon; with report by L. Harris. il Newsweek 63:27-8 My 25 '64
Hi-ho New Hampshire! Barry goes galloping in; with reports by P. O'Neil and M. Gart. il Life 55:28-35 N 1 '63

PRIMARIES—*Continued*
Honest injun, it's finally time to vote: New Hampshire Republicans; with report by R. Ajemian. il Life 56:28-33 Mr 6 '64
How democracy democs; New Hampshire primary. R. Moley. Newsweek 63:96 F 17 '64
How Goldwater won in California. B. Stout. Reporter 31:17-19 Jl 2 '64; Reply. B. M. Stave. 31:10+ Ag 13 '64
How to pick a presidential nominee; New Hampshire primary. D. Lawrence. U S News 56:124 Mr 23 '64
How to succeed in politics. Nation 198:546 Je 1 '64
It's up to the undecideds; New Hampshire presidential primary. D. F. O'Neil. Nat R 16:193-4 Mr 10 '64
Lessons from the Lone Ranger; Oregon's presidential primary. il Time 83:17-20 My 22 '64
Letter from Washington. R. H. Rovere. New Yorker 40:193-8 My 16 '64
Letter from Washington; losers in the New Hampshire primary. R. H. Rovere. New Yorker 40:178+ Mr 21 '64
Levitation of Lodge. Nation 198:405-6 Ap 27 '64
Lodge faces his big test in Oregon; with editorial comment. J. Skow. il Sat Eve Post 237:15-19, 84 My 16 '64
Lodge is Oregon's bride by mail. R. B. Frazier. New Repub 150:9-10 My 9 '64
Lodge livens up G.O.P. Life 56:4 Mr 20 '64
Mayor Wagner: a rise in political stock. U S News 56:21 Je 15 '64
More about the backlash; Maryland presidential primary. Time 83:21-2 My 29 '64
More of the backlash; Indiana's presidential primary. Time 83:37 My 15 '64
Nation's primary primary; New Hampshire primary. D. F. Ford. il Reporter 30:37-9 F 27 '64
New Hampshire. Commonweal 80:4 Mr 27 '64
New Hampshire campaign. il Time 83:25 F 21 '64
New Hampshire poll: write-in fever gains. il Newsweek 63:18-21 Mr 9 '64
New Hampshire switch. K. Crawford. Newsweek 62:36 N 25 '63
New York: who won? il Newsweek 62:32 S 16 '63
News from New Hampshire. il Time 83:19-21 Mr 20 '64
Next: the showdown primary; California. U S News 56:58 Je 1 '64
Night Barry Goldwater lost. M. Kempton. New Repub 150:4-6 Mr 21 '64
On the '64 campaign trail. Sr Schol 84:33 Ap 3; 17 My 1 '64
On, Wisconsin! Reporter 30:14 Ap 23 '64
On Wisconsin? coming Maryland primary. Cato. Nat R 16:349 My 5 '64
Opening the big campaign; Republican primary in New Hampshire. il Bsns W p28-9 F 29 '64
Presidential primaries: useful or wasteful? pro and con discussion. il Sr Schol 84: 8-9 F 7 '64
Primary nonsense. R. Moley. Newsweek 62: 108 N 4 '63
Primary report. J. Caravan. Nat R 16:448 Je 2 '64
Racism rejected; two congressional primaries in Ohio. Reporter 30:11 Je 4 '64
Racism wasn't the issue in Tennessee. B. Kovach. Reporter 31:37-8 S 24 '64
Reflections on California. Nat R 16:477-9 Je 16 '64
Republican rupture; Wisconsin presidential primary. New Repub 150:4 Ap 18 '64
Salinger vs. Murphy; California's Democratic senatorial primary. il Newsweek 63:28 Je 15 '64
Showdown in California. Reporter 30:10 My 21 '64
Showdown in California: big crisis for Goldwater; with editorial comment. R. Evans and R. Novak. il Sat Eve Post 237:15-19, 74 My 30 '64
State of Maryland. M. Kempton. New Repub 150:6-8 My 23 '64
Surprises in the primaries; California and Illinois. New Repub 150:6-8 Ap 11 '64
Sweepstakes in the snow; New Hampshire primary. J. Skow. il Sat Eve Post 237:17-23 Mr 14 '64
Switching to Rocky; How the West was won? il Newsweek 63:21-2 Je 1 '64
Trailing a curious political animal; California primary. E. Burdick. il N Y Times Mag p 10+ My 31 '64
Tried-&-true technique; Louisiana Democrats gubernatorial primary. Time 83:14 Ja 24 '64
Two big fights start shaping up. R. Ajemian. Life 56:22 Mr 27 '64
Two down, three to go. New Repub 150: 3-4 Mr 21 '64
Uninvited guest; Maryland primary. il Time 83:24 My 22 '64
Wallace in Alabama and in Maryland. New Repub 150:4-5 My 16 '64
Wallace in Indiana; with editorial comment. G. Englehart. Nation 198:449, 451-3 My 4 '64
Wallace victory. America 110:558 Ap 25 '64
Wallace's Wisconsin, 264,100 votes. il Newsweek 63:33-4 Ap 20 '64
Warning from Wisconsin. Nat R 16:306-7 Ap 21 '64
What do primaries really mean? D. Lawrence. U S News 56:108 Mr 16 '64
What New Hampshire said. Nat R 16:218-21 Mr 24 '64
What Wallace vote proved in North; with views of Maryland editors and Governor Wallace. il U S News 56:29-32+ Je 1 '64
What Wisconsin meant. Time 83:37 Ap 17 '64
When Florida voted on civil-rights issue; gubernatorial primary. U S News 56:8 Je 8 '64
Who's Wallace? il Time 83:22 Ap 24 '64
Winners. il Newsweek 63:32-3 My 18 '64
Winning without winning; Maryland presidential primary. il Newsweek 63:17+ Je 1 '64
Wisconsin primary; resistance to integration in the North. Commonweal 80:133 Ap 24 '64
See also
Nominations for office

PRIMARY batteries. See Electric batteries

PRIMARY education. See Education, Elementary

PRIMARY elections. See Primaries

PRIMATES
Chromosome complements of two species of primates: cynopithecus niger and presbytis entellus. R. N. Ushijima and others. bibliog il Science 146:78-9 O 2 '64
Evolution of facial expression. R. J. Andrew. bibliog il Science 142:1034-41 N 22 '63
Gastric content of fasted primates: a survey. D. A. Brodie and R. W. Marshall. bibliog il Science 141:174-5 Jl 12 '63
Primate biology; planning meeting; report on meeting of scientists to discuss the possibility and desirability of cooperative efforts between the United States and Japan in the study of primates. L. Carmichael and A. J. Riopelle. Science 146:1078+ N 20 '64
Pyramidal tract: a comparison of two prosimian primates. J. A. Jane and others. bibliog il Science 147:153-5 Ja 8 '65
See also
Lemurs
Monkeys

PRIMATICCIO, Francesco
Francesco Primaticcio's Ulysses and Penelope. A. Frankfurter. il Art N 63:27 Ja '65

PRIME ministers
See also
Great Britain—Prime ministers

PRIME ministers conferences
Commonwealth: farce or force? il Newsweek 64:38-9 Jl 20 '64
How to keep alive. Time 84:32-3 Jl 24 '64
Letter from London; Commonwealth premiers' conference. M. Panter-Downes. New Yorker 40:67-9 Ag 1 '64
Sort of success. il Newsweek 64:37-8 Jl 27 '64
Who needs mother? Commonwealth prime ministers' meeting. il Time 84:28 Jl 17 '64

PRIMEAU, Ernest J. bp
Xavier Rynne book. America 108:906 Je 29 '63; Discussion. 109:30 Jl 13 '63

PRIMERS
Why Jonny can read. Time 81:52 Mr 8 '63

Bibliography

Improvement in basic textbooks. R. Kirk. Nat R 15:569 D 31 '63

PRIMITIVE and early church. See Church history—Primitive and early church

PRIMITIVE art; Primitive medicine; etc. See Art; Primitive; Medicine, Primitive; etc.

PRIMITIVES, American. See Painting, American

PRIMROSE, Archibald Philip, 5th earl of Rosebery. See Rosebery, A. P. P.

PRIMROSES
California's own primroses. il Sunset 130: 92-7 Mr '63
Eloquent admirer of simple English primrose. D. Warren. il Horticulture 41:74-5 F '63
Primroses. il Flower Grower 51:48 My '64
Primroses for spring color. il Pop Gard 15:19 Ap '64

PRIMULAS. See Primroses

PRIMUS, Pearl
Everyman's African roots. D. Leddick. por Dance Mag 38:20-1 O '64

PRINCE, Alain Wood
Fishing was wild. Outdoor Life 131:45-7+ Je '63
Place for everything. pors Outdoor Life 134:52-3+ S '64

PRINCE, Georgiana M.
Report from Finland. Dance Mag 38:15-17 F '64

PRINCE, John S.
Meet GEVIC, the computer that flies. S. V. Jones. il por Sci Digest 55:76-7 Ja '64

PRINCE, William Wood
Armour cuts the meat in its diet. il por Bsns W p54+ My 9 '64

PRINCE EDWARD COUNTY, Va.
After four years with no schooling. il U S News 55:10 S 2 '63
Back to school. il Newsweek 62:70 Ag 26 '63
Catching up in Prince Edward. il Time 82:56 Ag 9 '63
Classes again soon for Prince Edward Negroes. U S News 55:11 Ag 26 '63
Court says reopen schools; but will they be integrated? il U S News 56:37 Je 8 '64
Dickie's decision. il Time 82:56-7 S 27 '63
Eight days make a miracle. J. Callwood. il McCalls 91:34+ Ja '64
Four long years. il Sr Schol 85:1T N 11 '64
Kids in Prince Edward. M. Kempton. New Repub 149:14-15 O 5 '63
Lock begins to open. il Ebony 19:63-6+ N '63
Making haste slowly; Supreme court order to reopen public schools. Newsweek 63:52 Je 8 '64
Making history in Prince Edward County; Prince Edward free school association. N. V. Sullivan. il Sat R 47:59-61+ O 17 '64
Negroes in Prince Edward County. Sch & Soc 91:422 D 28 '63
Opening school doors. New Repub 150:5 Je 6 '64
Opening up Prince Edward; Free school association. Time 82:60 Ag 23 '63
Prince Edward County situation. W. V. Heuvel; N. V. Sullivan. il NEA J 53:12-15 Mr '64
Prince Edward free school system thrives; awaits Supreme ct. rule. Library J 89:930 F 15 '64
Prince Edward's injustice. America 110:328 Mr 14 '64
Schools for Negroes open in Prince Edward County. Christian Cent 80:1046 Ag 28 '63
Supreme court's new mood. Christian Cent 81:755-6 Je 10 '64
Ten thousand pennies. E. Moon. Library J 89:2297 Je 1 '64
Virginia ruling. Sr Schol 83:2T Ja 10 '64
When school bells ring after four years' silence. il U S News 55:41-3 S 30 '63

PRINCE GALLITZIN STATE PARK. See Pennsylvania—Parks and reserves

PRINCE GEORGES COUNTY memorial library, Hyattsville, Md.
Kennedy family's gentle suggestion: restore original name to Md. library. Library J 89:1211 Mr 15 '64
Prince Georges County commissioners cut off library board's buying power. Library J 88:4724 D 15 '63
Prince George's headquarters. E. B. Hage. il Library J 89:4722-4 D 1 '64

PRINCE Hall Masons. See Freemasons, Negro

PRINCE; story. See Vivante, A.

PRINCES, Education of. See Education of princes and princesses

PRINCES and princesses
And a nurse to tuck you in; Scandinavia's royal princes and princesses. il Time 84:26-38 Jl 3 '64
Cinderella princesses. R. Lecler. il Ladies Home J 81:52-3+ S '64
In Europe: the splash of grand and royal weddings, 1964. il Vogue 144:76-83 Ag 15 '64

PRINCESS ANNE, Md.
Dogs in Maryland; civil-rights sitdown. Newsweek 63:30 Mr 9 '64

PRINCESS too little; drama. See Nicholson, M. A.

PRINCESSES, Education of. See Education of princes and princesses

PRINCETON, N.J.
Isolating the causes of infiltration. A. T. Brokaw. il Am City 79:80-1 D '64
Princeton's lesson: school integration is not enough. P. Streit. il N Y Times Mag p 14+ Je 21 '64

PRINCETON club, New York. See New York (city)—Clubs

PRINCETON institute for advanced study. See Institute for advanced study, Princeton, N.J.

PRINCETON plan (school integration) See Public schools—Desegregation

PRINCETON theological seminary
Teen with a trowel; expedition to Petra, Jordan. C. Sayre. il Seventeen 22:118-19+ N '63

PRINCETON university
Designing with deference; undergraduate dormitories for Princeton. il Arch Rec 133:138-9 Mr '63
Engineering as a full partner in the university; excerpt from address, October 13, 1962. H. T. Heald. Sch & Soc 91:84-6 F 23 '63
Higher learning; host to racists: Malcolm X and Ross Barnett. Nat R 15:384 N 5 '63
No cheers for the rah-rah riot. G. Hechinger and F. M. Hechinger. il N Y Times Mag p33+ My 26 '63
Princeton building with colonaded facade; Woodrow Wilson school of public and international affairs. il Arch Rec 134:108-10 D '63
Profiles: W. W. Bradley, star of basketball team. J. McPhee. New Yorker 40:40-2+ Ja 23 '65
Rise of rep. il Time 83:61 F 14 '64

Libraries

Oral history project, John Foster Dulles library. Wilson Lib Bul 38:716 My '64
Princeton plans for the Scheide library. Wilson Lib Bul 38:722+ My '64

PRINCETON university press
Big scholar, little gypsy. D. Dempsey. Sat R 47:30-1 My 30 '64
Princeton starts own paperback series. Pub W 187:66-7 Ja 11 '65

PRINCETON university store. See College bookstores

PRINCIP, Gavrilo
Sarajevo fifty years after; consequences of the assassination of the archduke. V. Dedijer. bibliog f For Affairs 42:569-84 Jl '64
Sarajevo revisited, fifty years after. J. A. Barry. il por N Y Times Mag p 12-13+ Je 28 '64

PRINCIPAL; story. See Siegel, B.

PRINCIPALS, School. See School superintendents and principals

PRINGLE, John
Jamaica's Old Boy with the new ideas. C. Amory. il por Sat R 47:56-8 O 10 '64

PRINGLE, Larry
Hunting by air photos. Outdoor Life 131:50-1+ F '63
Mice in our forests. Am For 70:40-1+ N '64

PRINT collections. See Prints—Collectors and collecting

PRINT reader. See Reading machines

PRINTED circuits
Home-made printed circuits. T. J. Barmore. il Electr World 69:64 My '63
Making etched circuit boards. R. W. Bailey. bibliog il Electr World 69:38-9 Je '63
Printed board repair. G. McKinney. il Electr World 71:69 My '64

PRINTERS
See also
International typographical union
Strikes—United States—Printers

PRINTERS marks
Early printers' marks. W. Caxton, jr. il Am Artist 27:58-9+ F '63

PRINTING
Book craftsmen, N.Y, present Gresham's neoprint system. il Pub W 183:72+ My 6 '63
IPEX; new developments in the American printing industry. J. H. Winkler. il Pub W 184:78-84+ Ag 5 '63
Mangling a masterpiece; concerning typography of revised edition of Human action by L. von Mises. H. Hazlitt. Nat R 16:366-7 My 5 '64
Singapore to Istanbul: printing design and production from seven countries; with report by M. Glick and E. H. Glick. il Pub W 183:84-6+ Mr 4 '63
Sir Francis Meynell and the Nonesuch press. F. Johnson. il Am Artist 28:38-43+ F '64
Title page and the courteous typographer. P. Standard. il Pub W 185:118+ F 3 '64
Trends in typography; newspapers compete in Ayer cup typographical competition. R. L. Tobin. il Sat R 47:51-2 Je 13 '64
See also
Color printing
Lithography
Photomechanical processes
Type and typefounding
Typesetting
Typesetting machines

PRINTING—*Continued*

Design

Hermann Zapf: calligrapher, type designer, master of the book arts. P. A. Bennett. il Pub W 187:72-4+ Ja 4 '65
Letters from Denmark. P. Soederlund. il Horizon 5:120 Jl '63
P. J. Conkwright and University press book design; excerpt. J. Dreyfus. il Pub W 183: 78+ Mr 4 '63
See also
Type and typefounding

Exhibitions

Printing and the mind of man; exhibition, London, July 16-27. Pub W 184:67 Jl 1 '63

History

Bible and the development of printing. C. B. Grannis. Pub W 184:75 S 9 '63
King of typography: C. Plantin. il Time 81: 57 My 31 '63
Printing and the mind of man; reprint. il Wilson Lib Bul 38:392-6 Ja '64

Private presses

Colonial press expansion, new equipment to meet industry needs. R. R. Hackford. il Pub W 186:58-61 D 7 '64
Craft. New Yorker 39:18-19 Jl 27 '63
Morris's Kelmscott adventure revealed in Grolier club exhibit. P. A. Bennett. il Pub W 186:108-12 N 9 '64
Robert Frost: best-printed U.S. author, and his printer, Spiral press. P. A. Bennett. il Pub W 185:82-6+ Mr 2 '64
Saul and Lillian Marks and their Plantin press in Los Angeles. P. A. Bennett. il Pub W 186:114-18 Jl 6 '64

Study and teaching

Printers prepare for change; Colorado Springs center. il Bsns W p68-70 Ag 31 '63

PRINTING (photography) See Photography—Printing processes

PRINTING, Linoleum block. See Linoleum block printing

PRINTING, Offset
Letterset printing: some basic data. Pub W 185:98 Ja 6 '64

PRINTING industry
Fourth of July salute to American printing. S. Wecksler. Pub W 186:101 Jl 6 '64
Have to get something printed? il Changing T 18:20-2 Ag '64
IPEX; new developments in the American printing industry. J. H. Winkler. il Pub W 184:78-84+ Ag 5 '63
See also
Donnelly, R. R. and sons, company
Strikes—United States—Printers

Employees

Anti-discrimination pact signed in Philadelphia; action of Printing industres. Pub W 184:35 O 14 '63

Statistics

New records for publishing seen in Commerce survey; with editorial comment. Pub W 185:66-7, 74 F 3 '64

PRINTING machinery
High-speed electronic printer. A. W. Edwards. il Electr World 72:46-8 D '64
IPEX: machines and techniques; London exhibition, July 16 to 27, 1963. J. Dreyfus. il Pub W 184:78+ S 9 '63
Radiation, inc. builds high-speed printer. Aviation W 78:133 Je 10 '63
Untying the tongue; ultrahigh-speed printer. il Time 81:92 Je 7 '63
Westprint '64; items of book industry interest. L. D. Osborne. il Pub W 186:102-4+ Jl 6 '64
See also
Photocomposing machines
Typesetting machines

PRINTING paper (photography) See Photographic paper

PRINTS
Four seasons; from Chinese paintings. il Farm J 89:76 Ja '65
Frasconi the printmaker. F Getlein. New Repub 150:28-9 F 29 '64
Meeting with the West; first American residents by Japanese artists. C. H. Boehringer. il Am Heritage 14:16-31 Ag '63
Printmaking and the painter. F. Getlein. New Repub 149:31-3 O 5 '63
Prints of Edward Hopper. C. Zigrosser. il Am Artist 27:38-43+ N '63
See also
Linoleum block prints
Lithographs

Collectors and collecting

Antique autos; new collection of prints: Gallery of the American automobile. il Library J 88:2630-3 Jl '63
Prints of dancers; portfolio of twelve prints published by Dance collection of the New York public library. J. Anderson. il Dance Mag 38:42-3+ N '64

Exhibitions

Print on display. F. Getlein. New Repub 149: 35-6 Ag 31 '63
Prints at the Library; National exhibition at the Library of Congress. F. Getlein. New Repub 148:26-7 Je 1 '63

Technique

Bleach printing. R. Hufford. il Design 66:8-9 N '64
Cardboard printing. J. Lidstone. il Sch Arts 63:16-18 O '63
Cardboard printmaking; ed. by D. S. McIlvain. il Sch Arts 64:27-8 D '64 (to be cont)
Etchings of Sigmund Abeles. S. Hurwitz. il Am Artist 28:58-63+ S '64
Experiments in roller printing. il Design 64: 110-12 Ja '63
Gyotaku Japanese fish printing. P. Greenberg. il Sch Arts 63:21-2 Je '64
Ideas on loan; dazzling array of print techniques sent by one art school class to another. il Design 65:174-5 Mr '64
Mono-print printmaking. J. H. Casper. il Sch Arts 64:14-16 N '64
New intaglio technique. S. Hammer. il Am Artist 27:34-9+ F '63
Potato printing. J. Lidstone. il Sch Arts 62: 5-9 F '63
Print processes. H. Comstock. il Antiques 84: 294-301 S '63
Print; use of plastic weatherstrip cord to make blocks. H. R. Ringgenberg. il Sch Arts 64:13-15 Ja '65
Printmaking; beginning experience. R. Fennell and B. Storm. il Sch Arts 64:27-9 N '64
Prints and drawings. A. Hurwitz. il Sch Arts 62:16-18 Je '63
With inner tube and linoleum block; print making in the elementary school art program. A. Hurwitz. il NEA J 53:32-3 My '64

PRIP, John
John Prip and Reed & Barton. il Craft Horiz 24:51-2 Mr '64

PRISON architecture. See Prisons—Construction

PRISON camps

Russia

Denisovich: Russia's voice; novel of life in a labor camp. M. Koriakov. America 108:338-9 Mr 9 '63

PRISON chaplains. See Chaplains, Prison

PRISON education. See Education of prisoners

PRISON escapes. See Escapes

PRISON libraries
Correctional institutions helping the functionally illiterate. P. Chenault. bibliog f ALA Bul 58:804-9 O '64
Librarian plays the central role. C. J. Eckenrode. il ALA Bul 58:810-11 O '64
Service to inmates and staff. L. L. MacKenzie. ALA Bul 58:809 O '64

PRISON psychology
Okey-doke hokey-doke; self-help course at Illinois state penitentiary. il Newsweek 62:53 Jl 8 '63

PRISON publications
Insider's magazine; The atlantian. il Newsweek 62:78 Ag 12 '63
Journalists behind bars. J. F. Fixx. il Sat R 46:54-5+ Mr 9 '63

PRISON recreation
All the prisoners drove away; building a snow Cadillac at Dannemora. J. V. Whitey. New Yorker 39:80+ Ja 18 '64
Drama at San Quentin. J. N. Apostol. il Recreation 56:366-7 O '63
Gentlemen, place your bets; casino is in Nevada state prison. il Newsweek 62:25 Jl 1 '63

PRISON schools. See Education of prisoners

PRISON theatricals. See Prison recreation

PRISONERS
Boom town? disclosure by prisoner of buried nitroglycerin. Newsweek 63:34+ Mr 16 '64
Convict volunteers; for scientific research. T. B. Congdon, jr. il Sat Eve Post 236:62-4 Mr 2 '63
Cool look at the crime crisis. J. V. Bennett. Harper 228:123-7 Ap '64
Drug tests behind bars; Upjohn and Parke-Davis labs in Jackson, Mich. prison. il Bsns W p58-60+ Je 27 '64
On the outside; Richard Honeck after sixty-four years in jail. il Newsweek 62:18+ D 30 '63
Voice of the convict; excerpts from prize winning essays of Harper's contest. il Harper 228:164-70 Ap '64
Volunteers behind bars. il Time 82:72 Jl 12 '63
See also
Political prisoners

Legal status, laws, etc.

Bar behind bars. Time 83:88+ My 22 '64
Romance of Pewee Valley; Frankfort, Ky. R. Corns. Harper 229:32 S '64

Recreation

See Prison recreation

Rehabilitation

Half-way house; Brooklyn pre-release guidance center. M. Kempton. New Repub 148: 8-10 Mr 23 '63
To rehabilitate or to punish? prisons in Latin America and United States. R. Hill. il Américas 15:12-16 My '63
Without bars: some bold and some timorous experiments. G. Playfair. Harper 228:171-5 Ap '64

Treatment

Four and a half days in Atlanta's jails. G. W. Bishop. Atlan 214:68-70 Jl '64
In Arab hands. J. Lieber. il Nation 199:246-8 O 19 '64
Incident in Hattiesburg. H. Zinn. Nation 198: 501-4 My 18 '64; Discussion. 198:564 Je 8 '64

Germany (Democratic Republic)

Prisoners for sale; Bonn prisoners exchanged for butter, coffee, cocoa and sugar. il Time 84:41 O 16 '64

Syria

In Arab hands. J. Lieber. il Nation 199:246-8 O 19 '64

PRISONERS, Discharged
After sixty-four years, the prisoner comes home; R. Honeck. R. Gannon. il Sat Eve Post 237:38+ Mr 14 '64

Rehabilitation

After the stretch. M. Rudensky. Harper 228:180-2 Ap '64
Halfway houses. America 111:205 Ag 29 '64

PRISONERS, Education of. See Education of prisoners

PRISONERS, Political. See Political prisoners

PRISONERS, Women
In the Birmingham jail. B. Deming. Nation 196:436-7 My 25 '63
Romance of Pewee Valley; Frankfort, Ky. R. Corns. Harper 229:32 S '64

PRISONERS as authors
Combat novel from behind bars. R. B. Stolley. il Life 55:101-2+ D 6 '63

PRISONERS as fire fighters
Response of man to raw challenge. K. D. Flock. Am For 70:34-5 Jl '64

PRISONERS of war
See also
United States—History—Civil war—Prisoners and prisons

PRISONERS of war, Returned
Fortune's scapegoat; North Vietnamese return French prisoner after a decade. Newsweek 65:24 Ja 4 '65
Skinner's choice. R. L. Shayon. Sat R 46:16 S 7 '63

PRISONERS of war in Cuba
Americans; at least twenty-one languish in Castro's prisons. Sat Eve Post 236:18 F 2 '63
Cuban prisoner exchange. B. Lindeman. il Sat Eve Post 236:15-17+ F 2 '63
Epilogue to a failure; excerpts from Wine is bitter. M. Eisenhower. Time 82:20 Jl 26 '63
Furious footnote; excerpts from Wine is bitter. M. Eisenhower. Newsweek 62:42 Jl 29 '63
In time of need. Sat Eve Post 236:68 F 2 '63
Inside story of an amazing Cuba deal; excerpts from Wine is bitter. M. Eisenhower. U S News 55:23 Jl 29 '63
James Donovan and Castro. G. Samuels. Nation 196:299-302 Ap 13 '63
President Kennedy accepts custody of flag of Cuban brigade; remarks, December 29, 1962. J. F. Kennedy. Dept State Bul 48:88-90 Ja 21 '63
Prisoners in Cuba; summary of report. Américas 15:46 Jl '63
Roberto's story; forgotten young men; with editorial comment. W. F. Rickenbacker. il Nat R 15:94, 105-6 Ag 13 '63
Story behind the fat ransom. il Bsns W p84-6 F 9 '63
Swiss representatives visit Americans imprisoned in Cuba. Dept State Bul 48:137 Ja 28 '63

PRISONERS of war in Korea
Moral imperative; address, December 6, 1963. W. E. Mayer. Vital Speeches 29:266-70 F 15 '63
Skinner's choice. R. L. Shayon. Sat R 46:16 S 7 '63

PRISONERS of war in Russia
Father Ciszek's first public statement; with editorial comment. W. Ciszek. America 109:472, 475 O 26 '63
Loneliness of a long-distance Jesuit. W. J. Ciszek. America 111:514-17 O 31 '64

PRISONS

Construction

Inside the world's first pushbutton prison; Marion, Ill. C. Remsberg. il Pop Sci 182: 51-5+ Je '63

California

Drama at San Quentin. J. N. Apostol. il Recreation 56:366-7 O '63
See also
Alcatraz (island)

China (People's Republic)

U.S. doctor's five years in a red prison. J. N. Bell. il Todays Health 41:26-31 N '63

Cuba

Americans; at least twenty-one languish in Castro's prisons. Sat Eve Post 236:18 F 2 '63
Inside Castro's prisons. il Time 81:25 Je 7 '63

Delaware

Speaking out; bring back the whipping post! S. Lynch. Sat Eve Post 236:6+ Mr 30 '63

Illinois

Inside the world's first pushbutton prison; Marion, Ill. C. Remsberg. il Pop Sci 182: 51-5+ Je '63
Okey-doke hokey-doke; self-help course at Illinois state penitentiary. il Newsweek 62: 53 Jl 8 '63

Latin America

To rehabilitate or to punish? R. Hill. il Américas 15:12-16 My '63

Louisiana

Prison Perez style; ready for race demonstrators; Fort St Phillip, Plaquemines Parish. il U S News 55:16 N 4 '63

Maryland

Education in prison; Maryland state penitentiary. L. B. Dennis. New Repub 151:6 S 12 '64

Mexico

American in a Mexican death cell; Dykes Askew Simmons, jr. J. R. Phelan. il Sat Eve Post 236:81-5 S 21 '63

Michigan

Drug tests behind bars; Upjohn and Parke-Davis labs in Jackson, Mich. prison. il Bsns W p58-60+ Je 27 '64
See also
Detroit—Prisons and reformatories

Mississippi

Black Annie; lashings at Mississippi's Parchman penitentiary. Newsweek 61:33 Mr 18 '63

Missouri

Jefferson City: the pen that just grew; Missouri penitentiary for men. P. J. Buchanan. il Nation 199:355-7 N 16 '64

Nevada

Gentlemen, place your bets; casino is in Nevada state prison. il Newsweek 62:25 Jl 1 '63

New York (state)

All the prisoners drove away; building a snow Cadillac at Dannemora. J. V. Whitey. New Yorker 39:80+ Ja 18 '64

PRISONS—*Continued*

Portugal

What is Portugal hiding in its jails? Christian Cent 81:541 Ap 29 '64

United States

James V. Bennett's prisons. R. Goldfarb. New Repub 151:5 S 12 '64
Paroling the warden. il Time 84:64+ S 4 '64
To rehabilitate or to punish? R. Hull. il Américas 15:12-16 My '63
What can we do? white women's experiences in southern jails. I. H. Day and R. L. Day. Sat R 46:17 N 2 '63; Reply. A. E. Karro. 46:43 N 30 '63

See also
Alcatraz (island)
also subhead Prisons and reformatories under names of cities, e.g. Atlanta—Prisons and reformatories

Venezuela

Jail break; La Planta jail. Caracas. il Time 82:28 Ag 2 '63

PRISONS, Military
Author says he had plenty to yell about. J. R. McDermott. il Life 55:40+ Ag 16 '63

PRISTANE. See Hydrocarbons

PRITCHARD, John
Notes from abroad. C. Reid. por Hi Fi 13:24 F '63

PRITCHETT, Victor Sawdon
Across the vast land. Holiday 35:52-69+ Ap '64
Americans in my mind. Holiday 34:28-41+ Jl '63
Down the Seine. Holiday 34:62-7+ N '63
Fortunes and misfortunes of the famous Daniel Defoe. Horizon 7:40-9 Wint '65
Holland: the deftly governed. Holiday 35: 64-7+ Ja '64
Iran. Holiday 33:40-53+ Je '63
Irish character. Holiday 33:56-63+ Ap '63
Liars; story. New Yorker 40:58-63 N 21 '64
Secret people. Holiday 36:46-55+ O '64
Stranger in New York. Holiday 36:32-45+ Jl; 48-53+ Ag; 66-9+ S '64
Temptations of boredom. Holiday 37:8+ Ja '65

about

Appreciating Pritchett. L. Edel. New Repub 151:26+ Ag 8 '64
Reactions of a reading man. G. Hicks. Sat R 47:23-4 Je 27 '64
WLB biography. C. Barry. por Wilson Lib Bul 39:503+ F '65

PRITTIE, Terence
Again the issue of the two Germanys. N Y Times Mag p 10+ Ag 16 '64
Bomb shop in the Nile: target Israel. Atlan 214:37-40 Ag '64
Britain before the elections. Atlan 213:79-83 My '64
Nasser's German scientists. New Repub 148: 12-13 Ap 20 '63
No pipeline for Moscow. New Repub 148:9-10 Ap 6 '63
Old man won't let go. New Repub 148:9-10 Ap 27 '63
Paris-Bonn axis. New Repub 148:8-9 F 9 '63
Passing of work-obsessed Germany. N Y Times Mag p41+ Ap 21 '63
Stalemate in Germany. New Repub 148:10-11 F 2 '63
Table wines of Spain. Atlan 214:108-10 S '64
West Germany's next chancellor. New Repub 148:11-12 My 11 '63

PRIVACY
Assault on privacy. America 110:334-5 Mr 14 '64
Atrium expands builder house living area. il Arch Rec 135:108-11 mid-My '64
But can you do that? free press and the right of privacy. H. F. Pilpel. Pub W 183: 51-2 Ap 29 '63
Can public men have private lives? E. F. Goldman. il N Y Times Mag p 13+ Je 16 '63
Case for apartness. il House & Gard 124:254-9+ N '63
Case of the bugged bedroom. Time 85:38+ Ja 15 '65
Court agrees that there should be a remedy; Illinois suit brought by widow and son of Al Capone against Desilu productions, CBS and Westinghouse. H. F. Pilpel. Pub W 186:41 O 5 '64
Crescent house to encompass a lake view. il Arch Rec 133:98-101 mid-My '63
Four linked pavilions form builder house. il Arch Rec 135:92-5 mid-My '64
Invaders; rapid erosion of privacy. il Newsweek 63.81-2 Mr 9 '64
Invasion of privacy; excerpts from Naked society. V. Packard. Atlan 213:55-61 F '64
Laws of libel and privacy opposite on the see-saw. H. F. Pilpel. Pub W 186:295-6 Ag 31 '64
Leave me alone! J. P. Roche. Reporter 30:54-6 My 21 '64
Many-winged house on a big wooded lot has excellent zoning and quiet privacy. il Arch Rec 133:86-9 mid-My '63
Naked society, by V. Packard. Review
Pub W 185:66 Ja 6 '64
No place left to hide. D. Boroff. Sat R 47:47 Mr 21 '64
Notes and comment; problems of invasion of privacy. New Yorker 40:21 Je 27 '64
Open and shut case for privacy. il Am Home 67:44-5 Ap '64
Pin-wheel plan provides privacy without fences. il Arch Rec 135:153-6 Je '64
Please tap my wire. I like it! C. Fadiman. il Holiday 36:12+ Jl '64
Problem: privacy in the home for owners and guests. il Am Home 66:34-5 My '63
Protecting the right of privacy. P. B. Kurland. il PTA Mag 58:10-12 Mr '64
Receding walls give privacy to restricted site. il Arch Rec 135:84-7 mid-My '64
Right of privacy: an approach worth considering. H. F. Pilpel. Pub W 184:244-5 Ag 26 '63
Right to privacy; excerpt from Naked society. V. Packard. Atlan 213:71-5 Mr '64
Rocky road of HR 6386; privacy in housing survey; excerpts from testimony. R. Burgess. Nat R 15:429 N 19 '63
This H-shaped house is for people who believe in privacy. J. D. Bloodgood. il Bet Hom & Gard 41:56-7 Jl '63
Ubiquitous bugs and our privacy. Life 56:4 Je 12 '64
What happened to our privacy? R. Wallace. Life 56:11 Ap 10 '64
Whatever happened to my castle? M. A. Guitar. Am Home 67:40 O '64
When the only way to go is up. il House B 105:184-5+ S '63
Whole new world may open for use of subsidiary rights; New York law on the right of privacy. H. F. Pilpel. Pub W 185:63-4 F 3 '64

See also
Wire tapping

PRIVATE airplanes. See Airplanes—Private ownership

PRIVATE clubs. See Clubs

PRIVATE ear; drama. See Shaffer, P.

PRIVATE enterprise. See Free enterprise

PRIVATE eye (periodical)
Jaundiced eye. il Newsweek 61:62-3 Mr 18 '63
Public look at Private eye. M. Muggeridge. il Esquire 61:72-85+ F '64

PRIVATE flying
Danny Kaye. G. Casey and T. Nagle. il Flying 74:46+ Mr '64
Flying fling; roundtrip flight from Midland, Tex. to Toronto. B. K. Lindsay. il Flying 75:47-8 S '64
Flying in. il Time 81:66 Je 14 '63
Flying your own plane to Baja California. il Sunset 131:56+ N '63
Gentleman flier; symposium. il Esquire 61:82-5+ Je '64
I married an airplane. G. Barbor. il Read Digest 86:113-17 Ja '65
New lift in private aviation. il Bsns W p 118-20+ Ja 19 '63
One foot in the air. il Time 83:50-1 My 29 '64
Pilot report; go jump in the lake. A. H. Sanfelici. il Flying 74:40-1+ Je '64
Pour le sport. P. Franklin. il Flying 74:47+ Mr '64
Private lines. Aviation W 78:88 My 27 '63
Russians seek boost for private aviation. Aviation W 79:72+ D 2 '63
Troubles of private aviation under Russia's closed-sky policy. W. Cloud. Pop Sci 184:23-4+ Mr '64
Week-end pilot. F. K. Smith. See issues of Flying

PRIVATE libraries. See Libraries, Private

PRIVATE ownership. See Property

PRIVATE placement of securities. See Securities—Marketing

PRIVATE presses. See Printing—Private presses

PRIVATE property. See Property

PRIVATE rights. See Civil rights

PRIVATE school buildings. See School buildings
PRIVATE school libraries. See School libraries
PRIVATE schools
Ages three to fourteen in one school; Peninsula school, Menlo Park, Calif. il Arch Rec 133:177-9 My '63
Country day school has an expansible plan of linked units; Short Hills country day school, Summit, N.J. il Arch Rec 136:230-1 S '64
Education of a headmaster; Choate school, Wallingford, Conn; reprint. S. St John. il Library J 88:828-31 F 15 '63
Federal aid for parochial and private schools. W. S. Vincent. Sch & Soc 92:355-7 N 28 '64
Freedom or chaos? upstate New York's Lewis-Wadhams school, patterned on England's Summerhill. il Newsweek 63:83 Je 29 '64
Handbook of private schools, by P. Sargent. Review
Sat R 46:64 O 19 '63. P. Woodring; Discussion. 46:38 D 21 '63; 47:61 F 15 '64
Happy landing; tenth principal of Phillips Exeter academy. Newsweek 61:108 Je 24 '63
Horseback in the classroom; Foxcroft school. P. Downey. il Sports Illus 19:24-7 N 11 '63
Lake Forest antiques show. il Antiques 83:654 Je '63
Leadership and world society; LAWS program at Emma Willard boarding school for girls. A. L. Homan. il Sr Schol 83:11T S 27 '63
Modest architecture for a fine New England campus. M. F. Schmertz. il Arch Rec 134: 141-56 S '63
Modest dormitories for a country prep school; St Paul's school, Concord, N.H. il Arch Rec 133:125-32 Je '63
New England prep school. S. Birmingham. il Holiday 35:38-49+ F '64
Nonpublic schools: what must they teach? M. J. Stolee. bibliog f il Sch & Soc 92:274-6+ O 3 '64
Nursery through high school for girls; Greenwich academy, Greenwich, Conn. il Arch Rec 134:220-2 O '63
Off to Africa; resignation of W. G. Saltonstall from Phillips Exeter academy. il Newsweek 61:70 Mr 18 '63
On the slopes of Mt Ida; Emma Willard school. il Time 83:60 Je 26 '64
Private coeducational elementary school; Foote school, New Haven, Conn. il Arch Rec 133:184-6 My '63
Private school of fluid spaces; Moses Brown school, Providence, R.I. il Arch Forum 120: 122-3 My '64
Remodeling of a city school; Buckley school, N.Y. il Arch Forum 119:124-7 N '63
Science for schoolboys; St Mark's school of Texas. il Arch Forum 118:110-13 F '63
Something says yes; resignation of W. G. Saltonstall from Phillips Exeter academy. Time 81:61 Mr 15 '63
Summer scholars; Mount Hermon, Mass. il Newsweek 64:49 Jl 27 '64
Tackling man; new headmaster of Exeter. Time 81:59 Je 21 '63
Taft's third; Taft school, Watertown, Conn. Time 81:71-2 F 15 '63
This thing about Frank; Groton boy. J. Potter. New Yorker 39:70-4 Ag 10 '63
Warm-hearted guide to certain girls' schools. P. LaFarge. Harper 226:73-9 Ap '63
See also
Church schools

Attendance

Can public funds be constitutionally granted to private schools? address, January 9, 1963. R. F. Drinan. Vital Speeches 29:273-8 F 15 '63
Nonpublic high schools: fall 1963 enrollment and 1962-63 graduates; with tables. D. B. Gertler. Sch Life 47:32-5 O '64

Desegregation

As hard as ABC. il Time 84:68 Ag 21 '64

Finance

See School finance

Statistics

Statistics of nonpublic schools. D. B. Gertler. il Sch Life 46:31-6 O '63

Australia

Government finance for private schools in Australia. W. G. Smith. Sch & Soc 92:268-70 O 3 '64

France

School for wives; L'académie Maxim's. il Time 81:65 Mr 29 '63

Switzerland

Very private school; Le Rosey school, Switzerland. il Newsweek 63:109 Mr 16 '64

PRIVATE secretaries. See Secretaries
PRIVATE truck fleets. See Trucking—Private operations
PRIVATE wire systems. See Telegraph—Private wire systems
PRIVILEGES and immunities
Church ruled liable for damages; ruling against Holy Trinity Catholic church. Christian Cent 80:733 Je 5 '63
PRIZE fighting. See Boxing
PRO musica (organization) See New York pro musica antiqua (organization)
PROBABILITIES
Probability. M. Kac. il Sci Am 211:92-6+ bibliog(p269) S '64
Professor who breaks the bank. P. O'Neil. il Life 56:80-2+ Mr 27 '64
What can we predict? theory of mathematical probability. R. Yoshioka. il Sci N L 85:138-9 F 29 '64
See also
Chance
PROBATE law and practice
See also
Wills
PROBES, Space. See Space probes
PROBLEM children
Behavior: disturbed or disturbing? R. R. Kyllonen. NEA J 53:50-2 S '64
Delinquent: do we hate our children? R. Tunley. il Nation 199:5-6 Jl 13 '64; Reply. C. W. Tenney, jr. 199:inside cover Ag 10 '64
I can lick every person in this camp! a school social worker at a day camp. M. B. Crock. il NEA J 53:52-3 N '64
Little boy who couldn't learn. A. Lake. il Redbook 123:46-7+ Je '64
Problem children or problem parents. il Sci Digest 54:75-6 N '63
Reilly and I. B. Weiss. Commentary 35:302-11 Ap '63; Discussion. 36:166-9 Ag '63
School problem: attacks on teachers. il U S News 56:8 Mr 16 '64
Son's delinquency helps rebuild a marriage. D. C. Disney. Ladies Home J 80:52 Jl '63
Taming the neighborhood bully; with program for disscussion group, by M. Smart. S. H. Strait. il Parents Mag 38:44-5+. 140 Ap '63
See also
Juvenile delinquency
School children—Adjustment
Special classes and special schools
PROBLEM solving
Boost your problem-solving power. N. Stewart. Nations Bsns 52:122-4+ My '64
Get your money's worth from specialists. N. Stewart. Nations Bsns 52:96+ Ap '64
Let others solve your problems. J. G. Mason. il Nations Bsns 51:94-6 Je '63
Match decisions to your problems. N. F. Washburne. Nations Bsns 52:82+ O '64
Problem-solving. M. Scheerer. il Sci Am 208: 118-22+ Ap '63
Proposal for better business forecasting; adaptation of address. W. W. Leontief. Harvard Bsns R 42:166-7+ N '64
Science of being almost certain. G. A. W. Boehm. il Fortune 69:104-7+ F '64
Think your way to success. S. Schuler. il Nations Bsns 52:88-90+ Ap '64
PROBST, George E.
Cooperative education is first-rate education. PTA Mag 58:26-8 N '63
PROCAINE
Procaine action: antagonism by adenosine triphosphate and other nucleotides. A. S. Kuperman and others. bibliog il Science 144:1222-3 Je 5 '64
PROCEDURE (law)
And the Court said unto Gideon. Time 82:53 O 18 '63
Annals of law; Gideon case. A. Lewis. il New Yorker 40:144+ Ap 25; 108+ My 2; 150+ My 9 '64
See also
Criminal procedure
PROCESS
Artful pursuers of artful dodgers. T. Buckley. il N Y Times Mag p90+ S 8 '63
Summons instead of an arrest; Manhattan summons project. G. Samuels. il N Y Times Mag p 16+ Jl 26 '64
PROCESSIONS
Jesus for a night; Easter week processions in Corsica. Time 81:44 Ap 19 '63

PROCHNIK, Bruce
Tads. New Yorker 39:27-8 F 23 '63
PROCLAMATION of emancipation. See Emancipation proclamation
PROCLAMATIONS, Thanksgiving. See Thanksgiving proclamations
PROCOPIUS
Emperor's vices; excerpt from Secret histories, tr. by R. Atwater. Horizon 5:10 N '63
PROCRASTINATION
Don't do it now! C. Ford. il Read Digest 82:33-4+ F '63
PROCTER and Gamble company
Annals of business; Crest toothpaste. B. Bliven, jr. New Yorker 39:83-4+ Mr 23 '63
Behind P&G's marketing success. il Duns R 81:48-51+ My '63
P&G is told it must sell Clorox. Bsns W p82-3 D 21 '63
Profit teams of management. J. B. Weiner. il Duns R 84:36-7+ S '64
PROCUREMENT, Military. See United States—Armed forces—Procurement
PRODIGIES. See Children, Gifted
PRODIGIES, Musical. See Children as musicians
PRODUCERS and retailers cooperative, incorporated
New middleman co-op; marketing of eggs. L. M. Palmer. Farm J 87:69-70 Ap '63
PRODUCTION
Cultural lag in manufacturing. H. E. Klein. il Duns R 82:37-8+ Ag '63
Efficient economy. Time 82:85-6 Jl 12 '63
Golden key to production profits. H. E. Klein. il Duns R 81:50-2+ Ap '63
Running tide. il Fortune 68:49-50 D '63
Steep climb. il Fortune 67:39-40 F '63
Trend of business. J. Phillips. il Duns R 82:8-9 D '63
See also
Gross national product
Labor productivity
Supply and demand
Technocracy
Statistics
Facts and figures of the Americas; gross domestic product. Américas 16:42-3 Ja '64
Facts and figures of the Americas; gross national product in free world. il Américas 16:42-3 Ap '64
PRODUCTION, Agricultural
Food. N. S. Scrimshaw. il Sci Am 209:72-80 S '63
1963 feed grain program. F. Bailey, jr. and B. Brantley. il Suc Farm 61:69+ F '63
See also
Food supply
PRODUCTION, Theatrical. See Theatrical production
PRODUCTION code, Motion picture. See Moving picture censorship
PRODUCTION control
Concept of a production system. P. H. Thurston. il Harvard Bsns R 41:70-5 N '63
Diagnosing interdepartmental conflict. J. A. Seiler. bibliog f il Harvard Bsns R 41:121-32 S '63
Payoff from product management. B. C. Ames. il Harvard Bsns R 41:141-52 N '63
Reliability engineering. G. A. W. Boehm. il Fortune 67:124-7+ Ap '63
See also
Critical path analysis
PRODUCTION credit associations. See Finance companies
PRODUCTION line method. See Assembly line methods
PRODUCTION standards
Let's see Z.D. il Time 84:93-4 N 6 '64
See also
Work measurement
PRODUCTIVITY, Labor. See Labor productivity
PRODUCTS, Commercial. See Commercial products
PRODUCTS, New
Blessings in our time; portfolio. Esquire 60:140-3 D '63
Case of the unproductive products. S. A. Greyser. il Harvard Bsns R 42:20-2+ Jl '64
Inventions, patents, processes. See issues of Science digest
It's news to me! See issues of Better homes and gardens
Looking for gold in offbeat gadgets; housewares show in Chicago. il Bsns W p44-5 Jl 27 '63
Marketplace. Time 84:45 Jl 31 '64
New products. See issues of Business week
New products. See issues of Popular electronics
New products boom. P. Bart. Sat R 46:54 Je 8 '63
New products for summer. il Time 81:56 Ap 26 '63
Organizing for product innovation. J. W. Lorsch and P. R. Lawrence. il Harvard Bsns R 43:109-18+ Ja '65
Products & processes. See issues of Fortune
Products and processes. See issues of Missiles and rockets
ROI for new-product policy. P. A. Scheuble, jr. il Harvard Bsns R 42:110-20 N '64
Sales & distribution; need for new products. L. Morse. Duns R 81:79-80+ My '63
Short happy life. il Time 81:83 Mr 29 '63
What's newest. See issues of Newsweek
PRODUCTS, Quality of. See Quality of products
PROFACI gang. See Gangs
PROFANITY. See Swearing
PROFESSION, Choice of. See Vocational guidance
PROFESSIONAL attitudes. See Professionalism
PROFESSIONAL ball clubs. See Baseball clubs
PROFESSIONAL basketball. See Basketball
PROFESSIONAL basketball players. See Basketball players
PROFESSIONAL bowlers association
Guy named Smith is striking it rich. R. Boyle. il Sports Illus 19:36-8 N 25 '63
PROFESSIONAL ethics
See also
Business ethics
Engineers, Professional ethics for
Scientists, Professional ethics for
Teachers ethics
PROFESSIONAL football. See Football
PROFESSIONAL football clubs. See Football clubs
PROFESSIONAL football players. See Football players
PROFESSIONAL golf. See Golf
PROFESSIONAL golfers association
Payday on the senior circuit. R. Creamer. il Sports Illus 18:22-3 F 11 '63
PROFESSIONAL golfers' association championship. See Golf—Tournaments
PROFESSIONAL golfers' association seniors' tournament. See Golf—Tournaments
PROFESSIONAL sanctions. See Sanctions, Professional
PROFESSIONAL school of the Swiss hotel-keepers' association, Lausanne, Switzerland. See Hotel management—Study and teaching
PROFESSIONAL tennis. See Tennis
PROFESSIONAL workers
What is a pro? A. Dorne. Design 65:136 Mr '64
Salaries
Russia joins the war on poverty; pensions to collective farmers, pay increases to teachers and doctors. Bsns W p32 Jl 25 '64
PROFESSIONALISM
I want to be an amateur. M. A. Guitar. Mlle 57:152+ O '63
Local association studies ethics cases; readiness test. NEA J 53:24-5 F '64
Local associations build professional strength. R. H. Wyatt. il NEA J 53:18-20 F '64
PROFESSIONALISM (sports) See Amateurism (sports)
PROFESSIONS
Certification and professional autonomy; excerpt from Certification in education. L. B. Kinney. bibliog Sch & Soc 91:434-9 D 28 '63
Martyrs unlimited. P. F. Drucker. Harper 229:12+ Jl '64
Teacher-opinion poll, status of teaching as a vocation. il NEA J 53:56 My '64
See also
Occupations
Self employed
PROFESSOR Hobo; drama. See Huff, B. T.
PROFESSORS. See College professors and instructors
PROFFIT, William R. and Ackerman, J. L.
Fluoride: its effects on two parameters of bone growth in organ culture. bibliog Science 145:932-4 Ag 28 '64
PROFICIENCY and review tests. See Educational tests and measurements
PROFICIENCY examinations. See Examinations
PROFILE rocks. See Rock profiles
PROFILES. See Silhouettes

PROFIT
Basic principle of the free world; address, November 29, 1962. A. Ames. Vital Speeches 29:248-50 F 1 '63
Bright, dark spots in the profits picture; with chart. U S News 54:38 F 11 '63
Care and feeding of the profitable product; excerpts from Managing for results: economic tasks and risk-taking decisions. P. F. Drucker. Fortune 69:133-5 Mr '64
Corporate profit equation, for policy making by business, government, and labor. R. E. Speagle and H. R. Chace. il Harvard Bsns R 41:116-27 Mr '63
Earning a raise. il Time 82:85 N 8 '63
Experts see three bright years ahead; symposium. il Nations Bsns 51:41+ N '63
How much is enough? il Time 82:65 Ag 9 '63
How to get most from growth. C. A. Cerami. il Nations Bsns 51:34-5+ Jl '63
How world's biggest profit makes jobs; General motors' $2 billion expansion. il Nations Bsns 52:40-1+ Jl '64
Incentives marked by profit formulas; with editorial comment. W. Beller. il Miss & Roc 14:24-5, 54 Ja 20 '64
More power to them. Time 82:73 S 27 '63
No squeeze on profits. New Repub 148:6 My 4 '63
Profit phenomenon; General motors profits increase. il Time 81:75 F 8 '63
Profitless prosperity; address, May 23, 1963. J. D. Harper. Vital Speeches 29:566-9 Jl 1 '63
Profitless prosperity is on the way out. il Bsns W p54-5 Ja 4 '64
Profits in focus. il Fortune 69:32+ Je '64
Record earnings, but: do profit totals tell the whole story? il U S News 56:102-3 My 4 '64
Record profits now; but there's still a squeeze. il U S News 55:92-5 O 14 '63
Sales thrust will improve profit picture; views of key men. Nations Bsns 52:58+ Jl '64
Score on business profits: many gains reported, but— il U S News 54:84+ My 6 '63
Tooling up for profits; address, May 7, 1964. A. C. Daugherty. Vital Speeches 30:530-3 Je 15 '64
What is a fair profit? Duns R 83:31 Ap '64
What profit squeeze? Nation 196:170 Mr 2 '63
See also
Corporations—Finance

PROFIT sharing
Bigger melon, smaller slices; AMC for UAW. Bsns W p32 N 23 '63
New look at profit sharing. America 110:667-8 My 16 '64
Profit-sharing issues raises hob; American motors and UAW. Bsns W p48+ O 17 '64
Sharing the profits. Time 82:97 N 29 '63
What savings pay at GM, Ford. U S News 54:75 F 4 '63
See also
Savings-sharing plan in industry

PROFUMO, John Dennis
Britain's spy scandals; how they grow. il por U S News 54:46-8 Je 24 '63
Case of the sensitive osteopath. il por Time 81:29 Mr 29 '63
Crisis over Christine. E. Behr. il pors Sat Eve Post 236:77-85 Jl 13 '63
Doctor Stephen Ward returns. R. West. Esquire 62:141+ S '64
Embarrassed Establishment. Nation 196:538-9 Je 29 '63
Ineffectual but innocent; Lord Denning's report. il Time 82:40-1 O 4 '63
Is Super Mac to be undone by sex? il Newsweek 61:45-6 Je 24 '63
John Bull & John Profumo. J. Gross. Commentary 36:144-50 Ag '63
Letter from London; Profumo case. M. Panter-Downes. New Yorker 39:66-9 Je 29 '63
Mac the Slack. il por Newsweek 62:29 Jl 1 '63
Missing model. Newsweek 61:33 Ap 1 '63
New pornocracy. il Newsweek 62:35-6 Jl 8 '63
Pall on profumory; Ward-Keeler-Profumo scandal. C. Northcott. Christian Cent 80:1023 Ag 21 '63
Personal report on Britain's biggest scandal. L. Bergquist. il por Look 27:81-6 Jl 30 '63
Price of Christine. il por Time 81:32-3 Je 14 '63
Profumo affair. C. Brogan. Nat R 14:528-9+ Jl 2 '63
Profumo affair. J. M. Cameron. Commonweal 78:445-6 Jl 26 '63
Sagacious end of the affair; Denning report. Life 55:4 O 11 '63
Scandal that's rocking Britain; Profumo case. il por U S News 54:8 Je 17 '63
Temptress rocks the Empire; with report by P. Worsthorne. il pors Life 54:18-23 Je 21 '63
Thunder on the Thames; the British press and the Profumo case. J. Tebbel. il por Sat R 46:44-6 Jl 13 '63
Time of the trollop. il Time 81:24+ Je 21 '63
'What the hell. . .' il por Newsweek 61:38+ Je 17 '63
What would Queen Victoria say? Profumo scandal. B. Hollowood. N Y Times Mag p 7+ Je 30 '63
Word of Christine; concerning the Denning report. G. Playfair. New Repub 149:11-13 D 21 '63

PROGESTERONE
Whither the pill? R. A. McCormick. Cath World 199:207-14 Jl '64

PROGESTIN. See Progesterone

PROGNOSIS
Tocqueville and the problem of historical prognosis. E. T. Gargan. bibliog f Am Hist R 68:332-45 Ja '63

PROGRAM evaluation and budget committee. See American library association—Program evaluation and budget committee

PROGRAM evaluation and review technique. See Critical path analysis

PROGRAMMABLE film reader. See Calculating machines—Input-output equipment

PROGRAMMED teaching
Evaluation of programmed texts. R. L. Caulfield. Sch & Soc 91:116-17+ Mr 9 '63
Learn to read in thirty hours; Freeport, N.Y. il Sci Digest 56:5 O '64
Motivation in automated instruction. J. W. Moore and W. I. Smith. Sch Life 46:21-2 N '63
Other kind of teaching. E. Bender. Harper 230:48-55 Ja '65
Phase programming; sophomore English at Central high school, Columbus, Ohio. R. Marsh. il Sr Schol 83:7T N 15 '63
Programed help: in-service training program for librarians. W. Jones. Library J 89:4304 N 1 '64
Programmed learning and in-service training in libraries. T. C. Hines. bibliog ALA Bul 58:719-24 S '64
Programed materials; shall we let them in the library? T. C. Hines. il Library J 88:2055-8+ My 15 '63
Research on programed instruction at SDC. H. F. Silberman. il Sch Life 45:13-15+ Mr '63
Selection and use of programed learning materials. P. C. Lange. il NEA J 53:28-9 Ap '64
Special issue on programmed instruction; symposium, ed. by D. A. Cook and D. A. Sohn. bibliog il Sr Schol 84:6T+, 9T-15T Mr 13 '64
Strategies for using programed instruction. J. R. Murphy and I. A. Goldberg. bibliog f il Harvard Bsns R 42:115-32 My '64
There is a place for programmed instruction in the teaching of the visual arts. L. M. Quirke. il Sch Arts 63:31-3 Mr '64
What's happening in education? programmed instruction. W. D. Boutwell. PTA Mag 58:22 O '63
When publishers go public. W. Jovanovich. il Sat R 47:21-2+ My 16 '64
See also
Teaching machines

Anecdotes, facetiae, satire, etc.

Filling in the spaces. M. W. Lackey. Sat R 46:39 Ag 17 '63

PROGRAMMING (calculating machines)
Computer programs can be registered for copyright. Pub W 185:102 Je 8 '64
Computing ad absurdum. H. Schenck, jr. Nation 196:505-7 Je 15 '63
Imitation of man by machine. U. Neisser. bibliog Science 139:193-7 Ja 18 '63; Discussion. 140:212-14+ Ap 12 '63
Mixing math and motherhood; computer programming project. il Bsns W p86-7 Mr 2 '63
Wanted: 500,000 men to feed computers. S. L. Englebardt. il Pop Sci 186:106-9 Ja '65
Young wizard of computers. R. Bailey. il Life 57:107-13+ S 25 '64
See also
Programming languages (calculating machines)

PROGRAMMING languages (calculating machines)
Another Tower of Babel? D. S. Culbertson. bibliog Library J 88:940-3 Mr 1 '63; Reply. D. V. Black. 88:2164 Je 1 '63
Profiles; computer: analytical engine. J. Bernstein. il New Yorker 39:58-60+ O 19; 54-6+ O 26 '63
RCA action may herald move to standard program language. Aviation W 81:80-1 D 21 '64

PROGRESS
Art of being secure; address, January 21, 1964. R. M. Blough. Vital Speeches 30:282-6 F 15 '64
Progress through change. D. R. Watts. Wilson Lib Bul 38:413 Ja '64
Reasons for doing nothing. E. Dale. NEA J 52:11 N '63
Technological exploration; address, January 15, 1964. H. Ford, 2d. Vital Speeches 30: 246-9 F 1 '64
What is the key to progress? il Bsns W p 132+ My 16 '64
See also
Civilization
Inventions
Science and civilization
Social progress

PROGRESSIVE education
Family business in brief; traditional vs. progressive education. A. P. Eliasberg. il N Y Times Mag p39 Jl 26 '64
Freedom or chaos? upstate New York's Lewis-Wadhams school, patterned on England's Summerhill. il Newsweek 63:83 Je 29 '64
Urban school for progressive education. il Arch Rec 134:214-15 O '63

PROGRESSIVE movement in politics
Election of 1916. J. A. Huston. Cur Hist 47: 205-9+ O '64

PROGRESSIVE party
Social workers and the Progressive party, 1912-1916. A. F. Davis. bibliog f Am Hist R 69:671-88 Ap '64

PROHIBITION

India

Noble experiment, Indian style. T. F. Brady. il N Y Times Mag p24+ F 16 '64

Iowa

Drought ends in Iowa. D. Mabry. Reporter 29:27 Jl 4 '63

United States

How dry we were: prohibition revisited, by H. Lee. Review
Sat R 46:22 Je 1 '63. Q. Reynolds
Lean times in Boston; depression and the drys. C. W. Morton. Atlan 211:47-54 F '63
Thirty-five years ago; Chicago's gang wars. S. D. Smith. il N Y Times Mag p45+ F 9 '64
Thirty years ago; end of prohibition. G. Vincent. il N Y Times Mag p45-6+ D 1 '63

PROHIBITION party (United States)
Hangover. Newsweek 64:30 S 7 '64

PROJECT Apollo. See Space flight to the moon
PROJECT cloud gap. See Disarmament—Inspection
PROJECT Echo. See Communications satellites
PROJECT English. See English language—Study and teaching
PROJECT Fire. See Space vehicles—Atmospheric entry
PROJECT Gemini. See Space flight—Manned flights
PROJECT Haystack. See Radio antennas
PROJECT Haystaq. See United States—Patent office
PROJECT Mercury. See Space flight—Manned flights
PROJECT Mohole. See Mohole project
PROJECT needles. See Dipole orbital belts in space
PROJECT Ozma. See Life on other planets
PROJECT plowshare. See Atomic blasting
PROJECT Ranger. See Lunar probes
PROJECT Rover. See Rockets, Atomic powered
PROJECT sedan. See Atomic blasting
PROJECT; story. See Wood, M.
PROJECT Stratoscope. See Balloons—Use in research
PROJECT Telstar. See Communication satellites
PROJECT VELA. See Atomic bombs—Testing, Detection of
PROJECT West Ford. See Dipole orbital belts in space

PROJECTILES
See also
Bullets

PROJECTION, Moving picture. See Moving picture projection

PROJECTION apparatus
Action editor: how to buy one. L. Drukker. il Pop Phot 54:108-9+ F '64
Choosing the right projection screen. il Consumer Rep 29:232-4 My '64
Color clinic; eight-foot projected images. D. B. Eisendrath, jr. Pop Phot 54:10+ Ja '64
Color vision: an experiment. P. Farber. il U S Camera 27:50-1+ Ja '64; Discussion. 27: 16+ Ap '64
Directory of sound-slide systems. L. Lipton. il Pop Phot 55:84 O '64
Easel tracing-projector. M. Banister. il Pop Mech 120:130-4 Jl '63
Education's newest magic lantern; overhead projector; English at Stillwater, Minn, H.S. G. Erwin. il Sr Schol 84:28T-29T Mr 20 '64
Four closeups of movie projection. J. R. Gregory. il U S Camera 26:78-9+ My '63
Gaining new vision for social studies; overhead projectors and transparencies. R. A. Withey. il Sr Schol 85:18T Ja 21 '65
How bright your screen! R. Miller. il U S Camera 26:58+ My '63
How far have we gone? Kodascope B 16mm projector. G. Zygmund. il Mod Phot 27:100+ N '63
How to teach library skills without really being there; use of cartridge projectors in school libraries. V. S. Gerlach and I. Farnbach. il Library J 89:921-2 F 15 '64
HPI telescreen. L. Lachter. il U S Camera 26:93 F '63
Keppler on the SLR; depth of field. H. Keppler. il Mod Phot 28:18+ Ja '64
New movie projectors. B. Hering. il Pop Sci 184:162-5+ Mr '64
New projector does everything but applaud; 8mm projector. H. Luckett. il Pop Sci 185: 138-41 O '64
1965 photography directory and buying guide; showmanship. il Pop Phot 55:69-132 D '64
Photo bubble surrounds you at the Swiss national exposition in Lausanne. L. Barry. il Pop Phot 54:68 My '64
Project your color prints. N. Rothschild. il Pop Phot 52:62-3+ Mr '63
Projectors and enlarger lenses for sub-35. il Pop Phot 53:69 Ag '63
Projectors and screens. Consumer Rep 29:379-85 D '64
Teaching library skills with an overhead projector; school libraries. J. M. Landman. il Library J 89:923-4 F 15 '64
35mm. J. Wolbarst. Mod Phot 28:17+ Ap '64
Time projector; ceiling image of wristwatch. F. Johnson. il Pop Mech 120:133 D '63
Two new single-frame cameras and a slide projector. il Consumer Bul 47:29-31 Je '64
What makes projected 35mm slides unsharp? D. L. Miller. il Mod Phot 27:78-81 N '61
Your second projector. N. Rothschild. il Pop Phot 52:78-9 Mr '63
See also
Moving picture projection

PROJECTION of transparencies. See Transparencies—Projection

PROJECTIVE geometry. See Geometry, Projective

PROJECTORS. See Projection apparatus

PROJECTS (teaching)
Nature craft. J. Laury and J. Aiken. il Bet Hom & Gard 42:96 O; 121 N '64

PROKHOROV, Aleksandr M.
Nobel prize winners. por Sci N L 86:295 N 7 '64
Research on maser-laser principle wins Nobel prize in physics. J. P. Gordon. por Science 146:897-9 N 13 '64

PROKOF'EV, Sergei Sergeevich
Angel of fire (L'ange de feu) Criticism
New Yorker 40:62+ D 26 '64
At last, Prokofieff's Second symphony. J. Diether. por Am Rec G 30:1016-18 Jl '64
Celebration at seventy; Szigeti's Prokofiev; sonatas for violin and piano. A. Frankenstein. por Hi Fi 13:56-7 My '63
Long, twisting road. H. Weinstock. il pors Opera N 28:8-13 F 29 '64
Meanwhile, back at Symphony Hall. . . J. Lyons. il Am Rec G 30:1019 Jl '64
On records; War and peace. J. W. Freeman. Opera N 27:35 F 9 '63
Prokofiev, by L. Hanson and E. Hanson. Review
Opera N 29:34 D 26 '64. J. Honig
Prokofiev from Boston, a new series launched. A. Rich. il por Hi Fi 14:59-60 My '64

PROKOP, John
Arbor day, America's magic holiday. Am For 70:24-6+ Ap '64
Big squeeze in your back yard. Am For 69: 6-7+ Ap '63
Can forestry help? Am For 69:7+ Jl '63
Chief's first report. Am For 69:4+ S '63
Man in the middle. Am For 70:34-6+ My '64
Senator Ribicoff would end protest registration of insecticides. Am For 69:7+ O '63
This is a junkyard; color it green. Am For 71:14-17+ Ja '65
Well done, Mr Secretary! Am For 69:8+ Mr '63

PROKOVSKY, André
Andre Prokovsky. S. Goodman. pors Dance Mag 37:50-1 O '63

PROLACTIN
Circadian periodicity in the concentration of prolactin in the rat hypophysis. R. H. Clark and B. L. Baker. bibliog il Science 143:375-6 Ja 24 '64; Reply with rejoinder. J. D. Palmer. 145:296 Jl 17 '64

PROLETARIAN literature, American. See American literature

PROMENADE concerts. See Concerts

PROMISCUITY. See Sexual ethics

PROMOTERS and promoting
Boxing mess: why I want to get out. W. D. Fugazy. il Sat Eve Post 236:28-30+ Ap 6 '63
Dream: C. M. Clay. il Time 81:78-81 Mr 22 '63
Eleven men behind Cassius Clay. H. Horn. il Sports Illus 18:62-8+ Mr 11 '63
This death might kill boxing; death of Ernie Knox. R. H. Boyle. il Sports Illus 19:16-21 O 28 '63
To fight or not to fight? Clay-Liston rematch. R. H. Boyle. il Sports Illus 21:28-31 S 7 '64

PROMOTION, Sales. See Sales promotion

PROMOTION of employees. See Employees—Promotion

PROMS, School. See Student activities

PRONGHORN hunting
Antelope hunt with Ace Reid. B. Dalrymple. il Farm J 87:42-3+ O '63
I killed crooked horn. A. E. Hollemon. il Outdoor Life 133:68-9+ Ap '64
Pronghorn crawl. C. Elliott. il Outdoor Life 132:48-9+ S '63
Pronghorns for profit; reproductions of paintings by B. Kuhn. J. Linduska. Field & S 68:24-9 Ag '63

PRONGHORNS
Prairie drag race; catching antelope alive. T. Wilcox. il Outdoor Life 131:40-3+ Ja '63

PRONOUNCED clage and the tiger tooth; story. See Rhodin, E.

PRONUNCIATION
See also
English language—Pronunciation
Phonetics

PROPAGANDA
Dark doings; anti-Communist newsletter Tocsin fighting against right-wing. Nat R 14:396 My 21 '63
Epidemic of gooseflesh. G. W. Johnson. Atlan 212:43-6 D '63
For whom the bell rings. Nation 198:310 Mr 30 '64
Form council against rightist propaganda. Christian Cent 81:1229 O 7 '64
Free trade in ideas; excerpts from address. R. F. Kennedy. Sat R 46:43-4 F 16 '63
Fright peddlers fed on irresponsible charges; Senator Kuchel's warning against the extreme Right. J. N. Eller. America 108:734 My 25 '63
H. L. Hunt: portrait of a super-patriot; Life line. R. G. Sherrill. Nation 198:182-95 F 24 '64
New libel. Nation 199:234-5 O 19 '64
Package of political poison; analysis and criticism of None dare call it treason, by J. A. Stormer; reprint. R. W. Smith. Christian Cent 81:1263-4 O 14 '64
Plot!! to overthrow America!!! T. H. Kuchel. il N Y Times Mag p6+ Jl 21 '63
Propaganda and pornography. P. Revell. Library J 88:3562+ O 1 '63
Propaganda, by J. B. Whitton and A. Larson. Review
Sat R 47:42 Ap 4 '64. G. V. Allen
Propaganda gap, by W. Joyce. Review
Sat R 46:50 Jl 13 '63. J. F. Fixx
Propaganda, si in Cuba; photographs. N Y Times Mag p 12-13 Ap 12 '64
Strategy for a counterattack. J. F. Fixx. Sat R 48:74 Ja 9 '65
Will you join the dance? G. W. Johnson. New Repub 148:7 My 4 '63
See also
American committee for liberation
Foreign propagandists in the United States
Moving pictures—Propaganda films
Radio broadcasting—Propaganda
Rumor
Subversive activities

PROPAGANDA, American. See Propaganda

PROPAGANDA, Anti-Jewish. See Anti-Semitism

PROPAGANDA, Chinese
China's push in Africa. J. K. Cooley. Commonweal 79:424-6 Ja 10 '64
Myth who speaks for Mao; Lei Feng. J. Marcuse. il N Y Times Mag p30-1+ N 1 '64
Roots of Chinese ideology. S. Y. Dai. bibliog f Cur Hist 45:158-64+ S '63

PROPAGANDA, Communist
Anti-Americanism U.S. pays for. U S News 54:57 F 25 '63
Children's libraries; the Bulgarian way; Communist philosophy of juvenile literature. V. Haviland. Wilson Lib Bul 38:487 F '64
Foreign image. Commonweal 79:679-80 Mr 6 '64
Soviet foreign propaganda, by F. Barghoorn. Review
Science 144:675-7 My 8 '64. D. Lerner
Textbook factory: Volk und Wissen publishing company, East Berlin. H. Roske. Atlan 212:90-4 D '63
See also
Propaganda, Russian

PROPAGANDA, Fascist
Fascism for export: Italy and the United States in the twenties. A. Cassels. bibliog f Am Hist R 69:707-12 Ap '64

PROPAGANDA, German
Nazi propaganda, by Z. A. B. Zeman. Review
Sat R il 47:42 O 10 '64. J. Remak
Very educational; Bonn government propaganda film. Nation 196:319 Ap 20 '63

PROPAGANDA, Russian
My daddy can beat your daddy several centuries from now. il Time 84:30 Jl 31 '64
Soviet foreign propaganda, by F. C. Barghoorn. Review
New Repub 150:22-4 Je 6 '64. P. B. Mills
To meet the propaganda challenge. F. C. Barghoorn. il N Y Times Mag p 13+ Ja 19 '64

PROPAGATION of plants. See Plant propagation

PROPELLANTS, Rocket. See Rockets—Fuel

PROPELLERS
Facts and fancies about propellers. D. T. Abbott. il Yachting 115:90-1+ Ja '64
Prop is the thing. F. M. Paulson. il Field & S 68:120-4 Mr '64

PROPER motion of the stars. See Stars—Motion

PROPER names. See Names, Personal

PROPERTY
God, guilt and Goldwater. W. Stringfellow. Christian Cent 81:1079-83 S 2 '64; Discussion. 81:1338-9 O 28 '64
Mrs Murphy's private rights. W. J. Davis. America 109:454-6 O 19 '63
Play against Goldwater: private property, and civil rights bill. W. F. Buckley, jr. Nat R 15:13 Jl 16 '63
See also
Capitalism
Eminent domain
Wills

PROPERTY claims. See Claims

PROPERTY in foreign countries. See Investments, Foreign

PROPERTY insurance. See Insurance, Property

PROPERTY of hope; story. See Chappell, F.

PROPERTY rights. See Real property

PROPERTY tax
Death and taxes; Connecticut Public act 940. Nat Parks Mag 38:16 S '64
Miami taxpayers howl. il Bsns W p64+ Ag 22 '64
Your property taxes; do you know what you pay? il Changing T 17:7-11 O '63

PROPERTY values. See Land values

PROPHECIES
See also
Fortune telling

PROPHET movements. See Sects

PROPHETS
Prophets; the Lord's messengers changed all history. E. G. Kraeling. il Life 57:75-8+ D 25 '64

PROPORTION (architecture) See Architecture

PROPOSALS of marriage. See Marriage proposals

PROPRIETARY medicines. See Medicines, Patent, proprietary, etc.

PROPULSION, Jet. See Jet propulsion

PROPULSION, Rocket. See Rocket propulsion
PROSELYTISM. See Evangelistic work
PROSODY. See Versification
PROSPECTING
Back to the mines; new mining rush. il Time 83:90 Je 19 '64
Deep are the roots. Newsweek 61:90 Ap 8 '63
Mysterious maps to lost gold mines: Superstitution Mountains, Arizona; with report by R. B. Stolley. il Life 56:90-4+ Je 12 '64
Sourdoughs stake out new claim for survival. il Bsns W p30-1 Mr 28 '64
Treasure hunt at Timmins. il Newsweek 63:73-5 My 4 '64

Geophysical methods

New tools to map our hidden mineral wealth; seismic prospecting. J. M. Bruckshaw. il UNESCO Courier 17:28-32 Ja '64
World's greatest prospector. N. Carlisle. il Pop Sci 184:60-3+ My '64
See also
Petroleum—Prospecting—Geophysical methods
PROSPECTORS and developers association
Sourdoughs stake out new claim for survival. il Bsns W p30-1 Mr 28 '64
PROSPERITY
Abundance, threat or promise? R. Theobald. Nation 196:387-412 My 11 '63; Discussion. 196:inside cover Je 15 '63
Advent of abundance. G. Piel. il Bul Atomic Sci 19:2-6 Je '63
Affluence in U.S: the other side of the poverty story. il U S News 57:76-7 D 7 '64
Challenge of prosperity: symposium; presented with the Committee for economic development. il Sat R 48:23-32+ Ja 9 '65
Economic prosperity. il Sr Schol 85:16 S 23 '64
Indivisibility of world prosperity. il UNESCO Courier 16:27-9 Mr '63
Lasting prosperity? il Fortune 70:27-8+ Jl '64
Profitless prosperity; address, May 23, 1963. J. D. Harper. Vital Speeches 29:566-9 Jl 1 '63
Prosperity has continued unbroken; excerpts from address, October 16, 1964. L. B. Johnson. U S News 57:98 N 2 '64
Trend of business. J. Phillips. il Duns R 82:8-9 N '63
Uses of prosperity. B. Ward. il Sat R 47:27-9+ Ag 29 '64
What will bring back prosperity? symposium. il U S News 54:40-7 F 18 '63
See also
Business conditions
PROSTATE cancer. See Cancer
PROSTHESIS
Age of alloplasty; foreign materials used to replace the body's natural parts. il Time 85:54-5 Ja 1 '65
Electronic arm. il Time 82:74+ D 6 '63
Helping hand; thalidomide children. il Newsweek 62:62 S 9 '63
Medicine's frontier: rebuilding the human body. G. Astor. il Look 28:22-9 Je 30 '64
See also
Artificial limbs
PROSTITUTION
Anthology of pros. il Time 81:34 Ap 12 '63
Call wives; Long Island housewives. Newsweek 63:18 F 17 '64
Corrupt society. F. J. Cook. Nation 196:478 Je 1 '63
Jack the stripper; hunt for murderer of London prostitutes. Time 83:32+ My 8 '64
Murdering madams; sisters González Valenzuela. il Newsweek 64:60 N 2 '64
Seek new prostitution code. Christian Cent 81:1516 D 9 '64
Sisters of shame; Mexican white slavers. il Time 84:50 O 30 '64
Ten-dollar understanding: brothel behavior of the college boy. J. Richardson. Esquire 62:101+ S '64
Wolfenden report: report of the Committee on homosexual offenses and prostitution. Review
Christian Cent 80:1107 S 11 '63. A. A. Gross
PROTACTINIUM
Protactinium chemistry; report of symposium at Gatlinburg, Tenn. A. Chetham-Strode and D. E. Ferguson. Science 141:444 Ag 2 '63
Protactinium fluorides, the new class, $MPaF_6$. L. B. Asprey and R. A. Penneman. bibliog il Science 145:924 Ag 28 '64
PROTASS, Jay J. and others
Amino acid code in alcaligenes faecalis. Science 143:1174-6 Mr 13 '64
PROTEAS
Floral inheritance. E. Scholtz. il Natur Hist 72:26-31 My '63
PROTECTION (tariff) See Free trade and protection
PROTECTION of animals. See Animals—Protection
PROTECTION of birds. See Birds—Protection
PROTECTION of game. See Game protection
PROTECTION of plants. See Plants, Protection of
PROTECTION of the president. See Presidents—United States—Protection
PROTECTION of trees. See Trees, Care of
PROTECTION systems, Industrial
Portable eye spots intruders. Bsns W p 104 Ap 13 '63
PROTECTIVE coatings
Coat it with neoprene. V. L. Oertle. il Pop Mech 120:154-5 D '63
Scotch oven liner; spray-on material. Consumer Bul 48:34 F '65
Try a metal coating; longer-lasting protection for steel structures. A. P. Shepard. il Am City 79:99-101 N '64
See also
Plastic coating
PROTECTIVE coloration. See Color of animals; Color of insects
PROTECTIVE mechanisms (biology) See Defense mechanisms (biology)
PROTECTIVE mimicry. See Mimicry (biology)
PROTECTIVE paint. See Paint, Protective
PROTEIN deficiency. See Diet, Deficient
PROTEINASES
Enzymatic mechanism for the escape of certain moths from their cocoons. F. C. Kafatos and C. M. Williams. bibliog il Science 146:538-40 O 23 '64
See also
Enzymes
PROTEINS
Adhesion and emigration of leukocytes produced by cationic proteins of lysosomes. A. Janoff and B. W. Zweifach. bibliog il Science 144:1456-8 Je 19 '64
2-Aminoethylphosphonic acid in insoluble protein of the sea anemone metridium dianthus. L. D. Quin. bibliog il Science 144:1133-4 My 29 '64
Antibacterial and enzymic basic proteins from leukocyte lysosomes: separation and identification. H. I. Zeya and J. K. Spitznagel. bibliog il Science 142:1085-7 N 22 '63
Bee venom tolerance in white mice in relation to diet. A. W. Benton and others. bibliog il Science 145:1448-9 S 25 '64
Cell system in which rate and amount of protein synthesis are separately controlled. O. Landeros and H. M. Frost. bibliog il Science 145:1323-4 S 18 '64
Control of synthesis of RNA and protein in diapausing and injured cecropia pupae. S. J. Berry and others. bibliog il Science 146:938-40 N 13 '64
Cycloheximide: aspects of inhibition of protein synthesis in mammalian cells. H. L. Ennis and M. Lubin. bibliog il Science 146:1474-6 D 11 '64
Delayed appearance of labeled protein in isolated nerve endings and axoplasmic flow. S. H. Barondes. bibliog il Science 146:779-81 N 6 '64
Ergosomes at work: protein synthesis. Sci Am 209:66 Jl '63
Evaporation enhancement by protein films. L. K. James, jr. and D. J. O. Berry. bibliog il Science 140:312-14 Ap 19 '63
Evolving genes and proteins; report on symposium, September 17 and 18, 1964. V. Bryson and H. J. Vogel. Science 147:68-71 Ja 1 '65
4.5 billion years of protein molecules: what do we know now about how they are made? AAAS annual meeting, 26-31 December, Montreal. il Science 146:1076-7 N 20 '64
Genetic code. M. W. Nirenberg. il Sci Am 208:80-6+ bibliog(p 190) Mr '63
Growth control of nerve cells by a protein factor and its antiserum. R. Levi-Montalcini. bibliog il Science 143:105-10 Ja 10 '64
Inhibition of antibody synthesis by L-phenylalanine. W. L. Ryan and M. J. Carver. bibliog il Science 143:479-80 Ja 31 '64
Involvement of RNA in the synthesis of proteins. J. D. Watson. bibliog il Science 140:17-26 Ap 5 '63
Long-lived messenger RNA: evidence from cotton seed germination. L. Dure and L. Waters. bibliog il Science 147:410-12 Ja 22 '65

PROTEINS—*Continued*
Molecular model for protein synthesis. G. Zubay. bibliog il Science 140:1092-5 Je 7 '63
Precipitins in the rabbit produced by protein polysaccharide from bovine nasal cartilage. N. Di Ferrante. bibliog il Science 143:250-2 Ja 17 '64
Protein biosynthesis: some alternative considerations on the current hypothesis. R. W. Hendler. bibliog Science 142:402-5 O 18 '63
Protein-digesting enzymes; proteolytic enzymes. H. Neurath. il Sci Am 211:68-79 bibliog(p 154) D '64
Protein from petroleum. Sci Am 212:49-50 Ja '65
Protein purification by elution convection electrophoresis. S. Raymond. bibliog il Science 146:406-7 O 16 '64
Protein structure and function during differentiation; report of a symposium at Federation meetings of the American society of biological chemists. W. D. McElroy. Science 140:1427-30 Je 28 '63
Protein synthesis during development: control through messenger RNA. R. B. Scott and E. Bell. bibliog il Science 145:711-13 Ag 14 '64
Protein synthesis enhanced in the liver of rats force-fed a threonine-devoid diet. H. Sidransky and others. bibliog il Science 146:766-8 N 6 '64
Proteinpolysaccharide in connective tissue: inhibition of phase separation. H. Weinstein and others. bibliog il Science 142:1073-5 N 22 '63
RNA codewords and protein synthesis. M. Nirenberg and P. Leder. bibliog il Science 145:1399-407 S 25 '64
Steric factors in the chemistry of polypeptides, poly-α-amino acids and proteins. R. E. Whitfield. bibliog il Science 142:577-9 N 1 '63
Structural differences between two types of heavy chain disease proteins and myeloma globulins of corresponding types. K. Takatsuki and E. F. Osserman. bibliog il Science 145:499-500 Jl 31 '64
Subunit structure of proteins; report on annual symposium in biology. S. Lacks. Science 146:559-60+ O 23 '64
Thyroxine: effects on amino acid incorporation into protein in vivo. R. Michels and others. bibliog il Science 140:1417-18 Je 28 '63
Translational control of protein synthesis in a cell-free system directed by a polycistronic viral RNA. Y. Ohtaka and S. Spiegelman. bibliog Science 142:493-7 O 25 '63
Transplantation tolerance induced in adult mice by protein overloading of donors. P. Liacopoulos and J. H. Goode. bibliog il Science 146:1305-7 D 4 '64
Triplets unlocking code. W. Wingo. Sci N L 86:103 Ag 15 '64
Unusual aggregation of a nonfunctional tobacco mosaic virus protein. M. Zaitlin and W. R. Ferris. bibliog il Science 143:1451-2 Mr 27 '64
Vital protein produced from fungus tissue. Sci N L 83:383 Je 15 '63
See also
Amino acids
Collagen
Fibrinogen
Insulin
Lipoproteins
Myoglobin
Nucleoproteins
Tryptophan

PROTEINS, Blood. See Blood—Proteins

PROTEOLYTIC enzymes. See Enzymes

PROTESTANT church-owned publishers association
Church publishers begin seminars, plan convention. Pub W 186:90 S 28 '64
Protestant church publishers view role in communications. il Pub W 183:37-40 Mr 25 '63
Protestant publishers assn. holds 13th annual meeting. Pub W 185:34-5 Ap 13 '64

PROTESTANT churches
Way Protestants worship; excerpt from Ecumenical dialogue at Harvard. C. C. Richardson. Cath World 199:175-81 Je '64
See also
Church unity
Ecumenical movement
Protestantism

Clergy

See Clergy

Missions

See Missions

Relations

Catholic church

Catholic journal, Protestant columnist. R. M. Brown; reply with rejoinder. L. R. Keylock. Commonweal 77:621 Mr 8 '63
Dialogue in Portland. W. B. Cate. Christian Cent 80:745 Je 5 '63
German ecumenism: politics and the dialogue. H. Cox. Commonweal 77:635-9 Mr 15 '63
Unity we seek, ed. by W. S. Morris. Review Christian Cent 80:646 My 15 '63. L. J. Averill
Usefulness of anti-Catholicism. F. H. Littell. il Commonweal 78:422-4 Jl 12 '63

Jews

Lutherans repudiate deicide charge. Christian Cent 81:1452-3 N 25 '64

Theology

See Theology

England

See also
British council of churches

Germany

German ecumenism: politics and the dialogue. H. Cox. Commonweal 77:635-9 Mr 15 '63
See also
Evangelical church in Germany

Latin America

Latin American Protestantism: the coming crisis. T. Tschuy; discussion. Christian Cent 80:243-4 F 20 '63

Puerto Rico

Breakthrough in Puerto Rico. V. Clear. Christian Cent 80:1216-18 O 2 '63

Russia

American church dedicated in Moscow. Christian Cent 81:163 F 5 '64
Church in Moscow. il Time 83:65 F 7 '64

Spain

Delicate matter; broader rights for Protestants. Newsweek 61:78 Je 3 '63
Emancipation in Spain. Time 81:35 F 8 '63
Spain could be the test. Christian Cent 80:261 F 27 '63
Wait-and-see policy on Spanish freedom. Christian Cent 80:294 Mr 6 '63

United States

Call for an interdependent approach to metropolis. Christian Cent 80:996-7 Ag 14 '63
Disunion now; third annual consultation on church union. Newsweek 63:96-7 Ap 27 '64
Evangelical undertow. Time 82:57 D 20 '63
Ministerial health and unhealth; concerning articles in Saturday evening post and Look. R. N. Johnson. Christian Cent 80:706-8 My 29 '63
Ministry and institutional demands; concerning articles in Saturday evening post and Look; discussion. Christian Cent 80:335 Mr 13 '63
Protestant ecumenical dilemma. W. D. Wagoner; K. Bridston; W. Nicholls. Christian Cent 81:329-32 Mr 11 '64; Discussion. 81:642 My 13 '64
Reformation remembered. M. E. Marty. Christian Cent 80:1522+ D 4 '63
Southern white Protestantism at the turn of the century. K. K. Bailey. bibliog f Am Hist R 68:618-35 Ap '63
Ut unum sint . . . America 109:2 Jl 6 '63
See also
National council of the churches of Christ in the United States of America

PROTESTANT; Church and race problems; etc. churches and labor; Protestant churches and race problems; etc. See Church and labor

PROTESTANT, churches and labor; Protestant churches and race problems; etc. See Church and labor; Church and race problems; etc.

PROTESTANT Episcopal church
Brave new words; triennial general convention. Newsweek 64:91 N 2 '64
Catholic and reformed; study on confession and spiritual healing. America 111:471 O 24 '64
Ecclesiastical lightning rod. il Time 84:87-8 O 23 '64
Empty pews, full spirit. il Time 82:61+ Ag 16 '63
Episcopal dichotomy; 61st General convention of the Episcopal church. M. Frakes. Christian Cent 81:1390-2 N 11 '64

PROTESTANT Episcopal church—*Continued*
Episcopalians consider Megabagdad. J. M. Dabbs. Christian Cent 81:302-3 Mr 4 '64
Episcopalians: muddling through vs. creative outreach. C. K. Myers. Christian Cent 80: 1459-62 N 27 '63
Johnson at the altar rail; admission of non-Episcopalians to communion. il Time 83:60 Je 19 '64
Metabagdad; testing new methods of ministering. il Newsweek 64:44 Ag 3 '64
My people is the enemy, by W. Stringfellow. Review
Time 83:72 Je 5 '64
On the battle lines, ed. by M. Boyd. Review
Newsweek 63:71 Mr 30 '64
On the battle line; Episcopal church of the inner city. il Time 81:52-3 Ap 5 '63
Pike and prejudice; 61st general convention meeting. il Newsweek 64:75+ O 26 '64
P.B. steps down. Time 83:60 Ap 10 '64
Profiles; Church of St Matthew and St Timothy. R. Rice. il New Yorker 40:41-2+ Ag 1; 37-8+ Ag 8 '64
Talk with the 'PB'; interview, ed. by K. Woodward. J. E. Hines. Newsweek 65:70 F 1 '65
Union, not mere unity. Christian Cent 81: 323-5 Mr 11 '64
What's a Protestant? Time 84:76 O 30 '64
See also
Church of England
PROTESTANT monasticism. See Monasteries
PROTESTANT reformation. See Reformation
PROTESTANTISM
Connectionalism: the new polity? L. E. Schaller. Christian Cent 81:858-61 Jl 1 '64
Crisis in American Protestantism. R. Niebuhr. Christian Cent 80:1498-501 D 4 '63
Ecumenicity and entomology: new church problem. W. Stringfellow. Christian Cent 81:1239-41 O 7 '64
Episcopacy for our time; search for relevant polity. P. H. Pfatteicher. Christian Cent 81: 1361-4 N 4 '64; Discussion. 81:1559-60 D 16 '64
Faith and prejudice: intergroup problems in Protestant curricula, by B. E. Olson. Review
Commentary 35:455-60 My '63. M. E. Marty; Reply. B. E. Olson. 36:197-9 S '63
Is Anglicanism Protestant? excerpt from World Protestantism. W. H. Van De Pol. Cath World 200:95-9+ N '64
Joblessness: the coming challenge. L. E. Schaller. Christian Cent 80:171-3 F 6 '63
Modern Protestantism: aimless or resurgent? B. E. Meland. Christian Cent 80:1494-7 D 4 '63
Monoliths: existent and non-existent. R. M. Brown. Commonweal 77:596-7 Mr 1 '63
Moralism vs. Christianity. F. E. Stoeffler. Christian Cent 80:1299-302 O 23 '63; Discussion. 80:1520-1 D 4 '63
One Protestant voice? Christian Cent 80: 1291-2 O 23 '63
Protestant ecumenical dilemma. W. D. Wagoner; K. Bridston; W. Nicholls. Christian Cent 81:329-32 Mr 11 '64
Protestant renewal: a Jewish view. A. J. Heschel. Christian Cent 80:1501-4 D 4 '63
Protestantism and authority. R. M. Brown. Commonweal 81:69-71 O 9 '64; Reply with rejoinder. P. E. Meehl. 81:329-31 N 27 '64
Protestantism in American society; symposium. Commonweal 78:416-24 Jl 12 '63; Reply. M. E. Porter. 78:538-9 S 6 '63
Protestantism in American sociology. R. L. Means. Christian Cent 81:1554-6 D 16 '64
Speaking out; ecumenical movement threatens Protestantism. H. A. Buchanan and B. W. Brown. Sat Eve Post 237:10+ O 24 '64; Reply. G. Hinson. Christian Cent 81: 1592-5 D 23 '64
What young Protestants really believe. A. Whitman. il Redbook 123:45-7+ Ag '64
Within Protestantism, diversity. M. M. Shideler. Christian Cent 80:295-8 Mr 6 '63; Discussion. 80:498+ Ap 17 '63
World Protestantism, by W. H. van de Pol. Review
Cath World 200:185-6 D '64. J. V. Gallagher
See also
Fundamentalism
Sects
PROTESTANTS
Baptist intellectual's view of Catholicism. H. Cox; reply. P. Blanshard. Harper 226:14 Mr '63
PROTESTANTS and other Americans united for separation of church and state
Junipero Serra in overalls. America 111:370 O 3 '64
POAU in crisis. il Newsweek 64:102-3 O 5 '64
P.O.A.U. on trial; tempest over Der Stellvertreter. Christian Cent 80:1124 S 18 '63
POAU-WOW; annual meeting. Time 81:97 F 15 '63
Separationists confer. H. E. Fey. Christian Cent 81:166-7 F 5 '64
PROTESTANTS in Algeria
Relief in Algeria. G. Murray. Christian Cent 81:120-2 Ja 22 '64
PROTESTANTS in Cuba
Cuba revisited. J. A. MacKay. il Christian Cent 81:200-3 F 12 '64; Discussion. 81:402-6, 772 Mr 25, Je 10 '64
Fresh look at Cuba. J. A. Mackay. Christian Cent 81:983-7 Ag 5 '64; Discussion. 81:1308 O 21 '64
PROTESTANTS in France
European reaction to the Vatican council; France. Y. Chabas. Christian Cent 80:207-8 F 13 '63
For France resurgent; attitude towards nuclear arms. I. Chabas. Christian Cent 81:186-8 F 5 '64
PROTESTANTS in Germany
European reaction to the Vatican council; Germany. F. Luepsen. Christian Cent 80: 209 F 13 '63
Good news: steps in reconciliation; German Protestants to build repentance church at Dachau. Christian Cent 81:1583 D 23 '64
PROTESTANTS in Latin America
Latin American Protestantism: the coming crisis. T. Tschuy; discussion. Christian Cent 80:243-4 F 20 '63
PROTESTANTS in Spain
Aggiornamento in Spain; question of religious liberty. Christian Cent 82:7 Ja 6 '65
Non-Catholics in Spain; what rights can religious minorities in that country claim before the law? F. M. Castiella. il America 109:189-92 Ag 24 '63
Protestant status under discussion. Hispanicus. Christian Cent 81:1282 O 14 '64
Protestants in Spain. T. N. Davis. America 108:390 Mr 23 '63
Protestants in Spain; more freedom. America 110:300 Mr 7 '64
Spanish cardinal makes small concession. Christian Cent 81:165 F 5 '64
Spanish prelate dampens Protestant hopes. Christian Cent 80:734 Je 5 '63
PROTESTANTS in the United States
Divergent ethics. America 111:686-7 N 28 '64
Protestant establishment, by E. D. Baltzell. Review
Newsweek il 64:89 N 16 '64
Striking changes in the way Protestants & Catholics feel about each other. W. Goodman. Redbook 122:62-3+ Mr '64
What young Protestants really believe. A. Whitman. il Redbook 123:45-7+ Ag '64
PROTHROMBIN
Vitamin K induced prothrombin formation: antagonism by actinomycin D. R. E. Olson. bibliog il Science 145:926-8 Ag 28 '64; Correction. 147:66 Ja 1 '65
PROTITCH, Dragoslav
United Nations training programme for foreign service officers from newly independent countries. UN Mo Chron 1:67-71 N '64
PROTOCOL, Diplomatic. See Diplomatic etiquette
PROTON accelerators. See Accelerators (electrons, etc)
PROTON surgery. See Radiotherapy
PROTONS
Hydrogen energy levels: perturbation caused by proton structure. W. S. Porter. il Science 143:1324-5 Mr 20 '64
Nucleon structure; report of recent international conference at Stanford university. J. H. Fregeau. Science 141:548-9+ Ag 9 '63
Proton structure jelly-like. Sci N L 85:69 F 1 '64
Proton tunneling in radiation-induced mutation. R. Rein and F. E. Harris. bibliog il Science 146:649-50 O 30 '64
Tautomerism and protonation of guanosine. H. T. Miles and others. bibliog il Science 142:1458+ D 13 '63
Polarization
Polarized protons. Sci Am 208:74+ Mr '63
PROTOPLASM
See also
Cytoplasm
Mitochondria

PROTOPLASMIC streaming
Shuttle-streaming: synchronization with heat production in slime mold. R. D. Allen and others. bibliog il Science 142:1485-7 D 13 '63

PROTOZOA
See also
Foraminifera
Myxomycetes

Culture

In vitro culture of the flaggellate protozoan hexamita salmonis. J. R. Uzmann and S. H. Hayduk. bibliog Science 140:290-2 Ap 19 '63

PROULX, E. A.
All the pretty little horses: story. Seventeen 23:142-3 Je '64

PROUST, Marcel
Letter from Paris. Genêt. New Yorker 39:61 D 28 '63
Some Atget Paris pictures. R. Hattersley. Pop Phot 55:24+ O '64

PROUTY, Winston L.
Excerpt from address, April 10, 1963. Cong Digest 42:303+ D '63

PROVENCE, France
Provence. M. Goodman. il Atlan 214:110-12 Ag '64

PROVENSEN, Alice
Provensens; book artists for children. il por Pub W 186:111-12 Jl 13 '64

PROVENSEN, Martin
Provensens; book artists for children. il por Pub W 186:111-12 Jl 13 '64

PROVENZANO, Anthony
Life and times of Tony Pro. R. S. Gallagher and R. Semple. Reporter 29:37-40 S 12 '63
Outearning the boss. il por Time 81:25 F 22 '63
Postscript on Tony Pro. Reporter 31:8 D 31 '64
Tony Pro takes a tumble. il por Time 81: 20 Je 21 '63

PROVERBS
Parallel proverbs. M. Pei. Sat R 47:16-17+ My 2 '64
See also
Aphorisms and apothegms

PROVIDENCE, R.I.
New kind of city school for Providence. il Arch Forum 119:11 D '63

City planning

Downtown's dramatic comeback. D. B. Carlson. il Arch Forum 120:101 F '64
Urban renewal, our investment in tomorrow. J. Fawcett. il Am City 78:100-2 N '63

PROVIDENCIA (island). See Old Providence Island

PROVINCETOWN, Mass.
Sharks, go home; art in Provincetown. il Newsweek 64:78 Ag 24 '64

PROVINCETOWN art association
Sharks, go home. il Newsweek 64:78 Ag 24 '64
Where the artists are. K. Kuh. il Sat R 47: 34-5 S 26 '64

PROVINCIAL furniture, French. See Furniture, French

PROVINCIAL rights. See Federal and provincial relations (Canada)

PROVING grounds
ABRES firings going to PMR. F. G. McGuire. il Miss & Roc 12:12 Ap 15 '63
ARPA taking re-entry launches West. Miss & Roc 12:16 My 6 '63
Air force to manage PMR. Miss & Roc 13:13+ N 25 '63
Air force to take over PMR. F. G. McGuire. il Miss & Roc 13:12 Ag 12 '63
AMF tracking mount on job at PMR. W. Beller. il Miss & Roc 13:26 S 9 '63
Apollo hardware flights beginning at White Sands. il Miss & Roc 13:17 N 11 '63
Apollo testing to begin at White Sands. il Aviation W 79:281-3+ Jl 22 '63
Army limited war laboratory seeks to reduce research time; Aberdeen proving ground, Md. G. C. Wilson. Aviation W 80:27-8 Je 15 '64
Base in Maine called Blotner. W. S. Ellis. Harper 229:26+ S '64
Building for the moon launch, a study in speed and size. il Arch Forum 119:118-21 S '63
Buildings for the space program; how NASA deals with architects and engineers. il Arch Rec 133:147-54 Ja '63
Complex ready for Gemini-Titan II; Cape Canaveral. C. Butler. il Miss & Roc 13:21 O 28 '63
Eastern range's 1965 schedule shows sustained activity level. G. Alexander. Aviation W 82: 49 Ja 4 '65
Facilities cuts burden Wallops station sounding rocket program. il Miss & Roc 13:231-2 N 25 '63
Merritt Island support bids due. Aviation W 79:29 Ag 19 '63
Merritt Island telephone award to be reserved for Southern Bell. Aviation W 79:30 Ag 12 '63
Mississippi facility's first firing set for summer of '65. C. Butler. il Miss & Roc 13: 37-8 S 30 '63
NASA seen winning in AMR dispute. Miss & Roc 12:16 My 20 '63
NASA to control own launch area. il Aviation W 78:33 Ja 28 '63
Navy chafes to set up undersea test range; Atlantic underwater test & evaluation center of the Bahamas. il Bsns W p84+ Ap 27 '63
Outlook better for flight research center. Miss & Roc 13:16 Jl 8 '63
Pact clarifies NASA, DOD roles at Cape. G. Alexander. Aviation W 78:62 Mr 4 '63
President visits the big birds at Cape Canaveral and Merritt Island. il Bsns W p36 N 23 '63
Range instrumentation calls for more use of aircraft, new ground systems. il Miss & Roc 14:33-6 Je 1 '64
Second Scout launcher to speed research, training at Wallops. W. Beller. il Miss & Roc 13:41 S 16 '63
Space council to check DOD range plans. Aviation W 79:30-1 Ag 19 '63
Strike halts Merritt Island work. Aviation W 79:38 S 16 '63
TIROS launches to be moved to WTR; new Delta facility. H. Taylor. Miss & Roc 16:15 Ja 25 '65
Titan III program reappraised; Cape Canaveral. il Miss & Roc 12:12-13 F 25 '63
Transforming the Cape into a spaceport. il Bsns W p56-60+ Ap 6 '63
USAF building expanded range center; Cape Canaveral. il Aviation W 79:85+ S 16 '63
USAF to manage West Coast ranges. Aviation W 79:31 N 25 '63
Visit to Eglin. F. E. Hornaday. il Am For 70:19-21 Ag '64
Woomera readied for Blue Streak firing. H. J. Coleman. il Aviation W 79:66-7+ D 9 '63

PROVUS, Malcolm M.
Time to teach. NEA J 53:17-18 My '64

PROWITT, Renee Brown
Here's help in choosing books to give to children. Am Home 67:28 D '64
New books for the young. Am Home 66:20+ D '63

PROXIES
Proxy fighters; Thomas Mellon Evans and the Brown co. Newsweek 61:65 Mr 4 '63

PROXMIRE, Ellen
Double life of a senator's wife; excerpts from One foot in Washington. pors Redbook 122:66-74 Ja '64

PROXMIRE, William
Can small business survive? summary of address. por Pub W 185:41-2 Je 22 '64
Excerpt from address, September 25, 1963, and from debate, November 26, 1963. Cong Digest 43:57+ F '64
Glamour masks waste in space spending. por Nations Bsns 51:38-9+ N '63

PROXY; drama. See Hochhuth, R.

PROXY marriage. See Marriage law

PRPIC, George Jure
New breed behind the iron curtain. America 112:18-20 Ja 2 '65

PRUDDEN, T. M.
Remember? cars that ran on oatmeal and molasses. Sci Digest 55:80-5 Mr '64

PRUDENTIAL insurance company of America
Aiming at $2-million and under. il Bsns W p 151-2 N 21 '64
SEC hands Pru a blow. Bsns W p27-8 Ja 26 '63
That might pump, Prudential. R. Sheehan. il Fortune 69:98-103+ Ja '64

PRUETT, Gene
Cowboy's chronicle. il por Newsweek 62:60 S 16 '63

PRUFER, Olaf H.
Hopewell cult; with biographical sketch. Sci Am 211:20, 90-4+ D '64
Symbols by default. Art N 62:44-5+ O '63

PRUITT, William O. Jr
Arctic trail. Harper 226:44-50 Je '63
Cycle of living. Holiday 33:32+ F '63
Lichen, caribou and high radiation in Eskimos. il Audubon Mag 65:284-7 S '63
Some views concerning the development of Mount McKinley National Park. Nat Parks Mag 37:19 S '63

PRUITT-Igoe housing development. See St Louis—Housing

PRUNES
See also
Cookery—Fruit
PRUNING
Dormant garden care; pruning tools in action. R. L. Hering. il Pop Gard 16:44-5+ Ja '65
Give old plants a new lease on life. il Pop Gard 14:42 F '63
Guide to rose pruning. N. Gillespie. il Pop Gard 16:46-7 F '65
How our cover tree got that way. il Sunset 131:188-9 D '63
How to prune for mechanical harvest. il Farm J 87:83 F '63
How to prune your climbing roses. il Am Home 66:93 Jl '63
How to prune your modesto ash. Sunset 130: 294 Ap '63
It's about time to prune your fuchsias. il Sunset 132:226+ Mr '64
Our outdoor bonsai; Scotch pine. G. Harshbarger. il Flower Grower 51:20-1 Mr '64
Problem in pruning is people. A. N. Coit. Pop Gard 14:51+ Mr '63
Pruning primer. il Sunset 132:246-8+ Ap '64
Some spring pruning tips. B. A. Davis. Flower Grower 50:60 My '63
Summer pruning time is now. il Sunset 130: 222+ Je '63
Timely tips on spring pruning. E. F. Steffek. il Pop Gard 15:54-5 Mr '64
Tips on pruning. E. C. Richardson. Suc Farm 62:138 Mr '64
Tips on pruning roses. M. Costigan. il Horticulture 41:238 Ap '63
Two steps to proper pruning. il Flower Grower 51:20 F '64
We take the puzzle out of grape pruning. C. W. Gouget. il Pop Gard 14:46+ Mr '63
PRUNING apparatus and equipment
Big choice in pruning tools. S. M. Gallager. il Pop Sci 182:170-4 Mr '63
Gift to a gardener: shears or a saw. il Sunset 131:180-2+ D '63
PRUNUS subhirtella autumnalis. See Oriental flowering cherry
PRYCE-JONES, Alan
Art of Nabokov; excerpts. Harper 226:97-101 Ap '63
Bartlesville, Oklahoma. Vogue 144:54 D '64
Brecht in perspective. Theatre Arts 47:22-4 Je '63
British national theatre. Theatre Arts 47: 20-1+ N '63
Cleo in the Park. Theatre Arts 47:16-18 Jl '63
Evelyn Waugh. Commonweal 81:343-5 D 4 '64
Give opera back to the singers! Theatre Arts 47:14-16 Mr '63
Glories of glass. House & Gard 123:152-3 My '63
Max Frisch: the sage of Bahnhofstrasse. Theatre Arts 47:22-3 Ag '63
Nothing can erase Christmas. House & Gard 126:136-7 D '64
Openings, New York (cont) Theatre Arts 47: 10-13+ F; 57-9+ Mr; 10-13, 68-9 Ap; 12-15+ My; 10-13+ Je; 10-13 Jl; 10-15+ Ag; 10-13 D '63; 48:10-11+ Ja '64
Opinion, please, from New York. Mlle 57:40-1 O '63; 59:38+ Je '64
Plays that never get written. Theatre Arts 47:18-19 O '63
Sour grapes and peaches. Theatre Arts 47: 20-1 My '63
PRYCE-JONES, David
Israel's three cities. Commentary 35:52-61 Ja '63
PRYCHODKO, Marina
(tr) See Mayakosvky, V. Talk with a tax collector
PRYNNE, Michael
Our man in Spaxton. New Yorker 40:37-9 My 23 '64
PRYOR, Karen
They teach the joys of breast-feeding; excerpt from Nursing your baby. Read Digest 82:103-6 My '63
PRYOR, Madison E.
Bird man of Antarctica. il por Sci Digest 56: 48-9 D '64
PRYOR, Millard H. jr
Planning in a worldwide business. Harvard Bsns R 43:130-9 Ja '65
PSALMS. See Bible—Old Testament—Psalms
PSEUDOBULBAR paralysis. See Diseases
PSEUDOCOWPOX. See Cattle—Diseases and pests
PSEUDOMONAS
Alpha-ketoglutaric semialdehyde: a metabolic intermediate. R. M. M. Singh and E. Adams. bibliog il Science 144:67-8 Ap 3 '64
Indoleacetamide as an intermediate in the synthesis of indoleacetic acid in pseudomonas savastanoi. A. R. Magie and others. bibliog il Science 141:1281-2 S 27 '63
Toxic lysolipoid: isolation from pseudomonas pseudomallei M. S. Redfearn. bibliog il Science 146:648-9 O 30 '64
PSEUDOMONAS tabaci. See Tobacco—Diseases and pests
PSEUDONYMS
Whatever happened to Aaron Chwatt? il Esquire 62:128-9 S '64
PSILOCYBIN
Danger in happy drugs. E. Mirel. Sci N L 84:138 Ag 31 '63
PSITTACOSIS
Antibiotic for pet birds cuts parrot fever peril. Sci N L 85:152 Mr 7 '64
Nucleic acid metabolism in L cells infected with a member of the psittacosis group. E. M. Schechter and others. bibliog il Science 145:819-21 Ag 21 '64
PSORIASIS
Can those new drugs cure psoriasis? Good H 158:169 My '64
PSYCHIATRIC association, American. See American psychiatric association
PSYCHIATRIC hospitals. See Hospitals, Psychiatric
PSYCHIATRIC social work
Health planner: community psychiatry. New Yorker 40:22-3 Jl 11 '64
PSYCHIATRISTS
Couch & the stump; Fact questionnaire. Time 84:73 O 9 '64
Mental disease and the urban hospital. J. H. Knowles. il Atlan 214:107-11 Jl '64
Psychiatric training called malpractice. Sci N L 85:201 Mr 28 '64
Psychiatrist in the looking glass. C. Binger. Harper 228:62-7 Je '64
Psychiatrists and the poor. R. Coles. Atlan 214:102-6 Jl '64
PSYCHIATRY
Analyzing the analysts. il Newsweek 64:106+ O 12 '64
Inside psychiatry today. F. R. Schreiber and M. Herman. See issues of Science digest
Modern magician of the soul: A. Lambo, Nigerian psychiatrist. il Ebony 20:36-8+ D '64
People who fear sanity; anti-mental health movement. Sci Digest 55:75 F '64
Positive role of mental crisis; Dabrowski's theory of positive disintegration. J. Aronson. Sat R 47:82-4 D 5 '64
Psychiatric treatment; here and in England. W. Sargant. Atlan 214:88-95 Jl '64
Psychiatry. F. R. Schreiber and M. Herman. il Sci Digest 55:8-30 Je '64
Vital balance, by K. Menninger. Review
Sci Am 210:145-6+ Ap '64. E. G. Boring
What psychiatry can and cannot do. T. S. Szasz. bibliog Harper 228:50-3 F '64; Discussion. 228:11, 96+ Ap '64
See also
American psychiatric association
Mental illness—Therapy
Psychiatric social work
Psychology, Pathological
Caricatures and cartoons
Psychiatry it can be funny. Sci Digest 55:14-15 Je '64
Terminology
Speaking out; psychiatrists use dangerous words. K. Menninger. Sat Eve Post 237: 12+ Ap 25 '64
PSYCHIATRY, Forensic. See Forensic psychiatry
PSYCHIATRY, Industrial
How Dr Freud fares on production lines; mental health programs in industry. Bsns W p60 Ja 9 '65
PSYCHIATRY and religion
Do ministers really understand people? L. David and I. David. Good H 156:65+ Mr '63
On clinical pastoral training. R. J. Fairbanks. Christian Cent 80:556-9 Ap 24 '63
Protestant pastoral counseling, by W. E. Oates. Review
Christian Cent 80:430-1 Ap 3 '63. O. H. Mowrer
Psychiatric Catholic; right and wrong explanations of why Catholics prefer Catholic psychiatrists. P. R. Sullivan. America 108: 199-201 F 9 '63
Psychiatrist and moral values. S. J. Rowland, jr. Christian Cent 80:1613-14 D 25 '63
Psychiatry today. F. J. Braceland. Commonweal 80:172-4 My 1 '64
Religion and mental health. S. J. Rowland, jr. Christian Cent 80:684 My 22 '63
Sir, the word is moral! D. R. Kline. Christian Cent 81:455-8 Ap 8 '64; Discussion. 81:803-4 Je 17 '64

PSYCHICAL research
Lectures on psychical research, by C. D. Broad. Review
Sci Am 209:171-2+ N '63. G. A. Miller
Psychical research today, by D. J. West. Review
Sci Digest il 53:58 Je '63. H. Pryor

PSYCHOACOUSTICS. See Music—Acoustics and physics

PSYCHOANALYSIS
Books. L. Mumford. New Yorker 40:155-6+ My 23 '64
Computer age in psychoanalysis. F. R. Schreiber and M. Herman. Sci Digest 57:18-19 Ja '65
Fie upon Freud! psychoanalysis and composers. P. J. Pirie. il Hi Fi 14:31-3+ Jl '64
Home movies of early childhood: correlative developmental data in the psychoanalysis of adults. H. M. Serota. bibliog Science 143:1195 Mr 13 '64
Insight and responsibility, by E. H. Erikson. Review
Nation 199:438-40 D 7 '64. L. Abel
Life against death, by N. O. Brown. Review
Esquire il 59:100-2 Mr '63. T. B. Morgan
Neo-Freudianism & Erich Fromm. E. Z. Friedenberg; reply. C. Landesman. Commentary 35:78 Ja '63
They made our world: Freud. L. Rosten. Look 29:80-2 Ja 12 '65
To be a god. A. Wheelis. Commentary 36:125-34 Ag '63; Discussion. 37:10+ Ja '64
What killed Bob Lyons? executive's emotional problems. H. Levinson. il Harvard Bsns R 41:127-42+ Ja '63

Anecdotes, facetiae, satire, etc.

Freud frappé. R. Babcock. il Atlan 212:134-5 O '63
$25 hour. D. Newman and R. Benton. il Mlle 60:106+ N '64

PSYCHOANALYSIS and religion. See Psychiatry and religion

PSYCHOANALYTIC special; story. See Roth, P.

PSYCHOLINGUISTICS. See Language and languages—Psychology

PSYCHOLOGICAL counseling. See Counseling

PSYCHOLOGICAL examinations
Adventures of a test taker. J. Zola. Nat R 17:21-3 Ja 12 '65
Guide to using psychological tests. R. S. Barrett. Harvard Bsns R 41:138-46 S '63
Hawthorne effect; experiment at Ohio state university. Newsweek 61:106 Ap 15 '63
Snooping and testing; letter. J. E. Gordon. New Repub 152:28-30 Ja 9 '65
Snooping in the park; investigatory techniques. J. Ridgeway. New Repub 152:9-10 Ja 16 '65
Statistically defined displays and pattern detection of cerebral palsied children. C. F. Reed and A. Pollack. bibliog il Science 140:1331-3 Je 21 '63
Those school psychological tests. R. Kirk. Nat R 16:539 Je 30 '64
See also
Intelligence tests
Personality tests

PSYCHOLOGICAL medicine. See Medicine, Psychosomatic

PSYCHOLOGICAL quacks. See Quacks and quackery

PSYCHOLOGICAL research
Hawthorne effect; experiment at Ohio state university. Newsweek 61:106 Ap 15 '63
Hearing through skin. Sci N L 86:275 O 31 '64
Information-processing models in psychology. W. R. Reitman. bibliog Science 144:1192-8 Je 5 '64
See also
Animal experimentation

PSYCHOLOGICAL tests. See Psychological examinations

PSYCHOLOGICAL warfare
Changing cold war; symposium, ed. by D. F. Fleming. bibliog f Ann Am Acad 351:1-179 Ja '64

PSYCHOLOGISTS
Graduate preparation of educational psychologists; address, April 2, 1963. J. C. Stanley. Sch & Soc 91:354-5 N 16 '63
Proposals for state department of education certification of school psychologists; text of document. Sch & Soc 91:43-5 Ja 26 '63
Traits of eminent American psychologists. L. G. Wispé. bibliog il Science 141:1256-61 S 27 '63
See also
Jung, C. G.

PSYCHOLOGY
Games people play, by E. Berne. Review
Newsweek 64:47-8 Ag 31 '64
International relations and the psychologist. N. Jordan. Bul Atomic Sci 19:29-33 N '63; Discussion. 19:33-6+ N '63; 20:24 Mr '64
Scientific information exchange in psychology. W. D. Garvey and B. C. Griffith. il Science 146:1655-9 D 25 '64
Source book for Jungians. M. Philipson. New Repub 152:22-4 Ja 16 '65
World of psychology, ed. by G. B. Levitas. Review
Sci Am 209:159-60+ Jl '63. E. G. Boring
See also
Age (psychology)
Anxiety
Attitudes
Behavior (psychology)
Criminal psychology
Daydreams
Dreams
Fighting (psychology)
Laughter
Motivation (psychology)
Observation (psychology)
Psychiatry
Social psychology
also subheads Psychology; Psychological aspects under various subjects, e.g. Woman—Psychology; Moving pictures—Psychological aspects

Industrial applications

See Psychology, Industrial

Measurement

See Psychometrics

PSYCHOLOGY, Criminal. See Criminal psychology

PSYCHOLOGY, Educational
Becoming a nurse; a selective view. H. O. Mauksch. bibliog f il Ann Am Acad 346:88-98 Mr '63
Graduate preparation of educational psychologists; address, April 2, 1963. J. C. Stanley. Sch & Soc 91:354-5 N 16 '63
Harvard's Bruner and his yeasty ideas. A. T. Weil. Harper 229:81-6+ D '64
More positive expressions. J. Ciardi. Sat R 46:14 Ap 27 '63
More teacher authority is schools' basic need. F. Morley. Nations Bsns 52:27-8 Jl '64
Remember the piggy-back squirrel. Sister Mary Louis. NEA J 52:32 O '63
See also
Attention
Child study
Learning, Psychology of
Personality training and development
Readiness for school
Sex differences

Study and teaching

Basic four in psychology. E. P. Torrance. il NEA J 54:15-17 Ja '65

PSYCHOLOGY, Experimental
Could we be Nazi followers? Yale university tests. Sci Digest 55:81-2 Ja '64
Experiment perilous; attempt to discover the nature of blind obedience; Yale university. Sr Schol 83:2T N 15 '63
Prolonged immobilization of the body: changes in performance and in the electroencephalogram. J. P. Zubek and L. Wilgosh. bibliog Science 140:306-8 Ap 19 '63
See also
Stimulus and response

PSYCHOLOGY, Forensic
See also
Forensic psychiatry

PSYCHOLOGY, Industrial
Conflicts in human values. R. N. McMurry. Harvard Bsns R 41:130-6+ My '63
New findings will improve your decisions. il Nations Bsns 51:58-60+ Mr '63
See also
Psychiatry, Industrial

PSYCHOLOGY, Pathological
Of grace and nature; neurotic peculiarities which show up in religious life. Sister Mary Dominic. America 108:763 My 25 '63
Psychopathology of politicking. F. R. Schreiber and M. Herman. il Sci Digest 56:76-81 O '64
See also
Hypochondria—Anecdotes, facetiae, satire, etc.
Medicine, Psychosomatic
Mental illness

PSYCHOLOGY, Physiological
Harvard's Skinner, the last of the utopians. S. Klaw. Harper 226:45-51 Ap '63
Psychophysics of perceived intensity: a theoretical basis for Fechner's and Stevens' laws. D. M. MacKay. bibliog il Science 139:1213-16 Mr 22 '63
See also
Behaviorism
Brain—Localization of functions
Psychology, Experimental
Time perception

PSYCHOLOGY, Political. See Political psychology

PSYCHOLOGY, Prison. See Prison psychology

PSYCHOLOGY, Social. See Social psychology

PSYCHOLOGY of eating. See Eating, Psychology of

PSYCHOLOGY of learning. See Learning, Psychology of

PSYCHOMETRICS
Measurement of motivation. H. J. Eysenck. il Sci Am 208:130-4+ My '63
Nature and measurement of anxiety. R. B. Cattell. il Sci Am 208:96-104 Mr '63
What is your brain power? H. Earle. il Todays Health 41:50-5 O '63

PSYCHOMOTOR epilepsy. See Epilepsy

PSYCHONEUROSIS. See Neuroses

PSYCHOPATHOLOGY. See Psychology, Pathological

PSYCHOSES
Mental disease risk high after childbirth: puerperal psychosis. Sci N L 83:392 Je 22 '63
N-methylmetanephrine: excretion by juvenile psychotics. T. L. Perry. bibliog il Science 139:587-9 F 15 '63

PSYCHOSOMATIC medicine. See Medicine, Psychosomatic

PSYCHOTHERAPY
Psychiatrist and moral values. S. J. Rowland, jr. Christian Cent 80:1613-14 D 25 '63
TV therapy; family-group therapy sessions at Palo Alto's mental research institute taped for TV and played back. Newsweek 63:92+ My 11 '64
What is psychotherapy? G. G. Greer. Bet Hom & Gard 41:88 Ap '63
See also
Group psychotherapy
Psychiatry and religion

Anecdotes, facetiae, satire, etc.

Odyssey of a psychotherapist. H. A. Wilmer. il Science 145:902-3 Ag 28 '64

PSYCHOTROPIC drugs
See also
Hallucinogenic drugs

PSYCHROMETERS. See Hygrometers

PTERASPIS. See Ostracoderms

PTERIDINES
Pteridines as pigments in amphibians. M. Obika and J. T. Bagnara. bibliog il Science 143:485-7 Ja 31 '64

PTEROPODA. See Mollusks

PTEROPUS poliocephalus. See Bats

PUBERTY
Blindness: its relation to age of menarche. L. Zacharias and R. J. Wurtman. bibliog il Science 144:1154-5 My 29 '64
Coming of age on the Carob plantation; excerpt from Brown fountain pen. G. P. Elliott. Commentary 35:390-6 My '63
How puberty affects personality. il Sci Digest 55:65-6 My '64

PUBLIC address systems. See Loud speaking apparatus

PUBLIC advisory committee for trade negotiations. See United States—Public advisory committee for trade negotiations

PUBLIC affairs information service
Esoteric indexing crusade: inclusion of Superintendent of documents number with each government document entry; letter to the editor. R. B. Dennis. Library J 90:162 Ja 15 '65
Public affairs information service enters fiftieth year of operation. Library J 89:598 F 1 '64

PUBLIC affairs research council of Louisiana
Louisiana's wonderful invention. E. Kerr. Harper 227:94-6 O '63

PUBLIC buildings
As the federal capital spreads across the Nation; U.S. agencies and programs outside Washington area. il U S News 57:70-1 O 12 '64
Big government: how it spreads; federal government agencies spreading into Maryland and Virginia. il U S News 55:70-5 S 16 '63
Lean year for new buildings: Congress casts critical eye on NASA, PHS facilities requests. E. Langer. Science 142:471-2 O 25 '63
LBJ suite in a new federal building; Austin, Tex. il U S News 57:18 O 19 '64
President Johnson and public architecture: convictions on architect's role recalled. Arch Rec 135:10 Ja '64
Sequel to a spending dispute; Billings, Mont. il U S News 54:10 Ap 15 '63
Yasko cites execellence in new federal buildings. Arch Rec 137:23 Ja '65
See also
Capitols
Embassies (buildings)
Library architecture
Municipal buildings
also subhead Public buildings under names of cities, e.g. Washington, D.C.—Public buildings

PUBLIC buildings service. See United States—Public buildings service

PUBLIC debt (United States) See Debts, Public—United States

PUBLIC debts. See Debts, Public

PUBLIC defenders
Dearth of defenders. il Time 83:54 Je 19 '64
Justice for the poor; the banner of Gideon. R. G. Sherrill. il Nation 198:367-72 Ap 13 '64
Poor man in the scales. R. B. Ribman and S. M. Ribman. il Harper 228:150-4+ Ap '64
Rising to the defense. il Time 84:56+ Ag 7 '64

PUBLIC education association, New York
Braque festival: exhibition at four galleries. New Yorker 40:32 Mr 28 '64
Reading: help for underprivileged children. New Yorker 40:21-2 Ja 9 '65

PUBLIC eye; drama. See Shaffer, P.

PUBLIC finance. See Finance

PUBLIC health
Health physics; report of 1963 annual meeting of the Health physics society. A. P. Hull. Science 142:73-4 O 4 '63
Man and nature; address, October 12, 1964. D. Rusk. Dept State Bul 51:618-21 N 2 '64
See also
Air pollution
Medicine, Preventive
Sanitary engineering
Vaccination
Water pollution

Economic aspects

Economics of the Nation's health. R. Fein. il New Repub 149:7-9 N 9 '63
Planning for health. J. S. McKenzie-Pollock. New Repub 150:15-16 My 9 '64

International aspects

Health for peace and vice versa; address, September 27, 1963. H. Cleveland. Dept State Bul 49:676-81 O 28 '63
Health knows no boundaries. E. Schneider. il NEA J 53:70-1 Mr '64
Medical care for developing countries. C. E. Taylor. Atlan 213:75-6+ Ja '64
Overseas health aid basic. F. Marley. Sci N L 84:231 O 12 '63
See also
World health organization

Laws and legislation

Boat sanitation. E. Robberson. Yachting 116:52-5+ O '64
Health, education and welfare: the first decade. M. B. Folsom. Cur Hist 45:87-91+ Ag '63
New deal and national health. R. Lubove. bibliog f Cur Hist 45:77-86+ Ag '63

Social aspects

Anthropological perspective on medicine and public health. B. D. Paul. bibliog f Ann Am Acad 346:34-43 Mr '63

Africa

Africa's uphill struggle for maturity; ed. by A. Eisenberg and H. Eisenberg. Mrs G. M. Williams. il Ladies Home J 80:38+ O '63

Alaska

Acute diseases in Alaska now present the year round. Sci Digest 53:41 Ap '63

Caribbean Region

Outbreak of dengue. Time 82:42 O 25 '63

China (People's Republic)

Oriental renaissance in education and medicine. W. Penfield. bibliog il Science 141:1153-61 S 20 '63

PUBLIC health—*Continued*

Ethiopia

Little tooth decay found among Ethiopians. Sci N L 84:89 Ag 10 '63

France

Ma foi! mon foie! French liver trouble. il Time 82:22-3 D 27 '63

Great Britain

Britons vs. cigarettes: paradoxical behavior. U S News 55:86 D 2 '63
Health service: its first decade. A. Lindsey. bibliog Cur Hist 45:12-18 Jl '63

See also
Great Britain—National health service

India

India fights the big cough; with photographs. Sci Digest 55:74-7 Ap '64
Public medicine in India. P. Malhotra. bibliog f il Cur Hist 44:359-65+ Je '63

Ireland

Boston Irish vs. Dublin Irish. Sci Digest 56:55 Ag '64
Irishmen can eat fat, have low blood pressure. Sci N L 84:344 N 30 '63

Latin America

Sewage disposal plan seen helping 56 million. Sci N L 84:232 O 12 '63

See also
Pan American sanitary bureau

Russia

Soviets lag in dental care, mission reports. Todays Health 41:87 Ap '63

Tunisia

Battle of Tunisia. il UNESCO Courier 17:4-8 Ap '64

United States

Boston Irish vs. Dublin Irish. Sci Digest 56:55 Ag '64
Economics of national health; address, May 11, 1964. L. L. Terry. Vital Speeches 30:588-90 Jl 15 '64
Government and medicine in the United States; symposium. bibliog f il Cur Hist 45:65-114+ Ag '63
Is our environment poisoning us? R Brecher and E. Brecher. il Parents Mag 38:72-3+ O '63
LBJ's big health plan: cradle to grave; concerning first legislative message to the new Congress. il U S News 58:34-5 Ja 18 '65
Maternal and child health problems. A. Yankauer. bibliog f il Ann Am Acad 355:112-20 S '64
Physical and mental health in the city. E. J. Lieberman and L. J. Duhl. il Ann Am Acad 352:13-24 Mr '64
Program for reducing heart, cancer and stroke deaths. il U S News 57:6 D 21 '64
Stimulation of health research. J. H. Cassedy. bibliog Science 145:897-902 Ag 28 '64
Summing up: what can we do and what lies ahead. il New Repub 149:41-3 N 9 '63
U.S. people healthier this year than last. Sci N L 86:388 D 19 '64
What is a public-health physician? L. L. Terry. il Todays Health 41:54-7+ My '63
Where we stand as 1965 begins. M. Spencer. il Todays Health 43:20-5 Ja '65

See also
Negroes in the United States—Health and hygiene
New York (city)—Public health
Quarantine
United States—Public health service

Viet Nam (Republic)

Prefer western medicine. F. Marley. Sci N L 85:341 My 30 '64

PUBLIC health conferences
See also
World health assembly

PUBLIC health exhibits. See Health exhibits

PUBLIC health laboratories
See also
United States—Communicable disease center, Atlanta, Ga.

PUBLIC health service (United States) See United States—Public health service

PUBLIC health workers. See Health workers

PUBLIC houses (Ireland) See Bars and barrooms

PUBLIC housing. See Housing

PUBLIC housing administration. See United States—Public housing administration

PUBLIC housing projects. See Housing projects, Government

PUBLIC interest television programs. See Television programs, Public service

PUBLIC lands

United States

Battle for green acres. J. J. Shomon. il Audubon Mag 66:81 Mr '64
Lands we share; address, May 3, 1963. L. C. Binford. Am For 69:16-19+ Jl '63
Legislative needs for outdoor recreation; grants-in-aid program: excerpt from address. E. C. Crafts. il Am For 69:18-19+ Mr '63
LBJ's plan to beautify America. il U S News 58:28-30+ Ja 11 '65
Nature is murdered. B. Tufty. il Sci N L 84:90-1 Ag 10 '63
New land rush; government stakes its claims. il U S News 57:78-80 D 7 '64
Supply and demand. G. D. Butler. Recreation 56:120-2 Mr '63
West and its public lands; address, February 6, 1964. S. L. Udall. Vital Speeches 30:297-301 Mr 1 '64
Whose lands are these? R. Moley. Newsweek 61:104 Mr 11 '63

See also
Land grants
National forests
National parks and reserves—United States
United States—Land management, Bureau of

PUBLIC letter writers
Schoolboy in Sumer; prestige of the scribe; excerpt from History of mankind. L. Woolley. il UNESCO Courier 16:14-15 Je '63

PUBLIC libraries. See Libraries

PUBLIC library association. See American library association—Public library association

PUBLIC library of Cincinnati and Hamilton County
John F. Kennedy library exhibit; first display of tour. E. Cameron. il Wilson Lib Bul 39:63-5 S '64
Made in the house. E. Cameron. il Wilson Lib Bul 38:550-1 Mr '64
Staff meetings based on reading for an age of change series. M. A. Sanger. ALA Bul 58:526 Je '64

PUBLIC officers
Africa's new elites. D. Hapgood. Harper 227:43-9 D '63; Reply with rejoinder. E. J. Murphy. 228:11 Mr '64
Around the President. New Repub 149:5-6 D 7 '63
As Johnson really takes over... il U S News 56:31-3 Ap 6 '64
Austin-Boston axis. il Newsweek 63:19-20 Ja 13 '64
Bleed, but bleed, inwardly; reactions to outrageous criticism. B. H. Bakdikian. il N Y Times Mag p 10+ Ag 9 '64
Breeze through the corridors; LBJ men begin to move into the agencies. il Newsweek 63:79 My 25 '64
Brooke of Massachusetts; a Negro governor on Beacon Hill? E. R. F. Sheehan. Harper 228:41-7 Je '64
Businessman bureaucrats. Bsns W p 120 My 18 '63
Capital brotherhood; photographs. G. Tames. N Y Times Mag p96 My 5 '63
Closing the word gap? White House staff. il Newsweek 63:23 Ap 13 '64
Coming ADA government? J. Burnham. Nat R 16:954-9 N 3 '64
Crisis in staffmanship. Time 84:31 N 20 '64
Defense colossus. R. Moley. Newsweek 61:96 Je 17 '63
Does ADA run the New frontier? J. Burnham. il Nat R 14:355-62 My 7 '63
Epistles from the Eisenhower age. M. Kempton. Commentary 35:232-8 Mr '63
Herds. Reporter 28:14+ Mr 28 '63
Highest caliber U.S. candidates sought for international agencies; statement, with text of memorandum, August 15, 1964. L. B. Johnson. Dept State Bul 51:388-9 S 14 '64
How Mr Kennedy gets the answers; fact-finders and reporters. S. Hyman. il N Y Times Mag p 17+ O 20 '63
How the President keeps informed. H. Smith. il N Y Times Mag p 15+ Ag 30 '64
How White House is changing; Kennedy team adjusts to Johnson style. il U S News 55:34-6 D 23 '63
Johnson staff: new faces, new ways at the White House. il U S News 55:44 D 2 '63
Johnson takes over: the untold story. S. Alsop. il Sat Eve Post 237:17-23 F 15 '64

PUBLIC officers—*Continued*
Johnson's men: valuable hunks of humanity; White House staff. T. Wicker. il N Y Times Mag p 11+ My 3 '64
Key post for Negro; Jenkins gets Labor board job. U S News 55:24 Ag 5 '63
Law and order; responsibility of governors. America 108:796 Je 1 '63
Little man who's always there: J. Valenti. il Time 83:25 Ap 3 '64
LBJ's advisers: ins+outs=middle. il Newsweek 64:65-6 Jl 13 '64
Maggie's list; choices of M. C. Smith. il Time 81:21 Mr 1 '63
Marching orders; fitness of the White House staff. Newsweek 61:22 F 18 '63
Men Johnson will lean on. il Bsns W p27-8 N 30 '63
Men Lyndon likes. il Time 82:27-27A D 6 '63
Men who are close to Johnson. il U S News 55:43-5 D 9 '63
New appointments. il Time 85:16 Ja 8 '65
New generation in charge; old mistakes forgotten? il U S News 55:98-100 Ag 19 '63
New insiders; Johnson administration. il Newsweek 62:23-4 D 9 '63
New team; President Johnson's staff. il Time 83:18-19 My 29 '64
Nip-ups, anyone? fitness of White House staff. il Time 81:27 F 15 '63
Now, Harvard is out, and Texas is in. il U S News 55:6 D 9 '63
Ordeal of power, by E. J. Hughes. Review
Sat Eve Post 236:82 Ap 13 '63
Out of the catalyst into the fire; Pres. Johnson's science adviser. Bsns W p72+ D 14 '63
Outside insiders; economic advisers to the administration. il Time 84:109 N 13 '64
Pawns of the President. Nation 197:211 O 12 '63
Political virtuoso gathers the forces to take on the job. J. L. Steele. il Life 55:32-5 D 13 '63
President and the intellectuals. W. V. Shannon. Commonweal 79:386-7 D 27 '63
President's special consultant: J. Valenti. U S News 55:9 D 30 '63
Stevenson clan; New frontier appointees. New Repub 148:4 F 2 '63
Team's status. Time 83:15 Ja 17 '64
Texas Mafia moves in; Johnson's White House circle. S. Alsop. Sat Eve Post 237:14 Mr 21 '64
Type of people LBJ is appointing. il U S News 56:20 Mr 23 '64
U.S. steps up equal job opportunity. il Ebony 19:103-4+ S '64
Valet's view; with excerpts from Ordeal of power, by E. J. Hughes. il Time 81:17-19 Mr 22 '63
Washington's new set of White House VIPs. il Bsns W p32+ Mr 14 '64
What kind of monetary men? Time 84:100 D 11 '64
Who really makes U.S. foreign policy. il U S News 54:33-5 F 18 '63
Why there's trouble on the New frontier. S. Hyman. il Look 27:30+ Jl 2 '63
Young power: six couples on government work. il Vogue 142:108-11 Ag 1 '63
See also
Cabinet officers
Conflict of interests (public office)
Government employees
Governors
Legislators
Misconduct in office
Negro state officers
Political ethics
Public service
Women as public officers

Anecdotes, facetiae, satire, etc.
Day the news managers quit; fable of the New frontier. W. S. Just. Reporter 28:36-7 My 9 '63
Fun in Washington; annual dinner of Gridiron club. Time 81:63 Mr 22 '63
Husbands in crisis. N. H. Dickerson. McCalls 90:112+ Ag '63
Hyannis Port kid rides again; New frontieriana. J. Morressy. Nat R 15:483 D 3 '63

Appointment, qualifications, tenure, etc.
Better way to choose a president. D. Lawrence. U S News 54:120 Ap 8 '63
Hard-to-find quality. New Repub 149:5 O 12 '63
Which chaps will go wrong? il Sci Digest 54:39-40 S '63

Families
Twigs off the branch: sons & daughters in Washington. P. Mesta. il McCalls 92:34+ O '64

Gifts
Juggling that hot potato, the political gift. B. H. Bagdikian. il N Y Times Mag p 14-15+ Mr 22 '64

Salaries, allowances, etc.
As for expense accounts of government officials—. U S News 54:57 Ap 15 '63
Big pay boosts for U.S. leaders? il U S News 55:22 Ag 26 '63
CED's plan to nourish the top bureaucrats; establishment of Office of executive personnel. il Bsns W p70+ Jl 25 '64
Federal pay raises Congress is considering. il U S News 55:12 N 11 '63
Pay raise that blew up. il U S News 56:45 Mr 23 '64
Underpaid. Newsweek 61:20 Ap 29 '63
U.S. problem: low pay for top jobs; federal salaries. C. B. Randall. il N Y Times Mag p29+ S 15 '63
What price talent? Newsweek 62:19 Ag 26 '63

PUBLIC opinion
Abroad: praise, and doubts; Warren commission's version of the crime. U S News 57:62 O 12 '64
As others see us; ed. by J. F. Fixx. Sat R 47:31-3+ O 24; 35-7 N 7; 31-3 N 28; 43-4 D 12 '64; 48:33-4 Ja 2; 41-2 Ja 30 '65
Attitudes toward desegregation. H. H. Hyman and P. B. Sheatsley. il Sci Am 211:16-23 bibliog(p 142) Jl '64
First-hand report: new look at how U.S. rates in today's world. M. S. Johnson. il U S News 57:82-4 N 9 '64
Genie and the dinosaur; absence of an informed and active public opinion. N. Cousins. Sat R 46:22 My 25 '63
Goldwater: the world reacts. Newsweek 64:36-7 Jl 27 '64
How sorrowful bad; world reactions to assassination of President Kennedy. il Time 82:38-9 N 29 '63
How the world sizes up LBJ now. il U S News 57:33-5 D 14 '64
How the world sizes up the President. il U S News 56:54-5 My 18 '64
Mood abroad: let others worry. U S News 57:64 Ag 24 '64
New nuclear power: reaction abroad; explosion of a nuclear device by Communist China. il U S News 57:50 O 26 '64
On our quarrel with success; address, June 9, 1963. J. K. Galbraith. Dept State Bul 49:52-6 Jl 8 '63
Public opinion in the church; excerpts from pastoral letter. R. J. Cushing. Commonweal 78:426-7 Jl 12 '63
Re: extremism. Nat R 15:513-14 D 17 '63
Sky above, the mud below; American image. Newsweek 61:25 My 27 '63
Study of aspirations. H. Cantril. il Sci Am 208:41-5 bibliog(p 184) F '63
Sympathy & scrutiny; reactions to the assassination of J. F. Kennedy around the world. il Time 82:36-7 D 6 '63
Theory of public opinion, by F. G. Wilson. Review
Nat R 14:243-4 Mr 26 '63. W. Kendall
What's right with America; as observers abroad see it. il U S News 57:44-50 S 14 '64; Same abr. Read Digest 85:61-4 D '64
Who's got the button? U.S. prestige abroad. Time 81:17-18 Mr 1 '63
Whose opinion is world opinion? J. Burnham. Nat R 16:601 Jl 14 '64
Why the world-wide wave of anti-Americanism. il U S News 56:58-61 Mr 30 '64
World and LBJ; as the world sees it. U S News 55:41-2 D 9 '63
See also
Attitudes
Opinion research corporation
Public opinion polls

Anecdotes, facetiae, satire, etc.
Department of amplification; public opinion findings since the beagle flap; letter. E. J. Kahn, jr. il New Yorker 40:159-60+ Je 6 '64

Canada
Canadians answer a question; with discussion. C. Emmet. America 108:563-6 Ap 20 '63

Communist countries
As they see it. G. Bailey. Reporter 29:10+ D 19 '63

PUBLIC opinion—*Continued*

Europe, Eastern

Along the iron curtain: how people feel, what they say. A. Kucherov. il U S News 55: 37-42 Ag 19 '63

Europe, Western

American culture? qu'est-ce que c'est? L. F. Hannon. il N Y Times Mag p 10+ F 16 '64
Goldwater in the European mirror. J. Burnham. Nat R 16:1140 D 29 '64
How Europe sees it. J. Burnham. Nat R 14: 451 Je 4 '63

France

French people and de Gaulle. M. Gordey. il For Affairs 42:546-58 Jl '64
How de Gaulle rates with the home folks. U S News 54:19 F 18 '63
Letter from Paris; grief and shock at the assassination of President Kennedy. Genêt. New Yorker 39:133-4+ D 7 '63
Letter from Paris; our desegregation problem, little reaction among the French. Genêt. New Yorker 39:73 Jl 13 '63

Great Britain

American invasion, by F. Williams. Review New Repub 148:22-5 Mr 9 '63. B. DeMott
Blessing in disguise; British popular reactions to de Gaulle's veto. D. W. Brogan. America 108:262-3+ F 23 '63
British politics and Goldwater. A. Lejeune. Nat R 16:770 S 8 '64
Letter from London. M. Panter-Downes. New Yorker 39:196-8 D 7 '63
Thunderer thunders for press freedom. Christian Cent 80:453 Ap 10 '63

Latin America

When they shout, Yanqui, no! A. A. Berle. il N Y Times Mag p9+ Ja 26 '64

Nigeria

Pities U.S. Negroes more than Cubans; reactions to racial violence in Birmingham. Christian Cent 80:667 My 22 '63

Russia

Shock and grief in Russia; concerning assassination of President Kennedy. C. Foltz, jr. U S News 55:42 D 9 '63

United States

After Senator Dirksen decided White House mail was wrong. U S News 55:16 Ag 19 '63
America follows the middle of the road. A. Hacker. il N Y Times Mag p21+ My 5 '63
As the race ends: who'll win? Size-up: state by state; final look at the polls. il U S News 57:25-31 N 2 '64
Backlash issue; views on Negro's drive to improve his lot. L. Harris. il Newsweek 64:24+ Jl 13 '64
Beatlemania hits the U.S. Sr Schol 84:21 F 21 '64
Censorship begins at home; results of letters to the editor on Women strike for peace. M. J. Estren. Nat R 15:209-10 S 10 '63
Changing mood of America; what a nationwide survey shows. il U S News 55:36-45 Jl 29 '63
Chinese who? Time 84:15 D 25 '64
Citizen and foreign policy; address, September 30, 1963. K. Louchheim. Dept State Bul 49:681-4 O 28 '63
Citizen's role in foreign policy legislation; address, April 23,1964. R. J. Manning. bibliog f Dept State Bul 50:791-7 My 18 '64
Clues to the midwestern mind. M. Kniskern. il N Y Times Mag p33+ S 15 '63
Concerns of the Nation 1965. L. Harris. Newsweek 65:20 Ja 11 '65
Countrywide report on election race. il U S News 57:39-42 S 28 '64
Do polls tell the story? interview. G. Gallup. il U S News 57:52-4+ O 5 '64
Ethnic backlash? J. W. Carey. Commonweal 81:91-3 O 16 '64
Foreign interests. R. Steel. Commentary 37: 80-2 Mr '64
Foreign policy needs people, including you; remarks, January 20, 1964. W. J. Crockett. Dept State Bul 50:632 Ap 20 '64
From Washington straight. Cato. Nat R 14: 104 F 12 '63
Goldwater's chances now; what the political experts say. il U S News 57:27-31 Ag 3 '64
How strong is the hate vote? white backlash. B. H. Bagdikian. il Sat Eve Post 237:19-21 O 17 '64
How whites feel about Negroes: a painful American dilemma. il Newsweek 62:44-50+ O 21 '63
Into the '64 campaign homestretch. Sr Schol 85:8-11 O 28 '64
Is LBJ slipping? il Nat R 16:902-4 O 20 '64
Listening post: how the pros see the election. il Newsweek 64:20-2 Ag 31 '64
LBJ image. il Newsweek 64:27 Ag 31 '64
Making of foreign policy; television interview, January 11, 1964. D. Rusk; E. F. Goldman. Dept State Bul 50:164-76 F 3 '64
Members of Congress need your help. J. Miller. Suc Farm 61:78 F '63
Memo about a Dallas citizen. T. G. Harris. il Look 28:64+ Ag 11 '64
Mood of America in election year; what a national survey shows. il U S News 56: 68-73 Mr 30 '64
Mood of the land. il Time 82:9-10 D 20 '63
Mood of the South; a state-by-state report. il Newsweek 64:26 S 28 '64
No wonder they get away with it. W. F. Buckley. Nat R 14:103 F 12 '63
Notes and comment. New Yorker 40:49 O 10 '64
Political mood of U.S. now; what a nationwide survey shows. il U S News 57:54-63 Ag 24 '64
Polls and statistics; do they throw light or confusion? il Sr Schol 85:6-8+ O 21 '64
Reaction to killings. Sci N L 84:358 D 7 '63
Rights drive too fast? what a poll shows; New York times. il U S News 57:20-1 O 5 '64
Senator Goldwater as editors see him; excerpts from editorial comment. U S News 57:6 Jl 27 '64
Shelter owners pro-war. Sci N L 83:246 Ap 20 '63
Significant rumblings; U.S. policy in Vietnam. Newsweek 65:3-4 Ja 18 '65
Strange mood of America today. il U S News 54:31-3 F 25 '63
Survey finds: public support for business growing. Nations Bsns 51:114-16+ N '63
Tally; poll of all Goldwaters in Manhattan telephone directory. New Yorker 40:20-3 Ag 15 '64
Tax cut: now to spend that $11.5 billion il Life 56:46-7 Mr 6 '64
They hate Kennedy. S. Alsop. il Sat Eve Post 236:18 O 5 '63
Uncle Lyndon. S. Alsop. Sat Eve Post 237: 16 O 24 '64
Voices of moderation: days following the Republican convention; quotations. Nat R 16:675-6 Ag 11 '64
Way they feel; political sentiment in New York. M. Phelps. America 111:205 Ag 29 '64
What editors in the South say now; symposium. U S News 56:40-6 Je 29 '64
What northerners really think of Negroes. S. Alsop and O. Quayle. il Sat Eve Post 236:17-21 S 7 '63; Discussion. 236:4 O 5 '63
What polls tell about the mood of America. U S News 54:42-3 Je 10 '63
Who believes whom? R. Moley. Newsweek 61: 86 Ap 1 '63

PUBLIC opinion polls

Battle to call the winner; networks lean on pollsters and computers. il Bsns W p24-6 Je 6 '64
Big losers: the polls; Harris poll. il U S News 56:37 Je 15 '64
Do polls tell the story? interview. G. Gallup. il U S News 57:52-4+ O 5 '64
George Gallup looks at tomorrow's customer; interview. G. Gallup. il Nations Bsns 52: 68-70+ Mr '64
How accurate are polls in '64 elections? U S News 56:30 Je 1 '64
How accurate are the presidential polls? H. G. Earl. il Todays Health 42:36-9+ My '64
How right are the polls? with interview with G. Katona. il U S News 57:33-6 S 21 '64
How they say it's going; presidential election forecast. Time 84:19 Ag 14 '64
Intelligent woman's guide to political polls. E. Mazo. McCalls 92:80+ O '64
Johnson and the polls. S. Alsop. il Sat Eve Post 237:16 F 1 '64
Letter from Washington; Harris polls. Cato. Nat R 15:228 S 24 '63
Lyndon Johnson: will he win? story the polls tell. il U S News 57:44-7 S 7 '64
Politics and the polls. N. R. Hanson. Nation 199:331-2 N 9 '64
Polls: a year to be wary. Time 84:31 S 18 '64
Polls and statistics; do they throw light or confusion? il Sr Schol 85:6-8+ O 21 '64
Pollsters and politics: the California story. il Newsweek 63:26-8 Je 15 '64
Pollsters check and check again. Bsns W p32-3 S 12 '64

PUBLIC opinion polls—*Continued*
Private opinion on the polls; presidential election polls. S. M. Lipset. il N Y Times Mag p 14+ Ag 30 '64
248 questions for 1,260 Americans. il Newsweek 62:47 O 21 '63
Women's vote, how will it go? survey of political opinion. McCalls 91:70+ Mr '64
See also
Institute of student opinion
Scholastic research center

PUBLIC parking facilities. See Automobile parking

PUBLIC relations
Aimed folders find their targets; Dayton, Ohio. il Am City 79:116+ Jl '64
Baby-sitting for shoppers; Dearborn, Mich. il Am City 79:117-18 D '64
Better PR for public works; Memphis, Tenn; ed. by P. D. Eimon. il Am City 79:155-6+ Je '64
Eight cities, coast-to-coast, offer MPR patterns for 1964 action. Am City 79:117-19 Ja '64
Employee handbook promotes good parking relations; Wilmington, Del. il Am City 79:140 O '64
Festivals are communication. Am City 79:144+ My '64
Forums are successful in Akron. il Am City 78:136+ Mr '63
Hard sell in Washington. J. Tebbel. Sat R 47:51+ Jl 11 '64
Masters of the soft sell. il Am City 79:141+ Ag '64
Municipal purchasing and public relations. E. J. Brewer. il Am City 78:98-9 Ag '63
Ohio puts the personal touch into routine form letters by automatic typing. J. T. Ferguson. il Am City 78:113-14 Mr '63
Printing, planning and public relations. J. Cuffe. il Am City 78:102 N '63
Public relations. L. L. L. Golden. See second issue of each month of Saturday review
Public relations & the arts. A. H. Reiss. Mus Am 83:44-5 F '63
Some things that worry me about public relations; address, January 15, 1963. R. Van Riper. Vital Speeches 29:379-81 Ap 1 '63
Tax leaflet is a dollar stretcher. il Am City 78:122+ N '63
Tucson budget previews score with council, press, public. il Am City 78:133-4+ O '63
Under Marion Harper's big tent. S. H. Brown. il Fortune 69:128-32 My '64
Understanding the public. R. Roe. Am City 79:96-7 My '64
Unions need public acceptance, too. L. L. L. Golden. Sat R 46:63-4 D 14 '63
What makes a good PR man? L. L. L. Golden. Sat R 46:73 N 9 '63
See also
Customer relations
School and the community
service programs
also subhead Public relations under various subjects, e.g. Presidents—United States—Public relations

Bibliography

Books in communications. J. F. Fixx. See second issue of each month of Saturday review

PUBLIC relations society of America
Beginning steps; respecified code of ethics for financial public relations. L. L. L. Golden. Sat R 47:72 My 9 '64
Out in the open; Securities and exchange commission's report on corporate publicity and public relations. L. L. L. Golden. Sat R 46:52-3 Jl 13 '63

PUBLIC review board. See United automobile aircraft and agricultural implement workers of America—Public review board

PUBLIC roads, Bureau of. See United States—Public roads, Bureau of

PUBLIC school libraries. See School libraries

PUBLIC school teachers. See Teachers

PUBLIC schools
What's going on in schools & colleges. See issues of Changing times
See also
Courses of study
Education
Special classes and special schools

Attendance

See School attendance

Desegregation

Another noble experiment? reprint. D. Pickett. U S News 56:120 My 11 '64
As showdown nears on shifting of pupils. U S News 56:12 Mr 23 '64
As trouble spreads: ten years of mixed schools. il U S News 55:33-5 S 16 '63
Backlash in New York: PAT vs. Board of education. A. Croce. Nat R 16:816 S 22 '64
Balancing act; end to de facto segregation in the public schools. Newsweek 62:48 Jl 1 '63
Battle of the moms; members of Parents and taxpayers (P.A.T.) il Time 84:98 O 16 '64
Beyond tokenism. A. M. Bickel. New Repub 150:11-14 Ja 4 '64; Reply. R. Wilkins. 150:31 Ja 11 '64
Bitter end; end of official resistance in Mississippi. il Newsweek 64:25-6 S 14 '64
Boomerang. il Newsweek 62:24+ S 16 '63
Boundaries, buses and school boards. T. M. Quinn. il America 111:408-11 O 10 '64; Discussion. 111:574+ N 14 '64
Breakthrough in Dixie. Nation 199:149 S 28 '64
Breakthrough; New York city's public schools. Commonweal 77:633 Mr 15 '63
Brown decade; Brown v. Board of education. Nat R 16:433-4 Je 2 '64
Busing for racial balance is wrong; excerpts from address, October 16, 1964. B. M. Goldwater. U S News 57:97 N 2 '64
Civil rights act of 1964. Sch Life 47:13 O '64
Civil rights dominates NEA convention. il Sr Schol 85:2T-3T S 16 '64
Civil rights, will this summer tell? il Sr Schol 84:8-11 My 15 '64
Closing the gap. il Newsweek 64:70 S 21 '64
Common-sense compromise. Time 83:76+ My 22 '64
Compliments to the Court; refusal to grant certiorari to Court of appeals in Gary, Ind. case. Nat R 16:391 My 19 '64
Compulsory school busing and integration. W. W. Brickman. Sch & Soc 92:283 O 17 '64
Cooling it in the schools. il Time 84:77 S 11 '64
Court: 1954-1964; refusal to review the Gary case. Christian Cent 81:659-60 My 20 '64
Court says reopen schools; but will they be integrated? Prince Edward County, Va. il U S News 56:37 Je 8 '64
Courts & de facto. il Time 84:67 S 18 '64
Decision on zoning; New York state Supreme court. Sr Schol 84:2T+ Ap 3 '64
De facto segregation; summary of varying current views. B. Fielding. NEA J 53:11-14 My '64
Deliberate speed in D.C. S. McBee. New Repub 150:7-8 Je 20 '64
Desegregating city schools. J. H. Fischer. il PTA Mag 59:10-13 D '64
Desegregation creates problems, too. I. N. Berlin. Sat R 46:66-7 Je 15 '63
Desegregation decision; Brown v. Board of education, May 17, 1954. H. S. Ashmore. il Sat R 47:68-70+ My 16 '64
Desegregation in schools; Southern and border states. Library J 90:329-30 Ja 15 '65
Dialogue among pickets; segregation in Boston schools. H. Cox. Commonweal 79:245-6 N 22 '63; Reply with rejoinder. J. A. Murray. 79:485-6 Ja 24 '64
Discretion on de facto. il Time 84:90 O 30 '64
D.C. schools: 87.6 per cent Negro now. il U S News 57:10 N 23 '64
Drive for civil rights. Sr Schol 83:12-13 S 27 '63
Education of Big Ben; Negro demands for a loosening neighborhood-school pattern in Chicago. il Time 82:48 Ag 30 '63
Eight days make a miracle; Prince Edward County schools. J. Callwood. il McCals 91:34+ Ja '64
End in sight for neighborhood schools? il U S News 55:61 Jl 1 '63
Englewood and the northern dilemma. G. Walker. Nation 197:7-10 Jl 6 '63
Englewood, New Jersey: visitors in the classroom. S. Klaw. il Reporter 29:14-17 Jl 4 '63
Equal choices? D. Lawrence. U S News 54:108 Je 3 '63
Five who sued; plaintiffs in the five cases brought by the NAACP's legal defense fund in 1954. il Sat R 47:71 My 16 '64
Getting ready for fall; teachers, the key people. America 109:128 Ag 10 '63
How do the teachers feel? R. Coles. il Sat R 47:72-3+ My 16 '64
How not to integrate the schools; a personal testament. I. L. Gibel. Harper 227:57-60+ N '63; Discussion. 228:6 Ja '64
Human inequality; reprint. V. Royster. U S News 55:128 O 14 '63
In the South these children prophesy. R. Coles. il Atlan 211:111-16 Mr '63
Instant integration? New York schools. Newsweek 62:54 D 30 '63
Integrated: a tenth of South's Negro pupils. U S News 55:12 Ag 19 '63

PUBLIC schools—Desegregation—*Continued*
Integrated club. B. Baum. il Parents Mag 38: 62-3+ N '63
Integrating inferiority? Harlem schools. Newsweek 62:100+ N 25 '63
Integration. . . in reverse; middle-class white child in Negro slum school, San Francisco. G. B. Leonard. il Look 28:29-37 Ap 21 '64
Integration North and South. il Sr Schol 83:1T-2T+ S 20 '63
Integration; what happens to the kids? il Time 82:46+ Ag 16 '63
Is school integration a failure in New York? U S News 56:8 My 25 '64
Is segregation illegal, even if unintentional? in Orange and Englewood, N.J. U S News 54:10 My 27 '63
Kennedy children and integrated schools. il U S News 54:10-11 Je 17 '63
Letting George do it; public-school desegregation in Alabama. il Newsweek 62:33-4 S 23 '63
Little Rock finds a better way. J. A. Morris. Read Digest 83:142-6 S '63
Little Rock revisited, tokenism plus. G. Samuels. il N Y Times Mag p 13+ Je 2 '63
Lock begins to open; Prince Edward County. il Ebony 19:63-6+ N '63
Mandate against hypocrisy? desegregation in public schools in District of Columbia. D. Lawrence. U S News 57:112 N 23 '64
Mixed schools: as eleventh year begins. il U S News 57:37 Ag 31 '64
Mixed schools for Mississippi? il U S News 57:45 Jl 20 '64
Mixing schools: why one federal court refused; Savannah-Chatham County, Ga. F. M. Scarlett. il U S News 54:88-90 My 27 '63
More anticlimax than crisis. il Time 82:30 S 20 '63
More speed, less deliberation; Supreme court decisions in Virginia's Prince Edward County and Atlanta. Time 83:68 Je 5 '64
Negro & the New York schools. M. Decter. bibliog f Commentary 38:25-34 S '64; Discussion. 39:16 Ja '65
Negroes in Prince Edward County. Sch & Soc 91:422 D 28 '63
Neighborhood schools win a round in Supreme court. il U S News 56:56 My 18 '64
New program for desegregation. NEA J 53: 46 D '64
New York school boycott. M. Kempton. New Repub 151:6-7 S 26 '64; Discussion. 151:30 O 10; 30 O 24 '64
New York's Jim Crow schools: bleak facts and bright visions. B. Carter. il Reporter 31:23-6 Jl 2 '64
News and trends; theory and practice of integration. NEA J 53:4 S '64
No more parades? failure of the March for Democratic schools. M. Kempton. New Repub 150:5-7 My 30 '64
North and West have problems, too. G. W. Foster, jr. il Sat R 46:69-72+ Ap 20 '63
Now: a court ruling in defense of the neighborhood school; New York city. U S News 55:43 S 23 '63
Now, whites protest on a racial issue. il U S News 56:8 Mr 23 '64
On the integration front; reprints. Negro Hist Bul 27:20-2 O '63
One for the Court: cases concerning de facto segregation in the schools resulting from residential patterns. Nat R 16:1091 D 15 '64
Open door; Alabama's integrated schools. Newsweek 64:41 S 21 '64
Opening school doors. New Repub 150:5 Je 6 '64
Picking up speed. il Newsweek 64:71 Ag 31 '64
President vs. a governor: another school showdown; Alabama's Governor Wallace. il U S News 55:42-3 S 23 '63
Prince Edward County situation. W. V. Heuvel; N. V. Sullivan. il NEA J 53:12-15 Mr '64
Princeton's lesson: school integration is not enough. P. Streit. il N Y Times Mag p 14+ Je 21 '64
Pupil-transfer plan that is under fire. U S News 56:12 Je 15 '64
Racial crisis ahead for neighborhood schools; New York city. il U S News 55:46-8 Jl 8 '63
Racial integration in education; excerpt from Integration vs. segregation, ed. H. H. Humphrey. Sch & Soc 92:97-100 Mr 7 '64
Rearing children of good will; workshop on race prejudices. E. S. Ringold. il N Y Times Mag p61-2 S 22 '63
Says a white mother: we have rights, too, New York's school problems; with statements by three school authorities. il U S News 57:71-2+ O 26 '64
Scholastic teacher interview; ed. by H. Langer. J. H. Fischer. Sr Schol 85:8T-13T S 23 '64
School dispute, and parents arrested; sit-in against transfer of children from neighborhood school. il U S News 57:12 O 19 '64
School integration and civil rights; letter. J. E. Allen, jr. Sch & Soc 92:342 N 14 '64
School integration, or else. M. Weinberg. Commonweal 80:106-9 Ap 17 '64
Schools and the Negro: integration, then resegregation; Roosevelt high school, Washington, D.C. il U S News 55:80 N 25 '63
Schools in D.C. now 85.7 per cent Negro. U S News 55:12 N 18 '63
Shameful thing. il Time 82:26-7 S 13 '63
Since the Supreme court spoke; decision on school segregation. A. Lewis. il N Y Times Mag p9+ My 10 '64
So it goes. Nat R 15:221 S 24 '63
Southern school integration. America 111:339 S 26 '64
Supreme court's new mood. Christian Cent 81:755-6 Je 10 '64
Symposium on desegregation. il NEA J 52: 46-52 D '63
Teacher-opinion poll; de facto segregation. NEA J 53:30 N '64
Ten tragic years. D. Lawrence. U S News 56:120+ My 25 '64
This year's mixed schools: trouble in North, calm in South. il U S News 57:77-8 S 28 '64
Thou shalt not feel inferior! reprint. D. Lawrence. U S News 55:108 S 16 '63
Tokenism frustrates Negro hopes. Christian Cent 80:357 Mr 20 '63
U.S. court victory for neighborhood schools; Gary, Ind. U S News 56:50 Mr 16 '64; Same abr. with title What is a segregated school? Read Digest 84:128-9 Je '64
Unmoved: New Yorkers protest plan to bus children to racially mixed schools. il Newsweek 63:31 Mr 23 '64
Wallace notwithstanding. New Repub 149: 3-4 S 21 '63; Reply with rejoinder. M. Meltsner. 149:29-30 O 12 '63
What's a neighborhood? Time 83:76 Ap 10 '64
What's happening in education? neighborhood-school policy. W. D. Boutwell. PTA Mag 58:33-4 S '63
Where a state is breaking up the neighborhood schools; Orange and Englewood, N.J. il U S News 55:64-5 Ag 19 '63
Why a northern town fights school integration; Princeton plan. M. Gunther. il Sat Eve Post 237:66-7 S 19 '64
Why they fight for the P.A.T; pairing schools to obtain racial balance. P. Streit. il N Y Times Mag p20-1+ S 20 '64
Your child and prejudice. B. Spock. il Ebony 19:135-8+ O '64

See also
School boycotts

Bibliography

Public school desegregation; list of doctoral dissertations. F. Parker. Negro Hist Bul 26:228+ Ap '63

Finance

See School finance

Statistics

See Education—Statistics

United States

Background: the urban crisis. R. C. Weaver. il PTA Mag 59:18-20 O '64
Can the public school foster creativity? R. J. Mueller. il Sat R 47:48-9+ D 19 '64
Catholics and public schools. P. Scharper. Commonweal 79:533-8 Ja 31 '64
City schools. P. C. Sexton. bibliog f il Ann Am Acad 352:95-106 Mr '64
Critics of the schools never die, either. C. H. Wilson. il Sat R 47:51-3+ Je 20 '64; Discussion. 47:42 Jl 18 '64
Educational park: community vs. neighborhood. J. Barden. il Nation 198:388-91+ Ap 20 '64
Educationists' gadgetry produces poor teachers. F. Morley. Nations Bsns 51:27-8 Jl '63
Elementary school in the city: a conference report. Sch Life 45:26-34 Je '63
Enrollment, teachers, and schoolhousing; highlights from the fall 1962-63 survey of public schools. C. J. Hobson and S. Schloss. il Sch Life 45:14-17 Ja '63; 46:18-23 Ja '64

PUBLIC schools—United States—*Continued*
Function of schools in a changing society; excerpt from Public school in the American community. G. Graham. Sch & Soc 91: 257-60 Sum '63
Growth continues in U.S. public schools. il Sch Life 46:30 O '63
How severe is the school shortage? Parents Mag 38:46 Mr '63
How to judge a school system. S. Schuler. il Am Home 67:26+ My '64
In defense of the public school. A. Welsh. New Repub 148:12-13 Jl 29 '63; Discussion. 149:30-1 Ag 17 '63
Kind of public schools we want; address. F. Keppel. Vital Speeches 29:569-72 Jl 1 '63
Lighting a fire; conference sponsored by the National committee for the support of the public schools. il Newsweek 62:71 D 23 '63
Neutral schools. America 109:785 D 21 '63
One step closer to the ultimate answer. J. Scanlon. Sat R 47:59-60 F 15 '64
Our schools: battleground of conflicting interests; adapted from address, February 18, 1964. J. H. Fischer. il Sat R 47:66-7+ Mr 21 '64
Schoolhouse blues. America 109:285 S 21 '63
Schools for the sixties. il NEA J 53:37-52 Ja '64
What makes a school good. E. Youngert. Atlan 214:72-3 O '64
What's going on in schools & colleges. See issues of Changing times
What's happening in education? up-to-date sources on schools. W. D. Boutwell. PTA Mag 58:34 Ja '64
See also
Education—United States
High schools
Junior high schools
Rural schools—United States
School districts

PUBLIC schools (endowed)

England

Switch at Eton. Time 81:61 Mr 15 '63

Great Britain

Are Britain's Etons doomed to go? il Bsns W p 174-6+ S 19 '64

Scotland

Prince Charles: a schoolmate's view of a lonely boy; life at Gordonstown school. P. Pelham-Jones. il Redbook 122:72-3+ Ap '64

PUBLIC schools and religion
ABC's on prayers in school; questions and answers. U S News 55:41 Jl 1 '63
All others are invited; Bible-reading case. America 109:34 Jl 13 '63
Another kind of defiance; implementation of Supreme court decision on reading of prayers and the Bible. Time 82:16 Ag 16 '63
Baltimore prayer case; . . . to the Supreme court. America 108:245 F 23 '62
Becker's golden calf; constitutional amendment. M. E. Marty. Christian Cent 81:726-7 Je 3 '64
Behind the fight against school prayer; Christian view. H. B. Sissel. il Look 27: 25-9 Je 18 '63; Reply. America 108:874 Je 22 '63
Bible; better in school than in Court. Life 54:4 Mr 15 '63; Discussion. il 54:63-4+ Ap 12 '63
Bible reading in the public schools. A. W. Steinhilber. bibliog f Sch Life 46:13-16 O '63
Bible reading, prayers, and public schools. W. W. Brickman. Sch & Soc 91:272 O 5 '63
Can Bible reading be required in the public schools? U S News 54:8 Mr 4 '63
Catholics and the First; prayer amendment. Commonweal 80:281 My 29 '64
Chances for the prayer amendment. W. V. Shannon. Commonweal 80:283-4 My 29 '64
Children still pray in school; North Brookfield, Mass. defies Supreme court's ruling. il Life 55:53+ N 8 '63
Church and state, Bible-reading and recitation of the Lord's prayer in public schools. il Newsweek 62:48 Jl 1 '63
Churches rally to defense of High court. Christian Cent 81:1054 Ag 26 '64
Conducts loaded poll; Christian herald questionnaire. Christian Cent 81:1549 D 16 '64; Reply with rejoinder. D. Poling. 82:118 Ja 27 '65
Confusion on church and state. R. L. Gildea. Christian Cent 80:1381-2 N 6 '63
Conscience and the Constitution. T. Powell. il PTA Mag 58:10-12 N '63
Constitutional wonderland. America 108:351 Mr 16 '63
Court decides wisely; school prayer. Christian Cent 80:851 Jl 3 '63
Court on prayer. Commonweal 78:388-9 Jl 5 '63
Decision on the Lord's prayer and Bible reading. J. B. Sheerin. Cath World 197: 276-9 Ag '63
Dr Barth (Alan) on America's heart condition. Nat R 16:437 Je 2 '64
Does schoolroom prayer require a new amendment? il Time 83:62+ My 8 '64
Equal justice; Lord's prayer and Bible-reading cases. America 108:704 My 18 '63
Festivals and judges; two decisions. M. Himmelfarb. Commentary 35:67-70 Ja '63
Fourth R. Newsweek 61:24 Mr 11 '63
Furor over school prayers: latest in a growing debate; excerpts from testimony. E. H. Tuller; F. J. Sheen. U S News 56:72-4 My 11 '64
Goals of learning; address, February 11, 1963. A. W. Brustat. Vital Speeches 29:554-8 Jl 1 '63
God amendment. R. J. Dwyer. Nat R 16:494 Je 16 '64
God go home. Nat R 14:521 Jl 2 '63
God's little helpers; school-prayer issue. R. S. Gallagher. il Reporter 30:24-6 Je 4 '64; Discussion. 31:5 Jl 2 '64
Goldwater endorses school prayers. Christian Cent 81:1292 O 21 '64
Good King Wenslus-slus. F. Russell. Nat R 15:574-5 D 31 '63
Harassing the atheist; Baltimore prayer and Bible-reading case. America 108:386 Mr 23 '63
Here's what public schools can do about religion. A. S. Flemming. Good H 157:72+ O '63
High court rules as anticipated; religious exercises in public schools. Christian Cent 80:820 Je 26 '63
Implications of Supreme court decisions for contemporary church-state problems. W. B. Ball. Cath World 197:296-305 Ag '63
Jefferson's wall and the schools. H. L. Hurwitz. Sr Schol 84:9T F 7 '64
Legal religion in the schools. W. B. Ball. Cath World 197:366-71 S '63
Let us pray. Nation 198:358 Ap 13 '64
Loss to make up for; ban on religious observances in schools. il Time 81:13-14 Je 28 '63
Mr Becker and the bishops. America 111:79 Jl 25 '64
Mrs Murray's war on God. R. Liston. il Sat Eve Post 237:83-7 Jl 11 '64
Moral heritage and the law; prayers and Bible reading in the public schools. Life 54:4 Je 28 '63
Nation chooses sides in fight over prayer. il U S News 56:63-4 My 18 '64
Never say die! says Becker; prayer amendment bill. Christian Cent 81:852 Jl 1 '64
Nevertheless, God probably loves Mrs Murray. B. Shaw. il Esquire 62:110-112+ O '64
New uproar over school prayers. il U S News 56:12 My 4 '64
No time to lose; constitutional amendment proposed to counteract the Supreme court's ruling against prayer and Bible reading in the public schools. Christian Cent 81:691-2 My 27 '64
Opinion on the school prayers issue. Christian Cent 81:1454 N 25 '64
Organizing against the Supreme court; prayer and Bible-reading in public schools. R. Kirk. Nat R 16:406 My 19 '64; Discussion. 16:505 Je 16 '64
Outcast of Lebanon; case of J. N. Snavely. R. G. Hummerstone. il Nation 199:303-5 N 2 '64; Reply with rejoinder. E. U. Sowers, 2d. 200:inside cover Ja 11 '65
Point and counterpoint; federal funds and shared-time. J. O'Gara. Commonweal 78: 184 My 10 '63
Politics of religious equality. F. Canavan. America 108:664-7 My 11 '63
Prayer amendment. Commonweal 80:188-9 My 8 '64
Prayer amendments: a Catholic lawyer's view. W. B. Ball. Cath World 199:345-51 S '64
Prayer and the schools; Bible-reading decision. America 108:898 Je 29 '63
Prayer hearings; excerpts from statement before House judiciary committee. F. J. Becker. Sr Schol 84:13T My 15 '64
Prayer in school; attitude of the Catholic press. J. O'Gara. Commonweal 80:442 Jl 3 '64
Prayer or pluralism in the schools? J. Carr. Sat R 47:41 Jl 18 '64; Reply. V. T. LeSueur. 47:49 Ag 15 '64

PUBLIC schools and religion—*Continued*
Prayers in schools? concerning House judiciary committee hearings. Sr Schol 84:13-14 My 15 '64
Proposed amendment hit. Sr Schol 84:1T-2T Ap 3 '64
Reductio ad absurdum; New York prayer case. America 108:282 Mr 2 '63
Religion and public education. N. C. Nielsen, jr. America 108:830-1 Je 8 '63
Religion and public life. W. Herberg. Nat R 15:61 Jl 30 '63
Religion and schools. Sr Schol 82:1T-2T Mr 20 '63
Religion and the Court. J. O'Gara. Commonweal 78:391 Jl 5 '63
Religion and the schools. Sr Schol 83:4T D 6 '63
Religion and the schools, by P. Blanshard. Review
Sat R 46:82 N 16 '63. R. L. Hunt; Reply. T. E. Blackburn. 46:38 D 21 '63
Religion, education and the law; Law and society institute at the University of Kansas J. C. Bush. Christian Cent 81:1412-14 N 11 '64
Religion in education: a basis for consenus. W. B. Ball. America 108:528-30+ Ap 20 '63; Discussion. 108:640-3, 818; 109:15 My 4, Je 8, Jl 6 '63
Religion in state schools in Australia. R. Mathias. Christian Cent 81:1476-8 N 25 '64
Religion in the public schools; Catholic children at least can lose their faith. M. Novak. New Repub 148:16-18 Ap 13 '63
Religion in the schools; Bible-reading cases. America 108:894 Je 29 '63
Religion in the schools; constitutional issues involved, and the Court's decisions. J. Cass. Sat R 46:39-40 Jl 20 '63
Religion in the schools; opinion of Harvard law professor P. Freund. Time 84:59 D 11 '64
Religion, orthodoxy, public schools. C. M. Whelan. America 108:640-3 My 4 '63; Reply. T. B. McDonough. 108:818 Je 8 '63
Religious concern; prayer amendment. America 110:757 My 30 '64
Religious instruction: a natural right. R. Kirk. Nat R 16:234 Mr 24 '64; Discussion. 16:374-6 My 5 '64
Religious issues; in Florida and other areas of the country. Sr Schol 83:2T O 25 '63
Religious neutrality. J. J. Regan. America 110:74-6 Ja 18 '64
Religious scholarship and the Court. C. A. Holbrook. Christian Cent 80:1076-8 S 4 '63; Reply. S. E. Mead. 80:1342-3 O 30 '63
Religious schools and civic harmony. G. Weigel. Cath World 196:351-6 Mr '63
Republicans favor prayer amendment. Christian Cent 81:924 Jl 22 '64
Right to pray. D. Lawrence. U S News 56: 96 Mr 2 '64
Rights si, prayer no. Cato. Nat R 16:144 F 25 '64
Saving our children from God. L. B. Bozell. Nat R 15:19-22+ Jl 16 '63; Discussion. 15: 119 Ag 13 '63
School prayer battle. T. Powell. il Sat R 46:62-4+ Ap 20 '63; Discussion. 46:63 My 18 '63
School prayer referendum point system. Christian Cent 81:591 Ap 29 '64
School prayers and religious warfare. W. Berns. il Nat R 14:315-18 Ap 23 '63; Discussion. 14:421, 473 My 21-Je 4 '63
School prayers & the founding fathers. L. W. Levy; discussion. Commentary 35:76 Ja '63
School prayers decision. Sr Schol 83:9-11 S 13 '63
School prayers? the Presbyterians say no. U S News 54:10 Je 3 '63
School prayers: what's scheduled this autumn. U S News 55:11 Ag 19 '63
Schoolrooms and prayers. E. J. Hughes. Newsweek 62:15 Jl 1 '63
Schools and prayer. il Newsweek 62:82-3 S 9 '63
Schools react to Court decision. Christian Cent 80:1228 O 9 '63
Second Bible reading. Sr Schol 83:3T S 13 '63
Secular purpose: Supreme court's decision in the prayer and Bible-reading cases. America 109:127 Ag 10 '63
Shall we pray? il New Repub 148:4-6 Je 29 '63
Shared time argued in Chicago. Christian Cent 81:389 Mr 25 '64
Shared time; dual school enrollment. Christian Cent 81:819-20 Je 24 '64
Shared time experiment. J. G. Deedy, jr. il Commonweal 79:530-2 Ja 31 '64
Shared time; pro and con discussion. W. A. Anderson; T. Powell. NEA J 53:28-30 Mr '64
Supreme court and public prayer, by C. E. Rice. Review
America 111:49 Jl 11 '64 R. F. Drinan
Nat R 16:775-6 S 8 '64. L. B. Bozell
Supreme court decision on Bible reading and prayer recitation; with comments by lay and religious leaders. NEA J 52:55-6 S '63
Supreme court to hear Bible reading cases; Maryland and Pennsylvania. Christian Cent 80:198 F 13 '63
Teaching moral values. Christian Cent 81:164 F 5 '64
This month's feature: Congress & the school prayer decisions. Cong Digest 43:257-88 N '64
Tide reversed; church leaders endorse Supreme court's decision. Time 83:60+ Je 19 '64
To pray or not to pray, is that the question? F. Greenberg. il PTA Mag 58:22-5+ F '64
To prevent hysteria; Lord's prayer and Bible readings in Maryland and Pennsylvania. Christian Cent 80:485-6 Ap 17 '63; Discussion. 80:750 Je 5 '63
Unconstitutional prayers; letters to the editor. Nat R 15:163+ Ag 27 '63
Unfinished business; place of religion in public education. America 108:898 Je 29 '63
Vessels of Christ. M. Kempton. New Repub 150:13-14 My 16 '64
What prayer? Cato. Nat R 16:396 My 19 '64
Why clergymen are against school prayer. A. Eisenberg and H. Eisenberg. Redbook 124:38-9+ Ja '65

PUBLIC service
Men to match our problems; excerpts from address. L. J. Kroeger. il Recreation 57: 76-8 F '64
Official integrity. R. Moley. Newsweek 63:88 F 10 '64
See also
Civil service

Anecdotes, facetiae, satire, etc.

Field guide to government jargon. S. Klaw. Reporter 30:52 Ja 30 '64

PUBLIC service filming. See Moving pictures—Documentary films

PUBLIC service television programs. See Television broadcasting—Programs—Public service programs

PUBLIC speaking
Great speeches aren't necessarily good politics. D. S. Broder. il N Y Times Mag p7+ Mr 29 '64
Political speaking since the 1920's; address, August 20, 1963. J. L. Golden. bibliog Vital Speeches 29:763-7 O 1 '63
Speech and the community; address, April 5, 1963. R. T. Oliver. Vital Speeches 29: 459-62 My 15 '63
See also
Lectures and lecturing
Oratory
Stage fright

PUBLIC squares. See Plazas

PUBLIC utilities
Call on your utility company for help. M. R. Beasley. Am Home 66:72-3 O '63
How to regulate street openings. Am City 79:146+ Ag '64
Utility stock options: executive incentive v. public interest. L. Metcalf. il Nation 199: 151-4 S 28 '64
See also
Electric plants, Municipal
Pacific gas and electric company

Accounting

Consolidate your utility bills: Kirkwood, Mo. W. H. Pfitzinger. il Am City 78:80-1 Ag '63

Government ownership

See also
Electric utilities—Government ownership

Government regulation

See Public utilities—Regulation

Rates

See also
Water rates

Regulation

$500 million mistake; regulating AT&T the world's biggest business. A. Brynes. New Repub 151:11-14 S 26 '64
Regulating AT&T. A. Brynes. New Repub 151:11-14 O 3 '64

Securities

Utility stocks: worth looking into. il Changing T 18:34 Jl '64

PUBLIC welfare
See also
Social welfare

Law

See Social legislation—United States

California

Where relief grows and jobs go begging. U S News 57:16-17 O 19 '64

Germany (Federal Republic)

Maternity to eternity. Time 82:41 D 6 '63

Illinois

As thousands lined up for food handouts; Chicago and downstate. U S News 54:10 My 27 '63
Birth control, welfare funds, and the politics of Illinois; Illinois public aid commission. H. Bruno. il Reporter 28:33-5 Je 20 '63
Relief in Illinois. R. T. Cooper. New Repub 148:8 Je 15 '63

New York (state)

Crusade against the poor; relief chiselers in 1961, Newburgh, N.Y. F. M. Eckman. il Redbook 120:58-9+ F '63

Pennsylvania

Birth control and public aid. H. W. Fry. Christian Cent 81:438+ Ap 1 '64

United States

Deceit, corruption and scars of relief. M. Murphy. il Life 56:63 Ja 31 '64
Defense cuts release funds for humanity. Christian Cent 81:164 F 5 '64
Food subsidy for city folk; food stamp plan. il Bsns W p 164 Ap 11 '64
Goldwater's law; poverty and social welfare New Repub 150:4 F 1 '64
How much more of a welfare state for U.S.? il U S News 56:62-3 Ja 6 '64
Subsidiarity and welfare. America 111:477 O 24 '64
Wasted Americans, by E. May. Review
Commonweal 80:522-3 Jl 24 '64. N. Hentoff
Welfare abuses: how bad is the record? U S News 55:10 Ag 19 '63
Welfare mess. L. Chevalier. il Sat Eve Post 236:15-19 My 11 '63

Washington, D.C.

Continuing crisis. V. E. Lowder. Christian Cent 81:157-8 Ja 29 '64
Skeleton in the closet. S. D. Kean. Christian Cent 80:1148-9 S 18 '63

PUBLIC welfare workers. See Social workers

PUBLIC works
APW: a profit formula. E. P. Cliff. il Am For 69:28-30+ O '63
Better PR for public works; Memphis, Tenn; ed. by P. D. Eimon. il Am City 79:155-6+ Je '64
Headed for still loftier heights; public works spending. il Bsns W p 187-8+ O 19 '63
See also
Photography in public works

Federal aid

Accelerated public works, good or bad? Am City 78:7 S '63
Look what your federal taxes buy. il Nations Bsns 51:34-7+ O '63
Taxpayer's own diggers and builders. il Fortune 69:122-31 Ap '64
This month's feature: federal public works and unemployment. Cong Digest 43:225-56 O '64

Europe, Western

Public projects abroad offer U.S. big market. Nations Bsns 52:76+ My '64

PUBLIC works committee. See United States—Congress—House of representatives—Committees

PUBLIC works equipment. See Municipal equipment

PUBLIC works garages. See Garages, Municipal

PUBLIC works officers
Public-works men honored; top ten public works men-of-the-year. il Am City 79:34 O '64

PUBLICITY
Going public. A. W. Simon. Nation 199:219-21 O 12 '64
Goldfish bowl; ban on Catholic theologians. America 108:329 Mr 9 '63
See also
Government publicity
Photography in publicity
School publicity
Television in politics
also subhead Publicity under various subjects, e.g. Boxing—Publicity

PUBLISHERS adclub
Publishers' adclub to become two separate clubs. Pub W 183:29 Ap 8 '63

PUBLISHERS and libraries. See Libraries and publishers

PUBLISHERS and publishing
Book publishing today; interview, ed. by R. W. Apple, jr. M. Bessie. Writer 76:10-11+ F '63
Launching the first novel. P. R. Reynolds. il Sat R 47:56-8 S 12 '64
Off the cuff. W. C. Gault. Writer 77:7-8 My '64
Old imprint, a new author. H. Frankel. Sat R 46:18-19 S 7 '63
Production man's role: combatting confusion between publisher and manufacturer. L. Albert; F. Kleeberg. il Pub W 183:76+ My 6 '63
Publishing scene abroad; ABPC symposium. il Pub W 183:32-6 Je 3 '63; Correction. 183:41 Je 17 '63
Publishing the corporate book. W. Cross. Sat R 47:56+ Jl 11 '64
Role of the publisher's salesman in today's market. F. Watts. Pub W 187:121-4 Ja 18 '65
When publishers go public. W. Jovanovich. il Sat R 47:19-22+ My 16 '64
Year in retrospect. D. Dempsey. Sat R 46:18-19 D 21 '63
See also
American newspaper publishers association
Authors and publishers
Best sellers
Books—Advertising
Copyright
International publishers association
Music publishing
Newspaper publishing
Periodicals, Publishing of
Printing—Private presses
Royalties
Serial rights

Anecdotes, facetiae, satire, etc.

Stalking the muse on publishers' row. J. Leggett. il Harper 230:64-6 Ja '65

Art literature

At a price that allows us to publish the book; address. P. Grushkin. il Pub W 183:96-8 Mr 4 '63
Editorial; Buchmesse at Frankfort-on-the-Main. A. Frankfurter. Art N 62:21+ D '63
Focusing the foreign competition picture. S. Wecksler. Pub W 183:55 My 6 '63
See also
Shorewood publishing company, incorporated

Catholic literature

Catholic title production declined slightly in 1963. Pub W 185:30 Mr 16 '64
Chat with the publishers; reflections on the current state of Catholic books. D. L. Flaherty. America 108:256-7 F 23 '63

Childrens literature

Bobbsey twins at an orgy. W. J. Smith. Nation 198:633-5 Je 22 '64
Book publishing hits all-time high: juvenile books make greatest gains. Library J 88:840 F 15 '63
Frederic Melcher and children's books. R. Gagliardo. il ALA Bul 57:549-52 Je '63
Growth and growing pains in children's book publishing. C. B. Grannis. Pub W 183:136 F 18 '63
On publishing books for children. H. Schein. Horn Bk 39:629-31 D '63
Publishers' library editions: progress and problems viewed. Pub W 185:108+ F 3 '64

Consolidations and mergers

Building word power. il Bsns W p36 S 19 '64
Court puts five-year ban on McClurg-Parents merger. Pub W 183:90 F 11 '63
Encyclopaedia Britannica will buy G. & C. Merriam. il Pub W 186:36-7 S 21 '64
Meeting of minds; Encyclopaedia Britannica buys the Merriam-Webster dictionaries. il Time 84:100 S 18 '64

PUBLISHERS and publishing—Consolidations and mergers—*Continued*
Scientific American merges with Freeman textbook firm. Pub W 185:52 Ap 20 '64
Terms set for acquisition of Webster by McGraw-Hill. Pub W 183:90 F 11 '63

Finance

ABPC seminar: principles and procedures of credit in book publishing. Pub W 187:42-4 Ja 11 '65
Break-even point on novels: what cost factors are involved. Pub W 186:27-9 O 12 '64
Editor's easy chair; myths about publishing. J. Fischer. Harper 227:14+ Jl '63

International aspects

Book publishing and national development. P. S. Jennison. ALA Bul 57:512-16 Je '63
Books with an international accent; co-editions; adaptation of address. C. G. Benjamin. Sat R 47:39-41 Ag 8 '64
Overseas production; publishers report the pros and cons. Pub W 186:72-4+ S 7 '64
Un-cooperative productions. P. J. Rosenwald. Pub W 186:26-8 S 7 '64
World opens up for scholarly publishing. C. Kerr. il Sat R 47:28 My 30 '64

Limited editions

Making of a book; Chilmark press edition of The rime of the ancient mariner. P. Standard. il Pub W 186:78+ D 7 '64

Paperback books

ABA regionals: paperback books in the bookstore; summaries of panel discussions and addresses at Boston and Cleveland meetings. il Pub W 186:36-43 N 9 '64
Combined book exhibit program for communication between paperback book publishers and educational market. Wilson Lib Bul 38:31 S '63
New paperback lines. Sr Schol 82:25T Mr 13 '63
Paperbacks in religious book publishing. C. B. Grannis. Pub W 186:98 S 28 '64
Rand McNally reenters the paperback field. Pub W 185:70-1 Je 22 '64
Tarzan of the paperbacks. P. Mandel. il Life 55:11-12 N 29 '63
What's new in paperbacks? R. Beauchamp. il Sr Schol 83:22T Ja 17 '64
When publishers go public. W. Jovanovich. il Sat R 47:22+ My 16 '64

Public relations

They say no news is good news. H. Frankel. Sat R 47:32-3 Mr 7 '64

Religious literature

ABPC: religious publishers consider ecumenical books, general reviews. Pub W 183: 22-4 My 27 '63
Catholic title production increased 16 per cent in 1962. Pub W 183:35 Mr 18 '63
Directions: subject trends in religious book publishing. Pub W 183:84-5+ F 11 '63
Paperbacks in religious book publishing; Varied forms of religious communication. C. B. Grannis. Pub W 186:98 S 28 '64
Protestant church publishers view role in communications. il Pub W 183:37-40 Mr 25 '63
Religious press in America, by M. E. Marty and others. Review
Commentary 37:82-5 Mr '64. W. Coffey
RPG elects Wolfe, discusses paperback problems; symposium. il Pub W 185:49-52 Je 15 '64
RPG: how to integrate the promotion program; symposium. il Pub W 183:16-21 My 6 '63
RPG topic: how to reach denominational markets. Pub W 184:26-7 O 28 '63
RPG workshop; profit or loss in religious book publishing. Pub W 185:24-8 Ap 13 '64
Vitality in religious book publishing. C. B. Grannis. Pub W 185:82 F 10 '64
See also
Methodist publishing house, Nashville. Tenn.

Scientific literature

Can publishers pull the plug on copiers? Bsns W p 114 N 21 '64
Scientific publishing. T. Crowder. Science 144:633-7 My 8 '64; Discussion. 145:7-8, 534+ Jl 3, Ag 7 '64
See also
Publishers and publishing—Technical literature

Securities

Book publishing stock prices: a monthly report. See issues of Publishers' weekly
Textbook stocks. Duns R 84:88E+ S '64
Wall Street notes, 1963-64. il Pub W 185:95-8 Ja 20 '64; 187:93-6 Ja 18 '65

Statistics

American book title output; 1963-64: subject analysis of American title output. il Pub W 185:58-69 Ja 20 '64; 187:56-67 Ja 18 '65
Cooperative industry statistics: basis for business decisions. C. B. Grannis. Pub W 185:54 Ja 13 '64
New records for publishing seen in Commerce survey; with editorial comment. Pub W 185:66-7, 74 F 3 '64

Taxation

ABPC seminar: tax implications for book publishers. Pub W 186:27-30 N 23 '64; Reply. R. S. Helstein. 187:213 Ja 25 '65

Technical literature

High price of technical books. C. G. Benjamin. ALA Bul 59:61-4 Ja '65
Technical books and their sale examined at Denver ABA meeting; summary of addresses. M. Simons; J. Feyock. il Pub W 184:30-1 N 11 '63
Technical publishing and the international marketplace. il Pub W 184:57-60 N 11 '63

Textbooks

AIGA: the making and marketing of dual-purpose books; summary of addresses. B. R. McMillen; M. E. Rosenblum. Pub W 185:70+ Je 1 '64
ATPI annual meeting: expansion is keynote to meet crises and opportunities; with editorial comment. il Pub W 185:20-32, 44 My 18 '64
ATPI annual meeting: textbook research planned, major programs forecast; with editorial comment. il Pub W 183:16-28, 37 My 13 '63
Boom in youth. il Duns R 82:79-80 Jl '63
Federal, state, local economic developments; effect on schools and educational publishing; symposium at 1964 industry conference of the American textbook publishers institute; with editorial comment. il Pub W 185:14-24, 34 Ap 6 '64
New era for textbooks: roles of government, foundations and industry in education; symposium at 1963 industry conference of the American textbook publishers institute; with editorial comment. il Pub W 183:16-24, 34 Ap 8 '63
Publisher-manufacturer relations: textbooks; symposium. il Pub W 184:76-8+ O 14 '63
Schools and publishing: a partnership in transition; condensation of report. F. Redding. Pub W 183:22-5 Mr 18 '63
Textbook factory: Volk und Wissen publishing company, East Berlin. H. Roske. Atlan 212:90-4 D '63
Treatment of minority groups in textbooks; adaptation of address, October 2, 1964. A. J. McCaffrey. Pub W 186:22-7 O 12 '64
Two textbooks: a clinical report. il Pub W 185:100-2+ My 4 '64
When publishers go public. W. Jovanovich. il Sat R 47:19-22+ My 16 '64
See also
Textbooks

Africa

AAUP trips to Asia and Africa to view scholarly publishing needs. Pub W 186:42-50 Jl 20 '64

Asia

AAUP trips to Asia and Africa to view scholarly publishing needs. Pub W 186:42-50 Jl 20 '64

Australia

Australian book publishing up from schizophrenia; reprint. Pub W 185:20-2 Mr 16 '64; Discussion. 185:29 My 25; 186:24-5 S 7 '64

Canada

See also
University presses

Czechoslovakia

Visiting Prague publisher describes Czech book trade. Pub W 186:298-9 Ag 31 '64

England

See also
Oxford university press

PUBLISHERS and publishing—*Continued*

Europe, Western

Doing the Frankfurt scene. Pub W 184:28-30 S 16 '63

France

Book censorship in Paris. P. Lennon. Atlan 212:73-6 N '63
Creeping censorship. Newsweek 63:50+ Ap 20 '64
France's giant; Librairie Hachette. Time 82: 92-3 N 8 '63
Larousse's printing plant merges the old and the new. il Pub W 185:95-7 Ja 6 '64
Report on French publishing. G. Borchardt. il Pub W 184:33-5 Ag 12 '63; 186:29-31 Jl 27 '64

Germany (Democratic Republic)

Textbook factory; Volk und Wissen publishing company, East Berlin. H. Roske. Atlan 212:90-4 D '63

Germany (Federal Republic)

Looking backward; interest in the Hitler era. Newsweek 64:38-9 Ag 17 '64
Obituary note; Karl H. Ullstein of Ullstein verlag. Pub W 185:108 Ja 20 '64
Obituary; R. Ullstein, of Ullstein verlag. Pub W 185:81 F 10 '64
Springer-verlag starts American company. Pub W 186:91 S 28 '64

Great Britain

Britain survey service on orders. R. H. Smith. Pub W 184:49 Ag 5 '63
Cambridge press, England opens new, modern plant. il Pub W 184:58-60+ D 2 '63
Change of name for Grolier's British firm. Pub W 186:92 S 28 '64
First Aldus titles this fall; N.Y. office set. Pub W 186:26 Ag 17 '64
Grolier buys three reference divisions from British firm. Pub W 185:32 Ap 6 '64
Growth rate resumed in U.K. title production. il Pub W 185:105 Ja 20 '64
London's first World book fair: trade show or public fair? E. Moon. il Pub W 186:24-9 Jl 27 '64
One of a new breed: Paul Hamlyn of London. P. Rosenwald. il Pub W 183:41-5 F 4 '63
Scholastic expands language-teaching aids. il Pub W 185:33 Mr 30 '64
U.K. title production only slightly over '63 level. il Pub W 187:104 Ja 18 '65

See also
Nonesuch press
Pall Mall press, limited

Italy

Giangiacomo Feltrinelli: Italian publisher-bookseller pioneers to new book markets. P. J. Rosenwald. il Pub W 185:56-60 F 3 '64
Installment culture; Fabbri brothers. il Time 83:95 F 7 '64
Penalties of Italy's prosperity. S. Pacifici. Sat R 46:20-1 Jl 27 '63
Rizzoli editore plans extended U.S. operations. il Pub W 184:152-3 Jl 8 '63
Total recall; Castro's autobiography. il Newsweek 63:59 Ap 27 '64

Latin America

USIA's expanded Latin American book program. Pub W 186:29-31 Ag 10 '64

Rumania

New U.S.-Rumanian accord includes books. Pub W 185:52 Je 29 '64

Russia

Book publishing in the USSR. Review Wilson Lib Bul 37:786 My '63. F. M. Palmer
No censorship court battles in USSR! manuscripts don't get that far; summary of news conference. A. P. Rybin. Library J 88:2218-19 Je 1 '63
Soviet book delegation concludes visit to U.S.A; with editorial comment. il Pub W 183:25-6, 32 My 6 '63
U.S. book publishers report on book publishing in USSR. Library J 88:748 F 15 '63

Taiwan

Chinese reprinters and world copyright practice: a Chinese view and a U.S. publisher's reply. I. C. Loh; C. G. Benjamin. Pub W 185:22-9 Mr 30 '64
Formosa piracy: new pleas for a solution. R. H. Smith. Pub W 184:29 D 16 '63
Taiwan's best-selling pirates. C. Elliott. Life 55:8 N 15 '63

United States

Adclub on the advantages of summer publishing. Pub W 183:34-5 My 13 '63
All the customers are always right. D. Dempsey. Sat R 47:24-5 Mr 14 '64
ABA regional meetings: Denver, Dallas, New Orleans; summaries of panel discussions and addresses. il Pub W 184:18-40 N 18 '63
ABA regionals: book distribution and trade relations; summaries of panel discussions and addresses at Boston and Cleveland meetings. il Pub W 186:30-6 N 9 '64; Reply. L Epstein. 186:21-2 D 7 '64
ABPC: copyright, world trade, home markets, legislation and financial trends viewed at annual meeting; symposium. il Pub W 185:30-55 Je 15 '64
ABPC meeting: educational market, overseas ties, copyright revision explored; symposium. il Pub W 183:22-38 Je 3 '63
Avoid shipping delays: hire extra Xmas help. B. Schweid. Pub W 185:126-7 Ja 20 '64
Awake at last; publishing history of Call it sleep. H. Frankel. Sat R 47:29 N 21 '64
Congress debates the war on poverty; book publishing's role. R. H. Smith. Pub W 186:37 Ag 10 '64
Dex Libris, invisible bookseller. L. Meyer. Pub W 183:64-6 Mr 25 '63
Dissemination of print; address, May 1963. D. Lacy. il Wilson Lib Bul 38:54-64 S '63
Editor's easy chair; myths about publishing. J. Fischer. Harper 227:14+ Jl '63
Feffer and Simons to start cash-for-export plan. Pub W 183:53 Je 17 '63
Fiction, the publisher's Cinderella-child. L. Meyer. Pub W 184:53-4 S 23 '63
Goals for 1964; Book industry association president looks ahead; symposium. Pub W 185:46-9, 63 Ja 6 '64
Grand tradition. N. Cousins. Sat R 47:20 D 26 '64
How to succeed on company time; writing and publishing a company history. D. Dempsey. Sat R 47:28-9 Jl 18 '64
January books; some leading publishers' promotions. il Pub W 184:18-29 N 25 '63
January books: some major promotions announced by publishers. il Pub W 186:26-34 N 2 '64
Kennedy death affects publishing; new editions of books announced. Library J 89:334 Ja 15 '64
Lasser survey; step toward understanding; new era of bookseller- publisher communication. J. A. Duffy. Pub W 186:61 O 5 '64
More books but faster, faster please. J. A. Duffy. Pub W 185:119 Ja 20 '64
New light on order fulfillment. C. B. Grannis. Pub W 186:40 S 7 '64
NYU publishing course discusses going public. Pub W 185:48-9 My 4 '64
1963 publishing output soars in America and United Kingdom. Library J 89:584 F 1 '64
On the fringe. H. Frankel. Sat R 46:18-19 Ag 3 '63
One out of four comes back! how costly are returns to the bookseller and the publishers? F. Watts. Pub W 186:51-3 S 7 '64; Discussion. 186:55 S 21, 58-61 N 2 '64
Over the counter and out of the woods. D. Dempsey. Sat R 46:30 Ap 20 '63; Correction: 46:25 My 11 '63
Publishing revival in the second city; Chicago. C. R. Carner. il Library J 88:2435-8 Je 15 '63
Publishing then and now 1912-1964; excerpt from address, October 15, 1964. A. A. Knopf. Pub W 186:20-6 N 23 '64; Library J 89: 4312-14 N 1 '64; Sat R 47:21-3+ N 21; 17+ N 28 '64
Return of the personal publisher. D. Dempsey. Sat R 46:34-5 S 14 '63
Rights and permissions; non-marketing practices of large publishing houses. P. Nathan. Pub W 185:139 F 24; 48 Mr 23; 67 My 4 '64
Rival versions of Russian novel go down to the wire; reply. F. A. Praeger. Pub W 183: 36 F 4 '63
Short history of the ABA book buyer's handbook. G. Jennings. Pub W 186:57-8 N 2 '64
So you want to write a book; excerpt from The writing and selling of nonfiction. P. R. Reynolds. Sat R 46:48-50 Jl 13 '63; Reply. D. B. Sanborn. 46:43 Ag 10 '63
Soviets say contract for Solzhenitsyn novel is void. Pub W 183:48-9 F 4 '63
Take a bow: Michael Gross. il Pub W 184:22-8 D 30 '63
Thinking big in sixty-five. D. Dempsey. Sat R 48:24-5 Ja 16 '65

PUBLISHERS and publishing—United States —*Continued*
Too much, too soon, a study in timing: syndication and mass-market distribution. H. S. Klein. Pub W 185:124-5 Je 8 '64
US book totals soar ever higher; children's books climb steadily. Library J 89:927 F 15 '64
War on poverty. il Pub W 185:38-50 F 17; 32-43 My 4 '64; Discussion. 185:57 F 17; 38 Mr 30; 52 My 4 '64
War on poverty: challenge to publishing. R. H. Smith. Pub W 185:38 Mr 30 '64
Warren report in mass production. D. Dempsey. Sat R 47:25+ N 7 '64
We represent the library's interest: 19th century fiction of US and Britain; Tom Fool publishing company, Allagash, Me. Library J 89:4871 D 15 '64
What can be done about the distribution crisis? R. H. Smith. Pub W 184:49 N 18 '63
Wonderland of subsidiary rights. P. Nathan. Sat R 46:58-9+ D 14 '63
See also
American book publishers council
Protestant church-owned publishers association
University presses
also names of publishers, e.g. Praeger, Frederick A, incorporated

History

Gambler in publishing: Horace Liveright. L. Kronenberger. Atlan 215:94-104 Ja '65
Parnassus Corner: a life of James T. Fields, publisher to the Victorians, by W. S. Tryon. Review
Pub W il 184:26-30 Jl 29 '63. J. T. Winterich

Yugoslavia

Yugoslav publishers call for more translations. Pub W 185:69 Je 22 '64

PUBLISHERS book advertisements. See Books —Advertising

PUBLISHERS company, incorporated
Unfair competition charged in encyclopedia suit; suit against Publishers company, inc, of Washington. Pub W 186:50 N 16 '64

PUBLISHERS marks
See also
Colophons

PUBLISHERS of the year award
ABA establishes award for Publisher of the year. J A. Duffy. Pub W 185:48 Ap 13 '64

PUBLISHERS' publicity association
Publishers' adclub to become two separate clubs. Pub W 183:29 Ap 8 '63
Publishers' publicity assn. sets up first project. Pub W 184:32 O 14 '63
PPA to handle publicity for National book awards. Pub W 184:31 O 28 '63

PUBLISHERS trade exhibits. See Book exhibits

PUBLISHING. See Publishers and publishing

PUBLISHING of periodicals. See Periodicals, Publishing of

PUBS (Ireland) See Bars and barrooms

PUCCI, Emilio
High fashion, a low view of U.S. women. pors Life 57:69-70 O 16 '64
More's the Pitti. il Time 84:44 Jl 31 '64
Noble nose to the grindstone. il pors Life 57:63-4+ O 16 '64
Pucci; sportswear king of the world. E. Sheppard. il por Ladies Home J 80:55-61 Jl '63
Pucci the magnificent. V. Lawford. il pors Vogue 143:156-63 Mr 15 '64
Pucci's Africa: the pure wonder. il Vogue 145:106-11 Ja 1 '65

PUCCINI, Giacomo
La Bohème. Criticism
Opera N il 28:12-13 Mr 14 '64
Opera N il 28:17-20 Mr 14 '64
Sat R 47:23 Mr 28 '64
First opera in dynagroove: Madama Butterfly. P. L. Miller. il Am Rec G 29:684-5 My '63
From Angel, a remarkably successful new recording of La Bohème. P. L. Miller. il Am Rec G 30:1020-1 Jl '64
Gianni Schicchi. Criticism
Am Rec G il 29:420-1+ F '63
Leontyne Price as Tosca. P. L. Miller. il Am Rec G 30:92-4 O '63
On records; La Bohème. Opera N 28:37 Mr 14 '64
On records; La Bohème. Opera N 29:33 Ja 16 '65
On records; Il Trittico. C. J. Luten. Opera N 27:35 Mr 2 '63
On records; Madama Butterfly. C. J. Luten. Opera N 28:32 S 28 '63
On records; Manon Lescaut. Opera N 28:35 Ap 18 '64
On records; Tosca. Opera N 28:35 Ap 18 '64
On records; Tosca. Opera N 28:35 D 21 '63
On records; Turandot. Opera N 29:33 Ja 16 '65
Portrait of Manon. M. de Schauensee. Am Rec G 30:1100-1 Ag '64
Suor Angelica. Criticism
Am Rec G il 29:420-1+ F '63
Il tabarro. Criticism
Am Rec G il 29:420-1+ F '63
Tosca. Criticism
Mus Am 84:16-17 F '64
New Yorker 39:116 F 15 '64
Opera N 27:28 My 4 '63
Opera N 28:33 D 14 '63
Opera N il 28:17-20 Ap 18 '64
Sat R 47:57+ F 29 '64
Sat R 47:38 Ap 4 '64
Turandot. Criticism
New Yorker 38:78+ F 9 '63
Opera N il 29:17-20 Ja 16 '65
Sat R 48:22 Ja 30 '65

PUDDINGS
Fruit puddings. il Suc Farm 61:100+ Mr '63
Proving out the pudding. C. Claiborne. il N Y Times Mag p55-6 Ja 10 '65
Pudding and a pie using whey. Sunset 131: 169 S '63
Pudding and pie cook book. J. A. Beard. il House & Gard 124:169+ D '63
Puddings. il Good H 157:72-3+ D '63

PUEBLA pottery. See Pottery, Mexican

PUEBLO, Colo.

Hospitals

Rejuvenation and new growth restore usefulness to an older hospital. il Arch Rec 133:199-202 Mr '63

PUEBLO BONITO, N.Mex.
Pueblo Bonito: the place of the braced-up cliff. O. F. Oldendorph. il Nat Parks Mag 37:4-7 S '63

PUEBLO Indians
Ancient strength. O. La Farge. New Yorker 39:26-34 Ag 31 '63
Enduring life of the Pueblo Indians. P. S. Feibleman. Holiday 34:58-9+ Ag '63
Indian wampum builds an electronics plant. il Bsns W p74-6 My 23 '64
Pueblo gods and myths, by H. Tyler. Review
Sci Digest 55:84 Je '64. D. Cohen
20th-century Indians preserve customs of the cliff dwellers. il Nat Geog Mag 125:196-211 F '64

PUEBLO supermarkets, incorporated, Puerto Rico. See Supermarkets

PUENTE, Giuseppe del
Premier baritone. L. Saltzman. por Opera N 28:26-7 Ja 4 '64

PUERPERAL psychosis. See Psychoses

PUERTO maritimo. See Guayaquil

PUERTO RICANS
Puerto Rico: island at a crossroads. J. R. Moskin. il Look 28:26-34+ Mr 24 '64

PUERTO RICANS in the United States
I don't think the cop is my friend. G. Samuels. il N Y Times Mag p28+ Mr 29 '64
In New York you get swallowed by a horse. O. Lewis. Commentary 38:69-73 N '64
Puerto Rican tide begins to turn; migrants returning to their island now match the numbers moving to the island of Manhattan. A. W. Maldonado. il N Y Times Mag p84-5+ S 20 '64
Puerto Ricans. N. Glazer. Commentary 36: 1-9 Jl '63; Reply. W. P. Gillotti. 37:6 Ja '64
Puerto Rico: the migration reverses. A. W. Maldonado. il Nation 198:255-7 Mr 16 '64
Se habla espanol? J. Lelyveld. il N Y Times Mag p65-6+ Je 14 '64
Victims of welfare. S. Castan. il Look 27: 68-71 Mr 26 '63

PUERTO RICO
Poet in the Fortress: the story of Luis Muñoz Marín, by T. Aitken, jr. Review
Sat R il 47:40-1 O 17 '64. A. A. Berle
Puerto Rico: island at a crossroads. J. R. Moskin. il Look 28:26-34+ Mr 24 '64
Welcome to a new friend. il Time 85:24 Ja 8 '65
See also
Astronomical observatories—Puerto Rico
Elections—Puerto Rico
Forests and forestry—Puerto Rico
Housing—Puerto Rico
Protestant churches—Puerto Rico
San Juan
United Nations—Puerto Rico
Wages—Puerto Rico

PUERTO Rico—*Continued*

Description and travel

Adventure Cove; water-sports center. il Travel 119:8 F '63
Getting a charge up San Juan Hill. H. Sutton. il Sat R 46:24-6 F 2 '63
How a rave-notice travelog was made. T. Hirsch. il Pop Phot 52:94-5+ F '63
Under El Yunque; excerpt from Where the trade winds blow, a yachting guide to southern waters. B. Robinson. il Yachting 114:48-9+ O '63

Economic conditions

Booming Puerto Rico; success of Operation bootstrap. America 108:186 F 9 '63
Commonwealth of Puerto Rico. R. Picó. bibliog il Focus 14:1-6 O '63
Economic climate still beckons. il Bsns W p 150-2+ S 12 '64
Planning for what? America 108:387 Mr 23 '63
Solving the unsolvable. il Time 83:38 F 7 '64

Industries

Commonwealth of Puerto Rico. R. Picó. bibliog il Focus 14:1-6 O '63

Politics and government

Colonialism in Congress; House interior subcommittee on territorial and insular affairs. Reporter 28:11 Je 20 '63
Economic climate still beckons. il Bsns W p 150-2+ S 12 '64
Permit me to leave; L. Muñoz Marín stepping aside after four terms in office. il Time 84:35 Ag 28 '64

Religious institutions and affairs

News of the Christian world (cont) Christian Cent 81:25 Ja 1 '64
See also
Catholic church in Puerto Rico
Protestant churches—Puerto Rico

PUERTO RICO and the United States
Puerto Rico; the migration reverses. A. W. Maldonado. il Nation 198:255-7 Mr 16 '64

PUERTO VALLARTA, Mexico
Everybody's hideaway. il Time 82:42 N 1 '63
Hush-hush resort. W. W. Johnson. il Sat Eve Post 236:24-7 F 16 '63
Puerto Vallarta is changing, perhaps you should hurry. il Sunset 132:25-6+ Ja '64
Roughing it with the cognoscenti. H. Sutton. il Sat R 47:36+ Mr 14 '64
You can drive to Puerto Vallarta. il Sunset 131:72 O '63

PUFF pastry. See Pastry

PUFFERS
Formula of fugu: Japanese puffer fish. il Time 85:44 Ja 29 '65
Japanese puffer fish. Sci N L 86:139 Ag 29 '64
Tarichatoxin tetrodotoxin: a potent neurotoxin. H. S. Mosher and others. bibliog il Science 144:1100-10 My 29 '64

PUFFINS
Birds of the sea. A. Sprunt, 4th. il Motor B 112:29+ O '63

PUGET SOUND
Puget Sound; the climate, topography, tempo, life, but in particular, the boating. E. Crimmin. il Motor B 111:30-2+ My '63
See also
San Juan Islands, Wash.

PUGH, H. G.
Correlations of particles emitted in nuclear reactions. Science 147:177-9 Ja 8 '65

PUGH, James E. jr
Simplified audio impedance matching. Electr World 69:50-1+ Ap '63

PUGLIESE, Joseph
Sculptured door pulls of Ted Bielefeld. Craft Horiz 23:18-19 My '63

PUGWASH conferences on science and world affairs
Eleventh Pugwash conference; Dubrovnik, Yugoslavia. Bul Atomic Sci 19:46-8 N '63
Pugwash: a world movement on the responsibility of the scientist in world affairs. il UNESCO Courier 17:20-1+ N '64
Pugwash-Coswa: international conversations. E. Rabinowitch. Bul Atomic Sci 19:7-12 Je '63
Pugwash on scientific cooperation; reprint. Bul Atomic Sci 20:41-6 S '64
Pugwash XIII. Bul Atomic Sci 20:43-5 D '64
Pugwash XII; official statement. Bul Atomic Sci 20:45-8 Je '64
Reporter at large; eleventh conference in Dubrovnik, Yugoslavia. D. Lang. New Yorker 39:34-8+ D 21 '63

PUHARICH, Henry K.
Paper on intellectronics highlight for 25,000 at NEC exhibition. C. D. LaFond. Miss & Roc 15:34 O 26 '64

PUŁASKI, Kazimierz
General Pulaski's memorial day, 1964; proclamation, August 15, 1964. L. B. Johnson. Dept State Bul 51:354 S 7 '64
General Pulaski's memorial day, 1963; proclamation, August 27, 1963. J. F. Kennedy. Dept State Bul 49:460 S 23 '63

PULITZER, Lilly
Barefoot tycoon makes lillies bloom all over. il pors Life 54:105-9 F 8 '63

PULITZER prizes
Five 1963 Pulitzer awards in letters, no drama prize. il Pub W 183:29-31 My 13 '63
Judging the judges. Nation 198:498 My 18 '64
Just doing the job. il Time 83:84 My 15 '64
Loser take all. Time 81:75 My 17 '63
Mr Halberstam's prize. America 110:662 My 16 '64
Modern journalism. New Repub 148:5 My 18 '63
New deadline set for Pulitzers in letters. il Pub W 186:49-50 Jl 6 '64
1964 Pulitzer prizes omit fiction, drama awards. il Pub W 185:28-9 My 11 '64
Prize and prejudice? newspaper selections. il Newsweek 63:74+ My 18 '64
Pulitzer prizes. Wilson Lib Bul 37:820 Je '63
Who's afraid of what? Newsweek 61:67 My 20 '63

PULLEN, William R.
Georgia: the groves of academe. Wilson Lib Bul 38:278-80 N '63

PULLETS. See Poultry

PULLEYS
How to select pulley size. il Suc Farm 61:77 Je '63
Pulleys, lifting the east way; reprint. il Sci Digest 56:86-8 D '64

PULLIAM, Eugene
War whoop. Time 81:67 Mr 15 '63

PULLIAM, Lloyd
Statesmanship and obsolescence; a critique of the Conant proposals on teacher education. Sat R 47:54-5+ S 19 '64

PULLMAN porters. See Porters

PULMONARY edema. See Edema

PULMONARY embolism. See Embolism

PULMONARY emphysema. See Emphysema

PULP, paper and paperboard institute (U.S.A) incorporated
New paper trade organization formed. Pub W 185:113 My 4 '64

PULP and paper research institute of Canada
They know their target. D. B. Huyck. il Am For 71:18-21+ Ja '65

PULP wood industry. See Wood pulp industry

PULPY kidney disease. See Sheep—Diseases and pests

PULVER, Dorothy
Ordeal of Dorothy Pulver. T. Morris. il pors Redbook 122:58-9+ Mr '64

PUMA hunting
Cougar chase. K. Hueftle. il Outdoor Life 133:74-5+ Ap '64
Cougar for everybody. L. Miracle. il Outdoor Life 134:44-7+ D '64
Cougar nightmare; ed. by K. Crandall. E. B. Hilderbrand. il Outdoor Life 132:20-3+ Jl '63
Lions almost anytime. I. Morden. il Outdoor Life 131:46-9+ Ja '63
Lions beat them all; ed. by S. P. English, jr. G. Acosta. il Outdoor Life 131:64-7+ My '63

PUMAS

Capture

See Animals—Capture

PUMP priming. See Government spending policy

PUMP; story. See Humphrey, W.

PUMPHREY, Arthur
Portrait of gazelle. Theatre Arts 47:16-18 F '63

PUMPING engines. See Fire apparatus. Motor

PUMPING stations
Back to the river after seventy years; Lowell, Mass. E. J. Tierney and B. Cassidy. il Am City 78:74-6 Ag '63
Fallout filters; Oak Harbor, Wash. J. Buckner. il Am City 78:107-8 Je '63

PUMPING stations—*Continued*
Gas-fueled engine cuts pumping costs 58 per cent; Glendale, Ariz. il Am City 79:145 F '64
Simple control for a complex system; delivering Atoka reservoir water in Oklahoma City. D. B. Benham. il Am City 78:81-3 Ap '63
PUMPKIN faces. See Halloween
PUMPKINS
See also
Cookery—Vegetables
PUMPS
How to muffle a pool pump. il Sunset 133:90 Jl '64
New pump test center: Allis-Chalmers Norwood works. il Am City 78:90 D '63
Water pressure abroad; ten steps to choosing the right system; questions and answers. H. Holcomb. il Motor B 113:42-3 My '64
See also
Vacuum pumps
PUMPS, Fuel. See Fuel pumps
PUNCH (beverage)
Make a fragrant May-wine punch. Sunset 130:254 My '63
Punch. il Good H 157:92-3 D '63
Put punch in your entertaining. Am Home 66:18 D '63
Sparkling rose wine punch. il Ebony 18:188+ S '63
PUNCHED card systems
Fields for edge-punched filing cards. A. G. Newcombe. il Science 140:1312-13 Je 21 '63
PUNCHED tapes. See Data tapes
PUNCHES
Self-hammering layout punch. W. E. Burton. il Pop Sci 184:152-3 My '64
PUNCTUALITY
See also
Tardiness
PUNCTUATION
Emily Dickinson: poetry and punctuation. E. P. Stamm. il Sat R 46:26-7+ Mr 30 '63; Reply. T. Ward. 46:25 Ap 27 '63; Rejoinder. 46:23 My 25 '63
PUNCTUATION proclamation: drama. See Boiko, C.
PUNER, Helen
Homework for doting grandparents. Parents Mag 40:40-1+ Ja '65
Passing of Univac I; poem. N Y Times Mag p 104 O 20 '63
PUNISHMENT
Special supplement on crime and punishment; symposium. il Harper 228:121-36+ Ap '64; Discussion. 228:6+ Je '64
See also
Corporal punishment
PUNJAB, India
Pumping out the Punjab; world's largest irrigation project. Pop Sci 184:24+ Ja '64
PUPAE. See Insects—Development
PUPIL (eye)
Pupil size in relation to mental activity during simple problem-solving. E. H. Hess and J. M. Polt. bibliog il Science 143:1190-2 Mr 13 '64
PUPIL assistants in libraries. See School libraries—Student assistants
PUPILS letters. See Letters
PUPPETS and puppet plays
Cartons make rainy-day puppet stage. il Pop Mech 119:145 Ap '63
Hand puppets for Easter. il Sunset 130:151 Ap '63
Marionettes with music; Salzburg Marionettes at Town Hall. il N Y Times Mag p 126-7 D 13 '64
Moscow magic; Obratsov puppets. il Newsweek 62:77 O 14 '63
Playback puppetry; pre-recorded puppet shows. E. Welch. il Design 65:15 S '63
Puppet theatre from Moscow. F. Bowers. il Theatre Arts 47:24-5 O '63
Puppets in an hour by children. S. Salus. il Sch Arts 63:11-13 O '63
Scrap pile puppets. A. Mulbach. il Design 64:196-7 Je '63
Set the stage for make-believe with a marionette theatre you can build yourself. il House & Gard 126:250-1+ N '64
Theatre; Obratsov puppets. H. Clurman. Nation 197:268 O 26 '63
Three-cornered achievement. D. A. Paul. il Sch Arts 63:18-19 F '64
Will it go on B'way? Obraztsov puppet show. T. Prideaux. il Life 55:9+ S 13 '63
PURCELL, Edna Jean
Delightful daylilies. Pop Gard 15:32-3+ Ap '64
Summer is the big season for day-lilies. Flower Grower 50:28-9+ Jl '63
PURCELL, Henry
On records; Dido and Aeneas. Opera N 27:32 My 4 '63
Purcell's Dido and Aeneas freshly achieved. C. L. Osborne. il Hi Fi 13:71 F '63
PURCELL, J. Q.
Jimmy Bennett doesn't work here any more; story. New Yorker 40:38-9 Mr 14 '64
PURCELL, Pearl G.
National development and international education. Sch & Soc 92:209-10 My 2 '64
PURCELL, Theodore V.
Jesuit at Dartmouth. America 108:534-6+ Ap 20 '63
PURCELL, William L.
Buddhist chant. Am Rec G 30:806-8 My '64
Imperial court music of Japan. Am Rec G 31:118-19 O '64
Knock on the door. Library J 88:526+ F 1 '63
PURCHASING
See also
Consumers
Consumption (economics)
Quality of products
Shopping and shoppers
PURCHASING, County
Cooperative purchasing; Broward County, Fla. A. C. Dobay. il Am City 78:134+ My '63
Power-packed purchasing; Suffolk County, Riverhead, L.I, N.Y. S. P. Mitman. Am City 79:122-3 D '64
PURCHASING, Government
Certification for public purchasing agents; proposed at Governmental purchasing institute meeting. il Am City 80:91-2 Ja '65
$40 billion customer will buy more. Nations Bsns 53:38-9 Ja '65
See also
Contracts, Government
United States—Armed forces—Procurement
PURCHASING, Household
See also
Food—Prices
Quality of products

Terminology

Shopper's dictionary. il Changing T 18:27-32 Je '64
PURCHASING, Industrial
Buy by computer. J. W. Widing, jr. and C. G. Diamond. il Harvard Bsns R 42:109-20 Mr '64
Gentle art of stitch-in-timemanship; trade relations director. il Bsns W p74 My 11 '63
How to cut purchasing costs. L. Blumenthal. il Duns R 83:53-4+ Mr '64
Purchasing; From rags to riches. L. Morse. il Duns R 81:54-6+ My '63
When bottlenecks need to be broken. il Bsns W p47-8 Ag 29 '64
PURCHASING, Municipal
Biggest discount house in Virginia. G. L. Nunnally. Am City 79:98 S '64
Centralized purchasing system; El Dorado, Kan. G. L. Schrader. il Am City 78:108-9 S '63
Combine your purchases and save; Tacoma, Wash. L. A. Menconi. il Am City 78:83 D '63
Joint purchasing; Lower Makefield Township, Pa. W. H. Struwe. Am City 79:166+ Je '64
Just-right purchasing; DeLand, Fla. R. L. Kirchof. il Am City 79:136+ F '64
Little purchases cost lots; limited-purchase-order system; Philadelphia. O. R. Winter. Am City 79:150+ Ap '64
Low bid, generally not the best; Los Angeles, Calif. W. L. Lintz. il Am City 79:115-16 Mr '64
Master emergency dispatch systems. il Am City 79:197-8 Je '64
Municipal purchasing and public relations. E. J. Brewer. il Am City 78:98-9 Ag '63
Neighbor-to-neighbor purchasing plan; Pennsylvania. R. R. Moore. il Am City 79:160+ O '64
New government+centralized purchasing=increased efficiency; Elizabeth, N.J. S. H. Stone. il Am City 78:102-3 Ap '63
Purchasing for pennies a serving; Cincinnati, Ohio. J. G. Krieg. Am City 79:80 Jl '64
Purchasing forum attracts new bidders. O. R. Winter. il Am City 79:97 Ag '64
Purchasing manual is a must; Little Rock, Ark. A. M. Douthit and F. B. Peek. il Am City 78:89 N '63
Seven steps to better municipal purchasing; Middletown, Ohio. K. A. Jefferies. il Am City 79:118+ My '64

PURCHASING, Municipal—*Continued*
Two new purchasing procedures; Springfield, Mo. B. H. Jones and W. Kane. il Am City 78:117-18 Mr '63
Vendor-relations office; New York (city) R. J. Browne. Am City 78:153 O '63
Voluntary cooperative purchasing: Los Angeles County, Calif. V. W. Quam. Am City 79:92 Ja '64
We shopped around, and saved; Cincinnati, Ohio. J. G. Krieg. il Am City 78:99 Jl '63
What Tennessee cities are buying. il Am City 78:158+ Je '63

PURCHASING departments, Municipal. See Purchasing, Municipal

PURCHASING of water. See Water supply

PURDEY, James and sons, limited
Factory where time stands still. il Bsns W p84-7 Ap 13 '63

PURDIE, A. B.
Janua coeli; Domus aurea; poems. Cath World 199:27 Ap '64

PURDUE university, Lafayette, Ind.
Who believes whom? R. Moley. Newsweek 61:86 Ap 1 '63

Libraries

Purdue analyzes growth of ARL member libraries. Library J 89:4768 D 1 '64

PURDY, James Otis
Color of darkness; dramatization. See Violett, E.

about

James Purdy: American dreams. W. Schott. Nation 198:300-2 Mr 23 '64
WLB biography. E. Geller. por Wilson Lib Bul 38:572+ Mr '64

PURDY, Ken W.
End of an era at Indy. Sat Eve Post 237:60-2 My 30 '64
England. Atlan 211:118+ F '63
Look fast, think pink. Sat Eve Post 237:60-1 O 31 '64
Prince Philip: England's most misunderstood man. Look 28:30+ Ap 7 '64
Wankel. Atlan 215:109-10 Ja '65
(ed) See Moss, S. How to drive and survive
—See Moss, S. jt. auth.

PURDY, William
New Vatican approach to communism. Cath World 197:216-22 Jl '63

PURE oil company
Lure for pure. il Time 84:79 Jl 3 '64
New suitor bids for Pure oil's favors. il Bsns W p20 Jl 4 '64

PUREX corporation
Consumer reports vs. Purex: case dismissed. Consumer Rep 28:471 O '63
Guerrilla war on soap giants. il Bsns W p50-2 Ag 29 '64

PURIFICATION of water. See Water purification

PURINES
Actinomycin: correlation of structure and function of its complexes with purines and DNA. E. Reich. bibliog il Science 143:684-9 F 14 '64
Purine- and pyrimidine-specific antibodies: effect on the fertilized sea urchin egg. H. S. Rosenkranz and others. bibliog il Science 145:282-3 Jl 17 '64
See also
Adenine

I PURITANI; opera. See Bellini, V.

PURITANISM
See also
Puritans

PURITANS
Puritans against sex? no, says sociologist. Sci N L 85:20 Ja 11 '64

PUROMYCIN
Actinomycin and puromycin: effects on sequential gene activation by ecdysone. U. Clever. bibliog il Science 146:794-5 N 6 '64
Intestinal phosphatase activity; acceleration of increase by puromycin and actinomycin. F. Moog. bibliog il Science 144:414-16 Ap 24 '64
Memory in mice as affected by intracerebral puromycin. J. B. Flexner and others. bibliog il Science 141:57-9 Jl 5 '63
Puromycin effect on memory fixation in the goldfish. B. W. Agranoff and P. D. Klinger. bibliog il Science 146:952-3 N 13 '64
Reversal of thyroxine-induced hypermetabolism by puromycin. W. P. Weiss and L. Sokoloff. bibliog il Science 140:1324-6 Je 21 '63
Streptomycinoid antibiotics: synergism by puromycin. J. R. White and H. L. White. bibliog il Science 146:772-4 N 6 '64

PURPLE heart. See Decorations of honor

PURPLE martins. See Martins

PURPURA, Dominick P. and Waelsch, H.
Brain reflexes. Science 143:598+ F 7 '64
—See Goldensohn, E. S. jt. auth.

PURSES
Survival kit: the pick of the pocketbook. il Mlle 58:185 Ap '64

PURSGLOVE, S. David
A-power: creeping giant. Pop Mech 119:100-4+ Je '63
Cold war race for a missile killer. Pop Mech 121:122-5+ Ja '64
How space detectives rate Russia's moon probes. Pop Mech 119:89-93+ Mr '63
Look what those knucklehead machines are doing! Read Digest 82:278-80 Ap '63
Make sure your brake fluid won't kill you. Pop Mech 120:98-100+ S '63
Out of this world life detectors. Pop Mech 119:72-5 Je '63
Riddle of the black boxes. Pop Mech 120:86-91+ Ag '63
Sub rescues, four miles deep. Pop Mech 120:69-73+ Ag '63
War preventers. Pop Mech 119:106-11+ F '63
Will we pass up the moon for Mars? Pop Mech 120:104-8+ N '63

PURSHIA tridents. See Bitterbrush

PURTELL, Joseph
Business-wise editor. Sat Eve Post 236:74 Je 1 '63
SEC reforms to help, not hamstring. il por Newsweek 61:76+ Ap 15 '63

PURVES, Edmund Randolph
Edmund Randolph Purves dies at sixty-six. por Arch Rec 135:26 My '64

PURVIS, Hoyt H.
French higher education. Sat R 47:60-1+ Ag 15 '64

PUSEY, Nathan M.
University comes of age; adaptation of address, October 4, 1963. Sch & Soc 92:286-9 O 17 '64

PUSH button telephone. See Telephone, Push button

PUSHKIN, Aleksandr Sergeevich
Attaboy, Pushkin. por Newsweek 64:103+ N 30 '64
Letters of Alexander Pushkin, tr. with preface, introduction, and notes, by J. T. Shaw. Review
Sat R por 47:34-5 My 30 '64. E. J. Simmons
Smiling sigh. J. W. Stedman. Opera N 28:24-5 F 29 '64
Variations on a Russian verse. N. Rosen. il Sat R 47:25-6 N 28 '64; Discussion. 47:17 D 19 '64

PUSIE, Jean Baptiste
Hockey in the slapstick style. S. Fischler. il por Sports Illus 18:E3-4 F 11 '63

PUSS in boots; drama. See Thane, A.

PUSSY willow. See Willow

PUT-down (game) See Games

PUT it in writing; revue. See Musical comedies, revues, etc.—Criticisms, plots, etc.

PUTNAM, Carleton
Scientific racism; a reply. New Repub 148:29-31 F 23 '63

PUTNAM, Donald H.
Higher profit margin called avionics need; address. por Aviation W 81:105+ O 26 '64

PUTNAM, John F.
Information about dropouts: terms and computations. bibliog por Sch Life 45:24-9 My '63

PUTNAM, Judith. See Stokvis, I. E. jt. ed.

PUTNAM, Leon J.
To freeze or not to freeze. Christian Cent 81:1206+ S 30 '64

PUTNAM, Morris
Why I go-it-alone with broilers; ed. by J. Dyer. por Farm J 87:75 Jl '63

PUTNAM, Peter
If you had a choice. Sat R 46:29+ O 26 '63

PUTNAM, William Lowell
Mountain leadership on the trail. Recreation 56:240-2 My '63

PUTNAM'S, G. P, sons
Lancer edition starts Candy paperback scramble. Pub W 187:103-4 Ja 18 '65
Schlesinger protests use of quote in promotion of Buckley title. A. Schlesinger, jr. Pub W 183:12-13 Ap 22 '63; Reply with rejoinder. W. F. Buckley, jr. 183:31 Ap 29 '63

PUTTEN, Lodewijk van
Thymectomy: effect on secondary disease in radiation chimeras. bibliog Science 145:935-6 Ag 28 '64

PUTTERS (golf) See Golf clubs (sticks)

PUTTING (golf)
Pick a spot, then hit the putt firmly. J. Nicklaus. il Sports Illus 20:47 Ja 20 '64
Way under par in a parking lot; National putting championship. P. Downey. il Sports Illus 19:16-17 Jl 15 '63
Your putting stroke is fine for the short chip. J. Nicklaus. il Sports Illus 19:69 O 14 '63
PUTTING away childish things; story. See Schoen, B.
PUTZ, Louis J.
Unfinished reformation: a Catholic view. Christian Cent 81:109-21 Ja 22 '64
PUYALLUP, Wash.
Storm-sewer design factors. C. S. Seabrook. il Am City 79:76-8 Jl '64
PUYANA, Rafael
Recordings. M. Mayer. Esquire 61:38+ Je '64
PUZZLES
Art for puzzles' sake; Jackson Pollock jigsaw. il Newsweek 64:94 D 14 '64
Four-minute challenges. J. Leopold. il Read Digest 86:160B Ja '65
Hypnotic fascination of sliding-block puzzles. M. Gardner. il Sci Am 210:122+ F '64
See also
Anagrams
Crossword puzzles
PYE, Durwood T.
Judge Pye and the hundred sit-ins. B. M. Galphin. New Repub 150:8-9 My 30 '64
Shoofly Pye. il por Time 83:58 Ap 17 '64
Straws in the wind. Reporter 31:22+ S 24 '64
PYELONEPHRITIS. See Kidneys—Diseases
PYGMALION; drama. See Shaw, G. B.
PYGMIES
Little people; pygmy cemetery at Coshocton. H. C. Wolfe. Sat R 47:71 N 7 '64
PYGMY chameleon. See Chameleons
PYLE, Gene
(ed) Five photographers talk color & lenses. Pop Phot 54:82-91+ Ap '64
How to flatter your subject. il Pop Phot 53:138-9 N '63
PYLE, Howard
Apple of contentment; dramatization. See Thane, A.
Frank E. Schoonover: an exemplar of the Pyle tradition. H. C. Pitz. Am Artist 28: 64-9+ N '64
PYLE, William C. See Cohen, S. jt. auth.
PYLEE, M. V.
Challenge for Indian leadership. Cur Hist 46: 78-82+ F '64
PYM, John
Ice age; poem. Poetry 103:368-9 Mr '64
PYNCHON, Thomas
Secret integration; story. Sat Eve Post 237: 36-7 D 19 '64
PYRACANTHA. See Firethorns
PYRAMIDE, Vienne. See Restaurants—France
PYRAMIDS
Search for the first intellectual; hidden tomb of Imhotep. il Time 85:58 Ja 15 '65
PYRAZOLE
Interest grows in new Echo II pyrazole controlled-inflation scheme. M. Getler. il Miss & Roc 13:18 D 23 '63
PYRIMIDINES
Purine- and pyrimidine-specific antibodies: effect on the feritilized sea urchin egg. H. S. Rosenkranz and others. bibliog il Science 145:282-3 Jl 17 '64
PYROCERAM
Cookware tablemates for Centura settings. il Consumer Rep 29:4 Ja '64
Pyroceram for the table. il Consumer Rep 28: 461-2 O '63
PYROGENS
Endogenous pyrogen release from rabbit blood cells incubated in vitro with parainfluenza virus. E. Atkins and others. bibliog il Science 146:1469-70 D 11 '64
PYROXYLIN
Thin membranes of parlodion. N. Lakshminarayanaiah and A. M. Shanes. il Science 141:43-4 Jl 5 '63
PYRUS calleryana. See Chinese pear
PYRUVATE dehydrogenases. See Dehydrogenases
PYRUVATES
Pyruvate metabolism and control: factors affecting pyruvic carboxylase activity. A. D. Freedman and L. Kohn. bibliog il Science 145:58-60 Jl 3 '64
PYTHAGOREAN proposition
Clock paradox. J. Bronowski. il Sci Am 208: 134-6+ bibliog(p 186) F '63
Mathematical games; simple proofs of the Pythagorean theorem. M. Gardner. il Sci Am 211:118-20+ bibliog(p 144) O '64
PYTKOWICZ, Ricardo M. and Conners, D. N.
High pressure solubility of calcium carbonate in seawater. bibliog Science 144:840-1 My 15 '64

Q

Q meters. See Electric meters
QUAAL, Ward L.
Let's put America back to work; address, July 2, 1963. Vital Speeches 29:732-5 S 15 '63
QUACK grass. See Grasses
QUACKS and quackery
AMA, the FDA and quacks. J. Ridgeway. New Repub 149:31-3 N 9 '63
Biggest quackery racket. F. Marley. il Sci N L 84:291 N 9 '63
Crackdown on quackery; with report by O. Field. il Life 55:72B-81+ N 1 '63
Don't buy these remedies; arthritis quackery. il Sci Digest 55:60 Ja '64
Don't get trapped by a psychoquack. H. Kursh. il Todays Health 42:28-31+ Mr '64
Four horsemen of quackery: fear, gullibility, deceit, and deadlines. D. F. Ward. Todays Health 43:10+ Ja '65
Hucksters of pain; Ball clinic, Excelsior Springs, Mo. R. L. Smith. il Sat Eve Post 236:83-7 Ag 24 '63
Marriage counselors, helpers and hurters. P. Streit. il N Y Times Mag p26+ N 3 '63
Quack medical machines. J. P. McNeel. il Pop Mech 120:107-11+ O '63
Quackery gives vain hope. F. Marley. Sci N L 84:277 N 2 '63
Quacktitioners in the Old West; excerpts from Doctor on the frontier. R. Dunlop. il Todays Health 42:40-1+ N '64
Six myths of the health cults. S. S. Steinberg. Todays Health 42:8-10 Ja '64
Some pills and formulas that are under fire; Congress on medical quackery. U S News 55:10 N 4 '63
Strange world of mechanical quackery. R. L. Smith. il Todays Health 42:42-7+ N '64
What the health hucksters are up to. il Changing T 18:24-9 S '64
Writing an Rx on quacks; AMA and FDA national conference on quackery in medicine. il Bsns W p32-3 N 2 '63
QUADE, Quentin L.
Tension in U.S. politics. America 110:312-13 Mr 7 '64
World resounds: Milwaukee. America 109: 770 D 14 '63
QUADRIPLEGIA. See Paralysis
QUADRI-science, incorporated
Brains lay a nest egg; exchange of securities with EON corp. il Bsns W p74 D 28 '63
QUADROS, Jânio da Silva
Most dangerous man in Brazil. J. Dos Passos. il Nat R 15:53-7 Jl 30 '63
QUADRUPLETS
Fultz quads debut at Zeta cotillion. il Ebony 19:56-8+ Ap '64
Happy miracle in Lima, Ohio; Axe family. A. E. Farrell. il Good H 157:86-7+ S '63
How to be a loser with four aces; Axe family of Lima, Ohio. M. Cope. il Sat Eve Post 237:28-30 Je 6 '64
Nation's newest identical quads; Chicago's famous Harris quadruplets. il Ebony 19: 138-40+ N '63
Wide awake for quads; Axe family of Lima, Ohio. il Time 81:47 Mr 15 '63
QUAHOGS. See Clams
QUAIL pens
Quail recall pen. G. B. Evans. il Field & S 69:120-1+ N '64
QUAIL shooting
Florida quail cruise. C. Dickey. il Field & S 68:31-3+ N '63
I learn about quail. C. Dickey. il Outdoor Life 132:28-31+ N '63
I love a quail named Gambel. N. Riley. il Outdoor Life 132:50-1+ Ag '63
Oh, I'll never go there anymore. C. E. Gillham. il Field & S 67:50-2+ Ap '63
Quail guns and loads. J. O'Connor. il Outdoor Life 134:58-60+ N '64

QUAIL shooting—*Continued*
Quail shoot with a twist. P. Czura. il Field & S 69:48-9 Je '64
Tidewater quail. T. Janes. il Outdoor Life 134:28-9+ N '64
Tied up by topknots. J. Van Wormer. il Outdoor Life 132:62-3+ O '63
Upland shooting down on Florida's Gold Coast. V. Kraft. il Sports Illus 18:52+ Mr 4 '63
Valleys of the West. C. Conley. il Field & S 69:82-5 O '64

QUAILS
Backyard survey: how bobwhites form a covey. V. E. Davison. Audubon Mag 66:52-5 Ja '64
How to stock wild birds. A. MacBain. il Field & S 68:92-3 D '63
Rescuing the masked quail. Nat Parks Mag 37:17 Mr '63
Sex-linked albinism in the Japanese quail. J. K. Lauber. bibliog il Science 146:948-50 N 13 '64
What's happening to bob white? H. Babcock. il Field & S 68:34-6+ D '63
You can talk to quail. D. H. Chapman. il Field & S 69:8-9+ Ja '65

QUAISON-SACKEY, Alex
Human rights day 1964; message. UN Mo Chron 1:i D '64
about
Alex Quaison-Sackey, president of the General assembly. por UN Mo Chron 2:112 Ja '65
Ambassador from Ghana. New Yorker 39:20-2 Ag 3 '63
New U.N. president: critic of the U.S. il por U S News 57:22 D 14 '64
Something new. por Newsweek 64:29 D 14 '64
Topsy-turvy land. Nat R 15:90+ Ag 13 '63

QUAKERS. See Friends, Society of

QUALIFICATIONS of teachers. See Teachers—Qualifications

QUALITY control
Building in the old reliable; reliability engineering. il Bsns W p 178+ Mr 21 '64
Cosmic clinic for the moon rocket. C. B. Hicks. il Pop Mech 120:84-7+ S '63
Golden key to production profits. H. E. Klein. il Duns R 81:50-2+ Ap '63
Technique predicts reliability of avionics before initial system design work begins. P. J. Klass. il Aviation W 80:76-7+ Ja 6 '64
Zero defects campaign gets DOD impetus. K. Johnsen. Aviation W 81:63+ N 30 '64
See also
Sampling (statistical methods)

QUALITY of products
Advertising needs standards to prove claims. Consumer Bul 46:6-7 S '63
Business plans new sales surge; symposium. il Nations Bsns 52:33-5+ F '64
Buyer's lot is not always so unhappy. Consumer Rep 28:206-8 My '63
Buying guide issue. il Consumer Rep 29:1-432 D '64
Christmas amnesty. Consumer Rep 28:508-9 N '63
Consumers sue for defective products. Consumer Bul 47:43+ N '64
Do shoppers need help from the government? pro and con discussion. E. Peterson; R. H. Levi. il Changing T 18:7-12 Ag '64
Expensive tastes. Duns R 84:94 O '64
Guide to your buying guide (cont) il Consumer Rep 28:5-30 D '63
How do you pick the next winner? il Bsns W p81 My 16 '64
Important court decisions favor consumers. Consumer Bul 46:36-7 Mr '63
Important letters for prudent boatmen: YSB. B. Woodward. il Motor B 113:50-1 Mr '64
Imports will sharpen business skills; symposium. il Nations Bsns 51:36-7+ Ag '63
Institute report on. . . il Good H 158:6 My '64
NASA sets uniform reliability guidelines. Aviation W 79:72+ S 30 '63
Necessary rumpus: West Germany's DM magazine for rating consumer products. il Time 82:68-9 Ag 9 '63
Now they're selling quality! J. B. Weiner. il Duns R 82:59-60+ O '63
Quality at Kodak. T. R. Brooks. il Duns R 81:33-5+ Je '63
Quality is like money in the bank. Bet Hom & Gard 41:30+ My '63
Rating unknown power transformers. H. Q. Duguid. il Electr World 72:24-5 Jl '64
Reliability engineering. G. A. W. Boehm. il Fortune 67:124-7+ Ap '63
Roughing it around the world; Anglo-African trans-world safari. il Bsns W p48 Ja 26 '63
Scepter for king consumer; in California. il Bsns W p 106+ Mr 30 '63
Shopper's guide to bargain sales. il Changing T 17:7-11 F '63
Speaker for the house. C. Montgomery. See issues of Good housekeeping
Why don't they give the customer a break? il Changing T 17:7-12 S '63
Why spaceships work, tractors don't; Russian manufactures. U S News 54:46-7 My 6 '63
See also
Aerospace industries—Quality control
Consumers' research, incorporated
Quality control
Testing

QUALITY stabilization bill. See Price maintenance by industry

QUALTINGER, Helmut
Off Broadway; one-man show at Barbizon-Plaza. E. Oliver. New Yorker 39:94-5 N 2 '63
Profiles. J. Wechsberg. por New Yorker 39:53-4+ Ap 20 '63

QUAM, Victor W.
Voluntary cooperative purchasing. Am City 79:92 Ja '64

QUANG, Thich-tri-. See Thich-tri-Quang

QUANT, Mary
Adventurous ones. il por Vogue 142:75 Ag 1 '63

QUANTASOMES. See Chloroplasts

QUANTUM electrodynamics
Quantized magnetic flux in superconductors. R. D. Parks. bibliog il Science 146:1429-35 D 11 '64

QUANTUM theory
Giant quantum effect detected by scientists. Sci N L 85:159 Mr 7 '64
Quantum devices, how they work. J. R. Collins. il Electr World 70:39-41+ D '63
Understanding physics today. by W. H. Watson. Review
Sci Am 209:145-6+ O '63
See also
Mössbauer effect
Raman effect
Time reversal

QUARANTINE
Annals of medicine; inspection of the France by New York quarantine station. B. Roueché. New Yorker 39:174+ O 12 '63

QUARLES, Benjamin
Frederick Douglass; reprint. Negro Hist Bul 26:182+ Mr '63

QUARRELS
Fight promoter for the battle of the sexes. S. Alexander. il Life 54:102-4+ My 17 '63
How to win arguments with your parents. J. Hawkes. Seventeen 22:120-1+ N '63

QUARTERBACKS. See Football players

QUARTZ
Coesite and shocked quartz from Holleford Crater, Ontario, Canada. T. E. Bunch and A. J. Cohen. bibliog il Science 142:379-81 O 18 '63
Coesite and stishovite: stepwise reversal transformations. F. Dachille and others. bibliog il Science 140:991-3 My 31 '63

QUARTZ crystals
Quartz: anomalous weakness of synthetic crystals. D. T. Griggs and J. D. Blacic. bibliog il Science 147:292-5 Ja 15 '65
Understanding frequency-control crystals. R. L. Conhaim. il Electr World 71:36-8+ My '64

QUASARS. See Radio astronomy

QUASI-stellar objects. See Radio astronomy

QUASI-stellar radio sources. See Radio astronomy

QUAYLE, Oliver. See Alsop, S. jt. auth.

QUEBEC (city)
Queen & the chill. il Time 84:53 O 16 '64
Description
French touch: Quebec. R. Carson. il Holiday 35:72-3+ Ap '64
Wintertime, and the livin' is freezy. H. Sutton. il Sat R 46:22-5 F 9 '63

QUEBEC (province)
Atlantic report. Atlan 213:34+ Je '64
Bombers; Quebec liberation front (FLQ) Newsweek 61:49 Je 3 '63
Bombs in the quiet land. Time 81:20 My 31 '63
Can French Canada stand alone? M. Faribault. Atlan 214:135-9 N '64
Canada: a house dividing? il Sr Schol 84:8-10+ Ap 10 '64
Canada's crisis. M. R. MacGuigan. Commonweal 79:747-9 Mr 20 '64; Reply. R. A. Jones. 80:121-2 Ap 17 '64

QUEBEC (province)—*Continued*
Case for an independent Quebec. J. Moore. Harper 229:93-5+ O '64
De Gaulle's Canadian beachhead. J. D. Harbron. Commonweal 80:256-7 My 22 '64
Diefenbaker falls: did he jump or was he pushed? il Newsweek 61:36 F 18 '63
Fidel's disciple; Front de libération Québecois (FLQ) il Time 81:40 Je 14 '63
Fissionable material; raids by Army for the liberation of Quebec. il Newsweek 63:42+ Mr 9 '64
French Canada's strange revolt; role of FLQ (Quebec liberation front) L. Bergquist. il Look 27:90-4+ D 3 '63
French connection. il Time 82:42 O 25 '63
If Quebec secedes from Canada— il U S News 56:48 Mr 9 '64
In French Canada, vive la difference. il Bsns W p64-5+ O 12 '63
Letter from Quebec. M. Schleifer. Nation 199:386-9 N 23 '64
Now secession talk in Canada's biggest province. il U S News 54:60-1 Ap 1 '63
Quebec guerrillas; Canada faces secession. R. E. Spencer. il Nation 198:283-6 Mr 23 '64
Quebec in revolt. W. E. Griffith. For Affairs 43:29-36 O '64
Quebec revolution. A. Harrigan. il Cath World 199:109-15 My '64
Rallying round a flag. Time 83:33 My 29 '64
Reporter at large; an American's notes on Canadian culture. E. Wilson. il New Yorker 40:143-4+ N 28 '64
Rise of the separatists; raids by Quebec liberation army. Time 83:39 Mr 6 '64
Secessionists on the march. New Repub 149:10 Ag 31 '63
Trailer cruising northeast. E. R. Thornton. il Motor B 111:32-4+ Ap '63
Tremblant: big wilderness; ideal camping, fishing, boating. C. B. Colby. il Outdoor Life 133:22-4+ Je '64
Trouble with Quebec. G. Pelletier. il Atlan 214:115-18 N '64
Trying to blast a nation apart; Le Front de liberation Quebecois (FLQ) il Bsns W p 100+ Je 1 '63
Words, threats, death; Quebec liberation front. Newsweek 61:58 My 6 '63
See also
Anticosti island
French Canadians
Gaspé
Laurentian Mountains

QUEBEC Labrador airways. See Airlines—Canada

QUECHUA Indians. See Indians of South America—Peru

QUEEN bees. See Bees

QUEEN Elisabeth competition for pianists. See Music—Competitions

QUEEN Elisabeth violin competition. See Music—Competitions

QUEENS, N.Y.

Housing

Sam Lefrak; he builds them cheaper by the dozen; Lefrak City apartment project. D. B. Carlson. il Arch Forum 118:102-5 Ap '63

Negroes

Mason-Dixon line in Queens; Junction boulevard, between Jackson Heights and Corona. F. Powledge. il N Y Times Mag p 12+ My 10 '64

Stores

See also
Macy, R. H. and company

QUEENS borough public library
Operation head start. H. W. Tucker. il Library J 89:3382-3 S 15 '64

QUEENS college, New York
New facility provides five dining rooms. il Arch Rec 134:136-7 Ag '63

QUEEN'S gallery. See London—Galleries and museums

QUENNELL, Peter
First and last Rose. Sat R 47:26 D 26 '64
In the glow of the perfect patron. Horizon 5:62-71 Mr '63
Magpie's nest in a London mansion. Horizon 5:72-83 N '63
Shakespeare: mask and face. Mlle 58:74-5+ F '64

QUENTIN, Ames Rowe
Remarks to a depressed patient; poem. New Yorker 39:110 Je 15 '63

QUEREE, R. C.
My most unforgettable character. Read Digest 85:164-6+ N '64

QUERVELLE, Antoine Gabriel
Antiques. A. Winchester. Antiques 83:429 Ap '63
Philadelphia empire furniture by Antoine Gabriel Quervelle. R. C. Smith. il Antiques 86:304-9 S '64

QUESTION of honor; story. See Holland, B.

QUESTIONING
Learning through inquiry. J. R. Suchman. NEA J 52:31-2 Mr '63
Myths we live by; excerpts from address. L. Rosten. Redbook 122:35+ Ja '64

QUESTIONS, Childrens. See Childrens questions

QUESTIONS and answers
Ask a foolish question. E. G. Smith. Atlan 213:164-5 Mr '64

QUETICO provincial park. See Ontario—Parks and reserves

QUETICO-SUPERIOR wilderness region. See Wilderness areas

QUEZADA, Abel
Most powerful country in the world; excerpt from Best of impossible worlds. Atlan 213:100-1 Mr '64

QUICHE. See Pastry

QUICK breads. See Bread

QUICKSAND
Quicksand, nature's terrifying death trap. M. Gunther. il Read Digest 85:140-4 D '64

QUICKSILVER. See Mercury

QUIET Christmas; drama. See Hark, M. and McQueen, N.

QUIET island; story. See Bates, D.

QUIET night in jail; story. See Lorning, R.

QUIETUDE. See Silence

QUIGG, Floyd B.
Feel of the forest. Am For 69:28-31+ N '63
Sky fire: how science fights it. Am For 69:12-15+ O '63

QUIGG, Philip W.
Latin America: a broad-brush appraisal. For Affairs 42:399-412 Ap '64

QUIGLEY, Mike
(ed) See Sandburg, C. Carl Sandburg

QUIGLEY, Thomas B.
Do professional sports set a good example for our kids? Todays Health 42:16+ O '64

QUILES, Ismael
Man and the world. Américas 16:14-17 Ja '64
Twain shall meet. por Américas 17:6-9 Ja '65

QUILLEN, James H.
Excerpt from testimony, April 22, 1964. Cong Digest 43:278+ N '64

QUILTING
Quilting. il House & Gard 123:140-3 Mr '63

QUILTS
Virginia reel quilt, Americana for moderns. il Good H 157:162 S '63

QUIMBY, M. C. See Wolf, K. jt. auth.

QUIN, Louis D.
2-Aminoethylphosphonic acid in insoluble protein of the sea anemone metridium dianthus. bibliog Science 144:1133-4 My 29 '64

QUIN, Windham Thomas Wyndham-, 4th earl of Dunraven. See Dunraven , W. T. W.-Q.

QUINAULT, LAKE
Down the Quinault in a cedar dugout. il Sunset 130:22+ Je '63

QUINBY, Griffith E. See Dale, W. E. jt. auth.

QUINCES
See also
Cookery—Fruit

QUINCY, Fla.
Needed: more vote-ins. Nation 198:469-70 My 11 '64

QUINCY, Mass.

Historic houses, etc.

Peacefield; Adams mansion. il Travel 120:35-7 Jl '63

QUINE, W. V.
Foundations of mathematics; with biographical sketch. Sci Am 211:30, 112-16+ bibliog (p269) S '64

QUININE
Malformed by quinine. Sci N L 84:54 Jl 27 '63

QUINLAN, Seàn
World resounds: Washington. America 109:769 D 14 '63

QUINN, Anthony
Redbook dialogue. pors Redbook 120:54-5+ Mr '63
Visit. J. Hamilton. il pors Look 28:52-9 Je 16 '64

QUINN, Doris Kerns
What makes a good sentimental greeting? Writer 77:21-4+ O '64

QUINN, James Brian, and Cavanaugh, R. M.
Fundamental research can be planned; excerpts from studies. Harvard Bsns R 42:111-24 Ja '64
—and Mueller, J. A.
Transferring research results to operations. Harvard Bsns R 41:49-66 Ja '63

QUINN, John
Hot team in the old town; Philadelphia Phillies. W. Leggett. il por Sports Illus 18:18-21 Ap 29 '63

QUINN, John R.
1.2 seconds per bill. Am City 78:105 My '63

QUINN, John Robert
Even as the night; poem. America 109:771 D 14 '63
Now; poem. America 111:559 N 7 '64
On finding beggar's-lice on an old sweater; poem. Christian Cent 81:1615 D 30 '64
This timelessness; poem. Commonweal 81:196 N 6 '64

QUINN, Kevin, pseud.
Parish anti's. America 108:748+ My 25 '63

QUINN, Noël
Noël Quinn on watercolor; with biographical sketch. il por Am Artist 27:44-9+ My '63

QUINN, Robert J.
Chicago fire department jets around. Am City 79:89 Jl '64
Snorkel Bob: Chicago's champion fire fighter. K. Detzer. il por Read Digest 85:117-20 Ag '64

QUINN, Thomas M.
Boundaries, buses and school boards. America 111:408-11 O 10 '64

QUINONES
1,4-benzoquinone tetracarboxylic acid dianhydride, $C_{10}O_8$; a strong acceptor. P. R. Hammond. bibliog il Science 142:502 O 25 '63

QUINT, Beverly
To a dead turtle; poem. New Yorker 39:30 Je 29 '63
View; poem. New Yorker 40:73 Jl 25 '64

QUINTANILLA, countess of
Countess of Quintanilla. il pors Vogue 141:110-17+ Mr 15 '63
Madrid's best-dressed U.S. beauty. il pors Life 57:85-6 O 9 '64

QUINTO, Felice
Call me Daddy. J. Morris. il U S Camera 28:82-5 Ja '65

QUINTUPLETS
54,000,000 to 1; Prieto family of Maracaibo, Venezuela and Fischer family of Aberdeen, S.D. il Time 82:96 S 20 '63
Fischer quints at home; ed. by J. Bird; with photographs by John Zimmerman. M. A. Fischer. il Sat Eve Post 237:18-27 My 2 '64
Fischer quintuplets million-dollar babies. U S News 55:10 S 30 '63
Five came to Aberdeen. A. Lake. il McCalls 91:106-7+ D '63
Five plus five; Fischer and Prieto quintuplets. il Newsweek 62:71 S 23 '63
Historic birth. M. Acoca. il Life 55:38B-39 S 20 '63
Moderns hail quints; primitives not so sure. Sci N L 84:201 S 28 '63
Mom, doc and those quints are just fine; Fischer quintuplets. il Life 55:34-34A O 4 '63
Mystery quints of Argentina; Diligenti quintuplets. H. H. Martin. il Sat Eve Post 237:38-43 Ja 25 '64
One month old, the quints get a parade; Fischer quintuplets. il Life 55:50 O 25 '63
Other babies who broke the odds; Venezuelan quintuplets, ed. by H. H. Martin. E. L. Prieto Nava; I. C. de Prieto. il Sat Eve Post 237:19-27 Ja 18 '64
Our life will never be the same; ed. by J. Bird. A. J. Fischer. il Sat Eve Post 236:25-44 N 16 '63
Pride of Aberdeen; Fischer quintuplets. il Time 82:62 S 27 '63
Quints and quin-tinis; the Fischer babies. il Newsweek 62:27-8 S 30 '63
Quints, anyone? R. P. Crossley. il Pop Sci 185:53-5+ S '64
Quintuplet story; symposium. il pors Ladies Home J 80:55-74 D '63
Quintuplets and other news from Aberdeen, S.D. H. Jones. il Redbook 122:42-3+ Ja '64
Remember the Diligentis? with report by M. Acoca. il Life 55:77-80+ D 13 '63
They are like little bulls; Prieto quintuplets. H. H. Martin. il Sat Eve Post 237:68-72 O 3 '64
Those quints come wriggling in; Fischer babies. il Life 55:40-42B S 27 '63
What a year it has been! Fischer quintuplets; ed. by J. Bird. M. A. Fischer. il Sat Eve Post 237:25-31 S 26 '64

QUINTUPLETS, Dionne. See Dionne family

QUIRKE, Lillian Mary
There is a place for programmed instruction in the teaching of the visual arts. Sch Arts 63:31-3 Mr '64

QUIST, Veronica M.
Ancient flavors for foods of the present, edible alliums. Horticulture 41:272-3 My '63
Centaur flowers. Horticulture 41:338-9 Je '63
Grandifloras are grand roses. Horticulture 41:216-17 Ap '63
Marigolds, so bright, so satisfactory. Horticulture 41:368-9 Jl '63
Phlox. Pop Gard 15:26+ Mr '64
Spice is the variety of life. Horticulture 42:14-15 Ja '64
This lamb belongs in the garden. Flower Grower 50:61 My '63
Try little iris for big results. Horticulture 41:176 Mr '63

QUITO, Ecuador
Sounds of sites. W. Cross. Travel 119:32-3 Mr '63

QUIVER (archery) See Archery—Equipment

QUIZ shows. See Radio broadcasting—Quiz programs; Television broadcasting—Quiz shows

QUIZZES. See Information tests

QUMRAN scrolls. See Dead Sea scrolls

QUODDY project. See Passamaquoddy tidal power project

QUOIREZ, Françoise. See Sagan, F. pseud.

QUOTAS, Agricultural. See Agricultural administration—United States

QUOTAS, Immigration. See Immigration and emigration—United States

QUOTAS, Import. See Import quotas

QUOTATIONS
Addenda to a scrapbook. Christian Cent 81:1047 Ag 19 '64; Reply. J. B. Simpson. 81:1404 N 11 '64
Big bite; quotations; comp. by N. Mailer. Esquire 60:50+ O '63
In quotes; comp. by W. A. Weiss. Sat R 46:55 My 18; 50 Je 15 '63
Quotable quotes. See issues of Reader's digest
Quotable quotes; excerpts from National book awards acceptance speeches. Writer 76:22 Je '63
Quotes: labor; comp. by E. F. Murphy. N Y Times Mag p24 S 6 '64
Reading matter; bookish quotes in honor of National library week; comp. by E. F. Murphy. il N Y Times Mag p 128 Ap 14 '63
Straw for the fire: from his notebooks; ed. by D. Wagoner. T. Roethke. Poetry 105:113-18 N '64
Words JFK loved best; ed. by J. L. Kennedy. il Look 28:84-90 N 17 '64
See also subhead Quotations, maxims, etc. under various subjects, e.g. Spring—Quotations, maxims, etc.

Il QUOTIDIANO. See Rome (city)—Newspapers

R

RCA. See Radio corporation of America

REA. See United States—Rural electrification administration

REIT. See Real estate investment trusts

RERC. See Real estate research corporation

RFI. See Radio interference

Rh factors
How, when, and why is a baby threatened by Rh trouble? G. G. Greer. Bet Hom & Gard 41:110-11 F '63
Tapping for Rh-factor; preventing stillbirths. Sci N L 86:71 Ag 1 '64
Transfusions in the womb. il Time 85:43 Ja 15 '65

RIFT (reaction in-flight test) See Rockets, Atomic powered

RNA. See Ribonucleic acid

ROMBUS (reusable orbital module: booster and utility shuttle) See Rockets, Military transport

ROTC. See United States—Reserve officers training corps

RPI. See Rensselaer polytechnic institute, Troy, N.Y.

RTCA. See Radio technical commission for aeronautics

RABASSA, Gregory
Four centuries of Latin letters. Sat R 46:4(O 12 '63
(tr) See Galvao, H. Price of the Azores

RABB, Theodore K.
Sir Edwin Sandys and the Parliament of 1604. bibliog f Am Hist R 69:646-70 Ap '64

RABBET joints. See Joints (carpentry)

RABBIS
Modern rabbi. J. J. Petuchowski. Commentary 35:153-8 F '63; Discussion. 36:172 Ag '63
New elders; chief rabbis elected. il Time 83:60 Mr 27 '64

RABBIT cages. See Cages

RABBIT hunting
Best rabbit insurance. P. Czura. il Field & S 69:94-5+ Ja '65
Camouflaged bunnies. R. Camp. il Field & S 68:28-30+ N '63
Christmas hasenpfeffer. E. A. Bauer. il Outdoor Life 132:28-31+ D '63
Cottontails to spare. C. Dickey. il Outdoor Life 131:64-5+ Ap '63
Cross and doublecross. B. Geagan. il Outdoor Life 133:42-3+ Ja '64
Hippity hop and away we go; San Juan Island in Puget Sound. V. Kraft. il Sports Illus 21:40-2+ S 28 '64
I eat words, and rabbits. J. B. Gleason. il Outdoor Life 132:38-9+ N '63
My hare turns white. B. East. il Outdoor Life 134:50-2+ D '64
Picture yourself. H. F. Zeman. il Outdoor Life 132:44-7+ Ag '63
Reunion with rabbits. G. X. Sand. il Outdoor Life 132:32-5+ Jl '63
Soho! the beagles. J. MacVane. il Field & S 68:35-7+ Ja '64

RABBITS and hares
New papovavirus contaminating Shope papillomata. J. W. Hartley and W. P. Rowe. bibliog il Science 143:258-60 Ja 17 '64

RABE, Olive. See Fisher, A. jt. auth.

RABIES
Bite that can kill. il Bsns W p36-7 Jl 4 '64
One man's battle against rabies; Alaska. C. McClain. il Todays Health 42:56-9+ D '64
Rabies: cause and prevention. Good H 157:124 Jl '63
Rabies danger in wilds. Sci N L 83:196 Mr 30 '63

Immunity
Savior of Alaska's vital sled dogs; air force officer fights rabies in Arctic villages. il Ebony 19:118-20+ D '63
Should you be vaccinated for rabies? D. M. Cleary. Farm J 87:64 O '63

RABIES vaccine
Preventing the incurable. il Time 84:58 Ag 14 '64

RABIN, Arnold
Runaway Christmas stockings; story. Ladies Home J 80:138a D '63

RABINOVITZ, Aaron
Wholesaler questions NACS paperback jobbing scheme. Pub W 183:56-7 Je 10 '63

RABINOVITZ, David
How LBJ beat deadline in naming a judge. por U S News 56:8 Ja 20 '64
Merry Christmas Walter Reuther; two ex-union men as federal judges. W. Schulz. Nat R 15:484 D 3 '63
Senate problem: judgeships for two ex-union men? por U S News 55:12 N 11 '63

RABINOWITCH, Eugene
After Cuba: two lessons. Bul Atomic Sci 19:2-8 F '63
New Year's thoughts 1964. Bul Atomic Sci 20:2+ Ja '64
Pugwash-Coswa: international conversations. Bul Atomic Sci 19:7-12 Je '63
Scientific revolution; adaptation of addresses, 1963. Bul Atomic Sci 19:15-18 S; 11-16 O; 9-12 N; 14-17 D '63
Scientific revolution: man's new outlook; adaptation of address, 1963. Bul Atomic Sci 19:15-18 S '63; 20:34 Ap '64
Stop the world. Bul Atomic Sci 20:2-5 O '64
Turning back the clock. por Time 83:52-3 Ap 10 '64
—See Rubinstein, D. jt. auth.

RABINOWITZ, Alan
Realism in corporate real estate. bibliog f Harvard Bsns R 41:62-9 N '63

RABINOWITZ, Joni
Student's dividend in Georgia. New Repub 151:6-7 S 12 '64

RABINOWITZ, Lawrence. See Schmidt-Nielsen, B. jt. auth.

RABOVSKY, Istvan
Ballet, violins and shish kebab! Bihari. E. Caroll. il Dance Mag 37:27-8 D '63

RACCOON hunting
Coon fever, our favorite epidemic. S. James. il Pop Mech 119:117-20+ F '63
Coon hunter's life ain't easy. R. Rawlins. il Outdoor Life 131:80-1+ My '63

RACCOONS
Our most American animal. P. Redford. il Harper 227:47-50 O '63
Peripatetic reviewer. E. Weeks. Atlan 212: 152+ D '63
Raccoon comes to dinner. il Sunset 130:243-4 Mr '63
Rampant raccoons. M. Weston. il N Y Times Mag p29 Jl 21 '63
Rascal; condensation. S. North. il Read Digest 83:229-31+ S '63

RACE
Negro: how he's different. A. Hamilton. Sci Digest 54:6-11 O '63
Origin of races. by C. S. Coon. Review
Sat R 46:41 Je 22 '63. M. Mead
See also
Ethnic types

RACE and music. See Music and race

RACE attitudes. See Attitudes

RACE car drivers. See Automobile drivers

RACE cooperation. See Interracial cooperation

RACE differences. See Racial differences

RACE discrimination
After desegregation, what next? R. Wilkins. il Ebony 18:64-5 S '63
Are whites being discriminated against? U S News 54:8 Je 17 '63
Bread and butter side. L. Hughes. Sat R 46:19-20 Ap 20 '63
Church looks at television; alleged racial discrimination on television stations in Jackson, Miss. R. L. Shayon. Sat R 47:36 My 16 '64
Claim air wave rights for Negroes; United church of Christ petition to F.C.C. Christian Cent 81:725 Je 3 '64
Declaration on elimination of racial discrimination; with text of declaration. U N Rev 11:35-9+ Ja '64
Definitions of discrimination. il Newsweek 62: 18 Jl 29 '63
Discrimination charged; United church of Christ's petition to F.C.C. E. C. Parker. Christian Cent 81:1018+ Ag 12 '64
Draft on new convention on racial discrimination. U N Rev 11:39-40 Mr '64
Fulfilling our basic commitments as a nation; statement, July 10, 1963; with comments by nonwhite diplomats. D. Rusk. Dept State Bul 49:154-9 Jl 29 '63
Inalienable rights of all; address, July 10, 1963. W. J. Kenealy. Vital Speeches 29: 686-9 S 1 '63
NEA motion on discrimination in professional associations. NEA J 52:52 D '63
Negro's priorities: welfare or status. E. C. Ladd, jr. il Nation 199:243-6+ O 19 '64
New ruling: equal rights for whites; District of Columbia reformatory, Lorton, Va. il U S News 54:8 Je 3 '63
Racism, effects, origins, remedies. J. O. Lee. Christian Cent 80:907-9 Jl 17 '63
Rating the broadcaster; petition of United church of Christ to deny renewal of the licenses of two television stations in Jackson, Miss. R. L. Shayon. Sat R 47:21 Jl 11 '64
Recent trends in the study of minority and race relations. M. M. Gordon. bibliog f Ann Am Acad 350:148-56 N '63
Secretary Rusk's news conference of May 29, 1963; with excerpts from remarks on discrimination and U.S. foreign policy, May 27, 1963. D. Rusk. Dept State Bul 48:931-8 Je 17 '63
This is my country too; record of trip by an American Negro. J. A. Williams. il Holiday 36:30-3+ Ag; 58-9+ S '64; Discussion. 36:4+ O '64
Winning a war. il Ebony 18:112-13 My '63
See also
Discrimination in employment
Negroes in the United States—Segregation
Race prejudice

RACE equality. See Equality

RACE horses. See Horses

RACE improvement. See Eugenics

RACE prejudice
American dilemma. by G. Myrdal. Review
New Yorker 40:195-6+ Ap 18 '64. N. Bliven
Sci Digest 54:16-17 O '63. H. Pryor
Backlash; anti-Negro feeling and the coming election. T. H. White. il Life 57:100A-100B+ O 16 '64

RACE prejudice—*Continued*
Class, color and prejudice. B. Bettelheim. Nation 197:231-4 O 19 '63
Dialogue in a taxi. G. Ace. Sat R 47:9+ My 23 '64
First Negro family on Maple Terrace; with program for discussion group, by C. W. Mattuck. S. H. Strait. il Parents Mag 40:28+, 36-7+ Ja '65
Intelligence or prejudice? questions and answers. E. Van Den Haag. Nat R 16:1059-63 D 1 '64
Judgment on racism. America 110:470 Ap 4 '64
Must children pay the high price for prejudice? A. S. Flemming. Good H 157:41+ Ag '63
Must we hate? A. MacLeish. Atlan 211:79-82 F '63
My Negro problem, and ours. N. Podhoretz. Commentary 35:93-101 F '63; Discussion. 35:338-47, 430-8 Ap-My '63; New Repub 148:11-12 Mr 23; 7 Mr 30 '63
Negro father speaks. L. P. Jackson. Good H 156:79+ My '63
Negro: why whites fear him. S. Hirsh. il Sci Digest 54:12-15 O '63
Negroes also prejudiced. Sci N L 85:367 Je 6 '64
New bombing terrorists of the South call themselves Nacirema: American spelled backward. G. McMillan. Life 55:39-40 O 11 '63
Of many things. T. N. Davis. America 110: 583 My 2 '64
Panel of American women; with excerpts from a panel. S. S. Baker. il Ladies Home J 82:33-5+ Ja '65
Prejudice all around; attitudes among racial and ethnic groups in Chicago. America 110:838 Je 20 '64
Prejudice hurts everyone; with program for discussion group, by M. R. Sherwin. R. O. Dudley. il Parents Mag 38:38+, 72-3+ F '63
Prejudice: widespread and deep. il Newsweek 62:48-50 O 21 '63
Rising tide of Negro-Jewish tensions. R. C. Hertz. il Ebony 20:117-18+ D '64
Segregation in Sofia. il Newsweek 61:42 F 25 '63
Southern honor; views of the honest segregationist. R. J. Geurink. Commonweal 81:476-7 Ja 8 '65
Southerner appeals to the North: don't make our mistake! G. B. Leonard. il Look 28:15-19 Ag 11 '64
White man looks at the Negro. G. Cross. Look 27:60+ D 17 '63
Who likes whom; Chicago study. Time 83:24 Je 5 '64
Your child and prejudice. B. Spock. il Ebony 19:135-8+ O '64
See also
Negroes in the United States—Segregation
Race problems
Racism

RACE problems
Beatings in British Guiana, a bomb in Yemen, maybe gas? il Life 55:30-1 Jl 19 '63
Has race trouble tarnished U.S. image abroad? il U S News 55:66 Ag 19 '63
Is a race war shaping up? A. J. Toynbee. il N Y Times Mag p26+ S 29 '63
Race trouble: is it the same the world over? il U S News 55:32-8 Jl 1 '63; Same abr. with title Race discrimination: it's worldwide. Read Digest 83:163-4+ O '63
Reilly and I. B. Weiss. Commentary 35:302-11 Ap '63; Discussion. 36:166-9 Ag '63
Whites. Nation 197:61 Ag 10 '63
Who likes whom; Chicago study. Time 83:24 Je 5 '64
See also
Business and race problems
Church and race problems
Intermarriage of races
Interracial cooperation
Minorities
Negro race
Race prejudice
Race relations
also subhead Race problems under names of continents, countries, etc. e.g. Africa—Race problems

RACE relations
Calculated risk; Negro leadership. il Newsweek 64:26-8 Ag 10 '64
Case for the new South. T. Sanford. il Look 28:81-4+ D 15 '64
Crisis in race relations; symposium. il U S News 57:23-40 Ag 10 '64
Hear the voice of racial justice. Life 57:4 Ag 7 '64
Talk is race. il Time 84:17-18 Ag 7 '64
We saw you a stranger. M. M. Shideler. Christian Cent 81:1585-8 D 23 '64
Who will overcome? G. Hills. Nat R 16:818-20 S 22 '64; Correction 16:881 O 6 '64

RACE riots. See Riots

RACE track betting. See Book making (betting)

RACE tracks
Beauty and the tax collector. Sports Illus 18:8 Ap 22 '63
Bluegrass spring; photographs by J. L. Stage. Sports Illus 18:28-32 Ap 29 '63
Confessions of a racetrack flack; Cranwood race course. J. O'Keeffe. Esquire 61:112-13+ Ap '64
Del Miller's magic carpet; world's first synthetic racetrack, The Meadows, Pennsylvania. il Sports Illus 19:50-1 Jl 8 '63
Distance is the truest test; Belmont stakes at Aqueduct. W. Tower. Sports Illus 18:51 Je 10 '63
Fast trot; Roosevelt raceway. il Newsweek 64:50 Ag 31 '64
Golden days at the dentist's; Santa Anita, America's best racetrack. W. Tower. il Sports Illus 22:22-3 Ja 11 '65
Most beautiful racetrack in the world; Photographs of Chantilly. J. Cooke. Sports Illus 20:44-51 Je 8 '64
Muddy track; scandal at Berkshire Downs, Mass. il Newsweek 61:33+ Mr 18 '63
New York's unrecognized park lands. N. Ashby. il Am For 69:12-15 Jl '63
Saratoga racing centennial; reproductions of paintings. P. Davis. Sports Illus 19:34-9 Ag 5 '63
Soft sell brings a million-dollar gate. il Sports Illus 18:21 My 6 '63
Third race; Aqueduct. New Yorker 39:32-4 My 11 '63
Winning, and losing, big; Roosevelt raceway, Westbury, N.Y. Newsweek 62:76 N 18 '63
See also
Speedways

RACES of man. See Ethnology

RACHEL Carson memorial fund for research. See National Audubon society

RACHLIS, Eugene, and Marqusee, J. E.
Big deal. Esquire 59:98-9+ My '63

RACHMAN, Peter
Letter from London. M. Panter-Downes. New Yorker 39:67-8 Ag 3 '63
Saga of Polish Peter. por Time 82:28 Jl 26 '63

RACHMANINOFF, Sergei
Rachmaninoff by Graffman and Bernstein. J. Diether. il Am Rec G 31:451 Ja '65

RACHOW, Louis A.
Walter Hampden memorial library. Wilson Lib Bul 38:656-9 Ap '64

RACIAL differences
Erythrocyte acid phosphomonoesterase and glucose-6-phosphate dehydrogenase deficiency in Caucasians. F. A. Oski and others. bibliog il Science 139:409-11 F 1 '63
Giving the Olympics an anthropological once-over. M. Smith. il Life 57:81-2+ O 23 '64
Jennifer. C. Illig. Mlle 56:61+ F '63
Negro: how he's different. A. Hamilton. Sci Digest 54:6-11 O '63
Race and reason, by C. Putnam. Review New Repub 147:23-4 S 10 '62; 148:9-10 Ja 5 '63. D. C. Simmons; Discussion. 148:30 Ja 19; 29-31 F 23 '63
Races: what science says. il Newsweek 62: 50+ O 21 '63
Racial differences and the future. D. J. Ingle. bibliog Science 146:375-9 O 16 '64; Discussion. 146:1415-18, 1526-30; 147:6-7 D 11-18 '64, Ja 1 '65
Racial differences in skin resistance. L. C. Johnson and N. L. Corah. bibliog il Science 139:766-7 F 22 '63
Science and the race problem; report of the AAAS committee on science in the promotion of human welfare. bibliog Science 142: 558-61 N 1 '63; Discussion. 142:1419; 143:306-8, 913-15; 144:365 D 13 '63, Ja 24, F 28, Ap 24 '64
Treat race scientifically. Sci N L 84:22 Jl 13 '63

RACIAL discrimination. See Race discrimination

RACIAL doctrine. See Racism

RACIAL equality. See Equality

RACIAL extinction. See Genocide

RACINE, Wis.

Bridges

Many hands saved this deck. W. J. Chadwick. il Am City 78:76-7 Jl '63

RACING. See Automobile racing; Boat racing; Running; and similar headings

RACING cars. See Automobiles, Racing

RACING fans. See Sports fans

RACING yachts. See Yachts and yachting

RACISM

Episcopal argument obscures warning on racism. Christian Cent 81:1356 N 4 '64

I'm talking to you, white man; excerpt from autobiography of Malcolm X, by Alex Haley and Malcolm X. Malcolm X. il Sat Eve Post 237:30-2+ S 12 '64

Nazi mind. America 110:329 Mr 14 '64; Reply with rejoinder. P. W. Mullen. 110:498 Ap 11 '64

Portrait of an extremist; C. Lynch. T. Armbrister. il Sat Eve Post 237:80-3 Ag 22 '64

Race: the history of an idea in America, by T. F. Gossett. Review
Time il 83:102 Mr 13 '64

Racialism is an African sickness, too. G. T. Kimble. il N Y Times Mag p38-9+ O 11 '64

Racism, effects, origins, remedies. J. O. Lee. Christian Cent 80:907-9 Jl 17 '63

Racism on the left. New Repub 149:4 O 26 '63

Racism: the Nation's false religion. Christian Cent 80:166 F 6 '63

Rightists, racists, and separatists: a white bloc in the making? D. Danzig. Commentary 38:28-32 Ag '64

White sin. America 109:760 D 14 '63

See also

Race prejudice

RACKETEERING

Federal viewpoint on combating organized crime. H. J. Miller, jr. bibliog f Ann Am Acad 347:93-103 My '63

How criminals solve their investment problem; crime in business. il U S News 56:74-6 Mr 30 '64

Organized crime; a business enterprise. T. Sellin. bibliog f Ann Am Acad 347:12-19 My '63

Waterfront revisited. B. Schulberg. il Sat Eve Post 236:28-32+ S 7 '63

RACKHAM, Thomas W. See Kopal, Z. jt. auth.

RACKOWE, Alec

Girl next door; story. Good H 158:56-7 Ja '64

Grasshopper; story. Redbook 123:54-5 O '64

Love affair; story. Ladies Home J 81:74-8 S '64

RACKS. See Shelves

RACKS, Gun. See Gun racks

RACKS, Magazine. See Magazine stands, racks, etc.

RACKS, Spice. See Spice racks

RACKS, Wine. See Wine racks

RACQUET club. See Sports clubs

RADANT, Else

Here liveth fortune. Hi Fi 13:46-9+ Mr '63

RADAR

Experimenting with sonar. D. Meyer. il Pop Electr 21:41-5+ S '64

Measuring plasma density of the magnetosphere. K. L. Bowles. bibliog il Science 139:389-91 F 1 '63

Watching bird flights by radar. P. E. Hughes. il Audubon Mag 66:182-4 My '64

Antennas and scanning mechanisms

DOD funds $15 million for laser R&D. Aviation W 78:75 Ap 8 '63

Firm makes low-profile high-efficiency antennas. Miss & Roc 14:36 Mr 2 '64

Haystack antenna may go on in July. M. Getler. il Miss & Roc 14:26-8 Mr 23 '64

Haystack will advance radar precision. P. J. Klass. il Aviation W 78:80-2 F 4 '63

Haystack's needle-thin beam; air force's giant new antenna system. il Bsns W p66+ O 17 '64

Long Beach defense system radars shown. il Aviation W 79:110 N 25 '63

Multi-mode helicopter radar developed. B. Miller. il Aviation W 81:88-9+ O 26 '64

New radar telescope to map ionosphere. P. J. Klass. il Aviation W 79:84-5+ Ag 19 '63

New type radar probing surface of moon. P. J. Klass. il Aviation W 78:91 My 6 '63

Observatory in Puerto Rico will far surpass existing big dishes; Arecibo ionospheric observatory. C. D. LaFond. il Miss & Roc 13:24-5 N 11 '63

Promising array developed, successfully tested, then dropped. C. D. LaFond. il Miss & Roc 14:33-5 Mr 9 '64

Radar systems guard ICBM bases: Doppler principle. R. Lindsey. il Miss & Roc 12:33-4 Mr 11 '63

Radar warning system can see over horizon. Sci N L 86:216 O 3 '64

Unique monopulse antenna developed. C. D. LaFond. il Miss & Roc 12:35 Mr 11 '63

World's largest radar telescope; Arecibo, Puerto Rico. il Electr World 71:45+ F '64

Meteorological applications

See Radar meteorology

Military applications

Anti-satellite weapons tested; SPADATS. J. Trainor. Miss & Roc 15:10-11 S 28 '64

Autonetics designs advanced radar line. B. Miller. il Aviation W 78:90-1+ Je 17 '63

Chirp, a new radar technique. D. Lancaster. bibliog il Electr World 73:42-3+ Ja '65

Radar warning system can see over horizon. Sci N L 86:216 O 3 '64

Satellite tracker keeps sky vigil; SPADATS. Sci N L 86:265 O 24 '64

Super-power radar nears testing. R. Lindsey. il Miss & Roc 12:28 F 25 '63

See also

Semi-automatic ground environment system

RADAR altimeters. See Altimeters

RADAR defense network

Anti-satellite weapons tested; over-the-horizon radar. J. Trainor. Miss & Roc 15:10-11 S 28 '64

Bertrand Russell on the sinful Americans; exchange of letters. B. Russell; J. Fischer. Harper 226:20+ Je '63; Discussion. 227:8+ Ag '63

DEW line communications. W. A. Stocklin. Electr World 71:8 Ap '64

First AMR tracking ship begins checkout. G. Alexander. il Aviation W 78:28-9 My 6 '63

Here the U.S. fights the coldest war; with report by C. Mydans. il Life 54:18-27 Mr 1 '63

Mass air attack seen unlikely; defenses shifted, radars closed. Aviation W 79:24 Jl 8 '63

Radicians at the DEW line. W. A. Stocklin. il Electr World 71:48-9+ My '64

Russians believed to have radar with over-the-horizon capabilities. P. J. Klass. Aviation W 81:19 S 28 '64

See also

Ballistic missile early warning system

Guided missiles—Defenses

RADAR echoes. See Radar in astronomy

RADAR fire control systems. See Airplanes, Military—Armaments

RADAR in astronomy

Arecibo ionospheric observatory. W. E. Gordon. bibliog il Science 146:26-30 O 2 '64

JPL using two radar techniques to prepare map of surface of Venus. R. Pay. Miss & Roc 15:35 D 21 '64

New radar telescope to map ionosphere. P. J. Klass. il Aviation W 79:84-5+ Ag 19 '63

Radar observations of Jupiter. R. M. Goldstein. bibliog il Science 144:842-3 My 15 '64

Radar observations of Mars. R. M. Goldstein and W. F. Gillmore. il Science 141:1171-2 S 20 '63

Radar observations of Mars and Mercury. Sky & Tel 25:191+ Ap '63

Radar observations of Mercury. R. L. Carpenter and R. M. Goldstein. bibliog il Science 142:381 O 18 '63

RADAR in aviation

Air traffic control blueprint. P. J. Klass. il Aviation W 80:52-4+ Ja 20; 90-1+ Ja 27; 87-91+ F 3 '64

All-weather aircraft landing; ILS and PAR approach systems. F. B. Brady. Sci Am 210:25-35 Mr '64

Autonetics designs advanced radar line. B. Miller. il Aviation W 78:90-1+ Je 17 '63

Compact Doppler designed for helicopters. P. J. Klass. il Aviation W 80:79+ Je 8 '64

Dielectric rod produces radar echo gain. P. J. Klass. il Aviation W 79:88-9 N 4 '63

Doppler study holds promise of improved space navigation. R. Pay. Miss & Roc 13:24-5 O 14 '63

FAA, military evaluate HF grid antenna. B. Miller. il Aviation W 79:80-1+ S 2 '63

Flying the Atlantic without a navigator. R. E. Smallman. il Pop Sci 182:86-8+ Ap '63

Flying the beam when the fog rolls in. C. Leedham. il N Y Times Mag p22+ My 24 '64

FM/CW radar altimeter is flight tested. B. Miller. il Aviation W 80:55-6 Mr 30 '64

Model of pigeon's eye may assist radar. B. Miller. il Aviation W 81:55+ S 28 '64

Multi-mode helicopter radar developed. B. Miller. il Aviation W 81:88-9+ O 26 '64

RADAR in aviation—*Continued*
Optical radar employs multiple lasers. B. Miller. il Aviation W 80:62-3+ Mr 9 '64
Target simulator checks F-104G radars. B. Miller. il Aviation W 79:99+ N 25 '63
Traffic control is focus of FAA budget; Project beacon. R. H. Cook. Aviation W 80:52 Ja 27 '64
TSQ-47 traffic system undergoes test; Air force communications service. P. J. Klass. il Aviation W 79:69+ N 11 '63
Velocity sensors apply Mossbauer effect. P. J. Klass. il Aviation W 79:89+ S 9 '63
See also
Transponders

RADAR in navigation
Small-boat radar, now and tomorrow. F. E. Lawton. il Motor B 112:44-7 N '63
Taking the curse out of fog. F. T. Moss. il Yachting 116:48-50+ Ag '64

RADAR in space flight
Accuracy of Canoga radar tracking system is six feet in 30,000 miles. R. Pay. il Miss & Roc 14:31+ F 17 '64
Radar work to aid lunar explorers. C. D. LaFond. il Miss & Roc 12:22-3 Ap 8 '63
Spaceborne radar aimed at rendezvous guidance. M. Getler. il Miss & Roc 12:27-8 F 4 '63
Velocity sensors apply Mossbauer effect. P. J. Klass. il Aviation W 79:89+ S 9 '63
Westinghouse outlines design of Gemini radar. Miss & Roc 13:36-7 Ag 19 '63

RADAR meteorology
How the weatherman can listen in on thunderstorms; SPARSA (sferic pulse azimuth range spectrum analyzer) W. Cloud. Pop Sci 185:23+ O '64

RADAR simulators. See Simulators

RADAR technicians. See Electric workers

RADAR telescope. See Radar—Antenna and scanning mechanisms

RADATZ, Dick
Bring on The Monster. por Time 82:68 Jl 5 '63
Monster who puts out fires. T. Cohane. il pors Look 28:64-6 My 19 '64
Rally wrecker. H. L. Masin. por Sr Schol 82:36 Ap 3 '63

RADCLIFFE, E. B.
Cincinnati's May festival. Theatre Arts 47:67-8 My '63

RADCLIFFE, Woodward
Cast your own patio slabs. Pop Mech 119:164-5 My '63
Monstera for your shelf. Flower Grower 51:23 Ja '64
Sculptured look in garden seats. il Flower Grower 51:58-9 Ja '64
Stage plants dramatically. il Flower Grower 50:42-4 N '63

RADCLIFFE college, Cambridge, Mass.
Royal co-ed Christina prepares to enter Radcliffe. E. Behr. Sat Eve Post 236:78-9 S 28 '63

RADFORD, Edward P. jr, and Hunt, V. R.
Polonium-210; a volatile radioelement in cigarettes. bibliog Science 143:247-9; 144:366-7; 146:87 Ja 17, Ap 24, O 2 '64

RADHAKRISHNAN, Sir Sarvepalli
President of India sees United Nations giving conscience to world community; excerpts from address, June 10, 1963. U N Rev 10:51 Jl '63
—See Kennedy, J. F. jt. auth.

RADIAL ply tire (fabric) See Tire fabrics

RADIAL saws. See Saws

RADIATION
Cross-linking of polymers by radiation; with glossary. G. Adler. bibliog il Science 141:321-9 Jl 26 '63
Piggyback explorers will study radiation. Miss & Roc 13:14 Ag 12 '63
Rise in radiation. New Repub 148:4-5 Je 15 '63
Sandia tests revamping data about radiation damage to transistors. Miss & Roc 15:37 N 16 '64
Transistors face new radiation hazard; initial blackout of Telstar 1. P. J. Klass. il Aviation W 78:85-6+ Ja 21 '63
Weather in space; reprint. J. S. Butz, jr. il Sci Digest 55:67-72 Je '64
See also
Cosmic rays
Electronic apparatus and appliances—Radiation effects
Gamma rays
Mössbauer effect
Rayleigh radiation
Spectrum analysis
Stars—Radiation
Van Allen radiation belts
X rays

Accidents and injuries
Atomic dangers overrated. Sci N L 86:149 S 5 '64
New industrial hazard in cathode-ray machines. Sci N L 83:345 Je 1 '63

Industrial applications
What radiation can do for the production line. G. A. W. Boehm. il Fortune 70:140-3+ D '64

Measurement
Detection of nuclear radiation by semiconductors. H. S. Renne. bibliog il Electr World 70:39-42+ Ag '63
Global distribution of the net energy balance of the atmosphere from Tiros radiation data. S. I. Rasool. bibliog il Science 143:567-9 F 7 '64; Reply. R. Wexler and W. K. Widger, jr. 145:1206 S 11 '64
Infrared radiation from the atmosphere over the Arctic Ocean. W. B. Murcray. bibliog il Science 141:802-4 Ag 30 '63
Measure body radiation with hypodermic needle. Sci N L 85:184 Mr 21 '64
Radiation in the natural environment; symposium at William Marsh Rice university, Houston, Tex. J. A. S. Adams and W. M. Lowder. Science 141:365-6 Jl 26 '63
SAC U-2s modified for fallout sampling. C. M. Plattner. il Aviation W 79:72-3+ Ag 12 '63
WU-2 role in fallout detection. Aviation W 79:77 Ag 12 '63
West Ford dipole belt: optical detection at Palomar. A. Sandage and C. Kowal. il Science 141:797-8 Ag 30 '63
West Ford dipole belt: photometric observations. W. G. Tifft and others. il Science 141:798-9 Ag 30 '63
Wiesner, Charyk ordered Starad secrecy. L. Booda. Aviation W 78:26-7 Ap 15 '63

Physiological effects
Biological complexity and radiosensitivity. H. S. Kaplan and L. E. Moses. bibliog il Science 145:21-5 Jl 3 '64
Deoxycytidine in urine of humans after whole-body irradiation. H. K. Berry and others. bibliog il Science 142:396-8 O 18 '63
Diploid and endoreduplicated cells: measurements of DNA. A. G. Bell. il Science 143:139 Ja 10 '64
Erythropoietin production following gamma irradiation and hemorrhage in dogs. N. Pesic and others. bibliog il Science 143:49-50 Ja 3 '64
Examination of diurnal variation in lethally irradiated rats. R. L. Straube. il Science 142:1062 N 22 '63
β-Galactosidase: inactivation of its messenger RNA by ultraviolet irradiation. P. A. Swenson and R. B. Setlow. bibliog il Science 146:791-4 N 6 '64
Health physics; report of 1963 annual meeting of the Health physics society. A. P. Hull. Science 142:73-4 O 4 '63
Hot wasp nests; yellow-and-black daubers use radioactive mud. Time 84:35 Ag 14 '64
Ionizing radiation: effect on genetic transcription. E. C. Pollard. bibliog il Science 146:927-9 N 13 '64
Irradiation of the blood: method for reducing lymphocytes in blood and spleen. B. A. Barnes and others. bibliog il Science 145:1188-9 S 11 '64
Leukemia, multiple myeloma, and aplastic anemia in American radiologists. E. B. Lewis. bibliog il Science 142:1492-4 D 13 '63
Mice-bombarded with high-energy radiations. Sci N L 84:296 N 9 '63
Muscle-equivalent environmental radiation meter of extreme sensitivity. J. Kastner and others. bibliog il Science 140:1100-1 Je 7 '63
New discoveries on radiation of mice. Sci N L 84:264 O 26 '63
Overlap of photoreactivation and liquid holding recovery in escherichia coli. B. A. Castellani and others. bibliog il Science 143:1170-1 Mr 13 '64
Polonium-210; a volatile radioelement in cigarettes. E. P. Radford, jr. and V. R. Hunt. bibliog il Science 143:247-9 Ja 17 '64; Discussion. 143:917; 144:366-7, 952-3; 146:86-7 F 28, Ap 24, My 22, O 2 '64
Radiation accidents and emergencies; report on symposium. L. H. Lanzl and J. H. Pingel. Science 143:1352-6 Mr 20 '64

RADIATION—Physiological effects—*Continued*
Radiation action on DNA in bacteria: effect of oxygen. E. C. Pollard and P. M. Achey. bibliog il Science 146:71-3 O 2 '64
Radiation-chemical oxidation of peptides in the solid state. W. M. Garrison and others. bibliog il Science 146:250-2 O 9 '64
Radiation damage to artemia cysts: effects of water vapor. W. C. Snipes and W. Gordy. bibliog Science 142:503-4 O 25 '63
Radiation-induced mouse leukemia: consistent occurrence of an extra and a marker chromosome. N. Wald and others. bibliog il Science 143:810-13 F 21 '64
Radiation won't kill the race; results of a six-year study of the effects of radiation on mice. Time 84:65 Jl 3 '64
Relationship between nuclear volumes, chromosome numbers, and relative radiosensitivities. A. H. Sparrow and others. bibliog il Science 141:163-6 Jl 12 '63
Schistosomiasis: age of snails and susceptibility to X-irradiation. A. P. Szumlewicz. bibliog il Science 144:302-4 Ap 17 '64
Spleen-colony formation in anemic mice of genotype WW. E. A. McCulloch and others. bibliog il Science 144:844-6 My 15 '64
Thymus: its limited role in the recovery of homograft response in irradiated mice. M. L. Tyan and others. bibliog il Science 142:584 N 1 '63
Transplantation of rat bone marrow in irradiated mice: effect of exposure rate. N. Gengozian. bibliog il Science 146:663-4 O 30 '64

See also
Plants, Effect of radiation on
Space flight—Radiation hazards

Safety devices and measures

Fallout lollipops; A doctor tries to lick radiation. il Life 54:53-4+ F 8 '63
Overlap of photoreactivation and liquid holding recovery in escherichia coli. B. A. Castellani and others. bibliog il Science 143:1170-1 Mr 13 '64
Radiation accidents and emergencies; report on symposium. L. H. Lanzl and J. H. Pingel. Science 143:1352-6 Mr 20 '64
Radiation exposure records. H. Blatz. Science 140:770 My 17 '63
Radiation tolerance high. Sci N L 86:309 N 14 '64
Selenoamino acids: decrease of radiation damage to amino acids and proteins. F. Shimazu and A. L. Tappel. bibliog il Science 143:369-71 Ja 24 '64

RADIATION, incorporated
Gemini digital command system readied by Radiation, inc. M. Getler. il Miss & Roc 13:32-3 Jl 22 '63
Microcircuit plant to serve in-house need. P. J. Klass. il Aviation W 80:66-9 Mr 9 '64

RADIATION, Solar. See Solar radiation

RADIATION belts
Charting the earth's radiation belts. il Sky & Tel 28:212-13 O'64
IMP discovers new radiation belt. W. Beller. il Miss & Roc 14:22-3 Mr 23 '64
Radiation bulge detected. Sci N L 85:179 Mr 21 '64
Shock corridor; space around earth. Newsweek 63:69 Mr 23 '64

See also
Van Allen radiation belts

RADIATION belts, Artificial
Artificial belt may last ten years. Van Allen tells Goddard session. W. C. Wetmore. Aviation W 78:26 Mr 25 '63
Charting the earth's radiation belts. il Sky & Tel 28:212-13 O '64
Facts about the 1962 space bomb. J. Lear. il Sat R 46:45-8 Ap 6 '63; Reply with rejoinder. S. F. Singer. 46:50-1 My 4 '63
Hitch in the belt. Newsweek 61:47 Ap 1 '63
Lesson; Starfish test. Nation 196:258 Mr 30 '63
Microcircuit radiation problems probed. B. Miller. il Aviation W 79:93-4+ Ag 19 '63
Radiation belt decreases. Sci N L 83:279 My 4 '63
Radiation belt intensity dispute grows; summary of study presented at meeting of the American physical society; ed. by W. C. Wetmore. W. L. Brown. il Aviation W 78:60-1+ F 4 '63
Radiation belts. B. J. O'Brien. il Sci Am 208:84-96 My '63; Reply with rejoinder. S. F. Singer. 209:8+ Jl '63
Radiation belts, natural and artificial. C. E. McIlwain. bibliog il Science 142:355-61 O 18 '63
Recent nuclear blasts boost space radiation hazard. il Sci Digest 53:56-63 Ap '63
Transient radiation effects on avionics systems. Aviation W 79:97 Ag 19 '63

RADIATION biology. See Radiobiology

RADIATION chemistry. See Radiochemistry

RADIATION counters. See Counters (electrons, ions, etc)

RADIATION detectors. See Radiation—Measurement

RADIATION in the body. See Radioactive substances in the body

RADIATION medicine. See Radiology, Medical

RADIATION shielding. See Shielding (radiation)

RADIATION sickness
See also
Atomic bomb casualty commission

Therapy

Radiation accidents and emergencies; report on symposium. L. H. Lanzl and J. H. Pingel. Science 143:1352-6 Mr 20 '64

RADIATION sterilization
See also
Food, Effect of radiation on

RADIATION systems, incorporated
Promising array developed, successfully tested, then dropped. C. D. LeFond. il Miss & Roc 14:33-5 Mr 9 '64

RADIATION therapy. See Radiotherapy

RADIATOR solutions. See Anti-freeze solutions

RADIATORS
Masking an eyesore. R. Treves. il Pop Mech 120:170-1 N '63

RADICAL right conservatives. See Conservatism

RADICALS (chemistry)
Amateur scientist; free radicals. F. Swift. il Sci Am 209:146-7+ Jl '63
Free radicals and reactive molecules in clathrate cavities. P. Goldberg. bibliog il Science 142:378-9 O 18 '63
Free radicals and unstable molecules. S. N. Foner. bibliog il Science 143:441-50 Ja 31 '64
Free radicals; report of sixth international symposium on free radicals. C. K. Jen. Science 142:261-2+ O 11 '63
Mass spectral studies of surface catalysis: the production of free radicals at 40° C. T. W. Martin and R. E. Rummel. bibliog il Science 143:797-9 F 21 '64
Scavenger probe sampling: a method for studying gaseous free radicals. R. M. Fristrom. bibliog il Science 140:297-300 Ap 19 '63

RADICALS and radicalism
Peace agitator, by N. Hentoff. Review
Commentary 37:88-90 My '64. H. Dienstfrey

RADICIANS. See Electric workers

RADIMER, Carl A.
Strike in the Canadian woods. Nation 196:224-5 Mr 16 '63

RADIN, Eileen
Stained glass. Sch Arts 63:14-15 D '63

RADINOVSKY, Syd
Cannibal of the pond. Natur Hist 73:16-25 N '64

RADIO

Bibliography

Book reviews (cont of) Technical books. See issues of Electronics world

History

Birth of worldwide communication. Sr Schol 85:5 D 9 '64
Real beginning of radio. O. B. Young. il Sat R 47:48-50 Mr 7 '64; Discussion. 47:47 Ap 4 '64

Nomenclature

New nomenclature; standard prefixes. E. G. Louis. il Pop Electr 19:71 S '63

RADIO, Military. See Radio communication, Military

RADIO, Police. See Police radio

RADIO, Single sideband. See Radio transmission—Single sideband system

RADIO advertising
And now, a brief word from our sponsors. . .; bill prohibiting FCC regulation of broadcast advertising. D. Rapoport. Reporter 30:26-8 Je 4 '64
Chairman Henry on target; FCC's attempt to regulate commercial time standards. R. L. Shayon. Sat R 46:43 O 19 '63
Commercials for God; Freberg's spiritual ads. Time 82:50 Jl 12 '63
Commercials unlimited? New Repub 149:4 N 23 '63

RADIO advertising—*Continued*
Diode rings in a Dixie belle. il Bsns W p70 Ap 4 '64
Don't tell Szell; Cleveland summer orchestra's recorded radio commercial. Newsweek 62: 50 Jl 8 '63
Fewer commercials. New Repub 148:4-5 Ap 13 '63; Reply. W. Gore. 148:37 My 4 '63
Forecast for the FCC. R. L. Shayon. Sat R 47:51 Ja 11 '64
Forty-three cheers; dissenting vote on bill prohibiting the FCC from limiting number and frequency of commercials on the air. R. L. Shayon. Sat R 47:30 Ap 18 '64
Freedom of the air. New Repub 149:6 D 14 '63
Hard sell; hard-liquor commercials on WQXR. Newsweek 63:74 Mr 30 '64
Help quiet commercials. Sci N L 83:118 F 23 '63
Morning people; Klavan and Finch. il Newsweek 63:88+ My 4 '64
Moving the spirits; whisky commercials. Time 83:80 Mr 27 '64
Radio pirates try abducting audiences; shipboard radio stations off the coast of Great Britain. il Bsns W p47-8+ My 2 '64
Sales & distribution; WMCA: a radio station that sells through controversy. L. Morse. Duns R 83:63 Mr '64
Singing saleswoman. il Ebony 19:143-4+ Ap '64
TV commercials; the government ducks the issue. D. Smith. Nation 198:286-9 Mr 23 '64
Twenty-two straight commercials. Newsweek 61:87 Ap 15 '63
WQXR to broadcast liquor ads. Christian Cent 81:454 Ap 8 '64

RADIO aids to aviation. See Radio in aviation

RADIO aids to navigation. See Radio in navigation

RADIO altimeters. See Altimeters

RADIO amateur civil emergency service. See Radio stations, Amateur

RADIO amateurs. See Radio operators, Amateur

RADIO and television. See Radio broadcasting and television

RADIO antennas
AF starts tests of its most perfect antenna; Haystack. Miss & Roc 15:30 O 19 '64
Antenna advice. R. C. Beard. il Motor B 113:64 Ap '64
Antennas for business radio. H. H. Rice. il Electr World 69:33-5+ Mr '63
Antennas for FM-stereo reception. il Consumer Bul 46:25-8 O '63
Auxiliaries can get more from their radios. H. C. Lawrence. il Motor B 112:40-1+ N '63
Build a turnstile for stereo. F. J. Haines. il Pop Electr 19:68-9 N '63
Compact BCB DX antennas; loop antennas. F. J. Bauer, jr. il Pop Electr 22:75-6 Ja '65
Finding a needle with a Haystack. il Time 84:78 O 16 '64
Haystack radar-radio telescope dedicated. il Sky & Tel 28:349-51 D '64
Haystack's needle-thin beam; air force's giant new antenna system. il Bsns W p66+ O 17 '64
Huge antenna could spot marble 1,000 miles away; Haystack Hill, Tyngsboro, Mass. il(p241) Sci N L 86:249 O 17 '64
Hula Hoop; new hamor CB antenna; Directional discontinuity ring radiator. R. E. Pafenberg. il Pop Electr 19:25-30+ Jl '63
Indoor FM antenna; little Gallo. il Consumer Bul 47:2+ F '64
Indoor horn for TV-FM reception. B. V. K. French. bibliog il Electr World 70:50-1+ D '63
Indoor powered antennas; PM tests and reports. il Pop Mech 121:196 Ap '64
Non-miracle at a high price; indoor antenna. il Consumer Rep 28:148-9 Ap '63
Power line antenna adapter. L. Garner. il Pop Electr 19:50 S '63
Simple antenna boosts FM reception. J. Richards. il Pop Mech 120:199 N '63
Super sky spy; Haystack system. il Sci Digest 56:2 D '64
12-foot transformer for CB. D. T. Geiser. il Pop Electr 18:90 Mr '63
Two halos stacked for 2 meters. B. Sargent. il Pop Electr 22:65-6 Ja '65

RADIO apparatus
Adapt for FM stereo at one-third the cost. L. Feldman. il Pop Mech 120:116-18 Jl '63
Build the MPX. A. B. Otis, jr. il Pop Electr 18:63-6 Ap; 69-73+ My '63 (to be cont)
Stereo s'lector. A. B. Otis, jr. il Pop Electr 21:73-5 S '64
SCA: background-music demultiplexer. G. P. Kuntz. il Electr World 72:44-5 S '64
Wireless re-broadcaster; how to broadcast from your hi-fi, FM tuner, or TV set to every AM radio in the house. K. Dobler. il Pop Electr 22:47-9+ Ja '65
See also
Radio instruments

Medical applications
See Radio in medicine

RADIO apparatus industry and trade
Directory of importers and manufacturers of Japanese transistor radios. Electr World 69:38-9+ My '63; Correction. 70:82 S '63

RADIO apparatus on aircraft
Cessna to market new ARC radio. il Aviation W 79:103 O 28 '63
Extortion; radio license fee. F. K. Smith. il Flying 75:102 S '64
See also
Radio aids to aviation

RADIO apparatus on ships, boats, etc.
Electronic boating aids. E. Robberson. il Yachting 114:51-3+ Jl '63
Marine radio. E. Robberson. il Yachting 115:60-2+ Je; 116:54-6+ Jl '64
See also
Radio telephone on ships, boats, etc.

RADIO astronomy
According to Hoyle; galactic explosions. Newsweek 61:47 Ap 1 '63
Amazing new objects in the sky. B. H. Frisch. il Sci Digest 56:54-61 S '64
Arecibo ionospheric observatory. W. E. Gordon. bibliog il Science 146:26-30 O 2 '64
CTA. . .CTA. . .come in; distant sources of radio waves. Newsweek 64:90 N 9 '64
Channel 37 or the cosmos? Sky & Tel 25:307+ Je '63
Closing window; channel 37: Sci Am 209: 65 Jl '63
Component shapes in double radio sources. A. T. Moffet. bibliog il Science 146:764-5 N 6 '64
Cosmic electromagnetic radiation. E. M. Hafner. bibliog il Science 145:1263-71 S 18 '64
Cosmic X-ray sources. S. Bowyer and others. bibliog il Science 147:394-8 Ja 22 '65
Dallas conference on super radio sources. L. C. Green. il Sky & Tel 27:80-4 F '64
DX'ing Jupiter! S. Gibson. il Pop Electr 21: 41-3+ Ag '64
Explorations with the Hale telescope; adaptation of address, May 15, 1964. I. S. Bowen. il Science 145:1391-8 S 25 '64
Faraday rotation on decametric radio emissions from Jupiter. J. W. Warwick and G. A. Dulk. bibliog il Science 145:380-3 Jl 24 '64
Farthest object; quasi-stellar radio sources. Sci Am 210:59 My '64
Galactic radicals. Sci Am 211:60 N '64
Ground-based astronomy. P. H. Abelson. Science 146:1255 D 4 '64
Ground-based astronomy: a ten-year program; summary of report. Science 146:1641-8 D 25 '64
Heavens' new enigma; quasi-stellars. A. Rosenfeld. il Life 56:11-12 Ja 24 '64; Same abr. with title What are those quasi-stellars out there? Read Digest 84:207-8+ My '64
Heavy stars possible source of X-rays. Sci N L 86:47 Jl 18 '64
Hello, CTA-21, is anyone there? I. Asimov. il N Y Times Mag p52+ N 29 '64
Infrared astronomy by balloon. J. Strong. il Sci Am 212:28-37 bibliog(p 134) Ja '65
Jodrell bank observatory. V. K. McElheny. il Science 144:520-3 My 1 '64
Life and death of the universe. il Newsweek 63:63-7 My 25 '64
Lunar occultation of X-ray emission from the crab nebula. S. Bowyer and others. bibliog il Science 146:912-17 N 13 '64
Mariner-2 microwave observations of Venus. A. H. Barrett and E. Lilley. il Sky & Tel 25:192-5 Ap '63
More about X-rays from the Crab nebula. Sky & Tel 28:139 S '64
Most accurate measurement of Mercury. Time 81:59 Je 7 '63
Most distant object: quasi-stellar source. Sky & Tel 27:286-7 My '64
Mystery from way out; radio sources, CTA-21 and CTA-102. il Time 84:38 N 6 '64
New energy for earth? quasars. Sci N L 87:22 Ja 9 '65
New planetary facts for old; concerning Mercury and Venus. Sci Am 211:60 O '64
Observational neutrino astronomy. J. N. Bahcall. bibliog il Science 147:115-20 Ja 8 '65

RADIO astronomy—*Continued*
Odd-ball quasars may be closer than they seem. Sci N L 86:167 S 12 '64
Oldest rocks found; half the age of Milky way galaxy. il Sci N L 87:7 Ja 2 '65
Oscillations of quasars. G. C. McVittie. il Science 146:259-60 O 9 '64
Probe will measure cosmic noise levels. D. E. Fink. il Aviation W 80:68-9 Ja 6 '64
Quasar defined. Miss & Roc 14:8-9 My 4 '64
Quasar hypotheses. Sci Am 211:38-9 Ag '64
Quasars are crazy. A. Ewing. il Sci N L 86:106 Ag 15 '64
Quasi-stellar diameters and intensity fluctuations. J. Terrell. bibliog Science 145:918-19 Ag 28 '64; Reply. B. Hoffmann. 145:1336 S 18 '64
Quasi-stellar radio sources. J. L. Greenstein. il Sci Am 209:54-62 bibliog(p 178) D '63
Quest for QSS. Newsweek 64:41 D 28 '64
Questions of quasars. il Time 85:52 Ja 8 '65
Radar observations of Venus' rotation. Sky & Tel 28:341 D '64
Radio astronomy explorer program approval regarded as imminent. Miss & Roc 15:92-3 N 30 '64
Radio astronomy: FCC purposes compromise to share frequencies with UHF television broadcasters. D. S. Greenberg. Science 140: 164 Ap 12 '63; Discussion. 140:1174; 141:593-4 Je 14, Ag 16 '63
Radio astronomy merger; Cornell-Sydney university astronomy center. Sky & Tel 28: 274 N '64
Radio astronomy; report on symposium of the Northeast electronics research and engineering meeting. S. J. Goldstein, jr. Science 146:1605-6 D 18 '64
Radio astronomy: TV's rush for UHF threatens use of channel. D. S. Greenberg. Science 139:393 F 1 '63
Radio-emitting flare stars. B. Lovell. il Sci Am 211:13-19 bibliog(p 116) Ag '64
Radio map of the Andromeda galaxy. J. M. MacLeod. bibliog il Science 145:389-91 Jl 24 '64; Reply. H. C. Arp. 145:952 Ag 28 '64
Radio observations of Jupiter's rotation. il Sky & Tel 28:63+ Ag '64
Radio spectrum allocations to astronomy. il Sky & Tel 27:85 F '64
Radio stars identified. Sci N L 83:293 My 11 '63
Radio waves from Jupiter. K. L. Franklin. il Sci Am 211:34-42 bibliog(p 142) Jl '64
Reaching out. il Newsweek 63:82 Ap 13 '64
Repeatability of Jupiter's decametric radio emission. J. W. Warwick. bibliog il Science 140:814-16 My 17 '63
Satellite I and radio noise from Jupiter. G. S. Mumford. il Sky & Tel 29:27 Ja '65
Slow fade: neutron star hypothesis. Sci Am 211:86+ S '64
Solar symposium at Sydney. M. Minnaert. il Sky & Tel 27:151-3 Mr '64
Source of radio waves discovered in Cygnus. Sci N L 85:24 Ja 11 '64
Spare that channel. Time 81:51 My 10 '63
Strange celestial objects newly named: quasars. Sci N L 85:297 My 9 '64
Twinkling quasars. Sci Am 211:58 N '64
U.S. delegate reports on space radio communication conference; statement, November 8, 1963. J. McConnell. Dept State Bul 49:835-7 N 25 '63
Way of a galaxy. il Time 81:58+ F 8 '63
X-ray astronomy. Sci Am 209:67-8 D '63
X-ray astronomy. H. Friedman. il Sci Am 210:36-45 Je '64
See also
Radio telescope

RADIO astronomy observatory. See Artificial satellites—Astronomical applications

RADIO attenuators
Three handy attenuators. C. Henry. il Pop Electr 20:43-4 Ap '64

RADIO audiences
See also
Radio broadcasting—Program rating

RADIO-autography. See Autoradiography

RADIO batteries. See Storage batteries

RADIO broadcasting

Advertising applications

See Radio advertising

Book programs

ALA and CBS radio plan literary discussion series. Pub W 184:63 N 11 '63

Comedy

See Radio broadcasting—Humor

Conversation programs

Beeping Toms; live-conversation programs. il Newsweek 63:74 Mr 30 '64
Bosses make lousy lovers; H. G. Brown's talk show. J. Didion. il Sat Eve Post 238: 34+ Ja 30 '65
Talk man; B. Crandall's talk show. il Time 83:80 My 1 '64

Documentary programs

Radio that soars; Voice of America documentary about communication satellites. R. L. Shayon. Sat R 47:21 Jl 18 '64
Sustained scene; WBAI's Freedom now. L. Shayon. Sat R 46:38 Jl 20 '63

Drama

Aargh! Green Hornet! you here again? C. Osborne. Life 57:16 Ag 14 '64
Gothic revival; Shadow transcriptions of the '40s. il Time 84:59-60 S 4 '64
Reprise: WJRZ series of old-time dramas. New Yorker 40:23-4 Ag 22 '64
See also
Radio plays

Election results

Eight-inning final scores. Reporter 30:12 Je 18 '64
On election night: you be the expert. il Changing T 18:12-14 O '64
Quickie results could sway the election. R. Bendiner. il Life 57:125-6+ S 18 '64

Frequency allocation

See Radio frequency allocation

Frequency modulation

See Radio frequency modulation

Humor

Critics. G. Ace. Sat R 47:13 N 28 '64
Rent-a-pigeon; J. Coyle and M. Sharpe on KGO radio, San Francisco. il Newsweek 63:42 Ja 13 '64

Illegal applications

See also
Radio stations, Illegal

International aspects

See also
Radio broadcasting—Propaganda

Multiplex system

Build the MPX. A. B. Otis, jr. il Pop Electr 18:63-6 Ap; 69-73+ My '63 (to be cont)
MPX meter. F. Blechman. il Pop Electr 19: 41-4+ N '63
SCA; background-music demultiplexer. G. P. Kuntz. il Electr World 72:44-5 S '64
SCA background-music multiplexer. R. W. Winfree. il Electr World 70:42-5 D '63
Transistorized FM-stereo demodulator; multiplex adapter. J. W. Englund and others. il Electr World 72:34-5+ D '64
Wireless re-broadcaster; how to broadcast from your hi-fi, FM tuner, or TV set to every AM radio in the house. K. Dobler. il Pop Electr 22:47-9+ Ja '65

Music

Grand ole opry says so long to four stars. il Life 54:32-3 Mr 22 '63
Lady of the intermissions: Geraldine Souvaine. G. Souvaine. il Opera N 29:12-15 D 5 '64
Lay listener; Metropolitan opera broadcasts. C. J. Hurlock. il Opera N 29:16 D 5 '64
Letter from Europe. E. Helm. Mus Am 83: 271+ D '63
Metropolitan opera broadcasts 1931-64. Opera N 29:32 D 5 '64
Opera in the air; Texaco-Metropolitan opera broadcast. il Opera N 28:19-22 N 16 '63
Partners in excellence; Texaco sponsors Metropolitan broadcasts. A. C. Long il Opera N 29:8-11 D 5 '64
Radio and the Philharmonic: hitting a hip 1,000. il Sr Schol 82:12-13 Mr 20 '63
Radio-TV (cont) il Mus Am 83:212 Ja; 49 F; 50 Mr; 53 Ap; 41 My '63
Signs of opera; Texaco-Metropolitan opera broadcast. il Opera N 29:17-20 N 14 '64
Switch in time; unprecedented broadcast change. F. Stevenson. il Opera N 27:13-16 Mr 9 '63

News

Anybody out there? M. Mannes. Esquire 62: 54+ N '64
Covering the tragedy; President Kennedy's assassination. il Time 82:84 N 29 '63
Warning to pirates; Pennsylvania Supreme court's injunction against WPAZ. Time 82: 40 Jl 19 '63

RADIO broadcasting—News—*Continued*
What the voice of America tells the world. Good H 158:161 My '64
When the press shapes the news. H. Brucker. il Sat R 47:75-7+ Ja 11 '64; Discussion. 47: 46-7 F 8; 123+ Mr 14 '64
See also
Radio broadcasting—Election results

Opera

See Radio broadcasting—Music

Program rating

Shadow strikes again. R. L. Shayon. Sat R 46:51 Jl 13 '63
TV ratings rated low by Congress. Sr Schol 82:17-19 My 8 '63

Programs

Audiences did a lot of the work; past programs. S. Moore. Life 57:19 N 13 '64
Coffee break: Breakfast club. il Newsweek 61: 80 Je 3 '63
Gothic revival; Shadow transcriptions of the '40s. il Time 84:59-60 S 4 '64
Heh-heh-heh-heh; The Shadow knows. Newsweek 61:92 Ap 22 '63
Life radio review. C. Osborne. Life 57:16 Ag 14 '64
Look and listen; ed. by P. Dilts. See issues of Senior scholastic
Looking and listening. P. Dilts. See issues of Senior scholastic
See also
National association for better radio and television

Propaganda

Disarming the air waves: western censorship of BBC, Radio in the American sector of Berlin, Voice of America, and Radio free Europe. E. Schlosser. Nat R 16:1014-15 N 17 '64
H. L. Hunt: portrait of a super-patriot; Life line. R. G. Sherrill. Nation 198:182-95 F 24 '64
Know your rights. Nation 199:151 S 28 '64
Other government; North Viet Nam's Radio liberation. Time 83:29-30 Ja 31 '64
Radio right: hate clubs of the air. F. J. Cook. il Nation 198:523-7 My 25 '64
T.R.B. from Washington; preachers of fear: radio and television programs of COPE, and Life lines. New Repub 150:2 Ja 4 '64; Discussion. 150:30 Ja 25; 30 F 8 '64
See also
American committee for liberation

Quiz programs

Time to stump the experts: Information please on the air; excerpt from Not under oath. J. Kieran. il Horizon 6:106-11 Autumn '64

Religious programs

Across the airwaves. E. C. Parker. Christian Cent 80:724-5 My 29 '63
Prime time; United Presbyterian church on the meaning of Thanksgiving. Newsweek 62:92 D 2 '63
Reformation or defamation? 20th century reformation hour. R. G. Kemper. Christian Cent 80:465-6 Ap 10 '63
Religion and the FCC. M. Cohn. il Reporter 32:32-4 Ja 14 '65
Transistorized mission; United Presbyterian church's venture into radio jingles. R. L. Shayon. Sat R 46:36 Ag 24 '63

Sports

El As is the voice of America; broadcasts world series in Spanish. R. H. Boyle. il Sports Illus 19:33-4+ O 14 '63
Joe to behold! baseball announcer. H. L. Masin. il Sr Schol 83:24 S 20 '63
Memoirs of a short-wave prophet; listening to baseball broadcasts in Mississippi. W. Morris. New Yorker 39:117-18+ N 30 '63
Talk me out of the ball game. R. Schoenstein. Sat R 47:82 Ap 11 '64

Stereophonic transmission

FM on the threshold. L. Marcus. il Hi Fi 14:65-7+ N '64

Subscription programs

Plight of subscription radio. R. L. Shayon. Sat R 47:31 N 7 '64

Time signals

See Time signals, Radio

Weather forecasts

New Great Lakes weather code. il Motor B 113:94+ Je '64
New way to get your weather. R. P. Davis. il Motor B 113:40-3+ Je '64
Radio weathercasts, 1964. il Motor B 113: 49-54 Je '64
Radio weathercasts 1963; AM radio stations and their weathercast schedules. il Motor B 111:46-51 Je '63
Tornado alley's emergency net. L. Hunter. il Pop Electr 20:37-8+ Ap '64
Weather by the minute. E. D. Fales, jr. il Yachting 114:40-2+ Jl '63
WXCVR; tuning in FAA automatic radio weather broadcasts. H. B. Smith. il Pop Electr 20:63-5+ Ja '64

Canada

See also
Canadian broadcasting corporation

France

Letter from Paris; radio and television coverage for G. Defferre. Genêt. New Yorker 40:144-6 Mr 7 '64
Unequal time; allowance for presidential candidates. Time 83:39 Mr 13 '64

Germany (Federal Republic)

Dear Sister Bertha; West Berlin's RIAS (Radio in the American sector) Newsweek 61:80 Je 3 '63

Great Britain

Report of the committee on broadcasting, by H. Pilkington and others. Review Commentary 35:264-8 Mr '63. P. Breslow
See also
British broadcasting corporation

Luxembourg

Beaming with success. il Bsns W p64-6 Je 1 '63

Russia

What Soviet broadcasts say about the U.S. now. U S News 56:6 My 18 '64

United States

American radio today: the listener be damned. D. Smith. il Harper 229:58-63 S '64; Same abr. with title American radio: an insult to the public? Read Digest 85: 115-18 D '64; Discussion. Harper 229:6+ N '64
Coincidence or not; opportunities for presentation of viewpoints on any controversial issue. Nat R 15:382-4 N 5 '63
Editorials on the air. R. L. Shayon. Sat R 46:71 S 14 '63
Hi ho, the hierarchy. O. M. Verona. Esquire 62:74-5 O '64
New age of radio. A. Bester. il Holiday 33: 56-65+ Je '63
Turned up high. Time 84:102 S 18 '64
See also
National association of broadcasters
United States—Federal communications commission

RADIO broadcasting, Short wave
Calling all SWL DX'ers. G. L. Dexter. il Pop Electr 19:39-42+ S '63
Memoirs of a short-wave prophet; listening to baseball broadcasts in Mississippi. W. Morris. New Yorker 39:117-18+ N 30 '63
Short-wave broadcast predictions (title varies) S. Leinwoll. See issues of Popular electronics

RADIO broadcasting, Stereophonic. See Radio broadcasting—Stereophonic transmission

RADIO broadcasting and television
Onward and upward with the arts: British broadcasting corporation, Third programme. V. Mehta. New Yorker 39:98+ My 18 '63

RADIO broadcasting stations. See Radio stations

RADIO broadcasting stations, Amateur. See Radio stations, Amateur

RADIO capacitors
Filter capacitor replacement, think ahead. L. A. Harlow. il Pop Electr 20:79-80 Je '64

RADIO circuits
Designing the I.F. circuit. J. Tartas. il Electr World 72:46-9 S '64
New citizens band circuits. L. Buckwalter. il Electr World 69:48-9+ Ap; 32-3 Je; 70: 41+ S; 36+ N '63; 71:32-3+ Ja; 46-7+ Mr; 46-7+ My; 72:34-5+ Jl; 54-5+ O '64; 73: 50-1 Ja '65
Quieting audio switching transients. R. L. Ives. il Electr World 72:51 N '64
Revamp your CB for better noise limiting; conversion to the Makino circuit. R. L. Winklepleck. il Pop Electr 20:53-4 Ap '64

RADIO circuits—*Continued*
60-cycle repulsion coil-resonance engine. W. B. Ford. il Pop Electr 20:41-5+ Mr '64
What is Q? measure of power in tuned circuits. J. Tusinski. il Electr World 70:94+ O '63

RADIO City music hall. See New York (city)—Radio City music hall

RADIO coils
Coil-winding nomogram. A. L. Teubner. il Electr World 69:33 Ap '63

RADIO communication
Eavesdropping on satellites. T. Lamb. il Pop Electr 18:52-3+ F '63
Para-kiting: dawn of the human antenna. J. Joseph. il Pop Electr 18:94 F '63
See also
Dipole orbital belts in space
Intercommunicating systems
Space flight—Communication problems

Interference

See Radio interference

International aspects

Antarctic treaty countries hold meeting on telecommunications. Dept State Bul 49:107-8 Jl 15 '63

RADIO communication, Military
Army order: sound on! Sci N L 84:372 D 14 '63
South Vietnam's 40 megacycle intercom. A. F. Gonzalez, jr. il Pop Electr 18:41-5+ Ap '63
TSQ-47 traffic system undergoes test; Air force communications service. P. J. Klass. il Aviation W 79:69+ N 11 '63
Two documents will assist ECAC in solving military RFI problems. M. Getler. Miss & Roc 14:17-18 Mr 9 '64
See also
United States—Air force—Communication systems
World war, 1939-1945—Radio, radar, etc.

RADIO communication, Short wave
New look in microwaves. L. G. Sands. il Electr World 72:60-2 Ag '64
State-police microwave. M. Lincoln. il Electr World 71:48-50 F '64
Why not U.H.F. two-way radio. H. H. Rice. il Electr World 71:42-3 Mr '64
See also
Citizens radio service
Radio broadcasting, Short wave
Radio receiving apparatus, Short wave
Radio transmission, Short wave
Radio transmitters, Short wave
Tropospheric radio wave propagation

RADIO communication, Underground
Messages may be sent through earth's crust. Sci N L 84:13 Je 6 '63

RADIO condensers. See Radio capacitors

RADIO control
Radio-controlled garage-door openers. il Consumer Rep 28:378-82 Ag '63
See also subhead Radio control under various subjects, e.g. Airplane models—Radio control

RADIO converters
Bandspreading the ARC-5. E. H. Marriner. il Pop Electr 20:66+ Je '64
Eavesdropping on satellites; NASA 136. T. Lamb. il Pop Electr 18:52-3+ F '63
Noise figures of V.H.F. amateur converters. W. Connelly. il Electr World 72:34-5+ S '64
Transistorized six-meter converter. R. C. Hejhall. il Electr World 71:46-7 F '64

RADIO corporation of America
Attraction of opposites; Radio corporation of America offers to absorb Prentice-Hall inc. Time 84:58 D 25 '64
Big white room assembly raises ICBM reliability. il Miss & Roc 12:46 My 27 '63
Color prices lower. Newsweek 63:80+ My 25 '64
Going after the leader; IBM's System 360 and RCA's Spectra 70. il Bsns W p 122+ D 12 '64
New Tiros wheel design studied. M. Getler. il Miss & Roc 12:17 Je 3 '63
RCA takes aim on big computer sales. C. D. LaFond. il Miss & Roc 15:32-3 D 14 '64
RCA talking merger with Prentice-Hall. Pub W 186:44-5 D 28 '64
RCA's signal: coming in strong. il Bsns W p 110-12+ Je 29 '63

Astro-Electronics division

Moon shot technician. il Ebony 20:45-6+ D '64

RCA Victor division

Change of chairs; interviews, ed. by S. Fleming. il Hi Fi 14:28+ Ja '64
Da capo; complete numerical listing of RCA Victor Red seal albums. S. Smolian. Am Rec G 30:892-5, 1002-4, 1056-8; 31:82-4, 165-7, 271-3 My-Jl, S-N '64
Debut of dynagroove and some repercussions. R. D. Darrell. Hi Fi 13:37 My '63
First opera in dynagroove: Madama Butterfly. P. L. Miller. il Am Rec G 29:684-5 My '63
High quality classics at half price; Victrola records. P. Hart. Hi Fi 13:96 S '63
RCA Victor introduces dynagroove and Columbia calls it a backward step. G. Lieberson. il Am Rec G 29:600-1+ Ap '63
Second look at dynagroove. R. D. Darrell. Hi Fi 13:92 Ag '63

Research laboratories

RCA makes new type of small microcircuit. Aviation W 78:104 F 11 '63

RADIO direction finders. See Radio aids to navigation

RADIO equipment in taxicabs. See Taxicabs—Radio equipment

RADIO filters
Adjustable speech filter. D. Meyer. il Pop Electr 20:49-52 My '64
Low-pass audio filters for increased talk-power. R. A. Genaille. il Electr World 70:47-9 S '63
19-Kc. filter. T. E. Reamer. il Electr World 69:62-3 F '63
Tunable phase-shift audio filter. R. L. Ives. bibliog il Electr World 69:48-50 My '63

RADIO flying. See Aviation—Instrument flying

RADIO free Europe
Radio free Europe; remarks, December 2, 1964. L. B. Johnson. Dept State Bul 51:876-7 D 21 '64
Who knows? F. D. Elmer, jr. Christian Cent 80:783 Je 12 '63

RADIO frequency
Accurate audio frequency measurement. A. W. Edwards. il Electr World 70:46-7+ Ag '63
Army to use computers to simulate radio frequency interference problems. C. D. LaFond. il Miss & Roc 14:26-7 Je 22 '64
Frequency synthesizers. I. Math. il Electr World 73:27+ Ja '65
How we're using rock-bottom radio. W. S. Bacon and E. Nanas. il Pop Electr 19:51-4+ D '63
Precise measurement of radio frequencies. J. R. Johnson. il Electr World 72:47-50 Ag '64
Pros and cons of wideband response. N. Eisenberg. il Hi Fi 14:39-42+ My '64
R.F. coil frequency-finder. L. A. Wortman. il Pop Electr 20:60-1 F '64
R.F. response measurement. J. Tusinski. il Electr World 71:37+ F '64
Very-low-frequency radio waves and the ionosphere; report of symposium at the Central radio propagation laboratory, National bureau of standards, Boulder, Colo. D. D. Crombie. Science 142:508+ O 25 '63

Allocation

See Radio frequency allocation

Control

Unijunction c.w. monitor. J. F. Cleary. bibliog il Electr World 71:62+ Ap '64

RADIO frequency allocation
Banding together. il Newsweek 62:98 O 21 '63
Clearing the air; citizens band violations. il Newsweek 64:78-9 Ag 17 '64
New FCC rules in effect. L. G. Sands. il Electr World 71:30+ My '64
Precision of U.S. frequency standard. il Electr World 72:78 Jl '64
Tuning up on the new 460-Mc. police frequencies; with list of police stations on 450-460 Mc. K. Greenberg. il Pop Electr 20:56-8+ My '64

RADIO frequency meters. See Radio instruments

RADIO frequency modulation
Faithful sound; FM radio reception. R. Freas. Esquire 62:68+ N '64
FM on the threshold. L. Marcus. il Hi Fi 14:65-7+ N '64
FM: radio's problem child. J. Tebbel. Sat R 48:67-8 Ja 9 '65
Medium still unexplored. Hi Fi 14:35 My '64
See also
Radio receiving apparatus—Frequency modulation receivers
Radio stations, Frequency modulation

RADIO frequency signal generators. See Signal generators
RADIO generators. See Signal generators
RADIO in aviation
After the revolution, a King; navcom equipment. W. J. Kendall. il Flying 74:42-3+ My '64
Airports get new spotter; Servo-FAA aircraft direction finder. Bsns W p 122 N 30 '63
All-weather aircraft landing; ILS and PAR approach systems. F. B. Bardy. il Sci Am 210:25-35 Mr '64
Decca to show improved system in U.S. P. J. Klass. il Aviation W 81:88-9+ S 21 '64
Economy ILS aids readied for evaluation at two airports. P. J. Klass. il Aviation W 80:68-9+ Mr 2 '64
FAA endorses crash locator beacon use. Aviation W 80:47 Ja 27 '64
FAA testing extended-range radio link. P. J. Klass. il Aviation W 78:103+ Je 24 '63
Jet transport communications. R. L. Conhaim. il Electr World 70:27-30+ N '63
Landing device shows runway image in fog; Microvision. Sci N L 86:89 Ag 8 '64
Precision VOR gives improved accuracy. P. J. Klass. il Aviation W 80:82-3+ Ap 20 '64
Runway lights that aren't really there; microvision. il Sci Digest 56:63-4 O '64
Skyway crash preventers. K. Brown. il Pop Mech 120:106-10+ D '63
Suitcase-size localizer undergoes tests; aircraft being equipped with VOR receivers. B. Miller. il Aviation W 82:74-5 Ja 25 '65
System offers private-line radio service. P. J. Klass. il Aviation W 78:115+ My 13 '63
RADIO in fire protection
Wildfires in Alaska. D. E. Hess and others. il Am For 70:24-7+ F '64
RADIO in medicine
Deep body temperature of untethered dolphin recorded by ingested radio transmitter. R. S. Mackay. bibliog il Science 144:864-6 My 15 '64
RADIO in meteorology
Radio observation of the electromagnetic emission from warm clouds. J. D. Sartor. bibliog il Science 143:948-50 F 28 '64
RADIO in navigation
ABC's of the RDF. R. H. Sutherland. il Motor B 111:53+ My '63
Automatic direction finders. E. Robberson. il Yachting 115:76-8+ Ja '64
Consolan classroom. J. Martenhoff. il Motor B 113:24-5+ Je '64
Great way to spend the day, calibrate your rfd. H. M. Anthony. il Motor B 112:30-1 Ag '63
Landfall on a single radio beacon. G. Nichols, jr. Yachting 115:148-9 F '64
RDF: a navigator's best friend; Consol-Consolan line of position. J. Martenhoff. il Motor B 112:48-51+ N '63
See also
Radio apparatus on ships, boats, etc.
RADIO in politics
Candidates on air: new ruling from FCC. U S News 57:13 O 12 '64
See also
Radio broadcasting—Election results
Radio broadcasting—Propaganda
RADIO in rescue work
Request assistance! my estimated position is. H. M. Anthony. il Motor B 112:32-3 Ag '63
RADIO industry. See Radio apparatus industry and trade
RADIO instruments
C bridge. F. A. Parker. il Pop Electr 19:65-6+ N '63
Code bander. H. B. Smith. il Pop Electr 19:45-8 Ag '63
Crystal super calibrator. R. A. Scheidel. il Pop Electr 19:51-4+ N '63
Direct-reading audio-frequency meter. R. C. Apperson, jr. il Electr World 73:88-9 Ja '65
Monitor your code. I. C. Chapel. il Pop Electr 18:56-7+ Ap '63
MPX meter. F. Blechman. il Pop Electr 19:41-4+ N '63
Music/speech discriminator. F. D. Gross. il Electr World 69:36-8+ Ap '63
R.F. coil frequency-finder. L. A. Wortman. il Pop Electr 20:60-1 F '64
Signal stethoscope. L. E. Greenlee. il Pop Electr 19:59-61+ Jl '63
Which channel is it? measuring frequencies with heterodyne or deviation-type frequency meter. L. G. Sands. il Electr World 71:40+ F '64
Wide-range wow & flutter meter. F. J. DiElsi. il Electr World 71:76-8 Je '64
See also
Oscillators
RADIO interference
Design cure advocated for radio frequency interference problems. Miss & Roc 15:38-9 Jl 6 '64
FCC and 11 meters: a CBer's view. D. T. Geiser. il Pop Electr 20:59-60+ Je '64
Hum from crossed connections. J. A. Risse. il Electr World 71:86 F '64
Hum interference in car radios. D. T. Geiser. il Electr World 70:80 D '63
Interference stopper for AM sets. J. D. Amorose. Electr World 69:73 Je '63
Marine radio: receivers and operating. E. Robberson. il Yachting 116:54-6+ Jl '64
Noise figures of V.H.F. amateur converters. W. Connelly. il Electr World 72:34-5 S '64
Quieting audio switching transients. R. L. Ives. il Electr World 72:51 N '64
Radio & TV interference. T. R. Haskett and J. D. Blount. il Electr World 71:39-41 My; 40-1+ Je '64
Revamp your CB for better noise limiting. R. L. Winklepleck. il Pop Electr 20:53-4 Ap '64
Sure cure for ham, CB mobile noise. J. D. Lenk. il Pop Electr 19:65-6 O '63
Two documents will assist ECAC in solving military RFI problems. M. Getler. Miss & Roc 14:17-18 Mr 9 '64
RADIO jingles. See Radio advertising
RADIO laws and regulations
Sad sack agency. Nation 198:2-3 Ja 4 '64
See also
Radio frequency allocation
United States—Federal communications commission
RADIO liberty (agency) See American committee for liberation
RADIO loud speakers. See Loud speaking apparatus
RADIO Luxembourg. See Radio broadcasting—Luxembourg
RADIO measurements
See also
Radio frequency
RADIO meteorology
Radio meteorology; report on conference at the National bureau of standards, Boulder, Colo. laboratories, September 14-18, 1964. J. W. Herbstreit. Science 147:76-8 Ja 1 '65
RADIO modulators. See Modulators
RADIO operators
Licenses
Extortion; radio license fee. F. K. Smith. il Flying 75:102 S '64
FCC establishes fees for radio licenses. Electr World 70:69 Ag '63
How you can get a license to operate a student experimental radio station. D. T. Geiser. il Pop Electr 19:69-70+ S '63
Why won't they renew my radiotelephone license? B. G. Cato. Motor B 113:158+ My '64
RADIO operators, Amateur
Across the ham bands. H. S. Brier. See issues of Popular electronics
K7UGA will get the ham vote. A. Whitman. il N Y Times Mag p64+ S 13 '64
Monthly short-wave report. H. Bennett. See issues of Popular electronics
Radio hams tune up. Sci N L 84:11 Jl 6 '63
Rx for the amateur SWL. il Pop Electr 20:67-8+ F '64
Short-wave samaritans; medical aid gets through in emergencies, thanks to amateur radio operators. D. E. Logan, jr. il Todays Health 42:40-1+ Je '64
Anecdotes, facetiae, satire, etc.
Interview with KN3NOB. D. Harbaugh. il Pop Electr 18:82-3 Mr '63
RADIO phonograph combination. See Radio receiving apparatus—Phonograph combination
RADIO plays
Canterville ghost; ed. by W. Hackett. Plays 23:85-94 Mr '64
Canterbury tales; dramatization of poem by G. Chaucer. L. Olfson. Plays 22:97-107 My '63
Christmas every day; dramatization of story by W. D. Howells. J. McGowan. Plays 23:87-95 D '63
Crowning of King Arthur; dramatization of Morte d'Arthur by T. Malory. L. Olfson. Plays 24:87-96 D '64

RADIO plays—*Continued*
Five weeks in a balloon; dramatization of story by J. Verne. L. Olfson. Plays 23:87-95 Ap '64
Invisible man; dramatization of story by H. G. Wells. L. Olfson. Plays 24:83-93 N '64
Marmalade overture. C. Boiko. Plays 24:79-81 N '64
Romeo and Juliet; drama, ed. by L. Olfson. W. Shakespeare. Plays 23:87-98 My '64
Sherlock Holmes and the stockbroker's clerk; dramatization of story by A. C. Doyle. L. Olfson. Plays 23:85-95 O '63
Swiss family Robinson; dramatization of story by J. Wyss. L. Olfson. Plays 23:85-96 F '64
See also
Radio broadcasting—Drama

RADIO program rating. See Radio broadcasting—Program rating

RADIO programs. See Radio broadcasting—Programs

RADIO receiving apparatus
AM clock radios. il Consumer Rep 29:242-5 My '64
A.G.C. for receiver audio. J. L. Lanterman. il Electr World 71:78 Ap '64
Build a modern crystal set. W. T. Boyd. il Pop Electr 21:53-5+ Jl '64
Code bander. H. B. Smith. il Pop Electr 19:45-8 Ag '63
Converting your first command receiver. E. H. Marriner. il Pop Electr 18:45-8+ Je '63
FM table-model radios. il Consumer Rep 28:329-31 Jl '63
Multiplex muse; a critical listing of new hardware for listening. J. M. Conly. Reporter 31:42+ D 17 '64; Reply with rejoinder. W. H. Thomas. 32:8 Ja 14 '65
Radios and phonographs. Consumer Bul 29:90-106 D '64
Shopping the home entertainment circuit. R. Freas. il Am Home 67:85-7 D '64
Single-frequency receiver. W. B. Kincaid. il Electr World 71:44-5+ Ap '64
Soup up that AM broadcast receiver. F. J. Bauer, jr. il Pop Electr 20:56-7 Je '64
Tunnel diode receiver. R. D. Grimm. il Pop Electr 18:62-5+ Je '63
$2.98 clock radio. J. W. Spencer. il Pop Mech 120:183 D '63
Your leisure. Consumer Rep 28:356-65 D '63
See also
Magnavox company

Control

Build your own radio remote control. H. G. McEntee. il Pop Sci 185:108-11 Ag '64

Frequency modulation receivers

Design trends in receiver frequency control. J. Kyle. il Electr World 72:52-4+ D '64
Faithful sound; FM radio reception. R. Freas. Esquire 62:68+ N '64
Upgrading simple FM tuners. E. W. Cassaday. Electr World 69:80 My '63

History

Restoreth thy relic radio. T. M. Hannah. il Pop Electr 20:31-5+ My '64

Phonograph combination

Build the tune-table. H. L. Davidson. il Pop Electr 20:49-50 Je '64
Faithful sound; radio phonographs. R. Freas. il Esquire 60:59+ N '63

Power supply

High power vs. low power. H. S. Brier. il Pop Electr 20:67-8+ Je '64

Repairing

See also
Radio receiving apparatus, Portable—Repairing

Tuning

Low-down on hi-fi stereo tuners; FM multiplex tuners. C. P. Gilmore and H. Luckett. il Pop Sci 185:102-5+ S '64
MPX meter. F. Blechman. il Pop Electr 19:41-4+ N '63
Tune away rock-bound CB receiver. R. L. Winklepleck. il Pop Electr 20:47-50 Ap '64
Update your Eico 760. M. Moses. il Pop Electr 20:52 Ap '64
Upgrading simple FM tuners. E. W. Cassaday. Electr World 69:80 My '63

RADIO receiving apparatus, Portable
Airline eavesdropper. G. L. Downs. il Pop Electr 18:46-7 Ap '63
Being tiny is not enough; Panasonic R-8 and Sony AM-FM. il Consumer Rep 29:518-19 N '64
Build the AUX-9. T. H. Charters. il Pop Electr 21:65-7+ O '64
Directory of importers and manufacturers of Japanese transistor radios. Electr World 69:38-9+ My '63; Correction. 70:82 S '63
Full-sized portable am radios. il Consumer Rep 29:550-3 N '64
Haydn in the park. I. Berger. il Sat R 46:53+ My 25 '63
Miniature I.F. module superheterodyne pocket receiver. C. Caringella. il Pop Electr 21:49-52+ D '64
New circuits for FM portables. il Electr World 71:64 My '64
Personal radios. il Consumer Rep 28:220-4 My '63
Portable radio in thirty minutes. L. Steckler. il Pop Mech 119:135-7 Ap '63
Punch for portables; add-on amplifier and speaker. A. Kennedy. il Pop Mech 121:196-8 Ja '64
Run your radio on solar power. D. S. Halacy, jr. il Pop Sci 185:138-9 N '64
Small wonder; Tokyo's Sony corp. il Time 82:91 Jl 12 '63
Transistor radios. il Consumer Bul 47:6-9 Ja '64
Twosome; miniature speaker system for pocket transistor radio. L. A. Wortman. il Pop Electr 18:57 F '63
Vacation with music: take console sound in a suitcase. R. Freas. il Am Home 67:21+ Jl '64
What to consider when buying a transistor radio. Bet Hom & Gard 42:124 N '64
Wherever she goes; Greyhound bus company to install transistor radios above each seat. Time 82:69 N 15 '63

Repairing

Troubles with servicing. Consumer Bul 46:36-7 Ap '63

RADIO receiving apparatus, Short wave
Broadcast band DX getting started. T. R. Haskett. il Pop Electr 21:53-6+ N '64
Rx for the amateur SWL. il Pop Electr 20:67-8+ F '64
Simple superhet for 6. C. Green. il Pop Electr 18:58-61 Ap '63
Tune in on air traffic. M. Lincoln. il Pop Electr 21:58-9+ S '64
Two-meter simple superhet. C. Green. il Pop Electr 19:43-6+ S '63
VHF adventurer. J. G. Lee. il Pop Electr 19:41-6 O; 57-63 N; 61-6+ D '63
VHF listener. W. Henry. il Pop Electr 20:52-6+ Mr '64
Zener receiver muter. I. C. Chapel. il Pop Electr 21:88 Ag '64

RADIO receiving apparatus, Stereophonic
Guide to stereo shelving. L. Buckwalter. il Hi Fi 14:50-2+ Je '64
How to arrange for big entertainment. il Bet Hom & Gard 41:94+ S '63
Medium still unexplored. Hi Fi 14:35 My '64
Stereo receivers. il Consumer Rep 29:273-9 Je '64
Stereo s'lector. A. B. Otis, jr. il Pop Electr 21:73-5 S '64
Stereo table radios; AM/FM/MX. il Consumer Rep 28:434-7 S '63

RADIO receiving apparatus, Superheterodyne
Miniature I.F. module superheterodyne pocket receiver. C. Caringella. il Pop Electr 21:49-52+ D '64
Two-tube superhet for 80 meters. C. Green. il Pop Electr 20:45-8+ Ja '64

RADIO receiving apparatus, Superregenerative
Compact 6-meter transceiver. M. Leibowitz and C. Pappas. il Electr World 69:43-5 Ap '63

RADIO reception
See also
Radio antennas

RADIO relay league, American. See American radio relay league

RADIO service shops
Mac's electronics service. J. T. Frye. See issues of Electronics world to April 1963

RADIO servicemen
Proposal to the FCC; a citizens radio technician license. R. L. Conhaim. Electr World 69:48-9 Mr '63

RADIO sponsors. See Radio advertising

RADIO stars. See Radio astronomy

RADIO stations
Carl McIntire's radio station; application for transfer of radio station WXUR in Media, Pa. to the Faith theological society. America 111:765-6 D 12 '64
Crusader; WMCA and Supreme court decision for reapportionment. New Yorker 40:24-6 Je 27 '64

RADIO stations—*Continued*
Hard sell; hard-liquor commercials on WQXR. Newsweek 63:74 Mr 30 '64
Hidden TV test signals. L. Solomon. il Electr World 71:34-5 Ap '64
Listening without guilt: WINS. R. L. Shayon. Sat R 46:57+ Mr 9 '63
Moving the spirits; whisky commercials. Time 83:80 Mr 27 '64
New age of radio. A. Bester. il Holiday 33: 56-65+ Je '63
New facilities for WWVB and WWVL. il Electr World 71:39 Ja '64
Radio station throws party to prove a point; WCAU in Philadelphia. il Bsns W p56-7 S 5 '64
Reformation or defamation? WHHH. Warren. Ohio. R. G. Kemper. Christian Cent 80:465-6 Ap 10 '63
Warning to pirates; Pennsylvania Supreme court's injunction against WPAZ. Time 82:40 Jl 9 '63

RADIO stations, Amateur
How you can get a license to operate a student experimental radio station. D. T. Geiser. il Pop Electr 19:69-70+ S '63
Race against blindness; ham radio operators and eye surgeons join forces. M. Gunther. il Sat Eve Post 237:36-7 My 30 '64
Tornado alley's emergency net; Radio amateur civil emergency service. L. Hunter. il Pop Electr 20:37-8+ Ap '64
See also
Citizens radio service

RADIO stations, Frequency modulation
FM on the threshold. L. Marcus. il Hi Fi 14: 65-7+ N '64
Networks for FM. M. Williams; discussion. Sat R 46:51+ F 23; 72 Mr 30 '63
Tonic for the gin. il Newsweek 61:100+ My 27 '63

RADIO stations, Government
Radio marathon broadcasts truth to Cuba! W. I. Orr. il Pop Electr 19:58-9+ Ag '63

RADIO stations, Illegal
Caroline calling: pirate radio ship off coast of England. Newsweek 63:88 My 4 '64
Not cricket, Caroline! M. E. Pooley. il Pop Electr 21:38 Jl '64
Radio pirates try abducting audiences; shipboard radio stations off the coast of Great Britain. il Bsns W p47-8+ My 2 '64

RADIO stations, Military
How we're using rock-bottom radio. W. S. Bacon and E. Nanas. il Pop Electr 19:51-4+ D '63
Naval observatory time signals. H. C. Wood. il Electr World 70:30+ Ag '63

RADIO stations, Portable
Business radio report. L. G. Sands. il Electr World 71:51-4 Ja '64

RADIO stations, Short wave
Broadcast band DX getting started. T. R. Haskett. il Pop Electr 21:53-6+ N '64
Monthly short-wave report. H. Bennett. See issues of Popular electronics
New voice from Africa. G. L. Dexter. il Pop Electr 18:69 Je '63

RADIO technical commission for aeronautics
RTCA seeks simplified system in examining ATC problems. Aviation W 80:28 Je 22 '64
Technicians score FAA on traffic control. Aviation W 79:36-7 Jl 15 '63

RADIO telemetry. See Telemeter (physiological apparatus)

RADIO telephone
Companion 6-meter transmitter. C. Green. il Pop Electr 21:53-7 S '64
New citizens band circuits; new transceivers. L. Buckwalter. il Electr World 72:54-5+ O '64
New rules to govern CB. Pop Electr 21:55 O '64
Two-way radio; Fort Worth, Tex. J. I. Koski. il Am City 79:151-2 My '64
Wipe out vibrator hash. R. L. Winklepleck. il Pop Electr 19:41-5 D '63
See also
Police radio

RADIO telephone, Portable
Army order: sound on! Sci N L 84:372 D 14 '63
Choosing a two-way radio system. H. H. Rice. il Electr World 70:50-2 N; 52-3+ D '63
Community takes to the airways. W. J. Fletcher. il Suc Farm 61:124 Ap '63
Golf goes walkie-talkie. A. Coya. il Pop Electr 21:70 Jl '64
Ham-band walkie-talkies the easy way. H. B. Smith. il Pop Electr 20:61-4 Ap '64
Martin gets award for further work on Random access discrete address; portable mobile field radio telephone system. C. D. LaFond. il Miss & Roc 15:23 S 14 '64
Selective calling for two-way radio. M. Golden. il Electr World 69:41-4+ Je '63
Suddenly everybody wants a two-way radio. il Pop Sci 184:136-40 My '64
Transistors versus tubes for two-way radio. H. H. Rice. il Electr World 72:48-50 N '64
Two-way CB radios. L. Buckwalter and L. Steckler. il Pop Mech 120:92-5 Jl '63
Unique walkie-talkie a $19.95 kit. il Pop Electr 20:65 Ap '64
Walkie-talkie as a photo accessory. H. Friedman. il Pop Phot 55:78+ O '64
Walkie-talkie kits useful in many ways. Consumer Bul 46:43+ Je '63

RADIO telephone connections. See Telephone—Radio telephone connection

RADIO telephone licenses. See Radio laws and regulations

RADIO telephone on automobiles
Business radio report. L. G. Sands. il Electr World 71:51-4 Ja '64
Extra-feature two-way radio; use in routine water-service operations. L. B. Hertzberg. il Am City 78:144+ O '63
Suddenly everybody wants a two-way radio. il Pop Sci 184:136-40 My '64

RADIO telephone on motor vehicles
Choosing a two-way radio system. H. H. Rice. il Electr World 70:50-2 N; 52-3+ D '63
Why not U.H.F. two-way radio. H. H. Rice. il Electr World 71:42-3 Mr '64

RADIO telephone on ships, boats, etc.
Auxiliaries can get more from their radios. H. C. Lawrence. il Motor B 112:40-1+ N '63
CBers note! the rules have changed. E. S. Maloney. il Motor B 11:82+ N '64
Do you need a radiotelephone on board? H. C. Lawrence. il Motor B 113:32-3+ Ap '64
High seas calling. E. H. Marriner. il Pop Electr 21:52-4 O '64
High seas radiotelephone. P. R. Bartlett. Yachting 113:212+ My '63
Radiotelephone tips. R. C. Beard. il Motor B 111:88+ Je '63
V.H.F. marine radiotelephony. L. G. Sands. il Electr World 70:48-9+ Jl '63
What radiotelephone? E. Robberson. il Yachting 117:80-2+ Ja '65
Why won't they renew my radiotelephone license? B. G. Cato. Motor B 113:158+ My '64

Anecdotes, facetiae, satire, etc.

I'm bashful! S. Sawyer. il Motor B 112:42+ N '63

RADIO telescope
Arecibo observatory in Puerto Rico. il(p313) Sky & Tel 26:315+ D '63
Big dish: how haste and secrecy helped navy waste $63 million in race to build huge telescope. D. S. Greenberg. Science 144: 1111-12 My 29 '64
Biggest ear ever: Arecibo telescope. il Life 55:119+ N 8 '63
Data from a big dish; radio telescope at Arecibo. il Time 82:62 N 8 '63
Haystack radar-radio telescope dedicated. il Sky & Tel 28:349-51 D '64
Jodrell bank observatory. V. K. McElheny. il Science 144:520-3 My 1 '64
Large radio telescope of Ohio state university. J. D. Kraus. il Sky & Tel 26:12-16 Jl '63
Largest radio-radar telescope unveiled; Arecibo, Puerto Rico. Sci N L 84:323 N 23 '63
Observatory in Puerto Rico will far surpass existing big dishes; Arecibo ionospheric observatory. C. D. LaFond. il Miss & Roc 13: 24-5 N 11 '63
1,000-foot eye starts peering into space; Arecibo, Puerto Rico. il Pop Sci 184:88-9 F '64
Outer limits; Arecibo ionospheric observatory. il Newsweek 62:73 N 11 '63
Radio telescope operates with microwaves. Sci N L 84:14 Jl 6 '63
Radio telescopes: past, present & future. A. Giddis and L. Maggi. il Electr World 72:19-23+ Jl '64
Some current programs at Arecibo. C. A. Federer. il Sky & Tel 28:4-8, 73-7 Jl-Ag '64
Space explorers build their dream telescope; radio-radar telescope at Arecibo. il Fortune 70:127-9 Ag '64
300-foot radio telescope at Green Bank. J. W. Findlay. il Sky & Tel 25:68-75 F '63

RADIO time signals. See Time signals, Radio

RADIO transmission
Standing waves: do they? F. Blechman. il Pop Electr 20:61-4+ Je '64
See also
Radio antennas
Radio waves—Scattering

Double sideband system

DSB and the citizens bander. B. E. Packham. il Electr World 72:38-40 Ag '64

Single sideband system

Single sideband simplified. R. E. Baird. il Electr World 69:52-4+ F '63

RADIO transmission, Short wave
CM range nomogram. G. Karlin. il Electr World 71:29 Ja '64

RADIO transmitters
Marine radio: transmitting. E. Robberson. il Yachting 115:60-2+ Je '64
Monitor your code. I. C. Chapel. il Pop Electr 18:56-7+ Ap '63
Self-tuning transmitter clarifies space messages. Sci N L 83:118 F 23 '63

Frequency modulation transmitters

Modulation circuits for solid-state CB transmitters. W. A. Rheinfelder. il Electr World 71:28-30+ F '64

RADIO transmitters, Portable
Space-age tracking; radio tracking of wildlife. W. Bever. il Outdoor Life 132:47 O '63
Top band goes mobile. J. E. Rohen. il Pop Electr 18:55-8+ Je '63

RADIO transmitters, Short wave
Compact 6-meter transceiver. M. Leibowitz and C. Pappas. il Electr World 69:43-5 Ap '63
Companion 6-meter transmitter. C. Green. il Pop Electr 21:53-7 S '64
Double CB talk power. W. H. Minor. il Pop Electr 20:54-7 Ap '64
Double-duty EICO 772. R. Clark-Duff. il Pop Electr 19:49-51+ Jl '63
Low-pass audio filters for increased talk-power. R. A. Genaille. il Electr World 70:47-9 S '63
Messenger III; CB transceiver. il Pop Electr 21:50 Jl '64
Modulation circuits for solid-state CB transmitters. W. A. Rheinfelder. il Electr World 71:28-30+ F '64
R.F. power output measurements. R. L. Conhaim. bibliog il Electr World 70:53-6+ O '63
Solid-state 3-watt CB-ham transmitter. T. J. Barmore. il Electr World 70:46-7+ O '63
V.H.F. marine radiotelephony. L. G. Sands. il Electr World 70:48-9+ Jl '63

RADIO tubes. See Vacuum tubes

RADIO waves
Marine radio: transmitting. E. Robberson. il Yachting 115:60-2+ Je '64
New kind of whistler in high atmosphere. Sci N L 85:313 My 16 '64
Radio waves and light. Sky & Tel 28:71 Ag '64
Standing waves: do they? F. Blechman. il Pop Electr 20:61-4+ Je '64
Whistling noises give news from atmosphere. Sci N L 83:311 My 18 '63
See also
Ionospheric radio wave propagation
Microwaves
Radio frequency
Radio meteorology

Scattering

Tropospheric scatter: a bridge to Alaska. il Pop Electr 19:49 O '63

RADIOACTIVATION analysis
Atomic energy, ace detective. J. E. Roper and D. Robinson. il Read Digest 85:122-6 S '64
Atomic fingerprints; neutron activation analysis. il Time 84:58 Ag 7 '64
History revealed in ancient glass. R. W. Smith. il Nat Geog Mag 126:346-69 S '64
Most sensitive analysis. Sci N L 83:197 Mr 30 '63
Neutron activation analysis of fluid inclusions for copper, manganese, and zinc. G. K. Czamanske and others. bibliog il Science 140:401-3 Ap 26 '63
Nuclear activation analysis. R. E. Wainerdi and N. P. DuBeau. bibliog il Science 139: 1027-33 Mr 15 '63
Nuclear activation analysis; report on conference, 27-28 August 1964. V. P. Guinn and R. E. Wainerdi. Science 147:415-16+ Ja 22 '65
Quick, Watson the Geiger counter! neutron activation analysis. C. Remsberg. il Pop Mech 119:97-100 Ap '63

RADIOACTIVE dating
Ages of the Sikhote alin iron meteorite. D. E. Fisher. bibliog il Science 139:752-3 F 22 '63
Chronology of the galaxy. D. D. Clayton. bibliog il Science 143:1281-6 Mr 20 '64
Geological dating by fossil tracks. il(p401) Sci N L 83:404 Je 29 '63
Geomagnetic polarity epochs. A. Cox and others. bibliog Science 143:351-2 Ja 24 '64
Happy birthday. Newsweek 61:81 My 6 '63
Radiogenic strontium-87 as an index of geologic processes. C. E. Hedge and F. G. Walthall. bibliog il Science 140:1214-17 Je 14 '63
Relative dating of Arlington Springs man. K. P. Oakley. il Science 141:1172 S 20 '63
Tritium-hydrologic research: some results of the U.S. geological survey research program. C. W. Carlston. bibliog il Science 143:804-6 F 21 '64
See also
Radiocarbon dating

RADIOACTIVE fallout
Cesium-134 in Alaskan Eskimos and in fallout. H. E. Palmer and R. W. Perkins. bibliog il Science 142:66-7 O 4 '63
Children in fallout path science group contends. Sci N L 84:329 N 23 '63
Children's treaty. Sci Am 209:64-5 N '63
DOD prepares for nuclear effects tests. K. Johnsen. Aviation W 80:24 Mr 30 '64
Fallout and countermeasures. L. D. Hamilton. Bul Atomic Sci 19:36-40 S '63
Fallout, food, and man; report of symposium at meeting of Federation of American societies for experimental biology. M. S. Read and H. S. Olcott. Science 140:1341-2+ Je 21 '63
Fall-out hazards now and yesterday. A. M. Kuzin. il UNESCO Courier 17:11-13 N '64
Fallout: how much is too much? il Bsns W p27 Je 8 '63
Fallout in our food. il Consumer Rep 28:190-3 Ap '63
Fallout in the food chain; contaminated caribou diet of Nunamiut Eskimos. il Time 82:36 S 13 '63
Fallout 1963, an interim report. il Consumer Rep 28:448-9 S '63
High 1963 fallout no cause for concern. Sci N L 83:373 Je 15 '63
I can look my children in the eye again. il Newsweek 62:16-17 Ag 12 '63
Iodine-131 fallout from underground tests. E. A. Martell. bibliog il Science 143:126-9 Ja 10 '64
Iodine-131 in the thyroids of North American deer and caribou: comparison after nuclear tests. W. C. Hanson and others. bibliog il Science 140:801-2 My 17 '63
Lichen, caribou and high radiation in Eskimos. W. O. Pruitt. il Audubon Mag 65: 284-7 S '63
Nature rises from the ashes; Bikini and Eniwetok atolls. il Bsns W p 116-18 O 10 '64
No hot peril in tests. W. Wingo. Sci N L 84:133 Ag 31 '63
Nuclear tests and the fallout debate. il Sr Schol 82:10-13 Ap 3 '63
Nuclear weapons and world sanity; excerpts from address. L. Pauling. il UNESCO Courier 17:6-10 N '64
Particle size fractionation of airborne gamma-emitting radionuclides by graded filters. B. Shleien and others. bibliog il Science 147:290-2 Ja 15 '65
Rhodium-102 fallout: variations in deposition and concentrations in precipitation. M. W. M. Leo and A. Walton. bibliog il Science 140:1398-400 Je 28 '63
Underground test hazards. Sci N L 85:54 Ja 25 '64
See also
Atomic bomb shelters

Measurement

Environmental radiation: measurements of dose rates. P. F. Gustafson and others. bibliog il Science 145:44-7 Jl 3 '64
Fallout in food. il Consumer Rep 29:352-3; 30:33 Jl '64, Ja '65
Iodine-131 in Utah during July and August 1962. R. C. Pendleton and others. bibliog il Science 141:640-2 Ag 16 '63
Radioactive particle in sediment from the Columbia River. N. Cutshall and C. Osterberg. bibliog il Science 144:536-7 My 1 '64
Radioactivity up, but not dangerous. Am City 79:45 Ag '64
Replacement rates for human tissue from atmospheric radiocarbon. W. F. Libby and others. bibliog il Science 146:1170-2 N 27 '64

RADIOACTIVE fallout—*Continued*
Nevada
Nevada fallout: past and present hazards. L. Matison and R. Daly. il Bul Atomic Sci 20:41-5 Ap '64; Reply with rejoinder. G. M. Dunning. 20:29-30 S '64
RADIOACTIVE food contamination. See Food contamination
RADIOACTIVE iodine. See Iodine—Isotopes
RADIOACTIVE iodine in milk. See Milk contamination
RADIOACTIVE isotopes. See Radioisotopes
RADIOACTIVE particles. See Particles (nuclear physics)
RADIOACTIVE substances
Gamma emitters in marine sediments near the Columbia River. C. Osterberg and others. bibliog il Science 139:916-17 Mr 8 '63
Particle size fractionation of airborne gamma-emitting radionuclides by graded filters. B. Shleien and others. bibliog il Science 147:290-2 Ja 15 '65
See also
Radioisotopes
Radium poisoning
Thorium
Manipulators
See Manipulators
RADIOACTIVE substances in soils
Radiogeology and population exposure to background radiation in northern New England. A. Segall. bibliog il Science 140:1337-9 Je 21 '63
Strontium fixation by lime contained in soils. R. Mokady and M. Gal. bibliog il Science 145:154-5 Jl 10 '64
RADIOACTIVE substances in the body
Alaskan Eskimos have hot radioactive bodies. Sci N L 84:249 O 19 '63
Measure body radiation with hypodermic needle. Sci N L 85:184 Mr 21 '64
RADIOACTIVE tracers
Microtus: a simple method of recording time spent in the nest. R. W. Barbour. il Science 141:41 Jl 5 '63
Precaution in the use of iodine-125 as a radioactive tracer. Y. S. Bakhle and others. il Science 143:799-800 F 21 '64
RADIOACTIVE waste disposal
New process measures radioactive wastes. Sci N L 87:8 Ja 2 '65
Underground storage for radioactive wastes. Sci N L 86:312 N 14 '64
RADIOACTIVITY
Coal-powered stations release radioactivity. Sci N L 85:281 My 2 '64
Life after bomb; study of Eniwetok and Bikini atolls. Sci N L 86:67 Ag 1 '64
Radioactivity, atoms with too much energy. il Sci Digest 57:90-4 Ja '65
See also
Autoradiography
Beta rays
Decontamination (from gases, chemicals, etc)
Gamma rays
Plutonium
Accidents and injuries
Operation Red Dog; radiological assistance teams. K. N. Anderson. il Todays Health 43:64-9 Ja '65
Experiments
In a restless universe constants can vary; Westinghouse physicists prove rate of radioactive decay can be altered. Time 83:74 Je 19 '64
Industrial applications
X rays for engine innards; isotopic inspection. il Time 84:33 D 25 '64
Measurement
Atmospheric circulation from fission-product radioactivity in surface air. D. O. Staley. bibliog il Science 140:667-70 My 10 '63
Meteorological evaluation of the sources of iodine-131 in pasteurized milk. R. J. List and others. bibliog il Science 146:59-64 O 2 '64
Radioactivity in the atmospheric effluents of power plants that use fossil fuels. M. Eisenbud and H. G. Petrow. bibliog il Science 144:288-9 Ap 17 '64
Radioactivity measurements in Alaskan Eskimos in 1963. H. E. Palmer and others. bibliog il Science 144:859-60 My 15 '64
Strontium 90: estimation of worldwide deposition. H. L. Volchok. bibliog il Science 145:1451-2 S 25 '64
Strontium-90 in plants and animals of Arctic Alaska, 1959-61. D. G. Watson and others. bibliog il Science 144:1005-9 My 22 '64
See also
Counters (electrons, ions, etc.)
Geiger-Müller counters
Radiometers
Physiological effects
Antigenic material; persistence in hypersensitive cells. R. S. Speirs. bibliog il Science 140:71-2 Ap 5 '63
Can life survive the bomb? survey of Bikini and Eniwetok atolls. il Time 84:67 O 30 '64
Detection and quantitation of fallout particles in a human lung. A. V. Wegst and others. bibliog il Science 143:957-9 F 28 '64
Genetic effects. L. Pauling. Bul Atomic Sci 19:30-2 S '63
Inhaled radioactive particles and gases; report on symposium. W. J. Bair. Science 146:440+ O 16 '64
Permissible exposure to ionizing radiation. K. Z. Morgan. bibliog il Science 139:565-71 F 15 '63
Prenatal irradiation: effects on the development of the central nervous system and postnatal behavior; report on workshop conference. J. Werboff. Science 144:84-6 Ap 3 '64
Radioiodine: its nature and effects; report of symposium at the Hanford laboratories, Richland, Wash. L. K. Bustad. Science 142:510+ O 25 '63
Replacement rates for human tissue from atmospheric radiocarbon. W. F. Libby and others. bibliog il Science 146:1170-2 N 27 '64
Six years after H-bomb blasts; survey of Bikini and Eniwetok atolls. il U S News 57:64-5 N 2 '64
What the nuclear test ban means to your child's bones, blood, and future health. E. Ubell. McCalls 91:200-1 N '63
See also
Radioactive fallout
United Nations—Scientific committee on the effects of atomic radiation
Safety devices and measures
Fallout candy. Newsweek 61:91 Mr 18 '63
Operation Red Dog; radiological assistance teams. K. N. Anderson. il Todays Health 43:64-9 Ja '65
Radioprotection by pressor amidines. W. E. Rothe and others. il Science 141:160 Jl 12 '63
See also
Decontamination (from gases, chemicals, etc)
War use
See Radiological warfare
RADIOACTIVITY in milk. See Milk contamination
RADIOACTIVITY in time measurement. See Radioactive dating
RADIOBIOLOGY
Health physics; report of 1963 annual meeting of the Health physics society. A. P. Hull. Science 142:73-4 O 4 '63
Mutations: incidence in drosophila melanogaster reared on irradiated medium. M. S. Swaminathan and others. bibliog il Science 141:637-8 Ag 16 '63
Proton tunneling in radiation-induced mutation. R. Rein and F. E. Harris. bibliog il Science 146:649-50 O 30 '64
RADIOCARBON dating
Accuracy of radiocarbon dates. W. F. Libby. bibliog il Science 140:278-80 Ap 19 '63
Ancient cotton boll sets American identity. Sci N L 85:136 F 29 '64
Ancient oyster shells on the Atlantic continental shelf. A. S. Merrill and others. bibliog il Science 147:398-400 Ja 22 '65
Dating the past with radioactivity. il Sci Digest 57:92-3 Ja '65
Fluted projectile points: their age and dispersion in the New world. C. V. Haynes, jr. bibliog il Science 145:1408-13 S 25 '64
Harappa culture: new evidence for a shorter chronology. D. P. Agrawal. bibliog il Science 143:950-2 F 28 '64
Ontogeny of a salt marsh estuary. A. C. Redfield. bibliog il Science 147:50-5 Ja 1 '65
Pleistocene wood rat middens and climatic change in Mohave Desert: a record of juniper woodlands. P. V. Wells and C. D. Jorgensen. bibliog il Science 143:1171-4 Mr 13 '64
Radiocarbon and soil evidence of former forest in the southern Canadian tundra. R. A. Bryson and others. bibliog il Science 147:46-8 Ja 1 '65

RADIOCARBON dating—*Continued*
Radiocarbon dating: a case against the proposed link between river mollusks and soil humus. W. Broecker. bibliog il Science 143:596-7 F 7 '64; Reply. M. L. Keith and G. M. Anderson. 144:890 My 15 '64
Radiocarbon dating: fictitious results with mollusk shells. M. L. Keith and G. M. Anderson. bibliog il Science 141:634-7 Ag 16 '63
Radiocarbon dating of a late paleolithic culture from Egypt. P. E. L. Smith. bibliog il Science 145:811 Ag 21 '64
Radiocarbon dating of bone and shell from their organic components. R. Berger and others. bibliog Science 144:999-1001 My 22 '64

RADIOCHEMISTRY
Ionic intermediates and energy transfer in radiation chemistry; report of Faraday society discussion on fundamental processes in radiation chemistry. R. A. Holroyd and I. A. Taub. Science 142:1196-7 N 29 '63
Pulse radiolysis: fast reaction studies in radiation chemistry. L. M. Dorfman. bibliog il Science 141:493-8 Ag 9 '63
Radiation chemistry: aqueous media; report of conference at Gatlinburg, Tenn. E. J. Hart. Science 141:195-6+ Jl 12 '63
Radiation chemistry of the fixation of nitrogen. P. Harteck and S. Dondes. bibliog il Science 146:30-5 O 2 '64
Radiation-induced gelation of dilute aqueous pectin solutions. I. J. Wahba and others. bibliog il Science 139:1297-8 Mr 29 '63
Radiochemical methods of analysis; report on symposium by the International atomic energy agency in Salzburg. W. W. Meinke. Science 147:182-3 Ja 8 '65
See also
Isotope separation

RADIOGRAPHY
Gonadal dosages in investigative radiography. S. M. Garn and others. bibliog il Science 143:1039-40 Mr 6 '64
Microradiography of fossilized teeth. R. W. G. Wyckoff and others. il Science 140:78-80 Ap 5 '63
X-ray analysis of hemoglobin. M. F. Perutz. bibliog il Science 140:863-9 My 24 '63; Reply. G. S. Eadie and G. R. Gale. 142:343 O 18 '63
X-ray diffraction pattern of nerve myelin: a method for determining the phases. M. F. Moody. bibliog Science 142:1173-4 N 29 '63
See also
Autoradiography

RADIOIODINE. See Iodine—Isotopes

RADIOISOTOPE gages. See Gages

RADIOISOTOPES
Air concentrations of twelve radionuclides from 1962 through mid-1964. R. W. Perkins and others. bibliog il Science 146:762-4 N 6 '64
AEC frees another batch of isotopes. il Bsns W p68+ Je 13 '64
Autoradiographic distribution of radioactive sodium in rat kidney. P. F. Mercer and R. H. Wasserman. bibliog il Science 143:695-6 F 14 '64
Cosmic-ray exposure age of the Farmington meteorite from radioactive isotopes. J. DeFelice and others. bibliog il Science 142:673-4 N 8 '63
Density-gradient separation of organic particles by centrifugation. W. T. Lammers. bibliog il Science 139:1298-9 Mr 29 '63
Energy for remote areas. J. G. Morse. bibliog il Science 139:1175-80 Mr 22 '63
Engine inspectors use radioactive isotopes. Aviation W 80:65 Je 22 '64
Gamma-emitting radionuclides in newborns, infants, and children. N. S. MacDonald and others. bibliog il Science 141:1033-5 S 13 '63
How isotopes aid medicine in tracking down your ailments. J. Foster. il Todays Health 42:40-5+ My '64
Isotopes; different yet the same. il Sci Digest 55:78-80 Ap '64
New impetus is coming from industry. il Bsns W p50+ Ja 19 '63
Particle size fractionation of airborne gamma-emitting radionuclides by graded filters. B. Shleien and others. bibliog il Science 147:290-2 Ja 15 '65
Radioactive particle in sediment from the Columbia River. N. Cutshall and C. Osterberg. bibliog il Science 144:536-7 My 1 '64
Radium-226, radium-228, lead-210, and fluorine in persons with osteogenic sarcoma. H. F. Lucas., jr. and others. bibliog il Science 144:1573-5 Je 26 '64
Theoretical basis for logarithmic correlations of fractionated radionuclide compositions. E. C. Freiling. il Science 139:1058-9 Mr 15 '63
See also
Radioactive tracers
Radiology, Medical
also isotopes under names of chemical elements, e.g. Strontium—Isotopes

Industrial applications

See Radioactivity—Industrial applications

Medical applications

See Radiotherapy

RADIOLARIA
Radiolarians; construction of spherical skeleton. I. J. Smalley. bibliog il Science 140:396-7 Ap 26 '63

RADIOLOGICAL assistance teams. See United States—Atomic energy commission

RADIOLOGICAL warfare
Cobalt dusting would defeat own purpose; no effect on airplanes or troops. Sci N L 85:265 Ap 25 '64

RADIOLOGY, Medical
How isotopes aid medicine in tracking down your ailments. J. Foster. il Todays Health 42:40-5+ My '64
Radioisotope scanning; symposium by the International atomic energy agency, Athens, Greece. R. M. Kniseley. Science 145:416+ Jl 24 '64

RADIOMETERS
Dosimetry of atomic bomb radiation in Hiroshima by thermoluminescence of roof tiles. T. Higashimura and others. bibliog il Science 139:1284-5 Mr 29 '63
Infrared surveys of Hawaiian volcanoes. W. A. Fischer and others. bibliog il Science 146:733-42 N 6 '64
Use of infrared testing technique grows. P. J. Klass. il Aviation W 80:82+ My 4 '64

RADIONUCLIDES. See Radioisotopes

RADIOTELESCOPE. See Radio telescope

RADIOTHERAPY
Brain damage detected by radioactive isotopes. Sci N L 86:233 O 10 '64
Chilling during radiation aids cancer treatment. Sci N L 85:8 Ja 4 '64
Now, knifeless brain surgery; proton radiation in treating Parkinson's disease. il Sci Digest 55:71-2 Mr '64

RADISHES
Grow the delectable radish for all it's worth. W. A. Buck. House B 105:214-16 My '63
Radish roses. il Bet Hom & Gard 42:91 Ap '64

RADITSA, Bogdan
Idealism of Milovan Djilas. Commentary 35:149-53 F '63

RADIUM
Radium-226 and polonium-210 in leaf tobacco and tobacco soil. T. C. Tso and others. bibliog il Science 146:1043-5 N 20 '64
Radium-226 in human diet and bone. N. A. Hallden and others. bibliog il Science 140:1327-9 Je 21 '63
See also
Polonium

RADIUM poisoning
Keeping watch on luminous dials. Consumer Rep 29:271 Je '64
Some further words on luminous dials. Consumer Rep 29:413-14 S '64

RADKE, Helen
Local control: secret of schools' success; interview. por Nations Bsns 52:68-70+ F '64
School boards spokesman. G. Dapper. por Sat R 47:73+ Mr 21 '64

RADKE, William H.
State parks recreation menu. por Recreation 57:272-4 Je '64

RADNITZ, Robert B.
On creating films for children. Horn Bk 40:415-17 Ag '64

RADUGA dancers. See Ballet companies

RADZIWILL, Lee (Bouvier) princess
Jackie Kennedy's perplexing sister. B. Walters. por Good H 156:30+ Mr '63
Law's delay; annulment of first marriage. il por Time 83:62 F 28 '64

RAEBURN, Christopher
Pierre Monteux, the absolute professional. Hi Fi 14:41 S '64

RAEDER, Ruth
Hill-top gardening. Horticulture 41:79 F '63

RAFFEL, Burton
Bolsheviks in Bali. Sat R 46:34+ Mr 9 '63

RAFFERTY, Keen A. jr
Spontaneous kidney tumors in the frog: rate of occurrence in isolated adults. bibliog Science 141:720-1 Ag 23 '63

RAFFERTY, Max Lewis
Scholastic teacher interviews: Dr Max Rafferty; ed. by H. Langer. por Sr Schol 83: 5T-7T+ S 20 '63
Today's challenge in education; address, February 28, 1963. Vital Speeches 29:450-4 My 15 '63
What's wrong in the schools; educator speaks out; excerpts from address, December 6, 1963. por U S News 55:78-9 D 30 '63
about
Comments on Rafferty; letters to editor. Sr Schol 83:4T O 25; 6T N 8 '63
Max Rafferty of California. P. Woodring; discussion. Sat R 46:60+ F 16 '63
Max's maxims. il por Newsweek 63:72-3 Mr 30 '64
New hope of the far Right. G. Marine. il Nation 198:89-92 Ja 27 '64
Readin', ritin', and Rafferty. F. M. Hechinger. Reporter 30:46-8 Ap 9 '64

RAFTERY, Gerald
Confer with sages here. NEA J 54:25 Ja '65
Notes for an introduction to school libraries. Library J 89:4985 D 15 '64

RAFTS
Buying or building docks, piers and floats. G. Daniels. il Pop Mech 120:152-7 Ag '63
How to survive at sea. K. Brown. il Pop Mech 120:112-17+ N '63

RAGETLI, H. W. J. and Weintraub, M.
Immuno-osmophoresis, a rapid and sensitive method for evaluating viruses. bibliog Science 144:1023-4 My 22 '64

RAGHAVAN, V.
Differentiation in fern gametophytes treated with purine and pyrimidine analogs. bibliog Science 146:1690-1 D 25 '64

RAGMAN'S daughter; story. See Sillitoe, A.

RAGO, Henry
Praise of comedy: a discourse; poem. Poetry 103:82-4 O '63

RAGOUT. See Stew

RAGUSA. See Dubrovnik, Yugoslavia

RAGUSE, R. F.
Driving Opel's new Kadette. Pop Mech 120: 107 Jl '63

RAHMAN, Abdul, tunku
Malaya sees Sukarno as danger for southeast Asia; interview. por U S News 54:80-1 Mr 18 '63
Prime Minister of Malaysia visits Washington; exchange of greetings and toasts, July 22, 1964. Dept State Bul 51:190-2 Ag 10 '64
about
Malaysia's baptism of fire. il Sr Schol 83:10-13 N 1 '63
Man who. il por Time 81:43-5 Ap 12 '63
Notes of a new nation. J. M. Van der Kroef. il Nat R 15:390-2 N 5 '63
Our far-flung correspondents; Federation of Malaysia. R. Shaplen. il New Yorker 39: 130+ Ap 6 '63

RAHNER, Karl
Committed Christian in the modern world; excerpt from The Christian commitment. Cath World 198:144-50 D '63

RAHULA, Walpola
Anagarika Dharmapala, Buddhist missionary and educator. Sch & Soc 92:383-5 D 12 '64

RAIATEA
Backwater bacchanalia. H. Sutton. il Sat R 47:38+ My 9 '64

RAIDS
Another Cuban fiasco? il U S News 54:33-6 Ap 29 '63
Another side of the Cuban crisis. il Newsweek 61:21-2 Ap 8 '63
Caribbean commandos. il Newsweek 61:26-7 Ap 15 '63
Coming: new effort to topple Castro? il U S News 56:39 My 11 '64
Cuban crisis gets hotter. il U S News 54:4 Ap 8 '63
Game of irritation; anti-Castro sea raiders. Time 81:31 Ap 5 '63
Stronger Castro with U.S. help? with statement by President Kennedy. il U S News 54:35-7 Ap 15 '63
U.S. acts to prevent raids on Cuba from U.S. territory; joint statement by the Department of state, March 30, 1963. Dept State Bul 48:600-1 Ap 22 '63
Vamos! the buccaneers attack the Soviet prey. A. St George. il Life 54:18-25 Ap 12 '63

RAIL fences. See Fences

RAIL freight rates. See Railroads—Rates

RAIL mergers. See Railroads—Consolidations and mergers

RAILROAD accidents. See Railroads—Accidents

RAILROAD brotherhoods. See Trade unions—United States

RAILROAD cars. See Railroads—Cars

RAILROAD consolidation. See Railroads—Consolidations and mergers

RAILROAD construction. See Railroad engineering

RAILROAD employees. See Railroads—Employees

RAILROAD engineering
Gandy-dance to moon; spur line to connect Merritt Island launch area with Florida East Coast ry. il Bsns W p68+ Ap 18 '64

RAILROAD law
Arbitration board's award in railroad dispute; excerpts from text. Mo Labor R 87:36-43 Ja '64
Does rail labor law need a new timetable? government control delays settlements. Bsns W p82-3 Ja 9 '65
End in sight for Railway labor act? U S News 55:93-4 Jl 22 '63
High court ruling opens way for showdown in rules dispute; between carriers and operating brotherhoods. Bsns W p104 Mr 9 '63
Moonport stalled by rail strike. il Bsns W p64+ F 15 '64
Rail mediators throw a switch; rap bargaining methods of both sides. Bsns W p92 O 31 '64
Railroads' views on arbitration. U S News 54:106 Ap 22 '63
Showdown ahead on the railroads; strike or end of featherbedding? U S News 54:101 Mr 18 '63
Showdown soon on rail jobs. U S News 54: 106-7 Ap 15 '63

RAILROAD management. See Railroads— Management

RAILROAD models
So you want to be a railroad president. J. E. Demlow. il Hobbies 68:118-19 F '64
Which gauge should you choose? H. B. Comstock. il Pop Sci 184:169-71+ F '64
See also
Railroads, Toy

RAILROAD passengers. See Railroad travel; Railroads—Passenger traffic

RAILROAD porters. See Porters

RAILROAD rates. See Railroads—Rates

RAILROAD retirement benefits. See Pensions, Industrial

RAILROAD securities. See Railroads—Securities

RAILROAD stations. See Railroads—Stations

RAILROAD strikes. See Strikes—United States —Railroads

RAILROAD ties. See Railroads—Ties

RAILROAD travel
Across the vast, silent land called Siberia; trans-Siberian trek from Japan to Moscow. R. Hughes. il N Y Times Mag p 12-13+ My 31 '64
I like whistlestops. E. Kimbrough. Travel 122:34-5+ Jl '64
Special treat for steam fans. il Sunset 130: 48 My '63
Touring the redwood country by rail car. il Sunset 130:24+ Mr '63
You travel on rails, behind steam. il Sunset 131:34 Ag '63
See also
Railroads—Passenger traffic

RAILROAD watches. See Watches

RAILROAD work rules. See Railroads—Work rules

RAILROAD workers. See Railroads—Employees

RAILROADS
World route to super-railroads; address, January 16, 1964. J. N. Sites. Vital Speeches 30:252-5 F 1 '64
See also
Locomotives

Accidents
Runaway train. W. R. Young. il Life 54:79-80+ Mr 29 '63
Wrecking crew; boys rewire signal for Southern Pacific passenger train near LA. Newsweek 62:23-4 Jl 22 '63

Automatic train control
Pushbutton trains go automatic on Southern Pacific. il Pop Sci 185:107 S '64

Bibliography
Gift nominees: the new crop of train books. il Sunset 131:48+ D '63

RAILROADS—*Continued*

Buildings and structures

See also
Railroads—Stations

Cars

Air-conditioned transit fleet. il Am City 79: 138 O '64
Back on the rails. Time 84:76+ Ag 28 '64
Budd pulls a switch; bid on stainless steel subway cars. Bsns W p26 Jl 6 '63
See also
Railroads—Freight cars

Competitive transportation

Can the railroads be saved? railway situation in twenty-five countries; excerpts from Quest for crisis. J. N. Sites. Nat R 16: 971-3 N 3 '64
Transportation; address, January 14, 1963. D. P. Loomis. Vital Speeches 29:322-5 Mr 15 '63

Consolidations and mergers

Another big railroad merger takes shape; splitting the Chicago, Rock Island & Pacific railroad. il U S News 54:14 My 27 '63
As rail lines merge: pattern of future takes shape. il U S News 57:86-7 Jl 27 '64
Battle for a mighty good road; Union Pacific and North Western covet Rock Island line. il Bsns W p 119-20+ N 2 '63
Big if. Newsweek 61:80 Ap 29 '63
Broader view; control of the Baltimore & Ohio railroad by the Chesapeake & Ohio. Newsweek 61:67-8 Ap 8 '63
Dream coming true; proposed merger that would create nation's longest railroad. il Time 84:91 S 4 '64
Given first-round approval: merger plan for longest U.S. rail line; Great Northern Pacific & Burlington lines. il U S News 57: 8 S 7 '64
Green light for big merger: Norfolk & western, Nickel plate, Wabash. il U S News 54:14 Ap 29 '63
Green light for rail mergers? Seaboard-Coast line tie-up. il Bsns W p82 D 21 '63
Green lights for two big mergers; Norfolk & Western, Pennsy-NYC. il U S News 57:16 S 28 '64
Kennedy no to one big rail merger; Pennsylvania and New York central railroads. U S News 55:8 O 14 '63
Key man behind railroad mergers. il U S News 57:114-15 O 12 '64
Merger highball; Norfolk & Western railway and New York, Chicago & St Louis. il Newsweek 64:67 Jl 27 '64
Merger on the track; Rock Island stockholders vote for Union Pacific merger. Newsweek 65:71 Ja 25 '65
Merger spooks and spitballs: a look behind the moratorium mirage; address, June 22, 1963. D. P. Loomis. Vital Speeches 29:622-5 Ag 1 '63
Mergers: a new look by the New frontier. U S News 54:11 Mr 18 '63
Monkey wrench in rail merger plans. Bsns W p204 O 19 '63
New merger plan stuns railroads; Pennsy-Central consolidation opposed. Bsns W p27 O 5 '63
New railroad mergers in mind. il Newsweek 62:95 O 14 '63
Pennsy takes a gamble; sells holdings in the Norfolk & Western and the Wabash. Bsns W p31 S 19 '64
Red light in Washington; Pennsy-Central plan. Time 82:93 O 11 '63
Tough line on rail, air mergers; from intergovernmental committee. Bsns W p 140 Mr 16 '63
Toward a big three; Norfolk & Western's petition to take over the Nickel plate, the Wabash and three connecting roads. il Time 84:78 Jl 24 '64
Tracks coming together. Time 82:77 D 20 '63
Unlocking the door; ICC recommendation for merger of Great northern railway, Northern Pacific railway and Chicago, Burlington & Quincy railroad. il Newsweek 64:64 S 7 '64
Where the rails stand in merger movement. il Bsns W p60-2 Ag 3 '63
Why not merge and survive? W. T. Rice. Ann Am Acad 345:103-8 Ja '63
Why the Reading is a Wall Street belle; hope of merger enhances railroad's value. il Bsns W p 118+ O 17 '64
Wooing the Rock Island. Newsweek 62:72 Jl 8 '63
Worried suitors; proposed New York Central and Pennsylvania merger. Newsweek 61:79 F 25 '63

Dining cars

Imitation meal. C. W. Morton. il Atlan 214: 106 Ag '64
Meal-A-Mat. Newsweek 62:78 S 30 '63

Employees

Arbitration board's award in railroad dispute; excerpts from text. Mo Labor R 87:36-43 Ja '64
As rail dispute neared a crisis. U S News 55:69 S 2 '63
Back on the sidetrack again; President's plan. il Time 82:10-11 Ag 2 '63
Beyond the last mile. il Time 82:13-16 Jl 26 '63
Breakdown in Chicago. Newsweek 61:84 Mr 25 '63
Case of the elderly firemen; contempt-of-court charges brought by Locomotive firemen's union against Southern railway. U S News 55:125 N 18 '63
Deadline near in rail rules dispute. Bsns W p65-6 Je 29 '63
Firemen survive cutbacks. Bsns W p 105-6 My 16 '64
History of a law. H. Hazlitt. Newsweek 62: 75 S 16 '63
Labor month in review. Mo Labor R 86:III-IV Ag '63
Latest turn in rail dispute; what it all means. U S News 55:82 Ag 26 '63
Lumps in the featherbed. Newsweek 61:76 Mr 18 '63
Manpower, a prime resource. E. W. Williams, jr. bibliog f Ann Am Acad 345:122-9 Ja '63
Master strategist of the railroad settlement. M. H. Zim. il Fortune 70:164-6+ Jl '64
New round of stalemate: dispute between the railroad industry and the unions. B. J. Widick Nation 197:68-70 Ag 10 '63
New showdown on the railroads. U S News 57:73 N 2 '64
New trouble on rail work rules. U S News 55:123 O 7 '63
1963 railroad arbitration act. Mo Labor R 86:1187-8 O '63
No bed of feathers; work of a steam locomotive fireman. G. Burck. Life 55:23 S 27 '63
Off the rails; railroad settlement. New Repub 149:6 D 28 '63
Off-train rail unions itchy; demand wage boosts and other contract gains. Bsns W p68 S 28 '63
One for the roads. il Time 81:92+ Mr 15 '63
Rail-job cuts begin: how deep? locomotive firemen. U S News 56:96 My 11 '64
Rail strike: strategy still is to delay. il Bsns W p22-3 Jl 27 '63
Rail strike that reaches into space. il Bsns W p46+ O 26 '63
Railroad hires new firemen, but . . . il U S News 55:75 Ag 12 '63
Rails close ranks in bargaining. Bsns W p52+ F 16 '63
Railway dispute. il New Repub 149:7-8 Jl 20 '63
Seesaw to settlement. Newsweek 62:55-6 Ag 26 '63
That's railroadin'; firemen on the Southern. Time 82:16 Ag 9 '63
Toward the end of the line. il Time 82:15-17 Jl 19 '63
Train crews: firings delayed; concerning appeal of Locomotive firemen's union to Supreme court. U S News 56:95 Mr 16 '64
Unions switch: let U.S. run rails. il Bsns W p 122+ Ja 23 '65
When automation comes and workers stay on; Southern Pacific railway. U S News 54:88-9 Ap 1 '63
Work rules dispute. Commonweal 78:468 Ag 9 '63
See also
Featherbedding (industrial relations)
Porters
Railroads—Wages and hours
Strikes—United States—Railroads

Exhibitions

New life on the tracks; American railway progress exposition. il Bsns W p 120-2+ O 19 '63

Finance

Can the railroads be saved? railway situation in twenty-five countries; excerpts from Quest for crisis. J. N. Sites. Nat R 16: 971-3 N 3 '64
Clarification of transportation-policy goals. G. M. Harrison. Ann Am Acad 345:22-31 Ja '63
Comeback for railroads; how long will it last? il U S News 55:99-101 O 28 '63
Green light for the rails. il Duns R 83:pt2 106-9+ Je '64

RAILROADS—Finance—*Continued*
Highballing on new wheels; profitable year. il Time 85:82 Ja 15 '65
Outlook: brighter. il Time 82:81 Jl 5 '63
Pennsy's road ahead. T. O'Hanlon. il Duns R 83:36-8+ F '64
Profits & perils. il Time 82:112 D 6 '63
Railroads have quit slumbering. C. D. Buford. Ann Am Acad 345:58-65 Ja '63
Shade worse then bankrupt; plight of the New Haven. il Bsns W p 130+ My 9 '64
Why the rails are hot. il Fortune 67:203-4+ Je '63
See also
Railroads—Securities

Freight

Fast track for the rails. S. Nicholson. il Duns R 81:pt2 S113-15+ Je '63

Freight cars

Bonanza in bulk shipping. T. J. O'Hanlon. il Duns R 82:41-3+ O '63
Boxcars go to battle for Southern. il Bsns W p76-80+ Je 8 '63
Fighting off the pirates. Time 81:96+ My 3 '63
Pulling and hauling on the rails; annual seasonal boxcar shortage. Bsns W p54+ Ag 22 '64
Suddenly, there's a boom. il Bsns W p 178+ O 10 '64
See also
Railroads—Freight service

Freight rates

See Railroads—Rates

Freight service

Going thing. il Time 82:96 O 25 '63
There's money in freight again. il Bsns W p35-6 D 28 '63

Government ownership

See Railroads and state

Government regulation

See Railroads and state

History

Golden spike and the iron horse. il Sr Schol 84:7+ My 8 '64
Overland limited; excerpts from Central Pacific and the Southern Pacific railroads. L. Beebe. il Am Heritage 15:54-7+ D '63
See also
National railway historical society

Law

See Railroad law

Management

Hell of a different way to run a railroad. H. B. Meyers. il Fortune 68:100-9+ S '63
Staying on the rails; with editorial comment. Bsns W p23, 144 Jl 13 '63
See also
Railroads—Employees

Passenger traffic

Fewer, and far between. il Bsns W p 117-18+ S 26 '64
Happy commuters! il Newsweek 61:79 F 25 '63
Test high-speed rail; jet car passenger service. Sci N L 87:34 Ja 16 '65
See also
Commuters

Rates

Clarification of transportation-policy goals. G. M. Harrison. Ann Am Acad 345:22-31 Ja '63
Freight rates go up piecemeal; on less-than-carload business. Bsns W p32 Mr 30 '63
How the railroads are recapturing business; closing of coal pipeline. U S News 54:11 My 20 '63
Intricacies of rate-making. Bsns W p56 Ag 22 '64
New turn in the battle of the ports. U S News 54:11 Je 3 '63
Railroads give coal big break; lower rates for unitized train shipments. il Bsns W p34+ Mr 9 '63
There's money in freight again. il Bsns W p35-6 D 28 '63
See also
Railroads and state—United States

Securities

Why the Reading is a Wall Street belle; hope of merger enhances railroad's value. il Bsns W p 118+ O 17 '64

Sleeping cars

Wagons-lits rides into age of mass travel; Trans-European express. il Bsns W p 108-10 O 31 '64

Stations

Depot; with photographs by David Plowden. O. Jensen. Horizon 6:42-51 Sum '64

Strikes

See Strikes—United States—Railroads

Ties

Railroad ties; function in the garden. il Sunset 131:124+ N '63

Train speed

Comeback try for rail travel. il U S News 58:68 Ja 25 '65
Japan's fast train: how it's working out; new Tokaido line between Tokyo and Osaka. il U S News 58:69-70 Ja 25 '65
Speed, new hope for railroads. B. H. Frisch. il Sci Digest 56:50-5 D '64

Trains

Leaving on that New River train. J. Walsh. Hobbies 69:120-4 O '64

Wages and hours

Rail peace gets the go signal. Bsns W p 124+ N 28 '64
Wage chronology: railroads, nonoperating employees, 1961-62. bibliog f il Mo Labor R 86:409-10 Ap '63

Work rules

Another strike, another truce; why rail dispute goes on. U S News 56:77-80 Ap 20 '64
LBJ brand on the bargaining table; success in rail settlement; with editorial comment. Bsns W p89-91, 124 My 2 '64
On the track ahead; a new crisis; railroad work rules. il Bsns W p 108-10+ Ap 11 '64
Permissive anarchy. D. Lawrence. U S News 56:124 Ap 27 '64
Rail work rule: still an issue. U S News 56:93 My 18 '64
Railroad dispute: Johnson swings a red lantern; with editorial comment. il Bsns W p25-6, 202 Ap 18 '64
Trains keep running; settlement of the 4½-year-old featherbedding dispute. Bsns W p29 Ap 25 '64
What railroads want from LBJ now. il U S News 56:95-6 My 11 '64
Who won what in the rail dispute; How a five-year-old fight was settled in thirteen days. il U S News 56:76-7 My 4 '64
Work rules controversy in perspective. Mo Labor R 87:III-IV Mr '64

Africa, East

Express to the Mountains of the Moon. D. Reed. il Read Digest 85:234-40 S '64

Arabia

Cleaning up after Lawrence. Time 82:112 N 15 '63
Matter of duty; Hejaz railway. il Newsweek 62:60 D 9 '63

Argentina

Trolley named disaster. Time 85:31 Ja 22 '65

Cameroon

Mr Coffin represents U.S. at Cameroon railroad ceremony. Dept State Bul 51:722 N 16 '64

Canada

See also
Canadian Pacific railway
Great Slave Lake railway

Europe

Wagons-lits rides into age of mass travel; Trans-European express. il Bsns W p 108-10 O 31 '64

Europe, Western

See also
Railroads and state—Europe, Western

France

Why can't we run our railroads like the French? H. B. Comstock. il Pop Sci 183:82-6+ N '63

Germany (Federal Republic)

Love those rails; Deutsche Bundesbahn. il Time 84:84 Ag 21 '64
Moneymaking train for money-makers; Rheingold express. il Fortune 68:141-3 D '63

RAILROADS—*Continued*

Great Britain

Atlantic report; double-decker railroads. Atlan 213:26+ Mr '64
Beeching plan. Newsweek 61:68 Ap 8 '63
Clearing the track; Beeching's plan. Time 81: 98 Ap 5 '63
Goodbye, Puffing Billy. L. T. C. Rolt. il Horizon 6:72-7 Autumn '64
Letter from London. M. Panter-Downes. New Yorker 39:179 My 4 '63
Loco motivation; train spotting. il Newsweek 64:41 Jl 6 '64
New blow to the chin; resignation of chairman of the British railways board. Time 85: 66 Ja 1 '65
Victorian England; Beeching report. A. Burnet. New Repub 148:9-10 Ap 13 '63

Italy

Our man on the Settebello. New Yorker 40:41-4 Ap 18 '64

Japan

Arrow through the heart of Japan. il Fortune 70:150-1 N '64
Fast ride to Osaka. il Time 84:94 S 4 '64
Getting there is not much fun. il Time 81:31 F 8 '63
Japan's fast train: how it's working out; new Tokaido line between Tokyo and Osaka. il U S News 58:69-70 Ja 25 '65
Japan's track stars. il Bsns W p 124+ S 26 '64
Our far-flung correspondents; Bullet train, Tokyo-Osaka line. E. J. Kahn. New Yorker 40:155-6+ N 21 '64
Rapid transit: Japan shows way. il U S News 54:86-9 Je 3 '63
Riding Japan's super-express train. J. Pickerell. il Pop Sci 185:50-1 S '64
Speed, new hope for railroads; new Tokaido line. B. H. Frisch. il Sci Digest 56:50-5 D '64
United States delegations to international conferences; ECAFE study of Tokaido railway. Dept State Bul 48:660 Ap 29 '63

Mexico

Little trains out of Mexico City. il Sunset 130:68+ Mr '63
Mexico's new rail thrill: Ferrocarril Chihuahua al Pacifico. W. Kane. il Travel 119:34-7 F '63
Rail adventure trip across Mexico's Sierra Madre. il Sunset 132:34-6+ Mr '64

Russia

Rails curtailed in move to boost Aeroflot. Aviation W 79:41 Jl 1 '63

United States

Affluent railroads. D. Smith. Nation 197:312-14 N 16 '63
Automation in railroads. W. Wingo. Sci N L 84:54 Jl 27 '63
Big trim. Newsweek 63:72 My 11 '64
Call it schmaltz but it broke a long rail-road-union deadlock: President wins a fifteen-day truce. il Newsweek 63:91 Ap 20 '64
Comeback for railroads: how long will it last? il U S News 55:99-101 O 28 '63
Comeback try for rail travel. il U S News 58:68 Ja 25 '65
Deciding on the featherbed; railroad featherbedding fight. il Bsns W p67 S 28 '63
Decline of the railroads. America 109:506-7 N 2 '63
Featherbed fencing: presidential emergency board seeking solution to featherbedding issue. il Newsweek 61:76 My 13 '63
Hope dims for rail settlement: work-rules dispute. Bsns W p24 Ag 3 '63
Kept on the track; rail strike barred. Bsns W p 19 Ag 31 '63
Labor month in review. Mo Labor R 86:III-IV Ag '63
Last mile. America 108:387-8 Mr 23 '63
1963 railroad arbitration act. Mo Labor R 86: 1187-8 O '63
Our run-down railroads. C. Pell. New Repub 150:11-14 My 2 '64
Out of the tunnel. il Time 83:98 Je 12 '64
Pleading beyond reason? President's appeal for postponement of scheduled railroad strike. il Time 83:33-4 Ap 17 '64
Rail board offers peace plan: guidelines for settlement dispute over railroad work rules. Bsns W p 172 My 18 '63
Rail ruling points a way for others. Bsns W p 132+ D 7 '63
Rail settlement: a coup for LBJ. il Newsweek 63:67-8 My 4 '64
Railroads have quit slumbering. C. D. Buford. Ann Am Acad 345:58-65 Ja '63
Railway bargaining. New Repub 150:5 Ap 25 '64
Saving the railroads. C. Pell. Commonweal 79:249-50 N 22 '63
Showdown over featherbedding. il Sr Schol 83:14-16+ S 27 '63
Tale of two crises; address, November 5, 1963. J. H. Wright. Vital Speeches 30:122-5 D 1 '63
Time runs out for railroads. Bsns W p26 Jl 20 '63
Toward the end of the line. il Time 82:15-17 Jl 19 '63
Trouble with the railroad is... S. Berge. Changing T 18:6 Ap '64
Where the rails stand in merger movement. il Bsns W p60-2 Ag 3 '63

See also

Association of American railroads
Railroads—Consolidations and mergers
Railroads—History
Railroads, Short line
Railroads and state—United States
United States—Interstate commerce commission
also names of railroads, e.g. Florida East Coast railway

Viet Nam (Republic)

Most dangerous railroad in the world. il Newsweek 63:28 Je 8 '64
Slow train through Viet Nam's war. H. Sochurek. il Nat Geog Mag 126:412-44 S '64

RAILROADS, Narrow gage

See also

Edaville railroad
Silverton narrow gauge railroad

RAILROADS, Short line

Little lines that could. il Time 83:64-5 Ja 10 '64

See also

Wanamaker, Kempton and Southern railroad

RAILROADS, Single rail

Japan's track stars. il Bsns W p 124+ S 26 '64
Monorail: a one-track controversy. J. N. Bell. il Sat Eve Post 237:81-2 My 9 '64
Monorail for the New York world's fair. il Am City 78:111 D '63
Monorails; will they ever get off the ground? J. N. Bell. il Pop Mech 120:69-74+ D '63
Speed, new hope for railroads. B. H. Frisch. il Sci Digest 56:50-5 D '64

RAILROADS, Toy

Another way to landscape a train board. il Sunset 132:80+ Ja '64
Better model control for $5.50. H. L. Davidson. il Pop Electr 19:66-7 S '63

See also

Lionel corporation

RAILROADS and state

Can the railroads be saved? railway situation in twenty-five countries; excerpts from Quest for crisis. J. N. Sites. Nat R 16: 971-3 N 3 '64

Europe, Western

When governments run the railroads. il U S News 54:79-80 Mr 4 '63

United States

All right then, let's nationalize the RR's. Nat R 16:344-5 My 5 '64
Deadline near in rail rules disptue. Bsns W p65-6 Je 29 '63
Foot in the door; Munn v. Illinois. C. P. Magrath. il Am Heritage 15:44-8+ F '64
Johnson's first labor crisis: threat of a railroad strike. U S News 56:104 F 17 '64
Matter of necessity; independent tribunal to adjudicate labor disputes; address, April 2, 1964. A. F. Arpaia. Vital Speeches 30:477-80 My 15 '64
Meaning of the rail settlement. A. H. Raskin. Reporter 30:24-6 My 21 '64; Discussion. 30:6 Je 18 '64
New threat of rail strike as unions lose another round. il U S News 55:110-11 D 9 '63
Now that the railroads have compulsory arbitration. U S News 55:95-6 S 9 '63
Rail strike? not right away. U S News 56:85 F 3 '64
Solution that pleased nobody; forestalling of a national railway strike. Time 82:16 S 6 '63
They have no Hoffa. Reporter 30:20+ Ja 30 '64

RAILROADS and state—United States—*Cont.*
Unhappy precedent. Time 82:17 Ag 30 '63
Unions switch: let U.S. run rails. il Bsns W p 122+ Ja 23 '65
See also
Railroad law
Railroads—United States
United States—Interstate commerce commission
RAILS (birds)
Clapper clapper clapper. C. Conley. il Field & S 68:35-7+ S '63
Clapper rail. G. Santillo. il Outdoor Life 132:66-8+ S '63
RAILWAY accidents. See Railroads—Accidents
RAILWAY clerks. See Railroads—Employees
RAILWAY excursions. See Excursions
RAILWAY express agency, incorporated
Greyhound bids for a new outlet. Bsns W p25 F 29 '64
RAILWAY labor act. See Railroad law
RAILWAY regulation. See Railroads and state
RAILWAY ties. See Railroads—Ties
RAILWAYS. See Railroads
RAIMON, Alexandre
Alexandre the great. K. Whitehorn. il pors Ladies Home J 80:148-53 N '63
RAIN and rainfall
Anatomy of raindrops studied by scientists. il(p305) Sci N L 84:317 N 16 '63
Anonymous rainmaker. Newsweek 62:25+ Ag 12 '63
Pollen wettability as a factor in washout by raindrops. J. E. McDonald. bibliog il Science 143:1180-1 Mr 13 '64
Rainmaker, rainmaker, go away: Tulsa, Okla. il Time 82:17 Ag 9 '63
Strontium-90 accumulation on plant foliage during rainfall. R. G. Menzel and others. bibliog il Science 142:576-7 N 1 '63
See also
Droughts
Rain forests
RAIN forests
Life under 150 inches of rain. A. V. Barwood. il Sci Digest 54:18-21 O '63
See also
Olympic National Park
RAIN in Laredo; story. See Horgan, P.
RAIN making
Area coating makes rain. Sci N L 83:78 F 2 '63
Artificial rain compound tested in Australia: metaldehyde. Sci N L 84:104 Ag 17 '63
Computer grows clouds and produces rain. Sci N L 83:72 F 2 '63
Experiments in hurricane modification; seeding clouds with silver iodide. R. H. Simpson and J. S. Malkus. il Sci Am 211:27-37 bibliog(p 154) D '64
Firing up a rainstorm. il Pop Sci 185:47 Ag '64
Modification experiments on tropical cumulus clouds. J. S. Malkus and R. H. Simpson. bibliog il Science 145:541-8 Ag 7 '64; Same abr. with title Seeded clouds explode. Sci N L 86:115 Ag 22 '64
RAINAT, Joyce
Conch ain't got no bone. Motor B 112:34+ D '63
RAINBOOTS. See Shoes, Rubber, plastic, etc.
RAINBOW, Lunar
Rainbow of moonbeams and a high cloud ring of mystery. il Life 54:111-12 My 17 '63
RAINBOW BRIDGE NATIONAL MONUMENT
Last chance for Rainbow. A. W. Smith. Nat Parks Mag 37:2 Mr '63
Rainbow Bridge: record and requiem. A. W. Smith. Nat Parks Mag 37:2+ My '63
Road-block to Rainbow. P. M. Tilden. Nat Parks Mag 37:15 D '63
RAINBOW natural bridge. See Bridges, Natural
RAINBOW trout. See Trout
RAINCOATS
Singing? hardly. il Time 83:76+ Ap 17 '64
RAINDROPS. See Rain and rainfall
RAINE, Kathleen
Ancestral vision. Poetry 101:272-4 Ja '63
Concert; poem. New Yorker 40:60 O 31 '64
Epic poet. Poetry 101:426-30 Mr '63
Hollow hill; poem. Poetry 102:1-7 Ap '63
Key to William Blake: Mellon lectures at the National gallery of art, Washington. M. W. Hess. Christian Cent 80:1027-8 Ag 21 '63
Six poems: Old paintings on Italian walls; Puer aeternus; Statues; Natura naturans; Daisies of Florence; Images. New Yorker 40:32-3 Ja 16 '65
RAINES, Robert A.
Deficient in ferment. Christian Cent 81:864 Jl 1 '64
RAINEY, Lawrence
Strange, tight little town, loath to admit complicity. D. Nevin. il por Life 57:38-9 D 18 '64
RAINIER III, prince of Monaco
Memoirs of Monaco; ed. by S. Fliegers. pors McCalls 90:81-5+ Ap '63
about
Grace of Graustark; hour-long telecast, A look at Monaco. il por Time 81:42 F 22 '63
Grace of Kelly. R. Massie. il pors Sat Eve Post 236:18-19 Je 8 '63
RAINIER, MOUNT
Mount Rainier; testing ground for Everest. B. S. Bishop. il Nat Geog Mag 123:688-711 My '63
Our own Rainier. H. Sutton. il Sat R 46:36-8 N 9 '63
To the top of Rainier. il Sunset 131:26 Jl '63
See also
Mount Rainier National Park
RAINMAN, Eva Schindler-. See Schindler-Rainman, E.
RAINY day in Newark; drama. See Teichmann, H.
RAIZISS, Sonia
(tr) See Palchi, A. de. After many deaths
(tr) See Palchi, A. de. Winter that kills
RAJAKOVICH, Erich
Anne's executioner? Newsweek 61:40+ Ap 29 '63
End of the chase. por Time 81:35-6 Ap 26 '63
RAJAN, Sundar
Goa: a case of indigestion. Reporter 31:22 Jl 2 '64
RAKE'S progress; opera. See Stravinsky, I.
RAKESTRAW, W. Vincent
Famous hotel now college dorm. Negro Hist Bul 27:140-1 Mr '64
RALEY, Robert L.
History in houses; Hampton in Baltimore County, Maryland. il Antiques 84:434-8 O '63
RALLY; story. See Vivante, A.
RALSTON, Dennis
American twist; Davis cup matches. il Time 83:47 Ja 3 '64
Dennis is his own menace. J. Olsen. il pors Sports Illus 19:10-15 Ag 26 '63
High time for a U.S. victory. W. Tower. il por Sports Illus 20:18-21 Ja 6 '64
Menace. Newsweek 62:77 S 2 '63
RALSTON, Edgar L.
What you can do about aching feet; interview. McCalls 90:46 Ap '63
RALSTON, H. J. See Guillery, R. W. jt. auth.
RALSTON purina company
Turkeys put on beef. il Bsns W p68 Ap 4 '64
RAM jet propulsion. See Jet propulsion
RAMA RAU, Santha
Countess; story. Ladies Home J 80:102-4 D '63
Pacific adventures; a dictionary from Australia to Zamboanga. Vogue 142:106-11+ O 15 '63
Softly; story. por Sat Eve Post 236:51-3 D 7 '63
Ubiquitous spoon. House & Gard 124:118-19 Ag '63
What did you want most at seventeen? ed. by A. Ebert. por Seventeen 22:132-3 S '63
RAMADAN
Fasting and feasting. il Newsweek 61:57 F 25 '63
RAMAN effect
Interaction of light with light. J. A. Giordmaine. il Sci Am 210:38-49 bibliog(p 156) Ap '64
RAMBERT, Marie
Marie Rambert; midwife to the muses. C. Barnes. pors Dance Mag 37:42-3 Mr '63
RAMBIN, J. Howard, jr
Rambin of Texaco. il por Fortune 70:43 N '64
RAMEAU, Jean Philippe
Musical events; concert performance of Rameau's Castor and Pollux in Philharmonic Hall by Concert opera association. W. Sargeant. New Yorker 40:116-17 Ja 23 '65
Nature's harmonist. K. Hoover. il pors Opera N 28:8-13 Ja 4 '64
RAMEY, James T.
New merry-go-round; excerpts from address. Aviation W 82:11 Ja 11 '65
Requirements merry-go-round; excerpts from remarks. Aviation W 80:21 My 18 '64
Requirements merry-go-round: must need precede development? Bul Atomic Sci 20:12-15 N '64
about
Merry-go-round. W. J. Coughlin. Miss & Roc 16:46 Ja 18 '65

RAMJET airplane engines. See Jet airplane engines

RAMJET engines (rocket) See Rocket engines

RAMJET propelled airplanes. See Airplanes, Jet propelled

RAMO, Simon
What life will be like when the machines take over; interview. por U S News 54: 64-8 Je 24 '63

RAMO Wooldridge, incorporated. See Thompson Ramo Wooldridge, incorporated

RAMÓN Y CAJAL, Santiago
Science milestone. J. McMillan. il por Sci Digest 53:81-7 Ap '63

RAMOS, Maria
Festival in Penedo. Américas 15:32-4 N '63

RAMOS, Sugar
Death of a champion. M. Sharnik. il pors Sports Illus 18:18-21+ Ap 1 '63
Sugar daddy with a bongo beat. L. Griggs and R. D. Lozano. por Sports Illus 20:66-7 Mr 16 '64

RAMPART CANYON DAM (proposed) See Dams—Alaska

RAMPONE, Alfred J. and Shirasu, M. E.
Temperature changes in the rat in response to feeding. bibliog Science 144:317-19 Ap 17 '64

RAMS. See Sailing vessels

RAMS (animals). See Sheep

RAMSES to Rembrandt to Wright; story. See Black, S. M.

RAMSEY, Arthur Michael, abp
For freedom under establishment; interview. Christian Cent 81:853 Jl 1 '64
Reply by the Archbishop of Canterbury; reprint. por Horizon 5:107 S '63

about

Archbishop is a Protestant. por Time 84:54 Jl 31 '64
Empty pews, full spirit. il por(cover) Time 82:58-61+ Ag 16 '63
England's puckish prelate. L. Hannon. il pors Sat Eve Post 236:74+ My 4 '63

RAMSEY, Elizabeth M. and others
Cineradioangiographic visualization of the venous drainage of the primate placenta in vivo. bibliog Science 141:909 S 6 '63

RAMSEY, Frank
Smart moves by a master of deception; ed. by F. Deford. Sports Illus 19:57-63 D 9 '63

RAMSEY, J.
Pipe-fitting light stand. Pop Mech 120:146-7 Jl '63

RAMSEY, Jack
Results of a scholarship program. Wilson Lib Bul 37:571+ Mr '63

RAMSEY, Paul
Heraclitus; poem. Christian Cent 82:70 Ja 20 '65
Morgenthau on nuclear war. Commonweal 78: 554-7 S 20 '63

RAMSEY, Robert C.
Microphone sensitivity rating. Electr World 71:31+ My '64

RAMUS, Michael
Funny little people of Mike Ramus. G. P. Hunt. il por Life 57:3 Ag 14 '64

RANATRA fusca. See Water scorpions

RANCH houses
Getting back to the ranch. G. O'Brien. il N Y Times Mag p80-1 Ag 23 '64
Living with antiques; Colorado ranch of Mr and Mrs Royal B. Hassrick. E. Gaines. il Antiques 84:162-4 Ag '63

RANCH life
LBJ down on the farm. T. Wicker. Esquire 62:90-3+ O '64
Ranch wife looks at her heritage; Mary Hansen Mead, Teton County, Wyo. L. Lane. il Farm J 88:44-5+ Jl '64

RANCHES
Change rides the range. P. Friggens. il Read Digest 85:182-4+ Ag '64
Cowboys and Indians; visit to the U.S. by managers of a dude ranch in France. New Yorker 39:35-6 S 28 '63
88,000 golden acres waiting for the dust to settle; Irvine ranch, Calif. S. Freedgood. il Fortune 68:142-7+ N '63
Home on the range; working a typical ranch in LBJ country. J. C. Stewart. il U S News 55:64 D 23 '63
Life on the ranch; a day at home with LBJ. J. P. Sutherland. il U S News 56:67-8 Ap 13 '64
LBJ white house. J. B. Young. il Am Home 67:5-6 Mr '64
November in Wickenburg: the dudes are gathering. il Sunset 131:66+ N '63
Our day with President Johnson. il Suc Farm 62:41-3+ Mr '64
President's big sky country; with photographs by G. Silk. il Life 56:54-65 F 14 '64

RANCK, James B. Jr
Synaptic learning due to electroosmosis: a theory. bibliog Science 144:187-9 Ap 10 '64

RAND, Ayn
Goldwater people; excerpts from statement. por Look 28:53 N 3 '64

RAND, Christopher
Our far-flung correspondents (cont) New Yorker 39:31-2+ Ag 10 '63
Profiles. New Yorker 39:49-50+ My 11 '63; 40:43-8+ Ap 11; 57-8+ Ap 18; 55-6+ Ap 25 '64
Reporter at large (cont) New Yorker 40: 109-11+ N 7 '64

RAND, William
New breed in transportation. G. R. Rosen. por Duns R 83:pt2 100-2+ Je '64

RAND corporation
Planners for the Pentagon; with editorial comment. il Bsns W p56-8+, 144 Jl 13 '63
RAND: after nearly two decades of success, R&D nonprofit faces new tasks, new rivals. J. Walsh. il Science 144:1205-7 Je 5 '64
Rand corporation and our policy makers. S. Friedman. Atlan 212:61-8 S '63
Rand: R&D nonprofit pioneered a new kind of organization, served as a model for others. J. Walsh. Science 144:1112-14+ My 29 '64

RAND daily mail. See Newspapers—South Africa

RAND McNally and company
Rand McNally to buy Robert O. Law company. Pub W 185:106 Ja 20 '64

RANDAL, Vera
Alice Blaine; story. New Yorker 40:33-8 Jl 4 '64
Coming back; story. Sat Eve Post 237:54-61 S 12 '64
Going away; story. Sat Eve Post 237:36-7 S 5 '64

RANDALL, Charles
Bowling in the classroom. por Sci Digest 56: 24-5 S '64

RANDALL, Charles Edgar
Crazy blazes. Am For 69:8+ Jl '63
Fernow, the man who brought forestry to America. Am For 70:14-16+ Ap '64
Rags-to-riches forest. Am For 70:12-15+ Je '64
Toast to a tree. Am For 70:22-4+ My '64
White pine trees made history. Am For 69: 12-14+ Ap '63

RANDALL, Clarence Belden
Should Americans invest in South Africa? por Duns R 81:44-6 Ja '63
South Africa needs time. Atlan 211:77-80 My '63; Same abr. with title Why South Africa needs time. Read Digest 83:151-5 Ag '63
U.S. problem: low pay for top jobs. N Y Times Mag p29+ S 15 '63

about

Thoughts while shaving. por Newsweek 63:64+ Ja 20 '64

RANDALL, Dudley
Augury for an infant; poem. Negro Hist Bul 28:14 O '64

RANDALL, Florence Engel
Close by my side; story. Good H 156:82-3 Ap '63
Coconut on top. Writer 77:15-17 Ag '64
Friendship; story. Redbook 123:72-3 S '64
Heart of the house; story. Good H 157:78-9 S '63
Heirloom; story. Redbook 120:56-7 F '63
I was looking for you; story. Good H 157: 64-5 Ag '63
Man who didn't want to go home; story. Good H 156:80-1 F '63
Meeting place; story. Redbook 121:72-3 My '63
Newcomer; story. Redbook 121:52-3 S '63
Night life; story. Redbook 121:18-19 Ag '63
No beginning, no end; story. Redbook 122:70-1 Mr '64
Please call the office; story. Redbook 122: 40-1 D '63
What women know best; story. Good H 158:88-9 F '64
Where did it go? Redbook 122:80-1 Ap '64

RANDALL, John E. 2d
Voyage north. Yachting 115:47-9+ F '64

RANDALL, Lyman K.
Federal fetters for featherbedders. Harvard Bsns R 41:82-97 Ja '63

RANDALL, Margaret
For Gregory; poem. Poetry 102:93 My '63

RANDALL, Richard H. Jr
Benjamin Gerrish, brazier. Antiques 85:320-1 Mr '64
Sources of the empire style. Antiques 83: 452-3 Ap '63
—and McElman, Martha
Ebenezer Hartshorne, cabinetmaker. Antiques 87:78-9 Ja '65
RANDALL, Robert
Folklore of American taxation. New Repub 150:22-3 Mr 14 '64
RANDALL, Teresa Stich-. See Stich-Randall, T.
RANDALL, Tony
Funnyman changes face. il por Life 55:139-41 O 18 '63
RANDALL, Walter. See Nieder, P. C. jt. auth.
RANDOLPH, A. Philip
Filibuster of the people. N Y Times Mag p92-3 S 29 '63
If I were young today. por Ebony 18:82 Jl '63
March: what Negroes expected, what they want next: address, August 26, 1963. por U S News 55:82-5 S 9 '63
about
A. Philip Randolph. M. Kempton. New Repub 149:15-17 Jl 6 '63
Better day for brother Randolph. T. R. Brooks. Reporter 29:23 D 5 '63
Organized labor and the Negro worker. M. Bain. Nat R 14:455 Je 4 '63
People of the week. U S News 55:24 S 9 '63
Three Negroes receive 1964 Presidential freedom medal. C. W. Thomas. por Negro Hist Bul 28:58-9 D '64
RANDOLPH, Jennings
Citizen and his public responsibilities; address, September 12, 1963. Vital Speeches 30:9-11 O 15 '63
Excerpt from debate, September 8, 1964. Cong Digest 43:310+ D '64
RANDOM house, incorporated
Random house annual meeting optimistic. Pub W 186:33 Ag 10 '64
Random house sells Blaisdell to Ginn. Pub W 184:44 Ag 5 '63
RANDOM numbers. See Sampling (statistical methods)
RANDOM tetrahedral network. See Chemical bonds
RANEY, William
Obituary
Pub W 186:35 O 12 '64
RANGANATHAN, S. R.
S. R. Ranganathan, one American view. J. Shera. Wilson Lib Bul 37:581-2 Mr '63
RANGE finder cameras. See Cameras
RANGE finders. See View finders
RANGER (space vehicle) See Space vehicles
RANGER project. See Lunar probes
RANGES. See Stock ranges
RANGES, Kitchen. See Electric stoves; Gas stoves; Stoves
RANGES, Missile. See Proving grounds
RANGOON
Burma: gentle neighbor of India and red China. W. R. Moore. il Nat Geog Mag 123: 153-65 F '63
RANIS, Gustav
Crisis in foreign aid: a proposal. Yale R 53: 522-32 Je '64
RANK organization, limited
Rank progress. il Time 84:108 S 18 '64
RANKEN, Howard B.
Language and thinking: positive and negative effects of naming. bibliog Science 141: 48-50. 1240 Jl 5. S 27 '63
RANKIN, Allen
Because Amalia wanted to dance. Theatre Arts 47:60-3 O '63; Same abr. with title Born to dance. Read Digest 83:234-40 O '63
Billions of dollars unclaimed! Read Digest 84:77-81 My '64
Romantic Rio: city of a thousand delights. Read Digest 86:181-2+ Ja '65
RANKIN, James Lee
Assassination inquiry: slow, careful. il por U S News 56:49 Ja 27 '64
People of the week. il por U S News 55:10 D 30 '63
RANKIN, John
Rankin house; stop on underground railroad. M. E. Aber. Negro Hist Bul 26:253 My '63
RANNEY, Austin
Book for one reader. Reporter 28:48-50+ Mr 14 '63
RANNEY, Helen M. See Nagel, R. L. jt. auth.
RANSOHOFF, Daniel J.
Communicating a community service; D. J. Ransohoff's photographs of social conditions. M. R. Weiss. Sat R 46:72-3 S 14 '63
RANSOHOFF, Martin
Nudity for art's sake. por Newsweek 63:83 F 10 '64
RANSOM, Harry Howe
Away from the brink of war. Sat R 47:23-4 Jl 25 '64
How central is our intelligence? Sat R 47:25-6 Je 27 '64
Man and method: which is master? Sat R 47:48 S 26 '64
That's the way the money goes. Sat R 47: 60 Ja 11 '64
RANSOM, John Crowe
Culture and gallantry. il por Newsweek 63:79-80 Ja 27 '64
Equilibrist. il por Time 83:102 Ap 3 '64
RANSOM
Cuban prisoner exchange. B. Lindeman. il Sat Eve Post 236:15-17+ F 2 '63
In the black; aid in ransoming Bay of Pigs prisoners. Time 81:16 Mr 29 '63
James Donovan and Castro. G. Samuels. Nation 196:299-302 Ap 13 '63
Modern Mercedarian. N. McKenty. America 111:101 Ag 1 '64
Story behind the fat ransom; sway Bay of Pigs prisoners for U.S. goods. il Bsns W p84-6 F 9 '63
RANSTEAD, Donald D.
Chile turns left. Commonweal 80:594-6 S 4 '64
RANUNCULUS. See Buttercups
RAO, A. M. V. K. See Appa Rao. M. V. K.
RAO, Shanta
Mystery and the wonder: Shanta Rao. F. Bowers. il pors Dance Mag 37:46-9 O '63
Shanta Rao at 92nd street Y. M. Marks. Dance Mag 37:30+ N '63
RAPAPORT, Felix T. and Chase, R. M. Jr
Homograft sensitivity induction by group A streptococci. bibliog il Science 145:407-8 Jl 24 '64
RAPAPORT, Ionel
Art of the mentally retarded child. Sch Arts 63:13-17 Ja '64
RAPHAEL, Frederic
Yes, but you won't catch me going again; story. Yale R 53:416-27 Mr '64
RAPID-American corporation
Rapid-American trouble hinted by McCrory shift. Bsns W p 168 My 18 '63
Who's to blame for Riklis? Riklis? S. H. Brown. il Fortune 68:136-7+ O '63
RAPID transit
Can transportation systems put our cities back together again? D. B. Carlson. il Arch Forum 119:62-7 O '63
Commuter scooter? il Travel 120:37 S '63
Computer commuter? F. Riley. il Travel 121: 41 Mr '64
Experts debate ways to finance transit. Arch Forum 120:11 Mr '64
Highways to profit. Nation 196:539 Je 29 '63
Mass-transit bill, who can use it? Am City 79:7 Ag '64
Mass transit to the rescue. Bsns W p 182 O 10 '64
Monorail: a one-track controversy. J. N. Bell. il Sat Eve Post 237:81-2 My 9 '64
New concept in low-cost rapid transit; Transit expressway. il Am City 78:114-15 S '63
Rapid transit: the neglected highway. H. A. Williams. Nation 196:367-70 My 4 '63
Resurgence of rapid transit; excerpts from address, April 25 and April 26, 1963. R. L. Lich. il Am City 79:95 Mr '64
Salvaging mass transportation in urban areas. Am City 79:148-9 Ap '64
Sic transit transit. E. Goble. Arch Rec 133:9 Ap '63
Urban transit's new pep pill. H. B. Meyers. Fortune 70:166-7+ N '64
Urban transportation criteria. H. Fagin. Ann Am Acad 352:141-51 Mr '64
Wandering paths of a transit bill. V. J. Burke. il Reporter 31:31-3 Jl 16 '64
See also
Motor buses
Street cars
Subways
also subhead Rapid transit under names of cities, e.g. Philadelphia—Rapid transit

Fares

Demand and trends in prices for urban transit. G. Faux. bibliog f il Mo Labor R 87: 277-84 Mr '64

Finance

Vapid transit. Nat R 14:309 Ap 23 '63

RAPIDS shooting. See Boats and boating
RAPOPORT, Anatol
Armers and disarmers; con. Nation 196:175-7+ Mr 2 '63
Getting off the limb. Nation 196:271-2 Mr 30 '63
RAPOPORT, Daniel
And now, a brief word from our sponsors. Reporter 30:26-8 Je 4 '64
Mr Blatnik plans a purge. Reporter 31:32-4 D 3 '64
RAPP, Fred, and Benyesh-Melnick, Matilda
Plaque assay for measurement of cells infected with zoster virus. bibliog Science 141:433-4 Ag 2 '63
RAPP, George
Utopia, limited; excerpt from Vanishing America. W. E. Wilson. il por Am Heritage 15:64-72 O '64
RAPP, Herbert J. and Borsos, Tibor
Complement and hemolysis. Science 141:738-40 Ag 23 '63
RAPP, Marvin A.
Bridge and the wall; address, February 15, 1963. Vital Speeches 29:665-8 Ag 15 '63
Challenge to leadership; address, July 14, 1964. Vital Speeches 30:654-7 Ag 15 '64
RAPPAPORT, Anna Maria
Individualists; Mlle's annual Merit awards. por Mlle 58:76 Ja '64
RAPPOPORT, Solomon
Dybbuk. Criticism
Newsweek 63:90 F 17 '64
RARE book collections. See Libraries—Special collections
RARE books. See Book rarities
RARE books section. See Association of college and research libraries—Rare books section
RARE earths. See Earths, Rare
RARE gases. See Gases, Rare
RARICK, Joseph R.
Trees are my hobby. Horticulture 41:122 Mr '63
RAS, Norberto
Technology is not enough. Américas 17:10-15 Ja '65
RASCOVICH, Mark R.
Platinum tuna. Field & S 68:50-3+ Ap '64
RASKIN, A. H.
AFL-CIO; a confederation or federation? which road for the future? Ann Am Acad 350:36-45 N '63
Approach to automation: the Kaiser plan. N Y Times Mag p20-1+ N 3 '63
Automation: road to lifetime jobs? Sat R 47:14-16+ N 28 '64
Big strike: a thing of the past? Sat R 46:20-2+ N 16 '63
Civil rights: the law and the unions. Reporter 31:23-8 S 10 '64
Generalissimo of the war on poverty. N Y Times Mag p39+ N 22 '64
Is Hoffa finished? Reporter 30:22-4 Mr 26 '64
John L. Lewis and the mine workers. Atlan 211:53-8 My '63
Labor's crisis of public confidence. Sat R 46:21-5+ Mr 30 '63
Labor's mutinous mariners. Atlan 214:72-8 N '64
Labor's welfare state; the New York electrical workers. Atlan 211:37-44 Ap '63
Meaning of the rail settlement. Reporter 30:24-6 My 21 '64
Mr Meany's curse. Reporter 29:20-2 D 5 '63
Nonstop talks instead of nonstop strikes. N Y Times Mag p 12+ Jl 7 '63
Now Cole takes on automation. N Y Times Mag p26+ Ap 5 '64
Obsolescent unions. Commentary 36:18-25 Jl '63
Power of James R. Hoffa. Atlan 213:39-45 Ja '64
Report (favorable) on a teamsters local. N Y Times Mag p53-4+ N 1 '64
Rumbles from the rank and file. Reporter 32:27-30 Ja 28 '65
Speaking out. por Sat Eve Post 236:10+ O 12 '63
Walter Reuther's great big union. Atlan 212:85-90+ O '63
RASKIN, Anita
Girlsong; poem. McCalls 90:158 Je '63
RASKIN, Eugene
Motel comes to town. Nation 196:197-9 Mr 9 '63
RASKIN, Judith
Quote-unquote; interview, ed. by R. Jacobson. por Mus Am 84:21 N '64
RASKIN, Marcus
Books. Sci Am 211:109-10+ Ag '64
Bridge to disarmament. Bul Atomic Sci 19:25 Je '63
RASKOLNIKS
Old Believers. il Newsweek 61:62 My 6 '63
RASMUSSEN, A. E.
Big Muddy's first sewage plant. Am City 78:81-3 Jl '63
Digesters beat incineration. Am City 79:100-1 D '64
RASMUSSEN, George Stanley
Odd saga of the big Bahamas spenders. T. Armbrister. il por Sat Eve Post 237:30+ Ag 8 '64
RASMUSSEN, Howard, and others
Actinomycin D and the response to parathyroid hormone. bibliog Science 144:1019-21 My 22 '64
RASOOL, S. I.
Global distribution of the net energy balance of the atmosphere from Tiros radiation data. bibliog Science 143:567-9 F 7 '64
RASPBERRIES
Black raspberries for an edible hedge. I. C. Brown. il Horticulture 41:62 F '63
RASPONI, Lanfranco
Cyprus, where saints and goddesses meet. Vogue 141:162-3+ Ap 1 '63
Going places, finding things along the Spanish coast. House & Gard 123:46-9+ Ap '63
RASPS. See Files and rasps
RASSWEILER, Clifford F.
Speaking out. por Sat Eve Post 238:12+ Ja 30 '65
RAT. See Rats
RAT poisons
Bad news for brother rat; Raticate. P. Friggens. Read Digest 86:126-9 Ja '65
One hundred million rats against us. F. Powledge. il N Y Times Mag p36+ O 18 '64
Safe killer; Raticate. Newsweek 64:100 S 21 '64
RAT virus. See Viruses
RATCLIFF, John Drury
Ailment nobody mentions. Read Digest 85:77-80 S '64
Are you a hypochondriac? Read Digest 82:151-2+ Ap '63
Art from the looms of Aubusson. Read Digest 82:208-12 F '63
Bangkok's wonderful Dr Pierra. Read Digest 85:206-8+ S '64
Case of the vanishing monsters. Read Digest 85:254-6+ N '64
Cholesterol: guilty or not guilty? Read Digest 85:81-4 N '64
Facts about breast cancer. Read Digest 82:68-71 Mr '63
Lifesaving triumphs of arterial surgery. Read Digest 84:101-4 My '64
Lifesaving wonders of high-pressure oxygen. Read Digest 85:77-81 Jl '64
Man's best friend, the beefsteak. Todays Health 41:30-4 Je '63
New search for the fountain of youth. Read Digest 83:69-74 D '63
New timers for faulty hearts. Read Digest 83:169-70+ N '63
Nitrogen: industrial Cinderella. Sci N L 86:90-1 Ag 8 '64; Same abr. with title Nitrogen: the marvelous stuff that does nothing. Read Digest 85:122-4 O '64
Our amazing reflexes. Read Digest 83:136-8 O '63
Prostate cancer: needless killer. Read Digest 83:147-50 S '63
Sony turns small things into big profits. Read Digest 84:201-4 Je '64
Surgeons now repair or replace your damaged arteries. Todays Health 42:58-9+ My '64; Same abr. with title Lifesaving triumphs of arterial surgery. Read Digest 84:101-4 My '64
Triumph of Archy the Cockroach. Read Digest 82:37-8+ My '63
What EKG tells the doctor about your heart. Read Digest 82:91-4 Je '63
World's most bountiful store of drugs. Read Digest 83:97-101 Jl '63
Your liver's chemical magic. Todays Health 41:22-3+ D '63; Same abr. with title What your liver does for you. Read Digest 84:119-22 F '64
Your other circulatory system. Todays Health 42:30-1 D '64; Same abr. with title Our amazing white bloodstream. Read Digest 86:175-6+ Ja '65
(ed) See Best, C. H. How we discovered insulin
(ed) See Best, C. H. Victory over the sugar sickness
(ed) See Rutstein, D. D. Why do we let these babies die
RATCLIFFE, H. L. and Snyder, R. L.
Myocardial infarction; a response to social interaction among chickens. bibliog Science 144:425-6 Ap 24 '64

RATE regulation. See Insurance, Fire—Rates
RATES. See Telephone—Rates
RATH, Hildegard
My art is compulsive. il por Am Artist 27:34-9+ S '63
RATH, R. John
Carbonari: their origins, initiation rites, and aims. bibliog f Am Hist R 69:353-70 Ja '64
RATHBUN, Jess E.
Folding kayak. Pop Mech 119:152-5 Je '63
RATHNER, Herbert
Teen club forum. Recreation 57:518 D '64
RATICATE. See Rat poisons
RATING of automobiles. See Automobiles—Rating
RATING of executives. See Executives—Rating
RATING of products. See Quality of products
RATING of station wagons. See Station wagons—Rating
RATING of structures. See Valuation
RATING of teachers. See Teachers—Rating
RATING of television programs. See Television broadcasting—Program rating
RATING scales. See Educational tests and measurements
RATIONALISM
Rationalism in politics, by M. Oakeshott. Review
Commentary 35:168-72 F '63. G. Lichtheim
Nat R 15:360-2 O 22 '63. H. V. Jaffa
Toynbee dilemma. M. W. Hess. Christian Cent 81:8-9 Ja 1 '64
Tyranny of professorial rationalism. R. Kirk. Nat R 14:115 F 12 '63
RATIONING, Consumer
Cuba
Cuba now: shortages everywhere, even food rations can't be met. il U S News 54:47-8 My 27 '63
RATLIFF, L. Stanley. See Beach, F. F. jt. auth.
RATNER, Herbert
Rock book; Catholic viewpoint. Commonweal 78:392-5 Jl 5 '63
RATNER, Victor M. See Mandelbaum, B. jt. auth.
RATNOFF, Oscar D. See Davie, E. W. jt auth.
RATS
Artificial feeding of neonatal rats. S. A. Miller and H. A. Dymsza. bibliog il Science 141:517-18 Ag 9 '63
Common rat. Sci N L 86:95 Ag 8 '64
Diabetes mellitus in the sand rat induced by standard laboratory diets. K. Schmidt-Nielsen and others. bibliog il Science 143:689-90 F 14 '64
Early experience and emotional development. V. H. Denenberg. il Sci Am 208:138-40+ Je '63
Identical feeding and rewarding systems in the lateral hypothalamus of rats. D. L. Margules and J. Olds; reply with rejoinder. J. R. Brobeck. Science 140:218-20 Ap 12 '63
Infant handling; effects on avoidance learning, brain weight, and cholinesterase activity. J. T. Tapp and H. Markowitz. bibliog il Science 140:486-7 My 3 '63
Intrauterine foreign body: effect on pregnancy in the rat. L. L. Doyle and A. J. Margolis. il Science 139:833 Mr 1 '63; Reply with rejoinder. E. Eichner. 140:1136 Je 7 '63
Meet Mr Rat. B. Tufty. il(p289) Sci N L 83:298-9 My 11 '63
My friends, the rats. F. W. Nordsiek. il Sci Digest 53:79-83 Je '63
One hundred million rats against us. F. Powledge. il N Y Times Mag p36+ O 18 '64
Selective rat toxicant. A. P. Roszkowski and others. bibliog il Science 144:412-13 Ap 24 '64
Serum protein synthesis by the fetal rat. P. C. Kelleher and others. bibliog il Science 139:839-40 Mr 1 '63
Signal detection in the rat. M. H. Hack. bibliog il Science 139:758-60 F 22 '63
Strychnine: its facilitating effect on the solution of a simple oddity problem by the rat. W. J. Hudspeth. bibliog il Science 145:1331-3 S 18 '64
Tree rat, thamnomys surdaster surdaster, in laboratory research. M. Yoeli and others. bibliog il Science 142:1585-6 D 20 '63
War against the rats. Nation 198:63 Ja 20 '64
When they start playing footsie, it's time for a girl to quit; rats in Tokyo's main stem. Time 81:37 Mr 8 '63
RATS, Kangaroo. See Kangaroo rats
RATTÉ, Elizabeth H.
Foreign accents in the grades. PTA Mag 58:24-6 bibliog(p36) S '63
RATTÉ, John
American bishops at the first Vatican council. Commonweal 79:574-6 F 7 '64
Rich and lucid. Commonweal 79:82-3 O 11 '63
Simone Weil. Commonweal 77:669-70 Mr 22 '63
Splendid bishop. Commonweal 79:290-1 N 29 '63
RATTI, John
Hands in a family photograph; poem. Harper 226:92 Mr '63
Market man; poem. Harper 230:62 Ja '65
Women by the sea; poem. Poetry 103:372 Mr '64
RATTIGAN, Terence
Ross; text. por Theatre Arts 47:25-58 Ap '63
about
Man and boy. Criticism
New Yorker 39:143 N 23 '63
Newsweek 62:71 N 25 '63
Sat R 46:24 N 30 '63
Time 82:71 N 22 '63
RATTLE of a simple man; drama. See Dyer, C.
RATTLESNAKES
Never drop your guard. P. E. Allen. il Outdoor Life 131:44-7+ F '63
Rattleless rattlesnakes found on islands. Sci N L 86:105 Ag 15 '64
Rattling for tourists in northern Florida. J. O'Reilly. il Sports Illus 20:95-6+ Ap 13 '64
Snakebite ordeal; nineteen terrible hours. D. Utt. il Outdoor Life 135:37-9+ F '65
RATTNER, Abraham
Later Rattner; exhibition at Downtown gallery, New York City. F. Getlein. New Repub 150:36-7 Mr 28 '64
RAU, Santha Rama. See Rama Rau, S.
RAU, Simon and company, Bethlehem, Pa. See Drugstores
RAUDSEPP, Eugene
How to hire key people. Nations Bsns 51:54-9 S '63
RAUPE, Craig
Success of foreign aid; it must continue; address, March 3, 1964. Vital Speeches 30:406-9 Ap 15 '64
RAUSCHENBERG, Robert
Art. M. Kozloff. Nation 197:402-3 D 7 '63
Art pops in; with account by R. Constable. il por Life 57:65-6+ Jl 10 '64
Most happy fella. il por Time 84:84-7 S 18 '64
Pop goes the Biennale. il por Time 84:54 Jl 3 '64
Profiles. C. Tomkins. il New Yorker 40:39-40+ F 29 '64
Rauschenberg paints a picture. G. R. Swenson. il por Art N 62:44-7+ Ap '63
RAUSCHER, F. J. See O'Connor, T. E. jt. auth.
RAUSEN, Ruth G.
Best for teens and 'tweens. Sr Schol 84:20T-21T Mr 6 '64
Just something good. Sr Schol 84:18T-19T Mr 6 '64
RAUSHENBUSH, Esther
Mrs Raush. il por Newsweek 65:47 F 1 '65
RAUSHENBUSH, Stephen
Bridge Canyon Dam is not necessary. Nat Parks Mag 38:4-8 Ap '64
Water challenge of the Pacific Southwest. Nat Parks Mag 38:4-7 Je '64
RAVALLI refuge, Mont. See Bird Sanctuaries
RAVENSBRUECK lapins
Report on the ladies. N. Cousins. Sat R 46:22-3 F 16 '63
RAVENSWOOD power plant. See Atomic power plants
RAW materials
Can science offset the population explosion? excerpt from address. A. M. Weinberg. il Sci Digest 53:17-22 F '63
Chemistry in the raw; questions and answers. J. Daugherty and M. Daugherty. il Sci Digest 56:76-8 S '64
Shortages put new pressure on Russia. il Nations Bsns 51:72-3+ O '63
See also
Stockpiling
Prices
Costs stay in line as business expands. il Bsns W p43-4+ Jl 18 '64
Pressure grows for global price-fixing. il Nations Bsns 51:34-5+ My '63
RAWLINS, Robert
Coon hunter's life ain't easy. Outdoor Life 131:80-1+ My '63

RAWLINS, Stephen L.
Systematic error in leaf water potential measurements with a thermocouple psychrometer. bibliog Science 146:644-6 O 30 '64
RAWLINS, Winifred
Joy; poem. Christian Cent 80:878 Jl 10 '63
RAWLS, Betsy
Fairway woods: swing hard and be fearless; ed. by E. Shrake. il pors Sports Illus 21: 18-20+ Ag 3 '64
RAWLS, William A. Jr
Creative tank town. Recreation 56:380-1 O '63
RAWSON, Kenneth S. and Hartline, P. H.
Telemetry of homing behavior by the deermouse, peromyscus. bibliog Science 146: 1596-8 D 18 '64
RAY, Carleton
Locomotion in pinnipeds. Natur Hist 72:10-21 Mr '63
World's biggest, but for how long? N Y Times Mag p 123-5 D 13 '64
RAY, David
Card-players; poem. Nation 196:510 Je 15 '63
Mid-evening angst; poem. Yale R 54:237 D '64
This life; poem. Poetry 102:235 Jl '63
RAY, Gordon N.
Search for William Makepeace Thackeray. Sat R 47:20-1+ F 1 '64
RAY, Isabel
We gave a tasting party. por Farm J 87:78 D '63
RAY, Karl
Christmas in the paperback department. Pub W 184:39 Ag 19 '63
RAY, Man
An exciting ride in the van. R. Goldwater. por Sat R 46:19 Ag 17 '63
Grandada; exhibition at Manhattan's Cordier & Ekstrom gallery. il Time 81:90-1 My 17 '63
His heart belongs to dada. H. Kramer. Reporter 28:43-6 My 9 '63
Man; show of dadaist paintings. il por Newsweek 61:98-9 My 20 '63
Second fame: good food. N. Lyon. il por Vogue 145:186-8 F 1 '65
RAY, Manuel
Can't anyone here play this game? por Time 83:48 Je 12 '64
Playing for high stakes. il Newsweek 63:40 Je 1 '64
Unkept promise. por Newsweek 63:57 Je 15 '64
Visible CIA. Nation 198:613-14 Je 22 '64
War of nerves opens against Castro. por U S News 56:40 Je 1 '64
RAY, Oakley S. and Emley, Grace
Time factors in interhemispheric transfer of learning. bibliog Science 144:76-8 Ap 3 '64
RAY Surguine and company
Colorado paperback wholesaler moves, expands operation. il Pub W 184:41-2 N 18 '63
RAY weapons. See Weapons
RAYBURN House office building. See Washington, D.C.—Public buildings
RAYL, Dallas G.
Extended vacations at Timken. Mo Labor R 87:406 Ap '64
RAYL, Jimmy
Rayl gone guy! H. L. Masin. por Sr Schol 82: 28 F 13 '63
RAYLEIGH radiation
Light scattering by liquids at 6937 angstroms. J. L. Lundberg and others. bibliog il Science 145:1308-10 S 18 '64
RAYMOND, Jack
Do we need the draft? Look 27:17-20 Jl 30 '63; Same abr. Read Digest 84:119-20+ Mr '64
Vital new chapter in medical research is being written. Parents Mag 38:69+ O '63
Your son and selective service. Parents Mag 38:80+ S '63
RAYMOND, Marcel
Montreal botanical garden. Horticulture 42: 26-9 Jl '64
RAYMOND, Richard C.
Night landing; poem. Nation 196:534 Je 22 '63
RAYMOND, Samuel
Protein purification by elution convection electrophoresis. bibliog Science 146:406-7 O 16 '64
—See Weintraub, M. jt. auth.
RAYMOND and me that summer; story. See Perry, D.
RAYMONDA (ballet) See Ballets
RAYNAUD, Marylene
Addis Ababa abba-dabba; portfolio. Esquire 62:172-5 D '64
RAYNE, Max
Gain for Rayne. il Time 84:82 Ag 28 '64
RAYNOR, Vivien
Again the Village Picassos emerge. N Y Times Mag p26-7+ My 17 '64
RAYON flock. See Flock (fibers)
RAYON industry
Rescue for rayon. Time 83:86 F 14 '64
RAYS (fishes)
Never bedevil a devil fish! J. Fix. il Motor B 114:93+ N '64
RAYTHEON company
Doppler study holds promise of improved space navigation. R. Pay. Miss & Roc 13: 24-5 O 14 '63
Electronics field engineers around the world. C. J. Olson. il Electr World 70:42-3+ S '63
Flight by microwave. Time 84:38+ N 6 '64
Flying on the beam; Raytheon copter. il Newsweek 64:90 N 9 '64
RAZIK, Taher Abdul-. See Abdul-Razik, T.
RAZOR blades
Gillette faces the stainless-steel dragon. W. Guzzardi, jr. il Fortune 68:158-61+ Jl '63
Non-competitive razor blade sets standard; Wilkinson stainless-steel blades. Consumer Bul 46:43 S '63
Razor's edge; stainless-steel razor blade. il Newsweek 61:80-1 F 18 '63
Reluctant millionaires. il Time 83:92 My 1 '64
Revolution on the razor's edge; stainless-steel blades. E. T. Ewen. il N Y Times Mag p58+ O 6 '63
Stainless derby. il Consumer Rep 29:301 Je '64
Stainless; magic word intended to sell razor blades. il Consumer Bul 46:2+ N '63
Stainless steel razor blades. il Consumer Rep 28:470-1 O '63
Steelmakers' edge. il Time 82:93 S 20 '63
Swordsmith's razor blade; Wilkinson Super Sword-Edge. Consumer Rep 28:328 Jl '63
What about those stainless steel blades? Sci Digest 54:23 O '63
See also
Gillette company
RAZORS
Beauty gifts; electric shavers. il Seventeen 23:147 D '64
Men's electric shavers. il Consumer Bul 46: 6-9 D '63
Rechargeable and cordless shavers. il Consumer Bul 47:34-5 Ja '64
Women's electric shavers. il Consumer Bul 46:23-5 D '63
See also
Shaving
RE, Gerard F.
Re the Res; stock rigging. por Newsweek 62:70 Jl 22 '63
RE, Gerardo A.
Re the Res; stock rigging. por Newsweek 62: 70 Jl 22 '63
RE, Robert K.
Diodes regulate power supply. Electr World 70:66 O '63
RC filter chart. Electr World 70:25 Jl '63
Resistor power calculator. Electr World 69:37 Je '63
Tolerance calculator. Electr World 69:25 My '63
REA, D. G. and others
Interpretation of the 3- to 4-micron infrared spectrum of Mars. bibliog Science 141:923-7 S 6 '63
REA, James Edward
Book review. America 110:104-5 Ja 18 '64
REACH, James
What beginning writers want to know. Writer 76:10-12 O '63
REACTION motors division. See Thiokol chemical corporation
REACTIONARIES. See Conservatism
REACTORS, Nuclear. See Nuclear reactors
READ, Allen Walker
Desk dictionaries. Consumer Rep 28:547-50 N '63
Smaller dictionaries. Consumer Rep 29:145-7 Mr '64
That dictionary or the dictionary? Consumer Rep 28:488-92 O '63
READ, Sir Herbert
Anatomy of a nightingale. Sat R 46:33+ O 5 '63
Conversation with Sir Herbert Read; ed. by M. Y. Bassiouny. por Sch Arts 64:24-6 N '64
Good artist but a bad friend. Sat R 47:29+ Ap 4 '64
Two masters of modern art. Reporter 28:38-40 Je 6 '63
about
Man of four lives. por Time 81:94 Je 21 '63
Notes of a noble anarchist. J. Simon. Sat R 46:18 Ag 17 '63

READ, Sir Herbert—about—*Continued*
Remarkable bias in favor of man's unconscious self. D. Littlejohn. Commonweal 80: 92-4 Ap 10 '64
Sir Herbert Read on the teaching of art. J. S. Keel. bibliog por Sch Arts 63:19-21 D '63

READ, Hilton
My most unforgettable character. J. Helwig, jr. por Read Digest 84:129-33 My '64

READ, Leonard E.
Blessing of extremism; address, March 21, 1963. Vital Speeches 29:403-7 Ap 15 '63

READ, Merrill S. and Olcott, H. S.
Fallout, food, and man. Science 140:1341-2 Je 21 '63

READABILITY (literary style)
Gresham's law of literature; simplified books. A. Loftis and R. Marshall. il Sat R 46:64-5 S 21 '63

READERS (books)
Life is fun in a smiling, fair-skinned world; readers used in the elementary grades. O. Klineberg. bibliog il Sat R 46:75-7+ F 16 '63; Discussion. 46:56-7 Mr 23 '63
Modeled children. T. Orans. Commentary 36: 330-1 O '63; Reply with rejoinder. S. Adlen. 37:18 Mr '64
Redundancy in children's texts. E. C. Carterette and M. H. Jones. bibliog il Science 140:1309-11 Je 21 '63
Schoolman surveys concept of "the good life" in children's readers; excerpts from article. F. O. Wargny. Library J 88:4832-3 D 15 '63
See also
Primers

READER'S adviser (publication)
Reader's adviser, tenth edition; ed. by H. R. Hoffman. Review
Pub W 186:34-5 S 21 '64. D. M. Glixon

READERS and libraries. See Libraries and readers

READER'S digest
Foster parent for the Digest. il Time 85:48-9 Ja 1 '65
So it's all been done before. H. Rezatto. Writer 77:27-8+ N '64

READER'S digest association, incorporated
Reader's digest enjoined on cut-price claims for books. Pub W 185:239 Ja 27 '64

READERS' guide to periodical literature
Demand for dissent? public library practice in the selection of dissident periodicals; report. J. N. Berry, 3d. il Library J 89:3913-17 O 15 '64

READINESS for school
Early admission of able children to school; Warren demonstration project. J. W. Birch and others. bibliog Sch Life 46:7-9 Je '64
How to test their readiness for school; with study-discussion program. J. W. Kessler. bibliog il PTA Mag 58:15-17, 35 My '64
Preschools are not just for play. E. G. Neisser. il Parents Mag 39:72-3+ F '64
Seven signs of readiness for school. K. Kuperstock. il Parents Mag 38:56-7+ Je '63
That first day of school. L. Strong. il N Y Times Mag p57 Ag 30 '64
Time for tears. C. S. Waldrip. il NEA J 53:63 S '64
Viewpoint on school readiness; excerpt from School readiness: behavior tests used at the Gesell institute. F. L. Ilg and L. B. Ames. il Sch & Soc 92:397-402 D 26 '64
See also
Reading readiness

READING
See also
Books and reading
Childrens reading
International reading association
Readability (literary style)
Word perception

Readiness

See Reading readiness

Remedial teaching

Reading lab: Rx for better reading; Fairleigh Dickinson university, Rutherford, N.J. il Sr Schol 83:20T-21T O 4 '63
School library services for the culturally deprived child. R. L. Darling. bibliog f il Sch Life 46:18-20 O '63

Adults

Libraries: active agents in adult reading improvement. H. A. Robinson. bibliog f il ALA Bul 57:416-20 My '63
Reading improvement institute to be held in Chicago; Adult services division, ALA. Library J 88:1851 My 1 '63
Speed reading. E. N. Wood; E. Ehrlich. NEA J 52:44-6 Ap '63
Speed reading: can it be too fast? il Good H 157:139 Ag '63

Speed improvement

See Reading—Remedial teaching—Adults

Study and teaching

Bizarre alphabet teaches Johnny to read. G. Riemer. il Ladies Home J 81:70-1+ O '64
Book that sells books; Parent's guide to children's reading. Pub W 185:86 F 24 '64
Cracking the groen-ups' coed; Initial teaching alphabet. M. Gunther. il Sat Eve Post 237:34-5 Je 20 '64
Easier way to learn to read: i/t/a; Initial teaching alphabet. W. D. Boutwell. il PTA Mag 59:11-13 S; 11-13 O '64
Fight over phonics. il Life 56:105-6 Je 5 '64
First-grade reading under scrutiny. D. V. Gunderson. Sch Life 47:19-20 O '64
Helping parents to understand your reading program. R. C. Staiger. Sr Schol 85:13T N 18 '64
How Johnny can be taught to read, a new alphabet; Initial teaching alphabet. il U S News 56:76-7 My 18 '64
How three-year-olds teach themselves to read, and love it. M. Pines. il Harper 226: 58-64 My '63
Hunt, peck & read; teaching typewriter. il Time 84:56-7 Jl 24 '64
Individualized reading. L. Carlton and R. H. Moore. il NEA J 53:10-12 N '64
Janus face of reading; Initial teaching alphabet (i/t/a) C. Timm. il Wilson Lib Bul 39: 160-3 O '64
Learn to read in thirty hours; Freeport, N.Y. il Sci Digest 56:5 O '64
Learning to read. D. D. Durrell. Atlan 214: 87-8 S '64
Little children can learn to read; excerpts from How to teach your baby to read. G. J. Doman. il PTA Mag 59:30-2 Ja '65
New approach to reading; San Diego County reading study project. R. Van Allen. bibliog f il Wilson Lib Bul 39:154-9 O '64
On book-borne magic. F. G. Jennings. Sat R 46:66-7 O 19 '63
Phonics in beginning reading. W. G. Cutts. Sch Life 45:8-11 Ja '63
Primer for parents of first readers. P. Parish. il N Y Times Mag p 102 S 8 '63
Raising the level of literacy; adaptation of address, March 7, 1964. J. E. Fogarty. bibliog Sch Life 46:4-6 Je '64
Reading all of a sudden; Initial teaching alphabet. il Life 55:45-6+ N 1 '63
Reading: help for underprivileged children from Public education association volunteers. New Yorker 40:21-2 Ja 9 '65
Reading in basic education; excerpt from address, August 1, 1962. M. Smith. Sch & Soc 91:56-9 F 9 '63
Reading reform: look-say vs. phonics. R. Kirk. Nat R 16:974 N 3 '64
Reading scene; Initial teaching alphabet, or Augmented Roman. E. Geller. il Library J 89:4123-5 O 15 '64
Should parents teach reading? with study-discussion program. R. Strang. bibliog il PTA Mag 57:7-9, 34 Mr '63
Should the very young be taught to read? D. Durkin; W. D. Sheldon. bibliog il NEA J 52:20-4 N '63
Target: Dick and Jane; convention of Reading reform foundation. Nat R 15:267 O 8 '63
Teaching; Britain's initial teaching alphabet. il Time 83:52 Ap 3 '64
There's no magic formula for learning to r-r-r-r-read. E. H. Hanson. Parents Mag 38:56-7+ F '63
Too young to read? Glenn Doman system. il Life 57:107+ N 27 '64
Value of ITA; Initial teaching alphabet. J. Downing; I. Rose; W. G. Cutts. il NEA J 53:20-2 S '64
You can teach your baby to read. G. Doman and others. il Ladies Home J 80:62-3+ My '63
Your child and reading; reprint. il Todays Health 41:16 N; 16+ D '63; 42:60-1 Ja; 14 F; 62-3 Mr; 6 Ap '64
See also
Primers
Readers
Reading readiness

READING, Choice of. See Books and reading

READING aloud. See Books and reading—Reading aloud

READING and moving pictures. See Moving pictures and reading
READING and television. See Television and reading
READING by children. See Childrens reading
READING company
Why the Reading is a Wall Street belle; hope of merger enhances railroad's value. il Bsns W p 118+ O 17 '64
READING lists
ALA's young adult services division; list of interesting adult books for young people—1962. Wilson Lib Bul 37:730+ My '63
Booklists: bugaboo or boon? Shoreline high school, Seattle. P. V. Coffey. il Wilson Lib Bul 37:855-6 Je '63
Notes on high school book selection. M. K. Eakin; R. S. Alm. Library J 89:4603-5+ N 15 '64
Reviewing philosophy: adult books for young adults. L. Bulman. Library J 89:1878-9 Ap 15 '64
Those summer reading lists. T. M. Crager. Pub W 185:153-4 F 24 '64
See also
Books and reading—Best books
READING machines
Machine that reads writing. S. V. Jones. Sci Digest 55:52-3 F '64
Optical scanners; machines that read. K. Gilmore. il Electr World 72:33-7+ O '64
Philco corp. demonstrates multifont print reader. il Pub W 185:124-5 F 3 '64
READING readiness
Give slum children a chance; a radical proposal; excerpts from Crisis in black and white. C. E. Silberman. Harper 228:37-42 My '64; Discussion. 229:6 Jl '64
Parents, teachers, and early readers; televised series Preparing your child for reading by Denver public schools through National educational television services. D. DuBose. il Sr Schol 83:8T-9T N 1 '63
Preparing children for reading; reprint. A. Beery. il Todays Health 41:16+ D '63
Reading unreadiness in the underprivileged. W. G. Cutts. NEA J 52:23-4 Ap '63
Roots of reading. il Newsweek 64:76-7 Ag 17 '64
Should preschool children be taught the three R's? with study-discussion program. I. S. Black and J. W. Blos. bibliog il PTA Mag 59:24-6, 36 S '64
There's no magic formula for learning to r-r-r-r-read. E. H. Hanson. Parents Mag 38:56-7+ F '63
Too young to read? Glenn Doman system. il Life 57:107+ N 27 '64
What's happening in education? reading readiness. W. D. Boutwell. PTA Mag 58: 34 S '63
When are children ready to read? M. L. Kelley. il Sat R 46:58 Jl 20 '63
READING to children. See Books and reading—Reading aloud
READINGS, Dramatic. See Dramatic readings
READY-mixed concrete. See Concrete
READY or not, here comes the bride; story. See Worts, G. F.
READY-to-cook food. See Food—Ready-to-cook food
READY when you are, C.B! drama. See Slade, S.
REAGAN, Michael
For a guaranteed income. N Y Times Mag p20+ Je 7 '64
Fringe benefits. New Repub 148:7-8 Je 15 '63
Uncle Sam is really needed. N Y Times Mag p31+ S 13 '64
What 17 million shareholders share. N Y Times Mag p 11+ F 23 '64
REAGAN, Ronald
Republican party and the conservative movement. por Nat R 16:1055 D 1 '64
about
My technicolor senator. S. Alexander. Life 57: 30 D 4 '64
REAGENTS, Chemical. See Chemical reagents
REAL estate. See Real property
REAL estate advertising. See Real property—Advertising
REAL estate agents
Keeping the outsiders out. E. Richey. il Sat R 46:22-4 O 19 '63; Discussion. 46:23 N 30 '63
Michigan's ghetto buster. il Ebony 18:55-6+ F '63
Racist proposition: California on trial. D. Bess. Nation 199:179-82 O 5 '64
REAL estate boards, National association of. See National association of real estate boards
REAL estate business
Arizona: land for sale; business of Miss C. Collins. J. Roddy. il Look 27:32-5 O 8 '63
Back to normal. il Time 81:91 Je 7 '63
Bahamas for fun and profit. R. Joseph. il Esquire 62:121+ O '64
88,000 golden acres waiting for the dust to settle; Irvine ranch, Calif. S. Freedgood. il Fortune 68:142-7+ N '63
Foreign builders get a beachhead; newest look on U.S. skyline. il Bsns W p84-6+ My 11 '63
Hard sell in boom land; Florida real estate. A. Hirshberg. il Life 57:67-8+ N 13 '64
I sold a house to a Negro; Sarasota, Fla. E. Moore. il Ebony 18:92-4+ O '63
Land lords, by E. Rachlis and J. E. Marqusee. Review
New Repub 149:21-4 O 19 '63. D. M. Friedenberg
Millionaire: a self-portrait; interview, ed. by C. Sopkin. W. Johnson. Esquire 61:92-3+ F '64
My business is selling dreams. R. Morison. il Read Digest 83:110-12 S '63
New tactics in Florida land. il Bsns W p54-6+ Je 15 '63
Real-estate markets. il Fortune 67:84-8+ Mr; 98-101+ Ap; 128-32+ Je '63
Real estate syndicators retrench. il Arch Forum 118:9-10 My '63
Realism in corporate real estate. A. Rabinowitz. bibliog f il Harvard Bsns R 41:62-9 N '63
Still more gold in California land: speculative land investment. il Bsns W p 112-14 Ja 23 '65
They took her for a $20,000 ride; fast-talking real-estate promoters. il Changing T 18: 17-22 Ja '64
Vaguely realizing westward. il Time 81:58 F 15 '63
Where there's worry about credit. il U S News 56:76 Je 22 '64
See also
Corporations—Real estate operations
Location in business and industry
Tishman realty and construction company
Webb, Del E. corporation
Webb and Knapp, incorporated
REAL estate investment trusts
New road into real estate. D. Seligman and others. il Fortune 69:177-8 Ja '64
Prudent play in real estate. il Bsns W p 130+ Mr 28 '64
Realty trusts come under fire of IRS; Real estate investment trust act. Bsns W p56 Mr 2 '63
REAL estate research corporation
Brains behind the big deals; real estate researchers. il Bsns W p50+ Ag 15 '64
REAL estate taxes. See Local taxation; Real property and taxation
REAL property
How to find your cabin in the pines. C. Schoenfeld. il Field & S 67:43-5+ Mr '63
Key facts to know about joint ownership. il Good H 156:158 Je '63
One site saved; Merrywood. New Repub 149: 6 N 30 '63
Where to write for real estate information. Changing T 18:40-1 Ag '64
See also
Land speculation
Land values
Mortgages
Real estate business

Advertising

Don't buy land by mail! il Changing T 17: 7-11 Mr '63
Great land swindle. L. T. King. Commonweal 78:477-9 Ag 9 '63
Land frauds: look before you buy. T. Armbrister. il Sat Eve Post 236:17-23 Ap 27 '63

Europe, Western

Heavy spenders: West Germans snapping up property. il Newsweek 63:41 My 4 '64

Lebanon

Monopoly game. il Fortune 67:76 Je '63
REAL property and taxation
Architecture; tax abatement. W. McQuade. Nation 198:306-7 Mr 23 '64
How to ban architecture. Arch Forum 118:97 My '63; Discussion. 119:37 Jl '63
Is anybody covering this beat? Arch Forum 119:71 Jl '63
U.S. owners of Bulgarian property must file tax forms by June 15, 1963. Dept State Bul 48:905 Je 10 '63
REAL thing; story. See Ernst, P.
REAL wages. See Wages

REALISM in art
Art galleries; American scene. H. Rosenberg. New Yorker 39:147-8+ Mr 16 '63
Four realists: a review. F. Whitaker. Am Artist 28:54-61+ O '64
Magic realism of Gerald Mofchum. F. Whitaker. il Am Artist 27:24-9+ O '63
Pop goes the easel; pop art at New York's Guggenheim museum. il Newsweek 61:80 Ap 1 '63
See also
Trompe-l'œil
REALISM in literature
Children's libraries; postcript to a conference. D. M. Broderick. Wilson Lib Bul 38:209 O '63
Dearest freshness deep down things; excerpt from address, March 14, 1964. E. Cameron. il Horn Bk 40:459-72 O '64
Gates of horn: a study of five French realists, by H. Levin. Review
Reporter 28:42+ Je 20 '63. J. O'Brien
Heroics of realism. G. H. Hartman. Yale R 53:26-35 O '63
REALIST (periodical)
Man with a ho. il Newsweek 64:50-1 Ag 3 '64
REALITY
Art, science, and reality. G. R. Walker. Bul Atomic Sci 20:9-12 S '64
Daniel: dialogues on realization, by M. Buber; tr. by M. Friedman. Review
Sat R 47:26+ Ag 1 '64. R. B. Gittelsohn
Sense of reality. R. O. Johann. America 109:160 Ag 17 '63
REALS, Lucile F.
Answers to questions on antique samplers. Hobbies 68:51 My '63
Coverlet. Hobbies 69:28 Mr '64
On compiling a record for an antique. Hobbies 69:28+ O '64
REALTORS. See Real estate agents
REAMER, Thomas E.
Audio tone-burst generator. Electr World 70: 50-2+ O '63
FM multiplex signal generator. Electr World 69:55-8+ F '63
19-Kc. filter. Electr World 69:62-3 F '63
Phasemeter for audio frequencies. Electr World 70:43-6+ N '63
REANEY, James
Starling with a split tongue; poem. Atlan 214:146-7 N '64
about
Canadian chronicle. K. McRobbie. Poetry 103:269-70 Ja '64
REAPPORTIONMENT. See Apportionment (election law)
REAR view mirrors. See Automobiles—Equipment
REARDEN, Jim
Kodiak bear war. Outdoor Life 134:17-19+ Ag '64
Nomads of the North. Am For 69:8+ F '63
Too many caribou. por Outdoor Life 132:33-5+ S '63
REASON
Hoffa, Hegel, and Hoffer. N. Cousins. Sat R 46:26 Ap 20 '63
Men, apes, and termites. J. W. Krutch. Sat R 46:22-5 S 21 '63; Discussion. 46:29 O 12 '63
Reason in religion, by N. F. S. Ferré. Review
Christian Cent 81:115-16 Ja 22 '64. W. Gray
REASONING
See also
Problem solving
REAVEY, George
Now it can be told in Moscow. Sat R 46:27-9 F 9 '63
(tr) See Abramov, F. New life
(tr) See Evtushenko, E. A. Heirs of Stalin
(tr) See Evtushenko, E. A. Irreconcilable
(tr) See Evtushenko, E. A. Prologue
REAY, Billy
Rich bounty of mutiny. il por Sports Illus 19:72-4 D 2 '63
REAY, Devon
Garlic. Horticulture 41:228 Ap '63
Little berries that don't run. Flower Grower 50:67 Mr '63
Pines for winter protection and beauty all year. Flower Grower 50:33 N '63
REAY, M.
Burnet. Horticulture 41:99 F '63
REAY, Nina Butler
Mr Bates goes to the polls; drama. Plays 24:76-8 N '64
REBAY, Hilla
Baroness' income tax. il por Time 81:59 Mr 1 '63
REBENACK, John H.
Common fine. por Library J 89:4868-70 D 15 '64
REBHAN, John R.
Beauty up front. Flower Grower 50:32-3+ S '63
Saved trees mean so much. Flower Grower 52:30-1+ Ja '65
Two planning and planting ideas. Flower Grower 50:40-1 N '63
REBUILT automobiles. See Automobiles, Remodeled
RECAPPING of tires. See Tires, Rubber
RECATALOGING. See Cataloging
RECEIPTS (acknowledgements)
What papers should we keep? questions and answers. R. C. Cowan. PTA Mag 57:35 Je '63
RECEPTORS, Retinal. See Retina
RECEPTORS, Sensory. See Nervous system
RECESSION, Business. See Business depression
RECIPES. See Cookery
RECIPROCAL trade agreements. See United States—Commercial treaties and agreements
RECITALS, Dance. See Dance recitals
RECITALS, Musical. See Musical recitals
RECK, John
Hobbies à la carte. Pop Mech 119:118-19 Ap '63
RECKFORD, Kenneth J.
Death; poem. Commonweal 81:576 Ja 29 '65
RECKLESS, John
Weaknesses of the National health service. bibliog f Cur Hist 45:34-40 Jl '63
RECLAMATION, Bureau of. See United States—Reclamation, Bureau of
RECLAMATION of land
Mexico
See also
Chinampas
Netherlands
Clamshell dikes tame the ocean; Delta plan. G. B. Rubinstein. il Pop Mech 120:90-1 Jl '63
Dutch against the sea; twenty-five year program: Delta plan. H. Gilroy. il N Y Times Mag p96-7 S 15 '63
High wall of the Low Countries; delta plan. il UNESCO Courier 17:48-51 Jl '64
RECLASSIFICATION. See Classification
RECLINING chairs. See Chairs
RECLUSES
Last hermit. E. W. Smith. il Field & S 67: 56-8+ Ap '63
RECOGNITION (international law)
Nonrecognition; the diplomatic trap. R. A. Falk. il Nation 198:457-60 My 4 '64
RECOGNITION of words. See Word perception
RECOMBINATION of genes. See Crossing over (genetics)
RECOMMENDATIONS for positions
How to write a job reference. il Changing T 18:16 Jl '64
RECONNAISSANCE airplanes. See Airplanes, Military
RECONNAISSANCE rockets. See Rockets—Military applications
RECONNAISSANCE sensors. See Aeronautic instruments
RECONSTRUCTION (Civil war)
Tragic legend of reconstruction. K. M. Stampp. Commentary 39:44-50 Ja '65
W. E. B. Du Bois: pioneer reconstruction historian. D. Walden. bibliog f Negro Hist Bul 26:159-60+ F '63
RECORD (St Augustine, Fla)
Covering St Augustine. il Time 84:75 Jl 10 '64
RECORD changers. See Phonograph—Record changers
RECORD players. See Phonograph
RECORDER (musical instrument)
Drop thy pipe. J. G. Mitchell. il Atlan 213: 174+ Mr '64
Fossil woodwind. il Newsweek 62:67 Jl 29 '63
RECORDER music
See also
Phonograph records—Recorder music
RECORDING for the blind, incorporated
Books for the blind. il Newsweek 62:71 S 2 '63
Mind's ear; recorded textbooks. il Time 84: 36 Ag 14 '64
RECORDING instruments
See also
Magnetic recorders and recording
RECORDING of music. See Sound—Recording and reproducing
RECORDING studios. See Sound—Recording and reproducing

RECORDS
Archival product of a century of federal assistance to agriculture. H. T. Pinkett. bibliog f Am Hist R 69:689-706 Ap '64
See also
Business records
County records
Family records
Farm records
Fishing records
Personal records
Police records
Sports records

RECORDS, Phonograph. See Phonograph records

RECORDS, Preservation of. See Civilization—Preservation of records

RECORDS, School. See School reports and records

RECORDS, World. See World records

RECOVERY of lost articles. See Lost articles

RECREATION
Critical issues in recreation; report from the 46th National recreation congress. il Recreation 57:489-92+ D '64
Family and the community; excerpts from address. A. F. Wileden. Recreation 58:32 Ja '65
Guiding principles for program planning; excerpt from Recreation in American life. R. E. Carlson and others. Recreation 58:40-1 Ja '65
How to keep teens out of trouble; solution in Darien, Conn. R. Carson. il Parents Mag 39:48-9+ Je '64
None does his job alone; adaptation of address. J. A. Smith. Recreation 57:48 F '64
Recreation and urban development: a policy perspective; excerpts from Trends in American living and outdoor recreation. L. Wingo, jr. bibliog f Ann Am Acad 352:129-40 Mr '64
Recreation as a power for peace! G. O. Romney. Recreation 56:355 O '63
Recreation in low-cost housing projects. Recreation 57:79 F '64
Recreation site finders. L. Fox. il Recreation 56:92-3 F '63
Summer fun for the family. PTA Mag 57:7 Je '63
Two views on the Seattle watershed; recreation management, no! J. R. Heath. il Am For 68:9+ N '63
See also
Games
Hobbies
Industrial recreation
International recreation association
Leisure
Outdoor life
Parks
Physical education and training
Playgrounds
Pool rooms
Recreational therapy
Sports
Sports for children
Vacation projects

Activities

Art instruction in a summer program. V. Gregory. il Recreation 56:275 Je '63
Can community recreation meet the needs of youth? J. A. Wylie. il Recreation 56:406-8 N '63
Cornfield chemicals club. J. Castle. il Recreation 56:409-10 N '63
Creative magic for the senior citizen. S. W. Gross. il Recreation 57:234-5 My '64
Cultural activities go west; San Diego. R. Trembley. il Recreation 56:317-19 S '63
Cultural growth in capital letters! programs of cultural interests. J. Prendergast. il Recreation 57:440-1 N '64
Family unity and fitness too; Family day, Bedford, Mass; reprint. W. D. Godsoe. il Recreation 56:478 D '63
Leisure, its meaning and implications; excerpts from addresses. R. Theobald; C. K. Brightbill. Recreation 57:9-11 Ja '64
Making headlines; North Renfrew times, Deep River. J. A. Cropley. il Recreation 57:393+ O '64
Recreation out of necessity; excerpts from paper. J. A. Cropley. il Recreation 57:84-5+ F '64
Science through recreation, by W. Goodrich and C. M. Hutchins. Review
Recreation 57:303 Je '64
Seed of wonder; Vacation Bible school in the town of Cape May Court House, N. J. il Recreation 56:326-7 S '63
Space for the basic urge to be ornery. B. Furst. Recreation 56:163 Ap '63
State parks recreation menu; Kentucky state parks. W. H. Radke. il Recreation 57:272-4 Je '64
See also
Camping—Activities
Dancing
Handicraft
Picnics
Playground activities
Recreation for the handicapped

Administration

Behind the times; concerning report by the Community council of Greater New York. Recreation 56:324 S '63
Blueprint for organization; Los Angeles Department of recreation and parks. W. Frederickson, jr. il Recreation 57:410-14 O '64
Building a park and recreation department; Willamalane park and recreation district, Ore. R. M. Artz. il Recreation 57:442-5+ N '64
Good recreation management; address. H. Hines. Recreation 56:88-90+ F '63
How good is your board? R. E. Pike. il Recreation 58:33-5 Ja '65
New CPRS-NRA agreement; services of California park and recreation society and National recreation association combined. il Recreation 57:435-6 N '64
Notes for the administrator. Recreation 56: 91, 195, 382, 417; 57:82-3, 243, 311-12 F, Ap, O-N '63, F, My-Je '64
Park and recreation administrator. G. G. Eppley. Recreation 57:194-5+ Ap '64
Platform for conservation and outdoor recreation; adaptation of address. L. S. Rockefeller. il Recreation 57:446-8 N '64
Pooled facilities and services pay off: Pasadena, Calif. E. E. Bignell. il Recreation 57:346-7 S '64
Problem of priorities. L. R. Rockwood. Recreation 57:465-7 N '64
Public recreation: progress and problems. A. Todd. il Recreation 56:278-81 Je '63
State recreation services. R. J. Andrews. Recreation 56:404-5 N '63
Three R's of operation. H. J. Van Cott. il Recreation 56:378-9 O '63
To better advantage; new ways of extending playgrounds and recreation services; symposium. Recreation 57:188-90 Ap '64
Urban-oriented outdoor recreation; excerpts from address. L. F. Twardzik. il Recreation 56:470-3 D '63
See also
Recreation departments

Aims and objectives

Have you a recreation philosophy? E. F. Ziegler. Recreation 56:399-400 N '63
My philosophy of recreation. H. D. Edgren. Recreation 56:59-60 F '63
On recreation literacy; symposium. il Recreation 56:458-9+ D '63
Recreation and family needs; excerpts from Helping the family in urban society. R. S. Tefferteller. Recreation 56:423-4 N '63
Recreation's changing role. E. Schindler-Rainman. Recreation 58:12-13 Ja '65
Toward understanding leisure; outline for discussion. A. New. Recreation 58:36-7 Ja '65

Bibliography

Evaluation of outdoor areas; recent articles in Recreation. Recreation 56:473 D '63
New publications; Books & pamphlets received; Magazine articles. See issues of Recreation
Outdoor recreation for America. Recreation 56:361-3 O '63

Economic aspects

Sweden goes all out for the leisure boom. il Bsns W p32-3 S 7 '63

Federal aid

See Recreation and state

Finance

New paths to recreation space; symposium. il Recreation 57:12-26+ Ja '64
Reaching your publics. E. Lindsay. Recreation 58:14 Ja '65

History

Recreation out of necessity; excerpts from paper. J. A. Cropley. il Recreation 57:84-5+ F '64
Summertime revisited; portfolio. S. T. Cooper. Am Heritage 14:35-49 Je '63

RECREATION—*Continued*

International aspects

Broad horizons; Peace corps recreation workers. R. Schumm. il Recreation 56:356-8 O '63

Laws and regulations

Federal legislation for land acquisition; excerpts from address. J. P. Anderson. il Recreation 58:22-3 Ja '65
Pioneering legislation provides recreation for handicapped. F. M. Robinson. Recreation 56:403+ N '63

Public relations

Reaching your publics. E. Lindsay. Recreation 58:14 Ja '65

Publicity

How to get what you want; Opelika, Ala. W. J. Calhoun. il Recreation 57:521-2 D '64
Recreation has purpose; Parsons, Kan. il Recreation 57:350-1 S '64

Study and teaching

Not keeping pace. H. D. Sessoms. il Recreation 56:433 N '63
Recreation majors club; La Crosse state college. J. Christenson. Recreation 56:101 F '63

Japan

Japan today: golf and the country cottage. il U S News 57:66-9 S 14 '64
See also
Sports—Japan

United States

Army lakes float U.S. boatmen. J. Graham. il Motor B 112:34+ Ag '63
Big push for outdoor recreation. il Am For 69:14-16+ Mr '63
Big squeeze in your back yard. J. Prokop. il Am For 69:6-7+ Ap '63
Californian looks at California; address, February 27, 1963. J. K. Carr. il Am For 69:16-19 Ap '63
Federal intrusions anger states; providing outdoor-recreation opportunities. H. Titus. Field & S 68:20+ D '63
Hon dah (be my guest) J. Cook. il Am For 69:26-7+ Ap '63
How we manage good times all year long. B. Jobe and M. Longwell. il Farm J 88:106-7 Mr '64
Land and water conservation fund. il Recreation 57:449-50 N '64
Letting George do it won't do it. W. R. Catton, jr. il Nat Parks Mag 38:4-7 Mr '64
Mr Gillett's farm bureau talk; summary of address, December 9, 1963. C. A. Gillett. Am For 70:62 Ja '64
National agencies: two kinds. Recreation 56:119 Mr '63
New CPRS-NRA agreement; services of California park and recreation society and National recreation association combined. il Recreation 57:435-6 N '64
New horizons; address, September 23, 1964. L. S. Rockefeller. Am For 70:10-13 N '64
Park wilderness in danger? A. W. Smith. Nat Parks Mag 38:2 O '64
Plans for outdoor recreation; California public outdoor recreation plan. H. Broome. Liv Wildn 82:21-3 Wint '62
Private outdoor recreation industry; its management. G. W. Cornwell. il Am For 69:36-9+ O '63
Recreation's changing role. E. Schindler-Rainman. Recreation 58:12-13 Ja '65
Responsibilities in outdoor recreation. Am For 70:7 Mr '64
Should the outdoors be free? address. W. N. Aspinall. Am For 70:32-4+ Ap '64
So you want to entertain the public! private outdoor recreation industry. P. E. McDowell. il Am For 70:22-5+ Ja '64
Squeeze out! Recreation's abdication of responsibility; discussion. Recreation 56:56 F '63
State and local developments. E. Delany. See occasional issues of Recreation to May 1964
U.S. spends more on recreation than space. Sci N L 83:312 My 18 '63
Why we need the Land and water conservation fund bill. C. P. Anderson. Am For 70:24-7+ Mr '64
World enriched by our presence; report on the recent National conference on professional education for outdoor recreation. J. J. Shomon. Audubon Mag 66:354-5 N '64
See also
Forest recreation
National conference on outdoor recreation research
National recreation association
National recreation congress
Parks—United States
Prison recreation
Recreation, Rural
Recreation centers
Sports—United States
United States—Outdoor recreation resources review commission

RECREATION (periodical)
Evaluation of outdoor areas; recent articles. Recreation 56:473 D '63

RECREATION, Industrial. See Industrial recreation

RECREATION, Rural
All-year resort in a pasture. J. Russell. il Farm J 87:59 Ap '63
As the snow flies; cropland converted for winter recreation projects. H. E. Winkley. il Recreation 58:11 Ja '65
Building a park and recreation department; Willamalane park and recreation district, Ore. R. M. Artz. il Recreation 57:442-5+ N '64
Cash in on campsites. J. Bickers. il Farm J 88:28-9+ Je '64
Farm vacations; with editorial comment. J. B. Craig. il Am For 70:7, 8-11+ Jl '64
Fun on the farm. Changing T 17:6 My '63
How we get dad in on the fun. M. Felkner. Farm J 87:77+ Ap '63
Key to nature; address, August 1962. R. E. Carlson. il Recreation 56:64-6+ F '63
Policy for county parks and recreation; condensed statement. Recreation 57:270-1 Je '64
Recreation farming; look before you leap! F. Bailey, jr. Suc Farm 61:78+ Je '63
Recreation, farming's giant new crop. R. C. Davids. il Farms J 87:40-1+ F '63
Recreation harvest; farm at Cream Ridge, N.J. L. Fox. il Recreation 57:21-4 Ja '64
Rural recreation; report of the National seminar on rural family recreation. il Recreation 56:352 O '63

Finance

Recreation farming; how's it doing? B. Brantley. Suc Farm 62:42 Ag '64

RECREATION activities. See Recreation—Activities

RECREATION advisory council. See United States—President's recreation advisory council

RECREATION and state
Legislative needs for outdoor recreation; grants-in-aid program; excerpt from address. E. C. Crafts. il Am For 69:18-19+ Mr '63
New national recreation area system; with excerpts from testimony of Joseph Prendergast. Recreation 56:257-8 Je '63

RECREATION and the church. See Church work with youth

RECREATION areas
Recreation area standards: the city. L. Lynch. il Recreation 58:20-1 Ja '65
When is a recreation area a park? L. Lynch. il Recreation 57:394-6 O '64

RECREATION boards. See Recreation—Administration

RECREATION buildings
New forms and facades. il Recreation 58:26-8 Ja '65
Recreation buildings. il Arch Rec 134:145-52 Ag '63

RECREATION centers
Administrative offices and recreation center for YWCA; Pittsburgh, Pa. il Arch Rec 135:159-64 Mr '64
Air force assesses its recreation centers. A. Todd. Recreation 57:342-3 S '64
How to get a photo center in your city. S. Smoliar. Pop Phot 52:57+ My '63
In the swim in St Louis; Wohl recreation center. Mrs. E. G. Brungard. il Recreation 56:308-9+ S '63
New aquatorium on target; Commerce, Calif. A. J. Robles. il Recreation 56:413-16 N '63
Now a great place for teens; Nahunta, Ga. K. Davis. il Farm J 88:88-9 O '64
Shopping centers. R. Lambakis; discussion. Recreation 55:488; 56:108 D '62, Mr '63
Teen-age Olympics; Corral youth center serving LaGrange and Western Springs, Ill. H. Ehrlich. il Look 28:140-2 O 20 '64
Youth center from an old theater. il Arch Forum 118:152-3 My '63
See also
Recreation areas
School buildings as recreation centers

RECREATION clubs. See Clubs
RECREATION commissions reports. See Reports
RECREATION conferences
NRA district recreation conferences. Recreation 57:60-1+ F '64
World recreation congress, Japan 1964. T. E. Rivers. il Recreation 58:25 Ja '65
See also
National recreation congress
RECREATION departments
Third dimension; advisory councils. D. Jones. Recreation 56:282-4 Je '63
RECREATION education. See Recreation—Study and teaching
RECREATION for the aged
Action for aging; Training for leadership in senior citizens clubs, Austin, Tex. Mrs C. Clopton. il Recreation 57:300-1 Je '64
Adapting games for the handicapped. M. Thompson. Recreation 56:136-7 Mr '63
Brightening old age in Houston; Sheltering arms program. H. Whitman. il Todays Health 41:52-3 S '63
Challenge of leisure in old age. J. R. MacLean. Recreation 56:213 My '63
Crafts for aging; excerpts from introduction. D. Campbell. Craft Horiz 23:8-9 Ja '63
Creative magic for the senior citizen. S. W. Gross. il Recreation 57:234-5 My '64
Dancing enriches their retirement years; Sirovich day center in New York city. il Todays Health 41:64 Ag '63
Fun of retirement, by W. Peterson. Review Recreation 57:301 Je '64
How active are they? il Recreation 57:228-9 My '64
Recreation promotes health; excerpts from address, October 2, 1962. H. A. Rusk. Recreation 56:128-9 Mr '63
Senior citizens in suburbia. M. G. Hickerson. Recreation 56:220 My '63
Senior scholars; Institute for retired professionals. Newsweek 63:77 Ja 20 '64
RECREATION for the handicapped
Adapting games for the handicapped. M. Thompson. Recreation 56:136-7 Mr '63
Basketball for the physically handicapped; excerpts from Book of basketball. I. A. Leitner. il Todays Health 42:50-1+ Ja '64
Demonstration camp program for retarded. E. Wyant. Recreation 57:305 Je '64
Exploring a need; a survey of recreation in institutions for the mentally retarded. A. D. Cortazzo and A. R. Menefee. Recreation 57:304-5 Je '64
Finding buried treasure in the hospital; reprint. R. Sommer and I. Watson. Recreation 56:94-5 F '63
Fishing aplenty for the disabled. F. White. il Todays Health 42:50-1+ S '64
Goodwill recreation program; Dayton, Ohio. R. A. Steinbrunner. il Recreation 57:408-9 O '64
Marley's ghost. A. R. Doolittle. il NEA J 52:44-5 D '63
Pioneering legislation provides recreation for handicapped. F. M. Robinson. Recreation 56:403+ N '63
℞ for the ill & handicapped. M. Thompson. See issues of Recreation
Varsity and variety; Mansfield training school, Mansfield Depot, Conn. Recreation 57:28 Ja '64
Widen your doors. M. Thompson. Recreation 57:27-8 Ja '64
RECREATION month. See Special days, weeks, and months
RECREATION rooms
This family room is a theater at home. il Sunset 131:92 S '63
Three good details; basement conversion. il Am Home 67:90+ Ja '64
RECREATION workers
Congress faces. il Recreation 57:490-1 D '64
Have you a recreation philosophy? E. F. Ziegler. Recreation 56:399-400 N '63
Leaders of leisure. E. Kauffman. Recreation 57:463-4 N '64
Man of many talents; requirements for a college union director of today. K. G. Briscoe. Recreation 57:89-90 F '64
Park and recreation administrator. G. G. Eppley. Recreation 57:194-5+ Ap '64
People in the news (title varies) See issues of Recreation
Public relations on the playground. A. Howard. Recreation 56:169 Ap '63
Ready, willing, and able; symposium. Recreation 57:178-9 Ap '64
Staff relations. R. Andrews. Recreation 56:70 F '63
Take me to your leader. E. Drapela; J. A. Peterson. Recreation 57:196-8 Ap '64

Recruiting

Career day program; Sayre, Pa. F. N. Tokar. Recreation 56:108-9 Mr '63
How we fail in recruitment. L. F. Twardzik. il Recreation 57:468-9 N '64
Recruitment factors. B. C. Fernelius. Recreation 57:527 D '64
Student approach to recruitment. D. E. Sterle; T. M. Kavadas. il Recreation 57:318-19 Je '64

Supply and demand

Help wanted: female. M. B. Miller. Recreation 58:38+ Ja '65
Stream becomes a trickle. H. D. Sessoms. il Recreation 57:425 O '64

Training

Action for aging; Training for leadership in senior citizens clubs, Austin, Tex. Mrs C. Clopton. il Recreation 57:300-1 Je '64
Training for military programs; Lincoln air force base, Neb. R. M. Dula. Recreation 57:520 D '64
Trial and triump of training; playground supervisors, Ottawa, Ontario. A. D. Adie. Recreation 57:240-1 My '64
RECREATION workers, Volunteer
Starting from scratch; program at Indianola, Ia. J. Kerr. il Recreation 56:178+ Ap '63
RECREATIONAL therapy
Patient-planned program; South Florida state hospital. R. A. Prettyman. Recreation 57:407 O '64
Rehabilitative recreation in VA hospitals. C. C. Bream, jr. il Recreation 57:224-6 My '64
RECRUITING agencies. See Employment agencies
RECRUITING and enlistment. See United States—Army—Recruiting and enlistment
RECRUITING for business and industry. See Employment systems
RECRUITING of librarians; Recruiting of physicians; etc. See Librarians—Recruiting; Physicians—Recruiting; etc.
RECRUITING officer; drama. See Farquhar, G.
RECRUITMENT, Office for. See American library association—Library administration division
RECTAL glands. See Glands
RECTIFIERS. See Electric current rectifiers
RED Angus cattle. See Cattle—Breeds
RED Cloud
Surrender of Red Cloud; excerpt from memoirs. C. W. Taylor. por Am Heritage 15:111 Je '64
RED cross
Flag of mercy. Newsweek 62:42-4 S 16 '63
Red cross; a century of dedication. J. Wechsberg. il N Y Times Mag p22+ Ag 25 '63
Red cross; centenary of a universal banner. H. d'Havrincourt. il UNESCO Courier 16:20-5 Je '63

International committee, Geneva

Red cross; a century of dedication. J. Wechsberg. il N Y Times Mag p22+ Ag 25 '63

National blood program

See Blood donors

United States

Hard sell for mercy. il Bsns W p32+ My 16 '64
Red cross, a volunteer army. il N Y Times Mag p62-3 Mr 8 '64
RED drum fishing. See Bass fishing
RED foxes. See Foxes
RED RIVER OF THE NORTH
U.S. requests three IJC studies on water levels and pollution; text of letter, October 1, 1964. D. Rusk. Dept State Bul 51:599-600 O 26 '64
RED snapper fishing. See Snapper fishing
RED Sox (baseball) See Baseball clubs
RED spiders
Daily sensitivity rhythm of the two-spotted spider mite, tetranychus urticae, to DDVP. B. Polcik and others. bibliog il Science 145:405-6 Jl 24 '64
Spider mites and their cousins. Sunset 131:165 Jl '63
RED tape. See Bureaucracy
RED tide. See Fishes—Diseases and pests
RED WING, Minn.
Don't be just half-safe. R. Smith and others. il Am City 78:90-2 My '63
RED Wings (hockey team) See Hockey teams

REDBOOK magazine
JFK, the magazines, and peace. J. Tebbel. il Sat R 46:56-7 D 14 '63
Redbook's first sixty years. il Redbook 121: 74-86 My '63
Stein song. il Time 84:73 D 4 '64
REDDING, Frank
Schools and publishing: a partnership in transition; condensation of report. Pub W 183:22-5 Mr 18 '63
REDDING, Ruth
Indispensable daylilies. Pop Gard 14:36-7 Ap '63
REDDING, Saunders
Man against myth and malice. Sat R 47:48-9 My 9 '64
Sound of their masters' voices. Sat R 46:26 Je 29 '63
REDDY, John
Around the world with Bob Hope. Read Digest 82:140-4 Je '63
General who built the world's largest store. Read Digest 84:181-5 Ja '64
Great Gleason: TV's vast waistband. Read Digest 82:132-6 F '63
Mastah Freddy's modest miracle. Sat Eve Post 238:68+ Ja 30 '65
Stan the incredibly durable man. Read Digest 82:175+ Ap '63
Wild woild of Jimmy Durante. Read Digest 83:202-4+ N '63
REDECORATING. See House decoration
REDEEN, Robert L.
(ed) See Rusk, D. Secretary Rusk interviewed on Voice of America
REDEFER, Frederick L.
Chamber of educational horrors? Sat R 47:53 S 19 '64
Magnet for ideas. Sat R 47:20 Ag 8 '64
Teacher teaches better. NEA J 53:8-10 Ap '64
RÉDEI, G. P.
Somatic instability caused by a cysteine-sensitive gene in arabidopsis. bibliog Science 139:767-9 F 22 '63
REDEMPTION. See Salvation
REDEVELOPMENT, Urban. See City planning
REDEVELOPMENT program. See Economic assistance, Domestic
REDFEARN, M. S.
Toxic lysolipoid: isolation from pseudomonas pseudomallei. bibliog Science 146:648-9 O 30 '64
REDFIELD, Alfred C.
Ontogeny of a salt marsh estuary. bibliog Science 147:50-5 Ja 1 '65
REDFORD, Polly
Everglades skimmers. Motor B 112:44-5+ D '63
Our most American animal. Harper 227:47-50 O '63
Slow night au Relais. Atlan 212:120+ N '63
Small rebellion in Miami. Harper 228:96-8+ F '64
Vive les différences! Motor B 111:38-9+ Ap '63
REDICK, Thomas F. and others
Cerebrally active small moiety from taraxein-like blood fractions. bibliog Science 141: 646-7 Ag 16 '63
REDING, Georges R. and others
Sleep pattern of tooth-grinding: its relationship to dreaming. bibliog Science 145:725-6 Ag 14 '64
REDLICH, Don
Marion Scott, Don Redlich at 92nd street Y. M. Marks. Dance Mag 38:64 Mr '64
REDLICH, Norman
Counsel for the doomed. por Newsweek 61: 36-7 Mr 25 '63
Last chance on death row. H. Lavine. il por Sat Eve Post 236:76+ Je 29 '63
Warren's man. Cato. Nat R 16:528 Je 30 '64
REDMOND, James R.
Bohr effect; absence in a molluscan hemocyanin. bibliog Science 139:1294-5 Mr 29 '63
REDSKINS (football club) See Football clubs
REDUCING. See Corpulence
REDUCING diet. See Diet
REDUCING exercises. See Exercise
REDUCTION, Chemical
Hydrated electron: production and role in photobiology. G. W. Swenson and others. bibliog il Science 141:1042-3 S 13 '63
See also
Oxidation reduction reaction
REDUCTION of armaments. See Disarmament
REDWOOD
Anarchy among the redwoods. A. W. Smith. Nat Parks Mag 38:2 Mr '64
China's dawn redwood. il Sunset 133:150 Ag '64
Durability of redwood caused by fungus. Sci N L 83:264 Ap 27 '63
Finding the Mt Everest of all living things. P. A. Zahl. il Nat Geog Mag 126:10-51 Jl '64
Freeways versus redwoods. R. D. Butcher. il Nat Parks Mag 38:12-15 Je '64
President Johnson backs a Redwoods Park. C. W. Buchheister. Audubon Mag 66:282 S '64
Quiet crisis or lost cause? W. Stegner. Sat R 47:28+ S 19 '64
Redwood parks in peril. J. B. Craig. il(cover) Am For 70:8 Ap '64
Redwood totem. H. Gilliam. il Nation 199:91-3 S 7 '64
Redwoods and the fragile web of nature. R. D. Butcher. il Audubon Mag 66:172-4 My '64
Redwoods massacre. Audubon Mag 66:16 Ja '64
Redwoods National Park. P. M. Tilden. Nat Parks Mag 38:2 Ag '64
World's tallest tree discovered. M. B. Grosvenor. il Nat Geog Mag 126:1-9 Jl '64
World's tallest tree farm; follow-up for the future. E. A. Hofsted. il Am For 70:22-5+ S '64
See also
Sequoia
REDWOOD highway. See Roads—California
REDWOODS NATIONAL PARK (proposed) See National parks and reserves—United States
REE, Harry A.
Seven in the sixties. Sat R 46:35-6+ Ag 17 '63
REED, Mrs Alan
American dolls. Hobbies 69:40+ Ap '64
REED, Brita
Photography is possible. Sch Arts 62:11-13 Ap '63
REED, Charles F. and Pollack, Alan
Statistically defined displays and pattern detection of cerebral palsied children. bibliog Science 140:1331-3 Je 21 '63
REED, David
Battle against sleeping sickness. Read Digest 83:124-7 Jl '63
Colossus of rivers: the Amazon. il Read Digest 83:210-14+ S '63
Express to the Mountains of the Moon. Read Digest 85:234-40 S '64
Ghana: communism's new foothold in Africa. Read Digest 85:202-7+ Jl '64
Ivory Coast, Africa's big success story. Read Digest 86:107-12 Ja '65
Nigeria: black Africa's brightest hope. Read Digest 82:186-92 Mr '63
Ohio Valley, America's newest industrial empire. Read Digest 83:193-4+ D '63
REED, Donna
Donna Reed: fire and ice. D. Freeman. por Sat Eve Post 237:22-3 Mr 28 '64
Real life for the doctor's wife. A. Peters. il pors Todays Health 42:24-5+ Je '64
REED, Elizabeth Wagner
Solomon's seal and Jack-in-the-pulpit. Horticulture 41:182-3 Mr '63
Two wild flowers that adapt well to the regular garden. Horticulture 41:248 My '63
REED, Harold
High-gain low-hum module. Pop Electr 18:54 My '63
Multi-output zener voltage regulator. Electr World 71:94 F '64
REED, Henry
(tr) See Betti, U. Corruption in the palace of justice
REED, Henry Hope, jr
Department of amplification. New Yorker 39:163 Ap 20 '63
—and Bryant, H. S. jr
Plague; or, Contemporary traditional architecture in America. il Arch Forum 119:112-15 S '63
REED, Ione
Two unique western conifers. Horticulture 41:98 F '63
REED, J. O.
Africa's market literature. Nation 196:509-10 Je 15 '63
REED, Jim
Tornado; nature on a rampage. Todays Health 41:26-9+ My '63
REED, Kit
All the happy endings; story. Redbook 122: 64-5 N '63
Furnishing the rooms. Writer 77:20-1+ Mr '64
REED, Lester J. and others
Electron microscopic and biochemical studies of pyruvate dehydrogenase complex of escherichia coli. bibliog Science 145:930-2 Ag 28 '64

REED, Peter Hugh
More vintage Toscanini. Am Rec G 30:24-5 S '63
REED, Philip
Newbery and Caldecott runners-up. il Library J 89:1379 Mr 15 '64
REED, Richard
My father, the custodian. por Sr Schol 84:13T F 7 '64
REED, Roy
How to lynch a newspaper. Atlan 214:59-63 N '64
REED, Sarah R.
Apogees and perigees in library education. ALA Bul 58:589-90 Jl '64
Reinterpretation of standards. ALA Bul 57:247 Mr '63
REED, Stanley Foster
Entrepreneurship and the depressed area. Yale R 54:31-40 O '64
Inventor of the month. S. V. Jones. il por Sci Digest 54:52-3 S '63
REED, T. Edward
Assumptions in tests for meiotic drive. bibliog Science 139:406 F 1 '63
REED, W. A. and Fawcett, E.
High-field galvanomagnetic properties of metals. bibliog Science 146:603-10 O 30 '64
REED, Wayne O.
Implications of a renaissance in education; summary of address. por Pub W 185:39-41 F 17 '64
REED college, Portland, Ore.
Reed college arts center. H. Weese. il Arch Rec 133:136-7 My '63
REEDY, George
New man. il por Time 83:45 Mr 27 '64
People of the week. il por U S News 56:16 Mr 30 '64
REEDY, James R.
First flight across the bottom of the world. pors Nat Geog Mag 125:454-64 Mr '64
REEFS, Coral. See Coral reefs and islands
REEKIE, Gordon
Expositions, exhibits and today's museums. Natur Hist 73:20-9 Je '64
REELS, Fishing
See also
Fishing tackle
REEMTSMA, Keith, and others
Heterotransplantation of the kidney: two clinical experiences. Science 143:700-2 F 14 '64
RE-ENTRY problems (missile) See Guided missiles—Recovery
RE-ENTRY problems (space flight) See Space vehicles—Atmospheric entry
REES, Alan M.
New bottles for old wine: retrieval and librarianship. bibliog por Wilson Lib Bul 38:773-9 My '64
Special librarian: his future; bright or bleak? address, June 1964. bibliog por Library J 89:4288-94 N 1 '64
REESE, Seward
Emancipation proclamation; address, January 13, 1963. Vital Speeches 29:283-6 F 15 '63
REESE, W. J.
New booster system saves 50 per cent. Am City 79:92-3 Jl '64
REESE, William L.
Note on values. Sat R 47:24 D 12 '64
REEVE, E. B. and others
Plasma protein synthesis in the liver: method for measurement of albumin formation in vivo. bibliog Science 139:914-16 Mr 8 '63
REEVE, F. D.
Falls; poem. New Yorker 40:64 D 5 '64
Robert Frost confronts Khrushchev. Atlan 212:33-9 S '63
We settled by the lake; poem. New Yorker 40:48 S 26 '64
Writer versus bureaucrat in the Soviet Union. Atlan 213:69-74 Ja '64
REEVES, Hubert
Detection of solar neutrinos. Sky & Tel 27:276-8 My '64
REEVES, Katherine
Christmas gift; poem. Ladies Home J 81:83 D '64
REEVES, Nancy
Curious quest for womanpower. Nation 197:89-91 Ag 24 '63
REFEREES. See Umpires (sports)
REFERENCE books
Bedside reading: a reference book; excerpts from address. J. Barzun. Wilson Lib Bul 39:246-7 N '64
FAO lists titles in World intelligence service; new edition of catalog. Pub W 185:53-4 Ap 20 '64
Libros en venta issued, guide to Spanish books. Pub W 185:50 Ap 20 '64
See also
Encyclopedias

Bibliography

Basic reference books for the home. il Changing T 17:35-6 N '63
Best of references. D. M. Glixon. il Sat R 46:36-7+ Mr 23 '63
Current reference books, ed. by F. N. Cheney. See issues of Wilson library bulletin
If you want a book, any book: basic reference tools needed by booksellers. E. A. Geiser. Pub W 186:50-3 D 14 '64
Pick of the paperbacks; the reference shelf. il Sat R 46:38-9 Mr 23 '63
Reader's adviser, tenth edition; ed. by H. R. Hoffman. Review
Pub W 186:34-5 S 21 '64. D. M. Glixon
Reference books of 1963; recommendations of a committee of the Reference services division of the American library association. T. S. Shaw. Library J89:1667-75 Ap 15 '64
Reference books of 1962; accomodations of a committee of the Reference services division of the American library association; ed. by T. S. Shaw. Library J 88:1597-605 Ap 15 '63
Road map to the fields of learning. D. M. Glixon. il Sat R 47:37-9+ Mr 21 '64
REFERENCE departments. See Libraries—Reference departments
REFERENCE librarians, College. See College libraries—Reference work
REFERENCE services division. See American library association—Reference services division
REFERENCE work. See College libraries—Reference work; Libraries—Reference work
REFERENDUM
Off-track betting, from the horse's mouth; voting by New Yorkers. J. M. Willig. il N Y Times Mag p55+ N 3 '63
REFF, Theodore
Cézanne: the logical mystery. Art N 62:28-31 Ap '63
REFINERIES. See Oil refineries
REFINISHING furniture. See Furniture—Refinishing
REFLECTORS
Make a fan-fold umbrella light. F. L. Greenwald. il Pop Sci 185:132-4 N '64
REFLECTORS, Telescope. See Mirrors for telescopes
REFLEX action. See Reflexes
REFLEX cameras. See Cameras
REFLEXES
Bee sting starts a sequence of fast responses. R. Campbell. il Life 54:75A-75B Je 28 '63
Let it fall! let it fall! whatever it is. J. Tartas. il Pop Sci 182:97+ Je '63
Our amazing reflexes. J. D. Ratcliff. Read Digest 83:136-8 O '63
Stomach contraction upon central vagus stimulation. N. C. Jefferson and others. il Science 140:810-11 My 17 '63
See also
Conditioned response
REFORESTATION
Seed pines direct after forest fires. D. P. Simpson. il Farm J 88:48 D '64
See also
Forest planting
Forests and forestry
REFORM Judaism. See Judaism
REFORM of criminals. See Crime and criminals
REFORMATION
Reappraising the reformation. L. Swidler. Commonweal 81:156-8 O 30 '64
Twelve leaders and the Reformation. P. W. Schmidtchen. il Hobbies 69:106-7+ Mr '64
See also
Calvinism
REFORMATION Sunday
Ecumenical changes; concerning sermons. America 109:656-7 N 23 '63
Reformation remembered. M. E. Marty. Christian Cent 80:1522+ D 4 '63
REFORMATORIES
New ruling: equal rights for whites; District of Columbia reformatory, Lorton, Va. il U S News 54:8 Je 3 '63
Swinging prison priest; Lorton reformatory, Va. D. R. Maxey. il Look 28:24-9 D 29 '64
See also
Wiltwyck school for boys, Esopus, N.Y.
REFORMED church in America
Move toward union. Christian Cent 81:228 F 19 '64
REFORMED church in South Africa
Prophecy redefined. Christian Cent 80:1419 N 13 '63

REFORMED church in the Netherlands
Sinner of Elburg. il Time 84:92 D 4 '64
REFORMED churches
Reformed churches take strong stand on race. Crhistian Cent 81:1077 S 2 '64
World alliance of reformed churches. D. Macleod. Christian Cent 80:1083-4 S 4 '63
REFRACTION, Double
Strain-induced birefringence in fluoride films on uranium dioxide. W. P. Ellis. bibliog il Science 144:1570-2 Je 26 '64
REFRACTORY metals. See Heat resistant alloys
REFRESHMENT stands. See Concessions (food, etc)
REFRIGERATED cameras. See Cameras
REFRIGERATION and refrigerating machinery
See also
Thermoelectric cooling
REFRIGERATION therapy. See Cold—Therapeutic applications
REFRIGERATOR desserts. See Desserts
REFRIGERATORS

Safety devices and measures

Safety measures for discarded refrigerators. Good H 158:160 Mr '64
REFRIGERATORS, Electric
Coming, a new kind of refrigerator; thermoelectric refrigerator. Good H 158:161 F '64
General electric Americana refrigerator-freezer. il Consumers Bul 47:19-21 Ag '64
Heat pump keeps food hot or cold; thermoelectric refrigerator also a warming cabinet. il Pop Sci 184:106 Ja '64
Real cool coolers. il McCalls 91:34 Je '64
Refrigeration. il Consumer Rep 29:158-71 D '64
Refrigerator-freezer combinations. il Consumer Bul 46:6-15 Jl '63
Small-boat refrigeration: up from the ice age! G. P. Manning. il Motor B 115:76-9+ Ja '65
Some cold personal facts about your refrigerator. N. Engle. Am Home 66:82+ Jl '63
Timely refrigerator tips. B. G. Wadsworth. il Parents Mag 38:144 My '63
Two-door refrigerator-freezers. il Consumer Rep 29:368-75 Ag '64
Two thermoelectric refrigerators. il Consumer Rep 28:412-13 S '63
Upright freezers. il Consumer Rep 28:416-22 S '63
Very new refrigerators. G. V. Young. il Bet Hom & Gard 42:80 O '64

Defrosting

Another hurry-up refrigerator defroster; Red-E-Defrost. il Consumer Rep 28:149-50 Ap '63
Defroster devices for refrigerators and freezers; new electrical hazard. il Consumer Bul 47:9-11 My '64
Quicker, easier defrosting. E. Taylor. il Good H 158:186 My '64
To defrost or not to defrost. Consumer Rep 28:422 S '63
REFRIGERATORS, Portable
Man! here's a cool way to camp. il Pop Sci 183:128-9+ Jl '63
Portable cooler seals in quality. W. H. Hardy. il Farm J 87:64A+ O '63
Portable refrigerator. C. Conley. il Field & S 67:107-8 Mr '63
To improve your ice chest. il Sunset 132:108 Je '64
REFUELING of airplanes. See Airplanes—Refueling
REFUGEE children
Boy who survived Auschwitz. E. Papanek and E. Linn. il Sat Eve Post 237:34-41 Ap 11 '64
REFUGEE; story. See Malamud, B.
REFUGEES
Through the wire; US defectors. il Newsweek 61:42 My 20 '63

Resettlement

American investment pays off; Corbett family. T. Hudes. il Look 27:82a-82c Jl 2 '63
Surplus people. H. Bowser. Sat R 46:12 Ag 17 '63
REFUGEES, Algerian
Algerian aftermath. H. Giniger. il N Y Times Mag p32+ Mr 22 '64
REFUGEES, Arab
Arab refugee today. F. L. Hutchison. Christian Cent 81:823-6 Je 24 '64; Discussion. 81: 1016, 1339 Ag 12, O 28 '64
Arab refugees: a changing problem. D. Peretz. For Affairs 41:558-70 Ap '63
Hope for Palestine refugees. H. Walz. Christian Cent 80:306-7 Mr 6 '63; Discussion. 80:781-2 Je 12 '63
Reconciler resigns. Christian Cent 80:229 F 20 '63
U.N. asks conciliation commission to continue efforts with Arab refugees; statements, December 11, 14 and 18, 1962; with statement by E. Jackson, and text of resolution. C. T. Rowan. Dept State Bul 48: 99-104 Ja 21 '63
REFUGEES, Austrian
Thank you, America; Heidi Keir in Clay County, Iowa. il Farm J 86:89 N '63
REFUGEES, Chinese
Double defection; red Chinese defectors. Time 82:44 O 18 '63
Life and death of Precious Plum Flower. K. L. Stumpf and E. Gamarekian. il Sat Eve Post 237:66+ Ap 4 '64
Red China: one hour by train. C. Morrison. il Look 28:30-1 Je 16 '64
Refugee reports on red China. S. Karnow. il Reporter 29:39-42 Jl 18 '63
Return to the frontier. E. Chang. il Reporter 28:38-41 Mr 28 '63
U.S. grants aid to Chinese refugees in Hong Kong. Dept State Bul 52:41-2 Ja 11 '65
REFUGEES, Cuban
Another Cuban fiasco? il U S News 54:33-6 Ap 29 '63
Bitter, frustrated, divided: Cuba's refugees. M. Bracker. il N Y Times Mag p7+ Ap 21 '63
Blunted arrow's head. New Repub 148:6 Ap 13 '63
Coming: new effort to topple Castro? il U S News 56:39 My 11 '64
Cuban doctor's decision. B. Asbell. il Redbook 120:46-7+ Mr '63
Cuban exiles: the mirage of Havana; Revolutionary recovery movement. A. Burt. Nation 200:76-9 Ja 25 '65
Girl spy against Castro. A. St George. il Look 28:60-5 D 29 '64
Guerra! still the word in Miami. T. Szulc. il N Y Times Mag p9+ Jl 5 '64
Help us fight! cry the angry exiles. H. H. Martin. il Sat Eve Post 236:23-30+ Je 8 '63
I believe. W. Jordan. por Seventeen 22:23 Ap '63
Incredible escape. J. P. Blank. il Read Digest 84:159-62+ My '64
Iowa, si! training program for Spanish teachers. il Newsweek 62:75 Ag 19 '63
Keeping pace with the PTA; Operation simpático; Dade County, Fla. C. Marburgh. il PTA Mag 58:31-2 S '63
Man in Havana; J. B. Donovan. New Yorker 39:22-3 Jl 6 '63
Miami si, Castro no. il Sr Schol 82:8-9+ My 1 '63
Miami's Cuban refugee crisis. A. Morrison. il Ebony 18:96-100+ Je '63
New look at Cuba; exiles resume training. Nation 197:209 O 12 '63
Practice makes perfect. Nation 196:297 Ap 13 '63
Protestants to aid Catholic refugees. Christian Cent 80:702 My 29 '63
Pulling the tail; Manuel Artime's Revolutionary recovery movement. Time 84:28 S 11 '64
Refugee leader blames U.S. for broken promise; excerpts from statement, April 18, 1963. J. Miró Cardona. U S News 54:65-7+ Ap 29 '63
Safety in the stars. il Time 82:24 S 27 '63
That month; April's cruelty. il Time 81:21-2 Ap 26 '63
U.S. changes policy on Cuban refugees. Christian Cent 81:100 Ja 22 '64
U.S. outlines policy toward Cuban refugees; statement, May 22, 1963. E. M. Martin. Dept State Bul 48:983-90 Je 24 '63
Visible CIA. Nation 198:613-14 Je 22 '64
We should help the Cuban exiles find a leader. Life 54:4 My 3 '63
When Cuban exiles broke loose in Washington. il U S News 57:8 Ag 3 '64
See also
Cuban revolutionary council
Cubans in the United States
REFUGEES, German
Alt lang syne; reunion of Germans expelled from Communist Poland. il Time 81:30 Je 21 '63
Berlin: the great tunnel thriller; with report by L. Hall and R. Chelminski. il Life 57: 57-9+ O 16 '64
Block that midget. il Time 82:29 Ag 9 '63
Brave buddelers of Berlin. J. O'Donnell. il N Y Times Mag p32-3+ Ap 7 '63
Breaching the wall: the odds grow. A. J. Olson. il N Y Times Mag p 11+ Ag 9 '64

REFUGEES, German—*Continued*
Cad who came in from the cold. Time 84:36+ Jl 10 '64
East Germany; freedom tunnel. Time 84:41 O 16 '64
Gay life; fifty-seven escape through tunnel in Berlin. Newsweek 64:52 O 19 '64
Lower barrier? escape of jockey Michael Meyer. il Newsweek 64:50 S 28 '64
They keep coming. il Time 84:32 Jl 17 '64
Transplanted in liberty; Boesekendorfers. Newsweek 61:52-3 Je 17 '63
Two inches to safety; escape of Heinz Meixner and fiancée. il Time 81:36 My 17 '63

REFUGEES, Indian (East Indian)
Always the twain shall flee. il Time 83:34 Ap 10 '64
Asians v. Asians; India's newest dispossessed flock home from neighboring Burma. il Time 84:29 Jl 17 '64

REFUGEES, Jewish
Boy who survived Auschwitz. E. Papanek and E. Linn. il Sat Eve Post 237:34-41 Ap 11 '64
Friar who saved 5,000 Jews. W. I. Fischman. il Look 28:66+ D 1 '64

REFUGEES, Lao
Refugee problem in Laos; statement, with memorandum, January 25, 1963. Dept State Bul 48:567-72 Ap 15 '63

REFUGEES, Pakistani
Always the twain shall flee. il Time 83:34 Ap 10 '64

REFUGEES, Polish
Charlie and out; escape of Obacz family by private plane. il Newsweek 62:41 Jl 22 '63
Hedgehopping to freedom. il Time 82:26+ Jl 19 '63

REFUGEES, Russian
Family man. il Newsweek 61:52 Ap 29 '63
It started with stamps. Time 81:35 F 15 '63
Over the bridge; Chinese expel Russians from Sinkiang. il Newsweek 63:40+ Je 22 '64

REFUGEES, South African
Captain Nelson's freedom ferry. il Time 83:38 Ap 10 '64

REFUGEES, Sudanese
Sudan's shame. America 109:4 Jl 6 '63

REFUGES, Bird. See Bird sanctuaries

REFUNDING
Making money on refundings. Bsns W p 116+ Ja 26 '63

REFUNDS on income tax. See Income tax—Refunds

REFUSE, Utilization of
Unhappy record of composting. Am City 78:7 D '63

REFUSE and refuse disposal
Billboards, slobs and cemeteries. R. Starnes. Field & S 68:10+ Jl '63
Collect refuse, not complaints. J. W. Stephenson. il Am City 78:97-9 O '63
Coming struggle to breathe. T. O. Thackrey. Sat R 47:23-5+ O 10 '64
Composting; its role in European refuse disposal. E. F. Spitzer. il Am City 79:102-5 O '64 (to be cont)
Garbage down the hatch. il Sunset 130:147 My '63
Garden clubs get clean-up going; in Snohomish County, Wash. il Sunset 134:83 Ja '65
Good contract collection; Seattle, Wash. R. W. Morse. il Am City 78:191-2+ S '63
Harbor housecleaning by boat; Milwaukee. il Am City 78:148 D '63
Housewives' revolt; Los Angeles penalty for not separating tin cans from other garbage. il Newsweek 61:36 Mr 18 '63
How to make trash disappear with one easy motion. il House B 106:222 My '64
In the bag for keeps; refuse collection, College Park, Md. R. A. Edwards. il Am City 78:89-92 Ap '63
It's bad manners to litter. Parents Mag 39:142 S '64
Litter clean-up out of the ordinary; Portsmouth, Va, and Pleasant Hill, Calif. Am City 79:34 Ap '64
LBJ's plan to beautify America. il U S News 58:28-30+ Ja 11 '65
Motorized refuse collectors; Claremont, Calif. B. B. Johnson, jr. il Am City 79:103-4 F '64
No refuse refused; Waterbury, Conn. A. A. Mirto. il Am City 79:117-18 Ap '64
Picking up the pieces. H. G. Tapply. il Field & S 69:72 My '64
Prepacked refuse increases payload; Borough of Hammersmith, London, England. il Am City 78:82 Ag '63
Refuse collection and disposal. See issues of American city
Refuse disposal by contract extraordinary; St Petersburg, Fla. Am City 79:38 F '64
Refuse wranglers clean up the town; Scottsdale, Ariz. il Am City 79:99 S '64
Solid-waste-disposal challenge. Am City 79:25 Ja '64
Solid waste headache. Nation 198:615 Je 22 '64
Tote barrels; Middletown, Ohio. W. F. Cottrell and K. E. Young. il Am City 78:117-18 My '63
Unseasonable winter; brush collection; Nashville, Tenn. K. B. Stallings. il Am City 78:33 N '63
You must have a garbage-disposal unit; Thornton, Colo. D. J. Bretzke. Am City 79:177 Je '64
See also
Municipal dumps
Radioactive waste disposal
Refuse, Utilization of
Refuse incinerators
Refuse receptacles
Sewage disposal
Street cleaning
Water pollution

Apparatus
Truck-mounted chipper-container; Walla Walla, Wash. V. Tompkins. il Am City 79:18 D '64

REFUSE collection. See Refuse and refuse disposal

REFUSE collection trucks
Golden yellow for safety; New York city's trucks. F. J. Lucia. il Am City 78:27 Mr '63
Refuse trains bring three-way savings; Winston-Salem, N.C. G. W. Kilday. il Am City 80:88-90 Ja '65

REFUSE containers. See Refuse receptacles

REFUSE grinders
Pushbutton eating center; combination dining counter-dishwasher-disposal unit. il Pop Mech 120:96-8 Ag '63

REFUSE incinerators
Built to fit the site; Port Washington, N.Y. G. Gewecke. il Am City 78:120-1 Je '63
Burn brush without smoke; brush burner; Detroit, Mich. G. C. Richards and R. Schink. il Am City 78:34 S '63
Case of the disappearing household trash. V. T. Habeeb. il Am Home 66:52+ My '63
Electrostatic precipitators can solve the fly-ash problem in municipal incinerators. A. B. Walker. il Am City 79:148+ S '64
European incinerators. E. F. Spitzer. il Am City 79:85-7 N '64
For longer incinerator life; Philadelphia, Pa. R. A. Cotton. il Am City 78:92-4 N '63
Honeycomb armor protects tipping floors; Merrick, Long Island, N.Y. il Am City 79:26 Je '64
How to select an incinerator bucket. R. F. Chesarek. il Am City 79:80-2 Ag '64
Incinerator can be attractive; Wauwatosa, Wis. F. D. Kuckuck. il Am City 78:96-8 Mr '63
Mobile leaf burner; serves as trash burner rest of the year. M. Banister. il Pop Mech 120:184-7+ S '63
Noteworthy features of new incinerator; Garden City, N.Y. B. J. Gorman. il Am City 79:94-5 Jl '64
Ram-fed incinerator; Clearwater, Fla. il Am City 79:69-72 D '64
Regional approach to refuse disposal; New Haven, Conn. il Am City 79:94-5 Je '64
Residue tells the story; Greenwich, Conn. G. A. Hawkins. il Am City 78:104-6 S '63
Twice as big, better than new; Darien, Conn. A. W. Saburn. il Am City 78:91-3 F '63
We borrowed from the steel industry; incinerator maintenance; Oyster Bay, N.Y. V. J. Cerniglia and H. J. Campbell, jr. il Am City 79:89-91 My '64

REFUSE receptacles
Disposable bags. il Am City 78:32 O '63
Flyless refuse collection; Cedra Rapids, Ia. C. D. Smith. il Am City 78:81-2 D '63
Garbage goes underground to beat costs; Dunn, N.C. A. B. Uzzle, jr. and J. T. Jackson. Am City 79:34 Mr '64
In the bag for keeps; refuse collection, College Park, Md. R. A. Edwards. il Am City 78:89-92 Ap '63
It's in the bag for a second city; Riverdale, Md. W. Ford and J. Carswell. il Am City 79:22 My '64
Lively Louie; talking litter basket. il Am City 78:29 N '63
Now, community trash cans. il Farm J 88:64C F '64
Our merchants like big garbage cans; Denison, Tex. J. Smithen. il Am City 78:23 Jl '63

REFUSE receptacles—*Continued*
Paper-bag collection on request; Camden, Ark. G. G. Fox. il Am City 79:14 O '64
Rental containers become a popular item; Scottsbluff, Neb. L. Mortensen. il Am City 79:34 Ap '64
Unkempt, unswept label touches off a storm; installation of enclosed baskets; Indianapolis. R. G. Bredell. il Am City 79:114-15 O '64

REGAN, John J.
Religious neutrality. America 110:74-6 Ja 18 '64
Supreme court, obscenity and censorship. Cath World 200:142-8 D '64

REGATTAS
Alcohol burns in the Northwest; National outboard championship regatta. C. D. Strang. Motor B 112:112 Ag '63
Analysis of the one-of-a-kind. R. N. Bavier, jr. il Yachting 113:58-60+ My '63
Cadences of crew; reproduction of paintings. H. Schmidt. Sports Illus 18:42-50 Je 10 '63
Everyone goes to Santa Barbara; Semana nautica. B. Robinson. il Yachting 114:44-5 D '63
Extra season; Midwinter snipe regatta, Florida. B. Robinson. il Yachting 115:49-51+ My '64
He gave everything for the Big Red; Intercollegiate rowing association regatta. T. C. Brody. il Sports Illus 18:44-5 Je 24 '63
Life guide. il Life 55:7 Ag 2 '63
Month in yachting. See issues of Yachting
Mountain sailing; Huntington Lake, Calif. P. Harder. il Yachting 113:54-5+ Je '63
Operation sail; loomings and landfalls. F. Rohr. il Motor B 113:44-5+ Je '64
Right way to row is to head for Tokyo; tryouts for Tokyo Olympics. R. Lardner. il Sports Illus 18:53-4 My 27 '63
Scows on Okoboji. M. Wiley. il Yachting 115: 101-5+ Ja '64
Try fifty-three for laughs; Harvard vs Cornell. T. Mayer. Sports Illus 18:74-6+ Je 10 '63
Where Brittania never waives the rules; Cowes regatta. il Esquire 59:106-7 F '63
Yachting's One-of-a-kind regatta. B. Robinson. il Yachting 113:52-9+ Ap '63
See also
Rowing
Sailboat racing
Yacht racing

REGENERATION (biology)
Regenerating tissues from the cockroach leg: a system for studying in vitro. E. P. Marks and J. P. Reinecke. bibliog il Science 143: 961-3 F 28 '64
Thymus: its role in lymphoid recovery after irradiation. R. Auerbach. bibliog Science 139:1061 Mr 15 '63

REGENT'S park zoo. See London zoological gardens

REGGIE the ghost; drama. See Hall, M.

REGIONAL airports. See Airports

REGIONAL ballet companies. See Dance companies

REGIONAL libraries. See Libraries, Regional

REGIONAL organizations. See International organization—Regional organizations

REGIONAL plan association, New York
Five major issues. Recreation 57:80-1 F '64
Suburbanites cast their votes for city planning; survey by New York's regional plan assn. Arch Forum 119:84-5 D '63

REGIONAL planning
Architecture as total community: the challenge ahead. A. Mayer. bibliog f il Arch Rec 135:137-44 Mr; 169-78 Ap; 145-52 My; 141-6 Je; 136:129-38 Ag; 197-205 S; 139-48 O '64; Reply to O issue. E. Goble. 136:9 D '64
Big squeeze in your back yard. J. Prokop. il Am For 69:6-7+ Ap '63
Boston: shaping a region. il Arch Forum 120: 105 Je '64
Brand new city for Maryland. J. W. Anderson. Harper 229:100-2+ N '64
Community and privacy; toward a new architecture of humanism. by S. Chermayeff and C. Alexander. Review
Arch Forum il 119:106-7 D '63. D. B. Carlson
Community: could this be our town? W. Von Eckardt. il New Repub 151:17-24 N 7 '64; Discussion. 151:37-8 N 28 '64
Five major issues; New York city metropolitan region. Recreation 57:80-1 F '64
Man with the plan; Irvine ranch, Calif. il Time 82:68-72 S 6 '63
New frontier of higher education. D. Canty. il Arch Forum 118:96-103 Mr '63
New York state plans for regional development. il Arch Rec 136:23+ Ag '64
Planning for a hundred tomorrows; southern California. il Bsns W p74-5+ O 24 '64
Privately financed plan to tighten urban sprawl; Green Spring Valley and Worthington Valley, Md. il Fortune 70:212 N '64
Regional pattern for dispersal. C. S. Stein. Arch Rec 136:205-6 S '64
U.S. proposes town-centered planning for Asia; statement, March 4, 1964. K. T. Young. Dept State Bul 50:759-61 My 11 '64
See also
Cities and towns
City planning
Parks
Regional plan association, New York
Rural planning
Suburbs
Tennessee Valley authority

Great Britain

Cumbernauld: a citadel of many levels for both men and machines. il Arch Forum 121:206-7 Ag '64
New towns: and fresh in-city communities. A. Mayer. bibliog f il Arch Rec 136:129-38 Ag '64

Spain

Operation Badajoz; Spain's TVA. R. M. Elizalde. il Am For 69:24-7 F '63

United States

See Regional planning

REGIONAL theater. See Theater—Community and little theater movement

REGISTERS of births, etc.
Can you prove where you were born? Suc Farm 62:38 My '64

REGISTRATION of architects. See Architects —Licenses and registration

REGISTRATION of voters. See Voters, Registration of

REGULATION of body temperature. See Temperature, Animal and human

REGULATION of prices. See Price regulation by government

REGULATORS, Voltage. See Voltage regulators

REGULATORY commissions. See Independent regulatory commissions

REHABILITATION
Miracle boy revisited; David Posnett, Buckingham Valley, Pa. C. Brossard. il Look 28:38-41 O 20 '64
Return from the womb; case of Jerome Meyer. il Time 81:93-4 My 17 '63
Urban renewal for people. D. B. Carlson. il Arch Forum 120:86-9 Ja '64
What you can do with what you have; rehabilitation of a quadriplegic, with report by J. Mason. il Life 56:75-88 Je 19 '64
See also
Institutes for the achievement of human potential

Morocco

Mass Moroccan rehabilitation. J. Viorst. il Sci N L 83:218-19 Ap 6 '63

REHABILITATION centers
Center for visually handicapped, Chicago. H. Weese. il Arch Rec 133:132-3 My '63
Courts and classrooms aid rehabilitation. il Arch Rec 135:202-3 Ap '64
Here's the story of the best round-up in Texas; West Texas rehabilitation center. C. E. Ball. il Farm J 87:36J Ag '63
Retraining center exploits a sloping site. il Arch Rec 135:200-1 Ap '64
Where mentally retarded children start new lives; Warren G. Murray children's center, Centralia, Ill. H. G. Earl. il Todays Health 42:26-31 N '64

REHABILITATION of discharged prisioners. See Prisoners, Discharged—Rehabilitation

REHABILITATION of prisoners. See Prisoners —Rehabilitation

REHABILITATION of the insane. See Mentally ill—Rehabilitation

REHABILITATION of the mentally ill. See Mentally ill—Rehabilitation

REHBERGER, D. F.
14-watt transistor hi-fi amplifier. Electr World 69:46-7+ My '63

REHDER, R. M.
Les beaux arbres; poem. Yale R 52:561 Je '63

REHEARSAL club, New York
Anniversary. New Yorker 39:17-19 Jl 20 '63

REHEARSAL; drama. See Anouilh, J.

REHEARSALS, Theatrical. See Theatrical production

REHM, George
Cows, why I like them! excerpt from Requiem for twelve cows. Farm J 87:58X Ap '63
REHMANNIA
This aristocrat is worth looking for. il Sunset 131:204 S '63
REICH, E.
Actinomycin: correlation of structure and function of its complexes with purines and DNA. bibliog Science 143:684-9 F 14 '64
REICH, Melvin, and Mandel, H. G.
Uracil: failure to restore DNA synthesis while relieving 5-fluorouracil-induced inhibition. bibliog Science 145:276-7 Jl 17 '64
REICH, Wilhelm
World of Wilhelm Reich. P. Rieff. Commentary 38:50-8 S '64
REICH, Willi
New goals. Mus Am 84:17 O '64
REICHARDT, Richard
Baseball's richest rookie. N. Cope. il pors Sat Eve Post 237:68-9 S 19 '64
Richest bonus baby ever. E. Shrake. il pors Sports Illus 21:16-21 Jl 6 '64
200 grand kid. il pors Life 57:85-7 Jl 10 '64
REICHEL, Jules
Bring out the stretcher; football as the trainer sees it. W. J. McKean. il pors Look 28:28-32 O 6 '64
REICHELDERFER, Francis Wilton
Gentleman of the guard. J. Lear. por Sat R 46:36-9 Ag 3 '63
REICHERT, Elsa. See Reichart, R. J. jt. auth.
REICHERT, Gene
Launching a one-design class. Yachting 114:62-3+ Jl '63
REICHERT, Robert J. and Reichert, Elsa
Clear views on your binoculars. Audubon Mag 66:115-17 Mr '64
REICHSTAG fire
Will to believe. M. Kempton. New Repub 150:17-20 Ap 11 '64
REID, Al
Catamaran to Tahiti; ed. by R. Choy. Yachting 113:85-7+ Ap '63
REID, Alastair
Department of amplification. New Yorker 40:194-5 N 14 '64
Figures on the frieze; poem. New Yorker 38:32 F 9 '63
Geneva; poem. New Yorker 39:30 Ja 25 '64
Letter from Barcelona (cont) New Yorker 39:105-6+ My 4 '63
Letter from Edinburgh. New Yorker 40:103-4+ O 24 '64
Me to you; poem. New Yorker 39:36 D 21 '63
Poet's view of childhood. por Atlan 211:102-4 Mr '63
Reporter at large (cont) New Yorker 39:43-4+ S 7 '63
Spiral; poem. New Yorker 39:40 Ap 6 '63
Sporting scene. New Yorker 39:161-8+ Ap 13; 188+ O 19 '63
That dying; poem. New Yorker 40:46 Ap 25 '64
To a child at the piano; poem. Atlan 211:121 Mr '63
REID, B. L.
Last act and the action of Hamlet. Yale R 54:59-80 O '64
REID, Calvin G.
Phone call. Harper 228:164-6 Ap '64
REID, Charles
Britten at fifty a protean composer. N Y Times Mag p38-9+ N 17 '63
Notes from abroad. See issues of High fidelity
REID, Clyde H.
Let's stop building cathedrals! Christian Cent 81:797-9 Je 17 '64
Supervising seminary field work. Christian Cent 80:528-30 Ap 24 '63
REID, Everett G.
Why I'm raising other people's children. Parents Mag 38:78+ S '63
REID, Giorgina
I got a good straight fire-engine red. il Pop Phot 55:58-9+ S '64
REID, Hale C.
Freed time for in-service education. NEA J 52:54 N '63
REID, J. K. S.
Calvin's influence in Scotland and England. Christian Cent 81:699-701 My 27 '64
REID, James D.
Build the Reflectoflex speaker enclosure. Pop Electr 19:47-50 D '63
REID, Joseph H. See Glover, E. E. jt. auth.
REID, Ogden R. Jr
Newsman v. newsman. por Time 83:79 Mr 20 '64
REID, Robert H.
Fable for other times. Sch & Soc 92:227-8 Sum '64
REIDY, Clare
My retreat. por Redbook 121:6+ Jl '63
REIDY, John
Future techniques. See issues of U.S. camera
REIF, F.
Quantized vortex rings in superfluid helium; with biographical sketch. Sci Am 211:22, 116-22 bibliog(p 156) D '64
REIF, Rita
Home (cont) N Y Times Mag p96-7 O 20 '63
REIFLER, Sam
Two semesters at Wagner's inn; story. Esquire 59:109 Ap '63
REILLY, Alice F.
California: demonstrated success. por Library J 89:1683-7 Ap 15 '64
REILLY, Gerard D.
Labor experts urge new policies; interview. por Nations Bsns 51:66-8+ Ap '63
REILLY, John F.
Big brother is listening. B. H. Bagdikian. il Sat Eve Post 237:68-70 Je 6 '64
REILLY, Robert T.
Adam's image. America 108:746-8 My 25 '63
REIMAN, Ray
How to gear hog raising to new price trends. Suc Farm 61:32 N '63
Large cattle inventory dims long-term outlook. Suc Farm 61:103 Ap '63
Major changes here in beef cattle trends. Suc Farm 61:25 Je '63
Test-plot farming pays off. Suc Farm 62:36-7 Je '64
REIMAN, Roy J.
Big-power farming is coming fast. Suc Farm 63:46-7 Ja '65
Two hundred bushels twice, and he's aiming higher. Suc Farm 63:32-3+ Ja '65
—and Zeman, L. E.
Look what top management can do for rough land. Suc Farm 62:44-5+ N '64
REIN, Robert, and Harris, F. E.
Proton tunneling in radiation-induced mutation. bibliog Science 146:649-50 O 30 '64
REINCKE, Arno B.
He could take it; reprint. Read Digest 82:140-2 F '63
REINDEER
New era for an ancient business; modern herding practices of Sweden's Laplanders. il Bsns W p34-5 Ja 2 '65
REINECKE, John P. See Marks, E. P. jt. auth.
REINER, Carl
Enter laughing; dramatization. See Stein, J.
REINER, Fritz
Return of Reiner; interview. ed. by J. S. Harrison. por Mus Am 83:12-13 O '63

about

Fritz Reiner, 1888-1963. R. Dettmer. por Mus Am 83:272-3 D '63
Fritz Reiner: in memoriam. I. Kolodin. il pors Sat R 46:45-7 D 28 '63
Obituary
Opera N por 28:29 D 14 '63. P. Hart
Reiner in Chicago. P. Hart. por Hi Fi 14:42-6 Ap '64
Reiner retires. R. Dettmer. Mus Am 83:12-13 Jl '63
REINER, Gabriel
Scrambler. il por Newsweek 63:60 F 3 '64
REINER, Thomas
Defense in the economy. Bul Atomic Sci 19:34-5 S '63
REINES, Frederick
Neutrinos, old and new. bibliog Science 141:778-83 Ag 30 '63
REINGOLD, Edwin M.
Cuba: lost soul, new saints. Newsweek 61:26-7 F 4 '63
REINHARD, L. Andrew
L. Andrew Reinhard dies at seventy-two. Arch Rec 136:26 S '64
REINHARD, Lillian
Why do husbands. . . ? Ladies Home J 80:48+ O '63
REINHARD, Mary Jane
We went out to see. Sch Arts 64:5-9 Ja '65
REINHARDT, Adolph
Next revolution in art. Art N 62:48-9 F '64

about

Art. H. Kramer. Nation 196:533-4 Je 22 '63
REINHOLD, H. A.
Liturgy and the second Vatican council; constitution on the sacred liturgy. Cath World 198:347-56 Mr '64
Maria Laach revisited. Commonweal 78:497-500 Ag 23 '63
Mass of the future. Commonweal 80:565-8 Ag 21 '64
Tension between individualism and community in the church. Commonweal 79:724 Mr 13 '64

REINIKKA, Merle A.
Orchids under artificial lights. Horticulture 42:12-13 Ja '64
REINING, Conrad C.
Interdisciplinary effect in African studies. bibliog f Ann Am Acad 356:100-5 N '64
REINO, Mary L. See Vester, J. W. jt. auth.
REINOSO-SUÁREZ, F. See Camacho-Evangelista, A. jt. auth.
REINSURANCE. See Insurance—Reinsurance
REIS, Claire R.
(ed) Composers' letters. por Mus Am 83:14-17 Ja '63
REIS, Donald J. and Cuénod, Michel
Tonic influence of rostral brain structures on pressure regulatory mechanisms in the cat. bibliog Science 145:64-5, 1460 Jl 3, S 25 '64
REIS, Lillian
They call me Tiger Lil. A. G. Aronowitz. il pors Sat Eve Post 236:28+ O 26 '63
REIS, Ronald E.
Weekend amateur. il U S Camera 27:64-5 Je '64
REISCHAUER, Edwin Oldfather
Inevitable partners. por Life 57:27-8 S 11 '64
Union of two worlds. Sports Illus 19:50-4 D 23 '63
about
High noon. il por Newsweek 63:34+ Ap 6 '64
Our man in Japan. il pors Look 27:31-2+ S 10 '63
When a U.S. ambassador was stabbed. il por U S News 56:20 Ap 6 '64
REISCHAUER, Haru
Our man in Japan. il pors Look 27:31-2+ S 10 '63
REISCHE, Diana
Hollywood's J.F.K. Sr Schol 82:19 Ap 24 '63
REISS, A. M. and Plescia, O. J.
Fixation of complement to fragments of antibody. bibliog Science 141:812-13 Ag 30 '63
REISS, Alvin H.
Public relations & the arts. Mus Am 83:44-5 F '63
REISS, Franklin J.
How to update your lease. Suc Farm 61:104 O '63
What's ahead in farm leases? Suc Farm 61: 24 N '63
REISSIG, Herman F.
Too tenuous. Christian Cent 80:807 Je 19 '63
REISSMAN, Frank
Culturally deprived child: a new view; excerpt from address. Sch Life 45:5-7 Ap '63
REITER, Melvyn T.
Candid recording. Pop Phot 52:103+ Mr '63
Make your own accessory projector lens for less than a $1.50. Pop Phot 54:86+ Je '64
REITMAN, Walter R.
Information-processing models in psychology. bibliog Science 144:1192-8 Je 5 '64
REITZEL, Marques E.
Marques E. Reitzel describes his wet-in-wet method; with biographical sketch. por Am Artist 28:36-7+ Mr '64
REJECTED manuscripts. See Editors and editing
REKHI, Joginder Singh
Sikh discovers America. il pors Nat Geog Mag 126:558-90 O '64
REKOSH, Jerold. See Held, R. jt. auth.
RELATIVES
Art of in-lawship. il Todays Health 42:78 Ap '64
It's relative season! or How to get along with our nearest, dearest. Am Home 67:36 N '64
Should newlyweds live with their parents? excerpts from Grandparents and their families. F. H. Richardson. il Todays Health 42:54-5+ Ap '64
What newlyweds should know about in-laws. A. Balk. bibliog il Todays Health 42:56-7+ Ap '64
RELATIVITY (physics)
Bearing of philosophy on the history of science; address, December 29, 1963. A. Grünbaum. bibliog Science 143:1406-12 Mr 27 '64; Reply. E. M. Kelly. 144:1450 Je 19 '64
Clock paradox. J. Bronowski. il Sci Am 208: 134-6+ bibliog(p 186) F '63
Einstein shift, an unsettled problem. F. Schmeidler. il Sky & Tel 27:217-19 Ap '64
Einstein upheld. Sci Am 208:77-8 My '63
Einstein was right; reprint. Sci Digest 54:69-70 D '63
Test proposed to check on Einstein's theory. Sci N L 87:57 Ja 23 '65
Three million year trip in fifty-five years. A. Rosenfeld. il Life 54:34-8 My 24 '63
See also
Light—Velocity
Space and time
RELAXACIZOR. See Exercising machines
RELAXATION
Art of relaxation. W. A. Peterson. Read Digest 83:70 Ag '63
Septuagenarian's formula for fitness: learn to relax. J. Stewart-Gordon. il Todays Health 42:22-5 Ag '64; Same abr. with title Relax and get fit! Read Digest 85:75-8 Ag '64
Take a two-hour vacation when pressures build up. B. Todrin and P. D. White. Parents Mag 39:66+ N '64
See also
Rest
RELAY (artificial satellite) See Communications satellites
RELAY racing. See Running
RELAY running. See Running
RELAYS
See also
Electronic relays
RELEASED time for religious instruction. See Public schools and religion
RELIABILITY control. See Quality control
RELIABILITY of products. See Quality of products
RELICS and reliquaries
Rape of the lock; theft and return of hair of Mohammed. Time 83:32 Ja 10 '64
Rumble over a relic; return of supposed skull of Andrew, Greece's patron saint. Christian Cent 81:1197 S 30 '64
RELIEF (sculpture)
Relief-decorated ceramics. R. E. Taggart. il Antiques 83:430-3 Ap '63
See also
Rubbings
RELIEF maps
Army sells maps in 3-D; plastic relief models. il Sunset 133:19 D '64
Mapping the surface of the earth. M. M. Thompson and J. L. Speert. il Natur Hist 73:30-7 O '64
RELIEF models
Use models; city planning improvements, Manitowoc, Wis. B. Mattson. il Am City 79: 118-19 Mr '64
RELIEF work
Alaska digs out of disaster; federal aid is needed. il Bsns W p25-6 Ap 4 '64
Do-it-yourself foreign aid. il Changing T 18: 33-5 Je '64
Light in the Congo. America 112:68 Ja 16 '65
Relief in Algeria. G. Murray. Christian Cent 81:120-2 Ja 22 '64
U.S. interferes with Christian charity; question of help for churches in Cuba. Christian Cent 81:101 Ja 22 '64
See also
American friends service committee
Charities
Food relief
International voluntary workcamps
Medical relief work
Red cross
also subhead Relief work under names of continents, countries, etc. e.g. Hong Kong—Relief work
RELIGION
Age of prophets. M. D. Zeik. Commonweal 78:67-70 Ap 12 '63
Beast from the sea. B. Vawter. il Commonweal 80:253-6 My 22 '64
Good news. il Fortune 70:97-8 D '64
Holy Spirit and religion. R. Hazelton. Christian Cent 82:73-4 Ja 20 '65
On the eclipse of God. E. L. Fackenheim. Commentary 37:55-60 Je '64; Discussion. 38:24+ D '64
Second thoughts on the religious revival; excerpt from Religion and freedom in the modern world. H. J. Muller. Harper 228: 82-5+ F '64
See also
Atheism
Authority (religion)
Christianity
Colleges and universities—Religious life
Faith
God
Modernism
Mythology
Natural theology
Religions
Religious thought
Revelation
Secularism
Television broadcasting—Religious programs
Theology
Women and religion
Worship
Youth—Religion

RELIGION—*Continued*

Anecdotes, facetiae, satire, etc.

Pen-ultimates, by E. Marty and D. Peerman. Review
Christian Cent 80:1469 N 27 '63. K. A. Olsson

Bibliography

Books for Lenten reading. D. L. Flaherty. America 108:304-5 Mr 2 '63
Comparative religion, philosophy of religion bookshelf. H. Smith. Christian Cent 80:830-1 Je 26 '63; Reply. M. L. Snow. 80:1140 S 18 '63
Lenten reading. R. N. Zearfoss. Christian Cent 80:274 F 27 '63
Manna for the desert; list of spiritual reading. America 110:227-8+ F 15 '64
Religion: some spring books January through May. il Pub W 183:56-75 F 11 '63
Religious books: some fall highspots, September through December. il Pub W 186: 59-80 S 28 '64
Religious books; some spring highspots, January through May. il Pub W 185:48-66 F 10 '64
Religious books to come; ed. by I. E. Stokvis and J. Putman. Library J 88:3106-23+; 89: 138-51, 3190-204; 90:138-40+ S 1 '63, Ja 1, S 1 '64, Ja 1 '65
Report on special projects. M. E. Marty. Christian Cent 80:462 Ap 10 '63

Statistics

See Religious statistics

Study and teaching

Religion, a humanistic field, by C. A. Holbrook. Review
Christian Cent 81:210 F 12 '64. R. Lee
Religion and education. G. N. Shuster. Commonweal 79:504-7 Ja 31 '64
Religious studies on campus. R. J. Gerber. America 111:292-5 S 19 '64

RELIGION, Comparative. See Religions

RELIGION, Personal. See Christian life

RELIGION, Primitive
God's presence and absence; Africa's primitive religious cults. J. V. Taylor. Christian Cent 81:1136-8 S 16 '64

RELIGION and art. See Art and religion

RELIGION and business. See Business ethics

RELIGION and children. See Children—Religion

RELIGION and communism. See Communism and religion

RELIGION and democracy
Are we really teaching democracy? V. C. Blum. Cath World 197:21-7 Ap '63
Religion; future of America; address, March 1, 1964. W. P. Shofstall. Vital Speeches 30: 474-7 My 15 '64
Representing the community; analogy with democracy. C. Davis. America 111:353 S 26 '64

RELIGION and education. See Public schools and religion

RELIGION and higher education. See Church and education

RELIGION and labor. See Church and labor

RELIGION and language
Dead, yes! dying, no! P. S. Collins. America 109:648 N 23 '63
For us. Christian Cent 80:419 Ap 3 '63

RELIGION and law
Kant and Judaism. E. L. Fackenheim. Commentary 36:460-7 D '63
Libel, slander and religion. J. W. Giles. Christian Cent 80:1331-3 O 30 '63
On the side of life; question of blood transfusion authorized by judge for a Jehovah Witness. Time 83:76+ F 21 '64
Religion and law; conference at Jackson Lake, Wyo. M. E. Marty. Christian Cent 80: 902-3 Jl 17 '63
Religion, education and the law; Law and society institute at the University of Kansas. J. C. Bush. Christian Cent 81:1412-14 N 11 '64
Religious right to violate the law? W. Herberg. Nat R 16:579-80 Jl 14 '64; Discussion. 16:741-2, 783-4 Ag 25-S '64; Correction of S 8 issue. 16:794+ S 22 '64
Whose responsibility? S. E. Mead. Christian Cent 80:1342-3 O 30 '63

RELIGION and literature
Celebration of flesh: poetry in Christian life, by A. C. McGill. Review
Christian Cent 82:80-2 Ja 20 '65. S. J. Rowland, jr
Theology as literature. K. B. Cully. Christian Cent 81:237-8 F 19 '64

RELIGION and music
To carol is to dance. S. Aker. il Dance Mag 38:40-1 D '64

RELIGION and philosophy. See Philosophy and religion

RELIGION and politics. See Church and politics

RELIGION and psychiatry. See Psychiatry and religion

RELIGION and science
Atheism's resort to mendacity; falsehoods in Science and religion. D. A. Lowrie. Christian Cent 80:1513-16 D 4 '63
Catholics and the science explosion. W. A. Wallace. Cath World 200:109-15 N '64
Faith and science; address, February 5, 1963. K. W. Baker. Vital Speeches 29:437-9 My 1 '63
From Galileo to Paul VI. H. Taylor. Cath World 199:301-7 Ag '64
Future of God. J. Lear. il Sat R 47:173-5+ Ag 29 '64
One Galileo case is enough. J. J. Langford. Cath World 200:205-10 Ja '65
Priest who haunts the Catholic world. J. Kobler. il Sat Eve Post 236:42-51 O 12 '63; Reply. R. J. Roth. America 109:792-4 D 21 '63
Radiation and social ethics; conference of nuclear scientists and theologians, University of Chicago. A. P. Klausler. Christian Cent 80:199-200 F 13 '63
Radiation and social ethics; conference of nuclear scientists and theologians, University of Chicago. W. A. Wallace. America 108:880-3 Je 22 '63
Science and religion; address, December 18, 1963. L. A. Ferre. Vital Speeches 30:277-9 F 15 '64
Science and religion; examination of the prevalent Christian stance. J. R. Pleasants. il Commonweal 78:91-2 Ap 19 '63
Science at Vatican II. America 111:583 N 14 '64
Science, religion and student values; plea for a genuine encounter between church and university. O. H. Mowrer. Christian Cent 80:1200-2 O 2 '63; Discussion. 80:1442+ N 20 '63
Scientific intellectual: the psychological & sociological origins of modern science, by L. S. Feuer. Review
Sci Am 209:129-30+ Ag '63
Scientist-minister begins dual career. il Todays Health 41:84 D '63
Where religion and science meet. R. B. Gittelsohn. Sat R 46:23-4+ Mr 23 '63

RELIGION and sex. See Sex and religion

RELIGION and sociology
Key is crisis. T. Thompson. Christian Cent 81:586 Ap 29 '64
New Negro and the church. G. S. Wilmore, jr. Christian Cent 80:168-71 F 6 '63
Peter Berger's attack upon Christendom. Christian Cent 80:415 Mr 27 '63; Reply. P. L. Berger. 80:649 My 15 '63
Sociology of religion, by M. Weber. Review
Sat R 46:37-8 F 16 '63. J. K. Feibleman
See also
Sociology, Christian

RELIGION and state. See Church and state

RELIGION and technology
Christians in a technological era, by H. C. White, jr. Review
Cath World 200:57-8+ O '64. J. L. Walsh

RELIGION and war. See War and religion

RELIGION in literature
New Orpheus; ed. by N. A. Scott, jr. Review
Christian Cent 81:913 Jl 15 '64. R. Detweiler

RELIGION in periodicals. See Periodical literature

RELIGION in the public schools. See Public schools and religion

RELIGIONS
Christianity and the encounter of the world religions, by P. Tillich. Review
Christian Cent 80:273 F 27 '63. M. C. Ebersole
Ecumenics and non-Christians; new secretariat for non-Christians. bibliog America 110:753 My 30 '64
Estimated membership of the world's principal religions; table. (title varies) (cont) Sr Schol 83:44 O 4 '63; 85:48 O 7 '64
See also
Bahaism
Buddha and Buddhism
Theosophy

RELIGIOUS advertising
See also
Church advertising

RELIGIOUS architecture. See Church architecture

RELIGIOUS art. See Christian art and symbolism

RELIGIOUS book clubs. See Book clubs

RELIGIOUS books. See Religious literature

RELIGIOUS conferences
All-Africa Christianity; All-Africa conference of churches. E. C. Parker. Christian Cent 80:670-2 My 22 '63
Another Oberlin conference. D. L. Day. Christian Cent 80:1334-5 O 30 '63
Brethren and the church; second Theological study conference, July 20-24. R. A. Bollinger. Christian Cent 81:1062-3 Ag 26 '64
Cardinal of unity; Cardinal Bea at Harvard university's four-day Catholic-Protestant colloquium. W. M. Abbott. America 108:484 Ap 13 '63
Colloquium at Harvard. Commonweal 78:60 Ap 12 '63; Reply. R. E. Murphy. Commonweal 78:356 Je 21 '63
Conventions needn't be conventional. Christian Cent 80:923 Jl 24 '63
Ecumenical dialogue at Harvard, ed. by S. H. Miller and G. E. Wright. Review
Sat R 47:32 My 30 '64. D. A. Poling
Ecumenical or regional? permament European conference of churches proposed. C. Northcott. Christian Cent 81:1358 N 4 '64
Episcopalians retard COCU plans; consultation on church union. Christian Cent 81:1054 Ag 26 '64
Frankfurt: the ghost of unity; meeting of World Presbyterian and Reformed alliance. W. D. Wagoner. Christian Cent 81:1089-90 S 2 '64
Fusion at Oberlin; Consultation on church union. K. Haselden. Christian Cent 80:422-3 Ap 3 '63
Impressions from Helsinki, Rome and Montreal. G. A. Lindbeck. Cath World 198:272-80 F '64
Indian Christians hold peace talks. Christian Cent 80:701-2 My 29 '63
Methodists chill C.O.C.U; Consultation on church union, Princeton meeting. H. E. Fey. Christian Cent 81:599-600 My 6 '64; Discussion. 81:936-7 Jl 22 '64
N.A.E. on church-state. D. M. Kelley. Christian Cent 80:454-5 Ap 10 '63
Orthodox at Rhodes; third Pan-Orthodox conference. M. Rinvolucri. Commonweal 81:502 Ja 15 '65
Primitive ecumenical catechism; excerpts from reports and messages of major ecumenical conferences. R. French. Christian Cent 80:1505-8 D 4 '63
Prophet of the Kirchentag. C. Northcott. Christian Cent 80:933-4 Jl 24 '63
Separate but interacting; conference on church-state relationships, Columbus, Ohio. H. E. Fey. Christian Cent 81:231-2 F 19 '64
Slow march to unity; Britain's first Faith and order conference. C. Northcott. Christian Cent 81:1231-2 O 7 '64
Splendidly irrational; first British faith and order conference. America 111:506 O 31 '64
Together at Harvard; Roman Catholic-Protestant colloquium. J. O'Gara. Commonweal 78:90 Ap 19 '63
Trifaith conference; Protestant-Catholic-Jewish. A. P. Klausler. Christian Cent 81:1572-3 D 16 '64
Unity talks hit snag; Consultation on church union in Princeton. Christian Cent 81:542-3 Ap 29 '64
West Germany. F. Luepsen. Christian Cent 80:472-4 Ap 10 '63
See also
East Asia Christian conference
Methodist conference on human relations
Missionary conferences
World conference on faith and order
World council of churches

RELIGIOUS cooperation
Ecumenical footnote. J. E. Wilbur. America 108:845-6 Je 15 '63
Ecumenism in Buffalo. W. Folger. Christian Cent 81:58 Ja 8 '64
Geneva to Rome; resolution to establish with the Vatican a joint working committee on interfaith cooperation. il Time 85:89 Ja 29 '65
Good news from Dallas. Christian Cent 81:790 Je 17 '64
Operation understanding; New Orleans churches. America 112:154 Ja 30 '65
Practical ecumenism, donations to separated Christians. Commonweal 80:30-1 Ap 3 '64
Religious leaders allied for civic goals. R. G. Howes. Cath World 197:114-19 My '63
Roman radical in London. C. Northcott. Christian Cent 81:907-8 Jl 15 '64
See also
National council of the churches of Christ in the United States of America

RELIGIOUS denominations. See Sects

RELIGIOUS discrimination in college. See Colleges and universities—Discrimination

RELIGIOUS discussion. See Discussion

RELIGIOUS drama
Daniel and Job. F. Merkling. il Opera N 27:33 F 2 '63
See also
Drama, Medieval
Passion plays

RELIGIOUS education
Can public funds be constitutionally granted to private schools? address, January 9, 1963. R. F. Drinan. Vital Speeches 29:273-8 F 15 '63
Christian schools, secular subjects. Brother Fidelian. Commonweal 81:566-8+ Ja 29 '65
Faith and prejudice: intergroup problems in Protestant curricula, by B. E. Olson. Review
Christian Cent 80:617-19 My 8 '63. F. H. Littell; Reply B. E. Olson. 80:887 Jl 10 '63
Life-involvement learning; Lutheran long range program. il Time 84:65 S 25 '64
Newman apostolate. J. O'Gara. Commonweal 79:32 O 4 '63
Religion and education. G. N. Shuster. Commonweal 79:504-7 Ja 31 '64
Religion in the public schools; Catholic children at least can lose their faith. M. Novak. New Repub 148:16-18 Ap 13 '63
Religious schools and civic harmony. G. Weigel. Cath World 196:351-6 Mr '63
Talk it over. America 109:33 Jl 13 '63
Teaching our faith in God, by L. H. DeWolf. Review
Christian Cent 80:646-7 My 15 '63. B. F. Wade
$3 million religious program undertaken by Lutherans. Pub W 185:32-3 Mr 23 '64
See also
Catechetics
Children—Religion
Church and education
Confraternity of Christian doctrine
Mission schools
Moral education
Public schools and religion
Theological education

Bibliography

Religious education bookshelf. W. Fallaw. Christian Cent 80:1170-1 S 25 '63

RELIGIOUS experience. See Experience (religion)

RELIGIOUS faith. See Faith

RELIGIOUS films. See Moving pictures—Religious films

RELIGIOUS freedom. See Religious liberty

RELIGIOUS habit. See Religious orders—Habit

RELIGIOUS institutes and workshops
Religion, education and the law; Law and society institute at the University of Kansas. J. C. Bush. Christian Cent 81:1412-14 N 11 '64

RELIGIOUS institutions and affairs
News of the Christian world. See issues of Christian century
On the religious news front. Christian Cent 80:997 Ag 14 '63
See also subhead Religious institutions and affairs under names of countries, e.g. Turkey—Religious institutions and affairs

RELIGIOUS intermarriages. See Marriages, Mixed

RELIGIOUS liberty
Becker amendment. Christian Cent 81:475 Ap 15 '64
Becker amendment would imperil true religion. Christian Cent 81:629 My 13 '64
Catholic reform and religious liberty. K. Haselden. Christian Cent 80:1570-2 D 18 '63
Catholicism and freedom. H. A. MacDougall. America 110:486-7 Ap 4 '64
Civil rights should cover atheists. Christian Cent 81:541 Ap 29 '64
Committing religious suicide; attacks upon the First amendment. Christian Cent 81:420 Ap 1 '64
Conscience at the council. America 109:204 Ag 31 '63
Council and liberty. America 110:335 Mr 14 '64
Council's religious liberty document. J. B. Sheerin. Cath World 199:140-3 Je '64
Court upholds Sabbatarian. Christian Cent 80:854 Jl 3 '63

RELIGIOUS liberty—*Continued*
Ecumenical sadness and hope. M. Novak. Christian Cent 81:1518 D 9 '64
Letter from Vatican City; third session of Vatican council II. X. Rynne. il New Yorker 40:90-103 Ja 9 '65
Of note: Religious liberty; excerpts from address. F. H. Littell. Commonweal 81:486-8 Ja 8 '65
On religious liberty. J. C. Murray. America 109:704-6 N 30 '63
Prayer amendments: a Catholic lawyer's view. W. B. Ball. Cath World 199:345-51 S '64
Propose charter of religious freedom. Christian Cent 80:197 F 13 '63
Religious freedom. America 108:599 Ap 27 '63
Religious liberty: Buddhist protests and Catholic principles. J. B. Sheerin. Cath World 197:339-42 S '63
Restraints on American Catholic freedom. J. Victor. bibliog f Harper 227:33-9 D '63
Theological frame of religious liberty. J. D. Hughey. Christian Cent 80:1365-8 N 6 '63; Reply. J. H. Sherman. 81:14-15 Ja 1 '64
Third myth. K. Haselden. Christian Cent 80:1491-3 D 4 '63
This matter of religious freedom. J. C. Murray. America 112:40-3 Ja 9 '65
Vatican II, act III. M. Novak. New Repub 151:7-8 O 17 '64
See also
Church and state
Liberty of conscience

RELIGIOUS literature
Divine reading. America 108:247 F 23 '63
RPG panel: design of religious books for contemporary appeal. il Pub W 186:76-7 D 7 '64
Theology as literature. K. B. Cully. Christian Cent 81:237-8 F 19 '64
Typewriter as a pulpit. D. A. Womack. Writer 76:25-6 D '63
See also
Booksellers and bookselling—Religious literature
Protestant church-owned publisher's association
Publishers and publishing—Religious literature
Religious newspapers and periodicals

RELIGIOUS medals. See Medals, Devotional

RELIGIOUS music. See Church music

RELIGIOUS mysteries. See Mysteries, Religious

RELIGIOUS newspapers and periodicals
Are southern churches silent? S. Southard. Christian Cent 80:1429-32 N 20 '63
Opening the religious press; discussion. A. Gilbert; F. Canavan. America 108:336-7 Mr 9 '63
Politics in the pulpit; presidential campaign. il Time 84:63 O 9 '64
Religious press in America, by M. E. Marty and others. Review
Cath World 198:187-8 D '63. J. Magmer
Christian Cent 80:1612-13 D 25 '63. A. P. Klausler
Commonweal 79:488-9 Ja 24 '64. R. Hoyt
Sat R 46:74 S 14 '63. J. F. Fixx
See also
Ave Maria (periodical)
Christian century (periodical)
Theology today (periodical)

Anecdotes, facetiae, satire, etc.

Baptist beauties. Christian Cent 81:1319 O 21 '64; Reply. S. J. Allen. 81:1527 D 9 '64

RELIGIOUS orders
Of grace and nature; neurotic peculiarities which show up in religious life. Sister Mary Dominic. America 108:763 My 25 '63
Only a brother? C. J. McNaspy. America 108:744-5 My 25 '63
See also
Benedictines
Sisterhoods
Vocation (in religion)

Habit

Dior, what 've you done? design for new nun's habit. America 111:246 S 12 '64
Sisters' outfits; Ursulines experimental outfit. America 112:34 Ja 9 '65; Discussion. 112:152 Ja 30 '65

RELIGIOUS poetry
From the seventeenth century. E. Bowers. Poetry 104:120-1 My '64

RELIGIOUS prejudice. See Prejudice

RELIGIOUS publishers group. See American book publishers council

RELIGIOUS radio programs. See Radio broadcasting—Religious programs

RELIGIOUS records. See Phonograph records—Religious records

RELIGIOUS relics. See Relics and reliquaries

RELIGIOUS services. See Church services

RELIGIOUS statistics
By the numbers. Newsweek 63:91 My 11 '64

RELIGIOUS thought
Quest for honesty. D. Callahan. Commonweal 80:137-40 Ap 24 '64; Reply with rejoinder. D. P. Gray. 80:262-3 My 22 '64

RELIGIOUS toleration. See Toleration

RELIGIOUS vocation. See Vocation (in religion)

RELIQUARIES. See Relics and reliquaries

RELISHES. See Pickles and relishes

RELUCTANT dragon; drama. See Thane, A.

REMAK, Joachim
Goosestep at the waltz. Sat R 46:23-4 S 7 '63
Players in a political horror show. Sat R 47:42 O 10 '64

REMARQUE, Erich Maria
Night in Lisbon; novel. Good H 158:75-9 Mr; 74-5 Ap '64

REMARRIAGE
How America lives. B. H. Hoffman. il Ladies Home J 80:24+ Ap '63
How to be happy, the second time around! J. R. Gaver. il McCalls 90:54+ Ap '63
Rockefeller minister faces discipline; United Presbyterian church. Christian Cent 80:668-9 My 22 '63

REMBERT, John, jr
John junior. E. Peter, jr. New Repub 148:14 Je 29 '63

REMBRANDT Hermanszoon van Rijn
Bitten with acid by Rembrandt. J. Canaday. il por N Y Times Mag p72-3 Ap 5 '64
Rembrandt's Bible drawings. A. Werner. il Am Artist 28:52-8+ D '64

REMEDIAL reading. See Reading—Remedial teaching

REMEDIES (in medicine) See Medicine, Magic, mystic, etc.

REMEMBER; story. See Gordon, E. E.

REMENGESAU, Thomas
Trust Territory of the Pacific Islands; statement, May 28, 1964. Dept State Bul 50:1018-20 Je 29 '64

REMICK, Lee
Double image of Lee Remick. B. Davidson. por Sat Eve Post 236:38-9 My 18 '63
Two ways to skin a cat. E. Miller. il pors Seventeen 22:136+ My '63

REMIDDI, Maria
Vision of mankind transformed. UNESCO Courier 17:16-20 Ap '64

REMINGTON rifles. See Rifles

REMINISCENCE
Good old days are good. il Sci Digest 56:81 Jl '64
Mr Dunkenheimer; my fifth Christmas. A. Morrissett. il Redbook 122:12+ D '63
Muley's enchanted summer; vacation days of childhood. D. Connelly. il Sports Illus 19:52-8 Jl 8 '63
Our family Christmas. L. Frost. Redbook 122:45+ D '63
What holiday memories mean to children. B. Spock. Redbook 124:16+ D '64

REMLEY, A. L.
New director of advertising and promotion. por Wilson Lib Bul 37:886 Je '63

REMMER, H. and Merker, H. J.
Drug-induced changes in the liver endoplasmic reticulum: association with drug-metabolizing enzymes. bibliog Science 142:1657-8 D 27 '63

REMODELED furniture. See Furniture, Remodeled

REMODELED houses. See Houses, Remodeled

REMODELING (architecture)
Barn gives your soaring space you can't afford to build today. G. Henle. il House B 105:142-5+ S '63
Big ideas for improving your shop and home; symposium. il Pop Sci 183:97-108+ S '63
Deft, economical remodeling. il Arch Rec 135:126-7 Ja '64
Fresh surfaces and dramatic lighting brighten an old apartment lobby; Manhattan's London terrace. il Arch Forum 118:132-3 Ap '63
Rebuilding. See issues of Architectural forum to July 1964
Rejuvenation and new growth restore usefulness to an older hospital. il Arch Rec 133:199-202 Mr '63
So you want to convert an old barn. J. Trahey. il House B 106:72-7+ Jl '64

REMODELING (architecture)—*Continued*
Soaring interior; converting a garage to a house. il Sunset 131:70-3, 96 Jl '63
Split-level showcase in Manhattan; Design research, inc. il Arch Forum 120:118-21 Ap '64
See also
Houses, Remodeled
REMOTE control. See Electric control; Radio control
REMOTE indicating compass. See Compass
REMSBERG, Bonnie. See Remsberg, C. jt. auth.
REMSBERG, Charles
Accident fraud is highway robbery. Read Digest 84:201-4 F '64
Inside the world's first pushbutton prison. Pop Sci 182:51-5+ Je '63
Quick, Watson the Geiger counter! Pop Mech 119:97-100 Ap '63
St Louis' two-legged tower: tallest U.S. monument. Pop Sci 184:91-4 Ap '64
—and Remsberg, Bonnie
Aristocrats of crime. N Y Times Mag p9+ D 27 '64
Roll of dishonor. N Y Times Mag p69 Ja 26 '64
RENARD, Jean Claude
Poèmes (extraits) with English tr. by W. Fowlie. Poetry 104:310-21 Ag '64
RENARD, Jules
Between silence and rhetoric. G. Bree. Sat R 47:38+ N 7 '64
RENAUD, Madeleine
Letter from Paris; performance of Beckett's Oh les beaux jours. Genêt. New Yorker 40:102+ F 22 '64
RENAULT, Mary
WLB biography. M. L. Holton. por Wilson Lib Bul 38:353 D '63
RENDEL, John
Behind the National motor boat show. Yachting 115:507 Ja '64
Blue Jays are flying high. Yachting 114:41+ Ag '63
RENDEZVOUS (space) See Orbital rendezvous (space flight)
RENE, Natalia
Isadora Duncan and Constantin Stanislavsky. Dance Mag 37:40-3 Jl '63
RENÉ Fribourg collection. See Art—Private collections
RENEGOTIATION board. See United States—Renegotiation board
RENIN
Hypertensive vascular disease produced by homologous renin. G. M. C. Masson and others. bibliog il Science 145:178-80 Jl 10 '64
Renal baroceptor control of renin secretion. S. L. Skinner and others. bibliog il Science 141:814-16 Ag 30 '63
RENNE, Harold S.
Detection of nuclear radiation by semiconductors. bibliog Electr World 70:39-42+ Ag '63
Semiconductors strain gages. Electr World 70:36-8+ Jl '63
RENNELS, Edward G. and Hood, J. F.
Sialic acid concentrations in the pituitary glands of normal and ovariectomized rats. bibliog Science 144:416-17 Ap 24 '64
RENNERT, Maggie
Four-fourths; poem. Sat R 46:17 O 5 '63
RENOIR, Auguste
Cry of love; excerpt from Renoir, my father. J. Renoir. il por Read Digest 83:86-90 Ag '63
Incident and sequel; excerpt from Renoir, my father. J. Renoir. Read Digest 82:55-6 My '63
RENOIR, Jean
Cry of love; excerpt from Renoir, my father. Read Digest 83:86-90 Ag '63
Incident and sequel; excerpt from Renoir, my father. Read Digest 82:55-6 My '63
RENSING, Ludger
Daily rhythmicity of corpus allatum and neurosecretory cells in drosophila melanogaster (meig) bibliog Science 144:1586-7 Je 26 '64
RENSSELAER polytechnic institute, Troy, N.Y.
Chicago architects win R.P.I. contest. il Arch Forum 118:11 Mr '63
Design for mechanical learning; architectural competition. il Arch Rec 135:178-92 My '64
RENT
Should you rent your home? J. R. Vollman. il Am Home 66:11-13+ My '63
Vacation houses that pay for themselves. il House B 105:141-57+ My '63
RENT laws
Letter from London; hole in Rent act of 1957: Rachman empire. M. Panter-Downes. New Yorker 39:67-8 Ag 3 '63
RENTAL collections. See Libraries—Rental collections
RENTAL libraries. See Libraries, Rental
RENTAL services
Appliances you can rent. Good H 156:171 Ap '63
If you don't want to buy it, rent it! D. Engle. Am Home 66:23 N '63
New life on leasing. il Duns R 81:65-6+ Ap '63
Rent-a-scape; Landscape leasing, inc. Newsweek 64:39 D 28 '64
Report cites industry reliance on leasing. W. H. Gregory. il Aviation W 78:113+ Je 17 '63
Thriving in business without any sales. il Bsns W p 140-1+ Mr 23 '63
See also subhead Renting under various subjects, e.g. Boats—Renting
RENTING of automobiles. See Automobiles—Renting
RENTING of boats. See Boats—Renting
RENTING of farm machinery. See Agricultural machinery—Renting
RENTING of office buildings. See Office buildings—Renting
RENTING of phonograph records. See Phonograph records—Circulation, loans, etc.
RENTON, Bruce
Italian elections. Nation 196:414 My 18 '63
Letter from Italy. Nation 196:187-8 Mr 2 '63
RENTZEL, Delos W.
Airway tide in transportation. Ann Am Acad 345:73-80 Ja '63
REORGANIZATION (business) See Business management and organization
REOVIRUSES. See Viruses
REPAIR men. See Repairmen
REPAIR shops
See also
Automobile service stations
Motor trucks in repair service
REPAIRING
Clinic for homeowners (title varies) See issues of Popular mechanics
First aid for minor household ailments. R. Whitman. Am Home 68:76-7 Ja '65
How to take the hard work out of upkeep. Bet Hom & Gard 41:33-4+ N '63
Seven smart ideas for your home. il Pop Sci 185:124-5 S '64
Your second home: off-season care. il Am Home 67:30 Ap '64
See also
Calking
Houses—Maintenance and repair
also subhead Repairing under various subjects, e.g. Household appliances—Repairing
REPAIRMEN
Time-saving, money-saving advice from your repairman. R. M. Burnley. il Redbook 121:58-9+ Ag '63
REPARTEE. See Conversation
REPELLENTS, Animal. See Animal repellents
REPELLENTS, Bird. See Bird repellents
REPELLENTS, Insect. See Insect baits and repellents
REPENTANCE
See also
Confession
REPERTORY companies. See Theater—United States
REPERTORY theater. See Theater
REPERTORY theater, New York. See New York (city)—Theater
REPORT cards. See School reports and records
The REPORTER (periodical)
This liberal magazine, 1964. M. Ascoli. Reporter 30:12-14 My 7 '64
USIA; with editorial comment. E. R. Murrow. Reporter 28:6+ My 9 '63
REPORTERS and reporting
Advice from a millionaire publisher; address. J. H. Whitney. Sat R 47:71-3 D 12 '64; Discussion. 48:66 Ja 9 '65
Anatomy of a headline; how the diocesan press reported the announcement of the reform of the curia. A. V. Krebs, jr. America 109:662-4 N 23 '63; Discussion. 110:83-4 Ja 18 '64
Better council coverage; reporting of Vatican II. America 109:473 O 26 '63
Biggest story in the world; excerpts from address. J. Reston. New Repub 148:15-17 My 4 '63
Both sides & the middle; press correspondent in Cyprus injured. Time 84:52+ Ag 21 '64
Call on Castro; U.S. newsmen in Cuba. il Newsweek 64:62-4 Ag 10 '64
Campaign blur. Time 84:71 O 9 '64

REPORTERS and reporting—*Continued*
Campaign coverage; the Republicans & the reporters. Time 84:52 Ag 21 '64
Campaign issue: biased reporting? il U S News 57:40 Ag 3 '64
Catholics and Vietnam. Commonweal 79:244-5 N 22 '63; Reply with rejoinder. P. O'Connor. 79:427-8 Ja 10 '64
Communist at the White House; Polish reporter. Z. Broniarek. il Sat Eve Post 237:62-3 My 2 '64
Covering a pilgrimage. il Time 83:50 Ja 17 '64
Covering the tragedy; President Kennedy's assassination. il Time 82:84 N 29 '63
Dateline: Cyprus. il Newsweek 63:46 Mr 30 '64
Dateline, Saigon: war of words. il Newsweek 62:98-9 O 7 '63
Day Khrushchev died; false report. Time 83:59 Ap 24 '64
Day the press halted a war; with report by L. Chelminski. il Life 56:28-35 Ap 3 '64
Desert strike. W. V. Kennedy. America 110:866 Je 27 '64
Did press pressure kill Oswald? reprint. L. Grove. il U S News 56:78-9 Ap 6 '64
Dilemma of a guild reporter. M. Bracker; discussion. Reporter 28:10+ F 14 '63
Disillusion. Nation 198:406 Ap 27 '64
Drebby and Dan; sportswriting's most unforgettable characters. il Newsweek 63:54 Ap 13 '64
Echoes out of Saigon; concerning report of fact-finding mission to South Viet Nam. Time 83:58 Mr 6 '64
Foreign correspondence. by J. Hohenberg. Review
Nation 200:58-60 Ja 18 '65. J. Stolle
Foreign policy conference held for editors and broadcasters. Dept State Bul 49:644 O 21 '63
Founders of the Negro press. L. Bennett, jr. il Ebony 19:96-8+ Jl '64
Fourteen clues to Washington news. R. Baker. il N Y Times Mag p31+ Ap 7 '63
From Washington straight, misinformation on U.S. foreign policy. Cato. Nat R 15:385 N 5 '63
Getting the story in Vietnam. D. Halberstam. Commentary 39:30-4 Ja '65
Go-ahead for Bible scholars; new instruction of the pontifical commission for Biblical studies. America 110:754 My 30 '64
High times with a by-line. W. L. Rivers. Sat R 46:20 Ag 17 '63
Hildy Johnson's last scoop. H. A. Smith. Read Digest 85:227+ O '64
Honest quote: J. Mabley of Chicago's American. Time 84:61 Ag 7 '64
How to evade the issue. J. Tebbel. Sat R 47:79-80 Ja 11 '64
How to read the financial pages without going broke. P. Bart. Harper 227:31-5 Ag '63; Discussion. 227:6+; 230:14 O '63, Ja '65
How to spot a newsman. J. Hohenberg. Sat R 46:55 Je 8 '63
In pursuit of the sound; NBC correspondent killed in the Congo. il Newsweek 64:64 D 7 '64
In the peace pipe room; Goldwater and reporters. Newsweek 64:68 N 16 '64
Informing foreign journalists about America; World press institute. R. Kirk. Nat R 16:1017 N 17 '64
Inquiry; forthcoming study of the methods and resources now applied by the press to coverage of national defense. W. V. Kennedy. America 112:11 Ja 2 '65
Is the public getting the truth about the race issue? size-up by a panel of editors from North and South. il U S News 55:82-7 N 11 '63
Journalism and foreign affairs; address, March 13, 1964. R. J. Manning. Dept State Bul 50:541-9 Ap 6 '64; Same with title Press and the government. Vital Speeches 30:453-7 My 15 '64
Journalism of tomorrow. M. A. Guitar. il Mlle 56:162-3+ Mr '63
Journalism's challenge and answers. J. Tebbel. Sat R 46:50-1 Je 8 '63
Last men in Havana; foreign correspondents. il Time 82:40 S 27 '63
Laurence of Nagasaki. Newsweek 63:74 F 3 '64
Letter from the publisher. B. M. Auer. il Time 83:11 Ja 31 '64
Letter from the publisher; experience of Time's correspondent M. Garcia in British Guiana. B. M. Auer. Time 84:25 N 27 '64
Letters from Vatican City. by X. Rynne. Review
Commonweal 78:461-2 Jl 26 '63. J. Leo
Lewis's trumpet. Newsweek 64:53 Ag 24 '64
Liebling, libel, and the press. L. M. Lyons. Atlan 213:43-8 My '64
Little dignity; Jack Ruby trial. Newsweek 63:80 Mr 2 '64
Long seasons; J. Drebinger retires. il Time 83:53 Ap 10 '64
Maggie vs. May. Newsweek 61:23-4 Ap 8 '63
Managing the news; Time's criticism of the American corps of correspondents in South Vietnam. Nation 197:250-1 O 26 '63
Mismanaging the news. Sat Eve Post 237:80 Mr 7 '64
Mob of Dallas? Newsweek 63:76-7 Ap 27 '64
Modern journalism; Pulitzer prize. New Repub 148:5 My 18 '63
New pique; relations between the Pentagon and the press. il Newsweek 63:61 Je 29 '64
News managers. B. H. Bagdikian. Sat Eve Post 236:17-19 Ap 20 '63
Nhu deal. il Newsweek 62:65-6 N 25 '63
One man's facts are another man's prejudices. P. Lisagor. il Nations Bsns 52:23-4 O '64
Our man in Saigon; with introd. by D. Schoenbrun. G. J. W. Goodman. il Esquire 61:57-60+ Ja '64
Piecing together portraits, royal and otherwise. G. P. Hunt. Life 56:3 Mr 6 '64
Race beat. il Newsweek 63:88+ Je 15 '64
Report (limited) from Communist China. J. Marcuse. il N Y Times Mag p9+ My 24 '64
Reporting. by L. Ross. Review
Sat R 47:133 Mr 14 '64. J. F. Fixx
Saigon story. il Time 82:55 O 11 '63
Science of reporting; career of New York times's science editor. Time 82:32-3 D 27 '63
Self-reliance in Saigon; New York herald tribune's B. Deepe. Time 85:38 Ja 8 '65
Separate papers: S. Gruson and F. Lewis. il Newsweek 61:91 Ap 22 '63
Splasher; J. Anderson. Newsweek 61:94 My 13 '63
Sporting life; R. Lardner covers the world series from his bed. R. L. Tobin. Sat R 47:8+ Jl 11 '64
Suzy sasy; latest international gossip. P. Coffin. il Look 28:87-90+ Ag 11 '64
Sweet harmony in the southern skies; journalists covering Goldwater's campaign. M. McGrory. America 111:400 O 10 '64
There are 00 trees in Russia; the function of facts in newsmagazines. O. Friedrich. Harper 229:59-65 O '64
Traitor to my class; move from Washington, D.C. to Flordia. F. Knebel. il Look 28:32+ Ag 25 '64
Two-hatters; reporters who sell automobile advertising and cover the news beat. Newsweek 64:69 Ag 31 '64
Vatican beat. il Newsweek 64:102+ O 26 '64
Viet beat. il Newsweek 64:76 S 7 '64
Vietnam controversy. P. O'Connor. Commonweal 78:537-8 S 6 '63
View from Saigon. il Time 82:62 S 20 '63
War in Vietnam, Luce version. W. H. Hunter. New Repub 148:15-17 Mr 23 '63
Washington correspondents on Ike vs. JFK. Newsweek 61:59 Ap 8 '63
Washington press establishment. K. E. Meyer. Esquire 61:73-6+ Ap '64
When the press shapes the news. H. Brucker. il Sat R 47:75-7+ Ja 11 '64; Discussion. 47:46-7 F 8; 123+ Mr 14 '64
Who killed Diem and why? V. L. Borin. il Nat R 16:441-6 Je 2 '64
Why American political reporting is better than England's. D. E. Butler. Harper 226:14+ My '63
Write right; getting more conservatives into journalism. Newsweek 64:64 Ag 10 '64

See also
Journalism
Journalists
News
Newspaper court reporting
Nieman fellowships
Overseas press club of America
Press conferences
Radio broadcasting—Sports
Science news
Sports journalism
United Nations correspondents association
Women as reporters

Japan

Covering it like a tent; Cabinet shakeup. il Time 82:56 Jl 26 '63
Not so honorable club; newsmen's private press clubs. il Newsweek 64:96+ N 23 '64

REPORTING to employees. See Employees. Reporting to

REPORTS
Dear Chris; simplified annual report of Chicago's Bell & Howell co. Newsweek 63:88 Mr 23 '64
18,000,000 books nobody reads. R. Girdler. Sat R 46:71+ Ap 13 '63; Discussion. 46:54 My 11; 55 Jl 13 '63
How to compile a pictorial report. report of Mount Vernon, N.Y. recreation commission. Recreation 56:463 D '63
How's the annual report coming? S. W. Bryant. il Fortune 69:104-7+ Ja '64
Report on reports; Workshop on annual reports, by the Graphics institute. New Yorker 39:45-6 O 19 '63
Telling the whole tale; annual meeting report to stockholders. il Bsns W p42 Ag 1 '64
See also
Municipal reports
REPORTS, Library. See Library reports
REPORTS, School. See School reports and records
REPORTS, Scientific. See Scientific literature
REPORTS, Technical. See Technical literature
REPOTTING of plants. See Plants, Potted
REPPERT, Ralph
Catch me on-camera: excerpt from Ralph Reppert and his electric wife. Read Digest 85:188C Jl '64
Of Martians and mores. Read Digest 83:36B S '63
Why is everyone so helpful? excerpt from Ralph Reppert and his electric wife. Read Digest 86:160D-160E Ja '65
REPRESENTATIVE; drama. See Hochhuth, R.
REPRESENTATIVE government and representation
Challenge to representative self-government; address, January 23, 1964. M. A. Feighan. Vital Speeches 30:304-7 Mr 1 '64
Supreme court and the Republic; decisions on reapportionment. F. Morley. Fortune 70: 102+ Ag '64
See also
Apportionment (election law)
Democracy
Republics
REPRESENTATIVES, Congressional. See Congressmen
REPRESENTATIVES, Presidential. See Public officers
REPRINTS. See Books—Reprints
REPRINTS, Scientific. See Scientific literature
REPRODUCTION
Morphogenesis of syncytiotrophoblast in vivo: an autoradiographic demonstration. A. R. Midgley, jr. and others. bibliog il Science 141:349-50 Jl 26 '63
Original sex; a kind of sexual mating between caulobacter bacteria. Time 84:85 N 13 '64
See also
Artificial insemination, Human
Conception
Fertility, Human
Ovaries
Sex determination and control
Spawning
REPRODUCTION of catalog cards. See Catalog cards—Reproduction
REPRODUCTION of manuscripts. See Manuscripts—Reproduction
REPRONAR. See Photography—Apparatus and supplies
REPS, Paul
Signatures. R. Sward. Poetry 102:335-6 Ag '63
REPTILES
Anoxia: tolerance in reptiles. D. A. Belkin. bibliog il Science 139:492-3 F 8 '63
Reptilian thermoregulation: evaluation of field studies. J. E. Heath. bibliog il Science 146:784-5 N 6 '64
See also
Alligators
Crocodiles
Gila monsters
Lizards
Snakes
Turtles
REPUBLIC aviation corporation
Republic seeking diversification to backstop phaseout of F-105; summary of address. M. I. Peale. Aviation W 78:113 Ja 21 '63
SMS satellite program under way. M. Getler. Miss & Roc 12:27 F 25 '63
REPUBLIC OF CAMEROUN. See Cameroun
REPUBLIC OF CONGO. See Congo (capital Brazzaville)
REPUBLIC OF IRELAND. See Ireland
REPUBLIC OF THE PHILIPPINES. See Philippines
REPUBLICAN aviation corporation
Four horsemen; new management team. il Newsweek 64:92 S 21 '64
REPUBLICAN clubs. See Political clubs and associations
REPUBLICAN national committee. See Republican party
REPUBLICAN party
Abandoning the middle of the road. Bsns W p 148 Jl 25 '64
After the attack. Commonweal 80:408 Je 26 '64
After the deluge. K. Crawford. Newsweek 64:37 S 28 '64
After the election. America 111:589 N 14 '64
After the fall; a Republican's hopes for his party. M. C. Moos. New Repub 151:11-14 D 12 '64
After the fall: to the mainstream? Newsweek 64:31-2 N 9 '64
After the primaries. R. Moley. Newsweek 63:92 Je 22 '64
Against the Democrat Democrat. Time 81:19 Mr 22 '63
Alien reviews the election. E. M. von Kuehnelt-Leddihn. Nat R 16:1058 D 1 '64
Anatomy of the Goldwater boom. T. Wicker. il N Y Times Mag p7+ Ag 11 '63
Another upset victory for the Republicans; special election in California. U S News 54: 10 Je 24 '63
Anti-Burch society. Newsweek 65:24 Ja 18 '65
As Republican choice narrows for '64. U S News 54:43 Mr 18 '63
As Republicans close ranks. il U S News 57: 34-5 Ag 24 '64
As Republicans look over the field for '64. il U S News 55:64 Jl 1 '63
At 8:25 p.m: I'm going to run. il Newsweek 63:21-5 Je 22 '64
Atlantic report; Goldwater boom. Atlan 212: 4+ D '63
Back to work. New Repub 151:3-5 N 14 '64
Backlash vote is G.O.P. pitfall. Life 57:4 Jl 24 '64
Barry's summit. Newsweek 65:15 Ja 4 '65
Behind the Goldwater phenomenon. H. Brandon. Sat R 47:6+ Jl 11 '64
Beyond ideology; new national chairman. il Time 85:19-20 Ja 22 '65
Birds and the beasts were there; dinner to benefit liberal Republicans' magazine Advance. G. F. Hobart. Nat R 14:485 Je '63
Bleating of sheep. M. Kempton. New Repub 150:15-18 Je 20 '64
Bliss, Ford and the second party's job. Life 58:4 Ja 22 '65
Block Goldwater movement in the GOP. il Newsweek 62:19-20 Jl 22 '63
Bomb that was a bomb; Governor Rockefeller's attack on radical right elements. il Time 82:19 Jl 26 '63
Boring Republicans. S. Alsop. il Sat Eve Post 237:16 Ap 25 '64
Breakaways from Barry. il Time 84:19 Jl 31 '64
Bubbles, bubbles. M. Kempton. New Repub 149:15-16 Ag 17 '63
Burdened by Barry; Republican congressional candidates. Time 84:26-7 O 9 '64
Business, and the party platforms. T. O'Hanlon. il Duns R 84:55-7+ O '64
By the right flank, marched; California primary and National convention. Nat R 16:433 Je 2 '64
Bye, bye Burch? il Newsweek 64:19-21 D 21 '64
Campaign about fundamentals. Fortune 70: 99-100 Ag '64
Can anyone stop Goldwater now? il Newsweek 63:23-4+ Je 15 '64
Can Republicans come back? history shows this. il U S News 57:38-9 N 23 '64
Can Republicans make a comeback? with statements from congressmen and interview with G. R. Ford. il U S News 58:36-41 Ja 18 '65
Can the GOP survive Goldwater? R. Wilson. il Look 28:20-1 Jl 14 '64
Carping about a candidate: press reaction to Goldwater. Time 83:36 Je 19 '64
Case against the Republicans. H. S. Commager. il N Y Times Mag p9+ Ja 12 '64
Changing lineup for Republicans; New Hampshire primary vote; with statement by L. H. Bean. il U S News 56:39-41 Mr 23 '64
Choosing battlefield for GOP; congressional Republicans. il Bsns W p36 S 7 '63
Citizens for Goldwater. Nat R 16:758 S 8 '64

REPUBLICAN party—*Continued*
Civil rights and the GOP. Nation 197:21 Jl 13 '63
Clearing the underbrush. il Time 84:24 D 18 '64
Conservative future at stake; Goldwaterism. Life 57:4 Jl 17 '64
Conservative revolution. M. Ascoli. Reporter 31:28 S 24 '64
Conservatives strike up the band; politics in Connecticut. A. Brownell. Nat R 16:231-2+ Mr 24 '64
Cool off, Republicans! R. Moley. Newsweek 65:80 Ja 18 '65
Crossroads for the GOP. W. A. Rusher. il Nat R 14:109-12 F 12 '63; Reply. F. Barron. 14:331 Ap 23 '63
Crucial choice for the Republicans. A. Krock. il N Y Times Mag p5+ Jl 12 '64
Crucial four-letter word: duty. E. J. Hughes. Newsweek 63:15 Je 29 '64
D-day at Cleveland. Nation 198:614 Je 22 '64
Danger of extremism. Nation 199:21 Jl 27 '64
Decisions in Denver; Republican governors meeting; Inside at Hershey. il Newsweek 64:25-7 D 14 '64
Destiny's tot; seventeenth congressional district, Manhattan. R. G. Smith. il Nat R 16: 861-2 O 6 '64
District revamping poses new GOP woe. Bsns W p20+ D 26 '64
Draft-Goldwater drive: a progress report. W. A. Rusher. Nat R 15:185-7 S 10 '63
Draft Goldwater move starts, its meaning. il U S News 54:42-5 Ap 29 '63
Election decided in mid-July. E. T. Folliard. America 111:587 N 14 '64
End of an era; power shift. il Newsweek 65: 23-4 Ja 25 '65
End of era for Republicans, a conservative party again? il U S News 57:41-3 Jl 20 '64
End to Republican party in Mississippi. U S News 56:8 Mr 30 '64
Essential South. R. Moley. Newsweek 63:122 Ap 20 '64
Exclusive interview: Goldwater speaks his mind. B. M. Goldwater. il U S News 57: 46-9+ D 21 '64; Reply. New Yorker 40:23 Ja 2 '65
Explosive nucleus. Nation 196:537-8 Je 29 '63
Farce at Cleveland. R. Moley. Newsweek 63: 92 Je 29 '64
Fat cats' twilight. R. Moley. Newsweek 64:124 N 23 '64
Fiscal responsibility. New Repub 151:5 N 21 '64
For golf, money and love. New Repub 148:8-9 My 25 '63
From behind in the stretch; California's Republican presidential primary. il Time 83: 19-20 My 29 '64
From party leaders: Republican future; symposium. il U S News 57:68-70+ N 16 '64
From Washington straight. Cato. Nat R 14: 228: 17:55 Mr 26 '63. Ja 26 '65
From Washington straight: Cuba issue. Cato. Nat R 14:148 F 26 '63
From Washington straight; so-called moderates against the Goldwater GOP. Cato. Nat R 16:906 O 20 '64
Future of the Republican party. D. D. Eisenhower. il Sat Eve Post 238:21-5 Ja 30 '6.
Future of the Republican party, by R. J. Donovan. Review
New Repub 152:20 Ja 2 '65. G. W. Johnson
General had to dress for dinner. M. Kempton. New Repub 151:6 D 19 '64
Go, go, GOP. il Newsweek 62:38 N 11 '63
Go with Goldwater? K. Crawford. Newsweek 61:25 F 4 '63
Goldwater and the race issue. Nat R 15:45-6+ Jl 30 '63
Goldwater and the Republican party. Bsns W p 148 Je 13 '64
Goldwater bandwagon. M. Ascoli. Reporter 30:10+ Je 18 '64
Goldwater in '64. Nat R 16:570+ Jl 14 '64
Goldwater movement. W. Lippmann. Newsweek 62:13 Ag 5 '63; Reply. Nat R 15:223 S 24 '63
Goldwater on extremists. R. Moley. Newsweek 62:76 Jl 29 '63
Goldwater, the romantic regression. H. J. Morgenthau. Commentary 38:65-8 S '64
Goldwater threat. W. Lippmann. Newsweek 64:13 Jl 6 '64
Goldwaterism; the new ideology. C. McWilliams. Nation 199:68-71 Ag 24 '64
Goldwaterite revolution. W. D. Burnham. Commonweal 80:531-5 Ag 7 '64; Discussion 80:610-14 S 4 '64
Goldwater's Dirksen. K. Crawford. Newsweek 64:31 Jl 13 '64
Goldwater's nine; men who run his campaign and Republican national politics. C. Mohr. il N Y Times Mag p28-9 S 13 '64
Goldwater's problem and the G.O.P. Life 56:4 Je 19 '64
Governor Romney: why the Republican pros distrust him. F. Knebel. il Look 28:75-7 Mr 10 '64
Governor Scranton to the rescue. M. McGrory. America 110:860 Je 27 '64
GOP: a trunkful of troubles. il Newsweek 64:25-8 N 16 '64
G.O.P. against itself. P. Duke. Reporter 31: 12-15 Jl 2 '64
GOP and Rockefeller. E. J. Hughes. Newsweek 61:15 Je 3 '63
G.O.P. and the gap. M. Mannes. Reporter 31: 28-30 Ag 13 '64
GOP: can the moderates come back? M. Viorst. il Nation 199:217-19 O 12 '64
GOP chairmanship. R. Moley. Newsweek 65: 96: Ja 25 '65
GOP disestablishment. M. Kempton. New Repub 151:5-7 Jl 11 '64
G.O.P. has its convention prematurely. il Life 56:47-48A Je 19 '64
GOP heads into a dilemma. Nat R 16:898 O 20 '64
GOP in Mississippi. R. Moley. Newsweek 61:112 My 13 '63
G.O.P. in '64. W. V. Shannon. Commonweal 79:417-18 Ja 10 '64
GOP race: who's up, down, and out. il Newsweek 63:19-20 My 11 '64
GOP shuffle: so to REAP. Nat R 17:49 Ja 26 '65
GOP upsurge: new hopes for '64. il Newsweek 61:23-4 Mr 18 '63
G.O.P. wounds that can be healed. Life 57:4 N 27 '64
GOP's Chinese wing. E. J. Hughes. Newsweek 62:13 Jl 29 '63
GOP's Goldwater: busting out all over; Listening post: a head for Rockefeller but a heart for Goldwater. il Newsweek 61:28-32 My 20 '63
GOP's unmerry Christmas. E. J. Hughes. Newsweek 64:9 D 28 '64
Great G.O.P. logjam of presidential timber. il Life 56:28-31 F 7 '64
Grenier plan for the G.O.P. J. Ter Horst. Reporter 31:24-6 O 8 '64
Hand at the helm; chairman of National committee. Time 84:28A Jl 24 '64
Heads off. New Repub 150:2+ Je 20 '64
High winds, fresh air. Newsweek 61:24 F 25 '63
House Republican battle: Ford seeks to unseat Halleck. il U S News 58:13 Ja 4 '65
House Republicans drop the old guard; Rep. Ford of Michigan replaces Rep. Halleck of Indiana. il Bsns W p22-3 Ja 9 '65
How Republican leaders view the Negro. S. Booker. il Ebony 19:25-8+ Mr '64
How Republican race lines up. il U S News 56:33-5 Mr 16 '64
How Republicans expect to win. Nations Bsns 52:77-8+ Je '64
How the Republicans can win. A. Larson. Sat Eve Post 237:21-3 Ja 25 '64
How to beat a voting machine and a drive to make it honest; voting frauds in Chicago. il U S News 54:63 Ap 8 '63
If Goldwater gets it. New Repub 150:3-4 Je 13 '64
In the black and blue; campaign surplus. Newsweek 64:35-6 N 23 '64
In there fighting. il Time 84:38 N 13 '64
Johnson's Eisenhower premise. S. Rousseas. Nation 199:375-9 N 23 '64
Key Republican candidates. Sat Eve Post 237: 86 O 24 '64
Labels vs. policies. H. Hazlitt. Newsweek 64:85 N 30 '64
Left hook. Nat R 15:7+ Jl 16 '63
Lessons of the nomination drive. W. A. Rusher. Nat R 16:641-3 Jl 28 '64
Let's grow up, conservatives! followers of Barry Goldwater. il Newsweek 64:27-30 Jl 27 '64
Letter from Washington. R. H. Rovere. New Yorker 39:113-20 N 2 '63; 40:111-18 Je 13; 161-2 D 19 '64
Letter from Washington: losers in the New Hampshire primary. R. H. Rovere. New Yorker 40:178+ Mr 21 '64
Lincoln takeover. Time 81:24 F 22 '63
Los Angeles did it. K. Crawford. Newsweek 63:38 Je 15 '64
LBJ vs. —? il U S News 56:35-6 Je 8 '64
Many-membered GOP. R. Moley. Newsweek 65:82 Ja 11 '65
Meaning of San Francisco. E. Roper. Sat R 47:17+ Ag 22 '64

REPUBLICAN party—*Continued*
Memo to a future historian. T. H. White. il Life 57:32-5+ N 13 '64
Men around Goldwater. R. Evans and R. Novak. il Sat Eve Post 237:32-4 O 24 '64
Men behind Goldwater. R. G. Spivack. il Look 28:45+ N 3 '64
Middle ground of a Midwest Republican. R. Taft, jr. Sat R 47:14-16 Ag 22 '64
Mr Byrnes' views. R. Moley. Newsweek 64:100 D 14 '64
Mr Johnson defines his political creed; excerpts from statements. L. B. Johnson. U S News 55:114 D 9 '63
Moderates move to get GOP back in step. il Bsns W p36-7 N 7 '64
Morning after. C. McWilliams. Nation 199: 345-7 N 16 '64
Must conservatives be Republicans? J. Burnham. Nat R 16:1052 D 1 '64
My case for the Republican party, 1964. B. Goldwater. Sat R 47:21-3+ O 17 '64
Neither an echo nor a choice. M. Ascoli. Reporter 31:22-3 O 8 '64; Discussion. 31:6 N 5 '64
Never again. il Time 85:20 Ja 29 '65
New challenger to the Kennedy clan; C. Percy. W. Trombley. il Sat Eve Post 236: 38-9 S 28 '63
New conservative manifesto. T. G. Harris. il Look 28:19-23 D 29 '64
New G.O.P; interview, ed. by R. Manning. J. V. Lindsay. Atlan 215:39-43 Ja '65
New men; Goldwater party. New Repub 151: 3-5 Jl 25 '64
New, new guard of the GOP. V. E. Lewis and H. Chambers. Nation 199:85-8 S 7 '64
New thrust; Who are the Goldwaterites? The disenchanted. il Time 84:17-21 Jl 24 '64
Next president? il Newsweek 63:23 F 10 '64
Nixon's new role: what will it be? U S News 54:24 Mr 25 '63
No room at the top. New Repub 152:4 Ja 2 '65
Non-candidates. Time 83:13 Ja 24 '64
Now: unity for Republicans? il U S News 57: 44 Jl 27 '64
Ohio and Governor Rhodes. W. F. Fickenbaker. il Nat R 16:61-4 Ja 28 '64
One place where Republicans gained; gubernatorial contests. U S News 57:12 N 16 '64
Only 725 days. il Time 84:32 N 20 '64
Opening the big campaign; Republican primary in New Hampshire. il Bsns W p28-9 F 29 '64
Order of battle; a Republican's call to reason, by J. K. Javits. Review
Commentary 38:68-70 Ag '64. A. Hacker
Commonweal 80:373-4 Je 12 '64. W. D. Burnham
Nat R 16:544 Je 30 '64. W. A. Rusher
Time 83:24 My 1 '64
Party anarchy or party responsibility? D. Lawrence. U S News 57:84 Ag 3 '64
Party comes of age. R. Moley. Newsweek 61: 88 Je 3 '63
Party control. R. Moley. Newsweek 64:76 Ag 3 '64
Party of Ike. E. J. Hughes. Newsweek 63:15 My 4 '64
Party of the last part. K. Crawford. Newsweek 65:32 Ja 25 '65
Party re-alignment? Commonweal 81:315 N 27 '64
Party revolution. R. Moley. Newsweek 64:92 Jl 13 '64
Party's nine lives. R. Moley. Newsweek 64: 106 N 30 '64
Peek but don't peak. Newsweek 62:33-4 N 25 '63
Pen pal for Dean. Time 85:17 Ja 8 '65
Picture of the Republican party; address, July 15, 1964. D. D. Eisenhower. Vital Speeches 30:645-7 Ag 15 '64
Platform problem. K. Crawford. Newsweek 64:26 Jl 6 '64
Plight of the moderates. Nation 198:641 Je 29 '64
Political lemming. K. Crawford. Newsweek 63:39 My 18 '64
Political parties plan new strategies. il Nations Bsns 51:40-1+ D '63
Program of faith; address, July 13, 1964. M. O. Hatfield. Vital Speeches 30:652-4 Ag 15 '64
Pull of the right. J. O'Gara. Commonweal 81:410 D 18 '64
Putsch in the GOP. D. Bess. il Nation 198: 474-7 My 11 '64
Question now: Johnson vs. which Republican? il U S News 55:32-3 D 23 '63
Rampant right invades the GOP. T. G. Harris. il Look 27:19-25 Jl 16 '63
Realignment of parties? W. Lippmann. Newsweek 64:15 Jl 20 '64
Rebuilding from the ground up; with editorial comment. Bsns W p32, 200 N 14 '64
Rebuilding the G.O.P. Reporter 31:10 D 17 '64
Rebuilding the G.O.P. Sat Eve Post 237:76 N 28 '64
Recovering from Barry. W. D. Burnham. il Commonweal 81:319-22 N 27 '64
Republican agony. W. Lippmann. Newsweek 63:19 Je 22 '64
Republican campaign strategy. W. D. Burnham. Commonweal 80:287-90 My 29 '64; Reply. J. Russell. 80:452 Jl 3 '64
Republican choice: where Eisenhower stands; summary of interview. D. D. Eisenhower. U S News 56:20 Je 22 '64
Republican coalition; excerpts from address. W. Scranton. il Time 83:25 My 1 '64
Republican feud spreads to Congress. U S News 57:33 D 28 '64
Republican looks at extremism. D. R. Maxey. il Look 29:24-7 Ja 26 '65
Republican moderates. W. Lippmann. Newsweek 64:29 O 12 '64
Republican party and the conservative movement; symposium. Nat R 16:1053-6+ D 1 '64
Republican party has no future. R. H. Marz. New Repub 151:10-11 D 19 '64
Republican plan for fighting poverty. U S News 56:10 Mr 9 '64
Republican rupture; Wisconsin presidential primary. New Repub 150:4 Ap 18 '64
Republican search. E. J. Hughes. Newsweek 63:13 Ja 27 '64
Republican South. K. Crawford. Newsweek 64:42 N 16 '64
Republican success. W. Lippmann. Newsweek 63:13 Mr 30 '64
Republicans. See issues of Time during presidential campaign
Republicans and the empty track. E. T. Folliard. America 109:36 Jl 13 '63
Republicans and the South. Sat Eve Post 236:68 F 2 '63
Republicans: convention preview? il Newsweek 62:25 Jl 15 '63
Republicans: how they're running. il Time 82:24 O 25 '63
Republicans take a brand-new look at the candidates. il U S News 55:65-7 D 9 '63
Republicans take another look at Governor Scranton. U S News 55:82 D 16 '63
Revised conclusion of James Reston. P. R. Bushnell. il Nat R 14:449-50+ Je 4 '63
Road back for the G.O.P. J. K. Javits. il N Y Times Mag p28-9+ N 15 '64
Rockefeller and the GOP. W. Lippmann. Newsweek 61:15 Ap 1 '63
Root of the Republican disaster W. Lippmann. Newsweek 64:31 N 23 '64
Runaway Republicans. M. Ascoli. Reporter 31:26-7 Ag 13 '64
Russian diplomat's question; Goldwater movement. S. Alsop. Sat Eve Post 237:16 O 17 '64
Salvaging of Republicanism. E. J. Hughes. Newsweek 64:21 N 2 '64
Schizophrenia in the G.O.P. W. D. Burnham. il Commonweal 79:5-10 S 27 '63
Scranton's move. H. Brandon. Sat R 47:7-8 Jl 4 '64
Senator Goldwater and the backbiters. W. F. Buckley, jr. Nat R 17:16+ Ja 12 '65
Senators who are balking at Goldwater. il U S News 57:12 Ag 3 '64
Signs that point to '64. il U S News 55:48 N 4 '63
Six vs. LBJ: latest on the Republican scramble. il U S News 56:57-8 Ja 13 '64
Slugfest in California. W. F. Buckley, jr. Nat R 16:394 My 19 '64
Southern republicanism. R. Moley. Newsweek 61:108 My 27 '63
Spawning season for G.O.P. delegates. Life 56:4 My 8 '64
Speaking out; G.O.P. for white men only? J. Robinson. Sat Eve Post 236:10+ Ag 10 '63
Speaking out: G.O.P. invades the South. B. Goldwater. Sat Eve Post 236:10+ Ap 13 '63
Special duty for Republicans. J. V. Lindsay. Harper 227:94-5+ S '63; Reply. J. Goodspeed. 227:12+ N '63
Stop the press! young Republicans and journalism. Reporter 31:22 Ag 13 '64
Stronger role for Republican governors? U S News 57:11 D 14 '64
Suicide notes. K. Crawford. Newsweek 61: 34 Ap '63
Suite 3505. W. A. Rusher. Nat R 16:683-6 Ag 11 '64
T.R.B. from Washington; GOP and civil rights. New Repub 151:2 Jl 4 '64
Team that put Goldwater over. il U S News 57:15 Jl 27 '64

REPUBLICAN party—*Continued*

There was plenty of give and take; Goldwater's Republican unity conference. il Newsweek 64:19-20 Ag 24 '64

This president thing. il Time 81:26-31 Je 14 '63

Thruston Morton, the all-purpose Republican. R. L. Riggs. New Repub 150:8-10 Je 27 '64

Time to hear from Goldwater; summary of statement. N. A. Rockefeller. Life 55:4 Jl 26 '63

Together again: meeting of National committee. Newsweek 65:20-1 F 1 '65

Toward a broad view; meeting of the Republican governors' association. il Time 84:35 D 11 '64

Toward the target. il Newsweek 62:36+ O 21 '63

Two big fights start shaping up. R. Ajemian. Life 56:22 Mr 27 '64

Two indispensable men. R. Moley. Newsweek 61:96 F 11 '63

Varieties of disaster. Commonweal 80:384-5 Je 19 '64

Vive la différence? Nat R 15:50 Jl 30 '63

Voting system adds to election uncertainty. F. Morley. il Nations Bsns 52:27-8 S '64

War party. Nation 196:189-90 Mr 9 '63

What about Republicans? Keating takes another look; summary of interview. K. B. Keating. U S News 57:20 D 7 '64

What can save the G.O.P? G. R. Ford. il Fortune 71:140-1+ Ja '65

What hope for maintaining a conservative opposition? J. Dos Passos. Nat R 16:907-9 O 20 '64

What is liberal Republicanism? A. Larson. Sat R 47:14-17 F 29 '64

What it means; party revolution. R. Moley. Newsweek 64:84 Jl 27 '64

What mom wrought; L. Crane's television discussion program. W. F. Buckley, jr. Nat R 16:715 Ag 25 '64

What New Hampshire said. Nat R 16:218-21 Mr 24 '64

What next for conservatism? F. S. Meyer. Nat R 16:1057 D 1 '64

What price peace? il Newsweek 64:30 Ag 17 '64

What the defeated party can do. D. Lawrence. U S News 57:132 N 9 '64

What the GOP is doing in the South. V. Dabney. Harper 226:86-8+ My '63

What's ahead for the G.O.P? E. Mazo. il Sat Eve Post 263:36 D 14 '63

When leaders meet: Republicans size up their candidates. il U S News 56:76 Ja 20 '64

When Republicans take a closer look at election returns; with statements by leaders on future of party. U S News 57:41-2 N 23 '64

Whither the Republicans? R. Evans, jr. Reporter 28:32-4 F 28 '63

Who'll run against Kennedy in '64; survey of Republicans: governors, national committee, state chairmen. il U S News 54:53-8 My 20 '63

Who's ahead now in Republican race. il U S News 56:38-43 Ap 6 '64

Whose Republican party? C. Joyner. New Repub 150:10-11 Je 13 '64

Why Goldwater is gaining ground. il U S News 56:31-3 Ap 27 '64

Why G.O.P. should choose Scranton. Life 57:4 Jl 3 '64

Why I am a Republican. D. D. Eisenhower. Sat Eve Post 237:17-19 Ap 11 '64; Same abr. with title Policies I believe will strengthen this country. Read Digest 85:102-8 Jl '64

Why not me-tooism? K. Crawford. Newsweek 62:20 D 30 '63

Why Republicans chose Ray Bliss. il U S News 58:22 Ja 25 '65

Will it be Goldwater, Rockefeller, or—? poll of Republican leaders in fifty states. il U S News 55:46-8 O 7 '63

Will Republicans face the challenge? il Ebony 20:80-1 Ja '65

Will '64 election be a surprise? il U S News 54:42-4 Mr 11'63

Will the G.O.P. commit suicide? Sat Eve Post 237:90 Je 27 '64

Winning side, by R. De Toledano. Review Nat R 15:570 D 31 '63. J. G. Tower

Without portfolio. C. B. Luce. il McCalls 91:16+ Ag '64

Wraps are off: Rockefeller vs Goldwater. il Newsweek 62:41 Jl 29 '63

Young GOP in old Dixie. R. Moley. Newsweek 61:108 My 20 '63

See also

National conventions, Republican

Platforms, Political

Anecdotes, facetiae, satire, etc.

Tears for the grand old party. C. B. Luce. il Nat R 16:529-30+ Je 30 '64

History

GOP; liberal origins and the future. A. Larson. Nation 198:236-9 Mr 9 '64

Growth of the Republican party. W. H. Harbaugh. bibliog f Cur Hist 47:199-204+ O '64

REPUBLICS

How a Republic dies. R. Moley. Newsweek 62:80 Ag 26 '63

REQUIEMS

Day of the premiere; Verdi Requiem. F. Stevenson. il Opera N 28:13-16 Mr 28 '64

Dvorak revived; Musica aeterna's Requiem. C. J. McNaspy. America 110:351-2 Mr 14 '64

Messa da requiem. il Opera N 28:17-20 Mr 28 '64

Music to my ears; Dvorak's Requiem revived. I. Kolodin. Sat R 47:113 Mr 14 '64

Musical events: Berlioz's Requiem, performed by Philadelphia orchestra with Temple university choirs. W. Sargeant. New Yorker 40:98-100 Ap 11 '64

Musical events; Dvořák's Requiem mass performed by Musica aeterna; conducted by F. Waldman. W. Sargeant. New Yorker 40:171-3 Mr 7 '64

Sacred opera; Requiem mass. J. W. Freeman. il Opera N 28:24-6 Mr 28 '64

Splendidly untidy; Mozart's requiem at memorial mass for the late President Kennedy. C. J. McNaspy. America 110:174+ F 1 '64

See also

Phonograph records—Requiems

RERUM novarum. See Encyclicals

RESALE price fixing. See Price maintenance by industry

RESCUE at sea. See Survival (after airplane accidents, shipwrecks, etc)

RESCUE beacons. See Beacons

RESCUE; story. See Updike, J.

RESCUE trucks. See Fire apparatus, Motor

RESCUE work

Drama at the end of a rope; pulling a submerged automobile with an elderly couple to safety from River Dee, Scotland. il Life 55:97-100 O 18 '63

Lifesaving with a realistic touch. F. A. Lindeburg and F. D. Lewis. il Recreation 57:134-5 Mr '64

Snow convoy! New York state thruway. E. D. Fales, jr. il Pop Sci 184:69-74+ F '64

They find lost men; Search and rescue unit. B. East. il Outdoor Life 133:33-5+ Je '64

See also

Airplanes in rescue work

Animals—Protection

Helicopters in rescue work

Mine rescue work

Radio in rescue work

Space rescue work

Survival (after airplane accidents, shipwrecks, etc)

United States—Air force—Air rescue service

United States—Coast guard

RESEARCH

Broader outlook for research; letter. G. Nadler. Science 141:763 Ag 30 '63

Changing environment of science; adaptation of address, December 28, 1964. A. T. Waterman. Science 147:13-18 Ja 1 '65

Comparative failure in science. B. G. Glaser. bibliog Science 143:1012-14 Mr 6 '64

Future of research. Nation 197:311-12 N 16 '63

Grantitis. C. J. Flora; reply. J. Bennett. Science 139:1235 Mr 22 '63

Homo sapiens, that strange paradox; scientific research. D. Bovet. il UNESCO Courier 16:56-7 Jl '63

Into the world of the future. N. Semenov. il UNESCO Courier 16:58-63 Jl '63

Neglected scientific areas. W. Davis. Sci N L 85:19 Ja 11 '64

1963-1964 science review. Sci N L 84:389-94; 86:389-96 D 21 '63, D 19 '64

Nonprevalence of humanoids: excerpts from This view of life. G. G. Simpson. bibliog Science 143:769-75 F 21 '64; Discussion. 144: 245-6, 613-16, 954; 145:231 Ap 17, My 8, 22, Jl 17 '64

Peter J. W. Debye: an interview; March 5, 1964; ed. by D. R. Corson and others. P. J. W. Debye. il Science 145:554-9 Ag 7 '64

Profiles; center of a new world. C. Rand. il New Yorker 40:43-8+ Ap 11; 57-8+ Ap 18; 55-6+ Ap 25 '64

Research frontier. See issues of Saturday review

RESEARCH—*Continued*

Research gap; research and development spending in western Europe. Time 82:103-4 N 1 '63
Responsible scientific choice. P. H. Abelson. Science 141:999 S 13 '63; Discussion. 142: 914; 143:308, 429-30 N 15 '63, Ja 24-31 '64
Roots of scientific integrity. P. H. Abelson. Science 139:1257 Mr 29 '63
Science advances in 1963-1964. Sci N L 84: 387-8; 86:387-8 D 21 '63, D 19 '64
Science in the news. Sci Digest 53:91-5 Je '63
Science news & views. E. Mott. Sci Digest 53:12-15 F; 24-6 Mr '63
Scientific method; excerpt from Scientist. H. Margenau and D. Bergamini. il Fortune 70:100+ D '64
Serendipity in research. P. H. Abelson. Science 140:1177 Je 14 '63; Discussion. 141:862; 142:621; 143:196 S 6, N 8 '63; Ja 17 '64
Strong inference; address, September 1963. J. R. Platt. bibliog Science 146:347-53 O 16 '64; Discussion. 146:1635-6 D 25 '64
Tomorrow's pioneers. F. L. Phelps. il Américas 15:20-8 F '63
What are we looking for? P. A. Richmond. bibliog Science 139:737-9 F 22 '63
What it means to be a scientist; excerpts from address, May 5, 1964. G. T. Seaborg. Sci N L 85:314-15+ My 16 '64
World science will create; excerpt from Space: its impact on man and society, ed. by L. Levy. J. P. Stapp. il Nations Bsns 53:58-63 Ja '65

See also

Colleges and universities—Research
Communication in education
Communication in science
Documentation
Libraries and research
Physics—Research
Seminars

also Astronomical research; Industrial research; and similar headings

Anecdotes, facetiae, satire, etc.

Chaos in the brickyard; letter. B. K. Forscher. Science 142:339 O 18 '63
1965: herewith, a conversation with the mythical Grant Swinger, head of Breakthrough institute. D. S. Greenberg. Science 147:29-30 Ja 1 '65

Cost

Diller, a dollar, a very expensive scholar. J. Barzun. il Horizon 5:60-3 S '63
R&D, industry's maverick. S. Nicholson. il Duns R 81:63-4+ Ap '63
Stop! federal expenditures for science. il Newsweek 62:102 O 21 '63
Where billions for research go; with excerpts from address by M. Price. il U S News 55:72-4 N 25 '63

Economic aspects

Change ahead for labs. il Bsns W p92+ Ap 4 '64
Down-to-earth results of rocket research. Changing T 17:6 N '63
Foreign grants: U.S. reducing, but not ending, support program for research activities abroad. D. S. Greenberg. Science 145: 1160-1 S 11 '64
Foreign research: NIH, Defense, carrying out reductions of aid for work in laboratories abroad. D. S. Greenberg. Science 143:1017-18 Mr 6 '64
Global budgeting for science. J. Lear. Sat R 46:28 N 23 '63; Discussion. 47:95-6 Ja 4 '64
Morality in science: report on a crisis. J. Lear. il Sat R 46:49-54 Mr 2 '63; Discussion. 46:51-2 My 4; 37-8 Je 1; 46 Ag 3 '63
New versus the classical in science. E. Mayr. Science 141:765 Ag 30 '63; Reply. E. D. Hanson. 142:623 N 8 '63
Scientific complex: proceed with caution. J. F. Mahar and D. C. Coddington. il Harvard Bsns R 43:140-8+ Ja '65
Sensible shopping in the supermarket of science. P. M. S. Blackett. il UNESCO Courier 16:30-1 Jl '63
Technicians, equipment, and originality. I. H. Page. Science 140:451 My 3 '63

Federal aid

Aiming at the market instead of the moon. il Time 81:83 Je 21 '63
Astronomy: academy study urges ten-year, $224 million program of new telescope construction. D. S. Greenberg. Science 146: 899-900 N 13 '64
Basement science: what happens when a do-it-yourself scientist looks to Washington for support. D. S. Greenberg. Science 146: 621-3 O 30 '64; Discussion. 146:1251-2; 147. 109-10 D 4 '64, Ja 8 '65
Big picture: House committee hears views on basic problems of science-government relations. D. S. Greenberg. Science 142: 650-3 N 8 '63
Budget: $14.9 billion asked for research in fiscal 1964. J. Walsh. Science 139:394-5 F 1 '63
Budget: requests for R&D funds edge above $15 billion mark for a fiscal year of austerity. J. Walsh. il Science 143:337-8 Ja 24 '64
By 1970, a $20-billion plateau? government R&D spending. il Bsns W p64-6 Jl 25 '64
Career awards: no more new ones will be made under NIH program. J. Walsh. Science 146:1662 D 25 '64
Chemistry in the universities. P. H. Abelson. Science 144:251 Ap 17 '64; Reply. A. V. Grosse. 144:797 My 15 '64
Congress and research. P. H. Abelson. Science 139:305 Ja 25 '63
Congress and science: inquiries into R&D are currently quiet. D. S. Greenberg. Science 143:661-2 F 14 '64
Congress: new study shows federal education budget of $2.2 billion, $613 million of it for research. J. Walsh. Science 141:29-31 Jl 5 '63
Congress plans investigation of government-funded research. H. M. David. Miss & Roc 13:15 Ag 19 '63
Congressional rein on R&D defended. C. D. LaFond. Miss & Roc 15:18 S 21 '64
Crisis in research. J. R. Killian, jr. Atlan 211:69-72 Mr '63
Daddario unit seeking proper level of R&D aid; interview, ed. by H. M. David. E. Q. Daddario. Miss & Roc 15:26 Ag 10 '64
Demler warns of tight controls on R&D; with editorial comment. Miss & Roc 14:14, 46 Mr 23 '64
DOD may ease R&D cost-sharing rules. P. J. Klass. Aviation W 81:17 D 28 '64
Distribution of federal research funds. P. H. Abelson. Science 144:491 My 1 '64
Distribution of research funds. P. H. Abelson. Science 142:453 O 25 '63; Discussion. 142:1420+ D 13 '63
Elliott committee: basic research fares well as House group hears 38 on federal support of science. D. S. Greenberg. Science 142:1443-4 D 13 '63
Elliott committee: final reports issued as fifteen-month investigation of federal research comes to end. D. S. Greenberg. Science 147:131-2 Ja 8 '65
Elliott committee: first report should quell fears that inquiry has anti-scientific orientation. D. S. Greenberg. Science 143:791 F 21 '64
Federal expenditures and the quality of education; excerpts from address, March 21, 1963. H. Orlans. bibliog Science 142:1625-9 D 27 '63
Federal grants and small institutions; letter. H. R. Albrecht. Science 143:306 Ja 24 '64; Reply. P. E. Cloud, jr. 143:1121 Mr 13 '64
Federal R&D: Congress continues to boost budget, but increases are on last year's reduced scale. J. Walsh. Science 146:623-4 O 30 '64
Federal support of basic research. P. H. Abelson. Science 143:1397 Mr 27 '64
Federal support of science: a formula for co-operation; excerpts from Federal support of basic research in institutions of higher learning. Science 143:1300-3 Mr 20 '64; Discussion. 144:485-6 My 1 '64
Fermi prize money: congressional committee takes steps to assume control of annual $50,000 award. D. S. Greenberg. Science 143:1305 Mr 20 '64; Reply. D. O. Walter. 144:796 My 15 '64
15 per cent of budget for R&D; $6.1 billion budget for space research. W. Davis. Sci N L 83:67 F 2 '63
Foreign research: U.S. agencies take steps to limit their support for programs carried out abroad. D. S. Greenberg. Science 141: 138 Jl 12 '63
Geographic distribution of R&D funds. D. Wolfle. Science 147:361 Ja 22 '65
Goldwater: an effort to evaluate the effects that his election might have on scientific activity. D. S. Greenberg. Science 145:685-7 Ag 14 '64; Discussion. 146:171+ O 9 '64
Government and university research. J. L. Doob. Bul Atomic Sci 20:33 Ap '64

RESEARCH—Federal aid—*Continued*
Government research grants; effect of the new procedures on the individual investigator; letter. B. Commoner. Science 140:1048+ Je 7 '63
Graduate education: navy program in rocket astronomy opens new horizons to university scientists. J. Walsh. il Science 141:788-90 Ag 30 '63
Grant system: Elliott committee finds flaws, diversity in study of practices of federal agencies. D. S. Greenberg. il Science 145:795-8 Ag 21 '64
High-energy physics: budget cuts by House committees contrast with easing of funds for other fields. D. S. Greenberg. Science 144:1432-3 Je 19 '64
High-energy physics: major fight brewing as midwestern legislators take stand on MURA accelerator. D. S. Greenberg. Science 142:208-10 O 11 '63
House panel to begin scrutiny of government-funded basic research. H. M. David. il Miss & Roc 15:14 S 28 '64
House R&D subcommittee told federal funding reaching peak. H. M. David. Miss & Roc 13:18 O 21 '63
House unit outlines areas in R&D probe. Aviation W 80:71 Mr 9 '64
Indirect costs: Congress moves toward fixing a 20-percent ceiling on research overhead. J. Walsh. Science 142:211-12 O 11 '63
Information explosion, real or imaginary? national system of handling scientific and technical information. J. C. Green. Science 144:646-8 My 8 '64
Investigation: House unanimously approves comprehensive inquiry into federal support of research. D. S. Greenberg. il Science 141:1161-4 S 20 '63
Investigation: mixed motivations led to House decision to probe government support for research; with editorial comment. D. S. Greenberg. Science 141:1245, 1261-4 S 27 '63
Justifying basic research. P. E. Klopsteg. Science 147:11 Ja 1 '65
LBJ and science: policies marked by continuity, but a few events suggest developments for future. D. S. Greenberg. Science 143:939-40 F 28 '64
Midwest: new arrangement for Argonne holds promise of greater federal financial aid for region. D. S. Greenberg. Science 146:749-51 N 6 '64
MURA accelerator: compromise for the Mid-West. D. S. Greenberg. bibliog Science 143: 450-2 Ja 31 '64; Reply. D. W. Kerst 143: 1274 Mr 20 '64
Mixed band of sponsors propose investigation of federal research. J. Walsh. Science 141: 702-3 Ag 23 '63
Money, accounting, and research talent; letter. W. H. Brattain. Science 145:536 Ag 7 '64
Money for science: NAS studies likely to have large influence on future of government support; with editorial comment. D. S. Greenberg. Science 146:475, 508-9 O 23 '64
Moondoggle: letter. J. E. McDonald. Science 144:1086 My 29 '64; Reply. S. Garb. 145:109 Jl 10 '64
More defense, space R&D fallout sought. K. Johnsen. Aviation W 78:103+ Ap 22 '63
More for basic research. Sci N L 85:199 Mr 28 '64
Mutual irritations. Sci Am 210:58-9 My '64
National chamber fears federal research role. Sci N L 87:52 Ja 23 '65
NIH: moratorium on career awards for researchers called for blend of budgetary and policy reasons. J. Walsh. Science 145:1283-4 S 18 '64
Nationalization of U.S. science. S. Klaw. il Fortune 70:158-60+ S '64
New goal for U.S. research? Bsns W p28 O 26 '63
New overseers for federal science. J. Walsh. Science 142:210 O 11 '63
New regulations pertaining to research grants of the Public health service; letter. A. D. Welch. Science 141:1099-100+ S 13 '63
Patent rights under federal R&D contracts. il Harvard Bsns R 41:6-7+ S '63
Patents: industry, universities renew debate on who gets rights to U.S.-sponsored medical research. E. Langer. Science 147:134-5 Ja 8 '65
Pentagon and campus; the sullen marriage. W. Marx. il Nation 198:499-501 My 18 '64
Political good fortune of medical research. M. Veorst. il Science 144:267-70 Ap 17 '64
Politics and technology. E. T. Chase. Yale R 52:321-39 Mr '63
Politics: Johnson and Goldwater scientist groups show differing views on civilian technology. D. S. Greenberg. Science 146: 509+ O 23 '64
Post-Sputnik: relations between science, government now passing into more settled, mature stage. D. S. Greenberg. Science 145: 1281-3 S 18 '64
President Kennedy on science; excerpts from address, October 22, 1963. J. F. Kennedy. Science 142:1129 N 29 '63
Primary scientific publication and the federal government. B. W. Adkinson. bibliog Science 140:613-17 My 10 '63
Prime contractors retain R&D money. Bsns W p80 O 31 '64
Prodigious inventory-taking. P. H. Abelson. Science 143:1127 Mr 13 '64
R&D, and the relations of science and government; statement before a congressional subcommittee; with editorial comment. P. M. Gross. Science 142:625, 645-50 N 8 '63
R&D funds requested. A. Ewing. Sci N L 85:71 F 1 '64
Research: as the stakes go up, idea of a man in Washington considered by more universities. J. Walsh. Science 142:1043-5 N 22 '63
Research comes first; excerpt from address. D. F. Hornig. Sci N L 86:226 O 10 '64
Research competition: as budgetary pressures grow, Congress reveals concern about scientific choices. D. S. Greenberg. il Science 143:1149-51 Mr 13 '64
Research for building: the big battle rages in Washington. B. P. Spring. il Arch Forum 119:122-3+ S '63
Research grants, are they worth saving? letter on recommendations of the Committee on sponsored research of the American council on education. J. W. Mehl. Science 142:914-16 N 15 '63
Risks and returns of R&D spending. il Newsweek 62:68 S 2 '63
Science and federal programs: the continuing dialogue; adapted from address, April 28, 1964. J. A. Shannon. Science 144:976-8 My 22 '64
Science in policy, policy in science; excerpt from testimony before the House subcommittee on science, research, and development. J. B. Wiesner. Bul Atomic Sci 20:36-40 F '64
Scientific advice for Congress; excerpts from address, November 20, 1963. C. P. Anderson. Science 144:29-32 Ap 3 '64
Scientific advisers for Congress; letter. R. H. Lueck. Science 143:525 F 7 '64; Reply. R. Rossbacher. 144:363 Ap 24 '64
Scientific gloom: congressional actions have stirred pessimism but little of it is justified. D. S. Greenberg. Science 144:32-3 Ap 3 '64
Sixteen billions for science; where the money goes; interview. J. B. Wiesner. il U S News 56:72-6 F 3 '64
Slim pickings from NASA; study on Commercial applications of missile/space technology. Bsns W p55+ S 14 '63
Space science and the universities; address, May 7, 1963. F. Seitz. Science 141:614-18 Ag 16 '63
Spread of research money. Sci N L 85:254 Ap 18 '64
Sweeping probe of research spending; with editorial comment. Bsns W p26-7, 152 S 21 '63
Tightening federal budgets. D. Wolfle. Science 142:543 N 1 '63
Tobacco report: agencies ponder action; Congress takes the lead with a $5-million research plan. J. Walsh. Science 143:788-9 F 21 '64
Uncle Sam: big man on campus; government research and development spending. il Bsns W p90-2+ N 2 '63
U.S. patent policy and government research. R. L. Wright. il Bul Atomic Sci 19:9-13 D '63; Reply with rejoinder. M. A. Holman. 20:32-4 O '64
Washington: a new science trend. Sci Digest 57:28 Ja '65
Washington holds the purse; R&D funds. il Bsns W p60-1 Ja 11 '64
Washington ramble: news in brief on investigations, accelerators, anger in NSF, and other matters; with editorial comment. D. S. Greenberg. Science 142:919, 940-1 N 15 '63
When pure science meets pure politics. D. S. Greenberg. il Reporter 30:39-41 Mr 12 '64
When scientists testify. A. Etzioni. Bul Atomic Sci 20:23-6 O '64
Where the R&D dollars go. il Bsns W p54+ S 28 '63

RESEARCH—Federal aid—*Continued*
Who can do the job better? government study of national laboratories. il Bsns W p 194+ S 19 '64
Who gets the word? letter. G. E. Moore. Science 143:99 Ja 10 '64

Anecdotes, facetiae, satire, etc.

Pioneering; letter. P. L. Petrakis. Science 142:1019 N 22 '63

International aspects

See Science—International aspects

Canada

Report on Canadian science. J. H. Winchester. il Sci Digest 56:75-81 D '64
See also
National research council of Canada

Czechoslovakia

Biological research in Czechoslovakia. V. K. McElheny. il Science 145:799-802 Ag 21 '64

Europe, Western

Hot on the heels of the U.S. research and development spending. il Bsns W p92-4 N 9 '63
Research in biology: new pattern of support is developing. V. K. McElheny. Science 145:908-12 Ag 28 '64
Time of trial for European reserach cooperation. V. K. McElheny. Science 147: 280-2 Ja 15 '65

Germany (Federal Republic)

Revival of oceanography in Germany. V. K. McElheny. il Science 146:45-8 O 2 '64

Great Britain

Britain confronts its technical options. V. K. McElheny. il Science 146:1446-9 D 11 '64
U.K. concern grows over scientist exodus. H. J. Coleman. Aviation W 78:104+ Mr 25 '63

Italy

Research climate in Italy. V. K. McElheny. il Science 145:690-3 Ag 14 '64; Reply. H. B. Reisman. 145:1387 S 25 '64

Japan

Science in Japan; report on symposium at the AAAS meeting. L. Campbell. bibliog il Science 143:776-82 F 21 '64; Reply. H. B. Hamilton. 144:616 My 8 '64

Russia

No winner yet in the science race. R. E. Marshak. il N Y Times Mag p59-60+ O 11 '64
Reexamining the Soviet scientific challenge. R. E. Marshak. il Bul Atomic Sci 19:12-17 Ap '63
Russia's hidden science city. A. Parry. il Sci Digest 53:222-8 My '63
Soviet affairs. A. Parry. Miss & Roc 12:40 F 4; 46 Mr 11 '63
See also
Atomic research—Russia

United States

Basic research: capabilities of universities and other research organizations. L. C. Allen. Science 141:674 Ag 23 '63
Brain mines of tomorrow. J. H. Hollomon. Sat R 46:46-7 My 4 '63
Empiricism in latter-day behavioral science. V. E. Bixenstine. bibliog Science 145:464-7 Jl 31 '64; Reply. B. F. Skinner. 145:1385+ S 25 '64
Goose and the golden egg. W. J. Coughlin. Miss & Roc 13:46 N 18 '63
Government support of research. P. H. Abelson. Science 139:377 F 1 '63
House unit outlines areas in R&D probe. Aviation W 80:71 Mr 9 '64
How much is enough? Time 83:92 Je 12 '64
How things look in a big new U.S. industry; research and development; with chart. U S News 57:119 O 19 '64
How to survive in space business. il Bsns W p 102-4+ Ja 16 '65
Individual R&D productivity is declining; summary of address. J. H. Rubel. Aviation W 78:37 Mr 18 '63
Leisure of the theory class. M. Mayer. Esquire 59:16+ Mr '63
Man's dependence on the earthly atmosphere, ed. by K. E. Schaefer. Review
Nation 196:330-1 Ap 20 '63. C. Dreher
Mocked grants backed. W. Wingo. Sci N L 84:37 Jl 20 '63
Need free research. Sci N L 87:20 Ja 9 '65
No winner yet in the science race. R. E. Marshak. il N Y Times Mag p59-60+ O 11 '64
Real danger in fluoridated water. J. Lear. Sat R 46:77-9 D 7 '63
Reexamining the Soviet scientific challenge. R. E. Marshak. il Bul Atomic Sci 19:12-17 Ap '63
R&D and unemployment. W. A. Stocklin. Electr World 71:10 Ja '64
R&D funds requested. A. Ewing. Sci N L 85:71 F 1 '64
Research in America. J. Lear. See issues of Saturday review
Speaking out; oceans of ignorance. M. B. Schaefer. Sat Eve Post 236:8+ F 16 '63
Stop! federal expenditures for science. il Newsweek 62:102 O 21 '63
Trends in scientific research; excerpts from address, November 6, 1963. P. H. Abelson. Science 143:218-23 Ja 17 '64; Discussion. 143:1276; 144:244 Mr 20. Ap 17 '64
Vannevar Bush speaks; excerpts from statement, November 21, 1963. V. Bush. Science 142:1623 D 27 '63
View from a distant star, by H. Shapley. Review
Sci N L 84:230 O 12 '63
See also
Carnegie institution of Washington
Colleges and universities—Research
Hudson institute, incorporated
Rand corporation
Stanford research institute
United States—Scientific research and development, Office of

RESEARCH, Cooperative
Pooling drug research; Interpharm GmbH & co. il Bsns W p66-8+ O 26 '63
Time of trial for European research cooperation. V. K. McElheny. Science 147:280-2 Ja 15 '65

RESEARCH airplanes. See Airplanes, Experimental

RESEARCH associations. See Associations

RESEARCH centers. See Research laboratories

RESEARCH corporation
Corporation award goes to mathematicians. Sci N L 85:56 Ja 25 '64

RESEARCH foundations. See Foundations, Charitable and educational

RESEARCH in colleges. See Colleges and universities—Research

RESEARCH institute, Midwest. See Midwest research institute

RESEARCH institute of America, incorporated
If the machine wants our jobs, let's buy it. Life 57:4 Ag 14 '64

RESEARCH laboratories
Campus plan for a mountain-top research complex; Bethlehem steel company. il Arch Rec 134:121-5 D '63
Favorable environment for research. P. H. Abelson. Science 139:875 Mr 8 '63; Reply. W. H. Bradley. 141:232 Jl 19 '63
High mountain monastery for research; National center for atmospheric research. Boulder, Colo. il Arch Forum 120:82-5 Ja '64
Housing the creative mind. il Newsweek 61: 82-3 F 18 '63
How to remain in the laboratory though head of a department. E. C. Pollard. Science 145:1018-21 S 4 '64
Instead of an abandoned factory; Cambridge, Mass. il Am City 78:89 O '63
IBM lab taps European science skills. P. J. Klass. il Aviation W 78:76-8 Ap 8 '63
Monkey research center to cost about $2,000,000; Delta regional primate research center, Covington, La. Sci N L 84:269 O 26 '63
Need to know. W. J. Coughlin. Miss & Roc 13:46 S 2 '63
New AF/Mitre lab may alter concepts. M. Getler. il Miss & Roc 13:36-7 Jl 1 '63
New research park; Pittsburgh's Panther Hollow. il Sci N L 83:391 Je 22 '63
New think factories. il Duns R 81:pt2 S104-5 Mr '63
Scientific complex: proceed with caution. J. F. Mahar and D. C. Coddington. il Harvard Bsns R 43:140-8+ Ja '65
TAC designs new geology labs for Harvard. il Arch Rec 135:240 Ja '64
Who can do the job better? government study of national laboratories. il Bsns W p 194+ S 19 '64
See also
Atomic research laboratories
Battelle memorial institute, Columbus, Ohio
Bell telephone laboratories
Southwest research institute. San Antonio, Tex.

RESEARCH libraries
Academic and research libraries. F. H. Wagman. ALA Bul 58:533 Je '64
Credo reconsidered; excerpts from Libraries and universities. P. Buck. il Library J 89:4295-300 N 1 '64
Library of Congress: automation urged for bibliographic control but not prescribed as a panacea. J. Walsh. Science 143:452-5 Ja 31 '64
Of infinite remembrance; excerpts from address, October 18, 1963. J. D. Hart. il Library J 89:1179-83 Mr 15 '64
Unprovocative exactitude; excerpt from Future of the research library. V. W. Clapp. Library J 89:1502 Ap 1 '64
RESEARCH organizations. See Associations
RESEARCH ships. See Ships, Research
RESEARCH workers
Crisis in research. J. R. Killian, jr. Atlan 211:69-72 Mr '63
RESEARCH workers, Government. See Government employees
RESEGREGATION of schools. See Public schools—Desegregation
RESEMBLANCE, Protective. See Mimicry (biology)
RESEMBLANCES
Sweater boy; resemblance to Nikita Khrushchev. il Newsweek 62:88+ N 25 '63
RESENTMENT. See Anger
RESERPINE
Influence of methodology on electroencephalographic sleep and arousal: studies with reserpine and etryptamine in rabbits. W. G. Steiner and others. bibliog il Science 141:53-5 Jl 5 '63
Reserpine: its effect on silver-stained structures of the heart. T. Cooper and others. bibliog il Science 141:526-7 Ag 9 '63
RESERVATIONS, Indian. See Indians of North America—Reservations
RESERVE forces (United States) See United States—Armed forces—Reserves
RESERVE officers training corps. See United States—Reserve officers training corps
RESERVOIRS
About: the water we need. F. J. Cook. il N Y Times Mag p90+ N 24 '63
Home ponds create a problem for public water supplies; algae infestations. Am City 79:172 O '64
Reservoir roof supports a lake; Cincinnati. C. M. Bolton. il Am City 79:22 O '64
Store winter water for summer use; Long Branch, N.J. O. A. Newquist. il Am City 78:74-5 F '63
Two gigantic reservoirs; Springfield, Mass. P. C. Karalekas and C. A. Manganaro. il Am City 79:73-5 Jl '64
Water, water, everywhere; Newport News, Va. il Am City 79:73-4 Ja '64
Whiskeytown reservoir is ready for visitors. il Sunset 132:28+ Ap '64

Inspection

Underwater reservoir inspection. il Am City 79:34 Ja '64
RESETTLEMENT of refugees. See Refugees—Resettlement
RESIDENCE halls. See Dormitories
RESIDENTIAL hotels. See Apartment hotels
RESIDENTIAL zoning. See Zoning
RESINOUS materials
Carbonate rocks: cleaning with suspensions of hydrogen-ion exchange resin. S. F. Percival, jr. and others. il Science 142:1456 D 13 '63
RESINOUS products
Resin-testing methods pose standards problem; epoxy resins for filament winding. il Miss & Roc 13:34-5 Ag 12 '63
RESINS. See Gums and resins
RESISTANCE, Electric. See Electric resistance
RESISTANCE to disease. See Immunity
RESISTANCE to disease in plants. See Plants—Disease and pest resistance
RESISTANCE to government. See Government, Resistance to; Passive resistance to government
RESISTANCE to Negro segregation. See Negroes in the United States—Segregation, Resistance to
RESISTORS, Electric. See Electric resistors
RESLER, E. L. jr. See Bauer, S. H. jt. auth.
RESNICK, Linda E. and Jameson, D. L.
Color polymorphism in Pacific tree frogs. bibliog Science 142:1081-3 N 22 '63
RESNIK, Muriel
Any Wednesday. Criticism
America 110:466 Mr 28 '64
America 110:552 Ap 18 '64
Look il por 28:100-4 Je 16 '64
New Yorker 40:106 F 29 '64
Newsweek 63:56 Mr 2 '64
Sat Eve Post il 237:83-7 Ap 25 '64
Sat R 47:23 Mr 7 '64
Time il 83:61 F 28 '64
RESNIK, Regina
Necessary evil. Opera N 28:8-12 Mr 28 '64
Quote: unquote; interview, ed. by R. Jacobson. por Mus Am 84:32 Ap '64

about

Musical events; concert performance of R. Strauss's Elektra with the New York philharmonic. W. Sargeant. New Yorker 40:163 D 19 '64
RESONANCE
Low Q resonance. J. Tusinski. il Electr World 72:90-1 N '64
60-cycle repulsion coil-resonance engine. W. B. Ford. il Pop Electr 20:41-5+ Mr '64
RESONANCE, Magnetic. See Magnetic resonance
RESONANCE, Nuclear magnetic. See Nuclear magnetic resonance
RESORT hotels. See Hotels, taverns, etc; Summer resorts
RESORTS. See Health resorts, watering places, etc; Summer resorts; Winter resorts
RESOURCE centers. See High school libraries
RESOURCES, Conservation of. See Conservation of resources
RESOURCES, Natural. See Natural resources
RESOURCES for the future, incorporated
Plenty of resources if we use them right; report with charts. Bsns W p84-6 Ap 6 '63
RFF resources forecast shows qualified optimism; with charts. J. B. Craig. Am For 69:16-19+ My '63
Resources for 300 million; summary of report. W. Davis. Sci N L 83:227 Ap 13 '63
RESPECT
Is disrespect inevitable? with study-discussion program, by E. M. Duvall. R. M. Butler. bibliog il PTA Mag 57:24-6, 36 Mr '63
RESPECT; story. See Slate, J.
RESPIRATION
Breath-holding spells lower oxygen in blood. Sci N L 84:9 Jl 6 '63
Clearance of bacteria by the lower respiratory tract. G. A. Laurenzi and others. bibliog il Science 142:1572-3 D 20 '63
Cold bath for baby; chilling for the newborn. Time 84:53 D 25 '64
First breath. C. A. Smith. il Sci Am 209:27-35 O '63
Life-giving balancing act. R. Campbell. il Life 55:70-1 N 8 '63
Master switch of life. P. F. Scholander. il Sci Am 209:92-6+ bibliog(p 178) D '63
Methanol in normal human breath. S. P. Eriksen and A. B. Kulkarni. bibliog il Science 141:639-40 Ag 16 '63
Revolution in breathing: under water. W. Cloud. Pop Sci 182:29 Ap '63
Water-breathing rodents. Sci Am 208:83-4 Ap '63
RESPIRATION, Artificial
How to save a life. il Sci Digest 54:79-80 S '63
Life or death: demonstration mouth-to-mouth breathing. il Pop Sci 183:91-3 O '63
New fight against sudden death: mouth-to-mouth breathing, heart massage. A. Cutler. il Look 28:44-6+ D 1 '64
New life-saving method: mouth-to-mouth resuscitation and external heart massage. D. W. Larson. il Outdoor Life 132:48-9+ Ag '63
Teens revive strangling brother; mouth-to-mouth method, learn it now! il Todays Health 42:82 F '64
RESPIRATION gasmeter. See Respiratory apparatus
RESPIRATION of plants. See Plants—Respiration
RESPIRATORY apparatus
Chemical drift stopped by mask. B. C. Kilvert, jr. il Flower Grower 50:61 Ag '63
Gills for a hamster. il Life 57:55-6 N 6 '64
Now, human gills. il Sci Digest 56:10-11 D '64
Take it how easy? il Time 83:52 Ja 31 '64

RESPIRATORY organs

Diseases

Clearance of bacteria by the lower respiratory tract. G. A. Laurenzi and others. bibliog il Science 142:1572-3 D 20 '63
Deadly membrane; treatment for hyaline membrane disease. Time 84:68 O 30 '64
Infant's cause of death: hyaline membrane disease; case of Patrick Bouvier Kennedy. il Time 82:33 Ag 16 '63
Respiratory distress: relation to prematurity and other factors in newborn monkeys. W. F. Windle. bibliog il Science 143:1345-6 Mr 20 '64
Whys of caesareans; Patrick Bouvier Kennedy's death. il Newsweek 62:50+ Ag 19 '63

See also
Asthma
Bronchitis
Cold (disease)
Rhinitis
Tuberculosis

RESPIROMETERS
Differential respirometer of simplified and improved design. W. E. Gilson. il Science 141:531-2 Ag 9 '63

RESPONSES to stimuli. See Stimulus and response

RESPONSIBILITY
Am I my brother's keeper? man's inhumanity to man. Sat Eve Post 237:90 My 9 '64
Am I my brother's keeper? symposium. il Seventeen 23:102-5+ D '64
Better way to choose a president. D. Lawrence. U S News 54:120 Ap 8 '63
Chance for everyone to grow. V. Packard. Read Digest 83:114-18 N '63
Christian morality and race issues. Life 56:4 Mr 27 '64
Collective guilt in the U.S? take a look at the world; with excerpts from address by T. B. Morton. il U S News 55:72-4 D 23 '63
Commonwealth of human responsibility; address, June 15, 1964. W. W. Wirtz. Vital Speeches 30:610-12 Ag 1 '64
Documents of the struggle for public decency. E. Capouya. Sat R 47:13+ Jl 25 '64
Don't just stand there! J. Lyons. Parents Mag 39:32+ D '64
Double-purpose plan; social responsibility and self-realization. L. S. Vander Werf. Sch & Soc 91:213-14 My 4 '63
Education for responsible freedom. R. H. Wyatt. NEA J 52:41 S '63
Education for world responsibility. L. V. Edinger. NEA J 53:23 S '64
Efficacy of martyrdom. Nation 197:310-11 N 16 '63
Eichmann in Jerusalem, by H. Arendt. Review
New Repub 148:23-33 Je 15 '63. B. Bettelheim; Discussion. 148:29-31 Je 29; 149: 28-30 Jl 20 '63
Freedom's time of testing. W. Reuther. il Sat R 47:36+ Ag 29 '64
Frontier of service; address, June 8, 1964. R. S. Shriver. America 111:14-16 Jl 4 '64
Genie and the dinosaur; absence of an informed and active public opinion. N. Cousins. Sat R 46:22 My 25 '63
Great morality. D. Lawrence. U S News 57: 100 D 21 '64
How to handle a bigger job. H. R. Dressner. il Nations Bsns 51:68-71 Ag '63
Irresponsibles. Reporter 29:12 D 19 '63
Is business socially responsible? J. W. Clark. America 110:250-2 F 22 '64
Let's dare to be square. C. H. Brower. Read Digest 82:49-51 Ap '63
Man-computer relationship. D. L. Johnson and A. L. Kobler; discussion. Science 139: 1231-2+ Mr 22 '63
Memo about a Dallas citizen. T. G. Harris. il Look 28:64+ Ag 11 '64
Murder they heard; Kew Gardens incident. S. Milgram and P. Hollander. il Nation 198:602-4 Je 15 '64
No time for collective guilt; reprint. V. Royster. U S News 55:72 D 9 '63
Not getting involved. il Time 83:72+ My 15 '64
Pause of conscience. D. Lawrence. U S News 58:116 Ja 25 '65
Personal accountability. Duns R 83:37 Ja '64
Politics without malice; panel discussion, ed. by M. Hickey. il Ladies Home J 81:80+ Ap '64
Postscript on The deputy. R. M. Brown. Commonweal 80:174-6 My 1 '64
Power of one. M. E. Jenkins. PTA Mag 58:2-3 Ap '64
Priorities of the future; address. A. E. Summerfield. Vital Speeches 29:334-6 Mr 15 '63
Privatist ethic and self-fulfillment. H. Stroup. Christian Cent 81:1031-3 Ag 19 '64; Reply. W. D. Bonis. 81:1365-6+ N 4 '64
Responsibilities of the educated man; address, April 9, 1964. G. Kirk. Vital Speeches 30:471-4 My 15 '64
Responsibility: an escape and an approach. W. E. Olson. Bul Atomic Sci 19:2-6 Mr '63 '63; Discussion. 19:29-30 Je '63
Responsible individualism. D. Lawrence. U S News 57:128 O 12 '64
Return of the native. N. Cousins. Sat R 47: 14 Jl 4 '64
Saying I'm sorry is not enough. R. W. Bacmeister. il Parents Mag 38:60-1+ Mr '63
Squares America needs; reprint. C. H. Brower. il U S News 56:70-2 Ap 6 '64
Study of the sickness called apathy; concerning Catherine Genovese's murder. A. M. Rosenthal. il N Y Times Mag p24+ My 3 '64
Violence around us; excerpts from But will it sell? M. Mannes. McCalls 91:74+ F '64
Way to freedom. R. O. Johann. America 109: 568 N 9 '63
We are involved. America 110:506-7 Ap 11 '64
What are your ultimate objectives? address, September 6, 1963. H. F. Harding. Vital Speeches 29:757-60 O 1 '63
When silence is a crime. L. Nizer. McCalls 92:95+ O '64
Where America is weakest; interview. A. Burke. il U S News 57:66-70 Jl 13 '64
Who cares? L. Gross. il Look 28:17-19 S 8 '64; Same abr. with title Is there a Samaritan in the neighborhood? Read Digest 85:106-10 N '64
Whose fault was it? with introd. by S. F. Teele. Harvard Bsns R 42:107-10 Ja '64
Why murder is contagious; interview. F. Wertham. McCalls 91:136+ F '64
Word. V. P. McCorry. America 111:95-6 Jl 25 '64

RESPONSIBILITY (law) See Liability (law)

RESS, Paul Evan
Artistry in a bullring is not enough. Sports Illus 21:44-7 Ag 10 '64
Fight for life by the home team. Sports Illus 20:32-9 Ja 27 '64
Golf. Sports Illus 19:58-60 O 21 '63
Motor sports. Sports Illus 19:52-3 N 11 '63; 20:48-50 F 3; 51-2 Je 29 '64
Prince Karim Aga Khan. Sports Illus 21:58-67 Ag 10 '64
Sweet explosion in the air. Sports Illus 19:16-17 Jl 8 '63

REST
Restful quiz. J. Daugherty and M. Daugherty. il Sci Digest 55:5-7 Mr '64
See also
Relaxation
Sleep

REST homes. See Nursing homes

REST periods
Plea to let sleeping men lie. M. W. Lear. il N Y Times Mag p49+ S 27 '64

RESTAURANT associates, incorporated
Profiles. G. T. Hellman. il New Yorker 40:59-60+ O 17 '64

RESTAURANT guide books. See Guidebooks

RESTAURANT workers. See Restaurants—Employees

RESTAURANTS
Home-cooked country food that sells; Dolly Martin's tearoom, Jefferson County, Wis. N. Nichols. il Farm J 88:74-5 Ap '64
Need for a sidewalk cafe society. E. Kendall. il N Y Times Mag p 12-13+ Jl 5 '64
Sidewalk cafés. New Yorker 40:30-2 Je 13 '64
Want high cuisine? place to look is up. il Newsweek 62:70-1 Jl 8 '63
See also subhead Hotels, restaurants, etc. under names of cities, e.g. New York (city)—Hotels, restaurants, etc.

Employees

Wages in eating and drinking places, June 1963. G. L. Stelluto. il Mo Labor R 87:544-8 My '64

Finance

Big beef stew; effect of expense account cuts. il Newsweek 61:72 Mr 11 '63
Expense-account fiasco; its effects. il U S News 54:39-41 Mr 11 '63
Expense-account meals: what the rules really are. il U S News 54:96+ Mr 4 '63
Prove it and you're O.K; IRS regulation of expense account expenditures. Time 81: 76 Ap 5 '63

RESTAURANTS—*Continued*

Inspection

Inspector. New Yorker 39:18-19 Ag 24 '63

Music

Discord in the discotheque; musicians protest against accompanying phonograph records. il Bsns W p 156+ My 23 '64

Australia

Dining adventures in Australia. S. Spitzer. il Holiday 36:94-5+ N '64

Europe, Western

Chicken and strudel; Wienerwald (Vienna Woods) chain of restaurants. Newsweek 63: 92 My 25 '64
Europe's fine restaurants (cont) Holiday 35: 90-3 Ja '64
Europe's finest restaurants 1965. S. Spitzer and H. Spitzer. il Holiday 37:64-9 Ja '65
Let's travel to Europe. Mlle 56:106+ Mr '63

France

Gastronomic tour of France. W. Root. il House B 105:150-1+ Mr '63
Ketchup, yet! new wave in French eating habits. il Newsweek 65:36 F 1 '65
Profiles: Mme M. L. Point; manageress of Fernand Point's Restaurant de la Pyramide, in Vienne. J. Wechsberg. New Yorker 39:63+ O 5 '63
Star boarding in the French provinces. J. Egan. Atlan 211:100+ Ap '63
Three stars on none, quelle différence! Guide Michelin to France. P. E. Schneider. il N Y Times Mag p20+ Jl 19 '64

Greece, Modern

Greece: get your ambrosia here. R. Joseph. il Esquire 61:66-7+ Je '64

United States

Better batter, lotta butter; specialized pancake palaces. Time 82:59+ Jl 26 '63
Bistros up in arms; vs IRS rules. Bsns W p29 Mr 30 '63
Dining in/out with Esquire. il Esquire 59: 46A-46D Mr '63
Dining in, out with Esquire; Ridge terrace, East Lake George, N.Y. Esquire 61:56 Je '64
Dining out in America: eighty-four fine restaurants. S. Spitzer. Holiday 33:117-20+ Je '63
Eating your way south; along the Intracoastal. H. M. Winters. il Motor B 114:30-1+ S '64
Holiday annual restaurant awards (title varies) (cont) il Holiday 34:76-7 Jl '63; 36:70-3 Jl '64
Howard Johnson's new flavor; food management program. il Bsns W p 109-10+ O 19 '63
In the bag; taking the filet home to Fido. il Time 84:53 S 4 '64
Restaurants. il Arch Rec 136:207-16 S '64
Return to elegance. H. Sutton. il Sat R 47: 36+ O 24 '64
Summer dining tips from major restaurants; with recipes. G. Maddox. il Todays Health 41:34-7+ Ag '63
Three nights in another town. il Esquire 60: 71-4 Ag '63
What the men are having for lunch! famous foods from famous places; with recipes. M. Johnston. il Bet Hom & Gard 41:72-7+ Mr '63

RESTAURANTS, Government
Victual issue. il Newsweek 61:17 F 4 '63

RESTITUTION claims
Deadline for claims on Austrian persecutee fund is October 31. Dept State Bul 49:550 O 7 '63
Department welcomes amendment to Philippine war damage act; statement, with remarks by Roger Hilsman. Dept State Bul 49:301 Ag 19 '63
Netherlands compensation program for Nazi victims broadened. Dept State Bul 49:437 S 16 '63
Netherlands compensation program for Nazi victims; press release, July 1, 1963. Dept State Bul 49:142-3 Jl 22 '63
President signs Cuban claims bill; asks study of vesting provision; statement, October 17, 1964. L. B. Johnson. Dept State Bul 51: 674-5 N 9 '64
$10-billion conscience fund; payment by West Germany for Nazi crimes against the Jews. il U S News 57:58 Ag 10 '64
Unclaimed property of victims of Nazi persecution; executive order, February 26, 1963. J. F. Kennedy. Dept State Bul 48:618 Ap 22 '63
U.S. and Bulgaria sign agreement relating to financial questions; Department announcement with texts of the agreement and accompanying letters, July 2, 1963. Dept State Bul 49:138-41 Jl 22 '63

RESTON, James
Biggest story in the world; excerpts from address. New Repub 148:15-17 My 4 '63
Man on the moon, men on the dole; reprint. Aviation W 78:21 Ap 22 '63
To publish the news and raise hell. New Repub 148:15-16 Mr 30 '63
What ever happened to the beat generation? reprint. Sr Schol 84:12T Ap 24 '64
What was killed was not only the President but the promise. N Y Times Mag p24-5+ N 15 '64
What's he like? and how will he do? N Y Times Mag p8-9+ Ja 17 '65

about

Average newspaper is not a public utility. M. Kempton. New Repub 148:16-18 Mr 30 '63
Extremism in defense of the Democratic party. C. B. Luce. Nat R 16:719-21 Ag 25 '64
Revised conclusion of James Reston. P. R. Bushnell. il Nat R 14:449-50+ Je 4 '63
Something to hoot about. por Time 81:62 F 8 '63

RESTON, Va.
Community: could this be our town? W. Von Eckardt. il New Repub 151:17-24 N 7 '64; Discussion. 151:37-8 N 28 '64
Reston; answer to suburban sprawl. il Arch Rec 136:119-34 Jl '64
What is a new town? one answer is Reston. il Fortune 70:178+ D '64

RESTORATION of books. See Books—Conservation and restoration
RESTORATION of buildings. See Architecture—Conservation and restoration
RESTORATION of documents. See Documents—Conservation and restoration
RESTORED houses. See Houses, Restored
RESTORED villages. See Villages, Restored

RESTOUT, Denise
(tr) See Landowska, W. From the Landowska notebooks

RESTRAINT of trade
See also
Boycott

RESTRICTION of labor output. See Labor productivity
RESTRICTIONS on travel. See Travel regulations
RÉSUMÉS of employment. See Applications for positions
RESURFACING of pavements. See Pavements—Surface treatment

RESURRECTION
Easter and the keys of death. Christian Cent 81:387 Mr 25 '64
See also
Jesus Christ—Resurrection and ascension

RESUSCITATION
Immortality by freezing. F. Marley. Sci N L 85:389 Je 20 '64
Life after drowning; case of Roger Arntsen of Norway. il Time 81:66 My 31 '63
Prospect of immortality, by R. C. W. Ettinger. Review
Sci Digest 56:46 Ag '64. D. Cohen
Tilting out of trouble; resuscitation of a skindiving student. Time 82:60 Ag 30 '63
See also
Cardiac resuscitation
Respiration, Artificial

RETAIL clerks international association
When pickets are used to scare away customers. il U S News 54:74-5 F 4 '63

RETAIL credit. See Credit
RETAIL inventory method. See Inventories
RETAIL prices. See Prices

RETAIL trade
Brazil hails its king of credit. il Bsns W p 134+ N 14 '64
Business outlook. Bsns W p 19-20 Je 15 '63
Business outlook; retail sales. Bsns W p 19-20 Ag 17 '63
Buyers step up the pace again. il Bsns W p25-7 Mr 23 '63
Catching up with the facts. il Fortune 68:47-8 N '63
Coming up roses. il Bsns W p23-5 Mr 14 '64
Communist merchandise. New Repub 148:6-7 Je 1 '63

RETAIL trade—*Continued*
Consumer splurges for Easter. il Bsns W p32 Ap 20 '63
Doing fine and better days ahead. il Bsns W p25-6 Ag 24 '63
Dual distribution vs. the small retailer. T. J. Murray. il Duns R 84:28-9+ Ag '64
Europe goes shopping; increasing Americanization of taste. il Bsns W p58-60+ My 18 '63
Fourteen important ratios in twelve retail lines, 1962. il Duns R 82:38-9 N '63
Franchising, new scope for an old technique. W. P. Hall. il Harvard Bsns R 42:60-72 Ja '64
Giants plan to get still bigger. il Bsns W p 100-2+ Je 6 '64
Growing strength in small retailing. A. F. Doody and W. R. Davidson. bibliog f Harvard Bsns R 42:69-79 Jl '64
How people are spending their money. il U S News 56:104-6 Ap 27 '64
Ratios of retailing; with table. Duns R 84:46-7 S '64
Retail empire reaches across the prairie; from western Wisconsin to eastern Montana. il Bsns W p70-2+ Mr 7 '64
Trading up. Newsweek 63:67 Ja 20 '64
See also
Bargain sales
Canvassing
Chain stores
Christmas business
Discount houses (retail trade)
Drug trade
GEM international, incorporated
Grocery stores
Mail order business
Sears, Roebuck and company
Shopping centers
RETAIL, wholesale and department store union
Organizing the old folks; RWDSU's retired members. B. Carter. Reporter 30:31-2 Mr 12 '64
RETAIL workers
Wages and hours
Changes in employee earnings in retail trade, June 1961-June 1962. H. Schaffer. il Mo Labor R 86:802-7 Jl '63
Earnings in retail trade, June 1961. H. Schaffer. il Mo Labor R 86:44-51 Ja '63
RETAILERS. See Merchants
RETAILERS excise tax. See Excise tax
RETAINING walls
Rim your terrace with retainers. il Pop Gard 14:44-5 N '63
Slope-holding fact sheet. il Am Home 66:101-2 My '63
Steel wall saves a road; Contra Costa County, Calif. V. W. Sauer. il Am City 78:8 N '63
Ten retaining walls to dress up your yard. W. B. Eagan. il Pop Mech 119:160-2 My '63
RETARDED children. See Children, Backward
RETENTION (psychology)
Retention in rats: the effect of proactive interference. H. Gleitman and L. Jung. bibliog il Science 142:1683-4 D 27 '63
RETHBERG, Elisabeth
Friendly voice; interview, ed. by A. M. Lingg. pors Opera N 28:10-12 F 15 '64
RETICULAR formation, Brain. See Brain
RETICULOCYTES. See Erythrocytes
RETINA
Analysis in the retina. Sci Am 212:50 Ja '65
Bilateral differences in the human occipital electroencephalogram with unilateral photic driving. N. L. Freedman. bibliog il Science 142:598-9 N 1 '63
Directional movement and horizontal edge detectors in the pigeon retina. H. R. Maturana and S. Frenk. bibliog il Science 142:977-9 N 15 '63
Elusive pigments. Sci Am 209:68+ D '63
Foveal receptors of the monkey retina: fine structure. J. E. Dowling. bibliog il Science 147:57-9 Ja 1 '65
Human eyes see only three colors. Sci N L 85:249 Ap 18 '64
Primate retinal responses: slow changes during repetitive stimulation with light. P. Gouras and R. E. Carr. bibliog il Science 145:413-14 Jl 24 '64
Selective sensitivity to direction of movement in ganglion cells of the rabbit retina. H. B. Barlow and R. M. Hill. bibliog il Science 139:412-14 F 1 '63
Three-color vision. Sci Am 211:56-8 N '64
Three colors, three receptors. il Sci Am 210:60+ My '64
Three-pigment color vision. E. F. MacNichol, jr. il Sci Am 211:48-56 bibliog(p 154) D '64
Visual cortex of the brain; visual system of the cat. D. H. Hubel. il Sci Am 209:54-62 bibliog(p 186) N '63
Visual pigments in single rods and cones of the human retina. P. K. Brown and G. Wald. bibliog il Science 144:45-6+ Ag 3 '64; Reply. R. A. Weale. 145:1205-6 S 11 '64
Visual pigments of single primate cones. W. B. Marks and others. bibliog il Science 143:1181-3 Mr 13 '64
Why color-blind? Newsweek 64:64 O 19 '64
RETINE. See Cancer—Vaccines
RETIRED military officers
Few grey flannels for brass. il Bsns W p 143+ N 2 '63
What to do with Othello? problem of the retired officer. Nation 196:317-18 Ap 20 '63
RETIRED teachers. See Teachers, Retired
RETIREMENT from business, etc.
Before you move to Florida look both ways! E. T. Kienz. Consumer Bul 47:6-9 F '64
Down Mexico way. il Time 83:53 My 22 '64
Flexible versus compulsory retirement policies. F. Slavick and J. W. McConnell. il Mo Labor R 86:279-81 Mr '63
Go now, stay later. M. Gough. il House B 106:76-9+ Ja '64
More early retirement. Bsns W p 110 My 16 '64
New retirement plan. N. E. Harl. il Suc Farm 61:39+ O '63
Problems of retirement. America 110:625 My 9 '64
Push for early retirement. M. C. Bernstein. New Repub 151:23-4 Ag 22 '64
Putting the old out to pasture. il Bsns W p78+ O 10 '64
Reporter at large. C. Trillin. il New Yorker 40:120+ Ap 4 '64
Retire by climate. N. D. Ford. il Travel 121:28-32+ Ja '64
Special retirement provisions in industry; excerpt from Corporate retirement policy and practices. H. Fox and M. C. Kerpen. il Mo Labor R 87:781-5 Jl '64
They don't loaf in retirement. T. Irwin. il Today Health 41:28-9+ F '63
Traitor to my class; move from Washington, D.C. to Florida. F. Knebel. il Look 28:32+ Ag 25 '64
When executives retire. G. W. Chapman. il Duns R 82:63-4+ O '63
When you retire, three ways to go at it. il Changing T 18:7-11 Je '64
Where sick companies can turn for advice; Score project. il Bsns W p94+ Ag 15 '64
See also
American association of retired persons
Pensions, Industrial
Teachers, Retired
RETIREMENT homes. See Old age homes
RETIREMENT housing. See Aged—Housing
RETIREMENT income. See Income
RETIREMENT systems. See Municipal employees—Pensions; Pensions, Industrial
RETIREMENT villages. See Aged—Housing
RETOUCHING. See Photography—Retouching
RETRAINING programs. See Employees—Training
RETREATS, Spiritual
My retreat. C. Reidy. il Redbook 121:6+ Jl '63
Nuns for a day; group of Colorado housewives called Fransisters. il Newsweek 64:50 Ag 17 '64
RETRIEVER trials. See Field trials (dogs)
RETRIEVERS
Bonus: duck for a dog. D. M. Duffey. il Outdoor Life 132:140-2+ S '63
Do trials test real retrievers? J. Stetson. il Field & S 68:140+ Je '63
My dog Sam. H. Babcock. il Field & S 69:46-8+ S '64
Rough and ready Chesapeakes. D. M. Duffey. il Outdoor Life 134:90-2+ Jl '64
Tenacious retriever. J. Stetson. il Field & S 69:116-17 Jl '64
See also
Golden retrievers
Labrador dogs
Training
See Dogs—Training
RETTALIATA, John T.
Future and the Illinois institute of technology. Sch & Soc 92:272-4 O 3 '64
RETURN; story. See Kirch, P.
RETURN to innocence; story. See Lambert, E.

REUBEN, J. P. and others
Muscle: volume changes in isolated single fibers. bibliog Science 142:246-8 O 11 '63
REUBEN, Reuben; story. See DeVries, P.
REUBENS, Beryl L.
Five weeks to D-day. Library J 88:1101-2 Mr 15 '63
REULING, Karl F.
(ed) See Toye, F. Two hours before sunset
REUNIFICATION question, German. See Germany—Union (proposed)
REUNION at Thanksgiving; story. See Coffin, R. P. T.
REUNION in Gehenna; story. See Perelman, S. J.
REUNIONS, Family. See Family reunions
REUSCHLEIN, Harold Gill
Good-by to isolationism. por Cath World 198:28-32 O '63
REUSS, Henry S.
America gets an unexpected break. Harper 226:37-42 My '63
Ombudsman for America. N Y Times Mag p30+ S 13 '64
REUTER, Richard W.
President sends Food for peace report to Congress; accompanying memorandum, September 21, 1964. Dept State Bul 51:678-80 N 9 '64
REUTHER, Walter Philip
Bread-and-butter issues as Reuther reviews them; summary of address. por Newsweek 62:87 N 18 '63
Excerpt from statement submitted to Joint economic committee, February 15, 1963. Cong Digest 42:113+ Ap '63
Freedom's time of testing. Sat R 47:36+ Ag 29 '64
Labor-management relations; address, February 4, 1963. Vital Speeches 29:376-9 Ap 1 '63
Speaking out. por Sat Eve Post 236:10+ D 7 '63
When unions try to expand. U S News 55:124 N 18 '63
about
AFL-CIO showdown: Meany wins. U S News 55:116 O 21 '63
Auto workers' program. Commonweal 80:30 Ap 3 '64
Chrysler settles: what price peace? il por Newsweek 64:87-90 S 21 '64
Detroit talkathon: UAW contract time. il por Newsweek 64:61-2 Jl 6 '64
How Reuther maps demands. U S News 55:94-5 D 2 '63
Is this to be the year of a big strike in autos? issue of UAW with GM. il por U S News 56:93-5 Mr 16 '64
Look ahead to the auto negotiations. T. R. Brooks. il Reporter 30:27-9 My 21 '64
Meany vs. Reuther; clash on rights march. U S News 55:22 Ag 26 '63
People of the week. por U S News 55:16 N 25 '63
Plan for a flexible work week; thirty-five hour week at forty hours' pay. Bsns W p27 Mr 2 '63
President Reuther, meet President Johnson. por Newsweek 63:59-60 Mr 30 '64
Price of labor peace in the auto industry. il por U S News 57:82-5 S 21 '64
Real issue in autos, as industry sees it. il U S News 56:83-5 Ap 13 '64
Rhetoric of Walter Reuther. S. Levey. Reporter 28:26-8 Mr 14 '63
Target. Newsweek 64:64 S 7 '64
Walter Reuther's great big union. A. H. Raskin. il por Atlan 212:85-90+ O '63
What Reuther wants now from the auto industry. il por U S News 56:87-8 Ap 6 '64
When a union tries to break the U.S. wage barrier. il U S News 56:85-6 Mr 30 '64
Why union chose Chrysler as target for strike. il U S News 57:73-4 S 7 '64
Wider split in the AFL-CIO? U S News 54:91 F 11 '63
Will there be an auto strike? il por U S News 57:66-8 Ag 31 '64
REVEL, Michel, and others
Actinomycin D: an effect on rat liver homogenates unrelated to its action on RNA synthesis. bibliog Science 146:1311-13 D 4 '64
REVELATION
Scripture and tradition, by G. Moran. Review
Cath World 198:185-6 D '63. N. J. McEleney
See also
Mystery
REVELATION, Book of. See Bible—New Testament—Revelation
REVELL, Mary Margaret
Naiad in vaseline. il por Time 81:85 My 3 '63
REVELL, Peter
Propaganda and pornography. Library J 88:3562+ O 1 '63
REVELLE, Roger
Environment: land, air, water. New Repub 151:25-8+ N 7 '64
Mining the bottom of the sea; excerpts from study. por Sat R 47:60-1 O 3 '64
Water-resources research in the federal government; excerpts from report of the Task group on coordinated water-resources research of the Federal council for science and technology. bibliog Science 142:1027-33 N 22 '63
Water; with biographical sketch. Sci Am 209:24+, 92-100+ bibliog(p307) S '63
REVENUE, Municipal. See Municipal finance
REVENUE, State. See State finance
REVERBERATION. See Acoustics, Architectural
REVERE cartridge system. See Magnetic recorders and recording
REVERIE. See Daydreams
REVERSAL of time. See Time reversal
REVIEW of politics (periodical)
Review of politics. America 109:404 O 12 '63
REVIEWS of books. See Book reviews
REVIEWS of moving pictures. See Moving picture plays—Criticisms, plots, etc.
REVISION, Literary. See Authorship
REVIVALS
See also
Evangelistic work
REVOLT of the vegetables; drama. See Crichton, M. C.
RÉVOLUTION (periodical) See Periodicals—France
REVOLUTION, Social. See Social revolution
REVOLUTIONARY movement of the people. See Political parties—Cuba
REVOLUTIONARY war (United States) See United States—History—Revolution
REVOLUTIONS
On revolution, by H. Arendt. Review
New Yorker 40:210-14+ Ap 18 '64. N. Bliven
Reporter 28:42-3 My 9 '63. G. Steiner
Time 81:96 Mr 22 '63
Violence in Africa; developments in Togo, Brazzaville and Dahomey. T. P. Melady. America 109:734-5 D 7 '63
What Communist breakup means to us; interview. Z. Brzezinski. Nations Bsns 52:34-5+ Je '64
See also
France—History—February revolution, 1848
Government, Resistance to
REVOLVERS
Colt conversion revolvers. W. R. Orbelo. il Hobbies 68:125 D '63
Colt new model police pistol. W. R. Orbelo. il Hobbies 69:127 My '64
Colt Peacemaker. W. R. Orbelo. il Hobbies 68:115 Ag '63
1885 [i.e. 1855] root model Colt. C. G. Worman. il Hobbies 69:126-7 Mr '64
Samuel Colt and his revolver. W. R. Orbelo. Hobbies 68:113 Ap '63
Smith and Wesson model 1½ new issue revolver. W. R. Orbelo. il Hobbies 69:125 Jl '64
What and why is an Allen & Wheelock lipfire revolver? H. R. Mouillesseaux. il Hobbies 69:118-19 N '64
REVOLVING check-purchase plan. See Banks and banking—Check credit plans
REWALD, John
Birth of impressionism. Art N 62:30-1+ Mr '63
REWARDS, prizes, etc.
Akidemy awards: Homestead air force base, Fla. J. A. Turner. il Recreation 57:519-20 D '64
ALA awards and citations for 1963-1964. il Library J 88:3018-20; 89:2938-40 S 1 '63, Ag '64
ALA awards, citations, and scholarships for 1964-1965. Library J 88:4184-6; 89:4494-6 N 1 '63, N 15 '64
ALA invites application now for 1964 awards, scholarships. Library J 88:4834-6 D 15 '63
ALA invites nominations for awards and scholarships. Library J 89:4619-20 N 15 '64
Awards. See issues of Wilson library bulletin
Awards given to architects and engineers. Arch Rec 134:332 O '63
Bodoni and balance; Ayer cup awarded to the Valley news of Lebanon, N.H. il Newsweek 63:74 My 18 '64

REWARDS, prizes, etc.—*Continued*
Children's spring book festival awards given. Pub W 183:33 My 13 '63; 185:29 My 11 '64
David Brinkley and his golden key. C. S. Wren. il Look 28:44+ F 25 '64
First winners of the Danforth award for college teachers. il Sat R 46:65 Mr 23 '63
Fort Knox wins first Conservation special award. il Am For 69:35 Ag '63
French literary prizes, 1964. T. de Saint Phalle. il Pub W 186:35-7 D 28 '64
Golden tach award. il Hot Rod 17:105 Je '64
Good loud holler; cartoonist and teacher win Golden key awards. il NEA J 52:36-7 Mr '63
Grants, fellowships, and awards. See occasional issues of Science
Happiness is recognition; teachers awards. il NEA J 53:62-4 Ja '64
Helping hand for a literary upstart. J. Fischer. Harper 227:20+ S '63; Discussion. 227:10+ N '63
Herblock's golden key. J. Star. il Look 27: 62+ F 26 '63
Literary prize game. D. Dempsey. il Horizon 5:68-75 Jl '63
Literary prizes and awards, 1963-64. il Pub W 185:99-103 Ja 20 '64; 187:97-102 Ja 18 '65
Prize offers and awards. See issues of Writer
Prizes and awards. See issues of Publishers' weekly
Rocket research solid microrocket wins award. il Miss & Roc 12:34-5 Ap 29 '63
Ten cities, one county win merit certificates. il Am City 80:73-5 Ja '65
Twenty-two cities win certificates of merit. Am City 79:7+ F '64
Two $10,000 prizes awarded on Corfu; International literary prize and the Formentor prize. Pub W 183:39 My 20 '63
See also
Medals
National safety council
Solomon R. Guggenheim foundation
Sports illustrated (periodical)
also names of rewards, e.g. Pulitzer prizes

Anecdotes, facetiae, satire, etc.

Firsts and the mosts of 1964. Christian Cent 81:1639 D 30 '64

REX Oedipus: introducing Juney Potter; story. See Rhodin, E.

REXROTH, Kenneth
Blesse mee and thee. Nation 199:282 O 26 '64
Lady poetry. Nation 198:494-5 My 11 '64
Latin verse: a universe apart. Nation 198: 148-50 F 10 '64
Panelizing dissent. Nation 199:97-9 S 7 '64
Poet in a fugitive cause. Nation 199:382-3 N 23 '64
about
Good house. G. Sorrentino. Poetry 104:179-81 Je '64

REY, Sydor
Stella; story. Commentary 36:473-8 D '63

REYES, Frank F.
Minister who follows the migrants. M. Cope. il pors Sat Eve Post 237:34-6 Ja 4 '64

REYES, Ramon de los
Ballet espanol Alba, Reyes, 92nd street Y. J. Maskey. Dance Mag 38:64 Je '64

REYES, Rolando Santana. See Santana Reyes, R.

REYES, Salvador
Oases in the Atacama Desert. Américas 15: 10-16 S '63

REYES, Victor M.
Twentieth century Mexican painting. Américas 16:17-26 Ag '64

REYNAUD, Paul
When England offered everything to France; excerpt. por Sat R 46:26-8 Mr 16 '63

REYNOLDS, Billie
Oregon's Bohemia. Travel 119:41-5 My '63

REYNOLDS, Charles
Experimenting with film. Pop Phot 55:91+ S '64
Films '64-'65. Pop Phot 55:193 D '64; 56:168 Ja '65
Focus on Al Maysles. Pop Phot 54:128-31 My '64
Focus on Robert Freson. Pop Phot 54:74-81+ Je '64
Focus on Tony Schwartz. Pop Phot 53:58-61+ S '63
Guide to collecting classics in 8-MM. Pop Phot 52:104-7+ Mr '63
Movies to learn from. Pop Phot 52:122+ My '63
Publish your own, they did! Pop Phot 52:76-83+ My '63
Shoot for showing. Pop Phot 52:118+ Je '63
U.S.I.A. offers new jobs for apprentice filmmakers. Pop Phot 51:111+ D '62
What every film-maker should read. Pop Phot 52:117+ My '63

REYNOLDS, Clinton
Automotive milestones; the passing of Clinton Reynolds' strange car collection. L. Payne. il Motor T 16:80-3 Ja '64

REYNOLDS, Debbie
Debbie does it! ed. by E. Miller. pors Seventeen 23:80-1+ Jl '64
about
Hello, Debbie. por Newsweek 63:87 Je 29 '64
They couldn't sink Debbie either. il pors Life 56:108-11 Je 19 '64
Unsinkable Debbie Reynolds. R. W. Lewis. il pors Sat Eve Post 237:74-5+ Ag 22 '64

REYNOLDS, Don B.
Hoffa's name in Baker hearing; excerpts from testimony. U S News 56:86 F 3 '64
More on the Bobby Baker case: insurance, a stereo, and TV ads; excerpts from testimony. U S News 56:56-9 F 3 '64
about
Bobby Baker again. por Newsweek 64:22 S 14 '64
Enterprisers. K. Crawford. Newsweek 63:28 F 23 '64
Those confidential files. Nation 198:178 F 24 '64
White House leak. il Newsweek 63:15 F 17 '64

REYNOLDS, Fred
Strike up the bands for culture. Am Rec G 29:920-3+ Ag '63
Sweet and swinging. See issues of American record guide

REYNOLDS, G. S.
Potency of conditioned reinforcers based on food and on food and punishment. Science 139:838-9 Mr 1 '63

REYNOLDS, J. Francis
I learned about flying from that! Flying 74: 50+ Ja '64

REYNOLDS, James J. Jr
He fights the toughest battles. por Bsns W p 126+ Ja 16 '65
People of the week. por U S News 56:12 Mr 2 '64

REYNOLDS, John Fulton
General Reynolds and Dear Kate: reprint. M. R. Maloney. il por Am Heritage 15:62-5 D '63

REYNOLDS, Malvina
Out of tune. Nat R 16:221 Mr 24 '64
Tacky into the wind. il por Time 83:76 F 28 '64

REYNOLDS, Marc, and Silver, H. R.
Barbecue supreme. Esquire 62:54-7 Jl '64

REYNOLDS, Marion H.
Sparkling hues of tuberous begonias. Horticulture 41:146 Mr '63

REYNOLDS, Michael M.
Access to information. por Library J 89:1692-4 Ap 15 '64

REYNOLDS, Orr E. See Nicks, O. W. jt. auth.

REYNOLDS, Paul R.
Launching the first novel. Sat R 47:56-8 S 12 '64
Rights and royalties; excerpt from Writing and selling of non-fiction. Writer 77:13-15 Mr '64
Should every writer have an agent? excerpt from Writing and selling of fiction. Sat R 48:69-70+ Ja 9 '65
So you want to write a book; excerpt from The writing and selling of nonfiction. Sat R 46:48-50 Jl 13 '63

REYNOLDS, Quentin
Churchill at ninety: twilight of a hero. Sat Eve Post 237:15-17 N 28 '64
Mandate for murder. Sat R 46:33 My 4 '63
They knew what they wanted. Sat R 46:22 Je 1 '63
(ed) See Slater, S. My life inside the mob
(ed) See Tung, C. P. Red China
about
Quent. por Newsweek 61:82-3 Je 3 '63

REYNOLDS, Robert
Robert Reynolds; personality profile. R. Slater. por Flying 74:16+ Ja '64

REYNOLDS, Robert L.
Man of conscience. Am Heritage 14:20-3+ F '63

REYNOLDS, Robert W.
Pulmonary edema as a consequence of hypothalamic lesions in rats. bibliog Science 141:930-2 S 6 '63

REYNOLDS, Russell R. See Neelands, R. W. jt. auth.

REYNOLDS, Ted
Furtive free ride. Life 56:8 F 7 '64
REYNOLDS, Tim
Aubade; poem. Christian Cent 80:804 Je 19 '63
Photograph of a late poet; poem. Atlan 213: 82 F '64
Poem for Hermann Hesse. Poetry 101:395 Mr '63
Two-sided moon; poem. Sat R 47:30 Jl 18 '64
REYNOLDS, Vernon
Man of the woods. Natur Hist 73:44-51 Ja '64
REYNOLDS metals company
Fernandez wins 1963 Reynolds student prize. il Arch Rec 133:29 Mr '63
Glitter of real estate lures industry dollars. il Bsns W p32+ Mr 2 '63
Shortcut to sheet aluminum. il Bsns W p52+ Mr 9 '63
Third force in urban renewal. H. Kay. il Fortune 70:130-3+ O '64
REZATTO, Helen
Just an average lawyer. Read Digest 82:145-8+ My '63
One week of horror on the Great Plains. Read Digest 82:195-6+ Ap '63
So it's all been done before. Writer 77:27-8+ N '64
REZNIKOFF, Charles
Two poets of New York. G. Cambon. Poetry 102:226-8 Jl '63
RHEA, John
Science milestone; Lawrence Hargrave. Sci Digest 53:79-86 F '63
RHEEM manufacturing company
Renaissance at Rheem. J. B. Weiner. Duns R 83:35+ Ap '64
RHEINFELDER, William A.
Modulation circuits for solid-state CB transmitters. Electr World 71:28-30+ F '64
Noise performance of transistors in audio circuits. Electr World 73:31-3 Ja '65
RHEINFRANK, William J.
Solving street cleaning's toughest problem. Am City 79:94-5 Ap '64
RHENISH furniture. See Furniture, German
RHENIUM
Mononuclear and polynuclear chemistry of rhenium (III): its pronounced homophilicity. F. A. Cotton and others. bibliog il Science 145:1305-7 S 18 '64
Rhenium and osmium abundances in stony meteorites. J. W. Morgan and J. F. Lovering. bibliog il Science 144:835-6 My 15 '64
RHEOLOGY
Terminology
Glossary of rheological terms. Miss & Roc 16:34-5 Ja 11 '65
RHEO-OPTICS. See Optics
RHESUS factor. See Rh factors
RHESUS monkeys. See Monkeys
RHEUMATIC fever
Rheumatic fever can now be checked! E. Ubell. Parents Mag 38:91+ O '63
RHEUMATISM. See Arthritis
RHEUMATOID arthritis. See Arthritis
RHINE RIVER
Rhine. F. Russell. il Horizon 6:18-27 Spr '64
Rhine roam. D. Whitney. il Travel 120:43-7 S '63
You may hear Lorelei sing. il Sunset 131: 32 O '63
RHINE VALLEY
Maps
Panorama of the Rhine. Horizon 6:24, sup (folded map) Spr '64
RHINITIS
Allergy-caused sniffles continue through winter. Sci N L 86:249 O 17 '64
Breakthrough in hog rhinitis control! D. Seim. Farm J 87:32 Ag '63
Rhinitis-free feeder pigs on the way. D. Hagen. il Farm J 87:42 D '63
Rhinitis: new help is coming. J. Harvey. il Suc Farm 61:54-5 D '63
RHINOCEROS
Nature note. Sci N L 86:239 O 10 '64
Passion for rhinoceros. L. H. Lapham. il Sat Eve Post 237:66-8 F 1 '64
Rhinoceros. J. O'Connor. il Outdoor Life 135: 36-9+ Ja '65
World save-the rhino movement proposed. Sci N L 83:89 F 9 '63
RHIZOPHORA. See Mangrove
RHIZOPODA
See also
Radiolaria
RHOADES, Verne
Fashioning the cradle of forestry in America; excerpt from address. por Am For 70:34-5+ D '64

RHODE ISLAND
See also
Birds—Rhode Island
Fishing—Rhode Island
Libraries—Rhode Island
Music festivals—Rhode Island
Commission to encourage morality in youth
R.I. censors' activities ruled unconstitutional; with editorial comment. Pub W 183:42-3. 49 Mr 4 '63
Politics and government
Highly employable; Republican Governor J. Chafee re-elected. Time 84:41 N 13 '64
Religious institutions and affairs
News of the Christian world (cont) Christian Cent 80:218-20+, 721-2, 784+, 1314+; 81: 284+, 808-9, 1606 F 13, My 29, Je 12, O 23 '63, F 26, Je 17, D 23 '64
RHODE ISLAND commission to encourage morality in youth
Governor dissolves R. I. censorship commission. Pub W 185:100 Je 8 '64
RHODE ISLAND. University, Kingston
Small units comprise residence complex for U. of Rhode Island. il Arch Rec 134:15 N '63
RHODES, James A.
Austerity in Ohio. R. Giles. il Reporter 29:39-42 N 7 '63
Ohio and Governor Rhodes. W. F. Rickenbacker. il Nat R 16:61-4 Ja 28 '64
RHODES, Lawrence
Brief biography. S. Goodman. pors Dance Mag 38:50-1 Ja '64
RHODES, Philip H.
Spars, rigging and hardware. Yachting 115:46-7+ Ap '64
RHODES, Philip L.
Designer's role. Yachting 116:42-4 S '64
RHODES, Willard
This record is important: the innate musicality of Sandy Bull. Am Rec G 29:899 Jl '63
RHODES (island)
Rough map of Greece. P. L. Adams. il Atlan 214:56-60 Jl '64
Water for the village; Lindos. J. Martin. il Atlan 212:144+ D '63
RHODES scholars and scholarships
Christmas present; M. E. Smith, selected as a Rhodes scholar. Time 85:43 Ja 1 '65
Englishman's audit of Rhodes scholars. Elton. Harper 228:98-100+ My '64
RHODESIA
Foreign relations
Death of the Federation. T. Molnar. Nat R 16:353 My 5 '64
Politics and government
Another tea party? Newsweek 63:53-4 Ap 27 '64
Atlantic report. Atlan 214:10+ S '64
Bit of a breather. il Time 84:46 S 18 '64
Black and white. Newsweek 63:47 My 11 '64
Christmas postponed; proposed unilateral declaration of independence. Time 84:27-8 N 6 '64
Colonialism in reverse. Time 81:46+ Ap 19 '63
Davy rides again. New Repub 149:10 N 23 '63
Death of the Federation. T. Molnar. Nat R 16:353 My 5 '64
Deceptive calm. il Newsweek 61:52 Ap 16 '63
Defused? prospect of unilateral declaration of independence fades. il Newsweek 64:56 S 21 '64
Looking to London. il Newsweek 63:51-2 Mr 16 '64
New range boss. Time 83:35 Ap 24 '64
Rebellion in Rhodesia? R. W. Howe. New Repub 151:13-14 N 14 '64
Sir Roy's last throw. Newsweek 64:56 O 12 '64
Tougher line in Africa; Rhodesia gets a new leader. il U S News 56:15-16 Ap 27 '64
Two tough men; warning from Britain's new Prime Minister. il Newsweek 64:51 N 9 '64
White *uhuru*. il Time 84:39 S 4 '64
White supremacy. New Repub 150:8 My 2 '64
Will he, won't he, will he, won't he..? E. Huxley. Nat R 16:651-2 Jl 28 '64
Race problems
Where whites in Africa are ready to fight it out. il U S News 56:56-7 My 25 '64
Religious institutions and affairs
Bishop Dodge expelled by Southern Rhodesia Christian Cent 81:981 Ag 5 '64

RHODESIA AND NYASALAND (Federation)
Act of betrayal; secession of Northern Rhodesia. Newsweek 61:34 Ap 8 '63
Crumbling federation. il Time 81:43 Ap 5 '63
Deceptive calm. il Newsweek 61:52 Ap 16 '63
End of a dream in Southern Rhodesia. C. Sterling. il Reporter 28:29-33 My 9 '63
Last meeting. il Newsweek 62:34 D 23 '63
No flowers for Welensky's baby. E. Huxley. Nat R 16:65-6 Ja 28 '64
No squawks, please. il Time 81:31 F 22 '63
Rhodesian trap. A. Keppel-Jones. il Nation 197:111-13+ S 7 '63
Rhodesias and Nyasaland. F. M. G. Willson. Cur Hist 46:148-55+ Mr '64
River of tears. il Time 83:32 Ja 10 '64
Taps? Newsweek 62:39 Jl 8 '63
Trouble brewing; smuggling of hops into Southern Rhodesia. Time 81:38 F 15 '63
Welensky's phantom. Newsweek 61:40+ Mr 4 '63
Where Negroes have the whites on the run; interview. O. B. Bennett. il U S News 55:68-75 S 9 '63

RHODIN, Eric
Corrigan Frye and the FBI; story. Seventeen 22:106-7 Mr '63
Pronounced clage and the tiger tooth; story. Seventeen 22:138-9 S '63
Rex Oedipus: introducing Juney Potter; story. Seventeen 23:128-9 My '64

RHODIUM
Rhodium-102 fallout: variations in deposition and concentrations in precipitation. M. W. M. Leo and A. Walton. bibliog il Science 140:1398-400 Je 28 '63

RHODODENDRONS
Dependable rhododendrons. R. De Wilde, jr. il Horticulture 42:26-7+ Je '64
Dexter rhododendrons. S. Berns. il Horticulture 41:320 Je '63
Good culture increases rhododendron hardiness. J. H. Clarke. il Horticulture 41:150-1 Mr '63
Great past, greater future. M. C. Ohlander. il Flower Grower 51:46-9+ Ap '64
Rhododendrons that stay low. D. G. Leach. il Flower Grower 51:31+ S '64
Rhododendrons that stay small. C. M. Fitch. il Flower Grower 50:53-5 Ap '63
Rhododendrons you can buy. Sunset 132:296-8+ My '64
Species rhododendrons. B. Bovee. il Pop Gard 14:74-5 My '63
Success with rhododendrons. B. B. Brown. il Flower Grower 51:37+ F '64
They'll flower in a decade or so; tree rhododendrons. il Sunset 132:190+ F '64
You don't just grow a rhododendron, you live with it. il Sunset 132:120-5 My '64

RHODOSPIRILLUM rubrum
Coenzyme Q: intracellular distribution in rhodospirillum rubrum. A. F. Greene and J. P. Mascarenhas. bibliog il Science 144:1455-6 Je 19 '64

RHOME, Jerry
Playing catch. il por Time 84:68+ D 4 '64
Rise of Rhome. por Newsweek 64:75 N 23 '64
Sharp change in the game. D. Jenkins. il pors Sports Illus 21:28-31 N 16 '64

RHONE-Poulenc corporation. See France—Industries

RHUBARB
See also
Cookery—Rhubarb

RHYNE, Charles S.
Reforming decadent state legislatures; address, October 26, 1964. Vital Speeches 31:118-21 D 1 '64
Rule of law as a foreign policy; address, April 7, 1964. Vital Speeches 30:467-70 My 15 '64

RHYTHMIC phenomena. See Periodicity

RIB fractures. See Fractures

RIBAUT, Jean
Tragic dream of Jean Ribaut. S. Harris. il Am Heritage 14:8-15+ O '63

RIBBLE, Frederick D. G.
Farewell, groves of academe. por Time 82:81 Jl 12 '63

RIBES viburnifolium
Good looking all year long. il Sunset 133:190 S '64

RIBICOFF, Abraham
Senator's plan to end religious issue in school aid; excerpts from address, May 20, 1963. por U S News 54:100-2 Je 3 '63
Speaking out. por Sat Eve Post 237:6+ Mr 21 '64
Trade; the key to Atlantic maturity; address, May 17, 1964. Vital Speeches 30:514-16 Je 15 '64
We are poisoning the air. Look 27:131-2+ O 22 '63

about
Senator Ribicoff would end protest registration of insecticides. J. Prokop. il por Am For 69:7+ O '63

RIBMAN, Ronald B. and Ribman, S. M.
Poor man in the scales. Harper 228:150-4 Ap '64

RIBMAN, Samuel M. See Ribman, R. B. jt. auth.

RIBONUCLEASE
Chromosome puffs in drosophila induced by ribonuclease. F. M. Ritossa and R. C. Von Borstel. bibliog il Science 145:513-14 Jl 31 '64
Partial enzyme synthesis. Sci N L 83:214 Ap 6 '63

RIBONUCLEIC acid
Actinomycin D: and effect on rat liver homogenates unrelated to its action on RNA synthesis. M. Revel and others. bibliog il Science 146:1311-13 D 4 '64
Aminoacyl position in aminoacyl sRNA. C. S. McLaughlin and V. M. Ingram. bibliog il Science 145:942-3 Ag 28 '64
Antibody plaque formation by normal mouse spleen cell cultures exposed in vitro to RNA from immune mice. H. Friedman. bibliog il Science 146:934-6 N 13 '64
Antibody production by nonimmune spleen cells incubated with RNA from immunized mice. E. P. Cohen and J. J. Parks. bibliog il Science 144:1012-13 My 22 '64
Association of rapidly metabolized DNA and RNA. J. H. Cherry. bibliog il Science 146:1066-9 N 20 '64
Asynchronous synthesis of RNA in nucleoli of root meristem. A. K. Bal and P. R. Gross. bibliog il Science 143:808-10 F 21 '64
Base composition of the RNA of a reovirus variant. P. J. Gomatos and I. Tamm. bibliog il Science 140:997-8 My 31 '63
Breakdown of rat-liver ergosomes in vivo after actinomycin inhibition of messenger RNA synthesis. T. Staehelin and others. bibliog il Science 140:180-3 Ap 12 '63
Chemistry of memory. Newsweek 61:109 Je 24 '63
Chromatography of ribonuclease-treated myosin extracts from early embryonic chick muscle. E. F. Baril and others. bibliog il Science 146:413-14 O 16 '64
Chromosomal and nucleolar RNA synthesis in root tips during mitosis. N. K. Das. bibliog il Science 140:1231-3 Je 14 '63
Chromosome puffs. W. Beermann and U. Clever. il Sci Am 210:50-8 bibliog(p 156) Ap '64
Complementary RNA in nucleus and cytoplasm of mouse liver cells. B. H. Hoyer and others. bibliog il Science 140:1408-12 Je 28 '63
Control of synthesis of RNA and protein in diapausing and injured cecropia pupae. S. J. Berry and others. bibliog il Science 146:938-40 N 13 '64
Deoxyribonuclease sensitivity of ribonucleic acid synthesizing system from tobacco leaves. J. G. Shaw. bibliog il Science 139:924-5 Mr 8 '63
Double-stranded ribonucleic acid formation in vitro by MS 2 phage-induced RNA synthetase. C. Weissmann and P. Borst. bibliog il Science 142:1188-91 N 29 '63
Effect of bromination on the biological activities of transfer RNA of escherichia coli. C. T. Yu and P. C. Zamecnik. bibliog il Science 144:856-9 My 15 '64
Experimental cardiac hypertrophy: concentrations of RNA in the ventricles. L. Gluck and others. bibliog il Science 144:1244-5 Je 5 '64
β-Galactosidase: inactivation of its messenger RNA by ultraviolet irradiation. P. A. Swenson and R. B. Setlow. bibliog il Science 146:791-4 N 6 '64
Genetic code: emergence of a symmetrical pattern. R. V. Eck. bibliog il Science 140:477-81 My 3 '63
Hybridization of rapidly labeled nuclear ribonucleic acids. R. P. Perry and others. bibliog il Science 145:504-7 Jl 31 '64
Inhibition of adhesiveness and aggregation of dissociated cells by inhibitors of protein and RNA synthesis. M. H. Moscona and A. A. Moscona. bibliog Science 142:1070-1 N 22 '63
Involvement of RNA in the synthesis of proteins. J. D. Watson. bibliog il Science 140:17-26 Ap 5 '63
Is memory a matter of enzyme induction? C. E. Smith; discussion. Science 139:1090-2+ Mr 15 '63

RIBONUCLEIC acid—*Continued*
Long-lived messenger RNA: evidence from cotton seed germination. L. Dure and L. Waters. bibliog il Science 147:410-12 Ja 22 '65
Messenger RNA utilization during development of chick embryo lens. R. B. Scott and E. Bell. bibliog il Science 147:405-7 Ja 22 '65
Mitochondrion. D. E. Green. il Sci Am 210: 63-6+ bibliog(p 152) Ja '64; Reply with rejoinder. E. Rabinowitch. 210:10+ Ap '64
New biology and the nature of man; adaptation of address, 1963. G. W. Beadle. Bul Atomic Sci 20:13-17 Mr '64
Nucleolus: a center of RNA methylation. M. L. Birnstiel and others. bibliog il Science 142:1577-80 D 20 '63
Nucleotides: separation from an alkaline hydrolysate of RNA by thin-layer electrophoresis. F. M. DeFilippes. bibliog il Science 144:1350-1 Je 12 '64
Operon: on its third anniversary. G. S. Stent. bibliog Science 144:816-20 My 15 '64
Polypeptide synthesis in sea urchin embryogenesis: an examination with synthetic polyribonucleotides. M. Nemer and S. G. Bard. bibliog il Science 140:664-6 My 10 '63
Protein synthesis during development: control through messenger RNA. R. B. Scott and E. Bell. bibliog il Science 145:711-13 Ag 14 '64
Puffs heredity clue. W. Wingo. Sci N L 86:83 Ag 8 '64
RNA believed to be a director of heredity. Sci N L 84:67 Ag 3 '63
RNA codewords and protein synthesis. M. Nirenberg and P. Leder. bibliog il Science 145:1399-407 S 25 '64
RNA synthesis in rat seminal vesicles: stimulation by testosterone. W. D. Wicks and F. T. Kenney. bibliog il Science 144:1346-7 Je 12 '64
Reevaluation of assays used to show RNA induction of glucose-6-phosphatase in ascites cells. J. Imsande and B. Ephrussi. bibliog il Science 144:854-6 My 15 '64
Replication of the RNA of bacteriophage R17. M. L. Fenwick and others. bibliog il Science 146:527-30 O 23 '64
Ribonucleic acid: effect on conditioned behavior in rats. L. Cook and others. bibliog il Science 141:268-9 Jl 19 '63
Ribonucleic acid synthesis in protoplasts of escherichia coli: inhibition by actinomycin. D. B. Mach and E. L. Tatum. bibliog il Science 139:1051-2 Mr 15 '63
Ribonucleic acids of the ilyanassa embryo. J. R. Collier. bibliog il Science 147:150-1 Ja 8 '65
Ribosomal RNA in the developing chick embryo. M. A. Lerner and others. bibliog il Science 141:1187-8 S 20 '63
Ribosomal RNA on the surface of ribosomes. M. Santer. bibliog il Science 141:1049-50 S 13 '63
Ribosomes and ribonucleic acids in three morphological states of neurospora. H. R. Henney, jr. and R. Storck. bibliog il Science 142:1675-6 D 27 '63
Separation of microsomal RNA into five bands during agar electrophoresis. R. Bachvaroff and P. R. B. McMaster. bibliog il Science 143:1177-9 Mr 13 '64
Source of the third RNA. Sci Am 208:76 Mr '63
Structure of RNA. R. Langridge and P. J. Gomatos. bibliog il Science 141:694-8 Ag 23 '63
Synthesis of RNA in vitro stimulated in dipteran salivary glands by 1,1,3-tryicyano-2-amino-1-propene. J. Jacob and J. L. Sirlin. bibliog il Science 144:1011-12 My 22 '64
Thermal inactivation of the primer in DNA-dependent synthesis of RNA in animal tissue. J. J. Furth and P. Loh. bibliog il Science 145:161-2 Jl 10 '64
Thinking worm's molecule. W. Cloud. Pop Sci 182:32+ My '63
Toxic effect of pseudomonas tabaci on RNA metabolism in tobacco and its counteraction by kinetin. L. Lovrekovich and others. bibliog il Science 145:165 Jl 10 '64
Translational control of protein synthesis in a cell-free system directed by a polycistronic viral RNA. Y. Ohtaka and S. Spiegelman. bibliog Science 142:493-7 O 25 '63
Virus-specific double-stranded RNA in poliovirus-infected cells. D. Baltimore and others. bibliog il Science 143:1034-6 Mr 6 '64
Zinc stimulation of RNA and protein synthesis in rhizopus nigricans. W. S. Wegener and A. H. Romano. bibliog il Science 142: 1669-70 D 27 '63

RIBONUCLEOPROTEINS. See Nucleoproteins
RIBOSOMES. See Nucleoproteins
RICCHIUTI, N. V. See Gibbs, C. L. jt. auth.
RICCI, Marco
Violent Venetian. il Time 82:76 N 29 '63
RICCI, Matteo
Rites controversy. J. R. Rosenbloom. America 110:544-5 Ap 18 '64
RICCI, Ruggiero
Prodigy's return. por Newsweek 64:93-4 N 30 '64
RICE, Berkeley
Haiti; last act of a tragicomedy. Harper 226: 65-6+ My '63
RICE, Charles E. See Kellogg, W. N. jt. auth.
RICE, Charles Owen
Innocence of U.S. steel. Commonweal 80:504-6 Jl 24 '64
RICE, Dale W.
Hawaiian monk seals. Natur Hist 73:48-55 F '64
RICE, Elmer
Der Elmer. Newsweek 62:78-9 Ag 26 '63
Monotony report. Time 82:62+ Ag 30 '63
RICE, Howard H.
Antennas for business radio. Electr World 69:33-5+ Mr '63
Choosing a two-way radio system. Electr World 70:50-2 N; 52-3+ D '63
Transistors versus tubes for two-way radio. Electr World 72:48-50 N '64
Why not U.H.F. two-way radio? Electr World 71:42-3 Mr '64
RICE, Joseph P. jr
Education of subcultural groups. bibliog f Sch & Soc 92:360-2 N 28 '64
RICE, Norman S. and Halpin, J. H.
Joseph Warford, silversmith of Albany and Salem, New York. Antiques 85:429-31 Ap '64
RICE, Oliver
Poem: Wahai, grandfather. Poetry 102:233-4 Jl '63
RICE, Robert
Profiles (cont) New Yorker 40:41-2+ Ag 1; 37-8+ Ag 8 '64
Reporter at large. New Yorker 39:153-4+ O 19 '63
RICE, Theron J.
Other side of the coin; excerpts from letter. Aviation W 79:21 Ag 26 '63
RICE, William Thomas
Why not merge and survive? Ann Am Acad 345:103-8 Ja '63
RICE-DAVIES, Mandy
Dial S for squalor; Regina v. Stephen Thomas Ward. il Time 82:22+ Ag 2 '63
In Britain, a new Lady Hamilton? il por U S News 55:14 Jl 15 '63
Personal report on Britain's biggest scandal. L. Bergquist. il por Look 27:81-6 Jl 30 '63
Randy Mandy teufelsbraten. il por Time 83: 76 Ja 17 '64
RICE
Grain of rice is worth a drop of blood. B. B. Fall. il N Y Times Mag p 10-12+ Jl 12 '64
Oldest rice in the world; rice-terraces of the Ifugaos, Philippines. il Sci Digest 54:10 Jl '63
You can grow your own rice. il Sunset 130: 98-9 Mr '63
See also
Cookery—Rice
International rice research institute
RICE COUNTY, Kan.
U.S. aid, wanted or not: report on a well-to-do county; with excerpts from editorial by M. Moxley. il U S News 54:40-2 Ap 1 '63
RICE pudding. See Puddings
RICE university, Houston, Tex.
Breaking the founder's strings. il Bsns W p62-3 F 29 '64
Rice university conference develops five factory projects. S. L. Pittman. il Arch Rec 134:115-20 D '63
Rice university: the pangs of change. J. Graves. Holiday 35:76-7+ Je '64
RICH, Adrienne
Beyond the heirlooms of tradition. Poetry 105:128-9 N '64
For example; poem. Nation 197:352 N 23 '63
In the North; Sister; Peeling onions; Well in ruined courtyard; Apology; Peace; poems. Poetry 101:233-7 Ja '63
Mr Bones, he lives. Nation 198:538+ My 25 '64
Parting; poem. Nation 197:396 D 7 '63
Trees; poem. Nation 197:328 N 16 '63
Two songs; poems. Nation 200:90 Ja 25 '65

RICH, Alan
Faust symphony, the Lisztian fire aflame. Hi Fi 14:49-50 Jl '64
Four saints; humanity is the key word. Hi Fi 15:70-1 F '65
Handel's Water music, newly, and handsomely, afloat. Hi Fi 14:67-8 Ag '64
Metropolitan forum; reprint. Opera N 28:33 D 7 '63
Opera for the ears alone. Mus Am 84:10-11+ N '64
Prokofiev from Boston, a new series launched. Hi Fi 14:59-60 My '64
Twelfth-century miracle marvelously rekindled. Hi Fi 14:66 S '64
Up opera's ladder. Opera N 29:9-12 Ja 30 '65
Wilhelm Furtwangler, a luminous probing. Hi Fi 14:47-9+ S '64

RICH, Alexander
Polyribosomes. Sci Am 209:44-53 bibliog(p 178) D '63
—and Vinogradov, A. P.
Arctic disarmament. Bul Atomic Sci 20:22-3 N '64
—and others
Polyribosomes: size in normal and polio-infected HeLa cells. bibliog Science 142: 1658-63 D 27 '63

RICH, Daniel Catton
Painting where the action is. Sat R 48:48-9 Ja 23 '65
Reflections of a self-curious savant. Sat R 47:30-1 F 29 '64

RICH, Mark
Training for the urban ministry. Christian Cent 81:148-9 Ja 29 '64

RICH, Marvin A. and others
Chromosome aberrations: their role in the etiology of murine leukemia. bibliog Science 146:252-3 O 9 '64
—See Oroszlan, S. jt. auth.

RICH, Stuart U. and Portis, Bernard
Clues for action from shopper preferences. Harvard Bsns R 41:132-49 Mr '63

RICH, The
My debut a horror. B. Frazier. il Life 55:133-4+ D 6 '63
Onward and upward with the arts; can the rich write? G. T. Hellman. New Yorker 39: 46-8+ Je 8 '63
Profile of the rich. Time 83:89 Ap 3 '64
Wealthy American bum. R. Kirk. Nat R 14: 198 Mr 12 '63; Reply. R. W. Blair. 14:333 Ap 23 '63
See also
Capitalists and financiers
Millionaires

RICHARD III, king of England
Image of Richard III. R. Moley. Newsweek 61:112 Mr 25 '63

RICHARD, B.
Career guidance editorial, skills for America. See issues of Popular mechanics to April 1963

RICHARD, Cliff
More happy than Elvis. por Newsweek 61:63 F 25 '63

RICHARD, Jerry
From the inferno. Nation 199:411-12 N 30 '64

RICHARD III; drama. See Shakespeare, W.—Plays

RICHARDS, Gayne
Washington front. America 110:623; 111:768 My 9, D 12 '64

RICHARDS, Glenn C. and Behm, Donald
Economy street paving fills the gap. Am City 78:89-91 S '63

RICHARDS, Horace G. and Broecker, Wallace
Emerged holocene South American shorelines. bibliog Science 141:1044-5 S 13 '63

RICHARDS, I. A.
For Marianne Moore on her seventy-fifth birthday; poem. Poetry 101:410-11 Mr '63

RICHARDS, John
Grace at table. Read Digest 83:114-16 Ag '63

RICHARDS, Kenneth W. See McDonough, R. H. jt. auth.

RICHARDS, M. C.
Centering as dialogue; excerpt from Centering: in pottery, poetry, and the person. il Craft Horiz 24:31-3+ Jl '64

RICHARDS, Stanley
Theatre. Theatre Arts 47:64-5 F '63

RICHARDS, Tad
Support mental health, or I'll kill you; P.I; In reply; poems. Poetry 103:298-300 F '64

RICHARDS, Vincent
Cheap paperback is no country cousin (cont) Library J 88:1920 My 15 '63

RICHARDSON, Christine D. See Vanderzant, E S. jt. auth.

RICHARDSON, Cyril C.
Way Protestants worship; excerpt from Ecumenical dialogue at Harvard. Cath World 199:175-81 Je '64

RICHARDSON, Dow
Mr Chairman. . . Atlan 214:176-7 N '64

RICHARDSON, E. P.
Andrew Wyeth. Atlan 213:62-71 Je '64

RICHARDSON, Earl C.
Farm kids deserve a good education, too. Suc Farm 62:49+ Je '64
Save fruit trees from winter damage. Suc Farm 61:75 N '63
Thirty-one cows over 18,000 pounds, here's how. Suc Farm 62:133 Mr '64

RICHARDSON, Elinor
Teacher learns by TV in L.A. Sr Schol 85: 17T Ja 21 '65

RICHARDSON, Frank Howard
Are parents responsible for childhood fears? Todays Health 42:8+ O '64
Chicken pox: least serious of contagious childhood diseases. Todays Health 42:27 Ja '64
Cowpox: man's friendly disease. Todays Health 42:12+ F '64
Diphtheria: onetime child-strangler. Todays Health 42:12+ My '64
Measles: most contagious of the infectious diseases of childhood. Todays Health 41:44-5+ O '63
Mumps. Todays Health 41:6+ D '63
Should newlyweds live with their parents? excerpts from Grandparents and their families. Todays Health 42:54-5+ Ap '64
Whooping cough. Todays Health 42:36-7+ Je '64

RICHARDSON, Gloria
Gloria, Gloria. M. Kempton. il New Repub 149:15-17 N 16 '63
Gloria Richardson. il por Newsweek 62:26+ Ag 5 '63
Gloria Richardson. il pors Ebony 19:23-6+ Jl '64
People in a trap; Negro protest movement, Cambridge, Md. S. Alsop. il Sat Eve Post 237:12 Je 6 '64
Pinpoint portrait. J. H. Roy. Negro Hist Bul 27:18 O '63
State of Maryland. M. Kempton. New Repub 150:6-8 My 23 '64
Who can we surrender to? R. A. Liston. il pors Sat Eve Post 236:78-80 O 5 '63; Reply. 236:82 N 2 '63

RICHARDSON, H. Neil
Koinonia in deed. Christian Cent 81:206-7 F 12 '64

RICHARDSON, Howard
(tr) See Guerdon, D. Laundry

RICHARDSON, Jack
Mr Fisher is open. Esquire 60:158+ D '63
Noblest hustlers. Esquire 60:94+ S '63
Ten-dollar understanding. Esquire 62:101+ S '64
about
Lorenzo. Criticism
New Repub 148:29 Mr 9 '63
New Yorker 39:112+ F 23 '63
Newsweek 61:60 F 25 '63
Sat R 46:24 Mr 9 '63
Theatre Arts 47:13 Ap '63
Time 81:75 F 22 '63

RICHARDSON, John
Braque: pre-cube to post-Zen. Art N 63:29-31+ Ap '64

RICHARDSON, John Adkins
Solitude, modernity & art education. Sch Arts 63:34-7 S '63

RICHARDSON, John H.
Saigon and CIA. Newsweek 62:38+ O 21 '63

RICHARDSON, Marion B.
Who should teach engineering? letter. Science 143:916 F 28 '64

RICHARDSON, Marvis, and Dutton, R. W.
Antibody synthesizing cells: appearance after secondary antigenic stimulation in vitro. bibliog Science 146:655-6 O 30 '64

RICHARDSON, Robert S.
Reminiscences of E. C. Slipher. Sky & Tel 28:208-9 O '64

RICHARDSON, Stewart
Is the puff in danger? Pub W 184:22 Jl 22 '63

RICHARDSON, Tony
Director. New Yorker 39:47-8 O 12 '63
People are talking about. . . por Vogue 141: 78-9 F 15 '63

RICHARDSON-Merrell, Incorporated
Merrell's bitter pill; anti-cholesterol drug, MER-29. Bsns W p23 D 28 '63

RICHART, Ralph M. and Corfman, P. A.
Chromosome number and morphology of a human preinvasive neoplasm. bibliog Science 144:65-7 Ap 3 '64

RICHEY, Elinor
Keeping the outsiders out. Sat R 46:22-4 O 19 '63
Kenwood foils the block-busters. Harper 227:42-7 Ag '63
Splitsville, U.S.A. Reporter 28:35-8 My 23 '63
RICHIE, Donald
Letter from Burma. Nation 197:77-8 Ag 10 '63
Letter from Hamburg. Nation 197:96-8 Ag 24 '63
Letter from Pagan. Nation 197:166-8 S 21 '63
RICHLAND, Wash.
Plutonium town. Newsweek 63:82 Ap 20 '64
RICHLER. Mordecai
Canadiana: one man's view. Holiday 35:41+ Ap '64
Living legends. Vogue 145:128-9+ Ja 1 '65
RICHMOND, Earl
Born in a darkroom. il Design 65:80-1 N '63
RICHMOND, Phyllis Allen
What are we looking for? bibliog Science 139:737-9 F 22 '63
RICHMOND, Calif.
Safe spray banishes pool bugs. T. M. Wilson. il Am City 79:33 O '64
RICHMOND, Va.

Architecture

Plague; or Contemporary traditional architecture in America. H. H. Reed, jr. and H. S. Bryant, jr. il Arch Forum 119:112-15 S '63

Education

Schools of Richmond offer: a world of new possibilities. NEA J 54:26-8 Ja '65

Negroes

Richmond's quiet revolution. V. Dabney. Sat R 47:18-19+ F 29 '64
RICHTER, Anne J.
Frederic Melcher library of books about books. Library J 89:4118-20 O 15 '64
RICHTER, G. W.
Electron microscopy: proteins in experimental pathology. Science 141:834-5 Ag 30 '63
RICHTER, Karl
St John according to Richter. M. Bernheimer. por Sat R 48:51 Ja 30 '65
RICHTER, Max
Butterfly farmer. il pors Pop Mech 119:120-1 Mr '63
RICHTER, Sviatoslav Teofilovich. See Rikhter, S. T.
RICHTHOFEN, Manfred von
Our most worthy enemy. il pors Life 56:74-5 Mr 20 '64
RICKARD, Mrs R. B.
$4,000 borough hall. Am City 78:127-8 N '63
RICKENBACKER, Edward V.
Men and the planes: 1914-1918; six postscripts. Esquire 62:32 Ag '64
New frontiers without freedom; address, March 16, 1964. Vital Speeches 30:490-4 Je 1 '64

about

Private turbulence of Eastern air lines. I. Ross. il pors Fortune 70:172-4+ Jl '64
RICKENBACKER, William F.
CED: tycoon trap? Nat R 14:155-6 F 26 '63
Freedom, virtue, and the state. Nat R 15: 191-5 S 10 '63
House of horrors. Nat R 16:323-4 Ap 21 '64
Oh, it's a sad case, America is. Nat R 16:545-6 Je 30 '64
Ohio and Governor Rhodes. Nat R 16:61-4 Ja 28 '64
Roberto's story; forgotten young men. Nat R 15:105-6 Ag 13 '63
Visit to GHQ. por Nat R 16:354 My 5 '64

about

Rocky road of HR 6386; privacy in housing survey; excerpts from testimony. R. Burgess. Nat R 15:429 N 19 '63
RICKETT, H. W.
America's wild beauties; excerpts from Odyssey book of American wildflowers. Life 56:60-3 Ap 3 '64
RICKETTSIA
Intracellular infection and the carrier state. J. E. Smadel. bibliog il Science 140:153-60 Ap 12 '63
RICKEY, Branch
Return of the mahatma. F. Graham, jr. pors Sat Eve Post 236:66-8 Mr 9 '63
RICKEY, George
Art galleries; exhibition at the Staempfli R. M. Coates. New Yorker 40:164-5 N 7 64
RICKING, Myrl
Continuing battle. por ALA Bul 57:293-5 Ap '63
Recruitment. ALA Bul 57:267-9, 601-3, 670-1, 867-8, 1049-50; 58:236-7, 323, 567-9, 730-2 Mr, Je-Jl, O, D '63, Mr-Ap, Je, S '64
RICKMAN, Eric
Rooster tales. See issues of Hot rod
RICKOVER, Hyman George
Decline of the individual. por Sat Eve Post 236:11-13 Mr 30 '63
Never-ending challenge; excerpts from address, October 1962. U S News 54:38 Ap 22 '63
Program to improve our schools; excerpts from Education for all children. por Ladies Home J 80:20+ O '63

about

Fermi award: Rickover honored: selection signals some changes. J. Walsh. Science 146: 1149-50 N 27 '64
For Rickover: retirement or action by Congress? il por U S News 54:14 F 25 '63
Let's solve the Rickover problem. Sat Eve Post 236:80 Mr 16 '63
People of the week. por U S News 55:10 D 30 '63
Schoolmaster Rickover. C. Jencks. New Repub 148:14-16 Mr 2 '63; Reply with rejoinder. J. P. Meerman. 148:15-18 Ap 27 '63
RIDDLE airlines
Congress, CAB eye Riddle operations. R. H. Cook. Aviation W 79:47+ D 16 '63
RIDDLES
Guess who's playing Santa! il Good H 157: 100-1+ D '63
Horse race to Mecca and who owns the zebra? A. Gingrich. Esquire 60:8 S '63
RIDE from Mauch Chunk; story. See O'Hara, J.
RIDE into town; story. See Roueché, B.
RIDEAU CANAL
Home to the sea. W. C. Brewer, jr. il Motor B 113:114-15+ Ja; 24-5+ F; 52+ Mr '64
Rideau revisited. J. G. Robinson. il Yachting 114:38-40+ Ag; 52-3+ S '63
Rideau, with four apiece. H. L. Brun. il Motor B 114:28-9+ Jl '64
RIDGES, Ocean. See Ocean bottom
RIDGEWAY, James F.
AMA, the FDA and quacks. New Repub 149: 31-3 N 9 '63
Bang, bang, you're dead. New Repub 148:6 F 16 '63
Barry fights crime, but you'd never know it from the record. New Repub 151:9-11 O 3 '64
Birth control by surgery. Commonweal 151: 9-11 N 14 '64
Car design and public safety. New Repub 151:9-11 S 19 '64
Death on the Atchafalaya. New Repub 150:13-14 Ap 25 '64
Don't wait, buy a gun now! New Repub 150: 9-10 Je 6 '64
Down by the Styx. New Repub 149:8 Ag 31 '63
Fun with guns in the United States Senate. New Repub 150:6-7 F 22 '64
Great battle for Storm King. New Repub 151: 8-9 N 28 '64
Great odometer mystery. New Repub 152:10-11 Ja 23 '65
Gunboats on the Raritan. New Repub 148:17-19 Ja 1 '63
Last clean river. New Repub 151:5 D 12 '64
Look, lady, it's human. New Repub 149:8 O 5 '63
Midnight clam chase. New Repub 151:18 S 5 '64
More than a hundred ways to gyp McNamara. New Repub 150:6-7 My 2 '64
Nuclear power in private hands. New Repub 150:9-10 Ap 18 '64
One million abortions. New Repub 148:14-17 F 9 '63
Protecting the public; how independent is the FPC? New Repub 149:21-5 S 21 '63
Segregated food at the supermarket. New Repub 151:6-7 D 5 '64
Smokescreen. New Repub 152:5-6 Ja 9 '65
Snooping in the park. New Repub 152:9-10 Ja 16 '65
Snoops; private lives and public service. New Repub 151:13-17 D 19 '64
Speaking of reorganization. New Repub 151: 16 N 21 '64
That nine-foot channel. New Repub 151:12 D 26 '64
That super-quiet, squishy ride. New Repub 152:15-16 Ja 30 '65

RIDGEWAY, James F.—*Continued*
Tires and road safety. New Repub 151:8-10 O 17 '64
To bury the dead. New Repub 149:29-30 Ag 31 '63
To the rescue of the marine. New Repub 151:12 Jl 11 '64
Too old at forty-five? New Repub 151:22 Ag 22 '64
Washington rent strike. New Repub 150:10 F 8 '64
—See Kempton, M. jt. auth.
RIDGWAY, Agnes
Visit; story. Seventeen 22:98-9 O '63
RIDING. See Horsemanship
RIDLER, Anne
Uses of typology. H. Carruth. Poetry 101:424-6 Mr '63
RIDRUEJO, Dionisio
Spain's restless voices; interview. Cath World 197:88-94 My '63
RIEDEL, James A.
Boss and faction. bibliog f Ann Am Acad 353:14-26 My '64
RIEDEL, W. R. and others
Pliocene-pleistocene boundary in deep-sea sediments. bibliog Science 140:1238-40 Je 14 '63
RIEDESEL, Friederike Charlotte Luise (von Massow) freifrau von
Baroness on the battlefield; excerpts from Baroness von Riedesel and the American revolution, ed. and tr. by M. L. Brown. pors Am Heritage 16:64-79 D '64
RIEDESEL, Friedrich Adolph, freiherr von
Baroness on the battlefield; excerpts from Baroness von Riedesel and the American revolution, ed. and tr. by M. L. Brown. F. C. L. V. Riedesel. il por Am Heritage 16:64-79 D '64
RIEDL, Max
München: fun capital. U S Camera 27:82-3+ N '64
RIEFENSTAHL, Leni
Shame and glory in the movies. A. Berson and J. Keller. il Nat R 16:17-21 Ja 14 '64
RIEFF, Philip
World of Wilhelm Reich. Commentary 38:50-8 S '64
RIEHL, Herbert
On the origin and possible modification of hurricanes. bibliog Science 141:1001-10 S 13 '63
RIEKE, William O. See Kay, K. jt. auth.
RIEKER, Jane
Palm Beach: hopped up about Joey. Life 56:25 Ap 3 '64
RIEMER, George
Bizarre alphabet teaches Johnny to read. Ladies Home J 81:70-1+ O '64
Frank look at marital fidelity. Good H 158:49+ Ja '64
RIEMER, Henry
Near-perfect meter shop. Am City 78:81-3 N '63
RIENOW, Leona Train. See Rienow, R. jt. auth.
RIENOW, Robert, and Rienow, L. T.
Political frustration: cause and cure. Sat R 46:25-8 S 28 '63
RIENZI; opera. See Wagner, R.
RIES, S. K. See Donnalley, W. F. jt. auth.
RIES, Victor H.
Bulb planting. Horticulture 41:562-3 N '63
Put your garden to bed. Horticulture 41:608-9 D '63
RIESER, Carl
Great credit pump. Fortune 67:122-4+ F '63
Unfinished job at W. R. Grace. Fortune 68:108-13+ Ag '63
When the crowd goes one way Litton goes the other. Fortune 67:114-19+ My '63
RIESMAN, David
Containing ourselves; excerpt. New Repub 148:14-17 Ap 6 '63
What the Beatles prove about teen-agers; interview. U S News 56:88 F 24 '64
—and others
Tootle: a modern cautionary tale; excerpt from The lonely crowd. Wilson Lib Bul 38:160-1 O '63
RIESSMAN, Frank
Reassuring report about children with odd study habits. Redbook 124:59+ N '64
Teaching the culturally deprived. NEA J 52:20-2 Ap '63
—and Hannah, Arlene
Teachers of the poor. PTA Mag 59:12-14 N '64
RIETH, Theobald
Verdun revisited; Reconciliation over graves project. Time 82:19-20 Ag 16 '63
RIETZ, H. Lewis
Excerpts from addresses, May 8, 1962 and April 30, 1963. Cong Digest 42:221+ Ag '63
RIFAT, Gail
Dossier on a Washington beauty. il pors Mlle 58:132-5 Mr '64
RIFKIN, Alfred H.
Violence in human behavior. Science 140:904-6 My 24 '63
RIFLE practice. See Trap shooting
RIFLE ranges. See Shooting ranges
RIFLE shooting. See Shooting
RIFLE sights. See Firearms—Sights
RIFLE straps. See Hunting outfits
RIFLE targets. See Targets
RIFLES
Colt's new rifle; the M-16. il Time 82:86 N 22 '63
Four-in-one gun. il Pop Mech 121:122-3 F '64
GI guns that aren't. il Bsns W p 139-40 F 23 '63
Gun that broke the red-tape barrier; Armalite rifle. K. Warner. il Pop Mech 120:108-10+ S '63
How to buy a good used gun. E. Matunas. il Pop Mech 120:130-4 N '63
In atomic age, army seeks a better rifle. U S News 55:11 Jl 15 '63
Krag-Jorgensen. C. G. Worman. il Hobbies 69:125+ Ag '64
Lightest hunting rifle ever made. K. Warner. il Pop Sci 185:90+ N '64
New army rifle is on target; Colt AR-15. il Bsns W p 110 N 16 '63
New Remington and Weatherby rifles. J. O'Connor. il Outdoor Life 133:128+ Ap '64
New rifle can kill man behind concrete wall. Sci N L 85:78 F 1 '64
New rifles for '64. W. Page. il Field & S 68:114-18 Mr '64
Not just kid stuff; Daisy rifles. il Bsns W p88-90 Ja 25 '64
Putt-putt-putt. W. Page. il Field & S 69:78-81 Jl '64
Rifle called Daisy. J. D. Brown. il Sports Illus 18:58-64+ Ap 29 '63
Rifles for Africa. J. O'Connor. il Outdoor Life 132:54+ D '63
Sighting in for big game. J. O'Connor. il Outdoor Life 132:70+ S '63
Spencer repeater. W. R. Orbelo. il Hobbies 68:123 S '63
Stocks for hunting rifles. J. O'Connor. il Outdoor Life 134:54-8 D '64
Tomorrow's rifles. il Time 84:35 Ag 14 '64
.22 caliber autoloading rifles. il Consumer Rep 30:34-7 Ja '65
Varminter carbine. Field & S 67:102 Mr '63
What happened to the .256? W. Page. il Field & S 67:58-60 F '63
Winchester's new Model 70. J. O'Connor. il Outdoor Life 133:104-8 Mr '64
See also
Shooting—Competitions
RIFLES, Air. See Air guns
RIFT. See Rockets, Atomic powered
RIGA, Peter J.
Liturgy and action. Commonweal 81:445-8 D 25 '64
RIGA, MOUNT. See Taconic Mountains
RIGER, Robert
Baseball's power elite. Esquire 59:76-7+ Je '63
.4 of a second. Esquire 61:82-7 Ja '64
Greatest fights of the century. il Esquire 60:188-91 D '63
Sunny Jim's lament. Esquire 60:83-6 Ag '63
RIGG, K. B.
Lime: good or bad for your garden? Pop Gard 14:16+ Mr '63
RIGGING. See Masts and rigging
RIGGS, Dionis Coffin
Hummingbird's nest; poem. McCalls 90:168 My '63
RIGGS, F. Behn
World information center. Bul Atomic Sci 21:34-5 Ja '65
RIGGS, John L. and Lennette, E. H.
Simian virus 40: isolation of two plaque types. bibliog Science 147:408-9 Ja 22 '65
RIGGS, Robert L.
Thruston Morton, the all-purpose Republican. New Repub 150:8-10 Je 27 '64
RIGHT and left (political science)
Blessing of extremism; address, March 21, 1963. L. E. Read. Vital Speeches 29:403-7 Ap 15 '63
Cell 772, or Life among the extremists. W. Morris. Commentary 38:31-9 O '64
Extremism: letters to the editor. Christian Cent 81:1306-7 O 21 '64

RIGHT and left (political science)—*Continued*
Facing extremism. C. Banks. Christian Cent 81:1623 D 30 '64
Liberals and the right. Commonweal 81:372-3 D 11 '64
Speaking of extremists, who's playing right field? W. K. Wyant, jr. New Repub 151:12-16 S 19 '64; Reply. K. Friedberg. 151:29-30 O 10 '64
Strange tactics of extremism, by H. Overstreet and B. Overstreet. Review
Harper 229:20+ N '64. J. Fischer
Sat R 47:39 O 3 '64. R. Drummond
Sat R 47:95-6 O 10 '64. R. L. Tobin
What is an extremist? G. B. Leonard. Look 28:33-7 O 20 '64
See also
Conservatism
Liberalism
RIGHT- and left-handedness. See Left- and right-handedness
RIGHT and wrong. See Ethics
RIGHT kind of house; story. See Slesar, H.
RIGHT of assembly. See Assembly, Right of
RIGHT of asylum. See Asylum, Right of
RIGHT of counsel. See Right to counsel
RIGHT of privacy. See Privacy
RIGHT of way
See also
Eminent domain
RIGHT thing; story. See Watson, B. J.
RIGHT to counsel
Annals of law; Gideon case. A. Lewis. il New Yorker 40:144+ Ap 25; 108+ My 2; 150+ My 9 '64
Bar behind bars. Time 83:88+ My 22 '64
Confessions from suspects; Danny Escobedo's conviction reversed. Time 84:51 Jl 3 '64
Crime, wealth and justice. R. Goldfarb. New Repub 151:15-16 Ag 22 '64
Ex-con overturns the law; with report by M. Durham. il Life 56:83-4+ Je 12 '64
Gideon's echoes; right to counsel affirmed in trials for misdemeanor. Time 85:39+ Ja 29 '65
Gideon's trumpet, by A. Lewis. Review
New Repub 151:21+ Jl 4 '64. H. L. Packer
Sat R 47:28 Je 27 '64. W. B. Butler
Time il 84:118-19 S 18 '64
Rising to the defense. il Time 84:56+ Ag 7 '64
RIGHT to labor
Other rights battle. Time 83:100+ My 15 '64
See also
Labor laws and legislation—United States
Open and closed shop
RIGHT to travel. See Travel regulations
RIGHT to work laws. See Labor laws and legislation—United States
RIGHT wing conservatives. See Conservatism
RIGHT you are if you think you are; drama. See Pirandello, L.
RIGHTIST propaganda. See Propaganda
RIGHTS, Bill of (United States) See United States—Constitution—Bill of rights
RIGHTS, Civil. See Civil rights
RIGHTS, Natural. See Natural law
RIGHTS, Universal declaration of human. See Universal declaration of human rights
RIGHTS of women. See Woman—Equal rights
RIGOLETTO; opera. See Verdi, G.
RIHA, Jeanne
Triple revolution. America 112:162-4 Ja 30 '65
RIIS, Roger William
I am for the churches. Read Digest 84:135-8 Je '64
RIIS-HANSEN, Vagn
Marvellous food at Messel's. Vogue 142:136+ D '63
RIJN, Rembrandt Hermanszoon van. See Rembrandt Hermanszoon van Rijn
RIKER, Audrey. See Riker C. jt. auth.
RIKER, Charles, and Riker, Audrey
And baby makes three. Parents Mag 39:52-3+ Mr '64
RIKHOFF, James C.
Big on pigs. por Outdoor Life 134:34-5+ Ag '64
RIKHTER, Svîatoslav Teofilovich
Notes from abroad. P. Moor. Hi Fi 13:28+ Mr '63
RIKHYE, Indar Jit
U.N.'s new power; where will it be used next? il U S News 54:54-6 F 4 '63
RIKLIS, Meshulam
But when they voted. por Newsweek 62:104 O 14 '63
Caught in the rapids. por Time 82:93-4+ O 11 '63
Who's to blame for Riklis? Riklis? S. H. Brown. il por Fortune 68:136-7+ O '63
RILEY, Bridget
Something to blink at. il Time 83:75 My 1 '64
RILEY, Condon
Saint Anthony paintings of Frank Mason. Am Artist 28:62-7+ Je '64
RILEY, Frank
Computer commuter? Travel 121:41 Mr '64
RILEY, Gordon A.
Experimental marine ecology. Science 142:1685+ D 27 '63
RILEY, Marjorie Western
Dear, it's so nice of you to ask me, but; poem. McCalls 92:84 O '64
RILEY, Nord
Goof hunter's Bible. Outdoor Life 132:34-5+ D '63
I love a quail named Gambel. Outdoor Life 132:50-1+ Ag '63
RILEY, Robert, and others
Cellulose acetate membranes: electron microscopy of structure. bibliog Science 143:801-3 F 21 '64
RILEY, Vernon
Synergism between a lactate dehydrogenase-elevating virus and eperythrozoon coccoides. bibliog Science 146:921-3 N 13 '64
RILKE, Rainer Maria
Four German poets. L. Mueller. Poetry 101:291 Ja '63
Santa Claus of loneliness. por Time 83:118+ Je 12 '64
RIMBAUD, Arthur
Four poets and two dramatists. W. Fowlie. Poetry 104:190-1 Je '64
RIMSKII-KORSAKOV, Nikolaĭ Andreevich
From ultraphone, Rimsky-Korsakov's last opera. P. L. Miller. Am Rec G 31:452-3 Ja '65
RINEHART, Jonathan
Mothers without joy. Sat Eve Post 236:29-30+ Mr 23 '63; Same abr. Read Digest 83:83-7 Jl '63
RINEHART, Marion Sladky
Fringe benefit in Egypt. pors Wilson Lib Bul 39:52-5 S '64
RINES, Robert H.
Inventor of the month. S. V. Jones. il por Sci Digest 57:15 Ja '65
RINFRET, A. P.
Deep-freezing our heritage; excerpt from Cryogenic technology, ed. by R. W. Vance. por Sat R 46:62-3 O 5 '63
RING-billed gulls. See Gulls
RING culture. See Plants—Soilless culture
RING-neck doves. See Pigeons
RINGEL, William E.
Is it all right to break the law? por U S News 55:6 Ag 12 '63
RINGGENBERG, Harold R.
Print. Sch Arts 64:13-15 Ja '65
RINGLAND, Arthur
John Dennett Guthrie, Pinchot pioneer. Am For 69:23+ F '63
RINGLING brothers, Barnum and Bailey circus. See Circus
RINGLING brothers circus. See Circus
RINGOLD, Evelyn S.
Parent and child. N Y Times Mag p32 Je 30; 47-8 Ag 11; 61-2 S 22; 49-51 D 15 '63; 63-4 My 10 '64
(comp) Please write. N Y Times Mag p38 Je 23 '63
RINGS
If your husband wears a wedding ring. il McCalls 90:62 Je '63
Rings around your future; engagement rings. il Seventeen 22:66 My '63
RINGS, Vortex. See Vortex motion
RINGS of trees. See Tree rings
RINGWOOD, N.J.
Intellectual freedom; raising hell with the Legionnaires. E. T. Moore. ALA Bul 57:222-4 Mr '63
RINGWORM fungi. See Fungi, Pathogenic
RINKER, Floyd
English-communication; summary of address. Sr Schol 84:1T-2T F 28 '64
RINKS, Skating. See Skating rinks
RINZLER, Alan
No soul in Beatlesville. Nation 198:221-2 Mr 2 '64

RIO DE JANEIRO

Description

Going places, finding things in Brazil, Chile and Peru. D. Beal. il House & Gard 124: 270+ N '63
Romantic Rio: city of a thousand delights. A. Rankin. il Read Digest 86:181-2+ Ja '65
Why they're still flying down to Rio. R. Joseph. il Esquire 60:214-17 D '63

Galleries and museums

Museum in Rio conceived as fine arts center. il Arch Rec 133:149-52 Mr '63

Housing

New houses for Rio. V. Sanson. il Américas 16:32-3 D '64

Music

Brazil nuts; Teatro municipal's first international opera season in eight years. Newsweek 64:74 Ag 31 '64
Flying down to Rio. R. Kovacs. Opera N 28:32 D 14 '63

Social conditions

No easy answer; Rio's *favelas*. M. J. Kubic. il Newsweek 64:59 N 30 '64

Social life and customs

People of Rio. L. Gross. il Look 27:54-64 Je 4 '63

Theater

Theatre. S. Richards. il Theatre Arts 47:64-5 F '63

RIO GRANDE
Peace on the Rio Grande. New Repub 149:7 S 21 '63

RIO GRANDE VALLEY
Overlap land, gringo and Mexican meet in the Rio Grande country. J. Graves. Holiday 35:74-5+ Mr '64

RIO treaty. See Inter-American treaty of reciprocal assistance

RIOPELLE, Arthur J. See Carmichael, L. jt. auth.

RIOPELLE, Jean Paul
Riopelle: international speedscapes. F. O'Hara. il por Art N 62:32-4+ Ap '63
Rocket Riopelle. il por Newsweek 61:97-8 My 27 '63

RIOT act; drama. See Greene, W.

RIOTS
Anti-U.S. riots around the world: why. il U S News 57:11 D 7 '64
Around the world, reds burn U.S. books. il U S News 57:62-3 D 21 '64
As racial conflicts broke out anew. il U S News 54:8 Ap 29 '63
Cambridge, Md; Savannah, Ga; New York, N.Y. il Newsweek 62:21-3 Jl 22 '63
Campus riots: they got out of hand this year. il U S News 54:10 My 20 '63
Civil rights: it's a two-way street. il Newsweek 62:35 Jl 29 '63
College student behavior. W. W. Brickman. Sch & Soc 91:343 N 16 '63
Dangers of militancy; Negro outbursts. Time 82:17 Jl 19 '63
Day at the stadium; final match rugger world series; at Port Elizabeth South Africa. il Time 82:36+ S 20 '63
How the reds make a riot. E. H. Methvin. Read Digest 86:63-9 Ja '65
How to avoid a race riot. A. I. Waskow. Sat R 46:8-10+ Jl 6 '63
Is the public getting the truth about the race issue? size-up by a panel of editors from North and South. il U S News 55:82-7 N 11 '63
No cheers for the rah-rah riot. G. Hechinger and F. M. Hechinger. il N Y Times Mag p33+ My 26 '63
North and South, more race troubles. U S News 55:8 O 7 '63
Now, Birmingham violence up North: New York and Chicago. il U S News 55:4 Ag 12 '63
Other areas where race riots flared. il U S News 57:6 Ag 3 '64
Race riots: a world problem. U S News 57:24 Ag 10 '64
Race, riots and city administration. Am City 79:7 S '64
Race riots of the past: a worry for the future. il U S News 55:54-5 Jl 15 '63
Reporter at large; admission of Negro students to University of Georgia. C. Trillin. New Yorker 39:62-7 Jl 13 '63
Riotous fun; teen-age rioting. il Time 82: 80 S 13 '63
Thirty miles divide folly and reason; Cambridge and Salisbury, Md; with report by M. Durham. il Life 55:18-25 Jl 26 '63
Those do-it-yourself spontaneous riots; anti-American demonstrations. il Time 84:27-8 D 18 '64
Three USIS libraries attacked in Cairo, Jakarta, and Surabaya. Library J 90:80 Ja 1 '65
We was robbed! riots at Long Island's Roosevelt raceway. il Time 82:77 N 15 '63
When left-wingers went wild in Britain. il U S News 54:16 Ap 29 '63
When race tension became race strife. il U S News 55:6 Jl 22 '63
Where racial problems flared in North: New York and Cleveland. il U S News 56:4 F 10 '64
Who can we surrender to? R. A. Liston. il Sat Eve Post 236:78-80 O 5 '63
Why race troubles hit one city, spare another: a case study: Cambridge and Salisbury, Md. il U S News 55:78-80 Ag 5 '63

See also

Draft riots, 1863
Mob violence
also subhead Riots under names of countries and cities, e.g. India—Riots

RIOUX, J. William
School social work in the United States. Sch Life 46:9-10 Ag '64

RIPLEY, Robert LeRoy
Baffling black-and-white. M. R. Weiss. il Sat R 47:66 S 12 '64

RIPLEY, Sidney Dillon, 2d
American triangular turned chair? Antiques 85:104-6 Ja '64
Smithsonian head sees museum as lively spot; summary of address. Sci N L 85:120 F 22 '64

about

Modernizing the attic. il por Time 83:74-5 F 21 '64
Ripley revisited. New Yorker 40:19-21 Jl 11 '64
Smithsonian institution elects new secretary. por Sci N L 84:53 Jl 27 '63

RIPLEY, Miss.
Christmas carpenters; rebuilding Antioch Baptist church. il Newsweek 65:15-16 Ja 4 '65

RIPPLE, Ezra H.
Civil, and sometimes uncivil, war; excerpts from manuscripts with sketches by J. E. Taylor, ed. with introd. by B. Catton. Am Heritage 15:50-61 O '64

RISBERGS, Janis
That crazy Latvian. il por Newsweek 63:73-4 Mr 9 '64; Same abr. Read Digest 85:25-6 Jl '64

RISEN, Celia C.
Born with no place to go. Sat R 48:25-6 Ja 16 '65

RISING sun. See Tokyo—Newspapers

RISINGER, Gerald E. and Parker, P. N.
Thiamine: a novel conversion from thiochrome. Science 141:1280-1 S 27 '63

RISK capital. See Capital

RISKS (insurance) See Insurance—Risks

RISSE, Joseph A.
Hum from crossed connections. Electr World 71:86 F '64

RISSER, Paul G.
Somatic mitoses in cells of picea glauca cultivated in vitro. bibliog Science 143:591-2 F 7 '64

RITCHIE, Virginia
Have children, can travel! Sr Schol 84:8T-9T Mr 20 '64

RITCHIE, Ward
Ward Ritchie: designer, printer, publisher, man of books. P. A. Bennett. il por Pub W 186:84-8+ O 5 '64

RITES and ceremonies

See also

Marriage customs and rites
Processions

Congo (capital Leopoldville)

Atrocities seen as rites; cannibalism by Congolese rebels. B. Tufty. Sci N L 86:371 D 12 '64

Japan

Japanese New Year. il Travel 121:39-43 Ja '64

RITES of passage; story. See Blum, R.

RITOSSA, F. M. and Von Borstel, R. C.
Chromosome puffs in drosophila induced by ribonuclease. bibliog Science 145:513-14 Jl 31 '64

RITSOS, Yannis
Night of a solitary; Immobility of the voyage; Surpassing of danger; Rainy; Ultimate landing; Honest confrontation; Heard and the unheard; Estrangement; Recollection; Moment; Architect; poems, tr. by R. Dalven. Poetry 103:306-15 F '64
about
Note on Yannis Ritsos. R. Dalven. Poetry 103:334 F '64

RITTER, E. Jay
Long live the cockroach. Sci Digest 54:41-4 N '63
Sojourner Truth. Negro Hist Bul 26:254 My '63

RITTER, Hope, Jr
Defense of mate and mating chamber in a wood roach. Science 143:1459-60 Mr 27 '64

RITTER, Norman. See Pearson, D. jt. auth.

RIVALS; drama. See Sheridan, R. B.

RIVALS; story. See Baker, L.

RIVER boats. See Steamships and steamboats

RIVER fronts. See Water fronts

RIVER navigation. See Inland navigation

RIVER trips
Colorado jackpot. J. Olsen. il Sports Illus 19:52-9 S 2 '63
Colorado River cruise. V. L. Oertle. il Yachting 113:52-3 Mr '63
Cruising the Connecticut. B. Hawkins. il Motor B 113:30-1+ Ap '64
Cruising the upper Mississippi. F. M. Paulson. il Field & S 69:62-5+ Je '64
Desert boating; lower Colorado River. F. M. Paulson. il Field & S 69:57-9+ N '64
Exploring the Colorado: Lee's Ferry to Lake Mead. F. E. Masland, jr. il Nat Parks Mag 38:4-7+ My '64
Going places, finding things on a Mississippi paddle wheeler. M. C. Burke. il House & Gard 126:44-6+ N '64
In the wake of Daniel Boone. J. Gribbins. il Motor B 113:38-9+ Je '64
Inside Europe aboard Yankee. I. Johnson and E. Johnson. il Nat Geog Mag 126:157-95 Ag '64
Lady on a river of rock; Barranca de Cobre, Mexico, ed. by J. O'Reilly. M. E. O'Reilly. il Sports Illus 19:26+ O 21 '63
McKenzie River trip. W. F. Heald. il Travel 122:31-3 Jl '64
Missouri River cruise. R. J. Smith. il Yachting 116:40-3+ Jl '64
Try Florida's St Johns. C. R. Meyer. il Motor B 114:32-5 S '64
Upriver from Nawiliwili; Huleia River. il Sunset 131:61-2 O '63
You may hear Lorelei sing. il Sunset 131:32 O '63
See also
Canoe trips

RIVERA, Betty
Honesty. Horticulture 41:605 D '63
Witchery of witch hazel. Horticulture 41:181 Mr '63

RIVERA, Chita
She dances with marvelous joy. E. Palatsky. il pors Dance Mag 39:32-5 Ja '65

RIVERA, Diego
Fabulous life of Diego Rivera, by B. D. Wolfe. Review
Nation 198:18-19 Ja 4 '64. H. Kramer
Time il por 82:100+ N 22 '63
He mixed his paints with politics. W. G. Rogers. il Sat R 46:60 D 7 '63

RIVERDALE. See Bronx, N.Y.

RIVERDALE, Md.
It's in the bag for a second city. W. Ford and J. Carswell. il Am City 79:22 My '64

RIVERDALE, N.J.
International chef; Powder Horne mill. il Travel 119:38 Mr '63

RIVERDALE outdoor laboratories. See Nature study

RIVERHEAD, N.Y.
Incident in a rural slum. L. Long. Christian Cent 81:1088-9 S 2 '64

RIVERHEAD, N.Y, free library
Public library and the teen-age; Young adult book discussion group for past four summers. D. R. Watts. Wilson Lib Bul 38:299 N '63

RIVERS, Larry
Dear teen-age audience. por Seventeen 23:170+ N '64
Street scene. por Newsweek 62:75 S 2 '63

RIVERS, Thomas E.
World recreation congress, Japan 1964. Recreation 58:25 Ja '65

RIVERS, William L.
Focussing a wide angle lens on life. Sat R 46:24-5 Je 29 '63
High times with a by-line. Sat R 46:20 Ag 17 '63

RIVERS
Operation Badajoz: Spain's TVA. R. M. Elizalde. il Am For 69:24-7 F '63
Rivers of international concord. G. F. White. il UNESCO Courier 17:32-3+ Jl '64
Turn left at Spring Creek, Wyoming. M. Hagen. il Am For 70:30-1+ S '64
Twelve rivers under protection study. C. H. Callison. Audubon Mag 66:178 My '64
See also
Brooks, creeks, etc.
Deltas
Floods
Water pollution
also names of rivers, e.g. Danube River

Names

See Names, Geographical

Regulation

See also
Mississippi River—Regulation
Nile River

RIVERSIDE, Calif.
New maintenance center brings order out of chaos. R. W. Broffle. il Am City 79:93-5 O '64

RIVERSIDE Drive; drama. See Donovan, J.

RIVERSIDE yacht club. See Yacht clubs

RIVETING. See Rivets and riveting

RIVETS and riveting
Pop goes the rivet. J. Burroughs. il Pop Sci 185:156-7 N '64
Pop rivets; new riveting tool, Pop Rive Tool. il Hot Rod 17:52-3 D '64
Quick riveter; Marson rivet-all. C. Conley. il Field & S 69:91 Ag '64
Tool to make riveting easy; RiveTool. il Consumer Rep 29:214 My '64
Useful art of riveting. il Sunset 134:84-5 Ja '65

RIVIERA
Artful Riviera. H. Sutton. il Sat R 47:22-3 Ag 8 '64
How to rent a yacht on the Riviera. L. R. Hills. il Esquire 59:95-6+ Ap '63
Italian Riviera, land that winter forgot. H. Walker. il Nat Geog Mag 123:743-89 Je '63
Less expensive Riviera visit. Sunset 132:32 Ja '64
Little winkel of paradise on the *mittelmeer*. H. Sutton. il Sat R 47:19+ S 5 '64
See also
Saint-Tropez, France

RIVIERE, Bill
Pole your canoe. Field & S 68:50-3+ My '63

RIVKIN, Arnold
Nigeria: a unique nation; excerpts from African presence in world affairs. Cur Hist 45:329-34 D '63

RIVOYRE, Christine de
Jubilation; tr. by F. Frenaye. Vogue 144:238-9+ D '64

RIZZOLI, Angelo
Enough for one man. il por Newsweek 65:46-8 Ja 4 '65

RIZZOLI editore. See Publishers and publishing—Italy

ROACH, Irene
Our children made us stop smoking! Parents Mag 39:35+ Jl '64

ROAD accidents. See Traffic accidents

ROAD construction. See Highway engineering

ROAD is long; story. See Moser, E.

ROAD law. See Highway law

ROAD making machinery
What the road show has for urban streets. il Am City 78:98-102 F '63

ROAD maps, guides, etc.
How to read a road map. G. M. Schultz. il Todays Health 41:14-17+ Mr '63
Lost heroes of touring. R. Cantwell. il Sports Illus 20:60-2+ Je 22 '64

ROAD materials
See also
Aggregates (building materials)

ROAD models. See Roads—Models

ROAD signs
Across Europe with sign language. il Sunset 132:64-5 F '64
Sign uniformity still lagging. il Am City 79:104 D '64
Signs of our times. M. Lamm. il Motor T 15:60-3 Ag '63

ROAD to Bethlehem; drama. See DuBois, G.

ROAD traffic
Highway revolution. R. Moley. Newsweek 63: 96 My 4; 104 My 11 '64
Strange highway forces that louse up your driving; report from Purdue university. E. D. Fales, jr. il Pop Sci 184:94-7+ My '64
See also
Highway engineering
Street traffic
Television in traffic control
Traffic engineering
Traffic regulations
Traffic signs

Radar control

Radar vs. speeding; Montclair. N.J. H. Knowles. il Am City 79:119 Ap '64

Europe, Western

Get a horse. il Newsweek 63:44 Ap 13 '64
Traffic jams, too; how Europe fights them. il U S News 56:60-1 Ap 6 '64

France

Aux armes, automobilistes! il Time 83:26 Ja 31 '64

ROADS
See also
Culverts
Driveways
Streets
Trails

Contracts

Corrupt society. F. J. Cook. Nation 196:466-9 Je 1 '63

Federal aid

More billions for roads. Bsns W p36 Ag 29 '64

Finance

Higher cost for U.S. highway system. U S News 58:93 Ja 25 '65
Road costs go higher. il Bsns W p84 D 5 '64
See also
Toll roads

Intersections

Trapped in spaghetti. il Time 84:60 O 30 '64

Law

See Highway law

Lighting

Light touch on the freeway; Santa Monica freeway. il Am City 78:123 O '63
New lighting advances. il Am City 78:124+ O '63

Models

Pint-sized super highways. il Pop Mech 121:128-31 Mr '64

Radar control

See Road traffic—Radar control

Safety devices and measures

Country roads, they're not safe! L. J. Urben. Suc Farm 61:130 Ap '63

Superhighways

See Express highways

Traffic lines

See Traffic markings

Alaska

See also
Alaska highway

Arizona

Arizona's Pinal pioneer parkway. il Sunset 132:38+ Ja '64

Asia

Asian highway. il UN Mo Chron 1:67-74 O '64
Intelligence report; secret Chinese road-building. il Newsweek 61:34 Ap 29 '63

California

For back road collectors; Anderson grade. il Sunset 132:66+ Je '64
Freeways versus redwoods. R. D. Butcher. il Nat Parks Mag 38:12-15 Je '64
Instead of the freeway. il Sunset 130:86-91 Mr '63
Redwood highway: will it be parkway or freeway? il Sunset 131:23 S '63
Road ahead is mostly empty; Death Valley-Big Pine road. il Sunset 131:18 D '63
Up a tree; question of widening highway 101 or saving redwoods. il Newsweek 63:68-9 Ap 20 '64

Canada

Along the Trans-Canada highway with boys and station wagon. R. L. Ornauer. il Redbook 122:60-1+ F '64
For mountain road collectors. the Rogers Pass drive is ready. il Sunset 131:41+ Jl '63
Life guide; loafing spots along the Trans-Can. il Life 54:19 My 17 '63
Personal business: automobile tours. Bsns W p 101 Jl 6 '63

Central America

See also
Pan-American highway

China (People's Republic)

China s new roads: where do they lead? D. Warner. il Reporter 29:31-3 S 26 '63

Florida

On the edge of the Everglades; Tamiami trail. S. Akin. il Travel 122:32-4 O '64

Italy

Half-billion-dollar lace to tie the Italian boot. il Fortune 68:102-7 Ag '63

Jordan

In no man's land; disputed road. il Newsweek 64:52+ N 16 '64

Kentucky

We took the back way home. J. Stuart. il Am For 69:40-1+ N '63

Latin America

Facts and figures of the Americas. il Américas 15:42-3 Ap '63
See also
Pan-American highway

New York (state)

Highway robbery; proposed highway along banks of the Willowemoc and Beaver kill. Sports Illus 20:7 F 3 '64
Notes and comment; renaming New York state thruway. il New Yorker 40:23 F 29 '64
Snow convoy! New York state thruway. E. D. Fales, jr. il Pop Sci 184:69-74+ F '64

Pennsylvania

Uncorking a bottleneck; modernizing Pennsylvania turnpike. il Bsns W p 106 S 21 '63

United States

Blue Ridge parkway. J. T. Starr. il Atlan 211:120-1 My '63
Facts and figures of the Americas. il Américas 15:42-3 Ap '63
Highway program heads for new crisis. il Nations Bsns 52:34-5+ O '64
Highway revolution. R. Moley. Newsweek 63: 96 My 4; 104 My 11 '64
Highway robbery. J. Wright. il Sat Eve Post 236:19-23 N 30 '63
History along a U.S. byway; Virginia's Route 5. il Time 84:57-62 Jl 10 '64
Interstate highways: a progress report; with map. Changing T 18:23-5 Je '64
Let's clean up this highway mess. K. O. Gilmore. Read Digest 85:86-92 N '64
Let's rescue our roadsides now! M. Frome. Am For 69:10-11+ N '63
Route sixty-six; boulevard to the Golden West. H. E. Dark. il Todays Health 41: 28-9+ Je '63
Shenandoah trails; Skyline drive. J. T. Starr. il Am For 69:16-18+ Je '63
Sights on the shunpikes. il Time 84:56+ Jl 10 '64
Some scandals in the roads program. U S News 54:10 My 13 '63
This new sign could lead you to a whole new way of life. il House B 106:54-5+ Jl '64
See also
Billboards
Express highways
Roads—Federal aid
Toll roads

Utah

Logan Canyon road controversy: anatomy of a principle. J. H. Berryman. il Nat Parks Mag 37:12-15 Jl '63

Virginia

Improvement not needed. il Nat Parks Mag 38:16 Jl '64
Porpoising highway; Chesapeake Bay tunnel-bridge. il Pop Mech 119:94-5 Je '63

Western states

Personal business: automobile tours. Bsns W p 101 Jl 6 '63

ROADSIDE advertising. See Advertising, Outdoor

ROADSIDE improvement
Let's rescue our roadsides now! M. Frome. Am For 69:10-11 N '63

ROADSTERS. See Sports cars

ROALMAN, A. R.
Dogs can be fun and safe. Todays Health 42:20-2 Jl '64
These groups do something about high taxes! Suc Farm 62:32 Mr '64

ROALMAN, Pete
Prepare for the unexpected. Field & S 68:40-2+ D '63

ROAN, Peter R.
Value analysis. por Am City 79:101-2 Jl '64

ROANOKE, Va.

Education

School-within-a-school concept for Roanoke. il Arch Rec 135:158-9 F '64

ROARK, Garland
Non-fiction that reads like a novel. Writer 78:16-18 Ja '65

ROASTING. See Cookery—Meat; Cookery—Poultry

ROBB, Felix C.
Academic preparation of teachers: Conant's proposals. Science 141:1166-8 S 20 '63

ROBBE-GRILLET, Alain
Secret room; story. Esquire 59:79 F '63

about

Robbe-Grillet. New Yorker 40:24-5 Ja 9 '65

ROBBERIES and assaults
Amateurs; bank robberies in the U.S. Time 82:19 Ag 23 '63
Big deal on Casino street; robbery of Clerc's jewelry shop, Monte Carlo. Time 84:31 Jl 31 '64
Big rise in bank robberies and the FBI response. il U S News 54:14 Ap 15 '63
Bigger than Brinks; Royal mail robbery. il Newsweek 62:40+ Ag 19 '63
Biggest caper; New York jewel robbery. il Newsweek 62:36 N 18 '63
Britain's great train robbery; mystery unraveled. il U S News 56:46-9 Ja 6 '64
Cheddington caper; Royal mail robbery. il Time 82:21-2 Ag 16 '63
Day they shot it out at Maryknoll seminary. il Life 56:46-7 Mr 20 '64
Gigantic gem goof; Manhattan's jewel theft of November 8, 1963. P. Mandel. il Life 56: 84-6+ F 7 '64
Great British train robbery; seven million in cash. P. Hamill. il Sat Eve Post 237: 30-2+ S 19 '64; Same abr. with title Britain's great train robbery. Read Digest 85:134-9 D '64
Greatest jewel robbery; hold-up of a jewelry delivery station wagon in Manhattan. il Time 82:20 N 22 '63
Greatest train robbery; Glasgow-to-London mail train. il U S News 55:12 Ag 19 '63
Hilarious hunt for the highwaymen; Great Cape Cod mail robbery. E. M. Wylie and R. V. Leary. il Sat Eve Post 236:75-81 Ap 13 '63
Looting the loot; New York jewel robbery. il Newsweek 62:35-6 N 25 '63
New-style bank robber. F. Sondern, jr. il Read Digest 83:33-4+ D '63
Stop! for the greatest train robbery; with comment by E. Chapman. il Life 55:16-23 Ag 23 '63
Train robbery's sequel: covering the loss; $7-million holdup. il Bsns W p 108+ Ag 17 '63
Treasure hunt; theft of $7 million from the Glasgow-London Royal mail train. Newsweek 62:42-3 Ag 26 '63
Who robs banks and how much is taken. U S News 56:8 Mr 9 '64

See also
Burglary and burglars

ROBBERS. See Brigands and robbers

ROBBERSON, Elbert
Automatic direction finders. Yachting 115: 76-8+ Ja '64
Boat sanitation. Yachting 116:52-5+ O '64
Electrical and electronic. il Yachting 115:44-5+ Ap '64
Electronic boating aids. Yachting 114:51-3+ Jl '63
Get the most out of your binoculars. Yachting 115:57-9+ Mr '64
Marine radio. Yachting 115:60-2+ Je; 116:54-6+ Jl '64
Speedometers and logs. Yachting 116:44-6+ D '64
Transistorized electronic ignition systems. Yachting 114:63-5+ N '63
We build a boat. Yachting 115:38-40+ F '64
What radiotelephone? Yachting 117:80-2+ Ja '65
What you should know about alternators. Yachting 113:40-2+ F '63
(ed) Yachting asks about fiberglass boats. por Yachting 115:45-8+ My '64
(ed) Yachting asks about wooden boats; questions and answers. por Yachting 114: 60-3+ O '63

ROBBERSON, Winifred
Are you asking for more laws? Yachting 113: 164-5 Je '63
Yo ho! to the fair by boat. il Yachting 116: 164 Jl '64

ROBBERY insurance. See Insurance, Burglary

ROBBIA, Giovanni della
Antiques. A. Winchester. il Antiques 83:429 Ap '63

ROBBIA, Luca Della
Gallery for young people. C. B. Johnson. il Sch Arts 64:45 D '64

ROBBINS, Daniel
Gleizes: cubism as a way of life. Art N 63: 24-7+ S '64
Morris Louis: triumph of color. Art N 62:28-9+ O '63
Superart and superman. Art N 62:35-7+ Ap '63

ROBBINS, Eldon
Pack up and go. Pop Sci 184:145+ F '64

ROBBINS, Elliott, and Marcus, P. I.
Mitotically synchronized mammalian cells: a simple method for obtaining large populations. bibliog Science 144:1152-3 My 29 '64

ROBBINS, Emma B.
Imagement for catalog card reproduction. por Library J 88:3544-6 O 1 '63

ROBBINS, Jay H.
Tissue culture studies of the human lymphocyte. bibliog Science 146:1648-54 D 25 '64

ROBBINS, Jhan
Children who caused a crisis. Redbook 123:50-1+ Ag '64
I stayed after school with Theodore Roosevelt. Read Digest 85:76-80 O '64
Launching of J.J.C.B.C.Theophrastus. Read Digest 84:243+ Je '64
Visit to County Wexford, Ireland. Redbook 124:76-8 N '64
What are Americans like? Redbook 122:56-7+ D '63

—and Robbins, June
Convict who became a minister. Redbook 124:38-9+ D '64
John Glenn: aftermath of a bad year. Redbook 124:44-5+ Ja '65
New teenage medicine. Good H 157:70-1+ Ag '63
One man's war on war. Redbook 123:54-5+ My '64
One of our children is a pony. Good H 156: 66+ My '63
Psychic powers of Sam Benson. Read Digest 86:119-22 Ja '65
Success of women's success schools. Read Digest 83:115-18 D '63
Why didn't they hit back? Redbook 121:52-3+ Jl '63
Will Shakespeare's happy 400th birthday. Read Digest 84:23-4+ Ap '64

ROBBINS, June. See Robbins, Jhan, jt. auth.

ROBBINS, Mary Louise
Antigens. Science 141:443-4 Ag 2 '63

ROBBINS, Paul R.
Crop cost-cutting ideas that really work. Suc Farm 62:34-5 D '64

ROBBINS, Tom
Redbook dialogue: B. Russell and T. Robbins. por Redbook 123:66-7+ S '64

ROBERSON, Diane L.
Flower recipes for garden gourmets. Horticulture 41:174-5 Mr '63
Rose recipes. Horticulture 41:313 Je '63
Salad greens for your garden. Horticulture 41:222-3+ Ap '63

ROBERT, Henry Martyn
On the fringe. H. Frankel. Sat R 47:40 Mr 21 '64

ROBERT A. Taft sanitary engineering center. See United States—Public health service

ROBERT and Elizabeth; musical comedy. See Musical comedies, revues, etc.—Criticisms, plots, etc.

ROBERT C. Scull collection. See Art—Private collections

ROBERT Joffrey ballet (organization) See Ballet companies

ROBERT O. Anderson Aspen award. See Aspen institute for humanistic studies

ROBERT O. Law company. See Law, Robert O, company

ROBERT Woods Bliss collection of pre-Columbian art. See Art—Private collections

ROBERTO, Holden Alvaro
Our far-flung correspondents. T. Sterling. New Yorker 39:167-8+ N 16 '63
Truth about Angola. T. Molnar. Nat R 16:280 Ap 7 '64

ROBERTS, Aaron
Aaron Roberts and the southeastern Connecticut cabinetmaking school. H. Comstock. il Antiques 86:437-41 O '64

ROBERTS, Archie
Archie. por Newsweek 62:82+ O 14 '63
Look out, Mister Roberts. A. Wright. il por Sports Illus 21:34+ N 9 '64
Mr Wonderful. H. L. Masin. il pors Sr Schol 83:42-3 N 8 '63

ROBERTS, Arthur James
All-American saint. E. Linn. il por Sat Eve Post 237:72-3 N 21 '64

ROBERTS, Barbara. See Sheridan, B. jt. auth.

ROBERTS, Bobby
Why bands play on in Philly. il pors Bsns W p52-4 D 28 '63

ROBERTS, Bruce
Gettysburg 1963. il U S Camera 26:74-7+ Ag '63

about

Blur for realism. il U S Camera 28:40-3 Ja '65

ROBERTS, C. A.
How to train a motorcycle squad. Am City 79:99 F '64

ROBERTS, Chalmers M.
Nine men who control Congress. Atlan 213:63-8 Ap '64

ROBERTS, Charles T.
Realistic property accounting. por Sch Life 46:25-7 N '63

ROBERTS, Donald Verlin
Mission in Moscow. por Newsweek 63:55 F 10 '64

ROBERTS, Edward Glenn
Cool fireball named Roberts. B. Heilman. il pors Sport Illus 20:31-4+ F 10 '64

ROBERTS, Elizabeth Madox
Life is from within. R. P. Warren. por Sat R 46:20-1+ Mr 2 '63

ROBERTS, Elliott B.
From a peak in Darién. Américas 15:40-3 S '63
Where the williwaws blow. Américas 16:22-7 O '64

ROBERTS, Harold R. See Lechler, E. jt. auth.

ROBERTS, Henry L.
Area studies: Russia and eastern Europe. Ann Am Acad 356:93-9 N '64
(comp) Recent books on international relations. See issues of Foreign affairs

ROBERTS, Howard L.
Signal-generating equipment. Electr World 70:31-4+ Ag '63

ROBERTS, Hugh D.
Linley House in Bath. Antiques 83:570-3 My '63

ROBERTS, Kenneth
Mission to Malagasy. il Library J 89:4476-7 N 15 '64

ROBERTS, Morton S.
Hydrogen in galaxies. Sci Am 208:94-100+ Je '63

ROBERTS, Neil
All-round kid. Sports Illus 18:11 Ap 1 '63

ROBERTS, Patricia Easterbrook
Bouquets of tissue paper. Design 64:153+ Mr '63

ROBERTS, Philip
Just passing through; poem. Sat R 47:35 F 29 '64

ROBERTS, Rachel
Rex Harrison and his own fair lady. J. Hamilton. il pors Look 27:72-4+ Je 18 '63

ROBERTS, Ralph R.
Afternoon at the track. Nation 196:338 Ap 27 '63

ROBERTS, Robin
Whiz Kids are still going strong. W. Leggett. por Sports Illus 20:60+ Je 8 '64

ROBERTS, Thomas d'Esterre, abp
Gadfly. por Time 84:54 Jl 31 '64
Roberts ruling. America 111:100 Ag 1 '64

ROBERTSON, A. D. J. and Evans, C. R.
Single-unit activity in the cat's visual cortex: modification after an intense light flash. bibliog Science 147:303-4 Ja 15 '65

ROBERTSON, A. Willis
Excerpt from address, November 26, 1963. Cong Digest 43:47+ F '64
Key senator tells why ARA won't work; interview. por Nations Bsns 52:84-6 F '64

about

How a top Democrat would cut budget. por U S News 54:22 Mr 18 '63

ROBERTSON, Allan
Where do all the horses go? Pop Sci 185:48-9+ Jl '64

ROBERTSON, Anya
Good grief! Garbo? il pors Life 54:55-6+ Ap 5 '63

ROBERTSON, Archie
Fill yourself up, clean your plate. Am Heritage 15:56-66+ Ap '64
From bully! to vigah! Horizon 5:68-71 N '63
King and us. Horizon 6:18-25 Wint '64
Murder most foul. Am Heritage 15:90-104 Ag '64

ROBERTSON, Cliff
He likes to cook: Cliff Robertson; the movies' JFK. pors Bet Hom & Gard 41:78 Mr '63

about

He needed the President for his breakthrough. V. Kelly. il pors Look 27:52+ Je 18 '63
Hollywood's J.F.K. D. Reische. por Sr Schol 82:19 Ap 24 '63
Twenty years after: PT 109. il pors Life 54:98+ My 17 '63

ROBERTSON, Doug
Case of the killer grizzly. por Outdoor Life 134:29-31+ S '64

ROBERTSON, James H.
Why so many flunk out. N Y Times Mag p32+ My 5 '63

ROBERTSON, Nan
Lonely lady behind Barry. Sat Eve Post 237:36 O 24 '64
Our new First lady. Sat Eve Post 237:20-5 F 8 '64
Where the boys are not. Sat Eve Post 236:28-33 O 19 '63

ROBERTSON, S. Donald
Whitewash in Whitewater. Library J 89:2900+ Ag '64

ROBERTSON, Stewart
Race to Hawaii. Motor B 111:42+ My '63

ROBEY, George
New rig for balao salt water sensation. pors Outdoor Life 131:44-5+ Ja '63

ROBIN, Ralph
Examine this; poem. Christian Cent 81:80 Ja 15 '64
How could he tell? poem. Christian Cent 80:744 Je 5 '63
Into loutland; poem. New Repub 148:24 F 9 '63
Old addresses; poem. Christian Cent 82:15 Ja 6 '65
Watch carefully; poem. Christian Cent 81:1172 S 23 '64

ROBIN Hood
In defense of R. Hood. R. Payne. il por N Y Times Mag p48+ N 17 '63

ROBIN redbreast. See Robins

ROBINETT, G. C. Jr
Machine accounting stops deficit spending. Am City 79:100-1 Ag '64

ROBINS, Corinne
Wanderers. Commonweal 79:440-1 Ja 10 '64

ROBINS
Here come the robins! J. George. il Read Digest 84:217-20 Mr '64
Robins get around. E. A. Bauer. il Field & S 67:59+ Ap '63
When a state spray kills the state bird; Michigan's robin redbreast. A. G. Etter. il Audubon Mag 65:134-7 My '63

ROBINSON, Alice L.
School library: instruction's partner; address, November, 1962. Library J 88:823-5+ F 15 '63

ROBINSON, Anne T.
Laced pinks are for every garden. Horticulture 41:124-5 Mr '63
Look into the future of clematis. Horticulture 41:198 Ap '63

ROBINSON, B. W.
Tips for selecting cattle handling equipment. Suc Farm 62:71 Mr '64

ROBINSON, Barbara
All the summer's promise; story. Ladies Home J 80:104-5 Je '63
Beyond this moment; story. Good H 158:82-3 Ap '64
Clayborne Hill car pool; story. McCalls 91:70-1 S '64
Don't lick the stamp yet. Writer 76:11-13+ S '63
Girl everybody noticed; story. Good H 157:90-1 N '63
Honor thy father-in-law; story. McCalls 90:96-7 My '63

ROBINSON, Bert L.
Old man plants a tree; poem. Am For 71:48 Ja '65

ROBINSON, Bill
With the racing classes. See issues of Yachting

ROBINSON, Bill, 1918-. See Robinson, W. W.
ROBINSON, Bruce
Slocum society. Motor B 111:52+ Mr '63
ROBINSON, Christina
Boat club dance; drama. Plays 22:11-22 Ap '63
ROBINSON, Donald
Far right's fight against mental health. Look 29:30-2 Ja 26 '65
How safe is Fail-safe? Read Digest 82:91-4 My '63
—See Robinson, N; Roper, J. E. jt. auths.
ROBINSON, Donald W.
How sinister is the education establishment? Sat R 48:56-7+ Ja 16 '65
How well is history taught? Sat R 47:62-3 D 19 '64
ROBINSON, Doris J.
Date with a dish. Ebony 18:142+ Je; 110+ Ag; 134+ O '63
ROBINSON, Douglas
Hovering helicops. N Y Times Mag p 102-4 Ap 19 '64
ROBINSON, Francis
Daughter of the gods. Opera N 29:26-8 D 26 '64
Her own dear self. Opera N 28:27-9 Ja 18 '64
Rosa Ponselle: a grand tradition. Mus Am 83: 14-15 Ap '63
ROBINSON, Frank
Moody tiger of the Reds. M. Sharnik. il pors Sports Illus 18:32-4+ Je 17 '63
Player of the week; Cincinnati Reds outfielder. por Sports Illus 21:85 Ag 17 '64
ROBINSON, Frank M.
Pioneering legislation provides recreation for handicapped. por Recreation 56:403+ N '63
ROBINSON, Frederick B.
Eighth wonder of Erastus Field. Am Heritage 14:12-17 Ap '63
ROBINSON, Gertrude A. See Nelson, J. L. jt. auth.
ROBINSON, Gladys Reed
White-veined milk-thistle. Flower Grower 50:59 Ag '63
ROBINSON, H. Alan
Libraries; active agents in adult reading improvement. bibliog f por ALA Bul 57:416-20 My '63
ROBINSON, Helen M.
Problems; cause and cure. Todays Health 42:62-3 Mr '64
ROBINSON, Herbert
1040 and all that. Reporter 30:56 Mr 12 '64
ROBINSON, Jackie. See Robinson, J. R.
ROBINSON, Jacob
Hannah Arendt and her critics. M. Geltman. il Nat R 16:1007-12 N 17 '64
ROBINSON, James H.
Second emancipation; address, June 16, 1963. Vital Speeches 29:610-13 Ag 1 '63
ROBINSON, John Arthur Thomas, bp
God and the Bishop of Woolwich; excerpt from Honest to God. pors Horizon 5:4-7+ S '63

about

Bishop and the debate. M. E. Marty. Christian Cent 81:830-2 Je 24 '64
Bishop's heresy. por Newsweek 61:94-5 Ap 8 '63
Honest to God debate. T. Merton. il Commonweal 80:573-4+ Ag 21 '64
Honest to God reformation. H. G. Lewis. Christian Cent 81:736-8 Je 3 '64
Honest to marriage. Christian Cent 81:477 Ap 15 '64; Reply with rejoinder. J. A. T. Robinson. 81:738-9 Je 3 '64
Religionless Christianity. por Time 81:49-50+ Ap 12 '63
Religionless religion. G. Foley. Christian Cent 80:1096-9 S 11 '63; Discussion. 80:1277-8, 1341-2, 1472 O 16, 30, N 27 '63
ROBINSON, John G.
Rideau revisited. Yachting 114:38-40+ Ag; 52-3+ S '63
ROBINSON, John Roosevelt
Speaking out. por Sat Eve Post 236:10+ Ag 10 '63
There's only one way to beat the Yankees. por Life 55:106A-12 O 4 '63

about

Life goes to Jackie Robinson's jam session: $15,000 for civil rights. il por Life 55:79-81 Jl 5 '63
ROBINSON, John Thomas
Fishing boat captain. il pors Ebony 18:43-5 O '63
ROBINSON, Leonard Wallace
After the Yankees what? a TV drama. N Y Times Mag p44-5+ N 15 '64
Avoiding the no point system. N Y Times Mag p 19+ Ap 19 '64
Decision; story. Sat Eve Post 237:34-6 D 5 '64
English secretaries must have nous. N Y Times Mag p 16+ D 20 '64
Practice of an art; story. Sat Eve Post 237: 50-3 S 5 '64
We have more than five senses. N Y Times Mag p30+ Mr 15 '64
ROBINSON, Louie
Big man, big business. Ebony 19:57-8+ Ag '64
Blues becomes big business. Ebony 18:34-6+ Ap '63
Drug addicts who cure each other. Ebony 18: 116-18+ F '63
First Negro astronaut candidate. Ebony 18:71+ Jl '63
Kingdom of King Narcisse. Ebony 18:112+ Jl '63
Monterey, and all that jazz. Ebony 20:54-8+ D '64
Nancy Wilson. Ebony 19:40-2+ D '63
Thirty-eight years of serious music. Ebony 19:102-6 F '64
Willie Mays' new home. Ebony 18:88-92+ Ag '63
World's greatest diamond thief. Ebony 18: 35-6+ My '63
ROBINSON, Margaret K.
Physical oceanography: plans for U.S.-Japan cooperation. Science 146:1371-2 D 4 '64
ROBINSON, Nadine, and Robinson, Donald
Canal Zone motorboating. Motor B 111:44-5+ My '63
ROBINSON, Peter, and others
Late eocene multituberculates and other mammals from Wyoming. bibliog Science 145:809-11 Ag 21 '64
ROBINSON, Ray
(ed) See Kennedy, J. F. President Kennedy talks about you, your children and peace
ROBINSON, Ray Charles. See Charles, R.
ROBINSON, Robert. See Phipps, J. jt. auth.
ROBINSON, Roland I. and Bartell, H. R. jr
Uneasy partnership SEC/NYSE. Harvard Bsns R 43:76-88 Ja '65
ROBINSON, Sarita
Lighthouse. por Wilson Lib Bul 37:806 My '63
ROBINSON, Selma
After breast cancer: learning to live again. McCalls 91:32+ Ap '64
Going to Maxim's. McCalls 91:116-17+ Mr '64
ROBINSON, Spottswood William, 3d
Negro judge for D.C? President picks Robinson. por U S News 55:21 O 14 '63
ROBINSON, Stanley D. See Handler, M. jt. auth.
ROBINSON, Stephen H. and Brecher, George
Delayed incorporation of tritiated thymidine into DNA. bibliog Science 142:392-3 O 18 '63
ROBINSON, Sugar Ray
Long ago. il por Time 82:71 Jl 5 '63
Winchell v. Sugar Ray. Time 85:48 Ja 1 '65
ROBINSON, Ted
Car in the White House drive. Pop Sci 185: 80-2 S '64
ROBINSON, Theodore
Theodore Robinson, America's first impressionist. F. Lewison. il por Am Artist 27: 40-5+ F '63
ROBINSON, Thomas E.
What's so unreasonable about a teacher's wanting to participate in politics? NEA J 53:39-40 My '64
ROBINSON, W. O.
Test boars in crosses? ed. by J. Bickers. Farm J 88:44B Je '64
ROBINSON, Wilhelmena S.
In-service education of the teacher of African history; address, 1964. bibliog Negro Hist Bul 28:33-4+ N '64
ROBINSON, William Wheeler, 1918-
Under El Yunque; excerpt from Where the trade winds blow, a yachting guide to southern waters. il Yachting 114:48-9+ O '63
—and Van Dyck, S. A.
1000 miles without a rudder. il pors Yachting 114:58-60+ S '63
ROBINSON-Patman act. See Price discrimination
ROBISON, William C.
National parks in Australia. Nat Parks Mag 38:11-15 Jl '64

ROBLES, Arnold J.
New aquatorium on target. Recreation 56: 413-16 N '63
ROBLES, Luis González. See González Robles, L.
ROBLES, Marco Aurelio
Expected surprise. por Newsweek 63:54 My 25 '64
Panama winner Robles can he control the reds? il U S News 56:21 My 25 '64
Passing a test. il por Time 85:30 Ja 22 '65
Time to get rolling. il por Time 84:36+ O 9 '64
ROBOTS. See Automatons; Manipulators
ROBSJOHN-GIBBINGS, T. H.
Lost Greek look retrieved; how the Nicholas Goulandrises had the furniture of the fifth century, B.C. re-created for their new Athens flat. il Vogue 141:118-23+ F 15 '63
ROCA-GARCIA, Helen
Elderberry bush. Horticulture 41:458 S '63
Relatives of the flowering dogwood. Horticulture 41:165 Mr '63
ROCCA, Antonio
Gentleman's guide to barroom brawling. por Esquire 62:130 O '64
ROCCUS americanus. See White perch
ROCHAS, Hélène
Well-groomed panther. il por Time 83:92 Mr 20 '64
ROCHE, Anthony Dalton
Aussie for the future. F. Deford. il por Sports Illus 18:55-7 Ap 29 '63
ROCHE, John P.
Curbing of the militant majority. Reporter 29:34-8 Jl 18 '63
How a president should use the intellectuals. N Y Times Mag p 10+ Jl 26 '64
JFK: bricks and broken glass. Reporter 29: 48+ N 7 '63
Latter-day puritans from Erin. Reporter 30: 44 Mr 26 '64
Leave me alone! Reporter 30:54-6 My 21 '64
Touching tale of lost illusions. Reporter 28: 58+ Mr 28 '63
ROCHE, John Patrick
Are you a better gardener than your spouse? Pop Gard 15:10-11 Ja '64
ROCHE, Kevin
New Saarinen office. W. McQuade. il por Arch Forum 118:114+ Ap '63
ROCHE, Marcel
Humanities in the scientific curriculum. bibliog Science 141:698-700 Ag 23 '63
ROCHE, Mary, 1907-
Going places, finding things in New York state. House & Gard 124:44+ O '63
How to lead your child to music. House & Gard 126:182-3+ S '64
Italy where people garden for fun. House & Gard 123:162-3+ Ap '63
ROCHE, Mary Alice
Are you a better gardener that your spouse? Pop Gard 15:10-11 Ja '64
Do-it-yourself bonsai. Am Home 66:94+ My '63
Happiness is a thing called vegetable gardening. il Flower Grower 51:40-2+ Ja '64
Old roses for new gardens. Pop Gard 15:12-13 F '64
Sunny, peppery nasturtium. Flower Grower 50:54-5 Je '63
ROCHE, Paul
Note on Aeschylus. R. Kirk. Nat R 15:62 Jl 30 '63
ROCHE-COURBON, Chateau of. See France—Historic houses, etc.
ROCHESTER, N.Y.

City planning

Here's way to rebuild your city. il Nations Bsns 52:34-5+ My '64

Music

[Musical events] (cont) Mus Am 84:24-5 Jl '64

Negroes

Rochester: where a race riot hit a model city; with interview with F. J. Horton. il U S News 57:37-40 Ag 10 '64
Visit to Rochester. B. Carter. Reporter 31: 16+ Ag 13 '64; Discussion. 31:6+ S 10 '64

Police

Movies aid police work, reassure public. W. M. Lombard. Am City 79:52 Ap '64

Riots

Calculated risk; Negro leadership. il Newsweek 64:26-8 Ag 10 '64
Rage in Rochester. il Newsweek 64:20+ Ag 3 '64
Rochester: where a race riot hit a model city; with interview with F. J. Horton. il U S News 57:37-40 Ag 10 '64
Why race riots strike nice northern city. il Bsns W p24 Ag 1 '64
ROCHESTER, N.Y. University
Summer scientists; Rochester's summer research institute for radiation biology. Newsweek 64:81 S 7 '64
See also
Eastman school of music, Rochester, N.Y.
ROCHET, Waldeck
Letter from Paris. Genêt. New Yorker 40: 120+ My 30 '64
ROCK, Irvin, and Steinfeld, George
Methodological questions in the study of one-trial learning. bibliog Science 140:822-4 My 17 '63
—and Victor, Jack
Vision and touch: an experimentally created conflict between the two senses. Science 143:594-6 F 7 '64
ROCK, John
Speaking out. por Sat Eve Post 236:10+ Ap 20 '63
about
Birth control: Catholic opinion varies widely on Rock's new book. D. S. Greenberg. Science 140:791-2 My 17 '63
Birth control: the pill and the church. il por Newsweek 64:51-5 Jl 6 '64
Catholic doctor speaks up; with interview, ed. by J. Howard. il pors Life 54:40-40B My 10 '63
Catholic physician favors birth control. Christian Cent 80:699-700 My 29 '63
Doctor Rock show. America 110:133 Ja 25 '64
Soldiers of humanity. America 108:790 Je 1 '63
ROCK, Maxine A.
Needed: a permanent refuge for California's tule elk. Nat Parks Mag 38:8-11+ Je '64
Sounds of yesterday; poem. Nat Parks Mag 38:10 Ap '64
ROCK, Vincent P.
Men Johnson will need. Nation 199:348-9 N 16 '64
ROCK carvings. See Petroglyphs
ROCK CREEK park. See Washington, D.C.—Parks and playgrounds
ROCK garden plants. See Plants, Rock garden
ROCK gardens. See Gardens, Rock
ROCK ISLAND railway. See Chicago, Rock Island and Pacific railway
ROCK 'n' roll music. See Jazz music
ROCK paintings. See Cave drawings and paintings
ROCK pinks. See Wild pinks
ROCK profiles
Rocks or faces? J. Durniak. il Pop Phot 52: 61-3 F '63
ROCK rabbits. See Pikas
ROCK salt
Getting better results from salt. il Am City 78:32 Ag '63
ROCK sculpture. See Mountain sculpture
ROCK specimens. See Geological specimens
ROCK tumbler. See Tumbling barrels
ROCKEFELLER, Ann M.
Songbird secrets. Audubon Mag 66:119-23, 186-90 Mr-My '64
ROCKEFELLER, David
Challenge of leisure; address, February 17, 1964. Vital Speeches 30:379-81 Ap 1 '64
Formula for prosperity. Sat R 46:28 O 12 '63
Leisure: new national resource. por Recreation 57:390-2 O '64
Man is the central element; excerpts from address. por Fortune 68:78 N '63
New trends in the financial markets; address, December 12, 1963. Vital Speeches 30:267-9 F 15 '64
U.S. business image in Latin America; address, September 23, 1964. Vital Speeches 31:7-10 O 15 '64
about
Alliance that is making little progress. por U S News 54:40+ F 25 '63
Friend at the Chase; financial group to renew Lower Manhattan. il por Bsns W p24+ D 21 '63
Friend speaks out on banking. il pors Bsns W p83-4+ Ap 25 '64

ROCKEFELLER, David—about—*Continued*
National-bank policy attacked. por U S News 55:122-3 O 21 '63
Profiles. E. J. Kahn, jr. por New Yorker 40: 37-8+ Ja 9; 40-2+ Ja 16 '65
SR's businessman of the year. W. D. Patterson. por Sat R 48:39-40+ Ja 9 '65

ROCKEFELLER, John Davison, 1839-1937
Grand acquisitor. R. L. Heilbroner. il pors Am Heritage 16:20-5+ D '64
Rockefeller foundation; how it operates. G. Williams. il Atlan 213:106-18 Ap '64

ROCKEFELLER, John Davison, 1906-
Plea to the young Negro. N Y Times Mag p 16+ Ap 19 '64

about

Profession: philanthropy. il pors Bsns W p80-2+ Ja 16 '65
Visit with John D. Rockefeller 3rd. W. Clifford. il pors Look 28:78-80 S 8 '64

ROCKEFELLER, Mrs John Davison, 3d
People are talking about. . . por Vogue 143: 142-3 F 1 '64

ROCKEFELLER, Laurance Spelman
New horizons; address, September 23, 1964. por Am For 70:10-13 N '64
Platform for conservation and outdoor recreation; adaptation of address. por Recreation 57:446-8 N '64
What kind of America? excerpt from address, September 23, 1964. por Audubon Mag 66: 376-81 N '64

about

Laurance Rockefeller receives AFA award. il por Am For 69:4 D '63

ROCKEFELLER, Margaretta (Fitler)
After the Rockefeller wedding. il por U S News 54:22 My 20 '63
After the Rockefellers returned to New York. por U S News 54:20 Je 17 '63
And a lady called Happy Murphy. il pors Life 54:24-9 My 3 '63
Call me Happy. il por Newsweek 61:31-2 Je 17 '63
Divorce in Idaho. por Time 81:24 Ap 26 '63
Front-page secret; Mrs Murphy's divorce. il por Newsweek 61:21 Ap 29 '63
Governor's happy lady. J. D. Brown. il pors Sat Eve Post 236:15-19 Je 22 '63
Happy honeymoon. il por Time 81:31 My 17 '63
Home to father; Mrs Rockefeller loses fight for her children. il Newsweek 64:44 O 12 '64
How problems are piling up for Rockefeller. por U S News 54:48 My 6 '63
Judgment of Solomon. E. Balcomb. Christian Cent 82:106-10 Ja 27 '65
Picnic trial. il por Time 84:63 S 11 '64
Question of custody. il por Time 84:88+ O 9 '64
Rockefeller baby; how much political effect? il por U S News 56:20 Ja 13 '64
Rockefeller vs. Murphy; custody suit. il por Newsweek 64:29 Ag 31 '64
We have found happiness; with report by D. Nevin. il pors Life 54:41-2+ My 17 '63

ROCKEFELLER, Mary (French)
YWCA, international success story. pors Nat Geog Mag 124:904-33 D '63

ROCKEFELLER, Nelson Aldrich
Challenge of communism. por Look 28:27-9 Je 2 '64
For a united, nuclear Europe; summary of address. por Time 81:20 My 3 '63
Inter-continental unity; address, November 20, 1964. Vital Speeches 31:132-5 D 15 '64
Motivated by the pure desire for excellence. PTA Mag 57:19-20 F '63
Our foreign policy; what is it? address, March 3, 1964. Vital Speeches 30:402-6 Ap 15 '64; Excerpts. por U S News 56:85-7 Mr 16 '64
Time to hear from Goldwater; summary of statement. Life 55:4 Jl 26 '63
Timid tinkering; criticism of the President. Newsweek 62:24 S 9 '63
Where Rockefeller stands; interview. pors U S News 55:76-83 S 23 '63
World trade; address, May 7, 1964. Vital Speeches 30:494-7 Je 1 '64

about

After the Rockefeller wedding. il por U S News 54:22 My 20 '63
After the Rockefellers returned to New York. por U S News 54:20 Je 17 '63
All sorts of roads. il por Time 82:24 N 1 '63
Ambassador Lodge running strong. il por Newsweek 63:21-5 Mr 23 '64
And a lady called Happy Murphy. il pors Life 54:24-9 My 3 '63
Bad news from the oracles. il Time 81:23 Je 7 '63
Bomb that was a bomb; attack on radical right elements in the Republican party. il por Time 82:19 Jl 26 '63
Building a science center overnight. por Bsns W p32 Ja 26 '63
Caesar and his wife. Newsweek 61:89 My 20 '63
Call me Happy. il por Newsweek 61:31-2 Je 17 '63
Can anyone stop Goldwater now? il por Newsweek 63:23-4+ Je 15 '64
Can Rockefeller stop Goldwater? por U S News 55:34 Jl 29 '63
Candidate Rockefeller. por Newsweek 62:33-4 N 18 '63
Capital pursuit. por Newsweek 61:24 Ap 22 '63
Common cause. il por Newsweek 63:19-20 Mr 2 '64
Divorce in Idaho. Time 81:24 Ap 26 '63
Each is sure the triumph of the other will wreck the party; California primary. T. H. White. il por Life 56:26-31 My 29 '64
Elephants in Tammanyland; seventeenth congressional district, Manhattan. B. Carter. il Reporter 29:41-3 N 21 '63
Fight a little harder. il por Newsweek 62: 19 O 28 '63
Fingers crossed. il por Newsweek 63:40+ Je 8 '64
First hurrahs. il por Newsweek 63:16-17 Ja 13 '64
Full-dress challenge. il Newsweek 61:22 F 18 '63
Goldwater and Rockefeller. J. O'Gara. Commonweal 78:472 Ag 9 '63
Goldwater and the race issue. Nat R 15:45-6+ Jl 30 '63
Goldwater on extremists. R. Moley. Newsweek 62:76 Jl 29 '63
Goldwater, Rockefeller, and the Young Republicans. M. S. Evans. por Nat R 15:97-100+ Ag 13 '63
Governor and booze. Life 56:2 Ap 10 '64
Governor Rockefeller, a man apart. E. T. Folliard. America 108:524 Ap 20 '63
Governor Rockefeller's divorce. Commonweal 79:179 N 8 '63; Reply. T. Bourne. 79:350 D 13 '63
Governor's happy lady. J. D. Brown. il pors Sat Eve Post 236:15-19 Je 22 '63
GOP and Rockefeller. E. J. Hughes. Newsweek 61:15 Je 3 '63
GOP opens with a pair. por Bsns W p36 My 4 '63
Great society: Rockefeller style. il por U S News 58:20 Ja 18 '65
Happy day; marriage of Gov. N. A Rockefeller to Mrs Margaretta Fitler Murphy. il por Newsweek 61:29-30 My 13 '63
Happy honeymoon. il por Time 81:31 My 17 '63
Happy scandalmonger; San Francisco convention of the Young Republicans. Nat R 15:89-90 Ag 13 '63
He cared enough, and so did Oregon; with report by L. Harris. il por Newsweek 63: 27-8 My 25 '64
Home is where the hearth is. Time 83:27-8 Ap 3 '64
How Goldwater won in California. B. Stout. Reporter 31:17-19 Jl 2 '64
How problems are piling up for Rockefeller. pors U S News 54:48 My 6 '63
How to succeed in politics. Nation 198:546 Je 1 '64
I shall go to New Hampshire. Time 82:35 N 15 '63
If it's Rockefeller vs. Kennedy in 1964—. il pors U S News 54:56-8 F 11 '63
Is Nelson Rockefeller dead? S. Alsop. il pors Sat Eve Post 236:18 O 12 '63
It's up to the undecideds. D. F. O'Neil. Nat R 16:193-4 Mr 10 '64
Kicking the rock around. por Newsweek 63:20 Ap 6 '64
Kinfolk; backing of cousin, R. S. Aldrich. por Newsweek 61:39 Je 24 '63
Lessons from the Lone Ranger. il pors Time 83:17-20 My 22 '64
Letter from Washington. R. H. Rovere. New Yorker 39:115-20 N 2 '63
Long Rocky road. il por Bsns W p32+ N 16 '63
Most important marriage. il por Time 81:16 My 10 '63
Nelson Rockefeller. M. Kempton. New Repub 150:6-7 Ja 4 '64
New Hampshire: first test for the big divorce issue. M. Parker. il por Life 56:32-3 F 7 '64
New Hampshire poll; write-in fever gains. il por Newsweek 63:18-21 Mr 9 '64
One who is. Time 81:30 Ap 19 '63

ROCKEFELLER, Nelson Aldrich—about—*Cont.*
Political evolution of Nelson Rockefeller. W. Weaver. pors N Y Times Mag p 11+ F 16 '64
Politically unhappy marriage. Nat R 14:392-3 My 21 '63
Reporter at large. R. Harris. New Yorker 40:101-3+ S 12 '64
Revised conclusion of James Reston. P. R. Bushnell. il por Nat R 14:449-50+ Je 4 '63
Rockefeller and the GOP. W. Lippmann. Newsweek 61:15 Ap 1 '63
Rockefeller baby; how much political effect? il por U S News 56:20 Ja 13 '64
Rockefeller: down but not out. W. V. Shannon. Commonweal 78:341-2 Je 21 '63
Rockefeller: he has it if he wants it, and he does. M. Kempton. New Repub 148:11-14 Mr 2 '63
Rockefeller: into an uphill race. il pors U S News 55:26 N 18 '63
Rockefeller resolve. E. J. Hughes. Newsweek 62:23 S 23 '63
Rockefeller under fire. Bush urges that he withdraw; summary of address. P. Bush. il por U S News 54:20 Je 24 '63
Rockefeller vs Goldwater. J. Duscha. New Repub 149:13-14 O 26 '63
Rockefeller's candidacy. R. Moley. Newsweek 62:124 O 14 '63
Rockefeller's cool campaign. J. Desmond. por Nation 197:23-5 Jl 13 '63
Rockefeller's future: will liquor scandals hurt? U S News 54:20 Ap 29 '63
Rockefeller's triple-threat brain trust. A. L. Otten and C. B. Seib. Harper 227:74-9 Jl '63
Rocking their boat; Governors conference. il por Time 82:12 Ag 2 '63
Rocky in Miami Beach. New Yorker 39:48-9 N 23 '63
Rocky rocky road. Nat R 14:143 F 26 '63
Rocky wrecks the joint. J. Desmond. por Nation 197:63-5 Ag 10 '63
Rocky's running again. il pors Newsweek 62:20-2+ Ag 26 '63
Rocky's running start. Time 82:18 N 22 '63
Scent of gold water. Newsweek 62:36-7 S 23 '63
Showdown in California: big crisis for Goldwater; with editorial comment. R. Evans and R. Novak. il por Sat Eve Post 237:15-19, 74 My 30 '64
Slugfest in California. W. F. Buckley, jr. Nat R 16:394 My 19 '64
Still fishing. Newsweek 62:30 S 30 '63
Switching to Rocky; How the West was won? il por Newsweek 63:21-2 Je 1 '64
This president thing. il por Time 81:26-31 Je 14 '63
To Topeka and Omaha. il por Newsweek 61:31 Ap 15 '63
Two key decisions: Rocky's and GOP's. il por Newsweek 61:23-4 My 6 '63
View from defeat. E. J. Hughes. Newsweek 63:20-1 Je 15 '64
We have found happiness; with report by D. Nevin. il pors Life 54:41-2+ My 17 '63
Whisky and water. Newsweek 63:29-30 Ap 27 '64
Will it be Goldwater, Rockefeller, or—? poll of Republican leaders in fifty states. il por U S News 55:46-8 O 7 '63
Without portfolio; Governor Rockefeller's remarriage. C. B. Luce. McCalls 90:29+ S '63
Wraps are off; Rockefeller vs Goldwater. por Newsweek 62:41 Jl 29 '63

ROCKEFELLER, Winthrop
Arkansas anniversary. il pors Life 55:87-9+ S 6 '63
Arkansas: squire vs. demagogue. T. Dearmore. il Reporter 31:38-42 O 22 '64
Can Win win? por Time 84:38 O 16 '64
Coming up: a two-party fight in Arkansas. por U S News 56:20 My 4 '64
Help from brother. Newsweek 63:22 Je 1 '64
Market weekend for a farming Rockefeller. il pors Fortune 70:149-53 Jl '64
Showdown in Arkansas: Win Rockefeller vs. Orval Faubus. B. H. Bagdikian. il pors Sat Eve Post 237:75-7 S 19 '64
Squire of Petit Jean. il por Time 81:27 Mr 8 '63
Winthrop Rockefeller against Orval Faubus. P. J. Owens. New Repub 150:6-7 Ap 25 '64

ROCKEFELLER brothers
Profiles: D. Rockefeller. E. J. Kahn, jr. New Yorker 40:37-8+ Ja 9; 40-2+ Ja 16 '65
Rockefeller vs. Kennedy. il U S News 54:36-9 Ap 1 '63
Rockefellers' New York; with photographs by A. Newman. J. Peter. Look 27:82-5 Mr 26 '63

ROCKEFELLER foundation
Rockefeller foundation; how it operates. G. Williams. il Atlan 213:106-18 Ap '64
$266,900,000: private give-away, done by three men. A. Talmey. Vogue 141:103 Je '63

ROCKEFELLER institute for medical research, New York
Rockefeller institute. P. Lyon. il Holiday 36: 52-7+ S '64
Subway in the balance. Newsweek 63:57 Mr 9 '64
Subways and science: two N.Y. institutions consider meaning of coexistence in crowded Manhattan. E. Langer. il Science 143:789-90 F 21 '64

ROCKERS. See Chairs

ROCKET engines
Air-breathing boosters gain favor. W. Beller. il Miss & Roc 12:22-3+ Mr 18 '63
Cure engines in flight; rocket engine analyzer and decision instrumentation. Sci N L 85:395 Je 20 '64
Electric propulsion. M. L. Yaffee. il Aviation W 80:77-81+ Ja 27; 54-5+ F 3; 54-6+ F 10; 78-9+ F 17 '64
Electric propulsion of rockets. R. N. Watts, jr. il Sky & Tel 28:206-7 O '64
Engine may oust big booster; air turbo-exchanger. W. Beller. il Miss & Roc 12: 12-13 Ap 8 '63
F-1 troubles won't delay Saturn V. H. Taylor. il Miss & Roc 12:16 Mr 11 '63
Flight of M-1 delayed three years. H. Taylor. il Miss & Roc 12:16-17 Ap 22 '63
Gaseous-core rocket rapidly gaining support as feasible engine system. W. Beller. il Miss & Roc 14:26-7 My 4 '64
HITCO producing 120-in motor nozzles. I. Stone. il Aviation W 81:66-7 Jl 20 '64
Hybrid concept developing rapidly toward goal of tripropellant engine. J. F. Judge. il Miss & Roc 15:31-2+ N 9 '64
Late-starting rocket; development of hybrids. il Time 84:100 N 20 '64
Launch vehicle alarm system demonstrated; rocket engine analyzer and decision instrumentation. Aviation W 80:18 Je 8 '64
Marquardt exploring air augmentation. R. Hawkes. il Miss & Roc 15:28+ Ag 17 '64
NASA seeking $5.4 billion; big engine programs to OART. H. Taylor. il Miss & Roc 14:12 Ja 6 '64
NASA seen blocking electric propulsion; with definition of terms. W. Beller. Miss & Roc 14:24-5 F 10 '64
Non-eroding nozzle under development. J. F. Judge. il Miss & Roc 15:22-3 D 14 '64
Northrop ready to pick engines for M-2, HL-10 lifting body studies. R. Hawkes. il Miss & Roc 14:18+ Je 22 '64
120-in. boosts argument for solids. R. Lindsey. il Miss & Roc 14:27-8+ Ap 27 '64
Phoebus-powered second-generation engine to have 250,000 lbs. thrust. H. Taylor. Miss & Roc 15:17 O 12 '64
Rocket engine of future? il(p49) Sci N L 86: 50 Jl 25 '64
SA-6 shows engine-out capability following unscheduled shutdown. G. Alexander. il Aviation W 80:24-5 Je 8 '64
Scorpio engine heads jobs at Rocket propulsion laboratory. W. E. Wilks. il Miss & Roc 13:24-5+ D 9 '63
16-in. HARP booster nears flight. M. Getler. Miss & Roc 14:22 Ja 27 '64
Space demands boost propellant output. il Aviation W 81:64+ N 23 '64
Titan III-C stage zero role revamps UTC structure. R. Lindsey. il Miss & Roc 14: 34+ Ja 20 '64
Two new labs to sharpen Aerojet's solid, liquid capabilities. W. E. Wilks. il Miss & Roc 14:18+ Mr 23 '64
260-in. igniter fabrication detailed. il Miss & Roc 15:28 O 12 '64
U.S. rocket motors; specifications. Aviation W 80:197-8 Mr 16 '64
UTC studies refinements for advanced rocket motors. I. Stone. il Aviation W 78:54-5+ Je 17 '63
Vroom! out of this world engines: reprint. R. M. Loebelson. il Sci Digest 55:40-4 Ap '64
World's biggest nozzle delivered. il Miss & Roc 16:17 Ja 11 '65
X-12 engine series to follow X-8 tests. C. M. Plattner. il Aviation W 79:99+ N 11 '63
See also
Aerojet-General corporation
Ion engines
Space vehicles—Propulsion systems

Exhaust
Rocket fuels toxic to plants, animals. Sci N L 86:36 Jl 18 '64

ROCKET engines—*Continued*

Manufacture

Huge hydroclave works on massive Titan III exit cones. il Miss & Roc 13:28+ S 23 '63
Tapco now top U.S. nozzle producer. J. F. Judge. il Miss & Roc 12:44-5+ Ap 29 '63

Materials

Aerojet proves 260-in. case method. il Miss & Roc 15:23 Ag 17 '64
Air force admits big potential for boron filament structures. W. Beller. il Miss & Roc 14:22-3 Je 15 '64
Barrel staves likely for big booster cases; filament-wound plastic. il Miss & Roc 13:41 Ag 12 '63
Columbium thrust chamber is test-fired M. L. Yaffee. il Aviation W 80:47-8 Mr 30 '64
CEBM unit to check Polaris cases; filament-wound cases. il Miss & Roc 13:39-40 Ag 12 '63
Emerson offers a solution to nozzle problem; Thermo-Lag subliming material. il Miss & Roc 13:31 D 23 '63
Expandable nozzle skirts are tested. Aviation W 78:63 Mr 18 '63
Huge hydroclave works on massive Titan III exit cones; handling any reinforced plastic component. il Miss & Roc 13:28+ S 23 '63
Huge nozzles economically feasible. J. F. Judge. il Miss & Roc 12:26-8 Je 24 '63
Nickel alloy rings for 260-in. solid program impose stringent standards. J. F. Judge. il Miss & Roc 15:38-9 O 12 '64
Rocketdyne studying reductions in rocket case weight for USAF. Aviation W 79:37 S 30 '63
Thiokol motor to test paper as low-density, high-strength laminate. J. F. Judge. il Miss & Roc 15:28 Jl 20 '64

Testing

Aerojet proves 260-in. case method. il Miss & Roc 15:23 Ag 17 '64
Apollo service module engine beginning prequalification. C. M. Plattner. il Aviation W 81:42-6 Jl 27 '64
CEBM unit to check Polaris cases; filament-wound cases. il Miss & Roc 13:39-40 Ag 12 '63
ELDO third-stage model test scheduled. W. C. Wetmore. il Aviation W 79:73-4+ D 16 '63
F-1 engine needs 200 more test-firing successes. Miss & Roc 12:17 Ap 22 '63
Five-segment motor tested successfully. I. Stone. il Aviation W 79:52-3 Jl 29 '63
Gemini, Centaur shots due this week. Miss & Roc 15:15-16 N 30 '64
Hybrids studied for lunar landing engine. M. L. Yaffee. il Aviation W 80:23-4 Je 22 '64
Mighty F-1. S. Spillman. il Pop Sci 183:102-5+ O '63
Oxidizer additives may boost RL-10 power. il Miss & Roc 13:38+ Ag 26 '63
P&W studies small, high-thrust engines. G. Alexander. il Aviation W 79:73+ S 23 '63
SERT-1 flight shows ion engine potential. Aviation W 81:21 Jl 27 '64
Space moves down: air force rocket test chamber simulates atmospheric conditions. il Bsns W p70-2+ Mr 21 '64
Subscale motors to verify 260-in. design. C. M. Plattner. il Aviation W 80:40-1+ Je 22 '64
Test failures mar F-1 engine development. E. H. Kolcum. Aviation W 78:26 F 4 '63
Titan transtage restarted twice during first long-duration firing. Aviation W 79:27 Jl 29 '63

Thrust control

Lockheed refines jet tab technique. R. Hawkes. Miss & Roc 12:31 Ap 1 '63
NASA-USAF test thrust augmentation offered by air-scoop shroud. il Aviation W 79:64-5 O 21 '63
120-in. motor test termed successful; solid-propellant Titan 3C zero-stage booster motor. Aviation W 80:71 F 3 '64
Solid rocket thrust vectored by jet tabs. I. Stone. il Aviation W 78:57 F 4 '63
Students find new throttling method. W. S. Beller. il Miss & Roc 16:27-8 Ja 25 '65
Tapco producing Saturn attitude-control rockets. il Miss & Roc 12:47 Je 24 '63
Three firms developing hybrid thruster. M. L. Yaffee. il Aviation W 80:65+ Mr 23 '64
Thrust vectoring monitor demonstrated. R. D. Hibben. il Aviation W 79:115+ Ag 26 '63
Two thrust-termination ports eliminated in 120-in. solid motor. Aviation W 80:40+ Mr 9 '64
Use of jet tabs for thrust vector control being studied for large solid propulsion. C. M. Plattner. il Aviation W 80:48-9+ Mr 9 '64

ROCKET fuel. See Rockets—Fuel

ROCKET launchers
Saenger's final interview with M/R; ed. by W. Beller. E. Saenger. Miss & Roc 14:35+ F 24 '64
Second Scout launcher to speed research, training at Wallops. W. Beller. il Miss & Roc 13:41 S 16 '63

ROCKET propulsion
Electric propulsion. M. L. Yaffee. il Aviation W 80:77-81+ Ja 27; 54-5+ F 3; 54-6+ F 10; 78-9+ F 17 '64
Electric propulsion. W. E. Moeckel. bibliog il Science 142:172-8 O 11 '63
Electric propulsion of rockets. R. N. Watts, jr. il Sky & Tel 28:206-7 O '64
Hybrid rockets. il Miss & Roc 15:31-2+ N 9 '64
NASA seen blocking electric propulsion; with definition of terms. W. Beller. Miss & Roc 14:24-5 F 10 '64
No further SERT-type tests needed; $3-billion electrical system seen. Miss & Roc 15:32 S 7 '64
Propellant program shift is criticized. Aviation W 80:21 Je 8 '64
Propulsion know-how considered equal to needs of future weapons. il Miss & Roc 14:131-2+ Mr 30 '64
Russian propellant efforts parallel U.S. M. L. Yaffee. Aviation W 81:24-5 D 7 '64
Scorpio engine heads jobs at Rocket propulsion laboratory. W. E. Wilks. il Miss & Roc 13:24-5+ D 9 '63
Three firms developing hybrid thruster. M. L. Yaffee. il Aviation W 80:65+ Mr 23 '64
USAF rocket study to measure pilot's role in mission success. Aviation W 79:79 S 16 '63

See also
Rockets, Atomic powered
Solid propellant rockets

ROCKET research corporation
Rocket research solid microrocket wins award. il Miss & Roc 12:34-5 Ap 29 '63

ROCKET sleds
Saenger's final interview with M/R; ed. by W. Beller. E. Saenger. Miss & Roc 14:35+ F 24 '64

ROCKET to freedom; drama. See Fisher, A. and Rabe, O.

ROCKETDYNE division. See North American aviation, incorporated—Rocketdyne division

ROCKETS
Background on Egyptian rocketry. Miss & Roc 14:37 F 24 '64
Explosions for freedom. B. Tufty. il Sci N L 83:406-7 Je 29 '63
Fight rocket vibrations. Sci N L 85:359 Je 6 '64
Gaseous rockets could re-shape space transportation principles. Miss & Roc 15:15 N 16 '64
How to shoot down hail. P. Van Den Berg. il Sci Digest 53:42-5 My '63
Hybrid rockets. il Miss & Roc 15:31-2+ N 9 '64
Missiles and rockets' world missile/space encyclopedia, 1963-1964. il Miss & Roc 13:35-7+ Jl 29 '63; 15:39-46+ Jl 27 '64
Multipurpose field missiles are sought. G. Alexander. il Aviation W 78:154-5 Mr 11 '63
Sky-high pollution; exhaust gases from rockets. Newsweek 61:48 F 4 '63
U.S. spacecraft; International spacecraft; specifications. Aviation W 80:193-4 Mr 16 '64
Will marines go to war by rocket? il U S News 57:8 Jl 13 '64

See also
Liquid propellant rockets
Solid propellant rockets

Amateur experiments

Boy and his bird. il Life 57:133-4 S 25 '64
Do it yourself orbit. il Life 56:101-2+ Ap 24 '64

Anecdotes, facetiae, satire, etc.

What kids say about rockets. H. Dunn. il Sci Digest 54:65-8 O '63

Control

See also
Solid propellant rockets—Control

ROCKETS—*Continued*

Design

Why rockets have fins. W. Von Braun. il Pop Sci 185:68-9+ S '64

Fuel

Chemical-fuel engine feasibility studied. M. L. Yaffee. il Aviation W 80:81+ Je 15 '64
Emulsions win growing attention. J. F. Judge. Miss & Roc 16:34-6 Ja 11 '65
Fuel slosh poses major design problems. R. D. Hibben. il Aviation W 80:58-9+ Je 15 '64
Honeycomb propellant matrix could permit solid, liquid mating. il Miss & Roc 14:26+ Ja 20 '64
Hybrids work geared to lunar survey role. W. Burkett. Miss & Roc 14:38 Mr 9 '64
Hydrogen is headache for Saturn engineers. Sci N L 85:379 Je 13 '64
Keeping danger at arm's length; Hercules powder mixes and tests explosive rocket fuels. il Bsns W p77 Ag 10 '63
Lewis chemist makes magnetic rocket fuel. Aviation W 79:30 N 11 '63
Navy propellant mixer technique employs gas turbulence in porous tube. il Miss & Roc 15:22+ S 28 '64
Predict super rocket fuel. Sci N L 87:19 Ja 9 '65
Progress report on the moon race. il Fortune 69:142-5 Mr '64
Rocket fuel tablets. Sci N L 86:339 N 28 '64
Space demands boost propellant output. il Aviation W 81:64+ N 23 '64
UTC wins lunar landing hybrid rocket. M. L. Yaffee. il Aviation W 81:275 Jl 6 '64

Fuse

Three firms developing hybrid thruster. M. L. Yaffee. il Aviation W 80:65+ Mr 23 '64

History

How Lindbergh gave a lift to rocketry; excerpts from This high man: a biography of Dr Robert H. Goddard. M. Lehman. il Life 55:115-18+ O 4 '63

Launchers

See Rocket launchers

Launching

Athena scores first success. C. D. LaFond. il Miss & Roc 15:32-5 N 16 '64
Automatic checkout gives rockets the green light. W. Von Braun. il Pop Sci 184:58-60 Ja '64
Carrier to serve as rocket launch range. D. E. Fink. Aviation W 81:33 O 19 '64
Launch platforms gaining acceptance. J. F. Judge. il Miss & Roc 12:26-7+ Je 17 '63
New technique to end rocket blow-ups. Sci N L 86:104 Ag 15 '64
Why and how of the countdown. W. Von Braun. il Pop Sci 186:66-7+ Ja '65

Materials

Combustible rocket cases developed for Shillelagh, other programs. W. Beller. il Miss & Roc 14:31 Je 22 '64

Military applications

Bounce-back recon rocket under operational evaluation; Ping-Pong. il Miss & Roc 15:24 D 7 '64

Testing

Construction speeded at Johnston Island; Thor launch pads. Miss & Roc 14:16 Ap 20 '64
Cosmic clinic for the moon rocket. C. B. Hicks. il Pop Mech 120:84-7+ S '63
Dazzle flights slated to check instrumentation. M. Getler. il Miss & Roc 14:33 My 11 '64
First Blue Streak arrives in Australia for ELDO use. B. W. Poirier. il Miss & Roc 13:35 Ag 19 '63
Fourth successful Saturn. il Sky & Tel 25:260-1 My '63
Navy launches second DAC-Roc in rocket probe test series. Aviation W 79:56 D 30 '63

Transportation

Airship studied as booster carrier. F. G. McGuire. Miss & Roc 12:16 Mr 4 '63
Boeing 377(PG) undergoes flight tests. H. D. Watkins. il Aviation W 78:80-1+ Je 24 '63

Use in research

Circulation of the upper atmosphere. R. E. Newell. il Sci Am 210:62-72+ bibliog(p 152) Mr '64
Dazzle flights slated to check instrumentation. M. Getler. il Miss & Roc 14:33 My 11 '64
DOD stalls navy tactical probe. Miss & Roc 14:14 F 10 '64
Eclipse launches successful; Operation probe high. Miss & Roc 13:24+ Jl 29 '63
Graduate education: navy program in rocket astronomy opens new horizons to university scientists. J. Walsh. il Science 141:788-90 Ag 30 '63
Honeywell to develop passive-scan telescope. Aviation W 79:26 S 2 '63
Luster probe seeks lunar dust samples. B. Miller. il Aviation W 80:54-5+ Je 15 '64
Marquardt preparing for big sales of Roksondes. W. E. Wilks. il Miss & Roc 13:33-4 S 9 '63
Modular payload developed for probe. W. Beller. il Miss & Roc 15:24-5 N 23 '64
Noctilucent clouds. R. K. Soberman. il Sci Am 208:50-9 bibliog(p 188) Je '63
16-in. HARP booster nears flight. M. Getler. Miss & Roc 14:22 Ja 27 '64
Super-cooled paddles used in high altitude air sampler. C. M. Plattner. il Aviation W 82:44-5+ Ja 11 '65
U.S. research rockets; Leading international research rockets; specifications. Aviation W 80:200-1 Mr 16 '64
Where is science taking us? C. Y. Johnson. il Sat R 46:59-60 Mr 2 '63
X-ray astronomy. Sci Am 209:67-8 D '63
X-ray astronomy. H. Friedman. il Sci Am 210:36-45 Je '64

ROCKETS, Atomic powered

AEC likely to spend over $2 billion on rockets and auxiliary power units; NERVA engine system. il Miss & Roc 15:172-4+ N 30 '64
Atomic power for rockets. W. Von Braun. il Pop Sci 185:68-9+ Jl '64
Can ion engines conquer space? il Bsns W p 110+ Mr 30 '63
Gas core rockets promise cost benefits. il Aviation W 80:64-5+ F 3 '64
Gaseous-core rocket rapidly gaining support as feasible engine system. W. Beller. il Miss & Roc 14:26-7 My 4 '64
Hot rocket to nowhere; Project Rover. G. Bylinsky and W. E. Howard. il Sat Eve Post 236:78-81 N 9 '63
Housekeeping jobs that don't go begging; bidding for development of nuclear rockets. il Bsns W p 146+ Mr 9 '63
Jackass and the Kiwis. America 108:246 F 23 '63
Kiwi changes may stop vibration. M. L. Yaffee. Aviation W 79:32 N 25 '63
Materials problems hobbling gaseous-core nuclear rocket concept. il Miss & Roc 12:28, 31 Je 3 '63
Milestones near in nuclear rocket effort; RIFT, Rover and Kiwi programs. M. L. Yaffee. Aviation W 81:30+ N 9 '64
NASA plans post-Nerva follow-on study. I. Stone. Aviation W 78:53 Mr 18 '63
NASA seen blocking electric propulsion; with definition of terms. W. Beller. Miss & Roc 14:24-5 F 10 '64
Nerva space simulation-firing complex almost ready. E. J. Bulban. il Aviation W 80:54-5+ My 18 '64
Nuclear rocket backers bid for post-Apollo role. Miss & Roc 15:16 N 23 '64
Nuclear rocket by 1975. Sci N L 86:343 N 28 '64
Phoebus may yield 268-lb. reactor. F. G. McGuire. il Miss & Roc 12:16-17 Ap 8 '63
Phoebus-powered second-generation engine to have 250,000 lbs. thrust. H. Taylor. Miss & Roc 15:17 O 12 '64
Poodle interests Saturn officials; low-thrust radioisotope propulsion system. W. E. Wilks. il Miss & Roc 14:22-3 Je 8 '64
RIFT knocked out of Rover program. Miss & Roc 14:13 Ja 6 '64
Rover slips extra fourteen-sixteen months. F. G. McGuire. il Miss & Roc 12:14-15 Mr 11 '63
Search. W. J. Coughlin. Miss & Roc 14:54 Je 8 '64
Small nuclear engine developed; Project Poodle. Aviation W 80:22 Je 8 '64
Small nuclear explosions to propel rockets. Sci N L 85:46 Ja 18 '64
Trimming the atom; Project Rover. il Newsweek 63:86 Je 29 '64
Wernher Von Braun answers your questions. W. Von Braun. il Pop Sci 182:62-3+ Mr '63

Testing

Kiwi to be deliberately destroyed. Miss & Roc 16:15 Ja 11 '65
Plum Brook reactor tests to start in June. il Miss & Roc 12:56 Ap 29 '63
Upcoming tests may determine nuclear rocket reactor design. R. Lindsey. Miss & Roc 13:38 O 14 '63

ROCKETS, Military transport
1,200 men in a rocket; Ithacus and ROMBUS. il Sci Digest 56:75 O '64
Reusable rocket designed; ROMBUS. J. Eberhart. Sci N L 86:197 S 26 '64
Rockets to carry troops; ROMBUS or Ithacus. Sci N L 86:50 Jl 25 '64

ROCKETS, Sounding
Canada poised to enter sounding rocket market with Black Brants. il Miss & Roc 15: 31+ Jl 20 '64
Carrier to serve as rocket launch range. D. E. Fink. Aviation W 81:33 O 19 '64
Dornier is developing paraglider rocket. W. C. Wetmore. il Aviation W 80:65+ Ja 13 '64
Major international cooperative sounding rocket programs. Aviation W 81:74-5 Jl 6 '64
Marquardt preparing for big sales of Roksondes. W. E. Wilks. il Miss & Roc 13:33-4 S 9 '63
NASA program develops F-104A sounding rocket launch method. E. H. Kolcum. il Aviation W 78:57+ Mr 4 '63
Navy launches second DAC-Roc in rocket probe test series. Aviation W 79:56 D 30 '63
U.S. sounding rockets; specification (cont) Aviation W 78:195 Mr 11 '63

ROCKETTES. See Dancers

ROCKFORD college, Rockford, Ill.
Success story your schools can copy. il Nations Bsns 51:68-70+ F '63

ROCKING chairs. See Chairs

ROCKING horses. See Toys

ROCKOWER, Isabelle
Tensions; his and hers. McCalls 92:114+ N '64

ROCKS
Geological aspects of high-pressure research. F. R. Boyd. bibliog il Science 145:13-20 Jl 3 '64
Have some fun with garden rock. il Sunset 130:184+ F '63
Metamorphism in the act. Sci Am 208:75-6 My '63
See also
Aluminum silicates
Arches, Natural
Metamorphism

Age

Glauconite from the Precambrian belt series, Montana. R. A Gulbrandsen and others. bibliog il Science 140:390-1 Ap 26 '63

Analysis

Carbonate rocks: cleaning with suspensions of hydrogen-ion exchange resin. S. F. Percival, jr. and others. il Science 142:1456 D 13 '63
Chemical variations in a granitic pluton and its surrounding rocks. A. K. Baird and others. bibliog il Science 146:258-9 O 9 '64
Rubidium-strontium isochron study of the Grenville front near Lake Timagami, Ontario. J. A. Grant. bibliog il Science 146: 1049-53 N 20 '64

Collectors and collecting

Anatomy of a rock collector. H. D. Brown. il Hobbies 68:124 Mr '63

ROCKS, Igneous
Bendix simulating lunar magma in laboratory tests. J. F. Judge. il Miss & Roc 14: 36-7 Mr 23 '64
Composition of basalts from the Mid-Atlantic Ridge. A. E. J. Engel and C. G. Engel. bibliog Science 144:1330-3 Je 12 '64
Igneous rocks of the East Pacific rise. A. E. J. Engel and C. G. Engel. bibliog il Science 146:477-85 O 23 '64; Correction. 146:1637 D 25 '64
Origin of high-alumina basalt, andesite, and dacite magmas. W. Hamilton. bibliog il Science 146:635-7 O 30 '64

ROCKSTEIN, M. and Brandt, K. F.
Enzyme changes in flight muscle correlated with aging and flight ability in the male housefly. bibliog Science 139:1049-51 Mr 15 '63

ROCKVILLE, Conn.
Fluorescent City, U.S.A. L. B. Flaherty, jr. il Am City 78:124 Ap '63

ROCKVILLE, Md.
Within five years. il Am City 78:95 Mr '63

Education

Grouping by sex; Broome jr. high school. C. J. Fahrner and J. M. Cronin. il NEA J 52: 16-17 My '63

ROCKVILLE CENTRE, N.Y.
Inexpensive overlay replaces seal coat. R. C. Olton. il Am City 80:76-7 Ja '65

ROCKWELL, Eleanor
Spring in southern California; poem. New Repub 148:28 Ap 13 '63

ROCKWELL, F. A.
Beginning and the middle of your story. Writer 76:13-16+ O '63
Goals. Writer 77:19-21 S '64
Plot blueprints. Writer 77:16-21 My '64

ROCKWELL, F. F. and Grayson, E. C.
Home greenhouse. See issues of Flower grower

ROCKWELL, George Lincoln
Nazi mind. America 110:329 Mr 14 '64

ROCKWELL, Norman
I paint the candidates; with paintings. Look 28:50-3 O 20 '64
New Kennedy painting. il Look 28:60-1 Jl 14 '64
Norman Rockwell paints from the life of Lady Bird Johnson and Peggy Goldwater. il McCalls 92:102-5 N '64

about

Portrait sketches of Norman Rockwell. N. Kent. il por Am Artist 28:38-43+ S '64

ROCKWELL manufacturing company
R&D by the numbers. il Bsns W p59-61 Ag 24 '63

ROCKWELL-Standard corporation
Rockwell increases its thrust. il Bsns W p 146+ D 12 '64

ROCKWOOD, Linn R.
Problem of priorities. por Recreation 57:465-7 N '64

ROCKY MOUNTAIN goat hunting
Bargain goat hunt. E. A. Bauer. il Field & S 69:31-3+ Ag '64

ROCKY MOUNTAIN goats
Goat-watching in the Cascades. il Sunset 130: 54+ F '63

ROCKY MOUNTAIN NATIONAL PARK
Autumn trail trip in Rocky Mountain National Park. M. A. Hochman. il Nat Parks Mag 39:16-19 Ja '65
Rambling through the Never Summers. R. Fleck. il Nat Parks Mag 38:10-12 F '64

ROCKY MOUNTAIN sheep hunting. See Mountain sheep hunting

ROCKY MOUNTAIN spotted fever
Fleas, the ticks, spotted fever and me. R. Spencer. Sat R 46:47-9 N 2 '63

ROCKY MOUNTAINS
Bird islands in the prairies; Little Rocky Mountains. O. S. Pettingill, jr. il Audubon Mag 66:250-1 Jl '64
Flowers, trees, gardens and parks in the Rocky Mountains. G. W. Kelly. il Horticulture 42:34-5+ Ag '64
Rocky Mountains; symposium. il Holiday 34: 10+ Ag '63
Winding trip in the Rockies. il Sunset 130: 54-5 My '63
See also
Pikes Peak

Canadian Rockies

See also
Assiniboine, Mount

ROCOCO art. See Art, Rococo

RODAHL, Kaare
Nerve as a tissue. Science 147:414-15 Ja 22 '65

RODALE books, incorporated
FTC charges Rodale with making false ad claims. Pub W 185:40 My 18 '64

RODALE press, incorporated. See Rodale books, incorporated

RODBARD, S. and others
Induction of papillary growths in the heart. bibliog Science 143:1341-2 Mr 20 '64

RODDY, Joseph, and Cabot, H. B.
Impregnable Boston symphony: Mr Cabot meets the chorus crasher. Harper 227:35-8 Jl '63

RODE, Alex
Zeeb; story. Américas 15:18-20 N '63

RODELL, Fred
Tv or no TV in court? N Y Times Mag p 16+ Ap 12 '64
Warren court stands its ground. N Y Times Mag p23+ S 27 '64

RODENBERG, Richard
Almost perfect pilgrimage of Boop and his group; Cincinnati's basketball fans. W. Bingham. il pors Sports Illus 18:24-5 Ap 1 '63

RODENTS
See also
Lemmings
Pikas
Rats

RODENTS as carriers of infection
See also
Plague
RODEO sports news (periodical)
Cowboy's chronicle. il Newsweek 62:60 S 16 '63
RODEOS
Boley round-up time. il Ebony 20:100+ N '64
Braving the bulls. Time 85:60 Ja 29 '65
Bulldogger; J. Bynum. il Time 82:33-4 S 6 '63
Cheyenne's seven wild and woolly days in July; Frontier days celebration. il Bsns W p22-3 Ag 3 '63
It's round-up time this month in Pendleton. il Sunset 131:28+ S '63
Master of the bulls; photographs. B. Ballantine. Sat Eve Post 237:60-3 S 5 '64
Rider from Omaha; J. Houston. il Newsweek 64:61 D 14 '64
Rodeo clown; W. Peth. C. Lofting. il Life 55:37-8+ Jl 19 '63
Rodeo goes to college. B. Keating. il Holiday 35:134+ F '64
Rodeo just for kids. C. E. Ball. il Farm J 87:28-9+ Ag '63
Rodeo school; Thyrl Latting's rodeo school, Robbins, Ill. il Ebony 19:122-4+ Je '64
Sporting life. il Newsweek 62:80 N 11 '63
Texas trail ride; Negro cowboys. il Ebony 18:115-16+ My '63
RODGER, Patrick C.
Canny Scot. Newsweek 64:46 Ag 10 '64
Successor to Visser't Hooft. G. Murray. Christian Cent 81:1030 Ag 19 '64; Correction. 81:1148 S 16 '64
Who'll be head man? Time 84:65 S 25 '64
RODGERS, Calbraith Perry
Coast to coast in twelve crashes. S. Harris. il por Am Heritage 15:46-9+ O '64
RODGERS, Dorothy
My favorite things; excerpts. McCalls 91:120-5 My; 60+ Je; 102-3+ Jl; 34+ S; 92:28+ O '64
about
Domestic creature. il por Newsweek 64:39 D 28 '64
RODGERS, Mary Augusta
American family. November 1963. Redbook 124:69-71 N '64
For me? Redbook 124:31+ Ja '65
Hats. Redbook 121:15 My '63
Love story; story. Redbook 122:50-1 Mr '64
Pleasures of pack trips. Redbook 123:35-6+ O '64
Spur of the moment; story. Good H 156:90-1 My '63
Wyoming; wild and wonderful. Redbook 120:68-9+ Mr '63
RODGERS, Richard
Conversation with Richard Rodgers; interview. ed. by S. Chotzinoff. por Holiday 34:137-8+ D '63
Now the musical theater is enshrined. N Y Times Mag p20-3 Je 21 '64
RODGERS, Ruth
Tips for string savers. Pop Gard 14:24-5+ F '63
RODIN, Auguste
Heroic conception. il Newsweek 61:102+ My 13 '63
International comeback of a has-been titan of sculpture. il pors Life 55:86B-94 O 25 '63
Rodin: genius with giblets. P. M. Grand. il Art N 62:24-8 My '63
Rodin revolution; exhibition at the Museum of modern art. J. Canaday. il N Y Times Mag p36-7 Je 9 '63
Rodin's sculpture. B. Kaufman. Commonweal 78:436-7 Jl 12 '63
Sculptors of light and shadow. J. McAndrews. il Sat R 47:37-8 F 8 '64
RODITI, Edouard
Return of Europe's Jews. Commentary 36:63-8 Jl '63
RODMAN, Maia Wojciechowska
What did I say, dear? pors Library J 89:1385-6+ Mr 15 '64
RODMAN, Selden
After the children, the storm. Sat R 47:54+ N 14 '64
RODMAN public library, Alliance, Ohio
Alliance stays loose. A. C. Parsons. il Library J 88:4540-2 D 1 '63
RODRIGUES, Amália
You ain't been blue. por Time 83:68+ F 7 '64
RODRIGUEZ, Carlos Sosa-. See Sosa-Rodriguez, C.
RODRIGUEZ, Eduardo Barreiros. See Barreiros Rodriguez, E.
RODRIGUEZ, Jorge Alessandri
President of Chile addresses General assembly; summary of address. por U N Rev 10:39 Ja '63
RODRIGUEZ, Juan
Juan for the money. pors Newsweek 64:54 Ag 24 '64
Little Chi Chi's other side. D. Jenkins. il pors Sports Illus 21:34-6+ Ag 10 '64
RODRIGUEZ, Luis
All week long the word was Griffith. R. H. Boyle. il por Sports Illus 18:24-5+ Je 17 '63
King David and the Black Bull. H. Horn. il por Sports Illus 20:18-21 Je 22 '64
RODRIGUEZ, Marcos Armando
Deadly witness. Time 83:28 Ap 10 '64
Off-stride troika. Newsweek 63:38 Ap 13 '64
RODRIGUEZ, Rafael
Incredible escape. J. P. Blank. il Read Digest 84:159-62+ My '64
RODRIGUEZ Y SANCHEZ, Manuel Laureano. See Manolete
RODS, Curtain. See Curtain and drapery fixtures
RODS, Fishing. See Fishing tackle
ROE, Kenn Sherwood
Bodega: symbol of a national crisis. Am For 69:22-5 D '63
ROE, Richard D.
Flamboyant tigridia. Horticulture 41:360 Jl '63
These natives love the shade of summer. Flower Grower 51:51-2 My '64
Weather in the garden. Horticulture 41:412-13 Ag '63
Which is better spring or fall planting? Horticulture 41:506 O '63
Zinnias for brilliance all summer. Horticulture 41:214 Ap '63
ROE, Rowena, pseud.
Understanding the public. Am City 79:96-7 My '64
ROEDER, Kenneth D.
Night fighters in a sonic duel. Natur Hist 73:32-9 Ja '64
—See Dunning, D. C. jt. auth.
ROEMER, Milton I.
Changing patterns of health service; their dependence on a changing world. bibliog f Ann Am Acad 346:44-56 Mr '63
ROEPKE, Wilhelm
Keynes revisited. Nat R 14:239-41 Mr 26 '63
Letter from Geneva. Nat R 16:195-6 Mr 10 '64
about
Beyond the Common market. Nat R 15:137-8 Ag 27 '63
Economist in the grand tradition. L. M. Hacker. Nat R 14:532-3 Jl 2 '63
Laissez faire with a dash of Keynes. por Bsns W p72+ Ap 13 '63
ROER, Berniece
Contrast. Writer 77:23-4 Je '64
ROETGER, R. C.
Devil with deviation! Motor B 115:80-1 Ja '65
ROETHKE, Theodore
Abyss; poem. Harper 227:82-3 N '63
Chums; poem. Sat R 46:52 D 21 '63
Her convalescence; poem. Ladies Home J 81:124 Ap '64
Her longing; poem. Atlan 212:101 O '63
Her time; Infirmity; Meadow mouse; Wish for a young wife; Tranced; Moment; poems. New Yorker 39:50-1 O 19 '63
Pike; poem. Sat R 46:42 N 9 '63
Right thing; poem. Atlan 211:51 Mr '63
Rose; poem. New Yorker 39:26-7 Jl 6 '63
Song; My wrath. where's the edge. Harper 226:44 F '63
Straw for the fire: from his notebooks; ed. by D. Wagoner. Poetry 105:113-18 N '64
Supper with Lindsay; Song; Wheeze for Wystan; poems. Poetry 103:85-9 O '63
Thing; poem. Sat R 46:10 Mr 9 '63
about
Obituary
Pub W 184:40 Ag 12 '63
Requiem for God's gardener. H. Carruth. Nation 199:168-9 S 28 '64
Roethke: poet of transformations. S. Kunitz. New Repub 152:23-9 Ja 23 '65
Roethke's last poems. R. J. Mills, jr. Poetry 105:122-4 N '64
Theodore Roethke. J. Dickey. Poetry 105:119-22 N '64
Theodore Roethke: a passion and a maker. J. Ciardi. Sat R 46:13 Ag 31 '63
ROGALLO wing. See Airplane wings
ROGALLO wing paraglider. See Gliders (aeronautics)
ROGER, J. C. and others
Nicotinic acid analogs: effects on response of chick embryos and hens to organophosphate toxicants. bibliog Science 144:539-40 My 1 '64

ROGERS, Anne Hone
Best girl in the dog show. R. H. Boyle. il Sports Illus 20:40-2+ F 10 '64
ROGERS, Carl R.
Learning to be free. NEA J 52:28-30 Mr '63
ROGERS, Charles B.
Charles B. Rogers pleads for the spirit in art; with biographical sketch. il por Am Artist 27:42-3+ S '63
ROGERS, Frank Bradway
John Shaw Billings: 1838-1913. bibliog Library J 88:2622-4 Jl '63
Medical library association. Science 143:1240-1 Mr 13 '64
ROGERS, Fred G.
Rotary yacht squadron of Pennsylvania. Motor B 114:68 D '64
ROGERS, Gary
Getting closer to nature in the Tetons. Am For 69:12-14+ My '63
ROGERS, Ginger
Her school was the stage; interview, ed. by A. B. Haines. pors Dance Mag 37:32-4 N '63
ROGERS, Harold
Music at Harvard yesterday. Mus Am 83:6-7 Je '63
ROGERS, Howard G.
Instant color photography. W. Siegrist. il por Sci N L 83:250-1 Ap 20 '63
ROGERS, John
Build yourself a jet-drive aquaplane. Pop Sci 184:88-92 Je '64
ROGERS, John J. W. and Schubert, Carlos
Size distributions of sedimentary populations. bibliog Science 141:801-2 Ag 30 '63
ROGERS, Judith V. See Walters, G. C. jt. auth.
ROGERS, Lindsay
Line of succession. Reporter 29:20-2 D 19 '63
ROGERS, Millard F. Jr
New England glass company: some discoveries. Antiques 86:77-81 Jl '64
ROGERS, Richard
Richard Rogers: serious popular or popular serious. S. Green. por Mus Am 83:10-11 F '63
ROGERS, Rosemary
How your youngster learns to talk. Parents Mag 38:50-1+ Ap '63
ROGERS, Rutherford D.
Yung Lo encyclopedia presented to Library of Congress. Dept State Bul 49:740 N 11 '63
ROGERS, Ted
Sandwich fiberglass construction technique. Motor B 112:74+ O '63
ROGERS, Virgil M.
Automation. bibliog NEA J 52:50-2+ O '63
Does automation call for new solutions? PTA Mag 58:7-9 Je '64
Help wanted, 1964. NEA J 53:53 F '64
ROGERS, W. G.
He mixed his paints with politics. Sat R 46:60 D 7 '63
ROGERS, Warren, Jr
Reflections on the Bob and John show. New Repub 148:10-11 F 23 '63
ROGERS PASS highway. See Roads—Canada
ROGET, Peter Mark
On the fringe. H. Frankel. Sat R 47:40 Mr 21 '64
ROGGER, Hans
Soviet reform school. Cur Hist 47:292-8 N '64
ROGIN, Gilbert
At the Sea-Vue arms; story. New Yorker 40:56-63 O 24 '64
Blessed day; story. Mlle 59:146-7 S '64
Chico King: popular singer; story. Esquire 62:134 O '64
Description of a presumption. New Yorker 39:29 Ja 18 '64
1109 Klingenstein; story. New Yorker 40:45-8 Ap 18 '64
Ernest observes; story. New Yorker 39:44-7 O 26 '63
Fielding's progress; story. New Yorker 39:58-66 N 30 '63
Judging Keller; story. New Yorker 40:40-7 Mr 14 '64
Mr Blitz and the total vacation game. Sports Illus 19:48-59 Jl 1 '63
Night talk; story. Vogue 144:161 O 15 '64
Them apples; story. New Yorker 40:40 D 19 '64
Wolf whistle; story. Vogue 144:70 Ag 1 '64
about
Letter from the publisher. S. L. James. por Sports Illus 20:4 F 17 '64
ROGOFF, Gordon
Hamlet of brain and passion. Hi Fi 14:51-2 Jl '64
Homages to Shakespeare delights, and a few dangers. Hi Fi 14:91 S '64
Joan and the good guys. Reporter 31:52-4 N 19 '64
Olivier's Othello, coiling power and wounded majesty. Hi Fi 14:34+ D '64
Sean O'Casey's legacy. Commonweal 81:128-9 O 23 '64
Stage. Commonweal 80:176-7, 299-300 My 1, 29 '64
Streetcar named Kazan. Reporter 31:38+ D 17 '64
Theatre. Nation 198:153-4 F 10 '64
Trouble with Alice. Reporter 32:53-4 Ja 28 '65
ROGOWSKI, Theodore
Lee Wulff vs. Jock Scott transatlantic salmon challenge match. Esquire 59:100-3+ Je '63
ROGUE RIVER, Ore.
Sliding up a damp chute. B. Goldrath. il Field & S 68:46-7 Jl '63
There's a way to ride a river; conquering the wild, white Rogue. B. Goldrath. il Pop Mech 119:104-6 My '63
ROGUE RIVER CANYON, Ore. See Canyons
ROHDE, Barbara
Even the devil gets lonesome; story. Redbook 123:46-7 Jl '64
ROHDEA
Cousin of the aspidistra. il Sunset 133:162 D '64
ROHE, Ludwig Mies van der. See Mies van der Rohe, L.
ROHEN, James E.
Top band goes mobile. Pop Electr 18:55-8+ Je '63
ROHLF, John
(ed) Livestock. See issues of Farm journal
ROHOLT, O. A. and others
Antibody combining site: the B polypeptide chain. bibliog Science 141:726-7 Ag 23 '63
ROHR, Frank
How of those hopped-up sailboats. Pop Mech 121:108-12+ F '64
Operation sail. Motor B 113:44-5+ Je '64
SORC treasure to Doubloon. Motor B 111:164-5+ Ap '63
Tiny Burgoo big Bermuda winner. il Motor B 114:126-8+ Ag '64
ROHR corporation
World's biggest nozzle delivered. il Miss & Roc 16:17 Ja 11 '65
ROHRBACH, Heinrich
Borer-resistant pussy willows. Horticulture 41:502-3 O '63
Flowering dogwood for the North. Horticulture 41:556 N '63
ROHRKE, Martin C. See Leonard, M. jt. auth.
ROHWEDER, Ralph A.
Medical progress requires animal research. Todays Health 41:88 S '63
ROISUM, Bryant H.
How to recognize suicidal depression. Ladies Home J 81:26+ S '64
ROIZEN, Joseph
Helical video recorder for television. Electr World 72:47-9 O '64
ROJAS, Jorge
Farmer, city founder, and poet. L. Zalamea. il por Américas 15:36-9 N '63
ROJAS PINILLA, Gustavo
Dictator's comeback. por Time 84:29 Ag 14 '64
ROKEACH, Milton
Delusions. G. P. Elliott. Commentary 37:78-81 Je '64; Discussion. 38:6+ D '64
ROLAND, Stanley J. Jr
Dialogue on the moral crisis. Christian Cent 81:705 My 27 '64
ROLE playing. See Dramatization in education
ROLFE, John
John's royal wife. D. Garnett. il N Y Times Mag p 104-6 Ap 5 '64
ROLL bars. See Automobiles—Safety devices and measures
ROLL call; story. See Loeser, K.
ROLL-top desks. See Desks
ROLLEFSON, Ragnar
Science in the State department. W. M. Todd. Bul Atomic Sci 20:27-9 D '64
ROLLER painting. See Painting, Industrial and practical
ROLLIN, Betty
Eat: an unsettling experience with an Allan Kaprow environment. Vogue 143:124-5+ Ap 1 '64
New beat: topical folk singers, their songs. Vogue 144:60+ S 1 '64
ROLLING repair shops. See Motor trucks in repair service
ROLLING Stones. See Singers

ROLLINS broadcasting, incorporated
How a radio chain got into pest control. Bsns W p65-6+ Jl 11 '64

ROLLO, Pinkie
Furious fun of Pinkie and Pat. B. H. La-Fontaine. il por Sports Illus 21:20-1 Ag 24 '64

ROLLS. See Bread

ROLLS razor limited
Doomsday book. Time 84:94 S 4 '64
Rolls razor calls it quits. Bsns W p 114+ Jl 25 '64
Supa John. il Newsweek 63:67 Mr 2 '64
Trouble in never-never land. il Time 84:82 Jl 24 '64
Wilting Bloom. Newsweek 64:68 Jl 27 '64

ROLT, L. T. C.
Good-bye, Puffing Billy. Horizon 6:72-7 Autumn '64

ROLVAAG, Karl Fritjof
Minnesota's winter magic. por Travel 122:30-4 D '64

about

Minnesota winner, recount court picks Rolvaag. por U S News 54:16 Ap 1 '63

ROMAN, Lawrence
P.S. I love you. Criticism
Newsweek 64:92 N 30 '64

ROMAN art. See Art, Roman

ROMAN Catholic authors. See Catholic authors

ROMAN Catholic church. See Catholic church

ROMAN Catholics. See Catholics

ROMAN coins. See Coins

ROMAN cookery. See Cookery, Roman

ROMAN curia. See Catholic church—Roman curia

ROMAN emperors
Caesar the destroyer. R. Moley. Newsweek 62:84 S 2 '63

ROMAN empire. See Rome

ROMAN women. See Women—Rome

ROMANCE
Am I really in love? questions and answers. A. Wood. il Seventeen 23:136-7+ Je '64
Crushing season is on. J. Wescott. il Seventeen 23:14 S '64
How to make love in five languages; excerpts from How to marry a millionaire. D. Lilly. il McCalls 91:94-5 Je '64
I'll take romance. J. Didion. Nat R 15:246+ S 24 '63
Return of the femme fatale. M. Lerner. il Ladies Home J 80:80-1+ Je '63
Who killed romance? E. Kendall. Mlle 56: 125+ F '63; Same abr. Read Digest 82:103-4 Mr '63
Will I ever find a boy I really love? questions and answers. A. Wood. il Seventeen 22:156-7+ My '63

Anecdotes, facetiae, satire, etc.

Man talk. D. Newman and R. Benton. Mlle 59:98+ S '64

ROMANESQUE architecture. See Architecture, Romanesque

ROMANESQUE sculpture. See Sculpture, Romanesque

ROMANIA. See Rumania

ROMANIDES, John S.
Orthodox: arrival and dialogue. Christian Cent 80:1399-403 N 13 '63
U.S. Russian orthodoxy. Christian Cent 81: 993 Ag 5 '64

ROMANO, Antonio H. See Wegener, W. S. jt. auth.

ROMANTIC life of Alphonse A; story. See Donleavy, J. P.

ROMANTIC love. See Love

ROMANTICISM
Romanticism reconsidered, by N. Frye. Review
Christian Cent 80:1611-12 D 25 '63. F. Eversole

ROME
Caesar the destroyer. R. Moley. Newsweek 62:84 S 2 '63
Legacies of Julius Caesar and Rome. Sr Schol 84:5+ Mr 20 '64
Year one. M. I. Finley. il Horizon 6:4-17 Wint '64
See also
Women—Rome

ROME (city)
Notes from Rome. J. Cogley. Commonweal 78:469-71 Ag 9 '63

Airports

Rome airport displeases Alitalia, others. R. H. Cook. il Aviation W 80:46-8 F 3 '64

Antiquities

Father of letter forms: Trajan column. G. Barford. il Sch Arts 64:29-32 D '64

Art

Art news from Rome (cont) M. Gendel. il Art N 62:48+ Sum '63; 63:44-5+ Sum '64
New treasures uncovered in old Rome. M. Gendel. il Art N 62:34-5+ Sum '63

City planning

Rome builds a new forum for business. il Bsns W p 120-1+ D 5 '64

Description

Easy does it, as the Romans do. L. Barry. il Pop Phot 51:46+ D '62
Mr Handel slept here, too. W. Weaver. il Hi Fi 14:47-51+ Ap '64

Economic conditions

Letter from Rome. W. Murray. il New Yorker 40:92+ Je 27 '64

Historic houses, etc.

Palace for sale; Palazzo Poli. il Time 81:36 F 15 '63

History

Letter from Rome; exhibit commemorating centenary death of G. G. Belli. W. Murray. New Yorker 40:99-100+ Je 27 '64

Music

Mr Handel slept here too. W. Weaver. il Hi Fi 14:47-51+ Ap '64
Notes from our correspondents (cont of) Notes from abroad. W. Weaver. Hi Fi 13: 18+ My; 10+ O '63; 14:51 O '64; 15:27+ Ja '65

Newspapers

Press crisis in Italy; Il Quotidiano ceases publication. America 110:696 My 23 '64

Politics and government

Letter from Rome. W. Murray. il New Yorker 40:92+ Je 27 '64

St Peter's cathedral

Doors of death; new bronze doors for St Peter's, Rome. il Time 84:68-70 Jl 24 '64
Mea culpa; St Peter's great central dome. J. Updike. New Yorker 39:137-8+ N 16 '63

Street traffic

Eternal motorist. Newsweek 63:47-8 My 18 '64
Roads of Rome. il Time 83:77 My 15 '64
What to do about traffic? some answers from abroad. il U S News 54:86-90 F 4 '63

Streets

Via Veneto. Travel 119:21 Ap '63

Theater

Letter from Rome; Teatro dell'opera. W. Murray. New Yorker 40:96-7 Je 27 '64

ROME, Ga.
They hate Kennedy. S. Alsop. il Sat Eve Post 236:18 O 5 '63

ROMEO and Juliet; drama. See Shakespeare, W.

ROMEO and Juliet; story. See Masetto, A. D.

ROMER, Alfred S.
International congress of zoology. Science 140:1113-14+ Je 7 '63

ROMERA, Antonio R.
Monvoisin in South America. Américas 15:7-11 My '63

ROMERO, John
Judge's report. por Sports Illus 20:20-1 Je 22 '64

ROMERO, Pablo José Bush
Lost worlds of Don Pablo. C. Phinizy. il pors Sports Illus 21:80-4+ N 30 '64

ROMERO, Patricia
Trip to Virginia. Negro Hist Bul 27:96+ Ja '64

ROMERO, Vicente
To Carmen Amaya. Dance Mag 38:47 Ja '64

ROMERSTEIN, Herbert
Campaign against anti-communism. Nat R 14: 108 F 12 '63

ROMETSCH, Elly
Missile secrets; and Bobby Baker case. por U S News 57:14 O 12 '64

ROMIG, Mary F. and Lamar, D. L.
Strange sounds from the sky. Sky & Tel 28: 214-15 O '64

ROMIG, W. R. See Bayreuther, K. E. jt. auth.

ROMM, Mikhail
Russian art & anti-Semitism; address. Commentary 36:435-7 D '63

ROMNEY, G. Ott
Recreation as a power for peace! por Recreation 56:355 O '63
ROMNEY, George, 1734-1802
Drawings by George Romney at Yale. E. Sharp. il Antiques 86:598-603 N '64
ROMNEY, George, 1907-
How businessmen can serve their country; interview, ed. by B. Hibbs. por Read Digest 83:76-80 O '63
Where Romney stands; interview. por U S News 56:70-5 Mr 9 '64
about
Businessman in a political jungle. H. B. Meyers. il por Fortune 69:132-5+ Ap '64
Change of fortunes? por Newsweek 61:30 My 13 '63
Citizens' victory. Time 81:24 Ap 12 '63
For Romney: a win, a boost. il pors U S News 54:44-6 Ap 15 '63
George Romney gone bust. C. A. Ferry. New Repub 150:12-15 Ja 25 '64
Governor Romney: why the Republican pros distrust him. F. Knebel. il pors Look 28: 75-7 Mr 10 '64
Governor Romney's first labor crisis. por U S News 56:21 Je 8 '64
In the making: a Romney boom? il por U S News 54:19 My 13 '63
Interment in Michigan. por Time 82:18-19 N 22 '63
It ain't any fun. Newsweek 62:19-20 O 28 '63
Lightning strikes thrice. Time 83:25 My 8 '64
Living legends. A. Robin. Todays Health 41: 59 Je '63
Making their records. il por Time 82:29 S 13 '63
People of the week. por U S News 55:16 N 25 '63
Romney's trial run. New Repub 148:6 My 11 '63
State GOP slaps Romney. Bsns W p80+ N 16 '63
This president thing. il Time 81:26-31 Je 14 '63
Through the eye. Time 82:25 N 1 '63
Top Republican who survived. por U S News 57:19 N 16 '64
Trying to drape the albatross. il por Time 84:22 S 25 '64
Two Republican hopefuls. por Look 28:71 Mr 10 '64
Voters bought Romney. Newsweek 61:32+ Ap 15 '63
What happened when two noncandidates got together. por U S News 56:14 F 24 '64
ROMNEY, Golden
Questions to ask ourselves. Recreation 57:7-8 Ja '64
ROMPER room (television program) See Television broadcasting—Childrens programs
ROMUALDI, Serafino
Labor and the Alliance. Américas 15:18-21 Ag '63
ROMULO, Carlos P.
Freedom's other face. Sat R 47:16+ D 19 '64
Light in Diliman. il por Time 84:69 Jl 3 '64
Report on C.P.R. N. Cousins. Sat R 47:32 Ap 11 '64
RONA, Elizabeth
Geochronology of marine and fluvial sediments. Science 144:1595-7 Je 26 '64
RONAN, Colin A.
Galileo Galilei, 1564-1642. Sky & Tel 27:72-8 F '64
Phoenix of astronomers. Natur Hist 74:52-7 Ja '65
RONAN, Elena Vinadé
Palace for Picasso. Américas 16:32-7 Jl '64
RONAN, Margaret
Chip off the old block. Sr Schol 83:10 O 25 '63
RONCOLE VERDI, Italy
New day for Roncole; Verdi's birthplace. M. J. Matz. il Opera N 28:30-1 Ap 4 '64
RONEY, James G. Jr
Inverted indexing on edge-notched cards. bibliog Science 142:227-8 O 11 '63
ROOD, Ronald N.
And how are your little red constables? PTA Mag 59:31 O '64
Teacher to the president. PTA Mag 57:15 My '63
ROOF drainage. See Drainage, House
ROOF gardens
Boom at the top. il Newsweek 64:65 Ag 10 '64
Green grows my kudzu. P. Mandel. il Life 54:80+ My 31 '63
Hand of the gardener. I. Hayden. il Horticulture 42:46+ F '64
ROOF heliports. See Heliports
ROOF paint. See Paint
ROOF trusses. See Trusses
ROOFING
Application of a one-ply roofing system. E. G. Long. il Arch Rec 136:263-4 S '64
Fluid applied roofing for Houston stadium. il Arch Rec 137:185-6 Ja '65
Fluid roofing systems of synthetic rubber. il Arch Rec 135:177-8 Ja; 179-80 F; 215-16+ Mr '64
ROOFS
Bold roof line creates an exciting house inside and out. A. Borg. il Am Home 66:6 Ja '63
Choosing the right roof. Bet Hom & Gard 42:90 Jl '64
Experimental plywood roof in Seattle. il Arch Forum 118:122 Ap '63
Foamed plastics for flat roof insulation. R. E. Polson. il Arch Rec 133:197-8 Je '63
It's a truss and chain roof. il Sunset 132:103 F '64
Long-span structure: light folding trusses. B. P. Spring. il Arch Forum 120:114 F '64
More house for less money. A. J. Maher. il Pop Mech 120:140-3 N '63
Raising the roof of an old barn makes room for parties. il House & Gard 123:172-3 My '63
Roofs, design and pattern; photographs from The wonders of Europe. Design 66:37-9 N '64
Saddle shell roof for theater; movie house north of Chicago. il Arch Rec 135:155-8 Mr '64
Soaring laminated arches create dramatic interiors for a hilltop house. il Arch Rec 133:78-81 mid-My '63
Sod roof cool, green, and alive. il Sunset 133: 68-70 Ag '64
Support method for stressed-skin panels. il Arch Rec 133:168 Ja '63
Tension band prestresses pleated roof. il Arch Rec 133:209 Mr '63
Tests check roofing system for huge plant. F. Couch. il Arch Rec 137:175-8 Ja '65
This house has a wonderful hole in its head. il Sunset 133:76 Ag '64
What's happened to the built-up roof? R. M. Stafford. Arch Rec 136:176-8 D '64
See also
Shells (structural engineering)
Repairing
How to keep a roof over your head. Am Home 67:74-5 Je '64
Reroofing by the acre, while production continues; Lockheed-Georgia co. il Bsns W p76-7 N 23 '63
Wintertime leaky roofs. il Consumer Bul 47: 10-11+ Ja '64
ROOM; drama. See Pinter, H.
ROOM air conditioners. See Air conditioning equipment
ROOM at the bottom, room at the top; story. See Cuomo, G.
ROOM dividers. See Partitions
ROOM furnishings. See Household furnishings
ROOM painting. See Painting, Industrial and practical
ROOM III at Fusco's. See New York (city)—Hotels, restaurants, etc.
ROOMMATES
Houseful of roommates. C. S. Wren. il Look 28:66-71 Ja 14 '64
ROOMS
Atrium house. il House B 105:57-79 Ag '63
Comfort for a man. F. Byerly. il Bet Hom & Gard 41:46-51 Mr '63
Decorating ingenuity. G. O'Brien. il N Y Times Mag pt2 p52-3 S 29 '63
Enchanting rooms that fool the eye. il House & Gard 125:106-13 Ap '64
Engaging rooms that say welcome. il House & Gard 126:216-23 N '64
Finest rooms by America's great decorators, ed. by K. Tweed. Review
Antiques il 86:322-3 S '64
Garden rooms inaugurate a gay new trend in decoration. il House & Gard 127:110-17 Ja '65
H&G gives a house individuality with color inside and out; H&G colors for 1965. il House & Gard 126:150-73 S '64
How many ways could you use this room? il Bet Hom & Gard 41:68-9 F '63
How to stretch one room into two; How to make one big beautiful room out of three little ones. il House & Gard 125:184-7 My '64
How you can play variations on a space. il House & Gard 126:262-7+ N '64

ROOMS—*Continued*
Ideas international! il Bet Hom & Gard 42: 40-5 Ag '64
Illustrated history of furnishing, by M. Praz. Review
Antiques il 86:320-1 S '64
Increase your living space. il Ladies Home J 80:114 Mr '63
Introducing H&G colors for 1964; symposium. il House & Gard 124:121-45 S '63
Lavish a room with fabric for easy color scheming. il Bet Hom & Gard 41:55 S '63
Make room for an extra bed. il Good H 156: 108-15 Mr '63
Now four jobs can be done instead of one. il House B 105:210-11 S '63
Open plan family room-kitchen. il Sunset 133: 82-3 Jl '64
Roof hangs from light steel rods; garden room. il Sunset 131:112 N '63
Rooms; National decoration and design show. New Yorker 39:39-40 N 2 '63
Seven rooms men have asked for. il House & Gard 124:54-61 Jl '63
Stretch space. il Bet Hom & Gard 42:25-6+ F '64
Subject is privacy. il Am Home 67:43-9 O '64
Take-it-easy rooms; part-time homes. il House & Gard 123:92-7 Je '63
Teen-age room contest winner. il Bet Hom & Gard 41:70-1 O '63
Three ways to create a garden room for all seasons. il Am Home 68:84-5 Ja '65
See also
Basements and cellars
Bathrooms
Bedrooms
Childrens rooms
House decoration
Kitchens
Laundries
Living rooms
Music rooms and equipment
Nurseries
Parlors
Playrooms
Recreation rooms
Sewing rooms
Studies (rooms)

ROOMS, Miniature
Christmas in miniature. E. M. Parvin. il Hobbies 69:122-4 D '64
It's the little things that count; collection of Adele Braude, Chicago. V. R. Smith. il Hobbies 69:116-17+ My '64
Mrs Ingler's miniature creations. S. A. Parvin. il Hobbies 69:116+ Je '64
My miniature rooms. R. Poteet. il Hobbies 68: 116-17+ N '63
Thorne room at Phoenix art museum. S. A. Parvin. il Hobbies 68:116-17+ Ag '63

ROOMS, Remodeled. See Houses, Remodeled

ROONEY, Agnes Baldwin
Clear the path; story. Redbook 124:88-9 N '64
Lion in the refrigerator; story. Redbook 122: 38-9 D '63

ROONEY, Art
Winning ways of a thirty-year loser. G. Holland. il pors Sports Illus 21:90-4+ N 23 '64

ROONEY, Ed
Lights, action, camera! U S Camera 26:64-7+ N '63

ROONEY, Frank Leo
WLB biography. L. Ash. por Wilson Lib Bul 39:422 Ja '65

ROONEY, Fred B.
How Democrats held a congressional seat. il por U S News 55:6 Ag 12 '63

ROONEY, John J.
Guardian of the taxpayers' money; House appropriations subcommittee. por U S News 54:19 Je 17 '63
How to save money: an open letter to Congressman John J. Rooney. H. S. Villard. Harper 228:17+ Ja '64

ROONEY, Mickey
Judy and Mickey reunited. il pors Life 55: 47+ Jl 19 '63

ROONEY, Paul M.
Scholarship realities. Library J 89:2904+ Ag '64

ROONEY, Thomas P. and Kerr, P. F.
Chinoptilolite: a new occurrence in North Carolina phosphorite. Science 144:1453 Je 19 '64

ROONEY, Walter J.
Be realistic in space planning, architect advises special librarians; statement, April 25, 1963. Library J 88:2223 Je 1 '63

ROOPE, Clover
Observer at the dance notation conference. Dance Mag 38:13-15 Ag '64

ROOS/Atkins award
California clothing stores establish literary award. Pub W 184:31 O 28 '63

ROOSA, Robert Vincent
Money flows and balance-of-payments adjustment; address, October 8, 1964. Dept State Bul 51:669-73 N 9 '64
Reforming the international monetary system. For Affairs 42:107-22 O '63
about
Danger to the dollar; what Treasury wants to do about it. por U S News 55:81-2 Jl 22 '63
No. 1 dollar defender. por Bsns W p90+ Ag 3 '63

ROOSEVELT, Blanche, pseud. See Macchetta, B. R. T.

ROOSEVELT, Eleanor (Roosevelt)
I remember Hyde Park. por McCalls 90:71-3+ F '63; Same abr. Read Digest 82:95-100 Je '63
Tomorrow is now; excerpts from Foreword ed. by E. Denniston. por Ladies Home J 80: 39-45 S '63
about
Beloved agitator. il por Newsweek 64:121-2 N 23 '64
Eleanor Roosevelt: a lady for all seasons. A. Stevenson. por Sat R 47:26-7 O 10 '64
Eleanor Roosevelt; a lifetime of dedication to human rights; address, October 21, 1963. Thant. por UNESCO Courier 16:15 D '63
Eleanor Roosevelt memorial service held at Washington cathedral; remarks, November 15, 1962. D. Rusk. Dept State Bul 48:51 Ja 14 '63
Eleanor Roosevelt: my most unforgettable character. E. Bugbee. por Read Digest 83: 91-7 O '63
Homage to Eleanor Roosevelt. U N Rev 10:28 D '63
Mrs Roosevelt and children's books. H. Ferris. il por Library J 89:2149-51+ My 15 '64
Mrs Roosevelt does a TV commercial. T. L. Stix. Harper 227:104-6 N '63
Mrs Roosevelt, RIP; discussion. Nat R 14:173 F 26 '63
Mrs Roosevelt's legacy; report on the status of women. E. Peterson. por McCalls 91:84+ O '63
Thoughts as her travels ended. L. Smith. por Sat R 46:19-20 S 7 '63
Tribute to a great American lady. A. MacLeish. il pors N Y Times Mag p 17+ N 3 '63
United Nations pays tribute to memory of Mrs Roosevelt. por Dept State Bul 48:48-50+ Ja 14 '63

ROOSEVELT, Franklin D, Lake. See Grand Coulee power and reclamation project

ROOSEVELT, Franklin Delano, 1882-1945
Day the money stopped; March 6, 1933. C. Bird. il Look 27:84+ Mr 12 '63
F.D.R. and the Democratic triumph. J. T. Patterson. Cur Hist 47:216-20+ O '64
F.D.R. vs. the Democratic party. W. Myers. il por Esquire 59:115+ Mr '63
Ike's view: FDR policy prolonged the war; summary of interview, ed. by E. T. Folliard. D. D. Eisenhower. il por U S News 58:12 Ja 4 '65
Johnson and Roosevelt. R. Moley. Newsweek 65:80 F 1 '65
This thing about Frank. J. Potter. New Yorker 39:70-4 Ag 10 '63

ROOSEVELT, Franklin Delano, 1914-
Excerpt from testimony, July 23, 1963. Cong Digest 42:280+ N '63
Excerpt from testimony, May 5, 1964. Cong Digest 43:304+ D '64
about
Advise & consent; F. D. Roosevelt jr. before Senate commerce committee. por Time 81: 19 Mr 22 '63
Back in government; FDR, jr. gets commerce post. por U S News 54:16 F 11 '63
Last chance for Junior. B. Brower. por Sat Eve Post 236:32-3 Jl 27 '63
Nothing to hide. por Newsweek 61:26 Mr 25 '63
Poor political choice. Sat Eve Post 236:80 Mr 16 '63
Return of Roosevelt. New Repub 148:5 F 16 '63

ROOSEVELT, Franklin Delano, family
I remember Hyde Park: a final reminiscence. E. Roosevelt. McCalls 90:71-3+ F '63; Same abr. il Read Digest 82:95-100 Je '63

ROOSEVELT, James
After Sam's scalp. por Time 84:15 D 25 '64

ROOSEVELT, Julian K.
Olympic preview. Yachting 115:41-3 F '64

ROOSEVELT, Kermit
Leopard in large type. por Outdoor Life 133:50-3+ Ap '64

ROOSEVELT, Theodore
My dear Selous; letters. ed. by E. Hahn. por Am Heritage 14:40-2+ Ap '63

about

From bully! to vigah! A. Robertson. il pors Horizon 5:68-71 N '63
I stayed after school with Theodore Roosevelt. J. Robbins. il Read Digest 85:76-80 O '64
Mr Dooley's friends; excerpts from Mr Dooley remembers. F. P. Dunne. por Atlan 212:77-80+ S '63
Physical fitness on the New frontier. il por U S News 54:10 F 18 '63
TR, the strenuous life of a great American; excerpts from T.R: the story of Theodore Roosevelt. N. F. Busch. il pors Read Digest 83:237-43+ Jl '63
Was T.R. a drunk? J. G. Hayden. il Am Heritage 15:82-3 O '64
When gentlemen prepared for war. F. Russell. il Am Heritage 15:24-7+ Ap '64

ROOSEVELT CAMPOBELLO INTERNATIONAL PARK
Campobello agreement. Dept State Bul 50:206-8 F 10 '64
Mrs Johnson to participate in Campobello Park ceremonies. Dept State Bul 51:312 Ag 31 '64

ROOSEVELT estate, Hyde Park, N.Y. See Hyde Park, N.Y.—Roosevelt estate

ROOSEVELT memorial. See Washington, D.C.—Monuments, statues, etc.

ROOSEVELT raceway. See Race tracks

ROOSEVELT university, Chicago, Ill.
Annex for Louis Sullivan's auditorium. il Arch Rec 134:246 Ag '63

ROOT, Gladys Towles
Lady defender. il por Newsweek 63:22 Mr 2 '64

ROOT, John W. and others
Isotopic molecules: separation by recycle gas chromatography. bibliog Science 143:676-8 F 14 '64

ROOT, Robert
Scientists and survival. Christian Cent 81:673 My 20 '64
Some dare to die. Christian Cent 81:1623 D 30 '64

ROOT, Waverley
Gastronomic tour of France. House B 105:150-1+ Mr '63
How to make French dressing. House B 105:256+ N '63
How to read a menu. House B 105:179+ My '63

ROOT carving. See Carving (art industries)

ROOT celery. See Celeriac

ROOT cuttings. See Plant propagation

ROOT of all evil; story. See Greene, G.

ROOT pressure. See Roots

ROOTES motors, limited
Chrysler gets aboard British auto boom. Bsns W p54 Je 13 '64
Ford sells hot bundle to Britain; Rootes buys Fairlane. il Bsns W p32 N 2 '63

ROOTS, John McCook, and Entwistle, Basil
Defense of moral re-armament, and a reply to Russell Kirk. Nat R 16:969 N 3 '64

ROOTS
Labeled oxygen: increased diffusion rate through soil containing growing corn roots. C. R. Jensen and D. Kirkham. bibliog il Science 141:735-6 Ag 23 '63
Nematode-trapping fungi: evaluation of axenic healthy and galled roots as trap inducers. D. W. Iffland and P. V. Allison. bibliog il Science 146:547-8 O 23 '64
Partial synchronization of nuclear divisions in root meristems with 5-aminouracil. H. H. Smith and others. il Science 142:595-6 N 1 '63
Preservation of chlorophyll in leaf sections by substances obtained from root exudate. H. Kende. bibliog il Science 145:1066-7 S 4 '64
Root diseases biologically controlled; report of international symposium on factors determining the behavior of plant pathogens in soils. W. C. Snyder. Science 141:835-7 Ag 30 '63
Root hairs, cuticle, and pits. F. M. Scott and others. bibliog il Science 40:63 Ap 5 '63
Root pressure in conifers. J. W. O'Leary and P. J. Kramer. bibliog Science 145:284-5 Jl 17 '64

ROPE
Amazing plastic ropes, they splice themselves. G. Daniels. il Pop Sci 184:142-8 Je '64
Give a man enough rope. il Sunset 133:37-8+ D '64
Know your ropes. J. A. Emmett. il Outdoor Life 134:96+ N '64
Rope tangle. W. Andrews. il Yachting 113:76-8+ Ap '63
What's your line? E. Crimmin. il Motor B 113:86-9+ Ja '64
Will your rope let you down? W. Andrews. il Yachting 115:64-6+ My '64

ROPE Jumping
Rope skipping. R. A. Tapply. Recreation 57:175-6 Ap '64

ROPE; story. See Seager, A.

ROPER, Burns W.
Interview at gunpoint. Sat R 47:44 Ag 8 '64
—and Roper, Elmo
How big is the backlash? Sat R 47:24 O 3 '64

ROPER, Elmo
After the election. Sat R 47:12 N 28 '64
Americans look at the Atlantic future. Sat R 47:26-7 Ja 4 '64
Gallup on education. Sat R 47:78-9 Mr 21 '64
Getting close to home. Sat R 46:14+ Ag 31 '63
Meaning of San Francisco. Sat R 47:17+ Ag 22 '64
November 22: what did it mean? Sat R 47:28 My 9 '64
Weighing the campaign. Sat R 47:28 O 31 '64
Wheat sale and the public. Sat R 46:23 N 16 '63
Will Clayton: groundbreaker in ideas. Sat R 46:22-3 My 11 '63
—See Roper, B. W. jt. auth.

about

People's choice for L.B.J.'s V.P. E. Havemann. il Life 57:68-70+ Ag 14 '64

ROPER, Hugh Redwald Trevor-. See Trevor-Roper, H. R.

ROPER, James E.
Colossal new palace on Capitol hill. Read Digest 86:79-84 Ja '65
Robert Kennedy speaks his mind on living outdoors family style. Pop Gard 14:26-9 My '63
—and Robinson, Donald
Atomic energy, ace detective. Read Digest 85:122-6 S '64

RORABACHER, Louise E.
Appointment in the desert. Sat R 47:47-8 F 15 '64

ROREM, Ned
Song and singer; excerpt from lecture-recital. Am Rec G 30:468-70+ F '64

about

Best in American song: Ned Rorem. P. L. Miller. por Am Rec G 30:864-5 My '64

RORIMER, James Joseph
Best-loved art. Seventeen 22:154-5 My '63

about

Auction! excerpt. J. Brough. McCalls 90:112-13+ Ap '63
Mona Lisa. New Yorker 38:23-4 F 9 '63

ROSAN, Robert C. and others
Spectroscopic ultramicroanalysis with a laser. Science 142:236-7 O 11 '63

ROSARIO
Cousins. il por Newsweek 64:88-9 S 28 '64

ROSARY pea. See Crabs eye vine

ROSBAUD, Hans
Da capo; recordings. S. Smolian. Am Rec G 29:816 Je '63
Hans Rosbaud, 1895-1962. J. Evarts. por Mus Am 83:21 F '63

ROSBERG, Carl G. Jr, and Segal, Aaron
East African Federation. bibliog f Int Concil 543:4-72 My '63

ROSE of Lima, Saint
Sanctuary; for New World's first saint. il por Travel 120:41-3 D '63

ROSE, Biff
Fourth Rose. por Time 85:68 Ja 29 '65

ROSE, Billy
Girl named Fanny. por McCalls 90:52+ S '63
Rose is a rich Rose. il por Newsweek 61:80 My 27 '63

ROSE, Carl
Cartoonist at large in the Village. il N Y Times Mag p46-7 N 24 '63

ROSE, Charles R.
Poetry of art. Sch Arts 62:12 Mr '63

ROSE, Dixie E.
December embers. Horticulture 41:600-1 D '63
Homes for persecuted wildings. Horticulture 41:324-5 Je '63
Indian parsnip. Horticulture 41:132 Mr '63
Native orchid, lady's-slipper. Horticulture 41:291+ My '63
ROSE, Elinor K.
Light verse in depth. Writer 77:20-2 Ag '64
ROSE, François de
Atlantic relationships and nuclear problems. For Affairs 41:479-90 Ap '63
ROSE, Frank Anthony
Alabama quality. il por Time 81:80+ Je 14 '63
Nation's crisis crowds in on one man; with report by D. Nevin. il pors Life 54:77-8+ Je 14 '63
ROSE, Ivan. See Downing, J. jt. auth.
ROSE, Jerry A.
Elusive Viet Cong. New Repub 148:19-26 My 4 '63
I'm hit! I'm hit! I'm hit! il Sat Eve Post 236: 34-47 Mr 23 '63
Laos: the war that never stops. Sat Eve Post 236:78+ Ag 24 '63
We are going to change this damn world! Sat Eve Post 236:77-81 N 2 '63
We can't win, but we need not lose. New Repub 149:15-18 O 12 '63
Who's who in Asia. New Repub 150:13-15 Ap 4 '64
Will Cambodia go Communist? Sat Eve Post 237:68+ Mr 28 '64
ROSE, Leonard
Notes from abroad; interview, ed. by R. McMullen. por Hi Fi 14:12+ Ja '64
ROSE, Stephen C.
Churches and Mississippi. Christian Cent 81: 909-10 Jl 15 '64
N.C.C. visits Clarksdale. Christian Cent 80: 1104-6 S 11 '63
Test for nonviolence. Christian Cent 80:714-16 My 29 '63
ROSE, Virginia Brown
It could happen this Christmas. Farm J 88: 59+ D '64
ROSE, W. K.
Dark Lorelei. Nation 199:96-7 S 7 '64
ROSE clover. See Clover
ROSE cold. See Hay fever
ROSEANNE of yesterday; story. See Cavanaugh, A.
ROSEBERY, Archibald Philip Primrose, 5th earl of
Rosebery, by R. R. James. Review
Nat R 15:111 Ag 13 '63. S. Leslie
ROSEBUD cherry. See Oriental flowering cherry
ROSEBUD reservation, S.D. See Indians of North America—Reservations
ROSELIEP, Raymond
Family: on the night Robert Frost died; poem. Commonweal 77:559 F 22 '63
Kodachrome: Katherine Anne Porter; poem. Cath World 196:342 Mr '63
Put out a lunch for Christmas; poem. Commonweal 79:426 Ja 10 '64
Smoke smell of spring; Canticle; Singing lesson; poems. Poetry 104:91-2 My '64
Summer night at the Keohens; poem. Commonweal 81:388 D 11 '64
There's that flesh again, Hamlet; poem. America 111:255 S 12 '64
Wheels; poem. Nation 199:283 O 26 '64
Wish for Paolo; poem. Poetry 101:398 Mr '63
about
Americans and others. J. M. Morrison. Poetry 104:115 My '64
ROSEMARY for remembrance; drama. See Martens, A. C.
ROSEN, A. A. and Rubin, Meyer
Natural carbon-14 activity of organic substances in streams. bibliog Science 143: 1163-4 Mr 13 '64
ROSEN, Edgar R.
Italy's coalition government. Cur Hist 47:339-44 D '64
ROSEN, Frank L.
Role of the allergist in the battle against air pollution; address, March 1963. Consumer Bul 46:36-8 S '63
ROSEN, Fred, and others
Induction of several adaptive enzymes by actinomycin D. bibliog Science 146:661-3 O 30 '64
ROSEN, George
Required reading. por Newsweek 64:50-1 Jl 13 '64
ROSEN, Gerald R.
New breed in transportation. Duns R 83:pt2 100-2+ Je '64
ROSEN, Harold
Hypnosis: the fad and the facts. Todays Health 41:38-9+ O '63
ROSEN, Nathan
Variations on a Russian verse. Sat R 47: 25-6 N 28 '64
ROSEN, Norma
Sister Gertrude; story. Redbook 122:60-1 N '63
Thousand tears; story. Redbook 123:42-3 Je '64
What must I say to you? story. New Yorker 39:48-53 O 26 '63
ROSEN, Roslyn
Letter from Mexico City. Nation 198:200-3 F 24 '64
ROSEN, Samuel
Now hear this; difference in hearing between an American and a Mabaan. il por Newsweek 61:80 My 6 '63
ROSENBAUM, Samuel R.
Hydroponic culture; address, November 11, 1963. Mus Am 83:153 D '63
ROSENBERG, Barnett
Future techniques; electrically-charged picture-taking system. J. Reidy. U S Camera 26:12+ D '63
ROSENBERG, Bernard
New York politics & the liberal party. Commentary 37:69-75 F '64
ROSENBERG, Dorothy. See Rosenberg, M. jt. auth.
ROSENBERG, Eugene
Purine and pyrimidines in sediments from the experimental Mohole. bibliog Science 146:1680-1 D 25 '64
ROSENBERG, Harold
Art and the shared metaphor. Sat R 47:33-4 Ap 25 '64
Art establishment. Esquire 63:43-6+ Ja '65
Art galleries. See issues of New Yorker October 22, 1962 to November 2, 1963
Artist as family man. Sat R 46:37-8 Mr 9 '63
Barnett Newman. Vogue 141:134-5+ F 1 '63
Books. New Yorker 40:169-71+ Mr 14; 114-18+ Ag 22 '64
De Kooning. Vogue 144:146-9+ S 15 '64
Jasper Johns. Vogue 143:174-7+ F 1 '64
1914. Art N 63:38-41 O '64
ROSENBERG, James L.
(tr) See Frisch, M. Chinese wall
ROSENBERG, Marvin, and Rosenberg, Dorothy
There are no Indians left now but me. Am Heritage 15:18-23+ Je '64
ROSENBERG, Maurice
Warren commission. Nation 199:110-12 S 14 '64
ROSENBERG, Murray D.
Cell guidance by alterations in monomolecular films. bibliog Science 139:411-12 F 1 '63
ROSENBERG, P. E. and Holland, H. D.
Calcite-dolomite-magnesite stability relations in solutions at elevated temperatures. bibliog Science 145:700-1 Ag 14 '64
ROSENBERG, Seymour, and Cohen, B. D.
Speakers' and listeners' processes in a word-communication task. bibliog Science 145: 1201-3 S 11 '64
ROSENBERG, Shirley Sirota
Boy who thought pancakes were green. Parents Mag 38:70-1+ F '63
How tall will your child be? Parents Mag 40:42-3+ Ja '65
Should teachers wield the rod? Parents Mag 39:74-5+ F '64
Solving the mystery of birth defects. Parents Mag 39:36-7+ Ja '64
ROSENBERG, Stuart E.
Christians and Jews: a new rapprochement; excerpt from America is different. Christian Cent 81:295-8 Mr 4 '64
ROSENBLOOM, Joseph R.
Rites controversy. America 110:544-5 Ap 18 '64
ROSENBLUM, Louis A.
What do do about an ulcer. por Parents Mag 38:139-42 N '63
ROSENBLUM, M. Edward
AIGA; the making and marketing of dual-purpose books; summary of address. Pub W 185:72+ Je 1 '64
ROSENBLUM, Richard
What they might have said. Am Heritage 14:94-8 Ap '63
ROSENFELD, Albert
Atom-powered ship is national disgrace. Life 54:40-40A Je 14 '63
Get-together of fine fellows. Life 54:86+ F 8 '63
Heavens' new enigma. Life 56:11-12 Ja 24 '64; Same abr. with title What are those quasi-stellars out there? Read Digest 84:207-8+ My '64

ROSENFELD, Albert—*Continued*
Men in training to fly Dyna-Soar; six pilots whose mission may abort. Life 54:100A-100B+ F 22 '63
Pitfalls and perils out there. Life 57:112+ O 2 '64
Remembrance of a genius. Life 56:31 Je 12 '64
Seeing color with the fingers. Life 56:102-6+ Je 12 '64
Three million year trip in fifty-five years. Life 54:34-8 My 24 '63
What causes earthquakes, hopes for predicting them. Life 56:37-8 Ap 10 '64
—See Hills, A. jt. auth.

ROSENFELD, David
Sail repairs. il Yachting 114:46-7 Jl '63

ROSENFELD, Stephen S.
Soviet-American exchanges, tit-for-tat good-will. Science 143:1413-17 Mr 27 '64

ROSENFIELD, John
Texas roundup. Theatre Arts 47:23+ Mr '63

ROSENFIELD, Loyd
Dim view; poem. Atlan 214:127 Jl '64

ROSENHAUPT, Hans
Pusey on higher education. Sat R 46:84 N 16 '63

about

Fellowships. New Yorker 40:44-6 S 19 '64

ROSENHOUSE, Harvey
Brake on the Alianza. New Repub 150:19-21 Mr 28 '64

Der ROSENKAVALIER; opera. See Strauss, R.

ROSENKRANZ, H. S. and others
Purine- and pyrimidine-specific antibodies: effect on the fertilized sea urchin egg. bibliog Science 145:282-3 Jl 17 '64

ROSENMAN, Ray H.
They ran the heart study. il pors Bsns W p50-1+ D 12 '64

ROSENQUIST, James
What is pop art? interview; ed. by G. R. Swenson. il Art N 62:41+ F '64

about

Explosion of pop art: exhibition at the Guggenheim museum. A. B. Saarinen. il Vogue 141:134+ Ap 15 '63

ROSENSTOCK, Joseph
Wagner I know. por Opera N 28:8-11 D 14 '63

ROSENTHAL, Abraham Michael
Alarm rings in India. Read Digest 82:84-8 F '63
As Japan changes, so does the emperor. N Y Times Mag p 13+ My 19 '63
Purest of all the great cities. N Y Times Mag p52-3+ My 5 '63
Seeing the world through my children's eyes. por Ladies Home J 80:37+ N '63
Study of the sickness called apathy. N Y Times Mag p24+ My 3 '64

about

Legwork in megalopolis. il por Time 83:59-60 Ap 24 '64
Unapathetic book. New Yorker 40:23-4 Je 20 '64

ROSENTHAL, Abraham Michael, family
Seeing the world through my children's eyes. A. M. Rosenthal. il Ladies Home J 80:37+ N '63

ROSENTHAL, Alan
Cold crusade. Nation 196:361-4 Ap 27 '63
Could Kennedy budge the Congress? New Repub 148:13-15 My 4 '63

ROSENTHAL, Bernard
Wish granted. il por Newsweek 63:82 Ja 20 '64

ROSENTHAL, David
Remembering Dilys Laing; Overbrook sanatorium; poems. Poetry 102:94-5 My '63

ROSENTHAL, Harold L. and others
Strontium-90 content of deciduous human incisors. bibliog Science 140:176-7 Ap 12 '63

ROSENTHAL, M. L.
Enemy; poem. Reporter 30:44 Ap 9 '64
Jim Dandy; poem. Reporter 29:44 N 7 '63
Metaphysical; poem. Reporter 29:31 Jl 4 '63
Modern poetry. bibliog NEA J 53:54-7 Ja '64
My best love; poem. Reporter 29:62 O 10 '63
Not writ in water. Reporter 30:52-4 F 13 '64
Prospect of delight. Reporter 31:50+ S 10 '64
Something that might simply be. Reporter 29:54+ S 12 '63
Spark from Pasternak; poem. Nation 198:382 Ap 13 '64
Two elegiac poems: Song of dead friends; Psalm. Poetry 104:25 Ap '64

ROSENTHAL, Mel
Difficult birth. Nation 199:144+ S 21 '64

ROSENTHAL, Otto. See Eisenhardt, R. H. jt. auth.

ROSENTHAL, Philip
Design for a worldwide market. il pors Bsns W p47-8+ My 18 '63

ROSENTHAL porcelain. See Pottery, German

ROSENWALD, Lessing Julius, collection
Library of Congress given 700 rare books. Pub W 186:34 Ag 10 '64
Quiet beauty; exhibition of illustrated books at Washington's National gallery of art. il Newsweek 62:74 Ag 26 '63

ROSENWALD, Peter J.
Adclub session on European advertising and promotion; summary of address. Pub W 186:49 N 16 '64
Booksellers but no books. Pub W 186:22-3 Ag 3 '64
Frankfurt book fair, 1963. Pub W 184:18-25 N 4 '63
Giangiacomo Feltrinelli: Italian publisher-bookseller pioneers to new book markets. Pub W 185:56-60 F 3 '64
New World book fair set for London, June, 1964. por Pub W 184:23-4 Jl 22 '63
One of a new breed: Paul Hamlyn of London. Pub W 183:41-5 F 4 '63
Un-cooperative productions. Pub W 186:26-8 S 7 '64

ROSES
Carefree roses. D. C. Stemler. il Horticulture 42:34-5+ Ja '64
Climbing and pillar roses. K. P. Jones. il Horticulture 41:334-5 Je '63
Climbing roses. E. G. Pierce. il Pop Gard 14:36+ Mr '63
Differences between greenhouse and garden roses. J. Milton. il Horticulture 41:316-17 Je '63
Fairy, carefree rose for all. J. Milton. il Flower Grower 51:33 F '64
For 1965, the new roses. il Sunset 134:60-2 Ja '65
Fragrant old rose remains a favorite. M. Haislip. il Flower Grower 51:28-9 Mr '64
Future fragrance. il Flower Grower 50:31 Jl '63
Good roses often overlooked. Sunset 132:194 F '64
Grandifloras are grand roses. V. M. Quist. il Horticulture 41:216-17 Ap '63
Grow better roses. M. C. Ohlander. il Flower Grower 50:48-50 Ap '63
Growing roses in containers. il Sunset 130:228+ Je '63
Guide to rose pruning. N. Gillespie. il Pop Gard 16:46-7 F '65
Half dozen ways to use roses in your garden. P. F. Frese. il Pop Gard 14:24-5 S '63
H&G's gardener's month; how do you evaluate a new rose? il House & Gard 124:200-1 S '63
How to grow our rose selections. Bet Hom & Gard 42:102 F '64
John F. Kennedy memorial rose. il(cover) Flower Grower 52:8 Ja '65
Kinds of roses and their uses. H. Mason and L. Grove. il Bet Hom & Gard 41:60-5 F '63
Make mine old-fashioned roses. R. Thomson. il Pop Gard 14:30-1+ F '63
Modern roses at the United Nations. il Pop Gard 14:28-9 F '63
Modern roses belong in every garden. C. H. Perkins. il Pop Gard 14:34-5+ Mr '63
New and novelty roses. il Horticulture 42:54 F '64
New roses for everybody. H. R. O'Brien. il Pop Gard 15:32-4+ F '64
New roses to enjoy in 1964. Flower Grower 51:66 F '64
Nine new hybrid teas. il Sunset 132:62-4 Ja '64
Now, seventy-hour roses. Sci Digest 53:81 My '63
Old roses for new gardens. M. A. Roche. il Pop Gard 15:12-13 F '64
Readers vote for the most fragrant roses. Flower Grower 51:20 Je '64
Rose is born; Christian Dior of Meilland. S. B. Hutton. il Pop Gard 14:29-32 Jl '63
Rose of the future. H. Swim. il Pop Gard 15:19+ Jl '64
Rose on our cover, you will see it at the New York world's fair. il Flower Grower 51:23 Je '64
Rose standard. il House & Gard 123:74 F '63
Rosebushes tended now give more spring blooms. Sci N L 84:296 N 9 '63
Roses. il Seventeen 22:46 Mr '63
Roses. B. Black. il Pop Gard 15:24-6 S '64
Roses during their bloom peak. Sunset 132:276-7 My '64
Roses for fragrance. il Flower Grower 51:32 F '64
Roses for your garden. Am Home 67:98-100 Mr '64

ROSES—*Continued*
Roses from seed. E. W. Ferris. il Horticulture 41:276-7 My '63
Roses: how to grow America's favorite flowers. il Good H 158:166-7 Ap '64
Roses, how to select wisely. R. A. Browne. Flower Grower 51:32+ F '64
Sawdust mulch for roses. O. M. Cook. il Flower Grower 50:56 Jl '63
There's news in roses for '64. il Pop Gard 16:22-3+ F '65
There's nothing like a rose. I. McLendon. il Pop Gard 15:20-2 F '64
Tips on pruning roses. M. Costigan. il Horticulture 41:238 Ap '63
Two dozen roses. R. C. Allen. il Horticulture 42:18-19+ Ap '64
What is a rose? il Am Home 67:50-3 Mr '64
Wintering roses. A. C. Burrage. il Horticulture 42:40-2 O '64
See also
Jackson and Perkins company
Plants—All America selections

ROSES, Arrangement of
1963 winner of Sterling bowl. il Flower Grower 50:63 O '63

ROSES and meadows and blushes on cheeks; story. See Mounsey, B.

ROSES for dinner; story. See McWhirter, M.

ROSES in Burnt Oak; story. See Glanville, B.

ROSETTA stone inscription
Cleopatra & Ptolemy gave Champollion his missing clue. il UNESCO Courier 17:10-11 Mr '64

ROSEVILLE, Minn.
You can't beat electronic data processing. R. W. Turnlund. il Am City 78:97-8 Jl '63

ROSEWALL, Ken
Sporting scene. H. W. Wind. New Yorker 39:128+ F 23 '63

ROSHOLT, John N. and others
Isotopic fractionation of uranium in sandstone. bibliog Science 139:224-6 Ja 18 '63

ROSHWALD, Mordecai
International force. Bul Atomic Sci 19:24-7 Ap '63

ROSICRUCIAN Egyptian, Oriental museum and art gallery, San Jose, Calif.
Californias' museum of ancient mysteries. il Travel 121:45-7 Mr '64

ROSKE, Helmut
Textbook factory. Atlan 212:90-4 D '63

ROSKILL, Mark
Split worlds of Max Beckmann. Art N 63:46-8+ D '64

ROSKO, Milt
Blues around the clock. por Outdoor Life 134:60-1+ S '64

ROSLAVLEVA, Natalia
How large is Soviet ballet? Dance Mag 37:35-7+ N '63

ROSLIN, Norman
Reprise. New Yorker 40:23-4 Ag 22 '64

ROSLYN, N.Y.

Historic houses, etc.

Preservation notes. B. Snow. il Antiques 85:460 Ap '64

ROSS, Alan
Jamaica. Mlle 59:174-5+ My '64

ROSS, D. S. Carne-. See Carne-Ross, D. S.

ROSS, David
Records in a bookstore: a new look. Pub W 184:41-3 Ag 19 '63

ROSS, David, 1895-
Pleiades; Primavera; On a blue afternoon; poems. Poetry 102:88-9 My '63
Poems, books of poems, and character. J. Langland. Poetry 103:258-61 Ja '64

ROSS, David W.
Ferryboat farewell. Travel 119:41-3 Ap '63

ROSS, Elaine
Christmas cookie cook book. House & Gard 126:175-80 D '64
Hot hors d'oeuvre cook book. House & Gard 124:225+ O '63

ROSS, Eulalie Steinmetz
Folk-tale collections. Horn Bk 39:490-1 O '63
(comp) To tell a story; excerpt from Lost half-hour: a collection of stories. Horn Bk 39:253-8 Je '63

ROSS, G. S. and others
Polymorphism in isopropyl alcohol. bibliog Science 141:1043-4 S 13 '63

ROSS, Irwin
Beaverbrook: Britain's rambunctious press lord. Read Digest 84:155-6+ Mr '64
Bob Six's bag of tricks. Fortune 67:130-2+ F '63
Britain goes on a gambling spree. Read Digest 84:93-7 Ap '64
Congressmen and their conflicting interests. Read Digest 85:118-23 Jl '64
General aniline goes private. Fortune 68:127-9+ S '63
Master spy who almost got away. Harper 229:47-54 D '64
Negroes are moving up the job ladder. Read Digest 83:53-7 D '63
1900 auto show. Motor T 16:110-16 N '64
Private turbulence of Eastern air lines. Fortune 70:172-4+ Jl '64
Rescuing the forgotten prisoners. Sat R 48:17-18+ Ja 16 '65
Under the Channel by tunnel. Read Digest 85:35-6+ Jl '64
When you borrow, when you buy, watch those interest rates! Read Digest 83:157-8+ N '63

ROSS, James Edward
Combat novel from behind bars. R. B. Stolley. il pors Life 55:101-2+ D '63

ROSS, Lillian
Reporter at large. New Yorker 40:35-8+ Jl 18 '64

about

Books in communications. J. F. Fixx. Sat R 47:133 Mr 14 '64
Invisible observer. por Time 83:66+ My 1 '64

ROSS, Marvin C.
Scottish tobacco mulls in the Hillwood collection. Antiques 83:568-9 My '63

ROSS, Mary Ellen
Indoor campanulas. Horticulture 41:414 Ag '63

ROSS, Michael
Mexico's border towns. Travel 120:32-4 N '63
Stars in your eyes. Travel 119:38-40+ F '63

ROSS, Nancy Wilson
I went to the wedding at Sikkim. Vogue 141:114-15+ Je '63
In the high Himalayas an American becomes a royal princess. Sat Eve Post 236:20-5 My 11 '63

ROSS, Philip
Role of government in union growth. Ann Am Acad 350:74-85 N '63

ROSS, R. Dudley
Nearby Bahamas are rich in bird life. Audubon Mag 65:204-7 Jl '63

ROSS, Spencer
Pictures under glass. il Pop Phot 52:64-5+ Ap '63

ROSS, Stanley R.
Mexico: cool revolution and cold war. Cur Hist 44:89-94+ F '63

ROSS, T. Peter
Sukarno's lavish ganefo was mostly snafu. Sports Illus 19:28-31 D 2 '63

ROSS, Thomas B. See Wise, D. jt. auth.

ROSS, Wallace A.
Fifty-eight-second film festival. A. Levy. il Reporter 28:39-40+ Je 20 '63

ROSS, Wallace C.
Measuring one-design sails. Yachting 116:57-9+ Jl '64

ROSS, Walter
Cashing in the New York dollar. Esquire 61:66-7+ Ap '64
In search of the perfect tire. Esquire 59:92-3+ My '63
Where did Charles Lindbergh go? Esquire 60:85-8+ O '63; Same abr. with title What became of Charles Lindbergh? Read Digest 84:91-6 F '64

ROSS-SKINNER, Jean
Du Pont's financial acumen. Duns R 81:42-4+ F '63

ROSS; drama. See Rattigan, T.

ROSSANT, M. J.
Beleaguered pound and the threatened dollar. Reporter 32:30+ Ja 28 '65
Economic education of John F. Kennedy. Reporter 28:22-5 F 14 '63
President's calculated risk. Reporter 30:27-9 Ja 30 '64

ROSSELLI, John
Wingless sea gull. Reporter 30:34-5 Je 4 '64

ROSSET, Barnet Lee, 1922-
Gross and Rosset speak on paperbacks at Adclub. Pub W 183:50 F 4 '63

ROSSETTI, Christina
Who inspired her imagery? M. Peckham. por Sat R 46:41 D 28 '63

ROSSI, Luis Banchero
Who's who in foreign business. por Fortune 69:62 Mr '64

ROSSI, Mario
China in the wings. New Repub 149:9 N 2 '63
Paying the bill for peace. New Repub 148:8-9 Je 1 '63

ROSSI, R. M.
Clean sweep costs more. por Am City 79:114-15 Je '64

ROSSINI, Gioacchino
Barber of Seville (Il barbiere di Siviglia)
Criticism
Opera N 27:25-6 Mr 9 '63
Opera N il 27:17-20 Mr 9 '63
Opera N 27:34 Ap 13 '63
La Cenerentola. H. Glass. il Am Rec G 31:196-8 N '64
Conchita Supervia, a souvenir. M. de Schauensee. il Am Rec G 30:866 My '64
On London, Theresa Berganza at l'Italiana il Algeri. P. L. Miller. il Am Rec G 30:1012-13+ Jl '64
On records; Il barbiere di Siviglia. Opera N 28:35 Ja 18 '64
On records; Il barbiere di Siviglia. C. J. Luten. Opera N 27:36 Mr 9 '63
On records; La cenerentola. Opera N 29:35 D 5 '64
On records; La scala di seta. Opera N 28:35 F 8 '64
Otello. Criticism
New Yorker 40:97-9 Je 27 '64
La Scala di seta. P. L. Miller. Am Rec G 29:706-7 My '63
Serious Rossini. F. Toye. il por Opera N 27:8-12 Mr 9 '63
Victoria de los Angeles on three new recordings from Angel: Barber of Seville, Cavalleria rusticana, and Mélodies de France. il Am Rec G 30:184-7 N '63
ROSSIO, Joann
No trapped housewives here. por Redbook 123:6+ Ag '64
ROSSITER, Clinton
Excerpt from testimony, March 5, 1964. Cong Digest 43:150+ My '64
ROSSMAN, I. J.
Hospital care goes home. por Parents Mag 38:135+ D '63
Infant diarrhea. Parents Mag 39:140 Ap '64
—and Schein, C. J.
Gall bladder diseases. Parents Mag 39:133-4 O '64
ROSSO, Medardo
Moment caught. il Newsweek 62:106 O 7 '63
Rosso re-evaluated. il Time 82:80-1 O 11 '63
Sculptors of light and shadow. J. McAndrews. il Sat R 47:37-8 F 8 '64
ROSSOFF, Martin
Let them have books. Sat R 47:64-5+ N 21 '64
ROSS'S geese. See Geese
ROST, Tom
Fast cars, fancy targets. il Field & S 68:38-41 Mr '64
ROSTAND Claude
Night at the opera. Mus Am 84:26-7 Ja '64
ROSTAND, Edmond
Cyrano de Bergerac. Criticism
Theatre Arts il(p 15) 47:69 Ag '63
ROSTEN, Leo
Is New York a mess? an open letter to the Mayor of New York. Look 27:26-7 F 12 '63
Myths we live by; excerpts from address. Redbook 122:35+ Ja '64
They made our world. Look 27:65-7 Je 18; 52-3 Jl 30; 38-9 S 24; 126-7 O 22; 118-19 N 19; 34-5 D 31 '63; 28:100-1 F 25; 43 Ap 7; 94-5 Je 16; 60-1 Ag 25; 66-7 S 22; 112-13 D 15 '64; 29:80-2 Ja 12 '65
What television can, and cannot, do. Read Digest 82:143-4+ F '63
ROSTEN, Norman
Homage to a grade B movie; poem. New Repub 148:21 Je 1 '63
Los Angeles; poem. Sat R 46:101 O 12 '63
ROSTENBERG, Adolph, Jr, and Kass, Gus
Color her beautiful. Todays Health 42:14-17+ Ag '64; Same abr. with title Chemistry of hair coloring. Sci Digest 56:68-74 D '64
ROSTOW, Eugene Victor
New start for the Alliance. Reporter 28:23-9 Ap 25 '63
about
Case for Yale law school. il por Newsweek 61:100+ Je 10 '63
ROSTOW, Walt Whitman
Alliance for progress; address, March 10, 1964. Dept State Bul 50:496-500 Mr 30 '64
Alliance for progress: August 1964; address, August 7, 1964. Dept State Bul 51:306-11 Ag 31 '64
Atlantic agenda; address, March 16, 1964. bibliog f Dept State Bul 50:578-87 Ap 13 '64
Atlantic community: an American view; address, May 9, 1963. Dept State Bul 48:855-60 Je 3 '63
Challenge of democracy in developing nations; address, January 26, 1964. Dept State Bul 50:251-60 F 17 '64
Cold war, a look ahead; address, March 28, 1963. Dept State Bul 48:551-7 Ap 15 '63
Economic development; address, August 19, 1963. Vital Speeches 29:712-17 S 15 '63; Same. Dept State Bul 49:422-30 S 16 '63
Europe and the Atlantic alliance; address, June 24, 1964. Dept State Bul 51:38-43 Jl 13 '64; Same. Vital Speeches 30:617-20 Ag 1 '64
How to make a national market; address, October 1, 1963. Dept State Bul 49:667-73 O 28 '63
Nationalization of takeoff; address, May 2, 1963. Dept State Bul 48:824-9 My 27 '63
On working with history; address, June 5, 1964. Dept State Bul 50:961-6 Je 22 '64
Perspective on the tasks of the 1960's; address, May 11, 1964. Dept State Bul 50:864-7 Je 1 '64
Role of Germany in the evolution of world politics; address, September 18, 1963. Dept State Bul 49:536-42 O 7 '63
Shaping the future; address, January 9, 1964. Dept State Bul 50:177-83 F 3 '64; Same. Vital Speeches 30:260-4 F 15 '64
Some lessons of economic development since the war; address, October 7, 1964. Dept State Bul 51:664-9 N 9 '64
Test: are we the tougher? N Y Times Mag p21+ Je 7 '64
Third round. For Affairs 42:1-10 O '63
U.S. policy in a changing world; address, October 6, 1964. Dept State Bul 51:637-42 N 2 '64
United States tasks on the world scene; address, November 20, 1963. Dept State Bul 49:921-9 D 16 '63
about
New look. por Newsweek 63:54 My 25 '64
Rostow: the intellectual Fortinbras. L. J. Halle. New Repub 151:21-3 Jl 25 '64
ROSTROPOVICH, Mstislav
Quote: unquote; interview, er. by R. Uebel. por Mus Am 84:20 F '64
ROSZAK, Theodore
By love depressed. Nation 200:33-4 Ja 11 '65
Strategy and conscience. Nation 196:250-2 Mr 23 '63
ROSZKOWSKI, Adolph P. and others
Selective rat toxicant. bibliog Science 144:412-13 Ap 24 '64
ROTARY clubs
Wonderful, wide, backslapping world of Rotary. J. Bird. il Sat Eve Post 236:58-62 F 9 '63
ROTARY piston engines. See Automobile engines
ROTARY planers. See Planing machines
ROTARY yacht squadron of Pennsylvania. See Yacht clubs
ROTATION of crops
Continuous corn, are we headed for trouble? L. E. Zeman. il Suc Farm 61:36-7+ D '63
ROTATION of planets. See Planets—Rotation
ROTATION of stars. See Stars—Rotation
ROTATION of the earth. See Earth—Rotation
ROTBARD, Marvin
Sound ideas. Am Rec G 30:1130-1 Ag '64
ROTBERG, Robert I.
Teaching of African history. Am Hist R 69:47-63 O '63
ROTH, Alice
Snowshoe league. por Recreation 57:358 S '64
ROTH, Arnold
By the sea, by the beautiful sea; drawings. Sports Illus 21:22-8 Jl 27 '64
ROTH, Bernhard A.
Bewitching Blennerhassett. Travel 119:48-50 Ap '63
Irrigation water from a tidal creek. Farm J 87:54-5 D '63
Jet-age airport helps its neighbors. Am City 79:92-3 D '64
—and Fox, Lester
Do as farmers do. Pop Gard 14:22-3 My '63
ROTH, Cecil
He had a covenant to keep. Sat R 48:31+ Ja 30 '65
New light on the Dead Sea scrolls. Commentary 37:27-32 Je; 38:18+ D '64
ROTH, Charles A. See Saks, N. M. jt. auth.
ROTH, Ed
Drag racers' Big Daddy; with report by J. Bride. il pors Life 57:95-6+ O 16 '64
ROTH, Edwin
Forged metal in Germany; excerpts from Neue schmiedeformen, tr. by H. Wegener. il Craft Horiz 24:12-17+ Ja '64
ROTH, Emery, and sons (firm)
Emery Roth and sons marks 60th anniversary. il Arch Rec 133:26 My '63

ROTH, Fred W. See Pederson, J. H. jt. auth.
ROTH, Günter D.
Popular astronomy in Germany. Sky & Tel 27:8-11 Ja '64
ROTH, Harold L.
Plans and consultants. Library J 88:3027-8 S 1 '63
Protection and insurance. por Library J 88:4152-4; 89:426+ N 1 '63, F 1 '64
ROTH, Henry
Awake at last. H. Frankel. Sat R 47:29 N 21 '64
Belated success of Henry Roth. J. Howard. il pors Life 58:75-6 Ja 8 '65
ROTH, James A.
Precision globes of Mars. il Sky & Tel 27:19 Ja '64
ROTH, Jay S. and others
Inhibition of growth of chick embryo by inhibition of deoxycytidylate deaminase. bibliog Science 142:1473-4 D 13 '63
ROTH, Jesse, and others
Hypoglycemia; a potent stimulus to secretion of growth hormone. bibliog Science 140:987-8 My 31 '63
ROTH, Louis M. and Dateo, G. P. jr
Uric acid in the reproductive system of males of the cockroach blattella germânica. bibliog Science 146:782-4 N 6 '64
ROTH, Philip
Novelist advises teenagers that novels are bad for you. Library J 88:1738 Ap 15 '63
Philip Roth talks to teens. por Seventeen 22:170+ Ap '63; Excerpts. Library J 88:1738 Ap 15 '63
Psychoanalytic special; story. Esquire 60:106 N '63
Writing about Jews. Commentary 36:446-52 D '63; 37:16+ Ap '64

about

WLB biography. E. Geller. por Wilson Lib Bul 39:187+ O '64
ROTH, Robert E.
What's going on here? Recreation 57:118-20 Mr '64
ROTH, Robert H. See Giarman, N. J. jt. auth.
ROTH, Robert J.
Charles Sanders Peirce: 1839-1914. America 111:108-10 Ag 1 '64
Importance of matter. America 109:792-4 D 21 '63
ROTH, William M.
Industry role in trade negotiations; address, November 24, 1964. Dept State Bul 51:853-5 D 14 '64
ROTHBAUM, Melvin
Economic dilemmas of collective bargaining. bibliog f Ann Am Acad 350:95-103 N '63
ROTHBERG, Abraham
De Gaulle's double no, single yes. Christian Cent 80:334-5 Mr 13 '63
Gaullist view. Christian Cent 80:1427-9 N 20 '63
Hungary seven years later. Christian Cent 80:1174-6 S 25 '63
New look in Paris. Commonweal 77:514-15 F 8 '63
Pluto is the furthest planet; story. Yale R 54:219-33 D '64
Thousand doors; novel. Ladies Home J 81:78-9 N; 80-4 D '64; 82:50-1 Ja '65
Yugoslavia: after the Partisan generation. Yale R 53:221-32 D '63
ROTHÉ, Walter F.
Way out of the calendar mess. il Look 28:39+ D 1 '64
ROTHE, William E. and others
Radioprotection by pressor amidines. Science 141:160 Jl 12 '63
ROTHENBERG, Jerome
Slower music; poem. Poetry 103:367 Mr '64
ROTHENSTEIN, Sir John
Britain's liveliest museum. il por Time 83:70-4 Ja 10 '64
ROTHGARBER, Herbert
Magic yo-yo. Recreation 58:29+ Ja '65
ROTHMAN, Seymour
How to lose a good night's sleep. Read Digest 83:25-6 Ag '63
ROTHMAN, Stanley
Choice in Chile: left or far left? Reporter 31:26-9 Jl 2 '64
ROTHMAN, Stuart
NLRB job up for grabs. Bsns W p74 Ap 6 '63
ROTHNEY, John W. M. See Nelson, R. J. jt. auth.
ROTHSCHILD, Guy de, baron
New elan in an old clan. il pors Time 82:70-4 D 20 '63
ROTHSCHILD, Norman
Depth-of-field myths. por Pop Phot 52:90-1 My '63
Facts & fables about single-lens reflexes. por Pop Phot 52:111-13 Ap '63
Filters for color; control, correct, create. il Pop Phot 52:74-87 Je '63
Forty stocking stuffers. il Pop Phot 51:68-71 D '62
Guide to help you end the confusion in floodlamp sources. Pop Phot 52:134-6 Ja '63
Konica Domirex, a prototype. Pop Phot 54:65-7 Je '64
Norman Rothschild's guide to daylight color slide films. il Pop Phot 53:166-75 D '63
Project your color prints. Pop Phot 52:62-3+ Mr '63
Technical story; Polacolor process. Pop Phot 52:59+ Mr '63
Tests report: new master photoguide. Pop Phot 51:66-7+ D '62
Toning, gimmick or valuable tool? por Pop Phot 52:93-4 Mr '63
Two new color films: Kodachrome-X. Pop Phot 52:18-19+ Mr '63
What focal length is best? il Pop Phot 53:142-3+ N '63
Ye olde tintype. Pop Phot 52:120 Mr '63
Your second projector. il Pop Phot 52:78-9 Mr '63
ROTHSCHILD, Pauline, baronne de
Evangeline Bruce: her listening gaiety. Vogue 144:128-9+ S 15 '64

about

Vie de château: glimpses of a romantic woman. il pors Vogue 142:106-7 D '63
ROTHSCHILD, V. Henry, 2d
Business practices under the new T&E rules. Duns R 82:40-2+ N '63
ROTHSCHILD family
New elan in an old clan. il Time 82:70-4 D 20 '63
ROTHSTEIN, Arnold
Thirty-five years ago. S. D. Smith. il por N Y Times Mag p96-8 O 27 '63
ROTHSTEIN, Arthur
Color negative or transparency. U S Camera 26:39+ Ag '63
Creative color. See issues of U.S. camera
Next stop: inside Russia; latest in guided camera tours. M. A. Matzken. il Mod Phot 28:48+ F '64
Shooting with available light. il por Pop Sci 182:102-5+ Mr '63
ROTHSTEIN, Robert
People to people. U S Camera 27:62 Ap '64
ROTHWELL, Jack C.
Shorter workweek. Nation 197:382-7 O 7 '63
ROTISSERIE cooking. See Cookery
ROTOLO brothers
Can you see, my son, can you really see? cataracts removed from five Rotolo brothers; with report by J. Bonfante. il Life 57:32-41 N 20 '64
They see but what? il pors Life 58:56A Ja 29 '65
ROTOR ship models
Model rotor-sailing ship. R. L. Clough, jr. il Pop Mech 120:124-7 Ag '63
ROTOR ships
What ever happened to the rotor ship? E. S. Allen. il Motor B 111:116+ F '63
ROTORS
French firm static-tests jet-flap rotor; for reaction-powered helicopters. W. C. Wetmore. il Aviation W 81:57+ D 21 '64
Rotor study proposals requested for army heavy lift helicopter. Aviation W 81:21 Ag 31 '64
ROTPROOFING. See Cotton fabrics—Protection
ROTTENBERG, Simon
Labor monopoly policy reconsidered; excerpt from address. Mo Labor R 86:139 F '63
ROTTERDAM

Description

Gateway to Europe. il Time 81:87 Je 21 '63
What do you think of Rotterdam? L. Barry. il Pop Phot 54:18+ Je '64

Harbor

Busiest port in the world. il Fortune 70:148-50 Ag '64
ROTZ, Johnny
Touch of gold in the saddle. G. Holland. il pors Sports Illus 20:24-6+ Mr 23 '64
ROUART, Julie (Manet)
Great ones all painted us. pors Life 54:48-55 My 10 '63

ROUAULT, Georges
Arts; Rouault exposition at Perls galleries, New York. C. J. McNaspy. America 111: 760 D 5 '64
Bonanza split. il Time 82:52 Ag 9 '63
Two masters of modern art. H. Read. Reporter 28:38-40 Je 6 '63

ROUDIEZ, Leon S.
Evil and the ecstasy. Sat R 46:38-9 O 26 '63

ROUECHÉ, Berton
Annals of medicine (cont) New Yorker 39:34-6+ Ag 17; 174+ O 12 '63; 40:158+ S 12; 217-18+ N 7 '64
Another Saturday. New Yorker 39:68-9 D 21 '63
Consultation. New Yorker 39:62+ Ag 31 '63
Key; story. New Yorker 40:40-2 My 2 '64
Reporter at large (cont) New Yorker 39:48-50+ Ap 6 '63; 40:37-8+ D 26 '64
Ride into town; story. New Yorker 40:96 Ag 22 '64

ROUGE. See Cosmetics

ROUGEMONT, Denis de
Books; more love in the western world. J. Updike. New Yorker 39:90-4+ Ag 24 '63
By love depressed. T. Roszak. Nation 200:33-4 Ja 11 '65

ROUGH, James H.
Virtually every snowflake . . . Am City 78:71-3 Ag '63

ROUKE, Eve
Old song. Commonweal 80:394 Je 19 '64

ROULETTE; story. See White, W.

ROULSTON, Dan
Safe-stop lever. Hot Rod 17:108-9 O '64

ROUND buildings. See Buildings, Round

ROUNDTREE, John G.
Education and the Negro. bibliog Negro Hist Bul 27:106-8+ F '64

ROUNDUPS
See also
Rodeos

ROUQUETTE, Robert
Fresh orientation in the church. Cath World 196:343-50 Mr '63

ROURKE, Shaun
New genesis; poem. Horn Bk 40:210 Ap '64

ROUS sarcoma. See Sarcoma

ROUSE, Irving
Prehistory of the West Indies. bibliog Science 144:499-513 My 1 '64

ROUSE, James
Brand new city for Maryland. J. W. Anderson. Harper 229:100-2+ N '64
New approach to new-town planning. D. Canty. il Arch Forum 121:194-9 Ag '64

ROUSSEAS, Stephen
Johnson's Eisenhower premise. Nation 199: 375-9 N 23 '64
—and Farganis, James
Fences against power. Nation 196:343-6+ Ap 27 '63
Politics of the possible. Nation 196:240-4; 197:inside cover, 93 Mr 23, Ag 24 '63

ROUSSEAU, Henri, known as Le Douanier
Little father of all the primitives. il Art N 62:29+ My '63
Primitive. il Newsweek 61:92 My 6 '63

ROUSSEAU, Jean Jacques
Jean Jacques Rousseau; symposium. il pors UNESCO Courier 16:4-26 Mr '63
Solitary wanderer. J. C. Herold. bibliog il pors Horizon 6:94-103 Sum '64

ROUSSEAU, Richard W.
Change without fanfare. America 110:694 My 23 '64

ROUSSEL, Hubert
Sir John and the jubilee. Mus Am 84:22 Ap '64

ROUTING machines
Hitch a router to your lathe! R. J. De Cristoforo. il Pop Sci 183:116-18 Ag '63
Motorize your turning chisel; portable electric router. R. J. DeCristoforo. il Pop Mech 121: 184-7 Ja '64
PM tests new router with three-size chuck. il Pop Mech 120:165 S '63
Router. il Pop Sci 183:178+ D '63

ROUX, Edmonde Charles-. See Charles-Roux, E.

ROUX family
Dynasty of marine painters: the Roux family of Marseilles. J. Meissonnier. il Antiques 86:583-7 N '64

ROVANIEMI
Letter from Finland. J. Bainbridge. New Yorker 40:170+ O 3 '64

ROVER company
Rover all over. il Time 82:99-100 O 25 '63

ROVERE, Richard H.
Books (cont) New Yorker 39:195-6+ Mr 16; 119 My 11; 235-8 N 16 '63
Letter from Atlantic City. New Yorker 40:112-17 S 5 '64
Letter from San Francisco. New Yorker 40: 77-80+ Jl 25 '64
Letter from Washington. See issues of New Yorker
Loneliest place in the world. Am Heritage 15:28-32 Ag '64
Minds of Barry Goldwater. Harper 229:37-42 S '64
Our far-flung correspondents. New Yorker 39:76-8+ Jl 13 '63
Reporter at large. New Yorker 40:201-4+ O 3; 217-22+ O 17 '64
World is in his debt. Sat Eve Post 236:38-40 S 21 '63
about
Rumbles left and right, by W. F. Buckley, jr. Review
Nat R 14:367-8 My 7 '63. J. Chamberlain

ROVIT, Earl
Fathers and sons in American fiction. Yale R 53:248-57 D '63

ROW houses
Past-and-present house. G. O'Brien. il N Y Times Mag p 126-7 O 6 '63
Rental housing as architecture; Fairview Heights, Ithaca, N.Y. il Arch Rec 136:143-8 D '64
Staggered for privacy and view; sixteen-unit row house in Dallas. il Arch Rec 136:116-17 Ag '64

ROW spacing of plants. See Plants. Space arrangement of

ROWAN, Carl Thomas
Carl Rowan's advice: oust civil-rights quacks; excerpts from address, 1964. por U S News 57:14 Ag 17 '64
Rowan under fire; excerpts from statements. U S News 56:13 F 10 '64
U.N. asks conciliation commission to continue efforts with Arab refugees; statements, December 11, 14 and 18, 1962. Dept State Bul 48:99-103 Ja 21 '63
U.N. asks Secretary-General to take initiative on Hungary; statement, December 18, 1962. Dept State Bul 48:74-6 Ja 14 '63
USIA: building bridges of peace in a changing world; address, December 8, 1964. Dept State Bul 51:906-12 D 28 '64
USIA overseas libraries 1964. por Wilson Lib Bul 39:40-3+ S '64
Youth; address, August 24, 1964. Vital Speeches 30:721-5 S 15 '64
about
Ambassador. New Yorker 39:45-6 D 7 '63
Cover: Carl T. Rowan; top Negro in United States government. por(p 133) Negro Hist Bul 27:138-9 Mr '64
More racial strife? yes, warns a Negro envoy. por U S News 54:20 Je 3 '63
Murrow legacy. Reporter 30:12+ Mr 12 '64
Murrow resigns from USIA; Carl T. Rowan appointed. Pub W. 185:65 F 3 '64
New "Voice" of America. por Sr Schol 84:23 Mr 6 '64
Our man in Finland. W. Wiskari. il pors N Y Times Mag p63-4+ N 17 '63
Picked to tell the U.S. story abroad. por U S News 56:16 F 3 '64
Same wave length; new director. por Newsweek 63:17 F 3 '64
USIA, Murrow and Rowan. Nation 198:129 F 10 '64
Virtues of talking back. il por Time 83:19 Ja 31 '64
Youngest U.S. ambassador. il pors Ebony 19: 52-4+ Ja '64

ROWAN, Roy
Peking puts up a Congo command post. Life 57:66A-66B D 18 '64

ROWANS, Virginia, pseud. See Tanner, E. E, 3d

ROWE, Dorothy S.
Earning your life list; reprint. Audubon Mag 66:70-3 Mr '64

ROWE, James W.
Inflation and U.S. aid. Reporter 30:28-30 Ap 23 '64

ROWE, Wallace P.
Resistance of mice infected with Moloney leukemia virus to Friend virus infection. bibliog Science 141:40-1 Jl 5 '63
—See Hartley, J. W. jt. auth.

ROWELL, John
Pennsylvania: more bears than books. por ALA Bul 58:816+ O '64
What books for the young adult? por Library J 89:4103-6 O 15 '64

ROWEN, Herbert H.
(comp) Articles and other books received; Low Countries. See issues of American historical review

ROWEN, Hobart
Detroit, higher wages, cheaper cars? New Repub 150:17-18 Je 6 '64
Let's spend more. New Repub 148:13-16 My 25 '63
(ed) See Heller, W. Walter Heller's word for 1964: prosperous

ROWING
Agony and ecstasy. il Newsweek 61:92 My 13 '63
Anything that boys can do; Vesper boat club for Olympic berth. T. C. Brody. il Sports Illus 21:12-15 Jl 20 '64
Beauty part of rowing. W. G. Wing. il Harper 227:26+ S '63
Easy row on the road to Japan; Harvard crew. T. C. Brody. il Sports Illus 20:30-1 My 25 '64
Four x eight=crew of the decade; four crews of Olympic caliber. T. C. Brody. il Sports Illus 21:53-4 Jl 6 '64
Gently down the stream. il Esquire 59:112-13 Je '63
Long-haired crew; Harvard's eight. il Newsweek 63:78 Je 22 '64
One for the alumni; Vesper boat club to represent U.S. at the Olympics. il Time 84:72 Jl 17 '64
Race problem at Howard is how to win; first Negro institution to crash exclusive college rowing. H. Whall. Sports Illus 20:72+ Ap 27 '64
Row to Tokyo; Olympic rowing trials. il Newsweek 64:77 Jl 20 '64
Rowing (cont) il Sports Illus 18:56+ My 20; 53-4 My 27; 50+ Je 3; 44-5 Je 24 '63
Shovelful of victory college regattas. Newsweek 63:63 Je 29 '64
Two make ready but one to go; Intercollegiate rowing association regatta. il Time 83:44-5 Je 26 '64
See also
Regattas

ROWLAND, Stanley J. Jr
But God, you laugh; poem. Christian Cent 80:1131 S 18 '63
Octet. Christian Cent 81:939 Jl 22 '64
Poetry and theology: a poet's view. Christian Cent 82:80-2 Ja 20 '65
Prayer for Ash Wednesday. Christian Cent 81:199 F 12 '64
Psychiatrist and moral values. Christian Cent 80:1613-14 D 25 '63
Religion and mental health. Christian Cent 80:684 My 22 '63
To the police in Birmingham, Alabama; poem. Christian Cent 80:638 My 15 '63

ROWLEY, Peter
Divorce, New York style. Nation 199:461-3 D 14 '64
Paying for UN policing. New Repub 151:7 O 10 '64

ROWLEY, William. See Middleton, T. jt. auth.

ROWLINGSON, Donald T.
Interpreting the resurrection. bibliog f Christian Cent 80:459-61 Ap 10 '63

ROWNTREE, Diana
New architecture of Castro's Cuba. il Arch Forum 120:122-5 Ap '64

ROWSE, Alfred Leslie
A. L. Rowse solves Shakespeare's sonnets; interview. Pub W 184:31 S 30 '63
Cornishman looks at California. Mlle 59:124+ My '64
It is a Marlowe year also. N Y Times Mag p 15+ F 16 '64
about
A. L. Rowse: a study in versatility. R. Halsband. Sat R 47:57 Ja 11 '64
Bard game. Newsweek 63:65 Ja 6 '64
Historian. New Yorker 39:43-5 O 19 '63

ROY, Gregor
Beholding the rich panorama of Islam. Commonweal 81:142-3 O 23 '64
Dusk song for Trishna: a tone poem. Mlle 58:42 Ja '64
Movie of the month. Cath World 200:67-8 O '64
New books. Cath World 198:884+ Mr '64
Play of the month. Cath World 198:391-2; 199:263-4 Mr, Jl '64
Sean O'Casey: genius of the theater. Cath World 200:259-60 Ja '65

ROY, Jessie H.
Pinpoint portraits. Negro Hist Bul 26:176, 252; 27:18, 36, 92 F, My, O-N '63, Ja '64

ROY, Ralph Lord
Methodists: crisis of conscience. Nation 198:262-5 Mr 16 '64

ROY, Walter
Reaction of organized British teachers to crises; excerpt from Membership participation in the National union of teachers. Mo Labor R 87:1022-5 S '64

ROYAL, Darrell
Oklahoma-Texas football feud. T. Cohane. il por Look 27:85-7+ O 8 '63
When in doubt, punt. il por Time 82:50 N 22 '63

ROYAL ballet, Great Britain
Aurora and lesser companions. D. Hering. il Dance Mag 37:19-23+ Jl '63
Balletomanes rejoice! visit to the United States. il Seventeen 22:232 My '63
Britain's ballet on a new kick; photographs. S. Peck. N Y Times Mag p66-7 Ap 14 '63
England's Royal ballet; the seventh visit. il Dance Mag 37:39-43 Ap '63
Hottest little team in show biz. il Life 54:107-8 My 24 '63
Letter from Paris. Genêt. New Yorker 39:191 N 30 '63
Music to my ears; Elektra, with and without. I. Kolodin. Sat R 46:33-4 Je 1 '63
Music to my ears; Fonteyn, Nureyev, Ashton's Pigeon at the Metropolitan. I. Kolodin. Sat R 46:67 My 11 '63
Music to my ears; golden age of ballet. I. Kolodin. Sat R 46:24+ My 4 '63
Music to my ears; MacMillan week at the Royal ballet. I. Kolodin. Sat R 46:42 My 25 '63
Music to my ears; Symphony and Marguerite and Armand at Metropolitan opera house. I. Kolodin. Sat R 46:22 My 18 '63
Musical events; performance of Giselle. W. Sargeant. New Yorker 39:100-1 My 4 '63
Musical events; performance of Rite of spring. W. Sargeant. New Yorker 39:93-4+ My 18 '63
Musical events; performance of Sleeping Beauty. W. Sargeant. New Yorker 39:96+ Ap 27 '63
Musical events; performances of Elektra and The invitation. W. Sargeant. New Yorker 39:157 My 25 '63
New Nijinsky? il Newsweek 61:61 My 6 '63
Ninette de Valois retires as director. C. Barnes. il Dance Mag 38:42-6 Mr '64
Not quite it; Royal ballet at Metropolitan opera house. il Time 81:43-4 My 10 '63
Nureyev, plus and minus. J. Martin. il Sat R 46:48-9+ My 25 '63
Royal ballet's most uncommon commoner. J. Martin. il Sat R 46:55-6+ Ap 27 '63

ROYAL Bangkok sports club. See Sports clubs

ROYAL botanical gardens, Hamilton, Ontario. See Botanical gardens

ROYAL Canadian mounted police. See Canada—Royal Canadian mounted police

ROYAL Canadian navy. See Canada—Navy

ROYAL collection, Great Britain. See Art—Private collections

ROYAL commission on health services. See Canada—National health service

ROYAL commission on the press. See Newspapers—Great Britain

ROYAL Danish ballet
Festival season in Denmark. J. Martin. il Sat R 47:53-5 Je 27 '64

ROYAL Dutch-Shell group
New chemical hybrid; Italy's Montecatini and Royal Dutch/Shell oil combine. il Bsns W p70-3 Ja 11 '64
Stormy engagement; negotiations between Royal Dutch Shell and Italy's Montecatini complex. Time 82:89 N 22 '63

ROYAL family of Great Britain. See Great Britain—Royal family

ROYAL gambit; drama. See Gressieker, H.

ROYAL hunt of the sun; drama. See Shaffer, P.

ROYAL Kaanapali golf course. See Golf courses

ROYAL Ontario museum of archeology
Toronto treasures, universal and university; Royal Ontario museum draws a 50th anniversary show. J. S. Boggs. il Art N 61:32-4+ F '63

ROYAL opera, Stockholm. See Opera—Sweden

ROYAL philharmonic orchestra of London
Notes from our correspondents. F. Apraham-ian. il Hi Fi 14:29+ N '64
Troubles in Britain; report by M. Cooper. Mus Am 83:12 Ag '63

ROYAL Shakespeare theatre company
Double Will from England; productions of King Lear and Comedy of errors. il Time 83:49 My 29 '64
Howl! howl! productions of King Lear and Comedy of errors at Lincoln Center's New York state theater. il Newsweek 63:80-1 Je 1 '64

ROYAL Shakespeare theatre company—*Cont.*
In England: Richard II, King Henry IV, and Henry V at Stratford-upon-Avon. H. Popkin. Vogue 144:80 S 15 '64
Letter from London; performance of Persecution and assassination of Marat as performed by the inmates of the asylum of Charenton under the direction of the Marquis de Sade, by P. Weiss. M. Panter-Downes. New Yorker 40:204-6 S 19 '64
Letter from London; Royal Shakespeare company trilogy, Wars of the roses. M. Panter-Downes. New Yorker 40:116+ Ap 4 '64
Real royalty; Royal Shakespeare company at Lincoln Center's New York state theater. H. Hewes. Sat R 47:35 My 23 '64
Shakespeare company. G. Rogoff. Commonweal 80:398 Je 19 '64
Shakespeareland; presentation of Shakespeare's history plays at Stratford-upon-Avon. H. Hewes. Sat R 47:30 Je 6 '64
Theatre; performance of King Lear at New York state theatre. New Yorker 40:78 My 30 '64
Theater; productions of Comedy of errors and King Lear in New York. R. Brustein. New Repub 150:30-2 Je 13 '64

ROYAL Shakespeare theatre, Stratford-on-Avon
Letter from Stratford; seven historical plays: Richard II, Henry IV, Henry V and trilogy Wars of the roses. M. Panter-Downes. New Yorker 40:146-8+ My 23 '64
Play that never was; Wars of the Roses trilogy. il Time 82:37 Ag 2 '63

ROYAL theater, Copenhagen. See Opera houses

ROYAL theater, Madrid. See Opera houses

ROYAL Winnipeg ballet
Royal Winnipeg ballet, Boston arts festival, Jacob's pillow. D. Hering. Dance Mag 38:26-8 S '64

ROYALIST party (France) See Action française

ROYALITE. See Plastics, Laminated

ROYALL, Kenneth Claiborne
Truce team in Alabama. il por U S News 55:28 O 7 '63

ROYALTIES
Authors ask new policy on royalties and reprints. Pub W 186:36-8 Jl 27 '64
Fifty-fifty split; reprint and book club royalties. P. Nathan. Pub W 184:19-21 D 30 '63
Rights and permissions; reprint and book club royalties. P. Nathan. Pub W 184:42-3 O 21 '63
Rights and royalties; excerpt from Writing and selling of non-fiction. P. R. Reynolds. Writer 77:13-15 Mr '64
Royalties and advances: publishers cite some trends. Pub W 186:30-2 O 19 '64
See also
Oil lands—Royalties

ROYALTY. See Kings and rulers; Princes and princesses; *also* subhead Royal family under names of countries, e.g. Great Britain—Royal family

ROYERSFORD, Pa.
How to keep industry. H. J. Grossman. il Am City 78:122 S '63

ROYSTER, Vermont Connecticut
How to pick a pocket or two. Read Digest 82:126-7 Je '63
Human inequality; reprint. U S News 55:128 O 14 '63
No time for collective guilt; reprint. U S News 55:72 D 9 '63
Who's picking whose pocket? por Time 81:66 Mr 22 '63

ROZE, Janis A.
Pilgrim of the river. Natur Hist 73:34-41 Ag '64

ROZELLE, Alvin. See Rozelle, P.

ROZELLE, Pete
Bush-league scandal. Time 81:45 Ap 26 '63
Players are not just people. T. Maule. il por Sports Illus 18:22+ Ap 29 '63
Sportsman of the year. K. Rudeen. por Sports Illus 20:22-6+ Ja 6 '64
Why pro football must live with sin. T. Cohane. il Look 27:64-71 Jl 2 '63

ROZEN, Marvin E.
Some reflections on civil defense. Bul Atomic Sci 20:21-4 Je '64

ROZHDESTVENSKII, Robert
Cold shoulder. il por Time 84:61 D 11 '64

RUANDA-URUNDI. See Burundi; Rwanda

RUARK, Robert
Let's nix the sickniks. Sat Eve Post 236:38-9 Je 29 '63
My last safari. pors Sat Eve Post 236:76-81 Ap 27 '63
Why Spain is home. Sat Eve Post 237:28-33 Ap 4 '64

RUBADIRI, J. David
Africa: an African evaluation; address, April 11, 1964. bibliog f Ann Am Acad 354:84-90 Jl '64

RUBBER
Hexanedione from hydrocarbon polymer oxidation. E. M. Bevilacqua and P. M. Norling. bibliog il Science 147:289-90 Ja 15 '65

RUBBER, Artificial
Breathing air out of water; silicone membrane. il Time 84:78 O 16 '64
Coat it with neoprene. V. L. Oertle. il Pop Mech 120:154-5 D '63
Fluid roofing systems of synthetic rubber. il Arch Rec 135:177-8 Ja; 179-80 F; 215-16+ Mr '64
New rubber sealer is almost indestructible; silicone rubber. il Pop Sci 184:102 Mr '64
Synthetic elastomers. J. B. Campbell. bibliog il Science 141:329-34 Jl 26 '63

RUBBER, Sponge
Foam rubber fun. R. Von Hoorn. il Design 66:10-12 S '64

RUBBER asphalt pavements. See Pavements, Rubber asphalt

RUBBER boats. See Boats, Rubber

RUBBER industry and trade
How much can Akron tell Detroit? radial ply tire. il Bsns W p94-6+ Ag 8 '64
See also names of rubber companies, e.g. Firestone tire and rubber company

RUBBER-sheet geometry. See Topology

RUBBER tires. See Tires, Rubber

RUBBERS. See Shoes, Rubber, plastic, etc.

RUBBINGS
Crayon-cement prints; fourth graders. D. Beringer. il Sch Arts 63:39-40 My '64
Designs from rubbings. il Design 66:40-1 S '64
Grave rubbers; early New England gravestones. C. Willard. il Look 27:M6-M7 Ag 27 '63
Mortality writ in stone; early New England gravestones. S. Marsal. il Américas 16:22-30 S '64
New England gravestone rubbings. A. Parker and A. Neal. il Craft Horiz 23:16-19+ Jl '63
Reprints by rubbing; relief rubbed portraits. A. L. Ochs. il Design 66:16-18 N '64
Rubbings. E. M. Alexander. il Sch Arts 62:27-8 My '63
Rubbings are easy. il Sunset 133:58-9 Ag '64
Where the rub comes in; New England gravestones. il Time 81:72-3 Mr 22 '63

RUBBISH disposal. See Refuse and refuse disposal

RUBEL, John H.
Individual R&D productivity is declining; summary of address. Aviation W 78:37 Mr 18 '63

RUBELLA
Exposure to rubella unwise in pregnancy. Sci N L 84:169 S 14 '63
German measles danger. Sci N L 85:149 Mr 7 '64
German measles epidemic. Time 83:42 Ap 24 '64
Measles threat to unborn. Sci N L 86:194 S 26 '64
Rubella antibodies in human serum; detection by the indirect fluorescent-antibody technique. G. C. Brown and others. bibliog il Science 145:943-5 Ag 28 '64
Rubella virus: inhibition in vitro by amantadine hydrochloride. H. F. Maassab and K. W. Cochran. bibliog il Science 145:1443-4 S 25 '64
Rubella virus: neutralizing antibody in commercial gamma globulin. G. M. Schiff and others. bibliog il Science 142:58-60 O 4 '63
Spots all over; New York city epidemic. Newsweek 63:90 Ap 13 '64
Spreading across U.S; German measles. U S News 56:8 My 11 '64
Worst rash of measles; epidemic of German measles. Bsns W p98 Ap 4 '64

RUBEN, Laurens N. and Balls, Michael
Genetic disparity and cancer induction by normal tissue implants in amphibia. bibliog Science 146:1321-2 D 4 '64

RUBENS, Sir Peter Paul
Exuberant genius of Peter Paul Rubens. G. Kent. il por Read Digest 85:146-51 Ag '64
Regal hangings in a Quaker temple. il Art N 63:26-8 O '64

RUBENSTEIN, Beverly
Love stories: bibliography for young adults. Library J 88:837-9 F 15 '63

RUBENSTEIN, J. S.
Dylan Thomas as poet. Commonweal 79:642-3 F 21 '64

RUBENSTEIN, Martin
You don't have to be a hero. Field & S 68: 40-2+ F '64
RUBEROID company
Renewal gains from Ruberoid contest. il Arch Forum 119:7 S '63
Ruberoid award winners announced. il Arch Rec 134:10 S '63
Ruberoid competition gives New York ideas for urban renewal. il Arch Rec 134:14-15 O '63
RUBIDIUM
Metastable rubidium aluminum silicate with a hexagonal sheet structure. C. A. Sorrell and T. Negas. bibliog il Science 141:917 S 6 '63
RUBIDIUM magnetometers. See Magnetometers
RUBIN, Albert L. and others
Histocompatibility and immunologic competence in renal homotransplantation. bibliog Science 143:815-16 F 21 '64
RUBIN, Edward P.
Not much inflation this year; interview. por (p 55) U S News 56:60 Mr 2 '64
RUBIN, Hans Morten
From a European's perspective. Reporter 28: 19 Je 6 '63
RUBIN, Harry
Defective cancer virus; with biographical sketch. Sci Am 210:18, 46-52 Je '64
RUBIN, Hilda
Painting became my life. il por Am Artist 29: 46-51+ Ja '65
RUBIN, L. G.
New American traveler. Esquire 61:40+ My '64
RUBIN, Larry
Accident; For a poet-athlete; poems. Poetry 102:20-1 Ap '63
Betrayal; poem. Sat R 47:35 Ja 25 '64
Garden of delusion; poem. Harper 228:187 Ap '64
Gift of time; poem. Yale R 53:77 O '63
Kite; poem. Commonweal 79:285 N 29 '63
Letter to a Dutch friend (for Hans Memelink) poem. Commonweal 78:379 Je 28 '63
Saturday afternoon; poem. Sat R 46:84 My 18 '63
Souvenir (Poland) poem. Harper 226:94 My '63
RUBIN, Meyer, and Taylor, D. W.
Radiocarbon activity of shells from living clams and snails. bibliog Science 141:637 Ag 16 '63
—See Rosen, A. A. jt. auth.
RUBIN, Michael
Necessary evils; story. Redbook 123:52-3 My '64
RUBIN, Morton J.
Meteorology. Science 142:416 O 18 '63
RUBIN, Rick
Sunday morning; story. Esquire 60:129 N '63
RUBIN, Roxanne
Are you forgotten? Seventeen 23:43 S '64
RUBIN, William
Ellsworth Kelly: the big form. Art N 62:32-5+ N '63
RUBINKAM, Henry
Small boat ventilation. Yachting 115:150 F '64
RUBINSTEIN, Alvin Z.
Medical care in the Soviet Union. bibliog f Cur Hist 44:339-44 Je '63
On IAEA's future. Bul Atomic Sci 21:25-7 Ja '65
Soviet image of western Europe. bibliog f Cur Hist 47:280-5+ N '64
RUBINSTEIN, Anton
Rubinstein's Demon; substantially complete recording. H. Weinstock. Sat R 47:69 O 31 '64
RUBINSTEIN, Artur
Afternoon with Artur Rubinstein; interview, ed. by M. Wilcox; with editorial comment. pors Hi Fi 13:25, 26-30+ Jl '63
Artur Rubinstein talks to teens. por Seventeen 22:160+ My '63
Conversation with Artur Rubinstein; interview, ed. by S. Chotzinoff. por Holiday 33:74-5+ My '63
about
Conspiracy of conscience; concert in Nijmegen. il por Time 81:41-2 My 3 '63
Musical events: all Chopin program. W. Sargeant. New Yorker 39:124-6 F 15 '64
Rubinstein touch, untouched at seventy-five. H. C. Schonberg. pors N Y Times Mag p 12+ Ja 26 '64
That civilized man. il por Time 83:110 Ap 17 '64
RUBINSTEIN, Daniel, and Rabinowitch, Eugene
Fluorescence and absorption changes in chlorella exposed to strong light: the red band. bibliog Science 142:681-2 N 8 '63
RUBINSTEIN, G. B.
Clamshell dikes tame the ocean. Pop Mech 120:90-1 Jl '63
RUBINSTEIN, Helena
Tiny, tireless tycoon of beauty. il pors Life 56:117-18+ My 15 '64
RUBY, Jack
Ruby's fantasy. por Newsweek 63:23 My 11 '64
about
Belli for the defense: a flamboyant advocate. il Time 82:48 D 20 '63
By Jack Ruby. il Newsweek 63:79-80 F 10 '64
Dallas justice: the real story of Jack Ruby and his trial, by M. Belli and M. C. Carroll. Review
New Repub 151:19-22 N 21 '64. T. S. Szasz
Day in court. il por Newsweek 63:18 Ja 6 '64
Death penalty and fair trial. W. E. Oberer. Nation 198:342-4 Ap 6 '64
Defendant who wants attention. il Time 83: 23 F 21 '64
Dignity and justice. Nation 198:205 Mr 2 '64
Eye on that window. il Newsweek 63:32+ Je 22 '64
50,000-word leak. Time 84:40 Ag 28 '64
For the defense; testimony at bail hearing. Time 83:20-1 Ja 31 '64
I got principles. il pors Newsweek 62:44+ D 9 '63
Jack Ruby on trial. M. Kempton. New Repub 150:17-20 Mr 7 '64
Jack Ruby's strange trial; new chapter in assassination story. il por U S News 56:70 Mr 23 '64
Letter from Paris. Genêt. New Yorker 40: 159-60 Mr 21 '64
Man who killed Oswald. il por Time 82:34-5 D 6 '63
Others; year after the assassination of President Kennedy. il Time 84:33 N 27 '64
Possessed. Newsweek 63:66 Mr 23 '64
Ruby convicted. Sr Schol 84:32 Ap 3 '64
Ruby's fugue state. pors Newsweek 63:25-6 F 3 '64
Shame of Dallas, Texas. il Sat Eve Post 237:82 Ap 11 '64
Trying for the truth of it; question of a defense request for a sanity hearing. Time 83:26 My 8 '64
Untold story of Jack Ruby. E. Linn. il por Sat Eve Post 237:24-6+ Jl 25 '64
Was this man sane ? with report by E. Havemann. il pors Life 56:26-33 F 21 '64
What's your source? il por Newsweek 64:68-9 Ag 31 '64
RUBY trial. See Trials (murder)
RUBYTHROATS. See Hummingbirds
RUCHT, Karl
Karl Rucht: new arrival in U.S.A; interview. por Mus Am 83:49 Mr '63
RUCK sack. See Packs
RUCKER, Darnell
Liberal and the manual arts in education. Sch & Soc 91:350-2 N 16 '63
RUDA, Jose Maria
Work of the Sixth committee of the General assembly, scope and trends. UN Mo Chron 1:81-90 Ag '64
RUDD, Augustin G.
Symbols, traditions and liberty; address, October 24, 1962. Vital Speeches 29:256 F 1 '63
RUDD, Enid
Peterpat. Criticism
Time il 85:61 Ja 15 '65
RUDD, Hughes
Death of William Faulkner. Sat Eve Post 236:32-4+ Jl 13 '63
Uranium prospector; story. Sat Eve Post 236:50-7 D 21 '63
RUDD, Lloyd K.
He likes to cook. por Bet Hom & Gard 41: 80 Ap '63
RUDD, Margaret T.
Unamuno's hunger for immortality. Christian Cent 81:1589-92 D 23 '64
RUDD, Robert L.
Introduction to pesticides; excerpts from Pesticides and the living landscape. Audubon Mag 66:222-6 Jl '64
Long-range damage of pesticides; excerpts from Pesticides and the living landscape. Audubon Mag 66:361-6 N '64
RUDDERS
Development of the anchor and rudder. il Nat Geog Mag 123:523 Ap '63
RUDEEN, Kenneth
Automobiles (cont) Sports Illus 18:51-3 Ap 22 '63
College football. Sports Illus 20:44-6 Ja 13 '64

RUDEEN, Kenneth—*Continued*
Harness racing (cont) Sports Illus 18:80 My 20; 19:50-1 Jl 8 '63
Hockey (cont) Sports Illus 18:53-4 Mr 25 '63
Motor sports (cont) Sports Illus 18:47+ F 25; 36-8 Mr 4; 68-9+ Ap 1; 72-3 Ap 15 '63; 20:54-5 Je 22 '64

RUDEL, Julius
Julius imperator; interview, ed. by Q. Eaton. pors Opera N 28:14-16 F 29 '64
New York city opera sings for Julius. M. Mayer. il pors N Y Times Mag p38+ S 29 '63
Quote: unquote; interview, ed. by E. Helm. por Mus Am 83:25 O '63

RUDENESS. See Courtesy

RUDENSKY, Morris
After the stretch. Harper 228:180-2 Ap '64

RUDIN, Ellen
Ellen Rudin to leave SLJ for book editorial position. Library J 89:1394+ Mr 15 '64

RUDIN, Harry R.
Aftermath in the Congo. Cur Hist 45:341-6 D '63

RUDKIN, George T. and others
DNA contents of chromosome Ph[1] and chromosome 21 in human chronic granulocytic leukemia. bibliog Science 144:1229-32 Je 5 '64

RUDKIN, Margaret
Round little pig in a big square kitchen; excerpt from The Margaret Rudkin Pepperidge farm cookbook. McCalls 90:122-3+ S '63

about

Mrs Rudkin revisited. New Yorker 39:42-4 N 16 '63

RUDLOE, Jack J.
Science in action; the biological collector. Natur Hist 73:59-62 N '64

RUDNICK, Philip
Flip: an oceanographic buoy. bibliog Science 146:1268-73 D 4 '64

RUDOFSKY, Bernard
Hedonism for the destitute; excerpt from Kimono mind. Horizon 7:106-9 Wint '65
In praise of stairs. il Horizon 6:78-87 Autumn '64

about

Anonymous architecture; Architecture without architect, at the Museum of modern art. A. L. Huxtable. il N Y Times Mag p92-3 N 8 '64
Does the present measure up to the past in design? il por Fortune 71:192 Ja '65

RUDOLF, crown prince of Austria
Mayerling remains a mystery. R. Payne. il por N Y Times Mag p34-5+ Ja 26 '64

RUDOLPH, Dale
Boomerang. Pop Mech 121:156-8+ Ap '64

RUDOLPH, Jack
Peninsula eleven. Mus Am 83:21 O '63

RUDOLPH, L. C.
It just isn't so. Christian Cent 80:1107 S 11 '63

RUDOLPH, Lloyd I. and Rudolph, S. H.
India turns to a conciliator. N Y Times Mag p 11+ Je 14 '64

RUDOLPH, Marguerita
Children's literature in the Soviet Union. Horn Bk 40:646-50 D '64

RUDOLPH, Paul
Horrors! a handsome garage. E. Goble. Arch Rec 133:9 F '63
Paul Rudolph designs a place to park in downtown New Haven. il Arch Rec 133: 145-50 F '63
Rudolph calls students to task of urban design. il Arch Rec 135:23+ My '64
Rudolph's Roman road. W. McQuade. il Arch Forum 118:104-9 F '63
School for the arts at Yale. il Arch Rec 135: 111-20 F '64
Yale's School of art and architecture. il por Arch Forum 120:84-5 F '64

RUDOLPH, Susanne Hoebert
Notes from a maternity ward. Atlan 211:122-5 Mr '63
—See Rudolph, L. I. jt. auth.

RUDWICK, Martin J. S. See Harland, W. B. jt. auth.

RUE, Leonard Lee, 3d
Deer in a dishpan. il Outdoor Life 132:50-2 N '63

RUEDA, Lupo Hernández. See Hernández Rueda, L.

RUEDA, Manuel
Books. M. Valldeperes. Américas 15:41-2 D '63

RUETHER, Rosemary
Speaking out; Catholic mother tells, why I believe in birth control. por Sat Eve Post 237:12+ Ap 4 '64; Same abr. Read Digest 84:148-50+ Je '64

RUFE, Federico
Sweet and hot. Sat R 46:73 O 12 '63

RUFEISEN, Oswald
Dissent on Brother Daniel. M. Galanter. Commentary 36:10-17 Jl '63; Discussion. 37: 19-20+ Ja '64

RUFF, Beatrice
Eggshell giftware. Design 64:157 Mr '63
Stained glass jewelry. Design 65:75 N '63

RUFF, Ben
Cow country dress peddler. il pors Life 57: 56-7 Jl 31 '64

RUFFED grouse shooting. See Grouse shooting

RUFFIN, Emanuel, Jr
Only Negro lion tamer. il pors Ebony 19: 49-50+ O '64

RUFUS Robin's day in court; drama. See Rybak, R. K.

RUG pads
Carpet underlays. il Consumer Rep 29:432-4 S '64

RUG; story. See O'Brien, E.

RUGANTINO; musical comedy. See Musical comedies, revues, etc.—Criticisms, plots, etc.

RUGBY, Tenn.
Colony of younger sons. J. Keats. il Holiday 35:22+ F '64

RUGBY football
Sporting scene; England vs. Scotland. A. Reid. il New Yorker 39:161-8+ Ap 13 '63

RUGEL, Miriam
Sweet forever; story. Sat Eve Post 236:40-3 Je 15 '63

RUGG, Harold
Study of creativity. F. Parker. Sat R 46:49 Ag 17 '63

RUGGLES, Melville J.
Better read than dead. Sat R 46:23 Ag 10 '63

RUGH, Roberts, and others
X-rays: are there cyclic variations in radiosensitivity? bibliog Science 142:53-6 O 4 '63

RUGS and carpets
Bed rug in colonial America. M. D. Iverson. bibliog il Antiques 85:107-9 Ja '64
Carpet covers all. G. O'Brien. il N Y Times Mag p74-5 My 5 '63
Choosing and using area rugs. Bet Hom & Gard 41:89 Jl '63
Designing rugs. C. H. Larson. il Sch Arts 64:19-20 D '64
Exciting rug news. J. Ellestad. il House B 106:122-33 Je '64
Have you hooked a large one lately? M. Garrity. il Bet Hom & Gard 42:64-5 Mr '64
Hook yourself an heirloom. il Good H 156: 122+ Mr '63
Hooked rugs to make and to treasure. il House & Gard 125:160-1 My '64
Hooking in a hurry! M. Garrity. il Bet Hom & Gard 41:56-7+ N '63
How to buy carpeting. Am Home 68:104 Ja '65
How to choose carpeting with confidence. B. G. Wadsworth and N. Pierce. il Parents Mag 38:61+ Ag '63
How to design and make needlepoint rugs. il House & Gard 126:202-3+ O '64
More rugs the better. il Vogue 142:132-3 O 15 '63
Punch-needle hooking: easy and speedy way to make a rug. C. Brown. il House B 105: 114-19+ F '63
Shop talk. R. Davidson. il Antiques 83:372+ Ap '63
Spots on record carpet year. Bsns W p67 N 14 '64
Wall-to-wall carpeting in the bathroom. il Bet Hom & Gard 41:38 S '63
What's new in carpets for '63. il Good H 156:210+ Ap '63
World underfoot. G. O'Brien. il N Y Times Mag p50-1 Ja 19 '64

Care

Carpet upkeep pays off in wear. B. G. Wadsworth. il Parents Mag 38:100 Ag '63
How to care for carpets and area rugs. Bet Hom & Gard 43:120-1+ Ja '65
Rugs; floor covering versus floor coloring. Consumer Bul 47:27-8 Je '64

RUGS and carpets, Oriental
Mongol rugs in Chinese paintings; excerpts from book. M. S. Dimand. il Antiques 84: 714-17 D '63

RUHMANN, Karl
Ruhmann collection of decorative pewter. R. M. Vetter. il Antiques 83:690-3 Je '63

RUHR VALLEY
Changing Ruhr. il Time 83:66 Ja 31 '64
Ruhr scrubs the grime. il Bsns W p 100-2+ O 3 '64

RUINA, J. P.
Ruina taking top post at IDA. J. Trainor. por Miss & Roc 15:15 S 21 '64

RUIZ NOVOA, Alberto
New look. il Newsweek 64:47 Ag 17 '64

RUKEYSER, Muriel
Double dialogue homage to Robert Frost; poem. Sat R 47:44 F 29 '64
Fighting for roses; poem. Atlan 212:78 D '63
Poem as mask. Nation 198:336 Mr 30 '64

about

Closest permissible approximation. H. Carruth. Poetry 101:358-60 F '63
Poetry of three women. M. Swenson. Nation 196:164-6 F 23 '63

RULE, Betty-Jo
By popular request: branch building in Denver. Wilson Lib Bul 37:569-70 Mr '63

RULE, Colter
Travel well. See issues of Travel to September 1964

RULE, Jane
No more bargains; story. Redbook 121:68-9 S '63

RULE, Janice
Golden rule. C. R. Jennings. il por Sat Eve Post 237:72+ Je 13 '64

RULE, John T.
Must the colleges police sex? Atlan 213:55-8 Ap '64

RULE of law
America's efforts toward world order; address, August 12, 1964. L. B. Johnson. Dept State Bul 51:298-301 Ag 31 '64; Same with title Restraint and law. Vital Speeches 30:674-5 S 1 '64
Arms control and behavioral science; excerpts from address, September 2, 1963. W. H. Goodenough. bibliog Science 144:821-4 My 15 '64
Good-by to isolationism. H. G. Reuschlein. Cath World 198:28-32 O '63
Khrushchev-Johnson notes on the use of arms. N. Khrushchev; L. B. Johnson. Cur Hist 46:357-63 Je '64
Making of foreign policy; television interview, January 11, 1964. D. Rusk; E. F. Goldman. Dept State Bul 50:164-76 F 3 '64
Principles of international law concerning friendly relations and cooperation among states: peaceful settlement of disputes; address, November 19, 1963. E. F. Kelly. bibliog f Dept State Bul 50:57-66 Ja 13 '64
Rule of law, now; address, July 3, 1963. A. Chayes. Dept State Bul 49:162-7 Jl 29 '63; Same. Vital Speeches 29:696-9 S 1 '63

See also
World conference on world peace through law

RULERS. See Kings and rulers

RULES (instruments)
Know the rule; folding rulers. il Bet Hom & Gard 41:114B+ Mr '63

RULES committee. See United States—Congress—House of representatives—Committees

RULFO, Juan
Hill of the comadres; story. tr. by L. Kemp. Atlan 213:102-5 Mr '64
New novel in Mexico: a look at Juan Rulfo. H. Ferro. por Américas 16:40-1 O '64

RUM
Drum-beating for rum; Bacardi's comeback. il Bsns W p 102-4+ O 12 '63

RUMAKER, Michael
Sky is a runner; story. Seventeen 23:90-1 Jl '64

RUMANIA
Between East and West: a Rumanian visit. R. S. Elegant. il Newsweek 62:33-4 Ag 5 '63
Secretary-General visits Romania and Yugoslavia. il U N Rev 10:46-7 Je '63

See also
Airlines—Rumania
Bucharest
Communism—Rumania
Hotels, taverns, etc.—Rumania
Mamaia
Publishers and publishing—Rumania

Commercial treaties and agreements

Shopping list; U.S. and Rumanian economic pact. Newsweek 63:74 Je 15 '64

Cultural relations

U.S. and Rumania exchange notes on cultural and other exchanges; Department announcement, with text of notes, April 2, 1963. W. A. Crawford; P. Macovei. Dept State Bul 48:661-3 Ap 29 '63

Description and travel

Rolling out a red Carpathian. H. Sutton. il Sat R 46:18-19+ Jl 13 '63

Economic conditions

New strain on red empire: nationalism vs. communism. A. Kucherov. il U S News 54:100-2 Je 17 '63
Rumania: satellite out of orbit? il Sr Schol 85:14-16+ O 28 '64
Satellite veers off course. il Bsns W p 154+ My 16 '64

Economic policy

Rumania: another split in Communist ranks. P. Ben. il New Repub 149:10-13 O 19 '63

Economic relations

Independent satellite. il Time 84:31 Jl 24 '64
Reluctant satraps. il Time 83:26 Je 19 '64
United States and Rumania agree to broaden mutual relations; announcement of talks, with text of joint communique, June 1, 1964. Dept State Bul 50:924-6 Je 15 '64

Foreign relations

Boys from Bucharest; delegation in Peking. il Time 83:39 Mr 13 '64
Never mind about Marco Polo. il Time 84:40 S 4 '64
Rumania look west. M. M. Mestrovic. Commonweal 81:10-12 S 25 '64
Satellite looks West; Rumania's quiet revolution. il Newsweek 64:31-5 Ag 10 '64

Russia

Carrot and the stick; crisis in Soviet-Rumanian relations. Newsweek 64:47 Jl 20 '64
Dynamite; Rumanian declaration of independence. Newsweek 63:32 Je 1 '64
New red rebel. il Newsweek 62:32 Jl 15 '63
Rumania's Gheorghiu-Dej; another rebel red? U S News 57:22 Jl 20 '64
Russia's satellites in new orbits. A. Werth. Nation 200:27-9 Ja 11 '65

Nationalism

New strain on red empire: nationalism vs. communism. A. Kucherov. il U S News 54:100-2 Je 17 '63

Politics and government

Have you seen Brigitte. . ? il Newsweek 64:32-5 Ag 10 '64

Social conditions

Have you seen Brigitte. . ? il Newsweek 64:32-5 Ag 10 '64

RUMANIAN rite. See Byzantine rite

RUMEN
Ethanol accumulation in the rumen after overfeeding with readily fermentable carbohydrate. M. J. Allison and others. bibliog il Science 144:54-5 Ap 3 '64

RUMEN inflammation. See Cattle—Diseases and pests

RUMENITIS. See Cattle—Diseases and pests

RUMFORD, W. Byron
Proposition fourteen. il por Time 84:23 S 25 '64
Will California send a Negro to the Senate? il pors Ebony 19:25-8+ Ja '64

RUMMEL, Joseph Francis, abp
Archbishop Rummel dies. Christian Cent 81:1452 N 25 '64

RUMMEL, R. E. See Martin, T. W. jt. auth.

RUMMEL, Robert W.
TWA official examines SST economics; address. por Aviation W 82:59-60+ Ja 4 '65

RUMMY (game)
Case of gin in Vegas. C. Goren. il Sports Illus 20:90-1 Ap 6 '64

RUMOR
Rumors: their birth, growth and death. B. H. Bagdikian. il N Y Times Mag p 14+ Je 14 '64; Reply with rejoinder. R. Major. p2 Jl 5 '64
Wings of madness; Water moccasin episode. H. Bowser. Sat R 47:26 O 24 '64

RUMPELSTILTSKIN; drama. See Thane, A.

RUMSEY, Marian
But can he swim? Motor B 114:35-7 Jl '64
Never a dull moment. Motor B 112:27+ Ag '63

RUNAWAY boys and girls
Dominic Tucci slept here; New York world's fair. A. G. Aronowitz. il Sat Eve Post 237:20-1 Jl 25 '64
Why do children run away? B. M. Silverman. il Parents Mag 38:35+ Ag '63
Why they run away from home. E. S. Ringold. il N Y Times Mag p63-4 My 10 '64
RUNAWAY Christmas stockings; story. See Rabin, A.
RUNAWAY genie; drama. See Watts, F. B.
RUNAWAYS; story. See Mirvish, R. F.
RUNGE, DeLyle P.
St Petersburg at lakeside. Library J 89:4714-16 D 1 '64
RUNGE, Ted
Mister, are you clean? Pop Phot 55:138-9+ D '64
RUNK, Alfred E.
Listen to the mockingbird. Flower Grower 50:7 Ag '63
RUNK, Mrs C. Stanley
Bluebirds returning? Audubon Mag 66:56 Ja '64
RUNK, John
How work trousers hung in 1912. J. Szarkowski. il Pop Phot 54:72-3 Ap '64
RUNKEL, S. T.
Black plastic sheets control pond weeds. il Suc Farm 62:98 S '64
RUNNING
According to plan; indoor two-mile record. Time 81:78 Mr 15 '63
All alone & kinda slow. Time 84:51 N 27 '64
And now there are two. W. Bingham. il Sports Illus 18:14-17 Mr 18 '63
Brisk tuneup for the long season ahead; U.S. Olympic middle-distance runners. J. Underwood. il Sports Illus 20:64+ Je 1 '64
Classic foursome in the Vale of Tempe. T. Maule. il Sports Illus 18:59-62 My 13 '63
Dash of style for track and field. R. Terrell. il Sports Illus 18:12-15 Ja 28 '63
Everybody runs to Boston; Boston marathon. W. Bingham. il Sports Illus 18:12-17 Ap 29 '63
Fastest boy in the West challenges a champion; 17-year-old G. Lindgren. R. Creamer. il Sports Illus 20:66+ Ja 27 '64
Fastest is faster. G. Rogin. il Sports Illus 21:56-60+ O 5 '64
For glory, & for stew; Boston marathon. Time 83:47 My 1 '64
From humdrum to well-done in one easy mile; first sub-four minute mile. R. Creamer. il Sports Illus 20:46+ F 24 '64
How a man of spirit wrecked Igloi's computer. T. Maule. il Sports Illus 18:26-9+ Je 3 '63
How fast is the fastest man alive? Olympic prospect, Florida A&M B. Hayes. J. Underwood. il Sports Illus 20:26-9 My 18 '64
I'll run a record mile; ed. by J. N. Bell. J. Beatty. il Pop Mech 119:112-15 Ap '63
It hurts to run. B. Libby. il Sat Eve Post 236:54-5 F 2 '63
Jim Beatty: America's fastest miler. il Look 27:81 Ap 9 '63
Let them try; fastest mile ever run in the U.S. il Time 81:65 My 31 '63
Light (torch division) that failed; Olympic torch from Los Angeles to Detroit by relay of runners. H. Higdon. il Sports Illus 19:47-9 N 4 '63
Look! another record. il Time 81:50 F 22 '63
Looking for a challenger; Grambling college, sprint relay team. il Time 83:94+ My 15 '64
Magic of the Great Igloi; with report by J. Beatty. il Life 54:54B-9 Mr 1 '63
Man who broke the four-minute mile. A. Carthew. il N Y Times Mag p66+ Ap 19 '64
Nobody can help; dual meets and championship meets, cross country running. Newsweek 62:94 D 2 '63
Now, if O'Hara really tries: fastest indoor mile. T. C. Brody. il Sports Illus 20:68-9 Mr 16 '64
O'Hara burns up the mile. il Life 56:78-9 Mr 27 '64
On the run from dogs and people. H. Higdon. il Sports Illus 18:76-80+ Ap 15 '63
On the track; four-minute mile barrier cleared by schoolboy. il Newsweek 63:64 Je 15 '64
Our swiftest are the best anywhere; nationals in St. Louis. T. Maule. il Sports Illus 19:22-5 Jl 1 '63
Painful path to glory; B. Edelen, top marathon runner on the U.S. Olympic team. L. Shecter. il Sat Eve Post 237:76+ O 3 '64
Run for your health. L. Smith. il Todays Health 42:34-7 O '64
Run one, run all: the Boston. il Life 54:80A-83 My 3 '63
Running is such sweet torture. J. Underwood. il Sports Illus 20:26+ Je 22 '64
Snell's tortured race to a record mile. il Sports Illus 21:28-9 N 30 '64
Start's the thing; world's fastest human. Time 81:66+ Je 28 '63
Straight man in a twisty race. J. Lovesey. il Sports Illus 20:40-2+ Je 1 '64
Ten years after; new absolute limit for the mile. il Time 83:94 My 15 '64
3:48 mile? Newsweek 64:86-7 N 30 '64
Very fast crowd at the tape; California's Compton invitational. G. S. Brown. il Sports Illus 20:28-9 Je 15 '64
With Oyol on the front; indoor mile record beaten. Time 83:50 F 21 '64
Young druggist's sure Rx. R. Creamer. il Sports Illus 20:56+ F 10 '64
See also
Animal locomotion
Hurdle racing
RUNT disease. See Animals—Diseases and pests
RUNWAY lighting. See Airports—Lighting
RUNYON, Damon
Sentimental cynic. il por Time 84:71 N 13 '64
RUOFF, C. E.
Operation pickup. Pop Electr 18:33+ Je; 19:47-8+ O '63
RUPE, Billy D. and others
Stress modification of drug response. bibliog Science 141:1186-7 S 20 '63
RUPP, Adolph
Urbane Baron concocts another surprise. J. Underwood. por Sports Illus 20:24-5+ F 17 '64
RUPP, Richard H.
Flannery O'Connor. Commonweal 79:304-7 D 6 '63
RUPRECHT, Fred
Old-fashioned Roman Christmas; Forum of the twelve Caesars restaurant. il Esquire 60:228-31 D '63
RURAL areas development program. See Rural planning
RURAL community centers. See Community centers, Rural
RURAL education. See Rural schools
RURAL electric cooperatives. See Cooperative associations
RURAL electrification. See Electric service, Rural
RURAL electrification administration. See United States—Rural electrification administration
RURAL library service
Books for Osage: deposits in general store. I. Mothner. il Look 28:60+ Ap 21 '64
Federal government and rural book distribution. ALA Bul 57:531-3 Je '63
RURAL life. See Country life; Farm life
RURAL mail carriers. See Postmen
RURAL museums. See Folk museums
RURAL planning
Across the editor's desk. D. Hanson. Suc Farm 61:8 Mr '63
RURAL recreation. See Recreation, Rural
RURAL school children. See School children
RURAL schools
Rural disadvantaged. R. M. Isenberg. NEA J 52:27 Ap '63
United States
Education in depressed areas, ed. by A. H. Passow. Review
Sat R 46:75 Ap 20 '63. D. W. Dodson: Reply. R. A. Dentler. 46:63 My 18 '63
Farm kids deserve a good education, too; with editorial comment. E. C. Richardson. il Suc Farm 62:8, 49+ Je '64
RURAL youth
Are we selling education short? Suc Farm 61:76 Ag '63
In step together; report on National conference on problems of rural youth. Recreation 56:441 D '63
New federal program trains those leaving farms; Manpower development and training act. F. Bailey, jr. Suc Farm 61:92 F '63
See also
Negro youth
RUSCH, Richard B.
Magnetic core memories. Electr World 71:37-9 Ap '64
RUSH, Benjamin
American Hippocrates. il Todays Health 42:87 N '64
I gave him barks and saltpeter. P. R. Cutright. bibliog il por Am Heritage 15:58-61+ D '63

RUSH, Kenneth
Let's be realistic; address, November 17, 1964. Vital Speeches 31:171-4 Ja 1 '65

RUSHER, William A.
Crossroads for the GOP. Nat R 14:109-12 F 12 '63
Draft-Goldwater drive: a progress report. Nat R 15:185-7 S 10 '63
Lessons of the nomination drive. Nat R 16: 641-3 Jl 28 '64
Man who stands tall. Nat R 16:656-7 Jl 28 '64
On little cat feet. Nat R 15:200-1 S 10 '63
Suite 3505. Nat R 16:683-6 Ag 11 '64
Traveling. Nat R 16:979-80 N 3 '64
Trimming the Democratic turkey with Republican parsley. Nat R 16:544 Je 30 '64

RUSHFORTH, Norman B. and others
Behavior in hydra: contraction responses of hydra pirardi to mechanical and light stimuli. bibliog Science 139:760-1 F 22 '63
Behavior in hydra: inhibition of the contraction responses of hydra pirardi. bibliog Science 145:602-4 Ag 7 '64

RUSHMORE, Robert
Canterbury tale. Reporter 28:46-7 Ap 25 '63
Operatic Kembles. Opera N 29:6-11 Ja 23 '65

RUSK, Alice C.
Music and stories enrich a curriculum. ALA Bul 57:163 F '63

RUSK, Dean
Age of the rights of man; address, October 12, 1963. Dept State Bul 49:654-8 O 28 '63
Ambassadors asked to report on activities in promoting exports; letter, August 2, 1963. Dept State Bul 49:290 Ag 19 '63
America's brightest opportunities. por Nations Bans 51:76-8+ Je '63
Atlantic alliance; address, April 7, 1964. bibliog f Dept State Bul 50:650-5 Ap 27 '64
Atlantic and European unity; address, May 9, 1964. Dept State Bul 50:810-15 My 25 '64
Central treaty organization holds 11th ministerial meeting; statement, April 30, 1963. Dept State Bul 48:841-3 My 27 '63
Central treaty organization meets at Washington; address, April 28, 1964; with final communique. Dept State Bul 50:766-9 My 18 '64
Community of interest between the U.S. and Mexico; remarks, March 5, 1964. Dept State Bul 50:449-50 Mr 23 '64
David E. Bell becomes administrator of AID; statement, December 21, 1962. Dept State Bul 48:65-6 Ja 14 '63
Dean Rusk analyzes Alliance science progress; excerpts from remarks, October 5, 1964. Sci N L 86:258+ O 24 '64
Dedication of church center for the United Nations; address, September 22, 1963. Dept State Bul 49:570-3 O 14 '63
Department of state budget requests for fiscal 1965; statement, April 28, 1964. Dept State Bul 50:836-43 My 25 '64
Department urges Congress to revise immigration laws; statement, July 31, 1964. Dept State Bul 51:276-80 Ag 24 '64
Divided world of communism; interview, ed. by E. Abel, April 10, 1963. Dept State Bul 48:644-6 Ap 29 '63
East-West trade; statement, March 13, 1964. Dept State Bul 50:474-84 Mr 30 '64
Education for citizenship in the modern world; address, February 16, 1964. Dept State Bul 50:358-64 Mr 9 '64
Eighth meeting of SEATO council of ministers; statement, April 8, 1963. Dept State Bul 48:641-3 Ap 29 '63
Eleanor Roosevelt memorial service held at Washington cathedral; remarks, November 15, 1962. Dept State Bul 48:51 Ja 14 '63
Equal employment opportunity; Negro foreign service officers; remarks, March 12, 1964. Dept State Bul 50:629-31 Ap 20 '64
Excerpt from testimony, April 5, 1963. Cong Digest 42:174+ Je '63
First twenty-five years of the United Nations from San Francisco to the 1970's; address, January 10, 1964. Dept State Bul 50:112-19 Ja 27 '64
Foreign aid program; statement, April 5, 1963. Dept State Bul 48:664-71 Ap 29 '63
Foreign aid program for 1964; statement, June 11, 1963. Dept State Bul 49:19-28 Jl 1 '63
Foreign assistance program; statement, March 23, 1964. bibliog f Dept State Bul 50:595-601 Ap 13 '64
Foreign policy and the American citizen; address, December 10, 1963. bibliog f Dept State Bul 49:990-6 D 30 '63
Foreign policy aspects of U.S. immigration laws; statement, July 2, 1964. Dept State Bul 51:98-101 Jl 20 '64
Freedom and development; address, September 25, 1964. Dept State Bul 51:498-503 O 12 '64
Freedom in the postwar world; address, August 29, 1964. Dept State Bul 51:362-7 S 14 '64
Fulfilling our basic commitments as a nation; statement, July 10, 1963. Dept State Bul 49:154-8 Jl 29 '63
Gettysburg address and our commitment to freedom; address, November 17, 1963. Dept State Bul 49:842-4 D 2 '63
Howard university to conduct foreign affairs scholars program; statement, October 9, 1963. Dept State Bul 49:684 O 28 '63
International cooperation in space science; remarks, January 31, 1963. Dept State Bul 48:294-5 F 25 '63
International educational and cultural exchanges: a look back and a look ahead; address, October 24, 1963. Dept State Bul 49:742-4 N 11 '63
Laos and Viet-Nam, a prescription for peace; address, May 22, 1964. Dept State Bul 50: 886-91 Je 8 '64; Same with title International agreements. Vital Speeches 30:546-9 Jl 1 '64
Letter from Secretary Rusk to British ambassador, April 6, 1963. Dept State Bul 48:759 My 13 '63
Making of foreign policy; television interview, January 11, 1964. Dept State Bul 50:164-76 F 3 '64
Man and nature; address, October 12, 1964. Dept State Bul 51:618-21 N 2 '64
Marine corps and the foreign service: a working partnership; address, October 16, 1964. Dept State Bul 51:643-5 N 2 '64
Memorandum from Secretary Rusk. Dept State Bul 48:429-31 Mr 25 '63
Mr Rusk and Mr Harriman discuss nuclear test ban treaty; interview on television, July 28, 1963; ed. by M. Agronsky. Dept State Bul 49:240-5 Ag 12 '63
Mixed-manned demonstration ship visits Washington; remarks, October 20, 1964. Dept State Bul 51:661-2 N 9 '64
National interest, 1964; address, June 7, 1964. Dept State Bul 50:955-8 Je 22 '64
New NATO Secretary General assured of U.S. support; letter, August 1, 1964. Dept State Bul 51:275 Ag 24 '64
Ninth anniversary of SEATO; statement, September 6, 1963. Dept State Bul 49:464 S 23 '63
North Atlantic council meets at The Hague; statement, May 12, 1964, with communique. Dept State Bul 50:850-2 Je 1 '64
Nuclear test ban treaty: symbol of a new course; statement, August 12, 1963. Dept State Bul 49:350-6 S 2 '63. Same with title Test ban treaty. Vital Speeches 29:674-7 S 1 '63
OAS approves Rio treaty measures against Castro regime; statement, July 22, 1964. bibliog f Dept State Bul 51:174-9 Ag 10 '64
Parliamentary government and the Alliance for progress; address, February 5, 1964. Dept State Bul 50:305-7 F 24 '64
Present prospect; address, January 22, 1964. bibliog f Dept State Bul 50:190-5 F 10 '64; Same with title Our foreign policy. Vital Speeches 30:290-3 Mr 1 '64
President Johnson proclaims 1965 as International cooperation year; remarks at White House ceremonies, October 2, 1964; with text of proclamation. Dept State Bul 51:557-60 O 19 '64
Pursuit of peace; address, August 2, 1964. Dept State Bul 51:214-18 Ag 17 '64
Road ahead; address, February 13, 1963. Dept State Bul 48:311-16 Mr 4 '63
Role of international law in world affairs; remarks, November 14, 1964. Dept State Bul 51:802-3 D 7 '64
Science and development in Chile; address, October 9, 1964. Dept State Bul 51:634-7 N 2 '64
Secretary comments on Korean exchange rate system reform; statement, May 3, 1964. Dept State Bul 50:830 My 25 '64
Secretary deplores book burning and damage to U.S. embassies; statement, December 9, 1964. Dept State Bul 51:905 D 28 '64
Secretary discusses Berlin in filmed interview; ed. by J. Steele. Dept State Bul 48: 135-7 Ja 28 '63
Secretary inaugurates broadcasts to Latin America via Relay; statement, January 17, 1963. Dept State Bul 48:171 F 4 '63
Secretary Rusk addresses Advertising council; remarks, March 12, 1963; with questions and answers. Dept State Bul 48:467-75 Ap 1 '63

RUSK, Dean—*Continued*
Secretary Rusk discusses appropriation request before Senate committee; statement, July 16, 1963. Dept State Bul 49:260-4 Ag 12 '63
Secretary Rusk discusses the outlook for 1964 over Japanese television; interview, December 24, 1963. Dept Stat Bul 50:40-6 Ja 13 '64
Secretary Rusk holds press and radio news briefing:
Houston. Dept State Bul 48:388-93 Mr 18 '63
Los Angeles. Dept State Bul 48:361-8 Mr 11 '63
Secretary Rusk interviewed:
ABC's Issues and answers, July 26, 1964. Dept State Bul 51:231-7 Ag 17 '64
BBC's Encounter program, May 10, 1964. Dept State Bul 50:816-22 My 25 '64
CBS reports, November 11, 1964. Dept State Bul 51:771-2 N 30 '64
CBS reports program. Dept State Bul 50:4-7 Ja 6 '64
Columbia broadcasting system program, October 16, 1964. Dept State Bul 51:614-15 N 2 '64
December 23, 1964. Dept State Bul 52:34-41 Ja 11 '65
GFWC television program, April 13, 1963. Dept State Bul 48:698-703 My 6 '63
German television. Dept State Bul 51:106-8 Jl 27 '64
Issues and answers program, October 18, 1964. Dept State Bul 51:654-60 N 9 '64
Meet the press, August 30, 1964. Dept State Bul 51:394-400 S 21 '64
Meet the press, January 27, 1963. Dept State Bul 48:244-50 F 18 '63
NBC, August 5, 1964. Dept State Bul 51:268-70 Ag 24 '64
NBC's Today program, January 21, 1963. Dept State Bul 48:202-7 F 11 '63
Voice of America. Dept State Bul 50:330-6 Mr 2 '64
Washington reports to the people. Dept State Bul 48:440-3 Mr 25 '63
Secretary Rusk to Ambassador Tejera-Paris; note, August 12, 1963. Dept State Bul 49:365 S 2 '63
Secretary Rusk to Secretary Martin; notes, January 22, 1964. Dept State Bul 50:203-4 F 10 '64
Secretary Rusk urges Americans to join Books USA campaign; statement, May 1, 1963. Dept State Bul 48:806 My 20 '63
Secretary Rusk urges full appropriations for foreign aid; statement, December 12, 1963. Dept State Bul 49:999-1004 D 30 '63
Secretary Rusk's news conference:
January 2, 1964. bibliog f Dept State Bul 50:81-9 Ja 20 '64
February 1, 1963. Dept State Bul 48:235-43 F 18 '63
February 7, 1964. Dept State Bul 50:274-84 F 24 '64
February 27, 1964. Dept State Bul 50:403-9 Mr 16 '64
March 6, 1964. Dept State Bul 50:439-46 Mr 23 '64
March 8, 1963. Dept State Bul 48:432-9 Mr 25 '63
March 27, 1964. Dept State Bul 50:570-6 Ap 13 '64
April 3, 1964. Dept State Bul 50:608-14 Ap 20 '64
May 29, 1963. Dept State Bul 48:931-8 Je 17 '63
July 1, 1964. Dept State Bul 51:82-8 Jl 20 '64
July 31, 1964. Dept State Bul 51:221-8 Ag 17 '64
August 16, 1963. Dept State Bul 49:356-64 S 2 '63
September 10, 1964. Dept State Bul 51:426-32 S 28 '64
September 14, 1964. Dept State Bul 51:468-72 O 5 '64
October 8, 1964. Dept State Bul 51:575-81 O 26 '64
November 8, 1963. Dept State Bul 49:810-17 N 25 '63
Secretary sends good wishes on Latvia's national day; letter, November 15, 1963. Dept State Bul 49:932 D 16 '63
Security and freedom: a free-world responsibility; address, February 26, 1963. Dept State Bul 48:383-8 Mr 18 '63
Situation in the western Pacific; address, April 25, 1964. Dept State Bul 50:732-7 My 11 '64
Some current issues in U.S. foreign policy; remarks, April 18, 1963; with questions and answers. Dept State Bul 48:679-88 My 6 '63
Some thoughts on the conduct of foreign policy; remarks, July 23, 1964. Dept State Bul 51:185-8 Ag 10 '64
SEATO council of ministers meets at Manila; statement, April 13, 1964. Dept State Bul 50:690-3 My 4 '64
Stake in Viet Nam; address, April 22, 1963; with questions and answers. Dept State Bul 48:727-35 My 13 '63; Same. Vital Speeches 29:493-7 Je 1 '63
State of the North Atlantic alliance; address, July 12, 1963. Dept State Bul 49:190-8 Ag 5 '63
Statements, February 13, 1963. Dept State Bul 48:357 Mr 11 '63
Task of the O.A.S. Cuba; address, July 21-24, 1964. Vital Speeches 30:665-7 Ag 15 '64
Teaching the fundamentals of international understanding; address, September 8, 1964. Dept State Bul 51:437-41 S 28 '64
Tenth anniversary of SEATO; statement, September 5, 1964. Dept State Bul 51:400 S 21 '64
Toilsome path to peace; address, March 19, 1964. Dept State Bul 50:530-5 Ap 6 '64
Toward a new dimension in the Atlantic partnership; address, October 27, 1963. Dept State Bul 49:726-31 N 11 '63
Toward the brotherhood of man; address, October 19, 1964. Dept State Bul 51:650-2 N 9 '64
Toward victory for freedom; address, September 14, 1964. Dept State Bul 51:463-8 O 5 '64; Same. Vital Speeches 31:2-5 O 15 '64
Trade and the Atlantic partnership; address November 16, 1964. Dept State Bul 51:766-71 N 30 '64
Trade, investment, and peace; address, October 5, 1964. Dept State Bul 51:570-5 O 26 '64
Trade union movement and social progress in the western hemisphere; address, November 23, 1964. Dept State Bul 51:849-52 D 14 '64
Transmission from U.S. to Australia via Commonwealth cable opened; statement, December 2, 1963. Dept State Bul 49:969 D 23 '63
25th anniversary of the Department of state bulletin; statement. Dept State Bul 51:2 Jl 6 '64
Unfinished business; address, September 10, 1963. Dept State Bul 49:490-6 S 30 '63
United Nations in the fight for freedom; address, February 22, 1963. Dept State Bul 48:393-8 Mr 18 '63
United States and Japan: common interests in the building of a peaceful world; address, January 28, 1964. bibliog f Dept State Bul 50:230-5 F 17 '64
U.S. and Japan inaugurate television link via Syncom III; statement, October 7, 1964. Dept State Bul 51:592 O 26 '64
United States and Spain renew defense agreement. Dept State Bul 49:686-8 O 28 '63
U.S. comments on Peiping's nuclear capacity; statement, September 29, 1964. Dept State Bul 51:542 O 19 '64
U.S. efforts to achieve safeguarded test ban treaty; statement, March 11, 1963. Dept State Bul 48:485-9 Ap 1 '63
U.S.-Japan science committee concludes fourth meeting; remarks, June 23, 1964. Dept State Bul 51:61-3 Jl 13 '64
U.S. New Zealand, and Australia reaffirm ties of friendship; remarks, July 17, 1964. Dept State Bul 51:194-5 Ag 10 '64
U.S. reaffirms commitments to Taiwan and Viet-Nam; statements, April 16, 17 and 20, 1964. Dept State Bul 50:694-7 My 4 '64
U.S. requests three IJC studies on water levels and pollution; text of letter, October 1, 1964. Dept State Bul 51:599-600 O 26 '64
U.S. seeks solution to problem of tuna fishing off Ecuador; statement, June 5, 1963. Dept State Bul 48:976 Je 24 '63
U.S. supports full membership for Japan in OECD; statement, March 28, 1963. Dept State Bul 48:572 Ap 15 '63
U.S. supports preconditions for conference on Laos; U.S. statement, July 30, 1964. Dept State Bul 51:218-20 Ag 17 '64
United States takes measures to repel attack against U.S. forces in southeast Asia; statement, August 6, 1964. Dept State Bul 51:263-5, 267 Ag 24 '64
Universal appeal of the Declaration of independence. Dept State Bul 51:74-8 Jl 20 '64
White House holds conference on export expansion; address, September 17, 1963. Dept State Bul 49:599-601 O 14 '63
Why Laos is critically important; address, June 14, 1964. Dept State Bul 51:3-5 Jl 6 '64

RUSK, Dean—*Continued*
Why we treat different Communist countries differently; address, February 25, 1964. Dept State Bul 50:390-6 Mr 16 '64; Same. Vital Speeches 30:354-7 Ap 1 '64; Excerpts. U S News 56:55 Mr 9 '64
World transformed; excerpts from address at Time's anniversary dinner. por Time 81: 62 My 17 '63
Your stake in foreign aid; address, March 6, 1964. Dept State Bul 50:434-8 Mr 23 '64
—and McNamara, R. S.
Letter to members of House; August 17, 1963. Dept State Bul 49:399-400 S 9 '63
—and Muñiz, C. M.
U.S. and Argentina reaffirm traditional ties; joint statement, January 24, 1963. Dept State Bul 48:211-13 F 11 '63
—and Park, C. H.
Secretary Rusk holds talks with President of Korea; joint communique, January 29, 1964. Dept State Bul 50:238 F 17 '64
—and Schroeder, Gerhard
German Foreign Minister talks with Secretary Rusk; joint communique, November 26, 1964. Dept State Bul 51:847 D 14 '64

about

Atlantic report; Secretary Rusk. Atlan 214: 10 N '64
Dean Rusk and the President. W. V. Shannon. Commonweal 78:5-6 Mr 29 '63
Mild Mr Rusk. A. Campbell. New Repub 150:13-16 Ap 11 '64
Musings from State. Time 83:14-15 Ja 24 '64
Name in the game; question of shift in personnel. por Time 81:20-1 Mr 15 '63
Perfect format; talks with visiting statesmen at U.S. mission building. il pors Time 82: 39 O 4 '63
Quiet man. il por Time 82:24-7 D 6 '63
Rusk warns allies: do more for defense. por U S News 55:26 N 11 '63
Secretary Rusk heads delegation to SEATO council meeting. Dept State Bul 50:577 Ap 13 '64
Talking to Tito; Rusk's courtesy call. Time 81:27-8 My 10 '63

RUSK, Howard A.
Fluoridation fight in N.Y; reprint. Sci Digest 55:30-3 Ap '64
Recreation promotes health; excerpts from address, October 2, 1962. por Recreation 56: 128-9 Mr '63

RUSKAUFF, Bob
Aloha to the Transpac fleet. Motor B 112:135 Jl '63
Lake Elsinore's resurrection. Motor B 113: 52+ My '64
Off to the western races. Motor B 111:154-5 My '63
Prospects for the Pacific summer. Motor B 111:149-51 Ap '63
Salton Sea to the big bear. Motor B 115:204+ Ja '65
To aid hospitalized driver. Motor B 111:134-5 F '63
Westward ho! Motor B 112:97 O '63; 114:130 O; 118-19 N; 76 D '64; 115:236-7 Ja '65

RUSKIN, John
First and last Rose. P. Quennell. Sat R 47:26 D 26 '64
Genius of John Ruskin, ed. by J. D. Rosenberg. Review
Commonweal 80:64-7 Ap 3 '64. A. Kostelanetz
Rosie & the critic. por Time 85:70+ Ja 8 '65

RUSS, Lavinia
Blithe spirits: some children's books for adults to give adults. Pub W 186:28-31 S 14 64
Juvenile paperbacks or the curious case of Curious George. Pub W 185:44-5 Mr 16 '64
Let the children's books shout, or A plea for more window display. Pub W 186:93-5 Ag 24 '64

RUSSELL, Anna
Comediva. por Time 84:50 Jl 17 '64

RUSSELL, Bertrand Russell, 3d earl
After the test ban; letter. Nation 197:inside cover, 241 O 19 '63
Bertrand Russell on the sinful Americans; exchange of letters. Harper 226:20+ Je '63
Chemical warfare. Nation 197:inside cover Jl 6 '63
Chemical warfare in Vietnam. New Repub 149:30-1 Jl 6 '63
Genetic effects. Bul Atomic Sci 19:31-2 Je '63
Is communism a menace? Russell's answer. por N Y Times Mag p35+ Ap 7 '63
Redbook dialogue: B. Russell and T. Robbins. por Redbook 123:66-7+ S '64
Soviet anti-Semitism: an exchange. Commentary 39:35-7 Ja '65
US, the USSR, and Cuba. New Repub 150:29 My 23 '64

about

Bewitchment of Bertrand Russell. J. Mander. New Repub 149:20-2 Ag 17 '63; Reply. R. Schoenman. 149:38-9 O 5 '63
Down and down he goes. Nat R 14:310 Ap 23 '63

RUSSELL, Bill
I owe the public nothing. E. Linn. il pors Sat Eve Post 237:60-3 Ja 18 '64
Panic is on again. B. Ottum. il por Sports Illus 21:18-19+ N 9 '64
Russell of spring. H. L. Masin. Sr School 84: 22 F 28 '64
We are grown men playing a child's game. G. Rogin. il pors Sports Illus 19:74-8+ N 18 '63

RUSSELL, Cazzie
Cazzie Russell: sophomore cage phenom. il pors Ebony 19:101-2+ Ap '64
His hopes hang by an ankle. J. Underwood. il por Sports Illus 20:18-21 Mr 23 '64

RUSSELL, David H.
Your child and reading; reprint. Todays Health 41:16 N '63

RUSSELL, Donna Shinn
Meanest woman in the world. Opera N 28:26-8 Ja 11 '64

RUSSELL, Elizabeth S. See Craig, M. L. jt. auth.

RUSSELL, Francis
Four mysteries of Warren Harding. Am Heritage 14:4-9+ Ap '63
Men and manners. Nat R 16:612+, 877-8 Jl 14, O 6 '64
Merchants of death. Nat R 15:362-4 O 22 '63
Movies (cont) Nat R 14:167-9; 15:114+; 16: 77-9, 165, 367-70, 1156+; 17:31-2 F 26, Ag 13 '63, Ja 28, F 25, My 5, D 29 '64-Ja 12 '65
Only the little tramp matters. Nat R 16: 1066+ D 1 '64
Passing scene (cont) Nat R 15:494-6, 574-5 D 3, 31 '63
Rhine. Horizon 6:18-27 Spr '64
Sacco guilty, Vanzetti innocent? Am Heritage 13:4-9+ Je '62; 14:93 F '63
Sheiks and shebas, dance no more. Horizon 5:118-19 Jl '63
Strike that made a president. Am Heritage 14:44-7+ O '63
Theater (cont) Nat R 14:465-7 Je 4 '63
Then and now. Nat R 14:326+ Ap 23 '63
When gentlemen prepared for war. Am Heritage 15:24-7+ Ap '64

about

Only yesterday. J. Chamberlain. Nat R 16: 691-3 Ag 11 '64

RUSSELL, James E.
Why belong to NEA? letter. NEA J 53:35-7 N, 64; 54:7 Ja '65

RUSSELL, John
All-year resort in a pasture. Farm J 87:59 Ap '63
Narrow rows: the coming thing? Farm J 87:36-7+ Mr '63

RUSSELL, John, 1919-
Art news from London. See issues of Art news
Baroque pearls. Art N 63:51+ O '64
Castle tomorrow. Vogue 142:126-33 Ag 1 '63
Cellini, Houdon & others at the V.&A. Art N 63:30-1+ D '64
Max Ernst. Vogue 144:168-73+ S 1 '64
Monarchs as patrons. Art N 62:44-5+ D '63
1954-1964. Art N 63:35-7+ My '64
Swinging art dealers: the Marlborough boys in New York. Vogue 143:102-5+ Ja 1 '64

RUSSELL, John L. Jr
Bulbs in the deep South. Flower Grower 50: 69-70 Ap '63

RUSSELL, Liane Brauch
Mammalian X-chromosome action; inactivation limited in spread and in region of origin. bibliog Science 140:976-8 My 31 '63

RUSSELL, Lillian
Lillian Russell. A. Debus. il por Hobbies 69: 44-5 Jl '64

RUSSELL, Mary Jane
What ever happened to Mary Jane? interview, ed. by B. Clerke. pors Ladies Home J 80:82-3 Je '63

RUSSELL, Pee Wee
Jazz. W. Balliett. New Yorker 39:123-4 S 14 '63
New Pee Wee. por Newsweek 62:78 S 16 '63

RUSSELL, Richard Brevard
One plan to end race troubles: pay people to move; summary of address, March 16, 1964. por U S News 56:36-7 Mr 30 '64
Russell defends the filibuster. por N Y Times Mag p20+ Mr 15 '64
South states its case; statement, June 12, 1963. por U S News 54:78 Je 24 '63

RUSSELL, Richard Brevard—*Continued*

about

If a filibuster comes, Russell will be the manager. U S News 55:18 Jl 1 '63
Man who leads the southern senators. M. Greenfield. por Reporter 30:17-21 My 21 '64
Russell scores abandonment of bombers. G. C. Wilson. Aviation W 79:28-9 S 23 '63
Russell sounds call for civil-rights fight. U S News 56:8 F 3 '64
Senator Russell extends power; chairman of the Senate military appropriations subcommittee. Christian Cent 80:293 Mr 6 '63
Senator Russell in the last ditch. F. W. Collins. il por N Y Times Mag p 16+ O 20 '63
Senator Russell of Georgia: does he speak for the South? il por Newsweek 62:20-4 Ag 19 '63
Veteran spokesman for the Old South. por Bsns W p28-9 Ap 18 '64

RUSSELL, Robert
Pike fishing by bell. Atlan 214:75-8 Ag '64

RUSSELL, Robert D.
Alcohol. NEA J 53:66-7 Mr '64

RUSSELL, Roger H.
Build a hi-fi volume compressor expander. Pop Electr 21:41-5+ O '64

RUSSELL, Ronald M.
How to call ducks. Outdoor Life 133:44-7+ Ja '64

RUSSELL, Rusty
It's not too early to plan your color holiday cards. Pop Phot 53:66-7+ O '63

RUSSELL, William C. Jr
Town with a romantic past lights for the future. Am City 79:116 N '64

RUSSELL family
Russell coat-of-arms. H. K. Eilers. il Hobbies 69:126-7 D '64

RUSSELL Sage foundation
Social impact of standardized testing. D. A. Goslin. NEA J 52:20-2 O '63

RUSSETT, Bruce Martin
Britain, the Common market, and the challenge to western unity. Cath World 196: 299-305 F '63

RUSSIA
Appraisal of Khrushchev by Harriman; political and economic pressures behind agreement with the West. W. A. Harriman. il N Y Times Mag p 10+ Ag 25 '63
New Russia. P. Ben. New Repub 151:7-8 S 19 '64
Russia in 1964: report on a two-month visit. A. Werth. Nation 199:183-8 O 5 '64
Russia, revisited, is still a mystery. M. Frankel. il N Y Times Mag p34-5+ S 15 '63
Russia; symposium, with photographs by Burt Glinn. bibliog Holiday 34:16+ O '63
Soviet Union, 1963; symposium. bibliog f il Cur Hist 45:193-234+ O '63
Soviet Union, 1964; symposium. bibliog f il Cur Hist 47:257-302+ N '64

See also
Aerospace industries—Russia
Agricultural administration—Russia
Agriculture—Russia
Airlines—Russia
Americans in Russia
Aral Sea
Architecture—Russia
Architecture, Domestic—Russia
Art—Russia
Astronomical observatories—Russia
Atomic power—Russia
Atomic research—Russia
Aviation—Russia
Ballet—Russia
Banks and banking—Russia
Book industries and trade—Russia
Books and reading—Russia
Bukhara
Camps—Russia
Caspian sea
Censorship—Russia
Chemical industries—Russia
Childrens literature—Russia
Christmas—Russia
Collective farms—Russia
Colleges and universities—Russia
Communism—Russia
Courts—Russia
Crime and criminals—Russia
Education—Russia
Food supply—Russia
Foreign students in Russia
Foreign visitors in Russia
Gambling—Russia
Gold mines and mining—Russia
Housing—Russia
Investments, Foreign (in Russia)
Irrigation—Russia
Jazz music—Russia
Jews in Russia
Journalism—Russia
Justice, Administration of—Russia
Kazakhstan
Khabarovsk, Siberia
Labor laws and legislation—Russia
Leningrad
Libraries—Russia
Marriage—Russia
Medical service—Russia
Merchant marine—Russia
Moving pictures—Russia
Music—Russia
Names, Geographical—Russia
Natural resources—Russia
Oimyakon
Old age pensions—Russia
Opera—Russia
Prison camps—Russia
Publishers and publishing—Russia
Radio broadcasting—Russia
Research—Russia
Science—Russia
Secret service—Russia
Shopping and shoppers—Russia
Space research—Russia
Television industry—Russia
Theater—Russia
Tourist trade—Russia
Trials—Russia
Ukraine
United Nations—Russia
Volgograd
Wages—Russia
Women—Russia
World war, 1939-1945—Russia
Youth—Russia

Antiquities

Archeology in the Soviet Union. S. F. Starr. Yale R 54:311-20 D '64

Armed forces

Soviets parade missile arsenal; May day speech takes softer line. H. J. Coleman. Aviation W 78:36 My 6 '63
Soviets press technical modernization of military services. il Aviation W 78:92-5 Mr 11 '63

Forces in Cuba

Building up again? Russia's military presence in Cuba. il Time 81:32 F 8 '63
Hardening Soviet base in Cuba. il Time 81: 23 F 15 '63
How Russia is using its Cuban base. U S News 54:45 Mr 4 '63
Kenneth Keating, critic of our Cuban policy. J. Daniel. Read Digest 82:190-2+ My '63
Measuring the threat. Commonweal 77:551 F 22 '63
Pullout and pressures. Newsweek 61:18 Mr 4 '63
Real change in Cuba. R. Hotz. Aviation W 78:17 Mr 4 '63
Secretary Rusk appears on Meet the press; transcript of interview, January 27, 1963. D. Rusk. Dept State Bul 48:244-50 F 18 '63
Secretary Rusk's news conference of February 1, 1963. D. Rusk. Dept State Bul 48:235-43 F 18 '63
Up to the others; questions about Cuba. il Time 81:19-20 Mr 15 '63
When in due course. il Time 81:21 F 22 '63

Boundaries

Search for lebensraum? struggle between Russia and red China. il Time 84:40-1 S 18 '64
Sinkiang: Soviet rustlers in China's Wild West. S. Karnow. il Reporter 30:36-9 Je 18 '64
Where troops of red China and Soviet stand toe to toe. il U S News 56:53-4 Ja 6 '64

Commerce

ABC's of American wheat sales to the reds; with statement by J. F. Kennedy. il U S News 55:52-3 O 21 '63
As Russia goes shopping; outlook in the wheat belt. il U S News 55:42-4 O 14 '63
Deal in wheat? il Time 82:31 O 4 '63
Dialogue? yes; concessions? beware! A. A. Berle, jr. il N Y Times Mag p9+ O 20 '63; Discussion. p26+ N 10 '63; 19-20 Ja 19 '64
East-West: the new trade winds. il Newsweek 62:38-40 Ag 19 '63
From Washington straight. Cato. Nat R 15: 270 O 8 '63
How to deal with the Russians. J. Thackray. il Duns R 83:57-8+ My '64
How West bails out Khrushchev. il U S News 57:48 S 7 '64

RUSSIA—Commerce—*Continued*
No pipeline for Moscow. T. Prittie. New Repub 148:9-10 Ap 6 '63
Red insurance man; Garant insurance, Vienna. Time 82:91-2 D 13 '63
Red trade, red aid? Sr Schol 83:22-3 Mr 6 '64
Should the U.S. trade with enemies? R. K. Massie. Sat Eve Post 237:19-21 F 1 '64
Sino-Soviet economic relations, 1959-1962. O. Hoeffding. bibliog f il Ann Am Acad 349: 94-105 S '63
Soviet-bloc market: so big and yet so far. il Bsns W p53-4 O 19 '63
Talking trade; American businessmen discuss Soviet-American trade in Moscow. il Newsweek 64:79 N 30 '64
Temptation of trade; Bonn's cancellation of Soviet pipe order. Time 81:33 Ap 5 '63
Tricks and trials of working in Moscow; increased trade with Russia. il Bsns W p50-2 My 30 '64
Two for the money; British firms close trade deals with Russia. Newsweek 61:81 My 13 '63
200 million new customers for U.S? interview. E. M. Braderman. il U S News 55:40-3 N 4 '63
U.S. wheat for the Soviets? pro and con discussion. Sr Schol 83:8-9 O 25 '63
Welcome, capitalists. Time 84:108 S 18 '64
Wheat for reds; who's paying? il U S News 56:87-8 F 17 '64
Who'll profit from big wheat deal. il U S News 55:50 O 28 '63
Will the West bail out Russia with trade? il U S News 57:106-7 D 7 '64
Will the West now bail out Khrushchev? il U S News 55:36-8 D 30 '63

Cultural relations

Barghoorn has a new book due from Princeton in March. Pub W 184:32-3 N 25 '63
Soviet-American exchanges, tit-for-tat goodwill. S. S. Rosenfeld. Science 143:1413-17 Mr 27 '64
U.S. and U.S.S.R. sign agreement on exchanges for 1964-65; Department statement; with remarks by Ambassador Kohler, February 22, 1964. Dept State Bul 50:451-2 Mr 23 '64
Will the swaps keep on? Barghoorn incident. il Bsns W p28-9 N 23 '63
See also
Exchange of persons programs

Defenses

Khrushchev's losing fight with his marshals. V. Zorza. il Life 57:42-3+ N 6 '64
Khrushchev's paper bear. C. J. V. Murphy. Fortune 70:114-15+ D '64
Kosygin calls military fund cuts disarmament route, attacks MLF. Aviation W 81:16 D 28 '64
Military strategy (Voennaya strategiya) Review
Reporter il 28:34+ F 14 '63. R. L. Garthoff
New Soviet problem. R. Hotz. Aviation W 80:21 F 17 '64
New stalemate and new strategy; Secretary McNamara's testimony before the House armed services committee. Bsns W p28 F 2 '63
Paper bear. W. J. Coughlin. Miss & Roc 16:46 Ja 11 '65
Red dilemma. W. J. Coughlin. Miss & Roc 15:46 S 7 '64
Russia shows off its missiles; with report by R. Brigham. il Life 57:42-42B+ N 20 '64
Shifts in Soviet strategic thought. T. W. Wolfe. bibliog f For Affairs 42:475-86 Ap '64
Soviet claim of Polaris equivalent questioned; summary of report of Institute for strategic studies, London. Aviation W 79:77+ D 2 '63
Soviet military budget. T. Sosnovy. bibliog f il For Affairs 42:487-94 Ap '64
Soviet missile parade features anti-ICBM, wheeled carriers. il Aviation W 81:26-8 N 16 '64
Soviets display five new missiles in Red square anniversary parade. il Miss & Roc 15:16-18 N 16 '64
Soviets revert to ICBM emphasis. F. G. McGuire. Miss & Roc 13:18 D 2 '63
USSR blends diplomatic, military goals. il Aviation W 80:101 Mr 16 '64
United States military posture today. A. J. Cottrell. bibliog f Cur Hist 47:71-6+ Ag '64
U.S. Soviet strengths detailed; with editorial comment. J. Trainor. Miss & Roc 14:14, 46 Ap 20 '64
Where we stand on defense; excerpts from address, November 28, 1963. R. S. McNamara. il Duns R 83:53-4+ F '64; Same. Bul Atomic Sci 20:35-9 Mr '64
Who's ahead in missile race; what a British survey shows. il U S News 55:52-3 N 18 '63
Why LBJ holds the arms line. il Bsns W p28-9 Ja 23 '65
See also
Aeronautics, Military—Russia

Description and travel

How intourist took me in. K. Snow. Nat R 16:355-7 My 5 '64
Life guide: how to visit the Soviet Union. il Life 55:22-4 S 13 '63
My Russian journey. E. L. Grossen. il Sr Schol 84:12T Ap 17 '64
Sights on a 10,000-mile trip. il Life 55:24-30 S 13 '63
View of all the Russias. L. Van Der Post. il Holiday 34:58-70+ O '63

Diplomatic and consular service

Soviet attaché accused of improper activities; U.S. asks departure; note, July 1, 1963. R. H. Davis. Dept State Bul 49:137 Jl 22 '63
Then again, maybe *nyet*; proposed move of Soviet embassy to Chevy Chase. il Time 81:22 My 3 '63
United States and Soviet Union sign consular convention; statement, May 27, 1964, with text of convention, June 1, 1964. L. B. Johnson. Dept State Bul 50:979-85 Je 22 '64; Excerpts without statement. Cur Hist 47: 303-5 N '64

Economic conditions

Another big race the Russians are losing. il U S News 57:122-4 N 9 '64
Are Soviets on the road to capitalism? il U S News 57:14 Jl 27 '64
Big changes inside Russia. C. Foltz, jr. il U S News 56:54-65 Ja 20 '64
Big try for plenty. il Life 55:55-6+ S 13 '63
Economist diary; London editors' impressions. Newsweek 61:60 Je 10 '63
For Soviet women: a thirteen-hour day; average Russian wife. E. Whiteside. il N Y Times Mag p28-9+ N 17 '63
Going in the red? concerning report of Central intelligence agency's press conference. Sr Schol 84:20 F 7 '64
Growing troubles in Khrushchev's empire. il U S News 55:54-6 O 21 '63
Has Russia lost the cold war; is communism failing? il U S News 55:50-4 N 18 '63
Kosygin and the Russian consumer; with statements by U.S. academic experts. il Newsweek 64:73-4+ N 9 '64
Numbers game; CIA report. il Newsweek 63: 31-2 Ja 20 '64
Pressure on Khrushchev. P. Ben. New Repub 148:7-8 Mr 9 '63
Quality of life behind the Soviet statistics. H. A. Grunwald. il Fortune 69:146-7+ Mr '64
Report from Russia. P. Ben. New Repub 150: 16-18 Je 13 '64
Russia in deep trouble; will U.S. give help? interview. G. W. Nutter. il U S News 56: 50-7 Ap 13 '64
Russians get more pie. il Bsns W p50-2+ Jl 20 '63
Should the U.S. trade with enemies? R. K. Massie. Sat Eve Post 237:19-21 F 1 '64
Soviet economic developments; Khrushchev and after. O. Gass. bibliog f il Commentary 37:54-68 F '64; Reply with rejoinder. P. Goodman. 38:12-15 Jl '64
Soviet shadow economy; vast illegal network of undercover dealings. J. M. Hochstein. il Reporter 30:27-31 Ap 9 '64
Speaking out; we can make the Russians disarm. W. P. Reuther. Sat Eve Post 236: 10+ D 7 '63
Tomorrow is three suits. il Time 83:28-33 F 21 '64; Same abr. with title Khrushchev's monumental economic mess. Read Digest 84:69-73 Je '64
Trends in Soviet personal income components; excerpt of Recent trends in Soviet personal income and consumption. R. E. Golden. bibliog f il Mo Labor R 86:385-7 Ap '63
Visit to a Russian village. D. Whiteside. il N Y Times Mag p26-7+ D 8 '63
Wheat for Russia. New Repub 149:5 N 16 '63

RUSSIA—Economic conditions—*Continued*
Who's burying whom? concerning CIA report. Time 83:23 Ja 17 '64
Winter of communism's discontent. A. Shub. il Reporter 30:29-31 Ja 2 '64
See also
Agriculture—Russia
Food supply—Russia
Russia—Industries
Wages—Russia

Bibliography

Studies of the Soviet economy. H. Schwartz. Harvard Bsns R 41:6-8+ My '63

Economic policy

And back in the U.S.S.R; ideas borrowed from capitalism. Newsweek 64:72 S 28 '64
Big Soviet project gets the ax; hydroelectric-aluminum complex at Bratsk. il Bsns W p62+ Ja 25 '64
Centralization versus decentralization in mainland China and the Soviet Union. D. H. Perkins. bibliog f Ann Am Acad 349: 70-80 S '63
Economic controversy in the Soviet Union: Liberman's goals for economic reform. M. I. Goldman. For Affairs 41:498-512 Ap '63
Khrushchev eats his words. A. Werth. Nation 198:64-6 Ja 20 '64
Khrushchev hits Soviet industry planning. O. K. Antonov; N. S. Khrushchev. Aviation W 78:105+ Ja 21 '63
Khrushchev's paper bear. C. J. V. Murphy. Fortune 70:114-15+ D '64
Looking backward; consumer-goods factories to try supply-and-demand experiment. Time 85:25 Ja 22 '65
New trend in Russia: creeping capitalism. il U S News 57:119-20 S 28 '64
Patching up Russia's planned economy. J. M. Montias. Reporter 28:22-4 Ap 11 '63
Russia's latest plan: confession of a failure il U S News 55:44-5 D 23 '63
Shortages put new pressure on Russia. il Nations Bsns 51:72-3+ O '63
Soviet economic developments: Khrushchev and after. O. Gass. bibliog f il Commentary 37:54-68 F '64; Reply with rejoinder. P. Goodman. 38:12-15 Jl '64
Soviet strategy for economic growth, by N. Spulber. Review
Sat R 47:34 F 1 '64. H. Schwartz
Trends in the Soviet economy. M. T. Florinsky. Cur Hist 47:266-71 N '64
USSR 1965; address, December 10, 1964. A. N. Kosygin. il Vital Speeches 31:213-24 Ja 15 '65
What next in Soviet planning? L. Smolinski. bibliog f For Affairs 42:602-13 Jl '64
Why Russia downgrades planners. Bsns W p98-100+ O 31 '64
Why Russia may become tougher trade adversary. il Nations Bsns 51:86-7 F '63
See also
Communism—Russia

Economic relations

Tall building on Smolenskaya square. il Fortune 69:207-8+ Ap '64
Will the West now bail out Khrushchev? il U S News 55:36-8 D 30 '63

China (People's Republic)

Sino-Soviet economic relations, 1959-1962. O. Hoeffding. bibliog f il Ann Am Acad 349: 94-105 S '63

Cuba

Castro and Khrushchev: the ties that bind. Panatela. il Reporter 28:38-9 Mr 14 '63
Horse-trade in Moscow. Bsns W p25-6 My 4 '63

Egypt

Russia picks up a tab; finances Bokaro steel mill and Aswan High Dam. Bsns W p29 My 9 '64

Great Britain

Easy terms for Russia. Newsweek 64:94 S 21 '64
Russia exploits British-EEC breakdown. Bsns W p 126 F 16 '63

India

Russia picks up a tab; finances Bokaro steel mill and Aswan High Dam. Bsns W p29 My 9 '64

United States

Reappraisal of U.S.-U.S.S.R. trade policy; excerpts from address, March 12, 1964. H. J. Berman. Harvard Bsns R 42:139-44+ Jl '64
What it's like to trade with Russia. il Nations Bsns 52:36-7+ Ag '64

Foreign relations

After Khrushchev what? with report by K. Lachmann. il U S News 57:39-45 O 26 '64
Back of Russia's sudden soft line. il U S News 55:25-8 S 2 '63
Can we deal with Moscow? with editorial comment. G. F. Kennan. Sat Eve Post 236: 38+, 96 O 5 '63
Coexistence and the class struggle. R. Aron. New Repub 149:10-11 S 28 '63
Cold war and weapons control. L. W. Martin. Cur Hist 47:1-5+ Jl '64
Dispensing the word, Kremlin-style; summary of address. N. S. Khrushchev. il Sr Schol 82:16-17 Mr 13 '63
Egypt, the Soviet Union and Israel. New Repub 150:11-12 Je 6 '64
Fall of Nikita K; with comment on the world's news fronts. il Sr Schol 85:17-18+, 24 O 28 '64
Flowers, swallows & strangers; game of peaceful coexistence. il Time 84:28 Ag 7 '64
Iron grip falters. il Bsns W p74+ N 28 '64
Is Khrushchev Dr Strangelove? U S News 57:51 O 5 '64
Khrushchev at seventy. Nation 198:407 Ap 27 '64
Khrushchev at the crossroads. il Newsweek 62:29-30+ Jl 22 '63
Khrushchev mends some fences. C. Wassermann. Reporter 29:36-8 S 26 '63
Kosygin calls military fund cuts disarmament route, attacks MLF. Aviation W 81:16 D 28 '64
Mildly welcomed truce. E. J. Hughes. Newsweek 62:31 O 21 '63
Minuet of the powers. il Newsweek 64:46+ N 9 '64
Moscow: which way? S. Alsop. il Sat Eve Post 237:13 N 21 '64
New look at Russia from the inside; interview. I. D. Levine. U S News 55:92-3 Ag 26 '63
Of hope & skepticism. il Time 82:11 Jl 26 '63
On peace and war in the atomic age; address, April 5, 1963. M. S. Pap. Vital Speeches 29: 531-5 Je 15 '63
Place is Berlin, the problem is Peking; Khrushchev's visit to East Berlin. il Time 82:23 Jl 5 '63
Return to multilateral diplomacy. J. D. Singer. Yale R 53:36-48 O '63
Russia after Khrushchev. New Repub 151:3-4 O 24 '64
Russia, China, and the underdeveloped areas. H. Gelman. bibliog f Ann Am Acad 349: 130-42 S '63
Seven safeguards for dealing with reds. A. Dulles. Nations Bsns 51:66-7+ O '63
Soviet policy in the developing countries P. E. Mosely. For Affairs 43:87-98 O '64
Spirit of Moscow. il Time 82:22-3 Jl 26 '63
Stalin-Trotsky split: a lesson for Kremlinologists. J. A. Hough. Reporter 29:37-9 D 5 '63
Stalin's foreign policy reappraised, by M. D. Shulman. Review
New Repub 149:22+ Ag 3 '63. H. Seton-Watson
Step toward limbo. Newsweek 64:40 Ag 24 '64
To meet the propaganda challenge. F. C. Barghoorn. il N Y Times Mag p 13+ Ja 19 '64
USSR 1965; address, December 10, 1964. A. N. Kosygin. il Vital Speeches 31:213-24 Ja 15 '65
Will they take Aye? W. F. Buckley, jr. Nat R 15:51 Jl 30 '63
With Khrushchev on campaign. il U S News 56:15 Ap 20 '64
With test-ban treaty, has Khrushchev changed his ways? interview. Z. Brzezinski. U S News 55:72-3 S 30 '63
Without portfolio. C. B. Luce. il McCalls 92: 15 Ja '65
See also
Russia—Boundaries
United Nations—Russia

History

Third round. W. W. Rostow. For Affairs 42:1-10 O '63

Africa

Sino-Soviet competition in Africa. R. A. Scalapino. For Affairs 42:640-54 Jl '64

Asia

Moscow, Peking and the Communist parties of Asia. R. A. Scalapino. For Affairs 41: 323-43 Ja '63

RUSSIA—Foreign relations—*Continued*

China (People's Republic)

As Russia-China talks got under way. U S News 55:20 Jl 15 '63
Battle of the giants. J. O'Gara. Commonweal 77:654 Mr 22 '63
Bear-baiting. J. Burnham. Nat R 16:718 Ag 25 '64
Behind the big red rift. il Sr Schol 83:20-2+ S 13 '63
Behind the Russian-Chinese split; interview, ed. by M. Gordey. N. S. Khrushchev. il Look 27:32-3+ F 12 '63
Brinkmanship phase of Russian and Chinese diplomacy. il Newsweek 63:41 Ap 13 '64
China and Russia: on the brink? il U S News 55:8 S 16 '63
China vs. K: point of no return? il Newsweek 61:41-2 Mr 25 '63
China vs. Russia: the new game. il U S News 55:27-30 Jl 29 '63
Chinese come smiling to Moscow; rift widens. il Life 55:28-9 Jl 19 '63
Chinese-Soviet rift: origins and portents. P. E. Mosely. For Affairs 42:11-24 O '63
Cold war of the communisms. E. Crankshaw. il N Y Times Mag p25+ My 26 '63
Communist China and the Soviet bloc; symposium, ed. by D. S. Zagoria. bibliog f il Ann Am Acad 349:1-162 S '63
Communist schism. H. Brandon. Sat R 47:6+ Ag 1 '64
Confrontation; Chinese party delegation in Moscow; What they are fighting about. il Time 82:24-5 Jl 12 '63
Confusions of communism. il Newsweek 64:28 Jl 6 '64
Crisis in Soviet-Chinese relations; address, June 14, 1964. C. B. Luce. Vital Speeches 30:591-4 Jl 15 '64
Dealing with the Soviet Union. W. Lippmann. Newsweek 62:17 Jl 22 '63
Deciphering the code; Sino-Soviet negotiations. Newsweek 64:46+ N 23 '64
Era of many Romes. il Time 84:44-6 N 13 '64
Fine clothes, not highfalutin words. Newsweek 62:28 Jl 1 '63
Four years' news. il Newsweek 62:46 Jl 29 '63
Get out of here: Peking's delegation in Moscow. il Time 82:23-4 Jl 26 '63
Goulash, Mr Mao? revolution, Mr K. il Time 83:31-2 Ap 10 '64
How blows the East wind? J. Burnham. Nat R 16:230 Mr 24 '64
How red China shook the Kremlin. J. Alsop. Read Digest 83:129-30 O '63
How we can profit from the China-Soviet break. V. Zorza. il Look 27:49-50 N 19 '63
Inside report: how real is the Russia-China break? M. L. Harvey. il U S News 56:64-9 Je 15 '64
Khrushchev's dilemma in Cyprus and Vietnam. F. B. Stevens. U S News 57:43 Ag 31 '64
Kremlin tries to play it two ways. il Bsns W p27-8 N 14 '64
Little Georgie's task. Newsweek 63:49-50 Mr 16 '64
Madness of Mao Tse-tung. S. Alsop. il Sat Eve Post 236:12 O 26 '63
Moscow and Peiping; before and after the split; address, September 6, 1963. T. F. Tsiang. Vital Speeches 29:760-3 O 1 '63
Ne kulturny! il Newsweek 62:51+ S 23 '63
Near the breaking point? il Sr Schol 84:14 Ap 24 '64
Neither peace nor war. Newsweek 62:62+ D 2 '63
New Russo-Chinese equation. F. Kuh. Nation 199:294 N 2 '64
Nikita Khrushchev: Maoist. J. Burnham. Nat R 16:644 Jl 28 '64
Of bathers & borders; Sino-Soviet feud. Time 82:47 O 4 '63
Old times or new realities? il Newsweek 64:45 N 16 '64
On the borderline. il Newsweek 64:33-4 S 14 '64
Peculiar partnership. H. C. Hinton. il Commonweal 79:91-4 O 18 '63
Reaching for power. il Bsns W p20-1 Jl 6 '63
Recriminations in Moscow: Sino-Soviet loggerheads. A. Werth. Nation 197:43-6 Jl 27 '63
Red China and the U.S.S.R; transcript of television program State department briefing, broadcast February 11, 1963. Dept State Bul 48:271-83 F 25 '63
Russia and China. Commonweal 78:443-4 Jl 26 '63
Russia-China split: how real? il U S News 54:44-7 Mr 18 '63
Russia, China, the U.S. today. F. B. Stevens.
Russia vs. China: flames grow hotter. il U S News 57:59 N 23 '64
Russian-Chinese struggle over who will bury Newsweek 62:31 Jl 15 '63
us? with editorial comment. M. Frankel. il Sat Eve Post 236:30+. 82 Ap 13 '63; Same abr. with title Bitter feud that splits the Communist world; without editorial comment. Read Digest 83:138-44 Ag '63
Search for lebensraum? struggle between Russia and red China. il Time 84:40-1 S 18 '64
Sino-Soviet conflict in perspective. R. A. Scalapino. bibliog f Ann Am Acad 351:1-14 Ja '64
Sino-Soviet nuclear dialogue: 1963. A. L. Hsieh. bibliog Bul Atomic Sci 21:16-21 Ja '65
Sino-Soviet rift: an old, old story. J. P. Davies, jr. il Reporter 29:32-4+ Ag 15 '63
Sino-Soviet rift widens. il Sr Schol 83:18 O 18 '63
Sino-Soviet tensions; excerpts from Sino-Soviet relations: retrospect and prospect. P. S. H. Tang. bibliog f Cur Hist 45:223-9 O '63
Soviet-Chinese split looks permanent; red record: a forty year feud. Bsns W p24-5 Jl 13 '63
Split between Peiping and Moscow; address, May 6, 1964. T. F. Tsiang. Vital Speeches 30:516-20 Je 15 '64
Split between Russia and China. E. Crankshaw. Atlan 211:60-5 My '63
They are talking. Time 84:37 N 20 '64
Threat and opportunity in the Communist schism. Z. Brzezinski. For Affairs 41:513-25 Ap '63
Toward two red worlds? split in Communist camp. il Bsns W p31 Ap 11 '64
Tsars, mandarins, and commissars: a history of Chinese-Russian relations, by H. Schwartz. Review
Sat R 47:27 Ap 4 '64. P. E. Mosely
Two touchy borders; Sinkiang and Manchuria. New Repub 149:8 O 12 '63
Wait till next year; red China's delegation in Moscow. Time 82:24-5 Jl 19 '63
Warm-up time; China vs. Russia. Newsweek 62:46+ N 4 '63
What about the Sino-Soviet split? J. Monnerot. Nat R 14:447-9 Je 4 '63; Discussion. 14:541 Jl 2 '63
What the Russia-China split can mean; survey of views of experts in world capitals. il U S News 55:44-6 S 23 '63
When a dragon and a bear disagree. P. E. Mosely. Sat R 46:38-9+ N 23 '63
When comrades meet; Sino-Soviet conference. New Repub 149:3-4 Jl 6 '63
Who shall be master? J. Burnham. Nat R 16:688 Ag 11 '64
Widening gulf between Mao and Khrushchev. D. S. Zagoria. il Reporter 28:39-40 Ap 25 '63
Widening Sino-Soviet split. il Newsweek 61:50-2 Mr 18 '63

Cuba

Adopted son in revolt. Newsweek 62:51 S 16 '63
After the Cuban crisis. D. H. Wrong. Commentary 35:28-33 Ja '63
Castro, Khrushchev, and Mao. T. Draper. il Reporter 29:27-31 Ag 15 '63
Courting Comrade Castro: first visit to the Soviet Union. il Newsweek 61:43-4 My 13 '63
Cuba: between promise and decay. R. Eder. il N Y Times Mag p5+ Je 21 '64
Fidel in wonderland. il Time 83:18-19 Ja 24 '64
Further clarification; concerning interviews with Kennedy and Castro. J. Daniel. New Repub 149:6-7 D 21 '63
Kremlin climate: Castro's visit to Moscow. il Newsweek 63:38 Ja 27 '64
Raid 'em and weep. Time 81:19 Mr 29 '63
Soviet policies in Latin America. D. T. Cattell. bibliog f Cur Hist 47:286-91+ N '64
Unofficial envoy: an historic report from two capitals. J. Daniel. New Repub 149:15-20 D 14 '63
When Khrushchev and Castro get together. il U S News 54:37-9 My 13 '63

See also

Russians in Cuba

Egypt

Fatigued finish; Khrushchev's state visit to Egypt. Time 83:29 My 29 '64
Khrushchev's tour: no great triumph. il U S News 56:14 Je 1 '64

RUSSIA—Foreign relations—Egypt—*Continued*
K's African campaign. il Newsweek 63:52 My 18 '64
Postmortem; Khrushchev's tour. J. A. Morris, jr. il Newsweek 63:30+ Je 1 '64
Visit to the Land of the Sphinx; Khrushchev in Egypt. J. A. Morris, jr. il Newsweek 63: 41 My 25 '64

Europe, Eastern

Best laid plans. il Newsweek 64:35 Ag 3 '64
East Europe's second chance. V. E. Mares. bibliog f il Cur Hist 47:272-9+ N '64
How strong is the Soviet bloc? R. F. Staar. bibliog f il Cur Hist 45:209-15 O '63
Is Russia losing East Europe? C. Foltz, jr. il U S News 56:48-54 Ap 20 '64
Khrushchev's hidden weakness; captive nations; with editorial comment. R. M. Nixon. il Sat Eve Post 236:23-9, 88 O 12 '63; Same abr. without editorial comment. Read Digest 84:59-64 Ja '64
Weight of empire. Newsweek 63:37 Mr 9 '64

Europe, Western

Soviet image of western Europe. A. Z. Rubinstein. bibliog f Cur Hist 47:280-5+ N '64

France

Paris loves Moscow? Newsweek 63:41-2 Ap 13 '64

Germany (Democratic Republic)

Khrushchev's impossible man in Berlin. A. J. Olsen. il N Y Times Mag p37+ O 11 '64
Ordeal of coexistence, by W. Brandt. Review
Sat R 46:26-7 My 18 '63. W. H. Chamberlin

Germany (Federal Republic)

More talks with the Russians; American and Soviet leaders of public opinion meet in Leningrad. N. Cousins. Sat R 47:30 S 26; 30-1 O 10 '64
Ordeal of coexistence, by W. Brandt. Review
Sat R 46:26-7 My 18 '63. W. H. Chamberlin
Soviet soft line towards the West. G. F. Hudson. Cur Hist 45:230-4+ O '63

Hungary

Hungary: renaissance after revolt. D. Holden. il Sat Eve Post 237:38+ Ap 25 '64

India

India and the Soviet Union. S. Gupta. bibliog f Cur Hist 44:141-6 Mr '63

Indonesia

Visiting Armenian; Mikoyan. Time 84:38 Jl 3 '64

Iran

Neither protocol nor freedom. il Time 82: 45 N 29 '63

Japan

About face; Mikoyan's visit to Tokyo. Newsweek 63:30 Je 1 '64

Latin America

Soviet policies in Latin America. D. T. Cattell. bibliog f Cur Hist 47:286-91+ N '64

Middle East

Red bankroll; Middle eastern economic aid. il Time 85:30-1 Ja 15 '65

Norway

Reverse response; Khrushchev's visit to Norway. Time 84:36 Jl 10 '64

Poland

Gone hunting. il Newsweek 63:31 Ja 13 '64

Rumania

Carrot and the stick. Newsweek 64:47 Jl 20 '64
Dynamite; Rumanian declaration of independence. Newsweek 63:32 Je 1 '64
Satellite looks West; Rumania's quiet revolution. il Newsweek 64:31-5 Ag 10 '64

Scandinavia

Cool to Khrushchev. New Repub 150:9-10 Ap 4 '64

United States

After test ban: what is next. F. B. Stevens. il U S News 55:58-9 O 7 '63
Back to power politics; nationalism and looser alliances. il Bsns W p27-9 O 19 '63
Changes in Russia: U.S. size-up. U S News 57:53 O 26 '64
Cold war is a war. D. Lawrence. U S News 55:124 N 25 '63
Common action for the control of conflict, by V. P. Rock. Review
U S News il 55:64-6 N 18 '63
Easing of the cold war? U S News 54:8 Je 24 '63
East and and West enter a new phase. E. Crankshaw. il N Y Times Mag p 16+ Ag 30 '64
East-West thaw. il Bsns W p25-30 S 28 '63
Euphoria. D. Lawrence. U S News 55:132 O 7 '63
Good-by Mr Barghoorn, pleasant journey. il Newsweek 62:37-8 N 25 '63
Is a U.S. deal with Russia near? il U S News 55:27-9 Jl 22 '63
Is it to be a truce with Russia? il U S News 56:35-7 My 4 '64
K and LBJ: a time for taking stock. il Newsweek 62:33 D 16 '63
Llewellyn Thompson: JFK's no. 1 Russian expert. L. Bergquist. il Look 27:21-5 F 12 '63
Neither dead nor red; Cuban crisis. Earl of Home. Read Digest 82:69-71 F '63
New hopes in the race for peace. Bsns W p26-7 Ja 25 '64
Next step: playing it by ear. il Newsweek 62:29-30 O 7 '63
Notes on a 1963 visit with Khrushchev. N. Cousins. il Sat R 47:16-21+ N 7 '64
Object lesson for optimists. D. L. Flaherty. America 109:148 Ag 17 '63
On the autobahn; U.S. army convoy blocked at Marienborn checkpoint. il Newsweek 62:44+ N 18 '63
Openings for diplomacy; Cuba: catalyst of peace. L. Dewart. Nation 196:113-15 F 9 '63
Our relations with Russia; address, October 19, 1963. J. F. Kennedy. Vital Speeches 30:34-5 N 1 '63; Excerpts with editorial comment. il U S News 55:126-8 N 11 '63
President and Soviet leaders exchange New Year's messages. L. B. Johnson; N. S. Khrushchev and L. Brezhnev. Dept State Bul 50:121 Ja 27 '64
Russia and China view the United States. A. Dallin. bibliog f Ann Am Acad 349:153-62 S '63
Russia, China, the U.S. today. F. B. Stevens. U S News 57:59 N 23 '64
Snooping; Soviet boats near U.S. shores. Newsweek 61:30+ Mr 25 '63
Soviet-American relations; address, February 28, 1963. R. F. Starr. bibliog Vital Speeches 29:468-73 My 15 '63
Spirit of Moscow: turning tough again. U S News 55:4 N 25 '63
There's good politics in peace offensive; East-West agreements. Bsns W p22-3 Ja 11 '64
Third round. W. W. Rostow. For Affairs 42: 1-10 O '63
Tiger will bite. S. Alsop. il Sat Eve Post 236:18 O 19 '63
Unfinished business. D. Lawrence. U S News 56:100 Ja 27 '64
U.S.S.R. accepts U.S. proposal for direct communication link; statement, April 5, 1963. Dept State Bul 48:600 Ap 22 '63
U.S. and Soviet Union exchange notes on interference with ships; texts of notes, April 22, August 3, 5 and 18, and September 15, 1964. Dept State Bul 51:482-5 O 5 '64
U.S. and U.S.S.R. sign agreement for direct communications link: White House statement, June 20, 1963, with text of agreement. Dept State Bul 49:50-1 Jl 8 '63
U.S. disclaims responsibility for attacks on Soviet ships; note, April 3, 1963. Dept State Bul 48:599 Ap 22 '63
U.S. rejects Soviet charge of firing on trawler; U.S. note of March 14 and Soviet note of March 12, 1963. Dept State Bul 48: 475-6 Ap 1 '63
U.S.-Soviet thaw: a new treaty; provision for exchange of consulates. Newsweek 63:38 Je 8 '64
Unthawing the thaw; U.S. army convoy blocked at autobahn's Marienborn checkpoint. il Time 82:25-6 O 18 '63
Unthinkable detente. Nation 198:449 My 4 '64
Ways to peace. Commonweal 79:119-20 O 25 '63
Weighing the advantages; Soviet-American détente. H. Brandon. Sat R 46:16+ N 2 '63
Western powers reject Soviet charges on NATO nuclear defense; exchange of notes between the United States and the Soviet Union, May 12 and April 8, 1963. Dept State Bul 48:860-6 Je 3 '63
What Khrushchev is thinking; as reported from private conferences in Moscow. il U S News 55:42 D 16 '63

RUSSIA—Foreign relations—United States—*Continued*
What Nikita Khrushchev told U.S. businessmen touring Europe; excerpts from addresses, November 6 and November 7, 1963. N. Khrushchev. U S News 55:62 N 18 '63
Why? Barghoorn case. Nation 197:377 D 7 '63
Why Russia and China now fear U.S. il U S News 57:66-70 N 30 '64

Yugoslavia

Advice from the host; winding up of Khrushchev's state visit to Yugoslavia. il Time 82:29 S 6 '63
Billions in U.S. aid and Tito wants to bury capitalism. A. Kucherov. il U S News 55: 68-9 S 16 '63
Close-up of Khrushchev: less zip, more caution. il U S News 55:22 S 16 '63
Family problems; Khrushchev's visit to Yugoslavia. il Newsweek 62:38 S 2 '63
Horse trading; Tito in Leningrad. Newsweek 63:46 Je 22 '64
Khrushchev and Tito join forces to bury capitalism. il U S News 55:22 S 9 '63
Nikita in Titoland. U S News 55:12 S 2 '63
Tito of Yugoslavia: new role for an old rebel? il Sr Schol 83:12-15+ O 11 '63
Window on the West. il Newsweek 62:40+ S 9 '63

History

Chinese and the Russians; excerpt from Peking and Moscow. K. Mehnert. bibliog f Ann Am Acad 349:1-13 S '63
History of the USSR: from Lenin to Khrushchev, by L. Aragon. Review
Sat R 47:29 Ag 8 '64. H. Schwartz
Kremlin plays Russian roulette; fall of Khrushchev. H. E. Salisbury. il N Y Times Mag p25+ O 25 '64
Man like no other. R. Payne. il N Y Times Mag p79-80+ S 8 '63
On peace and war in the atomic age; address, April 5, 1963. M. S. Pap. Vital Speeches 29:531-5 Je 15 '63
Russia: a tormented history. H. E. Salisbury. il Holiday 34:37-8+ O '63
Survival's favorite son. I. Deutscher. Nation 199:494-6 D 21 '64
Was Lenin necessary? L. Schapiro. Commentary 38:57-60 D '64
See also
Ivan IV, the Terrible, czar of Russia
Russo-Japanese war, 1904-1905

Bibliography

Articles and other books received; Soviet Union, comp. by R. V. Allen. See issues of American historical review

Historiography

Consequences of the Stalin personality cult. Sch & Soc 91:225-6 My 4 '63
How to talk about communism; when it sets dogma above fact. H. Overstreet and B. W. Overstreet. il PTA Mag 57:16-18 My '63

Textbooks

Soviet second thoughts on tsarist colonialism. L. R. Tillett. bibliog f For Affairs 42: 309-19 Ja '64

Revolution, 1917-1921

People and life. 1891-1921, by I. Ehrenburg. Review
Commentary 35:179-82+ F '63. T. Frankel
Soviet revolution, 1917-1939, by R. R. Abramovich. Review
Commentary 35:84-6 Ja '63. R. V. Daniels

History, Naval

Coal for the fleet that had to die. L. J. R. Cecil. bibliog f Am Hist R 69:990-1005 Jl '64

Industries

Better things for better living through chemistry? Time 82:17-18 D 20 '63
Big Soviet project gets the ax; hydroelectric-aluminum complex at Bratsk. il Bsns W p62+ Ja 25 '64
Down at Kursk station; economic crimes. Time 83:33-4 Mr 6 '64
Heavy industry thriving but due for a face-lift. il Life 55:60 S 13 '63
Khrushchev hits Soviet industry planning. O. K. Antonov; N. S. Khrushchev. Aviation W 78:105+ Ja 21 '63
Proof of the Soviet plum pudding; fertilizer and chemical industry. Bsns W p 100 D 21 '63
Russia catch up? not for a long time. E. Crankshaw. il N Y Times Mag p 19+ Mr 1 '64
Russians drop a lap behind; lagging growth rate. il Bsns W p30-1 Ja 18 '64
Russia's new bosses reshape its industry. il Bsns W p 104+ O 31 '64
Sewing machines & spontaneity. il Time 85:23 Ja 8 '65
Soviet economic developments; Khrushchev and after. O. Gass. bibliog f il Commentary 37:54-68 F '64; Reply with rejoinder. P. Goodman. 38:12-15 Jl '64
Soviet Union: more chemicals. New Repub 149:12 D 28 '63
U.S.S.R. resources for heavy industry. C. D. Harris. bibliog il Focus 13:1-6 Mr '63
What bothers the boss in a Soviet factory. il Bsns W p45-6 Jl 13 '63
Why spaceships work, tractors don't; Russian manufacturers. U S News 54:46-7 My 6 '63
See also
Chemical industries—Russia

Intellectual life

After the coffee-break. G. Struve. New Repub 148:15-17 F 2 '63; Reply. Y. Zhukov. 148:6 Ap 27 '63
Case against Brodsky. Time 84:43 Jl 3 '64
Conscience of the thaw. P. Viereck. Sat R 47:38-9 My 16 '64
Cult of optimism: political and ideological problems of recent Soviet literature, by W. N. Vickery. Review
Sat R 46:23 Ag 10 '63. M. J. Ruggles
Cultural notes. H. Brandon. Sat R 47:12+ Je 20 '64
Dilemma of the Soviet intellectual. L. S. Feuer. il N Y Times Mag p 13+ Ag 18 '63
Echoes of Stalinism. A. Werth. Nation 196: 308-9 Ap 13 '63
From the second city. Time 81:32 Mr 29 '63
Lesson in dialectics; reimposition of strict controls. New Repub 148:7 Ap 6 '63
Letter from Paris. A. Werth. Nation 196: 104-6 F 2 '63
Marshaling the forces. il Newsweek 61:36 Ap 8 '63
Mr K's turn toward Stalinism. E. Griffiths. il Sat Eve Post 236:70-3 Je 1 '63
New men of the Soviet sixties. P. Johnson. il Reporter 28:16-21 My 9 '63
New Soviet man? M. Harrington. Commonweal 78:39-42 Ap 5 '63
Of firs, flies & fears; Khrushchev's blast against recent artistic expression. il Time 81:26 Mr 22 '63
Poem's progress. il Newsweek 62:39-40 S 2 '63
Poetry and policy. il Newsweek 61:37 Mr 4 '63
Report from Russia; new freedom and its limits. P. Ben. New Repub 150:15-17 Je 27 '64
Russia: poetry, politics, and the unpredictable. P. Johnson. il Reporter 29:44-8 N 21 '63
Screws are tightened again. A. Brumberg. il Reporter 28:21-4+ My 9 '63
Shades of Stalin; Khrushchev's warning to artists and intellectuals. il Newsweek 61: 42 Mr 25 '63
Specter haunts the Kremlin. E. Lyons. Read Digest 83:55-61 S '63
Trial of a poet. Newsweek 64:34+ S 14 '64
Weight of silence. Newsweek 62:26-7 D 23 '63
Word to the wise: clues to freedom permitted under Brezhnev and Kosygin. Newsweek 64:46 N 16 '64
Writer versus bureaucrat in the Soviet Union. F. D. Reeve. Atlan 213:69-74 Ja '64

Maps

All the Russias. Holiday 34:56-7 O '63
Map of Russia (cont) Sr Schol 83:25 O 4 '63; 85:29 O 7 '64

Navy

New four ocean challenge; address, September 18, 1963. J. S. McCain, jr. Vital Speeches 30:57-61 N 1 '63
See also
Russia—History, Naval

Submarine service

Red flag over the seven seas. H. W. Baldwin. Atlan 214:37-43 S '64
Sighted sub, surfaced same; U.S. destroyer Cecil & Soviet submarine incident during the Cuban crisis. il Time 81:18 Je 28 '63
Soviet submarine threat. H. W. Baldwin. il Reporter 31:39-42 S 24 '64

Politics and government

After Khrushchev what? with report by K. Lachmann. il U S News 57:39-45 O 26 '64
B after K? il Newsweek 62:26 D 23 '63

RUSSIA—Politics and government—*Continued*
Change and stability in the Soviet Union. M. T. Florinsky. Cur Hist 45:205-8+ O '63
Changes in Russia: U.S. size-up. U S News 57:53 O 26 '64
Communists in gray flannel suits. M. Frankel. New Repub 151:7-8 O 31 '64
Fall of Nikita K; with comment on the world's news fronts. il Sr Schol 85:17-18+, 24 O 28 '64
Khrushchev at seventy: the hidden dangers of success. il Newsweek 63:48-9 Ap 27 '64
Khrushchev backlash. il Newsweek 64:48+ N 2 '64
Khrushchev the terrible. Nation 199:289-90 N 2 '64
Khrushchev's sea of troubles. S. Alsop. il Sat Eve Post 237:18 Ja 25 '64
Kremlin chiefs pledge business as usual. il Bsns W p30-3 O 24 '64
Kremlin votes no confidence. A. Werth. Nation 199:291-5 N 2 '64
Marshaling the forces. il Newsweek 61:36 Ap 8 '63
Mixture as before. il Newsweek 64:40 D 21 '64
New look at Russia from the inside: interview. I. D. Levine. U S News 55:92-3 Ag 26 '63
New men at the top in the Kremlin. il U S News 57:21 O 26 '64
Nikita's fortunes. Newsweek 61:48-50 Ap 15 '63
Nikita's monologue. Newsweek 62:42+ N 18 '63
Notes on the Khrushchev ouster. J. Burnham. Nat R 16:952 N 3 '64
Policy debate in Moscow. R. C. Tucker. New Repub 150:7-8 My 16 '64
Political power: USA/USSR, by Z. Brzezinski and S. P. Huntington. Review
Commonweal 81:46-8 O 2 '64. W. V. O'Brien
New Repub 150:15-16+ My 23 '64. A. Buchan
Revolt in the Kremlin. il Time 84:28-31 O 23 '64
Room at the top. il Newsweek 63:52 F 17 '64
Russia, China and England; our basic policy remains unchanged; address, October 18, 1964. L. B. Johnson. Vital Speeches 31:34-6 N 1 '64; Same with title President reports on change in Soviet leadership, Chinese nuclear test, and new British government. Dept State Bul 51:610-14 N 2 '64
Russia: Khrushchev and after. O. Gass. bibliog f Commentary 36:353-63 N '63
Russian problems and U.S. politics. I. Deutscher. Nation 199:43-5 Ag 10 '64
Shuffle in the Kremlin. il Newsweek 64:37 Jl 27 '64
Soviet freedom: a balance sheet. J. R. Azrael. New Repub 148:18-20 Mr 2 '63
Successor confirmed; Khrushchev's heir apparent. Time 84:30 Jl 24 '64
What Khrushchev is thinking; as reported from private conferences in Moscow. il U S News 55:42 D 16 '63
What's bothering Khrushchev: crises at home and abroad. il U S News 54:75-6 Ap 1 '63
Who would succeed Mr K? F. B. Stevens. il U S News 56:53 Ap 27 '64
Will Khrushchev be forced out? U S News 54:43-4 My 6 '63
See also
Communism—Russia
Communist party (Russia)

Population

Soviet Union; head count. Newsweek 61:51 Je 24 '63

Race problems

Color bar. Newsweek 61:51-2 Je 17 '63

Religious institutions and affairs

Devil and Mr Nasser; Soviet Muslims. America 110:784 Je 6 '64
Freedom of atheism. America 110:355 Mr 21 '64
Fresh persecution in USSR. America 110:212 F 15 '64
From Russia, without love; new Institute of scientific atheism. Time 83:60 Mr 13 '64
New dimension in scientific atheism. R. H. Marshall, jr. il Cath World 199:238-44 Jl '64
Religion in Russia. P. Ben. New Repub 151: 15-16 D 26 '64
Religion in Russia today: a first-hand report. C. Foltz, jr. il U S News 56:56-7 F 10 '64
Religion in the Soviet Union. G. Bailey. il Reporter 31:25-9 Jl 16 '64
Religion in the Soviet Union. J. Panowski. Nat R 16:865-7 O 6 '64
Return from Russia. W. Ciszek. America 110: 408-11 Mr 28 '64
Soviet atheist's Sputnik; Atheist's companion. D. A. Lowrie. Christian Cent 80:177-9 F 6 '63
What sort of détente? Commonweal 79:211-12 N 15 '63
See also
Moscow—Religious institutions and affairs
Orthodox Eastern church, Russian

Social conditions

Behind the curtains, bamboo and iron. J. Massey-Stewart. il N Y Times Mag p 12+ Je 16 '63
Consumer in the Soviet Union and the United States; summary of paper presented at Conference on the economics of Soviet industrialization, May 1961. J. G. Chapman. il Mo Labor R 86:11-13 Ja '63
Quality of life behind the Soviet statistics. H. A. Grunwald. il Fortune 69:146-7+ Mr '64
Return from Russia. W. Ciszek. America 110: 408-11 Mr 28 '64
Russia catch up? not for a long time. E. Crankshaw. il N Y Times Mag p 19+ Mr 1 '64
Russians get more pie. il Bsns W p50-2+ Jl 20 '63
See also
Communism—Russia
Jews in Russia
Marriage law—Russia
Youth—Russia

Social life and customs

Bourgeois manners for the Bolshevik masses; excerpts from Continuing our discussion about the cultured man; tr. by L. Gottlieb. A. Perventzev. il Horizon 6:106-11 Wint '64
Figures in the apparatus. il Holiday 34:70-3 O '63
Meet the Lozovans of Moscow. il Life 55: 88B-99 S 13 '63
Salad days. Newsweek 63:41-2 Ap 6 '64
Tough time for puritans behind the iron curtain. C. Grenier. il N Y Times Mag p 14-15+ My 24 '64
What Russian girls are like. G. Frost. il N Y Times Mag p 16-17+ Ja 24 '65

Territorial expansion

How to talk about communism; when colonialism and anticolonialism are the subject. H. Overstreet and B. W. Overstreet. PTA Mag 57:8-10 Ap '63

Treaties

Sign of the times; Russia and East Germany sign treaty of friendship, mutual assistance, and cooperation. il Newsweek 63:44+ Je 22 '64
Sop for Walter; friendship pact between East Germany and the Soviet Union. Time 83:26 Je 19 '64
Soviet-East German friendship treaty; text. Cur Hist 47:363-4+ D '64
See also
Russo-German treaty, 1905

RUSSIA and Africa
Khrushchev in Africa, why he's making the trip. U S News 56:20 My 18 '64
Soviet Union and African countries; address, April 10, 1964; with questions and answers. N. Fedorenko. Ann Am Acad 354:1-8 Jl '64

RUSSIA and Europe
Russia and Europe. Z. Brzezinski. For Affairs 42:428-44 Ap '64
Russia's Europe; shifting satellites. A. Werth. il Nation 198:644-6 Je 29 '64

RUSSIA and the United States
Conflicts & affinities. R. V. Daniels. Commentary 38:86-8 S '64
Demise of NATO. R. Steel. Commentary 35: 397-402 My '63
Postwar disarmament negotiations. L. Jensen. Cur Hist 46:336-40+ Je '64
President renews hope for peace; concerning commencement address at American university. Christian Cent 80:822 Je 26 '63
Russian ships call at Boston; Soviet oceanographic vessels. il Bsns W p 120+ Ap 11 '64

RUSSIA in literature
Soviet political satire. G. Struve. New Repub 149:19-22 S 28 '63

RUSSIAN art. See Art, Russian
RUSSIAN art objects. See Art objects, Russian
RUSSIAN artists. See Artists, Russian
RUSSIAN athletes. See Athletes

RUSSIAN authors. See Authors, Russian
RUSSIAN church. See Orthodox Eastern church, Russian
RUSSIAN composers. See Composers, Russian
RUSSIAN cookery. See Cookery, Russian
RUSSIAN dancers. See Dancers
RUSSIAN drama
See also
Theater—Russia
RUSSIAN economic assistance. See Economic assistance, Russian
RUSSIAN fiction
Going to town and other stories, by Y. Kazakov, tr. by G. Azrael. Review
Sat R 47:39 F 1 '64. P. Viereck
It's a gloomy world, gentlemen; excerpts from introduction to Six Russian short novels. R. Jarrell. Atlan 211:76-82 Ap '63
RUSSIAN helicopters. See Helicopters
RUSSIAN historians. See Historians, Russian
RUSSIAN humor. See Humor, Russian
RUSSIAN inventors. See Inventors
RUSSIAN Jews. See Jews in Russia
RUSSIAN language

Alphabet

Transliteration of modern Russian; roles of American standards association sectional committee Z39 and British standards institution. J. Orne. il Library J 88:4157-60 N 1 '63

Study and teaching

Russian in two hours. L. A. Harlow. il Sci Digest 54:45-8 N '63
Surveying Russian technical publications: a brief course. J. G. Tolpin. Science 146:1143-4 N 27 '64
RUSSIAN literature
After the coffee-break. G. Struve. New Repub 148:15-17 F 2 '63; Reply. Y. Zhukov. 148:6 Ap 27 '63
Cult of optimism: political and ideological problems of recent Soviet literature, by W. N. Vickery. Review
Sat R 46:23 Ag 10 '63. M. J. Ruggles
Dissonant voices in Soviet literature, ed. by P. Blake and M. Hayward. Review
Reporter 28:49-50+ F 28 '63. R. W. Mathewson, jr
Gardens of today and yesterday. O. A. Carlisle. Nation 198:586-8 Je 8 '64
History of Soviet literature, by V. Alexandrova, tr. by M. Ginsburg. Review
Sat R 46:22 Ag 10 '63. L. N. Shapiro
Party of one. A. Kazin. bibliog il Holiday 34:16+ O '63
Poem's progress. il Newsweek 62:39-40 S 2 '63
Politics, poetry, and prose. M. Friedberg. Sat R 47:40+ My 16 '64
Predicaments of Soviet writing. I. Howe. New Repub 148:19-21 My 11; 19-22 My 18 '63
Smiling sigh; concerning Pushkin's Eugene Onegin. J. W. Stedman. Opera N 28:24-5 F 29 '64
Voices in the snow: encounters with Russian writers, by O. A. Carlisle. Review
Sat R 46:29-30 F 9 '63. H. E. Salisbury
RUSSIAN military assistance. See Military assistance, Russian
RUSSIAN opera. See Opera, Russian
RUSSIAN Orthodox church. See Orthodox Eastern church, Russian
RUSSIAN painting. See Painting, Russian
RUSSIAN peasants. See Peasantry—Russia
RUSSIAN poetry
Case against Brodsky. Time 84:43 Jl 3 '64

Translations into English

Babi Yar; tr. by M. Hayward. E. Evtushenko. Life 54:32-3 Ap 19 '63
By the Aral Sea; If you but knew; tr. by J. Weir. T. G. Shevchenko. UNESCO Courier 17:15-16 Je '64
Heirs of Stalin; tr. by G. Reavey. Y. Yevtushenko. Sat Eve Post 236:60 Ag 10 '63
Irreconcilable; tr. by G. Reavey. E. Evtushenko. Life 54:33 Ap 19 '63
Moscow; Century of the wolf; Leningrad; Fragments; Verses to the unknown soldier; tr. by R. Lowell. O. Mandelstam. Atlan 211:64-8 Je '63
Poems; tr. by R. Lowell. A. Akhmatova. Atlan 214:60-5 O '64
Prologue; tr. by G. Reavey. Y. Yevtushenko. Sat Eve Post 236:62 Ag 10 '63
RUSSIAN postage stamps. See Postage stamps
RUSSIAN propaganda. See Propaganda, Russian
RUSSIAN refugees. See Refugees, Russian
RUSSIAN RIVER
Shad come early to the Russian River. il Sunset 132:68+ Ap '64
RUSSIAN space probes. See Space probes, Russian
RUSSIAN spies. See Spies
RUSSIAN statesmen. See Statesmen
RUSSIAN strategy. See Strategy
RUSSIAN students
Sasha's creed: Russia right or wrong. G. Feifer. il N Y Times Mag p9+ Ap 28 '63
Soviet fathers and sons. G. Feifer. New Repub 148:11-13 Je 1 '63
RUSSIAN studies. See Area studies
RUSSIAN theater. See Theater—Russia
RUSSIAN track team. See Track athletics
RUSSIAN trawlers. See Fishing boats
RUSSIAN visitors in Australia. See Foreign visitors in Australia
RUSSIAN visitors in the United States. See Foreign visitors in the United States
RUSSIAN weddings. See Marriage customs and rites
RUSSIAN youth. See Youth—Russia
RUSSIANS
Chinese and the Russians; excerpt from Peking and Moscow. K. Mehnert. bibliog f Ann Am Acad 349:1-13 S '63
Drive with devils behind you; Russians at Monte Carlo rally. C. N. Barnard. il Sat Eve Post 237:64-5 Mr 7 '64
How intourist took me in. K. Snow. Nat R 16:355-7 My 5 '64
Is communism a menace? Russell's answer. B. Russell. il N Y Times Mag p35+ Ap 7 '63; Discussion. p4+ Ap 21 '63
New Soviet man? M. Harrington. Commonweal 78:39-42 Ap 5 '63
Rare new view at the top; Russian leaders. pors Life 55:72-9 S 13 '63
Russia; symposium, with photographs by Burt Glinn. bibliog Holiday 34:16+ O '63
Some eminent heroes. il Holiday 34:86-93 O '63
Visit to a Russian village. D. Whiteside. il N Y Times Mag p26-7+ D 8 '63
When a housewife goes shopping in Russia. C. Foltz, jr. il U S News 56:88-9 Ja 27 '64
Why we must put holes in the iron curtain. Life 55:4B S 13 '63
See also
Humor, Russian
RUSSIANS in Cuba
Comrade Blimp; Morozov letter. Newsweek 62:50 D 16 '63
RUSSIANS in the United States
Little red schoolhouse in Washington, D.C. C. Sadler. il McCalls 91:54+ S '64
Voyage pittoresque aux Etats-unis de l'Amérique par Paul Svignine; an appreciation. M. B. Davidson. Am Heritage 15:49-51+ F '64
When the Russians try to invade suburbia. A. Chamberlin. il Sat Eve Post 236:28-9 Ag 24 '63
RUSSIN, Robert I.
University bronze foundry. Am Artist 27:46-51+ D '63
RUSSO, Bob
Riverside 400. Hot Rod 16:104 O '63
RUSSO, Genco
Insider talks about the Mafia. R. Toporoff. il pors Look 27:110+ O 22 '63
RUSSO-German treaty, 1905
Coal for the fleet that had to die; Treaty of Bjoerko. L. J. R. Cecil. bibliog f Am Hist R 69:990-1005 Jl '64
RUSSO-Japanese war, 1904-1905
Coal for the fleet that had to die. L. J. R. Cecil. bibliog f Am Hist R 69:990-1005 Jl '64
RUSSWURM, John B.
Founders of the Negro press. L. Bennett, jr. il por Ebony 19:96-8+ Jl '64
RUST, James H. jr, and others
Plague toxin: its effect in vitro and in vivo. bibliog Science 142:408-9 O 18 '63
RUST, Robert
What changes in beef retailing mean to you. Suc Farm 62:93 F '64
RUST. See Corrosion and anticorrosives
RUSTIN, Bayard
Leftward march. Nat R 16:11-13 Ja 14 '64
Lone wolf of civil rights. M. Meyer. il pors Sat Eve Post 237:76-8 Jl 11 '64
Marchers' master plan; with editorial comment. W. R. Young and W. Lambert. il pors Life 55:4, 63-4+ Ag 23 '63
RUSTOW, Dankwart A.
Turkey's second try at democracy. Yale R 52:518-38 Je '63

RUSTS (botany)
Malate dehydrogenases in the rusted bean leaf. R. C. Staples and M. A. Stahmann. bibliog il Science 140:1320-1 Je 21 '63
Stomatal penetration of wheat seedlings by stem and leaf rust: effect of light and carbon dioxide. D. Yirgou and R. M. Caldwell. bibliog il Science 141:272-3 Jl 19 '63

RUTABAGAS
See also
Cookery—Vegetables

RUTENBERG, A. C.
Xenon fluorides; fluorine-19 nuclear magnetic resonance spectra. bibliog Science 140:993-4 My 31 '63

RUTGERS university, New Brunswick, N.J.

Graduate school of library service

Day at library school. J. N. Berry, 3d. il Library J 90:72-5 Ja 1 '65
Need and opportunity; concerning symposium by alumni association. E. Moon. Library J 89:1922 My 1 '64
Rutgers announces speakers for documentation seminars. Library J 88:3187 S 15 '63
Rutgers library school reports on its own documentation research. Library J 88:1966 My 15 '63
Rutgers plans series of seminars on systems for organizing information. Library J 88: 1642+ Ap 15 '63
Second Rutgers seminar presents SYNTOL discussion. Library J 89:214 Ja 15 '64
UDC dissected and discussed at first of Rutgers' seminars: Systems for the organization of information report. T. C. Hines. Library J 88:4592-4 D 1 '63

Libraries

Increase in library budget urged by Rutgers president. Library J 90:217 Ja 15 '65

RUTGERS university press
Rutgers university press aids foreign libraries. Library J 88:749 F 15 '63

RUTH Garver Gagliardo school library scholarship. See Library science—Scholarships and fellowships

RUTHERFOORD, Jim
Dynamite on Doe Creek. Field & S 69:84-6+ Ja '65
Rocks of the Roanoke River. Field & S 69:52-5+ My '64

RUTHERFORD, Margaret Taylor
Mrs John Bull, ltd. por Time 81:72 My 24 '63
Old girl still kicks up. il pors Life 55:55-6+ O 4 '63
Princess Margaret. por Newsweek 64:90A S 14 '64

RUTKOWSKI, Edwin H.
Federal aid for higher education. Commonweal 79:40-3 O 4 '63

RUTLEDGE, Aaron L.
Be yourself first; ed. by L. Lane. Farm J 87:73+ O '63

RUTLEDGE, Archibald
Beyond your valleys; poem. McCalls 91:187 My '64
Once to his love; poem. McCalls 91:172 Mr '64
Royal guest; poem. McCalls 91:155 Je '64
Source; poem. McCalls 90:161 Ap '63
Timing; poem. McCalls 91:190 Ap '64

RUTLEDGE, Bob
Comics are collectible. Hobbies 68:120-1 Je '63

RUTMAN, Mark
Washington's Christmastime crossing. Travel 120:49-50 D '63

RUTSALA, Vern
Fat man; poem. Nation 197:286 N 2 '63

RUTSTEIN, David D.
Why do we let these babies die? ed. by J. D. Ratcliff. Read Digest 85:56-60 Ag '64

RUZDAK, Vladimir
Soldier of fortune; interview. ed. by A. M. Lingg. por Opera N 28:30 Ja 4 '64

RUZICKA, Rudolph
Rudolph Ruzicka at eighty: an appreciation. P. A. Bennett. il por Pub W 184:92-5 Ag 5 '63

RWANDA
African slaughter. Commonweal 79:616 F 21 '64
Atlantic report; tribal groups. Atlan 213:26+ Je '64
Bodies in the lake. Time 83:21 Ja 24 '64
Chou En-lai and the Watusi. C. Sterling. il Reporter 30:22-4 Mr 12 '64; Reply. G. Nyangoma. 30:8 Ap 9 '64
Rwanda and Burundi. R. Y. Gildea, jr. and A. Taylor. bibliog il Focus 13:1-6 F '63

Native races

Africa's dilemma. V. S. Kearney. America 110:274 F 29 '64
Kill thy neighbor; Watusis murdered by Bahutu tribesmen. J. P. Nugent. il Newsweek 63:51 F 24 '64
Rise and fall of the Watusi; slaughter of Tutsi by Bahutu. E. Huxley. il N Y Times Mag p 10+ F 23 '64
Where black slaughters black: death of the Watusi; revolt of Bahutu. A. J. Meyers. il U S News 56:50-1 F 24 '64

RYAN, Bill
Lady of a vanished era. Yachting 115:186 Mr '64

RYAN, Cornelius
How two book-beset writers created a tandem library. il House & Gard 125:40-1 Ap '64

RYAN, E. Barry
Here the sport is going sour; ed. by W. Tower. por Sports Illus 20:34-8 Je 8 '64

RYAN, E. Nora, and McNeil, D. R.
Much ado about money. Parents Mag 39:44-5+ My '64

RYAN, Jack. See Miller, O. J. jt. auth.

RYAN, John A.
John A. Ryan: pioneer of Catholic social thought. J. Cogley. Commonweal 78:24-5 Mr 29 '63

RYAN, John Dale
Air-command change: Ryan succeeds Power as chief. por U S News 57:19 D 7 '64
New big gun. il pors Time 84:23 D 4 '64

RYAN, John L.
Planning Holy Cross for effective hospital care. Arch Rec 133:184-9 Mr '63

RYAN, Kathy
How two book-beset writers created a tandem library. il por House & Gard 125:40-1 Ap '64

RYAN, Kenneth J. and others
Estrogen-induced 16-hydroxysteroid dehydrogenase activity in rat kidney. bibliog Science 142:243-4 O 11 '63

RYAN, Leo Thomas, jr
Art in the sun. D. Carlson. il Sch Arts 63: 5-9 F '64

RYAN, M. P.
North to Antigua. Motor B 114:42-5 S '64

RYAN, Mary Perkins
Catholic asks: Are parochial schools the answer? excerpt from Are parochial schools the answer? U S News 56:75-6 Ap 13 '64
Modest proposal of Mary Perkins Ryan. J. A. O'Connor. por Cath World 199:216-23 Jl '64

RYAN, Pat
Harness racing. Sports Illus 19:70-2 O 14 '63; 21:52+ Ag 3; 58-9 Ag 31; 54+ S 14; 100-2 O 5 '64

RYAN, Ray
Two birds bet a million on a club in the bush. R. Coughlan. il por Sports Illus 18: 84-8+ My 20 '63

RYAN, Stephen P.
Play of the month. Cath World 197:79-80 Ap '63

RYAN, Wayne L. and Carver, M. L.
Inhibition of antibody synthesis by L-phenylalanine. bibliog Science 143:479-80 Ja 31 '64
—and Wells, I. C.
Homocitrulline and homoarginine synthesis from lysine. bibliog Science 144:1122+ My 29 '64

RYAN, William F.
Excerpt from address, April 11, 1963. Cong Digest 43:24+ Ja '64
Excerpt from debate, April 7, 1964. Cong Digest 43:184+ Je '64
Excerpt from remarks, August 19, 1964. Cong Digest 44:29+ Ja '65

RYAN, William Michael
Fifty years in the monkey house. L. Alexander. il McCalls 91:110-11+ F '64

RYBAK, Rose Kacherian
Election day in Spooksville; drama. Plays 24:29-39 O '64
Rufus Robin's day in court; drama. Plays 22:74-8, 82 Ap '63

RYBIN, Aleksandr Pavlovich
No censorship court battles in USSR! manuscripts don't get that far; summary of news conference. Library J 88:2218-19 Je 1 '63

RYCHETNIK, Joe
Should he shoot the Magnum? pors Outdoor Life 133:38-41+ F '64

RYDBECK, O. E. H.
Plasmas: wave interaction and dynamic nonlinear phenomena. Science 141:181-2+ Jl 12 '63

RYDELL, Bobby
Bobby Rydell: sing a song of show business. E. Miller. por Seventeen 22:158-9+ Ap '63

RYDEN, Arthur H.
What good does school counseling do? PTA Mag 58:28-30 bibliog(p37) O '63
RYDER, Meyer S.
Labor relations aspects of plant relocation. Mo Labor R 86:415-17 Ap '63
RYHINER, Peter
Passion for rhinoceros. L. H. Lapham. il por Sat Eve Post 237:66-8 F 1 '64
RYNEARSON, Edward R.
Let the hopelessly ill die? U S News 55:18 Jl 1 '63
RYNNE, Xavier, pseud.
Letter from Vatican City (cont) New Yorker 39:120+ My 11; 41-2+ Je 15; 74+ Jl 20; 179-86+ S 28; 123-4+ O 26; 144+ N 30 '63; 88+ Ja 18; 40:166+ S 19 '64; 90-103 Ja 9 '65
Magnum mysterium. Newsweek 62:77 Ag 12 '63
Open letter to the New Yorker. R. M. Brown. Christian Cent 80:956-7 Jl 31 '63; Reply. D. E. Faust. 80:1142-3 S 18 '63
RYOANJI, Brooklyn botanic garden. See Brooklyn botanic garden
RYRIE, Colin
Two silver, three bronze. Yachting 116:28-30+ D '64
RYSANEK, Leonie
Senta reborn; interview, ed. by G. Fitzgerald. por Opera N 27:15 F 2 '63
RYSKIND, Morrie
Dolph Menjou. Nat R 15:440 N 19 '63
Report on California. Nat R 16:968 N 3 '64

about

On the beach with Morrie Ryskind. E. McDowell. il Nat R 14:318-19 Ap 23 '63
RYUKYU ISLANDS
See also
Economic assistance in the Ryukyu Islands
RYUN, Jim
Kansas boy with a man-size task. T. O'Leary. il por Sports Illus 21:46-50+ S 14 '64
On the track. por Newsweek 63:64 Je 15 '64
RZEWSKI, Frederic
Is it music? il por Newsweek 62:53 S 2 '63

S

SAC. See United States—Air force—Strategic air command
SAFE (satellites for emergencies) See Artificial satellites
SAGE. See Semi-automatic ground environment system
SAO. See Secret army organization (Organisation de l'armée secréte)
SAS. See Scandinavian airlines system
SATAF. See United States—Air force—Site activation task force
SATAR (satellite for aerospace research) See Artificial satellites—Use in research
SBA. See United States—Small business administration
SBIC. See Small business investment companies
SCAPE suit. See Astronauts—Clothing
SCAR (International scientific committee of Antarctic research) See International union of geodesy and geophysics
SCAT (speed control of attitude and thrust) See Aeronautic instruments
S. C. Johnson and son. See Johnson, S. C, and son
SCIS. See Science curriculum improvement study
SCLC. See Southern Christian leadership conference
SCOR. See International council of scientific unions—Scientific committee on oceanic research
SCS. See United States—Soil conservation service
SCSD. See School construction systems development
SEATO. See Southeast Asia treaty organization
SEC. See United States—Securities and exchange commission
SEC-vidicon. See Television cameras
SECO (sequential decoding) See Calculating machines
SICA. See Italian society of agricultural colonization
SIM. See Student interracial ministry (organization)
SINA. See Society for indecency to naked animals
SIU. See Seafarers' international union of North America
SJVIS. See Fresno County, Calif, free library
SKF industries, incorporated
Tougher work rules save 600 jobs. Bsns W p 102 F 29 '64
SLA. See Special libraries association
SLR cameras. See Cameras
S-meters. See Electric meters
S-money. See Money—United States
SMPTE. See Society of motion picture and television engineers
SNAP (secondary nuclear auxiliary power) See Space vehicles—Atomic power plants
SNAP-50. See Space vehicles—Atomic power plants
SNAP 9-A. See Space vehicles—Atomic power plants
SNCC. See Student non-violent coordinating committee
SOM. See Skidmore, Owings and Merrill, architects and engineers
SPAR (seagoing platform • for acoustics research) See Ships, Research
SPARSA (sferic pulse azimuth range spectrum analyzer) See Radar meteorology
SPD (Social democratic party) See Political parties—Germany (Federal Republic)
SPIE. See Society of photo-optic instrumentation engineers
SPUR (space power unit reactor) See Space vehicles—Atomic power plants
SRAM (short-range attack missile) See Guided missiles—Launching from airplanes
SRC (Survey research center) See Michigan. University, Ann Arbor
S-66 (satellite) See Artificial satellites—Use in research
S. S. Kresge company. See Kresge, S. S, company
SSRS. See Society for social responsibility in science
STL. See Space technology laboratories, incorporated
STOL. See Airplanes, Short take-off and landing
STOL airplanes. See Airplanes, Short take-off and landing
SUB. See Supplemental unemployment benefits
SUNY (State university of New York) See New York state university
SV 40 (simian virus) See Cancer viruses
SWLA. See Southwestern library association
SAAL, Hubert
Yes, Virginia, there is a Miami. Sat R 47:76-9+ O 10 '64
SAAL, Rollene W.
Pick of the paperbacks. See issues of Saturday review
SAALBURG, Leslie
Leslie Saalburg, illustrator of mode. F. Whitaker. il por Am Artist 27:20-5+ F '63
SAARINEN, Aline B.
Explosion of pop art. Vogue 141:86-7+ Ap 15 '63
SAARINEN, Eero
Dulles international airport. Arch Rec 134:101-10 Jl '63

about

As hard as one can. R. Lynes. Harper 226:30-1 Mr '63
Designer for the corporate image. E. Kaufmann, jr. il Sat R 46:38 F 2 '63
Dream dorm or nightmare? L. Baron. il Mlle 60:109+ Ja '65
Father and son. W. Von Eckardt. New Repub 150:32-4 F 15 '64
Plowmen's palace; new headquarters of Deere and company. il Time 84:64-5 Ag 7 '64
Saarinen's dark tower: the CBS building and how it grew. E. Larrabee. il Harper 229:55-61 D '64
SAARINEN, Eero, and associates (firm)
New Saarinen office. W. McQuade. il Arch Forum 118:113-19 Ap '63
SAARINEN, Eliel
Father and son. W. Von Eckardt. New Repub 150:32-4 F 15 '64
SAASKI, Elric W.
Amateur scientist. Sci Am 211:137-8+ D '64
SAATJIAN, Boghos N.
Updated transistor ignition system. Electr World 71:51+ My '64
SAAVEDRA, Juan de la Cruz. See Cruz Saavedra, J. de la
SABAH. See North Borneo

SABARTÈS, Jaime
Palace for Picasso. E. V. Ronan. il por Americas 16:34-7 Jl '64
SABBATH
See also
Sunday legislation
SABBATICAL leave. See Leave of absence
SABENA (airline) See Airlines—Belgium
SABER saws. See Saws
SABIN, Albert Bruce
Breaking the impasse. Bul Atomic Sci 19:36 O '63
Sabin to do cancer study. Sci N L 83:274 My 4 '63
SABIN, Robert
Adele Marcus: the challenge of teaching. Mus Am 83:53 F '63
Arabella. Am Rec G 30:1084-7 Ag '64
Ariadne auf Naxos; June 11, 1944, Vienna festival performance. Am Rec G 30:188-91 N '63
Bach by Gould: incomparably the most fascinating. Am Rec G 31:211-12 N '64
Bright victory. Dance Mag 38:38-40 Ap '64
Daphne. Am Rec G 30:658-9 Ap '64
Final release of recordings by the late Bruno Walter. Am Rec G 30:488-91 F '64
First recordings of Debussy and Hindemith works for narrator and ensemble. Am Rec G 30:926-7 Je '64
Glenn Gould: a poet and a seeker. Am Rec G 30:292-3 D '63
Guest editorial: fifteen years with Mr Bing. Mus Am 84:4+ N '64
Hear America first. Mus Am 84:6-9 Mr '64
Hurok; adventurer in the arts. Dance Mag 38:40-6+ Ja '64
Keyboard miscellany. Am Rec G 29:566-9 Mr '63
Requiem by, and for, Paul Hindemith. Am Rec G 30:756-8 My '64
Three violinists, three internal perspectives. Am Rec G 31:114-16 O '64
Well-tempered clavichord. Am Rec G 30:574-5 Mr '64
SABIN vaccine. See Poliomyelitis—Vaccines
SABLE, Daniel
(comp) Guide to background music. Pop Phot 53:102+ S '63
SABLE, Jean Baptiste Pointe de. See Pointe de Sable, J. B.
SABOTAGE
Avoiding martyrdom; eight men convicted of sabotage in Africa. Time 83:25 Je 19 '64
I plead not guilty; trial of ten South Africans on charges of sabotage. S. Uys. New Repub 149:12-13 D 28 '63
SABURN, A. Walter
Twice as big, better than new. por Am City 78:91-3 F '63
SACASA, Guillermo Sevilla-. See Sevilla-Sacasa, G.
SACCHARIDES
Intestinal disaccharidases; absence in two species of sea lions. P. Sunshine and N. Kretchmer. bibliog il Science 144:850-1 My 15 '64
SACCHARIN
Sugar substitutes safe? cyclamate. Sci N L 86:196 S 26 '64
SACCO and Vanzetti; opera. See Blitzstein, M.
SACCO-Vanzetti case
Last letters home. B. Vanzetti. Nation 197: 86-8 Ag 24 '63
New light on Sacco and Vanzetti. B. H. Bagdikian. New Repub 149:13-17 Jl 13 '63
Sacco, guilty, Vanzetti innocent? F. Russell; reply with rejoinder. M. A. Musmanno. Am Heritage 14:92-3 F '63
Sacco-Vanzetti: the missing fingerprints. F. J. Cook; discussion. Nation 196:inside cover Ja 26; inside cover, 329 Ap 20 '63
Tragedy in Dedham, by F. Russell. Review
New Repub 148:25-30 Mr 2 '63. M. A. Musmanno; Discussion. 148:37-8 Mr 23 '63
SACHAR, Edward J.
Behavioral science and criminal law; with biographical sketch. Sci Am 209:30, 39-45 bibliog(p 186) N '63; 210:9 Ja '64
SACHS, Hans
Songs of life and love in ancient Nuremberg. D. Stevens. il Hi Fi 15:71 Ja '65
SACHS, Maurice
Sin along the Seine. L. LeSage. il Sat R 47: 34 Ag 8 '64
SACHS, Robert G.
Can the direction of flow of time be determined? bibliog Science 140:1284-90 Je 21 '63
Power of prediction, an example. Bul Atomic Sci 20:20-1 D '64
SACHS, Samuel, 2d
Reconstructing the Whirlwind of 26th street. Art N 61:26-9+ F '63
SACHTJEN, Wilbur M. See Clee, G. H. jt. auth.
SACHTLEBEN, Carl H.
Libraries of St Louis. por Library J 89: 2539-43 Je 15 '64
SACK, Saul
Secular tendency in church-related colleges in Pennsylvania; excerpt from History of higher education in Pennsylvania. bibliog f Sch & Soc 91:430+ D 28 '63
SACKETT, Gene P. and others
Choice behavior in rhesus monkeys: effect of stimulation during the first month of life. bibliog Science 147:304-6 Ja 15 '65
Food versus perceptual complexity as rewards for rats previously subjected to sensory deprivation. bibliog Science 141: 518-20; 142:1021-2 Ag 9, N 22 '63
SACKETT, Howard G.
Ambitious program for the 88th Congress. NEA J 52:32 F '63
SACKETT, K. E.
Full day's wages; story. Sat Eve Post 237: 50-4 My 2 '64
SACKETT, Russell
Old bird won't sell. Life 55:13 Ag 9 '63
SACKETT, Walter W. jr
Are we drinking too much milk? Sci Digest 53:19-25 Ap '63
SACKEY, Alex Quaison-. See Quaison-Sackey, A.
SACKS, Seymour. See Campbell, A. K. jt. auth.
SACKTOR, Bertram, and Dick, A. R.
Oxidation of extramitochondrial diphosphopyridine nucleotide by various tissues of the mouse. bibliog Science 145:606-7 Ag 7 '64
SACKVILLE, Thomas, 1st earl of Dorset. See Dorset, T. S.
SACKVILLE-WEST, Victoria
Evening with Virginia Woolf. E. Irons. New Yorker 39:115-16+ Mr 30 '63
For the pure joy of it. D. Warren. il Horticulture 41:401 Ag '63
SACRAMENT of penance. See Confession
SACRAMENTO, Calif.
Destiny rides again; new Sacramento Canal. il Newsweek 62:65 Jl 15 '63
Notes for a gazetteer. P. Hamburger. New Yorker 38:81-2+ F 2 '63

Galleries and museums

Museum that travels. Parents Mag 38:121 Ap '63
Pets on loan. W. Cross. il Parents Mag 38: 60-1 Ap '63
See also
E. B. Crocker art gallery

Governors mansion

See Governors mansions

Stores

Sacramento department store looks inward. il Arch Rec 133:168-9 Je '63
SACRAMENTO VALLEY astronomical society
Amateur astronomy at Sacramento. N. Leonard and M. C. Rohrke. il Sky & Tel 25:82+ F '63
SACRAMENTS
Art and sacrament; symbolism found in contemporary artistic creation. F. Eversole. Christian Cent 81:393-6 Mr 25 '64
Christ the sacrament of the encounter with God, by E. Schillebeeckx. Review
America 110:50+ Ja 11 '64. J. M. Powers
Cath World 198:320-1 F '64. H. D. Noyes
Christian Cent 81:211 F 12 '64. G. H. Kehm
Consecration of the layman, by M. Thurian. Review
America 110:608-9 My 2 '64. R. J. Bastian
Third absurdity; washing of feet. Christian Cent 81:227 F 19 '64
See also
Baptism
Marriage
SACRED college of cardinals. See Cardinals
SACRED cows. See Cows in religion, folklore, etc.
SACRED deer, child of the moon god: story. See Treviño, E. B.
SACRED Heart, Devotion to
Word. V. P. McCorry. America 108:892-3 Je 22 '63; 110:777-8 My 30 '64
SACRED Heart, Society of the. See Society of the Sacred Heart
SACRED music. See Church music
SACRED relics. See Relics and reliquaries

SACRED skull; story. See Buck, P. S.
SACRIFICE
See also
Atonement
SACRIFICE; story. See Singer, I. B.
SADDLES
Build your own pack saddle; burro packers. il Sunset 132:140 Mr '64
Victorian side-saddles. A. Hall. il(p 1) Hobbies 69:54 N '64
SADE, Donatien Alphonse François, comte de
Life and ideas of the Marquis de Sade, by G. Gorer. Review
Sat R 46:58+ S 28 '63
Time il por 82:101 Jl 12 '63
SADLER, Christine
Little red schoolhouse in Washington, D.C. McCalls 91:54+ S '64
Our very busy First lady. McCalls 91:79-81+ Mr '64
SADLER, Josie
Six comediennes. J. Walsh. il pors Hobbies 68:33-6 My; 33-5 Je '63
SADLER, Marion
Fasten executive belts. il por Time 84:100 O 23 '64
Sadler's back. Newsweek 64:92 O 26 '64
SADLER, William A. jr
Pastors and preaching. Christian Cent 81:582+ Ap 29 '64
Pessimism rejected. Christian Cent 80:1207 O 2 '63
Philosophical foursome. Christian Cent 80:1435-6 N 20 '63
SADLER'S Wells ballet. See Royal ballet, Great Britain
SADLER'S Wells theatre. See London—Theater
SADOFF, Simon
Meet Simon Sadoff. E. Palatsky. il por Dance Mag 37:19-20 D '63
SADOWSKI, J. L. See Copley, C. M. jr, jt. auth.
SADUSK, Joseph F. jr
Drugs; how safe is safe enough? new medical director of the U.S. Food and drug administration. W. R. Young. il por Life 57:37-40 Jl 3 '64
FDA: trouble-ridden medical unit gets new director after 2-year search to fill difficult position. E. Langer. por Science 143:1018-19 Mr 6 '64
SADWIN, Lippe D.
Explosive welding with nitroguanidine. bibliog Science 143:1164+ Mr 13 '64
SAENGER, Eugen
Saenger urges Germans to build space ships. por Miss & Roc 13:35 Jl 8 '63
Saenger's final interview with M/R; ed. by W. Beller. por Miss & Roc 14:35+ F 24 '64
SAFARI. See Hunting—Africa, East
SAFARI club, Kenya. See Sports clubs
SAFE deposit boxes
Law & your safe-deposit box. il Changing T 18:29-31 Mr '64
SAFE progress association. See Citizens associations
SAFELIGHTS. See Photography—Apparatus and supplies
SAFES
Outlet-box wall safe. D. E. Grant. il Pop Mech 120:153 D '63
Where they keep the money; portfolio. il Fortune 68:114-17 O '63
See also
Mosler safe company
SAFETY awards. See National safety council
SAFETY belts
Auto safety for children. il Consumer Rep 28:292-4, 319 Je-Jl '63
Belts have fastened. il Time 81:85 Mr 8 '63
Crash for safety. il Motor T 15:42-3 Jl '63
Fasten your seat belt; how to make an alarm for your car that reminds you. R. M. Benrey. il Pop Sci 183:87-9 Ag '63
Few seat belts get a better rating. il Consumer Rep 29:412-13 S '64
How the experts shop for seat belts. K. N. Anderson. il Todays Health 41:20-5+ Ap '63
Seat-belt know-how. Newsweek 61:76 Mr 4 '63
Seat belts. il Consumer Rep 29:332-6 Jl '64
Seat belts in the news. Consumer Rep 28:260 Je '63
Seat harnesses: a technological lag. Consumer Rep 28:148 Ap '63
So you don't use seat belts? P. W. Kearney. Read Digest 83:121-3 Jl '63
Some new news on seat belts. il Motor T 15:106-7 N '63
TV star credits safety belt with saving his life. il Todays Health 41:11+ Ap '63
Two more seat belts. Consumer Rep 28:316-17 Jl '63
Use those seat belts in the city too. Sci Digest 54:66 Jl '63
You belt your life. Motor T 15:42-3 Ag '63
SAFETY deposit vaults. See Vaults
SAFETY devices and measures
Better safe than sorry. Am Home 66:81 My '63
Get rid of those bathroom booby traps! J. Lentz. il Todays Health 42:71 N '64
How to build a hazard-free home. P. Neuhaus. il Todays Health 42:54-7 S '64
How to stay alive on a ladder. B. Gladstone. il Pop Mech 120:166-9 Ag '63
Know these gardening safety tips. Good H 158:163 My '64
List of safety tips every home should have. Bet Hom & Gard 41:115 Mr '63
Public safety. il Am City 79:36 Ag '64
Safety last. S. Blum. il Redbook 121:56-7+ S '63
Safety tips for young scientists. Parents Mag 38:175 O '63
Santa's safety list. Recreation 56:412 N '63
Some home safety hints. Consumer Bul 46:30 O '63
Stop! look! listen! B. C. Kilvert, jr. Flower Grower 50:30+ Jl '63
Twenty-minute safety tour can save you and/or your home. H. E. Dark. il Todays Health 41:36-7+ F '63
See also
Accidents—Prevention
Fire protection
Road signs
also subhead Safety devices and measures under various subjects, e.g. Aviation—Safety devices and measures
SAFETY education
Drownproofing. F. Lanoue. Recreation 57:132-3 Mr '64
Make your own safety sideshow; reprint. R. L. Meyer. il Recreation 57:200-1 Ap '64
Psychology for safety. il Sci Digest 54:74 Ag '63
Student accidents. NEA J 52:78 O '63
See also
Traffic regulations—Study and teaching
SAFETY engineering
He makes accidents obsolete. M. Stearns. il Pop Mech 120:101-4+ Ag '63
They take all the fun out of getting killed! N. Carlisle. il Pop Sci 183:74-6+ N '63
SAFETY glass. See Glass, Safety
SAFETY locks. See Automobile locks and keys
SAFETY-razor blades. See Razor blades
SAFETY stud tires. See Tires, Automobile
SAFEWAY stores, incorporated
Gourmet foods fill the supermarket cart. il Bsns W p47-8+ D 5 '64
SAFF, Donald
Dynamic design. Sch Arts 64:32-7 N '64
SAFFERMAN, Robert S. and Morris, M. E.
Algal virus; isolation. bibliog Science 140:679-80 My 10 '63
SAFIR, Aran
Blindness you can prevent. Parents Mag 39:132-3 Je '64
SAFIRE, William L.
Bookseller's public relations. Pub W 184:25-7 O 21 '63
SAGA of my seventeenth summer; story. See Seib, K. H.
SAGAN, Françoise, pseud.
Absolument, Mlle Bardot! interview, ed. by R. Grenier. por Ladies Home J 82:42-3+ Ja '65
Follow the fashion or leave the country. Vogue 141:120+ Mr 1 '63
I adore cars. Vogue 142:120-3+ N 1 '63
P.S. to summer; its singular French pleasures, tr. by F. Du Plessix Gray. Vogue 144:196+ S 1 '64
Woman of thirty. Vogue 142:32-5 Jl '63

about

Bonheur, impair et passe. Criticism
New Yorker 39:80+ Ja 25 '64
SAGE grouse shooting. See Grouse shooting
SAGER, Ruth
Genes outside the chromosomes; with biographical sketch. Sci Am 212:16, 70-9 bibliog(p 134) Ja '65
—and others
Coding ambiguity in cell-free extracts of chlamydomonas. bibliog Science 140:304-6 Ap 19 '63

SAGINAW, Mich.
Lighting
Fluorescents instead of ornaments. E. H. Potthoff, jr. and M. E. Peacock. il Am City 79:126+ O '64
SAGOFF, Maurice
Where art thou, muse? Horizon 6:121 Sum '64
SAGOFF, Sara E.
Switch-about shopkeepers; drama. Plays 22: 69-76 Mr '63
SAGRA musicale umbra. See Music festivals—Italy
SAGUARO. See Cactus
SAGUARO NATIONAL MONUMENT
New Saguaro road proposed. H. Melts. Nat Parks Mag 37:23 S '63
SAGUIER, Rubén Bareiro
Guaraní: proud mark of the Paraguayan. Américas 16:6-10 Mr '64
SAHARA DESERT
Diary of a hitchhike across the Sahara; Peace corps girls; with report by B. Kral. il Life 56:92-4+ Ap 17 '64
End of a legend: five Peace corps girls journey across the Sahara. il Newsweek 63:50 Mr 16 '64
Sahara; bridge or barrier? I. W. Zartman. bibliog il Int Concil 541:3-62 Ja '63
See also
Irrigation—Sahara Desert
SAHIAR, Khurshed, and Schwartz, R. S.
Inhibition of 19S antibody synthesis by 7S antibody. bibliog Science 145:395-7 Jl 24 '64
SAHL, Mort
Comic who'll never be in. E. Linn. pors Sat Eve Post 237:28-9 S 19 '64
SAHLINS, Marshall D.
Books. Sci Am 210:139-40+ My '64
SAHM-Chun-Li. See Dancing, Korean
SAHULA, Peter
Change of pace. il U S Camera 27:48-9 Je '64
SAIGON
As the lid comes off in Saigon. il U S News 55:20 N 18 '63
Eye of the hurricane. il Newsweek 63:27 Je 8 '64
Letter from Saigon. Nation 197:205-7 O 5 '63
Portrait of a city at war. R. P. Martin. il U S News 54:78-80 Je 10 '63
Saigon: explosion by a brazen enemy. il Life 58:28-9 Ja 8 '65
Saigon is calm, but the war is near; photographs. D. Halberstam. N Y Times Mag p 10-11 Ja 26 '64
Shaken city. il Time 84:20 Ag 14 '64
Sometimes it's bad, sometimes it's good; an American's first impressions. W. Tuohy. il Newsweek 65:29 Ja 18 '65
Newspapers
Permissiveness in Saigon. Time 82:70 D 13 '63
Riots
Land of despair. il Newsweek 64:46 D 7 '64
SAIL away innocent; story. See Capdevila, A.
SAILBOAT racing
Approach to the finish. J. Sutphen and A. Kostanecki. il Yachting 115:70-1+ Ap '64
Approach to the leeward mark. J. Sutphen and A. Kostanecki. il Yachting 115:39-41+ Mr '64
Approach to the weather mark. J. Sutphen and A. Kostanecki. il Yachting 115:50-2+ F '64
Destination: Bermuda. A. F. Loomis. il Yachting 115:50-2+ Je '64
Dinghies and the racing classes; Frostbiting. il Motor B 112:38+ Ag '63
Fanning out from Florida; Windmill, one-design class. W. P. McMillen. il Yachting 116:44-5+ N '64
Flying lady of the Flying Dutchman. A. Zich. il Sports Illus 18:43-4+ Ap 22 '63
French sailor first in ocean race. il Motor B 114:88-9 Ag '64
How the Frostbite dinghy found its future. W. J. H. Dyer. il Motor B 112:38+ Ag '63
I.O.D.'s, the big little class. M. H. Farnham. il Motor B 113:80-3+ Ja '64
International team racing. N. Beckner and J. Beckner. il Yachting 114:56-7+ S '63
Marblehead celebrates the 75th anniversary of its race week. B. D. Barker, 3d and L. M. Fowle. il Yachting 116:38-9+ Ag '64
Measuring one-design sails. W. C. Ross. il Yachting 116:57-9+ Jl '64
New England, U.S. dinghy cradle. il Motor B 112:36-7+ Ag '63
Oldest one-design? J. B. Trevor, jr. il Yachting 115:191 Mr '64
Our Olympic chances. G. D. O'Day. il Yachting 115:54-6+ Mr '64; Discussion. 115:35+ Je '64
Paul Elvstrom on racing and the Olympics; interview. il Yachting 116:27-8+ Ag '64
Race weeks; Larchmont's 65th; Marblehead's 74th. B. D. Barker, 3d; L. M. Fowle. il Yachting 114:51+ S '63
Sailor with but a single thought; racing a boat singlehanded. H. Whall. il Sports Illus 19:50-1 Ag 12 '63
Sails and their trim; excerpt from Cornelius Shields on sailing. C. Shields. il Yachting 116:51-3+ Ag '64
Selecting the Olympic classes. R. N. Bavier, jr. Yachting 115:62-3+ Ap '64
Stars that shine with Tokyo gold; Star class race. H. Whall. il Sports Illus 21:20-1 Ag 17 '64
Tiny Burgoo big Bermuda winner. F. Rohr. il Motor B 114:126-8+ Ag '64
Two Texans shoot it out with a pair of 55s. H. Whall. il Sports Illus 19:52-4 S 16 '63
Victory by design. il Time 82:68-9 S 27 '63
Win, lose or sink, the best were out sailing; sailing championship of North America. H. Whall. il Sports Illus 19:70-2 S 30 '63
With the racing classes. B. Robinson. See issues of Yachting
See also
Regattas
Accidents and injuries
See Sports—Accidents and injuries
Anecdotes, facetiae, satire, etc.
Sailsmanship; gentle art of winning without cheating. E. W. Himsworth. il Yachting 113:46-7+ My '63
SAILBOATS
Blue Jays are flying high. J. Rendel. il Yachting 114:41+ Ag '63
Fanning out from Florida; Windmill, one-design class. W. P. McMillen. il Yachting 116:44-5+ N '64
40-knot sailboat. B. Frisch. Sci Digest 55:30 My '64
How of those hopped-up sailboats. F. Rohr, jr. il Pop Mech 121:108-12+ F '64
Oldest one-design? J. B. Trevor, jr. il Yachting 115:191 Mr '64
Sailboats 64-65. il Motor B 113:150-5+ Ja '64; 115:146-51+ Ja '65
Sailing simplified. F. M. Paulson. il Field & S 69:80-3+ Ag '64
See also
Catamarans
Masts and rigging
Trimarans
Design
Aviza, a 1725 shallop. W. A. Baker. il Yachting 113:190-2 My '63
Designs. See issues of Yachting
Great American sailboats; Ensenada, a cutter in the wake of coot. B. Koelbel. il Motor B 113:102-4 Je '64
Great American sailboats: Erin. B. Koelbel. il Motor B 114:54+ Ag '64
Great American sailboats; Marie-Princess. B. Koelbel. il Motor B 114:50-1+ Jl '64
Look ma, no hands. H. Caufman. il Motor B 112:93 N '63
New look at the shapes we're in. il Motor B 111:28-37 F '63
Other man's boat; Westward. il Yachting Yachting 113:64-5+ Je '63
Equipment
Yachting's boat show. il Yachting 115:127-32+ Ja '64; 117:127-32+ Ja '65
SAILFISH fishing
Sailfish for excitement. G. Heinold. il Outdoor Life 134:30-1+ O '64
Sailfish on a fly. T. McNally. il Outdoor Life 134:34-5+ D '64
Something new in fishing tournaments at Palm Beach. M. Kane. il Sports Illus 18: 42-3 Ja 28 '63
SAILING
Bob Bavier on spinnaker handling; interview. ed. by B. Robinson. B. Bavier. il Yachting 116:29+ S '64
Feathering in heavy weather. L. S. Wright. il Yachting 115:206-7 My '64
Freegoing, seagoing family affair; the Badham family's ketch. il Life 54:81-4 Je 21 '63
Holiday handbook of small-boat sailing. W. P. Bradley. il Holiday 36:97-100 Ag '64
Importance of sail trimming. L. North. il Yachting 113:74-5+ Ap '63
Incident I'll never forget. H. A. Calahan. Yachting 115:218-19 My '64
Long way west. M. B. Peterson. il Motor B 111:35-7+ Ap; 38+ My '63

SAILING—*Continued*
Sailing is action, thrills, magic. M. Back. il Seventeen 23:74-5+ Jl '64
Sailing on the edge. L. Morgan. il Motor B 114:48-9 N '64
Sailing simplified. F. M. Paulson. il Field & S 69:80-3+ Ag '64
Single-handed passages; across the north Atlantic. F. Chichester. il Yachting 113: 43-5+ My '63
Twelve-meter spinnaker jibe. B. D. Barker, 3d. il Yachting 115:57-9+ Je '64
See also
Boats and boating
Cruising
Regattas
Sailboat racing
Yachts and yachting

Anecdotes, facetiae, satire, etc.
Anyone want a tow? T. W. Howland. il Yachting 114:67 O '63
Dark doings of suburban skippers; crew-stealing. C. B. Palmer. il N Y Times Mag p28+ Ag 4 '63
Slack off your sheet! J. F. Swan. il Yachting 117:108-9+ Ja '65

Study and teaching
Classroom under canvas. il Motor B 114:48-9 Ag '64
Learning by doing; Ardell's sailing school, Newport Beach, Calif. A. Lockabey. il Yachting 116:62-3+ Ag '64
Olympic training in southern California. R. Fenton. il Yachting 115:44-5+ Je '64
Organizing a junior sailing program; with introduction. L. M. Fowle and M. J. Hodges. il Sports Illus 18:30-8 Je 24 '63
Starting a junior sailing program. D. V. Smythe. il Yachting 115:54-6+ My '64

SAILING ships. See Sailing vessels

SAILING vessels
And all I ask is a tall ship; Lisbon to Bermuda windjammer race for student seamen; photographs by R. Meek; with account by A. Villiers. Sports Illus 21:22-9 Jl 20 '64
End of a great old ship; Bear. W. H. Taylor. il Yachting 113:198 My '63
Great American sailboats; Gundred; 40-foot ketch. B. Koelbel. il Motor B 114:36+ N '64
Great American sailboats; ketch Eric, descendant of a famous line of double-enders. W. H. Koelbel. il Motor B 113:111+ Ja '64
Great American sailboats; Little Ranger; offshore ketch. B. Koelbel. il Motor B 113: 34+ Mr '64
Inside Europe aboard Yankee; cruise on a ketch. I. Johnson and E. Johnson. il Nat Geog Mag 126:157-95 Ag '64
Last of the lake windjammers. Captain Jack. il Yachting 114:133-4 Ag '63
Man who stopped the rams. W. W. Wade. il Am Heritage 14:18-23+ Ap '63
New York sees ghosts of past. il Bsns W p29 Jl 25 '64
Niña II. E. C. Uriburu. il Américas 15:2-7 Ap '63
1,600 miles on a windjammer; Statsraad Lehmkuhl. D. C. Fales. il Pop Sci 185:74-7+ Ag '64
Operation sail. D. W. Dwyer. il Yachting 115: 64-6+ Ap '64
Operation sail; loomings and landfalls. F. Rohr. il Motor B 113:44-5+ Je '64
Opsail, once in a lifetime spectacle. il Motor B 114:86-7 S '64
Over the bounding main again; Lisbon to Bermuda windjammer race for student seamen; with photographs by E. Hartmann. Sat Eve Post 237:64-9 Jl 11 '64
Retire and cruise. C. Stoessel. il Motor B 113:38-9+ Ap '64
Tale of a tall ship; Indonesian barkentine Dewarutji. F. Rohr. il Motor B 114:90-2+ O '64
Tall ships; windjammers in Lisbon-Bermuda race promenade past the Manhattan skyline. il Life 57:54-65 Jl 24 '64
To the bear; steam barkentine. G. M. S. Tod. il Motor B 111:118 My '63
Virgin Isles adventure; Windjammer cruise on Maverick. W. M. Domin. il Travel 122: 35-8 D '64
Year that was. il Motor B 115:62-75 Ja '65
See also
Catboats
Junks
Schooners

Design
Other man's boat. A. E. Luders, jr. il 114:56-8+ Ag '63

History
Cleopatra's barge; America's first venture in building a seagoing yacht, or hermaphrodite brig. C. H. Jenrich. il Motor B 114:116-17 D '64

SAILMAKERS
When business is a breeze; Hood sailmakers, incorporated. il Bsns W p94-6+ S 26 '64
Yachting interviews; Ted Hood, a versatile sailmaker; ed. by B. D. Barker, 3d. F. E. Hood il Yachting 114:48-50 Jl '63

SAILORS. See Seamen

SAILORS reading. See Service mens reading

SAILPLANES. See Gliders (aeronautics)

SAILS
How come the spinnaker. R. M. Clancy. il Motor B 114:46-7+ Ag '64
Measuring one-design sails. W. C. Ross. il Yachting 116:57-9+ Jl '64
Olympic sails by computer. T. Vickery. il Motor B 114:48+ O '64
Permanent spinnaker net as used on the yawl Malay. H. DeFontaine. il Yachting 115: 80 Je '64
Sails. O. C. Torrey, jr. il Yachting 115:46-7+ Ap '64
Sails and their trim; excerpt from Cornelius Shields on sailing. C. Shields. il Yachting 116:51-3+ Ag '64
Synthetic sails are a skipper's best friend; nylon and dacron. J. Sutphen. il Yachting 113:38-9+ My '63
Twelve-meter sails. B. D. Barker, 3d. il Yachting 116:49+ S '64
Twelve-meter spinnaker jibe. B. D. Barker, 3d. il Yachting 115:57-9+ Je '64
Two sails in one. il Yachting 113:27 Je '63

Repairing
Sail repairs; photographs. D. Rosenfield. Yachting 114:46-7 Jl '63

SAIN, Johnny
Pitch like a pro; Yankee coach's ball-on-a-stick. il por Pop Sci 183:100-1 O '63
Positively Sain. H. L. Masin. il por Sr Schol 83:48-9 O 4 '63

SAINFOIN
Sainfoin given new appraisal. il Suc Farm 62:90 N '64

SAINSBURY, Wilfred J.
Jones collection and the American club in London. Antiques 85:185-9 F '64

ST ALBANS, Francis Bacon, viscount. See Bacon, F.

ST ANDREWS ISLAND
Coconuts, tourists, and pirate gold: San Andrés and Providencia. B. De Holguín. il Américas 15:39-41 Ap '63

ST ANDREWS Presbyterian college, Laurinburg, N.C.
Pavilion for dining and student center. il Arch Rec 134:134-5 Ag '63

ST AUGUSTINE, Fla.
Acid test; swim-integrators. il Newsweek 63:26-7 Je 29 '64
After dark in St Augustine. M. Waldron. il Nation 198:648-51 Je 29 '64
Anarchy in St Augustine. L. Goodwyn. il Harper 230:74-81 Ja '65
Critical test for the nonviolent way. J. Herbers. il N Y Times Mag p5+ Jl 5 '64
Forlorn hope in a city of trouble. il Life 56:38-38A Je 26 '64
King's targets. il Newsweek 63:26+ Je 22 '64
No man's land. il Newsweek 64:16-17 Jl 6 '64
Old slave market. Nation 198:594 Je 15 '64
Oldest city in the United States. G. de Zéndegui. il Américas 16:7-14 My '64
Portrait of an extremist; C. Lynch. T. Armbrister. il Sat Eve Post 237:80-3 Ag 22 '64
St Augustine's oldest store museum; Hamblen hardware store. C. Genovar. il Hobbies 68:51+ D '63
This time, things changed; racial violence. il Time 84:27 Jl 10 '64
Unsaintly St Augustine; hotbed of racial injustice and strife. il Ebony 19:92-4+ Ag '64
Where racial trouble keeps erupting. il U S News 57:6 Jl 6 '64
Why we went; symposium. Christian Cent 81:1061-2 Ag 26 '64
Worst yet; beatings, arson and murder. P. Watters. New Repub 150:6 Je 27 '64

ST AUGUSTINE record. See Record (St Augustine, Fla)

ST-BARTHÉLEMY (island)
Do not disturb. E. Boyd. il Travel 120:38-40 N '63

ST BARTHOLOMEW'S church, New York. See New York (city)—Churches

ST BENEDICT
Patron of Europe. America 111:542 N 7 '64
ST BERNARD. Hospice of. See Hospice of St Bernard
ST BERNARD PASS. See Great St Bernard pass
ST BERNARD tunnel. See Tunnels and tunneling
ST CATHERINE'S monastery, Sinai peninsula. See Monasteries
ST CHARLES, Ill.
Electronic dispatching gets 100 per cent response. il Am City 79:36 Ag '64
ST CROIX
Across to St Croix. M. M. Davis. il Travel 121:36-8+ Ja '64
ST CROIX RIVER
Last clean river; proposal to build power plants on the St Croix. J. Ridgeway. New Repub 151:5 D 12 '64
St Croix: who owns a river? A. D. Stedman. il Nation 199:490-3 D 21 '64
Taming a wild river. Nat Parks Mag 38:14 D '64
That nine-foot channel; Northern states power company proposes to build power plant. J. Ridgeway. New Repub 151:12 D 26 '64
ST DENIS, Ruth
Divine moment: interview, ed. by J. Fox. pors Dance Mag 37:34-5+ S '63

about

Denishawn. il pors Newsweek 64:50 Ag 24 '64
Milestone celebration at Jacob's Pillow. R. Stevenson. il pors Dance Mag 38:36-7 Ag '64
Sense of ministry. il por Time 84:42 Ag 21 '64
SAINT-DENIS. See Paris
SAINT-DENYS-GARNEAU, Hector de
Reporter at large. E. Wilson. New Yorker 40:74+ N 21 '64
ST FRANCIS DAM. See Dams—Failures
ST FRANCIS of Assisi. See Francis of Assisi, Saint
ST FRANCIS XAVIER university, Nova Scotia
Antigonish and the world. D. M. Connor and Z. Cameron. America 108:398-9 Mr 23 '63
ST GEORGE, Andrew
Vamos! the buccaneers attack the Soviet prey. il Life 54:18-25 Ap 12 '63
(ed) See Boegli, J. C. My life as a Peace corps girl
SAINT-GERMAIN-DES-PRÉS. See Paris
SAINT HELENS, MOUNT
Features and significance of the Mount Saint Helens cave area. W. R. Halliday. il Nat Parks Mag 37:11-14 D '63
ST HONORE cake. See Pastry
SAINT Joan; drama. See Shaw, G. B.
ST JOAN'S alliance
Women and the church. R. Lauer. Commonweal 80:151 Ap 24 '64
ST JOHN, Francis R.
Library service to neighborhood areas: summary of address. Wilson Lib Bul 37:743 My '63
Top library posts involved in two major job changes. Library J 88:4341 N 15 '63
ST JOHN, Jill
Hollywood's carefree child. R. W. Lewis. il pors Sat Eve Post 237:32-4 My 9 '64
Jill the beautiful kook. il pors Life 55:123-5 N 8 '63
Smoking toad. por Time 82:47 S 27 '63
ST JOHN, Seymour
Education of a headmaster; reprint. Library J 88:828-31 F 15 '63
ST JOHN, New Brunswick
Midas of the maritimes; Irving oil co. strike. il Time 83:67 Ja 31 '64
ST JOHN ISLAND
Island gunkholing paradise. B. D. Barker. 3d. il Yachting 114:38-40+ D '63
Over to St John. M. M. Davis. il Travel 120: 58-60 D '63
ST JOHNS, Adela (Rogers)
Heartbeat away; story. McCalls 90:110-11 My '63
ST JOHN'S college, Annapolis, Md.
St John's college: four years with the great books. D. Boroff. il Sat R 46:58-61+ Mr 23 '63; Discussion. 46:60 Ap 20 '63
St John's West; new campus in Santa Fe. Newsweek 61:90 Mr 11 '63
ST JOHNS RIVER
Along a lazy river. B. Thielen. il Holiday 35: 27-31+ F '64
Try Florida's St Johns. C. R. Meyer. il Motor B 114:32-5 S '64
Where lower is upper. E. White. il Yachting 114:61-2+ N '63
ST JOSEPH lead company
Built-in brakes for Ozarks boom. il Bsns W p 190-2+ N 21 '64
ST KITTS (island)
Sullenness under the sun. N. T. di Giovanni. Nation 196:287-9 Ap 6 '63
ST LAURENT, Yves Mathieu
All about Yves. il Time 82:46 Ag 9 '63
Rites of new fashion. il por Newsweek 62:48-51 Ag 12 '63
Sacrebleu! Time 81:95 Mr 22 '63
Voila! les girls return. E. Sheppard. il Sat Eve Post 236:30+ Mr 16 '63
Yves Saint Laurent. J. T. Stark. il pors Look 28:84-8 Jl 14 '64
ST LAWRENCE, GULF OF
See also
Anticosti Island
SAINT LAWRENCE ISLAND
See also
Gambell
ST LAWRENCE RIVER
Cruise to the sea. F. Mowat. il Yachting 113:57-9+ Je '63
ST LAWRENCE SEAWAY
Red flows the St Lawrence. Time 83:92 Mr 6 '64
St Lawrence Seaway after 4 years: success or failure? interview. J. H. McCann. il U S News 54:58 Ap 22 '63
Seaway flunks as a moneymaker. il Bsns W p55-6+ Ap 20 '63
U.S. and Canada exchange notes on St Lawrence Seaway tolls; Department announcement; with exchange of notes and memorandum of supplementary agreement, May 28-June 1, 1964. P. Martin; W. W. Butterworth. Dept State Bul 51:169-70 Ag 3 '64
ST LAWRENCE university, Canton, N.Y.
Rock doc; geology professor. C. Kocivar. il Look 27:M8+ N 5 '63
ST LOUIS
Gaslight square: comeback for St Louis slum. il Bsns W p29-31 Ag 17 '63
St Louis dresses up. il Life 55:133-9 N 15 '63
Spirit of St Louis. P. Deutsch and R. Deutsch. il Redbook 121:60-1+ Jl '63

Architecture

Steel reveals new strength. il Arch Forum 119:115-17 N '63

City planning

St Louis takes the cure; a case history for ailing cities. A. M. Watkins. il Harper 229: 66-70 Ag '64
To the brink & back. il Time 84:66 Jl 17 '64

Description

Night lights; guide to after-hours entertainment in St Louis. C. S. Davidson. il Library J 89:2544-6 Je 15 '64
Spirit of St Louis. B. K. Schwartz. il ALA Bul 58:507-11 Je '64
Walking tour of Greater St Louis. J. Farrington. il Wilson Lib Bul 38:855-9 Je '64

Education

Diploma-giving principal; St Louis's Charles Sumner high school. il Ebony 18:76+ Je '63
Education joins housing and welfare in coordinated federal effort. J. Mauch. il Sch Life 45:14-16 F '63
Sam Shepard's faith. P. Friggens. il PTA Mag 58:18-20+ Mr '64; Same abr. with title Is the Negro equal in intelligence and ability? Read Digest 84:83-7 Mr '64

Hotels, restaurants, etc.

Catfish and champagne; guide to dining highlights. M. O'Brien. il Library J 89: 2533-8 Je 15 '64

Housing

Education joins housing and welfare in coordinated federal effort; Pruitt-Igoe housing development. J. Mauch. il Sch Life 45: 14-16 F '63

Libraries

Bibliophile's itinerary of St Louis. L. Mead. il Wilson Lib Bul 38:860-4 Je '64
Libraries of St Louis. C. H. Sachtleben. il Library J 89:2539-43 Je 15 '64
Libraries of St Louis. E. K. Norman. il ALA Bul 58:512-18 Je '64
See also
Mercantile library association

Lighting

No more sickly purples. il Am City 79:106 Jl '64

ST LOUIS—*Continued*

Monuments, statues, etc.

Engineering of Saarinen's arch; Jefferson national expansion memorial. il Arch Rec 133:188-91 My '63

Incredible Gateway arch; Jefferson national expansion memorial. C. B. Hicks. il Pop Mech 120:86-90+ D '63; Same abr. Read Digest 84:169-70+ Mr '64

St Louis' two-legged tower: tallest U.S. monument; Gateway arch. C. Remsberg. il Pop Sci 184:91-4 Ap '64

Towering arch on the river front. il Am City 78:48 My '63

Music

[Musical events] Mus Am 84:22 Jl '64

Parks and playgrounds

City revitalized. Mrs E. G. Brungard. il Recreation 56:267+ Je '63

See also
St Louis zoological garden

Public health

Mosquito control for 4¼ cents per person. C. M. Copley, jr. and J. L. Sadowski. il Am City 78:128-9 Je '63

Recreation

In the swim in St Louis; Wohl recreation center. Mrs E. G. Brungard. il Recreation 56:308-9+ S '63

Religious institutions and affairs

Council in miniature; conference between laity, priests and archbishop. America 112:70-1 Ja 16 '65

Sanitary affairs

Sewer pushes through a bog. E. Maran. il Am City 79:171-2 S '64

Stores

Waving three flags brings in the buyers: Famous-Barr company. il Bsns W p86-7 O 3 '64

Streets

St Louis' slurry-seal experiment. A. H. Beck. il Am City 78:78-80 F '63

Welfare, Department of

Education joins housing and welfare in coordinated federal effort. J. Mauch. il Sch Life 45:14-16 F '63

ST LOUIS, Mich.
What it costs to clean a digester. R. M. Henneberger, jr and H. Bush. il Am City 78:105 Mr '63

ST LOUIS Cardinals (football club) See Football clubs

ST LOUIS citizens council. See White citizens councils

ST LOUIS COUNTY, Mo, library
Stained glass for St Louis; Lewis and Clark branch. E. K. Norman. il Library J 88:4551-2 D 1 '63

ST LOUIS encephalitis. See Sleeping sickness

ST LOUIS junior Catholic interracial council. See Catholic interracial councils

ST LOUIS planetarium. See Planetariums

ST LOUIS public library
Cover: the Julia Davis fund; rare collection of Negro literary works. il(p 157) Negro Hist Bul 27:162-3 Ap '64

ST LOUIS writers. See Authors, American

ST LOUIS zoological garden
Eureka! it's twins; baby hippos. il Life 54:84+ My 10 '63

SAINT LUCIA'S day. See Christmas—Sweden

ST MALO TIDAL DAM. See Dams—France

ST MARIES plywood company
Sending a plant back to school. Bsns W p65-6 N 28 '64

ST MARK'S school of Texas. See Private schools

ST MARTIN, Hardie
Poetry of Antonio Machado. Poetry 101:343-5 F '63

ST MARTIN (island)
St Maarten: a Caribbean find. J. Egan. il Atlan 213:106+ Ja '64

ST MARYS, Ohio
Maximum-minimum approach to civil-defense communications. G. A. Gerstner. il Am City 78:131-2 N '63

ST MARY'S thistles. See Milk thistles

ST MATTHEW'S and St Timothy's church. See New York (city)—Churches

ST MICHAEL'S MOUNT (island) England
Fabled Mount of St Michael. A. Villiers. il Nat Geog Mag 125:880-98 Je '64

ST MORITZ, Switzerland
Hardy St Moritz; paintings by A. François; with account by F. R. Smith. Sports Illus 22:34-9 Ja 25 '65

SAINT-NOM-LA-BRETÈCHE. See Golf courses

ST PATRICK'S college seminary, Cornwall, N.Y. See Theological schools

ST PATRICK'S day

Drama

Granny from Killarney. A. C. Martens. Plays 23:1-14 Mr '64

ST PAUL

Description

Land of the sky blue water. R. Deardorff. il Redbook 123:70-1+ S '64

Education

Africa, images and realities; summer Social studies institute program. J. Mather. il NEA J 52:33-5 Mr '63

St Paul's social studies institute. J. Engh. il Sr Schol 85:10T-11T Ja 14 '65

Stores

Downtown store with indoor parking; Dayton company department store. il Arch Rec 135:170-2 Je '64

SAINT Paul and the monkeys; story. See Kelley, W. M.

ST PAUL public library
Imagement for catalog card reproduction. E. B. Robbins. il Library J 88:3544-6 O 1 '63

SAINTPAULIAS. See African violets

ST PAUL'S cathedral. See London—St Paul's cathedral

ST PAUL'S school, Concord, N.H. See Private schools

ST PETER'S cathedral, Rome. See Rome (city) —St Peter's cathedral

ST PETERSBURG, Fla.

Lighting

Sunshine at night. L. H. Andrews. il Am City 78:111 Ag '63

ST PETERSBURG, Fla, public library
St Petersburg at lakeside. D. P. Runge. il Library J 89:4714-16 D 1 '64

ST PETERSBURG, Russia. See Leningrad

SAINT PHALLE, Therese de
French literary prizes, 1964. Pub W 186:35-7 D 28 '64

SAINT-PIERRE (island) Switzerland
Saint-Pierre: isle of blissful solitude. il UNESCO Courier 16:18-19 Mr '63

ST POLYCARP, Sister
My own personal patron saint. J. Trahey. il Read Digest 84:97-100 Mr '64

SAINT-SAËNS, Camille
. . . And a Samson from Saint-Saëns. C. L. Osborne. Hi Fi 14:66-7 Ja '64
First stereo recording of Samson et Dalila. M. de Schauensee. Am Rec G 30:497+ F '64
On records; Samson et Dalila. Opera N 28:32 Ap 11 '64
On records; Samson et Dalila. Opera N 29:35 D 26 '64
Samson and Delilah. Criticism
Mus Am il 84:22-3 N '64
Opera N 29:17-20 D 26 '64
Opera N il 29:24-5 D 26 '64
Sat R 47:35+ O 31 '64

ST SOPHIA. See Istanbul—Santa Sophia

ST THOMAS ISLAND
5:25 for St Thomas. G. Sloane. il Motor B 113:44-5+ Ap '64
Sparkling St Thomas. M. M. Davis. il Travel 120:28-31+ D '63

SAINT-TROPEZ, France
Rover boy at St Tropez. H. Sutton. Sat R 47:29-30 Ag 15 '64

SAINT (unknown) with two donors; story. See Warner, S. T.

ST VIRGINIA, Sister Mary. See Mary St Virginia, Sister

SAINTE-BEUVE, Charles Augustin
Back on the roost after Proust. L. Laurent. Sat R 46:33 Je 29 '63
Cher maitre. A. Kazin. Reporter 29:62-4 Ag 15 '63
Method of Sainte-Beuve. W. Fowlie. Poetry 103:183-4 D '63

SAINTE-MARIE, Buffy
Buffy Sainte-Marie: the Cree with a kink in her voice. B. Hogan. il pors Look 28:59+ D 15 '64

SAINTS
My own personal patron saint. J. Trahey. il Read Digest 84:97-100 Mr '64
Pope confers sainthood on twenty-two African martyrs. E. B. Thompson. il Ebony 20:23-6+ Ja '65
Uganda's black saints. il Time 84:57 Jl 17 '64
Who's who of saints; Analecta Bollandiana. il Time 81:60 My 31 '63
See also
Beatification
SAINTSAVER, Henri E.
Seven big how's for attracting songbirds. Audubon Mag 65:311-13 S '63
SAITO, Tsunemasa, and Be, A. W. H.
Planktonic foraminifera from the American oligocene. bibliog Science 145:702-5 Ag 14 '64
SAKAGUCHI, Bungo, and others
Interference between sex-ratio agents of drosophila willistoni and drosophila nebulosa. bibliog Science 147:160-2 Ja 8 '65
SAKAMOTO, Kyu
Rising son. por Newsweek 62:64 Jl 1 '63
SAKKARAH, Egypt. See Egypt—Antiquities
SAKOL, Jeanne
Going places, finding things in new fields for adventurous wayfarers. House & Gard 125: 22+ Ja '64
SAKS, Norman M. and Roth, C. A.
Ruby laser as a microsurgical instrument. bibliog Science 141:46-7 Jl 5 '63
SAKS, Toby
Look at the future. por Mus Am 83:10 Jl '63
SALAD dressings. See Salads
SALAD greens. See Greens, Edible
SALADS
Any-season salads; with recipes. il Farm J 88:75 My '64
Big-batch salad/dessert: frozen fruit salad. N. Nichols. il Farm J 88:76 D '64
Cold salad entrée is a midsummer night's treat. il Sunset 133:110-11 Ag '64
Crisp salads to eat outdoors. il Pop Gard 15:49 S '64
Dessert salads. M. Kaytor. il Look 28:64-5 Je 2 '64
Easy-to-fix holiday salads. il Bet Hom & Gard 42:68-9 D '64
Gallery of fifteen sensational summer salads and twenty-four special tips! il Bet Hom & Gard 41:60-5+ Jl '63
Great salads of all time. M. Johnston. il Bet Hom & Gard 42:60-5+ Ag '64
Guide to salad dressings. il Good H 156:151 Je '63
Hearty salads. il Suc Farm 61:61-2 Ag '63
Holiday salads. il Suc Farm 62:59-60 D '64
Hot skillet salads; with recipes. B. L. Henry. il Farm J 89:70-1 Ja '65
How to create vegetable fantasies. il House & Gard 126:118-19 Ag '64
How to make French dressing. W. Root. il House B 105:256+ N '63
How to wilt a green salad. Sunset 130:246 Ap '63
Ideas for autumn salads. Sunset 131:198 O '63
Informal meals for warm weather serving; meat, macaroni and cheese salad. D. J. Robinson. il Ebony 18:100+ Ag '63
Look and cook; gelatin salads and garden vegetables. il Bet Hom & Gard 41:84 Ag '63
Main dish salads for summer. il Ebony 19:106+ Ag '64
Make-ahead gelatin salads. il Bet Hom & Gard 42:82 Ap '64
Make-ahead magic. M. Johnston. il Bet Hom & Gard 41:70-5+ S '63
Making a salad the classic way. il Sunset 131:127 S '63
Midwinter salads. il Bet Hom & Gard 42:62 Ja '64
Old-fashioned perfection salad. il Bet Hom & Gard 41:78-9 F '63
Our chef's salad. il McCalls 91:108-9+ Je '64
Salad days. il McCalls 90:98-9+ Jl '63
Salad shenanigans; fresh herb mayonnaise salad. il Sunset 134:58-9 Ja '65
Salads in good form. il McCalls 91:126-7+ F '64
Secret of a low calorie salad; low in calories dressing. Sunset 132:198+ Mr '64
Secrets of shimmering molded salads; gelatin salads. il Am Home 67:60-2+ Je '64
Spanish America's fiesta dish; cold meats and vegetable salad. il Sunset 131:116 Jl '63
Spring molded salads. il Bet Hom & Gard 41:89-90 My '63
Spring salad specials. J. Figg. il Suc Farm 62:80-1 My '64
Spring salads. il Bet Hom & Gard 42:87 My '64
Successful recipes. il Suc Farm 61:51-2 D '63
Summer salad in seventeen flavors; with recipes. il Seventeen 23:146-7+ Je '64
Summer special, a platter salad. il Sunset 130: 188 Je '63
Summertime is green leaf time. C. Claiborne. il N Y Times Mag p56 Je 14 '64
Swingin' summer salads. V. T. Habeeb. il Am Home 66:44-5+ Jl '63
Top O'the summer to you; fruit salads. il McCalls 91:106-7+ Jl '64
Turn over a new leaf this summer; with recipes. H. Mills. il Redbook 123:62-3 Je '64
Two delicious vegetable salads. Sunset 131: 142 S '63
We scout the world for salads. M. E. Hoehener. il Good H 156:174 Je '63
Winter's the time to invent a hearty salad. Sunset 130:148+ F '63
You make them ahead of time. il Sunset 130: 190-1 Mr '63
SALAM, Abdus
Diseases of the rich and diseases of the poor. Bul Atomic Sci 19:3+ Ap '63
Pakistan: the case for technological development. Bul Atomic Sci 20:2-5 Mr '64
World security and developing nations. Bul Atomic Sci 20:6-8 S '64
SALAMANCA. University. See Colleges and universities—Spain
SALAMANDER stoves. See Stoves
SALAMANDERS
Dance of the salamanders. R. L. Scheffel. il Audubon Mag 66:168-71 My '64
Good salamanders. il Sunset 130:268+ Mr '63
Gynogenesis in salamanders related to amybstoma jeffersonianum. H. C. MacGregor and T. M. Uzzell, jr. bibliog il Science 143:1043-5 Mr 6 '64
Inulin and albumin absorption from the proximal tubule in necturus kidney. W. N. Scott and others. bibliog il Science 146:1588-90 D 18 '64
Salamander hormones clue to human growth. Sci N L 85:150 Mr 7 '64
See also
Newts
SALARIES
Equal pay for women, one view; summary of statement. W. B. Owen. U S News 54: 100 Ap 8 '63
Starting pay for college graduates; still headed up in most fields; chart. U S News 55:10 Jl 15 '63
U.S. seeks industry pay formula. Aviation W 78:26 My 6 '63
Western Europe; where the pay is. Time 83:86+ Je 5 '64
When women get paid as much as men. il U S News 54:97-8 Je 3 '63
Who earns what when? il Changing T 17:16 D '63
See also
Executives—Salaries, allowances, etc.
Librarians—Salaries
Non-wage payments
Professional workers—Salaries
Public officers—Salaries
Teachers—Salaries
SALASACA Indians. See Indians of South America—Educador
SALAZAR, António de Oliveira
Too late in the day; summary of address. por Time 82:24 Ag 23 '63
about
Defying the U.N; Salazar of Portugal. por U S News 55:24 S 9 '63
Portugal: little country with big troubles. il por U S News 55:46-8 Ag 26 '63
SALE, J. Kirk
Togo: the lesson for Africa. Nation 196:135-7 F 16 '63
SALE, Roger
Lonely Mr Green. New Repub 151:25-6 S 26 '64
SALEM, Mass.
Historic houses, etc.
Early New England homes with 20th-century owners. R. W. Houseman. il Am Home 66: 26-31 Mr '63
SALEM college, Winston-Salem, N.C.
Boon to the gifted; program for North Carolina's most brilliant and creative high school students. Time 81:63 Je 28 '63
SALERNO, James L.
No more communications failures. Am City 79:115 F '64
SALES, Art. See Art sales

SALES, Book. See Book sales

SALES forecasting. See Business forecasting

SALES managers

Sales managers must manage. R. O. Leon. il Harvard Bsns R 42:107-14 My '64

Ways to build stronger sales team; excerpts from How to tailor your sales organization to your markets. M. DeVoe. Nations Bsns 52:62-4+ F '64

SALES policies

Future challenges marketing. F. F. Mauser. Harvard Bsns R 41:172+ N '63

Magnavox goes its own golden way. S. H. Brown. il Fortune 69:112-15+ F '64

SALES promotion

Armstrong cork co.'s switch-hitting team. il Bsns W p 118+ S 12 '64

Art representative and you. Design 64:213 Je '63

Behind P&G's marketing success. il Duns R 81:48-51+ My '63

Children's market. il Time 82:86 Jl 12 '63

Coke tries new ways to refresh. il Bsns W p 100-1+ Ag 24 '63

Diaper service. M. W. Lear. McCalls 91:84-5+ Ja '64

IBM'S growth power. il Duns R 82:33-5+ Jl '63

Juvenile series promotion increases traffic, ups sales; North star books. il Pub W 183:155 F 18 '63

King and Tuchman speak on What to do with an author. Pub W 183:41 F 25 '63

New ways in marketing strategy. L. Morse. Duns R 83:42-4+ Ja '64

Sales & distribution; bizarre promotions. J. B. Weiner. Duns R 82:45-6+ S '63

Sales & distribution; trading stamps. L. Morse. Duns R 82:49-50+ Jl '63

Selling game. il Newsweek 61:86-7 Mr 18 '63

Selling goods through games; use of games in supermarkets. L. Morse. Duns R 84:49 Jl '64

Selling the other fellow's goods; Steel processing committee of Carbon products division. il Bsns W p 122+ Ja 16 '65

Something extra in selling. L. Morse. il Duns R 82:33-4+ S '63

Well-planned Crawford; promoting Pepsi-Cola. R. Oulahan. il Life 56:11-12 F 21 '64

See also

Coupons

Display of merchandise

Trading stamps

SALES tax

Bigger and noisier: New York's sales-tax proposal. il Newsweek 61:24-5 Ap 29 '63

Everything's up, up, up to date; opposition to sales tax. il Time 81:25 Ap 26 '63

Fighting the tax; city sales tax. New Yorker 39:34-5 Ap 27 '63

One more state joins sales-tax bandwagon; others boost rates. U S News 54:113 My 20 '63

Passed; city sales tax. New Yorker 39:31-2 My 11 '63

Real-estate taxes, sales taxes and lotteries. Am City 78:7 Jl '63

SALES techniques. See Salesmen and salesmanship

SALESMANSHIP. See Salesmen and salesmanship

SALESMEN and salesmanship

Birth of a salesman; representative of the Real silk hosiery mills, inc. of Indianapolis, Ind. H. B. Jacobs. New Yorker 39:209-12+ D 7 '63

Business plans new sales surge; symposium. il Nations Bsns 52:33-5+ F '64

Gone with the glad-hander; today's industrial salesman. il Time 82:96 S 13 '63

Hard sell in boom land; Florida real estate. A. Hirshberg. il Life 57:67-8+ N 13 '64

Informed selling. A. M. Sullivan. Duns R 84:94 S '64

New breed of salesman; not like Willy. il Newsweek 64:94-7+ O 5 '64

New rules of personal selling. E. B. Weiss. il Duns R 81:49-51+ F '63

Pitfalls in buying a vacuum cleaner. Consumer Bul 47:2 Ag '64

Role of the publisher's salesman in today's market. F. Watts. Pub W 187:121-4 Ja 18 '65

Salesman will call. R. L. Smith; reply with rejoinder. J. W. Dienhart. Nation 196:inside cover F 9 '63

Secrets of a supersalesman; automobile salesman. il Ebony 19:83-4+ Ag '64

Sound of a different drummer. L. Morse. Duns R 82:26-8 Ag '63

Wanted: salesmen. il Changing T 17:39-41 My '63

What makes a good salesman. D. Mayer and H. M. Greenberg. il Harvard Bsns R 42:119-25 Jl '64

See also

Booksellers and bookselling

Canvassing

Study and teaching

How to create a salesman. L. Morse. il Duns R 82:46-7+ D '63

SALGADO, Antonio

Philosophy in Hispano-America. Américas 15:17-22 Mr '63

SALINAS, Porfirio

L.B.J.'s favorite painter. J. Langguth. il N Y Times Mag p75+ Mr 15 '64

SALINE water. See Water, Saline

SALINE water conversion. See Sea water—Desalting

SALINGER, Jerome David

J. D. Salinger on education. A. W. Vogel. Sch & Soc 91:240-2 Sum '63

Salinger: an introduction. Christian Cent 80:287 F 27 '63

Salinger and Golding: conflict on the campus. F. E. Kearns; discussion. America 108:242+ F 23 '63

Salinger and his critics. D. P. Costello. il Commonweal 79:132-5 O 25 '63

Salinger; how to live without love. A. Chester. Commentary 35:467-74 Je '63; Reply. M. E. Parrish. 36:350 N '63

SALINGER, Pierre

Our stake in southeast Asia. pors Look 28:44+ O 20 '64

Photography in the White House; interview, ed. by O. Atkins. por U S Camera 26:12+ Mr '63

Redbook dialogue; Mannes and Salinger. pors Redbook 123:64-5+ O '64

about

Au revoir, Pierre. Time 84:26 D 18 '64

Candidate Salinger. il por Newsweek 63:28-9 Ap 27 '64

Departure of picturesque Pierre. M. McGrory. America 110:474 Ap 4 '64

Echoes. il por Newsweek 64:34+ O 19 '64

How Murphy upset Salinger. U S News 57:19 N 16 '64

No kidding. il por Time 83:25-6 My 8 '64

No place to go but up. il Newsweek 63:30 My 25 '64

Nomination by association. il por Time 83:36 Je 12 '64

People of the week. U S News 56:16 Ap 13; 22 Je 15 '64

Physical fitness on the New frontier. il por U S News 54:10 F 18 '63

Pierre goes west. il por Newsweek 63:16 Mr 30 '64

Pierre Salinger: inelegant, rotund, untiring, frank, tough, and witty. il pors Newsweek 61:60-1 Ap 8 '63

Pierre: the salty Senate candidate. L. Bergquist. il pors Look 28:112-16 My 19 '64

Pierre's round. il por Newsweek 63:24 Ap 6 '64

Plucky Pierre crashes the party. J. Phelan. il por Sat Eve Post 237:20-1 My 30 '64

Plus for Pierre. por Time 84:22 Ag 7 '64

Salinger and the Asians. il pors Look 28:42-3 O 20 '64

Salinger swings for Senate, there's bedlam in California. R. Ajemian. il por Life 56:43 Ap 3 '64

Salinger vs. Murphy. il por Newsweek 63:28 Je 15 '64

Senator Salinger: a controversial appointment. il por U S News 57:12+ Ag 17 '64

Senator Salinger? Newsweek 64:28 Ag 10 '64

Senator Salinger? por Time 83:16-17 Mr 27 '64

Up from the White House. Newsweek 64:34 Ag 17 '64

Who is the good guy? il pors Time 84:34-8 O 16 '64

SALINITY of soils. See Soils, Salts in

SALISBURY, Harrison E.

Dawn of darkness at noon. Sat R 46:48 D 14 '63

Encounter and discovery. Sat R 46:29-30 F 9 '63

Kremlin plays Russian roulette. N Y Times Mag p25+ O 25 '64

Opinion, please from New York. Mlle 60:13-14 Ja '65

Russia: a tormented history. Holiday 34:37-8+ O '63

Soviet press. Bul Atomic Sci 19:33-4 F '63

SALISBURY, John W. See Hunt, G. R. jt. auth.

SALISBURY, Conn.
Our far-flung correspondents; cabin on Mt Riga. C. Rand. New Yorker 39:31-2+ Ag 10 '63
Reporter at large. C. Rand. New Yorker 40: 109-11+ N 7 '64

SALISBURY, Md.
Machine-accounting benefits. W. M. Perkins. il Am City 78:134-5 Je '63
Small town moves into the big time. F. Deford. il Sports Illus 20:57-8 Mr 2 '64

Negroes

Lesson of Cambridge and Salisbury: was violence necessary? L. B. Bozell. Nat R 15: 145-7 Ag 27 '63
Thirty miles divide folly and reason; Cambridge and Salisbury, Md; with report by M. Durham. il Life 55:18-25 Jl 26 '63
Why race troubles hit one city, spare another; a case study: Cambridge and Salisbury, Md. il U S News 55:78-80 Ag 5 '63

SALISBURY, N.C.

Social life and customs

Fultz quads debut at Zeta cotillion. il Ebony 19:56-8+ Ap '64

SALISH Indians
Propose another Lake of Perfidy; high dam on Flathead River in Montana; reply. J. E. Nolan. Christian Cent 80:833 Je 26 '63

SALIVARY glands
Culture of insect salivary glands in a chemically defined medium. G. B. Cannon. bibliog Science 146:1063 N 20 '64
Histone staining with ammoniacal silver. M. M. Black and H. R. Ansley. bibliog il Science 143:693-5 F 14 '64
Synthesis of RNA in vitro stimulated in dipteran salivary glands by 1,1,3-tricyano-2-amino-1-propene. J. Jacob and J. L. Sirlin. bibliog il Science 144:1011-12 My 22 '64

SALIX. See Willow

SALK, Jonas Edward
Great new dream of Dr Salk. il pors Life 54: 78-84 F 8 '63

SALK institute for biological studies, San Diego, Calif.
Great new dream of Dr Salk. il Life 54:78-84 F 8 '63

SALK vaccine. See Poliomyelitis—Vaccines

SALLAL, Abdullah
Mess in Yemen. il por Time 82:39 S 13 '63
Our Yemen policy: pursuit of a mirage. P. Horton. il Reporter 29:28-35 O 24 '63

SALM, Alex
Ondine leads fleet into Hobart. Yachting 113: 58-9+ Mr '63

SALM, C. Luke
Is the Catholic college an apostolate? Cath World 200:211-17 Ja '65

SALM, Walter G.
Babylon battery. Pop Electr 21:51-2 Jl '64
Fabulous fuel cell. Pop Electr 21:47-50+ S '64

SALMAGGI, Alfredo
Salmaggi's stand. W. A. Storrer. Opera N 28:25 My 2 '64

SALMOIRAGHI, G. C. and Bloom, F. E.
Pharmacology of individual neurons. bibliog Science 144:493-9 My 1 '64

SALMON, Eugene N.
Resources in library technology. por Library J 89:1495-502 Ap 1 '64

SALMON, Robert
New look at Robert Salmon. J. Wilmerding. il Antiques 87:89-93 Ja '65

SALMON
Death of the salmon. R. Haig-Brown. il Atlan 213:57-9 Ja '64
Fall defined; excerpt from Fisherman's autumn. R. Haig-Brown. il Atlan 212:69-70 S '63
See also
Cookery—Fish

Migration

See Fishes—Migration

SALMON, Smoked. See Fish, Smoked

SALMON disease. See Dogs—Diseases and pests

SALMON fishing
Atlantic salmon in central Oregon. il Sunset 130:89+ My '63
Best single salmon pool anywhere; Norway's Malangsfoss pool. il Sports Illus 21:64-7 Ag 17 '64
Feast and a famine. il Bsns W p 116-18 S 14 '63
Fisherman's tour of Scotland. J. Brooks. il Outdoor Life 131:28-31+ Ja '63
Grilse of the Upsalquitch. B. S. Wright. il Field & S 67:68-9 Ap '63
Hog-wild chinooks. F. H. Ames. il Outdoor Life 132:50-2+ D '63
Land of ekaluk aluk. A. J. McClane. il Field & S 68:46-8+ Je '63
Landlocks deluxe. B. Warner. il Field & S 69: 37-9+ My '64
Lee Wulff vs. Jock Scott transatlantic salmon challenge match. T. Rogowski. il Esquire 59:100-3+ Je '63
Love letter to the Miramichi. C. T. Coiner. il Esquire 60:116-19+ S '63
New landlock salmon water. M. Terziev. il Outdoor Life 134:20-3+ Jl '64
Oregon's September madness. B. Behme. il Field & S 68:41-3 S '63
Peripatetic reviewer. E. Weeks. Atlan 211: 128+ My '63
River to the Arctic. B. Warner. il Field & S 68:78-80+ Ja '64
Salmon for everyone. E. A. Bauer. il Outdoor Life 135:40-3+ F '65
Salmon of Yucataw Rapids. F. Dufresne. il Field & S 69:68-9 S '64
There's always dames. C. Ford. il Field & S 68:6+ Ag '63
Tips for summer landlocks. W. Davis. il Outdoor Life 134:56+ Jl '64
When the kings run. W. W. Hunter. il Outdoor Life 133:56-7+ Je '64
Whoop-and-holler salmon. C. Chatfield. il Outdoor Life 134:36-9+ Ag '64

SALMON MOUNTAINS. See Klamath Mountains

SALMON RIVER
Wild ride down the Middle Fork of Idaho's Salmon. il Sunset 132:36-8+ Je '64

SALMONELLA. See Bacteria, Pathogenic

SALOMAN, A. J.
Property index number. por Am City 79:139+ N '64

SALOMON, Charlotte
Way to the depths. il Time 82:86 S 27 '63

SALOMON, I. L.
(tr) See Betocchi, C. Little diary on growing old (XVIII)
(tr) See Betocchi, C. Summer song

SALOMON, Julian H.
Planning camps. Recreation 56:139-41 Mr '63

SALOMON brothers and Hutzler
Fast and canny traders. il Bsns W p 118+ Je 27 '64

SALON du livre de Montréal. See Book exhibits

SALONICA international trade fair. See Exhibitions

SALOONS. See Bars and barrooms

SALSAMENDI, A.
Hot chocolate, stiff collar; story. Américas 16:33-8 Ag '64

SALSINGER, Harry
School bonds nixed. Sr Schol 85:1T-2T N 4 '64

SALT
Polygonal fracture and fold systems in the salt crust, Great Lake Desert, Utah. F. W. Christiansen. il Science 139:607-9 F 15 '63
Salt. A. Huxley. House & Gard 123:116-17 Mr '63
Salt incorporation in natural ices. A. W. Cobb. il Science 141:733 Ag 23 '63
Social influence of salt. M. R. Bloch. il Sci Am 209:88-96+ Jl '63
Sodium chloride: modification of crystal habit by chemical agents. R. S. Ploss. bibliog il Science 144:169-70 Ap 10 '64
Taste of sodium chloride solutions after adaptation to sodium chloride: implications for the water taste. L. M. Bartoshuk and others. bibliog Science 143:967-8 F 28 '64
See also
Morton salt company
Rock salt

Physiological effects

High level of sodium necessary in pregnancy. Sci N L 84:265 O 26 '63
Nasal salt excretion and the possible function of the cloaca in water conservation. K. Schmidt-Nielson and others. bibliog Science 142:1300-1 D 6 '63

SALT and pepper shakers
Century of salt shakers. A. G. Peterson. il Hobbies 68:86-8+ O '63

SALT free diet. See Diet in disease

SALT glands. See Glands

SALT in the body
Sodium chloride deprivation: development of sodium chloride as a reinforcement. W. Wagman. il Science 140:1403-4 Je 28 '63

SALT LAKE. See Great Salt Lake

SALT LAKE CITY
Notes for a gazetteer. P. Hamburger. New Yorker 40:222+ N 21 '64
Salt Lake City. D. Messinesi. Vogue 144:108 S 1 '64

SALT LAKE CITY—*Continued*
Lighting
City regains lighting greatness. E. W. Walton. il Am City 79:131+ Mr '64
Music
[Musical events] il Mus Am 84:14-15 F '64
SALT LAKE CITY public library
Stone face for Salt Lake. R. E. Thomas. il Library J 89:4719-21 D 1 '64
SALT marshes
Death of a salt pond; Cotuit, Mass. S. Cobb. Audubon Mag 65:70-2 Mr '63
Marshes prograding in Oregon: aerial photographs. C. L. Johannessen. bibliog il Science 146:1575-8 D 18 '64
Ontogeny of a salt marsh estuary. A. C. Redfield. bibliog il Science 147:50-5 Ja 1 '65
Salt marsh garden. E. N. Danenberg. il Horticulture 42:46-7 N '64
Wetlands lesson on Long Island; town of Hempstead. C. W. Buchheister. Audubon Mag 65:77 Mr '63
SALT rising bread. See Bread
SALT spreaders
Mix chemicals for faster melting. A. Engelhart. il Am City 78:16 O '63
SALT water. See Water, Saline
SALT water aquariums. See Aquariums
SALT water fishing
And there goes the whole weekend. il Sports Illus 19:24-5 S 9 '63
Big fish story. M. Wiley. il Yachting 115:40-4+ My '64
Blue water bargain. G. Casey. il Outdoor Life 133:60-3+ Je '64
Blues around the clock; off New Jersey, party-boat fishing. M. Rosko. il Outdoor Life 134:60-1+ S '64
Fifty-six minutes to paradise; southern New England. W. R. Miller. il Flying 75:42-4 Ag '64
First day blues. C. Conley. il Field & S 68:40-1+ Jl '63
Fishing boat captain. il Ebony 18:43-5 O '63
Fishing the tides. A. J. McClane. il Field & S 68:64-7 Ja '64
Fishing your way south. C. R. Meyer. il Motor B 112:30-3+ S '63
Florida's sturgeon spree. R. F. Burgess. il Outdoor Life 131:44-7+ Mr '63
Hemingway (the boatman) C. Meyer. il Motor B 114:21-3+ Jl '64
IQ of a blue. J. Guy. il Outdoor Life 132:52-3+ Ag '63
Is salt-water fishing doomed? F. T. Moss. il Field & S 69:10-11+ Jl '64
Mystery fish of the sea. J. Brooks. il Field & S 69:40-1+ Ag '64
New rig for balao salt water sensation. G. Robey. il Outdoor Life 131:44-5+ Ja '63
New sport: captain-fishing. V. Kraft. il Sports Illus 19:26-30+ S 2 '63
Old razormouth. A. J. McClane. il Field & S 68:96-8+ Ap '64
Pickup camper paradise. R. Cannon. il Field & S 67:70-3+ Ap '63
Pollock are powderkegs. G. Heinold. il Outdoor Life 131:78-9+ My '63
Sailfish on a fly. T. McNally. il Outdoor Life 134:34-5+ D '64
Salt water. G. Heinold. See issues of Outdoor life
Something new in fishing tournaments at Palm Beach. M. Kane. il Sports Illus 18:42-3 Ja 28 '63
Sportfishing. N. Benedict. See issues of Yachting
Striped fever. L. Green. il Outdoor Life 133:44-5+ My '64
Tailers. J. Brooks. il Outdoor Life 132:36-7+ N '63
Wahoo are sudden. J. Brooks. il Field & S 68:38-9+ N '63
We beat our drums. G. Heinold. il Outdoor Life 131:66-7+ Ap '63
Where the fish are; the Bahamas. F. T. Moss. il Motor B 114:29-32+ N '64
Whoop-and-holler salmon. C. Chatfield. il Outdoor Life 134:36-9+ Ag '64
Wicked kings. H. G. Boughton. il Outdoor Life 131:60-1+ Je '63
See also
Albacore fishing
Bonefish fishing
Mackerel fishing
Marlin fishing
Shark fishing
Swordfish fishing
Tarpon fishing
Tuna fishing
SALTER, George
Visit with George Salter; designer, calligrapher, illustrator and teacher. P. A. Bennett. il por Pub W 186:82-7 S 7 '64
SALTFORD, Herb
How to enjoy more nature activity. Audubon Mag 65:47-50 Ja '63
SALTMAN, Paul. See Charley, P. jt. auth.
SALTON, Gerard
Automatic information processing in western Europe. bibliog Science 144:626-32 My 8 '64
SALTON SEA
Drilling for power; geothermal resources. il Bsns W p60 Ja 18 '64
SALTONSTALL, Leverett
Text ban treaty; the military considerations: address, September 9, 1963. Vital Speeches 29:750 O 1 '63
SALTONSTALL, Richard, jr.
Seattle Sixes. Yachting 115:54-5+ F '64
SALTONSTALL, William Gurdon
Off to Africa. por Newsweek 61:70 Mr 18 '63
Something says yes. por Time 81:61 Mr 15 '63
Yankee idealist in Africa. il pors Life 56:51-4 Mr 20 '64
SALTS
Neutral salts: the generality of their effects on the stability of macromolecular conformations. P. H. Von Hippel and K. Y. Wong. bibliog il Science 145:577-80 Ag 7 '64
SALTWATER fishing. See Salt water fishing
SALTZMAN, Barbara. See Saltzman, J. jt. auth.
SALTZMAN, Joe, and Saltzman, Barbara
Long odds and sure things on the California ballot. Reporter 31:28-30 N 5 '64
SALTZMAN, Leopold
Premier baritone. Opera N 28:26-7 Ja 4 '64
SALUS, Sandra
Puppets in an hour by children. Sch Arts 63:11-13 O '63
SALUTE, Flag. See Flag salute
SALVADOR, Brazil
Sister Dulce. S. Seegers and K. Seegers. il Cath World 199:230-7 Jl '64
Treasury of sacred art. F. Borghini. il Américas 15:8-12 Ap '63
SALVADORI, Mario
Pier Luigi Nervi. Arch Forum 120:78-9 My '64
SALVADORI, Max
Partners in disaster. Reporter 28:50+ My 23 '63
SALVADORIAN poetry
Four Salvadorian poets; with poems. E. Odio. il Américas 16:27-31 Je '64
SALVAGE
Aquanauts skin-dive to retrieve missiles. il Pop Sci 185:108-9 N '64
Time bombs in the Mississippi. E. D. Fales jr. il Pop Sci 182:124-30+ Ap '63
See also
Submarine disasters
SALVAGE (boats) See Salvage (ships)
SALVAGE (ships)
Help, but at a price. J. P. Dunne. il Motor B 114:40-1+ S '64
Underwater furniture factory; out of Great Lakes shipwrecks. J. Grenard and J. Grenard. il Motor B 111:76-7+ Je '63
We bought a 55-foot yacht for $500. D. C. Siverts. il Pop Sci 184:74-6+ Ap '64
SALVAGE archeology. See Archeology
SALVAGE divers. See Diving, Submarine
SALVATION
Outside the camp; excerpt from Passion. K. A. Olsson. Christian Cent 80:264-7 F 27 '63
Word. V. P. McCorry. America 108:276, 507, 694; 109:84-5 F 23, Ap 13, My 11, Jl 20 '63
See also
Justification
SALVATION army
Steady as before. Time 82:86+ O 11 '63
SALVATION army bands. See Bands (music)
SALZBURG festival
Here liveth fortune. E. Radant. il Hi Fi 13:46-9+ Mr '63
Return from exile. E. Helm. il Mus Am 84:26-7 S '64
Salzburg success. D. A. Mackinnon. Opera N 29:27 N 14 '64
Salzburg tradition. F. Warnke. il Opera N 28:30 N 16 '63
SALZBURG marionettes. See Puppets and puppet plays
SALZBURG seminar in American studies
Seminar at Salzburg. A. Toffler. il Sat R 46:32-4 Ag 17 '63

SALZMAN, Eric
Benjamin Britten's War requiem. Hi Fi 13:51-2 Jl '63
Music from the electronic universe. Hi Fi 14:54-7 Ag '64
New musical conceptions realized by electronic means. Hi Fi 13:91 Ag '63
New Oedipus Rex brings more of Stravinsky's Stravinsky. Hi Fi 13:126-7 O '63
1963 hi-fi show. Mus Am 83:35+ O '63
Opera comes into its own, Bluebeard's castle twice more on discs. Hi Fi 13:60-1 Je '63
Portrait of Robert Craft. Hi Fi 14:24-6 Jl '64
Samson from Handel. Hi Fi 14:65-6 Ja '64
Scordatura; and the Mysteries of the rosary. Hi Fi 13:73-4 Ap '63
SAMADEN, Switzerland
Where Latin's still alive. W. J. Granberg. il Travel 122:28-31 O '64
SAMANT, Mohan
Chant of centuries; exhibition at Manhattan's World house galleries. il por Time 83:72-3 Mr 6 '64
SAMARASINGHE, Earle
Great step forward. Library J 89:4473-5 N 15 '64
SAMIOS, Nicholas P. See Fowler, W. B. jt. auth.
SAMMOND, Harry
Color slides; techniques. R. Miller. il U S Camera 26:24+ Jl '63
SAMOA, AMERICAN. See American Samoa
SAMOS, Greece
Tunnel of Eupalinus. J. Goodfield. il Sci Am 210:104-10+ Je '64
SAMOS (artificial satellite) See Artificial satellites—Military applications
SAMPLERS
Another American home kit. D. L. Brightbill. il Am Home 66:40+ Mr '63
Answers to questions on antique samplers. L. F. Reals. il Hobbies 68:51 My '63
Make your own Christmas sampler. P. B. Brunton. il Todays Health 42:40-1 D '64
See also
Needlework
SAMPLES (merchandising)
Reports from a battle front. Consumer Rep 29:212 My '64
SAMPLING (statistical methods)
Common sense in sampling. C. R. Wasson. Harvard Bsns R 41:109-14 Ja '63
Exploring the exploratory sample. R. A. Bauer. Harvard Bsns R 41:128-31 Mr '63
Science of being almost certain. G. A. W. Boehm. il Fortune 69:104-7+ F '64
Standard sampler for assay of airborne microorganisms; letter. P. S. Brachman and others. Science 144:1295 Je 12 '64
SAMPSON, Anthony
South Africa, the time bomb ticks. N Y Times Mag p 11+ Ap 12 '64
—and Makins, Virginia
X=the French power elite. Esquire 62:70-5+ Jl '64
SAMPSON, Dorothy Kidd
Divide plants now for bigger and better lily-of-the-valley flowers. il Flower Grower 50:19 Ag '63
SAMPSON, Edith (Spurlock)
People in trouble. A. Schiller. il Harper 228:145-9 Ap '64
SAMPSON, Richard T.
Sense and sensitivity in pricing. Harvard Bsns R 42:99-105 N '64
SAMSITES. See Guided missile bases
SAMSON and Delilah; opera. See Saint-Saëns, C.
SAMSON et Dalila; opera. See Saint-Saëns, C.
SAMTSOVA, Galina
Brief biography. S. Goodman. pors Dance Mag 38:52-3 Ap '64
SAMUEL, Aryeh H. and others
Large electron pulses in hydrocarbons. bibliog Science 144:839 My 15 '64
SAMUEL, Maurice
Maurice Samuel & Jewish letters. R. Alter. Commentary 37:50-4 Mr '64
SAMUELS, Gertrude
Alabama U: a story of two among 4,000. il N Y Times Mag p 12+ Jl 28 '63
British way with the junkie. N Y Times Mag p37+ O 18 '64
Death of a youth worker. Sat Eve Post 236:74-6 Ap 6 '63
Even more crucial than in the South. N Y Times Mag p 12-13+ Je 30 '63
Feud within the Black Muslims. N Y Times Mag p 17+ Mr 22 '64
German democracy; a reporter's notebook. il N Y Times Mag p 17+ Ja 5 '64
I don't think the cop is my friend. N Y Times Mag p28+ Mr 29 '64
In search of a cure for the alcoholic. N Y Times Mag p51+ O 27 '63
James Donovan and Castro. Nation 196:299-302 Ap 13 '63
Jews in Germany today. Harper 228:45-50 My '64
Little Rock revisited, tokenism plus. N Y Times Mag p 13+ Je 2 '63
Meditation of U Thant. N Y Times Mag p32-3+ D 13 '64
People versus Baby. N Y Times Mag p40-1+ Ja 17 '65
Summons instead of an arrest. N Y Times Mag p 16+ Jl 26 '64
Two ways: Black Muslim and N.A.A.C.P. N Y Times Mag p26-7+ My 12 '63
Who shall judge a policeman? N Y Times Mag p8+ Ag 2 '64
SAMUELS, H. J.
Extra-special moose. pors Outdoor Life 132:33-5+ O '63
Suddenly there was a bear. por Outdoor Life 133:58-9+ Je '64
SAMUELSON, Lorene
Every child's valentine. Sch Arts 62:10 F '63
SAMUELSON, Paul Anthony
Case against Goldwater's economics. N Y Times Mag p28+ O 25 '64
What the future holds for business; interview. por U S News 57:64-8+ D 14 '64
When old virtues may be modern sins; excerpts from book. por U S News 54:38 Mr 4 '63
SAN ANDREAS fault. See Faults (geology)
SAN ANDRES (island). See Saint Andrews Island
SAN ANDRÉS Y PROVIDENCIA
Unspoiled speck. il Time 84:16-17 D 25 '64
SAN ANTONIO, Tex.
Near-perfect meter shop. H. Riemer. il Am City 78:81-3 N '63
Architecture
Setting a style for Texas. il Bsns W p 132+ Ag 15 '64
Music
[Musical events] (cont) Mus Am 83:15 F '63; 84:15+ F '64
San Antonio ore. J. Rosenfield. Opera N 27:33-4 Ap 13 '63
See also
San Antonio symphony orchestra
Recreation
Interservice showcase; variety shows by Inter-service recreation athletic council (ISRAC) il Recreation 56:60 F '63
SAN ANTONIO, Tex. public library
For circus fans only! K. Sexton. il ALA Bul 57:251-5 Mr '63
SAN ANTONIO grand opera festival. See Music festivals—Texas
SAN ANTONIO symphony orchestra
Gold and silver waltz; two Texas anniversaries. E. Lewis. il Mus Am 83:14-15+ O '63
Other Puritans; Merry mount. G. Ashford. Opera N 29:31 Ja 23 '65
SAN ANTONIO'S HemisFair. See Exhibitions
SANASARDO, Paul
Paul Sanasardo dance company at Hunter college playhouse. J. Maskey. Dance Mag 38:64 Mr '64
Paul Sanasardo dance company, 92nd street Y. M. Marks. Dance Mag 38:139-40 D '64
SANATORIUMS
See also
Health resorts, watering places, etc.
SAN BERNARDINO, Calif. County free library
California library uses form to alleviate censorship pressure. Library J 88:4179 N 1 '63
SAN BLAS, Mex.
Boat into the jungles around San Blas. il Sunset 130:81-2+ Ap '63
SANCES, Anthony, Jr, and others
Electronarcosis and evoked cortical responses. bibliog Science 141:733-5 Ag 23 '63
SÁNCHEZ, Manuel Laureano Rodríguez y. See Manolete
SÁNCHEZ O, Eduardo, pseud.
Industrial prize for Colombian novelists. Américas 16:31-2 S '64
SÁNCHEZ VILELLA, Roberto
Welcome to a new friend. il por Time 85:24 Ja 8 '65
SANCTIONS, Professional
Professional sanctions: where, when, and how. R. B. Kennan. NEA J 52:37-8 D '63
Strikes, sanctions, and the schools. J. Scanlon. il Sat R 46:51-5+ O 19 '63; Discussion. 46:39 D 21 '63

SANCTITY. See Holiness
SANCTUARIES, Bird. See Bird sanctuaries
SAND, George, pseud. of Mme Dudevant
Honeymoon in a monastery. F. Grunfeld. Reporter 28:33-6 Je 6 '63
SAND, George X.
Bay of Pigs. Field & S 67:54-5 Mr '63
Hunting the Pennsylvania hearthlands. Field & S 68:27-9+ O '63
Reunion with rabbits. Outdoor Life 132:32-5+ Jl '63
SAND, N. L. S.
Remedy; poem. Reporter 30:49 Ja 16 '64
Youth is impatient; poem. Reporter 31:56 O 8 '64
SAND, Paul
Off Broadway. E. Oliver. New Yorker 39:146-7 N 23 '63
SAND
Study surf sand by color; Fernandina Beach, Fla. Sci N L 83:221 Ap 6 '63
See also
Quicksand
SAND bass fishing. See Bass fishing
SAND blast
Make your own sandblaster. M. Banister. il Pop Mech 120:191-5+ O '63
SAND buggies. See Motor vehicles
SAND casting. See Casting (sculpture); Molds (for casting); Plaster work (craft)
SAND dunes
Geometry of Bermuda calcareous dune cross-bedding. F. T. Mackenzie. il Science 144: 1449-50 Je 19 '64
Indian summer for the Indiana dunes? il Am For 69:20-1+ Mr '63
Sand + oil=trees. E. J. Long. il Am For 70:46-8 Ja '64
SAND filtration. See Sewage disposal—Filtration
SAND painting
Sand art; project for elementary grades. P. Greenberg. il Sch Arts 64:5-9 D '64
SAND sculpture
Sand art; project for elementary grades. P. Greenberg. il Sch Arts 64:5-9 D '64
SANDAGE, Allan, and Kowal Charles
West Ford dipole belt: optical detection at Palomar. Science 141:797-8 Ag 30 '63
SANDAGE, Allan R.
Exploding galaxies. Sci Am 211:38-47 N '64
—and Miller, W. C.
Exploding galaxy M82: evidence for the existence of a large-scale magnetic field. bibliog Science 144:405-9 Ap 24 '64
SANDALS
On the beaten track; sandals are hottest of all. il Time 83:52 Je 19 '64
SANDBURG, Carl
Carl Sandburg; interview, ed. by M. Quigley. por Ebony 18:158-9 S '63
Just a hundred years ago. Nat Geog Mag 124:1-3 Jl '63
about
In the Sandburg tradition. W. Stafford. Poetry 102:388-9 S '63
Visit with Sandburg at sunset; with photographs by J. Mahan. H. Sandburg. Sat Eve Post 237:62-5 Je 6 '64
SANDBURG, Helga
Freedom; story. Redbook 121:66-7 Jl '63
Innocent; story. Redbook 120:64-5 Ap '63
Skip it. Horn Bk 40:86-7 F '64
Visit with Sandburg at sunset. Sat Eve Post 237:62-5 Je 6 '64
SANDE, Vivian
Your health. Redbook 121:130 S '63
SANDEEN, Ernest
Keeping time; poem. Nation 196:312 Ap 13 '63
SANDER, Willy
How to select a closed-circuit Tv camera. Electr World 70:41-3+ O '63
SANDERS, Barkev S.
Federal health estimates, 300 per cent wrong. por Nations Bsns 52:31-3+ N '64
SANDERS, Carl E.
Excerpt from testimony, July 30, 1963. Cong Digest 42:273+ N '63
about
Progress goes marching through Georgia. B. Hibbs. il por Sat Eve Post 236:69-73 F 16 '63
SANDERS, Charles L.
Cleveland's living legend in law. Ebony 19: 48-50+ N '63
Louis Armstrong, the reluctant millionaire. Ebony 20:136-8+ N '64
Playing hooky for freedom. Ebony 19:153-62 Ap '64
President who hurt Negroes most. Ebony 19:110-12+ My '64
Requiem for Queen Dinah. Ebony 19:146-8+ Mr '64
SANDERS, Dora
Stage door brigade. Dance Mag 37:22+ S '63
SANDERS, Gladys
All my beautiful darlings; story. Seventeen 22:130-1 N '63
SANDERS, H. E.
Cloud sentinel. Pop Electr 19:56-8+ O '63
SANDERS, Howard L.
Oceanography of the western South Atlantic. Science 147:183-4 Ja 8 '65
SANDERS, J. A.
To tell the truth. Christian Cent 81:763-6 Je 10 '64
SANDERS, Marion K.
Case of the vanishing spinster. N Y Times Mag p34+ S 22 '63
How an idealist won a two-front war. Harper 226:111 Je '63
Issues girls, club ladies, camp followers. N Y Times Mag p38+ D 1 '63
Next mayor of New York? Harper 226:33-41 F '63
Sweden's remedy for police brutality. Harper 229:132+ N '64
SANDERS, Peggy
Hats from paper junk. Design 65:152-3+ Mr '64
New faces for common places; Christmas tree cones. il Design 65:61-3 N '63
SANDERS, Ronald
Israel in fiction. Nation 196:122-3 F 9 '63
SANDERS, Sol W.
For U.S: it's war with one arm. U S News 57:46-8 Jl 20 '64
SANDERS, Theodore M.
What doctors can do to cut the cost of medical care. Harper 228:16+ My; 229:10 Jl; 11 Ag '64
SANDERS, Thomas G.
Do we need public Protestantism? Christian Cent 81:1424-6 N 18 '64
Religious freedom; the Court expands a concept. Nation 197:25-8 Jl 13 '63
SANDERS, William
Expanding fabric of our common interest. Américas 16:1-5 Jl '64
SANDERS. See Sanding machines
SANDERSON, Judson
Desert strip. Flying 75:45 Jl '64
Port in a storm. Flying 75:24-8 Ag '64
SANDERSON, Sibyl
Massenet's choice; first Manon at Met. il por Opera N 28:28-9 D 21 '63
SANDHILL cranes. See Cranes (birds)
SANDIA corporation
Small memory for large numbers; ceramic memory units. il Time 83:53 Mr 27 '64
SAN DIEGO, Calif.
Place to stay. il Time 85:36 Ja 22 '65
Education
Film trips: excursions unlimited. J. F. Wilson. Sr School 85:21T Ja 21 '65
San Diego's listening and viewing centers. C. A. Lazzaro. il Sr Schol 85:20T Ja 21 '65
Hotels, restaurants, etc.
Dining pavilion over water. il Arch Rec 136: 208-9 S '64
Libraries
San Diego science libraries form cooperative association; Associated science libraries of San Diego. Library J 88:4181 N 1 '63
Recreation
Cultural activities go West. R. Trembley. il Recreation 56:317-19 S '63
Theater
San Diego's cultural center. O. Maynard. Dance Mag 38:148-9 D '64
SAN DIEGO ballet. See Ballet companies
SAN DIEGO Chargers (football club) See Football clubs
SAN DIEGO city college
California library's experiment supports abolition of fines. Library J 88:4339 N 15 '63
SAN DIEGO COUNTY, Calif.
New approach to reading. R. Van Allen. bibliog f il Wilson Lib Bul 39:154-9 O '64
SAN DIEGO zoological garden
Living pair of dragons at San Diego zoo. il Life 55:57-8 S 27 '63
SANDING
Sanding simplified. G. F. Stillwell. il Motor B 113:27+ Mr '64
SANDING belts. See Belting

SANDING machines
Belt-disk sander. H. R. Clark. il Pop Mech 121:193-5 Ja '64
Belt-disk sander: a tool to own. P. McCafferty. il Pop Sci 182:122-6 F '63
Belt sander that works on its side. B. Burk. il Pop Sci 185:162-3 N '64
Finishing sanders; belt sander. il Pop Sci 183: 172+ D '63
From armature to sander; contour sander. C. B. Dombrowski. il Pop Mech 121:163 Ja '64
Handyman how-to; portable electric sanders. il Bet Hom & Gard 41:33-4 O '63
Power sanders. il Pop Sci 183:168+ N '63
Sanding simplified. G. F. Stillwell. il Motor B 113:27+ Mr '64
What! polish with a belt sander? H. B. Comstock. il Pop Sci 185:166-7 O '64

SANDLER, Irving H.
Al Held paints a picture. Art N 63:42-5+ My '64
James Brooks and the abstract inscape. Art N 61:30-1+ F '63

SANDO, Francis A.
C.P.M: what factors determine its success? Arch Rec 135:211-16 Ap; 202-4 My '64

SANDOE, James
Mystery, detective, suspense (cont) Library J 88:579, 1028, 1550+, 1906, 2276, 2732-3+, 3105, 3648-50, 4239-41, 4666-7 F 1, Mr 1, Ap 1, My 1, Je 1, Jl, S 1, O 1, N 1, D 1 '63

SANDOW, Alexander
Neuromuscular function. Science 139:198-200 Ja 18 '63
—and Preiser, Hanna
Muscular contraction as regulated by the action potential. bibliog Science 146:1470-2 D 11 '64
—and others
Electrochemical coupling in potentiation of muscular contraction. bibliog Science 143: 577-9 F 7 '64

SANDROCK, David H.
Design of simple Q meter. Electr World 72: 84-6 S '64

SANDS, Diana
Sisters under their skins. il por Time 83:96 Je 5 '64

SANDS, Leo G.
Business radio report. Electr World 71:51-4 Ja '64
Electronic scanning simplifies telemetry. Electr World 72:36-7+ Jl '64
New FCC rules now in effect. Electr World 71:30+ My '64
New look in microwaves. Electr World 72:60-2 Ag '64
Upgrade from CB to business radio. Electr World 70:33 Jl '63
V.H.F. marine radiotelephony. Electr World 70:48-9+ Jl '63
Which channel is it? Electr World 71:40+ F '64

SANDS, Matthew
Monitoring a test ban. Bul Atomic Sci 19: 12-15 Mr '63

SANDSON, John, and Hamerman, David
Binding of an alpha globulin to hyaluronate-protein in pathological synovial fluids. bibliog Science 146:70-1 O 2 '64

SANDSTORMS. See Dust storms

SANDSTROM, Richard
Cardboard printmaking; junior high school. Sch Arts 64:27-8 D '64

SANDUSKY, Ohio
Organizing to fight the snow. R. L. Bushman. il Am City 79:38 N '64

SANDVIK steel company. See Sweden—Industries

SANDWICH glass. See Glassware

SANDWICHES
Beer break. M. Kaytor. il Look 27:46 Jl 16 '63
Cheese sandwiches hot off the griddle! il Bet Hom & Gard 41:94 O '63
Great sandwich, wasn't it? il McCalls 91:140-1+ My '64
Ideas for hot sandwiches. Sunset 132:180 Mr '64
Keeping cook cool. C. Claiborne. il N Y Times Mag p 18 Jl 5 '64
Knife and fork sandwich, eight decks high. il Sunset 130:232 My '63
Lucky seven sandwiches. Parents Mag 38:97 Ag '63
Mexican main dish sandwich. il Sunset 130: 176 Ap '63
Open-face sandwiches for cool summer eating. il Sunset 130:172 Je '63
Quick holiday sandwiches. Sunset 131:120 D '63
Sandwiches. il Suc Farm 61:62+ Ag '63
Sandwiches, hot and cold. il Bet Hom & Gard 42:73-4 Ag '64
Sandwiches that make a meal. il Redbook 121:72-3+ Jl '63
Three course sandwich. il McCalls 91:152 My '64
You can reach for these and not worry. il Sunset 130:120 F '63

SANDY HOOK, N.J.
New look into the sea. R. H. Boyle. il Sports Illus 20:58-62+ Mr 9 '64

SANDYS, Duncan
Picking up the pieces. Newsweek 62:49 Jl 22 '63
Tough guy. Newsweek 63:32+ F 3 '64

SANDYS, Sir Edwin
Sir Edwin Sandys and the Parliament of 1604. T. K. Rabb. bibliog f Am Hist R 69:646-70 Ap '64

SANDYS, Stuart Fuller-. See Fuller-Sandys, S.

SANE (organization) See National committee for a sane nuclear policy

SAN FERNANDO VALLEY, Calif.
Valley of compassion; Valley aid for cancer program. D. Gregory. il Look 27:116-18+ O 22 '63

SAN FERNANDO VALLEY times
Toot! toot! Time 82:56-7 O 11 '63

SANFORD, Alexandra
Sea room for the impressionable years. Horn Bk 40:475-84 O '64

SANFORD, Nevitt
New approach to liberal education. Sat R 47: 62-4 Ja 18 '64

SANFORD, Terry
By their own free choice; tobacco and cancer; address, April 6, 1964. Vital Speeches 30:463-7 My 15 '64
Case for the new South. por Look 28:81-4+ D 15 '64

SANFORD family
Sanford coat-of-arms. H. K. Eilers. il Hobbies 69:126 Ag '64

SAN FRANCISCO
Tourism is getting bigger. il Am City 78: 152+ Je '63

Airports

San Francisco airport expansion started. R. H. Cook. il Aviation W 78:41+ Je 24 '63

Architecture

Sky line. L. Mumford. New Yorker 39:143-4+ D 7 '63

Art

Art news from San Francisco. J. Coplans. il Art N 63:21+ Ja '65
Art news from San Francisco. J. Magloff. il Art N 62:51-2 Ja '64
Reviews: San Francisco. J. Magloff. il Art N 63:20 Mr; 20+ Ap; 20+ My '64
Sculptor who embarrasses San Francisco; B. B. Bufano. il Harper 226:53-7 F '63

Churches

Monumental cathedral for the modern age; new Roman Catholic cathedral. il Arch Forum 120:11 Mr '64

City planning

Downtown's dramatic comeback. D. B. Carlson. il Arch Forum 120:103 F '64
New main street for San Francisco. il Arch Forum 118:11 F '63
Sky line. L. Mumford. New Yorker 39:143-4+ D 7 '63
Under the knife, or all for their own good. il Time 84:66+ N 6 '64

Clubs

To the Grove: Bohemian club. il Newsweek 64:19-20 Ag 10 '64
Walden West: members of Bohemian club. il Time 84:21 Ag 7 '64

Description

Magic of California's golden city. R. Dunlop. il Todays Health 42:32-5+ Je '64
San Francisco. L. Lee. il Mlle 57:50+ Je '63
Travel tips. P. P. Coleman. Sr Schol 83:11T N 15 '63

Earthquake and fire, 1906

When San Francisco shook to pieces. il Sr Schol 84:5 Ap 17 '64

Education

Integration. . . in reverse; middle-class white child in Negro slum school. G. B. Leonard. il Look 28:29-37 Ap 21 '64
Man who taught too well; case at Mills high school. D. Bess. Nation 196:507-8+ Je 15 '63
San Francisco's PALS starts them young; Polytechnic high school. A. Corona and R. Corona. il Pop Electr 19:55-6 D '63

SAN FRANCISCO—*Continued*

Galleries and museums

You can go on board San Francisco's floating ship museum October 5. il Sunset 131:18-19+ O '63

See also

M. H. De Young memorial museum, San Francisco

San Francisco museum of art

Historic houses, etc.

Inside story of San Francisco. C. Kellogg. il Ladies Home J 80:62-5 Je '63

History

Mark Twain's San Francisco. B. Taper. il Am Heritage 14:50-3+ Ag '63

Hospitals

Thoughtful layouts for efficient nursing; French hospital. il Arch Rec 136:181-3 O '64

Hotels, restaurants, etc.

Little wonder restaurants of San Francisco. S. Spitzer. Holiday 34:92-3+ N '63

Housing

San Francisco renewal. il Arch Forum 120:72-3 Mr '64

Music

[Musical events] (cont) Mus Am 83:12 Je '63; 84:22 Ja; 11 F; 25 Ap; 20 Jl '64

San Francisco interim. A. Boucher. il Opera N 29:26-7 S 26 '64

San Francisco spring. A. Boucher. il Opera N 28:29 S 28 '63

Show goes on; dispute between Opera association and Musicians union. Newsweek 64:84-5 S 14 '64

See also

San Francisco opera company

San Francisco symphony orchestra

Negroes

There isn't any time. Fortune 70:127-8 Jl '64

Newspapers

What to read in the Cow palace. il Time 84:74-5 Jl 10 '64

See also

San Francisco chronicle

Police

San Francisco's peacemakers; special training for police pays off in smooth handling of civil rights disorders. A. Ogle. America 111:232-3 S 5 '64

Rapid transit

First new rail rapid transit. il Am City 79:108-9 My '64

Recreation

Finest public photographic facilities. F. M. Levy. il Am City 78:28 Jl '63

Social life and customs

Perle Mesta's party notebook. P. Mesta. il McCalls 91:30+ N '63

Stores

Gump's: one of a kind. il Bsns W p46-8+ D 21 '63

Theater

Health in an ailing profession; Actor's workshop. R. Brustein. New Repub 152:32-5 Ja 30 '65

I don't wanna play. H. Blau. il Sat R 47:32+ F 22 '64

Rise of rep. il(p59) Time 83:61 F 14 '64

Theatre; Actor's workshop of San Francisco. H. Clurman. Nation 197:98-9 Ag 24 '63

SAN FRANCISCO ballet

Ballet '63 hits the big time. D. Duncan. il Dance Mag 37:20-1 S '63

San Francisco ballet, Walt Whitman theatre. D. Hering. Dance Mag 38:29-30 Ap '64

SAN FRANCISCO BAY

Steamboat on San Francisco Bay. C. Darlington. il Motor B 111:50+ My '63

SAN FRANCISCO BAY REGION

World of the Bay; drawings by Darrell McClure. J. Mower. Yachting 115:53-6 Je '64

SAN FRANCISCO chronicle

Battle by the bay. il Time 81:75-6 My 17 '63

SAN FRANCISCO examiner

Battle by the bay. il Time 81:75-6 My 17 '63

SAN FRANCISCO federal reserve bank. See Federal reserve banks

SAN FRANCISCO Giants (baseball) See Baseball clubs

SAN FRANCISCO international film festival. See Moving picture festivals

SAN FRANCISCO museum of art

Semper Fi. Newsweek 61:90 Je 10 '63

SAN FRANCISCO opera company

Coming of age in San Francisco. Time 82:64 S 27 '63

Instant opera; four new productions. A. Bloomfield. il Mus Am 84:48-9 D '64

Musical events. W. Sargeant. New Yorker 40:172+ O 10 '64

San Francisco (cont) A. Boucher. il Opera N 28:32 N 16; 31-2 D 7 '63; 29:30-1 N 14; 30 D 19 '64

San Francisco postscript; photographs. Opera N 29:32-3 D 26 '64

San Francisco talent. A. Boucher. Opera N 27:32 Mr 23 '63

Stravinsky and San Francisco. A. Frankenstein. il Theatre Arts 47:22+ Mr '63

SAN FRANCISCO photography center

Finest public photographic facilities. F. M. Levy. il Am City 78:28 Jl '63

SAN FRANCISCO public library

Mishandled, but a landmark. W. R. Holman. il Library J 88:4698-700 D 15 '63

SAN FRANCISCO symphony orchestra

San Francisco discord. Newsweek 63:79 My 18 '64

SAN FRANCISCO Warriors (basketball team) See Basketball teams

SAN GENNARO, Feast of. See Fasts and feasts

SANGER, Clyde

Toward unity in Africa. For Affairs 42:269-81 Ja '64

SANGER, Margaret Anne

Staff meetings based on reading for an age of change series. ALA Bul 58:526 Je '64

SANGRE DE CRISTOS MOUNTAINS

Green-forested, the cloud-haunted Sangre de Cristos. J. Schaefer. Holiday 34:66-7+ Ag '63

SANGSTER, Margaret E.

Ghosts; poem. McCalls 92:106 Ja '65

Such tiny joys; poem. McCalls 91:132 Ag '64

SANGSTER, W. E.

No wonder! Read Digest 82:126-8 Mr '63

SANGUISORBA officinalis. See Burnet

SANITARY affairs. See subhead Sanitary affairs under names of countries, states, cities, e.g. Dayton, Ohio—Sanitary affairs

SANITARY engineering

Odor of chlorine. Am City 78:7 My '63

See also

Pipe laying

Public health

Sewage disposal

Sewer cleaning

Sewerage

Street cleaning

SANITARY engineering center. See United States—Public health service

SANITARY fills. See Filling (earthwork)

SANITARY inspection

See also

Sewer inspection

SANITARY laws. See Public health—Laws and legislation

SANITATION

Are you giving houseroom to health hazards? E. M. Wylie. Am Home 66:14+ Ap '63

See also

Barns and stables—Sanitation

Sanitary engineering

SANITATION, Household

See also

Plumbing

SANITATION garages. See Garages, Municipal

SANITY. See Mental hygiene

SAN JACINTO tramway. See Cableways

SAN JOAQUIN VALLEY information service. See Fresno County, Calif, free library

SAN JOSE, Calif.

Notes for a gazetteer. P. Hamburger. New Yorker 39:148+ My 4 '63

Galleries and museums

See also

Rosicrucian Egyptian, Oriental museum and art gallery

Newspapers

Plum in the valley; Ridder newspaper group. il Time 83:48 My 8 '64

Social conditions

San Jose discovers how it feels to be rich. il Bsns W p70-2+ S 26 '64

SAN JOSÉ, Costa Rica
Ash-covered capital; Irazú's eruption. il Time 83:33 Ja 17 '64
Sky is falling; Irazú eruption. T. Armbrister. il Sat Eve Post 237:20-5 Ap 11 '64
Spectacular Irazú. C. J. Cordero. il Américas 16:21-7 Ap '64
Volcano on a rampage: the tragedy of Costa Rica; Irazú. il U S News 56:71-3 Je 29 '64

SAN JOSÉ PURUA. See Zitácuaro, Mexico

SAN JOSE state college. See California state college. San Jose

SAN JUAN, Puerto Rico

Description

San Juan: the new Havana. W. J. Dorvillier. il Sat R 48:41+ Ja 2 '65
Wondrous San Juan. M. M. Davis. il Travel 120:30-3+ O '63

Hotels, restaurants, etc.

San Juan sequel. M. M. Davis. il Travel 121: 15 Ja '64

Social conditions

Unbeatable mayor of San Juan. il Life 57:65-6+ S 25 '64

Transportation

Packaged fares cut bus operating costs. il Am City 79:133 S '64

SAN JUAN ISLANDS, Wash.
Fifty-four forty or compromise. H. Sutton. Sat R 47:30+ O 17 '64
Hippity hop and away we go. V. Kraft. il Sports Illus 21:40-2+ S 28 '64
North to the islands. B. Robinson. il Yachting 115:68-70+ Ja '64

SAN JUAN RIVER
San Juan turns a corner. il Sunset 133:27 Ag '64

SANKALIA, H. D.
Middle stone age culture in India and Pakistan. bibliog Science 146:365-75 O 16 '64

SAN MARTIN DE PORRES. See Cities and towns—Colombia

SAN MATEO, Calif.

Architecture

Prestige branch bank with an atrium. il Arch Rec 135:128-9 Ja '64

SAN MATEO COUNTY, Calif.
New pattern of disease. Time 86:62-3 N 22 '63

SAN MIGUEL DE ALLENDE, Mexico
Going places, finding things in central Mexico. E. Sheridan. il House & Gard 126:60+ O '64
Today's art in yesterday's city. G. de Zéndegui. il Américas 15:23-6 Mr '63

SAN MIGUEL ISLAND, Calif. See Santa Barbara Islands, Calif.

SANNES, Sanne
Women, wives & witches. M. Orovan. il U S Camera 27:68-71 Ag '64

SAN NICOLAS ISLAND. See Santa Barbara Islands. Calif.

SAN QUENTIN prison. See Prisons—California

SAN REMO, Italy
Little winkel of paradise on the *mittelmeer*. H. Sutton. il Sat R 47:19+ S 5 '64

SAN SALVADOR ISLAND
San Salvador seen first; by Columbus. B. Tufty. Sci N L 86:294 N 7 '64

SANSOM, William
Dreamscape of Connemara. Holiday 33:41-2+ Ap '63
Europe enjoyed: the grand tour today. Holiday 37:38-51+ Ja '65
Gulp-in-the-mouth love; story. Vogue 142: 179 D '63
Magical moments on shipboard. N Y Times Mag p36+ My 10 '64
Montenegro. Holiday 36:54-7+ Ag '64
Sarcophagi and skyscrapers. Holiday 35:62-73+ Mr '64
Smiling land. Holiday 36:58-63+ O '64
Traveling with Mlle: the truant fancy. Mlle 58:123-5 F '64

SANSON, Vitorino
New houses for Rio. Américas 16:32-3 D '64

SANTA ANA, Calif.
Back into Orange County's past; Charles W. Bowers memorial museum. il Sunset 131:34 N '63

SANTA ANITA race track. See Race tracks

SANTA BARBARA, Calif.

Newspapers

How to retire in Santa Barbara; sale of News-press. il Time 83:44 Mr 27 '64
Reader relations. Newsweek 63:61 Mr 16 '64

SANTA BARBARA, Calif, public library
California librarians protest Santa Barbara library situation. Library J 88:4597-8 D 1 '63
Library board issues statement on Santa Barbara situation. Library J 88:3813-14 O 15 '63
Paperbacks in public libraries. W. E. Hinchliff. Sr Schol 82:12T Mr 13 '63
Santa Barbara librarian resigns after clash with deputy. Library J 88:3182-4 S 15 '63; Reply. 88:4104 N 1 '63

SANTA BARBARA city college, Calif.

Library

School for ninety-day wonders. P. Gebhard. il Library J 88:2198-200 Je 1 '63

SANTA BARBARA ISLANDS, Calif.
Cruising the Santa Barbara Channel Islands; Anacapa, Santa Rosa and San Miguel. J. Bugay. il Yachting 113:40-2+ My '63
Offshore California: the Channel Islands. W. P. Crowe. il Yachting 117:106-7+ Ja '65
Waterworks indicates West Coast Indian site. Sci N L 83:216 Ap 6 '63

SANTA BARBARA mission
Mission tour at Santa Barbara. il Sunset 132: 42+ Ap '64

SANTA BARBARA news-press. See Santa Barbara. Calif.—Newspapers

SANTA CATALINA ISLAND
By U-drive boat along Catalina's lee. il Sunset 130:50 Ap '63
Catalina. J. H. Winchester. il Travel 121:24-9 Je '64

SANTA CLARA, Calif.
For God, country and the Santa Clara swim club. W. Trombley. il Sat Eve Post 237: 66-71 Jl 25 '64

Parks and playgrounds

Make your parks people-pleasers. E. Carmichael. il Am City 79:104-6 Ap '64

SANTA CLARA COUNTY, Calif.

Hospitals

Architects employ hospital staff as consultants for unusual design. il Arch Rec 133: 196-8 Mr '63

SANTA CLARA VALLEY, Calif.
San Jose discovers how it feels to be rich. il Bsns W p70-2+ S 26 '64

SANTA CLAUS
Business is awful. A. Buchwald. il McCalls 91:52 D '63
Guess who's playing Santa! il Good H 157: 100-1+ D '63
This ho-ho-ho- business; Santa Claus school, Albion, N.Y. A. Levy. il Sat Eve Post 237: 20-1 D 12 '64
Where Santa comes by troika; in Russia. T. Frankel. McCalls 92:62 D '64
See also
Christmas

Anecdotes, facetiae, satire, etc.

Claus. T. Meehan. New Yorker 40:26-7 Ja 9 '65

SANTA CLAUS and the three polar bears; drama. See Bennett, R.

SANTA CRUZ ISLAND, Calif. See Santa Barbara Islands, Calif.

SANTA ELENA, FORT. See Fort Santa Elena

SANTA FE, N.Mex.
Notes for a gazetteer. P. Hamburger. New Yorker 40:206+ O 17 '64

SANTA FE opera association
Lulu arrives. G. Martin. il Opera N 28:8-12 S 28 '63
Lulu arrives; American stage premiere. A. Young. Mus Am 83:30-1 S '63
Lulu, Daphne, and an uncertain sky. P. J. Smith. il Hi Fi 14:68-71 N '64
New Mexican myth. A. Young. Opera N 29:24 O 17 '64
Santa Fe at seven. G. Martin. il Opera N 28: 28-31 Ap 11 '64
Strauss in Santa Fe. il Newsweek 64:47 Ag 10 '64
Strauss out West; first stage performance in America of Daphne. U. Lucas. Mus Am 84:19 S '64

SANTAMARIA, Carlos Sanz de
Up-beater. Newsweek 63:45 F 3 '64

SANTA MONICA, Calif.
No federal aid for this municipal bus line. E. N. Mobley. il Am City 79:173-4 Je '64
Parking-lot program that leaves the motorist smiling. E. N. Mobley. il Am City 78:147 Je '63

SANTA MONICA city college, Calif.
Excellence in junior college. W. W. Brickman. Sch & Soc 91:297 O 19 '63
SANTANA REYES, Rolando
So it goes; Cultural attaché of the Cuban embassy in Uruguay. R. Peter. Nat R 15: 566 D 31 '63
SANTA ROSA ISLAND, Calif. See Santa Barbara Islands, Calif.
SANTA SOPHIA. See Istanbul—Santa Sophia
SANTAYANA, George
Natural and ultimate religion. por Nat R 15: 561-2 D 31 '63
about
Cool world. por Time 82:114+ N 1 '63
Santayana and the task ahead. A. Danto. Nation 197:437-40 D 21 '63
Santayana, the later years, by D. Cory. Review
Commonweal 79:576-8 F 7 '64. D. Littlejohn
Sat R por 46:40-1 N 16 '63. G. W. Allen
SANTEE, Calif.
Reclaimed sewage becomes a community asset. J. Merrell and R. Stoyer. il Am City 79:97-101 Ap '64
SANTEE RIVER
Singing rivers and a sea of mud. E. White. il Sports Illus 19:66-8+ D 16 '63
SANTER, Melvin
Ribosomal RNA on the surface of ribosomes. bibliog Science 141:1049-50 S 13 '63
SANTIAGO, Chile
Description
Santiago, bright star of Chile. R. Llewellyn. il Holiday 34:76-81+ N '63
Hotels, restaurants, etc.
Portillo: ski incidentals in the Chilean Andes. il Vogue 142:174-5 N 15 '63
SANTILLO, George
Clapper rail. il por Outdoor Life 132:66-8+ S '63
SANTLEY, Sir Charles
Kurz, d'Andrade, Santley, Van Rooy. A. Favia-Artsay. por Hobbies 68:30-1 My '63
SANTO DOMINGO, Dominican Republic
Baroque in Santo Domingo. D. Suro. il Américas 16:15-21 Je '64
Reader's choice. E. Bohan. Travel 121:13 Ja '64
SANTO DOMINGO church. See Lima, Peru—Churches
SANTOS, Vincente N.
Trust Territory of the Pacific Islands; statement, June 5, 1963. Dept State Bul 49:219-22 Ag 5 '63
SAN VITO DE JAVA
Italian colonists in Costa Rica. D. G. Cole. il Américas 15:38-41 Je '63
SANYAL, H. N.
Question of confidence. por Newsweek 64:49-50 S 21 '64
SÃO PAULO (city), Brazil
Brazilian bright spot. il U S News 55:68-9 Ag 12 '63
São Paulo, city of promise. R. Llewellyn. il Holiday 33:68-77+ F '63
Theater
Theatre. S. Richards. il Theatre Arts 47:64-5 F '63
SÃO PAULO biennial. See Art—Exhibitions
SÃO SALVADOR. See Salvador, Brazil
SAP
How sap moves in trees. M. H. Zimmermann. il Sci Am 208:132-8+ bibliog(p 192) Mr '63
SAPORITI, Piero
He caught her eye at the bullfights. Life 56: 40B F 21 '64
SAPOTES
Sapote makes a good impression. il Sunset 132:280+ Ap '64
SARA, pseud.
So I'm not Lady Chatterley, so better I should know it now; story. Commentary 35:44-51 Ja '63
SARABHAI, Mrinalini
Dance is my beloved. il pors Dance Mag 38: 54-7 Ja '64
SARAF, D. N. and others
Diffusion coefficients of hydrocarbons in water: method for measuring. bibliog Science 142:955-6 N 15 '63
SARAGAT, Giuseppe
At last! il por Newsweek 65:39 Ja 11 '65
Red votes end Italian impasse. por Bsns W p22 Ja 2 '65
SARAH Lawrence college, Bronxville, N.Y.
Mrs Raush; new president Mrs E. Raushenbush. il Newsweek 65:47 F 1 '65
SARAH; story. See Hamer, M. J.
SARAIVA, Antonio José
Portuguese Sancho Panza in the Far East. UNESCO Courier 16:14-19 Ap '63
SARAJEVO, Yugoslavia
Local, personal affair; assassination of Archduke Franz Ferdinand. C. G. Pepper. il Newsweek 64:37-8 Jl 13 '64
Sarajevo revisited, fifty years after. J. A. Barry. il N Y Times Mag p 12-13+ Je 28 '64
SARASOTA, Fla.
Education
Master plan for consolidated public school. il Arch Rec 135:154-5 F '64
Theater
What price theater? Asolo theater. H. Hewes. Sat R 47:36 S 19 '64
SARATOGA race track. See Race tracks
SARATOGA SPRINGS, N.Y.
Centennial summer. il Newsweek 62:55 Ag 19 '63
100-year binge. il Time 82:43 Ag 9 '63
100-year spree at Saratoga; with report by M. Smith. il Life 55:52B-61 Jl 26 '63
Saratoga racing centennial; reproductions of paintings. P. Davis. Sports Illus 19:34-9 Ag 5 '63
Saratoga Springs. R. Kelley. il Travel 120: 50-2 Ag '63
Sporting scene. R. Angell. New Yorker 40: 185-8+ S 12 '64
SARAWAK
Our far-flung correspondents; Federation of Malaysia. R. Shaplen. New Yorker 39:155-8 Ap 6 '63
Rajah's return. il Time 81:41-2 My 17 '63
Roadblock; inclusion of North Borneo and Sarawak. Newsweek 62:45-6 S 2 '63
Sarawak; Peace corps volunteer. E. C. Price, jr. il Nat Geog Mag 126:334-7 S '64
Troubles of becoming a nation; the story of Malaysia. R. P. Martin. il U S News 54: 80-1 Ap 15 '63
Tunku yes, Sukarno no. Time 82:24 S 6 '63
SARAZANI, Fabrizio
Arab-Venetian: a pleasure dome. Vogue 142: 186-91 S 15 '63
SARCOMA
Chromosome abnormalities in vitro in human leukocytes associated with Schmidt-Ruppin Rous sarcoma virus. W. W. Nichols and others. bibliog il Science 146:248-50 O 9 '64
Defective cancer virus; Rous sarcoma virus. H. Rubin. il Sci Am 210:46-52 Je '64
Defective virus; Rous sarcoma virus. Sci Am 208:74+ Je '63
Growth inhibition of sarcoma and carcinoma cells of homozygous origin. K. E. Hellström. bibliog Science 143:477-8 Ja 31 '64
Low malignancy of Rous sarcoma cells as evidenced by poor transplantability in turkeys. V. V. Bergs and V. Groupe. bibliog il Science 139:922-3 Mr 8 '63
Radium-226, radium-228, lead-210, and fluorine in persons with osteogenic sarcoma. H. F. Lucas, jr. and others. bibliog il Science 144:1573-5 Je 26 '64
Rous sarcoma in Chinese hamsters. C. G. Ahlström and others. bibliog il Science 144: 1232-3 Je 5 '64
Sarcomas in cotton rats inoculated with Rous virus. G. J. Svet-Moldavsky and I. A. Svet-Moldavskaya. bibliog Science 143:54-5 Ja 3 '64
Tumors induced in primates by chicken sarcoma virus. J. S. Munroe and W. F. Windle. bibliog il Science 140:1415-16 Je 28 '63
SARCOPHAGA. See Flies
SARDINES
Night-caught and day-caught larvae of the California sardine. J. D. Isaacs. bibliog il Science 144:1132-3 My 29 '64
Sardines. il Changing T 18:47 F '64
SARDINIA
Escape to the sun. il Holiday 37:70-3 Ja '65
Sardinia. il Vogue 141:106-9 Ap 15 '63
Sardinia, how to share the renaissance of a lovely island. H. Barnes. il House B 105: 54+ Ag '63
Sardinia incidentals; practical, specific. Vogue 141:26 Ap 15 '63
SARDIS
Digs expose ancient Lydian capital. G. M. A. Hanfmann. il Natur Hist 72:18-27 D '63
Golden Sardis. G. M. A. Hanfmann. il Horizon 5:82-9 S '63
SARFATY, Regina
Quote: unquote: interview. ed. by R. Jacobson. por Mus Am 84:29 Ja '64

SARGANT, William
Psychiatric treatment; here and in England. por Atlan 214:88-95 Jl '64

SARGASSO SEA
Strontium content and variable strontium-chlorinity relationship of Sargasso sea water. F. T. Mackenzie. bibliog il Science 146:517-18 O 23 '64

SARGEANT, Winthrop
Books (cont) New Yorker 39:208+ O 26 '63; 40:122+ F 22 '64
Crucible. Am Rec G 29:508-9+ Mr '63
Musical events. See issues of New Yorker
Profiles (cont) New Yorker 39:49-50+ My 4 '63; 40:49-50+ Je 6 '64

SARGENT, Bob
Two halos stacked for 2 meters. Pop Electr 22:65-6 Ja '65

SARGENT, E. N.
Santos: tempo rumba; poem. New Yorker 39:46 Ap 13 '63

SARGENT, Herb
How to face the move to California. Esquire 59:70 My '63

SARGENT, John Singer
Instead of paughtraits. il Time 83:114-16 Ap 17 '64
John Singer Sargent and decoration. D. F. Hoopes. il Antiques 86:588-91 N '64
John Singer Sargent; his private world. N. Lansdale. il Am Artist 28:58-63+ N '64

SARGENT, Martin van Buren
Reach for young rebels. il por Time 85:61 Ja 22 '65

SARIDELE. See Soybean products

SARIT Thanarat
Death of a man. il por Time 82:18 D 20 '63
Hard to replace. Newsweek 62:30 D 23 '63
Legacy of Sarit Thanarat. D. Warner. Reporter 31:42-4 S 24 '64
Marshal's minor wives & major tickel; question of misappropriation of public funds. il por Time 84:30 Jl 17 '64
Sarit's legacy. il Time 83:22 Mr 27 '64
Where did all that money come from? S. Karnow. il pors Sat Eve Post 237:62-3+ O 31 '64

SARKISSIAN, Karekin
Interview with the Armenian observer at the council; ed. by E. M. Jung. Cath World 197:258-63 Jl '63

SARMIENTO, Domingo Faustino
Sarmiento, the educator. E. Correas. il por Américas 16:27-32 Ag '64

SARNOFF, David
By the end of the twentieth century. Fortune 69:116-19 My '64
Promise of the future. por Seventeen 23:240+ Ag '64
Storing sparks tomorrow; excerpt from Promise and challenge of the computer. Sat R 48:95 Ja 2 '65

about

David Sarnoff's vision. H. H. Martin. por Sat Eve Post 236:56+ F 16 '63
RCA's signal: coming in strong. il por(cover) Bsns W p 110-12+ Je 29 '63

SARNOFF, Robert W.
Television journalism: address, December 7, 1964. Vital Speeches 31:174-7 Ja 1 '65

about

Sarnoff fights back. P. Goodman. New Repub 148:25-7 Ap 20 '63

SAROYAN, Aram
Extension of content. Poetry 104:45-7 Ap '64
Six poems: I have spent a year mostly alone; Bad dreams; At a bus stop; My friends one by one; Talking to you; Facts. Poetry 104:20-2 Ap '64

SAROYAN, William
Alive; story. Ladies Home J 81:65-6 Ag '64
Americans in Paris, 1929. New Repub 148:26-8 F 9 '63
Around the world, and death, and back again. Reporter 30:31-4 Je 4 '64
Best angel God ever saw. por Sat Eve Post 236:94-5 N 16 '63
Dusty, smeared, musty, moldy, tattered life of P. T. Barnum. Sat Eve Post 237:70-1 Je 13 '64
Event of enormous beauty. Sat Eve Post 237:84-5 Ag 8 '64
Four plays: Playwright and the public; Handshakers; Doctor and the patient; This I believe. Atlan 211:50-2 Ap '63
Funny business of marriage. por Sat Eve Post 236:44-5 O 5 '63
It's me, O Lord! por Sat Eve Post 237:75-6 Ap 18 '64
Me. Sat Eve Post 236:54-9 Mr 9 '63
Miraculous phonograph record. Sat Eve Post 236:84-5 O 19 '63
Oldest story; story. Sat Eve Post 236:54-60 My 11 '63
Shout Armenia wherever you go. Sat Eve Post 237:74+ N 21 '64
Sons and fathers. Reporter 31:52-3 S 24 '64
Wild boy. Sat Eve Post 237:32+ Ja 25 '64

SARRAUTE, Nathalie
Books; instruments. R. Adler. New Yorker 40:181-3 My 2 '64
Salon saboteur. V. Mercier. Nation 198:217-18 Mr 2 '64

SARRIS, Andrew
Farthest-out moviegoers. Sat R 47:14-15 D 26 '64

SARTON, May
House in winter; poem. New Yorker 39:65 Ja 4 '64
Joanna & Ulysses; story. Ladies Home J 80:70-2 S '63

SARTOR, J. Doyne
Radio observation of the electromagnetic emission from warm clouds. bibliog Science 143:948-50 F 28 '64

SARTRE, Jean Paul
Jean-Paul Sartre speaks; interview, ed. by J. Piatier. Vogue 145:94-5+ Ja 1 '65
Making of a writer; excerpt from The words, tr. by B. Frechtman. Harper 229:49-57 S; 101-4+ O '64

about

Books. J. Stafford. Vogue 144:98 O 15 '64
Childhood of a leader. G. Elliott. Nation 199:118-19 S 14 '64
Existentialism; with report by F. Kappler. il pors Life 57:86-96+ N 6 '64
Existentialist self-analysis. L. LeSage. por Sat R 47:34-5+ S 12 '64
First installment of Sartre's autobiography. G. Greene. Commonweal 81:75-6 O 9 '64
La force des choses, by S. de Beauvoir. Review
New Yorker 39:88-91 Ja 11 '64. Genêt
Lauréat malgré lui. por Newsweek 64:52-3 N 2 '64
Letter from Paris. Genêt. New Yorker 39:142+ N 16 '63; 40:170 My 16 '64
Letter from Paris; concerning a lecture on literature. Genêt. New Yorker 40:68-70 D 26 '64
Nobel committee and Sartre. W. F. Buckley, jr. Nat R 16:1004 N 17 '64
Pen is not the sword. il por Time 84:112+ O 9 '64
Prophet of nevertheless. il por Time 84:44 O 30 '64
Question of fidelity; excerpts from Force of circumstance, tr. by R. Howard. S. de Beauvoir. Harper 229:57-64 N; 111-14+ D '64
Sartre: fragments of an autobiography. J. Daniel. New Repub 151:19-21 O 10 '64
Sartre: French philosopher is model of literary intellectual by two cultures definition. J. Walsh. Science 146:900-2 N 13 '64
Sartre: nothing but nothing. Christian Cent 80:479 Ap 10 '63
Sartre resartus. J. O'Brien. Reporter 31:47-8 N 5 '64
Self-made man. por Newsweek 64:124 O 5 '64
Two good choices. Nation 199:319 N 9 '64

SARTWELL, Frank
Mariner scans a lifeless Venus. Nat Geog Mag 123:732-42 My '63

SASIDHORN, Nibondh. See Smythe, H. H. jt. auth.

SASKATCHEWAN
See also
Zoology—Saskatchewan

SASLOW, George
Cardiovascular disease. Science 142:601+ N 1 '63

SASS, Daniel B.
Paleontology. Science 143:166+ Ja 10 '64

SASSA, Atsuyuki
New light on the assassination: a secret agent's story; excerpts from interview, ed. by G. Troelstrup. U S News 56:38-9 Je 8 '64

SASSAFRAS
Toast to a tree. C. E. Randall. il Am For 70:22-4+ My '64

SASSOON, H. F. and Parsons, M. H. C.
Brownian movement in color photomicrography. Science 139:1285-6 Mr 29 '63

SASTRY, Krishna K. S. and Muir, R. M.
Gibberellin: effect on diffusible auxin in fruit development. bibliog Science 140:494-5 My 3 '63

SATAN. See Devil

SATELLITE for aerospace research. See Artificial satellites—Use in research

SATELLITE states. See Communist countries

SATELLITES
Galileo's first records of Jupiter's satellites; reprint. J. Meeus. il Sky & Tel 27:105-6 F '64
Jupiter, largest of the planets, has twelve known satellites. S. D. Gossner. il Natur Hist 72:54-5 My '63
See also
Artificial satellites

SATIE, Erik
Man with a mask. E. Helm. il por Hi Fi 13:54-6+ D '63
Music marathon; Satie's Vexations repeated 840 times. Newsweek 62:95 S 23 '63
Shoot the piano player; Satie's Vexations played 840 times in succession. por Time 82:54 S 20 '63

SATIRE
Anti-establishmentarians. R. Brustein. New Repub 148:28-9 F 23 '63
British satirists are a bloody bore. J. G. Dunne. Life 56:18 Ap 24 '64
From Alice to Animal farm: getting students to appreciate and write satire. S. Cochell. il Sr Schol 85:10T S 16 '64
Letter from London. C. Marowitz. Nation 196:313-14 Ap 13 '63
Mad: wild oracle of the teenage underground. J. Skow. il Sat Eve Post 236:62-5 D 21 '63
Over and out; Village vanguard series of Speak outs. New Yorker 40:29-31 D 19 '64
Sour grapes and peaches. A. Pryce-Jones. il Theatre Arts 47:20-1 My '63
This is the satire that is; concerning British satire and humor. B. Hollowood. il N Y Times Mag p 13+ Jl 7 '63
See also
Caricatures and cartoons
Parodies

SATO, Eisaku
Japan, the U.S, and war in South Vietnam; interview, ed. by R. P. Martin. por U S News 58:42-3 Ja 11 '65

about

Final act. por Newsweek 64:54 N 23 '64
Pilgrim on flight 800. por Time 85:24 Ja 15 '65
Pro-U.S. premier; anti-U.S. riots. il por U S News 57:20 N 23 '64
Who is Mr Sato? il por Newsweek 65:44-5 Ja 25 '65

SATO, Satoru
Susuki and dragonflies; poem. Poetry 105:165 D '64

SATTERFIELD, John Creighton
Excerpt from address, January 30, 1964. Cong Digest 43:93+ Mr '64
Government by intimidation is emerging in U.S. por U S News 55:122-3 O 14 '63

SATTLER, Harald
Shah was not amused. Time 85:26 Ja 22 '65

SATTLEY, Helen R.
Elementary school library growth in New York city. ALA Bul 58:482-8 Je '64

SATURDAY evening post
Balm for a gloomy bear; settlement of libel actions against the Saturday evening post. Time 83:51 F 14 '64
Butts reverses field to try for full $3,060,000. Pub W 185:77 F 10 '64
Campaign reflections by a family magazine. W. F. Buckley, jr. Nat R 16:854-5 O 6 '64
Curtis fight over; Post reduced to twenty-six issues. Pub W 186:31-2 N 23 '64
Days of decision; Bryant libel suits. Newsweek 63:65 F 17 '64
Debatable football scandal in the Southeast; Georgia-Alabama game. D. Jenkins. il Sports Illus 18:18-21 Mr 25 '63
Dramatic moment; case of W. Butts vs. Curtis publishing company. il Sports Illus 19:26-7 Ag 26 '63
Fix or fiction? W. Butts. il Time 82:38+ Ag 16 '63
High cost of libel; W. Butts v. Curtis publishing co. il Newsweek 62:72-3 S 2 '63
How much can coach Butts keep? 3-million-dollar libel award. U S News 55:6+ S 2 '63
I call on Joe Culligan. P. Martin. Esquire 59:84-6+ Mr '63
It's not the money, it's the vindication; with editorial comment. R. H. Boyle. il Sports Illus 19:5, 46-7 S 2 '63
Keeping posted; new 1965 schedule. Newsweek 64:51 Ag 3 '64
Libel judgement against Curtis reduced to $460,000. Pub W 185:239 Ja 27 '64
Look at the past and the future; change to biweekly publication. Sat Eve Post 237:84 D 12 '64
Money for the Post. Time 83:43 Ja 24 '64
Post and integration; editorial. Sat Eve Post 236:70 Mr 2 '63
So sue me. il Time 81:51 Mr 29 '63
Somebody's lying; report of alleged conspiracy to rig Georgia-Alabama game. Newsweek 61:51 Ap 1 '63
Sophisticated muckraking; W. Butts's libel suit. il Time 82:34 Ag 23 '63
$3,060,000 worth of guilt. il Time 82:37+ Ag 30 '63

SATURDAY review
Beyond make-believe; second annual SR-U.S. national student association magazine contest. S. B. Chickering. Sat R 47:28-9 O 10 '64
Dr Canby and his team. M. Cowley. il Sat R 47:54-5+ Ag 29 '64
Saturday review: a birthday salute. C. B. Grannis. Pub W 186:302 Ag 31 '64
SR's eleventh-twelfth annual advertising awards. W. D. Patterson. il Sat R 46:62-7 Ap 13 '63; 47-73-6+ Ap 11 '64; Discussion of Ap 11 issue. 47:60 My 9 '64
Three years later; Saturday review and McCall corporation. N. Cousins. Sat R 47:20+ F 29 '64
Trade winds; special anniversary column. B. Cerf. il Sat R 47:10+ Ag 29 '64
See also
Amy Loveman national award
Anisfield-Wolf awards

SATURDAY review moral adoption program. See Adoption

SATURDAY review of literature. See Saturday review

SATURN (planet)
Infrared Saturn photograph. il Sky & Tel 26:10 Jl '63
Laboratory exercises in astronomy, the rotation of Saturn and its rings. O. Gingerich. il Sky & Tel 28:278-9 N '64
Like a diamond in the sky. il Time 81:47 Mr 22 '63
Saturn, second largest planet, has a unique system of rings. S. D. Gossner. il Natur Hist 72:52-3 Je '63
Saturn's rings less than one foot thick. Sci N L 83:168 Mr 16 '63
Studies of Jupiter and Saturn. il Sky & Tel 28:133 S '64
Wondrous rings of Saturn. T. D. Nicholson. il Natur Hist 73:50-2 O '64

SATURN (space vehicle) See Space vehicles

SATURN booster. See Space vehicles—Propulsion systems

SATZ, Janet Maas
Art of Janet Maas Satz. W. Caxton, jr. il por Am Artist 28:26-31+ My '64

SAUBERT, Jean
Extracurricular. il por Newsweek 63:58 Ja 20 '64
Gamin with a world of guts. D. Jenkins. il por Sports Illus 20:12-15 Ja 20 '64
Undeniably a girl. il por Time 83:74 Ja 17 '64

SAUCERS, Flying. See Flying saucers

SAUCES
Brown saucery; with recipes. C. Claiborne. il N Y Times Mag p98+ N 3 '63
Coquettish croquettes. il McCalls 92:138-9+ O '64
Dessert sauces. Am Home 67:77 N '64
Golden succulent turkey and smooth gravy. Am Home 66:68-9 N '63
Happy marriage: asparagus with hollandaise. il McCalls 91:38 Je '64
How to slice, dice, boil, broil, stuff, puff, wash, squash, cream, steam, prepare and care for vegetables. il Am Home 67:54-5+ Ap '64
Make your own barbecue sauce. Sunset 130:198 My '63
Marinades and bastes. il Am Home 67:62+ My '64
Sauce marvels are easy, using a blender. il Sunset 130:210 Mr '63
Sauce that's saucier; vinaigrette sauce. C. Claiborne. il N Y Times Mag p49-50 Je 2 '63
Sauce up lamb for spring; with recipes. il Bet Hom & Gard 42:112-13 Ap '64
Sauces vive la différence! il Am Home 67:66+ O '64
Successful recipes; ice cream and sauces. il Suc Farm 62:57-8 Je '64
Ways to sauce spaghetti; with recipes. Sunset 132:180-1 Ap '64

SAUD, king of Saudi Arabia (abdicated 1964)
Acting for the king. Newsweek 63:47 Ap 13 '64
Ailing, failing king. por Time 81:38 My 24 '63
Brother act. por Newsweek 63:34 Ja 13 '64
Crown prince. Newsweek 64:50+ N 16 '64
Long linger the King. Time 81:34 Ap 5 '63

SAUD, king of Saudi Arabia—*Continued*
No place like home. Time 82:34 S 27 '63
Out of the Arabian nights into the 20th century. il por U S News 55:83-4 N 25 '63
Reformer replaces a big spender. por U S News 56:16 Ap 13 '64
Silent monarch. il Time 83:40 Ja 3 '64
Tough all over. il por Newsweek 62:43 Jl 22 '63
Two more kings in trouble. il pors U S News 54:96-7 My 6 '63
SAUDER, E. R.
Instruments for engines that generate power. Am City 79:121-2 S '64
SAUDI ARABIA
See also
Slavery—Saudi Arabia
Economic conditions
Re-emergence of Saudi Arabia. il Sr Schol 82:8-11+ Ja 30 '63
Foreign relations
At cross-purposes in the sands of Yemen. D. Holden. il Reporter 28:37+ F 14 '63
Politics and government
Acting for the king. Newsweek 63:47 Ap 13 '64
Allah's choice; Prince Feisal becomes regent. Time 83:33-4 Ap 10 '64
Brace of kings. il Time 84:43-4 N 20 '64
Brother act. il Newsweek 63:34 Ja 13 '64
Crown prince; Faisal is new king. Newsweek 64:50+ N 16 '64
Decisive weeks. Newsweek 62:37-8 S 30 '63
Faisal modernizes but with caution. D. A. Schmidt. il N Y Times Mag p38+ N 1 '64
No place like home. Time 82:34 S 27 '63
Out of the Arabian nights into the 20th century. il U S News 55:83-4 N 25 '63
Re-emergence of Saudi Arabia. il Sr Schol 82:8-11+ Ja 30 '63
Reformer replaces a big spender. il U S News 56:16 Ap 13 '64
Silent monarch. il Time 83:40 Ja 3 '64
Where a friend of the West runs things now. U S News 57:20 N 16 '64
SAUER, Louis W.
Your child's health. See issues of PTA magazine
SAUERBRATEN. See Cookery—Meat
SAUERKRAUT
See also
Cookery—Vegetables
SAUL, Margaret
Business of book buying, as special librarians see it. Library J 88:2636-9 Jl '63
NACS: management seminar studies how to measure, control pilferage. Pub W 186:30-3 S 21 '64
SAUL, Peter
Discredited merchandise. il por Newsweek 64:94+ N 9 '64
SAULNIER, Raymond J.
People of the week. por U S News 54:20 My 13 '63
SAULT SAINTE MARIE, Ontario
They find lost men; Search and rescue unit. B. East. il Outdoor Life 133:33-5+ Je '64
SAUNA. See Baths, Vapor
SAUNDERS, Alexander, Jr
Workshop: casting in the ceramic shell. Craft Horiz 23:50-1 Jl '63
SAUNDERS, James
Next time I'll sing to you; dramatization of Hermit disclosed, by R. Trevelyan. Criticism
Commonweal 79:404 D 27 '63
New Yorker 39:131-2 D 7 '63
New Yorker 39:148+ My 25 '63
Sat R 46:25 D 14 '63
SAUNDERS, Jennifer
Globular cluster Omega Centauri. Sky & Tel 26:133-7 S '63
SAUNDERS, Joseph F.
Water molecule in biological systems. Science 147:179-81 Ja 8 '65
SAUNDERS, Josephine
Ill and exiled to the desert; poem. New Yorker 39:134 My 18 '63
SAUNDERS, R. A.
Overqualified. New Repub 151:22 Ag 22 '64
SAUNDERS, Robert
INSEA 1963. Sch Arts 63:18 D '63
SAUNDERS, Silvia
American exhibits at England's famous Chelsea flower show. Pop Gard 14:6+ My '63
SAUNDERS, Stuart Thomas
Businessmen in the news. por Fortune 68:69 Ag '63
Key man behind railroad mergers. il por U S News 57:114-15 O 12 '64
No. one railroad job: it goes to a merger expert. por U S News 55:21 Jl 8 '63
Outlook: brighter. il por Time 82:81 Jl 5 '63
Pennsy's road ahead. T. O'Hanlon. il por Duns R 83:36-8+ F '64
Switch of tracks. por Newsweek 62:72-4 Jl 8 '63
SAUROMATUM
Lizard to grow in the garden. V. Greiff. il Flower Grower 50:80 Ag '63
SAUSAGE
Art of sausage making. Sunset 134:114+ Ja '65
Inside facts about sausages. il Good H 157: 163 O '63
Potato sausages are easy to make. Sunset 132:176 Ap '64
See also
Cookery—Game
Cookery—Meat
SAUSAGE festival. See Festivals—Texas
SAUSALITO, Calif.
On a wooded California slope with a view. il Arch Rec 135:150-3 Ja '64
SAUTÉING. See Frying
SAUTER, Van G.
According to Hoiles. New Repub 150:5 F 22 '64
SAUVAGE, Leo
Oswald affair. Commentary 37:55-65 Mr '64
Oswald in Dallas: a few loose ends. Reporter 30:24-6 Ja 2 '64
SAVAGE, Mildred
In vivo; story. Good H 158:83-5 My '64
SAVAGE, Richard
Control of character. Writer 76:7-9 Ag '63
SAVAGE, W. Sherman
George Washington of Centralia Washington. bibliog Negro Hist Bul 27:44-7 N '63
SAVANG Vatthana, king of Laos
Around the world with Savang Vatthana. il por Time 81:25 Mr 8 '63
SAVANNAH, Ga.
Historic houses, etc.
Southern mansion with timeless ideas; Owens-Thomas House. il House & Gard 124:148-51 S '63
SAVANNAH (ship) See Ships, Atomic powered
SAVANNAH RIVER
U.S. undercuts own job-making goal. il Nations Bsns 51:40-1+ Jl '63
SAVANYU, Jean
Curl up and read. Seventeen 22:79 Ag '63; 23:94+ Ap '64
SAVARESE, Julia
Side lights. Am Home 66:64+ Je; 12+ Jl; 20-1 S '63
SAVE me a place at Forest Lawn; drama. See Yerby, L.
SAVE the children federation
Self-help in Appalachia. H. Gunther. il Sr Schol 85:11T O 21 '64
SAVIDIS, George
Note on Takis Sinopoulos. Poetry 105:43 O '64
(tr) See Elytis, O. Axion esti: The genesis
(tr) See Sinopoulos, T. Magda; Sophia etc; Sight and vision; Ioanna's invitation; One of Constantine's nights; Beheading
SAVIGNAC, Raymond
Visual haymakers. il por Newsweek 63:76+ Ap 13 '64
SAVILE, D. B. O.
Spore discharge in basidiomycetes: a unified theory. bibliog Science 147:165-6 Ja 8 '65
SAVILL gardens. See Gardens—England
SAVING and savings
Consumer saving. Fortune 68:44+ O '63
Drift to thrift. D. Seligman and others. il Fortune 68:261-2+ Jl '63
Family financial program. il Changing T 17: 39-43 Ag; 41-5 S; 41-5 O; 39-43 N '63
How can you start saving? Bet Hom & Gard 42:91 Ja '64
Insure savings to $25,000? U S News 54:110-11 Ap 15 '63
Low finance; questions and answers. J. Goodsell. il Ladies Home J 80:42 Ap '63
150,000 at GE share $110-million payout. Bsns W p80 Mr 16 '63
Safety is family investor's goal as stocks hit record highs. U S News 55:113 S 23 '63
Savings of Americans grow past trillion-dollar mark; summary of report. U S News 56:98 Ap 13 '64
Shift in saving habits. U S News 56:97-8 Mr 9 '64
Time to borrow. Time 85:80 Ja 15 '65
Tug-of-war for tax savings; savings institutions vs merchandisers; with editorial comment. il Bsns W p34, 192 Mr 21 '64

SAVING and savings—*Continued*
What people are doing with their savings. il U S News 54:107-8 Mr 18 '63
What's happening to savings. il U S News 54:105 Je 10 '63
Where people are putting money. U S News 55:92-3 Jl 15 '63
Where people are putting their extra money. il U S News 57:75-6 Ag 10 '64
Where people keep their savings, and why. il Changing T 18:33-6 D '64
Where savings now earn most. il U S News 57:72-4 D 21 '64
Where tax-cut money ended up. U S News 57:88-9 S 21 '64
Your nonfarm assets; what are they worth? il Suc Farm 61:35 O '63
See also
Finance, Personal
Investment clubs
Investments
Postal savings banks

SAVING grace; drama. See Blum, E. H.

SAVINGS and loan associations
Borderline vs. outright; indictment of West Coast savings & loan association. Newsweek 62:76 S 30 '63
California's S.&L.'s: the boom the bankers knock. H. Kay. il Fortune 70:118-23+ Ag '64
Detective from the city room. Time 83:44+ Mr 27 '64
Easier borrowing for builders? U S News 56:99 Ja 27 '64
Going up again: interest rates on savings; role of mutual savings banks. il U S News 55:103-4 S 16 '63
Growing pains. Time 83:83-4 Mr 27 '64
In works: new bank controls. U S News 54: 112-13 My 6 '63
Man who makes S&Ls toe the mark; FHLBB's J. P. McMurray. il Bsns W p72-4+ Ja 18 '64
Money comes in faster than it goes out. il Newsweek 62:70-2 S 16 '63
More on savings-loan clampdown. U S News 55:129-31 N 18 '63
New curb for savings-loan firms. U S News 56:86 Ja 20 '64
New U.S. rules for savings and loans: what 1964 will bring. U S News 55:94-5 N 4 '63
Official worry: rate war for the savings dollar. il U S News 55:113-15 O 14 '63
Policeman who pounds California's S&L beat. il Bsns W p40-1 Jl 4 '64
Rate war. Newsweek 62:74 Jl 8 '63
S&Ls at the $1-billion crossroads. R. Nason. il Duns R 82:43-5+ D '63
Savings and loans: lots of money and problems. U S News 54:103-4 My 27 '63
Savings & loans: more rate cuts. U S News 54:106 Je 3 '63
Savings and loans' rate war and what can come of it. il U S News 55:91-2 Jl 15 '63
Shift in savings and loan rate? U S News 55:87 Jl 1 '63
Twelvefold increase. Time 82:56 Ag 30 '63

Holding companies
Fight brewing on S&L holding companies. Bsns W p54 Mr 2 '63
S&L watchdogs growl louder; tighter controls over dividend policies. Bsns W p45 O 26 '63
S&Ls on coast close ranks. Bsns W p76+ Ag 22 '64

Securities
Executive investor; undervalued S&Ls? il Duns R 81:73-74E Je '63

SAVINGS banks
Going up again: interest rates on savings; role of mutual savings banks. il U S News 55:103-4 S 16 '63

SAVINGS bonds. See Bonds, Government

SAVINGS-sharing plan in industry
Appraisal of Kaiser's sharing plan. C. A. MacIlvaine. Mo Labor R 87:401-4 Ap '64
Approach to automation: the Kaiser plan. A. H. Raskin. il N Y Times Mag p20-1+ N 3 '63
Breakthrough at Kaiser; automation and unemployment. L. T. King. Commonweal 78: 11-12 Mr 29 '63
Cutting Kaiser's melon. America 108:659 My 11 '63
Fruits of Kaiser plan taste sweet to all; share cost savings. il Bsns W p47-8 S 21 '63
Group incentive; Kaiser plan. T. R. Brooks. Duns R 81:47E-8 Mr '63
How workers benefit when costs are cut. il U S News 54:91-2 My 6 '63
Kaiser plan passes first test; savings sharing plan. il Bsns W p48+ My 4 '63
Kaiser's melon; long-range sharing plan payoff. Newsweek 61:76 My 6 '63
Landmark in labor relations; Kaiser-United steelworkers agreement. H. Malmgren. New Repub 148:7 Mr 16 '63
Long range sharing plan for Kaiser steel corp. employees; text of the plan. Mo Labor R 86:154-60 F '63
Managing your manpower; Kaiser's long range sharing plan. T. R. Brooks. Duns R 84:65 Jl '64
Outsiders keep peace at Kaiser. Bsns W p 105 O 24 '64
Profit sharing for workers: troubles of a noble experiment; American motors and United auto workers. il U S News 57:117+ O 26 '64
Profit sharing: what union won; United auto workers and American motors corporation. U S News 57:72 N 2 '64
Second look at profit sharing; American motors, Kaiser steel. U S News 56:78-9 Je 22 '64
Sharing plans: two reports; Kaiser steel, American motors. U S News 56:86 Ap 13 '64
When workers join in cutting costs; who gains; sharing of savings at Kaiser steel corporation. il U S News 55:113-15 O 21 '63

SAVIO, Mario
Savio onstage. il por Newsweek 64:71 D 21 '64

SAVOIE, Leonard M.
Accounting improvement: how fast, how far? bibliog f Harvard Bsns R 41:144-50+ Jl '63

SAVOY Plaza (hotel) See New York (city)—Hotels, restaurants, etc.

SAVOYARDS. See D'Oyly Carte opera company

SAW horses. See Sawhorses

SAWAKO, Ariyoshi
Prayer; story, tr. by J. Bester. Redbook 121: 133-42 Ag '63

SAWDUST mulching. See Mulching

SAWHORSES
Knockdown sawhorses. il Pop Sci 184:101 Ja '64
Sawhorses the easy way. il Sunset 133:166 N '64

SAWING
How to saw good, like all of us should. R. J. DeCristoforo. il Pop Sci 184:104-7 Je '64

SAWMILLS
Wages and hours
Wages in southern sawmills and planing mills, June 1962. G. L. Stelluto. il Mo Labor R 86:151-3 F '63

SAWS
Bike saw. F. L. Anderson. il Pop Mech 121: 186 F '64
Copper overcoats for saw blades. R. J. De Cristoforo. il Pop Mech 120:124-5+ O '63
DeWalt's new direct-drive table saw. R. J. De Cristoforo. il Pop Sci 185:160-1 N '64
Four special jobs for a saber saw. W. E. Burton. il Pop Sci 182:148-50 F '63
Hacksaws are getting more versatile. il Pop Mech 120:38 Ag '63
Homemade power hacksaw for less than $20. W. E. Burton. il Pop Sci 184:162-6+ F '64
How to keep a chain saw biting. L. H. Moore. Farm J 87:60C N '63
Little big saw. il Pop Mech 120:150-1 D '63
New, larger, and heavier sabre saws. il Consumer Bul 47:31-3 F '64
New radial saw has three speeds. il Pop Mech 120:182 S '63
Portable circular saw; saber saw. il Pop Sci 183:164+ D '63
Saber saws. il Consumer Rep 29:60-6 F '64
Sabre saws for the home craftsman. il Consumer Bul 46:28-33 D '63
Table saw; Radial-arm saw; Bandsaw. il Pop Sci 183:159-60+ N '63
Things you never knew about handsaws; hacksaws. il Pop Sci 184:160-2+ Ja '64
Toolkraft's new high-speed table saw. H. Walton. il Pop Sci 185:158-9 N '64
See also
Jigsaws

SAWTOOTH PRIMITIVE AREA, Idaho. See Wilderness areas

SAWYER, Charles
Education of the craftsman, its changing role. Craft Horiz 23:10-13+ My '63

SAWYER, Helen
Painting in oil on paper. il por Am Artist 28:44-9 Ja '64

SAWYER, Jack
How can psychology contribute? Bul Atomic Sci 19:35-6+ N '63

SAWYER, Kenneth
Wall: mosaic tiles. Craft Horiz 23:20-3+ My '63

SAWYER, Ruth
Precious herbs of Christmas; story. Horn Bk 39:635-41 D '63
This is the Christmas. Horn Bk 40:666-73 D '64

SAWYER, Stan
I'm bashful! Motor B 112:42+ N '63

SAWYER, W. W.
Algebra; with biographical sketch. Sci Am 211:28, 70-8 bibliog(p269) S '64

SAXE, Bacon and O'Shea
Roy Cohn. M. Kempton. New Repub 148:15-17 Ap 20 '63

SAXON, James J.
Are banks behind the times? the case for broad changes; interview. por U S News 55:90-3 N 25 '63

about

Bankerly feud. por Newsweek 63:60 Mr 30 '64
Banking's newcomers face tougher going. il Bsns W p52+ O 31 '64
Easier credit? dispute is on; quality of bank credit. U S News 55:128-9 O 7 '63
Fed hits back in the Saxon feud; concerning control of national banks. por Bsns W p 171-2 S 14 '63
National-bank policy attacked. por U S News 55:122-3 O 21 '63
Rift on control of banking: nationally chartered banks vs state-chartered banks. il por Bsns W p47-8+ F 23 '63
Saxon and the Fed cross swords again; concerning corporate savings in national banks. Bsns W p21 Ja 4 '64
Saxon crusade. il por Time 82:101 O 18 '63
Sharp pencils and sharp tongues. por Bsns W p85-6 Je 29 '63
State bank men tee off on Saxon. por Bsns W p54+ My 11 '63
What the banks hold in trust; comptroller's study report. il Bsns W p 124+ Je 20 '64
Why small bankers are unhappy with Washington. por U S News 54:112+ My 13 '63

SAYÃO, Bidú
Bidú; interview, ed. by G. M. Eby. por Opera N 29:10-11 Ja 2 '65

SAYERS, Frances Clarke
Margin for surprise. Horn Bk 40:640-1 D '64

SAYERS, Gale
Gale of hurricane force! H. L. Masin. por Sr Schol 85:22 O 21 '64

SAYINGS. See Aphorisms and apothegms; Proverbs

SAYLE, Edward
Actors stage rent blitz. il pors Bsns W p200+ My 18 '63

SAYLES, Leonard R.
Executives need this skill. Nations Bsns 52:48-50 Ag '64

SAYRE, Constance
Teen with a trowel. pors Seventeen 22:118-19+ N '63

SAYRE, Francis B. Jr
Sermon that caused a political furor; excerpts. por U S News 57:23 S 28 '64

about

Chaplain to the New frontier. R. Massie. il pors Sat Eve Post 236:70-2 S 21 '63

SAYRE, Joel
Glance at Billingsgate. Holiday 33:34+ My '63

SAYRE, Ruth Buxton
Who's been doing your thinking lately? Farm J 88:79+ O '64

SAYRE, Woodrow Wilson
Commando raid on Everest. pors Life 54:58-66+ Mr 22 '63
It's publish or perish. Life 58:66 Ja 22 '65
Moriturus publicabo. Time 83:78 My 22 '64
One against Tufts. Newsweek 63:58 Ap 13 '64
One way to live. por Newsweek 63:78-9 Mr 30 '64
Should tenure go? C. M. Curtis. Nat R 16:864 O 6 '64
Threshold of what? il por Time 83:86+ Ap 24 '64
Why pick on a fine teacher? Life 56:4 My 15 '64

SCAFFOLDING
Get off the ground on scaffolding. D. C. Fales and E. D. Fales. il Pop Sci 185:130-4 S '64

SCALAPINO, Robert A.
Moscow, Peking and the Communist parties of Asia. For Affairs 41:323-43 Ja '63
Sino-Soviet competition in Africa. For Affairs 42:640-54 Jl '64
Sino-Soviet conflict in perspective. bibliog f Ann Am Acad 351:1-14 Ja '64

SCALE insects
Heterochromatic chromosomes in the coccids. S. W. Brown and U. Nur. bibliog il Science 145:130-6 Jl 10 '64
Synergism between a lactate dehydrogenase-elevating virus and eperythrozon coccoides. V. Riley. bibliog il Science 146:921-3 N 13 '64

SCALES (weighing instruments)
Bathroom scales. il Consumer Bul 47:14-18 S '64
Inexpensive postal scales. il Consumer Bul 47:23-4 N '64

SCALI, John
Cuban crisis: how close we were to war; excerpts from Politics of policy-making: the Kennedy years. R. Hilsman. il por U S News 57:59-60 Ag 17 '64; Excerpts. Look 28:19-21 Ag 25 '64
Man in the middle. por Newsweek 64:80-1 Ag 17 '64

SCALLOPS
St James scallop. A. G. Melvin. il Hobbies 68:130+ Ja '64
See also
Cookery—Fish

SCAMMELL, Michael
(tr) See Nabokov, V. Luzhin defense
(tr) See Nabokov, V. Lyre

SCAMMON, Richard M.
What's ahead in the population boom; interview. por U S News 54:68-71 My 6 '63
Why one third of us don't vote. N Y Times Mag p36+ N 17 '63

SCANDINAVIA
And a nurse to tuck you in. il Time 84:26-38 Jl 3 '64
Scandinavia today. J. H. Wuorinen. Cur Hist 47:350-4+ D '64
See also
Architecture—Scandinavia
Arts and crafts—Scandinavia
Space research—Scandinavia

Description and travel

Delight around Denmark. W. Britton. il Motor B 111:90-2+ F; 126+ Mr '63
Friendly flight to northern Europe. L. B. Johnson. il Nat Geog Mag 125:268-93 F '64
Going places, finding things in Scandinavia. B. Pepis. il House & Gard 123:36+ Mr '63
Northern places. M. Mannes. il Reporter 29:55-8+ Ag 15 '63
Travel's picture portfolio. Travel 122:50-5 D '64

Economic conditions

What Lyndon Johnson found next door to Russia. R. W. Ruth. il U S News 55:73-4 S 23 '63

Foreign relations

Cool to Khrushchev. New Repub 150:9-10 Ap 4 '64
What Lyndon Johnson found next door to Russia. R. W. Ruth. il U S News 55:73-4 S 23 '63

Maps

Progress in Viking land; new map of Scandinavia. il Nat Geog Mag 123:492-3, sup(folded map) Ap '63

SCANDINAVIAN airlines system
SAS places first DC-8-62 order. Aviation W 81:30 D 7 '64
Tough management spurs SAS recovery. L. L. Doty. il Aviation W 82:39+ Ja 18 '65

SCANDINAVIAN cookery. See Cookery, Scandinavian

SCANDINAVIAN princes and princesses. See Princes and princesses

SCANDINAVIANS
Northern places. M. Mannes. il Reporter 29:55-8+ Ag 15 '63

SCANDUR, Leonard
Traffic courts; cash register justice. Nation 198:144-5 F 10 '64

SCANIA-vabis. See Automobile industry and trade—Sweden

SCANLON, John
Aspen: a new day for the humanities. Sat R 46:40-1+ D 21 '63
Can the Christian life be taught? Sat R 47:77 Mr 21 '64
Luther Foster of Tuskegee. Sat R 47:76+ My 16 '64
Report card. See issues of Saturday review
Strikes, sanctions, and the schools. Sat R 46:51-5+ O 19 '63

SCANLON, John J.
What one top company wants; excerpts from address. Nations Bsns 52:68+ Ap '64

SCANLON, Wayne W.
Intermetallic compounds. bibliog Science 142:1265-9 D 6 '63

SCANNERS, Horizon. See Aeronautic instruments
SCANNING electron microscope. See Electron microscope and microscopy
SCAPIN; drama. See Molière, J. B. P.
SCAPINO ballet. See Ballet—Netherlands
SCAPTURA, G. F.
Machine accounting. Am City 79:103 Ap '64
SCARBROUGH, Marilyn
Cupid on the couch. Seventeen 22:156 F '63
SCARECROW'S hat; drama. See Urban, C.
SCARLETT, Frank M.
Mixing schools: why one federal court refused. por U S News 54:88-90 My 27 '63
SCARPELLI, D. G. See McConnell, D. G. jt. auth.
SCARPINO, Mary L.
New adventures with glass. Sch Arts 64:34-5 Ja '65
SCARSDALE, N.Y.
Education
Upgrading existing school facilities: high school. S. Leggett. il Arch Rec 133:163-71 F '63
Parks and playgrounds
Citizens on the alert. W. L. Foley. Recreation 57:14-15 Ja '64
SCATCHARD, George. See Freeman, D. H. jt. auth.
SCATTER radio communications. See Ionospheric radio wave propagation
SCATTER rugs. See Rugs and carpets
SCATTERGUNS. See Shotguns
SCATTERING (physics)
Light scattering by liquids at 6937 angstroms. J. L. Lundberg and others. bibliog il Science 145:1308-10 S 18 '64
Molecular beam scattering at thermal energies. R. B. Bernstein. bibliog il Science 144:141-50 Ap 10 '64
See also
Radio waves—Scattering
SCENARIO writing. See Moving picture authorship
SCENE designers. See Designers
SCENEDESMUS obliquus. See Algae
SCENERY. See Nature
SCENERY, Preservation of. See Preservation of landmarks, scenery, etc.
SCENERY, Stage. See Theater—Stage scenery
SCENIC areas. See Preservation of landmarks, scenery, etc.—United States
SCENT. See Perfumery
SCENTED candles. See Candles
SCENTED-leaved geraniums. See Geraniums
SCENTS. See Odcrs
SCHAAL, Albert A.
You & your diet (cont) Good H 156:183-6 F; 175-8 Mr; 197-200 Ap '63
SCHACHTER, David, and others
Vitamin D_3: direct action on the small intestine of the rat. bibliog Science 143:143-4 Ja 10 '64
SCHAEFER, George
Letting George do it. il por Newsweek 65:53 F 1 '65
SCHAEFER, Henry
Ox hunt for moose. Outdoor Life 134:36-9+ S '64
SCHAEFER, Jack
Green-forested, the cloud-haunted Sangre de Cristos. Holiday 34:66-7+ Ag '63
SCHAEFER, Milner B.
Speaking out. por Sat Eve Post 236:8+ F 16 '63
SCHAEFER, Victor A.
Notre Dame's mosaic tower. Library J 89:4743-5 D 1 '64
SCHAEFFER, Charles
Politics of air pollution. Nation 196:421-3 My 18 '63
SCHAETZEL, J. Robert
Atlantic alliance; United States and Europe; address, October 21, 1963. Vital Speeches 30:78-81 N 15 '63
Atlantic partnership as viewed from the U.S.A.: address, October 21, 1963. Dept State Bul 49:731-6 N 11 '63
Tides of change; address, February 12, 1963. Dept State Bul 48:322-8 Mr 4 '63
SCHAFER, Elizabeth Paine
Picture window. NEA J 54:18 Ja '65
SCHAFER, Horst
Impact! M. A. Matzkin. il Mod Phot 27:60-5 N '63
SCHAFER, Mary C.
Thanksgiving. Horticulture 41:566-7 N '63
SCHAFER, Milton
Art of Wilhelm Kempff. Mus Am 84:58-9 O '64
SCHAFER, Roger
221d3: the key to moderate-income housing? Arch Forum 118:85 Ap '63
SCHAFFER, Roy
Ecumenical in Erie. Christian Cent 80:863-4 Jl 3 '63
SCHALK, Adolph
Foam rubber lion? Commonweal 79:368-70 D 20 '63
Germans and Berlin: one wall, many views. Commonweal 78:63-5 Ap 12 '63
Jews in Germany. Commonweal 79:185-7 N 8 '63
My friend, the Titoist. Commonweal 80:542-4 Ag 7 '64
SCHALL, James V.
Christmas and the world. Commonweal 79:389-92 D 27 '63
SCHALLER, George B.
Mountain gorilla displays. il Natur Hist 72:10-17 Ag '63
SCHALLER, Lyle E.
Churches enter the housing business. Christian Cent 80:1263-5 O 16 '63
Connectionalism: the new polity? Christian Cent 81:858-61 Jl 1 '64
Joblessness: the coming challenge. Christian Cent 80:171-3 F 6 '63
SCHANE, H. Philip, and Leonard S. L.
Phosphorylase α activity in uterine muscle: stimulation by ethylenediaminetetraacetic acid. bibliog Science 140:811-12 My 17 '63
SCHAPIRO, J. Salwyn
Plaster of Paris patriots. Sat R 46:43-4 Je 22 '63
SCHAPIRO, Leonard
Was Lenin necessary? Commentary 38:57-60 D '64
What's really gone wrong in Russia; interview, ed. by J. Fromm. por U S News 54:46-8 Je 10 '63
SCHAPPER, Beatrice
Buckle up for a safe flight. Todays Health 42:46-7+ D '64
Research and interviewing techniques; excerpt from Prose by professionals, ed. by T. Morris. Writer 77:20-3 Ja '64
SCHARDT, Arlie W.
High voltage on the Detroit ice. Sports Illus 18:24-32 Ja 28 '63
SCHARF, Mary
Separate vacations beat none. Farm J 87:25+ Je '63
SCHARLOCK, Donald P. and others
Auditory discrimination by the cat after neonatal ablation of temporal cortex. bibliog Science 141:1197-8 S 20 '63
SCHARPER, Philip
Catholics and public schools. Commonweal 79:533-8 Ja 31 '64
SCHARY, Dore
With a cast of thousands. J. S. Zimmer. il McCalls 91:130-3+ N '63
SCHAUER, Blase
Aggiornamento on the campus. C. Stevens. America 112:122-3 Ja 23 '65
SCHAWLOW, Arthur L.
Advances in optical masers; with biographical sketch. Sci Am 209:28, 34-45 bibliog(p 170) Jl '63
How the ruby laser works. Pop Sci 185:65 N '64
SCHEAR, Rillmond
Right-wing retreat in Seattle. Reporter 31:35-6 D 3 '64
SCHECHTER, Esther M. and others
Nucleic acid metabolism in L cells infected with a member of the psittacosis group. bibliog Science 145:819-21 Ag 21 '64
SCHEDULES
Critical path method of scheduling. E. R. McCamman. il Arch Rec 133:155-8 Ja '63
See also
Critical path analysis
Anecdotes, facetiae, satire, etc.
Everything on schedule. Christian Cent 81:383 Mr 18 '64
SCHEDULES, Household. See Home economics
SCHEDULES, School
Flexible class scheduling by computer. Sch & Soc 92:220+ Sum '64
SCHEER, George F.
Why Washington stood up in the boat; with reproduction of painting and memoir by W. Whittredge. Am Heritage 16:17-19 D '64
SCHEER, Milton D. and Klein, Ralph
Oxygen atom reactions with condensed olefins. bibliog Science 144:1214 Je 5 '64

SCHEERER, Martin
Problem-solving. Sci Am 208:118-22+ Ap '63
SCHEERINGA, Jack H.
When pickets are used to scare away customers. il por U S News 54:74-5 F 4 '63
SCHEFFEL, R. L.
Dance of the salamanders. Audubon Mag 66:168-71 My '64
SCHEIB, Winifred H.
Magic of mistletoe. Sci Digest 54:61-3 D '63
SCHEIBER, W. A.
Codes cover an experimental house. Am City 78:83-4 Ag '63
SCHEIDEL, R. A.
Crystal super calibrator. Pop Electr 19:51-4+ N '63
SCHEIN, C. J. See Rossman, I. J. jt. auth.
SCHEIN, Edgar H.
How to break in the college graduate. Harvard Bsns R 42:68-76 N '64
SCHEIN, Herman
On publishing books for children. Horn Bk 39:629-31 D '63
SCHEINER, Seth M.
Early career of T. Thomas Fortune. 1879-1890. bibliog Negro Hist Bul 27:170-2 Ap '64
SCHEJTER, Abel, and others
Stoichiometry of hemoglobin reactions. bibliog Science 141:784-8 Ag 30 '63
SCHELL, Erwin Haskell
Apple for the teacher. por Bsns W p 104 S 28 '63
SCHELLING, T. C.
Signals & feedback in the arms dialogue. Bul Atomic Sci 21:5-10 Ja '65
SCHELLSBURG, Pa.
Turning four churches into one; United church of Schellsburg. il Time 84:75 N 20 '64
SCHENBECK, Fred A.
Spring I remember best; story. Farm J 87:62F Mr '63
SCHENCK, Hilbert, Jr
Computing ad absurdum. Nation 196:505-7 Je 15 '63
Myth-image of the scientist. Nation 197:140-2 S 14 '63; Same abr. with title Scientific freedom, hah! Sci Digest 54:43-7 D '63
Project Apollo: wasteful spectacular. Nation 197:339-41 N 23 '63
SCHENCK house. See New York (city)—Historic houses, etc.
SCHENDEL, Gordon
New wild West. Esquire 60:140-1+ O '63
SCHENECTADY, N.Y.

Finance

Value analysis. P. R. Roan. il Am City 79:101-2 Jl '64

Politics and government

Boss and faction. J. A. Riedel. bibliog f il Ann Am Acad 353:14-26 My '64
SCHENK, Gretchen Knief
(ed) Extending library service. See issues of Wilson library bulletin
SCHENKEL, Christopher Eugene
Voice. il por Newsweek 62:100 O 7 '63
SCHERAGO, Earl J.
(comp) Guide to scientific instruments. Science 142:697+ N 8 '63
SCHERCHEN, Hermann
Musical past and the electronic future; tr. by M. Bernheimer. por Sat R 47:63-5+ O 31 '64

about

Herr doktor. il por Time 84:76 N 27 '64
More Scherchen. M. Bernheimer. Sat R 47:65-6 N 28 '64
Music to my ears; Scherchen at the Academy. I. Kolodin. Sat R 47:52 N 14 '64
Musical events; concert in Philharmonic Hall. W. Sargeant. New Yorker 40:233 N 21 '64
Musical events; concert in Philharmonic Hall with the Philadelphia orchestra. W. Sargeant. New Yorker 40:231-3 N 14 '64
Music's Faust. pors Newsweek 64:90 N 16 '64
Scherchen on discs. R. Freed. Sat R 47:65 O 31 '64
SCHERER, James A.
Diary with a design. Christian Cent 81:1040 Ag 19 '64
SCHERER, W. F. and others
Venezuelan equine encephalitis virus in Veracruz, Mexico, and the use of hamsters as sentinels. Science 145:274-5 Jl 17 '64
SCHERMAN, David E.
Everybody blows up! Life 54:49-50 Mr 8 '63
He slashes at the spiteful heirs of Stalin. Life 54:36-7 Ap 19 '63
It's bye! bye! blackjack. Sport Illus 20:18-20+ Ja 13 '64; Same abr. Read Digest 84:223-6 Je '64
Let's pep up those old classics. Life 57:22 O 9 '64
Life theater review. Life 58:14 Ja 8 '65
From photographer to writer to editor. G. P. Hunt. il por Life 58:3 Ja 15 '65
SCHERMAN, Thomas
Gentleman explorer; interview, ed. by A. M. Lingg. pors Opera N 28:30-1 F 15 '64
SCHERY, Robert W.
Flower grower's turf tips. Flower Grower 51:41+ Ap '64
Live with your lawn and like it! Flower Grower 50:34-5+ S '63
Many varieties of Kentucky bluegrass. Horticulture 41:568-9 N '63
SCHEUBLE, Philip A. Jr
ROI for new-product policy. Harvard Bsns R 42:110-20 N '64
SCHEUER, Sidney H.
Trade with the reds? N Y Times Mag p26+ N 10 '63
SCHEVILL, James
Always we walk through unknown people; poem. Sat R 46:23 F 16 '63
Bashir was my name; poem. Sat R 47:178 Ag 29 '64
Fury of music; poem. Nation 196:532 Je 22 '63
In the Theatre of the absurd; poem. Nation 196:514 Je 15 '63
Poets ascend the technical trend. Sat R 47:30-3 Jl 4 '64

about

Poetry chronicle. R. Howard. Poetry 102:187-8 Je '63
Something that might simply be. M. L. Rosenthal. Reporter 29:56 S 12 '63
SCHEVILL, William E. and others
Underwater sounds of pinnipeds. bibliog Science 141:50-3 Jl 5 '63
SCHICK, Béla
Great baby doctor. G. Naismith. il pors N Y Times Mag p 109 N 24 '63
SCHICK, F. B.
Aerospace in the nuclear age. Bul Atomic Sci 19:46-9 D '63
SCHICK, Frank L.
International standardization of library statistics. ALA Bul 58:1011-13 D '64
Professional library manpower. ALA Bul 58:315-17 Ap '64
SCHICKEDANZ, Gustav
Who's who in foreign business. por Fortune 70:60 S '64
SCHICKEL. Richard
Big money writers. Life 57:58-60+ Jl 31 '64
Life movie review. Life 56:14 My 8; 57:21 Jl 17; 12 Ag 21 '64
Nureyev: top male dancer who quit the Soviets dazzles the West. Look 27:26-8+ Jl 16 '63
P.S. 165. Commentary 37:43-51 Ja '64
Raymond Chandler, private eye. Commentary 35:158-61 F '63
SCHICKELE, Peter
About the awful. Nation 198:588-9 Je 8 '64
SCHIFF, Dorothy
New York: break in the ranks. il por Time 81:44 Mr 8 '63
Wayward press. A. J. Liebling. New Yorker 39:173-6+ Mr 16 '63
SCHIFF, Gilbert M. and others
Rubella virus: neutralizing antibody in commercial gamma globulin. bibliog Science 142:58-60 O 4 '63
SCHIFF, Medad
Isaac bound; story. Commentary 37:59-62 Ap '64
SCHILLEBEECKX, Edward
Church and mankind's future on earth; excerpt from address. por Cath World 200:218-23 Ja '65
Procreation and human dignity; interview, ed. by P. Wesseling and C. Enkelaar. Commonweal 80:331-2 Je 5 '64
SCHILLER, Andrew
Coming revolution in teaching English. Harper 229:82-4+ O '64
People in trouble. Harper 228:145-9 Ap '64
SCHILLER, Anita R.
Survey of salary surveys. por ALA Bul 58:279-86 Ap '64
SCHILLER, Herbert I.
Sovereign state of Comsat. Nation 200:71-6 Ja 25 '65
SCHILLER, Hillel
Panel urges schools to incorporate paperbacks; striking cases cited. Library J 88:844-5 F 15 '63
What is MEDLARS? Library J 88:949-53 Mr 1 '63

SCHILLER, Lawrence
Football's grind and glitter. il Sat Eve Post 236:32-7 O 5 '63
Sedans, rails and gassers. il Sat Eve Post 237:58-61 Ja 4 '64

about

Nhu deal. il Newsweek 62:65-6 N 25 '63

SCHILLING, Earl
How I learned to be a teen-age gas saver. por Pop Sci 184:58-61+ Je '64

SCHILLING, George
Judge they have to tell it to. E. Havemann. il por Sports Illus 21:38+ N 16 '64

SCHILPP, Paul Arthur
Toward a super-conscious tomorrow. Sat R 47:32-3 D 19 '64
Toward a warless world. Christian Cent 81: 212-14 F 12 '64

SCHIMPL, Anneliese, and others
Cyanamide formation under primitive earth conditions. bibliog Science 147:149-50 Ja 8 '65

SCHINDLER, David W. See Comita, G. W. jt. auth.

SCHINDLER-RAINMAN, Eva
Recreation's changing role. Recreation 58: 12-13 Ja '65

SCHINNELLER, James
Misunderstandings denying the appreciation of modern art. Sch Arts 62:25-8 Ap; 21-3 My '63

SCHINNERER, Paul
Cadillac V-16. Motor T 15:64-7 S '63

SCHIOTZ, Fredrik Axel
Pastor for the Federation. por Time 82:48 Ag 23 '63

SCHIPA, Tito
Quote-unquote; interview, ed. by J. Ardoin. por Mus Am 84:32 S '64

SCHIPHOL, See Amsterdam, Netherlands—Airports

SCHIPPERS, Thomas
I've hypnotized lions and people; interview, ed. by J. Howard. por Life 55:68 D 6 '63

about

Matinee idol maestro. il pors Life 55:57-8+ D 6 '63
Music to my ears; Beethoven by Schippers and Serkin. I. Kolodin. Sat R 48:22 Ja 30 '65
Musical events; Barber's Andromache's farewell performed by New York philharmonic. W. Sargeant. New Yorker 39:154 Ap 13 '63
Professional tool, a source of enjoyment. il pors Hi Fi 13:66-7 S '63
Schippers festival. por Time 82:81-2 O 25 '63

SCHIRRA, Walter Marty, 1923-
Schirra reports on MA-8 flight success. por Aviation W 78:55+ F 11 '63

about

Astronauts may become artists. R. Hawkes. Miss & Roc 13:21 Jl 8 '63
Schirra had blood disorder after flight. Miss & Roc 12:15 F 11 '63

SCHISGAL, Murray
Luv. Criticism
Commonweal 81:389 D 11 '64
Life il 58:79-81+ Ja 8 '65
Nation 199:415 N 30 '64
New Repub 151:20 D 12 '64
New Yorker 40:143 N 21 '64
Newsweek il 64:102 N 23 '64
Sat R 47:29 N 28 '64
Time il 84:81 N 20 '64
Vogue 145:68 Ja 1 '65
Tiger. Criticism
Commonweal 77:665 Mr 22 '63
Nation 196:166-7 F 23 '63
New Yorker 38:116 F 16 '63
Newsweek 61:56 F 18 '63
Time il 81:63 F 15 '63
Typists. Criticism
Commonweal 77:665 Mr 22 '63
Nation 196:166-7 F 23 '63
New Yorker 38:114+ F 16 '63
Newsweek 61:56 F 18 '63
Time 81:63 F 15 '63

SCHISGALL, Oscar
Banks that build new businesses around the world. Read Digest 82:128-31 F '63
Grasp the nettle, now! Read Digest 85:43-4+ N '64
Israel's new waterline: will it bring war? Look 27:82+ Ap 9 '63
Our defense secrets are for sale cheap. Look 27:78-80 Ag 27 '63
Settled out of court. Read Digest 84:25-6+ Mr '64
Techniques and style in article writing; excerpt from Prose by professionals, ed. by T. Morris. Writer 76:14-16 S '63
Too many government investigations! Read Digest 82:135-8 Mr '63

SCHISLER, D. Gale
Teacher-politician. il NEA J 53:69 D '64

SCHISTOSOMES
Schistosoma mansoni: development of challenge infections in mice exposed to irradiated cercariae. A. P. Szumlewicz and L. J. Olivier. bibliog il Science 140:411-12 Ap 26 '63
Schistosome ova: rapid separation from mouse tissue by digestion with pinguinain. E. Toro-Goyco and others. bibliog il Science 142:407 O 18 '63

SCHISTOSOMIASIS
Annals of medicine. B. Roueché. New Yorker 40:217-18+ N 7 '64
Ecological design of irrigation canals for snail control. W. R. Jobin and A. T. Ippen. bibliog il Science 145:1324-6 S 18 '64
Immunity seen possible to snail-carried disease. Sci N L 83:297 My 11 '63
Schistosomiasis: age of snails and susceptibility to X-irradiation. bibliog il Science 144:302-4 Ap 17 '64
Snail's plague. il Time 82:66 Jl 5 '63
Wage war against snail; using marisa against australorbis. Sci N L 85:302 My 9 '64

SCHIZOPHRENIA
Behavior disruption in cebus monkeys as a function of injected substances. D. C. Ferguson and A. E. Fisher. bibliog il Science 139:1281-2 Mr 29 '63
Endogenous metabolic factor in schizophrenic behavior. H. H. Berlet and others. bibliog il Science 144:311-13 Ap 17 '64
Inside psychiatry today; new view of schizophrenia. F. R. Schreiber and M. Herman. Sci Digest 56:69-71 Ag '64
Link mental disease to protein factor. Sci N L 86:359 D 5 '64
Schizophrenic child. il Sci Digest 55:40 Mr '64
Schizophrenics in the sun. R. Littell. Read Digest 82:201-2+ My '63
Secrets of schizophrenia. il Sci Digest 55:83-4 Ja '64
Space-child ten years later. F. R. Schreiber and M. Herman. Sci Digest 56:86-7 N '64
Wave of psychosis: characteristic brain-wave pattern. il Newsweek 62:68 O 7 '63

SCHLAEGER, Gerald J.
American airlines; history on the wing. Flying 74:40-1+ Ja '64
Fine art of design improvement. Flying 74: 46-7+ Ja '64
Hot start. Flying 75:52-4 S '64
Pilot report. Flying 74:42-3+ Ap '64
Pilot report; Bede BD-1. Flying 74:34-5+ F '64
Pilot report; Champion Lancer. Flying 74: 45+ Ja '64
Pilot report; room for one more. Flying 74: 36-7+ Je '64
Used aircraft pilot report. Flying 74:36-7+ Mr '64

SCHLAFLY, Phyllis
Excerpt from testimony, August 27, 1963. Cong Digest 43:221+ Ag '64

SCHLAGEL, Walter
How we reduced electric rates. Am City 78:136+ N '63

SCHLAMM, William S.
Eastman's loves and revolutions. Nat R 17: 65-6 Ja 26 '65

SCHLAMME, Martha
Broadway postscript; World of Kurt Weill in song. H. Hewes. Sat R 46:33 Ag 10 '63
Quote . . . unquote. H. Yurchenco. por Mus Am 83:18 Jl '63
Welcome interloper. por Time 81:46 Je 21 '63

SCHLEGEL, David E. See Smith, S. H. jt. auth.

SCHLEH, Edward C.
Fallacy in measuring management. Duns R 82:49-50+ N '63

SCHLEIFER, Marc
Letter from Havana. Nation 198:442-5 Ap 27 '64
Letter from Quebec. Nation 199:386-9 N 23 '64
Sepia deb ball. Nation 198:665-6 Je 29 '64

SCHLEISNER, William H.
Memorial exhibit, New York botanical garden. il Pop Gard 14:12 Ap '63

SCHLEMM, Betty Lou
Betty Lou Schlemm engages her subject. il por Am Artist 28:30-1+ F '64

SCHLESINGER, Arthur, 1917-
America and the world revolution; ed. by N. Podhoretz. Commentary 36:278-96 O '63
Eulogy: John Fitzgerald Kennedy. Sat Eve Post 236:32-32a D 14 '63
Historian and history. For Affairs 41:491-7 Ap '63
Historian as artist. Atlan 212:35-41 Jl '63
Hopes for world order. New Repub 152:24 Ja 9 '65
Schlesinger at the White House; ed. by H. Brandon. Harper 229:55-60 Jl '64
Schlesinger protests use of quote in promotion of Buckley title. Pub W 183:12-13 Ap 22; 31 Ap 29 '63
What kind of president will Johnson make now? interview. por U S News 57:53-5 N 16 '64

about

Violation of Arthur. W. F. Buckley, jr. Nat R 14:271 Ap 9 '63

SCHLESINGER, Ina
Soviet education in 1962. bibliog f Sch & Soc 91:197-8 Ap 20 '63
Soviet education in 1963. bibliog f Sch & Soc 92:204-5 My 2 '64

SCHLESINGER, John
His father's son. il por Time 82:64-5 Ag 2 '63

SCHLESINGER, Michael, and Mark, Raymond
Wasting disease induced in young mice by administration of cortisol acetate. bibliog Science 143:965-6 F 28 '64

SCHLIEMANN, Heinrich
Science milestone. D. Cohen. il por Sci Digest 53:79-86 Mr '63

SCHLIEREN apparatus
Amateur scientist; how to photograph air currents in color and build an accurate Foucault pendulum. R. Walan. il Sci Am 210:132-3+ F '64

SCHLINDWEIN, Harold F.
Centrifugal casting in the high school. Sch Arts 64:36-8 S '64

SCHLINK, Edmund
Doctor Schlink warns Vatican council. Christian Cent 80:1425 N 20 '63

SCHLITZ, Joseph, brewing company
How they put gusto into Schlitz. W. Bowen. il Fortune 70:106-9+ O '64
Selling suds like soap. R. Uihlein. il Bsns W p60-2+ Ag 8 '64

SCHLOSS, Samuel. See Hobson, C. J. jt. auth.

SCHLOSSER, E. pseud.
Disarming the air waves. Nat R 16:1014-15 N 17 '64

SCHLOTTMANN, Jeanette
Dancers' bookshelf. Dance Mag 38:36 Jl '64

SCHLUETER, Paul
Faith in a secular age. Christian Cent 80:805 Je 19 '63
Not unlike Job. Christian Cent 81:1216-17 S 30 '64

SCHMALZ, Robert F. and Chave, K. E.
Calcium carbonate: factors affecting saturation in ocean waters off Bermuda. bibliog Science 139:1206-7 Mr 22 '63

SCHMECK, Harold M. jr
(comp) Science marches on. N Y Times Mag p46 My 24 '64

SCHMECKEBIER, Laurence Eli
Figure paintings of A. Henry Nordhausen. Am Artist 29:34-9+ F '65
Trade marks of M. Peter Piening. Am Artist 29:52-7 Ja '65

about

New appointment. por Am Artist 27:6+ S '63

SCHMEER, M. Rosarii
Growth-inhibiting agents from mercenaria extracts: chemical and biological properties. bibliog Science 144:413-14 Ap 24 '64

SCHMEIDLER, F.
Einstein shift, an unsettled problem. il Sky & Tel 27:217-19 Ap '64

SCHMELZLEE, Robert
Are we losing bright failing students? Sch & Soc 92:189-90 Ap 18 '64

SCHMERTZ, Mildred F.
Architectural drawing for printing by halftone. Arch Rec 133:133-40 Je '63
Architectural drawing for printing processes. Arch Rec 133:137-44 F '63
Architecture at the New York world's fair. il Arch Rec 136:143-50 Jl '64
Better architecture for the performing arts. Arch Rec 136:115 D '64
Wasmuth's great portfolio on Wright reprinted. Arch Rec 135:84+ Ja '64

SCHMID, John C.
New wonder camera for nature close-ups. il Audubon Mag 65:266-8 S '63

SCHMID, Peter
Letter from Formosa; tr. by W. J. Dannhauser. Commentary 37:68-70 Ap '64
Lion of Malawi. Reporter 32:20-2 Ja 14 '65
Portugal's last stand in Mozambique. Reporter 30:37-40 My 21 '64
Somalia's instant army. Reporter 31:48-50 S 24 '64
Tshombe's four hundred. Reporter 31:25-6 D 17 '64

SCHMIDLING, Gilbert T.
Luminous. New Yorker 40:24-6 Je 20 '64

SCHMIDT, Albert C.
Romanesque runaround. Reporter 32:36-8 Ja 14 '65

SCHMIDT, Beverly
Beverly Schmidt and Anneliese Widman at Judson Hall. D. Hering. Dance Mag 37:55-6 F '63
Beverly Schmidt and company, 92nd street Y. J. Maskey. Dance Mag 38:67 Je '64

SCHMIDT, Clarence
Miracle on a mountain. D. L. Goodrich. il pors Sat Eve Post 237:22-7 S 12 '64

SCHMIDT, Dana Adams
Al Baath challenges Nasser. N Y Times Mag p42+ O 6 '63
Faisal modernizes but with caution. N Y Times Mag p38+ N 1 '64

SCHMIDT, Emerson P.
Excerpt from statement submitted to Joint economic committee, February 15, 1963. Cong Digest 42:119+ Ap '63

SCHMIDT, Harvey
Cadences of crew. il Sports Illus 18:42-50 Je 10 '63

SCHMIDT, Joe
Joe Schmidt: king of the red doggers. I. R. McVay. il pors Look 27:62+ S 24 '63

SCHMIDT, Larrie Henry
Plot that flopped. P. Swank. il por Look 29:28-9 Ja 26 '65

SCHMIDT, Lars
Hardly anybody knows him. D. J. Hamblin. il pors Life 57:133-4+ O 16 '64

SCHMIDT, Maarten
Questions of quasars. il por Time 85:52 Ja 8 '65

SCHMIDT, Marjorie G.
Colorful shrub for West Coast gardens. Flower Grower 50:16-17+ O '63
Striking California natives: the bush poppies. Horticulture 41:420 Ag '63

SCHMIDT, Paul O. and Tessmer, Leslie
Single-basin flexibility. Am City 79:88-9 F '64

SCHMIDT, Richard A. and Cohen T. J.
Particle accretion rates: variation with latitude. bibliog Science 145:924-6 Ag 28 '64

SCHMIDT, Ruth A. M.
Pleistocene marine microfauna in the Bootlegger Cove Clay, Anchorage, Alaska. bibliog Science 141:350-1 Jl 26 '63
—and others
Surface features of metallic spherules. bibliog Science 142:581-2 N 1 '63

SCHMIDT-NIELSEN, Bodil, and Rabinowitz, Lawrence
Methylurea and acetamide: active reabsorption by elasmobranch renal tubules. bibliog Science 146:1587-8 D 18 '64
—and Schrauger, C. R.
Amoeba proteus: studying the contractile vacuole by micropuncture. bibliog Science 139:606-7 F 15 '63

SCHMIDT-NIELSEN, Knut, and others
Diabetes mellitus in the sand rat induced by standard laboratory diets. bibliog Science 143:689-90 F 14 '64
Nasal salt excretion and the possible function of the cloaca in water conservation. bibliog Science 142:1300-1 D 6 '63

SCHMIDTCHEN, Paul W.
Books. See issues of Hobbies

SCHMITT, Hans A.
European communities. bibliog f Cur Hist 45:257-63+ N '63
Germany's search for identity. bibliog f Cur Hist 47:326-31 D '64

SCHMITT, Karl M.
(comp) Articles and other books received; Latin America. See issues of American historical review

SCHMITT, Ronald W. See Bean, C. P; Hart, H. R. jr. jt. auths.

SCHMOKEL, Wolfe W.
German aid to Africa. Cur Hist 44:219-25 Ap '63
Germany and the Common market. bibliog f Cur Hist 45:283-8 N '63

SCHNABEL, Artur
Artur Schnabel, a legend reëmergent. P. Hart. pors Hi Fi 13:65-8+ N '63
Artur Schnabel: the complete Beethoven piano sonatas. R. Kammerer. pors Am Rec G 30:378-80+ Ja '64

SCHNABEL, Artur—*Continued*
Notes from our correspondents. R. Gelatt. Hi Fi 14:24+ F '64
Schnabel & Beethoven. J. S. Harrison. il por Mus Am 83:274+ D '63
Schnabel reappraised. S. Stele. por Sat R 47:48 Ja 25 '64
SCHNEEBELI, Herman T.
Why businessmen make good politicians; interview. por Nations Bsns 51:94-8+ N '63
SCHNEIDAU, John D. jr
Pigeons and cryptococcosis; letter. Science 143:525 F 7 '64
SCHNEIDER, Alan
A B B of Alan Schneider. A. Levy. il pors N Y Times Mag p27+ O 20 '63
SCHNEIDER, Elsa
Health knows no boundaries. NEA J 53:70-1 Mr '64
What part will the schools play? Sch Life 46:18 Ag '64
SCHNEIDER, Gerald
Conservation and the Fort Ord complex. Am For 70:22-3+ Ag '64
SCHNEIDER, Hans Joseph
FRF, the supreme lens test. U S Camera 27:34+ N '64
SCHNEIDER, I. R. and others
Blue-green algal virus LPP-1: purification and parital characterization. bibliog Science 144:1127-9 My 29 '64
SCHNEIDER, J. Thomas
General Pershing & I. pors Sat Eve Post 236:70+ Ap 27 '63
SCHNEIDER, Joseph
Capture the look that goes too soon. il Am Home 67:104 S '64
SCHNEIDER, Liliane
Schneider affair. il por Time 82:108 O 11 '63
SCHNEIDER, Pierre E.
Art news from Paris. See issues of Art news
Great French recipe, for the Folies. N Y Times Mag p 18+ Ap 28 '63
Maeghts' glorious adventure in art. Vogue 144:186-9+ O 15 '64
Now the crime of art-napping. N Y Times Mag p36-7+ Ap 7 '63
Oh! what a dizzy and dolce vita. N Y Times Mag p39+ N 15 '64
Painting is stronger than Picasso? Art N 63:35+ Mr '64
Public muse. Art N 63:46-8+ O '64
Rome becomes a system of roads. Art N 62:50-1+ S '63
Seventy-five, and still a one-man show. N Y Times Mag p34-5+ S 8 '63
Spanish genius: contradiction and tradition. Art N 62:26-7 Mr '63
300,000 French students can't be wrong. N Y Times Mag p 16-17+ F 9 '64
Three stars or none, quelle différence! N Y Times Mag p20+ Jl 19 '64
SCHNEIDER, R. G. and others
Hemoglobin G_{Coushatta}: a new variant in an American Indian family. bibliog Science 143:697-8 F 14 '64
SCHNEIDER, Rita Marie, and Young, G. V.
So many fresh ways to go with kitchen color. Bet Hom & Gard 41:66-9 Ap '63
SCHNEIDER, Romy
Arrivederci, Romy. G. Talese. por Esquire 60:112-13 N '63
Lovely Romy goes home. il pors Life 54:45+ Je 14 '63
Romy Schneider. C. R. Jennings. il pors Sat Eve Post 236:36-8 N 23 '63
SCHNEIDER, Ronald M.
Continent discovered. Reporter 30:58 Ja 30 '64
Five years of Cuban revolution. bibliog f Cur Hist 46:26-33 Ja '64
U.S. in Latin America. bibliog f Cur Hist 48:1-8+ Ja '65
SCHNEIDERMAN, Howard A. and Gilbert, L. I.
Control of growth and development in insects; excerpts from address, December 28, 1962. bibliog Science 143:325-33 Ja 24 '64
SCHNEIDERMAN, Marvin A. and others
Toxicity, the therapeutic index, and the ranking of drugs. bibliog Science 144:1212-14 Je 5 '64
SCHNEIDERS, Alexander
Tyranny of guilt feelings; excerpt from The anarchy of feeling. Cath World 198:40-5 O '63
SCHNEIRLA, T. C.
Determined ant. G. Laycock. il Field & S 68:61+ My '63
SCHNITZER, Robert C.
Professional theatre at Ann Arbor. L. Cook. il por Theatre Arts 47:29-31 Ag '63
SCHODDE, Stephen C.
College students speak out. Sch & Soc 91:358+ N 16 '63
—See Covert, E. R. jt. auth.
SCHODER, Raymond V.
Ancient Cumae; with biographical sketch. Sci Am 209:28+, 108-21 D '63
SCHOEBERLEIN, Marion
Basket of summer; poem. Nat Parks Mag 38:10 Jl '64
February River; poem. Nat Parks Mag 38:12 F '64
Man at the clavichord; poem. Atlan 211:85 Je '63
Squirrel; poem. Horn Bk 39:484 O '63
SCHOECH, W. A.
Western Pacific; address, May 17, 1963. Vital Speeches 29:584-6 Jl 15 '63
SCHOECK, Helmut
Why socialized health schemes fail. por Nations Bsns 51:40-1+ Mr '63
SCHOEFFLER, Oscar E.
Fashions. Esquire 59:43 Je '63; 61:161 My; 62:109 Ag; 55 O '64
SCHOEN, Barbara
I wouldn't twist with just anyone; story. Seventeen 23:144-5 N '64
Putting away childish things; story. Seventeen 23:66-7 Jl '64
Suffer finks gladly; story. Seventeen 23:138-9 My '64
SCHOENBAUM, David
Politics of German wheat. Nation 197:447-9 D 28 '63
SCHOENBERG, Arnold. See Schönberg, A.
SCHOENBERG, Carl
Adoption: the created family. bibliog f Ann Am Acad 355:69-74 S '64
SCHOENBERG, M. D. and others
Cytoplasmic interaction between macrophages and lymphocytic cells in antibody synthesis. bibliog Science 143:964-5 F 28 '64
SCHOENBRUN, David Franz
Casebook of a southern senator. Esquire 60:104-8+ S '63
Feathers and fun. Newsweek 62:65 Jl 8 '63
Le grand David. por Newsweek 61:90 F 18 '63
SCHOENFELD, Clay
How to find your cabin in the pines. Field & S 67:43-5+ Mr '63
How to write about science; excerpts from Publicity media and methods. Writer 77:22-5 F '64
SCHOENFELD, Mrs David
Pleasure Island. Wilson Lib Bul 37:683-4 Ap '63
SCHOENFELD, Robert L. and Milkman, Norman
Digital computors in the biological laboratory. bibliog Science 146:190-8 O 9 '64
SCHOENKNECHT, Walt
Scamp of the ski slope; Mount Snow, Vermont. il pors Life 54:93-4 F 8 '63
SCHOENSTEIN, Ralph
Eine kleine nachtnoise. Sat R 46:41 Je 29 '63
Sing along with Bach. Sat R 46:60 N 30 '63
60,000,000 projections can't be wrong. Sat R 46:56 Je 8 '63
Talk me out of the ball game. Sat R 47:82 Ap 11 '64
They couldn't resist the title. Sat R 47:53 F 8 '64
What time does the coffee go on? Sat R 46:17 D 28 '63
Will the real Columbus please stand up! Sat R 46:90 O 12 '63
SCHOETERS, Georges
Fidel's disciple: Front de libération québecois (FLQ) il por Time 81:40 Je 14 '63
SCHÖFFLER, Paul
Master singer; interview, ed. by A. M. Lingg. por Opera N 28:32-3 Mr 14 '64
SCHOLANDER, P. F.
Master switch of life; with biographical sketch. Sci Am 209:28, 92-6+ bibliog(p 178) D '63
SCHOLANDER, Sven
Richard Dyer-Bennet; interview, ed. by S. Fleming. R. Dyer-Bennet. il Hi Fi 13:16+ Mr '63
SCHOLARS
See also
College professors and instructors
SCHOLARSHIP. See Learning and scholarship
SCHOLARSHIPS and fellowships
American academy gives first traveling fellowship; Doubleday establishes writing fellowships. Pub W 183:39 My 27 '63
ALA awards, citations, and scholarships for 1964. Library J 88:4184-6 N 1 '63
ALA awards, citations, and scholarships for 1965. Library J 89:4494-6 N 15 '64
ALA invites application now for 1964 awards, scholarships. Library J 88:4834-6 D 15 '63

SCHOLARSHIPS and fellowships—*Continued*
ALA invites nominations for awards and scholarships. Library J 89:4619-20 N 15 '64
Dollars for scholars; grants for secondary schools in Pittsburgh scholars program. Sr Schol 84:4T F 7 '64
Five athletes, 500 scholarships. il Ebony 19: 57-61 O '64
Government finance for private schools in Australia. W. G. Smith. Sch & Soc 92:268-70 O 3 '64
Grantsmanship. J. O'Reilly. Mlle 58:90-1+ D '63
Lane Cooper scholarships; Cornell, Rutgers, and Yale universities. Sch & Soc 91:162 Ap 6 '63
Life guide; a lot of scholarship dollars. il Life 55:13 S 27 '63
Lifetime sabbaticals. Duns R 83:46 Ja '64
Money for education. America 112:9-10 Ja 2 '65
Need for scholarship in teacher education. W. W. Brickman. Sch & Soc 92:122 Mr 21 '64
New award, fellowships made for science writing; Richard Prentice Ettinger program for creative writing. Pub W 184:66 N 11 '63
Nominations for human rights fellowship requested. U N Rev 10:13 Mr '63
NATO announces 1964-65 research fellowships. Dept State Bul 49:998 D 30 '63
Scholarship realities; Buffalo and Erie County public library, letter to the editor. P. M. Rooney. Library J 89:2904+ Ag '64
Scholarships: a new study on who gets them and who needs them by American council on education. J. Walsh. Science 141:413-14 Ag 2 '63
Scholarships for college undergraduates. Sch & Soc 91:347 N 16 '63
Today's Marshall plan. il Time 81:51 Mr 8 '63
While school keeps; Citizens' scholarship foundation. J. Cass. Sat R 46:84 F 16 '63
With strings; eccentrically conditioned scholarships. il Time 84:78+ N 13 '64
See also
African scholarship program of American universities
College students—Aid
National merit scholarship corporation
National scholarship service and fund for Negro students
Nieman fellowships

SCHOLASTIC ability. See Ability

SCHOLASTIC institute of student opinion. See Scholastic research center

SCHOLASTIC magazines, incorporated
At our corner: new durable bindings for Scholastic paperbacks. Sr Schol 85:25T D 2 '64
Foreign language periodicals for youth. Wilson Lib Bul 39:107 O '64
1963 Scholasitc magazines art awards. il Sr Schol 82:10-11 My 15 '63
Presenting the 1963 Scholastic awards. il Sr Schol 82:8 My 15 '63
Presenting the 1964 Scholastic awards. il Sr Schol 84:16-22+ My 15 '64
Scholastic magazines starts new research division. Pub W 186:37 S 14 '64
Scholastic teacher travel awards. il Sr Schol 84: 8T-12T Mr 20; 10T-12T Ap 17 '64
Scope: for retarded readers and the culturally deprived. Library J 89:4130 O 15 '64
SCOPE: it's new! il Sr Schol 85:5T S 16 '64

SCHOLASTIC research center
As high school students see it. il Sr Schol 85:11 O 28 '64
Great expectations; college. il Sr Schol 82: 1T Ap 17 '63
How teen-agers look at drinking; results of poll by Institute of student opinion; table. Sr Schol 85:19 D 2 '64
Life plans. il Sr Schol 82:1T My 1 '63
Lodge, Kennedy top ISO poll. il Sr Schol 84: 1T My 8 '64
Scholastic magazines starts new research division. Pub W 186:37 S 14 '64
Student opinions. Sr Schol 84:23 My 8 '64
Students' choice. Sr Schol 85:1T O 28 '64

SCHOLASTIC scope (periodical) See Childrens periodicals

SCHOLASTICISM
See also
Thomism

SCHOLEM, Gershom
Martin Buber's Hasidism. bibliog f Commentary 32:305-16 O '61; 33:162-3 F '62; 37: 18-20 F '64
Religious authority & mysticism; excerpts from On the kabbalah and its symbolism. Commentary 38:31-9 N '64

SCHOLES, Arthur
Flightless birds face extinction. Sci N L 85:26 Ja 11 '64

SCHOLES, Kenneth
Recovery; poem. New Yorker 40:109 Je 13 '64

SCHOLL, S. E.
New plates save an old bridge. Am City 78:110-11 My '63
Precasting culvert prevents traffic hold-up. Am City 79:89 D '64

SCHOLL, William M.
What you can do about your aching feet; interview. McCalls 90:46 Ap '63

SCHOLLANDER, Don
Dominant swimmer for a dominant country. G. S. Brown. il Sports Illus 21:30-3 O 26 '64
Water babies; five world records by American team in Tokyo. por Time 82:43 Ag 30 '63
Who's afraid of an old troll? C. Phinizy. por Sports Illus 21:16-17 Ag 10 '64

SCHOLTZ, Elizabeth
Floral inheritance. Natur Hist 72:26-31 My '63

SCHOMER, Howard
Toward peace and justice. Christian Cent 80:703-6 My 29 '63

SCHON, Donald A.
Champions for radical new inventions. bibliog f Harvard Bsns R 41:77-86 Mr '63

SCHöN, Miguel A. and Arends, Tulio
Transferrin: variations in blood serum of red howler monkeys. bibliog Science 146: 774-5 N 6 '64

SCHöNBERG, Arnold
Eisler on Schoenberg; interview, ed. by W. Lowenfels. Sat R 46:33-4 Ag 31 '63
Erwartung by Pilarczyk. I. Kolodin. Sat R 46:55 F 23 '63
Listening to Schoenberg. P. Heyworth. pors Hi Fi 13:51-4+ Ag '63
Music of Arnold Schoenberg. A. Cohn. il Am Rec G 30:192-4 N '63
Music of Arnold Schoenberg: now, volume II. A. Cohn. por Am Rec G 30:394-5 Ja '64
Not one but three new versions of Pierrot Lunaire. J. Diether. Am Rec G 29:643-4+ Ap '63
Schoenberg from Pelléas to Genesis. A. Frankenstein. por Hi Fi 13:68-9 D '63

SCHONBERG, Harold C.
Chess nut is a helpless pawn. N Y Times Mag p67+ N 29 '64
From Leschetizky to Gabrilowitsch; twenty pianists on piano rolls. Hi Fi 14:67-8 Mr '64
Metropolitan forum; reprints. Opera N 28:33 D 7; 33 D 21 '63
Rubinstein touch, untouched at seventy-five. N Y Times Mag p 12+ Ja 26 '64
Sight of music. Harper 230:110-14 Ja '65
Speaking out. por Sat Eve Post 236:10+ Jl 13 '63
Verdi is heard over Wagner's thunder. N Y Times Mag p 14-15+ My 19 '63
—See Krokover, R. jt. auth.
about
Childe Harold in New York; question of acoustics. il por Time 82:36+ S 6 '63

SCHöNIG, Heinz Peter
Father Schönig: circus priest extraordinary. G. Kent. il Read Digest 84:74-8 Je '64

SCHOODIC POINT. See Acadia National Park

SCHOOL activities. See Student activities

SCHOOL administration. See School management and organization

SCHOOL administrators. See School superintendents and principals

SCHOOL advertising. See School publicity

SCHOOL age
Cutback in Russia. Time 84:69 Ag 21 '64
Early admission of able children to school; Warren demonstration project. J. W. Birch and others. bibliog Sch Life 46:7-9 Je '64
Two more years of enforced schooling? U S News 56:8 Mr 9 '64
See also
Readiness for school

SCHOOL and social and economic problems
Attack on poverty. C. G. Norris. bibliog Horn Bk 40:364-9 Ag '64
Chaos of urban schools. R. Kirk. Nat R 16: 495 Je 16 '64
City schools. P. C. Sexton. bibliog f il Ann Am Acad 352:95-106 Mr '64
Demonstration project to combat poverty; Fulton County, Ga. Sch Life 46:4 Ag '64
Do you dig all jive? G. Weinstein. il Sr Schol 85:13T-14T Ja 14 '65
Education of subcultural groups. J. P. Rice, jr. bibliog f Sch & Soc 92:360-2 N 28 '64

SCHOOL and social and economic problems—*Continued*
Education: President's message outlines program concentrated on aiding the disadvantaged. J. Walsh. Science 147:382-3 Ja 22 '65
Elementary school in the city: a conference report. Sch Life 45:26-34 Je '63
Investment in people. H. M. Phillips. il UNESCO Courier 17:8-11+ O '64
Language and the dignity of youth. C. J. Calitri. il Sat R 46:46-7+ Jl 20 '63
Operation understanding; Columbus school, Baltimore. J. Epstein. il NEA J 53:22-4 Mr '64
Preparing the city child for his school. G. C. Fusco. bibliog f il Sch Life 46:5-8 My '6
Rope to jump, a well to dig. T. Parrish. il Reporter 31:37+ N 19 '64
Rural kids in big cities; Rural education association convention. Sr Schol 83:3T N 15 '63
Scholastic teacher interviews: Dr John H. Fischer; ed. by H. Langer. J. H. Fischer. Sr Schol 85:8T-13T+ S 23 '64
School dropout and the family; adaptation of address, November 8, 1963. R. D. Strom. Sch & Soc 92:191-2 Ap 18 '64
Slums and suburbs, by J. B. Conant. Review Parents Mag 39:129 My '64
Statement on values; concerning document, Some intergroup factors influencing the teaching of American social values. Sr Schol 84:1T-2T My 8 '64
Stepping-stones from the slums. L. Velie. il Read Digest 83:175-80 O '63
Teacher, by S. Ashton-Warner. Review Sat R il 46:45 O 5 '63. L. S. Mitchell
To be continued: story of Baltimore early school admissions project. A. C. Harding. il NEA J 53:30-2 S '64
War on poverty; book publishing's role in adult education, job retraining; symposium; with editorial comment. il Pub W 185: 38-50, 57 F 17 '64
War on poverty: impact on education. il Sr Schol 85:1T Ja 14 '65
Warring on poverty; summary of address. J. K. Galbraith. Sr Schol 84:4T F 7 '64
See also
School social work
Socially handicapped children—Education

SCHOOL and society (periodical)
Fiftieth year of School and society. W. W. Brickman. Sch & Soc 92:23 Ja 25 '64
Quarter-century of the Society for the advancement of education. T. A. Distler. Sch & Soc 92:261 O 3 '64
Status of School and society, 1962-63. W. W. Brickman. Sch & Soc 91:207 My 4 '63
Status of School and society, 1963-64. W. W. Brickman. Sch & Soc 92:216 Sum '64

SCHOOL and the community
Beauty around our town; art show at Moorpark elementary school, Calif. J. Stillion. il Sch Arts 63:22-4 F '64
Citizens and their schools. J. Cass. Sat R 47:55-6 N 21 '64; Reply. R. I. Coun. 47: 44 D 19 '64
Editor's notebook; giving of themselves. M. S. Fenner. NEA J 52:64 D '63
Great art of public relations. W. H. Fisher. Sch & Soc 92:47 F 8 '64
How to win the fight for a new school. H. Mehling. il Redbook 122:48-9+ Ja '64
Is the curriculum our business? with a study-discussion program, by D. B. Harris and E. S. Harris. A. H. Marckwardt. bibliog il PTA Mag 58:7-9, 35-6 Ap '64
Local control: secret of schools' success; interview. Mrs F. A. Radke. il Nations Bsns 52:68-70+ F '64
Operation understanding; Columbus school, Baltimore. J. Epstein. il NEA J 53:22-4 Mr '64
School referenda; case of Rich Township district, Ill. J. M. Patterson. Vital Speeches 29:463-5 My 15 '63
What's happening in education? speeding up the adoption of new and better methods of education. W. D. Boutwell. PTA Mag 58: 18 F '64
Whole town's talking; about school program and finance seminars, Columbus, Ohio. J. L. Davis. il NEA J 52:26-7 O '63
Widening a world; program providing cultural opportunities in Hebbronville, Tex. P. B. Sexton. Wilson Lib Bul 38:852-4 Je '64
See also
Teachers and the community

SCHOOL and the home
Helping parents to understand your reading program. R. C. Staiger. Sr Schol 85:13T N 18 '64
Parent meets teacher. A. P. Eliasberg. il N Y Times Mag p 112+ N 1 '64
Preparing the city child for his school. G. C. Fusco. bibliog f il Sch Life 46:5-8 My '64
Teachers and parents work together in depressed neighborhoods. G. C. Fusco. il Sr Schol 84:13T-14T Ap 24 '64
What to do? America 109:223 S 7 '63
Working with parents; symposium. il NEA J 52:8-23 D '63
See also
Home study
Parents and teachers associations

Caricatures and cartoons

Parents' day. Saxon. New Yorker 39:50-3 N 16 '63

SCHOOL architecture. See School buildings

SCHOOL art. See Art—Study and teaching

SCHOOL art exhibits. See Childrens art—Exhibitions

SCHOOL arts (periodical)
Reader survey, highlights & insights. H. E. Hoffa. il Sch Arts 63:33-4 D '63

SCHOOL athletics
High school of champions; McClymonds of Oakland, Calif. il Ebony 18:25-8+ Ap '63
See also
Basketball
Football
Physical education and training

SCHOOL attendance
Compulsory high school attendance? pro and con discussion. D. E. Winchell; R. Meckley. il NEA J 53:10-12 F '64
Falsifying attendance figures. NEA J 54:68 Ja '65
51 million and more; school enrollments. il Sch Life 46:17 O '63
Financial health of education. Sch & Soc 92: 350 N 28 '64
Five-year-olds in school. R. M. Walker. il Sch Life 46:20 N '63
Future school enrollments. il Sch & Soc 91: 343+ N 16 '63
Rate of enrollment rises. il Sch Life 47:16 O '64
See also
Colleges and universities—Class attendance
Junior colleges—Attendance
Private schools—Attendance
Student withdrawals

SCHOOL bags. See Bags

SCHOOL boards
Are school boards necessary? H. B. Holt. Sch & Soc 91:349-50 N 16 '63
Board-staff negotiations. J. P. Steffensen. Sch Life 47:6-8 O '64
Denver achieves professional negotiations. R. Newlon and B. J. Lee. il NEA J 52:14-16 F '63
Local control: secret of schools' success; interview. Mrs F. A. Radke. il Nations Bsns 52:68-70+ F '64
Our schools: battleground of conflicting interests; adapted from address, February 18, 1964. J. H. Fischer. il Sat R 47:66-7+ Mr 21 '64
Rights of teachers. New Repub 148:5-6 Je 1 '63
School board fight in Indianapolis; Citizens school committee vs Non-partisans of better schools. Christian Cent 81:598 My 6 '64
Who's in charge? il Time 83:44+ My 8 '64
See also
National school boards association

SCHOOL bonds. See School finance

SCHOOL book fairs. See Book fairs

SCHOOL books. See Textbooks

SCHOOL boycotts
As race trouble erupted in the North. il U S News 56:6 Mr 9 '64
Better schools are the real goal of integration. Life 56:4 F 21 '64
Beyond tokenism. A. M. Bickel. New Repub 150:11-14 Ja 4 '64; Discussion. 150:31 Ja 11; 38 F 15 '64
Boycott in Chicago. Newsweek 63:30-1 Mr 9 '64
Boycott in New York? Newsweek 63:45 Ja 6 '64
Boycott picture; New York city. il Sr Schol 84:2T+ F 21 '64
Boycotts. Time 83:82 Mr 6 '64
Boycotts and bargaining; excerpts from address, February 1964. J. H. Fischer. Sr Schol 84:4T Mr 20 '64
Bus the children? school boycotts. R. A. Graham. America 110:160-1 F 1 '64
Circle of futility. P. Schrag. Commonweal 79:685-8 Mr 6 '64

SCHOOL boycotts—*Continued*
Cross-busing, now it's here; Princeton plan. il Life 57:44-46C S 25 '64
De facto segregation; school boycott of February 3, 1964. Commonweal 79:583-4 F 14 '64
Great New York boycott; what will happen if the cry for better schools fails? C. Jencks. New Repub 150:12-14 F 15 '64
Hooky; school boycott. il Newsweek 63:62 F 17 '64
Neighborhood school system in danger? il U S News 56:48-52 Mr 16 '64
New wave. il Newsweek 63:24+ F 10 '64
N.Y.C. school boycott; Parents and taxpayers coordinating council and Joint council for better education. il Sr Schol 85:1T S 30 '64
New York dilemma; Negro boycott against segregated schools. il Time 83:49 F 7 '64
New York school boycott. M. Kempton. New Repub 151:6-7 S 26 '64; Discussion. 151:30 O 10; 30 O 24 '64
New York's boycott: what did it prove? T. R. Brooks. il Reporter 30:32-4 F 27 '64
One step closer to the ultimate answer. J. Scanlon. Sat R 47:59-60 F 15 '64
Playing hooky for freedom. C. L. Sanders. il Ebony 19:153-62 Ap '64
Public schools; the spreading boycott; New York city's problem. il Time 83:40+ F 14 '64
School boycott. Sr Schol 84:2T Ja 31 '64
School boycotts are signs of frustration. Christian Cent 81:198 F 12 '64; Discussion. 81:376 Mr 18 '64
School boycotts: your city may be next. il U S News 56:6+ F 17 '64
Schools boycotted; New York and other cities. il Sr Schol 84:19-20 F 21 '64
Standing P.A.T. Time 84:44 S 25 '64
White boycott; Parents and taxpayers coordinating council and the Joint council for better education. Reporter 31:18+ O 8 '64
White walkout; two-day school boycott in New York city. il Newsweek 64:87-8 S 28 '64

SCHOOL buildings
Biggest states tackle school shortage. il Arch Forum 119:5 S '63
Building types study (cont) il Arch Rec 133: 159-62 F; 134:199-222 O '63; 135:145-64 F; 136:225-48 S '64
California to get school-components bid. Arch Rec 134:36 N '63
Carpets & clusters; schools that look like wheels and circus tents at Greeley, Colo. il Time 84:44 S 25 '64
Components program for California schools. il Arch Rec 135:167-9 Ja '64
False economies in schoolhouse construction. W. W. Caudill. il Sat R 46:72-4+ My 18 '63
Four schools. il Arch Forum 120:115-23 My '64
Gores of E.F.L. notes changing standards for size and location of big city schools. Arch Rec 135:23 Mr '64
How to launch a school building program. M. Mayer. Bet Hom & Gard 42:120+ S '64
Lightweight partitions cut school costs. il Arch Rec 133:212 Mr '63
Midwest preparatory school in a monastic mood; St John's preparatory school, Collegeville, Minn. il Arch Forum 119:108-13 D '63
Modest architecture for a fine New England campus; Phillips academy, Andover, Mass. M. F. Schmertz. il Arch Rec 134:141-56 S '63
New kind of city school for Providence. il Arch Forum 119:11 D '63
New schools for the suburbs. il Arch Forum 119:56-67 Ag '63
New York state offers stock school plans. Arch Rec 134:36 N '63
Our new school. J. O. Mitchell. il Sch Arts 63:10-11 N '63
Pei tackles the city school problem. il Arch Forum 118:7 Mr '63
Plug-in schools: next step in educational design? B. P. Spring. il Arch Forum 119: 68-73 Ag '63
Realistic property accounting. C. T. Roberts. il Sch Life 46:25-7 N '63
Rocky beats a dead horse; stock school plans in New York state. il Arch Forum 119:75-6 N '63
School building boom follows rising enrollments to high school. M. B. Ayre. il Arch Rec 133:18 My '63
School costs cut by new components. B. P. Spring. il Arch Forum 120:112-17 F '64
Science for schoolboys; St Mark's school of Texas. il Arch Forum 118:110-13 F '63
Special schools; building types study. il Arch Rec 133:167-86 My '63
Swiss school is a lesson in concrete; School for economic and social studies, St Gallen. il Arch Forum 120:78-81 Ja '64
Team teaching and school construction. H. C. F. Arnold. il Arch Rec 134:18 O '63
Urban schools. il Arch Forum 119:77-99 N '63
What can you do about rising school taxes? S. Schuler. il Am Home 67:10+ Ap '64
See also
Classrooms

Air conditioning

Air-conditioning, architecture and education; symposium, ed. by H. Wright. Arch Rec 135:146-50 F '64
Air-conditioning for a twelve-month program. il Arch Rec 135:151-3 F '64
Air conditioning: modular rooftop units. B. P. Spring. il Arch Forum 120:116 F '64
Budget design for a flexible school with air conditioning. il Arch Rec 136:244-5 S '64
Ceiling units for school air conditioning. il Arch Rec 136:163-4 Ag '64

Cost

Facing up to costs. E. Goble. Arch Rec 133:9 Ja '63
School component designs, costs revealed; California's program. il Arch Rec 135:166-72 F '64
School costs cut by new components. B. P. Spring. il Arch Forum 120:112-17 F '64
Trimming builders' school bills; California educators and architects. il Bsns W p62-3 Ja 4 '64

Heating and ventilation

Lights, people heat a Wisconsin school; Kimberly high school. il Arch Rec 134:194-5 N '63
School floors warmed by electric heating. R. E. Barnes. il Arch Rec 134:165-6 Jl '63

SCHOOL buildings, Bombproof. See Building, Bombproof

SCHOOL buildings, Portable
Portable school program for Pittsburgh. J. Pekruhn. il Arch Rec 133:176-8 F '63
Portable school that can be moved intact; Dearborn, Mich; New Jersey studies a deployable school. il Arch Rec 133:173-5 F '63

SCHOOL buildings, Prefabricated
Component systems for schools. il Arch Rec 133:180-1 F '63
School component designs, costs revealed; California's program. il Arch Rec 135:166-72 F '64

SCHOOL buildings, Remodeled
High school rehabilitated; Community high school, Evergreen Park, Ill. il Arch Forum 119:128-9 N '63
Remodeling of a city school; Buckley school, N.Y. il Arch Forum 119:124-7 N '63

SCHOOL buildings as recreation centers
Guide for joint use of facilities: school and recreation facilities, Austin, Tex. Recreation 56:322-3+ S '63

SCHOOL bus transportation. See School children—Transportation

SCHOOL buses
See also
School children—Transportation

SCHOOL camping
Adventures in nature. W. Bly. Recreation. 57:115 Mr '64

SCHOOL children
First day of school! photographs. R. C. Davids. Farm J 87:32 S '63
Good-by, little boy! H. G. Green. il Read Digest 83:79-82 S '63
Grouping and human values; excerpt from address. J. W. Gordon. il Sch Life 45:10-15 Jl '63
Rural disadvantaged. R. M. Isenberg. NEA J 52:27 Ap '63
See also
Children, Backward
High school students
Intelligence tests
Negro school children
Problem children
Readiness for school
Teachers and students

Adjustment

Are school psychologists helping or hurting your child? il Redbook 122:76-7+ Ap '64
Big brothers to troubled children; Whittier school, Washington, D.C. C. M. Bloomberg and C. H. Troupe. il NEA J 53:22-5 Ja '64

SCHOOL children—Adjustment—*Continued*
First day of school. il Am Home 66:22 S '63
First grade and first worries; with study-discussion program, by R. Strang. M. Marston. bibliog il PTA Mag 57:14-16, 34 Ap '63
In the South these children prophesy. R. Coles. il Atlan 211:111-16 Mr '63
Moving? what to do about schools. il Good H 157:129 Jl '63
New girl. M. Cousins. il Good H 157:74-85 Ag '63
New town, new school, new problems. G. L. Wyatt. il Parents Mag 39:68-9+ S '64
Saburo's native land. C. B. Gross. il Read Digest 82:107-9 F '63
That first day of school. L. Strong. il N Y Times Mag p57 Ag 30 '64
When a child's afraid of school; with program for discussion groups, by M. R. Sherwin. J. M. Toolan. il Parents Mag 38:48+, 80-1+ O '63
See also
High school students—Adjustment

Anecdotes, facetiae, satire, etc.
Culprit in the convent; condensation of Life with Mother Superior. J. Trahey. il Read Digest 83:221-3+ Ag '63

Health
See Children—Care and hygiene

Medical inspection
Should schools give physical checkups? il Good H 158:165 F '64
What the schools do (and don't do) to protect children's health. G. G. Greer. Bet Hom & Gard 43:14 Ja '65

Migration
See Children of migrant laborers

Nutrition
See Children—Nutrition

Punishment
See School discipline

Reading
See Childrens reading

Transportation
Compulsory school busing and integration. W. W. Brickman. Sch & Soc 92:283 O 17 '64
Free riders; Missouri's refusal to provide buses for parochial pupils. il Newsweek 61: 32 My 20 '63
Missouri shows them; transportation of parochial as well as public school children. J. O'Gara. Commonweal 78:272 My 31 '63
Neighborhood schools win a round in Supreme court. il U S News 56:56 My 18 '64
Protest in Missouri. America 108:729 My 25 '63
Should Catholic pupils get free bus rides? U S News 54:10 My 20 '63
Slums and suburbs, by J. B. Conant. Review Parents Mag 39:129 My '64

SCHOOL children and strangers. See Children and strangers
SCHOOL childrens uniforms. See Uniforms
SCHOOL clothes. See Clothing and dress—Children
SCHOOL construction. See School buildings
SCHOOL construction systems development
Trimming builders' school bills; California educators and architects. il Bsns W p62-3 Ja 4 '64
SCHOOL counselors
Classroom incident; symposium. NEA J 54: 54-5 Ja '65
Should vocational guidance be junked? pro and con discussion. il NEA J 52:30-2 D '63
Special counseling for the young student. il Good H 158:125 Ja '64
What good does school counseling do? with study-discussion program, by E. M. Duvall. A. H. Ryden. bibliog PTA Mag 58:28-30, 36-7 O '63
SCHOOL custodial workers. See Janitors
SCHOOL dances. See Student activities
SCHOOL day
Eight hour school day? Sr Schol 83:1T O 25 '63
Eight-to-five schooling? Sr Schol 83:1T-2T O 11 '63; Discussion. 83:4T N 1; 4T N 15 '63

SCHOOL decoration
Color affects performance. Sci N L 85:141 F 29 '64
SCHOOL discipline
Children look at their own behavior. R. Lippitt and others. il NEA J 53:14-16 S '64
Classroom incident. NEA J 53:33-4 S; 25-6 O; 24-5 N; 55-6 D '64
Discipline? follow the yellow brick road. R. Agnew. il NEA J 53:52-4 O '64
First aid for discipline problems. R. E. Muuss. NEA J 52:8-11 S '63
School crisis in the Nation's capital; interview. C. F. Hansen. il U S News 54:62-8 Mr 11 '63
Secondary school discipline: with comments by F. D. Bartlett; M. Luney; K. Larson. il NEA J 52:12-17 S '63
Should teachers wield the rod? S. S. Rosenberg. il Parents Mag 39:74-5+ F '64
Teacher-opinion poll; classroom discipline. il NEA J 53:25 S '64
See also
Corporal punishment
SCHOOL districts
Inter-district cooperation. M. W. Bierbaum and R. Sperreng. NEA J 52:56 Mr '63
New schools in federally affected areas. il Sch Life 47:14-15 O '64
School assistance in federally affected areas: Public law 815 and Public law 874. il Sch Life 46:8-9 My '64
When a community votes no. E. Zimbel. il Sat R 48:54-5 Ja 16 '65
SCHOOL enrollment. See School attendance
SCHOOL entrance age. See School age
SCHOOL equipment. See School furniture, equipment, etc.
SCHOOL excursions
Class trip. D. C. Koch. il NEA J 53:17-20 Ap '64
Film trips: excursions unlimited; San Diego city schools. J. F. Wilson. Sr Schol 85:21T Ja 21 '65
Urban art program; Downtown community school, New York city. P. Greenberg. il Sch Arts 64:7-9 N '64

Anecdotes, facetiae, satire, etc.
Bus 23, where are you? J. M. Lynch, jr. il NEA J 53:23 Ap '64
SCHOOL exhibits
Humanities fair; Woodward school for boys, Washington, D.C. il NEA J 53:44-5 D '64
See also
Childrens art—Exhibitions
SCHOOL expenses. See School finance
SCHOOL finance
Bonds for educational purposes, sales, interest rates, et cetera; public schools. E. C. Deering. See issues of School life
Can public funds be constitutionally granted to private schools? address, January 9, 1963. R. F. Drinan. Vital Speeches 29:273-8 F 15 '63
Educational expenditures. F. W. Harrison and E. P. McLoone. il Sch Life 46:21-3 O '63
Financial health of education. Sch & Soc 92: 350 N 28 '64
Financial status of the public schools, 1964. E. L. Lindman. il NEA J 53:38-9 N '64
Government finance for private schools in Australia. W. G. Smith. Sch & Soc 92:268-70 O 3 '64
Local control: secret of schools' success; interview. Mrs F. A. Radke. il Nations Bsns 52:68-70+ F '64
Money makes a difference. F. Keppel. Parents Mag 39:80+ F '64
School bonds nixed; Detroit. H. Salsinger. Sr Schol 85:1T-2T N 4 '64
School bonds, sales, interest rates, et cetera. E. C. Deering. See issues of School life to March 1963
School finance workshop; teachers of Quincy, Ill. R. E. Meyer. NEA J 53:54 D '64
School referenda; case of Rich Township district, Ill. J. M. Patterson. Vital Speeches 29:463-5 My 15 '63
Schools and money. Sr Schol 83:2T N 8 '63
What can you do about rising school taxes? S. Schuler. il Am Home 67:10+ Ap '64
What's happening in education? up-to-date sources on schools. W. D. Boutwell. PTA Mag 58:34 Ja '64
When a community votes no. E. Zimbel. il Sat R 48:54-5 Ja 16 '65

SCHOOL finance—*Continued*
Where there's a crisis in the schools. U S News 57:8 D 28 '64
Whole town's talking; about school program and finance seminars, Columbus, Ohio. J. L. Davis. il NEA J 52:26-7 O '63
See also
Colleges and universities—Finance
Education and state
Schools—Accounting

SCHOOL for jesters; drama. See Whitman, C.

SCHOOL for scandal; drama. See Sheridan, R. B. B.

SCHOOL forests
Dream for our schools. F. Lape. il Am For 70:8-11+ Ag '64

SCHOOL furniture, equipment, etc.
Billions for Johnny; record $1.7 billion for school equipment and supplies. il Time 84:80 Ag 21 '64
It's a two-faced school board. il Sunset 132:166+ My '64

SCHOOL health service. See School children—Medical inspection

SCHOOL houses. See School buildings

SCHOOL janitors. See Janitors

SCHOOL journalism. See College and school journalism

SCHOOL laws and legislation
Health, medical care, and education. il Sr Schol 85:25 O 28 '64
What's happening in education? W. D. Boutwell. PTA Mag 58:13-14 Mr '64

United States

Books to benefit from expansion of education act. Pub W 186:35 N 2 '64
Bulwarks against federal control. A. W. F. Ford. Sr Schol 82:16T Mr 20 '63
Congress; decision to break up comprehensive education bill, act on parts, taken in House. J. Walsh. Science 140:620 My 10 '63
Education Congress. il Sr Schol 83:1T Ja 10 '64
Education legislation 1964-65. Sr Schol 85: 6T O 7 '64
Education: President's program provides more room at top. J. Walsh. Science 139:474-5+ F 8 '63
Exclusive Thanksgiving convention reports; discussion of National defense education act. il Sr Schol 85:1T+ D 9 '64
Federal aid for school libraries: NDEA, Vocational education act, Economic opportunity act. F. Keppel. Library J 90:293-5 Ja 15 '65
Five years of NDEA. Sch Life 46:12 O '63
Four education bills reported in Senate. Pub W 184:32 O 14 '63
Health professions assistance act. Sch Life 46:16 N '63
Higher education as a national resource: a proposed federal program; text of document, January 17, 1963. Sch & Soc 91:218-21 My 4 '63
Higher education facilities act of 1963. il Sch Life 46:13-22 My '64
House subcommittee okays NDEA extension, amendment. Pub W 186:52-3 Jl 20 '64
Housing act and higher education. L. G. Burns. bibliog f Sch & Soc 91:211-12 My 4 '63
Loyalty oath: 1964-65. T. Kaser. Sat R 47: 60+ N 21 '64; Reply. H. A. Bedau. 48: 46 Ja 16 '65
NDEA amended by P.L.88-665. G. Krettek and E. D. Cooke. ALA Bul 58:985 D '64
NDEA for humanities. Sr Schol 85:1T O 21 '64
National defense education act of 1958; the new amendments. il Sch Life 46:16-24 Mr '64
NDEA loans to private schools. G. C. Decker. il Sch Life 45:19-21 Ap '63
National defense school library institutes for 1965. G. Krettek and E. D. Cooke. ALA Bul 59:22 Ja '65; Same. Wilson Lib Bul 39:417+ Ja '65
NEA and the hill. R. Anderson. il NEA J 52:36-9 Ap '63
New NDEA to help school librarians. Library J 89:3406 S 15 '64
Next steps in federal aid. R. H. Wyatt. NEA J 53:35-6 Mr '64
Nonpublic schools: what must they teach? M. J. Stolee. bibliog f il Sch & Soc 92: 274-6+ O 3 '64
Occupational plans of student borrowers under NDEA. R. C. Hall. il Sch Life 45: 26-9 Ja '63
One step closer to the ultimate answer. J. Scanlon. Sat R 47:59-60 F 15 '64
President asks $1.5 billion for aid to education; with editorial comment. Pub W 187: 273-4, 280 Ja 25 '65
President Johnson signs amended, expanded NDEA; excerpts from address, October 16, 1964. L. B. Johnson. Library J 89:4990 D 15 '64
President's program for education; summary of proposals. il Sat R 46:68-9 Mr 23 '63
Provisions for handicapped children: P.L. 88-164. Sch Life 46:5 D '63
Q and A on NDEA: provision for audio-visual materials. il Sr Schol 85:13T Ja 21 '65
Role of the NDEA. D. D. Walsh. il Sat R 46:73-4 F 16 '63
Senate and House pass NDEA bill, including school librarians. ALA Bul 58:697 S '64
Summary of the administration's bill for education. Sch Life 45:27-8 F '63
This month's feature: Congress and aid to higher education. Cong Digest 42:35-64 F '63
Top of the agenda; Johnson's comprehensive education bill. il Newsweek 65:56-7 Ja 25 '65
Vocational education act of 1963. il Sch Life 46:3-12 Mr '64
While school keeps; National defense education act. J. Cass. Sat R 46:75 N 16 '63
Will Congress pay for education? C. Jencks. il New Repub 150:11-14 Ja 11 '64
See also
Federal aid to education

SCHOOL leaving age. See School age

SCHOOL librarians
Educating for flexibility. E. Dale. ALA Bul 57:131-4 F '63
Librarian at work with teachers; symposium; with introd. by S. I. Fenwick. ALA Bul 57: 153-69 F '63
New NDEA to help school librarians. Library J 89:3406 S 15 '64
Principal and the school librarian. M. G. Bowden. Wilson Lib Bul 37:572-3+ Mr '63
School librarian builds a public image: adaptation of address. D. F. Walker. Library J 88:3258-60 S 15 '63
School library: instruction's partner; address, November, 1962. A. L. Robinson. Library J 88:823-5+ F 15 '63
Senate and House pass NDEA bill, including school librarians. ALA Bul 58:697 S '64
Teacher or librarian? summary of address. E. C. Saltus; discussion. Library J 88: 814, 1194, 2044 F 15, Mr 15, My 15 '63
This task is ours; superintendent's philosophy about school libraries; excerpts from address, April 5, 1963. C. E. Brown. il Library J 88:4434-6 N 15 '63
See also
American association of school librarians

Education

Frick commission is benefactor in Pa. elem. ln. training project. Library J 88:2094 My 15 '63

Recruiting

See Librarians—Recruiting

Salaries

School librarians would gain by pending tax legislation. Library J 89:2160+ My 15 '64

SCHOOL libraries
Automating the school library: an advanced report; Brentwood public schools, Brentwood, L.I. C. A. Vertanes. il Wilson Lib Bul 37:864-7 Je '63
Big push. E. Geller. Library J 90:282 Ja 15 '65
California starts two-year study of school libraries statewide. Library J 89:927+ F 15 '64
Creative elementary school library; ed. by J. Lowrie. See issues of Wilson library bulletin to June 1963
Demonstration school libraries. Sch & Soc 91:163-4 Ap 6 '63
Education of a headmaster; Choate school, Wallingford, Conn; reprint. S. St John. il Library J 88:828-31 F 15 '63
Elementary school library growth in New York city. H. R. Sattley. il ALA Bul 58: 482-8 Je '64
Eye of the octopus; library and team teaching in an eight-arm school; Vale elementary school, Cashmere, Wash. M. Brooks and E. Elledge. il Library J 89:320-1+ Ja 15 '64
Help needed; Washington, D.C. E. Rudin. Library J 88:1291 Mr 15 '63
Individual study carrels; excerpts from School library, facilities for independent study in the secondary school. R. E. Ellsworth and H. D. Wagener. il Arch Rec 134:233-4 O '63

SCHOOL libraries—*Continued*
Information retrieval for students; with profile of Education centre library. Toronto. Library J 88:4412 N 15 '63
Information retrieval for students; with profile of Education centre library, Toronto. L. H. Freiser. il Library J 88:1121-3 Mr 15 '63; Discussion. 88:1566+, 1922+, 2372, 3251-3 Ap 15, My 15, Je 15, S 15 '63
IMC in the continuous progress school. J. Berry. il Library J 89:4599-602 N 15 '64
Librarian at work with teachers; symposium; with introd. by S. I. Fenwick. ALA Bul 57:153-69 F '63
Libraries inadequate; summary of report by Educational facilities laboratories. Sr Schol 83:5T O 4 '63
Lj surveys library progress '64. Library J 90:320+ Ja 15 '65
Louisiana pl is host to school lns; Texas schools use pl staff in seminar. il Library J 88:4827-8 D 15 '63
NLW backs better school libraries. Library J 88:842 F 15 '63
N. Carolina school libs. growing. Library J 89:339 Ja 15 '64
Notes for an introduction to school libraries. G. Raftery. Library J 89:4985 D 15 '64
Planning school library quarters; symposium. bibliog f il ALA Bul 58:103-11+ F '64
School libraries. See every other issue of Wilson library bulletin beginning September 1963
School libraries. F. K. Johnson. See issues of Wilson library bulletin to May 1963
School libraries; two new Washington, D.C. elementary schools. Sr Schol 85:7T O 7 '64
School library: instruction's partner; address, November, 1962. A. L. Robinson. Library J 88:823-5+ F 15 '63
School library reporter. M. H. Mahar. Sch Life 46:29-30 O; 19 D '63; 22-3 My; 13 Jl '64
School library reporter. R. L. Darling. Sch Life 46:19 N '63; 41-2 Ja; 27 Mr; 6 Je '64
School library services for the culturally deprived child. R. L. Darling. bibliog f il Sch Life 46:18-20 O '63
Schools without libraries: our national disgrace. F. Keppel. il McCalls 92:116+ N '64; Discussion. Library J 89:4576 N 15 '64; Pub W 186:28 O 26 '64
Socio-economic factors in library service to students; excerpts. M. L. Jones. il ALA Bul 58:1003-6 D '64
Story of a Hilda Maehling fellow; project coordinating library services with the summer school program in Mesa, Ariz. J. Stocker. NEA J 53:45 O '64
Student needs: response to challenge; symposium. il Wilson Lib Bul 39:383-401+ Ja '65
They can't learn without books. L. G. Carson. il Parents Mag 39:74+ Ap '64
This task is ours; superintendent's philosophy about school libraries; excerpts from address, April 5, 1963. C. E. Brown. il Library J 88:4434-6 N 15 '63
Wayne County library establishes resource center for school libraries. Library J 89:2305-6 Je 1 '64

See also
High school libraries
Libraries and schools

Acquisitions

Institutional market. E. Yungmeyer. Wilson Lib Bul 38:577 Mr '64
Is it habit or law? cutting the red tape of library book buying. N. Paige. Library J 89:909-13 F 15 '64; Discussion. 1286 Mr 15 '64

Anecdotes, facetiae, satire, etc.

Confer with sages here. G. Raftery. NEA J 54:25 Ja '65

Automation

Automated bibliography; Staples high school, Westport, Conn; letter to the editor. E. R. Savitzky. Library J 89:4954 D 15 '64
Brave new school libraries. R. N. Case. Wilson Lib Bul 38:763-5 My '64

Bibliographic services

Automated bibliography; Staples high school, Westport, Conn; letter to the editor. E. R. Savitzky. Library J 89:4954 D 15 '64

Bibliography

Short bibliography on planning school library quarters. ALA Bul 58:128 F '64

Book losses

See Libraries—Book losses

Book selection

See Book selection

Censorship

Attempt at censorship; Carlsbad, Calif, high school. J. T. Halligan. Library J 88:4002-3 O 15 '63
Book censors; what to do about them. G. Soule. Sr Schol 85:26T O 7 '64
Censors and their tactics; excerpts from address, November 7, 1963. J. Nelson. Library J 88:4809-12+ D 15 '63
Writer warns school librarians against creeping censorship; summary of address. J. Nelson. Library J 88:4445 N 15 '63

Circulation, loans, etc.

Streamlining essential routines; Fulton County school libraries, Atlanta, Ga. V. McJenkin. Wilson Lib Bul 37:680-1 Ap '63

Classification

See Classification

Designs and plans

Case studies in school library planning; five school libraries. il ALA Bul 58:116-22 F '64

Finance

Caught Knapping; two winners of grants under Knapp foundation. R. L. Chisolm. Library J 88:3272-3 S 15 '63
Federal aid for school libraries. F. Keppel. Library J 90:293-5 Ja 15 '65
Immediate applications invited for phase two of Knapp project. Library J 88:3573 O 1 '63
Knapp project names three schools in second phase of five year program. Library J 89:2160 My 15 '64
Knapp project names two schools in first phase of 5-year goal. Library J 88:3276 S 15 '63
Knapp-sack of progress; visits to two schools selected for Knapp school libraries project. P. Sullivan. il Wilson Lib Bul 39:392-6 Ja '65
Librarian's dream come true; Knapp school libraries project, Marcus Whitman elementary school, Richland, Wash. P. Sullivan. il NEA J 53:46-7 S '64
Phase 1 of Knapp project under way; applicants must apply by April first. Library J 88:841 F 15 '63
Underway: the Knapp project's first year. P. Sullivan. Library J 89:2143-5 My 15 '64

Instruction in use

See Libraries—Instruction in use

Paperback books

N.J. paperback study. Sr Schol 83:4T Ja 17 '64
N.J. to conduct statewide survey on school use of trade paperbacks. Library J 88:4005 O 15 '63
Panel urges schools to incorporate paperbacks; striking cases cited. H. Schiller. Library J 88:844-5 F 15 '63
Paperbacks in school and public libraries; symposium. il Sr Schol 82:9T-10T+ Mr 13 '63; Summary. Wilson Lib Bul 37:734 My '63
Paperbacks in the HS library. M. Cheeseman. Library J 88:2044 My 15 '63
Plainview welcomes paperbacks: high school library's experience. D. Cohen. bibliog il Library J 90:306-8 Ja 15 '65
Special issue on paperbacks; symposium, ed. by M. Bogart. il Sr Schol 85:17T-26T+ D 2 '64
Special issue on paperbacks; symposium, ed. by R. Beauchamp. il Sr Schol 83:21T-35T Ja 17 '64

Phonograph and phonograph records

See Libraries—Phonograph and phonograph records

Public relations

School library promotion. J. Jahnke. il Wilson Lib Bul 39:478-9 F '65

Reference work

Scholars can be made as well as born. C. L. Baron. Wilson Lib Bul 39:261+ N '64

Statistics

Surveys of school library statistics published by USOE. Library J 89:4614+ N 15 '64

SCHOOL libraries—*Continued*

Student assistants

Intellectual laboratory for children; Horace Mann elementary and junior high school, laboratory school at Northwest Missouri state college, Maryville. C. S. Peterson. il Wilson Lib Bul 39:403-5 Ja '65
Library aide program. M. Moss. Wilson Lib Bul 38:298 N '63
Student helpers in the elementary school library. L. S. Cohen; reply. E. G. Williams. Library J 88:1196 Mr 15 '63

Technical processes

Panacea or Pandora's box? a look at central processing in New York state. V. J. Aceto. Library J 89:322-4+ Ja 15 '64; Discussion. 89:1284 Mr 15 '64
Streamlining essential routines; Fulton County school libraries, Atlanta Ga. V. McJenkin. Wilson Lib Bul 37:680-1 Ap '63

Volunteer workers

Parents help with audio-visual aids. M. Bise. Wilson Lib Bul 37:787-8+ My '63

SCHOOL libraries and art. See Libraries and art
SCHOOL libraries and audio-visual materials. See Libraries and audio-visual materials
SCHOOL libraries and social and economic problems. See Libraries and social and economic problems
SCHOOL library architecture. See Library architecture
SCHOOL library catalogs. See Catalogs, Library
SCHOOL library conferences. See Library conferences
SCHOOL library journal
Anniversary. E. Rudin. Library J 88:3274 S 15 '63
SCHOOL library surveys
California starts two-year study of school libraries statewide. Library J 89:927+ F 15 '64
Panacea or Pandora's box? a look at central processing in New York state. V. J. Aceto. Library J 89:322-4+ Ja 15 '64; Discussion. 89:1284 Mr 15 '64
Surveys of school library statistics published by USOE. Library J 89:4614+ N 15 '64
SCHOOL lockers. See Lockers
SCHOOL management and organization
Educational records are useful in making decisions. A. R. Lichtenberger. Sch Life 47:20-2 N '64
See also
Classroom management
School boards
School discipline
School districts
School superintendents and principals

Teacher participation

Democracy, teachers, and educational decision-making. A. R. Dykes. Sch & Soc 92:155-6 Ap 4 '64

SCHOOL newspapers. See College and school journalism
SCHOOL of American ballet, Incorporated
Open letter: about the Ford foundation's SAB program of services to ballet students and teachers. O. Maynard. Dance Mag 38:22-4 Jl '64
SCHOOL of general studies, Columbia university. See Columbia university—School of general studies
SCHOOL of hotel administration. See Cornell university, Ithaca, N.Y.
SCHOOL of performing arts. See New York (city)—Education
SCHOOL officials. See State superintendents of public instruction
SCHOOL orchestras
Teen-agers tune up; photographs. A. Rich. N Y Times Mag p80+ My 5 '63
SCHOOL organization. See School management and organization
SCHOOL papers. See College and school journalism
SCHOOL plays. See College and school drama
SCHOOL prayer. See Public schools and religion
SCHOOL prayer decision. See United States—Supreme court—Decisions
SCHOOL principals. See School superintendents and principals
SCHOOL psychologists. See Psychologists
SCHOOL publicity
Education in newspaper advertisements. G. Gerbner. Sch & Soc 92:363-5 N 28 '64

SCHOOL readers. See Readers
SCHOOL reports and records
Educational records are useful in making decisions. A. R. Lichtenberger. Sch Life 47:20-2 N '64
My parents, my teacher, and me. E. F. DeRoche. il NEA J 52:16-17 D '63
Report on reports. il NEA J 52:14-15 D '63
Reporting in depth; new report card system at Evanston, Ill. il Newsweek 61:91 F 25 '63
Restoration of report cards; symposium, ed. by P. J. Misner; with study-discussion program, by D. B. Harris and E. S. Harris. bibliog il PTA Mag 58:10-12, 36 F '64
What report cards don't tell. O. Palmer. il Parents Mag 39:50-1+ Je '64
SCHOOL science library program. See American association for the advancement of science—School science library program
SCHOOL sessions. See School day
SCHOOL shelters. See Atomic bomb shelters
SCHOOL shops

Safety devices and measures

Space age schools have shop health hazards. Sci N L 84:344 N 30 '63

SCHOOL social work
School social work in the United States. J. W. Rioux. Sch Life 46:9-10 Ag '64
SCHOOL; story. See O'Hara, J.
SCHOOL subjects. See Courses of study
SCHOOL superintendents and principals
Denver achieves professional negotiations. R. Newlon and B. J. Lee. il NEA J 52:14-16 F '63
Education of a headmaster; Choate school, Wallingford, Conn; reprint. S. St John. il Library J 88:828-31 F 15 '63
Education of a school superintendent. W. W. Brickman. Sch & Soc 91:232 Sum '63
Educational statesmanship. P. Woodring. Sat R 46:55 Mr 23 '63; Discussion. 46:60 Ap 20 '63
Our schools: battleground of conflicting interests; adapted from address, February 18, 1964. J. H. Fischer. il Sat R 47:66-7+ Mr 21 '64
Personal attention; New York's new superintendent of schools. New Yorker 39:15-16 Je 29 '63
Principal and the school librarian. M. G. Bowden. Wilson Lib Bul 37:572-3+ Mr '63
School administrator's need for inservice education. F. F. Beach and L. S. Ratliff. Sch Life 45:16-17 Mr '63
This task is ours; superintendent's philosophy about school libraries; excerpts from address, April 5, 1963. C. E. Brown. il Library J 88:4434-6 N 15 '63
What's happening in education? board of education selecting superintendent. W. D. Boutwell. PTA Mag 57:15 F '63
See also
National association of secondary-school principals
National education association—Department of elementary school principals
State superintendents of public instruction
SCHOOL supplies. See School furniture, equipment, etc.
SCHOOL surveys. See Educational surveys
SCHOOL teachers. See Teachers
SCHOOL transportation. See School children—Transportation
SCHOOL vacations. See Vacations
SCHOOL visitations. See School and the home
SCHOOL year
Air-conditioning for a twelve-month program. il Arch Rec 135:151-3 F '64
Our schools should be open all year. A. S. Fleming. Good H 156:46 Ap '63
SCHOOLEY, Susan
Beauty is a tree; poem. Horn Bk 40:663 D '64
SCHOOLHOUSES. See School buildings
SCHOOLMENS week. See Educational conferences
SCHOOLROOMS. See Classrooms
SCHOOLS
See also
American schools abroad
Law schools
Military post schools, American
Mission schools
Parochial schools, Catholic
Private schools
School buildings
Vocational education

SCHOOLS—*Continued*

Accounting

Needed, better school financial accounting. B. K. Adams and J. A. Perkins, jr. Sch Life 45:11-12 My '63
Realistic property accounting. C. T. Roberts. il Sch Life 46:25-7 N '63

Colombia

Colombia's extraordinary teacher-builder. S. Seegers and K. Seegers. Read Digest 82: 111-15 Mr '63

England

Scandal for schools; buildings problem. il Newsweek 61:86 F 11 '63

Great Britain

Art & craft in the British primary school. J. R. Milsome. il Sch Arts 64:16-17 Ja '65

Hawaii

Legacy of a princess; Kamehameha schools. il Time 83:76 My 22 '64

Norway

Impromptu teaching in Norway. E. R. Branson. il Sr Schol 84:12T-13T Mr 20 '64

United States

See also
Education—United States
Public schools—United States
Rural schools—United States

Wales

Scandal for schools; buildings problem. il Newsweek 61:86 F 11 '63

SCHOOLS, Elementary. See Education, Elementary

SCHOOLS, Experimental
Dewey's labs. Newsweek 61:75 Je 3 '63
School run by children; Summerhill. C. Brossard. il Look 27:28-33 N 19 '63

SCHOOLS, Traveling
See also
Colleges and universities, Traveling

SCHOOLS and libraries. See Libraries and schools

SCHOOLS and social and economic problems. See School and social and economic problems

SCHOOLS for American dependents abroad. See American schools abroad

SCHOOLS for dogs. See Dogs—Training

SCHOOLS of business. See Business education

SCHOOLS of education. See Colleges and universities—Education departments

SCHOONERS
Back to the schooners. Sports Illus 19:8 Ag 5 '63
Great American sailboats; Little maid of Kent; 30 foot schooner. W. H. Koelbel. il Motor B 112:52+ D '63
Jamie, the deadrise coaster. F. F. Kaiser. il Motor B 113:112-13+ My '64
Last of the Lakes windjammers; Northwest. il Yachting 115:188+ Mr '64
Saga of the Curlew. D. Skellon. il Yachting 113:38-9+ F '63; Reply. A. Forward. 114:120 Ag '63

Design

Great American sailboats; a skipjack schooner; Coot. B. Koelbel. il Motor B 113:68D+ Ap '64
Great American sailboats; Island Princess. J. Atkin. il Motor B 112:28-9+ Ag '63
Little Maid of Kent, in steel! J. Atkin. il Motor B 113:35-6 Mr '64

SCHOONHOVEN, L. M.
Spontaneous electrical activity in the brains of diapausing insects. Science 141:173-4 Jl 12 '63

SCHOONMAKER, Frank
Language of wine. bibliog Sat R 47:40-2+ O 24 '64
Wine lovers dictionary. See occasional issues of House beautiful

SCHOONOVER, Frank E.
Frank E. Schoonover: an exemplar of the Pyle tradition. H. C. Pitz. il pors Am Artist 28:64-9+ N '64

SCHOONOVER, Shirley W.
Old and country tale; story. Atlan 212:55-64 Ag '63

SCHOONOVER observatory, Lima, Ohio. See Astronomical observatories

SCHORER, Mark
All bone. Reporter 30:42-4 Ja 2 '64

SCHORR, Daniel
Shadows on the success of Der Alte. Reporter 28:27-8 F 28 '63
(ed) See Adenauer, K. Old warrior looks back

SCHORRE, Charles
Portfolio of drawings by Charles Schorre. il Am Artist 27:30-5 N '63

SCHORY, Dick
Dick Schory; interview, ed. by S. Fleming. por Hi Fi 13:20 Jl '63

SCHOSSBERGER, Emily
University presses, 1965. America 112:45+ Ja 9 '65

SCHOTT, Webster
James Purdy: American dreams. Nation 198:300-2 Mr 23 '64
Leaves of glass. Nation 199:74-6 Ag 24 '64
Stillborn America. Nation 199:440-2 D 7 '64

SCHRADER, G. L.
Centralized purchasing system. Am City 78: 108-9 S '63

SCHRAG, Peter
Circle of futility. Commonweal 79:685-8 Mr 6 '64
Light touch. NEA J 52:13 My '63
Searching for certitudes. Commonweal 79:36-40 O 4 '63

SCHRAGE, Chuck
Fifty years for the U.S. power squadrons. Yachting 115:64+ Ja '64
Ladies' auxiliaries. Yachting 117:58+ Ja '65
With the power squadrons. See issues of Yachting

SCHRAGE, Samuel
Maccabees ride again. A. G. Aronowitz. il por Sat Eve Post 237:32+ Je 27 '64

SCHRAUGER, Carolyn Ruth. See Schmidt-Nielsen, B. jt. auth.

SCHREIBER, Daniel
Low-down on dropouts. PTA Mag 58:4-6 bibliog(p37) N '63

SCHREIBER, Flora Rheta
Our first ninety days in the White House. Good H 158:86-9+ My '64
Sentences, a clue to your child's development. Todays Health 41:26-9+ Ap '63
(ed) See Smith, W. L. I believe
(ed) See Wilbur, C. B. Homosexual men and women
(ed) See Williams, R. J. Key to health: your heredity
—and Herman, Melvin
Inside psychiatry today. See issues of Science digest
Psychiatry. il Sci Digest 55:8-30 Je '64

SCHREKER, Franz
Distant sound. E. Balogh. por Opera N 29: 6-7 D 19 '64

SCHREMMER, Fritz
Centipede's spiral is live shelter. Natur Hist 72:42-5 My '63

SCHRIER, Allan M. See Blough, D. S. jt. auth.

SCHRIER, William
World wants you; address, June 6, 1963. Vital Speeches 29:597-600 Jl 15 '63

SCHRIFTGIESSER, Karl
Blueprint for political plenty. Sat R 46:57-8+ S 28 '63
For free and fair enterprise. Sat R 46:31 My 11 '63

SCHRöDER, Gerhard
Deadlock, or deathblow? il por Time 81:34 My 17 '63
—See Rusk, D. jt. auth.

SCHROEDER, Dorothy
Bonsai. Horticulture 41:200-1 Ap '63
For flavor and fragrance grow herbs. Horticulture 41:464-5 S '63

SCHROEDER, Eva M.
Hosta for foliage. Flower Grower 51:33+ Ag '64
Orchid cactus, exotic of the cactus world. Horticulture 41:415 Ag '63

SCHROEDER, Henry A.
Hard water is best for health. Consumer Bul 46:2+ Mr '63
—and Balassa, J. J.
Cadmium: uptake by vegetables from superphosphate in soil. bibliog Science 140:819-20 My 17 '63

SCHROEDER, Peter
Panoramic camera for under $40. il Pop Phot 54:54-5+ F '64

SCHROEDER, R. J.
Theatre. Nation 199:312 N 2 '64

SCHROEDER, Richard C.
Soul for the Alliance. Américas 15:2-6 O '63

SCHROEDER, Robert E.
Photographing the night creatures of Alligator Reef. il Nat Geog Mag 125:128-54 Ja '64

SCHROTEL, Stanley R.
Will city streets ever be safe again? interview. por U S News 54:80-3 Ap 8 '63

SCHROTH, Raymond A.
James Baldwin's search. Cath World 198: 288-94 F '64

SCHUBERT, Carlos. See Rogers, J. J. W. jt. auth.

SCHUBERT, Franz Peter
And another Schwanengesang: Fischer-Dieskau. P. L. Miller. Am Rec G 30:487 F '64
Art of Elisabeth Schumann. G. Breuer. Am Rec G 29:780-1 Je '63
Confirmation and exploration: three Schubert song recitals by Prey and Souzay. H. Glass. il Am Rec G 30:482-3+ F '64
For Schubert, dissimilar excellences. H. Goldsmith. il Hi Fi 14:70-1 Ap '64
Hotter's third and best Winterreise. H. Glass. Am Rec G 29:561-3 Mr '63
Important documentation of a great artist. P. L. Miller. Am Rec G 31:455 Ja '65
On records; Die winterreise; Schwanengesang. Opera N 28:35 F 1 '64
Toscanini and Schubert: Philadelphia, November 1941; Symphony no. 9. il Am Rec G 30:18-21 S '63
Two Wanderers, one of them colossal. R. Kamerer. Am Rec G 30:682 Ap '64
With the Philadelphians in 1941, Toscanini's Schubert Ninth. H. Goldsmith. Hi Fi 13: 125-6 O '63

SCHUBERTH, Christopher
Geological jaunt. New Yorker 40:35 My 9 '64

SCHUCHMAN, Robert M.
Psychiatrist at the bar. Nat R 16:201-3 Mr 10 '64

SCHUCK, John R. and others
Luminous figures: factors affecting the reporting of disappearances. bibliog Science 146:1598-9 D 18 '64

SCHUETTE, Marie, and Müller-Christensen, Sigrid
German and Italian embroidery of the middle ages; excerpts from Pictorial history of embroidery. Craft Horiz 24:23-7 N '64

SCHUH, Harry
Schuh-Schuh, baby! H. L. Hasin. por Sr Schol 85:28 O 28 '64

SCHULBERG, Budd
How are things in panicsville? Life 55:79-82+ D 20 '63; Same abr. with title Hollywood, where are you? Read Digest 84:68-72 Mr '64
Waterfront revisited. por Sat Eve Post 236: 28-32+ S 7 '63

SCHULER, Stanley
Before selecting a nursery school: stop, look & listen. Ladies Home J 80:60+ O '63
Can we save our play space? Am Home 67: 48-9 Ja '64
Coming: new jobs, new titles. Nations Bsns 51:40-1+ Je '63
House cleaners to the rescue. Am Home 67: 102+ Ja '64
How to cope with problem executives. Nations Bsns 52:78-80+ S '64
How to judge a school system. Am Home 67:26+ My '64
Is your town prepared for disaster? Am Home 67:12+ O '64
Take a second look at those new community health proposals. Am Home 67:16+ Jl '64
Think things through. Nations Bsns 51:86-8 Ag '63
Think your way to success. Nations Bsns 52:88-90+ Ap '64
Water, a most precious commodity. Am Home 67:76-8 Mr '64
What can you do about rising school taxes? Am Home 67:10+ Ap '64
Where you can cut costs next. Nations Bsns 51:58-60+ O '63
Worst pet in the world. Pop Sci 184:124-6+ Ap '64
You can cut your upkeep costs. Nations Bsns 52:94-6 My '64
You can get ahead faster. Nations Bsns 51: 76-9 F '63

SCHULKE, Flip
When & how to shoot 35mm RFDR. P. Caulfield. il Mod Phot 27:64-9 My '63

SCHULLER, John J. Jr
Teaching children to swim. NEA J 52:55-6 Mr '63

SCHULMAN, Alan R.
Siege warfare in Pharaonic Egypt. Natur Hist 73:12-21 Mr '64

SCHULMAN, Charles E.
Zionism and Judaism. Christian Cent 80:858-60 Jl 3 '63

SCHULMAN, Irwin J.
Case against the fireside chat. N Y Times Mag p 10+ Je 14 '64

SCHULMAN, Robert
Alaska: can it survive as a state? Sat Eve Post 236:78+ O 12 '63

SCHULT, Veryl
New look at the old mathematics. NEA J 53:12-15 Ap '64
—and Abell, T. L.
Inservice education of mathematics teachers. Sch Life 45:29-36 Jl '63

SCHULTE, Vivian Reade
Can you tell food fact from fiction? Parents Mag 38:92+ O '63

SCHULTE-HILLEN, K. H.
My search to find the drug that crippled my baby. pors Good H 156:94-102 My '63

SCHULTHEIS, Virginia
Former child objects. Wilson Lib Bul 37:552 Mr '63

SCHULTZ, C. Bertrand, and others
Paleontologic investigations at Big Bone Lick State Park, Kentucky: a preliminary report. bibliog Science 142:1167-9 N 29 '63

SCHULTZ, George P.
Unemployment and labor market policy; excerpt from address. Mo Labor R 86:808-10 Jl '63

SCHULTZ, Gwen M.
Food taboos. Todays Health 42:28-32 F '64
How to read a road map. Todays Health 41: 14-17+ Mr '63

SCHULTZ, Harald
Indians of the Amazon darkness. il Nat Geog Mag 125:736-58 My '64

SCHULTZ, James L.
Where to find new leaders. Nations Bsns 52:38-9+ O '64

SCHULTZ, Morton J.
All about transistorized ignition. Pop Mech 120:172-7+ S '63
Getting to know your alternator. Pop Mech 119:174-9+ Mr '63
Keep the fuel flowing. Pop Mech 119:158-63+ Je '63
Keep the power in power steering. Pop Mech 120:166-70 D '63
Keep your headlights on the beam. Pop Mech 120:157-61 Jl '63
Know your car's cooling system. Pop Mech 119:170-3+ Ap; 166-71 My '63
Lifting the lid on power brakes. Pop Mech 121:178-82+ F; 174-7 Mr '64
Motor that starts the motor. Pop Mech 120: 158-62+ Ag '63
℞ for rough idle. Pop Mech 119:172-5+ F '63
Seal out winter drafts. Am Home 67:87-8 N '64
Should you lay a hand on your carburetor? Pop Mech 121:176-80+ Ap '64 (to be cont)
Stop that costly drip! Am Home 67:88-9+ Ap '64
Valve nobody knows. Pop Mech 120:178-81 O '63
What to do if your heating system quits. Am Home 67:76+ Ja '64
Why bother with winter battery care. Pop Mech 120:180-4+ N '63
Your emergency road service chart. Pop Mech 121:105 F '64
—and Dark, H. E.
Hot tips for cold starts. Pop Mech 121:176-82+ Ja '64

SCHULTZ, Robert S.
Profits, prices, and excess capacity. bibliog f Harvard Bsns R 41:68-81 Jl '63

SCHULTZ, T. W.
Let's invest in people not land. Suc Farm 61:33 Jl '63

SCHULTZE, Klaus
Klaus Schultze; tr. by A. Adams. I. Meinecke. il Sch Arts 64:16-18 D '64

SCHULTZE, Mildred
Experimental weaving. Sch Arts 63:18-19 S '63

SCHULWEIS, Harold M.
Bias against man. Christian Cent 81:361-4 Mr 18 '64

SCHULZ, Charles M.
Charlie Brown's Christmas stocking. il Good H 157:129-44 D '63
Christmas is together-time; excerpt. McCalls 92:118-19 D '64
What is the most wonderful feeling in the world? excerpts from Security is a thumb and a blanket. il McCalls 91:66 O '63

about

Good grief, Charlie Schulz! C. R. Jennings. il por Sat Eve Post 237:26-7 Ap 25 '64
Gospel according to Peanuts, by R. L. Short. Review
Time il 85:45 Ja 1 '65

SCHULZ, Harold A.
Militia Christi. Christian Cent 81:1173 S 23 '64
Wisdom's direction; poem. Christian Cent 80:1607 D 25 '63

SCHULZ, Richard W.
Building a science curriculum. NEA J 53:21-3 O '64
SCHULZ, William
Legislative news. Nat R 16:196 Mr 10 '64
Merry Christmas Walter Reuther. Nat R 15: 484 D 3 '63
U.S. students in Cuba: how far left? Nat R 15:229 S 24 '63
SCHULZE, Franz
Art news from Chicago (cont) Art N 62: 19+ Mr; 48 My; 48 Sum; 20 N '63; 53-4 Ja; 63:48 Sum '64
SCHUMACH, Murray
Bright diamond. N Y Times Mag p80-1 My 26 '63
SCHUMACHER, Max
Portrait of a dragonfly driver. P. E. Hansen. il pors Flying 74:46-7+ My '64
(ed) See Friml, R. Pox on Broadway
SCHUMAN, Frederick L.
Wasted decades: 1899-1939. bibliog f Cur Hist 46:326-30 Je '64
SCHUMAN, Robert
Man of Europe. por Time 82:42 S 13 '63
Man of the border. Newsweek 62:44-5 S 16 '63
Mr Europe dies. America 109:276 S 21 '63
Obituary
Nat R 15:226 S 24 '63. W. F. Rickenbacker
SCHUMAN, William
Arts in our colleges. Mus Am 83:5 Je '63
Case for a Center; questions from Opera news answered. por Opera N 29:6-11 S 26 '64
Have we culture? yes, and no. N Y Times Mag p21+ S 22 '63
Inside job. il Newsweek 64:74-5 D 21 '64
Lincoln Center situation. E. Palatsky. il por Dance Mag 37:36-8 My '63
Mixing business and art. il pors Bsns W p42-5 Ag 3 '63
Shiny new image. por Newsweek 65:84-5 Ja 25 '65
SCHUMANN, Elisabeth
Art of Elisabeth Schumann. G. Breuer. por Am Rec G 29:780-1 Je '63
Elisabeth Schumann. A. Favia-Artsay. il pors Hobbies 68:30-1 Ap '63
On records: Schubert songs. C. J. Luten. Opera N 27:32 My 4 '63
SCHUMANN, Robert Alexander
For Schumann, a sonic replacement; for Rubinstein, artistic vindication. H. Goldsmith. Hi Fi 13:71-2 Ag '63
SCHUMER, Janet
Reader's choice. Travel 121:15 Ap '64
SCHUMM, Ruth
Broad horizons. Recreation 56:356-8 O '63
SCHUNK, Evaline
Humphrey the Humpher. por Wilson Lib Bul 39:164 O '64
SCHUR, Peter H. and Becker, E. L.
Complement-fixing properties of pepsin-treated rabbit and sheep antibodies. bibliog Science 141:360-2 Jl 26 '63
SCHUR, Sylvia
Jewish cooking. Sat Eve Post 236:64-6 F 16 '63
SCHURMANN, Franz
Economic policy and political power in Communist China. bibliog f Ann Am Acad 349: 49-69 S '63
SCHURR, Sam H.
Economics of atomic power. Bul Atomic Sci 21:22-5 Ja '65
Energy; with biological sketch. Sci Am 209: 26, 110-14+ bibliog(p307) S '63
SCHURZ, Carl
Beginning of action: Carl Schurz and John Wesley Powell; excerpt from The quiet crisis. S. L. Udall. il por Am For 69:20-3+ O '63
Man of conscience. R. L. Reynolds. il pors Am Heritage 14:20-3+ F '63
SCHUSCHNIGG, Kurt von
Where are they now? pors Newsweek 61:20 Mr 25 '63
SCHUSTER, Edward J.
How much unity for Africa? Cath World 198:215-22 Ja '64
SCHUSTER, M. L. and others
Starch formation induced by a plant parasitic nematode. bibliog Science 143:1342-3 Mr 20 '64
SCHUSTER, Richard P. Jr
Information for arms control. Bul Atomic Sci 19:35-6 F '63
Orbital war unexplained. Bul Atomic Sci 19: 32-3 My '63
SCHUTZ, Roger
Latin America: testing ground of ecumenism; excerpt from Unity: man's tomorrow. Cath World 197:28-35 Ap '63
SCHUTZER, A. I.
Lady-killer. Am Heritage 15:36-9+ O '64
SCHUTZER, Paul
Faces of the satellites. il por Life 55:102-14 N 15 '63
SCHUYLER, Donna Jo
Inattention; poem. McCalls 91:172 Mr '64
SCHWAB-FELISCH, Hans
Theatre in West Germany today. Theatre Arts 47:16-21 Je '63
SCHWABACHER, Albert E. Jr
Women & money; excerpt from Man and civilization: the potential of woman. Vogue 141:94-7+ Ap 1 '63
SCHWALB, Harry M.
Underwater guinea pigs help scientists study life. Sci Digest 53:6-11 F '63
SCHWALBERG, Bob
It wasn't here! U S Camera 26:59+ Je '63
SCHWALBERG, Carol
Architect's photographer. U S Camera 26: 66-9+ Mr '63
Photographer is a rabbi. U S Camera 26:66-9+ O '63
They always get the picture. U S Camera 26:46-9+ Jl '63
What do these pictures have in common? U S Camera 28:60-3+ Ja '65
Your health. Redbook 120:20+ Mr; 121:12 Jl; 122:118 D '63
Your prints on other people's walls. U S Camera 26:40+ Mr '63
SCHWANN catalogs. See Phonograph records—Catalogs
SCHWARTZ, Abba P.
Foreign and domestic implications of U.S. immigration laws; address, April 3, 1964. Dept State Bul 50:675-82 Ap 27 '64
SCHWARTZ, Alvin
No fears, no tears at the dentist's. Parents Mag 39:54-5+ N '64
Parent's guide to childhood pleasures; excerpt from Fun for children and parents. Redbook 123:75-82 Ag '64
Play is child's work. Parents Mag 38:74-5+ N '63
SCHWARTZ, Arthur
Ambulatory Arthur Schwartz. M. Esterow. Mus Am 83:16-17 O '63
SCHWARTZ, Beatrice K.
Spirit of St Louis. por ALA Bul 58:507-11 Je '64
SCHWARTZ, Benjamin
Sino-Soviet relations, the question of authority. bibliog f Ann Am Acad 349:38-48 S '63
SCHWARTZ, Bert
Is it really higher education? Sat R 47:52-4+ D 19 '64
SCHWARTZ, C. M. See Young, A. P. jt. auth.
SCHWARTZ, Daniel
Pennsylvania. il Fortune 69:84-91 F '64
SCHWARTZ, Eugene J.
Why babies cry; ed. by W. J. Schwartz. Todays Health 41:26-8 S '63
SCHWARTZ, Fred
Art education and the crafts. Craft Horiz 24:8 Jl '64
SCHWARTZ, George
Consider the horse; or, A study of U.S. capitalism. N Y Times Mag p20+ O 4 '64
Keynes formula sweeps on. N Y Times Mag p32+ S 8 '63
SCHWARTZ, Harry
Communist uses of capital. Sat R 47:34 F 1 '64
If Lenin were alive today. N Y Times Mag p 14+ Jl 14 '63
Insider's story on Moscow. Sat R 47:29 Ag 8 '64
Studies of the Soviet economy. Harvard Bsns R 41:6-8+ My '63
SCHWARTZ, Harry W.
If discounters threaten, don't panic, fight back. Pub W 185:30-1 Mr 30 '64
SCHWARTZ, Herbert S. and others
Mitomycin C: chemical and biological studies on alkylation. bibliog Science 142:1181-3 N 29 '63
SCHWARTZ, Herman
Wiretapping: yes or no? Christian Cent 82: 77-9 Ja 20 '65
SCHWARTZ, Judith N. and Ubell, Earl
New Jersey modern dance school inspires a foundation into existence. Dance Mag 37: 18-19 Mr '63
SCHWARTZ, Julia
Beginning teacher. Sch Arts 63:46 S '63; 48 My '64
SCHWARTZ, Leonard
New paperback revolution; retail sales upsurge. Pub W 184:25-6 S 30 '63

SCHWARTZ, Leonard E.
Control of outer space. Cur Hist 47:39-46 Jl '64
When is international space cooperation international? Bul Atomic Sci 19:12-18 Je '63
SCHWARTZ, Lynne Sharon
Wizard of Oz; dramatization of story by L. F. Baum. Plays 22:83-96 Ap '63
SCHWARTZ, Marvin D.
Jan Martense Schenck house in the Brooklyn museum. Antiques 85:421-8 Ap '64
Treasures in English silver from the Morrison collection. Antiques 85:570-4 My '64
SCHWARTZ, Maurice
Amateur scientist. Sci Am 208:168-70+ Ap '63
SCHWARTZ, Robert L.
Case for fast drivers. Harper 227:65-70 S '63; Same abr. with title What are the real causes of auto crashes? Read Digest 84: 181-2+ Ap '64
SCHWARTZ, Robert S. and Beldotti, Lorraine
Homologous disease reactivation by X-radiation. bibliog Science 140:171-2 Ap 12 '63
—See Sahiar, K. jt. auth.
SCHWARTZ, Tony
Sound. See issues of Popular photography

about

Focus on Tony Schwartz. C. R. Reynolds. il pors Pop Phot 53:58-61+ S '63
Sound. New Yorker 40:49-50 N 21 '64
SCHWARTZ, W. J.
(ed) See Schwartz, E. J. Why babies cry
SCHWARTZ, William F.
Venereal disease. NEA J 53:64-5 Mr '64
SCHWARZ, Boris
Baroque for bow and strings. Sat R 46:65+ O 26 '63
Brahms of Francescatti and Heifetz. Sat R 46:57 D 28 '63
Corelli, Torelli, Locatelli. Sat R 47:66 Je 27 '64
Heifetz's Beethoven again. Sat R 46:43 Jl 27 '63
Mis-tuned violin. Sat R 46:39 Ag 31 '63
Soviet music since Stalin. Sat R 46:55-6+ Mr 30 '63
SCHWARZ, C. W. See Burmeister, W. L. jt. auth.
SCHWARZ, Eugene
Dragon; tr. by E. R. Hapgood. Criticism
Commonweal 78:196 My 10 '63
New Yorker 39:96+ Ap 20 '63
Newsweek 61:90 Ap 22 '63
Sat R 46:27 Ap 27 '63
Theatre Arts il(p 11) 47:64 Je '63
SCHWARZ, F. A. O. (toy store) See New York (city)—Stores
SCHWARZ, Solomon M.
Soviet Jewish minority. Cur Hist 47:299-302+ N '64
SCHWARZKOPF, Elisabeth
Quote: unquote; interview, ed. by R. Jacobson. por Mus Am 83:44 S '63

about

Back to back; Metropolitan debut. il por Newsweek 64:100 O 26 '64
Everything in its time. G. Breuer. por Opera N 29:26-8 D 19 '64
Method and manner of Elisabeth Schwarzkopf. E. Greenfield. il pors Hi Fi 14:60-4+ N '64
Music to my ears; Schwarzkopf's Marschallin. I. Kolodin. Sat R 47:35+ O 31 '64
SCHWASSMANN-Wachmann comet. See Comets
SCHWEBEL, Milton
Students, teachers, and the bomb. NEA J 52: 46-8 Mr '63
SCHWEBEL, Stephen M.
United Nations and the challenge of a changing international law; address, April 25, 1963. Dept State Bul 48:785-9 My 20 '63
SCHWEID, Bernard
Avoid shipping delays: hire extra Xmas help. Pub W 185:126-7 Ja 20 '64
SCHWEIGER, E. and others
Endogenous circadian rhythm in cytoplasm of acetabularia: influence of the nucleus. bibliog Science 146:658-9 O 30 '64
SCHWEIGHAUSER, Charles A.
New skies for St Louis. Sky & Tel 25:316-20 Je '63
SCHWEITZER, Albert
Albert Schweitzer: an anachronism. J. Randal. il por Time 81:35 Je 21 '63
Contagious spirit. R. Steele. Christian Cent 82:54 Ja 13 '65
God bless all living beings. E. Anderson. il pors Ladies Home J 80:26-8 D '63
Jungle doctor go home. N. Cousins. Sat R 46:30 Mr 16 '63; Same with photographs. Sci Digest 54:44-52 Jl '63
Schweitzer on race. por Newsweek 61:95 Ap 8 '63
To Schweitzer on his ninetieth. Christian Cent 82:38 Ja 13 '65
Verdict on Schweitzer, by G. McKnight. Review
Christian Cent 81:966 Jl 29 '64. M. L. Brown
Nat R 16:657-8 Jl 28 '64. O. von Habsburg
SCHWEITZER, Edna R.
Music fun for all. Recreation 57:302-3 Je '64
SCHWEITZER, Gertrude
So many voices; story. Redbook 123:151 S '64
Uncle Cholly; story. Ladies Home J 81:88-90 Ap '64
SCHWEITZER, Glenn
Moscow embassy: officer named to fill science liaison post. D. S. Greenberg. Science 140: 283 Ap 19 '63
SCHWEITZER, Louis
Bail-bond scandal. D. Oberdorfer. il por Sat Eve Post 237:66-7 Je 20 '64
SCHWEITZER, Pierre Paul
Towards an expanding world economy. UN Mo Chron 1:63-6 N '64

about

From banque to bank. por Newsweek 62:55 Jl 1 '63
General practitioner. por Time 81:78+ Je 28 '63
IMF feels impact of stronger Europe. por Bsns W p 150-2+ Je 15 '63
Monetary fund outlook: new chief, but few changes. por U S News 55:18 Jl 1 '63
Schweitzer approach. por Fortune 68:75-6+ S '63
SCHWENDINGER, Richard B. and Erdman, J. G.
Carotenoids in sediments as a function of environment. bibliog Science 141:808-10 Ag 30 '63
Sterols in recent aquatic sediments. bibliog Science 144:1575-6 Je 26 '64
SCHWEPPES, limited
Everything is schwell. il Time 81:92 Je 14 '63
SCHWERNER, Armand
On unperfect actors. E. Capouya. Sat R 46: 40-1 D 14 '63
SCHWERNER, Michael
Recollection of Michael Schwerner. R. Woodley. Reporter 31:23-4 Jl 16 '64
SCHWERTMANN, U. and Jackson, M. L.
Hydrogen-aluminum clays: a third buffer range appearing in potentiometric titration. bibliog Science 139:1052-4 Mr 15 '63
SCHWETZINGEN festival. See Music festivals —Germany (Federal Republic)
SCHWINGEN. See Wrestling
SCHWIRKMANN, Horst
Fumigating the fumigator. Time 84:25 S 25 '64
Joker. Newsweek 64:48+ S 28 '64
SCHWITTERS, Dan L.
You and your dealer. Suc Farm 63:68 Ja '65
SCHWITTERS, Kurt
Art news from London; amends to Schwitters. J. Russell. Art N 62:47 My '63
Collage by Kurt Schwitters. K. Kuh. il Sat R 46:37 F 23 '63
Take a meat grinder; retrospective exhibition at London's Marlborough gallery. Newsweek 61:100 Ap 15 '63
SCIACCA, Thomas P. and Lipschutz, M. E.
Electron microscopy of meteoritic and artificially shocked graphite. bibliog Science 145: 1049-50 S 4 '64
SCIATIC nerves. See Nerves
SCIATICA
Shots against sciatica. Newsweek 63:54 Ja 27 '64
SCIENCE
Are we retrogressing in science? M. K. Hubbert. bibliog il Science 139:884-90 Mr 8 '63; Discussion. 140:570+; 141:232 My 10, Jl 19 '63
Century of science, by W. Davis. Review
Sci N L 84:214 O 5 '63
Changing environment of science; adaptation of address, December 28, 1964. A. T. Waterman. Science 147:13-18 Ja 1 '65
Coming changes in American science. N. W. Storer. bibliog Science 142:464-7 O 25 '63; Reply. W. Spieth. 143:197 Ja 17 '64
Doctor Killian's warning; excerpts from address. J. R. Killian, jr. Aviation W 80:21 Ap 27 '64
Empiricism in latter-day behavioral science. V. E. Bixenstine. bibliog Science 145:464-7 Jl 31 '64; Reply. B. F. Skinner. 145:1385+ S 25 '64

SCIENCE—*Continued*
Ethics and science, by H. Margenau. Review
Sci N L 86:287 O 31 '64
Fashion and competition in science; letter. G. C. McVittie. Science 146:341-2 O 16 '64; Discussion. 147:237-8 Ja 15 '65
Fifth estate in the seventh decade; excerpts from address, December 28, 1963. P. M. Gross. Science 143:13-20 Ja 3 '64; Discussion. 143:917; 144:1086-7 F 28, My 29 '64
From freedom's herald to prophet in chains; excerpt from The scientific intellectual. L. S. Feuer. Sat R 46:42-3 Jl 6 '63
Homo sapiens, that strange paradox; scientific research. D. Bovet. il UNESCO Courier 16:56-7 Jl '63
Little science, big science, by D. J. de S. Price. Review
Nation 197:14-16 Jl 6 '63. C. Dreher
Sci Digest il 54:42 Ag '63. B. H. Frisch
Mass production of knowledge. P. R. Zilsel. Bul Atomic Sci 20:28-9 Ap '64
Neglected scientific areas. W. Davis. Sci N L 85:19 Ja 11 '64
New scientist: essays on the methods and values of modern science, ed. by P. C. Obler and H. A. Estrin. Review
New Yorker 39:66+ Ag 31 '63. J. Bernstein
1963-1964 science review. Sci N L 84:391; 86:392-3 D 21 '63, D 19 '64
On the history of science; excerpts from address. J. T. Wilson. Sat R 47:50-1 My 2 '64
President Kennedy on science; excerpts from address, October 22, 1963. J. F. Kennedy. Science 142:1129 N 29 '63
Science forecast for 1964-1965. W. Davis. il Sci N L 84:402-3; 86:402-3 D 28 '63, D 26 '64
Science in less-developed countries; letter. J. B. Calhoun. Science 146:717 N 6 '64
Science interest at peak. Sci N L 84:274 N 2 '63
Science: the glorious entertainment, by J. Barzun. Review
New Repub 150:19-20+ Ap 18 '64. W. E. Boggs
Talk in Chicago; address, June 13, 1963. R. Oppenheimer. Bul Atomic Sci 19:4-6 O '63
Technology, prediction, and disorder. A. Wohlstetter. il Bul Atomic Sci 20:11-15 O '64
U.S. science entering new era; interview. D. F. Hornig. il Nations Bsns 52:40-1+ Je '64
World science will create; excerpt from Space: its impact on man and society, ed. by L. Levy. J. P. Stapp. il Nations Bsns 53:58-63 Ja '65
Your science ABC's. See issues of Science digest

See also
Communication in science
Inventions
Psychology
Technology

Bibliography

Book reviews. See issues of Science
Necessity of popular science. P. Siekevitz. Nation 198:146-8 F 10 '64
Science and math; paperbacks. D. M. Laux. Sr Schol 85:28T D 2 '64
Science, technology: some outstanding titles. il Pub W 183:44-66 Ap 15; 184:36-56 N 11 '63; 185:28-48 Ap 20; 186:28-48 N 16 '64
Scientific, technical, and medical books to come; ed. by I. E. Stokvis and J. Putnam. Library J 88:4247-75; 89:1126-60+, 2835-70, 4399-436 N 1 '63, Mr 1, Jl, N 1 '64
Scientific, technical and medical books to come; ed. by M. Cooley and I. E. Stokvis. Library J 88:1040-78 Mr 1 '63
Summer scientific, technical and medical books; ed by I. E. Stokvis and J. Putnam. Library J 88:2739-69 Jl '63

Exhibitions

Life guide; science exhibits. il Life 56:17+ F 7 '64
Science at the fair. il Sr Schol 84:12-13+ Ap 3 '64

See also
Seattle—Pacific science center

Experiments

Make a dime fly; excerpt from Fun with scientific experiments. M. Freeman and I. Freeman. il Sci Digest 54:82 Ag '63
Safety tips for young scientists. Parents Mag 38:175 O '63

See also
Electricity—Experiments
Physics—Experiments

Federal aid

See Research—Federal aid

Fiction

See Science fiction

History

Bearing of philosophy on the history of science; address, December 29, 1963. A. Grünbaum. bibliog Science 143:1406-12 Mr 27 '64
History of microbiology; report. R. N. Doetsch. Science 146:956 N 13 '64
How history is made; letter. A. Ore. Science 143:1276 Mr 20 '64
Our heritage from Galileo Galilei; address, May 21, 1964. R. E. Gibson. il Science 145:1271-6 S 18 '64; Discussion. 146:997-8; 147:8 N 20 '64, Ja 1 '65
Scientific intellectual, by L. S. Feuer. Review
Commentary 37:88-9 F '64. J. Maddox

Information services

National bureau of standards to administer new reference system; National standard reference data system. Library J 88:2858 Ag '63
Need information center; testimony before the Ad Hoc subcommittee of the House committee on education and labor, July 18, 1963. W. Davis. Sci N L 84:70-1 Ag 3 '63
Storehouse of facts; Standard reference data center. W. Davis. Sci N L 84:6 Jl 6 '63
World information center. F. B. Riggs. Bul Atomic Sci 21:34-5 Ja '65

International aspects

And quiet shines the sun. R. Lewis. Bul Atomic Sci 20:30-2 Ja '64
Biologist looks at world co-operation in science. N. M. Sissakian. il UNESCO Courier 16:10-16 My '63
Breaking the ice in Antarctica. J. Lear. il Sat R 46:43-5 N 2 '63
Common ground. G. T. Seaborg. Bul Atomic Sci 19:42-4 D '63
Dean Rusk analyzes Alliance science progress; excerpts from remarks, October 5, 1964. D. Rusk. Sci N L 86:258+ O 24 '64
Foreign grants: U.S. reducing, but not ending, support program for research activities abroad. D. S. Greenberg. Science 145:1160-1 S 11 '64
IBM lab taps European science skills. P. J. Klass. il Aviation W 78:76-8 Ap 8 '63
International competition and cooperation; adaptation of statement. A. T. Waterman. Science 145:1261 S 18 '64; Reply. S. V. Hart. 146:865-6 N 13 '64
International competition in science. P. H. Abelson. Science 140:773 My 17 '63
International cooperation in science; symposium. Bul Atomic Sci 21:32-9 Ja '65
Mental health. D. J. Lagmanovich. il Américas 15:1-5 Mr '63
Military safety, and cooperation with Russian science; interview, ed. by W. Beller and F. G. McGuire. T. Von Karman. Miss & Roc 12:22-3 F 25 '63
NAS celebrates 100th year; summary of address. J. F. Kennedy. il Sci N L 84:274 N 2 '63
Our common enterprise. Bul Atomic Sci 19:24 S '63
Our common enterprise: a non-apocalyptic view. M. Todd. Bul Atomic Sci 20:27-9 F '64
Physical oceanography: plans for U.S.-Japan cooperation; report on planning meeting on physical oceanography. M. K. Robinson. Science 146:1371-2 D 4 '64
Primate biology; planning meeting; report on meeting of scientists to discuss the possibility and desirability of cooperative efforts between the United States and Japan in the study of primates. L. Carmichael and A. J. Riopelle. Science 146:1078+ N 20 '64
Promise of science and technology; address, November 12, 1964. A. E. Stevenson. Dept State Bul 51:810-15 D 7 '64
Pugwash on scientific cooperation; reprint. Bul Atomic Sci 20:41-6 S '64
Science and international cooperation; address, October 22, 1963. J. F. Kennedy. Dept State Bul 49:778-82 N 18 '63
Science in the service of man. A. T. Waterman. Bul Atomic Sci 19:3-6 My '63
Scientific revolution; the beginning of world community; adaptation of address, 1963. E. Rabinowitch. Bul Atomic Sci 19:14-17 D '63
Unesco science and technology; summary of report. Bul Atomic Sci 20:31-4 N '64

SCIENCE—International aspects—*Continued*
U.S.-Russia cooperate in 1964 Antarctic program. Sci N L 84:184 S 21 '63
U.S. scientists profit from overseas research. Sci N L 84:100 Ag 17 '63
See also
International geophysical year
Joint United States—Japan committee on scientific cooperation
United States—State, Department of—International scientific affairs, Office of

Juvenile literature

See Scientific literature for children

Nomenclature

Scientific nomenclature. K. E. Boulding; discussion. Science 131:1566; 142:11 My 20 '60, O 4 '63

Periodicals

Basic research journals. D. Wolfle. Science 146:869 N 13 '64; Reply. A. M. Russell. 147:110 Ja 8 '65
Challenges to editors of scientific journals; address, March 19, 1963. J. R. Porter. bibliog Science 141:1014-17 S 13 '63
Citations in popular and interpretive science writing; letter. E. Garfield. Science 141:392 Ag 2 '63
100 new periodicals in science, technology, medicine; comp. by staff of Ulrich's international periodicals directory. il Library J 89:1036-41 Mr 1 '64; Correction. 89:2262 Je 1 '64
Science-technology periodicals; Science and technology division, New York public library. G. S. Bonn. il Library J 88:954-8 Mr 1 '63
See also
Bulletin of the atomic scientists
International science and technology (periodical)

Philosophy

Biology and the nature of science. G. G. Simpson; discussion. Science 140:762+ My 17 '63
Decision theory in law, science, and technology. T. A. Cowan. bibliog Science 140:1065-75 Je 7 '63; Reply. I. Kraft. 143:99-100 Ja 10 '64
Little science, big science, by D. Price. Review
Science 140:639-41 My 10 '63
Scientific explanation; adaptation of address, September 24, 1963. W. Weaver. Science 143:1297-300 Mr 20 '64
World without a logos. H. Marcuse. Bul Atomic Sci 20:25-6 Ja '64
See also
Nature, Laws of
Physics—Philosophy

Popularization

See Science news

Quotations, maxims, etc.

Science marches on; comp. by H. M. Schmeck, jr. il N Y Times Mag p46 My 24 '64

Scholarships and fellowships

Dollars and scholars. Newsweek 61:47 F 4 '63
Fellowships: White House prods federal agencies to increase, and harmonize graduate support. D. S. Greenberg. Science 139:818 Mr 1 '63
Grants, fellowships, and awards. See occasional issues of Science
Predoctoral and postdoctoral fellowships. P. H. Abelson. Science 144:1181 Je 5 '64; Discussion. 145:1124; 1258 S 11-18 '64
Scientists abroad. A. J. A. Elliott. UNESCO Courier 16:65-6 Jl '63

Social aspects

Diseases of the rich and diseases of the poor. A. Salam. Bul Atomic Sci 19:3+ Ap '63
Emotion versus intelligence in public support of science; letter. W. H. Freeman. Science 143:433 Ja 31 '64
How science is to change daily life; interview. Todd. il U S News 55:70-4 N 11 '63
Interdependence of science and society. A. V. Topchiev. Bul Atomic Sci 19:7+ Mr '63
Literature and science, by A. Huxley. Review
Sci Am 210:141-2+ Mr '64. M. Black
New Year's thoughts 1964. E. Rabinowitch. Bul Atomic Sci 20:2+ Ja '64
Nth culture problem. S. A. Lakoff. Bul Atomic Sci 20:21-3 My '64
Political consequences of the rise of science. B. de Jouvenel. il Bul Atomic Sci 19:2-8 D '63; Discussion. 20:32 Ap '64
Promise of science and technology address, November 12, 1964. A. E. Stevenson. Dept State Bul 51:810-15 D 7 '64
Public image of science important to nation. Sci N L 85:6 Ja 4 '64
Rationality of modern society. R. Aron. Bul Atomic Sci 20:23-4 Ja '64
Role of science in charting course for the world of tomorrow; text of message, February 4, 1963. U Thant. U N Rev 10:15-17 F '63
Science in the service of man. A. T. Waterman. Bul Atomic Sci 19:3-6 My '63
Science in the suburbs: private research unit discovers flaws in dependence on the local community; Waldemar medical research foundation. E. Langer. il Science 146:39-42 O 2 '64; Reply. L. Gross. 147:9 Ja 1 '65
Scientific intellectual: the psychological & sociological origins of modern science, by L. S. Feuer. Review
Sci Am 209:129-30+ Ag '63
Scientific revolution: man's new outlook; adaptation of address, 1963. E. Rabinowitch. Bul Atomic Sci 19:15-18 S '63; Reply. A. L. Mottet, jr. 20:34 Ap '64
Scientific statesmanship; adaptation of address, December 10, 1963. B. Commoner. Bul Atomic Sci 19:6-10 O '63
Scientists and public affairs: though world has changed, they remain preoccupied with the bomb. D. S. Greenberg. Science 142:1635 D 27 '63; Discussion. 143:430+; 144:366, 954; 145:7 Ja 31, Ap 24, My 22, Jl 3 '64
Scientists and their images. A. T. Waterman. Science 143:311 Ja 24 '64; Discussion. 143:1120; 144:246 Mr 13, Ap 17 '64
Successor to democracy; warning against science S. A. Coblentz. Christian Cent 81:78-80 Ja 15 '64; Reply. E. S. Scott. 81:341-2 Mr 11 '64
Talk in Chicago; address, June 13, 1963. R. Oppenheimer. Bul Atomic Sci 19:4-6 O '63
Third scientific revolution; excerpts from address, May 6, 1964. M. S. Eisenhower. Sci N L 85:322+ My 23 '64
Unhappy arbiters of values, standards, and tastes. J. Barden. Bul Atomic Sci 19:34-6 D '63; Reply with rejoinder. G. Mann. 20:30-2 O '64
View from a distant star, by H. Shapley. Review
Sci N L 84:230 O 12 '63
Where is science taking us? R. Bellman. Sat R 47:56 Ap 4 '64; Reply. Mrs H. S. Zim. 47:72 N 7 '64
World of the future. N. N. Semenov. il(cover) Bul Atomic Sci 20:10-15 F '64
See also
Society for social responsibility in science

Study and teaching

Academic organization in physical science. H. G. Booker. Science 146:35-7 O 2 '64
Building a science curriculum. R. W. Schulz. il NEA J 53:21-3 O '64
Can your school afford the new science programs? W. J. Gruver. Sch Life 46:5-7 Ja '64
Course content improvement, British style. D. Wolfle. Science 142:1263 D 6 '63
Curriculum reform. J. Walsh. Science 144:642-6 My 8 '64; Discussion. 145:1385; 146:866; 147:8 S 25, N 13 '64, Ja 1 '65
Dig in; science training program in astronomy and anthropology, Brooklyn, New York, children's museum. Recreation 57:121 Mr '64
Education: Wiesner asks action on pre-college science teaching, offers fairly modest proposals. J. Walsh. Science 140:1292-3 Je 21 '63
Face-lift for the science curriculum. J. B. Wiesner. il UNESCO Courier 16:32-6 Jl '63
How is science being taught? with study-discussion program, by D. Harris and E. Harris. A. Calandra. bibliog il PTA Mag 59:4-6, 35 D '64
Newton in third grade; new science program, Experikit. il Newsweek 64:98-100 N 9 '64
On scientific literacy; symposium. il NEA J 52:32-5+ Ap '63
On the history of science; excerpts from address. J. T. Wilson. Sat R 47:50-1 My 2 '64
Parent learns with child; experimental program at Howard university, Washington, D.C. il Sci N L 86:278 O 31 '64
Science: a tool of culture; address. C. Bibby. Sat R 47:51-3 Je 6 '64
Science and higher education. W. W. Brickman. Sch & Soc 91:391 D 14 '63
Science and method; elementary school science instruction. Sr Schol 82:2T-3T F 20 '63
Science class; nine to eleven year olds at Columbia's School of engineering and applied science. New Yorker 39:22-3 Ja 4 '64

SCIENCE—Study and teaching—*Continued*
Science education programs in Georgia high schools. W. M. Brogdon and C. L. Koelsche. Sch & Soc 91:195-7 Ap 20 '63
Science for the citizen: an educational problem. J. H. Mathewson; discussion. Science 139:678-80+ F 15 '63
Science in the elementary school. P. E. Blackwood. il Sch Life 47:13-15+ N '64
Science 100, 1963-64. H. H. J. Nesbitt and J. Hart. Science 146:895-6 N 13 '64
Science workshops; Los Angeles. il Ebony 18:66-8+ Ag '63
Scientists in the classroom; excerpts from Where, when, and why. M. Mayer. Commentary 35:312-19 Ap '63; Reply with rejoinder. R. Hyman. 36:195-6 S '63
Soviets pushing to be first in science. Sci N L 86:152 S 5 '64
Talented Chinese youth. Sci N L 83:100 F 16 '63
Teaching junior high school science; opinions differ. D. W. Stotler; A. F. Eiss. il NEA J 52:54-6 O '63
Teaching science in Turkey; letter. C. C. Zimmerman. Science 144:364 Ap 24 '64
330 million brains for a new era; science teaching. R. Maheu. il UNESCO Courier 16:24-9 Jl '63
Time to pause and regroup? P. B. Sears. Science 144:1297 Je 12 '64; Discussion. 145: 767-8, 1387 Ag 21, S 25 '64
See also
Nature study
Science curriculum improvement study
Science students
Scientific education

Projects

Science boosters unlimited. M. Golin. il Todays Health 41:50-1+ My '63

Terminology

Abuse of words; letter. E. Shaw. Science 145: 874+ Ag 28 '64

Canada

Report on Canadian science. J. H. Winchester. il Sci Digest 56:75-81 D '64

Chile

Science and development in Chile; address, October 9, 1964. D. Rusk. Dept State Bul 51:634-7 N 2 '64
Science in Chilean life. Sci N L 86:258 O 24 '64

China (People's Republic)

Beyond ideology; 1964 Peking symposium of sciences. il Newsweek 64:56 S 7 '64
Scientific enigma of Communist China; excerpts from Scientific revolution and world politics. C. P. Haskins. Sat R 47:58-60 Je 6 '64

Germany (Federal Republic)

Genetics at Cologne. V. K. McElheny. il Science 146:904-7 N 13 '64

Great Britain

Great Britain: science and labor's squeak-in. V. K. McElheny. Science 146:506-8 O 23 '64
New goals for science in Britain. P. H. Abelson. Science 143:919 F 28 '64
Science policy shapes up as issue in coming British election. J. Maddox. il Science 143:1146-8 Mr 13 '64
Scientific migration: Britain agitated anew by research team's decision to move to United States. J. Maddox. Science 143:786-8 F 21 '64

Italy

Research climate in Italy. V. K. McElheny. il Science 145:690-3 Ag 14 '64; Reply. H. B. Reisman. 145:1387 S 25 '64

Japan

Science in Japan; report on symposium at the AAAS meeting. L. Campbell. bibliog il Science 143:776-82 F 21 '64; Discussion. 144: 616; 145:344 My 8, Jl 24 '64
Sciences in Japan; special symposium at the AAAS annual meeting, December 26-30, 1963. Science 142:604-5 N 1 '63

Latin America

Science, technology, and development; first Inter-American meeting of science and technology. J. D. Perkinson. il Américas 16:1-5 Mr '64

Russia

Can Soviet scientists break through the iron curtain? E. Mott. il Todays Health 41:29-33+ S '63
Interdependence of science and society. A. V. Topchiev. Bul Atomic Sci 19:7+ Mr '63
Lysenko: attacks on his theories renewed in U.S.S.R. in aftermath of Khrushchev's removal from power. D. S Greenberg. Science 146:1024-5 N 20 '64
See also
Research—Russia

United States

See Science

SCIENCE (periodical)
Birthdays of Science. D. Wolfle. Science 145: 11 Jl 3 '64
By scientists for scientists. P. H. Abelson. Science 142:1427 D 13 '63
Clipping and conflict; letter. D. D. Jensen. Science 142:341+ O 18 '63; Discussion. 142: 1621 D 27 '63
Indexes to our journal; letter. F. Henritz. Science 144:1178 Je 5 '64
Instructions for contributors. Science 141: 305-6 Jl 26 '63; Reply. G. M. Clemence. 141: 1131 S 20 '63
Letters to the editor. P. H. Abelson. Science 143:201 Ja 17 '64
Seven years of progress. P. H. Abelson. Science 141:491 Ag 9 '63

SCIENCE, Ethics of. See Scientists, Professional ethics for

SCIENCE, Freedom of
Myth-image of the scientist. H. Schenck, jr. Nation 197:140-2 S 14 '63; Same abr. with title Scientific freedom, hah! il Sci Digest 54:43-7 D '63

SCIENCE adviser, Office of. See United States —State, Department of—International scientific affairs, Office of

SCIENCE advisory committee. See United States—President's science advisory committee

SCIENCE and art. See Art and science

SCIENCE and civilization
Abacus and the rose; a dialogue after Galileo. J. Bronowski. il Nation 198:4-17 Ja 4 '64
Atomic age, ed. by M. Grodzins and E. Rabinowitch. Review
New Yorker 40:136-41 Je 13 '64. J. Bernstein
Biopolitics: science, ethics, and public policy. L. K. Caldwell. Yale R 54:1-16 O '64
By the end of the twentieth century. D. Sarnoff. il Fortune 69:116-19 My '64
Cognitive dissonance: its use in science. E. G. Boring. bibliog Science 145:680-5 Ag 14 '64; Discussion. 146:471-2 O 23 '64
Coming changes in American science. N. W. Storer. bibliog Science 142:464-7 O 25 '63; Reply. W. Spieth. 143:197 Ja 17 '64
Communication and comprehension of scientific knowledge; address, October 23, 1963. R. Oppenheimer. Science 142:1143-6 N 29 '63
Politics of the space age; excerpt from Space: its impact on man and society, ed. by L. Levy. L. B. Johnson. il Sat Eve Post 237: 22-3 F 29 '64
Rationality of modern society. R. Aron. Bul Atomic Sci 20:23-4 Ja '64
Science: a tool of culture; address, reprint from Nature. C. Bibby. Sat R 47:51-3 Je 6 '64
Science and the general welfare in a democracy. P. H. Abelson. Science 144:957 My 22 '64; Reply. S. C. Mohr. 145:660 Ag 14 '64
Science and the new humanism; excerpts from address. H. Hoagland. bibliog Science 143:111-14 Ja 10 '64; Discussion. 143:1121-3; 144:1293 Mr 13, Je 12 '64
Science in the new political climate. P. H. Abelson. Science 146:345 O 16 '64
Science: the glorious entertainment, by J. Barzun. Review
Commentary 38:73-4 Ag '64. A. R. Louch
Holiday 35:18-19 My '64. C. Fadiman
New Yorker 40:236+ N 21 '64. J. Bernstein
Science year: 1965 designated by Johnson for stressing efforts directed toward human welfare. D. S. Greenberg. Science 144:1433 Je 19 '64
Scientific revolution: the new content of politics. E. Rabinowitch. Bul Atomic Sci 19:11-16 O '63
Scientific statesmanship; adaptation of address, December 10, 1963. B. Commoner. Bul Atomic Sci 19:6-10 O '63
Society and science; adaptation of address. V. R. Potter. bibliog Science 146:1018-22 N 20 '64
Speaking out; does our space research threaten life on earth? B. Lovell. Sat Eve Post 237:10+ F 22 '64
Speaking out; who's that tampering with my clock? H. A. Smith. il Sat Eve Post 236: 10+ Ag 24 '63

SCIENCE and civilization—*Continued*
Successor to democracy; warning against science. S. A. Coblentz. Christian Cent 81:78-80 Ja 15 '64; Reply. E. S. Scott. 81:341-2 Mr 11 '64
Teaching and the expanding knowledge. A. Szent-Györgyi. Science 146:1278-9 D 4 '64

SCIENCE and economics
S.T.P: index of prosperity. V. A. Kovda. il UNESCO Courier 16:18-23 Jl '63

SCIENCE and industry. See Industrial research

SCIENCE and literature. See Literature and science

SCIENCE and philosophy. See Philosophy and science

SCIENCE and religion See Religion and science

SCIENCE and religion (periodical) See Periodicals—Russia

SCIENCE and state
America's new policy makers: the scientists' rise to power, by D. W. Cox. Review
Science 143:1156 Mr 13 '64. R. N. Kreidler; Reply. D. W. Cox. 144:798 My 15 '64
Big dish: how haste and secrecy helped navy waste $63 million in race to build huge telescope. D. S. Greenberg. Science 144:1111-12 My 29 '64
Big picture: House committee hears views on basic problems of science-government relations. D. S. Greenberg. Science 142:650-3 N 8 '63
Bill providing science advisory staffs for House and Senate may be a step in a new direction. J. Walsh. Science 140:1293-4 Je 21 '63
Biopolitics: science, ethics, and public policy. L. K. Caldwell. Yale R 54:1-16 O '64
Britain confronts its technical options. V. K. McElheny. il Science 146:1446-9 D 11 '64
Budget: requests for R&D funds edge above $15 billion mark for a fiscal year of austerity. J. Walsh. il Science 143:337-8 Ja 24 '64
Can only scientists make government science policy? E. G. Mesthene. Science 145:237-40 Jl 17 '64; Reply. C. W. Sherwin. 145:990 S 4 '64
Challenge of bureaucratized science. H. Wheeler. Bul Atomic Sci 20:14-17 Ja '64
Congress and science: Daddario study casts doubts on proposals to establish advisory service. D. S. Greenberg. Science 145:904-5 Ag 28 '64
Congress and science: Senate seeks review of government's program in fields of science and technology. E. Langer. Science 139:817-18 Mr 1 '63
Congress: hearings on science advisory staff reveals interest, but no strong inside demand. J. Walsh. Science 142:1446 D 13 '63
Congress plans technical advisory corps. Aviation W 78:93+ Je 24 '63
Congressional frustration. D. Wolfle. Science 141:865 S 6 '63
Democratic platform: science section stresses work in space, oceanography, and atomic energy. D. S. Greenberg. Science 145:1161-2 S 11 '64
Devil's advocates. P. H. Abelson. Science 140:1365 Je 28 '63; Reply. E. W. Radoslovich. 144:364-5 Ap 24 '64
Effective use of scientific advice. P. H. Abelson. Science 140:939 My 31 '63
Elliott committee: latest study calls for improvement in data on scientific manpower problems. D. S. Greenberg. Science 146:234 O 9 '64
Federal scientist-administrator. E. S. Uyeki and F. B. Cliffe, jr. bibliog il Science 139:1267-70 Mr 29 '63
Great Britain: science and labor's squeak-in. V. K. McElheny. Science 146:506-8 O 23 '64
High-energy physics: panel proposes construction, operation program to run through 1981. D. S. Greenberg. Science 140:958-9 My 31 '63
Hot on the heels of the U.S. research and development spending. il Bsns W p92-4 N 9 '63
Interfaces between science and public policy excerpts from address, March 1964. C. P Haskins. Science 144:801 My 15 '64
Johnson or Goldwater, two scientists explain their choice. G. B. Kistiakowsky; E. Teller. Science 146:380-2 O 16 '64
Legislation: in first session, 88th Congress shows itself to be more critical patron of science. J. Walsh. Science 143:27-8 Ja 3 '64
LBJ and science: policies marked by continuity, but a few events suggest developments for future. D. S. Greenberg. Science 143:939-40 F 28 '64
Management of science in the public interest: adaptation of address. C. W. Sherwin. Bul Atomic Sci 20:9-12 Je '64; Reply. F. Forscher. 20:23 D '64
Manpower: Senate study describes how scientists fit into scheme of things in red China, Soviet Union. J. Walsh. Science 141:253-5 Jl 19 '63
Mohole: the project that went awry. D. S. Greenberg. il Science 143:115-19, 223-7, 334-7 Ja 10-24 '64; Discussion. 143:994, 1274-6, 1393-4 Mr 6, 20-27 '64
NAS study: public policy group offers prescription to promote science-government cooperation. D. S. Greenberg. Science 143:1304-5 Mr 20 '64
National academy: public policy group, headed by Kistiakowsky, seems bound for important role; Committee on science and public policy. D. S. Greenberg. Science 141:27-8 Jl 5 '63
Nationalization of U.S. science. S. Klaw. il Fortune 70:158-60+ S '64
New administration: indications are it will bring few changes for scientific, academic worlds. D. S. Greenberg. Science 142:1277-8 D 6 '63
Nobel winners endorse Johnson and Humphrey; Two eminent scientists disagree on candidates. Sci N L 86:280 O 31 '64
Only one side of the question. P. H. Abelson. Science 145:347 Jl 24 '64; Same with title Exorbitant cost of dissent. Sat R 47:62 O 3 '64
Policy and legacy. J. Walsh. Science 142:1151-3 N 29 '63
Policy and the scientists. L. A. DuBridge. For Affairs 41:571-88 Ap '63
Political consequences of the rise of science. B. de Jouvenel. il Bul Atomic Sci 19:2-8 D '63; Discussion. 20:32 Ap '64
Post-Sputnik: relations between science, government now passing into more settled, mature stage. D. S. Greenberg. Science 145:1281-3 S 18 '64
PT boat government. Aviation W 78:21 Ap 1 '63
President's science adviser. P. H. Abelson. Science 142:1025 N 22 '63; Discussion. 142:1257; 143:427-9 D 6 '63, Ja 31 '64
R&D, and the relations of science and government; statement before a congressional subcommittee; with editorial comment. P. M. Gross. Science 142:625, 645-50 N 8 '63
Research competition: as budgetary pressures grow, Congress reveals concern about scientific choices. D. S. Greenberg. il Science 143:1149-51 Mr 13 '64
Same old gang? advisory boards and committees. D. Wolfle. Science 141:677 Ag 23 '63
Science advice: new division for science policy research set up in LRS to aid Congress. J. Walsh. Science 145:1162-4 S 11 '64
Science advisory staffs for House and Senate: letter. B. E. Knox. Science 141:593 Ag 16 '63
Science and federal programs: the continuing dialogue; adapted from address, April 28, 1964. J. A. Shannon. Science 144:976-8 My 22 '64
Science and government: a survey of some of the major elements in growing, troubled relationship. D. S. Greenberg. Science 141:338-40 Jl 26 '63
Science and government: OECD ministers for science compare experiences on national policies. E. Langer. Science 142:372-3 O 18 '63
Science and international cooperation; address, October 22, 1963. J. F. Kennedy. Dept State Bul 49:778-82 N 18 '63; Excerpt. Bul Atomic Sci 19:42 D '63
Science and politics, by Q. M. Hogg. Review
New Repub 151:23-4 S 26 '64. D. S. Greenberg
Science 140:622-3 My 10 '63. D. K. Price
Science goes to Washington. M. Greenfield. il Reporter 29:20-6 S 26 '63; Same. Science 142:361-7 O 18 '63; Discussion. Reporter 29:8+ O 24 '63
Science in government. H. Pryor. Sci Digest 56:46-7 O '64
Science in policy, policy in science; excerpt from testimony before the House subcommittee on science, research, and development. J. B. Wiesner. Bul Atomic Sci 20:36-40 F '64
Science planks and party platforms. R. E. Lapp. Science 143:195 Ja 17 '64
Science policy; report on informal meeting at the University of Sussex, England. R. H. Bolt. Science 144:1047 My 22 '64
Science under Johnson. Sci N L 84:359 D 7 '63

SCIENCE and state—*Continued*
Scientific advice for Congress; excerpts from address, November 20, 1963. C. P. Anderson. Science 144:29-32 Ap 3 '64
Scientific gloom; congressional actions have stirred pessimism but little of it is justified. D. S. Greenberg. Science 144:32-3 Ap 3 '64
Scientific revolution: the new content of politics. E. Rabinowitch. Bul Atomic Sci 19:11-16 O '63
Scientist and national policy; address, December 27, 1962. M. Bundy. Science 139: 805-9 Mr 1 '63
Scientists and national policy-making, ed. by R. Gilpin and C. Wright. Review Science 144:1438-9 Je 19 '64. A. T. Waterman
Scientists, seers and strategy. A. Wohlstetter. bibliog f For Affairs 41:466-78 Ap '63
Sensible shopping in the supermarket of science. P. M. S. Blackett. il UNESCO Courier 16:30-1 Jl '63
Snow affair. M. S. Simpson. Bul Atomic Sci 19:28-32 Ap '63
U.S. science entering new era; interview. D. F. Hornig. il Nations Bsns 52:40-1+ Je '64
When scientists testify. A. Etzioni. Bul Atomic Sci 20:23-6 O '64
Who gets the word? letter. G. E. Moore. Science 143:99 Ja 10 '64
See also
Research—Federal aid
United States—National science foundation

History

State and science five centuries ago. T. H. Stevenson. Bul Atomic Sci 21:28-9 Ja '65

SCIENCE and technology center, New York. See New York state university—Center of science and technology (proposed)

SCIENCE and the humanities
Case for balance; liberal arts; address, October 3, 1963. T. J. Watson. Vital Speeches 30:118-21 D 1 '63
Curricular balance in the university. Sch & Soc 91:31 Ja 26 '63
Future-mindedness. K. Nott. Commentary 36:49-54 Jl '63
Human challenge; address, September 2, 1964. J. M. Hester. Vital Speeches 30:746-9 O 1 '64
Humanities in the scientific curriculum. M. Roche. bibliog Science 141:698-700 Ag 23 '63
Literature and science, by A. Huxley. Review Sci Am 210:141-2+ Mr '64. M. Black
Manpower needs and higher education; summary of report with editorial comment. W. W. Brickman. Sch & Soc 91:110 Mr 9 '63
Modern science and the old Adam. T. H. Von Laue; discussion. Bul Atomic Sci 19: 33-4 Ap; 30 Je; 28-9 S '63
Needs of the humanities. D. Wolfle. Science 143:1279 Mr 20 '64
New culture emerging. Sci N L 85:388 Je 20 '64
Nth culture problem. S. A. Lakoff. Bul Atomic Sci 20:21-3 My '64
On the history of science; excerpts from address. J. T. Wilson. Sat R 47:50-1 My 2 '64
One campus, two cultures. L. Lafore. Science 145:790-5 Ag 21 '64; Discussion. 146:472; 597-8 O 23-30 '64
Poet's investigation of science: from the 1963 Arthur D. Little lecture. R. Graves. Sat R 46:82-8 D 7 '63
Pomp and circumstance: C. P. Snow. R. Adams. Atlan 214:95-8 N '64
Science and the humanities. P. H. Abelson; discussion. Science 139:677-8, 682 F 15 '63
Science and the humanities: a new level of symbiosis. G. T. Seaborg. bibliog il Science 144:1199-203 Je 5 '64; Discussion. 145:231 Jl 17 '64
Science as a servant of historical knowledge; summary of address. G. T. Seaborg. New Repub 150:11-13 F 22 '64
Science, the humanities, and education. W. W. Brickman. Sch & Soc 91:159 Ap 6 '63
Snow affair. M. S. Simpson. Bul Atomic Sci 19:28-32 Ap '63
Speech education, a terrible responsibility. G. A. Yeomans. Vital Speeches 30:348-52 Mr 15 '64
Two cultures. America 108:632-3 My 4 '63
Two cultures reaffirmed. Sci Am 209:67 D '63
Unhappy arbiters of values, standards, and tastes. J. Barden. Bul Atomic Sci 19:34-6 D '63; Reply with rejoinder. G. Mann. 20: 30-2 O '64

SCIENCE and war. See War and science

SCIENCE aptitude tests. See Aptitude tests

SCIENCE as a profession
Career decisions of very able students. R. C. Nichols. il Science 144:1315-19 Je 12 '64; Discussion. 144:1535; 145:533-4 Je 26, Ag 7 '64; Wilson Lib Bul 39:489+ F '65
Careers decided early. Sci N L 85:263 Ap 25 '64
Comparative failure in science. B. G. Glaser. bibliog Science 143:1012-14 Mr 6 '64
Compleat botanist; adaptation of address, December 30, 1963. A. J. Sharp. bibliog Science 146:745-8 N 6 '64
Prestige. P. H. Abelson. Science 145:771 Ag 21 '64
Promise of the future. D. Sarnoff. Seventeen 23:240+ Ag '64
Science in the public interest. C. W. Sherwin. Sat R 47:38-9 Ag 1 '64

SCIENCE as recreation. See Recreation—Activities

SCIENCE books for children. See Scientific literature for children

SCIENCE camps. See Camps

SCIENCE citation index
Science citation index. il Wilson Lib Bul 38: 750-1 My '64
Science citation index. T. C. Hines. il Library J 89:2735-7 Jl '64

SCIENCE city. See Akademgorodok, Siberia

SCIENCE clubs
News from science clubs. Sci N L 83:206, 251, 367 Mr 30, Ap 20, Je 8 '63

SCIENCE clubs of America
Science clubs of America. Sci N L 86:128 Ag 22 '64
Science youth program; Science clubs of America. Sci N L 84:125 Ag 24 '63

SCIENCE curriculum improvement study
Science curriculum group seeks publisher contacts. Pub W 186:50-1 N 16 '64

SCIENCE drawing. See Drawing

SCIENCE education. See Scientific education

SCIENCE fairs
Argentine science fair; First Uruguayan science fair surprises in variety. W. Davis. il Sci N L 84:311 N 16 '63
Fairs: national, local. il Sci N L 84:126 Ag 24 '63
Fairs: national, local; National science fair-international. il Sci N L 86:127 Ag 22 '64
Fourteenth annual NSF-I. il Sci N L 83:295 My 11 '63
Health awards winners. Sci N L 85:311 My 16 '64
Owl exhibit on conservation. C. Stapleton. il Audubon Mag 66:152-3 My '64
Science exhibits; at Seattle fair, federal funds, scientists helped, New Yorkers try a different tack. J. Walsh. il Science 140: 960-2 My 31 '63
Science fair award winners; Health awards winners; special honors at fair. il Sci N L 83:325-9+ My 25 '63
Science fair award winners; Special award winners. il Sci N L 85:323-7+ My 23 '64
Science fair in Spain. il Sci N L 85:279 My 2 '64
Science fair in Sweden. Sci N L 83:294 My 11 '63
Science fairs. D. Wolfle. Science 140:1055 Je 7 '63; Discussion. 141:1132+ S 20 '63
220 fairs join NSF-I; Three sisters, six wins. Sci N L 83:247 Ap 20 '63
U.S. science fair winners to show projects in Japan. Sci N L 84:281 N 2 '63
Uruguay holds first National science fair. Sci N L 84:280 N 2 '63
Winners enter science. Sci N L 86:135 Ag 29 '64

SCIENCE fiction
Barnum of the space age. P. O'Neil. il Life 55:62-4+ Jl 26 '63
Computers in science fiction. M. Ascher. bibliog f Harvard Bsns R 41:40-2+ N '63
Evolution of monsters; adapted from Faust revisited. M. Fishwick. Sat R 46:32+ S 14 '63
Inspirational value of science fiction. Sci Digest 53:34 Mr '63
Mark Twain science writer. R. Bass. Sci Digest 54:47 Ag '63
Martians in the classroom. S. Cochell. Sr Schol 82:9T-10T Mr 6 '63
Science fact, science fiction. J. W. Campbell. Writer 77:26-7 Ag '64
Sword of Achilles. I. Asimov. Bul Atomic Sci 19:17-18 N '63; Same with title SF: clue to creativity. il Library J 89:914-17 F 15 '64
See also
Moving pictures—Science fiction
Television broadcasting—Science fiction

SCIENCE in criminal investigation. See Criminal investigation

SCIENCE in literature
See also
Science fiction
SCIENCE information. See Communication in science
SCIENCE information exchange. See Smithsonian institution—Science information exchange
SCIENCE kits. See Scientific apparatus and instruments
SCIENCE literature. See Scientific literature
SCIENCE museums
See also
American museum of natural history, New York
SCIENCE news
AAAS meeting and the press; letter. R. A. Bruner. Science 143:763 F 21 '64; Reply. S. Lambert. 144:486 My 1 '64
Citations in popular and interpretive science writing; letter. E. Garfield. Science 141:392 Ag 2 '63
Communication and comprehension of scientific knowledge; address, October 23, 1963. R. Oppenheimer. Science 142:1143-6 N 29 '63
Communication of science information. P. H. Tannenbaum. bibliog il Science 140:579-83 My 10 '63
Hugh Downs column. H. Downs. Sci Digest 56:50-3 S '64
Pressures for publicity. Sci N L 83:228 Ap 13 '63
Science in the news. See issues of Science digest
Science journalism: the coming age. L. Lessing. Bul Atomic Sci 19:23 D '63
Science news & views. E. Mott. Sci Digest 53:12-15 F; 24-6 Mr '63
Science newsfront. W. Cloud. See issues of Popular science monthly
Science reporting. P. H. Abelson. Science 139:177 Ja 18 '63; Discussion. 139:1098+ Mr 15 '63
Scientific paperback revolution. H. Cirker. Science 140:591-4 My 10 '63; Discussion. 141:483-4+; 142:148+, 1619-20 Ag 9, O 11, D 27 '63
SCIENCE research associates, Chicago
IBM goes to school. Newsweek 63:55-6 Ja 6 '64
Science research assoc. sold to IBM for $62 million. Pub W 184:33 D 30 '63
SCIENCE service, incorporated
Science boosters unlimited. M. Golin. il Todays Health 41:50-1+ My '63
Science youth program. Sci N L 86:128 Ag 22 '64
See also
Science clubs of America
SCIENCE students
Careers decided early. Sci N L 85:263 Ap 25 '64
How young scientists get started. W. Davis. il Sci N L 84:250 O 19 '63
New TV show stars science fair winners. il Sci N L 84:319 N 16 '63
Presidential scholars, 1964. il Sch Life 46:2-4 Jl '64
Science fair winners get close-up look at nuclear energy at work; week-long visit at Argonne national laboratory. il Todays Health 43:8-9 Ja '65
Science youths start younger. S. Moore. il Sci N L 84:170-1+ S 14 '63
Teen science brain force. W. Davis. Sci N L 87:21 Ja 9 '65
Teen scientists honored in state talent searches. Sci N L 84:120 Ag 24 '63
Undergraduate institutions and the production of scientists. A. W. Astin. bibliog il Science 141:334-8 Jl 26 '63; Reply. F. A. Sieverts. 141:762 Ag 30 '63
See also
Science talent search
SCIENCE talent search
Science talent search. il Sci N L 84:127; 86:126 Ag 24 '63, Ag 22 '64
Science youth program; Science clubs of America. Sci N L 84:125 Ag 24 '63

1963 (22d)

School rivalry in STS. Sci N L 83:133 Mr 2 '63
STS scholarship winners. il Sci N L 83:166-7 Mr 16 '63
Washington trip winners; 22nd Science talent search; with sampling of test. Sci N L 93:68-9, 74 F 2 '63
Winners' science projects. Sci N L 83:103 F 16 '63
Winning science projects. Sci N L 83:119 F 23 '63

1964 (23d)

Million science projects. il Sci N L 85:278 My 2 '64
Remarks at talent search. C. E. Scripps; C. H. Weaver. Sci N L 85:164 Mr 14 '64
Science scholarship winners. il Sci N L 85:163 Mr 14 '64
Science talent search winners. Sci N L 85:86 F 8 '64
STS winners' projects. Sci N L 85:103 F 15 '64
Search for scientists at high school level. Sci N L 84:207 S 28 '63
Talent search honors. Sci N L 85:71 F 1 '64
Winners enter science. Sci N L 86:135 Ag 29 '64
Winners' science projects. Sci N L 85:119 F 22 '64

1965 (24th)

Talent search is on. Sci N L 86:182 S 19 '64
SCIENCE teachers
Equal opportunity; letter. D. W. Pierson. Science 142:154 O 11 '63
Mathematics and science teachers in U.S. high schools; excerpt from report. K. E. Brown and E. S. Obourn. il Sch Life 45:24-5 Ja '63

Certification

Standards for science teachers. D. Wolfle. Science 141:235 Jl 19 '63
SCIENCE teaching. See Science—Study and teaching
SCIENCE writers, National association of. See National association of science writers
SCIENCE writing. See Scientific literature
SCIENCE youth month. See National science youth month
SCIENTIFIC apparatus and instruments
ACHEMA, world's largest chemical engineering congress, shows scientific instruments of twenty-three nations. T. L. Campbell. il Science 145:1026-35 S 4 '64
Amazing apparatus of the gay nineties. C. A. Phillips. il Pop Electr 22:39-42+ Ja '65
Guide to scientific instruments; comp. by E. J. Scherago. il Science 142:697+ N 8 '63
Instrument issue; symposium. bibliog il Science 142:161+; 146:177-200+ O 11 '63, O 9 '64
New products. See issues of Science
Science for Santa's sack. F. Snakenberg. il Sci N L 86:314-15 N 14 '64
Splendor of old scientific instruments: a cabinet de mathématiques. il Fortune 69:148-53 Ap '64
What's new in research instruments. T. L. Campbell. bibliog il Science 144:892-8 My 15 '64
See also
Astronomical instruments
Biological apparatus and supplies
Medical instruments and apparatus
Meteorological instruments
Microscope and microscopy
SCIENTIFIC-Atlanta, incorporated
One way to do it. il Time 81:80+ Ap 26 '63
SCIENTIFIC committee on oceanic research. See International council of scientific unions—Scientific committee on oceanic research
SCIENTIFIC committee on the effects of atomic radiation. See United Nations—Scientific committee on the effects of atomic radiation
SCIENTIFIC conferences
ACHEMA, world's largest chemical engineering congress, shows scientific intruments of twenty-three nations. T. L. Campbell. il Science 145:1026-35 S 4 '64
Can Soviet scientists break through the iron curtain? E. Mott. il Todays Health 41:29-33+ S '63
Creative chat; Conference on education for creativity in the sciences. New Yorker 39:24-5 Je 15 '63
Meetings. See issues of Science
Obese degeneration of scientific congresses. G. E. W. Wolstenholme. Science 145:1337-9 S 18 '64; Reply. I. H. Page. 146:1001 N 20 '64
Proper accounting. P. H. Abelson; reply. J. W. Still. Science 139:676 F 15 '63
Proper public accounting for science. P. H. Abelson. Sat R 46:51-2 F 2 '63
When and where. See issues of Missiles and rockets
See also
Inter-American meeting of science and technology
International conference on the peaceful uses of atomic energy, 3d, Geneva, 1964
United Nations conference on the application of science and technology for the benefit of the less developed areas

SCIENTIFIC education
Approaching ceilings in the supply of scientific manpower; excerpts from address, February 19, 1963. W. R. Brode. bibliog il Science 143:313-24 Ja 24 '64
Churchill college, a modern university college. J. Cockcroft. Science 146:502-4 O 23 '64
Education: President's program provides more room at top. J. Walsh. Science 139:474-5+ F 8 '63
Equal opportunity; letter. D. W. Pierson. Science 142:154 O 11 '63
Experiment in industry-education; address, September 13, 1963. S. Shenberg. Vital Speeches 30:90-3 N 15 '63
Graduate aid: poll of educators suggests that needs vary widely in scientific disciplines. D. S. Greenberg. Science 140:35-7 Ap 5 '63
NASA and education; fast growth stirs Senate committee to place brakes on new university grants. D. S. Greenberg. Science 142:1042 N 22 '63; Reply. H. L. Dryden. 143:427 Ja 31 '64
NSF: new program aims to speed process for transforming good institutions into excellent ones. D. S. Greenberg. Science 144:154-5 Ap 10 '64
No secret formula for making scientists. L. C. Eiseley. il N Y Times Mag p66+ O 18 '64
Science and the small college: to compete with the universities, colleges decide to hang together. J. Walsh. Science 142:564-6 N 1 '63
Science education need stressed by Johnson. Sci N L 87:51 Ja 23 '65
Scientific age: the impact of science on society, by L. V. Berkner. Review
Sat R 47:72-3 N 21 '64. R. Gross
Scientists in the classroom; excerpts from Where, when, and why. M. Mayer. Commentary 35:312-19 Ap '63; Reply with rejoinder. R. Hyman. 36:195-6 S '63
Stairway to the stars. R. M. White. il NEA J 52:9-10 Ap '63
Training the creative scientist; address, May 7, 1963. G. T. Seaborg. Sci N L 83:314-17 My 18 '63
Writing in the sky. M. E. Jenkins. PTA Mag 57:2-3 Ap '63
See also
Engineering education
Science—Study and teaching
SCIENTIFIC exhibitions. See Science—Exhibitions
SCIENTIFIC expeditions
See also
American museum of natural history. New York—Expeditions
Archeological expeditions
National geographic society—Expeditions
New York botanical garden—Expeditions
SCIENTIFIC information. See Communication in science
SCIENTIFIC instruments. See Scientific apparatus and instruments
SCIENTIFIC laboratories. See Research laboratories
SCIENTIFIC laboratory, Los Alamos, N.Mex. See United States—Scientific laboratory, Los Alamos, N.Mex.
SCIENTIFIC libraries
Plan automated libraries; scientific data. W. Davis. Sci N L 85:371 Je 13 '64
See also
New York public library—Science and technology division
SCIENTIFIC literature
By scientists for scientists. P. H. Abelson. Science 142:1427 D 13 '63
Challenges to editors of scientific journals; address, March 19, 1963. J. R. Porter. bibliog Science 141:1014-17 S 13 '63
Ethics of scientific publication. D. J. de S. Price. bibliog Science 144:655-7 My 8 '64; Reply. G. R. Wendt. 145:110+ Jl 10 '64
Houston list. E. G. Holley. il Library J 88:959-61 Mr 1 '63
How to write about science; excerpts from Publicity media and methods. C. Schoenfeld. Writer 77:22-5 F '64
Is the literature worth keeping? J. Maddox. il Bul Atomic Sci 19:14-16 N '63
Is the scientific paper fraudulent? excerpt from Experimental method. P. B. Medawar. Sat R 47:42-3 Ag 1 '64; Discussion. 47:44-6 S 5 '64
Keepingupmanship. Newsweek 63:92 Je 15 '64
Language of scientific reports; letter. R. K. Dewar. Science 142:11 O 4 '63
Multiple authorship trends in scientific papers. B. L. Clarke. bibliog il Science 143:822-4 F 21 '64; Discussion. 144:798 My 15 '64
Primary scientific publication and the federal government. B. W. Adkinson. bibliog Science 140:613-17 My 10 '63
Rate your company's research productivity. M. H. Hodge, jr. bibliog f il Harvard Bsns R 41:109-22 N '63
Reports live only decade. Sci N L 83:150 Mr 9 '63
Reprints: a proposal; letter. A. F. Hofmann and others. Science 146:1251 D 4 '64
Science citation index, a new dimension in indexing. E. Garfield. bibliog Science 144:649-54 My 8 '64
Science fact, science fiction. J. W. Campbell. Writer 77:26-7 Ag '64
Science writing: a growing profession. P. C. Fraley and E. Ubell. il Bul Atomic Sci 19:19-22 D '63
Scientific information and the government; concerning the Committee on scientific information, and the Weinberg reports. G. S. Bonn. il Library J 88:4164-6 N 1 '63
Surveying Russian technical publications: a brief course. J. G. Tolpin. Science 146:1143-4 N 27 '64
System for reporting symposium discussions. A. R. Weinhold and K. F. Baker. Science 144:1474 Je 19 '64
300 years of storing words: scientific communication; excerpt from address. J. R. Porter. il Sat R 48:92-5 Ja 2 '65
See also
Blaisdell publishing company
Publishers and publishing—Scientific literature
Science—Periodicals
Science news
Translating
See Translations and translating
SCIENTIFIC literature for children
Christmas survey of new books about science for young readers (title varies) J. R. Newman. Sci Am 209:161-2+ D '63; 211:143-9 D '64
Editors, authors, librarians and scientists weigh science books; institute at Rutgers university. P. H. Allen. Library J 88:4828-30 D 5 '63
Paperbacks in an age of science. H. J. Deason. Sr Schol 83:31T Ja 17 '64
Science books for the young reader. C. B. Grannis. Pub W 185:62 Ap 20 '64
Science books with souls. E. Stamm. Library J 88:1299-30 Mr 15 '63
Science: the wonder ingredient in science books. N. Long. Library J 89:325-7 Ja 15 '64
Survey of young people's science books published in 1963-1964 (title varies) Natur Hist 72:4-17 D '63; 73:4-15 N '64
Bibliography
Views on science books. I. Asimov. See issues of Horn book magazine
SCIENTIFIC management, International congress for. See International congress for scientific management
SCIENTIFIC method
Potential theory of adsorption; authority in science. M. Polanyi. bibliog Science 141:1010-13 S 13 '63; Reply. G. A. Louis. 142:1257 D 6 '63
Scientific method; excerpt from Scientist. H. Margenau and D. Bergamini. il Fortune 70:100+ D '64
Strong inference; address September 1963. J. R. Platt. bibliog Science 146:347-53 O 16 '64; Discussion. 146:1635-6 D 25 '64
What are we looking for? P. A. Richmond. bibliog Science 139:737-9 F 22 '63
SCIENTIFIC names of plants. See Botany—Nomenclature
SCIENTIFIC news. See Science news
SCIENTIFIC periodicals. See Science—Periodicals
SCIENTIFIC personnel, Government. See Government employees
SCIENTIFIC photography. See Photography—Scientific applications
SCIENTIFIC reports. See Scientific literature
SCIENTIFIC research. See National research corporation; Research
SCIENTIFIC societies
See also names of scientific societies, e.g. National academy of sciences
SCIENTIFIC terms. See Science—Terminology
SCIENTIFIC theories. See Science
SCIENTIFIC toys. See Toys
SCIENTIFIC workers. See Scientists
SCIENTIFIC writing. See Scientific literature

SCIENTISTS
Are young scientists less creative than artists? Sci Digest 53:31 Mr '63
Better use of scientists. Sci N L 86:34 Jl 18 '64
Bigotry in science. P. H. Abelson. Science 144:371 Ap 24 '64
Changing environment of science; adaptation of address, December 28, 1964. A. T. Waterman. Science 147:13-18 Ja 1 '65
Creativity in the sciences. P. H. Abelson. Science 140:1271 Je 21 '63
Fellowship expansion: presidential plan criticized at hearing before House science, space committee. D. S. Greenberg. Science 139:392-3 F 1 '63
Fifth estate in the seventh decade; excerpts from address, December 28, 1963. P. M. Gross. Science 143:13-20 Ja 3 '64; Discussion. 143:917; 144:1086-7 F 28, My 29 '64
From freedom's herald to prophet in chains; excerpt from The scientific intellectual. L. S. Feuer. Sat R 46:42-3 Jl 6 '63
Genetic effects; with reply by B. Glass. B. Russell. Bul Atomic Sci 19:31-2 Je '63
Get-together of fine fellows. A. Rosenfeld. il Life 54:86+ F 8 '63
Goddard's technical manpower. R. W. Hutchison. il Electr World 71:62-3 Je '64
Hero worship in science. Sci N L 84:134 Ag 31 '63
Manpower: academy study presents proposals for better utilization of scientists and engineers. D. S. Greenberg. Science 145:252-3 Jl 17 '64
Measure for crackpots. F. J. Gruenberger. il Science 145:1413-15 S 25 '64; Reply. H. Schenck, jr. 146:718 N 6 '64
Myth-image of the scientist. H. Schenck, jr. Nation 197:140-2 S 14 '63; Same abr. with title Scientific freedom, hah! il Sci Digest 54:43-7 D '63
New scientist: essays on the methods and values of modern science, ed. by P. C. Obler and H. A. Estrin. Review
New Yorker 39:66+ Ag 31 '63. J. Bernstein
No secret formula for making scientists. L. C. Eiseley. il N Y Times Mag p66+ O 18 '64
On the history of science; excerpts from address. J. T. Wilson. Sat R 47:50-1 My 2 '64
Poet's investigation of science: from the 1963 Arthur D. Little lecture. R. Graves. Sat R 46:82-8 D 7 '63
Potpourri and gallimaufry. P. E. Klopsteg. Science 140:594-8 My 10 '63
Radiation and social ethics. A. P. Klausler. Christian Cent 80:199-200 F 13 '63
Reaction to Snow: scientists' role in public affairs draws increasingly heavy criticisms. D. S. Greenberg. Science 142:34-5 O 4 '63; Discussion. 142:13; 143:7, 638, 764 O 4 '63, Ja 3, F 14-21 '64
Revitalizing the mature scientist. P. H. Abelson. Science 141:597 Ag 16 '63
Science worries about the world. il Bsns W p24-5 Ja 4 '64
Scientist by several other names. E. L. Klingelhofer. Science 142:1123 N 29 '63; Reply. F. Costin. 145:8 Jl 3 '64
Scientist in biography. H. I. Sharlin. Bul Atomic Sci 19:27-8 N '63
Scientists and Jesuits, gypsies and Jews; letter. M. Amrine. Science 142:913 N 15 '63; Reply. R. B. Davis. 143:763-4 F 21 '64
Scientists and their images. A. T. Waterman. Science 143:311 Ja 24 '64; Reply. D. T. Brancato. 143:1120 Mr 13 '64
Scientists urge a broader view. Bsns W p96-7 Ja 9 '65
Skeptical look at scientific experts. D. E. Lilienthal. il N Y Times Mag p23+ S 29 '63; Discussion. p6 O 20 '63
Successor to democracy; warning against science. S. A. Coblentz. Christian Cent 81:78-80 Ja 15 '64; Reply. E. S. Scott. 81:341-2 Mr 11 '64
Training the creative scientist, address, May 7, 1963. G. T. Seaborg. Sci N L 83:314-17 My 18 '63
What it means to be a scientist; excerpts from address, May 5, 1964. G. T. Seaborg. Sci N L 85:314-15+ My 16 '64

See also
Astronomers
Chemists
Mathematicians
Physicists
Science as a profession
Society for social responsibility in science
Women as scientists

Ethics

See Scientists, Professional ethics for

Political activities

America's new policy makers, by D. W. Cox. Review
Christian Cent 81:673 My 20 '64. R. Root
Can only scientists make government science policy? E. G. Mesthene. Science 145:237-40 Jl 17 '64; Reply. C. W. Sherwin. 145:990 S 4 '64
Election: partisan activity of scientists unlikely to sow discord in scientific community. D. S. Greenberg. Science 146:232-4 O 9 '64
Management of science in the public interest; adaptation of address. C. W. Sherwin. Bul Atomic Sci 20:9-12 Je '64; Reply. F. Forscher 20:23 D '64
Money for science: NAS studies likely to have large influence on future of government support; with editorial comment. D. S. Greenberg. Science 146:475, 508-9 O 23 '64
Nobel laureates issue statement supporting Johnson and Humphrey. E. Langer. Science 146:578 O 23 '64
Nobel winners endorse Johnson and Humphrey; Two eminent scientists disagree on candidates. Sci N L 86:280 O 31 '64
Only one side of the question. P. H. Abelson. Science 145:347 Jl 24 '64; Same with title Exorbitant cost of dissent. Sat R 47:62 O 3 '64
Policy and the scientists. L. A. DuBridge. For Affairs 41:571-88 Ap '63
Politics: Johnson and Goldwater scientist groups show differing views on civilian technology. D. S. Greenberg. Science 146:509+ O 23 '64
Professionals emerge as political force; Scientists and engineers for Johnson. Aviation W 81:26 O 12 '64
Science and the 1964 election. P. H. Abelson. Science 146:17 O 2 '64
Science planks and party platforms. R. E. Lapp. Science 143:195 Ja 17 '64
Scientists and national policy-making, ed. by R. Gilpin and C. Wright. Review
Bul Atomic Sci 20:25-7 N '64. E. G. Mesthene
Science 144:1438-9 Je 19 '64. A. T. Waterman
Scientists and the public weal. P. Siekevitz. Nation 197:271-3 N 2 '63
Scientists for Goldwater. Sci N L 86:254 O 17 '64
Scientists for Johnson. Sci N L 86:143 Ag 29 '64
Scientists, seers and strategy. A. Wohlstetter. bibliog f For Affairs 41:466-78 Ap '63
Skeptical look at scientific experts. D. E. Lilienthal. il N Y Times Mag p23+ S 29 '63
Strauss, Teller, Libby to serve on Goldwater science task force. Science 145:1417 S 25 '64
Venture into politics: scientists and engineers in the election campaign. D. S. Greenberg. Science 146:1440-4, 1561-3 D 11-18 '64
Whiz kids vs. military men: who is shaping defense? il U S News 54:46-7 Mr 4 '63

Salaries

Consulting: advice for a price has become an important factor in finances of many scientists. D. S. Greenberg. Science 145:1416-17 S 25 '64

Supply and demand

Aid to the U.S. D. Wolfle. Science 139:803 Mr 1 '63
Approaching ceilings in the supply of scientific manpower; excerpts from address, February 19, 1963. W. R. Brode. bibliog il Science 143:313-24 Ja 24 '64
Brain drain; loss of scientific and technical talent to the U.S. Time 81:98 Mr 15 '63
Goose and the golden egg. W. J. Coughlin. Miss & Roc 13:46 N 18 '63
Great need for scientists. Sci N L 83:100 F 16 '63
Help wanted; future shortage of scientists. Newsweek 63:88+ Ap 13 '64
How guard our diversity in science? C. P. Haskins. Science 140:141 Ap 12 '63
Lost scientists. Sci Am 208:81-2 Ap '63
Manpower: activist administration finds Congress hard to convince on bigger investment in people. J. Walsh. Science 139:815-17 Mr 1 '63
Manpower: Senate study describes how scientists fit into scheme of things in red China, Soviet Union. J. Walsh. Science 141:253-5 Jl 19 '63
PT boat government. Aviation W 78:21 Ap 1 '63
Plug asked for drain of scientists to U.S. Sci N L 85:132 F 29 '64

SCIENTISTS—Supply and demand—*Continued*
Scientific migration: Britain agitated anew by research team's decision to move to United States. J. Maddox. Science 143:786-8 F 21 '64
Scientists and engineers, 1960-70; supply and demand. H. V. Stambler. il Mo Labor R 86: 1275-82 N '63
Single office proposed to combat shortage of scientists and engineers. H. M. David. il Miss & Roc 15:21 O 5 '64
Technical personnel shortage. Electr World 70:75 D '63
Today's job market, and tomorrow's. D. Wolfle. Science 145:665 Ag 14 '64
U.K. concern grows over scientist exodus. H. J. Coleman. Aviation W 78:104+ Mr 25 '63
When exchange is not really exchange. E. Broda. Bul Atomic Sci 20:23-5 N '64

SCIENTISTS, African
Raising number of African scientists. Sch & Soc 92:328 N 14 '64

SCIENTISTS, Amateur
Basement science: what happens when a do-it-yourself scientist looks to Washington for support. D. S. Greenberg. Science 146:621-3 O 30 '64; Discussion. 146:1251-2; 147:109-10 D 4 '64, Ja 8 '65
Go dig up a fossil. il Changing T 17:11-12 Ap '63
Wanted: ten million amateur scientists; excerpts from Wanted: amateur scientists. R. Froman. il Pop Sci 184:82-5+ Ap '64

SCIENTISTS, American
Creative scientists of today. J. A. Chambers. bibliog il Science 145:1203-5 S 11 '64; Discusssion. 147:66-7 Ja 1 '65
Emotion versus intelligence in public support of science; letter. W. H. Freeman. Science 143:433 Ja 31 '64
Scientists and public affairs: though world has changed, they remain preoccupied with the bomb. D. S. Greenberg. Science 142: 1635 D 27 '63; Discussion. 143:430+; 144:366, 954; 145:7 Ja 31, Ap 24, My 22, Jl 3 '64
Scientists organize for peace. E. Mirel. Sci N L 84:117-18 Ag 24 '63
U.S. science-technology manpower is 2.7 million. Sci N L 84:137 Ag 31 '63
See also
Federation of American scientists

SCIENTISTS, British
Better to be British? leading scientists leave Britain for the U.S. il Time 83:74 F 21 '64
Brain drain; loss of scientific and technical talent to the U.S. Time 81:98 Mr 15 '63
British brain explains the brain drain. B. Lovell. N Y Times Mag p 13+ Mr 22 '64
Lost scientists. Sci Am 208:81-2 Ap '63
Manhunters: British minister blames American recruiters for emigration of scientists. D. S. Greenberg. Science 139:893 Mr 8 '63
Not just the lolly; emigration of scientists to US. il Newsweek 61:66 Mr 11 '63
Top scientists flee Britain. Bsns W p89 Mr 2 '63
U.S.-Britain: battle of the brains; British scientists to U.S. Sr Schol 82:23 Mr 27 '63
Why Britain is losing brains to the U.S. U S News 56:9 F 24 '64

SCIENTISTS, Exchange of. See Exchange of persons programs

SCIENTISTS, German
Nasser's hired Germans; Israelis fight to stop missiles being built. S. de Gramont. il Sat Eve Post 236:60-1+ Jl 13 '63
Trackdown of the German scientist. A. J. Olsen. il N Y Times Mag p30+ S 22 '63

SCIENTISTS, Professional ethics for
Ethical code for scientists? letter. L. Cranberg. bibliog Science 141:1242 S 27 '63; Discussion. 142:916, 1257 N 15, D 6 '63
Ethical problems: an invitation. D. Wolfle. Science 143:435 Ja 31 '64; Discussion. 145: 873 Ag 28 '64
Ethics for the scientist. J. Haybittle. Bul Atomic Sci 20:23-4 My '64
Ethics of scientific publication. D. J. de S. Price. bibliog Science 144:655-7 My 8 '64; Reply. G. R. Wendt. 145:110+ Jl 10 '64
Scientist speculates; an anthology of partly-baked ideas, ed. by I. J. Good. Review
Bul Atomic Sci 19:30-1 My '63. H. Born
When scientists testify. A. Etzioni. Bul Atomic Sci 20:23-6 O '64

SCIENTISTS and engineers for Johnson (organization)
Scientists for Johnson. Sci N L 86:143 Ag 29 '64

SCIENTISTS' institute for public information
Science for the citizen. Sci Am 208:74-5 My '63

SCIENTISTS on survival (organization)
Scientists on survival: second annual meeting quiet, fruitful in contrast to earlier affair. D. S. Greenberg. Science 140:1291-2 Je 21 '63
War without killing. E. Mirel. Sci N L 83: 405 Je 29 '63

SCIENTOLOGY
Have you ever been a boo-hoo? J. Phelan. il Sat Eve Post 237:81-5 Mr 21 '64

SCILLY ISLANDS
Blimey, it's balmy! N. Braybrooke. il Sat R 46:42+ Ap 13 '63
England's own South Sea Islands. M. Goodman. il House B 105:48+ N '63

SCIOMYZIDS
Deadly larva, deadly snails. il Time 82:59-60 S 20 '63

SCION. See Grafting

SCISM, Mack
Mummers theatre of Oklahoma City. A. J. Treanor. il por Theatre Arts 47:55-9 D '63

SCISSORS and shears
Very sharp scissors and shears. il Bet Hom & Gard 42:17 Ap '64

SCISSORS work. See Paper work

SCIURUS kaibabensis. See Squirrels

SCLANDERS, Ian
Bonus for babies. Nation 198:167-8 F 17 '64
Diefenbaker vision. Nation 198:387-8 Ap 20 '64
Peace corps: nursery for diplomats. Nation 199:31-3 Jl 27 '64
Politics: the rich man's game. Nation 198: 215-16 Mr 2 '64

SCLAR, C. B. and Carrison, L. C.
Phase composition of commercial ammonium carbonate. bibliog Science 140:1205-7 Je 14 '63
—and others
High-pressure metallic indium telluride: preparation and crystal structure. bibliog Science 143:352-3 Ja 24 '64
Stishovite: thermal dependence of the crystal habit. bibliog Science 144:833-5 My 15 '64

SCLARENCO, Carl
What to do about a drafty house. Bet Hom & Gard 42:125 N '64

SCLERAL lenses. See Contact lenses

SCLEROSIS
Study Soviet virus claim; amyotrophic lateral sclerosis or Lou Gehrig's disease getting further study by U.S. scientists. Sci N L 87:30 Ja 9 '65

SCLEROSIS, Multiple
Human uses seen in multiple sclerosis study. Sci N L 84:141 Ag 31 '63
MS; crippler of young adults. R. N. DeJong. Todays Health 42:36-7 N '64
Possible MS vaccine; demyelinating diseases research. F. Marley. Sci N L 85:67 F 1 '64

SCLEROTIZATION. See Insects—Development

SCOBELL, John
John Scobell, Union spy in Civil war; excerpts from Eyes and ears of the Civil war. G. A. Foster. il Ebony 19:135-8+ D '63

SCOBEY, Joan
Best of both worlds. Mlle 57:171-3+ My '63

SCOFIELD, John
India in crisis. il Nat Geog Mag 123:599-661 My '63

SCOFIELD, John B.
Wanted: strong parents. Parents Mag 38:53+ Je '63
Why kids rebel. Read Digest 82:130-3 Je '63

SCOGGIN, Margaret C.
(comp) Outlook tower. See issues of Horn book magazine

SCOLLON, Kenneth M.
Why art in education? Sat R 47:70-2+ F 15 '64

SCONES
Hot scones and fresh strawberry jam. il Sunset 132:206 My '64
Sweet scones from sourdough. il Sunset 131: 142 Jl '63

SCOOTERS. See Ice boats and ice boating

SCOPE calibrators. See Calibrators

SCOPES. See Telescopic sights

SCOPITONE. See Jukeboxes

SCORDATURA
Scordatura; and the Mysteries of the rosary. E. Salzman. Hi Fi 13:73-4 Ap '63

SCORE project. See United States—Small business administration

SCOREBOARDS
Mets think big; seven-story gimmick, sing-along scoreboard. il Sports Illus 20:17 Ap 13 '64

SCORPIONS
Ancient scorpions found. il Sci N L 85:226 Ap 11 '64
Desert arachnids emerge. R. H. Wright. il Natur Hist 74:54-7 F '65

SCORPIONS, Fossil
Anatomy of decay as preserved in shale. L. Størmer. il Natur Hist 73:20-5 D '64

SCOTCH
Letter from Edinburgh. A. Reid. il New Yorker 40:103-4+ O 24 '64

SCOTCH in Canada
Scotch in Canada; excerpts from Scotch. J. K. Galbraith. il Harper 228:35-40 Je; 229: 79-84 Jl; 77-80 Ag '64

SCOTCH pine. See Pine

SCOTCH tape. See Adhesive tape

SCOTCH whiskey. See Whiskey

SCOTLAND
Atlantic report. Atlan 214:40+ N '64
Scotland; the dour and the beautiful with photographs by I. Penn. R. Douglas-Home. Vogue 143:132-45+ Ap 15 '64
See also
Aberdeen
Banks and banking—Scotland
Bass Rock
Gardens—Scotland
Perth
Public schools (endowed)—Scotland
Skye, Isle of

Antiquities
See also
Callernish

Description and travel
Letter from Edinburgh. A. Reid. il New Yorker 40:103-4+ O 24 '64
New good move for travellers: Vogue 143:8+ Ap 15 '64
Scotland for outsiders. H. Fast. il Esquire 61: 69+ F '64

Industries
See also
Distilling industries

Religious institutions and affairs
News of the Christian world (cont) Christian Cent 80:308+, 720-1, 888-90+, 1182-3, 1414; 81:60-2, 442-4, 648-9, 1377 Mr 6, My 29, Jl 10, S 25, N 13 '63, Ja 8, Ap 1, My 13, N 4 '64

Social life and customs
Scotland is a state of mind. J. Stewart-Gordon. il Read Digest 82:234-6+ My '63

SCOTLAND and England. See England and Scotland

SCOTT, Amoret, and Scott, Christopher
Old dummy board figures. Antiques 83:564-7 My '63

SCOTT, Chris
Nine months later. Nat R 15:478 D 3 '63

SCOTT, Christopher. See Scott, A. jt. auth.

SCOTT, David
Bass bugs made easy. Outdoor Life 134:52 Ag '64
First home TV tape recorder. Pop Sci 183: 94-6+ O '63
This walking wheel turns itself. Pop Sci 185: 44-6 Jl '64

SCOTT, Don
Don Scott clicks on TV bowling show. il pors Ebony 20:87-8+ D '64

SCOTT, Dred
Black pawn on a field of peril. B. Catton. il por Am Heritage 15:66-71+ D '63

SCOTT, Edward L.
He turned the poles to gold. P. Downey. il por Sports Illus 18:E5-8 Mr 11 '63

SCOTT, F. M. and others
Root hairs, cuticle, and pits. bibliog Science 140:63 Ap 5 '63

SCOTT, George C.
Great Scott. B. Davidson. il pors Sat Eve Post 236:88-9 N 16 '63

SCOTT, George L.
Foot in the door; Munn v. Illinois. C. P. Magrath. il Am Heritage 15:44-8+ F '64

SCOTT, H. H. incorporated
Split personality spells success. il Bsns W p 156+ Mr 16 '63

SCOTT, Hugh
Speaking out. por Sat Eve Post 237:8+ My 9 '64

SCOTT, Jack Denton
King of beasts makes his last stand. Read Digest 84:193-4+ F '64
To see September. Read Digest 85:221-4 S '64
Trouper of the treetops. Read Digest 82:210-11+ My '63

SCOTT, Jock
Lee Wuff vs. Jock Scott transatlantic salmon challenge match. T. Rogowski. il pors Esquire 59:100-3+ Je '63

SCOTT, John
Unshaped anguish. Christian Cent 80:831 Je 26 '63

SCOTT, John Jay
Is antitrust hurting growth? address. Duns R 83:55-6+ My '64

SCOTT, John Paul
Critical periods in behavioral development. bibliog Science 138:949-58; 139:1115-16 N 30 '62, Mr 15 '63

SCOTT, Kenneth
Black nativity at Philharmonic Hall. M. Marks. Dance Mag 37:56 F '63

SCOTT, Marion
Marion Scott, Don Redlich at 92nd street Y. M. Marks. Dance Mag 38:64 Mr '64

SCOTT, Meredith A.
Look again, old-timer! il Motor B 112:41-3+ Jl '63

SCOTT, Michelle
Littlest scene stealer: United Nations children's choir of Los Angeles. il pors Ebony 18:63-4+ Jl '63

SCOTT, Nathan A. Jr
Dialogue with deity. Sat R 47:41 Mr 7 '64

SCOTT, Peter
We mean to take it back; America's cup. por Sports Illus 21:27-31 Ag 24 '64

about
Guarding against indolence. il pors Time 84: 90 S 18 '64
Ornithologist at Sovereign's helm. il pors Life 57:53+ S 18 '64
Peter Scott: a man for all reasons. il pors Esquire 62:136-7 S '64

SCOTT, Robert B. and Bell, Eugene
Messenger RNA utilization during development of chick embryo lens. bibliog Science 147:405-7 Ja 22 '65
Protein synthesis during development: control through messenger RNA. bibliog Science 145:711-13 Ag 14 '64

SCOTT, Ruth Boyer
Check your traveling shoes. Sci Digest 54: 21-2 Ag '63
Cooking has changed. Todays Health 41:48-51+ S '63
Could you deliver a baby? reprint. Sci Digest 56:63-6 D '64

SCOTT, Steve
Wenderski-Winkel dragster. il Hot Rod 17: 52-4 Jl '64

SCOTT, Susan
Two good cooks are better than one; ed. by R. Behnke. por Farm J 88:76-8 My '64

SCOTT, Thomas R. and Powell, D. A.
Measurement of a visual motion aftereffect in the rhesus monkey. bibliog Science 140: 57-9 Ap 5 '63

SCOTT, Tom K. and Jacobs, W. P.
Auxin in coleus stems: limitation of transport at higher concentrations. bibliog Science 139:589-90 F 15 '63

SCOTT, Vernon
Elvis: ten million dollars later. McCalls 90: 90-1+ F '63
Gregory. McCalls 90:104-5+ S '63
Kim Novak vs. the code. Sat Eve Post 237: 16-17 S 5 '64
Saga of Lassie. Sat Eve Post 237:24-7 O 3 '64
Stars, second generation. McCalls 90:68-9+ Jl '63

SCOTT, Sir Walter, bart
Wizard of the North. J. W. Stedman. il por Opera N 29:23-7 D 5 '64

SCOTT, Walter N. and others
Inulin and albumin absorption from the proximal tubule in necturus kidney. bibliog Science 146:1588-90 D 18 '64

SCOTT, Wendell G.
Cancer; address, August 31, 1964. Vital Speeches 30:762-6 O 1 '64

SCOTT, William D.
Liquid temperature controller. Electr World 72:46-7 N '64

SCOTT, Winfield Townley
Child's morning; poem. Sat R 46:34 O 26 '63
Listening for the different voice. Sat R 46: 36-8 O 26 '63
Summer-house; poem. Sat R 46:19 S 28 '63
Touching sacred objects. W. Stafford. Poetry 102:115-16 My '63

SCOTT-HILL, W. I.
Flying clubs, there; western Europe. Flying 74:54+ Je '64

SCOTT COUNTY, Ia.
Priceless gift of better speech; rural school districts. R. E. Shine and others. NEA J 53:36A-36B Ja '64

SCOTT paper company
Keeping executives healthy. S. W. Bryant. il Fortune 67:122-3+ Ap '63

SCOTT'S (restaurant) See London—Hotels, restaurants, etc.

SCOTTSDALE, Ariz.
Refuse wranglers clean up the town. il Am City 79:99 S '64

SCOTTSDALE, Ariz, All-Arabian horse show. See Horse shows

SCOUGALL, Stuart, and Gifford, P. C.
Aboriginal art and mythology. Natur Hist 74:46-53 bibliog(p70) F '65

SCOULLER, J. Donald
Special report from S.M.P.T.E.'s Los Angeles convention. il Pop Phot 55:92+ Ag '64

SCOUR in swine. See Swine—Diseases and pests

SCOURING powders. See Cleaning compositions

SCOUTING, Basketball. See Basketball scouting

SCOUTING, Football. See Football scouting

SCOUTS, Girl. See Girl scouts

SCOUTTEN, E. F.
American free enterprise system; address, November 21, 1963. Vital Speeches 30:269-73 F 15 '64

SCOVELL, Esther
America warns its youth. America 108:451 Ap 6 '63

SCOVILL manufacturing company
Cutting back middle management: new shine to Scovill. J. B. Weiner. il Duns R 84:34-5+ Jl '64

SCOVILLE, Herbert, jr
New science head for disarmament agency. E. Langer. Science 142:1045 N 22 '63

SCOVOTTI, Jeanette
Echo; interview, ed. by A. M. Lingg. por Opera N 27:15 F 16 '63
Quote: unquote; interview, ed. by M. Brozen. por Mus Am 84:25 My '64

SCRANTON, William Warren
Free enterprise; address, February 21, 1964. Vital Speeches 30:326-8 Mr 15 '64
Republican coalition; excerpts from address. por Time 83:25 My 1 '64
Tribute to Abraham Lincoln; address, November 19, 1963. Vital Speeches 30:132-3 D 15 '63

about

Against the Democrat Democrat. Time 81:19 Mr 22 '63
At 8:25 p.m: I'm going to run. il pors Newsweek 63:21-5 Je 22 '64
Back to the wars. Newsweek 64:20+ Jl 6 '64
Barry's blitz. il por Newsweek 64:28+ Jl 13 '64
Bigger push to run. por Bsns W p30-1 Mr 21 '64
Bill Scranton, a reluctant candidate. J. Bird. il pors Sat Eve Post 237:73-7 Ja 18 '64
Bleating of sheep. M. Kempton. New Repub 150:15-18 Je 20 '64
Boomlet for Bill Scranton: how to succeed without trying. il pors Newsweek 63:19-20+ Ja 27 '64
Can Scranton still win? il por U S News 57:45 Jl 6 '64
Champion of the moderates. Christian Cent 81:819 Je 24 '64
Closer now to an open race. por U S News 56:16 Mr 30 '64
Crisis at the Cow palace. S. Alsop. il pors Sat Eve Post 237:17-21 Jl 11 '64
Enter Scranton. il por Newsweek 62:16 D 30 '63
Fifteen days to go, the Scranton campaign. il pors N Y Times Mag p8-9 Je 28 '64
Governor Scranton: is he really reluctant? H. Ehrlich. il pors Look 28:72-4 Mr 10 '64
Governor Scranton to the rescue. M. McGrory. America 110:860 Je 27 '64
Governor Scranton's delicate situation. M. McGrory. America 110:562 Ap 25 '64
GOP in San Francisco: Alabama casts twenty votes for. . . Delegates: a grand old party. il por Newsweek 64:16-21 Jl 20 '64
He didn't say yes but he didn't say no. il por Time 83:37-9 Ap 17 '64
Hey, look me over. il por Newsweek 63:19-20 Je 29 '64
I am a candidate. il pors Time 83:13-15 Je 19 '64
I do not wish to run. pors Newsweek 63:35-6 Ap 20 '64
If not Rockefeller or Goldwater, here are two dark horses. por U S News 54:48-9 Je 3 '63
In home stretch: can Scranton make it? il por U S News 56:31-3 Je 29 '64
Interview with Governor Scranton; ed. by J. Kraft. Harper 229:94+ Jl '64
Let's not kid ourselves. il Time 84:17-18 Jl 3 '64
Logical candidate. S. Alsop. por Sat Eve Post 237:15 Ja 18 '64
Luncheon in Philadelphia. Time 82:19 N 22 '63
Making their records. il por Time 82:29 S 13 '63
Mission: a winner's image. il por Time 83:18-19 Je 26 '64
More on that non-candidate. il por Time 83:21 My 29 '64
Now, a Scranton challenge for the nomination. por U S News 56:19 Je 22 '64
On a cross of falsehoods. Time 83:26 F 21 '64
Out of the doldrums. il Time 84:60 Jl 3 '64
Portrait of a not-so-dark horse. J. Welsh. il pors N Y Times Mag p 12+ Ja 12 '64
Quite a few things to say. por Time 83:26 Mr 13 '64
Republicans. il por Time 82:17 D 27 '63
Republicans take another look at Governor Scranton. por U S News 55:82 D 16 '63
Scranton. New Repub 150:3-4 Je 27 '64
Scranton: now a favorite son for '64. por U S News 55:17 Jl 1 '63
Scranton of Pennsylvania. M. Kempton. New Repub 148:9-12 F 16 '63
Scranton of Pennsylvania. R. A. Smith. por Fortune 69:80-4+ F '64
Scranton on automation. Sci N L 86:35 Jl 18 '64
Scranton's move. H. Brandon. Sat R 47:7-8 Jl 4 '64
Scranton's off-again on-again boom. por Life 56:48B Je 19 '64
Sharpening the spikes. por Newsweek 62:23-4 Jl 1 '63
Some facts of history. il Time 84:19 Jl 10 '64
Squire Scranton bides his time. T. H. White. il pors Life 56:63-8+ F 28 '64
Still in there fighting. il por Time 84:21-2 Jl 10 '64
Sudden magnificence of William W. Scranton. M. E. Evans. Nat R 16:269-70+ Ap 7 '64
Talk with Governor Scranton. H. Brandon. il Sat R 47:12-13 Ap 4 '64
Tender moment on the short steep uphill trail: with just three weeks to go Scranton makes the sparks fly; with report by R. Ajemian. il pors Life 56:28-37 Je 26 '64
This president thing. il Time 81:26-31 Je 14 '63
Two Republican hopefuls. por Look 28:71 Mr 10 '64
Waiting game of William W. Scranton. P. Duke. por Reporter 30:30-2 F 27 '64
What happened when two noncandidates got together. por U S News 56:14 F 24 '64
Why G.O.P. should choose Scranton. Life 57:4 Jl 3 '64

SCRANTON, William Warren, family
Room at the top: the Scrantons of Scranton. il Newsweek 63:25-7 Ja 27 '64

SCRANTON, Pa, public library
Federal prosecution of fraudulent dealers. ALA Bul 58:304 Ap '64
Former Scranton (Pa) librarian charged with embezzlement. Library J 88:2472 Je 15 '63
Investigation of alleged frauds. Wilson Lib Bul 38:604+ Ap '64

SCRAP metal
Scrappy market. il Time 81:98+ My 3 '63
Unburied dead on the roads: discarded cars. il Bsns W p34 Mr 28 '64

SCRAP metal sculpture. See Metal sculpture

SCRATCHBOARD drawing
Scratchboard. il Design 66:14-15 S '64
Scratchboard illustration. B. Cooney. il Horn Bk 40:162-5 Ap '64

SCRATCHING
Fine art of scratching; interview, ed. by H. G. Earl. S. Ayres, jr. il Todays Health 43:38-41+ Ja '65

SCREECH owls. See Owls

SCREEN houses. See Garden houses, shelters, etc.

SCREEN printing. See Silk screen printing

SCREEN writing. See Moving picture authorship

SCREENS (doors, windows, etc)
Nested hurricane screens shield windows. il Arch Rec 135:186 Je '64
Shoji screen hides unsightly window. R. Kotrba. il Pop Mech 119:147 My '63

SCREENS (fences) See Fences

SCREENS (furniture)
Panel door decor. il Pop Mech 120:144-5 S '63

SCREENS (photography) See Projection apparatus

SCREENS (sun)
Add comfort with shade on your terrace. il Pop Gard 15:44-5 Ap '64
Built-in shade. J. B. Brimer. il Flower Grower 51:22-3 S '64
Controlling the color of daylight. il Sunset 131:62-3 Ag '63

SCREENS (sun)—*Continued*
Design against sun and glare; home office, Humble oil and refining company, Houston, Tex. il Arch Rec 134:173-8 O '63
Here is an extension sunshade. il Sunset 130:134 Je '63
Sectional patio screens. il Pop Mech 119: 134-5 Je '63
Soaring sun roofs create a shade garden. il Sunset 130:100-1 Je '63
Sun canopy is a cool idea. V. W. Kondra. il Pop Sci 184:149 Ap '64
They used lumber in slender strips. il Sunset 132:116 Ap '64
Three breezy ways to beat the sun! F. Glass and P. Lindberg. il Bet Hom & Gard 41: 62-3+ Je '63
Typhoon-proof louvers screen tropical sun; Philippine American life insurance office building, Manila. il Arch Rec 134:139-41 D '63
SCREENS, Moving picture. See Moving picture screens
SCREENS, Projector. See Projection apparatus
SCREVANE, Paul R.
Next mayor of New York? M. K. Sanders. il por Harper 226:33-41 F '63
SCREW drivers
Things you never knew about screwdrivers. il Pop Sci 184:156+ Ja '64
SCREWS
Wood screw holding-power calculator. il Pop Sci 185:154 N '64
SCRIBES. See Public letter writers
SCRIMSHAW, Nevin S.
Food; with biographical sketch. Sci Am 209: 24, 72-80 S '63
SCRIMSHAW
Scrimshaw collector. C. Barnes, jr. and C. Bowen. il Am Heritage 15:8-13 O '64
Souvenirs of the seas. C. Z. Spriggs. il Hobbies 68:28-9+ Ap '63
SCRIPPS, Charles E.
Remarks at talent search. Sci N L 85:164 Mr 14 '64
SCRIPPS-Howard newspapers
Apartness in Cincinnati. Time 83:82 Je 12 '64
SCRIPT writing. See Television authorship
SCRIPTA Technica, incorporated. See Translations and translating
SCRIPTO, incorporated
Scripto on strike; the race-wage picket line. C. J. Levy. Nation 200:31-2 Ja 11 '65
SCRIPTS, Moving picture. See Moving picture authorship
SCRIPTS, Television. See Television scripts
SCRIPTURE studies. See Bible study
SCRIVER, Bob
Bob Scriver: western sculptor. M. Strachan. il por Am Artist 28:50-2+ S '64
SCROLLS (decorative design)
Sequential drawing activity & the scroll. J. W. Cataldo. il Sch Arts 62:34-5 Je '63
SCROLLS from the Dead Sea. See Dead Sea scrolls
SCRUTINY (periodical)
Books. H. Rosenberg. New Yorker 40:169-71+ Mr 14 '64
Importance of scrutiny, ed. by E. Bentley. Review
Commonweal 81:457-8 D 25 '64. B. McCabe
Passion of Scrutiny. J. G. Weightman. Nation 197:393-4 D 7 '63
Scrutiny: a quarterly review, 1932-1953, ed. by F. R. Leavis and others. Review
Sat R 46:27+ N 2 '63. M. Peckham
Scrutiny bound. R. Gottlieb. New Repub 149:21-4+ D 7 '63
SCUBA. See Diving apparatus
SCULL, Robert
At home with Henry; R. C. Scull's collection of pop art. il por Time 83:68-71 F 21 '64
Can this be art? E. Genaur. il por Ladies Home J 81:151-5 Mr '64
SCULL, Robert C, collection. See Art—Private collections
SCULLING. See Rowing
SCULLY, Ed
Washington, D.C. U S Camera 27:70-4 Ap '64
SCULLY, James
Fantasy of little waters; poem. New Yorker 39:44 N 2 '63
Gibraltar; poem. New Yorker 39:36 Mr 2 '63
Search for passion. Nation 197:329-30 N 16 '63
(ed) See Corso, G. Audience swam for their lives
(ed) See Gilbert, J. Audience swam for their lives
SCULLY, Vin
Transistor kid. R. Creamer. il por Sports Illus 20:96-8+ My 4 '64
SCULLY, Vincent
Architecture and man at Yale. Sat R 47:26-9 My 23 '64
Athens Hilton: a study in vandalism. Arch Forum 119:100-3 Jl '63
Life World's fair review. Life 57:9 Jl 31 '64
Light, form, and power: new work of Louis Kahn. Arch Forum 121:162-70 Ag '64
Mailer vs. Scully. por Arch Forum 120:96-7 Ap '64
SCULPTORS
Reviews and previews: new names this month. See issues of Art news
Sculptors of light and shadow. J. McAndrews. il Sat R 47:37-8 F 8 '64
SCULPTORS materials. See Artists materials
SCULPTURE
Beware of sculpture. K. Kuh. Vogue 141:26+ Mr 1 '63
Marisol's magic mixtures; exhibition at the Stable gallery, New York. L. Campbell. il Art N 63:38-41+ Mr '64
Mud-flat museum. il Time 84:89 Ag 28 '64
On sculpture. G. Stark. il Sch Arts 63:27-30 Mr '64
Perpetual motion. F. Getlein. New Repub 151: 33-4+ O 3 '64
Sculpture. M. F. Andrews. bibliog il NEA J 53:58-61 S '64
Statues in silhouette; sculpture garden, Museum of modern art, New York. il N Y Times Mag p44-5 O 18 '64
Through the ages with the thinker. il Nat Parks Mag 37:20 D '63
See also
Animal sculpture
Bronzes
Carving (art industries)
Casting (sculpture)
Ceramic sculpture
Decoration and ornament, Architectural
Garden ornaments
Ice sculpture
Metal sculpture
Monuments
Mountain sculpture
Plaster casts
Plaster sculpture
Portrait sculpture
Statues
Stone carving
Wire sculpture
Wood carving

Exhibitions

Art galleries; exhibitions of modern sculpture at Whitney and Sidney Janis. R. M. Coates. New Yorker 40:152-5 D 19 '64
Enter: young American sculptors; Whitney museum of American art. J. Canaday. il N Y Times Mag p44-5 D 6 '64
Era of the object; Manhattan's Whitney museum biennial exhibit. il Time 84:84-5 D 11 '64
Spectrum of sculpture; recent shows. M. Kozloff. Nation 199:312-13+ N 2 '64
William Accorsi's toy sculpture. il Craft Horiz 23:24-5 N '63

Private collections

See Art—Private collections

Study and teaching

Materials

Coat hanger sculpture. F. Major. il Design 65:98-9 Ja '64
Plaster sculpture; ninth grade. R. Vislosky. il Sch Arts 64:7-9 O '64
Plowshares into sculpture. Y. Chomicky. il Sch Arts 62:22-4 Mr '63
Prophet, furnace cement sculpture. F. L. Marlow. il Sch Arts 64:20-1 O '64
SCULPTURE, African
Tribal art from Africa. C. M. Turnbull. il Natur Hist 73:46-53 Mr '64
See also
Sculpture, Bini
SCULPTURE, American
American sculpture: the collection of James H. Ricau. il Antiques 86:291-8 S '64
Disrespectful hand-maiden; chaos in 1962-64 sculpture at the Whitney. T. B. Hess. il Art N 63:38-9+ Ja '65
Four sculptors, four styles. il Art N 62:36-7 Sum '63
Image in the round; Whitney museum's every-other-year show. New Repub 148:37-9 Mr 2 '63
Is sculpture a step-child? a colloquy. P. Agostini; R. Mallary; M. Friedman. il Art N 63:40-2+ S '64
Possible futures; Whitney museum biennial. il Newsweek 65:74 Ja 18 '65

SCULPTURE, American—*Continued*
Sculpture at Winterthur. F. H. Sommer. il Antiques 85:182-4 F '64
Steel mistletoe. T. B. Hess. il Art N 61: 46-7+ F '63
Survey of American sculpture. Hobbies 69: 84+ Jl '64
See also
Agostini, P.
Arnold, A.
Baizerman, S.
Baskin, L.
Berks, R.
Biederman, C.
Bleifeld, S.
Bontecou, L.
Bufano, B. B.
Calder, A.
Collie, A.
De Lue, D.
Gage, M.
Hague, R.
Hare, D.
Hosmer, H.
Hunt, R.
Ihlenfeld, K.
Jonas, L. P.
Lachaise, G.
Lippold, R.
Lipton, S.
Lopez, G.
McCullough, G.
Maldarelli, O.
Marans, M.
Miller, E.
Muir, W.
Nakian, R.
Nevelson, L.
Noguchi, I.
Oldenburg, C.
Ortlieb, R.
Portanova, J.
Rickey, G.
Scriver, B.
Smith, D.
Spaventa, G.
Sullivan, M.
Voulkos, P.
Zogbaum, W. M.
SCULPTURE, Animal. See Animal sculpture
SCULPTURE, Architectural. See Decoration and ornament, Architectural
SCULPTURE, Bini
Africa: the face behind the mask. B. Davidson. il Horizon 5:44-53 Mr '63
Art of Benin. il Ebony 18:91-4 F '63
SCULPTURE, British
See also
Epstein, J.
Hepworth, B.
Moore, H.
Paolozzi, E.
SCULPTURE, Buddhist
Buddha in situ and in New York; Asia House show. J. G. Mahler. il Art N 62:36-7+ My '63
Theme & gentle variations; exhibition at Asia House in Manhattan. il Time 81:76-8 Je 7 '63
SCULPTURE, Ceramic. See Ceramic sculpture
SCULPTURE, Eskimo. See Eskimos—Art
SCULPTURE, French
See also
Barye, A. L.
Houdon, J. A.
Ipousteguy, J.
Lachaise, G.
Lipchitz, J.
Maillol, A.
Pevsner, A.
Rodin, A.
SCULPTURE, German
Colossal for the medium: Meissen porcelain sculptures. C. C. Dauterman. il Antiques 85:214-17 F '64
SCULPTURE, Greek
Gift of beauty. il Life 55:52-67 Jl 19 '63
SCULPTURE, Greek (modern)
See also
Capralos, C.
SCULPTURE, Indian (East India)
Entranced anatomy; Indian sculpture collected by the Cleveland museum of art. il Time 84:80-1 O 30 '64
SCULPTURE, Italian
Horrors of Bomarzo; interview, ed. by M. L. B. Ambrosini. G. Borghese. il Harper 228: 66-71 Ap '64
See also
Manzù, G.
Michelangelo Buonarroti
Pisano, G.
Rosso, M.
SCULPTURE, Japanese
See also
Nagare, M.
SCULPTURE, Metal. See Metal sculpture
SCULPTURE, Mobile. See Mobiles
SCULPTURE, Primitive
See also
Sculpture, African
SCULPTURE, Religious. See Christian art and symbolism
SCULPTURE, Romanesque
Leo de Garius fecit, 1179. A. de Egry. il Art N 62:34-7+ Ja '64
SCULPTURE, Snow. See Snow modeling
SCULPTURE, Soap. See Soap sculpture
SCULPTURE, Spanish
See also
Gonzalez, J
Leodegari
SCULPTURE, Sumerian
Worshippers of Sumer; excerpt from History of mankind. L. Woolley. il UNESCO Courier 16:18-19 Je '63
SCULPTURE, Swiss
See also
Giacometti, A.
Kemeny, Z.
Müller, R.
SCULPTURE, Ukrainian
See also
Archipenko, A.
SCULPTURE, Venezuelan
See also
Escobar, M
SCULTHORP, Elsie Louise
Best ground covers to use with bulbs. House B 105:250-2 O '63
How to enhance the natural beauty of rock. House B 106:176-9+ Ap '64
Why a garden needs more than plants. House B 106:80-7 Ag '64
SCURR, J. W. Reginald
From a silk handkerchief. por Library J 88:2439-45 Je 15 '63
SEA. See Ocean
SEA anemones
2-Aminoethylphosphonic acid in insoluble protein of the sea anemone metridium dianthus. L. D. Quin. bibliog il Science 144: 1133-4 My 29 '64
SEA beaches. See Beaches
SEA bears. See Seals (animals)
SEA birds. See Water birds
SEA cows. See Manatees
SEA drum fishing. See Drumfish fishing
SEA elephants. See Elephant seals
SEA food
Let the sea nourish your health. E. Ubell. il House B 105:122-3 Je '63
See also
Clams
Cookery—Fish
Fish as food
Oysters
SEA gulls. See Gulls
SEA Hawk (destroyer escort) See Warships—United States
SEA-level canal. See Canals—Central America
SEA level changes
Recent high relative sea level stand near Recife, Brazil. T. H. Van Andel and J. Laborel. bibliog il Science 145:580-1 Ag 7 '64
Sea level and climate of the past century. W. L. Donn and D. M. Shaw. bibliog il Science 142:1166 N 29 '63
Sea level changes in the past 6000 years: possible archeological significance. F. P. Shepard. bibliog il Science 143:574-6 F 7 '64
Seas rise upon land. Sci N L 85:236 Ap 11 '64
SEA lions. See Seals (animals)
SEA OF CORTÉZ. See California, Gulf of
SEA otters
Recovery of a fur bearer. K. W. Kenyon. il Natur Hist 72:12-21 N '63
SEA planes. See Seaplanes
SEA power
Fighting ship still sails the sea. H. W. Baldwin. il N Y Times Mag p 14-15+ Ja 26 '64
New four ocean challenge; address, September 18, 1963. J. S. McCain, jr. Vital Speeches 30:57-61 N 1 '63
Seapower and the mid-South; address, May 21, 1963. F. Lee. Vital Speeches 29:690-3 S 1 '63
SEA products. See Marine resources
SEA shells. See Shells (conchology)

SEA shore. See Seashore

SEA sickness. See Seasickness

SEA sounds. See Ocean sounds

SEA turtles. See Turtles

SEA urchins
- Bending waves of the posterior flagellum of ceratium. C. J. Brokaw and L. Wright. bibliog il Science 142:1169-70 N 29 '63
- Cholinergic action of homogenates of sea urchin pedicellariae. E. G. Mendes and others. bibliog Science 139:408-9 F 1 '63
- Primitive heart in the echinoid strongylocentrotus purpuratus. R. A. Boolootian and J. L. Campbell. bibliog il Science 145:173-5 Jl 10 '64

SEA walls
- Asphalt promenade; Cape May, N.J. J. P. Sweitzer. il Am City 78:95-6 N '63

See also

Dikes (engineering)

SEA water
- Calcium carbonate: factors affecting saturation in ocean waters off Bermuda. R. F. Schmalz and K. E. Chave. bibliog il Science 139:1206-7 Mr 22 '63
- Electrolytic conductance of sea water: effect of calcium carbonate dissolution. K. Park. bibliog il Science 146:56-7 O 2 '64
- High pressure solubility of calcium carbonate in seawater. R. M. Pytkowicz and D. N. Conners. bibliog il Science 144:840-1 My 15 '64
- Mining the bottom of the sea; excerpts from study. R. Revelle. il Sat R 47:60-1 O 3 '64
- Noble gases in sea water. R. Bieri and others. bibliog il Science 146:1035-7 N 20 '64
- Scraping the bottom; new deposits of metals on the ocean floor. Newsweek 61:66 Ap 15 '63
- Sea water: saturation with apatites and carbonates. J. R. Kramer. bibliog il Science 146:637-8 O 30 '64
- Strontium content and variable strontium-chlorinity relationship of Sargasso sea water. F. T. Mackenzie. bibliog il Science 146:517-18 O 23 '64
- Suspended clay in a water sample from the deep ocean. J. J. Groot and M. Ewing. Science 142:579 N 1 '63
- Vast treasures untapped in the restless sea. Sci N L 85:118 F 22 '64

Desalting
- Big atom; solving the water shortage. C. Dreher. il Nation 197:451-4 D 28 '63; Same abr. with title A-power can end the water shortage. Sci Digest 56:57-60 Ag '64
- Boiling point; how atom can draw water and power from the seas. il Newsweek 63:68 Mr 16 '64
- Desalination of water. P. H. Abelson. Science 146:1533 D 18 '64
- Desalinization serves an island; Virgin Islands; electrodialysis plant in Buckeye, Ariz. il Am City 79:18 S '64
- How navy will desalt water in Cuba. il U S News 56:13 F 24 '64
- International symposium on water desalination to be held in 1965. Dept State Bul 51:417-18 S 21 '64
- Ion-exchange removal of sodium chloride from water with calcium hydroxide as recoverable regenerant. K. Popper and others. bibliog il Science 141:1038-9 S 13 '63
- Now, a drink from the sea. T. Willets. il Motor B 113:90-1+ Ja '64
- Politics of fresh water. D. E. Pesonen. il Nation 200:49-51 Ja 18 '65
- President moves to advance program on desalting of water. Dept State Bul 51:230-1 Ag 17 '64
- Reactor to desalt water. Sci N L 84:82 Ag 10 '63
- Report released on program to develop desalination; statement, October 25, 1964. L. B. Johnson. Dept State Bul 51:723-4 N 16 '64
- Rushing a Cuban water cure; Guantanamo. il Bsns W p34-5 Jl 4 '64
- Saltwater made fresh. Sci N L 85:381 Je 13 '64
- Squeezing sea water may solve the fresh-water shortage. W. Cloud. Pop Sci 185:21+ D '64
- U.S. and Israel to share cost of detailed survey on desalting; memorandum of understanding, statement, with text of memorandum; and report of joint team of experts. L. B. Johnson. Dept State Bul 51:724-6 N 16 '64
- U.S. and U.S.S.R. hold talks on desalting of sea water; joint memorandum, July 16, 1964; with list of U.S, U.S.S.R. representatives. Dept State Bul 51:144:5 Ag 3 '64
- U.S. and U.S.S.R. to cooperate in field of desalination; Department announcement with text of agreement. Dept State Bul 51:828-9 D 7 '64
- Water for Guantanamo. B. Tufty. il Sci N L 85:131 F 29 '64
- Water to order; Guantanamo naval base. E. J. Long. il Am For 70:25+ My '64
- Where we stand with water desalting. R. S. Fenton. il UNESCO Courier 17:28-31 Jl '64
- World is getting thirstier; hope to turn salt water into fresh. L. Galton. il N Y Times Mag p94+ S 27 '64

Pollution
- Aquatic pollution; report on symposium held by the Aquatic biology group of American society for microbiology. J. A. J. McLaughlin. Science 146:281+ O 9 '64

SEA water temperature. See Ocean temperature

SEA waves. See Waves

SEA waves, Seismic. See Seismic sea waves

SEABAUGH, Judy
- Please stop telling me that I have to have a baby. por Redbook 121:6+ My '63

SEABEE (airplane) See Airplanes, Amphibious

SEABOARD world airlines
- Construction will start in March on Seaboard's Kennedy terminal. J. W. Carter. Aviation W 81:26 D 28 '64

SEABORG, Glenn T.
- Age of nuclear power; excerpts from statement. por Sci N L 86:178 S 19 '64
- Common ground. Bul Atomic Sci 19:42-4 D '63
- Conference on peaceful uses of atomic energy opens at Geneva; statement, August 29, 1964. Dept State Bul 51:408-11 S 21 '64
- International atom; address, October 27, 1964. bibliog f Dept State Bul 51:779-86 N 30 '64
- Nuclear energy for the benefit of man; statement, September 15, 1964. Dept State Bul 51:519-24 O 12 '64
- Our heritage of the elements; address, October 19, 1964. Vital Speeches 31:90-4 N 15 '64
- Science and the humanities: a new level of symbiosis. bibliog Science 144:1199-203 Je 5 '64
- Science as a servant of historical knowledge; summary of address. New Repub 150:11-13 F 22 '64
- Statement, July 3, 1963. Dept State Bul 49:168-9 Jl 29 '63
- Training the creative scientist; address, May 7, 1963. Sci N L 83:314-17 My 18 '63
- Value of exchange. Bul Atomic Sci 19:25 S '63
- What it means to be a scientist; excerpts from address, May 5, 1964. Sci N L 85:314-15+ My 16 '64

—and Fritsch, A. R.
- Synthetic elements; with biographical sketches. Sci Am 208:38, 68-78 bibliog(p200) Ap '63

—and McNamara, R. S.
- Letter to the President from Chairman of Atomic energy commission and Secretary of defense, May 18, 1964. Dept State Bul 51:94-5 Jl 20 '64

about
- As plutonium fades, AEC calls industry in. il por Bsns W p58-60+ D 26 '64
- Franklin medal to Seaborg. Sci N L 84:242 O 19 '63
- Red carpet out for Seaborg; findings on visit to Russia. pors Bsns W p 100-2+ Je 15 '63
- Science and the general welfare in a democracy. P. H. Abelson. Science 144:957 My 22 '64; Reply. S. C. Mohr. 145:660 Ag 14 '64

SEABROOK, C. S.
- Storm-sewer design factors. por Am City 79:76-8 Jl '64

SEABURY, Paul. See Lipset, S. M. jt. auth.

SEABURY, Samuel
- Man who rode the tiger, by H. Mitgang. Review
  - Am Heritage 14:100-1 Je '63
  - Sat R 46:43 Mr 30 '63. R. A. Low

SEABURY investigation. See New York (city) —Politics and government

SEAFARERS' international union of North America
- Battle of the Great Lakes. W. J. Eaton. il Reporter 29:38-40 N 21 '63
- Canada gets the ships moving, at a price. Bsns W p51+ N 2 '63
- Canadian judge drops bomb on sea unions; proposal for government take-over of maritime unions. Bsns W p85 Jl 20 '63
- Great Lakes labor war. H. Bruce. il Nation 197:298-300 N 9 '63

SEAFARERS' international union of North America—*Continued*
Labor's mutinous mariners. A. H. Raskin. il Atlan 214:72-8 N '64
Lakes open up, but for how long? labor dispute threatens. Bsns W p 125 Mr 28 '64
Mutiny on the Great Lakes. T. R. Brooks. Commonweal 79:278-80 N 29 '63
Peace plan for the Lakes; trusteeship to run Canadian unions. Bsns W p50 Ag 10 '63
Trouble on the waterfront. Time 83:30 Mr 27 '64
Union row roiling Great Lakes again. Seafarers international union and Canadian maritime union. il Bsns W p 100 Je 8 '63
Why unions are at war on the Great Lakes; SIU vs. Canadian maritime union. il U S News 55:91-2 S 23 '63

SEAFARING life
See also
Whaling

SEAGER, Allan
Cure; story; excerpt from Frieze of girls. Atlan 213:62-8 F '64
Precocious champions. Holiday 35:110+ Je '64
Rope; story. Atlan 215:79-82 Ja '65

SEAGER, Ralph W.
First day after Christmas; poem. McCalls 92:109 Ja '65
Love has both eyes open; poem. McCalls 91:140 Ja '64
Trailing arbutus; poem. McCalls 90:166 Ag '63

SEAGOING platforms for acoustic research. See Ships, Research

SEAGULLS. See Gulls

SEAL BEACH Leisure World, Calif. See Aged —Housing

SEAL hunting
My Eskimo adventure. G. M. Daetz. il Outdoor Life 131:48-9+ F '63

SEAL rescue operation. See Military training

SEALAB-I. See Underwater structures

SEALE, Patrick
Arab against Arab. New Repub 149:11-13 D 14 '63
Arab unity evaporating. New Repub 149:11-12 Jl 13 '63
Emergence of the Ba'ath. New Repub 148:7-8 Mr 23 '63
Syria in flux. New Repub 149:9-10 S 14 '63

SEALING compositions
New epoxy stops leaks. J. Joseph. il Pop Sci 183:107-9+ Ag '63
New rubber sealer is almost indestructible; silicone rubber. il Pop Sci 184:102 Mr '64
Useful sealants & adhesives. B. Cobb, jr. Yachting 115:178-9 Je '64

SEALOCK, Richard B.
New ALA officer. J. C. Shipman. por ALA Bul 57:661-2 Jl '63

SEALS (animals)
Diving depths of the Weddell seal. A. L. DeVries and D. E. Wohlschlag. bibliog il Science 145:292 Jl 17 '64
Glimpse of Eden; friendship between a woman and a wild seal. N. W. Hooke. il Sat Eve Post 237:30-1 N 14 '64
Hawaiian monk seal; Leeward Islands. D. W. Rice. il Natur Hist 73:48-55 F '64
Lobos Island; home of two kinds of sea lions: hair seals and fur seals (sea bears) E. C. Uriburu. il Américas 15:33-7 Je '63
Locomotion in pinnipeds. C. Ray. il Natur Hist 72:10-21 Mr '63
Male sea lion shows little father love. Sci N L 85:152 Mr 7 '64
Seals are about gone. J. Van Nostrand. il Am Heritage 14:10-17+ Je '63
Seals in Antarctica are record deep-sea divers; Weddell seal. Sci N L 86:72 Ag 1 '64
Sonar signals of the sea lion. T. C. Poulter. Science 139:753-5 F 22 '63
See also
Elephant seals
North Pacific fur seal commission

SEAMAN, Elwood A.
American fisheries society. Science 143:1237-40 Mr 13 '64

SEAMANS, Robert C. jr
Post-Apollo programs detailed; summary of interview, ed. by H. Taylor. Miss & Roc 15:14 O 26 '64

SEAMANSHIP. See Navigation

SEAMEN
Crew life in Newport. E. B. Morris. il Yachting 116:46-8+ S '64
Developing a 12-meter crew. E. B. Morris. il Yachting 116:44-6+ Jl '64
Hands and berths; story of the Corinthians. M. H. Farnham. il Motor B 111:47+ F '63
How to organize a crew bank. E. A. Walker. il Yachting 115:220-1 My '64
If there were two ships, it was a race. A. Villiers. il Sports Illus 21:27-9 Jl 20 '64
Men and the boats; portfolio. Yachting 116:50-9 S '64
See also
National maritime union of America

Wages and hours

Our strike-strangled merchant marine. R. S. Strother. Read Digest 82:75-9 F '63

SEAPLANES
Beriev urges 2,000-passenger seaplane. il Aviation W 79:127+ S 23 '63
PBY water bombers battle forest fires in Quebec. D. A. Brown. il Aviation W 81:66-8+ Ag 3 '64
Pilot report; go jump in the lake. A. H. Sanfelici. il Flying 74:40-1+ Je '64
When boats had wings. W. S. Griswold. il Pop Sci 182:71-9+ Je '63
See also
Airboats
Airplanes, Amphibious
Ground effect machines

Landing

Smooth landing on smooth water. W. F. Gabella. il Flying 74:47+ Je '64

SEAPORTS. See Ports

SEARCH and rescue unit. See Rescue work

SEARCH for a man; story. See Harrington, J.

SEARCHES and seizure
Cops v. the courts; standards of police search and seizure. Time 84:59-60 Ag 28 '64
Protecting the right of privacy. P. B. Kurland. il PTA Mag 58:10-12 Mr '64
U.S. protests to Soviet Union on incident involving U.S. vessel; Department statement, July 17, 1964. Dept State Bul 51:145 Ag 3 '64

SEARES, Frederick H.
Obituary
Sky & Tel por 28:123+ S '64

SEARLE, Ronald
Mush, mush, a brisk look at the Snowshoe state. il Holiday 34:44-53 Jl '63
Out in the sun again. il Sports Illus 20:16-23 Mr 2 '64

SEARLES, John E.
Brasilia. Sch Arts 63:24-8 O '63

SEARLES, Sidney Z.
Bulldozers at your door. Read Digest 83:83-7 S '63

SEARLS, Hank
Pilgrim project; story. Sat Eve Post 237:44-6 Ap 11; 52-3 Ap 18 '64

SEARS, Eleonora
Bostonian unique; Miss Sears. C. Amory. por Vogue 141:80-3 F 15 '63

SEARS, Gerald W. See Donn, B. jt. auth.

SEARS, Paul B.
Pacific tropical botanical garden. Science 147:241 Ja 15 '65
Time to pause and regroup? Science 144:1297 Je 12 '64
Vegetation, climate, and coastal submergence in Connecticut. bibliog Science 140:59-60 Ap 5 '63

SEARS, Stephen W.
Trail blazer of the Far West. Am Heritage 14:60-4+ Je '63

SEARS, Roebuck and company
Art at Sears. F. Getlein. New Repub 148:27-8 Ap 20 '63
Buy fund shares in supermarkets? U S News 55:120 D 9 '63
Four Ms of Sears. il Time 83:62+ Ja 31 '64
General who built the world's largest store. J. Reddy. Read Digest 84:181-5 Ja '64
How Sears, Roebuck plans for the future. N. Buckley. il Duns R 82:44-6+ O '63
Mail-order chic. il Life 56:57+ Mr 20 '64
Sears makes it look easy. J. McDonald. il Fortune 69:120-7+ My '64
Sears recants fund plan. Bsns W p 130 F 23 '63
Sears, Roebuck calls the doctor; Community medical assistance program. L. L. Golden. Sat R 47:75 D 12 '64
Sears tries the big time. G. Moore. il Motor T 16:58-9 Ap '64
Way being cleared for Sears mutuals. Bsns W p 134 Mr 9 '63
See also
Allstate enterprises, incorporated

SEASHORE, Stanley E. See Likert, R. jt. auth.

SEASHORE
Life guide; spectacular seashores. Life 54:16 Je 14 '63
Season for seashore and seaports. M. Gough. il House B 105:46+ Jl '63
World by the sea. B. Thielen. il Holiday 35: 72-7+ My '64
See also
Beaches
Sand dunes
SEASHORE houses. See Beach architecture
SEASHORE vegetation
Waterside gardening. F. F. Rockwell. il Flower Grower 50:49-51 S '63
SEASICKNESS
Seasickness. J. Henderson. il Motor B 111: 42-3+ Ap '63
SEASIDE resorts
See also
Blackpool, England
Summer resorts
SEASON in Spain; story. See Toney, R.
SEASONAL labor
Now the White House controls summer jobs. U S News 54:8 Mr 4 '63
U.S. summer jobs: pull vs. merit. U S News 54:10 Ap 22 '63
See also
Migrant labor
SEASONINGS
Add a dash and taste the difference! il Bet Hom & Gard 41:102-3 O '63
Flavor, the secret of good cooking. M. Johnston and P. McBride. il Bet Hom & Gard 42:66-7+ Mr '64
Gourmet travel kit: seasonings, flavorings, drink additives. M. Kaytor. il Look 28:88-9 My 5 '64
See also
Capers
Monosodium glutamate
SEASONS
How to live with the four seasons. M. E. Falter. House & Gard 126:28+ S '64
See also
Autumn
Spring
Summer
Winter
SEAT belts. See Safety belts
SEATS
Color-coded seats prevent delay; Long Beach arena. W. Hanssen. il Am City 78:95 Ag '63
How does your seat rate? il Sci Digest 54: 43-4 Ag '63
See also
Automobiles—Seats
Boats—Seats
SEATS, Chair. See Chair seats
SEATTLE
Airports
What happened at Seattle? R. Bach. il Flying 74:33 Ap '64
Architecture
Unusual structural wall for IBM in Seattle. il Arch Rec 134:104-7 D '63
Art
Eighteenth-century porcelain in Seattle. il Antiques 85:80-5 Ja '64
Seattle sketches of Mark Tobey. il Am Artist 27:56+ My '63
Century 21 exposition, 1962
Librarians' image improved, says report on Library 21. Library J 88:2222 Je 1 '63
Library 21 goes home. Wilson Lib Bul 37:836 Je '63
Library 21 report. Wilson Lib Bul 37:830 Je '63
Library 21: what was its meaning? C. Field. Library J 88:831 F 15 '63
Reverie on Puget Sound. R. Stokes. Library J 88:974 Mr 1 '63
Science exhibits; at Seattle fair, federal funds, scientists helped, New Yorkers try a different tack. J. Walsh. il Science 140: 960-2 My 31 '63
Description
Seattle after the ball. H. Sutton. il Sat R 46: 53-4 O 5 '63
Education
Seattle: when nonachievers shun the library; Garfield high school. V. Smith. ALA Bul 58:817-19 O '64
Traveling study collections: museums into the classroom. F. Cochran. Sr Schol 85: 21T Ja 21 '65
Electric power
Power lines go underground. A. C. Tyler. il Am City 79:105-6 Ag '64
Galleries and museums
World wide antique artifacts; Seattle art museum. H. D. Brown. il Hobbies 69:123+ Ap '64
Gardens
But not everyone needs or wants a lawn. il Sunset 131:76-7 S '63
Hotels, restaurants, etc.
South Pacific long house on waterfront. il Arch Rec 136:216 S '64
Lighting
Keeping 40,000 lights in good repair. J. M. Nelson. il Am City 79:147+ Je '64
Music
[Musical events] (cont) Mus Am 83:74+ D '63; 84:23-4 Ap; 63-4 D '64
Pacific science center
Pacific science center. D. Wolfle. Science 142: 345 O 18 '63; Reply. R. S. Weiss. 143:639 F 14 '64
Police
Tall in the cockpit; Seattle harbor police. E. Crimmin. il Motor B 113:24-5+ My '64
Rapid transit
Safer transit system. E. J. Slingerland. il Am City 79:105 Ja '64
Sanitary affairs
Good contract collection. R. W. Morse. il Am City 78:191-2+ S '63
Social life and customs
Families by the boatload; Seattle's boating family of the year. E. Crimmin. il Motor B 111:106+ Ap '63
Theater
New Rainier; Seattle repertory theater. Time 82:73 N 29 '63
Rise of rep. il Time 83:54-5+ F 14 '64
Water supply
Water insurance pays dividends; Tolt River project. E. J. Allen. il Am City 79:100-2 My '64
SEATTLE center playhouse. See Seattle—Theater
SEATTLE public library
Seattle goes Scandinavian; Ballard branch. R. Mostar. il Library J 88:4553-4 D 1 '63
SEATTLE yacht club. See Yacht clubs
SEAVER, Edwin
Solving the human enigma. Sat R 46:27-8 My 18 '63
SEAVEY, Joseph S.
Tennis boom. Recreation 57:282 Je '64
SEAWALLS. See Sea walls
SEAWEED. See Kelp
SEBACEOUS glands
What medical science can do about acne. B. H. Frisch. Sci Digest 57:61-4 Ja '65
SEBERG, Jean
Innocence abroad. por Newsweek 61:95 My 6 '63
Jean Seberg. P. Hamill. pors Sat Eve Post 236:22-3 Je 15 '63
Jean Seberg revisited. E. Miller. il por Seventeen 22:130-1+ Mr '63
Under the locusts; Lilith on location. New Yorker 39:23 Ag 17 '63
SECHENOV, I. M.
Brain reflexes. D. P. Purpura and H. Waelsch. Science 143:598+ F 7 '64
SECHZER, Jeri A. and Brown, J. L.
Color discrimination in the cat. bibliog Science 144:427-9 Ap 24 '64; Summary. Sci Am 210:59 Je '64
SECKEL, Margaret
Great art in the elementary library. Library J 88:4813-16 D 15 '63
SECOND advent
Trumpeter of doomsday; Millerites. H. A. Larrabee. il Am Heritage 15:34-7+ Ap '64
Word. V. P. McCorry. America 109:690 N 23 '63
SECOND chance; story. See Freeman, J. T.
SECOND committee of the General assembly. See United Nations—Economic and financial committee
SECOND glance; story. See Cavanaugh, A.
SECOND time around; story. See Fisher, M. F. K.
SECONDARY batteries. See Storage batteries

SECONDARY education. See Education, Secondary

SECONDARY school teachers. See Teachers

SECONDHAND boats. See Boats, Used

SECONDHAND cameras. See Cameras, Used

SECONDS. See Time measurements

SECOR (artificial satellite) See Artificial satellites—Mapping applications

SECRET agents. See Spies

SECRET army organization (Organisation de l'armée secrète)
L'affaire Argoud. Time 81:33 Mr 8 '63
Better than the firing squad; life sentence for Curutchet. il Time 84:35 Jl 10 '64
Demned elusive. . . BBC-TV interview with G. Bidault. il Newsweek 61:48+ Mr 18 '63
Determined ones. il Time 81:40 Mr 15 '63
Finis for S.A.O? il Time 81:32 Ap 5 '63
Kidnaped. A. Argoud. Nat R 15:15-16 Jl 16 '63; Reply. J. Soustelle. 15:209 S 10 '63
Man in the middle. Time 83:29 Ja 10 '64
No blindfold; execution of Lt. Col. Jean-Marie Bastien-Thiry. il Newsweek 61:47 Mr 25 '63
Package of treason. Newsweek 61:40+ Mr 11 '63
Partial remission; de Gaulle grants pardons to former OAS members. Newsweek 65:27 Ja 4 '65

SECRET defense information. See Defense information, Classified

SECRET integration; story. See Pynchon, T.

SECRET place; story. See Stern, R. M.

SECRET police, Russian. See Secret service—Russia

SECRET room; story. See Robbe-Grillet, A.

SECRET service
Craft of intelligence. A. Dulles. il Harper 226:128-74 Ap '63
See also
World war, 1939-1945—Secret service

France
Kidnaped. A. Argoud. Nat R 15:15-16 Jl 16 '63; Reply. J. Soustelle. 15:209 S 10 '63

Germany (Federal Republic)
Espionage; costly baby: spies for Russia in West Germany. Newsweek 62:40-1 Jl 22 '63
Failure of intelligence; Gehlen organization. Newsweek 62:34 Ag 5 '63
Triple double. il Time 82:26 Jl 19 '63

Great Britain
And then there were three. il Time 82:27 Jl 12 '63
Anticlimax; the Denning report. Newsweek 62:51 O 7 '63
Blushing James Bond. A. Burnet. New Repub 149:9-10 Ag 17 '63
Ineffectual but innocent; Lord Denning's report. il Time 82:40-1 O 4 '63
New uproar in Britain over security; summary of Denning report. il U S News 55:8 O 7 '63
Sagacious end of the affairs; Denning report. Life 55:4 O 11 '63
Theydunit. Newsweek 62:22+ Jl 15 '63

Russia
Big brother is still watching. E. Crankshaw. il N Y Times Mag p8+ D 29 '63
Composite portrait of the Soviet spy. H. M. Hyde. il N Y Times Mag p 14+ F 16 '64
Gumshoe. Newsweek 63:38 Ja 27 '64
KGB, your friendly agent. Newsweek 65:26 Ja 4 '65
Key defector. Sr Schol 84:18 Mr 13 '64
Mystery of a Russian who fled to the west. il U S News 56:8 F 24 '64

United States
Craft of intelligence. A. Dulles. il Harper 226:128-74 Ap '63
Facts about the Secret service; report. il U S News 55:62 D 16 '63
Mr Q mystery; case against agent Bolden. il Newsweek 63:20 Je 1 '64
Moment of tragedy. il U S News 55:6 D 2 '63
See also
Presidential candidates—Protection
Presidents—United States—Protection
United States—Central intelligence agency
Vice-Presidents—United States—Protection

SECRET societies
See also
Ku Klux klan
Mafia

South Africa
See also
Broederbond (League of brothers)

SECRET tournament; story. See Sourian, P.

SECRET writing. See Ciphers

SECRETARIES
English secretaries must have nous; British secretaries in New York. L. W. Robinson. il N Y Times Mag p 16+ D 20 '64
Executive's long right arm. il Bsns W p42-4+ Ag 8 '64
Really, now; ban on English secretaries in New York city. Newsweek 64:74 Jl 13 '64
Reverse English; British secretaries barred entry to New York city. il Time 84:91 Jl 10 '64

SECRETARIES, Association of council. See Association of council secretaries

SECRETARIES, Legal
Job no young lawyer can afford to turn down. il Time 83:66-7 Je 5 '64

SECRETARIES of defense (United States)
Centralization forces reorganization. il Miss & Roc 12:95-7+ Mr 25 '63

SECRETARIES of state (United States)
How would you like to be secretary of state? M. W. Childs. NEA J 53:57 S '64

SECRETARY General of the United Nations. See United Nations—Secretary General

SECRETARYS manuals. See Office manuals

SECRETIONS
Electrophysiologic indications of the osmoregulatory role of the teleost urophysis. K. Yagi and H. A. Bern. bibliog il Science 142:491-3 O 25 '63
Trans-2-dodecenal and 2-methyl-1, 4-quinone produced by a millipede. J. W. Wheeler and others. bibliog Science 144:540-1 My 1 '64
See also
Bile
Pheromones

SECRETS, Book of. See Manuscripts, Hebrew

SECRETS, Official. See Official secrets

SECRETS, Trade. See Trade secrets

SECRIST, John, collection. See Phonograph records—Collectors and collecting

SECTS
Africa's prophet movements. R. C. Mitchell. Christian Cent 81:1427-9 N 18 '64
Black Jews of Harlem: Negro nationalism and the dilemmas of Negro leadership, by H. Brotz. Review
Commentary 38:77-9 O '64. N. Glazer
Future of the denominations in an ecumenical era; excerpt from What's ahead for the churches. M. E. Marty. Cath World 200:34-41 O '64
Kingdom of King Narcisse. L. Robinson. il Ebony 18:112+ Jl '63
Peace churches as communities of discernment. J. L. Burkholder. Christian Cent 80:1072-5 S 4 '63
West meets East; self-realization fellowship. il Time 82:45 Ag 30 '63
See also
Church of God
Church unity
Churches of Christ
Jehovah's Witnesses
Mennonites
Plymouth brethren
Shakers

SECULAR institutes
See also
Opus Dei

SECULARISM
Catholic science textbooks? V. E. Smith. America 110:78-80+ Ja 18 '64; Discussion. 110:208, 270 F 15, 29 '64
Charles Bradlaugh and the secularists. W. S. Smith. Christian Cent 80:331-4 Mr 13 '63
Dilemma of modern belief, by S. H. Miller. Review
Christian Cent 80:1206 O 2 '63. A. P. Klausler
Facing the secular. H. Cox. Commonweal 79:619-22 F 21 '64
Faith in a secular age. P. Schlueter. Christian Cent 80:805 Je 19 '63
Interfaith dialogue and church-state issues. B. J. Coughlin. America 108:900-3 Je 29 '63

SECURITIES
Fed cuts long-term buying; operation nudge. Bsns W p54 My 11 '63
See also
Bonds
Investments
Investments, Foreign
Municipal bonds
also subhead Securities under various subjects, e.g. Eelctric utilities—Securities

SECURITIES—*Continued*

Advertising

U.S. pitch at British investors stirs the city; Merrill Lynch's advertising. il Bsns W p 134+ Ap 13 '63

Marketing

Deadlock on the floor; controversy over floor trading. Newsweek 63:69 Ap 6 '64
How they raise money without much of a fuss; private placement of debt issues. il Bsns W p 164+ O 17 '64
M.I.P. variations; New York stock exchange's monthly investment plan. Fortune 69:205 Mr '64
New York; criminal infiltration of the securities industry. L. J. Lefkowitz. Ann Am Acad 347:51-7 My '63
On the floor; controversy between New York stock exchange and Securities and exchange commission over floor trading. Newsweek 63:101-2 Ap 20 '64
Private route to new capital; direct placements. J. Ross-Skinner. il Duns R 81:35-6+ Ja '63
Second thoughts on going public; management research survey. Bsns W p 114 F 16 '63
Two horses; position of Stock exchange specialist. Newsweek 63:66 F 3 64
Wall Street musters its defenses; SEC's study of floor trading and stock specialists. il Bsns W p84-6 Jl 27 '63
Wall Street's main event: SEC vs. the specialists. T. A. Wise. il Fortune 69:149-52+ My '64

Private placement

See Securities—Marketing

Regulation

Breathing spell on SEC action. Bsns W p 170+ Ap 20 '63
Choir of approval; proposed changes in U.S. securities laws. Newsweek 61:74 Je 17 '63

SECURITIES, Fraudulent
Re the Res; stock rigging. Newsweek 62:70 Jl 22 '63
Scrap paper. Newsweek 61:76 My 13 '63

SECURITIES, Privately placed. See Securities —Marketing

SECURITIES, Tax exempt
Opening tax-exempts to smaller investors; tax-exempt bond funds. il Bsns W p72-4+ D 21 '63
See also
Taxation, Exemption from

SECURITIES, Unclaimed
Billions of dollars unclaimed! A. Rankin. Read Digest 84:77-81 My '64

SECURITIES and exchange commission. See United States—Securities and exchange commission

SECURITY. See Internal security; International security; Social and economic security

SECURITY and consular affairs, Bureau of. See United States—State, Department of—Security and consular affairs, Bureau of

SECURITY and insecurity (psychology)
Art of being secure; address, January 21, 1964. R. M. Blough. Vital Speeches 30: 282-6 F 15 '64
Everybody's lonesome. D. G. Francisco. il Parents Mag 38:136 Ap '63
Meaning of security. M. Wolf. il Parents Mag 38:64+ D '63
Touch of reassurance; with study-discussion program, by R. Strong. D. K. Osborn and P. P. W. Knapp. bibliog il PTA Mag 58: 10-12, 35 D '63
What parents ask about children's fears. M. J. E. Senn. il McCalls 90:74+ Ap '63

SECURITY classification (government documents)
New turmoil over security; Otepka case. il U S News 55:48 N 25 '63
Q-clearance: the development of a personnel security program. H. P. Green. il Bul Atomic Sci 20:9-15 My '64
Those confidential files. Nation 198:178 F 24 '64
Top-secret mania. L. A. Stevens. il Nation 197:218-21 O 12 '63
See also
Defense information, Classified

SECURITY clearance program. See United States—Atomic energy commission

SECURITY council of the United Nations. See United Nations—Security council

SECURITY service. See Secret service

SEDATIVES
See also
Barbiturates
Tranquilizing drugs

SEDIMENTATION and deposition
Age and accumulation rate of dolomite-bearing carbonate sediments in South Australia. H. C. W. Skinner and others. bibliog Science 139:335-6 Ja 25 '63
Carotenoids in sediments as a function of environment. R. B. Schwendinger and J. G. Erdman. bibliog il Science 141:808-10 Ag 30 '63
Genesis of hydrocarbons of low molecular weight in organic-rich aquatic systems. J. D. Mulik and J. G. Erdman. bibliog il Science 141:806-7 Ag 30 '63
Ionene: a thermal degradation product of β-carotene. W. C. Day and J. G. Erdman. bibliog il Science 141:808 Ag 30 '63
Marine sediments: effects of a tube-building polychaete. E. W. Fager. bibliog il Science 143:356-9 Ja 24 '64
Periodic phenomena observed with spherical particles in horizontal pipes. D. G. Thomas. bibliog il Science 144:534-6 My 1 '64
Pile of ocean dregs under Argentine basin. Sci N L 85:104 F 15 '64
Pollen accumulation rates: estimates from late-glacial sediment of Rogers Lake. M. B. Davis and E. S. Deevey, jr. bibliog il Science 145:1293-5 S 18 '64
Size distributions of sedimentary populations. J. J. W. Rogers and C. Schubert. bibliog il Science 141:801-2 Ag 30 '63
Sonar probing in Narragansett Bay. H. E. Edgerton and others. il Science 146:1459-60 D 11 '64
Sterols in recent aquatic sediments. R. B. Schwendinger and J. G. Erdman. bibliog il Science 144:1575-6 Je 26 '64
Time's traces in sediment. D. B. Ericson and G. Wollin. il Natur Hist 72:52-61 F '63
Varved marine sediments in a stagnant fjord. M. G. Gross and others. bibliog il Science 141:918-19 S 6 '63
See also
Deep sea deposits

SEDITION
Assorted enemies. Reporter 29:14+ S 26 '63
See also
Trials (sedition)

SEDUMS
Sedum cauticolum. D. Klaber. il Pop Gard 14: 17 My '63
Sun & rock lovers. E. W. Finch. il Flower Grower 50:36-7+ Ag '63

SEDWICK, Frank
Figaro's forebears. Opera N 27:25-6 Mr 9 '63

SEE, Elliot, jr
How much light in earthshine? Life 55:86B S 27 '63

SEE, Richard
Mechanical translation and related language research. bibliog Science 144:621-6 My 8 '64

SEED boxes (horticulture) See Flats, etc (horticulture)

SEED catalogs. See Catalogs, Seed and plant

SEED potatoes. See Potatoes

SEED spreaders. See Garden tools, equipment and supplies

SEEDING
Best time of year: spring planting. B. Black. il Pop Gard 14:28-32 Mr '63
Flower grower's home garden notebook. J. B. Brimer. il Flower Grower 51:35-6 Jl '64
Timely planting boosts yields. L. E. Zeman. il Suc Farm 62:96 F '64
See also
Corn—Seeding

SEEDING, Indoor. See Flats, etc (horticulture)

SEEDLINGS
Culture of small barley embryos on defined media. K. Norstog and J. E. Smith. bibliog il Science 142:1655-6 D 27 '63
Fine seedlings deserve the best care. K. S. Taylor. il Horticulture 42:38-9+ Ap '64
How to establish late summer seedlings. Suc Farm 61:35 Ag '63
To keep heat off young seedlings. il Sunset 130:283 Ap '63
See also
Flats, etc (horticulture)

SEEDS
Dehydration of seeds in intact tomato fruits. W. J. McIlrath and others. il Science 142: 1681-2 D 27 '63
Glucose transfer from adenosine diphosphate-glucose to starch in preparations of waxy seeds. O. E. Nelson and C. Y. Tsai. bibliog il Science 145:1194-5 S 11 '64
Make sure seed is tops. G. W. McKee. Suc Farm 62:58-9 F '64
Trees and shrubs from seed. il Sunset 133: 252+ N '64

SEEDS—*Continued*
You can still sow seeds: month of November. Sunset 131:278+ N '63
Your own dried herbs and seeds. il Sunset 131:176 Ag '63
See also
Flowers—Seed
Germination
Pine—Seed

Dispersal

Seed discharge in arceuthobium: a photographic study. T. E. Hinds and others. bibliog il Science 140:1236-8 Je 14 '63

Germination

See Germination

SEEDS, Effect of radioactivity on. See Plants, Effect of radioactivity on

SEEGER, Daniel Andrew
Conscience and religion. America 111:771 D 12 '64
Religious agnostic. por Newsweek 63:27-8 F 3 '64
Supreme being clause held invalid. Christian Cent 81:197-8 F 12 '64

SEEGER, Pete
Pete Seeger talks to teens. por Seventeen 22:148+ N '63
about
Minstrel with a mission. il pors Life 57:61-2+ O 9 '64
Under two flags. Nation 196:279 Ap 6 '63

SEEGERS, Kathleen Walker
Brazil's big dust bowl. Read Digest 83:212-16+ Jl '63
—See Seegers, S. W. jt. auth.

SEEGERS, Scott, and Seegers, K. W.
Colombia's extraordinary teacher-builder. Read Digest 82:111-15 Mr '63
Sister Dulce. Cath World 199:230-7 Jl '64

SEEMAN, Bernard
Sleep for sale? Todays Health 42:22-3+ S '64

SEFERIADES, Giorgos Stylianou
From Mythistorema; excerpts from poems. Life 56:76+ Ja 17 '64
King of Asine: poem. Sat R 46:19 N 30 '63
Letter to a foreign friend; tr. by N. Valaorites. Poetry 105:50-9 O '64
Santorini; Salamis in Cyprus; Three mules; poems, tr. by E. Keeley and P. Sherrard. Poetry 105:44-9 O '64
about
Contemporary Greek. D. S. Carne-Ross. Poetry 101:285-6 Ja '63
George Seferis. K. Friar. por Sat R 46:16-20 N 30 '63
Giorgos Seferiades wins 1963 Nobel prize. Pub W 184:27-8 N 4 '63
Greek poet's odyssey; with report by R. Warner. il pors Life 56:75-6+ Ja 17 '64
Harsh and tender greatness. por Newsweek 62:52 N 4 '63
Letter from Athens; tr. by K. Hourmousiades. V. Vassilikos. Poetry 105:60-4 O '64

SEFERIS, George. See Seferiades, G. S.

SEGAL, Aaron
Israel and Zionism. Nation 197:293-6 N 9 '63
—See Rosberg, C. G. jr, jt. auth.

SEGAL, Bernard
Young artists exhibit. Sch Arts 64:38-9 Ja '65

SEGAL, David I.
Requiem. Commonweal 79:262-3 N 22 '63

SEGAL, Evalyn F. and Holloway, S. M.
Timing behavior in rats with water drinking as a mediator. bibliog Science 140:888-9 My 24 '63

SEGAL, George
Him. il por Newsweek 64:101A+ N 9 '64
Modern plaster master. il pors Life 56:103-4+ Je 19 '64
People are talking about. . . il por Vogue 143:98-9 Mr 15 '64
Segal's vital mummies. A. Kaprow. il por Art N 62:30-3+ F '64
They paint; you recognize. il por Time 83:74-5+ Ap 3 '64

SEGAL, Lore
Beating of the girl; story. Sat Eve Post 236:46-7 N 23 '63
Other people's houses (cont) New Yorker 40:36-46 Mr 21; 39-44+ Je 13; 30-8+ Jl 25 '64

SEGAL, Stanton, and others
Galactose metabolism by rat liver tissue: influence of age. bibliog Science 142:1311-13 D 6 '63

SEGALL, Ascher
Radiogeology and population exposure to background radiation in northern New England. bibliog Science 140:1337-9 Je 21 '63

SEGALL, Marshall H. and others
Cultural differences in the perception of geometric illusions. bibliog Science 139:769-71; 140:422+ F 22, Ap 26 '63

SEGNI, Antonio
Atlantic partnership; address, January 15, 1964. Vital Speeches 30:258-60 F 15 '64
President Segni of Italy visits the United States; exchange of greetings, January 14, 1964. Dept State Bul 50:196 8 F 10 '64
about
Scramble for succession. Newsweek 64:37 D 21 '64
Workweek; visit to Washington. il por Newsweek 63:16 Ja 27 '64

SEGOVIA, Andrés
Legend behind the guitar. M. Mayer. il por N Y Times Mag p36+ F 16 '64

SEGREGATION, Social
Are we segregating our children? with program for discussion group, by M. R. Sherwin. D. Dodson. il Parents Mag 38:52, 70-1+ S '63
How ghettos destroy people. Sci Digest 54:74-5 Ag '63
See also
Discrimination in housing
Negroes in the United States—Segregation

SEGREGATION in education
Dimensions of democracy in education; address, October 23, 1964. C. A. Thomas. Vital Speeches 31:74-8 N 15 '64
Facts of de facto. il Time 82:30-1 Ag 2 '63
Lag in some schools; specific proposals to aid in solving the problems of minority-group education. L. M. Grande. America 108:438-9 Mr 30 '63
Racial balance in schools. R. F. Drinan. America 110:158-60 F 1 '64
Racial integration in education; excerpt from Integration vs. segregation, ed. by H. H. Humphrey. Sch & Soc 92:97-100 Mr 7 '64
What's happening in education? neighborhood-school policy. W. D. Boutwell. PTA Mag 58:33-4 S '63

SEGREGATION of libraries. See Libraries and Negroes

SEGREGATION of Negroes. See Negroes in the United States—Segregation

SEIB, Charles B.
New business spokesman urges positive approach. Nations Bsns 52:42-3+ My '64
Regulators pinpoint new targets. Nations Bsns 51:38-9+ F '63
White House gears up for campaign year. Nations Bsns 51:40-1+ O '63
Who framed the tax plan. Nations Bsns 51:32-3+ Ap '63
—See Otten, A. L. jt. auth.

SEIB, Kathleen Hurst
Saga of my seventeenth summer; story. Seventeen 22:74-5 Je; 96-7 Jl '63

SEIBERLING, Dorothy
Artist has some answers. Life 56:83 Ja 31 '64
Scarred, scrubbed, remade, they can't let it alone. Life 55:36 Ag 9 '63
about
Art editor with a biblical mission. G. P. Hunt. por Life 57:5 D 25 '64

SEIBU of Los Angeles (store) See Los Angeles—Stores

SEICHES
Alaskan earthquake of 27 March 1964: remote seiche stimulation. W. L. Donn. bibliog il Science 145:261 Jl 17 '64

SEIDEL, Frederick
Verse. L. Bogan. New Yorker 39:210-11 O 12 '63

SEIDEL, Harris
Empty water mains; condensed report. Am City 78:33 Ap '63

SEIDENBAUM, Art
AH: making of My fair lady. McCalls 92:96-8+ O '64
—See Dickert, L. jt. auth.

SEIDENSTICKER, Edward
Reasons for travel. Atlan 212:122+ Jl '63
(tr) See Yamakawa, M. Talisman

SEIDMAN, Joel
Liberals and the labor movement. Mo Labor R 87:132-3 F '64
Union agenda for security. Mo Labor R 86:636-44 Je '63

SEIFERT, Harvey
False faces for freedom. Christian Cent 81:1265-7 O 14 '64

SEIFERT, Walt
Lake Erie's living legend. Field & S 69:34-5+ Ag '64

SEILER, John A.
Diagnosing interdepartmental conflict. bibliog f Harvard Bsns R 41:121-32 S '63
SEIM, Dick, and Braun, Dick
Now color helps sell eggs. Farm J 87:26-7+ Je '63
SEINE RIVER
Down the Seine. V. S. Pritchett. il Holiday 34:62-7+ N '63
SEINEMEYER, Meta
Historical records; Richard Strauss memorial. A. Favia-Artsay. il por Hobbies 69:31+ S '64
SEISMIC petroleum prospecting. See Petroleum—Prospecting—Geophysical methods
SEISMIC prospecting. See Prospecting—Geophysical methods
SEISMIC sea waves
Alaskan earthquake of 27 March 1964: remote seiche stimulation. W. L. Donn. bibliog il Science 145:261 Jl 17 '64
Chaos at dawn! Alaskan tidal wave hits Los Angeles. H. Luray. Yachting 115:215-17 My '64
Danger: tidal wave! S. V. Jones. il Sci Digest 56:83-7 Jl '64
Forests, a natural defense against seismic waves. C. D. Whitesell and R. E. Daehler. il Am For 70:38-9 N '64
Quakes, winds and great waves. D. Cort. il Nation 198:363-5 Ap 13 '64
SEISMOGRAPHS
Riddle of the black boxes. S. D. Pursglove. il Pop Mech 120:86-91+ Ag '63
Seismic measurements on the ocean bottom. H. Bradner. bibliog il Science 146:208-16 O 9 '64
See also
Seismometers
SEISMOLOGY
Earthquake source mechanisms. H. Benioff. bibliog il Science 143:1399-406 Mr 27 '64
Explosion seismology. E. W. Carpenter. bibliog il Science 147:363-73 Ja 22 '65
Our trembling earth. J. Lear. il Sat R 47: 41-7 My 2 '64
Seismic measurements on the ocean bottom. H. Bradner. bibliog il Science 146:208-16 O 9 '64
Shocks follow quake. B. Tufty. Sci N L 86: 327 N 21 '64
Silent music of the earth. M. H. Thompson. il UNESCO Courier 17:21-3 Ap '64
SEISMOMETERS
Undersea sensors planted near USSR. M. Getler. Miss & Roc 15:17 S 7 '64
SEITZ, Frederick
Space science and the universities; address, May 7, 1963. Science 141:614-18 Ag 16 '63
SEITZ, Kenneth H.
Cold weather warm-up. Flower Grower 51: 30-2 O '64
SEITZ, William
Rise and dissolution of the avant-garde. Vogue 142:182-3+ S 1 '63
(ed) See Duchamp, M. What's happened to art
SEIZE the day; drama. See Otis, M.
SEIZURES. See Searches and seizures
SEIZURES, Audiogenic. See Neuroses, Experimental
SEKERIS, C. E.
Sclerotization in the blowfly imago. bibliog Science 144:419 Ap 24 '64
—and Mergenhagen, D.
Phenoloxidase system of the blowfly, calliphora erythrocephala. bibliog Science 145: 68-9 Jl 3 '64
SEKULER, Robert William, and Ganz, Leo
Aftereffect of seen motion with a stabilized retinal image. bibliog Science 139:419-20 F 1 '63
SELA, Michael, and others
Specific immunologic unresponsiveness to synthetic polypeptide antigens. bibliog Science 139:342-3 Ja 25 '63
SELANDER, Robert K. See Johnston, R. F. jt. auth.
SELBREDE, Bob
Special-interest cars. Motor T 16:74 N '64
SELBY, Anne. See Selby, E. jt. auth.
SELBY, Earl, and Selby, Anne
Wyoming tightens up on happy-time money. Read Digest 86:53-7 Ja '65
SELBY, Herbert, Jr
Call me Cubby. H. Frankel. Sat R 48:40-1 Ja 23 '65
SELBY, Hubert
Stillborn America. W. Schott. Nation 199: 440-2 D 7 '64
SELBY, Stuart A.
Film for the classroom. Pop Phot 51:114+ D '62
SELBY, Suzanne R.
Madison avenue methods. Sr Schol 85:7T O 14 '64
No picnic in the beginning. Sr Schol 84:10T-11T Ap 24 '64
SELDEN, Armistead I. Jr
What the squabble in Panama is all about; interview. por U S News 56:34-7 Ja 27 '64
SELDEN, William K.
Where do they go to college? Sat R 46:72-3 Je 15 '63
Whither the university? Sat R 46:80+ N 16 '63
SELDES, Gilbert
Destruction in a little black book. Sat R 47:34-5 N 14 '64
SELECTION of students. See Student selection
SELECTIVE service, Military. See Military service, Compulsory
SELENIUM
Selenoamino acids: decrease of radiation damage to amino acids and proteins. F. Shimazu and A. L. Tappel. bibliog il Science 143:369-71 Ja 24 '64
SELENOGRAPHY. See Moon—Surface
SELEY, Jason
Synaesthesia. New Yorker 39:20-2 Ja 25 '64
SELF, H. L.
In the feed lot. Suc Farm 61:30 D '63
SELF
Mortal no: death and the modern imagination, by F. J. Hoffman. Review
Commonweal 81:76-9 O 9 '64. B. Murchland
Person; what it means to be a person. R. O. Johann. il America 110:606 My 2 '64
Peter Sellers talks to teens. P. Sellers. Seventeen 23:92+ Jl '64
See also
Personality
SELF allergy. See Allergy
SELF analysis. See Self evaluation
SELF assurance. See Self reliance
SELF confidence. See Self reliance
SELF consciousness. See Bashfulness
SELF-contained underwater breathing apparatus. See Diving apparatus
SELF control
Never the small stuff. W. W. Ward. Read Digest 83:23-4 Ag '63
Want to be a real pro? C. F. Moore, jr. Read Digest 83:56-8 Ag '63
SELF culture
Challenge of leisure; address, February 17, 1964. D. Rockefeller. Vital Speeches 30:379-81 Ap 1 '64
Make yourself a better manager. J. G. Mason. il Nations Bsns 52:80-2 F '64
Self-development; excerpts from Self-renewal: the individual and the innovative society. J. W. Gardner. Science 143:641 F 14 '64
SELF defense
Right of self-defense. il Time 83:43 Je 26 '64
When in doubt, yell and run. L. Strong. il N Y Times Mag p92 Mr 22 '64
SELF defense for women
Are hatpins enough? case of Arlene Del Fava in New York. il Time 84:62-3 Jl 17 '64
Case of the switchblade; New York's Sullivan law. Newsweek 64:34 Jl 27 '64
First scream, then scram. il U S News 54: 58-9 Ap 1 '63
How good are those self protection devices? il Good H 158:161 F '64
Tears for men; pengun for women. il Time 82:79 O 11 '63
SELF denial
Word. V. P. McCorry. America 110:204-5 F 8 '64
SELF dependence. See Self reliance
SELF-determination, National
Africa and the world: problems of today and tomorrow; address, August 24, 1963. G. M. Williams. Dept State Bul 49:432-6 S 16 '63
Age of the rights of man; address, October 12, 1963. D. Rusk. Dept State Bul 49:654-8 O 28 '63
Our stake in the United Nations; address, October 24, 1963. J. J. Sisco. Dept State Bul 49:773-7 N 18 '63
Unfinished business; address, September 10, 1963. D. Rusk. Dept State Bul 49:490-6 S 30 '63
United States explains position on Portuguese territories; statements, July 26 and July 31, 1963; together with the text of a resolution adopted by the Council on July 31, 1963. A. E. Stevenson. Dept State Bul 49: 303-9 Ag 19 '63
SELF development. See Self culture
SELF discipline. See Discipline; Self control

SELF education. See Self culture
SELF employed
Flurry in private pension plans; Keogh law. Bsns W p 167-8 N 16 '63
New retirement plan. N. E. Harl. il Suc Farm 61:39+ O '63
Pensions for the self-employed; Keogh act. il Changing T 17:7-12 My '63
Personal business; HR-10 plan. Bsns W p 133 S 28 '63
Self-employed: it's time to act on pensions; Self-employed individuals tax retirement act. il U S News 55:118-20 N 11 '63
Self-employment in the United States, 1948-62. J. E. Bregger. il Mo Labor R 86:37-43 Ja '63
SELF evaluation
How well-adjusted are you? excerpt from Wisdom of your subconscious mind. J. K. Williams. Read Digest 85:136-7 S '64
Know yourself! excerpt from address, January 21, 1963. J. W. Gardner. Read Digest 83:72-4 N '63
Power to see ourselves. P. J. Brouwer. Harvard Bsns R 42:156-62+ N '64
Yourself as others see you; sensitivity training program. il Bsns W p 160+ Mr 16 '63
SELF feeders, Cattle. See Cattle self feeders
SELF government. See Autonomy; Democracy
SELF government in education
Student-faculty council revisited; campus government. P. A. Bloland. Sch & Soc 91:216-18 My 4 '63
SELF help. See Self reliance
SELF help activities. See Cooperative associations
SELF improvement. See Self culture
SELF incrimination
Extending the Fifth: to state courts. Time 83:43 Je 26 '64
Freedom on non-speech. Newsweek 63:21 Je 29 '64
SELF insurance. See Insurance—Self insurance
SELF knowledge. See Self evaluation
SELF-medication. See Medicine
SELF realization
Double-purpose plan; social responsibility and self-realization. L. S. Vander Werf. Sch & Soc 91:213-14 My 4 '63
To save the life of "I." M. Mannes. Vogue 144:172-3 O 1 '64
SELF realization fellowship. See Sects
SELF reliance
Challenge of confident living; condensation. R. O'Brien. Read Digest 84:211-13+ Ap '64
Growth of self-reliance; H. E. Gruber and M. Weitman. Sch & Soc 91:222-3 My 4 '63
On self-help and foreign aid; address, April 2, 1963. F. S. Okotie-Eboh. Vital Speeches 29:502-3 Je 1 '63
Put self-doubt on your payroll. W. Kemsley. Writer 77:30-2 My '64
SELF respect
Help your child like himself; with study-discussion program, by C. W. Mattuck. S. Blau. il Parents Mag 38:37-8, 62-3+ D '63
SELF restraint. See Self control
SELF service restaurants. See Cafeterias
SELF that walks like a cat; story. See Hurlbut, K.
SELIG, Henry
Xenon hexafluoride complexes. bibliog Science 144:537 My 1 '64
—and others
Chemistry of the noble gases; with biographical sketches. Sci Am 210:22+, 66-77 bibliog(p 150) My '64
Xenon tetroxide: preparation and some properties. bibliog Science 143:1322-3 Mr 20 '64
SELIGMAN, Ben B.
Automation & the state. Commentary 37:49-54 Je; 38:24 D '64
Disarmament and the economy. Commentary 35:369-77; 36:196-7 My, S '63
Those dark, satanic mills. Commentary 38: 69-71 Jl '64
Underclass. Commentary 37:91-2 F '64
SELIGMAN, Daniel
Belated rise of advertising. Fortune 69:120-3+ Mr '64
FTC presents: the great sandpaper shave. Fortune 70:130-3+ D '64
Future of the office-building boom. Fortune 67:84-8+ Mr '63
Move to apartments. Fortune 67:98-101+ Ap '63
—and Wise, T. A.
New forces in the stock market. Fortune 69: 92-5+ F '64
—and others
Big disappearing act. Fortune 68:231-2 D '63
Personal investing. See issues of Fortune
SELIGMANN, Kurt L.
Dance without the dancer. il Time 83:44-5+ Ja 31 '64
SELIGSON, Lou
Jordan waters; when Israel turns the tap. Nation 198:622-4 Je 22 '64
SELLA, André
Small, proud, cream-colored hotel; Hotel du Cap. J. Bryan, 3d. Holiday 34:62-3+ S '63
SELLERS, Jack
Letter from Kentucky. Nat R 14:399 My 21 '63
SELLERS, James
Our reluctant laity and the seminaries. Christian Cent 81:551-2+ Ap 29 '64
Vigilance is needed. Christian Cent 80:617 My 8 '63
SELLERS, Peter
Peter Sellers talks to teens. por Seventeen 23:92+ Jl '64
Redbook dialogue: Peter Sellers & Carol Burnett. por Redbook 122:60-1+ D '63
about
Come on out, Pete. il por Newsweek 64:98+ N 2 '64
Sellers' last role; almost; with account by S. Alexander. il pors Life 57:27-8+ Jl 31 '64
This man says he's Peter Sellers. J. Krantz. pors McCalls 90:42+ Ag '63
Ubiquitous, multifarious Sellers. F. Lewis. il pors N Y Times Mag p20+ Je 23 '63
Weird world of Peter Sellers. C. Brossard. il pors Look 28:M5-M7 Ja 28 '64
Which one's real? E. Miller. il pors Seventeen 22:48+ N '63
World of Sellers. il por Newsweek 62:90 S 9 '63
SELLERS, Rose Z.
College library recruits with an exhibit and a symposium. por Library J 88:1105-7 Mr 15 '63
SELLIN, Thorsten
Organized crime; a business enterprise. bibliog f Ann Am Acad 347:12-19 My '63
SELLING. See Marketing; Salesmen and salesmanship
SELLS, Bruce H. See Slotnick, I. J. jt. auth.
SELLS, C. J. See VanArsdel, P. P. jr. jt. auth.
SELLTIZ, Claire
Social contacts of foreign students with Americans; excerpt from Attitudes and social relations of foreign students in the United States. bibliog Sch & Soc 91:261-6 Sum '63
SELMA, Ala.
Aim: registration; attempt by Negroes to register. il Time 85:20-1 Ja 29 '65
Shades of Bull Connor; Negroes attempt to register. il Newsweek 65:21-2 F 1 '65
SELOUS, Frederick Courteney
My dear Selous: letters, ed. by E. Hahn. T. Roosevelt. por Am Heritage 14:40-2+ Ap '63
SELTZER, Leon, and Ingle, Harold
Report on scholarly publishing in Asia; summary. pors Pub W 186:43-7 Jl 20 '64
SELTZER, Louis Benson
Too much power for labor? excerpts from address, February 12, 1963. por U S News 54: 97 F 25 '63
about
Replying in spades. il por Time 81:50 My 31 '63
SELVA, James
Positive force: Jimmy Selva. W. Como. il pors Dance Mag 37:48-50+ F '63
SELWAY-Bitterroot wilderness area. See Wilderness areas
SELWYN, George Augustus
Extraordinary life and times of George Selwyn. by O. Sherwin. Review
Newsweek il 63:84+ Ja 20 '64
SELYE, Hans
New search for the fountain of youth. J. D. Ratcliff. por Read Digest 83:69-74 D '63
—and others
Calciphylaxis: passive transfer. bibliog Science 143:365-6 Ja 24 '64
SEMAN, Khalil
Fired scholar brings suit against Library of Congress. Library J 88:1636+ Ap 15 '63
SEMANA nautica. See Regattas

SEMANTICS
Analytic philosophy and educational thought; excerpt from Foundations of education. G. F. Kneller. bibliog f Sch & Soc 1:61+ F 9 '63
Milk, beads, thongs, and the spiral nebulae. B. Evans. il Atlan 214:126-7 Jl '64
Notes and comment; misunderstanding: negotiate vs. discuss during the Panama crisis. New Yorker 39:27 F 8 '64
See also
Analysis (philosophy)

SEMEN
Acceptance or rejection of male skin by isologous female mice: effect of injection of sperm. G. F. Katsh and others. bibliog il Science 143:41-2 Ja 3 '64
Prezygotic selection in ABO blood groups. E. Matsunaga and Y. Hiraizumi; discussion. Science 137:861-2; bibliog 139:406-7 S 14 '62, F 1 '63
Spermatogenesis in man; an estimate of its duration. C. G. Heller and Y. Clermont. bibliog il Science 140:184-6 Ap 12 '63

SEMENENKO, Serge
Getting Curits off the spot; straight term-loan bank financing. por Bsns W p96 Ag 17 '63
How can a banker help? il por Newsweek 62:62-3 D 23 '63
Optimism at Curtis. il por Time 82:31 D 20 '63

SEMENOV, Nikolai Nikolaevich
Into the world of the future. UNESCO Courier 16:58-63 Jl '63
World of the future. por Bul Atomic Sci 20:10-15 F '64

SEMI-AUTOMATIC ground environment system
NATO plans SAGE-type system; NADGE; with other infrastructure projects. W. Beller. Miss & Roc 15:14-15 O 12 '64

SEMICONDUCTOR diodes. See Diodes

SEMICONDUCTORS
Avionics demands spur microcircuit sales. B. Miller. il Aviation W 79:63-5+ D 23 '63
Competition to tighten in semiconductors. B. Miller. il Aviation W 79:56-9+ S 23 '63
Design seen as interim solution to circuit irradiation. M. Getler. Miss & Roc 14:37-8 Mr 2 '64
Detection of nuclear radiation by semiconductors. H. S. Renne. bibliog il Electr World 70:39-42+ Ag '63
Domestic replacements for foreign semiconductors. J. Eimbinder. il Electr World 70:26-8 Jl '63
Electron beam technique makes, inspects semiconductor microcircuits. P. J. Klass. il Aviation W 79:80-1+ S 23 '63
Growth, at a price, for transistors. Bsns W p 102+ Ap 6 '63
Micro electronics manufacturers; five firms top burgeoning field. il Miss & Roc 14:31-3+ F 3 '64
Microcircuit plant to serve in-house need. P. J. Klass. il Aviation W 80:66-9 Mr 9 '64
New product, old problem. Bsns W p63 Ap 4 '64
Not yet solid in the solid state. Bsns W p26-7 My 16 '64
Semiconductor lasers. B. Lax. bibliog il Science 141:1247-55 S 27 '63
Semiconductors for power supplies. F. W. Gutzwiller. il Electr World 72:27-30+ N '64
Semiconductors strain gages. H. S. Renne. il Electr World 70:36-8+ Jl '63
Study forecasts microcircuitry growth. B. Miller. il Aviation W 78:84+ F 25 '63
Superconducting semiconductors. Sci Am 210:56+ Je '64
Thin-film transistor research pressed. B. Miller. il Aviation W 78:68-9+ F 4 '63
Unijunction transistor. D. L. Pippen. il Electr World 71:46-7+ Ja '64
See also
Electric current rectifiers
Indium antimonide

Testing

Simple tests for semiconductors. C. D. Todd. il Electr World 70:36-8 D '63

SEMI-DETACHED; drama. See Turner, D.

SEMINARIANS. See Theological students

SEMINARIES. See Theological schools

SEMINARS
Columbia's unorthodox seminars. P. Goodman. Harper 228:72-5+ Ja '64
Existing law and measures to improve the status of women in the western hemisphere. G. A. Tillett. Dept State Bul 51:128-32 Jl 27 '64
Harvard seminar for freshmen. Sch & Soc 91:208 My 4 '63
Sunshine seminars; Institute for humanistic studies in Aspen, Colo. il Newsweek 64:48 Jl 27 '64
Whole town's talking; about school program and finance seminars, Columbus, Ohio. J. L. Davis. il NEA J 52:26-7 O '63

SEMINOLE Indians
Do these Indians really own Florida? R. Bongartz. il Sat Eve Post 237:62-3+ F 1 '64
On the Seminole peace path. H. Sutton. il Sat R 46:21-3 D 14 '63

SEMPLE, Ronald. See Gallagher, R. S. jt. auth.

SEMROW, Harry H.
Biggest thank you party. il pors Ebony 19:55-6+ F '64

SEN, Binay Ranjan
Need to solve problems of hunger and malnutrition; address. por U N Rev 10:35-6+ N '63
Our half hungry world. por Parents Mag 39:32+ Ag '64
about
Lauds church aid to the hungry. Christian Cent 80:262 F 27 '63

SENATE (United States) See United States—Congress—Senate

SENATE committees. See United States—Congress—Senate—Committees

SENATE investigations. See Government investigations

SENATE office building. See Washington—D.C.—Public buildings

SENATORIAL candidates. See Candidates, Political

SENATORS
Adequate number of Democrats. il Time 85:16-20 Ja 15 '65
L'affaire Baker. K. Crawford. Newsweek 62:35 N 4 '63
Casebook of a southern senator. D. Schoenbrun. il Esquire 60:104-8+ S '63
Chorus of angels; question of opening their financial books to public view. Time 84:21-2 Ag 7 '64
Making senators lift lid, a little, on wealth. Bsns W p 18 Jl 4 '64
New chairman and a new senator. U S News 55:13 S 2 '63
Plea to the South; southern senators cease to obstruct passage of the civil rights bill. America 110:592 My 2 '64
Presidents and president-makers. W. S. White. NEA J 53:27 O '64
Race politics enters pact ratification issue; test ban treaty before Senate. Christian Cent 80:1124 S 18 '63
Secrets of the Senate. Newsweek 61:23-4 Ap 22 '63
Senate: a crisis in leadership. il Newsweek 62:29-30 N 18 '63
Senate generals in the rights battle. il U S News 56:12 Mr 2 '64
War whoopers. Nation 196:238 Mr 23 '63
What makes a great senator? N Y Times Mag p 15+ Je 14 '64
When is a majority a majority? il Time 83:22-6 Mr 20 '64
When senators started calling each other names. il U S News 55:8 N 18 '63
See also
United States—Congress—Senate

Election

Interviews with winners and losers: how they explain what happened. il U S News 57:63-4+ N 16 '64
Now there are two Senators Kennedy; Other Senate races. il Newsweek 64:35-8 N 9 '64
Senate races: who won, who lost. U S News 57:45 N 16 '64
Senate shift. Cato. Nat R 16:860 O 6 '64
Two Kennedys sweep two states; old man Young topples Taft. R. Ajemian. il Life 57:38-9 N 13 '64

SENATORS (baseball) See Baseball clubs

SENATORS wives. See Congressmens wives

SENDAI virus. See Viruses

SENDAK, Maurice
Caldecott award acceptance; address, June 30, 1964. il Horn Bk 40:344-51 Ag '64
about
Maurice Sendak. L. Wolfe. il por Horn Bk 40:351-4 Ag '64
Maurice Sendak. U. Nordstrom. il por Library J 89:1374-6 Mr 15 '64
Maurice Sendak: an artist best understood by children. F. N. Chrystie. il por Pub W 185:87-9 F 24 '64

SENDAK, Maurice—about—*Continued*
Maurice Sendak, illustrator of the child's world. J. H. Michel. il Am Artist 28:44-9+ S '64
Newbery and Caldecott winners: Emily Neville, Maurice Sendak. il por Pub W 185: 30-2 Mr 9 '64
Newbery-Caldecott awards. por Wilson Lib Bul 38:617 Ap '64

SENDER, Ramón J.
Ephemeral Amazon kingdom. Américas 15: 28-32 My '63

SENDERS, John W.
Information storage requirements for the contents of the world's libraries. bibliog Science 141:1067-8 S 13 '63

SENECA Indians
Exporting the American idea; Quaker technology among the Senecas. A. Wallace. Sat R 46:54-6 Ap 6 '63
Is fair treatment a civil right? Christian Cent 81:510 Ap 22 '64
Lake of Perfidy; Allegheny reservoir. New Repub 150:5 Ap 18 '64
Senecas suffer another blow. Christian Cent 81:1421 N 18 '64
Senecas to be flooded out; Kinzua Dam project. Sr Schol 84:17 Mr 20 '64

SENEGAL
Atlantic report. Atlan 211:32-5 Mr '63
Briefly sympathetic. Time 81:42 My 17 '63
Colored rulers. G. C. Turner. Negro Hist Bul 26:222 Ap '63
Jitters in Dakar. New Repub 149:8 N 2 '63
Only one hat. il Time 81:45 Mr 15 '63
Senegal. R. J. H. Church. bibliog il Focus 15:1-6 S '64
See also
United Nations—Senegal

SENEGALESE poetry

Translations into English

Midnight elegy; For kôra, tr. by C. Guenther. L. S. Senghor. Poetry 103:179-81 D '63

SENESCENCE in plants. See Age (plants)

SENESI, Mauro
Breach; story, tr. by E. Maclachlan. Atlan 213:88-90 My '64
Father and son; story, tr. by E. Maclachlan. Atlan 213:87-9 F '64

SENFL, Ludwig
Ludwig Senfl. J. W. Barker. il Am Rec G 30:666-7 Ap '64

SENFT, Craig T.
Postscript: a fable. Pub W 185:37-8 My 18 '64

SENGHOR, Léopold Sédar
Femme noire; poem, with English tr. by C. Guenther. Reporter 29:41 D 5 '63
Midnight elegy; For kôra; poems, tr. by C. Guenther. Poetry 103:179-81 D '63

about

Colored rulers. G. C. Turner. Negro Hist Bul 26:222 Ap '63
In praise of négritude. por Newsweek 64: 80 Jl 27 '64
Note on Léopold Sédar Senghor. C. Guenther. Poetry 103:199 D '63
Only one hat. il por Time 81:45 Mr 15 '63

SENIOR, Clarence
Case for birth control. Parents Mag 38:84-5+ O '63

SENIOR citizen month. See Special days and weeks

SENIOR citizens clubs. See Recreation for the aged

SENIOR scholastic (periodical)
Letters to the editor; with editorial comment. Sr Schol 83:18 Ja 10 '64

SENIOR services corporation
Never too old to buy. Bsns W p 170-1 My 23 '64

SENIORITY, Employee
Job tenure of American workers, January 1963. H. R. Hamel. il Mo Labor R 86:1145-52 O '63

SENIORS, High school. See High school students

SENN, Milton John Edward
Are teen-agers people? McCalls 90:74+ S '63
Child care in Russia: better than ours? McCalls 90:40+ Mr '63
Child's-eye view of life and death. McCalls 91:64+ Ap '64
Let's stop scaring our children. McCalls 92: 74+ O '64
Storm over childbirth. McCalls 90:40+ F '63
TB; the far-from-dead disease. por McCalls 91:88+ O '63
We must stop contaminating our water; ed. by E. M. Wylie. Am Home 66:44-5+ Ja '63
What parents ask. See issues of McCall's
Winter enemy no. 1; the flu. por McCalls 91:84+ N '63

SENSATION. See Senses and sensation

SENSE of humor. See Humor

SENSE organs
See also
Eye
Senses and sensation

Fishes

Don't let H.O. spoil your fishing. D. Bowers. il Field & S 69:38-40 N '64

Insects

Fine structure of the interpseudotracheal papillae of the blowfly. J. R. Larsen. bibliog il Science 139:347 Ja 25 '63

SENSES and sensation
Early concepts of the senses and the mind. A. C. Crombie. il Sci Am 210:108-16 My '64
Mystery of our sixth senses. R. Platt. Read Digest 83:75-8 S '63
No wonder! W. E. Sangster. Read Digest 82: 126-8 Mr '63
Plasticity in human sensorimotor control. R. Held and S. J. Freedman. bibliog il Science 142:455-62 O 25 '63
Psychophysics of perceived intensity: a theoretical basis for Fechner's and Stevens' laws. D. M. MacKay. bibliog il Science 139:1213-16 Mr 22 '63
Touching quiz. J. Daugherty and M. Daugherty. Sci Digest 55:5-7 Je '64
Vision and touch: an experimentally created conflict between the two senses. I. Rock and J. Victor. Science 143:594-6 F 7 '64
We have more than five senses. L. W. Robinson. il N Y Times Mag p30+ Mr 15 '64
See also
After images
Brain
Hearing
Pain
Perception
Smell
Taste
Time perception
Touch

SENSING, Thurman
Excerpt from address, May 24, 1964. Cong Digest 43:280+ N '64

SENSORAMA simulators. See Simulators

SENSORS, Fluid. See Aeronuatic instruments

SENSORS, Horizon. See Aeronautic instruments

SENSORS, Infrared. See Aeronautic instruments

SENSORS, Reconnaissance. See Aeronautic instruments

SENSORY deprivation
Cutaneous sensitivity after prolonged visual deprivation. J. P. Zubek and others. bibliog il Science 144:1591-3 Je 26 '64
Electroencephalographic changes during and after fourteen days of perceptual deprivation. J. P. Zubeck and others. bibliog il Science 139:490-2 F 8 '63
Food versus perceptual complexity as rewards for rats previously subjected to sensory deprivation. G. P. Sackett and others. bibliog il Science 140:518-20 Ag 9 '63; Reply with rejoinder. W. A. Hillix. 142:1021-2 N 22 '63
Get away from it all? Don't! Sci Digest 54: 83 O '63
Plasticity in human sensorimotor control. R. Held and S. J. Freedman. bibliog il Science 142:455-62 O 25 '63
Self-maintained visual stimulation in monkeys after long-term visual deprivation. R. H. Wendt and others. bibliog il Science 139: 336-8 Ja 25 '63
Sight loss heightens sense of touch. Sci N L 86:56 Jl 25 '64
Two-week isolation affects brain activity. Sci N L 83:120 F 23 '63
Visual hallucinations during sensory deprivation: a problem of criteria. P. Suedfeld and J. Vernon. bibliog il Science 145:412-13 Jl 24 '64

SENSORY receptors. See Nervous system

SENTER, Raymond D. pseud.
Air force candidate Goldwater. New Repub 151:8 S 5 '64
Anti-missile dilemma. New Repub 148:6-7 Mr 9 '63
Banning bombs in orbit; can the US and USSR get together? New Repub 149:16-18 O 5; 31 N 16 '63
Barry's bomber gap. New Repub 151:9-10 S 12 '64

SENTER, Raymond D. pseud—*Continued*
Democracy's military establishment. New Repub 150:21-2 Ap 25 '64
Dilemma of the military. Bul Atomic Sci 19:24-7 D '63
End of the manned bomber. New Repub 48: 19-20 F 9 '63
Goldwater and the bomber-gap. New Repub 150:10-12 Ja 25 '64
I spy, you spy, it's alright. New Repub 150: 7-8 Je 13 '64
Khrushchev, the generals and Goldwater. New Repub 151:8-9 N 21 '64
Rebellion in the air force? New Repub 149: 13-15 S 28; 54+ N 9 '63
That attack from space. New Repub 148:17-19 My 4; 30 Je 8 '63

SENTIMENTALITY
New sentimentality. D. Newman and R. Benton. il Esquire 62:25-31 Jl '64

SEOANE, Manuel
Anniversary of the Alliance. Américas 15:1 Ag '63

SEPARATION (chemistry)
Separation and fractionation of macromolecules and particles. A. Tiselius and others. bibliog il Science 141:13-20 Jl 5 '63

SEPARATION of isotopes. See Isotope separation

SEPARATION of powers
Trip to Moscow and beyond. J. N. Eller. America 109:149 Ag 17 '63
World challenge to Mr Johnson. L. J. Halle. il N Y Times Mag p 17+ Ap 5 '64

SEPTEMBER
In September; anniversaries, events and other dates coming up next month (title varies) (cont) il N Y Times Mag p 17 S 1 '63; 18 Ag 30 '64
To see September. J. D. Scott. il Read Digest 85:221-4 S '64

SEPTIC tanks
If you plan to install a septic tank. il Sunset 132:110+ Je '64

SEPTICEMIC plague. See Plague

SEPULCHRAL monuments
Grave rubbers; early New England gravestones. C. Willard. il Look 27:M6-M7 Ag 27 '63
Mortality writ in stone; early New England gravestones. S. Marsal. il Américas 16:22-30 S '64
New England gravestone rubbings. A. Parker and A. Neal. il Craft Horiz 23:16-19+ Jl '63
Selecting a cemetery memorial. Consumer Bul 47:37-8 My '64
Stone carving in New England graveyards. A. Ludwig. il Antiques 86:87-91 Jl '64

SEQUINS
Magic glitter; from the days of King Tut to the age of stroblites. W. Como. il Dance Mag 37:56-7 Je '63

SEQUOIA
Fire ecology of the giant sequoias; controlled fires one solution to survival. R. J. Hartesveldt. il Natur Hist 73:12-19 bibliog(p67) D '64
See one big tree, and you want to see another. il Sunset 131:30-2 Jl '63
See also
Redwood

SEQUOIA NATIONAL PARK
Walk up Moro Rock. il Sunset 131:48 Jl '63

SEQUOIO, Ron
Brief biography. S. Goodman. pors Dance Mag 37:42-3 F '63

SERBIAN folk tales. See Folk literature, Serbian

SERBIN, Max
Gentile influence in Jewish music. Am Rec G 30:770-2+ My '64
Reflections on Gustav Holst's The hymn of Jesus. Am Rec G 29:512-14 Mr '63

SEREBNICK, Judith
(ed) First novelists, spring 1964; statements by the writers. Library J 89:661-9 F 1 '64
(ed) First novelists, spring-summer, fall, 1963. Library J 88:580-93, 2277-83, 3651-7 F 1, Je 1, O 1 '63

SEREBRIAKOFF, Victor Vladimir
Bread with the big brain. il pors Life 57:73-4+ Jl 24 '64

SERENA. See Birth control—Canada

SERENGETI NATIONAL PARK. See National parks and reserves—Tanganyika

SERENITY
Search. A. Gordon. Read Digest 82:137-8 Ap '63

SERENY, Gitta
Woman's special happy time. Good H 156: 72+ Mr '63

SERGE, Victor
Broken eggs of the Soviet omelet. N. Weyl. Nat R 16:75-7 Ja 28 '64
Conscience & revolution. H. Kramer. Commentary 37:85-7 Ap '64
Dawn of darkness at noon. H. E. Salisbury. Sat R 46:48 D 14 '63
Memoirs of a revolutionary, 1901-1941, by V. Serge; tr. and ed. by P. Sedgwick. Review
New Repub 150:30-2 Mr 7 '64. I. Howe

SERGEANT Cuff, pseud. See Winterich, J. T.

SERGEANT fish
How to outsmart cobia. G. Heinold. il Outdoor Life 134:10-11+ Jl '64

SERGEANT fish fishing
Mystery fish of the sea. J. Brooks. il Field & S 69:40-1+ Ag '64

SERGEEV, Konstantin
Friendly visit. J. Anderson. il pors Dance Mag 38:18-21+ N '64
Prince of a Cinderella. I. Kolodin. Sat R 47: 33+ S 26 '64

SERGEI Vavilov (ship) See Ships, Research

SERIAL publications
Automating the serial record. J. Becker. ALA Bul 58:557-60 Je '64
U.S. periodicals and serial services; cost indexes for 1964. il Library J 89:2746-9 Jl '64

SERIAL rights
Rights and permissions; White House years: mandate for change 1953-1956. P. Nathan. Pub W 184:61 N 18 '63

SERIALS (moving pictures) See Moving pictures—Serial films

SERIALS (novels) See Fiction in periodicals and newspapers

SERIES, Book
Nuts to excelsior. C. M. Craig. Library J 89: 4989 D 15 '64
Replacements for blacklisted series offered by small libraries project. Library J 89: 4996 D 15 '64

SERIGRAPHY. See Silk screen printing

SERMONS
One thing worse than this; sermon delivered at Northaven Methodist church, Dallas, November 24, 1963. W. A. Holmes. Christian Cent 80:1555-6 D 11 '63

SEROFF, Victor
Alkas' Katerina. Sat R 47:64 Mr 28 '64
Double Dargomyzhsky. Sat R 47:50+ F 29 '64
Opera for Christmas. Sat R 47:57 D 12 '64
Posthumous Tchaikovsky. Sat R 47:48 Jl 25 '64
Where is Russian opera? Opera N 27:8-11 Ap 6 '63

SEROTA, Herman M.
Home movies of early childhood: correlative developmental data in the psychoanalysis of adults. bibliog Science 143:1195 Mr 13 '64

SEROTONIN
Alteration in learning ability caused by changes in cerebral serotonin and catechol amines. D. W. Woolley and T. van der Hoeven. bibliog il Science 139:610-11 F 15 '63; Reply with rejoinder. D. E. McMillan. 145:952 Ag 28 '64
Behavioral-neurochemical correlation in reactive and nonreactive strains of rats. H. S. Sudak and J. W. Mass. bibliog il Science 146:418-20 O 16 '64
Behavioral response rates in pigeons: effect of α-methyl-m-tyrosine. J. N. Hingtgen and M. H. Aprison. bibliog il Science 141: 169-71 Jl 12 '63
Prevention of a mental defect of phenylketonuria with serotonin congeners such as melatonin or hydroxytryptophan. D. W. Woolley and T. van der Hoeven. bibliog il Science 144:1593-4 Je 26 '64
Serotonin binding to nerve-ending particles of the rat brain and its inhibition by lysergic acid diethylamide. R. M. Marchbanks and others. bibliog il Science 144:1135-7 My 29 '64
Serotonin deficiency in infancy as one cause of a mental defect in phenylketonuria. D. W. Woolley and T. van der Hoeven. bibliog il Science 144:883-4 My 15 '64
Serotonin rhythm in the pineal organ: control by the sympathetic nervous system. V. M. Fiske. bibliog il Science 146:253-4 O 9 '64
Teratogenic effect of 5-hydroxytryptamine in mice. E. Poulson and others. bibliog il Science 141:717 Ag 23 '63

SERPENTINE
Ocean crust composition. Sci N L 83:338 Je 1 '63

SERPENTS. See Snakes

SERRA, Junipero
Junipero Serra in overalls. America 111:370 O 3 '64
SERT, José Luis
Place on the Riviera. il por Time 84:64 Ag 7 '64
Sert on the Riviera. il Time 82:54 Ag 16 '63
SERT (space electric rocket test) See Artificial satellites
SERUM
Blood groups of chimpanzees: demonstrated with isoimmune serums. J. Moor-Jankowski. bibliog il Science 145:1441-3 S 25 '64
Canine antiserums analogous to human allergic and blocking antiserums. J. I. Tenenbaum and others. bibliog Science 142: 589-90 N 1 '63
Complement and hemolysis; report of workshop at the National institutes of health. Bethesda, Md. H. J. Rapp and T. Borsos. Science 141:738-40 Ag 23 '63
Contamination of commercial rabbit albumin preparations by bovine albumin. W. D. Linscott. il Science 142:1170-2 N 29 '63
Differences in complement titers of serums from spaced bleedings in guinea pigs. L. J. Brenner and E. E. Ecker. bibliog il Science 145:400-1 Jl 24 '64
Killing of cultured rabbit fibroblasts with isoimmune serum. D. A. Pious and S. E. Mills. bibliog il Science 142:52-3 O 4 '63
Photosensitizing substance in human serum: effect on HeLa cells. W. B. Wheeler and A. C. Hollinshead. bibliog il Science 141: 1279-80 S 27 '63
Rubella antibodies in human serum: detection by the indirect fluorescent-antibody technique. G. C. Brown and others. bibliog il Science 145:943-5 Ag 28 '64
Serum factor in renal compensatory hyperplasia. L. M. Lowenstein and A. Stern. bibliog il Science 142:1479-80 D 13 '63
Transferrin: variations in blood serum of red howler monkeys. M. A. Schön and T. Arends. bibliog il Science 146:774-5 N 6 '64
SERUM albumin. See Blood—Proteins
SERUM globulins
Molecular and submolecular localization of two isoantigens of mouse immunoglobulins. R. I. Mishell and J. L. Fahey. bibliog il Science 143:1440-2 Mr 27 '64
New serum group, Gm(p) M. Waller and others. bibliog il Science 142:1321-2 D 6 '63
Sonic energy effects in bovine serum albumin solutions. E. L. Hess and others. bibliog il Science 143:1176-7 Mr 13 '64
SERUM proteins. See Blood—Proteins
SERVAAS, Beurt R.
Editorial. Design 66:4 S '64
SERVANT problem; story. See Kelley, W. M.
SERVANTS. See Household employees
SERVATIUS, Robert
Reporter at large; Eichmann trial. H. Arendt. New Yorker 38:40-2+ F 16; 39:40-2+ F 23; 40-2+ Mr 2; 58-60+ Mr 16 '63
SERVICE
Anecdotes, facetiae, satire, etc.
T.L.C. keep your paws off me! T. Caldwell. Nat R 15:103-4 Ag 13 '63; Discussion. 15: 163 Ag 27 '63
SERVICE (in industry)
How to choose a service dealer. il Suc Farm 62:66-7 Ja '64
SERVICE, Community. See Community service
SERVICE, Public. See Public service
SERVICE, Volunteer. See Volunteer service
SERVICE corps of retired executives. See United States—Small business administration
SERVICE de régulation des naissances. See Birth control—Canada
SERVICE hatches. See Pass-throughs
SERVICE industries
Why service workers are less productive. Bsns W p 156 N 14 '64
See also
Willmark service system
Securities
Executive investor. il Duns R 83:117-19 F '64
SERVICE men
See also
Soldiers
Pay, allowances, etc.
See United States—Armed forces—Pay, allowances, etc.
Recreation
See United States—Armed forces—Recreation
SERVICE men, Discharged
Bonus march; Bonus expeditionary force. J. D. Weaver. il Am Heritage 14:18-23+ Je '63
Benefits
Needed: a new GI bill; the neglected vets. N. Levin. Nation 196:171-3 Mr 2 '63; Reply. J. A. Drayton. 196:inside cover Mr 23 '63
See also
Pensions, Military—United States
Education
Another anniversary; GI bill of rights. R. Moley. Newsweek 64:80 Jl 6 '64
Bargain bill. Newsweek 64:73 Jl 6 '64
Cold war GI bill? W. V. Kennedy. America 108:822 Je 8 '63
Fair deal for the cold war soldier. R. W. Yarborough. Harper 230:82-3 Ja '65
They also served; question of conscientious objectors. Christian Cent 81:790 Je 17 '64
See also
Servicemen's readjustment act of 1944
Organizations
Speaking out; let's say no to the veterans. E. P. Neilan. Sat Eve Post 236:8+ N 30 '63
SERVICE men, Negro. See Negro service men and women
SERVICE mens bonuses
Soldier's work between two wars; the Bonus march. D. MacArthur. il Life 57:61-2+ Jl 3 '64
SERVICE mens families
Lonely life of an air force wife; family of Capt. Richard Davis of the Tactical air command. il Look 27:20-6 Je 4 '63
Ordinary life of Americans in Saigon. P. Grose. il N Y Times Mag p26-7+ S 27 '64
SERVICE mens graves
Verdun revisited; Reconciliation over graves project. Time 82:19-20 Ag 16 '63
See also
National cemeteries, American
SERVICE mens pets. See Mascots
SERVICE mens reading
Sailors are readers; navy survey concludes. Library J 88:4342+ N 15 '63
SERVICE mens widows. See Widows
SERVICE stations. See Automobile service stations
SERVICEBERRIES
Downy serviceberry. G. R. Trimble, jr and J. Larmoyeux. il Horticulture 41:515 O '63
SERVING carts
Barbecue cart or garden carry-all. il Sunset 130:98-9 Ap '63
Build yourself a barbecue cart. il Bet Hom & Gard 41:20 Ag '63
Make one trip do the work of six. il House B 105:108-11 Je '63
Prefinished party cart. D. Swartwout. il Pop Mech 121:146-9 F '64
Rolling cart, the new household work horse. il House B 105:172-3+ Ap '63
Two homemades for your house; tea cart. S. Kallenbach. il Pop Sci 183:100-1 D '63
SERVING equipment. See Tableware
SERVING of papers. See Process
SERVING pantries. See Pantries
SERVO corporation of America
Airports get new spotter; Servo-FAA aircraft direction finder. Bsns W p 122 N 30 '63
SESQUIOXIDES. See Oxides
SESSIONAL papers. See Great Britain—Government publications
SESSIONS, Roger
Bland giant. il Time 83:50 My 8 '64
Montezuma and the Messiah; West Berlin premiere. H. Joachim. il Mus Am 84:20 My '64
SESSOMS, H. Douglas
Not keeping pace. por Recreation 56:433 N '63
Stream becomes a trickle. por Recreation 57:425 O '64
SESTINAS
Yes, wow! the riddle of the sestina. J. Ciardi. Sat R 46:15+ My 25 '63
SETHUNSA, Khotso
South Africa's black millionaire. il pors Ebony 18:73-6 My '63
SETLOW, R. B. and others
Thymine dimers and inhibition of DNA synthesis by ultraviolet irradiation of cells. bibliog Science 142:1464-6 D 13 '63
—See Swenson, P. A. jt. auth.

SETON, Mother Elizabeth Ann (Bayley)
American mother moves next to sainthood. il pors Life 54:38-38B Mr 29 '63
Blessed Elizabeth Seton. J. LaFarge. America 108:371 Mr 16 '63
From Pope John: praise for Americans. por U S News 54:16 Ap 1 '63
Jet-age pilgrimage. il Newsweek 61:72-3 Mr 25 '63
Making of a saint. T. Congdon. il por Sat Eve Post 236:74-8 Mr 23 '63
Saint for the U.S. il por Time 81:82 Mr 22 '63

SETON, Cynthia
Danger! teen-agers. McCalls 92:95+ N '64
Educated housewife's bill of rights. Redbook 123:47+ My '64

SETON-WATSON, Hugh
Stalin's trend in foreign policy. New Repub 149:22+ Ag 3 '63

SETSER, J. L. See Ehmann, W. D. jt. auth.

SETTERS
Dog man from Oregon. F. Dufresne. il Field & S 69:52-3+ N '64
Making of a setter. D. B. Hague. il Field & S 68:28-31 D '63

SEURAT, Georges Pierre
Gallery for young people. C. B. Johnson. il Sch Arts 62:49 Ap '63

SEUSS, Dr. pseud. See Geisel, T. S.

SEVAREID, Eric
Affluent slumland. por Recreation 58:4 Ja '65
Man who invented Panama. Am Heritage 14:106-10 Ag '63
Mountain and the garden. NEA J 53:16 Ap '64
So they say; interview. por Mlle 57:236-7 Ag '63
They're closing in on the great open spaces! Read Digest 82:196-8+ F '63
(ed) See Lippmann, W. Walter Lippmann, 1964

About

Sense of history. R. L. Shayon. Sat R 47:28 Je 6 '64

SEVENTEEN (periodical)
Making of a model. il Seventeen 22:84-5+ Jl '63
On-the-town spree! winners of annual Seventeen competitions. il Seventeen 22:34+ S '63

SEVENTEEN-nation disarmament conference, Geneva, 1962. See Conference of the Eighteen-nation committee on disarmament, Geneva, 1962-

SEVENTH fleet. See United States—Navy

SEVERE local storm warning center. See United States—Weather bureau

SEVERED head; drama. See Murdoch, I. and Priestley, J. B.

SEVERN wildfowl trust. See Bird sanctuaries

SEVERNY, A. B.
Solar magnetic fields; summary of address. por Sky & Tel 28:264 N '64

SEVERO, Richard
Automation and the news strike. Reporter 28:29-30+ Mr 14 '63

SEVILLA-SACASA, Guillermo
President Johnson receives chiefs of diplomatic missions; reply, December 13, 1963. Dept State Bul 49:997 D 30 '63

about

Dean of the corps. il pors Time 82:20 Jl 19 '63

SEVILLE, Spain
Stars of the Feria. il Vogue 144:80-5 Jl '64

SEVIN. See Insecticides

SÈVRES porcelain
Vincennes-Sèvres porcelain at the Cleveland museum of art. H. Hawley. il Antiques 85:322-5 Mr '64

SEWAGE
Activated carbon treatment. D. S. Davies and R. A. Kaplan. il Am City 80:78-81 Ja '65
Reclaiming used water; Whittier Narrows plant in Los Angeles County. J. D. Parkhurst. il Am City 78:83-5 O '63
Water reuse by design. R. R. Fleming. bibliog il Am City 78:106-8 O '63
See also
Sewerage

SEWAGE disposal
Biodegradation of alkylbenzene sulfonate in a simulated septic tank and drain field. A. E. Straus. bibliog il Science 142:244-5 O 11 '63
Industry's view on water and sewerage facilities; survey of Illinois industrialists. il Am City 79:102+ N '64
Inter-city water-sewerage agreements; Fort Worth, Tex. P. Holley. il Am City 79:73-5 D '64
Lather over detergents; anti-pollution campaigners push for laws. Bsns W p 104 F 16 '63
Little city gets sewage treatment; Heath, Ohio. C. F. Bird. il Am City 79:85-7 F '64
New methods to remove foam wastes found; fighting detergents with detergents. Sci N L 83:363 Je 8 '63
New sludge-disposal method; Lynnwood, Wash. il Am City 79:110-11 F '64
No special district for these cities; Phoenix, Ariz. metropolitan area. L. E. Goodall. il Am City 79:27 Ap '64
Sewerage and sewage purification. See issues of American city
Synthetic detergents in water and sewage systems; report of Society for industrial microbiology; annual meeting. W. J. Payne. Science 139:197-8 Ja 18 '63
Treat sewage as an area problem; Minneapolis-St Paul metropolitan area. A. W. Leslie. Am City 78:169-70+ Je '63
We are beating water pollution; North Dakota. W. V. Heuvelen. il Am City 78:34 Jl '63
What to watch for in sludge-cake storage. il Am City 79:35 F '64
Where is science taking us? detergent waste problem. M. A. Benarde. il Sat R 46:53 Ap 6 '63
See also
Septic tanks
Sewage lagoons
Water pollution

Activated sludge method

Everything under control in Dixon. C. K. Willett. il Am City 79:112-13 Ap '64

Filtration

Don't be just half-safe; Red Wing, Minn. R. Smith and others. il Am City 78:90-2 My '63
From septic tanks to secondary treatment; Cayey, Puerto Rico. R. M. Guzman. il Am City 78:103-4 N '63
Most complete waste-water treatment plant in the world; South Tahoe public utility district serving Bijou, Calif.-Lake Tahoe area. W. Priday and others. il Am City 79:123+ S '64
They all want to see the vacuum filters; waste-water-treatment plant, Ogden, Utah. il Am City 79:93-5 S '64
Triple-treatment sewage plant; Yorktown Heights, N.Y. A. Crew. il Am City 79:96-8 Mr '64

SEWAGE disposal plants
Big Muddy's first sewage plant; Sioux City, Ia. A. E. Rasmussen. il Am City 78:81-3 Jl '63
Concentric-circle design; Owatonna, Minn. R. Smith and others. il Am City 78:92-4 Mr '63
Construction cost index for sewage plants. Am City 79:27 Ja '64
Digesters beat incineration; Sioux City, Ia. A. E. Rasmussen. il Am City 79:100-1 D '64
Don't be just half-safe; Red Wing, Minn. R. Smith and others. il Am City 78:90-2 My '63
Everything under control in Dixon. C. K. Willett. il Am City 79:112-13 Ap '64
From septic tanks to secondary treatment; Cayey, Puerto Rico. R. M. Guzman. il Am City 78:103-4 N '63
How the sewage plants grow. Am City 79:30 My '64
It looks like a school; sewage-purification plant; Lawrenceburg, Ind. E. R. Hamilton. il Am City 79:98-100 O '64
One plant replaces four; control of waste-water purification; Greenwich, Conn. W. B. Van Riper. il Am City 79:110-12 O '64
Our good neighbor, the sewage-purification plant; Lakeland, Fla. G. McElhenney. il Am City 78:94-6 F '63
Sewage problems respect no political boundaries; Baton Rouge, La. G. S. Covert. il Am City 78:71-3 F '63
Sewerage and sewage purification. See issues of American city
They all want to see the vacuum filters; waste-water-treatment plant, Ogden, Utah. il Am City 79:93-5 S '64
This sewage plant gains friends; Great Neck, Long Island, N.Y. W. F. Cosulich and T. Keevan. il Am City 78:78-80 N '63
Triple-treatment sewage plant; Yorktown Heights, N.Y. A. Crew. il Am City 79:96-8 Mr '64

SEWAGE disposal plants—*Continued*
We doubled in area to solve our sewerage problem; Springfield, Ore. F. R. Smiley. il Am City 78:108-9 My '63
What you need to operate a waste-treatment plant. il Am City 78:101-3+ D '63
Where to put small sewage plants; Ohio's revised rules. Am City 79:23+ F '64

Power

How to estimate kilowatts in sewage-digester gas. W. A. O'Leary and V. Greiff. il Am City 78:92-4 Jl '63

SEWAGE flow
Isolating the causes of infiltration; Princeton, N.J. A. T. Brokaw. il Am City 79:80-1 D '64

SEWAGE gas
How to estimate kilowatts in sewage-digester gas. W. A. O'Leary and V. Greiff. il Am City 78:92-4 Jl '63

SEWAGE lagoons
Double-duty hog lagoon. C. F. Marley. il Suc Farm 61:104 Ap '63
Reclaimed sewage becomes a community asset; Santee, Calif. J. Merrell and R. Stoyer. il Am City 79:97-101 Ap '64

SEWAGE rentals. See Sewage disposal

SEWAGE sludge gases. See Sewage gas

SEWAGE systems. See Sewerage

SEWAGE tanks
Steel-lined for safety's sake; Owls head and Hunts Point, N.Y. il Am City 78:120 S '63
What it costs to clean a digester; St Louis, Mich. R. M. Henneberger, jr. and H. Bush. il Am City 78:105 Mr '63

SEWAGE treatment plants. See Sewage disposal plants

SEWANEE college. See University of the South, Sewanee, Tenn.

SEWELL, William H.
Some recent developments in socialization theory and research. bibliog f Ann Am Acad 349:163-81 S '63

SEWER cleaning
Clean sewers at half the cost; Walla Walla, Wash. P. H. Meyer. il Am City 78:27 N '63
Clean sewers on schedule; Dayton, Ohio. J. A. Chifala. il Am City 78:110-11 Je '63
Four-way program of sewer rehabilitation; Fairview Park, Ohio. E. J. Baugh. il Am City 79:117 Mr '64
Know when to holler for help; television inspection of sewer system, Hopkins, Minn. R. Brubacher. il Am City 79:92-3 My '64
No need for emergencies; Dearborn, Mich. J. M. Dick. il Am City 79:103-4 My '64

SEWER inspection
Four-way program of sewer rehabilitation; Fairview Park, Ohio. E. J. Baugh. il Am City 79:117 Mr '64
Isolating the causes of infiltration; Princeton, N.J. A. T. Brokaw. il Am City 79:80-1 D '64
Know when to holler for help; television inspection of sewer system, Hopkins, Minn. R. Brubacher. il Am City 79:92-3 My '64
Largest sewer photo inspection; Anchorage, Alaska. C. E. Cannon. il Am City 80:98-9 Ja '65
Late, late show; Owatonna, Minn. R. Pecore. il Am City 78:34 Ap '63
TV and chemical grout; stop sewer problems in Wichita, Kan. G. Wilton. il Am City 78:78-9 Ag '63
TV sewer inspection; Hartford, Conn. R. H. Brindley. il Am City 79:87-9 Ja '64

SEWER pipe laying. See Pipe laying

SEWER pipes
Plea for short sewers. R. L. Smith. il Am City 79:25 N '64
Storm-sewer design factors; Puyallup, Wash. C. S. Seabrook. il Am City 79:76-8 Jl '64
This line will change duties; Spartanburg, S.C. R. A. McCoy, jr. il Am City 79:116-17 Je '64
Upside-down wells; Dunn, N.C. A. B. Uzzle, jr. il Am City 79:30 My '64
See also
Sewer cleaning

Leakage

Seal sewer leaks from the inside. R. Nooe. il Am City 79:91-2 Je '64
Steel bands stop joint leakage. E. A. Janssen. il Am City 78:149 My '63

Repairing

Scuba divers replace missing pipe; Decatur, Ill. A. Van Praag, jr. il Am City 78:84-5 D '63
Steel bands stop joint leakage. E. A. Janssen. il Am City 78:149 My '63
TV and chemical grout; stop sewer problems in Wichita, Kan. G. Wilton. il Am City 78:78-9 Ag '63

SEWERAGE
Coded signal warns of sewer surcharge; Milwaukee. W. L. Burmeister and C. W. Schwarz. il Am City 78:96-7 S '63
No more storm-water worries; Middletown, Ohio. C. W. Thompson. il Am City 78:93-4 Ag '63
Sewer construction takes a dip; Upper Darby, Pa. J. E. Kirk and P. McHale. il Am City 78:25 Mr '63

Maintenance and repair

Don't wait for stoppages; Nassau County, N.Y. E. F. Gibbons and J. H. Peters. il Am City 79:79-81 N '64
Isolating the causes of infiltration; Princeton, N.J. A. T. Brokaw. il Am City 79:80-1 D '64
Look right into your sewer problems. J. A. Kern. il Am City 79:84-5 Ag '64

Statistics

Facts and figures of the Americas. il Américas 16:43 D '64

SEWERS. See Sewerage

SEWGOLUM, Papwa. See Sewgolum, S.

SEWGOLUM, Sewsunker
Papwa's championship play. E. Shirley. por Sports Illus 18:49 F 18 '63

SEWING
Home sewing; questions and answers (cont) M. Carter. Redbook 120:36 Mr; 50 Ap; 121:47 My; 22 Jl; 10 Ag '63
Short-order Christmas gifts. il Ladies Home J 80:32 D '63
Teaching your daughter to sew. M. C. Martin. il Parents Mag 40:44-5+ Ja '65
See also
Dressmaking
Mending

SEWING centers. See Sewing rooms

SEWING equipment
Outfitting a sewing corner. Am Home 67:105 N '64
What's new to help you sew. C. D. Legg. il Farm J 87:57 S '63

SEWING machines
Automatic stitch zigzag sewing machines. il Consumer Bul 48:43+ Ja '65
Automatic zigzag sewing machines. il Consumer Rep 28:105-12 Mr '63
Get the name and address of the maker!! if you can't, don't buy. Consumer Bul 46:40 O '63
Here is a new-old sewing machine; use cabinet of an old treadle sewing machine for a modern, electric model. il Sunset 133:102 S '64
How to get the most from your sewing machine. C. Houck. il Parents Mag 40:16 Ja '65
Japan sews up a market; sewing machine industry. il Bsns W p76+ Ag 3 '63
Straight-stitch sewing machines. il Consumer Bul 47:22-6 Ag '64
Trouble shooter; the electric sewing machine serviceman. T. Petrehn. il McCalls 90:134 Je '63
What makes an appliance automatic? Consumer Bul 46:32-3 Jl '63
Zigzag sewing machines. il Consumer Bul 47:22-6 S '64
See also
Singer manufacturing company

SEWING rooms
Bookshelf sewing center. il Pop Mech 121:146-8 Ap '64
Design your own room to sew. il Seventeen 22:83+ Je '63
Sewing center. H. Sibley. il Pop Mech 119:143 Ap '63
Sewing center's double life. il Sunset 134:56-7 Ja '65

SEX
Boys and girls together; excerpt from Moving into manhood. W. W. Bauer. il Todays Health 41:73+ S '63
Common sense sex code. R. E. Fitch. Christian Cent 81:1233-5 O 7 '64; Excerpts. Time 84:91 O 16 '64
Let's stamp out sex. J. Lubold. il Read Digest 83:73-5 O '63
New approach to sex. Sci Digest 54:71 D '63
Puritans against sex? no, says sociologist. Sci N L 85:20 Ja 11 '64

SEX—*Continued*
Realization of the sex nature; excerpt from Ethics of sex. H. Thielicke. Christian Cent 81:73-7 Ja 15 '64; Discussion. 81:304 Mr 4 '64
Sexual revolution; excerpts from Children for adoption. P. S. Buck. il Ladies Home J 81: 43-5+ S '64
What wives don't know about sex; ed. by J. Younger; reprint. A. Stone. Read Digest 84:78-80 Mr '64
What your doctor probably doesn't know about sex. H. I. Lief. Harper 229:92-6 D '64

SEX (biology)
See also
Hermaphroditism

SEX and law
Homosexuality: sin or disease? W. Overholser. Christian Cent 80:1099-101 S 11 '63; Discussion. 80:1304 O 23 '63
New pressure to ease morals laws; statutes regulating sexual practices and morals in New York state. U S News 57:12 D 7 '64
Sex vs. the law: a study in hypocrisy. H. F. Pilpel. il Harper 230:35-40 Ja '65

SEX and religion
Liberty of love; premarital sex. G. Foley. Christian Cent 81:826-9 Je 24 '64
New Protestant debate over sex. H. Cox; R. E. Fitch. Redbook 123:56-7+ O '64
One flock, no shepherd; Christian case for abstinence from sexual intercourse before marriage. America 110:784, 857 Je 6, 27 '64
Pornography, sex and the church. R. A. Cannon. Christian Cent 80:576-9 My 1 '63
Swedish bishops condemn premarital intercourse. Christian Cent 81:822 Je 24 '64

SEX attractants (insects) See Insect sex attractants

SEX behavior
Dance of the salamanders. R. L. Scheffel. il Audubon Mag 66:168-71 My '64
Defense of mate and mating chamber in a wood roach. H. Ritter, jr. Science 143:1459-60 Mr 27 '64
Feminine behavior in neonatally castrated and estrogen-treated male rats. H. H. Feder and R. E. Whalen. bibliog il Science 147:306-7 Ja 15 '65
Genotype and sex drive in intact and in castrated male mice. T. E. McGill and G. R. Tucker. bibliog il Science 145:514-15 Jl 31 '64
Hormones and sexual behavior. W. C. Young and others. bibliog il Science 143:212-18 Ja 17 '64
I'm sorry, dear; excerpt from Ways of the will. L. H. Farber. Commentary 38:47-54 N '64
Induction of conjugation by cell-free preparations in paramecium multimicronucleatum. A. Miyak. bibliog Science 146:1583-5 D 18 '64
Mirror display in the squirrel monkey, saimiri sciureus. P. D. MacLean. bibliog il Science 146:950-2 N 13 '64
Original sex; a kind of sexual mating between caulobacter bacteria. Time 84:85 N 13 '64
Playing cupid is a tough problem for a zookeeper. P. Hunt. il Life 57:54A Ag 21 '64
Sex behavior neglected. Sci N L 83:322 My 25 '63
Sexuality in crisis. L. J. Averill. Christian Cent 80:1196-9 O 2 '63
Suppression of the development of female mating behavior by estrogen administered in infancy. R. E. Whalen and R. D. Nadler. il Science 141:273-4 Jl 19 '63
See also
Courtship of insects

SEX censorship. See Censorship

SEX chromosomes. See Chromosomes

SEX control. See Sex determination and control

SEX crimes
My problem and how I solved it: our child was molested. il Good H 158:10+ Ja '64; Same abr. Read Digest 84:98-102 Ap '64
When the police welcome false alarms; child molesters. G. Marten. PTA Mag 57:30-1 My '63

SEX determination and control
Predicting the sex of the unborn infant. Good H 158:164 Je '64
Sex by sedimentation. Time 84:55 Jl 17 '64

SEX differences
Are we minimizing differences between the sexes? B. Spock. Redbook 122:20+ Mr '64
Boys weaker than girls. Sci N L 84:223 O 5 '63
Estrogen administered neonatally affects adult sexual behavior in male and female rats. S. Levine and R. Mullins, jr. bibliog il Science 14:185-7 Ap 10 '64
Grouping by sex; Broome jr. high school, Rockville, Md. C. J. Fahrner and J. M. Cronin. il NEA J 52:16-17 My '63
How men feel about sex. D. R. Mace. Read Digest 82:70-2 Je '63
Male and female; excerpts from Children tell stories; an analysis of fantasy. E. G. Pitcher. il Atlan 211:87-91 Mr '63
Need sex desegregation. W. Davis. Sci N L 86:22 Jl 11 '64
Sex-associated differences in serum proteins of mice. E. Espinosa and others. bibliog il Science 144:417-18 Ap 24 '64
What's happening in education? sex differences in children's learning behavior. W. D. Boutwell. PTA Mag 57:25 Je '63
What's the difference between boys and girls? il Todays Health 42:85 N '64

SEX education. See Sex instruction

SEX hormones. See Hormones, Sex

SEX in literature
Anatomy of Playboy. B. De Mott; discussion. Commentary 35:71-4 Ja '63
Compulsory sex scene. P. H. Johnson. Vogue 145:134-5 Ja 1 '65
Confessions of a square. J. W. Krutch. Sat R 47:23-6 My 9 '64
If it's shocking, will it sell? E. G. Patterson. Writer 76:17-19 Jl '63
Lady Chatterley goes to college. N. Lynch. Mlle 57:224-5+ Ag '63
Mary McCarthy and the group. M. Darrell. il Look 28:106-8+ F 25 '64
Pornography, sex and the church. R. A. Cannon. Christian Cent 80:576-9 My 1 '63
Predicts puritan revolution. Christian Cent 81:1076-7 S 2 '64
Varieties of love. E. Capouya. Nation 197: 457-9 D 28 '63

SEX in plants. See Plants, Sex in

SEX instruction
Adolescent sexual behavior; whose responsibility? excerpts from address, May 1964. M. S. Calderone. il PTA Mag 59:4-7 S '64
All about the birds and the beans. N. Spofford. il Redbook 121:6+ S '63
Child's questions about sex; with study-discussion program by R. Strang. H. H. Comly. il PTA Mag 59:7-9, 35 Ja '65
How I learned to answer the questions my daughter couldn't ask me. il Good H 157: 10+ Ag '63
Modesty is back in style; with program for discussion group, by M. Smart. S. Blau. Parents Mag 38:42, 51+ Mr '63
My problem and how I solved it: our child was molested. il Good H 158:10+ Ja '64; Same abr. Read Digest 84:98-102 Ap '64
Parent's guide to sex education; with study discussion program, by E. G. Neisser. M. B. Hoover. bibliog il Parents Mag 39: 27-8+, 60-3+ Ap '64
Problem in teen-age education. F. L. Filas. America 111:594-5+ N 14 '64
Sex in Russia. il Newsweek 64:106 O 19 '64
Sexplosion: disregard of moral restraints. R. E. Fitch. Christian Cent 81:136-8 Ja 29 '64; Discussion. 81:372+ Mr 18 '64
What teen-agers don't know about sex. S. H. Fraiberg. Parents Mag 38:35+ Jl '63

SEX perversion
See also
Homosexuality

SEX ratio
Inherited male-producing factor in an insect that produces its males from unfertilized eggs. A. Wilkes. bibliog il Science 144:305-7 Ap 17 '64; Reply with rejoinder. S. E. Flanders. 145:726-7 Ag 14 '64
Interference between sex-ratio agents of drosophila willistoni and drosophila nebulosa. B. Sakaguchi and others. bibliog il Science 147:160-2 Ja 8 '65

SEX relations
Conjugal love and conjugal morality. R. A. McCormick. America 110:38-42 Ja 11 '64
Eros denied: sex in western society, by W. Young. Review
Sat R 47:41-2 Je 6 '64. E. Capouya
Great symbol; sexual intercourse in marriage. C. Davis. America 111:803 D 19 '64
How men feel about sex. D. R. Mace. Read Digest 82:70-2 Je '63
Husbands and love. V. Cadden. Redbook 120: 62-3+ Ap '63
I'm sorry, dear; excerpt from Ways of the will. L. H. Farber. Commentary 38:47-54 N '64

SEX relations—*Continued*
Is it immature loving? F. M. Wessling. il America 110:594-6 My 2 '64; Discussion. 110: 768-70 My 30 '64
Love and sex. M. S. Calderone. Redbook 122: 39+ F '64; Same abr. with title There are no shortcuts to marriage. Read Digest 85:68-70 Ag '64
Must the colleges police sex? J. T. Rule. il Atlan 213:55-8 Ap '64; Discussion. 213:42+ Je '64
My problem and how I solved it: my husband was unfaithful. il Good H 156:10+ Mr '63
Sex problems after ten years of marriage. M. Davis. McCalls 90:50+ My '63
Speaking out; eroticism, sex and love. J. B. Priestley. Sat Eve Post 236:10+ Ap 27 '63

SEXTON, Anne
Last believer; story. Vogue 142:76 N 15 '63
Love song. Harper 227:83 O '63
Sylvia's death; poem. Poetry 103:224-6 Ja '64
Three green windows; poem. New Yorker 40:44 Je 6 '64
about
Five poets. R. Howard. Poetry 101:413-14 Mr '63
Poetry of three women. M. Swenson. Nation 196:164-6 F 23 '63

SEXTON, Brendan
Liberals and the labor movement. Mo Labor R 87:133-4 F '64

SEXTON, Kathryn
For circus fans only! ALA Bul 57:251-5 Mr '63

SEXTON, Patricia Cayo
City schools. bibliog f Ann Am Acad 352:95-106 Mr '64

SEXTON, Peggy B.
Widening a world. por Wilson Lib Bul 38: 852-4 Je '64

SEXUAL behavior. See Sex behavior

SEXUAL diseases. See Venereal diseases

SEXUAL ethics
Adolescent sexual behavior; whose responsibility? excerpts from address, May 1964. M. S. Calderone. il PTA Mag 59:4-7 S '64
College morals mirror our society. G. Hechinger and F. M. Hechinger. il N Y Times Mag p22+ Ap 14 '63
Colleges and public decency. R. Kirk. Nat R 16:112 F 11 '64; Discussion. 16:248 Mr 24 '64
Common sense sex code. R. E. Fitch. Christian Cent 81:1233-5 O 7 '64; Excerpts. Time 84:91 O 16 '64
Conjugal love and conjugal morality. R. A. McCormick. America 110:38-42 Ja 11 '64
Contraception is easier. America 112:6 Ja 2 '65
David Susskind's banned program: Sexual revolution in America. il Mlle 57:112-13+ O '63
Dialogue on the moral crisis; discussion at the annual meeting. S. J. Roland, jr. Christian Cent 81:705 My 27 '64
Dolce vita in a colder climate. M. Muggeridge. il Esquire 60:96-7+ N '63
Extramarital sex and the pill. P. A. Bertocci. Christian Cent 81:267-70 F 26 '64; Discussion. 81:499 Ap 15 '64
Failure of the sexual revolution in southern California. N. Morgan. il Esquire 62:57-8+ Ag '64
If they had only waited. Read Digest 86:85-9 Ja '65
Lady Chatterley goes to college. N. Lynch. Mlle 57:224-5+ Ag '63
Modesty is back in style; with program for discussion group, by M. Smart. S. Blau. Parents Mag 38:42, 51+ Mr '63
Morals on the campus. Newsweek 65:74 Ja 11 '65
Morals revolution on the U.S. Campus. il Newsweek 63:52-6+ Ap 6 '64
More on campus mores. D. A. Eldridge. il Sat R 47:57-9+ Je 20 '64
New Protestant debate over sex. H. Cox; R. E. Fitch. Redbook 123:56-7+ O '64
Of love and the like, teen-age division. M. Weston. il N Y Times Mag p 109-10+ O 11 '64
Privatist ethic and self-fulfillment. H. Stroup. Christian Cent 81:1031-3 Ag 19 '64; Reply. W. D. Bonis. 81:1365-6+ N 4 '64
Quaking morals; British Quakers report. Newsweek 61:77 Mr 4 '63
Realization of the sex nature; excerpt from Ethics of sex. H. Thielicke. Christian Cent 81:73-7 Ja 15 '64; Discussion. 81:304 Mr 4 '64
Second sexual revolution. il Time 83:54-9 Ja 24 '64
Sermonizing on sex: views of chaplain of Baltimore's Goucher college. Newsweek 64: 45 D 21 '64
Sex and hypocrisy. America 111:504 O 31 '64
Sex and the college girl. G. Greene; A. Montagu. il McCalls 90:106-7+ S '63
Sex and the college girl, by G. Greene. Review
New Repub 150:18-21 Ap '64. C. Jenks; Discussion. 150:28-9 Ap 18; 37-8 My 16 '64
Sex on the campus. Newsweek 62:75 Ag 12 '63
Sex on the campus; evaded problem. L. A. Kirkendall. Nation 198:165-7 F 17 '64
Sex on the campus: the real issue. M. Mead; discussion. Redbook 120:16 Mr '63
Sex text antidote. America 110:501 Ap 11 '64
Sexplosion: disregard of moral restraints. R. E. Fitch. Christian Cent 81:136-8 Ja 29 '64; Discussion. 81:372+ Mr 18 '64
Sexual morality and the young. J. Bingham. Mlle 57:126+ S '63
Sexual revolution. America 108:526 Ap 20 '63; Reply. R. F. Charles. 108:625-6 My 4 '63
Sexuality in crisis. L. J. Averill. Christian Cent 80:1196-9 O 2 '63
Six boys discuss dating and morals; symposium. il Seventeen 23:86-9+ Jl '64
Ten-dollar understanding; brothel behavior of the college boy. J. Richardson. Esquire 62: 101+ S '64
Too much sex on campus. J. L. Barron. il Ladies Home J 81:48+ Ja '64; Same abr. Read Digest 84:59-62 My '64
See also
Illegitimacy
Marriage
Sex and religion
Sex relations

SEXUAL maturity. See Puberty

SEXUAL sterilization. See Sterilization, Sexual

SEYCHELLES (islands)
Authentic paradise. il Newsweek 64:58 N 9 '64

SEYDOUX, Roger
Ambassador Seydoux. New Yorker 39:15-16 Jl 13 '63

SEYMOUR, Charles
End of a friendship. Am Heritage 14:4-6 Ag '63
Obituary
Nat R 15:142 Ag 27 '63

SEYMOUR, Dan
Comet. por Newsweek 63:71 Je 29 '64

SEYMOUR, George Dudley
(ed) Last days and valiant death of Nathan Hale; excerpts from Documentary life of Nathan Hale. Am Heritage 15:5-1 Ap '64

SEYMOUR, James K.
You can make money at trucking. il por Bsns W p 134+ F 16 '63

SEYMOUR, Lynn
Brief biography. S. Goodman. pors Dance Mag 37:54-5 Je '63

SEYMOUR, Whitney North, jr
Plea to curb the bulldozer. N Y Times Mag p80-1+ O 13 '63

SEYMOUR family
Seymour coat-of-arms. H. K. Eilers. il Hobbies 68:126-7 Ap '63

SEYNES, Philippe de
Application of science, technology to quicken economic development; statement, September 27, 1963. por U N Rev 10:28-33 N '63
Industrialization, vital key for progress in Asia and the Far East; address, March 11, 1963. U N Rev 10:19-22 Ap '63
International trade and African trade problems; text of statement. U N Rev 10:9-13 Mr '63
Latin American problems in today's world economy; text of statement. por U N Rev 10:18-20+ Je '63

SHAARA, Michael
Two roads to Petra: story. Sat Eve Post 236:60-2 Jl 27 '63

SHABAD, Steven
Amerikanets in a Moscow school. pors N Y Times Mag p44+ Je 9 '63

SHABAD, Theodore
Behind the smile on Krokodil. N Y Times Mag p22-3+ Je 7 '64

SHAD
See also
Cookery—Fish

SHAD fishing
Delaware shad. C. Conley. il Field & S 68: 61-3 Mr '64
Maytime is shad time. L. R. Green. il Outdoor Life 131:82-4+ My '63
Pulling the plug that killed a great shad stream; Delaware River. J. S. Martin. Sports Illus 18:50 My 27 '63

SHAD fishing—*Continued*
Shad are back. D. R. Crandall. il Outdoor Life 133:44-5+ Mr '64
Shad come early to the Russian River. il Sunset 132:68+ Ap '64
When the shad come home from the sea; reproductions of paintings by F. Golden; with account by D. Barnes. Sports Illus 20:40-51 Mr 16 '64
SHADBLOWS. See Serviceberries
SHADBOLT, Maurice
In storied lands of Malaysia. por Nat Geog Mag 124:734-83 N '63
SHADE
For barbecue fun; relax in cool refreshing shade. K. Smith. il Pop Gard 14:60-2 Jl '63
Shade for beef cattle. W. N. Garrett. Suc Farm 61:67 Ag '63
See also
Screens (sun)
SHADE houses. See Shelters (agriculture)
SHADE plants. See Plants. Shade
SHADE trees. See Trees; Trees in cities
SHADEGG, Stephen C.
Barry's tactician. il Newsweek 64:20+ Ag 10 '64
Men behind Goldwater. R. G. Spivack. il Look 28:45+ N 3 '64
SHADES. See Window shades
SHADES and shadows
Shadows. New Yorker 40:43-4 O 3 '64
Ten ways to lighten shadows. il Pop Phot 54:94-5 Ja '64
SHADING of plants. See Plants. Shading of
SHADOWGRAMS
Our footloose correspondents; to Moscow with a shadowgrapher. V. Perera. New Yorker 39:144+ Ap 27 '63
Photograms: why & how. A. Francekevich. il Pop Phot 53:22+ O '63
SHADOWS. See Shades and shadows
SHAFER, Burr
Through history with J. Wesley Smith. il Sat R 47:148 Ag 29 '64
SHAFER, Elizabeth
Grandfather's letter to God; poem. McCalls 92:169 N '64
SHAFFER, Bernard L. See Tasch, P. jt. auth.
SHAFFER, Kenneth R.
Teenage elysium: our own delusion; reprint. por Library J 89:4976-8 D 15 '64
SHAFFER, Peter
Private ear. Criticism
America 109:752 D 7 '63
Nation 197:306 N 9 '63
Newsweek 62:104 O 21 '63
Theatre Arts il 48:65 Ja '64
Time 82:76+ O 18 '63
Public eye. Criticism
America 109:752 D 7 '63
Newsweek 62:104 O 21 '63
Sat R 46:32 O 26 '63
Theatre Arts 48:65 Ja '64
Time 82:76+ O 18 '63
Royal hunt of the sun. Criticism
Vogue 144:112 O 1 '64
SHAFFER, Roy
East Africa's one-man peace corps. il pors Todays Health 41:20-5 Je '63
SHAFFER, Samuel
Hubert Humphrey comes on strong. N Y Times Mag p 11+ Ag 25 '63
SHAFTING
See also
Cranks and crankshafts
SHAFTING, Flexible
Three power take-offs for a flexible shaft. J. Burroughs. il Pop Mech 121:190-1 Ap '64
SHAH, B. P.
Analog computation. Science 141:448 Ag 2 '63
SHAH, Krishna. See Paton, A. jt. auth.
SHAHN, Ben
Letter and the spirit. F. Getlein. New Repub 150:25-6 Ja 25 '64
SHAKER cookery. See Cookery, American
SHAKER furniture. See Furniture, American
SHAKERS
Shaker form & function. W. R. Stewart. bibliog il Sch Arts 63:26-8 Ap '64
SHAKESPEARE, William
Romeo and Juliet; drama. ed. by L. Olfson. Plays 23:87-98 My '64
about
Britain that Shakespeare knew. L. B. Wright. il Nat Geog Mag 125:613-65 My '64
Brush up your Shakespeare. N. Braybrooke. il Sat R 47:92+ Mr 14 '64
Burton Hamlet. J. Diether. il Am Rec G 30:1092-5 Ag '64
Come, woo me. J. Diether. Am Rec G 30:990-1 Je '64
Curl up and read. J. Savanyu. por Seventeen 23:94+ Ap '64
For the quadricentennial; the tragedie of Hamlet, prince of Denmarke. J. Diether. il por Am Rec G 30:778-81+ My '64
Homages to Shakespeare delights, and a few dangers. G. Rogoff. Hi Fi 14:91 S '64
How Shakespeare spent the day. I. Brown. il Sat R 47:14-17+ Ap 4 '64
London that was Shakespeare's; excerpts from Shakespeare of London. M. Chute. il pors UNESCO Courier 17:14-17+ My '64
Not of an age but for all time. B. Ward. il N Y Times Mag p 17+ Mr 15 '64
Ode to an impudent upstart. S. O'Casey. il N Y Times Mag p20+ Ap 19 '64
Out, out . . . ! D. Martin. Sat R 47:59 Ap 18 '64
Shakespeare at 400. il Life 56:58-99 Ap 24; 80A-88+ My 1 '64
Shakespeare boom; a 400-year success story; interview. L. B. Wright. il pors U S News 56:68-71 Ap 27 '64
Shakespeare had an aye for women. L. B. Wright. NEA J 53:34 N '64
Shakespeare: mask and face. P. Quennell. il por Mlle 58:74-5+ F '64
Shakespeare our contemporary, by J. Kott. Review
Life 57:24 O 16 '64. T. Prideaux
So-called Shakespeare dictionary. P. W. Schmidtchen. il por Hobbies 68:106-7 O '63
Special issue on Shakespeare; symposium, ed. by J. Mersand. il por Sr Schol 84:13T-16T+ F 21; 8T-11T F 28 '64
Tragedy of Coriolanus. J. Diether. Am Rec G 30:345-6 D '63
Who was Shakespeare? P. Milward. America 110:566-7 Ap 25 '64
William Shakespeare: year four hundred. il UNESCO Courier 17:12-13 My '64

Anecdotes, facetiae, satire, etc.

Lost weekend of Willielmum Shaxpere. R. Joseph. il Esquire 61:120-3 Mr '64
Shakespeare exposed. J. Glashan. il Holiday 35:58-63 Je '64
Shakespeare on photography. G. Gilbert. por U S Camera 27:15 Ja '64

Anniversaries, etc.

Administrator's view; library promotion, Greenwich, Conn. J. W. Bryant. il Wilson Lib Bul 39:464-7 F '65
After four centuries; Britain's observances in honor of Shakespeare's anniversary. J. Coll. America 110:567-9 Ap 25 '64
Bard in Britain; anniversary year performances, comp. by B. Coletti. Sat R 47:95-6 Mr 14 '64
Cake with 400 candles on it. L. Lerman. il Mlle 58:76-80+ F '64
Letter from Stratford; 400th anniversary exhibition. M. Panter-Downes. New Yorker 40:148-50 My 23 '64
London's Shakespeare year. il Sat R 47:97 Mr 14 '64
Much ado about Will; Bardmania in England. il pors Newsweek 63:99-101 Ap 27 '64
Shakespeare in Maryland; Enoch Pratt free library, Baltimore. D. Sinclair. il Wilson Lib Bul 39:480-1 F '65
Shakespeare schedule; anniversary year performances in USA and Europe. R. Meyer, jr. Sat R 47:98-9 Mr 14 '64
Shakespeare year. W. Houlton. il NEA J 53:60-2 F '64
Shakespeare's England. A. Cutler. il Travel 121:34-40 Mr '64
Three Stratfords. P. P. Coleman. il Sr Schol 84:22T F 21 '64
Will Shakespeare's happy 400th birthday. J. Robbins and J. Robbins. por Read Digest 84:23-4+ Ap '64
World rendezvous in Stratford: 400th anniversary exhibition. il por UNESCO Courier 17:18-19 My '64

Appreciation

Culture for the savages; a mother's way of introducing her children to Shakespeare. G. Goff. il Redbook 120:6+ Ap '63
Shakespeare and the garden. F. C. Coulter. il Pop Gard 15:14+ S '64
Shakespeare in present-day perspective; symposium. bibliog il Christian Cent 81:481-92 Ap 15 '64
This side idolatry. L. F. Doyle. por Cath World 199:182-7 Je '64
Why bother with the bard? T. Guthrie. il Seventeen 23:148-9+ S '64

SHAKESPEARE, William —*Continued*

Authorship

History's biggest literary whodunit. D. J. Hamblin. il Life 56:69-70+ Ap 24 '64; Same with title Who wrote Shakespeare? por Read Digest 85:95-9 Jl '64

Bibliography

Bard in paper. R. L. Hillier. il Library J 89:193-8 Ja 15 '64
Brush up your Shakespeare! R. Hart. Wilson Lib Bul 38:653-5 Ap '64
New books on Shakespeare. Christian Cent 81:494-8 Ap 15 '64
Problems in Shakespearian scholarship; reprint. L. Marder. Wilson Lib Bul 38:660-3+ Ap '64
Vision and reality: Shakespeare to Calvin Coolidge. P. Pickrel. Harper 228:113-14+ My '64

Biography

Happy birthday, whoever you are. D. Littlejohn. Reporter 31:56+ S 24 '64

Characters

Creator of clowns and kings: his magic and power. il Life 56:78A-85+ Ap 24 '64
Forebears of Falstaff; Shakespeare's Merry Wives of Windsor. G. McElroy. Opera N 29:24-5 Ja 23 '65
Ten favorites from Shakespeare; photographs. T. Guthrie. N Y Times Mag p 18-19 Mr 15 '64

Collections

Another part of the forest; symposium. il por Wilson Lib Bul 38:628-44+ Ap '64

Criticism and appreciation

Shakespeare our contemporary, by J. Kott, tr. by B. Takorski. Review
Nation 199:94-6 S 7 '64. O. LeWinter

Criticism and interpretation

Last act and the action of Hamlet. B. L. Reid. Yale R 54:59-80 O '64
Opinion, please from London. A. Brien. Mlle 58:30+ F '64
Shakespeare and the choreographer. W. Sorell. il Dance Mag 38:43-5+ My '64
Shakespeare in present-day perspective; symposium. bibliog il Christian Cent 81:481-92 Ap 15 '64

Film strips

On film and filmstrip. P. E. Silberstein. il Sr Schol 84:20T-21T F 21 '64

Illustrations

Shakespeare. D. Stock. il Look 28:50-8 Ap 7 '64
Thurber on Avon. J. Thurber. Horizon 7: 118-20 Wint '65

Language

Thank you, William Shakespeare! G. Wright. Read Digest 85:82 Ag '64

Law

Bard & the bar. il Time 83:78 My 1 '64

Maps

New-old map re-creates the Britain of the Bard. Nat Geog Mag 125:666-7, sup(folded map) My '64

Moving pictures

On film and filmstrip. P. E. Silberstein. il Sr Schol 84:20T-21T F 21 '64

Music

Music for Shakespeare. S. Popper. il Opera N 28:8-12 My 2 '64
Music for Shakespeare; twentieth century approach. C. S. Susa. il Mus Am 84:46-7 S '64
Music of Shakespeare's time; and also Shakespeare music of more recent times. Am Rec G 30:1026-7 Jl '64
Musical events; Promenade concert at Philharmonic Hall. W. Sargeant. New Yorker 40:132-3 Je 13 '64
Shakespeare and music. C. J. McNaspy. America 110:581-2 Ap 25 '64

Philosophy

Bottom: on Shakespeare, by L. and C. Zukofsky. Review
Nat R 16:874-6 O 6 '64. G. Davenport

Plays

Enjoy the recorded riches of complete Shakespeare plays. E. Kinard. House B 106:38+ Mr '64
Letter from London; Royal Shakespeare company trilogy, Wars of the roses. M. Panter-Downes. New Yorker 40:116+ Ap 4 '64
Letter from Stratford; seven historical plays: Richard II, Henry IV, Henry V and trilogy Wars of the roses; performed by Royal Shakespeare theatre. M. Panter-Downes. New Yorker 40:146-8 My 23 '64
Shakespeare: still modern after 400 years. W. Johnson. il Sr Schol 84:4-5+ Ap 24 '64
Spoken word. E. Wagenknecht. Hi Fi 14:90+ Ag '64
Traveling with Mlle: the truant fancy. W. Sansom. il Mlle 58:123-5 F '64

Anecdotes, facetiae, satire, etc.

Three variations on a Shakespearean theme. T. Meehan. Mlle 58:81-3 F '64

Antony and Cleopatra

Antony and Cleopatra; production of Shakespeare festival in Central park. America 109:62-3 Jl 13 '63
New York; Shakespeare festival presentation. A. Pryce-Jones. il Theatre Arts 47:10 Ag '63
Stage seen on small screen; Central park production of Antony and Cleopatra televised. H. Hewes; R. L. Shayon. Sat R 46: 17 Jl 6 '63
Up in Central park. il Newsweek 62:60-1 Jl 1 '63

Comedy of errors

Double Will from England; Royal Shakespeare company's production at Lincoln Center's New York state theater. Time 83:49 My 29 '64
Howl! howl! Royal Shakespeare co. production. il Newsweek 63:80-1 Je 1 '64
Real royalty; Royal Shakespeare company at Lincoln Center's New York state theater. H. Hewes. Sat R 47:35 My 23 '64
Shakespeare with a few tears; Royal Shakespeare company's version. R. Brustein. New Repub 150:30-2 Je 13 '64
Stratford, Connecticut. A. Pryce-Jones. il(p 12) Theatre Arts 47:14+ Ag '63
Stratford, Ontario. A. Pryce-Jones. il(p 15) Theatre Arts 47:69 Ag '63
Theatre; Royal Shakespeare company's production in New York. H. Clurman. Nation 198:592 Je 8 '64

Hamlet

Anatomy of Burton's melancholy. H. Hewes. Sat R 47:24+ Ap 25 '64
Antic Hamlet; First quarto version at New York's 13th street theatre. R. J. Schroeder. Nation 199:312 N 2 '64
Burton's Hamlet. J. McLaughlin. Cath World 199:308-12 Ag '64
Creator of clowns and kings; his magic and power. il Life 56:78A-85+ Ap 24 '64
Crowning irony; John Gielgud's production. il Newsweek 63:78 Ap 20 '64
Electronovision first: Hamlet in 1,000 cities. L. Alterman. il Sr Schol 85:36 S 16 '64
Everything's up to date in Elsinore. T. Prideaux. il Life 56:91-2+ Ap 24 '64
First night in Minneapolis. L. Kirstein. Nation 196:437-8 My 25 '63
Gide's Hamlet. J. O'Brien. Reporter 31:38-9 Jl 16 '64
Hamlet; Richard Burton as Hamlet. T. Lewis. America 110:657 My 9 '64
Hamlet's castle; Kronborg castle. J. H. Preston. il Holiday 35:24+ Ja '64
I know not seems; Gielgud production. T. F. Driver. Reporter 30:43-4 My 21 '64
Last act and the action of Hamlet. B. L. Reid. Yale R 54:59-80 O '64
London openings. A. Brien. il Theatre Arts 48:30-1 Ja '64
Men, women and children; Hamlets all. G. Eells. il Theatre Arts 48:18-21+ Ja '64
New Dane in town; New York Shakespeare festival production. il Newsweek 63:80 Je 29 '64
People's choice; New York Shakespeare festival production. H. Hewes. Sat R 47:18 Jl 4 '64
Prince of thought; R. Burton's Hamlet. Time 83:65 Ap 17 '64
Revised standard Dane; new Hamlet of F. Zeffirelli. il Time 82:38 D 27 '63
Shakespeare with a few tears; Sir John Gielgud's production. R. Brustein. New Repub 150:30-2 Je 13 '64
Stage. G. Rogogg. Commonweal 80:176-7 My 1 '64
Stage and state; first offering of the British national theater. il Newsweek 62:62 N 4 '63
Theatre; John Gielgud's production at Lunt-Fontanne. J. McCarten. New Yorker 40: 108 Ap 18 '64

SHAKESPEARE, William—
Plays—Hamlet—*Continued*
Theatre; John Gielgud's production at the Lunt-Fontanne theatre. H. Clurman. Nation 198:465-6 My 4 '64
Theater; R. Burton's New York performance. G. Wills. Nat R 16:458-9 Je 2 '64
Theatre; Richard Burton's Hamlet. H. Popkin. Vogue 143:40 Je '64
View from the East; Tyrone Guthrie theatre opening. R. Gilman. Commonweal 78:282-3 My 31 '63

Henry V

Hit & miss in Minnesota; Tyrone Guthrie theater. il Time 83:64 My 22 '64
Stratford, Connecticut. A. Pryce-Jones. il(p 12) Theatre Arts 47:68 Ag '63
Tyrone Guthrie theatre. H. Clurman. Nation 199:59-60 Ag 10 '64

King Lear

As flies to wanton boys; Royal Shakespeare theatre production. T. F. Driver. il Reporter 28:44-6 Mr 14 '63
Broadway postscript; good company; Stratford, Conn. festival. H. Hewes. Sat R 46:21-2 Je 29 '63
Company way; Stratford, Ontario, production. H. Hewes. Sat R 47:28 Ag 15 '64
Double Will from England; Royal Shakespeare company's production at Lincoln Center's New York state theater. il Time 83:49 My 29 '64
Everyman's disasters; Connecticut's triumph. Time 82:44 Ag 16 '63
Howl! howl! Royal Shakespeare co. production. il Newsweek 63:80-1 Je 1 '64
King Lear; Royal Shakespeare company at Lincoln Center's New York state theatre. T. Lewis. America 110:852-3 Je 20 '64
King Lear; Royal Shakespeare company production. Vogue 144:30 Ag 1 '64
King Lear; Royal Shakespeare company's production. R. A. Duprey. Cath World 199:327-8 Ag '64
Real royalty; Royal Shakespeare company at Lincoln Center's New York state theater. H. Hewes. Sat R 47:35 My 23 '64
Shakespeare company; Peter Brook-Paul Scofield King Lear. G. Rogoff. Commonweal 80:398 Je 19 '64
Shakespeare with a few tears; Royal Shakespeare company's version. R. Brustein. New Repub 150:30-2 Je 13 '64
Stratford, Connecticut. A. Pryce-Jones. Theatre Arts 47:14 Ag '63
Theatre; performance by Royal Shakespeare company at New York state theatre. New Yorker 40:78 My 30 '64
Theatre; Peter Brook-Paul Scofield production at New York state theater. H. Clurman. Nation 198:591-2 Je 8 '64
We came crying hither: an essay on some characteristics of King Lear. M. Mack. Yale R 54:161-86 D '64

Othello

Divorce, moorish style; New York Shakespeare festival presentation. H. Hewes. Sat R 47:20 Ag 1 '64
In London: Othello: Sir Laurence Olivier plays the lead. H. Popkin. Vogue 144:102 S 1 '64
Letter from London; National theatre production at Old Vic. M. Panter-Downes. New Yorker 40:98 Je 13 '64
Off Broadway; New York Shakespeare festival's production indoors at Martinique. E. Oliver. New Yorker 40:93-5 O 24 '64
Olivier's Othello. H. Hewes. Sat R 47:25 My 30 '64
Ordinary Othello; New York Shakespeare festival. il Newsweek 64:49 Jl 27 '64
Two Moors an ocean apart; one in London, the other in New York. T. Prideaux. Life 57:23 D 11 '64

Richard III

Black intelligence; American Shakespeare festival's production. il Newsweek 63:80 Je 29 '64

Taming of the shrew

Off Broadway; Phoenix production at Anderson theatre. E. Oliver. New Yorker 39:137-8 Mr 16 '63
Openings, New York; presentation at Phoenix theatre, New York. Theatre Arts 47:71-2 My '63

Timon of Athens

Broadway postscript; Stratford, Ontario, production. H. Hewes. Sat R 46:27 Ag 17 '63
Duke in Athens; Canada's Stratford Shakespearean festival. Newsweek 62:52 Ag 12 '63

Troilus and Cressida

Broadway postscript; Stratford, Ontario, production. H. Hewes. Sat R 46:27 Ag 17 '63
Letter from Paris; performance in French, at Théâtre de France. Genêt. New Yorker 40:142-3 Mr 7 '64
Stratford, Ontario. A. Pryce-Jones. il(p 15) Theatre Arts 47:68 Ag '63

Political and social views

If Tom is half as old as Will. . . W. B. Blakemore. Christian Cent 81:489-92 Ap 15 '64

Quotations

Shakespeare; photographic tribute on 400th anniversary. D. Stock. il Look 28:50-8 Ap 7 '64
Shakespeare views the fair; comp. by D. Curtis. il Travel 122:42-3 Ag '64

Religion and ethics

Shakespeare and man's salvation. R. E. Fitch. il Christian Cent 81:486-8 Ap 15 '64

Sonnets

A. L. Rowse solves Shakespeare's sonnets; interview. A. L. Rowse. Pub W 184:31 S 30 '63
Mr W. H. by L. Hotson. Review
New Repub 151:16-19 N 28 '64. P. M. Kendall
Rest is still silence. B. Grebanier. Sat R 47:56-7 Ja 11 '64
Trouble with the Bard. C. Sykes. Nation 198:101+ Ja 27 '64
William Shakespeare, by A. L. Rowse. Review
Newsweek por 63:65 Ja 6 '64
Time il 83:83 Ja 10 '64

Staging and acting of plays

Avoiding a method. P. Hall. Theatre Arts 47:24-5 Ag '63
Creator of clowns and kings: his magic and power. il Life 56:78A-85+ Ap 24 '64
Everything's up to date in Elsinore. T. Prideaux. il Life 56:91-2+ Ap 24 '64
Great Sir Laurence; interview, ed. by R. McDowall. L. Olivier. il Life 56:80A-88+ My 1 '64
Little mummers render the Bard; Mrs Cartwright's childrens' production in Salt Lake City. il Life 55:120+ S 20 '63
Much ado about Shakespeare: three summer festivals. J. Novick. il Harper 228:64-71 My '64
Play's the thing, not the raiment. H. Taubman. il N Y Times Mag p22-3+ Ag 9 '64
Scholastic teacher interviews: James Allen Jones; ed. by H. Langer. J. A. Jones. il Sr Schol 84:10T-11T F 28 '64
Shakescene; selective survey of productions in the U.S. and Canada. il Time 84:52-3 Jl 31 '64
Shakespeare in present-day perspective; symposium. bibliog il Christian Cent 81:481-92 Ap 15 '64
Shakespeare is to hear. V. Voss. Mlle 58:122+ F '64
Shakespeare with a few tears. R. Brustein. New Repub 150:30-2 Je 13 '64
See also
Royal Shakespeare theatre company
Shakespeare festivals

Study and teaching

In the secondary schools. J. Mersand. il Sr Schol 84:14T-15T F 21 '64
Why bother with the bard? T. Guthrie. il Seventeen 23:148-9+ S '64
William to Tucker to Jess. J. Shera. Wilson Lib Bul 38:677 Ap '64

Translations

Translating Hamlet: version in modern English. J. Ciardi. Sat R 46:13 Ag 3 '63; Discussion. 46:16+ S 28 '63

SHAKESPEARE festival, Stratford-on-Avon
Learning about Shakespeare in his hometown. Sister Mary Sylvia. il Sr Schol 84:8T-9T F 28 '64
Letter from Stratford. M. Panter-Downes. New Yorker 40:145-50 My 23 '64
See also
Royal Shakespeare theatre company

SHAKESPEARE festival, Stratford, Ontario
Broadway postscript; Grecian yearns. H. Hewes. Sat R 46:27 Ag 17 '63
Company way. H. Hewes. Sat R 47:28 Ag 15 '64

SHAKESPEARE festival, Stratford, Ontario —*Continued*
Duke in Athens; Canada's Stratford Shakespearean festival. Newsweek 62:52 Ag 12 '63
If a theater is to prosper. T. Guthrie. il N Y Times Mag p7+ Jl 28 '63
Stratford, Ontario; productions, 1963 season. A. Pryce-Jones. il(p 15) Theatre Arts 47:68-9 Ag '63
Stratford wedding. R. Ubriaco. il Opera N 29:23 O 17 '64
SHAKESPEARE festivals
400 minus one; productions of Ashland and San Diego festivals. H. Hewes. il Sat R 46:16-17 Ag 31 '63
Much ado about Shakespeare: three summer festivals. J. Novick. il Harper 228:64-71 My '64
Quadricentennial. Holiday 35:146-7 Mr '64
Reviewer's notebook; New York's Shakespeare festival. T. Lewis. America 111:392 O 3 '64
Sceptered isle in holiday humor; Shakespeare's 400th birthday. il Bsns W p 146-8 Ap 18 '64
Shakespeare events this summer in Britain. il NEA J 53:63 F '64
Shakespeare festivals. Theatre Arts 47:72-3 Je '63
Shakespeare in the U.S. and Canada, 1964. Sat R 47:18-19 Ap 4 '64
Show and gaze o' the time. J. T. Shawcross. il Christian Cent 81:481-4 Ap 15 '64
Travel notes. R. Joseph. Esquire 61:39-40+ Mr '64
See also
American Shakespeare festival theatre and academy, Stratford, Conn.
New York Shakespeare festival
Shakespeare, W.—Anniversaries, etc.
Shakespeare festival, Stratford, Ontario
SHAKESPEARE library, Washington. See Folger Shakespeare library, Washington, D.C.
SHAKESPEARE memorial theatre. See Royal Shakespeare theatre, Stratford-on-Avon
SHAKESPEARE on phonograph records. See Phonograph records—Spoken records
SHAKESPEAREAN actors and actresses. See Actors and actresses
SHAKESPEARIAN music. See Shakespeare, W.—Music
SHAKHBUT bin Sultan, sheik of Abu Dhabi
O Long of Life drinks camel milk and runs on oil. T. Green. il pors Life 54:50+ My 3 '63
Sheik jackpot. il por Time 81:36 My 3 '63
Sheik of Abu Dhabi; world's richest man? il por U S News 57:54-6 Jl 6 '64
SHALE oil. See Oil shales
SHALIT, Gene
Books for children and playful adults. McCalls 91:48+ D '63
Children's books. McCalls 91:92+ My '64
Children's books for Christmas giving. McCalls 92:90+ D '64
SHALL we gather at the river? story. See McKinley, G.
SHALOM-Stolt Dagali collision. See Collisions at sea
SHALOWITZ, Elaine Langerman
Our school is trying team teaching. NEA J 53:45-6 My '64
SHAMAN, Harvey
Basic lighting rigs. il Pop Phot 53:136-7 N '63
Electronic flash studio in a 19-inch case. il Pop Phot 51:76-9+ D '62
Problems, solutions. il Pop Phot 54:106-9 Ja '64
T system. Pop Phot 53:64-7 Jl '63
(ed) See Forscher, M. Committee for a sane policy in automation
SHAMBURGER, Page
Bahamas treasure hunt. Flying 74:45 F '64
SHAMMA, Geraldine
I was Castro's prisoner; ed. by B. Lindeman. pors Sat Eve Post 236:78-81 My 18 '63
SHAMPOOS
Developing a shampoo for babies. E. M. McCabe. il Parents Mag 38:24+ Jl '63
SHANE, Harold G. See Buffie, E. G. jt. auth.
SHANE, Ted
Roamer's ramblings. See issues of Travel
SHANES, Abraham M.
Membrane permeability: monolayer relationships. bibliog Science 140:824-5 My 17 '63
Quantitative molecular approach to the permeability changes of excitation. bibliog Science 140:51-3 Ap 5 '63
—See Lakshminarayanaiah, N. jt. auth.
SHANET, Howard
En garde, Vanguard! Sat R 47:118 Mr 14 '64

SHANGHAI
Description
Shanghai. P. Durdin. il Sat R 48:42-3+ Ja 2 '65
SHANK, Edwin Gerald, Jr
Captain's last letters from Vietnam; excerpts. pors U S News 56:46-9 My 4 '64; Life 56: 34B-34D+ My 8 '64
SHANKAR, Ravi
And now the sitar. il por Time 84:84+ N 6 '64
SHANKLAND, R. S.
Michelson-Morley experiment. Sci Am 211: 107-14 N '64
SHANKLIN, H. A.
I learned about flying from that. Flying 75: 54+ Jl '64
SHANKLIN, John F.
Expanding use of industrial forest land; excerpts from address, January 1963. Recreation 57:18-19+ Ja '64
Recreation under the microscope. Am For 69: 32-5 Jl '63
SHANKLIN, Richard G. Jr, and Cuevas, R. A.
Supplemental water plant came first. Am City 79:153-5+ O '64
SHANNON, Claude E.
Man-machines may talk first to Dr Shannon. B. Brower. por Vogue 141:88-9+ Ap 15 '63
SHANNON, James A.
Science and federal programs: the continuing dialogue; adapted from address, April 28, 1964. Science 144:976-8 My 22 '64
You'll live longer; interview. por Nations Bsns 52:104-6+ Mr '64
SHANNON, James P.
This New generation. America 109:384-5 O 5 '63
SHANNON, William V.
Cuba and the administration. Commonweal 77:585-6; 78:51 Mr 1, Ap 5 '63
Elder Kennedy. New Repub 151:21-2 D 26 '64
Future of a noble lady. Good H 158:76-81+ Ap '64
Philippine war claims. New Repub 148:10-12 My 18 '63
Reforming the House, a four-year term? N Y Times Mag p22-3+ Ja 10 '65
Washington report. See issues of Commonweal
Who owns the Senate? New Repub 148:5-6 Mr 2 '63
Why Humphrey gets taken for granted. New Repub 151:10-12 Jl 4 '64; Correction. 151: 37 Ag 8 '64
SHANNON airport. See Airports—Ireland
SHAPERS
Shaper. il Pop Sci 183:183 N '63
SHAPIRA, Moses Wilhelm
Shapira affair, by J. M. Allegro. Review Sat R 48:30-1 Ja 30 '65. T. H. Gaster
SHAPIRO, Charles
Denial of the big dream? Sat R 46:28 Je 29 '63
Rebel with a craft. Sat R 46:34 O 26 '63
SHAPIRO, David
Group learning of speech sequences without awareness. bibliog Science 144:74-6 Ap 3 '64
SHAPIRO, Fred C.
Bedford-Stuyvesant. New Yorker 40:23-6 Ag 1 '64
SHAPIRO, Frieda S.
Your income tax deductions. NEA J 53:65 Ja '64
SHAPIRO, Harry L.
Books in review. Natur Hist 73:4+ O '64
Man grows bigger if not better. N Y Times Mag p 13+ D 15 '63
SHAPIRO, Harvey
Master and teacher; poem. Nation 196:216 Mr 9 '63
On some words of Ben Azzai; Modern poetry and the tradition; poems. Poetry 102:22 Ap '63
Writer; Beyond the demonic element; Purities; Distances; poems. Poetry 105:183-4 D '64
SHAPIRO, Irvin
Non-partisan, transistorized candidate. New Repub 150:11-12 Mr 28 '64
SHAPIRO, J. Erwin
Unvarnished trash upheld by N.Y. Supreme court judge. Library J 88:3812 O 15 '63
SHAPIRO, Jay R. See Lutwak, L. jt. auth.
SHAPIRO, Karl
End paper: Balcony scene; Vacation; Antipoem; Death of a student; Basement apartment; Witches are flying; Teamsters union; poems. Poetry 103:90-6 O '63
Library, asylum, platform for uninhibited leaps; address, February 15, 1963. por Wilson Lib Bul 37:661-9 Ap '63

SHAPIRO, Karl—*Continued*

about

Leaves of glass. W. Schott. Nation 199:74-6 Ag 24 '64
Verse. L. Bogan. New Yorker 40:238+ N 7 '64

SHAPIRO, Ludmilla N.
Quiet flows their prose. Sat R 46:22 Ag 10 '63

SHAPIRO, Milton J.
Spahn sues for $175,000 over fictionalized biography. Pub W 185:70 F 3 '64
Warren Spahn wins $10,000 over fictionalized book. Pub W 185:100 Je 8 '64

SHAPIRO, Samuel
Dissent, si; dissenter, no; discussion. Nation 196:inside cover F 16 '63
Explaining Fidel Castro. New Repub 148:23-4 Ap 20 '63

SHAPIRO, family
At Maryland cup, it's nepotism all the way. il Bsns W p 102-3 S 7 '63

SHAPLEN, Robert
Letter from Manila. New Yorker 39:136-40+ Je 8 '63
Letter from Saigon. New Yorker 39:201-4+ D 14 '63; 40:37-8+ Jl 11; 179-86+ S 19 '64
Our far-flung correspondents. New Yorker 39:130+ Ap 6 '63; 40:150+ Ap 18 '64
Reporter at large. New Yorker 39:50-2+ S 28 '63; 40:78+ Ja 16 '65

SHAPLEY, Harlow
Life on unseen planets. por Sci Digest 53:59-64 F '63

SHAPLIN, Judson T.
Antecedents of team teaching; excerpt from Team teaching. bibliog f Sch & Soc 91:393-407 D 14 '63

SHARED time (public and parochial schools)
See Educational cooperation

SHARED time for religous instruction. See Public schools and religion

SHAREHOLDERS. See Stockholders

SHARF, Frederic A. See Hennessy, W. G. jt. auth.

SHARIF, Omar
Bad role for Omar the actor. C. Goren. il Sports Illus 21:82 O 19 '64

SHARK fishing
Duel with a hammerhead. G. Heinold. il Outdoor Life 131:8-9+ Ja '63
Tiger by the tail. A. J. McClane. il Field & S 69:70-4+ Ja '65

SHARKEY, A. G. jr. See Friedel, R. A. jt. auth.

SHARKS
Electrocardiographic studies of free-swimming sharks. P. W. Gilbert and S. D. Douglas. bibliog il Science 140:1396 Je 28 '63
Fascinating shark. A. C. Clarke. il Holiday 36:116 S '64
Menace sharks may pose. Good H 157:144 Ag '63
Pack strikes; deaths of capsized boat passengers off Philippines. Newsweek 61:42 Je 3 '63
Rectal glands of marine and fresh-water sharks: comparative histology. M. Oguri. bibliog il Science 144:1151-2 My 29 '64
Shark finds food fast by underwater sound. Sci N L 86:200 S 26 '64
Sharks attracted by low pulsing sounds. Sci N L 84:345 N 30 '63
Sharks: attraction by low-frequency sounds. D. R. Nelson and S. H. Gruber. bibliog il Science 142:975-7 N 15 '63
Sharks: sense and nonsense. A. Hamilton. il Sci Digest 54:53-6 Jl '63
See also
Dogfish

SHARLET, Robert S.
Russia's courts of public pressure. Nation 200:55-7+ Ja 18 '65

SHARLIN, Harold I.
Scientist in biography. Bul Atomic Sci 19:27-8 N '63

SHARNIK, Morton
College football. Sports Illus 19:52+ N 18 '63
Death of a champion. Sports Illus 18:18-21+ Ap 1 '63
Four who baffled Liston. Sports Illus 20:60-2+ F 10 '64
Green Bay blocks to win. Sports Illus 21:76-9+ S 7 '64
You can't keep a bad boy down. Sports Illus 19:18-19 D 16 '63

SHARP, A. J.
Compleat botanist; adaptation of address, December 30, 1963. bibliog Science 146:745-8 N 6 '64
—See Wagner, W. H. jr, jt. auth.

SHARP, Dolph
You can't do that in church! Read Digest 85:247-8+ N '64

SHARP, Ellen
Drawings by George Romney at Yale. Antiques 86:598-603 N '64

SHARP, H. Rodney
Living with antiques; Hacienda, Florida residence of H. R. Sharp. J. A. L. Hyde. il Antiques 85:76-9 Ja '64

SHARP, Harold S.
Special library convinces management that the library is not a luxury. Library J 88:1107-8 Mr 15 '63

SHARP, Henry S.
Cades Cove and Chief Mountain: symbols of our restless earth. Nat Parks Mag 37:8-10 S '63

SHARP, J. S.
Ten steps to a healthier downtown. Am City 79:97-8 F '64

SHARP, R. Farquharson
(tr) See Ibsen, H. Doll's house

SHARP, Thomas H.
Only the box stays the same. il Bsns W p 130-2+ Je 20 '64

SHARP, Ulysses Simpson Grant, 1906-
Imperturbable admiral. Time 84:14 Ag 14 '64

SHARPE, Helen S.
Eggs, something to crow about! Parents Mag 38:69+ Ap '63

SHARPE, Malcome
Rent-a-pigeon. il por Newsweek 63:42 Ja 13 '64

SHARPENING
How to sharpen everything; all kinds of saws. H. Walton. il Pop Sci 185:144-9+ S '64
How to sharpen everything; cold chisels, screwdrivers, cutting pliers, tin snips, and countersinks. H. Walton. il Pop Sci 186:138-41+ Ja '65
How to sharpen everything; drill bits. H. Walton. il Pop Sci 185:136-9+ D '64
How to sharpen everything; knife-edged wood-cutting tools. H. Walton. il Pop Sci 185:148-53 N '64
How to sharpen everything; knives and scissors. G. Daniels. il Pop Sci 185:174-7+ O '64
How to sharpen everything; yard and garden tools. G. Daniels. il Pop Sci 185:136-40+ Ag '64
See also
Grinding machines
Pencil sharpeners

SHARPLESS, Joseph B.
Track and field development. por Recreation 57:230-1 My '64

SHARPLESS, Ti-Grace A.
Freedom, absolute and infinitely exhilarating. Art N 62:36-9+ N '63

SHARTZER, Whitney
Everybody pitches in. Am City 78:90-1 N '63

SHASTA, MOUNT
Climbing Mount Shasta by rail. il Sunset 132:70 Je '64

SHASTA CAVERNS. See Caves

SHASTA daisies
These all are shastas. il Sunset 130:238+ Mr '63

SHASTRI, Lal Bahadur
After Shastri, who? il Time 84:31 Jl 10 '64
Architect. por Time 83:22 Ja 24 '64
Back with the rain. Time 84:30+ Ag 7 '64
Blessed contact; new brand of neutralism for India. il Time 84:58 O 2 '64
Close to the soil. il por Time 83:29 Je 19 '64
In Nehru's steps. por Newsweek 63:39 F 3 '64
India turns to a conciliator. L. I. Rudolph and S. H. Rudolph. il por N Y Times Mag p 11+ Je 14 '64
India without Nehru. il por Sr Schol 85:12-14+ O 14 '64
Iron in his soul. il por Newsweek 63:39-40 Je 29 '64; Same abr. with title India after Nehru, will it work? Read Digest 85:141-2 S '64
Man of silk & steel. Time 83:40-1 Je 12 '64
Nehru's choice: Shastri. por U S News 56:21 Je 15 '64
Nehru's mantle falls on middle-of-roader. il por Bsns W p 131-2+ Je 6 '64
Nehru's successor? Gandhi disciple moves up. por U S News 56:14 F 3 '64
New initiatives. il Newsweek 64:34-5 Ag 31 '64
New man in India's spotlight. por Bsns W p68 F 1 '64
Next prime minister. New Repub 150:8 F 15 '64
Not-so-innocent Shastri. il pors N Y Times Mag p32-3 O 18 '64
Problems of inheritance. Newsweek 64:60+ O 26 '64
Quiet man takes over. por Newsweek 63:42+ Je 15 '64

SHASTRI, Lal Bahadur—*Continued*
Shastri at helm. Sr Schol 85:32 S 23 '64
Shastri takes over. M. Orshefsky. por Life 56:44F Je 12 '64
Stricken leader. por Newsweek 64:42 Jl 13 '64
Uneasy truce among Nehru's heirs. R. Knox. il Reporter 31:19-21 Jl 2 '64
SHATTER-proof glass. See Glass, Safety
SHATTUCK, John
Putting waste to work. il por Bsns W p 137-8 Mr 23 '63
SHATTUCK, Louise
Vegetables that sing of spring. Parents Mag 39:81+ Ap '64
SHAVER, LAKE
Hardest working water in the world; Big Creek development with playground Camp Edison. A. S. Green. il Am For 70:28-30 Je '64
SHAVERS, Electric. See Razors
SHAVING
Advice for women who shave. il Todays Health 42:36-7+ Jl '64
All about shaving. Sr Schol 84:45 Ap 10 '64
Shaving aids: la différence. il Mlle 57:22 Jl '63
What happens when you shave. J. H. Winchester. il Sci Digest 54:22+ O '63
What you should know about shaving your legs. il Good H 156:154 F '63
SHAW, Archibald B.
Censorship of textbooks; what can the superintendent do? NEA J 52:22-3 My '63
SHAW, Arnold
Gitars, folk songs, and halls of ivy. Harper 229:33-4+ N '64
SHAW, Artie
Grounds for divorce; story. McCalls 91:120-1 Ap '64
SHAW, Bernard. See Shaw, G. B.
SHAW, Bynum
Nevertheless, God probably loves Mrs Murray. Esquire 62:110-12+ O '64
SHAW, Callie
Pass the salt. por Time 82:31 O 11 '63
SHAW, Charles R. and Koen, A. L.
Hormone-induced esterase in mouse kidney. bibliog Science 140:70-1 Ap 5 '63
SHAW, Charlotte (Payne-Townshend)
Mrs G.B.S. by J. Dunbar. Review
Sat R por 46:33 Je 8 '63. S. Weintraub
Time por 82:83-4+ Jl 26 '63
SHAW, Clara
What happened after the award. ALA Bul 57:337-8 Ap '63
SHAW, Dale
Bungalow barges, fish bats, and bass. por Field & S 69:48-51 My '64
Hot tips from the tank men. Field & S 68:58-9+ F '64
SHAW, Darla
Art for enjoyment's sake. Recreation 58:31 Ja '65
SHAW, David M. See Donn, W. L. jt auth.
SHAW, Denis
Horse at Islamabad villa; story. Horizon 7: 54-5 Wint '65
SHAW, George Bernard
Candida. Criticism
McCalls 90:28+ Mr '63
GBS and the fair sex; quotations, with introduction by T. C. F. Lowry. il por Ladies Home J 81:128+ Ja '64
GBS in filmland. V. Delacorte. il por Esquire 62:150-1+ D '64
GBS on the USSR. R. Ohmann. Commonweal 80:519 Jl 24 '64
Man and superman. Criticism
Life 58:10 Ja 15 '65
Nation 199:522-3 D 28 '64
New Repub 152:33 Ja 30 '65
New Yorker 40:66+ D 19 '64
Sat R 47:33 D 26 '64
Mrs G.B.S. a portrait. by J. Dunbar. Review.
Sat R por 46:33 Je 8 '63. S. Weintraub
Time por 82:83-4+ Jl 26 '63
Mrs Warren's profession. Criticism
New Yorker 39:93 My 4 '63
Notes and comment. New Yorker 39:23 Je 1 '63
Playwright, plays and byplay. R. B. Dooley. pors Sat R 46:47-9 N 23 '63
Pygmalion. Criticism
Vogue il 144:152-5+ N 1 '64
Religion of Bernard Shaw. W. S. Smith. Christian Cent 80:1266-9 O 16 '63
Religious speeches of Bernard Shaw, ed. by W. S. Smith. Review
Christian Cent 81:17 Ja 1 '64. J. A. Davidson
Saint Joan. Criticism
Nation 199:60 Ag 10 '64
Time 83:64 My 22 '64
Shavian paradise lost. P. E. Mosely. Sat R 47:32 Jl 18 '64
Too true to be good. Criticism
America 108:591 Ap 20 '63
Nation 196:275 Mr 30 '63
New Repub 148:29 Mr 30 '63
New Yorker 39:73 Mr 23 '63
Newsweek 61:97 Mr 25 '63
Theatre Arts 47:69 My '63
Time il 81:74+ Mr 22 '63
SHAW, Herbert R.
Hydrogen-water vapor mixtures: control of hydrothermal atmospheres by hydrogen osmosis. bibliog Science 139:1220-2 Mr 22 '63
SHAW, Irwin
Goldilocks at graveside; story. Esquire 62: 32-4 Jl '64
My chancy life as a moviemaker. Vogue 142: 162-3+ S 1 '63
Snowy, snowy Alps. Mlle 58:154+ N '63
Tittle fading back. Esquire 63:31-4+ Ja '65
about
Children from their games. Criticism
New Yorker 39:96 Ap 20 '63
Newsweek 61:90 Ap 22 '63
Sat R 46:27 Ap 27 '63
Theatre Arts il 47:65 Je '63
SHAW, John G.
Deoxyribonuclease sensitivity of ribonucleic acid synthesizing system from tobacco leaves. bibliog Science 139:924-5 Mr 8 '63
SHAW, Lawrence
Georgeham: 1984. America 111:214-16 Ag 29 '64
SHAW, Mildred S.
Paper mosaics. Sch Arts 63:33 F '64
SHAW, Ralph R.
Information retrieval. bibliog Science 140: 606-9 My 10 '63
Too much, too fast. por Library J 88:4688-90 D 15 '63
SHAW, Richard Gregory
$250,000 bonanza. R. Lemon. il pors Sat Eve Post 237:70-1+ N 14 '64
SHAW, Rima
First time she saw Paris. P. Coffin. il pors Look 27:88-92 Jl 2 '63
SHAW, Robert
Method writer. il por Newsweek 64:94 D 7 '64
SHAW, Spencer G.
Children's libraries. por Wilson Lib Bul 39: 179 O '64
SHAW, Thomas Shuler
Reference books of 1962-1963. por Library J 88:1597-605; 89:1667-75 Ap 15 '63, Ap 15 '64
SHAW, Wally
Lip-synchronized sound. Pop Phot 54:150-1 Ja '64
SHAWCROSS, John T.
Show and gaze o' the time. Christian Cent 81:481-4 Ap 15 '64
SHAWN, Donald
Range-finder pilotage. Motor B 111:38+ Je '63
SHAWN, Ted
Changes I've seen. por Dance Mag 37:26-7 Je '63
Denishawn. il pors Newsweek 64:50 Ag 24 '64
Milestone celebration at Jacob's Pillow. R. Stevenson. il pors Dance Mag 38:36-7 Ag '64
Sense of ministry. il por Time 84:42 Ag 21 '64
SHAYON, Robert Lewis
Audio/video. Sat R 46:57 F 9; 57+ Mr 9; 76 Ap 13; 59 My 11; 52 Je 8; 51 Jl 13; 51 Ag 10; 71 S 14; 53 O 12 '63; 47:41 Ag 8 '64
High cost of indecision. Sat R 47:176 Ag 29 '64
TV and radio. See issues of Saturday review
SHAZAR, Schneor Zalman
Man without enemies. Time 81:30 My 31 '63
SHE laughs last; drama. See Paradis, M. B.
SHE loves me; musical comedy. See Musical comedies, revues, etc.—Criticisms, plots, etc.
SHEA, Dick
Toward a universal non-language. N Y Times Mag p62+ N 22 '64
SHEA, George W.
Garbled text. America 109:249 S 14 '63
SHEA, J. M. jr
Memo about a Dallas citizen. T. G. Harris. il pors Look 28:64+ Ag 11 '64
Memo from a Dallas citizen. por Look 28:88+ Mr 24 '64
SHEA stadium. See Stadiums
SHEARER, Marjorie
You've got to listen. Read Digest 85:237-8 O '64
SHEARER, Marva
Art of having (or being) a house guest. House B 106:92-5+ Jl '64

SHEARER, Thomas E.
Brave new world? address, May 29, 1964. Vital Speeches 30:670-2 Ag 15 '64
SHEARING, George
Players and popularizers. M. Williams. il por Sat R 47:45 Ag 22 '64
SHEARS, David
When Congress tries to rule the waves. New Repub 150:8-9 Je 6 '64
SHEARS. See Scissors and shears
SHEARWATERS
Birds of the sea. A. Sprunt, 4th. il Motor B 112:41+ Ag '63
SHEATSLEY, Paul B. See Hyman, H. H. jt. auth.
SHECTER, Leonard
Baleful look of a new Liston. Sports Illus 19:76-82+ O 14 '63
Painful path to glory. Sat Eve Post 237:76+ O 3 '64
Rational rebel in pinstripes. Sports Illus 18: 76-8+ My 13 '63
SHEDESKY, Pat
Foliage and texture in the garden. Horticulture 41:376-7 Jl '63
SHEDS
It's a garden storage wall. il Sunset 132:92 F '64
See also
Agricultural machinery—Storage
SHEEAN, Vincent
Best of braggarts. Opera N 28:27-9 Mr 21 '64
Made to be Otello. Opera N 28:26-8 F 15 '64
Massenet's choice. Opera N 28:28-9 D 21 '63
Tangled romance of Sinclair Lewis and Dorothy Thompson; excerpt from Dorothy and Red. por Harper 227:121-72 O '63
SHEED, Wilfrid
Enemies of Catholic promise. Commonweal 77: 560-3 F 22 '63
Heavenly junkyard. Commonweal 80:296-8 My 29 '64
One man's fancy. Commonweal 78:23-4, 145-6, 245-6, 402-4, 535-6; 79:17-18, 136+, 434-5, 570-1, 691-2; 80:15-16, 296-8, 448-9, 560-8; 81:16-17 Mr 29, Ap 26, My 24, Jl 5, S 6, 27, O 25 '63, Ja 10, F 7, Mr 6, 27, My 29, Jl 3, 24, S 25 '64
Salesman, sell thyself. Commonweal 79:223-4 N 15 '63
Speaking out. por Sat Eve Post 237:6+ Je 13 '64
Theater of the undiscussable. Commonweal 81:454-5 D 25 '64
SHEEHAN, Arthur T.
Austrian apocalypse. America 112:81 Ja 16 '65
SHEEHAN, Edward R. F.
Brooke of Massachusetts; a Negro governor on Beacon Hill? Harper 228:41-7 Je '64
Not peace, but the sword. Sat Eve Post 237: 20-32+ N 28 '64
Rise and fall of a Soviet agent. Sat Eve Post 237:30-2+ F 15 '64; Same abr. Read Digest 84:82-91 My '64
SHEEHAN, Ethna
America balances books for the children. America 109:634-8+ N 16 '63
Books for boys and girls. America 110:848-51 Je 20 '64
Children's books for Christmas giving. America 111:664-73 N 21 '64
Some spring books for boys and girls. America 108:804-7 Je 1 '63
SHEEHAN, Neil
When the rains come to Vietnam. N Y Times Mag p 12-13+ Je 14 '64
SHEEHAN, Robert
Conoco's widening world. Fortune 69:113-17+ Ap '64
Great day in the morning for Texas gulf sulphur. Fortune 70:136-40+ Jl '64
How General motors did it. Fortune 67:96-111+ Je '63
New report card on the business schools. Fortune 70:148-50+ D '64
That mighty pump, Prudential. Fortune 69: 98-103+ Ja '64
Thompson Ramo Wooldridge: two wings in space. Fortune 67:94-9+ F '63
Turnaround year for Monsanto. Fortune 70: 124-9+ S '64
What's rocking those rocks, the banks. Fortune 68:108-13+ O '63
—See Nickel, H. jt. auth.
SHEEHAN, Wilfred J.
State associations work closely with locals. NEA J 53:20-1 F '64
SHEEHY, Emma Dickson
(comp) Records for your children & you. See issues of Parents' magazine & better homemaking

SHEELER, Charles
Old precisionist; works on view in Manhattan's Downtown gallery. Time 85:82 Ja 29 '65
SHEEN, Fulton John, bp
Court exceeds its competency. por U S News 56:73-4 My 11 '64
Marriage is neither heaven nor hell but what is it? por Todays Health 42:60-1+ Ap '64
about
Bishop Sheen distorts the truth. Christian Cent 80:996 Ag 14 '63
In God we trust. Christian Cent 81:719 My 27 '64
Let the hopelessly ill die? por U S News 55: 18 Jl 1 '63
SHEEP
Depth perception in sheep: effects of interrupting the mother-neonate bond. W. B. Lemmon and G. H. Patterson. bibliog il Science 145:835-6 Ag 21 '64
Maternal facilitation of sucking drive in newborn lambs. G. Alexander and D. Williams. bibliog il Science 146:665-6 O 30 '64
Ram testing stations. il Suc Farm 61:44 Jl '63
Thirteen steps to good ewe management. Suc Farm 61:28 Jl '63
What's new and outlook for. See issues of Successful farming

Diseases and pests

How to protect lambs against overeating disease; enterotoxemia, pulpy kidney. J. W. Bailey. Suc Farm 61:102 N '63
See also
Worms, Intestinal and parasitic

Feeding

Ethanol accumulation in the rumen after overfeeding with readily fermentable carbohydrate. M. J. Allison and others. bibliog il Science 144:54-5 Ap 3 '64

Performance records and registration

Now they're progeny-testing rams. B. Fowler. il Farm J 87:40 S '63
SHEEP breeding
How to help yourself to a bigger lamb crop. J. W. Bailey. Suc Farm 62:74D Ap '64
Red clover may cause lamb birth decline. Sci N L 86:84 Ag 8 '64
These ideas save lambs. il Suc Farm 62:91 Mr '64
Three ways to boost your lamb crop. Farm J 88:50A My '64
SHEEP farms
Shepherd is a lady. il Ebony 19:68-70+ Jl '64
SHEEP grazing. See Grazing
SHEEP'S-bit
Jasione perennis. R. C. Hands. il Horticulture 41:419 Ag '63
SHEEPSHEAD fishing
Convict fish. G. Heinold. il Outdoor Life 135: 14-15+ F '65
SHEEPSKIN coats. See Coats
SHEERIN, John B.
Editorials. See issues of Catholic world
(ed) See Küng, H. Interview with Hans Küng
(ed) See Oberman, H. Interview with Dr Heiko Oberman
SHEET metal work
Androforming process comes of age; dieless metalworking method. J. F. Judge. il Miss & Roc 12:22-3 F 4 '63
Shortcut to sheet aluminum. il Bsns W p52+ Mr 9 '63
See also
Stretching

Projects

Hammer crafting sheet metal. W. E. Burton. il Pop Mech 119:140-2 Ap '63
SHEETS, Millard
Millard Sheets: the story of a giant. F. Whitaker. il Am Artist 28:32-7+ D '64
SHEETS
Bedding isn't what it used to be. il House B 106:81-99 F '64
Dreams of glory; stars and stripes. il Time 83:75 Je 26 '64
How to fold fitted sheets. il Good H 156: 180n Mr '63
Save decorating dollars with sheets and pillowcases. il Am Home 66:76-7 O '63
Sheets. il Consumer Bul 47:29-33+ Ja '64
Sheets and pillowcases; shop by price not by brand. il Consumer Rep 29:11-15 Ja '64

SHEFFER, Isaiah
Theatre of Peretz; dramatization of short stories by I. L. Peretz. Criticism
Commentary 37:71-3 Ja '64; Discussion. 37:25-7 Ap '64
SHEFFIELD, Isaac
Isaac Sheffield, Connecticut limner. E. deN. Mayhew. il Antiques 84:589-91 N '63
SHEFFIELD, Neal, jr
Simple slave strobe sync. Pop Electr 20:59-61+ My '64
SHEFFIELD corporation
Grinding a part from start to finish; abrasive machining. il Bsns W p76 F 9 '63
SHEFT, Irving, and others
Xenon hexafluoride: preparation of pure form and melting point. bibliog Science 145:701-2 Ag 14 '64
SHEHAB, Fakhri
Kuwait: a super-affluent society. For Affairs 42:461-74 Ap '64
SHEHAN, Lawrence Joseph, cardinal
Parochial school. America 110:478-81 Ap 4 '64
about
Baltimore story. America 109:256 S 14 '63
Heart of the matter; pastoral letter officially banning racial discrimination. Nation 196:218 Mr 16 '63
SHEILA (Annie Chancel)
Hooray for the Yé-Yé girls. il pors Life 56:42 My 29 '64
SHEININ, Yuri
Soviet scientist looks at disarmament. Bul Atomic Sci 20:19-22 Ja '64
SHELBURNE, Mary Willis
My father; poem. America 109:487 O 26 '63
Painting by an unknown artist; poem. America 109:50 Jl 13 '63
Seals; poem. America 110:605 My 2 '64
Truce; poem. America 111:69 Jl 18 '64
SHELBURNE museum, Shelburne, Vt.
Beach gallery opens at Shelburne museum. il Hobbies 68:52 S '63
Shelburne museum. il Travel 122:35-7 O '64
SHELBY, Carroll
It was snakebite day at Sebring. H. Whall. il por Sports Illus 20:20-3 Mr 30 '64
SHELBY COUNTY, Tenn.
County recording in three easy steps. G. Bates. il Am City 80:100-1 Ja '65
SHELDON, Craig T.
Alpha 66 Nat R 14:172 F 26 '63
SHELDON, Don
Busiest pilot in the bush. L. Elliott. il por Read Digest 82:255-7+ My '63
SHELDON, Donald Edward
Bush pilot's deadly, daily game. D. Moser. il pors Life 57:112-14+ N 27 '64
SHELDON, Eleanor Bernert. See Cottrell, L. S. jr. jt. auth.
SHELDON, Roger
30,000 boys and a merit badge. Am For 70:21+ My '64
SHELDON, William D.
Should the very young be taught to read? bibliog NEA J 52:20-2 N '63
SHELDON, Ill.
And was it a silent spring? C. B. Hicks. il Pop Mech 119:85-8+ Je '63
SHELEPIN, Aleksandr
Two Russians who are moving to the top. por U S News 57:20 N 30 '64
SHELL craft. See Shellwork
SHELL houses. See Building industry; Houses, Prefabricated
SHELL model. See Atomic nuclei
SHELL money
Money cowry. A. G. Melvin. il Hobbies 69:130+ D '64
Shell money. A. G. Melvin. il Hobbies 68:130 Ap '63
SHELL oil company
Compromise ends Shell deadlock. Bsns W p46 Ag 10 '63
Oil strikers get global support; IFPW back OCAW. il Bsns W p60+ My 25 '63
Sponsored films for schools. L. L. L. Golden. Sat R 47:80+ Ja 11 '64
SHELL work. See Shellwork
SHELLEY, Percy Bysshe
Tips; Esdaile notebook to be published. Pub W 185:51 Mr 9 '64
SHELLFISH
See also
Cookery—Fish
Oysters
Shrimps
SHELLS (architectural engineering)
Shells soar in Formosa; Luce memorial chapel at Tunghai university. il Arch Forum 121:136-9 Ag '64
SHELLS (conchology)
Amino acids in the proteins from aragonite and calcite in the shells of mytilus californianus. P. E. Hare. bibliog il Science 139:216-17 Ja 18 '63
California shell ornaments. C. Miles. il Hobbies 68:112+ Ag '63
Cone shells say "Hi". A. G. Melvin. il Hobbies 69:130 O '64
Radiocarbon activity of shells from living clams and snails. M. Rubin and D. W. Taylor. bibliog il Science 141:637 Ag 16 '63
Sea-shell at the Library of Congress. A. G. Melvin. il Hobbies 68:130 S '63
Seashells at the New York world's fair. A. G. Melvin. il Hobbies 69:130+ S '64
Shells for window panes. A. G. Melvin. il Hobbies 68:130 Jl '63
Triton shell. A. G. Melvin. il Hobbies 69:130+ Ap '64
West Coast rock shells. A. G. Melvin. il Hobbies 67:130+ F '63
See also
Cowries
Mollusks
Collectors and collecting
Pair that got hooked hunts specimens in distant reefs. il Life 57:54A Jl 10 '64
Shells available to collectors. A. G. Melvin. il Hobbies 69:130+ Ja '65
Unique shell collection. A. G. Melvin. Hobbies 69:130+ Mr '64
Photographs
Shells; with photographs by N. Leen. Life 57:46-53+ Jl 10 '64
SHELLS (projectiles) See Cartridges
SHELLS (structural engineering)
Plywood: new shapes yield new strength. il Arch Forum 120:126-31 Ap '64
Structural design of a free-form shell; Eastman Kodak pavilion for the 1964-1965 New York world's fair. il Arch Rec 134:222-4 S '63
Suspension roof frees arena from column obstructions. il Arch Rec 135:185 Je '64
Two new forming methods for shells. il Arch Rec 133:166 Ja '63
SHELLS, Fossil. See Mollusks, Fossil
SHELLS; story. See Wilson, R.
SHELL'S wonderful world of golf. See Golf—Tournaments
SHELLWORK
Shellcraft. A. G. Melvin. il Hobbies 68:130 N '63
SHELTERING arms agency. See Social agencies, Voluntary
SHELTERS
New entry and car shelter. il Sunset 132:116 Mr '64
Take-along shelters. il House & Gard 125:118-23 Je '64
SHELTERS (agriculture)
Lath house will protect shade lovers from hot sun. J. B. Brimer. il Flower Grower 50:22-3 Ag '63
SHELTERS, Air raid. See Air raid shelters
SHELTERS, Atomic bomb. See Atomic bomb shelters
SHELTERS, Garden. See Garden houses, shelters, etc.
SHELTON, Betty-Carol, and Davenport, Beulah
Top apple desserts. Farm J 88:80-1 O '64
SHELTON, C. R. and Colgrove, Melba
When & how to quit a job. Nations Bsns 52:96-8+ O '64
SHELTON, G. C.
What you need to know about beef cattle internal parasites. Suc Farm 62:106 F '64
SHELTON, Isabelle
Mad day with LBJ. por U S News 56:46+ Mr 2 '64
SHELTON, Robert
Alessio De Paolis. Mus Am 83:12-13+ N '63
Freedom songs. Nation 197:57-8 Jl 27 '63
Imperial wizard explains the klan. M. Long. il por N Y Times Mag p8+ Jl 5 '64
SHELTON, William R.
Embattled boss of Chicago's schools. Sat Eve Post 236:26-7 O 19 '63
SHELVES
Buffet shelf folds away. il Sunset 132:128 Ap '64
Buying guide to shelving materials. il Good H 158:169 Ap '64
Family room wall of convenient places for everything. il Bet Hom & Gard 41:56 S '63
Lazy-susan hardware rack. J. Canine. il Pop Mech 120:171 O '63

SHELVES—*Continued*
Perk up that plain wall; shadow-box window shelf. H. Sibley. il Pop Mech 120:128-9 Ag '63
Show-off shelves so decorative and practical. il Am Home 66:20+ O '63
See also
Bookcases
SHELVING, Library. See Library furniture and equipment
SHELVING systems (libraries) See Libraries—Shelving systems
SHEN, James C. Y.
Along the Yellow River; story. Yale R 53: 85-99 O '63
SHENANDOAH NATIONAL PARK
Shenandoah trails. J. T. Starr. il Am For 69: 16-18+ Je '63
SHENANDOAH VALLEY
Virginia's Shenandoah. W. W. Hubbard. il Travel 121:30-6 My '64
SHENBERG, Samuel
Experiment in industry-education; address, September 13, 1963. Vital Speeches 30:90-3 N 15 '63
SHENKER, Israel
Curls and cold steel. Sports Illus 20:40-1 Ja 27 '64
Great improviser. Life 55:81+ S 13 '63
They could be good if they tried. Sports Illus 19:18-19+ Jl 29 '63
SHENOY, G. Keshav
Indian teacher in America. NEA J 53:50 D '64
SHEPARD, A. P.
Try a metal coating. Am City 79:99-101 N '64
SHEPARD, Alan Bartlett, 1923-
Astronaut and investor; Alan Shepard turns banker. por U S News 55:16 N 4 '63
Ayes and ears. il Newsweek 63:94-5 Ap 27 '64
SHEPARD, Charles C.
Capreomycin: activity against experimental infection with mycobacterium leprae. bibliog Science 146:403-4 O 16 '64
SHEPARD, Francis P.
Sea level changes in the past 6000 years: possible archeological significance. bibliog Science 143:574-6 F 7 '64
—and others
Submarine geology by diving saucer. bibliog Science 145:1042-6 S 4 '64
SHEPARD, Hortense O.
Pilgrim's progress: Horace Bundy and his paintings. Antiques 86:445-9 O '64
SHEPARD, Mark
Iguassú Falls. Travel 120:34-7 D '63
SHEPARD, Richard F.
Etiquette of the executive lunch. Esquire 60: 142-3+ N '63
SHEPARD, Samuel
Sam Shepard's faith. P. Friggens. il PTA Mag 58:18-20+ Mr '64; Same abr. with title Is the Negro equal in intelligence and ability? Read Digest 84:83-7 Mr '64
SHEPHEARD'S. See Night clubs
SHEPHERD, Elizabeth
Adopting Negro children. New Repub 150: 10-12 Je 20 '64
SHEPHERD, George W. Jr
Loyalties in the emerging nations. Christian Cent 80:206-7 F 13 '63
SHEPHERD, Gordon Brook-. See Brook-Shepherd, G.
SHEPHERD, Jack
Birth control and the poor: a solution. Look 28:63-7 Ap 7 '64; Same abr. Read Digest 85:111-14 Ag '64
SHEPHERD, Jean
I hear America singing or leaves of grass revisited, like. Mlle 59:243+ Ag '64
SHEPHERD, Mabel E.
All about bananas. Horticulture 42:36 F '64
SHEPHERD, Massey H. Jr
Worship, liturgy and devotion bookshelf. Christian Cent 81:144-6 Ja 29 '64
SHEPHERD, Tryon Mason
Ghosts of silver. Hobbies 69:44 Ja '65
SHEPHERD kings. See Hyksos
SHEPHERD; story. See Lofts, N.
SHEPHERD'S-scabious. See Sheep's-bit
SHEPLER, Dwight
Down East; drawings. Yachting 114:47-9 Ag '63
SHEPPARD, Eugenia
Pucci; sportswear king of the world. Ladies Home J 80:55-61 Jl '63
So they say; interview. por Mlle 57:236-7 Ag '63
Voila: les girls return. Sat Eve Post 236:30+ Mr 16 '63
SHEPPARD, Lila
If your child can't spell. Parents Mag 38:151 O '63
SHEPPARD, Richard
On from antiquity; Churchill college at Cambridge. il Time 84:114-16 O 2 '64
SHEPPARD, Samuel
Reprieve for Dr Sam. il por Newsweek 64: 32+ Jl 27 '64
Sheppard case reopened. C. Welles. il pors Life 57:24D Jl 31 '64
SHEPPARD, Mrs Samuel. See Tebbenjohanns, A.
SHEPPTON mine disaster. See Coal mines and mining—Accidents and explosions
SHERA, Jesse H.
Dimensions of the Master's program. bibliog f ALA Bul 58:519-22 Je '64
(ed) [Libraries and automation] bibliog Wilson Lib Bul 38:740-79+ My '64
O! medium, O! media. por Library J 88:4149-51 N 1 '63
Toward a new dimension for library education; statement at session of ALA commission on national plan for library education, February 1963. ALA Bul 57:313-17 Ap '63
Without reserve. See issues of Wilson library bulletin
SHERATON, Mimi
Hong Kong. Mlle 56:98+ Ap '63
How to get him to marry you; excerpt from Seducer's cookbook. Mlle 57:148-9 O '63
SHERATON, Thomas
Thomas Sheraton. E. H. Bjerkoe. il Hobbies 69:90-1 Ag '64
SHERATON corporation of America
Wonderland economics of Sheraton corp. J. Thackray. il Duns R 83:3-4+ Je '64
SHERATON furniture. See Furniture, English
SHERBET. See Ice cream, ices, etc.
SHERBURNE, Edward G. Jr
Science and television. Science 143:792-3 F 21 '64
SHERIDAN, Bart
(ed) Sight & sound. See issues of McCall's to December 1963
—and Roberts, Barbara
There's a break in the dam! we've got to get out! McCalls 91:91-2+ Ap '64
—See Benjamin, L. jt. auth; jt. ed.
SHERIDAN, C. B. company
Harris-Intertype acquires Sheridan co. for $6,346,000. Pub W 185:39 My 18 '64
SHERIDAN, Ellen
Going places, findings things in central Mexico. House & Gard 126:60+ O '64
SHERIDAN, John D.
Junior capitalists, arise! excerpt from While the humour is on me. Read Digest 84:36C Ap '64
SHERIDAN, Maureen
Art enrichment. Sch Arts 63:19-20 My '64
SHERIDAN, Nina
Ballet child. Dance Mag 37:21-3 Je '63
SHERIDAN, Philip H.
General whose cry was: come on! E. T. Folliard. America 112:8 Ja 2 '65
SHERIDAN, Richard Brinsley Butler
Rivals; drama, ed. by L. Olfson. Plays 22: 87-96 Mr '63

about

From Command, Sheridan's The school for scandal. J. W. Barker. il Am Rec G 29:42-3+ F '63
School for scandal. Criticism
Commonweal 77:542 F 15 '63
Life il 54:47-8 F 22 '63
Nation 196:126-7 F 9 '63
New Repub 148:29 F 23 '63
New Yorker 38:69 F 2 '63
Sat R 46:20 F 9 '63
Sat R il 46:52 F 23 '63
Theatre Arts il 47:57-8 Mr '63
SHERIFFS
Desert is my beat; Pima County, Ariz. sheriff's deputy. il Ebony 19:134-6+ Ap '64
SHERIFFS deputies. See Sheriffs
SHERIN, Ray
Now it's ice-scratchers, it beats walking. Outdoor Life 131:50-1 Ja '63
SHERLOCK, John
Bleak little inn fit for any king. Sat Eve Post 236:39-41+ N 30 '63
SHERLOCK, Philip
Prospects in the Caribbean. For Affairs 41: 744-56 Jl '63
SHERLOCK Holmes (literary character) See Characters in literature
SHERLOCK Holmes and the stockbroker's clerk; drama. See Olfson, L.
SHERMAN, Alfred
Jacobs affair. Commentary 38:60-4 O '64
Nasser's decade. Commentary 36:151-7 Ag '63
Zionism and after. Commentary 38:63-4 Jl; 26+ N '64

SHERMAN, Allan
Song for dropouts. Time 83:76 Ap 10 '64
Spoofmaster. M. Zolotow. il pors Sat Eve Post 236:26-7 Ap 20 '63
SHERMAN, Allie
Pedantic professor who likes to buck long odds. T. Maule. il pors Sports Illus 21:53-7 S 7 '64
SHERMAN, Bennett
Are RFDR viewfinders accurate? Mod Phot 27:70-1+ My '63
SLR finders. Mod Phot 27:52-5+ Ap '63
Techniques tomorrow. See issues of Modern photography
SHERMAN, Constance
(tr) See Dorst, J. Secrets of migration
SHERMAN, George
Nonintervention: a shield for Papa Doc. Reporter 28:27-9 Je 20 '63
—See Allan, D. A. jt. auth.
SHERMAN, John
Ninety-four hour week. por Library J 89:1198-200 Mr 15 '64
SHERMAN, John H.
True religious liberty. Christian Cent 81:14-15 Ja 1 '64
SHERMAN, Robert
Recordings reports (cont) Sat R 46:68 Ap 27; 76 S 28; 58 N 30; 56 D 28 '63; 47:56 Ja 25; 44 Jl 11; 72 N 14; 60 N 28 '64
Sing a song of freedom. Sat R 46:65-7+ S 28 '63
SHERMAN, Susan
Definition; poem. Nation 197:396 D 7 '63
Dimension; poem. Nation 198:382 Ap 13 '64
Form of poem; poem. Nation 198:40 Ja 6 '64
Palace of the lowest moon; poem. Poetry 105:85-8 N '64
SHERMAN, William D.
On the death of W. C. Handy; poem. Negro Hist Bul 27:13 O '63
SHERMAN, William Tecumseh
While we were marching through Georgia; excerpt from Centennial history of the Civil war. B. Catton. il N Y Times Mag p28-9+ N 1 '64
SHERMAN antitrust law. See Trusts, Industrial —Law
SHERP, Raymond
I'm ugly; story. Seventeen 22:130-1 My '63
SHERPAS
Highest school in the world: Sir E. Hillary's latest conquest in the Himalayas. R. J. Spector. il UNESCO Courier 17:12-17 O '64
SHERRARD, Philip
Byzantium: the other half of the world. Horizon 5:4-34 N '63
(tr) See Seferis, G. Santorini; Salamis in Cyprus; Three mules
SHERRILL, Elizabeth
(ed) See Wilkerson, D. Cross and the switchblade
SHERRILL, John
(ed) See Wilkerson, D. Cross and the switchblade
SHERRILL, Joya
Tunisian breast of veal. F. DeKnight. il por Ebony 18:104+ F '63
SHERRILL, Robert G.
Florida's railroad war; a few sticks of dynamite. Nation 198:227-30 Mr 9 '64
H. L. Hunt: portrait of a super-patriot. Nation 198:182-95 F 24 '64
Justice for the poir; the banner of Gideon. Nation 198:367-72 Ap 13 '64
Power game: George Smathers, the golden senator from Florida. Nation 199:426-37 D 7 '64
Wallace and the future of Dixie. Nation 199:266-72 O 26 '64
SHERROD, Robert
Angry welcome for a Queen. Sat Eve Post 237:19-23 O 10 '64
Day in a former President's busy life. Sat Eve Post 237:16 Je 13 '64
Marines landed too. Sat Eve Post 236:30+ Ap 27 '63
(ed) See Nasser, G. A. Violent and vital world of Nasser
SHERWIN, Chalmers W.
Management of science in the public interest; adaptation of address. Bul Atomic Sci 20:9-12 Je '64
Science in the public interest. Sat R 47:38-9 Ag 1 '64
SHERWIN, K. H.
Laser gun sparks lectures. Pop Sci 185:64 N '64
SHERWIN, May Reynolds
How preschoolers learn to cope with problems. Parents Mag 39:48-9+ Ag '64
Try praise for preschoolers. Parents Mag 38:44-5+ Jl '63
SHERWOOD, Charles H.
Answers to your house plant questions. Suc Farm 62:100-1 Ja '64
SHERWOOD, Elizabeth Julia
Obituary
Wilson Lib Bul 38:29 S '63
SHERWOOD, Jean S.
Weeds. Pop Gard 14:99+ My '63
SHERWOOD, Robert Emmet
Abe Lincoln in Illinois. Criticism
Commonweal 77:543 F 15 '63
Nation 196:125-6 F 9 '63
New Yorker 38:69-70 F 2 '63
Sat R 46:20 F 9 '63
Theatre Arts il 47:58-9+ Mr '63
SHERWOOD, Suzanne R.
Maryland house & garden pilgrimage. Hobbies 69:91-2 My '64
SHERWOOD FOREST
On the trail of Robin Hood. il Travel 121:45-7 My '64
SHEVCHENKO, Taras
By the Aral Sea; If you but knew; poems, tr. by J. Weir. por UNESCO Courier 17:15-16 Je '64
Delights of the engraver's art; excerpt from diary, June 26, 1857. il UNESCO Courier 17:12-13 Je '64
Encounter on a summer night; story; excerpt from The painter, tr. by J. Weir. UNESCO Courier 17:17-22 Je '64
Poetry of faces; reproductions of paintings. UNESCO Courier 17:18-19 Je '64

about

Rebel with a cause. D. Pavlychko. por UNESCO Courier 17:10-12 Je '64
Shore of exile. R. Caillois. il UNESCO Courier 17:14-15 Je '64
SHEVELOVE, Burt
Too much Johnson; adaptation. See Gillette, W.
SHIAWASSEE national wildlife refuge, Mich. See Wildlife sanctuaries
SHIBUYA, Sachiko. See Shibuya, T. jt. auth.
SHIBUYA, Tatsuaki
Dissociation of olfactory neural response and mucosal potential. bibliog Science 143:1338-40 Mr 20 '64
—and Shibuya, Sachiko
Olfactory epithelium; unitary responses in the tortoise. bibliog Science 140:495-6 My 3 '63
SHIDELER, Mary McDermott
We saw you a stranger. Christian Cent 81:1585-8 D 23 '64
Within Protestantism, diversity. Christian Cent 80:295-8 Mr 6 '63
SHIELDING (heat)
Cavity injection explored for hypersonic cooling use. M. L. Yaffee. il Aviation W 82:36-8 Ja 4 '65
Cornell tests aim at base-heating guidelines. M. Getler. il Miss & Roc 13:24-5+ Ag 19 '63
Emerson offers a solution to nozzle problem; Thermo-Lag subliming material. il Miss & Roc 13:31 D 23 '63
Heat-halting material developed for spaceships. Sci N L 86:24 Jl 11 '64
Langley studying advanced heat shields. W. J. Normyle. il Aviation W 80:26-7 My 25 '64
Martin facility testing ablatives. W. Beller. il Miss & Roc 15:35-6 Ag 24 '64
Natural cork providing ablative protection for Minuteman, Polaris, Scout. J. F. Judge. il Miss & Roc 13:32-3+ O 28 '63
New spacecraft window design proposed for Apollo; compound reflective system. M. Getler. il Miss & Roc 13:26-7+ Ag 5 '63
Silicon-boron shielding protects ASSET vehicle during re-entry. J. F. Judge. il Miss & Roc 13:22+ D 23 '63
Spacecraft protection needs get increased Douglas R&D attention. W. E. Wilks. il Miss & Roc 14:24-5 Je 29 '64
Tantalum-tungsten alloy used in Agena vehicle. J. F. Judge. il Miss & Roc 13:28, 31 Jl 8 '63
Test complex simulates Polaris re-entry heat. J. N. Steinmetz, jr. il Miss & Roc 14:24-5 Ja 6 '64
Water recovery could dictate redesign of Apollo heat shield. Aviation W 80:28 Mr 2 '64
SHIELDING (radiation)
Russians report progress in developing chemicals to protect man against radiation. Bsns W p54 Ja 19 '63
Telstar II equipped to handle radiation. il Miss & Roc 12:17 My 6 '63

SHIELDING (radiation)—*Continued*
TIMM components work throughout high-intensity radiation bombardment. R. Kiefer. Miss & Roc 15:34 Ag 24 '64
See also subhead Shielding (radiation) under various subjects, e.g. Artificial satellites—Shielding (radiation)

SHIELDS, Cornelius
Sails and their trim; excerpt from Cornelius Shields on sailing. il por Yachting 116:51-3+ Ag '64
Tricks of match racing; excerpt from Cornelius Shields on sailing. Sports Illus 20:38-47 Je 29 '64
Weather omens; excerpt from Cornelius Shields on sailing. Atlan 213:124 Je '64
Word on local weather. Yachting 115:140-2 F '64

SHIELDS, John Potter
Miniature regulated power supply. Electr World 71:74-5 F '64
Simple square-wave pulse adapter. Electr World 71:77-8 Mr '64
Variable electronic gain control. Electr World 70:101 O '63

SHIELDS, William S. jr
Where the antelope play. il Sports Illus 21:46-51 O 12 '64
William S. Shields, jr. describes his painting technique. il por Am Artist 28:42-3 Ja '64

SHIFRISS, Oved, and George, W. L. jr
Sensitivity of female inbreds of cucumis sativus to sex reversion by gibberellin. bibliog Science 143:1452-3 Mr 27 '64

SHIINA, Etsusaburo
U.S. and Japan inaugurate television link via Syncom III: statement, October 7, 1964. Dept State Bul 51:592-3 O 26 '64

SHIKLER, Aaron
Four realists: a review. F. Whitaker. il Am Artist 28:54-61+ O '64

SHILS, Edward B.
Transportation's labor crisis. bibliog f Harvard Bsns R 42:84-98 My '64

SHIMAZU, F. and Tappel, A. L.
Selenoamino acids: decrease of radiation damage to amino acids and proteins. bibliog Science 143:369-71 Ja 24 '64

SHIMER college, Mount Carroll, Ill.
Unknown, unsung & unusual. il Time 81:76 Ap 19 '63

SHIMKIN, Michael B.
Personnel selection in academic institutions; letter. Science 143:637 F 14 '64

SHIMOMURA, Osamu, and others
Microdetermination of calcium by aequorin luminescence. bibliog Science 140:1339-40 Je 21 '63

SHINE, Richard E. and others
Priceless gift of better speech. NEA J 53:36A-36B Ja '64

SHINER, Don
Double-barreled planter. Design 65:214 My '64
Ice flies for panfish jigging. Pop Mech 119:160-4 F '63
Look what you can do with driftwood. il Design 65:210-11 My '64
New two-eyed target sharpens your aim. Pop Sci 182:96-7 Je '63

SHINING ROCK wild area. See Wilderness areas

SHINN, Roger L.
1963 First amendment conference; statement. por(p306) Cath World 197:308-10 Ag '63

SHIP and boat models
Ship models and ship modeling. E. D. Collins. il Hobbies 69:28-9 My '64
See also
Rotor ship models

SHIP building. See Shipbuilding

SHIP CANAL, Florida. See Florida Ship Canal project

SHIP canals. See Canals

SHIP figurehead. See Figureheads of ships

SHIP island; story. See Spencer, E.

SHIP libraries. See Libraries, Ship

SHIP masts. See Masts and rigging

SHIP signals. See Signals and signaling

SHIPBUILDING
At low tide; U.S. tenth among world shipbuilders. il Time 84:98+ S 11 '64
Automated yard builds ships indoors; Gothenburg, Sweden. il Pop Sci 183:96-7 N '63
I did it all; Verolme shipyards, Netherlands. il Time 81:110 Ap 19 '63
Shipbuilder to the world; Japan's boom. il Time 83:76-7 Ja 3 '64
Ships through the ages; a saga of the sea. A. Villiers. il Nat Geog Mag 123:496-545 Ap '63
Squeezing ships out of an assembly plant; Gotaverken shipyard, Sweden. il Bsns W p60-2 F 8 '64
See also
Naval architecture
Shipyards
Webb institute of naval architecture

Anecdotes, facetiae, satire, etc.

So you're going to build an ocean liner? J. H. Slate. il Atlan 214:122+ D '64

Wages and hours

Wage chronology: Pacific Coast shipbuilding: 1959-64. il Mo Labor R 87:1051-60 S '64

SHIPLEY, T.
Auditory flutter-driving of visual flicker. bibliog Science 145:1328-30 S 18 '64

SHIPMAN, Joseph C.
New ALA officer. ALA Bul 57:661-2 Jl '63

SHIPMASTERS
Captain's table. R. Joseph. il Esquire 59:86-8 My '63
Fishing boat captain. il Ebony 18:43-5 O '63
New sport: captain-fishing. V. Kraft. il Sports Illus 19:26-30+ S 2 '63

SHIPMENT of books
Is it cheaper to ship books by common carrier? A. Epstein. il Pub W 186:50-2 Ag 10 '64

SHIPMENT of goods
Closing in on the customer. L. Morse. il Duns R 81:pt2 S100-3+ Je '63
New boom in material handling. T. O'Hanlon. il Duns R 82:50-1+ D '63
New nerve centers of distribution. il Duns R 81:pt2 S104-6+ Je '63
Why some toys must be assembled. Good H 157:175 D '63

SHIPMENT of works of art. See Transportation of works of art

SHIPP, Joseph C. and others
Oxidation of carbon-14-labeled endogenous lipids by isolated perfused rat heart. bibliog Science 143:371-3 Ja 24 '64

SHIPPING
End of the lean years. il Fortune 68:84+ D '63
Tax law sparks a modern odyssey; Greek shipowners leaving U.S. il Bsns W p43-4 Ap 6 '63
Today's port, a trade and transport hub. H. C. Brockel. Ann Am Acad 345:95-102 Ja '63
See also
Panama Canal

Automation

Courts in conflict. T. R. Brooks. Duns R 82:74B D '63

Federal aid

Turn-around to efficiency. il Time 83:86 My 8 '64

International aspects

Fifteen nations to exchange shipping information; text of a joint Department of state-Federal maritime commission statement, December 15, 1964. Dept State Bul 52:13 Ja 4 '65
Foreign policy and the regulation of international shipping; statement, August 11, 1964. G. G. Johnson. Dept State Bul 51:314-17 Ag 31 '64
Making it hot for rate fixers; Uncle Sam attacks international shipping conferences. il Bsns W p60+ Ap 18 '64
U.S, Japan, and ten European nations end shipping talks; joint announcement, May 15, 1964. Dept State Bul 50:913-14 Je 8 '64
When Congress tries to rule the waves. D. Shears. New Repub 150:8-9 Je 6 '64

Rates

Flood tide for the barges. il Bsns W p48-51 Ag 1 '64
Foreign policy and the regulation of international shipping; statement, August 11, 1964. G. G. Johnson. Dept State Bul 51:314-17 Ag 31 '64
Freight rates go up piecemeal; on less-than-carload business. Bsns W p32 Mr 30 '63
Making it hot for rate fixers; Uncle Sam attacks international shipping conferences. il Bsns W p60+ Ap 18 '64
No care for profit; East-bloc ships underbid established rates. Time 83:101 F 28 '64
Ocean freight rates head into a gale. il Bsns W p96-7 Ag 31 '63
Tramps reap the harvest; Russian demand for ships to carry Canadian wheat. Bsns W p28 S 28 '63
U.S, Japan, and ten European nations end shipping talks; joint announcement, May 15, 1964. Dept State Bul 50:913-14 Je 8 '64
When Congress tries to rule the waves. D. Shears. New Repub 150:8-9 Je 6 '64

SHIPPING—*Continued*

Canada

Canada gets the ships moving, at a price. Bsns W p51+ N 2 '63
Trouble on the waterfront. Time 83:30 Mr 27 '64

Greece, Modern

N fleet for sale. il Time 84:103 O 9 '64
Negotiations with Niarchos. il Time 85:70-1 Ja 22 '65

Spain

See also
Freight vessels

United States

Breach in the dike; Jones act amendment. il Time 81:82 F 22 '63
Grain opens up Odessa again; U.S. wheat shipments. il Bsns W p32-4 Mr 21 '64
LBJ's first union showdown; how wheat strike came out. il U S News 56:89-90 Mr 9 '64
Next job: moving the wheat; handling Soviet grain. Bsns W p28-9 N 16 '63
Sailors on wheels. E. S. Allen. Motor B 113: 148-51 Mr '64
Shipping king comes ashore. il Bsns W p88-92+ N 23 '63
Taking the heat off wheat; end of ILA boycott. Bsns W p24-5 F 29 '64
To the rescue of the marine. J. Ridgeway. New Repub 151:12 Jl 11 '64
Triumph by telephone; boycott on loading ships with wheat for Russia. Newsweek 63:71 Mr 9 '64
Wheat for sale. New Repub 150:6 Ja 25 '64
Will American ships be forced off the seas? il U S News 54:75-7 Ap 22 '63

See also
Inland water transportation
Merchant marine—United States

SHIPPING, Inland water. See Inland water transportation

SHIPPING companies

Is Niarchos heading for port? il Bsns W p 110+ O 24 '64
Resigning over rates. Time 83:92 Ap 3 '64

See also
American export and Isbrandtsen lines
Grace lines, incorporated
Kulukundis lines, incorporated
Lykes brothers steamship company
Matson navigation company

SHIPPING conferences. See Shipping—Rates

SHIPPING containers. See Containers for shipping

SHIPS

Electronic jungle goes to sea; General H. H. Arnold, world's largest missile tracking ship. il Sci Digest 55:51 Ja '64
Life guide: historic ships. il Life 54:8 Mr 29 '63

See also
Constitution (frigate)
Figureheads of ships
Freight vessels
Motor ships
Ocean liners
Rotor ships
Sailing vessels
Salvage (ships)
Steamships and steamboats
Training ships

Control

Automated ships. il Electr World 72:55 N '64

Crews

See Seamen

Electronic equipment

See also
Ships—Control

Fires and fire protection

All risks removed; Lakonia's fire. il Newsweek 63:30 Ja 6 '64
Holiday I'll never forget; Lakonia disaster. R. Burca. il Read Digest 84:64-8 Je '64
Lakonia burns at sea. il Life 56:10-21 Ja 3 '64
Last voyage of the Lakonia. il Time 83:38-9 Ja 3 '64
Last voyage of the Lakonia. P. Hamill and F. Lee. il Sat Eve Post 237:72-5 F 1 '64
Thirty years ago; Morro Castle disaster. S. D. Smith. il N Y Times Mag p74+ S 13 '64

Food service

See also
Freight vessels—Food service

History

Ships through the ages; a saga of the sea. A. Villiers. il Nat Geog Mag 123:496-545 Ap '63

Loading and unloading

See Loading and unloading

Registration and transfer

Beaching the NLRB. Newsweek 61:62 Mr 4 '63
U.S. unions thwarted on foreign-flag ships. Bsns W p 122 F 23 '63
U.S. vs. the U.S (cont) R. Moley. Newsweek 61:84 F 4 '63

Safety devices and measures

For those in peril on the sea. D. Woodward. il UNESCO Courier 16:4-9 My '63

Signals and signaling

See Signals and signaling

Water supply

Now, a drink from the sea. T. Willets. il Motor B 113:90-1+ Ja '64

SHIPS, Atomic powered

Alice in atomland; world's first nuclear-powered merchant ship, the N.S. Savannah. il Newsweek 61:74+ Je 17 '63
At last, a maiden voyage for a nuclear ship; N.S. Savannah. il U S News 56:6 My 18 '64
Atom-powered ship is national disgrace: NS Savannah. A. Rosenfeld. il Life 54:40-40A Je 14 '63
Atom ship becalmed by pay row; engineers quit on Savannah. Bsns W p 176+ My 18 '63
Coming: nuclear ships for profit. il Sci Digest 57:23 Ja '65
Historic world cruise; but it's under wraps. il U S News 57:18 O 5 '64
Incorrect, illogical, etc; concerning congressional committee report. il Time 83:31 Ja 3 '64
Iron men and atomic ships; nuclear merchant marine. il Bsns W p 114-16 Je 8 '63
Is the first atomic cargo ship a flop? Savannah. il U S News 54:10 Ap 29 '63
N.S. Savannah: nine years after inception it is uncertain if ship is a boon or a boondoggle. E. Langer. Science 145:33-4 Jl 3 '64
N.S. Savannah: trouble-ridden nuclear ship gets under way with new crews and high spirits. E. Langer. il Science 144:1559-60+ Je 26 '64
On the Savannah. R. Burkhardt. New Repub 151:13 Jl 11 '64
Savannah finally sails. il Bsns W p 174-6+ My 16 '64
Savannah to sea. Newsweek 62:73 Jl 15 '63
Should U.S. build more atomic-powered ships? U S News 56:6-7 Ja 6 '64
U.S. nuclear ship: success or flop? trouble with the N.S. Savannah? il U S News 55: 86-8 Jl 15 '63
When to expect more atomic ships. U S News 56:12 My 25 '64
Why engineers tied up America's nuclear ship; Savannah and Marine engineers beneficial association. il U S News 54:74-5 My 27 '63

See also
Ice breaking vessels
Warships, Atomic powered

Design

Science does not travel alone. A. Kleihauer. il Sch Arts 62:29-32 My '63

SHIPS, Hospital. See Hospital ships

SHIPS, Model. See Ship and boat models

SHIPS, Motor. See Motor ships

SHIPS, Research

Acoustics research drone tests to aid navy's detection efforts. W. Beller. il Miss & Roc 15:27+ Ag 3 '64
Flip: an oceanographic buoy. P. Rudnick. bibliog il Science 146:1268-73 D 4 '64
Floating biology class; Stanford university's Te Vega. il(p385) Sci N L 83:386 Je 22 '63
Gone fishing; oceanographic ships, Albatross IV. il Newsweek 61:60 Je 17 '63
New mapper of the deep; Atlantis II. il Sci Digest 53:65 Je '63
Ocean ship launched for research studies; Eastward. Sci N L 85:328 My 23 '64
Russian ships call at Boston; Soviet oceanographic vessels. il Bsns W p 120+ Ap 11 '64
SPAR goes to sea. il Miss & Roc 15:18 D 21 '64

SHIPS, Training. See Training ships

SHIPS as weather stations. See Meteorological stations

SHIPS captains. See Shipmasters

SHIPS flags. See Flags—United States

SHIPS in art
Ship painters of the Mediterranean. J. Meissonnier. il Antiques 83:304-8 Mr '63

SHIPWORKERS
See also
Shipbuilding—Wages and hours

SHIPWORMS
Teredo. A. G. Melvin. il Hobbies 69:130+ N '64

SHIPWRECKS
Atlantic peril; British freighter Ambassador. il Newsweek 63:32 Mr 2 '64
Brave deed as a ship dies; rescue of crewman from British freighter, Ambassador. il Life 56:40-40A Mr 6 '64
Coast guard's worst week. R. Petrow. il Pop Sci 182:78-83+ Mr '63
Death of a ship; the Bear. il Newsweek 61:22+ Ap 1 '63
End of a great old ship; Bear. W. H. Taylor. il Yachting 113:198 My '63
Great glug downward; sinking of Chinese merchant ship, Leap Forward. Newsweek 61:53 My 13 '63
Great leap overboard; Communist China's Yüeh Chin. Time 81:34 My 10 '63
Naval trilogy; coastal minesweeper U.S.S. Grouse, and two coast guard accidents. il Newsweek 62:34-5 O 14 '63
Sulphur Queen's end. Newsweek 61:29 Mr 4 '63
To the Bear. G. M. S. Tod. il Motor B 111:118 My '63
We got to hang on; ed. by B. Fellows, K. Crosby and J. Dumas. il Life 55:19-20 O 25 '63
See also
Collisions at sea
Salvage (ships)
Submarine disasters
Survival (after airplane accidents, shipwrecks, etc)

SHIPYARDS
Full speed ahead in the doldrums; New Orleans shipyards il Bsns W p80-2+ O 12 '63
Wondering where the navy went; gloom grows at Brooklyn's navy yard. il Bsns W p30-1 O 17 '64
See also
Shipbuilding

SHIRAGIAN, Sonia
Visit to Armenia; story. New Yorker 39:44-8 Ap 27 '63

SHIRASU, Myron E. See Rampone, A. J. jt. auth.

SHIRK, James S. and others
Sinton bands: evidence for deuterated water on Mars. bibliog Science 147:48-9 Ja 1 '65

SHIRLEY, Ernest
Golf. Sports Illus 18:49 F 18 '63
Tennis. Sports Illus 19:98-9 D 23 '63

SHIRLEY, Isabel
Round face in the square frame. U S Camera 26:18+ My '63

SHIRTS
Knit shirts for boys to grow out of. il Consumer Bul 47:35-8+ Je '64
Men's shirts; wash-and-wear. il Consumer Rep 28:517-19 N '63
Men's T-shirts. il Consumer Rep 30:16-18 Ja '65
See also
Collars

SHISH kebab cookery. See Cookery—Meat

SHISHEKLY, Adib
Vengeance for the Druzes. il por Time 84:34 O 9 '64

SHISKIN, Julius
Signals and noise. Fortune 69:66 F '64

SHISTER, Joseph
Outlook for union growth. bibliog f Ann Am Acad 350:55-62 N '63

SHIVER, Ray A.
Oscilloscope photography in industry. Electr World 69:53-6+ Mr '63
Transducers for industrial instrumentation. Electr World 72:49-52 Jl '64

SHIVERING
Microvibrations in man and dolphin. M. Haider and D. B. Lindsley. bibliog il Science 146:1181-3 N 27 '64

SHKLOVSKY, I. S.
Exploding stars and evolution; excerpt from Cosmic radio waves. Sat R 47:41 Jl 4 '64

SHLAUDEMAN, Harry W.
(tr) See Bosch, J. Indelible spot

SHLEIEN, Bernard, and others
Particle size fractionation of airborne gamma-emitting radionuclides by graded filters. bibliog Science 147:290-2 Ja 15 '65

SHNEIDMAN, Edwin S. See Farberow, N. L. jt. auth.

SHOCK
Excess lactate: an index of reversibility of shock in human patients. G. Broder and M. H. Weil. bibliog il Science 143:1457-9 Mr 27 '64
What shock is. Newsweek 64:54 Jl 20 '64
See also
Electric shock

SHOCK absorbers
Breaking the bumper brakes the vehicle; shock absorber for spaceships. Sci N L 85:216 Ap 4 '64
Shock-absorbing shotgun. it saves your shoulder. K. Warner. il Pop Sci 185:38-9 Jl '64

SHOCK therapy
Electric shock on purpose. E. Bukestein. il Electr World 69:29-32+ F '63

SHOCK tubes
Chemical kinetics in shock tubes. S. H. Bauer. bibliog il Science 141:867-79 S 6 '63
Shock waves and high temperatures. M. McChesney. il Sci Am 208:109-19 bibliog (p 185) F '63

SHOCK waves
Ban the boom? tests in Oklahoma City. il Newsweek 64:52 Jl 27 '64
Boom & bust; White Sands tests. Time 84:76+ D 11 '64
Boom in a ghost town. Bsns W p29 D 12 '64
Boom restrictions may swell SST costs. il Aviation W 81:38-9+ Ag 3 '64
Boom town; Oklahoma City tests effect of flights by supersonic transport aircraft. Time 83:27 Mr 13 '64
Detonation-wave phenomena. D. D. Abernathy. Science 146:1635 D 25 '64
Era of supersonic morality; BONGO experiment to obtain public reaction to sonic boom. J. Lear. Sat R 47:49-50 Je 6 '64; Discussion. 47:46-7 Jl 4 '64
IMP finds magnetosphere shock wave. Aviation W 80:23 Mr 23 '64
Measuring the sonic boom. J. Kyle. il Electr World 72:58-60+ O '64
Shock waves and high temperatures. M. McChesney. il Sci Am 208:109-19 bibliog (p 185) F '63
Sonic boom town; Oklahoma City. R. Burkhardt. New Repub 151:5-6 Ag 22 '64
Sonic booms to test structures, sleepers. Aviation W 81:36 N 16 '64
Stishovite: synthesis by shock wave. P. S. De Carli and D. J. Milton. bibliog il Science 147:144-5 Ja 8 '65
Test sonic booms are stronger than from SST. Sci N L 87:25 Ja 9 '65

SHODA, Michiko. See Michiko, crown princess of Japan

SHOE dyes. See Dyes and dyeing

SHOE industry. See Shoes—Trade and manufacture

SHOE leather. See Leather

SHOEMAKER, Eugene M.
Geology of the moon. Sci Am 211:38-47 D '64
Moon close up. por Nat Geog Mag 126:690-707 N '64

SHOEMAKER, Frank R.
Flash calculator. U S Camera 26:30+ Ag '63

SHOEMAKER, Ted
Electric eye counts 300 flights a day by parent birds. Audubon Mag 66:90 Mr '64

SHOEMAKER, W. J. and Bruce, J. A.
Relighting downtown Denver. Am City 78:93-4 D '63

SHOEMAKER, Willie
Scent of roses. il por Time 83:65-6 Ap 24 '64
Sweet revenge; Preakness. Time 81:60 My 24 '63

SHOES
ABC's of children's shoes. il Good H 157:173+ S '63
Active young feet step out in leather shoes. il Parents Mag 38:110-11 Ap '63
Capsule history of shoes. G. Kahn. Holiday 33:54-5 Je '63
Check your traveling shoes. R. B. Scott. il Sci Digest 54:21-2 Ag '63
Children's sneakers. il Consumer Rep 29:217-21 My '64
Combat pumps? high-heeled shoes. il Newsweek 61:91 My 6 '63
Don't let your feet defeat you. L. D. Kirk. il Parents Mag 38:46 F '63
Fashions for legs and feet. il Vogue 143:68-73 F 15 '64

SHOES—*Continued*
Remake of the Scottish ghillie. il Esquire 59: 92-3 Ap '63
Right shoe. il Redbook 121:22+ My '63
Ski boots; selection and evaluation of. P. Idleman. il Consumer Bul 46:9-13+ O '63
Vogue's eye view: the greatest legs. il Vogue 144:53-9 Ag 15 '64
Which footwear for camp? C. B. Colby. Outdoor Life 131:78-9+ Ja '63
See also
Ballet slippers
Leather
Sandals

Care

What's available in shoe care products. il Good H 156:151 Je '63

Dyeing

See Dyes and dyeing

Trade and manufacture

Cobbler caters to ski crowd; Rudolph Haderer boot shop, Kitzbuhel, Austria. il Bsns W p32-3 Mr 9 '63
Earnings in footwear manufacturing, April 1962. F. W. Mohr. il Mo Labor R 86:168-70 F '63
Shoemakers look to their sales last. Bsns W p46+ F 29 '64
Shoes that come to your door; Charles C. Eaton co; Brockton, Mass. il Bsns W p86+ Ag 22 '64
Wage chronology: International shoe co (cont) il Mo Labor R 86:536-7 My '63
Wage chronology: Massachusetts shoe manufacturing; 1963-64. bibliog f il Mo Labor R 87:313-15 Mr '64
See also
Bata shoe company

SHOES, Rubber, plastic, etc.
Boots, boots, boots; fashionable footgear of American women. il Time 83:46 Ja 3 '64
Keeping your children's feet warm and dry. E. M. McCabe. il Parents Mag 38:30+ D '63
Outdoor footwear. H. Kanzler. il Field & S 68:50-1+ S '63
Singing? hardly. il Time 83:76+ Ap 17 '64
Synthetic shoes. Time 81:92+ Ap 5 '63

SHOFSTALL, W. P.
Bridge; case for fraternities; address, July 4, 1963. Vital Speeches 29:724-7 S 15 '62
Religion; future of America; address, March 1, 1964. Vital Speeches 30:474-7 My 15 '64
Ten delusions of youth; address, February 14, 1963. Vital Speeches 29:400-3 Ap 15 '63

SHOLTO-DOUGLAS, Patrick
Brigadier tells about the fight; interview, ed. by W. Smith. por Life 56:44D F 7 '64

SHOMAN, Abdul Hameed
Prosperous peddler. por Time 81:86 Ap 26 '63

SHOMON, Joseph J.
Battle for green acres. Audubon Mag 66:81 Mr '64
Goal: 2000 nature centers by the year 2000. Audubon Mag 66:148-9 My '64
Guidelines for a nature center. Audubon Mag 65:384-5 N '63
How Virginia preserves natural areas. il Audubon Mag 65:106-7 Mr '63
Nature centers and delinquency. Audubon Mag 66:14-15 Ja '64
Nature centers are spreading fast. il Audubon Mag 65:295 S '63
Nature centers gaining momentum. Audubon Mag 65:44-5 Ja '63
Naturealm. Audubon Mag 66:212-15 Jl '64
Some emerging concepts of natural areas and nature centers. Audubon Mag 65:176-7 My '63
World enriched by our presence. Audubon Mag 66:354-5 N '64
—See Batts, H. L. jr, jt. auth.

SHONFIELD, Andrew
After Brussels. For Affairs 41:721-31 Jl '63

SHOOTING
Basics of bowhunting. G. H. Gillelan. il Outdoor Life 134:114+ S '64
Doing what comes naturally. H. Babcock. il Field & S 67:32-3+ F '63
Fast cars, fancy targets; reproductions of paintings by T. Rost; text by W. Pages. Field & S 68:38-41 Mr '64
First steps in wingshooting. T. Trueblood. il Field & S 69:16+ Ag '64
G. I. earps. Time 81:45 Mr 1 '63
Hunting (cont) il Sports Illus 18:52+ Mr 4 '63
Practicing for wingshooting. G. H. Gillelan. il Outdoor Life 131:16-19+ Je '63
Shooters' problems; ed. by J. O'Connor. See issues of Outdoor life
Shooting. J. O'Connor. See issues of Outdoor life
Shooting; ed. by W. Page. See issues of Field & stream
Tips for shotgunners. W. C. Lammey. il Pop Mech 120:154-5 O '63
See also
Archery
Game preserves
Geese, Wild
Shooting—Competitions
Skeet (game)
Targets
Trap shooting
also Pigeon shooting; and similar headings

Accidents and injuries

Dodge City syndrome. S. Meisler. Nation 198: 460-1 My 4 '64
Surest gun; accidental killing of daughter by marksman. il Newsweek 62:33 S 16 '63

Competitions

Dodge City syndrome. S. Meisler. Nation 198: 460-1 My 4 '64
Month of bull's-eyes and Maggie's drawers; National rifle and pistol matches. il Sports Illus 21:28-33 Ag 10 '64

Study and teaching

Duffer to sharpshooter in ninety minutes; sight shooting. G. X. Sand. il Pop Mech 120:82-3 D '63
Long shots that aren't long. J. O'Connor. il Outdoor Life 134:70+ O '64
Quail shoot with a twist. P. Czura. il Field & S 69:48-9 Je '64
Shotgun primer. P. Czura. il Field & S 68: 42-5 Jl '63
Should he shoot the Magnum? J. Rychetnki. il Outdoor Life 133:38-41+ F '64
Straight-shooting teens; Whitehaven, Tenn, rifle club. D. Cipnic. il Parents Mag 39:44-5+ Ja '64
When your daughter wants to hunt. R. Starnes. il Field & S 67:12-14+ F '63
See also
Firearms—Safety devices and measures

SHOOTING clubs. See Sports clubs
SHOOTING preserves. See Game preserves
SHOOTING ranges
Dual-purpose range. R. Lowe. Recreation 57: 359 S '64
How to make a living-room rifle range; photocell target. T. W. Sikes. il Pop Sci 183:145-8+ S '63

SHOP benches. See Work benches
SHOPGIRLS. See Department stores—Employees
SHOPLIFTING
Putting the label on stealing. S. Withers. il N Y Times Mag p49 Jl 21 '63
Shoplifting; our white-collar scandal. D. Wharton. Read Digest 82:73-7 Ap '63

SHOPPERS information service, incorporated
Shopping made easy, it says here. Consumer Rep 28:205 My '63

SHOPPING and shoppers
Bazaar of bizarre bargains; items at the World's fair. H. Carlton. Life 57:18 Jl 17 '64
Booty from the Himalayas. B. F. Krainin. il Holiday 35:34 My '64
Free delivery service and telephone ordering are assets. R. H. Smith. Pub W 184:89 Ag 19 '63
George pleasures them with groceries; Publix markets, Florida. T. G. Harris. il Look 28: 102+ My 5 '64
How I learned to be an expert bargainer. G. Gaskill. il Read Digest 82:228-9+ Mr '63
Shop along with baby. M. Bernath. il Parents Mag 39:48-50+ Ja '64
Shopping; an Irish eye for value. D. Guinness. Holiday 33:106+ Ap '63
Super eating from supermarket specials. il Am Home 67:62-3+ O '64
There's more than one reason for going to Zurich. E. Gordon. House B 106:99+ Jl '64
What women hate about buying clothes. il Redbook 122:62-3+ F '64
See also
Christmas shopping
Purchasing, Household

Anecdotes, facetiae, satire, etc.

Walk on the wild side. W. M. Gibb. Atlan 211:132-4 Ap '63

Europe, Western

Shops of Europe. N. Barry. il Holiday 37: 117-22 Ja '65

SHOPPING and shoppers—*Continued*

Russia

Service with a snarl. il Newsweek 64:52 D 7 '64
When a housewife goes shopping in Russia. C. Foltz, jr. il U S News 56:88-9 Ja 27 '64

SHOPPING bags
High fashion in shopping bags? design winner by Xalco. il Design 65:173 Mr '64

SHOPPING by telephone. See Telephone in business

SHOPPING centers
Case of the lonesome loan; symposium. il Harvard Bsns R 42:6-8+ N '64
Casual elegance in a shopping center. il Arch Rec 136:210-11 S '64
Color and texture brighten a compact shopping center; Monmouth shopping center, Eatontown, N.J. il Arch Rec 135:174-6 Je '64
Confidence index gauges retail blight. Am City 79:98 F '64
Free space: can public libraries receive it? report of survey of branch libraries in shopping centers by Wichita, Kan, city library. R. Waters. ALA Bul 58:232-4 Mr '64
More convenient than a shopping center; Janesville, Wis. J. Lustig. il Am City 79: 116-17 S '64
New buildings at Northland in Detroit. il Arch Rec 133:166-7 Je '63
New curiosity shop; Pittsburgh's Shadyside. il Bsns W p 118-20+ Ja 18 '64
Shopping center as nucleus. D. Haskell. il Arch Forum 118:142 Je '63
Shopping centers. R. Lambakis; discussion. Recreation 55:488; 56:108 D '62, Mr '63
Southwest center reminiscent of old Mexico; Vista plaza shopping center, Chula Vista, Calif. il Arch Rec 133:176-7 Je '63
Squeeze on shopping centers. K. Hamill. il Fortune 68:116-18+ S '63
Unified variety on a fountained mall; Oakbrook center, Oak Brook, Ill. il Arch Rec 135:166-9 Je '64
Utilities set on the roof of Phoenix shopping center. il Arch Rec 134:136-8 D '63
White on white; new Texas shopping center, Fort Worth, Tex. il Arch Forum 119:96-9 Jl '63
See also
Business districts

England

Will it go in Britain? first suburban shopping center. il Bsns W p86-9 Ja 9 '65

Germany (Federal Republic)

Germans park and buy; Main-Taunus-Zentrum regional shopping center on outskirts of Frankfort. il Bsns W p58-60+ Ag 15 '64

SHOR, Franc
Conquest of the Holy City. Nat Geog Mag 124:839-55 D '63
Crusader road to Jerusalem. il Nat Geog Mag 124:797-837 D '63

SHOR, George G. jr, and Pollard, D. D.
Seismic investigations of Seychelles and Saya de Malha Banks, Northwest Indian Ocean. bibliog Science 142:48-9 O 4 '63

SHOR, Rachel
WLB biography (cont) Wilson Lib Bul 38:202, 411+ O '63, Ja '64

SHORE, Stephen
Angry young man with a camera; interview. il U S Camera 26:52-3 Je '63

SHORE, Wilma
It was different with Cinderella; story. Sat Eve Post 236:66-8 Ag 24 '63
May your days be merry and bright; story. Sat Eve Post 236:44-5 D 21 '63

SHORE. See Seashore

SHORE birds
Winter watching for shore birds. il Sunset 132:73-4 Mr '64

SHORE lines
See also
Coast changes

SHORE protection
Stemming the tide with turf. il Pop Sci 182:114 Je '63
See also
Sea walls

SHORE vegetation. See Seashore vegetation

SHOREWOOD publishing company, incorporated
Shorewood wins Carey-Thomas for Great drawings. Pub W 183:130 F 18 '63

SHORIKI, Matsutaro
Bigger & better than anyone. il por Time 81: 57-8 My 24 '63

SHORR, Ray
Lighting for duffers. Pop Phot 52:40-2+ Ja '63

SHORT, Bobby
Welcome home, Bobby. il pors Ebony 19:64-6+ Je '64

SHORT, Judith
Choicest co-ed. por Esquire 60:75 S '63

SHORT, Robert
Peanuts and the Bible. Américas 16:16-20 Ap '64

SHORT brothers and Harland, limited
Belfast makes successful maiden flight; turboprop freighter. il Aviation W 80:39 Ja 13 '64

SHORT cake. See Shortcake

SHORT circuits
Short circuits and fuses. B. Francois. il Motor B 111:37-8+ Mr '63

SHORT girls. See Stature

SHORT line railroads. See Railroads, Short line

SHORT-range attack missile. See Guided missiles—Launching from airplanes

SHORT selling. See Stocks—Short selling

SHORT stories
American short story, by W. Peden. Review
Sat R 47:31 Ag 22 '64. W. Bower
Awards to the new tale-tellers. R. Hughes. Sat R 46:27 Jl 20 '63
Furnishing the rooms. K. Reed. Writer 77: 20-1+ Mr '64
It pays to write confession stories. H. Withrow. Writer 77:17-21 F '64
Let's build a story. E. S. Fox. Writer 77:17-20+ Je '64
Lonely voice: a study of the short story, by F. O'Connor. Review
Sat R 46:26 Jl 20 '63. W. Bower
Pop art and the short story. W. J. Smith. Commonweal 80:508-10 Jl 24 '64
Prize stories 1963: the O. Henry awards, by R. Poirier. Review
Sat R 46:28-9 Jl 20 '63. H. Frankel
Twenty-three modern stories. ed. by B. Howes. Review
Sat R 46:21+ Ap 13 '63. G. Hicks
Twists, angles, and gimmicks. M. Corson. Writer 76:18-20+ My '63
View from the upstairs porch. S. F. Ciulla. Writer 76:9-11 N '63
Wayward reader. C. Fadiman. Holiday 36:26+ N '64
Writing the commercial short story. J. T. Freeman. Writer 77:10-15+ D '64
See also
Christmas stories
Detective and mystery stories
Fiction—Technique

SHORT subject films. See Moving pictures—Short subject films

SHORT-take-off and landing airplanes. See Airplanes, Short take-off and landing

SHORT wave radio. See Microwaves; Radio broadcasting, Short wave; Radio receiving apparatus, Short wave

SHORT wave radio stations. See Radio stations, Short wave

SHORT wave radio transmitters. See Radio transmitters, Short wave

SHORTCAKE
Fruitful endeavors. il Redbook 122:88-9+ Ap '64
Old-fashioned strawberry shortcake. il McCalls 91:54 Jl '64
Strawberry shortcake. B. M. Stover. il Parents Mag 39:66 Je '64
Summer shortcake. il McCalls 90:96-7+ Jl '63

SHORTEN, Monica
Introduced menace. Natur Hist 73:42-9 bibliog(p67) D '64

SHORTHAIRED pointers, German. See German shorthaired pointers

SHORTHAND
Shorthand: 60 B.C. to 1884. B. I. Blackstone. Sch Life 47:12 N '64

SHORTIA galacifolia. See Oconee bells

SHORTIA uniflora. See Oconee bells

SHORTRIDGE, John
Man with a mission. il Newsweek 61:60 F 18 '63

SHOSTAKOVICH, Dmitrii Dmitrievich
Dmitri's Lady; performance of Shostakovich's Katerina Ismailova at Covent Garden. il por Newsweek 62:61 D 16 '63
First recordings of two Shostakovich symphonies. J. Diether. por Am Rec G 30:1124-5 Ag '64
Katerina Ismailova. Criticism
Time 82:65 D 13 '63
Musical events; Shostakovich's Fourth symphony by Philadelphia orchestra. W. Sargeant. New Yorker 39:94+ Mr 2 '63

SHOSTAKOVICH, Dmitriĭ Dmitrievich—*Cont.*
Nose. Criticism
Sat R 47:65 Je 13 '64
Rehabilitation. Newsweek 61:63 F 25 '63
Shostakovich without ideology. P. Heyworth. il pors Hi Fi 14:96-100+ O '64
Soviet music since Stalin. B. Schwarz. por Sat R 46:55-6+ Mr 30 '63
Two recordings of Shostakovich's Quartet no. 8. A. Cohn. Am Rec G 30:585 Mr '64

SHOT putting
Aannnnghhh! Coliseum relays in Los Angeles. J. Underwood. il Sports Illus 20:84+ My 25 '64
Prince of put; Dallas Crutcher Long III smashes the world record. il Time 83:79 Je 12 '64

SHOTGUN gauges. See Gages

SHOTGUNS
All-around shotgun. J. O'Connor. il Outdoor Life 132:70+ O '63
Factory where time stands still. il Bsns W p84-7 Ap 13 '63
Fallen Lady. H. Babcock. il Field & S 69:68-70+ My '64
Gentlemen, choose your weapons. il Esquire 62:118-19 O '64
Guns for gobblers. W. Page. il Field & S 67:96-100 Mr '63
Inventor takes the kick out of shooting; Hydro-Coil. D. Barnes. il Sports Illus 19:89+ S 9 '63
Mid-continent roosters. W. Page. il Field & S 68:130-2+ Ap '64
Mystery of the 16 gauge? W. Page. il Field & S 69:68-70+ Ag '64
New guns flood country. W. Page. il Field & S 67:130-4 Ap '63
Quail guns and loads. J. O'Connor. il Outdoor Life 134:58-60+ N '64
Shock-absorbing shotgun, it saves your shoulder. K. Warner. il Pop Sci 185:38-9 Jl '64
Shotgun shooter's manual. W. Page. il Field & S 69:56-64 S '64
Tips for shotgunners. W. C. Lammey. il Pop Mech 120:154-5 O '63
Up and down guns. W. Page. il Field & S 68:70-4 S '63
Winchester scatterguns. W. Page. il Field & S 69:68-70+ N '64

SHOULDER dislocations. See Dislocations

SHOUT from the rooftops; drama. See Gregg, J.

SHOVE, Gene, and Andrew, Frank
Maintaining quality of stored grain. Suc Farm 61:43 Jl '63

SHOW (periodical)
Enthusiasts. il Newsweek 62:109 O 21 '63
Show goes on. il Time 83:82 Je 12 '64
Show sold. Time 84:71 N 13 '64

SHOW cases. See Exhibition cases

SHOW girls. See Actors and actresses

SHOW rooms. See Showrooms

SHOW windows
Store windows and in-store display. T. Huntington. Pub W 185:76-8 Ja 6 '64
Wilderness; display of New York state departments of conservation and commerce at Manhattan savings bank. New Yorker 39:34-5 Je 8 '63

SHOWER baths
Why not a hot shower right in camp? il Sunset 133:84 Jl '64

SHOWER gifts. See Gifts

SHOWER of gold; story. See Barthelme, D.

SHOWERS (parties) See Entertaining

SHOWROOMS
Elegant showroom for a Paris square. il Arch Forum 118:118-19 F '63
One of New York's thrills: showroom sightseeing. il House B 106:50 Jl '64

SHOWS, Thomas B. Jr, and others
Erythrocyte glucose-6-phosphate dehydrogenase in Caucasians: new inherited variant. bibliog Science 145:1056-7 S 4 '64

SHOWY ladys slipper. See Ladys slippers

SHRAG, Peter
Newton: pipeline from Harvard. Sat R 48:49-50+ Ja 16 '65

SHRAKE, Edwin
Everyone for backgammon. Sports Illus 20:42-4+ My 4 '64
Golf. Sports Illus 20:52+ Mr 2 '64
Pro football. Sports Illus 21:66+ O 26 '64
Richest bonus baby ever. Sports Illus 21:16-21 Jl 6 '64
(ed) See Rawls, B. Fairway woods: swing hard and be fearless

SHREDDING machinery
This shredder made this garden grow. I. McLendon. il Flower Grower 51:27 O '64

SHREINER, Charles W.
Lord helps Charly, and vice versa. B. Hibbs. Read Digest 85:140-4 Ag '64

SHREWS
Minks, shrews and men in a winter swamp. B. Gilbert. il Sports Illus 18:38-42+ Mr 18 '63

SHREWSBERRY, Reynard C. and Musulin, Boris
Raoult's law study of vanadium pentafluoride in uranium hexafluoride. bibliog Science 145:1452-4 S 25 '64

SHREWSBURY laboratories. See Worcester foundation for experimental biology

SHRIKES
Contrapuntal bird songs; courtship duet by African shrike. Sci Am 208:80+ My '63

SHRIMPS
Cultured prawns; the kuruma prawn. il Time 81:43+ Mr 29 '63
See also
Cookery—Fish

SHRINERS. See Freemasons

SHRINERS' hospitals for crippled children. See Children—Hospitals

SHRINES
See also
Lourdes, France

SHRIVER, Robert Sargent, 1915-
Ambassadors of good will; the Peace corps. pors Nat Geog Mag 126:297-345 S '64
Challenge with a difference. Sat R 47:30 D 5 '64
Close look at the Peace corps and its volunteers; interview. por U S News 56:38-41 Ja 6 '64
Frontier of service; address, June 8, 1964. America 111:14-16 Jl 4 '64
I have the best job in Washington. por N Y Times Mag p34+ Je 9 '63
Message to American librarians. Wilson Lib Bul 38:833 Je '64
Moral force of sport. por Sports Illus 18:30-1+ Je 3 '63
Peace corps: frontier for youth. Parents Mag 38:46-7+ Jl '63
Talk with Sargent Shriver: how to fight the poverty war; interview, ed. by R. T. Stout. pors Newsweek 64:72-3 D 14 '64
Two years of the Peace corps. For Affairs 41:694-707 Jl '63
When Peace corps teachers return. NEA J 52:13-14+ Mr '63
about
Band-aid program? war on poverty. il por Newsweek 63:35-6+ F 17 '64
Essential Sargent Shriver. M. Kempton. New Repub 150:12-14 Mr 28 '64
Field marshal in poverty war. il por Bsns W p28-9 Mr 7 '64
Generalissimo of the war on poverty. A. H. Raskin. il por N Y Times Mag p39+ N 22 '64
Handsome, busy, hot government property; with report by R. B. Stolley. il pors Life 56:40-2+ My 1 '64
Into the stratosphere. il por Time 83:15 Ja 17 '64
Into the trenches; anti-poverty measures. Newsweek 63:17-18 Mr 30 '64
It is almost as good as its intentions. il pors Time 82:18-22 Jl 5 '63
Peace corps after two years. il Sr Schol 82:6-9 Mr 13 '63
People of the week. U S News 56:16 Ja 20 '64
Sargent Shriver: a candid portrait, by R. A. Liston. Review
New Repub 151:30-1 Jl 25 '64. G. W. Johnson
Shriver moves into the front rank. A. Lewis. il pors N Y Times Mag p21+ Mr 15 '64
War on poverty; the first shots. il Newsweek 64:71-4+ D 14 '64
What next for Sargent Shriver? I. Mothner. pors Look 28:77-8+ Je 16 '64
Where $1-billion will go; LBJ's anti-poverty program. por Bsns W p29-30 Mr 21 '64

SHROUD, Holy. See Holy Shroud

SHROUT, Bill. See Shrout, K. jt. auth.

SHROUT, Kathy, and Shrout, Bill
Deer hunt country style. Field & S 68:54-7+ O '63

SHROVE Tuesday. See Carnival

SHRUB. See Beverages

SHRUBS
Add color dash with trees and shrubs. R. R. Thomasson. il Pop Gard 15:24-7 F '64
Arboretum et fruticetum Britannicum, The trees and shrubs of Britain, by J. C. Loudon. Review
Am For il 69:8-9+ Ag '63. H. W. Dengler
Best roses, trees, and shrubs for 1964. H. Mason. il Bet Hom & Gard 42:64-9 F '64
Deciduous shrubs worth knowing. il Sunset 132:122 Ja '64
Double duty from shrubs and trees. S. W. Plimpton. il Horticulture 41:518-19 O '63
New for '63. Pop Gard 14:71+ F '63
Nine shrubs that give bountiful bloom. il Flower Grower 51:30-1 My '64
Shrubs for all seasons. M. J. Dietz. il Flower Grower 50:30-2 Mr '63
Shrubs for winter color. il Pop Gard 16:30-1 Ja '65
Shrubs in Florida. P. Dempsey. il Horticulture 42:18-21 N '64
Summer propagation; flowering trees and shrubs. R. G. Coggeshall. il Horticulture 42:40-1 Je '64
Trees & shrubs for all season color. F. F. Rockwell and E. C. Grayson. il Flower Grower 50:45+ O '63
Two planning and planting ideas. J. R. Rebhan. il Flower Grower 50:40-1 N '63
Variety, the spice of your garden; flowering shrubs. J. Fanning. il Pop Gard 15:24-7 N '64
Volatile growth inhibitors produced by aromatic shrubs. C. H. Muller and others. il Science 143:471-3 Ja 31 '64; Reply with rejoinder. P. V. Wells. 144:889-90 My 15 '64
Why not have a shrub-cutting garden? E. L. Sculthorp. House B 105:67-8+ S '63
See also
Evergreens
Hedges
Pruning
also names of shrubs. e.g. Firethorns

Planting

Shrub aristocrats. M. Costigan. il Horticulture 42:32-3 F '64
Six planting do's and don'ts. C. Lisle. il Pop Gard 14:42-3 Ap '63

SHTEPPA, Konstantin
How to talk about communism; when it sets dogma above fact. H. Overstreet and B. W. Overstreet. il PTA Mag 57:16-18 My '63

SHUB, Anatole
Moscow's satellites; in and out of orbit. N Y Times Mag p22-3+ Mr 15 '64
Winter of communism's discontent. Reporter 30:29-31 Ja 2 '64

SHUBERT, Jacob J.
J.J. Newsweek 63:61 Ja 6 '64

SHUBIK, P. See Lijinsky, W. jt. auth.

SHUBIN, Seymour
In time of sorrow: the gift of your presence. Read Digest 84:240-2 Je '64

SHUFFLEBOARD
Shuffleboard scorer. E. H. Berg. il Pop Sci 184:156 F '64

SHUGART, Ralph
Pediatrician. il pors Life 57:48A-55 Jl 31 '64

SHUGG, Roger W.
Multiversity press; summary of annual report. por Pub W 186:40-4 Jl 6 '64

SHUI-JEN. See Tankas

SHULA, Don
How the Colts met triumph, and disaster; ed. by T. Maule. por Sport Illus 22:24-9 Ja 11 '65
Road to the title in the West; ed. by T. Maule. Sports Illus 22:42-4+ Ja 18 '65

SHULDINER, Herbert
Flying jeep. Pop Sci 185:45-7+ D '64
Keep your pipe in good spirits. Pop Sci 184:155-7 Ap '64
New home for the Mets. Pop Sci 184:86-8 Ap '64
Was John Glenn injured in space? Pop Sci 186:55-9+ Ja '65

SHULENBERGER, Arvid
Henry James as minor novelist. Nat R 14:166 F 26 '63
OK novelists today. Nat R 16:115-16 F 11 '64

SHULL, Fremont A. and Miller, D. C.
Help the man in the middle. Nations Bsns 51:36-7 F '63

SHULMAN, Daniel
Girl-watching. Seventeen 22:92-3+ Je '63

SHULMAN, Label
Abraham and Rigoletto. Opera N 28:6 F 22 '64

SHULMAN, Marvin Oscar
Taxes. Dance Mag 37:129 D '63

SHULMAN, Sidney, and others
Antibody response to immunization by different routes. bibliog Science 145:815-17 Ag 21 '64

SHULTZ, Dyson P.
Artistic marriage? Sch Arts 62:27 F '63

SHULTZ, George P.
Fort Worth project of the Armour automation committee; excerpt of report. Mo Labor R 87:53-7 Ja '64

SHUMAN, Charles B.
Which is better for wheat growers? por Farm J 87:33+ Mr '63

SHUMAN, John T.
Educating for industry. Atlan 214:90-4 D '64

SHUMWAY, F. Ritter
Charting the Great Lakes for yachtsmen. por Motor B 113:98+ F '64

SHUPP, Cleo
Speaking out. por Sat Eve Post 236:12+ Je 29 '63

SHURTLEFF, Mal, and Fieght, J. J.
How to control alfalfa and clover diseases. Suc Farm 62:52-3+ My '64
Small grain diseases; how to control them. Suc Farm 62:46-7+ Ag '64

SHUSTAK, Lawrence
With an SLR? shooting techniques. P. Caulfield. il Mod Phot 27:56-63 Ap '63

SHUSTER, Alvin
Back to the woods. N Y Times Mag p32+ Ag 18 '63
Jokes with the LBJ brand. N Y Times Mag p 100+ S 13 '64
Our 398 millionaires; a new breed. N Y Times Mag p37 S 15 '63
Stamps for art's sake. N Y Times Mag p30+ S 20 '64
Swifter completion of their rounds. Sat R 47:17-19+ Mr 21 '64
—and Franklin, B. A.
How a race riot happened. Sat Eve Post 236:15-19 My 4 '63

SHUSTER, Benjamin H.
Dizziness: your body's warning light; ed. by L. S. Hutchison. Today Health 41:50+ F '63

SHUSTER, George N.
Averages obscure the differences. Sat R 47:71 Ap 18 '64
Looking hard for answers. Sat R 46:80 My 18 '63
Maisie Ward's journey. Commonweal 81:123-5 O 23 '64
New statistics on an old problem. Commonweal 79:436 Ja 10 '64
Religion and education. Commonweal 79:504-7 Ja 31 '64

SHUTE, Barbara E. See O'Keefe, J. A. jt. auth.

SHUTTERS, Camera. See Camera shutters

SHY, G. M. and Gonatas, N. K.
Human myopathy with giant abnormal mitochondria. bibliog Science 145:493-6 Jl 31 '64

SHYER, Marlene Fanta
All my own; story. Good H 158:88-9 Mr '64
Difficult part; story. Redbook 123:54-5 Je '64
Once upon a weekend; story. Redbook 123:68-9 S '64

SHYNESS. See Bashfulness; Timidity

SHYRE, Paul
Child buyer; dramatization of novel by J. Hersey. Criticism
Life 56:16 Ap 3 '64
New Yorker 40:58-9 Ja 2 '65
Time il 85:53 Ja 1 '65

SIALIC acids
Sialic acid concentrations in the pituitary glands of normal and ovariectomized rats. E. G. Rennels and J. F. Hood. bibliog il Science 144:416-17 Ap 24 '64
Sialic acid-containing glycopeptide from chlorella. D. L. Correll. bibliog Science 145:588-9 Ag 7 '64

SIAM. See Thailand

SIAMESE fighting fishes. See Fighting fishes

SIAMESE twins
How medical progress has hastened the passing of the side show. J. Lentz. il Todays Health 42:48-51 Mr '64

SIBBALD, John R.
Apple pie without apples; with recipes. Am Heritage 15:114 Ap '64

SIBELIUS, Jean Julius Christian
Sibelius from an old hand and a new one. J. Diether. il por Am Rec G 30:586-7 Mr '64
Two views of the Sibelius First. J. Diether. Am Rec G 30:1126-7 Ag '64

SIBERIA
Return from Russia. W. Ciszek. America 110:408-11 Mr 28 '64
See also
Akademgorodok
Khabarovsk
Novosibirsk

SIBERIA—*Continued*

Description and travel

Across the vast, silent land called Siberia; trans-Siberian trek from Japan to Moscow. R. Hughes. il N Y Times Mag p 12-13+ My 31 '64

SIBLEY, Antoinette
Antoinette Sibley. S. Goodman. pors Dance Mag 37:52-3 S '63

SIBLEY, Hi
Build this cook-out counter for your patio. Pop Sci 183:110-12 Ag '63
Dress up your eggs for Easter. Pop Mech 119:160-1 Ap '63
You can make this birdbath for a song. Pop Mech 120:74 S '63

SIBLINGS
Boys and other beasts; excerpts. B. Lang. McCalls 91:68+ F; 74+ Mr; 78+ Ap '64
Brotherly love? E. J. LeShan. il N Y Times Mag p 114+ N 22 '64
How one mother solved the jealousy problem. il Todays Health 42:74-7 Ja '64
Mommy does it hurt to have a baby? B. Wertheimer. il Parents Mag 39:110+ N '64
New baby. L. Miller. il Redbook 120:56-7+ Ap '63
Our Johnny-come-lately baby. P. Buck. il Parents Mag 38:52-3+ D '63
Tail-end Charlie. E. Wahleen. il PTA Mag 58:19 Ja '64

SICHER, Frederic
Indiana Dunes National Lakeshore. Nat Parks Mag 38:4-7+ Jl '64

SICILY
See also
Geology—Sicily
Poor—Sicily

Economic conditions

Gandhi of Sicily. G. D. Kumlien. Commonweal 79:745-6 Mr 20 '64
Waiting is a way of life. Time 82:46 N 15 '63

Social conditions

Small candle of Danilo Dolci. A. Winston. Christian Cent 81:1109-10 S 9 '64

Social life and customs

Lampedusa in Sicily; the lair of the leopard. A. Colquhoun. Atlan 211:91-3+ F '63

SICK, The
At the hospital: mother is part of the cure. R. Kramer. il N Y Times Mag p85-6 Ap 5 '64
Family in health and illness; some neglected areas. C. E. Vincent. bibliog f Ann Am Acad 346:109-16 Mr '63
Hospitals worry patients. F. Marley. Sci N L 84:151 S 7 '63
How to amuse a shut-in child. il Todays Health 42:26-9 D '64
How to help your hospital. Sister Mary Ferdinand. il Todays Health 42:74-6 F '64
I believe; ed. by A. Armstrong. L. Veach. Seventeen 22:22 D '63
Letter to a useless friend. Christian Cent 80:323-4 Mr 13 '63
Mama, you're pretty inside; housekeeping from a bed. G. H. Land. il Redbook 123:12+ S '64
Meeting patients' psychosocial needs in the general hospital. E. L. Brown. Ann Am Acad 346:117-25 Mr '63
One long night in a baby hospital; Babies hospital in New York city. E. M. Wylie. il Good H 158:84-9+ Je '64
Pack a beauty kit for that hospital stay. L. D. Kirk. il Parents Mag 38:44 My '63
Sick, and tired of it. G. Hechinger. il N Y Times Mag p71-2 Ja 12 '64
Wake-up war between patient and nurse. H. B. Jacobs. il N Y Times Mag p 19+ My 10 '64
What to do when your child is sick. E. P. Duffy. il Parents Mag 39:44-6+ N '64
Why can't mothers stay in hospitals with their children? M. Wessel and N. Simon. il Redbook 121:41+ Ag '63
See also
Incurables
Physicians and patients

Recreation

See Recreation for the handicapped

SICKLE cell anemia. See Anemia

SICKLEMIA. See Anemia

SICKNESS
Turn your sickness into an asset. L. E. Bisch. Read Digest 83:90-3 D '63
See also
Sick, The

SICKNESS absence. See Absenteeism

SICKNESS benefit plans. See Employees benefit plans

SICKNESS insurance. See Insurance, Health

SICRE, José Gómez-. See Gómez-Sicre, J.

SIDE-saddles. See Saddles

SIDEWALK cafes. See Restaurants

SIDEWALK games. See Games

SIDEWALK superintendents. See Building

SIDEY, Hugh
Departure of a deputy president. Life 56:105-6+ Mr 6 '64
Journey out of grief: R.F.K.'s mission to Asia. Life 56:32-3 Ja 31 '64

about

Care and feeding of the Kennedy image. il U S News 55:92-3 S 9 '63

SIDIS, William James
Devourers of genius. H. Bowser. Sat R 47:34 F 22 '64

SIDLE, Jimmy
Boy meets quarterback; showing the World's fair to an All American. il pors Look 28:M8-10 F 11 '64

SIDMAN, Richard L. and others
Mutant mice, quaking and jimpy, with deficient myelination in the central nervous system. bibliog Science 144:309-11 Ap 17 '64

SIDNEY, John
Back of beyond. Travel 119:44-7 Ap '63
Nature thought of it first. Sci Digest 54:44-7 O '63
Nature's weirdest inventions. Sci Digest 53:12-16 My '63
When an elephant sleeps. Sci Digest 54:19-22 S '63

SIDNEY on skis; story. See Brown, J.

SIDRANSKY, Herschel, and others
Protein synthesis enhanced in the liver of rats force-fed a threonine-devoid diet. bibliog Science 146:766-8 N 6 '64

SIE, Hsien-gieh, and Fishman, W. H.
Glycogen synthetase: its response to cortisol. bibliog Science 143:816 F 21 '64

SIEDLER, Wolf Jobst
Building and rebuilding of Berlin. Atlan 212:103-9 D '63

SIEGEL, Benjamin
Principal; story. Redbook 121:125-56 Je '63

SIEGEL, Bernard J.
Fruit of the golden bough. Sat R 46:54 D 7 '63

SIEGEL, Dorothy
When you take the youngsters to Europe. Parents Mag 38:58-9+ Je '63

SIEGEL, Edward B.
Ski safe! address. Recreation 57:32 Ja '64

SIEGEL, Laurence, and others
Burgeoning university enrollments and academic quality. Sch & Soc 91:336-8 N 2 '63

SIEGEL, Maurice
Island of yesterday afternoon. Sat R 46:55+ O 12 '63

SIEGEL, Seymour
Totem in the tephillin and tallis. Sat R 47:37 Je 6 '64

SIEGFRIED: opera. See Wagner, R.

SIEGLE, Peter E.
Education, automation, and competency. Sch & Soc 92:309-10 O 31 '64

SIEGMEISTER, Elie
From CRI, Elie Siegmeister's Symphony no. 3; truly worth attention. A. Cohn. Am Rec G 31:255 N '64

SIEGRIST, William
Instant color photography. Sci N L 83:250-1 Ap 20 '63

SIEKEVITZ, Philip
Necessity of popular science. Nation 198:146-8 F 10 '64
Scientists and the public weal. Nation 197:271-3 N 2 '63

SIEKMAN, Philip
Battle for the kitchen. Fortune 69:108-11+ Ja '64
Hoover's well-vacuumed world. Fortune 69:143-6+ Je '64
When executives turned revolutionaries. Fortune 70:147-9+ S '64

SIEPI, Cesare
Siepi face to face; interview, ed. by F. Stevenson. por Opera N 28:30-1 D 28 '63

SIEPMANN, Charles A.
What is wrong with TV, and with us. N Y Times Mag p 13+ Ap 19 '64

SIERRA Aranzazu (ship) See Freight vessels

SIERRA club
Call of the wild. il Time 83:54 Mr 27 '64

SIERRA LEONE
Teaching through trial and error. L. F. Bailey. Sr Schol 84:10T-11T Ap 17 '64
See also
Presidents—Sierra Leone
SIERRA NATIONAL FOREST. See National forests
SIERRA NEVADA, Calif.
High Sierra in spring; with photographs by G. Silk. Life 56:48-61 My 29 '64
Rescue on the rocks; airborne posse saves lives in High Sierras. W. S. Griswold. il Pop Sci 184:74-5+ Mr '64
SIESTAS. See Rest periods
SIGAL, Albert E.
New York plans protection for children. Arch Rec 133:172 F '63
SIGAL, Clancy
Two scenes of English life. Commentary 38: 55-7 Jl '64
What is theater? New Repub 151:20-3 S 26 '64
SIGEL, M. Michael
Immunologic phenomena: cold-blooded vertebrates. Science 141:543+ Ag 9 '63
Interferon. Science 146:956-7 N 13 '64
SIGHT
Adaptation to displaced vision: visual, motor, or proprioceptive change? C. S. Harris. bibliog il Science 140:812-13 My 17 '63
Auditory flutter-driving of visual flicker. T. Shipley. bibliog il Science 145:1328-30 S 18 '64
Autokinetic movement: selective manipulation of directional components by image stabilization. L. Matin and G. E. MacKinnon. bibliog il Science 143:147-8 Ja 10 '64
Contour interaction and visual resolution: contralateral effects. M. C. Flom and others. bibliog il Science 142:979-80 N 15 '63
Depth perception loss with local monocular suppression: a problem in the explanation of stereopsis. J. Hochberg. bibliog il Science 145:1334-6; 146:800 S 18, N 6 '64
Disappearance of luminous designs. J. P. McKinney. bibliog il Science 140:403-4 Ap 26 '63; Discussion. 144:1359-60 Je 12 '64
Eyesight of newborn well developed at birth. Sci N L 84:361 D 7 '63
How's your eye-Q? visual problems of teachers. J. R. Gregg. il Sr Schol 84:14T Ap 10 '64
Hue-wavelength relation measured by color-naming method for three retinal locations. R. M. Boynton and others. bibliog il Science 146:666-8 O 30 '64
Inhibition in visual systems. D. Kennedy. il Sci Am 209:122-4+ Jl '63
Interference in visual recognition. J. S. Bruner and M. C. Potter. bibliog il Science 144:424-5 Ap 24 '64
Mom! mom! I can see! highpowered spectacles for legally blind. T. Irwin. il Sat Eve Post 236:71-2 My 25 '63
Pattern vision in newborn infants. R. L. Fantz. bibliog il Science 140:296-7 Ap 19 '63
Receptors of human color vision; with appendix by W. S. Stiles. G. Wald. bibliog il Science 145:1007-17 S 4 '64
Responses of single cells in visual system to shifts in the wavelength of light. R. L. De Valois and others. il Science 146:1184-6 N 27 '64
Sensitivity of visual receptors of carotenoid-depleted flies: a vitamin A deficiency in an invertebrate. T. H. Goldsmith and others. bibliog il Science 146:65-7 O 2 '64
Stop, look, and see! J. K. Lagemann. il Read Digest 83:128-31 Jl '63
View from the capsule; astronaut Cooper's vision. Newsweek 63:60 F 17 '64
Vision and touch: an experimentally created conflict between the two senses. I. Rock and J. Victor. Science 143:594-6 F 7 '64
Visual evoked potentials as a function of flash luminance and duration. J. D. Wicke and others. bibliog il Science 146:83-5 O 2 '64
Visual experience in infants: decreased attention to familiar patterns relative to novel ones. R. L. Fantz. bibliog il Science 146:668-70 O 30 '64
See also
After images
Color sense
Eye—Movements
Flicker phenomena
Night vision
Optical illusions
Space perception
SIGHT (animals)
Inhibition in visual systems. D. Kennedy. il Sci Am 209:122-4+ Jl '63
Single-unit activity in the cat's visual cortex: modification after an intense light flash. A. D. J. Robertson and C. R. Evans. bibliog il Science 147:303-4 Ja 15 '65
Vision in frogs. W. R. A. Muntz. il Sci Am 210:110-15+ Mr '64; Reply with rejoinder. D. J. Merrell. 210:10+ My '64
Visual cortex of the brain; visual system of the cat. D. H. Hubel. il Sci Am 209:54-62 bibliog(p 186) N '63; Reply. M. Nadler. 210: 12+ F '64
Visual motion detection in the cat. G. Baumgartner and others. bibliog il Science 146:1070-1 N 20 '64
SIGHT (birds)
Complex visual concept in the pigeon. R. J. Herrnstein and D. H. Loveland. il Science 146:549-51 O 23 '64
SIGHT conservation. See Eye—Care and hygiene
SIGHT-seeing helicopters
Helicopter sightseeing. H. Wilson. il Travel 121:55-7 My '64
New copter at the fair. il Sci Digest 56:53-6 Jl '64
SIGHT shooting. See Shooting
SIGHTS. See Firearms—Sights
SIGHTS, Telescopic. See Telescopic sights
SIGHTS for bows. See Bow sights
SIGMON, Carl
All-American prima donna. Mus Am 83:18-19 Ja '63
SIGN in Sidney Brustein's window; drama. See Hansberry, L.
SIGN painting
See also
Lettering
SIGNAC, Paul
Letter from Paris; exhibition at the Louvre. Genêt. New Yorker 39:56-7 D 28 '63
SIGNAL generators
Additional notes on audio sweep generator. F. J. Manus. Electr World 72:112 N '64
Audio tone-burst generator. T. E. Reamer. il Electr World 70:50-2+ O '63
FM multiplex signal generator. T. E. Reamer. il Electr World 69:55-8+ F '63
R. F. response measurement. J. Tusinski. il Electr World 71:37+ F '64
Signal-generating equipment. H. L. Roberts. il Electr World 70:31-4+ Ag '63
Simple signal generator. C. Henry. il Pop Electr 20:44-5 Ap '64
Simple square-wave pulse adapter; converts sine waves to square waves. J. P. Shields. il Electr World 71:77-8 Mr '64
Transistorized color-TV pattern generator. J. K. Stewart. il Electr World 72:96-9 N '64
TD/RFG: tunnel diode, radio frequency generator. S. E. Bammel. il Pop Electr 18:44-7+ F '63
SIGNAL lights, Automobile. See Automobiles—Signal lights
SIGNAL oil and gas company
Garrett, Signal propose to merge after Curtiss-Wright raises offer. Aviation W 79:33 O 28 '63
SIGNAL tracers. See Radio instruments
SIGNALS and signaling
Flags; when and how to fly them. C. F. Chapman. il Motor B 113:97-104 Ja '64
See also
Navigation aids
SIGNATURES (writing)
See also
Autographs
SIGNIFICANT experience; story. See Griffin, G.
SIGNPOST; drama. See Clapp, P.
SIGNS and signboards
Breaking the sign barrier; International committee for breaking the language barrier. il Newsweek 63:97A-97B Je 8 '64
Toward a universal non-language. D. Shea. il N Y Times Mag p62+ N 22 '64
See also
Billboards
Posters
Road signs
Traffic signs
SIGUR, Alexander
Crisis in the colleges. America 109:711-12+ N 30 '63
SIH, Paul K. T.
Our China policy; a reappraisal. por Cath World 200:84-90 N '64
SIHANOUK, Norodom. See Norodom Sihanouk
SIK, A. E.
How to read a weather map. Motor B 112: 48-51+ S '63
Winds. bibliog Motor B 112:39-41+ O '63

SIKES, Thomas W.
How to make a living-room rifle range. Pop Sci 183:145-8+ S '63

SIKHS
History of the Sikhs, by K. Singh. Review
Christian Cent 81:242 F 19 '64. P. H. Ashby

SIKKIM
American queen: the new Maharani of Sikkim. il U S News 55:26 D 16 '63
From debutante to the deities. il Time 82:33 D 13 '63
Grace and Hope; wedding of Prince Palden Thondup Namgyal. il Newsweek 61:52 Mr 25 '63
His fair lady; marriage of Maharaj Kumar of Sikkim, Palden Thondup Namgyal and Hope Cooke. il Newsweek 61:37 Ap 1 '63
I went to the wedding at Sikkim. N. W. Ross. Vogue 141:114-15+ Je '63
In the high Himalayas an American becomes a royal princess. N. W. Ross. il Sat Eve Post 236:20-5 My 11 '63
Post-debutante marries Palden Thondup Namgyal. il Life 54:34-5 Ap 5 '63
Sikkim. D. Doig. il Nat Geog Mag 123:398-429 Mr '63
To be a princess; ed. by M. V. Thayer. Hope Namgyal, princess of Sikkim. il McCalls 90:86-91+ S '63
Wedding of two worlds. L. E. Battaglia. il Nat Geog Mag 124:708-27 N '63
Where there's Hope. il Time 81:30 Mr 29 '63
Yankee queen. il Newsweek 62:44 D 16 '63

SIKORSKY, Igor I.
Salute to Igor Sikorsky. R. Hotz. Aviation W 81:11 O 5 '64
They call him Mr Helicopter. A. Dawydoff. il por Flying 74:30+ F '64

SIKORSKY aircraft division. See United aircraft corporation—Sikorsky aircraft division

SILAGE
All-in-one silage works for calves, too. Farm J 87:43 N '63
Continuous corn silage, why not? D. Seim. il Farm J 87:51-2 Ap '63
Corn silage cuts beef feeding costs. Farm J 87:32 Je '63
Double rows make more silage. B. Hardy. il Farm J 88:37+ My '64
Dozen new feeds from your silos. L. M. Palmer. il Farm J 87:30-1+ Jl '63
Faster gains from fertilized silage. D. Seim. Farm J 87:49 My '63
Grass silage tricks from Europe. Farm J 87:60A N '63
Haylage tops corn silage for steers. il Farm J 88:46 My '64
He uses silos year-round. J. Everly. il Suc Farm 62:38 Ap '64
How to make good corn silage; interview, ed. by L. Zeman. W. F. Hueg. Suc Farm 61:39+ S '63
Lime boosts silage value; cuts spoilage. J. Mills. Farm J 87:64 Ap '63
Low-moisture silage for beef cattle. T. W. Perry. il Suc Farm 61:98 My '63
Make corn silage in December? Farm J 88:29 Ag '64
New: center-cut silage. il Farm J 87:33+ F '63
Ten keys to success with high-moisture corn. B. Brantley. il Suc Farm 61:44-5 Ag '63
Ways to make richer silage; corn silage. C. F. Marley. il Farm J 88:42D N '64
What about silage additives? E. W. Klosterman. il Suc Farm 61:43 Ag '63

SILAGE handling
Head house for silos. B. Hardy. il Farm J 87:30-1 S '63
New machines for richer silage. D. K. O'Brien. il Farm J 87:24+ Ag '63
Rigs that speed up silage-making. il Farm J 87:36H Ag '63

SILARD, John
Case against MLF. Bul Atomic Sci 20:18-20 S '64
Introduction. Bul Atomic Sci 20:6-7 Ap '64

SILAS, Paul
Silas is golden! H. L. Masin. por Sr Schol 83:28 D 13 '63

SILBER, Irwin
Basic library of U.S. folk music. por Library J 88:1835-8 My 1 '63

SILBERFARB, Edward J.
Who will mediate the mediators? Reporter 28:23-6 Mr 14 '63

SILBERLING, Edwyn
Case for a national lottery. McCalls 90:68+ S '63

SILBERMAN, Charles E.
Businessman and the Negro; excerpt from Crisis in black and white. Fortune 68:97-9+ S '63
Chattel law and the Negro; excerpts from Crisis in black and white. Fortune 69:142-3+ My '64
Give slum children a chance; excerpts from Crisis in black and white. Harper 228:37-42 My '64
Real news about automation. Fortune 71:124-6+ Ja '65
Up from apathy, the Woodlawn experiment; excerpts from Crisis in black and white. Commentary 37:51-8 My; 38:20+ O '64

SILBERMAN, Harry F.
Research on programed instruction at SDC. Sch Life 45:13-15+ Mr '63

SILBERMAN, Lee
Critical examination of SEC proposals. Harvard Bsns R 42:121-32 N '64

SILBERSTEIN, Paula E.
On film and filmstrip. Sr Schol 84:20T-21T F 21 '64

SILENCE
Brain aroused by silence. Sci N L 86:198 S 26 '64
Need for silence. F. R. Schreiber and M. Herman. Sci Digest 56:87-8 N '64
Poets and mystics. J. Fandel. Commonweal 79:309-10 D 6 '63
Shh, the need for do-nothing quietude. B. Chapin. il Recreation 57:437-8 N '64

SILENCE; story. See Davis, C.

SILENT films. See Moving pictures—Silent films

SILENT miaow; story. See Gallico, P. W.

SILHOUETTES
Seen profiles. S. Gruenberg. il Sch Arts 63:8-9 N '63

SILICA
Silica; annual symposium of the American ceramic society. A. R. Cooper. Science 143:395+ Ja 24 '64
Site of preference energy and selective uptake of transition-metal ions from a magma. R. G. Burns and W. S. Fyfe. bibliog il Science 144:1001-3 My 22 '64
See also
Novaculite
Soils—Silica content

SILICA gel
Thoughts on drying flowers in silica. D. L. Zakon. il Horticulture 41:470-1 S '63

SILICATES
Coesite and stishovite: stepwise reversal transformations. F. Dachille and others. bibliog il Science 140:991-3 My 31 '63
See also
Serpentine

SILICON
Crystal structures at high pressures of metallic modifications of silicon and germanium. J. C. Jamieson. bibliog il Science 139:762-4 F 22 '63
Two new forms of silicon. R. H. Wentorf, jr. and J. S. Kasper. bibliog il Science 139:338-9 Ja 25 '63
Xenon fluorosilicate and related compounds. A. F. Clifford and G. R. Zeilenga. bibliog Science 143:1431 Mr 27 '64

SILICON carbide
Laser that produces non-stop. Bsns W p 114 S 7 '63

SILICON compounds
Meteoritic mineral; *sinoite*. Sky & Tel 28:340 D '64
Silicon oxynitride: a meteoritic mineral. C. A. Andersen and others. bibliog il Science 146:256-7 O 9 '64

SILICON controlled rectifiers. See Electric current rectifiers

SILICON diodes. See Diodes

SILICON oxynitride. See Silicon compounds

SILICON rectifiers. See Electric current rectifiers

SILICON solar batteries. See Solar batteries

SILICON transistors. See Transistors

SILICONE membrane. See Membranes (technology)

SILICONE paint. See Paint

SILICONE rubber. See Rubber, Artificial

SILICONES
Dow Corning tailoring silicone work to meet individual needs of buyers. J. F. Judge. il Miss & Roc 14:27-8 My 18 '64

SILK, George
High Sierra in spring; photographs. il Life 56:48-61 My 29 '64
President's big sky country. il Life 56:54-65 F 14 '64
Pure pleasure of being half killed. il Life 54:73-4 My 24 '63

SILK screen printing
Gummed label art; paper labels make offbeat screen print motif. il Design 65:56 N '63
Random register serigraphs. B. Wasserman. il Sch Arts 64:35-8 O '64
Silk-screen printing for panels. R. W. Bailey. il Electr World 70:73 Jl '63
Silk screening. il Design 66:31-3 S '64
Silk screening. il House & Gard 127:100-1+ Ja '65
Workshop: the direct photographic silk screen. J. Cloonan. il Craft Horiz 23:54-5 N '63

SILKWORMS
Diglyceride release from insect fat body: a possible means of lipid transport. H. Chino and L. I. Gilbert. bibliog il Science 143:359-61 Ja 24 '64

SILL, MacDonald
Inventor of the month. S. V. Jones. il por Sci Digest 56:84 S '64

SILLING, C. E. and associates
Small office with a large view. il Arch Rec 134:217-20 S '63

SILLIPHANT, Stirling
Fingers of God. por Time 82:60-1 Ag 9 '63

SILLITOE, Alan
Ragman's daughter; story. New Yorker 39:30-6 Ag 3 '63

about

WLB biography. L. Ash. por Wilson Lib Bul 38:203 O '63

SILLOWAY, Stuart F.
Businessmen in the news. por Fortune 70:27 Ag '64

SILO gases. See Gases, Asphyxiating and poisonous

SILONE, Ignazio
Return to Fontamara. Reporter 31:42-4+ O 22 '64

SILOS
Don't abandon that leaky silo. W. F. Bear. il Suc Farm 62:100 My '64
See also
Silage

SILOS, Missile. See Guided missiles—Launching pads

SILVA, Michel
Saturday's silent heroes. Life 57:59-60+ N 6 '64

SILVA, Ruth
Excerpt from testimony, February 28, 1964. Cong Digest 43:155 My '64

SILVA CASTRO, Raúl
World of Eliana Simón. Américas 15:40-1 Jl '63

SILVER, Cathy S.
Hatofsky: emerging expressionist. Art N 62:50-1+ F '64

SILVER, George A.
Are cigarettes necessary? Nation 196:379-80 My 4 '63

SILVER, H. Richard. See Reynolds, M. jt. auth.

SILVER, Horace
Tenacious craft of Horace Silver. M. Williams. por Sat R 46:52-3 S 14 '63

SILVER, James Wesley
Campus scourge at Ole Miss; with observations; ed. by S. O'Quin. pors Life 57:74A-74B Jl 17 '64
Mississippi must choose. N Y Times Mag p8+ Jl 19 '64

about

Closed society. por Newsweek 62:66+ N 18 '63
Closed society. por Time 82:37 N 15 '63
Old times there are not forgiven. R. Dugger. Nation 198:659-60 Je 29 '64
Professor's book may cause dismissal from Ole Miss. Pub W 185:50-1 Je 29 '64
Silver of Ole Miss. Nation 197:358 N 30 '63
Two southern liberals. J. Epstein. Commentary 38:73-4+ D '64

SILVER, Philip
Taking a stand in Vermont; poem. Harper 229:46 O '64

SILVER, Sidney L.
Capacitance transducer systems. Electr World 72:38-40+ S '64
Distributed-amplifier techniques. Electr World 73:28-40 Ja '65
Electromagnetic delay lines. Electr World 69:46-9+ F '63
Magnetic modulators. Electr World 71:65-9 Je '64
Vibration instrumentation. Electr World 72:56-8+ N '64

SILVER
Electrolytic growth of silver dendrites. W. A. Ainsworth. bibliog il Science 146:1294-5 D 4 '64
Silver from Ur of ancient Mesopotamia. J. W. Mellichamp and M. Levey. il Science 142:44-5 O 4 '63
See also
Silverware

Prices

Not-so-free silver. Fortune 68:232+ O '63

SILVER All-America awards. See Sports illustrated silver anniversary All-America

SILVER as money
Cloud that really had one. Bsns W p 148 Mr 23 '63
Coinage crisis. H. Hazlitt. Newsweek 64:84 D 7 '64
Decline and fall of silver coins. D. R. Maxey. il Look 28:55-7 D 29 '64
Expert tells why silver coins must go; excerpts from address, 1964. V. Clain-Stefanelli. il U S News 57:100-3 D 7 '64
Future of U.S. coinage; address, October 20, 1964. V. Clain-Stefanelli. Vital Speeches 31:85-8 N 15 '64
No more silver money? changes ahead in dimes, quarters, half dollars. il U S News 57:57-9 O 19 '64
Not-so-free silver. Fortune 68:232+ O '63
One man's search for free silver. M. Kitman. il Sat Eve Post 236:78+ O 26 '63
Silver: an era ends. il Bsns W p76+ Je 1 '63

SILVER-bell trees
Tree of bells. il Flower Grower 51:19 F '64

SILVER certificates. See Paper money—United States

SILVER collection. See Newberry library, Chicago

SILVER halides
Photochromic silicate glasses sensitized by silver halides. W. H. Armistead and S. D. Stookey. bibliog il Science 144:150-4 Ap 10 '64

SILVER iodide
High-pressure polymorphs in the silver iodide phase diagram. B. L. Davis and L. H. Adams. bibliog il Science 146:519-21 O 23 '64
Modification experiments on tropical cumulus clouds. J. S. Malkus and R. H. Simpson. bibliog il Science 145:541-8 Ag 7 '64
Pressure-induced trapping phenomenon in silver iodide. H. C. Duecker and E. R. Lippincott. bibliog il Science 146:1295-7 D 4 '64

SILVER plate. See Silverware

SILVER question. See Silver as money

SILVER salmon fishing. See Salmon fishing

SILVER SPRINGS, Md.

Hospitals

Planning Holy Cross for effective hospital care. J. L. Ryan. il Arch Rec 133:184-9 Mr '63

SILVERBERG, Robert
... And be sure to pack a tape recorder. Hi Fi 13:31-4 Jl '63
Whole man from Moravia. Hi Fi 13:55-7+ Mr '63

SILVERFISH
Nature note. Sci N L 85:45 Ja 18 '64

SILVERMAN, Betsey Marden
Can three generations live together? Parents Mag 38:43+ Ap '63
Why do children run away? Parents Mag 38:35+ Ag '63

SILVERMAN, Burton
Four realists: a review. F. Whitaker. il Am Artist 28:54-61+ O '64

SILVERMAN, M. D. and Browning, W. E. jr
Fibrous filters as particle-size analyzers. bibliog Science 143:572-3 F 7 '64

SILVERMAN, S. Richard
Educating deaf children; adaptation of address. Sch Life 46:24-8 Ja '64

SILVERS, Herbert Ferber
Caged action. il Time 81:74 Ap 12 '63

SILVERS, Phil
Frenzied world of Phil Silvers. A. Gillespie. il pors Good H 158:30-2+ Ja '64

SILVERSMITHING
Craftsman & teacher. N. Griner. il Sch Arts 63:28-9 S '63
John Prip and Reed & Barton. J. Prip. il Craft Horiz 24:51-2 Mr '64

SILVERSMITHS
Joseph Warford, silversmith of Albany and Salem, New York. N. S. Rice and J. H. Halpin. il Antiques 85:429-31 Ap '64
Silversmiths of Barnstable, Massachusetts. R. McCulloch and A. Beale. il Antiques 84:72-4 Jl '63
Some Franco-American silversmiths and jewelers. F. J. Dallett. il Antiques 84:706-9 D '63

SILVERSTEIN, Arthur M.
Ontogeny of the immune response. bibliog Science 144:1423-8 Je 19 '64
—and others
Homograft rejection in the fetal lamb: the role of circulating antibody. bibliog Science 142:1172-3 N 29 '63
SILVERSTEIN, Josef
From democracy to dictatorship in Burma. bibliog f Cur Hist 46:83-8+ F '64
SILVERSTONE, Marilyn
Royal wedding at Jaisalmer. il Nat Geog Mag 127:66-79 Ja '65
about
Focus on Marilyn Silverstone. L. Barry. il por Pop Phot 56:130-5+ Ja '65
SILVERTON narrow gauge railroad
Behind steam to Silverton. il Sunset 130:34-6 Je '63
Steam still has a day. il Bsns W p60-2 Ag 22 '64
SILVERWARE
A. Michelsen Christmas spoons. P. Owen. il Hobbies 68:45 D '63
Best-loved silver; popular patterns in America. il Seventeen 23:166-7 Ap '64
Cannon of sterling; miniature guns of British artillery regiment. W. B. Edwards. il Hobbies 68:116-17+ Jl '63
Design in regency silver. J. Banister. il Antiques 86:299-303 S '64
England, Russia, and Virginia; seventeenth-century ties in wood and silver. C. Oman. il Antiques 83:317-19 Mr '63
English and Irish cream jugs. J. Stone. Antiques 87:94-8 Ja '65
Ghosts of silver; table implements of the last 100 years. T. M. Shepherd. il Hobbies 69:44 Ja '65
Home-bred or Huguenot? J. Banister. il Antiques 84:288-93 S '63
How to monogram contemporary silver. il House & Gard 126:190-1+ S '64
Joseph Warford, silversmith of Albany and Salem, New York. N. S. Rice and J. H. Halpin. il Antiques 85:429-31 Ap '64
Late classical styles in American silver, 1810-1830. B. B. Tracy. il Antiques 86:702-6 D '64
Long-lasting love, silver. il McCalls 90:102-9 My '63
Midnight portrait of silver. W. Murch. il Vogue 142:172-5 N 1 '63
Museum accessions in American silver. R. Davidson. il Antiques 84:84+ Jl '63
Museum acquisitions in English silver. R. Davidson. il Antiques 84:324+ S '63
Nine colonial sugar boxes. K. Buhler. il Antiques 85:88-91 Ja '64
Recent museum accessions in American silver. R. Davidson. il Antiques 85:704 Je '64
Sheffield plate. H. Comstock. il Antiques 85:209-13 F '64
Silver at hand; painting by W. Murch. Vogue 144:212-13 O 1 '64
Silver by Alexandra Watkins. A. Meisel. il Craft Horiz 23:26-7+ N '63
Silver for every day. il Seventeen 22:122-3 N '63
Silver to have and to hurl. J. Didion. Vogue 143:60 Ap 1 '64
Tarnish-free ways to store silver. il House B 106:210-11 My '64
Treasures in English silver from the Morrison collection. M. D. Schwartz. il Antiques 85:570-4 My '64
What do you want in silver? il Seventeen 23:146-7 N '64
See also
Spoons
Care
How to care for your silver. il Am Home 67:84-5 N '64
Keeping silver tarnish-free. E. Taylor. il Good H 156:258 Ap '63
Silver light, silver bright; special covers. il Seventeen 22:196 Ap '63
SILVERWARE, Miniature
Silver in miniature. R. Davidson. il Antiques 85:706 Je '64
SILYBUM marianum. See Milk thistles
SIMAZINE. See Herbicides
SIMBERG, Jack
Muntz makes it: comeback from bankruptcy. il por Bsns W p70+ N 9 '63
SIMENON, Georges
Simenon's mosaic. J. Jacobs. Reporter 32:38-40 Ja 14 '65
SIMEONE, F. A.
Hemorrhagic shock: metabolic effects. Science 141:536+ Ag 9 '63
SIMERL, L. H.
Is the single-litter hog system for you? Suc Farm 61:132 F '63
SIMES, Jack, 3d
Lure of the wild white noise. B. Ottum. il pors Sports Illus 21:22-5 S 14 '64
SIMIAN virus. See Cancer virus
SIMIONATO, Giulietta
Music to my ears; Bellini's Capuletti performed by American opera society. I. Kolodin. Sat R 47:35 My 16 '64
SIMISON, Frank M.
Trailer treks. Travel 119:40-4 Mr '63
SIMJIAN, Luther G.
Inventor of the month. S. V. Jones. por Sci Digest 54:56 D '63
SIMKIN, William E.
Fewer strikes ahead in U.S? interview. por U S News 56:78-81 Mr 23 '64
SIMMERMAN, Nancy L. See Dahlgren, G. jt. auth.
SIMMONDS, W. Austin
Trinidad and Tobago. Américas 15:8-13 Mr '63
SIMMONS, Billy
New way out of debt. M. T. Bloom. Read Digest 85:134-7 Ag '64
SIMMONS, Charles
Poets in search of a public. Sat R 46:46-8 Mr 30 '63
Rhyme from academe. Sat R 47:42-3 My 30 '64
SIMMONS, Curt
Whiz Kids are still going strong. W. Leggett. por Sports Illus 20:60+ Je 8 '64
SIMMONS, Ernest J.
Real life on the edge of dreams. Sat R 47:29-30 Ag 22 '64
Wonderful friend of the Czar. Sat R 47:34-5 My 30 '64
SIMMONS, Florence Leech
Instructional resource center. ALA Bul 57:170-4 F '63
SIMMONS, Gene, and Bell, Peter
Calcite-aragonite equilibrium. bibliog Science 139:1197-8 Mr 22 '63
SIMMONS, Henry, and Goodwin, Irwin
On the move. Newsweek 63:72-3 F 10 '64
SIMMONS, J. Edgar
Address to a cannon; poem. New Repub 148:24 Je 15 '63
I sought my love in caverns of ice; poem. New Repub 150:18 F 8 '64
Light everlasting; poem. Commonweal 81:480 Ja 8 '65
Resurrection; poem. Nation 196:253 Mr 23 '63
SIMMONS, Marilyn
New way out of debt. M. T. Bloom. Read Digest 85:134-7 Ag '64
SIMMONS, Nevah
Peonies. Pop Gard 15:28-9 My '64
SIMMONS, Stanford L.
Spooking up on chucks. Outdoor Life 133:64-5+ Mr '64
SIMON, Anne W.
Going public. Nation 199:219-21 O 12 '64
It's a new world; excerpts from Stepchild in the family. McCalls 91:78-9+ F; 66+ Mr; 76+ Ap; 86+ My '64
SIMÓN, Eliana
World of Eliana Simón. R. Silva Castro. il por Américas 15:40-1 Jl '63
SIMON, Eric J.
Inhibition of bacterial growth by drugs of the morphine series. bibliog Science 144:543-4 My 1 '64
SIMON, Howard
On predicting space weather. Sat R 46:52 Ap 6 '63
SIMON, Irving B.
AIGA's fifty books as seen by a production man. por Pub W 185:78-9+ My 4 '64
SIMON, John
The deputy and its metamorphoses. Nation 198:270-2 Mr 16 '64
Notes of a noble anarchist. Sat R 46:18 Ag 17 '63
On Broadway and off; a midseason view of the current plays. Harper 226:98-100+ Mr '63
Opinion, please, from New York. Mlle 59:48+ My '64
SIMON, Kate
Cozumel. Mlle 59:188 My '64
Dalmatian montage. Vogue 144:8 N 15 '64
Holiday handbook. Holiday 34:99-104 Jl '63
Insider's New York from A to Z. Holiday 36:111-16 Jl '64
Mexico's man. Sat R 46:74-6+ O 12 '63
SIMON, Leroy
Get close for zoo stoppers! P. Caulfield. il por Mod Phot 27:82-7 Je '63
SIMON, Mina Lewiton
Flute solo with figured bass; story. New Yorker 39:44-7 Mr 9 '63

SIMON, Neil
Barefoot in the park. Criticism
America 109:753 D 7 '63
Commonweal 79:226 N 15 '63
New Yorker 39:93 N 2 '63
Newsweek il 62:62 N 4 '63
Sat R 46:32 N 9 '63
Theatre Arts il(p9) 48:68 Ja '64
Time il 82:74 N 1 '63
West, north & south of Broadway. por Time 82:68+ N 29 '63
SIMON, Nina
Bride in Boystown. B. Gary. il pors Mlle 57: 290-1+ Ag '63
SIMON, Nisa. See Wessel, M. A. jt. auth.
SIMON, Norton
Abstract businessman. il por Time 83:90-5 Je 5 '64
Another string to Simon's bow. por Bsns W p 178 N 21 '64
Blast from Simon. il por Time 84:59 D 25 '64
Exit Lord Pengo. il por Newsweek 63:61 My 4 '64
Hunt for the best. por Time 83:92 Ap 24 '64
Outsider tries his hand at firing up a lagging steelmaker. il por Bsns W p 18-19 D 26 '64
Simon says. Newsweek 63:88 My 25 '64
Tomato philosopher. il por Time 82:64-5 Ag 23 '63
Watch that man. Time 84:57 N 20 '64
SIMON, Oliver
Very private squirrel. Redbook 121:19-20 My '63
SIMON, Paul
Illinois legislature: study in corruption; ed. by A. Balk. Harper 229:74-8 S '64
SIMON, Robert E. jr
What is a new town? one answer is Reston. il por Fortune 70:178+ D '64
SIMON, Samuel L.
Labor: a target for NLW? por Library J 88: 1109-11 Mr 15 '63
SIMON, Walter A.
Diplomat with an artistic touch. il pors Ebony 20:88-9+ N '64
SIMON family
Stained glass; 400 years in one family. P. Almasy. il UNESCO Courier 16:17-20 My '63
SIMON Boccanegra; opera. See Verdi, G.
SIMON Rau and company, Bethlehem, Pa. See Drugstores
SIMONDS, Edith
Children can learn from politics. Parents Mag 39:45+ O '64
SIMONE, Kirsten
Kirsten Simone. S. Goodman. pors Dance Mag 37:58-9 My '63
SIMONE, Nina
Simmering down. Newsweek 62:82 S 30 '63
SIMONS, Elwyn L.
Early relatives of man; with biographical sketch. Sci Am 211:14, 50-62 bibliog(p 142) Jl '64
Some fallacies in the study of hominid phylogeny. bibliog Science 141:879-89 S 6 '63
SIMONS, Gustave
Mexican divorce, will it stand up in court? McCalls 91:52+ N '63
SIMONS, Margaret
Technical books and their sale examined at Denver ABA meeting; summary of address. por Pub W 184:30 N 11 '63
SIMONSEN, Mario Henrique. See Baer, W. jt. auth.
SIMONSON, William N.
(comp) Articles and other books received; Latin America. Am Hist R 69:1207-10; 70: 315-17 Jl, O '64
SIMONT, Marc
Stratford on fifty-yard line. il Sports Illus 19: 32-5 N 25 '63
Those who watch golf bear watching. il Sports Illus 20:40-4 Ap 6 '64
SIMPKINS, John J.
Best in show. il Flower Grower 50:38-42 Je '63
Color from your garden brightens the indoors. il Flower Grower 50:71 Ag '63
Compact camera for home and abroad. Flower Grower 50:71 Ap '63
Do you shoot in the shade? Flower Grower 50: 63 Je '63
Flash for your garden. Flower Grower 50:65 My '63
How-to-photographs. Flower Gorwer 50:68-9 Mr '63
Man who will grow 363,800 flowers for the fair. Flower Grower 51:36 Ja '64
Photography season starts at the flower show. il Flower Grower 51:59 Mr '64
Picture the wonders in your own back yard. Flower Grower 50:56 O '63
Practice your shooting! Flower Grower 50:13 Jl '63
SIMPLES. See Botany, Medical
SIMPLICIA, Sister Mary. See Mary Simplicia, Sister
SIMPSON, Alan
Man for Vassar. il por Time 81:63 Je 28 '63
Mr Simpson of Vassar. J. Lelyveld. il pors N Y Times Mag p30-1+ D 13 '64
Oxford to Vassar. por Newsweek 62:49 Jl 1 '63
SIMPSON, Bob
Living aboard, a way of life. il Yachting 115:57+ My '64
Oil, your engine's lifeblood. Motor B 113: 188-9 My '64
SIMPSON, George Gaylord
Biology and the nature of science. Science 139:81-8; 140:764+ Ja 11, My 17 '63
Nonprevalence of humanoids; excerpts from This view of life. bibliog Science 143:769-75 F 21 '64
Organisms and molecules in evolution; adaptation from paper. bibliog Science 146:1535-8 D 18 '64
SIMPSON, Howard W.
Engineering genius of the modern automatic transmission. il por Motor T 16:82-5 O '64
SIMPSON, James H. jr
Inventor of the month. S. V. Jones. il por Sci Digest 54:78-9 N '63
SIMPSON, Johnny
Winner from the wrong side of the barn. P. Ryan. il Sports Illus 21:54+ S 14 '64
SIMPSON, Lesley Byrd
(tr) See Gómara, F. L. de. City of the living god
SIMPSON, Louis
Constant lover; poem. New Yorker 40:38 Ap 11 '64
Poet in war: Battle; Ash and the oak; poems. N Y Times Mag p 122 D 6 '64
Sailors; poem. New Yorker 39:39 Je 15 '63
Terminations, revelations. W. Stafford. Poetry 104:104-5 My '64
Way it was in the Bulge. N Y Times Mag p27-9+ D 6 '64
SIMPSON, Mary S.
Snow affair. Bul Atomic Sci 19:28-32 Ap '63
SIMPSON, Maxwell Stewart
Paintings of Maxwell Stewart Simpson. F. Whitaker. il por Am Artist 27:32-7+ My '63
SIMPSON, Milward L.
Rise and fall of Cuba; address, May 20, 1964. Vital Speeches 30:520-2 Je 15 '64
SIMPSON, Robert H.
Hurricanes and tropical meteorology. Science 141:935-6+ S 6 '63
—and Malkus, J. S.
Experimental in hurricane modification: preliminary results. Science 142:498 O 25 '63
Experiments in hurricane modification; with biographical sketches. Sci Am 211:20, 27-37 bibliog(p 154) D '64
—See Malkus, J. S. jt. auth.
SIMPSON college, Indianola, Ia.
Simpson's catalytic action; Dunn library. W. W. Garton. il Library J 89:4758-60 D 1 '64
SIMS, Fay M.
How much do you know about your farm business? Farm J 87:104 F '63
SIMS, James Marion
J. Marion Sims, M.D. women's medical emancipator. T. F. Walsh and S. T. Donohue. por Todays Health 42:30-1+ Je '64
SIMS, Lydel
Autumn in Tennessee. Holiday 34:22+ N '63
SIMULATORS
Feely is here; Sensorama simulator. L. H. Lapham. il Sat Eve Post 237:28-9 Ap 18 '64
First man on moon will not drown in dust; lunar environment chamber. Sci N L 83: 249 Ap 20 '63
Machine simulates muscles in operation. M. L. Yaffee. il Aviation W 81:64-5 Ag 31 '64
Martian environment. Sci N L 83:386 Je 22 '63
Mating behavioral science and simulation. R. A. Bauer and R. D. Buzzell. il Harvard Bsns R 42:116-24 S '64
New ASW trainer improves readiness of Canadian fleet. M. Getler. il Miss & Roc 13:26-7 D 16 '63
New driving simulator varies to suit driver. Sci N L 85:360 Je 6 '64
Now step into a movie Sensorama. L. Lipton. il Pop Phot 55:114+ Jl '64

SIMULATORS—*Continued*
Profit in make-believe; Link simulators. il Time 81:86 Je 21 '63
Target simulator checks F-104G radars. B. Miller. il Aviation W 79:99+ N 25 '63
See also
Flight simulators
Space station simulators
SIMULATORS, Flight. See Flight simulators
SIN
Sir, the word is moral! D. R. Kline. Christian Cent 81:455-8 Ap 8 '64
Word. V. P. McCorry. America 109:180-1 Ag 17 '63
See also
Guilt
SIN of pride; story. See Stewart, N.
SINANOGLU, Oktay
Precocious prof. il por Time 81:39 My 31 '63
SINATRA, Frank, 1917-
And Sinatra tangles with the law. R. Oulahan and T. Thompson. il por Life 55:93-5 S 27 '63
Chairman of the board. por Newsweek 62:60 O 28 '63
King of the birds. il pors Time 83:48 My 22 '64
New role for Sinatra-san. il pors Life 57:80+ Jl 3 '64
Where the king of the world goes. D. Newman. il por Esquire 61:120-1+ Ap '64
SINATRA, Frank, 1944?
Frank Sinatra's son comes on singing like his old man. il pors Life 55:77-9 Ag 23 '63
Kidnaper who panicked. Time 82:17-18 D 27 '63
My state of mind was fear. il por Time 83:25 F 28 '64
Sinatra caper. il por Newsweek 62:20-2 D 23 '63
Slobber, slobber. il por Newsweek 62:96 S 23 '63
There's nothing to be sorry for. il por Time 82:14-15 D 20 '63
SINATRA, Frank, family
Frankie's kids. G. Christy. il Good H 158:80-1+ Je '64
SINATRA, Frank, jr, kidnaping case. See Kidnaping
SINCE last time; story. See Hickler, H. W.
SINCERITY
Literature and sincerity. by H. Peyre. Review
Nation 197:222-4 O 12 '63. V. Mercier
SINCLAIR, Andrew
Why should I travel when I'm already here? Mlle 36:138-9+ Ap '63
SINCLAIR, Bruce
DeGaulle curbs US trade talks with Europe. New Repub 150:12-14 Mr 7 '64
SINCLAIR, Charles, and Lachenbruch, David
Hi-fi, stereo buying guide for families with children. Parents Mag 38:75+ My '63
SINCLAIR, Dorothy
Shakespeare in Maryland. Wilson Lib Bul 39:480-1 F '65
SINCLAIR, Max
Big-game smoked sausage. Outdoor Life 134:10-11 N '64
SINCLAIR, T. C.
Electronic pumps: a new approach to vacuum generation. Electr World 73:44-5 Ja '65
SINCLAIR, Upton
All roads led to reform. Sat R 47:35 F 1 '64
My anti-headache diet. Harper 227:40-2 D '63
SINCLAIR, W. K. See Yu, C. K. jt. auth.
SINCLAIR oil corporation
Day of the dinosaur; Sinclair refining's exhibit at World's fair. il Bsns W p34-5 O 19 '63
Getting there is half the fun; dinosaur models for Sinclair's New York world's fair exhibit. H. B. Comstock. il Pop Sci 183:50-3 S '63
How to find oil the modern way. il Time 82:98 S 13 '63
Monsters arrive for the World's fair: the dinosaurs invade. il Life 55:87-8+ D 6 '63
Wage chronology: Sinclair oil companies, 1963. il Mo Labor R 86:1442-3 D '63
SINDEN, John A. See Sinden, L. B. jt. auth.
SINDEN, Lynn B. and Sinden, J. A.
Camping in Great Britain; Americans! you never had it so good! Am For 71:34-7+ Ja '65
SINDONA, Michele
Beating the cycle. il por Time 84:92 S 25 '64
He's building a business bridge. il pors Bsns W p 128-30+ O 10 '64
SINÉ, Maurice
Massacre man. il por Newsweek 61:49 Mr 4 '63
SINE-wave generators. See Signal generators
SINEY, Marion C.
British official histories of the blockade of the central powers during the First World war. bibliog f Am Hist R 68:392-401 Ja '63
SING low, sweet Harriet; story. See Preston, B. B.
SINGAPORE
Crackdown at dawn. il Time 82:50 O 4 '63
Troubles of becoming a nation; the story of Malaysia. R. P. Martin. il U S News 54:78-9 Ap 15 '63
Housing
Housing: one way to fight reds in Asia. R. P. Martin. il U S News 55:64-7 O 28 '63
Politics and government
Atlantic report. Atlan 213:14+ F '64
Riots
Amok but not asunder. il Time 84:29 Jl 31 '64
SINGER, Helen
At Higginbotham's doorway, Madras; Boom and bust beneath the bo tree; Of H. J. asking directions at Windsor; To Calif. a concession; Neighbor boy diving; If I believe my eyes; Unkept, unweeded garden; animism undermined; Taking the dust; Across this landscape; poems. Poetry 102:359-67 S '63
SINGER, I. J.
Converts; story. Commentary 38:46-8 D '64
SINGER, Isaac Bashevis
Blood; story. Harper 229:87-94 Ag '64
Cunegunde: story. Esquire 62:135 D '64
Esther Kreindel the second; story. Sat Eve Post 237:50-2 O 17 '64
Interview; ed. by J. Blocker and R. Elman. Commentary 36:364-72; 37:20 N '63; Mr '64
My father's courthouse; stories. Sat Eve Post 236:38-41 My 4 '63
Rootless mysticism. Commentary 39:77-8 Ja '65
Sacrifice; story. Harper 228:61-4 F '64
Taibele and Hurmizah; story. tr. by M. Ginsburg. Commentary 35:132-8 F '63
Three tales; story. tr. by R. Whitman and C. Hemley. Commentary 38:40-5 O '64
Wedding in Brownsville; story. Commentary 37:43-9 Mr '64
about
Isaac Bashevis Singer. L. Kahn. Commonweal 81:538-40 Ja 22 '65
Last of the line. W. Miller. Nation 200:15-16 Ja 4 '65
SINGER, J. David
Armers and disarmers; pro. Nation 196:174-5 Mr 2 '63
Peace research, peace action. Bul Atomic Sci 19:13-17 Ja; 36 My '63
Return to multilateral diplomacy. Yale R 53:36-48 O '63
SINGER, Jacques
Jacques Singer. conductor Portland symphony, Oregon. A. Fried. por Mus Am 83:9 My '63
SINGER, Maxine F. and Tolbert, George
Specificity of potassium-activated phosphodiesterase of escherichia coli. bibliog Science 145:593-5 Ag 7 '64
SINGER, Milton
Social sciences in non-western studies. bibliog f Ann Am Acad 356:30-44 N '64
SINGER, Robert A.
Amateur scientist. Sci Am 209:133-6+ O '63
SINGER, Ronald
Reviews. Natur Hist 72:4 My '63
SINGER, S. Fred
Space vehicles in an ionized medium. Science 147:74-6 Ja 1 '65
about
Facts about the 1962 space bomb. J. Lear. il Sat R 46:45-8 Ap 6 '63
SINGER, S. J. See Metzger, H. jt. auth.
SINGER company
Conversion of Singer installation to be completed within eighteen months; Singer-Metrics. C. D. LaFond. il Miss & Roc 15:41-2 Ag 10 '64
SINGER manufacturing company
It's a spryer Singer. E. K. Faltermayer. il Fortune 68:144-8+ D '63
SINGER-Metrics. See Singer company
SINGERS
Big folk singers on campus: Peter, Paul & Mary. I. Mothner. il Look 27:59-62 Jl 2 '63
Bright acts to fill the tables. il Life 57:68+ Jl 24 '64

SINGERS—*Continued*
Cabbage number one; Sylvie Vartan. il Time 83:43-4 Je 19 '64
Cast. See issues of Opera news to November 28, 1963
Cast of the characters; Last savage. G. Fitzgerald. il Opera N 28:13-15 F 8 '64
Controversy in song; Chad Mitchell trio. R. Hemming. il Sr Schol 82:18 My 8 '63
Divas in movieland. P. V. Beckley. il Opera N 29:8-13 D 19 '64
Dramatic accent: singing-actor. A. Williamson. il Hi Fi 14:53-5+ Mr '64
Dumb sound; weird noises teen-agers call music. A. G. Aronowitz. il Sat Eve Post 236:88, 91-5 O 5 '63
Folk singers and their fans. S. Castan. il Look 27:49-50+ Ag 27 '63
Folk singers for the love of it; Il folk studio in Rome. il Time 83:80 Ap 10 '64
Folk-singing ambassadors; in tune with their times; S. Addiss and B. Crofut. il Sr Schol 83:17 S 27 '63
Gianninis: musical Philadelphia family. M. De Schauensee. il Opera N 28:14-16 Ap 11 '64
Gitars, folk songs, and halls of ivy. A. Shaw. il Harper 229:33-4+ N '64
Give opera back to the singers! A. Pryce-Jones. pors Theatre Arts 47:14-16 Mr '63
Greatest pretender. Time 84:61 Jl 17 '64
Hiram and the Animals; comparison with the Beatles. New Yorker 40:40-3 S 12 '64
Hooray for the Yé-Yé girls. il Life 56:39-40+ My 29 '64
Jazz; concert performed by Swingle singers, at Carnegie Hall. W. Balliett. New Yorker 40:147-8 N 7 '64
Jazz concerts; deep-country blues singers at Hunter college. W. Balliett. New Yorker 40:133-5 My 30 '64
Jazz records; B. Holiday and M. Bailey. W. Balliett. New Yorker 39:86-9 Ag 24 '63
Just playin' folks; photographs by J. Launois. Sat Eve Post 237:24-9 My 30 '64
Lassalle and others on LP. A. Favia-Artsay. il Hobbies 69:31-3 Ag '64
Listen to the folk singers! il Read Digest 82:39-40+ F '63
Little Peggy hits the big time. C. S. Wren. il Look 27:Z4+ O 22 '63
Long trail a-winding; S. Addiss and B. Crofut. il Newsweek 61:53 Ap 29 '63
Magic dragon; folk-singing group, Peter Paul and Mary. il Newsweek 61:88 Ap 8 '63
Metropolitan forecast; 1963-64 Metropolitan repertory. Opera N 27:13 My 4 '63
Metropolitan season; scene and costume sketches in color for 1963-64, with complete roster. Opera N 28:17-20 O 19 '63
Necessary evil; Metropolitan auditions. R. Resnik. il Opera N 28:8-12 Mr 28 '64
New beat; topical folk singers, their songs. B. Rollin. Vogue 144:60+ S 1 '64
Oratorios for industry; world's most successful singers of TV commercials. il Time 84:42 Jl 24 '64
People are talking about M. Jagger, a British Rolling Stone rocker. Vogue 144:72-3 Jl '64
Popular records. D. Watt. New Yorker 39:92-4 Je 1 '63
Reviews; folk. Mus Am 83:266 D '63
Reviews: folk. H. Yurchenco. il Mus Am 83:266 D '63; 84:43 F; 49 My; 42-3 N '64
Revolutionary etudes; round table of Chénier characters. F. Stevenson. pors Opera N 27:14-15 Mr 2 '63
Singers of imperial Russia. A. Favia-Artsay. il Hobbies 69:30-1 My '64
Singers' opera; Metropolitan repertory. J. Gutman. il Opera N 27:8-12 Mr 2 '63
Singing barn; who's who in folk music? quiz yourself. il Seventeen 22:86-7+ D '63
Souvenirs of opera and song. A. Favia-Artsay. il Hobbies 69:30-1+ Mr '64
Spring tour casts. Opera N 28:32 Mr 28 '64
Stars of San Gennaro; four singers on a holiday in Little Italy; photographs. Opera N 28:13-15 N 16 '63
Swing, swung, Swingled; Swingle singers. Time 84:83-4 N 6 '64
Three's company: Peter, Paul and Mary. A. G. Aronowitz and M. Blonsky. il Sat Eve Post 237:30+ My 30 '64
Togetherness; folk singing Weavers. il Newsweek 61:95 My 13 '63
Up opera's ladder. A. Rich. il Opera N 29:9-12 Ja 30 '65
Womenfolk; all-girl folk singing quintet. il Ebony 19:182-5 Je '64
Yanks in Deutschland. il Newsweek 64:118+ O 5 '64
See also
Beatles
Choirs
Singing
also names of singers, e.g. B. Dylan

Anecdotes, facetiae, satire, etc.

Missing record; reprint. R. Lawrence. il Mus Am 84:12-13+ N '64

SINGERS, Negro. See Negro musicians

SINGH, Raizada M. M. and Adams, Elijah
Alpha-ketoglutaric semialdehyde: a metabolic intermediate. bibliog Science 144:67-8 Ap 3 '64

SINGH, Swaran
Modest Mr Singh. Newsweek 64:30 Ag 3 '64

SINGING
Harvard hootenanny; folk singers at Harvard club of New York. New Yorker 40:29-30 Mr 21 '64
I sing a gentle song, folk singing. O. Smith. il Seventeen 23:20 Ja '64
Question of style; bel canto tradition. R. Bonynge. Mus Am 84:44-5 D '64
Revival of bel canto. M. Davenport. il Opera N 28:8-13 Ja 11 '64
Singing Verdi; address. G. Martinelli. il Mus Am 83:14-15+ Mr '63
See also
Tone deafness
Vibrato

Competitions

Auditions 1963-1964. A. M. Lingg. il Opera N 27:16-17 My 4 '63; 28:24 My 2 '64
Competition in Bulgaria; International young operatic singers competition, Sofia. K. Adler. il Opera N 28:6-7 O 19 '63
Metropolitan auditions. il Mus Am 83:15 My '63
Music to my ears; Metropolitan auditions. I. Kolodin. Sat R 46:31 Ap 13 '63
Necessary evil; Metropolitan auditions. R. Resnik. il Opera N 28:8-12 Mr 28 '64
Slave market; auditioning for singing jobs in Rainbow. il Newsweek 61:70 My 13 '63

SINGING, Congregational. See Church music

SINGING commercials. See Radio advertising; Television advertising

SINGING nun. See Luc Gabrielle, Sister

SINGING nuns. See Choral groups and societies

SINGING silence; story. See Wuorio, E. L.

SINGLE frame cameras. See Cameras

SINGLE-handed Trans-Atlantic race. See Yacht racing

SINGLE-lens reflex cameras. See Cameras

SINGLE men. See Bachelors

SINGLE rail railroads. See Railroads, Single rail

SINGLE sideband system. See Radio transmission—Single sideband system

SINGLE women
Case of the vanishing spinster. M. K. Sanders. il N Y Times Mag p34+ S 22 '63
How come a nice girl like you isn't married yet? A. Van Buren. il McCalls 90:51+ Jl '63
How to travel alone, and like it. H. Dolson. Redbook 123:65+ My '64

Anecdotes, facetiae, satire, etc.

Spinster's survival kit. G. Greene. il Mlle 57:90+ Je '63

SINGLETON, Henry E.
Infant with a giant appetite. il por Bsns W p66-8 Ja 11 '64

SINHALESE art. See Art, Sinhalese

SINKIANG PROVINCE, China (People's Republic)
Over the bridge; Chinese expel Russians from Sinkiang. il Newsweek 63:40+ Je 22 '64
Sinkiang: Soviet rustlers in China's Wild West. S. Karnow. il Reporter 30:36-9 Je 18 '64

SINKS
Stainless-steel sinks. il Consumer Bul 46:2+ My '63
Which new sink for your new kitchen? il Sunset 130:122+ Mr '63

SINN, Marty
Marty's memories of a long cold race. por Life 56:66+ Mr 6 '64

about

Girl named Sinn. G. Rogin. il pors Sports Illus 21:58-64 Ag 24 '64
Sunny mermaid of the marathon. il pors Life 56:61+ Mr 6 '64

SINNETTE, Elinor D. See Brown, H. B. jt. auth.
SINOITE. See Silicon compounds
SINO-PAKISTAN air agreement. See Aviation —International aspects
SINOPOULOS, Takis
Magda; Sophia etc; Sight and vision; Ioanna's invitation; One of Constantine's nights; Beheading; poems, tr. by E. Keeley and G. Savidis. Poetry 105:36-42 O '64
about
Note on Takis Sinopoulos. G. Savidis. Poetry 105:43 O '64
SINOR, Denis
Uralic and Altaic: the neglected area. Ann Am Acad 356:86-92 N '64
SINSHEIMER, Robert L. See Burton, A. jt. auth.
SIODMAK, Alex
A & B roll editing. U S Camera 26:80-1+ Ap '63
SIOUX CITY, Ia.
Digesters beat incineration. A. E. Rasmussen. il Am City 79:100-1 D '64
This water main can bend. W. Murphy. il Am City 78:90-1 Mr '63
Sanitary affairs
Big Muddy's first sewage plant. A. E. Rasmussen. il Am City 78:81-3 Jl '63
Street cleaning gets assembly-line techniques. W. D. McElwee. il Am City 78:126-7 Je '63
SIOUX Indians. See Dakota Indians
SIPHONOPHORA
Carbon monoxide production by a bathypelagic siphonophore. G. V. Pickwell and others. bibliog il Science 144:860-2 My 15 '64
Siphonophores and the deep scattering layer. E. G. Barham. bibliog il Science 140:826-8 My 17 '63
SIPPEL, Robert F. and Glover, E. D.
Fission damage in calcite and the dating of carbonates. bibliog Science 144:409-11 Ap 24 '64
SIPPLE, Horace L.
Good eating for all ages. Todays Health 42: 64-5+ F '64
SIQUEIROS, David Alfaro
Art and activism. il por Newsweek 64:46 Jl 27 '64
Paintings from prison. il por Time 83:68 F 21 '64
Siqueiros. R. Winnett. New Repub 148:7 Mr 2 '63
SIR John Soane's museum. See London—Galleries and museums
SIRE, Glen, and Sire, Jane
Friend from Nebraska; story. Ladies Home J 81:84 O '64
Lavender scarf; story. Redbook 121:56-7 Ag '63
Loss; story. Redbook 124:84-5 N '64
SIRE, Jane. See Sire, G. jt. auth.
SIRENS. See Whistles
SIRI, Giuseppe, cardinal
Truth first and always; interview. ed. by W. M. Abbott. America 108:434-5 Mr 30 '63
SIRIWARDENA, Subada
Ceylon: silent victory. UNESCO Courier 17: 7-12 S '64
SIRLIN, J. L. See Jacob, J. jt. auth.
SIRMIONE, Italy
Visit to Sirmione. D. Dodge. il Holiday 33: 28+ My '63
SIROS (Island) See Syros (Island)
SIROTO, Leon
From African anvils. Horizon 6:122-4 Sum '64
SIRULNICK, Sid
Reprise. New Yorker 40:23-4 Ag 22 '64
SISAKIAN, Norair Martirosovich
Biologist looks at world co-operation in science. UNESCO Courier 16:10-16 My '63
SISCO, Joseph J.
Our stake in the United Nations; address, October 24, 1963. Dept State Bul 49:773-7 N 18 '63
Resurgence of the United Nations Security council; address, June 18, 1964. Dept State Bul 51:55-9 Jl 13 '64
United Nations role in political disputes; address, March 11, 1963. Dept State Bul 48: 529-35 Ap 8 '63
SISCO, Robert D.
Swimming pools by subscription. Am City 78:99-101 My '63
SISK, B. F.
Excerpt from testimony, April 24, 1964. Cong Digest 43:271 N '64
SISK, Glenn
Contemporary situation of: the Negro in Atlanta. Negro Hist Bul 27:174-5 Ap '64
Economic condition of the Negro in Atlanta. bibliog Negro Hist Bul 27:87-90 Ja '64
Negro health in Atlanta. bibliog Negro Hist Bul 27:65-6 D '63
Negro in Atlanta politics (1870-1962) bibliog Negro Hist Bul 28:17-18 O '64
SISK, John P.
Close to the madding crowd. Commonweal 77: 544 F 15 '63
Fear of immorality. Commonweal 81:415-18 D 18 '64
Mirrors of advertising. Commonweal 79:707-10 Mr 13 '64
Sorokin: the lone wolf's stubbornness. Commonweal 79:608-10 F 14 '64
SISK, Phil A.
Sequential program to develop textural sensitivity. Sch Arts 63:21-6 Ja '64
SISKINS. See Finches
SISSEL, H. B.
Behind the fight against school prayer. Look 27:25-9 Je 18 '63
SISSMAN, L. E.
Henley, July 4: 1914-1964; poem. New Yorker 40:55 Jl 4 '64
Three Cambridge poems: Birdman of Cambridge, Mass; Footnote: Mrs Circassian, Lowell R-54; Stillman infirmary. New Yorker 40:60 O 24 '64
SISTER cities. See Intercommunity cooperation
SISTER Gertrude; story. See Rosen, N.
SISTER teachers
Education
See Teachers—Education
SISTERHOODS
Dear Mother Superior; letters to the Superior. Sister Alice Carlene. America 110: 488-9 Ap 4 '64
Emerging nuns. America 111:79 Jl 25 '64
General Reynolds and Dear Kate; Sister Hildegardis of Sisters of charity, Emmitsburg, Md; reprint. M. R. Maloney. il Am Heritage 15:62-5 D '63
Girl sets out to be a nun; with report by B. Cummiskey. il Life 54:66-79 Mr 15 '63
Hong Kong doctor with 1,000 patients; Our Lady of Maryknoll hospital in Hong Kong. C. Morrison. il Look 28:24-9 Je 16 '64
Less risk with nuns; study of nuns' health records. D. R. Campion. America 110:665 My 16 '64
Let your light shine, sister. M. G. Lacey. America 109:302-5 S 21 '63; Reply. M. Walsh. 109:618 N 16 '63
New era for the nun in the world. A. McCormack. il Cath World 199:144-51 Je '64
Nuns for the 21st century; educational standards of teaching nuns. il Time 84:43 Jl 17 '64
Nuns in the wide, wide world. J. P. Fisher; H. Smith. il America 110:282-5 F 29 '64; Discussion. 110:440-3 Mr 28 '64
Nuns in the world. M. Novak. Commonweal 79:274-8 N 29 '63; Discussion. 79:457-61 Ja 17 '64
Nuns I've known. P. S. Cronin. America 108: 710-11 My 18 '63
That convent wall. R. R. Bremner. America 111:456-7 O 17 '64
Vanishing nun. J. Star. il Look 27:41-5 O 22 '63
SISTERS; story. See Graham, E.
SISTERS; story. See Painter, C.
SISTINE chapel. See Vatican—Sistine chapel
SIT-in demonstrations. See Negroes in the United States—Segregation, Resistance to
SITAR
And now the sitar. il Time 84:84+ N 6 '64
SITATUNGA hunting. See Antelope hunting
SITE activation task force. See United States —Air force—Site activation task force
SITE planning. See Housing projects—Site planning
SITE values. See Land values
SITES, James N.
Can the railroads be saved? excerpts from Quest for crisis. Nat R 16:971-3 N 3 '64
Trail to super transport service; address, March 18, 1963. Vital Speeches 29:441-4 My 1 '63
World route to super-railroads; address, January 16, 1964. Vital Speeches 30:252-5 F 1 '64
SITES, Building. See Building sites
SITES, Historic. See Historic houses, etc.
SITES, Industrial. See Location in business and industry

SITKA spruce. See Spruce

SITTERLY, Bancroft W.
Symposium on abundances of elements in stars. Sky & Tel 29:11-14 Ja '65

SITTING. See Posture

SITTING Bull (Indian chief)
There are no Indians left now but me. M. Rosenberg and D. Rosenberg. il pors Am Heritage 15:18-23+ Je '64

SITTON, Claude
Inquiry into the Mississippi mind. N Y Times Mag p 13+ Ap 28 '63
Not token freedom, full freedom. N Y Times Mag p21+ Je 9 '63
Once more the K.K.K. il N Y Times Mag p8-9 Ag 11 '63
Southern Negro drives for the vote. N Y Times Mag p28-9 S 29 '63

SITUATION; story. See Modisane, B.

SITWELL, Dame Edith
Facade; entertainment with poems. J. Diether. il Am Rec G 31:304-7 D '64
Friend to peacocks. por Time 84:33 D 18 '64
Obituary
Pub W 186:53 D 28 '64
Peacock poetry. por Newsweek 64:57 D 21 '64

SITWELL, Sir Osbert
Farewell to Carlyle square. por Atlan 213: 76-8 Mr '64
Too late to save Bohemia; excerpt from Pound wise. Horizon 6:119-20 Wint '64

SIVARD, Robert
Fantasy in reality; show at Manhattan's Midtown galleries. il Time 81:77 F 15 '63
Side-street painter; or, Shopping with Sivard. il Horizon 5:84-91 N '63

SIVERTS, Donald C.
We bought a 55-foot yacht for $500. Pop Sci 184:74-6+ Ap '64

SIX, Robert Forman
Bob Six's bag of tricks. I. Ross. il pors Fortune 67:130-2+ F '63
Highflying Robert Six. R. L. Whearley. il por Sat Eve Post 236:82+ F 23 '63

SIX characters in search of an author; drama. See Pirandello, L.

SIXTH fleet. See United States—Navy

SIZE
510-pound strongboy. il Ebony 19:103-8 My '64
Letter from Stan Delaplane; larger sizes of today. S. Delaplane. Todays Health 41:50+ Mr '63
See also
Clothing and dress—Size

SIZER, Theodore R.
Harvard's thirty-one-year-old dean. por Time 83:44+ Mr 20 '64

SJÖBERG, Leif
(tr) See Hammarskjöld, D. Markings
(tr) See Hammarskjöld, D. Poems from Markings

SKAGIT RIVER
Out for sea-run Dolly Varden. il Sunset 132:73-4 Ap '64

SKATEBOARDING
Here come the sidewalk surfers. il Life 56:89-90 Je 5 '64

SKATES
Sharpen your skates on a circular saw. il Pop Mech 121:156-7 Ja '64

SKATES (fishes)
Hawk that swims; excerpt from Shadows in the sea. H. W. McCormick and others. il Sat R 46:66 O 5 '63

SKATING
America on ice. D. Button. il Am Heritage 14:38-49 F '63
Bashful barber and a worldly kid from Smoke Rise. H. Horn. il Sports Illus 20:20-1 F 17 '64
Curls and cold steel. I. Shenker. il Sports Illus 20:40-1 Ja 27 '64
Figure skating: a lifetime activity. M. F. Maroney. il Recreation 57:29 Ja '64
Flash of fire on the ice. J. Bell. il Sports Illus 20:52-3 Ja 27 '64
Good sports go places; excerpt from Seventeen book of etiquette and entertaining. E. A. Haupt. Seventeen 23:32 N '64
How to succeed by trying; world's figure-skating championship. il Time 81:78 Mr 15 '63
I believe; champion figure skating; ed. by J. Ellenzweig. L. Hanlon. il Seventeen 23:213 F '64
Skating. L. Griggs. Sports Illus 18:49 Mr 4 '63
So I go to Walden a-skating; excerpts from Journal, ed. by M. Meltzer. H. D. Thoreau. il N Y Times Mag p 11 D 29 63

SKATING rinks
Artificial ice rinks (cont) il Am City 78:82-3 F '63
Build your own skating rink. il Pop Sci 183: 141 O '63
Ice rinks: construction and operation. D. A. Parkhurst. Recreation 56:377-8 O '63
Ice skaters enjoy heat breaks; Dearborn, Mich. O. L. Hubbard and R. K. Archer. il Am City 87:86-7 D '63
Ice skating in Mississippi. il Am City 78:93 Ap '63
Iceman cometh! V. Green. il Recreation 57: 416-17 O '64
Oak Park ice rink. W. Norman. il Recreation 57:472-3 N '64
Skaters hail the modern artificial ice age. il Am City 79:82-4 N; 90-1 D '64
Smooth skating. R. Lachance. Recreation 57: 356 S '64
Three R's of operation. H. J. Van Cott. il Recreation 56:378-9 O '63

SKEBBINS, Gerald J.
Is Goldwater moving left? Nat R 15:337-8 O 22 '63

SKEET (game)
Crazy skeet. B. Kreh. il Outdoor Life 131: 74-5+ Ap '63
How to get started in trap and skeet: the sport for sharpshooters. H. Bradshaw. il Pop Sci 185:142-6+ O '64

SKELETON
Want to build an elephant? il Life 54:77-8 My 24 '63

SKELLON, David
Saga of the Curlew. por Yachting 113:38-9+ F '63

SKELTON, Robin
Three poems for Ireland: Queens; Parnell, eighteen-ninety; Spring race meeting. Poetry 102:231-2 Jl '63
Two memorials; poem. Poetry 104:31-5 Ap '64

SKETCHES (drama) See Skits (drama)

SKETCHING. See Drawing

SKEWER cooking. See Cookery

SKI boots. See Shoes

SKI bum; story. See Gary, R.

SKI cabins. See Cabins

SKI clothing. See Clothing and dress—Sports clothes

SKI jumping. See Skis and skiing

SKI-kites. See Kites

SKI lodges. See Lodges (architecture)

SKI poles. See Skis and skiing—Equipment

SKI resorts. See Winter resorts

SKIBINE, George
Can it be true? interview, ed. by L. Joel. por Dance Mag 38:40-1 Ag '64

SKIDDING of automobiles. See Automobiles—Skidding

SKIDMORE, Owings and Merrill (firm)
New ways in architecture. H. Kramer. Reporter 29:58-60+ D 5 '63

SKIER'S progress; story. See Williams, T.

SKIFFS. See Boats and boating

SKIING. See Skis and skiing

SKIING, Water. See Water skis and skiing

SKILLETS
Is there a perfect frying pan? no. il Sunset 133:88-91 N '64

SKIN
Burns and other skin lesions; microcirculatory responses in man during healing. J. G. Zimmer and D. J. Demis. bibliog il Science 140:994-6 My 31 '63
Can wrinkles be prevented? Good H 157:137-8 Ag '63; Same with title What you can do about wrinkles. Sci Digest 54:75-8 D '63
Chromaffin cell: electron microscopic identification in the human dermis. M. H. McGavran. bibliog il Science 145:275-6 Jl 17 '64
Hearing through skin. Sci N L 86:275 O 31 '64
Life-giving balancing act. R. Campbell. il Life 55:76-7 N 8 '63
Racial differences in skin resistance. L. C. Johnson and N. L. Corah. bibliog il Science 139:766-7 F 22 '63
Skin impedance and phase angle as a function of frequency and current. R. Plutchik and H. R. Hirsch. bibliog il Science 141: 927-8 S 6 '63
Skin resistance levels and galvanic skin response: unilateral differences. P. A. Obrist. bibliog Science 139:227-8 Ja 18 '63
What's fragile skin; what isn't. il Vogue 141: 116-17 F 15 '63
See also
Sunburn

Care and hygiene

Beauty bulletin; American face race. il Vogue 143:178-81+ F 1 '64
How to baby your skin. il Redbook 120:70-1+ F '63

SKIN—Care and hygiene—*Cont.*
Peaches and cream, etc. il Seventeen 22: 150-1+ Ap '63
Skin care. il Mlle 59:132-3 S '64
Summer suggestions to save your own skin. McCalls 90:130 Jl '63
Your skin and the sun. L. D. Kirk. il Parents Mag 39:104-5 Je '64

Diseases

What your skin tells about you. G. H. Millet. il Parents Mag 38:40-1+ Ag '63
See also
Acne
Allergy
Psoriasis

SKIN cancer. See Cancer

SKIN diving. See Diving, Submarine

SKIN grafting. See Transplantation of organs, tissues, etc.

SKIN temperature
Thermography of the human body. R. B. Barnes. bibliog il Science 140:870-7 My 24 '63
Trouble with hot spots. il Time 81:78-9 Je 14 '63

SKINNER, Burrhus Frederic
Behaviorism at fifty. bibliog Science 140:951-8 My 31 '63
about
Adventurous ones. por Vogue 142:76 Ag 1 '63
Christian's dilemma. J. Collignon. il por Sat R 47:14-16 Je 27 '64
Harvard's Skinner, the last of the utopians. S. Klaw. por Harper 226:45-51 Ap '63

SKINNER, C. Wickham
Management of international production; excerpts from research report. Harvard Bsns R 42:125-36 S '64

SKINNER, Carlton
Self-government in the South Pacific. For Affairs 42:137-47 O '63

SKINNER, Constance Lindsay, award. See Constance Lindsay Skinner award

SKINNER, Cornelia Otis
Let me explain. . . Read Digest 83:79-81 Ag '63
about
Cornelia and the Loves of Charles; dramatic monologues. J. Ciardi. por Sat R 46:35 Ap 13 '63

SKINNER, H. C. W. and others
Age and accumulation rate of dolomite-bearing carbonate sediments in South Australia. bibliog Science 139:335-6 Ja 25 '63

SKINNER, Jean Ross-. See Ross-Skinner, J.

SKINNER, Knute
Man and the moon; poem. New Repub 148:23 Je 29 '63

SKINNER, Lowell D.
Skinner's choice. R. L. Shayon. Sat R 46:16 S 7 '63

SKINNER, Sandford L. and others
Renal baroceptor control of renin secretion. bibliog Science 141:814-16 Ag 30 '63

SKINNER, W. A. and Alaupovic, P.
Vitamin E oxidation with alkaline ferricyanide. bibliog Science 140:803-5 My 17 '63

SKIPPER, James
Association of research libraries concentrates on centralized cataloging. Library J 89: 2953 Ag '64

SKIPPING rope. See Rope jumping

SKIS and skiing
Alaska offers new ski thrills. C. McClain. il Todays Health 42:18-20+ Ja '64
Aspen's new silver lode. il Bsns W p30-1 Ja 25 '64
Champions by default; North American Alpine championships, Stowe, Vt. Sports Illus 18:10 Mr 25 '63
Deep powder skiing at Tod Mountain; new ski area in British Columbia. il Sunset 132:20+ Ja '64
Don't sell the U.S. ski team short. Life 56:4 F 21 '64
Expressway dirt builds ski slopes; Grosse Pointe Shores, Mich. T. K. Jefferis. il Am City 79:28 Jl '64
Fairy tale slalom. il Life 54:55-6 Mr 8 '63
Fight for life by the home team; downhill ski race. P. Ress. il Sports Illus 20:32-9 Ja 27 '64
.4 of a second; micro-measuring the difference between victory and defeat in next month's Olympic Alpine. R. Riger. il Esquire 61:82-7 Ja '64
Gamin with a world of guts. D. Jenkins. il Sports Illus 20:12-15 Ja 20 '64
Gold in the ski hills. D. Cort. Nation 198: 120-1 F 3 '64
Good sports go places; excerpt from Seventeen book of etiquette and entertaining. E. A. Haupt. Seventeen 23:32 N '64
In and out of a jam; U.S. ski coach B. Beattie. D. Jenkins. il Sports Illus 20:14-19 F 17 '64
Indoor ski resort; Tokyo. il Pop Mech 121: 113 F '64
Joyful school for city kids; snow classes in Alps and Pyrenees; with photographs by J. Marquis. Sports Illus 18:32-4+ Mr 25 '63
Let them eat slush; seedings of skiers. Time 82:40 D 27 '63
Let's go skiing. J. Martineau. il Am For 69: 36-9+ F '63
Let's not spoil their sport. A. M. Lawrence. il Sports Illus 20:18-20 F 3 '64
Lonely quest in Lapland; cross-country skiing. D. S. Connery. il Sports Illus 20:46-7+ Ja 27 '64
Maestro tunes his teen ski stars; with photographs by M. Kauffman. Sports Illus 18:24-30 F 11 '63
Man who jumps with the devil; Norway's T. Engan. J. Lovesey. il Sports Illus 20:42-5 Ja 27 '64
Moving up in the downhill; gathering of best skiers at Vail, Colo. for training. il Sports Illus 22:22-5 Ja 25 '65
New speed and old in skiing abroad; interview. J. Jay. Mlle 60:189+ N '64
New sugar in an old state; skiing in Vermont. H. Horn. il Sports Illus 19:30-4 N 18 '63
Norge's way; Norge ski club 60th annual meet. il Newsweek 65:71-2 F 1 '65
Oh, say, can you ski? S. Welton. il Parents Mag 38:66-7+ D '63
Olympic winter in the Tyrol; photographs; with report by R. Terrell. Sports Illus 19: 48-57 N 25 '63
On the laps of the snow gods; skiing in Norway. H. Kenner. Nat R 16:405+ My 19 '64
One man's molehill; Midwest ski hills. il Newsweek 63:74 Ja 20 '64
Our ski team flies high; with report by M. Smith. il Life 56:66-70+ Ja 10 '64
Personal bus for skiing. B. Kocivar. il Look 27:92a-92c Mr 12 '63
Personal business; winter holiday Alpine skiing. Bsns W p89-90 D 21 '63
Pointing for Innsbruck; top U.S. skiers and Olympic trials. il Time 81:55 Ap 12 '63
Rage to ski; with photographs by J. Zimmerman. Sat Eve Post 236:24-9 F 9 '63
Ski bums; the upland Bohemians. K. K. Waller. il Mlle 58:172-3+ N '63
Ski calendar: where to ski when all over the world. Vogue 142:176 N 15 '63
Ski safe! address. E. B. Siegel. il Recreation 57:32 Ja '64
Skier on a slope to glory; C. Ferries. R. Terrell. il Sport Illus 18:30-4+ Mr 11 '63
Skiers and non-skiers both like it in Aspen. il Sunset 132:53+ Mr '64
Skier's West. il Sunset 130:66-73 F '63
Skiing (cont) R. Terrell. il Sports Illus 18: 54-6+ Ap 15 '63
Skiing, a family affair. M. Cohen. il Redbook 122:28+ Ja '64
Skiing through history. R. McKee. il Recreation 57:33-4 Ja '64
Snow is blue; new plastic run. il Newsweek 62:75 O 7 '63
Snows of spring; spring skiing. il Time 81: 52 My 10 '63
Snowy, snowy Alps. I. Shaw. Mlle 58:154+ N '63
Social climbing on the slopes. G. Talese. il Sat Eve Post 236:30+ F 9 '63
Some spice for the sugar; excerpt from Book of American skiing. E. Bowen. il Sports Illus 19:37-8+ N 18 '63
Swiss skier surprises the Austrians; pre-Olympic ski meet in Austria. R. Terrell. il Sports Illus 18:18-21 F 25 '63
Teen travel talk. il Seventeen 22:42 N; 134 D '63; 23:86 N '64
There are no wet blankets at Snoqualmie. H. Horn. il Sports Illus 20:50-5+ Ja 6 '64
Throw away that stem; parallel skiing. il Sports Illus 21:46-51 N 23 '64
Tough Americans: winners? U.S. Olympic skiers. il Newsweek 63:73 F 3 '64
Undeniably a girl; J. Saubert. il Time 83: 74 Ja 17 '64
Vermont ski trails. N. Ashby. il Am For 70: 50-2 F '64
Washington ski time. R. Henley. il Travel 123:36-7 Ja '65
Where it never snowed before. il Time 85:43 Ja 1 '65

SKIS and skiing—*Continued*
World of white. R. L. Nelson. il Audubon Mag 66:92-6 Mr '64
Young team with a mission; Alpine team. il Sports Illus 19:22-7 D 2 '63
See also
Water skis and skiing

Accidents and injuries
See Sports—Accidents and injuries

Anecdotes, facetiae, satire, etc.
Honest ski is the best policy. E. J. Kahn. jr. Mlle 60:142-3+ D '64

Equipment
He turned the poles to gold. P. Downey. il Sports Illus 18:E5-8 Mr 11 '63
You need more than snow to go skiing. il Changing T 19:19-20 Ja '65

SKITS (drama)
Living premise. il Ebony 19:59-60+ N '63

SKITTLES
Anyone for skittles? C. B. Hicks. il Pop Mech 121:156-7 Mr '64

SKLANSKY, Morris, and Neisser, E. G.
What's behind those teen-age masks? Parents Mag 39:64-5+ Ap '64

SKLAR, Robert
Our literary Tocqueville. Reporter 31:50 N 5 '64

SKLARE, Marshall
Intermarriage & the Jewish future. Commentary 37:46-52 Ap '64

SKOBLIKOVA, Lidia
Curls and cold steel. I. Shenker. il por Sports Illus 20:40-1 Ja 27 '64

SKODA. See Automobile industry and trade—Czechoslovakia

SKOGSBERG, Alfred H.
Magic numbers of 7-8-9. NEA J 52:50-1 Mr '63

SKOKIE junior high school. See Winnetka, Ill. —Education

SKOLNIK, Sandra J. See Bessman, S. P. jt. auth.

SKOPLJE earthquake. See Earthquakes—Yugoslavia

SKORNIA, Harry J.
Uses of diversity. R. L. Shayon. Sat R 47:27 Je 20 '64

SKORUPSKI, John
Big improvement in operation Am City 79:78-9 Ag '64

SKOW, John
Bravery is not enough. Sat Eve Post 236:78-80 Ag 10 '63
Broadway's hottest playwright, Edward Albee. Sat Eve Post 237:32-3 Ja 18 '64
Funny side of the Bunny business. Sat Eve Post 236:56-7 Mr 2 '63
Lodge faces his big test in Oregon. Sat Eve Post 237:15-19 My 16 '64
Mad: wild oracle of the teenage underground. Sat Eve Post 236:62-5 D 21 '63
Mona Lisa. Sat Eve Post 236:22-3 F 16 '63
Nebraska fiasco: buy now, pay never. Sat Eve Post 237:66-8 F 29 '64
Showdown in Arkansas: no dice in Hot Springs. Sat Eve Post 237:78-9 S 19 '64
Small war in Westport. Sat Eve Post 237:18-19 N 28 '64
Speaking out. por Sat Eve Post 237:12+ My 23 '64
Sunday afternoon fox. Sat Eve Post 237:24-5 D 5 '64
Sweepstakes in the snow. Sat Eve Post 237:17-23 Mr 14 '64
Tale of fish and chips. Sat Eve Post 237:60-1 F 8 '64
Who wants a tidy calendar? Sat Eve Post 237:38-9 Mr 7 '64

SKOWRONSKI, Hella
Hella Skowronski. D. Normark. il Craft Horiz 24:18-21+ Ja '64

SKROWACZEWSKI, Stanislaw
Musical events; concert at Carnegie Hall performed by Philadelphia orchestra. W. Sargeant. New Yorker 40:187 Ap 18 '64

SKUAS. See Gulls

SKUNK cabbages
Nature note. Sci N L 85:127 F 22 '64

SKUNKS
Little animal, big stink. W. Curtis. il Field & S 68:49+ Je '63
Loner. J. Stuart. il Am For 71:6+ Ja '65
Up the little finger. D. J. Anderson. il Field & S 69:24-6+ Ja '65

SKVARLA, John J. and Larson, D. A.
Nature of cohesion within pollen tetrads of typha latifolia. bibliog Science 140:173-5 Ap 12 '63

SKY diving. See Parachuting

SKY is a runner; story. See Rumaker, M.

SKYE, ISLE OF
Reader's choice. H. E. Gubbins. Travel 119:39 Mr '63

SKYHOOKS. See Balloons

SKYLIGHTS
Controlling the color of daylight. il Sunset 131:62-3 Ag '63
Easy way to build a skylight. D. Huff. il Pop Sci 185:144-5 Ag '64
How to control a bubble skylight. Sunset 130:150 My '63
Skylights for studios. il Arch Forum 118:84-5 Mr '63

SKYLINE drive. See Roads—United States

SKYSCRAPERS
CBS building. il Arch Forum 121:116-17 Ag '64
Coming: hanging skyscrapers. il Arch Forum 119:104-5 Jl '63
Different kind of skyscraper; First Pasadena state bank. il Arch Forum 120:122-5 Mr '64
Granite skyscraper for a Detroit loan association. il Arch Rec 133:202-4 Ap '63
Higher and lower. New Yorker 39:46-7 D 7 '63
Japanese show off structural skills. il Arch Forum 118:114-15 Mr '63
Logistics of vertical transport. il Fortune 67:89-95 Mr '63
Office building boom is going nationwide. il Arch Forum 118:114-19 My '63
Saarinen's dark tower: the CBS building and how it grew. E. Larrabee. il Harper 229:55-61 D '64
Skyscrapers go home! height limitations in Washington. D. Haskell. il Arch Forum 119:132 S '63
Skyscrapers; World trade center. New Yorker 39:21-2 F 1 '64
Unusual structural wall for IBM in Seattle. il Arch Rec 134:104-7 D '63
Up goes London. G. Kent. il Read Digest 82:213-16 Ap '63
Vest-pocket skyscraper in Hollywood. il Arch Forum 120:114-17 Ap '64
Will hanging tower attract exchange? il Arch Forum 118:116 Mr '63
World's biggest skyscrapers have New York up in the air; World trade center. il Arch Forum 120:118-21 Mr '64
Yamasaki's first skyscraper: headquarters for Consolidated gas company, Detroit. J. S. Hornbeck. il Arch Rec 133:143-50 My '63
See also
Eiffel tower
Office buildings

SLABS, Concrete. See Concrete slabs

SLACKS, Mens. See Clothing and dress—Men

SLACKS, Womens. See Clothing and dress

SLADE, Susan
Ready when you are, C.B! Criticism
New Yorker 40:66 D 19 '64
Newsweek 64:75 D 21 '64
Sat R 48:32 Ja 2 '65
Time il 84:86 D 18 '64

SLAGLE, Alton
Theatre USA. Theatre Arts 48:70-1+ Ja '64

SLANDER. See Libel and slander

SLANG
Beyond the ears of the Greys; Negro slang. il Time 82:14 Ag 2 '63
Do you dig all jive? G. Weinstein. il Sr Schol 85:13T-14T Ja 14 '65
Here's your Jenny Lee to London's odd dickey birds! D. Gunston. Travel 119:51-2+ F '63
Jazz lexicon, by R. Gold. Review
New Repub 151:34-6 N 28 '64. A. Goldman
Last word from Soul city; slang in Harlem. J. Griffin. il N Y Times Mag p62+ Ag 23 '64
Month at random; concerning obscenities in Dictionary of American slang. Wilson Lib Bul 38:22 S '63
Not for finks; sub-teen lingo. M. A. Guitar. il N Y Times Mag p50+ N 24 '63
Now everyone is hip about slang. B. Evans. N Y Times Mag p22+ Mr 22 '64
Salt in our talk. J. Martenhoff. il Motor B 113:19+ F '64
Slang bag; this winter's college slang. il Time 85:57 Ja 1 '65
Space-age guide for social astronauts. E. Auchincloss. Mlle 56:173+ Ap '63
War of words, obscenities in Dictionary of American slang. Newsweek 62:69 Jl 29 '63

SLAPSTICK moving pictures. See Moving pictures—Comedy

SLATE, George L.
Grapes for the home vineyard. Horticulture 41:208-9 Ap '63
Look at the future of lilies. Horticulture 42: 26-9 Ag '64
Plum. Horticulture 41:90 F '63
Unusual fruits. Horticulture 42:26-7+ Ap '64
Variety in the bramble patch. Horticulture 41:268-9 My '63

SLATE, John
Warning impulse timing and computing haversack. Fortune 69:157-8+ My '64

SLATE, John H.
So you're going to build an ocean liner? Atlan 214:122+ D '64

SLATE, Joseph
Respect; story. New Yorker 40:140-2 D 19 '64

SLATEN, Arthur Wakefield
Moncure Daniel Conway at South place chapel. W. S. Smith; reply. S. D. Wakefield. Christian Cent 80:468 Ap 10 '63

SLATER, Charles C. See Mainer, R. jt. auth.

SLATER, John V. and others
Temperature dependence of wing abnormality in tribolium confusum. Science 140:408-9 Ap 26 '63

SLATER, Mary. See Horn, H. jt. auth.

SLATER, Philip E. and Bennis, W. G.
Democracy is inevitable. bibliog f Harvard Bsns R 42:51-9 Mr '64

SLATER, Ralph
Robert Reynolds; personality profile. Flying 74:16+ Ja '64
Washington clipboard. See issues of Flying

SLATER, Sidney
My life inside the mob; ed by Q. Reynolds. pors Sat Eve Post 236:38-43+ Ag 24 '63

SLATON, Nellie Becker
Plague of Florida and California. Sci Digest 56:9-13 N '64

SLATON, William, Jr
Help yourself learning; special science classes in Los Angeles. il por Time 81:62+ Mr 15 '63

SLATTED barn floors. See Barns and stables—Floors

SLATTERY, Margaret E.
King in the kitchen; drama. Plays 23:53-9 Mr '64
Peppermint Easter egg; drama. Plays 22:35-42 Ap '63
Stolen cook; drama. Plays 24:67-75 N '64

SLAUGHTER, L. W.
On time. See issues of Hobbies

SLAVE; drama. See Jones, L.

SLAVE trade
Black cargoes: a history of the Atlantic slave trade, by D. P. Mannix. Review
Am Heritage 14:106-7 F '63
Merchandise was human; excerpt from Great Sahara. J. Wellard. Horizon 7:110-17 Wint '65

SLAVEN, Bob
Tartar. Yachting 113:54-5+ My '63

SLAVERY
Convention on abolition of slavery; text. Dept State Bul 49:323-6 Ag 26 '63
See also
Slave trade

Saudi Arabia
Emancipation. Newsweek 62:40 Jl 8 '63
Slavery lives on. America 108:481 Ap 13 '63

United States
American Civil war as a constitutional crisis. A. Bestor. bibliog f Am Hist R 69:327-52 Ja '64
Chattel law and the Negro; excerpts from Crisis in black and white. C. E. Silberman. Fortune 69:142-3+ My '64
Leaders of the first freedom movement. L. Bennett, jr. il Ebony 19:68-70+ Ag '64
Maybe it's time to look at the antislavery amendment; Thirteenth amendment. A. Avins. il U S News 56:82-4 My 11 '64
Myth and reality. H. N. Meyer. Commonweal 79:202-3 N 8 '63; Reply with rejoinder. H. Dienstfrey. 79:406-7 D 27 '63; Same. Negro Hist Bul 27:178-9 Ap '64
Second American revolution. C. Green. bibliog Negro Hist Bul 27:103-5 F '64
Slavery in the cities: the South 1820-1860, by R. C. Wade. Review
Nation 200:38-9 Ja 11 '65. E. D. Genovese
See also
Abolitionists
Dred Scott case
Emancipation proclamation

Fugitive slaves
Escape of valuable slave; Tom Stowe. J. R. Phillips. Negro Hist Bul 26:215 Ap '63
See also
Underground railroad

SLAVERY and slaves in literature
Annotated Uncle Tom's cabin, ed. by P. V. Stern. Review
Nation 198:666-8 Je 29 '64. Q. P. Stadler

SLAVES of the Immaculate heart of Mary
Slaves of Leonard Feeney. il Time 85:45 Ja 1 '65

SLAVIC languages
Alphabet
See also
Cyrillic alphabet

SLAVICK, Fred, and McConnell, J. W.
Flexible versus compulsory retirement policies. Mo Labor R 86:279-81 Mr '63

SLAVIN, Raymond G. and Garvin, J. E.
Delayed hypersensitivity in man: transfer by lymphocyte preparations of peripheral blood. bibliog Science 145:52-3 Jl 3 '64

SLAVITT, David R.
Lemmings; poem. New Repub 148:21 Ap 6 '63
New films in review (cont) Yale R 52:627-35; 53:309-15, 616-24; 54:299-307 Je, D '63, Je, D '64

SLAWECKI, Leon M. S.
Two Chinas in Africa. For Affairs 41:398-409 Ja '63

SLAYMAKER, S. R. 2d
Bass for the asking. Outdoor Life 132:24-7+ N '63
Hatch matching made easy. por Outdoor Life 133:66-7+ Ap '64

SLAYTON, Donald
We believe they should leave the flying to us. por Life 55:90 S 27 '63

SLAYTON, William
Design goals for urban renewal. Arch Rec 134:149-52 N '63
Cong Digest 43:112+ Ap '64
Federal housing agencies encouraging good design. Arch Rec 136:109 Ag '64
Urban renewal; address, February 14, 1964. Vital Speeches 30:376-8 Ap 1 '64; Excerpt.
Urban renewal; address, June 25, 1964. Vital Speeches 30:631-4 Ag 1 '64

SLEDD, James
Standard is a trademark. Consumer Rep 28: 551-2 N '63

SLEDDING. See Coasting

SLEDDING, Dog. See Dog sleds and sledding

SLEDS
Children's sleds. il Consumer Rep 28:535-7 N '63
Outrigger ski sled. H. B. Dabkowski. il Pop Mech 121:152-3 F '64
Year 'round fun from a sled. M. Price. il Pop Mech 119:146-7 Ap '63

SLEDS, Motor. See Motor sleds

SLEE, O. B. and others
Visual and radio observations of flare stars. Sky & Tel 25:83-6 F '63

SLEEP
Bedtime story; how much sleep do you need? il Mlle 56:152-3+ Mr '63
Blood pressure changes during human sleep. F. Snyder and others. bibliog il Science 142:1313-14 D 6 '63
Dialysis of sleep and waking factors in blood of the rabbit. M. Monnier and L. Hösli. bibliog il Science 146:796-8 N 6 '64
Do you need eight hours sleep? A. Hamilton. il Sci Digest 56:24-7 Jl '64
Eleven days without sleep; Randy Gardner. il Life 56:71-2 F 14 '64
How much sleep past sixty? il Time 84:50 Ag 7 '64
How to stay alert when you need sleep. C. Schwalberg. Redbook 122:118 D '63
If you have trouble getting enough sleep; interview. H. L. Williams. il U S News 55: 76-80 O 28 '63; Same abr. with title Do you have trouble sleeping? Read Digest 84:117-20 Ja '64
No more bedtime battles. M. Bernath. il Parents Mag 39:54-5+ Je '64
Paradoxical phase of sleep: its artificial induction in the cat by sodium butyrate. M. Matsuzaki and others. bibliog il Science 146: 1328-9 D 4 '64
Pontine reticular formation: relation to lateral geniculate nucleus during deep sleep. E. Bizzi and D. C. Brooks. bibliog il Science 141:270-2 Jl 19 '63
Sleep. L. Lessing. il Fortune 69:122-5+ Je '64

SLEEP—*Continued*
Sleep and wakefulness, by N. Kleitman. Review
Time il 83:44-6 F 14 '64
Sleep: cortical and subcortical recordings in the chimpanzee. W. R. Adey and others. bibliog il Science 141:932-3 S 6 '63
Sleep tendencies: effects of barometric pressure. W. B. Webb and H. Ades. il Science 143:263-4 Ja 17 '64
UCLA scientists induce sleep with bell. Sci N L 84:197 S 28 '63
Vestibular nuclei: activity of single neurons during natural sleep and wakefulness. E. Bizzi and others. bibliog il Science 145:414-15 Jl 24 '64
See also
Insomnia
SLEEP baths. See Baths
SLEEP habits of animals. See Animals—Habits and behavior
SLEEP walking. See Somnambulism
SLEEPERS. See Railroads—Ties
SLEEPERS (clothing) See Clothing and dress —Children
SLEEPING bags
Sleeping bags. il Consumer Rep 28:216-19 My '63
Toxic vapors from coin-op dry cleaning. Consumer Rep 29:317 Jl '64
SLEEPING BEAR NATIONAL PARK (proposed) See National parks and reserves—United States
SLEEPING cars. See Railroads—Sleeping cars
SLEEPING garments. See Nightgowns, pajamas, etc.
SLEEPING medicines. See Barbiturates
SLEEPING pills. See Barbiturates
SLEEPING sickness
Deadly female; Houston encephalitis epidemic. il Newsweek 64:58 S 7 '64
Encephalitis. il Life 57:125-6+ O 16 '64
Encephalitis hits more women than men; New Jersey. Sci N L 86:280 O 31 '64
Encephalitis subsiding; Houston, Tex. Sci N L 86:237 O 10 '64
Search for the night biter; Houston's outbreak. il Time 84:54 S 4 '64
Spreading: disease without a cure; St Louis type of encephalitis. il U S News 57:9 S 7 '64
SLEEPING sickness, African. See Trypanosomiasis
SLEEPLESSNESS. See Insomnia
SLEEPWALKING. See Somnambulism
SLEIGHT of hand; story. See Baldwin, F.
SLEIGHTHOLME, J. D.
No stone unturned. il Yachting 116:74-5+ S '64
SLEPIAN, Edward L.
Put a dragon in your galley. Motor B 115:88-91+ Ja '65
SLESAR, Henry
Right kind of house; story. excerpt from Clean crimes and neat murders. Read Digest 82:196-9 Mr '63
SLESNICK, Irwin L.
When science is fun. Sci Digest 55:73-4 Je '64
SLESSINGER, Seymour
Trading with the Communists. Commonweal 79:710-13 Mr 13 '64
SLESSOR, Sir John
Control of nuclear strategy. For Affairs 42:96-106 O '63
SLEVIN, Joseph R.
Washington desk. See issues of Dun's review and modern industry
SLEZAK, Edward J.
Fifty suggestions for a safe over-night. Recreation 56:130 Mr '63
Fifty suggestions for safe trips by canoe or boat. Recreation 57:137 Mr '64
SLEZAK, Walter
He likes to cook. por Bet Hom & Gard 42:106 O '64
SLICERS. See Kitchen utensils
SLIDE film projectors. See Projection apparatus
SLIDE projectors. See Projection apparatus
SLIDE rule
Smart stick. J. Martenhoff. il Motor B 113:40-1+ Ap '64
SLIDES, Childrens. See Playgrounds, Home—Equipment
SLIDES, Color. See Transparencies
SLIDES, Microscopic. See Microscopic slides
SLIDING block puzzles. See Puzzles
SLIDING doors. See Doors, Sliding
SLIEPCEVICH, Elena M.
School health education study. NEA J 53:60-1 Mr '64
SLIGH, Charles R. Jr
Your partner; the federal government; address, September 25, 1963. Vital Speeches 30:51-4 N 1 '63
SLIGHT ache; drama. See Pinter, H.
SLIME molds. See Myxomycetes
SLINGERLAND, E. J.
Safer transit system. Am City 79:105 Ja '64
SLINGSHOTS
Sharpest slingshooter. il Pop Mech 120:123 O '63
SLIP covers
Quick-change color. il House & Gard 125:142-9 Mr '64
Shift seasons with new slip covers. il Suc Farm 62:78-9 My '64
Slip cover care. Am Home 67:132 Jl '64
Spruce up with slip covers. il Am Home 67:50-3 My '64
Today's slipcovers. il Good H 158:122-6+ Mr '64
See also
Textile fabrics
SLIP forms. See Concrete construction—Forms
SLIPHER, Earl C.
Reminiscences of E. C. Slipher. R. S. Richardson. il pors Sky & Tel 28:208-9 O '64
SLIPS (clothing) See Underwear
SLIPYI, Josyf, abp
Kremlin and Vatican. America 108:283 Mr 2 '63
Kremlin cooperation. il por Time 81:70 F 22 '63
Touching consolation; release from Soviet prison. America 108:247 F 23 '63
SLIVKA, Rose
American craftsman, 1964. Craft Horiz 24:10-11+ My '64
SLO break basketball. See Basketball
SLOAN, Alfred Pritchard, Jr
General motors bonus system: an indispensable incentive. Fortune 69:125+ Ja '64
My years with General motors. por Fortune 68:135-42+ S; 145-8+ O; 167-70+ N; 149-52+ D '63; 69:123-6+ Ja; 123-6+ F '64
about
Alfred Sloan's success story. C. Kaysen. New Repub 150:21-3 F 29 '64
Last say on the company way. C. C. Brown. Sat R 47:55 F 22 '64
Mr General Motors. por Newsweek 63:73 Ja 27 '64
Strategist of success. por Time 83:62-4 Ja 24 '64
SLOAN, Irving J.
Inside social studies. Sat R 46:79 Je 15 '63
SLOAN, Jacob
(tr) See Amer, M. Yoke of the Torah
SLOAN, Mary Kay
Grand slam doubled. pors Outdoor Life 131:68-71+ Ap '63
(ed) See Sloan, S. R. 3d. Going for broke
SLOAN, Sam Ross, 3d
Going for broke; ed. by M. K. Sloan. pors Outdoor Life 131:72-5+ My '63
SLOAN-Kettering institute for cancer research
Human experimentation: cancer studies at Sloan-Kettering stir public debate on medical ethics. E. Langer. Science 143:551-3 F 7 '64; Discussion. 144:486; bibliog 145:768 My 1, Ag 21 '64
SLOAN valve company
Clean, quiet foundry almost runs itself. il Bsns W p52-3 Ap 13 '63
SLOANE, Eric
Sound of bells. Am Heritage 15:100-1 Je '64
SLOANE, Gloria
5:25 for St Thomas. il Motor B 113:44-5+ Ap '64
SLOANE, Louise
Fun for the hostess, too! Am Home 67:24 Je '64
There are children in your house. Am Home 67:24+ S '64
Vacation shopping for decorating treasures. Am Home 67:110+ Jl '64
SLOANE, Robert A.
Tree program restricts elm losses. Am City 79:165-6 O '64
SLOCUM, Joshua
Slocum society. B. Robinson. por Motor B 111:52+ Mr '63
SLOCUM society sailing club. See Yacht clubs
SLOGANS
Challenge to political shibboleths. P. Lisagor. il N Y Times Mag p39+ N 24 '63
From Tippecanoe to Scranton, too. H. F. Graff. il N Y Times Mag p 11+ Jl 5 '64

SLOGANS—*Continued*
Labels vs. policies; political catchwords. H. Hazlitt. Newsweek 64:85 N 30 '64
Slogan society. il Time 84:96+ O 16 '64
Words against words: political catchwords. H. Hazlitt. Newsweek 64:67 Ag 3 '64

SLOMAN, Joel
Blue woman; poem. Nation 199:224 O 12 '64
Part of a longer poem. Nation 197:328 N 16 '63

SLOOP racing. See Yacht racing

SLOOPS
Bahamian sailing craft; Bahama sloop. W. R. Johnson, jr. il Yachting 114:49-51+ N '63
Great American sailboats; Captain Cicero; cruising yacht. W. H. Koelbel. il Motor B 113:47+ F '64
Great American sailboats; Jerry Colemore. B. Koelbel. il Motor B 114:52+ D '64
Kialoa II; all-aluminum 73' sloop. P. Harder. il Yachting 115:62-3+ My '64
Profiles; two-week cruise aboard sloop Merrywend, around Long Island Sound. M. M. Hunt. il New Yorker 40:37-40+ Ag 22; 37-8+ Ag 29; 37-40+ S 5 '64
Shallow sea cruise; Dutch sloop. R. C. Weller. il Motor B 111:158-60 Ap '63

SLOT car racing. See Automobile models—Racing

SLOT machines. See Pinball machines

SLOTNICK, Irving J. and Sells, B. H.
Actinomycin resistance in bacillus subtilis. bibliog Science 146:407-8 O 16 '64

SLOTTED barn floors. See Barns and stables—Floors

SLOTTED floors (swine houses) See Swine houses—Floors

SLOW, Ralph
Improvement of student writing. Sch & Soc 91:175-7 Ap 6 '63

SLOW dance on the killing ground; drama. See Hanley, W.

SLOW learning children. See Children, Backward

SLOYAN, Gerard S.
Progress report on the liturgy. America 111: 179-83 Ag 22 '64

SLUDGE gas. See Sewage gas

SLUICE gates. See Gates, Hydraulic

SLUM children. See Children—Social and economic status

SLUM clearance. See Slums

SLUMS
Are we committing urban suicide? L. Hazard. Harvard Bsns R 42:152-4+ Jl '64
As the slum goes, so goes the Alliance; shantytowns of Latin America. J. Gross. il N Y Times Mag p 12-13+ Je 23 '63
Big city Christmas. J. O'Gara. Commonweal 79:388 D 27 '63
Biography of a tenement; from pasture to squalor. P. S. McGhee. il Nation 198:293-6 Mr 23 '64
Book focuses Republican attention on the slums; Let in the sun, by W. Klein. Pub W 186:45 N 9 '64
Close-up on poverty; O'Haires of Boston. M. Harrington. il Look 28:64-72 Ag 25 '64
Exploiting urban decay. Christian Cent 81:195-7 F 12 '64; Discussion. 81:431-3, 774 Ap 1, Je 10 '64
Harlem goes to war against the slumlords. R. K. Massie. il Sat Eve Post 237:71-5 F 29 '64
Housing and slum clearance: elusive goals. W. G. Grigsby. bibliog f il Ann Am Acad 352:107-18 Mr '64
Let in the sun, by W. Klein. Review
Reporter 31:54+ O 22 '64. C. W. Griffin, jr
Man's struggle for shelter in an urbanizing world, by C. Abrams. Review
Nation 199:199-201 O 5 '64. D. Gurin
No easy answer; Rio's *favelas*. M. J. Kubic. il Newsweek 64:59 N 30 '64
Patterns of decay. J. Berendt. il Esquire 59:96-9 Je '63
People of the slums. J. Colebrook. New Repub 148:18-22 Je 15; 15-18 Je 29 '63

SLURRY seal. See Pavements—Surface treatment

SLUSH hydrogen. See Hydrogen, Liquid

SMADEL, Joseph E.
Intracellular infection and the carrier state. bibliog Science 140:153-60 Ap 12 '63

SMALL, Millie
Britain's exciting new singer. il pors Ebony 19:48-50+ S '64

SMALL, Parker A. jr, and others
Polypeptide chains of rabbit gamma globulin. bibliog Science 142:393-4 O 18 '63
—See Baxter, J. H. jt. auth.

SMALL, Peter
35mm techniques; covering a 1,000-foot dive off Catalina. P. Stackpole. U S Camera 26:15+ Mr '63

SMALL business
Best of both worlds. J. Scobey. il Mlle 57: 171-3+ My '63
Businesses you can go into. il Changing T 17:41-4 Ap '63
Buying and selling a small business. Review
Pub W 187:82 Ja 11 '65
Dual distribution vs. the small retailer. T. J. Murray. il Duns R 84:28-9+ Ag '64
Exporting the dream. il Time 83:98 Ap 10 '64
Harvardmen vs. big business. R. Nason. il Duns R 83:41-2+ Ja '64
House urges more small business awards. Aviation W 82:93 Ja 25 '65
How to start a business. A. Poinsett. il Ebony 19:85-6+ Jl '64
Practical planning for small business. R. A. Golde. bibliog f il Harvard Bsns R 42:147-55+ S '64
Psychoanalyzing the small businessman. il Bsns W p90+ S 19 '64
R&D is more efficient in small companies. A. C. Cooper. bibliog f Harvard Bsns R 42:75-83 My '64
Risk takers. H. Hazlitt. Newsweek 62:62 Jl 29 '63; Same abr. with title Where jobs come from. Read Digest 83:195-6 O '63
Small business pacts continue decline. H. M. David. Miss & Roc 16:16 Ja 11 '65
That uneven tide. Time 84:76 Jl 24 '64
University studies disclose: this federal program destroys jobs. il Nations Bsns 52:36-7+ Ap '64

See also
Exclusive agencies
Self employed

Finance

Borrowing and the small businessman. R. Nason. il Duns R 82:61-2+ O '63
Encourage private capital to aid American industry; address, June 6, 1963. F. G. Binswanger. Vital Speeches 29:689-90 S 1 '63
Government as a banker: easy way to get money. il U S News 57:105-7 O 19 '64
How wage law hit small shop. U S News 57:75 Ag 17 '64
Making of a Negro middle class; Small business opportunities corporation (SBOC) Philadelphia. H. Lees. il Reporter 31:41-4 O 8 '64
Profit-planning accounting for small firms. J. Dearden. Harvard Bsns R 41:66-76 Mr '63
Small firms face tight financing period. W. Wright. Aviation W 78:89+ Je 3 '63
Trouble in Lilliput; small manufacturers. Time 82:89 S 20 '63

SMALL business administration. See United States—Small business administration

SMALL business investment companies
Are SBICs doing their job? S. L. Hayes and D. H. Woods. il Harvard Bsns R 41:6-8+ Mr '63
Borrowing and the small businessman. R. Nason. il Duns R 82:61-2+ O '63
Congress eases rein on SBICs. Bsns W p48 F 22 '64
For SBICs, a new flexibility. Bsns W p94 D 26 '64
Freeze on forming new SBICs. Bsns W p34+ Jl '64
SBICs: rocky road looms ahead. il Bsns W p66-7 Jl 20 '63
Small firms face tight financing period. W. Wright. Aviation W 78:89+ Je 3 '63

SMALL cause for alarm; story. See Gordon, E. E.

SMALL claims courts
Quick justice, no red tape. il Changing T 18:11-13 Mr '64

SMALL farms. See Farms, Small

SMALL hotel; story. See Knowlton, R. A.

SMALL in the eyes of a tiger; story. See Arnaldi, J.

SMALL libraries project. See American library association—Small libraries project

SMALL loan companies. See Finance companies

SMALL loans. See Loans, Personal

SMALL town life. See City and town life; Village life

SMALLEY, I. J.
Radiolarians: contruction of spherical skeleton. bibliog Science 140:396-7 Ap 26 '63

SMALLEY, Robert L. and Dryer, R. L.
Brown fat: thermogenic effect during arousal from hibernation in the bat. bibliog Science 140:1333-4 Je 21 '63

SMALLMAN, Robert E.
Flying the Atlantic without a navigator. Pop Sci 182:86-8+ Ap '63
House you'll build from four boxes. Pop Sci 183:102-4 D '63
How to prefab a vacation cabin in a home shop. il Pop Sci 184:100-6 Ap '64
You can save money tenting on two wheels. Pop Sci 184:124-5 My '64
SMALLMOUTH fishing. See Bass fishing
SMALLPOX
Against smallpox. Time 82:96+ S 20 '63
Needless agony of smallpox. R. M. Hendrickson. il Todays Health 41:22-3+ Mr '63
See also
Vaccination
SMALLWOOD, David M. and Michaels, Abraham
Clean-street bug is catching. Am City 78:98-100 S '63
SMART, Mollie
Magic of mothering. Parents Mag 40:35+ Ja '65
SMATHERS, George A.
Key senator urges better help for the aging. por Nations Bsns 52:36-7+ Jl '64
Power game: George Smathers, the golden senator from Florida. R. G. Sherrill. il por Nation 199:426-37 D 7 '64
SMEARS, Political. See Presidential campaigns
SMELL
Dissociation of olfactory neural response and mucosal potential. T. Shibuya. bibliog il Science 143:1338-40 Mr 20 '64
How a nose smells. il Sci Digest 55:86-7 My '64
Inquiline roach responds to trail-marking substance of leaf-cutting ants. J. C. Moser. il Science 143:1048-9 Mr 6 '64
Smell governed by electrical process. Sci N L 86:328 N 21 '64
Smell, sex and survival in animals. K. Von Frisch. il Sci Digest 53:65-72 F '63
Smelling is believing, or is it? Sci Digest 55:39 Ap '64
Stereochemical theory of odor. J. E. Amoore and others. il Sci Am 210:42-9 bibliog(p 152) F '64
SMELL of bread; story. See Kazakov, Y.
SMELSER, Marshall
Senator Eugene McCarthy: how to succeed by ignoring your well-wishers. Harper 228:76-8 Je '64
SMELT fishing
Catching smelt with a two-man net. il Sunset 130:26+ Je '63
Gentle art of catching smelts. E. R. Choate. il Atlan 214:93-4 N '64
Smelt have me hooked. H. F. Blaisdell. il Outdoor Life 131:30-1+ F '63
SMETANA, Bedřich
Bartered bride. il Am Rec G 30:662-3 Ap '64
On records: The bartered bride. Opera N 29:34 Ja 2 '65
SMILES
Smiles of men and monkeys. Sci Am 210:56+ Ja '64
Why men smile; reprint. il Sci Digest 57:79-82 Ja '65
SMILEY, Frank R.
We doubled in area to solve our sewerage problem. por Am City 78:108-9 My '63
SMILEY, Marjorie B.
Who would teach here. PTA Mag 58:16-19 S '63
SMIRNOFF, Dimitri
On records; Dimitri Smirnoff. J. W. Freeman. Opera N 27:32 My 4 '63
SMISSAERT, H. R.
Cholinesterase inhibition in spider mites susceptible and resistant to organophosphate. bibliog Science 143:129-31 Ja 10 '64
SMIT, A. J. Haagen-. See Haagen-Smit, A. J.
SMITH, A. J. M.
Something that might simply be. M. L. Rosenthal. Reporter 29:56+ S 12 '63
SMITH, A. P, manufacturing company
Case that cleared the way; unrestricted gift of $1,500 to Princeton university. L. L. L. Golden. Sat R 47:59 S 12 '64
SMITH, Alexander
In praise of winter; excerpt from Dreamthorp. Read Digest 85:53-5 D '64
SMITH, Alice Upham
Landscaping good enough to eat. Pop Gard 15:22-4 My '64
SMITH, Anthony Wayne
Hunting in our national parks? Audubon Mag 65:6-9 Ja '63
Jambo gasbag safari in Africa. pors Sat Eve Post 236:40-7 N 9 '63
SMITH, Barbara
What it's like in Cuba. New Repub 148:21-4 Ap 13 '63
SMITH, Bernard, jr
Life at section A, post two. il por Fortune 69:152+ My '64
SMITH, Beulah Fenderson
I shall forget; poem. McCalls 91:137 Jl '64
Return; poem. McCalls 91:220 O '63
SMITH, Beverly, jr
Yank returns to Oxford. por Sat Eve Post 236:70+ Mr 23 '63
SMITH, Beverly Bush
More cheese, please. Parents Mag 38:95+ O '63
Summer is berry nice. por Parents Mag 39:63-5+ Je '64
SMITH, Bradford
View from the subcontinent. Sat R 46:29 My 25 '63
SMITH, Bradford, jr
Stressing the package. por Bsns W p64+ Je 6 '64
SMITH, Bradley
Entries in a logbook. Sat R 46:89 O 12 '63
SMITH, Brydon E.
Canaletto in Canada. Art N 63:26-9+ N '64
SMITH, Mrs Burrows
David Brinkley and his golden key. C. S. Wren. il pors Look 28:44+ F 25 '64
SMITH, C. Earle, jr, and MacNeish, R. S.
Antiquity of American polyploid cotton. bibliog Science 143:675-6 F 14 '64
SMITH, C. Lavett
Fishes and climates. Natur Hist 73:34-9 F '64
Hermaphroditism in Bahama groupers. Natur Hist 73:42-7 Je '64
SMITH, Carl D.
Flyless refuse collection. Am City 78:81-2 D '63
SMITH, Carol
How to split a second. Pop Phot 52:58-60+ F '63
Ten ways to blow a fuse. Pop Phot 52:57 Ja '63
SMITH, Charles H. See Bhattacharji, S. jt. auth.
SMITH, Charlie
Charlie Smith, 121 years young. il pors Ebony 19:131-2+ N '63
SMITH, Clement A.
First breath; with biographical sketch. il Sci Am 209:20, 27-35 O '63
SMITH, D. F.
Chlorine pentafluoride. Science 141:1039 S 13 '63
Xenon oxyfluoride. bibliog Science 140:899-900 My 24 '63
SMITH, D. H.
Operation bootstrap. Am City 78:78-80 Jl '63
SMITH, Datus Clifford, 1907-
Children's books in developing countries; address. Horn Bk 39:36-49 F '63
Ten years of Franklin publications. por ALA Bul 57:507-12 Je '63
SMITH, David
Art galleries; exhibition at the Marlborough-Gerson. R. M. Coates. New Yorker 40:165-6 N 7 '64
David Smith, a major American sculptor. R. Motherwell. il por Vogue 143:134-9 F 1 '65
David's steel goliaths. il pors Life 54:129-33 Ap 5 '63
Four sculptors, four styles. il Art N 62:36-7+ Sum '63
SMITH, Desmond
Affluent railroads. Nation 197:312-14 N 16 '63
American radio today: the listener be damned. Harper 229:58-63 S; 8+ N '64; Same abr. with title American radio: an insult to the public? Read Digest 85:115-18 D '64
Chain squeeze; power of big food. Nation 198:646-8 Je 29 '64
Pay or free? the coming TV war. Nation 198:504-6 My 18 '64
SOS from the merchant marine. Nation 199:406-8 N 30 '64
Sugar: market and supermarket. Nation 199:327-9, inside cover N 9, D 14 '64
TV and more TV. Nation 200:62 Ja 18 '65
TV commercials; the government ducks the issue. Nation 198:286-9 Mr 23 '64
TV's unnerving numbers game. N Y Times Mag p40+ Ag 18 '63
Welcome hoax. Nation 197:259-61 O 26 '63
SMITH, Dido
Arts of Byzantium. Craft Horiz 23:34-7+ My '63
Offhand glass blowing. Craft Horiz 24:22-3+ Ja '64
SMITH, Earl E. T.
Ambassador Smith's Cuban report. D. M. Friedenberg. Commonweal 77:622-4 Mr 8 '63
SMITH, Edgar
Strange case of Edgar Smith. D. G. M. Coxe. il por Nat R 15:273-8 O 8 '63

SMITH, Edmund Ware
Bush-queer canoe trip. Field & S 69:40-2+ My '64
I mean, after all. Redbook 121:15 Jl '63
Last hermit. Field & S 67:56-8+ Ap '63
Trout from still waters. Field & S 68:58-9+ O '63
SMITH, Edward Lucie-. See Lucie-Smith, E.
SMITH, Elinor Goulding
Ask a foolish question. Atlan 213:164-5 Mr '64
Me? a genius? Vogue 143:48-9 F 1 '64; Same abr. Read Digest 84:157-8 My '64
SMITH, Erik
Mozart on the menu. Hi Fi 13:58-60 N '63
SMITH, Erwin E.
Cowhand. O. L. McKeen. il pors Am Heritage 14:16-31 O '63
SMITH, Eugene A.
Navigation in the islands. por Motor B 112: 32-3+ D '63
SMITH, Eugene E.
New trucks for old. Am City 79:13 Ag '64
SMITH, Eugenia
Case of a new Anastasia. il pors Life 55: 104A-112 O 18 '63
SMITH, F. Robert
Reader's choice. Travel 120:13 D '63; 122:7 Jl '64
SMITH, Frances C.
For all boys. Writer 77:22-4 N '64
SMITH, Frank Ellis
Southern politician. Nation 199:132-4 S 21 '64

about

Race was to the racists. E. M. Yoder, jr. Sat R 47:41 O 10 '64
SMITH, Frank Kingston
Week-end pilot. See issues of Flying
SMITH, Fred R.
Sporting look (cont) Sports Illus 18:72-9 My 20 '63
Tokyo travel facts. Sports Illus 21:42-7 Jl 6 '64
Travel. Sports Illus 19:52 Ag 12 '63
SMITH, G. E. Kidder
New German theaters and concert halls. il Arch Rec 134:179-94 O '63
SMITH, G. Roysce
Paperbacks in the general bookstore. Pub W 186:43-5 O 19 '64
SMITH, George E. and Zeman, L. E.
Mixed fertilizers or bulk blends? Suc Farm 61:50-1 Ap '63
SMITH, Gerald R.
Project social studies, a report. Sch Life 45:25-7 Jl '63
SMITH, Gerard C.
Nuclear defense of NATO; address, April 22, 1964. bibliog f Dept State Bul 50:783-90 My 18 '64; Same with title Problems of foreign policy. Vital Speeches 30:526-30 Je 15 '64
SMITH, Gordon S. and Eckles, B. F.
Soil surveys ease growing pains. Am City 78:96-7 Ag '63
SMITH, H. Allen
Black death on the living-room floor. Sat Eve Post 237:28+ F 1 '64
Claude Fetridge's infuriating law. Read Digest 82:229-30+ Je '63
Contrary genius of Fidgets' Retreat. Read Digest 84:27-8+ Ja '64
Hildy Johnson's last scoop. Read Digest 85: 227+ O '64
Hold that habit! Read Digest 83:231-3 Jl '63
I'm absent in mind only; excerpt from Short history of fingers and other state papers. Read Digest 84:15-16+ Mr '64
Polynesian palmistry; excerpt from Two-thirds of a coconut tree. Sat R 46:70 Mr 16 '63
Speaking out. Sat Eve Post 236:10+ Ag 24 '63
Unsound and the fury. Sat Eve Post 236:62 Mr 9 '63
SMITH, Hamilton O. See Levine, M. jt. auth.
SMITH, Hannis S.
Consultants' column (cont) Library J 88: 4334+, 4719 N 15, D 15 '63
SMITH, Harmon
Hitting the road. Dance Mag 37:29-30 D '63
Lady, you bring romance. Dance Mag 38:62-3 Ap '64
One way to break into photography. U S Camera 27:58-9+ Ap '64
What's a dancer doing at Mr Kenneth's? Dance Mag 39:22-3 Ja '65
SMITH, Harold A.
Developing a good system of communications. por Wilson Lib Bul 38:535-9 Mr '64
SMITH, Harold H.
Neutron irradiations: biological effects. Science 143:1466+ Mr 27 '64
—and others
Partial synchronization of nuclear divisions in root meristems with 5-aminouracil. Science 142:595-6 N 1 '63
—See Curtis, H. J. jt. auth.
SMITH, Harry
Guy named Smith is striking it rich. R. Boyle. il por Sports Illus 19:36-8 N 25 '63
SMITH, Hartland B.
Code bander. Pop Electr 19:45-8 Ag '63
Fido's whistle-controlled flivvers. Pop Electr 21:47-51+ O '64
Ham-band walkie-talkies the easy way. Pop Electr 20:61-4 Ap '64
Idento-minder. Pop Electr 19:51-3 S '63
Lullaby box. Pop Electr 21:57-8 Jl '64
Tap tap temperature taker. Pop Electr 21: 39-43+ Jl '64
WXCVR. Pop Electr 20:63-5+ Ja '64
SMITH, Hedrick
How the President keeps informed. N Y Times Mag p 15+ Ag 30 '64
(comp) Laughs from Cairo. N Y Times Mag p 131 D 13 '64
SMITH, Hervey Garrett
America's cup races are illegal! Yachting 116:72+ S '64
SMITH, Hilary
Nuns in the wide, wide world. America 110: 284-5 F 29 '64
SMITH, Howard K.
Berlin/1964. Esquire 62:35-9 Jl '64
(ed) See Manning, R. J. Mr Manning interviewed on News and comment
SMITH, Howard Worth
Excerpt from address, May 9, 1962. Cong Digest 42:55+ F '63
Excerpt from debate, August 19,1964. Cong Digest 44:18+ Ja '65

about

Judge Smith moves with deliberate drag; chairman of the House rules committee. D. Oberdorfer. il pors N Y Times Mag p 13+ Ja 12 '64
Master in the House. il por Newsweek 63:19-20 Ja 20 '64
Slow-down Smith. M. Kempton. New Repub 149:8-9 D 14 '63
SMITH, Hughie Lee
Negro artist in America today. Negro Hist Bul 27:111-12 F '64
SMITH, Huston
Comparative religion, philosophy of religion bookshelf. Christian Cent 80:830-1 Je 26 '63
SMITH, Hyrum M. and Miller, L. M.
Doors were opened. Sch Life 46:8-10 Ja '64
SMITH, Ian Douglas
Another tea party? Newsweek 63:53-4 Ap 27 '64
Tougher line in Africa; Rhodesia gets a new leader. il por U S News 56:15-16 Ap 27 '64
Will he, won't he, will he, won't he. . ? E. Huxley. Nat R 16:651-2 Jl 28 '64
SMITH, Ida
Desert sanctuary. Nat Parks Mag 37:15-17 S '63
Walnut Canyon National Monument. Nat Parks 38:11-13 N '64
SMITH, J. Austin
None does his job alone; adaptation of address. por Recreation 57:48 F '64
SMITH, J. Frederick
Bright color under soft light. il U S Camera 27:35-7 My '64
More art than sex. il pors U S Camera 26: 62-3+ Jl '63
One photographer+one model=all women. J. Morris. il por U S Camera 26:64-71 My '63
SMITH, J. Russell
J. Russell Smith, geographer, educator, and conservationist, by V. M. Rowley. Review Am For 70:41+ D '64. M. Bush
SMITH, J. Winslow
Surveying a boat with diesel power. Motor B 114:32-3 O '64
SMITH, James C. and others
Motor responses of moths to low-intensity X-ray exposure. bibliog Science 140:805-6 My 17 '63
SMITH, James Steel
Jargon in the humanities. Harper 228:111-12 Mr '64
SMITH, Jean Edward
Bay of Pigs; the unanswered questions. Nation 198:360-3 Ap 13 '64
Berlin: the erosion of a principle. Reporter 29:32-3+ N 21 '63
CIA on trial. Reporter 30:53-6 Je 18 '64

SMITH, Jedediah
Trail blazer of the Far West. S. W. Sears. il Am Heritage 14:60-4+ Je '63
SMITH, Jerome Irving
Dressed pictures. Antiques 84:694-7 D '63
SMITH, Joan Merriam
Shades of Amelia. il por Newsweek 63:20 Mr 30 '64
SMITH, John B. K. and Mines, Robert
Six ways to handle your anxiety. Sci Digest 54:19-24 N '63
Why so many of us are tired. Sci Digest 53: 87-91 My '63
SMITH, John E.
Ethics, love, and wisdom. Sat R 47:80 Ja 4 '64
SMITH, Joseph
Here is my home at last! C. Carmer. il Am Heritage 14:26-33+ F '63
SMITH, Josiah
Gradele of trobel. Am Heritage 14:112 Ap '63
SMITH, Joyce E. See Norstog, K. jt. auth.
SMITH, Justin C. See Munster, J. H. jr, jt. auth.
SMITH, Karl U. See Greene, P. M. jt. auth.
SMITH, Kelly Miller
Creative disruptions; race relations lecture at Vanderbilt university. W. A. Geier. Christian Cent 80:344 Mr 13 '63
SMITH, Kendall O. and Melnick, J. L.
Adenovirus-like particles from cancers induced by adenovirus-12 but free of infectious virus. bibliog Science 145:1190-2 S 11 '64
SMITH, Kenneth L.
Seabell; other man's boat. Yachting 115:72-3 Je '64
SMITH, Kirby D. and others
Xanthine dehydrogenase in drosophila: detection of isozymes. bibliog Science 142: 226-7 O 11 '63
SMITH, Kirk
For barbecue fun; let's have a cookout. Pop Gard 14:55-7 Jl '63
SMITH, Lafayette
Girls in the Olympics. Todays Health 42: 28-31+ O '64
Run for your health. Todays Health 42:34-7 O '64
SMITH, LeRoi
Glass buckets; photographs. Hot Rod 17:88-9 O '64
Triple-threat 'Vette. il Hot Rod 17:74-7+ O '64
SMITH, Leroy D. jr
Seven minute color prints in trays with machine chemicals. il Pop Phot 55:56-7+ S '64
SMITH, Lillian
Day it happens to each of us; excerpt from Our faces, our words. McCalls 92:124-5+ N '64
Thoughts as her travels ended. Sat R 46:19-20 S 7 '63
Too tame the shrew. Sat R 46:34+ F 23 '63
SMITH, Lillian H.
News from Narnia. Horn Bk 39:470-3 O '63
SMITH, Liz
Les hangouts. Esquire 60:140-1 N '63
Nudity cult. Sports Illus 22:34-9 Ja 18 '65
SMITH, Louis
Philadelphia, Pennsylvania: a process of fragmentation. H. Lees. il Reporter 29:18-20 Jl 4 '63
SMITH, Mabel G.
Return from the deaf. por Farm J 87:70 Jl '63
SMITH, Maggie
Maggie, Maggie. por Time 82:78+ N 22 '63
SMITH, Margaret
Homey type. il por Time 82:52-3 Ag 16 '63
Queen Margaret. il por Newsweek 62:54 S 9 '63
SMITH, Margaret (Chase)
Excerpt from address, March 24, 1962. Cong Digest 42:79+ Mr '63

about

Candidate Smith? Newsweek 62:34 N 18 '63
Hey, look me over. il Newsweek 63:19-20 F 24 '64
Lady from Maine: her record, her views. por U S News 56:16 F 3 '64
Lady in the New England snow. M. McGrory. America 110:246 F 22 '64
Lady of Maine. K. Crawford. Newsweek 63: 30 F 10 '64
Madam candidate. por Time 83:23 F 7 '64
Maggie vs. May. Newsweek 61:23-4+ Ap 8 '63
Maggie's list. il por Time 81:21 Mr 1 '63
Margaret Chase Smith: woman of courage, by F. Graham, jr. Review
Sat R por 47:42-3 Ap 18 '64. C. B. Luce
Mom and pop; Goldwater-Smith ticket. Reporter 29:24 N 21 '63
Twenty-four hours in the life of Margaret Chase Smith. H. Markel. il pors McCalls 91:116-17+ My '64
What is Maggie Smith up to? Mr. Cheshire. il pors Sat Eve Post 237:30-2 Ap 18 '64
Without portfolio. C. B. Luce. McCalls 91:18 Je '64
Woman for president? il pors U S News 56: 34-6 F 10 '64
Woman's right. por Newsweek 63:22-3 F 10 '64
SMITH, Marilynn
For goodness' sake, hold on. il por Time 83:56+ My 8 '64
SMITH, Marinobel
Mexican school for pilots. Américas 16:29-31 Mr '64
SMITH, Marshall
Downhill seconds before the disaster, then stillness. il Life 56:36-7 Ap 24 '64
Giving the Olympics an anthropological once-over. Life 57:81-2+ O 23 '64
Gone are rowdy roughing it days; today it's posh plus. Life 54:70-4+ Mr 29 '63
He bites people and spooks other horses. Life 55:129-30+ N 22 '63
Junk navy has a quietly perilous mission. Life 57:36-9 N 27 '64
Old man brings back a great day. Life 54: 35+ Je 21 '63
Room with ghost $4 and up. Life 57:134-6+ S 18 '64
Upper crust brought sin to the surface. il Life 55:54-7 Jl 26 '63
We'll do things the American way. Life 56: 70+ Ja 10 '64
SMITH, Mason Philip
Tate House in Stroudwater, Maine. il Antiques 84:172-4 Ag '63
SMITH, Merriman
Trends: Washington mood. See issues of Nation's business to December 1963
SMITH, Michael E.
Christmas present. por Time 85:43 Ja 1 '65
SMITH, Mike
Motorized action. il U S Camera 26:86-7 O '63
SMITH, Mitchell
Hands are for drawing. Sch Arts 63:21 F '64
SMITH, Mortimer
Reading in basic education; excerpt from address, August 1, 1962. Sch & Soc 91:56-9 F 9 '63
Scholastic teacher interviews: Mortimer Smith; ed. by H. Langer. por Sr Schol 84: 9T-12T My 1 '64
SMITH, Murphy D.
Preparing a manuscripts guide for a learned society; reprint. Hobbies 69:110-11+ My '64
SMITH, Ned
First moose at Mindedo. Outdoor Life 134: 60-1+ O '64
Why wait for spinach? Field & S 68:48-9+ My '63
SMITH, Nellene
Library board issues statement on Santa Barbara situation. Library J 88:3813-14 O 15 '63
Santa Barbara librarian resigns after clash with deputy. Library J 88:3182-4 S 15 '63; Reply. 88:4104 N 1 '63
SMITH, Norbert
Build the Blipper. Pop Electr 21:51-2 S '64
SMITH, Orriel
I sing a gentle song. por Seventeen 23:20 Ja '64
SMITH, Orville A. jr. See Stebbins, W. C. jt. auth.
SMITH, Pat
One photographer+one model=all women. J. Morris. il pors U S Camera 26:64-71 My '63
SMITH, Patrick J.
Covent Garden's friends. Opera N 29:29 D 19 '64
Everyman's guide to discmanship. Hi Fi 14: 17-18 O '64
Greatest opera? Opera N 28:23-4 D 28 '63
Lulu, Daphne, and an uncertain sky. Hi Fi 14:68-71 N '64
Paradox of late Strauss. Hi Fi 14:36-8+ Je '64
Riddle of Turandot. Opera N 29:24-5 Ja 16 '65
Strauss's Arabella as sung on the Munich stage. Hi Fi 14:68-9 Ag '64
SMITH, Paul
Dublin's lusty theater. Holiday 33:119-20+ Ap '63
Ways in which authors and booksellers can cooperate to sell books. Pub W 186:14-17 Ag 17 '64

SMITH, Paul C.
Collier's affair: a rueful memoir; excerpt from personal file. pors Esquire 62:132-5+ S '64
SMITH, Paul H.
Increasingly rear-guard. Christian Cent 81: 179 F 5 '64
SMITH, Peter Duval
(ed) See McCarthy, M. Mary McCarthy said
(ed) See Nabokov, V. What Vladimir Nabokov thinks of his work, his life
SMITH, Philip
Democracy in relation to education; excerpt from Philosophy of education: introductory studies. bibliog f Sch & Soc 92:414-18 D 26 '64
SMITH, Philip E. L.
Radiocarbon dating of a late paleolithic culture from Egypt. bibliog Science 145:811 Ag 21 '64
Solutrean culture; with biographical sketch. Sci Am 211:10, 86-94 Ag '64
SMITH, Philip R. jr
Memorial to an Indian Moses. Nat Parks Mag 37:13-15 F '63
SMITH, R. E.
Keeping a city in good shape. il pors Bsns W p 110-14 Je 6 '64
SMITH, Ralph J.
Missouri River cruise. Yachting 116:40-3+ Jl '64
SMITH, Ralph Lee
Hucksters of pain. Sat Eve Post 236:83-7 Ag 24 '63
Postal savings: America's poorest buy. Nation 199:140-1 S 21 '64
Salesman will call. Nation 196:8-10 Ja 5; inside cover F 9 '63
Strange world of mechanical quackery. Todays Health 42:42-7+ N '64
(ed) See Phelan, J. F. jr. It's tough to be a teen-ager
SMITH, Randolph, and others
Concentric-circle design. Am City 78:92-4 Mr '63
Don't be just half-safe. Am City 78:90-2 My '63
SMITH, Ray Winfield
History revealed in ancient glass. por Nat Geog Mag 126:346-69 S '64
SMITH, Raymond
Paul Tillich's concept of faith; condensation of Faith without belief. Cath World 200:162-3+ D '64
SMITH, Rhea Marsh
Spain emerges from isolation. Cur Hist 47: 345-9 D '64
SMITH, Richard Austin
How business failed Dallas. Fortune 70:156-60+ Jl '64
Now it's an agonizing reappraisal of the moon race. Fortune 68:124-9+ N '63
Onrushing auto makers. Fortune 68:96-8+ Ag '63
Scranton of Pennsylvania. Fortune 69:80-4+ F '64
$7-billion contract that changed the rules. Fortune 67:96-101+ Mr; 110-11+ Ap '63
SMITH, Richard Bensted-. See Bensted-Smith, R.
SMITH, Richard H.
Variation in the monoterpenes of pinus ponderosa laws. bibliog Science 143:1337-8 Mr 20 '64
SMITH, Richard S.
Return to Devil's Island. Travel 122:38-42 O '64
Tiger, and the unexpected. por Outdoor Life 135:44-7+ F '65
SMITH, Richmond W. jr, and Walker, R. R.
Femoral expansion in aging women: implications for osteoporosis and fractures. bibliog Science 145:156-7 Jl 10 '64
SMITH, Robert C.
Philadelphia empire furniture by Antoine Gabriel Quervelle. Antiques 86:304-9 S '64
Portuguese painted chairs. il Antiques 83:680-3 Je '63
Rhenish cabinet of the eighteenth century. Antiques 87:68-72 Ja '65
Summer exhibitions in Paris. Antiques 86: 194-5 Ag '64
SMITH, Robert E
Thermoregulatory and adaptive behavior of brown adipose tissue. bibliog Science 146: 1686-9 D 25 '64
—and Hock, R. J.
Brown fat; thermogenic effector of arousal in hibernators. bibliog Science 140:199-200 Ap 12 '63
SMITH, Robert G.
Destiny's tot. Nat R 16:861-2 O 6 '64
SMITH, Robert Paul
Appliance is something that gets attached to you. McCalls 91:98 Ap '64
Robert Paul Smith's attic. McCalls 92:90+ O '64
They don't make décor that way any more. McCalls 90:61 Je '63
They don't make fountain pens, or library paste, or hardly anything that way any more. McCalls 90:194+ S '63
They don't make ice boxes that way any more. McCalls 90:52 Ag '63
They don't make medicines that way any more. McCalls 90:114 Jl '63
They don't make Thanksgiving that way any more, or do they? McCalls 91:101+ N '63
They don't make them that way any more. McCalls 90:86-7+ My '63
SMITH, Robert W.
Package of political poison; analysis and criticism of None dare call it treason, by J. A. Stormer; reprint. Christian Cent 81: 1263-4 O 14 '64
SMITH, Roger
London area goes metro. Am City 79:124+ Ag '64
SMITH, Ruth B.
Calendar of coming events. See issues of Motor boating
SMITH, Ruth Newburn
Your baby's five senses and how they develop. Parents Mag 38:64-5+ S '63
SMITH, Ruth S.
Challenge of church libraries. bibliog por Library J 88:3000-3 S 1 '63
SMITH, Ruth Woodhull
Gardener; St Bartholomew's Episcopal church. New Yorker 39:34-6 S 21 '63
SMITH, Samuel H. and Schlegel, D. E.
Incorporation of uridine-H^3 into nuclei of virus-infected tobacco. bibliog Science 145: 1058-9 S 4 '64
SMITH, Sara Louise
Consumer health education. NEA J 53:62-3 Mr '64
SMITH, Sherwin D.
All wound up in tape. N Y Times Mag p54+ Ap 12 '64
Duel in the sun. N Y Times Mag p72-3 Ag 9 '64
Fifty years ago. N Y Times Mag p62-4 F 16 '64
Forty-two campaigns ago. N Y Times Mag p82+ O 25 '64
Forty years ago. N Y Times Mag p46+ N 3 '63
100 years ago. N Y Times Mag p50+ Je 7 '64
Subway saga. N Y Times Mag p48+ N 8 '64
Thirty-five years ago. N Y Times Mag p96-8 O 27 '63; 45+ F 9 '64
Thirty years ago. N Y Times Mag p50+ My 26 '63; 74+ S 13 '64 p45+ F 9 '64
When the big one (Hitler) got away. N Y Times Mag p86-8+ My 24 '64
SMITH, Stanley E.
Blow us something good, sirocco; story. Sat Eve Post 237:54-6 Mr 21 '64
Collecting: the modern shell game. Parents Mag 38:48-9+ Ag '63
We keep our weather eyes open. Parents Mag 39:44-5+ Ag '64
SMITH, Stephen Edward
Inscrutable Mr. Smith. L. Bergquist. il pors Look 27:28-30+ S 24 '63
Kennedy clansman nobody knows. A. L. Otten and C. B. Seib. il pors Sat Eve Post 236:69-70 S 7 '63
Name is Smith. T. Wicker. il pors N Y Times Mag p 11+ Jl 28 '63
One of the family. por Time 81:28 Ap 5 '63
People of the week. por U S News 54:20 My 13 '63
Stephen E. Smith. M. Kempton. New Repub 148:15-17 Mr 9 '63
SMITH, Stevie
Frog-prince; poem. Reporter 31:53 S 24 '64
Hymn to the seal. Atlan 214:78 N '64
Lord say and seal; Here lies; Miss Snooks, poetess; Northumberland house; Grange; poems. Poetry 105:109-12 N '64
Pretty; poem. Nation 198:246 Mr 9 '64
Tenuous and precarious; poem. Nation 199:40 Jl 27 '64

about

Dark Lorelei. W. K. Rose. Nation 199:96-7 S 7 '64
SMITH, Terry
Basketball's Irish czar. Sat Eve Post 237:54-5 F 8 '64
SMITH, Valerie Danby-. See Danby-Smith, V.
SMITH, Vincent E.
Catholic science textbooks? America 110: 78-80+ Ja 18 '64

SMITH, Virginia
Seattle: when nonachievers shun the library. por ALA Bul 58:817-19 O '64
SMITH, Virginia Ruth
It's the little things that count. Hobbies 69: 116-17+ My '64
SMITH, W. Eugene
Return of Eugene Smith! P. Stackpole. U S Camera 27:8 Ja '64
SMITH, W. G.
Government finance for private schools in Australia. Sch & Soc 92:268-70 O 3 '64
SMITH, Warren Sylvester
Astounding William T. Stead. Christian Cent 80:855-8 Jl 3 '63
Charles Bradlaugh and the secularists. Christian Cent 80:331-4 Mr 13 '63
George Tyrrell and the modernists. Christian Cent 80:490-2 Ap 17 '63
How pertinent is our theater? Christian Cent 81:1393-5 N 11 '64
R. J. Campbell at City temple. Christian Cent 80:1132-4 S 18 '63
Religion of Bernard Shaw. Christian Cent 80:1266-9 O 16 '63
Stewart Headlam and the Christian Socialists. Christian Cent 80:201-4 F 13 '63
Theosophist Helena Blavatsky. Christian Cent 80:1002-5 Ag 14 '63
Thomas Davidson and the New life fellowship. Christian Cent 80:642-5 My 15 '63
SMITH, Warrie Lynn
I believe; ed. by F. R. Schreiber. pors Seventeen 23:196-7 S '64
SMITH, Wendell I. See Moore, J. W. jt. auth.
SMITH, Wilbur J.
Strawberries & Linnaeus. Library J 89:2945-7 Ag '64
SMITH, William E.
Letter from the publisher. B. M. Auer. il por Time 83:11 Ja 31 '64
SMITH, William Gardner
Black man in Europe. Holiday 37:22+ Ja '65
SMITH, William James
Just a reporter, and then some. Commonweal 79:436-7 Ja 10 '64
Pop art and the short story. Commonweal 80:508-10 Jl 24 '64
SMITH, William Jay
Bobbsey twins at an orgy. Nation 198:633-5 Je 22 '64
Morels; poem. New Yorker 40:44 My 23 '64
My poetic career in Vermont politics. Harper 228:54-62 Ja '64
New poetry. Harper 227:106+ S '63
Petits chevaux: the twenties; poem. New Repub 148:22 F 9 '63
Some new poetry: from last August to this. Harper 229:99-103 Ag '64
Tin can; poem. Poetry 102:351-8 S '63
SMITH, William Raymond
Huxley the humanist. New Repub 150:28-30 Je 27 '64
SMITH, Willie
Have no fear and keep it clear, the jive is comin' and The Lion's here; excerpts from Music on my mind. por Esquire 61: 68-71+ Je '64
Music on my mind, by W. Smith with G. Hoefer. Review
Sat R il 47:50 S 12 '64. S. Dance
SMITH, Willie, sr
Player of the week; of Los Angeles Angels. por Sports Illus 21:69 Jl 6 '64
SMITH, Wray
Board of directors of Consumers union announces. C. E. Warne. por Consumer Rep 28:415 S '63
SMITH, Hinchman and Grylls associates, incorporated
How one large office uses construction cost estimates. W. B. Foxhall. il Arch Rec 135 106+ My '64
SMITH and Wesson revolvers. See Revolvers
SMITH brothers, incorporated (cough drops)
Brothers move on. il Time 83:86 F 21 '64
Trade and mark. Newsweek 63:68+ F 24 '64
SMITH college, Northampton, Mass.
Thomas C. Mendenhall: he keeps an eye on 2,300 girls. C. S. Wren. il Look 28:104-8 Je 2 '64
SMITH ISLAND
Island named Smith; quiet haven in Chesapeake Bay. R. Deardorff. il Travel 121: 42-5 Je '64
SMITH RIVER, Calif.
When winter storms roil the rivers, try the Smith for steelhead. il Sunset 132:19 Ja '64
SMITHERS, C. Francis
East Side house is grateful to Antiques magazine. Antiques 85:34 Ja '64; 87:50 Ja '65
SMITHSON, James
Professor Henry and his philosophical toys; with note by Mrs C. H. Danforth. M. Blow. il por Am Heritage 15:24-9+ D '63
SMITHSONIAN institution
Department of entomology opens. Hobbies 68:117 O '63
First ladies collection; Smithsonian institution's Dresses of the First ladies of the White House. Hobbies 68:51 Mr '63
Modernizing the attic. il Time 83:74-5 F 21 '64
Professor Henry and his philosophical toys; with note by Mrs C. H. Danforth. M. Blow. il Am Heritage 15:24-9+ D '63
Ripley revisited; eighth secretary. New Yorker 40:19-21 Jl 11 '64
Smithsonian head sees museum as lively spot; summary of address. S. D. Ripley, 2d. Sci N L 85:120 F 22 '64
Smithsonian preview. C. M. Watkins. il Antiques 85:86-7 Ja '64

Museum of history and technology

Hottest show in Washington. il U S News 56:77-9 My 11 '64
Letter from Washington. F. Gutheim. Nation 198:126-7 F 3 '64
Massive showcase for American history. il U S News 56:12 F 3 '64
New landmarks on the Washington horizon. E. J. Long. il Am For 70:20-1 Mr '64
New national monument; Museum of history and technology. E. Hall. il Sci N L 85:55 Ja 25 '64
Uncle Sam cleans out the attic; exhibits at Museum of history and technology. R. Smallman. il Pop Sci 184:34+ Ap '64
What are they doing with Gen. Sheridan's horse? A. Chamberlin. il Sat Eve Post 237: 70-3 My 9 '64

National air museum

Grounded and impounded. A. Dawydoff. il Flying 74:36-8+ Ja '64
Soaring air museum and an earthbound one. il Fortune 70:176-7 D '64

Science information exchange

Keeping up with current research: Science information exchange. M. E. Freeman and D. F. Hersey. Science 141:119 Jl 12 '63

Traveling exhibition service

Government in art. F. Getlein. New Repub 150:36-7 F 15 '64
SMITON, David R.
Value of independent drawing. il por Am Artist 28:52-7 N '64
SMITS, Lee
Retriever training clinic. Field & S 67:62-3 Mr '63
SMOG
Anti-smog kit. T. E. Stimson. il Pop Mech 120:125-7+ N '63
Atmospheric iodine abates smog ozone. W. F. Hamilton and others. il Science 140: 190-1 Ap 12 '63
Murk, smog, smoke, needed: fresh air. F. J. Cook. il N Y Times Mag p 10+ D 29 '63
New methods may remove smog poison. Sci N L 83:137 Mr 2 '63
Smog battle gets hot. C. N. Barnard. il Sat Eve Post 237:78+ Ap 25 '64
Smog devices tested by dynamometer system. Sci N L 85:152 Mr 7 '64
See also
Plants, Effect of smog on
also subhead Air pollution under names of cities, e.g. Los Angeles—Air pollution
SMOG neutralizers. See Automobile engines—Exhaust
SMOKE
Darkness at noon; Massachusetts, May 19, 1780. J. Ashbrook. bibliog Sky & Tel 27: 219 Ap '64
Overcoming smoke inhalation. il Am City 78: 26 D '63
See also
Smog
SMOKE flow research. See Aerodynamics
SMOKE houses. See Smokehouses
SMOKE jumpers. See Forest fire patrol, Aerial
SMOKE preventation
See also
New York (city)—Air pollution
Pittsburgh—Air pollution
SMOKED fish. See Fish, Smoked
SMOKED food. See Food, Smoked
SMOKEHOUSES
Fish, fowl and smoke; art of cooking with smoke. R. Cantwell. il Sports Illus 19:52-5 O 28 '63

SMOKELESS gunpowder. See Gunpowder, Smokeless

SMOKEY Bear. See Advertising characters

SMOKING

Athletes in smoke switch; series ads by the American cancer society. il Sr Schol 83:19 N 22 '63

Being nonchalant about smoking. Time 83:42 Ja 24 '64

Cancer education. Sr Schol 82:3T+ My 1 '63

Cigarette smoking and arteriosclerosis. S. L. Wilens and C. M. Plair; discussion. il Science 139:1096+ Mr 15 '63

Cigarette smoking harms lung tissue. Sci N L 83:399 Je 22 '63

Cigarette warning, the aftermath; reaction of smokers, congressmen, stock market. U S News 56:38-9 Ja 27 '64

College smoking; how come nobody's stopped? M. A. Guitar. Mlle 59:268-9+ Ag '64

Combating teen-age smoking. E. Corwin. il PTA Mag 58:4-6 Ap '64

Common sense about smoking, by C. M. Fletcher and others. Review
Nation 196:379-80 My 4 '63. G. A. Silver

Consumers union report on smoking and the public interest, by R. Brecher and others. Review
New Repub 149:15-16 S 21 '63. F. E. Kameny
Sat R il 46:38-9 Ag 24 '63. W. G. Cahan

Danger beyond smoking. N. Cousins. Sat R 47:22 Ja 25 '64; Same abr. Read Digest 84:41-2 My '64; Discussion. Sat R 47:31-2 F 15 '64

Dilemma of the problem smoker. L. M. Miller. Read Digest 84:63-8 My '64

Do ex-smokers live longer? Bsns W p67 N 16 '63

Ex-inhalers; pipes and cigars. il Bsns W p 124+ F 8 '64

Government report. il Time 83:42 Ja 17 '64

Hazards of judging. Newsweek 61:94 Mr 25 '63

Hazards of teen-age smoking; excerpts from Smoke screen: tobacco and the public welfare. M. B. Neuberger. il Parents Mag 39:51+ Ja '64

Here's the latest on tobacco and health. il U S News 56:44-5 Ja 20 '64

How to give up smoking; maybe. R. Brecher and E. Brecher. il N Y Times Mag p 16+ Ja 26 '64

How to stop smoking: guerrilla gambit or cruise cure? Newsweek 62:64 N 18 '63

If tobacco were spinach. Nation 197:359 N 30 '63

Irrational state. Nat R 16:97+ F 11 '64

Light up a petunia? Newsweek 62:62 S 9 '63

Most exhaustive survey on smoking & disease. il Time 82:40+ D 13 '63

New research on a stop smoking drug. il Good H 158:161 Mr '64

New way to cut out smoking; anti-smoking clinics in Great Britain. G. Emerson. Read Digest 83:100-4 O '63

One way to stop smoking; a kind of A.A. for smokers. Time 81:72 Mr 15 '63

One year later; effect of Surgeon General's report. Time 85:58 Ja 22 '65

Our children made us stop smoking! I. Roach. il Parents Mag 39:35+ Jl '64

San Francisco smoke; AMA 113th annual meeting in San Francisco. Newsweek 64: 56-7 Jl 6 '64

Science looks at tobacco; questions and answers. J. E. Gibson. il Todays Health 42: 33+ F '64

Semi-final word; delay in publication of government's report on cigarettes and lung cancer. Newsweek 62:81 O 14 '63

Smoke and fire; concerning report by Consumers union. il Newsweek 61:100+ Je 24 '63

Smokers' slowdown: how long will it last? U S News 56:6 F 24 '64

Smoking and cancer; a verdict; concerning Surgeon general's report. il Sr Schol 84: 4-7 F 21 '64

Smoking and health: the U.S. decision. il Newsweek 62:61-6 N 18 '63

Smoking as cancer risk. Sci N L 83:91 F 9 '63

Smoking fire burns hotter; health vs. industry. il Bsns W p32+ Ja 18 '64

Smoking habits: what Surgeon General says; remarks, January 11, 1965. L. L. Terry. U S News 58:14 Ja 25 '65

Smoking, health, and a giant industry. il U S News 55:84-6 D 2 '63

Smoking report. Sci Am 210:66-7 F '64

Smoking report; concerning Smoking to death? America 110:131 Ja 25 '64

Smoking scare? what's happened to it. il U S News 58:38-41 Ja 11 '65

Teacher opinion poll; student smoking on high school grounds. il NEA J 54:17 Ja '65

Teen-age smokers. il Sr Schol 84:7 F 21 '64

To alter smoking habit, stopping is best. Sci N L 83:249 Ap 20 '63

To smoke or not to smoke. Sr Schol 83:19 O 11 '63

To smoke, or not to smoke? il Newsweek 63:70-3 Ja 27 '64

To smoke or not to smoke; questions and answers; Tobacco institute replies. Sci N L 83:263+ Ap 27 '63

To teen-age smokers. Newsweek 61:86 Ap 8 '63

Tobacco: activity masks unrest in industry as government smoking study is prepared for release. E. Langer. Science 142:941-2 N 15 '63

Tobacco report: agencies ponder action; Congress takes the lead with a $5-million research plan. J. Walsh. Science 143:788-9 F 21 '64

Tobacco substitute fails. Sci N L 84:150 S 7 '63

Travel notes; pipe and cigar smoking on airplanes. R. J. Joseph. Esquire 60:88-91 D '63

Villain in smoke: a new view; excerpt from statement, January 29, 1964. L. Terry. U S News 56:61 F 10 '64

Wait and see; Surgeon General's one-year-later report on lethal effects of cigarette smoking. Nation 200:69-70 Ja 25 '65

Waiting for the smoke signal; report from U.S. government. il Bsns W p 150-2+ S 7 '63

Why people smoke. Sci Digest 53:61-2 Je '63

Why stop smoking? New Repub 150:6-7 Ja 25 '64

See also
Cigarettes
Cigars
Tobacco—Physiological aspects

SMOKING accessories

Tamper, rasp, and mull; wooden accessories for tobacco. E. H. Pinto. il Antiques 85: 690-4 Je '64

SMOKING of food. See Food—Smoking

SMOKY MOUNTAINS. See Great Smoky Mountains

SMOLEN, Michael

Another nasty stunt. il por Time 84:54 O 16 '64

SMOLIAN, Steven

Da capo. See issues of American record guide

SMOLIAR, Sophie

How to get a photo center in your city. Pop Phot 52:57+ My '63

SMOLINSKI, Leon

What next in Soviet planning? bibliog f For Affairs 42:602-13 Jl '64

SMOOT, Dan

Smoot's case. New Repub 151:5-6 O 31 '64

SMÖRGASBORD. See Cookery, Swedish

SMUCKLER, Edward A. and Benditt, E. P.

Carbon tetrachloride poisoning in rats: alteration in ribosomes of the liver. bibliog Science 140:308-10 Ap 19 '63

SMUGGLING

Art from nobody knows where; Mexican art treasures. W. J. Gill. il Sat Eve Post 237: 56-8 F 8 '64

Contrabando: big in Brazil; with report by M. J. Kubic. il Newsweek 62:46-7 Jl 8 '63

Great leveler; Latin American smugglers. il Time 83:32 Je 19 '64

Hooch in the hold; Royal Ceylon navy. Time 81:34 My 10 '63

Intellectual smugglers; thriving white-collar smugglers in West Germany. Time 82:115-16 D 6 '63

Opium must go through. S. Karnow. il Life 55:11-12 Ag 30 '63

Pirates of Teignmouth; English fishermen arrested. Newsweek 64:38+ Ag 31 '64

Seldom seen; illegal narcotics. Time 83:19 Mr 27 '64

Through the curtain, under the counter. Time 84:82+ Ag 21 '64

SMYLIE, James H.

Catholicism: molder of manpower. Christian Cent 80:1544-6 D 11 '63

Catholics and American goals. Christian Cent 81:140-3 Ja 29 '64

Catholics as immigrants. Christian Cent 80: 1396-9 N 13 '63

Presbyterians on church and state. Christian Cent 80:610-14 My 8 '63

Touch of casuistry. Christian Cent 80:1309 O 23 '63

SMYLIE, Robert E.

Leader of the posse. il por Newsweek 65:27 Ja 11 '65

SMYTH, Bernard John
In his own backyard; State news. il por Time 82:91 O 18 '63
SMYTH, David
Kaiser: model for Latin America. Nation 197: 415-17 D 14 '63
SMYTH, Henry D.
United States favors extension of IAEA safeguards system; statement, September 27, 1963. Dept State Bul 49:1019-21 D 30 '63
SMYTHE, D. Verner
Starting a junior sailing program. por Yachting 115:54-6+ My '64
SMYTHE, Hugh H. and Sasidhorn, Nibondh
Literacy and learning in Asia. Sch & Soc 91: 371-3 N 30 '63
SMYTHE, Reginald
'E's luv'ly. il Time 82:71+ N 1 '63
SNACK bars
Fund raising through refreshment operations. J. C. Evans. Recreation 56:233+ My '63
SNACKS. See Meals
SNAIL fever. See Schistosomiasis
SNAIL hawks. See Kites (birds)
SNAILS
Deadly larva, deadly snails. il Time 82:59-60 S 20 '63
Ecological design of irrigation canals for snail control. W. R. Jobin and A. T. Ippen. bibliog il Science 145:1324-6 S 18 '64
Polymorphism and population density in the African land snail, limicolaria martensiana. D. F. Owen. il Science 140:666-7 My 10 '63
See also
Cookery—Snails
Control
Killer snails pitted against crop pests. Sci N L 86:41 Jl 18 '64
Wage war against snail; using marisa against australorbis. Sci N L 85:302 My 9 '64
Diseases and pests
Schistosomiasis: age of snails and susceptibility to X-irradiation. A. P. Szumlewicz. bibliog il Science 144:302-4 Ap 17 '64
SNAILS, Effect of radiation on. See Radiation—Physiological effects
SNAITH, William T.
Building a new boat. il Yachting 114:42-5+ Ag; 42-4+ S '63
SNAKE bite. See Venom
SNAKE venom. See Venom
SNAKEROOT, Black. See Black snakeroot
SNAKES
First aid; poisonous snake bite. C. J. Potthoff. Todays Health 41:60 Je '63
How to tame a blacksnake. J. Stuart. Am For 70:18 F '64
Keep away from snakes. il Consumer Bul 47:27-9 Ag '64
New poison symbol irks snake expert; not all snakes are poisonous. Sci N L 86:120 Ag 22 '64
Snake attack; aesculape snakes. il Sci Digest 54:30-1 Ag '63
Snake hunt. il Sci Digest 56:47-51 Ag '64
Snakes are interesting; hognosed snakes. W. F. Heald. il Audubon Mag 65:218-21 Jl '63
Snakes; with photographs by N. Leen and account by P. Hunt. Life 54:37-49 Mr 1 '63
Vipers of Hmawza; with report by L. H. Tin Lat. Newsweek 64:50+ N 23 '64
See also
Rattlesnakes
Photographs
Snakes. N. Leen. Life 54:37-49 Mr 1 '63
SNAKES as pets. See Pets
SNAPPER fishing
Fishing for snapper blues. G. Heinold. il Outdoor Life 132:64+ Jl '63
Slugging red snapper. G. Heinold. il Outdoor Life 132:22+ S '63
SNAPPING turtles. See Turtles
SNAPSHOT albums. See Photographic albums
SNAPWEED. See Touch-me-nots
SNAVELY, Guy E.
Federal aid and higher education. Sch & Soc 91:86-8 F 23 '63
SNAVELY, James N.
Outcast of Lebanon. R. G. Hummerstone. il Nation 199:303-5 N 2 '64
SNEAD, Sam
Young Sam wins while old Mac sues. E. Shrake. por Sports Illus 20:52+ Mr 2 '64
SNEAKERS. See Shoes
SNEED, Larry
Can the cancer society combat the hidden persuaders? New Repub 150:12-13 F 8 '64
SNELL, David
Le grand snow job. Life 54:15 Ap 5 '63
SNELL, F. M. See Harmon, L. D. jt. auth.
SNELL, Peter
All alone & kinda slow. por Time 84:51 N 27 '64
Fastest is faster. G. Rogin. il por Sports Illus 21:56-60+ O 5 '64
How a man of spirit wrecked Igloi's computer. T. Maule. il por Sports Illus 18:26-9+ Je 3 '63
Let them try. il por Time 81:65 My 31 '63
Snell's tortured race to a record mile. il por Sports Illus 21:28-9 N 30 '64
3:48 mile? por Newsweek 64:86-7 N 30 '64
SNELLENBERGER, Earl G.
Expressive line and form. Design 66:42-3 S '64
Wonderful ways with color. Design 66:27-9 N '64
SNIDER, Arthur J.
Egg and Doctor Grabowski. Todays Health 41:80-1 N '63
How religion helps to heal. Sci Digest 56:6-13 Jl '64
Progress of medicine. See issues of Science digest
Why do we grow old? Todays Health 41:18-20 Jl '63
SNIDER, Faith
Directional line drawing for senior high school students. Sch Arts 64:18-19 Ja '65
SNIPE shooting
Two doubles a world apart. W. Chapman. il Sports Illus 19:100-2+ N 25 '63
SNIPES, Wallace C. and Gordy, Walter
Radiation damage to artemia cysts: effects of water vapor. bibliog Science 142:503-4 O 25 '63
SNIPES
Grand sportin' bird. W. Page. il Field & S 68:64-7 My '63
SNOBS and snobbishness
Aesthetics of snobbery; excerpt from Act of creation. A. Koestler. Horizon 7:50-3 Wint '65
Le snob-snob à l'etranger; excerpt from Snobissimo. P. Daninos. Harper 230:119 Ja '65
Snobs of Paris. P. Daninos. il Vogue 141: 124-7+ Ap 1 '63
SNODGRASS, Frank E.
Precision digital tide gauge. bibliog Science 146:198-200+ O 9 '64
SNODGRASS, Robert E.
Some mysteries of life and existence; excerpts. Hobbies 69:115 D '64
SNODGRASS, W. D.
Lobsters in the window; poem. New Yorker 38:36 F 2 '63
Lovers go fly a kite; poem. New Yorker 38:36 F 9 '63
Monet; Les nymphéas; poem. Atlan 211:83 F '63
—and Tolstoy, Tanya
Versions of Kozma Prutkov; poem. Poetry 104:203-9 Jl '64
SNOOK, Patrick K.
Backpacks and frames. Pop Mech 119:106-9 Je '63
Games for boaters. Pop Mech 120:106-9 Ag '63
Six bits of luxury for your boat. Pop Mech 121:152-3 Mr '64
—and Michaelson, Marc
Crisis kit for your boat. Pop Mech 121:154 Mr '64
SNOOK fishing
Big snook is disaster. W. Jacqmar. il Outdoor Life 131:40-1+ F '63
Place that Rocky knows; Ten Thousand Islands, Fla. E. White. il Sports Illus 20: 36+ My 25 '64
Where to catch snook. G. Heinold. il Outdoor Life 132:12+ N '63
SNOOPERSCOPES. See Viewers, Infrared
SNOQUALMIE, Wash.
There are no wet blankets at Snoqualmie. H. Horn. il Sports Illus 20:50-5+ Ja 6 '64
SNOVER, Robert
Signal corps escutcheon. Nation 198:207 Mr 2 '64
SNOW, Barbara
Christmas crèche figures: sculpture in miniature. Antiques 86:698-701 D '64
Living with antiques. Antiques 83:542-7 My '63
(ed) Preservation and urban renewal: is coexistence possible? Antiques 84:442-53 O '63
Preservation notes. Antiques 85:226, 460; 86: 100 F, Ap, Jl '64
SNOW, Brian C.
Light-controlled power supply, second thoughts. Pop Electr 21:70-2 S '64

SNOW, Charles Percy, baron Snow of Leicester.
See Snow of Leicester, C. P. S.

SNOW, George
High-energy physics. Science 146:809-10+ N 6 '64

SNOW, Kenneth
How Intourist took me in. Nat R 16:355-7 My 5 '64

SNOW, William B.
Throw away the collar; paper collars and dickies. il por Bsns W p67-8+ S 7 '63

SNOW of Leicester, Charles Percy Snow, baron
Affair; dramatization. See Millar, R.
Churchill. por Look 27:26-33 F 26 '63; Same abr. with title We must never deny our gratitude. Read Digest 82:66-71 My '63
Higher education in America. por NEA J 53: 11 Ap '64
Pat on the back; summary of address. Sr Schol 82:4T Mr 20 '63

about

C. P. Snow: corridors of power is novel about nuclear policy and politics, closed and open. J. Walsh. Science 146:234-6 O 9 '64
C. P. Snow: second thoughts on the two cultures likely to keep the pot boiling. J. Walsh. Science 142:653-4 N 8 '63
Dog that didn't bark. H. Corke. New Repub 148:27-30 Ap 13 '63; Discussion. 148:36-7 My 4 '63
Oh no, Lord Snow. M. Muggeridge. New Repub 151:27-9 N 28 '64
Politician in a nuclear quandary. G. Hicks. Sat R 47:33-4 S 12 '64
Pomp and circumstance: C. P. Snow. R. Adams. por Atlan 214:95-8 N '64
Reaction to Snow: scientists' role in public affairs draws increasingly heavy criticisms. D. S. Greenberg. Science 142:34-5 O 4 '63; Discussion. 142:13; 143:7, 638 O 4 '63, Ja 3, F 14 '64
Snow affair. M. S. Simpson. Bul Atomic Sci 19:28-32 Ap '63
Two cultures in the corridors. por Time 84: 102 N 20 '64
Two cultures reaffirmed. Sci Am 209:67 D '63
Walking the corridors of power. por Newsweek 64:25 D 28 '64

SNOW
Beauty in snow; ice crystals. il Natur Hist 72:28-9 D '63
Hunting in the snow. T. Trueblood. il Field & S 68:16+ D '63
Nature note. Sci N L 87:27 Ja 9 '65
Snow is what you make of it. J. Martineau. il Am For 70:38-41 F '64
Snowflake Bentley's magnificent obsession. D. Epstein and R. Epstein. il Read Digest 83:182-6 D '63
Splendor of winter. B. Tufty. il Sci N L 84: 378-9 D 14 '63
Water-tight pillows measure snowfall; Mount Hood, Ore. il Sci N L 86:405 D 26 '64

SNOW, Artificial
Where it never snowed before. il Time 85:43 Ja 1 '65

SNOW and ice removal
As soon as the first snowflake appears; snow removal in Metuchen, N.J. T. Eosso. il Am City 79:10 D '64
Blow snow off the bridges; Minneapolis. G. Bodien and L. C. Pratt. il Am City 79:71-2 Ja '64
Bubbles break the ice; in water tank, Kankakee, Ill. il Am City 78:112-13 O '63
Chemical snow removers are not the answer. Consumer Bul 48:20 F '65
Don't give away your snow shovel, ice chipper, or sand pail. Consumer Bul 47:28 F '64
Everybody pitches in; Dayton, Ohio. W. Shartzer. il Am City 78:90-1 N '63
Getting better results from salt. il Am City 78:32 Ag '63
Mix chemicals for faster melting. A. Engelhart. il Am City 78:16 O '63
Plows and plans for successful snow-fighting. R. R. Fleming. bibliog il Am City 79:75-7+ Ag '64
Salt, plow and haul; LaGrange, Ill. R. E. Meyer. il Am City 78:90-1 O '63
Should you use chemicals? where? how? E. D. Fales, jr. il Pop Sci 184:120-1+ F '64
Snow conference expands coverage. Am City 78:162+ Je '63
Snow-fighters get promise of better weather forecasts. A. Michaels. il Am City 79:106-7 Je '64
Snow melters: say good-bye to shoveling? J. Hand. il Pop Sci 184:120-1+ F '64
Snow removal (title varies) See issues of American city
Snow-removal costs; APWA research—foundation study. il Am City 78:76-7 D '63
Snowfighting with sirens; Prairie Village, Kan. R. E. Carroll. il Am City 79:92-3 F '64
Sprinkle brine for bare pavements; Logan, Ohio. il Am City 80:30 Ja '65
Sweepers whisk the snow away; Copenhagen. J. P. Horton. il Am City 79:76-7 D '64
Tips for tired snow fighters; Des Plains, Ill. E. R. Warnicke. il Am City 78:76-7 F '63
Upgrading a second-rate snow program; Grove City, Pa. F. E. Fisher. il Am City 79:108-9 O '64
Virtually every snowflake must be moved in Hibbing, Minn. J. H. Rough. il Am City 78: 71-3 Ag '63

SNOW blowers, throwers, etc.
Blow the snow away. J. H. Ingersoll. il Pop Gard 14:10-11 N '63
Blowing up a storm. il Newsweek 63:49 Ja 6 '64
Cold weather warm-up. K. H. Seitz. il Flower Grower 51:30-2 O '64
Cul-de-sacs demand special snow units; Rolling Meadows, Ill. J. McFeggan. il Am City 79:88-9 N '64
Directory of snow blowers. il Flower Grower 50:30-3 N '63
Get rid of snow the easy way. R. L. Hering. il Pop Gard 15:13-15 N '64
Hazards of removing snow by machine. Consumer Bul 48:9 F '65
Little maintenance goes a long way. il Pop Gard 15:16-17 N '64
Machines that shovel your snow. il Changing T 18:17-18 N '64
Snow removal equipment. il Consumer Bul 46:17-20 O '63
Snow thrower quickly clears walks and drives. B. C. Kilvert, jr. il Flower Grower 51:29-30 Ja '64
Take your pick of power. B. C. Kilvert, jr. il Flower Grower 51:30-2 N; 12-13 D '64
Twenty tips for snowblower buyers. J. Hand. il Pop Mech 120:96-100 D '63
What the new snow blowers can do for you. D. X. Manners and C. C. Calkins. il House B 105:242-3+ N '63
What's new at the hardware show; snow throwers. E. D. Fales, jr. il Pop Sci 183: 30-2+ D '63
Your guide to buying a snow thrower. E. F. Lindsley. il Pop Sci 185:144-7 D '64

SNOW crawlers. See Motor sleds

SNOW geese. See Geese, Wild

SNOW gun. See Snow machines

SNOW machines
Snow at the turn of a switch; snow gun. J. Hand. il Pop Sci 182:98-101+ Mr '63

SNOW modeling
Snow sculpture; excerpt. il Recreation 57: 498-9 D '64

SNOW plows
Plows and plans for successful snow-fighting. R. R. Fleming. bibliog il Am City 79:75-7+ Ag '64

SNOW removal equipment, Municipal
Blowers boost loading, drop costs; Arlington, Mass. F. N. O'Hara. il Am City 79:109-10 S '64
Eliminate the contract plowing; Newton, Mass. W. S. Pratt. il Am City 78:112-13 S '63
Small but powerful snow fighters; Pittsburgh, Pa. F. Ambrose. il Am City 78: 145 D '63
Upgrading a second-rate snow program; Grove City, Pa. F. E. Fisher. il Am City 79:108-9 O '64

SNOW scooters. See Motor scooters

SNOW sculpture. See Snow modeling

SNOW statue; story. See Toney, R.

SNOW throwers. See Snow blowers, throwers, etc.

SNOW tires. See Tires, Automobile

SNOW-White and Rose-Red; drama. See Bennett, R.

SNOWBERRIES
It just won't stay put. il Sunset 133:203 S '64

SNOWDEN, Donald
Reporter at large; First conference of the Arctic coöperatives at Frobisher Bay. E. Iglauer. New Yorker 39:188+ N 23 '63

SNOWDON, Antony Charles Robert Armstrong-Jones, 1st earl of
Nureyev; photographs. Life 57:92-102+ N 27 '64

SNOWDROP trees. See Silver-bell trees

SNOWDROPS
Snowflake or snowdrop? D. Klaber. il Pop Gard 15:23 F '64

SNOWFLAKES. See Snow
SNOWFLAKES (flowers)
Snowflake or snowdrop? D. Klaber. il Pop Gard 15:23 F '64
SNOWMOBILES. See Motor scooters
SNOWSHOE hare hunting. See Rabbit hunting
SNOWSHOES
Snowbird camping. C. B. Colby. il Outdoor 135:102-4 Ja '65
Snowshoe league; youth activities at Fort Wainwright, Alaska. A. Roth. Recreation 57:358 S '64
SNOWSTORMS
Don't panic. C. E. Jensen. il Field & S 68:30-2+ O '63
Japan battles off a banzai of white. il Life 54:36-7 F 8 '63
Snow convoy! New York state thruway. E. D. Fales, jr. il Pop Sci 184:69-74+ F '64
Thirteen days in a blizzard. G. J. Tucker. il Outdoor Life 133:20-3+ Ja '64
SNOWSUITS. See Clothing and dress—Children
SNOWTIRES. See Tires, Automobile
SNUFF
Snuff is not to be sneezed at. A. Carthew. il N Y Times Mag p90+ Mr 8 '64
SNUFFBOXES, snuff bottles, etc.
Scottish tobacco mulls in the Hillwood collection. M. C. Ross. il Antiques 83:568-9 My '63
SNYDER, A. P.
There's a long deep trail awinding. Am For 69:20-1+ Je '63
SNYDER, Frederick, and others
Blood pressure changes during human sleep. bibliog Science 142:1313-14 D 6 '63
SNYDER, Gary
Asleep on the train; poem. Nation 196:127 F 9 '63
Four from six years: February; July; August; November; poems. Poetry 103:97-101 O '63
Homer and the dragon: U.S. poetry before and after the beats. L. Holland. por Américas 16:28-32 Ja '64
SNYDER, John Avery
Stop the brush, I want to get off. Atlan 213:119-20 My '64
Superman in market. Atlan 215:110-11 Ja '65
SNYDER, John C.
What U.S. fruit growers can learn from Europe. il Farm J 87:77 Mr '63
SNYDER, John I. Jr
Automation: threat and promise. N Y Times Mag p 16+ Mr 22 '64
Does automation require a new economy? interview, ed. by T. R. Brooks. por Duns R 83:51-2+ F '64

about

Automation: problems and potentials in education. por Pub W 183:21-2 Ap 8 '63
Big labor hunts for the hard answers. K. Wheeler. il por Life 55:73+ Jl 19 '63
SNYDER, Louis L.
Putting a country together again. Sat R 46:34-5 D 28 '63
SNYDER, R. L. See Ratcliffe, H. L. jt. auth.
SNYDER, William
Days and nights of Beebee Fenstermaker. Criticism
Commonweal 78:247 My 24 '63
SNYDER, William C.
Root diseases biologically controlled. Science 141:835-7 Ag 30 '63
SO I'm not Lady Chatterley, so better I should know it now; story. See Sara, pseud.
SO long at the fair; drama. See Miller, H. L.
SO many voices; story. See Schweitzer, G.
SO much in common; story. See Pratt, H.
SOANE museum. See London—Galleries and museums
SOAP
See also
Cleaning compositions
SOAP industry and trade
Soap wars: a strategic analysis. S. Klaw. il Fortune 67:122-5+ Je '63
SOAP modeling. See Soap sculpture
SOAP operas. See Television broadcasting—Drama
SOAP sculpture
Have you tried carving soap? il Sunset 133:94 D '64
SOAPSTONE carvings, Eskimo. See Eskimos—Art
SOBERMAN, Robert K.
Noctilucent clouds; with biographical sketch. Sci Am 208:28, 50-9 bibliog(p 183) Je '63
SOBIN, Sidney S.
Blood flow through muscle. Science 140:702 My 10 '63
SOBRINHO, Francisco Matarazzo. See Matarazzo Sobrinho, F.
SOBY, James Thrall
About the cover: Nostalgia of the infinite; excerpt from Masters of modern art. Sat R 47:63 N 14 '64
Prophet in his own country. Sat R 46:21 N 2 '63
SOCCER
Big game; Dukla soccer club vs. West Ham United at Randalls Island stadium. New Yorker 39:16-18 Ag 24 '63
Color of the cup final; with photographs by Gerry Cranham. Sports Illus 20:48-52 Ap 27 '64
Cox's new kick. il Time 82:42 Ag 23 '63
Crashing of mountains; clash between Peru and Argentina. il Time 83:36 Je 5 '64
Global madness of soccer. B. Glanville. il Holiday 35:116+ Mr '64
Goal! World club soccer championship in Rio. il Time 82:37 N 29 '63
Happy afternoon at Wembley. Sports Illus 19:10+ N 4 '63
In the nonecumenical spirit; Catholic Celtics and Protestant Rangers. Sports Illus 18:14 My 27 '63
Pay-lay! il Time 81:55 Ap 12 '63
Six dreary days, then Saturday; the story of British football. J. Olsen. il Sports Illus 21:74-6+ O 12 '64
Sporting spirit; riot in Beirut. J. A. Morris, jr. Newsweek 65:36-7 Ja 11 '65
World's highest-paid athlete. il Ebony 18:62 4+ F '63
SOCCER fans. See Sports fans
SOCCER pools. See Gambling—Great Britain
SOCHOR, Eugene
Unesco in the decade of development. Sch & Soc 91:278-80 O 5 '63
SOCHUREK, Howard
American special forces in action in Viet Nam. il Nat Geog Mag 127:38-65 Ja '65
Crisis in photojournalism. Pop Phot 52:57+ Ap '63
Slow train through Viet Nam's war. il Nat Geog Mag 126:412-44 S '64
SOCIAL action department. See National catholic welfare conference
SOCIAL adjustment. See Adjustment, Social
SOCIAL agencies
Management of voluntary welfare agencies. E. Lippincott and E. Aannestad. Harvard Bsns R 42:87-98 N '64
SOCIAL agencies, Voluntary
Brightening old age in Houston; Sheltering arms program. H. Whitman. il Todays Health 41:52-3+ S '63
SOCIAL and economic security
Abundance, threat or promise? R. Theobald. Nation 196:387-412 My 11 '63; Discussion. 196:inside cover Je 15 '63
Again the issue of the welfare state. A. Hacker. il N Y Times Mag p9+ Mr 22 '64
Automation: road to lifetime jobs? A. H. Raskin. Sat R 47:14-16+ N 28 '64; Reply. P. E. Zwintscher. 47:21 D 26 '64
Bread without sweat; Ad hoc committee on the triple revolution. Christian Cent 81:451-2 Ap 8 '64
Building a great world society; address, June 10, 1964. L. B. Johnson. Dept State Bul 50:990-2 Je 29 '64; Excerpts. Sci N L 86:7 Jl 4 '64
Free men and free markets, by R. Theobald. Review
Sat R 46:57-8+ S 28 '63. K. Schriftgiesser; Reply. R. Theobald. 46:27 N 16 '63
Guaranteeing an income; new constitutional right for the developing post-industrial age. R. Theobald. il Commonweal 80:603-6 S 4 '64
How much more of a welfare state for U.S? il U S News 56:62-3 Ja 6 '64
If the machine wants our jobs, let's buy it. Life 57:4 Ag 14 '64
Is the welfare state obsolete? I. Kristol. Harper 226:39-43 Je '63; Same abr. with title Why the welfare state doesn't work. Read Digest 83:86-90 N '63; Discussion. Harper 227:6+ S '63
Pursuit of security; address, December 21, 1963. G. J. Lynch. Vital Speeches 30:504-6 Je 1 '64
Triple revolution. G. W. Johnson. New Repub 150:38-9 Ap 11 '64
Triple revolution. J. Riha. America 112:162-4 Ja 30 '65
Triple revolution; concerning report of the Ad hoc committee on the triple revolution. J. O'Gara. Commonweal 80:78 Ap 10 '64

SOCIAL and economic security—*Continued*
Unions' latest goal: lifetime jobs. il U S News 58:88+ Je 25 '65
We're moving deeper into welfare state; interview. V. Bush. Nations Bsns 51:36-7+ Mr '63
Worker security in a changing economy; symposium. bibliog f il Mo Labor R 86: 612-702 Je '63
See also
Inter-American conference on social security
Pensions, Industrial

New Zealand

Welfare state in New Zealand. D. P. O'Neill. America 110:286-8 F 29 '64

Sweden

When you abolish poverty; here's what life is like; welfare state. il U S News 56: 61-4 Mr 16 '64

SOCIAL aspects of science. See Science—Social aspects

SOCIAL attitudes. See Attitudes; Moral attitudes

SOCIAL behavior. See Manners and customs

SOCIAL change
Continuities in cultural evolution, by M. Mead. Review
Bul Atomic Sci 20:25-6 D '64. J. R. Platt
Culture by computer: Margaret Mead's ideas. il Sci Digest 53:51 My '63
Culture change and the planner. A. N. B. Garvan. Ann Am Acad 352:33-8 Mr '64
Diagnosing the American dream. M. W. Fishwick. il Sat R 46:8-11 D 21 '63
Era of radical change. M. Ways. il Fortune 69:112-15+ My '64
Evolution, organic and superorganic. T. Dobzhansky. Bul Atomic Sci 20:4-8 My '64; Reply. C. Hartshorne. 20:38 O '64
Foreign policy and the individual: identity in diversity; address, March 12, 1964. K. Louchheim. Dept State Bul 50:591-4 Ap 13 '64
Free men and fee markets, by R. Theobald. Review
Commentary 36:331-3 O '63. R. L. Heilbroner
Is this progress? photographs collected by Max Brandel. Horizon 6:106-7 Sum '64
July 1914—July 1964. W. H. McNeill. For Affairs 42:559-68 Jl '64
Literacy and learning in Asia. H. H. Smythe and N. Sasidhorn. il Sch & Soc 91:371-3 N 30 '63
Nation and world face sweeping changes; study of Technical military planning operation. il Nations Bsns 52:23-5+ Ja '64
One-dimensional man, by H. Marcuse. Review
Newsweek 63:80 Ja 27 '64
Planned cultural transition. M. Mead. Sci N L 83:143 Mr 2 '63
Science and the new humanism; excerpts from address. H. Hoagland. bibliog Science 143:111-14 Ja 10 '64; Discussion. 143:1121-3; 144:1293 Mr 13, Je 12 '64
Social change and medical organization in the United States; a sociological perspective. T. Parsons. bibliog f Ann Am Acad 346:21-33 Mr '63
Society seeks change. Sci N L 86:166 S 12 '64
Some recent trends in stratification theory and research. R. J. Murphy. bibliog f Ann Am Acad 356:142-67 N '64
Take a lesson from the dinosaur. B. Chisholm. il Parents Mag 39:55+ Ap '64
Uneven road to equality. W. Johnson. Sat R 47:53+ My 9 '64
Urban leadership during change. G. M. Kammerer and J. M. DeGrove. bibliog f Ann Am Acad 353:95-106 My '64
We may be rich but they are happy; transforming of prescientific communities. B. Ward. il N Y Times Mag p22-3+ My 5 '63
When thoughts are unthinkable. B. Dunham. il Nation 198:411-13 Ap 27 '64
See also
Acculturation
Social mobility
Social progress
Social revolution

SOCIAL classes
Some recent trends in stratification theory and research. R. J. Murphy. bibliog f Ann Am Acad 356:142-67 N '64
See also
Class distinction

SOCIAL commission of the United Nations. See United Nations—Social commission

SOCIAL conditions
U.S. foreign policy: problems and challenges for 1963; address, January 11, 1963. R. J. Manning. Dept State Bul 48:138-44 Ja 28 '63
World social situation; summary of introduction to United Nations Report on the social situation. U N Rev 10:27-8 Ap '63
See also
Civilization
Poverty
also subhead Social conditions under names of countries, states, cities, e.g. United States—Social conditions

SOCIAL conflict
Class, color and prejudice. B. Bettelheim. Nation 197:231-4 O 19 '63

SOCIAL correspondence. See Letter writing

SOCIAL credit party
Demagogue from Quebec. il Time 81:21 Mr 29 '63

SOCIAL development. See Social progress

SOCIAL diseases. See Venereal diseases

SOCIAL drinking. See Liquor problem

SOCIAL education
Take a lesson from the dinosaur. B. Chisholm. il Parents Mag 39:55+ Ap '64
See also
Citizenship, Education for
Family life, Education for
Sex instruction
Social sciences—Study and teaching

SOCIAL equality. See Equality

SOCIAL ethics
Are we post-Christian? America 108:394, 526 Mr 23, Ap 20 '63; Reply. R. F. Charles. 108:625-6 My 4 '63
Christian social ethics. E. J. Carnell. Christian Cent 80:979-80 Ag 7 '63; Reply. M. L. Stackhouse. 80:1219 O 2 '63
Psychology can't substitute for morality. B. Spock. Redbook 122:22+ Ja '64
Radiation and social ethics; conference of nuclear scientists and theologians, University of Chicago. W. A. Wallace. America 108:880-3 Je 22 '63
See also
Christian ethics
Church and race problems
Sexual ethics

SOCIAL evolution. See Social change

SOCIAL groups. See Groups (sociology)

SOCIAL history
Anarchists; excerpts. B. W. Tuchman. il Atlan 211:91-2+ My '63
See also subhead Social history under names of countries, states, etc. e.g. United States—Social history

SOCIAL insurance. See Insurance, Social

SOCIAL interaction
Group learning of speech sequences without awareness. D. Shapiro. bibliog il Science 144:74-6 Ap 3 '64
Myocardial infarction: a response to social interaction among chickens. H. L. Ratcliffe and R. L. Snyder. bibliog il Science 144:424-5 Ap 24 '64
Social stimulus to creativity; letter. E. G. Boring. Science 142:622-3 N 8 '63; Reply. S. Winokur. 143:526 F 7 '64

SOCIAL isolation. See Isolation, Social

SOCIAL justice
Social justice in the United States and in the hemisphere; address, November 4, 1964. T. C. Mann. Dept State Bul 51:775-8 N 30 '64
See also
Social ethics

SOCIAL legislation
See also
Unemployment—Relief measures

Canada

Bonus for babies. I. Sclanders. Nation 198: 167-8 F 17 '64

United States

Economic base and limits of social welfare. G. Colm. il Mo Labor R 86:695-700 Je '63
False faces for freedom. H. Seifert. Christian Cent 81:1265-7 O 14 '64
Federal legislation and programs for underprivileged young people; ed. by J. Lowrie. ALA Bul 58:705-11 S '64
Fresh funds for welfare; new congressional programs. Bsns W p31 O 12 '63
Uncle Sam is really needed; federal role in local affairs is necessary. M. D. Reagan. il N Y Times Mag p31+ S 13 '64
Welfare mess. L. Chevalier. il Sat Eve Post 236:15-19 My 11 '63
See also
Old age pensions—United States

SOCIAL life and customs
See also subhead Social life and customs under names of countries, states, cities, etc. e.g. United States—Social life and customs

SOCIAL mobility
Education and upward mobility. Sch & Soc 91:322 O 19 '63

SOCIAL news. See Newspapers—Society page

SOCIAL order (periodical)
Social order dies. America 110:32 Ja 11 '64

SOCIAL policy
See also
United States—Social policy

SOCIAL problems
Abandoned child. A. Henley. il McCalls 91:126-7+ My '64
American agenda; adaptation of address. J. W. Fulbright. Sat R 46:15-17+ Jl 20 '63; Reply. G. P. Kuiper. 46:13 Ag 17 '63
Research and development for social problems. J. R. Platt. Bul Atomic Sci 20:27-9 Je '64
See also
Church and social problems
Crime and criminals
Divorce
Family
Homosexuality
Juvenile delinquency
Libraries and social and economic problems
Marriage
Narcotic habit
Poor
Prostitution
Public health
Race discrimination
Race problems
School and social and economic problems
Slums
Sociology, Christian
Suicide
Unemployables
War
Woman—Social and moral questions

SOCIAL problems and art. See Art and society

SOCIAL problems in literature
Paperback pedagogy. V. Clear. Sat R 47:73 F 15 '64

SOCIAL progress
America and the world revolution; symposium, ed. by N. Podhoretz. Commentary 36:278-96 O '63; Discussion. 37:17-18 F '64
Good society; excerpts from address. N. Glazer. Commentary 36:226-31+ S '63; Discussion. 36:430 D '63
International aspects of development; address, April 5, 1963. Thant. il U N Rev 10:12-14 Ap '63
Social justice in the United States and in the hemisphere; address, November 4, 1964. T. C. Mann. Dept State Bul 51:775-8 N 30 '64
Tomorrow is here! Changing T 18:7-11 Jl '64
World of the future. N. N. Semenov. il(cover) Bul Atomic Sci 20:10-15 F '64
See also
Social change

SOCIAL psychology
Anthropological perspectives on medicine and public health. B. D. Paul. bibliog f Ann Am Acad 346:34-43 Mr '63
Is it time for the second step? remaining tasks in the search for peace. J. F. Wharton. Sat R 46:8-11+ Ag 17 '63
Problems of collaboration between social scientists and the practicing professions. L. S. Cottrell, jr. and E. B. Sheldon. Ann Am Acad 346:126-37 Mr '63
Reasonable adventurer, by R. Heath. Review Sat R 47:65-6 Ag 15 '64. D. Yount
Social standing; new science of proxemics. Newsweek 61:84 Ap 22 '63
What are people really like? il Changing T 18:31-3 Jl '64
See also
Adjustment, Social
Attitudes
Crowds
Groups (sociology)
Hate
Human relations
Leadership
Psychiatric social work
Social conflict
Stereotype (psychology)

SOCIAL research
Lost opportunities. D. Wolfle. Science 143:999 Mr 6 '64; Discussion. 144:951-2, bibliog 1407; 145:8, 343 My 22, Je 19, Jl 3, 24 '64
Research and development for social problems. J. R. Platt. Bul Atomic Sci 20:27-9 Je '64
Study of aspirations. H. Cantril. il Sci Am 208:41-5 bibliog(p 184) F '63

SOCIAL responsibility. See Responsibility

SOCIAL revolution
To salvage or to save; reflections on America's most pressing revolutions; address, May 9, 1963. J. Benitez. Vital Speeches 29:535-7 Je 15 '63

SOCIAL satire. See Satire

SOCIAL science research
Information retrieval in the social sciences. D. J. Foskett. bibliog il Wilson Lib Bul 38:755-62 My '64

SOCIAL science research council
See also
Joint committee on contemporary China of the American council of learned societies and the Social science research council

SOCIAL sciences
International relations and the psychologist: the scientific gulf. E. B. McNeil. Bul Atomic Sci 19:33-5 N '63
Mathematics in the social sciences. R. Stone. il Sci Am 211:168-72+ bibliog(p270+) S '64
Snow affair. M. S. Simpson. Bul Atomic Sci 19:28-32 Ap '63
Social sciences and society; excerpts. P. H. Odegard. Science 145:1127 S 11 '64
What's happening in social studies; summaries of periodical articles and reports, ed. by H. L. Hurwitz. Sr Schol 83:15T O 11; 10T N 1; 13T D 6 '63; 84:7T Ja 31; 7T F 28; 13T Ap 10; 85:8T O 14; 21T D 9 '64
See also
Behavioral sciences
Economics

Bibliography

New paperbacks in the social sciences. H. L. Hurwitz. Sr Schol 85:20T-22T D 2 '64
Paperbacks in the social sciences. V. J. Barone. Sr Schol 83:30T Ja 17 '64

Research

See Social science research

Study and teaching

Anecdote of the young lieutenant. L. H. Pollak. il PTA Mag 58:10-12 Ap '64
Comments on Rafferty; letters to editor. Sr Schol 83:4T O 25 '63
Gaining new vision for social studies; overhead projectors and transparencies. R. A. Withey. il Sr Schol 85:18T Ja 21 '65
How we rewrote our social studies curriculum; Leonia, N.J. public schools. K. J. Dunn. Sr Schol 85:8T-9T S 16 '64
It's never too early to learn the economic facts of life. J. K. Lagemann. il PTA Mag 59:4-7 N '64; Same abr. with title How children can learn the economic facts of life. Read Digest 85:65-9 D '64
Mass communication and the social sciences. C. S. Steinberg. Sch & Soc 92:105-6 Mr 7 '64
More social studies; concerning survey by Cooperative test division of ETS. il Sr Schol 84:2T-3T Ap 10 '64
New approach to citizenship. F. M. Hechinger. Parents Mag 38:49+ My '63
New approach to social studies. L. S. Kenworthy. il NEA J 52:44-5 Mr '63
New orbits in social studies; with study discussion program, ed. by D. Harris and E. Harris. J. Jarolimek. bibliog il PTA Mag 59:24-6, 36 O '64
Project social studies, a report; curriculum study centers at institutions of higher education. G. R. Smith. Sch Life 45:25-7 Jl '63
Roads make history. B. Zimo. il Sch Arts 63:18-20 Mr '64
St Paul's social studies institute. J. Engh. il Sr Schol 85:10T-11T Ja 14 '65
Scientists in the classroom; excerpts from Where, when, and why. M. Mayer. Commentary 35:312-19 Ap '63; Reply with rejoinder. R. Hymas. 36:195-6 S '63
Social sciences in non-western studies. M. Singer. bibliog f Ann Am Acad 356:30-44 N '64
Social sciences in two-year colleges. S. L. Guterman. Sch & Soc 91:200 Ap 20 '63
Social studies. W. Hill. Sch Life 45:19-20 Jl '63
Social studies curriculum: proposals for the future; report on the 1963 Cubberley conference, Standford university. R. E. Gross. Sr Schol 83:8T-9T O 25 '63
Social studies revision; New York city public school system. Sr Schol 85:2T+ O 21 '64
Some recent developments in socialization theory and research. W. H. Sewell. bibliog f Ann Am Acad 349:163-81 S '63
Stop playing blindman's buff. R. E. Gross and D. W. Allen. il Sr Schol 83:9T-12T O 11 '63

SOCIAL sciences—Study and teaching—*Cont.*
Survey of social studies teaching. Sch & Soc 92:302+ O 31 '64
Teacher and world affairs. B. B. Fall. NEA J 53:38 My '64
What's happening in education? California's recommendations for social studies. W. D. Boutwell. PTA Mag 57:14 Mr '63
Where, when and why: social studies in American schools, by M. Mayer. Review
Reporter 29:52+ Jl 18 '63. F. M. Hechinger
Sat R 46:79 Je 15 '63. I. J. Sloan
See also
National council for the social studies
Socially handicapped children—Education

Textbooks

Social science: a textbook for Soviet secondary schools, by G. K. Shakhnazarov and others. Review
Sr Schol 85:9T+ N 18 '64. H. Hurwitz

SOCIAL scientists
Social scientists featured as NLW workshop speakers. Library J 88:3568+ O 1 '63
Social scientists in the plant. L. L. Ferguson. il Harvard Bsns R 42:133-43 My '64

SOCIAL security. See Insurance, Social; Social and economic security

SOCIAL security act, 1935
See also
Old age, survivors' and disability insurance trust fund

SOCIAL security act amendments
Back of the questions about social security; with interview with R. M. Ball. il U S News 57:54-8+ D 7 '64
Clergymen have second chance for social security. Christian Cent 81:1422 N 18 '64
Drive for broader social security. il Bsns W p28+ Ja 9 '65
False promise of Medicare. R. Cubbedge. Read Digest 84:137-41 Ap '64
For Medicare: a new plan and a new outlook. U S News 57:77 Ag 31 '64
Forty-nine to forty-four for medicare; Senate vote. il Newsweek 64:22-3 S 14 '64
Great deception. R. Moley. Newsweek 64:128 O 5 '64
Health care for the aged: here are the two plans. il U S News 56:46-8 F 24 '64
How medicare was lost this year. M. Viorst. New Repub 151:6-7 O 17 '64
Income with freedom. R. Moley. Newsweek 64:116 S 21 '64
Is this the year for Medicare? P. Duke and S. Meisler. il Reporter 30:23-6 Ap 23 '64
Just for the record; Senate approves social security-financed medicare plan for the aged. Time 84:22-3 S 11 '64
Medical care and pensions: what the Senate voted. il U S News 57:8 S 14 '64
Medicare. Commonweal 80:624 S 18 '64
Medicare comes back; administration's medicare program vs Chmn. Mills of Ways & means. Bsns W p25 Je 8 '63
Medicaricature. Nat R 16:803-4 S 22 '64
New pension plan: who would get what. U S News 57:8-11 Jl 13 '64
New plan: raise pensions, taxes. il U S News 58:78 Ja 11 '65
New plans to take care of the old folks. il U S News 56:85-6 Je 1 '64
New U.S. health-care plan in brief. U S News 57:43 S 21 '64
Odds on aged health care. America 110:500 Ap 11 '64
Personal business; social security benefits. Bsns W p 109 Jl 18 '64
Price tag for old people's share of the Great society. il U S News 58:92-3 Ja 25 '65
Setbacks for LBJ; congressional action. Newsweek 64:29+ S 28 '64
Social security argument; issue in presidential campaign. il Time 84:25 O 23 '64
This month's feature: proposals to expand medicare for aged. Cong Digest 42:193-224 Ag '63
When surplus isn't all roses. il Bsns W p 150+ N 14 '64
Who pays for the care of the aged? controversy over government vs. private health insurance. Bsns W p68-9 N 23 '63
Who will be helped by medicare. il U S News 57:52-5 D 14 '64

SOCIAL security benefits. See Insurance, Social—United States; Old age pensions—United States

SOCIAL security conference, Inter-American. See Inter-American conference on social security

SOCIAL security numbering system. See Numbering systems

SOCIAL segregation. See Segregation, Social

SOCIAL service. See Social work

SOCIAL snobs. See Snobs and snobbishness

SOCIAL status
Keeping the poor in their place. A. Walinsky. New Repub 151:14-18 Jl 4 '64; Reply. R. Theobald. 151:36 Ag 8 '64
Society seeks change. Sci N L 86:166 S 12 '64
Status seekers, junior grade. M. A. Guitar. il N Y Times Mag p47-8 Ag 16 '64
See also
Middle classes
Social mobility

SOCIAL studies. See Social sciences

SOCIAL surveys
What makes a good community survey. M. F. Krughoff. Recreation 56:221-2, 264-6 My-Je '63

SOCIAL usage. See Etiquette

SOCIAL welfare
Grim state of welfare. J. Horwitz. il Look 27:72+ Mr 26 '63
Social-welfare planning. E. Wood. Ann Am Acad 352:119-28 Mr '64
Utopia in the sixties. D. J. Clark. il Cath World 196:357-63 Mr '63
Welfare society. America 111:249-50 S 12 '64
World we want. C. Anderson. il Ladies Home J 80:49 Ja; 57+ Mr; 53+ My '63

SOCIAL work
Little way; how to apply St Thérèse's method to social-action problems. E. Flexner. America 112:77-8 Ja 16 '65
Wasted Americans, by E. May. Review
Commonweal 80:522-3 Jl 24 '64. N. Hentoff
See also
Photography in social work

Work in schools

See School social work

SOCIAL work, Psychiatric. See Psychiatric social work

SOCIAL workers
Blind leader of the sighted; VA clinical social worker. il Ebony 19:60-2+ Mr '64
Social workers and the Progressive party, 1912-1916. A. F. Davis. bibliog f Am Hist R 69:671-88 Ap '64
Strike in a welfare state; workers in New York city's Welfare department. il Time 85:20-1 Ja 22 '65

SOCIALISM
Irving Howe, the socialist imagination. T. Solotaroff. Commentary 37:61-4 Je '64
Socialism re-examined, by N. Thomas. Review
Sat R 47:35+ F 1 '64. H. Swados
See also
Communism
Technocracy

Africa

This strange thing called African socialism. K. Kyle. il Reporter 28:27-9 Je 6 '63

Egypt

Nasser's brand of socialism. G. Gersh. Christian Cent 81:962-5 Jl 29 '64

Europe, Western

As Europe turns left. il U S News 54:62-4 Ap 29 '63
Socialists on the move. New Repub 149:12 O 5 '63

France

See also
Socialist party (France)

Great Britain

Lord Home got the job; But he won't keep it long. A. Waugh. Nat R 15:439 N 19 '63
Return of the Socialists: shaky course for Britain. il U S News 57:65-7 O 26 '64
Wilson defines British socialism. H. Wilson il N Y Times Mag p32+ S 15 '63
See also
Fabian society
Labor party (Great Britain)

United States

Socialism re-examined, by N. Thomas. Review
Newsweek 62:113+ N 18 '63
Why you oppose aid to education (the inside story) Nat R 14:349 My 7 '63

SOCIALISM, Christian
Stewart Headlam and the Christian Socialists. W. S. Smith. Christian Cent 80:201-4 F 13 '63

SOCIALIST parties

Europe, Western

European Socialists in evolution. E. v. Kuehnelt-Leddihn. Nat R 16:602 Jl 14 '64

SOCIALIST party (France)
Horizon 1980. Newsweek 63:51 F 17 '64
Rumblings on the left. E. Taylor. Reporter 30:15-19 Ja 2 '64

SOCIALIST party (Germany [Federal Republic])
Socialist without an issue. Time 83:30 My 8 '64
Socialists gaining. Time 84:34+ D 4 '64

SOCIALIST party (United States)
Socialist convention; lambs with a dream. J. Martin. Nation 198:595-7 Je 15 '64

SOCIALIZED medicine. See Medical service, State

SOCIALLY handicapped children
Deprived child. S. H. Wheeler. Wilson Lib Bul 39:342 D '64
I'm poor, and it hurts! questions and answers. A. Wood. il Seventeen 22:108-9 D '63
Our summer house guests. J. M. Jacobus. il Redbook 123:6+ Jl '64
Providing school library services for the culturally disadvantaged; ed. by J. Lowrie. bibliog il ALA Bul 58:523-6, 643-7, 705-11, 816-21, 1003-6; 59:49-53 Je-O, D '64-Ja '65
War on poverty; symposium, ed. with introd. by H. T. Drennan. il Library J 89: 3239-74+ S 15 '64. Discussion. 89:3274, 3354, 4674+ S 15, D 1 '64

Bibliography

Culturally disadvantaged child. R. F. Berneis. ALA Bul 59:53-7 Ja '65

Education

A for effort, and for new hope; Higher horizons program. il Bsns W p44-5 F 1 '64
Big break for poverty's children; New York city's program of educating preschool children; with account by P. Blake. il Life 56: 78B-89 Ap 3 '64
Big brothers to troubled children; Whittier school, Washington, D.C. C. M. Bloomberg and C. H. Troupe. il NEA J 53:22-5 Ja '64
Big-city schools, problems and prospects: help for children without. J. E. Stratten. il PTA Mag 59:16-18+ Ja '65
Culturally deprived child: a new view; excerpt from address. F. Reissman. Sch Life 45:5-7 Ap '63
Disadvantaged; symposium. il NEA J 52:16-30 Ap '63
Exclusive Thanksgiving convention reports. il Sr Schol 85:1T+ D 9 '64
Give slum children a chance; a radical proposal; excerpts from Crisis in black and white. C. E. Silberman. Harper 228:37-42 My '64; Discussion. 229:6 Jl '64
Helping our culturally impoverished children. L. W. Utter. NEA J 52:28-30 N '63
Let's stop mass-producing unemployables! L. Velie. Read Digest 85:59-63 Jl '64
Not like other children; slum children. B. Asbell. il Redbook 121:64-5+ O '63
Pilot lights: educating the underprivileged. New Repub 150:5-6 Ja 18 '64; Reply. J. den Boer. 150:30 F 22 '64
Poverty; target for education; address, February 15, 1964. F. Keppel. Vital Speeches 30: 510-12 Je 1 '64
Preparing the city child for his school. G. C. Fusco. bibliog f il Sch Life 46:5-8 My '64
School library services for the culturally deprived child. R. L. Darling. bibliog f il Sch Life 46:18-20 O '63
Schools, slums & Montessori. M. Mayer. Commentary 37:33-9 Je '64; Discussion. 38: 20+ N '64
Special issue: teaching the culturally deprived; symposium. il Sr Schol 84:5T-6T+ Ap 24 '64
Stars, smiles, and the hidden curriculum. M. Fantini and G. Weinstein. Sr Schol 85:14T S 30 '64
Teachers of the poor. F. Riessman and A. Hannah. il PTA Mag 59:12-14 N '64
Teaching the culturally deprived. F. Riessman. NEA J 52:20-2 Ap '63
Where an orange is a textbook. il Time 84:73 N 27 '64
Who would teach here. M. B. Smiley. il PTA Mag 58:16-19 S '63
Working with disadvantaged parents; Special project; District eleven, Chicago. L. G. Daugherty. NEA J 52:18-20 D '63
Your stake in better schools for all; with group discussion program, ed. by E. J. LeShan. H. Littledale. il Parents Mag 39:46, 57-9+ S '64

SOCIETIES
For inter-American understanding; Pan American societies in the United States. G. Meek. il Américas 15:27-34 Ag '63
Life guide; clubs for all sorts of joiners. il Life 54:15 F 8 '63
See also
Womens clubs and societies

SOCIETY. See Upper classes; *also* subhead Social life and customs under names of countries, states, cities, e.g. Washington, D.C.—Social life and customs

SOCIETY, Primitive
Does life end at sixty? A. Métraux. il UNESCO Courier 16:20-3 Ap '63
See also
Cannibalism
Nomads
Tribes and tribal system

SOCIETY and art. See Art and society

SOCIETY and law. See Jurisprudence

SOCIETY and literature. See Literature and society

SOCIETY and the individual. See Individual and society

SOCIETY for education in film and television.
Bang, bang, you're dead. A. W. Hodgkinson. New Repub 150:28+ Ap 25 '64

SOCIETY for indecency to naked animals
Bum steer. il Time 81:82 Mr 15 '63
Hart Schaffner & barks. Newsweek 61:36 Mr 18, 63

SOCIETY for social responsibility in science
Extension of concern. P. P. Moulton. Christian Cent 81:1022 Ag 12 '64

SOCIETY for the advancement of education
Bagley, Kandel, and the SAE. W. W. Brickman. Sch & Soc 92:258 O 3 '64
Quarter-century of the Society for the advancement of education. T. A. Distler. Sch & Soc 92:261 O 3 '64

SOCIETY ISLANDS
See also
Bora Bora
Raiatea

SOCIETY news reporting. See Reporters and reporting

SOCIETY of automotive engineers
SAE aerospace gathering covers broad spectrum. Miss & Roc 13:27+ S 30 '63

SOCIETY of brothers
Something long forgotten; Christian community. Christian Cent 81:1159 S 16 '64

SOCIETY of Friends. See Friends, Society of

SOCIETY of illustrators
Illustrators '63. il Am Artist 27:36-42+ O '63
Illustrators '63; moods and movements in book illustration. il Pub W 183:92-4 Je 3 '63

SOCIETY of Jesus. See Jesuits

SOCIETY of magazine writers
High cost of writing; Stern and Beinecke funds. J. F. Fixx. Sat R 47:53+ Je 13 '64

SOCIETY of motion picture and television engineers
Special report from S.M.P.T.E.'s Los Angeles convention. J. D. Scouller. il Pop Phot 55: 92+ Ag '64

SOCIETY of photographic instrumentation engineers. See Society of photo-optic instrumentation engineers

SOCIETY of photo-optic instrumentation engineers
BSD chief sees present photometric techniques at limit of development. C. D. LaFond. Miss & Roc 15:13 Ag 31 '64

SOCIETY of the Sacred Heart
Jubilation; memoir of a Sacred Heart education, tr. by F. Frenaye. C. de Rivoyre. Vogue 144:238-9+ D '64

SOCIETY page. See Newspapers—Society page

SOCIOLOGICAL analysis (periodical)
Sociological mainstream. America 111:246 S 12 '64

SOCIOLOGY
Beyond the ruling class, by S. Keller. Review
Commonweal 80:182-3 My 1 '64. R. M. Barry
New sociology, ed. by I. L. Horowitz. Review
Commonweal 80:643-5 S 18 '64. R. M. Barry
Protestantism in American sociology. R. L. Means. Christian Cent 81:1554-6 D 16 '64
Some recent trends in stratification theory and research. R. J. Murphy. bibliog f Ann Am Acad 356:142-67 N '64
What we don't know. America 110:273 F 29 '64
See also
Culture
Individualism
Leisure
Religion and sociology
Social psychology

SOCIOLOGY, Christian
Catholic social thought. J. O'Gara. Commonweal 79:684 Mr 6 '64; Reply. J. W. Phelps. 80:149-50 Ap 24 '64
Pope John's essay in inequality; Mater et magistra. B. L. Masse. America 108:368-71 Mr 16 '63
Problem of the Christian social sentimentalist. E. v. Kuehnelt-Leddihn. Nat R 16:403-4 My 19 '64
Religion of life insurance. A. Welsh. Christian Cent 80:1541-3, 1574-6 D 11-18 '63; Discussion. 81:118-19, 239-40 Ja 22, F 19 '64
Social change and Protestanism. K. Underwood. Commonweal 78:420-2 Jl 12 '63
See also
Christianity and economics
Religion and sociology

SOCIOLOGY, Industrial
Don Eugenio shows the way. G. W. Hill. Read Digest 82:245-6+ Je '63

SOCIOLOGY, Religious. See Religion and sociology

SOCIOLOGY, Rural
See also
Village life

SOCIOLOGY, Urban
City horizons; arresting of urban deterioration. Commonweal 81:501 Ja 15 '65
Sick cities, by M. Gordon. Review
Am Heritage 14:109-11 O '63. B. Catton
See also
Cities and towns
Urban renewal

SOCIOLOGY and science. See Science—Social aspects

SOCKS for athletes. See Clothing and dress—Sports clothes

SOCONY Mobil oil company
Socony trying insurance field. Bsns W p70 Mr 23 '63

SOCRATES
They made our world. L. Rosten. il por Look 27:65-7 Je 18 '63

SOD roofs. See Roofs

SODA bottles. See Bottles

SODALITIES
People of God; Boston sodality for priests and laymen. E. S. Stanton. America 110: 420-2 Mr 28 '64
What are sodalities? America 109:414 O 12 '63

SODIUM
Potassium vs. sodium; new heart disease treatment. Sci N L 86:309 N 14 '64

SODIUM bicarbonate
Sodium bicarbonate: increase in survival rate of rats inhaling oxygen. R. S. Matteo and G. G. Nahas. bibliog il Science 141:719-20 Ag 23 '63

SODIUM chloride. See Salt

SODIUM compounds
Paradoxical phase of sleep: its artificial induction in the cat by sodium butyrate. M. Matsuzaki and others. bibliog il Science 146:1328-9 D 4 '64
Sodium perxenate hexahydrate. A. Zalkin and others. bibliog il Science 142:501-2 O 25 '63

SODIUM in the body
Heart action potential: dependence on external calcium and sodium ions. R. K. Orkand and R. Niedergerke. bibliog il Science 146:1176-7 N 27 '64
Potassium and sodium content of tissues of hamsters and ground squirrels during hibernation. J. S. Willis. bibliog il Science 146:546-7 O 23 '64

SODOM, Israel
Progress in Sodom; economic boom. il Time 81:77 Mr 1 '63

SODOM and Gomorrah
Sins of Sodom. Time 82:54 S 6 '63

SOEDERLUND, Peter
Letters from Denmark. il Horizon 5:120 Jl '63

SOEKARNO. See Sukarno

SOFAS
Selecting a sofa bed. il Bet Hom & Gard 42: 22 Ja '64
Ugly duckling has become a swan; sofa beds. il House B 105:216-21 N '63
See also
Chaise longues
Day beds

SOFIA, Bulgaria
Letter from Sofia. G. LeCompte. Nation 197: 304-5 N 9 '63

Music

Competition in Bulgaria; International young operatic singers competition, Sofia. K. Adler. il Opera N 28:6-7 O 19 '63

SOFT drinks. See Beverages

SOFTBALL
Man with a golden arm; E. Feigner. il Time 82:41 Ag 23 '63
Snowshoe league; youth activities at Fort Wainwright, Alaska. A. Roth. Recreation 57:358 S '64
Twins; operatic Mets play softball. il Sports Illus 18:13 My 27 '63

SOFTENING of Mr Reub Simmons; story. See Crabb, A. L.

SOFTENING of water. See Water softening

SOFTENON. See Thalidomide

SOFTLY; story. See Rama Rau, S.

SOFTWOOD lumber. See Lumber

SOGETRAM school for training frogmen. See Diving. Submarine—Study and training

SOGNNAES, Reidar F.
Tooth destruction; report of symposium, AAAS section on dentistry. Science 139: 849-51 Mr 1 '63

SOHIO. See Standard oil company of Ohio

SOHN, David
Paperbacks in classroom; excerpts from Paperbacks in the schools. Sr Schol 83:23T Ja 17 '64
P.I: out of the clouds and into the classroom. Sr Schol 84:12T Mr 13 '64
—See Cook, D. A. jt. ed.
—See Leavitt, H. jt. auth.

SOHN, Louis B.
European security; interrelation of political, military, and economic factors. Bul Atomic Sci 20:16-18 D '64
Way to disarmament? New Repub 148:5-6 F 23 '63

SOHYO. See Trade unions—Japan

SOIL

Nitrogen content

Variations of nitrogen-15 abundance in soils. H. H. Cheng and others. bibliog il Science 146:1574-5 D 18 '64

SOIL acidity
Good soil mates. il Flower Grower 51:46-7 Ja '64
Lime your soil. B. Brinhart. il Horticulture 41:554-5 N '63
See also
Lime

SOIL aeration
Labeled oxygen: increased diffusion rate through soil containing growing corn roots. C. R. Jensen and D. Kirkham. bibliog il Science 141:735-6 Ag 23 '63
Most lawns need aerating. P. F. Frese. il Pop Gard 15:53 Ap '64
Soil air essential for good plant growth. B. Brinhart. il Horticulture 41:92-3 F '63

SOIL analysis. See Soils—Analysis

SOIL bank. See Agricultural administration—United States

SOIL cement pavements. See Pavements, Soil cement

SOIL conditioners
See also
Peat

SOIL conservation
California's half-million-acre greenhouse. J. N. Miller. il Read Digest 83:182-4+ Ag '63
New assignment for soil conservation districts. Farm J 87:46 Mr '63
New Garden of Eden? American farmer looks at Greece. J. Stuart. il Am For 69:14-17+ S '63; Reply. B. M. Lansdale. 70:6-7 Ja '64
New look at Penn's woods. V. C. Miles and G. V. Holmberg. il Am For 70:38-40 S '64
Rules for handling diverted acres. Suc Farm 61:123 F '63
Soil-use planning for individual and public goals. C. E. Kellogg. Bul Atomic Sci 20: 15-18 N '64
See also
Terraces (agriculture)

SOIL conservation service. See United States—Soil conservation service

SOIL deterioration
No such thing as worn-out soil. O. Bay. Farm J 87:40D Jl '63

SOIL disinfection
Toxic residues in soil nine years after treatment with aldrin and heptachlor. A. T. S. Wilkinson and others. il Science 143:681-2 F 14 '64

SOIL exhaustion. See Soil deterioration

SOIL fauna
Safari armed with microscopes; Unesco mission to the Congo. J. Balogh. il UNESCO Courier 17:24-7 O '64

SOIL fertility
Mixed fertilizers or bulk blends? G. E. Smith and L. E. Zeman. il Suc Farm 61:50-1 Ap '63
Rock and humus mingle to make the gardener's loam. il House & Gard 123:176-7+ Mr '63
See also
Green manuring
SOIL formation. See Soils
SOIL fungi. See Soil microbiology
SOIL insecticides. See Insecticides
SOIL maps. See Soil surveys
SOIL microbiology
Simazine: degradation by soil microorganisms. D. D. Kaufman and others. bibliog il Science 142:405-6 O 18 '63
SOIL moisture
Gold used to measure amount of water in soil. Sci N L 84:25 Jl 13 '63
Tips for growing crops in dry weather. Suc Farm 62:57 My '64
See also
Plants—Water requirements

Testing

Soil auger tool for testing soil moisture. J. Neurauter. il Pop Gard 14:67 Jl '63
SOIL pollution
Contamination of the environment; address, January 28, 1963. P. D. Kilburn. Vital Speeches 29:475-8 My 15 '63
Sitting on a volcano! J. B. Craig. Am For 70:11 S '64
SOIL salinity. See Soils, Salts in
SOIL surveys

United States

Recreation site finders. L. Fox. il Recreation 56:92-3 F '63
Soil surveys ease growing pains; Henrico County, Va. G. S. Smith and B. F. Eckles. il Am City 78:96-7 Ag '63
SOIL temperature
Factor of plant growth: soil temperature. B. Brinhart. il Horticulture 41:172 Mr '63
Silica source in soil solutions. R. O. Gifford and D. M. Frugoli. bibliog il Science 145: 386-8 Jl 24 '64
SOIL testing. See Soils—Analysis
SOILS
Biochemistry and soil science. A. D. McLaren. bibliog il Science 141:1141-7 S 20 '63
Crops and soils; ed. by R. D. Wennblom and G. W. Wormley. See issues of Farm journal
Soil. F. E. Bear. il Horticulture 42:30-1+ Jl '64
What's new and outlook for. See issues of Successful farming
Your own underground X-ray; soil sampling tube. il Sunset 133:66-7 Ag '64
See also
Clay
Fertilizers and manures
Forest soils
Gardening—Soil preparation
Irrigation

Analysis

Do as farmers do. B. A. Roth and L. Fox. il Pop Gard 14:22-3 My '63
Don't guess, test your soil. R. C. Hands. il Horticulture 42:8 F '64
Test your house plant soil. il Pop Gard 15: 63 F '64
Test your soil and be sure. R. C. Hands. il Horticulture 41:257 My '63
Test your soil for bigger crops. il Pop Gard 15:52-3 Mr '64
We tested our soil. H. S. Witty. il Flower Grower 51:44-5+ Mr '64

Mineral content

Are your crops hungry for micronutrients? L. E. Zeman. il Suc Farm 61:70-1+ Mr '63
Don't forget secondary elements. Suc Farm 61:96 F '63

Oxygen content

Labeled oxygen: increased diffusion rate through soil containing growing corn roots. C. R. Jensen and D. Kirkham. bibliog il Science 141:735-6 Ag 23 '63
Labeled oxygen: transport through growing corn roots. C. R. Jensen and others. il Science 144:550-2 My 1 '64

Potassium content

Corn down? find out why now. J. T. Murdock and L. E. Zeman. il Suc Farm 62:42-3+ O '64

Silica content

Silica source in soil solutions. R. O. Gifford and D. M. Frugoli. bibliog il Science 145: 386-8 Jl 24 '64

Strontium content

Strontium fixation by lime contained in soils. R. Mokady and M. Gal. bibliog il Science 145:154-5 Jl 10 '64

Temperature

See Soil temperature

Testing

See Soils—Analysis

Water content

See Soil moisture

Pennsylvania

New look at Penn's woods. V. C. Miles and G. V. Holmberg. il Am For 70:38-40 S '64

Tropics

Lateritic soils. M. McNeil. il Sci Am 211:96-102 N '64
SOILS, Alkali
Useless soil reclaimed with salt solutions; black alkali or sodic soil. Sci N L 84:31 Jl 13 '63
SOILS, Freezing of. See Frozen ground
SOILS, Liming of. See Lime
SOILS, Minerals in. See Soils—Mineral content
SOILS, Potting
New recipes for plant bed soil. L. Donelson. il Farm J 87:58F Ap '63
SOILS, Salts in
Infrared photos from air detect salt-damaged soil. Sci N L 84:98 Ag 17 '63
SOILS, Worn-out. See Soil deterioration
SOKA Gakkai (sect)
Buddha on the barricades. il Time 84:38-42+ D 11 '64
Creative Buddhism. America 110:857 Je 27 '64
Goodness, beauty & benefit; but for whom? religious society to enter the political field. il Time 83:42 My 22 '64
Japan's new religions and the Christian community. R. H. Drummond. Christian Cent 81:1521-3 D 9 '64
New faith called Soka Gakkai raises old problems in modern Japan. il Look 27:18-26 S 10 '63; Discussion. 27:13 O 22 '63
New religion disturbs Japanese politics; militant religion. Christian Cent 81:957 Jl 29 '64
SOKOLOFF, Leon
Elasticity of articular cartilage: effect of ions and viscous solutions. bibliog Science 141: 1055-7 S 13 '63
SOKOLOFF, Louis. See Weiss, W. P. jt. auth.
SOKOLOVSKII, Vasilii Danilovich
Manual of Soviet strategy. R. L. Garthoff. il Reporter 28:34+ F 14 '63
Straight from the horse's mouth; Soviet military strategy. W. D. Jacobs. il Nat R 15:68-70 Jl 30 '63
SOKOLOW, Anna
We work toward freedom; interview, ed. by W. Sorell. por Dance Mag 38:52-3+ Ja '64

about

Anna Sokolow dance company, 92nd street Y. M. Marks. il Dance Mag 38:66 Je '64
SOKOLOW, Diane
Raising two under two. Parents Mag 40:50-1+ Ja '65
SOLAL, Martial
Conversation with Martial Solal; interview, ed. by M. Williams. por Sat R 46:35-7 Jl 13 '63

about

Mister Solal. por Time 81:66+ Je 7 '63
SOLANUM tuberosum. See Potatoes
SOLAR, Lucio Garcia del. See Garcia del Solar, L.
SOLAR airlines
Third-level carrier considering Lear jet. Aviation W 81:31 D 14 '64
SOLAR atmosphere. See Sun—Atmosphere
SOLAR batteries
N-on-P solar cells gaining wider use. B. Miller. il Aviation W 78:88-9+ Mr 4 '63
New satellite design needs more solar cells. Sci N L 83:377 Je 15 '63
Run your radio on solar power; silicon solar cells. D. S. Halacy, jr. il Pop Sci 185:138-9 N '64
Solar cells continue in lead as most reliable solar energy conversion device. il Miss & Roc 14:52+ Je 1 '64
Solar clock. J. T. Rhamstine. il Pop Electr 19:56 D '63
SOLAR cells. See Solar batteries

SOLAR corona. See Sun—Corona

SOLAR eclipses. See Eclipses, Solar

SOLAR engines
Sun energizes EOS hydrogen engine. il Miss & Roc 13:35 N 18 '63

SOLAR flares
Flare and radio burst of V371 Orionis. Sky & Tel 27:86 F '64
Flares menace astronauts; Avoid lethal protons for best protection. W. Wingo. il Sci N L 85:99 F 15 '64
Lunar luminescence and solar flares. Z. Kopal and T. W. Rackham. il Sky & Tel 27:140-1 Mr '64
Physics of solar flares dissected at symposium. W. Beller. Miss & Roc 13:17 N 4 '63
Solar flare formation. Sky & Tel 27:147-8 Mr '64
Solar flare prediction progress. Aviation W 78:32 Mr 18 '63
Space condition forecasters. Time 82:48-9 Ag 2 '63
Sun flare story reported. Sci N L 84:295 N 9 '63

SOLAR furnaces
Thermal imaging techniques; report of conference at Acorn park, Cambridge, Mass. R. F. Walker. Science 140:504-5 My 3 '63

SOLAR heat collectors
Weather control: use of asphalt coatings to tap solar energy. J. F. Black. il Science 139:226-7 Ja 18 '63

SOLAR heaters
Solar heating. il Pop Sci 183:150 O '63

SOLAR heating
Solar heat without windows; poultry house. B. Hardy. il Farm J 87:71 Mr '63

SOLAR neutrinos. See Neutrinos

SOLAR photography. See Astronomical photography

SOLAR power
Thermionic flight experiment studied. M. Getler. il Miss & Roc 12:38+ Ap 29 '63
See also
Solar batteries

SOLAR probes. See Space probes

SOLAR radiation
Ionosphere used to study sun's cosmic rays. Sci N L 85:217 Ap 4 '64
Neutron and proton dosages in the upper atmosphere from solar flare radiation. E. J. Flamm and R. E. Lingenfelter. bibliog il Science 144:1566-9 Je 26 '64
Radar observations of the Corona and Mariner II measurements of the flux in the solar wind. J. C. Brandt. bibliog il Science 146:1671-2 D 25 '64
Radiation hazards in space. D. L. Dye and M. Wilkinson. bibliog il Science 147:19-25 Ja 1 '65
Radiation hazard in space from solar particles. P. Freier and W. R. Webber. bibliog il Science 142:1587-92 D 20 '63
Solar neutrons and the earth's radiation belts. R. E. Lingenfelter and E. J. Flamm. bibliog il Science 144:292-4 Ap 17 '64
Solar wind. Sky & Tel 27:287 My '64
Solar wind. E. N. Parker. il Sci Am 210:66-76 bibliog(p 156) Ap '64
Solar X-ray spectrum below 25 angstroms. R. L. Blake and others. il Science 146:1037-8 N 20 '64
Ultraviolet radiation from solar activity centers. Sky & Tel 26:83 Ag '63
See also
Van Allen radiation belts

SOLAR research. See Sun

SOLAR spectrum. See Spectrum, Solar

SOLAR system
Greatest challenge to man. B. Lovell. il N Y Times Mag p 12-13+ Ap 21 '63
Past and present theories on the origin of our solar system. S. D. Gossner. il Natur Hist 72:50-1 D '63
Recent findings about early solar system history. S. S. Huang. il Sky & Tel 28:13-15 Jl '64
Scientist in collision: was Velikovsky right? E. Larrabee. Harper 277:48-50+ Ag '63; Discussion. 227:12+ O; 83-7 D '63; 228:12 Ja '64
Why land on the moon? R. Jastrow and H. E. Newell. Atlan 212:41-5 Ag '63
See also
Planets

SOLAR telescope. See Telescope

SOLAR thermionic electric power system. See Space vehicles—Power supply

SOLDER and soldering
Many uses of solder. H. J. Entrican. Electr World 70:65 Jl '63
To solder or not to solder. L. A. Harlow. il Pop Sci 185:106 S '64
See also
Brazing

SOLDERING apparatus
Have gun, will solder. H. Luckett. il Pop Sci 182:163-5+ My '63

SOLDIERS
Draftee '63; Tony Princi of Medford, Long Island. J. Morschauser. il Look 27:21-5 Jl 30 '63
See also
Uniforms, Military

SOLDIERS, American. See United States—Army

SOLDIERS, English. See Great Britain—Army

SOLDIERS, Toy. See Toy soldiers

SOLDIERS bonuses. See Service mens bonuses

SOLDIERS letters. See Letters from service men

SOLDIERS pay. See United States—Army—Pay, allowances, etc.

SOLDIERS pets. See Mascots

SOLECKI, Ralph S.
Prehistory in Shanidar Valley, northern Iraq. bibliog Science 139:179-93 Ja 18 '63

SOLERI, Paolo
Highway sculpture: the fantastic bridges of Paolo Soleri. il Arch Forum 119:84-7 O '63
World of Paolo Soleri. por Arch Forum 118:13 Mr '63

SOLICH, Frank
Light man to do the heavy work. T. Brody. il Sports Illus 21:54-5 N 2 '64

SOLICITORS. See Lawyers

SOLID gasoline. See Gasoline, Solid

SOLID-liquid engines. See Rocket engines

SOLID propellant rockets
A. D. Little study probes solid propellant ignition. J. F. Judge. Miss & Roc 13:36 Jl 15 '63
Aerojet gambles on future of solids at Florida plant. J. Judge. il Miss & Roc 13:29-31 D 2 '63
Big-solid Saturn hopes discounted. W. E. Wilks. Miss & Roc 14:38 F 10 '64
Blue Scout jr. payload to gather frequency data above ionosphere. Aviation W 79:34 Ag 5 '63
Casual triumph; Lockheed solid-propellant booster. il Time 83:92 Je 12 '64
DOD considers further awards in 156-in. solid-rocket motor program. R. Hawkes. il Miss & Roc 15:16-17 D 21 '64
DOD proceeding with big solids. H. Taylor. Miss & Roc 13:16 Ag 26 '63
Five firms bidding in AF big solid motor program. Miss & Roc 12:15 F 25 '63
Gambling on finding a customer. il Bsns W p 128-30+ My 23 '64
Giant Florida complex will test solid fuels. il(p369) Sci N L 85:370 Je 13 '64
HITCO producing 120-in. motor nozzles. I. Stone. il Aviation W 81:66-7 Jl 20 '64
Hercules-ABL quench-tests Antares motors. il Miss & Roc 15:13 Jl 20 '64
Large solid motor bids sought. Aviation W 78:37 Ja 21 '63
Large solids feasibility awards due soon. il Aviation W 78:50-1+ F 11 '63
Lockheed refines jet tab technique. R. Hawkes. Miss & Roc 12:31 Ap 1 '63
156-in. motor firing successful. Aviation W 81:26 D 21 '64
156-in. solids adapted to multiple purposes. Aviation W 79:76 D 2 '63
120-in. boosts argument for solids. R. Lindsey. il Miss & Roc 14:27-8+ Ap 27 '64
120-in. motor test termed successful; solid-propellant Titan 3C zero-stage booster motor. Aviation W 80:71 F 3 '64
Rocket fuel tablets. Sci N L 86:339 N 28 '64
Rocket research solid microrocket wins award. il Miss & Roc 12:34-5 Ap 29 '63
Rocket studies stress solid propellants. il Aviation W 81:129-32 S 7 '64
Rohr completes ablative nozzle for Thiokol 156-in. solid motor. il Aviation W 82:25 Ja 4 '65
Smooth shift of large solids effort seen. D. E. Fink. Aviation W 80:30 Ja 13 '64
Solid motor clusters analyzed as possible S-1C substitutes. il Aviation W 80:71+ Ap 27 '64
Solid motor competition signifies missile, launch vehicle potential. I. Stone. il Aviation W 81:64-5 N 2 '64
Solid motor proponents seek new funds. il Aviation W 80:63+ My 25 '64

SOLID propellant rockets—*Continued*
Solid vs. liquid rockets? W. Von Braun. il Pop Sci 183:61-3 N '63
SRI composition formulations control combustion instability in solids. W. E. Wilks. Miss & Roc 14:36-7 Mr 9 '64
Subscale motors to verify 260-in. design. C. M. Plattner. il Aviation W 80:40-1+ Je 22 '64
Thiokol gets big-solids edge. F. G. McGuire. il Miss & Roc 12:14-15 Ap 22 '63
Thiokol monitors propellant behavior. il Miss & Roc 13:42 Ag 26 '63
Thiokol VP urges funding boost for space-storable propellants. J. F. Judge. Miss & Roc 14:18 Ap 20 '64
Titan III-C stage zero role revamps UTC structure. R. Lindsey. il Miss & Roc 14:34+ Ja 20 '64
Two firms planning solid Nova stage. Miss & Roc 12:14 F 4 '63
Two thrust-termination ports eliminated in 120-in. solid motor. Aviation W 80:40+ Mr 9 '64
USAF space, large solids efforts periled. L. Booda. Aviation W 79:18-19 Jl 8 '63
UTC to fire 120-in. Titan III motor. R. Lindsey. il Miss & Roc 12:36-8 F 18 '63
Use of jet tabs for thrust vector control being studied for large solid propulsion. C. M. Plattner. il Aviation W 80:48-9+ Mr 9 '64
Valveless control rockets developed. J. F. Judge. il Miss & Roc 15:18+ S 28 '64
Zierdt says propellants cost too much. J. F. Judge. Miss & Roc 12:35-6 F 11 '63

Control

Crab-oriented Gyro produced for Athena. B. Miller. il Aviation W 79:85-9 D 16 '63
Thiokol studies omni-axis nozzle control. I. Stone. il Aviation W 81:62-4+ D 14 '64

Launching

Athena rocket launches to begin in air force re-entry research. Aviation W 79:26 S 2 '63

Manufacture

ARC hard at work on development of beryllium powder. il Miss & Roc 12:27 My 27 '63
Canadian solid-fuel plant is completed. M. L. Yaffee. il Aviation W 79:91+ O 14 '63
McGregor plant boosts its capacity. J. F. Judge. il Miss & Roc 12:26-7 Ap 1 '63
156-in. solid motor center segment casting completed. C. M. Plattner. il Aviation W 80:52-3+ Mr 24 '64
Rocketdyne developing rugged grains. Miss & Roc 13:16 N 18 '63
Solid-rocket milling device offers cost reduction in labor, material. R. D. Hibben. il Aviation W 79:87-8 Jl 29 '63
Sud-aviation at work on family of five rockets. il Miss & Roc 13:25 Jl 8 '63
Thiokol's space booster plant takes shape in Georgia. J. F. Judge. il Miss & Roc 13:26-8 N 18 '63
Westinghouse know-how speeds flow of 120-in. cases for Titan III-C's. J. F. Judge. il Miss & Roc 15:32-3 S 14 '64

Materials

A-G finds filament-wound Minuteman cases would be lighter than expected. W. E. Wilks. il Miss & Roc 15:34-5 Jl 13 '64
Casing rockets in glass; cylindrical cases made of glass. il Bsns W p 108-10+ F 9 '63
$80,000 saving per case foreseen. R. Van Osten. il Miss & Roc 12:31 F 25 '63
Nickel alloy rings for 260-in. solid program impose stringent standards. J. F. Judge. il Miss & Roc 15:38-9 O 12 '64
156-in. solid motor center segment casting completed. C. M. Plattner. il Aviation W 80:52-3+ Mr 23 '64
260-in. booster insulation based on Minuteman, Polaris technique. J. F. Judge. il Miss & Roc 14:26-7 My 25 '64
Westinghouse know-how speeds flow of 120-in. cases for Titan III-C's. J. F. Judge. il Miss & Roc 15:32-3 S 14 '64
Wire-reinforced solid rocket test-fired. il Aviation W 81:58 O 26 '64

Testing

AF, NASA officials enthusiastic about LPC's 156-in. motor test. il Miss & Roc 14:25-6+ Je 8 '64
Apollo launch escape motor firing successful. il(p 113) Sci N L 83:125 F 23 '63
Controllable-impulse solid rockets tested. il Aviation W 82:81+ Ja 18 '65
Facility tests solids in environmental conditions. Miss & Roc 16:31 Ja 18 '65
First Athena veers off course. Aviation W 80:30 F 17 '64
First 156-in. solid motor readied by Lockheed for late spring firing. W. E. Wilks. il Miss & Roc 14:32-3+ Mr 16 '64
Five-segment motor tested successfully. I. Stone. il Aviation W 79:52-4 Jl 29 '63
NASA, USAF seek cause behind accidental motor ignition at Cape. Aviation W 80:29 Ap 20 '64
Partially buried, gimballed nozzle tested. il Aviation W 81:57 Ag 3 '64
Solid triumph. il Time 82:48 Ag 2 '63
Static discharge, shock studied as possible cape accident causes. Aviation W 80:35 Ap 27 '64
Titan II engine explodes during static test firing. R. Lindsey. il Miss & Roc 14:16 My 11 '64
Titan III program reappraised. il Miss & Roc 12:12-13 F 25 '63
Titan's solid booster romps through tests. il Bsns W p46 Jl 27 '63
UTC test fires Titan III booster. il Miss & Roc 13:15-16 Jl 29 '63
Wire-reinforced solid rocket test-fired. il Aviation W 81:58 O 26 '64

Transportation

AMF study cites solids handling needs. Miss & Roc 13:28 Ag 5 '63

SOLIDS
Infrared emission spectra of organic solids from 5 to 6.6 microns. W. A. Hovis, jr. il Science 143:587-8 F 7 '64
Mössbauer effect in chemistry and solid-state physics. G. K. Wertheim. bibliog il Science 144:253-9 Ap 17 '64
Organic solid state; report on symposium. P. L. Kronick. Science 145:730+ Ag 14 '64
Photosensitization in solids; report on international conference on photosensitization in solids. L. I. Grossweiner. Science 146:88-90 O 2 '64
Pressure and electronic structure. H. G. Drickamer. bibliog il Science 142:1429-35 D 13 '63
Solid-solid interaction studies by spectral reflectance. H. Zeitlin and others. bibliog il Science 141:423-4 Ag 2 '63
Solid-state physics; report on conference. D. N. Langenberg and R. F. Peart. Science 144:1365-6 Je 12 '64
Spectroscopy of solids in the far-infrared. M. Tinkham. bibliog il Science 145:240-7 Jl 17 '64

SOLIDS, Flow of. See Rheology

SOLITUDE
Just thinking. P. Wylie. il Ladies Home J 80:48+ N '63
Shh, the need for do-nothing quietude. B. Chapin. il Recreation 57:437-8 N '64
Solitude; who can take it and who can't. B. H. Frisch. il Sci Digest 55:12-18 Mr '64
To save the life of "I". M. Mannes. Vogue 144:172-3 O 1 '64

SOLOMON, A. K. See Damadian, R. jt. auth.

SOLOMON, Barbara Probst
Days and nights in Texas. Harper 227:94-7+ N '63
Franglais film. Nation 199:57-9 Ag 10 '64

SOLOMON, Charles
Yale's School of art and architecture. M. Burchard. il por Arch Forum 120:80-3 F '64

SOLOMON, Esther
Gourmet picnic. Sat Eve Post 236:74-5 S 7 '63

SOLOMON, Leonard
Crews of the Henriette. Yachting 113:195-7 My '63
East to Abaco. Motor B 114:36-9+ S '64
Great Lakes yachtsman takes a look at the Big Ocean. Motor B 111:28+ Je '63
Henriette V made the great circle. il Motor B 112:46-7+ O; 94+ N; 76-7+ D '63

SOLOMON, Maynard
Hardy independent. J. Tebbel. il por Hi Fi 14:46-8 F '64

SOLOMON, Seymour
Hardy independent. J. Tebbel. il por Hi Fi 14:46-8 F '64

SOLOMON, Stanley
Indispensable tape recorder. Sr Schol 85:6T N 18 '64
Learning resources de luxe! Sr Schol 83:13T-14T S 20 '63
Merriam's mirror of the language; Webster third revisited. Sr Schol 83:9T-10T S 13 '63
Round-the-world sabbatical. il Sr Schol 84:13T-14T Mr 20 '64
What can we learn from industry? Sr Schol 85:12T Ja 14 '65

SOLOMON R. Guggenheim foundation
Complex competition; Guggenheim international award exhibition. il Newsweek 63:53 Ja 27 '64
SOLOMON R. Guggenheim museum, New York
Fifty raps; sale of Kandinsky paintings. il Newsweek 64:60 Jl 13 '64
Kadinskys for sale. Newsweek 63:91 F 17 '64
Sweet and powerful; Van Goghs at New York's Guggenheim museum. Newsweek 63: 56 Ap 13 '64
SOLOMONS, Gus, jr
Brief biography. S. Goodman. pors Dance Mag 38:56-7 Je '64
SOLOMON'S seal
Solomon's seal and Jack-in-the-pulpit. E. W. Reed. il Horticulture 41:182-3 Mr '63
SOLON, John J.
What authors should know; excerpts from address. por(p37) Pub W 184:38-9 Jl 15 '63
SOLOTAROFF, Theodore
Irving Howe, the socialist imagination. Commentary 37:61-4 Je '64
Jewish camp. Commentary 37:76-8 Mr '64
Napoleon St and after. Commentary 38:63-6 D '64
SOLOVEICHIK, Samuel
More chemists die young; summary of address. Sci N L 84:199 S 28 '63
SOLOVIOFF, Nicholas
Buildings that inflamed the pride of the citizenry; drawings. Fortune 71:147-51 Ja '65
Drawings of Nicholas Solovioff. L. Hanson. il Am Artist 28:28-33+ O '64
SOLOW, Herbert
How NSF got lost in Mohole. Fortune 67:138-41+ My '63
Obituary
Fortune 71:118 Ja '65
SOLOWEY, Ben
Drawings of Ben Solowey. H. C. Pitz. il Am Artist 27:26-31 My '63
SOLTI, Georg
Special sound; interview. ed. by L. F. Loveday. por Opera N 27:14 Mr 23 '63
Verdi I know; ed. by A. M. Lingg. Opera N 28:8-11 D 7 '63
about
Music to my ears; a great Otello by Solti and McCracken. I. Kolodin. il Sat R 46:30-1+ Mr 23 '63
Music to my ears: Solti's Boris. I. Kolodin. Sat R 46:53 Mr 30 '63
Music to my ears; Solti's Figaro. I. Kolodin. Sat R 46:38+ Je 29 '63
Music to my ears; Solti's Tristan. I. Kolodin Sat R 46:47 F 23 '63
SOLTIS, Joseph D. and Beckham, C. H.
Story of gasoline. Motor T 16:106-9 N; 50-3 D '64; 17:58-61 Ja '65
SOLTOW, James H.
Recent developments in United States history. bibliog f Ann Am Acad 347:113-28 My '63
SOLTZ, Vicki. See Dreikurs, R. jt. auth.
SOLUTIONS
Applejack technique: new application of an old approach to solute concentration. H. M. Habermann. il Science 140:292 Ap 19 '63
Proteinpolysaccharide in connective tissue: inhibition of phase separation. H. Weinstein and others. bibliog il Science 142: 1073-5 N 22 '63
Radiation-induced gelation of dilute aqueous pectin solutions. I. J. Wahba and others. bibliog il Science 139:1297-8 Mr 29 '63
SOLUTREAN period. See Stone age
SOLZHENITSIN, Aleksandr
One day in the life of Ivan Denisovich: condensation of novel. tr. by M. Hayward and R. Hingley. por Sat Eve Post 236: 35-47+ F 9 '63
One day in the life of Ivan Denisovich; excerpts from Praeger and Dutton editions. Sat R 46:28+ F 9 '63
about
Denisovich: Russia's voice; novel of life in a labor camp. M. Koriakov. America 108: 338-9 Mr 9 '63
Russia's writers: after silence, human voices. il por Time 82:82-3+ D 20 '63
Soviets say contract for Solzhenitsyn novel is void. Pub W 183:48-9 F 4 '63
Three (at least) paperback Solzhenitsyns on the market. Pub W 183:38 F 25 '63
SOMALI language
Illiterate poets of Somalia. J. Contini. Reporter 28:36-8 Mr 14 '63
SOMALIA
Blood on the horn. il Time 83:25 F 14 '64
Communist block interest in Africa; address, November 18, 1963. G. M. Williams. Dept State Bul 49:929-32 D 16 '63
Communist bridgehead? il Newsweek 62:41 N 25 '63
Frontier troubles. Newsweek 61:52 Mr 25 '63
Illiterate poets of Somalia. J. Contini. Reporter 28:36-8 Mr 14 '63
King of kings; Ethiopia's frontier conflict with Somalia. New Repub 150:8 F 29 '64
Shades of the Mad Mullah; Somali-Ethiopian border fighting. il Newsweek 63:48 Ap 13 '64
Somali Republic. S. Touval. bibliog f il Cur Hist 46:156-62 Mr '64
Somalia's instant army. P. Schmid. il Reporter 31:48-50 S 24 '64
Weathering the wind of change. C. Miller. Sat R 47:33-4+ Je 13 '64
Who owns what? il Time 81:28 Mr 22 '63
Who will listen to the BBC? New Repub 148: 10 Mr 30 '63
See also
Elections—Somalia
Forests and forestry—Somalia
SOMALILAND. See Somalia
SOMALIS
Illiterate poets of Somalia. J. Contini. Reporter 28:36-8 Mr 14 '63
SOME effects of a hat; story. See Warner, S. T.
SOME legends of Christmas; story. See Benasutti, M.
SOME things about Miss America they don't show on television; story. See McCarthy, J.
SOMEONE has to say something; story. See Brown, J.
SOMEONE to share; story. See Gordon, E. E.
SOMERLOTT, Robert
Eskimo pies; story. Atlan 213:65-8 Ja '64
SOMERS, Anne Ramsay
Considerations for policy-makers; the European experience. New Repub 149:36-8 N 9 '63
SOMERS, Florence
Aloha on a budget. Redbook 121:36+ Ag '63
New movies. See issues of Redbook
Try Texas for family fun. Redbook 124:20-2 Ja '65
Vacation by the sea. Redbook 123:24 Ag '64
SOMERS, Gerald A.
Award-winning program for NLW. por Wilson Lib Bul 39:472-4 F '65
Librarian's syndrome; letter to the editor. Library J 89:4672+ D 1 '64
SOMERVILLE, Ted
Elk hunt in Virginia? ed. by G. H. Gillelan. pors Outdoor Life 135:42-3+ Ja '65
SOMETHING bright like a star; story. See Cavanaugh, A.
SOMETHING more! musical comedy. See Musical comedies, revues, etc.—Criticisms, plots, etc
SOMETHING new for Halloween; drama. See Newman, D.
SOMME, Battle of the. See European war, 1914-1918—Campaigns and battles
SOMMER, Elke
Elke Sommer: the movies' new wonder child. S. Gordon. il pors Look 27:70-3 O 22 '63
Elke's big blitz on Hollywood. pors Life 54: 74-6 My 31 '63
Packaged tomato. por Time 82:58 Jl 12 '63
Season of Sommer. J. Hyams. il pors Sat Eve Post 237:70-3 Ap 18 '64
SOMMER, Frank
John F. Watson: first historian of American decorative arts. Antiques 83:300-3 Mr '63
Sculpture at Winterthur. Antiques 85:182-4 F '64
SOMMER, Robert
Dark journey into Expertland. N Y Times Mag p 16+ Jl 28 '63
—and Watson, Irene
Finding buried treasure in the hospital; reprint. Recreation 56:94-5 F '63
SOMMER, Theo
For an Atlantic future. For Affairs 43:112-25 O '64
SOMMERS, Joseph
Novels of a dead revolution. Nation 197:114-15 S 7 '63
SOMMERS, Martin
Obituary
Sat Eve Post 236:88 Ag 24 '63
SOMNAMBULISM
Most sleep-walkers emotionally unstable. Sci N L 84:313 N 16 '63
Sleepwalkers wander when not dreaming. Sci N L 86:312 N 14 '64
SOMOROFF, Ben
Troublemakers. Esquire 60:78-9 S '63
SOMOZA, Luis
Cuban raiders; recruiting in Nicaragua. por Newsweek 62:33 S 30 '63

SON et lumière (sound and light)
Electronic drama; Independence Hall, Philadelphia. G. Loney. il Theatre Arts 47:27-8 Jl '63
Illuminations of history. il N Y Times Mag p20-1 Ag 4 '63
Letter from Paris; programs during eighth centenary of the Cathedral of Notre-Dame Genêt. New Yorker 39:84 Jl 27 '63
SON Ngoc Thanh
Our far-flung correspondents. R. Shaplen. New Yorker 40:158+ Ap 18 '64
SONAR
Acoustics research drone tests to aid navy's detection efforts. W. Beller. il Miss & Roc 15:27+ Ag 3 '64
Beast hears like bat. il(p81) Sci N L 86:87 Ag 8 '64
Detection, classification are key jobs. il Miss & Roc 15:46+ S 21 '64
Experimenting with sonar. D. Meyer. il Pop Electr 21:41-5+ S '64
Nature's counter-sonar. Time 85:35 Ja 22 '65
Noisy fish tracked by team of scientists; sonar-equipped fish. il Sci N L 86:261 O 24 '64
Search for the Thresher. F. N. Spiess and A. E. Maxwell. bibliog il Science 145:349-55 Jl 24 '64
Seeing with sound. il Time 82:79 N 1 '63
Siphonophores and the deep scattering layer. E. G. Barham. bibliog il Science 140:826-8 My 17 '63
Sonar probing in Narragansett Bay. H. E. Edgerton and others. il Science 146:1459-60 D 11 '64
Sonar sextants sight on sea bottom. il Pop Sci 184:74-5 My '64
Sonar signals of the sea lion. T. C. Poulter. Science 139:753-5 F 22 '63
SONATAS
See also
Phonograph records—Sonatas
SONDERN, Frederic, jr
Box that catches criminals. Read Digest 84:37-8+ Ap '64
Checks that never bounce. Read Digest 83:205-8 Ag '63
Jacksonville's jury of juvenile peers. Parents Mag 38:47+ Ag '63; Same abr. Read Digest 83:82-5 Ag '63
New-style bank robber. Read Digest 83:33-4+ D '63
Take the handcuffs off our police! Read Digest 85:64-8 S '64
Wonderful white stallions of Vienna. Read Digest 82:160-6 Ap '63
SONG, Yo Chan
Caged tiger. por Newsweek 62:37 Ag 26 '63
SONG writers. See Composers
SONGBIRDS. See Birds
SONGBOOKS
Bad bishop's book of love songs. il Horizon 6:26-31 Wint '64
SONGS
See also
Christmas carols
College songs
Folk songs
Hymns
Melodies
Phonograph records—Songs
SONGS (with music)
See also
Christmas carols (with music)
SONGS, American
Dolly's my sunflower; question of copyright infringement by composer of Hello, Dolly. Time 84:81 S 18 '64
Enduring songs of the 20th century. C. Morrison. il Look 29:36-43 Ja 12 '65
See also
Campaign songs
Folk songs, American
Negro songs
Yankee Doodle (song)
SONGS, Australian
Bouncing kangaroo; R. Harris, hardly the typical songwriter. Newsweek 62:50 Jl 8 '63
SONGS, Campaign. See Campaign songs
SONGS, German
Songs of life and love in ancient Nuremberg. D. Stevens. il Hi Fi 15:71 Ja '65
SONGS, Negro. See Negro songs
SONGS, Popular. See Music, Popular (songs, etc)
SONGS, Spanish
Strange songs of Spain find friends. W. M. Abbott. America 108:216 F 16 '63
SONGS of birds. See Birds—Song
SONIC boom. See Shock waves
La SONNAMBULA; opera. See Bellini, V.
SONNE, Niels H.
Salinger and John the Baptist. Library J 88:3031-3 S 1 '63
SONNEVILLE-BORDES, Denise de
Upper Paleolithic cultures in western Europe. Science 142:347-55 O 18 '63
SONS and fathers. See Parent-child relationship
SONTAG, Henrietta
Queen of song. Q. Eaton. Opera N 29:33 N 14 '64
SONTAG, L. W.
Your child's intelligence; reprint. Todays Health 41:90 O '63
SONTAG, Susan
Camp; summary of article in Partisan review. Time 84:75 D 11 '64
Feast for open eyes. Nation 198:374-6 Ap 13 '64
Man with a pain; story. Harper 228:72-5 Ap '64
about
Individualists; Mlle's annual Merit awards. il por Mlle 58:74-5 Ja '64
SONTHOFF, Herbert
What is the manager? bibliog f Harvard Bsns R 42:24-6+ N '64
SONY corporation. See Electronic apparatus industry and trade—Japan; Japan—Industries
SOOTHSAYERS. See Fortune telling
SOPHIA, Sister Mary. See Mary Sophia, Sister
SOPHIA. See Sofia, Bulgaria
SOPHIA, Santa. See Istanbul—Santa Sophia
SOPHIA university, Tokyo. See Colleges and universities—Japan
SOPHIE; musical comedy. See Musical comedies, revues, etc.—Criticisms, plots, etc.
SOPHOCLES
Electra. Criticism
America 111:266 S 12 '64
SOPKIN, Charles
(ed) See Johnson, W. Millionaire: a self-portrait
SORAYA, consort of Mohammed Reza Pahlevi, shah of Iran (divorced 1958)
Soraya: autobiography of a princess. pors McCalls 90:72-3+ Je '63
about
Imperial kiss. por Newsweek 64:98+ N 30 '64
SORBONNE. See Colleges and universities—France
SORCERER; story. See Nelson, D.
SORCERY. See Witchcraft
SORDARIA
Self-sterile auxotrophs and their relation to heterothallism in sordaria fimicola. A. S. El-Ani. bibliog il Science 145:1067-8 S 4 '64
SORE throat. See Throat—Diseases
SOREL, Claudette
Quote: unquote; interview, ed. by C. S. Susa. por Mus Am 84:21 F '64
SORELL, Walter
Appreciation of Jean Cocteau. Dance Mag 38:38-41 F '64
Louis Horst, 1884-1964; excerpt from address. Dance Mag 38:39 Mr '64
Modern dance festival in Toronto. Dance Mag 37:16+ My '63
Shakespeare and the choreographer. Dance Mag 38:43-5+ My '64
(ed) See Ailey, A. Style, essence, allusion
(ed) See Erdman, J. Coach to Spoleto
(ed) See Sokolow, A. We work toward freedom
SORENSEN, Theodore Chaikin
How the President makes a decision: excerpts from Decision-making in the White House. por Sat R 46:12-15+ Jl 27; 8-12+ Ag 3 '63
How the President runs the White House; excerpts from addresses, April 18 and May 9, 1963. U S News 54:70-2 Je 3 '63
about
Departure of a deputy president. H. Sidey. il pors Life 56:105-6+ Mr 6 '64
First man out. por Time 83:15 Ja 24 '64
JFK's alter ego. il por Newsweek 63:16-17 Ja 27 '64
Ted Sorensen of Nebraska. W. L. Miller. por Reporter 30:24-7 F 13 '64
SORENSEN, Virginia
Face: story. New Yorker 39:114 My 25 '63
SORENSON, James. See Cameron, J. R. jt. auth.
SORET spectrum. See Spectrum analysis
SOREX palustris. See Shrews

SORGE, Richard
Again the Sorge case. C. Johnson. il por N Y Times Mag p89-90+ O 11 '64

SORGHUM
Grow sorghum the way you do wheat? C. E. Ball. il Farm J 88:38-9+ Ap '64
See also
Milo

Diseases and pests
See also
Chlorosis (plants)

Hybrids
How to manage the new sudan-sorghum hybrids. il Farm J 88:30-1+ D '64
What we're learning about sorghum-sudan hybrids. L. E. Zeman. il Suc Farm 63: 34-5+ Ja '65

SORKIN, Dan
Stuntman of the air. por Newsweek 61:71 Mr 25 '63

SOROKIN, Pitirim Aleksandrovich
Anti-quantophrenia. por Newsweek 64:80+ S 7 '64
Sorokin: the lone wolf's stubbornness. J. P. Sisk. Commonweal 79:608-10 F 14 '64

SORRELL, Charles A. and Negas, Taki
Metastable rubidium aluminum silicate with a hexagonal sheet structure. bibliog Science 141:917 S 6 '63

SORRENTINO, Gilbert
Good house. Poetry 104:179-81 Je '64
Old soldiers never die; poem. Poetry 104:360 S '64
Silences; Two for Franz Kline; poems. Poetry 102:299-301 Ag '63
Thoreau runs out of sterno; Rugged individualist; poems. Nation 198:382 Ap 13 '64
Yorick's song for the New Year; poem. Nation 198:18 Ja 4 '64

SORROW
See also
Bereavement

SOSA-RODRIGUEZ, Carlos
U.N. General assembly holds memorial meeting; statement. Dept State Bul 49:892-3 D 9 '63
United Nations day 1963; excerpts from addresses. U N Rev 10:27+ N '63

about
Assembly president. il por U N Rev 10:6 O '63

SOSNOVY, Timothy
Soviet military budget. bibliog f For Affairs 42:487-94 Ap '64

SOTHEBY and company
Artful takeover; control of Manhattan's Parke-Bernet galleries. il Time 84:82 Jl 24 '64
Autograph letters and manuscripts at Sotheby's (1963-1964 season) K. V. Hostick. Hobbies 69:110-11 N '64
Fastest gavel in the West. il Life 55:60A-60B Jl 12 '63
Record price for abstracts; Guggenheim museum sells some Kandinskys. Time 84:70 Jl 10 '64
Rule Sotheby's; purchase of Parke-Bernet galleries. Newsweek 64:53 Jl 27 '64
Sale of the century; René Fribourg collection. il Newsweek 62:58 Jl 8 '63
Sotheby's buys controlling interest in Parke-Bernet. Pub W 186:34 Jl 27 '64
Takeover bid shakes art market; Sotheby's of London to win New York's Parke-Bernet. il Bsns W p 110+ Jl 11 '64

SOTOMAYOR, Carlos Martinez-. See Martinez-Sotomayor, C.

SOUERS, P. C. and Jura, G.
High pressure: effect on dysprosium. bibliog Science 145:575-7 Ag 7 '64
Negative temperature coefficient of resistance in bismuth I. bibliog Science 143:467-9 Ja 31 '64
Semiconducting region of ytterbium. bibliog Science 140:481-3 My 3 '63

SOUFFLES
Freezing & canning cookbook; excerpts. N. Nichols. il Farm J 87:94-7+ Ap '63
Soufflés, step by step. C. Claiborne. il N Y Times Mag p49 Je 28 '64

SOUL
By love depressed; D. de Rougemont's investigation of the western myths of love. T. Roszak. Nation 200:33-4 Ja 11 '65

SOULE, Carl
Xerox, the U.N. and I.C.Y. Christian Cent 81:1305-6 O 21 '64

SOULE, Claire Whitaker
Confessional; poem. Christian Cent 80:860 Jl 3 '63

SOULE, Gardner
Book censors. Sr Schol 85:26T O 7 '64
How the Wright brothers learned to fly. Pop Sci 183:51-7 D '63

SOUND
Hugh Downs column. H. Downs. Sci Digest 56:85-9 Ag '64
Search for perfect sound. Sci N L 85:294 My 9 '64
Sound of a diesel. R. P. Lister. Atlan 211:139-41 Mr '63
Sound originates in breakup of eddies. Sci N L 85:184 Mr 21 '64
See also
Acoustics, Architectural
Hearing
Music—Acoustics and physics
Noise
Phonetics
Phonograph records—Sounds
Ultrasonics
Voice

Apparatus
Audio components and tape recorders. il Consumer Bul 29:109-35 D '64
Audio level clippers & limiters. T. R. Haskett. il Electr World 71:51-4+ F '64
Audio: loudness compensation. H. Fantel. Opera N 29:35 Ja 23 '65
Build a hi-fi volume compressor expander. R. H. Russell. il Pop Electr 21:41-5+ O '64
Directory of sound-slide systems. L. Lipton. il Pop Phot 55:84 O '64
High fidelity. H. Fantel. Opera N 28:34 Ap 4 '64
Loudness control. R. A. Jacobs, jr. il Electr World 70:34-5+ D '63
Save that sound. A. Zuckerman. il Pop Phot 55:80+ O '64
Sleep-O-Mat; white noise generator. R. M. Voss. il Pop Electr 22:51-3 Ja '65
Sound advice. R. N. Angus. Mod Phot 28:86 Ap '64
Tape-recorder equalization curves. H. Burstein. il Electr World 72:38-40 Jl '64
See also
Earphones
Hydrophones
Loud speaking apparatus
Magnetic recorders and recording
Microphones
Sonar

Physiological effects
Origins of psychoacoustics; with editorial comment. S. J. London. Hi Fi 13:43, 44-7+ Ap '63
Reversible sonic inhibition of protein, purine, and pyrimidine biosynthesis in the living cell. V. W. Burns. bibliog il Science 146: 1056-8 N 20 '64
Sharks: attraction by low-frequency sounds. D. R. Nelson and S. H. Gruber. bibliog il Science 142:975-7 N 15 '63
Sonic energy effects in bovine serum albumin solutions. E. L. Hess and others. bibliog il Science 143:1176-7 Mr 13 '64

Recording and reproducing
Adding sound to slides & movies; questions and answers. J. A. Keel. il U S Camera 26: 70-1+ O '63
Distortion; the eternal enigma. A. Sterling. il Hi Fi 14:50-3+ S '64
Encores from the past; electric impulses from unique piano rolls. il Time 82:74+ S 13 '63
Fi gets higher. H. Kupferberg. il Atlan 211: 122+ My '63
High fidelity. H. Fantel. Opera N 28:34 Ja 25 '64
High fidelity newsfronts. N. Eisenberg. il Hi Fi 13:27+ My; 35+ D '63
Loudspeakers: the ideal and the possible. Hi Fi 13:27 Je '63
Photographer's guide to sound; symposium. il Pop Phot 55:73-84+ O '64
Photographer's guide to sound; symposium: with editorial comment. il Pop Phot 53:46, 49-65+ S '63
Prospects for psychoacoustics. I. M. Fried. Hi Fi 13:48-50+ Ap '63
Sound. J. Wesson. See issues of U.S. camera
Sound. T. Schwartz. See issues of Popular photography
Sound advice; sound effects. H. A. Manogian. Mod Phot 27:11+ Jl '63
Sound advice; your recorded voice. R. N. Angus. Mod Phot 27:18+ Je '63
Sound: highlights of the New York high fidelity show. J. Wesson. U S Camera 26:38-9 Ja '64
Sound; mixer in amateur filming. J. Wesson. U S Camera 26:26-7 N '63

SOUND—Recording and reproducing—Continued
Sound; recording studio. T. Schwartz. Pop Phot 53:28+ N; 32 D '63
Sound test report. il Pop Phot 56:34+ Ja '65
Sound with your pictures. G. W. Cushman. See issues of Popular photography to September 1963
Speakers: past, present, and future. N. Eisenberg. il Hi Fi 13:37-40+ Je '63
See also
Audio fairs
High fidelity sound systems
Magnetic recorders and recording
Moving picture sound recording
Moving pictures, Amateur—Sound effects
Phonograph records
Phonograph records—Recording

Bibliography

Books you can learn from. G. W. Cushman. Pop Phot 52:18+ Je '63

Stereophonic recording and reproducing

Checking stereo separation and phase. R. Glasgal. il Electr World 70:37+ O '63
Confessions of an illicit tape recordist. P. Moor. il Hi Fi 13:38-40+ Ag '63
FM stereo: an unfulfilled promise. P. Davies. Mus Am 84:47 O '64
Hi-fi, stereo buying guide for families with children. C. Sinclair and D. Lachenbruch. il Parents Mag 38:75+ My '63
High fidelity (title varies) (cont) Opera N 27:35 Mr 2; 28:34 D 28 '63
High fidelity newsfronts. N. Eisenberg. il Hi Fi 13:35 Ag '63
How to arrange for big entertainment. il Bet Hom & Gard 41:94+ S '63
Notes from abroad. P. Moor. Hi Fi 13:28+ Mr '63
Projecting with stereo sound. G. W. Cushman. il Pop Phot 53:28+ Ag '63
Room acoustics for stereo. D. P. Eisenman. il Hi Fi 13:50-3+ F '63
Turntables for stereo. J. Marshall. il Hi Fi 13:52-4+ Mr '63
See also
Magnetic recorders and recording—Stereophonic recorders

SOUND and light. See Son et lumière

SOUND conditioning. See Soundproofing

SOUND navigation and ranging. See Sonar

SOUND production by animals
Barking whales star on TV. il Pop Mech 119:99 F '63
Sonar signals of the sea lion. T. C. Poulter. Science 139:753-5 F 22 '63
Underwater sounds of pinnipeds. W. E. Schevill and others. bibliog il Science 141:50-3 Jl 5 '63
Vocal mimicry in tursiops: ability to match numbers and durations of human vocal bursts. J. C. Lilly. bibliog il Science 147:300-1 Ja 15 '65

SOUND production by fishes
Sea nocturnally noisy, fish talk more at night. Sci N L 85:56 Ja 25 '64

SOUND production by insects
Moth sounds and the insect-catching behavior of bats. D. C. Dunning and K. D. Roeder. bibliog il Science 147:173-4 Ja 8 '65
Sound communication in honeybees. A. M. Wenner. il Sci Am 210:116-22+ bibliog (p 156) Ap '64

SOUND ranging devices. See Hydrophones

SOUND suppressors
Sure cure for ham, CB mobile noise. J. D. Lenk. il Pop Electr 19:65-6 O '63

SOUND waves
Dig that third sound. Sci Digest 53:16 My '63
Mapping the air by sound. Time 82:52 Ag 30 63
Ocean waters studied for sound transmission. Sci N L 83:173 Mr 16 '63
355-foot seagoing cigar is automatic laboratory; SPAR (seagoing platform for acoustical research) measures sound transmission under water. Sci N L 86:139 Ag 29 '64
See also
Ultrasonic waves

SOUNDING (rockets.) See Rockets, Sounding

SOUNDING and soundings
See also
Depth indicators
Sonar

SOUNDING rockets. See Rockets, Sounding

SOUNDPROOFING
Cutting impact noise in apartment buildings. il Arch Rec 133:210-15 Ap '63
How to stop noise. B. Fader. il Am City 79:103-5 Je '64
Install sound-deadening ceiling tile. il Bet Hom & Gard 41:28 S '63
Noise: what to do about the biggest headache in most houses! Bet Hom & Gard 41:14 Ag '63
Now they're hushing up houses. il Changing T 18:38-40 My '64
Planning for quieter, sound-conditioned homes. L. S. Goodfriend and R. L. Cardinell. il Arch Rec 133:29+ mid-My '63
Sheet lead is superior soundproofing material. Sci N L 84:41 Jl 20 '63
Sound isolation between teaching spaces. W. R. Farrell. il Arch Rec 134:229-32 O '63
Your house can be quieter. Good H 156:147 Mr '63

SOUNDS of the sea. See Ocean sounds

SOUP mixes. See Food mixes

SOUPS
Aristocrats of soup. C. Claiborne. il N Y Times Mag p 117 N 8 '64
Caldo verde; with recipes. il Look 28:42-3 S 8 '64
Cold soups for a hot summer; with recipes. H. S. Witty. Flower Grower 51:17 Ag '64
Gazpacho, mucho gusto! il Bet Hom & Gard 42:80 Je '64
Hearty hot soups. il Suc Farm 61:90+ F '63
Here are five ideas for summer soups. Sunset 131:100+ Ag '63
It's an all-year summer soup. il Sunset 130:221 My '63
Last touch: broil the soup. il Sunset 131:199+ N '63
Salad soups from Spain and Mexico. il Sunset 133:108-9 Jl '64
Some like it cold. il Redbook 121:70-1+ Ag '63
Song of the soup kettle. N. C. Wood. il Ladies Home J 80:78-81+ Mr '63
Soup; non-alcoholic drinks appearing to be alcoholic drinks. New Yorker 40:40 Ap 18 '64
Soups of sturdy peasant stock. il McCalls 90:104-5+ Ag '63
Soup's on; frozen soup-sticks. il Ladies Home J 81:96-7 Jl '64
Soups that make a meal. il Redbook 122:56-7+ Ja '64
Sour grass soup. il N Y Times Mag p54 Je 16 '63
Successful recipes. il Suc Farm 63:93-4 Ja '65
Tempting uses of soup and juices. Good H 156:221 Ap '63
Yankee gumbo. C. Claiborne. il N Y Times Mag p79 My 26 '63
See also
Campbell soup company

SOUPS, Dry. See Food, Dried

SOUR cream. See Cream, Sour

SOURIAN, Peter
Secret tournament; story. Sat Eve Post 237:54-8 F 22 '64

SOURWINE, J. G.
New turmoil over security; Otepka case. il U S News 55:48 N 25 '63

SOUSA, John A. and Loconti, J. D.
Photoisomerism: a colorless photoinduced intermediate of *o*-nitrobenzylpyridine. bibliog Science 146:397-8 O 16 '64

SOUSTER, Raymond
All animals like me; poem. Atlan 214:164 N '64
Winter valley; Eddie Condon at the New colonial; Change; poems. Poetry 102:372-3 S '63

SOUTH
Curse & the hope; W. Faulkner's vision. il Time 84:44-8 Jl 17 '64
Dixieland reverie. E. M. Yoder, jr. il Sat R 47:39-40 My 30 '64
Idea of the South, ed. by F. E. Vandiver. Review
Commonweal 80:455-6 Jl 3 '64. L. F. X. Mayhew
Life guide; what's down South besides the sun. il Life 56:7 Ja 3 '64
Now, a Truman plan for the South; excerpts from address. H. S. Truman. U S News 55:15 S 30 '63
South and the southerner, by R. McGill. Review
Sat R 46:52+ Ap 20 '63. E. M. Yoder, jr
There are many Souths. America 108:459-60 Ap 6 '63
See also
Agriculture—Southern states
Appalachian Region
Confederate States of America
Crime and criminals—Southern states
Education—Southern states
Forests and forestry—Southern states
Gulf states
Law—Southern states
Libraries—Southern states
Negroes in the United States—South

SOUTH—*Continued*

Description and travel

Delightful Dixieland trail. il Bet Hom & Gard 42:119-22 Mr '64
Harbors of history: the Southeast heritage cruise. il Motor B 114:21-9 S '64
Places where spring seems lovelier. M. Gough. il House B 105:118+ Mr '63
Three-week honeymoon. J. Hamilton. il Look 28:74-9 My 5 '64

Economic conditions

Change in the mountains. B. Smith, jr. il Sat Eve Post 237:60-2 Mr 28 '64
Development of the U.S. South. A. Goldschmidt. il Sci Am 209:224-30+ bibliog(p310) S '63
Retraining and the South. J. E. Williams. il Mo Labor R 87:657-9 Je '64
Space crescent. W. S. Ellis. il Nation 199: 211-16, 239-43, 275-7+ O 12-26 '64

History

Southerner's answer to the Negro question. C. V. Woodward. il Reporter 30:39-44 F 27 '64
See also
Ku Klux klan
Negroes in the United States—History
Reconstruction (Civil war)
United States—History—Civil war

Industries

Space billions, now a boom? What's happening in five states. il U S News 57:64-9 Jl 20 '64
Study of the effects of unionism in southern plants. H. E. Steele and H. Fisher, jr. bibliog f il Mo Labor R 87:258-70 Mr '64
Unions still stumble on Dixie's stone wall. il Bsns W p49-50 Ap 25 '64
Why industry is moving South. il U S News 57:84-8 D 21 '64; Correction. 57:58 D 28 '64
See also
Agriculture—Southern states

Politics

Case for the southern progressive. R. McGill. Sat R 47:17-20 Je 13 '64
Civil rights, government money, and the vote in the South. il U S News 57:41-2 O 19 '64
Close look at the South and LBJ's home state. il U S News 57:45-6 O 12 '64
Crossroads in Dixie. J. J. Kilpatrick. Nat R 15:433-5 N 19 '63
Essential South. R. Moley. Newsweek 63:122 Ap 20 '64
Fare thee well, South. Nation 199:347 N 16 '64
Fixing the score in '64. E. Planer. Reporter 29:35-6 S 12 '63
Goldwater country. J. J. Kilpatrick. Nat R 14:281-2 Ap 9 '63
Is the South to be solid again? L. H. Bean. il U S News 56:34 Ja 20 '64
Lyndon and the South; to reapportion or not. Cato. Nat R 16:762 S 8 '64
New directions? Democrats loss of congressional seats to Republicans. il Newsweek 64:36 N 16 '64
New size-up of the South: what politicians are finding. il U S News 57:51-3 D 7 '64
On a poverty trip with LBJ. il U S News 56:58 My 25 '64
Party comes of age. R. Moley. Newsweek 61: 88 Je 3 '63
Politics and integration. R. Moley. Newsweek 61:112 Je 10 '63
Reporter at large; campaign: Goldwater in seven states of the confederacy and two border states. R. H. Rovere. New Yorker 40:201-4+ O 3 '64
Revolution in Dixie. K. Crawford. Newsweek 61:40 My 13 '63
Senator Thurmond: now he's a Republican. U S News 57:24 S 28 '64
'64 election: suppose the South does revolt. il U S News 54:44-5 Je 24 '63
South goes back up for grabs. J. J. Kilpatrick. il Nat R 15:523-4+ D 17 '63
Southern politician; with editorial comment. F. E. Smith. Nation 199:131, 132-4 S 21 '64
Southern politics and the Negroes. P. Duke. il Reporter 31:18-21 D 17 '64
Southern republicanism. R. Moley. Newsweek 61:108 My 27 '63
Speaking out; G.O.P. invades the South. B. Goldwater. Sat Eve Post 236:10+ Ap 13 '63
Stop Wallace. Nat R 16:577 Jl 14 '64
Straws in the south wind; Goldwater campaign. New Repub 151:13 Ag 22 '64
Twenty-three of thirty-six congressional chairmen are still southerners. U S News 58:14 Ja 4 '65
Uncertain South, by C. O. Lerche, jr. Review Sat R 47:29-30 Ag 1 '64. E. M. Yoder, jr.
Unions open new attack on conservatives; in South. il Nations Bsns 51:80-4 Mr '63
Vote in the South. Nat R 14:437 Je 4 '63; Reply. J. W. Daly. 15:121 Ag 13 '63
Wallace and the future of Dixie. R. G. Sherrill. Nation 199:266-72 O 26 '64
What the GOP is doing in the South. V. Dabney. Harper 226:86-8+ My '63
Will Goldwater sweep the South? il U S News 57:41-2 Ag 10 '64
Will the South bolt Kennedy in 1964? il U S News 54:76-7 My 27 '63
Young GOP in old Dixie. R. Moley. Newsweek 61:108 My 20 '63
See also
Southern governors conference

Prisons

See Prisons—United States

Race problems

See Negroes in the United States—South

Religious institutions and affairs

Southern white Protestantism at the turn of the century. K. K. Bailey. bibliog f Am Hist R 68:618-35 Ap '63

Social conditions

Southern establishment. S. Southard. Christian Cent 81:1618-21 D 30 '64

Social history

See also
Slavery—United States

SOUTH, University of the. See University of the South, Sewanee, Tenn.

SOUTH AFRICA
Blame me on history; excerpts. B. Modisane. Atlan 212:96-107+ N '63
His father's son: J. Schlesinger. il Time 82: 64-5 Ag 2 '63
Partial exclusion of South Africa from ILO meetings. U N Rev 10:59-60 Jl '63
See also
Airlines—South Africa
Basutoland
Bechuanaland
Botany—South Africa
Church and race problems in South Africa
Civil rights—South Africa
Gardens—South Africa
Gold mines and mining—South Africa
Immigration and emigration—South Africa
Law—South Africa
Newspapers—South Africa
Opera—South Africa
Transkei
United Nations—South Africa
Zambia

Commerce

Beating the ban. il Time 83:106 Je 12 '64

Description and travel

Travel notes. R. Joseph. Esquire 62:22+ N '64
Various pleasures of South Africa. R. Joseph. il Esquire 62:140-1 N '64

Economic conditions

South Africa: justice vs. money. il Newsweek 62:54-6 N 11 '63
Where there's a real boom in Africa. il U S News 56:108-9 My 11 '64

Foreign relations

Atlantic report. Atlan 213:34+ Ap '64
Cocky Boers. Newsweek 62:38 S 16 '63
Loneliness in the beloved country. C. W. De Kiewiet. For Affairs 42:413-27 Ap '64
South Africa: enclaves of trouble. J. Halpern. il Nation 197:49-52 Jl 27 '63
Whither the white belt? S. Uys. New Repub 148:12-14 Je 22 '63

Industries

South Africa's king of diamonds: H. Oppenheimer. G. Gaskill. Read Digest 84:197-8+ My '64
See also
Diamond mines and mining

Native races

Black pawns of Bantustan. T. Sterling. il Reporter 29:42-4+ O 10 '63
First step in the Transkei; Bantustan policy. T. Molnar. Nat R 16:155-6 F 25 '64; Reply with rejoinder. H. Suzman. 16:461 Je 2 '64

SOUTH AFRICA—Native races—*Continued*
South African fortnight. W. F. Buckley, jr; discussion. Nat R 14:127 F 12 '63
What makes Bantus buy. il Time 81:88 Je 21 '63
See also
South Africa—Race problems

Politics and government

Banning of Peter Brown. K. N. Carstens. Christian Cent 81:1274 O 14 '64
Black vote. Newsweek 62:36 D 16 '63
Loneliness in the beloved country. C. W. De Kiewiet. For Affairs 42:413-27 Ap '64
Overthrow of apartheid. P. Duncan. New Repub 148:9-10 Mr 9 '63
South Africa and world opinion. M. Benson. bibliog f Cur Hist 46:129-35+ Mr '64
South Africa: world's biggest race problem, but—. F. C. Painton. il U S News 56:58-61 Ja 6 '64
Whites in Africa; what is their fate? H. Foot. il(p 1) Sat R 47:10-12 Jl 25 '64

Race problems

A. W. Blaxall sentenced to six-month jail term; Johannesburg. Christian Cent 80:1324 O 30 '63
Alone; and so what? Newsweek 61:60 Je 10 '63
Apartheid a dangerous drift of events; Special committee reports to General assembly and Security council. il U N Rev 10:33-7 My '63
Apartheid in South Africa; Security council adopts two resolutions. UN Mo Chron 1:16-25 Jl '64
Apartheid in South Africa; work of special committee of UN. UN Mo Chron 1:3-9 N '64
Assembly adopts resolution on trial in South Africa; with text of resolution. U N Rev 10:8-10+ N '63
Blame me on history; excerpts. B. Modisane. Atlan 212:96-107+ N '63
Call for a dialogue in South Africa. D. V. Cowen. il N Y Times Mag p 19+ My 17 '64
Calls for world conference on racial problems; crusade of A. Walker. Christian Cent 80:1324 O 30 '63
Committee report on apartheid. U N Rev 10:24-6 Ag '63
Crossing the color line. il Time 81:39 My 24 '63
Dispensing with judges. il Time 81:32 My 10 '63
Double game in Africa. America 109:4 Jl 6 '63
Escape artists. Time 82:25 Ag 30 '63
Experiment in segregation. S. Uys. New Repub 148:10-11 My 4 '63
Family troubles. Time 82:33 Jl 19 '63
Fruits of apartheid. New Repub 150:21-2 My 16 '64
Gathering storm. Nation 196:498 Je 15 '63
Gathering storm; African independent states against Portuguese colonialism and South Africa's racial apartheid. Newsweek 62:47-8 Jl 29 '63
Hang they must not; trial at Rivonia, South Africa. Nation 198:470 My 11 '64
Hate against hate; terrorist organization. Newsweek 61:41+ Ap 8 '63
How to win & lose. Time 82:34 D 13 '63
In defense of apartheid. C. A. W. Manning. For Affairs 43:135-49 O '64
Jim Crow South African style. il Ebony 19:123-4+ My '64
Leading up to what Chief Poto told Chief Rusher; with letter by W. A. Rusher. Nat R 15:557-8 D 31 '63
Little more time for violence; with reply by C. Randall. D. Lowe. Atlan 212:24, 70-2 Jl '63
Loneliness in the beloved country. C. W. De Kiewiet. For Affairs 42:413-27 Ap '64
Measures to counter apartheid. U N Rev 10:25-8 D '63
Mission to South Africa. C. Northcott. Christian Cent 81:1550 D 16 '64
Official case for apartheid. H. Muller. il N Y Times Mag p28+ Je 7 '64
Papwa's championship play; Natal open in Durban, South Africa. E. Shirley. il Sports Illus 18:49 F 18 '63
Pressures on South Africa. V. C. Ferkiss. il Commonweal 79:591-4 F 14 '64
Reappraisal in South Africa. A. Vandenbosch. Yale R 53:11-25 O '63
Security council again condemns apartheid in South Africa; statement, with text of resolution. A. E. Stevenson. Dept State Bul 50:92-6 Ja 20 '64
Security council and South Africa. U N Rev 10:20-4 Ag '63
Security council calls for ban on sale of arms to South Africa; statements, with text of resolution. August 7, 1963. A. E. Stevenson; C. W. Yost. Dept State Bul 49:333-9 Ag 26 '63
Some stood up; African resistance movement. New Repub 152:7-8 Ja 2 '65
South Africa and world opinion. M. Benson. bibliog f Cur Hist 46:129-35+ Mr '64
South Africa: justice vs. money. il Newsweek 62:54-6 N 11 '63
South Africa needs time. C. B. Randall. il Atlan 211:77-80 My '63; Same abr. with title Why South Africa needs time. Read Digest 83:151-5 Ag '63
South Africa, the time bomb ticks; policy of apartheid. A. Sampson. il N Y Times Mag p 11+ Ap 12 '64
South Africa: world's biggest race problem, but—. F. C. Painton. il U S News 56:58-61 Ja 6 '64
South African fortnight. W. F. Buckley, jr; discussion. Nat R 14:127 F 12 '63
South Africa's tragic story. A. Walker. Christian Cent 81:406+ Mr 25 '64
Special committee adopts draft report. UN Mo Chron 1:32-7 D '64
Terror in Johannesburg; reprint. Nat R 16:727-8 Ag 25 '64
Thorn tree; amendment to give the government total control over the employment, place of residence and movements of African workers. Time 83:45-6 Ap 17 '64
Toward a world policy for South Africa P. Duncan. For Affairs 42:38-48 O '63
Two worlds of Jimmy Nkosi. J. A. Lukas. il N Y Times Mag p20-1+ Ja 3 '65
Unhappy apart. il Time 81:31-2 F 22 '63
U.N. condemns repression of opponents to apartheid; statement, October 11, 1963; with text of resolution. F. T. P. Plimpton. Dept State Bul 49:758-9 N 11 '63
U.N. Security council condemns apartheid in South Africa; sets up committee to study sanctions; statements, June 16 and June 18, 1964, with text of resolution. A. E. Stevenson. Dept State Bul 51:29-33 Jl 6 '64
West at bay. C. Legum. il Nation 197:70-3 Ag 10 '63
White South African's dilemma. B. Marais. Christian Cent 80:580-1 My 1 '63
Whites in Africa; what is their fate? H. Foot. il(p 1) Sat R 47:10-12 Jl 25 '64
Whose country? il Time 82:47 N 29 '63
See also
Church and race problems in South Africa
United Nations—South Africa

Religious institutions and affairs

Alan Walker in South Africa. H. Henderson Christian Cent 80:1410+ N 13 '63
Geyser wins appeal. Christian Cent 80:701 My 29 '63
News of the Christian world (cont) Christian Cent 80:444-5, 502, 990, 1084+, 1220-2, 1279, 1348-50, 1560-1; 81:120, 189, 839, 889-90, 1018, 1509-10; 82:120-1 Ap 3, 17, Ag 7, S 4, O 2, 16, 30, D 11 '63, Ja 22, F 5, Je 24, Jl 8, Ag 12, D 2 '64, Ja 27 '65
See also
Methodist church of South Africa

Social life and customs

Tell me, Josephine, ed. by B. Hall. Review Nat R il 16:498+ Je 16 '64. P. L. Buckley

Territorial expansion

Protectorates under the gun. S. Uys. New Repub 149:9-10 S 28 '63

SOUTH AFRICA in literature
Quartet: new voices from South Africa. ed. by R. Rive. Review
Sat R 46:43 N 16 '63. W. S. Lynch

SOUTH AFRICAN refugees. See Refugees, South African

SOUTH AMERICA
See also
Latin America

Economic conditions

See Latin America—Economic conditions

Education

See Education—Latin America

Politics

See Latin America—Politics

Population

Fastest growing area; tropical South America. Sci N L 86:37 Jl 18 '64

SOUTH AMERICA and the United States. See Latin America and the United States

SOUTH AMERICANS. See Latin Americans

SOUTH BEND, Ind.
Christmas gift for South Bend. U S News 56:68 Ja 6 '64
Holiday at South Bend; resurgence since Studebaker closure. Newsweek 65:45-6 Ja 4 '65
Pioneer in peril; Studebaker corporation. Sr Schol 83:19-20 Ja 17 '64
When a big company quits, the South Bend story. il U S News 55:76-8 D 23 '63

SOUTH branch of the Potomac. See Potomac River

SOUTH CAROLINA
See also
Fishing—South Carolina
Libraries—South Carolina
Unemployment—South Carolina
Water supply—South Carolina

History
Tragic dream of Jean Ribaut; flag of France on America's South Atlantic coast. S. Harris. il Am Heritage 14:8-15+ O '63

Politics and government
Notes from South Carolina. P. L. Buckley. Nat R 16:852 O 6 '64
Quiet South Carolina. R. Moley. Newsweek 63:100 Mr 23 '64

Race problems
Integration with dignity; with editorial comment. G. McMillan. il Sat Eve Post 236: 15-21, 80 Mr 16 '63
Smart southern politics. J. Frazier. New Repub 148:5 F 23 '63
South Carolina's moment of truth. H. J. Massaquoi. il Ebony 18:96-8+ My '63
Which way South Carolina? Christian Cent 80:165 F 6 '63

Religious institutions and affairs
News of the Christian world. Christian Cent 80:965; 81:1538-9 Jl 31 '63, D 9 '64

SOUTH DAKOTA
See also
Birds—South Dakota
Black Hills
Hunting—South Dakota

Race problems
Discrimination thrives in South Dakota (cont) Christian Cent 80:230 F 20 '63

SOUTH HUNTINGTON, N.Y.
Keep ahead of the water demand. O. A. Olsen. il Am City 79:167-8 S '64

SOUTH HUNTINGTON, N.Y, water district. See Water districts

SOUTH in literature
History, tragedy, and the imagination in Absalom, Absalom! C. Brooks. Yale R 52: 340-51 Mr '63

SOUTH KOREA. See Korea (Republic)

SOUTH MILWAUKEE, Wis.

Water supply
Big improvement in operation. J. Skorupski. il Am City 79:78-9 Ag '64

SOUTH PACIFIC commission
Self-government in the South Pacific. C. Skinner. il For Affairs 42:137-47 O '63

SOUTH SEA ISLANDS
Self-government in the South Pacific. C. Skinner. il For Affairs 42:137-47 O '63
See also
Bora Bora, Society Islands
Easter Island
Guam
Midway (islands)
Nauru (island)
Polynesia
Tahiti

SOUTH TYROL. See Tyrol

SOUTH VIET NAM. See Viet Nam (Republic)

SOUTH WARNER wild area. See Wilderness areas

SOUTH WEST AFRICA. See Southwest Africa

SOUTHAMPTON, N.Y.
Summer place. il Time 84:46 Ag 14 '64

SOUTHARD, Samuel
Are southern churches silent? Christian Cent 80:1429-32 N 20 '63
Southern establishment. Christian Cent 81: 1618-21 D 30 '64

SOUTHEAST ASIA. See Asia, Southeastern

SOUTHEAST ASIA treaty organization
Eighth meeting of SEATO council of ministers; statement, April 8, 1963; with communique. D. Rusk. Dept State Bul 48:641-4 Ap 29 '63
Grave concern; holding the line in Asia. il Newsweek 63:39 Ap 27 '64
Ninth anniversary of SEATO; statement, September 6, 1963. D. Rusk. Dept State Bul 49:464 S 23 '63
Secretary Rusk heads delegation to SEATO council meeting. Dept State Bul 50:577 Ap 13 '64
SEATO announces 1963-64 schedule of military defense exercises. Dept State Bul 49: 863-4 D 2 '63
SEATO council of ministers meets at Manila; statement; with text of communique, April 15, 1964. D. Rusk. Dept State Bul 50:690-3 My 4 '64
Tenth anniversary of SEATO; statement, September 5, 1964. D. Rusk. Dept State Bul 51:400 S 21 '64

SOUTHEASTERN regional ballet festival. See Dance festivals

SOUTHERN, Dodd A.
Cut-rate paving assessments. Am City 79:96 Ap '64

SOUTHERN, Terry
How I signed up at $250 a month for the big parade through Havana bla-bla-bla and wound up in Guatemala with the CIA. Esquire 59:67-8+ Je '63
Mickey Spillane as Mike Hammer. Esquire 60:74-6+ Jl '63
Twirling at Ole Miss. Esquire 59:100+ F '63
You're too hip, baby; story. Esquire 59:68-9 Ap '63
about
Creative capacity to astonish. J. Howard. il pors Life 57:39-40+ Ag 21 '64
Donkeyman by twilight. N. Algren. Nation 198:509-12 My 18 '64
No limits. por Newsweek 63:86+ Je 22 '64

SOUTHERN Baptist convention. See Baptists in the United States

SOUTHERN Baptists. See Baptists in the United States

SOUTHERN Bell telephone and telegraph company
Merritt Island telephone award to be reserved for Southern Bell. Aviation W 79:30 Ag 12 '63

SOUTHERN CALIFORNIA university, Los Angeles
Automated AV catalog; Department of cinema. Wilson Lib Bul 39:373 Ja '65

SOUTHERN Christian leadership conference
Hotter fires; friction between organizations; with report by K. Fleming. il Newsweek 62:19-21 Jl 1 '63
Scripto on strike; the race-wage picket line. C. J. Levy. Nation 200:31-2 Ja 11 '65

SOUTHERN company
Private power in TVA's backyard. il Bsns W p 176-8+ O 17 '64

SOUTHERN consumers' cooperative. See Cooperative associations

SOUTHERN corn rootworms. See Corn rootworms

SOUTHERN governors conference
Having wonderful time. Time 82:16-17 Ag 30 '63

SOUTHERN HIGHLANDS. See Appalachian Region

SOUTHERN ILLINOIS university, Carbondale
Art and the student teacher. L. B. Kennon and T. Markle. il Sch Arts 63:5-10 Ap '64
Big voice in Little Egypt. il Time 83:61 My 15 '64
New university campus is pre-planned for change: campus at Edwardsville. il Arch Rec 134:110-16 Ag '63

Library
Automated circulation procedure at Southern Illinois university. Library J 88:1133 Mr 15 '63

SOUTHERN PACIFIC railroad company
Jobs at stake in rail dispute; Southern Pacific railroad and Railway clerks union. U S News 54:96 Mr 11 '63
Overland limited; excerpts from Central Pacific and the Southern Pacific railroads. L. Beebe. il Am Heritage 15:54-7+ D '63
Rail arbitration: a pattern set? U S News 54:125 Mr 25 '63
When automation comes and workers stay on. U S News 54:88-9 Ap 1 '63

SOUTHERN pine beetles. See Pine—Diseases and pests

SOUTHERN Presbyterian church. See Presbyterian church in the United States (South)

SOUTHERN railway company
Boxcars go to battle for Southern. il Bsns W p76-80+ Je 8 '63
Case of the elderly firemen; contempt-of-court charges brought by Locomotive firemen's union. U S News 55:125 N 18 '63

SOUTHERN railway company—*Continued*
Hell of a different way to run a railroad. H. B. Meyers. il Fortune 68:100-9+ S '63
Rail firemen: fight flares again; feather bedding. U S News 58:71-2 Ja 11 '65
Railroad hires new firemen, but . . . il U S News 55:75 Ag 12 '63
That's railroadin'; firemen on the Southern. Time 82:16 Ag 9 '63
SOUTHERN RHODESIA. See Rhodesia
SOUTHERN states. See South
SOUTHERN transcontinental route. See Airways
SOUTHERN women. See Women—United States
SOUTHERNERS
He stands at the door. J. M. Dabbs. Christian Cent 81:359-60 Mr 18 '64
SOUTHEY, Robert
Story of the three bears and the man who didn't write it. J. M. Lexau. il Horn Bk 40:88-94 F '64
SOUTHWEST
Southwest; with report by H. Ehrlich. il Look 27:23-31 O 8 '63
See also
Hunting—Southwestern states
Water supply—Southwestern states
Description and travel
Great Southwest. C. Wolfe. il Flying 75:34-6+ S '64
Great Southwest. il Bet Hom & Gard 41:107-10 Ap '63
Land of adventure. A. De Dienes. il U S Camera 27:75-7+ Ag '64
Industries
Boom in the desert; why it grows and grows. il U S News 56:46-52 My 25 '64
Indian wampum builds an electronics plant. il Bsns W p74-6 My 23 '64
Politics
Goldwater; Southwest political story. F. Knebel. il Look 27:36-7 O 8 '63; Discussion. 27:18+ N 19 '63
SOUTHWEST AFRICA
Another Transkei. New Repub 150:11 Mr 7 '64
South West Africa. B. Kingsley. il Travel 119:50-4 Mr '63
South West Africa; timetable for freedom. P. Duncan. il Nation 198:265-7 Mr 16 '64
Territory of South West Africa. R. B. Ballinger. bibliog f Cur Hist 45:361-5 D '63
U.S. expresses continuing concern for future of South-West Africa; statement, October 30, 1963. S. R. Yates. Dept State Bul 49:946-8 D 16 '63
See also
United Nations—Southwest Africa
SOUTHWEST research institute, San Antonio, Tex.
It's solid gasoline. il Life 55:49-50 O 11 '63
SOUTHWEST TEXAS state teachers college, San Marcos
President's own. il Newsweek 62:54 D 30 '63
SOUTHWESTERN cookery. See Cookery, American
SOUTHWESTERN library association
Attempt to censure Bowker company fails at Southwestern LA meeting. Library J 89:4490 N 15 '64
SOUTHWICK, Albert B.
(ed) See Malcolm X. Malcolm X: charismatic demagogue
SOUTHWICK, Charles H.
Peromyscus leucopus: an interesting subject for studies of socially induced stress responses. bibliog Science 143:55-6 Ja 3 '64
SOUTHWORTH, Albert Sands
More living than the memory of the man. B. Newhall. Pop Phot 55:152-3+ N '64
SOUTINE, Chaim
Soutine: the impact of infighting. D. Sylvester. il por Art N 62:22-7+ O '63
SOUVAINE, Geraldine
Lady of the intermissions. pors Opera N 29:12-15 D 5 '64
SOUVANNA Phouma, prince of Laos, 1901-
Reporter at large. R. Shaplen. New Yorker 40:80+ Ja 16 '65
U.S.-backed neutrals. U S News 54:21 Ap 29 '63
SOUVENIR programs. See Theater programs
SOUVENIRS
Life guide: take-homes to tempt travelers. il Life 54:7 Je 21 '63
Vacation shopping for decorating treasures. L. Sloane. Am Home 67:110+ Jl '64
SOUZA, Cláudio Mello e. See Mello e Souza, C.
SOUZAY, Gerard
Quote: unquote; interview, ed. by J. Ardoin. por Mus Am 84:33 Ap '64
about
Master class with Souzay. il pors Mus Am 83:53 Mr '63
SOVEREIGNTY
Principles of international law concerning friendly relations and cooperation among states: sovereign equality of states; statement, December 3, 1963. E. F. Kelly. Dept State Bul 50:264-7 F 17 '64
SOVIET bloc. See Communist countries
SOVIET education. See Education—Russia
SOVIET embassy. See Embassies (buildings)
SOVIET government. See Russia—Politics and government
SOVIET literature. See Russian literature
SOVIET postage stamps. See Postage stamps
SOVIET studies. See Area studies
SOVIET theater. See Theater—Russia
SOVIET UNION. See Russia
SOVIET women. See Women—Russia
SOVIET writers. See Authors, Russian
SOVIET youth. See Youth—Russia
SOWDER, A. M.
Arbor day, our loveliest holiday. Am For 70:27+ Ap '64
Things you ought to know about Christmas trees. Am For 69:12-15+ D '63
SOWING. See Seeding
SOWS. See Swine
SOYA products. See Soybean products
SOYBEAN products
New foods and new hopes. il Newsweek 61:51 Je 17 '63
SOYBEANS
Chlorophyll content and growth of soybean plants: possible interaction of iron availability and day length. H. M. Benedict, and others. il Science 144:1134-5 My 29 '64
How to grow forty-bushel soybeans. Suc Farm 61:90 My '63
How two champions grow sixty-bushel soybeans. J. Russell. il Farm J 88:40-1 My '64
Ideas that bin more soybeans. il Farm J 87:44 My '63
Narrow rows; the coming thing? J. Russell. il Farm J 87:36-7+ Mr '63
Nature note. Sci N L 86:363 D 5 '64
New soybean resists cyst nematode. Farm J 87:40 Jl '63
Should pay to store corn and soybeans. T. A. Hieronymus. Suc Farm 61:33 S '63
Should you plant more soybeans? C. W. Gifford. Farm J 88:65-6 Ap '64
Soybean weed killers, they really work. J. Dyer. il Farm J 87:28-9 Je '63
Spray soybeans to set more pods? Farm J 88:32 Ag '64
Take off barley, hustle in soybeans. B. Hardy. il Farm J 87:36-7 Ap '63
They grow forty-bushel soybeans; Indiana farmers. L. E. Zeman. il Suc Farm 62:52-3 Ap '64
Thirty-five bu. beans top 100-bu. corn. Suc Farm 61:136 Mr '63
See also
Multipurpose food
SPAAK, Catherine
Stardom and boredom of Catherine Spaak. P. Hamill. il pors Sat Eve Post 237:58-60 My 2 '64
SPAAK, Paul Henri
Hold fast. For Affairs 41:611-20 Jl '63
New effort to build Europe. For Affairs 43:199-208 Ja '65
Year of special importance; address, October 2, 1963. Vital Speeches 30:37-41 N 1 '63
about
Congo; an attempt to go back. il por Time 83:27 Mr 27 '64
SPACE (architecture)
Here's a wonderful use of a front yard; space for playroom and pool. il Bet Hom & Gard 41:12 Ag '63
How to enlarge space without adding to it. il House & Gard 123:30+ Mr '63
Luxury of waste space. il Time 83:75 Mr 6 '64
Nine ways to increase your living space. il Ladies Home J 80:103-4+ Mr '63

SPACE, Outer
James Van Allen tells what space is really like; interview, ed. by W. Cloud. J. A. Van Allen. il Pop Sci 182:73-6+ Ap '63
Politics of outer space. L. P. Bloomfield. Bul Atomic Sci 19:12-14 My '63
Space: highlights of recent research. R. Jastrow and A. G. W. Cameron. bibliog il Science 145:1129-39 S 11 '64; Reply. E. A. Whitaker and W. K. Hartmann. 146:342 O 16 '64

International control

Closing in on a space pact; U.S. and Soviet Union make concessions on rules. Bsns W p60+ N 16 '63
Cooperation in outer space. R. N. Gardner. For Affairs 41:344-59 Ja '63
International cooperation in outer space; statement, October 27, 1964. F. T. P. Plimpton. bibliog f Dept State Bul 51:755-9 N 23 '64
Outer space. U N Rev 10:18 D '63

Law

See Space law

SPACE and information systems division. See North American aviation, incorporated—Space and information systems division

SPACE and time
Being and time, by M. Heidegger; tr. by J. Macquarrie and E. Robinson. Review
Christian Cent 79:1482-4 D 5 '62. W. Hordern; Discussion. 80:182-3 F 6 '63
We will now test the time machine. S. Spillman. il Sci Digest 54:57-60 O '63
See also
Ether (of space)
Relativity (physics)
Time reversal

SPACE arrangement of plants. See Plants, Space arrangement of

SPACE committee. See United States—Congress—Senate—Committees

SPACE detection and tracking system. See Radar—Military applications

SPACE division. See Chrysler corporation

SPACE environment chamber. See Testing laboratories

SPACE flight
Answers to your questions about space. W. Von Braun. il Pop Sci 182:92-4 F '63
Armchair astronauts. A. C. Clarke. Holiday 33:94-5+ My '63
Blue Gemini missions outlined by USAF. Aviation W 78:83 F 25 '63
Chronology of fiscal 1963-1964. Miss & Roc 13:200-2+ Jl 29 '63; 15:154-8+ Jl 27 '64
Coming up, though you may never hear it, a big roar over Dyna-Soar; with report by A. Rosenfeld. il Life 54:97-9+ F 22 '63
First unmanned Gemini flight will be orbital shot. W. Burkett. il Miss & Roc 13:16-17 Jl 15 '63
For Russia, a growing list of space flops. U S News 55:10 Jl 8 '63
Guidance and control; special report. C. D. LaFond. il Miss & Roc 13:31-6+ O 7 '63
Navigating the gravity wells of interplanetary space; a primer on the guidance of spaceships through the great unknown ocean sky. J. P. Hagen. il Sat R 47:48-51 Ap 4 '64; Discussion. 47:46 S 5; 64-5 O 3 '64
Saturn V is modern caravel; address, March 2, 1964. J. E. Webb. il Sci N L 85:165-7 Mr 14 '64
Space astronomy at the World's fair. P. A. Leavens. il Sky & Tel 27:332-4 Je '64
USAF keys space plan to three programs. E. H. Kolcum. il Aviation W 78:26-8 Ja 28 '63
USAF sees X-20 cancellation or cutback. E. H. Kolcum. Aviation W 78:26 F 25 '63
U.S. traffic to top 200 by 1976. il Miss & Roc 12:39 My 6 '63
See also
Calculating machines—Space flight applications
International astronautical federation
Navigation (space flight)
Orbital rendezvous (space flight)
Photography of space flights
Television in space flight
United States—National aeronautics and space administration

Communication problems

Aerospace uses seen for ear microphone. B. Miller. il Aviation W 81:53-4 Jl 27 '64
Apollo bio-telemetry system developed. B. Miller. il Aviation W 78:80-1 Mr 18 '63
Apollo communications details disclosed. P. J. Klass. il Aviation W 79:87+ O 21 '63
Apollo unified S-band network to cost minimum of $160-170 million. C. D. LaFond. il Miss & Roc 15:18+ Jl 20 '64
C-band link may aid in re-entry; Avco's Astrovoice. M. Getler. il Miss & Roc 12:28+ F 11 '63
Millimeter waves hold aerospace promise. B. Miller. il Aviation W 81:70-1+ Ag 24 '64
Motorola proposes combining Apollo communications into single system. R. Pay. il Miss & Roc 14:42-3 Ap 6 '64
S-band system subcontractors to Collins to be named this month. C. D. LaFond. il Miss & Roc 15:36-7 Ag 3 '64
Satellite communications and international understanding; statement, November 20, 1963. J. F. Kennedy. Dept State Bul 49:904 D 9 '63
Satellite tracking, telemetry, and communications. J. T. Mengel. il Electr World 71:58-60 Je '64
Study on lunar communications due. M. Getler. Miss & Roc 14:18 My 18 '64
Symposium stresses data compression. R. Pay. Miss & Roc 15:35 O 12 '64
U.S. delegate reports on space radio communication conference; statement, November 8, 1963. J. McConnell. Dept State Bul 49:835-7 N 25 '63
See also
Space telemetry

Economic aspects

Businessmen review the space effort. E. E. Furash. il Harvard Bsns R 41:14-16+ S '63
Costs and the choices. F. A. Lindsay. Atlan 212:51-4 Ag '63
Dark clouds in space; fourth national symposium. il Bsns W p 116+ My 9 '64
G&C market survey; market for balance of decade expected to approach $8.8 billion. il Miss & Roc 13:32-6 O 7 '63
Manned space flight funding. il Aviation W 79:70 Jl 22 '63
Priorities; funds for the Apollo program. Reporter 28:10 Je 6 '63
Race for the moon. R. Steel and W. Lineberry. Commonweal 78:321-3 Je 14 '63; Reply with rejoinder. E. J. Harrington. 78:427-9 Jl 12 '63
Race to the moon. New Repub 148:3-4 Ap 13 '63
Rites of spring. E. Diamond. Bul Atomic Sci 19:26-9 My '63
Space budget: opposition grows as scientists, congressmen, voice concern about lunar landing goal. D. S. Greenberg. Science 140: 790-1 My 17 '63; Discussion. 141:390; 142: 343 Ag 2, O 18 '63
Space technology: pay-off from spin-off. J. G. Welles and R. H. Waterman, jr. bibliog f il Harvard Bsns R 42:106-18 Jl '64
To moon or not to moon. il Time 81:53 My 31 '63
White House blocks Apollo slowdown. H. Taylor. Miss & Roc 13:16 D 9 '63

Food problems

Coverall seen as best thermal protector; menus for Gemini and Apollo. il Aviation W 81:72-3 N 23 '64
Diet that might wipe out malnutrition. il Time 82:62 N 22 '63
Edible space station material developed. Miss & Roc 12:35 Ap 15 '63
Edible space structure material tested. il Aviation W 78:34 Ap 22 '63
Manned spacecraft center combines food programs for Apollo, Gemini. Miss & Roc 14: 36 Je 8 '64
Pie in the sky: astronaut diet? Sci N L 86:84 Ag 8 '64
Space food harvest may be speeded up. Sci N L 83:169 Mr 16 '63
Space food problems. Sci N L 84:279 N 2 '63
Testing nutrition for space. il Todays Health 42:6-7 N '64

International aspects

Closing in on a space pact; U.S. and Soviet Union make concessions on rules. Bsns W p60+ N 16 '63
Control of outer space. L. E. Schwartz. Cur Hist 47:39-46 Jl '64
International organization and space law; address, May 1, 1963. A. Chayes. Dept State Bul 48:835-8 My 27 '63
Kennedy plan stirs attack on space funds. A. P. Alibrando. Aviation W 79:29-30 O 7 '63
Kennedy's offer stirs confusion, dismay; with editorial comment. A. P. Alibrando. Aviation W 79:21, 26-7 S 30 '63
Military role in space. G. C. Sponsler. Bul Atomic Sci 20:31-4 Je '64; Reply. D. W. Smythe. 20:37-8 O '64

SPACE flight—International aspects—*Cont.*
NASA denies Soviet moon proposal; with editorial comment. H. Taylor. Miss & Roc 13:21, 50 Ag 19 '63
NASA: talk of togetherness with Soviets further complicates space politics for the agency. J. Walsh. Science 142:35-8 O 4 '63
Outer space: problems of law and power; address, August 10, 1963. R. N. Gardner. Dept State Bul 49:367-71 S 2 '63
Redefinition of U.S. space goals planned; with editorial comment. A. P. Alibrando. Aviation W 79:21, 26-7 N 4 '63
Russia's space bobbles and what they mean. U S News 54:11 Ap 22 '63
Space: U.S and Soviet scientists get along on detailed planning for two cooperative projects. E. Langer. Science 140:39-40 Ap 5 '63
U.N adopts resolutions on cooperation in outer space; U.S. reaffirms offer to work with Soviet Union on manned lunar landing; statement, December 2, 1963; with texts of resolutions, December 13, 1963. A. E. Stevenson. bibliog f Dept State Bul 49:1005-14 D 30 '63
UN group will reconsider move to aid astronauts in distress. Aviation W 80:24 Ap 6 '64
U.S, Russia agree to swap data on space biology and medicine work. Miss & Roc 14:13 Je 15 '64
U.S.-Russian space agreement advances. W. J. Normyle. Aviation W 80:34 Je 15 '64
U.S. secrecy on Soviet launches scored. Aviation W 78:28 Je 3 '63
U.S.-USSR space plan covers direct exchange of weather data. Aviation W 78:36 Ap 1 '63
See also
United Nations—Committee on the peaceful uses of outer space

Manned flights

AF widens manned flight role. W. Burkett. Miss & Roc 14:12 Je 15 '64
Air force will have small role in Gemini. Aviation W 79:225+ Jl 22 '63
All aboard the Gemini; time 1984, or thereabouts. R. A. Heinlein. il Pop Mech 119: 112-16+ My '63
America's astronauts on the moon by 1970? il U S News 56:15 Ap 27 '64
Ames scientists advocate single earth-launch manned Mars mission. Miss & Roc 14:17-18 My 4 '64
Apollo, Gemini to cost $4 billion yearly. A. P. Alibrando. Aviation W 78:31 Ap 1 '63
Apollo-X spacecraft going into program definition next fiscal year. il Miss & Roc 15: 52-3+ N 30 '64
Astronauts can't be automated. J. W. Finney. il N Y Times Mag p24-5+ My 5 '63
Astronauts, top NASA leadership split over attempting MA-10 shot. il Miss & Roc 12: 16-17 My 27 '63
Can we ever go to the stars? W. Von Braun. il Pop Sci 183:63-5+ Jl '63
Collier trophy award; astronauts in Project Mercury. B. Kocivar. il Look 27:141-4+ O 22 '63
Coming: big space decision. W. Burkett. il Sci Digest 56:50-6 O '64
Cooper to de-pressurize MA-9 craft. H. M. David. Miss & Roc 12:30+ F 18 '63
Cooper's longest day; twenty-two orbits. il Newsweek 61:92 My 20 '63
DOD, NASA agree on Gemini experiments. W. H. Gregory. il Aviation W 80:38+ Je 1 '64
Early fourteen-day Voskhod flight is predicted. D. E. Fink. Aviation W 81:22-3 N 16 '64
Earth problems for space men. R. A. Pollard. il N Y Times Mag p28+ N 3 '63
Eight-day Soviet manned flight forecast. Aviation W 78:38 Ap 15 '63
First Gemini mission is key to initial two-man flight this year. H. Taylor. il Miss & Roc 14:16-17 Ap 6 '64
First manned Saturn 5 flight set for 1967. A. P. Alibrando. Aviation W 78:34 Mr 25 '63
First successful Gemini mission points to manned flight in 1964; Second Gemini flight set for August. G. Alexander. il Aviation W 80:29-30 Ap 13 '64
Flight coaches: astronauts, Glenn and Grissom. Newsweek 61:48 F 4 '63
Flight test of Gemini program nears, but role in post-Apollo plans remains cloudy. G. Alexander. il Aviation W 80:38-9+ Mr 30 '64
Fourth orbital spaceflight. il Sci N L 83:311 My 18 '63
Fubini urges military space role analysis. P. J. Klass. Aviation W 79:46+ S 2 '63
GT-5 astronaut will leave capsule. Miss & Roc 14:31-2 My 18 '64
GT-2 success brings go-ahead order for first manned Gemini. G. Alexander. il Aviation W 82:30-1 Ja 25 '65
Gemini, Apollo and beyond; special report. il Aviation W 81:48-9+ N 16; 48-9+ N 23 '64
Gemini design keyed to mission flexibility. G. Alexander. il Aviation W 78:52-5+ My 13 '63
Gemini evolves into operational program. il Aviation W 79:175-9+ Jl 22 '63
Gemini flight is still scheduled for 1963 despite many problems. Aviation W 79:29 O 21 '63
Gemini goals within reach despite delay in first flight. il Aviation W 81:76-8 N 23 '64
Gemini manned flight now year late. A. P. Alibrando. Aviation W 78:22 My 6 '63
Gemini; special report. il Miss & Roc 14:12-13+ Ap 13 '64
Go for Gemini. il Newsweek 65:52 F 1 '65
Grissom, Young selected for Gemini crew. W. J. Normyle. Aviation W 80:38-9 Ap 20 '64
Home base for spacemen; NASA's manned spacecraft center. il Bsns W p64-7+ My 30 '64
Is Russia leaving the moon to the U.S.? Bsns W p36+ N 2 '63
Kindergarten Gemini. Time 83:118 Ap 17 '64
Lessons of Project Mercury. R. Lewis. Bul Atomic Sci 19:51-3 D '63
LBJ wants post-Apollo plans. H. Taylor. il Miss & Roc 14:12 My 4 '64
MA-9 boosts hopes for tenth mission. il Miss & Roc 12:10+ My 20 '63
MA-9 experiments vital to rendezvous; plans for eighteen to twenty-two orbit flight. G. Alexander. Aviation W 78:55+ Ja 21 '63
Ma-10 ruled out; Project Mercury ends. Aviation W 78:36 Je 17 '63
Man to the moon. T. Alexander. il Pop Sci 185:60-5 Ag '64
Manned Gemini flight set for April. il Miss & Roc 16:13 Ja 25 '65
Manned project choices nearer; NASA plans. il Miss & Roc 12:14-15 F 18 '63
Manned space flight. il Electr World 17:56-7 Je '64
Manned Venus-Mars fly-by in 1970 studied. A. P. Alibrando. il Aviation W 78:56 Mr 4 '63
Mars mission study proposals evaluated. Aviation W 78:55 Ap 15 '63
Mercury showed value of pilot in space. il Aviation W 79:197-204 Jl 22 '63
Milestone for Gemini. Time 85:44 Ja 29 '65
Missile that will carry men; to fit Titan II ICBM for the Gemini spacecraft. il Bsns W p 136-8 O 12 '63
More cosmonaut trips expected. il Miss & Roc 12:14-15 Je 24 '63
NASA finalizes mission schedule for entire Gemini program. il Miss & Roc 15:12 Ag 24 '64
NASA fires a blast; Project Mercury. il Bsns W p30 O 12 '63
NASA/industry team wants future manned flights to use Apollo core. J. Trainor. il Miss & Roc 14:14-15 Je 8 '64
NASA presses for extended Apollo. H. Taylor. Miss & Roc 14:16 Ap 27 '64
NASA weighs MA-10 possibility. H. Taylor. il Miss & Roc 12:14 Ap 1 '63
NASA weighs MA-10; six-day flight urged. E. H. Kolcum. il Aviation W 78:22-3 My 27 '63
NASA weighs seventy-two-hr. mission after MA-9. E. H. Kolcum. Aviation W 78:34-5 My 13 '63
Navy-NASA program may yield scientist astronauts. H. M. David. Miss & Roc 12: 18 My 27 '63
New astronauts will fly second Gemini. Aviation W 81:24 Ag 3 '64
New time-in-orbit records set by Russians. Sci N L 83:408 Je 29 '63
Next in space: where added billions will go; Project Gemini. il U S News 58:38-9 Ja 4 '65
Next Soviet manned shot believed one year away. F. G. McGuire. Miss & Roc 14:33-4+ Je 22 '64
Nights of the iguana; stepped-up pace of the manned space-flight program. il Newsweek 64:84 Jl 13 '64
No Apollo slow-down; Webb; interview, with editorial comment by W. J. Coughlin and H. Taylor. J. E. Webb. il Miss & Roc 12:14-16, 46 Je 3 '63
Nova decision may be far away. R. Hawkes. il Miss & Roc 12:16-17 Ap 29 '63

SPACE flight—Manned flights—*Continued*
Our next adventure in space; reprint. E. Ubell and others. il Sci Digest 57:48-57 Ja '65
Pair picked for Gemini. V. Grissom; J. Young. il Life 56:113-14+ Je 5 '64
Paired up for Gemini; NASA announces the first crews. il Bsns W p70-2+ Ap 18 '64
Post-Apollo lunar-orbit experiment recommendations detailed in report. M. Getler. il Miss & Roc 15:22-3+ D 21 '64
Project Mercury concluded. R. N. Watts, jr. Sky & Tel 26:327-8 D '63
Schirra reports on MA-8 flight success. W. M. Schirra, jr. Aviation W 78:55+ F 11 '63
So we land on the moon, then what? with editorial comment. C. P. Gilmore. il Pop Sci 183:40, 59-61+ D '63
Soon: more space spectaculars; Project Gemini. il U S News 56:61 Ap 20 '64
Soviet space failures. Aviation W 78:39 Ap 15 '63
Space slowdown via defective parts? concerning final report on Project Mercury. Sr Schol 83:18 N 15 '63
Station holds key to USAF's man-in-space mission. D. Fink. il Aviation W 80:112-13+ Mr 16 '64
Tailored for the moon; space suit. il Newsweek 61:48 F 4 '63
Third manned Gemini will have rendezvous capability. R. Pay. Miss & Roc 15:21 Jl 6 '64
Titanic task. R. Hotz. Aviation W 81:11 N 2 '64
Trouble at the controls. il Newsweek 61:74 Je 3 '63
Two-man team named. il Sr Schol 84:19 My 1 '64
Under whose moon? il Time 81:15-16 My 31 '63
USAF may fly manned station in Titan 3 development program. Aviation W 80:28 F 10 '64
U.S. facing decisions on manned flight; with editorial comment. il Aviation W 79:68-9, 73-6 Jl 22 '63
U.S. space effort turns to Gemini, Apollo. E. H. Kolcum. il Aviation W 78:107-9+ Mr 11 '63
U.S. space program at funding plateau. il Aviation W 80:107-11 Mr 16 '64
Vehicle study for extended Mars mission calls for advances in varied technologies; manned Mars excursion module. H. D. Watkins. il Aviation W 80:54-5+ Ap 20 '64
Venus swingby would permit using Saturn hardware on manned Mars trip. W. E. Wilks. il Miss & Roc 15:24+ D 14 '64
Visit to the three Cape Kennedys. R. G. Whalen. il N Y Times Mag p34-5+ D 13 '64
Vostoks, Cosmos build Soviet space gains. E. Clark. il Aviation W 78:132-7 Mr 11 '63
Water recovery likely for Apollo flights. D. E. Fink. Aviation W 80:30-1 F 24 '64
Webb looks beyond Apollo. J. E. Webb. Aviation W 80:11 Mr 23 '64
Williams cites Mercury problems, contributions to future missions. Aviation W 79:74 Jl 1 '63
See also
Astronauts
Orbital rendezvous (space flight)
Space flight to Mars
Space flight to the moon

Anecdotes, facetiae, satire, etc.

What's for launch? P. Mandel. il Life 54:20 Je 14 '63

Bykovskii flight, 1963

After latest space test, is moon any nearer? il U S News 55:68-9 Jl 1 '63
Cosmonauts describe flights, experiments. S. Ramsey. Aviation W 79:28-30 Jl 1 '63
Hawk. il Newsweek 61:68 Je 24 '63
His and hers. il Newsweek 62:46 Jl 1 '63
Impressive failure; Vostoks 5 and 6. New Repub 148:7 Je 29 '63
Romanoff & Juliet. il Time 81:26+ Je 21 '63
Soviets push ahead in the space race. U S News 54:8 Je 24 '63
Theory of premature Vostok 5 separation is backed by NASA. P. J. Klass. il Aviation W 79:27-8 Jl 1 '63
Vostok 5 may have separated too early. P. J. Klass. il Aviation W 78:34-5 Je 24 '63
Vostok flights widen Soviet experience. il Aviation W 79:315-18 Jl 22 '63
Why Valentina flew. il Bsns W p26-8 Je 22 '63

Cooper flight, 1963

Cooper and his camera tell the great story. G. Cooper. il Life 54:26-35 Je 7 '63
Cooper flies almost-perfect twenty-two orbits; with editorial comment. il Aviation W 78:21, 26-31 My 20 '63
Cooper reports on details of MA-9 flight. G. Cooper. Aviation W 79:61-2+ O 14 '63
Cooper shows man can take it in space. il Bsns W p78+ My 25 '63
Cooper's contribution. W. J. Coughlin. Miss & Roc 12:72 My 27 '63
Cooper's flight prompts new studies. H. M. David. Miss & Roc 12:52+ Je 24 '63
Cooper's precise piloting of Faith 7 cited. G. Alexander. Aviation W 78:25-6 My 27 '63
Experts back Cooper sighting claims. Miss & Roc 13:14-15 O 14 '63
Finest hour for Atlas; booster does biggest job. il Bsns W p28-9 My 18 '63
He brings it in right on the old bazoo. il Life 54:28-33 My 24 '63
MA-9 pilot counters skeptics on sightings of small objects. Aviation W 79:31 Jl 1 '63
Man on the moon: how soon now? il U S News 54:35-9 My 27 '63
Man the whole world cheered. il U S News 54:24 My 27 '63
A man's victory; Great Gordo. il Time 81:17-21 My 24 '63
Mercury problems, successes reviewed. E. J. Bulban. Aviation W 79:29-30 O 14 '63
Nerve center; Goddard space flight center. New Yorker 39:30-2 My 25 '63
Notes and comment. New Yorker 39:23 Je 1 '63
On the bazoo. il Newsweek 61:61-4 My 27 '63
Rendezvous beacon in space. Sky & Tel 26:23 Jl '63
Scientists back Cooper's sighting claims. E. H. Kolcum. Aviation W 79:34 O 7 '63
Water, water. . . . Newsweek 61:70 Je 10 '63
Weightlessness effects on Cooper cited. W. C. Wetmore. il Aviation W 78:34-5 Je 17 '63

Komarov-Yegorov-Feoktistov flight, 1964

Bacterial compatibility stressed in selection of Voskhod crews. Aviation W 81:59 N 23 '64
Can U.S. catch up in space race? il U S News 57:58-60 O 26 '64
Cosmonauts' own story of epic three-man orbit; with US experts assessment, ed. by H. Suydam. V. Komarov and others. il Life 58:34-34C+ Ja 22 '65
Passenger service. il Newsweek 64:98-9 O 26 '64
Peaceful co-existence; address, October 19, 1964. L. I. Brezhnev. Vital Speeches 31:38-40 N 1 '64
Russians score again. il Bsns W p23-4 O 17 '64
Soviet success spurs U.S. space review; with editorial comment. W. J. Normyle. il Aviation W 81:21, 36-7 O 19 '64
Soviet three-man spaceship. R. N. Watts, jr. Sky & Tel 28:353-4 D '64
Soviets used Voskhod as orbital testbed. Aviation W 81:28-9 O 26 '64
Space shot significance. J. Eberhart. il Sci N L 86:259 O 24 '64
Sunrise with troika. il Time 84:51 O 23 '64
Trio return early. il Sr Schol 85:23 O 28 '64
Voskhod shows big Soviet lead; with editorial comment. H. Taylor. il Miss & Roc 15:13-14, 54 O 19 '64

Tereshkova flight, 1963

After lastest space test, is moon any nearer? il U S News 55:68-9 Jl 1 '63
And she didn't say, "my heavens!" J. Lear. Sat R 46:45 Jl 6 '63
Comely cosmonaut. E. Stevens. il Ladies Home J 80:60+ S '63
Cosmonauts describe flights, experiments. S. Ramsey. Aviation W 79:28-30 Jl 1 '63
His and hers. il Newsweek 62:46 Jl 1 '63
Impressive failure; Vostoks 5 and 6. New Repub 148:7 Je 29 '63
Three days in outer space. V. Tereshkova. il Sat Eve Post 237:62-3 Ja 4 '64
Vostok flights widen Soviet experience. il Aviation W 79:315-18 Jl 22 '63
Why Valentina flew. il Bsns W p26-8 Je 22 '63
Women are different. il Time 81:26+ Je 28 '63

Meteor hazards

Anti-meteoroid dust studied. Miss & Roc 13:29 N 25 '63
Meteoroid damage to spacecraft? Sky & Tel 27:150 Mr '64
Meteoroid detection satellite mock-up shown. C. D. LaFond. il Miss & Roc 12:32-3 Je 24 '63
Meteoroid protection developments aired at AIAA meeting. W. E. Wilks. Miss & Roc 14:29 My 25 '64

SPACE flight—Meteor hazards—*Continued*
Meteoroids and spacemen. Sci N L 85:15 Ja 4 '64
Meteoroids ruled out as space flight peril. Aviation W 79:107 N 11 '63
System detects holes caused by meteoroids. Aviation W 78:86 Ap 22 '63

Military applications

Air force space goals, projects defended by research staff chief. Aviation W 78:32 Je 3 '63
Apollo use in military programs proposed. Aviation W 81:27-9 N 9 '64
Apollo's military potential detailed. Miss & Roc 15:15 N 9 '64
Appeal to the President. W. J. Coughlin. Miss & Roc 12:46 Mr 18 '63
AEC military space funds voted. Aviation W 80:26 Je 22 '64
Banning bombs in orbit; can the US and USSR get together? R. D. Senter. il New Repub 149:16-18 O 5 '63; Reply with rejoinder. A. Frye. 149:30-1 N 16 '63
Battle for aerospace. J. Burnham. Nat R 15:346 O 22 '63
Brown views space for military support. Aviation W 78:109+ Ap 22 '63
Businessmen review the space effort. E. E. Furash. il Harvard Bsns R 41:14-16+ S '63
Can in the sky. W. J. Coughlin. Miss & Roc 13:54 D 16 '63
Congress seen key to military space role; Senate and House armed services committees. Aviation W 78:26-7 Mr 4 '63
DOD balks most military space expansion except in reconnaissance. il Aviation W 78:116-17+ Mr 11 '63
Fubini urges military space role analysis. P. J. Klass. Aviation W 79:46+ S 2 '63
Hope of increased DOD space funds slim. Aviation W 79:83-4+ N 4 '63
Johnson stress on military space seen. Aviation W 79:26-8 D 2 '63
LeMay sees offensive space force need. Aviation W 78:38 Mr 18 '63
McNamara spells out AF Gemini role; with editorial comment by W. J. Coughlin. F. G. McGuire. Miss & Roc 12:15, 46 Ap 1 '63
MOL studies to include army, navy tasks. Aviation W 79:32-3 D 16 '63
MOSS plans include military. W. E. Wilks. il Miss & Roc 12:14 My 13 '63
Military adaptability has early priority. Miss & Roc 14:24-5 Ap 13 '64
Military asks more of contractors. il Miss & Roc 12:34-40 My 20 '63
Military danger. A. Frye. Atlan 212:46-50 Ag '63
Military missions for X-20, Gemini under study. Aviation W 78:22 Mr 25 '63
Military role in space. G. C. Sponsler. Bul Atomic Sci 20:31-4 Je '64; Reply. D. W. Smythe. 20:37-8 O '64
Military space given new emphasis. H. M. David. Miss & Roc 12:15 F 11 '63
Military space program; address, February 5, 1964. A. C. Hall. Vital Speeches 30:361-5 Ap 1 '64; Excerpts. Aviation W 80:17 F 10 '64
Military space program; excerpts from address. E. Zuckert. Aviation W 78:17 Mr 25 '63
Military space requests were cut $607 million to avoid duplication. Aviation W 78:37 Ap 1 '63
NASA links efforts to defense to broaden appeal for support. A. P. Alibrando. Aviation W 79:32 Ag 19 '63
NASA losing ground within Congress. A. P. Alibrando. Aviation W 79:28 S 16 '63
NASA may get a military arm. H. M. David. Miss & Roc 13:14 Ag 5 '63
Navy feels its MOL experiment valid on military or NASA flight. D. E. Fink. Aviation W 81:13-14 D 28 '64
Politics of outer space. L. P. Bloomfield. Bul Atomic Sci 19:12-14 My '63
Proper focus, firm goals urged for U.S. military space program. Aviation W 78:27 Ap 29 '63
Receptive climate for military space growing. F. G. McGuire. Miss & Roc 12:18 Je 24 '63
Role of military in space could be expanded under President Johnson. H. M. David. Miss & Roc 13:16 D 2 '63
Satellite killer. New Repub 151:7 O 3 '64
Soviet space program. R. A. Kilmarx. Cur Hist 45:200-4+ O '63
Station holds key to USAF's man-in-space mission. D. Fink. il Aviation W 80:112-13+ Mr 16 '64
Survival in the space age; address. H. E. Newell. Aviation W 79:21 Ag 19 '63
That attack from space. R. D. Senter. New Repub 148:17-19 My 4 '63; Reply with rejoinder. P. Siekman. 148:30 Je 8 '63
Thinking matures on military's space role. il Aviation W 79:209-11+ Jl 22 '63
Titan III seen key to U.S. security. Miss & Roc 12:14 Ap 15 '63
U.N. calls on states to refrain from orbiting weapons; statement, October 16, 1963; with text of resolution. A. E. Stevenson. Dept State Bul 49:753-4 N 11 '63
Views of the presidential candidates on the future of the U.S. in space. L. B. Johnson; B. M. Goldwater. Miss & Roc 15:16-18 O 26 '64

Physiological aspects

Aging of space-traveling twin argument halted. Sci N L 83:229 Ap 13 '63
Air force investigating cardiovascular effects of zero-g. H. David. Miss & Roc 14:21 Mr 2 '64
AF will have special needs in Gemini. H. M. David. il Miss & Roc 12:31-2 Ap 8 '63
Anti-G drug research described. W. C. Wetmore. Aviation W 81:24 S 21 '64
Apollo environment attacked. R. Hawkes. Miss & Roc 12:14 My 6 '63
Automated evaluation of space performance. Sci N L 85:100 F 15 '64
Bacterial compatibility stressed in selection of Voskhod crews. Aviation W 81:59 N 23 '64
Basic Gemini ECS keyed to fourteen-day flight. H. D. Watkins. il Aviation W 79:52-3+ Ag 19 '63
Beckman defining biomedical tests for air force's MOL flight program. H. M. David. Miss & Roc 16:26-8 Ja 4 '65
Bioastronautics and space; report on third international symposium. J. Harmon. Science 147:314-15 Ja 15 '65
Bioastronautics: fundamental and practical problems; report on special astronautics symposium at the AAAS annual meeting. W. C. Kaufman. Science 143:1199+ Mr 13 '64
Biolabs evolving for NASA space stations. D. E. Fink. Aviation W 81:16-17 D 14 '64
Biomedical sensors improved for Gemini. W. H. Gregory. il Aviation W 80:69+ Je 8 '64
Bios 2 satellite to orbit primates, plants. B. Miller. Aviation W 78:79+ My 20 '63
Biotechnology research pushed by big companies. il Miss & Roc 13:83-4+ N 25 '63
Bones and Mercury 9. W. Cloud. Pop Sci 182:29-30 Ap '63
Cooper reports on details of MA-9 flight. G. Cooper. Aviation W 79:61-2+ O 14 '63
Cooper to de-pressurize MA-9 craft. H. M. David. Miss & Roc 12:30+ F 18 '63
Cooper's flight prompts new studies. H. M. David. Miss & Roc 12:52+ Je 24 '63
Cosmonauts describe flights, experiments. S. Ramsey. Aviation W 79:28-30 Jl 1 '63
Doctor in space an asset. Sci N L 86:260 O 24 '64
Emphasis urged for biomedical research. il Aviation W 81:54+ N 23 '64
Future bioastronautics research outlined. Aviation W 79:83 Jl 22 '63
Gemini, Apollo to demand tried-and-true instrumentation. H. M. David. Miss & Roc 13:37-8 S 9 '63
Gemini medical tests in space outlined. Sci N L 85:391 Je 20 '64
Gemini to be used as space medical lab. E. J. Bulban. Aviation W 78:79-80 F 25 '63
GD/A rotational test results are encouraging. il Miss & Roc 15:26 N 23 '64
GE test simulates orbiting lab. H. M. David. il Miss & Roc 13:31+ N 18 '63
Grumman tries to break 4-rpm limit. H. M. David. Miss & Roc 12:35+ Ap 15 '63
Hamilton standard starting manned tests of advanced Apollo suit design prototypes. D. E. Fink. il Aviation W 79:48-9+ O 28 '63
Human ability to judge objects from space supported by study. Aviation W 80:73-5 F 24 '64
Hydrogen reduction method praised. H. M. David. Miss & Roc 12:24 Mr 4 '63
Last barrier is man himself; with report by A. Rosenfield. il Life 57:102-12+ O 2 '64
MA-9 experiments vital to rendezvous; plans for eighteen to twenty-two orbit flight. G. Alexander. Aviation W 78:55+ Ja 21 '63
Man-chimp team urged in space satellite launch. Sci N L 84:182 S 21 '63
Military space given new emphasis. H. M. David. Miss & Roc 12:15 F 11 '63
Mumps gland could tell how astronaut fares. Sci N L 85:248 Ap 18 '64
NASA accelerates bioscience program. Aviation W 78:127 Mr 11 '63

SPACE flight—Physiological aspects—*Cont.*
NASA asks for bids on Biosatellite study. H. M. David. Miss & Roc 12:20 Mr 11 '63
NASA bioscience duties pinpointed. H. M. David. il Miss & Roc 12:32-3 F 4 '63
NASA defends oxygen atmosphere for Apollo. Miss & Roc 12:15 My 13 '63
NASA-DOD space medicine review due. D. E. Fink. Aviation W 80:35 Mr 2 '64
NASA pushes blood circulation work. H. M. David. Miss & Roc 15:23 O 12 '64
Navy gains in effort to control canal sickness. H. M. David. il Miss & Roc 15:26 Ag 31 '64
New booster raises biosatellite payload. D. C. Fink. il Aviation W 82:38-9 Ja 11 '65
Nine Gemini medical experiments picked. Aviation W 80:20 Je 1 '64
Opossum fetuses may yield zero-G data. K. J. Stein. il Aviation W 82:71+ Ja 18 '65
Orbital ills. il Newsweek 61:57-8 F 18 '63
Outer space enroached. W. Wingo. il(p 161) Sci N L 84:165 S 14 '63
Oxygen-helium atmosphere appears promising for manned space flight. H. M. David. Miss & Roc 15:32 Ag 3 '64
Physiological checklist suggested for crews. Aviation W 81:66 D 21 '64
Plasticity in human sensorimotor control. R. Held and S. J. Freedman. bibliog il Science 142:455-62 O 25 '63
Project forecast recommendations reshaping AF bioastronautics effort. H. M. David. Miss & Roc 15:27 O 19 '64
Prolonged spaceflight poses monotony problem. H. M. David. Miss & Roc 13:31-2 N 11 '63
Rangers may be launched unsterilized. H. Taylor. Miss & Roc 12:16 My 13 '63
Researcher proposes thirty-day oxygen tests. Miss & Roc 13:36-7 S 23 '63
Russians discuss space radiation findings at conference. H. David. Miss & Roc 13:34 O 21 '63
Schirra had blood disorder after flight. Miss & Roc 12:15 F 11 '63
Scientists debate effects of magnetic shielding on heart, blood cells. H. M. David. Miss & Roc 14:16 My 18 '64
Sex in orbit. Newsweek 63:47 Je 1 '64
Sick astronauts doctored. Sci N L 85:347 My 30 '64
Single-gas environment choice debated. B. Miller. Aviation W 78:85+ My 13 '63
Six-launch Bios series starts in '65. H. M. David. il Miss & Roc 13:34-5 S 2 '63
Solitude; who can take it and who can't. B. H. Frisch. il Sci Digest 55:12-18 Mr '64
Soviets reported improving space suits. C. Brownlow. Aviation W 79:33 O 14 '63
Soviets see helium use in spaceships. H. M. David. Miss & Roc 15:14-15 N 23 '64
Soviets seek cosmonaut behavior trends. E. J. Bulban. Aviation W 81:24-5 N 23 '64
Soviets used Voskhod as orbital testbed. Aviation W 81:28-9 O 26 '64
Space doctor who goes way out; Dr H. Strughold. il Bsns W p 106-8 N 28 '64
Step forward; coordinating space medicine. W. J. Coughlin. Miss & Roc 14:46 Mr 9 '64
Study long space trips. il Sci N L 85:115 F 22 '64
Study may ease rotation problems. H. M. David. il Miss & Roc 16:26-7 Ja 18 '65
Tolerance to acceleration tested; simulated landing impacts. il Aviation W 80:42 Mr 9 '64
UAC cyborg study in second phase. H. M. David. il Miss & Roc 12:41+ My 13 '63
USAF to simulate astronaut performance under stresses. il Aviation W 80:84 My 18 '64
U.S. Russia agree to swap data on space biology and medicine work. Miss & Roc 14:13 Je 15 '64
U.S.-Russian space agreement advances. W. J. Normyle. Aviation W 80:34 Je 15 '64
U.S. Russian space studies detailed. Aviation W 78:145 Je 10 '63
Use of drugs and servos urged to aid astronauts. W. Beller. il Miss & Roc 15:16-17 S 21 '64
Was John Glenn injured in space? H. Shuldiner. il Pop Sci 186:55-9+ Ja '65
Weighing man's survival in space; third International symposium on bioastronautics & the exploration of space, San Antonio. il Bsns W p98-100+ N 28 '64
Weightlessness effects on Cooper cited. W. C. Wetmore. il Aviation W 78:34-5 Je 17 '63
Weightlessness study program analyzed. H. D. Watkins. il Aviation W 80:52-3+ Mr 2 '64
What to breathe in space? W. Cloud. Pop Sci 183:13-14+ Ag '63
See also
Astronauts
Life support systems
Weightlessness

Psychological aspects

Astronauts studied for personality clashes. Sci N L 85:114 F 22 '64

Publicity

Answer lady of space; M. S. Niehaus. M. Clapp. il Todays Health 41:20-1+ O '63
How J. Gallagher O'Shay got the U.S. space program off the ground. J. Beatty, jr. il Esquire 62:96-8+ O '64
Singer urges early space project data. Aviation W 78:27 Ap 22 '63

Radiation hazards

Apollo astronauts are painstakingly protected from solar-flare protons. R. Pay. il Miss & Roc 15:22-3+ Jl 20 '64
Astronauts may need deeper lunar foxholes. Aviation W 79:73+ N 4 '63
Flares menace astronauts; Avoid lethal protons for best protection. W. Wingo. il Sci N L 85:99 F 15 '64
Gagarin outlines Soviet Union's rendezvous, lunar race goals. C. Brownlow. Aviation W 79:30-1 O 7 '63
IMP will warn of dangerous solar flares. R. D. Hibben. il Aviation W 79:28-9 N 4 '63
Neutron and proton dosages in the upper atmosphere from solar flare radiation. E. J. Flamm and R. E. Lingenfelter. bibliog il Science 144:1566-9 Je 26 '64
Radiation hazard in space from solar particles. P. Freier and W. R. Webber. bibliog il Science 142:1587-92 D 20 '63
Radiation hazards in space. D. L. Dye and M. Wilkinson. bibliog il Science 147:19-25 Ja 1 '65
Russians discuss space radiation findings at conference. H. David. Miss & Roc 13:34 O 21 '63
Solar flare warning system for astronauts considered possible. Aviation W 80:75 F 24 '64
Space shield of water. Sci N L 83:102 F 16 '63
Spacecraft radiation may boost tube use. P. J. Klass. il Aviation W 78:67+ Je 3 '63

Social aspects

Space technology: pay-off from spin-off. J. G. Welles and R. H. Waterman, jr. bibliog f il Harvard Bsns R 42:106-18 Jl '64

Terminology

Space-speak. il Seventeen 22:24 S '63

SPACE flight centers
Space program has infinite variety. il Arch Rec 133:151-8 Je '63

SPACE flight in art
I saw Atlas 9 take off! P. Calle. il Am Artist 27:58-9+ O '63

SPACE flight simulators
AC-2 Centaur pre-flight tests complete. il Aviation W 79:32 O 14 '63
AF pilots far exceed expected performance in military experiment; at GE Valley Forge space station simulation facility. H. M. David. Miss & Roc 15:26+ S 7 '64
Ames centrifuge to be most sophisticated. il Miss & Roc 15:33 Ag 31 '64
Apollo, Gemini simulator variety planned. E. J. Bulban. Aviation W 78:63+ Ap 15 '63
Apollo navigation simulator tests begin. il Aviation W 78:92 Ap 1 '63
Are you still there? ECHO chamber experiments. Newsweek 61:62+ Mr 11 '63
Astronaut classroom, simulator training. Aviation W 78:55 F 4 '63
Astronaut proficiency plan proposed. Miss & Roc 13:35-6 S 9 '63
Astronauts flying IBM simulators. C. D. LaFond. il Miss & Roc 14:31-2 Ja 6 '64
Chamber test to end this week. Aviation W 80:41 Mr 30 '64
Doff-and-don bag provides an emergency system for Apollo astronauts; safety in depressurization emergencies. il Aviation W 80:50-1 F 10 '64
Environmental testing spurs industry. il Miss & Roc 12:67-8+ My 20 '63
Facility will simulate 34,000-mph re-entries. J. F. Judge. il Miss & Roc 12:24-5 Je 10 '63
First Little Joe 2 launched successfully. il Aviation W 79:20-1 S 2 '63
Flies to the moon via cinerama; Ling-Temco-Vought simulator. il Pop Mech 119:95 My '63

SPACE flight simulators—*Continued*
Flight simulator readied for Gemini training at Cape Kennedy. C. Butler. il Miss & Roc 14:31 Mr 23 '64
Four GE engineers end thirty day chamber test. D. E. Fink. il Aviation W 79:32-3 N 18 '63
Gauging trails vacuum chamber capabilities. J. F. Judge. il Miss & Roc 15:36+ O 19 '64
Gemini egress-ingress procedures tested during conditions of zero-g. il Aviation W 80:72-3 Je 29 '64
Gemini evolves into operational program. il Aviation W 79:175-9+ Jl 22 '63
Gemini goals within reach despite delay in first flight. il Aviation W 81:76-8 N 23 '64
GD/A rotational test results are encouraging. il Miss & Roc 15:26 N 23 '64
Goddard seeks scaling laws to cut cost of environmental testing. W. Beller. il Miss & Roc 15:34-5 Jl 20 '64
Langley simulators perform lunar tasks. D. A. Brown. il Aviation W 80:54-5+ Ap 13 '64
Link to develop Apollo simulators for use at Houston center. AMR. Aviation W 78:25 My 6 '63
Long voyage in inner space. T. Flaherty. il Life 54:119-20 My 17 '63
MOL test subjects experience mild bends. Aviation W 80:21 Mr 30 '64
NAA building largest centrifuge; Rotational research facility. Miss & Roc 15:34-5 N 23 '64
NASA, Boeing resuming life-support tests. H. M. David. il Miss & Roc 14:28-9 Ja 27 '64
NASA center nears completion of launch-phase simulation facility. W. S. Beller. il Miss & Roc 15:18+ N 2 '64
Need cited for early Apollo re-entry tests. Aviation W 78:25 Ap 29 '63
Nerva space simulation-firing complex almost ready. E. J. Bulban. il Aviation W 80:54-5+ My 18 '64
Opossum fetuses may yield zero-G data. K. J. Stein. il Aviation W 82:71+ Ja 18 '65
Pilot's control of lifting body simulated. D. A. Brown. il Aviation W 80:56-7+ My 4 '64
Profit in make-believe; Link simulators. il Time 81:86 Je 21 '63
Simulator tests advanced recon systems. il Aviation W 78:99 My 27 '63
Simulators' shortcomings described. W. Beller. il Miss & Roc 15:18+ Ag 31 '64
Space comes to earth in huge laboratories. Sci N L 85:386 Je 20 '64
Space spectacles; with photographs by O. Gigli. R. Vaughan. Sat Eve Post 236:26-9 My 25 '63
Space vehicles in an ionized medium. S. F. Singer. Science 147:74-6 Ja 1 '65
Stress build-up ends isolation. Sci N L 83:280 My 4 '63
Test chamber art suffers from lack of information. il Miss & Roc 12:54-6+ My 20 '63
$30-million space test facility to allow Apollo mission simulation. Aviation W 78:65 F 18 '63
Three-man centrifuge to be new Ames research nucleus. R. Lindsey. il Miss & Roc 12:27 Je 3 '63
Tolerance to acceleration tested; simulated landing impacts. il Aviation W 80:42 Mr 9 '64
Trainer to simulate Gemini mission. W. Beller. il Miss & Roc 12:24-5 Ap 1 '63
USAF to simulate astronaut performance under stresses. il Aviation W 80:84 My 18 '64
Weightless workshop. R. Gannon. il Pop Sci 182:112-13+ Ap '63
Weird astronaut machines. N. Armstrong. il Life 57:137-40 S 25 '64
See also
Space station simulators

SPACE flight to Mars
Ames scientists advocate single earth-launch manned Mars mission. Miss & Roc 14:17-18 My 4 '64
Ames seeking industry analysis of Mars mission heat shielding. Aviation W 79:63-4 S 16 '63
ABL Mars landing may come in 1971. il Miss & Roc 15:15 Ag 24 '64
First manned landings on Mars now seen delayed until mid-'80s. H. D. Watkins. il Aviation W 79:97+ O 14 '63
General electric proposes nuclear-powered Mars vehicle for fifteen-month manned landing mission. il Aviation W 78:62-3 My 27 '63
Manned exploration of Mars? R. N. Watts, jr. il Sky & Tel 26:64-7+ Ag '63
Mariner 1966 Mars fly-by mission may be cancelled by NASA. H. Taylor. Miss & Roc 15:11 Jl 20 '64
Mars; are its canals full of water? is there really life there? W. Von Braun. il Pop Sci 183:18+ Ag '63
Mars exploration decisions due soon. il Miss & Roc 15:36 S 14 '64
Mars exploration seen delayed to 1980s. Aviation W 78:85+ Je 24 '63
Mars less hazardous. Sci N L 83:102 F 16 '63
Mars mission equipment, vehicles studied. I. Stone. Aviation W 78:59+ My 20 '63
Mars to be next space goal after moon. il Aviation W 79:84-6 Jl 22 '63
NASA near decision on whether to impact or fly by Mars in '66. H. M. David. il Miss & Roc 14:21 Ja 20 '64
NASA planning Mars expedition. W. Burkett. il Miss & Roc 12:34+ My 13 '63
NASA plans new spacecraft; unmanned Mars exploration vehicles. H. Taylor. Miss & Roc 14:15 Je 1 '64
Need clean spaceships. Sci N L 85:107 F 15 '64
Need for more accurate information sets planned landing back to 1985. il Miss & Roc 15:69-71+ N 30 '64
Northrop advocates parachute landing system for Mars Voyager. il Miss & Roc 15:26-7 D 7 '64
Preliminary studies completed on three-man Mars excursion module. il Aviation W 81:53-4+ N 16 '64
Ready, aim, wait! H. Hellman. il Sci Digest 54:35-9 D '63
750-950 day Mars round trips studied. I. Stone. Aviation W 81:71-3 S 28 '64
So you're going to Mars? what the inexperienced space traveler ought to know. A. C. Clarke. il Read Digest 86:131-5 Ja '65
Space: National academy panel recommends exploration of Mars as major goal in 1971-85 period. J. Walsh. Science 146:1025-7 N 20 '64
Thirty years to Mars. Sci N L 83:381 Je 15 '63
Vehicle study for extended Mars mission calls for advances in varied technologies. H. D. Watkins. il Aviation W 80:54-5+ Ap 20 '64
Venus swingby would permit using Saturn hardware on manned Mars trip. W. E. Wilks. il Miss & Roc 15:24++ D 14 '64
Will we pass up the moon for Mars? S. D. Pursglove. il Pop Mech 120:104-8+ N '63
See also
Space probes

SPACE flight to Mercury
Mercury missions seen more useful than Mars, Venus probes. D. M. Cole. il Miss & Roc 12:34+ Je 24 '63

SPACE flight to the moon
After latest space test, is moon any nearer? il U S News 55:68-9 Jl 1 '63
After moon landing, what next? NASA's dream projects. il Bsns W p 104+ Mr 28 '64
Apollo and its critics. R. Hotz. Aviation W 78:17 Ap 29 '63
Apollo astronauts are painstakingly protected from solar-flare protons. R. Pay. il Miss & Roc 15:22-3+ Jl 20 '64
Apollo chief, co-pilot to explore moon. D. E. Fink. il Aviation W 80:22-3 Mr 9 '64
Apollo date unchanged in funds crisis. A. P. Alibrando. Aviation W 79:28 D 23 '63
Apollo delay could cost $1 billion a year. D. E. Fink. Aviation W 80:25-6 F 10 '64
Apollo has trouble on earth; lunar landing program. il Bsns W p54-5 S 14 '63
Apollo in trouble despite increase. il Miss & Roc 14:17 Ja 27 '64
Apollo, JFK and General Eisenhower. E. T. Folliard. America 108:794 Je 1 '63
Apollo logistics system will be next manned space flight project. H. Taylor. Miss & Roc 14:16 My 25 '64
Apollo reflects technical skill of U.S. il Aviation W 79:107-9+ Jl 22 '63
Apollo-Saturn 5 may fly in 1966. Aviation W 80:35 F 10 '64
Apollo tracking ship accord reached. H. Taylor. Miss & Roc 13:17 D 16 '63
Astronauts will land standing up; questions and answers. W. Von Braun. il Pop Sci 184:82-3+ My '64
Back in orbit. il Newsweek 64:51-3 Ag 17 '64
Back seat for science? W. Wingo. il Sci N L 84:5 Jl 6 '63
Basic challenge; excerpt from message to Congress, May 25, 1961. J. F. Kennedy. Aviation W 79:25 D 2 '63

SPACE flight to the moon—*Continued*
Bell aerosystems alters LLRV design to better performance. M. Getler. il Miss & Roc 13:16-17 Ag 12 '63
Bendix seeks LEM landing contract. J. F. Judge. il Miss & Roc 12:26-7+ Mr 11 '63
Coincidence? opposition to the moon race. Nation 196:433 My 25 '63
Critical design phase ending on lunar excursion module. M. Getler. il Miss & Roc 13:22-3+ Jl 15 '63
De-accelerating; cut in NASA's manned space flight program. Newsweek 62:62 Jl 8 '63
Direct Saturn lunar support proposed. Aviation W 80:26 My 11 '64
Doff-and-don bag provides an emergency system for Apollo astronauts; safety in depressurization emergencies. il Aviation W 80:50-1 F 10 '64
Fantastic hazards of landing on the moon. A. Q. Maisel. Read Digest 83:103-7 S '63
Fifth Saturn 5 might launch men to moon. G. Alexander. il Aviation W 80:26-7 Mr 2 '64
FY '65 Apollo funds threatened; with editorial comment. Miss & Roc 13:14, 46 N 4 '63
$5.445 billion vital to moon goal. H. Taylor. il Miss & Roc 14:14-15 Ja 20 '64
Focus on space; Project Apollo. J. Finney. il N Y Times Mag p 10-11 Ja 12 '64
Footprints on the moon. H. L. Dryden. il Nat Geog Mag 125:356-401 Mr '64
Forgotten moon voyage of 1609; Kepler's Dream. J. Lear. il Sat R 46:39-44 My 4 '63; Discussion. 46:36-7 Je 1 '63
Gilruth supports Gemini as vital; elimination of some flights seen. Aviation W 79:32 S 23 '63
Goal for moon same. Sci N L 85:22 Ja 11 '64
Grandstands are emptying for the race to the moon. il Time 82:64-5 O 4 '63
Greatest challenge to man. B. Lovell. il N Y Times Mag p 12-13+ Ap 21 '63
How near the moon? U. S. moon program. il Newsweek 63:92 Je 8 '64
How 300,000 work for three moon men. il Newsweek 64:61-5 D 21 '64
Is the moon race on or off? joint U.S.-Russian moon expedition. Bsns W p29-30 S 28 '63
Is U.S. lagging in the moon race? with interview with A. R. Kantrowitz. il U S News 54:60-6 Ap 15 '63
Is U.S. running alone in the race to the moon? interview; ed. by J. Fromm. B. Lovell. il U S News 55:70-1 Ag 12 '63
Job for the next Congress: stop the race to the moon. B. Clark. Read Digest 84:75-9 Ja '64
JFK proposal threat to space funds; with editorial comment. H. Taylor. il Miss & Roc 13:25-6, 86 S 30 '63
Kennedy plan stirs attack on space funds. A. P. Alibrando. Aviation W 79:29-30 O 7 '63
Khrushchev puts Russia back into manned lunar landing race. A. P. Alibrando. Aviation W 79:29-30 N 11 '63
Landing men on moon dust. N. A. Weil. il Sci Digest 53:4-11 Mr '63
Langley simulators perform lunar tasks. D. A. Brown. il Aviation W 80:54-5+ Ap 13 '64
LEM flight schedule detailed; Program to include nine test articles; Lunar bug mission sequence outlined. Aviation W 79:145+ Jl 22 '63
LEM research facility nears completion. il Aviation W 79:83+ O 14 '63
Lunar landing abort techniques studied. E. J. Bulban. il Aviation W 78:53-4 My 27 '63
Lunar mission. il Aviation W 79:117-23 Jl 22 '63
Man in the moon suit. T. Alexander. il Esquire 60:104-5+ N '63
Man on the moon. W. E. Boggs. New Repub 149:6-7 Ag 3 '63; Reply with rejoinder. B. W. Bova 149:30 S 14 '63
Man on the moon: how soon now? il U S News 54:35-9 My 27 '63
Man on the moon, men on the dole; reprint. J. Reston. Aviation W 78:21 Ap 22 '63
Man to the moon. T. Alexander. il Pop Sci 185:60-5 Ag '64
Manned lunar landing. P. H. Abelson. Science 140:267 Ap 19 '63
Manned lunar landing defended. H. H. Hess. Science 140:1173-4 Je 14 '63
MSC plans five Apollo landings. Miss & Roc 13:16 Jl 15 '63
Martyrs on the moon? C. Dreher. Harper 226:33-8 Mr '63
Men and the moon. Newsweek 62:63 Jl 29 '63
Moon base cost set at $2 billion. W. Beller. Miss & Roc 14:17 My 11 '64
Moon industry; how big it is now. il U S News 57:60-3 O 5 '64
Moon madness. il Newsweek 61:81 My 6 '63
Moon minus one; resignation of D. B. Holmes. Newsweek 61:68 Je 24 '63
Moon, money, and men. W. W. Brickman. Sch & Soc 92:372 D 12 '64
Moon race blots out a town. R. Bailey. il Life 57:21 S 25 '64
Moon race: Russian disavowal of lunar-landing plans poses new problem for space program. D. S. Greenberg. Science 142:564 N 1 '63
Moon race with ourselves? Life 55:4 N 8 '63
Most rewarding lunar surveys sought by MSC for expeditions. I. Stone. Aviation W 79:81 N 4 '63
NASA considers use of aircraft for remote Apollo crew retrieval. Aviation W 78:65 Mr 18 '63
NASA denies Soviet moon proposal; with editorial comment. H. Taylor. Miss & Roc 13:21, 50 Ag 19 '63
NASA eyes Apollo follow-on systems; with detailed breakdown of FY '65 R&D budget request. H. Taylor. Miss & Roc 14:18-19 F 10 '64
NASA, industry define lunar landing plan. G. Alexander. il Aviation W 80:36-7 Mr 9 '64
NASA launch schedule to the moon. il Miss & Roc 13:110-11 N 25 '63
NASA may drop Surveyor lunar orbiter. A. P. Alibrando. Aviation W 78:25 Mr 4 '63
NASA: rein on budget may stiffen competition for funds between manned program space sciences. J. Walsh. Science 142:1636-7 D 27 '63
NASA RFP calls for lunar base by 1968. Miss & Roc 13:18 Ag 19 '63
NASA struggling to hold to 1970 man-on-moon schedule. H. M. David. Miss & Roc 13:15 D 23 '63
NASA studying lunar base feasibility. I. Stone. il Aviation W 79:71-3 Jl 1 '63
NASA tells Congress early plans for semipermanent base on moon. W. Beller. il Miss & Roc 14:26-7 Mr 16 '64
NASA weighs lunar logistics proposals. I. Stone. il Aviation W 80:52-3+ Ap 27 '64
NASA's Lunar logistics system likely to be postponed. H. Taylor. Miss & Roc 12:21 Je 24 '63
Now it's an agonizing reappraisal of the moon race. R. A. Smith. il Fortune 68:124-9+ N '63
On a Texas prairie, space city for 200,000. il U S News 54:66-9 F 18 '63
On mooning. J. Lear. Sat R 46:55-6 O 5 '63
On the bazoo. il Newsweek 61:63-4 My 27 '63
One-year Apollo delay cited. Aviation W 79:34 D 2 '63
Picking a way to the moon; guidance system for Apollo spacecraft. il Bsns W p82+ O 5 '63
Post-Apollo lunar-orbit experiment recommendations detailed in report. M. Getler. il Miss & Roc 15:22-3+ D 21 '64
Priorities; funds for the Apollo program. Reporter 28:10 Je 6 '63
Project Apollo. Commonweal 78:237 My 24 '63
Project Apollo: wasteful spectacular. H. Schenck, jr. Nation 197:339-41 N 23 '63
Public support of lunar mission debated. W. H. Gregory. Aviation W 80:75+ My 18 '64
Push to the moon: a one-horse race? il Bsns W p48 Jl 27 '63
Race for the moon. R. Steel and W. Lineberry. Commonweal 78:321-3 Je 14 '63; Reply with rejoinder. E. J. Harrington. 78:427-9 Jl 12 '63
Race that was. Commonweal 79:180 N 8 '63
Race to the moon. New Repub 148:3-4 Ap 13 '63
Red light. Newsweek 62:90 D 2 '63
Redefinition of U.S. space goals planned; with editorial comment. A. P. Alibrando. Aviation W 79:21, 26-7 N 4 '63
Redesigned lunar lander to fly in August. D. A. Brown. il Aviation W 80:75-7+ Ap 20 '64
Requests keep coming for moon flight seats. Sci N L 84:249 O 19 '63
Revolution isn't coming, it is already here. J. Dille. il Life 57:94-5+ S 25 '64
Russia's ladder to the moon; timetable for space. W. Wingo. il Sci N L 84:314-15 N 16 '63
Saturn IB/Centaur launch vehicle will be funded in FY '66. H. Taylor. Miss & Roc 14:17 My 18 '64
Scientific debate focuses on Apollo landings. Aviation W 79:74 Jl 22 '63

SPACE flight to the moon—*Continued*
Scientists on space: Senate group hears criticism and support for manned lunar landing program. D. S. Greenberg. Science 140: 1195-6 Je 14 '63
Senator Anderson questions Apollo schedule. Aviation W 80:29 Ja 20 '64
Senator Anderson, scientists rebut attacks on manned lunar landing. A. P. Alibrando. Aviation W 78:24 Je 3 '63
Seventy-two hours to the moon. il Sci Digest 53:37-40 Je '63
Sniping at NASA on space. il Bsns W p92-4+ My 11 '63
So we land on the moon, then what? with editorial comment. C. P. Gilmore. il Pop Sci 183:40, 59-61+ D '63
Soviet lunar plans helping NASA cause; with editorial comment. A. P. Alibrando. Aviation W 79:21, 28-9 O 21 '63
Soviets eye joint moon landing. H. Taylor. Miss & Roc 13:14 S 23 '63
Soviets plan manned circumlunar flight. Aviation W 79:29 Jl 1 '63
Space budget: opposition grows as scientists, congressmen, voice concern about lunar landing goal. D. S. Greenberg. Science 140: 790-1 My 17 '63; Discussion. 141:390; 142:343 Ag 2, O 18 '63
Space controversy: Senate committee to hear scientists on moon program, statement of eight scientists. M. L. Ewing and others. Science 140:1078 Je 7 '63
Space: formidable political base overshadows attempts to revise administration's lunar program. D. S. Greenberg. Science 145:137-9 Jl 10 '64
Space science, research effort grows but failures beset lunar missions. A. Alibrando. il Aviation W 78:124-5+ Mr 11 '63
Space: Senator Fulbright steps into lunar landing controversy. D. S. Greenberg. Science 142:470 O 25 '63
Study on lunar communications due. M. Getler. Miss & Roc 14:18 My 18 '64
Surveying surveyor. W. J. Coughlin. Miss & Roc 13:46 Ag 12 '63
Survivability of wire on moon tested. P. J. Klass. Aviation W 78:77+ My 27 '63
Tailored for the moon; space suit. il Newsweek 61:48 F 4 '63
Target: moon; photographs. N Y Times Mag p8-9 Ag 9 '64
To moon or not to moon. il Time 81:53 My 31 '63
U.S. to select orbiting lab or lunar base; report of NASA-Industry conference. E. H. Kolcum. Aviation W 78:32-4 F 18 '63
Visit to a small satellite? proposal for joint US-Soviet attempt. Newsweek 62:18-19 S 30 '63
Welsh urges civil lunar mission continuation for future benefits. C. M. Plattner. Aviation W 79:27 S 16 '63
What's happening in the race to the moon; interview. W. Von Braun. il U S News 56:54-7 Je 1 '64
Where is science taking us? il Sat R 46:80-1 D 7 '63
White House blocks Apollo slowdown. H. Taylor. Miss & Roc 13:16 D 9 '63
Whiteness of the moon. A. Welsh. New Repub 149:12-13 S 28 '63
Why land on the moon? R. Jastrow and H. E. Newell. Atlan 212:41-5 Ag '63
Why race to the moon? excerpts from report, by B. B. Hickenlooper and from address, by C. P. Anderson. il U S News 54:90-1 Je 10 '63
Why the moon is a must; interview. ed. by J. Steen. H. L. Dryden. il Pop Sci 183:92-4+ S '63
Without portfolio; Project Apollo. C. B. Luce. McCalls 91:18 Ap '64
World will be ruled from skies above. Life 54:4 My 17 '63
See also
Lunar probes
Space flight—Manned flights

Anecdotes, facetiae, satire, etc.

Man from the moon. T. Ungerer. il Holiday 36:76-83 D '64

Cost

Are we wasting billions in space? S. H. Loory. il Sat Eve Post 236:13-15 S 14 '63
NASA says Apollo date hinges on funds, fast budget action. il Aviation W 80:27-8 Ja 20 '64
Rail strike and the moon shot; Florida East Coast railway and moon-shot base near Cape Canaveral. U S News 55:86 O 28 '63
Still moonward bound. il Time 82:19-20 Jl 19 '63
That moon trip: debate sharpens. E. Diamond. il N Y Times Mag p 10+ Jl 28 '63
Why 20 billions to see more of the moon? il U S News 57:40-2 Ag 17 '64

International aspects

All systems gopak; joint U.S.-USSR lunar expedition. Nat R 15:265 O 8 '63
Can U.S. catch up in space race? il U S News 57:58-60 O 26 '64
End of the race? Sci Am 209:64-5+ D '63
How fast will the moon race pick up? il U S News 57:58-9 Ag 10 '64
How much gain from sending men to moon? summary of address, December 30, 1963. H. C. Urey. U S News 56:10 Ja 13 '64
How we can join in a moon trip. il Life 55: 100-3 O 11 '63
Is Russia leaving the moon to the U.S? Bsns W p36+ N 2 '63
Is U.S. running alone in the race to the moon? interview; ed. by J. Fromm. B. Lovell. il U S News 55:70-1 Ag 12 '63; Excerpts. Bul Atomic Sci 19:39 O '63
JFK proposal threat to space funds; with editorial comment. H. Taylor. il Miss & Roc 13:25-6, 86 S 30 '63
Kennedy's offer stirs confusion, dismay; with editorial comment. A. P. Alibrando. Aviation W 79:21, 26-7 S 30 '63
Khrushchev denies Russian pullout from lunar landing race; with editorial comment. Miss & Roc 13:15, 50 N 11 '63
Lunar proposal. W. J. Coughlin. Miss & Roc 13:52 O 14 '63; Discussion. 13:7 O 28 '63
Off to the moon with a Russian? il U S News 55:60 O 7 '63
On the road to the moon; more spectaculars ahead. il U S News 56:74-6 Ja 13 '64
Opposition to joint lunar offer repeated. D. E. Fink. Aviation W 79:28 D 9 '63
Progress report on the moon race. il Fortune 69:142-5 Mr '64
Race is over; Soviet Union out of race to moon. Newsweek 62:64 N 4 '63
Reasonable pace; President Kennedy's suggestion of a joint Soviet-American lunar expedition. W. J. Coughlin. Miss & Roc 13: 86 O 7 '63
Reversal of U.S. policy? proposal for joint U.S.-Soviet manned moon expedition. Sr Schol 83:18 O 11 '63
Right way to the moon; President Kennedy's proposal of Soviet-U.S. joint flight. Nation 197:209 O 12 '63
Soviets eye joint moon landing. H. Taylor. Miss & Roc 13:14 S 23 '63
Soviets out of moon race? Sr Schol 83:20 N 15 '63
Tandem to the moon? J. W. Finney. Reporter 29:36 O 10 '63
Together to the moon; question of US-Soviet cooperation. New Repub 149:3-4 O 5 '63
U.N. adopts resolutions on cooperation in outer space; U.S. reaffirms offer to work with Soviet Union on manned lunar landing; statement, December 2, 1963; with texts of resolutions, December 13, 1963. A. E. Stevenson. bibliog f Dept State Bul 49:1005-14 D 30 '63
U.S. shifts goals in space. il U S News 55:39-40 N 11 '63
Whither Apollo? New Repub 149:3-4 N 9 '63
Who's relaxing? Newsweek 63:69 Mr 30 '64
Why the moon race is slowing down. il U S News 55:38-41 O 28 '63

SPACE-General corporation
Electrochemical nerve cells under study. B. Miller. il Aviation W 78:103+ F 18 '63

SPACE heaters. See Heaters

SPACE industry. See Aerospace industries

SPACE law
Frontier is up. Time 82:54+ N 29 '63
Golden rule invalid in space: meaning of metalaw. E. Mirel. Sci N L 85:106-7 F 15 '64
Outer space: problems of law and power; address, August 10, 1963. R. N. Gardner. Dept State Bul 49:367-71 S 2 '63
Space junk damage poses legal problem. Sci N L 86:45 Jl 18 '64
Space law gets set for launching. il Bsns W p 109+ N 7 '64
Space law proposal moves forward; with text of U.S.-USSR draft in United Nations on peaceful uses of space. Miss & Roc 13:17 D 2 '63
To rule space: law or might? A. Gore. il N Y Times Mag p23+ N 10 '63
U.N. adopts resolutions on cooperation in outer space; U.S. reaffirms offer to work with Soviet Union on manned lunar landing; statement, December 2, 1963; with texts of resolutions, December 13, 1963. A. E. Stevenson. bibliog f Dept State Bul 49: 1005-14 D 30 '63

SPACE medicine. See Space flight—Physiological aspects
SPACE people. See Life on other planets
SPACE perception
Binocular depth perception without familiarity cues. B. Julesz. bibliog il Science 145: 356-62 Jl 24 '64
Cultural differences in the perception of geometric illusions. M. H. Segall and others. bibliog il Science 139:769-71 F 22 '63; Reply, with rejoinder. H. H. Spitz. 140:422+ Ap 26 '63
Depth perception loss with local monocular suppression: a problem in the explanation of stereopsis. J. Hochberg. bibliog il Science 145:1334-6; 146:800 S 18, N 6 '64
Induction of a stereoscopic depth effect. N. Pastore. il Science 144:888 My 15 '64
Maturation of performance with space-displaced vision. P. M. Greene and K. U. Smith. bibliog il Science 141:727-8 Ag 23 '63
Motor-sensory feedback and the geometry of visual space. R. Held and J. Rekosh. bibliog Science 141:722-3 Ag 23 '63
SPACE photography
Astronaut in orbit: shooting way out landscapes from far out space. M. A. Matzkin. Mod Phot 27:50+ Ag '63
Best lunar photographs yet. R. N. Watts, jr. il Sky & Tel 28:143-4 S '64
Camera may aid planetary terrain study. M. L. Yaffee. il Aviation W 79:69+ N 4 '63
Camera records staging sequence of Titan 2. il Aviation W 79:32 D 2 '63
Changing man's view: flight of Ranger VII. il Time 84:39-42 Ag 7 '64
Clear photos of moon. Sci N L 86:325 N 21 '64
Contraption that reconnoitered the moon; Ranger VII; with report by J. Hicks. il Life 57:30-36A Ag 14 '64
Do the moon photos change our plans? W. Von Braun. il Pop Sci 185:110-13+ N '64
Evaluating moon pictures will take three months. il (p97) Sci N L 86:101 Ag 15 '64
First closeup of the moon, space-age payoff for U.S. il U S News 57:8 Ag 10 '64
Four steps into space. L. Lipton. il Pop Phot 55:64-5 O '64
Future techniques; photographic miracles of the space age. J. Reidy. il U S Camera 26:38-9 F '63
GEC camera meets needs of Saturn test monitoring, lunar exploration. C. D. LaFond. il Miss & Roc 15:36+ D 7 '64
It's not green cheese; pictures Ranger VII sent back. il Bsns W p82-4+ Ag 8 '64
Latitudinal distribution of cloud cover from Tiros III photographs. A. Arking. bibliog il Science 143:569-72 F 7 '64; Reply. R. Wexler and W. K. Widger, jr. 145:1206 S 11 '64
Lunar orbiter stresses photo mission. il Aviation W 80:69+ My 25 '64
Mission on target; Ranger 7 on moon. il(p 19) Sr Schol 85:20 S 16 '64
Moon close up. E. M. Shoemaker. il Nat Geog Mag 126:690-707 N '64
Moon microscopy. il Sci Am 211:80-1 S '64
NASA lunar orbiter competition stirs broad interest in industry. E. H. Kolcum. Aviation W 79:29 S 9 '63
NASA may drop Surveyor lunar orbiter. A. P. Alibrando. Aviation W 78:25 Mr 4 '63
NASA seeks new lunar photo craft. H. Taylor. Miss & Roc 13:17 S 9 '63
NASA turns to incentives; procurement of the lunar orbiter photo spacecraft. Miss & Roc 13:28 O 7 '63
Next on moon: Surveyor. J. Eberhart. Sci N L 86:101 Ag 15 '64
Officials optimistic about Ranger VII returning first U.S. moon pictures. Miss & Roc 15:13 Ag 3 '64
Orbiter is first big NASA incentive job. R. G. O'Lone. Aviation W 79:32-3 O 7 '63
Ranger photos boost confidence in Apollo. H. D. Watkins. il Aviation W 81:19-23 Ag 10 '64
Ranger VII; briefing for Johnson brings out high level chit chat on various aspects of space. L. B. Johnson; H. E. Newell; D. F. Hornig. Science 145:563-5 Ag 7 '64
Ranger 7 colloquium. Sky & Tel 28:342-3 D '64
Ranger VII moon camera is successful; Could see auto on the moon. il Sci N L 86:85 Ag 8 '64
Ranger VII proves Apollo feasibility; with editorial comment. Miss & Roc 15:16+, 54 Ag 10 '64
Still cameras designed for lunar mission. W. Wright. il Aviation W 79:55-6+ N 25 '63
Survellance promises civil spin-off. Miss & Roc 14::44+ Je 1 '64
Taking the measure of the moon; success of Ranger 7. il Newsweek 64:15-18 Ag 10 '64
Techniques tomorrow; lunar surface photography. B. Sherman. il Mod Phot 28:12-13+ Ap '64
Techniques tomorrow; taking pictures of the earth from space. B. Sherman. il Mod Phot 28:14-15 Je '64
Why 20 billions to see more of the moon? il U S News 57:40-2 Ag 17 '64
See also
Photography of space flight
SPACE pollution. See Dipole orbital belts in space
SPACE power systems. See Space vehicles—Power supply
SPACE probes
Asteroids stir growing interest. D. M. Cole. il Miss & Roc 12:43+ F 25 '63
Balloon's eye view of Mars; Project Stratoscope II. il Bsns W p92-3+ Mr 9 '63
Better communications for Mars probe in 1964. Sci N L 83:312 My 18 '63
Boosters pace Mars life detection. R. Pay. Miss & Roc 16:32+ Ja 18 '65
Both upcoming mariners may pass behind Mars. R. Pay. Miss & Roc 15:62+ S 14 '64
Cold clouds over Venus. il Sci N L 83:149 Mr 9 '63
Digital television system is heart of Mariner spacecraft slated for November Mars flyby. R. Pay. il Miss & Roc 15:38+ Ag 3 '64
Dreams and responsibilities. W. Weaver. il Bul Atomic Sci 19:10-11 My '63
Eight planet-probe robots. B. Tufty. il (p225) Sci N L 84:227 O 12 '63
Eight vie for Pioneer solar probe. Miss & Roc 12:17 Mr 11 '63
Explore pathway to moon. il Sci N L 84:371 D 14 '63
Falling short. Newsweek 63:82 Ap 13 '64
First news from Venus. Sci Am 208:64-5 F '63
Fortunes of NASA; flight of the Mariner IV to Mars. Nation 199:478-9 D 21 '64
Fund limitations force Voyager Mars mission delay until 1971. J. Trainor. Miss & Roc 15:12 N 16 '64
Funds for new spacecraft expected to be included in FY '66 budget; Pioneer. il Miss & Roc 15:88-9 N 30 '64
Gulliver, ambassador to the microbes of Mars. C. P. Gilmore. il Pop Sci 183:60-1 D '63
How to find life on Mars. il Sci Digest 56:90 Ag '64
JPL facing Mariner C avionics problems. B. Miller. Aviation W 80:16-17 Je 29 '64
Journey to July; Mariner IV. il Newsweek 64:67 D 7 '64
Mariner design modified for Mars flyby. L. Stone. il Aviation W 78:50-1+ My 6 '63
Mariner 4 sensors relay excellent data. Aviation W 81:26-7 D 7 '64
Mariner goes wrong. Time 84:85 N 13 '64
Mariner 1966 Mars fly-by mission may be cancelled by NASA. H. Taylor. Miss & Roc 15:11 Jl 20 '64
Mariner reveals 800F Venus temperature. E. H. Kolcum. il Aviation W 78:30-1 Mr 4 '63
Mariner scans a lifeless Venus. F. Sartwell. il Nat Geog Mag 123:732-42 My '63
Mariner-2 microwave observations of Venus. A. H. Barrett and E. Lilley. il Sky & Tel 25:192-5 Ap '63
Mariner II: preliminary reports on measurements of Venus; symposium. bibliog il Science 139:905-11 Mr 8 '63
Mariner's course nearly optimum. Aviation W 81:26 D 14 '64
Mars-Mariner program. R. N. Watts, jr. il Sky & Tel 28:352-3 D '64
Mercury missions seen more useful than Mars, Venus probes. D. M. Cole. il Miss & Roc 12:34+ Je 24 '63
Mid-course correction decides Mariner fate. il Miss & Roc 15:12 D 7 '64
Mission to Mars; Mariner D. Time 84:51 D 4 '64
NASA near decision on whether to impact or fly by Mars in '66. H. M. David. il Miss & Roc 14:21 Ja 20 '64
NASA plans new Mars payload. Aviation W 81:32 S 7 '64
NASA speeds planetary program. Aviation W 78:39 Ap 15 '63
NASA studies advanced version of Pioneer solar probe. R. D. Hibben. il Aviation W 82:40-3+ Ja 4 '65
New Mariner planning pushed. H. Taylor. il Miss & Roc 12:12-13 Mr 4 '63
New space goal, Mars. Sci N L 86:339 N 28 '64

SPACE probes—*Continued*
Observatories in the sky. D. F. Nolan. il Sci N L 85:74-5 F 1 '64
On to the red planet; Mariner IV and Zond II. il Time 84:76 D 11 '64
One more chance to hit Mars. Bsns W p 121+ N 14 '64
Out of this world life detectors; Gulliver, astrorobot. S. D. Pursglove. il Pop Mech 119:72-5 Je '63
Phase 1 of billion-dollar Voyager development will begin next month. il Miss & Roc 15: 81-4+ N 30 '64
Philco labs developing protein detector to probe for life on Mars. Miss & Roc 14:26-7 Mr 2 '64
Pioneer program decisions expected in next few weeks. M. Getler. il Miss & Roc 13: 22-3+ S 9 '63
Plan advanced for landing probe on Mars in 1969 as urgent U.S. goal. H. M. David. il Miss & Roc 14:14-15 Ja 6 '64
Probe designed to give better horizon definition. C. D. LaFond. il Miss & Roc 16: 31+ Ja 25 '65
Probe will measure cosmic noise levels. D. E. Fink. il Aviation W 80:68-9 Ja 6 '64
Project Beagle Mars mission proposed. il Aviation W 81:48-9+ Jl 13 '64
Ranger 6, where are you? J. Joseph. il Pop Sci 182:64-8+ Je '63
Reconnaissance module proposals sought. B. Miller. Aviation W 78:36-7 My 20 '63
Rendezvous with Mars. il Sci Digest 57:24-7 Ja '65
Results from Mariner. R. N. Watts. Sky & Tel 26:195+ O '63
Results from Mariner 2. il Sky & Tel 25:89-90 F '63
Science academy wants post-Apollo priority for unmanned planetary shots. H. Taylor. Miss & Roc 15:11 N 2 '64
Scientists plan missions to comets. W. Beller. il Miss & Roc 12:22-3 My 6 '63
Scientists urge priority for Mars missions. il Aviation W 81:26-7 N 23 '64
Second Centaur shot planned next week. G. Alexander. Aviation W 79:41 N 11 '63
Second Mariner launch. il Sci N L 86:325 N 21 '64
Six-month lifetime predicted for Pioneer. L Stone. il Aviation W 80:69+ Ja 27 '64
Snowball in July; campaign for space probe visit to a comet. il Newsweek 62:64 N 4 '63
So we land on the moon, then what? with editorial comment. C. P. Gilmore. il Pop Sci 183:40, 59-61+ D '63
Soviet Mars probes due in November. Aviation W 81:24 Jl 13 '64
Space probes cheaper if launched from air. Sci N L 84:82 Ag 10 '63
Space sciences challenge. R. D. Hibben. il Aviation W 80:54-5+ Ja 27; 68-9+ F 10; 91-3+ F 17 '64
Three Mars craft. R. N. Watts, jr. Sky & Tel 29:29 Ja '65
Three Ranger hard-landing flights eliminated; four others delayed. E. H. Kolcum. Aviation W 79:17-18 Jl 29 '63
Two Mariner Mars spacecraft planned for launch in November. il Aviation W 81:30 Ag 24 '64
Two Mariner spacecraft poised for exploratory trip to Mars. R. Pay. il Miss & Roc 15: 14-15 N 2 '64
U.S. and Russia both launch probe to Mars. il Sci N L 86:375 D 12 '64
U.S. mission to Mars: Mariner speeds towards its date; with report by R. Bailey. il Life 58:41-2+ Ja 29 '65
U.S, Soviets ready spacecraft for Mars missions Nov. 4-Dec. 1. W. J. Normyle. Aviation W 81:22 N 2 '64
Unmanned interplanetary programs will get bigger funding in FY '65. il Miss & Roc 13:120-1+ N 25 '63
Unmanned probe studies due; NASA plans Miss & Roc 12:15 F 18 '63
Venus defined. Newsweek 61:62 Mr 11 '63
Voyage of Mariner II. J. N. James. il Sci Am 209:70-84 bibliog(p 171) Jl '63
Voyage to the morning star; findings of Mariner II. il Time 81:76-80 Mr 8 '63; Same abr. with title Voyage to Venus. Read Digest 82:120-5 Je '63
We need to know more about the sun; questions and answers. W. Von Braun. il Pop Sci 184:14+ Mr '64
What did we learn about Venus? W. Cloud. il Pop Sci 182:23+ My '63
What scientists hope to learn from Mars shot; Mariner IV. U S News 57:18-19 D 14 '64
With an eye on Canopus; U.S. Mariner IV. il Newsweek 64:58 D 14 '64
See also
Lunar probes

SPACE probes, Russian
How space detectives rate Russia's moon probes. S. D. Pursglove. il Pop Mech 119: 89-93+ Mr '63
Lunik 4 believed to have failed in mission. E. H. Kolcum. Aviation W 78:38 Ap 15 '63
Mars probe lost. Sky & Tel 26:23 Jl '63
New Russian shot at moon; unmanned lunar satellite, Moon IV. Bsns W p66 Ap 6 '63
Old devil moon; Lunik IV. il Newsweek 61: 62-3 Ap 15 '63
Soviet Zond 1. S. B. Kramer. Aviation W 80: 102 Je 1 '64
Soviets launch Lunik 4. Aviation W 78:33 Ap 8 '63
Soviets lose Mars probe contact. Aviation W 78:24 My 27 '63
Soviets may be using two Cosmos types. E. Clark. Aviation W 78:22-3 Ap 29 '63
Soviets planning new deep space probes. W. C. Wetmore. Aviation W 78:30-1 Je 10 '63
Zond to Venus. Newsweek 63:52 Je 22 '64

SPACE radiation. See Radiation

SPACE rescue work
How we'll answer an SOS from space. J. H. Winchester. il Sci Digest 54:81-5 S '63

SPACE research
Chronology of fiscal 1963-1964. Miss & Roc 13:200-2+ Jl 29 '63; 15:154-8+ Jl 27 '64
International space science symposium; report on fifth symposium. V. K. McElheny. il Science 144:1434-7 Je 19 '64
Many nations begin space science work. Aviation W 81:273-4 Jl 6 '64
National space research organizations. Aviation W 81:82 Jl 6 '64
1963-1964 science review. il(p385) Sci N L 84: 394; 86:396 D 21 '63, D 19 '64
Previews of space; symposium. il Bul Atomic Sci 19:7-29 My '63
Recent activity in space. R. N. Watts, jr. Sky & Tel 28:277 N '64
Space astronomy; summary of address. L. Goldberg. il Sky & Tel 28:264-6 N '64
Space science; address, December 26, 1962. H. E. Newell. bibliog il Science 139:464-71 F 8 '63
Unlocking sky secrets. Sci N L 84:7 Jl 6 '63
See also
Artificial satellites—Use in research
International council of scientific unions—Committee on space research
United Nations—Committee on the peaceful uses of outer space

International aspects

Access to international brainpower accrues from cooperative projects; NASA-ESRO collaboration. il Miss & Roc 13:149-50 N 25 '63
Are we wasting billions in space? S. H. Loory. il Sat Eve Post 236:13-15 S 14 '63
Cooperation with Europe. W. J. Coughlin. Miss & Roc 15:46 Jl 6 '64
Cosmos may have photographed U.S. Miss & Roc 12:18 Ap 1 '63
Europe begins joint effort into space. W. Wetmore. il Aviation W 80:116-17+ Mr 16 '64
German satellite contract due soon. W. Beller. il Miss & Roc 13:24-5 Ag 5 '63
How to do missile/space business in Europe. W. Beller. il Miss & Roc 13:22-5 Jl 22 '63
IAF stresses more cooperation. W. Beller. Miss & Roc 15:16-17 S 14 '64
International Comsat agency considered. C. Brownlow. Aviation W 80:34 F 17 '64
International cooperation in space science; remarks, January 31, 1963. D. Rusk. Dept State Bul 48:294-5 F 25 '63
International cooperation; with editorial comment. il Aviation W 81:68-9, 70-85+ Jl 6 '64
Military safety, and cooperation with Russian science; interview, ed. by W. Beller and F. G. McGuire. T. Von Karman. Miss & Roc 12:22-3 F 25 '63
NASA and western Europe agree on scientific satellite project: NASA announcement, July 21, 1964, with text of agreement. Dept State Bul 51:203-5 Ag 10 '64
On guard; terms of the first joint U.S.-Soviet research program in space. il Newsweek 61:47 Ap 1 '63
Rise and fall of the space age, by E. Diamond. Review
Miss & Roc 14:70 My 25 '64. W. J. Coughlin

SPACE research—International aspects—*Cont.*
Second Ariel in orbit. il Sky & Tel 27:288-9 My '64
Soviets block space data exchange pact. D. E. Fink. Aviation W 81:25 O 12 '64
Space meteorology and communications: a challenge to science and diplomacy; address, April 19, 1963. R. N. Gardner. Dept State Bul 48:740-6 My 13 '63
Speaking out; does our space research threaten life on earth? B. Lovell. Sat Eve Post 237:10+ F 22 '64
U.S. and Russia agree on publishing space data. Sci N L 85:392 Je 20 '64
U.S. and U.S.S.R. agree on implementation of cooperative space program; with exchange of letters and memorandum of understanding. A. A. Blagonravov; H. L. Dryden. Dept State Bul 49:404-10 S 9 '63
U.S. Canada to launch four satellites; Alouette and ISIS. Miss & Roc 14:16 Ja 20 '64
U.S. industry to profit from progress abroad. il Miss & Roc 15:106-7 N 30 '64
U.S. Soviets plan joint space projects. E. H. Kolcum. il Aviation W 79:64-5 Ag 12 '63
U.S.-U.S.S.R. relations: way cleared for frequency allocations, pact on legal principles for space. J. Walsh. Science 142: 1278-80 D 6 '63
Warsaw parley proposes joint lunar lab. W. C. Wetmore. Aviation W 81:34 S 14 '64
When is international space cooperation international? L. E. Schwartz. il Bul Atomic Sci 19:12-18 Je '63; Reply. A. W. Frutkin. 19:33-5 O '63

Argentina

Argentina continuing ionosphere probes at busy Chamical range. il Aviation W 81: 234-5 Jl 6 '64

Australia

Australia geared to Woomera operations. il Aviation W 81:251-3 Jl 6 '64

Austria

Funding lack restricts Austrian effort. Aviation W 81:207 Jl 6 '64

Belgium

Belgians to define long-term space goals. il Aviation W 81:197+ Jl 6 '64

Brazil

Brazil to launch first sounding rocket. il Aviation W 81:249-50 Jl 6 '64

Canada

Canadians seek coordinated, expanded space effort. il Aviation W 81:220-1+ Jl 6 '64

Czechoslovakia

Czechs seek national rocket launch site. il Aviation W 81:208-9+ Jl 6 '64

Egypt

Background on Egyptian rocketry. Miss & Roc 14:37 F 24 '64
Bomb shop in the Nile: target Israel. T. Prittie. Atlan 214:37-40 Ag '64
Egypt plans satellite launch within year. C. Brownlow. il Aviation W 79:32-3 S 9 '63

Europe, Eastern

Soviet bloc space work kept on ground. il Aviation W 81:215+ Jl 6 '64

Europe, Western

Cooperation keynotes meeting; third spaceflight symposium. W. Beller. Miss & Roc 12:14-15 My 27 '63
Europe begins joint effort into space. W. Wetmore. il Aviation W 80:116-17+ Mr 16 '64
Europe builds multilateral space effort. il Aviation W 81:100-1+ Jl 6 '64
Europe challenges in space. Bsns W p34 Ap 13 '63
ELDO participants report brisk pace. Miss & Roc 13:21 O 14 '63
Saenger urges Germans to build space ships. E. Saenger. Miss & Roc 13:35 Jl 8 '63
West Europe firms pushing space efforts. C. Brownlow. Aviation W 78:38-9 Ap 8 '63

France

France and Britain prepare to strike out into space on own. W. Beller. il Miss & Roc 12: 15-17 Je 17 '63
France plans to strengthen top position in Europe. il Aviation W 81:118-19+ Jl 6 '64
French government plans west Europe's most extensive space effort; with editorial comment. il Aviation W 78:21, 26-9 Je 17 '63
French Guiana space launch site approved as Hammaguir alternate. C. Brownlow. Aviation W 80:30 Ap 27 '64
French plan space research in new areas. C. Bronlow. il Aviation W 79:52-3+ Ag 12 '63
French to show off 66-ft. rocket. il Miss & Roc 12:21+ My 27 '63
IRBM work aids French space hopes. B. Poirier. il Miss & Roc 12:55 Ap 29 '63
Objectives slowed but unchanged by French civil space budget cut. Aviation W 79:27 S 23 '63

Germany (Federal Republic)

Dornier is developing paraglider rocket. W. C. Wetmore. il Aviation W 80:65+ Ja 13 '64
Fund cuts crimp German space push. F. G. McGuire. Miss & Roc 14:34 My 11 '64
German space effort waits new direction. il Aviation W 81:150-1+ Jl 6 '64
Germany links technical future to space. W. C. Wetmore. Aviation W 79:67+ S 9 '63
R&D, missile efforts are keys to Boelwok's major German space role. W. C. Wetmore. il Aviation W 79:58-9+ S 30 '63
Saenger's final interview with M/R; ed. by W. Beller. E. Saenger. Miss & Roc 14:35+ F 24 '64

Great Britain

Armchair astronauts. A. C. Clarke. Holiday 33:94-5+ My 63
British space efforts keyed to important fall elections. il Aviation W 81:128-30+ Jl 6 '64
British to shape national space program. Aviation W 81:30 S 14 '64
First ELDO Europa 1 booster hardware begins automated static testing program. il Aviation W 81:124-6 S 7 '64
France and Britain prepare to strike out into space on own. W. Beller. il Miss & Roc 12: 15-17 Je 17 '63
U.K. program to use Black Knights. F. G. McGuire. Miss & Roc 15:26 O 5 '64

India

India maintains major research program. il Aviation W 81:268-70 Jl 6 '64

Israel

Israel begins to apply theoretical work. il Aviation W 81:264-7 Jl 6 '64

Italy

Italians focusing on San Marco satellite. il Aviation W 81:170-1+ Jl 6 '64
San Marco satellite to probe air density. W. C. Wetmore. il Aviation W 79:76-7+ Ag 26 '63

Japan

Japan plans to develop, launch variety of space systems. il Aviation W 81:254-61 Jl 6 '64
Japan: soaring into space on a shoestring. il U S News 54:63 Ap 15 '63

Mexico

Mexico pushes to shape talent, facilities. il Aviation W 81:237-44 Jl 6 '64

Netherlands

Netherlands seeks broadly based national space plan. il Aviation W 81:192-3 Jl 6 '64

New Zealand

New Zealand programs keyed to research. Aviation W 81:263 Jl 6 '64

Pakistan

Pakistani effort keyed to poverty battle. il Aviation W 81:271-2 Jl 6 '64

Russia

Appeal to the President. W. J. Coughlin. Miss & Roc 12:46 Mr 18 '63
Cosmonauts to fly this year. W. Beller. Miss & Roc 12:14-15 Je 10 '63
Cosmos points to space spectacular. Aviation W 78:30 Ap 22 '63
Gagarin outlines Soviet Union's rendezvous, lunar race goals. C. Brownlow. Aviation W 79:30-1 O 7 '63
How space detectives rate Russia's moon probes. S. D. Pursglove. il Pop Mech 119: 89-93+ Mr '63
NASA leaders given intelligence data on Russian space activities. A. P. Alibrando. Aviation W 80:32-3 Ja 6 '64
Next Soviet manned shot believed one year away. F. G. McGuire. Miss & Roc 14:33-4+ Je 22 '64
Polyot and Peking. Newsweek 62:73 N 11 '63
Russian Cosmos flight objectives. Aviation W 78:22 Ap 29 '63
Russians describe space tests at Cospar. W. C. Wetmore. Aviation W 80:33-4 My 18 '64

SPACE research—Russia—*Continued*
Russia's ladder to the moon; timetable for space. W. Wingo. il Sci N L 84:314-15 N 16 '63
Scramble into space; 1963 space calendar; highlights of space age; comp. by W. Wingo. il(p 337) Sci N L 84:341-3 N 30 '63
Soviet aerospace program well-planned, closely military oriented. F. G. McGuire. il Miss & Roc 12:16-17 Je 10 '63
Soviet aims in astronomy and space research; reprint. B. Lovell. Bul Atomic Sci 19:36-9 O '63
Soviet circumlunar flight seen. Aviation W 80:77 My 18 '64
Soviet space program. R. A. Kilmarx. Cur Hist 45:200-4+ O '63
Soviets may not have extravehicular space experimentation capability. H. M. David. Miss & Roc 15:16-17 D 14 '64
Soviets planning extensive IQSY effort. Aviation W 81:65+ Ag 25 '64
Soviets reported improving space suits. C. Brownlow. Aviation W 79:33 O 14 '63
Space unit briefed on Soviets. Aviation W 80:30 Ap 20 '64
Titanic task. R. Hotz. Aviation W 81:11 N 2 '64
USSR's space effort hits economic snags. E. H. Kolcum. Aviation W 80:137+ Mr 16 '64
U.S.-Soviet space gap. il Sci Digest 56:23-5 D '64
Vostok flights widen Soviet experience. il Aviation W 79:315-18 Jl 22 '63

Scandinavia

Scandinavians advance ionosphere data. il Aviation W 81:180-1+ Jl 6 '64

Switzerland

Swiss seek academic support for space. Aviation W 81:205 Jl 6 '64

United Arab Republic

UAR plans follow-on to Star satellite. Aviation W 81:273 Jl 6 '64

United States

Aerojet is studying lunar oxygen system. Aviation W 79:107 N 11 '63
After moon landing, what next? NASA's dream projects. il Bsns W p 104+ Mr 28 '64
Aftermath. W. J. Coughlin. Miss & Roc 15:50 N 9 '64
AF outlines five-year research plan. D. C. Breasted. Miss & Roc 13:21 O 21 '63
AAAS deplores integrity erosion from pressures of space program. D. E. Fink. Aviation W 82:18 Ja 4 '65
Answers to your questions about space (title varies) (cont) W. Von Braun. il Pop Sci 182:92-4 F '63
Apollo use in military programs proposed. Aviation W 81:27-9 N 9 '64
Appeal to the President. W. J. Coughlin. Miss & Roc 12:46 Mr 18 '63
Barry Goldwater on space: GOP candidate wants military, not civilians, to run space program. E. Langer. Science 145:470-1 Jl 31 '64
Basic challenge; excerpt from message to Congress, May 25, 1961. J. F. Kennedy. Aviation W 79:25 D 2 '63
Basic Gemini ECS keyed to fourteen-day flight. H. D. Watkins. il Aviation W 79: 52-3+ Ag 19 '63
Bear trap. W. J. Coughlin. Miss & Roc 14:46 My 18 '64
Berkner outlines U.S. space goals, argues against program's critics; summary of address. L. V. Perkner. Aviation W 78:23 My 6 '63
Businessmen review the space effort. E. E. Furash. il Harvard Bsns R 41:14-16+ S '63
Coming back to earth; practical benefits of space research. Newsweek 62:56 S 30 '63
Common market and space program; address, June 17, 1963. J. M. Gavin. Vital Speeches 29:591-4 Jl 15 '63
Congress awaits LBJ space message. H. Taylor. il Miss & Roc 16:14 Ja 11 '65
Defense, space receiving Johnson mark. G. C. Wilson. Aviation W 81:18-19 Ag 31 '64
DDR&E ponders military Comsat future. I. Stone. il Aviation W 79:40-1+ S 2 '63
Dryden cites contributions of engineers; address. H. L. Dryden. Aviation W 78:67+ My 20 '63
Edwards proposes large five-year program. A. P. Alibrando. il Aviation W 79:77+ S 30 '63
15 per cent of budget for R&D; $6.1 billion budget for space research. W. Davis. Sci N L 83:67 F 2 '63
FY '65 missile/space money bills subject to minimal trimming so far. H. M. David. Miss & Roc 14:17 My 25 '64
FY '65 space request is $7.2 billion. Miss & Roc 14:15 Ja 13 '64
Footprints on the moon. H. L. Dryden. il Nat Geog Mag 125:356-401 Mr '64
Forty miles of information every day from space. L. Lessing. il Fortune 69:116-22+ Ja '64
Foundation for space progress; excerpts from address. E. C. Welsh. Aviation W 80:11 Je 22 '64
Future in space; excerpt from address. E. C. Welsh. Aviation W 81:17 N 9 '64
Gemini, Apollo and beyond; special report. il Aviation W 81:48-9+ N 16; 48-9+ N 23 '64
GE's space division thrives in adversity; General electric space technology center. il Bsns W p39-40+ D 19 '64
Glamour masks waste in space spending. W. Proxmire. il Nations Bsns 51:38-9+ N '63
GOP pledges more orderly space program, revitalized military R&D. H. M. David. Miss & Roc 15:12 Jl 20 '64
Growing power requirements accelerate research pace. M. L. Yaffee. il Aviation W 80:48-9+ My 25 '64 (to be cont)
G&C people and places; key contacts in NASA and military. Miss & Roc 13:73 O 7 '63
Hope of increased DOD space funds slim. Aviation W 79:83-4+ N 4 '63
Hornig outlines U.S. space mandate; interview, ed. by W. Beller. D. F. Hornig. Miss & Roc 14:34-5 Ap 20 '64
House unit to probe NASA fund shifts. A. P. Alibrando. Aviation W 78:38-9 F 18 '63
How haste in space makes waste. J. A. Morris. il Read Digest 85:82-7 Jl '64
How industry can adapt space inventions. il Sci Digest 56:32-3 D '64
Indelible mark; President John F. Kennedy. R. Hotz. Aviation W 79:21 D 2 '63
Late President, successor saw development of space program. il Aviation W 79:30-1 D 2 '63
LOC presses studies to keep abreast of growing launch problems. C. Butler. Miss & Roc 13:17 N 18 '63
Letter to the Colonel; reply to an article in Red star. W. J. Coughlin. Miss & Roc 12: 84 Je 24 '63
Lunik boosts NASA funding hopes. H. Taylor. il Miss & Roc 12:14-15 Ap 8 '63
LBJ wants post-Apollo plans. H. Taylor. il Miss & Roc 14:12 My 4 '64
Majority opinion; right or wrong? letter. P. D. Foote. Science 142:341 O 18 '63; Reply. D. W. Riley. 143:433 Ja 31 '64
Mars exploration seen delayed to 1980s. Aviation W 78:85+ Je 24 '63
Mars mission equipment, vehicles studied. I. Stone. Aviation W 78:59+ My 20 '63
Mars mission study proposals evaluated. Aviation W 78:55 Ap 15 '63
Mercury problems, successes reviewed. E. J. Bulban. Aviation W 79:29-30 O 14 '63
Message to company presidents. W. J. Coughlin. Miss & Roc 13:46 Jl 15 '63
MOL decision. W. J. Coughlin. Miss & Roc 15:46 D 14 '65; Reply. F. J. Howard. 16:4 Ja 25 '65
Moon race with ourselves? Life 55:4 N 8 '63
More defense, space R&D fallout sought. K. Johnsen. Aviation W 78:103+ Ap 22 '63
More space debate. R. Hotz. Aviation W 78: 17 Je 3 '63
Move to slash Apollo funds 10 per cent is narrowly defeated in Senate; with editorial comment. Aviation W 80:11, 25 Je 29 '64
NASA cites aircraft avionics research. Aviation W 79:121 S 16 '63
NASA links efforts to defense to broaden appeal for support. A. P. Alibrando. Aviation W 79:32 Ag 19 '63
NASA plans; special report. il Miss & Roc 12:14-18 F 18 '63
NASA: rein on budget may stiffen competition for funds between manned program space sciences. J. Walsh. Science 142:1636-7 D 27 '63
NASA, scientists divided on space goals. R. D. Hibben. Aviation W 78:24-5 Ap 29 '63
NASA technology utilization scrutiny due. A. P. Alibrando. Aviation W 79:28-9 Ag 5 '63
National space policy; excerpts from address. E. C. Welsh. Aviation W 80:21 Mr 2 '64
Need to know. W. J. Coughlin. Miss & Roc 13:46 S 2 '63
Now it's an agonizing reappraisal of the moon race. R. A. Smith. il Fortune 68: 124-9 N '63

SPACE research—United States—*Continued*
Observation in space; address, April 13, 1963. L. C. Meeker. Dept State Bul 48:746-51 My 13 '63
Only six NASA payloads orbited in 1963. A. P. Alibrando. Aviation W 79:30-1 N 18 '63
Our gamble in space; symposium. Atlan 212: 35-54 Ag '63
Outer space. Sr Schol 85:22 S 30 '64
Planning ahead. il Newsweek 61:98+ Mr 25 '63
Policy and legacy. J. Walsh. Science 142: 1152-3 N 29 '63
Post-Apollo goals, MOL fate imminent. D. E. Fink. Aviation W 81:24-5 N 9 '64
Post-Apollo programs detailed; summary of interview, ed. by H. Taylor. R. C. Seamans, jr. Miss & Roc 15:14 O 26 '64
Post-Apollo report due Sept 1; with editorial comment. H. Taylor. Miss & Roc 15:12, 46 Ag 24 '64
President will outline U.S. space goals. G. C. Wilson. Aviation W 82:16-17 Ja 11 '65
Price of the future. W. J. Coughlin. Miss & Roc 15:46 N 16 '64
Progress report on the moon race. il Fortune 69:142-5 Mr '64
Project definition technique to be applied to many more programs. J. Trainor. Miss & Roc 14:14-15 Mr 9 '64
Ranger VII; briefing for Johnson brings out high level chit chat on various aspects of space. L. B. Johnson; H. E. Newell; D. F. Hornig. Science 145:563-5 Ag 7 '64
Redefinition of U.S. space goals planned; with editorial comment. A. P. Alibrando. Aviation W 79:21, 26-7 N 4 '63
Report on space programs. il Bul Atomic Sci 19:18-25 My '63
Report stresses space structure reuse. R. D. Hibben. il Aviation W 79:71+ S 16 '63
R&D growth altering U.S. economy. W. Beller. il Miss & Roc 13:30-2 D 16 '63
Rise and fall of the space age, by E. Diamond. Review
Sat R 47:31+ My 9 '64. W. Hines
Russia's ladder to the moon; timetable for space. W. Wingo. il Sci N L 84:314-15 N 16 '63
Saturn V is modern caravel; address, March 2, 1964. J. E. Webb. il Sci N L 85:165-7 Mr 14 '64
Scramble into space; 1963 space calendar; highlights of space age; comp. by W. Wingo. il(p 377)) Sci N L 84:341-3 N 30 '63
Second Centaur shot planned next week. G. Alexander. Aviation W 79:41 N 11 '63
Second West Ford launch is successful. R. D. Hibbean. il Aviation W 78:34 My 20 '63
Six new NASA flight projects funded. il Miss & Roc 12:16-17 F 11 '63
Sorrowful year. W. J. Coughlin. Miss & Roc 12:72 F 25 '63
Space. il Life 57:79-91+ S 25; 74-81+ O 2 '64
Space: administration official says some harsh things about scientists opposing moon landing. D. S. Greenberg. Science 147:381 Ja 22 '65
Space age challenge to physicists; excerpts from address. H. L. Dryden. Aviation W 79:21 Ag 12 '63
Space and national priorities; address, October 17, 1963. J. W. Fulbright. Vital Speeches 30:41-4 N 1 '63
Space: formidable political base overshadows attempts to revise administration's lunar program. D. S. Greenberg. Science 145:137-9 Jl 10 '64
Space: highlights of recent research. R. Jastrow and A. G. W. Cameron. bibliog il Science 145:1129-39 S 11 '64; Reply. E. A. Whitaker and W. K. Hartmann. 146:342 O 16 '64
Space; its relationship to economic growth; address, May 14, 1964. H. B. Fancher. Vital Speeches 30:542-4 Je 15 '64
Space: National academy panel recommends exploration of Mars as major goal in 1971-85 period. J. Walsh. Science 146:1025-7 N 20 '64
Space program: results of poll of AAAS members. il Science 145:368 Jl 24 '64; Reply. A. T. Young. 145:989 S 4 '64
Space program: skepticism grows but in context of cold war it is hard for Congress to say no. D. S. Greenberg. Science 139: 890-1 Mr 8 '63; Reply with rejoinder. I. S. Menzies. 140:937 My 31 '63
Space program support to grow; with editorial comment. H. Taylor. Miss & Roc 13:14-15, 48 D 2 '63
Space research effects. Sci N L 83:199 Mr 30 '63
Space science and the universities; address, May 7, 1963. F. Seitz. Science 141:614-18 Ag 16 '63
Space sciences challenge. R. D. Hibben. il Aviation W 80:54-5+ Ja 27; 68-9+ F 10; 91-3+ F 17 '64
Space science, research effort grows but failures beset lunar missions. A. Alibrando. il Aviation W 78:124-5+ Mr 11 '63
Space Senator Fulbright steps into lunar landing controversy. D. S. Greenberg. Science 142:470 O 25 '63
Space technology: pay-off from spin-off. J. G. Welles and R. H. Waterman, jr. bibliog f il Harvard Bsns R 42:106-18 Jl '64
Space unit briefed on Soviets. Aviation W 80:30 Ap 20 '64
Speaking out; are we being too peaceful in space? H. W. Cannon. Sat Eve Post 236: 10+ Je 15 '63
Special report: test & checkout; with editorial comment by W. J. Coughlin. il Miss & Roc 12:19-26+, 92 My 20 '63
State of the Union. W. J. Coughlin. Miss & Roc 13:46 Jl 22 '63; Discussion. 13:7 Ag 12 '63
Structure problems of 70s listed. Miss & Roc 13:16-17 S 2 '63
Three Nova classes for 1970-80 unveiled. il Aviation W 78:34-6 Je 10 '63
Titanic task. R. Hotz. Aviation W 81:11 N 2 '64
USAF compiling space projections. Aviation W 78:31 My 27 '63
USAF keys space plan to three programs. E. H. Kolcum. il Aviation W 78:26-8 Ja 28 '63
USAF space, large solids efforts periled. L. Booda. Aviation W 79:18-19 Jl 8 '63
U.S. advances in space. il Sci N L 85:98 F 15 '64
U.S. alters advanced space plan focus; with editorial comment. D. E. Fink. Aviation W 81:17, 22 S 21 '64
U.S. facing decisions on manned flight; with editorial comment. il Aviation W 79:68-9, 73-6 Jl 22 '63
U.S. replies to Soviet charges against certain space activities; text of letter, June 6, 1963 to U.N. Secretary-General U Thant; with statement on Project West Ford. A. E. Stevenson. Dept State Bul 49:104-7 Jl 15 '63
U.S. shifts goals in space. il U S News 55:39-40 N 11 '63
U.S.-Soviet space gap. il Sci Digest 56:23-5 D '64
U.S. space activities. Sci N L 83:375 Je 15 '63
U.S. spurs international space research. il Aviation W 81:77-80 Jl 6 '64
U.S. to select orbiting lab or lunar base; report of NASA-Industry conference. E. H. Kolcum. Aviation W 78:32-4 F 18 '63
Urban conference hunts spin-off; space-research results applicable to urban problems; Oakland meeting. il Am City 78:166 S '63
Views of the presidential candidates on the future of the U.S. in space. L. B. Johnson; B. M. Goldwater. Miss & Roc 15:16-18 O 26 '64
Vital year in space. R. Hotz. Aviation W 82:17 Ja 18 '65
Vote by House will provide test of feeling toward space effort. D. E. Fink. Aviation W 80:17-18 Mr 23 '64
We are moving from preparation to fruition; with editorial comment. J. W. Webb. Miss & Roc 13:37, 262 N 25 '63
Webb looks beyond Apollo. J. E. Webb. Aviation W 80:11 Mr 23 '64
Welsh sees Soviet try at docking this year; summary of address. E. C. Welsh. Miss & Roc 12:35 Ap 8 '63
We're running the wrong race with Russia! F. V. Drake. Read Digest 83:49-55 Ag '63
Wernher Von Braun answers your questions (title varies) (cont) W. Von Braun. il Pop Sci 182:92-4 F; 183:63-5+ Jl '63
Who's relaxing? Newsweek 63:69 Mr 30 '64
Will space research pay off on earth? L. Galton. il N Y Times Mag p29+ My 26 '63
Women for space study. W. Wingo. Sci N L 84:103 Ag 17 '63
World ahead. W. J. Coughlin. Miss & Roc 15:168 Jl 27 '64
World will be ruled from skies above. Life 54:4 My 17 '63
Year of orderly progression toward our aspirations. J. E. Webb. Miss & Roc 15:39 N 30 '64

See also
United States—National aeronautics and space administration

SPACE station simulators
AF pilots far exceed expected performance in military experiment; at GE Valley Forge space station simulation facility. H. M. David. Miss & Roc 15:26+ S 7 '64
Crew-monitoring to have station priority. W. J. Normyle. Aviation W 81:71+ D 21 '64
Deaf personnel used in artificial-G test; space laboratory simulator. R. D. Hibben. Aviation W 81:117+ S 14 '64
Engineers emerge from eight days in centrifuge. il(p337) Sci N L 86:343 N 28 '64
Experiment simulates stay in space station. Aviation W 78:59 Mr 4 '63
GE test simulates orbiting lab. H. M. David. il Miss & Roc 13:31+ N 18 '63
GE, USAF simulate space station control. Aviation W 81:119-20 S 14 '64
Study may ease rotation problems. H. M. David. il Miss & Roc 16:226-7 Ja 18 '65

SPACE stations
Advanced Saturn guidance platform flies on successful Saturn I SA-5; ST-124 stabilized inertial platform. M. Getler. il Miss & Roc 14:26-8 F 10 '64
Advanced vehicle crew station proposals. Aviation W 79:64 S 16 '63
Aeronutronic studying automated bio lab; search for life on Mars. Aviation W 81:83+ S 28 '64
After the moon, this. F. McGuire. il Sci Digest 55:71-5 Ja '64
Agreement reached on MOL status, NASA to continue station studies. Aviation W 80:28 Ja 6 '64
Air force given space laboratory mission; with editorial comment. L. Booda. il Aviation W 79:25, 30-1 D 16 '63
Air force may be put in MODS driver's seat. Miss & Roc 12:15 My 27 '63
Air force, NASA at odds over MOL tracking requirements. J. Trainor. Miss & Roc 14:16 Je 29 '64
Air force seeks winged supply vehicle to link with MOL. H. M. David. il Miss & Roc 14:35-6 F 10 '64
Apollo-based station projected for 1970s; orbiting space station. Aviation W 81:46 D 7 '64
Apollo-type, six-man spacecraft designed to support twenty-four-man orbital space station. I. Stone. il Aviation W 79:72-3+ Ag 19 '63
Apollo-X presentation is first step toward NASA space station. H. Taylor. Miss & Roc 15:13 N 16 '64
Are Soviets taking military command of space? manned orbiting laboratory or MOL. il U S News 57:60 O 26 '64
Arizona compromise; MOL. R. Lewis. Bul Atomic Sci 20:45-7 Ap '64
Biolabs evolving for NASA space stations. D. E. Fink. Aviation W 81:16-17 D 14 '64
Brown outlines ultimate MOL. J. Trainor. Miss & Roc 14:15 F 24 '64
Congress initially favorable to air force management of MOL. H. M. David. Miss & Roc 13:16 D 16 '63
Cost edge indicated for large stations. il Aviation W 80:74+ Je 15 '64
Decision on manned orbiting space station now due late in 1964. il Miss & Roc 13: 113-14+ N 25 '63
DOD may manage national space station. E. H. Kolcum. Aviation W 79:26-7 S 16 '63
Design study shows zero-g space station potentialities. C. M. Plattner. il Aviation W 80:46-7+ Ap 6 '64
Douglas co. submits six-man MORL design. Aviation W 80:22 Je 1 '64
Douglas due to get new MORL award. Miss & Roc 15:60 N 30 '64
Douglas, GE, Martin start OSS studies. Aviation W 80:22 Je 8 '64
Douglas has NASA station study. Aviation W 79:37 D 9 '63
Douglas wins MORL follow-on study; manned orbital laboratory. Miss & Roc 13:21 D 9 '63
Edible space station material developed. Miss & Roc 12:35 Ap 15 '63
Energy for remote areas. J. G. Morse. bibliog il Science 139:1175-80 Mr 22 '63
Experiment choice paces MOL progress. W. Gregory. Aviation W 80:31 Ja 27 '64
Fire, rapid decompression pose hazards for MOL environment. Aviation W 80:48 Mr 30 '64
Flexible space station evolving at Langley; MORL. E. H. Kolcum. il Aviation W 81: 74-5+ O 19 '64
Getting a no, and a go; air force loses Dyna-Soar project, gets MOL. il Bsns W p76+ D 14 '63
Grumman tries to break 4-rpm limit. H. M. David. Miss & Roc 12:35+ Ap 15 '63
House trailer in orbit; Manned orbiting laboratory. il Time 82:54 D 27 '63
Inflatable space station escape vehicle under study. W. C. Wetmore. il Aviation W 78: 62-4+ My 6 '63
McNamara MOL decision due. H. Taylor. Miss & Roc 15:10 D 7 '64
Manned orbiting lab study bids sought. Aviation W 78:31 Ap 29 '63
MOL decision. W. J. Coughlin. Miss & Roc 15:46 D 14 '64; Reply. F. J. Howard. 16:4 Ja 25 '65
MOL requirements will be set by Jan. 1; with editorial comment. Aviation W 79:21, 26-7 D 23 '63
MOL studies to include army, navy tasks. Aviation W 79:32-3 D 16 '63
MOL study awards due soon. D. C. Breasted. Miss & Roc 13:14-15 D 16 '63
MOL to test man's space role. Aviation W 80:33 F 24 '64
MOL value, technical factors questioned. L. Booda. Aviation W 80:27-8 Ja 13 '64
MOL wins development okay. J. Trainor. il Miss & Roc 15:12-13 D 21 '64
MOSS may get extra year's study. H. Taylor. Miss & Roc 13:16 Ag 5 '63
MOSS planning faces slippage. H. Taylor. Miss & Roc 13:14 Jl 15 '63
MOSS plans include military. W. E. Wilks. il Miss & Roc 12:14 My 13 '63
Manned space station studies due in May. D. E. Fink. Aviation W 82:25 Ja 25 '65
Manned space stations could be Mars vehicle. Sci N L 86:360 D 5 '64
Military role in space. G. C. Sponsler. Bul Atomic Sci 20:31-4 Je '64; Reply. D. W. Smythe. 20:37-8 O '64
Military space planners insist MOL program not a race. il Miss & Roc 14:71-2+ Mr 30 '64
Military space station called critical. Aviation W 78:85 Je 24 '63
NASA building space station technology. il Aviation W 79:77-82 Jl 22 '63
NASA, DOD agree on space station. Aviation W 79:30 O 21 '63
NASA favors deployable stations for first-generation space study. Aviation W 78:61 Ap 15 '63
NASA flexible space station plan urged; National multipurpose space station. W. J. Normyle. Aviation W 81:22-3 O 12 '64
NASA/industry team wants future manned flights to use Apollo core. J. Trainor. il Miss & Roc 14:14-15 Je 8 '64
NASA picks large station design calling for three radial modules. R. Pay. il Miss & Roc 14:22-3 Ap 20 '64
NASA planning group approves Apollo X organizational structure. Aviation W 81:14 D 28 '64
NASA presses for extended Apollo. H. Taylor. Miss & Roc 14:16 Ap 27 '64
NASA seeks space station parameters. I. Stone. il Aviation W 78:70-3 Ap 1 '63
NASA starts manned station studies. H. Taylor. il Miss & Roc 12:18-19 Ap 29 '63
Navy feels its MOL experiment valid on military or NASA flight. D. E. Fink. Aviation W 81:13-14 D 28 '64
New gyros being sought for MORL. M. Getler. il Miss & Roc 16:31-3 Ja 11 '65
New type of spacesuit may be needed for MOL astronauts. H. M. David. Miss & Roc 15:22 D 7 '64
No Apollo slow-down: Webb; interview, with editorial comment by W. J. Coughlin and H. Taylor. J. E. Webb. il Miss & Roc 12:14-16, 46 Je 3 '63
Nuclear power studied for space stations. Aviation W 79:77+ Ag 19 '63
Off-the-shelf MORL packages seen. C. D. LaFond. il Miss & Roc 16:22-3 Ja 18 '65
Off we go; Gemini-Mol combination. il Newsweek 62:54 D 23 '63
Official says AF won't get MOSS. Miss & Roc 12:16 F 25 '63
OSS studies will start definition of the MOL. J. Trainor. il Miss & Roc 14:15 F 17 '64
Panel shaping space station. H. Taylor. il Miss & Roc 14:12 Mr 9 '64
Plan manned orbiting laboratory in space. Sci N L 84:394 D 21 '63
Plan space laboratory; MORL. Sci N L 86:77 Ag 1 '64
Post-Apollo goals, MOL fate imminent. D. E. Fink. Aviation W 81:24-5 N 9 '64
President will outline U.S. space goals. G. C. Wilson. Aviation W 82:16-17 Ja 11 '65
Pseudo-gravity space station proposed. W. C. Wetmore. il Aviation W 78:56-8 Ja 28 '63
Senate space head pushes MOL merger. D. E. Fink. Aviation W 81:16-17 D 7 '64

SPACE stations—*Continued*
Six astronauts picked for MOL; assignment to specialties planned. Aviation W 81:25 N 23 '64
Small space station planned for 1967-68. C. M. Plattner. il Aviation W 78:141+ Je 10 '63
Small space station seen most feasible. H. Taylor. Miss & Roc 14:15 Ap 20 '64
Soviet, NASA plans cloud MOL future. W. J. Normyle. Aviation W 81:26-7 O 26 '64
Soviet space station lead cited. Aviation W 79:27 S 23 '63
Soviet success spurs U.S. space review; reassessment of plans for MOL. W. J. Normyle. il Aviation W 81:36-7 O 19 '64
Space lab grounded? MOL program. Bsns W p 17 D 26 '64
Space telescope use with MORL proposed. R. D. Hibben. il Aviation W 80:71+ F 24 '64
Sperry Rand proposes cabling technique to simulate gravity. Aviation W 81:124-5+ S 14 '64
Station design funding to start next year. D. E. Fink. Aviation W 81:66+ D 21 '64
Study awards near for 3-module MOL. W. E. Wilks. Miss & Roc 14:32 My 11 '64
Study contracts for OSS delayed by reorientation to MOL program. Aviation W 80:31 My 25 '64
Study long space trips. il Sci N L 85:115 F 22 '64
Third phase of MORL study has ambitious experiment aims. R. Hawkes. Miss & Roc 15:28+ D 7 '64
Thirty-six-man space station seen after Apollo. il Aviation W 81:51+ N 16 '64
Three firms awarded space station studies. Aviation W 80:27 F 10 '64
USAF gives space station top priority. il Aviation W 79:214-15+ Jl 22 '63
USAF plans space station bid request. Aviation W 79:18 Jl 8 '63
Webb looks beyond Apollo. J. E. Webb. Aviation W 80:11 Mr 23 '64
Welsh reports MOL program is due to get program definition okay soon. H. Taylor. Miss & Roc 15:14-15 N 9 '64
Welsh says U.S. will build manned space stations. R. Hawkes. Miss & Roc 13:16-17 S 16 '63
When man steps out into space; drawings of GE's space program. R. Scarfo. N Y Times Mag p26-7 O 25 '64
When spacemen live in the sky. il Bsns W p32-3 Mr 16 '63

SPACE suits. See Astronauts—Clothing

SPACE systems division. See United States—Air force—Systems command

SPACE technology
Economics and space technology. W. H. Meckling. il Bul Atomic Sci 19:15-17 My '63
Electro-optics; report, comp. by C. D. LaFond. il Miss & Roc 14:23-31+ Je 1 '64
International cooperation; with editorial comment. il Aviation W 81:68-9, 70-85+ Jl 6 '64
Mystery duo; engineers behind the Soviet space effort. Newsweek 62:73 N 25 '63
New Soviet problem. R. Hotz. Aviation W 80:21 F 17 '64
Slim pickings from NASA; study on Commercial applications of missile/space technology. Bsns W p55+ S 14 '63
Space sciences challenge. R. D. Hibben. il Aviation W 80:54-5+ Ja 27; 68-9+ F 10; 91-3+ F 17 '64
Spacecraft technology and electronics packaging. il Electr World 71:54-5 Je '64
Vital year in space. R. Hotz. Aviation W 82:17 Ja 18 '65
World of missiles & spacecraft. W. J. Coughlin. Miss & Roc 13:212 Jl 29 '63

SPACE technology laboratories, incorporated
STL wins parallel LEM descent engine contract. J. F. Judge. il Miss & Roc 12:24-5 Je 3 '63
Systems integration contract forbids firm from bidding on hardware. Miss & Roc 15:16 N 9 '64

SPACE telemetry
Apollo bio-telemetry system developed. B. Miller. il Aviation W 78:80-1 Mr 18 '63
First flight of ELDO booster T/M components due next August. F. G. McGuire. il Miss & Roc 15:26-7 N 2 '64
Hardened telemetry system overcomes circuit design obstacles. Miss & Roc 15:39 Jl 6 '64
Highly advanced telemetry complex going in at Eastern test range. C. D. LaFond. il Miss & Roc 16:32-3 Ja 4 '65
Lockheed marketing new T/M system. Miss & Roc 13:15 Ag 12 '63
Lockheed T/M system may set trend. il Miss & Roc 12:36 Je 3 '63
Microcircuit plant to serve in-house need. P. J. Klass. il Aviation W 80:66-9 Mr 9 '64
Microminiature T/M system evolving. il Miss & Roc 12:48 My 6 '63
Miniature S-band units delivered. R. Pay. il Miss & Roc 15:33 S 28 '64
NASA, JPL seek cause of Ranger 6 failure. il Aviation W 80:22-5 F 10 '64
Our weakness in space. F. Drake. il Sat R 48:96-9 Ja 2 '65
Satellite tracking, telemetry, and communications. J. T. Mengel. il Electr World 71:58-60 Je '64
T/M chain collects real-time data. R. Pay. il Miss & Roc 14:33-4 Ja 6 '64
Understanding telemetry. W. H. Buchsbaum. il Electr World 71:25-8 Ap '64
Vestigial sideband offers increased T/M capability. C. D. LaFond. il Miss & Roc 13:24 Jl 8 '63

SPACE-to-ground link subsystem. See Space vehicles—Control systems

SPACE vehicle batteries. See Storage batteries

SPACE vehicle models
Minimal design changes appear in first all-metal mockup of LEM. D. A. Anderton. Miss & Roc 15:21 O 19 '64
NASA may increase scale model testing. R. D. Hibben. il Aviation W 80:36-7+ Je 8 '64

SPACE vehicle parts
Recent representative programs involving beryllium technology; table. Aviation W 81:70-1 N 9 '64
Space agency nears decision on adopting parts qualification list. Miss & Roc 14:17 Ap 20 '64

SPACE vehicles
Apollo-X spacecraft going into program definition next fiscal year. il Miss & Roc 15:52-3+ N 30 '64
Apollo's military potential detailed. Miss & Roc 15:15 N 9 '64
Can in the sky. W. J. Coughlin. Miss & Roc 13:54 D 16 '63
Defense may ease impact of X-20 loss; relationship of the cutback to Gemini. E. H. Kolcum. Aviation W 78:31 Mr 18 '63
Direct military value of Apollo questioned. Aviation W 81:25 Jl 20 '64
Eurospace outlines plans for joint aerospace transporter. F. G. McGuire. Miss & Roc 15:32-3 N 23 '64
First five years of the space age. Sky & Tel 25:148-50 Mr '63
Footprints on the moon. H. L. Dryden. il Nat Geog Mag 125:356-401 Mr '64
Funds for new spacecraft expected to be included in FY '66 budget; Pioneer. il Miss & Roc 15:88-9 N 30 '64
Gemini; special report. il Miss & Roc 14:12-13+ Ap 13 '64
Glowing future; chances of being hit by earthward-bound space-garbage. Nat Parks Mag 38:16 My '64
Lucky seven. R. Hotz. Aviation W 81:13 Ag 17 '64
Mariner design modified for Mars flyby. I. Stone. il Aviation W 78:50-1+ My 6 '63
Marshall studies advanced large vehicles. il Aviation W 79:33-4 D 2 '63
Missiles and rockets astrolog; current status of U.S. missile and space programs. See occasional issues of Missiles and rockets
Missiles and rockets' world missile/space encyclopedia, 1963-1964. il Miss & Roc 13:35-7+ Jl 29 '63; 15:39-46+ Jl 27 '64
NASA approves Voyager development. H. Taylor. Miss & Roc 16:13 Ja 4 '65
NASA plans new spacecraft; unmanned Mars exploration vehicles. H. Taylor. Miss & Roc 14:15 Je 1 '64
NASA: Ranger misfortunes attract attention of Congress to problems of spacecraft sterilization. J. Walsh. il Science 141:139-41 Jl 12 '63
NASA speeds planetary program. Aviation W 78:39 Ap 15 '63
New GE Apollo role may be challenged. A. P. Alibrando. Aviation W 78:28-9 Ap 22 '63
New Mariner planning pushed. H. Taylor. il Miss & Roc 12:12-13 Mr 4 '63
Next space capsule will have satellite inside; Pegasus. Sci N L 86:197 S 26 '64
1962 USAF space vehicle launches. il Aviation W 78:53 F 11 '63
Norair building re-entry test vehicles. il Aviation W 81:20-1 Jl 13 '64
Nova decision may be far away. R. Hawkes. il Miss & Roc 12:16-17 Ap 29 '63
Orbital tanker design concepts studied. I. Stone. Aviation W 81:55+ Ag 10 '64
RFP's trigger Voyager development. Miss & Roc 16:10 Ja 18 '65

SPACE vehicles—*Continued*
Ranger design and management criticized; reports. A. J. Kelley; E. D. Hilburn. Aviation W 80:56+ My 11 '64
Results from Mariner 2. il Sky & Tel 25:89-90 F '63
Rombus study keyed to post-Nova effort. il Aviation W 79:77 Jl 1 '63
Shuttle ferry to space stations, satellites seen; Astro. Sci N L 84:136 Ag 31 '63
Six-launch Bios series starts in '65. H. M. David. il Miss & Roc 13:34-5 S 2 '63
Space vehicle log. Aviation W 80:64 Ja 13; 135 Mr 16; 81:51 Jl 27 '64; 82:85 Ja 25 '65
Strange shapes of things to fly; with photographs by L. Schiller. Sat Eve Post 236:16-21 S 14 '63
Titan II-Centaur hybrid studied; modified Surveyor moon lander likely mission for booster. H. Taylor. il Miss & Roc 12:12-13 Mr 18 '63
U.S. space effort turns to Gemini, Apollo. E. H. Kolcum. il Aviation W 78:107-9+ Mr 11 '63
U.S. space program at funding plateau. il Aviation W 80:107-11 Mr 16 '64
U.S. spacecraft; International spacecraft; specifications. Aviation W 80:193-4 Mr 16 '64
U.S. spacecraft; specifications. Aviation W 78:189-90 Mr 11 '63
U.S. to select orbiting lab or lunar base; report of NASA-industry conference. E. H. Kolcum. Aviation W 78:32-4 F 18 '63
U.S. traffic to top 200 by 1976. il Miss & Roc 12:39 My 6 '63
USAF sees X-20 cancellation or cutback. E. H. Kolcum. Aviation W 78:26 F 25 '63
When spacemen live in the sky. il Bsns W p32-3 Mr 16 '63
See also
Lunar vehicles
Navigation (space flight)

Atmospheric entry

All-weather vehicles goal of structure design. il Miss & Roc 13:53+ N 25 '63
Army cites re-entry body advances by Materials research agency. M. Getler. il Miss & Roc 14:26-7 Je 29 '64
ASSET will become more sophisticated in X-20 substitute role; Aerothermodynamic/elastic structural systems environmental tests. D. C. Breasted. Miss & Roc 14:17 Ja 20 '64
Athena scores first success. C. D. LaFond. il Miss & Roc 15:32-5 N 16 '64
Facility will simulate 34,000-mph re-entries. J. F. Judge. il Miss & Roc 12:24-5 Je 10 '63
First ASSET launch scheduled in August. G. Alexander. Aviation W 78:34 Mr 18 '63
First ASSET transmits valuable data before disappearing in Atlantic. C. Butler. il Miss & Roc 13:18 S 23 '63
Former RAF Thors; made into boosters. W. E. Wilks. il Miss & Roc 14:31-2 Ap 6 '64
Fourth ASSET glider gathers flutter data. Aviation W 81:25-6 N 2 '64
Gemini photos may assist in re-entry wake research. R. Hawkes. il Miss & Roc 14:34 Ja 13 '64
Glider lost after ASSET shot succeeds. G. Alexander. il Aviation W 79:37 S 23 '63
Glider may be post-Apollo guinea pig. R. Hawkes. il Miss & Roc 12:26-7 F 11 '63
Liquid gas coolants studied for Dyna-Soar. Aviation W 79:100 S 30 '63
M-2 flight successes spur interest in lift re-entry. R. Hawkes. il Miss & Roc 13:14-15 S 9 '63
Multiple re-entry vehicles urged. Miss & Roc 13:37 O 21 '63
NASA studies FIRE re-entry heat data. G. Alexander. Aviation W 80:37 Ap 20 '64
New parachutes float spacecraft to earth; Cloverleaf. Sci N L 87:25 Ja 9 '65
Project Fire shot seeks re-entry data for Apollo. il Miss & Roc 14:20+ Ap 6 '64
Recoverable booster development must await bigger savings yields. J. Trainor. Miss & Roc 15:18 O 19 '64
Re-entry from Mars is major problem. M. Getler. Miss & Roc 15:41+ O 19 '64
Silicon-boron shielding protects ASSET vehicle during re-entry. J. F. Judge. il Miss & Roc 13:22+ D 23 '63
Sneaking up on earth would slow reentry. Sci N L 86:25 Jl 11 '64
Space hot rod launched; Project Fire. W. Wingo. il Sci N L 85:262 Ap 25 '64
Third ASSET launch results in recovery. Aviation W 81:24 Jl 27 '64
USAF seeks re-entry configuration data. I. Stone. il Aviation W 80:53+ Je 22 '64

Atomic power plants

Accumulation of error. Nation 198:567 Je 8 '64
AEC likely to spend over $2 billion on rockets and auxiliary power units; SNAP-50/SPUR program. il Miss & Roc 15:172-4+ N 30 '64
AEC readies destruct tests of SNAP-type reactors. Miss & Roc 13:26 S 30 '63
AEC sees off-the-shelf space-power packages. W. Beller. Miss & Roc 12:39 F 18 '63
Committee backs Snap 10A flight test. Aviation W 80:23 My 4 '64
General electric embarks on testing nuclear space power system dynamic components. J. F. Judge. il Miss & Roc 14:26-8 F 17 '64
Joint committee insisting on SNAP flight tests. Miss & Roc 14:14 F 17 '64
Joint committee raps DOD, AEC. W. Beller. il Miss & Roc 14:24-5 Mr 2 '64
Kiwi to be deliberately destroyed. Miss & Roc 16:15 Ja 11 '65
Lithium test aimed at SNAP-50/SPUR technology. R. D. Hibben. il Aviation W 81:58-9+ N 2 '64
Little reactors for space. W. Davis. il Sci N L 86:179 S 19 '64
Low-pressure potassium vapor powers two-stage turbine at GE. J. F. Judge. il Miss & Roc 15:23-4 Ag 3 '64
NASA seen blocking electric propulsion; with definition of terms. W. Beller. Miss & Roc 14:24-5 F 10 '64
Nuclear propulsion development pushed. Aviation W 80:47 Mr 9 '64
Power direct from fission. Sci N L 85:117 F 22 '64
Radiation escape may bring SNAP review. Aviation W 80:20 Je 1 '64
RCA delivers Snap 10A power modules. M. L. Yaffee. il Aviation W 81:53+ Jl 27 '64
Safe design of reactors is indicated. il Miss & Roc 14:17 Ja 13 '64
Satellite sought to flight-test Snap 10A. K. Johnsen. Aviation W 80:30 F 17 '64
SNAP mockup to burn up in re-entry. il Miss & Roc 12:32 Ap 15 '63
Snap-9A isotope generator powers navy transit navigation satellite. Aviation W 79:37 O 7 '63
SNAP plan is AEC bid for space role. K. Johnsen. Aviation W 80:31-2 Mr 2 '64
SNAP transit; SNAP 9-A. Newsweek 62:90 O 14 '63

Control systems

Acceptance testing under way on Honeywell Apollo flight display unit. C. D. LaFond. il Miss & Roc 14:26-7 F 24 '64
Apollo guidance computer design to permit checkout during flight. Aviation W 78:33 Ap 1 '63
Apollo optical-inertial guidance detailed. P. J. Klass. il Aviation W 79:32-3 S 30 '63
Attitude system is based on star-pair comparator. M. Getler. il Miss & Roc 12:31 Je 17 '63
Avionics changes included in Tiros wheel. K. J. Stein. il Aviation W 81:44-5+ Ag 3 '64
Basic Gemini ECS keyed to fourteen-day flight. H. D. Watkins. il Aviation W 79:52-3+ Ag 19 '63
Canopus star sensor will provide method to correct surveyor course. il Miss & Roc 15:36-7 Jl 6 '64
Chances appear good for more pilot control in Dyna-Soar flight. Miss & Roc 13:15 O 21 '63
Cockpit unit will allow Gemini astronauts to alter flight plan. il Miss & Roc 15:33 Ag 24 '64
Computers, integration top trends. il Miss & Roc 12:25-6+ My 20 '63
Dwarf to guide Apollo; G&N. V. Torrey. il Pop Mech 121:116-19+ F '64
First Apollo control prototype is readied. P. J. Klass. il Aviation W 80:91+ My 25 '64
First contracts let for U.S. standardized space guidance system. C. D. LaFond. Miss & Roc 14:17 Mr 2 '64
First Gemini computer model completed. R. D. Hibben. il Aviation W 79:58-9+ Jl 15 '63
First of some fifty block II Apollo G&N computers is due by mid-1965. R. Pay. il Miss & Roc 15:36-7 S 7 '64
Gemini digital command system exceeds reliability specifications. Miss & Roc 14:42-3 My 4 '64

SPACE vehicles—Control systems—*Continued*
Gemini digital command system readied by Radiation, inc. M. Getler. il Miss & Roc 13:32-3 Jl 22 '63
Gemini to test manual navigation systems. il Aviation W 80:39 Je 1 '64
GE develops satellite command unit. il Miss & Roc 12:34 F 4 '63
Guidance and control; special report. C. D. LaFond. il Miss & Roc 13:31-6+ O 7 '63
Guidance and navigation progress may come in detectors and read-out. il Miss & Roc 14:37-9 Je 1 '64
Guiding spacecraft to other worlds. W. Von Braun. il Pop Sci 182:14+ Je '63
High reliability servovalve design has parallel first-stage channels. il Aviation W 79:111+ Ag 19 '63
House probes Apollo guidance development. Aviation W 79:27 D 23 '63
ITT affiliate working on gas laser for guidance system use. il Miss & Roc 15:34-5 N 2 '64
Inventor of the month; how to steer in space. S. V. Jones. il por Sci Digest 56:84 S '64
Lightweight X-band radar proposed as sensor for space intercepts. M. Getler. Miss & Roc 14:41-2 My 4 '64
Man's capabilities affect design, mission of Gemini. il Aviation W 79:184-5+ Jl 22 '63
Mariner 4 sensors relay excellent data. Aviation W 81:26-7 D 7 '64
Mercury taught space pilot techniques. Aviation W 79:205 Jl 22 '63
Mid-course correction decides Mariner fate. il Miss & Roc 15:12 D 7 '64
More Apollo guidance flexibility sought. il Aviation W 81:71+ N 16 '64
Myoelectric servo control is developed. B. Miller. il Aviation W 78:69-70+ Mr 25 '63
NASA plans laser rendezvous guidance. B. Miller. il Aviation W 80:100-2+ My 18 '64
New Apollo guidance system could become standard for future. C. D. LaFond. il Miss & Roc 14:28+ Mr 16 '64
New inertial sensors show promise. W. Beller. il Miss & Roc 14:32-3 Je 29 '64
One ion rocket could hold satellite synchronous. Miss & Roc 13:31 Ag 5 '63
Photocell locked star with Mariner craft. Sci N L 86:375 D 12 '64
Pilot control of rendezvous stressed. R. Pay. Miss & Roc 13:56+ S 30 '63
Prototype ELDO guidance receiver to be delivered next June. F. G. McGuire. il Miss & Roc 15:32-3 O 26 '64
SA-6 shows engine-out capability following unscheduled shutdown. G. Alexander. il Aviation W 80:24-5 Je 8 '64
SSD plans space test of unified avionics. B. Miller. il Aviation W 81:42+ N 30 '64
Special report: advanced displays. il Miss & Roc 15:27-8+ O 5 '64
Spike use studied for hypersonic control. R. D. Hibben. il Aviation W 79:63 O 28 '63
Star-pattern recognition device urged. Miss & Roc 12:48+ Je 24 '63
Syncom II system opens new doors. il Miss & Roc 13:30 Ag 19 '63
System transfer azimuth from tower top to ground monitor. M. M. Merlen. il Miss & Roc 13:32-3 Jl 15 '63
USAF pushes micro-microwave efforts. P. J. Klass. il Aviation W 80:80-1+ Je 29 '64
See also
Inertial guidance systems
Television in space flight

Cooling

See also
Space vehicles—Thermal control

Cost

Spacecraft's R&D cost will top $700 million. il Miss & Roc 14:28+ Ap 13 '64

Design

AC-2 flight will test Centaur program. M. L. Yaffee. il Aviation W 79:75-7+ O 21 '63
Advanced space logistic systems studied. il Aviation W 79:54-5+ Jl 29 '63
AF can't agree on spacecraft design. W. E. Wilks. il Miss & Roc 12:16-17 Je 24 '63
Focus of LEM effort shifts to detailed refinements. W. J. Normyle. il Aviation W 80:20-3 Ap 6 '64
Gemini design keyed to mission flexibility. G. Alexander. il Aviation W 78:52-5+ My 13 '63
Hybrid spacecraft flies with no wings. il Bsns W p26-7 S 14 '63
Industry studies future concepts. il Aviation W 79:101 Jl 22 '63
Inflatable landing gear proposed to give LEM larger footprint. D. E. Fink. Aviation W 81:27 O 26 '64
LEM crushable landing pad design final. il Aviation W 81:61+ N 23 '64
Lunar mission. il Aviation W 79:117-23 Jl 22 '63
Lunar orbiter up for design review to meet delivery date in mid-'65. M. Getler. il Miss & Roc 15:35-7 O 26 '64
Meteoroid detection satellite mock-up shown. C. D. LaFond. il Miss & Roc 12:32-3 Je 24 '63
Nimbus C undergoes final design changes. Aviation W 82:41+ Ja 11 '65
Post-Apollo passenger, cargo types seen. Aviation W 79:81 Jl 8 '63
Ranger shows no changes needed in surveyor design. Miss & Roc 15:73-4+ S 14 '64
Report stresses space structure reuse. R. D. Hibben. il Aviation W 79:71+ S 16 '63
R&D, missile efforts are keys to Boelkow's major German space role. W. C. Wetmore. il Aviation W 79:58-9+ S 30 '63
Spacecraft protection needs get increased Douglas R&D attention. W. E. Wilks. il Miss & Roc 14:24-5 Je 29 '64
Three Nova classes for 1970-80 unveiled. il Aviation W 78:34-6 Je 10 '63
Vehicle study for extended Mars mission calls for advances in varied technologies. H. D. Watkins. il Aviation W 80:54-5+ Ap 20 '64

Electric equipment

Gemini fuel cell readied for GT-2 flight, now scheduled for September. M. Getler. il Miss & Roc 14:29-32+ Je 8 '64
Versatile vibrating-reed electrometer delivered to NASA. il Miss & Roc 15:51 S 14 '64

Electronic equipment

AF studying laser navigation sensors. M. Getler. il Miss & Roc 12:24-5 F 18 '63
Apollo communications details disclosed. P. J. Klass. il Aviation W 79:87+ O 21 '63
Apollo pre-modulation processor details given. Miss & Roc 14:34-5 Je 15 '64
Bendix star and planet tracker program locks on new detector device; channeltron. M. Getler. il Miss & Roc 13:24-5 O 21 '63
Circuits that heal themselves. il Time 83:50 Ja 3 '64
FEB joining-production plan evolving. M. Getler. Miss & Roc 12:37+ Mr 4 '63
Gravitational field sensor studied by Hughes to measure asteroids. Aviation W 82:73 Ja 25 '65
G&C advanced techniques; the wide-ranging search for tougher, lighter gyroscopes in space. il Miss & Roc 13:68-9+ O 7 '63
Hardened electronic systems urged. J. R. Crittenden. Miss & Roc 13:18-19 S 9 '63
Industry cautious in approach to manned spaceflight systems. C. D. LaFond and R. Pay. Miss & Roc 15:43+ O 5 '64
JPL facing Mariner C avionics problems. B. Miller. Aviation W 80:16-17 Je 29 '64
Military Comsat desires disclosed; concerning study presented at the Western electronics show and conference. Miss & Roc 13:26-8+ Ag 26 '63
Motorola proposes combining Apollo communications into single system. R. Pay. il Miss & Roc 14:42-3 Ap 6 '64
New horizon sensors planned for Agena D. B. Miller. il Aviation W 79:82-3+ S 30 '63
New inertial sensors show promise. W. Beller. il Miss & Roc 14:32-3 Je 29 '64
New non-coherent generator eyed for communications, missiles; Enertron. R. Pay. il Miss & Roc 13:26-7 O 21 '63
New space electronics products. See occasional issues of Missiles and rockets
New thin-film infrared sensor developed. P. J. Klass. il Aviation W 78:91+ My 20 '63
New type microwave transistor unveiled at components meeting. P. J. Klass. Aviation W 80:108-9 My 18 '64
Nucleonic sensor to gage spacecraft fuel. B. Miller. il Aviation W 80:74-5+ My 4 '64
Panel appraises outlook for microcircuits. P. J. Klass. il Aviation W 80:79+ Ap 6 '64
Radar work to aid lunar explorers. C. D. LaFond. il Miss & Roc 12:22-3 Ap 8 '63
Requirements for manned interplanetary journeys outlined. M. Getler. Miss & Roc 13:29-30+ O 14 '63
Satellites will test advanced avionics. B. Miller. il Aviation W 81:60-3+ Jl 20 '64
Silicone rubber sponge may encapsulate electronic components. J. F. Judge. il Miss & Roc 13:28 O 14 '63

SPACE vehicles—Electronic equipment—*Cont.*
SERT power requirement straining solid-state technology. il Miss & Roc 14:33-4 Ap 27 '64
Space parts specifications are prepared. B. Miller. Aviation W 79:111 Ag 5 '63
Spacecraft radiation may boost tube use. P. J. Klass. il Aviation W 78:67+ Je 3 '63
Spacecraft technology and electronics packaging. il Electr World 71:54-5 Je '64
TIMM components work throughout high-intensity radiation bombardment. R. Kiefer. Miss & Roc 15:34 Ag 24 '64
USAF pushes micro-microwave efforts. P. J. Klass. il Aviation W 80:80-1+ Je 29 '64
See also
Space telemetry

Equipment

BSD chief sees present photometric techniques at limit of development. C. D. LaFond. Miss & Roc 15:13 Ag 31 '64
Camera capsules aid Saturn program. il Miss & Roc 15:54+ S 14 '64
Careless use of redundant design can cause reduction in reliability. P. J. Klass. Aviation W 80:93-5 My 11 '64
Emphasis on space cryogenics advances at Linde. J. F. Judge. il Miss & Roc 13:22-4 S 23 '63
Epilogue to ineptitude. Time 82:30-1 O 11 '63
First color surveys of moon now expected in 1966. il Miss & Roc 15:27-8 Jl 6 '64
Fixed TV on Voyager could provide lander accuracy of 100 miles. Miss & Roc 15:66-7 S 14 '64
Gemini, Apollo to demand tried-and-true instrumentation. H. M. David. Miss & Roc 13:37-8 S 9 '63
Gemini potentiometer calibration test ended. Aviation W 80:51 Je 29 '64
GEC camera meets needs of Saturn test monitoring, lunar exploration. C. D. LaFond. il Miss & Roc 15:36+ D 7 '64
Gravity gradient device orients satellite. il Aviation W 80:57 F 24 '64
Gravity gradient feasibility test planned. P. J. Klass. il Aviation W 79:79+ N 25 '63
Integration, reliability, checkout emerge as key Apollo challenges. il Aviation W 79:290-1+ Jl 22 '63
Moon shot technician. il Ebony 20:45-6+ D '64
NASA, JPL seek cause of Ranger 6 failure. il Aviation W 80:22-5 F 10 '64
NASA weighs lunar logistics proposals. I. Stone. il Aviation W 80:52-3+ Ap 27 '64
OAO experiment unit delivered to NASA. R. D. Hibben. il Aviation W 80:55-6 Je 29 '64
Picture capability increased for Ranger 7. R. D. Hibben. il Aviation W 81:22-3 Jl 20 '64
Pioneer program decisions expected in next few weeks; magnetic cleanliness major design problem. M. Getler. il Miss & Roc 13:22-3+ S 9 '63
Plane to aid spacecraft radioaltimeter. Sci N L 87:29 Ja 9 '65
Power tool for astronauts. il Pop Mech 121:115 Ap '64
Ranger fixes aimed at June launch date. D. E. Fink. Aviation W 80:26-7 Ap 13 '64
Ranger 7 cameras removed, flight slips. D. E. Fink. Aviation W 80:29 F 17 '64
Ranger TV performed near design point. K. J. Stein. il Aviation W 81:100-1+ Ag 17 '64
Receiving kits may widen Tiros data use. G. Alexander. Aviation W 79:26 D 30 '63
SA-5 cameras recovered in Cook electric capsules. il Miss & Roc 14:18 F 3 '64
Scientific instruments in space exploration. R. L. Heacock. bibliog il Science 142:188-95 O 11 '63
Soviets describe equipment for Elektron. W. C. Wetmore. il Aviation W 80:49-50 Je 8 '64
Space telescope use with MORL proposed. R. D. Hibben. il Aviation W 80:71+ F 24 '64
Space tool for Apollo can deliver 50 ft.-lbs. of work. il Miss & Roc 14:37 Ja 13 '64
Where components must be improved. il Miss & Roc 12:40-1 Je 17 '63
See also
Life support systems
Television cameras

Escape devices

Apollo passes test; launch escape system. Sci N L 87:6 Ja 2 '65
Ballute device tested as Gemini mission recovery aid. M. L. Yaffee. il Aviation W 80:40-1+ Ap 6 '64
Gemini's horizontal-ejection escape system reported more than adequate. W. E. Wilks. il Miss & Roc 15:24-5 N 2 '64
Space ejection system designed around B-58 crew escape capsule. il Aviation W 81:81+ N 23 '64

Fuel

Test of positive expulsion device planned; expulsion system for rocket propellants. M. L. Yaffee. il Aviation W 81:59+ O 5 '64

Heat control

See Space vehicles—Thermal control

Instrument boards

Industry cautious in approach to manned spaceflight systems. C. D. LaFond and R. Pay. Miss & Roc 15:43+ O 5 '64

Landing systems

Air force picks three sites for space landings; Edwards, Holloman, Wendover. il Miss & Roc 12:34 Je 10 '63
Astronauts will land standing up; questions and answers. W. Von Braun. il Pop Sci 184:82-3+ My '64
Space agency invites twenty-nine firms to bid on two subsonic lifting body gliders based on M-2, HL-10. il Miss & Roc 14:17 F 24 '64

Mars

Ames seeking industry analysis of Mars mission heat shielding. Aviation W 79:63-4 S 16 '63
First manned landings on Mars now seen delayed until mid-'80s. H. D. Watkins. il Aviation W 79:97+ O 14 '63
Northrop advocates parachute landing system for Mars Voyager. il Miss & Roc 15:26-7 D 7 '64
Preliminary studies completed on three-man Mars excursion module. il Aviation W 81:53-4+ N 16 '64
Vehicle study for extended Mars mission calls for advances in varied technologies; manned Mars excursion module. H. D. Watkins. il Aviation W 80:54-5+ Ap 20 '64

Moon

Apollo chief, co-pilot to explore moon; lunar excursion module. D. E. Fink. il Aviation W 80:22-3 Mr 9 '64
Apollo experiment deadline nears; moon landings. Miss & Roc 14:16 Je 22 '64
Apollo logistics system will be next manned space flight project. H. Taylor. Miss & Roc 14:16 My 25 '64
Bell aerosystems alters LLRV design to better performance. M. Getler. il Miss & Roc 13:16-17 Ag 12 '63
Bell aerosystems studies lunar maneuvering system for NASA. I. Stone. Aviation W 81:65 S 21 '64
Bendix seeks LEM landing contract. J. F. Judge. il Miss & Roc 12:26-7+ Mr 11 '63
Bendix selects four-wheeled vehicle for mobile lunar lab. D. E. Fink. il Aviation W 81:38-9+ D 7 '64
Cloth rocket engine to land men on moon. Sci N L 85:392 Je 20 '64
Countdown for space flight. E. P. Aksenov and others. il UNESCO Courier 17:24-7 Ja '64
Critical design phase ending on lunar excursion module. M. Getler. il Miss & Roc 13:22-3+ Jl 15 '63
Direct Saturn lunar support proposed. Aviation W 80:26 My 11 '64
Equipment for intensive moon studies will be developed within fifteen months. il Miss & Roc 15:62+ N 30 '64
Focus of LEM effort shifts to detailed refinements. W. J. Normyle. il Aviation W 80:20-3 Ap 6 '64
Free-flight lunar landing model tested. C. M. Plattner. il Aviation W 78:77+ Ap 22 '63
Grumman selecting major components for LEM test program. il Aviation W 80:72-3 Ap 13 '64
How a moon shot works: a primer for you. T. Turner. il Esquire 62:204-7 D '64
Inflatable landing gear proposed to give LEM larger footprint. D. E. Fink. Aviation W 81:27 O 26 '64
Langley simulators perform lunar tasks. D. A. Brown. il Aviation W 80:54-5+ Ap 13 '64
Latest LEM configuration shown. il Aviation W 81:24 O 12 '64
Logistics version of lunar bug proposed to NASA by Grumman. il Aviation W 79:163+ Jl 22 '63
LEM can land even on pockmarked moon. Sci N L 86:101 Ag 15 '64

SPACE vehicles—Landing systems—Moon—*Continued*
LEM crushable landing pad design final. il Aviation W 81:61+ N 23 '64
LEM design changes keep weight within goals. Miss & Roc 14:15 F 10 '64
LEM design is nearly frozen. il Miss & Roc 14:26 Ap 6 '64
LEM design rapidly nearing completion. il Aviation W 80:33-4 Mr 2 '64
LEM design weight rises despite efforts at curtailment. M. L. Yaffee. il Aviation W 81:30-1 O 19 '64
LEM research facility nears completion. il Aviation W 79:83+ O 14 '63
LEM subs to be chosen by summer. H. Taylor. il Miss & Roc 12:14 F 25 '63
LEM's the name; lunar excursion module. il Newsweek 63:81 Ap 6 '64
Lunar landing abort techniques studied; Lunar excursion module. E. J. Bulban. il Aviation W 78:53-4 My 27 '63
Lunar surface experiment awards near. E. J. Bulban. il Aviation W 81:53+ O 26 '64
Lunar surface exploration gear analyzed. il Aviation W 81:69-71 N 16 '64
Minimal design changes appear in first all-metal mockup of LEM. D. A. Anderton. Miss & Roc 15:21 O 19 '64
Model photos show LEM configuration details. il Aviation W 78:34 Ja 21 '63
Moon base cost set at $2 billion. W. Beller. Miss & Roc 14:17 My 11 '64
Moon project: building the astronauts' lunar bug. il U S News 57:64-5 O 5 '64
Most rewarding lunar surveys sought by MSC for expeditions. I. Stone. Aviation W 79:81 N 4 '63
NASA, industry define lunar landing plan. G. Alexander. il Aviation W 80:36-7 Mr 9 '64
NASA studies lunar exploration concepts. il Aviation W 80:79 My 18 '64
NASA weighs lunar logistics proposals. I. Stone. il Aviation W 80:52-3+ Ap 27 '64
NASA's Lunar logistics system likely to be postponed. H. Taylor. Miss & Roc 12:21 Je 24 '63
Paraglider test problems affect Gemini. Aviation W 78:55 Ja 28 '63
Preliminary design frozen on lunar bug; LEM. il Aviation W 79:141-3+ Jl 22 '63
Project Apollo makes progress; lunar excursion module. R. N. Watts, jr. il Sky & Tel 27:249-51 Je '64
Proposals requested for first study of lunar base systems. Miss & Roc 14:13 Mr 23 '64
Reaction control system for LEM tested. H. D. Watkins. il Aviation W 81:83-4+ N 9 '64
Recovery site selection debated; Edwards AFB, Calif. Holloman AFB, N.Mex. and Wendover AFB, Utah. F. G. McGuire. Miss & Roc 13:14-15 Jl 8 '63
Redesigned lunar lander to fly in August. D. A. Brown. il Aviation W 80:75-7+ Ap 20 '64
Scientific debate focuses on Apollo landings. Aviation W 79:74 Jl 22 '63
Small space station seen most feasible; lunar excursion module saddlebags concepts. H. Taylor. Miss & Roc 14:15 Ap 20 '64
STL wins parallel LEM descent engine contract. J. F. Judge. il Miss & Roc 12:24-5 Je 3 '63
Spacecraft sterilization relaxed; lunar landing. Aviation W 79:34 S 16 '63
Twenty-nine firms seek role in Apollo logistics; LEM truck. Aviation W 80:24 Ap 6 '64
Surveying surveyor. W. J. Coughlin. Miss & Roc 13:46 Ag 12 '63
Ugly, unearthly bug; lunar excursion module. P. Conrad. il Life 57:85-6+ O 2 '64

Launching

AC-4 achieves primary flight objectives. G. Alexander. Aviation W 81:24 D 21 '64
Air force, navy pressing NASA to improve reliability of Scout. Aviation W 79:34 N 11 '63
Air force stressing operational economy of Titan 3 launch system. C. M. Plattner. il Aviation W 79:54-5+ S 9 '63
Apollo launch escape test due. il Miss & Roc 15:13 D 7 '64
At last U.S. takes the lead in big rockets; triumph of Saturn I. il U S News 56:44-5 F 10 '64
Atlas LV-3 launch record. Aviation W 81:19 Ag 3 '64
Centaur flies successfully. R. N. Watts, jr. il Sky & Tel 27:28-9 Ja '64
Centaur flight hailed as successful. C. Butler. il Miss & Roc 13:15 D 9 '63
Centaur flight in fall will be stringent test. C. Butler. Miss & Roc 13:19 S 9 '63
Centaur, IMP planned this week. Aviation W 79:30 N 25 '63
Countdown for space flight. E. P. Aksenov and others. il UNESCO Courier 17:24-7 Ja '64
Douglas developing improved Delta. W. E. Wilks. il Miss & Roc 15:33 Ag 10 '64
Eastern range's 1965 schedule shows sustained activity level. G. Alexander. Aviation W 82:49 Ja 4 '65
Fifth Saturn 5 might launch men to moon. G. Alexander. il Aviation W 80:26-7 Mr 2 '64
First flight of ELDO booster T/M components due next August. F. G. McGuire. il Miss & Roc 15:26-7 N 2 '64
First Titan 2 booster for Gemini delivered to NASA for checkout. Aviation W 79:39 N 4 '63
First unmanned Gemini flight will be orbital shot. W. Burkett. il Miss & Roc 13:16-17 Jl 15 '63
Five launchings at once. J. Eberhart. il Sci N L 86:51 Jl 25 '64
Floxed Atlas phase I approved. H. Taylor. il Miss & Roc 14:14 Je 22 '64
Four Gemini launches planned next year. Aviation W 81:21 N 30 '64
Gemini launch data target is mid-March. G. Alexander. il Aviation W 80:38-9 Ja 27 '64
Ground tests credited in Centaur success; with editorial comment. G. Alexander. il Aviation W 79:21, 30-2 D 9 '63
Haggle develops over Ranger failure. H. M. David. Miss & Roc 14:14-15 My 4 '64
Hottest rocket passes test; hydrogen-fueled Centaur. il Bsns W p58-60 D 7 '63
Hovercraft missile transporter seen. M. Getler. il Miss & Roc 15:18+ Ag 17 '64
I saw Atlas 9 take off! P. Calle. il Am Artist 27:58-9+ O '63
Launch of Mariner 4 scheduled this week. Aviation W 81:27 N 23 '64
Launch vehicle dynamics. R. D. Hibben. il Aviation W 80:36-7+ Je 8; 58-9+ Je 15 '64
Low-latitude noctilucent cloud of 15 June 1963. A. B. Meinel and others. il Science 141:1176-8 S 20 '63
Manned Gemini shots top schedule; with NASA launch record. H. Taylor. il Miss & Roc 15:14 D 21 '64
Man's leap into space; with 1964 space calendar. J. Eberhart. il(p369) Sci N L 86:373-4 D 12 '64
Marshall studies advanced large vehicles. il Aviation W 79:33-4 D 2 '63
NASA assessing GT-2 damage at Cape. Miss & Roc 15:17 Ag 24 '64
NASA, Chrysler trimming weight of S-1. G. Alexander. il Aviation W 79:54-7+ S 16 '63
NASA satellites to make detailed ionosphere study; Topside sounder, Ionosphere. il Miss & Roc 14:13 Mr 16 '64
NASA testifies that Rogallo wing is probably dead in Gemini program; Rogallo wing paraglider. H. M. David. Miss & Roc 14:21 F 24 '64
New Agena D checkout system in at Vandenberg. il Miss & Roc 13:42+ O 28 '63
Next Saturn is scheduled for this month. il Aviation W 80:70-1 Ja 6 '64
Officials optimistic about Ranger VII returning first U.S. moon pictures. Miss & Roc 15:13 Ag 3 '64
Only six NASA payloads orbited in 1963. A. P. Alibrando. Aviation W 79:30-1 N 18 '63
Photo sequence follows SA-6 liftoff. il Aviation W 81:80-1 Jl 20 '64
Poor man's launcher may encourage non-space nations. W. Beller. il Miss & Roc 13:43+ S 30 '63
Presidential decision is sought for Nova. E. H. Kolcum. Aviation W 78:26 Ap 29 '63
Ranger 7 completes early mission tests. H. D. Watkins. il Aviation W 81:18-20 Ag 3 '64
SA-5 orbit boosts U.S. prowess. C. Butler. il Miss & Roc 14:17-18 F 3 '64
SA-5 staging followed by flight, ground cameras. il Aviation W 80:76 F 24 '64
Saturn, Centaur launches slip; NASA says problems are minor. Aviation W 79:33 Ag 26 '63
Saturn makes it five for five. il Bsns W p77 F 1 '64
Saturn I decision will delay Apollo. H. Taylor. il Miss & Roc 13:15 N 4 '63
Saturn SA-5, both stages live, sends record payload to orbit; with editorial comment. G. Alexander. il Aviation W 80:17, 34 F 3 '64
Saturn SA-5, Tiros 8 readied for flights. Aviation W 79:39 D 16 '63

SPACE vehicles—Launching—*Continued*
Scout launches Explorer 19. il Aviation W 79:24 D 30 '63
Second OSO flight scheduled next week. W. J. Normyle. Aviation W 82:77+ Ja 25 '65
Secret fraternity; space registry maintained by the United Nations. Newsweek 61:58 F 18 '63
Space leadership hinges on SA-5 shot success. il Miss & Roc 13:18 D 16 '63
Theory of premature Vostok 5 separation is backed by NASA. P. J. Klass. il Aviation W 79:27-8 Jl 1 '63
Two Mariner Mars spacecraft planned for launch in November. il Aviation W 81:30 Ag 24 '64
U.S. takes space lead; launching of Saturn I, Echo II and a Ranger spacecraft. il Sr Schol 84:7 F 14 '64

Launching pads

Bids asked for Saturn 5 launch towers. Aviation W 78:35 Ap 1 '63
Construction speeded at Johnston Island; Thor launch pads. Miss & Roc 14:16 Ap 20 '64
Navy designs seagoing pad to launch satellites at sea. il Pop Sci 182:64-5 My '63

Launching sites

Building for the moon launch, a study in speed and size. il Arch Forum 119:118-21 S '63
French Guiana space launch site approved as Hammaguir alternate. C. Brownlow. Aviation W 80:30 Ap 27 '64
Hybrid Nova launch complex favored at Launch operations center. il Miss & Roc 13:186-91 N 25 '63
LOC presses studies to keep abreast of growing launch problems. C. Butler. Miss & Roc 13:17 N 18 '63
Team wins contract for Saturn V VAB; Kennedy space center. Miss & Roc 14:16 Ja 13 '64
These doors are 45 stories high; structure for Cape Canaveral. il Sci Digest 53:17 My '63

Lubrication

AFSC cites lubrication research needs. E. J. Bulban. Aviation W 78:71+ My 6 '63
Central information source urged; missile and space lubrication. J. F. Judge. il Miss & Roc 12:27+ My 13 '63

Maintenance and repair

How we'll answer an SOS from space. J. H. Winchester. il Sci Digest 54:81-5 S '63
In-flight maintenance stressed in manned missions beyond Apollo. W. E. Wilks. Miss & Roc 15:18 O 12 '64
LTV developing space repair guide for NASA. Aviation W 79:71 N 18 '63
Portable EB welding may get space role. J. F. Judge. il Miss & Roc 14:28+ Je 29 '64
Tools for space mechanics. R. Gannon. il Pop Sci 184:114-15+ Ap '64

Manufacture

Apollo funding stresses fabrication. H. Taylor. il Miss & Roc 12:16-17 F 4 '63
Apollo spacecraft boilerplate production advances. il Aviation W 78:30-1 Ap 8 '63
Apollo takes shape. il Bsns W p32-3 Ap 13 '63
Critical Apollo test modules produced. il Aviation W 79:124-31+ Jl 22 '63
Epilogue to ineptitude. Time 82:30-1 O 11 '63
First unmanned Apollo nears completion. C. M. Plattner. il Aviation W 81:40-1+ O 5 '64
Integration, reliability, checkout emerge as key Apollo challenges. il Aviation W 79: 290-1+ Jl 22 '63
Lockheed boosting its NASA Agena output. R. Lindsey. Miss & Roc 13:32 Ag 19 '63
MA know-how may be boon for future. R. Hawkes. Miss & Roc 13:15 Jl 22 '63
Michoud Saturn plant nears completion. il Aviation W 79:71 S 30 '63
Moon project: building the Apollo spaceship. il U S News 57:64-5 O 5 '64
NASA backs industry's Mercury record. A. P. Alibrando. Aviation W 79:31 O 14 '63
NASA lauds industry performance in Project Mercury production tasks. il Miss & Roc 13:14-16 O 14 '63
Plague of bugs; NASA criticism of contractors and technicians for shoddy work. il Newsweek 62:90 O 14 '63
Titan III buy must be decided to avoid cost hike, reliability drop. J. Trainor. Miss & Roc 14:14 Ap 13 '64
Titan III contract highly advanced. J. Trainor. Miss & Roc 14:13 My 4 '64

Materials

Advanced space logistic systems studied. il Aviation W 79:54-5+ Jl 29 '63
Aerojet moves into basic glass. J. F. Judge. il Miss & Roc 12:34-5 Mr 18 '63
All-weather vehicles goal of structure design. il Miss & Roc 13:53+ N 25 '63
Army cites re-entry body advances by Materials research agency. M. Getler. il Miss & Roc 14:26-7 Je 29 '64
Critical Apollo test modules produced. il Aviation W 79:124-31+ Jl 22 '63
Dow Corning tailoring silicone work to meet individual needs of buyers. J. F. Judge. il Miss & Roc 14:27-8 My 18 '64
Edible space structure material tested. il Aviation W 78:34 Ap 22 '63
Emphasis on space cryogenics advances at Linde. J. F. Judge. il Miss & Roc 13:22-4 S 23 '63
Labs race for space materials. il Bsns W p 120-1 Je 8 '63
New chemical theory. Sci N L 85:403 Je 27 '64
Report stresses space structure reuse. R. D. Hibben. il Aviation W 79:71+ S 16 '63
Silicone rubber sponge may encapsulate electronic components. J. F. Judge. il Miss & Roc 13:28 O 14 '63
Structural applications of beryllium grow. M. L. Yaffee. il Aviation W 81:64-5+ N 9 '64
Thermal control in space vehicles. A. L. Alexander. bibliog il Science 143:654-60 F 14 '64
See also
Shielding (heat)
Shielding (radiation)

Parts

See Space vehicle parts

Power supply

Apollo fuel cell progress termed sound. A. P. Alibrando. il Aviation W 80:32-3 Ja 20 '64
Apollo subsystems for service module delivered by Beech. il Aviation W 80:67 My 4 '64
Avco aims MHD generator at space role. R. D. Hibben. il Aviation W 80:62+ Ap 27 '64
Battery reliability ensures continued use. M. L. Yaffee. il Aviation W 80:49+ Je 1 '64
Chemical, solar, nuclear dynamic space vehicle power systems. Aviation W 80:82-3 Je 15 '64
Fuel cell prototypes accepted by NASA. il Sci N L 85:19 Ja 11 '64
Fuel cell readied for orbital test. il Miss & Roc 13:34+ Ag 26 '63
Gemini power systems. Aviation W 78:59 My 13 '63
GE seeking practical MHD space system. M. L. Yaffee. il Aviation W 81:55+ Jl 13 '64
Growing power requirements accelerate research pace. M. L. Yaffee. il Aviation W 80:48-9+ My 25 '64 (to be cont)
Mariner has enough gas. Sci N L 87:29 Ja 9 '65
NAA gets production-type Apollo engine. il Miss & Roc 14:18 My 4 '64
New non-coherent generator eyed for communications, missiles; Enertron. R. Pay. il Miss & Roc 13:26-7 O 21 '63
New spark to fuel cells. H. Klein. il Duns R 82:47+ O '63
N-on-P solar cells gaining wider use. B. Miller. il Aviation W 78:88-9+ Mr 4 '63
Piston engine space powerplant designed. W. Wright. il Aviation W 78:119+ F 18 '63
Power biggest problem. Sci N L 86:375 D 12 '64
Power direct from fission. Sci N L 85:117 F 22 '64
Power is problem in Voyager lander. il Miss & Roc 15:13 N 23 '64
Rapid-charge space battery developed. M. Getler. il Miss & Roc 14:28 Ja 6 '64
Representative space vehicle solar cell power systems. il Aviation W 80:60-1 My 25 '64
SERT power requirement staining solid-state technology. il Miss & Roc 14:33-4 Ap 27 '64
Space power from fuel cells. W. Von Braun. il Pop Sci 185:80-1+ Ag '64
Space power systems. M. L. Yaffee. il Aviation W 80:48-9+ My 25; 49 +Je 1; 55+ Je 8; 81+ Je 15 '64
Steam concept interests air force; ASTEC (advanced solar turbo electric concept) W. Beller. il Miss & Roc 14:24-5 Ap 27 '64; Reply. J. F. Coneybear. 14:6 Je 8 '64
Sun energizes EOS hydrogen engine. il Miss & Roc 13:36 N 18 '63
Thermionic cell generates A-C power. W. Beller. il Miss & Roc 12:18-19 F 11 '63
Vroom! out of this world engines; reprint. R. M. Loebelson. il Sci Digest 55:40-4 Ap '64
See also
Space vehicles—Atomic power plants

SPACE vehicles—*Continued*

Propulsion systems

AC-3 launch meets most goals. Aviation W 81:276 Jl 6 '64
AC-4 achieves primary flight objectives. G. Alexander. Aviation W 81:24 D 21 '64
Actuator modified for Gemini booster. Aviation W 81:21 D 28 '64
Aerojet's Miami facility nears completion. G. Alexander. il Aviation W 78:54+ Ap 29 '63
ASSET vehicles to fill part of Dyna-Soar gap. il Miss & Roc 12:30 Ap 29 '63
Air-breathing boosters gain favor. W. Beller. il Miss & Roc 12:22-3+ Mr 18 '63
AF, Martin recommend development of Titan III non-man-rated version. il Miss & Roc 15:11 Ag 31 '64
AF, NASA in tentative agreement on launch vehicle family. H. Taylor. Miss & Roc 14:14 My 11 '64
AF's Orion program getting NASA scrutiny. Miss & Roc 13:34-6 N 4 '63
Another successful Saturn. R. N. Watts, jr. Sky & Tel 27:163 Mr '64
Apollo-Saturn 5 may fly in 1966. Aviation W 80:35 F 10 '6
Apollo service module engine beginning prequalification. C. M. Plattner. il Aviation W 81:42-6 Jl 27 '64
Apollo testing to begin at White Sands. il Aviation W 79:281-3+ Jl 22 '63
Atlas-Centaur redeems itself, somewhat. Sci N L 87:6 Ja 2 '65
Atlas LV-3 launch record. Aviation W 81:19 Ag 3 '64
Atlas missile has a variety of missions. il Sci N L 86:374 D 12 '64
Big one for '64; Saturn I's first-stage booster. il Bsns W p32-3 Je 1 '63
Big test table for Saturn S-1C tops rigorous Boeing specifications. J. F. Judge. il Miss & Roc 15:24-5 Jl 6 '64
Booster re-use found practical in study. W. J. Normyle. il Aviation W 81:40-1 D 28 '64
Cape facilities for Saturn 5/Apollo, Titan 3 keyed to delivery of flight-ready boosters. G. Alexander. il Aviation W 78:54-5+ Ap 8 '63
Centaur flight hailed as successful. C. Butler. il Miss & Roc 13:15 D 9 '63
Centaur moon rocket, a success after all? U S News 57:12 Jl 13 '64
Centaur officials hopeful of successful second launching. Miss & Roc 13:15 N 18 '63
Centaur to carry surveyor model. Aviation W 81:18 N 30 '64
Chemical space engine development lags. Aviation W 81:58+ Jl 13 '64
Congress prods NASA's propulsion development. Miss & Roc 14:12 Mr 23 '64
Cornell tests aim at base-heating guidelines; Saturn booster program. M. Getler. il Miss & Roc 13:24-5+ Ag 19 '63
Cosmic clinic for the moon rocket. C. B. Hicks. il Pop Mech 120:84-7+ S '63
Crucial booster hearings start soon. H. M. David. Miss & Roc 14:13 Je 8 '64
Cryogenic system using RLIO considered for Apollo backup. Aviation W 80:36 Ja 20 '64
Delta launches Syncom 3; thrust-augmented Delta rocket used to boost the television satellite into orbit. W. McCann. il Sci N L 86:133 Ag 29 '64
DOD curtailment of solids work dropped due to stout opposition. L. Booda. Aviation W 79:27-8 Ag 26 '63
Different missions altering basic S-4B. H. D. Watkins. il Aviation W 79:48-9+ D 23 '63
Douglas developing improved Delta. W. E. Wilks. il Miss & Roc 15:33 Ag 10 '64
Douglas proposes an intercontinental ballistic transport for 1,200 troops. W. E. Wilks. il Miss & Roc 14:35 F 17 '64
Engine may oust big booster; air turbo-exchanger. W. Beller. il Miss & Roc 12:12-13 Ap 8 '63
F-1 troubles won't delay Saturn V. H. Taylor. il Miss & Roc 12:16 Mr 11 '63
Fifth Saturn 5 might launch men to moon. G. Alexander. il Aviation W 80:26-7 Mr 2 '64
Finest hour for Atlas; booster does biggest job. il Bsns W p28-9 My 18 '63
First ELDO Europa 1 booster hardware begins automated static testing program. il Aviation W 81:124-6 S 7 '64
First S-2 flight stage build-up scheduled. I. Stone. il Aviation W 80:50-1+ My 11 '64
First TAD set to launch NASA's Syncom III satellite in mid-August. C. Butler. Miss & Roc 15:14 Jl 20 '64
First Titan 3A vehicle fails to achieve orbit. Aviation W 81:32 S 7 '64
Five launchings at once. J. Eberhart. il Sci N L 86:51 Jl 25 '64
Former RAF Thors made into boosters. W. E. Wilks. il Miss & Roc 14:31-2 Ap 6 '64
Gaseous rockets could re-shape space transportation principles. Miss & Roc 15:15 N 16 '64
Gemini, Centaur shots due this week. Miss & Roc 15:15-16 N 30 '64
General dynamics proposes up-rated Atlas as Titan III-X competitor. il Miss & Roc 15:28+ N 16 '64
Greater emphasis on mission in large launch vehicle concept studies. il Miss & Roc 13:141+ N 25 '63
Ground tests credited in Centaur success; with editorial comment. G. Alexander. il Aviation W 79:21, 30-2 D 9 '63
Hatching our giant space birds; Saturn boosters of Michoud plant. il Bsns W p57-61 Ja 4 '64
Higher thrust potential planned for aerojet M-1 engine. il Aviation W 78:33 Ap 15 '63
Hottest rocket passes test; hydrogen-fueled Centaur. il Bsns W p58-60 D 7 '63
How to bring a booster back alive. P. Bono. Pop Sci 183:80-1 Jl '63
Improved Saturn IB would orbit 30 tons. H. Taylor. Miss & Roc 14:15 Mr 2 '64
Inside Gantry 37B; Saturn rocket. il Sci Digest 55:48-51 Je '64
Instability absent in recent F-1 engine test series. C. M. Plattner. il Aviation W 78:48-9+ My 27 '63
Intricate mechanism of Saturn V. il Life 57:95 S 25 '64
J-2, M-1 engine designed details reported. D. A. Anderton. il Aviation W 78:56-9 My 6 '63
Large reusable booster designs studied; report presented at American astronautical society meeting; ed. by C. M. Plattner. P. Bono. il Aviation W 78:52-3+ F 4 '63
Large vehicles alter handling concepts. il Aviation W 79:303+ Jl 22 '63
Largest load; Saturn SA-5. il Time 83:58-9 F 7 '64
Launch vehicle jockeying begins. il Miss & Roc 15:14 N 16 '64
Little Joe success will trigger Apollo test program soon. il Miss & Roc 13:15 S 2 '63
Long future seen for SLV 3B booster. R. Van Osten. il Miss & Roc 12:16-17 Ap 15 '63
Mighty F-1. S. Spillman. il Pop Sci 183:102-5+ O '63
Military's new rocket: Titan III by air force. il U S News 57:56-7 Ag 31 '64
Moon project: building the Saturn blast-off rocket. il U S News 57:62-3 O 5 '64
Motor failure dooms first TAT launching. Aviation W 78:36 Mr 18 '63
NAA gets production-type Apollo engine. il Miss & Roc 14:18 My 4 '64
NASA asks proposals to up-rate Saturn 5. Aviation W 80:22 Je 22 '64
NASA, Chrysler trimming weight of S-1. G. Alexander. il Aviation W 79:54-7+ S 16 '63
NASA considers recoverable lifting body boost vehicle. G. Alexander. il Aviation W 80:38-9+ Je 29 '64
NASA must decide Orion future. W. E. Wilks. il Miss & Roc 15:12-14 D 14 '64
NASA outlines reusable booster studies. E. H. Kolcum. il Aviation W 78:65+ My 27 '63
NASA plans post-Nerva follow-on study. I. Stone. Aviation W 78:53 Mr 18 '63
NASA plans to FLOX Atlas. Miss & Roc 13:14 N 11 '63
New NASA management concept aims for higher Centaur reliability. Aviation W 78:37 Ja 21 '63
Nova, post-Nova studies submitted to NASA. Aviation W 78:33 Ap 1 '63
Nova studies focus on radical designs. il Aviation W 79:89-91+ Jl 22 '63
On the move. H. Simmons and I. Goodwin. il Newsweek 63:72-3 F 10 '64
120-in. boosts argument for solids. R. Lindsey. il Miss & Roc 14:27-8+ Ap 27 '64
120-in. motor test termed successful; solid-propellant Titan 3C zero-stage booster motor. Aviation W 80:71 F 3 '64
Orbital tanker design concepts studied. I. Stone. Aviation W 81:55+ Ag 10 '64
Original Titan vehicle to launch Gemini 2. Aviation W 81:37 S 14 '64
Post-Saturn V development awaits high-priority manned Mars effort. il Miss & Roc 15:76-8 N 30 '64

SPACE vehicles—Propulsion systems—*Cont.*
P&W completes liquid test complex. il Miss & Roc 12:36 Ap 8 '63
Propellants, propulsion systems studied to boost Apollo capability. Aviation W 79:88 Ag 5 '63
Propulsion know-how considered equal to needs of future weapons. il Miss & Roc 14:131-2+ Mr 30 '64
Propulsion research aims at developing new fuel combinations. il Miss & Roc 13:62-4+ N 25 '63
Recoverable booster development must await bigger savings yields. J. Trainor. Miss & Roc 15:18 O 19 '64
Representative Karth urges U.S. sell boosters; interview, ed. by W. Beller; with editorial comment. J. E. Karth. Miss & Roc 13:21-2, 60 Ag 26 '63
Reusable rocket designed; ROMBUS. J. Eberhart. Sci N L 86:197 S 26 '64
S-1C heavy tooling installed at Marshall; center to begin building four stages soon. G. Alexander. il Aviation W 78:50-1+ Mr 25 '63
S-4B all-systems test vehicle eliminated. H. D. Watkins. Aviation W 81:23 D 21 '64
SA-5 orbit boosts U.S. prowess. C. Butler. il Miss & Roc 14:17-18 F 3 '64
SA-5 to fly first live S-4 upper stage. G. Alexander. il Aviation W 78:56-7 Ap 15 '63
SA-7 carrying Apollo boilerplate. il Miss & Roc 15:20 S 14 '64
SA-7 flies near-perfect mission. Aviation W 81:27 S 28 '64
Saturn-Apollo test. R. N. Watts, jr. il Sky & Tel 28:22-3 Jl '64
Saturn booster useful beyond moon program. Sci N L 85:395 Je 20 '64
Saturn engine stars in tests; F-1 engine. Bsns W p 122 Je 8 '63
Saturn I decision will delay Apollo. H. Taylor. il Miss & Roc 13:15 N 4 '63
Saturn IB/Centaur launch vehicle will be funded in FY '66. H. Taylor. Miss & Roc 14:17 My 18 '64
Saturn SA-5, both stages live, sends record payload to orbit; with editorial comment. G. Alexander. il Aviation W 80:17, 34 F 3 '64
Saturn shows one-engine-out capability. G. Alexander. Aviation W 78:32 Ap 1 '63
Saturn stage firing scheduled. Aviation W 79:39 D 23 '63
Saturn V slippage in certain. H. Taylor. il Miss & Roc 14:10-11 Mr 16 '64
Senate unit to probe separate booster efforts by NASA, DOD. Aviation W 80:37 Je 15 '64
Solid motor clusters analyzed as possible S-1C substitutes. il Aviation W 80:71+ Ap 27 '64
Space leadership hinges on SA-5 shot success. il Miss & Roc 13:18 D 16 '63
STL wins parallel LEM descent engine contract. J. F. Judge. il Miss & Roc 12:24-5 Je 3 '63
STL wins parallel LEM engine contract. C. M. Plattner. il Aviation W 78:30-1 Je 3 '63
Spacecraft re-usability emphasized at Douglas. Miss & Roc 14:35 My 11 '64
Stehling cites urgent propellant needs. J. F. Judge. il Miss & Roc 12:36 F 25 '63
Surveyor engine in final development. J. F. Judge. il Miss & Roc 16:18+ Ja 25 '65
SPO officer voices confidence in future of Titan III program; remarks. R. M. Herrington. Miss & Roc 12:13 Mr 18 '63
Test program for Saturn S-4B stage being reassessed. H. D. Watkins. il Aviation W 81:50-2+ S 21 '64
Thermionic flight experiment studied. M. Getler. il Miss & Roc 12:38+ Ap 29 '63
Titan 3A, 3C tests scheduled for eight different objectives. il Aviation W 81:17 Ag 31 '64
Titan 3C transtage successfully tested. Aviation W 78:31 Ap 29 '63
Titan three launches to begin in fall, 1964. G. Alexander. il Aviation W 78:27-8 F 25 '63
Titan 3 may have Comsat role. Aviation W 80:32 My 25 '64
Titan II carefully groomed for new role. il Miss & Roc 14:26-7 Ap 13 '64
Titan II-Centaur hybrid studied. H. Taylor. il Miss & Roc 12:12-13 Mr 18 '63
Titan transtage restarted twice during first long-duration firing. Aviation W 79:27 Jl 29 '63
Two getting ready, maybe only one to go; Air force's Titan III and Saturn IB by NASA. il Bsns W p49-50 Je 6 '64
U.K. program to use Black Knights. F. G. McGuire. Miss & Roc 15:26 O 5 '64
U.S. launch vehicles; International launch vehicles; specifications. Aviation W 80:195-6 Mr 16 '64
U.S. launch vehicles; specifications (cont) il Aviation W 78:191-2 Mr 11 '63
USAF modifies Thor for third ASSET. Aviation W 81:76-7+ Jl 20 '64
UTC test fires Titan III booster. il Miss & Roc 13:15-16 Jl 29 '63
Use of Centaur on Titan 2 studied as possible booster for surveyor. Aviation W 78:31 Ap 29 '63
Vroom! out of this world engines; reprint. R. M. Loebelson. il Sci Digest 55:40-4 Ap '64
Westinghouse know-how speeds flow of 120-in. cases for Titan III-C's. J. F. Judge. il Miss & Roc 15:32-3 S 14 '64
Will astronauts fly rocket boosters? W. Von Braun. il Pop Sci 184:72-3+ Je '64

See also
Ion engines
Liquid propellant rockets
Rocket engines
Solid propellant rockets
Space vehicles—Atomic power plants

Recovery

ADDPEP parachute shot due. il Miss & Roc 13:28 N 11 '63
Air-snatch technique speeds data acquisition at AMR. il Miss & Roc 13:48 O 28 '63
Apollo command module safely recovered in escape system evaluation. R. Pay. il Miss & Roc 14:21 My 25 '64
Ballute device tested as Gemini mission recovery aid. M. L. Yaffee. il Aviation W 80:40-1+ Ap 6 '64
Five-month test of Gemini paraglider paves way for operational development. C. M. Plattner. il Aviation W 79:60-1+ D 16 '63
How we'll answer SOS from space. J. H. Winchester. il Sci Digest 54:81-5 S '63
M-2 research craft landed seven times. il Aviation W 79:34 S 9 '63
Maneuverable re-entry vehicle program test planned in June. Aviation W 82:99 Ja 18 '65
NASA favors gliding parachutes for land recovery of spacecraft. Aviation W 81:61 D 14 '64
NASA seeks proposals for recovery gear. Aviation W 79:72 S 30 '63
NASA studies recovery systems to be used with future vehicles. Aviation W 78:69 My 27 '63
NASA testifies that Rogallo wing is probably dead in Gemini program; Rogallo wing paraglider. H. M. David. Miss & Roc 14:21 F 24 '64
Para-sail drop tests with full-scale Gemini capsules due. R. D. Hibben. il Aviation W 81:50-2+ Ag 31 '64
Parasail to be proposed for Gemini. R. Pay. il Miss & Roc 15:22-3 Ag 31 '64
Water recovery could dictate redesign of Apollo heat shield. Aviation W 80:28 Mr 2 '64
Water recovery likely for Apollo flights. D. E. Fink. Aviation W 80:30-1 F 24 '64

Safety devices and measures

Anti-meteoroid dust studied. Miss & Roc 13:29 N 25 '63
Astronaut distress plan expected. Aviation W 80:22 Mr 23 '64
Biomedical sensors improved for Gemini. W. H. Gregory. il Aviation W 80:69+ Je 8 '64
Can an astronaut bail out and live? W. Von Braun. il Pop Sci 183:14+ S '63
Doff-and-don bag provides an emergency system for Apollo astronauts; safety in depressurization emergencies. il Aviation W 80:50-1 F 10 '64
Gemini ejector sled tests set. Aviation W 78:65 Ap 29 '63
Inflatable space station escape vehicle under study. W. C. Wetmore. il Aviation W 78:62-4+ My 6 '63
IMP will warn of dangerous solar flares. R. D. Hibben. il Aviation W 79:28-9 N 4 '63
Lifeboat for space. il Todays Health 41:34 Ap '63
Zero-G tether tests seek pilot restraint. Aviation W 79:61 O 28 '63

See also
Space vehicles—Escape devices

Shielding from heat

See Shielding (heat)

Shielding from radiation

See Shielding (radiation)

SPACE vehicles—*Continued*

Stability and stabilizers

Agena-D satellites will test Nortronics attitude-stabilization gyro. C. D. LaFond. il Miss & Roc 13:34-5 Jl 1 '63
Gravity gradient device orients satellite. il Aviation W 80:57 F 24 '64
Gravity gradient feasibility test planned. P. J. Klass. il Aviation W 79:79+ N 25 '63
G&C NASA systems; new satellite systems demand accurate attitude controls. il Miss & Roc 13:65-7 O 7 '63
One ion rocket could hold satellite synchronous. Miss & Roc 13:31 Ag 5 '63
RCA unveils Stabilite at AIAA. il Miss & Roc 14:34-5 Je 29 '64
See also
Gyroscope

Sterilization

ARC studying contaminant removal. Miss & Roc 14:35 Ap 13 '64
Decontamination and sterilization of lunar and planetary spacecraft; letter. O. W. Nicks and O. E. Reynolds. Science 142:539-40 N 1 '63
Mars pollution unlikely with sterilized probes. Sci N L 85:185 Mr 21 '64
Microbe survivability on Mars simulated. W. C. Wetmore. Aviation W 80:75-6+ Je 29 '64
Need clean spaceships. Sci N L 85:107 F 15 '64

Testing

AC-2 flight will test Centaur program. M. L. Yaffee. il Aviation W 79:75-7+ O 21 '63
AIAA asks better space system testing. G. Alexander. Aviation W 78:27-8 Mr 25 '63
Apollo boilerplate test program cut. Aviation W 78:58 Ja 28 '63
Apollo command-service modules pass first boilerplate abort test. Aviation W 80:32 My 18 '64
Apollo hardware flights beginning at White Sands. il Miss & Roc 13:17 N 11 '63
Apollo nears critical ground test phase. il Aviation W 81:60-1+ N 16 '64
Big test table for Saturn S-1C tops rigorous Boeing specifications. J. F. Judge. il Miss & Roc 15:24-5 Jl 6 '64
Booster orbital piggyback pod studied. C. M. Plattner. il Aviation W 78:57-8+ Mr 18 '63
Centaur flight in fall will be stringent test. C. Butler. Miss & Roc 13:19 S 9 '63
Centaur flight stage readied for delivery. Aviation W 79:86 Ag 5 '63
First ASSET transmits valuable data before disappearing in Atlantic. C. Butler. il Miss & Roc 13:18 S 23 '63
First Gemini mission is key to initial two-man flight this year. H. Taylor. il Miss & Roc 14:16-17 Ap 6 '64
First S-2 flight stage build-up scheduled. I. Stone. il Aviation W 80:50-1+ My 11 '64
Five-month test of Gemini paraglider paves way for operational development. C. M. Plattner. il Aviation W 79:60-1+ D 16 '63
Flight test of Gemini program nears, but role in post-Apollo plans remains cloudy. G. Alexander. il Aviation W 80:38-9+ Mr 30 '64
Gemini capsule testing reaches high level as flight phase nears. D. E. Fink. Aviation W 80:30 Ja 20 '64
Gemini, Centaur shots due this week. Miss & Roc 15:15-16 N 30 '64
Gemini mission vehicle goes on mock flights. Sci N L 84:280 N 2 '63
Gemini model readied for water recovery testing. Miss & Roc 14:16 Ja 13 '64
Gemini spacecraft makes successful tests. il Sci N L 85:246 Ap 18 '64
General electric embarks on testing nuclear space power system dynamic components. J. F. Judge. il Miss & Roc 14:26-8 F 17 '64
Glider lost after ASSET shot succeeds. G. Alexander. il Aviation W 79:37 S 23 '63
Ground tests credited in Centaur success; with editorial comment. G. Alexander. il Aviation W 79:21, 30-2 D 9 '63
House space committee slates Ranger probe. H. M. David. Miss & Roc 14:15 Ap 13 '64
Joint committee insisting on SNAP flight tests. Miss & Roc 14:14 F 17 '64
Little Joe success will trigger Apollo test program soon. il Miss & Roc 13:15 S 2 '63
Meteoroid satellite passes crucial tests on way to mid-64 flight. C. D. LaFond. il Miss & Roc 14:22-3 F 17 '64
NASA may increase scale model testing. R. D. Hibben. il Aviation W 80:36-7+ Je 8 '64
Reaction control system for LEM tested. H. D. Watkins. il Aviation W 81:83-4+ N 9 '64
Robots' space ride. Sci N L 86:405 D 26 '64
SA-6 telemetry points to fatigue as cause of gearbox malfunction. Aviation W 81:26 Jl 13 '64
SA-7 flies near-perfect mission. Aviation W 81:27 S 28 '64
Satellite sought to flight-test Snap 10A. K. Johnsen. Aviation W 80:30 F 17 '64
Saturn V slippage is certain. H. Taylor. il Miss & Roc 14:10-11 Mr 16 '64
Special report: test & checkout; with editorial comment by W. J. Coughlin. il Miss & Roc 12:19-26+, 92 My 20 '63
Surveyor may slip six months. Aviation W 80:51 Je 22 '64
Test program for Saturn S-4B stage being reassessed. H. D. Watkins. il Aviation W 81:50-2+ S 21 '64
Third Centaur flight will test jettisoning of insulation panels. Aviation W 80:22 Je 22 '64
Titan 2 makes successful flight. Aviation W 79:37 Ag 26 '63
Twin success; impressive performance of Titan and Gemini. il Newsweek 63:82 Ap 20 '64
Unmanned X-20 could fly by July, 1965. G. Alexander. Aviation W 79:34 Ag 19 '63

Thermal control

Thermal control in space vehicles. A. L. Alexander. bibliog il Science 143:654-60 F 14 '64

Tracking

Accuracy of Canoga radar tracking system is six feet in 30,000 miles. R. Pay. il Miss & Roc 14:31+ F 17 '64
Air force, NASA at odds over MOL tracking requirements. J. Trainor. Miss & Roc 14:16 Je 29 '64
AF research aircraft zero in on tracking system noise. M. L. Yaffee. il Aviation W 79:78-9+ N 11 '63
Air force solving tracking ship problems. G. Alexander. Aviation W 80:63+ My 18 '64
AMF tracking mount on job at PMR; Mobile photographic tracking station. W. Beller. il Miss & Roc 13:26 S 9 '63
Apollo tracking ship accord reached. H. Taylor. Miss & Roc 13:17 D 16 '63
Apollo unified S-band network to cost minimum of $160-170 million. C. D. LaFond. il Miss & Roc 15:18+ Jl 20 '64
Fifteen nations serve as tracking site hosts. il Aviation W 81:88-9+ Jl 6 '64
Firm makes low-profile high-efficiency antennas. Miss & Roc 14:36 Mr 2 '64
Floating spacecraft tracking stations. R. LaCoste. il Electr World 72:17-19+ Ag '64
GT-10 to carry laser voice transmitter. il Miss & Roc 15:15 Ag 17 '64
Guidance and navigation progress may come in detectors and read-out. il Miss & Roc 14:37-9 Je 1 '64
Guiding spacecraft to other worlds. W. Von Braun. il Pop Sci 182:14+ Je '63
Highly advanced telemetry complex going in at Eastern test range. C. D. LaFond. il Miss & Roc 16:32-3 Ja 4 '65
How space detectives rate Russia's moon probes. S. D. Pursglove. il Pop Mech 119:89-93+ Mr '63
Manned network gets major push. Miss & Roc 14:18-19 F 17 '64
Mission control begins new space art. il Aviation W 79:274-5+ Jl 22 '63
NASA considers use of aircraft for remote Apollo crew retrieval. Aviation W 78:65 Mr 18 '63
NASA plans laser rendezvous guidance. B. Miller. il Aviation W 80:100-2+ My 18 '64
NASA requests $267.9 million for tracking, data net expansion. il Aviation W 80:235-6 Mr 16 '64
NASA to expand tracking network for Gemini and Apollo missions. il Aviation W 78:231+ Mr 11 '63
New Houston control facility may direct Gemini sooner than planned. M. Getler. Miss & Roc 13:32-4 Jl 8 '63
100 eyes to the sky; JPL command center. il Pop Electr 21:56 O '64
S-band system subcontractors to Collins to be named this month. C. D. LaFond. il Miss & Roc 15:36-7 Ag 3 '64
Satellite tracking, telemetry, and communications. J. T. Mengel. il Electr World 71:58-60 Je '64

SPACE vehicles—Tracking—*Continued*
Solid-state system to track X-20. il Miss & Roc 13:39-40 O 28 '63
Special report: advanced displays. il Miss & Roc 15:27-8+ O 5 '64
System could improve orbit gauging. Miss & Roc 13:16 N 4 '63
See also
Television in space flight

Transportation

Airship studied as booster carrier. F. G. McGuire. Miss & Roc 12:16 Mr 4 '63
Apollo-Saturn crawler due in late 1964. Aviation W 78:37 F 18 '63
Boeing 377(PG) undergoes flight tests. H. D. Watkins. il Aviation W 78:80-1+ Je 24 '63

Viewports

Gemini windows almost eye-shaped. Sci N L 83:199 Mr 30 '63
New spacecraft window design proposed for Apollo; compound reflective system. M. Getler. il Miss & Roc 13:26-7+ Ag 5 '63

SPACE vehicles, Atomic powered
General electric proposes nuclear-powered Mars vehicle for fifteen-month manned landing mission. il Aviation W 78:62-3 My 27 '63
NASA must decide Orion future. W. E. Wilks. il Miss & Roc 15:12-14 D 14 '64
Nuclear carrier to take men into orbit designed. Sci N L 83:88 F 9 '63
Nuclear flight programs canceled as President trims FY '65 budget. Aviation W 79:22 D 30 '63
Nuclear propulsion championed; meeting of the American nuclear society and atomic industry. Miss & Roc 13:20+ N 25 '63
Nuclear systems development to be dominated by electric engines. il Miss & Roc 13:74-6+ N 25 '63

SPACEMEN. See Astronauts
SPACEWOMEN. See Women as astronauts
SPACHE, George D.
Your child and reading; beyond the elementary years. Todays Health 42:6 Ap '64
SPACKS, Barry
Observation of the husband in the marketplace; poem. Yale R 52:415 Mr '63
SPADARO, Louis M.
Causes of boom and bust. Nat R 16:456-8 Je 2 '64
SPADATS (space detection and tracking system) See Radar—Military applications
SPAETH, Merrie
New faces in a smash new movie; ed. by E. Miller. pors Seventeen 23:132-3+ Je '64
about
Merrie and Tippy. New Yorker 40:35-6 My 23 '64
SPAETH, Sigmund
Ten nights club. por Opera N 28:6-7 Ap 11 '64
SPAGHETTI sauce. See Sauces
SPAHN, Warren Edward
At twice twenty-one. Time 82:41 Ag 23 '63
Grand old arm. il por Time 81:60 My 24 '63
Spahn sues for $175,000 over fictionalized biography. Pub W 185:70 F 3 '64
Warren Spahn: king of the hill. T. Cohane. il pors Look 27:67-70 Ap 23 '63
Warren Spahn wins $10,000 over fictionalized book. Pub W 185:100 Je 8 '64
SPAIN
Spain emerges from isolation. R. M. Smith. Cur Hist 47:345-9+ D '64
Spain's restless voices; interview. D. Ridruejo. Cath World 197:88-94 My '63
See also
Airlines—Spain
Atomic power—Spain
Barcelona
Church and state in Spain
Churches—Spain
Colleges and universities—Spain
Courts—Spain
Festivals—Spain
Jews in Spain
Marbella
Music festivals—Spain
Palma de Mallorca
Regional planning—Spain
Seville
Strikes—Spain
Tariff—Spain
Tourist trade—Spain
Trade unions—Spain
Trials—Spain

Air force

Spain plans purchase of 70 Northrop F-5s. Aviation W 82:26 Ja 18 '65

Colonies

Conquest and the cross; summary of address. L. Hanke. il Am Heritage 14:4-19+ F '63
Conquistadors in North American history, by P. Horgan. Review
Reporter 28:52+ Ap 25 '63. W. T. Hagan

Commerce

Remember the alcazar; veto against Spain's joining Common market. Nat R 16:307 Ap 21 '64

Commercial treaties and agreements

Trade agreement signed by U.S. and Spain. il Dept State Bul 48:146 Ja 28 '63

Description and travel

By rocking chair across Spain. A. Atkinson. il Holiday 34:70-4+ S '63
Eclipse of the fun. K. Tynan. Esquire 59:82+ My '63
Going places, finding things along the Spanish coast. L. Rasponi. il House & Gard 123:46-9+ Ap '63
Spain. E. Scully. il U S Camera 28:14-15 Ja '65
Spain; photographs by H. Cartier-Bresson; with report by H. Tracy. Vogue 143:122-32+ Je '64
Why Spain is home. R. Ruark. il Sat Eve Post 237:28-33 Ap 4 '64
See also
Escorial

Economic conditions

Closer to Europe. il Time 83:104 Je 12 '64
Embryo of a miracle. il Fortune 68:93-4+ N '63
Gain in Spain. R. J. Fitzpatrick. il America 111:656-8 N 21 '64
Letter from Barcelona. A. Reid. New Yorker 39:105-6+ My 4 '63
Next miracle country. F. Painton. il U S News 54:71-5 My 20 '63
Now on the road to prosperity, Spain. A. Zanker. il U S News 57:54-6 Jl 27 '64
Spain: headed up and aiming higher. il Bsns W p 118 D 7 '63
Spain turns charm on investors; four-year development called El plan. il Bsns W p 133-4+ O 17 '64
See also
Wages—Spain

Economic policy

Operation Badajoz; Spain's TVA. R. M. Elizalde. il Am For 69:24-7 F '63

Economic relations

Spain outside the door. Time 83:40+ Ap 3 '64

Foreign relations

Grand alliance: United States and Spain. Nation 199:317-18 N 9 '64
Making haste slowly. Newsweek 62:43-4 Ag 26 '63
Spain's long, hard look at tomorrow. il Sr Schol 82:9-11 Mr 20 '63

Cuba

Franco apes de Gaulle. New Repub 150:8 F 8 '64

France

DeGaulle and Franco. New Repub 149:13-14 D 14 '63
Europita. il Newsweek 61:34+ F 25 '63
New chums. Newsweek 63:50 Je 15 '64

United States

Europita. il Newsweek 61:34+ F 25 '63
Spain: playing it cool. New Repub 149:5 O 5 '63
Triumph for Franco. Nation 197:251 O 26 '63
United States and Spain renew defense agreement; exchange of notes and letters; with Department announcement and texts of documents. D. Rusk; F. M. Castiella. Dept State Bul 49:686-8 O 28 '63

History

Bibliography

Articles and other books received; Spain and Portugal, comp. by C. J. Bishko. See issues of American historical review

Ferdinand and Isabella, 1479-1516

Castles and the crown, by T. Miller. Review
Sat R 46:39 S 21 '63. H. Livermore

SPAIN—History—*Continued*

19th century

Phantom war of 1804. J. C. Fernández. il Américas 15:23-8 Je '63

Civil war, 1936-1939

Twenty-five years ago in Madrid. il Newsweek 63:42-3 Ap 13 '64

Industries

Spain turns charm on investors; four-year development called El plan. il Bsns W p 133-4+ O 17 '64

Politics and government

After twenty-five years, Franco is still a sphinx. P. Hofmann. il N Y Times Mag p21+ Ap 19 '64
Atlantic report. Atlan 214:24+ O '64
Change in Spain; a wider liberty. America 108:821 Je 8 '63
Forces at work in today's Spain. F. D. Wilhelmsen. America 109:306-14 S 21 '63
Franco, Congress and the Pentagon. C. McWilliams. Christian Cent 80:298-300 Mr 6 '63
Franco's Spain and the new Europe. R. Alan; reply with rejoinder. W. A. Miele. Commentary 35:164-5 F '63
Letter from Barcelona. A. Reid. New Yorker 39:105-6+ My 4 '63
Liberalism vs. the Spanish pavilion. R. Kirk. Nat R 16:774 S 8 '64
Spain: the big change is yet to come. New Repub 149:8-10 O 19 '63
Spain's long, hard look at tomorrow il Sr Schol 82:9-11 Mr 20 '63
Spanish pavilion: triumph for Franco? Christian Cent 81:1228-9 O 7 '64
Twenty-five years ago in Madrid. il Newsweek 63:42-3 Ap 13 '64
See also
Elections—Spain
Spain—Royal family

Religious institutions and affairs

Ecumenism in Spain. America 110:503 Ap 11 '64
News of the Christian world. Christian Cent 80:438-40, 1527-8; 81:190, 520-2, 1538 Ap 3, D 4 '63, F 5, Ap 22, D 9 '64
Non-Catholics in Spain; what rights can religious minorities in that country claim before the law? F. M. Castiella. il America 109:189-92 Ag 24 '63
See also
Catholic church in Spain
Protestant churches—Spain
Protestants in Spain

Royal family

Don Juan of Spain. J. Bryan, 3d. il Holiday 33:96-9+ My '63
Prevalence of pretenders. Time 83:44+ My 15 '64
Three kings; claimants to vacant Spanish throne. il Newsweek 63:48 My 18 '64

Social life and customs

In a Spanish village; excerpts from Spanish notebook. H. Tracy. Holiday 35:56-7+ My '64
Remains of Spain are mainly a strain. P. K. Brooks. Sat R 46:93+ O 12 '63

SPAITH, Rose Ann
Halloween masks you can make. Farm J 88:99 O '64

SPALDING, A. G. and brothers, incorporated
Tinkertoy, a wonderful wooden Christmas toy. J. Martineau. il Am For 70:30-1+ D '64
Toy that won't die; Tinkertoy. il Bsns W p 134-6+ S 12 '64

SPALDING, George H.
Los Angeles state and county arboretum at Arcadia. Horticulture 42:38-41 N '64

SPANI, Hina
Rococo presents. A. Favia-Artsay. Hobbies 68:30-1 Ja '64

SPANIARDS
Spaniard and his inferiority complex, by J. J. López-Ibor. Review
America 110:771 My 30 '64. C. A. Irizarry
Why Spain is home. R. Ruark. il Sat Eve Post 237:28-33 Ap 4 '64

SPANIARDS in the United States
Diary to a newly married poet; J. R. Jiménez in New York and New England. R. Gullón. il Américas 16:11-15 Mr '64

SPANIELS
All-around gun dog. D. M. Duffey. il Outdoor Life 134:144-50 O '64
Cocker national. J. Stetson. il Field & S 67:116+ F '63
English springer national trial. D. M. Duffey. il Outdoor Life 133:138-40+ Mr '64
National springer championship. J. Stetson. il Field & S 67:146-7+ Mr '63
National springer spaniel stake. D. M. Duffey. il Outdoor Life 131:120-2+ Mr '63
Springer spaniel championship. J. Stetson. il Field & S 68:162-3+ Mr '64

SPANISH. See Spaniards

SPANISH AMERICAN war. See United States —History—Spanish American war, 1898

SPANISH AMERICANS in the United States. See Latin Americans in the United States

SPANISH art. See Art, Spanish

SPANISH colonies in America. See Spain—Colonies

SPANISH cookery. See Cookery, Spanish

SPANISH dancing. See Dancing, Spanish

SPANISH explorers. See Explorers, Spanish

SPANISH furniture. See Furniture, Spanish

SPANISH HARLEM. See New York (city)—Harlem

SPANISH house decoration. See House decoration, Spanish

SPANISH language
Se habla espanol? J. Lelyveld. il N Y Times Mag p65-6+ Je 14 '64

SPANISH language in Mexico
Little now. C. Darlington. Atlan 214:167-8 N '64

SPANISH literature

Bibliography

Libros en venta; hispanic bibliography. M. C. Turner. il Library J 89:2559-61 Je 15 '64

SPANISH opera. See Opera, Spanish

SPANISH painting. See Painting, Spanish

SPANISH poetry

Translations into English

Cloud-music; Bull; tr. by A. Kerrigan. M. De Unamuno. Poetry 101:319-21 F '63
Elegy for Ramón Sijé; The unending lightning; tr. by E. Honig. M. Hernández. Poetry 101:325-8 F '63
From the apocryphal songbook: Abel Martín; tr. by B. Belitt. A. Machado. Poetry 101:312-18 F '63
Inventory of the dark; tr. by A. Kerrigan. C. J. Cela. Poetry 101:322-4 F '63
Official poster of green; tr. by D. M. Pettinella. J. C. Andrade. Nation 198:102 Ja 27 '64
To José María Palacio; Draw-wheel; Ephemeral past; O luminous late day! Grey olives; Proverbs and canticles; Winter sun; tr. by C. Tomlinson. A. Machado. Poetry 101:303-11 F '63

SPANISH riding school, Vienna. See Vienna—Spanish riding school

SPANISH science fair. See Science fairs

SPANISH wines. See Wine

SPANKING. See Corporal punishment

SPANN, James F. jr, and others
Reduction of cardiac stores of norepinephrine in experimental heart failure. bibliog Science 145:1439-41 S 25 '64

SPARE time. See Leisure

SPARERIBS. See Cookery—Meat

SPARGUR, Ronn
Peter to a cock; poem. Christian Cent 80:1303 O 23 '63
Poems for Holy week: Anointing; Entré; Crucifixion; Ascension. Christian Cent 81:392 Mr 25 '64
Shepherd's thoughts; poem. Christian Cent 81:1584 D 23 '64
Thomas, Thomas, feel my wounds; poem. Christian Cent 81:638 My 13 '64

SPARK, Muriel
Card party; poem. New Yorker 39:30 D 28 '63
Gentile Jewesses; story. New Yorker 39:31-4 Je 22 '63
Girls of slender means; story. Sat Eve Post 236:50-8 D 14 '63
On the lack of sleep; poem. New Yorker 39:58 D 7 '63
Quest for lavishes ghast. Esquire 62:216+ D '64

SPARK plugs
Fouled spark plug detector. J. F. Agee. il Pop Electr 20:82 Ja '64
Spark plug. R. E. Jennings. il Motor T 16:40-5 Je; 66-9 Jl; 64-7 Ag '64
Spark plug diagnosis. G. E. Melvin. il Suc Farm 62:47 My '64

SPARKMAN, John
Excerpt from address before National housing conference, February 24, 1964. Cong Digest 43:108+ Ap '64
Excerpt from address, June 26, 1963. Cong Digest 43:270+ N '64

SPARKMAN, Palmer
America's cup defense; special report. Motor B 113:34-5+ Ap '64
Cup boats in construction. Motor B 113:114-15+ Je '64
New course. Motor B 114:22-3 Ag '64
Twelve-meter team. Motor B 114:32-5 Ag '64

SPARKS, Fred
As it happens. Sat R 47:71 My 9; 28 My 16; 11 My 23; 8 My 30; 23 Je 6; 14 Je 20; 8 Jl 4; 10 Jl 11; 130 Ag 29; 8 S 5; 8 N 28; 48 D 5 '64; 48:16 Ja 9 '65
Cat with a telephone number. Read Digest 83:21+ Jl '63
Hotels I have known. Sat R 47:39-40+ Ja 4 '64
I'm in love with our 50th state. Read Digest 85:125-8 O '64
Recollections of an Olympic torchbearer. Sat R 47:100-3 Mr 14 '64
They don't make drivers like they used to. Read Digest 84:21-2+ Je '64

SPARKS, Will
Justice and the Canal. Commonweal 79:564-6 F 7 '64
Mr Minow's wasteland. Commonweal 78:7-10 Mr 29 '63

SPARROCK, J. M. B. See Barlow, H. B. jt. auth.

SPARROW, Arnold H. and others
Relationship between nuclear volumes, chromosome numbers, and relative radiosensitivities. bibliog Science 141:163-6 Jl 12 '63

SPARROWS
Anatomy of a nest; English sparrows nest. J. K. Terres. il Audubon Mag 66:356 N '64
Evolution of sparrows in North America. Sci N L 85:377 Je 13 '64
House sparrows: rapid evolution of races in North America. R. F. Johnston and R. K. Selander. bibliog il Science 144:548-50 My 1 '64
St Louis is proud of its European sparrow. J. E. Comfort. il Audubon Mag 65:381-3 N '63
White-throated sparrow. J. K. Terres. il Pop Gard 15:12 S '64

SPARS. See Masts and rigging

SPARTA
Sparta's iron way. Life 54:75-6+ Mr 8 '63

SPARTANBURG, S.C.
Machine accounting stops deficit spending. G. C. Robinett, jr. il Am City 79:100-1 Ag '64

SPAS. See Health resorts, watering places, etc.

SPATHELF, Victor F.
Some plain talk about higher education; address, October 2, 1964. Vital Speeches 31:40-3 N 1 '64

SPATIAL perception. See Space perception

SPAULDING, Seth
Channels of communication (cont) Sch Life 45:12-13 Ja; 18-19 Mr; 12-13 Ap; 19-20 My; 32-3 Je; 9 Jl '63

SPAVENTA, George
Introducing the sculpture of George Spaventa. F. O'Hara. il por Art N 63:44-7 Ap '64

SPAWNING
Spawning of starfish: action of gamete-shedding substance obtained from radial nerves. H. Kanatani. bibliog il Science 146:1177-9 N 27 '64

SPEAGLE, Richard E. and Chace, H. R.
Corporate profit equation. Harvard Bsns R 41:116-27 Mr '63

SPEAKEASIES. See Bootlegging

SPEAKERS (House of representatives) See United States—Congress—House of representatives—Speakers

SPEAKING in tongues. See Gift of tongues

SPEAR fishing
Why waste winter? D. W. Larson. il Outdoor Life 133:24-7+ Ja '64

SPEARMAN, Walter
Light on a southern exposure. Sat R 46:42-3 N 16 '63

SPEARS, Sir Edward
De Gaulle. por Look 27:68-70+ My 7 '63

SPEARS, Harold
What sort of school day is it? Sr Schol 85:8T N 4 '64

SPECIAL classes and special schools
Approach to the severely disturbed child; League school, Brooklyn. H. S. Arnstein. il N Y Times Mag p 119-20 O 6 '63
Art classes for aphasic children. J. B. Helms. il Sch Arts 63:35-6 Ja '64
Opening school doors to the brain-damaged; San Mateo County, Calif. S. Welton. il Parents Mag 39:78-9+ F '64
P.S. 165; New York city elementary school. R. Schickel. Commentary 37:43-51 Ja '64; Reply. E. F. Bondi. 37:16 My '64
See also
Mentally handicapped children—Education

SPECIAL collections in libraries. See Libraries—Special collections

SPECIAL committee of twenty-four on colonialism. See United Nations—Special committee on situation with regard to implementation of declaration on granting of independence to colonial countries and peoples

SPECIAL days, weeks, and months
American landmarks celebration seeks to preserve nation's heritage. C. W. Thomas. il Negro Hist Bul 28:24+ O '64
April is teaching career month. il NEA J 53:85-6 Ja '64
Challenge of leisure in old age. J. R. MacLean. Recreation 56:213 My '63
Changing face of teaching; theme for Teaching career month. il NEA J 54:61 Ja '65
Daze to come; Chases' calendar of annual events. Newsweek 64:98 D 7 '64
Editor's notebook. M. S. Fenner. NEA J 52:72 F '63
General Pulaski's memorial day, 1964; proclamation, August 15, 1964. L. B. Johnson. Dept State Bul 51:354 S 7 '64
Kudos for the House judiciary committee; National youth for Christ week. Christian Cent 80:1124 S 18 '63
Leif Erikson day, 1964; proclamation. L. B. Johnson. Dept State Bul 51:401 S 21 '64
Lesson taught by a shoelace; National safe boating week. E. Crimmin. il Motor B 114:54+ Jl '64
Let's travel on a vacation; vacation planning week. il Mile 57:48-50 Je '63
May is Senior citizens month. Recreation 56:223+ My '63
National freedom from hunger week, 1964; proclamation, August 15, 1964. L. B. Johnson. Dept State Bul 51:388 S 14 '64
One man's battle against poison; National poison prevention week. H. E. Dark. il Todays Health 42:43+ Mr '64
Senior citizens month; proclamation by the President of the United States. J. F. Kennedy. Sch Life 45:23 Ap '63
Tested ideas for recreation month. Recreation 56:396 N '63
Texas dog days. C. A. Nicholson. il Field & S 69:44-6 D '64
Third Sunday in May; Senior citizen Sunday. W. D. Pfost. Recreation 57:236-7 My '64
United States international aviation month, 1964; proclamation, July 28, 1964. L. B. Johnson. Dept State Bul 51:314 Ag 31 '64
Von Steuben day; proclamation, September 15, 1964. L. B. Johnson. Dept State Bul 51:472 O 5 '64
Warsaw uprising day; proclamation, July 31, 1964. L. B. Johnson. Dept State Bul 51:271 Ag 24 '64
Why a national forest products week? B. West. il Am For 69:44+ N '63
World trade week, 1964; proclamation, May 8, 1964. L. B. Johnson. Dept State Bul 50:935 Je 15 '64
World trade week, 1963; proclamation, April 20, 1963. J. F. Kennedy. Dept State Bul 48:758 My 13 '63
See also names of special days, weeks and months, e.g. World health day

SPECIAL edition: drama. See Fisher, A.

SPECIAL-effects box. See Photography—Apparatus and supplies

SPECIAL fund. See United Nations—Special fund

SPECIAL librarians. See Librarians

SPECIAL libraries. See Libraries, Special

SPECIAL libraries association
Fifty-fifth time; annual meeting. T. C. Hines. il Library J 89:2954-6 Ag '64
Four goals by 1970. Wilson Lib Bul 37:747 My '63
Mile-high conference. T. C. Hines. il Library J 88:2842-4 Ag '63
NSF grant awarded for expansion of SLA classification center. Library J 88:4181 N 1 '63
New York chapters of ADI and SLA hold joint meeting to honor Luhn. Library J 90:80-1 Ja 1 '65
SLA-ADI venture to implement technology information availability. Library J 88:2858 Ag '63
SLA conference footnotes. Library J 88:2859-60 Ag '63

SPECIAL libraries association—*Continued*
SLA schedules participation in CIOS management congress. Library J 88:3186 S 15 '63
SLA sets its sights on 1970 goals. Library J 88:1971 My 15 '63
SLA translations center gets financial aid. Pub W 187:65 Ja 11 '65
SPECIAL one; story. See Whedon, J.
SPECIAL; story. See Peterson, O.
SPECIAL teachers. See Teachers, Special
SPECIALISTS
Dark journey into Expertland. R. Sommer. il N Y Times Mag p 16+ Jl 28 '63
Double talk cuts egghead's value to business. G. S. Odiorne. il Nations Bsns 51:92-4 Ap '63
Get your money's worth from specialists. N. Stewart. Nations Bsns 52:96+ Ap '64
SPECIALISTS, Medical. See Specialization in medicine
SPECIALISTS, Stock. See Securities—Marketing
SPECIALIZATION
See also
Specialists

Anecdotes, facetiae, satire, etc.
Down from Valhalla: specialization among library pages. W. Jones. Library J 89:580 F 1 '64
SPECIALIZATION in agriculture. See Farm management
SPECIALIZATION in education
Plotting your course through college; choice of a major. D. Klein. il Seventeen 23:114-15 Ap '64
Where will they go after high school? H. A. Littledale. il Parents Mag 38:58-9+ Ap '63
SPECIALIZATION in medicine
G.P. is still needed. L. Lasagna. il N Y Times Mag p 18+ Ap 19 '64
Impediments to the acquisition and use of medical knowledge; letter. R. D. Baldwin. Science 141:1237-8 S 27 '63; Discussion. 143:8-9 Ja 3 '64
What is an internist? S. T. Donohue. il Todays Health 41:48-53+ Ap '63
Where rural patients get air-age care. H. G. Earl. il Todays Health 42:14-16 My '64
Who should treat your aches and pains? T. Berland. il Redbook 121:44+ My '63
SPECIES
Exponential values for the species-area relation. P. D. Kilburn. bibliog il Science 141:1276 S 27 '63
See also
Phylogeny
SPECIFIC dyslexia. See Word blindness
SPECIFIC gravity
Amateur scientist; Cavendish's experiment for determining the constant of gravity. C. L. Stong. il Sci Am 209:267-8+ S '63
Fresh water: temperature of maximum density calculated from compressibility. H. Eklund. bibliog il Science 142:1457-8 D 13 '63
SPECIFIC pathogen-free swine program. See Swine
SPECIFICATIONS
See also
Automobiles—Specifications
SPECIMENS, Biological. See Biological specimens
SPECTACLES. See Eyeglasses
SPECTACULARS (signs) See Electric signs
SPECTATOR (periodical)
Iain's in. Newsweek 62:81 N 18 '63
SPECTOR, Ivar
Human irritants of an immortal. Sat R 46:61 S 28 '63
To be monarch was her mission. Sat R 48:47 Ja 23 '65
SPECTOR, R. J.
Highest school in the world. UNESCO Courier 17:12-17 O '64
SPECTOR, Robert D.
Poet's other voices, other rooms. Sat R 47:36-8 F 1 '64
SPECTOR, Sidney, and others
Norepinephrine synthesis from tyrosine-C^{14} in isolated perfused guinea pig heart. bibliog Science 139:1299-301 Mr 29 '63
SPECTROFLUOROMETERS. See Spectrometers
SPECTROGRAPH
Optical spectra from fast ion beams. il Sky & Tel 28:201-2 O '64
World's largest spectrograph probes secrets of life: Argonne national laboratory, Chicago. H. G. Earl. il Todays Health 42:74-6 S '64
SPECTROGRAPH, Mass. See Mass spectrometry
SPECTROMETERS
Absolute spectrofluorometer. G. K. Turner. bibliog il Science 146:183-9 O 9 '64
See also
Mass spectrometry
SPECTROMETERS, Mass.
Mass spectrometry; report on twelfth annual conference on mass spectrometry. A. B. King. Science 146:90-1 O 2 '64
SPECTROPHOTOMETRY
Spectrophotofluorometry: biological techniques; report of extramural activity of the new Instituto di ricerche farmacologiche Mario Negri in Milan, Italy; lectures and demonstrations. R. L. Bowman. Science 142:267-8+ O 11 '63
SPECTROSCOPE
See also
Spectrograph
SPECTROSCOPY. See Spectrum analysis
SPECTRUM
See also
Stars—Spectra

Absorption spectra
See Absorption spectra

Fluorescence spectra
Absolute spectrofluorometer. G. K. Turner. bibliog il Science 146:183-9 O 9 '64
SPECTRUM, Coronal. See Spectrum, Solar
SPECTRUM, Infrared
Infrared spectroscopy and catalysis research. R. P. Eischens. bibliog il Science 146:486-93 O 23 '64
Infrared study of the OH groups in expanded kaolinite. R. L. Ledoux and J. L. White. bibliog il Science 143:244-6 Ja 17 '64
Spectroscopy of solids in the far-infrared. M. Tinkham. bibliog il Science 145:240-7 Jl 17 '64
Thermal reduction of bicarbonate to formate. I. C. Hisatsune and K. O. Hartman. bibliog il Science 145:1455-6 S 25 '64
SPECTRUM, Solar
In the light of the sun. A. C. Clarke. il Horizon 5:48-55 N '63
Is the sun metal rich? Sky & Tel 26:84 Ag '63
Rare-earth metals in the sun. R. N. Watts, jr. Sky & Tel 26:328 D '63
Solar observations in the extreme ultraviolet. il Sky & Tel 27:213-14 Ap '64
Solar X-ray spectrum below 25 angstroms. R. L. Blake and others. il Science 146:1037-8 N 20 '64
SPECTRUM analysis
Air concentrations of twelve radionuclides from 1962 through mid-1964. R. W. Perkins and others. bibliog il Science 146:762-4 N 6 '64
Dynamic reflectance spectroscopy; a new thermal technique. W. W. Wendlandt. bibliog il Science 140:1085-7 Je 7 '63
Fast-neutron spectroscopy. L. Cranberg. il Sci Am 210:79-86+ Mr '64
Molecular structure and spectroscopy; report of symposium. V. W. Laurie. Science 141:654+ Ag 16 '63
Mössbauer spectrum of iron-57 in iron metal at very high pressures. M. Nicol and G. Jura. bibliog il Science 141:1035-8 S 13 '63
Nuclear magnetic resonance spectroscopy in superconducting magnetic fields. F. A. Nelson and H. E. Weaver. bibliog il Science 146:223-32 O 9 '64
Optical spectra from fast ion beams. il Sky & Tel 28:201-2 O '64
Spectra of deoxygenated hemoglobin in the Soret region. R. Benesch and others. bibliog il Science 144:68-9 Ap 3 '64
Spectroscopic ultramicroanalysis with a laser. R. C. Rosan and others. il Science 142:236-7 O 11 '63
Spectroscopy; report of Mid-America spectroscopy symposium. J. E. Forrette. Science 141:442-3 Ag 2 '63
See also
Absorption spectra
Raman effect
Spectrum, Infrared
SPECULATION
Betting on the future. Time 82:74 S 27 '63
Bubble burst. il Newsweek 62:74+ D 2 '63
Commodities: the troubled markets. il Newsweek 63:51-4 Ja 6 '64
Fever camera: thermograph stock. Newsweek 62:96+ O 14 '63
Offbeat profits on Wall Street. N. Buckley. il Duns R 82:37+ S '63

SPECULATION—*Continued*
$150 million in oil, all gone! soybean oil swindle. P. Mandel. il Life 56:90-2+ Ap 3 '64
Sorry, wrong number. Newsweek 62:88 S 23 '63
Two for speculation. Duns R 83:83-4 Mr '64
See also
Investments
Land speculation
Stock exchange
SPEECH
Sound of speech. T. Schwartz. Pop Phot 54:28+ Mr '64
William Gargan's finest role; esophageal speech. C. B. Wall. Read Digest 83:49-54 S '63
See also
Children—Language
Conversation
Language and languages
Voice
Study and teaching
See Speech education
SPEECH, Freedom of. See Free speech
SPEECH, Liberty of. See Free speech
SPEECH clipper. See Sound—Apparatus
SPEECH compression apparatus. See Sound—Apparatus
SPEECH correction. See Speech therapy
SPEECH defects
How to help stroke victims regain speech. Todays Health 42:66 D '64
How your youngster learns to talk. R. Rogers. il Parents Mag 38:50-1+ Ap '63
Identifying speech disorders in the classroom. N. E. Wood. bibliog Sch Life 45:6-8 Mr '63
See also
Aphasia
Palate, Cleft
SPEECH education
Speech as a liberal study. M. Kinnane. Sch & Soc 91:330+ N 2 '63
Speech education, a terrible responsibility. G. A. Yeomans. Vital Speeches 30:348-52 Mr 15 '64
SPEECH research
Markovian model of time patterns of speech. J. Jaffe and others. bibliog Science 144:884-6 My 15 '64
Speakers' and listeners' processes in a word-communication task. S. Rosenberg and B. D. Cohen. bibliog il Science 145:1201-3 S 11 '64
Speech durations of astronaut and ground communicator. J. D. Matarazzo and others. bibliog il Science 143:148-50 Ja 10 '64
Talking in circles. il Newsweek 62:43 D 30 '63
SPEECH therapy
Priceless gift of better speech; rural school districts, Scott County, I. R. E. Shine and others. NEA J 53:36A-36B Ja '64
They make child's play of speech therapy: Lake County, Indiana, speech and hearing clinic. C. R. Carner. il Todays Health 41:24-7+ Mr '63
SPEECH writing. See Authorship—Collaboration
SPEECH-writing assistants to the President. See Public officers
SPEECHES, addresses, etc.
As other Presidents took the oath; excerpts from inaugural addresses, comp. by D. S. Davis. N Y Times Mag p22+ Ja 17 '65
Busy ghosts. P. Bart. Sat R 46:78 S 14 '63; Reply. R. Gross. 46:49 O 12 '63
Excerpts from famous inauguration speeches of the past. il Sr Schol 85:12-13 Ja 21 '65
Mr Chairman... D. Richardson. Atlan 214:176-7 N '64
When Johnson plans a speech—. U S News 56:33 F 3 '64
See also
Public speaking
SPEED
Measurement
See also
Velocimeters
SPEED boat racing. See Motor boat racing
SPEED indicators
See also
Accelerometers
Logs (nautical instruments)
Tachometers
SPEED laws. See Traffic regulations
SPEED limits. See Traffic regulations
SPEED of animals. See Animals—Speed
SPEED of birds. See Birds—Flight
SPEED of light. See Light—Velocity
SPEED of trains. See Railroads—Train speed
SPEED reducers. See Electric motors—Control
SPEED variation
Physiological effects
When the traveler gets ahead of sound; SST, the Concorde, capable of 1,450 miles an hour. A. Hano. il N Y Times Mag p21+ My 17 '64
SPEEDLIGHT. See Photography—Apparatus and supplies
SPEEDOMETERS
Speedometers and logs. E. Robberson. il Yachting 116:44-6+ D '64
SPEEDWAYS
Cashing in on speed; Daytona 500. il Bsns W p30-1 F 29 '64
Daytona, a dream come true. M. Muhleman. il Motor T 15:40-3 Mr '63
Dry lakes; Southern California timing association. L. Smith. il Hot Rod 17:72-5 Ja '64
Gasoline alley; Indianapolis motor speedway. E. Rickman. il Hot Rod 17:72-5+ S '64
Mile high 250 miler; Continental Divide raceway. R. Brock. il Hot Rod 17:17 S '64
Race before the race at Indianapolis. J. A. Maxwell. il Reporter 30:40+ My 21 '64
SPEEDWELLS
Carefree veronicas. M. C. Dolton. il Horticulture 41:512-13 O '63
SPEERT, Julius L. See Thompson, M. M. jt. auth.
SPEICHER, John
Of toads and half-truths. Reporter 29:50+ O 10 '63
SPEICHER, John F.
Great crown rumble; story. Sat Eve Post 237:40-5 Ja 4 '64
SPEIRS, Jack
Boating '64. Pop Mech 121:133-40+ Mr '64
How the dragsters do it. Pop Mech 119:128-31+ Mr '63
(ed) See Peterson, H. I ski 106 mph
SPEIRS, Robert S.
Antigenic material; persistence in hypersensitive cells. bibliog Science 140:71-2 Ap 5 '63
How cells attack antigens; with biographical sketch. Sci Am 210:28, 58-64 bibliog(p 152) F '64
SPEISER, E. A.
Why Abraham went forth. Life 57:39-40+ D 25 '64
SPEISER, Jean
Moods of the Everglades. il Nat Parks Mag 38:12-15 Ag '64
SPEISER, Richard M.
Golf moves indoors, lifesize and real; Golf-O-Tron. il por Bsns W p54-5 Ag 31 '63
SPELEOLOGY. See Caves
SPELLING
If your child can't spell. L. Sheppard. Parents Mag 38:151 O '63
See also
Alphabet
SPELLMAN, A. B.
Air: Baltimore oriole; poem. Nation 199:413 N 30 '64
For my unborn & wretched children; poem. Nation 198:664 Je 29 '64
Twist; poem. Nation 197:464 D 28 '63
View from Harlem. Nation 198:656-7 Je 29 '64
SPELLMAN, Francis Joseph, cardinal
Cardinal Spellman calls for censorship group; summary of address. Pub W 185:68 Je 22 '64
about
Cardinal Spellman reminisces. Christian Cent 80:1531 D 4 '63
Cardinal Spellman's twenty-five years. America 110:529 Ap 18 '64
Pastor-executive. il pors Time 83:54 My 15 '64
Unlocking the icebox; Christmas services in Antarctica. il por Time 83:41 Ja 3 '64
SPELLMON, Fronzell L.
Negro beauty culturist goes eastern. Negro Hist Bul 28:15 O '64
SPELVIN, George
Criticizing the critics (cont) Theatre Arts 47:32-3 Jl '63
Critics: TV or not TV. Theatre Arts 47:64-5 Ap '63
SPENCE, Sir Basil
Squires at large. il por Esquire 61:55 Ja '64
SPENCE, Kenneth W.
Cognitive factors in the extinction of the conditioned eyelid response in humans. Science 140:1224-5 Je 14 '63

SPENCER, Elizabeth
Fishing lake; story. New Yorker 40:24-5 Ag 29 '64
Ship island; story. New Yorker 40:52-6 S 12 '64
SPENCER, Frederick J.
British doctor. Cur Hist 45:25-31+ Jl '63
SPENCER, John M.
Flaw. por Newsweek 63:22+ Ja 20 '64
SPENCER, Mildred
Where we stand as 1965 begins. Todays Health 43:20-5 Ja '65
SPENCER, Robert J.
Test equipment control center. Pop Electr 18:73-4 F '63
SPENCER, Rolf E.
Pearson loses round one. Nation 198:43-6 Ja 13 '64
Quebec guerrillas. Nation 198:283-6 Mr 23 '64
SPENCER, Roscoe
Fleas, the ticks, spotted fever and me. por Sat R 46:47-9 N 2 '63
SPENCER, Steven M.
Be home soon, doctor. Ladies Home J 80:72-3 D '63
Medical team was ready. Sat Eve Post 236:37 N 16 '63
Medicine's miracle chamber. Sat Eve Post 237:70-2 S 19 '64
Spare-parts surgeons. Sat Eve Post 236:68-70 S 14 '63
SPENCER memorial Presbyterian church. See Brooklyn—Churches
SPENCER rifle. See Rifles
SPENDER, Stephen
How much should a biographer tell? Sat R 47:16-19 Ja 25 '64
How to identify a poet. Sat R 47:14-17 Ag 8 '64
1943: to be or not to be? Sat R 46:26+ Je 1 '63
One more new botched beginning; poem. New Yorker 40:42 My 2 '64
Poets and critics: the forgotten difference. Sat R 46:15-18 O 5 '63
Songs of an unsung classicist. Sat R 46:25+ S 7 '63
about
Spender: the poet as critic. J. Berryman. New Repub 148:19-20 Je 29 '63
SPENDING. See Consumption (economics)
SPENGLER, Oswald
Complicity with Spengler. M. Peretz. Nation 197:203-5 O 5 '63
SPERMATOZOA
Lactic and malic dehydrogenases in human spermatozoa. E. Goldberg. bibliog il Science 139:602-3 F 15 '63
See also
Sea urchins
SPERMINE
New discovery blocks resistance to drugs. Farm J 87:59 Mr '63
SPERRING, Robert. See Bierbaum, M. W. jt. auth.
SPERRY, R. W.
Great cerebral commissure; with biographical sketch. Sci Am 210:18, 42-52 bibliog(p 152) Ja '64
SPERRY and Hutchinson company
Sperry & Hutchinson's very successful stagnation. S. H. Brown. il Fortune 70:156-9+ N '64
SPERRY gyroscope company
Brain for most tools. il Bsns W p 116 F 8 '64
Sperry gyro gets new spin; Information & communications div. il Bsns W p45-6 O 12 '63
SPERRY Rand corporation
Sperry Rand proposes cabling technique to simulate gravity. Aviation W 81:124-5+ S 14 '64
Spin at Sperry. Time 84:80 Jl 3 '64
Systems group improve Sperry's competitive position with DOD. M. Getler. il Miss & Roc 15:24-5+ Ag 24 '64
SPESSIVTZEVA, Olga
Olga Spessivtzeva today. A. Dolin. il pors Dance Mag 37:34-8 Ap '63
SPHAGNUM moss. See Peat moss
SPHERES, Attraction of. See Gravitation
SPHERULES. See Meteorites
SPICE cake. See Cake
SPICE pinks. See Pinks
SPICE racks
Early American spice rack. A. J. Canada. il Pop Mech 121:160-1 Mr '64
Make this delightful spice of life gourmet rack. D. L. Brightbill. il Am Home 66:18+ Ja '63
SPICER, Betty Coe
New help for the monthly blue. Ladies Home J 80:16 Mr '63
There's a doctor in the house. Ladies Home J 80:49+ Je '63
SPICER, Carol
Address book can get awfully crowded. House B 106:137 My '64
SPICER, Stanley T.
Nova Scotia's sailor artist. Motor B 113:116-17+ Ja '64
SPICES
Cooking with herbs and spices. Am Home 66:68+ Mr '63
Herbs and spices: the secret key to flavor; with recipes. V. T. Habeeb. il Am Home 66:42-3+ Mr '63
Spices make the difference. J. Figg. il Suc Farm 62:92-3+ O '64
Which is which? McCalls 91:90+ My '64
See also
Cardamon
Cinnamon
Clove
Curry
Pepper
SPICOLA, Tony
Rare, the car, the setting and the atmosphere. il Hot Rod 17:86-7 Jl '64
SPIDER mites. See Red spiders
SPIDER webs
Adhesiveness of spider silk. T. Eisner and others. bibliog il Science 146:1058-61 N 20 '64
Amateur scientist; how to collect and preserve webs of spiders. L. B. Lougee. il Sci Am 208:159-60+ F '63
Spider webs studied. Sci N L 85:258 Ap 25 '64
Spider's victims retaliate by escaping sticky web. Sci N L 87:53 Ja 23 '65
SPIDERS
Cholinesterase inhibition in spider mites susceptible and resistant to organophosphate. H. R. Smissaert. bibliog il Science 143:129-31 Ja 10 '64
Predator nets a sugar ant; Australian netting spider. il Natur Hist 73:54-5 Mr '64
Spare that spider! it's eating our insects. Sci N L 83:377 Je 15 '63
See also
Tarantulas
SPIDERS, Red. See Red spiders
SPIEGEL, Sam
Emperor. il por Time 81:67-8 Ap 19 '63
SPIEGELMAN, S.
Hybrid nucleic acids; with biographical sketch. Sci Am 210:22, 48-56 bibliog(p 150) My '64
—See Ohtaka, Y. jt. auth.
SPIELMAN, Andrew
Swamp mosquito, culiseta melanura: occurrence in an urban habitat. bibliog Science 143:361-2 Ja 24 '64
SPIELMAN, Henry
Strictly a beep fleeter. il pors Am For 69:4-5 My '63
SPIER, Franklin
Former ad chiefs' advice: describe the book; summary of address. por Pub W 185:54-5 F 17 '64
New look in university press advertising. Pub W 184:22-30 O 7 '63
SPIERINGS, Tim
Far and near. Natur Hist 72:60-3 Ap '63
SPIES
Attaché case; four Western military attachés on Trans-Siberian railway trip. il Time 84:42+ O 16 '64
Boxed in; kidnaped spy discovered in trunk. il Newsweek 64:50+ N 30 '64
Britain's scandalous spy case. C. Brogan. il Nat R 14:195-6+ Mr 12 '63
Britain's spy scandals; how they grow. il U S News 54:46-8 Je 24 '63
Case of the Red Eagle; S. Wennerstrom of Sweden. il Time 83:30 My 8 '64
Case of the talking trunk. D. J. Hamblin. il Life 57:86A-86B+ N 27 '64
Class reunion; Philby joins Guy Burgess and Donald Maclean in Russia. Newsweek 62:33 Ag 12 '63
Composite portrait of the Soviet spy. H. M. Hyde. il N Y Times Mag p 14+ F 16 '64
D for Dolnytsin; spies for Britain and Russia. Newsweek 62:40 Jl 22 '63
De-briefing process for the U.S.S.R's defectors. il Newsweek 63:40-1 F 24 '64
Defector; Yuri Ivanovich Nosenko. Time 83:34+ F 21 '64
Doctor Stephen Ward returns. R. West. Esquire 62:138+ S '64

SPIES—*Continued*
Double duty in Canada; Ottawa based Vasily Vasilievich Tarasov correspondent for Izvestia, expelled as a spy. Time 84:49 My 8 '64
Fear at the top; execution of O. Penkovsky. Newsweek 61:60-1 Je 10 '63
Fumigating the fumigator. Time 84:25 S 25 '64
Gentleman spy: S. E. C. Wennerstrom. Time 82:26 Jl 5 '63
Giggle of Juan Ramirez. R. Plant. New Yorker 39:162+ N 2 '63
Girl spy against Castro. A. St George. il Look 28:60-5 D 29 '64
Great Britain; a surfeit of spies. New Repub 148:10 My 11 '63
Harriet Tubman. L. Bennett, jr. il Ebony 20:148+ N '64
Hell of a nice guy: S. E. C. Wennerström. Newsweek 62:36-7 Jl 8 '63
How a Soviet spy made Britain look slipshod. U S News 54:8 My 6 '63
How many Soviet spies in U.S. agencies? summary of statement, March 2, 1964. M. Goleniewski. U S News 56:10 Mr 16 '64
I gave them all; G. J. Gessner. il Time 83:21 Je 19 '64
Idealist; S. Wennerström convicted of gross espionage. Time 83:25 Je 19 '64
Illegals; Baltch-Egorov case. il Newsweek 62:21 Jl 15 '63
In from the cold; exchange of G. Wynne and Konon Trofimovich Molody. il Time 83:33 My 1 '64
Include the women. il Time 84:34 D 11 '64
Invisible man; J. Dunlap. il Newsweek 62:43 O 21 '63
Is Britain becoming a sick nation? Profumo scandal. U S News 55:10 Jl '63
John Scobell, Union spy in Civil war; excerpts from Eyes and ears of the Civil war. G. A. Foster. il Ebony 19:135-8+ D '63
Joker; Schwirkmann incident. Newsweek 64:48+ S 28 '64
Justice for Captain Kauffman. Nation 198:3 Ja 4 '64
Letter from London; Vassall case. M. Panter-Downes. New Yorker 39:146-8 My 25 '63
Man with the cosmic view; G. Paques. Time 82:42 O 4 '63
Master spy who almost got away; Swedish air force Colonel Wennerström. I. Ross. Harper 229:47-54 D '64
Midsummer dragnet; secret agents throughout the world. Time 82:25 Jl 19 '63
Mistaken identities. Time 82:26 Jl 26 '63
Modern spy extends his arena. C. Felix. il N Y Times Mag p24+ Je 9 '63
Name that tune; Bulgaria's Georgiev. Time 83:37 Ja 3 '64
New case cracked; three members of Soviet mission to the United Nations, U.S. citizen and a Soviet chauffeur. il Sr Schol 83:20 N 22 '63
One solitary flaw. il Newsweek 63:38 My 11 '64
Ordeal of Captain Kauffman. F. J. Cook. Nation 197:123-38 S 14 '63
Playboy sergeant who spied for Russia; Jack Dunlap. D. Oberdorfer. il Sat Eve Post 237:40+ Mr '64
Price to pay; I. A. Georgiev. il Newsweek 63:32 Ja 6 '64
Profumo affair. C. Brogan. Nat R 14:528-9+ Jl 2 '63
Quiet, conspiracy at work. W. F. Buckley, jr. Nat R 14:188 Mr 12 '63
Quiet man; J. W. Butenko. il Newsweek 62:44+ N 11 '63
Red spy's secret: first win the wives. U S News 57:12 D 7 '64
Rise and fall of a Soviet agent; Kim Philby. E. R. F. Sheehan. il Sat Eve Post 237:30-2+ F 15 '64; Same abr. Read Digest 84:82-91 My '64; Reply. D. Astor. Sat Eve Post 237:4-5 Mr 21 '64
Road to Khabarovsk; seizure of British and U.S. military attachés in Russia. il Newsweek 64:56 O 19 '64
Snapshots of a Soviet spy. K. Detzer. il Read Digest 83:210-14 N '63
Spies' demise; Igor Ivanov and John W. Butenko convicted. Time 84:15 D 25 '64
Spies we caught and what they were after. il U S News 55:8+ Jl 15 '63
Spy case dropped; A. Sokolov and J. A. Baltch. Sr Schol 85:16 O 14 '64
Spy scandal that concerns the U.S. and at the U.N. U S News 55:8 Jl 8 '63
Spy, spy, spies. il Time 82:23 Jl 12 '63
Spy thriller from a Moscow courtroom; Penkovsky trial. il U S News 54:8 My 20 '63
Spy who came in from the trunk. il Time 84:39 N 27 '64
Spying for peace, by J. Kimche. Review Nat R 14:534-5 Jl 2 '63. A. Lunn
Strangers on a bridge; excerpt. J. B. Donovan. il Sat Eve Post 237:30-2+ Mr 28 '64
Swedish spy details Soviet ICBM gamble. G. C. Wilson. Aviation W 81:22-3 D 14 '64
That spy loophole: a deal or a goof? Time 84:69-70 O 16 '64
Third man in the Burgess-Maclean case. U S News 55:10 Jl 15 '63
Tomorrow is forever. Newsweek 63:31 Ja 13 '64
Traders: Wynne for Molody. il Newsweek 63:40 My 4 '64
Undercover Talleyrand; French spy Georges Pâques. Time 84:31 Jl 17 '64
Waiting for the firing squad. A. Ladas. il Harper 229:87-90 N '64
What Soviet spies are up to in the U.S. U S News 54:10 Je 17 '63
Why Britain returned a master Soviet spy; exchange of Gordon Lonsdale for Greville Wynne. U S News 56:12 My 4 '64
With all due modesty; G. Pâques. Newsweek 62:58+ O 7 '63
Woman who saved the Union navy; M. Louvestre. G. A. Foster. il Ebony 19:48-50+ Jl '64

See also
Abel, R. I.
Espionage
Sorge, R.
World war, 1939-1945—Secret service

SPIES, Industrial
Cloak & camera in Detroit. il Time 84:61-2 Ag 14 '64
Corrupt society. F. J. Cook. Nation 196:475-6 Je 1 '63
Who stole the formula? J. Kobler. il Sat Eve Post 236:82+ Je 29 '63

SPIES in literature
Inside job? hero of The spy who came in from the cold. Newsweek 63:80 F 3 '64

SPIESS, F. N. and Maxwell, A. E.
Search for the Thresher. bibliog Science 145:349-55 Jl 24 '64

SPIGELGASS, Leonard
Dear me, the sky is falling; dramatization of story by G. Berg and J. Yaffe. Criticism
Commonweal 78:47 Ap 5 '63
Nation 196:254 Mr 23 '63
New Yorker 39:132 Mr 9 '63
Newsweek 61:69 Mr 18 '63
Sat R 46:28 Mr 23 '63
Theatre Arts il 47:10-12 Ap '63
Time il 81:70 Mr 15 '63
Mrs Merriweather's black nightgown; story. Ladies Home J 81:72-3 S '64
Start from scratch. Ladies Home J 80:50+ D '63

SPIKE, Robert W.
Bookshelf on the daily life of the church. Christian Cent 80:958-9 Jl 31 '63
United church: in search of a special calling. Christian Cent 80:234-7 F 20 '63

SPILHAUS, Athelstan Frederick
Athelstan's world; no-nonsense science strip. il por Newsweek 61:86 F 18 '63
Man in the sea. Science 145:993 S 4 '64
Oceanography: a wet and wondrous journey. Bul Atomic Sci 20:11-15 D '64

SPILLANE, James M.
Language institutes show the way. NEA J 53:25-6 My '64

SPILLANE, Mickey
I, the actor. il por Time 81:51 Je 7 '63

about
Mickey Spillane as Mike Hammer. T. Southern. il pors Esquire 60:74-6+ Jl '63

SPILLER, Burton L.
Fishing's forgotten spot. Field & S 67:96-8+ F '63

SPILLER, D.
Insecticide resistance: effects of WARF antiresistant on toxicity of DDT adult houseflies. bibliog Science 142:585-6 N 1 '63

SPILLER, Robert E.
Poet's life in six stanzas. Sat R 46:50-1 N 9 '63

SPILLMAN, Sandy
Mighty F-1. Pop Sci 183:102-5+ O '63
Now, a hormone that melts away fat. Sci Digest 57:71-4 Ja '65
We will now test the time machine. Sci Digest 54:57-60 O '63

SPINACH
Too much spinach bad if taking anticoagulants. Sci N L 85:56 Ja 25 '64

See also
Cookery—Vegetables

SPINAGE, C. A.
Animals on camera; excerpt from Animals of East Africa. il N Y Times Mag p 174-5 Ap 7 '63

SPINAL cord
Bioelectric activity in long-term cultures of spinal cord tissues. S. M. Crain and E. R. Peterson. bibliog il Science 141:427-9 Ag 2 '63
Pyramidal tract: a comparison of two prosimian primates. J. A. Jane and others. bibliog il Science 147:153-5 Ja 8 '65
Synapse arising at central node of Ranvier, and note on fixation of the central nervous system. D. Bodian and N. Taylor. bibliog il Science 139:330-2 Ja 25 '63
What can go wrong; the spinal cord. R. Campbell. Life 54:78+ Je 28 '63

SPINAL meningitis. See Meningitis

SPINDLER, George D.
Anthropology. bibliog NEA J 52:28-31 S '63

SPINDLER, Laurence
Special-interest cars. Motor T 16:75 N '64

SPINE
Anatomy for the ballet teacher; interview, ed. by W. Como (cont) R. Gelabert. il Dance Mag 37:64-7 F '63
See also
Spinal cord

Abnormities and deformities

Spinal defects repeated in families, study shows. Sci N L 84:329 N 23 '63

Wounds and injuries

Canvas cast; Foster bed. il Newsweek 64:56 Jl 6 '64
Very special patient. il Time 84:46 Jl 3 '64

SPINELLO, Matt P.
On the citizens band. See issues of Popular electronics

SPINGARN, Lawrence, P.
Run of three. J. M. Morrison. Poetry 101: 279-80 Ja '63

SPINGARN, Natalie Davis
Meet our medical FBI: excerpts from To save your life. Parents Mag 38:78-9+ O '63

SPINNAKERS. See Sails

SPINNING, James M.
Corporal punishment? NEA J 52:19-20 S '63

SPINNING lines. See Fishing tackle

SPINNING reels. See Fishing tackle

SPINNING tackle. See Fishing tackle

SPINNING tops. See Tops

SPINSTERS. See Single women

SPIRAL growth and movement
What makes a tree trunk spiral? O. A. Lindquist. il Am For 69:15 Je '63; Discussion. 69:40-1 Ag '63; 70:3 Ja '64

SPIRAL press. See Printing—Private presses

SPIRAL stairways. See Stairways

SPIRIDIGLIOZZI, Nunzio
Copper enameling on clay. Sch Arts 64:38 N '64

SPIRIT, Holy. See Holy Spirit

SPIRITS. See Ghosts

SPIRITUAL exercises
Season of renewal; Lenten reading. D. J. O'Hanlon. Commonweal 77:643-5 Mr 15 '63

SPIRITUAL healing. See Faith cure

SPIRITUAL life
Everyone must have an island; excerpts from address. H. Hanson. Recreation 56:449 D '63
Is there a tragic sense of life? L. Abel. Commentary 38:35-40 D '64
Questions to ask ourselves. G. Romney. Recreation 57:7-8 Ja '64
Varieties of stupidity. America 108:899 Je 29 '63
See also
Christian life
Holiness

SPIRITUAL retreats. See Retreats, Spiritual

SPIRITUAL values. See Worth

SPIRO, Herbert J.
Political stability in the new African states; address, April 11, 1964; with questions and answers. Ann Am Acad 354:97-109 Jl '64

SPITSBERGEN. See Svalbard

SPITZER, Elroy F.
Composting; its role in European refuse disposal. Am City 79:102-5 O '64 (to be cont)
European incinerators. Am City 79:85-7 N '64
Good water is not enough. Am City 78:112-14 My '63

SPITZER, Helen. See Spitzer, S. jt. auth.

SPITZER, Jeffrey C. and Steelink, Cornelius
Acetylene ester from aster spinosus. bibliog Science 146:1460-1 D 11 '64

SPITZER, Silas
Adventures in home cooking. Holiday 34:99-104 S '63
Dining adventures in Australia. Holiday 36: 94-5+ N '64
Dining adventures in the South Seas. Holiday 35:82-3+ Je '64
Dining out in Chicago. Holiday 35:121-4 F '64
Little wonder restaurants of San Francisco. Holiday 34:92-3+ N '63
—and Spitzer, Helen
Europe's finest restaurants 1965. Holiday 37: 64-9 Ja '65

SPITZNAGEL, John K. See Zeya, H. I. jt. auth.

SPIVACK, Robert G.
Man behind Goldwater. Look 28:45+ N 3 '64

SPIVACKE, Harold
National archives of sound recordings? por Library J 88:3783-8 O 15 '63

SPIVEY, Cleo
Crop that never fails us; ed. by J. D. Boyd. Farm J 88:36-7+ N '64

SPJELDNAES, Nils, and Henningsmoen, K. E.
Littorina littorea; an indicator of Norse settlement in North America? bibliog Science 141:275-6; 142:1022 Jl 19, N 22 '63

SPLEEN cells. See Cells

SPLICES. See Knots and splices

SPLICING of moving pictures. See Moving pictures—Editing

SPLIETHOFF, Herbert O.
Stretching the recreation day. Am City 78: 163-4 S '63

SPLINTS (surgery)
Balloons for broken bones. il Life 57:93-4+ O 30 '64
Blowing up a splint. il Time 84:97 O 2 '64
Emergency splints. C. Conley. il Field & S 68:69 Ja '64

SPLIT brain research. See Brain

SPLIT-level houses. See Architecture, Domestic

SPLIT-up of stocks. See Stocks—Split-up

SPLIT-vacations. See Vacations

SPOCK, Benjamin
Anger and rivalry in children. Redbook 124: 34-5+ Ja '65
Are we minimizing differences between the sexes? por Redbook 122:20+ Mr '64
Bottle, blanket and thumb; comfort or bad habit? por Redbook 122:26+ F '64
Children and death. por Redbook 122:36+ Ap '64
Children and discrimination. por Redbook 123: 30+ S '64
Difficulties in breast feeding. por Redbook 123:16+ Je '64
Discipline: where fathers fail. pors Redbook 123:48-9+ Jl '64
Doctor Spock talks with mothers. See issues of Ladies' home journal to September 1963
How my ideas have changed. pors Redbook 121:51-5+ O '63
If fateful issues are to be decided wisely. PTA Mag 57:19 F '63
Learning to live in a troubled world. por Redbook 123:26+ Ag '64
Medical care for the aged, what young families should know. por Redbook 123:34+ My '64
Playing with toy guns. por Redbook 124:24+ N '64
Protecting children from the harm of discrimination. por Redbook 123:26+ O '64
Psychology can't substitute for morality. por Redbook 122:22+ Ja '64
Ticking away. il Newsweek 63:68-9 Mr 23 '64
Toilet training. por Redbook 122:38+ N '63
What holiday memories mean to children. por Redbook 124:16+ D '64
What toys mean to children. Redbook 122:46-7+ D '63
Your child and prejudice. por Ebony 19:135-8+ O '64

SPOFFORD, Nancy
All about the birds and the beans. Redbook 121:6+ S '63

SPOILING of children. See Children—Management and training

SPOILS system
See also
Civil service

SPOKEN phonograph records. See Phonograph records—Spoken records

SPOLETO festival. See Music festivals—Italy

SPONGE boats. See Fishing boats

SPONGE room; drama. See Waterhouse, K. and Hall, W.

SPONGE rubber. See Rubber, Sponge

SPONONO; drama. See Paton, A. and Shah, K.

SPONSLER, George C.
Military role in space. Bul Atomic Sci 20:31-4 Je '64

SPONSORED television programs. See Television advertising

SPONSORS, Advertising. See Television advertising

SPOOLCRAFT. See Spools

SPOOLS
Yule spools. il McCalls 91:94-5+ D '63

SPOON RIVER; drama. See Aidman, C.

SPOON-thermometer. See Kitchen utensils

SPOONS
A. Michelson Christmas spoons. P. Owen. il Hobbies 68:45 D '63
Heavenly starters. il Seventeen 22:126-7 Ap '63
Ubiquitous spoon. S. Rama Rau. House & Gard 124:118-19 Ag '63

SPORANGIOPHORES
Sporangium discharge in pilobolus: a photographic study. R. M. Page. bibliog il Science 146:925-7 N 13 '64

SPORES (botany)
Spore discharge in basidiomycetes: a unified theory. D. B. O. Savile. bibliog il Science 147:165-6 Ja 8 '65
Spore discharge mechanism in basidiomycetes. L. S. Olive. bibliog il Science 146:542-3 O 23 '64

SPORN, Eugene M. See Wayner, M. J. jr. jt. auth.

SPORN, Michael B. and Dingman, C. W.
Histone and DNA in isolated nuclei from chicken brain, liver, and erythrocytes. bibliog Science 140:316-18 Ap 19 '63
—See Dingman, C. W. jt. auth.

SPORN, Philip
We're the most enterprising utility in this country. H. Kay. il por Fortune 69:138-41+ My '64

SPORT buses. See Station wagons

SPORT fishing boats. See Fishing boats

SPORT knives. See Knives

SPORT parachuting. See Parachuting

SPORT trophies. See Trophies, Sport

SPORT trucks. See Motor trucks

SPORTING goods
Catalog cache: with list of mail-order specialists. il Sports Illus 21:54-60 N 16 '64
How to buy tennis and golf equipment. il Seventeen 22:42 Je '63
Miniature McCoy; sporting gear in girl-and-boy size. il Sports Illus 19:46-51 D 2 '63
What's new. See issues of Outdoor life
See also
Hunting outfits

SPORTS
Moral force of sport. S. Shriver. il Sports Illus 18:30-1+ Je 3 '63
SR/1965 world travel calendar. R. E. Meyer, jr. il Sat R 48:47-8+ Ja 2 '65
Scoreboard. Time 81:83 Je 7 '63
Sport: the changing scene. il Holiday 34:115+ D '63; 35:134+ F; 116+ Mr; 122+ My; 110+ Je; 36:122+ Jl; 151-2+ N; 158+ D '64
You get trimmer every day! il Seventeen 23:104-5 Je '64
See also
Aquatic sports
Athletes
Games
Olympic games
Sports for children
Sports journalism
Television broadcasting—Sports
Track athletics
also names of sports, e.g. Football

Accidents and injuries

Baseball is inviting a beanball homicide. T. Cohane. il Look 28:74-6+ Ag 11 '64
Big spill; Santa Anita Derby. il Sports Illus 18:16-20 Mr 11 '63
Bookies of doom; insurance salesmen. D. Jenkins. il Sports Illus 19:36-8+ N 4 '63
Bring out the stretcher; football as the trainer sees it; J. Reichel of Syracuse university. W. J. McKean. il Look 28:28-32 O 6 '64
Commonsense commission; California boxing commission. Sports Illus 20:7 Ja 6 '64
Day in the life of a pro-football doctor. A. F. Gonzalez, jr. il Todays Health 42:22-5+ O '64
Death of a champion; Moore-Ramos fight. M. Sharnik. il Sports Illus 18:18-21+ Ap 1 '63
Death takes no holiday; seven-car crash at the Indianapolis 500. il Newsweek 63:86 Je 8 '64
First aid for athletic injuries. Todays Health 42:49 O '64
For the want of a warning a pennant was lost; with editorial comment. R. Creamer. il Sports Illus 18:22-3, 68+ Je 17 '63
Graceful prelude to death: Buddy Werner and Barbara Henneberger; with report by M. Smith. il Life 56:34-9 Ap 24 '64
How a knockout kills. F. B. Byrom. il Sci Digest 54:23-7 S '63
I killed a man. R. Donoghue. il Sat Eve Post 236:65-6 Mr 23 '63
Incredible sequence as a racing car goes wild. il Life 56:46-7 Ap 24 '64
Indianapolis; 500-mile race. Sports Illus 20:17 Je 8 '64
Instant of terror as 500 goes up in flame; Indianapolis auto race. il Life 56:44-5 Je 26 '64
Kiss the guy or tackle him? M. Cope. il Sat Eve Post 236:76-7 O 26 '63
Knockdown! rough experience in an MORC. K. Klokke. il Yachting 117:73+ Ja '65
Last race: death of skiers, W. Werner and Barbi Henneberger. il Time 83:36 Ap 24 '64
Let them begin slowly; injuries and fatalities in high school football. Sports Illus 21:16 N 30 '64
Letter home. J. Jones. Esquire 62:22+ D '64
Magnificent and the macabre; Indianapolis 500; D. MacDonald and E. Sachs killed. B. Ottum. il Sports Illus 20:24-9 Je 8 '64
Mantle's breaks, and yours. D. Duncan. il Pop Sci 185:100-3+ O '64
My search for faith; ed. by J. Poppy. B. Sternberg. il Look 28:78-82+ Mr 10 '64
Search for ring safety. Sports Illus 18:16+ Ap 15 '63
Should professional boxing be banned? pro and con discussion. il Sr Schol 82:22-3 Ap 17 '63
Ski doctor. il Newsweek 61:60 F 4 '63
Slambang of baseball. il Sports Illus 18:38-44 Ap 8 '63
Something went wrong; broken neck of B. Steinberg. il Time 82:60 Jl 12 '63
Tenth death; Ernie Knox. il Time 82:84 O 25 '63
This death might kill boxing; death of Ernie Knox. R. H. Boyle. il Sports Illus 19:16-21 O 28 '63
Tragedy on the lake; Cleveland yachting club races. Sports Illus 19:5 Ag 26 '63
War on ferocity; injuries in pro football. W. Bingham. il Sports Illus 19:18-23 N 11 '63
Water, as in hard; racing high-speed powerboats. Sports Illus 18:14 Je 17 '63
What you can do with what you have; rehabilitation of a quadriplegic, with report by J. Mason. il Life 56:75-88 Je 19 '64
Year of the knees in the NBA. W. Leggett. Sports Illus 19:84-5 N 25 '63

Anecdotes, facetiae, satire, etc.

How to make a champion out of a four-year-old. P. Cummings. Sports Illus 18:E3-4 Ap 29 '63
Outdoor upsmanship. O. Godbout. Read Digest 84:24D Je '64
Sporting gesture. J. Wescott. il Seventeen 23:22 My '64

Fiction

How to forget baseball. T. Sturgeon. il Sports Illus 21:84-90+ D 21 '64
Second letter to sports writers. D. M. Broderick. Library J 89:4608-9 N 15 '64

History

Union of two worlds; Olympic games. E. O. Reischauer. il Sports Illus 19:50-4 D 23 '63

Insurance aspects

Bookies of doom; insurance salesmen. D. Jenkins. il Sports Illus 19:36-8+ N 4 '63

International aspects

Cozy show of coexistence; world speed skating championships at Karuizawa. L. Griggs. Sports Illus 18:49 Mr 4 '63
East succumbs to a western craze; Orient's fastest-growing sport: golf. A. Wright. il Sports Illus 19:86-91 N 25 '63
Politics makes strange sport; Jakarta games. Sports Illus 19:16 N 25 '63

Judging

All week long the word was Griffith; Griffith-Rodriguez fight. R. H. Boyle. il Sports Illus 18:24-5+ Je 17 '63
Judge they have to tell it to; G. Schilling. E. Havemann. il Sports Illus 21:38+ N 16 '64
Judge's report; Griffith-Rodriguez bout. J. Romero. il Sports Illus 20:20-1 Je 22 '64

SPORTS—*Continued*

Periodicals

See also
Sports illustrated (periodical)
World tennis (periodical)

Photographs

Football's grind and glitter. L. Schiller. Sat Eve Post 236:32-7 O 5 '63
Moments to remember: 1954-1964; Sports Illustrated tenth anniversary. Sports Illus 21: 31-57 Ag 17 '64
Sport in the Orient. D. Moore. Sports Illus 19:38-49 D 23 '63
Year's best sports photos. Look 27:28-32 Ap 9 '63; 28:92-6 Je 30 '64

Records

See Sports records

Asia

Living link to the people; mastery of the games of the West. il Sports Illus 19:56-9 D 23 '63
See also
Asiad (games)

Australia

Sporting scene; Laver vs Rosewall, professional matches. H. W. Wind. New Yorker 39:128+ F 23 '63

Bermuda

Travel notes. R. Joseph. Esquire 61:31+ Ap '64

Brazil

See also
Soccer

Cambodia

High scorer with either hand. A. Wright. il Sports Illus 19:60-5 D 23 '63

Dominican Republic

See also
Baseball

England

Old frontier sets an athletic pace; Britain's bankers athletics programs. il Bsns W p30-1 Ap 6 '63
Sporting scene; England vs. Scotland Rugby match. A. Reid. il New Yorker 39:161-8+ Ap 13 '63
See also
Cricket (game)
Soccer

Europe, Western

Wild world of European sports. R. Daley. il Sat Eve Post 236:60-1 F 16 '63

Far East

Sport in the Orient; photographs. D. Moore. Sports Illus 19:38-49 D 23 '63

France

Championship in a royal barnyard; French view of golf. P. E. Ress. il Sports Illus 19: 58-60 O 21 '63

Greece, Ancient

Glory of the Grecian games. R. Littell. il Read Digest 84:204R-204S+ Ap '64
Manslaughter born of a fixed race. A. Eliot. il Sports Illus 21:104-8+ O 5 '64

Japan

Cozy show of coexistence; world speed skating championships at Karuizawa. L. Griggs. Sports Illus 18:49 Mr 4 '63
Driven beyond dignity; Nichibo Kaizuka women's volleyball team. E. Whitehead. il Sports Illus 20:16-19 Mr 16 '64
Frantic lunge into sport; with report by L. Griggs. il Life 57:34-42 S 11 '64
Japan has a love affair with sports. R. Trumbull. il N Y Times Mag p30-1+ S 27 '64
Sewing up the game; Riccar sewing machine co. il Time 83:90 My 8 '64
Sportsman in Japan. R. Joseph. il Esquire 61:90-3+ Ja '64
Travel notes. R. Joseph. Esquire 61:14+ Ja '64
Very dry run in Tokyo; Japan rehearses for '64 Olympics. il Sports Illus 19:64-5+ O 28 '63

Mexico

Aztec basketball court unearthed in Mexico. Sci N L 85:312 My 16 '64
See also
Bullfights

Russia

Big jump: a Siberian champion tells his story. V. Brumel. il Sports Illus 18:38-41 F 4 '63
Flying start for the U.S.S.R. G. S. Brown. il Sports Illus 18:18-21 F 11 '63

Scotland

Sporting scene; England vs. Scotland Rugby match. A. Reid. il New Yorker 39:161-8+ Ap 13 '63

Spain

See also
Bullfights

Thailand

Mana and the King of Siam. S. Karnow. il Sports Illus 18:44 Ja 28 '63

United States

Champions who gave the year its flavor; photographs. Sports Illus 20:30-40 Ja 6 '64
Changing silhouettes in sport; symposium. il Recreation 56:328-30, 375-6 S-O '63
For the record. See issues of Sports illustrated
How sports helped break the color line. A. S. Young. il Ebony 18:114-16+ S '63
Je-ne-sais-quoits or horseshoes? A. Hano. il N Y Times Mag p96+ S 13 '64
Lot of gold in forty-eight hours. il Sports Illus 19:14-28+ S 16 '63
Municipal sports programs and policies; 1962 survey. il Recreation 56:214-18 My '63
New wave in sports. R. H. Boyle. Sports Illus 21:40-5 D 21 '64
Sports. H. L. Masin. See issues of Senior scholastic
Sports. See issues of Newsweek
True crisis. J. Underwood. il Sports Illus 18: 16-19+ My 20 '63

West Indies (Federation)

Sporting scene; test series: England vs. West Indies cricket matches. A. Reid. il New Yorker 39:188+ D 19 '63

SPORTS arenas. See Stadiums
SPORTS car club of America. See Automobile clubs
SPORTS car racing. See Automobile racing
SPORTS cars
Awful, awful, street roadster. L. Smith. il Hot Rod 16:46-50 Ag '63
Cars; photographs. See issues of Hot rod
Cheetah; new GT prowler. D. Francisco. il Hot Rod 17:70-5+ Mr '64
Chevy's Corsa: a European flair with a U.S. feeling. B. Ottum. il Sports Illus 21:96-7 S 21 '64
Chrysler's ramblin' rallywagons; Sports car club of America. B. Greene. il Hot Rod 17:78-81 Mr '64
Cobra Daytona coupe. il Motor T 16:27 Ap '64
Detroit sports cars will they replace the imports? il Motor T 17:22-3 Ja '65
Dodge Palomino sport pickup. C. Isica. il Motor T 16:78-9 Ap '64
Fastback coming back fast; Chrysler's Barracuda. il Time 83:94 Ap 10 '64
Ford turns the Mustang loose. il Bsns W p 152+ Ap 18 '64
Ford's young one; Mustang. il Time 83:92-102 Ap 17 '64
Inside Rogers' roadster. il Hot Rod 17:102-3 N '64
Instant roadster. L. Smith. il Hot Rod 17: 70-5+ F '64
Little red riding hood. il Hot Rod 17:32-5+ Jl '64
MT driver's report; EMPI's impish Sportster. B. McVay. il Motor T 15:30-5 Jl '63
Mustang. R. Brock. il Hot Rod 17:70-3 My '64
Mustang, a new breed out of Detroit. il Newsweek 63:97-101 Ap 20 '64
Mustang by Ford out of Thunderbird. il Consumer Bul 47:10-14 Jl '64
Mustang, for those who think young. D. Bartley. il Esquire 61:86-8 My '64
Pure joy of sports cars; with portfolio of paintings by Lemuel B. Line. Fortune 70: 167-71 Jl '64
Return of the classic Cord. H. E. Dark. il Pop Mech 120:82-4+ Ag '63
Robust roadster. il Hot Rod 17:90-1 D '64
Runaway; Mustang breaking sales records. il Newsweek 64:65 Ag 24 '64
Special cars: more for fun than for transportation; not tested by CU. Consumers Rep 28:183 Ap '63
Sports car for everyman; Ford's new Mustang. R. Grossman. il Sports Illus 20:38-40+ Ap 20 '64
Sports car for the masses; Ford Mustang. il Life 56:51-2+ Ap 17 '64
Spotlight on the MG Midget. J. Whipple. il Pop Mech 120:24+ D '63

SPORTS cars—*Continued*
Thunder T. il Hot Rod 17:36-7 D '64
Tiger, Tiger burning bright. D. Wells. il Hot Rod 18:44-7 Ja '65
Touring car called Apollo. P. Biro. il Hot Rod 17:74-7 Jl '64
Unmasking the Mustang. il Time 83:91 Mr 13 '64
Whatever happened to sports cars? D. Bartley. il Esquire 60:82-7+ S '63

Exhibitions

Seattle auto custom fair; 1963. L. Smith. il Hot Rod 16:70-3 O '63

Testing

Chevelle road test. B. McVay. il Motor T 16:38-43 Ja '64
CU's first look at the Ford Mustang. il Consumer Rep 29:320-1 Jl '64
Datsun SPL-310 road test. B. McVay. il Motor T 16:60-3 Mr '64
Fairlane Sports Coupe road test. J. Wright. il Motor T 16:50-5 Ja '64
MT road test; Corvette Sting Ray. J. Wright. il Motor T 15:22-7 My '63
MT road test; Fiat 1500. B. McVay. il Motor T 15:50-5 S '63
MT road test; MG sports sedan. J. Wright. il Motor T 15:50-5 Jl '63
MT road test; Nova SS, Chevy II sport coupe. B. McVay. il Motor T 15:62-7 My '63
MT road test; Triumph Spitfire road test. B. McVay. il Motor T 15:44-7 D '63
MT road test; Volvo 122-S and P-1800S. B. McVay. il Motor T 15:50-7 O '63
Plymouth Sports Fury road test. J. Wright. il Motor T 16:28-33 Ja '64
Road testing an American hybrid; AC Cobra. J. Wright. il Motor T 15:34-9 S '63

SPORTS cars, Foreign. See Automobiles, Foreign

SPORTS clothes. See Clothing and dress—Sports clothes

SPORTS clubs
Charlie's seventh heaven; Racquet club, Palm Springs, Calif. A. Wright. il Sports Illus 18:36+ Ap 15 '63
Club to suit a king's fancy; Royal Bangkok sports club; reproductions of paintings. F. McMahon. Sports Illus 19:78-85 D 23 '63
Down go the pigeons; Thunder Mountain club, N.J. il Bsns W p88-90 Je 6 '64
Swimming and tennis club in California. il Arch Rec 134:146-7 Ag '63
Two birds bet a million on a club in the bush; B. Holden and R. Ryan in Kenya. R. Coughlan. il Sports Illus 18:84-8+ My 20 '63
See also
Fishing clubs

SPORTS columns. See Newspapers—Sections, columns, etc.

SPORTS equipment. See Sporting goods

SPORTS fans
Augusta; where Georgia retaliates for Sherman's march. D. Jenkins. il Sports Illus 20:94-6+ Ap 6 '64
Bloody but unbowed: the golf buff. W. B. Furlong. il N Y Times Mag p24-5+ My 19 '63
Buffalo stands for the Bills. E. Shrake. il Sports Illus 21:32-3 O 5 '64
Disciples of St Darrell on a wild weekend; four football games in three days. D. Jenkins. il Sports Illus 19:72-80+ N 11 '63
Enter Adams' army. Sports Illus 21:8 Jl 27 '64
Race before the race at Indianapolis. J. A. Maxwell. il Reporter 30:40+ My 21 '64
Six dreary days, then Saturday; the story of British football. J. Olsen. il Sports Illus 21:74-6+ O 12 '64
Stadium notes: forward passage. J. Wescott. il Seventeen 23:22 N '64
Those who watch golf bear watching; reproductions of paintings. M. Simont. Sports Illus 20:40-4 Ap 6 '64
Watchers of the race; photographs. J. Cooke. Sports Illus 21:26-33 N 9 '64
See also
Baseball fans
Basketball fans

SPORTS for children
Fit sports for pre-teens. L. Marett. il Parents Mag 38:54-5 Je '63
Sports to last a lifetime. P. W. Goldman. il N Y Times Mag p47-8 Je 28 '64

SPORTS for women
Girls' track coach in Hawaii. il Ebony 18:53-4+ Mr '63
See also
Women as athletes

SPORTS illustrated (periodical)
Letter to the publisher; congratulations on 10th anniversary. H. R. Luce. il Sports Illus 21:4 Ag 17 '64
Moments to remember: 1954-1964. il Sports Illus 21:31-57 Ag 17 '64
Sportsman of the year: A. R. Rozelle. K. Rudeen. il Sports Illus 20:22-6+ Ja 6 '64
Sportsman of the year: Ken Venturi. A. Wright. il Sports Illus 21:32-9 D 21 '64
Tie for the top and a tribute to Bonnie; sportswear designers. J. A. Zill. il Sports Illus 18:48-50 My 6 '63

SPORTS illustrated silver anniversary All-America
Era shaped by war. R. Cantwell. il Sports Illus 21:36-8+ N 30 '64
Jerome Brud Holland wins Sports illustrated award. Negro Hist Bul 27:57-8 D '63
Silver anniversary. R. Cantwell. il Sports Illus 19:64-6 N 11 '63

SPORTS insurance. See Sports—Insurance aspects

SPORTS journalism
Makers of the sports page; ancient art of sportswriting. P. Knauth. il Sports Illus 19:34-6+ S 16 '63
My son the sportswriter; S. Povich. il Time 81:54+ F 22 '63

Anecdotes, facetiae, satire, etc.

New sportswriter. C. M. Curtis. il Atlan 214:120+ D '64

SPORTS museums. See Museums

SPORTS promoting. See Promoters and promoting

SPORTS records
Go, Bobby! go, to beat the magic 50; left winger of the Black Hawks, B. Hull. W. Leggett. il Sports Illus 22:14-17 Ja 25 '65
Olympic records, where will they end? B. H. Frisch. il Sci Digest 56:6-14 O '64
Why sports records are being broken: science or supermen? R. Gannon. il Pop Sci 182:58-62+ My '63

SPORTS reporting. See Reporters and reporting

SPORTS uniforms. See Uniforms, Sports

SPORTSMANSHIP
Bible in the bullpen. J. Devaney. il Sat Eve Post 237:28-9 My 2 '64
I believe. M. Woodward. Seventeen 22:168 F '63
Lesson from Boston; rivalry in sports. Sports Illus 18:6 Mr 4 '63
Little leaguers have big problems, their parents. J. Brosnan. il Atlan 211:117-20 Mr '63
Old man McGurkin. E. Allison. il Field & S 68:38-9+ Je '63
Sport is education; excerpts from address, October 28, 1963. R. Maheu. il UNESCO Courier 17:4-9 Ja '64; Reply. D. R. Wills. 17:64-5 Jl '64
Sportsmen don't happen. D. M. Duffey. il Outdoor Life 135:64-5+ F '65

SPORTSMEN
Across the years. C. Ford. il Field & S 69:6+ Jl '64
Lake Erie's living legend. W. Seifert. il Field & S 69:34-5+ Ag '64
Overreachers; portfolio. G. Talese. Esquire 60:152-7 D '63
See also
Hunters

SPOTS, Removal of. See Cleaning

SPOTTED fever. See Rocky Mountain spotted fever

SPOTTED horses in art. See Horses in art

SPOTTED weakfish fishing. See Weakfish fishing

SPOTTING. See Photography—Printing processes

SPRAGUE, G. F. and others
Virus as a mutagenic agent in maize. bibliog Science 141:1052-3 S 13 '63

SPRAGUE, Henry
Sailor with but a single thought. H. Whall. il por Sports Illus 19:50-1 Ag 12 '63

SPRAGUE, Howard B.
Medicine. Ladies Home J 81:43 O '64

SPRAGUE, James I.
Big western feed lots. Suc Farm 61:64-5+ F '63

SPRAINS
Sprains; first aid. C. J. Potthoff. Todays Health 42:62 F '64

SPRANGER, Eduard
Obituary
Sch & Soc 92:65+ F 22 '64

SPRATTLING, Willis, jr
Rocket test team boss. il pors Ebony 19:46-8+ My '64

SPRAY-on starch. See Starch (for clothes)

SPRAY residue on fruits, vegetables, etc.
Sonic bath washes off spray residues. Farm J 87:44D S '63
SPRAYING and dusting
Bug- and disease-proof your garden. B. Hering. il Pop Gard 15:60-3 My '64
Fruit tree spraying. P. P. Pirone. il Horticulture 43:38-9 Ja '65
Give old plants a new lease on life. il Pop Gard 14:43 F '63
How to poison bugs, but not yourself. J. Hyypia. il Pop Sci 182:106-9+ Je '63
New beetle has toe hold in Corn Belt; cereal leaf beetle. J. Russell. il Farm J 87:25 Jl '63
Questions & answers about dormant sprays. L. M. Vasvary. il Flower Grower 51:28-9+ F '64
Spray ripens tomatoes at one time; chemical mendok. Farm J 89:54 Ja '65
Tree program restricts elm losses; Grosse Point Park, Mich. R. A. Sloane. il Am City 79:165-6 O '64
See also
Airplanes in agriculture
Airplanes in insect control
Fertilizers and manures—Spray applications
Fungicides
Helicopters in insect control
Insecticides
Pesticides
SPRAYING and dusting apparatus
Johnny, get your calking gun. S. J. Howard. il Pop Mech 120:156-60 N '63
New machine spreads weedkiller granules. L. Donelson. il Farm J 87:64E F '63
Plastic sprayer weighs little. B. C. Kilvert, jr. il Flower Grower 50:58 O '63
Power to spare: do's & don'ts of dusting and spraying. B. C. Kilvert, jr. il Flower Grower 51:38-9 My '64
Sprayers & dusters. il Pop Gard 14:76-8 My '63
Three ideas for using chemicals. il Suc Farm 61:84 My '63
See also
Aerosols
SPRAYING materials. See Insecticides
SPREADERS, Fertilizer. See Fertilizer spreaders
SPREITZER, Elmer A.
On the road to Washington. America 109:426-7 O 12 '63
SPRIGGS, C. Z.
Souvenirs of the seas. pors Hobbies 68:28-9+ Ap '63
SPRING, Bernard P.
Plug-in schools: next step in educational design? Arch Forum 119:68-73 Ag '63
Research for building: the big battle rages in Washington. Arch Forum 119:122-3+ S '63
School costs cut by new components. Arch Forum 120:112-17 F '64
Technology: methods and machines to shape the future. Arch Forum 119:88-93 O '63
SPRING, Eleanor
Summer loves; story. Ladies Home J 81:60-1 Jl '64
SPRING
April magic in the ocean deeps. J. George. il Read Digest 82:107-11 Ap '63
Frost recedes north. Sci N L 83:235 Ap 13 '63
Mystery of spring. R. M. Carleton. il Todays Health 41:18-19+ Ap '63
Outdoors. V. Bourjaily. Esquire 61:168-70 Ap '64
Spring has many meanings. B. Tufty. il(p 177) Sci N L 83:183 Mr 23 '63
Spring 1964: bloom and boom. il Newsweek 63:15-16 Mr 30 '64
Spring, return to life. B. Tufty. il Sci N L 85:186-7 Mr 21 '64
What is spring? S. Churchill. Read Digest 84:182C My '64
Poetry
Dawn; Slippers for the wind; Corn shuck dolls. J. Stuart. Am For 70:37 Ap '64
Truth & poetry; ed. by H. V. Wilson. Flower Grower 51:80 Mr '64
Unwelcome guests. R. Benton. Am For 70:37 Ap '64
Quotations, maxims, etc.
Spring! comp. by E. F. Murphy. il N Y Times Mag p62 Ap 7 '63
SPRING and Mrs Malloy; story. See Henderson, R.
SPRING cleaning. See House cleaning
SPRING I remember best; story. See Schenbeck, F. A.
SPRING MOUNTAINS
Easy detour from Las Vegas. Sunset 131:58 O '63
SPRING star flowers
Plant these more often. R. C. Hands. il Horticulture 41:425 Ag '63
SPRINGEL, Hans Otto
Special report: new records from Germany. Mus Am 83:37 F '63
SPRINGER, Georg F. and others
Galactosidase action on human blood group B active escherichia coli and ox red cell substances. bibliog Science 146:946-7 N 13 '64
SPRINGER, Lois E.
Bells. See issues of Hobbies
SPRINGER spaniels. See Spaniels
SPRINGER-verlag, West Germany. See Publishers and publishing—Germany (Federal Republic)
SPRINGER-verlag New York, incorporated
Springer-verlag starts American company. Pub W 186:91 S 28 '64
SPRINGERLE cookies. See Cookies
SPRINGFIELD, Ill.
Politics and government
Percy's purge. J. L. McDowell. New Repub 150:8 Je 27 '64
SPRINGFIELD, LAKE. See Lakes, Artificial
SPRINGFIELD, Mass.
Education
See also
Springfield college
Water supply
Two gigantic reservoirs. P. C. Karalekas and C. A. Manganaro. il Am City 79:73-5 Jl '64
SPRINGFIELD, Mo.
Two new purchasing procedures. B. H. Jones and W. Kane. il Am City 78:117-18 Mr '63
SPRINGFIELD, Ore.
Summer pool dons a winter coat. R. M. Artz. il Am City 79:94-6 Ag '64
We doubled in area to solve our sewerage problem. F. R. Smiley. il Am City 78:108-9 My '63
SPRINGFIELD college, Springfield, Mass.
Glenn Olds, innovator at Springfield. M. K. Harvey. Sat R 47:67 F 15 '64
Spirit, mind, body. R. H. Boyle. il Sports Illus 19:76-8+ D 2 '63
SPRINGS
Florida springtime. L. Harris. il Travel 120:26-30 S '63
See also
Hot springs
SPRINGS (mechanism)
See also
Automobiles—Springs and suspension
SPRINKLERS
Everybody loves the water. il Pop Gard 15:48-9 Jl '64
Lawn sprinklers. il Consumer Bul 47:30-3 Ag '64
New robot rainmakers for wall-to-wall lawns. H. Walton. il Pop Sci 183:102-5+ Ag '63
Set-and-forget sprinkler systems; underground sprinklers. B. Gladstone. il Pop Mech 120:150-6 Jl '63
Sprinkling skyrockets hourly peaks. il Am City 79:101-2 Je '64
Watering devices. il Pop Gard 14:67+ Jl '63
See also
Watering of gardens, lawns, etc.
SPRINTING. See Running
SPROUL, Allan
Use and abuse of economic policy. Sat R 48:36+ Ja 9 '65
about
Sproul urges deficit attack. Bsns W p74 Je 29 '63
SPRUCE
Sitka spruce, Alaska's new state tree. A. S. Harris. il Am For 70:32-5 Ag '64
Two unique western conifers. I. Reed. il Horticulture 41:98 F '63
SPRUCE budworms
Control
Operation budworm: Maine. J. Milton. il Am For 69:26-7+ S '63
Operation budworm: Washington. T. Burrier. il Am For 69:28-9 S '63
SPRUNT, Alexander, jr
Wild flamingoes on parade. Audubon Mag 65:352-5 N '63

SPRUNT, Alexander, 4th
Bald eagles aren't producing enough young; summary of address, November 10, 1962. Audubon Mag 65:32-5 Ja '63
Birds of the sea. Motor B 112:46-7 Jl; 41+ Ag; 45+ S; 29+ O; 54+ N; 35+ D '63
SPUR of the moment; story. See Rodgers, M. A.
SPURIA irises. See Irises
SPURWINGED geese. See Geese, Wild
SPY-ban pact; story. See Ellis, H. F.
SPYING. See Spies
SQUALIDAE
See also
Dogfish
SQUARE D company
Very round profits of Square D. S. Mahoney. il Fortune 70:136-9+ Ag '64
SQUARE-wave generators. See Signal generators
SQUARES (instrument) See Carpenters squares
SQUARES, Public. See Plazas
SQUASH (game)
Sporting scene; H. Khan vs. M. Khan, United States Open championship. H. W. Wind. il New Yorker 39:87-90+ F 1 '64
SQUASHES
See also
Cookery—Vegetables
SQUAT Betty; drama. See Waterhouse, K. and Hall, W.
SQUERI, Robert
Survival by design. Sch Arts 63:12-15 S '63
SQUIBB, E. R, and sons
Building a new kind of bone bank; calf cartilage for surgical use, called Boplant. Bsns W p22 Ja 2 '65
SQUIDS
Intracellular perfusion of Chilean giant squid axons. I. Tasaki and M. Luxoro. bibliog il Science 145:1313-15 S 18 '64
SQUIRE, Christi
Garden furniture. Pop Gard 14:50-5 My '63
SQUIRE, James R.
Five rules for sequence. NEA J 53:14-16 N '64
Re-renewing: the future of NCTE. Sch & Soc 92:52-3 F 8 '64
Ways of the spirit and mind. Sch & Soc 91: 101 F 23 '63
SQUIRES, Donald F.
Modern tools probe deep water. Natur Hist 72:22-9 Je '63
SQUIRES, Raymond
Cost of conformity. PTA Mag 58:4-6 bibliog(p36) Mr '64
SQUIRREL hunting
Calling all fox squirrels. H. Bradshaw. il Field & S 69:65-7+ S '64
Primer on squirrel hunting. C. Patterson. il Outdoor Life 131:62-3+ Je '63
Squirrel dogs. D. M. Duffey. il Outdoor Life 132:98-100 Jl '63
Team for squirrels. R. Tinsley. il Outdoor Life 134:54-5+ S '64
SQUIRRELS
Assault on common sense; eight-day open season on rare Kaibab squirrel. Nat Parks Mag 38:16 Ag '64
Introduced menace; American gray squirrel threat to British woodlands. M. Shorten. il Natur Hist 73:42-9 bibliog(p67) D '64
My friend the squirrel. J. K. Terres. il Flower Grower 50:20-1+ D '63
Nature note; flying squirrel. Sci N L 85:79 F 1 '64
Night gliders of the woodlands; flying squirrels. I. Muul and J. W. Alley. il Natur Hist 72:18-25 My '63
Seagoing squirrel; photographs. R. C. Bloomfield. Field & S 68:117 My '63
Trouper of the treetops. J. D. Scott. il Read Digest 82:210-11+ My '63
Very private squirrel. O. Simon. il Redbook 121:19-20 My '63
Why shoot the Kaibab squirrel? sciurus kaibabensis. C. W. Buchheister. il Audubon Mag 66:359-60 N '64
SQUIRRU, Eduardo
Latin America and the Atlantic culture. Américas 15:13-17 N '63
SQUIRRU, Rafael
Architect of peace. Américas 16:2-4 Ap '64
Death has taken away a friend; poem, tr. by R. Connally. Américas 15:inside cover D '63
Deeper reality. Américas 16:1 Ja '64
I have faith in the new man. Américas 15:1 Je '63
Pop art or the art of things. Américas 15:15-21 Jl '63
Tamayo. Américas 15:23-9 O '63
Two draftsmen. Américas 16:42 Jl '64

SRINIVASAN, P. R. and Borek, Ernest
Enzymatic alteration of nucleic acid structure. bibliog Science 145:548-53 Ag 7 '64
SRNEC, Jiří
Balletomime. il por Time 83:65 Mr 13 '64
STAACK, Hagen
Pulpit in the home. il por Time 83:65 F 7 '64
STAAR, Richard
How strong is the Soviet bloc? bibliog f Cur Hist 45:209-15 O '63
Profile of Poland. bibliog f Cur Hist 44:257-64 My '63
STABILITY, Emotional. See Emotional stability
STABILIZATION of prices. See Price regulation by government
STABILIZERS, Automobile. See Automobiles—Stability and stabilizers
STABLES. See Barns and stables
STACHYS
This lamb belongs in the garden. V. M. Quist. il Flower Grower 50:61 My '63
STACK, John
Supersonic airliner coming; is U.S. losing out to Europe? interview. por U S News 54:50-2 Je 24 '63
STACKPOLE, Edouard A.
Figureheads the glory of the prow. Motor B 112:48-9+ D '63
STACKPOLE, Henrietta
Planets, palms, and numbers. Mlle 60:50-1+ Ja '65
STACKPOLE, Peter
35mm techniques. See issues of U.S. camera
STADDON, J. E. R.
Reinforcement as input: cyclic variable-interval schedule. bibliog Science 145:410-12 Jl 24 '64
STADER, Maria
Maria Stader's latest: do not miss this record! H. Glass. Am Rec G 29:463 F '63
STADIUMS
Atlanta tries to hit one into the stands. il Bsns W p44 N 7 '64
Big league lawn; Yankee stadium. B. C. Kilvert, jr. il Flower Grower 50:46-7 O '63
Biggest dome of all, for Texas, of course; lamella trusses for roof of Houston stadium. il Bsns W p56-8+ O 5 '63
Call them Mickey's mice or Pluto's pups; Los Angeles Angels. M. Durslag. il Sports Illus 21:44-5 Jl 20 '64
Chez Shea; William A. Shea stadium opened. il Newsweek 63:73 Ap 27 '64
Color-coded seats prevent delay; Long Beach arena. W. Hanssen. il Am City 78:95 Ag '63
Domed stadium for air-conditioned baseball; Houston stadium. il Pop Sci 185:70-1 Jl '64
Football; Polo Grounds, New York. New Yorker 39:140+ N 30 '63
Home run heaven; Minnesota's Metropolitan stadium. F. Deford. il Sports Illus 20:22-5 My 18 '64
Houston's big new bubble. il Sports Illus 21: 26-7 Ag 10 '64
How I'd build the perfect ball park. B. Veeck. il Pop Sci 184:94-5+ Mr '64
Ice skating in Mississippi. il Am City 78:93 Ap '63
Life-dome auditorium; Brownwood, Tex. J. Clary. il Am City 78:100-1 O '63
New home for the Mets; Shea stadium. H. Shuldiner. il Pop Sci 184:86-8 Ap '64
Notes and comment; end of the Polo Grounds. New Yorker 40:39 Ap 25 '64
Oops, there goes another old shrine; Sportsman's park, St Louis. R. Creamer. Sports Illus 19:46-7 Jl 8 '63
Quaint cult of the Mets; baseball in the Polo Grounds. R. Creamer. Sports Illus 18: 61-3 My 6 '63
Sport moves under a big top: domed structures on campus. il Sports Illus 22:40-7 Ja 11 '65
Sporting scene; Mets at William A. Shea stadium. R. Angell. il New Yorker 40:96+ My 30 '64
Sporting scene; the Mets at the Polo Grounds. R. Angell. il New Yorker 39:132+ My 25 '63
Stadiums. il Arch Forum 119:96-103 S '63
Stadiums: city status symbol. il Newsweek 62:74-5 S 30 '63
Under the big dome in Houston; Colt's new air-conditioned dome. il Newsweek 64:68-70 Ag 17 '64
STADLER, Quandra Prettyman
Light in Tom's eye. Nation 198:666-8 Je 29 '64
STAEHELIN, Theophil, and others
Breakdown of rat-liver ergosomes in vivo after actinomycin inhibition of messenger RNA synthesis. bibliog Science 140:180-3 Ap 12 '63

STAFFA, Dino, abp
Clear it with the Vatican. por Time 82:72 S 20 '63
STAFFORD, D. W. and Iverson, R. M.
Radioautographic evidence for the incorporation of leucine-carbon-14 into the mitotic apparatus. bibliog Science 143:580-1 F 7 '64
STAFFORD, Edward Peary
My most unforgettable character. por Read Digest 84:64-9 Ap '64
STAFFORD, Jean
Books. Vogue 143:27 Ja 15; 70 Mr 15; 56 Ap 15; 61 My; 144:32 Jl; 39 Ag 15; 78 S 15; 108 O 1; 98 O 15; 78 N 1; 148 D '64; 145:67 Ja 1; 97 F 1 '65
Ordeal of Conrad Pardee; story. Ladies Home J 81:58-9 Jl '64
STAFFORD, Robert M.
What's happened to the built-up roof? Arch Rec 136:176-8 D '64
STAFFORD, Thomas
They said, go to Harvard. Life 55:86B+ S 27 '63
STAFFORD, William
Address to the vacationers at Cape Lookout; poem. New Yorker 40:94 Ag 22 '64
Animal that drank up sound; poem. Atlan 213:85 Je '64
Day I got the good idea; Collector; Human condition; Across Kansas; poems. Poetry 102:174-6 Je '63
During the evening news; poem. Sat R 46:30 D 28 '63
Fifteen; poem. Atlan 213:68 F '64
First war; poem. Sat R 36 N 21 '64
In the Sandburg tradition. Poetry 102:388-9 S '63
Judgments; poem. Harper 229:74 D '64
Man from the Alaska highway; poem. Harper 228:50 Ap '64
Maybe alone on my bike; poem. New Yorker 40:94 Ap 4 '64
Rescued year; Growing up: mother; Family turn; How I escaped; poems. Poetry 104:238-42 Jl '64
Service of friendliness. Poetry 102:323-4 Ag '63
Some short poems. Harper 229:70 Ag '64
Terminations, revelations. Poetry 104:104-8 My '64
Touching sacred objects. Poetry 102:115-18 My '63
War monuments; poem. Sat R 46:78 My 11 '63

about

Powers, Edel, Stafford win National book awards. Pub W 183:30-1 Mr 18 '63
Think what's got away. . . R. Creeley. Poetry 102:44-5 Ap '63
STAFFORDSHIRE ware
Staffordshire and steam. R. J. LeBoeuf, jr. il Antiques 85:666-70 Je '64
STAG beetles. See Beetles
STAG hunting. See Deer hunting
STAGE. See Actors and actresses; Theater
STAGE costume. See Costume, Theatrical
STAGE food. See Theatrical production
STAGE fright
Always in the wings, the shakes. L. Funke. il N Y Times Mag p20+ My 17 '64
How to cope with stage fright. S. Blau. il Parents Mag 38:66-7+ My '63
What stage fright? W. F. Miksch. Atlan 213:126 Je '64
STAGE names. See Pseudonyms
STAGE photography. See Photography, Theatrical
STAGE props. See Theatrical production
STAGE scenery. See Opera—Stage scenery; Theater—Stage scenery
STAGECRAFT. See Theater—Stage scenery
STAGER, R. A. and Drickamer, H. G.
Ytterbium; effect of pressure and temperature on resistance. bibliog Science 139:1284 Mr 29 '63
STAGG, Anne
Delights of the Swiss fair. House & Gard 126:234-7+ O '64
STAHL, N. and Mayer, A. M.
Experimental differentiation between phototaxis and motility in chlamydomonas snowiae. bibliog Science 141:1282-4 S 27 '63
STAHMANN, Mark A. See Staples, R. C.; Weber, D. J. jt. auths.
STAHR, Alden
Why tough kids go straight. Parents Mag 38:56-7+ D '63
STAIGER, Ralph C.
Helping parents to understand your reading program. Sr Schol 85:13T N 18 '64

STAINED glass. See Glass painting and staining
STAINER, Sir John
On records; Crucifixion. Opera N 28:35 D 28 '63
STAINLESS steel. See Steel, Stainless
STAINLESS steel blades. See Razor blades
STAINLESS steel coins. See Coins
STAINLESS-steel sinks. See Sinks
STAINLESS steel tableware. See Tableware, Stainless steel
STAINS, Removal of. See Cleaning
STAINS and staining (biology)
Histone staining with ammoniacal silver. M. M. Black and H. R. Ansley. bibliog il Science 143:693-5 F 14 '64
Nerve fibers and terminals: electron microscopy after nauta staining. R. W. Guillery and H. J. Ralston. bibliog il Science 143:1331-2 Mr 20 '64
Reserpine: its effect on silver-stained structures of the heart. T. Cooper and others. bibliog il Science 141:526-7 Ag 9 '63
STAIRCASES. See Stairways
STAIRWAYS
Architecture; photographic exhibition at the Museum of modern art, New York. W. McQuade. Nation 197:332-3 N 16 '63
Big idea: floating basement stairs. il Pop Sci 183:123 S '63
In praise of stairs. B. Rudofsky. il Horizon 6:78-87 Autumn '64
Spirals are space-saves and spirals are fun. il Sunset 132:104-9 Ap '64
Stairs; a critical test of the builder's skill. il House & Gard 123:114-17 F '63
Where every inch counts, use a circular stairway. il House B 105:200 S '63
See also
Garden steps
STAKES
See also
Garden stakes and staking
STAKING of plants. See Garden stakes and staking
STALACTITES
Sculpture with water. il UNESCO Courier 17:18-19 Jl '64
Stalagmites and stalactites; Diamond cave. E. O'Donnell. il Natur Hist 73:22-5 My '64
STALAGMITES
Sculpture with water. il UNESCO Courier 17:19-19 Jl '64
Stalagmites and stalactites; Diamond cave. E. O'Donnell. il Natur Hist 73:22-5 My '64
STALEY, A. E, manufacturing company
Staley's greener corn. il Bsns W p48 Ja 11 '64
STALEY, Allen F.
Radical romantics. Art N 63:32-4+ My '64
STALEY, D. O.
Atmospheric circulation from fission-product radioactivity in surface air. bibliog Science 140:667-70 My 10 '63
STALEY, Jane Goss
Planning a successful bazaar. Bet Hom & Gard 41:98-9 S '63
STALIN, Iosif
Listening to Ivan Denisovich. N. Cousins. Sat R 46:18+ F 9 '63
Long look at Stalin, ten years after. E. Crankshaw. il pors N Y Times Mag p30+ Ap 7 '63
On the anniversary; tenth anniversary of death. Time 81:43 Mr 15 '63
Stalin-Trotsky split: a lesson for Kremlinologists. J. A. Hough. Reporter 29:37-9 D 5 '63
Stalin's foreign policy reappraised. by M. D. Shulman. Review
New Repub 149:22+ Ag 3 '63. H. Seton-Watson
STALINGRAD, Battle of, 1942-1943
Battle that turned the Nazi tide. H. W. Baldwin. il N Y Times Mag p23-5+ Ap 14 '63
Paulus and Stalingrad, by W. Goerlitz. Review
Newsweek il 63:77 Ja 13 '64
Red ran the tide of the Volga. A. Werth. Sat R 47:29+ Mr 14 '64
STALINISM. See Communism—Russia
STALKING of game. See Tracking and trailing
STALLINGS, Laurence
Bloody Belleau Wood; excerpts from Doughboys. Am Heritage 14:65-77 Je '63
STALLIONS
See also
Lipizzan horses
STALLS, Loafing. See Barns and stables—Equipment
STALLWORTH, Dave
He's a shocker! H. L. Masin. il por Sr Schol 85:24 Ja 14 '65

STAMFORD, Conn.

Education

School convertible to future team teaching. il Arch Rec 134:206-9 O '63

Libraries

See also
Ferguson library, Stamford, Conn.

STAMLER, Jeremiah
How to avoid a heart attack. Sci Digest 54: 43-7 S '63
—See Blakeslee, A. L. jt. auth.

STAMM, Edith Perry
Emily Dickinson: poetry and punctuation. Sat R 46:26-7+ Mr 30; 23 My 25 '63
Portrait of poetic justice. Sat R 46:44 O 5 '63

STAMM, Edward P.
Obituary
Am For il por 71:8-9 Ja '65

STAMM, Esther
Science books with souls. Library J 88:1299-30 Mr 15 '63

STAMMERING
Children's problems that go away. P. W. Goldman. il N Y Times Mag p58 Ja 10 '65
Stuttering: causes and treatment. Good H 156:152 F '63

STAMP collecting. See Postage stamps—Collectors and collecting

STAMPP, Kenneth M.
Tragic legend of reconstruction. Commentary 39:44-50 Ja '65

STAMPS, Food. See Food relief

STAMPS, Postage. See Postage stamps

STANCHIONS. See Barns and stables—Equipment

STANDARD, Paul
Making of a book. Pub W 186:78+ D 7 '64
Title page and the courteous typographer. Pub W 185:118+ F 3 '64

STANDARD and Poors corporation
Assessing gilt; nation's three bond-rating services. il Time 84:58 D 25 '64

STANDARD catalog for high school libraries
Satisfied conscience. E. Moon. Library J 89: 2045 My 15 '64

STANDARD dream; story. See Corcoran, B.

STANDARD of living
Buying power, more gains coming; interview. E. Clague. il Nations Bsns 52:31-3+ Ap '64
Consumer in the Soviet Union and the United States; summary of paper presented at Conference on the economics of Soviet industrialization, May 1961. J. G. Chapman. il Mo Labor R 86:11-13 Ja '63
Consumer's day dawns in Land of Rising Sun. il Bsns W p 128-30+ Mr 21 '64
U.S. living standard leads world. il Nations Bsns 52:66-9 S '64
Workers' wealth and family living standards; with reply by E. D. Hollander. H. H. Lamale. il Mo Labor R 86:674-86 Je '63
See also
Budget, Household
Food consumption
Income
Poverty

STANDARD oil companies
Grand acquisitor. R. L. Heilbroner. il Am Heritage 16:20-5+ D '64

STANDARD oil company of New Jersey
Italy turns now to West for oil. Bsns W p47-8 Mr 30 '63
Jersey Standard's corporate longevity. il Duns R 81:28-30+ Mr '63

STANDARD oil company of Ohio
Outside track at Standard oil co. of Ohio research laboratory. Newsweek 61:81 Ap 8 '63
Sohio Project moonbeam. R. W. Burhans. il Sky & Tel 25:128-31 Mr '63

STANDARD time. See Time—Systems and standards

STANDARDIZATION
Piper studying standardized parts plan. il Aviation W 79:99 O 28 '63
School costs cut by new components. B. P. Spring. il Arch Forum 120:112-17 F '64
See also
American standards associations
Quality of products

STANDARDIZATION (sociology)
See also
Conformity

STANDARDS (ethics) See Ethics

STANDARDS, Electric. See Electric standards

STANDARDS, International
One nation's tuck is another's drag. Time 84:106+ D 4 '64

STANDARDS, Library. See Libraries—Standards

STANDARDS, National bureau of. See United States—Standards, National bureau of

STANDARDS in education. See Education—Standards

STANDARDS of length
Should we abolish the inch? R. Nason. il Duns R 82:35-6 S '63

STANDARDS of production. See Production standards

STANDEN, Edith A.
Grand tour. Antiques 83:660-4 Je '63

STANDING congressional committees. See United States—Congress—Committees

STANDISH, Robert
Life is the raw material. Writer 77:20-1+ Jl '64

STANDPIPES
Good style in water storage. il Am City 79: 87-8 My '64
New alloys produce savings in standpipes; Phoenix, Ariz. il Am City 79:24 My '64
Umbrella standpipe doubles storage; Dennis, Mass. G. A. Barker. il Am City 78:14 Je '63

STANFORD, Ann
Motion toward noon; Messenger; poems. Poetry 102:378-9 S '63
Umbrella; poem. New Yorker 39:98 Je 22 '63

STANFORD, Don
Day in spring; story. Redbook 121:24 Ag '63

STANFORD, George S.
Civil defense again. Bul Atomic Sci 20: 35-6 Ap '64

STANFORD, John, jr
Home in Texas. R. Dugger. New Repub 150: 6 Mr 28 '64

STANFORD, Neal
Last days of the Panama Canal. Sci Digest 54:29-31 Jl '63

STANFORD, Peter
Why not go racing? Yachting 113:184-6 Mr '63

STANFORD electronics laboratories
Stanford electronics labs pursues laser, ion-propulsion studies. R. Pay. il Miss & Roc 13:24-5 S 16 '63

STANFORD research institute
Aerospace firms chafe at government control. Miss & Roc 12:21 Je 10 '63
Focusing farther and sharper; long-range planning. il Bsns W p54+ Je 1 '63
Honeycomb propellant matrix could permit solid, liquid mating. il Miss & Roc 14:26+ Ja 20 '64
Stanford: boom in electronics in the San Francisco Bay area was ignited down on the farm. J. Walsh. Science 143:1305-7 Mr 20 '64
SRI composition formulations control combustion instability in solids. W. E. Wilks. Miss & Roc 14:36-7 Mr 9 '64

STANFORD university, Stanford, Calif.
Anti-anythingarians. il Newsweek 63:67 Mr 23 '64
Not that wind; founding of conservative Winds of freedom foundation. Nat R 14: 440 Je 4 '63
Ripping up the campus for an atom gun: Stanford linear accelerator center. il Bsns W p24-5 F 1 '64
What one college freshman found: far from home. J. Dotson. il Seventeen 24:108-9 Ja '65

Graduate school of business

Bared by a B-school; Stanford students at Boise Cascade corp. il Bsns W p90+ Mr 14 '64
Where experts are worlds apart; Stanford conference. il Bsns W p74+ N 7 '64

School of education

Stanford university's School of education. J. W. McKenney. il NEA J 53:46-8 Ap '64

STANG, Joanne
Day our block burned down. Good H 157: 72-3+ Ag '63
Verbal cartoons. N Y Times Mag p 120+ N 3 '63

STANGBYE, Thomas
Disappearing act. il por Newsweek 63:68-9 Je 1 '64

STANGE, Douglas C.
Note on Daniel A. Payne. Negro Hist Bul 28:9-10 O '64

STANGE, Kenneth N. See Nunes, M. E. jt. auth.

STANGEL, Paul J.
New way to apply fertilizer: by air; interview. Suc Farm 62:38+ Je '64

STANGOHR, Clarence
At a Russian monastery. Commonweal 78: 501-3 Ag 23 '63

STANISLAVSKII, Konstantin Sergeevich
Leaves from Stanislavsky's notebooks; excerpts. por UNESCO Courier 16:20-2 N '63
My life in art; excerpts. pors UNESCO Courier 16:15+ N '63

about

Actor with a hundred faces. il pors UNESCO Courier 16:16-19 N '63
Isadora Duncan and Constantin Stanislavsky; with excerpts from letters. N. Rene. il Dance Mag 37:40-3 Jl '63
Stanislavsky; revolutionary of the modern theatre. G. Kristi. il pors UNESCO Courier 16:12-14 N '63

STANISLAVSKI system. See Acting

STANLEY, Aileen
Six comediennes. J. Walsh. il pors Hobbies 68:32-4 O; 32-4 N; 32-4+ D '63; 32-4 Ja '64

STANLEY, Alexander O.
How to go international; excerpts from Handbook of international marketing. Nations Bsns 51:90-2+ S '63
International markets. See issues of Dun's review and modern industry to June 1963

STANLEY, Mrs Ferrell
Fingertip sight. il por Newsweek 62:55 D 30 '63

STANLEY, Henry Morton
Greatest African explorer of all time. D. Peattie and L. Peattie. il Read Digest 82: 258-60+ Je '63

STANLEY, Jackson
Rebel with many causes. New Repub 149:22-4 Jl 13 '63

STANLEY, James
Mail-order psychology. Mlle 59:94-5+ Je '64

STANLEY, John
Indignation as a passionate form of love. Commonweal 80:615-16 S 4 '64

STANLEY, Jon G. and Fleming, W. R.
Excretion of hypertonic urine by a telecost. bibliog Science 144:63-4 Ap 3 '64

STANLEY, Julian C.
Graduate preparation of educational psychologists; address, April 2, 1963. Sch & Soc 91:354-5 N 16 '63

STANLEY, Timothy W.
Gall of Monsieur Gallois. Bul Atomic Sci 19: 27-30 O '63

STANLEY, Wendell M.
Nobelist offers hope. Sci N L 86:214 O 3 '64

STANLEY steamer. See Automobiles, Steam

STANLEYVILLE massacre. See Congo massacre, 1964

STANLY, Jack
Kid from Kentucky. D. Duncan. il pors Dance Mag 37:26-8 Mr '63

STANOVNIK, Janez
Aid, trade and economic development; the changing political context. For Affairs 42: 242-54 Ja '64

STANSGATE, Anthony Neil Wedgwood Benn, 2d viscount. See Benn, A. N. W.

STANTON, Edward S.
Books to be noted; religion. America 109: 675-6+; 110:642-4; 111:712-14 N 23 '63, My 9, N 28 '64
Ecumenics and laymen in the pew. America 109:210-12 Ag 31 '63
People of God. America 110:420-2 Mr 28 '64

STANTON, Frank
Case for political debates on TV. N Y Times Mag p 16+ Ja 19 '64

STANTON, Will
Bombs bursting in air! McCalls 91:71+ Jl '64
Dear Abby; poem. McCalls 91:212 Ap '64
Deck the halls with boughs of whatchamacallit. McCalls 92:122-3+ D '64
Father in the first grade. McCalls 91:82-3+ F '64
Fathers don't stand a chance. Good H 156: 54+ F '63
Friends of Sammy; story. McCalls 91:72-3 Ja '64
Girl in the curio shop; story. Ladies Home J 80:58-9 Mr '63
Golden evenings; story. McCalls 92:54-5 Ja '65
Great outdoors; story. Redbook 123:52-3 Ag '64
Imperfect listener; story. Ladies Home J 80: 106 Je '63
Life TV review. Life 56:10 Je 12 '64
Myra; story. McCalls 91:102-3 Mr '64
Remember me to what's his name. Sat R 46:27-8 Ag 24 '63; Same abr. Read Digest 83:121-2 O '63
To all a good-night; story. McCalls 91:80-1 D '63
Tool catalogs, a critical appraisal. Life 56: 12+ My 1 '64
Where there's smoke. McCalls 91:28+ Ag '64
You know how it is with women; story. Ladies Home J 80:84-5 Ap '63

STAPHYLOCOCCI
Apocatalase of catalase-negative staphylococci. J. Jensen and M. O. Hyde. bibliog il Science 141:45-6 Jl 5 '63
Effect of cold on the presence of staphylococcus aureus in the external nares of the rat. R. H. Poe and others. bibliog il Science 143:487 Ja 31 '64
Inhibition of synthesis of the cell wall of staphylococcus aureus by cephalothin. T. W. Chang and L. Weinstein. bibliog il Science 143:807-8 F 21 '64
Outwit those stay-around staph germs. L. F. Nichols. il Parents Mag 38:74-5+ O '63
Staphlococcal alpha-hemolysin: detection on the erythrocyte membrane by immunofluorescence. A. S. Klainer and others. bibliog il Science 145:714-15 Ag 14 '64
Staphylococcus aureus UC-18: agent of nosocomial infections. R. B. Kundsin and others. Science 145:1322-3 S 18 '64

STAPHYLOCOCCIC mastitis. See Mastitis

STAPHYLOLYTIC enzymes. See Enzymes

STAPLES, James T.
Camper on the beach; poem. Nat Parks Mag 38:13 D '64

STAPLES, Richard C. and Stahmann, M. A.
Malate dehydrogenases in the rusted bean leaf. bibliog Science 140:1320-1 Je 21 '63

STAPLES and stapling machines
Nailing down home sales of staplers. il Bsns W p48 Ap 6 '63
Those speed-work stapling tools. J. Hand. il Pop Sci 184:138-41 Je '64

STAPLETON, Bill
Pictures under pressure. il Pop Phot 52:44-7+ F '63

STAPLETON, Cathy
Owl exhibit on conservation. por Audubon Mag 66:152-3 My '64

STAPP, John Paul
World science will create; excerpt from Space: its impact on man and society, ed. by L. Levy. por Nations Bsns 53:58-63 Ja '65

STAR charts. See Astronomy—Charts, diagrams, etc.

STAR class race. See Sailboat racing

STAR clusters. See Stars—Clusters

STAR flite, limited
Odd saga of the big Bahamas spenders. T. Armbrister. il Sat Eve Post 237:30+ Ag 8 '64

STAR ISLAND, N.H. See Isles of Shoals, Me. and N.H.

STAR measurements. See Astronomical measurements

STAR of Bethlehem (flower)
Ornithogalum. N. E. Dupee. il Flower Grower 42:34-5 N '64

STAR of Bethlehem; drama. See Martens, A. C.

STAR spangled banner festival. See Festivals —Maryland

STARBUCK, George
I dreamt I went shooting fish in my bare chest; poem. Harper 226:77 Ap '63
Out in the cold; poem. New Yorker 39:41 Ap 20 '63
Pit viper; poem. New Yorker 40:121 Ap 11 '64
Starry night; poem. New Yorker 39:42 My 11 '63

STARBUCK, George E.
Librarian fights dismissal in Buffalo court case. Library J 89:1050 Mr 1 '64

STARBUCK, James
Dancing along with Mitch. S. Goodman. il pors Dance Mag 37:30-3+ S '63

STARCH
Glucose transfer from adenosine diphosphate-glucose to starch in preparations of waxy seeds. O. E. Nelson and C. Y. Tsai. bibliog il Science 145:1194-5 S 11 '64
Starch formation induced by a plant parasitic nematode. M. L. Schuster and others. bibliog il Science 143:1342-3 Mr 20 '64
Starch synthesis in excised lemon fruit tissue growing in vitro. H. A. Kordan. bibliog il Science 142:971 N 15 '63

STARCH (for clothes)
Spray starches. il Consumer Rep 29:126-7 Mr '64

STARCH electrophoresis. See Electrophoresis

STARDUST hotel. See Las Vegas, Nev.—Hotels, restaurants, etc.

STARE, Fredrick J.
Sense and nonsense about nutrition. Harper 229:66-70 O '64; Same abr. with title Sense and nonsense about the food we eat. Read Digest 86:58-62 Ja '65
What's your question? questions and answers. por Seventeen 22:160-1+ S '63
—See Trulson, M. F. jt. auth.

STARFISH test. See Atomic bombs—High altitude explosions
STARFISHES
Spawning of starfish: action of gamete-shedding substance obtained from radial nerves. H. Kanatani. bibliog il Science 146:1177-9 N 27 '64
STARK, Freya
Excitement of travelling with a civilized companion. Vogue 143:148-9+ Je '64
On traveling with a notebook. Atlan 214:95-6 D '64
Saying what one means. Atlan 212:102-3 O '63
STARK, George
On sculpture. Sch Arts 63:27-30 Mr '64
STARKER, Janos
Sad hero. il por Time 84:80 O 16 '64
STARKEY, Lycurgus M. Jr.
Christians and the gambling mania. Christian Cent 80:267-70 F 27 '63
Not by pedigree. Christian Cent 81:339 Mr 11 '64
STARKIE, Walter
Carmen and the tarots. Am Rec G 31:4-9 S '64
STARKS, Grady
Through a black man's eyes; ed. by E. Dunbar. pors Look 27:31-5 D 17 '63
STARLETS (actresses) See Moving picture actors and actresses
STARLINGS
Hot foot for birds on inaugural route. il Bsns W p34 O 31 '64
STARNES, Richard
Americanization of Axel. por Field & S 69:10-11+ Ja '65
Anti-gun extremists are at it again. por Field & S 68:12+ Ap '64
Appalachia. Field & S 69:30-3 Jl '64
Billboards, slobs and cemeteries. por Field & S 68:10+ Jl '63
Black with crows. Field & S 67:40-2+ Mr '62
Breakthrough. por Field & S 69:16+ N '64
How to shoot skeet and stay solvent. por Field & S 68:16+ Mr '64
Invitation to a fish fry. por Field & S 69:21-2+ O '64
Is there a cure for the common scold? por Field & S 68:12+ N '63
Lament in a dry climate. por Field & S 68:12+ F '64
On the trail of the wily special interest. por Field & S 69:14+ My '64
Plot to disarm Washington. por Field & S 68:18+ S '63
Predators on the Potomac. por Field & S 67:12+ Mr '63
Rampart we watch. por Field & S 68:12+ Ag '63
Rockahominy project. por Field & S 68:12+ My '63
Shotgunner's mystique. por Field & S 69:14+ D '64
Stewart Udall and the quiet crisis. por Field & S 68:18+ Je '63
Sweet revenge of Mr Toad Clay. Field & S 68:12+ D '63
Think, and live. por Field & S 68:12+ O '63
We're losing the war against slobs. por Field & S 69:12-15 Jl '64
What, me buy a farm? por Field & S 69:20+ Je '64
When you are the hunted. por Field & S 68:14+ Ja '64
When your daughter wants to hunt. por Field & S 67:12-14+ F '63
You might call it CBS distorts. por Field & S 69:20+ S '64
Your right to own a gun; will it be challenged by new restrictions? yes. por Pop Mech 121:94-9+ F '64
STAROVERI. See Raskolniks
STARR, Blaze
Blaze Starr in nighttown. T. B. Morgan. il pors Esquire 62:58-62+ Jl '64
STARR, Isidore
Reapportionment, big issue for the 60's. Sr Schol 85:6T-7T S 30 '64
STARR, John T.
Blue Ridge parkway. Atlan 211:120-1 My '63
Moosehead: Thoreau's North Woods lake. Am For 70:20-3 Je '64
Mount Desert; where the forest meets the sea. Am For 69:36-9 N '63
New England's arctic mountain; Mt Washington. Am For 71:22-5+ Ja '65
Shenandoah trails. Am For 69:16-18+ Je '63
STARR, Kathleen Riordan
Howard Zahniser; poem. Liv Wildn 85:7 Wint '64
STARR, Richard F.
Soviet-American relations; address, February 28, 1963. bibliog Vital Speeches 29:468-73 My 15 '63
STARR, Ricki
Meet Ricki Starr; wrestler with a gimmick. E. Palatsky. il por Dance Mag 37:27 My '63
STARR, S. Frederick
Archeology in the Soviet Union. Yale R 54:311-20 D '64
STARR, Wilmarth
Teaching of foreign languages; current issues and the future; condensation of address. Sch Life 46:7-10 N '63
STARRETT, Agnes Lynch
Agnes Lynch Starrett honored by colleagues. por Pub W 186:54-5 Jl 20 '64
STARRETT, Robert
Photography in the fine arts. IV. Am Artist 27:44-9+ S '63
STARS
Astronomy. J. Stokley. See issues of Science news letter
Black holes in space; dying stars or white dwarfs. A. Ewing. Sci N L 85:39 Ja 18 '64
Deep-sky wonders. W. S. Houston. See issues of Sky and telescope
From whence cometh our light. J. Moorhead. PTA Mag 59:2-3 D '64
Two neutron stars seen. A. Ewing. Sci N L 85:291 My 9 '64
See also
Astrology
Eclipses, Stellar
Galactic systems
Magellanic clouds
Milky way
Occultations
Planets
Universe

Age

New star dating method; measurements of lithium. Sci N L 83:278 My 4 '63

Atmospheres

Atmosphere of cool stars contains water vapor. Sci N L 86:22 Jl 11 '64
Symposium on abundances of elements in stars. B. W. Sitterly. il Sky & Tel 29:11-14 Ja '65

Brightness

See Stars—Magnitudes

Catalogs

Fundamental star positions. Sky & Tel 27:86-7 F '64
Not observed or existing. J. Ashbrook. il Sky & Tel 26:80-1 Ag '63

Classification

Laboratory exercises in astronomy, spectral classification. O. Gingerich. il Sky & Tel 28:80-2 Ag '64

Clusters

Chronology of the galaxy. D. D. Clayton. bibliog il Science 143:1281-6 Mr 20 '64
Globular cluster in Hercules occupies vast volume of space. T. D. Nicholson. il Natur Hist 74:32-5 Ja '65
Globular cluster Omega Centauri. J. Saunders. il Sky & Tel 26:133-7 S '63
How long does a star cluster last? Sky & Tel 27:148 Mr '64
Inside a globular star cluster. A. Boyko. il Sky & Tel 28:269-71 N '64
Planetary systems associated with main-sequence stars. H. Brown. bibliog il Science 145:1177-81 S 11 '64
Rotation of the globular cluster Omega Centauri. Sky & Tel 28:274 N '64

Constitution

Lithium and star aging. Sky & Tel 26:82 Ag '63

Distance

Getting acquainted with astronomy. il Sky & Tel 28:280-1 N '64
Magnitude-distance nomograph; parallax. Sky & Tel 25:139 Mr '63

Magnitudes

Magnitude-distance nomograph. Sky & Tel 25:139 Mr '63
Magnitude scale of stellar brightness had its origin in 120 B.C. T. D. Nicholson. il Natur Hist 73:40-3 Ja '64
Oscillations of quasars. G. C. McVittie. il Science 146:259-60 O 9 '64
Quasi-stellar diameters and intensity fluctuations. J. Terrell. bibliog Science 145:918-19 Ag 28 '64; Reply. B. Hoffmann. 145:1336 S 18 '64
Stellar brightnesses in the far ultraviolet. il Sky & Tel 27:216 Ap '64

Measurements

See Astronomical measurements

STARS—*Continued*

Motion

Automatic measurement of star photographs; determination of accurate proper motions. il Sky & Tel 27:286 My '64
Einstein shift, an unsettled problem. F. Schmeidler. il Sky & Tel 27:217-19 Ap '64
Orbits in the solar and stellar systems; report on International astronomical union symposium 25 on the theory of orbits in the solar system and in stellar systems. D. Brouwer. Science 146:1602-3 D 18 '64
Proper motion survey. Sky & Tel 27:17 Ja '64

Observations

Visual and radio observations of flare stars. O. B. Slee and others. il Sky & Tel 25:83-6 F '63

Parallax

See Parallax, Stellar

Radiation

Visual and radio observations of flare stars. O. B. Slee and others. il Sky & Tel 25:83-6 F '63
Where is science taking us? revision of a paper describing attempt to establish pattern of X-ray emission from the Crab nebula. H. Friedman. il Sat R 47:44-5 Jl 4 '64
X-rays and neutron stars. il Sky & Tel 27: 215-16 Ap '64
X rays in the unknown. il Time 82:79 N 1 '63

Rotation

Oscillations of quasars. G. C. McVittie. il Science 146:259-60 O 9 '64
Rotation of stars. H. A. Abt. il Sci Am 208: 46-53 bibliog(p 184) F '63

Spectra

Ancient stars discovered. A. Ewing. Sci N L 83:98 F 16 '63
Changing spectrum of Deneb. il Sky & Tel 28:132 S '64
Interpretation of the 3- to 4-micron infrared spectrum of Mars. D. G. Rea and others. bibliog il Science 141:923-7 S 6 '63
Laboratory exercises in astronomy, spectral classification; Henry Draper catalogue. O. Gingerich. il Sky & Tel 28:80-2 Ag '64
New spectra of symbiotic stars. il Sky & Tel 27:214 Ap '64
Rotation of stars. H. A. Abt. il Sci Am 208: 46-53 bibliog(p 184) F '63
Twinkle, twinkle 3C-273. Time 81:85-6 Ap 5 '63

STARS, Double

Barnard's star as an astrometric binary. P. Van de Kamp. il Sky & Tel 26:8-9 Jl '63
Companion of Procyon: some prediscovery reports. J. Ashbrook. Sky & Tel 28:72 Ag '64
Mu Cassiopeiae as a double star. Sky & Tel 28:274 N '64

Eclipses

Algol, still a demon star! K. C. Chou. il Sky & Tel 27:24-6 Ja '64

STARS, Dwarf

Barnard's star as an astrometric binary. P. Van de Kamp. il Sky & Tel 26:8-9 Jl '63
Black holes in space; dying stars or white dwarfs. A. Ewing. Sci N L 85:39 Ja 18 '64
Smallest white dwarf? Sky & Tel 27:17-18 Ja '64

STARS, Flare. See Stars, Variable

STARS, Multiple

Planetary systems associated with main-sequence stars. H. Brown. bibliog il Science 145:1177-81 S 11 '64

STARS, New

Astronomical sleuthing finds two star nova; Nova Sagittae. Sci N L 86:342 N 28 '64
Did American Indians see the guest star? discovery of prehistoric drawings. W. C. Miller. il Sat R 47:37-9 Jl 4 '64; Reply. R. Plank. 47:58-9 O 3 '64
Distant supernova remnant. Sci Am 209:59-60 O '63
Dwarf novae (cont) S. Mumford, 3d. il Sky & Tel 26:190-3 O '63
Early spectral changes of Nova Herculis 1963; with Roundup. D. B. McLaughlin. il Sky & Tel 25:206-8 Ap '63
Exploding star visible in early morning sky Sci N L 83:123 F 23 '63
New star of 1572 is still exploding. C. D. Hellman. il Sat R 47:39-43 Jl 4 '64
New supernova theory; search for a neutron star in the crab nebula. A. Ewing. Sci N L 86:53 Jl 25 '64
Nova Puppis 1963. Sky & Tel 27:211 Ap '64
Nova Ursae Minoris 1956. Sky & Tel 26:11 Jl '63
Supersupernova. Sci Am 208:78 Mr '63
Supersupernova confirmed? Sci Am 209:86 S '63
Wild atomic reactions. Sci N L 85:83 F 8 '64

STARS, Photography of. See Astronomical photography

STARS, Subdwarf

Life on unseen planets; lilliputian stars. H. Shapley. il Sci Digest 53:59-64 F '63

STARS, Variable

Algol, still a demon star! K. C. Chou. il Sky & Tel 27:24-6 Ja '64
Bamberg search for bright variable stars. W. Strohmeier. il Sky & Tel 26:264-5 N '63
Eclipsing stars and their periods. R. Szafraniec. il Sky & Tel 28:20-1 Jl '64
Eclipsing variable star observations. il Sky & Tel 27:58-9; 28:244-5 Ja '64, O '64
New observations of AE Aquarii. M. F. Walker. il Sky & Tel 29:23-5 Ja '65
1962 minimum of R coronae borealis. L. J. Robinson. il Sky & Tel 25:94-5 F '63
Observations of eclipsing variable stars. il Sky & Tel 27:316-18 My '64
Observations of eclipsing variables. il Sky & Tel 26:153-4 S '63
R Coronae borealis still active. il Sky & Tel 27:125 F '64
Radio-emitting flare stars. B. Lovell. il Sci Am 211:13-19 bibliog(p 116) Ag '64
Stellar explosion; variable star in Ursa Minor discovered. Sky & Tel 25:135 Mr '63
SZ Herculis observations wanted. il Sky & Tel 25:277 My '63
Variable star notes; investigations by commission of the International astronomical union. il Sky & Tel 29:21-2 Ja '65
Visual and radio observations of flare stars. O. B. Slee and others. il Sky & Tel 25:83-6 F '63
See also
Cepheids

STARTECH cameras. See Cameras

STARTERS, Automobile. See Automobiles—Starting devices

STARTERS, Electronic. See Electronic apparatus and appliances

STARVATION

Dieting the most drastic way; effects of total starvation. il Time 83:31 Ja 24 '64
Starving for science. D. Cort. il Nation 199: 329-31 N 9 '64
See also
Fasting

STASSEN, Harold

Dignified loser drops one more. L. Wainwright. Life 56:27 Mr 20 '64
Most intrepid candidate. Sat Eve Post 237: 78 F 15 '64
Stassen has no time for small talk. N. N. Eller. America 110:813 Je 13 '64

STATE, Heads of. See Heads of state

STATE, The

Memorials, yes: this one no: President Kennedy's inaugural summons. J. Ciardi. Sat R 47:20 S 5 '64
See also
Individual and state
Sovereignty

STATE aid to libraries. See Libraries and state

STATE and agriculture. See Agricultural administration

STATE and art; State and church; etc. See Art and state; Church and state; etc.

STATE and municipal relations

Cities attack problems with new powers. Nations Bsns 52:102+ Ap '64
From bossism to cosmopolitanism: changes in the relationship of urban leadership to state politics. W. C. Havard. bibliog f Ann Am Acad 353:84-94 My '64
State vs. the city: the painful politics of obstruction; Boston. D. B. Carlson. il Arch Forum 120:106-7 Je '64
Supreme court vs. farmer legislatures. Am City 79:7 Jl '64

STATE banks. See Banks and banking—United States

STATE bar associations. See Bar associations

STATE bonds

Ballots for borrowing. Time 84:114 N 13 '64

STATE candidates. See Candidates, Political

STATE colleges. See Colleges and universities, State

STATE control of education. See Education and state

STATE conventions, Political. See Political conventions

STATE courts. See Courts, State

STATE debts. See State finance

STATE department (United States) See United States—State, Department of
STATE departments of education. See Education, State departments of
STATE elections. See Elections—United States
STATE employment service
Job referral is a proper state function. Christian Cent 80:901 Jl 17 '63
STATE encouragement of science, literature and art
Art, non-art: the curse of official culture. R. Brustein. il New Repub 151:85-8+ N 7 '64
Government and art; concerning report, The arts and the national government. W. V. Shannon. Commonweal 78:493-4 Ag 23 '63
New patron; proposed national foundation of the arts. Nation 200:42 Ja 18 '65
President and the arts; remembering JFK. A. Heckscher. Sat R 46:6+ D 14 '63
See also
Art and state
STATE finance
Can the state live on crumbs? federal-state fiscal relations. J. Anderson. il Sat R 48: 31-2+ Ja 9 '65
Fifty states with one big problem, money. il Sr Schol 82:8-10 F 6 '63
Funds for the states; Heller plan. Commonweal 81:436-7 D 25 '64
How to raise money without really trying. il Time 81:29 Ap 5 '63
Road to Washington. America 108:431-2 Mr 30 '63
State-local debt shoots up. U S News 58:75 Ja 4 '65
States: tax, tax; owe, owe. il Time 84:35 N 27 '64
Subsidizing the states; the Heller plan. E. L. Dale, jr. New Repub 151:11-12 N 28 '64; Discussion. 151:29 D 12; 29-30; D 19; 29-30 D 26 '64
Why states and cities are crying for help. il U S News 58:108-9 Ja 25 '65
See also
Taxation, State
STATE flowers
Minnesota, your lady's-slipper is showing. B. Bengston. il Audubon Mag 66:227 Jl '64
Your state flower: bluebonnet Texas. L. Krelove. il Flower Grower 51:46 My '64
Your state flower; California-poppy, California. L. Krelove. il Flower Grower 50:26 My '63
Your state flower: hawthorne, Missouri. L. Krelove. il Flower Grower 50:46 S '63
Your state flower: hibiscus, Hawaii. L. Krelove. il Flower Grower 51:65 Ap '64
Your state flower: orange blossom, Florida. L. Krelove. Flower Grower 50:27 Mr '63
Your state flower: pine cone, Maine. L. Krelove. il Flower Grower 51:66 F '64
Your state flower: sunflower, Kansas. L. Krelove. il Flower Grower 50:46 Jl '63
STATE forestry associations. See Forestry societies
STATE forests. See Forests, State
STATE government investigations. See Government investigations
STATE governments
Case of disappearing power? il Sr Schol 84: 33-5 F 14 '64
How to put the states back in business. E. G. Brown. Harper 229:98+ S '64
Our quaint political folkways. J. Ellison. Nation 197:323-5 N 16 '63
State governments better shape up; the Heller plan. Life 57:4 D 18 '64
Why bail out the states? the Heller plan. C. Jencks. New Repub 151:8-10 D 12 '64; Discussion. 151:28-9 D 26 '64
See also
Governors
STATE governments, Council of. See Council of state governments
STATE hospitals, Psychiatric. See Hospitals, Psychiatric
STATE institutions
See also
Mentally ill—Care and treatment
STATE labor legislation. See Labor laws and legislation—United States
STATE legislation. See Legislation—United States
STATE legislators. See Legislators
STATE legislatures
Citizen views the legislature; address, August 21, 1963. T. H. Hamilton. Vital Speeches 30:26-8 O 15 '63
Democratic sweep: in legislatures, too. U S News 57:10 N 16 '64
Equality in representation: congressional districts. Christian Cent 81:291-2 Mr 4 '64
House Nebraska built. D. Janson. Harper 229:124+ N '64
Ins and outs at State houses. il Newsweek 64:40-2 N 9 '64
Let's put a price tag on our laws; mounting costs of state government. J. N. Miller. il Read Digest 85:217-18+ O '64
My poetic career in Vermont politics. W. J. Smith. il Harper 228:54-62 Ja '64; Discussion. 228:6+ Mr '64
New charter for state legislatures. il Time 83:22-3 Je 26 '64
One man, one vote. Commonweal 80:441 Jl 3 '64
Reapportionment and the courts. A. M. Bickel. New Repub 150:7 Je 27 '64
Reforming decadent state legislatures; address, October 26, 1964. C. S. Rhyne. Vital Speeches 31:118-21 D 1 '64
Shape of the legislatures. il Time 84:43 N 13 '64
Supreme court vs. farmer legislatures. Am City 79:7 Jl '64
U.S. voting map: a year of change. il Newsweek 61:28-30 Mr 25 '63
See also subhead Legislature under names of states, e.g. Texas—Legislature
STATE libraries. See Libraries, State
STATE library associations. See Library associations
STATE library surveys. See Library surveys
STATE liquor authority, New York
Bringing back your own; tax-free liquor. Newsweek 61:57 Ap 8 '63
Bunny money. Newsweek 61:23-4 Ap 29 '63
Corruption uncorked in New York. P. Welch and others. il Life 54:22-31+ Ap 5 '63
Empires of toothpicks; Playboy club's liquor license. Nation 196:366 My 4 '63
Great liquor scandal. Time 81:24-5 Ap 12 '63
More to come? Time 81:18 F 8 '63
Rockefeller's future: will liquor scandals hurt? U S News 54:20 Ap 29 '63
Stiff shot; grand jury investigation. Newsweek 62:35-6 N 18 '63
Thirteenth man; Hyman D. Siegel charged in the liquor scandal. il por Newsweek 61:21 Je 3 '63
To Topeka and Omaha. il Newsweek 61:31 Ap 15 '63
STATE lotteries. See Lotteries
STATE medicine. See Medical service, State
STATE officers
See also
Negro state officers
STATE ownership. See Government ownership
STATE parks and reserves
Parks in your backyard. C. L. Wirth. il Nat Geog Mag 124:647-707 N '63
State park camping facilities. il Recreation 56:127 Mr '63
See also subhead Parks and reserves under names of states, e.g. Tennessee—Parks and reserves
STATE planning
See also
Regional planning
STATE regulation of industry. See Industry and state
STATE rights
Attacks on 14th amendment exposed. Christian Cent 80:732 Je 5 '63
Change the Constitution? Warren urges great debate. U S News 54:19 Je 3 '63
Latest idea for breaking the power of the states. il U S News 54:56-7 My 6 '63
Noted jurist says, repeal the Fourteenth amendment. R. N. Wilkin. U S News 57 72-4 Ag 24 '64
Reaction's refuge; proposed constitutional amendments. K. Crawford. Newsweek 61:31 Je 3 '63
States' rights amendments. il Time 81:22 Je 7 '63
States' rights? proposed amendments. Commonweal 78:269 My 31 '63
To form a much less perfect union. H. S. Commager. il N Y Times Mag p5+ Jl 14 '63
See also
Federal and state relations
STATE superintendents of public instruction
Scholastic teacher interviews: Dr Max Rafferty; ed. by H. Langer. M. Rafferty. Sr Schol 83:5T-7T+ S 20 '63
STATE taxation. See Taxation, State
STATE trees
Sitka spruce, Alaska's new state tree. A. S Harris. il Am For 70:32-5 Ag '64
STATE universities. See Colleges and universities, State
STATE university of New York. See New York state university
STATE visits. See Visits of state

STATEN ISLAND
Relocation of big mains. B. J. Feitelson. il Am City 79:108-10 Mr '64

STATES (United States)
Chart of the fifty states (cont) Sr Schol 83:19-20 O 4 '63; 85:25-6 O 7 '64
See also
Council of state governments
State governments

STATES, Ideal. See Utopias

STATES, New
Africa is poised on the razor's edge. W. A. Nielsen. il N Y Times Mag p11+ F 9 '64
Developing nations' greatest need. C. Bowles. il N Y Times Mag p 15+ Ap 12 '64
Developing nations of the world: necessity of working together; address, December 6, 1963. Prince Bernhard. Vital Speeches 30: 229-33 F 1 '64
Evolution of rising responsibility; address, December 13, 1964. H. Cleveland. Dept State Bul 52:7-12 Ja 4 '65
Frank exchange: private conference of high officials of African nations at Corning, N.Y. New Yorker 40:20-2 Jl 18 '64
How they take their independence. E. Monroe. New Repub 150:20+ Mr 14 '64
Morning after: a study of independence, by B. Crozier. Review
Commentary 38:71-3 Ag '64. R. Owen
1963's new nations. il Sr Schol 83:13 O 4 '63
Political stability in the new African states; address, April 11, 1964; with questions and answers. H. J. Spiro. Ann Am Acad 354:97-109 Jl '64
Reallocation of world responsibilities; address, January 31, 1964. G. W. Ball. Vital Speeches 30:293-6 Mr 1 '64; Same. Dept State Bul 50:287-93 F 24 '64
Results of empire: new problems for old. Newsweek 63:32+ Ja 27 '64
Sweep of nationalism in Africa; address, April 11, 1964; with questions and answers. T. P. Melady. Ann Am Acad 354:91-6 Jl '64
True story of black Africa and its future; interview. G. H. T. Kimble. il U S News 54:72-9 F 11 '63
See also
Malawi
Underdeveloped areas

Economic conditions

Poorer nations face a debt crisis; repaying creditors. il Bsns W p 110+ D 7 '63

History

Newly independent states; with list of states and previous sovereignty. G. E. Pearcy. il Focus 15:1-6 D '64

Politics

Military in the political development of new nations; with basic data on armed forces. M. Janowitz. Bul Atomic Sci 20:6-10 O '64

STATES rights. See State rights

STATESMEN
From friend and foe in America: sense of shock and dismay at the despicable act; statements. U S News 55:49 D 2 '63
Living link to the people; mastery of the games of the West. il Sports Illus 19:56-9 D 23 '63
Most likely to succeed; public officers in China, Russia & western Europe; symposium. il N Y Times Mag p 10-11 Ap 28 '63
See also
Heads of state
Politicians

STATESVILLE prison, Joliet. See Prisons—Illinois

STATIC. See Electricity, Static

STATION wagons
Dodge's new little wagon, how does it compare? V. L. Oertle. il Pop Sci 185:62-4+ Jl '64
How owners rate their new Chevelles. il Pop Mech 121:87-91+ F '64
Kaiser Jeep Wagoneer, 6-passenger. il Consumer Bul 46:22-3 Ag '63
New station wagons raise the roof. Pop Mech 121:116-17 Mr '64
1965 station wagons. Changing T 18:12 D '64
1964 station wagons. il Changing T 17:12 D '63
1963 station wagons. il Consumer Bul 46:16-18 Jl '63
Olds F-85 Vista cruiser wagon. J. Wright. il Motor T 16:20-1 Mr '64
Station wagons. il Consumer Rep 29:292-300 Je '64
Your next new car, sedan or wagon. Bet Hom & Gard 42:44+ N '64

Camping equipment

Station wagon camp boxes. il Sunset 132: 50+ F '64

Equipment

Personal bus for skiing. B. Kocivar. il Look 27:92a-92c Mr 12 '63
Rover's conversion; equipment for explorer-cameraman. H. Zipkin. il Field & S 68: 156-8 Ap '64
Tailgate box increases storage in station wagon. W. J. Jahoda. il Pop Mech 119:180 Mr '63

Prices

Prices, engines and gearing specifications for all U.S. wagons. il Motor T 16:46-9 Jl '64

Rating

Ratings of station wagons. il Consumer Rep 28:302-5 Je '63

Specifications

Prices, engines and gearing specifications for all U.S. wagons. il Motor T 16:46-9 Jl '64

Testing

Fiat 1100 station wagon road test. B. McVay. il Motor T 16:72-5 D '64
Four compact wagons. D. Francis and A. Markovich. il Pop Sci 184:50-3+ Je '64
MT road test; Cortina GT and Estate wagon. J. Wright. il Motor T 16:80-5 Ap '64
MT road test; Opel Kadett & Caravan 1000. M. Lamm. il Motor T 16:42-6 Ap '64
MT road test: room at the top Buick Skylark wagon. J. Wright. il Motor T 16:22-5 Mr '64
Station wagons. il Consumer Rep 28:295-301 Je '63
Toyota land cruiser station wagon road test. B. McVay. il Motor T 16:66-9 Mr '64
World of wagons; Chevrolet Impala; Ford Country Squire; Rambler Classic V-8; Falcon Six; Chevy II Nova Six; Fairlane Ranch Wagon; Plymouth Fury; Pontaic Safari; Dodge 440; Rambler American. il Motor T 16:22-45 Jl '64

STATION wagons, Foreign
Fiat 1100 station wagon road test. B. McVay. il Motor T 16:72-5 D '64
Foreign station wagons. Changing T 18:26 Ja '64
Spotlight on the Opel Kadett. E. Nelson. il Pop Mech 121:40+ Ap '64

STATIONERY
Dear pen pal. il Seventeen 23:184 S '64
Embossing stationery. Consumer Bul 47:22 D '64
For belles lettres. il House & Gard 123:196-9 My '63
Well-dressed letter. House & Gard 124:25+ O '63
What counts in quality stationery. Good H 157:173 D '63
See also
Letterheads

STATIONS, Railroad. See Railroads—Stations

STATIONS in space. See Space stations

STATIONS of the cross
Subway stations of the cross. C. B. Egan. America 110:367-9 Mr 21 '64

STATISM
Issue of statism. H. Hazlitt. Newsweek 64: 68 Jl 27 '64

STATISTICAL methods
See also
Sampling (statistical methods)

STATISTICS
Not so vital statistics; comp. by H. Helfer. il N Y Times Mag p90 D 1 '63; 40 S 13 '64
Qui numerare incipit errare incipit; excerpts from On the accuracy of economic observations. O. Morgenstern. il Fortune 68:142-4+ O '63; Reply. J. Shiskin. Fortune 69:66 F '64
See also
Religious statistics
also subhead Statistics under various subsubjects, e.g. Cancer—Statistics

STATISTICS coordinating project. See American library association—Statistics coordinating project

STATISTICS of sampling. See Sampling (statistical methods)

STATUARY. See Statues

STATUE of liberty
Mighty woman with a torch. il Sr Schol 85: 7 O 28 '64

STATUES
Horsemanship; statue of Rhodes returned to British South Africa co. Time 84:33 D 18 '64

STATUES—*Continued*
Shapes from the ancient earth. il Horizon 5:66-7 N '63
See also
Monuments
Plaster casts
Portrait sculpture

STATURE
Can you predict how tall a child will grow? il Good H 156:156-7 Je '63
Hormone gives girls boost in height. Sci Digest 53:33 My '63
How tall will your child be? S. S. Rosenberg. Parents Mag 40:42-3+ Ja '65
King-size kids; Japanese getting taller. il Newsweek 64:50+ O 12 '64
Man grows bigger if not better. H. L. Shapiro. il N Y Times Mag p 13+ D 15 '63
Tall girl meets tall boy; Elinor Provonsha and Bill Barbour. S. Gordon. il Look 27: 56-8+ My 21 '63

STATUS (law)
See also
United States—Armed forces—Legal status, laws, etc.

STATUS, Social. See Social status

STATUS of forces agreements. See United States—Armed forces—Legal status, laws, etc.

STATUTE of limitations. See Limitations (law)

STAUBACH, Roger Thomas
Dick Smith's roommate. por Newsweek 62: 105-6 O 21 '63
Jolly Roger. il pors Time 82:92-4+ O 18 '63
Navy's S bomb. H. L. Masin. por Sr Schol 83: 22 N 15 '63
Setting for greatness at Philadelphia; Army-Navy football game. D. Jenkins. il pors Sports Illus 19:32-4+ D 2 '63
Showdown for a quarterback. M. Cope. il Sat Eve Post 237:28-9 O 17 '64
Staubach of navy: humility under pressure. T. Cohane. il pors Look 28:68-73 S 22 '64

STAUDACHER, Frank Lester
Staudacher: man with a mission. E. Crimmin. il pors Motor B 115:109-11+ Ja '65

STAUDACHER, Les
Water, as in hard; racing high-speed powerboats. Sports Illus 18:14 Je 17 '63

STAUDINGER, Else
Else Staudinger's 100-million-dollar gift to Uncle Sam. M. T. Bloom. Read Digest 85:189-90+ Ag '64

STAUFFENBERG, Claus Schenk von
Men who tried to kill Hitler; excerpts, ed. by J. Naar. R. Manvell and H. Fraenkel. il por Look 28:50-2 D 15 '64
When the big one (Hitler) got away. S. D. Smith. il por N Y Times Mag p86-8+ My 24 '64

STEAD, Bill
Hell's angels fly again. J. N. Bell. il Sat Eve Post 237:28-31 N 7 '64

STEAD, Frank W.
Tritium distribution in ground water around large underground fusion explosions. bibliog Science 142:1163-5 N 29 '63

STEAD, William T.
Astounding William T. Stead. W. S. Smith. Christian Cent 80:855-8 Jl 3 '63

STEAK. See Beef

STEALING
Couple apprehended with stolen documents in Detroit. Pub W 185:136 F 24 '64
Couple convicted in stolen documents case. Pub W 186:54 Jl 20 '64
Crook's tour. H. Pask. Travel 119:51+ Ap '63
Girl's best friend; diamond-switching theft at Winston's and Tiffany's. Newsweek 65: 32 Ja 25 '65
Great gem caper; theft of gems from American museum of natural history. il Newsweek 64:38+ N 16 '64
He who steals my purse steals my credit cards. Time 83:53 Je 19 '64
Hi' Joe, where are you? racing greyhound stolen. J. Lovesey. il Sports Illus 22:20-1 Ja 25 '65
Ice-blue ending; Star of India returned. il Newsweek 65:24+ Ja 18 '65
Museum jewel robbery; gems taken from New York city's American museum of natural history. il Time 84:23 N 6 '64
NACS: management seminar studies how to measure, control pilferage. M. Saul. il Pub W 186:30-3 S 21 '64
Never on Thursday; A. K. Madsen's jewel thefts. Newsweek 61:33 My 6 '63
Night they stole the Star of India; gem theft, New York's American museum of natural history. il Life 57:77-80 N 13 '64
Open locker 0911; clues to recovery of gems taken from New York city's American museum of natural history. il Time 85:23 Ja 15 '65
Pilferage and some methods of controlling it; college stores. F. J. Worthington; J. R. Shaw; D. Staggs. Pub W 185:33-5 My 25 '64
Sea-going dragnet; theft and recovery of Chee Chee V. P. Handelman. il Yachting 114:130 D '63
Thieves meet match in waterfront game; G-men fences. il Bsns W p 118+ F 23 '63
$350,000 loot in a 25¢ locker; recovery of jewels looted from the American museum of natural history. M. Acoca. il Life 58:30-3 Ja 22 '65
32nd-story men; office thievery. Time 82:36 Ag 16 '63
See also
Art thefts
Automobiles, Theft of
Boats, Theft of
Book thefts
Embezzlement
Shoplifting
Thieves

STEAM, Natural
Drilling for power; geothermal resources. il Bsns W p60 Ja 18 '64
Uncorking earth's steam kettle. il Sci N L 86:154-5 S 5 '64

STEAM automobiles. See Automobiles, Steam

STEAM barkentines. See Sailing vessels

STEAM baths. See Baths, Vapor

STEAM carriages
See also
Automobiles, Steam

STEAM engines
Steam engine (cont) M. Banister. il Pop Mech 119:196-9 F '63
See also
Locomotives

History

Origins of the steam engine. E. S. Ferguson. il Sci Am 210:98-107 bibliog(p 152) Ja '64

STEAM generators. See Boilers

STEAM locomotives
See also
Locomotives

STEAM-spray irons, Electric. See Electric irons

STEAM yachts. See Yachts and yachting

STEAMBOATS. See Steamships and steamboats

STEAMSHIP lines
Dream of domination; state-owned Italian line. il Time 81:88+ Mr 29 '63
Fleet's in. J. H. Winchester. il Travel 122: 41-3 S '64
Italy bids to rule the waves; North Atlantic passenger service. il Bsns W p 148-50+ F 23 '63
To the sea in ships; increase in passenger traffic. Bsns W p31 Ja 26 '63
See also
American export lines
Cunard steamship company
Hamburg-American line
Lykes brothers steamship company
United States lines

STEAMSHIPS and steamboats
All steamed up. il Newsweek 63:76 Mr 2 '64
Down river in a Mark Twain idyl; aboard river boat Admiral Jones, sternwheeler. il Life 55:91-2 Jl 19 '63
Going places, finding things on a Mississippi paddle wheeler. M. C. Burke. il House & Gard 126:44-6+ N '64
Staffordshire and steam. R. J. LeBoeuf, jr. il Antiques 85:666-70 Je '64
Steamboat on San Francisco Bay. C. Darlington. il Motor B 111:50+ My '63
See also
Naval architecture
Ocean liners
Steamship lines

Automation

Piping all hands to the pushbuttons; automation at sea. il Bsns W p92-4 Ja 25 '64
When machines replace seamen; mechanized ships. il Bsns W p 100+ Ja 25 '64

Food service

Dining adventures in the South Seas; luxury cruise on S.S. Monterey. S. Spitzer. il Holiday 35:82-3+ Je '64

History

Steamboat's charter of freedom; Gibbons v. Ogden. G. Dangerfield. il Am Heritage 14: 38-43+ O '63

STEARNS, Jean. See Stearns, M. W. jt. auth.

STEARNS, John F.
Referral relationships. por Library J 89:1011-14+ Mr 1 '64

STEARNS, Marshall W.
Jazz (cont) Mus Am 83:134 Ja; 41-2 F; 25-6 Mr; 45 My; 34 O; 49 N; 281-2 D '63; 84:53-4 F; 55 Mr; 63 Ap; 57 My; 54 Jl; 57 S; 46-7 O; 270 D '64
Jazz in New York. Mus Am 83:35 F '63
—and Stearns, Jean
Little background on tap dancing. Esquire 62:192-3+ D '64
STEARNS, Myron
He makes accidents obsolete. Pop Mech 120: 101-4+ Ag '63
How your pocket may be picked. Read Digest 85:48-50 Ag '64
STEARNS, Peter N.
Patterns of industrial strike activity in France during the July monarchy. bibliog f Am Hist R 70:371-94 Ja '65
STEARNS, Richard
Stars that shine with Tokyo gold. H. Whall. il por Sports Illus 21:20-1 Ag 17 '64
STEBBINS, Doris E.
Add a row of mint. Pop Gard 14:82-3 My '63
Bed of mint. Horticulture 41:254-5 My '63
Gardening on a dime. Horticulture 41:308-9 Je '63
Green and white accents. Horticulture 41: 380 Jl '63
Herbs in the teapot. Horticulture 41:402 Ag '63
How to succeed with sweet peas. Horticulture 42:14-15 F '64
Perennials for color through August. Horticulture 41:224-5 Ap '63
STEBBINS, Fred
How to play tennis on the wall. il Todays Health 42:46-8 O '64
STEBBINS, Richard P.
Global goblins and good fairies. Sat R 47:34-6 Ag 15 '64
STEBBINS, William C. and Smith, O. A. Jr
Cardiovascular concomitants of the conditioned emotional response in the monkey. bibliog Science 144:881-3 My 15 '64
STECHLER, Gerald
Newborn attention as affected by medication during labor. bibliog Science 144:315-17 Ap 17 '64
STECKEL, Anita
Mom art. il Esquire 60:134-5 O '63
STECKLER, Larry. See Buckwalter, L. jt. auth.
STEDMAN, Alfred D.
St Croix: who owns a river? Nation 199:490-3 D 21 '64
STEDMAN, Jane W.
Most ingenious paradox. Opera N 27:24-7 F 16 '63
Smiling sigh. Opera N 28:24-5 F 29 '64
Un-sound principle? Opera N 28:12 Ja 25 '64
Wagner in travesty. Opera N 27:24-7 F 23 '63
Wizard of the North. Opera N 29:23-7 D 5 '64
STEEBNER, R. E.
Good lighting spells progress. Am City 79: 82-3 Jl '64
STEEGMULLER, Francis
Books. New Yorker 39:114-16 Ja 18 '64
Ciao Fabrizio. New Yorker 40:205-8+ O 10 '64
In the lobby; story. New Yorker 40:228 N 28 '64
STEEL, Ronald
Britain and Europe: the lesson of Skybolt. Commonweal 77:507-9 F 8 '63
De Gaulle on Vietnam. Commonweal 80:141-3 Ap 24 '64
De Gaulle's deadline. Commonweal 81:412-14 D 18 '64
Demise of NATO. Commentary 35:397-402 My '63
Disintegrating alliance. Commonweal 78:127-9 Ap 26 '63
Eyestrain at Cannes. Commonweal 80:361-4 Je 12 '64
Foreign interests. Commentary 37:80-2 Mr '64
Fortress America. Commentary 36:119-24 Ag '63
In place of NATO. New Repub 151:19-22 N 14 '64
Is Congress obsolete? Commentary 38:59-64 S '64
Movies. Christian Cent 80:1137-8, 1550-2+ S 18, D 11 '63
Speaking out; excerpt from End of alliance por Sat Eve Post 237:10+ Mr 28 '64; Same abr. with title Is NATO obsolete? Read Digest 85:152-4 S '64
Venice observed. Commonweal 81:97-9 O 16 '64
(ed) See Fraser, D. M. Congress in the atomic age
(ed) See McDade, J. M. Congress in the atomic age
—and Lineberry, William
Race for the moon. Commonweal 78:321-3, 428-9 Je 14, Jl 12 '63

STEEL
High-strength steels. il Sci N L 84:46-7 Jl 20 '63
New horizons for steel boatbuilding. S. F. Manning. il Motor B 114:40-1 D '64
Take a good look at steel; and discover the beautiful things it can do in and around a house. il House & Gard 125:94-7 Ja '64
See also
Nickel steel

Anecdotes, facetiae, satire, etc.

Be the first on your block to have a ton of steel. M. Kitman. il Sat Eve Post 237:26-7 Ap 4 '64

Cold working

Contact-bend-stretch rolling. Sci Am 210:64 My '64

Prices

Big steel. New Repub 148:5 Ap 20 '63
Can price rise help steel? il U S News 54: 35-7 Ap 22 '63
Competition keeps the price boosts down. Bsns W p29-30 My 4 '63
Dumping dispute. Time 81:86 Ap 26 '63
It's spelled Steele. Time 81:103 Ap 19 '63
Latest chapter in the story of steel prices. il U S News 54:40-1 Ap 29 '63
Letting the market decide the price. Bsns W p204 Ap 20 '63
LBJ and the rise. Newsweek 65:64 Ja 11 '65
Now, only a murmur. il Time 81:22 Ap 26 '63
Politics of steel. il Nat R 15:380 N 5 '63
Price control by warning. H. Hazlitt. Newsweek 61:81 Ap 29 '63
Price hikes ahead? Time 84:95 O 9 '64
Price rise chorous swells in steel. Bsns W p 120 O 24 '64
Problem remains. Nation 196:337 Ap 27 '63
Raising the price. Sr Schol 85:23 Ja 14 '65
Roger Blough on the problems of steel pricing. R. Blough. Fortune 71:139 Ja '65
Speaking out. Time 83:83 My 8 '64
Steel: another day, another JFK. Newsweek 61:67-8 Ap 29 '63
Steel price hike. Commonweal 78:156 My 3 '63
Steel price increases prompt antitrust probe. Bsns W p25 O 26 '63
Steel prices hiked. il Sr Schol 82:18 My 1 '63
Steel prices hit with the big one; Justice dept's trustbusters charging producers with price-fixing. il Bsns W p27-8 Ap 11 '64
Steel; the price-fixing charges. Time 83:102+ Ap 17 '64
Steele's crucial decision; recover costs, make a profit. il Newsweek 61:71-2 Ap 22 '63
Steel's folly. New Repub 148:5 Ap 27 '63
This time they make it stick. il Bsns W p33-4 Ap 20 '63
U.S. grand jury probes steel prices. Sr Schol 83:5-6 N 8 '63
Up, steel! Nat R 14:347 My 7 '63
Wall Street shrugs off steel price rises. il Bsns W p 112+ My 4 '63
Wheeling tests the water. Bsns W p27 Ap 13 '63
See also
Government investigations—Steel industry and trade

Stockpiling

See Stockpiling

Strength

New alloy for some tough jobs: maraging steel. il Bsns W p87-8 Ap 18 '64

STEEL, Stainless
From razor blades to rockets. D. Fossen. Pop Sci 183:126-7 O '63
Guide to stainless steel finishes. D. W. Pettigrew. il Arch Rec 133:217-18 Mr '63
How to use stainless steel for flashing. il Arch Rec 134:201-2 N '63
Stainless; magic word intended to sell razor blades. il Consumer Bul 46:2+ N '63
Steel that shaves the world; Sweden's Sandvik steel supplies stainless to Gillette. il Bsns W p63-4+ O 5 '63
Steelmakers' edge: Sweden's stainless blade market. il Time 82:93 S 20 '63
STEEL alloys
Strength of steel. V. F. Zackay. il Sci Am 209:72-82 bibliog(p 140) Ag '63
See also
Nickel steel
STEEL ball: story. See Bongartz, R.
STEEL castings
Continuous casting of steel. L. V. Gallagher and B. S. Old. il Sci Am 209:74-88 bibliog(p 178) D '63
New cast in steel. il Fortune 70:235-6 N '64

STEEL castings—*Continued*
New shortcut for specialty steels: pressure casting. Bsns W p54 F 29 '64
Steel without ingots. Bsns W p36 Mr 16 '63
Tower of steel. Time 81:87 Mr 29 '63
See also
Continuous casting

STEEL construction
Adaptable house dramatizes use of steel. il Arch Rec 135:58-61 mid-My '64
Bold and direct, using metal in a strong, basic way. il Arch Rec 136:135-42 Jl '64
Crisp design with steel components. il Arch Forum 118:118-19 Mr '63
Development house built of an architect-designed steel component system. il Arch Rec 133:82-5 mid-My '63
Emhart: a bold, pragmatic structure of concrete and steel. il Arch Forum 119:88-95 Jl '63
Guide to stainless steel finishes. D. W. Pettigrew. il Arch Rec 133:217-18 Mr '63
High-rise apartment structures of steel. R. M. Gensert. il Arch Rec 136:206-9 N '64
Metal shielding used as wall form. il Arch Rec 134:160 Jl '63
Nine buildings receive A.I.S.C. awards. il Arch Rec 134:14-15 S '63
Rhythm and symmetry in a steel-framed house. il Arch Rec 135:48-53 mid-My '64
Steel reveals new strength. il Arch Forum 119:115-17 N '63
Tallest steel bearing walls; New York's proposed World trade center. il Arch Rec 135:194-6 My '64
Tension band prestresses pleated roof. il Arch Rec 133:209 Mr '63
Two-story house using a system of steel components. il Arch Rec 133:126-9 mid-My '63

STEEL framing. See Framing (building)

STEEL furniture. See Furniture, Metal

STEEL industry and trade
Dumping dispute. Time 81:86 Ap 26 '63
Excess capacity, new trade challenge. il Nations Bsns 51:56-8 Ag '63

Finance

Tax changes replenish the till. il Bsns W p64 F 9 '63
Wall Street shrugs off steel price rises. il Bsns W p 112+ My 4 '63
Watch on prices. Newsweek 62:81 N 4 '63
Why steel foresees a feast: with tables. Bsns W p20-1 D 28 '63

International aspects

War over steel. il Time 82:66 Ag 23 '63

Wages and hours

Hard-hit Erie forge tries a pay cut ploy. Bsns W p50 S 14 '63
Is the lid coming off for bigger pay increases? il U S News 57:95-7 O 19 '64
Labor month in review; steel settlement. Mo Labor R 86:III-IV Jl '63
New-style contract in steel; meaning for other industries. il U S News 55:77 Jl 1 '63
Next step for sabbaticals. Bsns W p35-6 Ag 3 '63
Next wage test; steel to outdo autos? il U S News 57:92+ O 5 '64
Of cars and steel and tottering guideposts. T. R. Brooks. il Reporter 31:23-5 D 17 '64
Pay cut ratified, 1,200 jobs saved. U S News 55:87 O 28 '63
Satisfactory steel settlement. il Time 81:74 Je 28 '63
Settlement in steel. T. R. Brooks. Commonweal 78:449-52 Jl 26 '63
Steel accord near? Bsns W p27 Je 15 '63
Steel prices hiked. il Sr Schol 82:18 My 1 '63
Steel settlement without a raise? U S News 54:100 Je 10 '63
Steel settlement without crisis? now industry, union are hopeful. U S News 54:108 My 13 '63
Steel settles. Bsns W p23 Je 22 '63
Steel talks start icily. il Bsns W p 116 D 19 '64
Steel-wage talks: industry's position. U S News 57:74-5 D 28 '64
Steel's Abel to raise Cain; imminent collective bargaining sessions between the United steelworkers (USW) and the basic steel industry. H. Kasper. New Repub 152: 11-13 Ja 16 '65
Steel's harder face. Bsns W p 102 D 12 '64
USW nears time of decision. Bsns W p30 Mr 16 '63
Wages in the basic iron and steel industry, March 1962. L. E. Lewis. il Mo Labor R 86: 289-92 Mr '63
Where wages are heading in 1963. il U S News 54:93-4 Ap 29 '63

Canada

Steel: old giant with new tricks. I. Wolfert. il Read Digest 82:228-30+ F '63

Europe, Western

Uncommon authority: Common market's tariff raised. Time 83:84 Ja 17 '64
See also
European coal and steel community

France

France's no. 2 is trying harder; Pont-a-Mousson industrial holding company. il Bsns W p45-6+ Ja 23 '65

Great Britain

Letter from London; debate in Commons on nationalization. M. Panter-Downes. New Yorker 40:198-200 N 21 '64
Struggle for steel; debate over nationalization. il Time 85:70 Ja 22 '65

India

Key test of U.S. aid: socialized steel for India. il U S News 54:75-6 Ap 15 '63
Why a steel mill for India hit a foreign-aid roadblock. il U S News 55:42 S 2 '63

Japan

New no. three in steel. il Time 84:82 Jl 17 '64

United States

Backlog of decisions. Time 85:73A+ Ja 29 '65
Big change comes to steel; from open hearth furnace to oxygen furnace and computers. il Bsns W p78-81+ Ag 15 '64
Big change in steelmaking. W. Cloud. il Pop Sci 185:72-5+ D '64
Big steel. New Repub 148:5 Ap 20 '63
Blast from Simon; management of West Virginia's Wheeling steel. il Time 84:59 D 25 '64
Can steel keep up its pace in 1965? il Bsns W p32-3 D 5 '64
Collective bargaining; big steel passes a big test. il Newsweek 62:51-4 Jl 1 '63
Competition moving inland. Time 84:100+ D 11 '64
Counterattack. il Newsweek 62:82 O 7 '63
Dry run for steel talks. il Bsns W p92 Ja 19 '63
Dumping. Newsweek 61:76 F 25 '63
Feast or famine. il Newsweek 62:72 Jl 8 '63
Five-letter word for progress; address, November 17, 1964. L. T. Johnston. Vital Speeches 31:185-8 Ja 1 '65
Glitter returns to steelmen's treasuries. il Bsns W p84+ F 15 '64
Good old days are back again. il Bsns W p29 Je 6 '64
Grassroots militance in steel; model labor pact threatened. Bsns W p 118+ Ag 22 '64
Human attitude in steel talks. il Newsweek 61:81-2 Je 24 '63
Increasing tempo. Newsweek 63:83 Je 8 '64
Indictment; charges of conspiracy by Federal grand jury. il Newsweek 63:93-4 Ap 20 '64
Nonstop talks instead of nonstop strikes; steel's Human relations committee. A. H. Raskin. il N Y Times Mag p 12+ Jl 7 '63
Now, only a murmur. il Time 81:22 Ap 26 '63
Out for a bigger steel bite. il Bsns W p82-3+ F 16 '63
Outsider tries his hand at firing up a lagging steelmaker; N. Simon, new chairman of Wheeling steel. il Bsns W p 18-19 D 26 '64
Pinch is on in steel plate. Bsns W p27 My 23 '64
Price-fix charged; indictment by Federal grand jury. Sr Schol 84:20 My 1 '64
Price of profits. Newsweek 64:81-2 N 9 '64
Rising profits & prices. il Time 82:97 N 1 '63
Small ones; smaller companies prosper by producing just a few kinds of steel. il Time 84:92 S 4 '64
Steel: a big comeback for a growth industry. il U S News 56:97-9 Je 22 '64
Steel: another day, another JFK. Newsweek 61:67-8 Ap 29 '63
Steel gets hit with the big one; Justice dept.'s trustbusters charging producers with price-fixing. il Bsns W p27-8 Ap 11 '64
Steel hedging starts. il Bsns W p36-7 S 26 '64
Steel: old giant with new tricks. I. Wolfert. il Read Digest 82:228-30+ F '63
Steel price increases prompt antitrust probe. Bsns W p25 O 26 '63
Steel reopening uncertain; industry-USW human relations committee. Bsns W p 172 My 18 '63
Steel rolls toward a new record. Bsns W p31 Ag 29 '64

STEEL industry and trade—United States —*Continued*
Steel surprises its own prophets. il Bsns W p80-2 O 19 '63
Steel: the bargaining talks begin. il Newsweek 64:45 D 28 '64
Steel: the giant under fire. D. R. Jones. il Sat Eve Post 237:21-9 Je 27 '64
Steel will set bargaining pace. Bsns W p46 Ja 2 '65
Steel without strikes; with editorial comment. il Bsns W p25-6, 124 Je 29 '63
Steel's cautious hopes. il Time 81:85 Mr 22 '63
Surge of steel. il Newsweek 64:77-9 S 28 '64
This time they make it stick. il Bsns W p33-4 Ap 20 '63
USW sees no strike; credit to Human relations committee. il Bsns W p29 F 23 '63
When steel seeks help from Uncle Sam: steel's case against imports. il Bsns W p80-1 F 15 '64
Why steelmen raise the ante; capital spending boom. il Bsns W p 144+ N 16 '63
See also
Strikes—United States—Steel industry and trade
also names of steel companies, e.g. Kaiser steel corporation

STEEL metallurgy
Big change comes to steel; from open hearth furnace to oxygen furnace and computers. il Bsns W p78-81+ Ag 15 '64
Big change in steelmaking; oxygen process. W. Cloud. il Pop Sci 185:72-5+ D '64
Counterattack; basic-oxygen furnaces. il Newsweek 62:82 O 7 '63
Strength of steel; Ausform and Maraging processes. V. F. Zackay. il Sci Am 209:72-82 bibliog(p 140) Ag '63
See also
Steel castings

STEEL scrap. See Scrap metal

STEEL sculpture. See Metal sculpture

STEEL strikes. See Strikes—United States—Steel industry and trade

STEEL water tanks. See Water tanks

STEEL workers
In steel: no strike, longer vacations, longer contracts. il U S News 54:86 Je 24 '63
Second battle of Homestead. J. G. Colangelo, jr. il Reporter 29:29-31 Jl 18 '63
Two young steelworkers make New York new; with photographs by J. H. Karales. C. Brossard. Look 27:30-3 Mr 26 '63
See also
Steel industry and trade—Wages and hours
United steelworkers of America

STEEL works
New glow in steel technology; with paintings by J. R. Clift. Fortune 71:128-35 Ja '65

STEELE, Duane
Special-interest cars. Motor T 16:76 N '64

STEELE, H. Ellsworth, and Fisher, Homer, jr.
Study of the effects of unionism in southern plants. bibliog f Mo Labor R 87:258-70 Mr '64

STEELE, James P.
Where rural patients get air-age care. H. G. Earl. il por Todays Health 42:14-16 My '64

STEELE, John L.
Political virtuoso gathers the forces to take on the job. Life 55:32-5 D 13 '63
(ed) See Rusk, D. Secretary discusses Berlin in filmed interview

STEELE, Jonathan
Mississippi comes North to Harlem. New Repub 152:10-11 Ja 30 '65

STEELE, Max
Cat and the coffee drinkers. New Yorker 39:105-6+ My 11 '63

STEELE, Peter
Your competitors; address, November 21, 1963. Vital Speeches 30:373-6 Ap 1 '64

STEELE, Robert
Contagious spirit. Christian Cent 82:54 Ja 13 '65

STEELE, Thomas S.
Twice around in Adios. Yachting 116:34-6+ D '64; 117:98-100+ Ja '65

STEELE, William
Programmed instruction from teacher viewpoints. Sr Schol 84:9T-10T Mr 13 '64

STEELHEAD trout fishing. See Trout fishing

STEELINK, Cornelius. See Spitzer, J. C. jt. auth.

STEELWORKERS union. See United steelworkers of America

STEEN, Charles Augustus
What became of Pick and Steen? Fortune 69:164 F '64

STEEPLECHASING. See Horse racing

STEER wrestling. See Rodeos

STEERE, Ralph E. jr
Preparing for IR. Duns R 82:pt2 107-9+ S '63

STEERE, Russell L.
Tobacco mosaic virus; purifying and sorting associated particles according to length. bibliog Science 140:1089-90 Je 7 '63

STEERE, William C.
Plant hunter goes in search of Alaska's arctic plants. il por Flower Grower 51:22-3 Mr '64

STEERING gear
See also
Motor boats, Outboard—Steering gear
Rudders

STEERING gear, Automobile. See Automobiles—Steering gear

STEET, Marion L.
Teaching in the big city. NEA J 53:18-20 D '64

STEFANELLI, Vladimir Clain-. See Clain-Stefanelli, V.

STEFANILE, Felix
Catalogue of nine. Poetry 103:324-9 F '64
Ode for Pindar for William Carlos Williams; Fortune hunter; Cartoon for Aristotle; My long lost brother; poems. Poetry 102:147-51 Je '63

STEFANO, Giuseppi di
Halftone crisis; La Scala opera company. Time 81:60 F 8 '63

STEFANO, Joseph
Monster-of-the-month; Outer limits. il Newsweek 63:55 Ja 27 '64

STEFFEK, Edwin F.
Budding. Pop Gard 14:68+ Jl '63

STEFFENS, Lincoln
How I made a crime wave; excerpt from Autobiography of Lincoln Steffens. Read Digest 85:160D+ D '64

STEFFENSEN, James P.
Board-staff negotiations. Sch Life 47:6-8 O '64

STEGER, John Lee
Beautiful gamble for Johnny. A. Lake. i McCalls 91:62+ S '64

STEGNER, Wallace
Born a square: the westerners' dilemma Atlan 213:46-50 Ja '64
Creative writer as an image maker; excerpt from Creative writing. Writer 76:24 O '63
Megalopolis and the country all around. Liv Wildn 82:23-4 Winter '62
Ordeal at Devil's Gate. Esquire 61:100-1+ Je '64

STEGNER, Walter
Quiet crisis or lost cause? Sat R 47:28+ S 19 '64

STEHLI, F. G. and Helsley, C. E.
Paleontologic technique for defining ancient pole positions. Science 142:1057-9 N 22 '63

STEHLIK, Antoninus
Collaborationist priests. America 110:621-2 My 9 '64

STEHLIN, Paul
Evolution of western defense. For Affairs 42:70-83 O '63

STEICHEN, Edward
Life in photography; excerpts. il Look 27:28-37 N 5 '63
Steichen and his sound; interview. ed. by T. Schwartz. por Pop Phot 55:18 S '64
Steichen talking; excerpts from A life in photography. por Vogue 142:160-1 N 15 '63
about
Critics at large. D. Vestal. il Pop Phot 55:22+ Jl '64
Edward Steichen way out; photographs from Steichen: a life in photography. H. Keppler. Mod Phot 28:74-7 F '64
Steichen. il pors Vogue 142:156-9 N 15 '63
Steichen: a life in photography. M. R. Weiss. il Sat R 46:23-5 N 2 '63
Steichen, Atget. il Newsweek 62:100-1 N 4 '63

STEIG, Jeremy
Creative thing. New Yorker 40:46-7 O 17 '64

STEIG, William
Some notes on affectation; excerpt. il Vogue 141:114-15 F 15 '63
X-ray pen; excerpts from Continuous performance. il Sat R 46:20-1 F 16 '63

STEIGER, Rod
Steiger, the Pawnbroker. por Newsweek 62:75 D 23 '63

STEIN, Clarence S.
Regional pattern for dispersal. Arch Rec 136:205-6 S '64

STEIN, Edith
Manner is contemporary. Sister Mary Catherine. America 109:214-15 Ag 31 '63
Simone Weil and Edith Stein: modern mystic-martyrs. N. Braybrooke. Christian Cent 81:1461-3 N 25 '64

STEIN, Emanuel
Dilemma of union democracy. bibliog f Ann Am Acad 350:46-54 N '63
STEIN, Gabriel, and Forgacs, Chaim
Permselective membranes: spectroscopic and conductivity effects. Science 142:953-4 N 15 '63
STEIN, Gerald
All creatures great and small; story. Redbook 124:36-7 Ja '65
For I have wept; story. Sat Eve Post 237:46-50 Ja 4 '64
STEIN, Gertrude
What happened. Criticism
Commonweal 79:227 N 15 '63
What is remembered, by A. B. Toklas. Review
Time il por 81:97-8 Mr 22 '63
STEIN, Joseph
Enter laughing; dramatization of novel by C. Reiner. Criticism
Commonweal 78:47 Ap 5 '63
Nation 196:333 Ap 20 '63
New Yorker 39:74 Mr 23 '63
Newsweek 61:98 Mr 25 '63
Sat R 46:40 Ap 6 '63
Theatre Arts 47:72 My '63
Time il 81:77 Mr 22 '63
STEIN, Kenneth J.
Relay 2 designed for enhanced reliability. Aviation W 79:53+ D 9 '63
STEIN, Lawrence
Inorganic fluorine chemistry. Science 143:1058-60 Mr 6 '64
STEIN, Louis
You have to change to grow. il por Bsns W p48-9+ Mr 2 '63
STEIN, Manfred
Little boy at the wall. il pors Look 27:30-5 Je 18 '63
STEIN, Richard S.
Rheo-optics of polymers; report on conference. Science 144:1252-3 Je 5 '64
STEIN, Robert
Proof that money isn't everything. Sat R 46:40 N 23 '63

about

JFK, the magazines, and peace. J. Tebbel. il Sat R 46:56-7 D 14 '63
STEIN, Theodore
Automation & library systems; excerpts from Strengthening and coordinating reference and research library resources in New York state. bibliog por Library J 89:2723-34 Jl '64
STEIN, Toby
Carrousel; poem. Cath World 197:379 S '63
STEIN and Day, incorporated
Stein and Day: it's like a personal bookshop. il Pub W 186:40-1 N 2 '64
Stein & Day to publish for Lincoln Center theatre. Pub W 184:46-7 N 18 '63
Stein and Day to publish Olympia press series. Pub W 186:39-40 S 21 '64
STEINBECK, John
John Steinbeck's acceptance speech. Vogue 141:16 Mr 1 '63
Travels with Charley; condensation. Read Digest 84:275-8+ Je '64

about

Living legends. A. Robin. Todays Health 41:5 Ap '63
Our man in Helsinki. New Yorker 39:43-5 N 9 '63
STEINBERG, Alfred
Heavenly way to run a railroad. Read Digest 82:175-80 My '63
STEINBERG, Arthur G. and Wilson, J. A.
Hereditary globulin factors and immune tolerance in man. bibliog Science 140:303-4 Ap 19 '63
—See Polmar, S. H. jt. auth.
STEINBERG, Charles S.
Mass communication and the social sciences. Sch & Soc 92:105-6 Mr 7 '64
STEINBERG, David
Newarker speaks up for Noork. N Y Times Mag p99-100 O 20 '63
STEINBERG, Hy
Before you buy a portable drill. Am Home 67:86+ Ja '64
Big shift to electric heat. Am Home 67:82+ Mr '64
How to handle the finances for your custom-built home. Am Home 66:42-3 N '63
STEINBERG, Malcolm S.
Reconstruction of tissues by dissociated cells. bibliog Science 141:401-8 Ag 2 '63
STEINBERG, Michael
Bach, Major, and Minor. Sat R 46:36 Ap 13 '63
Brandenburgs by Klemperer. Sat R 46:72 O 26 '63
STEINBERG, Philip Orso
If baby could talk when you take his picture. il Farm J 88:62-3 Ja '64
STEINBERG, Rafael
Gems that grow on command. Sat Eve Post 237:70-3 Je 27 '64
Hello! wonderful! the world is one. Reporter 31:26-8 D 31 '64
Lonely line of armistice. Sat Eve Post 236:24-31 Jl 27 '63
Mr Hilton opens a hotel. Sat Eve Post 236:68-9 N 2 '63
Proud new jazzy age. Sat Eve Post 237:76-8+ O 17 '64
STEINBERG, Saul
Steinberg at the races. il Sports Illus 19:40-7 N 11 '63

about

For eloquence and precision. Pub W 183:71 Je 3 '63
STEINBERG, Sheldon S.
Cancer, a new look at what's happening. Suc Farm 61:92+ Ap '63
Get a medical checkup, it may save your life. Suc Farm 62:63 O '64
Six myths of the health cults. Todays Health 42:8-10 Ja '64
What you should know about health insurance. Suc Farm 62:84 O '64
STEINBERG, William
Leader of equals. il por Time 84:48 S 11 '64
Music to my ears; Steinberg's Bruckner. I. Kolodin. Sat R 47:40 D 5 '64
Pittsburgh's Steinberg. por Mus Am 83:24 Ag '63
Recordings. M. Mayer. Esquire 62:66+ O '64
Steinberg's programming. H. Kupferberg. il Atlan 214:134+ O '64
STEINBRUNNER, Richard A.
Goodwill recreation program. por Recreation 57:408-9 O '64
STEINEM, Gloria
Crazy legs; or, The biography of a fashion. N Y Times Mag p58+ N 8 '64
James Baldwin, an original. Vogue 144:78-9+ Jl '64
Mrs Kennedy at the moment. Esquire 62:125-7+ O '64
1964, won't you please come in? Ladies Home J 81:41-2+ Ja '64
Visiting Englishmen are no roses. N Y Times Mag p63-4 Mr 29 '64
STEINER, Clyde
Travel darkroom? Pop Phot 54:134-7 Ap '64
STEINER, George
Building a monument. Reporter 30:37-9 My 7 '64
Lafayette, where are we? Reporter 28:42-3 My 9 '63
Literature under a deadline. Reporter 28:50+ Ja 17; 10+ F 28 '63
Nerve of Günter Grass. Commentary 37:77-80 My '64
On Paul Goodman. Commentary 36:158-63 Ag '63
Thought in a green shade. Reporter 31:35-6 D 31 '64
STEINER, Ralph
Dangerous necessity to dramatize. Pop Phot 54:48-9+ F '64
STEINER, Stan
Always be thankful when you catch whales. Horizon 6:64-5 Sum '64
American Indian; ghettos in the desert. Nation 198:624-7 Je 22 '64
STEINER, W. G. and others
Influence of methodology on electroencephalographic sleep and arousal: studies with reserpine and etryptamine in rabbits. bibliog Science 141:53-5 Jl 5 '63
STEINFELD, George. See Rock, I. jt. auth.
STEINFELS, Peter
Testing the conscience of the church. Commonweal 81:244-6 N 13 '64
STEINHARDT, Carol
Summer action, sailing. U S Camera 26:58-9+ Ag '63
STEINHILBER, August W.
Bible reading in the public schools. bibliog f por Sch Life 46:13-16 O '63
STEINIGER, Edward L.
How to find oil the modern way. il por Time 82:98 S 13 '63
STEINMANN, Jean
Book reviews. J. A. Fitzmyer. America 109:597-8 N 9 '63
STEINMANN, Marion
Ultrasonic surgery to save a boy's eye. Life 58:46 Ja 15 '65
STEINMETZ, Joseph N. Jr
Test complex simulates Polaris re-entry heat. Miss & Roc 14:24-5 Ja 6 '64
STEINMETZ, Lucile Evans
What's biting you? Sci Digest 54:69-71 Ag '63

STEIRMAN, Hy
Publishing paper & ink. Time 82:32 D 27 '63
STELE, Sanford
Schnabel reappraised. Sat R 47:48 Ja 25 '64
STELLA, Sister Maris. See Maris Stella, Sister
STELLA, Joseph
Art galleries; memorial exhibition at the Whitney museum. R. M. Coates. New Yorker 39:184-7 N 23 '63
Consistent inconsistency of Joseph Stella. E. C. Baker. il Art N 62:46-7+ D '63
New York was his wife. il Time 82:70 N 8 '63
STELLA; story. See Rey, S.
STELLAR aberration. See Aberration (optics)
STELLAR eclipses. See Eclipses, Stellar
STELLAR-inertial guidance systems. See Guided missiles—Control
STELLAR magnitudes. See Stars—Magnitudes
STELLAR motion. See Stars—Motion
STELLAR parallax. See Parallax, Stellar
STELLAR radiation. See Stars—Radiation
STELLAR systems. See Stars—Clusters
STELLE, Charles C.
Balanced approach to disarmament; statement, October 29, 1963. Dept State Bul 49:793-8 N 18 '63
—See Tsarapkin, S. K. jt. auth.
Der STELLVERTRETER; drama. See Hochhuth, R.
STELOFF, Frances
Wise men fish here: the Gotham book mart. L. Caine. il pors Pub W 187:38-42 Ja 11 '65
STEM rust. See Rusts (botany)
STEMKE, G. W.
Allotypic specificities of A- and B-chains of rabbit gamma globulin. bibliog Science 145: 403-5 Jl 24 '64
STEMLER, Dorothy C.
Carefree roses. Horticulture 42:35-6+ Ja '64
STENBERG, Henning
Make mine toneline! U S Camera 26:64-5 Mr '63
STENCIL work
Modern art of stenciling. G. O'Brien. il N Y Times Mag p 112-13+ D 1 '63
Stencils are in style. J. Peter. il Look 27:42 S 24 '63
See also
Silk screen printing
STENDER, Ron
Two timer. Hot Rod 17:54 Ag '64
STENGEL, Casey
Stengel ponders, The year of the Berra. L. Koppett. il pors N Y Times Mag p21+ Ap 12 '64
STENGEL, Charles Dillon. See Stengel, C.
STENGREN, B.
Monster that moves by night. Am City 78: 84-5 N '63
STENMAN, Alex
Men and machines cut one-third off sweeping bill. Am City 79:111-12 Mr '64
STENNIS, John C.
People of the week. por U S News 54:20 Je 3 '63
STENODUS beetles. See Beetles
STENOGRAPHY. See Shorthand
STENT, Gunther S.
Operon: on its third anniversary. bibliog Science 144:816-20 My 15 '64
STENZEL, H. B.
Aragonite and calcite as constituents of adult oyster shells. bibliog Science 142:232-3 O 11 '63
Oysters: composition of the larval shell. bibliog Science 145:155-6 Jl 10 '64
STEP pyramids. See Pyramids
STEP stools. See Stools
STEPAN, Alfred
Religion, revolution and reform. Commonweal 81:547-9 Ja 22 '65
STEPANCHEV, Stephen
Library guard; poem. Sat R 46:10 N 30 '63
Lizard in the sun; poem. Nation 197:96 Ag 24 '63
STEPCHILDREN
It's a new world; excerpts from Stepchild in the family. A. W. Simon. McCalls 91:78-9+ F; 66+ Mr; 76+ Ap; 86+ My '64
STEPHEN, Edith
Edith Stephen and dance company, 92nd street Y. M. Marks. Dance Mag 38:70 Ap '64
STEPHENS, Alan
Doctor Williams and tradition. Poetry 101: 360-2 F '63
My friend the motorcyclist; Side-gallery for some insects; poems. Poetry 102:80-4 My '63
Terminations, revelations. W. Stafford. Poetry 104:105-6 My '64
STEPHENS, Claude O.
Great day in the morning for Texas gulf sulphur. R. Sheehan. il por Fortune 70:135-40+ Jl '64
STEPHENS, Mae Webb
Garden in a basket. Flower Grower 50:15-16 Je '63
Perennials from a mandarin's garden. Horticulture 41:378 Jl '63
STEPHENS, Olin
Yachting interviews: Olin Stephens, ed. by B. Robinson. por Yachting 116:47+ D '64
about
To keep the cup, get a man who knows how. H. Whall. il por Sports Illus 20:42-5 Ja 6 '64
STEPHENS, Peggy. See Stephens, W. jt. auth.
STEPHENS, William, and Stephens, Peggy
Romance of pearls. Read Digest 83:45-6+ O '63
STEPHENS college, Columbia, Mo.
Person-to-person teaching; Amplified telephone project. C. F. Madden. il Sat R 47: 50-1+ Jl 18 '64
Library
Stephens college library instruction program. B. Bartlett. ALA Bul 58:311-14 Ap '64
STEPHENSON, J. Gregg
Satellites: scientific mission and design. Science 139:776+ F 22 '63
STEPHENSON, J. W.
Collect refuse, not complaints. Am City 78:97-9 O '63
STEPHENSON, Sir William Samuel
Room 3603, the story of the British intelligence center in New York during World war II, by H. M. Hyde. Review
Nat R 15:159-60 Ag 27 '63. G. Morgenstern
STEPINAC, Aloysius, cardinal
Stepinac: lest we forget. America 109:35 Jl 13 '63
STEPPARENTS
How to be a stepparent. J. Cook. il N Y Times Mag p86+ Ap 19 '64
It's a new world; excerpts from Stepchild in the family. A. W. Simon. McCalls 91:78-9+ F; 66+ Mr; 76+ Ap; 86+ My '64
STEPPING stones. See Garden walks
STEPS, Garden. See Garden steps
STERBA, Monica
Walk in the forest; story. Harper 229:79-84 S '64
STEREO amplifiers. See Amplifiers
STEREO loud speakers. See Loud speaking apparatus
STEREO recorders. See Magnetic recorders and recording
STEREO vision. See Space perception
STEREOPHONIC phonograph. See Phonograph—Stereophonic equipment
STEREOPHONIC phonograph records. See Phonograph records—Stereophonic records
STEREOPHONIC pickup. See Phonograph—Stereophonic pickup
STEREOPHONIC radio receiving apparatus. See Radio receiving apparatus, Stereophonic
STEREOPHONIC recorders. See Magnetic recorders and recording—Stereophonic recorders
STEREOPHONIC sound. See Sound—Stereophonic recording and reproducing
STEREOPHOTOGRAPHY
Coming 3-D revolution. J. Tebbel. Sat R 47: 127-8 Mr 14 '64
Creative color; scoop on 3D. A. Rothstein. U S Camera 27:10+ Je '64
Laser revolution in 3D photography. il Sci Digest 57:8-9 Ja '65
Look's illusion; parallax panoramagram. il Time 83:66 F 21 '64
3D. il Look 28:102-5 F 25 '64
Three-dimensional photography without viewing aids. A. Rothstein. U S Camera 27:12+ Ja '64
See also
Stereoscope
STEREOSCOPE
Through the stereoscope. J. Walsh. il Hobbies 68:24-5+ Ag; 26-7 S; 28 O '63; 69: 28-9 Jl; 28 N '64
STEREOSCOPIC photography. See Stereophotography
STEREOSCOPIC viewers. See Stereoscope
STEREOSCOPY
Binocular depth perception without familiarity cues. B. Julesz. bibliog il Science 145: 356-62 Jl 24 '64

STEREOTYPE (psychology)
Ghosts of dead stereotypes. E. Blake, jr. Negro Hist Bul 26:212-14 Ap '63
STEREOTYPE characters. See Characterization
STERILITY
Flat-chested opinion; Strassmann's theory of relationship between brains and bosoms. Newsweek 64:61 S 14 '64
Making parenthood possible. R. Franklin. Redbook 124:50+ N '64
Overcoming infertility; excerpts from Planning your family. A. F. Guttmacher. Parents Mag 39:46-7+ Ag '64
Self-sterile auxotrophs and their relations to heterothallism in sordaria fimicola. A. S. El-Ani. bibliog il Science 145:1067-8 S 4 '64
STERILITY in insects
Cytoplasmic sterility in drosophila paulistorum which is ultimately dependent on nuclear genes. L. Ehrman. bibliog Science 145:159 Jl 10 '64; Reply with rejoinder. V. G. Meyer. 145:1460 S 25 '64
Insect fertility: inhibition by folic acid derivatives. M. M. Crystal. bibliog il Science 144:308-9 Ap 17 '64
See also
Chemosterilants
STERILIZATION
Ethylene oxide sterilization of tissue culture media. B. L. Brown and R. Fuerst. bibliog il Science 142:1654-5 D 27 '63
Life in a life island. il Time 83:52 My 29 '64
See also
Space vehicles—Sterilization
STERILIZATION, Sexual
Birth control by surgery. J. Ridgeway. New Repub 151:9-11 N 14 '64
Sterilization; facts and arguments. A. F. Guttmacher. Nation 198:344-7 Ap 6 '64
Voluntary sterilization. Time 85:43-4 Ja 15 '65
See also
Chemosterilants
Vasectomy
STERILIZATION of defectives, criminals, etc.
Difficulties of getting desterilized; case of Miguel Vega Andrade in California Supreme court. il Time 84:88 N 13 '64
STERILIZING chemicals. See Chemosterilants
STERLE, David E.
Student approach to recruitment; college students. por Recreation 57:318 Je '64
STERLING, Albert
Amplifier power: how much is enough? Hi Fi 13:54-7+ N '63
Distortion: the eternal enigma. Hi Fi 14:50-3+ S '64
Headphones up to date. Hi Fi 14:52-5 Ap '64
Stereo cartridges. Hi Fi 15:52-5+ Ja '65
What to listen for, and why. Hi Fi 13:41-3+ Je '63
STERLING, Carlos Márquez
Henry Clay: forerunner of Pan-Americanism. Américas 16:1-6 My '64
STERLING, Claire
Apertura a sinistra: second round. Reporter 29:28-32 N 21 '63
Can the Congo go it alone? Reporter 30:27-31 Je 18 '64
Chou En-lai and the Watusi. Reporter 30:22-4 Mr 12 '64
Cyprus: the archbishop can't lose. Reporter 30:12-16 Je 4 '64
End of a dream in Southern Rhodesia. Reporter 28:29-33 My 9 '63
Harold Wilson's hour. Reporter 31:17-20 N 5 '64
Italian elections: even worse than before. Reporter 28:22-5 My 23 '63
Italian tightrope act. Reporter 30:30-2 F 13 '64
Kenya discovers the perils of *uhuru.* Reporter 30:26-9 My 7 '64
Miracle is over: Italy's morning after. Reporter 31:33-4+ S 24 '64
Never-ended war of the Middle East. Reporter 29:24-8+ Jl 18 '63
One-man rule in Algeria. Reporter 29:32+ O 10 '63
Six move toward union. Reporter 32:25+ Ja 14 '65
Tanganyika: the tribulations of a good man. Reporter 30:21-5 Ap 9 '64
Tortuous way of Palmiro Togliatti. Reporter 31:35 S 24 '64
When will the Congo be ready for independence? Reporter 28:25-8 Ap 11 '63
STERLING, Clarence
Crystal structure of weddellite. bibliog Science 146:518-19 O 23 '64
STERLING, John
Natural heritage. Recreation 57:112-14 Mr '64
STERLING, Thomas
Black pawns of Bantustan. Reporter 29:42-4+ O 10 '63
Nigeria: the waking land. Holiday 34:32+ D '63
On being naked. Holiday 36:8+ Ag '64
Osagyefo thinks deep. Reporter 31:30-2 N 5 '64
Our far-flung correspondents. New Yorker 39:162+ N 16 '63
STERLING (money) See Money—Great Britain
STERLING and Francine Clark art institute, Williamstown, Mass.
Forain: genius at the periphery. il Art N 62:43+ Ap '63
Rococo master in Williamstown. Art N 63:44+ S '64
STERLING bowl tournament. See Roses. Arrangement of
STERLING Forest gardens. See Gardens—New York (state)
STERLING municipal library, Baytown, Tex.
Determination in Baytown. H. J. Blasick. il Library J 88:4538-40 D 1 '63
STERLING silver. See Silverware
STERN, Arnold. See Lowenstein, L. M. jt. auth.
STERN, Bert
Topsy-turvy flashbacks to yesteryear's films: big stars take old roles; photographs. Life 55:54-67 D 20 '63
STERN, Curt
(tr) See Baltzer, F. Theodor Boveri
STERN, Daniel
His letters hid a secret life. Sat R 47:43-4 S 12 '64
STERN, Edith M.
Do you fight about money? Parents Mag 38:54-5+ My '63
Something new for campers. Parents Mag 39:58-9+ Mr '64
You do marry the family. Parents Mag 39:70-1+ Ap '64
STERN, Elizabeth, and others
Hormone excretion patterns in breast and prostate cancer are abnormal. bibliog Science 145:716-19 Ag 14 '64
STERN, Evelyn
(tr) See Baltzer, F. Theodor Boveri
STERN, Hans
Man of many facets. il por Time 84:104-6 S 11 '64
STERN, Isaac
Notes from abroad; interview, ed. by R. McMullen. por Hi Fi 14:12+ Ja '64
STERN, J. David
National debt and the peril point. Atlan 213:35-8 Ja; 40 Mr '64
STERN, James L.
Automation; end or a new day in unionism? bibliog f Ann Am Acad 350:25-35 N '63
STERN, Karl
Prototype of the modern European. Commonweal 79:326-8 D 6 '63
STERN, Laurence, and Knoll, Erwin
Congress: when the private life of a lawmaker becomes a public affair. Esquire 61:82-6 Ap '64
—See Knoll, E. jt. auth.
STERN, Lothar
Science of vanishing electronics. Sci Digest 55:44-7 Je '64
SCR: silicon controlled rectifiers: new applications in the home. Electr World 70:27-30+ O '63
STERN, Louis
Collector's double-takes. il por Life 54:68A-68B+ Ap 26 '63
STERN, Marina
Talkie pop. il Time 84:68 Jl 24 '64
STERN, Philip M.
Machines are more important than people (yes or no?) N Y Times Mag p33+ D 1 '63
Russell Long's tax plan. New Repub 149:8-9 N 16 '63
Slow, quiet murder of tax reform; excerpts from Great Treasury raid. Harper 227:63-8 D '63; 228:11 Ap '64
Tax deviates; excerpt from The great Treasury raid. New Repub 150:11-13 F 1 '64
about
Some deductions. D. T. Bazelon. Commentary 38:67-8 Ag '64
STERN, Philip M, family fund. See Philip M. Stern family fund
STERN, Richard G.
Orvieto dominos, Bolsena eels; story. Harper 228:68-70 Je '64
Witty way with life. G. Hicks. Sat R 47:35-6 D 12 '64
STERN, Richard Martin
Cherishing kind: story. Good H 157:58-9 D '63
One day it's different; story. Good H 156:90-1 F '63
Secret place; story. Redbook 124:163-86 N '64

STERN, Robert
Behind the headlines. Sat R 47:38 N 14 '64

STERN, Robert M.
Policies for trade and development. bibliog f Int Concil 548:3-63 My '64

STERN, Walter E.
Eight ways to pitch a tarp; reprint. Recreation 56:123 Mr '63

STERN, William L. and Eyde, R. H.
Fossil forests of Ocú, Panama. Science 140: 1214 Je '63

STERN drives. See Marine engines

STERN gang. See Jews in Palestine—Resistance movement

STERN-Istomin-Rose trio. See Trios, Instrumental

STERNBACH, Richard
Feeling no pain; studies of the mechanisms of pain at the Massachusetts mental health center. il por Newsweek 62:61 Jl 8 '63

STERNBERG, Brian
My search for faith; ed. by J. Poppy. pors Look 28:78-82+ Mr 15 '64
Something went wrong. il por Time 82:60 Jl 12 '63
Trampoline tragedy. Newsweek 62:57 Jl 15 '63

STERNBERG, Hilgard O'Reilly
Brazil: complex giant. For Affairs 43:297-311 Ja '65

STERNBERGIA
For flowers in early autumn. il Sunset 133: 148 Ag '64

STERNCO industries, incorporated
Tropical fish take the profit hook. il Bsns W p84+ N 14 '64

STERNE, Laurence
Shandy's Sterne. R. Payne. il por N Y Times Mag p 118-20 N 24 '63

STERNGLASS, E. J.
Cancer; relation of prenatal radiation to development of the disease in childhood. bibliog Science 140:1102-4 Je 7 '63

STEROID hormones. See Hormones, Sex

STEROLS
Sterol induction of reproduction and stimulation of growth of pythium and phytophtora. J. W. Hendrix. bibliog il Science 144:1028-9 My 22 '64
Sterols in recent aquatic sediments. R. B. Schwendinger and J. G. Erdman. bibliog il Science 144:1575-6 Je 26 '64

STESSIN, Lawrence
Business goes on a manhunt. N Y Times Mag p37+ N 8 '64
New look at arbitration. N Y Times Mag p26+ N 17 '63

STETHOSCOPE
Discoverer of the stethoscope. il Todays Health 42:68 Mr '64

STETSON, Harlan True
Obituary
Sky & Tel 28:340 D '64

STETSON, Joe
(ed) Gun dogs. See issues of Field & stream

STETSON, Paul W.
Care and culture of tropical water lilies in the North. Horticulture 41:262-3 My '63

STEUBEN, Friedrich Wilhelm von
Von Steuben day; proclamation, September 15, 1964. L. B. Johnson. Dept State Bul 51:472 O 5 '64

STEUBEN glass. See Glassware

STEUBEN glass, incorporated
Poetry in three dimensions; Poetry in crystal exhibition. J. Ciardi. il Sat R 46:22-5 Ap 20 '63

STEVEDORES. See Longshoremen

STEVEN, William P.
Improving the product in Houston. por Time 82:36 Ag 23 '63

STEVENS, Christian
On the death of Father James Kittleson; poem. Commonweal 78:401 Jl 5 '63

STEVENS, Dana
Circusiana. See issues of Hobbies

STEVENS, David
Great opera houses: Prague. Opera N 28:25-9 D 28 '63
Notes from abroad. Hi Fi 13:40+ S; 30+ O '63

STEVENS, Denis
Songs of life and love in ancient Nuremberg. Hi Fi 15:71 Ja '65
Soupçon of vibrato. Hi Fi 14:53-5+ Ja '64
Struggle for perfection: conductors' rehearsals on record. Hi Fi 14:80+ O '64

STEVENS, Edmund
Comely cosmonaut. Ladies Home J 80:60+ S '63
Love and marriage, Soviet style. N Y Times Mag p 16-17+ Ap 26 '64
—See Alsop, S. jt. auth.

STEVENS, Frank A.
Challenge to the publisher; excerpts from address, October, 1964. bibliog f por Library J 89:4966-8 D 15 '64

STEVENS, George
Greatest story ever told; filming in Utah desert. W. Trombley. il por Sat Eve Post 236:34-40+ O 19 '63

STEVENS, Harold
Made of gummed paper tape; excerpts from Ways with art. Design 65:26-9 S '63

STEVENS, Inger
Inger Stevens. R. W. Lewis. il pors Sat Eve Post 237:20-1 Ja 4 '64

STEVENS, J. E. company
J. & E. Stevens co. F. H. Griffith. Hobbies 68:44 Mr '63

STEVENS, J. P. and company
Durable threads of J. P. Stevens. R. J. Whalen. il Fortune 67:102-9+ Ap '63
J. P. Stevens seeks a future beyond textiles. il Bsns W p98-9+ Mr 23 '63

STEVENS, James
Forest giant. por Am For 70:3 N '64

STEVENS, Janet R. T.
Pratt's service to students. por Wilson Lib Bul 39:384-8 Ja '65

STEVENS, Leonard A.
Top-secret mania. Nation 197:218-21 O 12 '63

STEVENS, Risë
Quote: unquote; interview, ed. by C. S. Susa. por Mus Am 84:20 O '64

about

American singer. A. M. Lingg. il pors Opera N 28:14-16 Mr 7 '64

STEVENS, Roger L.
President's arts adviser speaks at annual meeting of book committee; excerpts from address, December 10, 1964. Library J 90: 210 Ja 15 '65

STEVENS, Ruth
Sun dance; poem. Horn Bk 39:95 F '63

STEVENS, Ruth W.
Band concerts in the park. Recreation 56: 332 S '63

STEVENS, S. S. and Guirao, Miguelina
Scaling of apparent viscosity. bibliog Science 144:1157-8 My 29 '64

STEVENS, Stella
Fair young Hollywood girls. R. W. Lewis. por(p23) Sat Eve Post 236:24-5 S 7 '63

STEVENSON, Adlai Ewing
Accomplishments of 18th session of the U.N. General assembly; statement, December 18, 1963. bibliog f Dept State Bul 50:130-3 Ja 27 '64
Action by the United Nations; address, October 22, 1964. Vital Speeches 31:98-101 D 1 '64
Albanian proposal to change U.N. representation of China rejected; statement, October 16, 1963. Dept State Bul 49:755-8 N 11 '63
Anatomy of world leadership; address, April 3, 1964. bibliog f Dept State Bul 50:615-21 Ap 20 '64
Cooperation in outer space; statement, December 2, 1963. bibliog f Dept State Bul 49:1005-14 D 30 '63
Dedication of church center for the United Nations; address, September 22, 1963. Dept State Bul 49:573-4 O 14 '63
Eleanor Roosevelt: a lady for all seasons. Sat R 47:26-7 O 10 '64
Emerging consensus on economic and social development; statement, July 10, 1963. Dept State Bul 49:265-72 Ag 12 '63
Excerpt from address, November 15, 1961. Cong Digest 43:206+ Ag '64
Fifteenth anniversary of Universal declaration of human rights; statement, December 9, 1963. bibliog f Dept State Bul 50: 19-20 Ja 6 '64
Hard kind of patriotism. Harper 227:31-4 Jl '63
Human rights; address, January 28, 1964. Vital Speeches 30:323-6 Mr 15 '64
India and Pakistan urged to make new effort on Kashmir problem; statement, February 14, 1964. Dept State Bul 50:425-6 Mr 16 '64
Kenya and Zanzibar admitted to United Nations membership; statement, December 16, 1963. bibliog f Dept State Bul 50:32 Ja 6 '64
No apologies; excerpts from address. Sr Schol 85:18-19 Ja 7 '65
No mission but peace, no enemy but war. McCalls 92:112-13+ O '64
Our hemisphere; the long and short views; address, April 15, 1963. Dept State Bul 48: 704-9 My 6 '63. Excerpts Américas 15:44 Je '63
Pace-setters; interview. por Mlle 59:280 Ag '64

STEVENSON, Adlai Ewing—*Continued*
Promise of science and technology: address, November 12, 1964. Dept State Bul 51: 810-15 D 7 '64
Prospects for democracy around the world; address. Vital Speeches 29:305-9 Mr 1 '63
Security council again condemns apartheid in South Africa; statement, December 4, 1963. Dept State Bul 50:92-5 Ja 20 '64
Security council calls for ban on sale of arms to South Africa; statement, August 2, 1963. Dept State Bul 49:333-7 Ag 26 '63
Security council considers Southern Rhodesian question; statement, September 11, 1963. Dept State Bul 49:559-61 O 7 '63
Security council continues debate on Cambodian complaint; two statements, May 26, 1964. Dept State Bul 50:937-41 Je 15 '64
Security council continues U.N. force in Cyprus; statement, September 17, 1964. Dept State Bul 51:561-3 O 19 '64
Security council hears U.S. charge of North Vietnamese attacks; statement, August 5, 1964. Dept State Bul 51:272-4 Ag 24 '64
Security council team to examine Cambodia-Viet-Nam border areas; statement, June 4, 1964. Dept State Bul 50:1002-4 Je 29 '64
Security council votes extension of peace-keeping force in Cyprus; statement, June 19, 1964. Dept State Bul 51:64-7 Jl 13 '64
17th session of the U.N. General assembly: major accomplishments; statement, December 21, 1962. Dept State Bul 48:147-52 Ja 28 '63
Situation in Panama: statements, January 10, 1964. Dept State Bul 50:153-5 F 3 '64
Soviet Union vetoes U.S.-U.K. resolution in Security council on Israel and Syrian complaints; statement, August 28, 1963. Dept State Bul 49:520-2 S 30 '63
Statement on financial situation of the United Nations, June 21, 1963. Dept State Bul 49: 181-2 Jl 29 '63
Strengthening the machinery for peace; address, June 2, 1964. Dept State Bul 50: 966-71 Je 22 '64
Trained intelligence: the Nation's greatest weapon; address, June 12, 1963. Vital Speeches 29:581-4 Jl 15 '63
U.N. calls on states to refrain from orbiting weapons; statement, October 16, 1963. Dept State Bul 49:753-4 N 11 '63
U.N. General assembly holds memorial meeting; statement. Dept State Bul 49:894-5 D 9 '63
United Nations: hope for the future; address, October 24, 1963. Dept State Bul 49:766-73 N 18 '63. Same Vital Speeches 30:68-72 N 15 '63
United Nations: its value to the United States; statement, March 13, 1963. Dept State Bul 48:522-8 Ap 8 '63
United Nations pays tribute to memory of Mrs Roosevelt; statement, November 9, 1962. Dept State Bul 48:48-50+ Ja 14 '63
U.N. security council adopts resolution on Cyprus; statement, March 4, 1964. Dept State Bul 50:465 Mr 23 '64
U.N. Security council calls for ceasefire in Cyprus; statement, August 9, 1964. Dept State Bul 51:318 Ag 31 '64
U.N. Security council condemns apartheid in South Africa; sets up committee to study sanctions; statements, June 16 and June 18, 1964. Dept State Bul 51:29-33 Jl 6 '64
U.S. calls for constructive approach to Congo problem; statements, December 22 and December 24, 1964. Dept State Bul 52:43-6 Ja 11 '65
U.S. calls for frontier patrol to help prevent border incidents between Cambodia and Viet-Nam; statement, May 21, 1964. bibliog f Dept State Bul 50:907-13 Je 8 '64; Same. Vital Speeches 30:483-7 Je 1 '64
U.S. calls for negotiation of Malaysia-Indonesia dispute; statement, September 10, 1964. Dept State Bul 51:448-50 S 28 '64
U.S. cites illegal interference in support of Congo rebellion; statement, December 14, 1964. Dept State Bul 52:15-24 Ja 4 '65
U.S. comments on U.N. mission's Cambodia-Viet-Nam report; letter, September 9, 1964. Dept State Bul 51:527-9 O 12 '64
United States explains position on Portuguese territories; statements, July 26 and July 31, 1963. Dept State Bul 49:303-8 Ag 19 '63
U.S. expresses regret regarding expulsion of Greeks from Istanbul; statement, September 11, 1964. Dept State Bul 51:564-5 O 19 '64
U.S. favors peacekeeping force for Cyprus; statement, February 9, 1964. Dept State Bul 50:374-6 Mr 9 '64
U.S. informs U.N. of withdrawal of Congo rescue mission; text of letter to the president of the Security council, December 1, 1964. Dept State Bul 51:891 D 21 '64
U.S. informs U.N. security council on Cuban fishing boat incident; letter to President of the U.N. security council, February 7, 1964. Dept State Bul 50:279 F 24 '64
U.S. regrets Soviet veto of U.N. resolution on Malaysia complaint; statement, September 17, 1964. Dept State Bul 51:489-91 O 5 '64
U.S. replies to Cuban charges in U.N. General assembly; statement, December 11, 1964. Dept State Bul 52:24-6 Ja 4 '65
U.S. replies to Soviet charges against certain space activities; text of letter, June 6, 1963 to U.N. Secretary-General U Thant. Dept State Bul 49:104-7 Jl 15 '63
United States urges restraint on Israel and Syria; statement, December 3, 1964. Dept State Bul 52:27-9 Ja 4 '65
U.S. welcomes inquiry of Cambodian charge of chemical operations; text of letter, August 14, 1964. Dept State Bul 51:319 Ag 31 '64

about

City disgraced; demonstrators in Dallas. il Time 82:26 N 1 '63
Dallas image unveiled. J. C. Evans. Christian Cent 80:1438-40 N 20 '63
Mr Ambassador; with editorial comment. P. Lyon. pors Holiday 33:35, 36-9+ Je '63
Rededication; with excerpts from Statement on apartheid, by A. E. Stevenson. New Yorker 39:47-9 D 16 '63
Stevenson at the U.N. S. Gervis. Commonweal 77:591-3 Mr 1 '63
Thursday; reception celebrating admission of Kuwait to the United Nations. New Yorker 39:32-3 My 25 '63
White man is scared, says Harlem congressman; summary of address, May 19, 1963. A. C. Powell. il U S News 54:20 Je 3 '63

STEVENSON, Adlai Ewing, 3d
Twenty-four hours in the life of Adlai E. Stevenson, 3rd. T. Meehan. McCalls 92:80+ N '64

STEVENSON, Charles
Is this the way to fight the war against poverty? Read Digest 84:51-8 My '64
Let's stop sending U.S. dollars to aid our enemies. Read Digest 83:71-8 Ag '63
Real truth about the federal budget. Read Digest 82:49-54 My '63
When the bubble burst in Crockett, Texas. Read Digest 85:197-8+ S '64

STEVENSON, Coke R.
Story of eighty-seven votes that made history. il por U S News 56:46-50 Ap 6 '64

STEVENSON, Florence
Angel of mirth. Opera N 27:26-7 Mr 16 '63
Arabian knights. Opera N 28:24-5 F 15 '64
Born for tragedy. Opera N 27:8-13 F 9 '63
Day of the premiere. Opera N 28:13-16 Mr 28 '64
Flight of witches. Opera N 28:24-5 Ja 4 '64
Fun for the Philistines. Opera N 29:14-15 D 26 '64
Ignoble Romans. Opera N 28:8-12 O 19 '63
She was Tosca. Opera N 28:24-5 Ap 18 '64
(ed) See Fabiani, A. In this corner: Aurelio Fabiani

STEVENSON, Gordon
A-V avant-garde. Library J 88:3022-3 S 1 '63
Classification chaos. por Library J 88:3789-94 O 15 '63
Don't ignore the gifted listener. por Library J 88:519-22 F 1 '63
Dynamic inaction. Library J 88:3804, 4502+ O 15, D 1 '63
Practical record selector: a plaine and easie introduction. por Library J 88:1818-22 My 1 '63
(ed) Recordings. Library J 88:1809-40, 3783-804+ My 1, O 15 '63

STEVENSON, Grace T.
Library adult education activities in public libraries of Germany, Denmark, and England: report. ALA Bul 57:643-54 Jl '63
State library associations and National library week. ALA Bul 58:37-8 Ja '64
Where does ALA leadership come from? ALA Bul 57:105 F '63

STEVENSON, James
Apartment exhibit. New Yorker 40:27 Je 27 '64

STEVENSON, Noel C. and Hoyt, Murray
Strange wedding of Widow Ward. Read Digest 82:93-6 Ap '63

STEVENSON, Richard
Milestone celebration at Jacob's Pillow. Dance Mag 38:36-7 Ag '64

STEVENSON, Robert
First new-world opera. Américas 16:33-5 Ja '64

STEVENSON, Thomas H.
State and science five centuries ago. Bul Atomic Sci 21:28-9 Ja '65

STEW
For hungry skiers; hotch-potch. il Sunset 132:106 Ja '64
Goulash. il Sunset 130:162-4 Mr '63
Meaty stews. il Bet Hom & Gard 42:93-4 F '64
Pot-au-feu; soup and main course all in one. M. Kaytor. il Look 28:44-5 Mr 24 '64
Real old-fashioned oxtail ragout. il McCalls 91:108-9+ Ag '64
Stew season; with recipes. il McCalls 90:108-9+ F '63
Stews! il Good H 157:130-3 O '63
Successful recipes. il Suc Farm 63:93-4 Ja '65

STEWARD, F. C.
Control of growth in plant cells; with biographical sketch. Sci Am 209:22, 104-13 O '63
—and others
Growth and development of cultured plant cells. bibliog Science 143:20-7 Ja 3 '64

STEWARDESSES, Air. See Airlines—Hostesses

STEWART, A. C.
History of long, hot summers. Sat R 47:25-6 Ag 22 '64

STEWART, Albert B.
Discovery of stellar aberration; with biographical sketch. Sci Am 210:22, 100-8 bibliog(p 152) Mr '64

STEWART, Alexander
This was my father; interview, ed. by F. Miller. J. Stewart. il por McCalls 91:130-1+ My '64

STEWART, Alva W.
Feminine city managers. Am City 79:154+ My '64
North Carolina's gag law. Christian Cent 81:1336-8 O 28 '64
Open-door policy. Wilson Lib Bul 37:860-2 Je '63

STEWART, Charles E.
Correcting the image of Negroes in textbooks; address, 1964. por Negro Hist Bul 28:29-30+ N '64

STEWART, Charles T. Jr
Peace trend will bring better business. Nations Bsns 52:66-8+ Je '64
When inflation runs wild. Nations Bsns 53:78-82 Ja '65

STEWART, D. C. See Diamond, H. jt. auth.

STEWART, D. J.
Elbow room for the eye. Nat R 16:1072 D 1 '64

STEWART, David C.
College in the islands. Sat R 47:50-1 Ag 15 '64

STEWART, Desmond
Kassem's legacy. Nation 196:222-4 Mr 16 '63
Tremors in the Near East. Nation 198:23-5 Ja 6 '64

STEWART, Donald
Ballade. New Yorker 39:46 Ap 6 '63

STEWART, Evelyn Seeley
Big question of creativity. Parents Mag 38:62-3+ Je '63

STEWART, George R.
Good new West. Nation 197:10-17 Jl 6 '63

STEWART, Ian
British lions. New Repub 151:14-15 S 5 '64
Happiness says Mao is a hard day's work. N Y Times Mag p34+ S 27 '64
Lines by China's poet laureate. N Y Times Mag p 12+ Mr 29 '64
—and Wheaton, T. A.
l-Octopamine in citrus: isolation and identification. bibliog Science 145:60-1 Jl 3 '64

STEWART, J. George
Architect of the Capitol in trouble? por Arch Forum 119:11 Ag '63

STEWART, James
This was my father; interview, ed. by F. Miller. por McCalls 91:130-1+ My '64

about

Coddled commandos. il por Newsweek 63:28-30 F 10 '64

STEWART, James K.
Transistorized color-TV pattern generator. Electr World 72:96-9 N '64

STEWART, James Seth
I have the most dramatic job in the world. Read Digest 82:62-5 My '63

STEWART, Jane
Letter from Anchorage. Pub W 185:21 Ap 13 '64

STEWART, John Massey-. See Massey-Stewart, J.

STEWART, Mary
Setting and background in the novel. Writer 77:7-9 D '64

STEWART, Natacha
Acacias; story. New Yorker 39:30-40 Je 1 '63
In the middle of nowhere; story. New Yorker 40:29-36 Ja 9 '65
Sin of pride; story. New Yorker 40:53-60 S 19 '64
Talisman against insomnia; story. New Yorker 38:28-32 F 2 '63

STEWART, Nathaniel
Boost your problem-solving power. Nations Bsns 52:122-4+ My '64
Free the man who's boxed in. Nations Bsns 52:82-4+ Jl '64
Get your money's worth from specialists. Nations Bsns 52:96+ Ap '64
How to head off trouble. Nations Bsns 52:68-70+ Ag '64
How to spot comers. Nations Bsns 51:82-4+ N '63
Keep your business in balance. Nations Bsns 52:90-2+ N '64
You can keep morale high. Nations Bsns 51:70-2+ Mr '63

STEWART, Nellie M.
You write what you are. Writer 76:25 Ap '63

STEWART, Omer C.
Need to popularize basic principles; address, November 23, 1963. Vital Speeches 30:255-6 F 1 '64

STEWART, Robert
Father Pierre's Christmas mass; poem. America 111:801 D 19 '64
God, you baffler; poem. America 108:669 My 11 '63
Litany; poem. America 111:44 Jl 11 '64
Rite du printemps; poem. America 110:545 Ap 18 '64
Water; poem. America 110:219 F 15 '64

STEWART, Robert P.
New York: the system framework. bibliog Library J 89:1676-9 Ap 15 '64

STEWART, Shan
Three private gardens in Hong Kong. Pop Gard 14:36-7 Jl '63

STEWART, Thomas Dale
Physical anthropology. Science 141:177-8 Jl 12 '63

STEWART, Wally
Paul Bunyan moves North. Am For 70:54-6 F '64

STEWART, William
Painting, a fundamental art experience for children. Sch Arts 63:21-3 N '63
Shaker form & function. bibliog Sch Arts 63:26-8 Ap '64

STEWART-GORDON, James
Bargain vacations in paradise. Read Digest 84:217-18+ My '64
Flight into the unknown. Read Digest 82:120-5 Mr '63
Hookie Bell versus Graf Spee. Read Digest 85:180-2+ D '64
King Tut's golden hoard. Read Digest 84:198-204 Ap '64
London to Brighton, or bust. Read Digest 83:217-20 N '63
Scotland is a state of mind. Read Digest 82:234-6+ My '63
Septuagenarian's formula for fitness: learn to relax. Todays Health 42:22-5 Ag '64; Same abr. with title Relax and get fit! Read Digest 85:75-8 Ag '64

STEWS. See Stew

STICH-RANDALL, Teresa
Quote: unquote; interview, ed. by J. Ardoin. por Mus Am 83:17 Je '63
Singing Strauss. por Mus Am 84:16-17 Jl '64

STICHWEH, Rollie
Stitch in time is the Army's best weapon. D. Jenkins. il Sports Illus 21:73-4 O 5 '64

STICKERS. See Labels

STICKLAND, Peter
Crocodiles in the cellar. J. Atwater. il pors Sat Eve Post 237:32-3 S 26 '64

STICKNEY, P. B.
Polymers: thermal stability. Science 143:704 F 14 '64

STIEGLITZ, Alfred
Stieglitz burial. B. Downes. Pop Phot 51:62 D '62
Stieglitz's experiments in life. D. Norman. il por N Y Times Mag p 12-13 D 29 '63

STIGLER, George J.
Intellectual and the market place. Nat R 15:473-4+ D 3 '63

STIKA, Andrew J. See Ford, W. A. jt. auth.

STILBESTROLS
Beef additives. W. Burroughs and S. A. Ewing. il Suc Farm 61:100 N '63
Cheaper ways to winter beef cows. D. Seim. Farm J 87:40 D '63

STILES, Lindley J.
Conant's credentials; excerpt from Dr Conant and his critics. Sat R 47:56 S 19 '64

STILES, Lindley J.—*Continued*
International orientation for college administrators. Sch & Soc 91:356-8 N 16 '63

STILES, W. S.
Foveal threshold sensitivity on fields of different colors. bibliog Science 145:1016-17 S 4 '64

STILL, Clyfford
Aloof abstractionist. il por Time 82:76-7 N 29 '63
Art; exhibition at new Institute of contemporary arts at the University of Pennsylvania. M. Kozloff. Nation 198:39-40 Ja 6 '64
Freedom, absolute and infinitely exhilarating. T. A. Sharpless. il Art N 62:36-9+ N '63
In the right hands. Time 83:60 My 29 '64
Still on fire; extended loan at Buffalo's Albright-Knox art gallery. il por Newsweek 61:92 F 25 '63

STILL, James W.
Find that line for sure. Am City 79:99-100 Jl '64

STILL, Joseph W.
Zone of peace. Bul Atomic Sci 19:29-30 S '63

STILL, William Grant
Thirty-eight years of serious music. L. Robinson. il pors Ebony 19:102-6 F '64

STILL life painting
Nineteenth-century still-life painting in New Jersey. W. H. Gerdts. il Antiques 86:718-21 D '64
Still life stimulus. J. Stoker. il Sch Arts 62:29 Je '63

STILL life photography. See Photography—Still life

STILLBIRTH
Tapping for Rh-factor. Sci N L 86:71 Ag 1 '64

STILLION, John
Beauty around our town. Sch Arts 63:22-4 F '64

STILLMAN, Damie
Robert Adam's Grand tour. Antiques 83:670-4 Je '63

STILLMAN, Edmund
Free world split will widen. Nations Bsns 52:34-5+ Ap '64
Sarajevo; the end of innocence. Horizon 6:4-6+ Sum '64

STILLWATER, Minn.
That nine-foot channel; Northern states power company proposes to build power plant. J. Ridgeway. New Repub 151:12 D 26 '64

STILLWELL, Glen F.
Sanding simplified. Motor B 113:27+ Mr '64
Snap starting in winter. il Suc Farm 61:149 F '63
Ten timesaving tips. Motor B 111:152+ Ap '63
Updating your old phono. Pop Mech 119:177-9 My '63

STILLWELL, Hamilton
Adult education in an urban age. Sch & Soc 91:46-7 Ja 26 '63

STILTS
New design for stilts. il Pop Mech 121:160 Ap '64
Stilts for fun. B. Gilmore. il Pop Sci 184:144-5 Ap '64

STILWELL, Hart
My first doe. Field & S 68:36-7+ O '63

STILWELL, Robert L.
Art schooled in adversity. Sat R 47:64 D 5 '64
Monologues of a philolog. Sat R 47:34+ Je 13 '64
Reaching for the ends of being. Sat R 47:48-50 My 30 '64

STILWILL, Lois
Pleasures of convenience foods. Ladies Home J 80:133 N '63

STIMPFLING, J. H. See Cudkowicz, G. jt. auth.

STIMSON, Philip Moen
Common contagious diseases. Parents Mag 39:139-42 Mr '64
Shots that save. Parents Mag 39:47+ N '64

STIMSON, Thomas
Anti-smog kit. Pop Mech 120:125-7+ N '63
Try to stop this mechanized billy goat. Pop Mech 120:92-4+ Ag '63

STIMULANTS
Pill to fight mental depression; Eutonyl. Bsns W p76+ Ap 13 '63
Purple heart drug; young addicts. Sci N L 85:402 Je 27 '64

STIMULUS and response
Adaptation to displaced vision: visual, motor, or proprioceptive change? C. S. Harris. bibliog il Science 140:812-13 My 17 '63
Altruism or arousal in the rat? J. J. Lavery and P. J. Foley. il Science 140:172-3 Ap 12 '63
Arithmetic behavior in chimpanzees. C. B. Ferster. il Sci Am 210:98-104+ My '64
Attack elicited by stimulation of the thalamus cats. M. F. MacDonnell and J. P. Flynn. bibliog il Science 144:1249-50 Je 5 '64
Attention, vigilance, and cortical evoked-potentials in humans. M. Haider and others. bibliog il Science 145:180-2 Jl 10 '64
Aversive stimulation of the rat: long-term effects on subsequent behavior. G. C. Walters and J. V. Rogers. bibliog il Science 142:70-1 O 4 '63
Behavior: confinement, adaptation, and compulsory regimes in laboratory studies. J. L. Kavanau. bibliog Science 143:490 Ja 31 '64; Reply with rejoinder. J. D. Hawkins. 145:1460-2 S 25 '64
Behavior in hydra: contraction responses of hydra pirardi to mechanical and light stimuli. N. B. Rushforth. bibliog Science 139:760-1 F 22 '63
Behavior: persistence of shock-induced aggression. R. E. Ulrich and W. H. Craine. bibliog il Science 143:971-3 F 28 '64
Behavioral and electroencephalographic arousal to contrasting novel stimulation. N. M. Weinberger and D. B. Lindsley. bibliog il Science 144:1355-7 Je 12 '64
Behavioral response rates in pigeons: effect of α-methyl-m-tyrosine. J. N. Hingtgen and M. H. Aprison. bibliog il Science 141:169-71 Jl 12 '63
Cardiovascular concomitants of the conditioned emotional response in the monkey. W. C. Stebbins and O. A. Smith, jr. bibliog il Science 144:881-3 My 15 '64
Cat's ability to discriminate oblique rectangles. N. S. Sutherland. bibliog Science 139:209-10 Ja 18 '63
Cerebral heterostimulation in a monkey colony. J. M. R. Delgado. bibliog il Science 141:161-3 Jl 12 '63
Changes in intensity of punishment; effect on running behavior of rats. E. B. Karsh. bibliog il Science 140:1084-5 Je 7 '63
Conditioned anxiety and punishment effects on operant behavior of goldfish (carassius auratus) I. Geller. bibliog il Science 141:351-3 Jl 26 '63
Cortical evoked potentials and perception of paired flashes. E. Donchin and others. bibliog il Science 141:1285-6 S 27 '63
Dissociation and recovery of a response learned under the influence of chlorpromazine or saline. L. S. Otis. bibliog il Science 143:1347-8 Mr 20 '64
Early arousal and imprinting in chicks. W. R. Thompson and R. A. Dubanoski. bibliog il Science 143:1187-8 Mr 13 '64
Effects of cutaneous and muscle sensory nerve volleys in awake cats: a study in perception. J. E. Sweet and others. bibliog il Science 145:1071-3 S 4 '64
Electroconvulsive shock, retroactive amnesia, and the single-shock method. D. J. Leonard and A. Zavala. bibliog il Science 146:1073-4 N 20 '64
Electroencephalograms of sharks. P. W. Gilbert and others. bibliog il Science 145:949-51 Ag 28 '64
Escape and avoidance learning in newly hatched domestic chicks. H. James and C. Binks. bibliog il Science 139:1293-4 Mr 29 '63
Evolution of intelligence. M. E. Bitterman. il Sci Am 212:92-100 Ja '65
Eye fixation aspect of attention to visual stimuli in infant chimpanzees. G. Berkson and F. L. Fitz-Gerald. bibliog il Science 139:586-7 F 15 '63
Eyeball retraction: classical conditioning and extinction in the albino rabbit. E. B. Deaux and I. Gormezano. bibliog il Science 141:630-1 Ag 16 '63
Following and imprinting: effects of light and social experience. J. M. Polt and E. H. Hess. bibliog il Science 143:1185-7 Mr 13 '64
Following-response initiation in ducklings: age and sensory stimulation. G. Gottlieb. bibliog il Science 140:399-400 Ap 26 '63
Force of response during ratio reinforcement. D. E. Mintz; reply with rejoinder. M. F. Halasz. Science 139:1128-9 Mr 15 '63
Gravitational stress: changes in cortical excitability. A. N. Nicholson. bibliog il Science 145:1458-9 S 25 '64
Habituation of responses to novel stimuli in monkeys with selective frontal lesions. C. M. Butter. bibliog il Science 144:313-15 Ap 17 '64
Inhibition of evoked potentials by striatal stimulation and its blockage by strychnine. G. M. Krauthamer. bibliog il Science 142:1175-6 N 29 '63

STIMULUS and response—*Continued*
Interaction of positive and negative reinforcing neural systems. E. S. Valenstein and T. Valenstein. bibliog il Science 145:1456-8 S 25 '64
Intracranial reward delay and the acquisition rate of a brightness discrimination. R. E. Keesey. bibliog il Science 143:702-3 F 14 '64
Intracranial self-stimulation in man. M. P. Bishop and others. bibliog il Science 140:394-6 Ap 26 '63
Maternal deprivation: its influence on visual exploration in infant monkeys. P. C. Green and M. Gordon. il Science 145:292-4 Jl 17 '64
Mechanisms of receptor adaptation. M. Mendelson and W. R. Loewenstein. bibliog il Science 144:554-5 My 1 '64
Neuromimes: action of a reciprocally inhibitory pair. L. D. Harmon. bibliog il Science 146:1323-5 D 4 '64
Postsynaptic potentials and spike patterns during augmenting responses in cat's motor cortex. M. R. Klee and K. Offenloch. bibliog il Science 143:488-9 Ja 31 '64
Prediction of discrimination from generalization after variations in schedule of reinforcement. A. Haber and H. I. Kalish. bibliog il Science 142:412-13 O 18 '63
Preference aversion in mice to bitter substance. R. P. Warren. bibliog il Science 140:808-9 My 17 '63
Punishment and shock intensity. J. B. Appel. bibliog il Science 141:528-9 Ag 9 '63
Radiation-induced aversion to alcohol. L. J. Peacock and J. A. Watson. bibliog il Science 143:1462-3 Mr 27 '64
Radio control of minds. Sci N L 84:50 Jl 27 '63
Reaction time to cortical stimulation. J. Miller and M. Glickstein. bibliog il Science 146:1594-6 D 18 '64
Reinforcement as input: cyclic variable-interval schedule. J. E. R. Staddon. bibliog il Science 145:410-12 Jl 24 '64
Responses of single cells in visual system to shifts in the wavelength of light. R. L. De Valois and others. il Science 146:1184-6 N 27 '64
Ribonucleic acid: effect on conditioned behavior in rats. L. Cook and others. bibliog il Science 141:268-9 Jl 19 '63
Running as both a positive and negative reinforcer. A. G. Hundt and D. Premack. bibliog Science 142:1087-8 N 22 '63
Selective sensitivity to direction of movement in ganglion cells of the rabbit retina. H. B. Barlow and R. M. Hill. bibliog il Science 139:412-14 F 1 '63
Self-maintained visual stimulation in monkeys after long-term visual deprivation. R. H. Wendt and others. bibliog il Science 139:336-8 Ja 25 '63
Self-presentation and self-termination of a conflict-producing stimulus. E. Hearst and M. B. Koresko. bibliog il Science 146:415-16 O 16 '64
Sensitivity of the head to X-ray. J. Garcia and others. bibliog il Science 144:1470-2 Je 19 '64
Signal analysis of evoked potentials recorded from cats during conditioning. E. R. John and others. bibliog il Science 141:429-31 Ag 2 '63
Signal detection in the rat. M. H. Hack. bibliog il Science 139:758-60 F 22 '63
Signal duration as a factor in vigilance tasks. C. H. Baker. il Science 141:1196-7 S 20 '63
Simultaneous recordings of scalp and epidural somatosensory-evoked responses in man. E. F. Domino and others. bibliog il Science 145:1199-200 S 11 '64
Somatic inheritance of habituation of responses to light in planarians. R. A. Westerman. bibliog il Science 140:676-7 My 10 '63
Speech durations of astronaut and ground communicator. J. D. Matarazzo and others. bibliog il Science 143:148-50 Ja 10 '64
Startle reaction: modification by background acoustic stimulation. H. S. Hoffman and M. Fleshler. bibliog il Science 141:928-30 S 6 '63
Stimulus generalization of a positive conditioned reinforcer. D. R. Thomas and J. L. Williams. bibliog il Science 141:172-3 Jl 12 '63; Reply with rejoinder. T. K. Landauer. 142:9 O 4 '63
Synchronous sensory bombardment of young rats: effects on the electroencephalogram. W. Heron and H. Anchel. il Science 145:946-7 Ag 28 '64
Technique for sustaining behavior with conditioned reinforcement. J. Zimmerman. bibliog il Science 142:682-4 N 8 '63
Test of Deutsch's drive-decay theory of rewarding self-stimulation of the brain. S. S. Pliskoff and T. D. Hawkins. bibliog il Science 141:823-4 Ag 30 '63; Reply with rejoinder. J. A. Deutsch. 142:1125-6 N 29 '63
Timing behavior after lesions of zona incerta and mammillary body. P. Ellen and E. W. Powell. bibliog il Science 141:828-30 Ag 30 '63
Timing behavior in rats with water drinking as a mediator. E. F. Segal and S. M. Holloway. bibliog il Science 140:888-9 My 24 '63
Unit responses in the frog's tectum to moving and nonmoving visual stimuli. U. Grüsser-Cornehls and others. bibliog il Science 141:820-2 Ag 30 '63
Visual problem-solving in a bottlenose dolphin. W. N. Kellogg and C. E. Rice. bibliog il Science 143:1052-5 Mr 6 '64
Visual reinforcement in Siamese fighting fish. T. I. Thompson. bibliog il Science 141:55-7 Jl 5 '63
Word association: common and original response. F. R. Fosmire and H. E. Tryk. bibliog il Science 139:415-16 F 1 '63

STINEBRING, Warren R. See Youngner, J. S. jt. auth.

STING rays. See Rays (fishes)

STINGAREES. See Rays (fishes)

STINGO, John R. pseud.
Honest rainmaker. por Newsweek 64:67 N 16 '64
Reporter at large. A. J. Liebling. New Yorker 39:95-8+ Ja 11 '64

STINGS, insect. See Insect bites and stings

STINNES, Hugo, jr
Perilous swaying; Stinnes' cash-shy empire, West Germany. por Time 82:111+ O 18 '63
Shoring up an empire. il por Bsns W p34+ O 12 '63

STINNETT, Caskie
Under cover. Ladies Home J 81:17-18 Jl; 16 Ag; 17-18 S; 33-4 N; 26+ D '64

STISHOVITE
Stishovite; synthesis by shock wave. P. S. De Carli and D. J. Milton. bibliog il Science 147:144-5 Ja 8 '65
Stishovite: thermal dependence of the crystal habit. C. B. Sclar and others. bibliog il Science 144:833-5 My 15 '64

STITCHERY. See Embroidery

STITCHES (surgery) See Sutures

STIVENS, Dal
Compleat camel. Sci Digest 56:25-7 N '64

STIX, Harriet
Books on the women's pages of Times and Tribune; summary of address. Pub W 184:32-3 D 2 '63

STIX, Thomas L.
Mrs Roosevelt does a TV commercial. Harper 227:104-6 N '63

STOBO, Robert
Fantastic adventures of Captain Stobo. R. C. Alberts. il Am Heritage 14:65-77 Ag '63

STOCK, Brian C.
Why young men leave. Atlan 214:113-14 N '64

STOCK, Dennis
Shakespeare. Look 28:50-8 Ap 7 '64

STOCK, Michael. See Braceland, F. J. jt. auth.

STOCK, Noel
Is Lenin's face red? Nat R 16:25 Ja 14 '64

STOCK, Robert
After Troy; poem. Poetry 104:227 Jl '64

STOCK averages. See Stocks—Price indexes and averages

STOCK breeding. See Cattle breeding

STOCK brokers. See Brokers

STOCK-car racing. See Automobile racing

STOCK certificates. See Stocks—Certificates

STOCK control. See Inventories; Stores or stock-room keeping

STOCK dividends. See Dividends

STOCK exchange
Aging stock. il Fortune 69:75-6 My '64
But we're providing liquidity; floor trading. Newsweek 62:56 Jl 29 '63
Close look at the stock market surge. il U S News 55:44-6 S 30 '63
Executives and their stocks: now they're buying again. il U S News 54:101-3 Mr 4 '63
Is a bull market in stocks in the making? what investment advisers say; symposium. il U S News 54:40-5 Ap 22 '63
Making self-regulation work. Bsns W p 112 Ag 24 '63
Modernizing the market; concerning SEC report. il Time 82:71-2 Jl 26 '63
New forces in the stock market. D. Seligman and T. A. Wise. il Fortune 69:92-5+ F '64
Stock market nervously bullish. il Newsweek 63:61-2+ F 10 '64

STOCK exchange—*Continued*
Stock market's own report: what happened in crisis of '62. U S News 54:135 Mr 25 '63
Stocks surge, but where's the public? il Newsweek 61:73-4+ Ap 29 '63
They're confident of the market's momentum. il Newsweek 61:75 Ap 29 '63
Up from the depths. il Bsns W p25-6 Ap 13 '63
Urgent questions about the stock market: implications of controversial SEC study. R. F. Murray. bibliog f Harvard Bsns R 42:53-9 S '64
Watchdog of Wall Street. New Repub 148:7-8 My 25 '63
Western Europe; the medieval capital markets. il Time 83:90 F 14 '64
What investment advisers now see ahead; symposium. il U S News 56:54-60 Mr 2 '64
What's causing the new rise in the stock market; as investment authorities see it, symposium. il U S News 55:46-52 S 16 '63
What's next in the stock market? il U S News 54:36-9 F 25 '63
When presidents get sick or die; impact on the stock market. U S News 55:98 D 2 '63
Where the stock market is heading. il U S News 54:66-9 My 27 '63
Year for caution, but not for alarm; symposium. il Bsns W p56-8 Ja 2 '65
See also
Government investigations—Stock exchange
Speculation
United States—Securities and exchange commission

Crisis, October 1929

America's great depression, by M. N. Rothbard. Review
Nat R 16:456-8 Je 2 '64. L. M. Spadaro

Regulation

Adding up the damage of SEC market study. il Bsns W p88+ Ag 17 '63
Critical examination of SEC proposals. L. Silberman. Harvard Bsns R 42:121-32 N '64
Dampening the fire before it starts; Fed's clampdown on margin requirements. Bsns W p 114 N 9 '63
Heavy buying of stock on credit? application of margin rule. U S News 55:100-1 Ag 26 '63
Housekeepers; practices of brokerage firms. Fortune 69:242+ Ap '64
Japanese lose yen for stocks; falling prices point to economic woes, government acts. il Bsns W p 134-6+ O 31 '64
Job left undone. Bsns W p 140 F 15 '64
Laws that SEC wants. Bsns W p 116 My 4 '63
Market that serves the pros. il Bsns W p 163-4+ S 19 '64
New cop on big board beat; not immune from antitrust laws. Bsns W p28 My 25 '63
New reason to list; government's new authority to regulate stocks traded both on and off the exchanges. Time 84:74 Ag 28 '64
Reform gets final wrap-up; market reform bill has SEC blessing. Bsns W p74+ Ag 8 '64
Room at the top; margin requirements raised. il Time 82:103 N 15 '63
SEC head urges: do it yourself; Wall Street rules. Bsns W p 140 D 5 '64
SEC's swipe at specialists; disorderly market after Kennedy assassination. Bsns W p73 F 1 '64
Silent market. Fortune 70:90+ Jl '64
Stock market reform gets a shove. il Bsns W p91-2 F 8 '64
Straight and narrow Wall St; new rules governing the securities industry. Bsns W p 118+ Ag 15 '64
Tightening up on Wall Street. Bsns W p 164 Ap 13 '63
Wall Street can live with the new rules. Bsns W p 120+ O 3 '64
Wall Street's main event: SEC vs. the specialists. T. A. Wise. il Fortune 69:149-52+ My '64
Who controls NYSE's wires? case before Supreme court. Bsns W p76 Mr 2 '63

Europe, Western

Bears on the bourse. Time 84:85 Jl 3 '64
Doldrums abroad. il Newsweek 64:69 Jl 13 '64
Where inflation fails to boost stocks. il Bsns W p 150+ Ap 11 '64

London

Along Throgmorton street. il Fortune 67:70+ Ap '63

Luxembourg

Where Europe's dollar bonds find a market. il Bsns W p 156-8+ O 10 '64

New York (city)

Adding up the damage of SEC market study; Funds under fire. il Bsns W p88+ Ag 17 '63
Agree on floor trading rule; SEC and New York exchange. Bsns W p 158 Ap 11 '64
Annals of finance; Ira Haupt & co. affair. J. Brooks. New Yorker 40:160+ N 14 '64
Annals of finance; 1962 crisis. J. Brooks. New Yorker 39:35-6+ Ag 31 '63
Big board is under fire; special study of the securities markets. il Bsns W p23-4 Jl 20 '63
Big board takes on assembly line look. il Bsns W p 110-11+ N 14 '64
Brokers split on fee hike. Bsns W p20 Ja 2 '65
Case of nerves. Time 84:61 Ag 14 '64
Commodities: soybeans and salad oil; the greatest scandal in the history of Wall Street is still going on. P. Vanderwicken. il Esquire 61:91-3+ Ap '64
Commodity blow-up shuts big brokerage; Ira Haupt & co. closes. il Bsns W p96+ N 30 '63
Critical examination of SEC proposals. L. Silberman. Harvard Bsns R 42:121-32 N '64
Deadlock on the floor; floor trading. Newsweek 63:69 Ap 6 '64
Debate over floor traders; SEC vs New York exchange. Bsns W p 166 Mr 21 '64
For Wall Street; tighter rules, fewer secrets; special study of securities markets. il Bsns W p23-5 Ap 6 '63
Gaudy façade? Securities and exchange commission report. il Newsweek 63:75-7 My 4 '64
Important, but not all-powerful; institutional investors. il Bsns W p92-4 Jl 18 '64
In stock prices: big buyers stage a private boom. il Bsns W p23-4 F 16 '63
In wake of Haupt failure; second thoughts on commodities dealing. Bsns W p 128 D 7 '63
Is the little investor always wrong? il Changing T 18:21-3 S '64
It's been frantic; market climbs in a summer rally. il Newsweek 64:63 Jl 20 '64
It's harder to play follow the leader. il Bsns W p87-8 Jl 20 '63
Johnson boom; with reservations. il Bsns W p 125-6 D 7 '63
Johnson boomlet in stocks. il Bsns W p27 Ja 18 '64
Lessons from the Haupt affair. Fortune 69:74+ Ja '64
LBJ market. Newsweek 64:79-80 S 28 '64
May milestone. Newsweek 61:76+ Je 10 '63
Money, bears & bulls; a look at Wall Street. W. Manchester. il Holiday 35:42-53+ Mr '64
M.I.P. variations; New York stock exchange's monthly investment plan. Fortune 69:205 Mr '64
Neither all bad nor all good; Cohen report on the Nation's securities markets. il Newsweek 62:64-7 Ag 19 '63
On the floor. Newsweek 63:101-2 Ap 20 '64
On toward 880. il Time 83:99 My 15 '64
100-million-dollar mystery? attempt to aid Ira Haupt and co. by New York stock exchange. il U S News 55:109-10 D 16 '63
Personal business; how to follow the market from faraway places. Bsns W p 137-8 Je 20 '64
Policeman's lot is not a happy one. il Newsweek 63:63-4 Je 22 '64
Quiet rebellion moves into the open. Bsns W p 120 Je 20 '64
Relaxed and confident. il Newsweek 62:56 Ag 26 '63
Rescue operation. il Newsweek 62:80+ D 9 '63
Restraint on the floor. il Time 83:104 Ap 17 '64
Scandal in salad oil gets bigger every day; with editorial comment. il Bsns W p32+, 160 D 14 '63
Skeptical SEC eye on Wall Street. il Newsweek 62:55-6+ Jl 29 '63
Skittish bulls. Newsweek 63:77 My 11 '64
Some of the skeptics are sold at last. il Bsns W p 109-10 Ap 25 '64
Stock yields: a study of thirty-five years; common stocks on New York stock exchange. U S News 55:110-11 D 9 '63
Stocks and the public. New Repub 149:5-6 Ag 3 '63
Straight and narrow Wall St; new rules governing the securities industry. Bsns W p 118+ Ag 15 '64
Strength in the clutch; reaction to momentous events of the past week. il Time 84:99 O 23 '64
Taking great care it will never happen again; DeAngelis' scandal. Bsns W p 166 Ap 18 '64

STOCK exchange—New York (city)—*Cont.*
Tax plan: Wall Street is wary. il Bsns W p64-5 F 2 '63
1066 & all that; market has climbed. il Time 84:87 Jl 10 '64
Testing a new high. Time 85:73 Ja 29 '65
Trend right now is up. il Newsweek 62:65 S 16 '63
Two horses: trading during minutes following President Kennedy's assassination. Newsweek 63:66 F 3 '64
Uneasy partnership SEC/NYSE. R. I. Robinson and H. R. Bartell, jr. Harvard Bsns R 43:76-88 Ja '65
Wall Street: a slight case of nerves. il Newsweek 62:63 Jl 15 '63
Wall Street musters its defenses; SEC's study of floor trading and stock specialists. il Bsns W p84-6 Jl 27 '63
Wall Street revives fast after the crisis. il Bsns W p28-9 N 30 '63
Wall Street shrugs off steel price rises. il Bsns W p 112+ My 4 '63
Wall St talks. See issues of Business week
Wall Street today: highs go higher. il Newsweek 62:89-92 N 11 '63
Wall Street watches stocks break records. il Bsns W p31 S 7 '63
Wall Street wonders; is the ball over? il Bsns W p22 D 19 '64
Wall Street's main event: SEC vs. the specialists. T. A. Wise. il Fortune 69:149-52+ My '64
Wall Street's view: a modest price gain. il Bsns W p70-2 D 28 '63
War scare; effect of Vietnamese crisis. Newsweek 64:62+ Ag 17 '64
Watching brush fires on Wall Street; Syntex stock. il Bsns W p 110-12 Ja 25 '64
What safeguards are there for today's investors? U S News 55:81-2 D 23 '63
Where is the stock market headed? il Changing T 18:7-11 O '64
Who controls NYSE's wires? case before Supreme court. Bsns W p76 Mr 2 '63
Why brokers yearn to merge. Bsns W p78-80 Ag 31 '63
Why did Wall Street go off the track? il Bsns W p 118+ Je 13 '64

Tokyo

Japan woos U.S. investors. il Bsns W p76+ Ap 6 '63
Japanese lose yen for stocks; falling prices point to economic woes, government acts. il Bsns W p 134-6+ O 31 '64
Pleasing the ancestors. il Time 81:87-8 Je 21 '63

Toronto

Canada is riding a homemade boom. il Bsns W p66-7 Ag 1 '64
Las Vegas in Toronto; Texas Gulf sulphur's mineral strike at Timmins. il Bsns W p 113-14 Ap 25 '64
Windfall that fell. il Time 84:64 Ag 14 '64
STOCK exchange, American. See American stock exchange
STOCK exchange specialists. See Securities—Marketing
STOCK margin requirements. See Stock exchange—Regulation
STOCK market. See Stock exchange
STOCK market charts. See Stocks—Price indexes and averages
STOCK market clubs. See Investment clubs
STOCK market letters. See Investments—Advisers
STOCK purchase options
Option play. Newsweek 61:68+ Mr 4 '63
Personal business: stock options are better than cash. Bsns W p 183 My 18 '63
Pulling the rug from stock options. Bsns W p 104+ Ja 11 '64
Solid fringe. il Time 83:88 Mr 6 '64
Stock options at the crossroads. J. C. Baker. Harvard Bsns R 41:22-4+ Ja '63
Stock options lose a lot of luster. Bsns W p 104+ Mr 14 '64
Stock options: tighter rules? U S News 54: 105-6 Mr 11 '63
Tightening tax laws on stock options. Bsns W p74 Mr 2 '63
STOCK ranges
Crusade for rangeland restoration. J. F. Arnold. il Am For 69:28-32 My '63
Grazers set policy. il Am For 69:46-7 My '63
Home on the range; wild horse range in southern Nevada. il Newsweek 62:30+ S 2 '63
New hope for public land watersheds; range conservation. R. E. Getty. il Am For 70: 14-19 D '64
Ravelling watersheds; grazing lands must be restored. C. L. Forsling. il Am For 60:12-14+ F '63
Well done, Mr Secretary! with editorial comment. J. Prokop. il Am For 69:8-9+ Mr '63
What are we doing to our land? O. J. Murie. Am For 69:15 F '63
STOCK-room keeping. See Stores or stock-room keeping
STOCK specialists. See Securities—Marketing
STOCK splits. See Stocks—Split-up
STOCK ticker machines
Ticker. New Yorker 40:22-3 Jl 18 '64
STOCKBROKERS. See Brokers
STOCKDALE, Alice Boyd
Magpies; poem. McCalls 91:64 Mr '64
STOCKDALE, F. and others
5-bromodeoxyuridine: effect on myogenesis in vitro. bibliog Science 146:533-5 O 23 '64
STOCKDALE, Harold J.
Make best use of back rubbers for beef. Suc Farm 61:46 Jl '63
STOCKER, Hilda L.
Paperbacks in the classroom. Library J 89: 318-19+ Ja 15 '64
STOCKER, Joseph
Story of a Hilda Maehling fellow. NEA J 53:45 O '64
STOCKER, Stanley W.
Factors affecting camping facilities. Recreation 56:142 Mr '63
STOCKERT, Hank
How to anodize aluminum. Pop Sci 182:144-6 F '63
STOCKERT, Henry A.
Dim your lights at home, too. Pop Mech 119: 154-7+ F '63
STOCKHAMER, Rose
Day camp for the mentally retarded. Recreation 56:236-7 My '63
STOCKHAUSEN, Karl Heinz
Father; music without instruments or electronic music. New Yorker 39:25-6 Ja 18 '64
Stockhausen's Kontakte on DGG; a telling experience. A. Cohn. Am Rec G 29:952+ Ag '63
Stockhausen's non-lecture. M. Bernheimer. Sat R 47:44+ Ja 25 '64
STOCKHOLDERS
Are stockholders ranks thinning? il Bsns W p72-3 F 1 '64
C&O's happy holders; Greenbrier house parties promote loyalty. il Bsns W p96-8 D 7 '63
Financial goals: management vs. stockholders. G. Donaldson. bibliog f il Harvard Bsns R 41:116-29 My '63
Full disclosure; stockholder relations. L. L. L. Golden. Sat R 46:56 O 12 '63
Getting a line on stockholders; report by Wharton school. il Bsns W p 168+ S 14 '63
Important, but not all-powerful; institutional investors. il Bsns W p92-4 Jl 18 '64
Is the little investor always wrong? il Changing T 18:21-3 S '64
It pays to buy out small stockholdings. Bsns W p 144 D 5 '64
Minority owners can avoid squeeze-outs. F. H. O'Neal. Harvard Bsns R 41:150-2+ Mr '63
One for the books; Transitron stockholders' suit. il Fortune 67:191-2+ Mr '63
Personal business; how to follow the market from faraway places. Bsns W p 137-8 Je 20 '64
Proxy fighters; Thomas Mellon Evans and the Brown co. Newsweek 61:65 Mr 4 '63
So you're about to become a stockholder. il Changing T 18:17-19 Ap '64
Telling the whole tale; annual meeting report to stockholders. il Bsns W p42 Ag 1 '64
What safeguards are there for today's investors? U S News 55:81-2 D 23 '63
What 17 million shareholders share. M. D. Reagan. il N Y Times Mag p 11+ F 23 '64
See also
Executives as stockholders
Women as investors
STOCKHOLDERS meetings
Annual meetings cut frills. il Bsns W p88-90 Ap 20 '63
Crowell-Collier holds stormy annual meeting. Pub W 183:69-70 Ap 15 '63
Most are gone, but not the hecklers; this year's annual meetings. il Bsns W p66-7 My 9 '64
What's the annual meeting worth? symposium il Duns R 82:36-7+ Jl '63
With a little stock and a lot of cheek. Time 84:100 O 30 '64
STOCKHOLM

City planning

War spared the city, but builders won't. il Bsns W p24-6 Jl 6 '63

STOCKHOLM—*Continued*

Music

Notes from our correspondents. F. Hedman. Hi Fi 14:28+ F '64

STOCKHOLM festival. See Music festivals—Sweden

STOCKINGS. See Hosiery

STOCKLIN, William A.
For the record. See issues of Electronics world

STOCKMANN's store. See Helsinki—Stores

STOCKPILING
Another run-up in tin prices. Bsns W p30 N 2 '63
$8.7 billion stockpile. New Repub 148:6 Mr 30 '63
GM jolts steelmen; stockpiling steel. il Bsns W p28 F 23 '63
High cost of uncertainty; GM stockpiling steel. Bsns W p 100 Mr 2 '63
Metals pinch speeds drive to tap stockpile; price-supply bind, of copper, lead and zinc. Bsns W p34 Ja 23 '65
Stockpile still increasing. Sci N L 85:38 Ja 18 '64
Stockpiled aluminum up for sale. Bsns W p34 Ap 13 '63
Uproar over stockpiles: a committee's report. U S News 55:10 O 7 '63

STOCKS
Aerospace stocks regaining strength. M. Getler. il Miss & Roc 14:31-3 Ap 20 '64
Big disappearing act. D. Seligman and others. il Fortune 68:231-2 D '63
Buying stocks the dollar averaging way. il Good H 156:156 F '63
Calculating the return. il Newsweek 62:80 D 9 '63
Close look at some of the growth stocks of today. il Duns R 82:121-3 N '63
Companies' stocks; as their officials size them up. il U S News 57:100-2 O 19 '64
Executive investor; new Japanese stocks. Duns R 81:74E+ Je '63
Executive investor; proved growth stocks. il Duns R 81:127-8 Ap '63
Executive investor; the market in 1963. Duns R 81:89-90+ Ja '63
Executives and their stocks: buying and selling both rise. il U S News 55:70-2 Jl 29 '63
Experts analyze investment outlook. C. M. Bliss; A. P. Haake, jr; J. C. Bickford. il Nations Bsns 52:106-8+ Je '64
Experts predict stock market outlook; symposium. il Nations Bsns 51:56-8+ Je '63
How common stocks fit our savings program. J. H. Fithian. il Suc Farm 62:71+ Ag '64
How the big funds are investing their money. il U S News 55:79-80 Ag 12 '63
How to handle your money now; as experts see it; symposium. il U S News 58:44-8 Ja 4 '65
How to look up a stock; reference books. il Changing T 17:31-3 My '63
Institutions begin to hedge. il Bsns W p 140+ Je 15 '63
Random walk in Wall Street. Fortune 67:204 F '63
Senior securities, boon for banks? C. M. Williams. il Harvard Bsns R 41:82-94 Jl '63
So you're about to become a stockholder. il Changing T 18:17-19 Ap '64
Stock split by AT&T: meaning for shareholders. U S News 55:98-9 D 2 '63
Stock yields: a study of thirty-five years; common stocks on New York stock exchange. U S News 55:110-11 D 9 '63
Stocks the big funds are buying now. il U S News 56:93-4 Je 8 '64
Ten stocks for specific investment aims. Duns R 83:107-8+ Ap '64
Too much buying of stocks on credit? il U S News 55:127+ N 18 '63
Twenty freedom from worry stocks. il Duns R 83:81-3 Mr '64
Two high flyers. Newsweek 62:86+ S 23 '63
Ups and down. New Repub 149:5 S 28 '63
Wall Street in Europe. il Time 83:88+ Mr 6 '64
What investment funds are doing with their money. U S News 54:92+ F 11 '63
What's causing the new rise in the stock market; as investment authorities see it, symposium. il U S News 55:46-52 S 16 '63
Why buy growth stocks? L. G. Colt; J. W. Hazard; J. F. Dewhurst. il Changing T 18:7-11 F '64
Year of the white chips? il Newsweek 65:57 F 1 '65
See also
Bonds
Corporations
Saving and savings
Securities
Speculation
Stock exchange
Stockholders
also subhead Securities under various subjects, e.g. Banks and banking—Securities

Certificates

Are those old stock certificates worth anything? Changing T 18:19-20 N '64

Marketing

Comsat in orbit over Wall Street. il Newsweek 63:73 Je 15 '64
Executive investor; dollar averaging and some promising growth stocks. il Duns R 83:77-9 Je '64
Market that serves the pros. il Bsns W p 163-4+ S 19 '64
Monopoly on Front street; National quotation bureau, source of price quotations for over-the-counter stocks. Fortune 68:232+ S '63
Personal investing; SEC reaches over the counter. il Fortune 67:231-2 My '63
Pressure is off. Fortune 69:63 Je '64
Ride on the rails. il Fortune 68:231-2 O '63
Stocks in the boondocks; Argentina's Deltec organization. il Time 83:85 Ja 17 '64
Third market; discount selling. il Newsweek 64:82 O 26 '64
Third market; discount trading. il Time 84:99-100 O 23 '64
Way out of a dilemma? report by special committee of the New York stock exchange. Newsweek 65:70 Ja 11 '65
What price what? Newsweek 64:78 N 2 '64
Where are the people? Fortune 67:208 Je '63
See also
National association of securities dealers

Odd lots

Odd-lot buyers step up action. U S News 56:84-5 My 4 '64

Price indexes and averages

Annals of finance; 1962 crisis. New York stock exchange. J. Brooks. New Yorker 39:35-6+ Ag 31 '63
As investors weigh the chances today. il U S News 56:92-4 Ja 13 '64
Battling toward 900; magic mark on the Dow-Jones index. il Bsns W p26 Ja 23 '65
Big buyers are still optimistic. Bsns W p 143-4 My 23 '64
Bull, bear or bearull? Time 83:83 F 21 '64
Bulls break through. il Time 82:95 S 13 '63
Bulls get a little edgy. il Bsns W p 118+ O 3 '64
Can the tax cut keep it perking? il Bsns W p23 F 29 '64
Case of the jitters. il Bsns W p23 Jl 6 '63
Charts point a rising course. il Bsns W p73-4 Je 1 '63
Gains, but not up to averages. il Bsns W p82+ Ja 11 '64
Hot new issue that burned the pros; Comsat stock price. il Bsns W p 112 Ag 22 '64
In stock prices: big buyers stage a private boom. il Bsns W p23-4 F 16 '63
It's harder to play follow the leader. il Bsns W p87-8 Jl 20 '63
Japanese lose yen for stocks; falling prices point to economic woes, government acts. il Bsns W p 134-6+ O 31 '64
Johnson boom; with reservations. il Bsns W p 125-6 D 7 '63
Markets weather bad news. Bsns W p30 N 28 '64
One reason stock prices stay high. il U S News 56:115-17 Ap 27 '64
Pale blue; stocks hitting new highs. Fortune 69:239 Ap '64
Playing it safe but profitably; mutual funds vs the averages. il Bsns W p72+ Ag 8 '64
Pros step back; small investors come back. il Bsns W p 111-12 Jl 25 '64
Random character of stock market prices, ed. by P. H. Cootner. Review
Fortune 70:70 O '64
Some of the skeptics are sold at last. il Bsns W p 109-10 Ap 25 '64
Stock market trends to watch. M. Nadler. Nations Bsns 52:90+ D '64
Stocks and calamities. Fortune 69:82 My '64
Stocks with highest yields; with chart. U S News 56:83-4 Je 22 '64
Street consensus: new highs lie ahead. il Bsns W p 122+ S 21 '63
Swift comeback for stocks. il Bsns W p25 My 18 '63
Wall Street looks, then leaps ahead. il Bsns W p31 N 21 '64

STOCKS—Price indexes and averages—*Cont.*
Wall Street pays a price. il Bsns W p25 D 5 '64
Wall Street watches stocks break records. il Bsns W p31 S 7 '63
Wall Street wonders; is the ball over? il Bsns W p22 D 19 '64
What stock averages don't show; with chart. U S News 57:86 S 14 '64
What's next in the stock market? il U S News 54:36-9 F 25 '63
Where is the stock market headed? il Changing T 18:7-11 O '64
Whistling past a crisis. il Bsns W p35 O 24 '64
Why did Wall Street go off the track? il Bsns W p 118+ Je 13 '64
Winners & losers. il Time 85:82 Ja 15 '65
Year of the white chips? il Newsweek 65:57 F 1 '65
See also
National quotation bureau, incorporated

Anecdotes, facetiae, satire, etc

Year of the bull in worthless Chinese bonds. M. Kitman. il Sat Eve Post 237:72-3 Ag 22 '64

Short selling

Rise of the shorts. il Fortune 67:205-6+ Ap '63

Split-up

Mother Bell's children. Newsweek 64:68 Ag 24 '64
Splitting with pride. Time 83:94+ Ap 10 '64

Taxation

See Taxation of bonds, securities, etc.

Valuation

See Corporations—Valuation

STOCKS, Fraudulent. See Securities, Fraudulent

STOCKTON, Allen
Sportiest Alfa. Motor T 16:80-1 O '64

STOCKTON, Charles G.
Operation on President McKinley. S. Adler. il Sci Am 208:118-30 Mr '63

STOCKTON, Frank R.
Old Pipes and the Dryad; dramatization. See Thane, A.

STOCKWELL, Charles W.
Mekong madness. Outdoor Life 132:12-13+ Jl '63

STOCKWOOD, Mervyn
South bank religion. il por Time 82:66-7 Jl 26 '63

STOCKYARDS, Chicago. See Chicago—Stockyards

STODDARD, Charles H.
Forester to head BLM. J. B. Craig. il pors Am For 69:4-5+ Je '63
Take a look at the land you own. C. H. Callison. il Audubon Mag 66:302-3 S '64

STODELLE, Ernestine
College or career for dancers? Bennington's answer. Dance Mag 38:40-5 S '64

STOEFFLER, F. Ernest
Moralism vs. Christianity. Christian Cent 80:1299-302 O 23 '63

STOERKER, C. Frederick
Peace corps: no longer an experiment. Christian Cent 81:1396-8 N 11 '64

STOESSEL, Catherine
Retire and cruise. pors Motor B 113:38-9+ Ap '64

STOESSINGER, John G.
UN crisis: the politics of money. Nation 199:263-6 O 26 '64

STOFFEL, Frederick E.
Teaching in overseas schools. NEA J 53:8-9 My '64

STOFFEL, Lester L.
Scenic showcase for Oak Park. Library J 89:4717-19 D 1 '64

STOKE, Harold W.
Current college curriculum; address, September 1962. Sch & Soc 91:88+ F 23 '63

STOKE, Harvey F.
Art of grafting. Pop Gard 14:54+ Mr '63

STOKELY, James. See Dykeman, W. jt. auth.

STOKER, James
Still life stimulus. Sch Arts 62:29 Je '63

STOKES, Edward L.
Have a good time, daughter. Read Digest 83:202-4 Ag '63

STOKES, G. W.
Development of complete homozygotes of tobacco. bibliog Science 141:1185 S 20 '63

STOKES, Roy
On the grindstone (cont) Library J 88:524-5, 974, 1430-1, 1842+, 2212-13, 2648, 2850, 3036, 3808-9, 4168, 4588 F 1, Mr 1, Ap 1, My 1, Je 1, Jl-S 1, O 15-N 1, D 1 '63

STOKES, Thomas L, award. See Thomas, L. Stokes award

STOKES, William Lee
Fossilized stomach contents of a sauropod dinosaur. Science 143:576-7 F 7 '64

STOKLEY, James, 1900-
Astronomy. See issues of Science news letter

STOKOWSKI, Leopold Anton Stanislaw
Musical events; concerts performed by American symphony orchestra in Carnegie Hall. W. Sargeant. New Yorker 39:117-18 Ap 6; 203 O 19 '63; 112-13 F 8 '64
Stokowski conducts a new life. E. Coleman. pors N Y Times Mag p72+ D 6 '64

STOKVIS, Irene E. and Putnam, Judith
(eds) Books to come. Library J 88:594-6+, 3658-93+; 89:670-2+, 2378-450, 3788-888 F 1, O 1 '63, F 1, Je 1, O 1 '64
(eds) Business books to come. Library J 88:4242-6; 89:1120-6, 2830-4, 4392-8 N 1 '63, Mr 1, Jl, N 1 '64
(eds) Paperbacks to come. Library J 88:3295-337; 89:346-81+, 2175-207, 3422-57; 90:336+ S 15 '63, Ja 15, My 15, S 15 '64, Ja 15 '65
(eds) Religious books to come. Library J 88:3106-23+; 89:138-51, 3190-204; 90:138-40+ S 1 '63, Ja 1, S 1 '64, Ja 1 '65
(eds) Scientific, technical, and medical books to come. Library J 88:4247-75; 89:1126-60+, 2835-70, 4399-436 N 1 '63, Mr 1, Jl, N 1 '64
(eds) Summer books to come. Library J 88:2284-351+ Je 1 '63
(eds) Summer business books. Library J 88:2734-8+ Jl '63
(eds) Summer scientific, technical and medical books. Library J 88:2739-69 Jl '63
—and others
(eds) Meet Ed Emberley. Library J 88:3991-5 O 15 '63
(ed) Paperback books to come. Library J 88:2105-32 My 15 '63
—See Cooley, M. jt. ed.

STOLBERG, Irving
C.O. sentenced to prison. Christian Cent 80:1229 O 9 '63

STOLEE, Michael J.
Nonpublic schools: what must they teach? bibliog f Sch & Soc 92:274-6+ O 3 '64

STOLEN automobiles. See Automobiles, Theft of

STOLEN cook; drama. See Slattery, M. E.

STOLLE, Fred
Another long chorus of waltzing Matilda. F. Deford. il por Sports Illus 21:93-5 S 21 '64
Outcasts are counted in. J. Lovesey. il por Sports Illus 21:22+ Jl 13 '64

STOLLE, Jane
Congo: a calculated confusion. Nation 196:252-4 Mr 23 '63
Reporter as hero. Nation 200:58-60 Ja 18 '65

STOLLEY, Richard
Battle to save his brain. Life 55:98+ S 27 '63
Beatles of Foggy Bottom. Life 56:38-38A Ap 3 '64
Combat novel from behind bars. Life 55:101-2+ D 6 '63
Despite four hard failures he wants one more crack. Life 56:94 Je 12 '64
Ev and Hubert, heroes of the historic session. Life 56:36-7 Je 19 '64
He's beginning to feel his oats; account of S. Shriver. Life 56:42+ My 1 '64
Justice falls on three duck lovers. Life 55:11 Ag 2 '63
Piling stone on stone takes a long time. Life 56:54+ Je 19 '64
Poignant tissue of white lies. Life 54:19 F 22 '63
Senator's pioneer mother talks about Barry and herself. Life 55:24-7 Jl 12 '63
Time bomb in a hole. Life 55:9+ O 11 '63
Triumphant ticket whoops it up and saddles up way down at the LBJ. Life 57:36-7 N 13 '64
(ed) Washington report. Life 57:25 D 18 '64; 58:32 Ja 8; 40D Ja 15; 34D Ja 22 '65
Will Congress nail together the Great society? Life 58:36-7 Ja 15 '65
Work, memories, old friends. Life 56:34B My 29 '64
World filled with tension and a high whine. Life 57:36-41 N 6 '64

about

Whatever happened to the wild blue yonder? G. P. Hunt. por Life 57:3 N 6 '64

STOLOFF, Carolyn
Dinosaurs: poem. New Yorker 40:30 F 29 '64

STOLPER, Wolfgang F.
Development of Nigeria; with biographical sketch. Sci Am 209:26+. 168-72+ bibliog (p308) S '63

STOLTZ, Jim
Fastest club in America. Motor B 111:43-4+ Je '63

STOLZ, Mary
Honorable profession. Sat R 47:45-6 N 7 '64
In their own good time; story. Redbook 122: 125-56 D '63
Love's season; story. Redbook 123:145 O '64

STOMACH
Antidromic inhibition accompanied by ventral root positivities. R. Werman. bibliog il Science 143:824-5 F 21 '64
Stomach contraction upon central vagus stimulation. N. C. Jefferson and others. il Science 140:810-11 My 17 '63
Window to the human stomach; strangest series of experiments in medical history. il Todays Health 43:88 Ja '65
See also
Rumen

Acidity

Acid indigestion: myth & mysteries. il Time 84:39 Ag 28 '64

Diseases

When your stomach signals trouble. G. G. Greer. Bet Hom & Gard 41:17-18+ N '63
See also
Digestive system—Diseases
Peptic ulcers

Secretions

See also
Gastric juice

Surgery

How much of the stomach should be cut out? il Time 83:48-9 Ja 3 '64

STOMACH ulcers. See Peptic ulcers

STOMMEL, Henry
Varieties of oceanographic experience. bibliog Science 139:572-6 F 15 '63

STONCIUS, Stanley
Opportunities in professional organization. NEA J 53:60 O '64

STONE, Abraham
What wives don't know about sex; ed. by J. Younger; reprint. Read Digest 84:78-80 Mr '64

STONE, Alma
Potato throwers; story. Reporter 28:40-2 F 28 '63

STONE, Benjamin
Archipelagic refuge. Natur Hist 72:32-9 N '63

STONE, C. Walter
Dean's dream. por Library J 89:2740-5 Jl '64

STONE, Don
Don Stone believes in thorough preparation. il por Am Artist 27:30-1+ D '63

STONE, Donald
Life at section A, post two. Fortune 69:152+ My '64

STONE, Edward Durell
Are most cities too ugly to save? interview. por U S News 57:82-8 N 30 '64
Modern architecture. bibliog il NEA J 53: 54-7 F '64
about
Architect's trend-setting home for the fair. J. Peter. il pors Look 28:42-4 F 11 '64
Building on the Wright foundation. A. Christ-Janer. il Sat R 46:36-7 F 2 '63
Open diplomacy; Roosevelt House, New Delhi. il Time 81:60-1 Ap 12 '63
Recent work of Edward Durell Stone; with introductory statement by Stone. il Arch Rec 136:149-60 O '64
Squires at large. Esquire 61:75 Je '64
Stone pares down his cultural clam shell. il por Life 56:50+ F 7 '64

STONE, George Winchester
MLA's experience; excerpts from address. por(p37) Pub W 184:39-40 Jl 15 '63

STONE, Harry
Dark corners of the mind: Dickens' childhood reading. Horn Bk 39:306-21 Je '63

STONE, Howard W.
Lighting devices from a New Hampshire collection. Antiques 86:82-3 Jl '64

STONE, James
Curl up and read. Seventeen 23:30 Je '64

STONE, Jan
Turkey's her meat. ed. by N. Nichols. por Farm J 87:80+ N '63

STONE, Jeremy J.
Arms race or disarmament? Bul Atomic Sci 20:20-4 S '64; 21:30 Ja '65

STONE, Jonathan
English and Irish cream jugs. Antiques 87: 94-8 Ja '65

STONE, Leslie
Eighteen-hour day of a British backbencher. N Y Times Mag p32-3+ Ja 10 '65

STONE, Marvin
(comp) Business books of 1962. por Library J 88:944-8 Mr 1 '63

STONE, P. W.
Preprinted insert. Sat R 47:38 Ag 8 '64

STONE, Ralph, and Wagner, P. L.
Diagnosis was harder than the cure. Am City 78:177+ S '63

STONE, Ralph A.
Search for Utopia. Reporter 30:54+ F 27 '64

STONE, Richard
Mathematics in the social sciences; with biographical sketch. Sci Am 211:30+, 168-72+ bibliog(p270+) S '64

STONE, S. Byron
Eight tips for better night color. Pop Phot 55:76-7 Jl '64

STONE, Sanford H. and others
Histamine: differences in amount available for release in lungs of guinea pigs susceptible and resistant to acute anaphylaxis. bibliog Science 146:1061-2 N 20 '64

STONE, Sidney H.
New government+centralized purchasing= increased efficiency. por Am City 78:102-3 Ap '63

STONE, Walker
Congo: the morning after; reprint. U S News 57:68 Ag 24 '64

STONE, William T.
Boating laws and regulations. Yachting 115: 49-51+ Ap '64
Washington report. See issues of Yachting

STONE age
Lunar notation on upper paleolithic remains. A. Marshack. il Science 146:743-5 N 6 '64
Neolithic city in Turkey. J. Mellaart. il Sci Am 210:94-104 Ap '64
Prehistory in Shanidar Valley, northern Iraq. R. S. Solecki. bibliog il Science 139:179-93 Ja 18 '63
Radiocarbon dating of a late paleolithic culture from Egypt. P. E. L. Smith. bibliog il Science 145:811 Ag 21 '64
Solutrean culture. P. E. L. Smith. il Sci Am 211:86-94 Ag '64
2,500 mile revolution; Neolithic revolution. Sci Am 211:40+ Ag '64
Upper Paleolithic cultures in western Europe. D. de Sonneville-Bordes. il Science 142:347-55 O 18 '63

STONE carving
Byfield stones, our earliest American sculpture? L. W. Watkins. il Antiques 84:420-3 O '63
Mortality writ in stone; early New England gravestones. S. Marsal. il Américas 16:22-30 S '64
Stone carving in New England graveyards. A. Ludwig. il Antiques 86:87-91 Jl '64

STONE crabs. See Crabs

STONE faces. See Rock profiles

STONE implements and weapons
Early man in the Andes. W. J. Mayer-Oakes. il Sci Am 208:116-22+ My '63
European relics. C. Miles. Hobbies 68:112+ N '63
Fluted projecticle points: their age and dispersion in the New world. C. V. Haynes, jr. bibliog il Science 145:1408-13 S 25 '64
Microscope reveals uses of stone age knives. Sci N L 85:264 Ap 25 '64
Middle stone age culture in India and Pakistan. H. D. Sankalia. bibliog il Science 146: 365-75 O 16 '64
Pleistocene chipped stone tool on Santa Rosa Island, California. P. C. Orr. bibliog il Science 143:243-4 Ja 17 '64
Recognizing the emergence of man; Tolchaco stone tool industry. R. Ascher and M. Ascher. bibliog il Science 147:243-50 Ja 15 '65
Stone edges. C. Miles. il Hobbies 69:112+ Jl '64
See also
Stone age

STONE knives. See Stone implements and weapons

STONE MOUNTAIN memorial
Will Robert E. Lee ride again? il Bsns W p 184-5+ S 26 '64

STONE mulching. See Mulching

STONE paintings. See Pictures

STONE rubbings. See Rubbings

STONE sheep hunting. See Mountain sheep hunting

STONE tools. See Stone implements and weapons

STONEBURNER, Tony
Farmer makes things grow; poem. Christian Cent 80:1368 N 6 '63
Mass, for a retreatant not in communion; poem. Christian Cent 81:796 Je 17 '64

STONECROPS. See Sedums

STONEFLIES
Stonefly aquatic in the adult stage. S. G. Jewett, jr. bibliog Science 139:484-5 F 8 '63
STONEHENGE, England
Secret of Stonehenge. G. S. Hawkins. il Harper 228:96-9 Je '64
Stones of time. Newsweek 62:103 N 18 '63
STONEHILL, Harry S.
Legacy of scandal. Newsweek 62:39 Ag 5 '63
STONER, Lee H. and Neteland, Edward
Current teacher education in Pakistan. Sch & Soc 91:174-5 Ap 6 '63
STONEWALL, Rock
Muscles are his business. il pors Ebony 20:147-50 D '64
STONEWALL, Tex.
This is LBJ's country. il U S News 55:60-4 D 23 '63
STONEWORK, Decorative. See Decoration and ornament, Architectural
STONG, C. L.
(ed) Amateur scientist. See issues of Scientific American
STOOKEY, S. D. See Armistead, W. H. jt. auth.
STOOLS
Camp stool. E. V. Traylor. il Pop Mech 120:164 Ag '63
How to keep your feet up in style. il House & Gard 124:42-3 N '63
Step stools; be safe when you reach! il Consumer Bul 47:10-13 Ap '64
STOOP, Bert
Tempest over Der stellvertreter. Christian Cent 80:980-1 Ag 7 '63
STOOP, Norma McLain
Selfish summer; poem. Christian Cent 80:1101 S 11 '63
STOOP ball. See Ball
STOOPS, Jack
Drawing. Sch Arts 63:29-31 Je '64
STOP here, my friend: story. See Gerber, M. J.
STOP the music! story. See Wells, R. W.
STOP watches
Electronic stop watch. F. Blechman. il Pop Electr 19:51-4+ O '63
STOPH, Willi
Coming man? por Newsweek 64:82 O 5 '64
Joy, not jubilation. il por Time 84:56 O 2 '64
STOPHLET, John J.
Land of the trembling earth. il por Nat Parks Mag 37:10-15 O '63
Night life on the desert. il Nat Parks Mag 38:12-15 Mr '64
STOPWATCHES. See Stop watches
STORAGE
There's a raisin box for everything. G. Danner. il Pop Electr 20:96 My '64
See also
Closets
Warehouses
also subhead Storage under various subjects, e.g. Boats—Storage
STORAGE batteries
Battery care pointers. Suc Farm 61:52 S '63
Car battery saver. R. C. Apperson, jr. il Pop Electr 20:33-6 Ap '64
Cordless battery-powered appliances. il Consumer Bul 47:26-7 F '64
Cordless tools & appliances. il Changing T 18:39-41 F '64; Same abr. with title Gadgets that run by themselves. Read Digest 85:155-6 O '64
Do pennies prevent battery corrosion? il Pop Sci 183:28-30 Jl '63
Modern batteries; primary and secondary batteries. J. R. Collins. il Electr World 70:34-6+ O '63
Rapid-charge space battery developed. M. Getler. il Miss & Roc 14:28 Ja 6 '64
Storage battery that won't leak. il Bsns W p93-4 S 12 '64
Why bother with winter battery care. M. J. Schultz. il Pop Mech 120:180-4+ N '63
Charging
Multiply radio battery life; with simple re-charger. F. Greenwald. il Pop Mech 120:192 S '63
Science of a dynamic advertisement. Consumer Bul 47:16-17 My '64
Your flashlight and other batteries; should they be recharged. il Consumer Bul 46:32-5 S '63
Testing
Auto voltmeter shows you'll go. J. Tartas. il Pop Electr 21:53-5+ D '64
STORAGE battery chargers
Battery charger uses an SRC. R. G. Dale. il Electr World 72:79 S '64
Go slow when you buy a charger for your auto battery. il Consumer Bul 46:33-5 Mr '63
Recharging made fast; GE's new cell uses third electrode. Bsns W p60 O 5 '63
X-line charger. O. P. Ferrell. il Pop Electr 20:47-51 Mr '64
STORAGE cabinets. See Cabinets (furniture)
STORAGE houses
Fruit storage for half the cost. B. Hardy. il Farm J 87:21+ Ag '63
STORAGE in the home
Accent on storage. il Bet Hom & Gard 42:102-3 Mr '64
Accessories to solve closet storage problems. Good H 156:153 Je '63
Best storage ideas we've seen. il Bet Hom & Gard 41:7+ Ap '63
Bonus storage. il Farm J 88:81 Ap '64
Built-in assets. G. O'Brien. il N Y Times Mag p42-3 Ag 16 '64
Four convenience projects. il Bet Hom & Gard 42:43-4 S '64
Four terrific projects you can build. F. R. Glass. il Bet Hom & Gard 41:54-5 Mr '63
Here are hiding places; storage for folding tables and chairs. il Sunset 132:139 Mr '64
Here is almost the ultimate in narrow-shelf storage. il Sunset 130:128 My '63
Hiding place for trunks. il Sunset 132:78 Ja '64
How to make every inch of space count; kitchen storage space. il House B 106:190-3+ My '64
How to set up: a movable storage wall, a home office for two, a one-piece music center. il House & Gard 124:180-3 O '63
How to stretch space for storing clothes. il House B 105:192-5 S '63
If you can't build in, build out! il Am Home 66:48-53 Ap '63
Instant storage for pots. il House & Gard 125:194-5 Ap '64
Linens deserve planned storage. il House B 105:48+ Mr '63
One, two, three and done! basement storage idea. il Bet Hom & Gard 41:22 S '63
Plan for specialized storage. J. Holmstrand. il Suc Farm 62:76-7 My '64
Plans in space. il Suc Farm 61:91 F '63
Solve a difficult kitchen storage problem. il Bet Hom & Gard 41:33 S '63
Space savers. il Pop Mech 121:140-1 Ap '64
Storage surprises. il Bet Hom & Gard 41:115 O '63
Stretch space. il Bet Hom & Gard 42:25-6+ F '64
Stylish storage! il Bet Hom & Gard 41:100 Ap '63
That big problem of too-little space. G. O'Brien. il N Y Times Mag p76-7 My 17 '64
These room dividers serve also as music center, magazine library. il Sunset 130:136 My '63
What gripes you about my housekeeping? J. Gillies. il Farm J 89:64 Ja '65
What's new in storage? wall-to-wall style! F. Byerly. il Bet Hom & Gard 41:58-9 My '63
See also
Closets
Cupboards
Kitchen cabinets
STORAGE of bulbs. See Bulbs—Storage
STORAGE tanks. See Water tanks
STORAGE walls
Accent on storage. il Bet Hom & Gard 42:102-3 Mr '64
Hobby wall. il Pop Mech 121:139 Ap '64
Movable storage wall fact sheet. il Am Home 66:51-2 Ap '63
One wall can hold so much. il House B 105:84 Ap '63
Outdoor storage walls. il House B 105:38 My '63
Personal, and portable. G. O'Brien. il N Y Times Mag p58-9 Je 9 '63
Remodel the fireplace wall, transform the room. il Sunset 130:184 My '63
Serious collector of playfulness, and how he lives; home of A. Girard. il House B 105:134-7 Ap '63
Space-making storage wall. il Farm J 87:64 Jl '63
This storage wall is specialized. il Sunset 132:148 My '64
Wow of a wall! D. Popplestone. il Bet Hom & Gard 41:82 My '63
STORCK, Roger. See Henney, H. R. jr, jt. auth.
STORE records. See Business records
STORER, Norman W.
Coming changes in American science. bibliog Science 142:464-7 O 25 '63

STOREROOM; story. See Henderson. R.
STORES
Building types study. il Arch Rec 135:157-76 Je '64
Shopping the import stores; western import stores. il Sunset 131:125-6+ O '63
Store building: faster growth this year? H. C. F. Arnold. il Arch Rec 135:26 Je '64
Stores; newest thinking on store design; symposium. il Arch Rec 133:159-82+ Je '63
See also
Department stores
Grocery stores
Retail trade
Sears, Roebuck and company
Supermarkets
Variety stores
also subhead Stores under names of cities, e.g. New York (city)—Stores

Equipment
Consider maintenance costs in choosing store materials. il Pub W 184:47-8 O 14 '63

Lighting
Consider maintenance costs in choosing store materials. il Pub W 184:47-8 O 14 '63
Light in the right place for stores. A. Makulec. il Arch Rec 133:187-9 Je '63

STORES, Self service
See also
Supermarkets
STORES or stock-room keeping
Vroman's stock control system is unwieldy but it is effective. D. Jamison. il Pub W 185:64-6 My 4 '64
See also
Inventories
STORIES. See Childrens stories; Fairy tales; Fiction; Parables; Short stories; Story telling
STORKE, Thomas More
Reader relations. Newsweek 63:61 Mr 16 '64
STORKS
Who brought the stork? white-bellied stork. E. K. Carruth. il Sci Digest 53:87-9 Mr '63
See also
Marabous
Wood storks
STORM, Bruce. See Fennell, R. jt. auth.
STORM doors. See Doors
STORM KING hydroelectric project. See Hydroelectric plants
STORM sewer systems. See Sewer pipes
STORM sewers. See Sewer pipes
STORM water. See Sewerage
STORM waves. See Waves
STORM windows. See Windows
STORMER, Leif
Anatomy of decay as preserved in shale. Natur Hist 73:20-5 D '46
STORMONT, Clyde, and others
Mosaic hemoglobin types in a pair of cattle twins. bibliog Science 145:600-1 Ag 7 '64
STORMPROOF construction. See Building, Stormproof
STORMS
Avalanche of rain; destruction and tragedy over the West coast. il Time 85:28 Ja 1 '65
How to defeat any gale. R. P. Davis. il Motor B 112:42-3+ O '63
Over, under and over again; yawl Doubloon battered by gale. H. Whall. il Sports Illus 20:32-3 Je 1 '64
Saga of the Curlew. D. Skellon. il Yachting 113:38-9+ F '63; Reply. A. Forward. 114:120 Ag '63
See also
Aviation—Storm hazards
Cloudbursts
Hail
Hurricanes
Thunderstorms
Tornadoes
STORMS, Magnetic. See Magnetic storms
STORMY petrels. See Petrels
STORROW, James J.
AFA honors two solid citizens. il por Am For 69:34-5 O '63
STORY for Teddy; story. See Swados, H.
STORY hour. See Story telling
STORY telling
Bilingual story hour program: NYPL branches. P. B. White. il Library J 89:3379-81 S 15 '64
Listening heart. J. B. Bradley. bibliog il Wilson Lib Bul 37:677-9+ Ap '63
Of storytelling, national dilemma, and human grace. E. D. Landau. Horn Bk 39:485 O '63
Story falls in the silence: Family evening story hours, Nassau library system. S. G. Shaw. il Wilson Lib Bul 39:179 O '64
Storytelling in Java. P. B. McVickar. il Horn Bk 40:596-601 D '64
Storytelling project for slow learners. J. Pressler. il ALA Bul 57:168-9 F '63
Sunshine in the memory. R. H. Vigures. Horn Bk 39:349 Ag '63
To tell a story; excerpt from Lost half-hour: a collection of stories, comp. by E. S. Ross. Horn Bk 39:253-8 Je '63
STORY telling records. See Phonograph records—Childrens records
STORYTELLING. See Story telling
STOTLER, Donald W.
Teaching junior high school science. NEA J 52:54-6 O '63
STOTT, Mary Roelofs
My most unforgettable character. Read Digest 82:124-8 Ap '63
STOTTS, Gene
Negro Paul Revere of Quantrill's raid; story. Negro Hist Bul 26:169-70 F '63
STOUFFER, Lloyd
Biggest thing since mass production. Read Digest 84:107-10 Ja '64
STOUT, Bill
California Democrats: battle royal for the Senate. Reporter 30:21-4 My 7 '64
How Goldwater won in California. Reporter 31:17-19 Jl 2 '64
STOUT, Irving W. See Langdon, G. jt. auth.
STOUT, Pola
Spirit of style. Sat R 47:45-7+ O 24 '64
about
Five designers, five approaches. P. Adler. il por Craft Horiz 24:44-5 Mr '64
STOUT, Rex
Authors league backs JFK, asking fairer tax treatment for writers. Pub W 183:27-9 Mr 11 '63
Man who came in from the cold. Mile 59:60-1 Jl '64
Why Nero Wolfe likes orchids. Life 54:108 Ap 19 '63
STOUTENBURG, Adrien
Avalanche; poem. New Yorker 40:224 O 31 '64
Brobdingnag; poem. New Yorker 39:26 Ja 25 '64
STOUTENBURGH, John L. jr
Museum world. See issues of Hobbies
STOVALL, Walter
Image. por Time 82:27 S 13 '63
Where integration led to intermarriage. por U S News 55:10 S 16 '63
STOVER, Blanche M.
Lunch almanac. See issues of Parents' magazine & better homemaking
My own cookbook. See issues of Parents' magazine & better homemaking
STOVES
Easier ways to cleaner ranges. il Am Home 67:96-7 O '64
Friendly stove. R. Davies. House & Gard 124:216-17 O '63
Just wait till you see the new ranges! il McCalls 91:36 Ap '64
Radiators for frozen skaters; salamander stoves; Akron, Ohio. A. T. Wilcox. il Am City 78:36 Mr '63
What makes a range good these days. Bet Hom & Gard 42:108 Ap '64
See also
Electric stoves
Gas stoves
STOVES, Alcohol. See Alcohol as fuel
STOVES, Outdoor. See Camp stoves
STOWAGE
Ventilation and stowage. A. W. Moffat. il Yachting 114:46+ Ag '63
STOWAWAYS
Furtive free ride. T. Reynolds. il Life 56:8 F 7 '64
Member of the wedding; trip from London to Perth in a crate. Newsweek 64:48 N 16 '64
Reluctant sailor: a self-portrait. C. Capone. il Esquire 61:100-1+ My '64
STOWE, David M.
What about mainland China? Christian Cent 82:44-6 Ja 13 '65
STOWE, Harriet Elizabeth (Beecher)
God was her co-author. por Newsweek 61:96 Ap 8 '63
In Uncle Tom are our guilt and hope. A. Haley. il N Y Times Mag p23+ Mr 1 '64
Mrs Stowe and the American imagination. K. S. Lynn. New Repub 148:20-1 Je 29 '63; Reply. H. A. Taylor. 149:31 Jl 13 '63
Rankin house; stop on underground railroad. M. E. Aber. Negro Hist Bul 26:253 My '63
Uncle Tom and predestination. D. Chaput. Negro Hist Bul 27:143 Mr '64

STOWE, Leland
Awesome challenge of Mt Aconcagua. Read Digest 84:106-11 Mr '64
Haiti's voodoo tyrant. Read Digest 83:222-6+ N '63
Miracle at Vicos. Read Digest 82:222-6+ Ap '63
STOYENOFF, Norma J.
Importance of being persistent. Writer 76:25+ My '63
STOYER, Ray. See Merrell, J. jt. auth.
STRACHAN, G. See Perkins, H. J. jt. auth.
STRACHAN, Mary
Bob Scriver: western sculptor. Am Artist 28:50-2+ S '64
STRADIVARIUS violin. See Violin
STRAIGHT, Dorothy
Wunder-kids. por Vogue 144:222-3 D '64
STRAIGHT, Michael
Raid on resources. New Repub 149:19-20 N 30 '63
STRAIGHT from the heart; drama. See Whitman, C.
STRAIGHT-stitch sewing machines. See Sewing machines
STRAIN gages
Semiconductors strain gages. H. S. Renne. il Electr World 70:36-8+ Jl '63
STRAINCHAMPS, Ethel
Advice for adult students. Sat R 47:66 Ag 15 '64
Offspring of Webster's Third. Sat R 46:68 Ap 20 '63
STRAINS and stresses
See also
Strain gages
Struts
Trusses
STRAIT, Suzanne Hart
First Negro family on Maple Terrace. Parents Mag 40:36-7+ Ja '65
Higher math for the lower grades. Parents Mag 38:60-1+ F '63
Manners are from the heart. Parents Mag 38:72-3+ bibliog(p42) N '63; Same abr. Read Digest 84:193-4 Je '64
Taming the neighborhood bully. Parents Mag 38:44-5+ Ap '63
STRAKOSCH, George R.
Elevatoring high-rise apartment buildings. Arch Rec 135:191-2+ Je '64
STRAKOSCH, Max
Romance a hundred years ago. M. E. Peltz. il por Opera N 28:12-15 F 22 '64
STRAND, Harold P.
Fun with a homemade thermopile. Pop Mech 119:186-8+ Mr '63
Homemade tile cutter. Pop Sci 182:120-1 F '63
How to make a Jacob's ladder. Pop Sci 184: 110-11 F '64
You can transform this transformer. Pop Mech 121:188-92 Ja '64
STRAND, Kaj Aage
Determination of stellar distances. bibliog Science 144:1299-309 Je 12 '64
New 61-inch astrometric reflector. por Sky & Tel 27:204-9+ Ap '64
STRAND, Mark
Map; poem. New Yorker 39:30 Jl 20 '63
Old people on the nursing home porch; poem. Yale R 53:76 O '63
Sailing to Italy; poem. Atlan 211:72 F '63
Standing still; poem. New Yorker 40:163 S 19 '64
Violent storm; poem. New Yorker 40:66 O 10 '64
Walking around; poem. Nation 196:358 Ap 27 '63
STRANG, Charles D.
Alcohol burns in the Northwest. Motor B 112:112 Ag '63
Drama at Detroit. Motor B 114:48-9+ S '64
Hail! the Hudson River marathon. Motor B 111:156 My '63
Racing and the A.P.B.A. por Motor B 115: 112-13+ Ja '65
Wiget's winning year. Motor B 111:122-3 F '63
With the outboarders. Motor B 111:98 Je '63
STRANG, Ruth
Should parents teach reading? PTA Mag 57: 7-9 bibliog(p34) Mr '63
They have to be taught to play. PTA Mag 58:32-4 bibliog(p35) N '63
STRANGE, Vivian
Ambassador of goodwill for police department. il pors Ebony 19:40-2+ Mr '64
STRANGE interlude; drama. See O'Neill, E. G.
STRANGE time; story. See McCullough, D.
STRANGER in town; story. See Gordimer, N.
STRANGER on the beach; story. See Collinge, P.
STRANGLER fig. See Figs
STRAP clamps. See Clamps
STRASBERG, Paula
Redbook dialogue. por Redbook 121:56-7+ Jl '63
STRASBERG, Susan
One battle I had to win; ed. by R. Hochstein. por Good H 156:88 My '63
STRASBOURG international festival. See Music festivals—France
STRASSBURGER, John. See Torgesen, J. L. jt. auth.
STRASSMANN, Erwin O.
Flat-chested opinion. Newsweek 64:61 S 14 '64
STRATEGIC air command. See United States—Air force—Strategic air command
STRATEGIC services, Office of. See United States—Strategic services, Office of
STRATEGY
After Cuba: two lessons. E. Rabinowitch. Bul Atomic Sci 19:2-8 F '63
America's strategy gap; address, December 4, 1962. M. R. Laird. Vital Speeches 29:245-8 F 1 '63
Arms and stability in Europe, by A. Buchan and P. Windsor. Review
New Repub 150:22-4 Ja 11 '64. H. Malmgren
Battlements of terror; fear as a deterrent? S. A. Coblentz. Christian Cent 81:1329-31 O 28 '64
Containing ourselves: some reflections on the enemy within; excerpt. D. Riesman. New Repub 148:14-17 Ap 6 '63
Control of nuclear strategy. J. Slessor. For Affairs 42:96-106 O '63
Fall of valor; new roles and doomed civilians. Nation 197:102 S 7 '63
Fate of counterforce. W. V. O'Brien. Commonweal 78:216-18 My 17 '63
Games of peace. L. Norman. il Newsweek 63:56-7 Ja 27 '64
Kill and overkill, by R. E. Lapp. Review
Bul Atomic Sci 19:26-7 Je '63. M. Kalkstein
McNamara discusses retaliatory forces; text of testimony before House armed services committee. R. S. McNamara. Aviation W 80:74-5+ Mr 2 '64
McNamara on strategy: a change in policy? excerpts from statement, January 30, 1963, with commentary by B. T. Feld. R. S. McNamara. il Bul Atomic Sci 19:36-9 Ap '63
Major defense challenges; address, August 8, 1963. W. F. McKee. Vital Speeches 29:702-4 S 1 '63
Military strategy (Voennaya strategiya) Review
Reporter il 28:34+ F 14 '63. R. L. Garthoff
Military value of missiles in Cuba. R. Hagan and B. Bernstein. il Bul Atomic Sci 19:8-13 F '63
Never again; McNamara's ground-forces plan. Newsweek 64:21 D 28 '64
New military strategy. G. H. Evans. bibliog f Cur Hist 47:77-80+ Ag '64
New strategy for survival. il Newsweek 61: 20-4 F 11 '63
NATO's nuclear dilemma. H. A. Kissinger. il Reporter 28:22-33+ Mr 28 '63
Pendulum is swinging too far. T. D. White. il Newsweek 63:22-3 F 24 '64
Perils of deterrence. W. C. Davidon and others. Bul Atomic Sci 19:28 Mr '63
Practice of partnership. D. Acheson. For Affairs 41:247-60 Ja '63
Return to multilateral diplomacy. J. D. Singer. Yale R 53:36-48 O '63
Russia's plans for the next war. M. S. Johnson. il U S News 54:52-5 Ap 8 '63
Shifts in Soviet strategic thought. T. W. Wolfe. bibliog f For Affairs 42:475-86 Ap '64
Soviet military strategy, ed. by V. D. Sokolovsky. Review
Newsweek 61:30 My 6 '63
Speaking out; strategy and the defense intellectuals. T. D. White. Sat Eve Post 236: 10+ My 4 '63
Straight from the horse's mouth; Soviet military strategy. W. D. Jacobs. il Nat R 15: 68-70 Jl 30 '63
Strategy of overkill. R. E. Lapp. Bul Atomic Sci 19:4-11 Ap '63
Studies of war, by P. M. S. Blackett. Review
Bul Atomic Sci 19:24-5 Mr '63. W. K. H. Panofsky
Nation 196:250-2 Mr 23 '63. T. Roszak
Test-ban treaty: atomic chess; positioning of military forces to serve purely political ends. T. D. White. Newsweek 62:23 S 9 '63
Why Europe fears us; excerpt from Great debate, tr. by E. Pawel. R. Aron. Atlan 214:47-52 D '64

STRATEGY—*Continued*
Wrangle over strategy. L. J. Halle. New Repub 150:19-21 Ja 18 '64
See also
Military art and science
United States—History—Civil war—Strategy
United States—History—Revolution—Strategy
World war, 1939-1945—Strategy

STRATEGY, Communist. See Communist strategy

STRATFORD, Conn, Shakespeare festival. See American Shakespeare festival theatre and academy, Stratford, Conn.

STRATFORD, Ontario, Shakespeare festival. See Shakespeare festival, Stratford, Ontario

STRATFORD-ON-AVON
Opening night in Stratford; the insider's game. C. Bingham. Vogue 143:199+ Ap 1 '64
Sceptered isle in holiday humor; Shakespeare's 400th birthday. il Bsns W p146-8 Ap 18 '64
Travel notes. R. Joseph. Esquire 61:39-40+ Mr '64
See also
Royal Shakespeare theatre, Stratford-on-Avon

STRATOSPHERE. See Atmosphere, Upper

STRATTEN, James E.
Big-city schools, problems and prospects. PTA Mag 59:16-18+ Ja '65

STRATTON, Charles Sherwood
Fairy-tale wedding, long long ago; General Tom Thumb's wedding to Lavinia Warren. M. Weston. il pors N Y Times Mag p66+ Ap 7 '63
Social notes: 100 years ago this month. il Am Heritage 14:112 F '63

STRATTON, Samuel S.
New York preliminaries. M. Kempton. New Repub 148:6 Je 8 '63; Reply. L. M. Levine. 149:30-1 Jl 13 '63

STRAUBE, Robert L.
Examination of diurnal variation in lethally irradiated rats. Science 142:1062 N 22 '63

STRAULMAN, Ann T.
Liturgy in English; letter. Commonweal 81:424 D 18 '64

STRAUS, A. E.
Biodegradation of alkylbenzene sulfonate in a simulated septic tank and drain field. bibliog Science 142:244-5 O 11 '63

STRAUS, Nathan, 3d
Speaking out. por Sat Eve Post 237:6+ Ag 8 '64

STRAUS, R. Peter
Crusader. New Yorker 40:24-6 Je 27 '64
Sales & distribution. L. Morse. Duns R 83:63 Mr '64

STRAUS, Robert
Role for behavioral science in a university medical center. bibliog f Ann Am Acad 346:99-108 Mr '63
—and Clausen, J. A.
Health, society, and social science. bibliog f Ann Am Acad 346:1-8 Mr '63
—See Clausen, J. A. jt. ed.

STRAUSS, Claude Levi-. See Levi-Strauss, C.

STRAUSS, Franz Josef
Giftie gie us; summary of newsletter. Nat R 16:1137 D 29 '64
Lion vs. the bull. Newsweek 63:36 Je 1 '64
Visitor's welcome. por Time 81:30 Je 7 '63

STRAUSS, George
Union bargaining strength: Goliath or paper tiger? bibliog f Ann Am Acad 350:86-94 N '63

STRAUSS, Johann, 1825-1899
Die fledermaus. Criticism
Opera N 27:25 Ap 13 '63
Opera N il 27:16-20 Ap 13 '63
Die fledermaus. H. Glass. il Am Rec G 31:208-10 N '64
On records; Die fledermaus. J. W. Freeman. Opera N 27:34 Ap 13 '63
Wonderful world of Johann Strauss. R. Freed. House B 105:270-3 N '63

STRAUSS, Lewis
Strauss heads scientists: Task force on science, space and the atom to aid Sen. Barry Goldwater. Sci N L 86:235 O 10 '64

STRAUSS, Morris
My most unforgettable character. E. Guttmann. por Read Digest 83:117-22 Ag '63

STRAUSS, Richard
Another for Straussians: the Richmond Salome. G. Kossodo. Am Rec G 30:191 N '63
Arabella. R. Sabin. il Am Rec G 30:1084-7 Ag '64
Ariadne auf Naxos. Criticism
Opera N 27:17-20 F 16 '63
Opera N il 27:30 F 2 '63
Opera N il 27:24-7 F 16 '63
Opera N il 27:28-9 F 16 '63
Sat R 47:65 Ja 11 '64
Sat R 47:40 F 15 '64
Ariadne auf Naxos, as Strauss heard it just before the bombs fell. C. L. Osborne. Hi Fi 13:72-3 Ag '63
Ariadne auf Naxos; June 11, 1944, Vienna festival performance. R. Sabin. il Am Rec G 30:188-91 N '63
Bouquet for Strauss. I. Kolodin. il pors Sat R 47:55-7 My 30 '64
Case of hard-earned bread; Strauss's tours in America. R. Breuer. il pors Hi Fi 14:42-5+ Je '64
Crash at the start. F. V. Grunfeld. Reporter 30:36-8 Je 4 '64
Daphne. Criticism
Newsweek il 64:47 Ag 10 '64
Daphne. R. Sabin. Am Rec G 30:658-9 Ap '64
Elektra. Criticism
Opera N 28:32 D 14 '63
Elektra revisited. G. Fitzgerald. Opera N 29:31 Ja 23 '65
Die frau from Munich. M. Bernheimer. il Sat R 47:65 S 26 '64
Die frau ohne schatten. Criticism
New Yorker 40:186 O 10 '64
Die frau ohne schatten. G. L. Mayer. il Am Rec G 31:96-101 O '64
From Rococo, Strauss by Schlusnus, Lehmann, Destinn, Jeritza, Pauly, et al. P. L. Miller. por Am Rec G 30:1090 Ag '64
Furtwängler radio performances on DGG. Am Rec G 30:570-1+ Mr '64
Hero's life? il pors Newsweek 63:76-7 Je 22 '64
Historical records; Richard Strauss memorial. A. Favia-Artsay. il Hobbies 69:30 S '64
Intermezzo. Criticism
Opera N 27:32 Mr 23 '63
Kahn, Morgan, and Salome. O. H. Kahn. Sat R 47:60 My 30 '64
Munich and its (sometimes) favorite son. P. Moor. il por Hi Fi 14:46-9+ Je '64
Musical events; concert performance of R. Strauss's Die frau ohne schatten in Philharmonic Hall, by Concert opera association. W. Sergeant. New Yorker 40:148+ Mr 28 '64
On Eurodisc, three for Straussians. P. L. Miller. Am Rec G 31:101-2 O '64
On records; Arabella. Opera N 29:35 D 19 '64
On records; Ariadne auf Naxos. J. W. Freeman. Opera N 27:35 F 16 '63
On records; Ariadne auf Naxos; Daphne. Opera N 28:35 D 14 '63
On records; Der Rosenkavalier. Opera N 29:35 D 19 '64
On records; Die fledermaus. Opera N 29:35 Ja 9 '65
Ormandy's Don Quixote, romantic intensity and satirical thrust. J. Diether. il Am Rec G 30:1088-9 Ag '64
Paradox of late Strauss; with editorial comment. P. J. Smith; G. R. Marek. il pors Hi Fi 14:35, 36-41+ Je '64
Return to Richard. por Time 83:100+ My 22 '64
Richard Strauss: a centennial discography. Sat R 47:62-3+ My '64
Der Rosenkavalier. Criticism
Mus Am il 84:22-3 N '64
New Yorker 40:184+ O 10 '64
New Yorker 40:221 O 24 '64
Opera N il 29:17-20 D 19 '64
Sat R 47:35 O 31 '64
Singing Strauss. T. Stich-Randall. Mus Am 84:16-17 Jl '64
Strauss and his contemporaries. R. Breuer. Sat R 47:64-5 My 30 '64
Strauss and his interpreters. il pors Sat R 47:61 My 30 '64
Strauss and the electronic future. G. Gould. il Sat R 47:58-9+ My 30 '64
Strauss bookshelf; a selective bibliography; comp. by B. Bernheimer. Sat R 47:65 My 30 '64
Strauss in Munich. D. Stevens. Opera N 28:28-9 My 2 '64
Strauss, Krauss, and Capriccio. R. Breuer. il por Sat R 46:60-1 O 26 '63
Strauss; 20th century classicist. W. Mann. Mus Am 84:14-15+ Jl '64
Strauss's Arabella as sung on the Munich stage. P. J. Smith. il Hi Fi 14:68-9 Ag '64
Szell's Strauss, stunning, supreme. R. Sabin. Am Rec G 31:109 O '64

STRAVINSKY, Igor Fedorovich
Interview with Stravinsky. ed. by C. J. McNaspy. America 109:219-20 Ag 31 '63
about
New Oedipus Rex brings more of Stravinsky's Stravinsky. E. Salzman. por Hi Fi 13:126-7 O '63
Nightingale. Criticism
New Yorker 39:122+ O 12 '63
Notes from our correspondents. S. Fleming. Hi Fi 14:12+ Ap '64

STRAVINSKY, Igor Fedorovich—about—*Cont.*
On records; Oedipus Rex. Opera N 28:36 Ja 4 '64
Rake's progress. Criticism
Hi Fi por 15:69-70+ Ja '65
Records. B. Boretz. Nation 200:94-6 Ja 25 '65
Song of Caesarea. il por Newsweek 64:79 S 7 '64
Stravinsky at home. V. Stravinsky. pors Mus Am 83:10-11 Ja '63
Stravinsky scrapbook. il pors Mus Am 83: 12-13 Ja '63
Stravinsky talks with Khrushchev; excerpts from Dialogues and a diary. R. Craft. il por Vogue 142:134-5+ N 1 '63
Stravinsky's Abraham and Isaac. B. Boretz. Nation 200:39-40 Ja 11 '65
When a just man dies; song composed in memory of J. F. Kennedy. Newsweek 63:75 Ap 20 '64
STRAVINSKY, Vera
Stravinsky at home. Mus Am 83:10-11 Ja '63
STRAWBERRIES
Alpine strawberries. M. Carpenter. il Horticulture 42:16-17 F '64
Home grown strawberries taste so good. B. C. Kilvert, jr. il Flower Grower 51:45 Ap '64
Little berries that don't run. D. Reay. Flower Grower 50:67 Mr '63
New strawberry grows faster than average. Sci N L 83:376 Je 15 '63
Strawberries for profit. J. D. Black. il Pop Gard 15:8-9+ Ap '64
Strawberries, pick them from your garden. F. F. Rockwell. Flower Grower 50:64 My '63
See also
Cookery—Fruit
STRAWBERRY shortcake. See Shortcake
STRAWFLOWERS
Flowers that last. B. Nichols. il Pop Gard 14: 11 Mr '63
Straw flowers are everlastings. il Sunset 130:305+ My '63
STRAWN, Bernice
Detergent dilemma. Bet Hom & Gard 41:94-5 Ap '63
Smart housekeeping for very busy gals. Bet Hom & Gard 42:78+ Ap '64
STREAM pollution. See Water pollution
STREAMING, Protoplasmic. See Protoplasmic streaming
STREAMS. See Brooks, creeks, etc.
STREATFEILD, Noel
Album and the artist. Horn Bk 40:159-61 Ap '64
STRECKER, Zelda
Five designers, five approaches. P. Adler. il por Craft Horiz 24:44 Mr '64
STREET, Donald
South to the Islands. Yachting 116:54-6+ Ag '64
STREET, James H.
What's wrong with the Alianza? Reporter 28:25-9 F 14 '63
STREET, Joseph C.
DDT antagonism to dieldrin storage in adipose tissue of rats. bibliog Science 146:1580-1 D 18 '64
STREET accidents
Prevention
See Streets—Safety devices and measures
STREET cars
Clang dies out; New Orleans street railway system. il Bsns W p84-6 D 14 '63
Do not talk to the motorman while the streetcar is in motion. D. Perry. il Read Digest 83:247-8+ O '63
Trolley museum; Branford, Conn. il Travel 120:45-7 Ag '63
STREET cleaning
Clean-street bug is catching; Philadelphia. D. M. Smallwood and A. Michaels. il Am City 78:98-100 S '63
Clean sweep costs more; Riverside, Calif. R. M. Rossi. il Am City 79:114-15 Je '64
Dirty streets have no place in our cleanest city; East Orange, N.J. R. P. English and others. il Am City 78:93-5 My '63
How to cut street-cleaning costs; El Paso, Tex. R. Hickok. il Am City 79:90-1 Jl '64
If it works in New York city. F. J. Lucia. il Am City 78:96-8 D '63; 79:100-2 Ja '64
Removing oil at 25° below; Mankato, Minn. E. G. Hill. il Am City 78:30 Je '63
Street cleaning. See issues of American city
Street cleaning gets assembly-line techniques; Sioux City, Ia. W. D. McElwee. il Am City 78:126-7 Je '63
Street-cleaning revolution. J. P. Horton. bibliog il Am City 78:106-8 Mr; 104-6 Ap '63
Stretching the street dollar; Lawrence, Kan. G. Williams and A. T. Hodges. il Am City 78:102-3 O '63
Sweepers are part of the parade; Phoenix, Ariz. J. A. Stokely. il Am City 78:36 S '63
We flush and sweep for better results; Palm Springs, Calif. T. W. Essen. Am City 78: 36 Ag '63
See also
Snow and ice removal
STREET cleaning apparatus
Flushers fill the gap; Mount Vernon, N.Y. A. Annunziata. Am City 79:8 My '64
Follow-up sweeper vacuums up dirt; Tucson, Ariz. H. L. Danforth. il Am City 79:8 My '64
Four times as costly; six times greater service; polypropylene brushes for Minneapolis street-sweeping machines. il Am City 78:44 My '63
Hand sweeping loses; street vacuum sweepers. C. M. Thelin. il Am City 78:20 Jl '63
How sweepers really perform. R. R. Fleming. bibliog il Am City 79:113-15 My '64
Men and machines cut one-third off sweeping bill; Fresno, Calif. A. Stenman. il Am City 79:111-12 Mr '64
Pool filters bow to a catch-basin cleaner; method used in Appleton, Wis. R. W. Bues. il Am City 79:25 F '64
Small city enjoys big-sweeper economy; Canonsburg, Pa. W. W. Buckley. il Am City 79:177-8 O '64
Solving street cleaning's toughest problem; vacuum-pick-up system; Milwaukee, Wis. W. J. Rheinfrank. il Am City 79:94-5 Ap '64
Street cleaning. See issues of American city
Street cleaning gets assembly-line techniques; Sioux City, Ia. W. D. McElwee. il Am City 78:126-7 Je '63
Street-cleaning revolution. J. P. Horton. bibliog il Am City 78:106-8 Mr; 104-6 Ap '63
See also
Refuse collection trucks
STREET flushing. See Street cleaning
STREET lighting
Choosing the right street-lighting luminaire. F. M. Neal. il Am City 79:94-6 D '64
City relights its core area. P. J. Bailey. il Am City 79:113 Ja '64
Dusk-to-dawn lighting; Pine City, Minn. W. W. Challeen, sr. il Am City 79:134 S '64
5,000 years of lighting. il Am City 78:129-30 F '63
From June bugs to fluorescents; Little Falls, Minn. D. L. Norgren. il Am City 79:127 F '64
Good lighting spells progress; Midland, Pa. R. E. Steebner. il Am City 79:82-3 Jl '64
Light for a world-famous small-city downtown; Grand Junction, Colo. J. M. Lacy. il Am City 79:115 D '64
Modern lighting sells itself; Grove City, Pa. F. E. Fisher. il Am City 79:111+ D '64
New lighting a real bargain; Emmaus, Pa. O. T. Iobst. il Am City 78:131 O '63
One-sided lighting story; Hattiesburg, Miss. C. F. Pittman, jr. il Am City 79:104 Jl '64
Out of the dark; Osseo, Minn. V. Joyner. il Am City 78:111 N '63
Outdoor lighting. See issues of American city
Seven-year relighting program. O. Lites. il Am City 78:129 My '63
Status of residential lighting. Am City 78: 122+ Ag '63
29 per cent rate increase buys 72 per cent more light; Dover, N.H. D. E. Chick. il Am City 79:132 F '64
Women's clubs help cities to advance street lighting. J. P. Heck. il Am City 79:114-15 S '64
See also
Electric lamps, Mercury vapor
also subhead Lighting under names of cities, e.g. Syracuse, N.Y.—Lighting
STREET lighting fixtures
Choosing the right street-lighting luminaire. F. M. Neal. il Am City 79:94-6 D '64
Colonial lighting adds beauty and safety; Lexington, Ky. il Am City 78:145 Je '63
Retire the relics; Covington, Ga. J. H. Bryan. il Am City 78:117 D '63
STREET markings. See Traffic markings
STREET of bugles; story. See Tyler, A.
STREET of the prophets; story. See Goldreich, G.
STREET openings
How to regulate street openings. Am City 79:146+ Ag '64
STREET paving. See Pavements
STREET railroads
Clang dies out; New Orleans street railway system. il Bsns W p84-6 D 14 '63

STREET repairing. See Streets—Maintenance and repair

STREET signs
Steel strapping cuts sign-mounting costs; New York city. H. A. Barnes. il Am City 79:137 Ap '64

STREET sweepers. See Street cleaning apparatus

STREET sweeping. See Street cleaning

STREET trades
Dreamsicle merchants. Newsweek 62:46-7 Ag 5 '63
Early, early show in Los Angeles; produce and flower markets. il Sunset 133:17 O '64
Everything under the sun; Chicago's Maxwell street. il Bsns W p28-9 Jl 13 '63
Matriarchs of the market. il Time 83:32+ Ja 3 '64
Place for all things; African markets. P. Bohannan. il Natur Hist 73:54-61 O '64

STREET traffic
Downtown snarl: a case for sorting, stacking, and storing. il Arch Forum 119:78-83 O '63
Full speed ahead on a dead-end road; excerpt from Heart of our cities. V. Gruen. il Horizon 6:66-71 Sum '64
Keep 'em rolling to the final jam. P. O'Neil. il Life 57:98-100+ N 13 '64
Let the computer tabulate your traffic counts. D. H. Johnson. il Am City 78:135 Mr '63
Out of the jam? Buchanan report. Newsweek 62:59 D 16 '63
Traffic in towns; concerning British report. F. Gutheim. Arch Rec 135:78+ Je '64
What to do about traffic? some answers from abroad. il U S News 54:86-90 F 4 '63
See also
Pedestrians
Television in traffic control
Traffic engineering
Traffic signs
also subhead Street traffic under names of cities, e.g. Rome (city)—Street traffic

Automatic control

Underground traffic detectors; Palo Alto, Calif. J. Taylor. il Am City 79:140+ S '64

STREET trees. See Trees in cities

STREET vacuum sweepers. See Street cleaning apparatus

STREET vendors. See Street trades

STREETER, Carroll P.
What farmers think of their future; present farm program; address, June 11, 1963. Vital Speeches 29:600-2 Jl 15 '63

STREETER, Edward
Fourth bride; story. McCalls 90:94-5 Je '63
You can't run away from Christmas; story. McCalls 92:112-13 D '64

STREETS
Where the cars are. il Time 82:64 N 1 '63
See also
Gutters
Pavements
Street cleaning

Lighting

See Street lighting

Maintenance and repair

Cement-stabilized aggregate wins; Grandview, Mo. L. W. Weller. il Am City 78:75-7 N '63
Don't compromise on quality; Kingsport, Tenn. M. L. West and S. K. Addington. il Am City 78:87-8 Mr '63
Economy street paving fills the gap; Detroit. G. C. Richards and D. Behm. il Am City 78:89-91 S '63
Hot-patch box saves cold cash; Fresno, Calif. M. J. Carozza. il Am City 78:9 Jl '63
Inexpensive overlay replaces seal coat; Rockville Centre, N.Y. R. C. Olton. il Am City 80:76-7 Ja '65
Match the treatment to street conditions. C. H. McDonald. il Am City 80:102-4 Ja '65
Resourceful street maintenance; Newark, N.J. R. G. Caprio and F. Crann. il Am City 78:96-7 Ap '63
Soil cement streets for six cents a day; Chickasha, Okla. B. Sullivan. il Am City 78:88-9 D '63
Street maintenance, then and now; Wayne County, Mich. O. Pommerening. il Am City 78:8 F '63
Stretching the street dollar; Lawrence, Kan. G. Williams and A. T. Hodges. il Am City 78:102-3 O '63
Switch to slurry seal; Waco, Tex. C. Hoge. il Am City 79:104-5 Mr '64
See also
Pavements—Surface treatment

Safety devices and measures

High-visibility colors; fluorescent color safety program. il Am City 78:96-8 My '63
See also
Traffic markings

Traffic lines

See Traffic markings

STREETS along the way; story. See Albee, G. S.

STREETS of New York; musical comedy. See Musical comedies, revues, etc.—**Criticisms, plots, etc.**

STREETT, J. C. Jr
Bile duct restoration in rana pipiens after ligation of the hepatoduodenal ligament. bibliog Science 143:592-4 F 7 '64

STREHLER, Allen F.
What's new about the new math? Sat R 47:68-9+ Mr 21 '64

STREIBIG, Don
Children's game. Pop Phot 54:141+ Ja '64
Film ideas. Pop Phot 53:184-5+ N '63
Ideas & scripts. Pop Phot 53:203-4 D '63; 54:141 My; 121 Je; 55:115 Jl; 94 Ag; 92 S; 109 O '64
Pro goes the amateur way. Pop Phot 54:111+ Mr '64

STREIGEL, Edward
Signals off. por Newsweek 63:30 F 10 '64

STREIKER, Lowell D.
Churchly mendacity. Christian Cent 81:805 Je 17 '64
Monologue. Christian Cent 80:1375-6 N 6 '63
Obligation ignored. Christian Cent 81:886-8 Jl 8 '64

STREISAND, Barbra
Barbra. S. Alexander. il pors Life 56:51-2+ My 22 '64; Same abr. with title Barbra Streisand, funny girl. Read Digest 85:51-5 Ag '64
Barbra Streisand: new singing sensation. C. Brossard. pors Look 27:M12+ N 19 '63
Barbra Streisand show. L. Lerman. il pors Mlle 59:158-9 My '64
Barbra Streisand: singing, swinging show stopper! E. Miller. pors Seventeen 22:108-9+ O '63
Barbra Streisand: that's enough. R. Gilman. Commonweal 80:147 Ap 24 '64
Bea, Billie, and Barbra. por Newsweek 61:79 Je 3 '63
Follow a star. C. Taylor. il por Seventeen 24:76+ Ja '65
Full throttle. por Newsweek 63:76-7 Ap 6 '64
Girl. il pors Time 83:62-7 Ap 10 '64
Good-bye Brooklyn, hello fame. P. Hamill. pors Sat Eve Post 236:22-3 Jl 27 '63
I remember Barbra. J. Weidman. por Holiday 34:123-5+ N '63
Individualists; Mlle's annual Merit awards. pors Mlle 58:75 Ja '64
Kook from Madagascar. J. S. Wilson. pors Hi Fi 14:43-5+ My '64
Money girl. il por Newsweek 64:48 Jl 6 '64
Nielsen's newest. Time 84:62 Jl 3 '64
On the rue Streisand. por Time 83:54 Ap 3 '64
People are talking about. . . pors Vogue 143:118-19 Mr 1 '64
Playbull. Theatre Arts 47:9 N '63
Success is a baked potato. pors Life 55:112+ S 20 '63
Wonderful year of Barbra Streisand. por Vogue 144:220-1 D '64

STREISSLE, Gert, and Maramorosch, Karl
Reovirus and wound-tumor virus; serological cross reactivity. bibliog Science 140:996-7 My 31 '63

STREIT, Clarence
Clarence Streit & Atlantica. Esquire 59:19-20+ Ap '63
Clarence Streit may yet be right. A. Gingrich. Esquire 59:6+ F '63

STREIT, Peggy
Go ye therefore, and teach all nations. N Y Times Mag p 12+ Mr 22 '64
It's easier to adopt a baby. N Y Times Mag p48+ Ag 23 '64
Marriage counselors, helpers and hurters. N Y Times Mag p26+ N 3 '63
Parent and child. N Y Times Mag p53+ Ja 24 '65
Princeton's lesson: school integration is not enough. N Y Times Mag p 14+ Je 21 '64
Walk through Arlington, and history. N Y Times Mag p9+ D 22 '63
What is courage? N Y Times Mag p30-1+ N 24 '63
Why they fight for the P.A.T. N Y Times Mag p20-1+ S 20 '64

STRENG, A. G. and Grosse, A. V.
Acid of krypton and its barium salt. bibliog Science 143:242-3 Ja 17 '64

STRENGELL, Marianne
Marianne Strengell. A. Adams. il Craft Horiz 23:34-6+ Ja '63

STRENGTH, Muscular. See Muscular power

STRENGTH of materials
High-strength steels. il Sci N L 84:46-7 Jl 20 '63
Strength of steel. V. F. Zackay. il Sci Am 209:72-82 bibliog(p 140) Ag '63
See also
Steel—Strength
Struts

STREPP, Hans G.
Rudolf Diesel; the man and his engine. Motor B 114:25-7+ O '64

STREPTOCOCCI
Biosynthesis of streptococcal cell walls; a rhamnose polysaccharide. L. D. Zeleznick and others. bibliog il Science 140:400-1 Ap 26 '63
Dentist checks children's throats; prevention of rheumatic fever. Sci Digest 56:57 N '64
Fructose-1,6-diphosphate requirement of streptococcal lactic dehydrogenases. M. J. Wolin. bibliog il Science 146:775-7 N 6 '64
Invader; cases of enterococcus infection at New Rochelle hospital. Newsweek 61:80 My 6 '63
Ravages of strep; classification of streptococci. il Time 84:68 O 30 '64
Throat cultures at home advised by researchers. Sci N L 86:214 O 3 '64

STREPTOCOCCUS sore throat. See Throat—Diseases

STREPTOMYCIN
Phenotypic repair of RNA-bacteriophage mutants by streptomycin. R. C. Valentine and N. D. Zinder. bibliog il Science 144:1458-9 Je 19 '64
Radioactive myoinositol: incorporation into streptomycin. H. Heding. bibliog il Science 143:953-4 F 28 '64
Sensitivity of cultured mammalian cells to streptomycin and dihydrostreptomycin. M. Moskowitz and N. E. Kelker. bibliog il Science 141:647-8 Ag 16 '63
Streptomycin and the genetic code. Sci Am 211:44-6 Jl '64
Streptomycin as an antiviral agent: mode of action. T. D. Brock and S. O. Wooley. bibliog il Science 141:1065-7 S 13 '63
Streptomycinoid antibiotics: synergism by puromycin. J. R. White and H. L. White. bibliog il Science 146:772-4 N 6 '64

STRESS (physiology)
Are you tense? here's why. il Sci Digest 53:85-90 Je '63
Case of the screaming silence. D. Naylor. il NEA J 53:61 Ja '64
Children's stresses and distresses; with study discussion program, ed. by R. Strang. L. B. Murphy. il PTA Mag 59:14-16, 35 O '64
Early developmental stress and later behavior. M. W. Lieberman. bibliog il Science 141:824-5 Ag 30 '63
Elastic membrane: effect of increasing tension on the absorptive capacity. J. H. Lunseth. bibliog il Science 141:438 Ag 2 '63
Gastric erosions in the rat: effects of immobilization at different points in the activity cycle. R. Ader. bibliog il Science 145:406-7 Jl 24 '64
Helping children cope with stress; with study-discussion program, by R. Strang. E. J. LeShan. bibliog il PTA Mag 58:7-9, 35 Ja '64
How to handle stress: learn to enjoy it; report of symposium at the University of California medical center, San Francisco, il Time 82:52-3 N 29 '63
Life inside a paper bag. R. Winkler. il Harper 227:44-5 S '63
Long-term isolation stress in rats. A. Hatch and others. bibliog il Science 142:507 O 25 '63
More strain on driver than astronaut in orbit. il Sci Digest 53:23-5 F '63
New troops march on headaches; tension and migraine research. Bsns W p72+ Je 20 '64; Same with title New attack on headaches. il Sci Digest 56:75-8 N '64
Peromyscus leucopus: an interesting subject for studies of socially induced stress responses. C. H. Southwick. bibliog il Science 143:55-6 Ja 3 '64
Poliomyelitis in monkeys: decreased susceptibility after avoidance stress. J. T. Marsh and others. bibliog il Science 140:1414-15 Je 28 '63
Stress affects success. Sci N L 86:23 Jl 11 '64
Stress modification of drug response. B. D. Rupe and others. bibliog il Science 141:1186-7 S 20 '63
Success game; concerning the report, Life stress and mental health, by Thomas S. Langner and others. Newsweek 62:88 D 2 '63
Tension can be an asset: if management deals with it constructively. D. W. Ewing. bibliog f Harvard Bsns R 42:71-8 S '64
Tensions; his and hers. I. Rockower. il McCalls 92:114+ N '64
Truth about executive stress. M. R. Feinberg. il Duns R 84:34-6+ Ag '64

STRETCH fabrics. See Textile fabrics, Synthetic

STRETCH fibers. See Textile fibers, Elastic

STRETCHING
Putting new stretch in tough metal; Metal flo corp.'s secret process. il Bsns W p34+ D 26 '64

STREUBEL, Don
Biggest black ever killed; ed. by B. East. por Outdoor Life 133:46-8+ My '64

STREYFFERT, Thorsten
Economics of sustained yield forestry in Sweden. por Am For 69:36-8+ Jl '63

STRICKHAUSEN, Harry
In the open. Poetry 102:391-2 S '63
Of the real world; Shadow and image; poems. Poetry 104:156-8 Je '64
Recent criticism. Poetry 104:264-7 Jl '64

STRICKLAND, A. C.
British physics journals. Science 144:986 My 22 '64

STRICKLAND, Remus James
Florida's sinner safari; Johns committee. E. Peter, jr. New Repub 148:13-15 Ap 27 '63

STRICKLAND, Roger
Roger the Rifle. H. L. Masin. por Sr Schol 82:26 Ja 30 '63

STRICOM. See United States—Armed forces—Strike command

STRIETELMEIER, John. See Hoffmann, V. jt. auth.

STRIKE command. See United States—Strike command

STRIKE the young hawk gently; story. See Brooks, W.

STRIKER, Richard Caine
Sound on file. Sat R 46:47-9 N 30 '63

STRIKES
See also
Arbitration, Industrial
Labor disputes

Economic aspects

Strike costs put at 190 millions; New York. U S News 54:99 Ap 8 '63

History

Strike and discontent. J. W. Bloch. Mo Labor R 86:645-51 Je '63

Australia

Striking country. Time 83:98+ Ap 24 '64

Belgium

At any cost; end of the doctors' strike. Newsweek 63:40+ Ap 27 '64
Back where they started; Belgian doctors' strike. Time 83:36 Ap 24 '64
Do doctors have a right to strike? il U S News 56:10 Ap 20 '64
Doctors go on strike; doctors vs socialized-medicine in Belgium. P. Hamill. il Sat Eve Post 237:79-83 My 16 '64
Doctors' remedy. il Newsweek 63:54+ Ap 20 '64
Doctors strike. il Sr Schol 84:15 Ap 24 '64
Physician, see thyself. il Time 83:43-4 Ap 17 '64
℞: strike; of physicians. Time 83:32 Ap 10 '64
Why 10,000 doctors went on strike. U S News 56:8 Ap 13 '64

Bolivia

Bolivia's revolution comes of age; strike in tin mines. J. D. Bowen. Reporter 29:34-6 S 26 '63

British Guiana

Admission of failure; Cheddi Jagan's agricultural workers' union. Time 84:29 Ag 14 '64
British Guiana strike settlement. Mo Labor R 86:1069-70 S '63

Canada

Midas of the maritimes; Irving oil co. strike, St John, New Brunswick. il Time 83:67 Ja 31 '64
Murder in the north. Newsweek 61:53 F 25 '63
Strike in the Canadian woods. C. A. Radimer. Nation 196:224-5 Mr 16 '63

STRIKES—*Continued*

Dominican Republic

Another chance; strike by taxi drivers and longshoremen. il Newsweek 63:54 My 18 '64

France

Back to work for French coal miners. il Sr Schol 82:20 Ap 17 '63
Black mugs' revolt. Newsweek 61:46+ Mr 18 '63
De Gaulle and the French strikes. A. Werth. Nation 196:239-40 Mr 23 '63
De Gaulle and the strike. J. Daniel. New Repub 148:10-11 Ap 13 '63
De Gaulle's labor policy on trial; what the French strikes are about. il U S News 54:90-1 Ap 1 '63
Fresh out; dairy farmers strike. Newsweek 64:57 O 12 '64
Give us some sous. il Time 81:24-5 Mr 22 '63
How de Gaulle came out in showdown with miners. il U S News 54:105-6 Ap 15 '63
How de Gaulle handles his labor problems. il U S News 54:100 Mr 18 '63
In the not so united Europe; French milk strike. E. Taylor. Reporter 31:12+ O 8 '64
Labor vs. de Gaulle; miners march on Paris. il Bsns W p78-80+ Mr 23 '63
Letter from Paris. Genêt. New Yorker 39:86+ Jl 27 '63
Letter from Paris; strikes in Paris transport system and on farms. Genêt. New Yorker 39:70 Jl 13 '63
Letter from Paris; twenty-four-hour general strike. Genêt. New Yorker 40:62 D 26 '64
Letter from Paris; university students all over France. Genêt. New Yorker 39:158-61 D 14 '63
Money talks; de Gaulle refused to budge when coal miners strike. il Newsweek 61:31-2 Ap 1 '63
Patterns of industrial strike activity in France during the July monarchy. P. N. Stearns. bibliog f Am Hist R 70:371-94 Ja '65
To the mines! Time 81:40+ Mr 15 '63
See also
Student strikes

Germany (Federal Republic)

Arbitration by Erhard. Newsweek 61:73-4 My 20 '63
Endangered miracle. il Time 81:93 My 10 '63
Erhard's decisive action; Baden Wurttemberg metalworking strike. il Bsns W p43-4+ My 11 '63
German labor strife avoided. U S News 54:90 My 20 '63
Walkouts and lockouts; metalworkers' union. il Newsweek 61:81 My 13 '63
Why the strikes in Germany. U S News 54:107 My 13 '63

Great Britain

Letter from London; postmen and post-office staffs. M. Panter-Downes. New Yorker 40:69-70 Ag 1 '64

Hawaii

Matter of motive; newspaper strike. il Time 82:40 Jl 19 '63

Italy

Chasing birds; Italian metalworkers. Newsweek 61:62+ Mr 4 '63
Striking figure. il Newsweek 64:27 D 28 '64

Japan

Ikeda averts wide strike. Bsns W p56+ Ap 25 '64

Spain

Trouble this summer? Time 81:36 Ap 26 '63

United States

Big strike: a thing of the past? A. H. Raskin. Sat R 46:20-2+ N 16 '63
Fewer strikes ahead in U.S? interview. W. E. Simkin. U S News 56:78-81 Mr 23 '64
Going up: cost of strikes. U S News 56:81 Je 29 '64
Hard times. il Time 81:13-17 Mr 1 '63
In the public interest. Commonweal 77:480 F 1 '63
Labor month in review; labor-management disputes. Mo Labor R 86:III-IV F '63
Labor's crisis of public confidence. A. H. Raskin. il Sat R 46:21-5+ Mr 30 '63
Now beginning: an era of costlier strikes? U S News 54:37-8 F 4 '63
Review of work stoppages during 1962-1963. L. R. Nolan. il Mo Labor R 86:796-801; 87:749-55 Jl '63, Jl '64
Right to publish; question of violence and vandalism during strikes. H. Hazlitt. Newsweek 61:78 Ap 8 '63
Story of two strikes: what unions are running up against; oil refinery in Texas, telephone company in Florida; Oil workers union. U S News 55:97 Ag 19 '63
Strike deadlocks go critical. Bsns W p34 F 9 '63
Strike threat will decline. S. W. Gellerman. il Nations Bsns 51:36-7+ Jl '63
Strike wanes as a weapon. il Bsns W p43-4 O 10 '64
Strikes and the public. H. Malmgren. New Repub 148:6 Ap 20 '63
Striking facts. J. O'Gara. Commonweal 77:556 F 22 '63
Two strikes: automobile workers and longshoremen. il Time 84:95 O 9 '64
Way out of our strike dilemma. M. Lerner. Look 27:84+ Ap 23 '63; Same abr. with title Our strike dilemma. Read Digest 83:75-8 Jl '63
When strikes hit plants: employers' newest answer. il U S News 56:89-90 Je 15 '64
Where strike wave is spreading. U S News 54:76 F 4 '63
Why strikes are on the rise il U S News 57:35-6 N 30 '64
Work stoppages; tables. See issues of Monthly labor review

Aerospace industries

Compulsory defense arbitration law urged. Aviation W 78:33 Ja 21 '63

Airlines

Airline mutual aid agreement renewed. Aviation W 81:30 Jl 20 '64
Pan Am-TWU pact ends one-day strike. Aviation W 81:29 Ag 31 '64

Automobile industry and trade

Autos: will strikes cut off the boom? with address by H. Ford. il U S News 57:71-3, 77-8 Jl 6 '64
Betting on a short one; with editorial comment. il Bsns W p25-7, 156 O 3 '64
Brush fires plague auto industry. Bsns W p54 N 14 '64
Detroit goes back to work. Bsns W p 128 N 28 '64
Detroit: out on one strike. Bsns W p28-9 O 31 '64
GM strike end is near. Bsns W p96+ O 24 '64
Hair tonic and dignity; UAW strike against General motors. il Newsweek 64:86+ O 12 '64
Little things behind a big strike. il U S News 57:89-91 O 12 '64
Only local disputes left to settle at GM. il Bsns W p89 O 31 '64
Real issue in the auto strike: demand for union power. il U S News 57:91-2 O 5 '64
Right to work; United auto workers against General motors. il Time 84:111 O 2 '64
Strike toll. il Time 84:97 O 30 '64
There they go again; U.A.W. workers at Ford launch their own strike. Time 84:110 N 13 '64
Walkout in Detroit; UAW strike at General motors. Newsweek 64:93-4 O 5 '64
Walter gives the word; General motors strike ended. Newsweek 64:78 N 2 '64
What happens when a big strike drags on. U S News 57:70-2 N 2 '64
What the auto strikes cost. U S News 57:88 D 7 '64
Why a big auto strike seems unlikely. U S News 57:92 Ag 24 '64
Will there be an auto strike? il U S News 57:66-8 Ag 31 '64

Chemical workers

Scripto on strike; the race-wage picket line. C. J. Levy. Nation 200:31-2 Ja 11 '65

Electric workers

Rocks at dusk; violence in Hillsdale, Mich. Newsweek 63:76 Je 8 '64

Farmers

This little piggy; National farmers organization meat-withholding action. Newsweek 64:72-3 S 7 '64
Violence off the streets; livestock-farmer's market boycott. il Time 84:38 S 18 '64
Vow; NFO holding action. il Newsweek 64:90 S 21 '64
When farmers go on strike. J. Bird. il Sat Eve Post 237:30+ N 21 '64

Government employees

Strikes of government employees, 1942-61. L. R. Nolan and J. T. Hall, jr. il Mo Labor R 86:52-4 Ja '63

STRIKES—United States—*Continued*

Government intervention

Can trains be kept running? Bsns W p26 Ag 24 '63
Cruelty. D. Lawrence. U S News 54:108 F 25 '63
Florida's railroad war; a few sticks of dynamite. R. G. Sherrill. il Nation 198:227-30 Mr 9 '64
LBJ and big strikes; is rail fight a pattern? il U S News 56:99-101 Ap 27 '64
Managers have to manage. C. P. Ives. Nat R 14:157-8 F 26 '63
Passing the buck. D. Lawrence. U S News 54:120 Ap 22 '63
Shippers give in but blast panel. il Bsns W p34 Ja 26 '63
Staying on the rails; with editorial comment. Bsns W p23, 144 Jl 13 '63
Time runs out for railroads. Bsns W p26 Jl 20 '63
Who will mediate the mediators? E. J. Silberfarb. il Reporter 28:23-6 Mr 14 '63
Why strikes are worrying union leaders. il U S News 54:86-8 Mr 4 '63

Grocery trade

Bite for Baltimore; food chains shut down. il Bsns W p87 Je 6 '64
Life without supermarkets; Retail clerks union vs Acme chain. U S News 56:82 Je 29 '64

Guided missile industry

Missile sites: less time lost. U S News 54:90 Je 17 '63

Lumber workers

Rival unions team up on plywood's Big six. Bsns W p74+ Je 15 '63

Maritime workers

Another strike on the docks: why? U S News 57:92-3 O 12 '64
Atom ship becalmed by pay row; engineers quit on Savannah. Bsns W p 176+ My 18 '63
Crippling dock strike settled. il Sr Schol 82:22 F 6 '63
Dock strike gets T-H treatment. Bsns W p48 O 10 '64
Dockers take a second look at pact. Bsns W p 124 Ja 23 '65
Dockwallopers' switch. il Newsweek 65:58 F 1 '65
Expensive education; new contract. Time 85:73A Ja 29 '65
Longshoremen boxed-in. W. McCann. Sci N L 86:246 O 17 '64
Our strike-strangled merchant marine. R. S. Strother. Read Digest 82:75-9 F '63
Shippers give in but blast panel. il Bsns W p34 Ja 26 '63
Swiss view of U.S. strikes: you lose orders, and jobs. K. Küng. il U S News 54:37 F 4 '63
They'd rather strike than work. il Time 85:66-7 Ja 22 '65
Unthinking man's strike. il Newsweek 65:67 Ja 25 '65
Up anchor. il Newsweek 61:70+ F 4 '63
Why dock settlement backfired. il Bsns W p28 Ja 16 '65
Why dockworkers closed down shipping. il U S News 58:6 Ja 25 '65

Newspapers

After a three-month shutdown, what striking printers got. U S News 54:98 Mr 18 '63
And the presses roll. Nat R 14:221+ Mr 26 '63
Automation and the news strike. R. Severo. il Reporter 28:29-30+ Mr 14 '63
Battle lines in Detroit. il Time 84:71-2 Jl 24 '64
Beyond toleration? Newsweek 61:48-9 Mr 4 '63
Bitter and the bright. Newsweek 61:87 F 25 '63
Blacked out; Detroit strike. Newsweek 64:77 S 7 '64
Blight begins to spread; New York newspaper strike. il Bsns W p30-2 Ja 19 '63
Challenging the strike record; the Youngstown, Ohio, vindicator. Time 85:44 Ja 22 '65
City without newspapers. New Repub 148:4 F 23 '63
Constitutional right to publish; excerpts from address, May 1, 1963. A. J. Goldberg. U S News 54:120 My 13 '63
Costly settlement; New York's newspaper strike. il Time 81:67 Mr 15 '63
Crisis for the independent daily. J. Tebbel; reply. L. F. Kent. Sat R 46:63 F 9 '63
Cruelty. D. Lawrence. U S News 54:108 F 25 '63
Deadlock in Detroit. Time 84:72 S 4 '64
Detroit's newspaper troubles; seven strikes in less than nine years. U S News 57:63 Ag 3 '64
Dilemma of a guild reporter. M. Bracker; discussion. Reporter 28:10 F 14 '63
During the blackout; what local government without newspapers can mean. G. Britt. New Repub 148:6-7 Ap 13 '63
Economics and the press. il Sr Schol 82:12-15 Mr 27 '63
Fallout from a strike; effects of New York's newspaper strike. Time 83:60 F 7 '64
15th week in Detroit; Detroit's newspaper strike. Time 84:92 O 30 '64
For newspapers, new roadblocks; New York. U S News 54:124 Mr 25 '63
Hard times. il Time 81:13-17 Mr 1 '63
Here we go again; prolongation of strike by photoengravers. il Time 81:80-1 Ap 5 '63
How idled workers get by when a strike stops their jobs; Detroit. U S News 57:120+ O 26 '64
How the Constitution was violated; reprint. D. Lawrence. U S News 54:124+ My 6 '63
Legalized labor chaos. H. Hazlitt. Newsweek 61:82 F 25 '63
Let's arbitrate communications strikes. Sat R 46:47-8 F 9 '63; Discussion. 46:50-1 Mr 9 '63
Life without the Times. M. Ascoli. Reporter 28:22 Mr 14 '63
Longest strike out; Detroit settlement. Newsweek 64:64 N 30 '64
Mayor again is frustrated. Bsns W p34 Mr 30 '63
Mayor smiled; settlement of New York newspaper strike. il Newsweek 61:62 Mr 18 '63
Modest proposal; concerning the blackout of daily news of art. A. Frankfurter. Art N 62:21+ Mr '63
Money & other things; biggest obstacle to a settlement. Time 81:63-4 Mr 22 '63
New look at the New York newspaper strike. il U S News 54:50-2 Mr 4 '63
New record for stubborness: Detroit's newspaper strike. Time 84:65 N 27 '64
New York: break in the ranks. il Time 81:44 Mr 8 '63
New York finds it can live without papers. Bsns W p34 Mr 2 '63
New York gets back a paper; New York post. il Bsns W p28 Mr 9 '63
New York newspaper strike has little effect on book reading. Library J 88:531-2 F 1 '63
No-strike moves by newspapers. U S News 54:92 My 6 '62
Notes and comment. New Yorker 38:23 F 9 '63
Notes and comment; New York times. New Yorker 39:33-8 Ap 13 '63
Now: a strike over a computer; Post-times in West Palm Beach and News-journal in Pensacola, Fla. U S News 55:110 N 25 '63
Paradoxes of a news strike. Nation 196:218-19 Mr 16 '63
Post time. il Newsweek 61:60-1 Mr 11 '63
Public pressure in Detroit. Time 84:69 N 13 '64
Right to know vs. the right to strike. J. Reston; M. Kempton. New Repub 148:15-18 Mr 30 '63
Right to publish. H. Hazlitt. Newsweek 61:78 Ap 8 '63
Rolling again. Newsweek 61:64+ Ap 15 '63
Score on strikes at newspapers; in Cleveland and New York. U S News 54:95-6 F 25 '63
Settlement on premium pay; Pressmen's union and the Paper and platehandlers union vs. Detroit free press. U S News 57:82-3 N 23 '64
Solidarity: forever? Newsweek 61:57 F 4 '63
Something to hoot about. Time 81:62 F 8 '63
Still no news in New York. Bsns W p24-5 F 16 '63
Strike costs put at 190 millions; New York. U S News 54:99 Ap 8 '63
Strike nobody won. W. L. White. Read Digest 83:155-8+ S '63
Strike seven; Detroit newspaper strike. Newsweek 64:71 Jl 27 '64
Strike two; Cleveland's newspaper strike. Time 81:59 Ap 12 '63
Strikers oppose a union shop; Cleveland U S News 54:86 F 18 '63
Strike's impact; New York and Cleveland newspaper strikes. il Time 81:76 F 8 '63
Striking cost. Newsweek 61:72 My 6 '63
Sussman talks on newspaper strike & book advertising. Pub W 183:134-5 F 18 '63
That Cleveland newspaper strike. J. Barden. Nation 196:159-61+ F 23 '63
To talk of many things; Musical America's Emergency weekly edition. M. Esterow. Mus Am 83:58 Ap '63

STRIKES—United States—Newspapers—*Cont.*
Too much power for labor? excerpts from address, February 12, 1963; with excerpts from letter by members of American newspaper guild. L. B. Seltzer. U S News 54:97 F 25 '63
Union kicks over the applecart; New York typographers reject strike settlement. il Bsns W p32-3 Mr 23 '63
Wayward press. A. J. Liebling. New Yorker 39:143-52 Ap 13 '63
Wayward press; reappearance of the Post. A. J. Liebling. New Yorker 39:173-6+ Mr 16 '63
What's going on? Detroit newspaper strike. Newsweek 64:102 O 26 '64
Where are the reformers? W. F. Buckley, jr. Nat R 14:227 Mr 26 '63

Office workers

US book exchange employees strike for higher wages. Library J 88:3812 O 15 '63

Paper trade

Strike closes Oxford's Rumford, Maine, mill. Pub W 186:36 S 14 '64

Petroleum industry and trade

Oil strikers get global support; IFPW back OCAW. il Bsns W p60+ My 25 '63

Printers

Kingsport loses challenge to union representation. Pub W 186:151-2 Jl 13 '64
Kingsport press strike goes on and on. Pub W 185:37 Je 1 '64
Kingsport unions backed by AFL-CIO; firm states view. il Pub W 184:28-30 D 2 '63
NLRB authorizes union election at Kingsport. Pub W 185:31 Mr 23 '64
No settlement in sight for Kingsport press strike. Pub W 184:26-7 N 4 '63
One for the unions; Kingsport press. Bsns W p 154+ Mr 21 '64
Unions explain their side of Kingsport strike. il Pub W 184:43-4 S 2 '63

Railroads

Arbitration board's award in railroad dispute; excerpts from text. Mo Labor R 87:36-43 Ja '64
Back of the dynamite. Nation 198:254 Mr 16 '64
Big rail strike? the prospects. U S News 54:89 My 20 '63
Blowup; Florida East Coast railway labor war. il Newsweek 63:67-8 F 24 '64
Business bets on no rail strike. il Bsns W p26-7 Jl 20 '63
Can trains be kept running? Bsns W p26 Ag 24 '63
Court dents longest rail deadlock. Bsns W p 104+ D 12 '64
Cruel deception. Newsweek 62:63-4 S 2 '63
End of the line? il Newsweek 62:64 Jl 15 '63
FBI enters case; against Florida East Coast railway. il Sr Schol 84:18 Mr 20 '64
Florida rail strike halted. Bsns W p52 N 16 '63
Florida Ry. hits a new roadblock; court orders to abandon cost-saving changes in work rules and pay rates. Bsns W p98 Mr 7 '64
Florida's railroad war; a few sticks of dynamite. R. G. Sherrill. il Nation 198:227-30 Mr 9 '64
If there's a railroad strike: effects on U.S. il U S News 55:30-1 Jl 22 '63
Jobs at stake in rail dispute; Southern Pacific railroad and Railway clerks union. U S News 54:96 Mr 11 '63
Mean & getting meaner; sabotage against the Florida East Coast railway & at Cape Kennedy. il Time 83:26 F 21 '64
Moonport stalled by rail strike. il Bsns W p64+ F 15 '64
New impasse in rail dispute; Florida East Coast railway. U S News 56:67 Ja 6 '64
New strike threat hangs over rails; job security dispute of nonoperating unions. Bsns W p68 Ag 15 '64
Next trouble spots: railroads and steel? il U S News 54:35-6 Mr 18 '63
On the track ahead; a new crisis; railroad work rules. il Bsns W p 108-10+ Ap 11 '64
One way to run a railroad and meet work-rule problems; Florida East coast. il U S News 55:67-9 S 2 '63
Rail arbitration: a pattern set? Southern Pacific railroad. U S News 54:125 Mr 25 '63
Rail dispute delays work at Cape. Aviation W 80:37 F 17 '64
Rail ruling points a way for others. Bsns W p 132+ D 7 '63
Rail strike and the moon shot; Florida East Coast railway and moon-shot base near Cape Canaveral. U S News 55:86 O 28 '63
Rail strike that reaches into space. il Bsns W p46+ O 26 '63
Railroad dispute: Johnson swings a red lantern; with editorial comment. il Bsns W p25-6, 202 Ap 18 '64
Railroad firemen get a warning. U S News 56:90 My 25 '64
Railroad strike: what are the chances? il U S News 54:43-4 My 27 '63
Railroad that defies the unions. T. Armbrister. il Sat Eve Post 237:84-9 F 22 '64
Ride on the rails. il Fortune 68:231-2 O '63
Showdown ahead on the railroads; strike or end of featherbedding? U S News 54:101 Mr 18 '63
Showdown soon on rail jobs. U S News 54:106-7 Ap 15 '63
Thirteen-month rail strike heats up; Florida East Coast railway. il U S News 56:116 F 24 '64
Unions switch: let U.S. run rails. il Bsns W p 122+ Ja 23 '65
When rail strike hit at moon shot; informational pickets sent to Cape Canaveral, Fla. moon-shot project, by Telegraphers union. U S News 55:98 S 30 '63
When the U.S. had a nationwide rail strike. U S News 55:93 Jl 22 '63
Where rail workers are on strike and trains are running; Florida East Coast railway. il U S News 54:93-6 Mr 11 '63
Why the country can't take a long railroad strike. il U S News 56:37-8 Ap 27 '64

Social workers

Strike in a welfare state; workers in New York city's Welfare department. il Time 85:20-1 Ja 22 '65

Steel industry and trade

As steel union gets set for new demands. il U S News 54:93-5 F 25 '63
Next trouble spots: railroads and steel? il U S News 54:35-6 Mr 18 '63
Steel locals turn restive. Bsns W p90 N 7 '64

Teachers

Course in defiance; New York's teachers vote to strike. il Time 82:90 S 13 '63
New look at teachers' strikes. U S News 55:92 S 23 '63
N.Y. strike averted. Sr Schol 83:2T+ S 27 '63
Scholastic teacher interviews: Carl J. Megel; ed. by H. Langer. C. J. Megel. Sr Schol 83:24T-26T O 4 '63; Discussion. 83:6T D 6 '63
Strikes, sanctions, and the schools. J. Scanlon. il Sat R 46:51-5+ O 19 '63; Discussion. 46:64 N 16; 39 D 21 '63
Teachers get a hand in running New York: strike threat. il Time 82:51 S 20 '63
Teachers' right to strike. Sch & Soc 92:93-4 Mr 7 '64
Teachers' strike issue. Sr Schol 83:1T-2T N 1 '63
Teachers strike: New York city's public school teachers. America 109:225 S 7 '63

Teamsters

Now Hoffa has the power to call a nationwide strike. U S News 56:94-5 Ja 27 '64

Telephone workers

How a company keeps going despite strike, sabotage; General telephone company of Florida. il U S News 55:77+ Ag 26 '63
Sabotage in Tampa; strike against the General telephone co. of Florida. il Time 82:65-6 Ag 16 '63

STRIKING clocks. See Clocks

STRING ensembles
Lucerne festival strings. S. Fleming. Hi Fi 13:24 My '63

STRING musicians shortage. See Musicians—Supply and demand

STRING quartet music
See also
Phonograph records—String quartet music

STRING quartets
Conversation of strings; Juilliard string quartet at Tanglewood. Time 82:56-7 Ag 23 '63
Music to my ears; Koeckert quartet. I. Kolodin. Sat R 46:47 F 23 '63

STRINGED instruments
Mother of a new family of fiddles. il Life 55:61-2 N 29 '63
See also names of stringed instruments. e.g. Guitar

STRINGER, William H.
Dream of the Nile. Sat R 46:18 Je 1 '63

STRINGFELLOW, William
Corny if not profane. Christian Cent 80:1135-6 S 18 '63

STRINGFELLOW, William—*Continued*
Ecumenicity and entomology: new church problem. Christian Cent 81:1239-41 O 7 '64
God, guilt and Goldwater. Christian Cent 1079-83 S 2 '64
Just so they be there. Christian Cent 80: 431-2 Ap 3 '63
about
Episcopal argument obscures warning on racism. Christian Cent 81:1356 N 4 '64
STRIP mining. See Coal mines and mining—Stripping operations
STRIPED bass fishing. See Bass fishing
STRIPTEASE acts. See Vaudeville
STRITAR, Jeffrey A. See Edwards, J. O. jt. auth.
STROBOSCOPE
Low-power stroboscope. S. Auyer. il Pop Electr 21:61-3+ N '64
STROBOSCOPIC instruments
Simple slave strobe sync. N. Sheffield, jr. il Pop Electr 20:59-61+ My '64
STROCK, Lester W.
Electroluminescence: theory and practice. Electr World 73:23-6+ Ja '65
STRODE, A. Chetham-. See Chetham-Strode, A.
STROESSNER, Alfredo
Our man in Paraguay. B. M. Lando. por Nation 196:157-9 F 23 '63
We will show them. il por Time 83:36 My 8 '64
STROETZEL, Donald S.
Building blocks, dirt cheap. Read Digest 84: 234-8 My '64
Earth bricks by the millions. Américas 16: 5-9 Ap '64; Same abr. with title Building blocks, dirt cheap. Read Digest 84:234-8 My '64
He helps workers become capitalists. Read Digest 84:181-5 F '64
They experiment in international living. Parents Mag 39:37+ Ap '64; Same abr. with title Winning the peace is a family job. Read Digest 84:205-7+ Ap '64
STROH, Ruth K.
Chartreuse enchantment. Flower Grower 50: 24-5 Je '63
Widen your house plant horizon. Pop Gard 15:22-3 N '64
STROHM, John
Farmers vote for freedom. Read Digest 83: 95-9 S '63
—and Ganschow, Cliff
Great pesticide controversy. Read Digest 83: 123-8 O '63
—and Lyons, Eugene
Food, the Achilles Heel of communism. Read Digest 84:246-7+ My '64
STROHMEIER, W.
Bamberg search for bright variable stars. Sky & Tel 26:264-5 N '63
STROKES, Apoplectic. See Cerebral hemorrhage
STROKES, Cardiovascular. See Heart—Diseases
STROLLERS (infants) See Baby carriages
STROM, Robert D.
School dropout and the family; adaptation of address, November 8, 1963. Sch & Soc 92: 191-2 Ap 18 '64
STROMMEN, Merton P.
Exhausting. Christian Cent 81:1086 S 2 '64
STRONG, Arline
Exploration at the pond. il Natur Hist 73: 44-5 Ap '64
STRONG, Dwight S.
New England; the refined Yankee in organized crime. bibliog f Ann Am Acad 347:40-50 My '63
STRONG, Frank E.
Fatty acids: in vivo synthesis by the green peach aphid, myzus persicae (Sulzer) bibliog Science 140:983-4 My 31 '63
STRONG, John
Infrared astronomy by balloon; with biographical sketch. Sci Am 212:16, 28-37 bibliog(p 134) Ja '65
STRONG, Kendrick
Sunday in East Berlin. Christian Cent 81: 1500+ D 2 '64
STRONG, Lydia
Do you take time to enjoy the season? Am Home 67:4 D '64
Parent and child. N Y Times Mag p67 Ag 18; 89-90 O 20 '63; 48 Ja 26; 53-4 F 16; 92 Mr 22; 97-8 Je 7; 57 Ag 30; 97-8 S 20; 142+ N 15 '64
Privacy vs. secrecy. Am Home 67:38-9 O '64
STRONGYLOCENTROTUS purpuratus. See Sea urchins
STRONTIUM
Strontium and calcium uptake by the green alga, oocystis eremosphaeria. N. R. Kevern. bibliog il Science 145:1445-6 S 25 '64; Reply with rejoinder. L. G. Williams. 146:1488 D 11 '64
Strontium content and variable strontium-chlorinity relationship of Sargasso sea water. F. T. Mackenzie. bibliog il Science 146:517-18 O 23 '64
Isotopes
Fallout and countermeasures. L. D. Hamilton. Bul Atomic Sci 19:36-40 S '63
Isotopic composition of lead and strontium from Ascension and Gough Islands. P. W. Gast and others. bibliog il Science 145:1181-5 S 11 '64
New Orleans tops in strontium count. Sci N L 84:248 O 19 '63
Radiogenic strontium-87 as an index of geologic processes. C. E. Hedge and F. G. Walthall. bibliog il Science 140:1214-17 Je 14 '63
Strontium and calcium reabsorption in renal tubules of the newt, triturus pyrrhogaster. R. Ichikawa and others. bibliog il Science 144:53-4 Ap 3 '64
Strontium 90: estimation of worldwide deposition. H. L. Volchok. bibliog il Science 145:1451-2 S 25 '64
Strontium-90 in plants and animals of Arctic Alaska, 1959-61. D. G. Watson and others. bibliog il Science 144:1005-9 My 22 '64
STRONTIUM in diet
Fallout in food. il Consumer Rep 29:352-3; 30:33 Jl '64, Ja '65
Fallout in the diet through mid-1963. il Consumer Rep 29:7 Ja '64
Fallout 1963, an interim report. il Consumer Rep 28:448-9 S '63
Lichen, caribou and high radiation in Eskimos. W. O. Pruitt. il Audubon Mag 65:284-7 S '63
STRONTIUM in the body
Strontium-90 content of deciduous human incisors. H. L. Rosenthal and others. bibliog il Science 140:176-7 Ap 12 '63
Strontium-90 in hair. B. J. Hopkins and others. bibliog il Science 139:1064-5 Mr 15 '63
STRONTIUM 90 in food. See Food contamination
STRONTIUM 90 in milk. See Milk contamination
STROTHER, Robert S.
Costly chaos in cotton, time to end it! Read Digest 82:149-50+ Je '63
He measured the speed of light. Read Digest 85:193-4+ Jl '64
Our strike-strangled merchant marine. Read Digest 82:75-9 F '63
Sad little story of Wink. Read Digest 85:97-100 O '64
STROUP, Herbert
Privatist ethic and self-fulfillment. Christian Cent 81:1031-3 Ag 19 '64
STROUSE, Norman H.
Book committee chairman reports survey on housewives' reading; excerpts from address, December 10, 1964. Library J 90:212-13 Ja 15 '65
STROUT, Donald E. and Strout, R. B.
Malady lingers on. Library J 89:2547-55 Je 15 '64
Word is more. Library J 88:2451-7 Je 15 '63
STROUT, Richard Lee
Democrats and business. New Repub 151:26-8 S 19 '64
Mr Lincoln also spoke. New Repub 149:14 N 23 '63
Our four-party system. New Repub 148:24-6 F 2 '63
Rise of the Irish. New Repub 150:22-4 Ja 18 '64
STROUT, Ruth B. See Strout, D. E. jt. auth.
STRUB, Charles
Golden days at the dentist's. W. Tower. il Sports Illus 22:22-3 Ja 11 '65
STRUCTURAL clay products research foundation
Bricks without straw bosses. J. Lear. il Sat R 47:45-9 F 1 '64
STRUCTURAL engineering
Architectural details. il Arch Rec 135:121-36 F '64
Beauty of 20th century engineering; exhibition at Museum of modern art; photographs. Sci Digest 56:14-19 N '64
C.P.M: what factors determine its success? F. A. Sando. il Arch Rec 135:211-16 Ap 202-4 My '64
Engineering of Saarinen's arch; Jefferson national expansion memorial. il Arch Rec 133:188-91 My '63

STRUCTURAL engineering—*Continued*
Look at the future of structural design; adaptation of address, October 1964. P. Weidlinger. Arch Rec 137:172-4 Ja '65
Merits of two model testing techniques. D. P. Billington and others. il Arch Rec 134:225-8 S '63
Moses builds a fair. il Arch Forum 120:64-75 Ja '64
School costs cut by new components. B. P. Spring. il Arch Forum 120:112-17 F '64
Structure plays leading role in latest Yamasaki designs. il Arch Rec 134:103-10 D '63
Typhoon-proof louvers screen tropical sun; Philippine American life insurance office building, Manila. il Arch Rec 134:139-41 D '63
Walls become columns, and vice versa. W. C. Wing. il Arch Rec 135:202-4 Mr '64
See also
Shells (structural engineering)
STRUCTURE of the American literary establishment (game) See Games
STRUCTURES, Underground. See Underground structures
STRUCTURES, Underwater. See Underwater structures
STRUDEL. See Pastry
STRUGHOLD, Hubertus
Space doctor who goes way out. il pors Bsns W p 106-8 N 28 '64
STRUNK, Orlo, jr
Hiroshima reflection; poem. Christian Cent 80:951 Jl 31 '63
STRUTHER, Jan
Choice; poem. McCalls 91:182 F '64
Cinderella; poem. McCalls 91:160 Ap '64
Cobwebs; poem. McCalls 90:168 F '63
Freedom; poem. McCalls 91:202 O '63
Golden touch; poem. McCalls 90:124 Ag '63
Marriage of true minds; poem. McCalls 92:159 N '64
Reason; poem. McCalls 92:155 D '64
STRUTS
Testing
Field facility speeds tests of Atlas silo struts. il Miss & Roc 12:30 Ap 1 '63
STRUVE, Gleb
After the coffee-break. New Repub 148:15-17 F 2 '63
Soviet political satire. New Repub 149:19-22 S 28 '63
STRUVE, Otto
Local system of stars. Sky & Tel 25:78-81 F '63
Some thoughts on Olbers' paradox. Sky & Tel 25:140-2 Mr '63
Story of U Cephei. Sky & Tel 25:199-201 Ap '63
about
Companion of Procyon: some prediscovery reports. J. Ashbrook. Sky & Tel 28:72 Ag '64
Obituary
Sky & Tel 25:247 My '63
Otto Struve as an astrophysicist. C. Payne-Gaposchkin. il pors Sky & Tel 25:308-10 Je '63
STRUVE, Walter
West Germany's economic miracle. Cur Hist 44:231-6+ Ap '63
STRUVE, Wilhelm
Crucial years of Wilhelm Struve. J. Ashbrook. il por Sky & Tel 25:326-7 Je '63
STRUWE, William H.
Joint purchasing. Am City 79:166+ Je '64
STRYCHNINE
Inhibition of evoked potentials by striatal stimulation and its blockage by strychnine. G. M. Krauthamer. bibliog il Science 142:1175-6 N 29 '63
Strychnine: its action on spinal motoneurons of cats. M. G. F. Fuortes and P. G. Nelson. bibliog il Science 140:806-8 My 17 '63
Strychnine: its facilitating effect on the solution of a simple oddity problem by the rat. W. J. Hudspeth. bibliog il Science 145:1331-3 S 18 '64
STUART, Dabney
Fair; poem. Poetry 103:169-72 D '63
Seven poets and a playwright. Poetry 104:258-64 Jl '64
STUART, Dick
Old Stonefingers, best show around Boston in years. R. Creamer. il por Sports Illus 19:42+ S 2 '63
STUART, Doris T.
Gourds. Pop Gard 14:73+ My '63
STUART, Jane
City of the dead blue wind; poem. Am For 69:55 O '63
Dawn; Slippers for the wind; Corn shuck dolls; poems. Am For 70:37 Ap '64
STUART, Jesse
Both barrels; story. Esquire 62:134 D '64
Every morning in Cairo. Sr Schol 84:9T-10T My 8 '64
Gratitude; poem. Am For 70:61 F '64
How to tame a blacksnake. Am For 70:18 F '64
Loner. Am For 71:6+ Ja '65
New Garden of Eden? Am For 69:14-17+ S '63
Or they perish. Am For 69:18-20 D '63
We took the back way home. il Am For 69:40-1+ N '63
about
New and selected, and a first volume. D. C. DeJong. Poetry 102:125-6 My '63
STUART, Neal Gilkyson
Journey; story. Redbook 124:40-1 Ja '65
Life, love and laughter of Carol Burnett. Ladies Home J 80:72-3+ Ap; 34+ My '63
We let our kids read comic books. Read Digest 85:124-6 Jl '64
(ed) See Aynes, E. A. Coming scandal in nursing
STUART, Mrs Robert J.
New political power of women. Ladies Home J 81:68+ S '64
STUBER, Stanley I.
Vatican dialogue. Christian Cent 81:1405 N 11 '64
STUD poker. See Poker
STUDEBAKER corporation
Christmas gift for South Bend. U S News 56:68 Ja 6 '64
End in South Bend: then there were four. il Newsweek 62:59-60 D 23 '63
High cost of quitting. Time 83:86 F 21 '64
Made in Canada from now on; move from South Bend, Ind. to Hamilton, Ont. il Bsns W p28-9 D 14 '63
Now there are four; dropping of auto production in the U.S. il Time 82:77 D 20 '63
Pioneer in peril. Sr Schol 83:19-20 Ja 17 '64
'64 cars. il Motor T 15:94-7 N '63
Studebaker: a span of history. il U S News 55:59 D 23 '63
Studebaker comes out of a skid. il Bsns W p66+ Mr 9 '63
Studebaker: end of a dream. B. J. Widick. il Nation 198:29-30 Ja 6 '64
Studebaker hangs on. Time 84:106 O 23 '64
Studebaker puts on new face. Bsns W p26 S 14 '63
Studebaker's problems. il Newsweek 62:92+ N 25 '63
Studebaker's year of decision. il Time 82:89-90 S 20 '63
Switch at Studebaker. Newsweek 62:83 D 9 '63
Troubles at Studebaker. Time 82:87 N 22 '63
What happens to retirees when a plant shuts down? Bsns W p50 N 21 '64
When a big company quits, the South Bend story. il U S News 55:76-8 D 23 '63
Why Studebaker? M. Lamm. il Motor T 16:42-5+ Mr '64
STUDENT achievements
Columbia college: report to headmasters, principals and counselors, 1962. H. S. Coleman. Sch & Soc 91:148-9 Mr 23 '63; Reply. A. L. Goren. 91:271 O 5 '63
Creative writing and school achievement. K. Yamamoto. bibliog f il Sch & Soc 91:307-8 O 19 '63
Entering levels and college courses in freshman mathematics. C. B. Lindquist. il Sch Life 45:14-17 Ap '63
My son, the underachiever. J. W. Kessler. il PTA Mag 57:12-14 Je '63
Student performance in new high school biology programs. H. Grobman. bibliog il Science 143:265-6 Ja 17 '64
What you can do about an underachiever. M. Grant. il Parents Mag 38:56-7+ Mr '63
When children don't achieve. L. Strong. il N Y Times Mag p 142+ N 15 '64
STUDENT activities
Freshness of the headlong years; with photographs by Farrell Grehan. Life 55:66-79 S 27 '63
Prom notes; themes from musical shows. Seventeen 23:188 Ap '64
Sixteen point plan for making good on college and prep school weekends. E. A. Haupt. Seventeen 22:60-1 Ap '63
What's in the wind for student activities? G. M. Van Pool. il PTA Mag 57:25-7 Ap '63
See also
Bands, College
Camera clubs
College students—Political activities

STUDENT aid
See also
Scholarships and fellowships
Student loans
STUDENT assistants
See also
School libraries—Student assistants
STUDENT conferences
See also
United States national student association
STUDENT councils. See Self government in education
STUDENT counselors. See School counselors
STUDENT demonstrations
Battle of Sproul Hall: protest against ban on political activities at University of California, Berkeley, with report by J. M. Russin. il Newsweek 64:44+ D 14 '64
Berkeley: does that banner still wave? Free speech movement. G. A. Harrison. New Repub 151:7-8 D 19 '64
Campus agitation vs. education. Life 58:4 Ja 22 '65
Campus uproar that is blamed on reds; University of California, Berkeley. il U S News 57:12 D 14 '64
Climate at Berkeley; discipline and the issue of political protests. il Time 84:30 D 25 '64
Escalation in California. N. Cousins. Sat R 48:20 Ja 30 '65
Extremism in the defense of... R. E. Fitch. Christian Cent 82:11-15 Ja 6 '65
Freedom to learn but not to riot; demonstrations at the Berkeley campus of the University of California. S. Hook. il N Y Times Mag p8-9+ Ja 3 '65
Lesson of Berkeley. S. M. Lipset and P. Seabury. il Reporter 32:36-40 Ja 28 '65
No fair! the students strike at California. G. Marine. il Nation 199:482-6 D 21 '64; Discussion. 199:477-8 D 21 '64; 200:inside cover Ja 11 '65
Panty raids? no! tough campus revolt; on the University of California campus at Berkeley. il Life 57:46A-46B D 18 '64
Revolt and retreat on the campus. Christian Cent 81:1612-13 D 30 '64
To prison with love; student sit-in at University of California, Berkeley. il Time 84:60 D 11 '64
What happened at Berkeley. J. Cass. il Sat R 48:47-8+ Ja 16 '65
When & where to speak. il Time 84:68-9 D 18 '64
When students try to run a university; University of California, Berkeley. il U S News 57:43 D 21 '64
Why the students revolt. B. Ward. il Nation 200:81-5 Ja 25 '65
You don't shoot mice with elephant guns; free speech movement at the University of California. S. Alexander. Life 58:27 Ja 15 '65
STUDENT drinking. See Liquor problem—United States
STUDENT drivers. See Automobile drivers
STUDENT employment
Chicago's answer for dropouts; Education-employment program. il Ebony 18:81-2+ O '63
Employment of school age youth, October 1963. H. R. Hamel. il Mo Labor R 87:767-73 Jl '64
Employment of school-age youth, October 1962. C. Rosenfeld. il Mo Labor R 86:907-13 Ag '63
Finding jobs for foreign students. D. O'Shea. America 108:558-62 Ap 20 '63
Holiday cure for bored teen-agers. A. Gillette. il UNESCO Courier 16:24-7 Ap '63
Money manners; excerpt from Seventeen book of etiquette and entertaining. E. A. Haupt. Seventeen 23:26 Ap '64
Summer service jobs for teens who care. il Good H 156:162-3 My '63
That summer job. il Sr Schol 82:24-5 Ap 3 '63
Those lazy, hazy days; summer jobs. il Time 81:57 Je 28 '63
What will your teen-ager do this summer? A. Q. Maisel. Read Digest 82:133-4+ My '63
Your first job: how to get it. B. Donahue. il Seventeen 22:78-9+ Je '63
See also
College students—Employment
High school students—Employment
STUDENT enrollment. See School attendance
STUDENT ethics
Campus rules on sex: an ex-envoy joins the debate; excerpts from letter. J. K. Galbraith. U S News 55:18 N 25 '63
Mach the knifers. Newsweek 64:98+ O 19 '64
Matter of attitude: girls in boys' bedrooms. Time 82:82 N 8 '63
Morality of college youth. Sch & Soc 92:258 O 3 '64
Woman and man at Harvard. America 109:620 N 16 '63
STUDENT exchange programs. See Students, Interchange of
STUDENT forums. See Forums (discussion and debate)
STUDENT government. See Self government in education
STUDENT gypsy, or The Prince of Liederkranz; musical comedy. See Musical comedies, revues, etc.—Criticisms, plots, etc.
STUDENT health. See College students—Health and hygiene
STUDENT interracial ministry (organization)
Doing is the difference. America 112:33 Ja 9 '65
STUDENT life
Bigger and better parietals? Harvard students. Nat R 15:427-9 N 19 '63
But where are the chaperons? M. W. Lear. il N Y Times Mag p22+ F 23 '64
Campus rules on sex: an ex-envoy joins the debate; excerpts from letter. J. K. Galbraith. U S News 55:18 N 25 '63
Clarification at College Park; low moral standards among fraternity members. V. E. Lowder. Christian Cent 81:500-2 Ap 15 '64
Colleges and public decency. R. Kirk. Nat R 16:112 F 11 '64; Discussion. 16:248 Mr 24 '64
Matter of attitude: girls in boys' bedrooms. Time 82:82 N 8 '63
Most invaluable freedom of them all; Britain and America from viewpoint of higher education. K. Tynan. Seventeen 23:148+ Mr '64
Something to talk about on campus. R. Arnon. il Mlle 59:320-2 Ag '64
Too much sex on campus. J. L. Barron. il Ladies Home J 81:48+ Ja '64; Same abr. Read Digest 84:59-62 My '64
See also
College students
Student activities
STUDENT loans
Beg, borrow, and bargain. il Newsweek 64:67 N 30 '64
Beware the college credit loan shark. Sr Schol 82:18 Ap 24 '63
College bound? you can study now, pay later. il U S News 57:52-4 Ag 10 '64
College on credit. Sr Schol 82:1T F 6 '63
Learn now, pay much later; Shapiro's plan. Time 81:59 Je 21 '63
Loan program that helps you become a doctor: Education and research foundation loan guarantee program. H. Earle. il Todays Health 41:36-41 Jl '63
Loans for college. il Changing T 17:24-5 My '63
Now you can get paid for going to college; report. il U S News 57:58 N 2 '64
Occupational plans of student borrowers under NDEA. R. C. Hall. il Sch Life 45:26-9 Ja '63
PCA loans for college. D. Hagen and J. Bickers. il Farm J 87:24 N '63
See also
United student aid funds, incorporated
STUDENT non-violent coordinating committee
Battle-scarred youngsters. H. Zinn. Nation 197:193-7 O 5 '63
Black Belt, Alabama. J. DeMuth. Commonweal 80:536-9 Ag 7 '64
Buy-in. Newsweek 63:22 Ja 6 '64
Food for Greenwood. R. Wulbert. New Repub 149:7 Jl 13 '63
Hattiesburg and central Illinois. J. Moore. Christian Cent 81:340-1 Mr 11 '64
Hotter fires; friction between organizations; with report by K. Fleming. il Newsweek 62:19-21 Jl 1 '63
Ivy-league integrationists. R. W. Apple, jr. il Reporter 28:32-4 F 14 '63
Mandate from history; fourth leadership training conference. E. Sutherland. il Nation 198:30-3 Ja 6 '64
Meeting; concerning reports to New York branch of plans of Mississippi branch. New Yorker 40:33-6 Ap 11 '64
Mississippi; from conversion to coercion. C. Jencks. New Repub 151:17-21 Ag 22 '64
Race: results instead of reasons. R. McGill. Sat R 48:52 Ja 9 '65
Roots of Negro militancy. S. Lynd. New Repub 150:5 F 22 '64
SNCC: the new abolitionists, by H. Zinn. Review
Christian Cent 81:1464 N 25 '64. A. R. Brockway
South's war against Negro votes. J. Poppy. Look 27:38+ My 21 '63

STUDENT non-violent coordinating committee
—*Continued*
Summer in Cambridge, Maryland. R. Brown. Horn Bk 40:315-19 Je '64
Voting in the Black Belt. C. Mabee. il Negro Hist Bul 27:50-6 D '63

STUDENT opinion
Children's war revisited. E. B. McNeil. Bul Atomic Sci 19:22-4 F '63
5,000 Vietnamese students study in Paris. M. Clos. il N Y Times Mag p38-9+ D 6 '64
From the academy; academic rights of students. R. Kirk. Nat R 16:606 Jl 14 '64
Mexico's youth speaks; excerpts from a poll, comp. by E. K. Culhane. America 109:408 O 12 '63
Personalists. il Time 82:44+ N 22 '63
Political profile of a university class; survey. D. Vinyard. il Sch & Soc 92:291-3 O 17 '64
Teen-agers distrust brilliant students. Sci Digest 53:25 F '63
Teen-agers speak out on teen-age drinking; discussion. il Sr Schol 82:12-14 Ja 30 '63
See also
New York herald tribune forum for high schools

STUDENT publications. See College and school journalism

STUDENT residences. See College students—Housing; Dormitories

STUDENT riots. See Riots

STUDENT selection
Burgeoning university enrollments and academic quality. L. Siegel and others. il Sch & Soc 91:336-8 N 2 '63
Chaos in college admissions. il Changing T 17:17-20 Ag '63
How do you rate as a dean of admissions? J. C. Palmer. il Sat R 47:74-5 Mr 21 '64
Test uses and limitations. B. A. Thresher. il NEA J 52:16-19 O '63
See also
College entrance examination board

STUDENT strikes
300,000 French students can't be wrong. P. E. Schneider. il N Y Times Mag p 16-17+ F 9 '64

STUDENT teachers
Art and the student teacher. L. B. Kennon and T. Markle. il Sch Arts 63:5-10 Ap '64

STUDENT teaching
Research and college teaching by students. Sch & Soc 91:135-6 Mr 23 '63

STUDENT tours. See Travel study courses

STUDENT travel. See Travel

STUDENT tutors. See Tutors and tutoring

STUDENT unions
Designing with deference; Bowdoin college senior center. il Arch Rec 133:142-4 Mr '63
Man of many talents; requirements for a college union director of today. K. G. Briscoe. Recreation 57:89-90 F '64
Pavilion for dining and student center. il Arch Rec 134:134-5 Ag '63
Students finance an activities center. il Arch Rec 134:132-3 Ag '63

STUDENT volunteer service. See Volunteer service

STUDENT withdrawals
Are we cheating twenty million students? problem of high-school dropouts. G. B. Leonard. il Look 27:36-40+ Je 4 '63
Are we losing bright failing students? R. Schmelzlee. il Sch & Soc 92:189-90 Ap 18 '64
Chicago's answer for dropouts. il Ebony 18:81-2+ O '63
College enrollments and dropouts. W. W. Brickman. Sch & Soc 93:3 Ja 9 '65
College majority; dropouts. J. Keats. il Life 54:70-4+ Je 21 '63
Compulsory high school attendance? pro and con discussion. D. E. Winchell; R. Meckley. il NEA J 53:10-12 F '64
Day our boy quit school, and how we got him back in! il Farm J 88:33+ My '64
Doors were opened; a commentary on the 1963 dropout campaign. H. M. Smith and L. M. Miller. Sch Life 46:8-10 Ja '64
Dropout campaign; exchange of letters between President Kennedy and Commissioner Keppel; September 5 and September 15, 1963. F. Keppel; J. F. Kennedy. Sch Life 46:2-3 O '63
Dropout: schools search for clues to his problems. L. M. Miller. bibliog il Sch Life 45:5-7+ My '63
Dropouts. P. Woodring. Sat R 46:59-60 F 16 '63
Dropouts and the draft. New Repub 149:3-4 Ag 17 '63; Reply with rejoinder. 149:36+ S 21 '63
Dropouts: high school. N. Buchheimer. Sr Schol 84:1T-2T Ap 17 '64
Employment of high school graduates and dropouts in 1962. J. Schiffman. il Mo Labor R 86:772-9 Jl '63
Employment of high school graduates and dropouts in 1963. V. C. Perrella. il Mo Labor R 87:522-9 My '64
Facts about school dropouts. U S News 55:10 Ag 26 '63
High school dropouts; with excerpts from statement by J. F. Kennedy. il Sr Schol 83:14-15+, 41 N 8 '63
How to spot a dropout. W. C. Kvaraceus. il Sr Schol 83:10T N 8 '63
Ideology of school withdrawal; summary of address, December 1962. E. Z. Friedenberg. Commentary 35:492-500 Je '63; Discussion. 36:270+ O '63
Information about dropouts: terms and computations. J. F. Putnam. bibliog Sch Life 45:24-9 My '63
Low-down on dropouts; with study-discussion program, by E. M. Duvall. D. Schreiber. bibliog PTA Mag 58:4-6, 36-7 N '63
Manpower planning and the new pariahs. E. M. Brandes. il Reporter 30:17-19 Mr 26 '64
No room at the bottom; paid work and school study programs. L. Velie. il Read Digest 84:169-70+ Ap '64
Out-of-school youth, February 1963. T. E. Swanstrom. il Mo Labor R 87:1416-24 D '64
Out-of-school youth, February 1963. V. C. Perrella and F. A. Bogan. il Mo Labor R 87:1260-8 N '64
Preventing college crack-ups. V. Balaban and H. F. French. Parents Mag 38:64+ F '63
Remarkable story of the dropouts and the college students. A. Fontaine. McCalls 91:36+ Mr '64
Renewed effort to solve the problem of dropout. M. Bayley. il Sch Life 46:11-16 D '63
Scholastic ability of school dropouts; with tables. O. R. Warner. bibliog Sch Life 47:21-2 O '64
School dropout and adult education. W. W. Brickman. Sch & Soc 92:179 Ap 18 '64
School dropout and the family; adaptation of address, November 8, 1963. R. D. Strom. Sch & Soc 92:191-2 Ap 18 '64
School dropouts in big cities. Sch & Soc 92:326 N 14 '64
School dropouts; summary of study. P. V. Williams. il NEA J 52:10-12 F '63
Six quitters: dropouts doing well today. il Esquire 62:102-3 S '64
Song for dropouts. Time 83:76 Ap 10 '64
Studies in success: course for potential high school dropouts, Mount Miguel H.S. San Diego County, Calif. K. Hopkins. il Sr Schol 84:27T Mr 20 '64
Teacher-opinion poll: adults and out-of-school youth. il NEA J 53:77 F '64
They help boys want to be educated; Chicago boys clubs. A. Q. Maisel. Read Digest 83:100-4 D '63
When junior seeks a job; with study-discussion program, by E. M. Duvall. W. W. Wirtz. bibliog il PTA Mag 57:12-14, 37 My '63
Why drop-outs drop out. Sci Digest 57:20 Ja '65
Why so many flunk out. J. H. Robertson. il N Y Times Mag p32+ My 5 '63

Anecdotes, facetiae, satire, etc.

In Xanadu, U.S.A. R. L. Darbonne. NEA J 53:51-2 F '64
Letter home from an anonymous co-ed. Esquire 62:104 S '64

STUDENTS
See also
Catholic students
College students
Foreign students in the United States
High school students
Medical students
Negro students
Venezuelan students

Employment

See Student employment

Grading and promotion

See Grading and marking (students)

Strikes

See Student strikes

STUDENTS, Interchange of
I believe; Negro high school exchange student in Farmington, Conn. from Birmingham, Ala. B. Donahue. Seventeen 22:46+ O '63

STUDENTS, Interchange of—*Continued*
President speaks to American field service students; remarks, July 20, 1964. L. B. Johnson. Dept State Bul 51:189 Ag 10 '64
Wine-tasting jobs and others not so dull; international AIESEC congress. R. Hoffmann. il Mlle 58:112-13+ F '64
See also
American field service
Experiment in international living (organization)
Foreign students in the United States
STUDENTS, Married
See also
College students, Married
High school students, Married
STUDENTS, Mentally superior. See College students, Mentally superior; High school students, Mentally superior
STUDENTS and teachers. See Teachers and students
STUDENTS letters. See Letter writing
STUDENTS songs. See College songs
STUDIES (rooms)
Dreamproof your study corner. il Seventeen 23:188-9 Ag '64
STUDIOS
Skylights for studios. il Arch Forum 118:84-5 Mr '63
Studio retreat, high on a hill. il Sunset 130: 137 Je '63
See also
Artists studios
STUDIOS (music)
See also
Music rooms and equipment
STUDIOS, Recording. See Sound—Recording and reproducing
STUDY
How to teach your child to remember. H. Pollan. il Parents Mag 39:54-5+ Mr '64
See also
Home study
STUDY carrels. See School libraries
STUDY guides
Great adventure; special TV study guides. bibliog il NEA J 53:75-8 Ja; 71-3 F; 79-82 Mr; 65-7 Ap '64
STUDY tours. See Travel study courses
STUDY-work plan. See Education, Cooperative
STUFFED toys. See Toys
STUFFING. See Cookery—Poultry
STUHLDREHER, Mary
High-heeled recruiter and a mama's boy. Sports Illus 19:72-6 S 23 '63
STUIVER, Minze, and Daddario, J. J.
Submergence of the New Jersey coast. bibliog Science 142:951 N 15 '63
—See Bloom, A. L.; Turekian, K. K. jt. auths.
STUMP removal
Getting rid of tree stumps. Consumer Bul 46:19 Ag '63
STUMPF, Karl Ludwig, and Gamarekian, Edward
Life and death of Precious Plum Flower. Sat Eve Post 237:66+ Ap 4 '64
STUNT flying. See Aviation—Stunt flying
STUNTING virus diseases. See Corn stunt disease virus
STURANI, Emmapaola, and others
Regulation of enzyme activity by specific reversal of feedback inhibition. bibliog Science 141:1053-4 S 13 '63
STURDEVANT, William D.
Carving in native woods. il pors Am Artist 28:59-63+ D '64
STURGEON, Theodore
How to forget baseball; story. Sports Illus 21:84-90+ D 21 '64
STURGEON electric company
Estimating bids by computer; Estimat. il Bsns W p80+ N 23 '63
STURGEON fishing
Florida's sturgeon spree. R. F. Burgess. il Outdoor Life 131:44-7+ Mr '63
Heavy devils of Hell's Canyon. C. Ormond. il Outdoor Life 133:58-9 My '64
STURKIE, Paul D. See Vogel, J. A. jt. auth.
STURM, Fred Gillette
Authenticity and other persons. Christian Cent 80:340-2 Mr 13 '63
STURROCK, Jock
'67 challenge; interview. por Motor B 114: 102-3 N '64
STURT, Charles
Ghastly blank; first exploration of Australia; excerpt from Cooper's Creek. A. Moorehead. il por Atlan 213:100-14 F '64
STUTTERING. See Stammering
STUTTGART, Germany

Music

[Musical events] il Mus Am 84:28 Jl '64
STUTTGART ballet festival. See Dance festivals
STUTZ, Geraldine Veronica
Female bearcat named Stutz. S. J. Daly. il pors Sat Eve Post 236:60-2 Ap 13 '63
STYCOS, J. Mayone
Outlook for world population. Science 146: 1435-40 D 11 '64
STYLE, Literary
Against the American grain. by D. Macdonald. Review
Commentary 35:351-3 Ap '63. S. Marcus
Constabulary style. C. Williams. il Esquire 62:106-7+ N '64
Golden words at Dartmouth; D. Lambuth's Golden book on writing. Time 82:36 D 27 '63
Is the literature worth keeping? J. Maddox. il Bul Atomic Sci 19:14-16 N '63
Let's lower sights and raise the caliber of student writing. A. L. Klein. NEA J 53: 17-18 N '64
Matter of style. Christian Cent 81:95 Ja 15 '64
Of style and the stylist. E. Cameron. Horn Bk 40:25-32 F '64
Saying what one means. F. Stark. Atlan 212: 102-3 O '63
Sermon notes: text I: Nothing is really hard but to be real. Sat R 47:12 Ap 25 '64
Style of Milton's epic. D. R. Pearce. Yale R 52:427-44 Mr '63
Techniques and style in article writing; excerpt from Prose by professionals, ed. by T. Morris. O. Schisgall. Writer 76:14-16 S '63
This business of style. F. F. Bond. Writer 77:27-8 Jl '64
See also
Words
STYLE in dress. See Fashion
STYLE shows. See Fashion shows
STYLING, Automobile. See Automobiles—Design
STYLUSES, Phonograph. See Phonograph needles
STYROFOAM
Fastest way to build a model plane. R. L. Clough. il Pop Sci 182:137-9 Mr '63
STYRON, William
Two writers talk it over. por Esquire 60:57-9 Jl '63
SUÁREZ, F. Reinoso-. See Reinoso-Suárez, F.
SUASSUNA, Ariano
Folk theater in northeastern Brazil. Américas 16:18-23 N '64
SUBCOMMITTEE of Senate on internal security. See United States—Congress—Senate—Committees
SUBCONTRACTING
Another setback for employers. U S News 55:85 Jl 15 '63
Courts in conflict. T. R. Brooks. Duns R 82:74B D '63
Issue that stalls steel pact; contracting-out dispute. Bsns W p 104-5 Je 8 '63
See also
Contracts, Government—Subcontracting
SUBJECT cataloging. See Cataloging
SUBJECT headings
Medical subject headings revised: cross reference guide to the Index medicus. Wilson Lib Bul 39:373 Ja '65
SUBJECT to approval; story. See Oppenheimer, M.
SUBJECT was roses; drama. See Gilroy, F. D.
SUBJECTS, Literary. See Literature—Themes
SUBMARINE archeology. See Archeology, Submarine
SUBMARINE bases. See Navy yards and naval stations
SUBMARINE boats
Aluminaut & aquanauts; world's first aluminum submarine. il Time 84:85 S 11 '64
Aluminum sub launched for deep-sea exploration; Aluminaut. il Sci N L 86:166 S 12 '64
Aluminum sub readied; Aluminaut. B. Tufty. il Sci N L 85:181 Mr 21 '64
Deep-down submarines. il Time 83:57 Je 5 '64
First two-man sub to study ancient wrecks Sci N L 85:89 F 8 '64
Harnessing the ocean depths; address, September 2, 1964. P. H. Nitze. Vital Speeches 30:749-51 O 1 '64
Jeeps in the deep; exploring inner space at 4,500 fathoms. W. Cloud. il Pop Sci 185: 42-6+ Ag '64
Mesoscaph subs seeks Gulf Stream mysteries. Sci N L 86:265 O 24 '64
Months underwater seen for non-atomic subs. Sci N L 85:248 Ap 18 '64
New inner space ships. il Sci Digest 56: 14-15 Ag '64

SUBMARINE boats—*Continued*
Propulsion research far more secret than work in related materials area. il Miss & Roc 15:74-6 S 21 '64
Sea beneath us. il Bsns W p48+ My 16 '64
Stalking fish in an oddball sub. il Pop Sci 184:98-9 My '64
Sub rescues, four miles deep. S. D. Pursglove. il Pop Mech 120:69-73+ Ag '63
Three below; Aluminaut. il Newsweek 64:83 S 14 '64
U-drive U-boat. J. Roe. il Pop Sci 184:134-5 Ja '64
Your own private submarine; Perry cubmarine. il Sci Digest 55:inside cover Mr '64
See also
Submarine warfare

Accidents

See Submarine disasters

Airplane combination

Navy seeking aid in components design for triphibious vehicle; flying submarine. Aviation W 80:28 Ap 13 '64
Search for the Flub; flying submersible vehicle. il Newsweek 63:89 Ap 13 '64

Detection

Detection, classification are key jobs. il Miss & Roc 15:46+ S 21 '64
Inventor of the month; how to spot a sub. S. V. Jones. il Sci Digest 57:15 Ja '65
Silent war in liquid space; anti-submarine warfare. J. P. McNeel. il Pop Mech 120: 122-7+ D '63

Materials

Propulsion research far more secret than work in related materials area. il Miss & Roc 15:74-6 S 21 '64

SUBMARINE boats, Atomic powered
Britain to spend billion on Polaris. Miss & Roc 12:13 Ap 15 '63
Checking out the Thresher's replacement: USS Dace, SSN 607. W. Cloud. Pop Sci 185:15-16 Jl '64
Deep submergence project calls for five-year expenditure of $200 million; long-endurance experimental research submarine. il Miss & Roc 15:28+ D 21 '64
Dive in a Thresher sub. H. Pryor. il Sci Digest 56:48-52 Jl '64
Invulnerable deterrent; Polaris missile and nuclear submarine. il N Y Times Mag p 18-19 Ap 5 '64
Missiles at sea: most dependable deterrent of all? Polaris submarines. il U S News 56:44-5 Ja 27 '64
Navy faces reorganization of forces, procurement structure. il Aviation W 78:80-1+ Mr 11 '63
Never-ending challenge; excerpts from address, October 1962. H. G. Rickover. U S News 54:38 Ap 22 '63
President Johnson commissions U.S.S. Sam Rayburn; remarks, December 2, 1964. L. B. Johnson. Dept State Bul 51:877 D 21 '64
Soviet proposal of nuclear-free zone in Mediterranean rejected; U.S. note of June 24, and Soviet note of May 20, 1963. Dept State Bul 49:83-6 Jl 15 '63
Underneath in the Ethan Allen. il Time 81:22 Mr 15 '63

Anecdotes, facetiae, satire, etc.

Turtle gap. Nation 198:178-9 F 24 '64

Control

Navigating under the sea. il Bsns W p 148-50+ Mr 16 '63
Navy standardizes Polaris SINS system. Aviation W 80:16 My 4 '64

Crews

Life aboard an atomic submarine. il N Y Times Mag p8-9 Ap 21 '63
Most rigorous service. W. Davis. Sci N L 83:244 Ap 20 '63
Polaris sub prowls the sea. R. Brigham. il Life 54:22-31 Mr 22 '63
Wanted: crews for A-subs. Bsns W p29 Je 8 '63

Safety devices and measures

How to prevent another Thresher; ultrasonic inspection technique. Bsns W p76+ Ag 17 '63
Surgery for a sub. il Newsweek 63:64 Ja 6 '64

SUBMARINE boats, Russian. See Russia—Navy—Submarine service
SUBMARINE cables. See Cables. Submarine
SUBMARINE detection and ranging devices. See Sonar

SUBMARINE disasters
Another unsolved mystery of the sea; Thresher. il U S News 54:67-9 Je 3 '63
At bottom of the sea, pictures of a death sub; Thresher. il U S News 57:16 O 12 '64
Back to the hunt; search for nuclear submarine Thresher. il Newsweek 61:31 Je 10 '63
Death of a submarine; Thresher. il Bsns W p36-7 Ap 20 '63
Did carelessness sink the Thresher? il U S News 58:10 Ja 18 '65
Epitaph for Thresher. il Newsweek 62:59 S 16 '63
Farther than she was built to go; U.S.S. Thresher. il Time 81:27-8 Ap 19 '63
First clues in mystery of the Thresher. il Life 54:36-9 Je 7 '63
How the Thresher died. Newsweek 62:26 Jl 1 '63
How to prevent another Thresher; ultrasonic inspection technique. Bsns W p76+ Ag 17 '36
Mystery of the Thresher; first loss to the atom fleet. il U S News 54:38-9 Ap 22 '63
Navy abandons search for Thresher; oceanographer blames sub's fate on storm. il Bsns W p60 S 14 '63
Nuclear sub loss stirs investigation to locate Thresher. il Sr Schol 82:18-19 My 1 '63
Ocean defeats man; Thresher accident. Sci N L 83:244 Ap 20 '63
Postmortem; Thresher. il Newsweek 61:22 Ap 29 '63
Satisfactory, or "satisfactory"? hearings into the death of the nuclear submarine Thresher. Time 81:24-5 My 3 '63
Sea enshrouds the silent; USS Thresher dives to doom in first nuclear sub disaster; with report by P. Mandel. il Life 54:38-44 Ap 19 '63
Search for the Thresher. il Newsweek 61:34 My 27 '63
Search for the Thresher. F. N. Spiess and A. E. Maxwell. bibliog il Science 145:349-55 Jl 24 '64
Thresher found? metal fragments photographed on ocean floor. il Bsns W p34 My 25 '63
Thresher inquiry. F. N. Karmatz. New Repub 148:7-8 Je 1 '63
Thresher post-mortem. Sci Am 209:66+ N '63
Thresher tragedy spurs deep-sea research. J. H. Wakelin, jr; D. L. Keach; E. A. Link. il Nat Geog Mag 125:759-86 Je '64
Thresher's troubles before disaster. U S News 54:14 Ap 29 '63
U.S.S. Thresher. il Newsweek 61:26-8 Ap 22 '63
Untested Thresher; Joint committee on atomic energy disclosures. Newsweek 65:72 Ja 18 '65
What really happened to the Thresher. R. Gannon. il Pop Sci 184:102-9+ F '64; Same abr. Read Digest 84:111-16 My '64
What sank Thresher, the A-sub? ed. by J. Lear. C. O. Iselin. il Sat R 46:57-60 O 5 '63; Reply. J. Lear. 47:62 N 7 '64
You can do anything when you know you're not alone; ed. by M. Drury. I. Harvey. il McCalls 90:100-3+ S '63; Same abr. Read Digest 84:71-6 F '64

SUBMARINE diving. See Diving, Submarine
SUBMARINE geology
Age of the ice age. il Time 81:51-2 F 22 '63
Basaltic cone suggests constructional origin of some guyots; Mono Lake, Calif. M. N. Christensen and C. M. Gilbert. bibliog il Science 143:240-2 Ja 17 '64
Basalts dredged from the northeastern Pacific Ocean. C. G. Engel and A. E. J. Engel. bibliog il Science 140:1321-4 Je 21 '63
Composition of basalts from the Mid-Atlantic Ridge. A. E. J. Engel and C. G. Engel. bibliog il Science 144:1330-3 Je 12 '64
Cretaceous, paleocene, and pleistocene sediments from the Indian Ocean. Y. Herman. bibliog il Science 140:1316-17 Je 21 '63
Crustal uplift southwest of Montague Island, Alaska. R. J. Malloy. il Science 146: 1048 N 20 '64
Guinea fracture zone in the equatorial Atlantic. D. C. Krause. bibliog il Science 146: 57-9 O 2 '64
Palynological investigation of a core from the Biscay abyssal plain. J. J. Groot. bibliog Science 141:522-3 Ag 9 '63
Pleistocene marine microfauna in the Bootlegger Cove Clay, Anchorage, Alaska. R. A. M. Schmidt. bibliog il Science 141:350-1 Jl 26 '63
Seismic investigations of Seychelles and Saya de Malha Banks, Northwest Indian Ocean. G. G. Shor, jr. and D. D. Pollard. bibliog il Science 142:48-9 O 4 '63

SUBMARINE geology—*Continued*
Submarine geology by diving saucer. F. P. Shepard and others. bibliog il Science 145: 1042-6 S 4 '64
Vegetation, climate, and coastal submergence in Connecticut. P. B. Sears. bibliog il Science 140:59-60 Ap 5 '63
SUBMARINE navigation. See Navigation, Submarine
SUBMARINE oil well drilling. See Oil well drilling, Submarine
SUBMARINE photography. See Photography, Submarine
SUBMARINE sounds. See Ocean sounds
SUBMARINE structures. See Underwater structures
SUBMARINE target simulators. See Simulators
SUBMARINE warfare
ASW contract stresses current hardware. Aviation W 81:19 D 14 '64
ASW; special report; with editorial comment. il Miss & Roc 15:24-6+, 82 S 21 '64
Navy, TRW ready ASW management pact. C. Brownlow. Aviation W 81:19-20 N 2 '64
Sea Hawk system may appear gradually; anti-submarine destroyer escort system. J. Trainor. Miss & Roc 15:16 Ag 24 '64
Silent war in liquid space; anti-submarine warfare. J. P. McNeel. il Pop Mech 120: 122-7+ D '63
Soviet submarine threat. H. W. Baldwin. il Reporter 31:39-42 S 24 '64
Torpedoes and concerts; joint maneuvers in South American waters. C. E. Erbsen. il Américas 15:35-8 Ag '63
See also
European war, 1914-1918—Submarine operations
Guided missiles—Launching from submarine boats
Torpedoes
SUBMERSION
Life underwater; diving response of elephant seal. il Newsweek 63:57 Mr 9 '64
Men under pressure; underwater living. il Newsweek 64:56 Ag 24 '64
Ocean-bottom homes for skin divers. J. Y. Cousteau. il Pop Mech 120:98-103+ Jl '63
Room at the bottom of the sea; Sealab divers, photographs. J. Atwater and R. Vaughan. Sat Eve Post 237:18-25 S 5 '64
Home under the sea; Sealab I. il Life 57: 74-8 S 4 '64
SUBMINIATURE cameras. See Cameras
SUBPOENA. See Process
SUBRAHMANYAN, V. and others
Ammonia: possible use for preserving fish. bibliog Science 142:233-4 O 11 '63
SUBROC (guided missile) See Guided missiles —Launching from submarine boats
SUBSCRIPTION books
Reviewing decline; concerning reviews of subscription books; reprint. M. K. Goggin and L. M. Sealberg. Library J 89:1687 Ap 15 '64
SUBSCRIPTION radio programs. See Radio broadcasting—Subscription programs
SUBSCRIPTION television, incorporated
Battle of Santa Monica; Subscription television, inc. R. L. Shayon. Sat R 47:37+ My 9 '64
Battling big odds for pay TV. il Bsns W p 139-40+ Je 27 '64
Box; will it revolutionize TV? P. O'Neil. il Life 57:43-4+ Jl 17 '64
California's cross-channel battle; Subscription television co. dispute. il Newsweek 63: 92+ Mr 23 '64
Death of STV. Time 84:72 N 13 '64
No Pat solutions; problems of Subscription television, inc. Newsweek 63:74-5 Je 22 '64
Pay or free? the coming TV war. D. Smith. Nation 198:504-6 My 18 '64
Pay-TV, set for wake, refuses to lie down. il Bsns W p34 N 14 '64
Proposition fifteen. America 111:683 N 28 '64
Stupid question, stupid answer; California's Proposition fifteen. Life 57:4 N 20 '64
Turning STV off; Proposition fifteen defeats pay-TV in California. Newsweek 64:67 N 16 '64
Where pay TV faces big showdown soon. il U S News 56:12 Ap 20 '64
Why suppress pay-TV? the fight in California. S. L. Weaver, jr. Atlan 214:55-9 O '64; Reply with rejoinder. C. de Young Thieriot. 215:34 Ja '65
SUBSCRIPTION television programs. See Television broadcasting—Subscription programs
SUBSIDENCES, Mine. See Mine subsidences
SUBSIDIES
Great uranium glut. H. B. Meyers. il Fortune 69:108-11+ F '64
King subsidy: for domestic textile mills. New Repub 149:7-8 D 14 '63
Politics, 1964: can anyone beat 100 billion dollars? il U S News 57:47-8 S 28 '64
Where U.S. subsidies are rising sharply. il U S News 57:86-7 S 21 '64
See also
Agricultural administration—United States
Family allowances
SUBSIDIES, Music. See Music and state
SUBSTITUTE products
See also
Meat substitutes
SUBSTITUTE teachers
Ten ways to help your substitute. M. Kaminsky. Sr Schol 85:9T O 14 '64
Why substitute? J. L. Hyek. NEA J 53:45 S '64
SUBSTITUTES
See also
Milk substitutes
SUB-SUBDWARF stars. See Stars, Subdwarf
SUBSURFACE structures. See Underground structures
SUB-TEEN slang. See Slang
SUBTERRANEAN houses. See Architecture, Domestic
SUBTERRANEAN termites. See Termites
SUBURBAN houses. See Architecture, Domestic
SUBURBAN life
Neighbours, by H. Bracey. Review
Newsweek il 64:81+ Ag 24 '64
Quit picking on suburbia. il Changing T 17: 34-6 O '63

Anecdotes, facetiae, satire, etc.

Okay-dokay, Rosita, I tell you about life in the U.S.A. K. Nelson. il Good H 156:40+ Mr '63
SUBURBAN matron's story; story. See Cousins, M.
SUBURBAN offices. See Location in business and industry
SUBURBS
Call for an interdependent approach to metropolis. Christian Cent 80:996-7 Ag 14 '63
Can cities compete with suburbia for family living? C. B. Wurster. il Arch Rec 136: 149-56 D '64
Challenge to leadership; address, July 14, 1964. M. A. Rapp. Vital Speeches 30:654-7 Ag 15 '64
Cluster zoning: one step toward a better suburbia. G. D. Lloyd. il Am Home 67:46-7 Je '64
Clusters instead of slurbs. A. L. Huxtable. il N Y Times Mag p36-7+ F 9 '64
France's landmark in urban design. il Arch Forum 118:108-11 Je '63
Housing message calls for aid to suburbs. Arch Rec 135:32 Mr '64
Quit picking on suburbia. il Changing T 17:34-6 O '63
Speaking out; the suburbs are a mess; excerpt from God's own junkyard. P. Blake. Sat Eve Post 236:14+ O 5 '63
Suburbs to slurburbs; Nashville, Tenn. New Repub 150:7 Je 6 '64
Tomorrow's suburbs: better living for less money. il Changing T 18:23-4 Ap '64
Ugly American. C. W. Griffin, jr. Reporter 30:53-4+ Ja 30 '64
When the Russians try to invade suburbia. A. Chamberlin. il Sat Eve Post 236:28-9 Ag 24 '63
See also
Regional planning
SUBVERSIVE activities
Cuba; the subversion airlift. il Time 81:19 Mr 29 '63
See also
Communism—United States
Internal security
SUBWAY cars. See Railroads—Cars
SUBWAYS
Going underground, the cities dig deep. il Newsweek 64:74-6 S 14 '64
See also subhead Subways under names of cities, e.g. Toronto—Subways

Cars

See Railroads—Cars
SUCCESS
How companies will win success; interview. Nations Bsns 52:26-7+ Ja '64
How men get ahead. R. M. Powell. il Nations Bsns 52:56-8+ Mr '64
How to be a failure. C. H. Brower. Read Digest 86:44-5 Ja '65
In one era and out the other; excerpts from Profession housewife. P. McGinley. il Ladies Home J 81:42+ Ap '64

SUCCESS—*Continued*
New business spokesman urges positive approach. C. B. Seib. il Nations Bsns 52:42-3+ My '64
Quality of rudeness. N. Pileggi. Esquire 61:98 Ja '64
Ragged Dick in the last lap. H. Swados. Nation 199:13-14 Jl 13 '64
Three millionaires tell how they did it; excerpts from Money talks! ed. by C. Sopkin. P. J. Sagona; W. P. Lear, sr; W. G. Riley. il Nations Bsns 52:106-8+ Ap '64
What it takes to be successful; symposium. il Nations Bsns 51:66-8+ Je '63
What you can learn from success. A. Uris. il Nations Bsns 51:76-8 Jl '63
Why men & nations seek success; interview. D. C. McClelland. il Nations Bsns 51:32-3+ S '63
Will success spoil your marriage? T. Howard. il McCalls 90:88-9+ Jl '63
You can get ahead faster. S. Schuler. il Nations Bsns 51:76-9 F '63
See also
Conduct of life

SUCCESSFUL farming (periodical)
Our mission for you. D. Hanson. Suc Farm 62:2B O '64
Want more vacation help? SF travel department. Suc Farm 62:32 Ag '64

SUCCESSION, Presidential. See Presidents—United States—Succession

SUCCESSION to the crown. See Great Britain—Royal family

SUCCINIC acid
Inducing resistance to freezing and desiccation in plants by decenylsuccinic acid. P. J. C. Kuiper. bibliog il Science 146:544-6 O 23 '64
Reduction of transpiration of leaves through stomatal closure induced by alkenylsuccinic acids. I. Zelitch. bibliog il Science 143:692-3 F 14 '64
Water transport across root cell membranes: effect of alkenylsuccinic acids. P. J. C. Kuiper. bibliog il Science 143:690-1 F 14 '64

SUCCULENT plants
Exploit the beauty of succulents in arrangements. R. M. Peters. il Pop Gard 16:38-9 Ja '65
Growing succulents for miniature landscapes. il Sunset 134:132-3 Ja '65
How to multiply succulents. il Sunset 130: 272+ My '63
If your hobby is succulents. il Sunset 131:168 Ag '63
Roosting place for hens and chickens; plants growing in trunks of date palms. il Sunset 131:300 N '63
See also
Aloes
Echeveria
Jade plants
Kalanchoes

SUCHMAN, J. Richard
Learning through inquiry. NEA J 52:31-2 Mr '63

SUCKER fishing
It's hooking-up time. D. R. Crandall. il Outdoor Life 131:36-7+ Ja '63

SUCKER; story. See McCullers, C.

SUCROSE. See Sugars

SUDAK, Howard S. and Maas, J. W.
Behavioral-neurochemical correlation in reactive and nonreactive strains of rats. bibliog Science 146:418-20 O 16 '64

SUDAN
See also
Christians in Sudan
Hunting—Sudan
Missions—Sudan
Negroes in the Sudan
Refugees, Sudanese

Native races
Now hear this; difference in hearing between an American and a Mabaan. il Newsweek 61:80 My 6 '63
Old Africa's people of the village; Meban tribe. A. Leipzig. il Natur Hist 73:10-19 Ap; 38-45 My '64

Politics and government
Bringing down father; rebellion in Negro provinces. il Time 84:28 N 6 '64
Deadly insects. E. Marsden. il Newsweek 65: 32-3 F 1 '65
General's exit. Newsweek 64:52+ N 30 '64
New deal in the Sudan. America 111:681 N 28 '64
Storm on the Nile; coalition government set up. Newsweek 64:52 N 9 '64

Public health
Old Africa's people of the village; Meban tribe. A. Leipzig. il Natur Hist 73:38-45 My '64

Religious institutions and affairs
Human rights in the Sudan. America 110:705 My 23 '64
Need for an inquiry. Commonweal 77:553 F 22 '63
Revolt in the Sudan; persecution of non-Muslims. America 109:758 D 14 '63
Sundown on Christianity in the Sudan. V. J. Dunigan. il Cath World 199:245-52 Jl '64
This side of the curtain. Commonweal 79: 704 Mr 13 '64
What about the Sudan? America 109:695 N 30 '63

Riots
Where Negroes and Arabs are clashing. il U S News 57:6 D 21 '64

Social life and customs
House of the Lady Aziza. C. Wagner. Reporter 30:35-6 Ja 2 '64

SUDAN grass

Hybrids
See Sorghum—Hybrids

SUDBURY, Ontario

Parks and playgrounds
Leadership by association. G. Kormos. il Recreation 57:191 Ap '64

SUEDE leather. See Leather

SUEDFELD, Peter, and Vernon, Jack
Visual hallucinations during sensory deprivation: a problem of criteria. bibliog Science 145:412-13 Jl 24 '64

SUEHSDORF, Adolph
Cats in our lives. Nat Geog Mag 125:508-41 Ap '64

SUEKER, Keith H.
Transistor Williamson stereo power amplifier. Electr World 72:42-6 O '64

SUELTENFUSS, E. A. and Pollard, Morris
Cytochemical assay of interferon produced by duck hepatitis virus. bibliog Science 139:595-6 F 15 '63

SUENENS, Léon Joseph, cardinal
Cardinal Suenens on the church; interview. ed. by W. M. Abbott. America 108:360-1 Mr 16 '63
about
Cardinal in the press. America 108:821 Je 8 '63
Cardinal Suenens in America. W. M. Abbott. America 110:701 My 23 '64
New era for the nun in the world. A. McCormack. il Cath World 199:144-51 Je '64
Pope's emissary. America 108:781 My 25 '63

SUEOKA, Noboru. See Cheng, T. Y. jt. auth.

SUEZ CANAL
Paid in full. Newsweek 61:36 F 4 '63
Suez sails on without its canal; Compagnie financiere de Suez. il Bsns W p60-2+ F 22 '64

SUEZ crisis. See Egypt—History—Invasion, 1956

SUFFER finks gladly; story. See Schoen, B.

SUFFERING
Beyond grief. R. O. Johann. il America 112: 76 Ja 16 '65
Cup of suffering. Christian Cent 81:355 Mr 18 '64
Word. V. P. McCorry. America 110:805-6 Je 6 '64

SUFFOCATION. See Asphyxia

SUFFOLK COUNTY, N.Y.
Power-packed purchasing. S. P. Mitman. Am City 79:122-3 D '64
Triple-benefit waterfront projects. H. L. Dennison. il Am City 78:110-12 Mr '63

SUFFRAGE
See also
Voters, Registration of
Voting

United States
Don't blame the American voter. W. G. Andrews. il N Y Times Mag p42-3+ O 18 '64
Eight million disfranchised Americans. Sat Eve Post 237:80 Ja 4 '64
Factor X for '64; stay-at-homes; with charts. il U S News 57:32-3 Ag 17 '64
G.I. vote in Texas. Time 84:63-4 S 11 '64
How your right to vote was won. A. Balk. Todays Health 42:52-4 F '64
If good men do nothing. R. L. Tobin. Sat R 47:16 Ag 1 '64

SUFFRAGE—United States—*Continued*
Should eighteen-year-olds vote? pro and con discussion. il Sr Schol 84:38-9 F 14 '64
Should we lower the voting age? G. J. Hecht. Parents Mag 39:39+ Mr '64
Speaking out; stay home and don't vote. J. Keats. Sat Eve Post 236:8+ O 26 '63
Universal voting at eighteen? pro and con discussion. il Sr Schol 85:10-11 O 21 '64
Votes for eighteen-year-olds. Newsweek 62:16 D 30 '63
What voting rights does the Constitution guarantee? H. G. Earl. Todays Health 42:32-3+ S '64
Who should be qualified to vote? H. Earl. il Todays Health 42:18-21+ Ag '64
Why don't more Americans vote? A. Balk. il Todays Health 42:28-31+ Ja '64; Correction. 42:84 Mr '64
Why one third of us don't vote; kept away by political and mechanical barriers. R. M. Scammon. il N Y Times Mag p36+ N 17 '63
Without portfolio. C. B. Luce. il McCalls 91:16+ Ag '64
See also
Negroes in the United States—Politics and suffrage
Washington, D.C.—Politics and government
Woman suffrage—United States
SUFFRAGE amendment. See Woman suffrage—United States
SUGAR
Taste sense of children for sweetness tested. Sci N L 85:207 Mr 28 '64
That extra something is brown sugar. il McCalls 91:98-9+ Ja '64
Manufacture and refining
How to get blood from a beet. il Bsns W p58+ D 21 '63
Physiological effects
Chelation of calcium by lactose: its role in transport mechanisms. P. Charley and P. Saltman. bibliog il Science 139:1205-6 Mr 22 '63
Sugar, coronaries linked. F. C. Livingstone. Sci N L 86:131 Ag 29 '64
Prices
Coping with the high price of sugar. il Fortune 68:215 Ag '63
Hoarding, speculating inflate sugar prices. il Bsns W p34 Je 1 '63
Sugar bubble and how it burst. il U S News 54:9 Je 10 '63
SUGAR beets
Beans and beets in the same field. J. Russell. Farm J 88:49 Ja '64
How to get blood from a beet. il Bsns W p58+ D 21 '63
SUGAR-bowl dream; story. See Bittle, C. R.
SUGAR bowl parade. See New Orleans—Parades
SUGAR bowls, etc.
Nine colonial sugar boxes. K. Buhler. il Antiques 85:88-91 Ja '64
SUGAR cane fibers. See Bagasse
SUGAR in the body
Phospholipid-sugar complexes in relation to cell membrane monosaccharide transport. P. G. LeFevre and others. bibliog il Science 143:955-7 F 28 '64
SUGAR industry and trade
Bet that failed; Olavarria and Galban Lobo file under Bankruptcy act. Bsns W p70+ Ag 1 '64
Cuba runs low on sweetening. Bsns W p26 My 4 '63
Cuba: salvation through sugar. J. O'Connor. il Nation 197:212-14+ O 12 '63
Five years of Castro's Cuba. T. Draper. bibliog f Commentary 37:25-37 Ja '64; Discussion. 37:8+ My '64
Hoarding, speculating inflate sugar prices. il Bsns W p34 Je 1 '63
SAM's song; Cuba's move into the world market. il Time 83:38 My 8 '64
Soaring sugar. Time 81:83 Mr 29 '63
Sugar as a weapon. Nation 196:413 My 18 '63
Sugar binge. Time 81:96 Je 7 '63
Sugar: market and supermarket. D. Smith. il Nation 199:327-9 N 9 '64; Reply with rejoinder. E. T. MacHardy. 199:inside cover D 14 '64
Sweet and sour; sugar prices. il Newsweek 61:74 My 20 '63
Winners and losers in sugar. il Fortune 68: 209-10+ Ag '63
SUGAR LOAF MOUNTAIN, Md.
Stronghold: story of a man and a mountain. J. H. Caldwell. Nat Parks Mag 37:16 Ag '63
SUGAR refining. See Sugar—Manufacture and refining
SUGAR substitutes
Sugar substitutes safe? cyclamate. Sci N L 86:196 S 26 '64
SUGARBUSH VALLEY, Vt.
Social climbing on the slopes. G. Talese. il Sat Eve Post 236:30+ F 9 '63
Some spice for the sugar; excerpt from Book of American skiing. E. Bowen. il Sports Illus 19:37-8+ N 18 '63
Tsoo-gaarr-boosch! skiing from your mountain doorstep; Sugarbush Valley. il Newsweek 64:48-51 D 28 '64
SUGARMAN, Daniel, and Hochstein, Rollie
Does a good date make a good mate? Seventeen 23:148-9+ Ap '64
SUGARS
Sucrose: precise determination of crystal and molecular structure by neutron diffraction. G. M. Brown and H. A. Levy. bibliog il Science 141:921-3 S 6 '63
See also
Fructose
Glucose
SUGGESTION
See also
Hypnotism
SUGGESTION systems
Employee suggestions; Kalamazoo, Mich. S. Kelley. il Am City 79:95 Ja '64
Power of suggestion. il Time 83:86 Je 19 '64
20,000,000 bucks in the suggestion box. E. D. Fales, jr. il Pop Sci 183:67-70+ D '63
See also
Technological innovations
SUICIDE
Can we stop suicides? N. L. Farberow and E. S. Shneidman. Todays Health 41:59+ D '63
Decision to die. S. Alexander. il Life 56:74-6+ My 29 '64
Doctors' wives tackle the suicide problem. M. Benson. il Todays Health 42:60-3 My '64
End of the glow; new suicides in Saigon. il Time 82:32 D 13 '63
Girls outnumber boys in suicide attempts. Sci N L 84:328 N 23 '63
High dive; leaps from Eiffel tower. Newsweek 61:52 My 20 '63
I'm going to kill myself. A. Hamilton. il Sci Digest 54:57-63 S '63
Jobless suicides. Sci Am 209:68 Jl '63
Mortal statistics. K. Nott. Commentary 38: 64-8 O '64
Psychiatrist examines suicide, questions and answers; excerpts from Encyclopedia of mental health. P. Friedman. il Todays Health 41:56-9+ D '63; Correction. 42:87 Ja '64
Suicide and jobless rates closely related. Sci N L 83:296 My 11 '63
Suicide and Scandinavia, by H. Hendin. Review
Nation 198:606-8 Je 15 '64. D. Horowitz
Suicide in childhood and adolescence. M. Clark. il NEA J 53:32-3+ N '64
Suicide in many forms; South Viet Nam. Time 82:32+ Jl 19 '63
Symbolic suicide; Nguyen Tuong Tam. Newsweek 62:43-4 Jl 22 '63
What killed Bob Lyons? executive's emotional problems. H. Levinson. il Harvard Bsns R 41:127-42+ Ja '63
Why people can't take it. F. R. Schreiber and M. Herman. il Sci Digest 56:66-9 S '64
Women suicides increase due to social pressures. Sci N L 85:271 Ap 25 '64
SUICIDE prevention center, Los Angeles
I'm going to kill myself. A. Hamilton. il Sci Digest 54:57-63 S '63
SUICIDE; story. See Connell, E. S. jr
SUIT like new; story. See Fontaine, R.
SUITS at law. See Actions and defenses
SUKALAC, Peter
Modified circuit. il Hot Rod 17:46-51 F '64
Offy answers back. il Hot Rod 17:46-51+ Mr '64
SUKARNO, 1901-
Talk with Sukarno: I am Indonesia; interview, with B. Krisher. por Newsweek 64:84 O 5 '64
about
Adventurer. Newsweek 62:46 O 7 '63
Can another $1 per person save a country from communism? il por U S News 55:86-8 Jl 29 '63
Clouds in the South Seas; with report by R. K. McCabe. il por Newsweek 61:42-4 Mr 4 '63
How Sukarno keeps his revolution spinning. D. Warner. Reporter 30:33-6 Ap 23 '64
I will eat you. J. Burnham. Nat R 16:60 Ja 28 '64
In dreamland. il por Newsweek 63:34 My 4 '64

SUKARNO—about—*Continued*
In the Far East: still no real peace. il por U S News 56:6 F 3 '64
Indonesia steps closer to the brink. il pors Bsns W p52-4+ Ja 16 '65
Indonesia takes a walk. il Sr Schol 85:18-19 Ja 21 '65
Malaya sees Sukarno as danger for southeast Asia; interview. A. Rahman. il por U S News 54:80-1 Mr 18 '63
Malaysia's baptism of fire. il Sr Schol 83: 10-13 N 1 '63
Mission to Malaysia. Sr Schol 84:7 F 14 '64
New sea of trouble in southeast Asia. il por U S News 54:46-8 F 11 '63
New world battleground in Asia? il por U S News 58:8 Ja 18 '65
Next war. Nation 199:150 S 28 '64
Notes of a new nation. J. M. Van der Kroef. il por Nat R 15:390-2 N 5 '63
Power balance in Indonesia. A. Vandenbosch. il Cur Hist 46:95-100 F '64
Punch-drunk. New Repub 150:13 Ja 18 '64
Robert Kennedy's aim: prevent a Sukarno war. por U S News 56:15 Ja 27 '64
Sukarno: back for more Kremlin arms? il por U S News 57:24 O 12 '64
Sukarno: on the road to disaster? por U S News 56:74 My 18 '64
Sukarno: regional bully. B. Grant. il Nation 198:111-14 F 3 '64
Sukarno stirs up another Asian storm. S. S. King. il por N Y Times Mag p 14-15+ Ja 19 '64
Sukarno's lavish ganefo was mostly snafu. T. P. Ross. il por Sports Illus 19:28-31 D 2 '63
Sukarno's sweet touch of fury. il por Life 58:34-5 Ja 29 '65
Sukarno's war; will it involve U.S? il por U S News 57:63 S 21 '64
We are going to change this damn world! J. A. Rose. il pors Sat Eve Post 236:77-81 N 2 '63
What we got for pampering Sukarno. D. Warner. il Reporter 31:30-2 O 8 '64

SULA bassana. See Gannets

SULFATES
Sulfate particulates: size distribution in Pittsburgh air. M. Corn and L. DeMaio. bibliog il Science 143:803-4 F 21 '64
Sulfate transport in human red cells: inhibition by some uncouplers of oxidative phosphorylation. A. Omachi. bibliog il Science 145:1449-50 S 25 '64

SULFIDES
See also
Methyl sulfide

SULFOXIDES
See also
Methyl sulfoxide

SULFUR
Isotopes
Fractionation of sulfur and carbon isotopes in a meromictic lake. E. S. Deevey, jr. and others. bibliog il Science 139:407-8 F 1 '63

SULFUR bacteria
Cytochrome in thiobacillus thiooxidans. J. London. bibliog il Science 140:409-10 Ap 26 '63

SULLENGER, D. B. See Phipps, K. D. jt. auth.

SULLIVAN, Aloysius Michael
At Santa Susanna's; poem. Cath World 197: 358 S '63
Awakening; poem. America 108:373 Mr 16 '63
Kerry Dan; story. Cath World 196:370-6 Mr '63
Reviewing stand. See issues of Dun's review and modern industry

SULLIVAN, Bill
Soil cement streets for six cents a day. Am City 78:88-9 D '63

SULLIVAN, Ed
Ed Sullivan screens Europe's entertainment; ed. by F. Kish. pors Travel 121:37-41 My '64

SULLIVAN, Frances A.
Let's try a tesser. PTA Mag 57:30-1 Je '63
Password is book. PTA Mag 58:28-30 Je '64

SULLIVAN, Frank
Greetings, friends! poem. New Yorker 39:30 D 21 '63; 40:29 D 26 '64
Insurance claims racket. Motor T 15:116-17 N '63

SULLIVAN, Howard A.
Old librarian and his almanack. por Library J 89:1188-92 Mr 15 '64

SULLIVAN, James
Ceremonial; poem. Commonweal 81:75 O 9 '64
Half moon sailing; poem. Commonweal 80: 449 Jl 3 '64
Strauss; poem. Commonweal 79:227 N 15 '63

SULLIVAN, Joanna
Reading lab: Rx for better reading. por Sr Schol 83:20T-21T O 4 '63

SULLIVAN, John L.
Duel in the sun. S. D. Smith. il por N Y Times Mag p72-3 Ag 9 '64

SULLIVAN, L. B.
Libel landmark. il Newsweek 63:74 Mr 23 '64

SULLIVAN, Leon
Hail pastor as OIC founder. il pors Ebony 19:35-6 My '64
Self-help in Philadelphia. H. Lees. il Reporter 31:15-17 D 17 '64

SULLIVAN, Leonor K.
Excerpt from debate, April 7, 1964. Cong Digest 43:180+ Je '64

SULLIVAN, Milton
Sculptor & teacher; interview, ed. by L. D. Jean. il por Sch Arts 63:25-7 F '64

SULLIVAN, Neil V.
Making history in Prince Edward County. por Sat R 47:59-61+ O 17 '64
Prince Edward County situation. por NEA J 53:13+ Mr '64

SULLIVAN, Peggy Anne
Interpreting children's literature for teachers. ALA Bul 57:156-7 F '63
Knapp-sack of progress. por Wilson Lib Bul 39:392-6 Ja '65
Librarian's dream come true. NEA J 53:46-7 S '64
School libraries. Wilson Lib Bul 38:793 My '64
Underway: the Knapp project's first year. Library J 89:2143-5 My 15 '64

about
Peggy Anne Sullivan. E. Rudin. Library J 88:1287 Mr 15 '63

SULLIVAN, Philip R.
Psychiatric Catholic. America 108:199-201 F 9 '63

SULLIVAN, Richard
Time is a commodity; regional library service in eastern Massachusetts. D. Nyren. por Library J 88:1943-5 My 15 '63

SULLIVAN, Robert J.
Boating manners. Motor B 112:46+ D '63

SULLIVAN, Walter, jr
Cave man gets a new look; reprint. Sci Digest 57:58-60 Ja '65
Communication with other planets; excerpt from We are not alone. Sat R 47:78-9 D 5 '64
Year of the quiet son. W. Jonathan. por Sat R 47:56 F 1 '64

SULLIVAN, Wilson
Miracle on Twelfth street. Sat R 47:48-9+ F 8 '64
Other side of the canvas. Sat R 46:18-19 Je 8 '63
Van Wyck Brooks: a bibliography. Sat R 46:19 My 25 '63
Weekly newspaper: commitment in suburbia. Sat R 46:74-5 N 9 '63
Whole world inside. Sat R 47:124-5+ Mr 14 '64

SULLIVAN, Wynn E.
Forestry in Ireland. Am For 70:31 Ap '64

SULLY, Alfred
General Sully reports; excerpts from letters, with reproductions of sketches and paintings, ed. by L. Sully. por Am Heritage 16:52-63 D '64

SULLY, Francois
Vietnam between the poles. Nation 197:421-2 D 14 '63

SULLY, Langdon
(ed) See Sully, A. General Sully reports

SULPHUR mines and mining
Canada
See also
Texas Gulf sulphur company

SULZBERGER, Arthur Ochs
Family enterprise. il por Time 81:58 Je 28 '63
Pleased Punch; new publisher. Newsweek 62: 41 Jl 1 '63

SUMERIAN inscriptions. See Cuneiform inscriptions

SUMERIAN literature
O ye daughters of Sumer! S. N. Kramer. il Horizon 5:108-9 Jl '63

SUMERIAN sculpture. See Sculpture, Sumerian

SUMERIANS
Schoolboy in Sumer; prestige of the scribe; excerpt from History of mankind. L. Woolley. il UNESCO Courier 16:14-15 Je '63

SUMITS, William J.
Automatic eyes. por Pop Phot 52:87 My '63
Bits & pieces. por Pop Phot 54:101 Mr '64
Darkrooms of the future. por Pop Phot 54: 107 Ap '64

SUMITS, William J.—*Continued*
Daylight color films only? por Pop Phot 53:73 Jl '63
Informal newsletter. por Pop Phot 53:187 D '63
New format: 46-mm? por Pop Phot 52:91 Mr '63
On learning electronics. por Pop Phot 52:107 Ap '63
Photography & common sense. por Pop Phot 52:75-6 F '63
Photography: the Rube Goldberg business. por Pop Phot 55:107 S '64
Thoughts on the Instamatic. por Pop Phot 53:91 S '63
What they might have done. por Pop Phot 53:54 O '63

SUMMER, C. E. and Peterson, Chester, jr
Feed on pasture. Suc Farm 61:62-3 Jl '63

SUMMER
Gardens, children and the good old summertime. J. B. Geddes. il Pop Gard 15:22-3 Jl '64
How to capture that lovely indolence of summer. il House B 105:89-121+ Je '63
Make work lighter for summer living. B. G. Wadsworth. il Parents Mag 39:138 Je '64
P.S. to summer. F. Sagan; F. Du Plessix Gray; S. Delaney. Vogue 144:196-7+ S 1 '64
Sumer is icumen in. B. Tufty. il(p369) Sci N L 83:378-9 Je 15 '63
Summer living. il Changing T 18:32 Ag '64
Summer secrets. B. Tufty. il Sci N L 85:394-5 Je 20 '64
Summer to remember. il Am Home 67:24 Jl '64
See also
August
Hot weather

Quotations, maxims, etc.
Truth & poetry; ed. by H. V. Wilson. Flower Grower 50:72 Ag '63

SUMMER activities. See Vacation projects
SUMMER at Strandhill; story. See McGahern, J.
SUMMER by the sea; story. See Gasperini, B.
SUMMER cabins. See Cabins
SUMMER camping. See Camping
SUMMER camps. See Camps
SUMMER cookery. See Cookery
SUMMER drinks. See Beverages
SUMMER entertaining. See Entertaining
SUMMER furniture. See Furniture, Outdoor
SUMMER games; story. See Price, R.

SUMMER homes
Camp Nikita; Khrushchev's seaside hide-away. il Time 82:19 Ag 16 '63
Honeycomb house for all seasons. il Sports Illus 20:40-5 Mr 23 '64
Houses that unsquare the cube. F. R. Smith. il Sports Illus 19:40-5 Jl 29 '63
Island home take full advantage of the outdoors. il Am Home 67:38-41 Ap '64
Leisure-time living. G. O'Brien. il N Y Times Mag p92-3 N 3 '63
Like to buy a vacation home? il Changing T 18:43-5 Je '64
Living with antiques; the Pavilion, Fort Ticonderoga. A. Winchester. il Antiques 84:52-6 Jl '63
Mr — builds his dream house. il Horizon 5:102-3 S '63
Personal business; vacation homes in Florida and Caribbean Region. Bsns W p81 Mr 2 '63
Vacation house good for all seasons. J. D. Bloodgood. il Bet Hom & Gard 42:48-9 Ap '64
Vacation houses: fun for all seasons. A. C. Borg. il Am Home 66:23-33 Je '63
Vacation houses that pay for themselves. il House B 105:141-57+ My '63
Vacationing in style. G. O'Brien. il N Y Times Mag p56-7 Jl 21 '63
Want to get away from it all? il Changing T 18:37-9 Ag '64
What a second home can do for you. Am Home 67:35 Ap '64
Yacht in a meadow; the Long Island house of Mrs De Menocal Simpson. il Vogue 141:178-81 My '63
Your second home. il Am Home 67:16+ Ap '64
See also
Cottages

SUMMER housekeeping. See Home economics
SUMMER houses. See Garden houses, shelters, etc.
SUMMER husband; story. See Gordon, E. E.
SUMMER in a shell; story. See Boles, P. D.

SUMMER Institute of linguistics
Apostle of the alphabet. il Time 82:25 S 27 '63

SUMMER institutes. See Teachers institutes
SUMMER jobs. See Seasonal labor
SUMMER jobs for students. See Student employment
SUMMER loves; story. See Spring, E.
SUMMER menus. See Menus
SUMMER music camps. See Music camps
SUMMER of Daisy Miller; drama. See Greene, B.
SUMMER out of season; story. See Delman, D.
SUMMER reading projects. See Libraries, Childrens—Projects

SUMMER resorts
Case for the passé resort. J. P. Harman. il Travel 121:48-50+ Je '64
Ebony's annual vacation guide. il Ebony 18:132-3 Je '63
Gentleman flier's own backyard. il Esquire 61:92-3 Je '64
Making the summer weekend scene. T. Meehan. Mlle 58:191-2+ Ap '64
Our changing resorts. D. D. Miller. il Travel 122:48-52 N '64
Photographic program featured at Vermont resort: The Silos. L. Lachter. il U S Camera 26:17 F '63
Summertime revisited; portfolio. S. T. Cooper. Am Heritage 14:35-49 Je '63
Velvet Europe. F. Morton. il Holiday 33:58-71+ My '63
See also
Atlantic City
Newport, R.I.

SUMMER schools
Boon to the gifted; program for North Carolina's most brilliant and creative high school students. Time 81:63 Je 28 '63
College scene this summer. il Dance Mag 38:14-19 Ap '64
Family campus on the mountaintop; University of southern California's Idyllwild campus. il Recreation 57:299+ Je '64
New American traveler. L. G. Rubin. Esquire 61:40+ My '64
1964 world guide to summer study. il Sr Schol 84:17T-25T Mr 20 '64
1963 world guide to summer study. Sr Schol 82:7T-9T+ Mr 20 '63
St Paul's social studies institute. J. Engh. il Sr Schol 85:10T-11T Ja 14 '65
Summer scholars. il Time 84:41 Jl 31 '64
Summer scholars; Mount Hermon, Mass. il Newsweek 64:49 Jl 27 '64
They challenge our top students; Mark Twain summer institute, Clayton, Mo. P. Friggens. il PTA Mag 57:4-7 My '63; Same abr. with title Here's a new kind of summer school. Read Digest 82:157-8+ Je '63
We set high standards and then lived up to them; summer institute in St Louis. il NEA J 53:28-9 O '64
See also
Idyllwild school of music and the arts
Salzburg seminar in American studies

SUMMER theater. See Theater—United States
SUMMER vacations. See Vacations
SUMMER work camps. See Labor camps

SUMMERFIELD, Arthur E.
Priorities of the future; address. Vital Speeches 29:334-6 Mr 15 '63

SUMMERHILL school, England. See Schools, Experimental
SUMMERHOUSE; story. See Boles, P. D.

SUMMERS, C. E.
Are you forcing your cattle to diet? Suc Farm 62:66 O '64
Changing beef cattle rations? Suc Farm 62:35 Ja '64
How to balance a feeder ration. Suc Farm 61:12 N '63
These beef specialists answer your twenty-one most asked questions. por Suc Farm 61:46-7 My '63

SUMMERS, Elaine
Fantastic gardens. Judson memorial church. J. Maskey. Dance Mag 38:30 Ap '64

SUMMERS, Hollis
At the Shaw gardens in St Louis; poem. Sat R 46:30 Mr 9 '63
Catalogue tells you what you are interested in; poem. Sat R 47:139 Mr 14 '64
Meeting; poem. Sat R 47:56 My 9 '64

SUMMIT, N.J. public library
Shop and library team up in book promotion plan. Pub W 184:171 Jl 8 '63

SUMMIT conferences. See International conferences
SUMMONSES. See Process

SUMO. See Wrestling
SUN
Create sun matter. W. Wingo. Sci N L 85:359 Je 6 '64
In the light of the sun. A. C. Clarke. il Horizon 5:48-55 N '63
International years of the quiet sun, 1964-65. M. A. Pomerantz. bibliog il Science 142:1136-43 N 29 '63
Noisy quiet sun. Sci Am 211:62 D '64
Solar symposium at Sydney. M. Minnaert. il Sky & Tel 27:151-3 Mr '64
Sun, moon, and planets this month. See issues of Sky and telescope
Sun never sets on Cleveland; solar simulators. Sci N L 83:310 My 18 '63
Tourist crop grows under midnight sun; Sweden, Norway, and Finland compete for tourists. il Bsns W p30-1 Jl 18 '64
We need to know more about the sun; questions and answers. W. Von Braun. il Pop Sci 184:14+ Mr '64
See also
Eclipses, Solar
International years of the quiet sun
Solar radiation
Spectrum, Solar
Sunspots

Atmosphere

Challenge of chromospheric physics. R. G. Athay. bibliog il Science 143:1129-38 Mr 13 '64
Motions in the solar atmosphere. J. W. Evans. il Sky & Tel 25:321-5 Je '63

Corona

Detect cool spot on sun. Sci N L 85:339 My 30 '64
First flight of Coronascope II. G. Newkirk, jr. and J. D. Bohlin. il Sky & Tel 28:16-19 Jl '64
Motions in the solar atmosphere. J. W. Evans. il Sky & Tel 25:321-5 Je '63
Radar observations of the Corona and Mariner II measurements of the flux in the solar wind. J. C. Brandt. bibliog il Science 146:1671-2 D 25 '64
Solar wind. E. N. Parker. il Sci Am 210:66-76 bibliog(p 156) Ap '64
What makes the shadows hot. Time 83:80 My 29 '64

Spectrum

See Spectrum, Solar

SUN (newspaper)
New Sun, small hello. il Time 84:43 S 25 '64
SUN, Photography of. See Astronomical photography
SUN burn. See Sunburn
SUN CITY, Ariz.
Reporter at large. C. Trillin. il New Yorker 40:120+ Ap 4 '64
SUN dials. See Sundials
SUN gas. See Helium
SUN glasses
And even in the dark. il Bsns W p30-1 Je 6 '64
In the dark. il Newsweek 63:106 My 25 '64
Instant sunglasses. S. M. Gallager. il Pop Sci 184:84-6+ F '64
Living in shadow; sunglasses stand for glamour and social status. B. Day. il N Y Times Mag p42+ Ap 12 '64
Notes and comment: winter of the dark glasses. il New Yorker 40:29 Mr 28 '64
Russian eye doctor uses spectacles with holes; stenopaic glasses. Sci N L 86:88 Ag 8 '64
Sunglasses. il Consumer Bul 47:13-15+ Je '64
SUN god. See Sun worship
SUN in art
Sun; excerpt from Sun in art. W. Herdeg. il Natur Hist 72:38-47 Ap '63
SUN oil company
Nightmare for oil marketers. Bsns W p66 Ja 19 '63
Strange case of Sun oil, which is damned if it does and damned if it doesn't. M. R. Lefkoe. il Fortune 68:117+ Ag '63
SUN roses
Sun roses simply like the sun. il Sunset 133:292 O '64
SUN screens. See Screens (sun)
SUN spots. See Sunspots
SUN stroke. See Sunstroke
SUN tan. See Tan
SUN tan preparations. See Cosmetics
SUN-times, Chicago. See Chicago sun-times
SUN up! drama. See Boiko, C.

SUN VALLEY, Idaho
Divorce in Sun Valley. il Newsweek 63:75-6 Mr 2 '64
Into the Valley of fun. B. Ottum. il Sports Illus 22:52-9 Ja 4 '65
Sun Valley notes. D. Messinesi. Vogue 144:116 N 1 '64
SUN worship
Sunlight creates an Egyptian god. J. K. Van der Haagen. il Sci Digest 53:48-58 Mr '63
SUNBURN
Beware-too much sun. il Good H 157:62-3+ Jl '63
Sun also burns. il Time 81:43 Je 21 '63
Sun tan safely. J. Henderson. il Motor B 114:52+ Jl '64
See also
Tan
SUNDAES. See Ice cream, ices, etc.
SUNDARALINGAM, M. See Jensen, L. H. jt. auth.
SUNDAY
American Sunday. America 109:723 D 7 '63
SUNDAY legislation
Blue Sunday. il Time 82:54+ O 25 '63
Closing law upheld; Kentucky's law. C. Courteau. Christian Cent 80:834 Je 26 '63
Fair Sabbath in practice. America 109:443 O 19 '63
Festivals and judges; two decisions. M. Himmelfarb. Commentary 35:67-70 Ja '63
Lord's day controversy; Maritime Provinces. R. S. Clarke. Christian Cent 80:440-2 Ap 3 '63
Practical lawmaking; fair-Sabbath bill for New York city. America 108:519 Ap 20 '63
SUNDAY mirror, London
Filling in the blanks; Boothby and the Sunday mirror. Time 84:52 Ag 14 '64
Sex, sensation & significance. il Time 81:55 My 10 '63
Smeared peer revenged; Lord Boothby and Sunday mirror. il Newsweek 64:40 Ag 17 '64
SUNDAY morning; story. See Rubin, R.
SUNDAY newspaper editions. See Newspapers—Sunday editions
SUNDAY opening of libraries. See Libraries—Hours of opening
SUNDAY pictorial. See Sunday mirror, London
SUNDAY school buildings. See Church architecture
SUNDAY suppers. See Suppers
SUNDAY supplements. See Newspapers—Sunday editions
SUNDBACK, Gideon
Fifty years of zip. S. V. Jones. il N Y Times Mag p 108-9 Ap 28 '63
SUNDE, Peggy. See Bernheimer, M. jt. comp.
SUNDIALS
Amateur scientist: sundial that tells clock time. C. J. Merchant. il Sci Am 210:136+ Mr '64
Making portable sundials. R. N. Mayall. il Sky & Tel 28:9-12 Jl '64
Shadows. New Yorker 40:43-4 O 3 '64
Sun time with a dial you mount on a wall. il Sunset 132:146+ Je '64
Sundials, by R. K. Marshall. Review
Sci Digest il 53:84 Je '63. B. H. Frisch
SUNFISH fishing
All about. . . ah. . . brim. C. Vinson. il Outdoor Life 131:82-3+ Ap '63
Ice fisherman's favorite. W. Davis. il Outdoor Life 135:76+ F '65
SUNGLASSES. See Sun glasses
SUNKEN treasure. See Treasure trove
SUNLEY, Edith
All about teething. Parents Mag 38:36-7+ Ag '63
How to care for a sick baby. Parents Mag 38:76-7+ O '63
Safety on all fours. Parents Mag 39:46-7+ O '64
Your baby doesn't need a clock. Parents Mag 38:52-3+ Mr '63
SUNLIGHT
Skin cancer and sunlight; report on conference. H. F. Blum. Science 145:1339-40 S 18 '64
SUNRISE
Day begins. . . H. Borland. il Read Digest 85:210-12 O '64
SUNSET (periodical)
Sunset way. il Time 82:73 N 1 '63
SUNSHINE, Philip, and Kretchmer, Norman
Intestinal disaccharidases: absence in two species of sea lions. bibliog Science 144:850-1 My 15 '64
SUNSPOTS
Drawings of sunspots aid solar understanding. Sci N L 83:121 F 23 '63
Signs of new solar cycle. Sci N L 84:263 O 26 '63

SUNSPOTS—*Continued*
Solar activity during the first six months of the International years of the quiet sun. H. W. Dodson and others. il Science 145: 1050-2 S 4 '64
Solar minimum and the International years of the quiet sun. H. W. Dodson and E. R. Hedeman. bibliog il Science 143:237-40 Ja 17 '64
Sunspot and granulation photography at Sacramento Peak. P. S. McIntosh. il Sky & Tel 27:280-2 My '64
SUNSTROKE
Sun tan safely. J. Henderson. il Motor B 114:52+ Jl '64
SUOR Angelica; opera. See Puccini, G.
SUPER markets. See Supermarkets
SUPER valu stores, incorporated
Supermarket chain that isn't a chain; Midwest food wholesaler. il Bsns W p80-2+ Ag 22 '64
SUPERCHARGERS
See also
Automobile engines—Superchargers
SUPERCONDUCTING plastics. See Plastics
SUPERCONDUCTIVE magnets. See Magnets
SUPERCONDUCTIVITY
New superconductors: making superconducting alloy by ultrarapid cooling. Sci Am 211:88 S '64
Nonlinear magnetics and superconductivity; report on 2nd International conference on nonlinear magnetics. G. C. Feth. Science 145:838 Ag 21 '64
Physics of high-field superconductors. C. P. Bean and R. W. Schmitt. bibliog il Science 140:26-35 Ap 5 '63
Quantized magnetic flux in superconductors. R. D. Parks. bibliog il Science 146:1429-35 D 11 '64
Superconducting indium antimonide. S. Geller and others. bibliog Science 140:62 Ap 5 '63
Superconducting metastable compounds. H. L. Luo and others. bibliog il Science 145:581-3 Ag 7 '64
Superconducting semiconductors. Sci Am 210: 56+ Je '64
Superconductivity. P. W. Anderson; B. T. Matthias. bibliog il Science 144:373-81 Ap 24 '64
Superconductivity; report on International conference on the science of superconductivity. H. R. Hart, jr. and R. W. Schmitt. Science 143:57-8+ Ja 3 '64
Superconductor forecast at room temperature. Sci N L 86:200 S 26 '64
SUPERHETERODYNE receivers. See Radio receiving apparatus, Superheterodyne
SUPERHIGHWAYS. See Express highways
SUPERINTENDENTS, School. See School superintendents and principals
SUPERIOR NATIONAL FOREST. See National forests
SUPERIOR students. See College students, Mentally superior; High school students, Mentally superior
SUPERIORITY complex, National. See Nationalism
SUPERMARKET blues; drama. See Fontaine, R.
SUPERMARKETS
Food chain with a Latin flair; Pueblo supermarkets, inc; Puerto Rico. il Bsns W p93-4+ My 16 '64
George pleasures them with groceries; Publix markets, Florida. T. G. Harris. il Look 28: 102+ My 5 '64
Heavenly supermarket. W. Marx. Nation 198: 372-3 Ap 13 '64
Life without supermarkets; Retail clerks union vs Acme chain. U S News 56:82 Je 29 '64
New textbook for supermarkets. il Bsns W p 156+ O 26 '63
Sales and distribution. L. Morse. Duns R 83: 61-3 Ap '64
Sales & distribution; trading stamps. L. Morse. Duns R 82:49-50+ Jl '63
Segregated food at the supermarket. J. Ridgeway. New Repub 151:6-7 D 5 '64
Selling goods through games. L. Morse. Duns R 84:49 Jl '64
Stamp fight is on in Britain. il Bsns W p88-9 Ag 3 '63
Super investigation. New Repub 150:5 My 16 '64
Supermarket shoppers put it on the cuff. il Bsns W p 117 Je 15 '63
Supermarket's big change. il Time 83:97 Je 12 '64
Truth in packaging. P. A. Hart. il Nation 196:542-3 Je 29 '63
Two unusual California supermarkets. il Arch Rec 133:172-3 Je '63
Why she really goes to market. H. H. Martin. il Sat Eve Post 236:40-3 S 28 '63; Same abr. with title When a woman goes to market. Read Digest 84:115-18 Mr '64
See also
Safeway stores, incorporated
Super valu stores, incorporated

Anecdotes, facetiae, satire, etc.

Superman in market. J. A. Snyder. il Atlan 215:110-11 Ja '65

Lighting

Lighting effects in the supermarket. Consumer Rep 29:52 F '64
SUPERNATURAL
See also
Ghosts
SUPERNOVAE. See Galactic systems; Stars, New
SUPERPHOSPHATES. See Phosphates
SUPERREGENERATIVE receivers. See Radio receiving apparatus, Superregenerative
SUPERSONIC aerodynamics. See Aerodynamics, Supersonic
SUPERSONIC air travel. See Air travel
SUPERSONIC airplane engines

Lubrication

See Jet airplane engines—Lubrication
SUPERSONIC airplanes. See Airplanes, Supersonic
SUPERSTITION
Boat is an island; tribulations of soothing the boating gods. N. J. Lays. il Motor B 115:94-7+ Ja '65
H_2\$; money-tossing vogue. S. D. Kohn. il N Y Times Mag p 121-2 S 13 '64
Picking some bones. Christian Cent 80:1255 O 9 '63
Protestant fetishes, anyone? Christian Cent 81:1479 N 25 '64
Superstitions? silly! (knock on wood) P. Tabori. il N Y Times Mag p34-5+ My 26 '63
Take any number. G. Vincent. il N Y Times Mag p44+ O 13 '63
Tunnel men shun women. E. Hall. Sci N L 84:53 Jl 27 '63
Wonderful white weasel. R. Beck. il Outdoor Life 135:48-9+ Ja '65
See also
Charms
Evil eye
Mythology
Voodooism
SUPPERS
Elegance for supper; with recipes. J. Hewitt. il N Y Times Mag p49 Ja 5 '64
Midnight supper on Halloween for sixteen; with recipes. il Seventeen 22:136+ O '63
Party-best recipe: campaign roll-ups. il Seventeen 23:180 S '64
Summer Sunday supper from the garden for four; with recipes. il Vogue 144:134 Ag 15 '64
Supper clubs, simple and such fun! il Good H 157:180 O '63
SUPP-HOSE. See Hosiery
SUPPLEMENTAL unemployment benefits
Detroit tries to level employment swings; system of scheduling to avoid layoffs. Bsns W p43-4 Mr 2 '63
Extended vacations at Alcoa. E. D. Mairs. Mo Labor R 87:404-6 Ap '64
SUPPLEMENTARY employment
Akron moonlighters: a special breed. il Bsns W p68+ D 5 '64
Are moonlighters the villains? B. L. Masse. America 110:631-2 My 9 '64
Managing your manpower; look at moonlighting. T. R. Brooks. Duns R 81:69-70+ Ja '63
More moonlighters; Labor dept. survey. Bsns W p 153 Mr 21 '64
Multiple jobholders in May 1963. F. A. Bogan and H. R. Hamel. bibliog f il Mo Labor R 87:249-57 Mr '64
Multiple jobholders in May 1962. J. Schiffman. il Mo Labor R 86:516-23 My '63
Rise in moonlighting. T. R. Brooks. Duns R 84:66+ Jl '64
SUPPLEMENTARY employment of teachers. See Teachers—Supplementary employment
SUPPLY and demand
Profits, prices, and excess capacity. R. S. Schultz. bibliog f il Harvard Bsns R 41: 68-81 Jl '63
See also
Consumption (economics)

SUPPLY and demand of scientists; Supply and demand of teachers; etc. See Scientists—Supply and demand; Teachers—Supply and demand; etc.
SUPPORT hosiery. See Hosiery
SUPREME court of the United States. See United States—Supreme court
SURE thing; story. See Hunter, E.
SURECK, David
(ed) See Thant. Interview with the Secretary-General
(ed) See Thant. U Thant speaks his mind
SURF fishing. See Salt water fishing
SURF riding
Australia, where surf-riding is flying on wings of foam. R. Cameron. Vogue 143: 119-20+ My '64
Champion of the heavies. il Time 85:35 Ja 8 '65
Fad and fascination of surfing. C. Mitchell. il Holiday 35:122+ My '64
High surfdom. J. Maisel. il Sports Illus 20: 60-5 My 18 '64
New sport, boat surfing. il Motor B 114:82 Jl '64
New wave; first annual U.S. invitational surfing championships. il Newsweek 63:81 Mr 9 '64
Pier roulette, new form of surfboard suicide. il Pop Mech 119:127 F '63
Riders of the surging sea. C. Phinizy. il Sports Illus 18:26-30 F 18 '63
Riding the wild waves; with report by G. Silk. il Life 54:56-69+ My 24 '63
Shooting the tube. il Time 83:57 Ja 10 '64
Surfin' craze. il Sr Schol 83:22-3+ S 20 '63
Surfing in tandem. il Life 57:68-70 Jl 3 '64
Surfing pizza-style; pypo-boarding. il Life 57:47-9 Ag 7 '64
Surf's up! il Time 82:49 Ag 9 '63
They ride the big surf. E. Burdick. il Read Digest 83:224-30 Jl '63
Wave of the future. il Newsweek 64:59 Jl 13 '64
West Coast surfers. I. Bauer. il Look 28: 54-7 Je 30 '64
You vs. the wave. Newsweek 63:71 Ja 13 '64
SURFACE, Bill
Golf. Sports Illus 18:60-2 Je 10 '63
Last days of Rogers Hornsby. Sat Eve Post 236:72+ Je 15 '63
Let's make this an honest election! Read Digest 85:53-7 S '64
Lively market in lame ducks. Sat Eve Post 237:66-7 Je 6 '64
Making money. N Y Times Mag p86+ O 18 '64
Sequel to the Bay of Pigs: four U.S. pilots; they died while serving their country. Life 54:44 Mr 15 '63
Winners often lose. N Y Times Mag p96-8+ Ap 19 '64
SURFACE chemistry
Low-energy electron diffraction; improved experimental methods provide new information on the structure of surfaces of solids. A. U. MacRae. bibliog il Science 139:379-88 F 1 '63
Surface phenomena; report on second annual symposium on fundamental phenomena in the material sciences. L. J. Bonis and H. H. Hausner. il Science 145:955-6+ Ag 28 '64
Surface physics; report of symposium at Washington state university. E. E. Donaldson. Science 141:364-5 Jl 26 '63
Surface physics; report on second annual Surface physics symposium. E. E. Donaldson. Science 145:1471-2+ S 25 '64
Vacuum: sputtering, desorption, and surface physics: report on annual Sherwood vacuum conference. S. O. Dean. Science 144:1251-2 Je 5 '64
SURFACE contamination
Surface contamination; report on first international symposium. S. K. Friedlander. Science 145:1076 S 4 '64
SURFACE phenomena. See Surface chemistry
SURFACE physics
Sea-to-air transport of surface active material. D. C. Blanchard. bibliog il Science 146:396-7 O 16 '64
SURFACE tension
Electric fields across water-nitrobenzene interfaces. M. Blank and S. Feig. bibliog il Science 141:1173-4 S 20 '63
Surface tension is energy source. R. Hawkes. il Miss & Roc 15:24-6 S 7 '64
SURFACE to air missiles. See Guided missiles
SURFACE treatment of pavements. See Pavements—Surface treatment
SURFACE treatment of playgrounds. See Playgrounds—Surface treatment
SURFACES, Fermi. See Fermi surfaces
SURFBOARDS
Set a sail on a surfboard; craft known as Sunfish and Sailfish. H. Whall. il Sports Illus 19:34-6+ D 16 '63
SURFING. See Surf riding
SURGEON general's office. See United States—Surgeon general's office
SURGEONS
Making of a surgeon. J. Star. il Look 28: 58-62+ Mr 24 '64
See also
Women as surgeons
SURGERY
Advanced surgery at NIH. il Sci N L 84:194 S 28 '63
Age of alloplasty; foreign materials used to replace the body's natural parts. il Time 85:54-5 Ja 1 '65
Best hope of all; with colored photographs of seven major operations. il Time 81:44-60 My 3 '63
Bleeding gullet; surgical report on Douglas MacArthur. il Time 83:79 Ap 3 '64
Bowel bypass. il Time 82:50 N 8 '63
Case of the Kelly clamp; surgical blunder at Toronto East general hospital. Newsweek 64:54-5 Jl 20 '64
Cold knife; surgery by freezing: cryosurgery. Newsweek 64:58 S 7 '64
Forerunner in vascular surgery; J. Hunter. Todays Health 42:65 Ap '64
Medicine's frontier: rebuilding the human body. G. Astor. il Look 28:22-9 Je 30 '64
Most radical operation; pelvic exenterations. il Time 84:49 Jl 31 '64
New miracles of baby surgery. L. David. Good H 156:76-7+ Ap '63
New surgical advances. Sci N L 86:242 O 17 '64
Opening the door to safer surgery. il Todays Health 41:71 Je '63
People who love operations. A. J. Snider. Sci Digest 54:56 O '63
Repair of a pitching arm. il Time 84:95 N 20 '64
Verdict on a surgeon; case of the Kelly clamp. Newsweek 64:72 Jl 27 '64
You can guard against needless surgery. Good H 156:145-7 F '63
See also
Cesarean section
Malpractice
Orthopedia
Sutures
Transplantation of organs, tissues, etc.
also subhead Surgery under names of organs and regions of the body, e.g. Brain—Surgery
History
Barber of the battlefield; Ambroise Paré. il Todays Health 41:88 N '63
Surgery 1860. il Sci Digest 54:28-9 S '63
SURGERY, Aseptic and antiseptic
Germ-free isolators. P. C. Trexler. il Sci Am 211:78-80+ Jl '64
SURGERY, Cosmetic. See Surgery, Plastic
SURGERY, Cost of. See Medical service, Cost of
SURGERY, Facial
New plastic promises better facial repairs; room temperature vulcanizing silastic. Sci N L 85:43 Ja 18 '64
SURGERY, Plastic
Cancer from plastics? Sci N L 87:55 Ja 23 '65
Complete chart of plastic surgery. McCalls 91:56+ Ag '64
Facts and fancies about plastic surgery. H. B. Thale. il Todays Health 41:54-5+ Ap '63
Plastic and reconstructive surgery for children. L. W. Sauer. PTA Mag 58:33-4 Ap '64
Report on plastic surgery. il Sci Digest 56:18-19 D '64
Uplift operations; the female breast. Time 83:48 Mr 27 '64
See also
Surgery, Facial
SURGERY, Primitive
See also
Trephining
SURGICAL dressing
Gold prevents adhesions; use of electrostatistically charged leaves in surgery or medicine. F. Marley. il Sci N L 86:211 O 3 '64
Out of the box: a layer of skin; polyvinyl plastic, Ivalon for burn victims. il Time 82:66 Jl 5 '63
SURGICAL instruments
Air drill used in surgery. il Sci N L 87:55 Ja 23 '65
Institute for experimental surgical instruments in Moscow. T. Takaro. bibliog il Science 142:195-9 O 11 '63

SURGICAL operations. See Surgery
SURGICAL shock. See Shock
SURINAM
See also
Fishing—Surinam
Hunting—Surinam

Description and travel

Going places, finding things in new fields for adventurous wayfarers. J. Sakol. il House & Gard 125:22+ Ja '64

SURNAMES. See Names, Personal
SURO, Dario
Baroque in Santo Domingo. Américas 16:15-21 Je '64
Stuart Davis, 1894-1964. Américas 17:30-1 Ja '65

SURPLUS products
Base in Maine called Blotner. W. S. Ellis. Harper 229:26+ S '64
GI guns that aren't. il Bsns W p 139-40 F 23 '63
How to buy a good used gun; war surplus. E. Matunas. il Pop Mech 120:130-4 N '63
How to identify surplus gear. K. Greenberg. il Pop Electr 20:66-8 Ja '64
Odd saga of the big Bahamas spenders. T. Armbrister. il Sat Eve Post 237:30+ Ag 8 '64
Surpluses and surpluses. J. L. Vizzard. Commonweal 79:361-2 D 20 '63
Technical manuals for surplus equipment. E. E. Kelley. Electr World 69:79 Je '63
War surplus. J. Ciardi. Sat R 46:20+ N 9 '63; Discussion. 46:30 D 7 '63; 47:30 Ja 4; 8 Ja 18 '64

SURPLUS products, Agricultural
Our dairy surplus, we import a chunk of it; with editorial comment. M. Norton. Farm J 87:34, 126 My '63
Problem of surplus; address, October 14, 1963. D. Paarlberg. Vital Speeches 30:152-5 D 15 '63
Seek restructured overseas relief; Public law 480. Christian Cent 81:453 Ap 8 '64
Surpluses and surpluses. J. L. Vizzard. Commonweal 79:361-2 D 20 '63
U.S. grain: surplus now, shortage soon? U S News 55:9 D 2 '63
Vanishing surplus: what it means to you. F. Bailey, jr. Suc Farm 62:80+ Mr '64

SURREALISM (art)
Dali reapproached. New Yorker 39:23 F 15 '64
Poetic shock; P. Delvaux's paintings. il Time 81:60-1 Je 28 '63

SURREY, Stanley Sterling
Tax program in perspective; address, February 28, 1963. Vital Speeches 29:354-60 Ap 1 '63

about

Stanley Surrey: architect of tax reforms. por U S News 54:21 Mr 18 '63
Who framed the tax plan. C. B. Seib. il por Nations Bsns 51:32-3+ Ap '63

SURRIDGE, Ronald
British public libraries in search of standards. por Library J 88:1950-5 My 15 '63

SURTEES, John
From a wild race in Mexico: a surprise champion. S. Moss. il por Sports Illus 21:60-2 N 2 '64
With a nudge for luck. il por Time 84:42 N 6 '64

SURVEY research center. See Michigan. University, Ann Arbor

SURVEYING
Great surveys of the American West, by R. A. Bartlett. Review
Natur Hist 72:4+ Mr '63. N. D. Newell
How to measure land, in armchair or field. F. Bailey, jr. il Suc Farm 62:50 Ja '64

SURVEYING, Aerial
Infrared surveys of Hawaiian volcanoes. W. A. Fischer and others. bibliog il Science 146:733-42 N 6 '64
Modified A-26 used for African surveys. C. Brownlow. il Aviation W 82:85-7 Ja 18 '65
Support concept cuts surveying costs; Quebec Labrador airways. D. A. Brown. il Aviation W 81:103-5 N 9 '64
World's greatest prospector. N. Carlisle. il Pop Sci 184:60-3+ My '64
See also
Mapping, Aerial

SURVEYING instruments
See also
Theodolites

SURVEYOR (space probe) See Lunar probes
SURVEYS. See Library surveys; Television surveys and similar headings
SURVEYS, Educational. See Educational surveys

SURVIVAL (after airplane accidents, shipwrecks, etc)
Couple who wouldn't die. T. Whiteside. il Sat Eve Post 236:56-65 Je 22 '63
Don't panic. C. E. Jensen. il Field & S 68:30-2+ O '63
Duel with nature; U.S. air force survival and special training school. P. Czura. il Field & S 69:52-3+ Jl '64
Fishermen reel in a U.S. flier; with report by H. Lavallee. il Life 55:49-52 S 13 '63
Fit survive; case of R. Flores and H. Klaben. il Newsweek 61:27 Ap 8 '63
Girl behind a frozen scream; H. Klaben's forty-nine day ordeal in the Yukon. D. J. Hamblin and W. Jarvis. il Life 54:68B-73+ Ap 12 '63
Hey, I'm alive! excerpt. H. Klaben and B. Day. il Good H 158:52-5+ Ja '64
How long people can last without food. il U S News 54:20 Ap 8 '63
How to survive at sea. K. Brown. il Pop Mech 120:112-17+ N '3
If your car goes in the water. J. M. Liston. il Pop Sci 182:45-8+ Je '63
Morning Star mystery. A. F. Loomis. il Yachting 114:25+ Ag '63
Rescue-aid satellites? SAFE (satellites for emergencies) Sci N L 86:219 O 3 '64
Saga of My Gal Sal. il Life 57:106B-116 N 20 '64
They watched for ravens gathering. B. East. il Outdoor Life 133:40-3+ Mr '64
Think, and live. R. Starnes. Field & S 68:12+ O '63
Thirteen days in a blizzard. G. J. Tucker. il Outdoor Life 133:20-3+ Ja '64
Trapped in the desert. G. Beeman. il Read Digest 85:100-5 Ag '64
Two faces recall the Yukon. il Life 54:36 Ap 5 '63

SURVIVAL diet. See Diet in exploration, shipwreck, etc.
SURVIVAL hikes. See Walking
SURVIVAL of man. See Man—Survival
SURVIVAL of nations
Take a lesson from the dinosaur. B. Chisholm. il Parents Mag 39:55+ Ap '64

SURVIVOR; story. See Jacobson, D.
SUSA, Conrad S.
Music for Shakespeare; twentieth century approach. Mus Am 84:46-7 S '64

SUSANNAH; opera. See Floyd, C.
SUSLOV, Mikhail
As Russia-China talks got under way. por U S News 55:20 Jl 15 '63
Confrontation; Chinese party delegation in Moscow. il por Time 82:24 Jl 12 '63
Two old hands at surviving purges. por U S News 57:14 N 2 '64

SUSPENDED animation. See Anabiosis
SUSPENSION bridges. See Bridges, Suspension
SUSPENSION of atomic bomb testing. See Atomic bombs—Testing, Suspension of
SUSQUEHANNA RIVER
River drowned under bay. E. Hall. Sci N L 84:86 Ag 10 '63

SUSSEX university. See Colleges and universities—England
SUSSKIND, David
Battle cries. Newsweek 61:69 My 13 '63
Closed end. Time 81:83 My 10 '63
Do-gooder. Newsweek 64:62 N 30 '64
Little David abroad. por Newsweek 62:56 S 9 '63

SUSSMAN, Aaron
Sussman talks on newspaper strike & book advertising. Pub W 183:134-5 F 18 '63

SUSSMAN, Cornelia, and Sussman, Irving
Modern artists encounter Christ. America 111:548-51 N 7 '64

SUSSMAN, Irving. See Sussman, C. jt. auth.
SUSSMAN, Leonard R.
Do minorities tyrannize American life? address, November 15, 1963. bibliog Vital Speeches 30:125-8 D 1 '63
Judaism for all seasons. Christian Cent 80:427-9 Ap 3 '63

SUSSMAN, M.
Growth of the cellular slime mold polysphondylium pallidum in a simple nutrient medium. bibliog Science 139:338 Ja 25 '63

SUTCLIFFE, Alys
Small plants for special uses. Horticulture 42:30-5 Mr '64

SUTCLIFFE, James H.
Germany East and West. Opera N 29:23-4 S 26 '64

SUTCLIFFE, Walter J.
Looking forward. por Motor B 113:46 F '64

SUTER, Rufus
Galileo in Padua; reprint. Sky & Tel 27:99-100 F '64

SUTHERLAND, Charles F. Jr
Ford's forest. Am For 69:18-19+ S '63
SUTHERLAND, Don
Hunting a new movie target? B. Knight. il por U S Camera 27:72-3 Jl '64
SUTHERLAND, Elizabeth
Cat and mouse game. Nation 199:105-8 S 14 '64
Mandate from history. Nation 198:30-3 Ja 6 '64
Theatre of the meaningful. Nation 199:254-6 O 19 '64
SUTHERLAND, Graham
Harsh ecology. il por Time 83:72-3+ My 22 '64
Painter. New Yorker 40:23-4 My 30 '64
SUTHERLAND, Joan
Bel canto revival. Discus. Harper 228:124-5 My '64
Boadicea in Walthamstow: with editorial comment. R. Kotlowitz. il pors Hi Fi 15:41. 52-6 F '65
Joan Sutherland; Command performance. P. L. Miller. Am Rec G 29:849 Jl '63
Joan Sutherland in La sonnambula. P. L. Miller. il por Am Rec G 29:596-8 Ap '63
Music to my ears; concert version of Handel's Alcina. I. Kolodin. Sat R 48:38 Ja 23 '65
Music to my ears; Sutherland on the heights in Sonnambula. I. Kolodin. Sat R 46:29 Mr 9 '63
Music to my ears; Sutherland's Violetta. I. Kolodin. Sat R 46:44+ D 28 '63
Musical events. New Yorker 40:125-6 F 29 '64
Musical events; performance of Bellini's I Puritani. W. Sargeant. New Yorker 39:98 Ap 27 '63
Musical events; performance of Bellini's La sonnambula. W. Sargeant. New Yorker 39: 228 D 14 '63
Musical events; performance of Verdi's La Traviata. W. Sargeant. New Yorker 39:67 D 28 '63
Notes from abroad. C. Reid. Hi Fi 13:14+ O '63
Pitch of perfection. il por Newsweek 61:78 Mr 4 '63
Prima donna. E. Coleman. por Opera N 29: 12-13 O 17 '64
Question of majesty. W. Cecil. por Sat R 47: 56-7+ Ap 25 '64
Sutherland in I Puritani. P. L. Miller. il por Am Rec G 30:656-7+ Ap '64
La Traviata. P. L. Miller. Am Rec G 30:95 O '63
SUTHERLAND, Kathleen
Painter. New Yorker 40:23-4 My 30 '64
SUTHERLAND, Millie
Hunting a new movie target? B. Knight. il por U S Camera 27:72-3 Jl '64
SUTHERLAND, N. S.
Cat's ability to discriminate oblique rectangles. bibliog Science 139:209-10 Ja 18 '63
SUTHERLAND, R. H.
ABC's of the RDF. Motor B 111:53+ My '63
SUTHERLAND, Sandy
Figure sketching in watercolor. il Am Artist 27:50-3+ O '63
SUTHERLAND, W. C.
Institute on community organization. Recreation 57:242 My '64
SUTIN, Helen Gorn
Crime and punishment; poem. McCalls 91: 154 F '64
Phony problem and solution; poem. McCalls 91:209 My '64
SUTPHEN, Jack
Synthetic sails are a skipper's best friend. Yachting 113:38-9+ My '63
—and Kostanecki, Andrew
Approach to the finish. Yachting 115:70-1+ Ap '64
Approach to the leeward mark. Yachting 115: 39-41+ Mr '64
Approach to the weather mark. Yachting 115: 50-2+ F '64
SUTTERFIELD, B. Glenn
Purple martin, harbinger of spring. Audubon Mag 65:178-9 My '63
SUTTON, Doris C. and Dwyer, K. R.
Cerium-144 and cesium-137 measurements in the 1963 United States wheat crop and milling products. bibliog Science 145:486-7 Jl 31 '64
SUTTON, Dwight, and Miller, J. M.
Implanted electrodes; cable coupler for elimination of movement artifact. Science 140: 988-9 My 31 '63
SUTTON, Sir Graham
Micrometeorology; with biographical sketch. Sci Am 211:18, 62-70+ bibliog(p 142) O '64
SUTTON, Horace
Bahamas. por McCalls 90:34+ My '63
Booked for travel. See issues of Saturday review
Confessions of a Hawaii fancier. Sat R 47: 50-2+ O 10 '64
Far-out side of Paradise. Sat R 46:52+ Mr 16 '63
It's a woman's world's fair. McCalls 91:40+ Ap '64
1964: a year-long jamboree for wanderers. Sat R 47:33-5+ Ja 4 '64
Palm Springs: the new Karlsbad. Sat R 48: 45+ Ja 2 '65
Return to elegance. Sat R 47:36+ O 24 '64
Roughing it with the cognoscenti. Sat R 47: 36+ Mr 14 '64
See Canada and live. McCalls 90:166-7+ Mr '63
Stop & go with Horace Sutton. See issues of McCall's
SUTTON, Lee
Actors can be teachers. Theatre Arts 47:64-5 Ag '63
SUTTON, Myron
Where to go in '64. pors Am For 70:16-19+ Ja '64
SUTTON, Robert B.
Historical report from Madras. Sch & Soc 92:231-2 Sum '64
SUTTON, Walter
Importing revolution. Nation 198:589-91 Je 8 '64
SUTURES
Sewn silk sutures infect. Sci N L 86:242 O 17 '64
SUVA, Fiji
British in Capricorn. H. Sutton. il Sat R 47: 34 My 16 '64
SUYDAM, Henry
Eighteen year hunt to find his father's killer. Life 55:58-60+ Ag 2 '63
Hoffa: how they nailed him. Life 56:20-5 Mr 13 '64
SUYIN, Han
Onward and upward with the arts. New Yorker 39:38-40+ D 28 '63
SUZUKI, Hiromi, and Kilgore, W. W.
Mitomycin C: effect on ribosomes of escherichia coli. bibliog Science 146:1585-7 D 18 '64
SUZUKI, Shinichi
Fiddling legions. il Newsweek 63:73 Mr 23 '64
How to lead your child to music. M. Roche. il House & Gard 126:182-3+ S '64
SVAGLIC, Martin J.
Light on Newman. Commonweal 78:204-6 My 10 '63
SVALBARD
Dinosaurs of the Arctic. E. H. Colbert. il Natur Hist 73:20-3 Ap '64
Spitsbergen: oasis in the Arctic. G. Gaskill. il Read Digest 84:224-6+ F '64
SVANHOLM, Set
Obituary
Opera N por 29:28-9 D 5 '64. Q. Eaton
SVEC, Harry J. and Flesch, G. D.
Thermochemical properties of xenon difluoride and xenon tetrafluoride from mass spectra. bibliog Science 142:954-5 N 15 '63
SVEHAG, Sven-Erik
Antibody formation in vitro by separated spleen cells: inhibition by actinomycin or chloramphenicol. bibliog Science 146:659-61 O 30 '64
SVENSKA salpeterverken, ab. See Fertilizer factories
SVERBEYEFF, Elizabeth
Home (cont) N Y Times Mag p94-5 D 8 '63; 82-4 My 24; 104-5 S 20; 84-5 D 13 '64
SVET-MOLDAVSKAIA, I. A. See Svet-Moldavskiĭ, G. J. jt. auth.
SVET-MOLDAVSKIĬ, George J. and Svet-Moldavskaîa, I. A.
Sarcomas in cotton rats inoculated with Rous virus. bibliog Science 143:54-5 Ja 3 '64
SVEVO, Italo
Svevo: news from the past. R. Gilman. New Repub 149:19-23 N 2 '63
SVININ, Paul
New nation through Russian eyes; reproduction of water colors. Am Heritage 15:52-63 F '64
Voyage pittoresque aux Etats-unis de l'Amérique par Paul Svignine; an appreciation. M. B. Davidson. por Am Heritage 15: 49-51+ F '64
SWADOS, Harvey
Freedom now. Commentary 36:406-8 N '63
My Coney Island uncle; story. Sat Eve Post 237:60-2 O 17 '64
New reasons for an old cause. Sat R 47:35+ F 1 '64
Ragged Dick in the last lap. Nation 199:13-14 Jl 13 '64
Revolution on the march. Nation 197:104-7 S 7 '63
Story for Teddy; story. Sat Eve Post 236: 58-60 N 23 '63

about

Real world. I. Howe. Commentary 37:80+ Ap '64

SWADOS, Harvey—about—*Continued*
Rebel with a craft. C. Shapiro. por Sat R 46:34 O 26 '63

SWAIN, Charles V.
Interchangeable parts in early American pewter. Antiques 83:212-13 F '63

SWAINSON, John Burley
Power ploy. Newsweek 61:25 F 18 '63

SWALLOWED objects. See Accidents; Foreign bodies (surgery)

SWALLOWS
Nature note. Sci N L 85:156 Mr 7 '64

SWALLOWTAILS. See Butterflies

SWAMINATHAN, M. S. and others
Mutations: incidence in drosophila melanogaster reared on irradiated medium. bibliog Science 141:637-8 Ag 16 '63

SWAMP antelopes. See Antelopes

SWAMP mosquitoes. See Mosquitoes

SWAMPERNIKS. See Trailers

SWAN, Mrs James
Bulfinch's houses for Mrs Swan. J. Kirker. il por Antiques 86:442-4 O '64

SWAN, Jon
City of speech. New Yorker 39:125-6+ Ap 6 '63
Common prayer; poem. New Yorker 40:56 N 7 '64
March weather; poem. New Yorker 39:42 Mr 9 '63
Portable gallery of pastoral animals; poem. New Yorker 39:44 My 4 '63
Report; poem. New Yorker 40:48 Ap 4 '64

SWAN, Joyce Ferris
My homemade remedy for lump-in-the-throat. Farm J 87:61 S '63
Slack off your sheet! Yachting 117:108-9+ Ja '65

SWAN, Lawrence W.
Aeolian zone. bibliog Science 140:77-8 Ap 5 '63
Ecology of the heights. Natur Hist 72:22-9 Ap '63

SWAN, Lester A.
Pest destroyers: excerpt from Beneficial insects. bibliog Audubon Mag 67:46-51 Ja '65
Pest-eating insects; excerpt from Beneficial insects. bibliog f Audubon Mag 66:314-19 S '64

SWAN, Thor
So far my film has cost me $20,000 and I'm not finished! por Pop Phot 55:190-2+ D '64

SWAN ISLANDS
Rare animals of the Swan Islands. Hobbies 68:129 F '64

SWAN LAKE federal waterfowl refuge. See Bird sanctuaries

SWANBERG, William A.
Was the Secretary of war a traitor? Am Heritage 14:34-7+ F '63

SWANK, Patricia
Plot that flopped. Look 29:28-9 Ja 26 '65

SWANK, Raynard C.
Six items for export; address, October 1962. por Library J 88:711-17 F 15 '63

SWANKER, Esther M.
On the care and feeding of volunteers. Library J 88:1728-9 Ap 15 '63

SWANS
Long fight to save the trumpeter swan; excerpt from Trumpeter swan. W. E. Banko. il Audubon Mag 65:373 N '63
On shooting swans and cranes. C. W. Buchheister. il Audubon Mag 65:356-7 N '63
Royalty of the bird kingdom. D. Peattie and L. Peattie. Read Digest 82:252C-252D+ Ap '63
Swan comeback. B. East. il Outdoor Life 133:99 F '64
Wild swans risk crash landings for corn; whistling swans, Shiawassee National wildlife refuge. P. Innis. il Audubon Mag 66:304-5 S '64

SWANSON, Don R.
D.R.S. to the G.L.S. J. Shera. Wilson Lib Bul 37:687+ Ap '63

SWANSON, Donald F.
Andrew Mellon on tax cuts. New Repub 148:22 Mr 23 '63

SWANSON, J. Chester
Whither vocational education? NEA J 52:58-60 O '63

SWANSON, Steve
Temptation; poem. Christian Cent 81:236 F 19 '64

SWARD, Robert
Desperater man than most. Poetry 104:380-1 S '64
My father, with wings; Terminal theater; Nazarucks; Ghosts; poems. Poetry 103:234-5 Ja '64
Signatures. Poetry 102:335-40 Ag '63

SWARTHMORE college, Swarthmore, Pa.
Rosemary's discovery; colleges summer-study programs for high school students. il Newsweek 64:74 Ag 24 '64
Swarthmore at 100. il Newsweek 63:58 My 4 '64
Swarthmore's 100th. il Time 83:81-2 Mr 6 '64

SWARTWOUT, David M.
Lawn party lamps. Pop Mech 119:138-42 Je '63
Make your yard a Christmas card. Pop Mech 120:138-43 D '63
Prefinished party cart. Pop Mech 121:146-9 F '64
Project-a-plan instant signs. Pop Mech 120:144-6 O '63

SWAZILAND
Atlantic report. Atlan 213:34+ Ap '64
High commission territories of southern Africa. B. S. Young. bibliog il Focus 14:1-6 D '63
Protectorates under the gun. S. Uys. New Repub 149:9-10 S 28 '63
South Africa: enclaves of trouble. J. Halpern. il Nation 197:49-52 Jl 27 '63
See also
United Nations—Swaziland

SWEARER, Howard R.
After Khrushchev: what next? bibliog f Cur Hist 47:257-65 N '64

SWEARING
Unhappy talk. H. B. Jacobs. Harper 226:95-7 Mr '63

SWEARINGEN, John E.
Executive decision; address, April 24, 1964. Vital Speeches 30:506-8 Je 1 '64

SWEARINGIN, Marvin
How good is single-cross corn? interview. Suc Farm 62:44-5 Ja '64

SWEAT socks. See Clothing and dress—Sports clothes

SWEATER from a distant place; story. See Boles, C.

SWEATERS
How to buy a sweater. il Seventeen 22:67 Ag '63
Sweaters. H. Obolensky. il Redbook 123:80-1 Jl '64

SWEATING. See Perspiration

SWEDEN
See also
Airplanes, Military—Sweden
Architecture—Sweden
Atomic power—Sweden
Banks and banking—Sweden
Christmas—Sweden
Churches—Sweden
Colleges and universities—Sweden
Copper mines and mining—Sweden
Dalecarlia
Forests and forestry—Sweden
Gardens—Sweden
Housing—Sweden
Insurance, Health—Sweden
Lapland
Libraries—Sweden
Liquor traffic—Sweden
National parks and reserves—Sweden
Opera—Sweden
Taxation—Sweden
Warships—Sweden
Women—Sweden

Antiquities

Bronze age seen in granite. H. Arbman. il Natur Hist 73:36-43 N '64

Description and travel

Photography afloat in Sweden; Gota Canal voyage. L. Barry. il Pop Phot 55:32+ Jl '64
Sweden, quiet workshop for the world. A. H. Brown. il Nat Geog Mag 123:451-91 Ap '63
Sweden: that middle way. F. Russell. il Nat R 16:877-8 O 6 '64

Economic conditions

Thirty years without recession: how Sweden does it. il U S News 57:100-2 N 23 '64

Economic policy

How the Swedes do it. P. Hirsch. New Repub 149:9 Jl 20 '63

Industries

Arms and the working men: Bofors. il Newsweek 65:66 Ja 11 '65
Biggest employer; the Wallenbergs. il Time 82:98 N 29 '63
Growing Grangesberg: exporter of iron ore. il Bsns W p 140+ Mr 21 '64
More buck for less bang; Bofors entry into pharmaceuticals. il Bsns W p 111+ O 26 '63
Nobel's old company: still dynamite. il Bsns W p60+ D 12 '64
Seemly success. il Time 81:98 Je 7 '63

SWEDEN—Industries—*Continued*
Steel that shaves the world; Sweden's Sandvik steel supplies stainless to Gillette. il Bsns W p63-4+ O 5 '63
Steelmakers' edge. il Time 82:93 S 20 '63
Sweden, quiet workshop for the world. A. H. Brown. il Nat Geog Mag 123:451-91 Ap '63
See also
Shipbuilding

Labor policy

Recommendation on Swedish wage policy. Mo Labor R 86:171-2 F '63

Moral conditions

Goodbye to summer. D. Fennell. Nat R 14:273-8 Ap 9 '63; Discussion. 14:421+ My 21 '63

Religious institutions and affairs

Disestablishment for the Church of Sweden? Christian Cent 81:901-2 Jl 15 '64
Goodbye to summer. D. Fennell. Nat R 14:273-8 Ap 9 '63; Discussion. 14:421+ My 21 '63
Lady in the pulpit; Barbro Stahl of Stockholm. il Time 81:83 Mr 22 '63
See also
Lutheran church in Sweden

Social conditions

Sweden: that middle way. F. Russell. il Nat R 16:877-8 O 6 '64
Taking sex seriously. Time 83:35 Mr 6 '64
See also
Social and economic security—Sweden

SWEDEN and the United States
Vice President Johnson visits northern Europe; address, September 4, 1963. L. B. Johnson. Dept State Bul 49:583-5 O 14 '63

SWEDENBORG, Emanuel
New Jerusalem. il Time 83:53 Je 26 '64

SWEDENBORGIANISM. See New Jerusalem church

SWEDISH cookery. See Cookery, Swedish

SWEDISH library association
Biblioteksţjänst (Library service inc) G. Ostling. il Library J 88:4323-5 N 15 '63
Swedish library cooperation. G. Ottervik. Library J 88:4316-18 N 15 '63

SWEDISH poetry

Translations into English

From Birgitta suite; tr. by T. Vance and V. Vance. S. Dagerman. Poetry 103:231-3 Ja '64

SWEDISH science fair. See Science fairs

SWEDISH spies. See Spies

SWEENEY, Daryl
Dopamine: its occurrence in molluscan ganglia. bibliog Science 139:1051 Mr 15 '63

SWEENEY, Francis
In memoriam: T. S. Eliot. America 112:120-1 Ja 23 '65

SWEENEY, James Johnson
Gaudí. Vogue 141:78-81+ Je '63
Living frame for sculpture. House & Gard 126:110-15+ Ag '64
San Lorenzo head; reprint. Am Artist 28:67-73 Mr '64

about

Sweeney's way. il Time 81:74 Je 14 '63

SWEENEY, John A. H.
Living with antiques. Antiques 85:542-7 My '64

SWEENEY, Richard J.
Warehousing and shipping: costs and solutions. por(p65) Pub W 184:68+ N 4 '63

SWEENEY, Richard M.
From a troop carrier; poem. Sat R 46:85 Je 15 '63

SWEEP generators. See Signal generators

SWEEPERS, Carpet. See Carpet sweepers

SWEEPERS, Lawn. See Lawn sweepers

SWEEPERS, Street. See Street cleaning apparatus

SWEEPSTAKES. See Lotteries

SWEET, Herman R.
Start an orchid collection. Horticulture 42:36-7+ N '64

SWEET, Marion
Below decks. Yachting 115:48+ Ap '64

SWEET, Ossian H.
You can't live there. A. Whitaker. Negro Hist Bul 26:223-4 Ap '63

SWEET, Walter C. See Weiss, M. P. jt. auth.

SWEET alyssum
Fragrance that grows and grows and grows. il Flower Grower 50:44-5 Ap '63

SWEET chariot. See Night clubs

SWEET forever; story. See Rugel, M.

SWEET peas
How to grow sweet peas. M. C. Ohlander. il Flower Grower 51:34-5 F '64
How to succeed with sweet peas. D. E. Stebbins. il Horticulture 42:14-15 F '64
Now's the time to plant sweet peas. Sunset 133:152 Ag '64

SWEET potatoes
Ceratocystis infection in sweet potato: its effect on proteins, isozymes, and acquired immunity. D. J. Weber and M. A. Stahmann. bibliog il Science 146:929-31 N 13 '64
Sweet potatoes from scratch. L. Eisman. il Horticulture 41:383 Jl '63
Sweets must have water, plant food. L. Donelson. Farm J 87:58D-58E Ap '63
Yams, cortisone source, now grown in U.S. Sci N L 83:201 Mr 30 '63
See also
Cookery—Vegetables

SWEET rocket. See Dames violets

SWEET tea viburnum. See Viburnums

SWEET williams
Charmer: wee willie. E. Markley. Flower Grower 50:27 Mr '63

SWEETENING agents. See Sugar substitutes

SWEETLY sings the donkey; story. See Delaney, S.

SWEETS. See Candy; Confectionery

SWEEZY, Paul M.
Viewing U.S. economy with a Marxist glass. por Bsns W p67-8+ Ap 13 '63

SWEGLE, Wayne
How to go boating with hardly any water Pop Sci 185:94-6 Jl '64
Our first year in boating. Pop Sci 184:134-6+ F '64
Right winter lay-up for a spry boat next spring. Pop Sci 185:116-20 O '64

SWEITZER, Jack P.
Asphalt promenade. Am City 78:95-6 N '63

SWENSON, G. R.
Rauschenberg paints a picture. Art N 62:44-7+ Ap '63
(ed) What is pop art? Art N 62:24-7+ N '63; 40-3+ F '64

SWENSON, George W. and others
Hydrated electron: production and role in photobiology. bibliog Science 141:1042-3 S 13 '63

SWENSON, May
All that time; poem. Nation 198:102 Ja 27 '64
Japanese breakfast; Italian sampler; poems. Poetry 101:329-30 F '63
Kite; poem. New Yorker 39:36 My 18 '63
Notes made in the Piazza San Marco; poem. New Yorker 38:32 F 2 '63
Poet as anti-specialist; adaptation of address. Sat R 48:16-18+ Ja 30 '65
Poetry chronicle. Poetry 102:118-25 My '63
Poetry of three women. Nation 196:164-6 F 23 '63
Secret in the cat; poem. Harper 228:59 My '64
Southbound on the freeway; poem. New Yorker 38:32 F 16 '63
Underestimations. X. J. Kennedy. Poetry 103:330-1 F '64
While seated in a plane; poem. Nation 198:19 Ja 4 '64
Yellow circle; poem. New Yorker 40:177 My 16 '64

SWENSON, P. A. and Setlow, R. B.
β-Galactosidase: inactivation of its messenger RNA by ultraviolet irradiation. bibliog Science 146:791-4 N 6 '64
—See Lieberman, E. M. jt. auth.

SWETS, John A.
Information retrieval systems. bibliog Science 141:245-50 Jl 19 '63

SWETT, John E. and others
Effects of cutaneous and muscle sensory nerve volleys in awake cats: a study in perception. bibliog Science 145:1071-3 S 4 '64

SWIDLER, Joseph C.
Extra-high-voltage at the FPC. il por Bsns W p72-4+ S 21 '63

SWIDLER, Leonard
Catholic colleges: a modest proposal. Commonweal 81:559-62 Ja 29 '65
Reappraising the reformation. Commonweal 81:156-8 O 30 '64

SWIFT, Ernest
Tale of two rivers. Am For 70:32-5+ Je '64
Transitions in forestry; address, March 26, 1963. por Am For 69:22-3+ Je '63
Why recreation depends on taxation: reprint. Am For 71:32-3 Ja '65

SWIFT, Fred
Amateur scientist. Sci Am 209:146-7+ Jl '63

SWIFT, Hewson. See Hruban, Z. jt. auth.

SWIFT, Hildegarde Hoyt
Power of a child's book. Sat R 46:43 My 11 '63

SWIFT, Joan
Our fortunes told; poem. Atlan 212:45 Jl '63
SWIFT, Jonathan
Jonathan Swift by N. Dennis. Review
Time il 85:90+ Ja 15 '65
SWIFT and company
Wage chronology: Swift & co, 1961-63. J. Griest. il Mo Labor R 86:1048-57 S '63
SWIFTIES. See Word games
SWIM, Herb
Rose of the future. por Pop Gard 15:19+ Jl '64
SWIMMER; story. See Cheever, J.
SWIMMING
Amphibious man. A. Whitman. il N Y Times Mag p96-7+ My 17 '64
Chet stream; Chet Jastremski of Indiana university. il Newsweek 61:51 Ap 1 '63
Dawn keeps churning along. W. Tower. il Sports Illus 20:26-8+ F 17 '64
Doctor who makes agony and fun pay off; Dr J. Counsilman of Indiana university. R. Lardner. il Sports Illus 20:48+ Mr 23 '64
Dominant swimmer for a dominant country; American swimming team at Olympics. G. S. Brown. il Sports Illus 21:30-3 O 26 '64
Flag flies high in Tokyo. il Life 57:74B-81 O 30 '64
Formula: hurt, pain, agony; best in the Big ten. il Time 82:42 Ag 23 '63
Four of a kind; National amateur athletic union championships. il Newsweek 64:55 Ag 17 '64
Girl named Sinn. G. Rogin. il Sports Illus 21:58-64 Ag 24 '64
How they chose the best team of all time; Olympic trials. H. Weiskopf. il Sports Illus 21:58-9 S 14 '64
Long voyage home; Amarillo's YMCA 50-mile swim. Sports Illus 19:8+ S 16 '63
Look out, Tokyo, California's coming. il Time 84:45 Ag 14 '64
Marty's memories of a long cold race. M. Sinn. Life 56:66+ Mr 6 '64
Naiad in vaseline; first person to swim the Messina Strait both ways. il Time 81:85 My 3 '63
Olympian at the fair. S. Gordon. il Look 28: 98-100+ F 11 '64
Powerful surge for Olympic gold; with report by D. de Varona. il Life 57:102-9 O 9 '64
Precocious champions. A. Seager. il Holiday 35:110+ Je '64
Scotch and a little water; Olympic swimming hope, B. McGregor. J. Lovesey. il Sports Illus 21:34-7 Jl 20 '64
Somebody's gonna break a record; in Tokyo. il Time 84:61-2 O 23 '64
Swimming (cont) il Sports Illus 18:43-4+ Mr 25; 67 Ap 1 '63
Water babies; five world records by American team in Tokyo. il Time 82:43 Ag 30 '63
Water etiquette. Am Home 67:46 Jl '64
Who let them in? coed swimming squad. il Life 54:89-90 Mr 22 '63
Who's afraid of an old troll? C. Phinizy. Sports Illus 21:16-17 Ag 10 '64
See also
Diving

Safety devices and measures

Can you swim well enough to survive? C. F. Grover. il Motor B 112:34-5+ Jl '63
Drownproofing. F. Lanoue. Recreation 57: 132-3 Mr '64
Even good swimmers drown. il Good H 158: 164 Je '64
Should you swim right after eating? il Good H 157:131 Jl '63
Swimming pool safety for your family. Good H 157:131 Jl '63

Study and teaching

But can he swim? M. Rumsey. il Motor B 114:35-7 Jl '64
Don't spoil the kids, throw them in. il Life 54:89-90 My 10 '63
Gray-flannel émigré from the East builds an empire out West; swimming coach LAAC and USC. C. Phinizy. il Sports Illus 18:43-4+ Mr 25 '63
Learn to swim in twenty min. il Ebony 18: 93-4+ Ap '63
Teaching a toddler to swim. T. D. Topping. il Redbook 121:34 Jl '63
Teaching children to swim when there are no school facilities. J. J. Schuller, jr. il NEA J 52:55-6 Mr '63
SWIMMING clubs
For God, country and the Santa Clara swim club. W. Trombley. il Sat Eve Post 237:66-71 Jl 25 '64
SWIMMING ladders. See Ladders

SWIMMING pools
Backyard swim pools must be disinfected. Sci N L 85:344 My 30 '64
Come up & sue me; swimming-pool laws. il Time 84:50 Ag 14 '64
CPM opens a pool ten months early; West Hartford, Conn. S. Moses. il Am City 79: 78-9 D '64
Doing your own pool maintenance. Sunset 131:78-9 Ag '63
Earth moving: sometimes it's the only way. il House B 106:76-9 Ag '64
Everybody loves the water. il Pop Gard 15:48-9 Jl '64
Get your pools out of the red. R. H. Beatie. il Am City 78:84-5 Jl '63
Good sense of a screened pool. G. Henle. il House B 106:140-7 Je '64
Hallmark house; atrium with swimming pool. il House & Gard 125:100-1 F '64
Hillside pools. il Sunset 133:90-1 O '64
How to cut pool operating costs. Sunset 130: 127 Je '63
In the swim in St Louis: Wohl recreation center. Mrs E. G. Brungard. il Recreation 56:308-9+ S '63
Ingenuity did it. il Sunset 131:66-7 Jl '63
Is a swimming pool a wise investment? R. Charles. il Parents Mag 39:67-70+ Mr '64
It's a swimming pavilion. il Sunset 130:130 My '63
Let's go swimming at home. il Pop Gard 15:36-9 F '64
Most-wanted pool features. R. Everly. il Am City 80:84-6 Ja '65
New allure of swimming pools. il House & Gard 123:100-5 Je '63
New aquatorium on target; Commerce, Calif. A. J. Robles. il Recreation 56:413-16 N '63
New way to build a swimming hole. il House & Gard 123:138-9 Mr '63
New ways to maintain swimming pools. D. X. Manners. House B 105:182+ Ap '63
Ol' swimmin' hole goes modern; automatic chlorination; Morristown, N.J. G. E. Burke. il Am City 79:100-1 Mr '64
Pool cover peels back; Hershey, Pa. il Am City 79:28 D '64
Pool filters bow to a catch-basin cleaner; method used in Appleton, Wis. R. W. Bues. il Am City 79:25 F '64
Pool should be more than a body of water for swimming. il House B 105:162-71+ Ap '63
Poured-concrete pool wallops gunite alternate by 50 per cent; Williston Park, N.Y. N. Bartilucci. il Am City 79:96-8 Je '64
Remodeled pool is bigger and better; Seashore pool, Kokomo, Ind. J. W. Miller. il Am City 79:94-6 F '64
Retractable housing opens pool in summer; Hershey sports center ride on wheels. il Arch Rec 134:142-3 D '63
Robot cleans this pool. il Sunset 132:171 My '64
Summer pool dons a winter coat. R. M. Artz. il Am City 79:94-6 Ag '64
Swimming and tennis club in California. il Arch Rec 134:146-7 Ag '63
Swimming at home in comfort. il Sunset 133: 72-4 Jl '64
Swimming at home under a roof. il Sunset 133:72-5 S '64
Swimming pools. Review
Consumer Bul 47:39 Jl '64
Swimming pools by subscription; Livingston, N.J. R. D. Sisco. il Am City 78:99-101 My '63
Swimming pools treated with iodine preferred. Sci N L 83:363 Je 8 '63
They got in the swim. il Farm J 87:51 Jl '63
This cabaña kneels to cover a pool. il Sunset 132:144 My '64
What you should know about swimming pools. House & Gard 123:157-8 Je '63
When you carve a pool into your backyard. J. R. Rebhan. il Pop Gard 14:65 My '63
Why not your own swim club? J. Fithian. il Farm J 88:26-7 Ag '64
Winterize your swimming pool. J. H. Ingersoll. il Pop Gard 15:35 N '64

Cleaning

Quick clean up for swimming pools. Sunset 131:114 S '63

Equipment

Swimming pool filters. S. Hedwall. il Recreation 56:418-20 N '63

Safety devices and measures

Delicate art of swimming pool guest control. H. C. Woltjen. Pop Gard 15:50 Jl '64
Have bikini, will sit; pool sitter. il Time 82: 41 Ag 2 '63
This swimming pool safety fence rolls away. il Sunset 131:86+ Jl '63

SWIMMING suits. See Bathing suits
SWINDLER, Daris R. and McCoy, H. A. Calcification of deciduous teeth in rhesus monkeys. bibliog Science 144:1243-4 Je 5 '64
SWINDLER, William F. See Mason. A. H. jt. auth.
SWINDLERS and swindling. See Fraud
SWINE
He combined two new ideas; SPF hogs and slotted floors. il Suc Farm 61:33 My '63
Here's how to get boars for free. Farm J 87:42 N '63
Hog news. See issues of Farm journal
I pay my rent in hogs. W. Messerly. il Suc Farm 61:50 Mr '63
Keep piggy sows on slats too; confinement on slats. D. Seim and J. Russell. il Farm J 88:36-7+ Ja '64
Now ultrasonics move to the hog farm! il Suc Farm 61:148 Mr '63
Pig tale. E. R. Choate. il Atlan 214:81-4 S '64
Under what conditions should you switch to SPF hogs? W. Messerly and J. Harvey. il Suc Farm 61:40-1 O '63
Victoria: a pig in a pram. M. E. Chase. il McCalls 91:114-15+ O '63
What's new and outlook for. See issues of Successful farming
See also
Woods hogs

Diseases and pests

First TGE vaccine ready for farm tests. D. Seim. Farm J 88:50 Mr '64
Hogs drink new erysipelas vaccine. D. Hagen. Farm J 88:35 Je '64
Incidence of gastric ulcers in swine. T. W. Perry and others. il Science 139:349-50 Ja 25 '63
1918 influenza epidemic continues in swine. Sci N L 83:370 Je 15 '63
Vets stop scours by testing for right drug. J. Russell. Farm J 87:42 D '63
See also
Brucellosis in swine
Hog cholera
Rhinitis
Trichina and trichinosis

Feeding

Best place for hog feed, water? D. Hagen. il Farm J 87:51 Mr '63
Can you afford to limit-feed hogs? T. W. Perry. il Suc Farm 62:34-5 Je '64
Don't discount oats for growing pigs. R. C. Wahlstrom. il Suc Farm 61:69 Ag '63
Don't overlook hogging-down corn. J. W. Bailey. il Suc Farm 61:74 S '63
Feed market hogs less. J. A. Rohlf. il Farm J 87:36-7+ S '63
Feeder pigs: management. B. Brantley and J. Harvey. il Suc Farm 61:40-1 S '63
Floor-feeding cuts disease troubles. D. Seim. Farm J 88:52 F '64
Here's the score on copper sulfate. J. Russell. Farm J 88:75 F '64
I get 100 lbs. pork from 331 lbs. feed. G. McGraw. il Suc Farm 61:42 Ag '63
Limited feeding for finishing hogs. J. Harvey and D. E. Becker. il Suc Farm 61:62-3+ Mr '63
Look how they're hamming up hogs. il Farm J 88:31 Jl '64
My sows never see pasture. J. Harvey. il Suc Farm 62:44-5 Ap '64
Now, limit the feed with self-feeders. D. Seim. Farm J 88:46 Ja '64
One stop grain handling, hog feeding. R. E. Geyer. il Suc Farm 61:32-3+ Je '63
Pelleting saves feed during finishing. D. Seim. Farm J 88:48 My '64
Spike pigs' water instead of feed? D. Hagen. il Farm J 88:36 D '64
3,000 hogs per year, not a sow on the place. J. Harvey. il Suc Farm 62:42-3 Je '64
When should you wean pigs for most profit? D. Hagen. Farm J 88:48 Ap '64
Why I stick with pasture. D. Seim. il Farm J 88:42-42A+ Ap '64
Why it pays to limit-feed sows in stalls. J. Harvey. il Suc Farm 61:52-3 Ap '63
Why they like limited feeding. il Suc Farm 62:13 Mr '64
See also
Swine self feeders

Grading and standardization

Feeder pigs you'd be proud to finish. J. Russell and D. Hagen. il Farm J 88: 34-5+ N '64
How to get paid for quality hogs. M. B. Kirtley. il Suc Farm 62:40-1 Ag '64

Marketing

Bargaining that might succeed. Farm J 89: 102 Ja '65
Feeder pigs you'd be proud to finish. J. Russell and D. Hagen. il Farm J 88:34-5+ N '64
How to get paid for quality hogs. M. B. Kirtley. il Suc Farm 62:40-1 Ag '64
How to get $2 more for feeder pigs. K. Copeland. Farm J 88:58B My '64
Just how dependable are hog cycles and ratios? J. Ferris. Suc Farm 61:55 Mr '63

Prices

Does scramble for gilts mean lower prices? D. Wolf. Farm J 88:48 Ap '64
How much for hogs in '65? economists we asked see another good year ahead! B. Brantley. il Suc Farm 62:46 O '64
How to gear hog raising to new price trends. R. Reiman. il Suc Farm 61:32 N '63
Just how dependable are hog cycles and ratios? J. Ferris. Suc Farm 61:55 Mr '63
SWINE, Care of
Twelve sure ways to cut baby pig losses. J. Harvey. il Suc Farm 61:68-9+ Mr '63
SWINE, Cooling of. See Livestock, Cooling of
SWINE, Wild. See Woods hogs
SWINE breeding
Coming: gilt replacements bred to order. D. Seim. il Farm J 87:34+ Jl '63
Test boars in crosses? ed. by J. Bickers. W. O. Robinson. Farm J 88:44B Je '64
See also
Artificial insemination
SWINE dysentery. See Swine—Diseases and pests
SWINE erysipelas. See Swine—Diseases and pests
SWINE farms
Double-duty hog lagoon. C. F. Marley. il Suc Farm 61:104 Ap '63
Feeder pigs; management. B. Brantley and J. Harvey. il Suc Farm 61:40-1 S '63
Hog raising tips to cut costs in half. A. G. Mueller and H. Guither. il Suc Farm 62: 102-3 F '64
Ideas that help me raise 1,200 hogs. il Suc Farm 61:94 N '63
Mind your hog farm visiting manners! H. Guither and D. Walker. il Suc Farm 61: 112+ F '63
On a rented 160 acres, Dennis Clark plans to stay in hogs. W. Messerly and J. Harvey. il Suc Farm 63:36-7 Ja '65
3,000 hogs per year, not a sow on the place. J. Harvey. il Suc Farm 62:42-3 Je '64

Equipment

One-man pig factory; swine farm near Moscow. Sci N L 86:142 Ag 29 '64
SWINE farrowing crates and pens
Best ideas of Geo. Brauer's newest hog house. J. Harvey. il Suc Farm 62:36-7 D '64
Close confinement for sows? D. Seim. il Farm J 88:40+ Mr '64
Floor-feeding cuts disease troubles. D. Seim. Farm J 88:52 F '64
His horse barn earns its keep. J. Harvey. il Suc Farm 62:58 O '64
How to cope with confinement problems. J. R. Pickard. il Suc Farm 61:39 Je '63
Is the single-litter hog system for you? L. H. Simerl. Suc Farm 61:132 F '63
My sows never see pasture. J. Harvey. il Suc Farm 62:44-5 Ap '64
New farrowing ideas for old buildings. W. Messerly. il Suc Farm 61:130 F '63
New finishing house; here's how it works. J. Harvey. il Suc Farm 61:50-1+ My '63
New hog system in an old barn. J. Harvey. il Suc Farm 62:46-7 N '64
Profit-planned hog housing. J. Harvey and A. J. Muehling. il Suc Farm 61:43-7 N; 33-5 D '63; 62:42-3+ Ja; 48-51 F; 44-5 Mr '64
They designed their own farrowing house. il Suc Farm 62:92 N '64
Twelve sure ways to cut baby pig losses. J. Harvey. il Suc Farm 61:68-9+ Mr '63
Why it pays to limit-feed sows in stalls. J. Harvey. il Suc Farm 61:52-3 Ap '63
SWINE house floors. See Swine houses—Floors
SWINE houses
Big change in hog housing. J. Harvey. il Suc Farm 62:50-1 S '64
Five ideas from one hog system. W. Messerly. il Suc Farm 62:98 N '64
New finishing house; here's how it works. J. Harvey. il Suc Farm 61:50-1+ My '63
New hog system in an old barn. J. Harvey. il Suc Farm 62:46-7 N '64
Pig nursery with a grown-up look. il Suc Farm 61:138 Mr '63

SWINE houses—*Continued*
Profit-planned hog housing. J. Harvey and A. J. Muehling. il Suc Farm 61:43-7 N; 33-5 D '63; 62:42-3+ Ja; 48-51 F; 44-5 Mr '64
Slats pay for themselves in six months. D. Wolf. il Farm J 87:34-5+ F '63
They designed their own farrowing house. il Suc Farm 62:92 N '64
They swapped hog house ideas; converting useless barns to modern hog buildings. W. J. Fletcher. il Suc Farm 62:48-9 O '64
Twice the hogs under one roof. D. Seim. il Farm J 88:76 Mr '64
What slotted floors will and won't do for you. A. H. Jensen and J. A. Hoefer. il Suc Farm 61:66-7 F '63
See also
Swine farrowing crates and pens

Equipment

New way to manage pigs. J. Harvey. il Suc Farm 62:90 Ap '64

Floors

Keep piggy sows on slats too; confinement on slats. D. Seim and J. Russell. il Farm J 88:36-7+ Ja '64
Now; slotted floors for nursery pigs. J. Harvey. il Suc Farm 62:92 Ap '64

Heating and ventilation

How to cool a farrowing house. J. Harvey. il Suc Farm 62:40-1 Jl '64

SWINE self feeders
He has a new way to feed hogs. J. Harvey. il Suc Farm 62:54-5 My '64
Profit-planned hog housing. J. Harvey and A. J. Muehling. il Suc Farm 62:44-5 Mr '64

SWINERS, John Louis
Cat's-eye view. il U S Camera 26:56-7 F '63

SWINFEN, Ann
Self-feeding's so easy a baby can do it. Parents Mag 38:60-1+ N '63

SWING (golf)
Crisp shot for soggy sand. J. Nicklaus. il Sports Illus 19:50 N 11 '63
Fairway woods: swing hard and be fearless; ed. by E. Shrake. B. Rawls. il Sports Illus 21:18-20+ Ag 3 '64
Pitcher's motion helps you hit a hook. J. Nicklaus. il Sports Illus 21:49 Ag 31 '64
Start right and you will finish right. J. Nicklaus. il Sports Illus 21:48 Ag 24 '64
Swing with the rhythm of a metronome. J. Nicklaus. il Sports Illus 21:65 O 12 '64
Unusual swing helps solve an unusual difficulty. J. Nicklaus. il Sports Illus 21:62 S 28 '64
Upright swing. J. Nicklaus. il Sports Illus 19:78 S 23 '63
You can learn from a telltale divot mark. J. Nicklaus. il Sports Illus 21:56 N 30 '64

SWING bands. See Bands (music)
SWING music. See Jazz music
SWINGING clocks. See Clocks
SWINGLINE, incorporated
Nailing down home sales of staplers. Bsns W p48 Ap 6 '63

SWINGS
Kid-powered jet swing. H. R. Pfister. il Pop Sci 184:146-7 Mr '64
Tot seat for back-yard swing. H. J. Kennard. il Pop Mech 120:128 Jl '63

SWISS air force. See Switzerland—Air force
SWISS chard. See Chard
SWISS cookery. See Cookery, Swiss
SWISS family Robinson; drama. See Olfson, L.
SWISS furniture. See Furniture, Swiss
SWISS music. See Music, Swiss
SWISS national exposition. See Exhibitions
SWISS spies. See Spies
SWISS watches. See Watches
SWISSAIR. See Airlines—Switzerland
SWITCH-about shopkeepers; drama. See Sagoff, S. E.
SWITCHES, Electric. See Electric switches
SWITCHES, Hair. See Wigs
SWITHINBANK, Charles W.
Ice movement of valley glaciers flowing into the Ross Ice Shelf, Antarctica. bibliog Science 141:523-4 Ag 9 '63

SWITZ, Theodore M.
Laborer for the harvest. Christian Cent 81:1369 N 4 '64

SWITZERLAND
Influence of the Swiss; an ABC of Swiss life. F. Nourissier. il Vogue 142:174-81+ O 1 '63
See also
Airlines—Switzerland
Airports—Switzerland
Alps
Banks and banking—Switzerland
Bern (city)
Geneva
Gstaad
Hotels, taverns, etc.—Switzerland
Humlikon
Montreux
Music festivals—Switzerland
Newspapers—Switzerland
Ouchy
Private schools—Switzerland
St Moritz
Saint-Pierre (island) Switzerland
Samaden
Space research—Switzerland
Tourist trade—Switzerland
Verbier
World war, 1939-1945—Switzerland
Zermatt
Zurich

Air force

Only a mirage; scandal over cost of planes. Newsweek 64:52+ O 19 '64

Description and travel

Camera guide to Switzerland. L. Barry. il Pop Phot 52:94-5+ Je '63
Going places, finding things in Switzerland. D. Beal. il House & Gard 124:16-17+ Jl '63
Let's travel. il Mlle 57:170+ Ag '63
Swiss know how to live and ski and eat and have fairs. R. Joseph. Esquire 60:20+ Jl '63
Well traveled camera. il Mod Phot 28:52+ Je '64

Economic conditions

Alarm against foreigners. il Time 83:96+ F 7 '64
Swiss turn. Newsweek 63:66 F 10 '64

History

Bibliography

Articles and other books received; Germany, Austria, and Switzerland. comp. by A. H. Price. See issues of American historical review

Religious institutions and affairs

News of the Christian world (cont) Christian Cent 80:590+; 81:948 My 1 '63, Jl 22 '64
See also
Catholic church in Switzerland

SWOONING. See Fainting
SWOPE park zoological gardens, Kansas City, Mo. See Zoological gardens
SWORDFISH fishing
High cost of not catching swordfish. D. Barnes. il Sports Illus 21:46-7 Jl 20 '64

SWORDS
Excalibur, ltd; interview, ed. by F. Stevenson. O. Kolombatovich. il Opera N 28:12-13 Ap 11 '64
Now swords are drawn for status; Wilkinson sword, ltd. il Bsns W p50-2 F 8 '64
Sword: badge of the gentleman. A. Duggan. il Holiday 34:32+ N '63

SYBARIS
Magnetism locates ruins. Sci N L 86:358 D 5 '64
Two ancient cities found. Sci N L 84:93 Ag 10 '63

SYDEMAN, William
Pioneer service to two young composers. R. Sabin. Am Rec G 30:971 Je '64

SYDNEY, John
Nature's creepiest freaks. Sci Digest 55:5-7 My '64

SYDNEY, Australia
Skyline rises in Sydney. il Bsns W p72+ N 21 '64

Music

[Musical events] Mus Am 84:31 S; 94 D '64

SYDNEY-Hobart race. See Yacht racing
SYER, Warren B.
Notes from our correspondents. il Hi Fi 14:17 Ap '64

SYKES, Christopher
Fine art of self-appraisal. Nation 199:310-11 N 2 '64
Nothing wasted except lives. Nation 197:94 Ag 24 '63
Trouble with the Bard. Nation 198:101+ Ja 27 '64

SYKES, Stephen
Do it yourself skyscraper. il pors Ebony 18:75-6+ Mr '63

SYKES, Velma West
Christmas parable. Farm J 87:83 D '63
Tell me. Bathsheba; poem. Christian Cent 80:1403 N 13 '63
Les SYLPHIDES (ballet) See Ballets
SYLVESTER, Arthur
Captain Shank's letters. Life 56:30 Je 5 '64
Sylvester's reply. Aviation W 78:118 Ja 28 '63
about
Don't swallow everything. il por Time 81:51 Mr 29 '63
Foot-to-mouth existence. por Newsweek 61:26 Mr 25 '63
Never say lie; grilling by the House information subcommittee on managed news. Time 81:81 Ap 5 '63
Official spokesman for managed news. il por U S News 54:14 Ap 1 '63
Service chiefs must detail news contacts. Aviation W 80:20-1 Je 8 '64
Sylvester, senators clash on TFX probe. Aviation W 78:28 Mr 18 '63
SYLVESTER, David
Enter Bacon, with the Bacon scream. N Y Times Mag p24-5+ O 20 '63
Soutine: the impact of infighting. Art N 62:22-7+ O '63
(ed) See Moore, H. Genius of Michelangelo as seen by Moore
SYLVIA, Sister Mary. See Mary Sylvia, Sister
SYMBIOSIS
Bull-horn acacia; Mexican ant acacia. V. N. Argo. il Natur Hist 74:22-7 Ja '65
Symbiosis: on the role of algae symbiotic with hydra. L. Muscatine and H. M. Lenhoff. bibliog il Science 142:956-8 N 15 '63
Symbiotic behavior among fishes from temperate ocean waters. F. H. McCutcheon and A. E. McCutcheon. bibliog il Science 145:948-9 Ag 28 '64
SYMBOLISM
See also
Cross and crosses
SYMBOLISM of numbers
Planets, palms, and numbers. H. Stackpole. il Mlle 60:50-1+ Ja '65
SYMBOLS
Greek alphabet quiz. R. P. Balin. il Pop Electr 19:73+ D '63
Trade marks of M. Peter Piening. L. Schmeckebier. il Am Artist 29:52-7 Ja '65
See also
Emblems
Guided missiles
SYMINGTON, Stuart
Symington cites weapons control in backing ban on nuclear tests. K. Johnsen. Aviation W 79:29 S 23 '63
SYMONETTE, Robert H.
Blue-water honors to Ondine. pors Motor B 111:56+ F '63
SYMPATHETIC nervous system. See Nervous system, Sympathetic
SYMPATHY, Letters of. See Letters
SYMPHONIC poems
See also
Phonograph records—Symphonic poems
SYMPHONIES
See also
Phonograph records—Symphonies
SYMPHORICARPOS. See Snowberries
SYMPOSIUM on library functions in the changing metropolis. See Library conferences
SYNAGOGUES
Big temple for Baltimore; Temple Oheb Shalom. il Arch Rec 135:147-52 Je '64
Major synagogue by Belluschi; Temple B'rith Kodesh in Rochester, N.Y. il Arch Rec 134:143-8 N '63
Synagogue by Yamasaki, Glencoe, Ill. il Arch Rec 136:191-6 S '64
Synagogue distinguished by expandable sanctuary for high holidays; Congregation temple Israel, Creve Coeur, Mo. il Arch Rec 134:146-50 Jl '63
Where Jews worship; exhibition at New York's Jewish museum. il Newsweek 62:92 N 4 '63
SYNANON House, Santa Monica, Calif.
Drug addicts who cure each other. L. Robinson. il Ebony 18:116-18+ F '63
Mutual aid in prison. il Time 81:45 Mr 1 '63
Where is science taking us? new criminal: a report on the hip killer. L. Yablonsky. il Sat R 46:54-6 F 2 '63
SYNAPSES
Acetylcholine and cholinacetylase content of synaptic vesicles. E. De Robertis and others. bibliog il Science 140:300-1 Ap 19 '63
Synapse. J. Eccles. il Sci Am 212:56-66 bibliog(p 134) Ja '65
SYNCHRONOUS meteorological satellite. See Artificial satellites—Meteorological applications
SYNCOM C (artificial satellite) See Communications satellites
SYNCOM I (artificial satellite) See Communications satellites
SYNCOM III (artificial satellite) See Communications satellites
SYNCOPE. See Fainting
SYNDICATE, Chicago. See Chicago—Crime
SYNDICATE material, Newspaper. See Newspapers—Syndicate service
SYNDROMES
Lincoln look, an inherited disorder? Marfan syndrome. Sci Digest 55:32 Je '64
SYNERGISM
Synergism between a lactate dehydrogenase-elevating virus and eperythrozoon coccoides. V. Riley. bibliog il Science 146:921-3 N 13 '64
SYNNESTVEDT, Sig
Red drive in Cuba. bibliog f Cur Hist 45:216-22+ O '63
SYNODS. See Councils and synods
SYNTAGMATIC organization language system. See Information storage and retrieval systems
SYNTEX corporation
Watching brush fires on Wall Street. il Bsns W p 110-12 Ja 25 '64
SYNTHESIS
Control of synthesis of RNA and protein in diapausing and injured cecropia pupae. S. J. Berry and others. bibliog il Science 146:938-40 N 13 '64
See also
Biosynthesis
SYNTHETIC detergents. See Cleaning compositions
SYNTHETIC diamonds. See Diamonds, Artificial
SYNTHETIC drugs. See Drugs
SYNTHETIC food. See Food substitutes
SYNTHETIC fur. See Fur, Artificial
SYNTHETIC insulin. See Insulin
SYNTHETIC intelligence machine. See Automatons
SYNTHETIC quartz crystals. See Quartz crystals
SYNTHETIC resins. See Resinous products
SYNTHETIC rubber. See Rubber, Artificial
SYNTHETIC textile fabrics. See Textile fabrics, Synthetic
SYNTOL (Syntagmatic organization language system) See Information storage and retrieval systems
SYPHILIS
Large syphilis increase in fifteen to nineteen age group. Sci N L 83:214 Ap 6 '63
Shocking facts about teenage venereal disease. Good H 158:168 Je '64
Syphilis. Consumer Rep 28:498-9 O '63
Vicious chain. F. Warshofsky. il Todays Health 41:24-9 Ag '63; Same abr. with title V.D. the vicious chain. Read Digest 83:107-10 D '63
Diagnosis
AMA gives syphilis tests. Sci N L 83:403 Je 29 '63
More syphilis tests advised in hospitals. Sci N L 84:325 N 23 '63
SYRACUSE, N.Y.
Airports
Syracuse airport shows earning power. il Am City 79:93 Ap '64
Housing
Presidential Plaza. il Arch Rec 134:198-9 S '63
Lighting
Residents asked for more. V. J. Moore. il Am City 78:125 S '63
Music
Upstate Tosca. J. Browning. Opera N 28:33 Mr 7 '64
Street traffic
How Syracuse selected its parking meters. W. F. Walsh. il Am City 78:86-8 Ap '63
SYRACUSE university
Libraries
For whom the books are collected; Lena R. Arents rare book room; reprint. K. V. Hostick. Hobbies 69:110 Ap '64
Syracuse univ. to develop model information center. Library J 89:4308 N 1 '64

SYRACUSE university—*Continued*

Newhouse communications center

Little Sam's big gift. il Time 84:52 Ag 14 '64
Nachas for Sam; Newhouse foundation finances new quarters for the Syracuse school of journalism. il Newsweek 64:56 Ag 17 '64

SYRETT, Robert
Notes from our correspondents. Hi Fi 14:22+ S '64

SYRIA
See also
Government ownership—Syria
Jordan River
Prisoners—Syria
United Arab Republic
United Nations—Syria
United States—Foreign relations—Syria

Boundaries

Anger in the Council; emergency session concerning Israeli-Syrian frontier incident. Time 82:29 S 6 '63
Jets over the Jordon; Israeli-Syrian border clash. Newsweek 64:48 N 23 '64
United States urges restraint on Israel and Syria: statement, December 3, 1964. A. E. Stevenson. Dept State Bul 52:27-9 Ja 4 '65
Water war; Syrian-Israeli dispute. Time 84:40 N 27 '64

Foreign relations

Another first step; Syrian-Iraqi pact. Newsweek 62:46 S 16 '63

Politics and government

Arab unity. Commonweal 77:655 Mr 22 '63
Cure for sick brothers. il Time 83:28 My 1 '64
Defying Nasser; Michel Alfaq and the Ba'ath party. il Newsweek 61:50 Ap 15 '63
Emergence of the Ba'ath. P. Seale. New Repub 148:7-8 Mr 23 '63
From God, or Nasser. Time 81:37 My 24 '63
Ham-handed in Cairo. New Repub 148:8 Ap 13 '63
Nasser: on the march again? il Newsweek 61:40 Mr 18 '63
Pacifier; anti-government unrest. Newsweek 63:36+ My 4 '64
Spreading infection. il Time 81:38-9 Mr 15 '63
Syria coup move toward Arab unity? il Sr Schol 82:21 Mr 27 '63
Syria in flux. P. Seale. New Repub 149:9-10 S 14 '63
Syria: test of Arab unity. G. LeCompte and L. Hamalian. Nation 196:375-6+ My 4 '63
Throwing away the script. Time 82:26 Jl 26 '63
Unity by disunion. Time 81:40 My 17 '63

SYRINGAS. See Mock oranges

SYROP, Konrad
(tr) See Mrozek, S. Birthday party
(tr) See Mrozek, S. Four fables from Poland

SYROS (island)
Two islands. E. Taylor. il Mlle 59:176-8+ S '64

SYRUPS
Glossary of popular syrups. Good H 157:164 N '63
Luscious berry syrups. N. Nichols. il Farm J 87:63 Je '63

SYSTEM development corporation
Research on programed instruction at SDC. H. F. Silberman. il Sch Life 45:13-15+ Mr '63
Scrambling for sales in war on poverty; to test and sell theories and products. Bsns W p32 Jl 11 '64

SYSTEMIC insecticides. See Insecticides

SYSTEMS engineering
Concept of a production system. P. H. Thurston. il Harvard Bsns R 41:70-5 N '63
How Pert-cost helps the general manager. H. W. Paige. il Harvard Bsns R 41:87-95 N '63
System theory and physiological processes; excerpts from addresses. R. W. Jones; J. S. Gray. Science 140:461-6 My 3 '63

SYSTEMS management
Can management information be automated? J. Dearden. Harvard Bsns R 42:128-35 Mr '64
Coordinating for productivity. il Duns R 84: pt2 104-5+ S '64
Improve your profits day by day! F. O. Hoffman. Harvard Bsns R 41:59-67 Jl '63
Manager's job: a systems approach. S. Tilles. bibliog f Harvard Bsns R 41:73-81 Ja '63
Top management and computer profits. J. T. Garrity. Harvard Bsns R 41:6-8+ Jl '63

SZAFRANIEC, Rozalia
Eclipsing stars and their periods. Sky & Tel 28:20-1 Jl '64

SZARKOWSKI, John
Creative color; interview, ed. by A. Rothstein. U S Camera 26:8-9 My '63
How work trousers hung in 1912. Pop Phot 54:72-3 Ap '64
Photographer's eye at modern museum. D. Vestal. il Pop Phot 55:54+ N '64

SZASZ, Suzanne
Child is born. il Parents Mag 39:50-1 Mr '64
Children's pictures, for a cause. il Pop Phot 52:72-5+ Mr '63

SZASZ, Thomas S.
Criminal insanity: facts or strategy. New Repub 151:19-22 N 21 '64
Psychiatry's threat to civil liberties. Nat R 14:191-3 Mr 12 '63
What psychiatry can and cannot do. bibliog Harper 228:50-3 F; 100 Ap '64

SZELL, George
Intangible and misunderstood; interview. Mus Am 83:6 My '63
Mixture of instinct and intellect; interview, ed. by P. H. Lang. pors Hi Fi 15:42-5+ Ja '65

about

Glorious instrument. il pors Time 81:58-60+ F 22 '63; Same abr. Read Digest 82:261-3+ My '63
Music to my ears; music's idea man. I. Kolodin. Sat R 47:25 Mr 7 '64
Music to my ears; Szell at the Philharmonic. I. Kolodin. Sat R 46:94 Mr 16 '63
Musical events; concert at Carnegie Hall performed by Cleveland orchestra. W. Sargeant. New Yorker 38:151-2 F 16 '63
Szell, still storming after fifty years. M. Mayer. il pors N Y Times Mag p 13+ F 2 '64

SZENT-GYÖRGYI, Albert
Brain, morals, and politics. Bul Atomic Sci 20:2-3 My '64
Teaching and the expanding knowledge. Science 146:1278-9 D 4 '64
—and others
Cancer therapy: a possible new approach. bibliog Science 140:1391-2 Je 28 '63

about

Nobelist's cancer theory; balance between promine and retine. W. Wingo. Sci N L 84:19 Jl 13 '63
Promote & retard. il por Time 82:43 Ag 2 '63

SZERYNG, Henryk
Henryk Szeryng; interview, ed. by S. Fleming. por Hi Fi 13:34+ Ap '63
Szeryng's (and Rubinstein's) Brahms. N. Lang. Am Rec G 29:444-5 F '63

SZIGETI, Joseph
Celebration at seventy; Szigeti's Prokofiev; sonatas for violin and piano. A. Frankenstein. Hi Fi 13:56-7 My '63

SZILARD, Leo
Minimal deterrent vs. saturation parity. Bul Atomic Sci 20:6-12 Mr '64

about

Fight over the A-bomb. F. Knebel and C. W. Bailey. Look 27:19-23 Ag 13 '63; Reply. A. K. Smith. Bul Atomic Sci 19:33 O '63
Leo Szilard, 1898-1964. E. Rabinowitch. por Bul Atomic Sci 20:16-20 O '64
Leo Szilard: the conscience of a scientist. T. Coffin. pors Holiday 35:64-7+ F '64
Remembrance of a genius. A. Rosenfeld. por Life 56:31 Je 12 '64
Scientists in politics: Council founded by Szilard brings cash and sophistication to lobbying. E. Langer. por Science 145:561-3 Ag 7 '64

SZILASI, A.
Receiving tube grid current. Electr World 69:50-1+ F '63

SZOGYI, Alex
(tr) See Gorky, M. Lower depths

SZONY, Francois
Glamorous paradox. E. Palatsky. il pors Dance Mag 37:30-3 Ag '63

SZUKALSKI, Stanislav
Mute singer; story. Atlan 214:61-6 Jl '64

SZULC, Tad
After Trujillo, a reformer with a mission. N Y Times Mag p30+ S 8 '63
Beautiful, cruel, explosive, Haiti. N Y Times Mag p26-7+ Je 9 '63
Capricorn uncensored. Sat R 46:64+ O 12 '63
Guerra! still the word in Miami. N Y Times Mag p9+ Jl 5 '64

SZUMLEWICZ, Alina Perlowagora
Schistosomiasis: age of snails and susceptibility to X-irradiation. bibliog Science 144:302-4 Ap 17 '64
—and Olivier, L. J.
Schistosoma mansoni: development of challenge infections in mice exposed to irradiated cercariae. bibliog Science 140:411-12 Ap 26 '63
SZYBALSKI, Waclaw. See Iyer, V. N. jt. auth.

T

T-groups. See Executives—Training
T party; drama. See Boiko, C.
T-shirts. See Shirts
TADC. See Toledo area development corporation
TFF. See Tools for freedom (organization)
TFX. See Airplanes, Military—United States
TFX contract investigation. See Government investigations—Government contracts
TGE virus. See Swine—Diseases and pests
TIRC. See Tobacco industry and research committee
TMRBM (transportable medium range ballistic missile) See Guided missiles
TTX. See Trailor train company
TV guide (periodical)
Tougher at ten. il Newsweek 62:58 S 9 '63
TVA. See Tennessee Valley authority
TVOR (terminal omnirange) See Radio aids to aviation
TWA. See Trans World airlines
TABAK, May Natalie
Zogbaum makes a sculpture. Art N 63:42-5+ D '64
TABARLET, B. E.
Are Swiss submarines better than ours? Sat R 47:72 Mr 21 '64
Labels, logic, and communism. Sch & Soc 91:224-5 My 4 '63
TABARLY, Eric
French sailor first in ocean race. il por Motor B 114:88-9 Ag '64
Il TABARRO; opera. See Puccini, G.
TABEL, William G.
Classroom on the Sound. Motor B 112:82 Ag '63
TABER, Fanny T.
Will there be any free Americans left? excerpts from letter. U S News 56:14 Je 8 '64
TABER, Gladys
That certain feeling. Writer 77:14-16 F '64
TABLE, The. See Table setting
TABLE decoration
All about buffets, and tables, too. E. D. Craster. il Bet Hom & Gard 41:62-7 N '63
Anything tastes better when it's beautifully served. il McCalls 90:74-9 F '63
Be an artist party. B. Stover. il Parents Mag 39:76-7 Mr '64
Birthday merry-go-round party. B. Stover. il Parents Mag 39:78 Mr '64
Candy evergreen tree. Good H 157:188 D '63
Catch a cloud in a teaspoon. il House B 105:96-107 Je '63
Centerpieces for your holiday table. J. E. Dwyer. il Pop Gard 15:38 N '64
Color magic for party tables. il House & Gard 125:130-5 Mr '64
Come to a candy cane mixer, a party for pint-size people. V. Stanton. il House B 105:152-3+ D '63
Dining rooms and centerpieces for autumn. il McCalls 92:128-33 N '64
Everlasting centerpiece. il House & Gard 126:174-5 S '64
Feast your eyes. M. Johnston. il Bet Hom & Gard 41:74-7+ Ap '63
Festive garnish for hall and buffet. il House & Gard 124:130-1 D '63
Mystery guests. il Seventeen 22:124-7+ F '63
Party-pretty ice bowl; centerpiece. il Seventeen 23:252 Ag '64
Place-mat parties. il Bet Hom & Gard 42:102-3 Ap '64
Real and ribbon roses to deck a wedding table. il Bet Hom & Gard 41:82 Je '63
Red and green spice for a Christmas table. il House & Gard 124:126-7 D '63
Right settings for the right times. R. W. Houseman. il Am Home 66:42-5 Je '63
Summery tables. il McCalls 91:86-93 Je '64
Table ideas from the Far East. il Good H 156:158 Mr '63
Three for the table in the spirit of the season. il Good H 157:229 D '63
Tips on tempting tables. Bet Hom & Gard 41:114A Ap '63
Witty centerpieces from the fruits of the harvest. il Am Home 66:34-5 N '63
You make it with ti leaves. il Sunset 131:175 Jl '63
See also
Party favors
TABLE games. See Games
TABLE gardens. See Gardens, Miniature
TABLE legs. See Tables
TABLE linen
For a carefree summer, use carefree things. il House B 105:120-1 Je '63
Gala revivals. il House & Gard 123:148-51 My '63
New fashions for tables. M. White. il Ladies Home J 81:70-3 My '64
One-of-a-kind tablecloths that make a party. il House & Gard 123:112-15 Mr '63
Take care of your table linens. Am Home 67:78 Je '64
Tricks in time keep table linens fine. B. G. Wadsworth. il Parents Mag 38:34 F '63
TABLE manners. See Etiquette
TABLE mats, tiles, etc.
Place mats by the yard. M. Garrity. il Bet Hom & Gard 41:58-9 F '63
TABLE saws. See Saws
TABLE setting
All about buffets, and tables, too. E. D. Craster. il Bet Hom & Gard 41:62-7 N '63
All set for fun. il Seventeen 23:144-5 O '64
Anything tastes better when it's beautifully served. il McCalls 90:74-9 F '63
Catch a cloud in a teaspoon. il House B 105:96-107 Je '63
Four tables, all small rule-breakers. il Vogue 141:130-1+ Ap 15 '63
Gala revivals. il House & Gard 123:148-51 My '63
Holiday tables sparkling with color. il Am Home 66:38-9 D '63
How they entertain in Hawaii. il House B 106:80-1 Ja '64
How to set holiday tables. il Am Home 67:44-5 D '64
It's an art. C. Kellogg. il Ladies Home J 80:92-7 Ap '63
Little things make my life interesting; ed. by R. Martens. A. Kracht. il Farm J 87:106-7 F '63
Mystery guests. il Seventeen 22:124-7+ F '63
New fashions for tables. M. White. il Ladies Home J 81:70-3 My '64
Right settings for the right times. R. W. Houseman. il Am Home 66:42-5 Je '63
Round the world parties; for a world of fun. il Seventeen 23:148-51 F '64
Set the scene for easy summer entertaining. il Am Home 67:50-3 Je '64
Set with taste and imagination. il Am Home 67:44-7 N '64
Seventeen reasons to give a party! il Seventeen 22:132-3 O '63
Tables dressed in their Christmas best. il McCalls 92:128-9+ D '64
Taste-setter winners. il Seventeen 23:112+ Ag '64
Tips on setting your table. il Am Home 66:62 Je '63
TABLE silver. See Silverware
TABLE stoves. See Electric stoves
TABLE tennis
Champ of the chop and loop. B. La Fontaine. il Sports Illus 20:54-6+ My 11 '64
TABLECLOTHS. See Table linen
TABLES
Cover old accidents (or prevent new ones) with vinyl fabric on your coffee table. il Bet Hom & Gard 41:30 S '63
Double your dining space. J. Holmstrand. il Suc Farm 62:80-1 S '64
For adults: games and tables. J. Peter. il Look 28:79 O 20 '64
For barbecue fun; custom-made for comfort. K. Smith. il Pop Gard 14:58 Jl '63
For Japanese-style dinners. il Sunset 133:88 Ag '64
Furniture with a built-in bonus. il House B 105:222-3 O '63
Furniture with a future: the tray-top table. il House & Gard 125:54-5 Mr '64
Gate-leg dining tables. S. Ellingson. il Pop Mech 121:170-2 Ap '64
It's a play table that folds up. il Sunset 133:150+ N '64
Its stripes are odds and ends. il Sunset 130:164 My '63

TABLES—*Continued*
Little tables with important talents. il House & Gard 125:30-1 My '64
New flexibility in furniture, thanks to bunching and nesting. il House B 105:224-5 O '63
Picnic hamper-table tailor-made to fit car trunk. E. Capper. il Pop Mech 119:132 My '63
Picnic tables; with shopping guide. C. Squire. il Pop Gard 14:55 My '63
Roll-away table for ping-pong. R. J. De Cristoforo. il Pop Sci 183:152-4 O '63
Shorty legs raise status of the card table. A. R. Tanner, jr. il Pop Sci 184:158-9 Ap '64
Sturdy table and stiff umbrella. il Sunset 131:111-12 S '63
Sympathetic, serviceable tea table. J. Ellestad. il House B 105:220-1 O '63
Table talk. il McCalls 91:146-51 N '63
This handsome table is willow. il Sunset 131:165 N '63
Up for light, down for railroading. il Sunset 134:80 Ja '65
What to look for when choosing tables and chests. il Bet Hom & Gard 41:124-5 Ap '63
When is a table not a table? il House B 105:62+ O '63
See also
Work tables
TABLEWARE
Dinnerware: plain & fancy. il Good H 157:122-9 O '63
Dishwasher-proof dinnerware. J. Holmstrand. il Suc Farm 62:52-3 Jl '64
Fine dinnerware. il Consumer Bul 46:18-19 Ap '63
Gilt-edged investments for entertaining. il House & Gard 124:194-99 O '63
It's an art. C. Kellogg. il Ladies Home J 80:92-7 Ap '63
Parents' magazine previews new elegance for family dining. B. G. Wadsworth and N. Pierce. il Parents Mag 39:63+ My '64
Party pack. M. Davidson. il Ladies Home J 80:102+ N '63
Platter that makes the feast. il House & Gard 125:180-1 Ap '64
See also
Pyroceram
TABLEWARE, Plastic
For a carefree summer, use carefree things. il House B 105:120-1 Je '63
Guarantee of non-staining properties; Brookpark plastic dishes. il Consumer Bul 46:32 O '63
Melamine dinnerware. il Consumer Rep 29:554-7 N '64
TABLEWARE, Stainless steel
President asks for tariff study on stainless steel flatware. Dept State Bul 51:63 Jl 13 '64
TABOGA ISLAND
Tale of two isles. H. Sutton. Sat R 46:33-4+ My 18 '63
TABORI, George
(tr) See Frisch, M. Andorra
TABORI, Paul
Of apples and other myths. N Y Times Mag p 182+ Ap 7 '63
Superstitions? silly! (knock on wood) N Y Times Mag p34-5+ My 26 '63
TABS (boats)
Does your boat's tail drag? try the new trim tabs. J. Martin. il Pop Sci 183:122-3+ Ag '63
Trim tabs. R. W. Hobbs. il Yachting 115:44-5+ F '64
TACHOMETERS
Electronic tachometers. J. Kyle. il Electr World 71:34-5+ My '64
Transistorized tachometer for automobile or boat engine. C. D. Todd. il Electr World 70:66-7+ N '63
X-line tachometer. C. Caringella. il Pop Electr 20:41-4 Ja '64
TACKLE, Fishing. See Fishing tackle
TACKLE boxes. See Boxes, cases, etc.
TACKLE; story. See O'Hara, J.
TACOMA, Wash.
Combine your purchases and save. L. A. Menconi. il Am City 78:83 D '63
Tacoma's Fort Nisqually. il Sunset 130:39 Mr '63
Finance
How to win a bond program. B. Bond. il Am City 79:120-1 Mr '64
TACOMA outboard club. See Boat clubs
TACONIC MOUNTAINS
Our far-flung correspondents; cabin on Mt Riga, Conn. C. Rand. New Yorker 39:31-2+ Ag 10 '63
TACONITE
Iron amendment; taconite on the Mesabi, Minnesota. il Newsweek 64:74+ N 16 '64
TACTICAL air command. See United States—Air force—Tactical air command
TACTUAL perception. See Touch
TAFT, Bruce A. See Knauss, J. A. jt. auth.
TAFT, Charles P.
Chief justice William H. Taft. America 112:30 Ja 9 '65
TAFT, Kingsley A. Jr
TVA at work; better hardwoods for the future. Am For 71:26-9+ Ja '65
TAFT, Philip
Interplant transfers in the automobile industry. Mo Labor R 86:276-8 Mr '63
Is there a crisis in the labor movement? no. Ann Am Acad 350:10-15 N '63
TAFT, Robert Alphonso, 1917-
Middle ground of a Midwest Republican. por Sat R 47:14-16 Ag 22 '64
Son of Mr Republican. il por Time 84:43B O 2 '64
Taft vs. Young. il pors Newsweek 64:36-8 O 26 '64
What beat Taft. Time 84:40 N 13 '64
Why, oh, why oh? Reporter 31:18+ N 19 '64
TAFT, William H.
Chief justice William H. Taft. C. P. Taft. America 112:30 Ja 9 '65
TAFT family
American family, by I. Ross. Review
Sat R 47:24 N 28 '64. E. E. Morison
TAFT-Hartley law. See Labor laws and legislation—United States—Taft-Hartley law
TAFT sanitary engineering center. See United States—Public health service
TAFT school, Watertown, Conn. See Private schools
TAGETES. See Marigolds
TAGGART, Ross E.
Relief-decorated ceramics. Antiques 83:430-3 Ap '63
Wares of Thomas Whieldon. Antiques 83:207-11 F '63
TAGGING of animals. See Animal tagging
TAGGING of fish. See Fish tagging
TAGLIABUE, John
From a Shakespeare notebook; poem. Poetry 102:166-8 Je '63
From an outdoor Blake festival; poem. Poetry 104:222-3 Jl '64
TAGS, Radioactive. See Radioactive tracers
TAHITI
Catamaran to Tahiti; ed. by R. Choy. K. Murphy; A. Reid. il Yachting 113:36-8+ Mr; 85-7+ Ap '63
Death for Tahiti; proposed testing ground for nuclear weapons. H. Capet. Atlan 212:73-4 Jl '63
Magic eye of Dan Budnik. il U S Camera 26:64-9 Ap '63
New Tahiti. H. Sutton. il Sat R 47:35-6+ Ap 11 '64
Tahiti bound. P. Stackpole. U S Camera 27:12+ My '64
Tahiti in July, a photographic wonderland. P. Stackpole. U S Camera 26:10+ N '63
Tahitian interlude; photographs. Travel 122:43-5 N '64
Test site in Tahiti. Newsweek 62:35-6 Ag 5 '63
35mm techniques; photo tour. P. Stackpole. U S Camera 27:14-15 N '64
TAHOE, LAKE
Open sesame. il Time 81:60 Ap 12 '63
TAI chi (exercise) See Exercise
TAIBELE and Hurmizah; story. See Singer, I. B.
TAIL lights. See Automobiles—Lighting
TAILORS
Anecdotes, facetiae, satire, etc.
Prsty of my tailor. J. Wechsberg. il Esquire 61:96-7+ Mr '64
TAILWHEELS. See Airplanes—Wheels
TAIMUTY, S. I. and others
X-ray-induced bulk photovoltaic effect in insulators. Science 144:173 Ap 10 '64
TAIWAN
Abnormal hemoglobin studies in Taiwan aborigines. R. Q. Blackwell and J. T. H. Huang. bibliog Science 139:771 F 22 '63
Atlantic report. Atlan 213:13-14+ Je '64
Chiang still dreams his dream. T. Durdin. il N Y Times Mag p 18-19+ Mr 22 '64
China 1965: counter-offensive and national recovery: address, December 31, 1964. K. S. Chiang. Vital Speeches 31:198-200 Ja 15 '65
Formosa: a success story. il Time 81:94 Mr 8 '63
Letter from Formosa; tr. by W. J. Dannhauser. P. Schmid. Commentary 37:68-70 Ap '64

TAIWAN—*Continued*
Our strongest ally in the Pacific. Fortune 68: 130+ Jl '63
Sword at the belly of red China. D. Norton-Taylor. il Fortune 68:150-3+ Jl '63; Same abr. Read Digest 83:127-31 S '63
Up from limbo. New Repub 148:8-9 Mr 2 '63
See also
Architecture—Taiwan
Birth control—Taiwan
Copyright—Taiwan
Economic assistance in Taiwan
Education—Taiwan
Elections—Taiwan
Investments, Foreign (in Taiwan)
Publishers and publishing—Taiwan
United States—Foreign relations—China

Commercial treaties and agreements

U.S. and Republic of China conclude textile arrangement; Department announcement, October 22, 1963, with exchange of notes between Ambassador Jerauld Wright and the Chinese Minister of foreign affairs. il Dept State Bul 49:789-92 N 18 '63

Economic conditions

China that is really thriving. R. P. Martin. il U S News 57:52-5 Ag 3 '64
Taiwan, the joyous and proud. P. L. Buckley. Nat R 14:152-3 F 26 '63

Foreign relations

Two Chinas. P. M. A. Linebarger. Cur Hist 47:162-5 S '64

Industries

Other China builds up. il Bsns W p 120-2 Jl 13 '63

Politics and government

Chiang Kai-shek: the crumbling facade. S. Karnow. il Sat Eve Post 236:101-5 D 7 '63
Chiang Kai-shek's silent enemies. A. Axelbank. Harper 227:46-50+ S '63; Discussion. 227:10+ D '63
Free China's next chief? Chiang Ching-kuo tours U.S. il U S News 55:26 S 23 '63
Heir apparent: Chiang Ching-kuo. Time 85: 23 Ja 22 '65
Son of Chiang. il Newsweek 62:47 S 23 '63
Taiwan, the joyous and proud. P. L. Buckley. Nat R 14:152-3 F 26 '63

Social conditions

Return to the frontier. E. Chang. il Reporter 28:38-9 Mr 28 '63

TAIZÉ monastery. See Monasteries

TAKAEZU, Toshiko
Four ceramists of Hawaii. J. Lovoos. il por Am Artist 27:66-73+ Je '63

TAKAHASHI, Taro, and Bassett, W. A.
High-pressure polymorph of iron. bibliog Science 145:483-6 Jl 31 '64

TAKARO, Timothy
Institute for experimental surgical instruments in Moscow. bibliog Science 142:195-9 O 11 '63

TAKATSUKI, Kiyoshi, and Osserman, E. F.
Structural differences between two types of heavy chain disease proteins and myeloma globulins of corresponding types. bibliog Science 145:499-500 Jl 31 '64

TAKE her, she's mine; drama. See Ephron, P. and Ephron, H.

TAKEDA, Hiroshi. See Donnay, J. D. H. jt. auth.

TAKEDA, James Tetsuzo
Hymns in haiku. Time 81:54+ Mr 15 '63

TAKEMORI, Shigeki, and King, T. E.
Coenzyme Q: reversal of inhibition of succinate cytochrome c reductase by lipophilic compounds. bibliog Science 144:852-3 My 15 '64

TAKESHITA, Hitoshi, and Anchel, Marjorie
Production of oosporein and its leuco form by basidiomycete species. bibliog Science 147:152-3 Ja 8 '65

TAKEYAMA, Kenzaburo
Wanted: more quake-proof buildings. UNESCO Courier 16:30-2 O '63

TALAL, Norman, and Tomkins, G. M.
Allosteric properties of glutamate dehydrogenases from different sources. bibliog Science 146:1309-11 D 4 '64

TALAVERAN pottery. See Pottery, Mexican

TALBERT, Anne
Parable of the no talents; poem. Christian Cent 80:903 Jl 17 '63

TALBERT, Bill
Way to better net play. pors Sports Illus 21: 28-33 Jl 13 '64
about
Advantage Talbert. Sports Illus 18:10 My 6 '63

TALBERT, William F.
One-two punch for the prettiest. Sports Illus 18:48-53 Ap 15 '63

TALBOT, Phillips
Some reflections on the United States in the United Nations; address, October 23, 1964. Dept State Bul 51:700-5 N 16 '64
United States in the United Nations; address, October 23, 1964. Vital Speeches 31:71-4 N 15 '64

TALBOT family
Talbot coat-of-arms. H. K. Eilers. il Hobbies 69:120-1+ Mr '64

TALENT
See also
Genius

TALENT agents. See Theatrical agencies

TALENT for delight; story. See Boles, P. D.

TALENTED children. See Children, Gifted

TALES of Hoffmann; opera. See Offenbach, J.

TALESE, Gay
Accommodation, Italian style. Esquire 59:88-93+ F '63
Aftermath Esquire 59:61-2+ Je '63
Arrivederci, Romy. Esquire 60:112-13 N '63
Bridge. Esquire 62:136-44+ D '64
Looking for Hemingway. Esquire 60:44-7+ Jl '63
Loser. Esquire 61:65-8+ Mr '64
Lost little rich girl. Sat Eve Post 236:40-2 Ag 10 '63
One year later, still no bomb. Esquire 59:76-7 My '63
O'Toole on the Ould Sod. Esquire 60:76-8+ Ag '63
Overreachers. Esquire 60:152-7 D '63
Social climbing on the slopes. Sat Eve Post 236:30+ F 9 '63
Soft psyche of Joshua Logan. Esquire 59: 82-5+ Ap '63
White man in Harlem. Esquire 62:123 S '64

TALISMAN against insomnia; story. See Stewart, N.

TALISMAN; story. See Yamakawa, M.

TALISMANS. See Charms

TALK. See Children—Language; Conversation

TALKING books
Books for the blind; tape recording. il Newsweek 62:71 S 2 '63
It's like this, cat, to appear soon in braille and talking-book editions. il Library J 89: 1839-40 Ap 15 '64
See also
Libraries—Work with blind
Recording for the blind, incorporated

TALKING litter baskets. See Refuse receptacles

TALL, Robert E.
FCC report. See issues of Popular electronics to December 1963

TALL girls. See Stature

TALL men. See Stature

TALL stranger; drama. See Dias, E. J.

TALLER, Herman
Federal jury indicts four over Calories don't count. Pub W 185:30 Mr 23 '64

TALLET, Jorge, and Fenyvesi, C. T.
Next step in Cuba. Nat R 16:397-8 My 19 '64

TALLMAN, Frank
Pilot report; Boeing P-12. por Flying 75:54-6+ Ag '64
Pilot report illustrated; Fokker E III. pors Flying 74:36-9+ My '64
Pilot report: S.E.5. por Flying 74:34-5+ Ja '64
Mad, mad world of the stunt flier. R. Vaughan. il pors Sat Eve Post 236:26-7 My 18 '63

TALLMANTZ, incorporated
Tallmantz on-stage. R. Bach. il Flying 74: 39+ Ja '64

TALLROTH, Tore
Consul-general. New Yorker 39:23-4 F 1 '64

TALMADGE, Herman
Excerpts from statements, July 31 and November 20, 1963. Cong Digest 43:83+ Mr '64

TALMAGE, David W. See Claman, H. N. jt. auth.

TALMEY, Allene
Art is the core. Vogue 144:116-23+ Jl '64
Cornucopia life of the Whitneys; Mr and Mrs J. H. Whitney, and their New York house. Vogue 145:140-5+ F 1 '65
Leningrad notes. Vogue 144:154+ D '64
$266,900,000: private give-away, done by three men. Vogue 141:102-3 Je '63

TALOUMIS, George
Before you leave on vacation. Pop Gard 14:65+ Jl '63
Bottlebrush buckeye. Pop Gard 15:11-12 N '64
Hanging baskets for summer color. Horticulture 41:372-3 Jl '63
Italy. Horticulture 43:36-7 Ja '65
Planting ideas that make for easy upkeep. Pop Gard 14:44-5+ Mr '63
Pots. Horticulture 42:20-1 Mr '64
Pots for plants. il Flower Grower 50:32-5 Jl '63
Stylish streets wear flowering trees. Flower Grower 50:55-7 My '63
There's a place in every garden for yews. Pop Gard 14:22-3+ S '63
Window boxes on Boston's Beacon Hill. il Pop Gard 14:42-4+ My '63

TALWANI, Manik. See Thompson, G. A. jt. auth.

TAM, Nguyen tuong. See Nguyen tuong Tam

TAMAGNO, Francesco
Made to be Otello. V. Sheean. il pors Opera N 28:26-8 F 15 '64

TAMARIND lithography workshop, Los Angeles
Because water hates grease. il Time 83:82-3+ Ap 10 '64

TAMAYO, Rufino
Gallery for young people; Fruit vendors. C. B. Johnson. il Sch Arts 63:40 Je '64
Tamayo: Mexican par excellence. R. Squirru. il Américas 15:23-9 O '63

TAMBLYN, R. T.
Bootstrap heating works in chilly Toronto. Arch Rec 133:184-6 Je '63

TAMBOURINES to glory; drama. See Hughes, L.

TAMES, George
Capital brotherhood. il N Y Times Mag p96 My 5 '63

TAMIAMI trail. See Roads—Florida

TAMING of the shrew; drama. See Shakespeare, W.—Plays

TAMM, Igor
With the cold season upon us, the mystery of the virus; interview. por U S News 57:78-80 O 19 '64

—and Eggers, H. J.
Specific inhibition of replication of animal viruses. bibliog Science 142:24-33; 143:196 O 4 '63, Ja 17 '64
—See Gomatos, P. J. jt. auth.

TAMMANY Hall
New face at Tammany. Newsweek 64:27 D 14 '64
Plain words from truthful George: excerpts from Plunkitt of Tammany Hall. il Am Heritage 14:98-9 Je '63

TAMPA, Fla.
Sabotage in Tampa; strike against the General telephone co. of Florida. il Time 82:65-6 Ag 16 '63

TAMURA, Miwako. See Marler, P. jt. auth.

TAN
Be bright about sunlight. L. D. Kirk. il Parents Mag 38:92 Jl '63
Beware-too much sun. il Good H 157:62-3+ Jl '63
How to protect your skin from the sun. C. Schwalberg. Redbook 121:12 Jl '63
Mlle plots the perfect tan. il Mlle 59:40-1 Jl '64
Suntan; suntan or sunban? a dermatologist talks on the safe and savvy way of handling the sun. Vogue 143:159 My '64
Your skin and the sun. L. D. Kirk. il Parents Mag 39:104-5 Je '64

TANAKA, Tokutaro
White egrets of Sagiyama. il Audubon Mag 65:298-305 S '63

TANCREDI
Tancredi. 1927-1964. M. Gendel. Art N 63:35-6 Ja '65

TANDEM bicycle. See Bicycles

TANEY, Roger Brooke
Black pawn on a field of peril. B. Catton. il por Am Heritage 15:69-71+ D '63

TANG, Peter S. H.
Sino-Soviet tensions; excerpts from Sino-Soviet relations: retrospect and prospect. bibliog f Cur Hist 45:223-9 O '63

T'ANG painting. See Painting, Chinese

TANGANYIKA
Brigadier tells about the fight; interview, ed. by W. Smith. P. Sholto-Douglas. il Life 56:44D F 7 '64
But which is the tail? Tanganyika. Newsweek 63:40 My 4 '64
Colored rulers. G. C. Turner. Negro Hist Bul 26:249 My '63
Festival time. E. A. Hawley. Christian Cent 81:1182-3 S 23 '64
Tanganyika: African new frontier. M. Gellhorn. Atlan 212:40-5 S '63
Tanganyika; Peace corps volunteer. R. E. Dygert. il Nat Geog 126:320-3 S '64
Who is safe? il Time 83:30-4+ Mr 13 '64
See also
East African Federation (proposed)
English in Tanganyika
Hunting—Tanganyika
National parks and reserves—Tanganyika
Tanzania
Zoology—Tanganyika

Economic conditions

Tanganyika's two years of independence. L. Cliffe. bibliog f il Cur Hist 46:136-41+ Mr '64

Foreign relations

President Nyerere of Tanganyika visits Washington; joint communique, July 16, 1963; with announcement of new Peace corps agreement. M. J. K. Nyerere and J. F. Kennedy. Dept State Bul 49:198-9 Ag 5 '63

Politics and government

Reporter at large; changeover. E. Hahn. il New Yorker 39:110+ Ap 27 '63
Tanganyika: the tribulations of a good man. C. Sterling. il Reporter 30:21-5 Ap 9 '64
Tanganyika's two years of independence. L. Cliffe. bibliog f il Cur Hist 46:136-41+ Mr '64

Race problems

Reporter at large; changeover. E. Hahn. il New Yorker 39:110+ Ap 27 '63

TANGANYIKA AND ZANZIBAR, United Republic of. See Tanzania

TANGIER

Banks

See Banks and banking—Morocco

TANGIER, Morocco
Last resort. il Newsweek 62:68 Ag 26 '63
Tangier: footnotes to a survey of the American socio-intellectual enclave; colored photographs by R. Fréson. W. Burroughs. il Esquire 62:114-19 S '64

TANGLEWOOD music festival. See Berkshire symphonic festival

TANGO (dance) See Dancing, Argentine

TANK airplanes
Air guard tankers to use surplus J47s. E. J. Bulban. il Aviation W 81:42-3 D 28 '64

TANK ships
Queen with the weak back; mystery of the Marine Sulphur Queen. Time 81:27-8 Mr 8 '63
Second try for a giant ship; SS Manhattan. il Bsns W p 160+ Ap 13 '63

TANK trucks
Gas stations cut the guesswork; electronic metering systems. il Bsns W p 116+ Ja 16 '65

TANKAS
Sea gypsies of China; Shui-jen, or Egg people. W. Menard. il Natur Hist 74:12-21 Ja '65

TANKERS. See Tank ships

TANKS
See also
Oil tanks
Water tanks

TANKS, Military
Tank battle: which is best? il U S News 55:16 Ag 26 '63

TANNENBAUM, Abraham J.
Brilliant student can be popular, if... PTA Mag 57:4-6 Je '63

TANNENBAUM, Frank
Columbia's unorthodox seminars. P. Goodman. Harper 228:72-5+ Ja '64

TANNENBAUM, Percy H.
Communication of science information. bibliog Science 140:579-83 My 10 '63

TANNENBAUM, Sheldon
My daughter on Good Friday; poem. Yale R 52:417 Mr '63

TANNER, Edward Everett, 3d
Joyous season; novel; condensation. Ladies Home J 82:44-5 Ja '65
What's in a name or two? H. Frankel. il Sat R 47:24-5 Ag 1 '64

TANNER, Henry
Communists in gray flannel suits. N Y Times Mag p 11+ Ag 2 '64
How to survive in the Kremlin. N Y Times Mag p26+ N 15 '64

TANNER, Ogden
Swiss build a thinking man's fair. il Arch Forum 121:92-9 Jl '64

TANNER, Virginia
Roots and wings; excerpts from address, June 2, 1963. por Dance Mag 37:16-17 N '63

TANNHÄUSER; opera. See Wagner, R.

TANNY, Vic
Tanny tumble. il Newsweek 62:60 D 23 '63

TANSEY, Anne
It was that kind of night; poem. Cath World 197:222 Jl '63
TANTALUM film. See Films, Metallic
TANTRUMS. See Temper
TANZANIA
Festival time. E. A. Hawley. Christian Cent 81:1182-3 S 23 '64; Reply. L. K. Painter. 81:1468 N 25 '64
Road to union is paved with good intentions. il Time 85:35 Ja 1 '65
Setback for communism in an African merger? Tanganyika and Zanzibar. il U S News 56:10 My 4 '64
Surprise merger; Tanganyika and Zanzibar. Sr Schol 84:23 My 8 '64
Tangibar; United Republic of Tanganyika and Zanzibar. il Time 83:30 My 1 '64
We are happy! United Republic of Zanzibar and Tanganyika. Newsweek 63:48 My 11 '64
TANZER, Marvin L. and Hunt, R. D.
Osteoclasts: organization in chick embryo bone. bibliog Science 141:1270-2 S 27 '63
TAO, Tien-wen
Phytohemagglutinin elicitation of specific anamnestic immune response in vitro. bibliog Science 146:247-8 O 9 '64
TAP dancers. See Dancers
TAP dancing
Big noise is jazz-tap. W. Como. il Dance Mag 37:20-1 N '63
Future for a tap company. P. Draper. Dance Mag 37:56-7 My '63
Ground hog; exhibition at the Village gate. New Yorker 40:47-9 D 12 '64
June Taylor dancers open with tap. il Dance Mag 37:42-3 Je '63
Tap series. P. Draper. See issues of Dance magazine to September 1963
Wonderful old-time hoofers at Newport. L. Jay. Dance Mag 37:18-19 Ag '63
TAPA cloth
Designing bark cloth. J. H. Wilding. il Sch Arts 64:39 S '64
TAPE
Household tapes: a guide to their use. il Good H 156:155 F '63
New tapes for old jobs; self-stick tapes. il House B 106:131+ F '64
Tackle it better with tape. G. Daniels. il Pop Sci 185:112-16+ Ag '64
See also
Adhesive tape
TAPE, Adhesive. See Adhesive tape
TAPE, Magnetic. See Magnetic tape
TAPE controlled machine tools. See Machine tools—Control
TAPE recorders and recording. See Magnetic recorders and recording
TAPE recordings
All wound up in tape. S. D. Smith. il N Y Times Mag p54+ Ap 12 '64
Anarchy and order; Dockstader's Eight electronic pieces. O. Daniel. Sat R 46:73 O 26 '63
File those sounds. A. Zuckerman. il Pop Phot 55:82+ O '64
High fidelity newsfronts. N. Eisenberg. il Hi Fi 13:35 Ag '63
Is tape really better than records? J. Wesson. U S Camera 27:24 S '64
Make sound-money. H. V. Fondiller. Pop Phot 55:81 O '64
New this month on tape. R. Freed. Sat R 46:63+ Ap 27 '63
Opera on tape, a midsummer bonanza. R. D. Darrell. il Hi Fi 14:108 Ag '64
Oral history project, Princeton university; Oral history collection, Columbia university. Wilson Lib Bul 38:716 My '64
Playback puppetry; pre-recorded puppet shows. E. Welch. il Design 65:15 S '63
Portraits in sound; audiobiographies. T. Schwartz. Pop Phot 54:30+ My '64
Pre-recorded tape at 3¾ ips. I. Kolodin. Sat R 47:47 D 26 '64
Pre-taped live show. H. Keppler. il Mod Phot 29:92+ Ja '65
Records and tapes. J. Muri. Sr Schol 85:8T-9T O 28; 10T N 4 '64
Records and tapes. R. Hemming. Sr Schol 82: 10T Ap 17; 11T My 8 '63
Reels, wheels, and economics. I. Berger. Sat R 47:73 My 30 '64
Sounds of history; recorded voices of 8,000 celebrities in National voice library. W. B. Furlong. il N Y Times Mag p72+ Mr 22 '64
Tape (cont) Mus Am 83:131 Ja; 40 F; 20-1 Ag; 50-1 S '63; 84:50 N '64
Tape deck. R. D. Darrell. See issues of High fidelity
Tape the unheard. H. V. Fondiller. Pop Phot 55:83 O '64
Tapes from the professionals; prerecorded tapes. R. D. Darrell. il Hi Fi 13:48-50 Ag '63
Tibbett on tape. F. Merkling il Opera N 28:6 D 21 '63
See also
Libraries—Tape recordings

Stereophonic recordings

Confessions of an illicit tape recordist. P. Moor. il Hi Fi 13:38-40+ Ag '63
Especially for Christmas. P. C. Pfunke and others. Am Rec G 30:352-4 D '63
Stereotape reviews. P. C. Pfunke and others. See issues of American record guide

Stereophonic records

Stereotape reviews. P. C. Pfunke and others. See issues of American record guide
TAPE recordings for the blind. See Talking books
TAPER, Bernard
Balanchine a biography; excerpts. Dance Mag 38:18-21+ F; 14-16+ Mr; 20-1+ Ap; 14-17+ My 18-19+ Je '64
Balanchine's return to Russia; excerpts from Balanchine. Harper 227:47-50+ N '63
Genius of Balanchine; excerpt from Balanchine. Theatre Arts 47:10-13+ N '63
Mark Twain's San Francisco. Am Heritage 14:50-3+ Ag '63
TAPESTRY
Art from the looms of Aubusson. J. D. Ratcliff. il Read Digest 82:208-12 F '63
Focus on tapestry. G. O'Brien. il N Y Times Mag p56-7 D 15 '63
Million dollars in woven beauty; Philadelphia museum unveils its rare tapestry collection. il Life 57:128-30 O 9 '64
New tapestry; with statements by new American weavers. R. Slivka. il Craft Horiz 23: 10-19 Mr '63
Nine tapestries on man in the atomic age; Le chant du monde (song of the world) by Lurçat. il UNESCO Courier 17:18-19 N '64
Peruvian tapestry warp. P. Hill. il Craft Horiz 23:22-6+ Jl '63
Regal hangings in a Quaker temple; Barberini tapestries by Rubens and P. da Cortona at Philadelphia museum. il Art N 63:26-8 O '64
TAPESTRY weaving
Peruvian tapestry warp. P. Hill. il Craft Horiz 23:22-6+ Jl '63
Weavers work with art and patience. il Life 57:133-4 O 9 '64
TAPEWORMS
See also
Cestoda
TAPP, Jack T. and Markowitz, Hal
Infant handling; effects on avoidance learning, brain weight, and cholinesterase activity. bibliog Science 140:486-7 My 3 '63
TAPPEL, A. L. See Shimazu, F. jt. auth.
TAPPER, Daniel N.
Cutaneous slowly adapting mechanoreceptors in the cat. bibliog Science 143:53-4; 144:891 Ja 3, My 15 '64
TAPPLY, H. G.
Sportsman's notebook. See issues of Field & stream
TAR pits, Los Angeles. See La Brea, Los Angeles
TAR sand. See Bituminous sand
TARANTA, Angelo. See Ovary, Z. jt. auth.
TARANTULAS
Nature note. Sci N L 87:45 Ja 16 '65
Tarantula! Sci N L 86:118 Ag 22 '64
TARASOV, Vladislaw S.
What a Russian found when he fled to U.S. U S News 55:11 S 30 '63
TARAXEIN. See Blood—Proteins
TARDINESS
Better never than late. J. K. Lagemann. House & Gard 125:110-11 F '64
What's so smart about being late? D. Wharton. Read Digest 82:171-4 Ap '63
TARGET simulators. See Simulators
TARGETS
New two-eyed target sharpens your aim. D. Shiner. il Pop Sci 182:96-7 Je '63
Why targets dodge. W. Page. il Field & S 68:54-8 Ja '64
TARICHATOXIN. See Toxins and antitoxins
TARIFF
Breakthrough; GATT negotiations on variable tariff cuts. Newsweek 63:68+ Mr 9 '64
Climate of world trade and U.S.-Canadian trade relations; address, September 15, 1963. G. G. Johnson. Dept State Bul 49:543-8 O 7 '63
De Gaulle curbs US trade talks with Europe. B. Sinclair. New Repub 150:12-14 Mr 7 '64

TARIFF—*Continued*
Europe, too, can have a farm problem; Kennedy Round of transatlantic tariff cuts. il Sr Schol 85:10-13 Ja 7 '65
First round of the Kennedy round. il Newsweek 63:78-82 My 11 '64
Industry role in trade negotiations; address, November 24, 1964. W. M. Roth. Dept State Bul 51:853-5 D 14 '64
Kennedy-round talks get down to business. Bsns W p30 N 21 '64
More tariff cuts coming. H. S. Piquet. Nations Bsns 52:110+ O '64
Question of exceptions; Kennedy round of tariff-cutting talks. Time 84:66 N 20 '64
Rising sales overseas. Nations Bsns 52:40-1+ F '64
Round and round; opening of the Kennedy round in Geneva. Newsweek 63:91 My 18 '64
Smoothing a rough road; Kennedy round trade talks in Geneva. Newsweek 64:82-3 N 30 '64
Stickler; negotiations on cutting of tariffs on agricultural products traded between U.S. and Common market. Newsweek 63: 79-80 Mr 16 '64
Toward the Kennedy round; plan to lower world tariffs. Time 83:95 Mr 6 '64
Tribute to perseverance; serious beginning of the Kennedy Round. Time 84:100 N 27 '64
World trade haggle; Kennedy round of world-trade talks. New Repub 151:6-7 N 28 '64
See also
General agreement on tariffs and trade

Belgium

Barriers within. Time 81:87 F 22 '63

Europe, Western

Barriers within. Time 81:87 F 22 '63
End of the chicken war. Time 82:98 N 29 '63
Gentlemen's agreement; chicken-tariff issue between US and EEC. Newsweek 62:79 O 28 '63
Playing chicken; agreement between the United States and the European economic community. New Repub 149:5 D 21 '63
Turnabout; European coal and steel community raises tariffs. Newsweek 62:75 D 16 '63
U.S. and EEC hold talks on poultry import fees; statement, May 31, 1963, and announcement, June 7, 1963. C. A. Herter. Dept State Bul 48:996-7 Je 24 '63
Yankee birds can't go to Common market. il Life 55:24-5 Ag 23 '63
See also
European economic community

Great Britain

Back to mercantilism; imposition of surcharge on imports. H. Hazlitt. Newsweek 64:84 N 9 '64
Books exempted from U.K. fifteen per cent import surcharge; with editorial comment. Pub W 186:31, 37 N 23 '64
Books' position unclear in U.K. 15 per cent tariff hike. Pub W 186:44 N 9 '64
Britain at bay; fifteen-per-cent surcharge on imports. America 111:591 N 14 '64
Britain in EFTA's doghouse. il Bsns W p31 N 28 '64
Exporters size up British surcharge. il Bsns W p 148 N 7 '64
Wilson swings the ax; remedies for balance-of-payments crisis; with editorial comment. il Bsns W p24-5, 168 O 31 '64

Spain

President proclaims protocol for Spain's accession to GATT; proclamation, September 6, 1963. J. F. Kennedy. Dept State Bul 49: 550-1 O 7 '63

United States

Appendix to U.S. tariff schedules on agricultural imports corrected; proclamation. L. B. Johnson. Dept State Bul 51:122 Jl 27 '64
Big business: is it too big? reprint. H. H. Humphrey. il Look 28:84-6 O 20 '64
Chicken war. America 109:380-1 O 5 '63
Coming to terms with the Common market; Trade expansion act. P. Forbath. il Reporter 28:24+ Je 20 '63
Feathering; retaliatory tariffs. il Newsweek 62:61-2 Ag 19 '63
First round of the Kennedy round. il Newsweek 63:78-82 My 11 '64
Foreign economic policy; address, January 7, 1963. T. B. Curtis. Vital Speeches 29:260-3 F 15 '63
Government pattern: can we breach EEC's wall? Bsns W p93-4 Je 15 '63
Kennedy round, progress and promise; address, July 17, 1963. W. T. Gossett. Dept State Bul 49:291-6 Ag 19 '63
Playing chicken; agreement between the United States and the European economic community. New Repub 149:5 D 21 '63
President amends regulations on imports of blue-mold cheese; proclamation, November 26, 1963. L. B. Johnson. Dept State Bul 49:970-1 D 23 '63
President concurs in findings on three escape-clause actions; duties on cotton typewriter-ribbon cloth, lead and zinc, and dried figs. Dept State Bul 48:145 Ja 28 '63
President sets up administration of Trade expansion act; executive order. J. F. Kennedy. Dept State Bul 48:180-2 F 4 '63
Readjusting United States foreign trade; address, April 5, 1963. L. Weiss. Dept State Bul 48:652-60 Ap 29 '63
Revised tariff schedules to be effective August 31, 1963. Dept State Bul 49:329 Ag 26 '63
Ruffled feathers; retaliatory tariffs against the Common market chicken-tariff hike. Time 82:70 Ag 16 '63
Streamlining the U.S. tariff system. Bsns W p42-4 Ja 19 '63
Tariff men do their homework. il Bsns W p49+ Mr 21 '64
Trade barriers; publishers ask tariff reduction, manufacturers seek retention. il Pub W 185:27-31 Mr 2 '64
U.S. raises duty on four articles imported from EEC countries; proclamation, December 4, 1963. L. B. Johnson. Dept State Bul 49:969-70 D 23 '63
United States tariff schedules made effective by President; proclamation, August 21, 1963. J. F. Kennedy. Dept State Bul 49: 478 S 23 '63
Ups and downs of tariffs. Sr Schol 83:10-11 S 27 '63
What the chicken war means. Farm J 87:110 S '63
See also
Duty free importation
United States—Commercial treaties and agreements

TARIFF, Exemption from. See Duty free importation
TARIFF commission. See United States—Tariff commission
TARKINGTON, Booth
Monsieur Beaucaire; dramatization. See Olfson, L.
TARLOFF, Frank
Heroine. Criticism
New Yorker 39:93 Mr 2 '63
Sat R 46:24 Mr 9 '63
TARO (game) See Tarot (game)
TAROM Romanian air transport. See Airlines—Rumania
TAROT (game)
Carmen and the tarots. W. Starkie. il Am Rec G 31:4-9 S '64
TARPAULINS
Eight ways to pitch a tarp; reprint. W. E. Stern. il Recreation 56:123 Mr '63
TARPON fishing
Angling's charmed circle; with editorial comment. L. Wulff. il Esquire 61:6, 96-7+ My '64
Fly rod tarpon. J. Brooks. il Field & S 67: 34-5 F '63
High-jump champs. G. Heinold. il Outdoor Life 132:10+ D '63
Mayhem in the mangroves. A. J. McClane. il Field & S 67:62-7 F '63
Southern pier fishing. G. Heinold. il Outdoor Life 135:14-15+ Ja '65
Tarpon are sissies. J. A. Knight. il Field & S 69:30-1+ Ja '65
Texas two-bit fishing. G. Getner. il Field & S 67:158-61+ Ap '63
Trail of the tarpon. D. M. Newell. il Field & S 68:56-7+ Mr '64
TARR, Cedric W. jr
Conventional weapons control. bibliog f Cur Hist 47:25-30 Jl '64
TARSCHYS, Rebecka
Aspen: International design conference. Craft Horiz 24:50 S '64
TARSIS, Valeriy
Soviet political satire. G. Struve. New Repub 149:19-22 S 28 '63
TART, Charles T. See Troffer, S. A. jt. auth.
TARTAR. See Calculi, Dental
TARTAS, Joseph
Auto voltmeter shows you'll go. Pop Electr 21:53-5+ D '64
Designing the I.F. circuit. Electr World 72: 46-9 S '64
6 meter 7 and 2 preamp. Pop Electr 21:53-4 Ag '64
Using hook-up wire. Electr World 72:36-8 D '64
Using slug-tuned coils. Electr World 71:48-50 Ap '64

TARTS
Holiday tart. il McCalls 91:124-5 F '64
On each Banbury tart is the Banbury cross. il Sunset 131:234 O '63
She's serving a fresh berry tart. il Sunset 130:238 My '63
Upside-down pie. C. Claiborne. il N Y Times Mag p87-8 Mr 22 '64
TARTU observatory. See Astronomical observatories—Estonia
TARTUFFE: drama. See Molière, J. B. P.
TARZAN (literary character) See Characters in literature
TARZWELL, Clarence M.
Pollution: it's deadlier than you think. G. Laycock. por Field & S 68:10-13 Ja '64
TASAKI, Ichiji, and Luxoro, Mario
Intracellular perfusion of Chilean giant squid axons. bibliog Science 145:1313-15 S 18 '64
TASCH, Paul
Identity of organized elements in carbonaceous chondrites; letter. bibliog Science 142:156+ O 11 '63
—and Shaffer, B. L.
Conchostracans: living and fossil from Chihuahua and Sonora, Mexico. bibliog Science 143:806-7 F 21 '64
—See Doumani, G. A. jt. auth.
TASHIAN, R. E. and others
Inherited variant of erythrocyte carbonic anhydrase in Micronesians from Guam and Saipan. bibliog Science 140:53-4 Ap 5 '63
TASHIRO, Kiyo
Is there a Dr Tashiro on the field? il pors Sports Illus 19:46-50 O 28 '63
TASHIRO, Shiro
Shiro Tashiro: American scientist. G. Eckstein. por Sat R 46:64-6 O 5 '63
TASHMAN, Nat
Whittled wooden jury rig prop brings boatman home safely. Motor B 113:372 Ja '64
TASS (news agency) See News agencies
TASTE
Duplexity theory of taste. G. Von Békésy. bibliog il Science 145:834-5 Ag 21 '64
Sour, salty foods make single taste in mouth. Sci N L 86:194 S 26 '64
Taste of sodium chloride solutions after adaptation to sodium chloride: implications for the water taste. L. M. Bartoshuk and others. bibliog Science 143:967-8 F 28 '64
Taste sense of children for sweetness tested. Sci N L 85:207 Mr 28 '64
Taste sensitivity to phenylthiourea in glaucoma. B. Becker and W. R. Morton. bibliog il Science 144:1347-8 Je 12 '64
TASTE, Musical. See Music—Appreciation
TASTEE-FREEZ corporation of America
Can franchises keep their flavor? Tastee Freez failure. Bsns W p62+ N 2 '63
TASTING party. See Entertaining
TATA, Jamsetji Nusserwanji
Remarkable house of Tata. J. E. Frazer. por Read Digest 82:248-52 Ap '63
TATE, Ernest C.
Bouqui and Malice, a folk tale of Haiti. Negro Hist Bul 26:176-7 F '63
TATE, James H. J.
Excerpt from statement, December 12, 1963. Cong Digest 43:246+ O '64

about

Democrats in a key city tell why they shifted votes. il U S News 55:56-7 N 25 '63
Philadelphia, Pennsylvania: a process of fragmentation. H. Lees. il Reporter 29:18-20 Jl 4 '63
TATE, Joan
(tr) See Edqvist, D. Bulango affair
TATE, William
Reporter at large. C. Trillin. New Yorker 39:59-67 Jl 13; 40+ Jl 20 '63
TATE gallery, London
Britain's liveliest museum. il Time 83:70-4 Ja 10 '64
Pictures and pounds. Newsweek 61:96 Mr 11 '63
TATUM, E. L. See Mach, B. jt. auth.
TAUB, Irwin A. See Holroyd, R. A. jt. auth.
TAUBE, Myron
Mess; story. Seventeen 23:156-7 S '64
TAUBER, Maurice F.
Documentation activities of associations. bibliog por Wilson Lib Bul 38:768-72 My '64
TAUBINGER, Laszlo M.
Doves and stoolpigeons. Nat R 16:1103-4 D 15 '64
TAUBMAN, Howard
Play's the thing, not the raiment. N Y Times Mag p22-3+ Ag 9 '64
TAVARD, George H.
Council, the press and theology; address. Cath World 199:337-44 S '64
Paul Tillich's system. Commonweal 79:566-8 F 7 '64
Scripture and tradition in pastoral perspective. Cath World 198:14-20 O '63
Theology in the Catholic college. Commonweal 78:273-5, 457 My 31, Jl 26 '63
TAVARES ESPAILLAT, Manuel
Then there were none. Time 84:29 Jl 10 '64
TAVES, Isabella
Cesarean births: how many are safe? Look 27:70-2+ Ag 27 '63
Commodore leaves the sea. Look 28:38-40+ Ap 21 '64
New advance in female fertility. Look 28:91-4 My 19 '64
Walter Cronkite: why won't he be himself on TV? Look 28:74+ Ag 25 '64
TAVISTOCK institute of human relations
British analysis goes deep; Tavistock institute study of automation. il Bsns W p 122+ O 26 '63
TAVOLGA, William N.
Psychophysics and hearing in fish. Natur Hist 73:34-41 Mr '64
TAWES, J. Millard
Maryland approves Assateague National Seashore. por Am For 69:6+ O '63
TAWNEY, R. H.
Echoes of an evolutionary. N. Fruchter. Nation 199:169-70 S 28 '64
TAX abatement. See Real property and taxation
TAX accountants. See Accountants
TAX agents. See Tax consultants
TAX billing. See Billing
TAX collection
Government files $1.2-million tax claim against Umbaugh aircraft. D. A. Brown. Aviation W 78:32 Ap 22 '63
Property index number; Cook County, Ill. A. J. Saloman. il Am City 79:139+ N '64
T-men join the Alliance; tax reform in Latin America. il Bsns W p68+ F 23 '63
See also
Tax returns
United States—Internal revenue service
Withholding tax
TAX consultants
Is taxpayers' revolt brewing? il U S News 54:37-9 Ap 8 '63
TAX deductions. See Income tax—Deductions
TAX delinquency. See Tax collection
TAX evasion
Baroness' income tax; using art to get dubious tax deductions. il Time 81:59 Mr 1 '63
Big bark bite; registrar of dogs for all Poland. Newsweek 61:36+ Ap 29 '63
Cold war and the income tax, by E. Wilson. Review
Nat R 16:71-4 Ja 28 '64. J. Dos Passos
Reporter 29:63-4 D 5 '63. G. Weales
Grand design; case of Leroy Joseph Deskin. Newsweek 61:23-4 F 18 '63
Nothing much to say. Newsweek 62:31 S 9 '63
Phantom tax swindlers. K. Wheeler. il Life 54:81-2+ Ap 12 '63
T-men join the Alliance: tax reform in Latin America. il Bsns W p68+ F 23 '63
Tax service's numbers game: it's not going so well. U S News 57:79-82 N 2 '64
$21 million mystery man. il Time 81:20 Mr 22 '63
TAX exempt securities. See Securities, Tax exempt
TAX exemption. See Taxation, Exemption from
TAX forms
Easier to file, harder to pay. il Bsns W p34 O 17 '64
Get going on your income tax. Changing T 19:16 Ja '65
Your income tax, all those forms and schedules. il Changing T 18:29-33 Ja '64
TAX planning
Year-end income tax tips. B. Brantley. Suc Farm 62:27+ D '64
TAX reduction. See Taxation—United States
TAX refunds
See also
Taxation—United States
TAX returns
Ahead, a tax return as simple as a check? with summary of plan approved by Senate finance committee. il U S News 55:75-6 D 30 '63
Are you wise about taxes? Bet Hom & Gard 42:92 Ja '64
Get going on your income tax. il Changing T 19:15-17 Ja '65
If you're worried about your tax number; requirement of social security numbers. il U S News 55:85-7 S 2 '63

TAX returns—*Continued*
Income-tax audit? the odds. U S News 57:78 Jl 13 '64
Income taxes: stick up for your rights! il Changing T 18:7-8 Ap '64
New tax detective: a gimlet-eyed machine. il Bsns W p96-7 F 8 '64
New tax form: what it's like; Tax returns: an easy plan. U S News 57:107-8 O 19 '64
Now you can estimate your '64 tax; official rates; with chart. U S News 56:124-5 F 24 '64
Personal business. Bsns W p65 Ja 4 '64
Phantom tax swindlers. K. Wheeler. il Life 54:81-2+ Ap 12 '63
Tax returns: changing patterns. U S News 56:98 Ja 27 '64
What happens to tax returns. U S News 56: 93-4 F 10 '64
What IRS will look for if they audit your tax return. F. Bailey, jr. Suc Farm 62:39 Ja '64
Your income tax, all those forms and schedules. il Changing T 18:29-33 Ja '64
Your income tax; questions and answers (cont) il Changing T 17:13-14 Ap '63
TAX write-off program. See Amortization deductions
TAXATION
If you think taxes in the U.S. are high; taxes lighter in six European countries, but heavier in Canada and Japan. il U S News 57:81-2 Ag 17 '64
Importing a tax from Europe; value added tax. Bsns W p 136+ Je 13 '64
See also
Poll tax
Tithes
also subhead Taxation under various subjects, e.g. Gifts—Taxation

Bulgaria

U.S. owners of Bulgarian property must file tax forms by June 15, 1963. Dept State Bul 48:905 Je 10 '63

Canada

Mr Gordon drops a shoe; U.S. investment in Canada. Fortune 69:56+ F '64

Great Britain

Britain gets a budget; tax cuts and higher spending. Bsns W p27 Ap 6 '63
Now Britain turns to a tax cut and big deficit. il U S News 54:109-10 Ap 15 '63

Italy

Embarrassing precedent; taxes the government had no right to collect. Newsweek 64:60 O 12 '64
Wild ones; annual tax game. il Newsweek 65: 40 Ja 11 '65

Latin America

T-men join the Alliance; tax reform in Latin America. il Bsns W p68+ F 23 '63

Monaco

Prince valiant. Time 81:25 My 31 '63

Nebraska

Churches feel tax squeeze. B. D. Kolasa. America 111:185-7 Ag 22 '64

Sweden

Progressive taxation. H. Hazlitt. Newsweek 61:88 My 13 '63

Underdeveloped areas

Will underdeveloped countries learn to tax? N. Kaldor. For Affairs 41:410-19 Ja '63

United States

After the tax cut. New Repub 150:3-4 F 15 '64
Ahead on the tax front: cuts and more cuts. il U S News 57:77-8 S 7 '64
Aid for small business. America 108:386 Mr 23 '63
Andrew Mellon on tax cuts. D. F. Swanson. il New Repub 148:22 Mr 23 '63
As a tax cut takes shape. U S News 55:80-1 Ag 12 '63
As tax-cut drive heats up; Kennedy vs. Republicans; excerpts from address, September 18, 1963; with reply by J. W. Byrnes, September 20, 1963. U S News 55:84-5 S 30 '63
At last you can see your tax cut; with charts. U S News 56:40-1 F 3 '64
Atlantic report; more flexible tax policy. Atlan 213:6+ Je '64
Authors league backs JFK, asking fairer tax treatment for writers. R. Stout. Pub W 183: 27-9 Mr 11 '63
Back of the urge for tax cuts. il U S News 54:37 Mr 18 '63
Back to fundamentals on taxes. Bsns W p 112 Je 22 '63
Backing for a tax cut, steel's Blough speaks out; summary of news conference. R. M. Blough. U S News 55:10 Ag 12 '63
Big break is almost here; tax reduction bill. il Bsns W p 104-6+ F 15 '64
Biggest tax cut ever? il Newsweek 62:19 Ag 26 '63
Boost from U.S. spending now, a drag later. il U S News 57:89-90 Jl 20 '64
Budget to include airways user tax plan. J. R. Ashlock. Aviation W 81:24 D 28 '64
Business and finance; state and local government levies. Newsweek 61:67 Ap 8 '63
Can the tax cut keep it perking? il Bsns W p23 F 29 '64
Case for tax reform. J. A. Pechman. Reporter 28:20-3 Je 6 '63
Chances for an early tax cut. U S News 55: 37-8 S 23 '63
Chances now of a tax cut. U S News 54:109-10+ My 6 '63
Choice: taxes or civil rights. Bsns W p30 S 28 '63
Clichés cost us our shirts; misuse of the term, federal funds. H. J. Taylor. Read Digest 84:165 Ja '64
Cold war and the income tax: a protest, by E. Wilson. Review
Sat R 47:60 Ja 11 '64. H. H. Ransom
Coming cut in excise taxes. Bsns W p204 N 21 '64
Congress moves, but stays in low gear. il Bsns W p21-2 D 7 '63
Congress vs. spenders. il Bsns W p25-6 F 23 '63
Congress votes tax cut. Sr Schol 84:15 F 28 '64
Cut-up tax cut. New Repub 148:3-4 Mr 2 '63
Cut your taxes even more. il Changing T 18: 17-20 Je '64
Dangers of tax cut as seen by Congress; with summary of message to Congress by J. F. Kennedy. il U S News 54:43-53 F 4 '63
Delay of tax cut puzzles the pros. J. N. Eller. America 109:344 S 28 '63
Dillon: a tax cut will help budget; excerpts from statement, September 1, 1963. D. Dillon. U S News 55:105 S 16 '63
Dillon: tax cuts or recession. il Newsweek 61:69 F 18 '63
Don't wait to cut the corporate tax. Bsns W p 116 Mr 30 '63
Down to fine print on the tax bill; Ways & means committee's version. il Bsns W p 191-2+ S 14 '63
Economic education of John F. Kennedy. M. J. Rossant. Reporter 28:22-5 F 14 '63; Discussion. 28:10+ Mr 14 '63
Effect of tax cut on business. il U S News 56:35-7 Mr 9 '64
Employment and taxes. Duns R 81:47 My '63
Fallacy behind the tax cut. J. Daniel. Read Digest 84:77-81 F '64
Fed chief supports a tax cut. Bsns W p26 D 14 '63
Federal, state, local economic developments: effect on schools and educational publishing; symposium at 1964 industry conference of the American textbook publishers institute; with editorial comment. il Pub W 185:14-24, 34 Ap 6 '64
First decisions on the new tax bill. U S News 54:105-6 Je 3 '63
First glimpse of a balanced budget. il Bsns W p 126+ My 16 '64
First things first in tax revision; Indian giving. Bsns W p 120 F 9 '63
Flat option. Newsweek 62:60 D 23 '63
For 1964: tax dates to remember. U S News 56:35 Ja 6 '64
For true tax reform. H. Hazlitt. Newsweek 61:89 Ap 15 '63
Ford formula cut '63 taxes, '64 spending; excerpts from address, July 8, 1963. H. Ford. U S News 55:16 Jl 22 '63
Gap between economist and politician. S. E. Harris. il N Y Times Mag p26+ Ap 14 '63
Government and the economy. il Sr Schol 84:14-15+ Mr 13 '64
Great Treasury raid, by P. M. Stern. Review
New Repub 150:22-3 Mr 14 '64. R. Randall
Reporter 30:56 Mr 12 '64. H. Robinson
Sat R 47:30-1 Ap 11 '64. H. S. Taylor
Growing echo in the states' vaults; with editorial comment. il Bsns W p 112+, 202 S 19 '64
Here's the tax bill. il Bsns W p23-5 Ja 26 '63
How good is the Kennedy style? Fortune 67: 91-2 Je '63

TAXATION—United States—*Continued*
How new law saves taxes for old folks. F. Bailey, jr. Suc Farm 62:72 My '64
How new tax plan affects investors. U S News 55:32-3 S 2 '63
How to cut taxes? cut the reforms. il Newsweek 61:23-4 Mr 11 '63
How to help the poor. H. Hazlitt. Newsweek 61:74 Mr 4 '63
How to rescue the tax cut. Life 54:4 Mr 1 '63
How to save the tax cut. il Fortune 67:79-80 Mr '63
How to solve the payments imbalance. il Newsweek 62:51 Ag 5 '63
How we choke incentive. H. Hazlitt. Newsweek 61:84 F 18 '63
If tax cut fails, what comes next? il U S News 56:35-8 My 11 '64
If taxes are cut; the chances of a boom. il U S News 54:32 F 11 '63
If there is a tax cut without reforms. il U S News 54:104-5 Mr 11 '63
In '64, a batch of new highs; with charts. Bsns W p 15-17 D 28 '63
In taxes: cuts but not much reform. il Bsns W p24-5 F 9 '63
In the end: will there really be a tax cut? il U S News 54:35-6 Mr 4 '63
Inflation is the cause. H. Hazlitt. Newsweek 62:71 Ag 12 '63
Instant tax cut. H. C. Wallich. Newsweek 65:82 Ja 25 '65
Is it time to write a whole new income tax law? R. A. Wormser. il U S News 54:60-4 Mr 18 '63
It won't be long now; tax cut bill. il Bsns W p27 F 8 '64
Jam in Congress: taxes and civil rights: dead for '63. U S News 55:74 N 18 '63
JFK's tax planners look to the open range. il U S News 54:64-6 Mr 25 '63
Just when you will get your tax cut; How tax changes affect you. il U S News 56:25-30 Mr 2 '64
Kennedy: cut taxes for our economic growth. il Bsns W p26-7 Mr 2 '63
Kennedy tax bill; Republican view; summary of statement. J. W. Byrnes. U S News 54:104 F 25 '63
Kennedy tells businessmen why a tax cut is needed now; remarks, September 10, 1963. J. F. Kennedy. il U S News 55:98-101 S 23 '63; Same with title Tax reduction. Vital Speeches 29:740-3 O 1 '63
Kennedy's committees. America 108:736 My 25 '63
Kennedy's formula for full employment. Bsns W p 110-13 Ja 26 '63
Kennedy's quarterback has his own ideas; Sen. R. Long. Bsns W p26 F 9 '63
Kennedy's tax may not be one to grow on. Life 54:4 F 8 '63
Lady of the House looks into taxes; with editorial comment. Bsns W p28-9, 180 My 23 '64
Let's back up and start over. Bsns W p 148 F 16 '63
Let's cut taxes again. Sat Eve Post 237:92 D 5 '64
Let's not lose the tax cut. Fortune 68:120 N '63
Long step toward a tax cut. il Time 82:15-17 Ag 23 '63
Look at the latest plan for tax cuts. il U S News 55:101 Ag 19 '63
Lower taxes, higher revenue; can LBJ do it? with summary of status in House and Senate finance committee. il U S News 56:84-5 Ja 20 '64
LBJ's pep pill for business; quick tax cuts in recessions; concerning State-of-the-Union message. il U S News 58:83-4 Ja 18 '65
Machines are more important than people (yes or no?) attitude test. P. M. Stern. il N Y Times Mag p33+ D 1 '63
Mobilizing business; with editorial comment. Bsns W p28-9, 148 My 4 '63
More delay for tax bill; deliberates. Bsns W p32 O 19 '63
More light on some of the President's tax reforms. il U S News 54:34-5 F 25 '63
More on the great tax myth. S. Alsop. Sat Eve Post 236:17 D 21 '63
More tax cuts coming. il Nations Bsns 52:38-41+ My '64
Need for a hot line. Fortune 68:119-20 N '63
New drive for tax cuts opens; even the hearings are under fire. Bsns W p34-6 Ap 20 '63
New tax bill and you. J. D. Bierman. Parents Mag 39:14+ Ap '64
New tax law; what it means to you. F. Bailey, jr. il Suc Farm 62:41+ My '64
New tax plan for investors. il U S News 54:106-9 Je 10 '63
Next, a floor fight; tax bill. il Newsweek 62:28-9 S 23 '63
Next tax bill can be even better. Fortune 69:105-6 Ap '64
Next turn in taxes. E. K. Faltermayer. il Fortune 70:104-7+ D '64
No help to the dollar. H. Hazlitt. Newsweek 62:62 Ag 5 '63
Of druthers & deficits. Time 82:15-16 S 27 '63
On cutting taxes. America 108:328 Mr 9 '63
Out of one pocket, and into another; federal tax reduction bill. il Bsns W p58-60 F 29 '64
Personal business. Bsns W p 113-14 Ja 16 '65
Personal business; new tax bill. Bsns W p 113-14 F 22; 113-14 F 29 '64
Phony tax cut. H. Hazlitt. Newsweek 63:81 F 24 '64
Plug for value added tax. Bsns W p28 Jl 25 '64
Power of free choice; address, December 3, 1963. C. G. Mortimer. Vital Speeches 30:214-16 Ja 15 '64
Preparing retreat on 5 per cent clause. il Bsns W p25 F 16 '63
President reaffirms high space priority. Aviation W 78:28 Ja 21 '63
Price is wrong; hearings of House ways and means committee. Time 81:17 Mr 29 '63
Prosperity insurance; address, September 18, 1963. J. F. Kennedy. Vital Speeches 29:738-40 O 1 '63
Pulling the rug from stock options. Bsns W p 104+ Ja 11 '64
Rail-pension tax: headed higher. U S News 55:122 O 7 '63
Real case for a tax cut. M. Ways. Read Digest 82:105-10 Mr '63
Reforms in the tax bill. America 110:334 Mr 14 '64
Report on taxes. K. Crawford. Newsweek 61:37 Mr 25 '63
Restraint on wage raises; Jacobsson's advice. Bsns W p 160 Mr 9 '63
Rich man's bill? il Newsweek 62:74+ O 28 '63
Running tide. il Fortune 68:49-50 D '63
Russell Long's tax plan. P. M. Stern. New Repub 149:8-9 N 16 '63
Senate rejects help for taxpayers on college costs. Pub W 185:51 F 17 '64
Senators propose instant tax relief; Senate finance committee. Bsns W p25 Ja 25 '64
$7,000 dividends tax-free: how? U S News 55:104 S 16 '63
Sham tax cut. H. Hazlitt. Newsweek 62:70 S 2 '63
Shape of the cut; House ways and means version of the bill. Time 82:27 S 20 '63
Share-the-revenue plan; domestic economic policy. R. L. Heilbroner. il N Y Times Mag p8+ D 27 '64
Shelve it! Nation 196:217 Mr 16 '63
Shortsighted tariff. H. Hazlitt. Newsweek 62:84 O 28 '63
Shortsighted taxes. H. Hazlitt. Newsweek 61:72 Je 3 '63
Should we tax incomes less? tax sales or manufacturing more; with editorial comment. il Bsns W p 150+ Je 20 '64
Slow, quiet murder of tax reform; excerpts from Great Treasury raid. P. M. Stern. Harper 227:63-8 D '63; Reply with rejoinder. H. F. Byrd. 228:8+ Ap '64
Some deductions. D. T. Bazelon. Commentary 38:67-8 Ag '64
Sooner than you think; speed tax bill. Bsns W p28+ F 1 '64
Spending habits are hard to break; with editorial comment. il Bsns W p27-8, 168 Je 6 '64
Spending into trouble; with editorial comment. D. D. Eisenhower. Sat Eve Post 236:15-19, 82 My 18 '63; Same abr. with title We are spending ourselves into trouble; without editorial comment. Read Digest 83:60-8 Jl '63
Stanley Surrey: architect of tax reforms. U S News 54:21 Mr 18 '63
State of the Union; address, January 14, 1963. J. F. Kennedy. Vital Speeches 29:226-30 F 1 '63; Same. Cur Hist 44:174-6+ Mr '63; Summary. il Sr Schol 82:15-17 Ja 30 '63
Stately pace for tax bill. Bsns W p26 My 25 '63
Still time in 1963 for a tax cut? il U S News 55:41-2 O 7 '63
Stop lights; huge loopholes. New Repub 150:2 Ja 11 '64
Students and taxes. America 110:838 Je 20 '64
Tax bill: not so bad for investors after all. U S News 54:105-6 Je 24 '63
Tax bill snarled. America 109:552 N 9 '63
Tax changes; what they mean to you. il U S News 55:34-7 S 30 '63

TAXATION—United States—*Continued*
Tax credits for education. V. C. Blum. il America 110:669-72 My 16 '64; Reply. J. F. Morse. 110:855 Je 27 '64; Rejoinder. 111:97 Ag 1 '64
Tax cut before tax reform? pro and con discussion. Sr Schol 82:10-11 Mr 27 '63
Tax cut comes closer; Ways & means approval of new rate scale, with editorial comment. il Bsns W p23-4, 124 Ag 17 '63
Tax cut comes first; concerning Kennedy's State of the Union and budget messages; business reaction. il Bsns W p23-6 Ja 19 '63
Tax cut: easy does it. Bsns W p28 Je 1 '63
Tax cut every year? T. G. Harris. Look 28:70+ O 20 '64
Tax cut experiment. Commonweal 77:479 F 1 '63
Tax cut harvest; what we can expect from the new bill. J. Tobin. New Repub 150:14-17 Mr 7 '64
Tax cut in '63? New Repub 149:5 O 26 '63; Reply. E. Seligman. 149:31 N 16 '63
Tax cut in wonderland. H. Hazlitt. Newsweek 62:90 N 4 '63
Tax cut: key to '64 growth. M. Nadler. il Nations Bsns 51:31-3+ O '63
Tax cut need not bring on boom and bust. Life 56:4 F 7 '64
Tax-cut plan: progress report. il U S News 54:75 Je 17 '63
Tax-cut proposal. H. Hazlitt. Newsweek 63:72 Ja 20 '64
Tax cut; Puritans vs. the New frontier. il Newsweek 61:67 F 11 '63
Tax cut, reforms, recession; Kennedy's latest views; questions and answers. J. F. Kennedy. il U S News 54:86-8 Mr 11 '63
Tax cut regardless? H. Hazlitt. Newsweek 62:52 D 30 '63
Tax cut that is in trouble. U S News 54:92+ F 18 '63
Tax cut; the sound and the fury. Sr Schol 82:15-16 Mr 20 '63
Tax cut: the triumph of an idea. il Bsns W p 180+ Ap 11 '64
Tax dilemma. D. Lawrence. U S News 54:104 F 18 '63
Tax less spend more? that's what Myrdal advises; summary of address, December 3, 1963. G. Myrdal. U S News 55:26 D 16 '63
Tax plan: business gives it a sour reception; Kennedy's tax cut proposals. il Bsns W p26-7 F 2 '63
Tax plan: deficit worries Congress; Kennedy's tax cut proposals. il Bsns W p25-6 F 2 '63
Tax plan from business leaders. U S News 54:106 Ap 29 '63
Tax plan: Wall Street is wary. il Bsns W p64-5 F 2 '63
Tax plan: where it will bite. il Bsns W p76-8 F 2 '63
Tax program in perspective; address, February 28, 1963. S. S. Surrey. Vital Speeches 29:354-60 Ap 1 '63
Tax rebate; tax cut vs. reform. Time 81:23 Mr 8 '63
Tax reduction; address, May 20, 1963. W. W. Heller. Vital Speeches 29:561-4 Jl 1 '63
Tax reduction and balanced budget; address, October 8, 1963. D. Dillon. Vital Speeches 30:44-7 N 1 '63
Tax-reduction bill; address. L. B. Johnson. Vital Speeches 30:322-3 Mr 15 '64
Tax reduction comes through at last. Bsns W p 132 F 22 '64
Tax revision. New Repub 148:6 Je 29 '63
Tax trimmers. R. Lekachman. Commentary 35:289-95 Ap '63
Tax triumph; Internal revenue act of 1964. L. T. King. Commonweal 80:111-13 Ap 17 '64
Taxes: a cut for '63, but no reform? il Newsweek 61:67 My 6 '63
Taxes and confusion; concerning House ways and means committee and new tax bill. Nat R 15:265+ O 8 '63
Taxes and consumer spending. Duns R 84:39 O '64
Taxes and prosperity; address, July 8, 1963. H. Ford. Vital Speeches 29:717-19 S 15 '63; Excerpts. U S News 55:16 Jl 22 '63
Taxes & spending. il Nations Bsns 51:32-41+ Ap '63
Taxes: the big date is March 13. il Newsweek 63:61 Mr 2 '64
Taxes: the Kennedy cuts. il Newsweek 61:67-70 F 4 '63
Taxes: the long view. H. Hazlitt. Newsweek 62:59 Jl 1 '63; Same abr. with title Progression: toward what? Read Digest 83:205+ S '63
Taxes; to cut or not to cut. il Sr Schol 82:5-7 Ja 30 '63
Taxing times. Reporter 28:16+ Mr 14 '63
That damned tax bill. Nat R 16:221-2 Mr 24 '64
That 1954 tax cut. R. Moley. Newsweek 61:108 Mr 18 '63
These groups do something about high taxes! A. R. Roalman. Suc Farm 62:32 Mr '64
$32-billion more to spend; with editorial comment. il Bsns W p23-5, 124 Mr 7 '64
This month's feature: President's tax revision program. il Cong Digest 42:99-107+ Ap '63
Tightening tax laws on stock options. Bsns W p74 Mr 2 '63
Tighter money ahead? il U S News 54:102-3 F 25 '63
Tighter tax rules for foundations? U S News 57:76 Ag 3 '64
Time for tax candor. Duns R 81:45 Ap '63
To the floor; administration's tax bill. Time 83:14 Ja 31 '64
To the people: President Kennedy's television talk. Newsweek 62:20 S 30 '63
Trend of business; tax cut. J. Phillips. il Duns R 83:8-9 Ap '64
Two cheers for the tax cut. Reporter 30:10+ Mr 12 '64
Up, if taxes go down; impact of a tax cut on U.S. business in 1964; McGraw-Hill capital spending survey. il Bsns W p28-9 N 9 '63
Victory and a half. Newsweek 63:15 F 17 '64
Walter Heller, Mr Tax Cut. T. G. Harris. il Look 27:81-2+ Je 18 '63
War on want, at home; concerning the State of the Union message; with editorial comment. il Bsns W p 19-21, 112 Ja 11 '64
Washington outlook; showdown on tax reduction. Bsns W p31-2 Ag 3 '63
Washington outlook; tax-cut outlook. Bsns W p43 Je 29 '63
Ways & means roughs out the new tax bill. Bsns W p78-9 Je 22 '63
What consensus? Time 81:18-19 Mr 1 '63
What tax cut can mean to you. U S News 56:46-8 Ja 27 '64
What the tax bill will do. il Time 83:21 F 28 '64
What the tax cut can do. F. B. Wilde. Sat R 47:30-2 Ja 11 '64
What your tax is to be in '64: with charts. U S News 55:32-5 Ag 26 '63
Where taxes are sure to keep on rising; social security tax. il U S News 55:67-9 N 11 '63
Who should get how much? F. B. Wilde. Sat R 48:34 Ja 9 '65
Who wants a tax cut? Time 81:26 F 15 '63
Why Kennedy's tax cut trouble gets deeper. Life 54:4 Mr 29 '63
Wilbur Mills grinds exceedingly fine. il Newsweek 62:61 Ag 19 '63
Wilbur Mills talks on taxes; interview. W. Mills. il Nations Bsns 52:30-1+ Ag '64
Will tax cut be stalled? il U S News 55:33-4 O 28 '63
Will taxes be raised in '65? U S News 57:87-8 D 14 '64
With the tax cuts; reforms. il Newsweek 61:75 Je 10 '63
You can almost start spending it now. il Time 83:13-14 F 14 '64
See also
Amusement tax
Excess profits tax
Excise tax
Income tax—United States
Local taxation
Property tax
Sales tax
Tax evasion
Taxation, State
Taxation of bonds, securities, etc.
United States—Internal revenue service
also subhead Taxation under various subjects, e.g. Insurance—Taxation

Anecdotes, facetiae, satire, etc.
Art Buchwald tax plan; excerpt from I chose capitol punishment. A. Buchwald. Read Digest 84:12H Mr '64
TAXATION, County
As cities and counties get frantic for cash. il U S News 57:79-80 S 14 '64
TAXATION, Double
Double taxation. H. Hazlitt. Newsweek 62:70 Ag 19 '63
Income tax convention with Sweden enters into force. Dept State Bul 51:452 S 28 '64
Income tax protocol enters into force with Netherlands. Dept State Bul 51:601 O 26 '64
Income tax protocol with Japan enters into force. Dept State Bul 51:401 S 21 '64

TAXATION, Double—*Continued*
Supplementary tax convention signed with Sweden. Dept State Bul 49:760 N 11 '63
Tax convention with Honduras continues in force. Dept State Bul 50:312 F 24 '64
United States and Greece sign estate tax protocol. Dept State Bul 50:385-6 Mr 9 '64
U.S. and Philippines sign income tax convention. Dept State Bul 51:601 O 26 '64
U.S.-Luxembourg income-tax convention enters into force. Dept State Bul 52:42 Ja 11 '65

TAXATION, Exemption from
Canadian issues to be exempt from interest equalization tax; executive order; September 2, 1964. L. B. Johnson. Dept State Bul 51:442 S 28 '64
Challenge to tax exemption. D. Wolfle. Science 146:175 O 9 '64
Churchmen defend the F.O.R. Christian Cent 80:733 Je 5 '63
Dodge to the right? Newsweek 62:25 Jl 1 '63
Faith without works? Commonweal 78:238 My 24 '63
Foundations as a tax dodge. F. J. Cook. Nation 196:321-5 Ap 20 '63; Reply. J. Williams. 196:inside cover My 18 '63
Foundations in business: report. U S News 55:104-5 O 28 '63
Foundations: Patman maintains pressure for tighter regulation of tax-exempt organizations. J. Walsh. Science 145:559-61 Ag 7 '64
Foundations: Patman plugs away at theme that growth, operations of tax exempts call for scrutiny. J. Walsh. Science 142:370-2 O 18 '63
Heat on foundations; abuses of tax exemption. Bsns W p38 S 19 '64
Heat on Hunt; investigation of tax-exempt foundations. Newsweek 64:23-4 S 14 '64
Industrial aid bonds: boon or bane? Duns R 81:pt2 S100 Mr '63
New war between the states: tax subsidies for industry; industrial band programs. il U S News 55:117-18 N 25 '63
Patman shoots again. Bsns W p 146+ O 26 '63
Personal business; tax-exempts. Bsns W p 141-2 Mr 14 '64
Realty trusts come under fire of IRS; Real estate investment trust act. Bsns W p56 Mr 2 '63
Revenue service revokes F.O.R.'s tax status. Christian Cent 80:357-8 Mr 20 '63
What price peace? Newsweek 61:28-9 My 27 '63
Why tax benefits for the clergy? Christian Cent 81:1230 O 7 '64
See also
Church property—Taxation

TAXATION, Municipal. See Local taxation

TAXATION, State
Empty tills. il Newsweek 61:24-5 Ap 8 '63
In states, cities: a cry for services, a revolt on taxes. U S News 55:102-4 O 28 '63
Keeping up with Uncle. il Time 85:21 Ja 22 '65
Making sense of state taxes; three-year study of state levies on business. Bsns W p54 Je 20 '64
1963: year of big jump in state, local taxes. il U S News 54:83-4 F 4 '63
Now it's a round of tax increases. U S News 56:93 My 25 '64
Painless taxes: new gimmicks for states, cities. il U S News 57:80+ Jl 27 '64
Setback for a dark horse; Romney tax plan rejected. U S News 55:16 N 25 '63
State, local taxes: up, up. U S News 56:87 Ap 20 '64
State taxes: little bits of liability floating all over. il Newsweek 63:67 Je 29 '64
State taxes, yours and others; up-to-date facts on every state. il Changing T 18:39-47 O '64
States bite harder. il Bsns W p 114+ Mr 9 '63
States: tax, tax; owe, owe. il Time 84:35 N 27 '64
Taxes that never stop going up. il U S News 57:95-6 N 30 '64
What relief? il Time 81:19-20 Mr 1 '63
When federal taxes go down, what about your state tax? U S News 56:95-6 Mr 9 '64
Your state & local taxes, up and up and up. il Changing T 18:25-9 Jl '64
See also
Sales tax

TAXATION of bonds, securities, etc.
Curbs on use of tax-free bonds? U S News 55:82-3 Jl 22 '63
President supports bill to impose interest equalization tax; letter to Representative W. Mills, February 25, 1964. L. B. Johnson. Dept State Bul 50:464 Mr 23 '64
Soon: tax check on stock profits. U S News 56:98 Mr 30 '64
Tax bill did its work while Congress mulled; interest equalization tax. il Bsns W p67 Jl 4 '64
Tax-selling vs. overall planning. il Duns R 84:141-2+ N '64
Tax tips for stockholders; questions and answers. il Changing T 18:43-5 Ag '64

TAXATION of corporations; Taxation of insurance; etc. See Corporations—Taxation; Insurance—Taxation; etc.

TAXATION of personal property
See also
Property tax

TAXATION of works of art
Gift is now a gift. Time 83:68 Je 19 '64

TAXCO, Mexico
Description
Climbing Taxco's cobbled streets. il Sunset 131:29 Ag '63

TAXICAB drivers
Poet, actor, painter: cabbie; New York cab drivers. E. T. Ewen. il N Y Times Mag p36+ O 27 '63
Why capital's taxi drivers stay home at night. U S News 56:8 F 3 '64
Anecdotes, facetiae, satire, etc.
Consultation. B. Roueché. New Yorker 39: 62+ Ag 31 '63

TAXICABS
Box that tailoring made. il Time 82:62 Ag 2 '63
For New Yorkers only. il Look 27:54b Mr 26 '63
Letter from Paris. Genêt. New Yorker 39: 192-4 N 30 '63
Fares
More than ten years of metered taxi fares; Charlotte, N.C. H. G. Cleveland. il Am City 78:115-16 My '63
$1.8 million taxi ride. Nation 199:131 S 21 '64
Radio equipment
WCAB: new closed-circuit FM radio station for cabdrivers and their passengers. New Yorker 40:24-5 Ja 2 '65

TAXIDERMY
Brothers under the skin; companies called Jonas bros. il Bsns W p 136-8+ O 26 '63

TAXIMETERS
More than ten years of metered taxi fares; Charlotte, N.C. H. G. Cleveland. il Am City 78:115-16 My '63

TAXONOMY. See Biology—Classification

TAXUS. See Yews

TAY-Sachs disease. See Amaurotic family idiocy

TAYLOR, Add. See Taylor, B. jt. auth.

TAYLOR, Alice, and Ahsan, S. R.
India's agricultural problems. bibliog Focus 14:1-6 S '63
—See Gildea, R. Y. jr; Guernsey, L. jt. auths.

TAYLOR, Arba S.
Phantom city; Bayway refinery. New Yorker 39:26-8 Ja 18 '64

TAYLOR, Betty
Light touch. NEA J 52:57 O '63
—and Taylor, Add
Down the Antilles. Yachting 116:49-51+ N '64

TAYLOR, Bill
How to sweeten a lemon. Pop Sci 186:88-91+ Ja '65

TAYLOR, Brie
Towards a plastic revolution. Art N 63:46-9+ Mr '64

TAYLOR, Carl E.
Medical care for developing countries. Atlan 213:75-6+ Ja '64

TAYLOR, Cecil
Cecil Taylor and the new tradition. J. Goldberg. por Sat R 46:42-3 F 9 '63

TAYLOR, Sister Cecily
Aftermath; poem. Commonweal 78:430 Jl 12 '63

TAYLOR, Charles H.
Ink experiments. Sch Arts 64:29-30 S '64

TAYLOR, Charles W.
Surrender of Red Cloud; excerpt from memoirs. Am Heritage 15:111 Je '64

TAYLOR, Curtice
Follow a star. por Seventeen 24:76+ Ja '65

TAYLOR, Dabney
Christmas in Euzkaldunak. Todays Health 42:18-19+ D '64
(ed) See Fong, K. I believe

TAYLOR, Duncan Norton-. See Norton-Taylor, D.

TAYLOR, Dwight W. See Rubin, M. jt. auth.

TAYLOR, Edmond
After Brussels. Reporter 28:29-32 F 14 '63
American investments in Europe. Reporter 31: 25-9 D 3 '64
Behind de Gaulle's veiled threats. Reporter 31:30+ N 19 '64
De Gaulle at Trier: the oracle speaks. Reporter 30:25-7 Je 18 '64
De Gaulle's Romanian gambit. Reporter 31: 41-3 Ag 13 '64
France: a third force? Reporter 30:24-6 F 27 '64
General and the miners. Reporter 28:14-18 Ap 11 '63
In the not so united Europe. Reporter 31:12+ O 8 '64
More cloak than dagger. Reporter 29:65-6 N 21 '63
New popular front? Reporter 28:13-19 Je 20 '63
Rumblings on the left. Reporter 30:15-19 Ja 2 '64
What price MLF? Reporter 31:12+ D 3 '64

TAYLOR, Edward Plunket
Man with many eyes; Argus corporation of Canada. pors Time 81:81-2 F 8 '63
Their hats are in the ring. W. Tower. il por Sports Illus 20:26-32 My 4 '64

TAYLOR, Elizabeth, 1912-
In the sun; story. New Yorker 40:49-56 Ap 18 '64
Mice and birds and boy; story. New Yorker 38:28-32 F 9 '63
Mr Wharton; story. New Yorker 39:36-40 Je 8 '63
Two islands. Mlle 59:176-8+ S '64
Voices; story. New Yorker 39:28-31 Jl 20 '63
Vron and Willie; story. New Yorker 40:34-9 Ja 16 '65

TAYLOR, Elizabeth, 1932-
Elizabeth and Liza; ed. by J. Hamilton. por Look 28:72-7 Ap 21 '64
Elizabeth Taylor talks about Cleopatra; ed. by J. Hamilton. pors Look 27:41-7+ My 7 '63
I refuse to cure my public image; interview, ed. by R. Meryman. pors Life 57:74-85 D 18 '64; Same abr. Time 84:36 D 25 '64
Around London with Liz; TV travelogue. il pors Life 55:89-91 Ag 16 '63
Boss makes $150,000, employe 2.4 million. U S News 54:10 Je 3 '63
Burton and the girls; with interview with R. Burton. il pors Look 28:40-2+ Ja 28 '64
Cleopatra; trials and tribulations of an epic film. W. Wanger and J. Hyams. il pors Sat Eve Post 236:28-38+ Je 1 '63
Dickenliz in Toronto. Newsweek 63:78 F 10 '64
Funny thing happened on the way to decorum. por Time 83:56 Ja 3 '64
Keats to the ducks; E. Taylor's London scheduled on CBS. por Newsweek 62:77 Jl 15 '63
Liz and Dick put iambics in the big time. T. Prideaux. Life 57:12 Jl 24 '64
Millionairess. il por Time 81:50 Je 7 '63
Miracle on 46th street. il Time 83:86+ Je 12 '64
Miss Taylor and family: an outside view. S. Elkin. il por Esquire 62:118-20+ N '64
Perils of Mexican divorce. il por Time 82: 34 D 27 '63
Return of the femme fatale. M. Lerner. por Ladies Home J 80:80-1+ Je '63
Something to write home about. il por Time 84:62 Jl 3 '64
We will dance. por Newsweek 64:73 D 21 '64

TAYLOR, Emily
Keeping house with Emily Taylor. See issues of Good housekeeping

TAYLOR, Eula May
Teacher influence in politics. NEA J 53:64 Ja '64

TAYLOR, Fan
Still small voice. Mus Am 83:12-13 F '63

TAYLOR, Frank J.
Airports: our newest billion-dollar business. Read Digest 85:192-4+ D '64
Call me 552. Read Digest 83:123-4 Ag '63
He's forever chasing rainbows. Sat Eve Post 236:70-1 N 30 '63
One man's crusade for everybody's freedom. Read Digest 84:139-42 Je '64
Three lives of David Starr Jordan. Read Digest 82:113-17 My '63

TAYLOR, Frederick Winslow
Revolutionary then, orthodox now. por Bsns W p94 Ap 20 '63

TAYLOR, Gardner C.
Why I believe there is a God. por Ebony 18: 86 F '63

TAYLOR, George
Informed neutrals score a triumph. por Bsns W p43-4+ My 9 '64

TAYLOR, George E.
Leadership of the universities. bibliog f Ann Am Acad 356:1-11 N '64

TAYLOR, Harold
Academic industry. Commentary 38:68+ D '64
Education of a modern girl. PTA Mag 58: 4-6 bibliog(p36) S '63
Higher education and the system. Commentary 35:450-4 My '63
Idea of a world college. Sat R 47:29-32+ N 14 '64
(ed) Teaching about peace and war. Sr Schol 83:9T+ N 22 '63
What the family isn't teaching. Sat R 46:17-19 My 18 '63

TAYLOR, Harold S.
On the slanting of the news. Nat R 16:489-90 Je 16 '64
Reform for form 1040. Sat R 47:30-1 Ap 11 '64

TAYLOR, Harrison
Interiors by Taylor. il pors Ebony 19:68-70+ Ap '64

TAYLOR, Henry J.
Clichés cost us our shirts. Read Digest 84: 165 Ja '64
Don't tread on whom? Read Digest 85:138-9 Ag '64

TAYLOR, Hobart, jr
Commemoration of 100th anniversary of Emancipation proclamation; with biographical sketch. por(p 181) Negro Hist Bul 26: 183-5 Mr '63
U.S. steps up equal job opportunity. il pors Ebony 19:103-4+ S '64

TAYLOR, Hugh
From Galileo to Paul VI. Cath World 199:301-7 Ag '64

TAYLOR, Jack
Underground traffic detectors. Am City 79: 140+ S '64

TAYLOR, James E.
Civil, and sometimes uncivil, war; sketches. Am Heritage 15:50-61 O '64

TAYLOR, James L.
Planning functional quarters for the school library. Sch Life 47:16-20 N '64

TAYLOR, Jeanette
Sometimes the dream comes true. Seventeen 23:66-7 Mr '64

TAYLOR, Jeff H.
Electronic candles dance and glow. Pop Electr 21:49-52 N '64
Field-effect transistor voltmeter. Pop Electr 21:45-8 Jl '64
Spookin' light. Pop Electr 21:67-9 S '64

TAYLOR, Joan
Front yards. Horticulture 42:16-17 Jl '64

TAYLOR, John F. A.
Humanities in land grant universities. Sat R 47:64-5+ Ap 18 '64

TAYLOR, John V.
God's presence and absence. Christian Cent 81:1136-8 S 16 '64

TAYLOR, June
June Taylor dancers open with tap. pors Dance Mag 37:42-3 Je '63

TAYLOR, Kamala (Purnaiya)
WLB biography. R. Montgomery. por Wilson Lib Bul 38:296 N '63

TAYLOR, Katharine
Nonsense makes sense to a child. Sat R 46: 55-6 D 21 '63

TAYLOR, Kathryn S.
Fine seedlings deserve the best care. il Horticulture 42:38-9+ Ap '64
Growing bulbs in pots indoors. Horticulture 42:24-7+ N '64

TAYLOR, L. B. jr
Bird that went into orbit. Read Digest 82: 224-5 F '63

TAYLOR, Lee
He's sharpening up for the speedboat record. il pors Pop Sci 184:59 My '64

TAYLOR, Mark M.
Celosia. Horticulture 41:246 My '63
Cobra lily. Horticulture 42:38-9 Ja '64
Hollies. Horticulture 41:604 D '63
Keep cool with landscaping. Horticulture 41: 459 S '63
Larkspur is better than ever. Pop Gard 15:8 F '64
Pacific madrona, a colorful tree. Horticulture 41:162-3 Mr '63
Poppies for color. Pop Gard 15:16-17 S '64
Tree of unusual merit. Horticulture 41:199 Ap '63

TAYLOR, Maxwell Davenport
Ambassador Taylor's news conference, September 9, 1964. Dept State Bul 51:433-5 S 28 '64
Excerpt from testimony, April 8, 1963. Cong Digest 42:188+ Je '63

TAYLOR, Maxwell Davenport—*Continued*
Military advice; its use in government; address, February 15, 1964. Vital Speeches 30:336-9 Mr 15 '64
Risks can be accepted; statement, August 14, 1963. por(p55) U S News 55:64-6 Ag 26 '63

about

Chips go down on South Vietnam. por Bsns W p31-2 Je 27 '64
Hour of decision. Nation 199:421 D 7 '64
Just a minute. il por Time 84:21-2 D 4 '64
Leavetaking; U.S. ambassador to South Viet Nam. il por Time 84:25-6 Jl 10 '64
Lowdown from the top U.S. command in Saigon. pors Life 57:46-46B+ N 27 '64
McNamara-Taylor report: a long, hard war in Vietnam. por U S News 56:21 My 25 '64
New coup, old crisis: Maxwell Taylor on the spot; with report by E. Weintal. il por Newsweek 64:43-5+ S 21 '64
No time limit; new U.S. ambassador to South Viet Nam. il por Time 84:30-1 Jl 17 '64
1,002nd way. il por Time 85:15 Ja 8 '65
Our new men in Saigon; M. Taylor to replace H. C. Lodge. por Time 84:15-16 Jl 3 '64
President reaffirms basic policy in Viet-Nam; White House statement, December 1, 1964. Dept State Bul 51:869-70 D 21 '64
Report from South Vietnam. il por U S News 55:21 O 14 '63
Search for answers; visit to South Viet Nam. il por Time 82:48 O 4 '63
Situation. Time 84:30-1 D 11 '64
Taylor tries a new start in Vietnam. P. Grose. il pors N Y Times Mag p 12-13+ Ag 9 '64
Trigger happiness. Nat R 16:1091 D 15 '64
Two officials under fire. por U S News 56:13 Ja 6 '64
Vietnam: never grimmer. il por Newsweek 64: 45 D 7 '64
Vietnam: soldier to Saigon. il por Newsweek 64:18-20 Jl 6 '64
What to expect of new American leaders in Vietnam. por U S News 57:12 Jl 6 '64
Why it's so hard to beat the Communists in Vietnam; McNamara-Taylor mission. R. P. Martin. il U S News 55:56-7 O 7 '63

TAYLOR, Mykia
Early spring; poem. McCalls 90:174 Ap '63

TAYLOR, Naomi. See Bodian, D. jt. auth.

TAYLOR, Neville
Fact & fancy; reporting the Vassall case. Time 81:62 F 8 '63

TAYLOR, Paul
Paul Taylor dance company at Little theatre. J. Maskey. Dance Mag 38:64 F '64

TAYLOR, Peter
Demons; story. New Yorker 39:30-4 Ag 24 '63
Two pilgrims; story. New Yorker 39:36-42 S 7 '63

TAYLOR, Prince A. bp
Welcome for Bishop Taylor. D. Macleod. Christian Cent 81:1317-18 O 21 '64

TAYLOR, Raymond L.
Eighth Philadelphia meeting. Science 139: 621-8 F 15 '63
Report of the seventh Cleveland meeting. Science 143:835-42 F 21 '64
Seventh Cleveland meeting. Science 140:907-12+; 141:279-81 My 24, Jl 19 '63
Third Montreal meeting. Science 144:1032-42; 145:297-9 My 22, Jl 17 '64

TAYLOR, Robert S.
Information sciences. por Library J 88:4161-3 N 1 '63
Professional reading: five reviews. Wilson Lib Bul 38:766-7+ My '64

TAYLOR, Robert Selby
Taylor for de Blank. D. M. Norman. Christian Cent 81:378-80 Mr 18 '64

TAYLOR, Roger C.
Jolly boating weather. Yachting 115:210-13 My '64

TAYLOR, Samuel
Beekman place. Criticism
New Yorker 40:108 O 17 '64
Sat R 47:30 O 24 '64
Time 84:77 O 16 '64

TAYLOR, Samuel Woolley
Four rules for the short story. Writer 76:7-9 F '63
Needle for Felix. Field & S 67:58-61 Mr '63

TAYLOR, Sandra
Sweet home; excerpt. Sr Schol 82:14-15 My 15 '63

TAYLOR, Stephen James Lake Taylor, baron
America's medical future; a Briton's view. Nation 197:177-9 S 28 '63
Deep analysis of the American mind. N Y Times Mag p9+ F 23 '64

TAYLOR, Theodore
Last and most blessed Christmas gift; story. McCalls 91:78-9 D '63
So simple, so treacherous. Sat Eve Post 237: 66-7 N 28 '64

TAYLOR, Thurston
Worcester's place of delight. Library J 88: 4535-7 D 1 '63

TAYLOR, Toni
Kids play while parents work. Parents Mag 38:65-7 F '63
—See Hymes, J. L. jt. auth.

TAYLOR, Mrs Vernon, 3d
Inventive skier's worldly wardrobe. il pors Life 58:49-50 Ja 29 '65

TAYLOR, Walter A.
Obituary
Arch Rec 135:43 F '64

TAYLOR, William H.
End of a great old ship. Yachting 113:198 My '63
Key West to Cedar Keys. Yachting 114:46-8+ N '63

TAYLOR, William J.
Little sawmill; poem. Am For 70:53 Je '64

TAYLOR, William L.
Civil rights: federal responsibility; address, November 14, 1964. Vital Speeches 31:143-6 D 15 '64

TAYLOR, Zachary
Faces from the past. R. M. Ketchum. por Am Heritage 14:52-3 O '63
Zachary Taylor, twelfth President 1849-1850. F. Freidel. il pors Nat Geog Mag 127:106-9 Ja '65

TAYLOR Allderdice high school. See Pittsburgh—Education

TAZIEFF, Haroun
Hidden world of volcanoes. UNESCO Courier 16:20-5 O '63

TCHAIKOVSKY, Peter Ilyitch
Eugene Onegin. Criticism
Opera N il 28:17-20 F 29 '64
Sat R 47:43-4 F 29 '64
First recording of Tchaikovsky's Iolantha. P. L. Miller. Am Rec G 30:972 Je '64
Introducing John Ogdon. R. Kammerer. Am Rec G 30:384 Ja '64
On records; Eugene Onegin. Opera N 28:34 F 29 '64

TCHELITCHEW, Pavel
Huntington Hartford's ivory tower. M. Grosser. Nation 198:403 Ap 20 '64
Tchelitchew: the melancholy of anatomy. P. Tyler. il Art N 63:36-8+ Ap '64

TEA
Gentle art of tiny teapot tea. P. Mooho. Esquire 62:180+ D '64
Herbs in the teapot. D. E. Stebbins. il Horticulture 41:402 Ag '63
Iced tea that won't cloud. Sunset 133:118 Jl '64
Perfect cup of tea. B. Zache. il Bet Hom & Gard 43:74 Ja '65

TEA, Afternoon. See Afternoon teas

TEA carts. See Serving carts

TEA drinking. See Manners and customs

TEA parties. See Entertaining

TEA rooms. See Restaurants

TEA roses. See Roses

TEA tables. See Tables

TEACHER education. See Teachers—Education

TEACHER librarians. See School librarians

TEACHER morale. See Morale

TEACHER participation in school administration. See School management and organization—Teacher participation

TEACHER pupil relations. See Teachers and students

TEACHER shortage. See Teachers—Supply and demand

TEACHERS
American public school teachers, 1960-61. il NEA J 52:48-51 Ap '63
Art of teaching: some minor heresies. D. Grumbach. Cath World 200:22-7 O '64
Board-staff negotiations. J. P. Steffensen. Sch Life 47:6-8 O '64
Classroom teachers in elementary and secondary schools; with tables. Sch Life 47: 25-7 O '64
Editor's notebook. M. S. Fenner. See issues of NEA journal
Elmon Ousley: teacher of the year. G. Zimmerman. il Look 27:98-100 My 7 '63
For elementary teachers; reports on meetings of NCGE, NCTE and NCSS. il Sr Schol 83:15T-16T D 13 '63
How to get the best teachers for your schools. M. Mayer. Bet Hom & Gard 42:16+ O '64

TEACHERS—*Continued*
Importance of teachers. E. Osgood. Sch & Soc 92:241 Sum '64
Lawana Trout: teacher of the year. G. Astor. il Look 28:33-7 My 19 '64
New militants. il Time 82:45 Ag 16 '63
Our teacher sees with her hands. S. Gordon. il Look 27:116a-116e Ap 23 '63
Rewards of a great teacher. R. Meryman. il Life 56:70-2+ Mr 13 '64
Right to read; religious sisters and brothers run the risk of becoming illiterate. America 109:250 S 14 '63
School library: instruction's partner; address, November, 1962. A. L. Robinson. Library J 88:823-5+ F 15 '63
School problem: attacks on teachers. U S News 56:8 Mr 16 '64
Society's scapegoat. Nation 197:150 S 21 '63
Teacher to the president. R. N. Rood. PTA Mag 57:15 My '63
Teachers and workers. New Repub 149:7-8 S 21 '63
When Peace corps teachers return. S. Shriver. il NEA J 52:13-14+ Mr '63
Who would teach here. M. B. Smiley. il PTA Mag 58:16-19 S '63
Who's the teacher? profile of the American public school teacher, by NEA research division. Sr Schol 84:4T Mr 6 '64
Why teachers are getting restless. il U S News 56:79-81 Je 1 '64
See also
American teachers in foreign countries
Art teachers
College professors and instructors
Foreign teachers in the United States
National education association
Negro teachers
Sanctions, Professional
School management and organization—Teacher participation
Substitute teachers
Teachers, Married
Teachers of the deaf
Teaching

Adjustment

Editor's notebook. M. S. Fenner. NEA J 54:82 Ja '65
Orientation, as seen by an experienced teacher and as seen by a second year teacher. M. W. Jones; S. Berger. il NEA J 53:46-8 O '64
Teaching in the big city. M. L. Steet. il NEA J 53:18-20 D '64
Welcome to the new teacher. il NEA J 52:8-10+ O '63
What the books don't tell you. J. T. Field. NEA J 53:58-9 O '64

Anecdotes, facetiae, satire, etc.

Emerging porpoise. R. Maegerlein. America 111:131-2 Ag 8 '64
Light touch. P. R. Tedesco. See issues of NEA journal

Applications for positions
See Applications for positions

Certification

Certification and professional autonomy; excerpt from Certification in education. L. B. Kinney. bibliog Sch & Soc 91:434-9 D 28 '63
Professional practice regulations; symposium. il NEA J 52:34-7 My '63
See also
Science teachers—Certification

Contracts

Advancing the welfare of members. F. L. Hipp. NEA J 53:19-20 Ja '64
Employment application forms. NEA J 53:55 My '64
Giving ample notice. NEA J 53:34 F '64
Local associations move toward professional negotiation. A. M. West. il NEA J 53:26-8 F '64
Local associations work for better teaching conditions. il NEA J 53:28-31 F '64
See also
College professors and instructors—Tenure

Duties

Teacher-opinion poll; duty-free lunch period. il NEA J 52:41 N '63

Education

Accreditation in teacher education. Sch & Soc 92:40 F 8 '64
Active voice. P. Woodring. Sat R 46:63 N 16 '63
American teachers association pushes activity in two vital areas; commission for improvement of teacher competency initiated. R. W. Hatch. Negro Hist Bul 27:150-2 Mr '64
Can American teachers teach? R. Bendiner. il Redbook 123:60-1+ O '64
Changes in Catholic schools. America 111:204 Ag 29 '64
Compulsory professional teacher training in England. H. K. Hutton. bibliog f Sch & Soc 92:358-9 N 28 '64
Conant follow-up; effects of publication of Education of American teachers. Sr Schol 83:1T D 6 '63
Conant seeks revolution; excerpts from address. J. B. Conant. Sr Schol 84:1T-2T Mr 13 '64
Conant teacher education reforms tested. Sr Schol 85:4T+ D 2 '64
Conant v. the establishment. Time 83:64 F 28 '64
Conant's recommendations; summary of last chapter of The education of American teachers. Sat R 46:56-7+ S 21 '63
Conant's report on teacher education. P. Woodring. Sat R 46:49-51 S 21 '63
Conclusions on educating America's teachers; excerpt from The education of American teachers. J. B. Conant. Sch & Soc 92:123-6 Mr 21 '64
Current teacher education in Pakistan. L. H. Stoner and E. Neteland. Sch & Soc 91:174-5 Ap 6 '63
Doctor Conant's bombshell. F. M. Hechinger. Reporter 29:44-6 S 26 '63
Education of American teachers, by J. B. Conant. Review
Commentary 37:85-7 Mr '64. R. S. Baker; Reply with rejoinder. R. Gross. 38:15 Jl '64
Commonweal 79:352-4 D 13 '63. J. McDermott
Life 55:4 S 20 '63
NEA J 52:64+ O '63. F. B. Stratemeyer
Newsweek il 62:92 S 23 '63
PTA Mag 58:14-15 N '63. W. D. Boutwell
Science 141:1166-8 S 20 '63. F. C. Robb
Sr Schol 83:1T S 27 '63
Time il 82:55-6 S 27 '63
Education of American teachers; excerpts from symposium on J. B. Conant's book. NEA J 53:49-53 Ap '64
Education of teachers; address, February 14, 1963. J. D. Koerner. Vital Speeches 29:412-16 Ap 15 '63
Educational exchange; education and library science. V. L. Jones. Library J 88:3178+ S 15 '63
Educationists' gadgetry produces poor teachers. F. Morley. Nations Bsns 51:27-8 Jl '63
Findings and prejudices in teacher education; excerpt from The miseducation of American teachers. J. D. Koerner. bibliog f Sch & Soc 92:127-34 Mr 21 '64
Higher standards. Sr Schol 82:1T F 27 '63
How not to teach teachers. J. D. Koerner. Atlan 211:59-63 F '63
Miseducation of American teachers, by J. D. Koerner. Review
Commentary 36:260-4 S '63. E. Z. Friedenberg
New Repub 149:21-5 Jl 6 '63. C. Jencks
Newsweek 61:96 My 13 '63
Sat R 46:77-9 My 18 '63. P. Woodring
Need for scholarship in teacher education. W. W. Brickman. Sch & Soc 92:122 Mr 21 '64
New and better teacher education. C. C. Travelstead. Sch & Soc 91:332-4 N 2 '63
New directions for India's teacher education. J. P. Lipkin. Sch & Soc 92:293-4 O 17 '64
Quarrel among educators; excerpt from The education of American teachers. J. B. Conant. il Sat R 46:53-5+ S 21 '63; Discussion. 46:50 O 19 '63
Quest for better teachers: a progress report on the Conant plan. A. Q. Maisel. Read Digest 85:241-4+ O '64
Speaking out; teachers get the worst education. J. D. Koerner. Sat Eve Post 236:8+ Je 1 '63
Standards for travel credit. E. Dyer. NEA J 53:68 F '64
Teacher education at Wisconsin. Sch & Soc 92:115+ Mr 21 '64
Teacher education for the next decade; adaptation of address, October 1, 1963. F. S. Chase. Sch & Soc 92:140-2 Mr 21 '64
Teacher education in Ethiopia. F. Klassen. Sch & Soc 91:96-8 F 23 '63
Teacher education: 1964; reactions to J. B. Conant's proposals; symposium. Sat R 47:51-2 S 19 '64

TEACHERS—Education—*Continued*
Teacher education through team teaching. J. L. Nelson and G. A. Robinson. Sch & Soc 91:409-10 D 14 '63
Teacher-opinion poll on teacher preparation. il NEA J 52:34 D '63
Teacher preparation. J. B. Whitelaw. Sch Life 46:11-13 Ja '64
Teaching is better with! M. Bennett. il Sat R 46:82-3 F 16 '63
Teaching of teachers: a national scandal? U S News 55:10 S 30 '63
Teaching through trial and error; NEA teach corps in Sierra Leone, West Africa. L. F. Bailey. Sr Schol 84:10-T-11T Ap 17 '64
To educate the educators. R. Kirk. Nat R 15: 24-5 Jl 16 '63
Unrealities in teacher education. I. N. Berlin. il Sat R 47:56-8+ D 19 '64
We want teachers who are educated. Time 81:74 My 10 '63
While school keeps; recommended changes in structure of NCATE. J. Cass. Sat R 46:70-1 Mr 23 '63
Why teacher can't teach. Life 54:4 Mr 22 '63
See also
Education—Study and teaching
Educational workshops
National council for accreditation of teacher education
Teachers colleges
Teachers institutes

Education in service

Freed time for in-service education; Cedar Rapids plan. H. C. Reid. NEA J 52:54 N '63
Inservice education of mathematics teachers; with suggestions for inservice programs in mathematics. V. Schult and T. L. Abell. Sch Life 45:29-36 Jl '63
Teacher education through team teaching. J. L. Nelson and G. A. Robinson. Sch & Soc 91:409-10 D 14 '63

Employment in business and industry

See Teachers—Supplementary employment

Ethics

See Teachers ethics

Health and hygiene

How's your eye-Q? J. R. Gregg. il Sr Schol 84:14T Ap 10 '64

Morale

See Morale

Oaths of allegiance, etc.

See Loyalty, Oaths of

Political activities

Boycotts and bargaining; excerpts from address, February 1964. J. H. Fischer. Sr Schol 84:4T Mr 20 '64
Education is a political enterprise. S. K. Bailey. NEA J 53:13 N '64
Political solicitations. NEA J 52:30 N '63
Teacher influence in politics; state of Washington. E. M. Taylor. NEA J 53:64 Ja '64
Teacher-opinion poll; politics. NEA J 53:72 Mr '64
Teacher-politician. il NEA J 53:69 D '64
Teacher's role in politics; as viewed by a Democrat and a Republican. C. Bielen; S. G. Crowe. NEA J 53:30-1 O '64
What's so unreasonable about a teacher's wanting to participate in politics? T. E. Robinson. NEA J 53:39-40 My '64

Public relations

See Teachers and the community

Qualifications

How good are our teachers? il Changing T 17:25-31 Je '63
NSF: new study on science, math teachers in high schools focuses on their education, assignment. J. Walsh. Science 140:880-1 My 24 '63
What students think of teachers; with study-discussion program, by E. M. Duvall. W. W. Wattenberg. bibliog il PTA Mag 58:4-6, 36-7 Ja '64
See also
College professors and instructors—Qualifications
Teachers—Certification

Rating

Can we measure good teaching objectively? A. W. Combs; H. E. Mitzel. NEA J 53:34-6+ Ja '64
City schools, a mixed report card. F. M. Hechinger. il N Y Times Mag p24+ Je 14 '64
Great teachers. D. Wolfle. Science 146:1421 D 11 '64
Teacher teaches better. F. L. Redefer. il NEA J 53:8-10 Ap '64

Reading

Teachers' professional reading. D. G. Petersen. Library J 88:1730-3 Ap 15 '63
To read or not to read; American history teachers in Indiana's public high schools. Sr Schol 85:4T O 7 '64

Recruiting

Teaching career? Sr Schol 83:1T N 8 '63
See also
Association for school, college, and university staffing

Salaries

Academic poker game. D. B. Johnson. il Sat R 46:70-1 Je 15 '63
Angry young men in teaching. S. M. Lambert. il NEA J 52:17-20 F '63; Discussion. 52:8-10 My '63
Beg, borrow, and bargain. il Newsweek 64:67 N 30 '64
Better way than merit pay. L. M. Collister. NEA J 53:37-8 My '64
City public school teachers' salaries, 1959-61. J. Griest. il Mo Labor R 86:411-15 Ap '63
Fringe benefits for teachers. J. H. Kleinmann and others. NEA J 52:17-18 N '63
Fringe benefits for teachers; Riverview Gardens, Mo. N. Estes and others. NEA J 53:24-5 S '64
Merit pay; the big question. J. H. Kleinmann. il NEA J 52:42-4 My '63
NEA works for teachers' salaries. il NEA J 52:11-14 O '63
Salaries: 1973; with chart. Sr Schol 83:1T+ O 11 '63
Salary justice for career teachers. E. L. Coons. il NEA J 53:34-5 O '64
Salary rebellion. Sr Schol 95:8T D 2 '64
State associations work closely with locals; Connecticut education association. W. J. Sheehan. NEA J 53:20-1 F '64
Teacher-opinion poll; merit pay. il NEA J 52:46 F '63
Teaching as a career, reports on salaries from the National education association. W. D. Boutwell. PTA Mag 58:26 D '63
What's happening in education? salaries in the United States. W. D. Boutwell. PTA Mag 57:11 Ap '63
See also
Strikes—United States—Teachers

Statistics

Facts on U.S. teachers from the census. Sch Life 46:4 Ag '64

Supplementary employment

Angry young men in teaching. S. M. Lambert. il NEA J 52:17-20 F '63; Discussion. 52:8-10 My '63
Moonlighters. il Newsweek 62:103 N 25 '63
Moonlighting? me too. il NEA J 52:48-50+ S '63

Supply and demand

Changing nature of the teacher shortage. R. C. Maul. il NEA J 52:41-2 N '63
Is there a teacher shortage? P. Woodring. Sat R 47:55-6 Ja 18 '64
New look at manpower needs in teaching. M. G. Stewart. bibliog f il Mo Labor R 87:639-44 Je '64
Teacher dropouts: still a dilemma. W. Wolf and W. C. Wolf, jr. Sch & Soc 92:193-4 Ap 18 '64
See also
Teachers—Recruiting

Tenure

Teacher dropouts: still a dilemma. W. Wolf and W. C. Wolf, jr. Sch & Soc 92:193-4 Ap 18 '64

Training

See Teachers—Education

TEACHERS, Interchange of
American host program. J. Cass. il Sat R 46: 76 Je 15 '63
Go Far East, young man. Sr Schol 85:2T Ja 7 '65
Indian teacher in America. G. K. Shenoy. NEA J 53:50 D '64
Would you like to teach overseas? T. E. Cotner. il Sr Schol 83:7T O 25 '63

TEACHERS, Married
What does marriage do to teaching? E. H. Hanson. il NEA J 52:8-10+ N '63

TEACHERS, New. See Teachers—Adjustment

TEACHERS, Retired
Earth being so good, would heaven seem best? E. Warren. il NEA J 53:8-10+ Mr '64

TEACHERS, Retired—*Continued*
Higher income for retired teachers. M. L. Ware. NEA J 53:14 F '64
Jackrabbit homesteading; retirement site from U.S. Department of the interior, Bureau of land management. S. Cochell. Sr Schol 84:12T F 7 '64
Plan now, retire later. L. Couch. NEA J 52:11-12 My '63

TEACHERS, Special
College and university programs for the preparation of teachers of exceptional children; with list of institutions. R. P. Mackie and others. Sch Life 45:29-35 Mr '63

TEACHERS aides
A+ for our lay readers. L. Freyman. il NEA J 53:19-20 N '64
Clerical help. W. W. Miller. NEA J 52:32 N '63
Noon-duty assistant program. R. F. Valdez. NEA J 53:63 Ap '64
Teachers' aides: a new way to help schools. il Good H 157:168 N '63

TEACHERS and libraries. See Libraries and schools

TEACHERS and students
Angels. S. Plapinger. il Ladies Home J 81: 47-51 My '64
Big hand, little hand; learning to tell time. N. H. Hartshorne. il Parents Mag 39:60-1+ S '64
Cipher in the snow. J. E. Mizer. NEA J 53: 8-10 N '64
Classroom incident. NEA J 53:25-6 O; 24-5 N '64
Conning the professor. il Time 82:56+ N 1 '63
Editor's notebook. M. S. Fenner. NEA J 53: 72 D '64
I'll remember you always! A. K. Healy. il NEA J 53:66 D '64
In Xanadu, U.S.A. R. L. Darbonne. NEA J 53:51-2 F '64
More teacher authority is schools' basic need. F. Morley. Nations Bsns 52:27-8 Jl '64
Not like other children; slum children. B. Asbell. il Redbook 121:64-5+ O '63
Paper angel; how to dispose of objects made by the entire class. E. D. Carlson. NEA J 53:25 D '64
Rock doc; geology professor at St Lawrence university, Canton, N.Y. C. Kocivar. il Look 27:M8+ N 5 '63
Special feature on classroom relationships; symposium. il NEA J 53:8-19 S '64
Student anxiety; excerpt from Anxiety as related to thinking and forgetting. F. F. Lighthall. il NEA J 53:26-8 D '64
Teacher and group processes. J. Luft. il NEA J 52:12-14 Ap '63
What students think of teachers; with study-discussion program, by E. M. Duvall. W. W. Wattenberg. bibliog il PTA Mag 58:4-6, 36-7 Ja '64
Why do I teach? L. DeBase. il Parents Mag 39:82 S '64
Year my children hated school. Redbook 123:6+ O '64

TEACHERS and the community
Local associations build professional strength. R. H. Wyatt. il NEA J 53:18-20 F '64
Local associations take responsibility for professional behavior. A. M. Pence. NEA J 53:22-3 F '64
Teaching in the big city. M. L. Steet. il NEA J 53:18-20 D '64

TEACHERS associations. See Educational associations

TEACHERS college, Columbia university
Doctorate at Teachers college. Sch & Soc 92:185 Ap 18 '64

New college

Utopia and rebellion: the New college experiment; excerpt from Innovation in education. G. Watson. bibliog Sch & Soc 92: 72+ F 22 '64

TEACHERS colleges
Expansion of British training colleges. W. James. Sch & Soc 91:309-10 O 19 '63
Profiles of teacher education institutions. il NEA J 53:73-6 Mr; 46-8 Ap; 20-2 My '64
See also names of teachers colleges, e.g. George Peabody college for teachers, Nashville, Tenn.

Entrance requirements

Characteristics of entering freshmen in a teachers college; Newark state college. W. P. Angers and others. il Sch & Soc 91:68-9 F 9 '63

Libraries

See also
New York state university—Teachers college at Cortland—Libraries

TEACHERS conferences. See Educational conferences

TEACHERS contracts. See Teachers—Contracts

TEACHERS credit unions. See Credit unions

TEACHERS ethics
Code of ethics for the education profession. NEA J 52:43+ Ap '63
Giving ample notice. NEA J 53:34 F '64
Implementing the code of ethics. M. M. Mitchell. NEA J 53:41 D '64
Intercommunication system. NEA J 53:61 N '64
Local association studies ethics cases; readiness test. NEA J 53:24-5 F '64
Local associations take responsibility for professional behavior. A. M. Pence. NEA J 53: 22-3 F '64
Political solicitations. NEA J 52:30 N '63
Schools are not factories. G. W. Denemark. NEA J 53:25-7 Mr '64
What's happening in education? Code of ethics of the education profession and guidelines for professional sanctions. W. D. Boutwell. PTA Mag 58:21 O '63
See also
National education association—Committee on professional ethics

TEACHERS in business and industry
Angry young men in teaching. S. M. Lambert. il NEA J 52:17-20 F '63

TEACHERS in literature
Teacher's image in children's literature. F. H. Hektoen. Sr Schol 83:13T+ O 4 '63

TEACHERS institutes
FTA summer experience; Northern Illinois university. E. M. Anglin and J. H. King. NEA J 53:31 My '64
NSF academic year institutes: a review of the program's success. Sch & Soc 92:222 Sum '64
Now's the time to act on those summer institutes. P. P. Coleman. Sr Schol 83:5T-6T N 22 '63
Summer institutes. Sr Schol 84:5T F 7 '64
Summer institutes '65. P. P. Coleman. il Sr Schol 85:4T O 28 '64
What ever happened to Euclid? mathematics at La Cantuta, Chosica, Peru. F. L. Phelps. il Américas 16:6-11 N '64
Why not study abroad? international summer school program at Oxford univ. H. McDonnell. il Sr Schol 85:13T Ja 7 '65

TEACHERS loyalty oath. See Loyalty, Oaths of

TEACHERS of the deaf
Training for teachers of the deaf. R. L. Hoag. il Sch Life 45:18-20 Ja '63

TEACHERS salaries. See Teachers—Salaries

TEACHERS strikes. See Strikes—United States—Teachers

TEACHERS unions
Advancing the cause of education. E. O. Melby. NEA J 52:29 F '63
Board-staff negotiations. J. P. Steffensen. Sch Life 47:6-8 O '64
Case for independent professional teachers' associations. S. Dorros. Mo Labor R 87:543 My '64
Collective bargaining for public school teachers. Mo Labor R 87:1297-8 N '64
NEA convention and the organizing of teachers. L. R. Klein. Mo Labor R 87:882-5 Ag '64
Public interest in how teachers organize; Educational policies commission report. NEA J 53:43-5 S '64; Same. il Sr Schol 85: 10T-11T N 18 '64
Reaction of organized British teachers to crises; excerpt from Membership participation in the National union of teachers. W. Roy. Mo Labor R 87:1022-5 S '64
Schools are not factories. G. W. Denemark. NEA J 53:25-7 Mr '64
Teachers' syndicate of the U.A.R. R. E. Markarian. Sch & Soc 91:373-5 N 30 '63
When teachers organize; appeal from an impasse, professional negotiation and collective bargaining. Mo Labor R 87:1295-6 N '64
Why teachers are getting restless. il U S News 56:79-81 Je 1 '64
See also
American federation of teachers
United federation of teachers

TEACHERS workshops. See Educational workshops

TEACHING
Antecedents of team teaching; excerpt from Team teaching. J. T. Shaplin. bibliog f Sch & Soc 91:393-407 D 14 '63
Art and uncertainty. D. F. Guillaume. il Sch Arts 63:23-4 Mr '64
Can we measure good teaching objectively? A. W. Combs; H. E. Mitzel. NEA J 53:34-6+ Ja '64

TEACHING—*Continued*
Classroom communiqué. Time 81:60 Mr 29 '63
Controlled environment for team teaching. il Arch Rec 135:162-4 F '64
Crackling excitement in school corridors; team teaching at Wayland, Mass. with report by E. J. Anderson. il Life 54:78-84+ Mr 22 '63
Eye of the octopus; library and team teaching in an eight-arm school; Vale elementary school, Cashmere, Wash. M. Brooks and E. Elledge. il Library J 89:320-1+ Ja 15 '64
Grouping children for instruction, a conference points the way; symposium. Sch Life 45:5-12+ Je '63
Hidden hazards in teaching. J. Crescimbeni and R. J. Mammarella. NEA J 54:31 Ja '65
How not to make an assignment. W. Van Til. NEA J 53:49-51 O '64
Is team teaching for your child? A. Hamilton. il PTA Mag 58:4-6 My '63; Same abr. with title Team teaching; how good is it? Read Digest 84:169+ My '64
Is team teaching the answer? W. E. Arnold. bibliog f Sch & Soc 91:407-9 D 14 '63
Last chance for our schools? with editorial comment. M. Mayer. il Sat Eve Post 236: 24-6+, 78 S 14 '63
Learning; symposium. il NEA J 52:19-32 Mr '63
Needed, a way to save curiosity. F. A. J. Ianni and L. Josephs. bibliog f Sch Life 46:23-4 N '63
Our school is trying team teaching; West Rockville junior high school, Md. E. L. Shalowitz. NEA J 53:45-6 My '64
Rewards of a great teacher. R. Meryman. il Life 56:70-2+ Mr 13 '64
Rewards of teaching. M. E. Chase. Ladies Home J 81:48+ N '64
Special feature on classroom relationships; symposium. il NEA J 53:8-19 S '64
Teacher, by S. Ashton-Warner. Review
Commonweal 79:410 D 27 '63. P. Deasy
Teacher-opinion poll, status of teaching as a vocation. il NEA J 53:56 My '64
Teaching as a second career, but not as second best. NEA J 53:48-50 S '64
Teaching is better with! M. Bennett. il Sat R 46:82-3 F 16 '63
Team teaching & art teaching. H. Hoffa; T. Fawcett. il Sch Arts 62:18-20 F '63
Team teaching at Dundee. H. J. Langer. il Sr Schol 82:5T-6T+ F 27 '63
Team teaching; how good is it? A. Hamilton. Read Digest 84:169+ My '64
There's more than one way to teach. S. Hook; C. F. Madden. il Sat R 47:48-51+ Jl 18 '64
What's happening in education? on introducing new programs. W. D. Boutwell. PTA Mag 58:25 D '63
What's happening in education? team teaching. W. D. Boutwell. PTA Mag 57:25-6 My '63
See also
Academic freedom
Audio-visual instruction
Classroom management
Colleges and universities—Teaching
Montessori method of education
Programmed teaching
Psychology, Educational
Questioning
School discipline
Teachers
Teachers—Education
also subhead Study and teaching under various subjects, e.g. Reading—Study and teaching

Aids and devices

Channels of communication (cont) S. Spaulding. Sch Life 45:12-13 Ja; 18-19 Mr; 12-13 Ap; 19-20 My; 32-3 Je; 9 Jl '63
Design for mechanical learning; architectural competition held by Rensselaer polytechnic institute. il Arch Rec 135:178-92 My '64
Dial-a-course. Time 84:69 Ag 21 '64
Franks had the right idea. J. D. Finn. il NEA J 53:24-7 Ap '64
Free and inexpensive materials. D. DuBose. Sr Schol 85:18T S 23 '64
Getting the most from the newer media. W. C. Miller and A. L. Goldberg. il NEA J 53: 30-1 Ap '64
New instructional materials for teaching poetry. C. Guss. NEA J 53:57 My '64
Packaged history; Jackdaw kits. il Time 83: 42 Ja 10 '64
Scrambling for sales in war on poverty; to test and sell theories and products. Bsns W p32 Jl 11 '64
Textbooks and teaching aids; with study-discussion program, by D. B. Harris and E. S. Harris. N. Larrick. bibliog il PTA Mag 58: 4-6, 35-6 D '63
See also
Audio-visual aids
Instructional materials centers
Magnetic recorders and recording—Educational applications
Phonograph in education
Tape recordings
Teaching machines
Telephone in education
Television in education

History

See Education—History

TEACHING, Freedom of. See Academic freedom
TEACHING-learning laboratory. See Chicago. University
TEACHING load
Once the professor was a teacher. J. G. Kemeny. il N Y Times Mag p 14+ Je 2 '63
Teacher-opinion poll; assigning the new teacher. il NEA J 53:68 O '64
See also
Class size
TEACHING machines
Automated teachers; computerized talking typewriter. il Newsweek 64:55 Jl 20 '64
Do teaching machines really teach? R. J. Margolis. il Redbook 121:51+ S '63
Education comes of age. D. Boroff. il Parents Mag 38:74+ F '63
Educational alcove; audiovisual student carrel. New Yorker 39:29 S 7 '63
How three-year-olds teach themselves to read, and love it. M. Pines. il Harper 226: 58-64 My '63
Hunt, peck & read; teaching typewriter. il Time 84:56-7 Jl 24 '64
Plug-in schools: next step in educational design? B. P. Spring. il Arch Forum 119:68-73 Ag '63
Programmed instruction: challenge or threat to art education? D. W. Ecker. bibliog il Sch Arts 63:3-6 O; 12-14 N; 8-10 D '63
Programmed learning: return to reality. N. Buckley. il Duns R 83:46-7+ My '64
Special issue on programmed instruction; symposium, ed. by D. A. Cook and D. A. Sohn. bibliog il Sr Schol 84:6T+, 9T-15T Mr 13 '64
Teaching machines and the mentally retarded L. S. Blackman. il Sch Life 46:10-12 N '63
Tomorrow: automated schools. R. E. Packer. il Sci Digest 53:34-8 My '63
When publishers go public. W. Jovanovich. il Sat R 47:21-2+ My 16 '64
See also
Programmed teaching

Anecdotes, facetiae, satire, etc.

MARY: teacher's pet; replacement of students with learning machines, Mechanical analogue response yielders. J. Biermann and B. Toohey. Wilson Lib Bul 39:402 Ja '65
TEAGARDEN, Jack
In praise of Jack Teagarden! M. Williams. il por Sat R 47:114-15 Mr 14 '64
Jazz. W. Balliett. New Yorker 39:132+ N 16 '63
Obituary
Newsweek por 63:78 Ja 27 '64
TEAGARDEN, Weldon John. See Teagarden, J.
TEAGUE, Perry O. See Friou, G. T. jt. auth.
TEAGUE, Walter Dorwin
Exploring the mystery of design. Sat R 47: 48+ O 24 '64
Twenty best industrial designs since World war II. Sat R 47:16-19 My 23 '64
TEALE, Edwin Way
Beneficent cannibalism. il Natur Hist 72:30-7 Ap '63
TEALL, Edna
Painted reveries from long ago. il por Life 57:124-7+ N 27 '64
TEALL, Kaye Moulton
Before we part: story. Redbook 123:58-9 O '64
TEAM teaching. See Teaching
TEAMS, Baseball. See Baseball clubs
TEAMSTERS union. See International brotherhood of teamsters, chauffeurs, warehousemen and helpers of America
TEAR gas
Tears for men; pengun for women. il Time 82:79 O 11 '63
TEAR sacs. See Lacrimal organs
TEARS
Tears and the lacrimal gland. S. Y. Botelho. il Sci Am 211:78-84+ bibliog(p 142) O '64
TEAS. See Afternoon teas

TEATRO dell'opera, Rome. See Rome (city)—Theater
TEATRO real, Madrid. See Opera houses
TEBALDI, Renata
Handmaid of genius; interview, ed. by G. Fitzgerald. por Opera N 27:14-15 F 9 '63
about
Angelic voice. J. Ferris. por Opera N 29:26-7 Ja 30 '65
Like being born again. por Newsweek 63:76 Ap 6 '64
Music to my ears; Tebaldi's Adriana. I. Kolodin. Sat R 46:41+ F 9 '63
Music to my ears; Tebaldi's return. I. Kolodin. Sat R 47:23+ Mr 28 '64
Renata's return. por Newsweek 61:79 F 4 '63
Tebaldi's new Desdemona. M. Bernheimer. Sat R 47:34 Ap 18 '64
Tebaldi's reward. F. Merkling. Opera N 27:35 Mr 9 '63
TEBBEL, John
Coming 3-D revolution. Sat R 47:127-8 Mr 14 '64
FM: radio's problem child. Sat R 48:67-8 Ja 9 '65
Hard sell in Washington. Sat R 47:51+ Jl 11 '64
Hardy independent. Hi Fi 14:46-8 F '64
Horatio Alger revisited; excerpt from From rags to riches, Horatio Alger, jr. and the American dream. Pub W 183:121-5 F 18 '63
How Europe fights commercial TV. Sat R 46:46-7 Ag 10 '63
How to evade the issue. Sat R 47:79-80 Ja 11 '64
JFK, the magazines, and peace. Sat R 46:56-7 D 14 '63
Journalism's challenge and answers. Sat R 46:50-1 Je 8 '63
Mitch's biggest pitch. Sat R 46:69-70+ N 9 '63
Music by mail. Hi Fi 13:42-5+ Mr '63
Newspapers and the culture beat. Sat R 46:61+ Ap 13 '63
Paperbacks: revolution or evolution? Sat R 47:62-3 Je 13 '64
Presidents and the press. Sat R 46:68-70+ S 14 '63
Publisher to an era. Sat R 47:131-3+ Ag 29 '64
Pulitzer idea: fifty years old. Sat R 46:52-3 Mr 9 '63
Putting the Times to bed. Sat R 47:67-8+ D 12 '64
Reporting the World's fair. Sat R 47:83-4 Ap 11 '64
Responsibility and mass media. Sat R 46:58-9 F 9 '63
They never left home. Sat R 46:56+ My 11 '63
Thunder on the Thames. Sat R 46:44-6 Jl 13 '63
What's happening to journalism education? Sat R 46:52-3 O 12 '63; 47:103-4+ O 10 '64
When movies joined the jet set. Sat R 47:78-9 N 14 '64
TEBBENJOHANNS, Ariane
Sheppard case reopened. C. Welles. il pors Life 57:24D Jl 31 '64
TECHNETIUM
No steel corrosion with nuclear by-product. Sci N L 83:264 Ap 27 '63
TECHNICAL animations, incorporated
Business-wise editor; case of J. Purtell formerly of Time. Sat Eve Post 236:74 Je 1 '63
TECHNICAL assistance
See also
Industrialization
Underdeveloped areas
United Nations—Technical assistance program
TECHNICAL assistance, American
American aid to education in Peru. L. C. Keating. Sch & Soc 92:206-8 My 2 '64
Development aid: address, April 4, 1963. J. de Cubas. Vital Speeches 29:499-502 Je 1 '63
Hungry nations, by W. Paddock. Review
Sci N L 87:13 Ja 2 '65. B. Tufty
Rub of cultures. F. E. Dart. For Affairs 41:360-71 Ja '63
See also
United States—Peace corps
TECHNICAL assistance, Israeli
Israel's training program for modernizing countries. W. Gerber. Mo Labor R 87:432-4 Ap '64
TECHNICAL assistance, Russian
New Communist sales pitch. il Sr Schol 82:12-14+ F 13 '63
TECHNICAL assistance in Africa
Developing Africa's human and material resources; address, January 20, 1963. G. M. Williams. Dept State Bul 48:208-11 F 11 '63
TECHNICAL assistance in Asia
See also
Colombo plan
TECHNICAL assistance in Brazil
Backland's capitalism; Project Asimow. Time 84:66 Ag 14 '64
TECHNICAL assistance in Honduras
My children will read and write. D. V. Jacobs. il NEA J 52:46-7 My '63
TECHNICAL assistance in Korea
Grandfather to half a million kids; C. Anderson in Korea. R. C. Davids. il Farm J 88:28-9+ Jl '64
TECHNICAL assistance in Latin America
Miracle at Vicos. L. Stowe. il Read Digest 82:222-6+ Ap '63
Technical assistance; summary of address, March 1963. J. A. Mora. il Américas 15:44-5 My '63
Technology is not enough. N. Ras. il Américas 17:10-15 Ja '65
TECHNICAL assistance in Mexico
Mexico and the Indian; role of National Indianist institute. A. C. Flores. il Américas 16:9-16 F '64
TECHNICAL assistance program. See United Nations—Technical assistance program
TECHNICAL conferences
See also
Inter-American meeting of science and technology
TECHNICAL documentation center. See United States—Commerce, Department of
TECHNICAL education
ACE study: higher education's aloofness from occupational education seems to be thawing. J. Walsh. Science 144:1321-2 Je 12 '64
Automation; we can handle it. T. G. Harris. il Look 29:58-62 Ja 12 '65
Better skills will improve job outlook; interview. J. C. Donovan. il Nations Bsns 52:66-8+ D '64
Coming, better agricultural jobs without college! training programs in technical agriculture. R. E. Geyer. Suc Farm 62:88 Ap '64
Community college and technical education. Sch & Soc 91:54 F 9 '63
Confrontation; analysis of scientific and engineering education by the OECD examiners. D. Wolfle. Science 139:1173 Mr 22 '63
Libraries for technical education programs. W. J. Brooking and M. H. Mahar. bibliog il Sch Life 47:9-13 O '64
Man, education and work, by G. Venn. Review.
Sat R 47:69-70 S 19 '64. A. H. Lass
Mexico's M.I.T. P. Duffett. il Sat R 46:40-2+ Ag 17 '63
Plea for better education. Sci N L 85:372 Je 13 '64
Specialized transport training needs cited. Aviation W 78:41 Mr 25 '63
Technical institute. R. E. Baird. Electr World 71:79-81 Mr '64
Technical schools, key to opportunity; post high school education. il Changing T 17:31-3 O '63
See also
Apprentices
Engineering education
Illinois institute of technology, Chicago
Massachusetts institute of technology, Cambridge
Vocational education
TECHNICAL high school libraries. See High school libraries
TECHNICAL information
Administration & management stresses better information distribution. Miss & Roc 14:93-5 Mr 30 '64
DOD acts to standardize data flow. Miss & Roc 14:14 Mr 23 '64
Information transfer and retrieval. P. H. Abelson. Science 141:319 Jl 26 '63
Think your way to success. S. Schuler. il Nations Bsns 52:88-90+ Ap '64
Too much freedom of information. D. Wolfle. Science 144:1091 My 29 '64; Reply. A. C. Blackman. 145:1123 S 11 '64
TECHNICAL institutes. See Technical education
TECHNICAL literature
Are you a potential electronics technical writer? C. Glickstein. Electr World 69:58-60+ My '63; Reply. H. L. Shimberg. 70:12 O '63
Expanded program and new format for NYPL's New technical books. Library J 88:534 F 1 '63

TECHNICAL literature—*Continued*
Houston list. E. G. Holley. il Library J 88: 959-61 Mr 1 '63
See also
Booksellers and bookselling—Technical literature

Anecdotes, facetiae, satire, etc.
High cost of writing. C. W. Morton. il Atlan 213:114 My '64

TECHNICAL processes in libraries. See Libraries—Technical processes
TECHNICAL progress. See Progress
TECHNICAL schools. See Technical education
TECHNICAL workers. See Technicians in industry
TECHNICAL writing. See Technical literature
TECHNICIANS, Electronic. See Electric workers
TECHNICIANS, Medical. See Medical workers
TECHNICIANS, Radar. See Electric workers
TECHNICIANS in industry
Coming: new jobs, new titles. S. Schuler. Nations Bsns 51:40-1+ Je '63
Corporation at war with itself. W. E. Moore. il Duns R 81:58-60 Ap '63
Education and training of technicians. H. V. Stambler and A. Lefkowitz. il Mo Labor R 87:1278-80 N '64
Engineering technician. A. B. Kazan. Pop Mech 119:30+ Ap '63
Goddard's technical manpower. R. W. Hutchison. il Electr World 71:62-3 Je '64
Integrated approach to technical staffing. E. D. Phelps and W. Gallagher. il Harvard Bsns R 41:122-9 Jl '63
Is there a job for you in aerospace? J. M. Liston. il Pop Sci 184:53-7+ Mr '64
Technical schools, key to opportunity; post high school education. il Changing T 17:31-3 O '63
That manpower shortage. W. J. Coughlin. Miss & Roc 15:46 Jl 13 '64
Water-supply shortage good manpower. Am City 79:7 Je '64
See also
Electric workers
Engineers

TECHNIQUE (art) See Prints—Technique
TECHNIQUE (music) See Piano—Instruction and study; Violin playing
TECHNIQUE (writing) See Fiction—Technique
TECHNOCRACY
Letter from France; the technocratic age. B. de Jouvenel. Bul Atomic Sci 20:27-9 O '64
TECHNOLOGICAL change
Technological change and demand; production shift analysis in bituminous coal mining; excerpt from address. W. A. Vogely. il Mo Labor R 87:891 Ag '64
TECHNOLOGICAL innovations
Automation and full employment; the problem of government, industry and labor; address, March 9, 1964. D. J. McDonald. Vital Speeches 30:409-12 Ap 15 '64
Blue collar elite. T. R. Brooks. il Duns R 83:pt2 121-2+ Mr '64
By the end of the twentieth century. D. Sarnoff. il Fortune 69:116-19 My '64
Champions for radical new inventions. D. A. Schon. bibliog f Harvard Bsns R 41:77-86 Mr '63
Detroit: proving ground for new technology. H. E. Klein. il Duns R 83:49-50+ Ap '64
$5-million search for answers; Harvard to begin a ten-year study, financed by IBM. il Bsns W p84+ Jl 4 '64
How to stay ahead of change; symposium. il Nations Bsns 51:65-8 Jl '63
Opportunity & threat in technological change. J. R. Bright. il Harvard Bsns R 41:76-86 N '63
Quiet revolution in mixed materials. H. E. Klein. il Duns R 84:32-3+ Ag '64
Real news about automation. C. E. Silberman. il Fortune 71:124-6+ Ja '65
Six challenges for tomorrow's manager. J. H. Healey. il Duns R 84:60-1+ O '64
Strike threat will decline. S. W. Gellerman. il Nations Bsns 51:36-7+ Jl '63
U.S. science entering new era; interview. D. F. Hornig. il Nations Bsns 52:40-1+ Je '64
Versatile production line. il Duns R 83:pt2 119-20+ Mr '64
Wonder industrial adhesives. H. E. Klein. il Duns R 84:53-4+ O '64

TECHNOLOGICAL research. See Industrial research
TECHNOLOGICAL unemployment. See Unemployment, Technological

TECHNOLOGY
Automation will make more jobs. il Nations Bsns 51:38-9+ Je '63
Brain mines of tomorrow. J. H. Hollomon. Sat R 46:46-7 My 4 '63
Doctor Killian's warning; excerpts from address. J. R. Killian, jr. Aviation W 80:21 Ap 27 '64
Politics and technology. E. T. Chase. Yale R 52:321-39 Mr '63
Technological exploration; address, January 15, 1964. H. Ford, 2d. Vital Speeches 30:246-9 F 1 '64
Technology and economic development. A. Briggs. il Sci Am 209:52-61 bibliog(p306) S '63
Technology and the investor. N. Calder. Bul Atomic Sci 20:47-8 Ap '64
Technology and urban life; address, October 30, 1963. E. T. Chase. Vital Speeches 30: 346-8 Mr 15 '64
Technology, prediction, and disorder. A. Wohlstetter. il Bul Atomic Sci 20:11-15 O '64
See also
Inventions
Technical literature
Technocracy

Bibliography
Science, technology: some outstanding titles. il Pub W 183:44-66 Ap 15; 184:36-56 N 11 '63; 185:28-48 Ap 20; 186:28-48 N 16 '64
Scientific, technical, and medical books to come; ed. by I. E. Stokvis and J. Putnam. Library J 88:4247-75; 89:1126-60+, 2835-70, 4399-436 N 1 '63, Mr 1, Jl, N 1 '64
Scientific, technical and medical books to come; ed. by M. Cooley and I. E. Stokvis. Library J 88:1040-78 Mr 1 '63
Summer scientific, technical and medical books; comp. by I. E. Stokvis and J. Putnam. Library J 88:2739-69 Jl '63
Technical books of 1962-1963; 100 outstanding titles for the average public or college library; comp. by G. S. Bonn. il Library J 88:933-9; 89:1015-21 Mr 1 '63, Mr 1 '64

Periodicals
100 new periodicals in science, technology, medicine; comp. by staff of Ulrich's international periodicals directory. il Library J 89:1036-41 Mr 1 '64
Science-technology periodicals; Science and technology division, New York public library. G. S. Bonn. il Library J 88:954-8 Mr 1 '63

TECHNOLOGY and civilization
Control and use of technology. N. Calder. il Nation 200:3-5 Ja 4 '65
Four days shalt thou labor? E. T. Chase. il N Y Times Mag p28+ S 20 '64
Heading toward postcivilization. P. Pickrel. Harper 229:122+ O '64
How to live with machines. F. Leiber. Sci Digest 53:26-30 Je '63
Lead time to Utopia. Nation 199:450-1 D 14 '64
Mass production of knowledge. P. R. Zilsel. Bul Atomic Sci 20:28-9 Ap '64
Now let man take over; excerpt from address, January 21, 1963. L. Mumford. New Repub 148:12-15 F 16 '63; Same abr. with title Are we selling our souls for progress. il Sci Digest 54:85-9 Jl '63
One-dimensional man, by H. Marcuse. Review
Nation 198:534-7 My 25 '64. A. Gorz
Opportunity & threat in technological change. J. R. Bright. il Harvard Bsns R 41:76-86 N '63
Person in a machine age. P. Tournier. Christian Cent 81:793-6 Je 17 '64
Promise of science and technology; address, November 12, 1964. A. E. Stevenson. Dept State Bul 51:810-15 D 7 '64
Prospect for humanity; excerpt from Design science. R. B. Fuller. Sat R 47:43-4+ Ag 29 '64
Science is amoral; need scientists be amoral, too? T. M. Hesburgh. Sat R 46:55-6 Mr 2 '63; Discussion. 46:48 Ap 6 '63
Technological society, by J. Ellul, tr. by J. Wilkinson. Review
Nation 199:249-52 O 19 '64. R. Theobald
Sat R 47:48 S 26 '64. H. H. Ransom
Technology's challenge to education; symposium. Sat R 47:21-5+ D 12 '64
Technology's impact on religion; correlation between family income and church membership. C. M. Cook. Christian Cent 81: 1083-5 S 2 '64
Tomorrow is here! Changing T 18:7-11 Jl '64
Understanding media: the extensions of man, by M. McLuhan. Review
Nation 199:194-6 O 5 '64. D. A. Holmes and G. Zabriskie

TECHNOLOGY and religion. See Religion and technology
TECHNOLOGY satellites. See Artificial satellites—Use in research
TECTITES. See Tektites
TECTONICS. See Geology, Structural
TEDESCHI, David H. and Fellows, E. J.
Monoamine oxidase inhibitors: augmentation of pressor effects of peroral tyramine. bibliog Science 144:1225-6 Je 5 '64
TEDESCO, Phyllis Reynolds
Light touch. See issues of NEA journal
TEDLAR. See Vinyl fluoride
TEEN-age audiences. See Audiences
TEEN-age automobile drivers. See Automobile drivers
TEEN-age buying. See Youth market
TEEN-age centers. See Recreation centers
TEEN-age codes. See Discipline
TEEN-age drinking. See Liquor problem—United States
TEEN-age drivers. See Automobile drivers
TEEN-age employment. See Youth—Employment
TEEN-age entertaining. See Entertaining
TEEN-age fads. See Fads
TEEN-age manners. See Courtesy
TEEN-age marriage. See High school students, Married
TEEN-age nightclubs. See Night clubs
TEEN-age parents. See Parents
TEEN-age parties. See Entertaining
TEEN-age periodicals. See Periodicals
TEEN-age reading. See Books and reading
TEEN-age singers. See Singers
TEEN-age slang. See Slang
TEEN-age smoking. See Smoking
TEEN-age spending. See Budget, Personal
TEEN-ager love; musical comedy. See Musical comedies revues, etc.—Criticisms, plots, etc.
TEEN-agers. See Adolescence; Youth
TEEN-agers food preferences. See Food preferences
TEES
Elevating thoughts about elevated tees. J. Nicklaus. il Sports Illus 21:62 D 14 '64
There are two sides to every tee. J. Nicklaus. il Sports Illus 22:50 Ja 25 '65
TEETH
Brace yourself; orthodontic treatment. il Newsweek 63:72+ My 18 '64
Collagenous layer covering the crown enamel of unerupted permanent human teeth. P. T. Levine and others. bibliog il Science 146: 1676-8 D 25 '64
Documenting the case against fluoridation. J. Lear. il Sat R 47:85-92 Ja 4 '64; Same abr. Sci Digest 55:34-9 Ap '64; Discussion. Sat R 47:49-53 F 1; 24-31 F 15; 51-3 Mr 7; 47-9 My 2; 44 Ag 1 '64
Fluorides for better bites. Time 84:95 N 20 '64
Molar size sequences and fossil taxonomy. S. M. Garn and others. bibliog il Science 142:1060 N 22 '63
Observation of internal structures of teeth by ultrasonography. G. Baum and others. il Science 139:495-6 F 8 '63
Sleep pattern of tooth-grinding: its relationship to dreaming. G. R. Reding and others. bibliog il Science 145:725-6 Ag 14 '64
Strontium-90 content of deciduous human incisors. H. L. Rosenthal and others. bibliog il Science 140:176-7 Ap 12 '63
Tooth destruction; report of symposium, AAAS section on dentistry. R. F. Sognnaes. Science 139:849-51 Mr 1 '63
Vertebrate hard tissues; report on special symposium of the section of vertebrate morphology of the American society of zoologists. C. Gans. Science 144:323-4 Ap 17 '64
Where is science taking us? effects of fluoride. R. E. Hanford. Sat R 47:54 Mr 7 '64
Your teeth: folklore and fallacies; reprint. il Todays Health 42:84-5 Ap '64
See also
Dental research
Dentistry
Dentition
Mouth hygiene
Orthodontics

Care and hygiene

Antibiotics may help stop tooth troubles. Sci N L 87:56 Ja 23 '65
Dental care before the baby is born. il Todays Health 42:61 Mr '64
Dental care during pregnancy. A. N. Cranin. Redbook 123:46+ S '64
Fourteen questions on dental health answered. Todays Health 41:39+ Ap '63
Hot light beam tried to prevent tooth decay. Sci N L 85:200 Mr 28 '64
Just what are the most common dental problems? G. G. Greer. Bet Hom & Gard 41: 34 Je '63
New ideas about preventing tooth decay. Good H 156:143 Mr '63
New magic with your old teeth; questions and answers. il Sci Digest 55:48-50 Ja '64
New ways to guard against tooth decay. Good H 158:130-1 Ja '64
See also
Dentifrices
Toothbrushes

Diseases

Cariostatic effect of phosphates. F. J. McClure. bibliog il Science 144:1337-8 Je 12 '64
Decay-producing germs isolated from hamsters' teeth. il Todays Health 41:82 My '63
Dental caries: a new look; report on conference 30 November-1 December 1964. J. F. Frederick. Science 147:419-21 Ja 22 '65
Destroy tooth decay with laser light beam. Sci N L 86:105 Ag 15 '64
Little tooth decay found among Ethiopians. Sci N L 84:89 Ag 10 '63
Mineral-treated cereal prevents tooth decay. Sci N L 85:183 Mr 21 '64
Now they say: sweets do not cause tooth decay. Sci Digest 53:36 Je '63
Study tooth enamel crystals for decay causes. il Todays Health 41:74 D '63
Tooth decay is plague. Sci N L 87:19 Ja 9 '65
Tooth decay not caused by sweets, study shows. Sci N L 83:216 Ap 6 '63
Tooth decay reduced by penicillin pills. Sci N L 85:248 Ap 18 '64
Tooth decay, solving the puzzle. il Changing T 17:23-4 Ap '63
TEETH (animals)
Calcification of deciduous teeth in rhesus monkeys. D. R. Swindler and H. A. McCoy. bibliog il Science 144:1243-4 Je 5 '64
New choppers save bossy. C. L. Stratton. il Farm J 88:54D Ap '64
TEETH (fishes)
Calcified ectodermal collagens of shark tooth enamel and teleost scale. M. L. Moss and others. bibliog il Science 145:940-2 Ag 28 '64
TEETH, Artificial
New choppers save bossy. C. L. Stratton. il Farm J 88:54D Ap '64
TEETH, Fossil
Microradiography of fossilized teeth. R. W. G. Wyckoff and others. il Science 140:78-80 Ap 5 '63
TEETH, Transplantation of. See Transplantation of organs, tissues, etc.
TEETHING. See Dentition
TEETOR, Dave
Airlines off course? Flying 75:64-6 S '64
—and DeRemer, Bernard
Industry. Flying 74:27+ My '64
TEFFERTELLER, Ruth S.
Recreation and family needs; excerpts from Helping the family in urban society. Recreation 56:423-4 N '63
TEFLON
Teflon: slippery, synthetic. il Motor T 15: 104-5 N '63
Unstickables. il Time 83:95 Mr 13 '64
Wife saver; coating for pots and pans. il Am Home 67:54-5+ Je '64
TEGUCIGALPA, Honduras
Empty water mains; condensed report. H. Seidel. Am City 78:33 Ap '63
TEHERAN

Hotels, restaurants, etc.

Let's travel. il Mlle 57:26 Jl '63

Riots

Progress at a price; riots. il Time 81:34-5 Je 14 '63
TEHRAN. See Teheran
TEHUACÁN, Mexico
Ancient Mesoamerican civilization. R. S. MacNeish. bibliog il Science 143:531-7 F 7 '64
Origins of New World civilization. R. S. MacNeish. il Sci Am 211:29-37 bibliog(p 154) N '64
TEICHMANN, Howard
Rainy day in Newark. Criticism
Newsweek 62:62 N 4 '63
Theatre Arts 48:68 Ja '64
TEILHARD DE CHARDIN, Pierre
Christian's dilemma. J. Collignon. il por Sat R 47:14-16 Je 27 '64
Noosphere around us. por Newsweek 64:70 Ag 31 '64
Noosphere revisited. por Time 84:91-2 O 16 '64

TEILHARD DE CHARDIN, Pierre—*Continued*
Priest who haunts the Catholic world. J. Kobler. il pors Sat Eve Post 236:42-51 O 12 '63; Discussion. America 109:440. 542-3, 792-4 O 19, N 9, D 21 '63
Teilhard's collectivist salvation. T. Molnar. Nat R 14:464-5 Je 4 '63
To the anthill with love. T. Molnar. por Nat R 16:1073-4 D 1 '64

TEITELBAUM, Philip, and Cytawa, Jerzy
Spreading depression and recovery from lateral hypothalamic damage. bibliog Science 147: 61-3 Ja 1 '65

TEIXEIRA, Bernardo
Massacre at Quitexe. Nat R 16:822-3 S 22 '64

TEIXEIRA DIREITO, F.
Lisbon's style. Opera N 29:26 S 26 '64

TEIXEIRA LEITE, José R.
Introduction to Brazilian painting. Américas 16:21-8 My '64

TEJERA-PARIS, Enrique
Ambassador Tejera-Paris to Secretary Rusk; note, July 22, 1963. Dept State Bul 49:365-7 S 2 '63

TEKTITES
Chunks off the moon. il Time 82:61 N 29 '63
Detrital mineral grains in tektites. V. E. Barnes. il Science 142:1651-2 D 27 '63
Hydrogen in a tektite vesicle. J. A. O'Keefe and others. Science 143:39 Ja 3 '64
Moon material on earth. il Sci N L 84:339 N 30 '63
Origin of tektites. J. A. O'Keefe and B. E. Shute. bibliog il Science 139:1288-90 Mr 29 '63
Pieces of the moon. il Sci Digest 55:5 F '64
Project Moon harvest. Sky & Tel 27:212 Ap '64
Rare-earth elements in tektites. L. Haskin and M. A. Gehl. bibliog il Science 139: 1056-8 Mr 15 '63
Spalled, aerodynamically modified moldavite from Slavice, Moravia, Czechoslovakia. E. C. T. Chao. bibliog il Science 146:790-1 N 6 '64
Teardrops from space. il Sci N L 86:327 N 21 '64
Tektites and impact fragments from the moon. J. A. O'Keefe. il Sci Am 210:50-7 bibliog(p 152) F '64
When the moon fell. Newsweek 62:98 D 2 '63

TEL AVIV, Israel
Israel's three cities. D. Pryce-Jones. Commentary 35:55-8 Ja '63

Hotels, restaurants, etc.

Synagogue with bedrooms; Hotel Deborah, world's largest strictly kosher hotel. il Time 83:85 Je 12 '64

Music

Two in Tel Aviv. A. Frankenstein. Opera N 29:31 D 26 '64

TELCAN. See Video tape recorders and recording

TELECOMMUNICATION
See also
Teletype in aviation

TELECOMMUNICATION union, International. See International telecommunication union

TELEDYNE, incorporated
Infant with a giant appetite. il Bsns W p66-8 Ja 11 '64

TELEGRAPH

Private wire systems

Dangerous decision at a desperate time; increase of rates for commercial users of leased telegraph and telephoto services. R. L. Tobin. Sat R 46:49-50 Mr 9 '63

TELEGRAPH companies
Cross talk on what cables should carry; fights between telephone and telegraph companies. il Bsns W p 116+ F 22 '64
See also
American telephone and telegraph company
Western union telegraph company

TELEGRAPHERS
Island of yesterday afternoon: the press telegrapher. M. Siegel. Sat R 46:55+ O 12 '63

TELELECTURES. See Telephone in education

TELEMACHUS Clay; drama. See Carlino, L. J.

TELEMETER
Electronic scanning simplifies telemetry. L. G. Sands. il Electr World 72:36-7+ Jl '64
See also
Space telemetry

TELEMETER (physiological apparatus)
Multiple births foretold; detecting heartbeats of unborn babies. Sci N L 84:338 N 30 '63
Telemetry of homing behavior by the deermouse, peromyscus. K. S. Rawson and P. H. Hartline. bibliog il Science 146:1596-8 D 18 '64

TELEMETRY, Space. See Space telemetry

TELEOSTS
Excretion of hypertonic urine by a teleost. J. G. Stanley and W. R. Fleming. bibliog il Science 144:63-4 Ap 3 '64

TELEPATHY
See also
Extrasensory perception

TELEPHONE
Beep line. il Time 82:54 O 18 '63
Bootleg bonanza; fad for reconditioned antique telephones. il Newsweek 65:64 F 1 '65
Challenger to princess. il Bsns W p78+ Ja 26 '63
Hello, I want to speak to the oven; some of the wonderful things your telephone will do for you today, tomorrow and someday. J. L. Block. House & Gard 126:208-9+ O '64
Hold the phone! il McCalls 90:90-3 My '63
Look what's happening to the telephone. Changing T 18:6 My '64
Save money on phone service. Changing T 18:22 F '64
Service; telephone services available around the globe. New Yorker 39:32-3 Ap 6 '63
Simon sez; darkroom accessory, automatic dialing telephone. S. Nathan. il U S Camera 26:38 My '63
Something is calling. Time 82:58 N 8 '63
Superphone. il Newsweek 62:53 D 30 '63
What's coming tomorrow from today's telephones. il U S News 56:60-4 Mr 9 '64
See also
Advertising mediums—Telephone
Communication and traffic
Emergency communications systems
Radio telephone
Radio telephone on ships, boats, etc.
Telephone in government

Anecdotes, facetiae, satire, etc.

Now Parkinson's telephone law. C. N. Parkinson. il N Y Times Mag p39-40 Ap 12 '64

Apparatus and supplies

Build a telephone beeper. F. Blechman. il Pop Electr 19:57-9+ D '63
Loud-hailer for the telephone. D. L. Wilcox. il Pop Electr 19:67-9 D '63
Pickup pranks; recording pickup, oscillator, and tachometer. F. Blechman. il Pop Electr 19:60-1+ Ag '63

History

Thanks to one Bell, the whole world rings. il Sr Schol 84:5 Mr 13 '64

Intercommunicating systems

See Intercommunicating systems

Radio telephone connection

Don't call us, we'll call you; Bellboy system. il Time 84:39 D 25 '64

Rates

Does the FCC have AT&T's number? D. Gottlieb and D. Gottlieb. New Repub 148: 17-19 Ap 6 '63
Nightoll; rate cuts. Newsweek 61:73-4 F 11 '63
Soon: coast-to-coast phone call for $1. U S News 54:10 F 11 '63
Soon: long-distance calls to cost less. U S News 57:18 D 7 '64
Wrong numbers for A.T.&T; reduction in long-distance telephone rates. Time 84:105 D 4 '64

Religious applications

Australia's Life line movement. A. Walker. Christian Cent 81:20-1 Ja 1 '64
Throwing out the Life line. il Time 83:34 Ja 24 '64

Television combination

Bell is ringing. il Time 83:74-8 My 29 '64
On the way: see-as-you-talk phone service. il U S News 56:16 My 25 '64
Picturephone. Sci Am 211:48 Jl '64
Picturephone developed for commercial use. Sci N L 86:73 Ag 1 '64

Wire tapping

See Wire tapping

TELEPHONE, Dial
Dial A for anything. Newsweek 62:76 S 16 '63
Dial, buzz and blink. A. Trauffer. il Pop Electr 20:64-5 F '64
Dial 2122428180. W. Marx. il Nation 197:334-6 N 23 '63
Dial your party line. New Repub 150:5 Je 27 '64; Discussion. 151:30 Jl 11 '64

TELEPHONE, Push button
Now, a new kind of telephone. il U S News 55:11 N 25 '63

TELEPHONE cables
Down to the sea with phone lines. il Bsns W p70-1 Jl 4 '64
Toothy; sheathing that resists gnawing by gophers. il Newsweek 62:56 Jl 8 '63
U.S. and Japan inaugurate transpacific telephone cable; exchange of remarks, June 18, 1964. L. B. Johnson; H. Ikeda. Dept State Bul 51:26 Jl 6 '64
See also
Cables, Submarine

TELEPHONE companies
Cross talk on what cables should carry; fights between telephone and telegraph companies. il Bsns W p 116+ F 22 '64
Diamond-studded coyote; Teléfonos de México. il Time 82:115 D 6 '63
See also
American telephone and telegraph company
Bell telephone system
General telephone and electronics corporation
Southern Bell telephone and telegraph company

Employees

How a company keeps going despite strike, sabotage; General telephone company of Florida. il U S News 55:77+ Ag 26 '63

Wages and hours

As Michigan goes. Bsns W p 154 S 19 '64

TELEPHONE company buildings
Bell builds cellar in the sky; New York telephone's skyscraper. il Bsns W p30-1 F 9 '63

TELEPHONE directories
Walking fingers; classified telephone directories. il Newsweek 63:78-9 Ap 13 '64

TELEPHONE exchanges
Great immortal machine: direct-dialing exchange. il Pop Electr 22:69-70 Ja '65

TELEPHONE in business
Supermarket without a store; Hemkop in Stockholm, Sweden. il Bsns W p 100-2 Ja 11 '64

TELEPHONE in education
Lectures on the phone; telelectures. il Time 82:37 Jl 19 '63
Person-to-person teaching; Amplified telephone project. C. F. Madden. il Sat R 47:50-1+ Jl 18 '64; Reply. B. Horel. 47:49 Ag 15 '64

TELEPHONE in government
Hot line to link to East-West? Sr Schol 82:17 Ap 24 '63

Anecdotes, facetiae, satire, etc.

Central, give me a (hot) line. P. Mandel. il Life 54:19 Ap 26 '63

TELEPHONE information service. See Information services

TELEPHONE numbers
What's my line? unlisted phone numbers. Time 81:90 Ap 19 '63

TELEPHONE workers. See Telephone companies—Employees

TELEPHOTO lenses. See Lenses, Photographic

TELEPHOTOGRAPHY
Keppler on the SLR; monocular vs telephoto lens. il Mod Phot 28:30+ Ag '64
New TelXtender triples SLR lens's focal length. L. Barry. il Pop Phot 55:98 S '64
Telescopic power tripled; simple device to photograph stars electronically. Sci N L 86:342 N 28 '64

TELEPRINTER. See Teletype

TELEREGISTER corporation
Inventor of the month; mechanical brain quotes stock levels. S. V. Jones. il Sci Digest 56:22 Ag '64

TELESCOPE
Amateur scientist; ed. by C. L. Stong. See issues of Scientific American
Amateur scientist; telescope for a home observatory and a light meter. F. Aime. il Sci Am 209:120-2+ Ag '63
Astronomy: academy study urges ten-year, $224 million program of new telescope construction. D. S. Greenberg. Science 146: 899-900 N 13 '64
Determination of stellar distances; navy's new telescope at Flagstaff, Ariz. K. A. Strand. bibliog il Science 144:1299-309 Je 12 '64
Generation of telescopes. Sci Am 212:48 Ja '65
Gleanings for ATM's; ed. by R. E. Cox. See issues of Sky and telescope
Honeywell to develop passive-scan telescope. Aviation W 79:26 S 2 '63
Image tubes soon available. G. S. Mumford. il Sky & Tel 29:26 Ja '65
Increase telescope power. Sci N L 86:21 Jl 11 '64
Key to other worlds; using a neutrino telescope. A. Ewing. il Sci N L 84:99 Ag 17 '63
Large new telescopes for the southern hemisphere. V. K. McElheny. Science 146: 755-7 N 6 '64
Lincoln laboratory's 48-inch reentry telescope; Cassegrain telescope. R. N. Watts, jr. il Sky & Tel 25:330-1 Je '63
Long-range planning for American astronomy; Large optical telescopes erected since 1945. il Sky & Tel 29:3+ Ja '65
Mighty scope for the long eyes. il Life 54:53-4+ Je 7 '63
NASA speeds to fill gap in availability of big telescopes. H. Taylor. Miss & Roc 15:17 S 21 '64
New dimensions for the stars. il Time 83:48 Ap 3 '64
New 61-inch astrometric reflector; U.S. naval observatory, Flagstaff, Ariz. K. A. Strand. il Sky & Tel 27:204-9+ Ap '64
Observatory aircraft proposed for better satellite inspection. R. Pay. Miss & Roc 15:36-7 N 16 '64
People with the long eyes. il Fortune 67:102-3 Mr '63
Refiguring the 82-inch McDonald reflector's optics. J. Texereau. il Sky & Tel 28:345-8 D '64
Small moderately-priced telescope. il Consumer Bul 46:23 Jl '63
Space telescope use with MORL proposed. R. D. Hibben. il Aviation W 80:71+ F 24 '64
Telescope will orbit. A. Ewing. Sci N L 86: 231 O 10 '64
Telescopes for the future. Sky & Tel 28:202-3 O '64
View in the dark; Bouwers telescope. il Time 81:51 Je 21 '63
Visiting Germany's largest telescope; Karl Schwarzschild observatory. S. Van Den Bergh. il Sky & Tel 27:268-72 My '64
See also
Coronagraph
Mirrors for telescopes
Radio telescope
Telescopic sights

History

Explorations with the Hale telescope; adaptation of address, May 15, 1964. I. S. Bowen. il Science 145:1391-8 S 25 '64

Photographic telescope

First flight of Stratoscope II called success. Miss & Roc 12:37 Mr 11 '63
Stratoscope II: sky-high and starry-eyed. R. Gannon. il Pop Sci 182:86-90+ F '63

TELESCOPE mirrors. See Mirrors for telescopes

TELESCOPIC photography. See Telephotography

TELESCOPIC sights
Battles by starlight; new night-seeing scope. Time 84:100 N 20 '64
Medium vari-X's. Field & S 68:135 Ap '64
Mounting the scope. J O'Connor. il Outdoor Life 133:92-6 F '64

TELETYPE
Dial K for Khrushchev; direct hot line between Kremlin and White House. Bsns W p36 Ap 13 '63
Hot line to Moscow: how it will work. il U S News 55:8 Jl 1 '63
More libraries using teletype for interlibrary loan service. il Library J 89:4880 D 15 '64
Open wire to Kremlin. il Bsns W p36 Je 29 '63
U.S.S.R. accepts U.S. proposal for direct communication link; statement, April 5, 1963. Dept State Bul 48:600 Ap 22 '63
U.S. and U.S.S.R. sign agreement for direct communications link; White House statement, June 20, 1963, with text of agreement. Dept State Bul 49:50-1 Jl 8 '63
See also
Hot line (Washington and Moscow)

TELETYPE in aviation
Airlines planning two-way Syncom tests; transmission of a teletypewriter message. P. J. Klass. Aviation W 81:34 D 7 '64

TELETYPESETTERS. See Typesetting machines
TELEVISION
Bibliography
Book reviews (cont of) Technical books. See issues of Electronics world
Technical books. See issues of Electronics world
Color
See Television, Color
Frequency allocation
See Television frequency allocation
History
Mummy case to Ben Casey. E. T. Ewen. il N Y Times Mag p42+ Ag 25 '63
Photographic aspects
As I see it: New York city news photography and live TV news. E. Hannigan. il U S Camera 26:32+ Jl '63
Behind the scenes. il Mod Phot 27:48+ D '63
Color slides; TV and photo techniques. R. Miller. U S Camera 27:10+ Jl '64
Instant movies. R. Miller il U S Camera 26:80 Jl '63
Photographers guide to television. S. Paley. il Pop Phot 55:186-9 N '64
Television photography today. W. P. Banner. il U S Camera 26:18-19+ Je '63
TV's journalism triumph. B. Downes. Pop Phot 53:68 D '63
35mm techniques; camera reporting on TV. P. Stackpole. U S Camera 26:32+ O '63
Social aspects
See Television broadcasting—Social aspects
TELEVISION, Closed circuit
Closed circuit TV at AASA. NEA J 52:35 Mr '63
How to select a closed-circuit TV camera. W. Sander. il Electr World 70:41-3+ O '63
Indianapolis; 500-mile race. Sports Illus 20:17 Je 8 '64
Look right into your sewer problems. J. A. Kern. il Am City 79:84-5 Ag '64
NAACP Freedom spectacular; all-star TV show. il Ebony 19:57-8+ Jl '64
Nineteen-inch supermarket; electronic marketing in Tucson, Ariz. il Time 83:63 Mr 20 '64
TV goes C-C. R. M. Lipsyte. il N Y Times Mag p 157+ Ap 7 '63
TV teachers: leading a company into space. il Bsns W p60-1+ Ag 29 '64
See also
Television in education
TELEVISION, Color
Black and white turns to color; Telehue brings color to black-and-white TV screen. Bsns W p 104+ Mr 16 '63
Color catches fire. S. Brown. il Sat Eve Post 236:74-5 Ag 10 '63
Color-pattern generators. W. J. Cerveny. il Electr World 69:50-2+ Mr '63
Color TV beginning to boom. il Changing T 18:33-5 F '64
Color TV set makers turn sales volume up; hoping for more shows in color on air. il Bsns W p 144-6 Ja 23 '65
Color TV's several images. il Fortune 69:199-200+ Mr '64
Colorful sales. Newsweek 61:82+ Je 24 '63
European color-TV developments. P. Halliday. Electr World 70:66-7 Jl '63
It looks like a boom starting in color TV. il U S News 55:60 D 2 '63
Maintaining TV color balance. il Electr World 72:61 Jl '64
Promise of the peacock; color programs. Consumer Rep 28:261 Je '63
Simplified Mexican color TV. L. Solomon. il Electr World 72:48+ Jl '64
Whose hue? three-way choice of color. il Newsweek 63:44 Ja 6 '64
TELEVISION academy of arts and sciences. See Academy of television arts and sciences
TELEVISION actors and actresses. See Television broadcasting—Performers
TELEVISION advertising
And now a brief message from. . . G. Ace. Sat R 47:10 Ap 25 '64
And now, a brief word from our sponsors. . ; bill prohibiting FCC regulation of broadcast advertising. D. Rapoport. Reporter 30:26-8 Je 4 '64
And now a word from our newscaster. R. L. Tobin. Sat R 46:47-8 Je 8 '63; Reply. D. Hewitson. 46:42 Jl 13 '63
Another brief message from . . . G. Ace. Sat R 47:9 My 2 '64
Ask the man who listens; Texaco's regular Saturday afternoon broadcast of the Metropolitan opera. L. L. L. Golden. Sat R 46:60 My 11 '63
Big difference in Anacin. il Consumer Rep 28:261-2 Je '63
Chairman Henry on target; FCC's attempt to regulate commercial time standards. R. L. Shayon. Sat R 46:43 O 19 '63
Clio, muse of huckstery; winners in American TV commercials festival. Time 81:47 My 31 '63
Clio's commercials. R. L. Shayon. Sat R 46:52 Je 8 '63
Daniel (bubblegum) Boone; tie-in television. R. L. Shayon. Sat R 47:18 S 5 '64
Down; Northeast airlines television commercials. New Yorker 40:30-2 Mr 21 '64
East meets West in cartoon venture; Japanese animated cartoons for Video crafts, New York. il Bsns W p 104-5 My 11 '63
Fewer commercials. New Repub 148:4-5 Ap 13 '63; Reply. W. Gore. 148:37 My 4 '63
Fifty-eight-second film festival; American TV commercials festival in the Waldorf-Astoria. A. Levy. il Reporter 28:39-40+ Je 20 '63
Forecast for the FCC. R. L. Shayon. Sat R 47:51 Ja 11 '64
Forty-three cheers; dissenting vote on bill prohibiting the FCC from limiting number and frequency of commercials on the air. R. L. Shayon. Sat R 47:30 Ap 18 '64
Guerrilla war on soap giants. il Bsns W p50-2 Ag 29 '64
Help quiet commercials. Sci N L 83:118 F 23 '63
How Europe fights commercial TV. J. Tebbel. il Sat R 46:46-7 Ag 10 '63; Discussion. 46:67 S 14; 48 O 12 '63
Image builders go back to print; ads in magazines again. il Bsns W p70 O 31 '64
Little station that won't; KWUN's refusal of cigarette commercials. R. L. Shayon. Sat R 47:24 F 8 '64
Magic minutes. il Newsweek 61:92 Ap 22 '63
Mrs Roosevelt does a TV commercial. T. L. Stix. Harper 227:104-6 N '63
Moppet market; aiming at the child as consumer. A. F. Gonzalez. Reporter 30:40+ Je 18 '64
Movies are older than ever. G. Ace. Sat R 47:14 Ag 15 '64
New kinds of television; where do we go from here? V. Packard. il Atlan 212:68-74 O '63
Nothing but ads. P. Goodman. New Repub 148:28-30 F 9 '63
One-commercial Bonanza. America 109:406 O 12 '63
Oratorios for industry; world's most successful singers of TV commercials. il Time 84:42 Jl 24 '64
Our timid watchdog: FCC. Consumer Rep 29:110-11 Mr '64
Peanut butter world. C. W. Morton. Atlan 211:129 Ap '63
Selling point. il Time 85:56-7 Ja 22 '65
Singing saleswoman. il Ebony 19:143-4+ Ap '64
Sixty-second go-round; policy regarding controversial commercials. Newsweek 64:76 S 21 '64
Smoke gets in your ears. G. Ace. Sat R 47:18 D 12 '64
Sponsors with tone. Newsweek 61:88 F 11 '63
Still on their own; FCC proposal to regulate the number and length of commercials. Newsweek 63:55 Ja 27 '64
TV addenda. V. Hill. il Atlan 213:126-7 Ap '64
TV commercials loud? Sci N L 85:198 Mr 28 '64
TV commercials; the government ducks the issue. D. Smith. Nation 198:286-9 Mr 23 '64
TV's prosperous pitchmen; performers in commercials. B. Davidson. il Sat Eve Post 236:26-7 Ag 24 '63
That same wax of Ball again. G. Ace. Sat R 47:14 My 16 '64
Toward a T.V. code of manners; report by Britain's Independent television authority. Christian Cent 80:1022 Ag 21 '63
Toys more like toys. il Bsns W p31 S 28 '63
Twenty-two straight commercials. Newsweek 61:87 Ap 15 '63
What is wrong with TV, and with us. C. A. Siepmann. il N Y Times Mag p 13+ Ap 19 '64
What's good for U.N. is good for Xerox; six non-commercial 90-minute films on TV concerning UN global activities. Bsns W p80+ Ap 18 '64

TELEVISION advertising—*Continued*
When the client is a candidate; five TV commercials for the Democrats. P. Hamill. il N Y Times Mag p30-1+ O 25 '64
Wife who wasn't there; leading actress of Bewitched not in closing commercial. R. L. Shayon. Sat R 47:27 O 17 '64

Anecdotes, facetiae, satire, etc.
Escape hatch: pay-TV. C. W. Morton. il Atlan 214:121 O '64
Hooray for commercials! A. Buchwald. il Read Digest 84:27-8 My '64
TV's supersalesman. C. W. Morton. il Atlan 213:123 Je '64

TELEVISION aids to space flight. See Television in space flight

TELEVISION and children. See Television broadcasting and children

TELEVISION and libraries. See Libraries and television

TELEVISION and radio broadcasting. See Radio broadcasting and television

TELEVISION and reading
Movies, TV, and paperbacks. J. M. Culkin. Sr Schol 83:28T-29T Ja 17 '64

TELEVISION announcers. See Television broadcasting—Announcing

TELEVISION antennas
Big wire; cable television. il Time 84:110-11 N 13 '64
CATV in Logansport. W. A. Stocklin. Electr World 73:12 Ja '65
Cable TV: on the move; community antenna television systems. C. S. Tepfer. il Electr World 71:40-1+ Ja '64
Cable TV plays for New York jackpot. il Bsns W p34+ D 12 '64
For the two-TV family, two-set couplers. il Consumer Rep 29:330-1 Jl '64
Harnessing the antenna; community antenna TV system. R. Jones. il Electr World 71: 46-7 Ap '64
Indoor horn for TV-FM reception. B. V. K. French. bibliog il Electr World 70:50-1+ D '63
Indoor powered antennas; PM tests and reports. il Pop Mech 121:196 Ap '64
Is pay-TV sneaking to success? community antenna television systems. il Bsns W p32-3 Ap 25 '64
Is your TV antenna out of date? R. M. Benrey. il Pop Sci 186:68-71+ Ja '65
Loss figures for 300-ohm twin-lead. M. L. Nelson. il Electr World 73:30 Ja '65
Power antenna for out yonder. il Pop Mech 119:138 Ap '63
Powerful new antenna for tv and fm, too. C. Tepfer. il Pop Sci 182:188-9 Mr '63
Some corrections on TV roof antennas. Consumer Rep 30:7 Ja '65
TV's best guarded secret: electronically right length for rabbit ears. L. A. Harlow. il Pop Electr 19:49-50 Ag '63
Television's lusty offspring: the boom and brawls of CATV. il Newsweek 65:62-4 F 1 '65
Two-set couplers for TV and FM. il Consumer Bul 48:6-7 F '65

TELEVISION apparatus
Inconspicuous new UHF converter; Blonder-Tongue ultraverter model BTD-44. il Consumer Rep 30:6 Ja '65
Maintaining TV color balance. il Electr World 72:61 Jl '64
Results of EW tests on U.H.F. converters. il Electr World 72:31-3 Jl '64
UHF converters; Blonder-Tongue BTC-99S and BTU-2T. il Consumer Rep 29:386-8 Ag '64
U.H.F. converters; circuits & design. L. Solomon. il Electr World 71:41-4 F '64
UHF reception. J. Beever. il Electr World 70:37-9+ N '63; Reply with rejoinder. A. Weiss. 71:80-1 Ap '64
See also
Cathode ray tubes
Signal generators
Video tape recorders and recording

Manufacture
Color TV from a kit. H. Luckett. il Pop Sci 184:110-13 Mr '64

TELEVISION apparatus industry and trade
New TV designs for 1964. W. H. Buchsbaum. il Electr World 71:51-4+ Mr '64

TELEVISION apparatus on automobiles
New sounds for your car. il Motor T 15:44-7 Ap '63
TV blackout for autos? pro and con discussion. il Sr Schol 82:14 Mr 20 '63

TELEVISION authorship
Cant and candor. G. Ace. Sat R 47:12 Ag 22 '64
Comedy writers. G. Ace. Sat R 48:10 Ja 23 '65
Fingers of God; S. Silliphant. Time 82:60-1 Ag 9 '63
Friendly lynching; M. Miller script for Calhoun. Newsweek 64:87 N 9 '64
How to get by on $10,000 a week. G. Ace. Sat R 47:18 F 8 '64
Only you, Dick Daring! by M. Miller and E. Rhodes. Review
Life 57:12 N 6 '64. M. Wylie
Sat R 47:34 O 31 '64. R. L. Shayon
Only you, Merle Miller; concerning script of TV series Calhoun. Time 84:72+ N 13 '64
Queen of the soaps. Newsweek 63:66-7 My 11 '64
That same wax of Ball again. G. Ace. Sat R 47:14 My 16 '64
Think young. G. Ace. Sat R 47:12 Je 27 '64
Why is it all so lousy? F. Fenton. Esquire 59:46+ F '63

TELEVISION awards. See Academy of television arts and sciences

TELEVISION broadcasting
Camera's glass-eye; sensation of actuality. P. Goodman. New Repub 148:24+ My 25 '63
Can TV be saved? symposium. Esquire 60: 210-11+ D '63
Critics: TV or not TV. G. Spelvin. il Theatre Arts 47:64-5 Ap '63
Jack Benny plus one. G. Ace. Sat R 47:21 Ag 29 '64
Priceless role. Newsweek 62:56 D 16 '63
Television: embarrassing moments of 1963. C. W. Morton. il Atlan 212:136+ D '63
See also
Television stations
Video tape recorders and recording

Advertising
See Television advertising

Anecdotes, facetiae, satire, etc.
How to get by on $10,000 a week. G. Ace. Sat R 47:18 F 8 '64
Son-of-a-gun. G. Ace. Sat R 47:10 My 30 '64

Announcing
Good evening, good night. G. Ace. Sat R 47:9+ Mr 28 '64

Art programs
Art of collecting; five private American collections shown on NBC. K. Kuh. il Sat R 47:37-52 Ja 18 '64
Art on TV: The Louvre. R. L. Shayon. Sat R 47:18 D 19 '64

Baseball
See Television broadcasting—Sports

Boxing
See Television broadcasting—Sports

Business programs
TV turns cameras on business. il Bsns W p 116-18 F 9 '63

Censorship
Non-commercial channels. P. Goodman. New Repub 148:32-4 Ap 13 '63; Reply. H. Zitzler. 148:37 My 4 '63

Children, Effect on
See Television broadcasting and children

Childrens programs
Beatle fatigue. G. Ace. Sat R 47:18 D 5 '64
Can a chipmunk teach the new math on TV? R. Atcheson. il Sat Eve Post 238:26-7 Ja 16 '65
Children's hour. America 110:507 Ap 11 '64
Don't disturb the children. P. Goodman. New Repub 148:28-30 Mr 16 '63
Facts of life; Discovery '63. Newsweek 62:57 S 9 '63
Ox bowl game; CBS's annual telecast of Metro-Goldwyn-Mayer's The Wizard of Oz. il Time 85:68 Ja 15 '65
Time out for television. See issues of PTA magazine
World's largest kindergarten; Romper room. il Time 82:71-2 S 13 '63

Comedy
See Television broadcasting—Humor

Conversation programs
Audition; new teen-age panel, The comers. il New Yorker 40:29-32 Mr 28 '64
Television's new bad boy; Les Crane show. B. Carey. il Look 28:111-14 N 3 '64

TELEVISION broadcasting—*Continued*

Court proceedings

See Television broadcasting—Trials

Crime programs

Free crime school? TV explosion. America 108:425 Mr 30 '63
Man inside The man from U.N.C.L.E. il Time 85:68 Ja 29 '65
Television: stimulant to violence. J. Ellison. Nation 197:433-6 D 21 '63
TV violence, the kids react. M. A. Guitar. il N Y Times Mag p24 D 27 '64

Criticism

See Television criticism

Dancing

Conversation corner; New York repertoire workshop. L. Joel. Dance Mag 37:18 F '63
Dancing along with Mitch. S. Goodman. il Dance Mag 37:30-3+ S '63
Ernie Flatt in action. E. Palatsky. il Dance Mag 38:42-5 D '64
June Taylor dancers open with tap. il Dance Mag 37:42-3 Je '63
Looking at television. A. Barzel. See issues of Dance magazine
View from the big eye; Hollywood's TV dancers. O. Maynard. il Dance Mag 39:40-3 Ja '65
Whirlwind Wednesday in Brooklyn; R. Nureyev and S. Beriosova on Bell telephone hour. il Dance Mag 37:40-5 O '63

Documentary programs

Chopper warfare; ABC's Letters from Vietnam. il Newsweek 64:84 S 14 '64
Come back, Nell Gwyn; NBC show, The stately ghosts of England. il Newsweek 65:70 Ja 18 '65
Congress and the Cosa nostra. R. L. Shayon. Sat R 46:34 N 9 '63
Crème de la Kremlin; NBC's tour of the Kremlin. il Time 81:48 My 31 '63
D-day, Ike hour. il Time 83:86 Je 12 '64
D-day reminder of the best of Ike. L. Wainwright. Life 56:29 Je 19 '64
Flags are not enough: Widening gap; excerpts from TV script; ed. by A. Cooke. S. Hearst. il UNESCO Courier 17:26-9+ Je '64
Grace of Graustark; hour-long telecast, A look at Monaco. il Time 81:42 F 22 '63
How to see it without going; New York world's fair. H. Downs. il Sci Digest 55:8-12 Ap '64
How to sell broccoli; The French chef. il Time 83:56 Mr 20 '64
Indians protest film on caste system; David Brinkley's journal. Christian Cent 80:515 Ap 24 '63
Lessons in documentary; Louisiana diary. R. L. Shayon. Sat R 47:22 Mr 28 '64
Making of a documentary; Making of the President 1960, on ABC network. R. L. Shayon. Sat R 47:23 Ja 18 '64
Missing pieces; Nobel prize awards, 1964. R. L. Shayon. Sat R 48:36 Ja 2 '65
Natives are restless; essay form of nonfiction television on ABC's Chicago station, WBKB. R. L. Shayon. Sat R 47:28 F 1 '64
Princess Grace: a new role; Look at Monaco. J. Hamilton. il Look 27:64-70 F 12 '63
Probing Little Moscow; TV's Chet Huntley reporting. il Sr Schol 82:39 Ap 17 '63
Return to Normandy. R. L. Shayon. Sat R 47:48 Je 27 '64
Roosevelt retrospective; ABC series called F.D.R. il Time 85:50 Ja 8 '65
Spy. Newsweek 64:51 D 14 '64
Straight from the wolf's mouth; television documentary film presented by CBS. R. L. Shayon. Sat R 46:28 Ap 27 '63
TV's journalism triumph. B. Downes. Pop Phot 53:68 D '63
Too hot to handle? President and the Attorney General during the integration crisis at the University of Alabama. Newsweek 62:67-8 Ag 5 '63
Truman's view: MacArthur tried for presidency; Truman's memoirs on television. H. S. Truman. U S News 57:22 N 30 '64
Two Indias. R. L. Shayon. Sat R 47:43 Je 13 '64
UN-precedented; six United Nations shows for TV. il Newsweek 63:72 Ap 20 '64
Viewing the unseeable; L. Howard's documentary on Cuba. Nation 198:407 Ap 27 '64
What's wrong with documentaries. R. L. Shayon. Sat R 48:55 Ja 23 '65

Drama

Air; Mr Novak, and East side, West side. J. Miller. New Yorker 39:119-20+ N 16 '63
Best/worst television can do; Book for burning, on The defenders. ALA Bul 57:377-8 My '63; Reply with rejoinder. L. T. Dinnan. 57:472, 477 Je '63
Book for burning. J. Shera. Wilson Lib Bul 37:790 My '63
Businessman as critic; NBC-MGM weekly film series Mr Novak. R. L. Shayon. Sat R 47:22 Mr 21 '64; Reply. J. R. Miles. 47:34 My 9 '64
Can TV be saved? T. Guthrie. il Esquire 60: 211+ D '63
The defenders defaults. Christian Cent 81: 1485 D 2 '64
Doctors, lawyers & other TV heroes. H. Dienstfrey. Commentary 35:519-24 Je '63; Discussion. 36:348+ N '63
Great adventure. J. T. Aubrey, jr. il NEA J 52:33-48 O '63
Great adventure; special TV study guides. bibliog il NEA J 53:75-8 Ja; 71-3 F; 79-82 Mr; 65-7 Ap '64
Hamlet at Elsinore; joint production of Danish television service and BBC. il Newsweek 62:78 O 14 '63
Hit at Elsinore; BBC television production of Hamlet. R. L. Shayon. Sat R 47:41 D 12 '64
Jefferson story; Hallmark hall of fame. il N Y Times Mag p 100-1 O 27 '63
Judgment on the new season. il Time 82:59+ O 18 '63
Letting George do it; NBC's Hallmark Hall of fame. il Newsweek 65:53 F 1 '65
Local rivulets; Repertoire workshop. R. L. Shayon. Sat R 46:22 F 2 '63
Market for ideas; Leviathan five. R. L. Shayon. Sat R 47:27 F 29 '64
Masters of illusion; Defenders television program Book for burning. America 108: 487 Ap 13 '63
Meet Mr Novak. il NEA J 52:32 S '63
Mia Farrow: an actress in search of a character; soap opera Peyton Place. S. Gordon. il Look 28:72-6 D 1 '64
My battle with Ben Casey. V. Edwards. il Seventeen 23:130-1+ F '64
Oops! wrong Hamlet! New York's WCBS-TV videotape of New York Shakespeare festival's performance. R. L. Shayon. Sat R 47: 19 Jl 4 '64
Please, doctor. P. Collinge. New Yorker 40: 136+ Ap 25 '64
Powerless hero; new CBS program, East side, West side. R. L. Shayon. Sat R 46:40 N 2 '63; Reply. Mrs. F. Decorato. 46:30 D 7 '63
Real gone; Bed-sitting-room. il Time 81:82 My 10 '63
Riches or ruin for theatre? group W's plan for theatre-TV production. G. Eells. Theatre Arts 47:27-32+ N '63
Ride with terror. America 109:759 D 14 '63
Soapy sex moves to prime time. G. Cameron. Life 57:17 D 4 '64
Still with us; The defenders. Commonweal 79:495-6 Ja 31 '64
Subways are for stabbing; Ride with terror. Time 82:69 D 13 '63
TV's first-nighters; tape recording of The advocate. il Bsns W p 146+ O 19 '63
Tune in on censorship; Sam Benedict show and Defenders. il Wilson Lib Bul 37:724+ My '63
25,000,000 viewers can be wrong. R. L. Shayon. Sat R 47:36 F 22 '64
Wasteland needs more wastebaskets. W. Stanton. Life 56:10 Je 12 '64
Wring cycle; detergent dramas. W. Holbrook. Read Digest 83:189-90+ D '63
See also
Television broadcasting—Westerns

Texts

See Television plays

Economic aspects

Is little TV possible? P. Goodman. New Repub 148:26-8 My 18 '63

Educational applications

See Television in education

Election results

Button, button, who's got the winner? computer services for election results. Time 83:96 Je 5 '64
Eight-inning final scores. Reporter 30:12 Je 18 '64
Election eyes. il Newsweek 64:64+ N 16 '64
Night of the GIGO. Newsweek 64:98 N 2 '64
On election night: you be the expert. il Changing T 18:12-14 O '64

TELEVISION broadcasting—Election results—*Continued*
One down, one to go. R. L. Shayon. Sat R 47:17 Jl 25 '64
Pooling, cronking & brinking; joint network election service. Time 83:44 Je 19 '64
Plunge and pool; election coverage. il Newsweek 63:86 Je 15 '64
Quickie results could sway the election. R. Bendiner. il Life 57:125-6+ S 18 '64
TV braces for the big count; networks pool resources for reporting the vote. il Bsns W p26-7 O 31 '64

Anecdotes, facetiae, satire, etc.

The week that will be. W. V. Shannon. Commonweal 80:409-10 Je 26 '64

Football

See Television broadcasting—Sports

Golf

See Television broadcasting—Sports

History

Looking backward. il Newsweek 61:90+ F 18 '63

Horror programs

TV's year of the monster. il Life 57:54B-57 Ag 21 '64
Those clean-living all American monsters. I. Mothner. il Look 28:50+ S 8 '64
Why they love monsters. M. A. Guitar. il N Y Times Mag p 109 O 25 '64

Humor

America's favorite TV wife; Dick Van Dyke show. S. Gordon. il Look 28:M9-M10+ Ap 21 '64
Caesar or Como, the laughs are by Ace. R. P. Hunt. il N Y Times Mag p42+ S 15 '63
Can TV be saved? A. Capp. il Esquire 60: 211+ D '63
Eliminate the racial slur! revival of the Amos 'n' Andy TV series. Christian Cent 81:757 Je 10 '64
Ernest Borgnine: TV's howling new success; McHale's navy. C. Brossard. il Look 27:32a-32b+ Jl 16 '63
Everyman at sea; ABC's McHale's navy. il Newsweek 61:89 Mr 11 '63
Golden hillbillies. R. W. Lewis. il Sat Eve Post 236:30+ F 2 '63
G.A.P. loves the Hillbillies. A. Hano. il N Y Times Mag p30+ N 17 '63
How to try in TV without really succeeding. G. Ace. Sat R 47:15 O 17 '64
Laugh! I thought they'd never start. G. Ace. Sat R 47:24 Je 13 '64
Lindy's law. A. Goldman. New Repub 150: 34-5 Je 13 '64
Lowdown on Loudon; Garry Moore show. G. Millstein. Sat Eve Post 236:70+ Ap 6 '63
Peeping Toms; Carson and Allen shows. il Newsweek 61:54 F 25 '63
Wednesday question: want to watch Danny Kaye? il pors Newsweek 62:43-5 D 23 '63

Interference

See Television interference

International aspects

Meeting in space: anniversary of the first Telstar broadcast. il Time 82:55 Jl 19 '63
On the town meeting; Town meeting of the world. il Newsweek 62:81 Jl 22 '63
President's rites viewed throughout the world. Sci N L 84:355 D 7 '63
Wishful shrinking; veto over the use of Telstar II. R. L. Shayon. Sat R 46:16 Ag 3 '63

Laws and regulations

See Television laws and regulations

Licenses

See Television laws and regulations

Medical programs

Bridge at West Point; The eleventh hour. R. L. Shayon. Sat R 46:41 My 25 '63

Moral aspects

Ethics for Tonight. R. L. Shayon. Sat R 46: 59 My 11 '63
Relevant question; is it right? R. L. Shayon. Sat R 46:23 D 14 '63
See also
Television broadcasting and children

Moving pictures

Any night at the movies, TV version, with commercials, station breaks and public service announcements. il Changing T 17: 40-2 D '63
Little films that make it big; Olde time movie club, Asheville, N.C. W. P. Banner. il U S Camera 27:60-1 Ja '64
Now the earlier, earlier show. H. Alpert. il N Y Times Mag p22-3+ Ag 11 '63
Old ironclads. il Time 81:47 Mr 1 '63
One man's method; problems of TV film production. R. L. Shayon. Sat R 47:26 Ap 25 '64
Screens and screams. R. L. Shayon. Sat R 46:44 Ap 20 '63

Anecdotes, facetiae, satire, etc.

Add hot water; serves fourteen million. T. Meehan. New Yorker 40:35-7 Mr 28 '64

Music

Bigger than baseball; the American cultural explosion and the mass media. Mus Am 83:7 Mr '63
Gain and loss; Bach's St Matthew passion. C. J. McNaspy. America 108:620-1 Ap 27 '63
Letter from Europe. E. Helm. Mus Am 83: 271+ D '63
Radio-TV (cont) il Mus Am 83:212 Ja; 49 F; 50 Mr; 53 Ap; 41 My '63
William B. Williams: the man who runs the Make believe ballroom. il Look 27:78a-78c F 12 '63

Musical comedies, revues, etc.

Off Broadway to TV; Fantasticks. il N Y Times Mag p 102+ O 11 '64

Nature programs

Fang & fin hour. il Time 84:81 D 4 '64

News

Being kind to the competition; press comment. il Time 84:68 Jl 17 '64
Can TV be saved? D. Pearson. il Esquire 60:210+ D '63
CBS and NBC: Walter vs. Chet and Dave. il Newsweek 62:62-5 S 23 '63
Covering the tragedy; President Kennedy's assassination. il Time 82:84 N 29 '63
David Brinkley and his golden key. C. S. Wren. il Look 28:44+ F 25 '64
Day of the documentary. R. L. Tobin. il Sat R 47:121-2 Mr 14 '64
Did press pressure kill Oswald? reprint. L. Grove. il U S News 56:78-9 Ap 6 '64
Discord, N.H; primary election coverage. il Newsweek 63:82 Mr 2 '64
Does TV crime reporting jeopardize justice? pro and con discussion. il Sr Schol 84: 6-7 Mr 20 '64
Elections by electronics. R. L. Shayon. Sat R 47:22 Mr 14 '64; Reply. A. Van Zee. 47:33+ Ap 11 '64
Esthetics and the news. R. L. Shayon. Sat R 46:53 O 12 '63
His crime was playing it straight; CBS replaces W. Cronkite. R. Oulahan. Life 57:13 Ag 28 '64
Moment of candor; newsmen on tv during newspaper strike. il Time 81:51 F 15 '63
On the news beat. il Newsweek 63:74-5 Je 1 '64
Reporter; G. Pressman covering local scene in person for WNBC. New Yorker 39:19-21 Ag 17 '63
Straws of an ill wind; bias in news presentation. R. L. Tobin. Sat R 46:41-2 Jl 13 '63
Television journalism; the shackled giant; address, December 7, 1964. R. W. Sarnoff. Vital Speeches 31:174-7 Ja 1 '65
TV now top source for news. Wilson Lib Bul 38:608-9+ Ap '64
Television's princess of the press corps; N. Dickerson, correspondent in NBC's Washington bureau. B. Gottehrer. il Sat Eve Post 237:36-7 O 31 '64
Two-prong attack; joint exposure by Chicago daily news and CBS WBBM-TV of slum conditions in the city. il Newsweek 61:82 Je 3 '63
Upstairs was unhappy. il Newsweek 64:44-5 Ag 10 '64
Voice: football commentator Schenkel. il Newsweek 62:100 O 7 '63
Walter Cronkite: why won't he be himself on TV? I. Taves. il pors Look 28:74+ Ag 25 '64
When the press shapes the news. H. Brucker. il Sat R 47:75-7+ Ja 11 '64; Discussion. 47: 46-7 F 8; 123+ Mr 14 '64
See also
Television broadcasting—Election results

Operas

Ask the man who listens; Texaco's regular Saturday afternoon broadcast of the Metropolitan opera. L. L. L. Golden. Sat R 46:60 My 11 '63
Day of the crisis; switch from Der fliegende Holländer to Ariadne auf Naxos. il Theatre Arts 47:24+ Mr '63
Great opera houses: NBC-TV. Q. Eaton. il Opera N 28:28-33 F 8 '64

TELEVISION broadcasting—Operas—*Cont.*
Lucia coast to coast; NBC-TV. P. Moed. il Opera N 28:32 Mr 7 '64
Lucia di Lammermoor. C. S. Susa. il Mus Am 84:42 F '64
Menotti opera runs riot with a flood of tricks: Labyrinth premiere on NBC-TV. T. Prideaux. il Life 54:46 Mr 8 '63
Menotti's hour; Labyrinth. il Time 81:46 Mr 8 '63
Menotti's maze; Labyrinth. Newsweek 61:87 Mr 11 '63
Musical events; Bach's St Matthew passion. W. Sargeant. New Yorker 39:154-5 Ap 13 '63
Musical events; Menotti's Labyrinth. W. Sargeant. New Yorker 39:148-9 Mr 9 '63
Saturday afternoon at the Met. il Mus Am 84:10-13 Ja '64

Performers

Crossing the bar. Time 82:68 N 8 '63
Ed Sullivan screens Europe's entertainment; ed. by F. Kish. E. Sullivan. il Travel 121:37-41 My '64
Inger Stevens; TV's Farmer's daughter. R. W. Lewis. il Sat Eve Post 237:20-1 Ja 4 '64
Life, love and laughter of Carol Burnett. N. G. Stuart. il Ladies Home J 80:72-3+ Ap '63
Living color on television; Negroes on the screen (cont) R. L. Shayon. Sat R 46:57 F 9 '63
Next season. il Newsweek 62:64-5 Jl 8 '63
No, no, Dutch. il Newsweek 62:64-5 S 30 '63
Personal business; sell yourself in front of tv camera. Bsns W p 101-2 F 9 '63
Rich rubes: the Beverly hillbillies. il Newsweek 62:56 S 9 '63
TV's prosperous pitchmen; performers in commercials. B. Davidson. il Sat Eve Post 236:26-7 Ag 24 '63
Women don't like to look at women. L. Graham. il N Y Times Mag p48+ My 24 '64
See also names of television performers, e.g. Silvers, P.

Political programs
See Television in politics

Program production

Book is thrown at television. G. Ace. Sat R 47:10 N 7 '64
Capturing the Kremlin. il Newsweek 61:91 My 20 '63
Fitness takes a beating on television; Dick Powell theater. H. Horn. il Sports Illus 18:84-8+ Ap 1 '63
How to get by on $10,000 a week. G. Ace. Sat R 47:18 F 8 '64
I'm Dr Kildare's doctor. P. M. Wright. il McCalls 90:70+ S '63
Long, long show; three-hour special on the American Negro's fight for equal rights. Newsweek 62:56 S 2 '63
Mother Lupino. il Time 81:42 F 8 '63
No rig, no fix and no quiz. C. Welles. il Life 55:133+ O 18 '63
Only you, Dick Daring! by M. Miller and E. Rhodes. Review
Sat R 47:34 O 31 '64. R. L. Shayon
Pilots and spinoffs; independent TV producers. il Newsweek 61:102+ Ap 15 '63
Skydiving chute-em-up. D. Zeitlin. il Life 54:91-3 Ap 12 '63
Story behind Crisis. il Pop Phot 53:179+ D '63
Where the action is; trip to Patagonia for ABC's Wide world of sports. Time 81:81 My 17 '63

Program rating

Beatle fatigue. G. Ace. Sat R 47:18 D 5 '64
Broadcast ratings lose spell; testimony before Rep. Oren Harris' Permanent investigations subcommittee. il Bsns W p30-1 Ap 13 '63
Con game? Newsweek 61:48 Ap 1 '63
Disenchantment. R. L. Shayon. Sat R 46:76 Ap 13 '63
Gadget; radio and TV rating services. il Newsweek 61:80 Ap 8 '63
Great sampler. Nation 196:366-7 My 4 '63
Here's your rating, what's your hurry? G. Ace. Sat R 47:15 Mr 7 '64
Just how is it done? Harris committee hearings. il Bsns W p34 Mr 16 '63
Mindsweeper; James Tanner's electronic system for surveying TV audiences. Time 83:62 Mr 13 '64
Nielsen vs. Quixote. America 109:657 N 23 '63
Notes and comment; Nielsen report. New Yorker 40:29 D 19 '64
Order of battle; national Nielsen ratings. il Newsweek 64:87 N 9 '64
Prime time. il Time 81:56+ Mr 22 '63
Puzzle: who knows who looks at TV? investigation by House commerce investigating subcommittee. il U S News 54:44-7 Ap 8 '63
Quick & the dead. il Time 82:68 N 8 '63
Rating, writing, and 'rithmetic. G. Ace. Sat R 47:10 F 29 '64
Restive researchers. P. B. Bart. Sat R 46:47 Jl 13 '63
Roulette wheel; Nielsen ratings. Newsweek 64:56 D 21 '64
Selling confusion. il Time 81:79-80 Ap 12 '63
Statistical scramble. il Newsweek 62:74-5 N 11 '63
Super snooper to rate TV: a watch truck is watching you; Tanner electronic survey tabulator. D. Zeitlin. il Life 57:57+ S 25 '64
Take a letter. G. Ace. Sat R 47:16 N 21 '64
Television ratings on trial. B. Lindeman and A. Patureau. il Sat Eve Post 237:13-17 F 8 '64
TV ratings rated low by Congress. Sr Schol 82:17-19 My 8 '63
TV's unnerving numbers game. D. Smith. il N Y Times Mag p40+ Ag 18 '63
Top of my head. G. Ace. See issues of Saturday review, February 29, 1964-
Wonderland? validity of TV ratings. Newsweek 61:64 Mr 18 '63
Year of the photo finish. il Time 84:70 D 18 '64

Anecdotes, facetiae, satire, etc.

Same old rate race. G. Ace. Sat R 47:21 N 14 '64
60,000,000 projections can't be wrong. R. Schoenstein. Sat R 46:56 Je 8 '63

Programming

No. 1 supplier of TV viewers; CBS-TV. il Bsns W p90-1+ Ap 25 '64
Reviving the ad lib; policies regarding time for controversial issues. R. L. Shayon. Sat R 46:38 My 18 '63

Programs

Air; 1492, and Golden age of Greece, parts of series. J. Miller. New Yorker 39:116+ N 16 '63
Biography's backyard; The story of . . . Sat R 46:22 Je 29 '63
Birth of a salesman; Europeans reaction to U.S.-produced television programs. Newsweek 63:42 Ja 13 '64
Britain's new wave of satire ebbs; That was the week that was. B. Hollowood. il N Y Times Mag p 17+ Ja 26 '64
British and American satire; That was the week that was. A. Goldman. New Repub 150:27-8 F 22 '64; Reply. H. J. Gans. 150:30 Mr 21 '64
Can Mr Novak keep the teachers happy? S. Gordon. il Look 28:111-13+ O 6 '64
Can TV be saved? M. Liebman. il Esquire 60:210+ D '63
Channels (cont) S. White. il Horizon 5:113-14 Mr; 112-13 My '63
CBC explores book use by educational broadcasters. Pub W 184:150-1 Jl 8 '63
Cookies for TV. America 109:405 O 12 '63
D-day plus twenty years. H. Mitgang. il Look 28:78-85 F 25 '64
Dead; end of many shows. Time 81:50 Je 28 '63
Dethroned; Queen for a day dropped by ABC-TV. Newsweek 64:78 S 7 '64
Doctor Kildare is a doll. M. Durslag. Sat Eve Post 236:14-15 Mr 30 '63
Doctor Rock show. America 110:133 Ja 25 '64
Everyone's in the kitchen with Julia; French chef. L. H. Lapham. il Sat Eve Post 237:20-1 Ag 8 '64
Fitness takes a beating on television; Dick Powell theater. H. Horn. il Sports Illus 18:84-8+ Ap 1 '63
Folknik show; ABC-TV series Hootenanny. il Newsweek 61:64 Mr 18 '63
For unsleepy people; Late late late late show. Time 81:73 My 3 '63
From the same tube; replacements of old shows. Time 82:47+ Jl 26 '63
Good scout; Dick Van Dyke show. il Time 81:54 Je 14 '63
Home-model witch; ABC's Bewitched. I. Mothner. il Look 29:75-9 Ja 26 '65
How the fall season shapes up. il Newsweek 64:68-9 Ag 3 '64
I think I'm gaining on myself; Andy Griffith show. D. Freeman. il Sat Eve Post 237:68-70 Ja 25 '64
I'm Dr Kildare's doctor. P. M. Wright. il McCalls 90:70+ S '63
Judgment on the new season. il Time 82:59+ O 18 '63
Lay off, Macduff; TW3. G. Ace. Sat R 47:16 O 24 '64

TELEVISION broadcasting—Programs—*Cont.*
Less the merrier. G. Ace. Sat R 47:10 D 19 '64
Life TV review. Life 56:14 Mr 27; 17 My 8; 10 Je 12; 57:13 Ag 28; 21+ S 18; 17 O 23; 17 D 4; 15-16 D 18 '64; 58:8+ Ja 22 '65
Long day's monotony of TV. B. Brower. il Sat Eve Post 237:76-8 S 26 '64
Look and listen; ed. by P. Dilts. See issues of Senior scholastic
Looking and listening. P. Dilts. See issues of Senior scholastic
Lords of fun and games; M. Goodson and B. Todman. G. Rogin. il Sports Illus 18:52-60 Je 24 '63
Missed opportunities; National educational television's African writers of today. R. L. Shayon. Sat R 47:34 My 23 '64
Mr Minow's wasteland. W. Sparks. Commonweal 78:7-10 Mr 29 '63
Mr Novak's second year. il NEA J 53:26-9 S '64
More bow! more bow! Heifetz master class on National educational television network. Newsweek 61:58 F 11 '63
Naked classroom; Mr Novak. il Time 82:116+ O 4 '63
Naked truth; Naked city. il Newsweek 61:79 Mr 4 '63
New look in villains; ABC new entertainment programs. R. L. Shayon. Sat R 47:34 O 10 '64
New season. il Time 84:73-4 S 25 '64
News from Telstar II; CBS news's Town meeting of the world. R. L. Shayon. Sat R 46:53 N 16 '63
Next season. il Newsweek 62:64-5 Jl 8 '63
On TV war is heck. G. Ace. Sat R 47:18 O 10 '64
Operation Hootenanny. H. L. Masin. il Sr Schol 84:34 My 15 '64
Order vs. liberty; NBC series Profiles in courage. R. L. Shayon. Sat R 47:22 D 26 '64
President's week; Badge of courage. il Time 84:70+ N 20 '64
Reunion on channel 13; anniversary of Franklin D. Roosevelt's first inauguration with excerpts from the program. H. Bowser. il Sat R 46:18-19+ Ap 6 '63
Second week premières; CBS's new shows. il Time 84:106-7 O 2 '64
Shindog. il Newsweek 64:56 D 21 '64
Sight and sound. See issues of McCalls
Skydiving chute-em-up; Ripcord. D. Zeitlin. il Life 54:91-3 Ap 12 '63
Soapy; ABC season. il Newsweek 64:65 S 28 '64
Susskind and Sevareid. P. Goodman. New Repub 148:24-6 F 23 '63
Tap day. il Newsweek 63:76 F 10 '64
Teacher image; NBC's Mr Novak. il Newsweek 62:100 D 2 '63
TV, a season for laughter. Changing T 18:6 Ag '64
TV is thrown into upside down panic; top twenty programs. il Life 57:49-50 N 6 '64
TV jumps gun on next season; schedules locked up. il Bsns W p45-8 Mr 9 '63
Television; programs of potential interest to teachers and students. NEA J 53:87 Ja '64
TV-radio. See issues of Newsweek
TV searches the business soul; lectures by professor of marketing at St Joseph college, Philadelphia. il Bsns W p99-100 Mr 28 '64
TV troubles of Judy Garland. R. W. Lewis. il Sat Eve Post 236:92-5 D 7 '63
TV's new combines flex their muscles; RKO and Metromedia in television programming. il Bsns W p 122+ Jl 18 '64
Ten years later; crime-and-violence. R. L. Shayon. Sat R 47:39 S 26 '64
TW3, U.S.A. il Newsweek 63:50 Ja 20 '64
That was weak, that was. il Time 83:76 Ja 17 '64
Time listings. See issues of Time
Time out for television. See issues of PTA magazine
Up-to-the-minute situation in Chaos; excerpt from What's going on here? New Repub 148:17 Je 8 '63
Wait till next year? il Newsweek 64:40 D 28 '64
Watch their smoke. C. W. Morton. Atlan 211:111 F '63
Weekly view of reel fiction; Camera three. G. Hicks. Sat R 46:21-2 Jl 6 '63
What is wrong with TV, and with us. C. A. Siepmann. il N Y Times Mag p 13+ Ap 19 '64
What to expect on TV; photographs. S. Peck. N Y Times Mag p96-7 Ag 23 '64
What's going on; weekly program of news satire. New Yorker 39:34-6 My 11 '63
Where was the glory of Greece? CBS program on Athens. R. L. Shayon. Sat R 46:43 S 28 '63

See also

National association for better radio and television
Television broadcasting—Drama
TV guide (periodical)
Television scripts

Anecdotes, facetiae, satire, etc.

Many unhappy returns. il Newsweek 64:74 O 12 '64

Titles

Rose by any other name. A. Goodman. Sat R 47:16 Ap 18 '64

Propaganda

T.R.B. from Washington; preachers of fear: radio and television programs of COPE, and Life lines. New Repub 150:2 Ja 4 '64; Discussion. 150:30 Ja 25; 30 F 8 '64

Psychological aspects

Effects of observing violence. L. Berkowitz. il Sci Am 210:35-41 bibliog(p 152) F '64; Reply with rejoinder. P. Goodman. 210:8 Je '64
Picture of violence; effect of filmed violence. il Newsweek 63:91 F 24 '64
Special effects; violence witnessed on the screen. R. L. Shayon. Sat R 47:22 My 2 '64
Two faces of TV. Nation 198:43 Ja 13 '64
Two faces of violence; CBS television drama series The reporter. R. L. Shayon. Sat R 47:28 O 24 '64

Public service programs

Birchbark curtain; John Birch society bulletin urging protest against U.N. television specials. R. L. Shayon. Sat R 47:29 O 3 '64
Cleopatra for another Christmas; concerning J. Gould's criticism of the Xerox TV special, Carol for another Christmas. G. Ace. Sat R 48:10 Ja 30 '65
They sang along with Mitch; Xerox series of entertainment films based on activities of social agencies of the United Nations. R. L. Shayon. Sat R 47:24 My 30 '64
Warm Scrooge, cold Grudge; Carol for another Christmas, presented on the ABC television network. R. L. Shayon. Sat R 48:39 Ja 16 '65
Xerox, the U.N. and I.C.Y. C. Soule. il Christian Cent 81:1305-6 O 21 '64

Quiz programs

Corrupt society. F. J. Cook. Nation 196:480-4 Je 1 '63
No rig, no fix and no quiz. C. Welles. il Life 55:133+ O 18 '63
Out of isolation: Stivers big-money quiz show, 100 grand. Newsweek 62:67 Ag 5 '63
Question of ethics. Nation 196:434 My 25 '63
Quiz is back in biz! J. Iams. il Sat Eve Post 236:64-5 S 14 '63

Religious programs

I am with you; Catholic hour program over NBC. America 108:629 My 4 '63
Look, brothers. P. T. Hartung. Commonweal 78:247-8 My 24 '63
Pulpit in the home; NBC's Frontiers of faith. il Time 83:65 F 7 '64
Religion and the FCC. M. Cohn. il Reporter 32:32-4 Ja 14 '65
Televising the mass. America 109:619 N 16 '63

Science fiction

Monster-of-the-month; Outer limits. il Newsweek 63:55 Ja 27 '64

Scientific programs

Science and television. E. G. Sherburne, jr. Science 143:792-3 F 21 '64; Reply. M. B. Mitchell. 144:246 Ap 17 '64
Science for citizens; National educational television series, Exploring the universe. R. L. Shayon. Sat R 46:32 Mr 2 '63
Science program for the concerned citizen links book, TV series and study groups; Exploring the universe. Library J 88:988 Mr 1 '63

Social aspects

NBC turns down a golden chance; cancelation of program about teenage venereal disease. R. L. Tobin. Sat R 47:61-2 D 12 '64
Television research uninhibited. R. L. Shayon. Sat R 46:17 Ag 31 '63
VD on TV? il Newsweek 64:62 N 30 '64

TELEVISION broadcasting—Social aspects—*Continued*
What television can, and cannot, do. L. Rosten. Read Digest 82:143-4+ F '63
See also
Television broadcasting—Psychological aspects

Sports

After the Yankees what? a TV drama. L. W. Robinson. il N Y Times Mag p44-5+ N 15 '64
Big, booming business of pro football. T. J. Murray. il Duns R 84:38-40+ S '64
Big numbers game. Newsweek 62:56 D 30 '63
Bowl exposure is growing longer; television coverage of all eight major bowl games. D. Jenkins. il Sports Illus 21:64-9 D 21 '64
Brave executives; Bullfight in Spain, on NBC. il Newsweek 61:80 F 4 '63
Clean bill; boxing and television. Sports Illus 21:11-12 S 21 '64
Everybody his own quarterback. J. R. McDermott. Life 57:15-16 D 18 '64
Fascinating world of galleries; Wonderful world of golf, with photographs by H. Power. Sports Illus 18:38-45 F 11 '63
In Miami nearly everybody hates Clure Mosher. J. Underwood. il Sports Illus 19:54-8+ Jl 15 '63
Joe to behold! baseball announcer. H. L. Masin. il Sr Schol 83:24 S 20 '63
Laugh off $11 million? Columbia broadcasting system buys New York Yankee baseball club. J. R. Tunis. New Repub 152:11-12 Ja 2 '65
NBC's Olympic hurdle; question of rights to transmission by satellite. il Bsns W p34 O 10 '64
New way to get rich quick, in football. il U S News 58:64-5 Ja 18 '65
Olympic TV has a chance; via satellite. Bsns W p 116 My 2 '64
Phi beta football; use of technical devices. il Time 85:50-1 Ja 8 '65
Razzle-dazzle; CBS football coverage. Newsweek 64:65 S 28 '64
Stratford on fifty-yard line; New York fans at San Francisco 49ers-N.Y. Giants game outside TV blackout curtain. M. Simont. il Sports Illus 19:32-5 N 25 '63
Talk me out of the ball game. R. Schoenstein. Sat R 47:82 Ap 11 '64
TV kayo; end of televised boxing. Newsweek 63:41 Ja 6 '64
TV takes over the T formation; football games. Bsns W p23 F 1 '64
Transistor kid; telecaster V. Scully. R. Creamer. il Sports Illus 20:96-8+ My 4 '64
Twenty-eight-million-dollar deal; CBS wins 1964-65 television rights to the NFL's regular season games. W. Leggett. il Sports Illus 20:16-17 F 3 '64
Why do they all have to play in my living room. M. Leavitt. Life 57:17 O 23 '64
Winter sports note. Sports Illus 21:5 Ag 3 '64

Anecdotes, facetiae, satire, etc.

L'après-midi d'un fan. R. Angell. New Yorker 40:48-50 O 17 '64

Subscription programs

Battling big odds for pay TV. il Bsns W p 139-40+ Je 27 '64
Big play for pay TV's $1.50 splendors. M. Mayer. il Sat Eve Post 237:71-5 My 2 '64
California referendum fifteen; prohibition of pay-TV in the state. W. F. Buckley, jr. Nat R 16:806 S 22 '64
Chavez and Chekhov. Newsweek 64:69-70 Ag 3 '64
Fee versus free. Sports Illus 21:9 Jl 27 '64
Guard pay-TV channels against knotholing. Sci N L 85:216 Ap 4 '64
Is pay-tv here? W. A. Stocklin. Electr World 69:6 Mr '63
Is pay-TV sneaking to success? community antenna television systems. il Bsns W p32-3 Ap 25 '64
Mr Minow's wasteland. W. Sparks. Commonweal 78:9-10 Mr 29 '63
New emperor of pay. il Time 84:52 Ag 7 '64
1963: subscription tv's first vintage year. R. L. Tobin; discussion. Sat R 46:48+ F 9 '63
Pay or free? the coming TV war. D. Smith. Nation 198:504-6 My 18 '64
Pay TV, where it stands. Changing T 18:5-6 Mr '64
Rocky road for toll TV. Bsns W p 131-2 Jl 13 '63
Stupid question, stupid answer; California's Proposition fifteen. Life 57:4 N 20 '64
What do they think of pay TV? E. D. Fales, jr. il Pop Sci 183:75-8+ Jl '63
Why suppress pay-TV? the fight in California. S. L. Weaver, jr. Atlan 214:55-9 O '64; Reply with rejoinder. C. de Young Thieriot. 215:34 Ja '65
See also
Subscription television, incorporated

Trials

Bar's side of Canon 35. J. H. Yauch. Sat R 46:61-2 Mr 9 '63
Free press & fair trial. il Time 84:72 D 18 '64
On trial; concerning articles in Television quarterly and Public opinion quarterly. R. L. Shayon. Sat R 47:30 N 28 '64
TV and the Supreme court. R. Goldfarb. Commonweal 81:150-1 O 30 '64
TV before the bar; possible TV coverage of Ruby's trial. il Time 82:82 D 13 '63
Television in the courtroom? pro and con discussion. J. McLaughlin; R. F. Drinan. America 112:72-5 Ja 16 '65
TV or no TV in court? F. Rodell. il N Y Times Mag p 16+ Ap 12 '64
Uses of diversity; concerning H. J. Skornia's speech on Television in the courtroom. R. L. Shayon. Sat R 47:27 Je 20 '64

Westerns

Destry rides again, and again, and again. J. D. Weaver. il Holiday 34:77-80+ Ag '63
Worldwide lure of Bonanza. J. Poppy. il Look 28:80+ D 1 '64

Austria

Profiles; H. Qualtinger. J. Wechsberg. New Yorker 39:53-4+ Ap 20 '63

Canada

See also
Canadian broadcasting corporation

Europe

Ed Sullivan screens Europe's entertainment; ed. by F. Kish. E. Sullivan. il Travel 121:37-41 My '64

France

Franc for France; network spoof brought to trial. Time 84:78 N 20 '64
Letter from Paris; radio and television coverage for G. Defferre. Genêt. New Yorker 40:144-6 Mr 7 '64
Letter from Paris; seventy-fifth anniversary of Tour Eiffel. Genêt. New Yorker 40:176 My 16 '64
Managed news; new law, an old complaint. Time 84:61 Jl 3 '64
Unequal time; allowance for presidential candidates. Time 83:39 Mr 13 '64

Great Britain

All honor Honor. A. Carthew. il N Y Times Mag p73-5 Mr 1 '64
Britain's new wave of satire ebbs; That was the week that was. B. Hollowood. il N Y Times Mag p 17+ Ja 26 '64
BBC's Bloomsday; James Joyce's Ulysses televised. il Newsweek 63:74 Je 22 '64
Case for televising Parliament, by R. Day. Review
Sat R 46:36 N 23 '63. R. L. Shayon
Hamlet at Elsinore; joint production of Danish television service and BBC. il Newsweek 62:78 O 14 '63
How Britain tracks TV pirates. P. Halliday. Electr World 69:68 Je '63
How to offend everybody; That was the week that was. R. L. Shayon. Sat R 46:26 N 30 '63
Letter from London; replacement for That was the week that was. M. Panter-Downes. New Yorker 40:63 Ja 2 '65
No kidding; BBC television's That was the week that was. R. L. Shayon. Sat R 46:31 D 7 '63
Report of the committee on broadcasting, by H. Pilkington and others. Review
Commentary 35:264-8 Mr '63. P. Breslow
Third channel for British telly; Independent television. A. Carthew. il N Y Times Mag p 13+ Mr 29 '64

Ireland

Irish television. R. McHugh. America 108:670 My 11 '63

Italy

Romanzo sceneggiato. America 108:699 My 18 '63

Japan

Hot *yoromeki*; soap opera with sex. il Newsweek 65:34 Ja 4 '65

Mexico

Simplified Mexican color TV. L. Solomon. il Electr World 72:48+ Jl '64

TELEVISION broadcasting—*Continued*

Netherlands

Pirate war livens up Dutch TV. il Bsns W p36-7 O 24 '64

South Africa

Other vast wasteland; no mass television. Time 84:40 20 N '64

United Nations

See United Nations—Publicity

United States

Action speaks loudest; conference on Local public service programing. R. L. Shayon. Sat R 46:29 D 21 '63
Air. J. Miller. New Yorker 39:115-16+ N 16 '63
As 175 million Americans watched; President's funeral. il Newsweek 62:88-90 D 9 '63
Breaking the TV schedule straitjacket. R. L. Tobin. il Sat R 47:53-4 S 12 '64; Discussion. 47:96 O 10 '64
Coincidence or not; opportunities for presentation of viewpoints on any controversial issue. Nat R 15:382-4 N 5 '63
Equal time: the private broadcaster and the public interest, by N. N. Minow. Review Nation 200:62 Ja 18 '65. D. Smith
Fame is a funny thing. G. Moore. il Look 28: 77+ S 22 '64
Government and TV. Commonweal 78:340-1 Je 21 '63
Hi ho, the hierarchy. O. M. Verona. Esquire 62:74-5 O '64
If you can keep your head when all about you: television and news magazine coverage of the Kennedy assassination story. R. L. Tobin. il Sat R 46:53-4 D 14 '63; Discussion. 47:74 Ja 11 '64
Important developments in communications; address, April 2, 1963. N. N. Minow. Vital Speeches 29:425-30 My 1 '63
Memorandum to a network. L. E. Craine and Mrs L. E. Craine. Sat R 46:28 D 28 '63
Mr Minow's wasteland. W. Sparks. Commonweal 78:7-10 Mr 29 '63
New kinds of television; where do we go from here? V. Packard. il Atlan 212:68-74 O '63
One world; people in current news as television stars. Reporter 29:24+ O 24 '63
Partial insight of Mr Minow. W. F. Buckley, jr. Nat R 14:442 Je 4 '63
People look at television: a study of audience attitudes, by G. A. Steiner. Review Sat R 46:29 Mr 23 '63. R. L. Shayon
Purposes and problems; Steiner report. R. L. Shayon. Sat R 46:41 Ap 6 '63
Sick beside the screen. P. Goodman. New Repub 148:28-30 Je 8 '63
Sight & the sound; coverage of President Kennedy's assassination. Time 82:32 D 20 '63
Sponsor for quality. New Repub 148:3-5 My 4 '63
Surveys of TV, 1949-62. P. Witty. bibliog f Sch & Soc 91:334-6 N 2 '63
Television. A. Goldman. New Repub 150:27-8 F 22; 31+ Ap 11; 34-5 Je 13 '64
Television. P. Goodman. New Repub 148: 24-6 F 23; 35-7 Mr 2; 28-30 Mr 16; 26-8 Mr 30; 32-4 Ap 13; 25-7 Ap 20; 26-8 My 18; 24+ My 25 '63
TV image; coverage of events until after the Kennedy funeral. P. T. David. Nation 197: 413-14 D 14 '63
Television: is it losing the battle for quality? pro and con discussion. il Sr Schol 84:12-14 Ja 31 '64
Television journalism: the shackled giant; address, December 7, 1964. R. W. Sarnoff. Vital Speeches 31:174-7 Ja 1 '65
TV sees it now, for seventy hours; assassination of Pres. Kennedy and succeeding events. il Bsns W p34 N 30 '63
TV's four days of history. J. H. Winchester. il Read Digest 84:204I-204J+ Ap '64
Top of my head. G. Ace. See issues of Saturday review, February 29, 1964-
Views of a death; coverage of President Kennedy's assassination, the cortege and funeral. J. Miller. New Yorker 39:63-4 D 28 '63
What to expect next in television; interview. E. W. Henry. il U S News 57:48-52 Jl 6 '64

See also

American broadcasting-Paramount theaters, incorporated
Columbia broadcasting system
United States—Federal communications commission
Westinghouse broadcasting company

TELEVISION broadcasting and children

Crime shows on TV; a federal crackdown coming? excerpts from report by Senate subcommittee on juvenile delinquency. il U S News 57:49-50 N 9 '64
Experiments with violence. A. Goldman. New Repub 150:31+ Ap 11 '64
Father television knows best. R. L. Shayon. Sat R 47:42 D 5 '64
Hop along, Oliver. V. Kurtz. il Redbook 120: 44 Ap '63
Parents vs. television. B. Bettelheim. il Redbook 122:54-5+ N '63
Sex and violence in books, magazines and television. B. Bettelheim. il Redbook 123: 60-1+ My '64
Surveys of TV, 1949-62. P. Witty. bibliog f Sch & Soc 91:334-6 N 2 '63
Television and the superior student. R. J. Nelson and J. W. M. Rothney. il Sch & Soc 92:385-7 D 12 '64
TV does not harm eyes but reduces sympathy. Sci N L 85:40 Ja 18 '64
Television: stimulant to violence. J. Ellison. Nation 197:433-6 D 21 '63
Television violence. America 111:177-8 Ag 22 '64; Reply. J. T. Klapper. 111:500+ O 31 '64
TV violence, the kids react. M. A. Guitar. il N Y Times Mag p24 D 27 '64
Those tired children. Time 84:76 N 6 '64
We're teaching our children that violence is fun; closer look at toys, TV and movies. E. Merriam. Ladies Home J 81:44+ O '64
What TV violence can do to your child. Look 27:46-8+ O 22 '63
What's happening in education? question of how to manage TV in the home. W. D. Boutwell. PTA Mag 58:33 Ja '64
Why they love monsters. M. A. Guitar. il N Y Times Mag p 109 O 25 '64

See also

Society for education in film and television
Television broadcasting—Childrens programs

TELEVISION broadcasting and reading. See Television and reading

TELEVISION broadcasting for children. See Television broadcasting—Childrens programs

TELEVISION broadcasting in court rooms. See Television broadcasting—Trials

TELEVISION broadcasting stations. See Television stations

TELEVISION broadcasting studios. See Television studios

TELEVISION camera tubes. See Television cameras

TELEVISION cameras

Avionics changes included in Tiros wheel. K. J. Stein. il Aviation W 81:44-5+ Ag 3 '64
Camera capsules aid Saturn program. il Miss & Roc 15:54+ S 14 '64
Digital television system is heart of Mariner spacecraft slated for November Mars fly-by. R. Pay. il Miss & Roc 15:38+ Ag 3 '64
Fixed TV on Voyager could provide lander accuracy of 100 miles. Miss & Roc 15:66-7 S 14 '64
For conventions, piggyback TV. il Sci Digest 56:inside front cover Jl '64
How to select a closed-circuit TV camera. W. Sander. il Electr World 70:41-3+ O '63
Image orthicon astronomy. J. A. Hynek and J. R. Dunlap. il Sky & Tel 28:126-30 S '64
Ranger VII moon camera is successful; Could see auto on the moon. il Sci N L 86:85 Ag 8 '64
Ranger TV performed near design point. K. J. Stein. il Aviation W 81:100-1+ Ag 17 '64
TV camera tube sees in dark; SEC-vidicon. il Miss & Roc 13:36 D 2 '63

TELEVISION channels. See Television stations; Television transmission

TELEVISION circuits

Add a TV D.C. restorer. C. E. Cohn. il Electr World 70:78+ O '63
Designing the I.F. circuit. J. Tartas. il Electr World 72:46-9 S '64

TELEVISION commentators. See Television broadcasting—News

TELEVISION commercials. See Television advertising

TELEVISION converters. See Television apparatus

TELEVISION copyright. See Copyright—United States

TELEVISION criticism

Businessman as critic. R. L. Shayon. Sat R 47:22 Mr 21 '64; Reply. J. R. Miles. 47:34 My 9 '64
Cactus Jack. il Time 82:58 O 11 '63
Cleopatra for another Christmas; concerning J. Gould's criticism of the Xerox TV special, Carol for another Christmas. G. Ace. Sat R 48:10 Ja 30 '65

TELEVISION criticism—*Continued*
Huck Finning; Dr Jonathan Miller to write for the New Yorker. Newsweek 62:64 S 30 '63
Man with the popular mind. il Time 84:50 N 20 '64
Required reading; Variety's Rosen. Newsweek 64:50-1 Jl 13 '64
TELEVISION drama. See Television broadcasting—Drama
TELEVISION frequency allocation
Banding together. il Newsweek 62:98 O 21 '63
FCC's bonanza to tuner makers. il Bsns W p39-40 Jl 6 '63
Last chance at a TV channel. R. L. Tobin. Sat R 46:41-2 Ag 10 '63
What you should know about the new TV channels. C. C. Calkins. il House B 106:174-5+ Ap '64
TELEVISION generators. See Signal generators
TELEVISION guides. See TV guide (periodical)
TELEVISION in education
Big brother's TV set. W. Benton. Esquire 61:98-9+ Mr '64
Books, rights and educational broadcasting. R. J. Walsh, jr. Pub W 184:30-3 S 23 '63
Breaking the permissions barrier; creative use of books on ETV. N. Paige. Library J 89:3404-5+ S 15 '64
Can a chipmunk teach the new math on TV? R. Atcheson. il Sat Eve Post 238:26-7 Ja 16 '65
Channels of communication. S. Spaulding. Sch Life 45:12-13 Ja '63
Closed-circuit TV in the school library. A. Apfel. ALA Bul 57:259-60 Mr '63
Denver preschool reading project: ETV plus parents' guidebook. Library J 89:4621 N 15 '64
Dial H for history. il Newsweek 63:76-7 Mr 2 '64
Education comes of age. D. Boroff. il Parents Mag 38:118+ F '63
ETV grants go to five agencies. Sch Life 46:39 O '63
ETV in South Carolina. S. Elam. New Repub 149:7 Ag 31 '63
ETV; views of a classroom teacher, a TV teacher, and a superintendent. P. J. Wright; E. M. Johnson; W. H. Pierce. il NEA J 53:32-4 Ap '64
Great adventure. J. T. Aubrey, jr. il NEA J 52:33-48 O '63
Great adventure; special TV study guides. bibliog il NEA J 53:75-8 Ja; 71-3 F; 79-82 Mr; 65-7 Ap '64
Growing up in Samoa; whole school system turned over to television. il Time 84:90-1 D 4 '64
Here's a new idea for teaching; airborne tv. R. C. Davids. il Farm J 87:76-7 F '63
How television is used in schools. il Good H 156:168 Ap '63
Life guide: educational TV. il Life 55:13 O 18 '63
New service to simplify ETV use of book properties. Pub W 186:150 Jl 13 '64
Non-commercial channels. P. Goodman. New Repub 148:32-4 Ap 13 '63
Off-camera close-up. K. K. Waller. il Mlle 56:114-15+ F '63
Portable TV recorder for student teachers. Sch & Soc 92:330 N 14 '64
Reading room to discuss space age on April 20, humor on April 27. Library J 88:1743 Ap 15 '63
Report from Hagerstown; first large-scale closed circuit television network exclusively designed for classroom instruction. Sat R 47:63 Ap 18 '64
Research on the context of instructional television. J. L. Hayman, jr. and J. T. Johnson, jr. il Sch Life 45:8-11 Ap '63
Schola videotica. P. Goodman. New Repub 148:26-8 Mr 30 '63
School with teacherless classrooms; University of Miami's University college. W. Hartley and E. Hartley. il Pop Mech 120:128-30 O '63
Show that wasn't there; play dealing with race relations banned from Michigan state university's educational television station. R. L. Shayon. Sat R 47:27 Ag 15 '64
Teacher learns by TV in L.A. E. Richardson. Sr Schol 85:17T Ja 21 '65
Television; address, January 27, 1964. R. Garry. Vital Speeches 30:273-7 F 15 '64
TV teacher to Philly tots. il Ebony 19:147-50 O '64
TV teachers: training plant bosses statewide; South Carolina companies. il Bsns W p64+ Ag 29 '64
Texas educational microwave project. R. C. Norris. Sch Life 45:11-13 Ja '63
There's more than one way to teach. S. Hook; C. F. Madden. il Sat R 47:48-51+ Jl 18 '64
What price ETV? analysis of basic equipment costs. D. L. Flaherty. America 108:491-3 Ap 13 '63; Discussion. 108:755+ My 25 '63
Which ETV for your school system? symposium. il NEA J 52:40-2+ F '63
See also
National educational television and radio center
Television stations, Educational
TELEVISION in politics
Are political spots on TV unfair? U S News 57:10 S 28 '64
Battle to call the winner; networks lean on pollsters and computers. il Bsns W p24-6 Je 6 '64
Campaign debating. W. Lippmann. Newsweek 64:13 Ag 31 '64
Candidate and the broadcasters. R. L. Shayon. Sat R 47:41 Ag 8 '64; Discussion. 47:55+ S 12 '64
Candidates on air: new ruling from FCC. U S News 57:13 O 12 '64
Case for political debates on TV. F. Stanton. il N Y Times Mag p 16+ Ja 19 '64
Case for televising Parliament, by R. Day. Review
Sat R 46:36 N 23 '63. R. L. Shayon
Coming attack on Lyndon Johnson; debate issue. S. Alsop. Sat Eve Post 237:15 Mr 28 '64
Election under the big eye. il Sr Schol 85:27-8 S 23 '64
Elections by electronics. R. L. Shayon. Sat R 47:22 Mr 14 '64; Reply. A. Van Zee. 47:33+ Ap 11 '64
Electronic olympics; coverage of Republican national convention. il Time 84:40+ Jl 24 '64
Equal sequel. Time 84:53 Ag 28 '64
Great debate. R. Bensen. il Pop Electr 21:76-7+ O '64
How not to watch political conventions. L. Lorrinson. America 111:227 S 5 '64
Ike sheds some light. W. V. Shannon. Commonweal 79:682-3 Mr 6 '64
In the Cow Palace: toads and Brinklies; TV coverage of Republican convention. il Newsweek 64:50-1 Jl 27 '64
Levitation of Lodge. Nation 198:405-6 Ap 27 '64
Mr President vs Mr Ed. G. Ace. il Sat R 47:17 Ap 11 '64
Mudtrout on the hook; coverage of Democratic convention. il Newsweek 64:77-8 S 7 '64
New comedy TV season. G. Ace. Sat R 47:14 O 3 '64
Not so equal; suspension of equal time provision for political candidates. Nation 197:23 Jl 13 '63
On with the show; The Ev and Charlie show. il Newsweek 61:26 Mr 11 '63
Palace warfare; TV on the convention floor. il Newsweek 64:48 Jl 6 '64
Political impact of TV. R. Kellerman. il Nation 200:24-6 Ja 11 '65
Same program, new sponsors: the return of Ev and Charlie. U S News 54:25 Mr 11 '63
Shopping trip. G. Ace. Sat R 47:8 Je 6 '64
Should a president be required to debate his election opponent on TV? pro and con discussion. il Sr Schol 84:16-17+ My 8 '64
Small screen, super weapon. il Newsweek 62:76+ Ag 19 '63
Speaking out; L.B.J. should debate on TV. R. M. Nixon. Sat Eve Post 237:12+ Je 27 '64
Spotting the candidates; political commercials. il Newsweek 64:76-7 S 21 '64
Television & Canadian culture; adaptation of address. N. Compton. Commentary 38:75-9 N '64
TV or not TV? cameras barred at Baker investigation by Senate rules committee. K. Crawford. Newsweek 63:32 Mr 9 '64
TV poll projections: do they interfere with the vote? pro and con discussion. il Sr Schol 85:14-15 S 30 '64
TV take-over: mismanaged convention? il U S News 57:28 S 7 '64
TV zooms in on GOP: national convention. Bsns W p32+ F 22 '64
TV's equal-time gag. il Bsns W p28 Ag 29 '64
What next from planet Lyndon? coverage of the 1964 Democratic national convention. il Time 84:59 S 4 '64
When the client is a candidate; five TV commercials for the Democrats. P. Hamill. il N Y Times Mag p30-1+ O 25 '64
Where the networks can't win; equal-time problem. Bsns W p40 O 24 '64
See also
Television broadcasting—Election results

TELEVISION in science
See also
Television broadcasting—Scientific programs
TELEVISION in sewer inspection. See Sewer inspection
TELEVISION in space flight
Digital computer-TV displays gaining favor for operations C&C use. C. D. LaFond and R. Pay. il Miss & Roc 15:38-9+ O 5 '64
TELEVISION in traffic control
Smile! your car's on TV. B. Cummins. il Motor T 15:58-61 Ap '63
TELEVISION industry

Russia

Television servicing. Soviet style. T. M. Hannah. il Electr World 71:78-80 Ja '64

United States

Breaking TV out of its box. L. Lessing. il Fortune 70:150-3+ S '64
Colorful sales. Newsweek 61:82+ Je 24 '63
David Sarnoff's vision. H. H. Martin. Sat Eve Post 236:56+ F 16 '63
See also
Government investigations—Television industry
TELEVISION interference
Exterminate TV sync-bug interference! W. I. Orr. il Pop Electr 19:52-3 Jl '63
Radio & TV interference. T. R. Haskett and J. D. Blount. il Electr World 71:39-41 My; 40-1+ Je '64
Reducing U.H.F. TV interference. il Electr World 72:69 S '64
That vile interference. F. Blechman. il Pop Electr 18:77-81+ Mr '63
Trouble-shooting TV ghosts. C. E. Cohn. il Pop Electr 20:36 Ap '64
TELEVISION laws and regulations
Mr Labunski and the Camp Fire girls; concerning FCC local television hearings in Omaha. R. L. Shayon. Sat R 46:41 F 23 '63
Rating the broadcaster; petition of United church of Christ to deny renewal of the licenses of two television stations in Jackson, Miss. R. L. Shayon. Sat R 47:21 Jl 11 '64
Sad sack agency. Nation 198:2-3 Ja 4 '64
TV's equal-time gag. il Bsns W p28 Ag 29 '64
See also
United States—Federal communications commission
TELEVISION photography. See Television—Photographic aspects
TELEVISION plays
Carol for another Christmas. il N Y Times Mag p 138-40 D 6 '64
Patriots: prize winning play comes to TV. il Sr Schol 83:5 N 15 '63
Wedding dress; a play for television. E. O'Brien. Mlle 58:134-5+ N '63
TELEVISION production. See Television broadcasting—Program production
TELEVISION program rating. See Television broadcasting—Program rating
TELEVISION programming. See Television broadcasting—Programming
TELEVISION programs. See Television broadcasting—Programs
TELEVISION receiving apparatus
All-channel TV sets. il Consumer Rep 29:22-5 Ja '64
All's quiet on the TV front. H. G. McEntee. il Pop Sci 182:140-4 Ap '63
Big change in TV; ultra high frequency channels. il Sci Digest 55:37-8 My '64
Buying guide for television sets. il Good H 157:154 S '63
Heath Hi-Fi TV kit. H. Luckett. il Pop Sci 182:96-8 My '63
Home entertainment. Consumer Rep 29:79-89 D '64
How to build in (or even hide) your TV. il Sunset 132:76 Ja '64
Inside the '65 TVs. A. Margolis and R. Benrey. il Pop Sci 185:66-71 D '64
New pay-TV system to start in July. il Electr World 72:30 Jl '64
New TV designs for 1964. W. H. Buchsbaum. il Electr World 71:51-4+ Mr '64
New TV receivers. il Consumer Bul 46:6-10 N '63
19-inch TV sets. il Consumer Rep 30:12-15 Ja '65
Shopping the home entertainment circuit. R. Freas. il Am Home 67:85-7 D '64
TV law that will cost you money. il U S News 56:49 Ap 13 '64
This above all, to thine own tube be true; H. Gernsback's conception of a multiplex video receiver. il Time 83:65 Mr 6 '64
Three ways to convert your TV to UHF. Consumer Rep 28:382-3 Ag '63
UHF converters; Blonder-Tongue BTC-99S and BTU-2T. il Consumer Rep 29:386-8 Ag '64
U.H.F. tuners for 1964 TV sets. W. H. Buchsbaum. il Electr World 71:28-30+ Je '64
Your leisure. Consumer Rep 28:373-9 D '63
See also
Muntz TV, incorporated

Anecdotes, facetiae, satire, etc.

Somewhere over the rainbow. G. Ace. Sat R 47:22 S 26 '64

Color receivers

At last! a color TV kit. il Pop Electr 20:81-3 My '64
Automatic degausser for color TV. W. H. Buchbaum. il Electr World 72:53 S '64
Cheaper color TV. Time 82:81 Jl 5 '63
Color catches fire. S. Brown. il Sat Eve Post 236:74-5 Ag 10 '63
Color prices lower. Newsweek 63:80+ My 25 '64
Color TV. il Consumer Rep 28:524-5 N '63
Color TV from a kit. H. Luckett. il Pop Sci 184:110-13 Mr '64
Color TV: has it arrived? Changing T 17:6 Mr '63
Color-TV in kit form. il Electr World 70:49 D '63
Color TV in pieces. C. P. Gilmore. il Pop Mech 121:194-5 F '64
Color TV; is it finally worth the money? C. P. Gilmore. il Pop Sci 183:80-3+ Ag '63
Color television receivers (cont) Consumer Bul 46:29 Jl '63
Color-TV retrace blanking. il Electr World 73:58 Ja '65
Color TV set makers turn sales volume up; hoping for more shows in color on air. il Bsns W p 144-6 Ja 23 '65
Compact color TV from Japan. H. Luckett. il Pop Sci 183:132 D '63
Fight goes worldwide for color TV sales; competition from Japan. il Bsns W p44+ My 30 '64
Inside the '65 TVs. A. Margolis and R. Benrey. il Pop Sci 185:66-71 D '64
It looks like a boom starting in color TV. il U S News 55:60 D 2 '63
Japanese color-TV has simple controls. il Electr World 71:68 Mr '64
Motorola's new color TV tube. il Consumer Rep 29:235 My '64
Nine-inch color-TV set. il Electr World 72:110 N '64
1965 television receivers. il Consumer Bul 48:6-11 Ja '65
Push for color TV. Time 84:111-12 O 2 '64
Report on color tv. B. H. Frisch. il Sci Digest 55:33-7 Je '64
Understanding color TV demodulators. W. H. Buchsbaum. il Electr World 70:44-7 Jl '63
Unique color-TV tubes & systems: color cathode-ray tubes. L. Solomon. il Electr World 71:34-8+ Ja '64
What to know before you buy a color television. Bet Hom & Gard 42:47 S '64
What's happening in color television. il Good H 158:165 Je '64

Control

Cheater cord de luxe; TV control box. J. A. Fred. il Pop Electr 19:73 O '63
Japanese color-TV has simple controls. il Electr World 71:68 Mr '64
Stabilizing vertical height. il Electr World 72:89 S '64

Picture tubes

Unique color-TV tubes & systems: color cathode-ray tubes. L. Solomon. il Electr World 71:34-8+ Ja '64

Repairing

Fix your own TV. L. A. Harlow. il Pop Mech 121:192-5 Ap '64
Shrunken raster: a puzzler. A. Widmann. il Electr World 70:92 N '63
Television servicing problems. Consumer Bul 46:13 D '63

Testing

Hidden TV test signals. L. Solomon. il Electr World 71:34-5 Ap '64

Tuning

FCC's bonanza to tuner makers. il Bsns W p39-40 Jl 6 '63
TELEVISION receiving apparatus, Portable
Eleven-inch Admiral: a new portable TV. il Consumer Rep 29:52 F '64
GE's 11-inch personal TV. il Pop Sci 183:168 O '63
Portable TV sets. L. Solomon. il Electr World 72:28-30+ D '64

TELEVISION receiving apparatus, Portable—*Continued*
Portable TV that's light, inexpensive, and pretty good; GE 12-pound set. il Consumer Rep 28:430-1 S '63
TV 16-inch lightweight portables. il Consumer Rep 28:188-9 Ap '63
Tiny TV powered by internal batteries. H. Luckett. il Pop Sci 183:128 D '63
Tinyvision TV sets stir interest in new market. il Bsns W p91 Je 22 '63
Two more truly portable television sets; Sony 9-304 UW and Panasonic Mitey-9A. il Consumer Rep 29:393-4 Ag '64
Two unusual TV receivers from Japan: Sony Micro and Symphonic. il Consumer Bul 46:6-8 Ag '63

TELEVISION reception
ABCs of UHF-TV. R. M. Benrey. il Pop Sci 185:104-7 Ag '64
Big change in TV; ultra high frequency channels. il Sci Digest 55:37-8 My '64
Quiet truce in UHF war. Bsns W p34 F 22 '64
UHF reception. J. Beever. il Electr World 70:37-9+ N '63; Reply with rejoinder. A. Weiss. 71:80-1 Ap '64
U.H.F. tuners for 1964 TV sets. W. H. Buchsbaum. il Electr World 71:28-30+ Je '64

TELEVISION repairing. See Television receiving apparatus—Repairing

TELEVISION script writing. See Television authorship

TELEVISION scripts. See Television authorship

TELEVISION service shops
How to find honest TV service. L. Steckler. il Pop Mech 120:76-80 D '63
Mac's electronics service. J. T. Frye. See issues of Electronics world to April 1963
Television servicing, Soviet style. T. M. Hannah. il Electr World 71:78-80 Ja '64

TELEVISION servicemen
Television servicing, Soviet style. T. M. Hannah. il Electr World 71:78-80 Ja '64

Anecdotes, facetiae, satire, etc.

Can you trust a drug store tube tester? A. Margolis. il Pop Electr 20:50-2+ Ja '64

TELEVISION stations
Another TV station for the Johnsons? KLFY-TV. U S News 57:14 D 14 '64
At work at WOOK. il Newsweek 61:88 F 11 '63
Breaking TV out of its box. L. Lessing. il Fortune 70:150-3+ S '64
Closing window; channel 37. Sci Am 209:65-6 Jl '63
FCC ruling that could aid the Johnsons. U S News 56:8 My 11 '64
How will U.H.F. TV affect you? S. C. Silver. il Electr World 69:21-4+ Je '63
LBJ and KTBC; a hot potato for the FCC. il Newsweek 63:83-4 Ap 27 '64
Olé away; KMEX-TV. il Newsweek 61:88 Je 17 '63
Quiet truce in UHF war. Bsns W p34 F 22 '64
Rival nets run CBS dead heat. il Bsns W p36 D 12 '64
TV jumps gun on next season; schedules locked up. il Bsns W p45-8 Mr 9 '63
TV: U and non-U. I. Berger. il Sat R 46:53 F 23 '63
TV's new combines flex their muscles; RKO and Metromedia in television programming. il Bsns W p 122+ Jl 18 '64
Things start looking up for TV's stepchild. Bsns W p36 O 3 '64
Ultra sport; first TV station devoted exclusively to sports. Sports Illus 22:8+ Ja 25 '65
See also
Columbia broadcasting system

TELEVISION stations, Amateur
Amateurs. il Time 81:83 Mr 15 '63

TELEVISION stations, Educational
Books, rights and educational broadcasting. R. J. Walsh, jr. Pub W 184:30-3 S 23 '63
ETV's copyright stand hit at broadcasters' convention. Pub W 186:44 N 9 '64
Educational TV: what it is, where it's going. Changing T 17:38-45 F '63
Life guide: educational TV. il Life 55:13 O 18 '63
New and future trends in the use of audio-visual materials; excerpts from address, July 14, 1963. R. B. Hudson. il ALA Bul 58: 40-2 Ja '64
Reports on library-TV cooperation; NYPL and television station, WNDT. ALA Bul 58:47-8 Ja '64
Segregationist pinch: entertainment on ETV in Georgia. R. L. Shayon. Sat R 46:47 S 21 '63; Discussion. 46:29 O 19 '63
TV's fascinating fourth network. M. Mannes. il Ladies Home J 80:800+ Jl '63
Tv's highbrow wing feeds on business cash. Bsns W p 112+ Ja 19 '63
Very educational; dismissal of WNDT-TV's general manager. R. Heffner. il Newsweek 61:86 Ap 29 '63
Which ETV for your school system? symposium. il NEA J 52:40-2+ F '63

TELEVISION studios

Air conditioning

Air conditioning of television studios. A. Greenberg. il Arch Rec 135:180-1 Je '64

TELEVISION study guides. See Study guides

TELEVISION surveys
People look at television, by G. Steiner. Review
Time 81:47 Mr 1 '63
Two-way stretch; Chicago's WBBM-TV program, Feedback. R. L. Shayon. Sat R 47: 26 Ja 25 '64

TELEVISION tape recording. See Magnetic recorders and recording—Visual recordings

TELEVISION test patterns. See Television receiving apparatus—Testing

TELEVISION towers
Tower for tv; 30,000 dead birds. C. A. Kemper. il Audubon Mag 66:86-90 Mr '64

TELEVISION transmission
How will U.H.F. TV affect you? S. C. Silver. il Electr World 69:21-4+ Je '63
Last chance at a TV channel. R. L. Tobin. Sat R 46:41-2 Ag 10 '63
New potential of UHF. R. L. Tobin. il Sat R 47:37-8 Ag 8 '64
Radio astronomy; FCC purposes compromise to share frequencies with UHF television broadcasters. D. S. Greenberg. Science 140: 164 Ap 12 '63; Discussion. 140:1174. 141:593-4 Je 14 Ag 16 '63
Radio astronomy: TV's rush for UHF threatens use of channel. D. S. Greenberg. Science 139:393 F 1 '63
TV law that will cost you money; regulation of sets for UHF channels. il U S News 56:49 Ap 13 '64
TV transmission on laser beam demonstrated by North American. il Aviation W 78:83 Mr 18 '63
TV: U and non-U. I. Berger. il Sat R 46:53 F 23 '63
UHF+VHF=82. il Newsweek 63:84 Ap 27 '64

Frequency allocation

See Television frequency allocation

Interference

See Television interference

TELEVISION writing. See Television authorship

TELFORD, Allan D. and Herman, S. G.
Chickadee helps check insect invasion. Audubon Mag 65:78-81 Mr '63

TELL es-Sa'îdîyeh. See Jordan—Antiquities

TELL me again; story. See Laughlin, V.

TELLER, Edward
Case for Goldwater. por Science 146:380-2 O 16 '64
Teller urges strong nuclear management; excerpt from Science, technology, and management. por Aviation W 78:92+ Ap 22 '63
Treaty will impede missile defense; excerpts from testimony, August 12, 1963. por(p55) U S News 55:59-64 Ag 26 '63

about

Favored few. il por Newsweek 63:58 Mr 9 '64
Man who challenges the President; chief opponent of test-ban treaty. U S News 55:12 S 2 '63
Man with a mission. por Newsweek 62:22 S 2 '63
Tangled drama and private hells of two famous scientists. R. Coughlan. il pors Life 55:87A-94+ D 13 '63
Trading blows on the test ban. il por Bsns W p27-8 Ag 24 '63
Undeserving. E. A. Cahill. Nation 196:inside cover Ap 27 '63

TELLER, Oscar
Picasso in the nursery. Library J 89:4986-8 D 15 '64

TELLER, Sanford
Where and what to shoot in Florida. U S Camera 27:70-1+ Ja '64

TELLER, Walter
Winter in Bucks County; excerpts from Private line in Bucks County. Atlan 211:78-81 Mr '63

TELLURIDES
High-pressure phase transition in tin telluride. J. A. Kafalas and A. N. Mariano. bibliog il Science 143:952 F 28 '64
See also
Indium telluride

TELLURIUM
Tellurium: a new sensitive test. H. W. Lakin and C. E. Thompson. bibliog il Science 141: 42-3 Jl 5 '63
Tellurium content of marine manganese oxides and other manganese oxides. H. W. Lakin and others. bibliog il Science 142: 1568-9 D 20 '63

TELLUROMETER
Earth distances measured. Sci N L 84:163 S 14 '63
Speedy electronics map a new city; Burnsville, Minn. il Am City 79:30 D '64

TELPAZ, Gideon
Grandma's funeral; story. Reporter 30:35-8 Mr 26 '64

TELSTAR. See Communications satellites

TEMCOR, Walter
Resistive load for hi-fi test. Pop Electr 19: 54-5 S '63

TEMKIN, S. D.
France's Lower East side. Commentary 37: 90-1 My '64

TEMKO, Allan
Buildings in the vernacular. Sat R 48:24-7+ Ja 23 '65

TEMPER
How to head off tantrums. I. T. Comfort. il Parents Mag 38:60-1+ D '63
If I had anyone to get mad at, I'd scream. J. Goodsell. il Good H 158:48+ Ap '64
Temper tantrums threatened their marriage. D. C. Disney. Ladies Home J 81:20+ Ap '64
What teens gripe about. il Seventeen 22:138-9+ F '63

TEMPERANCE
Life and times of the late demon rum, by J. C. Furnas. Review
Newsweek il 65:94 Ja 25 '65
Methodists' stand on abstinence; general board of Christian social concerns. Christian Cent 80:1293 O 23 '63
Vice vs. virtue, a Puritan remembrancer. il Am Heritage 15:72-9 D '63
See also
Alcoholics anonymous

TEMPERANCE in literature
Ten nights in a bar room; an account of Timothy S. Arthur's sensational tale and illustrative slides. W. M. Clark. Am Heritage 15:14-17 Je '64

TEMPERATURE
See also
Heat
Humidity
Ocean temperature
Soil temperature
Thermistors

Measurement

Fresh water: temperature of maximum density calculated from compressibility. H. Eklund. bibliog il Science 142:1457-8 D 13 '63
Temperature regime of deep lakes. L. Johnson. bibliog il Science 144:1336-7 Je 12 '64

Physiological effects

Animals grow faster in controlled temperatures. Sci N L 83:164 Mr 16 '63
Cardiovascular responses of the chicken to seasonal and induced temperature changes. J. A. Vogel and P. D. Sturkie. bibliog il Science 140:1404-6 Je 28 '63
Cytoecology of temperature; report of international symposium. J. Levitt and others. Science 141:1199-200+ S 20 '63
Temperature dependence of anesthesia in goldfish. A. Cherkin and J. F. Catchpool. bibliog il Science 144:1460-2 Je 19 '64
Temperature dependence of the activity of the antitumor factor in the common clam. A. Hegyeli. bibliog il Science 146:77-8 O 2 '64
Temperature dependence of wing abnormality in tribolium confusum. J. V. Slater and others. il Science 140:408-9 Ap 26 '63
See also
Heat—Physiological effects

Regulation

Liquid temperature controller. W. D. Scott. il Electr World 72:46-7 N '64
See also
Thermostats

TEMPERATURE, Animal and human
Brown fat: thermogenic effect during arousal from hibernation in the bat. R. L. Smalley and R. L. Dryer. bibliog il Science 140:1333-4 Je 21 '63
Brown fat; thermogenic effector of arousal in hibernators. R. E. Smith and R. J. Hock. bibliog il Science 140:199-200 Ap 12 '63
Deep body temperature of untethered dolphin recorded by ingested radio transmitter. R. S. Mackay. bibliog il Science 144:864-6 My 15 '64
Hot diagnosis. il Newsweek 61:92 Je 10 '63
Hypothalamic temperature in the cat during feeding and sleep. T. Adams. bibliog il Science 139:609-10 F 15 '63
Keeping cool in summer heat. il Sci N L 86: 10-11 Jl 4 '64
Life-giving balancing act. R. Campbell. il Life 55:76-7 N 8 '63
Reptilian thermoregulation: evaluation of field studies. J. E. Heath. bibliog il Science 146:784-5 N 6 '64
Shade for beef cattle. W. N. Garrett. Suc Farm 61:67 Ag '63
Snakes are interesting; thermoregulation. W. F. Heald. il Audubon Mag 65:218-21 Jl '63
Temperature changes in the rat in response to feeding. A. J. Rampone and M. E. Shirasu. bibliog il Science 144:317-19 Ap 17 '64
Temperature regulation and metabolism in Mexican freetail bats. C. F. Herreid, 2d. bibliog il Science 142:1573-4 D 20 '63
See also
Skin temperature

TEMPERATURE, Atmospheric. See Atmospheric temperature

TEMPERATURE, Planetary. See Planets—Temperature and radiation

TEMPERATURE controllers. See Temperature —Regulation

TEMPERATURE-humidity index. See Weather —Mental and physiological effects

TEMPERATURE of the earth. See Earth temperature

TEMPERATURE regulators. See Thermostats

TEMPERATURE sense
Thermoperiodism in sea-run cutthroat trout (salmo clarki clarki) W. G. Heath. bibliog il Science 142:486-8 O 25 '63

TEMPERATURES, High. See High temperatures

TEMPERATURES, Low. See Low temperatures

TEMPLE, Robert
Know your car (cont) il Motor T 15:66-71 F '63
Motor trend's rare car collection (cont) Motor T 15:76-7 F; 76-7 Mr; 76-7 Ap '63

TEMPLE, Robert W.
Beating the bounce; suspension systems: from buggy to Sting Ray. Pop Sci 185: 102-7+ D '64

TEMPLE, William, abp
Restoring Temple's good name. Christian Cent 80:1155 S 18 '63

TEMPLES
See also
Synagogues

Egypt

Egypt's antiquities. S. Fields. il Travel 123:30-5 Ja '65
See also
Abu Simbel, Temples of

Greece, Ancient

Rough map of Greece: Bassae. P. L. Adams. il Atlan 213:73-8 Ap '64

Japan

Inside the great building, the great Buddha. il Sunset 130:26-7 F '63

TEMPLES, Buddhist
See also
Borobudur, Java
Temples—Japan

TEMPLETON, Edith
Eighteenth of August; story. New Yorker 39:27-33 Ag 17 '63

TEMPLIN, Elaine M.
Manuscript and cursive writing. NEA J 53: 26+ N '64

TEMPO (music)
See also
Metronome

TEMPO (periodical) See Periodicals—United States

TEMPORARY national economic committee. See United States—Temporary national economic committee

TEMPTATION; story. See Holland, B.
TEMPURA. See Cookery, Japanese
TEMUJIN. See Jenghis Khan
TEN Downing street. See London—Historic houses, etc.
TEN nights club. See Clubs
TEN THOUSAND ISLANDS
Place that Rocky knows. E. White. il Sports Illus 20:36+ My 25 '64
TENAFLY, N.J.
Colonial town center goes modern. C. M. Pratt. il Am City 79:122 Mr '64
TENANCY. See Farm tenancy
TENANT farming. See Farm tenancy
TENANTS. See Landlord and tenant
TENEMENT houses
Biography of a tenement; from pasture to squalor. P. S. McGhee. il Nation 198:293-6 Mr 23 '64
TENENT, Rose
Persian cyclamen. Horticulture 41:66 F '63
TENG, Hsiao-ping
Confrontation; Chinese party delegation in Moscow. il Time 82:24 Jl 12 '63
Man to watch. il Newsweek 62:27-8 D 30 '63
TENN, William, pseud.
First family. Am Rec G 29:428-9 F '63
TENNANT, Edward
Can the press serve the council? Cath World 197:107-13 My '63
TENNENBAUM, James I. and others
Canine antiserums analogous to human allergic and blocking antiserums. bibliog Science 142:589-90 N 1 '63
TENNESSEE
See also
Birds—Tennessee
Booksellers and bookselling—Tennessee
Festivals—Tennessee
Fishing—Tennessee
Geology—Tennessee
Hunting—Tennessee

Description and travel

Autumn in Tennessee. L. Sims. il Holiday 34:22+ N '63

Parks and reserves

Southern wild flowers at their best. E. Lawrence. il Pop Gard 14:37+ Mr '63

Politics and government

Racism wasn't the issue in Tennessee. B. Kovach. Reporter 31:37-8 S 24 '64

Religious institutions and affairs

News of the Christian world (cont) Christian Cent 80:688+, 812-13, 1184-6, 1526-7; 81:90-3, 122-4, 249-50, 438, 588, 890-1, 1150 My 22, Je 19, S 25, D 4 '63, Ja 15-22, F 19, Ap 1, 29, Jl 8, S 16 '64
TENNESSEE VALLEY
Forests, lakes and black-eyed peas. J. Gribbins. il Motor B 111:30-1+ Je '63
TVA at work; better hardwoods for the future. K. A. Taft, jr. il Am For 71:26-9+ Ja '65
TENNESSEE VALLEY authority
CAP and TVA: Barry's fine distinction. D. Oberdorfer. Reporter 31:36-8 S 10 '64
Forests, lakes and black-eyed peas. J. Gribbins. il Motor B 111:30-1+ Je '63
Sell the TVA? W. F. Buckley, jr. Nat R 15:472 D 3 '63
Sell TVA? how much would it bring? il U S News 55:50 N 11 '63
Such a lovely green valley. il Time 81:27 Ap 26 '63
TVA at work; better hardwoods for the future. K. A. Taft, jr. il Am For 71:26-9+ Ja '65
Wilderness plan hits trouble in Kentucky. il U S News 57:68-70 S 21 '64
TENNEY, Edward A.
Detroit's Mickey Mouse: the driver education myth. Nation 198:395-7 Ap 20 '64
TENNEY, Meshach
Pious partners of success. M. Durslag. il por Sat Eve Post 236:28+ My 4 '63
TENNIS
Advantage Talbert. Sports Illus 18:10 My 6 '63
American twist; Davis cup matches. il Time 83:47 Ja 3 '64
Another long chorus of waltzing Matilda; R. Emerson and F. Stolle, Australian Davis cup team. F. Deford. il Sports Illus 21:93-5 S 21 '64
Better than fancy pants. J. Lovesey. il Sports Illus 19:12-15 Jl 15 '63
Bright shine on an old shoe. F. Deford. il Sports Illus 21:38+ S 7 '64
Cold and hot; Wimbledon. Newsweek 64:81 Jl 13 '64
Court tennis: the royal game. D. M. Davis. il Holiday 36:158+ D '64
Cups & robbers; Davis cup. il Time 84:80 O 2 '64
Dust off a place for the Davis cup; Australia's for thirteen years. E. Shirley. il Sports Illus 19:98-9 D 23 '63
Egg and the net; spectator tennis is sick, participant tennis is flourishing. R. S. Hewlett. il Sports Illus 18:14-17 F 18 '63
Failure of a winning formula; U.S. plan fails, Australians win the Davis cup. F. Deford. il Sports Illus 21:30-1 O 5 '64
First Negro Davis cupper. il Ebony 18:151-2+ O '63
Great Gonzales. W. Brinkley. Holiday 34:85-90+ Jl '63
High time for a U.S. victory; winning of Davis cup. W. Tower. il Sports Illus 20:18-21 Ja 6 '64
How to play tennis on the wall. F. Stebbins. il Todays Health 42:46-8 O '64
It was anybody's championship, until a Mexican with a deft touch made it his. W. Bingham. il Sports Illus 19:22-5 S 16 '63
Laver's progress. Sports Illus 18:5-6 Ap 8 '63
Legend dies on the court; P. Gonzalez bid to come back. W. Bingham. Sports Illus 19:18-19 Jl 8 '63
Net gain; Roberta Alison in intercollegiate matches. il Newsweek 61:84 Ap 8 '63
New seedlings; national championships at Forest Hills. il Time 82:33 S 6 '63
Nineteen-year-old Puerto Rican brings U.S. tennis new hope; C. Pasarell. J. R. Moskin. il Look 27:104a-104c+ Je 18 '63
Not quite all right, Jack; Davis cup matches in Bournemouth. R. Ball. il Sports Illus 19:56-8 O 7 '63
On to Adelaide; U.S. v. India in Davis cup. il Time 82:77 N 15 '63
One for the Yanks; Wimbledon matches. il Time 82:60 Jl 12 '63
Our Davis cup runneth over. R. Kahn. il Sat Eve Post 237:66-9 S 26 '64
Outcasts are counted in; Wimbledon tournament. J. Lovesey. il Sports Illus 21:22+ Jl 13 '64
Pingpong, anyone? U.S. collapse at Wimbledon. il Time 84:80 Jl 10 '64
Queen Margaret. il Newsweek 62:54 S 9 '63
Small town moves into the big time; National indoor championship, Salisbury, Md. F. Deford. il Sports Illus 20:57-8 Mr 2 '64
Sporting scene; Davis cup challenge round match, in Cleveland Heights, Ohio. H. W. Wind. il New Yorker 40:188+ O 10 '64
Sporting scene; Laver vs Rosewall, professional matches. H. W. Wind. New Yorker 39:128+ F 23 '63
Sporting scene; 1964 United States lawn tennis championships at Forest Hills. H. W. Wind. New Yorker 40:164+ S 26 '64
Sporting scene; 1963 United States lawn tennis championships at Forest Hills. H. W. Wind. il New Yorker 39:126+ S 28 '63
Sporting scene; United States professional tennis championship at Forest Hills. R. Angell. New Yorker 39:91-5 Jl 27 '63
Strategy of success; U.S. Davis cup competition. il Newsweek 63:41 Ja 6 '64
Surrounded by Latins; national championships at Forest Hills. Time 82:57 S 13 '63
Tennis (cont) il Sports Illus 18:57-9 Mr 18; 55-7 Ap 29; 54+ Je 17 '63
Tennis anyone? Wimbledon. il Newsweek 64:47 Jl 6 '64
Tennis boom; East Detroit, Mich. J. S. Seavey. il Recreation 57:282 Je '64
Tennis; its early charms and lasting joys. il Sports Illus 21:26-44+ Jl 13 '64
They waited a year to get their revenge; Mexican Davis cup team vs American team. W. F. Talbert. Sports Illus 19:13 Ag 26 '63
Trojan triumph over Troy; National collegiate athletic association championships. F. Deford. il Sports Illus 19:40-1 Jl 1 '63
Trouble with tennis; topflight players air their grievances. il Esquire 61:119-23 My '64
Twelfth for Harry; Davis cup matches. il Time 84:86-7 O 9 '64
U.S. tennis is back on the center court. J. Olsen. il Sports Illus 19:8-15 Ag 26 '63
Yank at Wimbledon. il Newsweek 62:57-8 Jl 15 '63
Young, fresh setting for old Davis cup; challenge round between Australia and the U.S. F. Deford. il Sports Illus 21:76-8 S 28 '64
See also
Paddle tennis

TENNIS—*Continued*

Study and teaching

Brainy plan for tennis; Dick Skeen's school. il Life 56:113-14 Ap 17 '64
Way to better net play. B. Talbert. il Sports Illus 21:28-33 Jl 13 '64
Year-round tennis; ed. by J. C. Bachman. M. Wade. il Recreation 56:174-6 Ap '63

TENNIS, Table. See Table tennis

TENNIS clubs. See Sports clubs

TENNIS courts
Please keep your dog off my court. E. J. Kahn, jr. il Sports Illus 21:40-4 Jl 13 '64
Tent tennis. il Time 83:39 Ja 31 '64

TENNIS courts, Indoor
Era of elegance; tennis courts of the great estates; with a personal memory by W. Tower. il Sports Illus 21:34-9 Jl 13 '64
Never called on account of rain; indoor tennis courts, Winnetka, Ill. G. B. Caskey. il Am City 79:29 Je '64

TENNIS players
Greatest tennis player of all time: Bill Tilden. A. Danzig. il N Y Times Mag p 19+ D 22 '63
Latin raid on U.S. titles. il Life 55:95-6+ S 20 '63
New seedlings. il Time 82:33 S 6 '63
Not quite all right, Jack; Davis cup matches in Bournemouth. R. Ball. il Sports Illus 19:56-8 O 7 '63
One-two punch for the prettiest. W. F. Talbert. il Sports Illus 18:48-53 Ap 15 '63
Sporting scene; Davis cup challenge round match, in Cleveland Heights, Ohio. H. W. Wind. New Yorker 40:188+ O 10 '64
Sporting scene; 1964 United States lawn tennis championships at Forest Hills. H. W. Wind. New Yorker 40:164+ S 26 '64
Sporting scene; 1963 United States lawn tennis championships at Forest Hills. H. W. Wind. il New Yorker 39:126+ S 28 '63
Sporting scene; United States professional tennis championship at Forest Hills. R. Angell. New Yorker 39:91-5 Jl 27 '63

TENNIS trophies. See Trophies, Sport

TENN-TEX land and cattle company
City cowmen lose shirts and cattle. C. E. Ball. Farm J 88:60H Mr '64

TENNYSON, Leonard B.
United States in the Atlantic community. Cur Hist 45:264-70+ N '63

TENONING jigs. See Jigs

TENSER, Rose Palmai-. See Palmai-Tenser, R.

TENSI, Steve
Two for a quarterback. H. L. Masin. por Sr Schol 85:26 N 18 '64

TENSION (psychology) See Stress (physiology)

TENSION, Surface. See Surface tension

TENT of tomorrow. See New York (city)—Worlds fair, 1964—Architecture

TENTING. See Camping

TENTS
Back-pack tents. C. B. Colby. il Outdoor Life 135:28+ F '65
Keeping cool in camp. C. B. Colby. il Outdoor Life 134:84-5+ Jl '64
Tips on tents. J. Krill. il Outdoor Life 132:90-1 Jl '63
Umbrella tents. il Consumer Rep 28:210-14 My '63

TENURE, Academic. See College professors and instructors—Tenure

TENURE, Security of. See Social and economic security

TENURE of land. See Land tenure

TEOTIHUACAN, Mexico
Bigger than Athens. il Time 81:22-3 Je 21 '63
Treasure of Teotihuacán, new archaeological discoveries; tr. by D. Heyden. I. Bernal. il Atlan 213:106-11 Mr '64

TEPFER, Charles S.
Back talk from your house wiring. Pop Sci 182:155-7 F '63
Cable TV: on the move. Electr World 71:40-1+ Ja '64
(ed) Electronic antenna. Electr World 69:41-4+ F '63
Powerful new antenna for tv and fm, too. Pop Sci 182:188-9 Mr '63
Tape changer: it's here at last. Pop Sci 182:91-4+ Je '63

TERASIMA, Toyozo, and Tolmach, L. J.
X-ray sensitivity and DNA synthesis in synchronous populations of HeLa cells. bibliog Science 140:490-2 My 3 '63

TERATOLOGY. See Abnormalities (animals)

TERBORGH, George
Importance of being on time. Fortune 69:136-7 My '64

TEREDOS. See Shipworms

TERESHKOVA, Valentina Vladimirovna
Three days in outer space. pors Sat Eve Post 237:62-3 Ja 4 '64
Adventurous ones. por Vogue 142:75 Ag 1 '63
Comely cosmonaut. E. Stevens. il pors Ladies Home J 80:60+ S '63
His and hers. il por Newsweek 62:46 Jl 1 '63
Individualists; Mlle's annual Merit awards. il por Mlle 58:72-3 Ja '64
She orbits over the sex barrier; with report by C. B. Luce. il pors Life 54:28-33 Je 28 '63
She's the sweetheart of Soviet sky. il pors Life 55:42-3 S 13 '63
Women are different. il por Time 81:26+ Je 28 '63
See also
Space flight—Manned flight—Tereshkova flight, 1963

TER HORST, Jerald
Grenier plan for the G.O.P. Reporter 31:24-6 O 8 '64

TERLEP, John J.
California's new Stony Ridge observatory. Sky & Tel 26:248-50 N '63

TERM insurance. See Insurance, Life—Policies

TERMAN, Frederick E.
Herbert Hoover, engineer. Science 147:125-7 Ja 8 '65

TERMINAL buildings
Trucking terminal and home office. il Arch Rec 134:130-1 D '63

TERMINAL buildings, Airport. See Airport buildings

TERMINAL education. See Junior colleges

TERMINAL GEYSER. See Geysers

TERMINOLOGY. See subhead Terminology under various subjects, e.g. Politics—Terminology

TERMITES
African underground movement; white ants. A. Carr. il N Y Times Mag p57-8+ S 20 '64
Build right and prevent decay and termites. A. B. Parker. il House B 106:112-13+ F '64
Note on termites. Consumer Bul 47:40 F '64
Termite control, facts for remodelers. House B 105:215-16 S '63
Termites; donation to Museum of natural history. New Yorker 39:23 Ja 18 '64
Terrible termites. Am Home 67:108-9 My '64
Worst pet in the world. S. Schuler. il Pop Sci 184:124-6+ Ap '64

TERMS and phrases. See English language—Terms and phrases

TERNS
Birds of the sea. A. Sprunt. il Motor B 112:46-7 Jl '63

TERNSTROEMIAS
Leaves glossy and darkest green. il Sunset 132:258 Ap '64

TERPENES
Variation in the monoterpenes of pinus ponderosa laws. R. H. Smith. bibliog il Science 143:1337-8 Mr 20 '64
See also
Catnip

TERRA cottas, Japanese
Statues that seem to talk; hanhwa. il Sci Digest 53:52-4 Je '63

TERRA incognita; story. See Nabokov, V.

TERRACE, H. S.
Errorless discrimination learning in the pigeon: effects of chlorpromazine and imipramine. bibliog Science 140:318-19 Ap 19 '63
Wavelength generalization after discrimination learning with and without errors. bibliog Science 144:78-80 Ap 3 '64

TERRACES (agriculture)
Terraces for modern farming. T. L. Willrich. il Suc Farm 62:36-7 Jl '64

TERRACES (outdoor living areas) See Outdoor rooms

TERRA-kart (motor vehicle) See Motor vehicles

TERRAL, Rufus
To kill a river. Bul Atomic Sci 20:35-7 S '64

TERRARIUMS
Bottle allows easy planting of terrarium. B. C. Kilvert, jr. il Flower Grower 51:49 F '64
Garden in a glass world. L. J. Goodyear. il Pop Gard 16:26-8 Ja '65
Have a garden in a bottle. il Sunset 134:140 Ja '65
It's his personal jungle. il Sunset 133:164 N '64
Preview of spring. Z. Boyd. il Pop Gard 15:67 Mr '64
Terrariums. J. Hersey. il Flower Grower 50:24-5+ N '63

TERRASSE, Charles
Nephew. New Yorker 40:50-1 N 7 '64

TERRELL, James
Quasi-stellar diameters and intensity fluctuations. bibliog Science 145:918-19 Ag 28 '64

TERRELL, Roy
Skiing (cont) Sports Illus 18:54-6+ Ap 15 '63

TERRÉS, Jaime García. See García Terrés, J.

TERRES, John K.
Anatomy of a nest. Audubon Mag 66:356 N '64
Audubon mystery. Audubon Mag 66:91 Mr '64
Birds in your garden. Pop Gard 15:12 S; 4 N '64; 16:8 Ja; 12 F '65
Birds strut, soar, sing and dance for a mate: excerpt from Encyclopedia of American birds. Audubon Mag 65:172-5 My '63
Helping hand to the bluebird. Flower Grower 51:24-5+ Je '64
Just out from under a rock. Sports Illus 20: 50-1+ My 4 '64
My friend the squirrel. Flower Grower 50: 20-1+ D '63
On the trail of our wandering birds. Audubon Mag 66:100-3 Mr '64
Welcome the winter birds. Pop Gard 14:26-7+ N '63

TERRESTRIAL magnetism. See Magnetism, Terrestrial

TERRESTRIAL rotation. See Earth—Rotation

TERRIBLE Terry's surprise; drama. See Boiko, C.

TERRIEN, Margaret
I, who never kissed your head: story. Redbook 121:54-5 Je '63

TERRIERS
Dog gods wept. C. E. Gillham. il Field & S 68:58-60 Je '63
Top dog with a topknot: Yorkshire terrier. il Life 57:101-2+ N 20 '64
See also
Airedale terriers

TERRILL, Ross
Conversation in Peking. Christian Cent 82:47-50 Ja 13 '65
Trip to China. New Repub 152:9-11 Ja 2; 13-15 Ja 16; 15-16 Ja 23 '65

TERRITORIAL expansion
Khrushchev-Johnson notes on the use of arms. N. Khrushchev; L. B. Johnson. Cur Hist 46:357-63 Je '64
See also subhead Territorial expansion under names of countries, e.g. Russia—Territorial expansion

TERRITORIAL waters
Red trawlers: encroaching fishermen. W. S. Ellis. il Nation 197:346-8 N 23 '63
U.S. informs U.N. security council on Cuban fishing boat incident; letter to President of the U.S. security council, February 7, 1964. A. E. Stevenson. Dept State Bul 50:279 F 24 '64
See also
Fishery laws and legislation
Oil lands

TERRORISM
French Canada's strange revolt; role of FLQ (Quebec liberation front) L. Bergquist. il Look 27:90-4+ D 3 '63
Massacre at Quitexe: northern Angola. B. Teixeira. Nat R 16:822-3 S 22 '64
My clothes were blood-soaked, but I never moved: American missionary among rebels in Kwilu province, Congo; ed. by B. Lindeman. R. Hege. il Sat Eve Post 237:84-5 O 3 '64
Now it's a war against Americans in Vietnam. il U S News 56:35 Mr 2 '64
Remember the Card! explosion of U.S. aircraft transport ship in Saigon. Time 83:31 My 8 '64
Saga of the Anzoátegui: hijacking of Venezuelan freighter by FALN agents. il Time 81:35 F 22 '63
Terror fails to stem Venezuela's vote. il Life 55:42-4 D 13 '63
Terror in Johannesburg; reprint. Nat R 16: 727-8 Ag 25 '64
Terror in Saigon: target, Americans. il Newsweek 63:31 Mr 2 '64
Terrorists at work; report from Argentina. R. Peter. Nat R 16:638 Jl 28 '64
Truce and consequences: FALN in Venezuela. il Newsweek 62:53-4 D 9 '63
Venezuela: piracy and violence. il Newsweek 61:48+ F 25 '63
Violence is inevitable; Quebec terrorists. Newsweek 64:46 S 14 '64
Will the terrorists get Betancourt? R. Peter. Nat R 15:482 D 3 '63

TERRY, Fernando Belaúnde. See Belaúnde Terry, F.

TERRY, Luther L.
Answers on filters. U S News 56:38 Ja 27 '64
Economics of national health; address, May 11, 1964. Vital Speeches 30:588-90 Jl 15 '64
Political virus smoked out; address. Sci N L 85:277 My 2 '64
Pollution of U.S. air and water: how serious? interview. por U S News 55:98-101 S 16 '63
Smoking habits: what Surgeon General says; remarks, January 11, 1965. U S News 58: 14 Ja 25 '65
Villain in smoke: a new view; excerpt from statement, January 29, 1964. por U S News 56:61 F 10 '64
What is a public-health physician? por Todays Health 41:54-7+ My '63

about

Here's the latest on tobacco and health. il U S News 56:44-5 Ja 20 '64
Irrational state. Nat R 16:97+ F 11 '64
Storm signals for tobacco; report from Advisory committee on smoking and health. Bsns W p72+ O 12 '63
U.S. sums it up: quit smoking; Surgeon General's report. il por Bsns W p42-4+ Ja 18 '64

TERRY, Walter
Cinderella of the opera. Opera N 27:8-13 Ap 13 '63
Paradox of the New York city ballet. Theatre Arts 47:14-17 N '63

TERRY, William D. and Fahey, J. L.
Subclasses of human γ_2-globulin based on differences in the heavy polypeptide chains. bibliog Science 146:400-1 O 16 '64

TERZIEV, Marc
New landlock salmon water. Outdoor Life 134: 20-3+ Jl '64

TESLA coils
Big TC. C. Caringella. il Pop Electr 21:29-32+ Jl '64
Li'l TC. E. N. Kaufman. il Pop Electr 21: 33-5 Jl '64

TESSMER, Leslie. See Schmidt, P. O. jt. auth.

TEST ban talks. See International conferences

TEST ban treaty. See Nuclear test ban treaty, 1963

TEST pilots. See Air pilots

TEST records. See Phonograph records—Test records

TESTES. See Testicles

TESTICLES
Lactate dehydrogenase in pigeon testes: genetic control by three loci. W. H. Zinkham and others. bibliog il Science 144:1353-4 Je 12 '64
Lactate dehydrogenase in testis: dissociation and recombination of subunits. W. H. Zinkham and others. bibliog il Science 142:1303-4 D 6 '63
Lactate dehydrogenases in human testes. A. Blanco and W. H. Zinkham. bibliog il Science 139:601-2 F 15 '63

TESTIMONIALS in advertising. See Advertising—Testimonials

TESTIMONY. See Evidence (law); Witnesses

TESTING
Physics and nondestructive testing; report on symposium. W. J. McGonnagle. Science 144: 195 Ap 10 '64
Test it, but don't break it. H. E. Klein. il Duns R 83:50-2+ Ja '64
Testing without breaking. il Time 81:77 Je 28 '63
See also
Quality of products

TESTING, Educational. See Educational tests and measurements

TESTING, Psychological. See Psychological examinations

TESTING instruments
Calibrating test equipment. W. H. Buchsbaum. il Electr World 70:43-5+ Ag '63
Crystal test meter. C. Caringella. il Pop Electr 18:61-3 My '63
Direct-reading instruments; electronic measuring instruments. F. Van Veen. il Electr World 70:23-7+ Ag '63
Hot-series test box. F. P. Fritz. il Pop Mech 119:191-3+ Mr '63
How to build your own portable auto analyzer. R. M. Benrey. il Pop Sci 184:94-9+ Je '64
How to prevent another Thresher: ultrasonic inspection technique. Bsns W p76+ Ag 17 '63
Measuring the sonic boom; using electronic instrumentation. J. Kyle. il Electr World 72:58-60+ O '64
Multiple meter test set. R. E. Pafenberg. il Pop Electr 19:59 O '63
1963 directory of kit test equipment. Electr World 70:54-6+ Ag '63

TESTING instruments—*Continued*
RF power capsule. I. C. Chapel. il Pop Electr 18:58-9+ F '63
SCR tester. T. E. Hopkins. il Electr World 71:56 Ja '64
Simple transistor tester. J. E. Content and B. K. Morse. il Electr World 71:50 My '64
Speed service with simple instruments. C. Henry. il Pop Electr 20:43-5 Ap '64
Test equipment control center. R. J. Spencer. il Pop Electr 18:73-4 F '63
Test equipment product report. See issues of Electronics world
Test it, but don't break it. H. E. Klein. il Duns R 83:50-2+ Ja '64
See also
Calibrators
Radio instruments

Repairing
Instrument calibration and repair technician; electronics technicians and engineers. G. C. Gedney and F. M. Winterburg. il Electr World 70:28-9 Ag '63

TESTING laboratories
Environment simulator under construction. il(p33) Sci N L 84:39 Jl 20 '63
Environmental testing spurs industry. il Miss & Roc 12:67-8+ My 20 '63
Gauging trails vacuum chamber capabilities. J. F. Judge. il Miss & Roc 15:36+ O 19 '64
Goddard seeks scaling laws to cut cost of environmental testing. W. Beller. il Miss & Roc 15:34-5 Jl 20 '64
NASA center nears completion of launch-phase simulation facility. W. S. Beller. il Miss & Roc 15:18+ N 2 '64
Space chamber fails in tryout. Bsns W p50 Jl 27 '63
Space moves down; air force rocket test chamber simulates atmospheric conditions. il Bsns W p70-2+ Mr 21 '64
Space spectacles; with photographs by O. Gigli. R. Vaughan. Sat Eve Post 236:26-9 My 25 '63
See also
Associated testing laboratories, incorporated
Good housekeeping institute
United States testing company

TESTIS. See Testicles
TESTS, Information. See Information tests
TESTOSTERONE
RNA synthesis in rat seminal vesicles: stimulation by testosterone. W. D. Wicks and F. T. Kenney. bibliog il Science 144:1346-7 Je 12 '64
Testosterone-induced incubation patches of phalarope birds. J. E. Johns and E. W. Pfeiffer. bibliog Science 140:1225-6 Je 14 '63
TESTS, Information. See Information tests
TETANUS
I survived tetanus; ed. by H. A. Johnson. C. Cox. Farm J 88:54G Ap '64
Rising threat of tetanus. S. Blumenfeld. il Parents Mag 39:129-30 Je '64
Second deadliest poison. R. M. Hendrickson. il Todays Health 41:56-9+ O '63
Tetanus immunization. C. J. Potthoff. Todays Health 41:60 My '63
Tetanus: the disease we can prevent but don't. J. D. Wassersug. il Sci Digest 55:85-9 Ja '64
TETANUS antitoxin
Second deadliest poison. R. M. Hendrickson. il Todays Health 41:56-9+ O '63
Shots for tetanus: immunity for all. Time 82:43 D 13 '63
Tetanus protection is important. A. L. Frechette. Horticulture 42:15 D '64
TETER, Park
Chicken feed. New Repub 149:5 O 5 '63
TETLOW, Edwin
Cuba: why Castro is feeling stronger. New Repub 151:9-10 Jl 11 '64
Is Cuba ripe for revolt? New Repub 148:8-9 F 23 '63
TETRACYCLINES
High antibiotic doses cause death in six. Sci N L 84:328 N 23 '63
Making cancer glow. il Time 84:50 Ag 7 '64
Producers declare war over a wonder drug; suit against McKesson & Robbins. Bsns W p26 Ag 15 '64
Tangled trail of tetracycline. il Bsns W p90-1+ D 5 '64
Tetracycline fluorescence in permeability studies of membranes around intracellular parasites. H. G. Du Buy and others. bibliog il Science 145:163-5 Jl 10 '64
Treatment increases disease organisms. Sci N L 86:105 Ag 15 '64

TETRAETHYL lead
Fuel lead found in ocean from auto engines burning antiknock gasoline. Sci N L 84:405 D 28 '63
TETRAHEDRAL networks. See Chemical bonds
TETRAHEDRITE. See Copper sulfantimonites
TETRALOGY of Fallat
High pressure chamber to save blue babies. Sci Digest 53:31 My '63
We gave Diane back her life; first blue baby operation. W. J. Potts. il Read Digest 85:97-100 N '64
TETRANYCHUS bimaculatus. See Red spiders
TETRAZZINI, Luisa
Path of roses. G. Fitzgerald. por Opera N 29:24-5 D 12 '64
TETRAZZINI. See Cookery, Italian
TETRODOTOXIN. See Toxins and antitoxins
TEUBNER, A. L.
Cathode-follower nomogram. Electr World 70:33 S '63
Coil-winding nomogram. Electr World 69:33 Ap '63
Delta-Y transformation nomogram. Electr World 71:31 F '64
Meter range-extension nomogram. Electr World 70:37-8 Ag '63
Negative-feedback nomogram. Electr World 70:31 D '63
Ripple-filter design chart. Electr World 70:31 O '63
TEUSCHER, Henry
Cultural requirements of container-grown plants. Horticulture 41:138-9 Mr '63
TE VEGA (ship) See Ships, Research
TEXACO, incorporated
Partners in excellence; Texaco sponsors Metropolitan broadcasts. A. C. Long. il Opera N 29:8-11 D 5 '64
Texaco's new chief; J. Howard Rambin jr. Time 84:111B O 2 '64
TEXACO experiment, incorporated
Engine may oust big booster; air turbo-exchanger. W. Beller. il Miss & Roc 12:12-13 Ap 8 '63
TEXANS
Disciples of St Darrell on a wild weekend. D. Jenkins. il Sports Illus 19:72-80+ N 11 '63
Famous Texans; past and present. il U S News 55:14 D 9 '63
Texas: two-fisted, three-party state. R. Dugger. il N Y Times Mag p24-5+ N 3 '63
Word in defense of Texas. W. Morris. il N Y Times Mag p23+ Ap 5 '64
TEXAS
Close to the land. il Time 83:16-20 Ja 17 '64
Texas: the roots of the agony. R. McGee. Nation 197:427-31 D 21 '63
This is Texas; close-up of the President's home state. il U S News 55:70-2 D 16 '63
Word in defense of Texas. W. Morris. il N Y Times Mag p23+ Ap 5 '64
See also
Architecture, Domestic—Texas
Birds—Texas
Booksellers and bookselling—Texas
Courts—Texas
Festivals—Texas
Fishing—Texas
Forests and forestry—Texas
Geology—Texas
Hunting—Texas
Music festivals—Texas
Ranches
Rio Grande Valley
Zoology—Texas

Boundaries
Chip off Texas? El Chamizal. Newsweek 61:28-9 Mr 4 '63

Description and travel
Overlap land, gringo and Mexican meet in the Rio Grande country. J. Graves. Holiday 35:74-5+ Mr '64
Try Texas for family fun. F. Somers. il Redbook 124:20-2 Ja '65

Economic conditions
LBJ down on the farm. T. Wicker. Esquire 62:90-3+ O '64

History
Hill country of Lyndon Johnson. M. Maverick, jr. New Repub 150:12 Mr 14 '64

Legislature
Legislating in Texas. W. Morris. Commentary 38:40-6 N '64

Parks and reserves
Longhorn Cavern State Park. W. H. Matthews. 3d. il Nat Parks Mag 37:10-13 Je '63
West Texas wonderland. W. F. Heald. il Travel 119:45-6 Mr '63

TEXAS—*Continued*

Politics and government

Bush grows in Texas. Newsweek 62:30 S 30 '63
Deep in the heart of it. Time 83:38 My 15 '64
Lyndon's boy wins. Newsweek 62:15 D 30 '63
Political outlook: how LBJ's state is changing. U S News 55:5 D 30 '63
Rebellion in Texas? Newsweek 62:32-3 N 25 '63
Story of eighty-seven votes that made history. il U S News 56:46-50 Ap 6 '64
Texas giant awakens: greater political influence for Mexicanos. T. B. Morgan. il Look 27:71-2+ O 8 '63
Texas: two-fisted, three-party state. R. Dugger. il N Y Times Mag p24-5+ N 3 '63
Texas wrangle. il Newsweek 63:23-4 F 24 '64
Vote in Texas: 1964 storm signal for JFK. U S News 55:6 N 25 '63
Whither Texas? New Repub 149:6-7 N 2 '63

Race problems

Other Texans; Mexicanos. il Look 27:68-70 O 8 '63; Discussion. 27:13+ N 19 '63
Texas giant awakens; greater political influence for Mexicanos. T. B. Morgan. il Look 27:71-2+ O 8 '63
These are the times: on being a southern liberal; excerpts from Black, white and gray. R. Dugger. Commentary 37:40-5 Ap '64; Reply. L. T. Denison. 38:28 O '64

Railroad commission

Oil transaction draws fire. Bsns W p37 Ap 20 '63

Religious institutions and affairs

News of the Christian world (cont) Christian Cent 80:374+, 658-60, 1036-8; 81:29-30, 716-18, 866, 1118+, 1568 Mr 20, My 15, Ag 21 '63, Ja 1, My 27, Jl 1, S 9, D 16 '64

Social life and customs

Days and nights in Texas. B. P. Solomon. Harper 227:94-7+ N '63

Suffrage

See Suffrage—United States

TEXAS agricultural and mechanical college system

Agricultural and mechanical college of Texas, College Station

Nuclear science center for teaching and research. il Arch Rec 134:188-9 S '63

TEXAS boys choir. See Choral groups and societies

TEXAS broadcasting corporation
Man who is the President; how L.B.J.'s family amassed its fortune. K. Wheeler and W. Lambert. il Life 57:62-6+ Ag 21 '64

TEXAS company. See Texaco, incorporated

TEXAS Gulf sulphur company
Big strike; discovery of zinc, copper and silver in the Timmins area of Ontario. Newsweek 63:88 Ap 27 '64
Billion-dollar plunge in the bush. il Life 56:36-41 My 15 '64
Canada is riding a homemade boom. il Bsns W p66-7 Ag 1 '64
Getting used to wealth; metals discovery, Timmins, Ont. Bsns W p32 My 9 '64
Great day in the morning for Texas gulf sulphur. R. Sheehan. il Fortune 70:136-40+ Jl '64
Las Vegas in Toronto; Texas Gulf sulphur's mineral strike at Timmins. il Bsns W p 113-14 Ap 25 '64
Texas gulf spread, all this and Timmins, too. il Fortune 70:141-5 Jl '64
Treasure hunt at Timmins. il Newsweek 63:73-5 My 4 '64

TEXAS instruments incorporated
Who are your motivated workers? M. S. Myers. il Harvard Bsns R 42:73-88 Ja '64

TEXAS leaf-cutting ants. See Ants

TEXAS observer
20,000 words a week about the state as it is. W. Morris. New Repub 151:6-7 D 26 '64

TEXAS railroad commission. See Texas—Railroad commission

TEXAS state library, Austin
World's fair, Schmorld's fair; San Antonio to have teen fair; State-library-sponsored bookmobile. Library J 89:1399+ Mr 15 '64

TEXAS towers. See Artificial islands

TEXAS. University, Austin
Bounty of Texas. M. Kempton. New Repub 150:6-8 My 9 '64
Cambridge on the range. D. Boroff. il Sat R 47:48-50+ Je 20 '64
Ford grants $750,000 for translation center. Pub W 187:65 Ja 11 '65
Renaissance at the University of Texas. W. Morris. il Harper 226:76-9+ Je '63; Reply with rejoinder. T. Hardie. 227:14+ S '63
What Johnny doesn't know; week as visiting resident. W. F. Buckley, jr. Nat R 16:14+ Ja 14 '64

Graduate school of library science

Aid for Latin American collections. Wilson Lib Bul 38:604 Ap '64
U. of Texas to prepare librarians for Latin American collections. Library J 89:1575 Ap 1 '64

TEXEREAU, Jean
Refiguring the 82-inch McDonald reflector's optics. por Sky & Tel 28:345-8 D '64

TEXTBOOK censorship. See Censorship

TEXTBOOK publishers institute, American. See American textbook publishers institute

TEXTBOOKS
ATPI annual meeting; shape of textbook research. Pub W 183:20-1 My 13 '63
Are your child's textbooks outdated? il Good H 157:162-3 O '63
Books promote progress; traveling book and drug salesmen. W. Davis. Sci N L 84:36 Jl 20 '63
Catholic science textbooks? V. E. Smith. America 110:78-80+ Ja 18 '64; Discussion. 110:208, 270 F 15, 29 '64
Censors and the schools, by J. Nelson and G. Roberts, jr. Review
 New Repub 148:30-2 My 4 '63. C. Jencks; Discussion. 148:31 My 18; 29-30 Je 1 '63
Censorship of textbooks; symposium. il NEA J 52:18-28 My '63
Doubleday launches textbook series on minority groups' contributions. Library J 89:4618 N 15 '64
Doubleday's new series dealing with minority groups. il Pub W 186:35-6 N 2 '64
Faith and prejudice; intergroup problems in Protestant curricula, by B. E. Olson. Review
 Christian Cent 80:617-19 My 8 '63. F. H. Littell; Reply. B. E. Olson. 80:887 Jl 10 '63
Gresham's law of literature; simplified books. A. Loftis and R. Marshall. il Sat R 46:64-5 S 21 '63
High school English textbooks: a critical examination, by J. J. Lynch and B. Evans. Review
 Sat R 46:54 D 21 '63. J. F. Warner
Integrated textbooks; Detroit series. Christian Cent 81:38 Ja 8 '64
New educational project from Wash. Square press. Pub W 184:31 D 2 '63
Of textbooks and trapped idealists. F. Jennings. Pub W 184:34-43 Ag 5 '63
On the roots of bias; American Jewish committee report on textbooks used in Roman Catholic parochial schools. T. Cooper. Christian Cent 81:770-1 Je 10 '64
Paperbacks as textbooks in Texas: a tentative no. Pub W 183:84+ F 4 '63
Politics of textbooks. B. Crick. Commentary 38:67-9 Jl '64
Serbonian bog of secondary-school textbooks. R. Kirk. Nat R 16:197 Mr 10 '64
Textbook stocks. Duns R 84:88E+ S '64
Textbooks and trapped idealists; excerpt from American reading public. F. G. Jennings. il Sat R 47:57-9+ Ja 18 '64
Three textbooks analyzed at an "ill-natured lunch"; Textbook clinic of the American institute of graphic arts luncheon program. il Pub W 187:97-9 Ja 4 '65
Time to get new schoolbooks; reprint. J. L. Jones. il U S News 54:71 Mr 25 '63; Discussion. 54:98 My 6 '63
Two textbooks: a clinical report. il Pub W 185:100-2+ My 4 '64
Will Rhode Island banish Roger Williams? textbooks for private and parochial school students. Christian Cent 80:294 Mr 6 '63

See also

Biology—Textbooks
Publishers and publishing—Textbooks
Readers
Social sciences—Textbooks
United States—History—Textbooks

Bibliography

Improvement in basic textbooks. R. Kirk. Nat R 15:569 D 31 '63

Exhibitions

See Book exhibits

Germany (Federal Republic)

German textbooks and the Nazi past. G. R. Conant. il Sat R 46:52-3 Jl 20 '63; Reply. M. M. Krug. 46:31 Ag 17 '63

TEXTBOOKS—*Continued*

India

Indian educators view low-cost college texts. il Pub W 183:32-3 Mr 18 '63

Mexico

Battle of the books. Newsweek 61:88+ F 25 '63

United States

See Textbooks

TEXTILE design
Designing bark cloth. J. H. Wilding. il Sch Arts 64:39 S '64
Five designers, five approaches. P. Adler. il Craft Horiz 24:42-8 Mr '64
Marianne Strengell. A. Adams. il Craft Horiz 23:34-6+ Ja '63

Study and teaching

Art on a sewing machine; Applique decorating with paste and a felt pen; adapted from Decorative wall hangings. D. B. Van Dommelen. il Design 64:113-15+ Ja '63

TEXTILE fabrics
Best fabrics for farm homes. R. Martens. il Farm J 87:82-4 Ap '63
Can you talk the language of man-made fabrics? M. Gough. il House B 106:148-9 Mr '64
Cutting budget corners with fabric. M. E. Monze. Am Home 66:84 Jl '63
Fabrics. il Craft Horiz 24:12-31 My '64
Fill the house with lively fabric. il Am Home 67:50-3 Ja '64
Fountain of Edwardian fabrics. il Ladies Home J 81:139 Ja '64
Know your fibers and fabrics; questions and answers. J. Daugherty and M. Daugherty. il Sci Digest 56:27-9 O '64
New wrinkle in no-wrinkle garb. il Bsns W p34+ N 21 '64
Once such fine fabrics needed an upstairs maid! il House B 106:128-9 Mr '64
Printmakers delight; paperlike art fabric offers tactile surface. il Design 65:196-9 My '64
Save decorating dollars with sheets and pillowcases. il Am Home 66:76-7 O '63
Step by step from a fabric to a perfect color scheme. F. Byerly. il Bet Hom & Gard 41:58-63 Ap '63
Take a small piece of fabric. il Am Home 66:12 N '63
Woolen window curtains; eighteenth-century wool textiles. A. Brightman. il Antiques 86:722-7 D '64
See also
Curtains and draperies
Paper textiles
Sheets

Coating

New woolen fabrics wash without shrinking; Wurlan coating process. Sci N L 85:251 Ap 18 '64

TEXTILE fabrics, Fur-like. See Fur, Artificial

TEXTILE fabrics, Synthetic
Best care for easy-care fabrics. J. Gillies. Farm J 87:84 Ap '63
Big s-t-r-e-t-c-h. il Newsweek 64:72-3 S 14 '64
Clothes that almost take care of themselves. il Good H 158:146+ Ap '64
Dynel, newest in overlay materials. M. Penzer. il Motor B 112:44-5 O '63
Good wash & wear: how to know what you're getting. il Good H 156:204+ My '63
In the stretch. il Time 84:62 O 16 '64
Miracle fabrics, yes, but how do you clean 'em? with cleaning guide. il Changing T 18:7-11 S '64
New stretch for men's clothing; stretch fabrics. il Bsns W p86-7 Ja 25 '64
New way to save an old boat; Dynel marine fabric. G. Daniels. il Pop Sci 182:127-30 F '63
Shipshape in the beach house; new decorating materials. G. O'Brien. il Sports Illus 18:48-9 Je 3 '63
Sporting look; stretch fabrics. il Sports Illus 20:42-8 Mr 9; 21:72+ O 19 '64
Story of the green sport shirt that once was tan. Consumer Bul 47:38 My '64
Stretch clothes. il Look 27:45-6 My 21 '63

TEXTILE fibers
Know your fibers and fabrics; questions and answers. J. Daugherty and M. Daugherty. il Sci Digest 56:27-9 O '64

TEXTILE fibers, Elastic
Spandex elastic fibers. E. M. Hicks, jr. and others. bibliog il Science 147:373-9 Ja 22 '65

TEXTILE fibers, Synthetic
New man-made fiber can carpet kitchen; Herculon. il(p273) Sci N L 85:280 My 2 '64
Spandex elastic fibers. E. M. Hicks, jr. and others. bibliog il Science 147:373-9 Ja 22 '65

TEXTILE industry
U.S. concludes textile agreements with Israel and U.A.R; Department announcements, with texts of U.S. notes. Dept State Bul 50:51-6 Ja 13 '64
See also
Cotton industry and trade
Rayon industry

Securities

Old industry with a new image. il Bsns W p 116+ N 28 '64

Wages and hours

Earnings in synthetic textile mills, May 1963. J. C. Bush. il Mo Labor R 87:677-9 Je '64
Wage chronology; Berkshire Hathaway inc, 1953-64. il Mo Labor R 87:423-8 Ap '64

Great Britain

See also
Viyella international, limited

Hong Kong

Weavers' boom. il Time 84:66 Ag 14 '64

United States

Congress cuts cloth to fit textile men. Bsns W p34+ Ap 18 '64
Textile troubles. il Time 81:84+ Mr 29 '63
Way things are spinning in textiles. il Newsweek 64:84-5+ N 2 '64
See also
American viscose corporation
Burlington industries, incorporated
Deering, Milliken and company
Stevens, J. P. and company

TEXTILE machinery
How to knit a yacht; Macqueen cybernetics ltd. il Time 81:77 Mr 15 '63

TEXTILE workers
Earnings in synthetic textile mills, May 1963. J. C. Bush. il Mo Labor R 87:677-9 Je '64
See also
Cotton mills—Employees
Textile industry—Wages and hours
Woolen and worsted mills—Wages and hours

TEXTILE workers union of America
Rebellion in steel. R. W. Gibbons. Commonweal 81:540-2 Ja 22 '65

TEXTILES. See Textile fabrics

TEXTRON, incorporated
How to manage a conglomerate making. S. H. Brown. il Fortune 69:154-7+ Ap '64
Textron forecasts rise in defense sales. il Aviation W 78:85+ F 18 '63
Weaving the payoff. il Bsns W p45-6+ Je 15 '63

TEXTURE
Every surface has pattern or texture. R. Ferragallo. il Sch Arts 63:8-11 Je '64

TEXTURED stockings. See Hosiery

TEXTURES of life; story. See Calisher, H.

THACKERAY, William Makepeace
Search for William Makepeace Thackeray. G. N. Ray. il Sat R 47:20-1+ F 1 '64
When Pickwick went to Vanity fair. A. Ashforth. il por N Y Times Mag p8+ D 22 '63

THACKRAY, John
Accounting for inflation. Duns R 84:39-40+ D '64
Civil war among the auditors. Duns R 83:42-4+ Ap '64
How to deal with the Russians. Duns R 83:57-8+ My '64
International air cargo: the battle ahead. Duns R 83:pt2 132-5+ Je '64
Junior mortgages: high yields for the wary. Duns R 83:46-8+ F '64
Management ways of General electric. Duns R 82:28-30+ N '63
Portrait of growth: California's startling Union bank. Duns R 84:44-5+ O '64
What's an acquisition worth? Duns R 83:36-8+ Mr '64
Wonderland economics of Sheraton corp. Duns R 83:32-4+ Je '64

THACKREY, T. O.
Coming struggle to breathe. Sat R 47:23-5+ O 10 '64

THADDEN, Reinold von
Prophet of the Kirchentag. C. Northcott. Christian Cent 80:933-4 Jl 24 '63

THAIBOK fabrics, limited
Five designers, five approaches. P. Adler. il Craft Horiz 24:44 Mr '64

THAILAND
Atlantic report. Atlan 214:13-14+ D '64
Land of the free. V. S. Kearney. il America 110:573 Ap 25 '64
Thailand: new red target. il Newsweek 61:53 Mr 25 '63
See also
Bangkok
Child welfare—Thailand
Economic assistance in Thailand
Education—Thailand
Forests and forestry—Thailand
Sports—Thailand
Women—Thailand

Defenses

In the vaccination stage; SEATO maneuvers, Thailand. il Time 81:34 My 24 '63

Description and travel

Far and near. T. Spierings. il Natur Hist 72: 60-3 Ap '63

History

King and us. A. Robertson. il Horizon 6:18-25 Wint '64

Politics and government

Contented faces. R. McCabe. Newsweek 64: 34+ S 7 '64
Death of a man. il Time 82:18 D 20 '63
Hard to replace. Newsweek 62:30 D 23 '63
Legacy of Sarit Thanarat. D. Warner. Reporter 31:42-4 S 24 '64
Letter from Bangkok. E. J. Kahn, jr. il New Yorker 40:165-6+ D 5 '64
Missing balance. New Repub 149:11 D 28 '63
Smiling through with Thanom of Thailand. J. Langguth. il N Y Times Mag p 12-13+ Ja 3 '65
Where did all that money come from? S. Karnow. il Sat Eve Post 237:62-3+ O 31 '64

Social life and customs

Club to suit a king's fancy; Royal Bangkok sports club; reproductions of paintings. F. McMahon. Sports Illus 19:78-85 D 23 '63

THAILAND and the United States
King and us. A. Robertson. il Horizon 6:18-25 Wint '64

THAJEB, Ismael
United Nations seen as best guarantee of assistance. por U N Rev 11:29-31 Ja '64

THALASSEMIA. See Anemia

THALE, Harold B.
Facts and fancies about plastic surgery. Todays Health 41:54-5+ Ap '63

THALER, Mike
Music hath charms. il Mus Am 83:112-13 Ja '63

THALICTRUMS. See Meadow rues

THALIDOMIDE
More thalidomide tests. Sci N L 84:3 Jl 6 '63
My search to find the drug that crippled my baby. K. H. Schulte-Hillen. il Good H 156: 94-102 My '63
Reward. J. Lear. Sat R 46:47 F 2 '63
Thalidomide baby gets his arms. il Life 54: 30-1 F 22 '63
Thalidomide birth control. F. Marley. Sci N L 83:231 Ap 13 '63
Thalidomide cancer cure? Sci N L 83:71 F 2 '63
Thalidomide causes deformities in mouse litters. Sci Digest 53:72 Ap '63
Thalidomide deformities could be due to fathers. Sci N L 85:296 My 9 '64
Thalidomide: effect upon pregnancy in the rhesus monkey. J. F. Lucey and R. E. Behrman. bibliog il Science 139:1295-6 Mr 29 '63
Thalidomide: effects on Ehrlich ascites tumor cells in vitro. J. A. DiPaolo and C. E. Wenner. bibliog Science 144:1583 Je 26 '64
Thalidomide: effects on enzymes of glutamic acid metabolism in mice. E. Hirschberg and others. bibliog il Science 143:1343-4 Mr 20 '64
Thalidomide syndrome in monkeys. C. S. Delahunt and L. J. Lassen. bibliog Science 146:1300+ D 4 '64
Tragedy at Liege; Vandeput's thalidomide baby. J. Gallahue. il Look 27:72-4+ Mr 12 '63; Discussion. 27:16 Ap 23 '63

THALIDOMIDE babies. See Deformities

THALLIUM poisoning
Deadly cookies. Time 81:72 F 22 '63

THANARAT, Sarit. See Sarit Thanarat

THANE, Adele
Aladdin and his wonderful lamp; drama. Plays 23:45-56 Ap '64
Apple of contentment; dramatization of story by H. Pyle. Plays 23:57-66 N '63
Jack and the magic beanstalk; dramatization of story. Plays 24:55-64 Ja '65
Old Pipes and the Dryad; dramatization of story by F. R. Stockton. Plays 23:49-58, 96 Ja '64
Puss in boots; dramatization of story by C. Perrault. Plays 23:59-69 My '64
Reluctant dragon; dramatization of story by K. Grahame. Plays 22:51-60 Mr '63
Rumpelstiltskin; drama. Plays 22:53-63 Ap '63
Toinette and the elves; dramatization of story by S. Coolidge. Plays 23:59-68 D '63
Tom Sawyer, pirate; dramatization of novel by S. L. Clemens. Plays 23:77-84 Mr '64
Twelve dancing princesses; dramatization of Grimms' fairy tale. Plays 24:37-46, 54 N '64

THANE, Elswyth
Bagpipes end the sound of battle. Sat R 46:46-7 N 16 '63

THANE, Eric
Montana's valley of hush. Travel 119:46-9 F '63

THANH, Son Ngoc. See Son Ngoc Thanh

THANK you, Peg Carpenter, for your many kindnesses; story. See Heinemann, A.

THANKFUL elf; drama. See Chaloner, G.

THANKSGIVING day
Day of Thanksgiving and praise. il Sr Schol 83:5 N 22 '63
Thanksgiving reunion everybody just loves. K. Davis. il Farm J 88:68-9 N '64
Tradition of giving thanks. B. Tufty. il Sci N L 84:282-3 N 2 '63

Drama

Turkey gobblers. M. Hark and N. McQueen. Plays 23:29-41 N '63

THANKSGIVING decorations. See Decoration and ornament

THANKSGIVING dinners
American masterpiece. E. Ward-Hanna. il Ladies Home J 80:68-70+ N '63
Early American Thanksgiving recipes. G. Maddox. il Todays Health 42:50-5 N '64
Easiest Thanksgiving feast you'll ever fix! with recipes. il Bet Hom & Gard 42:82-3+ N '64
Easy Thanksgiving dinner. il Ebony 20:174+ N '64
Easy way to manage a big Thanksgiving. il Sunset 131:96-9 N '63
Please come for Thanksgiving; symposium. il Farm J 87:70 N '63
Six ways to give thanks with game. W. Bar-Ilian. il Ladies Home J 81:144-6+ N '64
Table for two; menu and recipes. Ladies Home J 81:26 N '64
Thanksgiving. M. C. Schafer. il Horticulture 41:566-7 N '63
Thanksgiving dinner away from home. il Sunset 133:104-7 N '64
Thanksgiving dinner U.S.A. il Am Home 66:48+ N '63
Thanksgiving feast. il Bet Hom & Gard 41: 80-1+ N '63
Thanksgiving starts here! il McCalls 92:134-5+ N '64
They don't make Thanksgiving that way anymore, or do they? R. P. Smith. il McCalls 91:101+ N '63

THANKSGIVING proclamations
Thanksgiving with purpose. America 111:687 N 28 '64

THANNHAUSER, Justin K. collection. See Art—Private collections

THANOM Kittikachorn
Smiling through with Thanom of Thailand. J. Langguth. il por N Y Times Mag p 12-13+ Ja 3 '65

THANT, 1909-
Activities planned to meet objectives of the development decade; summary of report. U N Rev 10:47-9 Jl '63
Africa and the world community; address, February 4, 1964. U N Rev 11:13-15 Mr '64
All human beings have a common stake in progress and prosperity, as they have in peace and survival; address, November 11, 1963. por U N Rev 10:5-7 D '63
Building a peaceful world; excerpts from statement. Sci N L 86:178+ S 19 '64
Congo: an account of United Nations action, and a look ahead; text of a report, February 4, 1963. por U N Rev 10:6-13 F '63
East-West relations and the United Nations; address December 2, 1962. U N Rev 10:55-9 Ja '63
Education in our changing times; address, June 2, 1963. U N Rev 10:48-50 Je '63
Eleanor Roosevelt; a lifetime of dedication to human rights; address, October 21, 1963. UNESCO Courier 16:15 D '63
Human rights day 1964; message. UN Mo Chron 1:ii-iii D '64

THANT, 1909—*Continued*
International aspects of development; address, April 5, 1963. U N Rev 10:12-14 Ap '63
Interview with the Secretary-General; ed. by D. Sureck. pors U N Rev 11:5-10 Ja '64; Excerpt. Sat Eve Post 236:42-3 S 21 '63
Introduction to the annual report of the Secretary-General on the work of the organization. UN Mo Chron 1:43-70 D '64
League of Nations and the United Nations; address, April 2, 1964. UN Mo Chron 1: 70-5 My '64
Letter dated 16 September 1963 to the Prime Minister of the Republic of the Congo. U N Rev 10:47 O '63
Looking ahead; address, January 7, 1964. Vital Speeches 30:226-9 F 1 '64; Same. U N Rev 11:9-11+ F '64
Military disengagement in the Congo; report. U N Rev 10:44-7 O '63
Record of the month; withdrawal of ONUC; summary of Secretary-General's report. UN Mo Chron 1:30-5 Jl '64
Role of science in charting course for the world of tomorrow; text of message, February 4, 1963. U N Rev 10:15-17 F '63
Secretary-General U Thant addresses Canadian Parliament; summary of address, May 26, 1964. UN Mo Chron 1:55-7 Je '64
Secretary-General's report on organization of the Peace-keeping force; summary. U N Rev 11:35-6 Ap '64
[Secretary-General's report to Security council, September 10, 1964] UN Mo Chron 1:3-8 O '64
Secretary-General's statement on his discussions with main parties; February 25, 1964. U N Rev 11:7 Ap '64
Some major issues before the United Nations; address, March 5, 1963. Vital Speeches 29: 360-4 Ap 1 '63; Same abr. U N Rev 10:16-19 Mr '63; Excerpts. Sat R 46:26 Mr 23 '63
Strengthening of the United Nations; address, April 3, 1964. UN Mo Chron 1:76-84 My '64
Text of communication, August 8, 1963, to foreign ministers of Federation of Malaya, Republic of Indonesia and Republic of Philippines. por U N Rev 10:13 Ag '63
Tribute to President John F. Kennedy. U N Rev 10:i D '63
U Thant speaks his mind; interview, ed. by D. Sureck. por Sat Eve Post 236:42-3 S 21 '63
United Nations day address; text. UN Mo Chron 1:9-11 N '64
United Nations day 1963; excerpts from addresses. U N Rev 10:27+ N '63
U.N. General assembly holds memorial meeting; statement. Dept State Bul 49:893-4 D 9 '63
U.N. Secretary-General U Thant visits Washington; greeting, August 6, 1964. Dept State Bul 51:304 Ag 31 '64
United Nations stand-by peace force; address, June 13, 1963. U N Rev 10:54-7 Jl '63
Year's developments in review. U N Rev 10: 6-11 Ag '63

about

Bill collector at work. Time 84:33 Ag 7 '64
Meditation of U Thant. G. Samuels. il pors N Y Times Mag p32-3+ D 13 '64
New Secretary-General. H. J. Morgenthau. Commentary 35:63-5 Ja '63; Discussion. 35: 531-2 Je '63
Pope Paul and U Thant topic: religious persecution. il por U S News 55:16 Jl 22 '63
Secretary-General confers with world leaders; picture section. UN Mo Chron 1:91-8 Ag '64
Secretary-General visits Romania and Yugoslavia. il pors U N Rev 10:46-7 Je '63
Secretary-General visits three African countries. U N Rev 11:12-13+ Mr '64
Secretary-General's visit to Canada. UN Mo Chron 1:107-10 Je '64
Strength of U Thant. J. A. Joyce. Christian Cent 80:1047-50 Ag 28 '63
U Thant at the U.N. 10 A.M. to 8 P.M; photographs by S. Falk. W. R. Frye. N Y Times Mag p 18-19 O 20 '63
U Thant: inscrutable shepherd of the U.N. N. F. Busch. por Read Digest 84:63-7 Mr '64
U.N.'s new power: where will it be used next? il por U S News 54:54-6 F 4 '63
Visits to Europe, Africa and Asia. UN Mo Chron 1:43-6 Ag '64
World is in his debt. R. H. Rovere. il Sat Eve Post 236:38-40 S 21 '63

THATCHER, Madelaine
How public should the front entrance be? House B 105:222-7 N '63

THAWING
Particle sorting by repeated freezing and thawing. A. E. Corte. bibliog il Science 142:499-501 O 25 '63

THAYER, Charles W.
More sensible way to hunt. Sports Illus 19: 68-72+ O 28 '63

THAYER, Ernest Lawrence
Seventy-five years ago: Casey at the bat. A. Austin. il N Y Times Mag p51+ Je 9 '63

THAYER, Mary Van Rensselaer
Dear Mrs Kennedy. Ladies Home J 80:76-7 My '63
I do not want my name mentioned ever, with hers. McCalls 91:237 N '63
(ed) See Hope Namgyal, princess of Sikkim. To be a princess

THAYER, Philip S. and Kensler, C. J.
Cigarette smoke: charcoal filters reduce components that inhibit growth of cultured human cells. bibliog Science 146:642-4 O 30 '64

THEATER
Albee revisited: rehearsals of Tiny Alice; opening of Who's afraid of Virginia Woolf? all over the world. New Yorker 40:31-3 D 19 '64
Birds, beasts, and Bach; Originale by Karlheinz Stockhausen. il Newsweek 64:80 S 21 '64
Life of the drama. by E. Bentley. Review New Repub 151:20-3 S 26 '64. C. Sigal
Pictures and players. H. V. Fondiller. il Pop Phot 56:210+ Ja '65
Rise of rep. il Time 83:54-61 F 14 '64
Second balcony: a nostalgic ode; viewing a play from the gallery. A. Levy. il N Y Times Mag p20+ Je 16 '63
Sour grapes and peaches. A. Pryce-Jones. il Theatre Arts 47:20-1 My '63
Spotlight on the stage critic. N. Houghton. Sat R 47:44-5 O 10 '64
Stuffed bird at forty-eight sharp; Stockhausen's Originale at Manhattan's second annual Avant-garde festival. il Time 84:81 S 18 '64
See also
Actors and actresses
Audiences
Drama
Dramatic criticism
Opera
Pantomime
Vaudeville

Advertising

Strategy meeting; attempt by fellow theater people to save L. Hansberry's Sign in Sidney Brustein's window. New Yorker 40: 49-51 D 5 '64

Bibliography

Theatre bookshelf. See issues of Theatre arts

Community and little theater movement

Actor's workshop of San Francisco. S. Eichelbaum. il Theatre Arts 47:34-6+ Je '63
I don't wanna play. H. Blau. il Sat R 47: 32+ F 22 '64
Life guide: community theater. il Life 56: 9 F 28 '64
Mummers theatre of Oklahoma City. A. J. Treanor. il Theatre Arts 47:55-9 D '63

Economic aspects

Broadway on ice: the obsolete industry. R. Hector. il Nation 198:267-9 Mr 16 '64

Finance

Broadway disaster; reasons why. U S News 54:8 Je 3 '63
Dear me, the sky is falling; losses on Broadway. Time 81:50 Je 7 '63
Hard life of an angel. il Fortune 70:96+ N '64
New deal for the arts. P. Goodman. Commentary 37:68-71 Ja '64
Now angels wing along the Rialto; investors in Broadway productions. J. Keating. il N Y Times Mag p28+ D 8 '63

History

See also
Commedia dell' arte
Theater—United States—History

Jews

Yiddish theater. S. Kanfer. il Atlan 212:104-6+ O '63

Moral and religious aspects

Theatre; verbal indecencies on our stage. H. Clurman. Nation 196:166-7 F 23 '63

THEATER—*Continued*

Stage scenery

Foldaway theater. J. H. Miller. il Recreation 56:370-2 O '63
Hofstra's mechanized stagehand. G. Loney. il Theatre Arts 47:67-8 Je '63
Lighting the playwright's way; projection technique. H. Hewes. Sat R 46:38 S 28 '63
Scene designers: their art and their impact. H. Hewes. il Sat R 47:26-31 D 12 '64

Austria

See also
Vienna—Theater

Brazil

Theatre. S. Richards. il Theatre Arts 47:64-5 F '63

Czechoslovakia

Balletomime; stage-light trick used by Black theater of Prague. il Time 83:65 Mr 13 '64
Czech mate; Prague pantomime theater and Laterna Magika in New York. il Newsweek 64:76 Ag 17 '64
Laterna magika. Commonweal 80:609 S 4 '64
Laterna magika. G. Conover. Nation 199:79-80 Ag 24 '64
Laterna magika. T. Lewis. America 111:199 Ag 22 '64
Laterna magika; combined stage and cinema. il Time 83:67 My 8 '64
Reunion; G. Voskovec and J. Werich. New Yorker 39:20-1 Jl 27 '63
Trick but not a treat; Laterna magika in Manhattan's Carnegie Hall. Time 84:53 Ag 14 '64

Denmark

See also
Copenhagen—Theater

Finland

Report from Finland. G. M. Prince. il Dance Mag 38:15-17 F '64

France

Broadway postscript; Seine conclusions. H. Hewes. Sat R 46:41 Je 8 '63
Catch up with; Théâtre de France at Manhattan's City Center. L. Lerman. Mlle 58: 105 Mr '64
How to succeed in Paris; turning How to succeed in business without really trying into a French musical. il Time 83:78 F 28 '64
Off Broadway; performance of Offenbach's La vie parisienne by Tréâtre de France at City Center. E. Oliver. New Yorker 40:67 Mr 21 '64
Off Broadway; performances of Racine's Andromaque, Ionesco's Le piéton de l'air, and Salut à Molière by Théâtre de France at City Center. E. Oliver. New Yorker 40: 112+ Mr 14 '64
Theatre; successful engagement of Théâtre de France at the City Center. H. Clurman. Nation 198:307-8 Mr 23 '64
See also
Paris—Theater

Germany (Federal Republic)

Audience of critics. K. Tynan. Holiday 36: 111-16+ O '64
Theatre in West Germany today. H. Schwab-Felisch. il Theatre Arts 47:16-21 Je '63
See also
Hamburg—Theater

Ghana

Ghana's young theatre. A. Zeitlin. il Theatre Arts 47:65-7+ N '63

Great Britain

Britain's new actors; rougher, tougher, angrier. C. Barnes. il N Y Times Mag p44-5+ O 6 '63
British experiment in art for the masses; Center 42. D. Thompson. New Repub 151: 7-8 N 21 '64
British national theatre. A. Pryce-Jones. Theatre Arts 47:20-1+ N '63
England's national theatre. C. Barnes. Nation 197:399-400 D 7 '63
English look. L. Lerman. il Mlle 56:142-5 Ap '63
Great Britain's national. H. Clurman. Nation 199:18-20 Jl 13 '64
London openings: National theatre company. A. Brien. il Theatre Arts 48:29-32 Ja '64
New British drama. ed. by H. Popkin. Review
Commonweal 81:461-2 D 25 '64. S. Callery
New trick at the Old Vic. H. Hewes. Sat R 47:73 Ja 4 '64
Openings. Stratford-upon-Avon; Chichester. A. Brien. il Theatre Arts 47:26-8+ O '63
Operatic Kembles; England's most distinguished theater clan. R. Rushmore. il Opera N 29:6-11 Ja 23 '65
Stage and state. il Newsweek 62:62 N 4 '63
Theatre. H. Clurman. Nation 197:244-6 O 19 '63
Week of despondency. T. F. Driver. Christian Cent 80:239-41 F 20 '63
See also
London—Theater
Old Vic theatre company
Royal Shakespeare theater company

Hawaii

Theatre USA; East-West center; University of Hawaii; production of Kabuki plays. A. Slagle. il Theatre Arts 48:70-1+ Ja '64

Israel

Holy inheritance; Habimah theater on tour of U.S. Newsweek 63:90 F 17 '64
Theatre; Habimah company in New York. H. Clurman. Nation 198:204 F 24 '64

Italy

See also
Commedia dell' arte

Japan

Magic of masks. E. King. il Dance Mag 37: 34-7 Ag '63
See also
Japanese drama
Tokyo—Theater

Mexico

Mexico's performing arts. J. Dalrymple. il Travel 122:44-6 Ag '64

Poland

Theatre: Poland. L. Pilarski. il Theatre Arts 47:71-4 Jl '63
See also
Warsaw—Theater

Russia

Here and there. Holiday 34:158 O '63
Reporter at large. R. Blum. il New Yorker 39:55-6+ N 2; 59-60+ N 9; 59-60+ N 16 '63
Theatre. H. Clurman. Nation 197:17-19 Jl 6 '63

Sweden

Sweden is a summer festival. G. Loney. il Theatre Arts 47:62-3+ Ap '63

United States

Along nightmare alley. W. Kerr. Vogue 141: 119 Ap 1 '63
American theatre '64; its problems and promise. H. Hewes. il Sat R 47:27-9+ F 22 '64
Battle for the American stage. R. A. Duprey. Cath World 197:246-51 Jl '63
Challenge of the new theatres; repertory system. H. Clurman. Nation 198:122-4 F 3 '64
Don't they know it's a turkey? E. Kendall. il N Y Times Mag p27+ Ap 14 '63
From red barn to package and tent. E. Coleman. il N Y Times Mag p 12-13+ Jl 19 '64
Funny thing happened on the way to the printer; excerpts from Mister Abbott. G. Abbott. Time 82:84 D 6 '63
Grass roots touring. L. Harris. il Theatre Arts 47:26-8+ Ag '63
How pertinent is our theater? W. S. Smith. Christian Cent 81:1393-5 N 11 '64
My summer with stars; apprentices at Westport country playhouse, Conn. R. Westbrook. il Seventeen 23:124-5+ My '64
Plight of the play producer; excerpts from address. A. Cantor. il Cath World 200:103-8 N '64
Reviewer's notebook. T. Lewis. America 108: 595 Ap 20 '63
Rites of summer theater. il N Y Times Mag p22-3 Ag 18 '63
See America next. R. Gilman. Commonweal 77:619 Mr 8 '63
Show business. See issues of Time
Stratford-on-firestones; New York Shakespeare festival's caravan of trucks. il Time 84:76 Jl 10 '64
Summer for Susan; summer-theater revival of Time out for Ginger. C. S. Wren. il Look 27:101-4 S 24 '63
Summer theatres tryout for Broadway. Theatre Arts 47:29 Jl '63
Theatre. T. Lewis. See issues of America
Theatre arts calendar. See issues of Theatre arts
Theatre of politics; the Negro. L. Abel. Nation 196:351-4 Ap 27 '63; Reply. H. F. Winslow, sr. 196:inside cover My 11 '63
Theatre USA news. See issues of Theatre arts

THEATER—United States—*Continued*
Time of the mouse; star system. R. Alexander. Life 57:19 N 20 '64
We are two cultural nations. R. Brustein. New Repub 151:25-6+ N 21 '64
West of Broadway; theater outside New York. R. Gilman. Commonweal 79:663 F 28 '64
Where are the natives? R. Gilman. Commonweal 79:44 O 4 '63
Where are the new playwrights? waiting. H. Clurman. il N Y Times Mag p26-7+ Je 7 '64
See also
American national theatre and academy
Theater—Community and little theater movement
Theater, Negro
Theatre guild, incorporated
also subhead Theater under various names of cities, e.g. New York (city)—Theater
History
Curses, foiled again! E. M. Halliday. il Am Heritage 15:12-23 D '63
When summer stock was stock; Westchester playhouse, Mount Kisco. il Theatre Arts 47:21-6 Jl '63
THEATER, Childrens
Growing big; theater for children flourishing in the U.S. il Newsweek 64:55-6 D 28 '64
Little mummers render the bard; Mrs Cartwright's childrens' production in Salt Lake City. il Life 55:120+ S 20 '63
Paper bag players. M. Marks. il Dance Mag 38:52-5+ Je '64
Paper bag props for holiday fun; account by The paper bag players. il Parents Mag 39:48-9+ D '64
THEATER, Chinese
Openings, New York. A. Pryce-Jones. Theatre Arts 47:67 F '63
THEATER, Community. See Theater—Community and little theater movement
THEATER, Jewish. See Theater—Jews
THEATER, Negro
100 years of Negro entertainment. A. Morrison. il Ebony 18:122-4+ S '63
Theatre of the meaningful. E. Sutherland. Nation 199:254-6 O 19 '64
We still need Negro theatre in America. P. Lindsay. Negro Hist Bul 27:112 F '64
See also
Negro drama
THEATER, Open air
All the world's a stage when the arts move outdoors. il Sr Schol 82:10-11 My 1 '63
Lulu, Daphne, and an uncertain sky; opera at Santa Fe. P. J. Smith. il Hi Fi 14:68-71 N '64
See also
Amphitheaters
THEATER, Traveling
Pushing for S.R.O; extras to build box-office pull of dance attractions. D. Duncan. Dance Mag 38:33 D '64
What time does the bus leave? L. Funke. il Theatre Arts 47:61-3+ Je '63
You can't do that in church! Bishop's company. D. Sharp. il Read Digest 85:247-8+ N '64
THEATER angels. See Theater—Finance
THEATER architecture. See Theater buildings
THEATRE arts (periodical)
Magazines; missing and presumed dead. il Time 83:82 Je 12 '64
THEATER audiences. See Audiences
THEATER buildings
Building types study. il Arch Rec 136:115-42 D '64
Dramatic hall for the performing arts; Jesse H. Jones Hall, Houston, Tex. il Arch Rec 137:113-15 Ja '65
European theatres revisited. R. Gilder. il Theatre Arts 47:68-70 N '63
Grotto theater is part of Tokyo office block; Nissei theater. il Arch Forum 120:120-1 F '64
Letter from England; Chichester festival theatre. J. Novick. Nation 196:553-5 Je 29 '63
Many-faceted stage for the performing arts; Clowes memorial hall, Butler university, Indianapolis. il Arch Forum 119:98-105 D '63
New German theaters and concert halls; views from the audience. G. E. K. Smith. il Arch Rec 134:179-94 O '63
New York's newest showplace: New York state theater Lincoln Center. I. Kolodin. il Sat R 47:31+ F 22 '64
Temporary theatre, permanent example; new ANTA-Washington square theatre. E. F. Kook. il Sat R 47:30 F 22 '64
Theater glamour again; Lincoln Center's newest theater. il Arch Rec 135:137-44 My '64
What's wrong with the new theatres. D. Johnston. il Theatre Arts 47:16-18+ Ag '63
See also
Bayreuth festspielhaus
Moving picture theaters
THEATER center group, Dallas. See Dallas—Theater
THÉÂTRE de France. See Theater—France
THEATER festivals. See Drama festivals
THEATRE guild, incorporated
Riches or ruin for theatre? group W's plan for theatre-TV production. G. Eells. Theatre Arts 47:27-32+ N '63
Trade winds. J. G. Fuller. Sat R 46:10 F 9 '63; Correction. 46:27 Mr 23 '63
THEATRE library association
Collectors, speak up; reprint. S. C. Gross. il Library J 89:202-4 Ja 15 '64
Theatre library association and Broadside. S. C. Gross. Wilson Lib Bul 38:664 Ap '64
THÉÂTRE national de l'Opéra, Paris. See Opera houses
THEATRE of Peretz; drama. See Sheffer, I.
THEATER photography. See Photography, Theatrical
THEATER programs
Programs with personality; souvenir programs of ballet companies. D. Hering. il Dance Mag 37:50-1+ S '63
Walk to that exit. B. Friel. Holiday 34:48+ N '63
THEATER Royal. See Dublin—Theater
THEATER tickets
Iceman melteth; new codes of ethics covering ticket sales. Time 84:50 Jl 17 '64
Return of the iceman. Time 84:72 N 20 '64
Scalpers scalped. il Newsweek 62:46 D 23 '63
THEATERS. See Theater buildings
THEATRICAL agencies
Concert impresarios, the big three. il Dance Mag 37:52-3 D '63
Men who rule the stars; Hollywood agents. B. Davidson. il Sat Eve Post 237:81-5 O 24 '64
THEATRICAL costume. See Costume, Theatrical
THEATRICAL directors
Determined lady; interview, ed. by A. M. Lingg. M. Wallmann. il Opera N 29:14-15 O 17 '64
Reporter at large; rehearsals of Fifth column, by E. Hemingway in Russia. R. Blum. il New Yorker 39:55-6 N 2; 59-60+ N 9; 59-60+ N 16 '63
To Lawrence Langner. K. Hepburn; E. Norton. Theatre Arts 47:10-11+ My '63
See also
Littlewood, J.
Merrick, D.
Women as theatrical managers, etc.
THEATRICAL libraries
See also
Libraries—Theater collections
New York public library—Theater collection
Theatre library association
Walter Hampden memorial library
THEATRICAL literature
See also
Libraries—Theater collections
THEATRICAL make-up. See Make-up, Theatrical
THEATRICAL managers
See also
Theatrical directors
THEATRICAL photography. See Photography, Theatrical
THEATRICAL posters. See Posters
THEATRICAL production
A B B of Alan Schneider; Albee, Beckett and Brecht. A. Levy. il N Y Times Mag p27+ O 20 '63
Albee revisited: rehearsals of Tiny Alice. New Yorker 40:31-3 D 19 '64
Alexander H. Cohen: bigger than Barnum. R. Gehman. il Theatre Arts 47:20-2+ O '63
Balletomime; stage-light trick used by Black theater of Prague. il Time 83:65 Mr 13 '64
Broadway on ice; the obsolete industry. R. Hector. il Nation 198:267-9 Mr 16 '64
Broadway's hottest producers. il Bsns W p90-1 F 2 '63
Confessions of a Broadway alchemist; excerpt from Watchman, what of the night? (cont) J. Harris. Theatre Arts 47:22-4+ F '63
Director prepares. H. Clurman. il Theatre Arts 47:16-19+ Ap '63

THEATRICAL production—*Continued*
Dumpling mystery and other gastronomic fakes. T. Prideaux. il Life 56:111-12 Ap 3 '64
Golden boys: The boys from Syracuse. Newsweek 62:82 S 16 '63
How an angel picks a play; excerpt from Occupation: angel. M. Cullman. Theatre Arts 47:66-7+ Ap '63
I remember Barbra. J. Weidman. Holiday 34:123-5+ N '63
Miracle on Broadway; Any Wednesday. N. Poirier. il Sat Eve Post 237:83-7 Ap 25 '64
Mister Abbott; excerpts. G. Abbott. il Theatre Arts 48:26-8 Ja '64
Mostel revisited; production of Fiddler on the roof. New Yorker 40:25-7 Ja 2 '65
New producer; off Broadway revival, Boys from Syracuse. New Yorker 39:16-18 Ag 10 '63
Opening the old kit bag; producer-director, J. Littlewood. il Time 82:64-5 Jl 5 '63
Plight of the play producer; excerpts from address. A. Cantor. il Cath World 200:103-8 N '64
Show must go on; case of The deputy. America 109:224 S 7 '63
Soft psyche of Joshua Logan. G. Talese. Esquire 59:82-5+ Ap '63
Theatre: how production affects a play's content. H. Clurman. Nation 196:213-14 Mr 9 '63
Vacuum-packed theater; Peter Coe's production of Next time I'll sing to you. R. Gilman. Commonweal 79:404 D 27 '63
Where are the new playwrights? waiting. H. Clurman. il N Y Times Mag p26-7+ Je 7 '64
Would little Joan Littlewood were here! A. Bailey. Esquire 61:113-15 Ja '64
See also
Moving picture production and direction
Operatic production
Shakespeare, W.—Staging and acting of plays
Theatrical directors
Women as theatrical managers, etc.

Anecdotes, facetiae, satire, etc.

Trade winds. J. G. Fuller. Sat R 46:8-9 S 7 '63

THEATRICALS, Prison, See Prison recreation
THEFT. See Embezzlement; Stealing; Thieves
THEFT insurance. See Insurance, Burglary
THEIR quiet lives; story. See Warner, S. T.
THEISM
See also
God
THEM apples; story. See Rogin, G.
THEME writing. See English language—Composition
THEOBALD, Robert
Abundance threat or promise? Nation 196: 387-412 My 11 '63
Cybernated era; address, June 30, 1964. Vital Speeches 30:636-40 Ag 1 '64
Food, jobs and human rights; address, September 21, 1963. Vital Speeches 30:61-4 N 1 '63
Guaranteeing an income. Commonweal 80: 603-6 S 4 '64
House that homo sapiens built. Nation 199: 249-52 O 19 '64
Leisure, its meaning and implications; excerpts from address. por Recreation 57:9-10 Ja '64
Manpower revolution. Nation 196:519 Je 22 '63
On the lack of scarcity. Nation 197:183-5 S 28 '63
THEODOLITES
Perkin-Elmer theodolite system for Saturn tested at Cape Canaveral. M. Getler. il Miss & Roc 13:62+ S 30 '63
THEOLOGIANS
Authority and the theologian. D. Callahan. Commonweal 80:319-23 Je 5 '64; Discussion. 80:511-14 Jl 24 '64
Cambridge objectors. il Time 83:78 Mr 6 '64
Theology as literature. K. B. Cully. Christian Cent 81:237-8 F 19 '64
See also
Women as theologians
THEOLOGICAL education
For the world of tomorrow. R. C. Miller. Christian Cent 81:544-6 Ap 29 '64
Ideas of a seminary. Christian Cent 80:518-20 Ap 24 '63
Making of ministers, ed. by K. R. Bridston and D. W. Culver. Review
Christian Cent 81:1040+ Ag 19 '64. J. B. Coburn
Ministry as servanthood. R. Hazelton. Christian Cent 80:521-4 Ap 24 '63
Reforming the seminaries. J. O'Donoghue. Commonweal 81:194-6 N 6 '64; Discussion. 81:391-2, 466-7+, 554 D 11 '64, Ja 8, 29 '65
Supervising seminary field work; Biennial consultation on seminary field work. C. H. Reid. Christian Cent 80:528-30 Ap 24 '63
See also
Religious education
Theological schools
THEOLOGICAL libraries
See also
American theological library association
THEOLOGICAL school professors. See College professors and instructors
THEOLOGICAL schools
Ideas of a seminary. Christian Cent 80:518-20 Ap 24 '63
Joining the theologians for thrift & tolerance; union of seven divinity schools. il Time 84:50-1 N 6 '64
Our reluctant laity and the seminaries. J. Sellers. Christian Cent 81:551-2+ Ap 29 '64
Seminary of the future? Pope John XXIII national seminary for delayed vocations. America 109:547 N 9 '63
Seminary planned by archdiocese of New York; St Patrick's college seminary, Cornwall, N.Y. il Arch Rec 135:236 Ja '64
Seminary professors resign; Southeastern seminary, Wake Forest, N.C. Christian Cent 82:101-2 Ja 27 '65
Seminary training. Commonweal 79:497-8 Ja 31 '64
Southern Baptist seminaries. O. T. Binkley. Christian Cent 80:774-5 Je 12 '63
Tomorrow's priests. America 110:152 F 1 '64
Tomorrow's seminaries. S. Poole. America 110:86-8+ Ja 18 '64; Discussion. 110:423-6+, 723-9 Mr 28, My 23 '64
Training for the urban ministry. M. Rich. Christian Cent 81:148-9 Ja 29 '64
Updating seminaries. America 111:122 Ag 8 '64
See also names of theological schools, e.g. Princeton theological seminary

Attendance

Parish ministry losing lure; report by American association of theological seminaries. Christian Cent 80:1537 D 11 '63; Discussion. 81:151 Ja 29 '64

Curriculum

Freedom of priests. D. Callahan. Commonweal 79:95-8 O 18 '63; Discussion. 79:285-8, 373-5 N 29, D 20 '63
Toward a more scholarly ministry; Hartford seminary's new curriculum. P. L. Berger. Christian Cent 80:524-7 Ap 24 '63

Directories

Directory: seminary offerings. Christian Cent 80:533-57; 81:553-77 Ap 24 '63, Ap 29 '64

THEOLOGICAL students
Ministers of tomorrow. il Time 81:69 F 22 '63
Parish ministry losing lure; report by American association of theological seminaries. Christian Cent 80:1537 D 11 '63; Discussion. 81:151 Ja 29 '64
Supervising seminary field work; Biennial consultation on seminary field work. C. H. Reid. Christian Cent 80:528-30 Ap 24 '63
Training for the urban ministry. M. Rich. Christian Cent 81:148-9 Ja 29 '64
THEOLOGICAL study conference. See Religious conferences
THEOLOGY
After Moncure Daniel Conway. J. A. Davidson. Christian Cent 80:277 F 27 '63
America's Catholic community: increasing involvement. B. Cooke. Christian Cent 80: 360-2 Mr 20 '63
Bishop of Woolwich speaks for the growing edge of Christian thought in America as well as Europe. D. Auchincloss. il Horizon 5:8-9 S '63
Christian belief in God, by D. Jenkins. Review
Christian Cent 82:18-19 Ja 6 '65. L. Gilkey
Concern for theology. J. C. Bennett. Commonweal 78:418-20 Jl 12 '63
Define your theology! Christian Cent 80:484 Ap 17 '63
Doctrine of the church, ed. by D. Kirkpatrick. Review
Christian Cent 81:864 Jl 1 '64. R. A. Raines
Evangelical undertow. Time 82:57 D 20 '63

THEOLOGY—*Continued*
Honest to God, by J. A. T. Robinson. Review
Christian Cent 80:603-4 My 8 '63
Nat R 16:452-4+ Je 2 '64. H. O. J. Brown; Discussion. 16:472+ Je 16 '64
Important theology. W. A. Johnson. Christian Cent 81:337-9 Mr 11 '64
In search of honesty. J. Cogley. Commonweal 79:705-7 Mr 13 '64
Karl Barth's theological quest. D. J. O'Hanlon. Commonweal 77:520-1 F 8 '63
Later Heidegger and theology, ed. by J. M. Robinson and J. B. Cobb, jr. Review
Christian Cent 80:1273-4 O 16 '63. S. Laeuchli
Laugh or perish! appeal for scholarly sanity. R. G. Gruenler. Christian Cent 80:204-5 F 13 '63
Lay theologians in parishes. E. C. Bianchi. America 109:772-3 D 14 '63
Liberal theology reconstructed. D. D. Williams. Christian Cent 81:1494-6 D 2 '64
Logic and the logos; second consultation on hermeneutics at Drew university. R. W. Funk. Christian Cent 81:1175-7 S 23 '64
Luther's meditations on the gospels, tr. by R. H. Bainton. Review
Christian Cent 80:1030 Ag 21 '63. H. J. Grimm
Man as servant. J. I. Miller. Christian Cent 81:233-6 F 19 '64
Mircea Eliade and the dialectic of the sacred, by T. J. J. Altizer. Review
Christian Cent 81:179-80 F 5 '64. E. J. Jurji
Moncure Daniel Conway at South place chapel. W. S. Smith; reply. S. D. Wakefield. Christian Cent 80:468 Ap 10 '63
New search for the historical Jesus; Marburg disciples. il Time 81:68+ Je 21 '63
On keeping human life human. P. Lehmann. Christian Cent 81:1297-9 O 21 '64; Reply. P. Ramsey. 81:1529 D 9 '64
Paul Tillich's system. G. H. Tavard. Commonweal 79:566-8 F 7 '64
Pentecostal movement: hopes and hazards. K. Kendrick. Christian Cent 80:608-10 My 8 '63
Southern Baptists: need for reformulation, redirection. S. S. Hill, jr; discussion. Christian Cent 80:276-7 F 27 '63
Systematic theology, by P. Tillich. Review
Christian Cent 81:518-19+ Ap 22 '64. D. D. Williams
Teilhard's collectivist salvation. T. Molnar. Nat R 14:464-5 Je 4 '63
Theological asides. C. Davis. America 108:861; 109:98, 236, 457, 710; 110:91, 281, 514, 720; 111:42, 158-9, 353, 558, 803 Je 15, Jl 27, S 7, O 19, N 30 '63, Ja 18, F 29, Ap 11, My 23, Jl 11, Ag 15, S 26, N 7, D 19 '64
Theological frame of religious liberty. J. D. Hughey. Christian Cent 80:1365-8 N 6 '63
Theology is not American. N. F. S. Ferré; discussion. Christian Cent 80:244 F 20 '63
Theology of Emil Brunner: pro and con. R. H. Bryant. Christian Cent 81:81-4 Ja 15 '64
Thrust of "progressive" Catholicism. G. A. Lindbeck. Commonweal 79:105-7 O 18 '63
Time has come. D. W. Ferm. bibliog f Christian Cent 81:903-6 Jl 15 '64; Discussion. 81:1178-9 S 23 '64
Tradition, reformation and development. J. Pelikan. Christian Cent 82:8-10 Ja 6 '65
Union proposal two years later; excerpt from reply appended to The challenge to reunion, by R. M. Brown and D. H. Scott. E. C. Blake. Christian Cent 80:396-8 Mr 27 '63; Reply. H. F. Reissig. 80:807 Je 19 '63
Vatican II needs a new approach. F. X. Murphy. Cath World 198:302-7 F '64
When is doctrine pure? excerpt from Open church. M. Novak. Commonweal 80:233-5 My 15 '64; Reply with rejoinder. T. Molnar. 80:453-4 Jl 3 '64
See also
Authority (religion)
Calvinism
Catechetics
Christian life
Christianity
Church unity
Ethics
God
Grace (theology)
Heresy
Immortality
Justification
Mary, Virgin—Theology
Mysticism
Natural theology
Protestantism
Rationalism
Religion
Religion and science
Revelation
Sacraments
Salvation
Secularism
Worship

Bibliography

Bookshelf on the daily life of the church. R. W. Spike. Christian Cent 80:958-9 Jl 31 '63
History of Christian thought bookshelf. J. Pelikan. Christian Cent 80:711-13 My 29 '63
Pastoral theology bookshelf. W. E. Oates. Christian Cent 80:1055-6 Ag 28 '63
Systematic theology bookshelf. R. M. Brown. Christian Cent 80:400-2 Mr 27 '63
Worship, liturgy and devotion bookshelf. M. H. Shepherd, jr. Christian Cent 81:144-6 Ja 29 '64

Study and teaching

College theology: career for laymen. W. T. Patterson. America 110:412-16 Mr 28 '64
Layman teaches theology. V. C. Zamoyta. Cath World 199:22-7 Ap '64
Mining the precious ore; how one Catholic seminary tackles the problem of studying Protestant theology. G. R. Fitzgerald. America 109:292+ S 21 '63
Seminar in ecumenical trialogue; Greater Boston ecumenical seminar. N. Ehrenstrom. Christian Cent 81:579-81 Ap 29 '64
Seminary theology; excerpts. C. Davis. Commonweal 80:43-6 Ap 3 '64
Theology in the Catholic college. G. H. Tavard. il Commonweal 78:273-5 My 31 '63; Discussion. 78:455-7 Jl 26 '63
Toward a more scholarly ministry; Hartford seminary's new curriculum. P. L. Berger. Christian Cent 80:524-7 Ap 24 '63
See also
Theological schools

Terminology

Jargon that jars. Time 82:55+ N 8 '63
Theology: dead letter or living teacher? J. B. Sheerin. Cath World 197:4-7 Ap '63
THEOLOGY, Doctrinal
See also
Mary, Virgin—Theology
THEOLOGY, Liberal. See Modernism
THEOLOGY, Natural. See Natural theology
THEOLOGY today (periodical)
Theology today: lively guide. Christian Cent 81:263 F 26 '64
THEOSOPHY
Theosophist Helena Blavatsky. W. S. Smith. Christian Cent 80:1002-5 Ag 14 '63; Discussion. 80:1244-6 O 9 '63
THERAPEUTIC abortion. See Abortion
THERAPEUTIC index. See Therapeutics
THERAPEUTICS
Father of rational therapy. Todays Health 41:73 O '63
Toxicity, the therapeutic index, and the ranking of drugs. M. A. Schneiderman and others. bibliog il Science 144:1212-14 Je 5 '64
See also
Acupuncture
Electrotherapy
Fasting
Inhalation (therapeutics)
Occupational therapy
Recreational therapy
Ultrasonic waves—Medical applications
THERE was a time; story. See Levinson, N.
THERESA; story. See Hahn, E.
THÉRÈSE, Sister Mary. See Mary Thérèse, Sister
THERMAL reactors. See Atomic power plants
THERMAL recovery of petroleum. See Petroleum engineering
THERMAL sensitivity. See Temperature sense
THERMAL waters. See Hot springs
THERMIONIC converters
Thermionic flight experiment studied. M. Getler. il Miss & Roc 12:38+ Ap 29 '63
THERMISTORS
Electronics' new mighty midget; thermistor. il Bsns W p 118 N 30 '63
Temperature sensitive devices. J. R. Collins. il Electr World 72:50-2 O '64
THERMODYNAMICS
ASSET to test hypersonic theory. il Miss & Roc 12:28 My 27 '63
ASSET vehicles to fill part of Dyna-Soar gap. il Miss & Roc 12:30 Ap 29 '63

THERMOELECTRIC cameras. See Cameras
THERMOELECTRIC cooling
Magnetothermoelectricity. R. Wolfe. il Sci Am 210:70-6+ bibliog(p 140) Je '64
Refrigerated clothing for summer of future. Sci N L 86:121 Ag 22 '64
THERMOELECTRIC generators. See Electric generators
THERMOELECTRIC refrigerators. See Refrigerators, Electric
THERMOELECTRICITY
USAF effort aimed at thermoelectrics. M. L. Yaffee. il Aviation W 80:55+ Je 8 '64
See also
Thermionic converters
Thermoelectric cooling
THERMOGRAPHY, Infrared. See Photography, Infrared
THERMOGRAPHY, Medical. See Photography, Medical
THERMOMAGNETISM
Magnetothermoelectricity. R. Wolfe. il Sci Am 210:70-6+ bibliog((p 140) Je '64
THERMOMETERS, Clinical
President decides not to modify duty on clinical thermometers. Dept State Bul 49:646-7 O 21 '63
THERMOMETERS, Cooking
Temperature takers! il Bet Hom & Gard 41:113 O '63
THERMOMETERS and thermometry
Dial-type thermometers. il Consumer Bul 47:16-19 O '64
Tap tap temperature taker; electronic thermometer. H. B. Smith. il Pop Electr 21:39-43+ Jl '64
Temperatures in depth; Fish-O-Therm. C. Conley. il Field & S 68:79 Ag '63
Thermometer takes sea's temperature. il Sci N L 83:343 Je 1 '63
Thermometers for freezers and refrigerators. il Consumer Rep 28:493 O '63
Undercooling of liquids. D. Turnbull. il Sci Am 212:38-46 bibliog(p 134) Ja '65
THERMONIC emission
Early vacuum tubes. P. G. Watson. il Electr World 72:42-3+ D '64
THERMONUCLEAR reactions. See Nuclear fusion
THERMONUCLEAR war. See Atomic warfare
THERMOPILES
Fun with a homemade thermopile. H. P. Strand. il Pop Mech 119:186-8+ Mr '63
THERMOREGULATORY behavior. See Temperature, Animal and human
THERMOS containers
Picnic jugs. il Consumer Bul 46:2+ Ag '63
THERMOSTATS
Banish freeze-and-fry home heating. J. Goldman. il Pop Mech 120:172-7+ O '63
'64 Cadillac makes its own weather. D. Francis. il Pop Sci 183:66-8 N '63
Your thermostats. House & Gard 124:214+ N '63
THESES. See Dissertations, Academic
THEY'VE closed the Palais Royale; story. See Waldo, M. J.
THIAMIN. See Vitamins—Vitamin B_1
THIBODEAU, Jean
Collectors' items. Horticulture 42:28-30+ Ap '64
THICH-quang-Lien
Buddhist way in Vietnam. J. Langguth. il pors N Y Times Mag p29+ O 11 '64
THICH-tri-Quang
Thich Tri Quang gets ready. Nat R 16:800 S 22 '64
Ugly Americans of Vietnam; with editorial comment. M. Higgins. il America 111:376-82 O 3 '64
THICKNESS gages. See Gages
THIEBAUD, Wayne
They paint; you recognize. il por Time 83:74-5+ Ap 3 '64
THIEF in the night; story. See Chute, B. J.
THIELEN, Benedict
Along a lazy river. Holiday 35:27-31+ F '64
Bahamas, golden Archipelago. Holiday 36:60-73+ D '64
Birds of Cocoa Beach. Holiday 35:64-5+ Je '64
Florida rides a space-age boom. Nat Geog Mag 124:858-903 D '63
New look of old Cape Cod. Holiday 34:30-43 S '63
Ring around the Gaspé. Holiday 35:22+ Ap '64
World by the sea. Holiday 35:72-7+ My '64
THIELICKE, Helmut
Realization of the sex nature; excerpt from Ethics of sex. Christian Cent 81:73-7 Ja 15 '64

THIELKE, Rosemary
PTA program. America 108:556-7 Ap 20 '63
THIER, Samuel, and others
Cystinuria: in vitro demonstration of an intestinal transport defect. bibliog Science 143:482-4 Ja 31 '64
THIESSEN, D. D.
Varying sensitivity of C57BL/Crgl mice to grouping. bibliog Science 141:827-8 Ag 30 '63
THIESSEN, Val
Plausibility. Writer 76:21-3+ O '63
THIEVES
Don't let camera thieves spoil your vacation. R. Dale. il Pop Phot 54:132-3 Ap '64
How your pocket may be picked. M. M. Stearns. Read Digest 85:48-50 Ag '64
Memoirs of a contemporary cutpurse; interview, ed. by W. R. Morey. R. Dale. il Mlle 58:184-5+ Ap '64
See also
Burglary and burglars
Stealing
THILL, Walter E.
Tips on bearings. Hot Rod 16:102-3 Jl '63
THIMBLE SHOAL TUNNEL. See Tunnels and tunneling, Underwater
THIMET
You can use thimet to kill corn rootworms. Farm J 87:46 Mr '63
THIN film. See Films
THINKING. See Thought and thinking
THIOKOL chemical corporation
$80,000 saving per case foreseen. R. Van Osten. il Miss & Roc 12:31 F 25 '63
Facility will simulate 34,000-mph re-entries. J. F. Judge. il Miss & Roc 12:24-5 Je 10 '63
Gambling on finding a customer. il Bsns W p 128-30+ My 23 '64
Hybrid rockets. il Miss & Roc 15:39-41 N 9 '64
Thiokol dedicates big booster plant. il Miss & Roc 14:21 My 18 '64
Thiokol gets big-solids edge. F. G. McGuire. il Miss & Roc 12:14-15 Ap 22 '63
Thiokol VP urges funding boost for space-storable propellants. J. F. Judge. Miss & Roc 14:18 Ap 20 '64
Thiokol's space booster plant takes shape in Georgia. J. F. Judge. il Miss & Roc 13:26-8 N 18 '63
World's biggest nozzle delivered. il Miss & Roc 16:17 Ja 11 '65
THIRD market. See Stocks—Marketing
THIRST
Four months without water. Sci Digest 53:50 My '63
Lateral hypothalamic lesions: effects on drinking elicited by carbachol in preoptic area and posterior hypothalamus. G. Wolf and N. E. Miller. bibliog il Science 143:585-7 F 7 '64
THIRTEEN-month year. See Calendar
THIRTEENTH amendment. See United States—Constitution—Amendments
THIRTY-five hour week. See Hours of labor
35mm cameras. See Cameras
35mm films. See Photography—Films
35mm photography. See Photography
THIS much and more; story. See Drury, M.
THISTLE in my bed; drama. See Powers, G.
THISTLES
See also
Milk thistles
THOMAS AQUINAS, Saint
Pange lingua; poem. tr. by J. Moffitt. America 109:314 S 21 '63
THOMAS More, Saint. See More, T.
THOMAS, Alan
Complaints and answers; address, May 1962. por Library J 88:510-12 F 1'63
THOMAS, Alexander. See Chess, S. jt. auth.
THOMAS, Arthur
Man who will grow 363,800 flowers for the fair. J. J. Simpkins. por Flower Grower 51:36 Ja '64
THOMAS, Arthur N.
Our living world; Uncle Chris; poems. Liv Wildn 84:33 Sum '63
THOMAS, Bruce
Status, and all that. por Library J 89:2275-80 Je 1 '64
THOMAS, C. A. and Orellana, R. G.
Biochemical tests indicative of reaction of castor bean to botrytis. bibliog Science 139:334-5 Ja 25 '63
THOMAS, C. A. Jr. See MacHattie, L. A. jt. auth.
THOMAS, Caitlin
Mudbath of experience. por Newsweek 62:105-6 N 4 '63

THOMAS, Charles Walker
American landmarks celebration seeks to preserve nation's heritage. Negro Hist Bul 28:24+ O '64
Church catches up. Negro Hist Bul 28:19-20 O '64
Detroit acclaims James Frazier. Negro Hist Bul 28:28 N '64
Nobel peace prize goes to Martin Luther King. Negro Hist Bul 28:35 N '64
Reflections: annual meeting. por Negro Hist Bul 28:27-8 N '64
Three Negroes receive 1964 Presidential freedom medal. Negro Hist Bul 28:58-9 D '64

THOMAS, David C.
Filming with the Fairchild 8. Pop Phot 53: 99+ S '63
Periodic phenomena observed with spherical particles in horizontal pipes. bibliog Science 144:534-6 My 1 '64

THOMAS, David R. and Williams, J. L.
Stimulus generalization of a positive conditioned reinforcer. bibliog Science 141:172-3; 142:9 Jl 12, O 4 '63

THOMAS, David W. and Blumer, Max
Pyrene and fluoranthene in manganese nodules. bibliog Science 143:39 Ja 3 '64

THOMAS, Della
Three-point program. ALA Bul 58:408-10 My '64

THOMAS, Dylan
Christmas in Wales; excerpts from Child's Christmas in Wales. Look 27:42-6 D 31 '63

about

Alec Guinness as Dylan. por Am Rec G 30: 1143-4 Ag '64
Do not go gentle into that good night. O. B. Brummell. il por Hi Fi 14:65 Je '64
Dylan Thomas as poet. J. S. Rubenstein. Commonweal 79:642-3 F 21 '64
Me and my bike. Esquire 62:146-9+ D '64
Recent criticism. H. Strickhausen. Poetry 104: 266 Jl '64
Undying voice. il pors Newsweek 63:58-9 Ja 27 '64
Wild boy. W. Saroyan. pors Sat Eve Post 237:32+ Ja 25 '64

THOMAS, Elizabeth Marshall
Bushmen of the Kalahari. Nat Geog Mag 123:866-88 Je '63

THOMAS, Elizabeth W.
Not the laurel. Atlan 214:108 Ag '64

THOMAS, Eugene S.
Its record is brilliant. PTA Mag 57:21 F '63

THOMAS, Frank
Player of the week; Phillies' right-handed slugger. por Sports Illus 21:67 Ag 24 '64

THOMAS, Gertrude Z.
Living with antiques: Walnut Hill. Antiques 86:707-11 D '64

THOMAS, Gregory
Symposium; grand maitre of the Commanderie de Bordeaux. New Yorker 40: 19-20 F 22 '64

THOMAS, Gwyn
Joyful noise. Holiday 36:10+ D '64
Martin Luther: the new piety. Holiday 35: 62-3+ Ja '64
Quest for King Arthur. Holiday 36:34-9+ Ag '64
Tranquillity and warm beer. Holiday 35:80-1+ My '64

THOMAS, Harold E. and Leopold, L. B.
Ground water in North America. bibliog Science 143:1001-6 Mr 6 '64

THOMAS, Helen
Caroline's wonderful little White House school. Good H 157:84-5+ O '63
(ed) See Johnson, L. B. Luci B. Johnson talks about her life

THOMAS, J. O.
Canadian satellite: the topside sounder Alouette. Science 139:229-32 Ja 18 '63

THOMAS, James S. bp
Negro heads Iowa Methodists. P. B. Mather. Christian Cent 81:1044 Ag 19 '64

THOMAS, Jean
Two 4-H'ers you'd like to know. por Farm J 87:64 F '63

THOMAS, Jess
Knight errant; interview, ed. by F. Stevenson. por Opera N 27:14 F 16 '63
Quote-unquote; interview, ed. by R. Jacobson. por Mus Am 84:31 Jl '64

about

Music to my ears; Thomas's Parsifal. I. Kolodin. Sat R 47:61 Ap 11 '64

THOMAS, John
Return of the prodigy. il Time 83:85 F 7 '64

THOMAS, Lately
Operator and the emperors. Am Heritage 15:4-23+ Ap '64

THOMAS, Lauren
Why Negro history week. Negro Hist Bul 27: 154 Mr '64

THOMAS, Lowell
New Guinea. Read Digest 84:186-92+ Ja '64
Real Lawrence of Arabia. por Read Digest 84: 252-6+ Je '64
Today's adventurelands. Travel 121:44-6 Ja '64

THOMAS, Mack
Treats; story. Sat Eve Post 237:44-6 D 12 '64

THOMAS, Maurice J.
Understanding the role of education. Sch & Soc 91:284 O 5 '63

THOMAS, Norman
Excerpt from statement, July 26, 1963. Cong Digest 43:92+ Mr '64
When the left was always right. Sat R 46:26 N 2 '63

about

Norman Thomas, by H. Fleischman. Review Christian Cent 81:938 Jl 22 '64. H. E. Fey
Norman Thomas, by H. Fleischman. Review Sat R 47:35 F 1 '64. U. Sinclair
Two birthdays. Nat R 16:1138-9 D 29 '64

THOMAS, Ralph
Waste into energy. Sci N L 86:282-3 O 31 '64

THOMAS, Robert E.
Stone face for Salt Lake. Library J 89:4719-21 D 1 '64

THOMAS, Roderick G.
Floral induction and the stimulation of cell division in xanthium. bibliog Science 140: 54-6 Ap 5 '63

THOMAS, Tay Pryor
Alaskan family's night of terror. il pors Nat Geog Mag 126:142-56 Jl '64

THOMAS, Thomas M. and Hedlund, R. L.
Tropic of Cancer before the U.S. Supreme court; excerpts from brief. bibliog f ALA Bul 58:291-8 Ap '64

THOMAS, W. Lamar
Space-age traffic control. Am City 78:99-100 Mr '63

THOMAS, Winburn T.
Circuses without bread. Christian Cent 80:823 Je 26 '63
Consultation on church growth. Christian Cent 80:1083 S 4 '63

THOMAS Alva Edison award
Edison foundation presents twelve awards to books, tv, radio, films, for youth. Library J 88:846 F 15 '63
$3,000 Thomas A. Edison fellowship being offered. Sci N L 83:184 Mr 23 '63

THOMAS Alva Edison foundation
Edison foundation presents twelve awards to books, tv, radio, films for youth. Library J 88:846 F 15 '63

THOMAS L. Stokes award
Lynch wins Stokes conservation award. il Am For 70:27 Jl '64

THOMASON, Catherine Dennis
Junior high learning lab. NEA J 52:15-16 N '63

THOMASSON, R. R.
Add color dash with trees and shrubs. Pop Gard 15:24-7 F '64
Crab apples, attractive in flower, fruit and foliage. Horticulture 41:564-5 N '63
Franklinia. Pop Gard 15:54 S '64
Ozark chinkapin. Pop Gard 14:85+ F '63

THOMISM
Thomism today. R. Lauer. Commonweal 80: 39-42 Ap 3 '64; Reply with rejoinder. R. J. Miller. 80:261-2 My 22 '64

THOMPKINS, Abraham M.
Abraham M. Thompkins given service award. Negro Hist Bul 27:19 O '63

THOMPSON, Allen Cavett
Allen's army. il por Newsweek 63:30 F 24 '64

THOMPSON, Allen E.
Two views on the Seattle watershed; timber management. yes. Am For 69:8+ N '63

THOMPSON, Ariadne
Our octagonal world; condensation. Read Digest 82:279-99 My '63

THOMPSON, Arthur R.
Arthur Thompson honored upon his retirement. Pub W 185:133 F 3 '64

THOMPSON, Benjamin
New store. New Yorker 39:26 D 28 '63

THOMPSON, Betty
Methodist missions retooled. Christian Cent 81:1273 O 14 '64
Ordeal in the Phanar. Christian Cent 82:72 Ja 20 '65
—See Parker, E. C. jt. auth.

THOMPSON, Bruce
Colorful gloxinia. House B 105:120-1+ F '63

THOMPSON, C. E. See Lakin, H. W. jt. auth.

THOMPSON, C. W.
Foot patrolmen radio equipped. Am City 78:89 Mr '63
No more storm-water worries. Am City 78:93-4 Ag '63

THOMPSON, Carol
Murder by proxy. il Newsweek 62:28 D 16 '63
THOMPSON, Carroll
You can do something about prejudice. Christian Cent 81:138-40 Ja 29 '64
THOMPSON, Clem W.
Smoking. NEA J 53:66-9 Mr '64
THOMPSON, Dennis
British experiment in art for the masses. New Repub 151:7-8 N 21 '64
THOMPSON, Donnis
Girls' track coach in Hawaii. il pors Ebony 18:53-4+ Mr '63
THOMPSON, Doris, and Johnson, Martha
Don't sell books. Pub W 185:45+ Mr 16 '64
THOMPSON, Dorothy
Dorothy and Red, by V. Sheean. Review
Newsweek por 62:110 N 18 '63
Sat R 46:35-6 N 16 '63. G. Hicks
Time il por 82:119+ N 15 '63
Tangled romance of Sinclair Lewis and Dorothy Thompson; excerpt from Dorothy and Red. V. Sheean. il pors Harper 227:121-72 O '63; Reply. D. Argow. 227:4 D '63
THOMPSON, Dorothy Barclay
Are you entertaining more and enjoying it less? Am Home 67:38 N '64
Is Christmas just for children? Am Home 67:18+ D '64
Perfectionist. Am Home 68:28-9 Ja '65
Private life of a child. Am Home 67:30+ O '64
What is a creative child? Am Home 67:28+ S '64
THOMPSON, Dunstan
Ovid on the Dacian coast; poem. New Yorker 40:63 Ja 2 '65
THOMPSON, Era Bell
Love comes to Mahalia. Ebony 20:50-2+ N '64
Pope confers sainthood on twenty-two African martyrs. Ebony 20:23-6+ Ja '65
THOMPSON, Ernest T.
Ernest T. Thompson stresses directness and simplicity; with biographical sketch. il por Am Artist 28:38-9+ D '64
THOMPSON, Francis
Movie maker. M. A. Matzkin. Mod Phot 28: 34+ O '64
Movie man. New Yorker 40:49-52 O 10 '64
THOMPSON, Frank, Jr
Excerpt from radio debate, February 26, 1963. Cong Digest 42:208+ Ag '63
THOMPSON, George A. and Talwani, Manik
Geology of the crust and mantle, western United States. bibliog Science 146:1539-49 D 18 '64
THOMPSON, George I.
Guardian of western coastline. il pors Ebony 20:40-2+ Ja '65
THOMPSON, Helen
We take the critics to the conductors. Mus Am 83:8 My '63
THOMPSON, Hunter S.
Southern city with northern problems. Reporter 29:26-9 D 19 '63
THOMPSON, J. Walter
Mister J. Walter Thompson. J. W. Young. por Sat R 47:71+ Ap 11 '64
THOMPSON, J. Walter, company
Mister J. Walter Thompson. J. W. Young. Sat R 47:71+ Ap 11 '64
THOMPSON, John
Brothers; story. Esquire 60:98-104 Ag '63
THOMPSON, John Beauchamp
Eucharist; poem. Christian Cent 81:766 Je 10 '64
General confession; poem. Christian Cent 81: 454 Ap 8 '64
Shuttlesworth at Shechem; poem. Christian Cent 81:550 Ap 29 '64
Sine aqua non; poem. Christian Cent 81:1085 S 2 '64
Stigmata; poem. Christian Cent 81:792 Je 17 '64
THOMPSON, Kenneth W.
Around the world with portfolio. Sat R 46:30-1 N 30 '63
Parley, stockpile, and stalemate. Sat R 46: 21+ Ag 3 '63
THOMPSON, Larue
Halt in Hungary. Travel 120:31-3 S '63
THOMPSON, Llewellyn E. 1904-
Llewellyn Thompson: JFK's no. 1 Russian expert. L. Bergquist. il pors Look 27:21-5 F 12 '63
THOMPSON, Lucky
Jazz concerts: part of Jazz on Broadway series, at Little theatre. W. Balliett. New Yorker 40:174-5 Mr 7 '64
THOMPSON, M. J. See Bowers, W. S. jt. auth.
THOMPSON, Mattie Lee
God rest you merry, bookseller. Pub W 185: 94-5 F 3 '64
THOMPSON, May Hall
Silent music of the earth. UNESCO Courier 17:21-3 Ap '64
THOMPSON, Mickey
Slowdown for Mickey. Sports Illus 21:22 S 7 '64
THOMPSON, Morris M. and Speert, J. L.
Mapping the surface of the earth. Natur Hist 73:30-7 O '64
THOMPSON, Morton
Adapting games for the handicapped. por Recreation 56:136-7 Mr '63
℞ for the ill & handicapped. See issues of Recreation
Widen your doors. Recreation 57:27-8 Ja '64
THOMPSON, O. C.
Concrete step manufacturers; Thompson unit step co, Indianapolis. il pors Ebony 19: 146-9 D '63
THOMPSON, R. W.
Winston Churchill, the Yankee Marlborough. Vogue 142:134-7+ S 15 '63
THOMPSON, Robert Farris
African dancers at the fair. Sat R 47:37-9 Jl 25 '64
Bossa nova from the source. Sat R 47:42-3 Jl 11 '64
Clare Fischer: the Pan-American way. Sat R 47:46-7 N 28 '64
Jazz roots in Nigeria. Sat R 47:52-3 Ap 11 '64
THOMPSON, T. Eugene
Murder by proxy. il por Newsweek 62:28 D 16 '63
THOMPSON, Thomas
Assassin: the man held, and killed, for murder. Life 55:37-9 N 29 '63
Five-month ordeal, with a whole career at stake. Life 57:92-6 N 13 '64
Frankenstein founds a vast new industry. Life 57:58-9 Ag 21 '64
In Texas a policeman and an assassin are laid to rest too. Life 55:52B-52E D 6 '63
Life movie review. Life 56:12 Ap 10; 12+ Je 26; 57:7 S 4; 19+ S 18 '64; 58:13 Ja 8 '65
Life record review. Life 56:16 Je 5 '64
Life theater review. Life 56:17 My 15 '64
Life World's fair review. Life 56:17 My 22 '64
That's right, that's so right, or is it? Life 56:70 My 29 '64
Two roads to a deadly face-off. Life 55:17-18 N 22 '63
Wilder's dirty-joke film stirs a furor. Life 58:51-2+ Ja 15 '65
—See Oulahan, R. jt. auth.
THOMPSON, Tracy
Clearing in the woods; poem. Christian Cent 81:334 Mr 11 '64
Field of flowers; poem. Christian Cent 81: 1105 S 9 '64
I have lost my teeth for laughter; poem. Christian Cent 80:1493 D 4 '63
Ring; poem. Christian Cent 81:766 Je 10 '64
THOMPSON, Travis I.
Visual reinforcement in Siamese fighting fish. bibliog Science 141:55-7 Jl 5 '63
THOMPSON, Tyler
Another pilgrimage to Jackson. Christian Cent 81:511-12 Ap 22 '64
Key is crisis. Christian Cent 81:586 Ap 29 '64
THOMPSON, Wade
Degree circus; season of kudos. Nation 198: 580-1 Je 8 '64
THOMPSON, William D.
For Catholic pulpit renewal. Christian Cent 81:644 My 13 '64
THOMPSON, William R. and Dubanoski, R. A.
Early arousal and imprinting in chicks. bibliog Science 143:1187-8 Mr 13 '64
THOMPSON Ramo Wooldridge, incorporated
Bunker-Ramo: from under that mattress. C. J. V. Murphy. Fortune 69:76+ F '64
Tapco now top U.S. nozzle producer. J. F. Judge. il Miss & Roc 12:44-5+ Ap 29 '63
Tapco producing Saturn attitude-control rockets. il Miss & Roc 12:47 Je 24 '63
Thompson Ramo Wooldridge: two wings in space. R. Sheehan. il Fortune 67:94-9+ F '63
THOMS, Herbert, and Hungerford, M. J.
Best way to have a baby. Parents Mag 39: 56-9+ N '64
THOMS, Wayne
Dodge chargers. Hot Rod 17:48-51 Jl '64
Merc goes racing. Motor T 15:60-3+ Mr '63
MT road test; American Rambler. Motor T 15:30-3 F '63
MT road test; Dart GT. Motor T 15:44-7 S '63
MT road test; Mercury. Motor T 15:20-5 Mr '63
MT road test; Tempest Le Mans. Motor T 15:54-9 F '63

THOMS, Wayne—*Continued*
MT road test: VW 1500, 1200. Motor T 15:36-41 Ag '63
Volkswagen 1200 road test. Motor T 16:50-3 Ag '64
Why economy run drivers get grey. Motor T 16:66-7 Ap '64
THOMSON, David
Army up in arms. Nation 196:232-3 Mr 16 '63
THOMSON, Donald A.
Ostracitoxin: an ichthyotoxic stress secretion of the boxfish, ostracion lentiginosus. bibliog Science 146:244-5 O 9 '64
THOMSON, Elizabeth W.
In defense of Nassau. Library J 88:3166-8 S 15 '63
Some recommended records for children. por Pub W 184:19-20 D 9 '63
THOMSON, J. R.
Bionics: a new science looks at nature's secrets. Todays Health 42:44-9+ Ja '64
THOMSON, J. Richard
How to get started building hi-fi kits. Pop Sci 183:138-40 N '63
THOMSON, Jean
Children's libraries. Wilson Lib Bul 39:499 F '65
THOMSON, John
How the East was won. New Repub 150:19-21 F 22 '64
THOMSON, Richard
Make mine old-fashioned roses. Pop Gard 14:30-1+ F '63
THOMSON, Roy
Capitalistic invasion. por Time 81:54 F 22 '63
Man who snatched away a meal. Time 84:36-7 N 6 '64
Weekend in Moscow. il Newsweek 61:86 F 25 '63
THOMSON, Tom
Cover. N. Kent. il Am Artist 28:4 Ap '64
THOMSON, Virgil
Four saints: humanity is the key word. A. Rich. il Hi Fi 15:70-1 F '65
Return of Susan B.: presentation of Mother of us all at Carnegie Hall. J. W. Freeman. Opera N 28:27 My 2 '64
THON, William
Master of texture; excerpts from Painter and his techniques, by Alan D. Gruskin. Design 65:215-18 My '64
William Thon describes his watercolor technique. il pors Am Artist 28:34-7 S '64
THOR publishing company
Books and a barefoot publisher. H. Frankel. Sat R 47:30-1 F 1 '64
THORBECKE, Franz
He looks down on Europe. U S Camera 26:24 Ap '63
THORBORG, Kerstin
Goddess in retirement. E. H. Palatsky. pors Opera N 27:32-3 F 23 '63
THOREAU, Henry David
So I go to Walden a-skating; excerpts from Journal, ed. by M. Meltzer. N Y Times Mag p 11 D 29 '63
about
Camper in the back yard. W. Harding. il Horizon 6:32-9 Autumn '64
Thoreau and fellow mammals. G. Byron. il por Audubon Mag 65:374-5 N '63
Two Concord men in a boat. F. Tilden. por Nat Parks Mag 38:8-10 Jl '64
THOREZ, Maurice
Decline of Maurice. il por Time 83:28 My 29 '64
Letter from Paris. Genêt. New Yorker 40:191-2 Ap 18; 120+ My 30 '64
Pavlovian reflex. por Newsweek 63:48 My 25 '64
Turnout for Maurice. il Time 84:34 Jl 24 '64
THORIUM
Element thorium may be key to nuclear power. Sci N L 85:178 Mr 21 '64
THORNE, Thomas
Duchess and William Byrd. Antiques 84:562-5 N '63
THORNE rooms. See Rooms, Miniature
THORNHILL, Kate
My most unforgettable character. A. L. Bowes. por Read Digest 84:114-18 F '64
THORNTON, Charles Bates
Appetite for the future. il pors Time 82:104-8+ O 4 '63
THORNTON, Edward R.
Quebec's newest road to fishing. Field & S 69:46-9+ Jl '64
Rescue! Field & S 67:34-6+ Mr '63
Trailer cruising northeast. Motor B 111:32-4+ Ap '63
THORNTON, William H.
Positive-ground transistor ignition system. Electr World 71:85 Ja '64

THOROUGHBRED horses. See Horses
THORP, Edward O.
Hit me easy. il Newsweek 63:64 Ap 13 '64
It's bye! bye! blackjack. D. E. Scherman. il por Sports Illus 20:18-20+ Ja 13 '64; Same abr. Read Digest 84:223-6 Je '64
Professor who breaks the bank. P. O'Neil. il por Life 56:80-2+ Mr 27 '64
THORP, Willard Long
Willard L. Thorp elected chairman. Development assistance committee. Dept State Bul 48:417 Mr 18 '63
THORPE, Darrell. See Hejhall, R. C. jt. auth.
THORPE, Day
Wilfred Bain. Mus Am 84:18-19 Ap '64
THORPE, Jim
Sentiment in Mauch Chunk. Sports Illus 21:6-7 Ag 3 '64
THORSEN, Harry D. Jr
Philately of Baden-Powell. Hobbies 69:99+ N '64
THORSON, John
Dynamics of motion perception in the desert locust. bibliog Science 145:69-71 Jl 3 '64
THOUGHT and language
Free will, again. H. D. Aiken. Commentary 37:79-82 F '64
Language and thinking: positive and negative effects of naming. H. B. Ranken. bibliog il Science 141:48-50 Jl 5 '63; Reply with rejoinder. H. Baum. 141:1238+ S 27 '63
Most beautiful word. R. L. Tobin. Sat R 46:18 Jl 20 '63
Of order, abstraction, and language. S. Burckhardt. Yale R 53:533-50 Je '64
Psychological implications of word usage. J. C. Nunnally and R. L. Flaugher. bibliog il Science 140:775-81 My 17 '63
THOUGHT and thinking
Family business: thinking creatively. A. P. Eliasberg. il N Y Times Mag p94 O 13 '63
Men to match our problems; excerpts from address. L. J. Kroeger. il Recreation 57:76-8 F '64
Not so fast. N. Cousins. Sat R 46:14 Jl 6 '63; Discussion. 46:18 Jl 27 '63
Social stimulus to creativity; letter. E. G. Boring. Science 142:622-3 N 8 '63; Reply. S. Winokur. 143:526 F 7 '64
Uses of thinking. J. K. Feibleman. Sat R 46:18-19+ Mr 2 '63
When thoughts are unthinkable. B. Dunham. il Nation 198:411-13 Ap 27 '64
Word. V. P. McCorry. America 111:56 Jl 11 '64
See also
Ideas
Ideology
Intellect
Logic
Problem solving
Reason
THOURON, Henry A.
Thouron of Hercules powder. il por Fortune 67:51 Mr '63
THOUSAND clowns; drama. See Gardner, H.
THOUSAND doors; novel. See Rothberg, A.
THOUSAND tears; story. See Rosen, N.
THRACE
See also
Monoklisia
THREATS
Check violence threats. Sci N L 84:357 D 7 '63
THREE against Christmas; opera. See Imbrie, A.
THREE cats; story. See Warner, S. T.
THREE dimensional photography. See Stereophotography
THREE little kittens; drama. See Miller, H. L.
THREE-mile limit. See Territorial waters
THREE-point free-fall mooring. See Anchors
THREE sisters; drama. See Chekhov, A. P.
THREE tales; story. See Singer, I. B.
THREE wheel automobiles. See Automobiles, Three wheel
THREE women; story. See Foster, I.
THRELKELD, John
Camellias are moving north. Pop Gard 14:32-3+ F '63
Twelve steps to easy gardening. Pop Gard 15:24-5 Mr '64
THREONINE
Protein synthesis enhanced in the liver of rats force-fed a threonine-devoid diet. H. Sidransky and others. bibliog il Science 146:766-8 N 6 '64
THRESHER, B. Alden
Test uses and limitations. NEA J 52:16-19 O '63

THRESHER, Roberta
Go for action. Recreation 62:12-14 Je '63
THRESHER (submarine boat) See Submarine boats, Atomic powered; Submarine disasters
THRESHOLD of pain. See Pain
THRIFT
Thrift vs. borrowing, which way to good times? with excerpts from book by P. A. Samuelson. il U S News 54:37-9 Mr 4 '63
See also
Domestic finance
THROAT
Diseases
Sore throat can be serious. T. Berland. il Todays Health 43:26-7+ Ja '65
Throat cultures at home advised by researchers. Sci N L 86:214 O 3 '64
Surgery
Tonsillectomy. Consumer Rep 29:256-7 My '64
What parents ask about T and A. M. J. E. Senn. il McCalls 91:46 S '64
THROAT cancer. See Cancer
THROCKMORTON, Peter
Bronze-age ship; excerpt from Lost ships. por Atlan 213:96-7+ Je '64
THROMBIN
Blood clotting: enzymic activation; report on symposium. J. H. Ferguson. Science 144:1159 My 29 '64
THROWERS, Snow. See Snow blowers, throwers, etc.
THROWS. See Coverlets
THUC, Ngo-dinh. See Ngo-dinh-Thuc
THULIN, Ingrid
Ingmar's Ingrid. il por Time 83:76+ F 28 '64
THUMB, General Tom. See Stratton, C. S.
THUNDER Mountain (shooting club) See Sports clubs
THUNDERBIRD classic invitational. See Golf —Tournaments
THUNDERHEADS. See Clouds
THUNDERSTORM detectors. See Meteorological instruments
THUNDERSTORMS
Amateur scientist; thunderstorm detectors. T. P. Leary. il Sci Am 208:167-70+ My '63
How the weatherman can listen in on thunderstorms. W. Cloud. Pop Sci 185:23+ O '64
Thunderstorm, huge dynamo. M. J. Walker. il Sci N L 85:362-3 Je 6 '64
Thunderstorm violence. T. Neville. Sci N L 84:135 Ag 31 '63
THURBER, James
Glass in the field; excerpts from Fables for our time. Read Digest 82:168C Mr '63
Last flower. il UNESCO Courier 17:27-8 N '64
Thurber on Avon. il Horizon 7:118-20 Wint '65
about
Long time no see. Mrs J. Thurber. il por Ladies Home J 81:50-1+ Jl '64
Reading I've liked. C. Fadiman. Holiday 33:56-7 Mr '63
THURBER, Mrs James
Long time no see. Ladies Home J 81:50-1+ Jl '64
THURM, Ulrich
Mechanoreceptors in the cuticle of the honey bee: fine structure and stimulus mechanism. bibliog Science 145:1063-5 S 4 '64
THURMAN, Howard
Christ's message to the disinherited; excerpts from Jesus and the disinherited. por Ebony 18:58+ S '63
THURMOND, Strom
Debate on civil rights; March 18, 1964. por U S News 56:102-4 Mr 30 '64
Federal judiciary; the usurpation of power; address, July 3, 1964. Vital Speeches 30:677-70 Ag 15 '64
Our national relationship to God; address, January 25, 1964. Vital Speeches 30:357-61 Ap 1 '64
United States foreign policy; address, June 13, 1963. Vital Speeches 29:548-51 Jl 1 '63
Why a Democratic senator turned Republican; address, September 16, 1964. pors U S News 57:83-4 S 28 '64
about
Notes from South Carolina. P. L. Buckley. Nat R 16:852 O 6 '64
Senator Thurmond: now he's a Republican. por U S News 57:24 S 28 '64
Thurmond attacks the church. Christian Cent 81:421-2 Ap 1 '64
Thurmond joins GOP. Sr Schol 85:25 S 30 '64

THURROTT, Suzan
Going home; poem. McCalls 90:167 My '63
Mr Giuseppo's greenhouse; poem. McCalls 90:178 Mr '63
Swing low; poem. McCalls 90:136 F '63
THURSTON, Philip H.
Concept of a production system. Harvard Bsns R 41:70-5 N '63
THURSTONE, Thelma Gwinn
Your child's intelligence; reprint. Todays Health 41:59-60 My '63
THYMIDINE
Delayed incorporation of tritiated thymidine into DNA. S. H. Robinson and G. Brecher. bibliog il Science 142:392-3 O 18 '63
DNA segregation in escherichia coli: observations by means of tritiated thymidine decay. S. Person and M. Osborn. bibliog il Science 143:44-6 Ja 3 '64
Synergistic effect of 5-bromodeoxy-uridine and gamma rays on chromosomes. F. K. S. Koo. bibliog il Science 141:261-2 Jl 19 '63
Thymidine incorporation by mitochondria in physarum polycephalum. E. Guttes and S. Guttes. bibliog il Science 145:1057-8 S 4 '64
THYMUS gland
Disease development, thymus removal linked. Sci N L 85:120 F 22 '64
Humoral thymic factor in mice: further evidence. L. W. Law and others. bibliog il Science 143:1049-51 Mr 6 '64
Immune reactivity in mice thymectomized soon after birth: normal response after pregnancy. D. Osoba. bibliog il Science 147:298-9 Ja 15 '65
Little gland that keeps you well. M. Markham. Parents Mag 38:90+ O '63
Lymphocytic choriomeningitis infection in neonatally thymectomized mice bearing diffusion chambers containing thymus. R. H. Levey and others. bibliog il Science 142:183-5 O 25 '63
No blood barrier seen in thymus gland study. Sci N L 85:37 Ja 18 '64
Thymectomy: effect on secondary disease in radiation chimeras. L. M. van Putten. bibliog il Science 145:935-6 Ag 28 '64
Thymectomy: prolongation of immunological tolerance in the adult mouse. H. N. Claman and D. W. Talmage. bibliog il Science 141:1193-4 S 20 '63
Thymus abnormalities linked to muscle disease. Sci N L 85:260 Ap 25 '64
Thymus and the development of immunologic responsiveness. J. F. A. P. Miller. bibliog il Science 144:1544-51 Je 26 '64
Thymus gland blamed for causing leukemia. Sci N L 86:195 S 26 '64
Thymus hormone. R. H. Levey. il Sci Am 211:66-71+ bibliog(p 142) Jl '64
Thymus: its limited role in the recovery of homograft response in irradiated mice. M. L. Tyan and others. bibliog il Science 142:584 N 1 '63
Thymus: its role in lymphoid recovery after irradiation. R. Auerbach. bibliog Science 139:1061 Mr 15 '63
Thymus, leukemia linked. Sci N L 84:50 Jl 27 '63
Thymus: role in maturation of fetal lymphoid precursors. M. L. Tyan. bibliog il Science 145:934-5 Ag 28 '64
Thymus: role in resistance to polyoma virus oncogenesis. L. W. Law. bibliog il Science 147:164-5 Ja '65
THYROID extracts
Thyrocalcitonin: hypocalcemic hypophosphatemic principle of the thyroid gland. P. R. Hirsch and others. bibliog il Science 146:412-13 O 16 '64
THYROID gland
Aberrant thyroid tissue in the mouse. R. D. Hunt. bibliog il Science 141:1054-5 S 13 '63
Cancer, thyroid link. F. Marley. Sci N L 86:243 O 17 '64
Cysteine stimulation of glucose oxidation in thyroid tissue. J. A. Pittman and others. bibliog il Science 140:389 Ap 26 '63
Human lipoproteins: role in transport of thyroid hormones. E. Toro-Goyco and M. Cancio. bibliog Science 139:761-2 F 22 '63
Iodine-125 distribution between follicular colloid and colloid droplets in mouse thyroid gland. W. C. Bauer and J. S. Meyer. bibliog il Science 145:1431-2 S 25 '64
Protein-bound iodine in serum of rats breathing 99 percent oxygen. P. Felig and others. bibliog il Science 145:601 Ag 7 '64
Radioiodine metabolism in children and adults after the ingestion of very small doses. M. A. Van Dilla and M. J. Fulwyler. bibliog il Science 144:178-9 Ap 10 '64

THYROID gland—*Continued*
Reversal of thyroxine-induced hypermetabolism by puromycin. W. P. Weiss and L. Sokoloff. bibliog il Science 140:1324-6 Je 21 '63
Thyroid-emotion link. Sci N L 86:183 S 19 '64
Thyroid hormones: control of terminal oxidation. J. R. Bronk. bibliog il Science 141: 816-18 Ag 30 '63
See also
Thyroid extracts
Diseases
Genetic influence on experimental allergic thyroiditis in guinea pigs. P. R. B. McMaster and others. bibliog il Science 147: 157 Ja 8 '65
THYROPROTEINS
Red hot argument in dairying. D. Braun. il Farm J 88:35+ Mr '64
THYROXINE
Reversal of thyroxine-induced hypermetabolism by puromycin. W. P. Weiss and L. Sokoloff. bibliog il Science 140:1324-6 Je 21 '63
Thyroxine: effects on amino acid incorporation into protein in vivo. R. Michels and others. bibliog il Science 140:1417-18 Je 28 '63
TI plant
Exotic Hawaiian ti plant. B. Brinhart. il Horticulture 41:478-9 S '63
TIANT, Luis
Player of the week; Cleveland Indians righthander. por Sports Illus 21:65 Ag 3 '64
TIBBETT, Lawrence
Tibbett on tape. F. Merkling. il por Opera N 28:6 D 21 '63
TIBET
Reminder for Buddhists; Panchen Lama deposed. Time 85:24 Ja 15 '65
See also
Ladakh
Zoology—Tibet
TIBETANS
See also
Sherpas
TIBURON, Calif.
Park a boat at your doorstep. il Sports Illus 21:14-17 Ag 3 '64
TICKER machines, Stock. See Stock ticker machines
TICKET offices, Airline. See Airlines—Ticket offices
TICKET speculators. See Theater tickets
TICKETS
See also
Airlines—Tickets
Theater tickets
TICKS
Bird trap; measures against bird-borne disease-bearing ticks. il Sci Digest 56:64-8 N '64
Gltathioune as an inducer of feeding in ticks. R. Galun and S. H. Kindler. bibliog il Science 147:166-7 Ja 8 '65
Wood ticks still prevalent. Sci N L 84:66 Ag 3 '63
TICKTON, Sidney G.
Third force in college enrollments; adaptation of address. Sat R 47:70-2 Mr 21 '64
TICONDEROGA, Fort. See Fort Ticonderoga
TIDAL marshes. See Salt marshes
TIDAL power. See Tide power
TIDAL waves. See Seismic sea waves
TIDE power
Moon power over St Malo. H. Manchester. il Read Digest 84:37-8+ Je '64
See also
Passamaquoddy tidal power project
TIDES
Earth and moon: past and future. G. J. F. MacDonald. bibliog il Science 145:881-90 Ag 28 '64
Moving tides; excerpt from The sea around us. R. L. Carson. il Motor B 112:20-2+ Jl '63
Precision digital tide gauge. F. E. Snodgrass. bibliog il Science 146:198-200+ O 9 '64
Tides, the scientific view. S. D. Hicks. il Motor B 112:23+ Jl '63
See also
Earth tides
Seiches
TIDES, Atmospheric. See Atmospheric tides
TIE-in merchandise. See Merchandising
TIED and dyed work. See Dyes and dyeing
TIEN art. See Art, Chinese
TIEPOLO, Giovanni Battista
Look upward, angels; ceiling panels by Tiepolo discovered in London. il Time 85: 64 Ja 15 '65
Tiepolo drawing; analysis of Meeting of Abraham & Melchizedek. il Am Artist 28: 80-1+ Je '64
TIERNEY, E. J. and Cassidy, Brendan
Back to the river after seventy years. Am City 78:74-6 Ag '63
TIERRA DEL FUEGO
Tierra del Fuego; excerpts from The cloud forest. P. Matthiessen. il Américas 16:35-42 F '64
TIES, Railroad. See Railroads—Ties
TIFFANY, Louis Comfort
Louis C. Tiffany, rebel in glass, by R. Koch. Review
Nation 199:469-70 D 14 '64. R. Howard
TIFFANY and company
Tiffany's goes West. Newsweek 62:66+ S 16 '63
TIFFEAU, Jacques
Jacques hits the jackpot. il por Life 57:69-70 O 2 '64
TIFFEN, C. E.
British cities try municipal movie houses. Am City 79:154 Ap '64
Fluoridation stalemated in Great Britain. Am City 79:142+ Mr '64
TIFFT, W. G. and others
West Ford dipole belt: photometric observations. Science 141:798-9 Ag 30 '63
TIGER, Dick
Smile on the face of the Tiger; Dick Tiger, Gene Fullmer fight in Africa. J. Olsen. il pors Sports Illus 19:12-19 Ag 19 '63
TIGER, Lionel
Ghana: a charismatic nation. bibliog f Cur Hist 45:335-40 D '63
TIGER; drama. See Schisgal, M.
TIGER hunting
Mekong madness. C. W. Stockwell. il Outdoor Life 132:12-13+ Jl '63
My greatest trophy; tiger with an arrow; ed. by B. East. F. Bear. il Outdoor Life 134:40-3+ O '64
Night belongs to the tiger. H. Klein. il Field & S 68:38-40+ S '63
Tiger, and the unexpected. R. S. Smith. il Outdoor Life 135:44-7+ F '65
TIGER, tiger, burning bright; drama. See Feibleman, P. S.
TIGERFLOWERS
Flamboyant tigridia. R. D. Roe. il Horticulture 41:360 Jl '63
TIGERS
Tiger. J. O'Connor. il Outdoor Life 133:36-9+ My '64
TIGERS (baseball) See Baseball clubs
TIGNOR, Robert L.
Indianization of the Egyptian administration under British rule. bibliog f Am Hist R 68:636-61 Ap '63
TIGRIDIA. See Tigerflowers
TIGUE, Ethel Erkkila
Don't wait to write your novel. Writer 76:25-6 S '63
TIJUANA, Mexico
Company town. il Time 82:24-5 S 27 '63
TIKAL. See Mayas
TILAPIAS. See Mouthbreeders
TILDEN, Freeman
Acquaintance with Acadia. Nat Parks Mag 37:4-7 Jl '63
Frontier photographer; excerpts from Following the frontier. Am Heritage 15:22-35 O '64
Two Concord men in a boat. Nat Parks Mag 38:8-10 Jl '64
TILDEN, Paul Mason
Agate Fossil Beds National Monument. Nat Parks Mag 38:4-7 Ag '64
Nature in rock & mineral (cont) Natur Hist 72:63-7 F; 58-64 Ag '63; 73:59-63 Ja; 58-61 Ap '64
Washington newsletter (cont) Natur Hist 72: 63-8 Je; 63-7 D '63; 73:66-9 Je; 61-3+ D '64
—and Machler, N. L.
Development of Mount McKinley National Park. Nat Parks Mag 37:10-15 My '63
TILDEN, William Tatem
Greatest tennis player of all time. A. Danzig. il pors N Y Times Mag p 19+ D 22 '63
TILE floors. See Floors, Tile
TILE setting
Who says you can't lay ceramic tile? S. J. Howard. il Pop Mech 121:156-60+ F '64

TILES
Floor and ceiling tile calculator. il Pop Sci 185:119 S '64
Handmade tiles decorate this garden gate. il Sunset 130:196 F '63
I made this; planning and making a cement tile mural. J. Amato. il Sch Arts 63:17-20 Ap '64
Patterned tiles; the new faces of silence. il House & Gard 123:202-3 Ap '63
Shopping for tile in Mexico. Sunset 130:40 Ap '63

TILES, Floor
Floor and ceiling tile calculator. il Pop Sci 185:119 S '64
Put an accent in your floor. il Bet Hom & Gard 41:53 S '63

TILGHMAN family
Tilghman coat-of-arms. H. K. Eilers. il Hobbies 68:126-7+ My '63

TILL, Irene
Annals of legislation. R. Harris. New Yorker 40:48-50+ Mr 14 '64

TILL the sands of the desert grow cold; story. See De Vries, P.

TILLAGE
Let's plow on the level. J. B. Liljedahl. il Suc Farm 62:49 Ap '64
Plow early, then plant with one trip. K. Pyle. il Farm J 87:52I My '63

TILLAMOOK, Ore.

Galleries and museums

Tillamook's pioneer museum. il Sunset 130: 23 Ap '63

TILLER, Marguerite
Lots of cheer, mother dear. NEA J 53:27 My '64

TILLER, W. A.
Dendrites. bibliog Science 146:871-9 N 13 '64

TILLES, Seymour
How to evaluate corporate strategy. bibliog f Harvard Bsns R 41:111-21 Jl '63
Manager's job: a systems approach. bibliog f Harvard Bsns R 41:73-81 Ja '63

TILLET, Paul
Reflections on War, politics, and power. Bul Atomic Sci 20:28-9 My '64

TILLETT, Anne. See Tillett, L. R. jt. auth.

TILLETT, Gladys A.
Existing law and measures to improve the status of women in the western hemisphere. Dept State Bul 51:128-32 Jl 27 '64
Progress report on the status of women. Dept State Bul 49:145-50 Jl 22 '63

TILLETT, Lowell R.
Soviet second thoughts on tsarist colonialism. bibliog f For Affairs 42:309-19 Ja '64

—and Tillett, Anne
Reddest tape. Travel 121:33-5+ Ja '64

TILLICH, Paul
Ambiguity of perfection; excerpts from address at Time's anniversary dinner. por Time 81:69 My 17 '63

about

Paul Tillich's concept of faith; condensation of Faith without belief. R. Smith. por(cover) Cath World 200:162-3+ D '64
Paul Tillich's system. G. H. Tavard. Commonweal 79:566-8 F 7 '64
Tillich as apologist. P. Van Buren. Christian Cent 81:177-9 F 5 '64; Discussion. 81:343-4 Mr 11 '64

TILLINGHAST, Richard
If you were here; poem. Harper 227:82 Ag '63
September: last day at the beach; poem. New Repub 149:20 S 28 '63

TILLMAN, Allen D.
Phosphorus for beef cattle. Suc Farm 62:102 Mr '64

TILSON, Everett
Remodeling the mansion. Christian Cent 80: 302-4 Mr 6 '63

TILTON, G. R. and Hart, S. R.
Geochronology. bibliog Science 140:357-66 Ap 26 '63

TIM
Tim's whims. il por Newsweek 63:46 Ja 6 '64

TIMBER
See also
Woodlots

TIMBER land. See Forest land

TIMBER wolves. See Wolves

TIMBERLAKE, Clare H.
U.S. outlines verification measures to assure compliance with proposed freeze of strategic nuclear vehicles; statement, August 27, 1964. Dept State Bul 51:413-17 S 21 '64

TIMBUCTOO. See Timbuktu

TIMBUKTU
Mystery tour; visit by four U.S. congressmen. il Newsweek 64:32 D 21 '64

TIME
Big hand, little hand; learning to tell time. N. H. Hartshorne. il Parents Mag 39:60-1+ S '64
Can the direction of flow of time be determined? R. G. Sachs. bibliog il Science 140:1284-90 Je 21 '63
Happy whichever New Year. J. Ciardi. Sat R 47:10 Ja 25 '64
It's timely to consider still another inequality. F. Morley. il Nations Bsns 52:27-8 My '64
Time is now. R. O. Johann. il America 110: 191 F 8 '64
See also
Calendar
Geological time
International date line

Systems and standards

Daylight saving is one result of international time standard. T. D. Nicholson. il Natur Hist 73:54-6 Ap '64
For a second; proposed new official standard for measuring a second. Time 84:85 S 11 '64
Frequency & time standards. G. E. Hudson. il Electr World 72:20-3 Ag '64
Further notes on atomic time standard. Electr World 73:75 Ja '65

TIME (periodical)
Birthday party. New Yorker 39:32-3 My 18 '63
Century cover boon; Time cover jinx and Notre Dame's defeat. Christian Cent 81: 1575 D 16 '64
Famous faces of forty years; Time's 40th anniversary celebrations. il Life 54:77-82D+ My 17 '63
Honored by Time magazine; eight eminent Negroes. Negro Hist Bul 27:28 N '63
Leading up to what Chief Poto told Chief Rusher; with letter by W. A. Rusher. Nat R 15:557-8 D 31 '63
Letter from the publisher; circulation and advertising statistics. B. M. Auer. Time 85:11 Ja 15 '65
Letter from the publisher; election extra. B. M. Auer. Time 84:25 O 30 '64
Letter from the publisher; 40th birthday. B. M. Auer. Time 81:19 Mr 8 '63
Letter from the publisher; H. Donovan becomes editor-in-chief of Time. B. M. Auer. il Time 83:15 Ap 24 '64
No time like the present; excerpts from issues of Time magazine. il Esquire 59:58-9 Ap '63
Report or manifesto? cover story on Cardinal Cushing. America 111:228-9 S 5 '64
SEC reform to help, not hamstring. il Newsweek 61:76+ Ap 15 '63
Time at forty. Time 81:10-11 My 10 '63
Time refuses to back down; Catholic opposition to urban renewal in Chicago. Christian Cent 80:420 Ap 3 '63
Time's 40th anniversary party. il Time 81:59-68+ My 17 '63
War in Vietnam, Luce version. W. H. Hunter. New Repub 148:15-17 Mr 23 '63

TIME, Daylight saving. See Daylight saving

TIME, Incorporated
Business-wise editor. Sat Eve Post 236:74 Je 1 '63
First tycoon and the power of his press. J. Kobler. il Sat Eve Post 238:28-32+ Ja 16 '65
Succession; H. R. Luce takes post of editorial chairman. il Newsweek 63:76 Ap 27 '64

TIME, Use of
Free time; address, June 18, 1963. D. N. Michael. Vital Speeches 29:616-20 Ag 1 '63
Go it, tortoise. R. Henderson. New Yorker 39:39-40 S 28 '63
Quick look at instancy. R. Hochstein. il House & Gard 126:60-1 S '64
Time on whose hands? J. O. Fulton. il Read Digest 85:73-5 O '64

TIME and space. See Space and time

TIME bombs. See Bombs

TIME capsules. See Civilization—Preservation of records

TIME-delay switches. See Electric switches

TIME for silence; story. See Gaffron, C.

TIME-Life International book society. See Book clubs

TIME measurements
GUT issue; new way of counting time; Greenwich universal time. Newsweek 63:74+ Ap 13 '64
Hugh Downs column. H. Downs. il Sci Digest 56:60-3 Jl '64

TIME measurements—*Continued*
Scientists get a new way to measure time; vibration rate of cesium-133 atom. il Bsns W p84+ O 24 '64
See also
Sundials
Time—Systems and standards
TIME of the key; drama. See Erskine, M.
TIME payment sales. See Instalment plan
TIME perception
Animals can tell time, but how? A. Hills. il Life 54:41-2+ My 31 '63
Never have enough time? J. Daugherty and M. Daugherty. il Sci Digest 53:55-7 Je '63
Psychological time. J. Cohen. il Sci Am 211: 116-22+ bibliog(p 156) N '64
Variations in alpha voltage of the electro-encephalogram and time perception. J. Anliker. bibliog il Science 140:1307-9 Je 21 '63
TIME reversal
Fifth force? time-reversal invariance. Sci Am 211:62 D '64
Time: one-way street. A. Ewing. Sci N L 86: 99 Ag 15 '64
TIME sharing computers. See Calculating machines—Cooperative use
TIME signals, Radio
Naval observatory time signals. H. C. Wood. il Electr World 70:30+ Ag '63
New NBS facility for better time broadcasts. il (p65) Sci N L 83:75 F 2 '63
TIMERS. See Timing devices
TIMES, London
New thunderer. il Time 83:48-9 My 8 '64
Thunderer thunders for press freedom. Christian Cent 80:453 Ap 10 '63
TIMES, Los Angeles
Happy Chandlers. il Newsweek 63:93 Je 8 '64
Man who doesn't take sides. il Time 84:39 D 25 '64
Publishing giant takes a long step; Chandlers of Los Angeles. il Bsns W p72-5+ Mr 14 '64
Troubled Times; western edition of New York times. il Bsns W p26 Ja 11 '64
TIMES, New York. See New York times
TIMES literary supplement, London
Book selection: education or communication? with editorial comment. il Wilson Lib Bul 37:671 Ap '63
TIMES-Mirror company
Publishing giant take a long step; Chandlers of Los Angeles. il Bsns W p72-5+ Mr 14 '64
Times Mirror acquires World publishing co. Pub W 184:247 Ag 26 '63
TIMES of Vietnam. See Newspapers—Viet Nam (Republic)
TIMES square, New York city. See New York (city)—Times square
TIMIDITY
Help for a shy child. L. Marett. il Parents Mag 39:52-3+ O '64
TIMING devices
Brilliant flash times your engine; xenon flash lamps. R. Benrey. il Pop Sci 183:164-7 O '63
Build a stereo indicator. C. Caringella. il Pop Electr 19:63-5+ S '63
Build the audiotimer. L. E. Garner, jr. il Pop Electr 21:57-60 N '64
Enlarger-phototimer. il Electr World 72:102 O '64
Idento-minder. H. B. Smith. il Pop Electr 19:51-3 S '63
TIMM, Charlotte
Janus face of reading. por Wilson Lib Bul 39:160-3 O '64
TIMMINS, Ontario
Billion-dollar plunge in the bush. il Life 56: 36-41 My 15 '64
Great day in the morning for Texas gulf sulphur. R. Sheehan. il Fortune 70:136-40+ Jl '64
Red-hot copper; Texas Gulf sulphur announces discovery of copper lodes near Timmins, Ontario. il Time 83:97 Ap 24 '64
Treasure hunt at Timmins. il Newsweek 63: 73-5 My 4 '64
TIMMONS, Gerald D.
Story of fluoridation. por Parents Mag 38: 139+ N '63
TIMON of Athens; drama. See Shakespeare, W.—Plays
TIMPANOGOS CAVE NATIONAL MONUMENT
Mountain with a heavy heart. N. N. Dodge. il Nat Parks Mag 38:9-10 Ap '64
TIMUR, A. and Fatt, I.
Fluid flow in porous media studied by a nuclear magnetic resonance technique. bibliog Science 146:1162-3 N 27 '64

TIN
High-pressure phase transition in tin telluride. J. A. Kafalas and A. N. Mariano. bibliog il Science 143:952 F 28 '64
Indium antimonide: superconductivity of the metallic form. H. E. Bömmel and others. il Science 139:1301-2 Mr 29 '63
Indium antimonide the metallic form at atmospheric pressure. A. J. Darnell and W. F. Libby. bibliog il Science 139:1301 Mr 29 '63
U.S. makes interim modification of tin disposal program; Department statement, June 21, 1963. Dept State Bul 49:56-7 Jl 8 '63
X-ray diffraction studies on tin at high pressure and high temperature. J. D. Barnett and others. bibliog il Science 141: 1041-2 S 13 '63
See also
Tôle

Stockpiling

See Stockpiling
TIN cans
Thin tin gets rolling; battle between tin plate and aluminum. il Bsns W p66+ My 11 '63
Tin can rooster. il Design 65:155 Mr '64
Tin cans are antiques now. J. Mebane. il Hobbies 69:28-9 Je '64
Uncanny transformation. il Time 84:104+ O 16 '64
See also
Beer containers
TIN industry and trade
See also
International tin council
TIN mines and mining

Bolivia

Bolivia's revolution comes of age; strike in tin mines. J. D. Bowen. Reporter 29:34-6 S 26 '63
Hostages of a mob of miners; with report by M. Acoca. il Life 56:62-6 Ja 3 '64
TIN plate
Thin tin gets rolling; battle between tin plate and aluminum. il Bsns W p66+ My 11 '63
What the canmakers really got. Bsns W p31 Mr 9 '63
TIN ware. See Tinware
TINAYRE, Yves
Record hunter rediscovers Yves Tinayre. P. L. Miller. Am Rec G 30:885-6 My '64
TINBERGEN, Niko
Shell menace. il Natur Hist 72:28-35 Ag '63
TINGLEY rubber company
Keeping your children's feet warm and dry. E. M. McCabe. il Parents Mag 38:30+ D '63
TINKER, Chauncey B.
Obituary
Pub W 183:41 My 20 '63
TINKER, Frank A.
Diaries of destruction. Pop Mech 120:108-12+ Jl '63
Problems. Flying 74:28+ My '64
Rugged prep school for smoke jumpers. Pop Mech 119:134-7+ F '63
TINKERTOYS. See Toys
TINKHAM, M.
Spectroscopy of solids in the far-infrared. bibliog Science 145:240-7 Jl 17 '64
TINKLE, Lon
Making room for controversy. Sat R 47:49 Ap 18 '64
TINSLEY, Russell
Best bet for bass. Field & S 67:60-1+ Ap '63
Float into the past. Outdoor Life 132:17-19+ Ag '63
Grand awakening. por Outdoor Life 131:50-3+ Mr '63
Hats off to the cats. Outdoor Life 134:42-3+ N '64
LCRA spells fish! Travel 121:56-8 F '64
New Mexico's high country. Travel 122:48-9 S '64
Pothole catfish. por Outdoor Life 131:78-80+ Je '63
Summer's hottest fishing. por Field & S 68: 48-9+ Jl '63
Team for squirrels. pors Outdoor Life 134: 54-5+ S '64
Unique new fishing lake. Outdoor Life 134: 38-9+ O '64
TINTYPE
Foto facts; modern tintype. P. Farber. U S Camera 27:36 Mr '64
Ye olde tintype. N. Rothschild. il Pop Phot 52:120 Mr '63
TINWARE
Caring for your Mexican tinware. il Sunset 131:142 O '63

TINY Alice; drama. See Albee, E.
TIP toppers club. See Clubs
TIPPER, Donald J. and others
Staphylolytic enzyme from chalaropsis: mechanism of action. bibliog Science 146:781-2 N 6 '64
TIPPETT, Michael
Englishman looks at opera. por Opera N 29: 6-9 Ja 2 '65
Tippett: a genuinely stereophonic thrill. J. Diether. Am Rec G 29:810-11 Je '63
TIPPING
Speaking out; down with tipping. J. A. Patton. Sat Eve Post 237:6+ F 29 '64
Tips on tipping and tippees. M. J. Arlen. il N Y Times Mag p20+ My 31 '64
See also
Waiters and waitresses
TIPPIT, J. D.
Capture of a killer. il U S News 55:10 D 2 '63
In Texas a policeman and an assassin are laid to rest too. T. Thompson. Life 55:52B-52E D 6 '63
TIPPIT, Mrs J. D.
Others; year after the assassination of President Kennedy. Time 84:34 N 27 '64
TIPPIT, J. D, family
Odd fate of Oswald's other victims. F. X. Tolbert. il Sat Eve Post 237:68-9 Ag 22 '64
Story of generosity; contributions to J. D. Tippit family. il por U S News 56:46 Ja 20 '64
TIRE cord. See Tire fabrics
TIRE fabrics
How much can Akron tell Detroit? radial ply tire. il Bsns W p94-6+ Ag 8 '64
TIRE gages. See Gages
TIRE industry and trade
See also
Firestone tire and rubber company
Goodyear tire and rubber company
TIREDNESS. See Fatigue
TIRES, Automobile
After the battle in U.S. rubber's executive suite. W. J. Miller. il Fortune 70:116-23+ D '64
Balance your car's wheels. R. Day. il Pop Sci 185:128-30 D '64
Belted tires. R. Huntington. il Motor T 15: 26-9+ Jl '63
FTC kicks some tires. Bsns W p34 D 5 '64
Getting a grip when you slip; spiked tires. il Bsns W p24-5 D 7 '63
In search of the perfect tire. W. Ross. il Esquire 59:92-3+ My '63
New drag slick! L. Smith. il Hot Rod 17:46-7 Jl '64
New grip on the road; metal-studded snow tires. Time 85:65 Ja 1 '65
News for winter drivers: tires with built-in chains. P. W. Kearney. il Read Digest 85:103-5 N '64
Role of racing tire. R. Brock. il Hot Rod 16: 40-3 Mr '63
Sears tries the big time. G. Moore. il Motor T 16:58-9 Ap '64
Snow tires. Consumer Bul 47:35 Ja '64
Snow tires, they aren't all the same! E. F. Lindsley. il Pop Sci 185:92-6+ N '64
Special tires for winter driving. il Consumer Bul 48:2+ Ja '65
That super-quiet, squishy ride. J. Ridgeway. New Repub 152:15-16 Ja 30 '65
Tire studs run into roadblock. Bsns W p 134 N 21 '64
Tire with the built-in chains; safety stud tires. E. Nelson. il Pop Mech 120:24+ S '63
Tires, a buyer's jungle. il Changing T 18:25-30 My '64
Tires and road safety. J. Ridgeway. New Repub 151:8-10 O 17 '64
Tires, how professional buyers pick 'em. il Changing T 18:24 D '64
Truth about tires. B. H. Frisch. il Sci Digest 56:69-74 N '64
What tire pressure is safest? il Todays Health 42:34-5+ S '64
What's coming in auto tires. D. Francis. il Pop Sci 185:56-9+ S '64
See also
Tire fabrics

Prices

Rise of the cheapies. Time 83:97 Ap 10 '64

Testing

From track to turnpike. D. Francis. il Pop Sci 183:54-7+ S '63
Good year for Goodyear. G. Moore. il Motor T 16:74-7 F '64
Rubber battle at Indy; Firestone fires up! G. Moore. il Motor T 16:55-7 Mr '64
TIRES, Motor truck
More truck-tire mileage; for municipal fleet, Cleveland, Ohio. F. D. East. il Am City 79:86-8 Jl '64
TIRES, Rubber
Treat tires right. il Suc Farm 62:74 Ja '64
TIRES, Tractor
Big tires, less packing. il Suc Farm 61:32 My '63
Five ways to increase traction. S. Clark. il Suc Farm 63:64 Ja '65
Know your tires. W. J. Fletcher. il Suc Farm 63:62-3 Ja '65
TIRESIAS, pseud.
Ali, ali, anza free-o! Nat R 14:113-14+ F 12 '63
Why we are wrong on Latin America. Nat R 16:225-6+ Mr 24 '64
TIROL. See Tyrol
TIROS (satellites) See Artificial satellites—Meteorological applications
'TIS always the same; story. See O'Flynn, C.
TISCHE, Jim
Turkeys plus. pors Field & S 68:26-7+ D '63
TISCHER, R. G. See Moore, B. G. jt. auth.
TISDALE, D. E. W.
Reader's choice. Travel 120:8 Ag '63
TISELIUS, Arne
Biochemical laboratory at Uppsala. V. K. McElheny. il por Science 144:1323-5 Je 12 '64
—and others
Separation and fractionation of macromolecules and particles. bibliog Science 141:13-20 Jl 5 '63
TISHMAN realty and construction company
Over the tracks. il Newsweek 62:76-8 S 30 '63
TISSERANT, Eugène, cardinal
Open city, silent city. Time 83:65 Ap 3 '64
Paul's way and... il Newsweek 63:83 Ap 6 '64
TISSERAT, Barbara
Haiku; poem. Horn Bk 39:417 Ag '63
TISSUE metabolism
Cell differentiation: some aspects of the problem. R. A. Flickinger. bibliog il Science 141:608-14 Ag 16 '63
Collagenolytic activity of intact and necrotic connective tissue. E. R. Goldstein and others. bibliog il Science 146:942-4 N 13 '64
Galactose metabolism by rat liver tissue: influence of age. S. Segal and others. bibliog il Science 142:1311-13 D 6 '63
Inhibition of adhesiveness and aggregation of dissociated cells by inhibitors of protein and RNA synthesis. M. H. Moscona and A. A. Moscona. bibliog Science 142:1070-1 N 22 '63
Temperature regulation and metabolism in Mexican freetail bats. C. F. Herreid, 2d. bibliog il Science 142:1573-4 D 20 '63
TISSUES
Aortico-pulmonary glomus tissue distribution and blood supply in the adult cat. M. A. Verity and others. bibliog il Science 145: 172-3 Jl 10 '64
Proteinpolysaccharide in connective tissue: inhibition of phase separation. H. Weinstein and others. bibliog il Science 142:1073-5 N 22 '63
Reconstruction of tissues by dissociated cells. M. S. Steinberg. bibliog il Science 141:401-8 Ag 2 '63
See also
Bone
Muscle
Plant cells and tissues

Culture

Albumin replacement by fatty acids in clonal growth of mammalian cells. R. G. Ham. bibliog il Science 140:802-3 My 17 '63
Animal cell strains; report on Cell culture collection committee. bibliog Science 146: 241-3 O 9 '64
Bone cells: biochemical and biological studies after enzymatic isolation. W. A. Peck and others. bibliog il Science 146:1476-7 D 11 '64
Cell culture perfusion chamber: adaptation for microscopy of clonal growth. J. J. Freed. bibliog il Science 140:1334-5 Je 21 '63
Clonal analysis of myogenesis. I. R. Konigsberg. bibliog il Science 140:1273-84 Je 21 '63
Continuously cultured tissue cells and viral vaccines; report of a committee on tissue culture viruses and vaccines; discussion. bibliog Science 140:766+ My 17 '63
Culture of embryonic cells of drosophila melanogaster in vitro. M. Horikawa and A. S. Fox. il Science 145:1437-9 S 25 '64
Culture of insect salivary glands in a chemically defined medium. G. B. Cannon. bibliog Science 146:1063 N 20 '64

TISSUES—Culture—*Continued*
Fluoride: its effects on two parameters of bone growth in organ culture. W. R. Proffit and J. L. Ackerman. bibliog il Science 145:932-4 Ag 28 '64
Histochemical demonstration of uptake of exogenous norepinephrine by adrenergic fibers in vitro. E. T. Angelakos. bibliog il Science 145:503-4 Jl 31 '64
Insect tissue culture: use of blastokinetic stage of leafhopper embryo. H. Hirumi and K. Maramorosch. bibliog il Science 144: 1465-7 Je 19 '64
Intracellular infection and the carrier state. J. E. Smadel. bibliog il Science 140:153-60 Ap 12 '63
Lobuloalveolar differentiation in mouse mammary tissues in vitro. R. R. Ichinose and S. Nandi. bibliog il Science 145:496-7 Jl 31 '64
Phytohemagglutinin elicitation of specific anamnestic immune response in vitro. T. W. Tao. bibliog il Science 146:247-8 O 9 '64
Redifferentiation of connective tissue cells in serial culture. R. E. Priest and J. H. Priest. bibliog il Science 145:1053-4 S 4 '64
Tissue culture studies of the human lymphocyte. J. H. Robbins. bibliog il Science 146:1648-54 D 25 '64

TITANIUM
Aluminum barrier broken. il Sci N L 85:162 Mr 14 '64
Titanium comes closer to space-age promise. Bsns W p29 N 16 '63
Titanium is ready for a takeoff. il Fortune 70:227 Jl '64
Titanium: miracle metal for supersonic flight. il U S News 56:36 Mr 16 '64
Titanium's future. M. L. Yaffee. il Aviation W 79:48-9+ D 2; 98-9+ D 9 '63

TITHES
Phrenology updated; concerning the A.I.M.R. Special research report CP-64. Christian Cent 84:503 Ap 15 '64
Reflections on tithing. B. Vawter. Commonweal 78:560-3 S 20 '63
Tithing: toward a clarification. W. L. Guerin. America 108:354-5 Mr 16 '63; Reply. J. L. Cullather. 109:118-19 Ag 3 '63

TITHONIA
Tithonia. M. V. Willwerth. il Pop Gard 14: 102 My '63

TITLES, Moving picture. See Moving pictures —Titles

TITLES of books, stories, etc.
Indians had a word for it: how! How to books. Christian Cent 81:319 Mr 4 '64
Mouthful of mudlumps. Christian Cent 81:223 F 12 '64
No, but I read the book twice; renaming a book or putting suggestive cover on its dust jacket. Christian Cent 82:31 Ja 6 '65
Theologians wax profane. Christian Cent 80: 1223 O 2 '63

TITLES of honor and nobility
Arise, Sir George Meany. G. Hodgson. New Repub 149:11 Je 20 '63
Honorifics. A. Austin. il N Y Times Mag p 15-16 Ag 11 '63

TITLES of television programs. See Television broadcasting—Programs—Titles

TITMUSS, Richard M.
What British doctors really think about socialized medicine. Harper 226:16+ F '63

TITO
Exchange of greetings, October 17, 1963; with text of communique. Dept State Bul 49: 738-40 N 11 '63
Summary of address, October 22, 1963. por U N Rev 10:9-10 D '63

about

Active coexister visits us. D. Binder. il pors N Y Times Mag p24+ O 13 '63
Billions in U.S. aid and Tito wants to bury capitalism. A. Kucherov. il U S News 55: 68-9 S 16 '63
Cool toward Tito; five-week air tour of South and North America. il por Newsweek 62:32 S 30 '63
Courteous, correct & cold; President Tito's state visit. il por Time 82:26 O 25 '63
Fan of Henry Ford's; Khrushchev's visit to Yugoslavia. il por Time 82:22 Ag 30 '63
How to win job security. Time 81:38 Ap 19 '63
How well can we trust Marshal Tito? R. Sherrod. il pors Sat Eve Post 236:75-9 Je 22 '63
Khrushchev and Tito join forces to bury capitalism. il por U S News 55:22 S 9 '63
Letter from Belgrade. J. Wechsberg. New Yorker 39:130+ S 21 '63
Lifelong rule for King Tito. Sr Schol 82:20 My 1 '63
Man in the middle. por Newsweek 62:67 O 21 '63
Nikita in Titoland. U S News 55:12 S 2 '63
People of the week. U S News 55:26 O 21 '63
Small hello; visit to Latin America. il Time 82:56 O 4 '63
Social climber; Tito's trips abroad. Reporter 29:18+ N 7 '63
Tito and the cops. il por Newsweek 62:25-6 N 4 '63
Tito for life. Newsweek 61:38+ Ap 22 '63
Tito in the United States. M. M. Mestrovic. Commonweal 79:181 N 8 '63
Tito of Yugoslavia: new role for an old rebel? il por Sr Schol 83:12-15+ O 11 '63
Titoism in flux. F. W. Neal. Cur Hist 44:294-8+ My '63
Tito's date; visit to Washington. il por Newsweek 62:20 O 28 '63
Tito's visit. Commonweal 79:156 N 1 '63
Tito's visit: a worry for U.S. il por U S News 55:52 O 28 '63
Tour time. il Newsweek 64:34+ Jl 13 '64
Trouble in Hollywood. Newsweek 64:39-40 D 21 '64
Two kinds of reds to call on Kennedy. por U S News 55:24 S 23 '63
Whew! visit to the US. il por Time 82:24 N 1 '63
Yugoslavia: after the Partisan generation. A. Rothberg. Yale R 53:221-32 D '63

TITRATION
Differences in complement titers of serums from spaced bleedings in guinea pigs. L. J. Brenner and E. E. Ecker. bibliog il Science 145:400-1 Jl 24 '64

TITTLE, Y. A.
Always leave them limp; New York Giants vs. Pittsburgh Steelers at Yankee stadium. il Time 82:40 D 27 '63
Armchair vote for old Y.A. L. Wainwright. Life 57:28 N 27 '64
Giant story; New York Giants win Eastern division championship. T. Maule. il Sports Illus 19:22-9 D 23 '63
How they racked up the great Tittle. il por Life 57:141-2 O 2 '64
It's not magic, says Tittle. W. N. Wallace. il pors N Y Times Mag p48+ N 10 '63
Plan that worked; Cleveland Browns vs New York Giants. T. Maule. il Sports Illus 19:16-19 O 21 '63
Tittle fading back. I. Shaw. il por Esquire 63:31-4+ Ja '65
Y. A. Tittle is the best policy. T. Maule. il por Sports Illus 19:64-6 N 18 '63

TITUS, Harold
(ed) Conservation. See issues of Field & stream
Quality duck hunting. Field & S 69:56-8+ My '64
Red carpet for pheasant hunters. Field & S 68:47-9+ S '63

TIUTCHEV, Fedor Ivanovich
Tyutchev and Tomlinson. D. Galler. Poetry 101:418-20 Mr '63

TIVOLI, Italy

Hadrian's villa

Emperor's monumental folly. M. Cable. il Horizon 5:32-9 My '63

TIVOLI GARDENS. See Copenhagen—Parks and playgrounds

TIWI (Melville Island people)

Rites and ceremonies

Qualifications for adulthood. J. C. Goodale. il Natur Hist 72:10-17 Ap '63

TO all a good-night; story. See Stanton, W.
TO Broadway with love; musical comedy. See Musical comedies, revues, etc.—Criticisms, plots, etc.
TO call my own; story. See Knowlton, R. A.
TO Mary with love; story. See Williams, L.
TO my daughter Carol; story. See Ernst, P.
TO set our house in order; story. See Laurence, M.
TO steal the moment; story. See Maner, W.
TO the Chicago abyss; drama. See Bradbury, R.
TO the open water; story. See Ford, J. H.
TO the water tower; musical comedy. See Musical comedies, revues, etc.—Criticisms, plots, etc.

TOADS
See also
Frogs

TOADSTOOLS. See Mushrooms

TOAST
French toast. B. M. Stover. il Parents Mag 39:93 F '64

TOASTS
Toasting: a timely abecedary. il Esquire 63: 47-51 Ja '65

TOASTERS, Electric. See Electric toasters

TOBACCO
Deoxyribonuclease sensitivity of ribonucleic acid synthesizing system from tobacco leaves. J. G. Shaw. bibliog il Science 139: 924-5 Mr 8 '63
Development of complete homozygotes of tobacco. G. W. Stokes. bibliog il Science 141:1185 S 20 '63
More tobacco research. Sci N L 85:102 F 15 '64
Radioactivity in tobacco; polonium. Sci N L 85:70 F 1 '64
Radium-226 and polonium-210 in leaf tobacco and tobacco soil. T. C. Tso and others. bibliog il Science 146:1043-5 N 20 '64
Tobacco mosaic virus; purifying and sorting associated particles according to length. R. L. Steere. bibliog Science 140:1089-90 Je 7 '63
Tobacco pesticides safe? F. Marley. Sci N L 85:134 F 29 '64
See also
Snuff

Diseases and pests

Toxic effect of pseudomonas tabaci on RNA metabolism in tobacco and its counteraction by kinetin. L. Lovrekovich and others. bibliog il Science 145:165 Jl 10 '64

Physiological effects

By their own free choice; tobacco and cancer; address, April 6, 1964. T. Sanford. Vital Speeches 30:463-7 My 15 '64
Cigarettes: testing on mice; letter. W. J. Turner. Science 143:994 Mr 6 '64
Crash effort for a safer cigarette; concerning the report of Surgeon general's advisory committee on smoking and health. B. Davidson. il Sat Eve Post 237:19-23 Ap 18 '64
Dilemma of the problem smoker. L. M. Miller. Read Digest 84:63-8 My '64
Emphysema in lung macrosections correlated with smoking habits. A. E. Anderson, jr. and others. bibliog il Science 144:1025-6 My 22 '64
It is less hazardous. il Time 83:60 Ap 17 '64
Reporter at large. T. Whiteside. il New Yorker 39:67-8+ N 30 '63
Storm signals for tobacco; report from Advisory committee on smoking and health. Bsns W p72+ O 12 '63
Tobacco-smeared mice found to develop tumors. Sci N L 86:130 Ag 29 '64
Tumor-promoting activity of extracts of unburned tobacco. F. G. Bock and others. bibliog il Science 145:831-3 Ag 21 '64
See also
Cigarettes
Smoking

Quotations, maxims, etc.

Indian perfume, pernicious weed; some comments con and pro; comp. by E. F. Murphy. il N Y Times Mag p50-1 F 23 '64

TOBACCO habit. See Smoking

TOBACCO industry and trade
Back to high levels. il Time 84:89-90 N 6 '64
Cigarette lobby. New Repub 151:4-5 O 10 '64
Cigarette sales: a sharp drop, then signs of an upturn. U S News 56:12 Mr 30 '64
Cigarette smokers still puffing away. il Bsns W p 148-50 D 14 '63
Cigarettes; tried and found guilty. L. M. Miller and J. Monahan. Read Digest 84:71-6 Ap '64
Crash effort for a safer cigarette; concerning the report of Surgeon general's advisory committee on smoking and health. B. Davidson. il Sat Eve Post 237:19-23 Ap 18 '64
Fight for life. Newsweek 63:66 Mr 30 '64
Huffing and puffing. Newsweek 63:65-6 F 10 '64
It won't happen here; affects of Surgeon General's report on tobacco industry. Bsns W p29 F 15 '64
Label on the pack? Newsweek 64:62 Jl 6 '64
Smoke & ire; FTC requirement of health warnings on all cigarette packages. Time 84:78 Jl 3 '64
Smoke still swirls around cigarettes. Bsns W p 122 Je 29 '63
Smokers light up less, but habit bounces back. il Bsns W p88-9+ D 12 '64
Smoking fire burns hotter; health vs. industry. il Bsns W p32+ Ja 18 '64
Smoking, health, and a giant industry. il U S News 55:84-6 D 2 '63
Still smoking. il Time 83:61 Ja 24 '64
Storm signals for tobacco; report from Advisory committee on smoking and health. Bsns W p72+ O 12 '63
Symptoms of slump. Time 83:85 F 14 '64
To smoke, or not to smoke? il Newsweek 63: 70-3 Ja 27 '64
Tobacco: administration showing little enthusiasm for follow-up on Public health service report. D. S. Greenberg. Science 143:1417-19 Mr 27 '64
Tobacco: after publicity surge, Surgeon general's report seems to have little enduring effect. D. S. Greenberg. Science 145:1021-2 S 4 '64
Washington hearings on cigarette labeling. il Time 83:79-80 Mr 27 '64
See also
American tobacco company
Cigar industry
Cigarettes

Advertising

Big risk for pipe smokers. E. Havemann. il Sports Illus 20:32-4+ Ap 13 '64
Deciphering the cigarette code. W. Goodman. New Repub 151:14 D 5 '64
Warning on every pack; new FTC rule. Bsns W p36 Je 27 '64

TOBACCO industry research committee
TIRC speaks. C. C. Little. Newsweek 62:63 N 18 '63

TOBACCO mosaic virus
Equilibrium sedimentation of uniform rods of tobacco mosaic virus. F. N. Weber, jr. and others. bibliog il Science 140:1090-2 Je 7 '63
Genetic code of a virus. H. Fraenkel-Conrat. il Sci Am 211:46-54 bibliog(p 142) O '64
Incorporation of uridine-H^3 into nuclei of virus-infected tobacco. S. H. Smith and D. E. Schlegel. bibliog il Science 145:1058-9 S 4 '64
Nobelist offers hope; virus cancer research. Sci N L 86:214 O 3 '64
Tobacco mosaic virus: cytological evidence of the synthesis in the nucleus. T. Hirai and A. Hirai. bibliog il Science 145:589-91 Ag 7 '64
Tobacco mosaic virus; purifying and sorting associated particles according to length. R. L. Steere. bibliog Science 140:1089-90 Je 7 '63
Unusual aggregation of a nonfunctional tobacco mosaic virus protein. M. Zaitlin and W. R. Ferris. bibliog il Science 143: 1451-2 Mr 27 '64
Virus reproduction study. Sci N L 85:291-2 My 9 '64

TOBACCO pipes
Keep your pipe in good spirits. H. Shuldiner. il Pop Sci 184:155-7 Ap '64
Pipe this; pipe and cigar smoking women. W. K. Zinsser. il Sat Eve Post 237:58-9 My 30 '64
White steatite pipe. C. Miles. il Hobbies 68: 113-14 Jl '63

TOBAGO
Trinidad and Tobago. W. A. Simmonds. il Américas 15:8-13 Mr '63
See also
Trinidad-Tobago

TOBEY, Mark
Seattle sketches of Mark Tobey. il Am Artist 27:56+ My '63

TOBIN, James
Barry's economic crusade. New Repub 151:13-16 O 24 '64
How planned is our economy? N Y Times Mag p 18+ O 13 '63
Tax cut harvest. New Repub 150:14-17 Mr 7 '64

TOBIN, Richard L.
(ed) Communications. See issues of Saturday review
Man with the pencil of light. Sat R 47:138-9+ Ag 29 '64
Sporting life. Sat R 47:8+ Jl 11 '64
That was the year that was. Sat R 47:56-7 F 15 '64
Writer. Sat R 47:6 Ja 25 '64

TOCH, Ernst
Jubilee fare. O. Daniel. Sat R 46:71 Mr 30 '63
Obituary
Opera N por 29:34 Ja 9 '64

TOCQUEVILLE, Alexis de
Tocqueville and the problem of historical prognosis. E. T. Gargan. bibliog f Am Hist R 68:332-45 Ja '63

TOD, Giles M. S.
To the bear. Motor B 111:118 My '63

TODAI-JI temple. See Temples—Japan

TODD, A. L.
Capsule history of American hotels. Holiday 33:54-5 F 63
Luckless Library of Congress. Sat R 47:24+ Ap 11 '64

TODD, Alexander Robertus Todd, baron
How science is to change daily life; interview. por U S News 55:70-4 N 11 '63
TODD, Arthur
Air force assesses its recreation centers. por Recreation 57:342-3 S '64
Ambassadors of the dance. Américas 16:6-11 O '64
New company gets a Washington inauguration. Dance Mag 37:38-9+ Mr '63
Public recreation: progress and problems. por Recreation 56:278-81 Je '63
TODD, Carl David
Simple tests for semiconductors. Electr World 70:36-8 D '63
Tape-slide synchronizer. Electr World 70:50-2+ S '63
Transistorized tachometer. Electr World 70:66-7+ N '63
Tunnel diode high-resistance checker. Electr World 69:86-8 Je '63
TODD, Carol
Opera mother. il pors Look 27:116+ D 17 '63
TODD, Elizabeth Frances
Elizabeth and Liza; ed. by J. Hamilton. E. Taylor. il pors Look 28:72-7 Ap 21 '64
TODD, Hollis N. and Zakia, R. D.
Is it true? Pop Phot 52:24 Mr; 53:40 N '63; 54:11-12 My; 16 Je; 55:8 S '64
TODD, John M.
Luther and the Catholics. il por Newsweek 64:46 Ag 10 '64
TODD, Murray
Our common enterprise: a non-apocalyptic view. Bul Atomic Sci 20:27-9 F '64
TODD, Reginald Stephen Garfield
Black and white. por Newsweek 63:47 My 11 '64
TODD, W. Murray
Science in the State department. Bul Atomic Sci 20:27-9 D '64
TODMAN, William
Lords of fun and games. G. Rogin. il por Sports Illus 18:52-60 Je 24 '63
TODRIN, Boris, and White, P. D.
Take a two-hour vacation. Parents Mag 39:66+ N '64
TOE shoes. See Ballet slippers
TOEPFER, Edwin F.
Insuring entrance door lock security. Arch Rec 135:221-2 Ap '64
TOFFLER, Alvin
Don't knock U.S. culture; adapted from Culture consumers. Life 57:96-100+ O 30 '64
Passage to post-civilization. New Repub 151:17-18 D 12 '64
Seminar at Salzburg. Sat R 46:32-4 Ag 17 '63
What the husbands think. Ladies Home J 81:26+ Je '64
Woman behind Barry Goldwater. Good H 158:58+ My '64
TOFU. See Cookery, Japanese
TOGLIATTI, Palmiro
Doing what is possible. por Time 84:30 Ap 28 '64
Palmiro's prophecy; future of communism in Italy. Time 84:42 S 18 '64
Prayer for a Communist. America 111:225 S 5 '64
Tortuous way of Palmiro Togliatti. C. Sterling. Reporter 31:35 S 24 '64
We need you. por Newsweek 64:35 Ag 31 '64
TOGO
Arranging things. Time 81:34 My 10 '63
President of Togo assassinated. il Sr Schol 82:17 Ja 30 '63
Togo: the lesson for Africa. J. K. Sale. Nation 196:135-7 F 16 '63
Togo woman leader. il Ebony 18:44+ Mr '63
U.S. recognizes government of Republic of Togo; statement, June 6, 1963. Dept State Bul 48:969 Je 24 '63
Violence in Africa; developments in Togo, Brazzaville and Dahomey. T. P. Melady. America 109:734-5 D 7 '63
TOGO, Fumihiko
Consul. New Yorker 40:21-2 S 5 '64
TOGOLAND, FRENCH. See Togo
TOILET
Christmas beauties: $4 and under; $5 and up. il Seventeen 22:82-5 D '63
Little beauties: from $1; from $5. il Seventeen 23:86-9 D '64
See also
Baths
Beauty, Personal
TOILET; drama. See Jones, L.
TOILET preparations
Baby toiletries are good for mothers, too. L. D. Kirk. il Parents Mag 39:128 O '64
D. Boone would have been shocked; grooming aids. E. Kendall. il N Y Times Mag p43+ O 13 '63
Everyone enjoys a gift of beauty. L. D. Kirk. il Parents Mag 39:138-9 N '64
Say it with fragrance. il Redbook 122:22 D '63
Scalping the competition; Alberto-Culver products. il Time 82:88 Jl 12 '63
See also
Cosmetics
Deodorants
Shampoos
TOILET training. See Infants—Care and hygiene
TOILET water. See Perfumery
TOILETS. See Water closets
TOINETTE and the elves; drama. See Thane, A.
TOKAIDO line. See Railroads—Japan
TOKENS
Packaged fares cut bus operating costs: San Juan, Puerto Rico. il Am City 79:133 S '64
TOKLAS, Alice B.
Miss Toklas on her own. J. Barry. New Repub 148:21-3 Mr 30 '63
TOKUDA, S. See Gilden, R. V. jt. auth.
TOKYO
Fresh start; Japan prepares for the XVIII Olympiad. il Time 84:30 Jl 10 '64
Hello! wonderful! the world is one; effect of the Olympics. R. Steinberg. il Reporter 31:26-8 D 31 '64
Setting for a glorious Olympiad; photographs. P. Turner. Sports Illus 21:32-41 Jl 6 '64
Tribulation in Tokyo; preparations for Olympics. Sports Illus 18:12 F 11 '63
Very dry run in Tokyo; Japan rehearses for '64 Olympics. il Sports Illus 19:64-5+ O 28 '63
See also
Stock exchange—Tokyo

Architecture

Clean sweep in Olympics; National gymnasium and annex. il Arch Forum 121:158-61 Ag '64
Functional grid in Japan. il Arch Forum 121:130-5 Ag '64

City planning

Big spending, mad building; Japan prepares for Olympics. R. P. Martin. il U S News 55:69-71 D 2 '63
End of an era; Tokyo reborn. il Newsweek 64:36-8 S 7 '64
Reek of cement in Fuji's shadow; $2 billion to refurbish Tokyo for the Olympic games. il Time 84:30-9 S 11 '64
Tokyo's Olympian remodeling. il Newsweek 61:42-4 Ap 29 '63

Description

End of an era; Tokyo reborn. il Newsweek 64:36-8 S 7 '64
Getting around in Tokyo. il Sunset 133:20+ S '64
Letter from Sendagaya. J. M. Flagler. il New Yorker 40:58+ Jl 25 '64
Letter from Sendagaya. J. M. Flagler. il New Yorker 40:58+ Jl 25; 86+ Ag 15 '64
New Japan. R. Blackmon. il Vogue 144:84-5+ Ag 15 '64
Olympic report. il Travel 122:66 S '64
Purest of all the great cities. A. M. Rosenthal. il N Y Times Mag p52-3+ My 5 '63
Sporting scene; Tokyo Olympics. E. J. Kahn, jr. il New Yorker 40:110+ O 17 '64
Tokyo, the peaceful explosion. W. Graves. il Nat Geog Mag 126:445-87 O '64
Tokyo travel facts. F. R. Smith. il Sports Illus 21:42-7 Jl 6 '64

Hotels, restaurants, etc.

Wright's Tokyo masterpiece; Imperial hotel. il Sunset 130:50 Je '63

Moral conditions

How to keep the Olympics clean. il Time 82:44 D 6 '63

Music

Berlin in Tokyo. B. E. Martin. Opera N 28:32 F 1 '64
Notes from abroad. F. Fujita. Hi Fi 13:22+ Ag '63
Tokyo's best; Toho school of music. Newsweek 64:76 Jl 27 '64

Newspapers

Founder's daughter; editorial responsibility. Time 84:60-1 Jl 3 '64
It gives us light; Asahi Shimbun. il Newsweek 64:44-5 Jl 6 '64

TOKYO—*Continued*

Sanitary affairs

When they start playing footsie, it's time for a girl to quit; rats in Tokyo's main stem. Time 81:37 Mr 8 '63

Social life and customs

Way of all pleasure; Nichigeki building. il Newsweek 63:94+ My 11 '64

Street traffic

What to do about traffic? some answers from abroad. il U S News 54:86-90 F 4 '63

Theater

Eraiza and company; first American musical in Tokyo, My fair lady in Japanese. il Newsweek 62:82 S 16 '63

Grotto theater is part of Tokyo office block; Nissei theater. il Arch Forum 120:120-1 F '64

Japan's first Broadway musical: My fair lady. il Life 55:95-6 O 4 '63

TOLAND, John

Last days of Dillinger; excerpt from The Dillinger days. Look 27:79-80+ F 12 '63

TOLANSKY, S.

It isn't the heat; it's midsummer science; excerpts from Penguin science survey A 1963. Sat R 46:41-3 Ag 3 '63

TOLBERT, Frank X.

Odd fate of Oswald's other victims. Sat Eve Post 237:68-9 Ag 22 '64

What is Cactus Jack up to now? Sat Eve Post 236:26, 29 N 2 '63

TOLBERT, George. See Singer, M. F. jt. auth.

TOLBERT, Thomas

Meet Thomas Tolbert, 1963 principal of the year. por Negro Hist Bul 26:250 My '63

TOLCHACO stone tool industry. See Stone implements and weapons

TÔLE

Tôle painting. il House & Gard 123:166-7 My '63

TOLEDANO, Jose

Jose Toledano and his Ballet espanol at Town Hall. J. Maskey. Dance Mag 37:33 D '63

TOLEDO, Ohio

Harbor

See also

Toledo-Lucas County port authority

Industries

Toledo's play for industry; Fort industry industrial park. il Bsns W p 106-8 Ap 4 '64

TOLEDO, Ohio, museum of art

Museum evaluations. A. Frankfurter. il Art N 63:24-7+ Ja '65

TOLEDO, Ohio, public library

Divided we're not; letter to the editor. R. D. Franklin. Library J 89:4238 N 1 '64

TOLEDO, Spain

Galleries and museums

Regeneration at Toledo; Jewish museum and library to be opened in the Sinagogo del Transito. A. Frankfurter. Art N 63:25 My '64

Libraries

Regeneration at Toledo; Jewish museum and library to be opened in the Sinagogo del Transito. A. Frankfurter. Art N 63:25 My '64

TOLEDO area development corporation

Toledo's play for industry; Fort industry industrial park. il Bsns W p 106-8 Ap 4 '64

TOLEDO cathedral. See Cathedrals—Spain

TOLEDO-Lucas County port authority

Big deal in Toledo; purchase of C&O bulk-loading complex. il Bsns W p92+ N 16 '63

TOLEDO Tornadoes (football club) See Football clubs

TOLERANCE (engineering)

Tolerance calculator. R. K. Re. il Electr World 69:25 My '63

TOLERANCE. See Toleration

TOLERATION

Bigotry in science. P. H. Abelson. Science 144:371 Ap 24 '64; Discussion. 144:1529+; 146:342 Je 26, O 16 '64

Bigotry's shifting patterns. Christian Cent 81:1196 S 30 '64

Catholicism and freedom. H. A. MacDougall. America 110:486-7 Ap 4 '64

Ceylon cries foul. America 109:413 O 12 '63

Clergy looks at bigotry. J. Pelikan. Sat R 46:32 My 11 '63

Too busy to hate. K. Haselden. Christian Cent 80:392-3 Mr 27 '63

Too late for drums? J. Ciardi. Sat R 46:11 Jl 27 '63

Word. V. P. McCorry. America 111:363-4 S 26 '64

See also

Religious liberty

TOLIVER, Joan

Off with the pigtails. por Newsweek 64:46 Ag 3 '64

TOLKIEN, J. R. R.

On fairy-stories. Horn Bk 39:457 O '63

TOLL roads

Toll for tolls? il Newsweek 62:60 O 14 '63

Toll-road bonds the latest look. U S News 56:86+ Je 29 '64

Toll road turnstiles click a merry tune. il Bsns W p 112-13 S 5 '64

TOLMACH, L. J. See Terasima, T. jt. auth.

TOLPIN, J. G.

Surveying Russian technical publications: a brief course. Science 146:1143-4 N 27 '64

TOLSTOI, Lev Nikolaevich, graf

Tolstoy goes to a rehearsal; excerpt from What is art? por Opera N 29:6-7 D 26 '64

War and peace: dramatization. See Neumann, A. and others

TOLSTOY, Leo. See Tolstoĭ, L. N.

TOLSTOY, Tanya. See Snodgrass, W. D. jt. auth.

TOM Sawyer, pirate; drama. See Thane, A.

TOM Swifties. See Word games

TOM Thumb, General. See Stratton, C. S.

TOMASI, T. B. jr. See Chodirker, W. B. jt. auth.

TOMATIN

Isolation of an antihistaminic principle resembling tomatine from crown gall tumors. B. A. Kovacs and others. bibliog il Science 144:295-6 Ap 17 '64; Reply with rejoinder. P. R. White. 146:670 O 30 '64

TOMATOES

Care of tomatoes from transplanting to harvest. B. C. Kilvert, jr. il Flower Grower 50:42-4 Jl '63

Chewy tomato; Tomato X, 6-inch-long hybrid. Newsweek 64:111 O 5 '64

Dehydration of seeds in intact tomato fruits. W. J. McIlrath and others. il Science 142:1681-2 D 27 '63

Earlier crop, more income from tomatoes on trellises. R. Anderson. il Farm J 88:72-3 F '64

Early tomato that's so good. H. S. Witty. Flower Grower 51:32 Ap '64

Genetic activity in a heterochromatic chromosome segment of the tomato. G. S. Khush and others. bibliog il Science 145:1432-4 S 25 '64

Herbert Hoover's favorite. F. E. Mason. il Pop Gard 16:24 Ja '65

Is this your year for tomatoes? il Sunset 132:102-5 Mr '64

Magnets ripen tomatoes. Sci N L 84:37 Jl 20 '63

One plant tomato. A. J. Hall. il Horticulture 41:141+ Mr '63

Ring culture whips tomato diseases. B. Hardy. il Farm J 88:32F Ag '64

Spray ripens tomatoes at one time: chemical mendok. Farm J 89:54 Ja '65

Starting tomatoes from seed is easy and fun. B. C. Kilvert, jr. il Flower Grower 50:26-7 Ap '63

Tomato's timetable is baseball's. il Sunset 130:278 My '63

See also

Cookery—Vegetables

TOMB figures

Funerary figures of the Kafirs. D. Newton. il Natur Hist 72:40-7 Je '63

TOMB robberies

Lucrative paradise for grave robbers. D. J. Hamblin. il Life 57:118-20+ N 20 '64

TOMBALBAYE, Francois

Colored rulers. G. C. Turner. Negro Hist Bul 27:91 Ja '64

TOMBOYS. See Girls

TOMBROPOULOUS, Elias G.

Fatty acid synthesis by subcellular fractions of lung tissue. bibliog Science 146:1180-1 N 27 '64

TOMBS

Will the real Columbus please stand up! R. Schoenstein. Sat R 46:90 O 12 '63

TOMBSTONES. See Sepulchral monuments

TOMCOD fishing

Early season fishing. G. Heinold. il Outdoor Life 131:8+ Mr '63

TOMI. See Constanta, Rumania

TOMKINS, Calvin
Art or not, it's food for thought. Life 57: 143-4 N 20 '64
Profiles (cont) New Yorker 39:47-50+ Mr 30; 49-50+ S 21 '63; 40:39-40+ F 29; 64-6+ N 28 '64
Reporter at large. New Yorker 39:127-8+ S 14 '63

TOMKINS, Gordon M. See Talal, N. jt. auth.

TOMLINSON, Charles
American scenes: Two views of two ghost towns; Letters from Amherst; In Connecticut; At Barstow; Arizona highway; Through closed eyes; Cavern; poems. Poetry 103: 102-9 O '63
Miscellany. Poetry 102:341-5 Ag '63
Natural art. Poetry 105:125-8 N '64
Nightingale; poem. New Yorker 39:76 Je 1 '63
Wilfred Owen. Poetry 104:41-3 Ap '64
(tr) See Machado, A. To José María Palacio; Draw-wheel; Ephemeral past; O luminous late day! Grey olives; Proverbs and canticles; Winter sun

about

Abstruse considerations. H. Carruth. Poetry 104:243-4 Jl '64
Importing revolution. W. Sutton. Nation 198: 589-91 Je 8 '64
Tyutchev and Tomlinson. D. Galler. Poetry 101:418-20 Mr '63

TOMLINSON, Frank S.
New consul-general. New Yorker 40:47 N 14 '64

TOMORROW; story. See Potter, D.

TOMPKINS, Pauline
Change and challenge for the educated woman. Sat R 46:69-70+ My 18 '63

TOMPKINS, R. M.
Iron general shows his mettle. R. Wallace. il por Life 54:80 F 22 '63

TOMS, Zach
Businessmen in the news. por Fortune 67:75 My '63

TOMS RIVER, N.J.
Concrete trees for the beach. P. F. Losi and J. G. Woods. il Am City 78:92-4 O '63

TON-that-Dinh
Interview with Ton-that-Dinh. por Look 28: 36 Ja 28 '64
Is the U.S. better off after Vietnam coup? por Bsns W p31-2 N 9 '63

TONE
See also
Voice

TONE arm, Phonograph. See Phonograph—Tone arm

TONE compensators. See Sound—Apparatus

TONE deafness
Just what is tone deafness? il Good H 158: 126-7 Ja '64

TONEY, Richard
Season in Spain; story. Seventeen 22:86-7 Je '63
Snow statue; story. Seventeen 23:124-5 F '64

TONGA (islands)
Tourists are almost unknown in Tonga. il Sunset 131:74+ O '63

TONGAN stamps. See Postage stamps

TONGIORGI, E. See Longinelli, A. jt. auth.

TONGUES, Gift of. See Gift of tongues

TONKA beans
Glucosides of coumarinic and o-coumaric acids in the tonka bean. F. A. Haskins and H. J. Gorz. bibliog il Science 139:496-7 F 8 '63

TONKIN, Doris Farmer
Vancouver Island. Travel 121:54-6 Ap '64

TONKIN GULF, Battle of. See Vietnamese crisis, 1964

TONSILLECTOMY. See Throat—Surgery

TONSILLITIS. See Tonsils—Diseases

TONSILS

Diseases

Tonsillitis. E. T. Wilkes. Parents Mag 39:122 My '64

TONSOR, Stephen J.
Pragmatism on the Potomac? Nat R 15:400-1 N 5 '63

TONY awards. See American theatre wing

TOO beautiful, too good; story. See O'Faolain, S.

TOO late for anger; story. See Perera, P.

TOO many cooks; drama. See Huff, B. T.

TOO much Johnson; drama. See Gillette, W.

TOO true to be good; drama. See Shaw, G. B.

TOOHEY, Barbara
Somebody's mother; poem. Wilson Lib Bul 37:863 Je '63
—and Biermann, June
Age of the mass-produced gargoyle. Library J 89:3698-9 O 1 '64
—See Biermann, J. jt. auth.

TOOL boxes, racks, etc.
Big idea: tool turret in a compact shop. S. M. Gallagher. il Pop Sci 183:102-4 S '63
Double-purpose tool box. G. P. Manning. il Motor B 113:26+ Mr '64
Drill-press tool rack. R. J. De Cristoforo. il Pop Mech 120:180-1 S '63
How to build your own compact storage corner for hand and power tools. il Pop Sci 185:120-4 Jl '64
How to fit fine tools to a case. H. Walton il Pop Sci 185:130-1+ N '64
How to mold a rattle-free case for car tools. P. McCafferty. il Pop Sci 183:120-3 Jl '63
It's a toolbox on wheels. il Sunset 133:265 O '64
New ideas for your workshop; New York world's fair. S. M. Gallager. il Pop Sci 184:89-93 My '64
Tool cushion for your shop. W. E. Burton. il Pop Sci 184:114-15 Mr '64
Tool holder that takes you off your feet. A. J. Garinger. il Pop Sci 182:106 My '63

TOOL cases. See Tool boxes, racks, etc.

TOOL holders. See Holding devices (machine work)

TOOL houses. See Garden houses, shelters, etc.

TOOL racks. See Tool boxes, racks, etc.

TOOL sharpening. See Sharpening

TOOLAN, James M.
When a child's afraid of school. Parents Mag 38:80-1+ O '63

TOOLS
Additional low-priced tools. il Consumer Bul 46:30-1 Jl '63
Boatbuilding tools. E. C. Miller. il Motor B 111:42-4+ F; 42-3+ Mr '63
Boatman's tool kit. J. A. Emmett. il Outdoor Life 132:98-100 N '63
Buyer's guide to automobile tools. il Pop Sci 185:72-83 Jl '64
Easy start tool. H. L. Davidson. il Pop Electr 20:88-9 Ja '64
Here are two basic tool kits. il Sunset 131: 155-6 N '63
Home workshop tools you'll see tomorrow. il Pop Mech 119:106-9+ Ap '63
Household tools, a new gift item. Consumer Bul 48:24 Ja '65
Popular science buyer's guide to home shop tools. il Pop Sci 183:157+ N; 155-6+ D '63; 184:151-2+ Ja '64
Pry bars: lift five tons or pull a nail. G. Daniels. il Pop Sci 182:102-4+ Je '63
Seven tools you can make from lathe bits. il Pop Sci 185:123 N '64
Shop talk. S. M. Gallager. See issues of Popular science monthly
Shopping for tools. See issues of Popular mechanics
What's new at the hardware show. S. M. Gallager. il Pop Sci 183:31+ D '63
With tools, it's how you use 'em. H. A. Calahan. il Motor B 113:24-5+ Mr '64
Your leisure (cont) il Consumer Rep 28:346-51+ D '63
See also
Electric tools, Portable
Farm tools
Garden tools, equipment and supplies
Machine tools
Stone implements and weapons
also names of tools, e.g. Wrenches

Storage

See also
Tool boxes, racks, etc.

TOOLS for freedom (organization)
Foreign aid, business style; new and used machinery sent to foreign schools. il Bsns W p 118+ F 29 '64

TOOTH decay. See Teeth—Diseases

TOOTH powders and pastes. See Dentifrices

TOOTH transplantation. See Transplantation of organs, tissues, etc.

TOOTHBRUSHES
Automatic toothbrushes, boon or bane? Consumer Bul 48:23-4 Ja '65
Electric toothbrushes. il Consumer Bul 47: 22-7 Mr '64
Interim report on electric toothbrushes. il Consumer Rep 28:100-1 Mr '63
Power toothbrush: worth the money? il Changing T 17:37-8 N '63

TOOTHBRUSHES—*Continued*
Report on the electric toothbrush. B. H. Frisch. il Sci Digest 55:35-8 Mr '64
Summing up on electric toothbrushes. Consumer Rep 28:186-7 Ap '63
Toothbrush and family oral hygiene. E. M. McCabe. il Parents Mag 38:14+ My '63

Anecdotes, facetiae, satire, etc.

Stop the brush, I want to get off. J. A. Snyder. il Atlan 213:119-20 My '64

TOOTHPICKS
Made with toothpicks. M. Hoffhine. il Design 65:212-13 My '64

TOPCHIEV, Aleksandr Vasil'evich
Interdependence of science and society. Bul Atomic Sci 19:7+ Mr '63

about

A. V. Topchiev, 1907-1962. E. Rabinowitch. por Bul Atomic Sci 19:8-9 Mr '63

TOPEKA, Kan.

Stores

See also
Macy, R. H. and company

TOPIARY work
Fanciful world of topiary. C. Hodgson. il Horticulture 41:578-9 N '63

TOPJIAN, H. Joseph
Numbers game in American business. Duns R 82:pt2 114-15 S '63

TOPOGRAPHICAL maps. See Relief maps

TOPOGRAPHICAL models. See Relief maps

TOPOGRAPHICAL surveying
Mapping the surface of the earth. M. M. Thompson and J. L. Speert. il Natur Hist 73:30-7 O '64

TOPOLOGY
Evolution of an active mathematical theory; rubber-sheet geometry. A. M. Gleason. bibliog il Science 145:451-7 Jl 31 '64
Mathematical games; planar graphs. M. Gardner. il Sci Am 210:126+ Ap '64
Topology, the art of distortion; excerpt from Mathematics. G. Kalvin. il Design 66:26-7 S '64

TOPOLSKI, Feliks
Pope Paul in the land of Jesus. Vogue 143:120-3+ Mr 1 '64

TOPOROFF, Ralph
Insider talks about the Mafia. Look 27:110+ O 22 '63

TOPPEL, Harold
Food chain with a Latin flair. il Bsns W p93-4+ My 16 '64

TOPPIN, Edgar A.
Book review. Negro Hist Bul 28:69-70 D '64
Emancipation reconsidered; adaptation of address, February 12, 1963. bibliog Negro Hist Bul 26:233-6 My '63

TOPPING, Audrey R.
First in space, but not in femininity. N Y Times Mag p 10-11+ Je 30 '63
On sale at GUM, Moscow's super shop. N Y Times Mag p 13+ Jl 28 '63

TOPPING, Norman
Bill of obligations; balance is vital to us; address, June 13, 1963. Vital Speeches 29:634-6 Ag 1 '63

TOPPING, Seymour
Close view of the Kremlin boss. N Y Times Mag p20+ Ag 11 '63

TOPPING, Tinka D.
Your child. Redbook 121:34 Jl; 12 Ag; 16 S '63

TOPPS chewing gum, incorporated
Beatles vs. LBJ. Newsweek 64:72 S 14 '64
Bubble-gum trust. il Time 84:64 S 4 '64
Getting the picture, bubble-gum enclosures. G. Eskenazi. il N Y Times Mag p 101 Ap 19 '64

TOPS
Again it's the tops. E. Merriam. il N Y Times Mag p 14-15 D 22 '63
Spinning fool has lift-off launching handle. il Pop Mech 121:161 Ap '64

TOPSIDE sounder, ionosphere. See Artificial satellites—Use in research

TORCH lilies
Amazing dwarf torch lily. M. C. Dolton. il Horticulture 41:160 Mr '63

TORCHES
New hand-sized oxy-butane torch. H. Walton. il Pop Sci 185:126-8 Ag '64

TORDON. See Herbicides

TORGESEN, John L. and Strassburger, John
Growth of oxalic acid single crystals from solution: solvent effects on crystal habit. bibliog Science 146:53-5 O 2 '64

TORMÉ, Mel
Fog lifts. por Newsweek 63:47 Ja 6 '64
Out of the fog. por Time 81:68 Mr 1 '63

TORMEY, Robert W.
Wood and clay pots. Sch Arts 64:20 Ja '65

TORNABENE, Lyn
Contradicting the Hollywood image. Sat R 46:19-21 D 28 '63

TORNADOES
Clear facts about stormy weather. il Good H 157:142-3 Ag '63
Do-it-yourself tornado made in living room. Sci N L 84:251 O 19 '63
One week of horror on the Great Plains. H. Rezatto. il Read Digest 82:195-6+ Ap '63
Riding herd on the twisters; U.S. weather bureau's Severe local storm forecast center (SELS) J. H. Winchester. il Read Digest 85:158-60+ O '64
Tornado alley's emergency net. L. Hunter. il Pop Electr 20:37-8+ Ap '64
Tornado hunters. il Newsweek 61:97 Je 10 '63
Tornado; nature on a rampage. J. Reed. il Todays Health 41:26-9+ My '63
Tornadoes across U.S. Sci N L 83:191 Mr 23 '63
Tornadoes, vicious storms. A. Ewing. il Sci N L 85:282-3 My 2 '64

TORNILLO, Pat L. Jr
In Dade County, Florida. NEA J 52:51-2 D '63

TORO-GOYCO, E. and Cancio, Marta
Human lipoproteins: role in transport of thyroid hormones. bibliog Science 139:761-2 F 22 '63
—and others
Schistosome ova: rapid separation from mouse tissue by digestion with pinguinain. bibliog Science 142:407 O 18 '63

TORONTO
See also
Stock exchange—Toronto

Architecture

Precast patterns in Ontario. il Arch Forum 119:100-1 O '63

Description

Beneath Toronto's skyscrapers. A. R. Pastore, jr. il Travel 122:35-8 Ag '64

Education, Board of

Education centre library

Information retrieval for students; with profile of Education centre library, Toronto. L. H. Freiser. il Library J 88:1121-3 Mr 15 '63; Discussion. 88:1922+, 3251-3, 4412 My 15, S 15, N 15 '63

Galleries and museums

See also
Royal Ontario museum of archeology

Libraries

See also
Toronto—Education, Board of—Education centre library

Music

[Musical events] (cont) Mus Am 83:163-4+ D '63; 84:29 Jl; 102 D '64
Notes from our correspondents. R. Syrett. Hi Fi 14:22+ S '64
Toronto's moods. R. Ubriaco. Opera N 28:32 D 21 '63

Rapid transit

See also
Toronto—Subways

Stores

Shoppers pick pearls on the half shell; T. Eaton co, ltd. il Bsns W p 138-40 N 28 '64

Street traffic

Electronic genie speeds traffic through 1,001 lights. G. McCaffrey. il Pop Sci 185:76-7+ S '64

Subways

In Canada, subways are for building. il Bsns W p76+ Mr 9 '63
Toronto: how one city is working out mass transit. il U S News 56:68-9 Je 22 '64

Transportation

Computer out-thinks. S. Cass. il Am City 79:98-9 Ag '64

Water supply

Ten years of Metro water supply. R. L. Clark. il Am City 79:118-19+ Je '64

TORONTO Maple Leafs (hockey team) See Hockey teams

TORONTO public library
Comments from Canada; excerpts from report. H. C. Campbell. Library J 88:2468 Je 15 '63

Branches

Multi-lingual library. H. C. Campbell. il Wilson Lib Bul 38:68-9+ S '63
Toronto's historic collections; opening of new Boys and girls house. J. Thomson. Wilson Lib Bul 39:499 F '65

TORONTO stock exchange. See Stock exchange —Toronto
TORPEDO boats
PT boats make comeback as PTFs in navy. il Pop Sci 185:100-1 D '64
PT's ride again; excerpt from At close quarters. R. J. Bulkley, jr. il Motor B 112:28-31 Jl '63
TORPEDOES
Deep hunting; Mark-46 torpedo. il Time 85: 30 Ja 1 '65
Mk 45 ASTOR now in production at Westinghouse; underwater-to-underwater missile. il Miss & Roc 13:16-17 O 21 '63
Mark 46 ASW torpedo to be operational next summer; launch from aircraft, helicopters or surface ships. il Miss & Roc 15:15 D 21 '64
Stand-off weapon for Seahawk ships is sole big missile development seen. il Miss & Roc 15:65-9 S 21 '64
TORQUE converters
GM's new torque converter. R. Huntington. il Motor T 15:71+ D '63
TORQUE wrenches
Things to know about torque wrenches. il Pop Sci 185:78-9 Jl '64
Tighten the tiny ones too. T. Green. il Hot Rod 16:74-7 S '63
TORRANCE, E. Paul
Basic four in psychology. NEA J 54:15-17 Ja '65
TORRANCE, Thomas F.
Calvin and the knowledge of God. Christian Cent 81:696-9 My 27 '64
TORREJÓN Y VELASCO, Tomás de
First new-world opera. R. Stevenson. il Américas 16:33-5 Ja '64
TORRES, José
Fast hands and purple lights. E. Shrake. il por Sports Illus 21:30-1 D 7 '64
TORRES, Manuel
United States in 1850. Américas 16:1-8 F '64
TORREY, Owen C. jr
Sails. Yachting 115:46-7+ Ap '64
TORREY, Volta
Computerizings. Atlan 212:140-3 D '63
Dwarf to guide Apollo. Pop Mech 121:116-19+ F '64
TORSION balance
New twist for maps with old instrument. Sci N L 86:201 S 26 '64
TORT liability. See Liability (law)
TORTE. See Cake
TORTILLAS. See Cookery, Mexican
TORTOISES
Lichens on Galápagos giant tortoises. J. R. Hendrickson and W. A. Weber. Science 144:1463 Je 19 '64
TORTS
See also
Personal injuries
TORTURE
America's dirty war. C. Davidson. il Nation 199:299-303 N 2 '64; Discussion. 199:inside cover N 23 '64
TORY party (Great Britain) See Conservative party (Great Britain)
TOSCA; opera. See Puccini, G.
TOSCANINI, Arturo
Happy news on a tenth anniversary. Hi Fi 14:41 Ap '64
More vintage Toscanini. P. H. Reed. il Am Rec G 30:24-5 S '63
On records; overtures. C. J. Luten. Opera N 29:28 S 26 '64
This was Toscanini, by S. Antek. Review
Am Rec G pors 30:436-8 Ja '64. I. Kipnis
This was Toscanini; excerpts. S. Antek. por Opera N 28:26-7 N 16 '63
Toscanini and his Isolino. il pors Hi Fi 14: 56-7 Ap '64
Toscanini conducts overtures. C. J. Luten. por Am Rec G 30:660-1 Ap '64
TOSTADAS. See Cookery, Mexican
TOTALITARIANISM
Big bite. N. Mailer. Esquire 60:16+ Ag '63
Eichmann in Jerusalem, by H. Arendt. Review
New Repub 148:23-33 Je 15 '63. B. Bettelheim; Discussion. 148:29-31 Je 29; 149: 28-30 Jl 20 '63
God, guilt and Goldwater. W. Stringfellow. Christian Cent 81:1079-83 S 2 '64; Discussion. 81:1338-9 O 28 '64
Totalitarianism. W. Ebenstein. bibliog NEA J 53:59-62 Ap '64
TOTE bags. See Bags
TOTEM poles
How to read a totem pole. il Sunset 130:56 Je '63
Never underestimate an Indian village. C. Harris. il Horn Bk 39:156-61 Ap '63
Totem pole art. il Design 66:36-7 S '64
Totem poles: family trees. F. J. Dockstader. il Natur Hist 73:62-3 O '64
Try totem poles; cardboard mailing tube. F. M. Major. il Design 64:173 Mr '63
TOTH, John J.
School aid in Saskatchewan. America 110: 812 Je 13 '64
TOU, Julius T.
Information systems: learning, adaptation, and control. Science 141:1070+ S 13 '63
TOUAREGS. See Tuaregs
TOUCH
Finger sight for blind. D. F. Nolan. Sci N L 86:119 Ag 22 '64
Fingertip sight. il Newsweek 62:55 D 30 '63
Girl who's all eyes. W. Cloud. Pop Sci 183: 21 S '63
Midwestern woman sees colors through her fingertips. il Pop Mech 121:89 Ap '64
Seeing color with the fingers; dermo-optical perception. A. Rosenfeld. il Life 56:102-6+ Je 12 '64
Sees with fingers. E. Mirel. Sci N L 85:7 Ja 4 '64
Vision and touch: an experimentally created conflict between the two senses. I. Rock and J. Victor. Science 143:594-6 F 7 '64
Who says do not touch? J. K. Lagemann. Read Digest 84:125-8 Ja '64
Woman who tells color by touch; reprint. R. K. Plumb. il Sci Digest 55:5-7 Ap '64; Discussion. 56:4-5 Jl '64
TOUCH-me-nots
Impatiens for color in shade. W. Luten. il Pop Gard 14:36-7 My '63
Luminous color in the shade. il Sunset 131:179 Jl '63
Oliver's weed is a blooming wonder. il Sunset 132:270 Ap '64
TOUCH telephone. See Telephone, Push button
TOUCHSTONE, Joseph C. and others
Cortisol from human nerve. Science 141:1275 S 27 '63
TOUDOUZE, Anaïs
Fashion plates of Anaïs Toudouze. R. B. M. Askew. il Antiques 85:575-7 My '64
TOUGALOO Southern Christian college, Tougaloo, Miss.
Racists attack Tougaloo. Christian Cent 81:422 Ap 1 '64
TOUGE, N. A.
Guide write! Travel 120:50-2 O '63
TOUGH nut; story. See Moravia, A.
TOULOUSE, France

City planning

France's landmark in urban design. il Arch Forum 118:108-11 Je '63
TOULOUSE-LAUTREC, Maple, countess de
Tips. Pub W 186:44-5 N 30 '64
TOULOUSE-LAUTREC MONFA, Henri Marie Raymond de
Art galleries; centennial exhibition at Wildenstein. R. M. Coates. New Yorker 40: 127-8+ Mr 7 '64
Art; Wildenstein centennial exhibition. M. Kozloff. Nation 198:223-4 Mr 2 '64
Bizarre denizens of Lautrec's world. J. Canaday. il por N Y Times Mag p 14-15+ F 2 '64
Cover. il Am Artist 28:4 My '64
Lautrec, good show eh? what? Newsweek 63:74-5 F 10 '64
La plume de mon oncle. il Time 81:66 F 22 '63
Portraits of three painters. H. Kramer. il Reporter 31:35-6 D 17 '64
Toulouse-Lautrec paints a portrait. M. G. Dortu. il por Art N 62:24-7 F '64
Women in an artist's life. il pors Life 57: 82-8+ O 16 '64
TOUPEES. See Wigs
TOURÉ, Sékou
Guinea's first five years. D. Hapgood. bibliog f Cur Hist 45:355-60 D '63
Ugly American in dark Africa. W. D. Patterson. il por Sat R 46:18-20+ Je 22 '63
TOUREL, Jennie
Gist of Jennie. R. Jacobson. por Mus Am 83:32-3 Je '63
TOURGÉE, Albion W.
Birth of Jim Crow; Plessy v. Ferguson. C. V. Woodward. por Am Heritage 15:52-5+ Ap '64
TOURING. See Automobile touring
TOURING theatrical companies. See Theater—United States
TOURIST bureaus. See Information services
TOURIST trade
City succumbs to fair fever. il Bsns W p 120+ Mr 21 '64
Go now, stay later. H. Gough. il House B 106:76-9+ Ja '64
Going abroad? latest on costs and places to see. il U S News 56:54-60 Ap 27 '64

TOURIST trade—*Continued*
Look where you're going. M. Gough. il House B 105:132+ S '63
One export never leaves home. il Time 83: 86 Je 5 '64
Tourists, pawns, and pigeons; taxation of tourists. W. D. Patterson. Sat R 47:24+ Ag 15 '64
Vacation abroad, latest on where to go, what it costs. il U S News 54:78-84 Ap 22 '63
See also
Souvenirs
Travel—Economic aspects
Travel agencies

Alaska

Eskimos bounce high at Utkeagvik. il Sunset 130:58+ Mr '63

Bahama Islands

Travel notes. R. Joseph. Esquire 62:26+ O '64

Bali

Bedding down in Bali. Holiday 34:221 D '63

Bermuda

Bermuda's a place no one ever seems to forget. M. Gough. il House B 106:114+ Mr '64
On with the off-season. il Time 82:26 Ag 2 '63

Canada

Enchanting eastern Canada. il Bet Hom & Gard 41:107-10 Je '63

Caribbean Region

Caribbean tourist tips. K. Dunham. il Travel 121:50-3 F '64
Let's travel to the Caribbean. il Mlle 59:189-93 My '64
On with the off-season. il Time 82:26 Ag 2 '63

Europe, Western

In Europe, tourists beat the beaten paths. il Bsns W p32-3 My 25 '63
Let's travel: Europe, '64. Mlle 58:200-4 Mr '64
Let's travel to Europe. Mlle 56:106+ Mr '63
Mlle's European travel portfolio 1963. il Mlle 56:196-204 Mr '63
Now voyager, a little attention to ways and means. R. Joseph. il Esquire 61:60-5 F '64
Rush to out-of-the-way Europe. il Newsweek 61:68-71 Je 3 '63
Teen travel talk. il Seventeen 23:114 Ja '64
Tourism: it's more than just fun. il U S News 57:92 N 2 '64
Travel notes. R. Joseph. Esquire 61:16+ F '64
Where the action is in Europe. K. D. Fishman. il Mlle 58:189-99 Mr '64
Where the tourists went. il Time 84:96+ N 6 '64

France

Letter from Paris: Parisians on summer vacations. Genêt. New Yorker 39:59-60 Ag 17 '63
Lost art of civilized touring. S. Bedford. il Esquire 62:126-31+ N '64
Worm turns; tourists avoid travel in France. Newsweek 64:43+ S 7 '64

Great Britain

Shakespeare year. W. Houlton. il NEA J 53:60-2 F '64
See also
British travel and holiday association

Greece, Modern

Dream of marble, a symphony of light. R. Warner. il N Y Times Mag p78-9+ Ap 26 '64

Guatemala

Non-tourist industry. il Newsweek 65:38 F 1 '65

Hawaii

Hawaii, where progress is the big problem. il Sat Eve Post 236:24-9 F 2 '63
Outer islands are in. il Time 81:35 My 31 '63
Tourists from Tokyo. il Bsns W p29 F 22 '64

Ireland

Elegant life. R. Joseph. il Esquire 59:62-7 Ap '63
Gloamin', where and how to roam in it. Holiday 33:188 Ap '63
Isn't this a pleasant way to tour Ireland? U-drive caravan costs $45 a week plus oats. il Sunset 130:34-6 Mr '63
Shopping; an Irish eye for value. D. Guinness. Holiday 33:106+ Ap '63
Travel in Ireland. il Holiday 33:147-54 Ap '63
Travel notes: joy of living in Ireland. R. Joseph. Esquire 59:24+ Ap '63

Italy

Lost art of civilized touring. S. Bedford. il Esquire 62:126-31+ N '64

Jamaica

Jamaica's Old Boy with the new ideas. C. Amory. il Sat R 47:56-8 O 10 '64
Proclamation: whereby four commoners may abide in the homes of dukes, etc. R. Joseph. il Esquire 61:76-81 My '64

Japan

Fuji, the ever-changing mountain. L. Barry. il Pop Phot 54:24+ My '64
Travel notes. R. Joseph. Esquire 61:14+ Ja '64

Latin America

South America: travel's sleeping beauty. T. Moscoso. il Sat R 47:53-4+ O 10 '64

Mexico

Camera guide to Mexico. L. Barry. il Pop Phot 53:54+ N '63
Mexico city. il Sunset 131:42-57 Ag '63
Mexico's border towns. M. Ross. il Travel 120:32-4 N '63

Northern Ireland

Northern Ireland: industry hasn't destroyed its natural beauty. il Esquire 59:151-3 Ap '63

Panama

Lightning guide to Panama. R. Condon. Holiday 34:82-3 N '63

Russia

Next stop: inside Russia; latest in guided camera tours. M. A. Matzken. il Mod Phot 28:48+ F '64
Reddest tape. L. Tillett and A. Tillett. il Travel 121:33-5+ Ja '64
Travel in the Soviet Union. V. Louis and J. Louis. il Holiday 34:143-8 O '63

Spain

Going places, finding things along the Spanish coast. L. Rasponi. il House & Gard 123: 46-9+ Ap '63
Tourist boom in Spain: is it another Florida? il Bsns W p83 S 7 '63

Switzerland

Sportier tune for the yodel. il Bsns W p32-3 Ag 29 '64

Turkey

Thanksgiving for Turkey. R. Joseph. il Esquire 63:76-9 Ja '65

United States

Enjoying the Rockies. M. Frome. il Holiday 34:93-100 Ag '63
Families with children enjoy New Jersey vacations. il Parents Mag 38:156 My '63
How do we look to these foreign tourists? R. Littell. Read Digest 82:233-4+ Ap '63
How to make that family trip: by plane, train, bus, or car? S. A. Mix. il Todays Health 41:30-5+ F '63
Let's travel. Mlle 58:193-7+ Ap '64
Mississippi; down, around and upon it. Holiday 33:176 My '63
Redwood country. H. Papashvily. il Holiday 35:20+ Mr '64
Tourists from Tokyo. il Bsns W p28 F 22 '64
See also
United States—Travel service

TOURISTS. See Tourist trade; Travelers

TOURISTS and customs administration. See Customs service and tourists

TOURISTS bureaus. See Information services

TOURMALINES
Ferric tourmaline from Mexico. B. Mason and others. bibliog il Science 144:71-3 Ap 3 '64

TOURNAMENT of champions. See Golf—Tournaments

TOURNAMENT of roses. See Pasadena, Calif. —Parades

TOURNAMENTS
Charge, Sir Knight! Maryland state jousting tournament. S. James. il Pop Mech 121:120-1 Mr '64
When knighthood's flower wilted; excerpt from The knight and the umbrella. I. Anstruther. il Sports Illus 20:88-90+ My 18 '64
See also
Basketball tournaments
Bridge tournaments
Golf—Tournaments

TOURNIER, Paul
Person in a machine age. Christian Cent 81: 793-6 Je 17 '64

TOURNIQUETS
How to use a tourniquet. C. J. Potthoff. Todays Health 42:70 Ap '64

TOURS, Art. See Art tours

TOURS, European. See Europe, Western—Description and travel

TOURS, Garden. See Garden tours
TOURS, Industrial. See Industrial tours
TOURS, Package. See Travel
TOUSSAINT, Jeanne
Living legends. C. Beaton. il por Vogue 145:126-7+ Ja 1 '65
Mlle Toussaint, her extraordinary jewels, the animal kingdom she made famous. il por Vogue 143:112-13 Je '64
TOUSTER, Oscar
Biological control mechanisms; report of symposium sponsored by Medical sciences section at AAAS Philadelphia meeting. Science 139:926-8 Mr 8 '63
TOUSTER, Saul
Doorknob; Green apple: still life I; Green apple: still life II; Green apple: still life III; poems. Poetry 105:180-2 D '64
TOUVAL, Saadia
Somali Republic. bibliog f Cur Hist 46:156-62 Mr '64
TOVAR, Andrés Pardo-. See Pardo-Tovar, A.
TOVARICH; musical comedy. See Musical comedies, revues, etc.—Criticisms, plots, etc.
TOWBOATS. See Tugboats
TOWE, Kenneth M. and others
Invertebrate ferritin: occurrence in mollusca. bibliog Science 142:63-4 O 4 '63
TOWELS
Big news today is towels. il Am Home 66:34-5+ Je '63
Kitchen gifts: twice as useful in terry-towel wraps. il Good H 157:158 D '63
Monogramming R for bed and bath. il House & Gard 127:124-7 Ja '65
One person, one towel. Time 82:78 N 15 '63
TOWER, John G.
Excerpt from address, April 16, 1963. Cong Digest 42:175+ Je '63
Let's stop financing socialism in Latin America. Read Digest 84:121-4 Ja '64
Recipe for Republican victory. Nat R 15:570 D 31 '63
about
Know your rights. Nation 199:151 S 28 '64
TOWER, Whitney
Horse racing. See issues of Sports illustrated
Personal memory. Sports Illus 21:39 Jl 13 '64
about
Letter from the publisher. S. L. James. il por Sports Illus 20:6 Mr 9 '64
TOWER of London
Basketball and beefeaters. J. McPhee. New Yorker 39:186-90+ Mr 16 '63
TOWER of Pisa. See Pisa—Campanile (leaning tower)
TOWER trucks. See Motor trucks, Municipal
TOWERS
First tower at M.I.T. il Arch Rec 136:135-8 O '64
West Ireland has its own leaning tower; Round tower of Kilmacduagh. il Sunset 131:42 N '63
See also
Eiffel tower
Television towers
TOWING
How to get towed without getting took; automobile towing. E. D. Fales, jr. il Pop Sci 183:33-7+ Ag '63
1964 towing options. Motor T 15:30+ N '63
Technique of towing a trailer. il Changing T 18:15-16 Je '64
Your emergency road service chart; push and tow specifications chart. M. J. Schultz. Pop Mech 121:105 F '64
TOWING equipment. See Automobiles—Equipment
TOWN life. See City and town life
TOWN meeting
Town meeting; New England town meeting. Am City 78:154+ Je '63
TOWN names. See Names, Geographical
TOWN planning. See City planning
TOWNE, Anthony
Letter to Philemon; poem. Christian Cent 81:364 Mr 18 '64
TOWNES, Charles Hard
Maser man. il por Newsweek 64:89 N 9 '64
Nobel prize winners. por Sci N L 86:295 N 7 '64
Park-bench scientist, but. por Sci Digest 57:42-3 Ja '65
Research on maser-laser principle wins Nobel prize in physics. J. P. Gordon. por Science 146:897-9 N 13 '64
Split award. por Time 84:41 N 6 '64
TOWNS. See Cities and towns
TOWNSEND, Edward T.
Is there a crisis in the American trade-union movement? yes. Ann Am Acad 350:1-9 N '63
TOWNSEND, Francis Everett
Year of the old folks revolt. D. H. Bennett. il pors Am Heritage 16:48-51+ D '64
TOWNSEND, Lynn Alfred
Apostle of economic growth; address, November 1, 1963. Vital Speeches 30:111-14 D 1 '63
about
Common market for North America; address, February 20, 1964. Vital Speeches 30:381-4 Ap 1 '64
Chrysler makes its turn on to the road back. il por Bsns W p 116-18+ O 31 '64
Chrysler restyles top ranks. por Bsns W p32+ Ja 19 '63
TOWNSEND, Robert Chase
This executive has no secretary. T. J. Murray. il pors Duns R 84:49-50+ O '64
TOWNSEND, William Cameron
Apostle of the alphabet. il por Time 82:25 S 27 '63
TOWNSEND old age pension plan
Year of the old folks revolt; Old age revolving pension plan. D. H. Bennett. il Am Heritage 16:48-51+ D '64
TOWNSEND towers, Dearborn, Mich. See Aged —Housing
TOWNSHIP planning. See Regional planning
TOXICOLOGY. See Poisons
TOXINS and antitoxins
Atrophy of skeletal muscle in chick embryos treated with botulinum toxin. D. B. Drachman. bibliog il Science 145:719-21 Ag 14 '64
Bacterial endotoxins. A. I. Braude. il Sci Am 210:36-45 bibliog(p 152) Mr '64
Calotropin, a cytotoxic principle isolated from asclepias curassavica L. S. M. Kupchan and others. bibliog il Science 146:1685-6 D 25 '64
Diphtheria antitoxin: antigen-combining and toxin-neutralizing properties of papain fragments. J. J. Cohen and others. bibliog il Science 144:1585-6 Je 26 '64
Formula of fugu: Japanese puffer fish. il Time 85:44 Ja 29 '65
Identity of tarichatoxin and tetrodotoxin. H. D. Buchwald and others. bibliog il Science 143:474-5 Ja 31 '64; Discussion. 144:319; 145:72 Ap 17, Jl 3 '64
Interferon-like viral inhibitor in rabbits after intravenous administration of endotoxin. M. Ho. bibliog il Science 146:1472-4 D 11 '64
Nicotinic acid analogs: effects on response of chick embryos and hens to organophosphate toxicants. J. C. Roger and others. bibliog Science 144:539-40 My 1 '64
Ostracitoxin: an ichthyotoxic stress secretion of the boxfish, ostracion lentiginosus. D. A. Thomson. bibliog Science 146:244-5 O 9 '64
Plague toxin: its effect in vitro and in vivo. J. H. Rust, jr. and others. bibliog il Science 142:408-9 O 18 '63
Selective rat toxicant. A. P. Roszkowski and others. bibliog il Science 144:412-13 Ap 24 '64
Tarichatoxin: isolation and purification. M. S. Brown and H. S. Mosher. bibliog Science 140:295-6 Ap 19 '63
Tarichatoxin tetrodotoxin: a potent neurotoxin. H. S. Mosher and others. bibliog il Science 144:1100-10 My 29 '64
Toxic lysolipoid: isolation from pseudomonas pseudomallei. M. S. Redfearn. bibliog il Science 146:648-9 O 30 '64
Toxin from aspergillus flavus: production on food materials of a substance causing tremors in mice. B. J. Wilson and C. H. Wilson. bibliog Science 144:177-8 Ap 10 '64
See also
Antigens and antibodies
Tetanus antitoxin
TOY automobiles. See Automobiles, Toy
TOY industry
Christmas and Freud. D. Moller. il Sat Eve Post 236:38 D 7 '63
Gifts for gifted children: Center for the gifted child, inc. il Bsns W p 182 N 16 '63
Toys more like toys. il Bsns W p31 S 28 '63
Toys of the year (cont) il Pop Mech 120:98-102 N '63
Toys: something for the girls. il Newsweek 61:90-1 Mr 25 '63
Visions of dollars dance in their heads. Time 83:88 Mr 20 '64
See also
Fisher-Price toys
Mattel, incorporated
Securities
Playing the toys. Fortune 68:250 N '63

TOY railroads. See Railroads, Toy
TOY scout jamboree; drama. See Miller, H. L.
TOY soldiers
Down to size; new line of inch-high plastic Arab soldiers. Newsweek 63:36 My 4 '64
Miniature warriors make fighting fun; reprint. il Hobbies 69:122-4 S '64
See also
Military miniatures
TOY tinkers division. See Spalding, A. G. and brothers, incorporated
TOY trains. See Railroads, Toy
TOYE, Francis
Serious Rossini. Opera N 27:8-12 Mr 9 '63
Two hours before sunset; interview, ed. by K. F. Reuling. por Opera N 29:26-9 Ja 23 '65
Obituary
Opera N il por 29:26-9 Ja 23 '65
TOYNBEE, Arnold Joseph
Africa: birth of a continent. Sat R 47:27-9+ D 5 '64
Again nationalism threatens. N Y Times Mag p23+ N 3 '63
As a famed historian sees the world of the future; interview, ed. by J. Fromm. pors U S News 56:78-82 Mr 30 '64
Churchill, progress of a slow grower. N Y Times Mag p40-2+ N 1 '64
Conditions of survival. Sat R 47:24-6+ Ag 29 '64
Is a race war shaping up? N Y Times Mag p26+ S 29 '63
It is one world or no world. N Y Times Mag p 28+ Ap 5 '64
Why I dislike western civilization. N Y Times Mag p 15+ My 10 '64

about

Food and Prof. Toynbee; World food congress. America 108:875 Je 22 '63
Toynbee dilemma. M. W. Hess. Christian Cent 81:8-9 Ja 1 '64
TOYOTA motor company. See Automobile industry and trade—Japan
TOYS
Animal toys, make them from rope. il Farm J 87:92 N '63
Building a set of children's blocks and a container to house them. G. Lacy. il Design 66:33-6 N '64
Christmas machine. il Sunset 131:68-71 D '63
Christmas shoppers' science list. F. Snakenberg. il Sci N L 84:298-9 N 9 '63
Christmas shopping for next Christmas. il Bsns W p40-1 N 7 '64
Dear Santa. il Suc Farm 61:44-5 D '63
Electric cannon fires BBs. R. L. Clough, jr. il Pop Mech 120:162-3 N '63
For Christmas, science inspires new toys. B. H. Frisch. il Sci Digest 56:38-46 D '64
Frankenstein founds a vast new industry; monsters are becoming big business. T. Thompson. il Life 57:58-9 Ag 21 '64
Ghoul tools; plastic model monsters. il Newsweek 63:62 Je 1 '64
Gifts for gifted children. il Bsns W p 182 N 16 '63
Good toys are more than playthings. E. M. McCabe. il Parents Mag 39:50+ F '64
Guide to play and playthings. R. M. Goldenson. il Parents Mag 39:62-3+ O '64
High cost of playing: way to deal with toys that don't last. C. R. Kimble. il Redbook 124:10+ Ja '65
Innocent merriment that would charm a laugh from Scrooge; exhibits at the Museum of contemporary crafts in New York city. il House & Gard 126:138-9 D '64
Inventing toys is no mere child's play. il Bsns W p40-1+ D 21 '63
Lionel's flyer; hovering spaceship. il Newsweek 63:88 Mr 23 '64
Little digger; toy power shovel. R. Anderson. il Pop Mech 119:144-7 F '63
Memoirs of a hungry mechanical basset; Gaylord the Pup. il Consumer Rep 28:262-3 Je '63
Merry-go-spin. H. Sibley. il Pop Mech 119:144 Je '63
Monsters invade the toy market. il Ebony 20:152-4+ D '64
Monstrous Christmas to all. E. Merriam. il Nation 199:463-4 D 14 '64
New breed of toys; science and math toys. il Time 84:90 D 4 '64
New toys that will dismay Santa's helpers; stuffed toys. il Sat Eve Post 236:30-7 D 7 '63
On and off the avenue (cont) New Yorker 39:158+ D 7 '63; 40:204+ D 12 '64
Psychologist's view: children and toys. J. Star. il Look 27:107-14 D 17 '63
Quick-change cardboard play mounts. M. H. Slutz. il Pop Mech 119:149 Ap '63
Rag doll legislation; concern about the innards of stuffed toys, California. Consumer Rep 28:509-10 N '63
Raggedy Ann: still flouncy at fifty. il Life 57:4 D 18 '64
Railroading right at home; sitting, climbing, and rocking toy. il Sunset 133:126 O '64
Real-world toys. il Life 55:121-4 N 22 '63
Return of the monsters. il Look 28:46-7 S 8 '64
Shopping guide to educational toys. il Good H 157:169-71 D '63
Stableful of Christmas ponies. il Sunset 133:75-6+ D '64
Sturdy toys and play furniture. il Sunset 133:66-7 D '64
Teeter-go-round. B. Gilmore. il Farm J 88:51 N '64
Ticking away; childhood tensions and traumas. il Newsweek 63:68-9 Mr 23 '64
Tinkertoy, a wonderful wooden Christmas toy. J. Martineau. il Am For 70:30-1+ D '64
Toy fair, 1963: merchandise for booksellers. il Pub W 183:20-9 Ap 1 '63
Toy that won't die; Tinkertoy. il Bsns W p 134-6+ S 12 '64
Toyland, 1963: from monkeys to mouse traps; $1.2 billion. il Newsweek 62:66-7 D 23 '63
Toys and boys and Christmas. W. H. Honan. New Repub 149:7-8 D 21 '63
Toys are for playing. J. W. Levin. il N Y Times Mag p 105-6 D 1 '63
Toys for Christmas. il Consumer Bul 46:18-22 D '63
Toys for the young scientist or engineer. il Consumer Bul 47:13-15 N; 43+ D '64
Toys in the gallery; exhibition at Manhattan's Betty Parsons gallery. il Time 82:60 D 20 '63
Toys made of towels. il Design 65:110-12 Ja '64
Toys that kids like. P. L. Levin. il N Y Times Mag p89-90 D 6 '64
Treats from toyland. il House & Gard 124:246-7 N '63
What toys mean to children. B. Spock. il Redbook 122:46-7+ D '63
Why some toys must be assembled. Good H 157:175 D '63
William Accorsi's toy sculpture. il Craft Horiz 23:24-5 N '63
See also
Christmas gifts for children
Doll houses
Mattel, incorporated
Tops
Toy industry
Toy soldiers

Exhibitions

Super toy fair; exhibition at the Museum of contemporary crafts. B. Plumb. il N Y Times Mag p 144-5+ N 15 '64

Safety devices and measures

Chemistry sets are fun, keep them safe! il Good H 157:175 D '63
Tips for your home and family. E. Maxwell. Todays Health 42:61-2 D '64

Storage

Build a bright refuge for the animal kingdom. il House & Gard 124:146-7 D '63

Testing

Choose children's toys with eye to safety. Sci N L 84:376 D 14 '63
Toys of the year (cont) il Pop Mech 120:98-102 N '63
TOYS, Electric. See Electric toys
TOZER, Eliot
Hook-and-ladder helicopters. Pop Sci 184:114-16 F '64
TOZZI, Giorgio
Three American tsars. A. M. Lingg. por Opera N 27:25-7 Ap 6 '63
TRACE elements
Geology and trace elements: relation to nutrition; report on symposium at the annual meeting of the Geological society of America. H. L. Cannon. Science 143:704+ F 14 '64
TRACERS, Radioactive. See Radioactive tracers
TRACHOMA
Trachoma. G. H. Werner and others. il Sci Am 210:79-84+ Ja '64
Trachoma and inclusion conjunctivitis agents: adaptation to hela cell cultures. Y. Mitsui and others. bibliog il Science 145:715-16 Ag 14 '64

TRACHOMA virus
Trachoma. G. H. Werner and others. il Sci Am 210:79-84+ Ja '64
Trachoma agent: glucose utilization by purified suspensions. R. A. Ormsbee and E. Weiss. bibliog il Science 142:1077-8 N 22 '63
TRACHTENBERG, Alan
Technology, education, and human values. Sch & Soc 92:316-18 O 31 '64
TRACHTENBERG, Jakow
Any boy can be a computer; Trachtenberg speed system. il por Life 54:53-4 My 17 '63
TRACK athletes. See Athletes
TRACK athletics
All aboard for Tokyo. il Time 84:58 S 25 '64
America first; U.S.-Soviet track meet in Los Angeles. il Newsweek 64:66 Ag 10 '64
At last the girls are ours; women's Olympic track and field team. T. C. Brody. il Sports Illus 21:68-9 Ag 17 '64
Class wins over mass at Albuquerque; national collegiate track and field championships. T. Maule. Sports Illus 18:46-7 Je 24 '63
Din, the color, the mood of indoor track; reproductions of paintings. J. Martin. Sports Illus 20:34-9 F 24 '64
Favorites in Tokyo 1964. Sports Illus 21:64-9 O 5 '64
Flag flies high in Tokyo. il Life 57:82-4+ O 30 '64
Flying start for the U.S.S.R. G. S. Brown. il Sports Illus 18:18-21 F 11 '63
Girls' track coach in Hawaii. il Ebony 18: 53-4+ Mr '63
Joyful theme at the AAU: younger, higher and faster. G. S. Brown. il Sports Illus 21: 22-5 Jl 6 '64
Junior sports jamboree. F. Duis. Recreation 57:359+ S '64
Kansas boy with a man-size task; 135 athletes compete for sixty positions on the U.S. Olympic track and field team. T. O'Leary. il Sports Illus 21:46-50+ S 14 '64
Life guide; Olympic hopefuls and where to see them. il Life 56:17 F 21 '64
Look! another record. il Time 81:50 F 22 '63
Meal at Moscow. il Time 82:52-3 Ag 2 '63
New upsurge in women's track. il Ebony 18:115-16+ Je '63
Now if O'Hara really tries; fastest indoor mile. T. C. Brody. il Sports Illus 20:68-9 Mr 16 '64
Old sport, new boom; photographs by Neil Leifer. Sat Eve Post 236:76-7 Ap 20 '63
Our lackadaisical girls take a Soviet shellacking; meet in Moscow. il Life 55:26-26A Ag 2 '63
Our Olympic chances; interview, ed. by H. L. Masin. R. Johnson. Sr Schol 85:54 O 7 '64
Outrunning the Russians on winged feet; with report by G. Korobkov. il Life 57:20-7 Ag 7 '64
Raves for the young; US vs USSR track meet in Los Angeles. J. Underwood. il Sports Illus 21:8-13 Ag 3 '64
Red track; meet at Moscow's Lenin stadium. il Newsweek 62:69 Ag 5 '63
Slight blow for extremism in sport's cold war; U.S. vs Russia in Los Angeles. D. Bank. il Sports Illus 21:46-7 Jl 27 '64
They came out in gale force. J. Underwood. il Sports Illus 20:36+ My 4 '64
They could be good if they tried; U.S. track team in Moscow. I. Shenker. il Sports Illus 19:18-19+ Jl 29 '63
To Tokyo by inches; U.S. Olympic track and field team. J. Underwood. il Sports Illus 21:18-21 S 21 '64
Track and field development. J. B. Sharpless. il Recreation 57:230-1 My '64
Track (title varies) See issues of Sports illustrated
Who buried whom; defeat of Russians by U.S. men's and women's teams. il Time 84:45-6 Ag 7 '64
Why can't we beat this girl? photographs of European track stars by N. Leifer. Sports Illus 19:54-7 S 30 '63
Year of hope and devil-take-the-hindmost: indoor track season. G. S. Brown. il Sports Illus 22:52-4 Ja 18 '65
See also
Hurdle racing
Jumping
Running
Shot putting
Vaulting (sport)
Weight throwing
TRACKING and trailing
Make like an Indian. S. E. Brock. il Outdoor Life 133:40-3+ Je '64
More sensible way to hunt; stalking. C. W. Thayer. il Sports Illus 19:68-72+ O 28 '63
Smart dogs keep on the right track. V. Kraft. il Sports Illus 18:99-100+ Ap 8 '63
Sport of stalking. J. O'Connor. il Outdoor Life 132:52-5+ O '63
What whitetails taught me; stalking of deer. D. M. Lance. il Outdoor Life 134:30-1+ N '64
TRACTOR engines
Increased power for older tractors. M. E. Long. Suc Farm 62:80 Ja '64
Machinery maintenance saves dollars. F. N. Reece. il Suc Farm 62:54-5 Ja '64
Power take-off or separate engine? Suc Farm 62:62 Ja '64
Cooling
Tractor cooling system pointers. Suc Farm 62:84 Ja '64
Fuel
Select the right fuel. W. J. Fletcher. il Suc Farm 62:73 Ja '64
Which diesel fuel for you? Suc Farm 61:118 Ap '63
See also
Automotive fuel
TRACTOR industry and trade
Offbeat market lures farm tractor markets. il Bsns W p98+ Mr 16 '63
See also
Caterpillar tractor company
TRACTOR tires. See Tires, Tractor
TRACTORS
Backyard bulldozer. A. Maher. il Pop Mech 121:114-15 F '64
Buy, lease, or hire it done? machinery tax management. J. D. Keast. Farm J 88:22+ F '64
Garden tractors. R. L. Hering. il Pop Gard 16:40-3 F '65
Gentle bulldozers of Peoria. G. Cross. il Fortune 68:166-71+ Jl '63
It took a tractor to turn my gardening chores into a joy ride. E. McHutchison. il Flower Grower 51:30-1 F '64
Let's plow on the level. J. B. Liljedahl. il Suc Farm 62:49 Ap '64
New garden tractors: more heft, more hustle. P. Geraci. il Pop Sci 184:129-33 Ap '64
Small equipment for big farms; garden tractors. W. J. Fletcher. il Suc Farm 63:66 Ja '65
Swivel-hipped tractor. J. M. Liston. il Pop Sci 184:141-5 Mr '64
Teach your son tractor safety. R. G. Pfister. il Suc Farm 62:92 Mr '64
Tractor comfort. Suc Farm 62:76 Ja '64
Trailer for yard tracs. H. Adams. il Pop Mech 119:156-8 My '63
What's new at the hardware show; garden tractors. J. Hand. il Pop Sci 183:30+ D '63
Care
Cut machinery costs! W. J. Fletcher. il Suc Farm 61:67+ Mr '63
Safety devices and measures
New emblem may save your life. K. A. Harkness. il Suc Farm 61:9 Jl '63
Trailers
See Trailers
Transmission
How useful are four-wheel drives? W. J. Fletcher. il Suc Farm 61:92+ My '63
Power take-off or separate engine? Suc Farm 62:62 Ja '64
TRACTORS, Municipal
Better paving procedure; Greenville, S.C. R. H. Cureton. il Am City 79:93 Je '64
Low bid, generally not the best; Los Angeles, Calif. W. L. Lintz. il Am City 79:115-16 Mr '64
Rubber-tired loader reduces noise; Pasadena, Calif. C. O'Connor. il Am City 78:100-1 Ag '63
TRACTORS-for-freedom. See Prisoners of war in Cuba
TRACY, Berry B.
Late classical styles in American silver, 1810-1830. Antiques 86:702-6 D '64
TRACY, Dwight
Partridge are honest birds. Outdoor Life 134: 56-9+ O '64
TRACY, Honor
Flake of Spain; excerpt from Spanish notebook. Vogue 143:124+ Je '64
Hay de todo in the Prado; excerpt from Spanish leaves. Horizon 6:42-5 Autumn '64
In a Spanish village; excerpts from Spanish notebook. Holiday 35:56-7+ My '64
Words, words, words. New Repub 148:22-3 Mr 16 '63
TRACY, Robert Emmet, bp
Has the council lost its steam? America 110: 162-4 F 1 '64

TRADE. See Business; Commerce

TRADE agreements

After the strike: time for reflection; with editorial comment. il Bsns W p72, 108 Ap 6 '63
ALPA adopts diplomatic bargaining. J. R. Ashlock. Aviation W 79:49 S 23 '63
ALPA may reject pact with American. J. R. Ashlock. Aviation W 78:42 F 25 '63
All right then, let's nationalize the RR's. Nat R 16:344-5 My 5 '64
All right, Walter; UAW's Ford settlement. Newsweek 64:80-1 S 28 '64
Built-in pay raises: what they mean for '64. il U S News 56:65-6 Ja 6 '64
Coal contract: what's in it; United mine workers union. U S News 56:90 Ap 6 '64
Coal miners and the new coal contract. Mo Labor R 87:III-IV My '64
Collective bargaining contracts in India. il Mo Labor R 86:300-1 Mr '63
Contracts a la mode; U.A.W. obtains concessions. il Time 84:87 S 25 '64
Costly settlement; New York's newspaper strike. il Time 81:67 Mr 15 '63
Deferred increases due in 1965 and wage escalation. G. Ruben. il Mo Labor R 87:1381-4 D '64
Developments in industrial relations. See issues of Monthly labor review
Developments in manufacturing industries. R. W. Benny. il Mo Labor R 87:1401-7 D '64
Developments under major agreements. G. Ruben. il Mo Labor R 87:1-10 Ja '64
Developments under major agreements. il Mo Labor R 87:1393-400 D '64
Grassroots militance in steel; model labor pact threatened. Bsns W p 118+ Ag 22 '64
High court ruling opens way for showdown in rules dispute; between carriers and operating brotherhoods. Bsns W p 104 Mr 9 '63
Huh! Hoffa's demands for nationwide labor contract. Newsweek 62:87-8 N 18 '63
In steel: no strike, longer vacations, longer contracts. il U S News 54:86 Je 24 '63
Labor month in review; steel settlement. Mo Labor R 86:III-IV Jl '63
Landmark in labor relations; Kaiser-United steelworkers agreement. H. Malmgren. New Repub 148:7 Mr 16 '63
LBJ brand on the bargaining table; success in rail settlement; with editorial comment. Bsns W p89-91, 124 My 2 '64
Major agreement expirations and reopenings in 1964-1965. C. T. Ward. il Mo Labor R 86:1383-93; 87:1371-80 D '63, D '64
Managing your manpower. T. R. Brooks. Duns R 83:55-6+ Ap '64
Managing your manpower; new labor-management difficulty in rank-and-file upsets. T. R. Brooks. Duns R 81:101 My '63
Mayor smiled; settlement of New York newspaper strike. il Newsweek 61:62 Mr 18 '63
More power to you, Jimmy. Nat R 15:425+ N 19 '63
Nationwide strike averted. Sr Schol 84:21 My 8 '64
New-style contract in steel; meaning for other industries. il U S News 55:77 Jl 1 '63
N.Y. printers contract plans to halt discrimination. Pub W 184:21-2 D 9 '63
Pattern for truckers; trucking industry's new contract. Bsns W p 105-6+ Ja 25 '64
Peace at a price; Chrysler pact with UAW; with editorial comment. il Bsns W p27-9, 204 S 12 '64
Railroad settlement. Time 83:19 My 1 '64
Satisfactory steel settlement. il Time 81:74 Je 28 '63
Settlement in steel. T. R. Brooks. Commonweal 78:449-52 Jl 26 '63
Steel settles. Bsns W p23 Je 22 '63
Timing contracts. T. R. Brooks. Duns R 84:60+ N '64
Trains keep running; settlement of the 4½-year-old featherbedding dispute. Bsns W p29 Ap 25 '64
Union contracts: a new series of studies. J. W. Bloch. Mo Labor R 87:1184-5 O '64
Unions and automation: truce on the West coast. B. Bliven. il Reporter 29:35-8 N 7 '63
UAW breaches the bargaining guidelines. T. R. Brooks. Duns R 84:45 D '64
Wage and employment guarantees in major agreements. A. H. Anderson. il Mo Labor R 87:1287-90 N '64
Wage chronology: American viscose division, FMC corp; 1959-63. il Mo Labor R 86:1302-6 N '63
When Hoffa gets the power he wants; demand for a contract between trucking industry and teamsters union. il U S News 55:121 N 18 '63
Who won what in the rail dispute; How a five-year-old fight settled in thirteen days. il U S News 56:76-7 My 4 '64
Why Wichita said no; rejection of new contract between the Boeing co. and the International assn. of machinists. il Bsns W p 106 Ap 27 '63
Workers vote on final Boeing proposal. Aviation W 78:29 Ap 1 '63

TRADE associations

Single voice speaks for French business Bsns W p 116 D 5 '64
Trade associations and how they grew. L. L. L. Golden. Sat R 47:64 Je 13 '64
When you speak for the trade. I. S. Kogan. Sat R 46:52-3 F 9 '63; Discussion. 46:64 Mr 9; 78 Ap 13; 55 My 11 '63

TRADE balance. See Balance of payments

TRADE catalogs. See Catalogs, Trade

TRADE discount. See Discount, Trade

TRADE exhibits, Publishers. See Book exhibits

TRADE expansion act. See Tariff—United States; United States—Commerce

TRADE fairs. See Exhibitions

TRADE journals

Miracle on Twelfth street; Fairchild newspapers. W. Sullivan. il Sat R 47:48-9+ F 8 '64
Writing for trade magazines. D. D. Dreis. Writer 77:25-6 N '64

TRADE marks

For Humble: Esso or Enco? Bsns W p64 Jl 20 '63
Macabre trademarks. Newsweek 62:29 Jl 1 '63
Story behind. . . See issues of Changing times
Trade marks of M. Peter Piening. L. Schmeckebier. il Am Artist 29:52-7 Ja '65

TRADE names

Battle of the brands. L. Morse. il Duns R 83:53-4+ My '64
Sales & distribution: avoiding brand-name conflicts. T. J. Murray. Duns R 85:61-2 Ja '65
Story behind. . . See issues of Changing times
Women flunk identity test; of branded products. Bsns W p50+ Ap 6 '63

TRADE practices

Back scratching deals raise antitrust ire; reciprocity practices. il Bsns W p45-6 F 9 '63

TRADE regulation

See also

Export controls
Marks of origin

TRADE relations

Rise of the trade relations director. V. A. Adams. il Duns R 84:35-6+ D '64

TRADE school libraries. See High school libraries

TRADE schools

Technical schools, key to opportunity; post high school education. il Changing T 17:31-3 O '63

TRADE secrets

Annals of business; trade secrets in development of space suits issue in Goodrich vs D. W. Wohlgemuth case. J. Brooks. New Yorker 39:37-8+ Ja 11 '64
Back to the guild? il Newsweek 61:62 Je 3 '63
Legal hurdle for job-hoppers. Bsns W p95 Je 1 '63
Savants, sandwiches, and space suits. J. H. Munster, jr. and J. C. Smith. Science 145:1276-81 S 18 '64; Discussion. 146:865, 1636-7 N 13, D 25 '64
They've got a secret. il Time 81:87-8+ F 22 '63
When walls have ears, call a debugging man; business counter-espionage experts use electronic listening devices. il Bsns W p 154+ O 31 '64
Who owns what's in your head? W. Bowen. il Fortune 70:175-8+ Jl '64
Who stole the formula? J. Kobler. il Sat Eve Post 236:82+ Je 29 '63

TRADE shows. See Exhibitions

TRADE union banks. See Banks and banking, Trade union

TRADE union congress. See Trades union congress

TRADE unions

See also

Collective bargaining
Industrial relations
Libraries—Work with trade unions
Open and closed shop
Picketing
Strikes

Benefit funds

High finance worries the union top brass; investing union funds. il Bsns W p 120+ N 9 '63

TRADE unions—*Continued*

Bibliography

Labor looks back to see its future. Bsns W p52+ N 21 '64

Constitutions

Union disciplinary powers and procedures. bibliog f il Mo Labor R 86:125-32, 255-61, 378-84, 491-6 F-My '63

Dues, fees, etc.

For unions: new power over members; rulings on fines. il U S News 56:103 F 17 '64

Educational work

Cultural activities of West European organized labor. K. Braun. Mo Labor R 86:370-7 Ap '63

Elections

Democracy's way at the ITU; printers' latest election campaign. Bsns W p78+ Je 6 '64
Managing your manpower; employers' rights in union elections. T. R. Brooks. Duns R 82:81 O '63
Miners gear for double trouble. Bsns W p67 D 5 '64
Miners want the vote. Bsns W p 152+ S 19 '64
Political row perils steel peace. il Bsns W p45-6 N 14 '64
Power struggle alters USW's political course; D. McDonald vs. I. W. Abel. il Bsns W p78+ D 26 '64
Union chiefs face double trouble. il Bsns W p99 D 12 '64
Union elections of officers; report to ABA meeting. Mo Labor R 87:1177-9 O '64
Union leaders face growing revolt. Bsns W p54+ O 3 '64

Finance

Freewheeling finances of the teamsters union. il Duns R 83:48+ Ja '64
Hoffa's newest enemy: a law's fine print; Landrum-Griffin act. Bsns W p47-8+ Ap 4 '64
How a big union handles money; United mine workers. U S News 54:94 My 6 '63
How unions handle their money. il U S News 54:98-100 My 27 '63
Labor's controversial $6 billion. T. O'Hanlon. il Duns R 83:47+ Ja '64
More union money for housing; government-guaranteed mortgage. Bsns W p 102 F 29 '64
New investment plan for unions. U S News 56:91 Mr 9 '64
Pinch on union treasuries. il Bsns W p 148+ S 19 '64
When a big union gets into big business; banks and insurance business of Amalgamated clothing workers of America. il U S News 56:91-3 My 18 '64
Will pension trial bring Hoffa's ouster? Bsns W p53-4 Ap 25 '64

History

Historical relationship of liberals and intellectuals to organized labor in the United States. M. F. Neufeld. bibliog Ann Am Acad 350:115-28 N '63

International aspects

Agony of success; address, November 14, 1963. H. Cleveland. Dept State Bul 39:845-50 D 2 '63
Aid abroad from U.S. unions; program of housing developments in Latin America. il U S News 57:110 N 30 '64
Anglo-American trade union conference. Mo Labor R 87:925-7 Ag '64
Labor: a partner in American foreign policy? J. P. Windmuller. Ann Am Acad 350:104-14 N '63
Meddling in Latin America. S. Meisler. il Nation 198:133-8 F 10 '64; Reply. C. Jagan. 198:516 My 25 '64

Investments

High finance worries the union top brass; investing union funds. il Bsns W p 120+ N 9 '63
Marina City. J. M. Liston. il Pop Sci 182:82-5+ Ap '63
Union support of towers toppling. il Bsns W p 108 My 16 '64

Jurisdictional disputes

Transportation's labor crisis. E. B. Shils. bibliog f Harvard Bsns R 42:84-98 My '64
Who does what? at Esso's Fawley refinery in England. T. R. Brooks. Duns R 82:84+ O '63

Law

See Labor laws and legislation—United States

Management

AFL-CIO: a confederation or federation? which road for the future? A. H. Raskin. Ann Am Acad 350:36-45 N '63
Dilemma of union democracy. E. Stein. bibliog f Ann Am Acad 350:46-54 N '63
Eggheads are leaving unions. il Nations Bsns 51:34-5+ S '63
Is there a crisis in the American trade-union movement? yes. E. T. Townsend. Ann Am Acad 350:1-9 N '63
Managing your manpower; J. Hoffa's leverage technique. T. R. Brooks. Duns R 83:61-4 F '64
Road to the future: a trade-union commission for self-analysis. S. Barkin. Ann Am Acad 350:138-47 N '63
USW simmers as steal talks near. il Bsns W p47-8 N 21 '64

Membership

American trade union membership in 1962. H. J. Neary. il Mo Labor R 87:501-7 My '64
Challenge facing British unions. W. E. J. McCarthy. bibliog f Ann Am Acad 350:129-37 N '63
Downward trend of union rolls. U S News 55:107 D 16 '63
Is there a crisis in the American trade-union movement? yes. E. T. Townsend. Ann Am Acad 350:1-9 N '63
Labor month in review; decline in union membership. Mo Labor R 86:III-IV N '63
Managing your manpower; white collar employees. T. R. Brooks. Duns R 82:74A D '63
Organizing the old folks; RWDSU's retired members. B. Carter. Reporter 30:31-2 Mr 12 '64
Outlook for union growth. J. Shister. bibliog f Ann Am Acad 350:55-62 N '63
Prospects for organization of white-collar workers; engineering unions. J. W. Kuhn. Mo Labor R 87:129-31 F '64
Race and labor: Bronx plumbers' dispute. Commonweal 80:281-2 My 29 '64
Union membership up. T. R. Brooks. Duns R 84:49-50+ S '64
Union program for eliminating discrimination. Mo Labor R 86:58-9 Ja '63
Unionism as a social choice: the engineers' case. B. Goldstein and B. P. Indik. bibliog f il Mo Labor R 86:365-9 Ap '63
White collar unions abroad. T. R. Brooks. Duns R 83:64+ F '64

Negro membership

Better day for brother Randolph. T. R. Brooks. Reporter 29:23 D 5 '63
Black men, white unions. E. Dunbar. il Look 27:43-4+ D 17 '63
Civil rights; discrimination in labor unions; address, May 12, 1964. W. M. Young, jr. Vital Speeches 30:535-7 Je 15 '64
Civil rights: the law and the unions. A. H. Raskin. il Reporter 31:23-8 S 10 '64
Discrimination, unions and Title VII. G. R. Blakey. America 111:210-12 Ag 29 '64
Ethnic and economic minorities: unions' future or unrecruitable? R. Marshall. bibliog f Ann Am Acad 350:63-73 N '63
Meany heads bias fight. Bsns W p78+ Jl 27 '63
NLRB cracks down on union bias; failure to process a Negro's grievance of Hughes tool co, Houston. Bsns W p50 Jl 11 '64
Plumbers dispute opens long, hot summer. il Arch Forum 120:5+ Je '64
Right to a job. il Newsweek 62:51-2 Ag 5 '63
Unions feel growing pressure to take more Negroes. il U S News 56:86+ My 25 '64
See also
Negro American labor council

Officials

Actors' new boss; F. O'Neal of Actors' equity assn. il Ebony 19:58-60+ Je '64
Can they find courage to fight? teamster leaders against Hoffa. il Bsns W p28-9 Mr 14 '64
Dilemma of union democracy. E. Stein. bibliog f Ann Am Acad 350:46-54 N '63
Eggheads are leaving unions. il Nations Bsns 51:34-5+ S '63
Is there a crisis in the American trade-union movement? the trade unionists' views; survey of thirty-eight union presidents. S. Barkin and A. A. Blum. il Ann Am Acad 350:16-24 N '63
Johnson gives labor the word; union chiefs at White House. il Bsns W p25-6 My 9 '64
Labor unions are worth the price. M. Ways. il Fortune 67:108-13+ My '63; Discussion. 67:20 Je '63

TRADE unions—Officials—*Continued*
Labor's controversial $6 billion. T. O'Hanlon. il Duns R 83:47+ Ja '64
Labor's power to destroy. Duns R 81:25 Mr '63
Leadership factor in union growth; excerpts from address. J. Barbash. Mo Labor R 86: 133-6 F '63
Meet tomorrow's union leaders. il Nations Bsns 52:38-9+ Jl '64
Men who speak for UAW. il Bsns W p43-4+ Je 20 '64

Political activities

AFL-CIO aid for Democrats. U S News 57:84 S 14 '64
As labor sees LBJ now; AFL-CIO goals. U S News 58:90-1 Ja 25 '65
Before assassination: a union's poll. U S News 56:89 F 10 '64
Blow at unions' political power? U S News 54:101 My 27 '63
Corporation, the employee, and politics; presidents' panel report. G. R. Rosen. il Duns R 84:38-40+ Jl '64
Disappointed over Kennedy; AFL-CIO disenchantment. Bsns W p46 Mr 2 '63
Hoffa's voice on Capitol hill; S. Zagri. il Bsns W p45-6+ S 14 '63
How unions stand with Johnson now. U S News 57:101-3 N 16 '64
If Barry goes to White House: what labor can expect. U S News 57:76-7 Jl 27 '64
Is President Johnson in labor's corner? concerning State-of-the-Union message. il U S News 58:72-3 Ja 18 '65
Labor backlash? T. R. Brooks. Commonweal 81:93-5 O 16 '64
Labor drive for LBJ hits own backlash. il Bsns W p49-50+ S 12 '64
Labor flexes its muscle for the new Congress. il Bsns W p56 N 14 '64
Labor outlook hinges on government. il Nations Bsns 51:38-9+ D '63
Labor's price tag for election; it's up to LBJ; demands of AFL-CIO. il U S News 57:85-6 D 7 '64
Managing your manpower; stemming the backlash. T. R. Brooks. Duns R 84:65 O '64
New union target; the courts. il Nations Bsns 52:32-3+ Ja '64
Nowhere to go but to Johnson; oppose archfoe Goldwater. Bsns W p47-8 Jl 25 '64
Old order at bay. Nat R 15:513 D 17 '63
Organized labor and the city boss. L. L. Friedland. bibliog f Ann Am Acad 353:40-51 My '64
Riddle of the labor vote. H. Harris. Harper 229:43-9 O '64
Unionists counter Goldwater gains. U S News 57:69 Ag 10 '64
Unionists prime political pumps. il Bsns W p82-4+ Ag 29 '64
Unions get new role in Britain. Bsns W p95-6 O 24 '64
Unions open new attack on conservatives; in South. il Nations Bsns 51:80-4 Mr '63
Unions push biggest political campaign; interview. A. Barkan. il Nations Bsns 52:38-9+ Ag '64
Unions' war on Goldwater; AFL-CIO plans its strategy. il U S News 57:73-4 Ag 17 '64
What unions want in '65. il Nations Bsns 52: 36-7+ D '64
See also
American federation of labor and Congress of industrial organizations—Committee on political education

Trusteeships

Peace plan for the Lakes; trusteeship to run Canadian unions. Bsns W p50 Ag 10 '63

Welfare funds

See Trade unions—Benefit funds

Africa

Current structure of African trade unionism; excerpts from Directory of labor organizations: Africa. Mo Labor R 86:172-3 F '63

Argentina

Peronist sword cuts two ways; plant seizures by unions. Bsns W p52 Je 27 '64

Asia

Labor organizations in Asia and Australasia. M. F. Riche. Mo Labor R 87:283-5 Mr '64

Australia

Labor organizations in Asia and Autralasia. M. F. Riche. Mo Labor R 87:293-5 Mr '64

Belgium

Special bonuses for Belgian unionists. R. A. Senser. Mo Labor R 87:928-9 Ag '64

British Guiana

British Guiana strike settlement. Mo Labor R 86:1069-70 S '63

Canada

Battle of the Great Lakes. W. J. Eaton. il Reporter 29:38-40 N 21 '63
Bully Banks. Newsweek 62:61 Jl 29 '63
Canadian judge drops bomb on sea unions; proposal for government take-over of maritime unions. Bsns W p85 Jl 20 '63
Great Lakes labor war. H. Bruce. il Nation 197:298-300 N 9 '63
Labor war on the Great Lakes: its effect on U.S. and Canada. U S News 54:99 Je 10 '63
Mutiny on the Great Lakes. T. R. Brooks. Commonweal 79:278-80 N 29 '63
Still the boss. Newsweek 62:38 N 4 '63
Trustees to run warring unions? U S News 55:85 Jl 29 '63
Union row roiling Great Lakes again. Seafarers international union and Canadian maritime union. il Bsns W p 100 Je 8 '63
When Canada's Liberals crack down on unions. il U S News 55:88-90 N 4 '63
Why unions are at war on the Great Lakes; SIU vs. Canadian maritime union. il U S News 55:91-2 S 23 '63
See also
Canadian labor congress

Colombia

Unions and national development; OAS cosponsors training course in Colombia. G. Meek. il Américas 15:25-7 My '63

Europe, Western

Cultural activities of West European organized labor. K. Braun. Mo Labor R 86:370-7 Ap '63
Freedom of association in eight European countries. H. Brickman. bibliog f Mo Labor R 86:1020-5 S '63
White-collar unionism in western Europe. E. M. Kassalow. bibliog f Mo Labor R 86:765-71, 889-96 Jl-Ag '63

France

By any other name: Confédération française des travailleurs chrétiens. America 111:30 Jl 11 '64
Labor vs. de Gaulle; miners march on Paris. il Bsns W p78-80+ Mr 23 '63

Germany (Democratic Republic)

What Ulbricht doesn't know. K. Wismach. Atlan 212:114-17 D '63

Germany (Federal Republic)

Erhard's decisive action; Baden Württemberg metalworking strike. il Bsns W p43-4+ My 11 '63
When unions are put on boards of directors. il U S News 58:74-5 Ja 11 '65

Great Britain

British Ford unions hit. Bsns W p 162 Ap 20 '63
Challenge facing British unions. W. E. J. McCarthy. bibliog f Ann Am Acad 350:129-37 N '63
In Britain, no to guidelines. U S News 55: 94 S 16 '63
Unions get new role in Britain. Bsns W p95-6 O 24 '64
Why British unions are under fire. il Bsns W p 134-6+ Jl 13 '63
See also
Labor party (Great Britain)

Hawaii

Hawaii's unions get mainland look. il Bsns W p86+ S 7 '63
See also
International longshoremen's and warehousemen's union

Israel

Union that is big business. Time 85:66-7 Ja 1 '65

Japan

Ikeda averts wide strike. Bsns W p56+ Ap 25 '64
Japanese workers protest. America 109:445 O 19 '63

Latin America

Bringing Latin unions into the Alliance; Declaration of Cundinamarca. il Bsns W p 174 My 18 '63
Labor and the Alliance. S. Romualdi. il Américas 15:18-21 Ag '63

TRADE unions—Latin America—*Continued*
Labor in Latin America. V. Andrade. America 110:142-4 Ja 25 '64
Now U.S. is exporting union ideas to Latin America. A. W. Robinson. il U S News 54: 86+ My 20 '63

Mexico

Where the union is the boss. il Bsns W p 110-11 Je 13 '64

Spain

Pressing for change in Spain; government-controlled unions. il Bsns W p94-6 Mr 7 '64

United States

Agency shop setback; states have power to enforce curbs on unions. Bsns W p 136 D 7 '63
American labor in 1962; a retrospect. P. Groom. bibliog f Mo Labor R 86:14-23 Ja '63
Another boost for federal unions. U S News 54:99 Je 3 '63
Bargaining focus for 1964-1965. Bsns W p92-3 D 28 '63; 48-9 Ja 2 '65
Battle of the Great Lakes. W. J. Eaton. il Reporter 29:38-40 N 21 '63
Big strike: a thing of the past? A. H. Raskin. Sat R 46:20-2+ N 16 '63
Big year for unions, too? here's what they hope to get. il U S News 58:64-5 Ja 4 '65
Bitter medicine for labor; CED study of union powers. Bsns W p34 Ap 4 '64
Common thread of trouble: defiance of union leadership. il Time 84:57 N 20 '64
Crisis in the American trade-union movement; symposium, ed. by S. Barkin and A. A. Blum. bibliog il Ann Am Acad 350: 1-156 N '63
Decline of labor; unions within unions. S. Lens. Commonweal 80:391-4 Je 19 '64; Reply. W. Fogel. 80:485 Jl 10 '64
Developments in industrial relations. See issues of Monthly labor review
Disenchanted unionist, by P. E. Sultan. Review
Reporter 30:47-8 Mr 26 '64. R. S. Gallagher
Double standard builds union power; with views of six executives. W. H. Peterson. il Nations Bsns 51:69-72+ My '63
Hard times. il Time 81:13-17 Mr 1 '63
How LBJ's early-warning system works for pay, prices. il U S News 56:86-8 F 10 '64
How unions are doing in '64. U S News 56: 85 Ap 13 '64
Is labor's wage push more bark than bite? E. K. Faltermayer. il Fortune 69:100-3+ Je '64
Labor and the defense economy. Nation 196:518 Je 22 '63
Labor at the crossroads. il Sr Schol 82:4-6+ F 27 '63
Labor ducks the future. B. J. Widick. il Nation 197:389-90 D 7 '63
Labor in 1963. J. F. Strickland. bibliog f Mo Labor R 86:1398-404 D '63
Labor month in review. See issues of Monthly labor review
Labor tries a comeback. H. Bernstein. Nation 197:107-9 S 7 '63
Labor unions are worth the price. M. Ways. il Fortune 67:108-13+ My '63; Discussion. 67:20 Je '63
Laborers follow the leaders. M. R. Konvitz. Sat R 47:40-1 F 29 '64
Liberals and the labor movement. J. Seidman; B. Sexton; S. B. Gottlieb. Mo Labor R 87:132-5 F '64
Managing your manpower; independent unions try for a comeback. T. R. Brooks. Duns R 82:81-2+ O '63
Managing your manpower; unions on the way out? T. R. Brooks. Duns R 82:51 S '63
New and vital role for labor. T. R. Brooks. il Duns R 83:pt2 103-5+ Je '64
New wage-price spiral ahead? U S News 56: 82 Ap 20 '64
Obsolescent unions. A. H. Raskin. Commentary 36:18-25 Jl '63
On the labor front. J. O'Gara. Commonweal 78:43 Ap 5 '63
Organized labor in American history, by P. Taft. Review
Sat R 47:31 Ag 8 '64. M. R. Konvitz
Other four: railroad operating unions. Time 82:16 Jl 26 '63
Prospects for organization of white-collar workers; excerpt from address. A. A. Blum. bibliog f Mo Labor R 87:125-9 F '64
Reform for the union movement? three writers suggest ways. il U S News 54:88-9 Je 24 '63
Rise in white collar organizing. Duns R 81: 45 Mr '63
Rumbles from the rank and file. A. H. Raskin. il Reporter 32:27-30 Ja 28 '65
Search for a cause. Newsweek 62:78 S 23 '63
Security of worker institutions. G. W. Brooks. Mo Labor R 86:652-8 Je '63
State of the unions, by P. Jacobs. Review
Commentary 37:86-8 F '64. L. A. Coser
Study of the effects of unionism in southern plants. H. E. Steele and H. Fisher, jr. bibliog f il Mo Labor R 87:258-70 Mr '64
Tough bargaining, and not just in autos. Bsns W p47-8 Jl 11 '64
Trying out three-way organizing; store employees unions, Gimbels-Schusters, Milwaukee. il Bsns W p90-1 Ja 19 '63
Unions' demands for 1964. il U S News 56: 89-91 Ja 13 '64
Unions rally to Johnson. Bsns W p46+ N 30 '63
Unions spend millions on foreign aid program. Bsns W p46+ Ag 24 '63
Unions still stumble on Dixie's stone wall. il Bsns W p49-50 Ap 25 '64
Unions veer toward protectionism. Bsns W p 124+ N 9 '63
U.S. labor: affluence vs. influence; fifth biennial convention of the AFL-CIO. il Newsweek 62:85-8 N 25 '63
What's ahead for labor? N. W. Chamberlain. Atlan 214:34-7 Jl '64
When a friend of labor turned critic; criticism of railroad brotherhoods; excerpts from address, August 27, 1963. W. Morse. U S News 55:96 S 9 '63
When a worker bucks his union; excerpts from letter. U S News 56:80 Je 22 '64
When unions look ahead: will gains offset losses? il U S News 55:93-4 S 16 '63
When unions try to expand; summaries of reports. W. P. Reuther. U S News 55:124 N 18 '63
White House stand on wages and prices. il U S News 56:84-5 F 3 '64
Why labor lost the intellectuals. H. Harris. Harper 228:79-80+ Je '64; Discussion. 229:6 Ag '64
Worker security in a changing economy; symposium. bibliog f il Mo Labor R 86:612-702 Je '63
See also
Actors' equity association
Arbitration, Industrial—United States
Featherbedding (industrial relations)
National federation of independent unions (proposed)
Strikes—United States
Trade unions—Officials
United States—Labor policy
also names of unions, e.g. International typographical union

Bibliography

Labor at the crossroads. A. A. Blum. Harvard Bsns R 42:6-8+ Jl '64

TRADE waste
Economical plating-waste treatment; cyanide recovery. H. E. P. Barta. il Am City 79: 75-6 Ja '64
Pollution report: Bendetsen of Champion. J. B. Craig. il Am For 70:10-11+ O '64

TRADEMARKS. See Trade marks

TRADER, C. David, and others
Hemoglobin: molecular changes during anuran metamorphosis. bibliog Science 139:918-19 Mr 8 '63

TRADER Vic restaurants. See Restaurants—United States

TRADERS, Grain. See Grain trade

TRADES union congress
Why British unions are under fire. il Bsns W p 134-6+ Jl 13 '63

TRADESCANTIA fluminensis. See Inch plants

TRADING stamps
How much do trading stamps add to your grocery bill? Consumer Bul 47:14-15 O '64
New licks in the stamp act. il Time 82:86 N 8 '63
Sales & distribution. L. Morse. Duns R 82: 49-50+ Jl '63
Selling game. il Newsweek 61:86-7 Mr 18 '63
Sperry & Hutchinson's very successful stagnation. S. H. Brown. il Fortune 70:156-9+ N '64
Stamp fight is on in Britain. il Bsns W p88-9 Ag 3 '63
Stamp war; trading stamps in Great Britain. Time 81:114 My 17 '63
Stamps. New Yorker 39:34-5 Mr 23 '63
Sticky confetti? stamp invasion in Britain. Newsweek 62:93-4 N 11 '63
Trading stamp mystique. Nation 199:179 O 5 '64
Trading stamps. R. M. Lipsyte. Esquire 59: 90 Ap '63
Trading stamps? no, thanks! fund raising for church. Christian Cent 81:388-9 Mr 25 '64

TRADING stamps—*Continued*
Trading stamps, who gets what? A. Fontaine. Read Digest 82:66-9 Je '63
Welcome hoax. D. Smith. il Nation 197:259-61 O 26 '63
See also
Premiums

TRADITION (theology)
Scripture and tradition, by G. Moran. Review
Cath World 198:185-6 D '63. N. J. McEleney
That the church may be more fully Catholic; excerpts from address, May 5, 1963. J. Pelikan. Cath World 198:151-6 D '63
Tradition is a living message. W. F. Dewan. Cath World 197:238-45 Jl '63

TRAFFIC. See Road traffic; Street traffic

TRAFFIC, Airline. See Airlines—Traffic

TRAFFIC accidents
And now he (she) drives. B. Lang. il N Y Times Mag p 110+ N 8 '64
Auto age in Kuwait. il N Y Times Mag p 108-9 S 15 '63
Big fish, little fish; chance of surviving in a small car. Newsweek 64:77-8 D 14 '64
Can we get the sick drivers off the road? G. G. Greer. Bet Hom & Gard 42:21-2+ O '64
Case for fast drivers. R. L. Schwartz. Harper 227:65-70 S '63; Same abr. with title What are the real causes of auto crashes? il Read Digest 84:181-2+ Ap '64; Discussion. Harper 227:6 N '63
Cause and treatment of whiplash injuries. Good H 158:158 Mr '64
Cause of long-trip car crashes studied. Sci N L 87:56 Ja 23 '65
Crash! are small cars death traps? E. D. Fales, jr. il Pop Sci 185:50-3+ Ag '64
Danger rides two wheels. B. Magid. il Parents Mag 38:68-9+ S '63
Death on the highway. Commonweal 80:408 Je 26 '64
Disaster on a fogbound turnpike; New Jersey turnpike. il U S News 54:14 Je 10 '63
Emotion behind the wheel causes traffic accidents. Sci Digest 53:19-20 My '63
Highway toll; death record on the roads. Newsweek 61:36 F 11 '63
How to get towed without getting took. E. D. Fales, jr. il Pop Sci 183:33-7+ Ag '63
If you have an accident. P. W. Kearney. Read Digest 86:201+ Ja '65
Living memorial in strangers' eyes. Time 82:60 Ag 30 '63
Low-down on highways; conference in Boston, November 19-20. J. L. Hofford. Christian Cent 81:89-90 Ja 15 '64
My son, the defendant; case of G. Martinis. il Newsweek 62:26-7 Jl 15 '63
Shattering records and bodies; Memorial day deaths. il Time 81:21 Je 7 '63
Slaughter on the Tiber; Rome's traffic problem. Newsweek 62:38 Jl 8 '63
Suddenly you're involved! C. J. Potthoff. il Todays Health 42:26-9+ Je '64
Traffic toll and the teen-ager; forum discussion. il Sr Schol 83:20 S 27 '63; Discussion. 83:12-14 Ja 17 '64
Vision of a crashproof car. C. Leedham. il N Y Times Mag p34+ O 25 '64
When big meets small; experiment in automobile survival. il Time 83:73-4 Je 12 '64
Your ten responsibilities in an accident. Bet Hom & Gard 42:14 Je '64
See also
Automobile driving
Automobiles—Safety devices and measures
Drinking and traffic accidents
Insurance, Automobile
Survival (after airplane accidents, shipwrecks, etc)

Cases

Crash detective. il Motor T 15:42-3 D '63
Truth about fatal car crashes; Harvard fatal highway collisions project. M. Mann. il Pop Sci 183:92-7+ D '63

TRAFFIC congestion. See Street traffic

TRAFFIC control, Airport. See Airports—Traffic control

TRAFFIC control, Airway. See Air traffic control

TRAFFIC counting. See Street traffic

TRAFFIC courts
Traffic courts; cash register justice. L. Scandur. il Nation 198:144-5 F 10 '64
You can have decent traffic courts. J. P. Economos and A. Fontaine. Read Digest 84:129-32 Ja '64

TRAFFIC detectors. See Detectors

TRAFFIC engineering
Improved traffic flow can save many lives. Sci N L 85:121 F 22 '64
Vehicular traffic flow. R. Herman and K. Gardels. il Sci Am 209:35-43 D '63

TRAFFIC engineers, Institute of. See Institute of traffic engineers

TRAFFIC fines. See Fines (penalties)

TRAFFIC liners. See Motor trucks, Municipal

TRAFFIC markings
Fog-proof system; marker lights; Oakland, Calif. J. E. Austin. il Am City 79:113-14 Mr '64
4,500 miles of pavement marking; Nevada. il Am City 78:123 My '63
Instant traffic lines, inlaid, too; Kalamazoo, Mich. R. B. Carroll. il Am City 79:15 S '64
Monster that moves by night. B. Stengren. il Am City 78:84-5 N '63
Ready-marked pavements; Charlotte, N.C. H. Hoose. il Am City 78:117 Ag '63
Testing traffic paint; Cincinnati. J. G. Krieg. il Am City 79:92-3 N '64

TRAFFIC police
Computerized wolf pack. il Newsweek 61:35-6 Mr 25 '63

TRAFFIC regulations
Caution traffic tickets ahead. il Changing T 17:13-15 Jl '63
Scientific speed limits would make roads safer. Sci N L 87:3 Ja 2 '65
Slaughter on the Tiber; Rome's traffic problem. Newsweek 62:38 Jl 8 '63
Traffic control. See issues of American city
See also
Automobile trailers—Parking
Electronics in traffic control
Traffic courts

Study and teaching

Highway safety studied. Sci N L 85:139 F 29 '64
Safety town trains children; traffic-safety school, Dade County, Fla. il Am City 79:23 Jl '64
Teach your tots about traffic. R. VanderWerf. il Parents Mag 39:64-5+ S '64
Traffic school for preschoolers; Maple Heights, Ohio. A. Nagy, jr. il PTA Mag 57:21 Je '63

TRAFFIC signals

Control

Electronic traffic metering; Eisenhower expressway, Chicago. C. S. Michalski. il Am City 79:133 Je '64
Space-age traffic control; Orlando, Fla. W. L. Thomas. il Am City 78:99-100 Mr '63

TRAFFIC signs
Sign uniformity still lagging. il Am City 79:104 D '64
Signs of our times. M. Lamm. il Motor T 15:60-3 Ag '63

Anecdotes, facetiae, satire, etc.

Dynasty. G. Highet. Vogue 143:95+ F 15 '64

TRAFFIC surveys
Survey, plan, expedite and review; Decatur, Ill. J. F. Nolan. il Am City 78:85-7 Ag '63

TRAFFIC violations
Traffic courts; cash register justice. L. Scandur. il Nation 198:144-5 F 10 '64

TRAGEDY
Is there a tragic sense of life? L. Abel. Commentary 38:35-40 D '64
Metatheatre, by L. Abel. Review
Commentary 36:325-7+ O '63. R. Gilman

TRAGER, Frank N.
Importance of Laos in southeast Asia. biblog f Cur Hist 46:107-11+ F '64
Two angles on the Marxist vision. Sat R 47:31+ F 1 '64

TRAGICAL historie of Dr Faustus; drama. See Marlowe, C.

TRAHEY, Jane
Culprit in the convent; condensation of Life with Mother Superior. Read Digest 83:221-3+ Ag '63
My own personal patron saint. Read Digest 84:97-100 Mr '64
So you want to convert an old barn. House B 106:72-7+ Jl '64

TRAIL riders of the wilderness
Back to Glacier Peak! il Am For 69:6-7 F '63
Waters of the Allagash. H. Clepper. il Am For 70:14-18+ N '64

TRAIL scooters. See Motor scooters

TRAILER-boat camps. See Automobile trailer camps

TRAILER camps. See Automobile trailer camps

TRAILER parking. See Automobile trailers—Parking

TRAILER train company
Kingpin of wheels on wheels. il Bsns W p91-2 D 19 '64

TRAILERS
Mountain goat trailer defies hillsides; Swampernik. S. Churchill. il Farm J 88:32C Ag '64
Technique of towing a trailer. il Changing T 18:15-16 Je '64
See also
Automobile trailers

Transportation
Kingpin of wheels on wheels; Trailer train co. il Bsns W p91-2 D 19 '64
TRAILERS, Horse. See Horses—Transportation
TRAILING. See Tracking and trailing
TRAILS
Build a nature trail; Cortland college; Camp Raquette Lake, N.Y. E. C. Waldbauer. il Recreation 57:114 Mr '64
Life guide; ghosts of history on today's highways. il Life 55:10 Jl 5 '63
Life guide; trails to blaze on late-summer days. il Life 55:9 Ag 16 '63
Long trail; Vermont's 260-mile footpath. V. Birge. il Recreation 56:228-9 My '63
New courses for old paths. il Recreation 58:17-19 Ja '65
There's a long deep trail awinding; John Muir trail in Sierra National Forest. A. P. Snyder. il Am For 69:20-1+ Je '63
See also
Appalachian trail
Pacific Crest Trail system
TRAIN, George Francis
Faces from the past. R. M. Ketchum. por Am Heritage 14:38-9 Ap '63
TRAIN robberies. See Robberies and assaults
TRAIN speed. See Railroads—Train speed
TRAIN spotters. See Railroads
TRAIN travel. See Railroad travel
TRAINING airplanes. See Airplanes, Training
TRAINING camps. See Military training camps
TRAINING devices. See Simulators
TRAINING of children. See Children—Management and training
TRAINING of dogs. See Dogs—Training
TRAINING of plants. See Plants, Training of
TRAINING schools for teachers. See Teachers—Education
TRAINING ships
1,600 miles on a windjammer; Statsraad Lehmkuhl. D. C. Fales. il Pop Sci 185:74-7+ Ag '64
Operation sail. D. W. Dwyer. il Yachting 115:64-6+ Ap '64
Operation sail; loomings and landfalls. F. Rohr. il Motor B 113:44-5+ Je '64
Operation sail, 1964. A. L. Lonsdale. il Motor B 113:108-9+ Ja '64
TRAINOR, Francis R.
Zoospores in scenedesmus obliquus. bibliog Science 142:1673-4 D 27 '63
TRAINS. See Railroads—Trains
TRAINS, Model. See Railroad models
TRAINS, Toy. See Railroads, Toy
TRAITORS
Was the Secretary of a war a traitor? W. A. Swanberg. il Am Heritage 14:34-7+ F '63
See also
Treason
TRAITS of character. See Character analysis
TRAKL, Georg
Hold on life. H. A. Klein. Nation 196:123-4 F 9 '63
TRAMMELL, Archie
Airman's almanic. Flying 75:68+ Ag; 58 S '64
TRAMP ships. See Freight vessels
TRAMPS
Jalopy nomads. B. Carter. Reporter 30:31-3 My 7 '64
TRAMWAYS, Aerial. See Cableways
TRAN-van-Chuong
One world; people in current news as television stars. Reporter 29:24+ O 24 '63
Viet Nam: decisive battle of the cold war; address, May 6, 1964. Vital Speeches 30:628-30 Ag 1 '64
TRAN-van-Chuong, Mme
I do not want my name mentioned ever, with hers. M. V. Thayer. McCalls 91:237 N '63
TRAN-van-Huong
For Vietnam's Premier it's been hellish; interview, ed. by F. Sully. por Newsweek 65:32 Ja 18 '65
Tightwire man. Time 84:26-7 N 6 '64
TRANQUILIZING drugs
Are tranquilizers overused in hospitals? Sci Digest 54:75-6 Ag '63
Beware tranquilizer addiction. il Sci Digest 55:40-1 Mr '64
Dornwal in the dock. Newsweek 64:59 S 7 '64
How good are those non-prescription tranquilizers? Good H 157:159-61 O '63
How tranquilizers work is theme of animal study. Sci N L 85:393 Je 20 '64
Instant happiness. R. P. Goldman. il Ladies Home J 80:67-71 O '63
Of cheese and tranquilizers. Pop Sci 184:22 Ja '64
Pills to soothe tension. W. Wingo. Sci N L 84:178 S 21 '63
Too many tranquilizers? G. G. Greer. Bet Hom & Gard 41:46 My '63
Tranquillity and after. il Newsweek 63:110+ Ap 20 '64
Truth about brain drugs. J. Steen. il Pop Sci 182:70-3+ F '63
What tranquilizers have done. il Time 83:43-4 Ap 24 '64
Your guide to mind drugs. R. Mines. il Sci Digest 55:69 Ja '64
TRANSAMERICA corporation
Department store that sells money. Bsns W p45-6+ My 23 '64
TRANSATLANTIC cables. See Cables, Submarine
TRANSATLANTIC flights. See Aviation—Transatlantic flights
TRANSATLANTIC passenger traffic. See Ocean travel
TRANS-ATLANTIC race. See Yacht racing
TRANSATLANTIC voyages. See Ocean travel
TRANS-CANADA highway. See Roads—Canada
TRANSCEIVERS. See Radio telephone
TRANSCONTINENTAL flights. See Aviation—Transcontinental flights
TRANSDUCERS
High fidelity newsfronts; direct recording process using transducer element. N. Eisenberg. il Hi Fi 14:37 S '64
Precision digital tide gauge. F. E. Snodgrass. bibliog il Science 146:198-200+ O 9 '64
Transducers for industrial instrumentation. R. A. Shiver. il Electr World 72:49-52 Jl '64
TRANSFER of employees. See Employees, Transfer of
TRANSFERRIN
Transferrin: variations in blood serum of red howler monkeys. M. A. Schön and T. Arends. bibliog il Science 146:774-5 N 6 '64
Transferrins in Venezuelan Indians: high frequency of a slow-moving variant. T. Arends and M. L. Gallango. bibliog il Science 143:367-8 Ja 24 '64
TRANSFIGURATION of Christ. See Jesus Christ—Transfiguration
TRANSFLORIDA SHIP CANAL. See Florida Ship Canal project
TRANSFORMERS. See Electric transformers
TRANSFUSION of blood. See Blood—Transfusion
TRANSIENT; story. See Elkin, S.
TRANSISTOR circuits
Eight electronic experiments with a transistor breadboard. L. Buckwalter. il Pop Mech 120:200-3 N '63
Hybrid circuit for transistor power. R. E. Pafenberg. il Pop Electr 20:66-7 Ap '64
New circuits for FM portables. il Electr World 71:64 My '64
Stereo indicator light circuit. L. Blaser. il Electr World 69:72 My '63
See also
Printed circuits
TRANSISTOR radios. See Radio receiving apparatus, Portable
TRANSISTOR tape recorders. See Magnetic recorders and recording
TRANSISTOR vibrators. See Multivibrators
TRANSISTORS
Accent on transistors. C. Wright. il Pop Phot 54:108-9 Ap '64
Bargain page amplifier. D. Meyer. il Pop Electr 21:69-72 O '64
D.C. to A.C. transistor power supply. C. E. Diehl. il Electr World 69:66 Je '63
Domestic replacements for foreign semiconductors. J. Eimbinder. il Electr World 70:26-8 Jl '63
Faithful sound; radio phonographs. R. Freas. il Esquire 60:59+ N '63
Field-effect transistor. P. S. Green. il Electr World 70:66+ S '63
Gifts: equipment and recordings. M. Mayer. Esquire 60:110+ D '63
Growth, at a price, for transistors. Bsns W p 102+ Ap 6 '63

TRANSISTORS—*Continued*
High fidelity. H. Fantel. Opera N 28:35 Ap 18 '64
IBM developing optical transistor. il Miss & Roc 12:40 Ap 1 '63
Just what is a transistor? il Good H 156:170 Ap '63
Light-controlled power supply, second thoughts. B. C. Snow. il Pop Electr 21:70-2 S '64
Midget revolution. I. Berger. Sat R 46:58-9 S 14 '63
Most; metal oxide semi-conductor transistor. Newsweek 61:86 F 18 '63
New fundamental building block; insulated-gate transistor. il Miss & Roc 12:50 Mr 4 '63
New products. N. Eisenberg. il Hi Fi 13: 56-8+ S '63
New transistor uses light, not electricity; optical transistor. Sci N L 83:194 Mr 30 '63
New type microwave transistor unveiled at components meeting. P. J. Klass. Aviation W 80:108-9 My 18 '64
9-watt transistorized hi-fi amplifier. S. E. Bammel. il Electr World 69:46-7+ Mr '63
Perpetual transistor power package. L. E. Greenlee. il Pop Electr 20:53-5+ My '64
Regulated transistorized power supplies. J. R. Collins. il Electr World 69:40-2 Mr '63
Replacements for non-standard domestic transistors. J. Eimbinder. il Electr World 70:36+ S '63
Sandia tests revamping data about radiation damage to transistors. Miss & Roc 15:37 N 16 '64
Selecting high-frequency transistors. R. Hejhall and D. Thorpe. il Electr World 72:50-2+ S '64
Sound advice; transistors vs. vacuum tubes. L. Zide. Mod Phot 29:26+ Ja '65
Sound ideas. L. Zide. Am Rec G 29:754-5 My '63
Sound; transistors at N.Y. trade show. J. Wesson. U S Camera 28:32+ Ja '65
Sound; tubes or transistors, which should you choose? J. Wesson. U S Camera 27:28+ N '64
Substituting silicon for germanium transistors. W. O. Hamlin. il Electr World 72: 39-41+ D '64
Transistor. M. Mayer. il Esquire 59:123+ Je '63
Transistor replacement technique. R. E. Pafenberg. il Pop Electr 19:62 S '63
Transistor substitution directory. Electr World 69:45 F; 43 Mr; 52-4 Ap; 45+ Je '63
Transistor topics. L. Garner. See issues of Popular electronics
Transistors for hi-fi, panacea or pandemonium? D. R. Von Recklinghausen and others. il Electr World 70:37-40+ S; 38-40+ O '63
Transistors for music; hi-fi amplifiers. R. E. Furst and L. Zide. il Electr World 71:48-50 Mr '64
Transistors vs tubes for hi-fi. E. S. Miller and others. il Electr World 70:48-9 N '63
Transistors vs tubes for hi-fi. W. W. Chou. Electr World 71:36+ F '64
Transistors vs tubes for hi-fi. F. L. Mergner. Electr World 71:45+ Ja '64
Transistors vs tubes for hi-fi. R. S. Burwen. Electr World 70:85 D '63
Transistors versus tubes for two-way radio H. H. Rice. il Electr World 72:48-50 N '64
Unijunction transistor. D. L. Pippen. il Electr World 71:46-7+ Ja '64
When tiny parts must be moved just a bit. il Bsns W p 100-2 S 21 '63

Noise

Noise performance of transistors in audio circuits. W. A. Rheinfelder. il Electr World 73:31-3 Ja '65

Testing

Simple transistor checker. A. J. Molinara. il Electr World 69:94 F '63
Simple transistor tester. J. E. Content and B. K. Morse. il Electr World 71:50 My '64
Simple transistor tests. G. McKinney. il Electr World 72:63 Ag '64

TRANSIT (artificial satellite) See Artificial satellites—Navigational applications
TRANSIT expressway. See Rapid transit
TRANSIT fares. See Rapid transit—Fares
TRANSIT systems. See Rapid transit
TRANSITION in literature. See Fiction—Technique
TRANSITIONAL metals. See Metals
TRANSITRON electronic corporation
One for the books; Transitron stockholders' suit. il Fortune 67:191-2+ Mr '63

TRANSKEI
Black pawns of Bantustan. T. Sterling. il Reporter 29:42-4+ O 10 '63
First step in the Transkei; Bantustan policy. T. Molnar. Nat R 16:155-6 F 25 '64; Reply with rejoinder. H. Suzman. 16:461 Je 2 '64
How to win & lose. Time 82:34 D 13 '63
Whose country? il Time 82:47 N 29 '63
TRANSLATER satellites. See Communications satellites
TRANSLATING machines
Computer confession; Georgetown university mechanical translation. New Repub 150:6-7 Je 6 '64
Computer for translating. A. Code. il Sci N L 83:374 Je 15 '63
Machine translation of Chinese. G. W. King and H. W. Chang. il Sci Am 208:124-35 Je '63; Reply with rejoinder. A. G. Oettinger. 209:8+ O '63
Mechanical translation and related language research. R. See. bibliog Science 144:621-6 My 8 '64; Discussion. 145:6 Jl 3 '64
TRANSLATION, Opera. See Opera—Language
TRANSLATIONS and translating
Aristophanes in American. X. J. Kennedy. Poetry 102:56-60 Ap '63
Better vernacular needed; poverty of most English versions of the mass. America 111: 434 O 17 '64
Continuing barrier; translation & East-West communications. R. Collison. il UNESCO Courier 16:6-9 F '63
Cooling off the Pope; translations of Pope John's encyclical Pacem in terris (Peace on earth) challenged. Newsweek 61:91 My 27 '63
Crisis in Japanese translation. F. Bowers. New Repub 148:32-3 Mr 23 '63
Eraiza and company; first American musical in Tokyo, My fair lady in Japanese. il Newsweek 62:82 S 16 '63
Language of encyclicals. America 108:825 Je 8 '63
Language of Rome; papal documents. America 111:652 N 21 '64
Liturgy in English; letter. A. T. Straulman. Commonweal 81:424 D 18 '64
Note on Aeschylus. R. Kirk. Nat R 15:62 Jl 30 '63
Now it can be told in Moscow; two translations of One day in the life of Ivan Denisovich compared with each other and the original. G. Reavey. Sat R 46:27-9 F 9 '63
Oil for the lamps of knowledge; Franklin publications program for developing countries. J. E. Daily. il Library J 89:4483-7 N 15 '64
On translating encyclicals. America 108:732 My 25 '63
On translating Voznesensky. B. Koten. Nation 199:337-8 N 9 '64
Reporter at large; profession of conference translator and interpreter. A. Reid. New Yorker 39:43-4+ S 7 '63
Scripta Technica; translator of scientific materials. il Pub W 184:61-2 N 11 '63
Scripta Technica makes liaisons with foreign firms. Pub W 187:276 Ja 25 '65
Search for sample books; Franklin book programs, authorized translations of American books for developing countries. J. E. Daily. il Wilson Lib Bul 39:59-61+ S '64
Significant correction; norms to regulate interim work of the Second Vatican council. America 108:358-9 Mr 16 '63
Theatre and lyric. R. Dalven. Poetry 102: 54-5 Ap '63
Uncharted lands, neglected masterpieces in the world of translations. R. Caillois. il UNESCO Courier 16:4-5 F '63
Words to pray with? forthcoming translation of the liturgy. G. B. Harrison. America 110:508-10 Ap 11 '64; Discussion. 110: 676-8; 111:2 My 16, Jl 4 '64
See also
Opera—Language
Poetry—Translating

Anecdotes, facetiae, satire, etc.

Restaurant English. P. K. Brooks. Sat R 47: 35 Ap 11 '64

TRANSLATIONS center, Special libraries. See Special libraries association
TRANSLOCATION in plants. See Plants—Translocation
TRANSMISSION, Automobile. See Automobiles—Transmission
TRANSMISSION lines. See Electric lines
TRANSMISSION of heat. See Heat—Transmission
TRANSMISSION of pictures. See Phototelegraphy

TRANSMUTATION (chemistry)
See also
Alchemy
TRANSOM ladders. See Ladders
TRANSPACIFIC flights. See Aviation—Transpacific flights
TRANS-PACIFIC yacht race. See Yacht racing
TRANSPARENCIES
B&W from color. il Mod Phot 27:60-7 F '63
B&W from color, here's how. H. Keppler and E. Meyers. il Mod Phot 27:68-9 F '63
Color films for transparencies. il Consumer Bul 46:6-8 O '63
Color negative or transparency. A. Rothstein. U S Camera 26:39+ Ag '63
Color slides. R. Miller. See issues of U.S. camera
Color workshop. F. Bond. il Mod Phot 29:34-5 Ja '65
Create color by solarizing. H. Keppler and P. Caulfield. il Mod Phot 28:52-4 Ap '64
Don't let your travel slide show fail. C. Burger. Pop Phot 52:130+ Ap '63
Farewell to slides? color prints. A. Francekevich. il Pop Phot 55:16+ S '64
Gaining new vision for social studies: overhead projectors and transparencies. R. A. Withey. il Sr Schol 85:18T Ja 21 '65
How to print your slides. B. Pierce. Pop Phot 54:134-5 Ja '64
Make color prints. W. Lane. il Travel 120:56-7 S '63
Negative positive. A. Asnis. U S Camera 26:30-1 F '63
New ways to look at slides. B. Pierce. Pop Phot 55:47 Jl '64
No-work slide protection. N. Rothschild. Pop Phot 54:97-8 F '64
Norman Rothschild's guide to daylight color slide films. N. Rothschild. il Pop Phot 53:166-75 D '63
Now! use Kodak drum processor for fast color prints from slides. B. Pierce. Pop Phot 55:52+ N '64
Slides to prints and vice versa. R. Miller. U S Camera 26:50-1+ Ag '63
Solving half-frame problems. N. Rothschild. il Pop Phot 55:54-5 Ag '64
Super bright, super sharp, super color. P. Caulfield. il Mod Phot 27:64-7 Je '63
Three key pictures. J. Kinney and C. Kinney. il U S Camera 26:54-7+ My '63
Two new color slide films. il Consumer Bul 47:43 Ja '64
Unusual slide show. P. Stackpole. U S Camera 27:12 My '64
Vagabond camera. W. Lane. il Travel 122:70-1 N '64
Which film? H. Keppler. il Mod Phot 27:52-7+ F '63
Why prints differ from slides. D. B. Eisendrath, jr. Pop Phot 54:8+ Je '64
Woodcuts from color transparencies. M. Johnson. il Pop Mech 119:182-3 Mr '63

Copying

Slide duplicates with your camera. N. Rothschild. il Pop Phot 55:46-9+ Ag '64

Projection

Color clinic; eight-foot projected images. D. B. Eisendrath, jr. Pop Phot 54:10+ Ja '64
Color slides; how to keep your audience awake. R. Miller. U S Camera 26:30-1 N '63
Color slides, movies. R. Miller. il U S Camera 27:30-1+ My '64
Color vision: an experiment. P. Farber. il U S Camera 27:50-1+ Ja '64; Discussion. 27:16+ Ap '64
First aid for color slides; filter over projector lens. C. Wright. il Pop Phot 55:80-2 Ag '64
Sound/slides: new recorders make it easier. M. A. Matzkin. il Mod Phot 28:92+ S '64
35mm. J. Wolbarst. Mod Phot 28:17+ Ap '64
What makes projected 35mm slides unsharp? D. L. Miller. il Mod Phot 27:78-81 N '63

Sound accompaniment

Adding sound to slides & movies; questions and answers. J. A. Keel. il U S Camera 26:70-1+ O '63
Slide-show sound track. E. Nanas. il Pop Phot 53:62-3+ S '63
Sound, a big plus for your pictures. R. Miller. U S Camera 27:26-7 O '64
Sound advice; connect your slide projector to a tape recorder? H. Keppler. Mod Phot 27:34+ O '63
Sound way to showmanship. Pop Phot 55:79 O '64
Synchronization. J. R. Gregory. il U S Camera 26:72-3 O '63
Tape-slide synchronizer. C. D. Todd. il Electr World 70:50-2+ S '63
Three master sound-slide showmen. L. Lipton. il Pop Phot 55:74-5 O '64
Vagabond camera. W. Lane. il Travel 122:58-9 D '64

Storage

File awhile! B. Lister. il U S Camera 27:32+ Je '64

Titles

Color clinic; titling slide shows. D. B. Eisendrath, jr. Pop Phot 52:32 Ap '63
Color slides; adding spice to your slide shows. R. Miller. il U S Camera 27:28 Mr '64

Trimming, mounting, etc.

Color slides. R. Miller. U S Camera 26:32+ S '63; 27:32+ Ja; 14-15 Je '64
New looks for old slide shows. D. B. Eisendrath, jr. Pop Phot 54:10+ F '64
You can mount sub-35 yourself. il Pop Phot 53:68 Ag '63
TRANSPIRATION of plants. See Plants—Transpiration
TRANSPLANTATION of organs, tissues, etc.
Acceptance or rejection of male skin by isologous female mice: effect of injection of sperm. G. F. Katsh and others. bibliog il Science 143:41-2 Ja 3 '64
Animal-man transplants. F. Marley. Sci N L 85:35 Ja 18 '64
Antigens associated with a tumor virus; rejection of isogenic skin grafts from leukemic mice. E. J. Breyere and L. B. Williams. bibliog il Science 146:1055-6 N 20 '64
Artificial internal organs; report on annual meeting of the American society for artificial internal organs. J. F. Maher and S. A. Wesolowski. Science 145:76-7 Jl 3 '64
Bile duct restoration in rana pipiens after ligation of the hepatoduodenal ligament. J. G. Streett, jr. bibliog il Science 143:592-4 F 7 '64
Blood transfusion helps dog transplant take. Sci N L 86:117 Ag 22 '64
Calf to man; use of bone from calves. Newsweek 65:55 Ja 11 '65
Chimp supply meager. F. Marley. Sci N L 86:3 Jl 4 '64
Chimp to man; kidney transplants. il Newsweek 62:55 D 30 '63
Closing the gap; transplanted human teeth. il Newsweek 62:75 Ag 26 '63
Compatible organ transplants seen within decade. Sci Digest 53:42-3 F '63
Desperate gamble: organ transplants. L. Galton. il Pop Sci 185:94-6+ D '64
Dissociation of homograft response to allogeneic versus xenogeneic skin grafts in irradiated mice. M. L. Tyan and L. J. Cole. bibliog il Science 141:813-14 Ag 30 '63
Drug treatment prolongs human kidney transfers. Sci N L 83:389 Je 22 '63
Duck retains transplant from leghorn chicken. Sci N L 84:169 S 14 '63
Early grafting saves lives of severely burned. Sci N L 85:25 Ja 11 '64
Experimental reversal of germ cells in ovaries of fetal mice. C. D. Turner and H. Asakawa. bibliog Science 143:1344-5 Mr 20 '64
First heart transplant. Sci Digest 55:82-3 Ap '64
First heart transplant. Time 83:52 Ja 31 '64
Five-finger exercise; case of Everett (Red) Knowles. Newsweek 61:76-7 Ap 1 '63
Genetic disparity and cancer induction by normal tissue implants in amphibia. L. N. Ruben and M. Balls. bibliog Science 146:1321-2 D 4 '64
Hair transplants used in correcting baldness. Sci N L 86:344 N 28 '64
Having a baby on one kidney. il Time 82:44 Ag 23 '63
He takes a grip on life; boy who made medical history puts his sewed-on arm to work. J. Howard. il Life 55:29-30+ Ag 2 '63
Heart transplants years in future. F. Marley. il Sci N L 86:170-1 S 12 '64
Helping hand. il Time 83:42 Mr 6 '64
Heterotransplantation of the kidney: two clinical experiences. K. Reemtsma and others. il Science 143:700-2 F 14 '64
Histocompatibility and immunologic competence in renal homotransplantation. A. L. Rubin and others. bibliog il Science 143:815-16 F 21 '64
Homograft rejection in the fetal lamb: the role of circulating antibody. A. M. Silverstein and others. bibliog Science 142:1172-3 N 29 '63
Homograft sensitivity induction by group A streptococci. F. T. Rapaport and R. M. Chase, jr. bibliog il Science 145:407-8 Jl 24 '64

TRANSPLANTATION of organs, tissues, etc. —*Continued*
Homograft tolerance in mice: use of urethan and sublethal irradiation. W. E. Davis, jr. and L. J. Cole. bibliog il Science 140:483-4 My 3 '63
Homographs in thymectomized, irradiated mice: responses to primary and secondary skin grafts. W. E. Davis, jr. and others. bibliog il Science 145:394-5 Jl 24 '64
Hungarians question organs' biochemical characteristics. Sci Digest 53:53 My '63
Hybrid resistance to parental marrow grafts: association with the Kregion of H-2. G. Cudkowicz and J. H. Stimpfling. bibliog il Science 144:1339-40 Je 12 '64
Immunity and susceptibility toward check-pouch transplants of a mouse leukemia. R. A. Adams. bibliog il Science 146:944-5 N 13 '64
Inhibition of antibody plaque formation by sensitized lymphoid cells: rapid indicator of transplantation immunity. H. Friedman. bibliog il Science 145:607-9 Ag 7 '64
Kidney transplants fail if cadavers unrelated. Sci N L 84:217 O 5 '63
Leg nerves transplanted to restore hand function. Sci N L 83:339 Je 1 '63
Limitations of transplants; tooth transplants. il Time 83:55 My 8 '64
Liver transplant: battle against the odds. il Time 82:87-8 O 4 '63
Living memorial in strangers' eyes. Time 82:60 Ag 30 '63
Look who's on first! E. Knowles. jr. il Time 81:66 My 31 '63
Low malignancy of Rous sarcoma cells as evidenced by poor transplantability in turkeys. V. V. Bergs and V. Groupe. bibliog il Science 139:922-3 Mr 8 '63
Lung transplants hopeful as cancer treatment. Sci N L 84:367 D 7 '63
Lymphocyte interaction: a potential histocompatibility test in vitro. F. Bach and K. Hirschhorn. bibliog il Science 143:813-41 F 21 '64
Man of another kidney. Time 82:36 Ag 9 '63
Medicine's frontier: rebuilding the human body. G. Astor. il Look 28:22-9 Je 30 '64
Medicine's next big step, spare parts surgery; reprint. R. E. Winter. il Sci Digest 55:65-9 F '64
Mosaic histocompatibility of skin grafts from female mice. D. W. Bailey. bibliog il Science 141:631-3 Ag 16 '63
Needless transplants? Newsweek 63:74 Mr 2 '64
New, but limited: hair transplantation. il Todays Health 41:48-9 Ag '63; Excerpts Sci Digest 55:22 Mr '64
New hope for kidney transplants. il Ebony 20:119-20+ N '64
New life for old teeth. Sci Digest 56:56 Ag '64
New problems for surgery; excerpts from address, December 30, 1963. F. D. Moore. Science 144:388-92 Ap 24 '64
Next: nerve banks. Newsweek 61:62 Ap 29 '63
1963's brightest promise: organ transplants. M. Mann. il Todays Health 42:24-6 Ja '64
Noble failure loses a life but advances surgery; human lung transplant. A. Kerr. il Life 55:32-4 Jl 26 '63
Organ exchanging seen. Sci N L 83:259 Ap 27 '63
Other arm. il Newsweek 63:52 Mr 9 '64
Pluripotent stem cell function of the mouse marrow lymphocyte. G. Cudkowicz and others. bibliog il Science 144:866-8 My 15 '64
Predict transplant result; solving the rejection problem. F. Marley. Sci N L 85:259 Ap 25 '64
Questions of the heart; transplant from a chimpanzee to a dying man. il Time 84:64 Jl 17 '64
Regular transplants of human teeth foreseen. Sci N L 86:153 S 5 '64
Renal transplants succeed. Sci N L 87:39 Ja 16 '65
Sacrifice of Jill Rosean; bone tissue transplant. A. Hirshberg. il Good H 158:52+ Je '64
Serologic typing of human lymphocytes with immune serum obtained after homografting. R. L. Walford and others. bibliog il Science 144:868-70 My 15 '64
Setback; death of William Grigsby, first human to receive an apparently successful liver transplant. Newsweek 61:92 Je 10 '63
Sight from dog and dogfish; grafting corneas from animals to human patients. il Time 84:94+ O 23 '64
Spare parts from chimp to man. il Time 82:41 D 27 '63
Spare-parts surgeons; transplanting vital organs. S. M. Spencer. il Sat Eve Post 236:68-70 S 14 '63
Surgeon creates hips from knees. Sci N L 83:232 Ap 13 '63
Surgeons replace thumbs with fingers. Sci N L 85:7 Ja 4 '64
Surgery's new frontier; transplanting human organs. Bsns W p97-8 N 9 '63
They can see again. J. K. Lagemann. Read Digest 84:217-18+ F '64
Thymus: its limited role in the recovery of homograft response in irradiated mice. M. L. Tyan and others. bibliog il Science 142:584 N 1 '63
Tissue compatibility test applicable to humans. Sci N L 84:141 Ag 31 '63
Tolerance between host and donor tissue in birds. W. S. Lapp and others. bibliog il Science 141:818-20 Ag 30 '63
Tolerance by injection. Sci Am 208:71+ Je '63
Transplant from dead; kidney transplant. F. Marley. Sci N L 83:243 Ap 20 '63
Transplant of male gland lasts seventeen years in USSR. Sci N L 84:360 D 7 '63
Transplant progress: more bold advances. il Time 82:61-2+ O 25 '63
Transplant triumph; first initially successful liver transplant on record. Newsweek 61:69+ My 27 '63
Transplantation of rat bone marrow in irradiated mice: effect of exposure rate. N. Gengozian. bibliog il Science 146:663-4 O 30 '64
Transplantation tolerance induced in adult mice by protein overloading of donors. P. Liacopoulos and J. H. Goode. bibliog il Science 146:1305-7 D 4 '64
Twins bear children after kidney transplantation. Sci N L 84:121 Ag 24 '63
Typing for transplants. Time 83:82+ Mr 13 '64
Volunteer kidney; case of George Brost. il Newsweek 61:76 Mr 4 '63
Where are they now? Herrick twins. il Newsweek 61:12 Mr 4 '63
Wisdom tooth transplants; Transplant era held back by lack of spare parts. Sci N L 85:182 Mr 21 '64
Year of the transplant. il Newsweek 63:50+ F 10 '64

TRANSPLANTING
Confessions of a scavenger; excerpts from Joy of a small garden. J. Gillespie. House & Gard 123:217-20 My '63
Planting from a container. il Sunset 130:254-5 Ap '63
Transplanting seedlings indoors. R. Kersey. il Flower Grower 51:38-9+ F '64

TRANSPLANTING human organs. See Transplantation of organs, tissues, etc.

TRANSPLUTONIUM. See Plutonium

TRANSPOLAR flights. See Aviation—Transpolar flights

TRANSPONDERS
Military transponder plans implemented. Aviation W 81:60-2 Jl 27 '64
Submerged transponders would fix missile impact points. R. Pay. il Miss & Roc 14:18+ Mr 16 '64
Transponders are coming. W. J. Kendall. il Flying 75:49+ Ag '64

TRANSPORT planes, Military. See Airplanes, Military transport

TRANSPORT workers
Labor; the enigma of the unions. T. R. Brooks. il Duns R 81:pt2 S135-6+ Je '63
Manpower, a prime resource. E. W. Williams, jr. bibliog f Ann Am Acad 345:122-9 Ja '63
New and vital role for labor. T. R. Brooks. il Duns R 83:pt2 103-5+ Je '64

TRANSPORT workers union
Pan Am-TWU pact to cost airline $11.5 million during next two years. Aviation W 81:50 S 7 '64

TRANSPORTATION
Trail to super transport service; address, March 18, 1963. J. N. Sites. Vital Speeches 29:441-4 My 1 '63
Transportation renaissance; symposium, ed. by G. F. Mott. Ann Am Acad 345:1-142 Ja '63
Transportation: the age of the specialist; symposium. il Duns R 83:pt2 100-18+ Je '64
Where is science taking us? jet propulsion principles applied to the problems of land transportatiion. J. V. Foa. il Sat R 47:68-9 N 7 '64
Wings of the future. E. Hall. il Sci N L 85:298-9 My 9 '64

TRANSPORTATION—*Continued*
Year 2000; address, September 23, 1964. V. F. Caputo. Vital Speeches 31:10-15 O 15 '64
See also
Pack transportation
Railroads
Railroads—Freight service
Rapid transit
Shipping
Subways
also subhead Transportation under various subjects, e.g. Boats—Transportation

Bibliography

Executive bookshelf. Duns R 83:pt2 149+ Je '64

Federal aid

Needed: a prompt end to the old luxury of limited thinking. il Arch Forum 119:94-5 O '63
Point of no return. Duns R 81:pt2 S97 Je '63
Problem: rational and effective allocation of resources. K. T. Healy. il Ann Am Acad 345:39-46 Ja '63
Urban transit's new pep pill. H. B. Meyers. Fortune 70:166-7+ N '64
Washington; who's got the action? C. Levy. il Duns R 81:pt2 S137-8+ Je '63

Laws and regulations

Fulfilling our basic commitments as a nation; statement, July 10, 1963; with comments by nonwhite diplomats. D. Rusk. Dept State Bul 49:154-9 Jl 29 '63
Transportation: the political dimensions of an economic dilemma. W. B. Johnson. bibliog f Ann Am Acad 345:47-57 Ja '63
Unraveling the freight rate mess; transportation bill. Bsns W p56+ F 8 '64

Alaska

Gold rush begins for Alaska trade. il Bsns W p 186+ O 10 '64

Ecuador

Streetcar named Autoferro Ecuatoriano; a ride from Quito to Guayaquil. S. Meyer. il Sat R 46:94+ O 12 '63

Great Britain

Traffic in towns; concerning British report. F. Gutheim. Arch Rec 135:78+ Je '64
See also
Railroads—Great Britain

Japan

See also
Railroads—Japan

Netherlands

Holland: gateway to Europe? transportation center of Common market. il Duns R 84:44-5+ Jl '64

Oklahoma

Seaports for Oklahoma. il U S News 54:66-9 F 11 '63

United States

Back on the rails. Time 84:76+ Ag 28 '64
Business bets on no rail strike. il Bsns W p26-7 Jl 20 '63
Full speed ahead on a dead-end road; excerpt from Heart of our cities. V. Gruen. il Horizon 6:66-71 Sum '64
Hold your nose at Bobby's pork. Life 55:4 O 18 '63
How to make that family trip: by plane, train, bus, or car? S. A. Mix. il Todays Health 41:30-5+ F '63
If you plan to see the New York fair, and you don't want to drive. il Sunset 132:44-6+ My '64
Mass-transit muddle. R. Moley. Newsweek 61:100 My 6 '63
Transportation and the city; symposium. il Arch Forum 119:61-95 O '63
Transportation: breaking through the distribution barrier; symposium. il Duns R 81:pt2 S97-106+ Je '63
Transportation renaissance; symposium, ed. by G. F. Mott. Ann Am Acad 345:1-142 Ja '63
Transportation's labor crisis. E. B. Shils. bibliog f Harvard Bsns R 42:84-98 My '64
Unblock that merger track! Life 54:4 Ap 5 '63
See also
Air travel—United States
Commuters
Ferries
Railroads—United States

TRANSPORTATION, Automotive
Motor carriage: the long and short of it. J. F. Pinkney. Ann Am Acad 345:66-72 Ja '63
See also
Trucking

TRANSPORTATION, Military
See also
Airdrop
United States—Army—Transportation
United States—Military air transport service

TRANSPORTATION, Municipal. See Rapid transit

TRANSPORTATION of works of art
Calculated risk. N. Kent. Am Artist 28:3 Ap '64
Historic journey of the Pieta. il Life 56:83-5+ Ap 17 '64
Pieta gets ready for the fair. il Bsns W p32-3 Ap 11 '64
To Tokyo or bust; Venus de Milo crated for journey. il Life 56:126 Mr 6 '64

TRANSPORTATION tokens. See Tokens

TRANSPORTATION workers. See Transport workers

TRANS-SIBERIAN railroad trip. See Railroad travel

TRANSVAAL daisies. See Gereberas

TRANS WORLD airlines
Airlines oppose new Atlantic area plan. R. G. O'Lone. Aviation W 81:31 S 28 '64
American, TWA to swap engine overhaul. Aviation W 79:41 Ag 19 '63
CAB to demand appearance by Hughes. R. H. Cook. Aviation W 80:39-40 Je 15 '64
Coffee, tea or Doris Day; introduction of in-flight entertainment. il Time 84:103-4 O 16 '64
Court to review CAB ruling on control of TWA by Hughes. Aviation W 81:29-30 Ag 3 '64
Court voids CAB order on Toolco-TWA. J. W. Carter. Aviation W 81:30-1 D 14 '64
Flying the Atlantic without a navigator. R. E. Smallman. il Pop Sci 182:86-8+ Ap '63
Grabbing again for TWA controls. il Bsns W p 168+ My 16 '64
Howard Hughes; he is battling for control of a billion-dollar empire. J. R. Phelan. il Sat Eve Post 236:15-23 F 9 '63
Hughes appeals TWA default judgment. Aviation W 78:45 Je 3 '63
Hughes battles to avoid court appearance. J. R. Ashlock. Aviation W 78:39-40 F 11 '63
Hughes breaks a date in fight for TWA. Bsns W p26 F 16 '63
Hughes judgment appeal denied. Aviation W 80:34 Je 8 '64
Hughes makes new pass at TWA. Bsns W p32 O 10 '64
Hughes' silence is major issue in merger. Aviation W 78:47 F 4 '63
Hughes takes a trick; wins control of TWA. Bsns W p27 Jl 18 '64
Hughes to sell TWA debentures. il Aviation W 79:40 O 7 '63
In devious battle; Hughes to repurchase TWA? Newsweek 63:72+ My 11 '64
Italy hinders TWA all-cargo jet effort. R. H. Cook. Aviation W 80:49-50 Ja 20 '64
Last gasp of the tin goose; 1929 Ford trimotor. A. Chamberlin. il Sat Eve Post 236:26-7 Ag 10 '63; Same abr. Read Digest 83:151-5 D '63
Merger seen as competitive tool. Aviation W 79:39 Ag 12 '63
New U.S. air policy threatens merger. L. L. Doty. Aviation W 78:38 F 11 '63
N. Atlantic area concept urged. Aviation W 79:32 S 2 '63
Northeast, Hughes file trust agreement; step toward regaining Trans World airlines. J. W. Carter. Aviation W 81:34-5 O 12 '64
Pan Am attacks plan to divide transatlantic routes with TWA. J. R. Ashlock. Aviation W 79:41 Ag 5 '63
Pan Am, TWA choose kerosene to ease public JP-4 controversy. J. R. Ashlock. Aviation W 82:32 Ja 25 '65
Pan Am, TWA differ over Atlantic policy. Aviation W 81:38 S 21 '64
Pan Am, TWA seek early merger action. Aviation W 78:45 Mr 18 '63
Ruling shakes TWA financial supporters. J. R. Ashlock. Aviation W 81:28 Jl 20 '64
Seaboard president attacks case for Pan American-TWA merger; summary of address. R. M. Jackson. Aviation W 78:44 Ja 21 '63
Tiny airline with a sharp riposte; Swissair. il Bsns W p 108-10 Ja 11 '64
Transatlantic case delay creates dilemma on foreign competition. Aviation W 79:39 Ag 26 '63
Trans World, Continental discuss merger. L. L. Doty. Aviation W 79:34-5 O 28 '63
TWA appeals CAB decision on Hughes. Aviation W 81:28 Jl 27 '64
TWA enthusiasm for merger is wavering. L. L. Doty. Aviation W 78:33 Mr 4 '63
TWA goes on the road to get suppliers. il Bsns W p 138+ Ja 26 '63

TRANS WORLD airlines—*Continued*
TWA keys domestic gain hopes to introduction of 727 service. Aviation W 80:29 Mr 23 '64
TWA official examines SST economics; address. R. W. Rummel. il Aviation W 82: 59-60+ Ja 4 '65
TWA purchase of six 727s dims prospect of Caravelle 10A order. Aviation W 79:29 S 2 '63
TWA to pay $16 million interest on debt. J. R. Ashlock. Aviation W 80:34-5 My 25 '64
TWA will seek Hughes default order. J. R. Ashlock. Aviation W 78:49 F 18 '63
TWA's DC-9 order totals $86.2 million. Aviation W 81:31 Jl 27 '64

TRANSYLVANIA
Trouble over Transylvania. G. Bailey. il Reporter 31:25-30 N 19 '64

TRAP shooting
Biggest, loudest show in U.S. sport; Grand American trapshoot. V. Kraft. il Sports Illus 19:26-8+ S 9 '63
How to get started in trap and skeet: the sport for sharpshooters. H. Bradshaw. il Pop Sci 185:142-6 +O '64
How to shoot skeet and stay solvent. R. Starnes. Field & S 68:16+ Mr '64
Shooting (cont) Sports Illus 19:89+ S 9 '63
See also
Skeet (game)

TRAPPING
Cannons for turkeys; distributing gobblers throughout Florida. K. Musson. il Field & S 68:10-11 O '63
Prairie drag race; catching antelope alive. T. Wilcox. il Outdoor Life 131:40-3+ Ja '63
Up the little finger. D. J. Anderson. il Field & S 69:24-6+ Ja '65

TRAPS, Insect. See Insect traps

TRASH. See Refuse and refuse disposal

TRASH burners. See Refuse incinerators

TRASH cans. See Refuse receptacles

TRASK, Robert A.
Waiting time. Harper 228:168-9 Ap '64

TRAUFFER, Art
Boost box. Pop Electr 18:58-9 My '63
Dial, buzz and blink. Pop Electr 20:64-5 F '64
Microphone volume control. Electr World 69:72 Ap '63
Mono use of stereo phones having two plugs. Electr World 71:79 My '64
Novelty lamps. Pop Mech 121:161 F '64
Phono fillips. Pop Electr 20:56-7 Ja '64
What's what light. Pop Electr 19:62 Jl '63

TRAVEL
Assorted pleasures and palaces for people who are going places. M. Gough. il House B 105: 84+ Je '63
Baedeker of what not to see. J. Wechsberg. il N Y Times Mag p 14+ Je 30 '63
Basic wardrobe for vacation travel. il Good H 158:161 My '64
Bits & pieces. W. J. Sumits. Pop Phot 54:101 Mr '64
Booked for travel. H. Sutton. See issues of Saturday review
Booked for travel. P. K. Brooks. il Sat R 47:30-1 O 3 '64
Camera guide. L. Barry. il Pop Phot 52:76-7+ Mr; 94-5+ Je; 53:84-5+ O; 54+ N '63
Camera safari. il U S Camera 26:34-5 Ag '63
Fall & winter travel tips. il Changing T 18: 24-5 O '64
Footloose and fatigued. H. Sutton. il Sat R 47:161-4+ Ag 29 '64
Going places. N. Kent. Am Artist 27:3+ Ap '63
Grand tour. E. A. Standen. il Antiques 83: 660-4 Je '63
Here and there. See issues of Holiday
How to leave home and like it. M. Gough. See issues of House beautiful
How to make love in five languages; excerpts from How to marry a millionaire. D. Lilly. il McCalls 91:94-5 Je '64
How to travel alone, and like it. H. Dolson. Redbook 123:65+ My '64
If you plan to see the New York fair, and you don't want to drive. il Sunset 132:44-6+ My '64
Impact of international travel on U.S. balance of payments; statement, November 30, 1964. C. H. Mace. il Dept State Bul 51: 888-90 D 21 '64
In praise of travel. W. D. Patterson. Sat R 47:28-9 Ja 4 '64
Let's travel. il Mlle 85:126-7 F; 200-4 Mr; 193-7+ Ap '64
Let's travel on a vacation; vacation planning week. il Mlle 57:48-50 Je '63
Let's travel to Europe; student camping tours. il Mlle 59:90-1 Jl '64
Let's travel to ski. Mlle 58:182-7 N '63
Life travel. il Life 57:91-5+ Ag 14; 62-71+ O 23 '64
[Month] travel in and beyond the West. See issues of Sunset
My secret scenes off-stage. E. Williams. il Travel 122:53-5 N '64
New freedom. W. D. Patterson. Sat R 46:30 Ag 24 '63
New look in camera tours. M. A. Matzkin. il Mod Phot 27:92+ N '63
Notebook for the sophisticated traveler: symposium. il Harper 230:103-34 Ja '65
On traveling with a notebook. F. Stark. il Atlan 214:95-6 D '64
Pacific/Orient '63: scrutiny of the bounty. R. Joseph. il Esquire 60:42-53 Ag '63
Paragon traveller: how she prepares for the beauty snares. Vogue 143:88 Ap 1 '64
Photography and travel. B. Downes. Pop Phot 54:38 F '64
Reasons for travel. E. Seidensticker. il Atlan 212:122+ Jl '63
Roamer's ramblings. T. Shane. See issues of Travel
Roamin' the globe with Travel. See issues of Travel
Round-the-world sabbatical. S. Solomon. il Sr Schol 84:13T-14T Mr 20 '64
Rush to out-of-the-way Europe. il Newsweek 61:68-71 Je 3 '63
Should every student travel abroad? J. F. Fixx. il Sat R 46:46+ F 16 '63
Sixth annual travel photo handbook. il Pop Phot 52:131-46 Ap '63
Sixth-seventh annual travel photo handbook. il Pop Phot 52:131-46 Ap '63; 54:131-46 Ap '64
So you like to travel. A. N. D. Brooks. Negro Hist Bul 26:204+ Mr '63
Stop & go. H. Sutton. See issues of McCall's
Summertime is tourtime: package, all-expense, escorted tours. P. P. Coleman. il Sr Schol 84:9T Ap 17 '64
Take your wife on your next business trip? Bet Hom & Gard 43:24-5 Ja '65
Teen travel talk. il Seventeen 23:173 Mr '64
Ten tips on taking your camera traveling. J. R. Gregg. U S Camera 27:64 O '64
Those student tours to Europe: what really goes on. G. Bocca. il McCalls 90:92-3+ Jl '63
To travel is to live; with sketches by H. C. Andersen. M. Gough. House B 106:144+ My '64
Travel. Vogue 144:44 Ag 15; 108 S 1; 74 S 15; 80 O 1; 90 O 15; 30+ N 1; 8 N 15; 54 D '64; 145:121 Ja 15; 96 F 1 '65
Travel & camera. il U S Camera 27:32-3 F; 26-7 Mr '64
Travel digest. See issues of Travel
Travel enriches our Christmas. V. Buchanan. il Travel 122:47-9 D '64
Travel notes. R. Joseph. See issues of Esquire
Travel; precious few unspoiled spots. il Time 83:74-5 Je 26 '64
Travel tips. P. P. Coleman. il Sr Schol 84: 4T Ja 31; 5T My 8; 85:5T S 30 '64
Travel with a purpose; special-interest tours. il Changing T 18:25-9 F '64
Traveling with Mlle: the truant fancy. W. Sansom. il Mlle 58:123-5 F '64
Travellers' tips, far-flinging; some level-headed, some personal, some precisely aimed at Africa. I. Chase. Vogue 142:221-3 O 1 '63
Well traveled camera. D. L. Miller. il Mod Phot 27:38+ Je '63
World travel issue 1965; symposium. il Sat R 48:39-45+ Ja 2 '65
Your questions answered. il Changing T 18: 14 Ap '64
See also
Air travel
Art tours
Automobile touring
Cruising
Customs service and tourists
Excursions
Luggage
Ocean travel
Opera tours
Packing of luggage
Vacations
Youth hostels

Advertising

Where to go in '64; visit U.S.A. tour through Europe, 1961. M. Sutton. il Am For 70:16-19+ Ja '64

TRAVEL—*Continued*

Bibliography

Background for travel. il NEA J 53:64-6 F '64
Better books for traveling. E. Kiester, jr. il Redbook 120:32+ F '63
Big trends in travel books. P. Andrews. il Pub W 183:32-41 Mr 4; 25-7 Mr 11 '63
Party of one. P. Fleming. il Holiday 35:14+ Ja '64
Travel tips. P. P. Coleman. il Sr Schol 84: 22T Mr 6 '64
Traveler's tales. B. Coletti. Sat R 47:84-5 O 10 '64
Travelers' tales. B. D. Laschever. Sat R 46: 62-4+ Mr 16 '63
Who needs Herodotus? M. Gough. il House B 105:136+ My '63

Caricatures and cartoons

Mlle's European travel portfolio 1963. Mlle 56:196-204 Mr '63

Economic aspects

Case of the extravagant traveler. E. Perényi. il Harper 230:105-9 Ja '65
Europe: on $5 an hour? H. L. Hurwitz. il Sr Schol 85:10T-11T Ja 7 '65
What does it cost to travel by bus, train, car, and plane? Bet Hom & Gard 41:7+ Ag '63
See also
Tourist trade

Exhibitions

U.S. travel shows. B. Barkley. il Travel 121: 49-51 Ja '64

Health aspects

Travel well. C. Rule; E. N. Dye. See issues of Travel

Publicity

T for travel; Travelers insurance company, publicizes travel for employees. E. L. Ericson. il Recreation 57:506-7 D '64

Social aspects

How to be an economy-tour millionaire. R. Gray. il NEA J 52:53-6 F '63

TRAVEL (periodical)
See also
Mr Travel award

TRAVEL, Space. See Space flight

TRAVEL agencies
Air tickets brew a dogfight. il Bsns W p53-4 N 7 '64
Have job, will travel. M. A. Brice. Mlle 60: 168+ N '64
How intourist took me in. K. Snow. Nat R 16:355-7 My 5 '64
New look in camera tours. M. A. Matzkin. il Mod Phot 27:92+ N '63
Personal business. Bsns W p85-6 F 1 '64
Scrambler; New York's Cosmos travel bureau. il Newsweek 63:60 F 3 '64
Travel data for summer artists. il Design 64:187 Je '63

TRAVEL articles. See Periodical literature

TRAVEL bureaus. See Information services

TRAVEL films. See Moving pictures—Documentary films

TRAVEL game; drama. See Miller, H. L.

TRAVEL guides. See Guidebooks

TRAVEL information. See Successful farming (periodical)

TRAVEL literature
Excitement of travelling with a civilized companion; travel essays. F. Stark. Vogue 143:148-9+ Je '64
Let's try a tesser. F. A. Sullivan. il PTA Mag 57:30-1 Je '63
See also
Guidebooks

TRAVEL regulations
Castro's U.S. guests. il Time 82:31-2 Ag 9 '63
Long way home; U.S. students defiance of State department travel ban. il Time 82:30 S 6 '63
Man with a country; defense of the basic American right to travel; excerpt from What can a man do? M. Mayer. Harper 228:88-90+ Mr '64; Discussion. 228:6 My '64
Nailing up the back door; all travel between Mexico and Cuba. New Repub 148:11 Ap 20 '63
Passport barrier: it must come down. H. S. Commager. il N Y Times Mag p 12+ O 20 '63
RSVP: and fifty-nine came. Newsweek 62: 47 Jl 15 '63
Raucous caucus room; House committee on un-American activities hearings on students, rebels, and hangers-on who had journeyed to Castro's Cuba in defiance of State department ban. il Newsweek 62:30+ S 23 '63
Red junket to Cuba; ed. by R. Tunley. B. Hoffman. il Sat Eve Post 236:25-9 O 5 '63
Reddest tape. L. Tillett and A. Tillett. il Travel 121:33-5+ Ja '64
Right to privacy; excerpt from Naked society. V. Packard. Atlan 213:71-5 Mr '64
Right to travel. Commonweal 79:736 Mr 20 '64
To travel freely. H. Aptheker. Bul Atomic Sci 20:25 Mr '64
Tourists from Tokyo. il Bsns W p28 F 22 '64
Travel ban; new restrictions. New Repub 149:6 N 23 '63
Travel ban defied; investigation of students by House un-American activities committee. il Sr Schol 83:7-8 O 4 '63
Travel to Cuba; State department ban. Commonweal 79:4-5 S 27 '63
U.S. establishes closed areas for official personnel of Bulgarian, Czechoslovak, Hungarian, Polish, and Rumanian missions; Department announcement, with texts of U.S. notes November 12, 1963, and list of U.S. counties closed to travel. Dept State Bul 49:860-3 D 2 '63
U.S. protests Soviet interference with convoys to Berlin; November 6, 1963. Dept State Bul 49:818 N 25 '63
U.S. repeats warning on travel to Cuba. Dept State Bul 50:10-11 Ja 6 '64
U.S. revises areas closed to Soviet citizens; proposes mutual abolition or reduction of restrictions; Department announcement, with U.S. note, November 12, 1963, and enclosures. Dept State Bul 49:855-9 D 2 '63
U.S. warns validated passport is required for travel to Cuba. Dept State Bul 49:92 Jl 15 '63

TRAVEL study courses
Field trip to Europe; business school students from West coast. il Bsns W p 48-9 Jl 13 '63
International orientation for college administrators. L. J. Stiles. Sch & Soc 91:356-8 N 16 '63
New American traveler. L. G. Rubin. Esquire 61:40+ My '64
Notes for flying freshmen, sailing sophomores, journeying juniors, and sight-seeing seniors. K. Davis. Mlle 57:309+ Ag '63
Teen travel talk; high school study-travel programs. il Seventeen 23:26 O '64
Traveling classrooms. E. E. Henderson. NEA J 52:57 F '63
Why not study abroad? international summer school program at Oxford univ. H. McDonnell. il Sr Schol 85:13T Ja 7 '65
Year of the great migration; student tours abroad. J. F. Fixx. il Sat R 47:78-9 F 15 '64
See also
Colleges and universities. Traveling
Experiment in international living (organization)

TRAVEL trailers. See Automobile trailers

TRAVEL with children
Bridge to the past; visits to historic places. E. F. Hunter. il Parents Mag 38:64-6+ Mr '63
Car travel can be fun-but make it safe. il Good H 157:128 Jl '63
Feeding the young traveler. B. M. Stover. il Parents Mag 38:72+ My '63
Have children, can travel! V. Ritchie. il Sr Schol 84:8T-9T Mr 20 '64
How to be at home abroad. P. Langeweische. il House B 105:148-9+ Mr '63
How to keep the kids happy on a trip; games. E. Beaver. il Bet Hom & Gard 42:93-4 Jl '64
How to survive a family trip. B. Miles. il Parents Mag 38:42-3 Ag '63
How to travel with children in Europe, by L. Hadley. Review
Time il 83:57 Ja 17 '64
How we discovered America. L. Hillary. il Redbook 121:60-1+ Je '63
Is your car child-safe? H. Dark and P. Dark. il Todays Health 41:14-17 Jl '63
Seeing the world through my children's eyes. A. M. Rosenthal. il Ladies Home J 80:37+ N '63
Tips on family car trips. B. G. Wadsworth. Parents Mag 39:22 Jl '64
Travel abroad family style. J. R. Komaiko. il Parents Mag 38:56-7+ Ap '63
Traveling safely with children. J. Chandler. il Redbook 121:40-1 Jl '63

TRAVEL with children—*Continued*
Traveling with children. A. Vanderbilt. il Travel 121:42-4 Mr '64
Traveling with young eyes. M. J. Kempner. il Harper 230:128-30 Ja '65
We took our children to Europe. R. Zagoren. House B 106:10+ Jl '64
We took to the great outdoors with baby. E. Hayes. il Parents Mag 39:46-7+ Je '64
When you take the youngsters to Europe. D. Siegel. Parents Mag 38:58-9+ Je '63

TRAVEL with pets
Traveling with the pet set. P. O'Keefe. Am Home 67:76 Je '64

TRAVEL writers. See Authors

TRAVELERS
Compatible companions, or How to stay out of trouble when you choose friends for the trip. D. L. McFadden. House B 106:26+ Je '64
How to be an economy-tour millionaire. R. Gray. il NEA J 52:53-6 F '63
Lovely American. il Time 84:60 S 18 '64
Notebook for the sophisticated traveler; symposium. il Harper 230:103-34 Ja '65
Runner through the mist. J. McCormick. Atlan 211:63-8 Mr '63
She travels the fastest. J. Howard. Mlle 56:70+ F '63
Tourists, beware. America 108:359 Mr 16 '63
Tourists from Tokyo. il Bsns W p28 F 22 '64
Young grandees on tour. G. Bocca. il Sat R 46:58-60 Mr 16 '63
See also
Voyages

Anecdotes, facetiae, satire, etc.

Adrift in Jamais-Jamais land. M. Bennett. il Sat R 46:67 Mr 16 '63
Cruisemanship. V. M. Black. il Travel 120:35-7 N '63

TRAVELERS checks
Checks that never bounce. F. Sondern, jr. il Read Digest 83:205-8 Ag '63
Good as money, and profitable, too. il Bsns W p 150+ N 7 '64
Traveler's checks, private money. il Changing T 19:41-3 Ja '65

TRAVELERS insurance companies
New hands on the umbrella. il Time 84:98+ D 11 '64

TRAVELING exhibitions. See Exhibitions, Traveling

TRAVELING hoist. See Hoisting machinery

TRAVELING salesmen. See Commercial travelers

TRAVELING stores
How to succeed in business without an office; rolling repair shops and sales displays. H. Walton. il Pop Sci 182:64-7 Mr '63

TRAVELING theater. See Theater, Traveling

TRAVELING wave tubes
Comsat readies RFP's. M. Getler. Miss & Roc 13:35+ N 11 '63
GE develops single-reversal TWT. il Miss & Roc 13:34 Ag 5 '63
Traveling-wave tubes. J. H. Jarrett. bibliog il Electr World 71:25-8 Mr '64

TRAVELLER without luggage; drama. See Anouilh, J.

TRAVELS
See also
Travelers
Voyages

TRAVELSTEAD, Chester C.
New and better teacher education. Sch & Soc 91:332-4 N 2 '63

TRAVERS, John F.
Foreign affairs begin at home. Cath World 199:16-21 Ap '64

TRAVERS, Pamela Lyndon
Where did she come from? why did she go? por Sat Eve Post 237:76+ N 7 '64

about

Rose for Mary Poppins. H. Frankel. Sat R 47:24-5+ N 7 '64

TRAVERS-BALL, Ian
Challenged to reconcile. America 109:736-7 D 7 '63
India and the Negro question. America 109:44-5 Jl 13 '63
No magic key. America 108:673-4 My 11 '63

TRAVERSE rods (for curtains) See Curtain and drapery fixtures

La TRAVIATA; opera. See Verdi, G.

TRAVIS, Martin B. and Watkins, J. T.
Time bomb explodes. Nation 198:83-5 Ja 27 '64

TRAXLER, Arthur E.
Educational frontier. Sch & Soc 91:72 F 9 '63
Modern revolution in education. Sch & Soc 92:33 Ja 25 '64

TRAYNOR, George
Charter for laymen, 1822. Commonweal 81:418-21 D 18 '64

TRAYS
How to get carried away in great style. il Am Home 67:48-9+ My '64
Tray for travelers. il Sunset 131:98+ D '63

TREANOR, Aline Jean
Mummers theatre of Oklahoma City. Theatre Arts 47:55-9 D '63

TREASON
Treason in the twentieth century, by M. Boveri. Review
Nat R 15:112 Ag 13 '63. N. Weyl
See also
Sedition

TREASON trials. See Trials (treason)

TREASURE; story. See Boles, P. D.

TREASURE trove
Anyone for buried treasure? Cocos Island. J. Iams. il Sat Eve Post 237:64-6 Je 13 '64
Bonanza on the bottom; scuba divers on Florida beaches. Time 84:42-3 Ag 28 '64
Deep sea diver uncovers treasure; 16th-century Spanish ship on western Bermuda reef. Hobbies 69:121 N '64
Drowned galleons yield Spanish gold. K. Wagner. il Nat Geog Mag 127:1-37 Ja '65
Greatest recovery of treasure in centuries? exhibit at the National geographic society building. il U S News 57:10 D 28 '64
King John's lost treasure. J. Morris. il Sat Eve Post 237:64+ My 30 '64
Lost worlds of Don Pablo. C. Phinizy. il Sports Illus 21:80-4+ N 30 '64
Oak Island's mysterious money pit. D. MacDonald. il Read Digest 86:136-40 Ja '65
Spanish gold two fathoms deep; off Florida's coast. J. Atwater. il Sat Eve Post 237:66-71 D 12 '64
Toplitz mystery; Lake Toplitz in the Austrian Alps. Newsweek 62:61-2 N 11 '63
Treasure fever hits Florida coastline. il Bsns W p28-9 O 10 '64
Wacky search for gold. L. H. Lapham. il Sat Eve Post 236:66-71 D 14 '63

TREASURERS, Company. See Corporations—Treasurers

TREASURY department. See United States—Treasury department

TREAT, Ida
To celebes. New Yorker 39:152+ O 26 '63

TREATIES
Assembly opens multilateral treaties to new states. U N Rev 11:39-41 F '64
First step to what? Soviet proposal of a nonaggression pact. E. A. Gross. Reporter 29:30-2 S 12 '63
Non-aggression pact? W. C. McWilliams. Commonweal 79:191-3 N 8 '63
This century's peace pacts and what followed. F. B. Stevens. il U S News 55:44-5 Ag 19 '63
See also
Antarctic treaty, 1959
Diplomacy
Inter-American treaty of reciprocal assistance
Nuclear test ban treaty, 1963

TREATMENT of prisoners. See Prisoners—Treatment

TREATS; story. See Thomas, M.

TREATY of Moscow. See Nuclear test ban treaty, 1963

TREBITSCH-LINCOLN, Ignatius
Spy as anti-hero. H. Bowser. Sat R 46:30 S 14 '63

TRECATE, Luigi Ferrari
Uncle Tom's hut (Capana dello Zio Tom)
Criticism
Opera N 27:25 My 4 '63
Time il 81:39-40 Mr 22 '63

TREDUP, Alice M.
Another kind of camera. Horn Bk 39:30-5 F '63

TREE, Marietta
Art of welcoming visitors from abroad. por House & Gard 126:242-3 N '64
Story of progress in achieving international human rights. NEA J 52:50-3 N '63
U.S. views on U.N. subcommittee's report on South-West Africa; statement, October 30, 1964. Dept State Bul 51:760-2 N 23 '64

about

Come to the party. il pors Time 84:22 N 6 '64
Our top girl at the UN. H. Ehrlich. il pors Look 27:64-6 Mr 26 '63
Patrician with a mission. il pors Life 55:107-8+ O 25 '63

TREE angel; drama. See Christmas plays—Texts

TREE breeding
Freeze-dried pollen speeds tree-breeding. Farm J 87:64 Mr '63
Search for super-trees. A. C. Jensen. il Am For 70:16-18+ Ag '64
They are bringing back the chestnut tree. J. C. Furnas. il Read Digest 82:129-32 Ap '63
Why conservationists are missing a big bet! S. S. Chase. il Am For 70:14-16 My '64

TREE buds. See Buds

TREE cutters; story. See Jones, M. L.

TREE farms. See Forest management

TREE frogs and tree toads
Color polymorphism in Pacific tree frogs. L. E. Resnick and D. L. Jameson. bibliog il Science 142:1081-3 N 22 '63

TREE geraniums. See Geraniums

TREE grafting. See Grafting

TREE houses
For adventure build a tree house. il Pop Gard 15:48-9 Ja '64
Out on a limb. C. Morrison. il Look 28:M7-9 Ag 11 '64
You go inside to go up. il Sunset 133:90 Ag '64

TREE nurseries. See Nurseries (horticulture)

TREE peonies. See Peonies

TREE planting
Aruba's one-man resources department. M. Frome. il Am For 70:24-6+ Jl '64
Give your trees a good start. il Bet Hom & Gard 41:112 Ap '63
How to plant an English walnut. J. Krill. il Flower Grower 51:38 Mr '64
New way to fertilize trees. R. D. Wennblom. il Farm J 87:29 F '63
Sand + oil=trees. E. J. Long. il Am For 70:46-8 Ja '64
Six planting do's and don'ts. C. Lisle. il Pop Gard 14:42-3 Ap '63
These trees do well in containers. Sunset 130:260+ Mr '63
Which is better spring or fall planting? R. D. Roe. il Horticulture 41:506 O '63
See also
Arbor day

TREE propagation. See Plant propagation

TREE protection. See Trees, Care of

TREE rats. See Rats

TREE rings
Tree ring extremes. W. M. Harlow. il Am For 69:27 Mr '63

TREE roots. See Roots

TREE sculpture. See Wood carving

TREE surgery. See Trees, Care of

TREES
Add color dash with trees and shrubs. R. R. Thomasson. il Pop Gard 15:24-7 F '64
Arboretum et fruticetum Britannicum. The trees and shrubs of Britain. by J. C. Loudon. Review
Am For il 69:8-9+ Ag '63. H. W. Dengler
Best roses, trees, and shrubs for 1964. H. Mason. il Bet Hom & Gard 42:64-9 F '64
Doomsday book for big trees? Am For 70:9 My '64
Double duty from shrubs and trees. S. W. Plimpton. il Horticulture 41:518-19 O '63
Fast-growing trees. D. Wyman. Am Home 67:100-1 O '64
Keep cool with landscaping. M. M. Taylor. il Horticulture 41:459 S '63
Look twice before cutting. D. White. il Flower Grower 50:45+ Mr '63
Plant a forest in your garden. il Sunset 133:152-3 Jl '64
Say it with trees! J. B. Craig. Am For 70:11 Ja '64
Set your garden ablaze with autumn color. T. A. Weston. il Am Home 66:34-5 S '63
These trees all have curious-looking or handsome fruits. il Sunset 131:274 O '63
Trees & shrubs for all season color. F. F. Rockwell and E. C. Grayson. il Flower Grower 50:45+ O '63
Trees are my hobby. J. R. Rarick. il Horticulture 41:122 Mr '63
Two planning and planting ideas. J. R. Rebhan. il Flower Grower 50:40-1 N '63
Wood you know? questions and answers. J. Daugherty and M. Daugherty. il Sci Digest 56:93-5 D '64
Yes, trees to grow in your house. il Good H 158:128 Ja '64
See also
Arbor day
Arboretums
Botany
Burls
Christmas trees
Flowering trees
Forest ecology
Fruit trees
Landscape gardening
Leaves
Nut trees
Spiral growth and movement
Tree breeding
Woodlots
Woods
also names of trees, e.g. Oak

Diseases and pests

How to save a jacaranda. il Sunset 130:249-50 Mr '63
See also
Spruce budworms
Trees, Care of
also subhead Diseases and pests under names of trees, e.g. Elm—Diseases and pests

Growth

See Growth (plants)

Planting

See Tree planting

Poetry

Another parson's view. R. A. McDonald. Christian Cent 81:1595 D 23 '64
Beauty is a tree. S. Schooley. Horn Bk 40:663 D '64
Parson and the tree. D. A. Mordhorst. Christian Cent 81:1485 D 2 '64
Spruce tree. M. W. Andrews. il Am For 71:41 Ja '65
Trees. R. S. Gorski. il Am For 70:48 D '64

Pruning

See Pruning

Quotations, maxims, etc.

Of trees; comp. by E. F. Murphy. il N Y Times Mag p60 Je 7 '64

Roots

See Roots

Spraying

See Spraying and dusting

Wounds and injuries

Time to heal tree wounds. B. Brinhart. il Flower Grower 50:25-6 Mr '63

TREES, Age of
California's methuselah trees. W. F. Heald. il Am For 70:34-5 Mr '64
Chronology of a small glacier in eastern British Columbia, Canada. J. R. Bray. Science 144:287 Ap 17 '64

TREES, Care of
Beware! the woods are full of tree quacks. J. M. Haller. il Pop Sci 184:127-9+ My '64
How to treat the base of a tree. il Bet Hom & Gard 42:115 Je; 83 Jl '64
How to use cables to reduce wind stress on trees. il Sunset 134:138 Ja '65
Lightning need strike only once. il Pop Gard 15:89 Jl '64
Root feeding method effective in care of trees and shrubs. E. Daniels. il Flower Grower 50:58 Ag '63
Saved trees mean so much. J. R. Rebhan. il Flower Grower 52:30-1+ Ja '65
See also
Spraying and dusting
Trees—Wounds and injuries

TREES, Dwarf
Bonsai. D. Schroeder. il Horticulture 41:200-1 Ap '63
Bonsai briefs: how to collect, care for, create your own. il House & Gard 124:302-6 N '63
Bonsai in one day. R. E. Atkinson. il Flower Grower 50:50-4 O '63
Bonsai: nature in miniature. il House & Gard 124:264-7 N '63
Bonsai trees. il Design 66:21 N '64
Charm and the art of bonsai. il Am Home 67:96+ N '64
Do-it-yourself bonsai. M. A. Roche. il Am Home 66:94+ My '63
Dwarf evergreens in modern landscaping. H. Latimer. il Horticulture 41:520-1 O '63
How to make your own bonsai. il House & Gard 124:306-7 N '63
How to share the bonsai hobby. Sunset 132:236 Mr '64
Make a miniature marvel to display or give away. il Sunset 131:58-9 D '63
Meaning of bonsai. Y. Yoshimura. il Horticulture 42:16-19+ D '64
This bonsai is oregano. il Sunset 131:182 S '63
See also
Fruit trees, Dwarf

TREES, Effect of radiation on. See Plants, Effect of radiation on
TREES, Fossil
Fossil forests of Ocú, Panama. W. L. Stern and R. H. Eyde. il Science 140:1214 Je 14 '63
Radiocarbon and soil evidence of former forest in the southern Canadian tundra. R. A. Bryson and others. bibliog il Science 147:46-8 Ja 1 '65
TREES, Growth of. See Growth (plants)
TREES, Historic
Georgia's famous trees. M. Hunn. il Am For 70:42-5 N '64
Sad goodbye; Kilmer oak at Rutgers university. R. F. West. il Am For 69:12+ N '63
TREES, Petrified. See Petrified forests
TREES, State. See State trees
TREES, Training of
Bumper crop from little trees. H. M. Farkas. il Pop Gard 15:26-7 Ap '64
Espaliers: attractive space savers. Sunset 132:226-7 Je '64
TREES in cities
Creeping treelessness. J. P. Mansfield. Recreation 56:254 Je '63
Street trees. R. Walter. il Horticulture 42:18-20+ Jl '64
Stylish streets wear flowering trees. G. Taloumis. il Flower Grower 50:55-7 My '63
Trees for city deserts. L. C. Walker. il Am For 69:28-30 Mr '63
Woods move into cities; northeastern seaboard. B. Tufty. Sci N L 85:373 Je 13 '64
TREIMAN, Joyce
Salute to the singular. il por Time 83:72-3+ F 28 '64
TREJO, Paul E.
Space education and the Foothill planetarium. Sky & Tel 28:124-5 S '64
TREMBLEY, Ralph
Cultural activities go West. Recreation 56:317-19 S '63
TREMBLING. See Shivering
TREMOLO. See Vibrato
TREMORINE
Tremorine: its peripheral action on striated muscle. B. Csillik. bibliog il Science 146:765-6 N 6 '64
TRENCH, Anthony Chenevix-. See Chenevix-Trench, A.
TRENET, Charles
Revoir Paris. por Newsweek 63:84-5 Je 29 '64
TRENHOLM, H. Councill
Martyr on Alabama racial tightrope. A. N. D. Brooks. por(p229) Negro Hist Bul 26:230-2 My '63
TRENHOLME, A. K.
Brand new partnership. Sr Schol 85:14T-15T Ja 21 '65
TRENT, James W.
Progress and anxiety. Commonweal 81:40-2 O 2 '64
TRENT, William E. family
Many commencements of Callie Trent. W. P. Pitt. il Read Digest 84:49-53 Je '64
TRENT, William J. jr
Scholastic teacher interviews: William J. Trent, jr; ed. by H. Langer. por Sr Schol 83:9T-11T D 6 '63
TRENTON, N.J.
Housing
Movers and voters. il Newsweek 63:28+ Mr 9 '64
TREPANNING. See Trephining
TREPASSO, Joe
Penny-by-penny. por Recreation 57:500-1 D '64
TREPHINING
Science and secrets of early medicine, by J. Thorwald. Review
Sci Digest 55:72 F '64. D. Cohen
TREPONEMA pallidum. See Syphilis
TRESKOW, Laura
Meet England's number one dollologist. C. H. Fawcett. il Hobbies 69:36+ Ja '65
TRESS, Wallace R.
Speckled bird; poem. Commonweal 79:72 O 11 '63
TRESSLER, Georg
Children's game. D. Streibig. il por Pop Phot 54:141+ Ja '64
TRESSLER, Marcille
Clay modeling. Sch Arts 64:27-8 Ja '65
Masks. il Sch Arts 63:14-15 O '63
TREVELYAN, George Macaulay
Trevelyan: the muse or the museum? J. Clive. Nation 196:143-5 F 16 '63
TREVELYAN, Raleigh
Hermit disclosed; dramatization. See Saunders, J. Next time I'll sing to you
TREVES, Ralph
Masking an eyesore. Pop Mech 120:170-1 N '63
Tools you need for pipe jobs. Pop Sci 183:98-100+ Ag '63
TREVIÑO, Elizabeth (Borton)
Sacred deer, child of the moon god; story. excerpt from Nacar, the white deer. Horn Bk 39:523-9 O '63
TREVOR, John B. jr
Oldest one-design? il Yachting 115:191 Mr '64
TREVOR-ROPER, Hugh Redwald
Four faces of heresy. Horizon 6:8-17 Spr '64
Great confrontations: Mary, queen of Scots and John Knox. Horizon 5:28-32 Jl '63
History, or hysteria? por Newsweek 64:35-6 D 28 '64
Hitler: the legend that failed. Holiday 36:35+ O '64
Jewish & other nationalisms. Commentary 35:15-21 Ja '63
TREXLER, P. C.
Germ-free isolators; with biographical sketch. Sci Am 211:15, 78-80+ Jl '64
TREYNOR, Jack L.
How to rate management of investment funds. Harvard Bsns R 43:63-75 Ja '65
TREYZ, Joseph H.
Cards-with-books program. ALA Bul 57:433-4 My '63
TREZISE, Philip H.
Trade expansion program; address, March 8, 1963. Dept State Bul 48:497-500 Ap 1 '63
United States and the European economic community; address, June 3, 1963. Dept State Bul 48:971-6 Je 24 '63
TRI-X film. See Photography—Films
TRIAL; story. See Ford, J. H.
TRIAL by jury. See Jury; Women as jurors
TRIAL lawyers. See Lawyers
TRIAL practice. See Procedure (law)
TRIALS
Big money question; six suppliers overcharged Philadelphia electric and UGI. il Bsns W p 176+ Ap 18 '64
Cigarettes v. lollipops; case of Edwin M. Green suing the American tobacco co. Time 84:59 D 11 '64
Cohn on the defense. Newsweek 63:24+ Ap 6 '64
Empty room; attendance at public trials. Time 85:47 Ja 1 '65
Ensuring fair trials; the impropriety of publicity. R. Goldfarb. New Repub 150:11-14 F 29 '64
How Hoffa got Hoffa. L. Velie. Read Digest 85:101-6 D '64
Jury tampering in Tennessee. C. R. Mollenhoff. il Look 27:79-82 My 21 '63
Late late show; trial of seven members of after-party brawl at coming-out party of Philadelphia debutante Fernanda Wanamaker Wetherill. il Time 83:74 Ap 24 '64
My son, the defendant; case of G. Martinis. il Newsweek 62:26-7 Jl 15 '63
Picnic trial; case of Rockefeller v. Murphy concerning custody of children. il Time 84:63 S 11 '64
Price of getting involved; Hector Mangual. T. Armbrister. il Sat Eve Post 237:81-5 S 26 '64
Question of custody; Happy Rockefeller's suit. il Time 84:88+ O 9 '64
Reasonably safe smoking; lawsuit against American tobacco co. Newsweek 64:50 D 14 '64
Trial by press release. Nation 199:83 S 7 '64
See also
Evidence (law)
Jury
Newspaper court reporting
Nuremberg trials
Television broadcasting—Trials
Belgium
Tragedy at Liege; Vandeput's thalidomide baby. J. Gallahue. il Look 27:72-4+ Mr 12 '63; Discussion. 27:16 Ap 23 '63
Canada
Case of the Kelly clamp. Newsweek 64:54-5 Jl 20 '64
Verdict on a surgeon; case of the Kelly clamp. Newsweek 64:72 Jl 27 '64
Cuba
Deadly witness; Castro v. M. A. Rodriguez. Time 83:28 Ap 10 '64

TRIALS—*Continued*

France

Model of stability; Argoud trial. il Newsweek 63:32 Ja 13 '64
Trial of Marie Besnard. by M. Besnard. Review
Newsweek il 61:107 Ap 15 '63
Voltaire and the Calas case. by E. Nixon. Review
Commonweal 78:113-16 Ap 19 '63. L. F. X. Mayhew

Germany (Federal Republic)

Auschwitz business. il Time 83:24 Ja 17 '64
Auschwitz come alive again. il N Y Times Mag p 14-15 Ap 19 '64
Exposing the horrors; war crimes trials in Frankfurt. New Repub 150:7-8 F 15 '64
Justice since Nuremberg. il Newsweek 61:52 Je 10 '63
Painful purgative. Time 83:35 Mr 20 '64
Sickening past; Auschwitz. il Newsweek 63: 29+ Ja 20 '64
Time running out. Newsweek 62:54 S 23 '63
U.S. rejects Soviet allegations on court action in Berlin; U.S. note of December 17 and Soviet note of November 29, 1962. Dept State Bul 48:45-6 Ja 14 '63
Visit to Auschwitz. Newsweek 64:40+ Jl 6 '64

Ghana

Outrage at law. Time 82:21 D 20 '63

Great Britain

Dial S for squalor; Regina v. Stephen Thomas Ward. il Time 82:22+ Ag 2 '63
Letter from London; Vassall case. M. Panter-Downes. New Yorker 39:146-8 My 25 '63
One crowded hour; Ward trial. il Time 82: 26+ Ag 9 '63
Reward from a robbery rap; A. Hinds' libel case. il Time 84:51 Ag 14 '64
Trial; Stephen Ward. il Newsweek 62:36+ Ag 5 '63

Israel

See also
Eichmann trial

Malawi

Sir Edgar & the elders. il Time 81:43 Ap 5 '63

Russia

Great western spy net; G. Wynne and O. Penkovsky. il Time 81:35 My 17 '63
Meet Comrade Punkovsky; people's court pass judgment on three youths. Time 81:34 Je 7 '63
Moscow: a day in the people's court. G. Feifer. il Reporter 30:29+ My 21 '64
Spies in Moscow: more than meets the eye; G. Wynne and O. Penkovsky. il Newsweek 61:41 My 20 '63
Spy thriller from a Moscow courtroom; Penkovsky trial. il U S News 54:8 My 20 '63

South Africa

Accusing the accuser; nine men accused of trying to overthrow the government. Newsweek 63:47 Je 22 '64
Avoiding martyrdom; eight men convicted of sabotage. Time 83:25 Je 19 '64
I plead not guilty; trial of ten South Africans on charges of sabotage. S. Uys. New Repub 149:12-13 D 28 '63
Washington Franklin Kathrada. Nat R 16: 575 Jl 14 '64

Spain

Cheated of the kill; trial of the existentialists. il Newsweek 63:28+ Mr 30 '64

TRIALS (espionage)

Justice for Captain Kauffman. Nation 198:3 Ja 4 '64
Ordeal of Captain Kauffman. F. J. Cook. Nation 197:123-38 S 14 '63
Strangers on a bridge; excerpt. J. B. Donovan. il Sat Eve Post 237:30-2+ Mr 28 '64

TRIALS (fraud)

Act II in Hoffa trial. Bsns W p 102+ Jl 18 '64
Dardi's deals. Newsweek 61:78-80 F 18 '63
Eight years; Hoffa trial. Newsweek 63:28 Mr 23 '64
Hoffa trial. F. J. Cook. il Nation 198:415-39 Ap 27 '64
James R. Hoffa: the prosecution rests. R. Cooper. New Repub 151:6-7 Ag 8 '64
Longest trial; U.S. v. Samuel Garfield, et al. Time 81:25-6 F 22 '63
On trial in Chicago; government charges Hoffa with fraud. R. Cooper. New Repub 150:13-14 Je 6 '64
Two down, one to go; Justice dept. vs teamsters chief Hoffa. il Bsns W p62-3 Ag 1 '64
Verdict on Hoffa. il Newsweek 63:30-1 Mr 16 '64
Vincible Jimmy; Hoffa guilty. Newsweek 64: 30 Ag 10 '64

TRIALS (kidnaping)

Lady defender; Sinatra jr. kidnaping trial. il Newsweek 63:22 Mr 2 '64

TRIALS (libel)

Birchers lose; Goldmark case. P. Jacobs. New Rpub 150:5 F 8 '64
Fallout from the Times; defendants granted new trial. Time 84:44 D 18 '64
Fix or fiction? W. Butts against the Saturday evening post. il Time 82:38+ Ag 16 '63
High cost of libel; W. Butts v. Curtis publishing co. il Newsweek 62:72-3 S 2 '63
Limits of political invective; case of Sally & John Goldmark. il Time 83:58 Ja 31 '64
Lose one, win one; libel actions against the New York Times. il Time 84:74+ O 2 '64
Money for the Post. Time 83:43 Ja 24 '64
Ordeal of John Henry Faulk. J. P. Blank. il Look 27:80-2+ My 7 '63
Sophisticated muckraking; W. Butts's libel suit against the Saturday evening post. il Time 82:34 Ag 23 '63
$3,060,000 worth of guilt. il Time 82:37+ Ag 30 '63
Was T.R. a drunk? Roosevelt vs. Newett. J. G. Hayden. il Am Heritage 15:82-3 O '64
What's in a name? Drew Pearson v. Fairbanks, Alaska, News-Miner. il Time 84:62 D 11 '64

TRIALS (murder)

Another day in Dallas; trial of Jack Ruby. il Time 83:24-5 Mr 13 '64
Avenger; Ruby trial. il Newsweek 63:28+ Mr 23 '64
Beckwith mistrial. Sr Schol 84:17 F 28 '64
Beckwith trial. il Newsweek 63:27 F 10 '64
Casus Belli; Ruby trial. il Time 83:34+ Mr 27 '64
Cheated of the kill; trial of the existentialists. il Newsweek 63:28+ Mr 30 '64
Dallas justice: the real story of Jack Ruby and his trial. by M. Belli and M. C. Carroll. Review
New Repub 151:19-22 N 21 '64. T. S. Szasz
Death for Ruby. il Time 83:27-8 Mr 20 '64
Did Lloyd Miller kill Janice May? R. Applegate. il Sat Eve Post 237:75-9 Ja 25 '64
Double standard for murder? acquittals of white slayers of Negroes in Mississippi. H. Carter. il N Y Times Mag p20+ Ja 24 '65
Extreme case; state of Georgia v. J. H. Sims and C. W. Myers. il Time 84:23-4 S 11 '64
Good-by, Belli; dismissal by Jack Ruby. il Newsweek 63:19 Mr 30 '64
Hung jury; B. DeLa Beckwith trial. Newsweek 63:16-17 F 17 '64
Hung jury; trial of B. De La Beckwith, accused killer of Mississippi N.A.A.C.P. leader Medgar Evers. Time 83:20-1 F 14 '64
Jack Ruby on trial. M. Kempton. New Repub 150:17-20 Mr 7 '64
Jack Ruby's strange trial; new chapter in assassination story. il U S News 56:70 Mr 23 '64
Letter from Paris; coverage in Figaro of trial of J. Ruby. Genêt. New Yorker 40:159-60 Mr 21 '64
Like picking a wife; jurors for Ruby trial. il Time 83:53 F 28 '64
Little dignity; Jack Ruby trial. Newsweek 63:80 Mr 2 '64
Madam's mark; case of M. Fein. il Time 84: 34 N 20 '64
Not guilty; Klansmen acquitted in trial for slaying of Lemuel Penn. il Newsweek 64:24-5 S 14 '64
On camera; Ruby trial. il Newsweek 63:31-2 Mr 16 '64
Reprieve for Dr Sam. il Newsweek 64:32+ Jl 27 '64
Ruby convicted. Sr Schol 84:32 Ap 3 '64
Ruby trial: a chance to redeem a tragedy. S. Bedford. il Life 56:36-36B F 28 '64
Savage stalks at midnight; Winston Moseley. il Time 83:21-2 Je 26 '64
Sheppard case reopened. C. Welles. il Life 57:24D Jl 31 '64
Strange case of Edgar Smith. D. G. M. Coxe. il Nat R 15:273-8 O 8 '63
Tale of Manhattan; trial of M. Fein. il Newsweek 64:27 D 7 '64
To find his father's killer; Welby Lee vs. Grover Jones. il Time 84:78 N 20 '64
Trial by newspapers; case of Sam Sheppard. il Time 84:44 Jl 24 '64
Trial of Delay Beckwith; accused killer of N.A.A.C.P. leader M. Evers. H. H. Martin. il Sat Eve Post 237:77-81 Mr 14 '64
Two trials; Jack Ruby and the man accused of slaying Medgar Evers. Nation 198:82 Ja 27 '64

TRIALS (murder)—*Continued*
Untold story of Jack Ruby. E. Linn. il Sat Eve Post 237:24-6+ Jl 25 '64
Violence, froth, sob stuff; was justice done? trial of Jack Ruby. S. Bedford. il Life 56:32-34B+ Mr 27 '64
War of nerves; questioning of prospective jurors in Ruby trial. Newsweek 63:19 Mr 2 '64
See also
Sacco-Vanzetti case

TRIALS (obscenity)
Bruce's trial. Newsweek 64:76 Jl 20 '64
National decent literature chairman held in contempt at California trial. Library J 89: 4764 D 1 '64
Trial of Lenny Bruce. A. Goldman. New Repub 151:13-14 S 12 '64

TRIALS (perjury)
Assault on Whittaker Chambers. W. F. Buckley, jr. il Nat R 16:1098-102 D 15 '64; Discussion 17:4+ Ja 12 '65
Death in the family; Roy M. Cohn's mistrial. il Time 83:76 My 1 '64
Everybody's laughing; mistrial in Roy Cohn case. Newsweek 63:24+ My 4 '64
Fear of high places; two trials of R. Cohn. Time 84:44 Jl 24 '64
Rendezvous of the federal prosecutors. M. Kempton. New Repub 150:6-7 Ap 18 '64
Winner; R. M. Cohn acquitted. Newsweek 64:31-2 Jl 27 '64

TRIALS (sedition)
Ordeal of William Penn. F. Biddle. il Am Heritage 15:30-3+ Ap '64

TRIALS (treason)
King's trial; excerpt from Coffin for King Charles. C. V. Wedgwood. il Horizon 6:32-40 Sum '64

TRIALS, Dog. See Field trials (dogs)

TRIALS, War crime. See World war, 1939-1945 —War criminals

TRIALS of animals. See Animals, Prosecution and punishment of

TRIANGLE within circle; story. See Nabokov, V.

TRIANGLES
Mathematical games; on polyiamonds: shapes that are made out of equilateral triangles. M. Gardner. il Sci Am 211:124-8+ bibliog(p 156) D '64

TRIATOMA. See Kissing bugs

TRIBES and tribal system
African chief explains tribalism. S. O. Adebo. il N Y Times Mag p26-7+ Mr 1 '64
Clues to the African personality. E. Huxley. il N Y Times Mag p 18+ My 31 '64
Tribalism and social evolution in Africa; address, April 10, 1964; with questions and answers. C. M. Turnbull. bibliog f il Ann Am Acad 354:22-32 Jl '64

TRIBOLET, Harold W.
Binding and related problems; reprint. Hobbies 69:110-11+ Jl '64
Protect those documents. Hobbies 68:110-12+ Mr '63

TRIBOLIUM confusum. See Flour beetles

TRIBUNE (Chicago) See Chicago tribune

TRICHINA and trichinosis
Drug promises defeat of deadly pork disease. Sci N L 86:162 S 12 '64
Found at last: a drug cure for trichinosis. W. Cloud. Pop Sci 184:26 Ap '64
Human trichinosis cure. Sci N L 85:134 F 29 '64
Outbreak of trichinosis traced to pork sausage. Sci N L 83:344 Je 1 '63

TRICHOMONIASIS, Vaginal
New medical hope for an intimate problem. Good H 156:169 Ap '63

TRICHOSPORUM. See Blush worts

TRICK photography. See Photography, Trick

TRICK skiing. See Water skis and skiing

TRICKLING filters. See Sewage disposal—Filtration

TRICYANO-amino-propene
Synthesis of RNA in vitro stimulated in dipteran salivary glands by 1,1,3-tricyano-2-amino-1-propene. J. Jacob and J. L. Sirlin. bibliog il Science 144:1011-12 My 22 '64

TRIEM, Eve
Flame of five jays; Gull; poems. Poetry 101: 396-7 Mr '63
Hawthorn; poem. Nation 198:636 Je 22 '64

TRIENNALE, Milan. See Design, Industrial—Exhibitions

TRIESTE

Music

Great opera houses: Trieste. M. J. Matz. il Opera N 29:28-31 Ja 30 '65

TRIESTE (bathyscaphe) See Bathyscaphe

TRIGÈRE, Pauline
Chic country cooking; with recipes. J. Peter and M. Kaytor. il pors Look 27:106-7+ My 21 '63

TRIGGS, Matt
Excerpt from statement to subcommittee on National service corps, June, 1963. Cong Digest 43:27+ Ja '64
Excerpt from testimony, March 12, 1964. Cong Digest 43:249+ O '64

TRIGLYCERIDES. See Glycerides

TRILBY (literary character) See Characters in literature

TRILLIN, Calvin
Books. New Yorker 40:107-12 Ag 15 '64
For spacious skies and ample waves of green. New Yorker 39:24-5 Ja 4 '64
Letter from Jackson. New Yorker 40:80+ Ag 29 '64
Reporter at large. New Yorker 39:30-4+ Jl 13; 32-6+ Jl 20; 34-6+ Jl 27 '63; 40:120+ Ap 4; 41-2+ Je 20 '64

TRILLING, Diana
Marilyn Monroe. Redbook 120:54-5+ F '63
Reflections a year later. Redbook 124:71-5 N '64
Who's afraid of the culture elite? Esquire 60:69+ D '63

TRIM tabs. See Tabs (boats)

TRIMARANS
Trimaran for Nuka Hiva. L. Barber. il Yachting 114:130+ Ag '63
24-foot racing trimaran. il Motor B 111:70 F '63

TRIMBLE, G. R. jr, and Larmoyeux, Jack
Downy serviceberry. Horticulture 41:515 O '63

TRIMBLE, William C.
Economic development in Liberia; address, December 11, 1964. Dept State Bul 51:912-14 D 28 '64

TRIMESTER system. See College year

TRINIDAD (island)
In a palmy potpourri. H. Sutton. il Sat R 46: 31-2 Je 1 '63
Trinidad is one colorful surprise after another. il Sunset 130:30+ F '63
See also
Birds—Trinidad (island)

Description and travel

Trinidad. V. S. Naipaul. Mlle 59:187 My '64

Politics and government

Prospects in the Caribbean. P. Sherlock. For Affairs 41:744-56 Jl '63

TRINIDAD-TOBAGO
Trinidad and Tobago. W. A. Simmonds. il Américas 15:8-13 Mr '63
Two islands; one nation. G. Meek. il Américas 15:7-12 N '63
Year after. Time 82:49 D 6 '63

TRINITY
Ecumenical setback; sermon attacking the traditional Christian belief in the Blessed Trinity. America 111:246 S 12 '64
Word. V. P. McCorry. America 108:844-5 Je 8 '63

TRINITY ALPS. See Klamath Mountains

TRINITY college, Dublin. See Colleges and universities—Ireland

TRINITY college, Durham, N.C. See Duke university, Durham, N.C.

TRINITY college, Washington, D.C.
Trinity caters to taste; new library. Sister Helen. il Library J 88:4573-6 D 1 '63
Very attractive cooky cutter. J. O'Reilly; reply. J. P. Morrison. Mlle 57:100 My '63

TRINITY-Sergius monastery, Zagorsk. See Monasteries

TRIOS, Instrumental
Best in each; Stern-Istomin-Rose ensemble. il Newsweek 62:86 S 9 '63
Notes from abroad; Stern-Istomin-Rose trio; interview, ed. by R. McMullen. E. Istomin; I. Stern; L. Rose. il Hi Fi 14:12+ Ja '64
Revelers. il Time 83:56 My 15 '64

TRIPLE crown. See Horse racing

TRIPLETS
Sleek and straight and hide an eye; New York's Dees sisters. il Life 56:53-4+ My 8 '64

TRIPODS
Portable tripod. D. Hanson. il Outdoor Life 132:67 O '63
See also
Camera tripods

TRIPPETT, Frank
Account of some conversations on U.S. 45. por Newsweek 64:21-3 Jl 13 '64

TRIPS, Student. See School excursions

TRIPTYCHS
Boston museum buys a masterpiece of martyrdom. il Life 55:64-5 O 18 '63
Flemish anonymous; Martyrdom of St Hippolytus, at Boston's museum of fine arts. il Time 82:86-7 O 18 '63
TRISTAN DA CUNHA (island)
Annals of migration. T. Whiteside. il New Yorker 39:154+ N 9 '63
Back to Eden. Newsweek 61:33-4 Ap 1 '63
Far-off exiles of Tristan. C. Mydans. il Life 55:72-4+ Jl 12 '63
Home to lonely Tristan da Cunha. J. P. Blair. il Nat Geog Mag 125:60-81 Ja '64
TRISTAN und Isolde; opera. See Wagner, R.
TRITELEIA uniflora. See Spring star flowers
TRITIUM
Tritiated water as a tool for ecological field studies. F. W. Woods and D. O'Neal. il Science 147:148-9 Ja 8 '65
Tritium-hydrologic research: some results of the U.S. geological survey research program. C. W. Carlston. bibliog il Science 143:804-6 F 21 '64
See also
Water supply—Tritium content
TRITIUM autoradiography. See Autoradiography
TRITOMAS. See Torch lilies
TRIUMPH; novel. See Wylie, P.
TRIVETS
These trivets are kerfed. il Sunset 133:99-100 D '64
TRIZEC corporation
Zeckendorf retreats; Canadian property. Time 82:91 Jl 12 '63
TROFFER, Suzanne A. and Tart, C. T.
Experimenter bias in hypnotist performance. bibliog Science 145:1330-1 S 18 '64
TROIANO, Rick
Crop your way to better pictures. U S Camera 27:54-5+ Ja '64
TROILUS and Cressida; drama. See Shakespeare, W.—Plays
TROJAN women; drama. See Euripides
TROLLEY cars. See Street cars
TROMANHAUSER, Edward
Effects of radiation on electronic components. Electr World 70:76-7 Jl '63
TROMBLEY, William
Babies without homes. Sat Eve Post 236:15-21 F 16 '63
Big boom in bathing suits. Sat Eve Post 236: 30 Jl 13 '63
Dowser who finds oil wells. Sat Eve Post 236:88-9 D 7 '63
Edgar Kaiser, maverick in motion. Sat Eve Post 236:20-1 Je 22 '63
Exploding University of California. Sat Eve Post 237:22-9 My 16 '64
For God, country and the Santa Clara swim club. Sat Eve Post 237:66-71 Jl 25 '64
Greatest story ever told. Sat Eve Post 236:34-40+ O 19 '63
Have zoo, will travel. Sat Eve Post 237:72-3 Ag 8 '64
New challenger to the Kennedy clan. pors Sat Eve Post 236:38-9 S 28 '63
New role for legendary George. Sat Eve Post 237:22-3 My 30 '64
Small-budget triumph: David and Lisa. Sat Eve Post 236:56, 59-60 Mr 16 '63
They cared enough to give the most. Ladies Home J 81:32+ Ap '64
What are they doing to Big Sur? Sat Eve Post 237:24-9 F 15 '64
TROMPE-l'oeil
Flowers into art. il McCalls 91:80-5 Ag '64
TROPHIES, Sport
Alaska grizzlies regain record book status. B. East. il Outdoor Life 132:10-11+ O '63
If only it had ended Friday; US wins Walker cup. H. Longhurst. Sports Illus 18:54 Je 3 '63
Lift high the jug insurance. Sports Illus 18:9 Ap 29 '63
Lipton cup. D. Barker. il Yachting 113:210+ Ap '63
Outdoor life publishes new Grancel Fitz book: How to measure and score big-game trophies. Outdoor Life 132:59+ S '63
Royal trophy winner. W. Page. il Field & S 67:74-5 F '63
Women of the world, rejoice! Federation cup in tennis. J. Lovesey. Sports Illus 18:54+ Je 17 '63
TROPHOBLAST
Morphogenesis of syncytiotrophoblast in vivo: an autoradiographic demonstration. A. R. Midgley, jr. and others. bibliog il Science 141:349-50 Jl 26 '63
TROPICAL architecture. See Architecture and climate
TROPICAL fishes. See Fishes
TROPICAL fruits. See Fruit
TROPICAL plants
See also
Fairchild tropical garden, Coconut Grove, Fla.
TROPICAL rain forests. See Rain forests
TROPICS
See also
Agriculture—Tropics
Soils—Tropics
Climate
See also
Africa, West—Climate
TROPISM (botany)
Magnets ripen tomatoes. Sci N L 84:37 Jl 20 '63
TROPOSPHERE. See Atmosphere
TROPOSPHERIC radio wave propagation
Air force takes over Big Rally II communications system. C. D. La Fond. il Miss & Roc 15:24-5 O 12 '64
FAA testing extended-range radio link. P. J. Klass. il Aviation W 78:103+ Je 24 '63
TROSTL, Arturo, jr
Cookie! the wonder boy. D. R. Maxey. il pors Look 27:116-18+ D 3 '63
TROTSKY, Leon
Broken eggs of the Soviet omelet. N. Weyl. por Nat R 16:75-7 Ja 28 '64
Hell-black night. il por Time 83:84+ Ja 10 '64
Life of Trotsky. I. Howe. New Repub 150: 20-3 Mr 21 '64
Odyssey of an obsolete hero. S. Heitman. por Sat R 46:47 D 14 '63
Prophet outcast, by I. Deutscher. Review
Commentary 37:52-60 Ja '64. G. Lichtheim; Discussion, 37:32+ My '64
Nation 197:350-2 N 23 '63. H. Baverman
New Yorker 40:167-70+ Je 6 '64. N. Bliven
Stalin-Trotsky split: a lesson for Kremlinologists. J. A. Hough. Reporter 29:37-9 D 5 '63
Tragedy of Trotsky. M. A. Fitzsimons. Commonweal 79:598-600 F 14 '64
TROTTER, J. See Camerman, N. jt. auth.
TROTTERS. See Horses
TROTTERS SHOALS DAM (proposed) See Dams
TROTTING race. See Harness racing
TROUBADOURS
One-man peace corps; B. Bohn. il Time 81: 42+ F 8 '63
TROUBLE in tree-land; drama. See Boiko, C.
TROUBLE with Christmas; story. See Gordon, R.
TROUPE, Carolyn H. See Bloomberg, C. M. jt. auth.
TROUSERS
Pajama game; pants for women. il Time 84: 67 Jl 3 '64
Panting; new fall fashion line. il Newsweek 64:109+ O 12 '64
Women in pants. il Vogue 144:45-53 Jl '64
TROUT, Lawana
Silent voices falling on deaf ears. NEA J 53:17-19 S '64
about
Lawana Trout: teacher of the year. G. Astor. il pors Look 28:33-7 My 19 '64
TROUT, Robert
Fiesta of Pamplona. Atlan 211:142+ Mr '63
TROUT
Hepatomas in rainbow trout: descriptive and experimental epidemiology. H. Wolf. bibliog il Science 142:676-8 N 8 '63
He's forever chasing rainbows; Snake River trout ranch; Buhl, Idaho. F. J. Taylor. il Sat Eve Post 236:70-1 N 30 '63
Insecticides: effects on cutthroat trout of repeated exposure to DDT. D. Allison and others. bibliog il Science 142:958-61 N 15 '63
It's the world's largest trout farm; Snake River trout ranch in Idaho's magic valley. il Sunset 132:94 My '64
Migration in Maine; brook trout. P. J. Fournier. il Natur Hist 73:46-9 O '64
Outlets for troutlets. Time 83:48+ Mr 13 '64
See also
Cookery—Fish
Migration
See Fishes—Migration
TROUT fishing
Allagash story; wilderness trout trip. T. Janes. il Outdoor Life 134:32-3+ Ag '64
Amazing trout bug. H. G. Tapply. il Field & S 67:80 Ap '63
Another gorge to fish. H. L. Lawrence. il Outdoor Life 133:78-82 Ap '64
April trout look down. H. F. Blaisdell. il Outdoor Life 131:72+ Ap '63

TROUT fishing—*Continued*
Beartooth adventure. E. A. Bauer. il Outdoor Life 133:48-51+ Je '64
Best all-round trout fly; muddler minnow. J. Brooks. il Outdoor Life 132:64-5+ O '63
Best flies for big trout. A. J. McClane. il Field & S 69:88-94 Je '64
Big trout on the little T. H. L. Lawrence. il Field & S 68:42-3+ Ja '64
Blue ribbon waters. P. Czura. il Field & S 68:62-3+ My '63
Bright Angel brownies. C. Fletcher. il Field & S 69:42-3 D '64
Broken stream revives; Brodhead Creek, Monroe County, Pa. J. Hayes. il Outdoor Life 131:52-5+ Je '63
Canandaigua can-can. T. Janes. il Outdoor Life 134:40-3+ Jl '64
Casting's fun, but can you catch trout? W. Jacqmar. il Outdoor Life 131:17-19+ Mr '63
Cold weather trout. T. Trueblood. il Field & S 67:22+ Mr '63
Curves catch trout. W. Davis. il Outdoor Life 131:84+ Je '63
Deadliest fly; nymph fishing. W. Davis. il Outdoor Life 131:86+ My '63
Double haul for distance. A. J. McClane. il Field & S 69:66-70 Jl '64
Dynamite on Doe Creek. J. Rutherfoord. il Field & S 69:84-6+ Ja '65
Early conservation and the golden era of trout fishing; excerpts from This wonderful world of trout. C. K. Fox. il Am For 70:38-41+ Ja '64
Fine points for fly casters. W. Davis. il Outdoor Life 133:70-2 Je '64
Fish catches man; trout fishing. C. K. Fox. Esquire 59:44+ Ap '63
Fish the flat water. G. B. Gordon. il Outdoor Life 133:50-1+ My '64
Fisherman's tour of Scotland. J. Brooks. il Outdoor Life 131:28-31+ Ja '63
Fishing Utah by camper. B. Behme. il Field & S 68:36-9+ F '64
Fishing's forgotten spot. B. L. Spiller. il Field & S 67:96-8+ F '63
Flies for sophisticated trout. T. Trueblood. il Field & S 68:24+ My '63
Fly fishing in lakes. A. J. McClane. il Field & S 69:86-9 N '64
For a warm opening day. W. Davis. il Outdoor Life 133:70+ Mr '64
For midsummer trout: let it rain. W. Davis. il Outdoor Life 132:30-1+ Ag '63
For the finest fishing plan a hunting trip. C. Elliott. il Outdoor Life 134:48-9+ O '64
Gallatin glissade; Gallatin National Forest. J. Clark. il Field & S 68:21-3+ Jl '63
Get 'em while they're cold. V. L. Hoss. il Outdoor Life 131:70-1+ Je '63
Glow in the dark; for steelhead, fire flies. L. Green. il Outdoor Life 132:40-3+ O '63
Gold for fishermen. V. L. Hoss. il Outdoor Life 133:54-7+ Ap '64
Great steel rush. il Time 85:52 Ja 1 '65
Greatest rainbow trip. B. McPherson. il Outdoor Life 133:40-3+ My '64
Hatch matching made easy. S. R. Slaymaker, 2d. il Outdoor Life 133:66-7+ Ap '64
How to catch trout on opening day. B. East. il Outdoor Life 133:47-9+ Ap '64
How to net a fish. W. Davis. il Outdoor Life 134:76-7 D '64
Hudson Bay and back by canoe. D. Jarden. il Outdoor Life 132:36-9+ S '63
Hunters' holiday. W. Page. il Field & S 68:38-40 Ag '63
In praise of trout and also me. P. O'Neil. il Life 56:102-4+ My 8 '64
Kayak merry-go-round. J. Clark. il Field & S 69:32-5 Ja '65
Keep moving. J. Freeman. il Outdoor Life 132:48-9+ N '63
Lake trout lore. A. J. McClane. il Field & S 69:70-4 D '64
Lakers at 30 below. B. Cary. il Outdoor Life 135:40-1+ Ja '65
Look southward, angler. W. Davis. il Outdoor Life 133:33-5+ Mr '64
Mail-run adventure. J. Clark. il Outdoor Life 134:44-5+ Jl '64
Mighty trout of the Mighty Mo. J. Brooks. il Outdoor Life 131:56-9+ Ap '63
Minor league steelhead. J. Freeman. il Field & S 68:114-17+ F '64
Miracle of Whites Greek. J. Hayes. il Outdoor Life 134:24-7+ N '64
Most delightful fishing. T. Trueblood. il Field & S 68:14-15+ Ag '63
My no. 1 fishing spot. H. Andrews. il Outdoor Life 132:24-7+ Jl '63
Nebraska's never-fail lakes. P. Czura. il Field & S 69:116-20 S '64
New fishing for Easterners; Erie's spring rainbow run. J. Hayes. il Outdoor Life 131:40-1+ Mr '63
New ice-fishing ideas; Michigan's rainbows. H. F. Zeman. il Outdoor Life 135:48-9+ F '65
New land of strange trout. E. A. Bauer. il Field & S 68:35-7+ Ap '64
New Mexico's high country. R. Tinsley. il Travel 122:48-9 S '64
New road to Rocky Mountain trout. E. A. Bauer. il Outdoor Life 131:68-71+ My '63
New steelhead thrills. D. F. Brown. il Outdoor Life 134:42-3+ D '64
Old-fashioned trout trip. R. Bailey. il Outdoor Life 133:36-9+ Je '64
Out for sea-run Dolly Varden. il Sunset 132:73-4 Ap '64
Owens; never-fail trout river. J. Mears. il Field & S 67:31-3+ Mr '63
Perfect trout stream. J. B. Gleason. il Outdoor Life 132:50-2+ Jl '63
Pockets full of trout. W. Davis. il Outdoor Life 133:70+ My '64
Promise of the North. T. Trueblood. il Field & S 69:24+ Je '64
Rainbows of Flaming Gorge. H. Wixom. il Field & S 69:100-2+ Jl '64
Remote ponds near home. N. Bryant. il Outdoor Life 131:76-7+ My '63
Rio Muy Grande. B. Warner. il Field & S 69:27-9+ D '64
Shooting the Snake. J. C. Daniel. il Field & S 68:58-61 S '63
Skaters' waltz. J. Brooks. il Field & S 69:60-1+ My '64
Snowmobile lakers. H. Bradshaw. il Field & S 69:27-9+ Ja '65
Some spring secrets. R. L. Estes. il Outdoor Life 131:72-3+ Ap '63
Something for a rainy day. G. Laycock. il Outdoor Life 135:44-7+ Ja '65
Steelhead fly fishing. T. Trueblood. il Field & S 68:16+ O '63
Steelheading at Ishi Pishi. il Sunset 130:48+ F '63
Storm fish. M. Ellis. il Field & S 67:10-11 Mr '63
Strong-arm steelheads. F. H. Ames. il Outdoor Life 135:34-5+ Ja '65
Summer fishing eastern streams. R. Warner. il Field & S 68:92-4+ Jl '63
Topside togue. A. J. McClane. il Field & S 67:29-31+ F '63
Touch of wilderness. C. Elliott. il Outdoor Life 133:56-7+ My '64
Tricks for opening day. A. J. McClane il Field & S 67:104-6+ Ap '63
Trophy brook trout. A. J. McClane. il Field & S 68:82-5 N '63
Trouble-shoot for trout. H. Wixom. il Outdoor Life 133:48-51+ Mr '64
Trout after dark. N. Bryant. il Outdoor Life 132:44-5+ Jl '63
Trout find of the year. E. A. Bauer. il Outdoor Life 131:36-9+ Mr '63
Trout fishing: ritual, not rapture. F. Chappell. il Holiday 36:122+ Jl '64
Trout from still waters. E. W. Smith. il Field & S 68:58-9+ O '63
Trouting, where? D. Carpenter. il Am For 69:22-3+ Mr '63
Two weeks for steelhead. J. Freeman. il Field & S 67:48-51+ F '63
Vest-pocket fishing. A. J. McClane. il Field & S 68:58-62 Jl '63
Warden's way. D. Knight. il Field & S 69:46-7+ Je '64
We ran the blackwater. R. E. Landsburg. il Outdoor Life 132:40-3+ Ag '63
Wet-fly casting for steelhead; Klamath River, Calif. il Sunset 133:18 S '64
What makes Hot Creek hot? J. Mears. il Outdoor Life 134:32-5+ S '64
Wickiup browns. D. Murphey. il Field & S 69:49-51+ Ag '64
See also
Grayling fishing

TROUYET, Carlos
Diamond-studded coyote. il por Time 82:115 D 6 '63
Who's who in foreign business. por Fortune 70:54 O '64

TROVATO, Joseph S.
Armory show; pictures and sculptures from Show of 1913. New Yorker 39:35-6 Mr 30 '63

Il TROVATORE; opera. See Verdi, G.

TROW, William Clark
Imaginary advice to students on taking examinations. Sch & Soc 91:124-5 Mr 9 '63

TROY, George
La abuela; story. Sat Eve Post 237:56-7 N 28 '64

TROY
Fall of Homer; Troy may not have fallen Newsweek 61:95 Ap 22 '63
Science milestone: Heinrich Schliemann archaeologist extraordinary. D. Cohen. il Sci Digest 53:79-86 Mr '63
TROY, Mo.
Modern water witching. R. S. Miller. il Am City 78:105-6 N '63
TROY, N.Y.
Water supply
Unconventional way. J. P. Buckley. il Am City 79:96-8 Ja '64
TRUCCO, Victor
Obituary
Opera N 29:25 O 17 '64. F. Robinson
TRUCIAL OMAN. See Abu Dhabi
TRUCK and coach division. See General motors corporation—Truck and coach division
TRUCK campers. See Campers and coaches, Truck
TRUCK motels. See Motels
TRUCK terminals. See Terminal buildings
TRUCK traffic. See Street traffic
TRUCKING
Motor carriage: the long and short of it. J. F. Pinkney. Ann Am Acad 345:66-72 Ja '63
Trucking: one stop shopping for shippers. il Duns R 81:pt2 S110-12+ Je '63
Trucks roll on. il Duns R 83:pt2 114-18+ Je '64
See also
Associated transport, incorporated
Overnite transportation company
Finance
On the road, traveling fast; trucking companies. il Bsns W p 165-6+ My 18 '63
Private operations
Private carriage: the fifth method. N. Buckley. il Duns R 83;pt2 145-6+ Je '64
Rates
Shippers by truck face higher freight bills. il Bsns W p 134+ Jl 11 '64
TRUCKING, Private. See Trucking—Private operations
TRUCKS
See also
Motor trucks
TRUCKS, Book. See Library furniture and equipment
TRUEBLOOD, D. Elton
New departure: a Quaker seminary. Christian Cent 80:531-2+ Ap 24 '63
TRUEBLOOD, Ted, pseud.
Advice to cooks. Field & S 68:16+ N '63
Cold weather trout. Field & S 67:22+ Mr '63
Cooking kits. Field & S 68:16+ F '64
Decision in Oregon. Field & S 69:10-12+ N '64
Education of ruff. por Field & S 69:53-6+ S '64
First steps in wingshooting. Field & S 69:16+ Ag '64
Flies for sophisticated trout. Field & S 68:24+ My '63
How to call crows, coyotes, dogs, children, etc. Field & S 69:24+ S '64
How to choose a fishing rod. Field & S 68:24+ Mr '64
How to hide the truth. por Field & S 67:26+ Ap '63
How to hunt chukars. Field & S 69:24+ O '64
Hunting in the snow. Field & S 68:16+ D '63
Know your grouse. Field & S 68:44-6+ S '63
Low-down fly line. Field & S 69:24+ My '64
Most delightful fishing. Field & S 68:14-15+ Ag '63
Now is the time. Field & S 68:16+ Ja '64
Promise of the North. Field & S 69:24+ Je '64
Rough and ready feather merchants. Field & S 68:43-5+ My '63
Sonic fish dog. pors Field & S 69:27-9+ Jl '64
Steelhead fly fishing. Field & S 68:16+ O '63
Take it easy. Field & S 68:24+ S '63
Things I could kick myself for. Field & S 67:16+ F '63
Too many elk. Field & S 68:36-9+ Jl '63
Toward season's end. Field & S 69:12-13+ Ja '65
Trueblood kicks again. Field & S 68:16+ Jl '63
Vacation clothes. Field & S 68:24+ Je '63
Water temperature: key to fishing. por Field & S 69:16+ Jl '64
Wild, free days. por Field & S 69:16+ D '64
Wilderness reward. por Field & S 67:47-9+ Ap '63
TRUESDELL, A. H. and Pommer, A. M.
Phosphate glass electrode with good selectivity for alkaline-earth cations. bibliog Science 142:1292-4 D 6 '63
TRUESDELL, C.
Fluid mechanics before the Society for natural philosophy. Science 143:382 Ja 24 '64
TRUFFAUT, François
Truffaut. New Yorker 40:45-6 O 31 '64
TRUFFLES
Rare white truffle. N. Barber. Holiday 35:142+ Je '64
TRUITTE, James
Alvin Ailey dance theatre; Clark center for the performing arts. J. Maskey. Dance Mag 38:54 Ag '64
TRUJILLO, Rhadamés
Trujillos revisited. Time 84:35 Ag 7 '64
TRUJILLO MOLINA, Rafael Leonidas
How Trujillo died. N. Gall. New Repub 148:19-20 Ap 13 '63
Trujillo: the last Caesar, by A. Espaillat. Review
Nat R 15:530-1 D 17 '63. N. Weyl
TRULL, Don
Don Trull queues up and counts his money. E. Shrake. il pors Sports Illus 21:16-19 Ag 17 '64
TRULL, Samuel G.
Strategies of effective interviewing. Harvard Bsns R 42:89-94 Ja '64
TRULSON, Martha F. and Stare, F. J.
Great balancing act: eating vs. activity. Todays Health 41:35-7+ Je '63
TRUMAN, Bess (Wallace)
What three Presidents say about their wives; excerpt from Woman in the White House. M. Means. il por Good H 157:58+ Ag '63
TRUMAN, David B.
Changing character of undergraduate education; address, January 11, 1964. Sch & Soc 92:380-3 D 12 '64
TRUMAN, Harry S.
Emancipation proclamation centennial, statement. por Ebony 18:21 S '63
Excerpt from remarks, January 8, 1964. Cong Digest 43:156 My '64
My first eighty years. pors Sat Eve Post 237:15-19 Je 13 '64
Now, a Truman plan for the South; excerpts from address. por U S News 55:15 S 30 '63
Truman's view: MacArthur tried for presidency; excerpts from TV series. por U S News 57:22 N 30 '64
about
Day in a former President's busy life. R. Sherrod. por Sat Eve Post 237:16 Je 13 '64
Fight over the A-bomb. K. Knebel and C. W. Bailey. Look 27:19-23 Ag 13 '63; Reply. A. K. Smith. Bul Atomic Sci 19:33 O '63
MacArthur story; with interview with D. MacArthur and report by H. Handleman. il U S News 56:38-46 Ap 20 '64
One kind of patriot. il Time 81:29 Ap 26 '63
Ramble in the past with Mr Truman. L. Wainwright. Life 56:29 Ap 24 '64
Truman and Eisenhower: their administrations and campaigns. V. Albjerg. il Cur Hist 47:221-8 O '64
Truman at eighty: honors and memories. por U S News 56:20 My 18 '64
Truman vs. Kennedy: debate over William Walker. U S News 54:20 Ap 29 '63
Untold stories about Truman and Marshall; excerpts from Journals of David E. Lilienthal. D. E. Lilienthal. por U S News 57:22 N 9 '64
Walk through history with Harry Truman; with editorial comment. J. McCarthy. il pors Holiday 34:55, 56-61+ N; 96-7+ D '63
When the U.S. had a nationwide rail strike. U S News 55:93 Jl 22 '63
TRUMAN, Harry S. library. See Harry S. Truman library, Independence, Mo.
TRUMBULL, Robert
Japan has a love affair with sports. N Y Times Mag p30-1+ S 27 '64
TRUMPET blowing
Anecdotes, facetiae, satire, etc.
One hell of a duck hunt; amateur trumpeters as hunters. V. Bourjaily. il Esquire 60:98-100+ O '63
TRUMPETER swans. See Swans
TRUMPETS of the Lord; musical comedy. See Musical comedies, revues, etc.—Criticisms, plots, etc.
TRUNDLE beds. See Beds
TRUNKS
Hiding place for trunks. il Sunset 132:78 Ja '64

TRUSSES
Biggest dome of all, for Texas, of course; lamella trusses for roof of Houston stadium. il Bsns W p56-8+ O 5 '63
More house for less money. A. J. Maher. il Pop Mech 120:140-3 N '63
See also
Struts

TRUST companies
Singing for regulation; Canada trust co. il Bsns W p72-3 Ap 4 '64

TRUST funds. See Trusts and trustees

TRUST territory of Papua and New Guinea. See New Guinea, Territory of

TRUST TERRITORY OF THE PACIFIC ISLANDS
America's neglected colonial paradise; with editorial comment. D. Oberdorfer. il Sat Eve Post 237:24-34, 76 F 29 '64; Same abr. without editorial comment. Read Digest 84:232-4+ Je '64
Micronesia. R. S. Hopkins. bibliog il Focus 13:1-6 Je '63
Trust Territory of the Pacific Islands; statements, May 28, 1964. M. W. Goding; T. Remengesau. Dept State Bul 50:1007-20 Je 29 '64
Trust Territory of the Pacific Islands; statements, June 5 and June 17, 1963. M. W. Goding; V. N. Santos. Dept State Bul 49: 207-29 Ag 5 '63
Trusteeship council urges realistic target dates for Pacific Islands. U N Rev 10:21-4 Jl '63
United Nations mission visits Trust Territory of the Pacific Islands. U N Rev 11:40-1 Mr '64
U.S. survey mission to visit Pacific Island Trust Territory. Dept State Bul 48:946 Je 17 '63

TRUSTEES, Library. See Libraries—Trustees, boards, committees, etc.

TRUSTEESHIP council. See United Nations—Trusteeship council

TRUSTEESHIPS of trade unions. See Trade unions—Trusteeships

TRUSTS, Industrial
See also
Business consolidations and mergers

International trusts

Shaping the big stick; European common market's anticartel policy. Newsweek 61:71 Ap 29 '63

Law

Annals of legislation; background and history of Drug industry antitrust bill. R. Harris. New Yorker 40:48-50+ Mr 14; 75-6+ Mr 21; 46-8+ Mr 28 '64
Antitrust in America; Antitrust act of 1890; excerpts from The business establishment, ed. by E. F. Cheit. R. Hofstadter. Commentary 38:47-53 Ag '64; Reply with rejoinder. M. R. Lazere. 38:28 N '64
Antitrust law hits aluminum; Alcoa to divest itself of Rome cable corp. Bsns W p98 Je 6 '64
Antitrust laws for labor unions? il U S News 54:13 Ap 8 '63
Antitrust; the Mississippi tide. Time 83:93-4 Ap 24 '64
Antitrust trends and new constraints. J. W. Markham. bibliog f Harvard Bsns R 41:84-92 My '63
Back scratching deals raise antitrust ire; reciprocity practices. il Bsns W p45-6 F 9 '63
Bigger stick; antitrust laws and banks. Newsweek 62:54 Jl 1 '63
Blocking a merger in advance. Bsns W p92+ My 4 '63
Crisis in antitrust. R. H. Bork and W. S. Bowman, jr. Fortune 68:138-40+ D '63
Damaging suit. Time 83:98+ Je 12 '64
EEC antitrust action. Duns R 81:53-4 Mr '63
Fastener firms and officials fined. Aviation W 79:40 S 23 '63
Grand acquisitor. R. L. Heilbroner. il Am Heritage 16:20-5+ D '64
In defense of antitrust. H. M. Blake and W. K. Jones. Fortune 70:135+ Ag '64
Is antitrust hurting growth? address. J. J. Scott. il Duns R 83:55-6+ My '64
More power for trustbusters. Time 82:75 S 6 '63
New antitrust chief's goal: more power to police your business; interview W. H. Orrick, jr. Nations Bsns 51:38-9+ O '63
New step for antitrust appeals; through Courts of appeals. Bsns W p90 My 4 '63
New weapons against bigness. S. Marcus. Harvard Bsns R 43:100-8 Ja '65
New worry in government: not enough newspapers? il U S News 56:111-12 Je 15 '64
On the judging of mince pies. D. J. Fennelly. il Harvard Bsns R 42:77-86 N '64
Results of antitrust. H. Hazlitt. Newsweek 64:98 S 21 '64
Sharpening the law on antitrust. il Bsns W p32-4 O 5 '63
Shelving manufacturers plead nolo contendere in antitrust suit. ALA Bul 58:563 Je '64
Thunderbolt for bank mergers; ruling in Philadelphia case by Supreme court. Bsns W p80+ Je 22 '63
Too many antitrust trials? yes, says Du Pont chief; excerpts from address, August 13, 1963. U S News 55:21 Ag 26 '63
Troubles pile up for most sued union. il Bsns W p 121-2+ Ap 18 '64
U.S. antitrust action: big is bad? il Newsweek 63:72-3+ Je 29 '64
Why businessmen keep a worried eye on Washington. il U S News 54:55-7 Ap 1 '63
Will Lever bros. lose all? R. Goodman. Nation 196:138-9 F 16 '63
Your right to a car bargain. W. Marx. Nation 196:195-7 Mr 9 '63

Germany (Federal Republic)

Comeback of the combine; Thyssen-Phoenix combine. il Time 81:98 Ap 5 '63
Shoring up an empire. il Bsns W p34+ O 12 '63

United States

Is bigness a bar to expansion by merger? Justice dept. vs oil companies. Bsns W p26-7 Ap 18 '64
See also
United States—Justice, Department of—Antitrust division

TRUSTS, Investment. See Investment trusts

TRUSTS and trustees
In memory of. . . D. Wolfle. Science 141:1139 S 20 '63
More choice for the investor; common trust fund. il Bsns W p 162+ Mr 21 '64
Personal business; children as stockholders. Bsns W p 183 O 19 '63
Personal business; common trust fund. Bsns W p89-90 Ag 8 '64
Where trust assets are invested. U S News 57:58 D 28 '64

TRUTH, Sojourner
Sojourner Truth. E. J. Ritter. Negro Hist Bul 26:254 My '63

TRUTH
Fidelity to truth. R. O. Johann. America 110: 370 Mr 21 '64
Philosopher's notebook; the reasonable man. R. O. Johann. America 108:497 Ap 13 '63
See also
Honesty
Reality
Sincerity

TRYK, H. Edward. See Fosmire, F. R. jt. auth.

TRYPANIS, C. A.
Three from overseas. E. G. Burrows. Poetry 105:207-8 D '64

TRYPANOSOMIASIS
Battle against sleeping sickness. D. Reed. Read Digest 83:124-7 Jl '63
Chagas' disease vaccine. Sci N L 86:158 S 5 '64

TRYPSIN
Hereditary deficiency of serum α_1- antitrypsin. F. Kueppers and others. bibliog il Science 146:1678-9 D 25 '64
Macroglobulin from human plasma which forms an enzymatically active compound with trypsin. J. W. Mehl and others. bibliog il Science 145:821-2 Ag 21 '64

TRYPTOPHAN
Indoleacetamide as an intermediate in the synthesis of indoleacetic acid in pseudomonas savastanoi. A. R. Magie and others. bibliog il Science 141:1281-2 S 27 '63
Tryptophan- and indole-excreting bacterial mutants. P. G. Lim and R. I. Mateles. bibliog Science 140:388 Ap 26 '63
Tryptophan synthetase from neurospora: a modification in the reaction scheme. M. D. Garrick and others. bibliog Science 145:491-2 Jl 31 '64

TSAI, Chia Yin. See Nelson, O. E. jt. auth.

TSAR and carpenter; opera. See Lortzing, A.

TSARAPKIN, S. K. and Stelle, C. C.
Report of conference of Eighteen-nation committee on disarmament; text of the interim report. U N Rev 10:42-3 O '63

TSCHIRKY, L. Robert
Spain's Gibraltar. Travel 120:38-9 S '63

TSETSE flies
Tsetse fly puparia: a new collecting technique. Z. H. Abedi and M. J. Miller. Science 141:264 Jl 19 '63
See also
Trypanosomiasis

TSHOMBE, Moise
Tshombe talks about U.S. role in the Congo; interview, ed. by A. J. Meyers. por U S News 57:50-1 Ag 3 '64

about

Aftermath in the Congo. H. R. Rudin. Cur Hist 45:341-6 D '63
As an East-West war heats up in the Congo. il por U S News 58:28-9 Ja 4 '65
Back comes Moses the Beloved. il Time 84: 24 Jl 3 '64
Balancing act. il Time 84:29 Ag 7 '64
Central Africa: go down, Moses. New Repub 149:13 Jl 20 '63
Congo: best bet is Tshombe. Life 57:4 Jl 17 '64
Congo: hostages, mercenaries and the CIA. J. Hatch. il Nation 199:452-5 D 14 '64
Congo turns to the white man. F. B. Stevens. il por U S News 57:55 S 14 '64
Congolese chaos continues. il por Newsweek 64:31 D 21 '64
Congo's Tshombe: alternating current. il por Newsweek 64:44+ O 19 '64
Crisis in the Congo; its meaning. A. J. Meyers. il por U S News 57:39-41 D 14 '64
How Katanga fell; with editorial comment. B. Littell. il por Sat Eve Post 236:74-6+, 84 My 11 '63
Immorality play. Newsweek 64:59 N 2 '64
Look who's here again. Nat R 16:639 Jl 28 '64
Man who wasn't there. il por Time 84:45 O 16 '64
Moise Tshombe's Congo comeback. por U S News 57:21 Jl 20 '64
One of those weeks. Newsweek 64:54+ S 21 '64
Premier no. four. il Time 84:28-9 Jl 17 '64
Setback for U.S. in Congo. il por U S News 57:46 Jl 13 '64
Snake has all the lines. il por Time 84:33-4 Jl 24 '64
Take-over. Newsweek 64:39-40 Jl 20 '64
Tshombe and the brigadier. il Newsweek 61: 40 F 4 '63
Tshombe at bay. il por Newsweek 64:42 Ag 17 '64
Tshombe in wonderland. S. de Gramont. il pors Sat Eve Post 237:82+ O 3 '64
Tshombe returns. Sr Schol 85:30-1 S 23 '64
Tshombe squeeze. Newsweek 65:26 Ja 4 '65
Tshombe's Spanish hideaway. il pors Ebony 19:100-2+ Ag '64
Under the knife. il Time 82:31 Jl 5 '63
UN's idiot policy in the Congo. E. Van Den Haag. Nat R 17:61-2 Ja 26 '65
Why the Africans hate Tshombe. M. Clos. il pors N Y Times Mag p24-5+ Ja 10 '65

TSIANG, Tingfu F.
Chinese tradition and modern currents; address, October 31, 1964. Vital Speeches 31: 105-9 D 1 '64
Moscow and Peiping; before and after the split; address, September 6, 1963. Vital Speeches 29:760-3 O 1 '63
Split between Peiping and Moscow; address, May 6, 1964. Vital Speeches 30:516-20 Je 15 '64

TSIEN, Tsuen-hsuin
Bamboo and silk and the art of talking back. J. Shera. Wilson Lib Bul 37:870 Je '63

TSIRANANA, Philibert
President of Malagasy Republic visits Washington; exchange of greetings, July 27, 1964. Dept State Bul 51:229-30 Ag 17 '64

TSO, Paul O. P. See Bonner, J. jt. auth.

TSO, T. C. and others
Radium-226 and polonium-210 in leaf tobacco and tobacco soil. bibliog Science 146:1043-5 N 20 '64

TSOTSIS and the Pondos; story. See Delius, A.

TSUGARU, Hanako
Japanese Prince meets girl, by go-between. E. Chapin. il por N Y Times Mag p42+ Mr 22 '64

TSUKADA, Matsuo
Umbrella pine, sciadopitys verticillata: past and present distribution in Japan. bibliog Science 142:1680-1 D 27 '63

TSUNAMI. See Seismic sea waves

TSUYUKI, Henry, and Wold, Finn
Enolase: multiple molecular forms in fish muscle. bibliog Science 146:535-7 O 23 '64

TUAREGS
Blue men rise. il Time 83:34 Ja 10 '64
Walking Rosetta stone. Sci Digest 54:63 D '63

TUBA (musical instrument)
How to buy a tuba... the kind you hold in your lap. J. J. Faran, jr. il Horizon 5:97-9 N '63

TUBAC, Ariz.
Spaniards came here 212 years ago. il Sunset 132:69+ Mr '64

TUBBY, Roger W.
Geneva, a center of international cooperative efforts; excerpts from an address, September 22, 1964. Dept State Bul 51:740-7 N 23 '64

TUBBY, Ruth P.
Planning for the long haul toward meeting standards. ALA Bul 58:499+ Je '64

TUBE cutting
Low-cost swing cut-off. C. G. Johnson. il Pop Mech 120:179 S '63

TUBE pins. See Vacuum tubes

TUBERCULIN
Tuberculin hypersensitivity: studies with radioactive antigen and mononuclear cells. K. Kay and W. O. Rieke. bibliog Science 139:487-9 F 8 '63
Tuberculin reactivity of a carbohydrate component of unheated BCG culture filtrate. H. Baer and S. D. Chaparas. bibliog il Science 146:245-7 O 9 '64

TUBERCULOSIS
India fights the big cough; with photographs. Sci Digest 55:74-7 Ap '64
Poverty blamed for rise in urban tuberculosis. Sci N L 86:18 Jl 11 '64
TB after ulcer surgery. F. Marley. Sci N L 85:357 Je 6 '64
TB spread by singer; Many TB patients now treated at home. Sci N L 85:357 Je 6 '64
TB world's worst disease. F. Marley. Sci N L 85:149 Mr 7 '64

Prevention and control

Battle of Tunisia. il UNESCO Courier 17:4-8 Ap '64
Danger! TB is on the rise! D. Murray. Read Digest 84:79-82 Je '64
New war against TB; tine test. il Time 81:52 My 24 '63
Preventing TB in children. E. M. Lincoln. il Parents Mag 39:151-2 S '64
Skid Row's TB detectives; Chicago. il Todays Health 41:53-4 D '63
TB eradication program concentrates on children. Sci N L 84:40 Jl 20 '63
TB; the far-from-dead disease. M. J. E. Senn. McCalls 91:88+ O '63
White plague is still a menace. E. A. Piszczek. il Todays Health 41:52-5 D '63

Vaccines

Birth of a new vaccine; Bacillus Calmette Guérin. il UNESCO Courier 17:10-11+ Ap '64

TUBERCULOSIS bacilli
Capreomycin: activity against experimental infection with mycobacterium leprae. C. C. Shepard. bibliog il Science 146:403-4 O 16 '64
Super-bacilli: a new challenge to medicine. il UNESCO Courier 17:14-15 Ap '64

TUBERCULOSIS in cattle
Here's the new program for TB. Farm J 88:36D Je '64

TUBERCULOSIS research
Momentous look into the microscope; March 24, 1882. il UNESCO Courier 17:8-10 Ap '64
Nicotinamide adenine dinucleotidase activity in cells of tuberculous animals. A. Bekierkunst and others. bibliog il Science 145: 280-1 Jl 17 '64

TUBEROSES
To enhance your summer garden, plant fragrant tuberoses. R. C. Hands. il Horticulture 41:265 My '63

TUBEROUS begonias. See Begonias

TUBES, Vacuum. See Vacuum tubes

TUBMAN, Harriet
Harriet Tubman. L. Bennett, jr. il pors Ebony 20:148+ N '64

TUBMAN, William Vacnarat Shadrach
Uncle Shad forever? il por Time 83:27 Ja 17 '64

TUCHMAN, Barbara W.
Anarchists; excerpts. por Atlan 211:91-2+ My '63
Game, gentlemen, a game. Esquire 59:114-16+ My '63

TUCK, Richard
Tuck and nip. il por Newsweek 64:34 O 12 '64

TUCK, William M.
Excerpt from debate, August 19, 1964. Cong Digest 44:24+ Ja '65

TUCKER, Bette Kirby
More children, the more love. Bet Hom & Gard 41:105 Mr '63

TUCKER, Mrs Bill
What's happened to the family heirloom. por Suc Farm 61:66-9 My '63

TUCKER, Carole
Shepherd is a lady. il pors Ebony 19:68-70+ Jl '64

TUCKER, G. Richard. See McGill, T. E. jt. auth.
TUCKER, Gerald J.
Thirteen days in a blizzard. por Outdoor Life 133:20-3+ Ja '64
TUCKER, Harold W.
Access to libraries study; statement, September 30, 1963. ALA Bul 57:1042 D '63
Operation head start. Library J 89:3382-3 S 15 '64
—and Becker, Joseph
Library/USA. ALA Bul 58:29-31 Ja '64
TUCKER, Raymond R.
Excerpt from address, February 24, 1964. Cong Digest 43:118+ Ap '64
TUCKER, Richard
Musical events; performance of role of Radames in Aïda. W. Sargeant. New Yorker 40:116-17 Ja 16 '65
Tenor. il pors Newsweek 65:76-7 Ja 11 '65
TUCKER, Richard, family
Sabbath eve. il pors Opera N 28:27-9 F 22 '64
TUCKER, Robert C.
Policy debate in Moscow. New Repub 150: 7-8 My 16 '64
TUCKER, W. T.
How customers make decisions. Nations Bsns 52:34-5+ Ag '64
TUCKER corporation
Death of a dream. Newsweek 62:66-7 Ag 12 '63
TUCSON, Ariz.
Finance
Tucson budget previews score with council, press, public. il Am City 78:133-4+ O '63
Galleries and museums
How it was a century ago at Tucson; Fort Lowell. il Sunset 133:54+ O '64
Newspapers
Trustbusters in Tucson; Arizona daily star bought by the Daily citizen. Time 85:67 Ja 15 '65
Sanitary affairs
Follow-up sweeper vacuums up dirt. H. L. Danforth. il Am City 79:8 My '64
TUCSON, Ariz. public library
Dust-off in the desert: new branch library in the far east end; reprint. J. F. Anderson. il Library J 89:4705-8 D 1 '64
Humphrey the Humpher; gift to central children's room. E. Schunk. il Wilson Lib Bul 39:164 O '64
TUCSON MOUNTAIN PARK. See Arizona—Parks and reserves
TUDOR, Antony
Musical events. W. Sargeant. New Yorker 40:167-8 My 16 '64
TUDOR, Bethany
Tudors at Higbee's. il pors Pub W 184:22-3 D 2 '63
TUDOR, Tasha
Tudors at Higbee's. il pors Pub W 184:22-3 D 2 '63
TUFTE, Edward E.
Pay-as-you-go brings code-level lighting. Am City 78:114 D '63
TUFTS university, Medford, Mass.
Campbell and Aldrich win competition for Tufts university library. il Arch Rec 134: 12-13 O '63
Should tenure go? case of W. W. Sayre. C. M. Curtis. Nat R 16:864 O 6 64
Why pick on a fine teacher? case of W. Sayre. Life 56:4 My 15 '64
TUFTY, Barbara
Sea intelligence: the dolphin. Sci N L 86: 138-9 Ag 29 '64
Spring has many meanings. Sci N L 83: 183 Mr 23 '63
— and Walker, Michael
Filth covers the waterfront. Sci N L 85:154-5 Mr 7 '64
TUGBOATS
Toughest corks afloat; Holland's oceangoing tugs. J. N. Miller. il Read Digest 83:172-4+ D '63
TUGGLE, Robert A.
Growing up with opera. Opera N 27:32-3 Mr 9 '63
Man Verdi; review. Opera N 27:33 Mr 23 '63
Martin's Verdi. Opera N 28:7 D 7 '63
TUGWELL, Rexford
Rexford Tugwell and the New deal, by B. Sternsher. Review
New Repub 150:21-4 Mr 7 '64. A. A. Berle
Sat R por 47:33-4 Mr 7 '64. D. Brogan
TUKHACHEVSKII, Mikhail Nikolaevich
Tukhachevsky affair, by V. Alexandrov. Review
Sat R 47:135-6 Mr 14 '64. M. Kalb
TULANE drama review
Dramatically different. il Time 84:52-3 Ag 14 '64
TULANE university, New Orleans
Who let them in? coed swimming squad. il Life 54:89-90 Mr 22 '63
TULE elk. See Elk
TULI, V. and others
N^6-benzyladenine: inhibitor of respiratory kinases. bibliog Science 146:1477-9 D 11 '64
TULIP exhibits. See Flower exhibits
TULIP trees
This is the real tulip tree. il Sunset 131: 204 D '63
Tulip tree. il Bet Hom & Gard 42:127 O '64
TULIPS
Collectors' items: the smaller tulips and daffodils. J. Thibodeau. il Horticulture 42:28-30+ Ap '64
How to select tulips. O. K. Moore. il House B 105:214-15+ O '63
Pinpoint spring color with tulips. R. M. Peters. il Pop Gard 15:36-7 S '64
Try the fairy tulips, too! E. F. Steffek. il Pop Gard 15:66-7 S '64
Tulipomania. L. M. Bourne. il Horticulture 41:264 My '63
Tulips for color next spring. E. F. Steffek. il Pop Gard 14:26-7+ S '63
Tulips old and new at Sterling Forest. C. Lewis. il Horticulture 42:26-7+ My '64
Two months of glorious bloom from tulips. B. Black. il Pop Gard 15:8-10 N '64
When it's tulip time in Holland. J. H. Winchester. il Read Digest 84:146-50 Ap '64
TULLER, Edwin H.
Excerpt from testimony, April 29, 1964. Cong Digest 43:271+ N '64
Real danger of a state religion. por U S News 56:72-3 My 11 '64
TULLIUS, F. P.
Computer poetry or, Sob suddenly, the bongos are moving. Harper 227:24+ D '63
Glare into the future. New Yorker 40:24-5 Jl 11 '64
TULSA, Okla.
Anonymous rainmaker. Newsweek 62:25+ Ag 12 '63
Rainmaker, rainmaker, go away. il Time 82: 17 Ag 9 '63
Description
Two giants rising in the Southwest. il U S News 54:69 F 11 '63
Religious institutions and affairs
Unity in Oklahoma; Roman Catholic church in Tulsa joins the Tulsa council of churches. Newsweek 63:82 My 4 '64
TULSA, Okla. city-county library system
Triple for Tulsa; Nathan Hale, Broken Arrow, Suburban Acres branches. A. B. Martin. il Library J 89:4740-2 D 1 '64
TUMBLING barrels
Quart-size four-gang tumbler. il Pop Mech 120:194-6 N '63
Rock tumbling in a fruit jar. il Sunset 132: 104+ F '64
TUMOR viruses
Antigenic behavior of Moloney lymphomas: independence of virus release and immunosensitivity. G. Klein and E. Klein. bibliog il Science 145:1316-17 S 18 '64
Inhibition by 5-iododeoxyuridine of the oncogenic effects of adenovirus type 12 in hamsters. R. J. Huebner and others. il Science 142:488-90 O 25 '63
Polyoma virus genetic material in a virus-free polyoma-induced tumor. D. Axelrod and others. bibliog il Science 146:1466-9 D 11 '64
Spontaneous kidney tumors in the frog: rate of occurrence in isolated adults. K. A. Rafferty, jr. bibliog il Science 141:720-1 Ag 23 '63
TUMORS
Glycogen-containing cells of estrogen-induced renal tumors of the hamster. J. A. Arcadi. bibliog il Science 142:592-3 N 1 '63
Hepatomas in rainbow trout: descriptive and experimental epidemiology. H. Wolf. bibliog il Science 142:676-8 N 8 '63
Induction of papillary growths in the heart. S. Rodbard and others. bibliog il Science 143:1341-2 Mr 20 '64
Potentiation of 5-fluorouracil inhibition of Flexner-Jobling carcinoma by glucose. S. S. Kung and others. bibliog il Science 141: 627-8 Ag 16 '63
Spontaneous kidney tumors in the frog: rate of occurrence in isolated adults. K. A. Rafferty, jr. bibliog il Science 141:720-1 Ag 23 '63

TUMORS—*Continued*
Temperature dependence of the activity of the antitumor factor in the common clam. A. Hegyeli. bibliog il Science 146:77-8 O 2 '64
Tumors induced in hamsters by simian virus 40; persistent subviral infection. P. Gerber. bibliog il Science 140:889-90 My 24 '63
See also
Sarcoma
TUMORS, Malignant. See Cancer
TUMORS, Plant
Isolation of an antihistaminic principle resembling tomatine from crown gall tumors. B. A. Kovacs and others. bibliog il Science 144:295-6 Ap 17 '64; Reply with rejoinder. P. R. White. 146:670 O 30 '64
Somatic mitoses in cells of picea glauca cultivated in vitro. P. G. Risser. bibliog il Science 143:591-2 F 7 '64
TUNA fish
See also
Cookery—Fish
TUNA fish, Canned. See Canned food
TUNA fishing
Day Alfandre fought geronimo. F. T. Moss. il Outdoor Life 133:70-3+ Ap '64
Great tuna war; commercial seiners vs sport fishermen. F. T. Moss. il Field & S 68:10-12+ Je '63
New hotspot for tuna. V. C. Heilner. il Field & S 69:144-6 My '64
U.S. seeks solution to problem of tuna fishing off Ecuador; statement, June 5, 1963. D. Rusk. Dept State Bul 48:976 Je 24 '63
TUNE on a bass drum; story. See Freitag, G. H.
TUNED circuits. See Radio circuits
TUNELLITE
Boron-oxygen polyanion in the crystal structure of tunellite. J. R. Clark. bibliog il Science 141:1178-9 S 20 '63
TUNES. See Melodies
TUNG, Chi-ping
Red China; ed. by Q. Reynolds. por Look 28:21-7 D 1 '64
TUNGSTEN
Firm exploring uses for foamed tungsten. il Miss & Roc 14:35 My 4 '64
High-pressure synthesis of molybdates with the wolframite structure. A. P. Young and C. M. Schwartz. bibliog il Science 141:348-9 Jl 26 '63
TUNGUS catastrophe. See Explosions
TUNGUS meteorite. See Meteorites
TUNGUSKA catastrophe. See Explosions
TUNING
Piano tuning, the electronic way. F. Van Veen. il Electr World 72:56-7 S '64
TUNING, Radio. See Radio receiving apparatus—Tuning
TUNING, Television. See Television receiving apparatus—Tuning
TUNING fork clocks. See Clocks
TUNIS, John R.
Laugh off $11 million? New Repub 152:11-12 Ja 2 '65
TUNISIA
Secretary-General visits three African countries. U N Rev 11:12-13+ Mr '64
See also
Architecture, Domestic—Tunisia
Public health—Tunisia
TUNLEY, Roul
Danish Jews. Sat Eve Post 236:74-5+ F 23 '63
Delinquent: do we hate our children? Nation 199:5-6 Jl 13 '64
Democrat who took Vermont. Sat Eve Post 236:82+ N 23 '63
Haunting world of Andrew Wyeth. Read Digest 84:166-70 Ja '64
King of the discounters. Sat Eve Post 236:28-9 Ap 13 '63
Tragedy of a vertical slum. Sat Eve Post 236:89-93 Je 29 '63
(ed) See Hoffman, B. Red junket to Cuba
TUNNEL diodes
Amateur scientist; electronic chronometer utilizing tunnel diodes. R. L. Watters. il Sci Am 208:157-60+ Mr '63
TD/RFG; tunnel diode, radio frequency generator. S. E. Bammel. il Pop Electr 18:44-7+ F '63
Tunnel diode high-resistance checker. C. D. Todd. il Electr World 69:86-8 Je '63
Tunnel diode receiver. R. D. Grimm. il Pop Electr 18:62-5+ Je '63
TUNNELL, Emlen
Eyes and ears of the N.Y. Giants. il pors Ebony 19:58-60+ D '63
Sporting scene. H. W. Wind. il New Yorker 39:165-72+ D 14 '63
TUNNELS and tunneling
Easier than Hannibal; St Bernard tunnel. il Time 83:24+ Mr 27 '64
Now, a highway short cut under the Alps; Great St Bernard tunnel. il U S News 56:12 Mr 30 '64
Reporter at large; Mont Blanc tunnel. J. Wechsberg. il New Yorker 39:140+ My 18 '63
Snowplow, go home! new tunnel and covered highway in the Alps. il Pop Sci 182:98-9 F '63
Tunnel of Eupalinus. J. Goodfield. il Sci Am 210:104-10+ Je '64
Tunnel under the Alps: Grand Saint Bernard tunnel. R. Gelatt. Reporter 28:36-8 Ap 11 '63
Ventilation
Air key to ocean tunnel. E. Hall. il Sci N L 85:218 Ap 4 '64
TUNNELS and tunneling, Underwater
Crossing that defies the Atlantic; bridge-tunnel system across Chesapeake Bay. il Fortune 67:112-21 Ap '63
Driving across Chesapeake Bay. il Sci Digest 53:64-9 Mr '63
New shortcut for North-South travel: Chesapeake Bay bridge-tunnel. il U S News 55:72-3 Ag 5 '63
Over and under seventeen mi. of open sea; link Delmarva Peninsula and the Norfolk-Virginia Beach area. il Bsns W p46-8+ Mr 23 '63
Porpoising highway; Chesapeake Bay tunnel-bridge. il Pop Mech 119:94-5 Je '63
Tunnel men shun women; Chesapeake Bay bridge-tunnel. E. Hall. Sci N L 84:53 Jl 27 '63
See also
Chesapeake Bay bridge-tunnel
English Channel tunnel (proposed)
TUOMIOJA, Sakari
Cherub from Finland. il por Time 83:39 Ap 3 '64
Death of United Nations mediator. UN Mo Chron 1:20-1 O '64
TUPELOS
Beetlebung tree. P. Brady. il Am For 69:52 My '63
TURANDOT; opera. See Puccini, G.
TURBINES
See also
Gas turbines, Aircraft
TURBOFAN engines. See Gas turbines, Aircraft
TURBOJET automobile engines. See Gas turbines, Automotive
TURBOPROP airplane engines. See Gas turbines, Aircraft
TURBULENCE
See also
Atmospheric turbulence
TURCO, Lewis
Awaken, bells falling; poem. Poetry 103:247 Ja '64
Columbine and laurel; poem. Sat R 48:74 Ja 16 '65
I knew a man once; poem. Sat R 47:24 Jl 18 '64
November 22, 1963; poem. Poetry 105:84 N '64
about
Five poets. J. Engels. Poetry 102:403 S '63
TURCOTTE, E. L. and Feaster, C. V.
Haploids: high-frequency production from single-embryo seeds in a line of Pima cotton. bibliog Science 140:1407-8 Je 28 '63
TURECK, Rosalyn
Secure in the universe: Bach's modern interpreters. por Time 83:67 Ja 3 '64
TUREKIAN, Karl K. and Stuiver, Minze
Clay- and carbonate-accumulation rates in three south Atlantic deep-sea cores. Science 146:55-6 O 2 '64
TURENNE, Henri de
France's Faure. N Y Times Mag p29+ Ap 26 '64
TURF. See Lawns
TURGENEV, Ivan Sergeevich
Month in the country. Criticism
Commonweal 78:354 Je 21 '63
New Yorker 39:126 Je 8 '63
Theatre Arts 47:10-11 Ag '63
TURIN, Italy
Turin with a car thrown in. R. Joseph. il Esquire 60:110-13 O '63
City planning
City as a single structure. il Arch Forum 121:200-1 Ag '64
TURIN'S automotive designers. See Designers
TURKEL, Stuart S.
What psychiatry can do. Harper 228:96+ Ap '64

TURKEY
Turkey; Peace corps volunteers. N. Borton and J. W. Borton. il Nat Geog Mag 126:330-3 S '64
Turkey's internal crisis. S. Lens. Commonweal 80:629-31 S 18 '64
See also
Buyuk Island
Cappadocia
Economic assistance in Turkey
Istanbul
Kurds
Tourist trade—Turkey
Women—Turkey

Antiquities

Backward into prehistory; excavation at Çatal Hüyük. il Time 85:61 Ja 1 '65
Lost civilization; Nemrut Dag. il Sci Digest 53:47-9 My '63
Neolithic city in Turkey; Çatal Hüyük. J. Mellaart. il Sci Am 210:94-104 Ap '64
Out of the stone age; Cayonu digs. il Newsweek 64:66 N 2 '64
Primitive metallurgy; use of copper by people of Cayonu, 7000 B.C. Sci Am 211:62+ D '64
Site of Myceanean civilization discovered in Turkey. Sci Digest 53:59 Mr '63
Uncover ancient tomb; burial tomb of King Gyges. il Sci N L 86:323 N 21 '64
See also
Sardis

Army

Our far-flung correspondents. C. Frankel. il New Yorker 40:136+ Je 6 '64

Commercial treaties and agreements

Cotton textile agreements concluded with Turkey; Department announcement; with texts of U.S. notes, July 17, 1964. G. G. Johnson. Dept State Bul 51:292-4 Ag 24 '64

Description and travel

Reader's choice; Valley of Goreme. F. R. Smith. Travel 120:13 D '63

Economic conditions

Growing pains on the Bosporus. il Fortune 71:92+ Ja '65
New associate; Common market. il Time 82:79-80 S 27 '63

Foreign relations

Bid for independence; official Soviet mission on a visit. il Newsweek 65:39 Ja 25 '65
President Johnson expresses hope for end of strife in Cyprus; exchange of messages. C. Gursel; L. B. Johnson. Dept State Bul 50:90 Ja 20 '64
Toward the vortex; expulsion of Greek citizens. Newsweek 64:52+ S 21 '64

Politics and government

Democracy or revolution? New Repub 150:10 Ja 4 '64
How to stay in trouble. il Time 81:38 Ap 5 '63
Insurrection II. il Time 81:26 My 31 '63
Just any government at all. Time 82:35 D 13 '63
Our far-flung correspondents. C. Frankel. il New Yorker 40:136+ Je 6 '64
Problems of democracy. Newsweek 62:45-6 D 16 '63
Turkey in crisis; jungle of interrelated nightmares. G. Gersh. Christian Cent 80:231-3 F 20 '63
Turkey's second try at democracy. D. A. Rustow. Yale R 52:518-38 Je '63

Religious institutions and affairs

See also
Christians in Turkey
Orthodox Eastern church in Turkey

Social conditions

See also
Women—Turkey

Social life and customs

Every town has two faces. R. H. Latimer. il Harper 227:26+ N '63
See also
Women—Turkey

TURKEY, Frozen. See Poultry, Frozen
TURKEY as food. See Cookery—Poultry
TURKEY calling. See Bird calling
TURKEY carving. See Carving (meat, etc)
TURKEY gobblers; drama. See Hark, M. and McQueen, N.

TURKEY hunting
Cornfield gobbler. W. Page. il Field & S 68:57-9+ Ap '64
Gobbler goes west. W. Bever. il Outdoor Life 131:60-1+ My '63
Guns for gobblers. W. Page. il Field & S 67:96-100 Mr '63
How not to clobber a gobbler. C. Elliott. il Outdoor Life 133:54-5+ Mr '64
Monarch of wolf creek. C. Elliott. il Outdoor Life 131:48-9+ Mr '63
$10 turkey. C. E. Gillham. il Field & S 67:26-8+ F '63
Turkey on the wing. B. W. Dalrymple. il Outdoor Life 132:60-3+ S '63
Turkey talk. C. Conley. il Field & S 68:36-7+ N '63
Turkeys plus. J. Tische. il Field & S 68:26-7+ D '63

TURKEYS
Low malignancy of Rous sarcoma cells as evidenced by poor transplantability in turkeys. V. V. Bergs and V. Groupe. bibliog il Science 139:922-3 Mr 8 '63
Tradition of giving thanks. B. Tufty. il Sci N L 84:282-3 N 2 '63
Turkeys put on beef. il Bsns W p68 Ap 4 '64
When the turkeys walked. N. M. Clark. il Am Heritage 15:92-3 D '63

Diseases and pests

New turkey disease; round heart. Farm J 88:61 Mr '64

Marketing

Contract that makes money for flock owners; Central cooperative turkey producers assn. il Farm J 88:42H N '64
Sure-fire ways to make money on turkeys. D. Seim. Farm J 88:44E D '64

TURKEYS, Wild
Cannons for turkeys; distributing gobblers throughout Florida. K. Musson. il Field & S 68:10-11 O '63
See also
Turkey hunting
TURKEYS as food. See Cookery—Poultry
TURKISH cookery. See Cookery, Turkish
TURKISH Cypriotes. See Turks in Cyprus
TURKISH folk tales. See Folk literature, Turkish
TURKISH language

Study and teaching

Language study and the Middle East. C. A. Ferguson. Ann Am Acad 356:76-85 N '64
TURKISH painting. See Painting, Turkish
TURKO-Tataric languages
See also
Altaic languages
TURKS in Cyprus
Cyprus, island of hate and fear; closeup of Greeks and Turks, the deadly enemies. M. Wall. il N Y Times Mag p 13+ Mr 8 '64
Cyprus: who is right? is anyone? Time 83:29 My 1 '64
TURKS ISLANDS
See also
Grand Turk
TURLEY, Bob
How I know what pitchers will throw. Sports Illus 21:30-3 Jl 20 '64
TURNABOUT in time; drama. See Martens, A. C.
TURNBULL, Colin M.
Music, men and gods. Natur Hist 72:47-53 My '63
Reviews (cont) Natur Hist 73:5-7+ My '64
Tribal art from Africa. Natur Hist 73:46-53 Mr '64
Tribalism and social evolution in Africa; address, April 10, 1964; with questions and answers. bibliog f Ann Am Acad 354:22-32 Jl '64
TURNBULL, David
Undercooling of liquids; with biographical sketch. Sci Am 212:16, 38-46 bibliog(p 134) Ja '65
TURNBULL, Gael
Actress; poem. Nation 198:76 Ja 20 '64
Particles; poem. Nation 198:124 F 3 '64
Weather of the mind; poem. Nation 198:54 Ja 13 '64
TURNBULL, John W.
Note from Texas. Commonweal 79:337 D 13 '63
TURNCOATS
GI who chose communism; A. Belthomme. S. Karnow. il Sat Eve Post 236:104-7 N 16 '63
Model red; Tung Chi-ping seeks sanctuary with Americans. il Time 84:22-3 Ag 14 '64
Ordeal by defection; case of Y. A. Aseyev. Newsweek 63:44 Ap 20 '64
Regards from an outcast; case of O. Lenchevsky. Time 83:40 My 22 '64

TURNER, Ada B.
Begonias for beauty. Horticulture 41:346-7 Je '63

TURNER, Arthur C.
Commonwealth: evolution or dissolution? Cur Hist 46:257-62+ My '64

TURNER, C. Donnell, and Asakawa, Hiroshi
Experimental reversal of germ cells in ovaries of fetal mice. bibliog Science 143:1344-5 Mr 20 '64

TURNER, David
Semi-detached. Criticism
New Yorker 39:99 O 19 '63
Newsweek 62:104 O 21 '63
Sat R 46:32 O 26 '63
Theatre Arts 48:65 Ja '64

TURNER, Donald E. See Giannattasio, F. jt. auth.

TURNER, E. Robert
We had to try twice. Am City 78:122-4 Je '63

TURNER, Ewart E.
No letup for Der stellvertreter. Christian Cent 80:1269-70 O 16 '63

TURNER, Geneva C.
African ruler: Prime Minister Margai of Sierra Leone. Negro Hist Bul 28:13 O '64
Book review. Negro Hist Bul 28:37 N '64
Colored presidents and rulers (title varies) (cont) Negro Hist Bul 26:222, 249; 27:17, 35, 91, 153, 177; 28:36-7 Ap-My, O-N '63, Ja, Mr-Ap, N '64

TURNER, George K.
Absolute spectrofluorometer. bibliog Science 146:183-9 O 9 '64

TURNER, Gerry, and Major, F. M.
Floating designs. Design 65:104-7 Ja '64

TURNER, J. J. and Pimentel, G. C.
Krypton fluoride; preparation by the matrix isolation technique. bibliog Science 140:974-5 My 31 '63

TURNER, J. O.
Find the faults first. por Am City 79:94 N '64

TURNER, John A.
Akidemy awards. Recreation 57:519-20 D '64

TURNER, John H.
Don't forget the meter shop. por Am City 80:82-3 Ja '65

TURNER, Joseph Mallord William
Art; exhibition at Washington national gallery. M. Kozloff. Nation 197:246-7 O 19 '63
In the glow of the perfect patron. P. Quennell. il por Horizon 5:62-71 Mr '63
Turner's pictures of nothing. L. Gowing. il Art N 62:30-3+ O '63

TURNER, Lucy Mae
Kin of Nat Turner. por Negro Hist Bul 27:78 Ja '64

TURNER, Mary C.
Libros en venta. por Library J 89:2559-61 Je 15 '64

TURNER, Pete
Kitemaker; photographs. Sports Illus 21:28-35 Ag 3 '64
Masters. il Sports Illus 18:26-35 Ap 1 '63
Setting for a glorious Olympiad; photographs. Sports Illus 21:32-41 Jl 6 '64

about

Focus on Pete Turner. J. Durniak. il por Pop Phot 52:62-71+ My '63

TURNER, Robert C.
People are living better than ever, but . . : interview. por U S News 55:59-61 O 14 '63

TURNER, Rufus P.
A.C. negative-resistance devices. bibliog Electr World 70:50-1+ Jl '63
Electronic color matcher. Pop Electr 18:51-3 My '63
Inexpensive D.C.-variable inductor. Electr World 71:70 F '64
Simple photoelectric amplifier. Electr World 72:104-5 N '64

TURNER, Theodore N.
Bar behind bars. por Time 83:88+ My 22 '64

TURNER, Thomas C.
Novelist and his theme. Writer 76:12-14+ D '63

TURNER, Tom
How a moon shot works: a primer for you. Esquire 62:204-7 D '64

TURNER, W. Price
Some British poets. G. Baro. Poetry 102:193-8 Je '63

TURNER, Waco
Nobody loses at the Poor boy open. E. Shrake. il por Sports Illus 20:28-31 My 11 '64

TURNEY, Bill
Street rod under an Indy influence. il Hot Rod 17:84-7 Je '64

TURNING
See also
Lathes

TURNIPS
See also
Cookery—Vegetables

TURNIPSEED, Martha
Genesee and Birmingham. Christian Cent 80:1239 O 9 '63

about

Churchmen defend sit-in student. Christian Cent 80:821 Je 26 '63; Discussion. 80:1106 S 11 '63

TURNLUND, R. W.
You can't beat electronic data processing. Am City 78:97-8 Jl '63

TURNPIKES. See Express highways

TURNTABLES
See also
Phonograph—Turntables

TUROVLIN, Lenore
Lucky one; story. McCalls 90:88-9 Ap '63
Wife game; story. McCalls 90:70-1 Ag '63

TURPIN, James W.
Project concern; somebody has to care. il Ladies Home J 80:52 Ap '63
Two physicians named outstanding young men. il por Todays Health 41:5+ Mr '63

TURRO, Nicholas J. See Hammond, G. S. jt. auth.

TURTLE Back zoo, West Orange, N.J. See Zoological gardens

TURTLE doves. See Pigeons

TURTLE MOUNTAINS, N.D.
Bird islands in the prairies. O. S. Pettingill, jr. il Audubon Mag 66:250-1 Jl '64

TURTLE racing
Turtle trots. il Newsweek 62:71 Jl 29 '63

TURTLES
Blood group studies with turtles. W. Frair. bibliog il Science 140:1412-14 Je 28 '63
Camouflaged still-fishing. H. Hediger. il Natur Hist 72:18-21 Je '63
Circulatory adaptation to diving in the freshwater turtle. J. E. Millen and others. bibliog il Science 145:591-3 Ag 7 '64
Great turtle mystery. G. Laycock. il Field & S 68:10-12+ Mr '64
How the turtle gets along without air at the bottom of the pond. W. Cloud. Pop Sci 185:21-2 N '64
Intercellular channels in the salt-secreting glands of marine turtles. R. A. Ellis and J. H. Abel, jr. bibliog il Science 144:1340-2 Je 12 '64
Pilgrim of the river; arrau, freshwater turtle. J. A. Roze. il Natur Hist 73:34-41 Ag '64
Stump lot adventure. D. R. Crandall. il Outdoor Life 131:80-1+ Ap '63
Turtle watching is fun and turtles have good manners. il Sunset 133:64-5 Ag '64
We fought a fresh-water monster. E. Nowak, jr. il Outdoor Life 133:48-9+ Ja '64

TURTLES, Green
Green turtle; letter to the editor. A. Carr. Américas 16:48 N '64
Green turtles: tasty treasures of the sea. G. S. Fichter. Read Digest 82:212C-212D+ F '63
Nature note; green turtle. Sci N L 86:410 D 26 '64
Saving the Atlantic green turtle: a biological experiment. G. K. Zimmer. il Nat Parks Mag 38:11-13 D '64

TUSCALOOSA, Ala.
King's targets. il Newsweek 63:26+ Je 22 '64

TUSHINGHAM, Rita
People are talking about. . . por Vogue 141:78-9 F 15 '63

TUSIANI, Joseph
Movie of the month. Cath World 197:395-6 S '63
Plant; poem. Cath World 197:132 My '63
Sunshine and evening; poem. Cath World 196:284 F '63

TUSINSKI, Joseph
Low Q resonance. Electr world 72:90-1 N '64
R.F. response measurement. Electr World 71:37+ F '64
What is Q? Electr World 70:94+ O '63
What is skin effect? Electr World 69:80-1 Je '63

TUSKEGEE, Ala.
New voting pattern; two Negroes elected to city council. Newsweek 64:32 S 28 '64

Negroes

Coexistence Tuskegee. New Repub 151:6 O 3 '64

TUSKEGEE Institute
Luther Foster of Tuskegee. J. Scanlon. il Sat R 47:76+ My 16 '64

TUSSMAN, Malka Haifetz
Spoil; Play without words; By an abandoned house; poems. tr. by J. Hirschman. Poetry 102:381-3 S '63

about

Note on Malka Tussman. J. Hirschman. Poetry 102:406 S '63

TUSTISON, W. A. See Goodner, C. J. jt. auth.
TUTENKHAMUN, king of Egypt
King Tut's golden hoard. J. Stewart-Gordon. il Read Digest 84:198-204 Ap '64
Tutankhamen, by C. Desroches-Noblecourt. Review
Art N il 62:32-3+ Ja '64. K. Levin
Tutankhamun's golden trove. C. D. Noblecourt. il Nat Geog Mag 124:624-46 O '63
TUTIN, Dorothy
Queens. New Yorker 39:33-4 Mr 23 '63
TUTOR; drama. See Brecht, B.
TUTORS and tutoring
Peripatetic reviewer; experience as a student tutor. E. Weeks. Atlan 211:126+ Je '63
Tutor corps; Summer '64 tutor corps. il Time 84:56 Jl 24 '64
University will try British tutoring system; University of Minnesota. Sci N L 87:9 Ja 2 '65
TUTSI. See Burundi—Native races
TUTTLE, Ruthanne
Pace-setters; interview. por Mlle 59:282-3 Ag '64
TUTUOLA, Amos
WLB biography. N. Ackerly. por Wilson Lib Bul 38:81 S '63
TVARDOVSKII, Aleksandr Trifonovich
Poem's progress. il por Newsweek 62:39-40 S 2 '63
Stalinsville on the Styx. Time 82:22+ Ag 30 '63
TWAIN, Mark, pseud. See Clemens. S. L.
TWARDZIK, Louis F.
How we fail in recruitment. por Recreation 57:468-9 N '64
Urban-oriented outdoor recreation; excerpts from address. por Recreation 56:470-3 D '63
TWAYNE publishers, incorporated
Publication explosion; American authors. K. Vanderbilt. Nation 198:219-20 Mr 2 '64
TWELVE dancing princesses; drama. See Thane, A.
TWELVE-mile limit. See Territorial waters
TWENTIETH century
Brave new world? address, May 29, 1964. T. E. Shearer. Vital Speeches 30:670-2 Ag 15 '64
By the end of the twentieth century. D. Sarnoff. il Fortune 69:116-19 My '64
Dissent from despair. A. B. Hoag. il N Y Times Mag p21+ Ap 5 '64
Era of radical change. M. Ways. il Fortune 69:112-15+ My '64
It is one world or no world. A. J. Toynbee. il N Y Times Mag p28+ Ap 5 '64
Meaning of the twentieth century, by K. E. Boulding. Review
Sat R 47:33-4 D 19 '64. E. Capouya
New generation in charge; old mistakes forgotten? il U S News 55:98-100 Ag 19 '63
1913. il Life 55:71-88 N 22; 65-72B N 29 '63; 56:46-61 Ja 3 '64
On the road from Idlewild. Fortune 68:97-8+ O '63
Party of one; confessions of an anachronism. C. Fadiman. il Holiday 33:11+ F '63
Public into private and the new boom in unreal estate. A. Gingrich. Esquire 61:4 Ja '64
Since World war I: what fifty years have brought and what another fifty years may bring. il U S News 57:38-43 Jl 6 '64
Twentieth century; symposium. il Look 29: 15-28+ Ja 12 '65
See also
Nineteen hundred and sixty-four
TWENTIETH century-Fox film corporation
Can Cleo pay it back? il Bsns W p48-50 Je 8 '63
Can Fox keep Cleopatra afloat? Bsns W p25-6 My 16 '64
Cleo and the critics. il Bsns W p34 Je 15 '63
Cleopatra papers; excerpts. J. Brodsky; N. Weiss. il Esquire 60:33-7+ Ag '63
Darryl Zanuck: last of the movie moguls. E. Havemann. McCalls 91:134-5+ O '63
Fortunes of Cleopatra. il Newsweek 61:63-6 Mr 25 '63
Goldfarb case fought by anti-censorship forces. Pub W 187:105-6 Ja 18 '65
Goldfarb vs. Notre Dame. Newsweek 64:53 D 28 '64
Importance of an image; Notre Dame injunction against Twentieth century-Fox movie. il Time 84:69 D 18 '64
Notre Dame's Irish dander rises over a movie; case against Twentieth century-Fox. il Life 57:68+ D 18 '64
Right of privacy & property; injunction against the movie John Goldfarb, please come home. il Time 84:54 D 25 '64
20th century reformation hour. See Radio broadcasting—Religious programs
TWENTY-five-hour week. See Hours of labor
TWENTY-one (game) See Blackjack (game)
TWICE-blessed family; story. See Athanas, V.
TWIGHT, Susanne
Two seasons at Crater Lake. Nat Parks Mag 37:15 Ag '63
TWILIGHT glow. See Zodiacal light
TWIN beds in Rome; story. See Updike, J.
TWIN berries. See Partridge berries
TWIN Disc clutch company
Clutch that slips on purpose; modulated clutch. il Bsns W p81 Je 20 '64
TWIN LAKES, Colo.
Terror at Twin Lakes. il Pop Sci 182:114-17 F '63
TWIN-lens reflex cameras. See Cameras
TWINING, Edward Francis Twining, baron
Lord and the regalia. S. Hugh-Jones. il por Horizon 5:92-6 My '63
TWINS
Believe it or not: these girls are twins; Susan and Karen Olson. C. Morrison. il Look 28:M10-M13 O 20 '64
Bringing up two at once. E. Lazar and C. Klein. il N Y Times Mag p78+ My 24 '64
Heredity vs. environment a surprising new answer; Monozygotic twins. J. Kaplan and Mr J. Kaplan. il Sci Digest 56:59-62 D '64
How can anyone teach a class with seven sets of twins? il Life 54:63-6 Ap 19 '63
Mosaic hemoglobin types in a pair of cattle twins. C. Stormont and others. bibliog il Science 145:600-1 Ag 7 '64
My baby was different. il Good H 156:10+ F '63; Same abr. Read Digest 83:147-50 Ag '63
Nat King Cole twins. il Ebony 18:106-12+ Ag '63
Three sets of twins in three years. S. James and R. W. Goldfarb. il Redbook 121:58-9+ My '63
Twins who found each other; Tony Milasi and Roger Brooks. B. Lindeman. il Sat Eve Post 237:76-8 Mr 21 '64; Same abr. Read Digest 85:93-7 Ag '64
Why are twins so special? C. B. Hicks. il Todays Health 41:18-21+ D '63
See also
Siamese twins
TWINS; story. See Glanville, B.
TWISS, Eleanor
Eleanor Twiss. por PTA Mag 59:30 O '64
TWISS, Robert
Boeing steps up efforts in cryogenics research. Miss & Roc 16:36-7 Ja 11 '65
Challenge met in Minuteman management. Miss & Roc 13:36 Jl 22 '63
Minuteman cost-cutting aims outlined. Miss & Roc 12:40+ Je 24 '63
TWISTING (botany) See Spiral growth and movement
TWO family houses. See Houses. Two-family
2,4-D
Growth-regulating chemicals persist in plants: qualitative bioassay. T. J. Muzik and J. W. Whitworth. bibliog il Science 140:1212-13 Je 14 '63
Pulchritudinous pest. J. Fix. il Motor B 112: 47+ D '63
TWO-headed animals. See Abnormalities (animals)
TWO islands; story. See Browne, D.
TWO nice girls; story. See Patton, F. G.
TWO party system. See Party government
TWO pilgrims; story. See Taylor, P.
TWO roads to Petra; story. See Shaara, M.
TWO semesters at Wagner's inn; story. See Reifler, S.
TWO story houses. See Houses
TWO thousand (year)
U.S. by 2000 A.D. il U S News 54:7 Ap 8 '63
U.S. thirty-seven years from now. il U S News 54:70-1 F 11 '63
Year 2000; address, September 23, 1964. V. F. Caputo. Vital Speeches 31:10-15 O 15 '64

Anecdotes, facetiae, satire, etc.

Warning: new century ahead. H. B. Jacobs. New Yorker 39:138+ Ap 27 '63
TWO thousand and four
August 29, 2004. C. Amory. Sat R 47:16+ Ag 29 '64
TWO-way radio. See Radio telephone, Portable
TWO-year colleges. See Junior colleges
TWOMEY, Katherine
Iris. Pop Gard 14:38-9+ Jl '63

TWORKOV, Jack
Religious art without God. Art N 63:32-5+ N '64
Tworkov: radical pro. L. Finkelstein. il por Art N 63:32-5+ Ap '64
Tworkov: the central image. il Art N 62:29+ Mr '63
TYAN, Marvin L.
Thymus: role in maturation of fetal lymphoid precursors. bibliog Science 145:934-5 Ag 28 '64
—and Cole, L. J.
Dissociation of homograft response to allogeneic versus xenogeneic skin grafts in irradiated mice. bibliog Science 141:813-14 Ag 30 '63
—and others
Thymus: its limited role in the recovery of homograft response in irradiated mice. bibliog Science 142:584 N 1 '63
TYCO, incorporated
Critical report on Tyco probe spurs USAF research scrutiny. Aviation W 80:20 Mr 23 '64
Laser that produces non-stop. Bsns W p 114 S 7 '63
Tyco probe spurs AF contracting reform. G. C. Wilson. Aviation W 79:40-1 D 16 '63
TYER, Travis
Selling the teenager. por Library J 89:1815-17 Ap 15 '64
(ed) Special section on library service to teenagers. por Library J 89:1815-35+ Ap 15 '64
TYLER, A. Clifford
Power lines go underground. Am City 79:105-6 Ag '64
TYLER, Anne
I play kings; story. Seventeen 22:338-41 Ag '63
Street of bugles; story. Sat Eve Post 236:64-6 N 30 '63
Youth talks about youth. Vogue 145:85+ F 1 '65
TYLER, Gus
(ed) Combating organized crime. bibliog f Ann Am Acad 347:1-112 My '63
Interdisciplinary attack on organized crime. bibliog f Ann Am Acad 347:104-12 My '63
TYLER, H. Richard
Botulinus toxin: effect on the central nervous system of man. bibliog Science 139:847-8 Mr 1 '63
TYLER, Harry
Coverlet; trade-marks of H. Tyler. L. F. Reals. il Hobbies 69:28 Mr '64
TYLER, John
John Tyler, tenth President 1841-1845. F. Freidel. il por Nat Geog Mag 127:98-101 Ja '65
TYLER, Lee
Canine U: dog school; it's harder on the owners than the dogs. Am Home 67:23 Jl '64
TYLER, Mansfield
Reconstruction legislators in Alabama. C. A. Brown. bibliog Negro Hist Bul 26:199-200 Mr '63
TYLER, Nancy Carole
Carole talks. il por Newsweek 65:23 F 1 '65
TYLER, Parker
Tchelitchew: the melancholy of anatomy. Art N 63:36-8+ Ap '64
TYLER, Ralph W.
What should high schools accomplish? PTA Mag 59:22-4 bibliog(p37) N '64
TYLER, William R.
Atlantic alliance: constant objectives in a context of change; address, April 27, 1964. Dept State Bul 50:776-83 My 18 '64
Department supports discretionary authority for President on trade with Poland and Yugoslavia; statement, May 27, 1963. Dept State Bul 48:947-51 Je 17 '63
Effect of the projected European union on NATO; address, April 5, 1963. Dept State Bul 48:648-52 Ap 29 '63; Same with questions and answers. Ann Am Acad 348:65-72 Jl '63
North America, the open continent; address, June 16, 1963. Dept State Bul 49:93-7 Jl 15 '63
United States and a changing Europe; address, March 17, 1964. Dept State Bul 50: 587-90 Ap 13 '64
TYLER, Tex.
Personal bookshop in a department store; book department of Mayer & Schmidt. il Pub W 186:44-5 Ag 17 '64
TYLL, Al
Advice from an expert: trick skiing. por Motor B 114:30-3 Jl '64
TYLLER, Jorgo
Three masks of the deer dancer. O. Maynard. por Dance Mag 38:34-6+ Ja '64
TYNAN, Kenneth
Antic arts. Holiday 33:101-3+ F '63
Audience of critics. Holiday 36:111-16+ O '64
Culture in a democracy; address, November 11, 1963. Mus Am 83:155-6 D '63
Eclipse of the fun. Esquire 59:82+ My '63
In his talent, Shakespeare summoned up . . . por Life 56:101-3 My 1 '64
Joan of Cockaigne. Holiday 36:113+ N '64
Most invaluable freedom of them all. por Seventeen 23:148+ Mr '64
To divorce art from money-making. N Y Times Mag p35+ D 1 '63
TYPE and typefounding
Hermann Zapf's letters. F. Johnson. il Am Artist 28:42-7+ O '64
TYPESETTING
Clinic speakers examine computer composition; meeting of the Trade book clinic, American institute of graphic arts. Pub W 186:112-13 N 9 '64
Harris-Intertype computers made especially for type composition. il Pub W 185:62-5 Ap 6 '64
Signs of the future? use of computers to set type. il Newsweek 64:88 N 9 '64
Special computer for printers. il Bsns W p 102 Mr 7 '64
TYPESETTING machines
Automation and the news strike. R. Severo. il Reporter 28:29-30+ Mr 14 '63
Automation takes hold in printing industry. il Bsns W p56-8 Ja 19 '63
IPEX: machines and techniques; London exhibition, July 16 to 27, 1963. J. Dreyfus. il Pub W 184:78+ S 9 '63
See also
Photocomposing machines
TYPEWRITERS
Lily's machine; music typewriter. il Time 84:52 D 4 '64
Mergenthaler produces three-shift chemical formula typewriter. il Pub W 185:100 Ja 6 '64
Switching to a black ribbon; Olivetti Underwood corp. il Bsns W p 178+ O 24 '64
See also
Olivetti corporation
TYPEWRITERS, Automatic
Ohio puts the personal touch into routine form letters by automatic typing. J. T. Ferguson. il Am City 78:113-14 Mr '63
TYPEWRITERS, Electric
Electric typewriter has battery, will travel. J. Steen. il Pop Sci 183:34 N '63
TYPHA. See Cattails
TYPHOID carriers. See Carriers of infection
TYPHOID fever
Epidemic in the Alps. Newsweek 61:86 Ap 8 '63
First came rumors, fears, then the ugly truth: typhoid! C. McCarry. il Sat Eve Post 236:84-7 My 25 '63
Ghost city; typhoid epidemic in Aberdeen. il Newsweek 63:52 Je 15 '64
Sickness on the slopes; typhoid fever in Zermatt, Switzerland. il Time 81:34 Ap 5 '63
Typhoid angus; outbreak in Aberdeen, Scotland. Time 83:62 Je 12 '64
Typhoid carriers treated by a new penicillin. Sci N L 86:9 Jl 4 '64
Typhoid fever in U.S. Sci N L 83:219 Ap 6 '63
Typhoid from canned meat unlikely in U.S. Sci N L 85:375 Je 13 '64
Typhoid rate in U.S. low. Sci N L 85:391 Je 20 '64
When typhoid hit a thriving city; cases in Aberdeen, Scotland. il U S News 56:8 Je 15 '64
TYPISTS; drama. See Schisgal, M.
TYPOGRAPHIC errors. See Errors, Typographic
TYPOGRAPHICAL union, International. See International typographical union
TYPOGRAPHY. See Printing
TYRAMINE
Monoamine oxidase inhibitors: augmentation of pressor effects of peroral tyramine. D. H. Tedeschi and E. J. Fellows. bibliog il Science 144:1225-6 Je 5 '64
TYRANNY. See Dictatorship
TYREE, David M.
New era in the loneliest continent. Nat Geog Mag 123:260-96 F '63
TYRIAN purple. See Dyes and dyeing
TYROL
Blood on the Alps. il Newsweek 64:48 S 28 '64
Tirol: 1363-1963. G. N. Kates. il Art N 62:28-30+ S '63
See also
Innsbruck, Austria

TYRONE Guthrie theatre. See **Minneapolis—Theater**

TYROSINE
Norepinephrine synthesis from tyrosine-C^{14} in isolated perfused guinea pig heart. S. Spector and others. bibliog il Science 139: 1299-301 Mr 29 '63
Spectrophotometric titrations of human serum albumin and reduced carboxymethylated albumin. D. S. Eisenberg and J. T. Edsall. bibliog il Science 142:50-1 O 4 '63

TYRRELL, D. A. J. and Chanock, R. M.
Rhinoviruses: a description. bibliog Science 141:152-3 Jl 12 '63

TYRRELL, George
George Tyrrell and the modernists. W. S. Smith. Christian Cent 80:490-2 Ap 17 '63

TYRRELL, Susan. See Creamer, S.

TYSON, Brady
Catholicism in Brazil. America 110:764-6 My 30 '64

TYSON, Carroll
Tyson collection: a painter's eye on masterworks. H. H. F. Jayne. il Art N 63:28-30+ S '64

TYSON, Robert C.
Businessman's prescription for good times; excerpts from address, September 29, 1964. por U S News 57:74-6 N 2 '64

TYSON collection. See Art—Private collections

TYUTCHEV, Fedor Ivanovitch. See Tiutchev, F. I.

U

UAW. See United automobile, aerospace and agricultural implement workers of America

U-boat warfare. See European war, 1914-1918—Submarine operations

UCLA. See California. University—Los Angeles campus

UDC (universal decimal classification) See Classification, Decimal

UFT. See United federation of teachers

UHF (ultra high frequency) See Television transmission

UHF television stations. See Television stations

UMT (Universal military training) See Military training

UMW. See United mine workers of America

UN. See United Nations

UN parties. See Entertaining

UNCSAT. See United Nations conference on the application of science and technology for the benefit of the less developed areas

UNCTAD. See United Nations conference on trade and development

UNCURK. See United Nations—Commission for the unification and rehabilitation of Korea

UNEF (United Nations emergency force) See United Nations—Armed forces

UNESCO. See United Nations educational scientific and cultural organization

UNICEF (United Nations international children's emergency fund) See United Nations children's fund

UNRWA. See United Nations relief and works agency for Palestine refugees in the Near East

UNSCEAR. See United Nations—Scientific committee on the effects of atomic radiation

UPI. See United press international

URW. See United rubber, cork, linoleum and plastic workers of America

US Open. See Golf—Tournaments

USBE. See United States book exchange, incorporated

USDA. See United States—Agriculture, Department of

USES. See United States—Employment service

USIA. See United States—Information agency

USIS libraries. See American libraries abroad

USLTA. See United States lawn tennis association

USNSA. See United States national student association

USOE. See United States—Education, Office of

USP (United States pharmacopoeia) See Pharmacopoeias

USPS. See United States power squadrons, incorporated

USSR (Union of Soviet Socialist Republics) See Russia

USWA. See United steelworkers of America

UTC. See United technology corporation

U-2 (airplane) See Airplanes, Military—United States

UBELL, Earl
Rheumatic fever can now be checked! Parents Mag 38:91+ O '63
What the nuclear test ban means to your child's bones, blood, and future health. McCalls 91:200-1 N '63
—and Loory, S. H.
Death of Nike-Zeus. Sat Eve Post 236:15-19 Je 1 '63
—and others
Our next adventure in space; reprint. Sci Digest 57:48-57 Ja '65
—See Fraley, P. C; Schwartz, J. N. jt. auths.

UBELL, Shirley
New Jersey modern dance school inspires a foundation into existence. J. N. Schwartz and E. Ubell. il Dance Mag 37:18-19 Mr '63

UCHIDA, Yoshiko
Bookbinding by Florence Walter. Craft Horiz 24:28-30 Jl '64

UDALL, Ermalee Webb
Home is not obsolete. por Ladies Home J 81: 32+ Jl '64

UDALL, Morris K.
Udall takes his stand. New Repub 150:10-11 Ja 18 '64

UDALL, Stewart Lee
American tradition; four symbols. N Y Times Mag p30-1 D 1 '63
Arts as a national resource; address, November 11, 1963; Excerpts. Sat R 47:14-16 Mr 28 '64; Mus Am 83:154 D '63
Beginning of action: Carl Schurz and John Wesley Powell; excerpt from The quiet crisis. por Am For 69:20-3+ O '63
His anger is fully justified; R. H. Boyle's views. Sports Illus 21:84-6+ N 16 '64
Legacy of Rachel Carson. Sat R 41:23+ My 16 '64
Natural history chapter. Liv Wildn 83:24 Spring '63
Obsolete assumptions: excerpts from address, March 1963. por Recreation 56:359-61 O '63
Pinchot and the foresters; excerpt from The quiet crisis. Am For 69:24-7+ N '63
Quiet crisis: excerpts. Sat R 46:19-22+ N 23 '63; Field & S 68:32-3+ D '63; PTA Mag 58:20-2 My '64
To save wildlife and aid us, too. N Y Times Mag p44-5+ S 15 '63
West and its public lands: address, February 6, 1964. Vital Speeches 30:297-301 Mr 1 '64

about

Secretary Udall assaults Kilimanjaro. il pors Life 55:55-6+ O 11 '63
Secretary Udall named Conservationist of year. il por Am For 71:5 Ja '65
Stewart Udall and the quiet crisis. R. Starnes. Field & S 68:18+ Je '63
Water for thirsty Southwest. il Bsns W p20-1 Ag 31 '63
Well done, Mr Secretary! with editorial comment. J. Prokop. il por Am For 69:8-9+ Mr '63

UDELL, Harold F.
Water pollution report. Motor B 112:92-3+ Ag '63

UDENFRIEND, S. and Zaltzman-Nirenberg, P.
Norepinephrine and 3,4-dihydroxyphenethylamine turnover in guinea pig brain in vivo. bibliog Science 142:394-6 O 18 '63

UDIN, Anne
Autographing parties: a community service. Pub W 185:77-9 F 17 '64

UELAND, Mark
Architecture. Nat R 16:120-2 F 11 '64

UELSMANN, Jerry N.
Heliographers; new photographic movement. il U S Camera 27:61-5 My '64

UETAKE, Yo-Jo
Two guys named Joe jolt Ithaca. M. Kane. il por Sports Illus 20:28-9+ Ap 6 '64

UFFEN, Robert J.
Theorist in hardrock. W. Jonathan. por Sat R 46:36-7 Jl 6 '63

UFFIZI gallery, Florence
Phantom of the Uffizi. il Newsweek 65:85 Ja 25 '65
Purloined Pollaiuolo panels. il Time 81:85 Mr 15 '63
Wanton multilation in the Uffizi. il Life 58:72-3 Ja 29 '65

UGALDE, Martín de
God's will; story. Américas 16:32-7 Je '64

UGANDA
Mixed-marriage; disparate tribes. New Repub 148:10 My 18 '63
White man's hangover. il Time 83:40 Ja 3 '64
See also
East African Federation (proposed)
English in Uganda
Hunting—Uganda
Natural resources—Uganda

UGANDA—*Continued*

History

Uganda. D. N. McMaster. bibliog il Focus 14:1-6 Ja '64

Native races

Big week with a Watusi. L. Wainwright. Life 57:23 Jl 17 '64

Politics and government

From king to president. Newsweek 62:46 O 14 '63

Uganda: the politics of compromise. T. K. Hopkins. Cur Hist 46:169-74+ Mr '64

Race problems

Uganda: the politics of compromise. T. K. Hopkins. Cur Hist 46:169-74+ Mr '64

UGGAMS, Leslie

Growing up. por Newsweek 62:59 D 30 '63

Leslie Uggams: little girl grows up. G. Astor. il pors Look 28:42-4 Je 30 '64

UHLIG, Frank, jr

Great white fleet. Am Heritage 15:30-43+ F '64

UHLIR, Norman F.

Automotive milestones. Motor T 17:78-83 Ja '65

UHR, Jonathan W.

Actinomycin D: its effect on antibody formation in vitro. bibliog Science 142:1476-7 D 13 '63

Heterogeneity of the immune response. bibliog Science 145:457-64 Jl 31 '64

—See Finkelstein, M. S. jt. auth.

UIHLEIN, Robert August, 1916-

How they put gusto into Schlitz. W. Bowen. il por Fortune 70:106-9+ O '64

Selling suds like soap. il Bsns W p60-2+ Ag 8 '64

UKRAINE

Back to the beginning of the tumultuous life of Nikita Khrushchev. H. H. Martin. il Sat Eve Post 237:18-26 N 7 '64

UKRAINIANS in the United States

American investment pays off: Corbett family. T. Hudes. il Look 27:82a-82c Jl 2 '63

ULAM, Stanislaw M.

Computers; with biographical sketch. Sci Am 211:32, 202-8+ bibliog(p272) S '64

ULANOV, Barry

Broadway. Cath World 198:263-4 Ja '64

ULANOVA, Galina

Particular treasure; excerpts from Days with Ulanova, with editorial comment by D. Hering. A. E. Kahn. il pors Dance Mag 37:40-8 S '63

ULANSKY, Gene

Alain Locke, philosopher of the new Negro. bibliog Negro Hist Bul 26:240-3 My '63

ULBRICHT, Walter

Khrushchev's impossible man in Berlin. A. J. Olsen. il por N Y Times Mag p37+ O 11 '64

Stalinist rule in East Germany. C. G. Anthon. Cur Hist 44:265-72+ My '63

ULCERS

See also

Peptic ulcers

ULEXITE

Pentaborate polyanion in the crystal structure of ulexite, $NaCaB_5O_6(OH)_6.5H_2O$. J. R. Clark and D. E. Appleman. bibliog il Science 145:1295-6 S 18 '64

ULLMAN, James Ramsey

At the top and out of oxygen. Life 55:73+ S 20 '63

Into Wyoming's wilderness. Travel 122:54-6+ O '64

Tusitala. Writer 76:10-12 Jl '63

ULLMANN, Harrison J.

Urban renewal fever. Nat R 16:1155-6 D 29 '64

ULLMANN, Herbert S.

Most prosperous bird colony. il Audubon Mag 65:150-1 My '63

ULLMANN, John E.

Alternatives to armaments. Sat R 46:13 My 4 '63

ULLRICH, Carl

Laughing lion has finally begun to roar; Columbia's oarsmen. T. C. Brody. il por Sports Illus 18:50+ Je 3 '63

ULLSTEIN, Karl H.

Obituary

Pub W 185:108 Ja 20 '64

ULLSTEIN, Rudolf

Obituary

Pub W 185:81 F 10 '64

ULLSTEIN publishing house. See Publishers and publishing—Germany (Federal Republic)

ULM, Germany (Federal Republic)

Beckett & the theater of the concrete. il Time 81:48+ Je 28 '63

ULMAN, Lloyd

Choosing the objectives of national wage-price policy. Mo Labor R 86:274-5 Mr '63

ULRICH, R. E. and Craine, W. H.

Behavior: persistence of shock-induced aggression. bibliog Science 143:971-3 F 28 '64

ULRICK, Charles J.

Build hi-fi interlock. Pop Electr 21:49-51 Ag '64

ULSTER

See also

Northern Ireland

ULTRACONSERVATISM. See Conservatism

ULTRA-HIGH frequency television reception. See Television reception

ULTRA-HIGH frequency television stations. See Television stations

ULTRA-HIGH frequency television transmission. See Television transmission

ULTRAHIGH pressure. See Pressure

ULTRA-HIGH vacuum. See Vacuum

ULTRASONIC test equipment. See Testing instruments

ULTRASONIC waves

Cover story. il Suc Farm 61:75 Mr '63

Electronic grader now on the market. D. Wolf. il Farm J 88:50 Mr '64

Hypersonic sound waves. A. Ewing. il Sci N L 85:355 Je 6 '64

Kilomegacycle ultrasonics. K. Dransfeld. il Sci Am 208:60-8 bibliog(p 183) Je '63

New ultrasonics move to the hog farm! il Suc Farm 61:148 Mr '63

Observation of internal structures of teeth by ultrasonography. G. Baum and others. il Science 139:495-6 F 8 '63

Perception of ultrasound. A. V. Haeff and C. Knox. il Science 139:590-2 F 15 '63

Industrial applications

Advances in ultrasonics. C. Glickstein. il Electr World 71:39-41 Mr '64

Continuous extraction during treatment with ultrasound. J. A. Lott and A. E. DeMaggio. bibliog il Science 139:825-6 Mr 1 '63

Sonic bath washes off spray residues. Farm J 87:44D S '63

Medical applications

Diagnosing with sound; ultrasonic scanning. il Sci Digest 56:56-8 D '64

Draw body by sound. B. Tufty. Sci N L 83:343 Je 1 '63

Into the eye with ultrasound. il Time 84:96 O 2 '64

Pictures by sound; ultrasound diagnostic feats. il Time 83:82 My 22 '64

Silent sound works wonders. B. Tufty. il Sci N L 83:234 Ap 13 '63

Sonar look at an unborn baby; with report by M. Steinmann. il Life 58:45-6 Ja 15 '65

Ultrasonic treatment helps mental patients. Sci N L 84:20 Jl 13 '63

Ultrasound used to save eye of eight-year-old boy. Sci N L 86:217 O 3 '64

ULTRASONIC welding

Ultrasonic ring welding may yield truly leak-tight metal containers. H. L. McKaig, jr. and C. Zglenicki. il Miss & Roc 15:28+ Ag 31 '64

ULTRASONICS

Advances in ultrasonics. C. Glickstein. il Electr World 71:25-7 F; 39-41 Mr '64 (to be cont)

Experimenting with sonar. D. Meyer. il Pop Electr 21:41-5+ S '64

Ultrasonic Sniffer. D. Meyer. il Pop Electr 18:41-4+ Mr '63

Ultrasonics; report on symposium 14-16 October, Santa Monica, Calif. J. J. G. McCue. Science 147:309-10 Ja 15 '65

ULTRA SPEED Anscochrome. See Photography—Films

ULTRAVIOLET rays

Fluorescent gems from Davy Jones's locker. P. A. Zahl. il Nat Geog Mag 124:260-71 Ag '63

Ultraviolet radiation effects on low molecular weight inorganic phosphates of yeast. E. M. Lieberman and P. A. Swenson. bibliog il Science 142:1315-16 D 6 '63

See also

Plants, Effect of ultraviolet rays on

Physiological effects

Thymine dimers and inhibition of DNA synthesis by ultraviolet irradiation of cells. R. B. Setlow and others. bibliog il Science 142:1464-6 D 13 '63

Ultraviolet sensitivity of escherichia coli containing heat-inducible λ prophages. M. Lieb. bibliog il Science 145:175-6 Jl 10 '64

UMLVELING, Ralph A.
Detroit doubles into three. Library J 88: 4531-4 D 1 '63
Investigate before you inveigh. por Library J 88:4693-5 D 15 '63

UMBARGER, H. E.
Intracellular regulatory mechanisms. bibliog Science 145:674-9 Ag 14 '64

UMBAUGH aircraft corporation
Government files $1.2-million tax claim against Umbaugh aircraft. D. A. Brown. Aviation W 78:32 Ap 22 '63

UMBRELLA pine. See Pine

UMBRELLAS
Fantastic gift you can make; jewel decorated umbrella. il McCalls 92:120-1 D '64
Sturdy table and stiff umbrella. il Sunset 131:111-12 S '63
Umbrellas; festive, practical. J. R. Rebhan. il Pop Gard 14:66-7 My '63

UMESTAUSKAS, Barbara
Soviets fear the dead. America 110:212 F 15 '64

UMPIRES (sports)
Just a second; National league umpires enforce the balk rule. W. Leggett. il Sports Illus 18:14-15+ Ap 22 '63
Officiating mess in the National hockey league. D. Anderson and R. S. Hewlett. il Sports Illus 18:26-8+ Ap 8 '63

UNAMUNO Y JUGO, Miguel de
Cloud-music; Bull; poems, tr. by A. Kerrigan. Poetry 101:319-21 F '63
Lone heretic, by M. T. Rudd. Review
Time por 83:88 Ja 17 '64
Spain, Unamuno, and Hispanic America. G. Baquero. il por Américas 16:8-14 Je '64
Unamuno's hunger for immortality. M. T. Rudd. Christian Cent 81:1589-92 D 23 '64

UNAUTHORIZED reprints. See Copyright—Unauthorized reprints

UNCLAIMED bank deposits. See Bank deposits, Unclaimed

UNCLAIMED legacies. See Legacies. Unclaimed

UNCLAIMED securities. See Securities, Unclaimed

UNCLE Cholly; story. See Schweitzer, G.

UNCLE Hobey; story. See Fort, H.

UNCLE Oscar from Enköping; story. See Urn, A.

UNCLE Tom
In Uncle Tom are our guilt and hope. A. Haley. il pors N Y Times Mag p23+ Mr 1 '64
Negro history and the modern Uncle Tom. Negro Hist Bul 27:134-5 Mr '64
Right kind of Uncle Tom; Negro leadership. L. Wainwright. Life 57:17 Ag 7 '64
Uncle Tom and predestination. D. Chaput. Negro Hist Bul 27:143 Mr '64

UNCLE Tom. See Henson, J.

UNCLE Tom; opera. See Trecate, L. F.

UNCLE Tom's hut; opera. See Trecate, L. F.

UNCLE Vanya; drama. See Chekhov, A. P.

UNCLE Wiggily stories. See Garis, H. R.

UNCONSCIOUSNESS. See Coma

UNDERACHIEVEMENT, Student. See Student achievements

UNDERDEVELOPED areas
Activities planned to meet objectives of the development decade; summary of report. Thant. U N Rev 10:47-9 Jl '63
Aid, trade and economic development; symposium. For Affairs 42:210-54 Ja '64
America and the world revolution; symposium, ed. by N. Podhoretz. Commentary 36:278-96 O '63; Discussion. 37:17-18 F '64
Applied microbiology in developing countries; report on symposium, May 1964. M. Alexander. Science 145:613-14 Ag 7 '64
Atlantic alliance: constant objectives in a context of change; address, April 27, 1964. W. R. Tyler. Dept State Bul 50:776-83 My 18 '64
Challenge of democracy in developing nations; address, January 26, 1964. W. W. Rostow. Dept State Bul 50:251-60 F 17 '64
Challenge of modernisation, by I. R. Sinai. Review
Sat R 47:42+ S 19 '64. L. J. Walinsky
Challenge of under-development; address, September 26, 1964. P. Martin. Vital Speeches 31:30-2 O 15 '64
Christian responsibility and world poverty, ed. by A. McCormack. Review
Cath World 199:50-2 Ap '64. W. J. Gibbons
Claim against the West. B. Ward. il Commonweal 81:219-22 N 13 '64
Cold war, a look ahead; address, March 28, 1963. W. W. Rostow. Dept State Bul 48: 551-7 Ap 15 '63
Coming: new challenge to U.S. trade. il Nations Bsns 52:54-5+ D '64
Common problems of industrial and developing countries; statement, March 25, 1964. G. W. Ball. Dept State Bul 50:634-40 Ap 20 '64
Economic development through private enterprise. E. G. Collado. For Affairs 41:708-20 Jl '63
Export economies between East and West. J. Levin. Yale R 52:373-84 Mr '63
Flags are not enough: Widening gap; excerpts from TV script; ed. by A. Cooke. S. Hearst. il UNESCO Courier 17:26-9+ Je '64
Food, the good medicine. Sci N L 83:114 F 23 '63
Foreign aid has succeeded. B. Ward. il N Y Times Mag p9+ Jl 12 '64
Handicap for new nations; climate. G. H. T. Kimble. il N Y Times Mag p35+ S 29 '63
How to make a national market; address, October 1, 1963. W. W. Rostow. Dept State Bul 49:667-73 O 28 '63
How world trade will change. il Nations Bsns 52:38-9+ S '64
Human resources and economic development; excerpts from United States papers prepared for UNCSAT conference. P. M. Hauser; F. H. Harbison. Mo Labor R 86:262-7 Mr '63
Hungry nations, by W. Paddock and P. Paddock. Review
Sat R 48:53 Ja 9 '65. A. E. Burns
Ideals for export; excerpts from address, September 19, 1963. C. H. Malik. Harvard Bsns R 42:51-9 Ja '64
Increased special fund assistance for low-income countries. il U N Rev 10:18-22 F '63
Industrial development; proposed new organization within United Nations. il U N Rev 11:24-5 F '64
International trade and economic development; statement, May 27, 1963. I. Frank. Dept State Bul 49:173-8 Jl 29 '63
Israel's training program for modernizing countries. W. Gerber. Mo Labor R 87:432-4 Ap '64
Latin America, 1964; symposium. bibliog il Cur Hist 46:1-37+ Ja '64
Local community and world affairs; remarks, April 21, 1964. L. B. Johnson. Dept State Bul 50:746-9 My 11 '64
Major objectives of the foreign aid program; address, November 21, 1964. D. E. Bell. Dept State Bul 51:821-5 D 7 '64
Morning after, by B. Crozier. Review
Commonweal 79:464 Ja 17 '64. V. C. Ferkiss
Nationalization of takeoff; address, May 2, 1963. W. W. Rostow. Dept State Bul 48: 824-9 My 27 '63
New air transport. Sci N L 83:116 F 23 '63
New Communist sales pitch. il Sr Schol 82: 12-14+ F 13 '63
New world threats: poverty and race; with editorial comment. P. Mason. il Nation 198: 63, 68-71 Ja 20 '64
Our obligation to the family of man; address, November 8, 1963. J. F. Kennedy. Dept State Bul 49:806-10 N 25 '63
Planning of development. E. S. Mason. il Sci Am 209:235-6+ bibliog(p310) S '63
Poor become poorer. B. Tufty. Sci N L 83: 387 Je 22 '63
Poorer nations find a new bootstrap; private development banks financing over-all economy. Bsns W p63-4+ Mr 14 '64
Population myths. D. H. Wrong. Commentary 38:61-4 N '64
Pressure grows for global price-fixing. il Nations Bsns 51:34-5+ My '63
Problems of economic development; statement, October 3, 1963. J. B. Bingham. Dept State Bul 49:712-21 N 4 '63
Rub of cultures. F. E. Dart. For Affairs 41:360-71 Ja '63
Russia, China, and the underdeveloped areas. H. Gelman. bibliog f Ann Am Acad 349: 130-42 S '63
Science for progress; symposium. il UNESCO Courier 16:4-63+ Jl '63
Science in less-developed countries; letter. J. B. Calhoun. Science 146:717 N 6 '64
Second thoughts on the Common market. D. F. Dowd. Yale R 53:168-91 D '63
Secretary Rusk's news conference of March 8, 1963. D. Rusk. Dept State Bul 48:432-9 Mr 25 '63
Sharing the wealth of science; UN science conference. il Bsns W p89-90+ Mr 23 '63
Sino-Soviet balance sheet in the underdeveloped areas. C. P. FitzGerald. bibliog f Ann Am Acad 351:40-9 Ja '64
Soviet policy in the developing countries. P. E. Mosely. For Affairs 43:87-98 O '64

UNDERDEVELOPED areas—*Continued*
Structure of development. W. Leontief. il Sci Am 209:148-54+ bibliog(p307) S '63
Technology and economic development. A. Briggs. il Sci Am 209:52-61 bibliog(p306) S '63
Trade and the less developed areas. W. Butler. For Affairs 41:372-83 Ja '63
Trade development and trade policy; statement, November 21, 1963. S. Z. Westerfield, jr. Dept State Bul 50:101-4 Ja 20 '64
Training program in developing financing. il U N Rev 11:37-8 Mr '64
UN common knowledge market. W. Davis. Sci N L 83:99 F 16 '63
What Communist breakup means to us; interview. Z. Brzezinski. Nations Bsns 52: 34-5+ Je '64
What it's like to be underdeveloped; excerpt from The great ascent. R. L. Heilbroner. Read Digest 82:21+ F '63
What the newer nations need. Life 55:4 O 4 '63
Why foreign aid? B. L. Masse. America 108: 637-9 My 4 '63
Why foreign aid; address, April 24, 1963. C. Bowles. Dept State Bul 48:777-84 My 20 '63
World security and developing nations. A. Salam. il Bul Atomic Sci 20:6-8 S '64
World without want, by P. G. Hoffman. Review
America 108:202 F 9 '63. W. J. Gibbons
See also
Agriculture—Underdeveloped areas
Aviation—Underdeveloped areas
Economic assistance
Education—Underdeveloped areas
Food supply—Underdeveloped areas
Housing—Underdeveloped areas
Investments, Foreign (in underdeveloped areas)
Medicine—Underdeveloped areas
States, New
Taxation—Underdeveloped areas
United Nations conference on the application of science and technology for the benefit of the less developed areas
UNDERGRADUATES. See College students
UNDERGROUND, Anti-Communist. See Anti-Communist movements
UNDERGROUND atomic testing. See Atomic bombs—Testing, Underground
UNDERGROUND houses. See Architecture, Domestic
UNDERGROUND irrigation. See Irrigation, Underground
UNDERGROUND living
Living it up way down; underground dream-house in Texas. il Life 56:51+ Ap 24 '64
World's fair visitors view life underground. il Todays Health 42:12 S '64
UNDERGROUND power distribution. See Electric distribution—Grounding
UNDERGROUND railroad
Harriet Tubman. L. Bennett, jr. il Ebony 20: 148+ N '64
Rankin house; stop on underground railroad. M. E. Aber. Negro Hist Bul 26:253 My '63
Underground railroad in Michigan. B. Coggan. Negro Hist Bul 27:122-6 F '64
UNDERGROUND sprinklers. See Sprinklers
UNDERGROUND structures
Dig they must, find they what? New York's subterranean jungle of tubes, pipes, wires and cables. F. J. Cook. il N Y Times Mag p 19+ My 19 '63
Living it up way down; underground dream-house in Texas. il Life 56:51+ Ap 24 '64
UNDERGROUND water. See Water, Underground
UNDERHILL, Andrew M. Jr
What! no rudder? (cont) Yachting 113:54-6+ F '63
UNDERPRIVILEGED children. See Children—Social and economic status
UNDERSEA stations. See Underwater structures
UNDERSTANDING. See Comprehension
UNDERTAKERS and undertaking
American way of death, by J. Mitford. Review
America 109:285 S 21 '63
Nat R 15:362-4 O 22 '63. F. Russell; Discussion. 15:455-6 N 19 '63
New Repub 149:29-30 Ag 31 '63. J. Ridgeway
Newsweek 62:84 S 9 '63
Reporter 29:48-50 S 26 '63. K. S. Lynn
Sat R 46:21-2 Ag 31 '63. D. Cort; Discussion. 46:37 S 28 '63
American way of death; condensation. J. Mitford. il Good H 158:69-82 F '64
Balm for an embalmer. Christian Cent 80: 1287 O 16 '63
Breaking funeral director's monopoly. Christian Cent 81:423 Ap 1 '64
Burial business hears voices; concerning J. Mitford's American way of death. Bsns W p80+ N 9 '63
Business of dying. il Time 82:68+ S 20 '63; Same abr. Read Digest 84:144-6 Ja '64
Checking the burial bills; Senate hearings on burial business. Bsns W p36 Jl 11 '64
Furor over funerals; why the cry of scandal? bibliog il Changing T 17:7-12 N '63
Muckraker, 1963 style. Nation 197:230-1 O 19 '63
Outrage over the death business; with report by P. Blake. il Life 55:98B-105+ S 20 '63
Speaking out; Americans don't want fancy funerals. J. Mitford. Sat Eve Post 236:8+ N 23 '63
Undertakers' racket. J. Mitford. Atlan 211: 56-62 Je '63
Ways of death; concerning three books on funeral industry. J. Brooks. Consumer Rep 29:40-3 Ja '64
UNDERWATER archeology. See Archeology, Submarine
UNDERWATER cables. See Cables, Submarine
UNDERWATER moving picture theaters. See Moving picture theaters, Underwater
UNDERWATER oil well drilling. See Oil well drilling, Submarine
UNDERWATER photography. See Photography, Submarine
UNDERWATER physiology. See Submersion
UNDERWATER sounds. See Ocean sounds
UNDERWATER structures
At home in the sea. J. Y. Cousteau. il Nat Geog Mag 125:465-507 Ap '64
Deep submergence project calls for five-year expenditure of $200 million. il Miss & Roc 15:28+ D 21 '64
Home in the deep; underwater village on the floor of the Red Sea. il Time 82:40 Jl 26 '63
Home under the sea; Sealab I. il Life 57: 74-8 S 4 '64
Man in the sea. A. F. Spilhaus. Science 145: 993 S 4 '64; Discussion. 146:471, 1113 O 23, N 27 '64
Man's future beneath the sea. W. Johnson. il Sr Schol 85:6-9+ Ja 7 '65
Men beneath the sea. il Newsweek 64:56-7 Jl 20 '64
Men under pressure; Sealab-I. il Newsweek 64:56 Ag 24 '64
New undersea test facility to go operational in December, 1965; Atlantic undersea test and evaluation center. Miss & Roc 15:78-9 S 21 '64
Ocean-bottom homes for skin divers. J. Y. Cousteau. il Pop Mech 120:98-103+ Jl '63
Race for the bottom of the sea. W. Cloud. il Pop Sci 183:35-40+ Jl '63
Room at the bottom of the sea; Sealab divers, photographs. J. Atwater and R. Vaughan. Sat Eve Post 237:18-25 S 5 '64
Settlers at the bottom of the sea. C. Phinizy. il Sports Illus 20:22+ Je 29 '64
Submarine geology by diving saucer. F. P. Shepard and others. bibliog il Science 145: 1042-6 S 4 '64
Submerged ocean station. Sci N L 84:395 D 21 '63
Undersea laboratory aids space research. Sci N L 87:23 Ja 9 '65
UNDERWATER thermometers. See Thermometers and thermometry
UNDERWATER-to-underwater missiles. See Torpedoes
UNDERWATER tunnels and tunneling. See Tunnels and tunneling, Underwater
UNDERWEAR
Fresh-as-spring lingerie. Good H 156:208n Ap '63
Good housekeeping's guide to buying slips that look and wear well. Good H 156:180 Je '63
There's many a slip. il Redbook 121:66-9+ Je '63
See also
Brassieres
Carter, William, company
Foundation garments
UNDERWOOD, Benton J.
Forgetting; with biographical sketch. Sci Am 210:22, 91-4+ bibliog(p 152) Mr '64
UNDERWOOD, John
Basketball. Sports Illus 18:60-2 Mr 18 '63; 20:42+ F 24; 50-2 Mr 9 '64
Cincy goes for a third. Sports Illus 18:24-6+ Mr 11 '63
College football (cont) Sports Illus 19:69-70 D 19 '63; 21:65-7 N 30 '64
Gunners are after Cincy. Sports Illus 18:22-5 Mr 25 '63
In Miami nearly everybody hates Clure Mosher. Sports Illus 19:54-8+ Jl 15 '63

UNDERWOOD, John—*Continued*
Only game in Panguitch, Utah. Sports Illus 18:56-60+ Mr 4 '63
Ramblers wreck Cincy. Sports Illus 18:22-5+ Ap 1 '63
Track & field (title varies) Sports Illus 20: 84+ My 25; 64+ Je 1 '64
True crisis. Sports Illus 18:16-19+ My 20 '63

about

Letter from the publisher. S. L. James. por Sports Illus 20:4 Mr 16 '64

UNDERWOOD, Kenneth
Social change and Protestantism. Commonweal 78:420-2 Jl 12 '63

UNDERWOOD corporation. See Olivetti Underwood corporation

UNDERWORLD. See Crime and criminals

UNDERWRITERS, insurance. See Insurance agents

UNEMPLOYABLES
New class. Nation 196:151 F 23 '63
Second chance for the unemployables; training of slum youths. il Bsns W p34 Je 8 '63
Who are the unemployables? Michigan employment security commission. il Bsns W p68-70 F 9 '63

UNEMPLOYMENT
Great unemployment fallacy. E. L. Dale, jr. New Repub 151:10-12 S 5 '64; Discussion. 151:37-8 S 19; 27-30 S 26 '64
On the cause of unemployment. il U S News 54:79 Ap 8 '63
Suicide and jobless rates closely related. Sci N L 83:296 My 11 '63
Trade and jobs: a world view. J. Lomax. il Nation 198:365-7 Ap 13 '64

See also

Employment

Relief measures

Here's way to make more jobs; interview. H. R. Northrup. il Nations Bsns 52:36-7+ Mr '64
Subsidy for older jobless. Bsns W p 141 Jl 13 '63
Thawing icebound jobs; winter homebuilding in Canada. Bsns W p 112 N 23 '63
This month's feature: federal public works and unemployment. Cong Digest 43:225-56 O '64

See also

United States—Job corps

Statistics

How many workers are idle. Nations Bsns 52: 32-3 Jl '64
Jobless, and why. H. Hazlitt. Newsweek 62:99 N 18 '63
Prevalence of disabilities in the work force. D. K. Lewis. il Mo Labor R 87:1002-8 S '64
Unemployment among full-time and part-time workers. R. L. Stein and J. L. Meredith. il Mo Labor R 87:1009-13 S '64
Unemployment, the no. one worry; with charts Bsns W p82-4 Ja 25 '64
Why unemployment stays high; policy-makers debate; with editorial comment. il Bsns W p 133+, 204 N 16 '63
Work history, attitudes, and income of the unemployed. R. L. Stein. il Mo Labor R 86:1405-13 D '63
Worker absence due to illness. il Mo Labor R 87:1181-3 O '64

Canada

See also

Unemployment—Relief measures

Florida

Miami's Cuban refugee crisis. A. Morrison. il Ebony 18:96-100+ Je '63

Great Britain

Angry ones. il Time 81:32 Ap 5 '63
Jobless riots in Britain: wildest in years. il U S News 54:6 Ap 8 '63
We want work; sac Mac, sac Mac. il Newsweek 61:33-4 Ap 8 '63

Pennsylvania

Second battle of Homestead. J. G. Colangelo. jr. il Reporter 29:29-31 Jl 18 '63

South Carolina

Here's do-it-yourself unemployment cure. il Nations Bsns 51:62-8 S '63

United States

America the backward? New Repub 148:3-4 Mr 30 '63
American agenda; evaluation of our society; address, May 1, 1963. J. W. Fulbright. bibliog Vital Speeches 29:520-6 Je 15 '63
Automation and full employment; the problem of government, industry and labor; address, March 9, 1964. D. J. McDonald. Vital Speeches 30:409-12 Ap 15 '64
Can we make more jobs without inflation? symposium on employment; with editorial comment. il Bsns W p26-7, 132 F 29 '64
Celestial mechanics of unemployment. R. E. Flanders. il Duns R 82:65+ O '63
Challenge to affluence, by G. Myrdal. Review
Sci Am 210:141-2+ Ja '64. L. H. Keyserling
Characteristics of urban depressed areas; excerpt from federal aid to depressed areas. S. A. Levitan. il Mo Labor R 87:48-52 Ja '64
Coming test of American democracy. H. J. Morgenthau. Commentary 37:61-3 Ja '64; Reply. E. C. Hughes. 37:24 Ap '64
Deepest two inches. Newsweek 61:74+ F 4 '63
Facts are in. M. Harrington. Nation 198:582-3 Je 8 '64
Familiar voice with a new warning; excerpts from address, April 3, 1963. J. L. Lewis. U S News 54:20 Ap 15 '63
Five case studies of displaced workers. H. Hammerman. il Mo Labor R 87:663-70 Je '64
Five ways to cut unemployment. R. Newcomb. Nations Bsns 52:31-3+ Jl '64
From the capital to the Catskills; interview. E. Clague. il Sr Schol 84:8T-10T Ja 31 '64
Fulfilling a promise; economy gained in the summer. il Fortune 68:43-4 S '63
High-bracket jobless. Newsweek 64:63-4 Jl 20 '64
How bad is unemployment? with editorial comment. il Bsns W p76+, 164 Mr 16 '63
Income without work. H. Hazlitt. Newsweek 63:78 Je 29 '64
Invisible men. J. O'Gara. Commonweal 78: 160 My 3 '63
It's time to face the future; excerpts from Challenge to affluence. G. Myrdal. il Look 27:96+ N 19 '63
Joblessness: the coming challenge. L. E. Schaller. Christian Cent 80:171-3 F 6 '63
Jobs: our no. 1 economic problem; president's manpower report to Congress. il Newsweek 61:75 Mr 18 '63
Let's put America back to work; address, July 2, 1963. W. L. Quaal. Vital Speeches 29:732-5 S 15 '63
Nation's no. one problem: find 35 million jobs in ten years. il U S News 55:41 Jl 8 '63
New class. Nation 196:151 F 23 '63
New horizons in economics. R. L. Heilbroner. il Sat R 47:31-2+ Ag 29 '64
New lost generation: jobless youth. M. Harrington. il N Y Times Mag p 13+ My 24 '64
Our number-one domestic concern. Sat Eve Post 236:82 My 4 '63
Overtime crackdown: Rx for unemployment? il Bsns W p99-100 Ja 18 '64
Poultice; symposium on employment sponsored by the American bankers association. il Newsweek 63:70 Mr 9 '64
Poverty and profits; symposium; with editorial comment. bibliog f Harvard Bsns R 42:6-8+ S '64
President's manpower report. D. Wolfle. Science 140:15 Ap 5 '63
Proposal for a revolution. J. P. Lyford. il Sat R 46:19-22 O 19; 25-8+ O 26 '63
Prosperity and jobs. Commonweal 79:584 F 14 '64
Public policy and unemployment; address, June 6, 1964. J. F. Oates, jr. Vital Speeches 30:594-8 Jl 15 '64
R&D and unemployment. W. A. Stocklin. Electr World 71:10 Ja '64
Recent trends and impact of unemployment. Mo Labor R 86:249-54 Mr '63
Right to work. Commonweal 79:268 N 29 '63
Self-help brightens job outlook. il Nations Bsns 51:52-4 Ag '63
Speaking out; the country needs featherbedding. A. H. Raskin. Sat Eve Post 236: 10+ O 12 '63
Unemployed youth in our affluent society; address, September 3, 1964. R. F. Male. Vital Speeches 30:734-6 S 15 '64
Unemployment and the reading problem. Sat Eve Post 236:70 F 9 '63
Unemployment in America. il Newsweek 61: 58-60+ Ap 1 '63
Unemployment problem: how serious it really is. il U S News 55:101-3 O 14 '63
Unemployment remedies. Sci N L 85:246 Ap 18 '64
Unemployment: who's hurt, where, how serious. il U S News 57:91-2 Ag 24 '64
War on poverty. G. Myrdal. New Repub 150:14-16 F 8 '64

UNEMPLOYMENT—United States—*Continued*
War on poverty. New Repub 149:3-4 D 28 '63
War on poverty: the first skirmish. A. L. Malabre, jr. il Reporter 31:27-9 D 17 '64
Washington desk. J. R. Slevin. Duns R 82:5-6 Jl '63
When my husband lost his job; interview, ed. by H. Lees. K. Lober. il McCalls 90:68+ My '63
Where unemployment hits hardest. M. B. Folsom. il Sat R 47:21-6 Ja 11 '64
Who are the unemployed? a look at the facts behind the figures. L. Fertig. Read Digest 85:115-16 S '64
Why the pressure is off wages; unemployment is high. il Bsns W p 101-2+ Mr 9 '63
Why there's no boom. il U S News 54:77-9 Ap 8 '63
Will unemployment rise? L. Keyserling. New Repub 148:39 Je 15 '63
Young jobless. il Time 81:91 Mr 15 '63
See also
Labor supply—United States
Unemployment surveys

Yugoslavia

Yugoslavian unemployment trends. R. G. Livingston. bibliog f il Mo Labor R 87:756-62 Jl '64

UNEMPLOYMENT, Technological
Automation (cont) il Sr Schol 83:12-13+ N 8 '63; 85:14-16+ N 11 '64
Automation & the state. B. B. Seligman. Commentary 37:49-54 Je '64; Discussion. 38:23-4 D '64
Automation is not the villain. P. F. Drucker. il N Y Times Mag p26-7+ Ja 10 '65
Automation: threat and promise. G. Ackley; J. I. Snyder, jr. il N Y Times Mag p 16+ Mr 22 '64
Automation toll: how serious? U S News 55:103 O 14 '63
But automation spawns problems, too. il Newsweek 65:76-7 Ja 25 '65
Canada copes with automation. Bsns W p75 Ja 26 '63
Career planning for the age of automation. G. Davenel. il Parents Mag 39:74-6+ S '64
Defense cuts bring a new kind of job crisis. il U S News 56:80-3 My 18 '64
Does automation cost many jobs? U S News 55:92+ S 23 '63
Does automation require a new economy? interview, ed. by T. R. Brooks. J. I. Snyder, jr. Duns R 83:51-2+ F '64
Easing the stress of job losses; sessions of President's labor-management group. il Bsns W p87-8 My 30 '64
Fallacies and facts about automation. V. R. Fuchs. il N Y Times Mag p27+ Ap 7 '63
Five ways to cut unemployment. R. Newcomb. Nations Bsns 52:31-3+ Jl '64
Gauging impact of automation; fourteen-member study commission proposed. Bsns W p 126 Mr 14 '64
Handwriting on the wall. Nation 197:446 D 28 '63
Heart of the matter. Nation 197:122 S 14 '63
Is there a crisis in the American trade-union movement? the trade unionists' views; survey of thirty-eight union presidents. S. Barkin and A. A. Blum. il Ann Am Acad 350:16-24 N '63
Labor dilemmas, automation and image. il Newsweek 61:61 Mr 4 '63
Learning new jobs before old ones fade; United auto workers. il Bsns W p 114+ Ap 11 '64
Leisure, its meaning and implications; excerpts from addresses. R. Theobald; C. K. Brightbill. Recreation 57:9-11 Ja '64
Lifetime of education. N. W. Chamberlain. NEA J 53:11 Ja '64
Managing your manpower; automation dilemma. T. R. Brooks. Duns R 81:65-6+ F '63
Manpower revolution; call for debate. G. G. Kirstein. il Nation 198:140-4 F 10 '64
Mr Meany's curse; automation. A. H. Raskin. Reporter 29:20-2 D 5 '63
Pension mirage. M. C. Bernstein. Nation 198:597-9+ Je 15 '64
Point of no return for everybody; with report by K. Wheeler. il Life 55:68A-71+ Jl 19 '63
Real news about automation. C. E. Silberman[il Fortune 71:124-6+ Ja '65
Stupid questions about automation. M. Mann. il Pop Sci 184:100-3+ My '64
Tranquilizing myths; automation responsible for the loss of jobs. Newsweek 62:99 O 14 '63
Union bargaining strength: Goliath or paper tiger? G. Strauss. bibliog f Ann Am Acad 350:86-94 N '63
Unions and automation: truce on the West coast. B. Bliven. il Reporter 29:35-8 N 7 '63
What's happening in education? W. D. Boutwell. PTA Mag 58:23 My '64
When brains take over factories. il U S News 56:83 F 24 '64
Where automation's pinch will be; Labor dept.'s analysis. il Bsns W p 114-16+ My 30 '64
See also
Unemployment—United States

UNEMPLOYMENT compensation. See Insurance, Unemployment

UNEMPLOYMENT insurance. See Insurance, Unemployment

UNEMPLOYMENT surveys
Gauging impact of automation: fourteen-member study commission proposed. Bsns W p 126 Mr 14 '64
Who are the unemployables? Michigan employment security commission. il Bsns W p68-70 F 9 '63

UNESCO. See United Nations educational, scientific and cultural organization

UNESCO House. See United Nations educational, scientific and cultural organization—Headquarters

UNESCO institute for education. See United Nations educational, scientific and cultural organization—Institute for education

UNFINISHED furniture. See Furniture

UNGER, Howard
Put more accuracy in your predicted logging. Motor B 113:106-7 Ja '64

UNGER, Leonard
Laos. bibliog Focus 14:1-6 My '64
about
Circus of Dr Unger. il por Time 83:23 Je 19 '64

UNGERER, Tomi
Conjugal beach; drawings. Holiday 36:58-61 Ag '64
Man from the moon. Holiday 36:76-83 D '64
Mordant eye on pro football. il Sports Illus 21:32-6 N 16 '64
about
Biting the hand that feeds him; portfolio. il Esquire 60:194-5 D '63
Kitemaker; photographs. P. Turner. Sports Illus 21:28-35 Ag 3 '64
More human than people. H. Frankel. Sat R 47:40 My 23 '64

UNGRADED classes
Cape Kennedy's high school for sky-high learning. B. Asbell. il PTA Mag 58:14-16 Ja '64
Melbourne: ungraded high, Melbourne, Fla. H. Langer. il Sr Schol 83:18T-19T O 4 '63
Nongraded high school, by B. F. Brown. Review
Sat R 47:70-2+ Ja 18 '64. A. Lass; J. S. Bruner
Ungraded primary; Maple Park elementary school near Seattle, Wash. il Time 81:42 Mr 22 '63

UNHAPPINESS. See Happiness

UNICEF. See United Nations children's fund

UNIDENTIFIED flying objects. See Flying saucers

UNIFORMS
One father. J. Ciardi. Sat R 47:15 D 12 '64
Why uniforms? M. S. Myers. America 109:630-2 N 16 '63; Reply. B. Leeming. 110:46-7 Ja 11 '64

UNIFORMS, Civil
Take me to your leader. E. Drapela; J. A. Peterson. Recreation 57:196-8 Ap '64

UNIFORMS, Military
Regimental uniforms; British. il Esquire 62:154-5 D '64
Tom Lovell paints a Continental soldier of 1781. il Am Artist 27:24-7 Mr '63
See also
United States—Army—Clothing

UNIFORMS, Sports
Uniform can be a death trap; football uniforms and heatstroke cases. R. Lardner. il Sports Illus 19:41-4+ N 25 '63

UNILEVER, limited
Unilever's Levers. Time 82:66 Ag 23 '63

UNION agreements. See Trade agreements

UNION bank of California. See Banks and banking—United States

UNION carbide and carbon corporation
How computers did the job at Seadrift; Union carbide's ethylene plant. il Bsns W p 146+ N 9 '63
Selling the other fellow's goods; Steel processing committee of Carbon products division. il Bsns W p 122+ Ja 16 '65
Stretching distillation towers. Bsns W p 118+ N 30 '63
Thriving under fetters; Union carbide India, ltd. il Bsns W p58-60 N 7 '64

UNION catalog of Library of Congress. See United States—Library of Congress—Union catalog

UNION leader (Manchester) See Manchester union leader

UNION OF SOUTH AFRICA. See South Africa

UNION OF SOVIET SOCIALIST REPUBLICS. See Russia

UNION Pacific railroad company
Battle for a mighty good road; Union Pacific and North Western covet Rock Island line. il Bsns W p 119-20+ N 2 '63
Weakened spring of government: a study in nineteenth-century American history. W. D. Farnham. bibliog f Am Hist R 68:662-80 Ap '63

UNION security. See Open and closed shop

UNION shops. See Open and closed shop

UNION theological seminary, New York
Bennett elected Union president. Christian Cent 81:7 Ja 1 '64
Committed openness. America 110:560 Ap 25 '64
Right on the premises. Time 82:53 D 27 '63
Successful misunderstanding; H. P. Van Dusen's retirement. Time 81:70-1 My 24 '63
Union man. Newsweek 63:63 Ja 6 '64
Union seminary offers help to its alumni. Christian Cent 80:1022 Ag 21 '63

UNIONS, Engineers. See Engineers unions

UNIROYAL. See United States rubber company

UNITARIANISM
Religion that moves. Newsweek 63:73 My 25 '64

UNITED air lines
Class warfare. il Time 82:75-6 S 6 '63
Lots of class; United air lines three-class service. il Time 84:79 Jl 3 '64
Teaching airline pilots their ABCs; United air lines Denver training center. il Ebony 19:33-4+ Jl '64
Travel notes; Cloud college, United air lines stewardess school. R. Joseph. Esquire 62:19-20+ Ag '64
United adds to commuter flights. Aviation W 81:36 N 16 '64
United gives up on one class. Bsns W p36 Je 27 '64
United plans Caravelle-727 integration. J. R. Ashlock. il Aviation W 78:45+ Ap 15 '63
United recruits private pilots. Aviation W 80:41 Je 15 '64
United single-class fare causes concern. J. R. Ashlock. Aviation W 78:45+ Ap 8 '63
United study may trim small-city service. Aviation W 80:43 My 18 '64
United tries spice in promotion efforts. J. W. Carter. Aviation W 81:28-9 O 5 '64
United's winterizing cuts flight delay. J. W. Carter. il Aviation W 81:29-30 Jl 27 '64

UNITED aircraft corporation
Growth versions of PT6 being developed. D. A. Brown. Aviation W 81:79 N 2 '64
Hybrid rockets. il Miss & Roc 15:36-7+ N 9 '64
United aircraft: success with a wry twist. H. B. Meyers. il Fortune 68:110-15+ D '63
UTC test fires Titan III booster. il Miss & Roc 13:15-16 Jl 29 '63
UTC wins lunar landing hybrid rocket. M. L. Yaffee. il Aviation W 81:275 Jl 6 '64
See also
United technology corporation

Hamilton standard division
UAC cyborg study in second phase. H. M. David. il Miss & Roc 12:41+ My 13 '63

Sikorsky aircraft division
Marine CH-53A buy to hit $200 million. G. C. Wilson. Aviation W 81:31-2 N 16 '64
New York airways, Sikorsky sign conditional pact for S-61N sale. Aviation W 80:37 F 10 '64
Salute to Igor Sikorsky. R. Hotz. Aviation W 81:11 O 5 '64

UNITED aircraft of Canada, limited. See United aircraft corporation

UNITED ARAB airlines. See Airlines—Egypt

UNITED ARAB REPUBLIC
See also
Aeronautics, Military—United Arab Republic
Arab states
Egypt
Space research—United Arab Republic
United States—Foreign relations—United Arab Republic

Commercial treaties and agreements
Trade with Paraguay and the United Arab Republic; proclamation. L. B. Johnson. Dept State Bul 51:120-1 Jl 27 '64

Defenses
UAR building independent military force. il Aviation W 80:297-9+ Mr 16 '64

Foreign relations
Two more kings in trouble; of Jordan and Saudi Arabia. il U S News 54:96-7 My 6 '63
U.S.A. and U.A.R. crisis in confidence. J. S. Badeau. For Affairs 43:281-96 Ja '65

UNITED association of journeymen and apprentices of the plumbing and pipe fitting industry of the United States and Canada
Plumbers' paradise; union resort, Konocti harbor. il Newsweek 62:72-3 S 16 '63

UNITED automobile, aerospace and agricultural implement workers of America
All right, Walter; UAW's Ford settlement. Newsweek 64:80-1 S 28 '64
Auto bargaining takes on a new complexion. Bsns W p92+ N 7 '64
Auto talks open amid hope, worries. il Bsns W p64-6 Jl 4 '64
Autos: will strikes cut off the boom? with address by H. Ford. il U S News 57:71-3, 77-8 Jl 6 '64
Auto workers' program. Commonweal 80:30 Ap 3 '64
Bending the guidelines; U.A.W.-Chrysler settlement. il Time 84:29-30 S 18 '64
Betting on a short one; with editorial comment. il Bsns W p25-7, 156 O 3 '64
Breaking the logjam. il Bsns W p23-4 O 10 '64
Buoyant UAW likes the odds. Bsns W p 124 Mr 14 '64
Can automobiles be humanized? Christian Cent 81:899 Jl 15 '64
Chrysler settles: what price peace? il Newsweek 64:87-90 S 21 '64
Contracts a la mode; U.A.W. obtains concessions. il Time 84:87 S 25 '64
Decline of labor; unions within unions. S. Lens. Commonweal 80:391-4 Je 19 '64
Detroit, higher wages, cheaper cars? H. Rowen. New Repub 150:17-18 Je 6 '64
Detroit talkathon: UAW contract time. il Newsweek 64:61-2 Jl 6 '64
Effects of pay raises in autos: an employer gives his view; excerpts from letter. U S News 58:66 Ja 4 '65
Facing UAW and a long, hot summer. il Bsns W p 150-1+ My 23 '64
Formula is set. il Bsns W p 154+ S 26 '64
GM strike end is near. Bsns W p96+ O 24 '64
GM strike: prototype for more conflict. B. J. Widick. il Nation 199:349-52 N 16 '64
Getting a jump on '64 auto talks; joint committees to study complex issues. il Bsns W p 161 Ap 20 '63
Horse trading starts; Big three auto companies vs UAW. il Bsns W p23-4 Ag 22 '64
How Reuther maps demands. U S News 55:94-5 D 2 '63
Inflation: more money, less value; negotiations between UAW and auto industry. Sr Schol 85:18 O 14 '64
Is the lid coming off for bigger pay increases? il U S News 57:95-7 O 19 '64
Is this to be the year of a big strike in autos? issue of UAW with GM. il U S News 56:93-5 Mr 16 '64
Little things behind a big strike. il U S News 57:89-91 O 12 '64
Look ahead to the auto negotiations. T. R. Brooks. il Reporter 30:27-9 My 21 '64
Managing your manpower. T. R. Brooks. Duns R 83:55-6+ Ap '64
Men who speak for UAW. il Bsns W p43-4+ Je 20 '64
New road opens; pre-bargaining study committee. il Newsweek 61:68+ Ap 29 '63
New type of pension plan. U S News 56:81-2 Je 1 '64
Now that the auto industry knows what Reuther wants. il U S News 57:75-6 Jl 13 '64
Only local disputes left to settle at GM. il Bsns W p89 O 31 '64
Pay tops UAW's 1964 shopping list. Bsns W p80-1 D 21 '63
Peace at a price; Chrysler pact with UAW; with editorial comment. il Bsns W p27-9, 204 S 12 '64
President Reuther, meet President Johnson. Newsweek 63:59-60 Mr 30 '64
Price of labor peace in the auto industry. il U S News 57:82-5 S 21 '64
Profit sharing for workers: troubles of a noble experiment. il U S News 57:117+ O 26 '64
Profit-sharing issues raises hob. Bsns W p48+ O 17 '64
Profit sharing: what union won. U S News 57:72 N 2 '64

UNITED automobile, aerospace and agricultural implement workers of America—*Continued*
Profits, polemics & politics. Time 84:73 Ag 28 '64
Prospects for autos amazes even Detroit; years of negotiations. il Bsns W p 19 D 28 '63
Real issue in autos, as industry sees it. il U S News 56:83-5 Ap 13 '64
Real issue in the auto strike: demand for union power. il U S News 57:91-2 O 5 '64
Right not to work; United auto workers against General motors. il Time 84:111 O 2 '64
Sort of ending; United auto workers reach a national agreement with General motors. Time 84:104 O 16 '64
Target; Chrysler picked for strike action. Newsweek 64:64 S 7 '64
Target: Chrysler; possibility of an auto strike. Time 84:91 S 4 '64
There they go again; U.A.W. workers at Ford launch their own strike. Time 84:110 N 13 '64
Trail-blazing pact? Sr Schol 85:24 S 30 '64
Troubles not over in autos. U S News 57:105 N 9 '64
UAW breaches the bargaining guidelines. T. R. Brooks. Duns R 84:45 D '64
UAW changes target. il Bsns W p82+ S 5 '64
UAW guns for more of the same. Bsns W p 144+ S 19 '64
UAW leans hard on retirement. Bsns W p90 My 30 '64
UAW price for peace: a major breakthrough. Bsns W p30 Ag 29 '64
UAW seeks to turn apathy into zeal. Bsns W p48-9 Ag 10 '63
UAW urges joint studies. Bsns W p81 Mr 30 '63
UAW's collison course; lines drawn for bitter bargaining. il Bsns W p26-7 Mr 28 '64
UAW's 19th constitutional convention. L. A. O'Donnell. Mo Labor R 87:654-6 Je '64
UAW's push in Canada. Bsns W p90 O 31 '64
Victory on wages is labor's 1964 goal; also job security and shorter week. il Bsns W p88+ D 28 '63
Wage chronology: North American aviation, inc. il Mo Labor R 87:556-60 My '64
Wage chronology; the Boeing co. Washington plants, 1962-65. il Mo Labor R 87:900-3 Ag '64
Wages or fringes? UAW weighs the odds. il Bsns W p60+ F 15 '64
Walkout in Detroit; UAW strike at General motors. Newsweek 64:93-4 O 5 '64
Walter Reuther's big union. A. H. Raskin. il Atlan 212:85-90+ O '63
What happens to retirees when a plant shuts down? Bsns W p50 N 21 '64
What happens when a big strike drags on. U S News 57:70-2 N 2 '64
What Reuther wants now from the auto industry. il U S News 56:87-8 Ap 6 '64
When a big company quits, the South Bend story. il U S News 55:76-8 D 23 '63
When a union tries to break the U.S. wage barrier. il U S News 56:85-6 Mr 30 '64
Where workers complain about too much pay. il U S News 56:92-3 Ja 27 '64
Why a big auto strike seems unlikely. U S News 57:92 Ag 24 '64
Why union chose Chrysler as target for strike. il U S News 57:73-4 S 7 '64
Will there be a rush for early retirement? il U S News 57:106-8 S 28 '64
Will there be an auto strike? il U S News 57:66-8 Ag 31 '64

Public review board

UAW's own court sums up; review board. Bsns W p73-4 Je 15 '63

UNITED Bible society. See Bible societies

UNITED carbon company
Three-way oil deal waits on tax ruling; ABC deal. Bsns W p94+ F 9 '63

UNITED church of Canada
United church of Canada: perils of ecclesiasticism. E. M. Howse. Christian Cent 80:976-9 Ag 7 '63
Welcome from a new province; General council in St John's, Newfoundland. J. R. Mutchmor. Christian Cent 81:1378-9 N 4 '64

UNITED church of Christ
Claim air wave rights for Negroes; United church of Christ petition to F.C.C. Christian Cent 81:725 Je 3 '64
Discrimination charged; petition to F.C.C. E. C. Parker. Christian Cent 81:1018+ Ag 12 '64
Formula in flux: reformation for the Disciples of Christ? R. E. Osborn. Christian Cent 80:1163-6 S 25 '63
Meeting the people. il Newsweek 64:86 N 9 '64
Taking the church where the people are. il Time 84:50 N 6 '64
United church: in search of a special calling. R. W. Spike. Christian Cent 80:234-7 F 20 '63; Discussion. 80:587-8 My 1 '63
Uniting and marching; General synod. H. E. Fey. Christian Cent 80:926-7 Jl 24 '63
Work together now! Christian Cent 81:389 Mr 25 '64

UNITED church women (organization)
Laity in mission; tenth assembly. M. Frakes. Christian Cent 81:1294-6 O 21 '64

UNITED dye and chemical corporation
$5,000,000 swindle; case of V. D. Dardi. il Time 81:95 Mr 15 '63
Roy Cohn: is he a liar under oath? with report by K. Wheeler and W. Lambert. il Life 55:24-31+ O 4 '63

UNITED Europe (proposed) See United States of Europe (proposed)

UNITED federation of teachers
Case for teachers' unions; excerpt from address. G. Brooks. Mo Labor R 87:292 Mr '64; Reply. S. Dorros. 87:543 My '64
Course in defiance; New York's teachers vote to strike. il Time 82:90 S 13 '63
New militants. il Time 82:45 Ag 16 '63
N.Y. strike averted. Sr Schol 83:2T+ S 27 '63
Teachers and workers. New Repub 149:7-8 S 21 '63
Teachers get a hand in running New York. il Time 82:51 S 20 '63
Toward labor monopoly in teaching? NEA, AFT and UFT. R. Kirk. Nat R 15:241 S 24 '63
Union or guild? organizing the teachers. S. Elam. il Nation 198:651-3 Je 29 '64

UNITED foundation torch fund
Gathering of the green. Newsweek 62:23-4 O 28 '63

UNITED fruit company
Latin America; encouragement for investors; address, November 20, 1963. D. D. McConkey. Vital Speeches 30:209-14 Ja 15 '64
United fruit's experiment in international partnership; Associate producers program. P. Deutschman. il Read Digest 85:146-50 O '64

UNITED fund
Do you wonder? il Seventeen 23:28 O '64

UNITED mine workers of America
Coal contract: what's in it. U S News 56:90 Ap 6 '64
Coal miners and the new coal contract. Mo Labor R 87:III-IV My '64
Coal royalties; small mines win. U S News 57:93 Ag 24 '64
Coal: when machines took over. il U S News 54:69-73 Ap 29 '63
Gray spring in Hazard. S. Gervis. Commonweal 78:220-2 My 17 '63
How a big union handles money. U S News 54:94 My 6 '63
John L. Lewis and the mine workers. A. H. Raskin. Atlan 211:53-8 My '63
Miners gear for double trouble. Bsns W p67 D 5 '64
Miners' new leader works another seam. il Bsns W p 121-2 Mr 28 '64
Miners want the vote. Bsns W p 152+ S 19 '64
New UMW president; protégé of John L. Lewis. U S News 54:20 F 4 '63
Troubles pile up for most sued union. il Bsns W p 121-2+ Ap 18 '64
UMW faces a miner's revolt; independent mining is spreading. Bsns W p70+ Ag 15 '64
UMW gives the nod to Boyle. Bsns W p70+ Ja 26 '63
UMW seeks job security, safety. Bsns W p68 Ja 4 '64

District 50

Talking troubles out at the plant level; company-union dialogue idea. Bsns W p74+ O 19 '63

UNITED mine workers of America welfare and retirement fund
One pension plan where things are going from bad to worse. U S News 54:121-3 Mr 25 '63

UNITED NATIONS
Action by the United Nations; address, October 22, 1964. A. E. Stevenson. Vital Speeches 31:98-101 D 1 '64
Anatomy of world leadership; address, April 3, 1964. A. E. Stevenson. bibliog f Dept State Bul 50:615-21 Ap 20 '64
Can the United Nations keep world peace in the 1960's? address, April 20, 1964. L. C. Meeker. bibliog f Dept State Bul 50:797-802 My 18 '64
Can the U.N. survive? A. Drury. Read Digest 82:142-4+ Mr '63

UNITED NATIONS—*Continued*
Case for international law; addresses, April 25, 26 and 27, 1963. S. M. Schwebel; R. N. Gardner; F. T. P. Plimpton. Dept State Bul 48:785-800 My 20 '63
Collapse of disarmament conference seen. L. L. Doty. Aviation W 81:16-17 Ag 31 '64
Collapsing UN. G. Niemeyer. il Nat R 16: 313-16+ Ap 21 '64
Coming: a new challenge to U.S. trade. il Nations Bsns 52:54-5+ D '64
Communism and peaceful coexistence; address: October 1, 1963. Earl of Home. Vital Speeches 30:5-9 O 15 '63
Declaration of interdependence; encyclical Peace on earth; with excerpts. N. Cousins. il Sat R 46:18-20 My 4 '63
Dedication of church center for the United Nations; addresses, September 22, 1963. D. Rusk; A. E. Stevenson. Dept State Bul 49:570-4 O 14 '63
Double trouble. Sr Schol 85:22-3 Ja 14 '65
Eichmann and the UN; letter to the editor. R. M. Lamport, jr. Nat R 15:251 S 24 '63
Evolution of rising responsibility; address, December 13, 1964. H. Cleveland. Dept State Bul 52:7-12 Ja 4 '65
Financing the U.N: pressures and principles. H. G. Nicholas. il Reporter 31:17-18 D 31 '64
First twenty-five years of the United Nations from San Francisco to the 1970's; address, January 10, 1964. D. Rusk. Dept State Bul 50:112-19 Ja 27 '64
Focus on the United Nations. il Sr Schol 83: 21-2 O 4 '63; 85:44+ O 7 '64
Haile Selassie I, addresses General assembly; summary of address, October 4, 1963. Haile Selassie I. il U N Rev 10:4-5 N '63
History repeats itself. Nation 200:69 Ja 25 '65
Human rights and foreign policy; excerpts from In pursuit of world order. R. N. Gardner. Sat R 47:23-5+ S 19 '64
In pursuit of world order, by R. N. Gardner. Review
New Repub 152:24 Ja 9 '65. A. Schlesinger, jr.
Industrial development; proposed new organization within United Nations. il U N Rev 11:24-5 F '64
Interview with the Secretary-General; ed. by D. Sureck. Thant. il U N Rev 11:5-10 Ja '64; Excerpt. Sat Eve Post 236:42-3 S 21 '63
Introduction to the annual report of the Secretary-General on the work of the organization. Thant. UN Mo Chron 1:43-70 D '64
Looking ahead; address, January 7, 1964. Thant. Vital Speeches 30:226-9 F 1 '64; Same. U N Rev 11:9-11+ F '64
Meetings for [month] See issues of UN monthly chronicle
New opportunities in the search for peace; address, September 20, 1963. J. F. Kennedy. Dept State Bul 49:530-5 O 7 '63; Same with title Responsibilities of the United Nations. Vital Speeches 30:2-5 O 15 '63
News in review. See issues of United nations review
19th anniversary of United Nations; remarks, October 23, 1964. L. B. Johnson. Dept State Bul 51:697 N 16 '64
No mission but peace, no enemy but war. A. E. Stevenson. il McCalls 92:112-13+ O '64
Notes of the month. See issues of UN monthly chronicle
On disarmament issues: peacekeeping since 1946. B. G. Lall. il Bul Atomic Sci 20:37-40 My '64
Paul VI to U Thant. America 109:91-2 Jl 27 '63
Perfect format; talks with visiting statesmen at U.S. mission building. il Time 82:39 O 4 '63
Perils of the UN. New Repub 151:5-6 N 28 '64
President of India sees United Nations giving conscience to world community; excerpts from address, June 10, 1963. S. Radhakrishnan. U N Rev 10:51 Jl '63
Principles of international law concerning friendly relations and cooperation among states: international law and nonintervention; statement, December 3, 1963. F. T. P. Plimpton. bibliog f Dept State Bul 50: 133-43 Ja 27 '64
Principles of international law concerning friendly relations and cooperation among states: peaceful settlement of disputes; address, November 19, 1963. E. F. Kelly. bibliog f Dept State Bul 50:57-66 Ja 13 '64
Projected European union and American international prestige. Q. Wright. bibliog f Ann Am Acad 348:132-40 Jl '63
Roles and critics of the United Nations; excerpts from address, August 11, 1964. H. Cleveland. Dept State Bul 51:351-4 S 7 '64
Some major issues before the United Nations; address, March 5, 1963. Thant. Vital Speeches 29:360-4 Ap 1 '63; Same abr. U N Rev 10:16-19 Mr '63
Spy scandal that concerns the U.S. and at the U.N. U S News 55:8 Jl 8 '63
Stitching the world together; toward a global democracy. P. C. Jessup. Sat R 47:17-19+ F 1 '64
Strength of U Thant. J. A. Joyce. Christian Cent 80:1047-50 Ag 28 '63
Strengthening of the United Nations; address, April 3, 1964. Thant. UN Mo Chron 1:76-84 My '64
This is the U.N. at play. S. Massie and R. Massie. il Sat Eve Post 236:54-7 Mr 30 '63
Two kinds of politics; address, May 8, 1963. H. Cleveland. Dept State Bul 48:871-6 Je 3 '63
U.N. a superstate? D. Lawrence. U S News 54:136 Mr 25 '63
United Nations day address; text. Thant. UN Mo Chron 1:9-11 N '64
United Nations digest. See issues of United Nations review
United Nations: hope for the future; address, October 24, 1963. A. E. Stevenson. Dept State Bul 49:766-73 N 18 '63; Same. Vital Speeches 30:68-72 N 15 '63
United Nations in the fight for freedom; address, February 22, 1963. D. Rusk. Dept State Bul 48:393-8 Mr 18 '63
U.N.'s new power: where will it be used next? il U S News 54:54-6 F 4 '63
United Nations today; address, October 24, 1964. G. W. Ball. Dept State Bul 51:694-700 N 16 '64
United Nations tribute to Pope of unity and peace. il U N Rev 10:32-3 Je '63
U.N.'s uncertain teen years. Sr Schol 85: 12-16+ N 4 '64
United Nations, what it is, what it has done; address, March 21, 1963. A. Chayes. Dept State Bul 48:562-6 Ap 15 '63
U Thant: inscrutable shepherd of the U.N. N. F. Busch. Read Digest 84:63-7 Mr '64
U Thant speaks his mind; interview, ed. by D. Sureck. Thant. Sat Eve Post 236:42-3 S 21 '63
Uses of diversity; address, September 9, 1963. H. Cleveland. Dept State Bul 49:461-4 S 23 '63
Vietnam: miscalculations and alternatives. N. Cousins. Sat R 47:32 D 12 '64
Vitality of the United Nations. S. Windass. Yale R 53:481-96 Je '64
What every U.N. critic should know. A. Larson. Sat R 46:13-15+ Je 15 '63; Reply. L. R. Ward. 46:15 Jl 13 '63
What the U.N. can do, if it will. A. Larson. Sat R 47:20 Je 27 '64
Where all paths to peace must meet. P. Van Slyck. Sat R 48:28-9 Ja 30 '65
Which way the U.N? New York herald tribune forum discussion. il Sr Schol 82: 12-13 My 1 '63
Who are the racists? il Time 84:29-30 D 18 '64
Year's developments in review; annual report. Thant. U N Rev 10:6-11 Ag '63
See also
American association for the United Nations
Food and agriculture organization of the United Nations
International court of justice, The Hague
World federation of United Nations associations
World health organization

Advisory committee on the application of science and technology to development

Science and technology. U N Rev 11:28-30 Ap '64

Armed forces

Communications on United Nations peacekeeping operations; summary of memorandum from the USSR and reply by the United Kingdom. UN Mo Chron 1:41-3 Ag '64
Member of the parish; address, June 6, 1964. H. Cleveland. Dept State Bul 50:971-6 Je 22 '64
Peace forces; Soviet proposal. Commonweal 80:560-1 Ag 21 '64
Peace-keeping operations; question of financing. UN Mo Chron 1:46-57 O '64
Principles of international law concerning friendly relations and cooperation among states: threat or use of force; statement, November 11, 1963. F. T. P. Plimpton. Dept State Bul 49:973-83 D 23 '63

UNITED NATIONS—Armed forces—*Continued*
Protocol and peacekeeping; address, October 22, 1964. A. B. Duke. Dept State Bul 51: 736-9 N 23 '64
Role of the United Nations. M. H. McVitty. Cur Hist 46:331-5 Je '64
Scandinavia's peace-keeping forces for U.N. P. Haekkerup. For Affairs 42:675-81 Jl '64
Soviets propose a U.N. peace force. Christian Cent 81:924 Jl 22 '64
Special U.N. session votes peace funds. Christian Cent 80:876 Jl 10 '63
Strengthening the machinery for peace; address, June 2, 1964. A. E. Stevenson. Dept State Bul 50:966-71 Je 22 '64
Sudden conversion; Moscow's proposal. Newsweek 64:47-8 Jl 20 '64
Thirteenth alarm; address. March 21, 1964. H. Cleveland. Dept State Bul 50:622-6 Ap 20 '64
Toilsome path to peace; address, March 19, 1964. D. Rusk. Dept State Bul 50:530-5 Ap 6 '64
U.N. charter, the purse, and the peace; address, May 15, 1964. A. Chayes. Dept State Bul 50:900-6 Je 8 '64
UN crisis: the politics of money. J. G. Stoessinger. Nation 199:263-6 O 26 '64
UNEF appropriation for 1964. il U N Rev 11: 35-9 F '64
U.N. seeks new way to finance peacekeeping. il Bsns W p 156+ N 21 '64
U.N.'s new power: where will it be used next? il U S News 54:54-6 F 4 '63
United Nations stand-by peace force; address, June 13, 1963. Thant. U N Rev 10:54-7 Jl '63
U.S. makes proposal on financing peacekeeping operations of N.N; statement, September 14, 1964, with text of working paper. F. T. P. Plimpton. Dept State Bul 51:486-9 O 5 '64

Forces in Cyprus

Boys in blue. il Newsweek 63:25 Mr 30 '64
Cherub from Finland. il Time 83:39 Ap 3 '64
Cyprus: the archbishop can't lose. C. Sterling. il Reporter 30:12-16 Je 4 '64
Cyprus: the Turks strike back. il Newsweek 64:37-8 Ag 17 '64
NATO effort. il Newsweek 64:43 Ag 31 '64
Needed: a stand-by U.N. force to keep peace by military means. R. N. Gardner. il N Y Times Mag p 12+ Ap 26 '64
Record of the month; activities of United Nations peace-keeping force. il UN Mo Chron 1:18-24 Je; 3-16 Jl '64
Record of the month; call for cease-fire in Cyprus. il UN Mo Chron 1:3-18 Ag '64
Record of the month; establishment and operations of the United Nations peacekeeping force in Cyprus. il UN Mo Chron 1:4-14 My '64
Remembrance day. Newsweek 63:47 Ap 13 '64
Secretary-General U Thant addresses Canadian Parliament; summary of address, May 26, 1964. Thant. UN Mo Chron 1:55-7 Je '64
Secretary-General's report on organization of the Peace-keeping force; summary. Thant. U N Rev 11:35-6 Ap '64
[Secretary-General's report to Security council, September 10, 1964] Thant. UN Mo Chron 1:3-8 O '64
Security council continues U.N. force in Cyprus; statements, September 17 and September 25, 1964. A. E. Stevenson; C. W. Yost. Dept State Bul 51:561-4 O 19 '64
Security council extends UNFICYP. UN Mo Chron 2:23-8 Ja '65
Taking sides. Time 84:65 O 2 '64
U.N. force to Cyprus. Commonweal 80:4-5 Mr 27 '64
UN in Cyprus; photographs. UN Mo Chron 1:101-8 My '64
U.N. peace-keeping force in Cyprus. il U N Rev 11:5-15+ Ap '64
UNFICYP. Newsweek 63:44 Ap 6 '64
U.S. favors peacekeeping force for Cyprus; statement, February 9, 1964. A. E. Stevenson. Dept State Bul 50:374-6 Mr 9 '64
U.S. offers to help U.N. finance Cyprus peacekeeping force; Department statement, March 11, 1964. Dept State Bul 50:484 Mr 30 '64

Forces in the Congo

Assembly extends United Nations operation in the Congo. il U N Rev 10:37-40 N '63
Atrocities in Katanga. America 108:213 F 16 '63
Congo: plugging a sieve with pinheads. R. W. Howe. Reporter 29:37-8 O 10 '63; Reply. S. O. Adebo. 29:8+ N 7 '63
Costly Congo. Newsweek 62:39 S 9 '63
Military disengagement in the Congo; report by the Secretary-General; with exchange of letters between C. Adoula and U Thant, August 22 and September 16, 1963. Thant. U N Rev 10:44-7 O '63
Please don't go. Time 82:39+ S 20 '63
Prolonging the peace. Newsweek 62:46-7 O 14 '63
Record of the month; withdrawal of ONUC; summary of Secretary-General's report. Thant. UN Mo Chron 1:30-5 Jl '64
Report by the officer-in-charge of the United Nations operation in the Congo (cont) U N Rev 10:59-65 Ja; 69-75 F '63
United Nations and the Congo; three questions; address, January 17, 1963. H. Cleveland. Dept State Bul 48:165-70 F 4 '63
Worse than Laos? New Repub 150:4 Je 13 '64

Forces in Yemen

Hard-luck Horn; Egyptian-Saudi Arabian disengagement agreement. il Newsweek 62:40 S 9 '63

Budget

See United Nations—Finance

Capital development fund

Capital development fund. UN Mo Chron 1: 47-8 N '64
U.S. continues to oppose capital development fund; statement, September 9, 1963. J. B. Bingham. Dept State Bul 49:561-3 O 7 '63

Charter

General assembly resolutions on organizational changes. U N Rev 11:16-20+ Mr '64
League of Nations and the United Nations; address, April 2, 1964. Thant. UN Mo Chron 1:70-5 My '64
OAS, the UN, and the United States. I. L. Claude, jr. bibliog f Int Concil 547:3-63 Mr '64
Overtures to Peking. New Repub 149:10 N 16 '63; Reply. E. Schwelb. 149:30 D 28 '63
Principles of international law concerning friendly relations and cooperation among states: sovereign equality of states; statement, December 3, 1963. E. F. Kelly. Dept State Bul 50:264-7 F 17 '64

Commission for the unification and rehabilitation of Korea

United Nations aims in Korea reaffirmed by Assembly. U N Rev 10:33-8 Mr '63

Commission on human rights

Commission on human rights. il U N Rev 11: 26-7 Ap '64
Elimination of racial discrimination; a declaration is drafted; with text. il U N Rev 10:45-51, 67 My '63
Human rights and foreign policy; excerpts from In pursuit of world order. R. N. Gardner. Sat R 47:23-5+ S 19 '64
Need to solve problems of hunger and malnutrition; address. B. R. Sen. U N Rev 10:35-6+ N '63
Religious freedom. America 108:599 Ap 27 '63
Seminar considers role of police in protection of human rights. U N Rev 10:33-4 Je '63
Story of progress in achieving international human rights. M. Tree. il NEA J 52:50-3 N '63
See also
United Nations—Subcommission on prevention of discrimination and protection of minorities

Commission on international commodity trade

Commodity trade and economic development; statement, April 30, 1963. W. M. Blumenthal. Dept State Bul 48:844-8 My 27 '63

Commission on narcotic drugs

Fight against narcotics. J. F. Mabileau. il U N Rev 11:29-34 F '64
Record of the month; annual session in Geneva. UN Mo Chron 1:64-6 Je '64

Commission on the status of women

Progress report on the status of women; 17th session. G. A. Tillett. Dept State Bul 49: 145-50 Jl 22 '63
Seventeenth session of the Commission on the status of women. M. L. Urbina. U N Rev 10:40-2 My '63
Women's work has just begun; concerning report of the Commission on the status of women. Nation 197:270 N 2 '63

Committee for industrial development

Industrial development goals. U N Rev 10:51 Je '63

UNITED NATIONS—*Continued*

Committee of seventeen

See United Nations—Special committee on situation with regard to implementation of declaration on granting of independence to colonial countries and peoples

Committee of twenty-four

See United Nations—Special committee on situation with regard to implementation of declaration on granting of independence to colonial countries and peoples

Committee on information from non-self-governing territories

Progress of an historic movement. il U N Rev 10:41-3 Je '63

Committee on the peaceful uses of outer space

Aerospace in the nuclear age. F. B. Schick. Bul Atomic Sci 19:46-9 D '63
Assembly approves program for peaceful uses of outer space. il U N Rev 10:22-9+ F '63
Astronaut distress plan expected. Aviation W 80:22 Mr 23 '64
Building and strengthening international co-operation in outer space; with message to the subcommittee from U Thant. il U N Rev 10:38-40 Je '63
Cooperation in outer space. R. N. Gardner. For Affairs 41:344-59 Ja '63
Future work of outer space committee. U S Rev 10:22 Ap '63
International organization and space law; address, May 1, 1963. A. Chayes. Dept State Bul 48:835-8 My 27 '63
Key UN space group meetings to be held in New York, Geneva. Aviation W 78:30 Mr 25 '63
Peaceful uses of outer space; text of the October 17, 1963 resolution, and excerpts of the December 24, 1963 resolution. Cur Hist 46:364+ Je '64
Peaceful uses of outer space. UN Mo Chron 1:39-47 N; 10-16 D '64
Space law gets set for launching. il Bsns W p 109+ N 7 '64
Space law proposal moves forward; with text of U.S.-USSR draft in United Nations on peaceful uses of space. Miss & Roc 13:17 D 2 '63
UN acting as catalyst for international co-operation. Aviation W 81:84-5 Jl 6 '64
United Nations committee receives new Soviet space use proposal. W. Wright. Aviation W 78:29 Ap 22 '63
United Nations group fails to gain accord on space use rules. W. Wright. Aviation W 78:129 My 20 '63
UN group will reconsider move to aid astronauts in distress. Aviation W 80:24 Ap 6 '64
United Nations; space committee makes little headway developing international law for space. E. Langer. Science 140:621+ My 10 '63
United Nations: space committee sees test ban, U.S.-Soviet accord as new footing for negotiation. J. Walsh. Science 141:1164-5+ S 20 '63
U.N. subcommittee debates law for outer space; statement, May 3, 1963. L. C. Meeker. Dept State Bul 48:923-5 Je 10 '63

Delegates

Dark faces in the UN. A. Morrison. il Ebony 18:23-6+ F '63
Diplomats entertain. M. Cartwright. il Negro Hist Bul 26:187-8 Mr; 216-18 Ap '63

Disarmament commission

Disarmament at the U.N: the quiet Assembly. H. A. Jack. Bul Atomic Sci 19:39-40+ F '63
Outer space. U N Rev 10:18 D '63

Documents

See United Nations—Publications

Economic and financial committee

Economic and social development. U N Rev 10:38-9 D '63

Economic and social council

Economic and social council in 1963. R. Walker. il U N Rev 10:40-2 Ag '63
General assembly resolutions on organizational changes. U N Rev 11:16-20+ Mr '64
Housing needs in development decade. il U N Rev 11:31-4+ Mr '64
Problems of economic development; statement, October 3, 1963. J. B. Bingham. Dept State Bul 49:712-21 N 4 '63
United Nations seen as best guarantee of assistance. I. Thajeb. U N Rev 11:29-31 Ja '64

See also
United Nations—Technical assistance program

Meetings, 1963

Emerging consensus on economic and social development; statement, July 10, 1963. A. E. Stevenson. Dept State Bul 49:265-72 Ag 12 '63
New initiatives in economic and social matters. il U N Rev 10:9-12+ My '63

Meetings, 1964

Economic and social council holds summer session in Geneva; summary of adopted resolutions and endorsements. UN Mo Chron 1:50-5 Ag '64
Economic and social council in perspective. R. Walker. UN Mo Chron 1:77-80 Ag '64
Expanding and protecting human rights throughout the world; statement, July 30, 1964. F. H. Williams. Dept State Bul 51:418-22 S 21 '64
U.N. economic and social council meets at Geneva; statements, July 14 and July 23, 1964. H. Cleveland; F. H. Williams. Dept State Bul 51:241-52 Ag 17 '64

Economic commission for Africa

Africa Hall an inspiring symbol. U N Rev 10:40-2 F '63
African development; statement, February 22, 1963. W. M. Kotschnig. Dept State Bul 48:625-8 Ap 22 '63
African unity urged; fifth session of ECA. U N Rev 10:6-9+ Mr '63
Economic commission for Africa. U N Rev 11:31-3 Ap '64
United States supports economic cooperation in Africa. L. B. Johnson; J. W. Fredericks. Dept State Bul 50:509-13 Mr 30 '64

Economic commission for Asia and the Far East

Asian institute for economic development and planning. U N Rev 10:50 Jl '63
Asian population conference. F. C. Madigan. America 110:188-90 F 8 '64; Correction. 111:202 Ag 29 '64
ECAFE proposals for construction of standard coasting vessels. il U N Rev 10:40 Mr '63
Economic commission for Asia and the Far East. U N Rev 11:33-4 Ap '64
Economic strains slow progress in many developing countries; text of introduction to Economic survey of Asia and the Far East, 1962. U N Rev 10:20-3 Mr '63
Mekong River plan. G. F. White. il Sci Am 208:49-59 bibliog(p200) Ap '63
Steps toward a fuller life in Asia and the Far East. il U N Rev 10:16-18 Ap '63
U.S. proposes town-centered planning for Asia; statment, March 4, 1964. K. T. Young. Dept State Bul 50:759-61 My 11 '64
Vietnam: the fourth course; international co-operation in science. G. F. White. il Bul Atomic Sci 20:6-10 D '64

See also
United Nations conference of Asian economic planners

Economic commission for Europe

Economic commission for Europe, its important role and future work. U N Rev 10:30 Ap '63
New perspectives for Economic commission for Europe. il U N Rev 10:42-5+ My '63
Record of the month; report of nineteenth session. UN Mo Chron 1:63-7 My '64

Economic commission for Latin America

Rendezvous with reality. il U N Rev 10:14-18 Je '63

Emergency force

See United Nations—Armed forces

Employees

United Nations tour guide supervisor. il Ebony 18:34-8 Ag '63
What did he say? U.N. interpreters. R. Marossi. Esquire 59:14+ My '63

Expanded program of technical assistance

See United Nations—Technical assistance program

Finance

Assembly accepts Court's opinion on peacekeeping expenses; working group to study methods of financing future operations. U N Rev 10:46-55+ Ja '63
Bill collector at work; Russia's debt. Time 84:33 Ag 7 '64

UNITED NATIONS—Finance—*Continued*
Budget estimates for 1965. il UN Mo Chron 1:63-5 Ag '64
Budget estimates for 1964. U N Rev 11:40-6 Ja '64
Budget for the financial year 1963. U N Rev 10:106-7 Ja '63
Can the U.N. survive? A. Drury. Read Digest 82:142-4+ Mr '63
Easing the financial situation; General assembly's fourth special session on seven proposals submitted; with text of proposals. il U N Rev 10:6-15, 62-3 Jl '63
Fifth committee discusses U.N. budget estimates for 1964; statement, October 28, 1963. W. S. Mailliard. Dept State Bul 49:871-5 D 2 '63
Financial brinkmanship at the U.N. H. Brandon. Sat R 47:6+ N 28 '64
Financial situation considered by General assembly. il U N Rev 10:6-11+ Je '63
Financing the U.N: pressures and principles. H. G. Nicholas. il Reporter 31:17-18 D 31 '64
Fulcrum of the United Nations. Nation 199: 477 D 21 '64
Going for broke? Time 85:24-5 Ja 29 '65
Is the U.N. on the verge of a crack-up? il U S News 54:52-4 Je 10 '63
Lack of cash creates crisis in U.N. Sr Schol 82:17-18 Ap 3 '63
Lesson of Cyprus. Nation 198:281 Mr 23 '64
Money talks; dispute over arrears of Soviet Union. il Newsweek 64:50-1 D 7 '64
More trouble for the U.N. Commonweal 78:291 Je 7 '63
1964 budget estimates. il U N Rev 10:29 Ag '63
Paying for UN policing. P. Rowley. New Repub 151:7 O 10 '64
Paying the bill for peace. M. Rossi. New Repub 148:8-9 Je 1 '63
Peace-keeping operations; Working group of twenty-one. UN Mo Chron 1:46-57 O; 51-6 N '64
Perils of the UN. New Repub 151:5-6 N 28 '64
Poverty, it's awful. Newsweek 61:40+ My 27 '63
Price of peace. Newsweek 61:40 Ap 8 '63
Red, green or yellow; question of Russia's payments. Time 84:37-8 D 4 '64
Red riposte. Newsweek 61:47 Je 3 '63
Report on financial management and the U.N. system released. Dept State Bul 50:67 Ja 13 '64
Revelation on the East River. H. Bowser. Sat R 47:24 S 12 '64
Rule of law, now; address, July 3, 1963. A. Chayes. Dept State Bul 49:162-7 Jl 29 '63; Same. Vital Speeches 29:696-9 S 1 '63
Showdown that the U.N. must face. Life 57:4 N 27 '64
Strange bedfellows. Newsweek 62:37 Jl 8 '63
Strengthening the UN. America 108:657 My 11 '63
Supporting peace. Commonweal 77:657 Mr 22 '63
Two kinds of politics; address, May 8, 1963. H. Cleveland. Dept State Bul 48:871-6 Je 3 '63
U.N. charter, the purse, and the peace; address, May 15, 1964. A. Chayes. Dept State Bul 50:900-6 Je 8 '64
U.N. collision. Commonweal 81:340-1 D 4 '64
UN crisis: the politics of money. J. G. Stoessinger. Nation 199:263-6 O 26 '64
United Nations financial crisis; address, March 12, 1963. R. N. Gardner. Dept State Bul 48:535-40 Ap 8 '63
U.N. General assembly adopts seven resolutions on financing; statements, with texts of resolutions adopted in plenary session on June 27, 1963. F. T. P. Plimpton; A. E. Stevenson. Dept State Bul 49:178-86 Jl 29 '63
U.N. seeks new way to finance peacekeeping. il Bsns W p 156+ N 21 '64
United Nations, voting patterns and financing; address, April 27, 1963. F. T. P. Plimpton. Dept State Bul 48:796-800 My 20 '63
U.S. makes proposal on financing peace-keeping operations of U.N; statement, September 14, 1964, with text of working paper. F. T. P. Plimpton. Dept State Bul 51:486-9 O 5 '64
U.S. mission expresses views on question of U.N. financing. A. E. Stevenson; S. O. Adebo; F. H. Williams. Dept State Bul 51: 826-8 D 7 '64
U.S. offers to help U.N. finance Cyprus peacekeeping force; Department statement, March 11, 1964. Dept State Bul 50:484 Mr 30 '64
U.S. states position on financing of U.N. peacekeeping operations; statement by the U.S. mission, March 6, 1963. Dept State Bul 48:443 Mr 25 '63
United States submits memorandum on U.N. financial crisis; letter with text of U.S. memorandum, October 8, 1964. A. E. Stevenson. Dept State Bul 51:681-90 N 9 '64
What is due the UN. New Repub 150:3-4 Ap 11 '64
Wrong approach to the UN problem. Nat R 14:522-3 Jl 2 '63

General assembly

How to hold elections without really voting. Time 85:19-20 Ja 8 '65
UN chicken home to roost. J. Burnham. Nat R 16:106 F 11 '64
United Nations: its value to the United States; statement, March 13, 1963. A. E. Stevenson. Dept State Bul 48:522-8 Ap 8 '63
United Nations, voting patterns and financing; address, April 27, 1963. F. T. P. Plimpton. Dept State Bul 48:796-800 My 20 '63

Sessions (17th)

General assembly resolutions. U N Rev 10: 88-104+ Ja '63
General assembly's seventeenth session. il U N Rev 10:5-7 Ja '63
Marriage convention opened for signature; other measures in social and human rights fields adopted by Assembly. il U N Rev 10:24-9+ Mr '63
Politics of population: a blueprint for international cooperation; address, May 4, 1963. R. N. Gardner. Dept State Bul 48:906-14 Je 10 '63
Politics of population; concerning United Nations resolution on population growth and economic development. R. N. Gardner. il Sat R 46:10-12+ S 7 '63
17th session of the U.N. General assembly: major accomplishments; statement, December 21, 1962. A. E. Stevenson. Dept State Bul 48:147-52 Ja 28 '63
Trade and other economic problems considered by General assembly. B. Lewandowski. il U N Rev 10:43-5+ Ja '63
United Nations pays tribute to memory of Mrs Roosevelt; series of statements made in the United Nations General assembly on November 9, 1962. Dept State Bul 48:48-50+ Ja 14 '63
United Nations role in political disputes; address, March 11, 1963. J. J. Sisco. Dept State Bul 48:529-35 Ap 8 '63
Work of the General assembly; plenary action in brief, December 1-21, 1962. U N Rev 10:8-14 Ja '63

Sessions (18th)

Accomplishments of 18th session of the U.N. General assembly; statement, December 18, 1963. A. E. Stevenson. bibliog f Dept State Bul 50:130-3 Ja 27 '64
Agenda of the 18th regular session of the U.N. General assembly. Dept State Bul 49:556-8 O 7 '63
Assembly opens multilateral treaties to new states. U N Rev 11:39-41 F '64
Assembly's general debate. il U N Rev 10:11-25+ N '63
Balanced approach to disarmament; statement, October 29, 1963. C. C. Stelle. Dept State Bul 49:793-8 N 18 '63
Campaign for world literacy; Campaign against hunger and disease; Science and technology for development. U N Rev 11: 31-4 Ja '64
Ceylon cries foul. America 109:413 O 12 '63
Declaration on elimination of racial discrimination; with text of declaration. U N Rev 11:35-9+ Ja '64
18th General assembly: a testing ground of hopes and opportunities; address, September 11, 1963. R. N. Gardner. Dept State Bul 49:501-8 S 30 '63
18th General assembly: fair and a little warmer, with scattered thundershowers; address, September 15, 1963. H. Cleveland. Dept State Bul 49:553-6 O 7 '63
18th session. il Time 82:27-8 S 27 '63
Eighty-one on the agenda. Newsweek 62:48 S 23 '63
Four Presidents and a Prime Minister address the General assembly; summaries of addresses. U N Rev 10:8-10 D '63
General assembly opens eighteenth regular session. il U N Rev 10:4-6 O '63
General assembly resolutions on organizational changes. U N Rev 11:16-20+ Mr '64
Issues before the eighteenth General assembly. bibliog f il Int Concil 544:1-199 S '63
Main decisions of eighteenth session. il U N Rev 11:12-14 F '64
New problems, little money as U.N. meets; with excerpts from address by J. F. Kennedy. il U S News 55:57-61 S 30 '63
Opening of general debate. U N Rev 10:7-9+ O '63

UNITED NATIONS—General assembly—Sessions (18th)—*Continued*
Opening on a note of optimism. Sr Schol 83:17 O 11 '63
Tensions ease under the sign of the moon; President Kennedy addresses the U.N. General assembly. il Newsweek 62:17-18 S 30 '63
Too peaceful. Newsweek 62:23 D 30 '63
Tributes to President John F. Kennedy. il U N Rev 10:i-iv+ D '63
U.N. assembly keeps busy pace. Sr Schol 83:6 N 8 '63
U.N. calls on states to refrain from orbiting weapons; statement, October 16, 1963; with text of resolution. A. E. Stevenson. Dept State Bul 49:753-4 N 11 '63
U.N.'s eighteenth session. Commonweal 79:4 S 27 '63
Work of the General assembly in brief. U N Rev 10:25-6 N; 42-5 D '63; 11:47-50 Ja '64

Sessions (18th Special)

Easing the financial situation; General assembly's fourth special session on seven proposals submitted; with text of proposals. il U N Rev 10:6-15, 62-3 Jl '63

Sessions (19th)

Beset by problems. Sr Schol 85:18 D 9 '64
From New York: diplomatic game at the U.N. H. Margolis. Bul Atomic Sci 21:40-4 Ja '65
General assembly nineteenth regular session; notes on the provisional agenda. UN Mo Chron 1:87-114 O '64
General assembly to convene on November 10. il UN Mo Chron 1:95-6 Jl '64
General debate; summaries of representatives's statements. UN Mo Chron 2:37-104 Ja '65
How not to vote. Newsweek 65:39 Ja 11 '65
In limbo. il Time 84:36 D 11 '64
Issues before the nineteenth General assembly. bibliog f il Int Concil 550:5-205 N '64
New power at the U.N. voting bloc of African nations. il Newsweek 64:28 D 14 '64
Notes on the provisional agenda of the General assembly's nineteenth session. UN Mo Chron 1:88-90 N '64
Opening of nineteenth session. UN Mo Chron 2:3-6 Ja '65
Picture section. il UN Mo Chron 2:105-12 Ja '65
Provisional agenda of nineteenth session of U.N. General assembly. Dept State Bul 51:491-3 O 5 '64
Supplementary list of items proposed for U.N. agenda. Dept State Bul 51:789-90 N 30 '64

Headquarters

Che's explosive return; bazooka fired at UN building. il Newsweek 64:43 D 21 '64
Church center for U.N. dedicated. Christian Cent 80:1229-30 O 9 '63
Dedication of church center for the United Nations; addresses, September 22, 1963. D. Rusk; A. E. Stevenson. Dept State Bul 49:570-4 O 14 '63
Hot enemies & cool friends; demonstrations at U.N. plaza in Manhattan. il Time 84:34 D 18 '64
Major development is underway at U.N. plaza. il Arch Rec 135:256 Ja '64
Stained glass memorial unveiled at headquarters. UN Mo Chron 1:75 O '64

High commissioner for refugees

Mandate of High commissioner for refugees extended five years. U N Rev 10:29-31+ F '63
Programme of the United Nations High commissioner for refugees. UN Mo Chron 1:50 N '64

History

First twenty-five years of the United Nations from San Francisco to the 1970's; address, January 10, 1964. D. Rusk. Dept State Bul 50:112-19 Ja 27 '64

International law commission

Consular relations; convention unanimously adopted in Vienna. U N Rev 10:52-6 Je '63
International law commission. E. Jiménez de Aréchaga. il U N Rev 10:42-4 Ag '63
International law commission; 16th session. UN Mo Chron 1:68 Je; 69 Ag '64
Record of the month; sixteenth session. UN Mo Chron 1:68 Je '64
Work of the Sixth committee of the General assembly, scope and trends. J. M. Ruda. UN Mo Chron 1:81-90 Ag '64

Legal committee

Work of the Sixth committee of the General assembly, scope and trends. J. M. Ruda. UN Mo Chron 1:81-90 Ag '64

Library

International by definition: Dag Hammarskjöld library; interview, ed. by J. N. Berry, 3d. L. Vladimirov. il Library J 89:4469-72 N 15 '64
UN library revises Documents index. Library J 88:2225 Je 1 '63

Membership

Growing power of the Afro-Asians. U S News 55:7 D 30 '63
Kenya and Zanzibar admitted to United Nations membership; statement, December 16, 1963. A. E. Stevenson. bibliog f Dept State Bul 50:32 Ja 6 '64
Kenya, Zanzibar admitted to United Nations; with Secretary-General's statement. il U N Rev 11:12-13 Ja '64
Kuwait becomes 111th member of United Nations. Dept State Bul 48:884 Je 3 '63
Let 'em stand; emergent nations. Time 83:40 My 15 '64
Membership in United Nations: Security council recommendations. UN Mo Chron 1:14-16 N '64

Political and security committee

Test-ban treaty; first committee's recommendations. U N Rev 10:15-17+ D '63

Population commission

Intensification of demographic studies, research, and training; statement, April 3, 1963; with text of resolution. J. B. Bingham. bibliog f Dept State Bul 49:28-32 Jl 1 '63

Publications

UN library revises Documents index. Library J 88:2225 Je 1 '63
UN sales section prepares new campaigns. il Pub W 184:85-6 S 16 '63

Bibliography

Current U.N. documents: a selected bibliography. See occasional issues of Department of state bulletin
Documents; selected list. See issues of UN monthly chronicle
Recent publications; reviews. See issues of UN monthly chronicle

Publicity

Flags are not enough: Widening gap; excerpts from TV script; ed. by A. Cooke. S. Hearst. il UNESCO Courier 17:26-9+ Je '64
UN-precedented; six United Nations shows for TV. il Newsweek 63:72 Ap 20 '64
What's good for U.N. is good for Xerox; six non-commercial 90-minute films on TV concerning UN global activities. Bsns W p80+ Ap 18 '64

Scholarships and fellowships

See Scholarships and fellowships

Scientific committee on the effects of atomic radiation

Report of the United Nations scientific committee on the effects of atomic radiation. Review
Bul Atomic Sci 19:32-3 Ap '63 A. C. Upton

Secretary General

Letdown at the UN; Hammarskjöld as Secretary General. J. Kraft. Harper 230:84+ Ja '65
New Secretary-General. H. J. Morgenthau. Commentary 35:62-5 Ja '63; Discussion. 35:531-2 Je '63
Press conferences. UN Mo Chron 1:46-8 My; 57 Je; 47-50 Ag '64
Record of the month. See issues of UN monthly chronicle
World is in his debt. R. H. Rovere. il Sat Eve Post 236:38-40 S 21 '63

Security council

General assembly resolutions on organizational changes. U N Rev 11:16-20+ Mr '64
Overtures to Peking. New Repub 149:10 N 16 '63; Reply. E. Schwelb. 149:30 D 28 '63
Resurgence of the United Nations Security council; address, June 18, 1964. J. J. Sisco. Dept State Bul 51:55-9 Jl 13 '64
Security council and South Africa. U N Rev 10:20-4 Ag '63
Security council calls for ban on sale of arms to South Africa; statements, with the text of a resolution, August 7, 1963. A. E. Stevenson; C. W. Yost. Dept State Bul 49:333-9 Ag 26 '63
Security council urgently calls on Portugal. il U N Rev 10:14-19 Ag '63
Security council's action on Senegal's complaint against Portugal. il U N Rev 10:22-4+ My '63

UNITED NATIONS—Security council—*Cont.*
Table; between urgent meetings. New Yorker 40:19-20 Ag 15 '64

Meetings, 1963

Against the last white strongholds. il Time 82:30 Ag 9 '63
Anger in the Council; emergency session concerning Israeli-Syrian frontier incident. Time 82:29 S 6 '63
Arms ban; embargo on arms shipments to Portugal for use in her African territories. il Newsweek 62:36 Ag 12 '63
Haiti-Dominican Republic dispute considered by Security council. il U N Rev 10:35-7 Je '63
Security council adopts resolution on South Africa; with text of resolution on apartheid adoped by the Assembly. U N Rev 11:14-15+ Ja '64
Security council considers complaint. il U N Rev 11:4-6 F '64
United States explains position on Portuguese territories; statements, July 26 and July 31, 1963; with text of a resolution adopted by the Council on July 31, 1963. A. E. Stevenson. Dept State Bul 49:303-9 Ag 19 '63

Meetings, 1964

Apartheid in South Africa. UN Mo Chron 1: 16-25 Jl '64
Cambodia; Security council appoints mission. UN Mo Chron 1:25-30 Jl '64
Record of the month:
  Call for cease-fire in Cyprus. UN Mo Chron 1:3-18 Ag '64
  Congo. UN Mo Chron 1:8-10 D '64
  Consideration of British air attack on Yemeni territory. UN Mo Chron 1:14-20 My '64
  Consideration of Malaysia's complaint against Indonesia. UN Mo Chron 1:25-34 O '64
  Debate on Kashmir. il UN Mo Chron 1:2-12 Je '64
  Extension of the UN peacekeeping force in Cyprus for three months. UN Mo Chron 1:3-20 O '64
  Palestine question. U N Mo Chron 1:3-8 D '64
  Security council considers complaint by Cambodia of acts of aggression. UN Mo Chron 1:12-17 Je '64
Secretary-General's statement on his discussions with main parties; February 25, 1964. Thant. U N Rev 11:7 Ap '64
Security council resolution on Cyprus. il Cur Hist 46:305-6 My '64
Security council takes up complaint against the United States on January 10, 1964. il U N Rev 11:6-8+ F '64
Security council team to examine Cambodia-Viet-Nam border areas; statement, June 4, 1964; with text of resolution. A. E. Stevenson. Dept State Bul 50:1002-4 Je 29 '64
Security council's debate: statements by the representatives of Cyprus, Greece and Turkey. S. Kyprianou; O. Eralp; D. S. Bitsios. UN Mo Chron 1:9-13 O '64
U.N. Security council condemns apartheid in South Africa; sets up committee to study sanctions; statements, June 16 and June 18, 1964, with text of resolution. A. E. Stevenson. Dept State Bul 51:29-33 Jl 6 '64
United States complaint; attack on destroyer Maddox in the Gulf of Tonkin. UN Mo Chron 1:18-28 Ag '64

Sixth committee

See United Nations—Legal committee

Social commission

Social commission; its work and achievements. U N Rev 10:57-9+ Jl '63

Social, humanitarian and cultural committee

Marriage convention opened for signature; other measures in social and human rights fields adopted by Assembly. il U N Rev 10:24-9+ Mr '63

Special committee of twenty-four on colonialism

See United Nations—Special committee on situation with regard to implementation of declaration on granting of independence to colonial countries and peoples

Special committee on principles of international law concerning friendly relations and cooperation among states

Session in Mexico city. UN Mo Chron 1:57-8 O '64
Special committee on principles of international law; concerning deliberations and decisions at session in Mexico city. UN Mo Chron 1:56-8 N '64

Special committee on situation with regard to implementation of declaration on granting of independence to colonial countries and peoples

Committee of twenty-four adopts resolution on the Gambia. U N Rev 10:33-5 O '63
Committee on colonialism. U N Rev 10:30-9 Ag '63
Critical situation in South West Africa: with resolution on South West Africa. U N Rev 10:24-8 Je '63
Independence without delay urged by Assembly for all colonial peoples; recommendations by Committee of seventeen. U N Rev 10:14-16 Ja '63
Interim measure seeks to speed British Guiana's independence. il U N Rev 10:33-7 Jl '63
Progress achieved in the field of decolonization. S. Coulibaly. UN Mo Chron 1:85-91 Je '64
Report on granting of independence to colonial countries and peoples. U N Rev 10:24 D '63
Situation in Southern Rhodesia explosive committee warns; with text of resolution. il U N Rev 10:29-33 Jl '63
Southern Rhodesia. U N Rev 11:16-20+ Ap '64
Special committee of twenty-four. U N Mo Chron 1:21-40 My; 24-43 Je; 35-49 Jl; 32-40 Ag; 36-40 O; 16-39 N; 16-32 D '64; 2:32 Ja '65
Special committee proposes visit to Aden and protectorates; discusses United Nations review. il U N Rev 10:25-32+ My '63
Subcommittee on Aden says United Nations action urgently necessary. U N Rev 10:38 Jl '63

Special committee on the policies of apartheid of the government of the republic of South Africa

Apartheid a dangerous drift of events; Special committee reports to General assembly and Security council. il U N Rev 10:33-7 My '63
Committee report on apartheid. U N Rev 10:24-6 Ag '63
Special committee report on apartheid. U N Rev 10:35-9 O '63

Special fund

$85.2 million program of Special fund aid approved at the Hague. UN Mo Chron 1: 52-6 Jl '64
Forty-one new development projects approved by Special fund. il U N Rev 10:41-6 Jl '63
Increased special fund assistance for low-income countries. il U N Rev 10:18-22 F '63
Nations pledge contributions to EPTA and Special fund; with statement by the Secretary-General. il U N Rev 10:33-4 N '63
New special fund projects. il U N Rev 11:25-30 Mr '64
Role of the special fund in the U.N. development decade; statement, January 14, 1963. J. B. Bingham. Dept State Bul 48:258-63 F 18 '63
United Nations nobody knows; social and economic activities. P. G. Hoffman. Sat R 46:10-12+ D 28 '63
United Nations special fund; photographs. UN Mo Chron 1:99-106 Je '64
U.S. comments on activities of U.N. special fund; statement, June 3, 1963. J. B. Bingham. Dept State Bul 49:68-71 Jl 8 '63
U.S. position on U.N. special fund project in Cuba; statements. D. Rusk; R. N. Gardner. Dept State Bul 48:357-60 Mr 11 '63
War on want. P. Hoffman. UN Mo Chron 1:92-8 Je '64
World without want, by P. G. Hoffman. Review
  America 108:202 F 9 '63. W. J. Gibbons

Study and teaching

Mock U.N. on the campus; Fairleigh Dickinson university, Madison, N.J. il N Y Times Mag p 17 Ap 28 '63
Teaching about the United Nations. W. Goldstein. bibliog il Sr Schol 83:11T N 22 '63
What to teach about the United Nations. A. Larson. il NEA J 53:26-8 Ja '64

UNITED NATIONS—*Continued*

Subcommission on prevention of discrimination and protection of minorities

Draft on new convention on racial discrimination. U N Rev 11:39-40 Mr '64
Propose charter of religious freedom. Christian Cent 80:197 F 13 '63
Right to leave a country upheld. U N Rev 10:30-2 Mr '63

Technical assistance program

EPTA: 1963 program reaches record level. UN Mo Chron 1:56-8 Jl '64
Fifteen years, anniversary of a resolution. D. Owen. UN Mo Chron 1:78-84 Jl '64
More experts, fellowships, equipment; expanding use of technical assistance. il U N Rev 10:21-3 Je '63
Nations pledge contributions to EPTA and Special fund; with statement by the Secretary-General. il U N Rev 10:33-4 N '63
Pledging conference for expanded programme of technical assistance and special fund. UN Mo Chron 1:37-9 D '64
Training program in development financing. il U N Rev 11:37-8 Mr '64
U.N. technical assistance program for 1965-66; statement, November 24, 1964. F. H. Williams. Dept State Bul 51:920-1 D 28 '64
United Nations training programme for foreign service officers from newly independent countries. D. Protitch. UN Mo Chron 1:67-71 N '64
See also
Food and agriculture organization of the United Nations

Trusteeship council

Record of the month; thirty-first session. il UN Mo Chron 1:69-75 Je; 60-70 Jl '64
Three remaining trust territories; Pacific Islands; New Guinea; Nauru. il U N Rev 10:21-9+ Jl '63
Trust Territory of the Pacific Islands; statements, May 28, 1964. M. W. Goding; T. Remengesau. Dept State Bul 50:1007-20 Je 29 '64
UN and Captain Galvao. Nation 197:377-8 D 7 '63

Voting

Fair's fair; one-nation, one-vote system analysed. Newsweek 61:52 Je 17 '63
How nations aided by U.S. vote in the United Nations; chart. K. Mundt. il U S News 57:12 Ag 24 '64
Why U.N. looks different to the U.S. now; with chart. il U S News 57:42-3 D 14 '64

Womens participation

Lady is a diplomat. S. Massie. il Ladies Home J 81:117-21 Je '64

Aden

Record of the month; Special committee of twenty-four. UN Mo Chron 1:21-9 My; 24-30 Je '64
Representative government constitutional changes called for; with text of resolution. U N Rev 10:30-3 Ag '63

Africa

Africa and the world community; address, February 4, 1964. Thant. U N Rev 11:13-15 Mr '64
African issues at the United Nations; address, April 18, 1964. G. M. Williams. Dept State Bul 50:751-5 My 11 '64
Cartography in Africa; United Nations regional cartographic conference for Africa, Nairobi, Kenya, July 1-13, 1963. G. E. Pearcy. Dept State Bul 49:1014-18 D 30 '63
Dark faces in the UN. A. Morrison. il Ebony 18:23-6+ F '63
Irresponsible & repugnant; Africans' complaint concerning Stanleyville rescue operation. il Time 84:19-20 D 25 '64
No apologies; Congo rescue mission; excerpts from address, 1964. A. Stevenson. Sr Schol 85:18-19 Ja 7 '65
Role of Africa in the United Nations; address, April 11, 1964; with questions and answers. T. Hovet, jr. Ann Am Acad 354:122-34 Jl '64
United Nations and colonialism in Africa. R. Welensky. Ann Am Acad 354:145-52 Jl '64
United Nations and the new Africa; address, March 29, 1963. G. M. Williams. Dept State Bul 48:602-5 Ap 22 '63
Why do we take it? J. Burnham. Nat R 17:20 Ja 12 '65

Albania

D.P.'s at the U.N. Reporter 29:22+ O 24 '63

Angola

Assembly condemns colonial war in Angola. il U N Rev 10:42-9 F '63
U.S. withdraws proposal on Angola opposed by Afro-Asian group; statements, December 18 and December 20, 1962. A. Gore; J. B. Bingham. Dept State Bul 48:105-7 Ja 21 '63

Arab states

Longest truce; Arab-Jewish Palestine war. il Time 81:36 Je 14 '63

Asia

Dark faces in the UN. A. Morrison. il Ebony 18:23-6+ F '63

Asia, Southeastern

Back to Geneva? M. Ascoli. Reporter 30:10 Je 4 '64
Secretary Rusk's news conference of July 1, 1964. D. Rusk. Dept State Bul 51:85-8 Jl 20 '64
UN: peace and politics. D. Grant. Nation 199: 1-2 Jl 13 '64

Basutoland

United Nations observers proposed for guaranteeing independence; with text of resolution on Basutoland, Bechuanaland and Swaziland. U N Rev 10:38-9 Ag '63

Bechuanaland

United Nations observers proposed for guaranteeing independence; with text of resolution on Basutoland, Bechuanaland and Swaziland. U N Rev 10:38-9 Ag '63

British Guiana

Interim measure seeks to speed British Guiana's independence. il U N Rev 10:33-7 Jl '63
Record of the month; Special committee of twenty-four. UN Mo Chron 1:35-43 Jl '64

Cambodia

Cambodia; Security council appoints mission. UN Mo Chron 1:25-30 Jl '64
Record of the month; Security council considers complaint. UN Mo Chron 1:12-17 Je '64
Report of the Security council mission. UN Mo Chron 1:24-8 Ag '64
Security council continues debate on Cambodian complaint; two statements, May 26, 1964. A. E. Stevenson. Dept State Bul 50: 937-41 Je 15 '64
U.S. comments on U.N. mission's Cambodia-Viet-Nam report; letter, September 9, 1964. A. E. Stevenson. Dept State Bul 51:527-9 O 12 '64
U.S. welcomes inquiry of Cambodian charge of chemical operations; text of letter from Ambassador A. E. Stevenson, August 14, 1964. Dept State Bul 51:319 Ag 31 '64

Canada

Member of the parish; address, June 6, 1964. H. Cleveland. Dept State Bul 50:971-6 Je 22 '64

Chile

President of Chile addresses General assembly; summary of address. A. Rodriguez. il U N Rev 10:39 Ja '63

China (People's Republic)

Albanian proposal to change U.N. representation of China rejected; statement, October 16, 1963. A. E. Stevenson. Dept State Bul 49:755-8 N 11 '63
China and the United Nations. W. Levi. Cur Hist 47:149-55+ S '64
China in the wings. M. Rossi. New Repub 149:9 N 2 '63
Chinese puzzle in the U.N. B. Pilkington. Christian Cent 82:50-1 Ja 13 '65
De Gaulle, red China and the U.N. Sat Eve Post 237:76 F 29 '64
Keep red China out! condensation of address. W. H. Judd. Read Digest 85:114-18 N '64
Mainland China and U.S. security. B. G. Lall. Bul Atomic Sci 20:24-7 Ap '64
Red China and Russia: their position in the U.N; address, November 18, 1964. D. E. Johnson. Vital Speeches 31:141-3 D 15 '64
Representation of China; Assembly rejects proposal. U N Rev 10:11-14 D '63
U.N. seat for an atomic red China? pro and con discussion. Sr Schol 85:10-11 N 4 '64
U.N. seat for red China? pro and con discussion. Sr Schol 83:14-15 S 20 '63
What about mainland China? D. M. Stowe. Christian Cent 82:44-6 Ja 13 '65

UNITED NATIONS—*Continued*

Congo (capital Leopoldville)

Aftermath in the Congo. H. R. Rudin. Cur Hist 45:341-6 D '63
Another round in Katanga? concerning ANC (Congolese national army) C. Scott. Nat R 15:478 D 3 '63
Assembly extends United Nations operation in the Congo. il U N Rev 10:37-40 N '63
Beats of the heart of darkness. Nat R 14:268 Ap 9 '63
Civilian assistance to the Congo. U N Rev 10:27-9+ Ag '63
Communications to Security council. UN Mo Chron 1:8-10 D '64
Congo: a calculated confusion. J. Stolle. Nation 196:252-4 Mr 23 '63
Congo: an account of United Nations action, and a look ahead; text of a report, February 4, 1963. U. Thant. il U N Rev 10:6-13 F '63
Congo: what was wrong, what is and will be wrong. A. J. Meyers. il U S News 54: 59-61 F 4 '63
Everybody's problem child. R. Howe. New Repub 148:10-12 Ap 27 '63
Katanga and the Congo crisis. C. K. Yearley. Commonweal 77:483-6 F 1 '63
Katanga? who's that? Nat R 16:138-9 F 25 '64
Lesson of the Congo. E. Van Den Haag. Nat R 16:771-3+ S 8 '64
President Kennedy welcomes end of Katanga secession; statement, January 21, 1963. J. F. Kennedy. Dept State Bul 48:207 F 11 '63
Secretary appears on Washington reports to the people; interview, ed. by H. W. Flannery. D. Rusk. Dept State Bul 48:440-3 Mr 25 '63
Secretary Rusk's news conference of July 1, 1964. D. Rusk. Dept State Bul 51:82-3 Jl 20 '64
Security council adopts resolution calling for non-intervention. UN Mo Chron 2:7-23 Ja '65
Story of the Congo. W. Lippmann. Newsweek 61:15 Mr 4 '63
Summary chronology of United Nations action relating to the Congo (cont) U N Rev 10:65-7 Ja; 75-7 F; 44 Mr; 31 Ap; 52 My; 57 Je '63
To Katanga and back, by C. C. O'Brien. Review
America 108:568-71 Ap 20 '63. V. S. Kearney
New Repub 148:23-4+ Ap 6 '63. J. P. Lash
Sat R il 46:44-5 Mr 30 '63. D. Kurzman
Ugly face in Africa. J. Davenport. Fortune 67:84+ F '63; Discussion. 67:20 Ap '63
United Nations and the Congo; three questions; address, January 17, 1963. H. Cleveland. Dept State Bul 48:165-70 F 4 '63
U.N. General assembly adopts seven resolutions on financing; statements, with texts of resolutions adopted in plenary session on June 27, 1963. F. T. P. Plimpton; A. E. Stevenson. Dept State Bul 49:178-86 Jl 29 '63
UN's idiot policy in the Congo. E. Van Den Haag. Nat R 17:61-2 Ja 26 '65
United Nations in crisis; Cuba and the Congo; address, February 23, 1963. R. N. Gardner. Dept State Bul 48:477-81 Ap 1 '63
United Nations role in political disputes; address, March 11, 1963. J. J. Sisco. Dept State Bul 48:529-35 Ap 8 '63
UN mission accomplished? America 110:588 My 2 '64
U.N. victory. Christian Cent 80:163 F 6 '63
U.S. cites illegal interference in support of Congo rebellion; statement, December 14, 1964. A. E. Stevenson. Dept State Bul 52:: 15-24 Ja 4 '65
When will the Congo be ready for independence? C. Sterling. il Reporter 28:26-8 Ap 11 '63

Cuba

United Nations in crisis; Cuba and the Congo; address, February 23, 1963. R. N. Gardner. Dept State Bul 48:477-81 Ap 1 '63
Uproar; suggested UN agricultural experimental station in Cuba. Newsweek 61:25 F 25 '63

Cyprus

Atlantic report. Atlan 214:12+ O '64
Boomerang? Greek Cypriot assault on St Hilarion. Newsweek 63:40+ My 11 '64
Can the United Nations save Cyprus? S. Castan. il Look 28:36-7 Je 2 '64
Cyprus dispute goes to U.N. il Sr Schol 84: 22 Mr 6 '64
Holding action. il Newsweek 63:42-3 Mr 16 '64
Lesson of Cyprus. Nation 198:281 Mr 23 '64
Secretary-General's statement on his discussions with main parties; February 25, 1964. Thant. U N Rev 11:7 Ap '64
Security council considers complaint. il U N Rev 11:4-6 F '64
Security council resolution on Cyprus. il Cur Hist 46:305-6 My '64
Security council votes extension of peacekeeping force in Cyprus; statement, June 19, 1964; with text of resolution. A. E. Stevenson. Dept State Bul 51:64-7 Jl 13 '64
Security council's debate; statements by the representatives of Cyprus, Greece and Turkey. S. Kyprianou; O. Eralp; D. S. Bitsios. UN Mo Chron 1:9-13 O '64
Some reflections on the United States in the United Nations; address, October 23, 1964. P. Talbot. Dept State Bul 51:700-5 N 16 '64
U.N. force voted. Sr Schol 84:19 Mr 20 '64
UN: peace and politics. D. Grant. Nation 199: 1-2 Jl 13 '64
U.N. security council adopts resolution on Cyprus; remarks by President Johnson, press statement by A. E. Stevenson, March 4, 1964; with text of resolution. Dept State Bul 50:465-6 Mr 23 '64
U.N. Security council calls for cease-fire in Cyprus; statement by Ambassador Stevenson, August 9, 1964, with text of resolution. Dept State Bul 51:318 Ag 31 '64
UN's task in Cyprus. New Repub 150:7 Mr 21 '64
See also
United Nations—Armed forces—Forces in Cyprus

Dominican Republic

Haiti-Dominican Republic dispute considered by Security council. il U N Rev 10:35-7 Je '63

Fiji

Committee adopts resolution on Fiji. UN Mo Chron 1:19-26 D '64
New constitution and integration of communities sought; with text of resolution. U N Rev 10:33-5 Ag '63

Gambia

Committee of twenty-four adopts resolution on the Gambia. U N Rev 10:33-5 O '63

Gibraltar

Committee adopts consensus on Gibraltar. UN Mo Chron 1:23-6 N '64

Great Britain

See also
United Nations—Cyprus

Greece, Modern

See also
United Nations—Cyprus

Haiti

Haiti-Dominican Republic dispute considered by Security council. il U N Rev 10:35-7 Je '63

Hungary

Secretary-General asked to take any helpful initiative on question of Hungary. U N Rev 10:40-2+ Ja '63
U.N. asks Secretary-General to take initiative on Hungary; statement, December 18, 1962; with text of resolution. C. T. Rowan. Dept State Bul 48:74-7 Ja 14 '63
United States reserves position on Hungarian credentials at U.N; statement, June 5, 1963. C. W. Yost. Dept State Bul 49:32 Jl 1 '63

India

India-Pakistan question. il U N Rev 11:5-11+ Mr '64
See also
United Nations—Kashmir

Indonesia

Cassava, anyone? Indonesia's withdrawal from the United Nations. il Time 85:24-5 Ja 15 '65
Indonesia steps closer to the brink; withdrawal from UN. il Bsns W p52-4+ Ja 16 '65
Indonesia takes a walk. il Sr Schol 85:18-19 Ja 21 '65
Indonesia: waiting for a letter; secession from the U.N. il Newsweek 65:27 Ja 18 '65
Malaysia's complaint against Indonesia. UN Mo Chron 1:25-34 O '64
New world battleground in Asia? il U S News 58:8 Ja 18 '65
Sukarno's Indonesia quits U.N. Christian Cent 82:68 Ja 20 '65
U.S. calls for negotiation of Malaysia-Indonesia dispute; statement, September 10, 1964. A. E. Stevenson. Dept State Bul 51: 448-50 S 28 '64

UNITED NATIONS—*Continued*

Ireland

Visit to Ireland; address, June 28, 1963. J. F. Kennedy. Dept State Bul 49:128-32 Jl 22 '63

Israel

Longest truce; Arab-Jewish Palestine war. il Time 81:36 Je 14 '63
Security council considers dispute between Israel and Syrian Arab Republic. UN Mo Chron 1:3-8 D '64
Security council continues consideration of Israel-Syria dispute. UN Mo Chron 2:28-32 Ja '65
Soviet Union vetoes U.S.-U.K. resolution in Security council on Israel and Syrian complaints; statements, August 28 and September 3, 1963; with the text of a draft resolution. A. E. Stevenson; C. W. Yost. Dept State Bul 49:520-3 S 30 '63
Syria and Israel submit charges to United Nations. U N Rev 10:24-30 O '63
United States urges restraint on Israel and Syria; statement, December 3, 1964. A. E. Stevenson. Dept State Bul 52:27-9 Ja 4 '65

Japan

U.S. supports full membership for Japan in OECD; statement, March 28, 1963. D. Rusk. Dept State Bul 48:572 Ap 15 '63

Kashmir

Record of the month; India-Pakistan question. UN Mo Chron 1:45-6 My '64
Record of the month; Security council's debate on the India-Pakistan question. il UN Mo Chron 1:2-12 Je '64

Kenya

Independence without delay is hope for four territories. U N Rev 10:35-8 Ag '63
Kenya, Zanzibar admitted to United Nations; with Secretary-General's statement. il U N Rev 11:12-13 Ja '64

Korea

U.N. invites Republic of Korea to take part in debate; statement, December 11, 1962; with text of resolution. G. A. Allott. Dept State Bul 48:70-4 Ja 14 '63
See also
United Nations—Commission for the unification and rehabilitation of Korea

Kuwait

Kuwait becomes 111th member of United Nations. il U N Rev 10:30-1 Je '63
Solvency, it's wonderful; 111th member. Newsweek 61:45 My 27 '63
Thursday. New Yorker 39:32-3 My 25 '63

Malawi

Independence without delay is hope for four territories; with text of resolution on Northern Rhodesia and Nyasaland. U N Rev 10:35-8 Ag '63
Malawi, Malta, and Zambia admitted to U.N. membership; statement, December 2, 1964. A. E. Stevenson. Dept State Bul 51:919-20 D 28 '64
Security council recommends Malawi for U.N. membership; statement, October 9, 1964. C. W. Yost. Dept State Bul 51:680 N 9 '64

Malaysia

Federation of Malaysia; with Secretary-General's conclusions. il U N Rev 10:11-15 O '63
Malaysia or bust. Newsweek 62:40 S 9 '63
Malaysia's complaint against Indonesia. UN Mo Chron 1:25-34 O '64
Mission to Sarawak and North Borneo; with text of message, August 5, 1963, to Secretary-General U Thant. il U N Rev 10:12-13 Ag '63
U.S. calls for negotiation of Malaysia-Indonesia dispute; statement, September 10, 1964. A. E. Stevenson. Dept State Bul 51:448-50 S 28 '64
U.S. regrets Soviet veto of U.N. resolution on on Malaysia complaint; statement, September 17, 1964. A. E. Stevenson. Dept State Bul 51:489-91 O 5 '64

Malta

Independence urged for Malta at earliest possible date. U N Rev 10:28-9 Je '63
Malawi, Malta, and Zambia admitted to U.N. membership; statement, December 2, 1964. A. E. Stevenson. Dept State Bul 51:919-20 D 28 '64
Security council recommends Malta and Zambia for U.N. membership; statement, October 30, 1964. C. W. Yost. Dept State Bul 51:759 N 23 '64

Northern Rhodesia

Independence without delay is hope for four territories; with text of resolution on Northern Rhodesia and Nyasaland. U N Rev 10:35-8 Ag '63

Oman

Proposal on Oman rejected for second successive year. U N Rev 10:80-2 F '63
Question of Oman. U N Rev 11:17-21 F '64

Pakistan

India-Pakistan question. il U N Rev 11:5-11+ Mr '64
See also
United Nations—Kashmir

Panama

Security council takes up complaint against the United States on January 10, 1964. il U N Rev 11:6-8+ F '64

Portugal

Assembly condemns colonial war in Angola. il U N Rev 10:42-9 F '63
Assembly urges independence for Portuguese territories. il U N Rev 10:16-28 Ja '63
Boycott or death. il Newsweek 62:34-5 Ag 5 '63
Portugal: little country with big troubles. il U S News 55:46-8 Ag 26 '63
Portuguese territories. U N Rev 11:16-19 Ja '64
Portuguese territories and the United Nations. P. Wohlgemuth. bibliog f Int Concil 545:3-68 N '63
Security council urgently calls on Portugal. il U N Rev 10:14-19 Ag '63
Security council's action on Senegal's complaint against Portugal. il U N Rev 10:22-4+ My '63
Security council's attention drawn to situation in Portuguese territories; with resolution on Portuguese territories. U N Rev 10:9-11+ Ap '63
Territories under Portuguese administration. U N Rev 10:21-2 D '63
United States explains position on Portuguese territories; statements, July 26 and July 31, 1963; together with the text of a resolution adopted by the Council on July 31, 1963. A. E. Stevenson. Dept State Bul 49:303-9 Ag 19 '63

Puerto Rico

Thanks, but no thanks; proposed discussion of independence. Time 84:40 D 4 '64

Russia

At U.N: showdown, or a deal with reds? il U S News 57:33-4 D 7 '64
Financial brinkmanship at the U.N. H. Brandon. Sat R 47:6+ N 28 '64
Red China and Russia: their position in the U.N; address, November 18, 1964. D. E. Johnson. Vital Speeches 31:141-3 D 15 '64
Red, green or yellow; question of Russia's payments. Time 84:37-8 D 4 '64
Showdown that the U.N. must face. Life 57:4 N 27 '64
U.N. charter, the purse, and the peace; address, May 15, 1964. A. Chayes. Dept State Bul 50:900-6 Je 8 '64
U.N. collision. Commonweal 81:340-1 D 4 '64
UN crisis: the politics of money. J. G. Stoessinger. Nation 199:263-6 O 26 '64
United Nations and the challenge of a changing international law; address, April 25, 1963. S. M. Schwebel. Dept State Bul 48:785-9 My 20 '63
U.S. regrets Soviet veto of U.N. resolution on Malaysia complaint; statement; September 17, 1964. A. E. Stevenson. Dept State Bul 51:489-91 O 5 '64
U.S.-Russian showdown: will it wreck U.N? il U S News 57:39-40 N 30 '64

Senegal

Security council's action on Senegal's complaint against Portugal. il U N Rev 10:22-4+ My '63

South Africa

Apartheid and the United Nations. R. C. Malhotra. Ann Am Acad 354:135-44 Jl '64
Apartheid in South Africa. UN Mo Chron 1:44-50 Je; 16-25 Jl; 30-2 Ag; 3-9 N; 32-7 D '64
Assembly adopts resolution on trial in South Africa; with text of resolution. U N Rev 10:8-10+ N '63
Boycott or death. il Newsweek 62:34-5 Ag 5 '63

UNITED NATIONS—South Africa—*Continued*
D.P.'s at the U.N. Reporter 29:22+ O 24 '63
Gathering storm. Nation 196:498 Je 15 '63
Lone dissenter. Newsweek 62:71 O 21 '63
Record of the month; apartheid in South Africa. UN Mo Chron 1:44-50 Je '64
Record of the month; recommendations of expert group on South Africa; summary of report of the Special committee on apartheid. UN Mo Chron 1:40-5 My '64
Rededication; with excerpts from Statement on apartheid, by A. E. Stevenson. New Yorker 39:47-9 D 14 '63
Security council adopts resolution on South Africa; with text of resolution on apartheid adopted by the Assembly. U N Rev 11:14-15+ Ja '64
Security council again condemns apartheid in South Africa; statement, December 4, 1963, with text of resolution. A. E. Stevenson. Dept State Bul 50:92-6 Ja 20 '64
Security council and South Africa. U N Rev 10:20-4 Ag '63
Security council calls for ban on sale of arms to South Africa; statements, with the text of a resolution, August 7, 1963. A. E. Stevenson; C. W. Yost. Dept State Bul 49:333-9 Ag 26 '63
South Africa and the UN. Nation 197:22 Jl 13 '63
Unanimity; South African apartheid was condemned by a vote of 106-1. Nation 197: 270 N 2 '63
U.N. condemns repression of opponents to apartheid; statement, October 11, 1963; with text of resolution. F. T. P. Plimpton. Dept State Bul 49:758-9 N 11 '63
United Nations resolution on South Africa. Cur Hist 45:366 D '63
U.N. Security council condemns apartheid in South Africa; sets up committee to study sanctions; statements, June 16 and June 18, 1964, with text of resolution. A. E. Stevenson. Dept State Bul 51:29-33 Jl 6 '64
Verwoerd's blight. Newsweek 62:45 Ag 19 '63
Wrong remedy. Nation 197:81 Ag 24 '63

Southern Rhodesia

Black and white. Newsweek 63:47 My 11 '64
Committee adopts consensus on Southern Rhodesia. UN Mo Chron 1:16-23 N '64
Record of the month; appointment of subcommittee by Special committee of twenty-four. UN Mo Chron 1:30-2 Je '64
Record of the month; Special committee of twenty-four adopts thirteen-power resolution. UN Mo Chron 1:29-40 My '64
Record of the month; subcommittee reports on talks with United Kingdom government. UN Mo Chron 1:43-9 Jl '64
Security council considers Southern Rhodesia. il U N Rev 10:16-22 O '63
Security council considers Southern Rhodesian question; statement, September 11, 1963. A. E. Stevenson. Dept State Bul 49:559-61 O 7 '63
Situation in Southern Rhodesia explosive committee warns; with text of resolution. il U N Rev 10:29-33 Jl '63
Southern Rhodesia. U N Rev 10:19-21 D '63
Southern Rhodesia; special committee resumes consideration of question. U N Rev 11:16-20+ Ap '64
Southern Rhodesia subcommittee reports on talks with United Kingdom government. il U N Rev 10:29-30 Je '63
Special committee concerned over explosive situation in Southern Rhodesia. il U N Rev 10:6-8 Ap '63

Southwest Africa

Critical situation in South West Africa. U N Rev 10:24-8 Je '63
Effective United Nations presence proposed for South West Africa. U N Rev 10:29-38 Ja '63
Preliminary judgement on South West Africa. U N Rev 10:66-9 F '63
Record of the month; Special committee of twenty-four. UN Mo Chron 1:32-41 Je '64
South West Africa; General assembly adopts four resolutions. U N Rev 11:21-4 F '64
Territory of South West Africa. R. B. Ballinger. bibliog f Cur Hist 45:361-5 D '63
U.S. expresses continuing concern for future of South-West Africa; statement, October 30, 1963. W. R. Yates. Dept State Bul 49: 946-8 D 16 '63
U.S. views on U.N. subcommittee's report on South-West Africa; statement, October 30, 1964. M. P. Tree. Dept State Bul 51:760-2 N 23 '64

Swaziland

United Nations observers proposed for guaranteeing independence; with text of resolution on Basutoland, Bechuanaland and Swaziland. U N Rev 10:38-9 Ag '63

Syria

Security council considers dispute between Israel and Syrian Arab Republic. UN Mo Chron 1:3-8 D '64
Security council continues consideration of Israel-Syria dispute. UN Mo Chron 2:28-32 Ja '65
Soviet Union vetoes U.S.-U.K. resolution in Security council on Israel and Syrian complaints; statements, August 28 and September 3, 1963; with the text of a draft resolution. A. E. Stevenson; C. W. Yost. Dept State Bul 49:520-3 S 30 '63
Syria and Israel submit charges to United Nations. U N Rev 10:24-30 O '63
United States urges restraint on Israel and Syria; statement, December 3, 1964. A. E. Stevenson. Dept State Bul 52:27-9 Ja 4 '65

United States

Accomplishments of 18th session of the U.N. General assembly; statement, December 18, 1963. A. E. Stevenson. bibliog f Dept State Bul 50:130-3 Ja 27 '64
Anti-Americanism U.S. pays for. U S News 54:57 F 25 '63
At U.N: showdown, or a deal with reds? il U S News 57:33-4 D 7 '64
Embarrassed American; failure to ratify international human rights conventions. W. Korey. Sat R 47:24-5 O 31 '64
Embarrassed American; failure to ratify international human rights conventions. W. Korey. Sat R 47:24-5 O 31 '64; Reply. E. Schwelb. 47:19-20 N 28 '64
Financial brinkmanship at the U.N. H. Brandon. Sat R 47:6+ N 28 '64
History repeats itself. Nation 200:69 Ja 25 '65
In pursuit of world order, by R. N. Gardner. Review
New Repub 152:24 Ja 9 '65. A. Schlesinger, jr.
Lesson of the Congo. E. Van Den Haag. Nat R 16:773+ S 8 '64
Looking outward; years of crisis at the United Nations, by A. E. Stevenson. Review
Sat R 46:30-1 N 30 '63. K. W. Thompson
Mr Ambassador; with editorial comment. P. Lyon. Holiday 33:35, 36-9+ Je '63
Our stake in the United Nations; address, October 24, 1963. J. J. Sisco. Dept State Bul 49:773-7 N 18 '63
Peaceful revolution; address, December 17, 1963. L. B. Johnson. Vital Speeches 30: 162-4 Ja 1 '64; Same. U N Rev 11:11-12 Ja '64; Excerpts with editorial comment. Nat R 15:554-5 D 31 '63
Report on financial management and the U.N. system released. Dept State Bul 50:67 Ja 13 '64
Security council hears U.S. charge of North Vietnamese attacks; statement, August 5, 1964. A. E. Stevenson. Dept State Bul 51: 272-4 Ag 24 '64
Situation in Panama; White House statements, communiques, Security council debate, and exchange of letters, January 10-16, 1964. Dept State Bul 50:152-6 F 3 '64
Some reflections on the United States in the United Nations; address, October 23, 1964. P. Talbot. Dept State Bul 51:700-5 N 16 '64
Stevenson at the U.N. S. Gervis. Commonweal 77:591-3 Mr 1 '63
Two kinds of politics; address, May 8, 1963. H. Cleveland. Dept State Bul 48:871-6 Je 3 '63
UN chicken home to roost. J. Burnham. Nat R 16:106 F 11 '64
U.N. group celebrates; Nashville chapter of the American association for the United Nations. W. A. Geier. il Christian Cent 81:1444 N 18 '64
United Nations financial crisis; address, March 12, 1963. R. N. Gardner. Dept State Bul 48:535-40 Ap 8 '63
United Nations in crisis; Cuba and the Congo; address, February 23, 1963. R. N. Gardner. Dept State Bul 48:477-81 Ap 1 '63
United Nations: its value to the United States; statement, March 13, 1963. A. E. Stevenson. Dept State Bul 48:522-8 Ap 8 '63
United Nations reconsidered; ed. by R. A. Moore. Review
Science 141:512-13 Ag 9 '63. Q. Wright
U.N. Secretary-General U Thant visits Washington; exchange of greetings, August 6, 1964. L. B. Johnson; Thant. Dept State Bul 51:303-5 Ag 31 '64
U.S. and UN. Nation 196:190 Mr 9 '63
United States in the United Nations; address, October 23, 1964. P. Talbot. Vital Speeches 31:71-4 N 15 '64
U.S. informs U.N. security council on Cuban fishing boat incident; letter to President of the U.S. security council, February 7, 1964. A. E. Stevenson. Dept State Bul 50: 279 F 24 '64

UNITED NATIONS—United States—*Continued*
U.S. makes proposal on financing peace-keeping operations of U.N; statement, September 14, 1964, with text of working paper. F. T. P. Plimpton. Dept State Bul 51:486-9 O 5 '64
U.S. participation in the U.N. during 1963; message to Congress, August 20, 1964. L. B. Johnson. bibliog f Dept State Bul 51:349-50 S 7 '64
U.S.-Russian showdown: will it wreck U.N? il U S News 57:39-40 N 30 '64
United States submits memorandum on U.N. financial crisis; letter with text of U.S. memorandum, October 8, 1964. A. E. Stevenson. Dept State Bul 51:681-90 N 9 '64
U.S. welcomes inquiry of Cambodian charge of chemical operations; text of letter from Ambassador A. E. Stevenson, August 14, 1964. Dept State Bul 51:319 Ag 31 '64
Vietnam: miscalculations and alternatives. N. Cousins. Sat R 47:32 D 12 '64
What every U.N. critic should know. A. Larson. Sat R 46:13-15+ Je 15 '63; Reply. L. R. Ward. 46:15 Jl 13 '63
Why do we take it? J. Burnham. Nat R 17:20 Ja 12 '65
Why U.N. looks different to the U.S. now; with chart. il U S News 57:42-3 D 14 '64

Viet Nam (Democratic Republic)
Security council hears U.S. charge of North Vietnamese attacks; statement, August 5, 1964. A. E. Stevenson. Dept State Bul 51:272-4 Ag 24 '64

Viet Nam (Republic)
Echoes out of Saigon; concerning report of fact-finding mission to South Viet Nam. Time 83:58 Mr 6 '64
General assembly sends fact-finding mission to South Viet-Nam. U N Rev 10:6-8 N '63
International protection of human rights; visit by a United Nations mission. F. Volio-Jimenez. UN Mo Chron 1:75-81 D '64
Inviting a judgment. Time 82:43-4 O 18 '63
Report of the Security council mission. UN Mo Chron 1:24-8 Ag '64
U.S. comments on U.N. mission's Cambodia-Viet-Nam report; letter, September 9, 1964. A. E. Stevenson. Dept State Bul 51:527-9 O 12 '64
Vietnam: alternative to disaster. D. Grant. il Nation 198:521-3 My 25 '64
Vietnam: the UN peeks in. B. Pilkington. Nation 197:273-5 N 2 '63

West Irian
Transfer of authority over West New Guinea, West Irian. il U N Rev 10:6-8 My '63
Transition near in West New Guinea (West Irian) il U N Rev 10:29 Ap '63

Yemen
Another job for the U.N. Time 81:31-2 My 10 '63
Backing and filling; United Nations Yemen observation mission. il Newsweek 62:56 N 11 '63
Course of events in Yemen. U N Rev 10:22-4 O '63
Mess in Yemen. il Time 82:39 S 13 '63
Method to confusion. Newsweek 62:45-6 S 16 '63
Record of the month. UN Mo Chron 1:51-3 Je '64
Record of the month; consideration of British air attack on Yemeni territory by Security council. UN Mo Chron 1:14-20 My '64
Record of the month; Special committee of twenty-four. UN Mo Chron 1:21-9 My '64
Secretary-General's report on the functioning of observation mission; summary. UN Mo Chron 1:28-30 Ag '64
Secretary-General's report on the functioning of observation mission. Thant. UN Mo Chron 1:34-6 O '64
U.N. sends observation mission to Yemen; statement, June 11, 1963; with text of resolution. A. E. Stevenson. Dept State Bul 49:71 Jl 8 '63
War in the desert: big fight over a small country. il U S News 55:62-3 Jl 15 '63
Yemen observation mission. il U N Rev 10:16-20 Jl '63

Zambia
Malawi, Malta, and Zambia admitted to U.N. membership; statement, December 2, 1964. A. E. Stevenson. Dept State Bul 51:919-20 D 28 '64
Security council recommends Malta and Zambia for U.N. membership; statement, October 30, 1964. C. W. Yost. Dept State Bul 51:759 N 23 '64

Zanzibar
Independence without delay is hope for four territories. U N Rev 10:35-8 Ag '63
Kenya, Zanzibar admitted to United Nations; with Secretary-General's statement. il U N Rev 11:12-13 Ja '64

UNITED NATIONS center, New York. See United Nations—Headquarters

UNITED NATIONS children's choir of Los Angeles. See Choirs

UNITED NATIONS children's fund
Christmas story; UNICEF Christmas cards and the John Birch society in California. Newsweek 64:30 D 21 '64
Hallowing Halloween; UNICEF trick-or-treaters. Christian Cent 81:1231 O 7 '64
New experiment in education; picture section. UN Mo Chron 1:87-92 D '64
Record of the month. UN Mo Chron 1:59-60 Jl '64
UNICEF greeting cards (cont) il UNESCO Courier 16:28-9 N '63
UNICEF meeting in Bangkok. il U N Rev 11:35-6 Mr '64
World with our readers. Holiday 36:59 D '64

UNITED NATIONS conference of Asian economic planners
Conference of Asian economic planners meets in Bangkok. UN Mo Chron 1:87 N '64

UNITED NATIONS conference on consular relations
Consular relations; convention unanimously adopted in Vienna. U N Rev 10:52-6 Je '63

UNITED NATIONS conference on the application of science and technology for the benefit of the less developed areas
Haves and have-nots. Newsweek 61:87 F 25 '63
How to feed millions. W. Davis. Sci N L 83:131 Mr 2 '63
President expresses hope for success of U.N. science conference; statement, January 25, 1963; message to opening session. J. F. Kennedy. Dept State Bul 48:302 F 25 '63
Science and technology. U N Rev 11:28-30 Ap '64
Science for progress; symposium. il UNESCO Courier 16:4-63+ Jl '63
Sharing the wealth of science. il Bsns W p89-90+ Mr 23 '63
UN common knowledge market. W. Davis. Sci N L 83:99 F 16 '63
UNCSAT, a stock-taking conference on science and technology. il U N Rev 10:14-15 F '63
United States to participate in U.N. science conference; statement, January 7, 1963; with U.S. representatives. D. Rusk. Dept State Bul 48:188-9 F 4 '63
Use of population as weapon. W. Davis. il Sci N L 83:115 F 23 '63
Wasting the taxpayers' money; a senator's report. S. M. Young. U S News 54:14 Mr 4 '63

UNITED NATIONS conference on trade and development
After the U.N. trade conference: lessons and portents. S. Weintraub. For Affairs 43:37-50 O '64
Aid, trade and economic development; symposium. For Affairs 42:210-54 Ja '64
Better deal. New Repub 150:9 My 9 '64
Evaluation of the conference on trade and development; summary of report to the United Nations Secretary-General. R. Prebisch. UN Mo Chron 1:55-7 Ag '64
General assembly establishes new institutional machinery for international trade. UN Mo Chron 2:33-5 Ja '65
Geneva conference. G. de Zéndegui. Américas 16:inside cover Ap '64
Haves and have-nots. H. Miller. New Repub 150:6-7 Mr 28 '64
In Geneva: global collective bargaining. il Newsweek 63:31-4 Ap 6 '64
New forum for the have-nots. Bsns W p 146 Je 20 '64
Perspective on the United Nations conference on trade and development; address, February 21, 1964. G. G. Johnson. Dept State Bul 50:410-15 Mr 16 '64
Plans for international trade conference endorsed by Assembly. il U N Rev 10:31-9+ F '63
Policies for trade and development. R. M. Stern. bibliog f il Int Concil 548:3-63 My '64
Pushing for more trade help. il Bsns W p 122+ F 29 '64
Record of the month. il UN Mo Chron 1:48-62 My; 58-64 Je; 49-52 Jl '64

UNITED NATIONS conference on trade and development—*Continued*
Robin Hood at Geneva. Time 83:93 Ap 3 '64
Round one. Newsweek 63:37 Je 29 '64
Shift of the compass. Commonweal 80:440-1 Jl 3 '64
Spirit of conciliation. R. Prebisch. UN Mo Chron 1:71-7 Jl '64
Toward a new trade policy for development; condensation of report. R. Prebisch. U N Rev 11:21-3 Ap '64
Trade is people, too. B. Pilkington. Christian Cent 81:610+ My 6 '64
Trends at the trade conference. UN Mo Chron 1:85-100 My '64
Underdeveloped get together. il Time 83:89 F 21 '64
U.N. conference on trade and development. Dept State Bul 50:557 Ap 6 '64
United Nations conference on trade and development. il U N Rev 11:21-4 Mr '64
United Nations conference on trade and development adopts final act; preamble and recommendations adopted on June 16, 1964. bibliog f Dept State Bul 51:150-67 Ag 3 '64
United States delegations to international conferences; Preparatory committee. Dept State Bul 48:264-5 F 18 '63
When poor meets rich. il Time 83:89 Je 19 '64
World trade issues. Sr Schol 84:22+ Ap 10 '64

UNITED NATIONS correspondents association
United Nations correspondent's circle. M. Cartwright. il Negro Hist Bul 27:93-4 Ja '64

UNITED NATIONS day
United Nations day, 1964; messages. C. S. Rodriguez and Thant. UN Mo Chron 1:I-III O '64
United Nations day, 1964; proclamation. L. B. Johnson. Dept State Bul 50:803 My 18 '64
United Nations day 1963; excerpts from addresses. Thant; C. Sosa-Rodriquez. il U N Rev 10:27+ N '63
United Nations day, 1963; proclamation, April 20, 1963. J. F. Kennedy. Dept State Bul 48:806 My 20 '63

UNITED NATIONS educational, scientific and cultural organization
Cost of literacy. E. Moon. Library J 89:1515 Ap 1 '64
Education in the developing nations. R. Maheu; J. A. Joyce. il Sat R 47:52-7+ Ag 15 '64
Fight against illiteracy: towards a world campaign; with excerpts from resolution. R. Maheu. UN Mo Chron 1:82-6 D '64
History of mankind; excerpts. il UNESCO Courier 16:4-19 Je '63
International cooperation in education, science, culture; 12th general conference of UNESCO, Paris, November 9-December 12, 1962. L. D. Battle. Dept State Bul 48:954-7 Je 17 '63
International standardization of library statistics. F. L. Schick. ALA Bul 58:1011-13 D '64
International youth conference in France. il Sch & Soc 92:365-6 N 28 '64
Letter from Paris; report on UNESCO philosophical colloquy to mark the end of L'Annee Kierkegaard. Genêt. New Yorker 40:170 My 16 '64
Methods of teaching about human rights; excerpt from Teaching human rights. NEA J 52:53 N '63
Prehistory and the beginnings of civilization, by J. Hawkes and L. Woolley. Review
Nation 197:55-6 Jl 27 '63. G. Daniel
Progress report on UNESCO. W. Benton. il Sat R 47:16-18+ Mr 7 '64
Reports on UNESCO's expansion. Sch & Soc 91:368+ N 30 '63
Results of Unesco's 12th general conference. M. S. Adiseshiah. Sch & Soc 91:198-9 Ap 20 '63
True Unesco; address, November 15, 1962. R. Maheu. Sch & Soc 91:70-2 F 9 '63
UNESCO and human rights for all. il UNESCO Courier 16:6-11 D '63
UNESCO: assessment and promise, by G. N. Shuster. Review
Sat R 47:77-8 Ja 4 '64. R. H. Heindel
UNESCO: Director General stakes out broader responsibilities in applying research to development. J. Walsh. Science 142:470-1 O 25 '63
UNESCO expands its science programme. il UNESCO Courier 16:22-3 Jl '63
UNESCO general conference meets at Paris; U.S. delegates. Dept State Bul 51:715 N 16 '64
UNESCO in the Congo. G. Fullerton. il UNESCO Courier 16:4-11 N '63
Unesco in the decade of development. E. Sochor. Sch & Soc 91:278-80 O 5 '63
Unesco science and technology; summary of report. Bul Atomic Sci 20:31-4 N '64
Unesco's adult literacy program. Sch & Soc 93:4 Ja 9 '65
World programme for education, science and culture; 1963-1964. il UNESCO Courier 16:30-2 Mr '63
See also
International conference on public education
International music council
International voluntary workcamps
United States national commission for UNESCO

Division of libraries, documentation and archives
Great step forward. S. Samarasinghe. il Library J 89:4473-5 N 15 '64

Headquarters
Dig UNESCO must, for a better Paris. il Arch Forum 118:9 F '63

Institute for education
International evaluation of educational achievement. Sch & Soc 91:380-1 N 30 '63

UNITED NATIONS emergency force. See United Nations—Armed forces

UNITED NATIONS food and agriculture organization. See Food and agriculture organization of the United Nations

UNITED NATIONS general assembly. See United Nations—General assembly

UNITED NATIONS human rights day and week. See Human rights day and week

UNITED NATIONS international atomic energy agency. See International atomic energy agency

UNITED NATIONS international children's emergency fund. See United Nations children's fund

UNITED NATIONS international conference on the peaceful uses of atomic energy. See International conference on the peaceful uses of atomic energy, 3d, Geneva, 1964

UNITED NATIONS international school
UN international school. C. Holm. il Parents Mag 39:66-7+ F '64

UNITED NATIONS interpreters. See United Nations—Employees

UNITED NATIONS relief and works agency for Palestine refugees in the Near East
Arab refugee today. F. L. Hutchison. Christian Cent 81:823-6 Je 24 '64
Arab refugees: a changing problem. D. Peretz. For Affairs 41:558-70 Ap '63
Hope for Palestine refugees. H. Walz. Christian Cent 80:306-7 Mr 6 '63; Discussion. 80:781-2 Je 12 '63
Palestine refugees. il U N Rev 10:50-61 F '63
Palestine refugees in the Near East. U N Rev 10:39-40 D '63
Pledges for activities of UNRWA in 1964. il U N Rev 11:26-8 Ja '64
$32.5 million pledged for UNRWA. il U N Rev 10:62 F '63
U.N. asks concilation commission to continue efforts with Arab refugees; statements, December 11, 14 and 18, 1962; with statement by E. Jackson, and text of resolution. C. T. Rowan. Dept State Bul 48:99-104 Ja 21 '63

UNITED NATIONS review
Special committee of twenty-four discusses United Nations review. U N Rev 10:31-2 My '63

UNITED NATIONS science conference. See United Nations conference on the application of science and technology for the benefit of the less developed areas

UNITED NATIONS seminars. See Seminars

UNITED packinghouse, food and allied workers
Packing up an Armour packing plant, Sioux City. Bsns W p80+ Jl 20 '63

UNITED packinghouse workers of America. See United packinghouse, food and allied workers

UNITED Presbyterian church in the United States of America
Blake's second thoughts; possibility of union. il Time 85:89 Ja 29 '65
Church catches up. C. W. Thomas. Negro Hist Bul 28:19-20 O '64
Church keeps hospitals open. Cnristian Cent 80:1022 Ag 21 '63
Church strives to keep hospitals open. Christian Cent 80:854 Jl 3 '63

UNITED Presbyterian church in the United States of America—*Continued*
Clear light on church-state relations. H. E. Fey. Christian Cent 80:735-6 Je 5 '63
Drawing the line: between the proper powers of church and state. il Newsweek 61:78-9 Je 3 '63
In the van; Negro moderator. Time 83:70 My 29 '64
Presbyterians' choice; Negro minister elected as moderator. Newsweek 63:82 Je 1 '64
Presbyterians elect Negro moderator. Christian Cent 81:725 Je 3 '64
Presbyterians on church and state. J. H. Smylie. Christian Cent 80:610-14 My 8 '63
Rockefeller minister faces discipline. Christian Cent 80:668-9 My 22 '63
School prayers? the Presbyterians say no. U S News 54:10 Je 3 '63
Strong stands; General assembly in Des Moines. il Time 81:58 My 31 '63
United Presbyterian general assembly. P. R. Carlson. Christian Cent 81:812+ Je 17 '64
United Presbyterians: prophecy vs. tradition. J. R. Fry. Christian Cent 80:1235-7 O 9 '63: Discussion. 80:1518 D 4 '63

UNITED Presbyterian general assembly. See United Presbyterian church in the United States of America

UNITED press international
Quarterbacking a nation's news. J. F. Fixx. il Sat R 46:48-9 Ag 10 '63
Straws of an ill wind; bias in news presentation. R. L. Tobin. Sat R 46:41-2 Jl 13 '63

UNITED Republic of Tanganyika and Zanzibar. See Tanzania

UNITED rubber, cork, linoleum and plastic workers of America
Why the pressure is off wages; unemployment is high. il Bsns W p 101-2+ Mr 9 '63

UNITED society of believers. See Shakers

UNITED STATES
Affluent slumland; the American landscape. E. Sevareid. il Recreation 58:4 Ja '65
Ambassador Kohler makes Fourth of July address on Moscow TV; tr. of address. F. D. Kohler. Dept State Bul 51:108-9 Jl 27 '64
American character; address, December 5, 1963. J. W. Fulbright. Vital Speeches 30:164-7 Ja 1 '64
American image. See issues of Senior scholastic to September 27, 1963
American personality; excerpt from American aspects. D. W. Brogan. Sat R 48:34-5 Ja 2 '65
American way of life: as Lyndon Johnson sees it; interview. L. B. Johnson. il U S News 55:112-14 D 9 '63
As others see us; ed. by J. F. Fixx. Sat R 47:31-3+ O 24; 35-7 N 7; 31-3 N 28; 43-4 D 12 '64; 48:33-4 Ja 2; 41-2 Ja 30 '65
Attack on Leviathan, by D. Davidson. Review
Nat R 14:498 Je 18 '63. R. Kirk
Future that young people will face in America. il U S News 57:50-2+ Ag 17 '64
Goal of the United States; text of speech to have been delivered before the Dallas citizens council, Dallas, Tex, November 22, 1963. J. F. Kennedy. Vital Speeches 30:105-7 D 1 '63
Goals Johnson will set for the country. il U S News 55:36-7 D 9 '63
God's own junkyard, by P. Blake. Review
Commonweal 80:296-8 My 29 '64. W. Sheed
Great society. L. B. Johnson. il Sat Eve Post 237:30-1 O 31 '64
Have we learned our lessons? Kennedy's assassination. Christian Cent 80:1567-8 D 18 '63
How can we serve? address, July 4, 1964. R. Y. McGinnis. Vital Speeches 30:657-9 Ag 15 '64
Illusion of time stopped; mood following the elections. il Newsweek 64:33 N 23 '64
Johnson: three goals prosperity, justice, peace; address, September 7, 1964. L. B. Johnson. il U S News 57:115-16 S 21 '64; Same with title Wants of the people. Vital Speeches 30:742-3 O 1 '64
Just seven years from now: coming changes in America. il U S News 55:62-5 D 2 '63
Look at America eleven years from now. U S News 56:15 My 11 '64
Mood of the land. il Time 82:9-10 D 20 '63
New aim for America; address, February 4, 1964. P. Howard. Vital Speeches 30:339-43 Mr 15 '64
1965: another good year? il U S News 58:21-4, 54-63 Ja 4 '65
1964: the affluent year? il U S News 56:38-47, 64-72, 98-9 Ja 13 '64
1964's eventful non-event. Christian Cent 82:37 Ja 13 '65
Of man & the moon; most immediate challenges. il Time 84:17 Ag 7 '64
Oh, it's a sad case, America is. W. F. Rickenbacker. Nat R 16:545-6 Je 30 '64
Our national goals: the hard choices. L. Hazard. Harvard Bsns R 41:22-4+ My '63
Our system of government; address, November 28, 1963. L. B. Johnson. Vital Speeches 30:131-2 D 15 '63
Outlook for greatness. A. Nevins. il Sat R 47:51-3+ Ag 29 '64
Power and responsibility. America 109:761 D 14 '63
Power of free choice; address, December 3, 1963. C. G. Mortimer. Vital Speeches 30:214-16 Ja 15 '64
Sky above, the mud below; American image. Newsweek 61:25 My 27 '63
Spring without fever. il Bsns W p23-5 Mr 30 '63
State of the Union. il Newsweek 65:15-19 Ja 11 '65
Statement, October 26, 1963. J. F. Kennedy. Sr Schol 83:1T D 6 '63
Strengthening America's heritage; address, April 17, 1964. P. F. Osborn, 3d. Vital Speeches 30:600-3 Jl 15 '64
Thoughts over the Pacific. W. J. Dalton. America 111:383 O 3 '64
Toast to America; address, May 13, 1964. J. G. Chatham. America 110:718-19 My 23 '64
Trends: the state of the Nation. F. Morley. See issues of Nation's business
U.S.A. revisited. J. Dos Passos. Atlan 213:47-54 Ap '64
U.S. thirty-seven years from now. il U S News 54:70-1 F 11 '63
Way people live today. il U S News 55:56-61 N 11 '63
What kind of nation are we? American character. A. Hacker. il N Y Times Mag p23+ D 8 '63
What the future holds for America: as the President's idea men see it; symposium. il U S News 56:40-4+ Je 22 '64
What's eating us? L. J. Halle. New Repub 151:17-20 S 19 '64; Reply. D. R. Ayer. 151:38 O 3 '64
What's right with America; as observers abroad see it. il U S News 57:44-50 S 14 '64
What's right with America; as observers abroad see it. il U S News 57:44-50 S 14 '64; Same abr. Read Digest 85:61-4 D '64
Whence and whither. G. R. Wilson. Flying 74:24 Mr '64
See also
Americans
States (United States)
also names of sections, states, e.g. Northeastern states; *also* subhead United States under various subjects, e.g. Education—United States

Advanced research projects agency
See United States—Defense, Department of—Advanced research projects agency

Advisory commission on international, educational and cultural affairs
Advisory commission reports on exchange program; press release, April 5, 1963. Dept State Bul 48:617 Ap 22 '63
Advisory commission to survey Hawaii's East-West center. Dept State Bul 49:684 O 28 '63
Advisory group submits report on cultural presentations. Dept State Bul 48:46 Ja 14 '63
Larsen report on the East-West center recommendations. Sat R 47:46 Jl 18 '64

Advisory commission on narcotic and drug abuse
Bridge for addicts. America 110:213 F 15 '64

Advisory council on the arts
New national Advisory council on the arts. R. H. Smith. Pub W 184:44 Jl 1 '63

Agency for international development
AID: a new research director and an activated advisory apparatus relied on to get research moving. J. Walsh. Science 141:412-13 Ag 2 '63
AID: almost everyone favors research on development problems but going has not been smooth. J. Walsh. Science 140:792-5 My 17 '63
AID analysis; Viet Nam (Republic) New Repub 151:4 S 12 '64
AID closes mission in Haiti. Dept State Bul 49:297 Ag 19 '63
AID, diagnosed to death. H. H. Miller. New Repub 150:14-16 Ja 18 '64

UNITED STATES—Agency for international development—*Continued*
Aid for AID. Reporter 29:14+ S 12 '63
Aid for AID; cooperation of National academy of sciences. Newsweek 62:56-7 Jl 8 '63
AID requested to inform Congress of re-obligation of prior year funds; text of a memorandum to the Administrator, January 8, 1963. Dept State Bul 48:185-6 F 4 '63
AID summarizes position on 1964 budget figures; memorandum to Secretary Rusk, May 7, 1963. D. E. Bell. Dept State Bul 48:881-3 Je 3 '63
American forestry abroad. H. S. Kernan. Am For 70:38-9+ Ap '64
Anchor man for foreign aid; with editorial comment. Bsns W p50-1+, 116 My 11 '63
Betrayal of foreign aid; no surrender. America 110:66 Ja 18 '64
Brazilian brings home the bacon. il Bsns W p82+ Mr 30 '63
Can a poor nation grow on an empty stomach? not until food production is increased. il Bsns W p56-7 D 26 '64
David Bell and foreign aid. Atlan 211:8 Je '63
David E. Bell becomes administrator of AID; statements, December 21, 1962. D. Rusk; D. E. Bell. Dept State Bul 48:65-7 Ja 14 '63
Development financing and the Alliance for progress; statement, December 2, 1964. P. Glaessner. Dept State Bul 51:881-4 D 21 '64
Europe helps out in Latin America. Bsns W p 128 Ap 13 '63
Foreign aid and the liberal dissent. I. Frank. New Repub 152:17-22 Ja 23 '65
Foreign aid fiasco. P. Duke. il Reporter 30:20-5 Ja 16 '64; Discussion. 30:6 F 13; 6+ F 27 '64
Foreign aid is a good long-term policy tool. Life 54:4 Ap 12 '63
Foreign aid: saved by the bell? J. Kraft. Harper 226:73-6+ F '63
Foreign aid: the hard line. il Newsweek 61:27-9 Je 3 '63
Foreign aid: the Johnson round. P. Duke. Reporter 30:25-6 Mr 26 '64
Foreign programs for universities. D. Wolfle. Science 145:235 Jl 17 '64
Golden rule. A. Brynes. New Repub 148:20-1 Mr 9 '63
How AID gets its shows on the road. il Bsns W p78+ D 5 '64
Inter-American center at Loyola. C. J. Nc-Naspy. America 112:36 Ja 9 '65
Operation niños. G. Kroloff. il Sch Life 46:9-11 Je '64
Orange is squeezed; a report on one failure in Panama. M. Kempton. New Repub 150:15-18 Ja 25 '64
Peace corps for business; management aid overseas. Bsns W p66 N 23 '63
Population planning: missions told that U.S. is now receptive to requests for some assistance. D. S. Greenberg. Science 140:1291 Je 21 '63
Revamping foreign aid; Clay commission's report. Commonweal 78:36 Ap 5 '63
Struggle over foreign aid. V. C. Ferkiss. America 108:488-90 Ap 13 '63
This month's feature: Congress and the foreign aid program. Cong Digest 42:163-92 Je '63
What's ahead for foreign aid. il Bsns W p50-1 Jl 6 '63

Agriculture, Department of

Agriculture and USDA policy; address December 5, 1963. G. L. Mehren. Vital Speeches 30:155-7 D 15 '63
Archival product of a century of federal assistance to agriculture. H. T. Pinkett. bibliog f Am Hist R 69:689-706 Ap '64
Hard row to hoe. il Time 81:21-5 Ap 5 '63
Ill-advised secrecy; refusal to make public names of pesticides. Consumer Rep 28:365-6 Ag '63
Let's invest in people not land; with editorial comment. T. W. Schultz. Suc Farm 61:6, 33 Jl '63
Momentous problem; finding a place to live. Sci N L 84:301 N 9 '63
Now the non-farmer asks for parity. E. Higbee. il N Y Times Mag p 15+ Je 2 '63
Our man in Amsterdam; U.S. food and agriculture exhibition. New Yorker 39:24-6 D 21 '63
Senator Ribicoff would end protest registration of insecticides. J. Prokop. il Am For 69:7+ O '63
Wedding on the Potomac. P. M. Tilden. Natur Hist 72:64-6 Je '63

See also
United States—Agricultural research service
United States—Federal extension service
United States—Forest service
United States—Soil conservation service

Forest service

See United States—Forest service

Library

Agricultural library network; role of NAL or National agricultural library. K. B. Payne. bibliog il Library J 88:4143-8 N 1 '63

Agricultural research service

Unpalatable food for thought. P. M. Tilden. Nat Parks Mag 38:2 My '64

Air force

Air force candidate Goldwater. R. D. Senter. New Repub 151:8 S 5 '64
Air force coins a word: aerospace. D. Burnham. Reporter 28:32-3 Je 6 '63
Air force dedicates second ARIS. C. D. LaFond. il Miss & Roc 13:34-5 Jl 22 '63
Air force defends Minuteman program. F. G. McGuire. Miss & Roc 12:18 My 13 '63
Air force: getting down to new business. T. D. White. Newsweek 61:37 My 13 '63
Air force given space laboratory mission; with editorial comment. L. Booda. il Aviation W 79:25, 30-1 D 16 '63
Air force hopes to ease cutback for active reserve, guard units. C. Brownlow. Aviation W 81:18-19 D 21 '64
Air force launched fifty-six payloads last year. il Aviation W 80:53 F 10 '64
Air force picks three sites for space landings. il Miss & Roc 12:34 Je 10 '63
Air force to manage PMR. Miss & Roc 13:13+ N 25 '63
Air force to take over PMR. F. G. McGuire. il Miss & Roc 13:12 Ag 12 '63
AF widens manned flight role. W. Burkett. Miss & Roc 14:12 Je 15 '64
Air force will have small role in Gemini. Aviation W 79:225+ Jl 22 '63
AF will have special needs in Gemini. H. M. David. il Miss & Roc 12:31-2 Ap 8 '63
Airship studied as booster carrier. F. G. McGuire. Miss & Roc 12:16 Mr 4 '63
Army takes to the air. il Time 81:17 Mr 22 '63
Army, USAF testing air support roles. C. Brownlow. il Aviation W 81:77+ S 21 '64
Barry's bomber gap. R. D. Senter. il New Repub 151:9-10 S 12 '64
Can in the sky. W. J. Coughlin. Miss & Roc 13:54 D 16 '63
Challenge met in Minuteman management. R. Twiss. il Miss & Roc 13:36 Jl 22 '63
Compilation of summary reports due to begin in Project forecast. Aviation W 79:28 S 9 '63
Congress initially favorable to air force management of MOL. H. M. David. Miss & Roc 13:16 D 16 '63
DOD may manage national space station. E. H. Kolcum. Aviation W 79:26-7 S 16 '63
DOD relents; air force seeks pilots. Aviation W 79:27 N 18 '63
Fighting to keep foothold in space. Bsns W p29 Ap 13 '63
Forecasting the wild blue yonder. R. Hotz. Aviation W 78:17 My 6 '63
473L to aid in worldwide USAF control. B. Miller. il Aviation W 81:49+ Ag 3 '64
Goldwater and the bomber-gap. R. D. Senter. New Repub 150:10-12 Ja 25 '64
Hitchhikers; token participation in Gemini manned space flight program. Newsweek 61:48 F 4 '63
How to survive at sea; Sea survival school. K. Brown. il Pop Mech 120:112-17+ N '63
McNamara spells out AF Gemini role; with editorial comment by W. J. Coughlin. F. G. McGuire. Miss & Roc 12:15, 46 Ap 1 '63
Military recreation: a family affair; Aviano air base in Italy. E. L. Ericson. il Recreation 56:373-4 O '63
Need to know. W. J. Coughlin. Miss & Roc 13:46 S 2 '63
New AF/Mitre lab may alter concepts. M. Getler. il Miss & Roc 13:36-7 Jl 1 '63
New bomber money prospect improves. Aviation W 80:29 Mr 2 '64
New ESD laboratory tests data concepts. Aviation W 79:89+ D 16 '63
Our man in Saigon. il Ebony 18:121-2+ Je '63
Rebellion in the air force. R. D. Senter. New Repub 149:13-15 S 28 '63; Reply with rejoinder. J. F. Loosbrock. 149:52+ N 9 '63
Recovery site selection debated. F. G. McGuire. Miss & Roc 13:14-15 Jl 8 '63
Services delay satellite disclosure. Aviation W 79:25 Jl 29 '63
Station holds key to USAF's man-in-space mission. D. Fink. il Aviation W 80:112-13+ Mr 16 '64
Strike command to test air support plan. C. Brownlow. il Aviation W 81:63-4+ O 26 '64

UNITED STATES—Air force—*Continued*
SACked; air force weight regulation. Newsweek 63:74 Mr 2 '64
Symposium points to more AF emphasis on hardware. H. M. David. il Miss & Roc 12:34-5 Ap 1 '63
SPO officer voices confidence in future of Titan III program; remarks. R. M. Herrington. Miss & Roc 12:13 Mr 18 '63
TSQ-47 traffic system undergoes test; Air force communications service. P. J. Klass. il Aviation W 79:69+ N 11 '63
USAF, army air roles evolving slowly. L. Booda. Aviation W 78:30-1 My 27 '63
USAF battles for new manned aerial space systems. G. Wilson. il Aviation W 80:78-83 Mr 16 '64
USAF, DOD spar over advanced ICBMs. I. Stone. il Aviation W 80:143-5+ Mr 16 '64
USAF Electronics technology lab plans extensive bionics studies. Aviation W 78:109+ Je 24 '63
USAF gives space station top priority. il Aviation W 79:214-15+ Jl 22 '63
USAF implements headquarters changes. L. Booda. Aviation W 78:33 Ap 22 '63
USAF may fly manned station in Titan 3 development program. Aviation W 80:28 F 10 '64
USAF pushes Vietnamese pilot training. L. Booda. il Aviation W 80:94-5+ Ap 20 '64
USAF school trains future space pilots; Aerospace research pilot school. il Aviation W 79:253+ Jl 22 '63
USAF wages space, weapon fund battles. L. Booda. il Aviation W 78:76-9 Mr 11 '63
USAF will test ground support concepts. E. J. Bulban. Aviation W 80:23 Je 1 '64
Zuckert gives views on aerospace issues; interview. E. M. Zuckert. Aviation W 80:72-3 Mr 2 '64
See also
Air bases
Airplanes, Military—United States

Aerospace medical division

See United States—Air force—Systems command

Aerospace research, Office of

AF outlines five-year research plan. D. C. Breasted. Miss & Roc 13:21 O 21 '63

Air commando groups

Air force expands Air commando forces. L. Booda. il Aviation W 78:48-9+ Je 3 '63
Civic action by the air force; address, October 19, 1963. C. E. LeMay. Vital Speeches 30:150-2 D 15 '63

Air national guard

See United States—Air national guard

Air proving grounds

See Proving grounds

Air rescue service

Air rescue service pushes modernization to handle expanded search-recovery role. G. Alexander. il Aviation W 81:40-3+ D 21 '64
Hook-and-ladder helicopters. E. Tozer. il Pop Sci 184:114-16 F '64

Air training command

USAF plans civilian pilot training role. E. J. Bulban. Aviation W 81:23-4 Ag 3 '64

Appropriations and expenditures

AF details $1-billion R&D request. Miss & Roc 12:14 Mr 4 '63
DOD ponders new cut in solid funds. H. Taylor. Miss & Roc 13:16-17 Jl 8 '63
Extra RS-70, submarine money included in defense authorization. Aviation W 78:38-9 Mr 18 '63
GAO praises USAF for savings. Aviation W 79:32 Jl 15 '63
GAO says air force overstated plug needs. Aviation W 78:64-5 Je 3 '63
MMRBM faces new budget slash. H. M. David. Miss & Roc 14:14 F 17 '64
New bomber funds win early approval. K. Johnsen. Aviation W 80:26-7 F 24 '64
Reduced supervision credited for Agena D savings. Aviation W 78:179 Je 10 '63

Communication systems

Air force takes over Big Rally II communications system. C. D. LaFond. il Miss & Roc 15:24-5 O 12 '64

Education

Duel with nature; U.S. air force survival and special training school. P. Czura. il Field & S 69:52-3+ Jl '64
See also
United States air force academy

Forces in Europe

Cold-blooded murder; T-39 shot down by Russians. il Time 83:20-1 F 7 '64
Handover at Helmstedt; released U.S. fliers. il Newsweek 63:44 Ap 6 '64
120-mile error; reconnaissance bomber with crew of three, forced down in East Germany. Time 83:32 Mr 20 '64
Political pawns? shooting down of the three U.S. airmen over East Germany. Newsweek 63:22+ Mr 30 '64
Problems in navigation; crew of an RB-66 held by Russians. il Newsweek 63:38 Mr 23 '64
USAF expands East German buffer zone. Aviation W 80:19 Ap 6 '64
Very regrettable; T-39 jet-training plane shot down. il Newsweek 63:34 F 10 '64

Forces in Viet Nam (Republic)

American tragedy in Vietnam; why GI's die but can't win; with analysis by M. S. Johnson. il U S News 56:40-2 My 11 '64
Captain's last letters from Vietnam; excerpts. E. G. Shank, jr. il U S News 56:46-9 My 4 '64; Life 56:34B-34D+ My 8 '64; Discussion. 56:30 Je 5 '64
In the air, on the ground. il Newsweek 65:39-40 Ja 25 '65
McNamara cool toward COIN proposals; navy counter-insurgency aircraft program. G. C. Wilson. Aviation W 80:16-17 Je 1 '64
McNamara faces Vietnam aircraft probe. D. E. Fink. Aviation W 80:31-2 My 18 '64
Manner of speaking; concerning a report of Laurence Barrett in the Herald tribune. J. Ciardi. Sat R 47:15 Je 13 '64; Reply. L. Barrett. 47:16 Jl 25 '64
New concepts sought for aging hardware. C. Brownlow. il Aviation W 81:65+ O 19 '64
Peanut air force. Time 83:28 My 22 '64
Quiet escalation; U.S. air strikes in Laos. il Time 85:22 Ja 22 '65
Search for new plane. il Bsns W p34 My 23 '64
USAF girds for counterblow in Vietnam. il Aviation W 81:16-18 Ag 10 '64
Vinson backs DOD in aircraft probe. Aviation W 80:25 My 25 '64

History

This week in history. il Sr Schol 83:9 O 4 '63

Logistics command

USAF logistics evolves to meet change in weapons technology. il Aviation W 81:16-45+ mid-D '64

Management

AF officers to bolster Apollo management. W. J. Normyle. Aviation W 81:22 Ag 24 '64
Data-processing subsystem to refine air force's 473L Pentagon complex. R. Pay. il Miss & Roc 15:26-7 Ag 17 '64
Development, procurement roles split in USAF headquarters shift. L. Booda. Aviation W 78:34 F 11 '63
See also
United States—Air force—Systems command

Medical and sanitary affairs

Doctor with one foot in space. K. N. Anderson. il Todays Health 42:32-5+ D '64

Procurement

Air force minimized engineering changes on StarLifter. J. R. Ashlock. il Aviation W 79:68-9+ S 2 '63
Air force studies product-life warranty. W. H. Gregory. Aviation W 81:24 N 2 '64
AFSC seeks advanced programs streamlining. Aviation W 79:95+ O 28 '63
Air force weighs ultimate cost system. W. H. Gregory. il Aviation W 80:71+ Je 22 '64
DOD considers further awards in 156-in. solid-rocket motor program. R. Hawkes. il Miss & Roc 15:16-17 D 21 '64
Douglas has NASA station study. Aviation W 79:37 D 9 '63
Scorpio engine heads jobs at Rocket propulsion laboratory. W. E. Wilks. il Miss & Roc 13:24-5+ D 9 '63
Three firms awarded space station studies. Aviation W 80:27 F 10 '64
USAF contracts. See issues of Aviation week & space technology
USAF logistics evolves to meet change in weapons technology. il Aviation W 81:16-45+ mid-D '64
USAF seeks tighter pre-contracting work. Aviation W 81:71 O 26 '64

UNITED STATES—Air force—*Continued*

Recreation

Air force assesses its recreation centers. A. Todd. Recreation 57:342-3 S '64
Airforce launches new youth programs. H. Rathner; J. A. Turner; R. M. Dula. il Recreation 57:518-20 D '64

Relations with civilians

See United States—Armed forces—Relations with civilians

Scientific research, Office of

AFOSR awards (title varies) See occasional issues of Aviation week & space technology

Site activation task force

Proud men; Site activation task force. W. J. Coughlin. Miss & Roc 12:50 F 11 '63

Special investigation, Office of

Air force murder case; Nancy Johnson and her son. J. Foisie. Nation 196:285-7 Ap 6 '63
Innocent's grim ordeal; murder of wife of airman Alec Johnson, Mountain Home air force base, Idaho. J. R. Phelan. il Sat Eve Post 236:62-7 F 2 '63

Strategic air command

Death of the B-47. il U S News 55:66 O 21 '63
465L programming needs cause problems. P. J. Klass. Aviation W 81:14-15 Jl 13 '64
How safe is Fail-safe? D. Robinson. Read Digest 82:91-4 My '63
How the modern Minuteman guards the peace. J. Atwater. il Sat Eve Post 236:65-9 F 9 '63
Mixed strategic force; address. T. S. Power. Aviation W 81:17 N 16 '64
New Mexico: underground air force; Atlas complex no. 4, near Roswell, N.Mex. B. Kocivar. il Look 27:M5-7 O 8 '63
SAC C&C system tests beginning. M. Getler. il(p 1) Miss & Roc 15:18 Jl 13 '64
SAC seeking to maintain force mixture. W. H. Gregory. il Aviation W 80:80-1+ Ap 27 '64
SAC units bear closing brunt. Aviation W 81:34 N 23 '64
Tough Tommy Power, our deterrent-in-chief. J. G. Hubbell. il Read Digest 84:71-6 My '64
U.S. nuclear team; address, May 14, 1964. T. S. Power. Vital Speeches 30:552-5 Jl 1 '64

Systems command

Air force manual to bring tighter systems management. Miss & Roc 14:15 Mr 9 '64
AFSC preparing tech war plan. Miss & Roc 14:15 Mr 16 '64
AFSC systems management role growing. W. H. Gregory. Aviation W 78:99+ My 13 '63
AF to begin work on master guidance system. Miss & Roc 13:16 S 9 '63
Joint panels smooth gaps in interface. il Aviation W 81:21-2 mid-D '64
New reliability goals; excerpts from address. H. M. Estes. Aviation W 80:21 Ja 13 '64
Space computer techniques under study. B. Miller. il Aviation W 80:72-3+ Mr 23 '64
SSD will assume responsibility for aerospaceplane effort in July. I. Stone. Aviation W 80:29 My 11 '64
Step forward; coordinating space medicine. W. J. Coughlin. Miss & Roc 14:46 Mr 9 '64
USAF keys space plan to three programs. E. H. Kolcum. il Aviation W 78:26-8 Ja 28 '63

Tactical air command

I flew with TAC's top gun. K. V. Brown. il Pop Mech 120:118-22+ O '63
Lonely life of an air force wife; family of Capt. Richard Davis of the Tactical air command. il Look 27:20-6 Je 4 '63
Simulation grows in support analysis. Aviation W 81:47+ mid-D '64
TAC center tests fast delivery concepts. C. Brownlow. il Aviation W 81:65+ O 12 '64
TAC evaluates ground support capability in maneuvers. E. J. Bulban. il Aviation W 81:62-4 Ag 17 '64
TAC evaluates new hardware concepts. C. Brownlow. il Aviation W 81:68-9+ O 5 '64
USAF seeking improved reconnaissance aids to conduct demanding new missions. W. Wright. il Aviation W 80:88-9+ Ap 6 '64
We've got the planes, what about the men. F. V. Drake. Read Digest 82:110-14 F '63

Air force, Army

Air assault development. W. Wright. il Aviation W 80:54-5+ F 17; 61-3+ F 24 '64
Army AAFSS proposals due Nov. 23. C. M. Plattner. Aviation W 81:92-4 N 9 '64
Army asks for more airborne fire power. il Bsns W p31 D 5 '64
Army explores air mobility potential. W. Wright. il Aviation W 80:90-1+ Mr 16 '64
Army looks skyward again. W. Wingo. il Sci N L 87:26-7 Ja 9 '65
Army prepares to expand pilot training. L. Booda. Aviation W 78:35-6 F 4 '63
Army seeks greater mobility in added air capability. G. C. Wilson. il Aviation W 78:84-5+ Mr 11 '63
Army takes to the air. il Time 81:17 Mr 22 '63
Army, USAF testing air support roles. C. Brownlow. il Aviation W 81:77+ S 21 '64
Budget unit implementing Howze plans. L. Booda. Aviation W 79:26-7 Jl 15 '63
Next war: massed helicopters? il U S News 56:62-3 Ap 20 '64
USAF, army air roles evolving slowly. L. Booda. Aviation W 78:30-1 My 27 '63

Air force, Navy

Bureaucracy and Frank Ellis. J. Ciardi. Sat R 47:14-15 Je 13 '64
F-111 weight, drag increases alarm navy. G. C. Wilson. Aviation W 80:16-17 Mr 23 '64
Fight for survival of the supercarrier; fleet admirals vs Secretary McNamara. R. K. Massie. il Sat Eve Post 236:17-25 N 2 '63
Kennedy sees navy's Walleye, Shrike. F. G. McGuire. Miss & Roc 12:21 Je 17 '63
Navy develops new aerial weapons series. il Aviation W 79:84 Jl 1 '63
Navy faces reorganization of forces, procurement structure. il Aviation W 78:80-1+ Mr 11 '63
Navy pressed to enlarge anti-submarine capabilities. il Aviation W 80:84-5+ Mr 16 '64
Navy to deploy A-6A squadron next year. D. A. Brown. il Aviation W 81:46-7+ Ag 17 '64
Navy uses UH-46 in evaluation of vertical resupply concept. il Aviation W 81:72-3 Ag 10 '64
Navy VAL contract may total $1 billion. G. C. Wilson. il Aviation W 80:27-8 F 17 '64
Shrike program being pushed by navy. F. G. McGuire. il Miss & Roc 12:15 My 6 '63
Still in defense. J. Ciardi. Sat R 47:13 Jl 11 '64

Air national guard

Air force hopes to ease cutback for active reserve, guard units. C. Brownlow. Aviation W 81:18-19 D 21 '64
Air guard tankers to use surplus J47s. E. J. Bulban. il Aviation W 81:42-3 D 28 '64

Anti-Communist measures

See Communism—United States—Anti-Communist measures; United States—Foreign relations—Anti-Communist measures

Antiquities

Save U.S. history; from the floodwaters of modern dams. Sci N L 83:390 Je 22 '63

Appropriations and expenditures

Appropriations: the crtics of Congress often slight an inner redoubt of the system. J. Walsh. Science 143:548-51 F 7 '64
Budget reacts on plutonium. Bsns W p26-7 Ja 18 '64
Business leader stumps for higher morality; summaries of addresses. E. P. Neilan. U S News 55:11 S 16 '63
Courage and defense economy. W. J. Coughlin. Miss & Roc 15:46 D 7 '64
Despite frugality, the budget rises. Newsweek 62:21 D 16 '63
Easy money. Read Digest 83:129 N '63
Federal expenditures; address, December 3, 1963. F. B. Wilde. Vital Speeches 30:243-5 F 1 '64
FY '65 missile/space money bills subject to minimal trimming so far. H. M. David. Miss & Roc 14:17 My 25 '64
Forestry in the federal budget, fiscal year ending June 30, 1965. Am For 70:6 Mr '64
Fresh funds for welfare; new congressional programs. Bsns W p31 O 12 '63
George Mahon talks on spending; interview. G. Mahon. il Nations Bsns 52:32-3+ Ag '64
Government waste; an official report; summary. U S News 57:10-11 D 28 '64
Headed for still loftier heights; public works spending. il Bsns W p 187-8+ O 19 '63

UNITED STATES—Appropriations and expenditures—*Continued*
How to spot false budget cuts. V. J. Burke. il Nations Bsns 52:42-3+ F '64
How to survive in space business. il Bsns W p 102-4+ Ja 16 '65
Legislation: in first session, 88th Congress shows itself to be more critical patron of science. J. Walsh. Science 143:27-8 Ja 3 '64
Melman: Overkill critic finds a welcome reception in capital, but the reasons are complicated. D. S. Greenberg. Science 144:271-3 Ap 17 '64; Discussion. 145:232-3, 1257 Jl 17, S 18 '64
Now see the innards of a fat pig. K. Wheeler and others. il Life 55:20-7+ Ag 16 '63
Pork and the President. R. Moley. Newsweek 62:96 S 9 '63
Pork lovers are no credit to our democracy. Life 55:4 S 6 '63
Report on wasteland. R. Moley. Newsweek 61:112 Ap 15; 104 Ap 22; 96 Ap 29 '63
Secret life of the A-11. D. Cater. Reporter 30:16-17 Ap 23 '64
Stop! federal expenditures for science. il Newsweek 62:102 O 21 '63
Trimming the fat. R. Hotz. Aviation W 81:11 N 30 '64
Waiting game clips spending; Congress and federal spending. il Bsns W p23-4 O 26 '63
When pure science meets pure politics. D. S. Greenberg. il Reporter 30:39-41 Mr 12 '64
Winning the Weevils. il Time 82:36 O 4 '63
See also
Budget—United States
Government spending policy
United States—Economic policy
also subhead Appropriations and expenditures under names of government departments, e.g. United States—Air force—Appropriations and expenditures

Architecture

See Architecture—United States

Area redevelopment administration

APW: a profit formula. E. P. Cliff. il Am For 69:28-30 O '63
Characteristics of urban depressed areas; excerpt from federal aid to depressed areas. S. A. Levitan. il Mo Labor R 87:48-52 Ja '64
Depressed areas built to order. B. B. VanDusen. il Nation 200:79-81 Ja 25 '65
Federal aid to depressed areas, by S. A. Levitan Review
New Repub 150:3+ Je 27 '64. E. T. Chase
From Washington straight; Area redevelopment agency bill. Cato. Nat R 15:144 Ag 27 '63
Is this the way to fight the war against poverty? C. Stevenson. Read Digest 84:51-8 My '64
Key senator tells why ARA won't work; interview. A. W. Robertson. Nations Bsns 52:84-6 F '64
Library, waterworks, firehouse for your town? Changing T 17:6 S '63
U.S. aid, wanted or not: report on a well-to-do county, Rice County, Kans; with excerpts from editorial by M. Moxley. il U S News 54:40-2 Ap 1 '63
What's back of fight over ARA. Nations Bsns 51:74-6+ N '63
When the bubble burst in Crockett, Texas. C. Stevenson. Read Digest 85:197-8+ S '64

Armed forces

Armed might: where the U.S. has gained. U S News 57:14 Jl 13 '64
Challenge to military professionalism. R. N. Ginsburgh. bibliog f For Affairs 42:255-68 Ja '64; Excerpts. U S News 56:93 F 17 '64
Creative color; photographic activities of the army, navy and air force. A. Rothstein. U S Camera 27:8+ O '64
Dangerous mixture: the military and politics. T. D. White. Newsweek 64:33 O 19 '64
Draft: many threatened, few chosen. J. C. Esty, jr. il N Y Times Mag p 13+ O 20 '63
Irreparable loss; civilian authority. R. Moley. Newsweek 62:72 Jl 1 '63
Military career; address, May 13, 1964. K. P. Bergquist. Vital Speeches 30:562-5 Jl 1 '64
National security and world responsibilities; address, June 3, 1964. L. B. Johnson. Dept State Bul 50:950-2 Je 22 '64
National security strategy; address, August 29, 1963. W. F. McKee. Vital Speeches 30:21-4 O 15 '63
Salute to the armed forces; photographs. N Y Times Mag p22-3 My 12 '63
Services' relationship with directorate is improving steadily. Miss & Roc 14:47-8 Mr 30 '64
Test-ban treaty: atomic chess; positioning of military forces to serve purely political ends. T. D. White. Newsweek 62:23 S 9 '63
Then one day in Saigon. W. V. Kennedy. America 109:760 D 14 '63
What's wrong with civil-military relations. T. D. White. Newsweek 61:30 My 27 '63
Who runs America? an examination of a theory that says the answer is a military-industrial complex. D. S. Greenberg; discussion. Science 139:247-8+ Ja 18 '63
See also
Armed forces day and week
United States—Air force
United States—Army
United States—Defense, Department of
United States—Joint chiefs of staff
United States—Marine corps
United States—Navy
United States—Reserve officers training corps

Appropriations and expenditures

Aerospace budget. R. Hotz. Aviation W 80:21 Ja 20 '64
Alternatives to armament expenditures; excerpts from address, December 1962. W. Leontief. il Bul Atomic Sci 20:19-21 Je '64
Arms and the big money men. J. Duscha. il Harper 228:39-47 Mr; 59-65 Ap '64; Reply. W. J. Coughlin. Miss & Roc 14:46 Mr 16 '64
Arms and the big money men. J. Duscha. il Harper 228:39-47 Mr; 59-65 Ap; 56-62 My 64; Discussion of March issue. 228:10+ My '64; Miss & Roc 14:46 Mr 16 '64
Arms and the woman. Nation 196:110 F 9 '63
Basic defense, space efforts to continue. G. C. Wilson. Aviation W 82:16-17 Ja 4 '65
Budget reflects belief in U.S. arms edge; with editorial comment. G. C. Wilson. il Aviation W 80:21, 26-30 Ja 27 '64
Budget restorations urged by Defense dept. Aviation W 81:25 Jl 13 '64
Candidates' records on defense and space bills. il Miss & Roc 15:16 O 19 '64
Change in RDT&E budget structure could trigger far-reaching results. Miss & Roc 14:101-3 Mr 30 '64
Closer DOD, space fund scrutiny seen.. G. C. Wilson. Aviation W 79:26-7 D 9 '63
Coming cuts in defense spending: how big? il U S News 55:76-8 N 18 '63
Committee accepts ICBM reliability. H. M. David. Miss & Roc 14:17-18 Ap 27 '64
Congress approves $47.2 billion for DOD. Aviation W 79:27-8 O 14 '63
Construction funds for unnamed missile, space efforts allotted. Aviation W 80:21 Mr 23 '64
Cut in defense costs? what a top official says; summary of address, October 1963. R. L. Gilpatric. U S News 55:16 N 4 '63
Cut of twenty-five per cent in defense costs? U S News 56:16 Mr 30 '64
Cutting up the arms budget. Nation 198:21 Ja 6 '64
Defense appropriation totals $46.7 billion. il Aviation W 81:27 Ag 10 '64
Defense ax raises sparks; military base shutdowns. Bsns W p24 My 1 '64
Defense budget stresses tactical needs. Aviation W 82:22-4 Ja 25 '65
Defense cutbacks: how they'll work. U S News 55:6 D 23 '63
Defense cuts bring a new kind of job crisis. il U S News 56:80-3 My 18 '64
Defense dept. research and development money; tables. Aviation W 78:63+ Ja 28 '63
Defense spending: down by $1-billion a year. il Bsns W p34+ Ap 25 '64
DOD accepts fund cuts to ease passage. Aviation W 79:20-1 Jl 29 '63
DOD authorization bill may be history's biggest. Miss & Roc 14:15 Ja 20 '64
DOD curtailment of solids work dropped due to stout opposition. L. Booda. Aviation W 79:27-8 Ag 26 '63
DOD preparing crucial bid for MMRBM funds. Miss & Roc 14:21 Ap 27 '64
DOD seeks less for weapons, research. G. C. Wilson. il Aviation W 80:26 Ja 20 '64
DOD shifts stir ire of Congress, allies. il Aviation W 78:73-5 Mr 11 '63
DOD space position defended. F. G. McGuire. il Miss & Roc 12:12-14 F 4 '63
DOD stresses urgent limited war needs. G. C. Wilson. Aviation W 80:22-4 F 3 '64
Desperate drive to cut defense spending. C. J. V. Murphy. il Fortune 69:94-7+ Ja '64
Extra RS-70, submarine money included in defense authorization. Aviation W 78:38-9 Mr 18 '63
FY '65 budget; programs at a glance. il Miss & Roc 14:18-19 Ja 27 '64

UNITED STATES—Armed forces—Appropriations and expenditures—*Continued*
FY '65 DOD budget $50 billion. D. C. Breasted. Miss & Roc 14:14 Ja 13 '64
House action on FY 1964 budget requests; Department of defense appropriations. Miss & Roc 13:178-80 Jl 29 '63
House approves $46.8 billion for defense. G. C. Wilson. Aviation W 80:26-7 Ap 27 '64
House group increases aircraft funds, cuts R&D by $362 million. Aviation W 80:28 F 17 '64
House lops nearly two billion from DOD funds. H. M. David. Miss & Roc 13:17 Jl 1 '63
House yields to administration on RS-70. Aviation W 79:34-5 Jl 1 '63
If—. D. Lawrence. U S News 55:124 O 21 '63
Impact of possible DOD cut studied. H. M. David. Miss & Roc 13:18 D 9 '63
Joint chiefs fight MMRBM fund clash. Aviation W 79:26 Ag 26 '63
Kennedy asks $53.7 billion for defense; with editorial comment. G. C. Wilson. il Aviation W 78:21, 26-8 Ja 21 '63
Lower fiscal 1965 defense request seen. L. Booda. Aviation W 79:26-7 O 14 '63
LBJ asks for $16.38 billion; with editorial comment. il Miss & Roc 14:14, 46 Ja 27 '64
McNamara cites arms lead; sees defense budget leveling. K. Johnsen. Aviation W 79:29 N 25 '63
McNamara's ban on defense expenditures; with report by L. Norman. Newsweek 62:28 Jl 8 '63
Major national security problems confronting the United States; address, November 18, 1963. R. S. McNamara. Dept State Bul 49:914-21 D 16 '63
Military space requests were cut $607 million to avoid duplication. Aviation W 78:37 Ap 1 '63
Missile funds down, RDT&E up in FY '66 budget request. Miss & Roc 16:16 Ja 18 '65
Money in old-style munitions. il Bsns W p 144+ Jl 25 '64
New patterns for military spending. il Bsns W p24-5 Ag 31 '63
Operation bulldozer. Nat R 15:555-6 D 31 '63
Pentagon at crossroads: cut where, add where? M. S. Johnson. il U S News 56:40-1 Ja 20 '64
Planners now stress final results. il Miss & Roc 12:29-31 Mr 25 '63
Programming's role in defense; excerpts from address. C. J. Hitch. Aviation W 81:17 O 12 '64
Russell scores abandonment of bombers. G. C. Wilson. Aviation W 79:28-9 S 23 '63
Sales to top $8 billion by '70. il Miss & Roc 12:20-2 My 20 '63
Scratch in the surface. il Time 82:11 D 20 '63
Senate approval seen for $47.4-billion DOD budget. H. S. David. il Miss & Roc 13:16-17 S 23 '63
Senate committee okays $46.8 billion for defense. Miss & Roc 15:12 Ag 3 '64
Senate rejects economy moves; passes defense money bill, 77-0. G. C. Wilson. Aviation W 79:30 S 30 '63
Senate votes DOD $46.8 billion; most House cuts are confirmed. Aviation W 81:27 Ag 3 '64
Senate will cite test ban risks in move to restore DOD funds. Aviation W 79:29 S 16 '63
Softening the shock of defense spending cuts. Bsns W p38 N 2 '63
Spending is the clue; LBJ's strategy for U.S. M. S. Johnson. U S News 56:51 F 3 '64
Status of FY 1965 budget requests; Department of defense appropriations. il Miss & Roc 15:143-5 Jl 27 '64
Strategy for American security; symposium. il Sat R 46:10-17 My 4 '63
Strategy, politics, and defense budgets, by W. Schilling and others. Review
Bul Atomic Sci 19:31-3 F '63. R. P. Wolff
Swinging the ax. Newsweek 63:23 My 4 '64
Swords in plowshares. New Repub 150:3-4 Ap 25 '64
T.R.B. from Washington; defense cut. New Repub 150:2 Ap 4 '64
Their finest hour. Nation 196:81 F 2 '63
Tug-of-war: military budget. J. Greene. Nation 196:117-20 F 9 '63
U.S. scrapping arms of future? il U S News 54:35 Ap 1 '63
Vast impact seen in DOD spending shift. K. Johnsen. Aviation W 79:36 D 9 '63
Warfare state. F. J. Cook. bibliog f Ann Am Acad 351:102-9 Ja '64
What will take up the slack? shrinking of defense procurement; with editorial comment. il Bsns W p50+, 128 Jl 18 '64
Where Congress finds fat in the budget. U S News 55:4 O 21 '63
Where defense spending goes from here. il Nations Bsns 51:78-80+ O '63
Where the fifty billions for defense will go. il U S News 55:45-7 O 28 '63
Where the shrinkage stopped. Time 82:38 O 4 '63
Why LBJ holds the arms line. il Bsns W p28-9 Ja 23 '65
See also
United States—Navy—Appropriations and expenditures

Clothing

See also
United States—Army—Clothing

Dental service

Army dentists still treat arrow wounds. Sci N L 86:281 O 31 '64

Education

Armed forces; careers in uniform; with charts. Sr Schol 85:21+ N 11 '64
Armed forces; careers with Uncle Sam. il Sr Schol 83:33-4 N 8 '63
Military and education. il Sr Schol 84:1T-2T F 7 '64
Our mistaught GIs. W. H. Boyer. Nation 197:361-4 N 30 '63
West Point & all that; views of D. Boroff. il Time 81:49-50 F 8 '63

Equipment and supplies

See also
United States—Defense, Department of—Defense supply agency

Forces in Cyprus

Security council extends mandate of Cyprus peace force; statement, December 18, 1964, with text of resolution. C. W. Yost. Dept State Bul 52:26-7 Ja 4 '65

Forces in Europe

Big lift and the big letdown; second armored division flown to West Germany. il Newsweek 62:23-5 N 4 '63
Double standard; US forces in Germany. Time 82:38 N 8 '63
Easier to get in than out. Nation 197:289 N 9 '63
Impact of Eisenhower. S. Alsop. Sat Eve Post 236:14 N 9 '63
Let's be honest with ourselves; with editorial comment. D. D. Eisenhower. Sat Eve Post 236:26-7, 86 O 26 '63
Magic word; fatal brawl at U.S. airbase, Evreux. Time 82:41 S 20 '63
Notes and comment; another attempt to dictate the terms of allied access to West Berlin. New Yorker 39:41 N 16 '63
Sparring on the autobahn. New Repub 149:6 N 16 '63
U.S. troops abroad: switching signals. il Newsweek 62:51 N 11 '63
Why GI's don't come home; real story. il U S News 55:78 N 18 '63
Withdrawal from Europe? an illusion. D. Acheson. il N Y Times Mag p7+ D 15 '63
See also
United States—Army—Forces in Europe

Forces in foreign countries

American children: alien by birth. P. S. Buck. Ladies Home J 81:36+ N '64
Peace on earth? what look around the world shows. il U S News 57:20-2 D 28 '64

Forces in Korea (Republic)

$5,000,000 bingo parlor; Walker hill. il Time 81:46 Ap 19 '63
Hooch is not a home; Korean mistresses. il Time 84:48 O 16 '64
Korea: the forgotten front. il N Y Times Mag p 14-15 Ag 18 '63
Korean paralysis; mired troops and frozen policy. F. Church. Nation 198:347-8+ Ap 6 '64
Nothing for the boys; South Korea's pleasure dome. il Newsweek 61:46 Ap 22 '63
See also
United States—Army—Forces in Korea (Republic)

Forces in Laos

Going up in Laos. Nation 198:642-3 Je 29 '64

Forces in Southeast Asia

Is U.S. fighting reds in the wrong place? il U S News 55:8 Ag 12 '63

Forces in the Congo (capital Leopoldville)

Congo: new police job for the United States. il U S News 57:60-1 Jl 6 '64

UNITED STATES—Armed forces—*Continued*

Forces in Viet Nam (Republic)

Alert in Vietnam; symposium. il Life 57:30-46B+ N 27 '64
American special forces in action in Viet Nam. H. Sochurek. il Nat Geog Mag 127:38-65 Ja '65
America's dirty war. C. Davidson. il Nation 199:299-303 N 2 '64; Discussion. 199:inside cover N 23 '64
Anniversary present; attack on Bien Hoa airfield by Viet Cong guerrillas. il Newsweek 64:57 N 16 '64
As the Vietnam war gets bloodier. il U S News 58:8 Ja 11 '65
As U.S. battle casualties pile up. il U S News 57:46 Jl 27 '64
Blackmail in Vietnam. New Repub 151:4-5 Ag 8 '64
Bureaucrats' war over Vietnam. J. Kraft. Harper 228:108+ My '64
Can U.S. win in Vietnam? an inside report; interview. S. W. Sanders. il U S News 58:44-7+ Ja 11 '65
Chinese puzzle. R. Hotz. Aviation W 81:11 Ag 10 '64
Choice in Vietnam: get tough, or out. U S News 57:30-1 D 7 '64
Choices get grimmer in southeast Asia; with editorial comment. il Bsns W p26-7, 180 My 23 '64
Colonel Van and General Harkins. Nation 197:230 O 19 '63
Credibility gap. R. Hotz. Aviation W 80:21 Je 15 '64
Dead duck? General Maxwell Taylor's testimony. Time 83:22 Ap 24 '64
Decision near on expanding Viet air war. C. Brownlow. Aviation W 81:17-18 D 7 '64
De Gaulle and Asia. Nation 198:157 F 17 '64
Deeper and deeper. Nation 199:81-2 S 7 '64
DOD, industry facing Vietnam challenge. L. Booda. il Aviation W 80:93-5+ Ap 13 '64
Elusive Viet Cong. J. A. Rose. New Repub 148:19-26 My 4 '63
End of the play. Nation 199:261 O 26 '64
Escalating war. R. Hotz. Aviation W 81:11 Jl 20 '64
Facts explode propaganda line. Nations Bsns 51:84 Je '63
Familiar refrain. il Newsweek 61:43 Mr 11 '63
From bad to awful; war in South Viet Nam. il Time 83:27 Mr 6 '64
From Vietnam battlefront: while U.S. hesitates, reds carry war south. S. W. Sanders. il U S News 57:38-9 Ag 3 '64
Frustrated but firm. Time 83:39 F 21 '64
Hour of decision. Nation 199:421 D 7 '64
House approves military aid funds; Vietnam policy criticized. Aviation W 80:29 Je 15 '64
I fought in Vietnam; interview. R. L. Moore, jr. il U S News 56:40-7 Je 8 '64
I think about him all the time. S. Plapinger. il Ladies Home J 81:55-7+ O '64
If you wonder how U.S. got involved in Vietnam; questions and answers. il U S News 56:40-1 Je 15 '64
I'm hit! I'm hit! I'm hit! with editorial comment. J. A. Rose. il Sat Eve Post 236:34-47, 84 Mr 23 '63
In Vietnam it's more than guns. il Bsns W p82-3+ Ag 1 '64
Inheritor of a wretched war; General Westmoreland in Saigon. J. Langguth. il N Y Times Mag p27+ N 15 '64
Is the Vietnam war falling apart? il U S News 57:23 D 28 '64
Job for the peace movement. Nation 198:253 Mr 16 '64
Johnson weighing N. Vietnam air strikes. C. Brownlow. il Aviation W 81:22-3 N 30 '64
Lesson in Vietnam. W. V. Kennedy. America 110:401 Mr 28 '64
Little war, far away and very ugly; with photographs by A. Okamura. Life 56:34-43 Je 12 '64
McNamara-Taylor report: a long, hard war in Vietnam. il U S News 56:21 My 25 '64
Mr Johnson's war. Nation 198:518 My 25 '64
"My husband died for his country, and no one cares". N. M. Lobsenz. Redbook 121:56-7+ O '63
One mission too many; Major Charles Kelly shot. Time 84:40 Jl 10 '64
One who was belligerent; award to Captain R. H. C. Donlon. il Time 84:31 D 11 '64
Only war we've got. D. F. Ford. Nation 199:66-8 Ag 24 '64
Opening a new front in Vietnam. S. W. Sanders. il U S News 57:26-8 Ag 17 '64
Over the border. Nation 198:405 Ap 27 '64
Planes over Saigon: wings tear off. D. F. Ford. il Nation 199:3-5 Jl 13 '64
President discusses Viet-Nam on CBS and NBC news programs; September 2 and September 9, 1963. J. F. Kennedy. Dept State Bul 49:498-500 S 30 '63
President pledges continuing support to Republic of Viet Nam; message, December 31, 1963. L. B. Johnson. Dept State Bul 50:121-2 Ja 27 '64
Sea action: this is no drill. il Newsweek 64:19-20+ Ag 17 '64
Secretary Rusk's news conference of February 27, 1964. D. Rusk. Dept State Bul 50:403-9 Mr 16 '64
Self-management of the news. Nation 198:309 Mr 30 '64
Serpent in the garden. Nation 198:469 My 11 '64
Setback in Vietnam; defeat at Ap Bac. H. G. Fairbanks. Commonweal 77:593-5 Mr 1 '63
Showdown in Vietnam; all-out fight ahead? il Bsns W p28-9 F 8 '64
South Viet Nam. M. Gart. Time 82:19 D 20 '63
South Vietnamese raiders extending war. L. Booda. il Aviation W 80:16-19 Ap 6 '64
South Vietnam's 40 megacycle intercom. A. F. Gonzalez, jr. il Pop Electr 18:41-5+ Ap '63
Stake in Viet Nam; address, April 22, 1963; with questions and answers. D. Rusk. Dept State Bul 48:727-35 My 13 '63; Same. Vital Speeches 29:493-7 Je 1 '63
Story of an ad: protest from kin of Americans killed in Vietnam in Washington star. Nat R 16:435-6 Je 2 '64
This is our enemy; Vietcong guerrilla. S. Karnow. il Sat Eve Post 237:19-25 Ag 22 '64
Tough man, tough job. Time 83:26 My 8 '64
Toward the showdown? il Time 84:23-7 Ag 7 '64
True story of war in Vietnam. R. L. Moore, jr. il U S News 56:38-41 My 18 '64
Truth about a war Americans aren't winning. S. W. Sanders. il U S News 55:46-9 Ag 5 '63
UH-1Bs attack Viet Cong; aircraft buildup shown. il Aviation W 81:78-9 Ag 31 '64
Ugliest American in Vietnam. D. Halberstam. il Esquire 62:114-17+ N '64
U.S. bombers are blasted in Vietnam; Bien Hoa airbase. J. Flynn. il Life 57:50-1 N 13 '64
U.S. buildup in Vietnam: how it has grown in ten years. il U S News 57:10 Ag 10 '64
U.S. bungle in Vietnam? the inside story. R. P. Martin; S. W. Sanders. il U S News 57:56-8 S 14 '64
U.S. casualties in Vietnam, a growing toll. U S News 58:10 Ja 18 '65
U.S. change in Vietnam new general takes over. il U S News 56:18 Je 29 '64
U.S. makes a change: new general in Vietnam. il U S News 56:20 My 11 '64
United States policy in Viet-Nam; address, March 26, 1964. R. S. McNamara. Dept State Bul 50:562-70 Ap 13 '64; Same. Vital Speeches 30:394-9 Ap 15 '64; Excerpts. Aviation W 80:11 Mr 30 '64
U.S. stakes in Vietnam; excerpts from address, March 26, 1964. R. S. McNamara. Aviation W 80:11 Mr 30 '64
Unsung hero of Vietnam: the G.I. medic. A. Gonzalez, jr. il Todays Health 41:26-9 O '63
Up to November 4. Nation 198:225 Mr 9 '64
Viet Nam: decisive battle of the cold war; address, May 6, 1964. Tran-van-Chuong. Vital Speeches 30:628-30 Ag 1 '64
Vietnam: fact and fiction. Nation 196:169 Mr 2 '63
Vietnam: go north? S. Alsop. il Sat Eve Post 237:10 Je 20 '64
Vietnam hangs on U.S. determination. C. J. V. Murphy. il Fortune 69:159+ My '64
Vietnam hawks and doves. B. B. Fall. New Repub 152:7-8 Ja 16 '65
Viet Nam: in double jeopardy? il Sr Schol 85:13-17 D 2 '64
Vietnam: land without laughter. T. E. Ennis. il Cur Hist 46:101-6 F '64
Vietnam, resistance or withdrawal? O. Gass. bibliog f Commentary 37:37-45 My '64; Reply. B. B. Fall. 38:6+ S '64
Vietnam: school for U.S. guerrillas. P. Worthington. Nation 196:179-80 Mr 2 '63
Viet-Nam situation; address, August 25, 1963. T. J. C. Heavner. Dept State Bul 49:393-8 S 9 '63
Vietnam: the waiting game. S. Alsop. il Sat Eve Post 237:18 O 31 '64
War in Vietnam. W. V. Kennedy. America 109:504 N 2 '63
War is waiting. il Time 82:26 N 22 '63
We can win in Vietnam. H. C. Lodge. il N Y Times Mag p 14-15+ Ja 17 '65

UNITED STATES—Armed forced—Forces in Viet Nam (Republic)—*Continued*
We must leave Vietnam. W. Morse. il N Y Times Mag p 14-15+ Ja 17 '65
Week with Squadron 365. A. Harrigan. Nat R 17:59 Ja 26 '65
What Johnson faces in South Vietnam. S. Castan. il Look 28:19-30 Ja 28 '64
What the Pentagon tells Congress about Vietnam. il U S News 56:42 My 25 '64
Why are Americans in Vietnam? an admiral's letter to his sons. W. S. Guest. il U S News 57:132-3 O 19 '64
Why U.S. is losing in Vietnam, an inside story; interview. S. T. Williams. il U S News 57:62-4+ N 9 '64
With the redskins of Vietnam. D. F. Ford. Nation 199:29-31 Jl 27 '64
See also
United States—Air force—Forces in Viet Nam (Republic)

Insignia

This week in history. il Sr Schol 83:9 O 4 '63

International security affairs division

Disarmament: an agency in search of a policy. L. W. Martin. il Reporter 29:22-6 Jl 4 '63

Legal status, laws, etc.

Need for a GI bill: Status of forces treaty. Nat R 16:1047-8 D 1 '64

Management

New shape of U.S. defense. il Miss & Roc 12: 26-8 Mr 25 '63

Medical and sanitary affairs

Unsung hero of Vietnam: the G. I. medic A. Gonzalez, jr. il Todays Health 41:26-9 O '63
See also
United States—Armed forces—Dental service

Negroes

Dispute over army civil rights role. Sr Schol 83:16 O 25 '63
Georgia's Vinson: battling the Pentagon. U S News 55:16 S 30 '63
See also
United States—Navy—Negroes
United States—President's committee on equal opportunity in the armed forces

Officers

See also
Retired military officers

Pay, allowances, etc.

In the works: a pay hike for military. il U S News 57:10 Jl 27 '64
New pay scale for armed forces. il U S News 55:10 O 7 '63
Out of the barracks bag; new pay bill. L. Norman. Newsweek 61:20+ F 4 '63
Speaking out; we treat our military shabbily. M. T. Wood. Sat Eve Post 238:10+ Ja 16 '65

Political activities

Lingering questions of civilian-military balance. il Sr Schol 84:9-11+ Ap 17 '64
Military mind. G. M. Lyons. Bul Atomic Sci 19:19-22 N '63
New rules for GI demonstrators. il U S News 55:57 Jl 29 '63

Procurement

Admiral Anderson attacks Pentagon policies; excerpts from address. G. W. Anderson. Aviation W 79:39 S 9 '63
Admiral Anderson's dissent; excerpts from address. G. W. Anderson. Aviation W 79: 21 S 9 '63
California firms study contract warnings. H. D. Watkins. il Aviation W 79:74-7 Jl 29 '63
Centralization of defense. W. J. Coughlin. Miss & Roc 12:46 F 4 '63
Changes beginning to pay dividends. il Miss & Roc 12:32-4+ Mr 25 '63
Collision in Washington: McNamara vs. the Congress. Newsweek 61:25-6 Mr 25 '63
Command, control procurement shifted. L. Booda. Aviation W 79:33-4 N 25 '63
Contractor evaluation comments asked. Aviation W 78:32 Ap 15 '63
Contractors find flaws in new regime: Barbs come from Congress, military. il Miss & Roc 12:66-8 Mr 25 '63
Crackdown on employee welfare programs sought. H. M. David. Miss & Roc 15:27-8 S 14 '64
DOD accepts fund cuts to ease passage. Aviation W 79:20-1 Jl 29 '63
DOD list of FY 1963 100 top prime contractors. il Miss & Roc 14:26 Ja 6 '64
DOD lists biggest research contractors. il Aviation W 80:83-4+ Ja 13 '64
DOD performance system explained; Contractor performance evaluation. C. W. Borklund. il Miss & Roc 13:31-2+ S 16 '63
Department of defense lists top 100 prime contractors for fiscal 1963. il Aviation W 79: 60-3 D 30 '63
DOD plans more equitable contracting. F. G. McGuire. Miss & Roc 12:18 Je 3 '63
DOD plans new selection policy. Aviation W 78:29 My 13 '63
DOD seeks less for weapons. research. G. C. Wilson. il Aviation W 80:26 Ja 20 '64
DOD shifts stir ire of Congress, allies. il Aviation W 78:73-5 Mr 11 '63
Defense contractors who study conversion plans will be repaid. Aviation W 80:35 Ap 27 '64
Economic impact of defense shifts eyed. K. Johnsen. Aviation W 79:28-9 S 30 '63
Editorial; TFX. R. Hotz. Aviation W 78:21 My 13 '63
Effort urged to ease effect of DOD shifts. K. Johnsen. Aviation W 79:31 N 11 '63
First contracts let for U.S. standardized space guidance system. C. D. LaFond. Miss & Roc 14:17 Mr 2 '64
Free anything gets put off limits. il Bsns W p28-9 N 21 '64
Gilpatric cites knowledge of X-22A firms. G. C. Wilson. Aviation W 78:36-7 Je 24 '63
Government buying erodes management. P. F. Hannah. bibliog f Harvard Bsns R 42: 53-62 My '64
In defense of the Defense secretary. Fortune 67:81-2+ Ap '63
Industry mixed on DOD's profit system. W. H. Gregory. Aviation W 79:60-3+ S 2 '63
Kennedy asks $53.7 billion for defense; with editorial comment. G. C. Wilson. il Aviation W 78:21, 26-8 Ja 21 '63
Labor surplus area awards jump sharply. K. Johnsen. Aviation W 81:26 Ag 24 '64
McClellan dubious about legality of Rubel procurement proposals. G. C. Wilson. Aviation W 78:37 Je 10 '63
McClellan group's reaction mixed on Rubel procurement proposals. Aviation W 78:125+ Je 17 '63
McNamara details DOD cost cuts. il Miss & Roc 13:16-17 Jl 22 '63
McNamara details defense buying, R&D; summary of testimony before House armed services committee. R. S. McNamara. Aviation W 78:27-30 F 4 '63
McNamara says primacy of top leaders is main Pentagon issue. K. Johnsen. Aviation W 78:33 Ap 8 '63
Major DOD research contractors listed. il Aviation W 80:95+ Ja 20 '64
New tactical missile contract expected to yield billions for industry. il Miss & Roc 14:54-6 Mr 30 '64
Pendulum may swing back in DOD policy. il Aviation W 80:73-7 Mr 16 '64
Pentagon salesman's day is busy one. il Miss & Roc 12:64-5 Mr 25 '63
Performance edge stressed in TFX quiz. G. C. Wilson. Aviation W 78:28-30 Ap 15 '63
Politics and procurement. W. J. Coughlin. Miss & Roc 12:58 Mr 4 '63; Reply. J. E. Karth. 12:8 Mr 25 '63
Procurement mix changes. il Bsns W p72+ F 16 '63
Promise, problems seen in rating plan. Aviation W 79:37 S 16 '63
Recreation allowance review is sought. G. C. Wilson. Aviation W 81:16-17 Jl 27 '64
Senate report urges new missile buying approach. H. M. David. Miss & Roc 14:15 Ap 6 '64
Senate votes defense procurement cuts. G. C. Wilson. Aviation W 78:26-7 Ap 22 '63
$7-billion contract that changed the rules. R. A. Smith. il Fortune 67:96-101+ Mr; 110-11+ Ap '63
Shifts that stem from TFX feud. Bsns W p34 Ag 24 '63
Slow-down in the Pentagon. H. W. Baldwin. For Affairs 43:262-80 Ja '65
Smarter bargainer. Time 81:91-2 Mr 15 '63
Space & defense group seeks 10-15 per cent sales hike. Miss & Roc 12:35 My 27 '63
Studies of defense contracting. S. Marcus. bibliog f Harvard Bsns R 42:20-2+ My '64
Sweeping source selection changes sought. P. J. Klass. Aviation W 81:24 O 5 '64
Systems group improves Sperry's competitive position with DOD. M. Getler. il Miss & Roc 15:24-5+ Ag 24 '64
Too many generals at work on contracts? concerning report by Stanford research institute. il Bsns W p91 Je 15 '63

UNITED STATES—Armed forces—Procurement —*Continued*
Tug-of-war: military budget. J. Greene. Nation 196:117-20 F 9 '63
Unclassified defense contracts: awards by county, state, and metropolitan areas of the United States fiscal year 1962, by W. Isard and G. J. Karaska. Review
Bul Atomic Sci il 19:34-5 S '63. T. Reiner
Value engineers' proper role discussed. D. E. Fink. Aviation W 78:98-9 My 6 '63

Public relations

Credibility gap. R. Hotz. Aviation W 80:21 Je 15 '64
Service chiefs must detail news contacts. Aviation W 80:20-1 Je 8 '64
Where the cuts hurt. il Bsns W p56+ Jl 18 '64

Recreation

$5,000,000 bingo parlor; Walker hill. il Time 81:46 Ap 19 '63
Interservice showcase; variety shows by Inter-service recreation athletic council (ISRAC) il Recreation 56:60 F '63
Military recreation: a family affair; Aviano air base in Italy. E. L. Ericson. il Recreation 56:373-4 O '63
Nothing for the boys; South Korea's pleasure dome. il Newsweek 61:46 Ap 22 '63
On the military front; reprint. D. Kasperick. il Recreation 56:460-3 D '63

Recruiting and enlistment

See also
Military service, Compulsory—United States

Relations with civilians

Get your gun from the army. S. Meisler. il Nation 198:568-71 Je 8 '64
Melman: Overkill critic finds a welcome reception in capital, but the reasons are complicated. D. S. Greenberg. Science 144:271-3 Ap 17 '64; Discussion. 145:232-3, 1257 Jl 17, S 18 '64
Overkill of Melman. Nation 198:359 Ap 13 '64
Pentagon jumps into the race fight. il U S News 55:49-50 Ag 19 '63
When a military base closes; what happens to a city? naval air station at New Iberia, La. il U S News 56:43-4 My 11 '64

Reserves

Coddled commandos; VIP reservists. il Newsweek 63:28-30 F 10 '64
In the works: changed program for reservists. U S News 55:10 Jl 1 '63
McNamara bombshell: merger of reservists. il U S News 57:3 D 21 '64
Merge national guard and reserves? McNamara's plan. il U S News 57:61-2 D 14 '64
Pentagon payola; reserve commissions. Nation 197:41 Jl 27 '63
Pentagon's new plan for reservists. U S News 55:14 Ag 19 '63
Personal business; reserve officers face tough decisions. Bsns W p 125 D 19 '64
We've been asked: what happens now to reservists? questions and answers. U S News 57:27 D 28 '64
See also
United States—National guard

Statistics

As U.S. forces enter the missile age. il U S News 54:6 F 11 '63

Strike command

Stricom. J. R. Moskin. il Look 27:38-43 Ap 23 '63

Training

See Military training

Armed forces security agency

See United States—National security agency

Arms control and disarmament agency

ACDA: criticism of Arms agency increases, but Congress grows friendly and outlook brightens. E. Langer. Science 141:255-6 Jl 19 '63
Arms control and disarmament; transcript of the television program State department briefing: disarmament, first broadcast, January 14, 1963. Dept State Bul 48:115-27 Ja 28 '63
Arms control inspection tests set. J. Trainor. Miss & Roc 14:14 Je 15 '64
Congress and disarmament. J. S. Clark. Bul Atomic Sci 19:3-8 S '63; Reply. S. Gottlieb. 19:40-1 D '63
Disarmament agency: a new look in ACDA's research programs. E. Langer. Science 140:795-6 My 17 '63
Disarmament: an agency in search of a policy. L. W. Martin. il Reporter 29:22-6 Jl 4 '63
Information for arms control. R. P. Schuster, jr. Bul Atomic Sci 19:35-6 F '63
New science head for disarmament agency. E. Langer. Science 142:1045 N 22 '63
Peace research neglected. Sci N L 83:117 F 23 '63
Provocation factor of new arms studied. K. Johnsen. Aviation W 80:29 F 10 '64
Public will be unwilling to buy costly arms inspection system. R. Hawkes. Miss & Roc 15:22 Jl 13 '64
7277; public law. Nat R 14:484 Je 18 '63; Reply with rejoinder. R. Morris. 15:31 Jl 16 '63
This month's feature: U.S. & international control of arms. Cong Digest 43:193-224 Ag '64
Verification and response in disarmament agreements; excerpts from report. Bul Atomic Sci 19:44-8 Ap '63

Army

Army emphasizes close support missiles. G. Alexander. il Aviation W 80:157-8 Mr 16 '64
Army explores air mobility potential. W. Wright. il Aviation W 80:90-1+ Mr 16 '64
Army gives new Lance details. D. C. Breasted. il Miss & Roc 13:18 O 28 '63
Draftee's diary from the Mississippi front. C. Vanderburgh. il Harper 228:37-45 F '64
Fort Hood: Sparta goes suburban. D. Boroff. il Harper 228:46-53 Ja '64
How new atomic shell builds U.S. strength. il U S News 55:8 D 23 '63
Johnson stresses army missile strength. G. C. Wilson. il Aviation W 80:33-4 F 10 '64
Join the army and feel elite. Time 82:17-18 Jl 26 '63
New army; use of helicopters in ground war. il Newsweek 63:35-6 Ap 27 '64
Speaking out; we treat our military shabbily. M. T. Wood. Sat Eve Post 238:10+ Ja 16 '65
USAF will test ground support concepts. E. J. Bulban. Aviation W 80:23 Je 1 '64
See also
Military training camps
United States—Air force, Army

Administration

Army centralizes guidance R&D functions at Redstone. Miss & Roc 13:14 Ag 12 '63
Big man in biggest building. il Ebony 18:84+ Ap '63

Clothing

How to dress warmly in winter. B. H. Frisch. il Sci Digest 57:34-41 Ja '65
See also
Uniforms, Military

Commissariat

Same: breakfast, dinner, and supper for all enlisted men. New Yorker 40:24-5 Ag 22 '64

Corps of engineers

Army lakes float U.S. boatmen. J. Graham. il Motor B 112:34+ Ag '63
City under the ice cap; Camp Century, Greenland. L. D. Hamilton. il Am City 78:100-2 Jl '63
How to feed a beach; saving Greater Los Angeles beaches. il Time 81:51 F 22 '63
Labor requirements for army civil works. R. V. Murray. il Mo Labor R 87:532-5 My '64
Moon map to aid Apollo astronauts. Miss & Roc 14:18 Je 29 '64
Taxpayers' own diggers and builders. il Fortune 69:122-31 Ap '64

Education

Army's language school. A. Friendly, jr. il Sat R 46:72-3 F 16 '63
Class-rooms in the military, by H. F. Clark and H. S. Sloan. Review
Newsweek il 63:77 Ja 20 '64
Dropouts and the draft. New Repub 149:3-4 Ag 17 '63; Reply with rejoinder. 149:36+ S 21 '63
See also
United States military academy, West Point

Enlistment

See United States—Army—Recruiting and enlistment

Equipment and supplies

Air assault development. W. Wright. il Aviation W 80:61-3+ F 24 '64

UNITED STATES—Army—Equipment and supplies —Continued
Army limited war laboratory seeks to reduce research time; Aberdeen proving ground, Md. G. C. Wilson. Aviation W 80:27-8 Je 15 '64
1970 army. J. H. Winchester. il Sci Digest 56:71-5 S '64

Forces in Europe

Again the autobahn. G. Bailey. Reporter 29: 16+ N 7 '63
Berlin: the erosion of a principle. J. E. Smith. Reporter 29:32-3+ N 21 '63
Conflict over convoys; halt of U.S. army convoy to Berlin by Soviets. Sr Schol 83: 19 N 22 '63
Dance of the gooney birds; Russians hold up American convoy en route to Berlin. il Time 82:31-2 N 15 '63
GI's: their war in Europe. R. G. Martin and R. Harrity. il Look 27:72-6 F 26 '63
Just when Nikita seemed all smiles; halt of U.S. military convoy en route to Berlin by Soviet troops. il U S News 55:62-3 N 18 '63
On the autobahn; U.S. army convoy blocked at Marienborn checkpoint. il Newsweek 62: 44+ N 18 '63
Unthawing the thaw; U.S. army convoy blocked at autobahn's Marienborn checkpoint. il Time 82:25-6 O 18 '63

Forces in Korea (Republic)

As an old war heats up. R. P. Martin. il U S News 55:35 Ag 12 '63
Flare-up. il Time 82:20 Ag 9 '63
Lonely line of armistice. R. Steinberg. il Sat Eve Post 236:24-31 Jl 27 '63
U.S. troops in Korea: ready and confident; interview. G. S. Meloy, jr. il U S News 55:65 Jl 22 '63

Guard duty

Third regiment: the President's own. P. S. Catling. il Holiday 35:33-6 Mr '64

Insignia

American military insignia, 1800-1851, by J. D. Campbell and E. M. Howell. Review Hobbies 68:127 F '64

Medical and sanitary affairs

See also
United States—Surgeon general's office

Missile command

Army moves to simplify servicing. M. Getler. Miss & Roc 16:22 Ja 25 '65

Morale

Duty, honor, country; address, May 12, 1962. D. MacArthur. il Life 56:36-38A Ap 17 '64; Excerpts. U S News 56:64-5 Ap 20 '64

Negroes

Guerrilla trainer; southeast Asian jungles. il Ebony 19:47-8+ Ap '64
Little-known Negro Rough riders. J. R. Phillips. Negro Hist Bul 27:59 D '63

Officers

Making of a general; excerpts from George C. Marshall: education of a general. F. C. Pogue. il Look 27:45-58 S 24 '63
See also
Generals

Pay, allowances, etc.

More pay for military? who would get what; chart. U S News 54:8 F 11 '63

Procurement

Budget unit implementing Howze plans. L. Booda. Aviation W 79:26-7 Jl 15 '63
Rotor study proposals requested for army heavy lift helicopter. Aviation W 81:21 Ag 31 '64

Proving grounds

See Proving grounds

Publications

Mail-order spooks; army newspapers sent to Chinese spies. Time 83:35 F 7 '64

Recruiting and enlistment

Dropouts and the draft. New Repub 149:3-4 Ag 17 '63; Reply with rejoinder. 149:36+ S 21 '63
Saved by the bells. Newsweek 62:33 S 23 '63
Volunteer army. New Repub 150:6 Ja 18 '64; Reply. J. den Boer. 150:30-1 F 22 '64

Reserves

Another step for efficiency; disbanding of army's organized reserve. il Time 84:26 D 18 '64
Mac the knife; McNamara discloses further defense cuts. Newsweek 64:24+ D 21 '64
See also
United States—National guard

Training

See Military training

Transportation

Big airlift. W. V. Kennedy. America 109:622 N 16 '63
Big lift and the big letdown; second armored division flown to West Germany. il Newsweek 62:23-5 N 4 '63
Big lift: Hell on wheels vaults Atlantic. il Life 55:36-36A N 1 '63
Big lift; 2nd armored division transported to West Germany. il Time 82:28-9 N 1 '63
Douglas proposes an intercontinental ballistic transport for 1,200 troops. W. E. Wilks. il Miss & Roc 14:35 F 17 '64
Exercise big lift: opening a 5,700-mile air bridge to Europe; with analysis by M. S. Johnson. M. L. Stone and T. J. O'Halloran. il U S News 55:36-9 N 4 '63
Job of getting them there fast; Operation big lift. il Bsns W p 128-9 N 2 '63
Operation big lift: second armored division moved to West Germany. Sr Schol 83:5 N 8 '63
Subtle message; airlift from Texas. to West Germany in three days. Newsweek 62:57 O 7 '63

Army, Department of the

See also
Pentagon building, Arlington, Va.

Army language school

See United States—Army—Education

Art

See Art, American

Atomic energy commission

As plutonium fades, AEC calls industry in; private contractors lease Hanford works. il Bsns W p58-60+ D 26 '64
Asroc test in nuclear series is revealed. Aviation W 80:30 F 10 '64
AEC asks $5 million to end Pluto effort. Aviation W 81:21 Jl 20 '64
AEC; energetic bargaining brings agreement on university contract clauses on security, information. J. Walsh. Science 140:38-9 Ap 5 '63
AEC frees another batch of isotopes. il Bsns W p68+ Je 13 '64
AEC military space funds voted. Aviation W 80:26 Je 22 '64
AEC: mission completed? Newsweek 63:58-9 Mr 9 '64
AEC readies destruct tests of SNAP-type reactors. Miss & Roc 13:26 S 30 '63
AEC reports nuclear weapons expenditures topping $5 billion. Aviation W 81:56 N 30 '64
AEC sees off-the-shelf space-power packages. W. Beller. Miss & Roc 12:39 F 18 '63
Atomic energy commission; special report. il Miss & Roc 15:171-4+ N 30 '64
AEC to aid water project; nuclear power plant for pumping water. Bsns W p98 Ja 9 '65
AEC to seek increase in standby test funds; space requests level. il Aviation W 80:37 Ja 27 '64
Breeder reactor gets its fuel; Enrico Fermi atomic power plant. il Bsns W p 144-5+ My 18 '63
Budget cuts and the AEC. Bul Atomic Sci 20:39-40 Mr '64
Fermi prize: J. Robert Oppenheimer named to receive annual AEC award. H. Bethe. Science 140:161-3 Ap 12 '63
Great uranium glut. H. B. Meyers. il Fortune 69:108-11+ F '64
Ground R&D stressed, flight trimmed. Miss & Roc 14:21 Ja 27 '64
Hot rocket to nowhere; Project Rover. G. Bylinsky and W. E. Howard. il Sat Eve Post 236:78-81 N 9 '63
Is the AEC obsolete? J. W. Finney. il Reporter 31:44-6 N 19 '64; Reply. J. G. Palfrey. 31:6 D 17 '64
Joint committee gets more control of AEC. Miss & Roc 13:15 Jl 15 '63
Joint committee raps DOD, AEC. W. Beller. il Miss & Roc 14:24-5 Mr 2 '64
Journals of David E. Lilienthal. Review New Repub 151:24-5+ O 17 '64. J. W. Finney
Latest nuclear weapons; test series Operation Dominic. Sci N L 85:111 F 15 '64
Nuclear ditch-digging: AEC's Project carryall. il Bsns W p84-5 D 21 '63

UNITED STATES—Atomic energy commission —*Continued*
Operation Red Dog; radiological assistance teams. K. N. Anderson. il Todays Health 43:64-9 Ja '65
Outrage on Bodega Head. G. Marine. il Nation 196:524-7 Je 22 '63
Policy and the scientists. L. A. DuBridge. For Affairs 41:576-8 Ap '63
Project plowshare: AEC program for peaceful nuclear explosives slowed down by test ban treaty. E. Langer. Science 143:1153-5 Mr 13 '64
Q-clearance: the development of a personnel security program. H. P. Green. il Bul Atomic Sci 20:9-15 My '64
Reorientations hampered ANP program. K. Johnsen. il Aviation W 78:81-7 Ap 1 '63
SNAP plan is AEC bid for space role. K. Johnsen. Aviation W 80:31-2 Mr 2 '64
Space, military take bulk of AEC budget. Aviation W 78:31 Ja 21 '63
Tangled drama and private hells of two famous scientists. R. Coughlan. il Life 55:87A-94+ D 13 '63
U.S. and Euratom to cooperate on fast neutron reactors; Department announcement, May 27, 1964. Dept State Bul 50:941-3 Je 15 '64

See also
Fermi award

Attorney General

See United States—Justice, Department of

Boundaries

Bending the river. il Time 82:20 Jl 26 '63
Border dispute settled. il Sr Schol 83:8 S 20 '63
Border pact: what Mexico gains, what Texas loses. il U S News 55:6 D 30 '63
Ceremony at Mexican border marks settlement of Chamizal dispute; address, September 25, 1964. L. B. Johnson. Dept State Bul 51:545-9 O 19 '64
Remember El Chamizal. Newsweek 62:49 Jl 29 '63
Slice of Texas soon to go to Mexico. il U S News 55:12 Jl 22 '63
United States and Mexico agree to conclude convention for settlement of Chamizal boundary dispute; statement, July 18, 1963; with Department statement and joint memorandum of Department and Mexican Ministry of foreign relations, July 17, 1963. J. F. Kennedy. Dept State Bul 49:199-204 Ag 5 '63
U.S. and Mexico sign convention settling Chamizal boundary; Department statement; text of convention, August 29, 1963; and text of minute, International boundary and water commission, United States and Mexico, August 28, 1963. Dept State Bul 49:480-4 S 23 '63
United States ratifies Chamizal convention. L. B. Johnson; E. M. Martin. Dept State Bul 50:49-51 Ja 13 '64

Budget, Bureau of the

Yardstick for red tape. Bsns W p38 S 12 '64

Bureau of Indian affairs

See United States—Indian affairs, Bureau of

Cabinet

Cabinet shake-up coming? il U S News 57:60 N 16 '64
Changes to watch for in the Cabinet. U S News 55:42 D 2 '63
How the President makes a decision; excerpts from Decision-making in the White House. T. C. Sorensen. Sat R 46:12-15+ Jl 27; 8-12+ Ag 3 '63
Political virtuoso gathers the forces to take on the job. J. L. Steele. il Life 55:32-5 D 13 '63
President's chief advisers. il Sr Schol 84:13-14 F 14 '64
Question from the audience. H. Brandon. Sat R 47:10 O 3 '64
Reorganizing the presidency. D. Lawrence. U S News 55:112 D 16 '63
Shuffles. Time 84:39 N 13 '64

See also
Secretaries of state (United States)

Capitol

Architect of the Capitol in trouble? Arch Forum 119:11 Ag '63
Crumbling Capitol: in danger of collapse. il U S News 54:14 Je 17 '63
Nation's Capitol revealed as never before. C. Hayden. il Nat Geog Mag 125:1-3 Ja '64
Under the dome of freedom. L. Aikman. il Nat Geog Mag 125:4-59 Ja '64

Census

Economic census to be taken for 1963. Pub W 184:28-9 O 21 '63
Rocky road of HR 6386; privacy in housing survey; excerpts from testimony. R. Burgess. Nat R 15:429 N 19 '63

Central intelligence agency

After the Cuban crisis. D. H. Wrong. Commentary 35:29-33 Ja '63
Bay of Pigs, by H. Johnson and others. Review
New Repub 150:21-2 Je 27 '64. T. R. Fehrenbach
Reporter 30:53-6 Je 18 '64. J. E. Smith
Sat R 47:41+ My 16 '64. H. Lavine
Brightening the image; CIA meets the press. Nation 198:81 Ja 27 '64
CIA-baiting. Nat R 16:185-6 Mr 10 '64
CIA; battle for secret power. S. Alsop. il Sat Eve Post 236:17-21 Jl 27 '63; Same abr. with title Intelligence business; secret battle for power. Read Digest 83:114-20 O '63
CIA sees no cutback in Soviet spending for defense and space. Aviation W 80:37 Ja 20 '64
CIA: the case builds up. F. J. Cook. il Nation 198:616-18 Je 22 '64
Craft of intelligence; excerpt. A. Dulles. il Harper 226:128-74 Ap '63
Craft of intelligence, by A. Dulles. Review
Nat R 16:244+ Mr 24 '64. T. A. Lane
New Repub 150:20-2 F 15 '64. P. B. Mills
Reporter 29:65-6 N 21 '63. E. Taylor
Sat R 47:42 F 1 '64. W. Walker
U S News il 55:100 O 21 '63
Diplomats in uniform. New Repub 149:13-15 N 2 '63
Folly in Vietnam. New Repub 149:6-7 S 21 '63
Foundations as fronts. Nation 199:102 S 14 '64
Going in the red? concerning report of Central intelligence agency's press conference. Sr Schol 84:20 F 7 '64
Growing risks of bureaucratic intelligence. H. W. Baldwin. il Reporter 29:48-50+ Ag 15 '63; Discussion. 29:6 S 12; 8+ O 10 '63
Haiti and the CIA; Case of Andrew Adams. Nation 200:22-3 Ja 11 '65
Hogwash about the CIA. S. Alsop. il Sat Eve Post 237:15 F 15 '64
How President Kennedy upset Cuban invasion of April 1961. U S News 54:29-30+ F 4 '63
How Trujillo died. N. Gall. New Repub 148:19-20 Ap 13 '63
Incubus. Nation 198:42 Ja 13 '64
Inquiry into the darkness of the cloak, the sharpness of the dagger. J. V. Lindsay. Esquire 61:106-7+ Mr '64
Invisible government; excerpts. D. Wise and T. B. Ross. il Look 28:37+ Je 16; 77-8+ Je 30 '64
Invisible government, by D. Wise and T. B. Ross. Review
Commonweal 80:639-40+ S 18 '64. W. D. Burnham
Nat R 16:541 Je 30 '64. W. F. Buckley, jr
New Repub 150:19-21 Je 27 '64. G. A. Harrison
Sat R il 47:25-6 Je 27 '64. H. H. Ransom
Let's stop baiting the CIA. Life 56:4 Mr 6 '64
Lion tamers. Nation 197:211 O 12 '63
McCone's successor. New Repub 151:4 D 12 '64
Ministry of information; public assessment of Soviet economic achievement. New Repub 150:4-5 Ja 25 '64
Reds with arms and cash spreading out from Cuba; Intelligence report. U S News 54:69 Mr 11 '63
Roberto's story; forgotten young men; with editorial comment. W. F. Rickenbacker. il Nat R 15:94, 105-6 Ag 13 '63
Russians drop a lap behind; lagging growth rate. il Bsns W p30-1 Ja 18 '64
Saigon and CIA. Newsweek 62:38+ O 21 '63
Shooting from the lip. Nat R 16:802-3 S 22 '64
Sick elephant. Nation 198:130 F 10 '64
Slown-down in the Pentagon. H. W. Baldwin. For Affairs 43:267 Ja '65
Speaking out; the CIA is getting out of hand; meddles in foreign policy. E. McCarthy. Sat Eve Post 237:6+ Ja 4 '64
Taboo span. Nation 198:593 Je 15 '64
U.S. intelligence: is it good enough? il U S News 55:66-7 S 9 '63
Unsecretive report on the C.I.A. B. F. Bagdikian. il N Y Times Mag p 18+ O 27 '63
Visible CIA. Nation 198:613-14 Je 22 '64

Children's bureau

Saving battered children. il Time 85:43 Ja 8 '65

UNITED STATES—Children's bureau—*Cont.*

Church history

Lively experiment, by S. E. Mead. Review Christian Cent 80:1030 Ag 21 '63. E. S. Gaustad
Recovery of American religious history. H. F. May. bibliog f Am Hist R 70:79-92 O '64

Civil aeronautics board

Air fares will drop. il Bsns W p 121-2+ S 7 '63
ATA told to submit to scrutiny by CAB. Aviation W 80:37 F 10 '64
Big dogs, little dogs, and the air cargo bone. S. Freedgood. il Fortune 70:122-9+ O '64
Board proposes $1-million subsidy cut. R. G. O'Lone. Aviation W 81:42 S 7 '64
Board rebuffs planned reductions to ease West Coast fare battle. Aviation W 81:37 O 12 '64
Board unit proposes fare policy. Aviation W 81:41 S 14 '64
Boyd favors quality competition instead of quantity in some areas. Aviation W 79:31 S 2 '63
Boyd reappointment viewed as certainty. L. L. Doty. Aviation W 79:45 D 23 '63
Boyd sees jet turbulence ban unneeded. J. R. Ashlock. Aviation W 80:37-8 Ja 13 '64
Boyd warns of sterner CAB fare policy. J. R. Ashlock. Aviation W 80:42-3 Ja 27 '64
CAB bureau criticizes Toolco agreement. R. G. O'Lone. Aviation W 81:40 O 26 '64
CAB cargo ruling sparks court appeal. J. W. Carter. Aviation W 81:29-30 Ag 17 '64
CAB demands sweeping changes in air transport assn. activities. Aviation W 78:41 F 11 '63
CAB feels wind from Northeast; refusal to renew Northeast airlines' Florida certificate. il Bsns W p45-6+ O 5 '63
CAB goals report draws little support. Aviation W 78:36 Ap 29 '63
CAB must rule on Panagra ownership. Aviation W 78:42 Ja 21 '63
CAB nears economy fares case decision. R. G. O'Lone. Aviation W 81:38-9 O 19 '64
CAB plans cargo airline aid. Aviation W 80:41 F 3 '64
CAB rebuffed by Appeals court, must reconsider Northeast case. Aviation W 80:41 My 18 '64
CAB regional airport plan faces delay. R. H. Cook. Aviation W 80:45 Ap 20 '64
CAB rejects Northeast renewal in 3-2 decision on Florida route. J. R. Ashlock. Aviation W 79:43 O 14 '63
CAB reversal of Northeast ruling unlikely despite merger proposal. Aviation W 79:43 S 30 '63
CAB seeking accurate reduced fare analyses. Aviation W 79:46 N 11 '63
CAB seeks to end domestic fare chaos. L. L. Doty. Aviation W 80:34-6 Ja 13 '64
CAB South American case bogged. Aviation W 79:129 O 7 '63
CAB starts studying Western area routes. Aviation W 81:37 Ag 24 '64
CAB to demand appearance by Hughes. R. H. Cook. Aviation W 80:39-40 Je 15 '64
Court grants trunkline petitions, orders stay of CAB cargo policy. J. W. Carter. Aviation W 81:35-6 Ag 24 '64
Decision against Northeast. Time 82:64 Ag 23 '63
Expansion seen saving helicopter service. J. R. Ashlock. Aviation W 81:34-5 Ag 24 '64
Family fight over family fares; airlines fight over family fares. Bsns W p36 S 28 '63
How to fix prices. Nat R 14:439 Je 4 '63
Legislation is key to Pacific fares. R. G. O'Lone. Aviation W 81:29 D 21 '64
Legislators cool to CAB foreign rate plea. J. R. Ashlock. Aviation W 80:28-9 Je 8 '64
Little problem that wasn't there; no-show problem. Consumer Rep 28:100 Mr '63
Monroney supports all-cargo carriers. Aviation W 81:29 Jl 13 '64
Northeast case pressure seen as threat. L. L. Doty. Aviation W 79:40-1 S 9 '63
Northeast struggles to fend off CAB ax. Bsns W p 18 Ag 3 '63
Objections expected on CAB fare rejection. Aviation W 78:43 F 25 '63
Pressures mount on CAB over Northeast. L. L. Doty. Aviation W 79:42-3 S 23 '63
Record trunkline profits seen for 1963. L. L. Doty. Aviation W 79:44 N 11 '63
Ruling that may kill an airline; Northeast airlines. U S News 55:8 Ag 26 '63
Subsidy drop is shown in CAB budget; FAA seeks $810 million. L. L. Doty. Aviation W 78:41 Ja 21 '63
Who will fly the cargo? CAB vs trunk lines. il Bsns W p 102+ Ag 15 '64
Who will fly the charters? nonscheduled, supplemental carriers. il Bsns W p47-8+ Ja 16 '65
Why Northeast faces its worst crisis yet; half local service feeder line, half long-haul trunk carrier. il Bsns W p48-51 Ja 9 '65

Civil air patrol

Perfect host. Civil air patrol. D. Edwards. il Flying 75:72 Ag '64

Civil defense, Office of

Shelters again; incentive program. New Repub 148:6 My 25 '63
Winners named in competition for school shelters. il Arch Rec 135:26+ F '64

Civil rights commission

See United States—Commission on civil rights

Civil service commission

Application rejected; nepotism regulation. W. B. Morse. Am For 70:32+ Jl '64
Exam; Peace corps volunteers exam conducted by the Civil service commission, New York office. New Yorker 39:22-3 D 21 '63
Oh, Mister President! excerpt from The image of the federal service. F. P. Kilpatrick and others. Sat R 47:50-1 Mr 7 '64
Snooping in the park; investigatory techniques. J. Ridgeway. New Repub 152:9-10 Ja 16 '65

Civilian conservation corps

Back to the woods. A. Shuster. il N Y Times Mag p32+ Ag 18 '63
Youth corps bill gets fresh start; new version of New deal's CCC. il Bsns W p79-80 Mr 30 '63

Civilization

American agenda; adaptation of address. J. W. Fulbright. Sat R 46:15-17+ Jl 20 '63; Reply. G. P. Kuiper. 46:13 Ag 17 '63
American civilization; excerpts from address. L. B. Johnson. Time 83:18 My 29 '64
American dream and crisis; address, August 24, 1964. D. E. Walker. Vital Speeches 31:78-82 N 15 '64
American system; address, August 12, 1964. H. Humphrey. Vital Speeches 30:682-5 S 1 '64
Arts as a national resource. S. L. Udall. Sat R 47:14-16 Mr 28 '64
Audacious promise of a great society. Life 57:4 N 13 '64
Bandeirantes and pioneers, by V. Moog; tr. by L. I. Barrett. Review
Nat R 16:736-7 Ag 25 '64. E. M. von Kuehnelt-Leddihn
Blueprint for the great society; excerpt from address, May 22, 1964. L. B. Johnson. il Am For 70:33 Jl '64
Brightness in the air. il Time 84:46-58 D 18 '64
Can we survive the fun explosion? J. W. Krutch. Sat R 48:14-16 Ja 16 '65
Cold war; address, April 5, 1964. J. W. Fulbright. bibliog f Vital Speeches 30:422-7 My 1 '64
Cult of culture. C. J. McNaspy. il America 110:626-8 My 9 '64
Cultural pluralism in the United States and in the projected European union; address, April 5, 1963; with questions and answers. S. K. Padover. Ann Am Acad 348:25-33 Jl '63
Culture against man, by J. Henry. Review
Sat R 46:40 N 23 '63. R. Stein
Desire for beauty, the hunger for community; building the Great society; excerpt from address, May 22, 1964. L. B. Johnson. New Repub 151:32 N 7 '64
Dying Egypt, dying; U.S. declines contribution to the saving of the Abu Simbel temples. F. Getlein. New Repub 150:26-8 My 30 '64
Education for citizenship in the modern world; address, February 16, 1964. D. Rusk. Dept State Bul 50:358-64 Mr 9 '64
Everything nailed down is coming loose; condensation of address. M. W. Fishwick. Sat R 46:11-14 Je 29 '63
Foreign policy and the American citizen; address, December 10, 1963. D. Rusk. bibliog f Dept State Bul 49:990-6 D 30 '63
Forgotten milestones of the Great society. D. Lawrence. U S News 58:104 Ja 18 '65

UNITED STATES—Civilization—*Continued*
Freedom is not enough; address, August 6, 1964. E. Lamb. Vital Speeches 30:719-21 S 15 '64
Freedom's time of testing. W. Reuther. il Sat R 47:36+ Ag 29 '64
From Herbert Hoover on his 90th birthday. H. Hoover. Read Digest 85:143-4 S '64; Same abr. with title American virtue as seen at ninety. Life 57:4 Ag 21 '64
Great society still has to take shape. E. T. Folliard. America 111:733 D 5 '64
Here are Johnson's promises for a Great society; State-of-the-Union message, January 4, 1965. L. B. Johnson. il U S News 58:98-102 Ja 18 '65; Same. Vital Speeches 31:194-8 Ja 15 '65
Hod-carrier: notes of a laborer on an unfinished cathedral, by G. W. Johnson. Review
Sat R 47:43 My 16 '64. E. Capouya
Human challenge; address, September 2, 1964. J. M. Hester. Vital Speeches 30:746-9 O 1 '64
Influence of Africans on American culture. J. A. Davis. bibliog f Ann Am Acad 354: 75-83 Jl '64
Machine in the garden, by L. Marx. Review
Reporter 31:35-6 D 31 '64. G. Steiner
Sat R 48:32 Ja 16 '65. H. Cohen
Mr Lilienthal's worries. J. O'Gara. Commonweal 78:296 Je 7 '63
Mountain and the garden. E. Sevareid. NEA J 53:16 Ap '64
Mythmakers, by B. Nossiter. Review
Commentary 37:71-2 Je '64. R. Lekachman
New renaissance man. H. Brandon. Sat R 47:18+ Ag 29 '64
November 22: what did it mean? E. Roper. Sat R 47:28 My 9 '64
O strange new world, by H. M. Jones. Review
Commentary 39:86-8 Ja '65. S. Lynd
New Repub 151:30+ N 28 '64. A. Koch
Sat R 47:36-7 S 12 '64. A. Heckscher
On the road from Idlewild. Fortune 68:97-8+ O '63
President takes office: Johnson-the-inheritor yields to Johnson-on-his-own. il Sr Schol 85:6-9 Ja 21 '65
Principle of the Great society. W. Lippmann. Newsweek 65:13 Ja 18 '65
Ragged Dick in the last lap. H. Swados. Nation 199:13-14 Jl 13 '64
Restless temper. G. W. Pierson. bibliog f Am Hist R 69:969-89 Jl '64
Skyscrapers, cowboys and skinny blondes; child's-eye view of life in America. P. W. Goldman. il N Y Times Mag p94+ N 29 '64
Strength to be free; address, June 18, 1964. E. M. Clark. Vital Speeches 30:727-30 S 15 '64
Waiting for the end, by L. A. Fiedler. Review
Nat R 16:654-6 Jl 28 '64. H. Kenner
Who really wants the Great society? Nat R 17:50 Ja 26 '65
Whose values should be taught? M. Birnbaum. il Sat R 47:60-2+ Je 20 '64
See also
United States—Intellectual life
United States—Social conditions

Anecdotes, facetiae, satire, etc.

Defense manual for tourists. M. Mannes. Harper 230:125-7 Ja '65

Climate

Retire by climate. N. D. Ford. il Travel 121: 28-32+ Ja '64
See also
Middle West—Climate

Coast guard

Coast guard emerging with GEM control. Aviation W 81:45 O 26 '64
Coast guard's worst week. R. Petrow. il Pop Sci 182:78-83+ Mr '63
Go! said the navy; crunch! case of cutter 322. P. Mandel and R. Kennedy. il Life 55: 17+ O 4 '63
Just what is coast guard approved? safety requirements. H. R. Kaplan. il Motor B 111:48-9+ Mr '63
Naval trilogy; coastal minesweeper U.S.S. Grouse, and two coast guard accidents. il Newsweek 62:34-5 O 14 '63
Plotting tomorrow's course. B. Woodward. Motor B 113:37 Je '64
Request assistance! my estimated position is. H. M. Anthony. il Motor B 112:32-3 Ag '63
Semper paratus. C. Darlington. il Motor B 111:34-5+ Je '63
When Bobby cruised, coast guard was near. il U S News 54:24 Mr 25 '63
When you must ditch at sea; reprint. E. J. Long. il Sci Digest 56:38-42 O '64
See also
United States coast guard academy

Coast guard auxiliary

Free USCGAux classes in boat handling. il Motor B 113:353-4+ Ja '64
Seagoing silver anniversary for the USCG auxiliary 1939-1964; symposium. il Motor B 113:30-7+ Je '64
Speak up: there's a decal in the offering. B. Woodward. il Motor B 111:76+ Mr '63
Under the blue ensign. B. Woodward. See issues of Motor boating
U.S. Coast guard auxiliary. R. Birnn. See issues of Yachting
USCGAux free instruction courses. il Motor B 112:83-4 Ag '63; 114:105-6 S '64

Commerce

Ambassadors asked to report on activities in promoting exports; letter, August 2, 1963. D. Rusk. Dept State Bul 49:290 Ag 19 '63
America gets an unexpected break. H. S. Reuss. Harper 226:37-42 My '63; Reply. M. G. Johnson. 227:6+ Jl '63
Beef from abroad. America 111:208 Ag 29 '64
Big business: is it too big? reprint. H. H. Humphrey. il Look 28:84-6 O 20 '64
Britain will buy more U.S. goods; sales prospects in Britain, Japan, southeast Asia. il Nations Bsns 51:36-7+ My '63
Common market and the Kennedy round. il Sr Schol 84:9-11 Ap 24 '64
Common market: now, Le package deal? il Newsweek 62:70-3+ D 16 '63
Drive to hike exports. il Bsns W p31 S 21 '63
Europe: a major role for EFTA; letter from Geneva. M. A. Heilperin. il Fortune 69:61-2+ Mr '64
Export expansion and balance of payments, remarks, April 7, 1964. L. B. Johnson. Dept State Bul 50:663-4 Ap 27 '64
Exports pull out of their slump. il Bsns W p 100+ Ag 10 '63
Foreign economic policy; address, January 7, 1963. T. B. Curtis. Vital Speeches 29:260-3 F 15 '63
Geneva trade talks; Common market and U.S. Nat R 14:441 Je 4 '63
Grim reality of foreign trade. il Duns R 81: 73-4+ My '63
Hard sell abroad. L. Morse. il Duns R 81: 46-9+ Ap '63
Here's where you can sell abroad. il Nations Bsns 51:76-8+ Ap '63
How to sell more abroad. A. S. Beckley. il Nations Bsns 51:106-10+ Mr '63
Imports will sharpen business skills; symposium. il Nations Bsns 51:36-7+ Ag '63
Industry role in trade negotiations; address, November 24, 1964. W. M. Roth. Dept State Bul 51:853-5 D 14 '64
International markets; export picture still dismal. A. O. Stanley. Duns R 81:95 My '63
International markets; what we can expect in our world trade position in 1963. A. O. Stanley. Duns R 81:51-3+ Ja '63
Major trading nations remove restrictions on U.S. exports; Department announcement, January 10, 1964; with list of import liberalizations. Dept State Bul 50:214-18 F 10 '64
Paradise-re-examined. il Time 81:83 F 15 '63
President establishes Interagency committee on export expansion. L. B. Johnson. Dept State Bul 50:25-6 Ja 6 '64
President greets Public advisory committee for trade negotiations; remarks, April 21, 1964. L. B. Johnson. Dept State Bul 50:749-50 My 11 '64
President sets up administration of Trade expansion act; executive order. J. F. Kennedy. Dept State Bul 48:180-2 F 4 '63
Readjusting United States foreign trade; address, April 5, 1963. L. Weiss. Dept State Bul 48:652-60 Ap 29 '63
Rising sales overseas. Nations Bsns 52:40-1+ F '64
Role of labor cost in foreign trade. W. C. Shelton and J. H. Chandler. bibliog f il Mo Labor R 86:485-90 My '63
Sales talk from the White House. il Time 82:73 S 27 '63
Showcase for U.S. exports. il Fortune 69:67-8 Mr '64
Sturdy exports. il Fortune 68:36+ Ag '63
Supermarket to the world; U.S. farm exports. il Time 84:102 S 18 '64
Thorough approach to foreign markets; use of consultants in international commerce; address, June 18, 1963. L. V. Kleydorff. Vital Speeches 29:631-3 Ag 1 '63

UNITED STATES—Commerce—*Continued*

Trade expansion program; address, March 8, 1963. P. H. Trezise. Dept State Bul 48: 497-500 Ap 1 '63

Trade, investment, and peace; address, October 5, 1964. D. Rusk. Dept State Bul 51:570-5 O 26 '64

Trade surplus. il Fortune 69:28+ My '64

Trade; the key to Atlantic maturity; address, May 17, 1964. A. Ribicoff. Vital Speeches 30:514-16 Je 15 '64

Union problem: imports vs. jobs; changes demanded in Trade expansion act of 1962. U S News 55:95 S 16 '63

U.S. balancing act in world trade. il Sr Schol 84:14-16 Ap 17 '64

U.S. exports: 2,600 products equal $21.4 billion. il Fortune 67:92 My '63

United States trade policies; address, October 3, 1963. A. Chayes. Vital Speeches 30:47-51 N 1 '63

Washington desk. J. R. Slevin. Duns R 81: 5-6 F '63

What the traffic will bear; export costs. Time 82:66 Ag 9 '63

What's needed to boost sales abroad; symposium. il Nations Bsns 52:62-4+ Ja '64

White House holds conference on export expansion; addresses, September 17, 1963. J. F. Kennedy; D. Rusk; C. A. Herter. Dept State Bul 49:595-605 O 14 '63

World trade; national and corporate interests; address, November 19, 1963. L. D. Copeland. Vital Speeches 30:264-7 F 15 '64

Yankee salesmen. Time 83:91 Ap 24 '64

See also

Export controls
Insurance, Credit
Merchant marine—United States
Shipping—United States
Tariff—United States
United States—Commercial treaties and agreements
United States—Trade information committee
World trade week

History

English furniture exports to America, 1697-1830. E. T. Joy. il Antiques 85:92-8 Ja '64

Brazil

Terms of trade and the Brazilian balance of payments; address, January 29, 1963. L. Gordon. il Dept State Bul 48:284-93 F 25 '63

Bulgaria

Department states views on trade relations between U.S. and Bulgaria; Department statement, July 2, 1963. Dept State Bul 49: 141 Jl 22 '63

Canada

Auto trade heads for open road; unified market for US-Canadian cars. il Bsns W p32+ Ja 23 '65

Canadian-American relations construct a solid foundation for effective world trade; address, April 22, 1963. R. W. Macaulay. Vital Speeches 29:503-6 Je 1 '63

Now a common market for U.S.-Canadian cars. U S News 58:10 Ja 25 '65

Communist countries

Absurd new example of local vigilantism; books from Communist countries. C. B. Grannis. Pub W 183:61 Je 17 '63

Burying communism. New Repub 150:3-4 Ja 25 '64

Can you do business with the Communists. il Time 83:84 My 8 '64

Columbus anti-Communist ordinance unconstitutional. Pub W 184:36-7 N 25 '63

Columbus discovery; Communist imports. C. Chittenden. Nat R 14:379 My 7 '63

Communist market: hard facts on its value to U.S. il U S News 55:81-2 O 7 '63

Communist merchandise. New Repub 148:6-7 Je 1 '63

Department opposes restriction of credit to Communist nations; statement, November 21, 1963. G. W. Ball. Dept State Bul 49: 935-6 D 16 '63

Department supports discretionary authority for President on trade with Poland and Yugoslavia; statement, May 27, 1963. W. R. Tyler. Dept State Bul 48:947-51 Je 17 '63

In the wind: more U.S. trade with Communists. U S News 58:10 Ja 18 '65

More trade with reds. America 110:787 Je 6 '64

New President wins first test in Senate; defeat of Mundt bill. U S News 55:6 D 9 '63

New trade drive. il Time 85:85 Ja 15 '65

Red trade: green light? il Newsweek 65:59 Ja 18 '65

Thawing trade with the reds. il Bsns W p65-6 Ja 2 '65

This month's feature: U.S. trade relations with the red bloc. Cong Digest 43:37-45+ F '64

U.S. grain dealers to be allowed to sell wheat to Soviet Union and eastern Europe; statement by President Kennedy, and letter from Attorney General, October 9, 1963. J. F. Kennedy; R. F. Kennedy. Dept State Bul 49:660-7 O 28 '63

U.S. to sell wheat. il Bsns W p29 O 12 '63

With our tongues hanging out. Nation 197: 189 O 5 '63

Wrapping up the deal to sell Russia wheat. il Bsns W p30-1 O 19 '63

Europe, Eastern

East-West trade: the iron curtain eighteen years later; address, November 11, 1964. R. B. Wright. Dept State Bul 51:185-20 D 7 '64

Europe, Western

After de Gaulle. America 108:250-1 F 23 '63

Chicken armistice. Time 82:99 O 25 '63

Chicken war. il Time 81:92 Je 14 '63

Chicken war puts new strains on unity; EEC curbs on poultry; with editorial comment. Bsns W p25-6, 132 Ag 10 '63

Chicken-war stew; United States and the Common market. P. Hendry. Reporter 29: 30+ N 7 '63

Chickening out; poultry tariffs raised, U.S. exports cut. Newsweek 61:80 Je 10 '63

Common market at the crossroads; address, March 20, 1963. A. K. Watson. Vital Speeches 29:397-400 Ap 15 '63

Europeans as beef eaters; what's in it for U.S. il U S News 56:96 Je 15 '64

Foreign trade, the glow is bright; sales abroad hit a record level. il Bsns W p62-4 Ja 2 '65

Germany's Erhard talks about trade, tariffs, the U.S. dollars; interview, ed. by K. Lachmann and A. Zanker. L. Erhard. U S News 56:62-4 Je 8 '64

Rougher going on trade. il Bsns W p27-8 F 9 '63

Salad days for foreign sales; with charts. il Bsns W p56-8+ D 28 '63

United States trade relations with the new Europe; the challenge and the opportunities; address, January 10, 1963. D. MacArthur, 2d. Dept State Bul 48:174-9 F 4 '63

Urge for the Yankee label. il Time 84:58-9 Jl 31 '64

Where Europe is headed now. A. Zanker. il U S News 54:50-2 Je 3 '63

Will foreign cars share in the U.S. boom? il U S News 57:125-6 O 19 '64

Great Britain

How U.S. beef is selling in Britain. il U S News 57:66 Jl 6 '64

Italy

I flew with the calves; with editorial comment. L. M. Palmer. il Farm J 88:4, 30-1+ N '64

Japan

Pacific kingpin. America 108:246 F 23 '63

Latin America

Brighter opportunities ahead in Latin America. B. DeSoissons. il Nations Bsns 51:80-2+ S '63

Kaiser: model for Latin America. D. Smyth. il Nation 197:415-17 D 14 '63

What French salesman de Gaulle was selling in Latin America. il U S News 56:100 Ap 6 '64

Netherlands

Our man in Amsterdam; U.S. food and agriculture exhibition. New Yorker 39:24-6 D 21 '63

Poland

Trade benefits to be continued to Poland and Yugoslavia; memorandum from President Johnson, March 26, 1964; with text of statement. L. B. Johnson. Dept State Bul 50:626-8 Ap 20 '64

Russia

ABC's of American wheat sales to the reds; with statement by J. F. Kennedy. il U S News 55:52-3 O 21 '63

America's jobless and Russia's markets. J. Lomax. Nation 196:262-4 Mr 30 '63

Another October: another Gromyko meeting; Lot of dough from wheat. il Newsweek 62: 33-4 O 21 '63

As Russia goes shopping: outlook in the wheat belt. il U S News 55:42-4 O 14 '63

UNITED STATES—Commerce—Russia—*Cont.*
Big deal; wheat deal between the U.S. and Russia. Time 83:26 Ja 10 '64
Big wheat deal. il Time 82:35 N 15 '63
Canada wheat pours into Soviet ships; with editorial comment. il Life 55:4, 30-3 O 11 '63
Chicken feed. P. Teter. New Repub 149:5 O 5 '63
Deal in wheat? il Time 82:31 O 4 '63
Deal on wheat; grain sales to the Soviet bloc. New Repub 149:7-8 N 23 '63
Dialogue? yes; concessions? beware! A. A. Berle, jr. il N Y Times Mag p9+ O 20 '63; Discussion. p26+ N 10 '63; 19-20 Ja 19 '64
East-West: the new trade winds; expansion of trade with the Soviet bloc; with report by E. Griffiths. il Newsweek 62:38-40 Ag 19 '63
For and against the grain. Reporter 29:14+ O 10 '63
From Washington straight. Cato. Nat R 15: 270 O 8 '63
Great trade muddle. Sat Eve Post 237:82 Mr 14 '64
Great wheat deal. Time 82:27 O 18 '63
Half-baked; wheat deal between the U.S. Russia and European Communist countries. Time 83:22 Mr 13 '64
How to share in East-West trade? il Newsweek 62:71 S 30 '63
Like surfboarding: negotiation for wheat sale to Russia. Newsweek 62:90+ O 7 '63
LBJ's first union showdown; how wheat strike came out. il U S News 56:89-90 Mr 9 '64
Massive wheat sale to U.S.S.R. Sr Schol 83: 8-9 O 4 '63
More U.S. trade with Russia. il U S News 57:16 N 30 '64
Next job: moving the wheat; handling Soviet grain. Bsns W p28-9 N 16 '63
Piece of the action; wheat bound for Russia. il Time 83:28 Mr 6 '64
Profit and politics. Reporter 30:14+ Ja 16 '64
Relax trade policies with Communist-bloc nations. Christian Cent 80:1292-3 O 23 '63
Rush to trade with reds; will U.S. join it? il U S News 55:51-2 S 30 '63
Russia's grain is last straw; ILA boycott. il Bsns W p 106-7 F 22 '64
Should the U.S. trade with enemies? R. K. Massie. Sat Eve Post 237:19-21 F 1 '64
Surplus wheat to Russia. B. Tufty. Sci N L 84:245 O 19 '63
Talking trade. il Newsweek 64:79 N 30 '64
Trade with Russia? both ayes and nays; businessmen questioned; with editorial comment. Bsns W p29-30, 144 O 5 '63
Trading with Communists. B. L. Masse. il America 110:570-2 Ap 25 '64
Trading with the Communists. C. A. Cooper. New Repub 149:9-12 O 12 '63
200 million new customers for U.S? interview. E. M. Braderman. il U S News 55: 40-3 N 4 '63
U.S. wheat for the Soviets? pro and con discussion. Sr Schol 83:8-9 O 25 '63
Wheat, and what else? U.S. crops to Russia. il Bsns W p34+ N 9 '63
Wheat for reds; who's paying? il U S News 56:87-8 F 17 '64
Wheat leads the way; East-West thaw. il Bsns W p25-8 S 28 '63
Wheat mess. Nat R 15:334 O 22 '63
Wheat sale and the public. E. Roper. il Sat R 46:23 N 16 '63
Wheat to Russia. America 109:450 O 19 '63
When Americans make machines for reds; excerpts from testimony. J. P. Drago. U S News 54:8 Ap 1 '63
Who'll profit from big wheat deal. il U S News 55:50 O 28 '63
Will the West bail out Russia with trade? il U S News 57:106-7 D 7 '64

South Africa

Maybe Lord Home has a heart; promises to halt British shipment of weapons. New Repub 149:7 Ag 17 '63

Yugoslavia

Trade benefits to be continued to Poland and Yugoslavia; memorandum from President Johnson, March 26, 1964; with text of statement. L. B. Johnson. Dept State Bul 50:626-8 Ap 20 '64

Commerce, Department of

Administration & management stresses better information distribution. Miss & Roc 14:93-5 Mr 30 '64
Back in government; FDR, jr. gets Commerce post. U S News 54:16 F 11 '63
Brain mines of tomorrow; Commerce department's new program in support of civilian technology. J. H. Hollomon. Sat R 46:46-7 My 4 '63
Business hot line. Bsns W p56+ O 24 '64
Commerce post goes to Connor. Bsns W p30 D 19 '64
DOD acts to standardize data flow. Miss & Roc 14:14 Mr 23 '64
Enlarged data center; Technical documentation center. N. Lawson. Sci N L 85:199 Mr 28 '64
Industry's slide rule is updated by eleven years; new input-output table. il Bsns W p 166-8 N 21 '64
Your foreign showcase. il Bsns W p 104+ Ag 29 '64
See also
United States—Area redevelopment administration

Commercial policy

See United States—Economic policy

Commercial treaties and agreements

Agricultural commodities agreement signed with Poland; Department announcement; text of agreement. il Dept State Bul 48:303-5 F 25 '63
Canada's car push hits a roadblock; tariff rebate plan on auto parts challenged. Bsns W p91-2 Jl 25 '64
Certain U.S. trade agreement concessions enter into force. Dept State Bul 48:182 F 4 '63
Cotton textile agreements concluded with Greece and Turkey; Department announcement; with texts of U.S. notes, July 17, 1964. G. G. Johnson. il Dept State Bul 51: 290-4 Ag 24 '64
Cotton textile arrangement concluded with Jamaica; Department announcement, October 2, 1963; with text of agreement. il Dept State Bul 49:645-6 O 21 '63
Department supports discretionary authority for President on trade with Poland and Yugoslavia; statement, May 27, 1963. W. R. Tyler. Dept State Bul 48:947-51 Je 17 '63
International coffee agreement, 1962; statement, March 12, 1963. G. C. McGhee. Dept State Bul 48:493-7 Ap 1 '63
President issues order on trade agreements program administration; executive order, April 18, 1963. J. F. Kennedy. Dept State Bul 48:839 My 27 '63
President reports on operation of trade agreements program, September 23, 1964. L. B. Johnson. Dept State Bul 51:516-17 O 12 '64
Quotas and quarrels; Japanese-American cotton-textile pact. Newsweek 62:74+ S 9 '63
Ratifications of FEN treaty exchanged with Belgium. Dept State Bul 49:484 S 23 '63
Shopping list; U.S. and Rumanian economic pact. Newsweek 63:74 Je 15 '64
Trade agreement signed by U.S. and Spain. il Dept State Bul 48:146 Ja 28 '63
Trade with Paraguay and the United Arab Republic; proclamation. L. B. Johnson. Dept State Bul 51:120-1 Jl 27 '64
U.S. and Hong Kong announce cotton textile agreement. il Dept State Bul 51:517-18 O 12 '64
U.S. and Hong Kong conclude cotton textile agreement; joint announcement, November 15, 1963. Dept State Bul 49:933-4 D 16 '63
United States and India conclude cotton textile agreement; Department announcement; with exchange of notes effecting the agreement; exchange of notes concerning category thirty-six exports. il Dept State Bul 50:914-17 Je 8 '64
U.S. and Japan agree on exports of zipper chain from Japan; Department announcement, exchange of letters between Ambassador Ryuji Takeuchi and Assistant secretary of state for economic affairs G. Griffith Johnson, and attachment. Dept State Bul 49:449 S 16 '63
United States and Japan conclude arrangement for cotton textile trade, 1963-65; joint announcement, exchange of notes and letters between Ambassador Ryuji Takeuchi and Assistant secretary of state for economic affairs G. Griffith Johnson, and attachments. Dept State Bul 49:440-9 S 16 '63
United States and Japan sign compensatory trade agreements; Department announcement, December 31, 1962; with schedules. Dept State Bul 48:108-9 Ja 21 '63
United States and Japan sign consular convention. Dept State Bul 48:585 Ap 15 '63
U.S. and Philippines conclude cotton textile agreement; announcement of initialing, with U.S. note and square yard equivalent conversion factors. il Dept State Bul 50: 383-5 Mr 9 '64

UNITED STATES—Commercial treaties and agreements—*Continued*

U.S. and Poland sign agricultural commodities agreements; Department announcement, with texts of agreements, February 3 and February 4, 1964. il Dept State Bul 50:308-12 F 24 '64

U.S. and Republic of China conclude textile arrangement; Department announcement, October 22, 1963, with exchange of notes between Ambassador Jerauld Wright and the Chinese Minister of foreign affairs. il Dept State Bul 49:789-92 N 18 '63

United States and United Kingdom conclude grains agreement; statement, April 16, 1964. C. A. Herter. Dept State Bul 50:703-4 My 4 '64

U.S.-Canada brawl: a matter of capital. Bsns W p29-30 N 2 '63

United States concludes meat agreement with Ireland, State-Agriculture announcement; with exchange of notes, February 25, 1964. Dept State Bul 50:468-9 Mr 23 '64

U.S. concludes meat agreement with Mexico; State-agriculture announcement, with United States note, May 14, 1964. Dept State Bul 50:944-5 Je 15 '64

U.S. concludes meat agreements with Australia and New Zealand; State-Agriculture announcement, with exchange of notes, February 17, 1964. Dept State Bul 50:380-2 Mr 9 '64

U.S. concludes textile agreements with Israel and U.A.R; Department announcements, with texts of U.S. notes. Dept State Bul 50:51-6 Ja 13 '64

U.S. participation in long-term cotton textile arrangement; statement, December 3, 1963. S. Nehmer. Dept State Bul 50:96-101 Ja 20 '64

United States-Polish agricultural commodities agreement. il Cur Hist 44:305-6 My '63

Commission on civil rights

Angry language; interim report considers cutting off federal funds for Mississippi. Newsweek 61:25-6 Ap 29 '63

Cruel and unusual punishments. D. Lawrence. U S News 54:108 Ap 29 '63

Federal commission urges rights action. Sr Schol 83:19-20 O 18 '63

It makes people mad; complaints against Mississippi sent to the U.S. civil rights commission. Time 81:24-5 Ap 26 '63

Mississippi; suggested cut-off of federal funds. New Repub 148:3-4 Ap 27 '63

Not enough. New Repub 149:3-4 O 12 '63

Push for civil rights; newest official size-up. il U S News 55:110-12 O 7 '63

Role of the civil rights commission. B. Carter. il Reporter 29:10-14 Jl 4 '63

What has been done is prologue; carrying out the Civil rights act. A. M. Bickel. New Repub 152:16-18 Ja 9 '65

Word and substance; findings of Civil rights commission report. Newsweek 62:42 O 7 '63

Committee for economic development

See Committee for economic development

Committee to strengthen the security of the free world

See United States—President's committee to strengthen the security of the free world

Communicable disease center, Atlanta, Ga.

Eggs salmonella. Newsweek 62:59 Jl 22 '63

How we're fighting illness from animals. J. E. Bishop. il Sci Digest 53:54-7 My '63

Meet our medical FBI; excerpts from To save your life. N. D. Spingarn. il Parents Mag 38:78-9+ O '63

Community relations service

How silly can you get? confirmation of director-designate. il Time 84:26-7 Jl 17 '64

What has been done is prologue; carrying out the Civil rights act. A. M. Bickel. New Repub 152:16-18 Ja 9 '65

Comptroller general

See United States—General accounting office

Conciliation service

See United States—Federal mediation and conciliation service

Congress

Are there too many lawyers in Congress? A. Hacker. il N Y Times Mag p 14+ Ja 5 '64

Arms and the big money men. J. Duscha. il Harper 228:39-47 Mr; 59-65 Ap; 56-62 My '64; Discussion of March issue. 228:10+ My '64; Miss & Roc 14:46 Mr 16 '64

Art of politics. G. McGee. il NEA J 52:36-9 F '63

Attack on the Congress. F. S. Meyer. Nat R 16:109-10 F 11 '64

Blueprint for a stronger Congress. C. P. Case. il Sat R 46:23-4+ N 23 '63

British-eye view of Congress. M. Edelman. Holiday 34:54-5+ Jl '63

Cold war between the Hill and Foggy Bottom. F. G. Dutton. il N Y Times Mag p36+ S 15 '63

Congress against itself. W. A. Korns. New Repub 150:26+ Je 27 '64

Congress and disarmament. J. S. Clark. Bul Atomic Sci 19:3-8 S '63; Reply. S. Gottlieb. 19:40-1 D '63

Congress at work; symposium. il Sr Schol 82:6-18+ F 20 '63

Congress should police itself. Life 55:4 N 22 '63

Congress: the sapless branch, by J. S. Clark. Review
  Life 56:6+ My 29 '64. N. MacNeil

Congress: when the private life of a lawmaker becomes a public affair. L. Stern and E. Knoll. il Esquire 61:82-6 Ap '64

Congressional morals. America 109:694 N 30 '63

Contempt of Congress; bill to compel disclosure of income. Nation 198:22 Ja 6 '64

Critics of Congress. R. Moley. Newsweek 62:124 O 21 '63

Deliberate pace in Congress safeguards your rights. F. Morley. il Nations Bsns 51:27-8 Mr '63

Floor plans for both the Houses. L. W. Koenig. Sat R 47:29-30 Je 13 '64

Franco, Congress and the Pentagon. C. McWilliams. Christian Cent 80:298-300 Mr 6 '63

Has Congress a future? W. D. Burnham. il Nation 196:545-8+ Je 29 '63

Hidden change in Congress. J. Kraft. Harper 229:116+ O '64

How to spot false budget cuts. V. J. Burke. il Nations Bsns 52:42-3+ F '64

Insider rule for congressmen. Bsns W p 144 N 23 '63

Is the government ready for the future? R. Drummond. Sat R 47:56+ Ag 29 '64

LBJ maps an agenda, lines up the team. il Bsns W p34-6 N 7 '64

LBJ wants Congress to do these things. il U S News 55:46-7 D 9 '63

Members of Congress need your help. J. Miller. Suc Farm 61:78 F '63

Nation's lawmakers. il Sr Schol 84:16-19 F 14 '64

Needed: a hot line from military to Congress? M. S. Johnson. il U S News 55:70-1 S 23 '63

Nine men who control Congress. C. M. Roberts. il Atlan 213:63-8 Ap '64

No time left to legislate. L. W. Koenig. Sat R 47:41-2 F 1 '64

Non-legislative arts. D. T. Bazelon. Commentary 38:82-5 D '64

Observations of a freshman in Congress. C. D. Long. il N Y Times Mag p34+ D 1 '63

President's dilemma; plans for reorganization. K. Crawford. Newsweek 64:43 N 23 '64

Profiles of the 88th's leaders. Sr Schol 82:44 F 20 '63

Reasonable man. W. J. Coughlin. Miss & Roc 14:46 Mr 2 '64

Refusal to act is often in public interest. J. Craft. il Nations Bsns 52:25-6 F '64

Science advisory staffs for House and Senate; letter. B. E. Knox. Science 141:593 Ag 16 '63

Scientific advice for Congress; excerpts from address, November 20, 1963. C. P. Anderson. Science 144:29-32 Ap 3 '64

T.R.B. from Washington; Congress at fault. New Repub 150:2 My 30 '64

Teacher's view inside Congress. D. B Fleming, jr. il NEA J 53:69-72 Ja '64

Trouble with Congress is. . . il Changing T 19:37-40 Ja '65

Under the dome of freedom; United States Capitol. L. Aikman. il Nat Geog Mag 125:4-59 Ja '64

Vanities of Otto Passman. M. Kempton. New Repub 149:14-15 D 28 '63

What's right and wrong with Congress. R. K. Huitt. il Nations Bsns 52:40-1+ N '64

What's wrong here? K. Crawford. Newsweek 62:22 D 23 '63

UNITED STATES—Congress—*Continued*
White House vs. Congress: is power balance shifting? excerpts from address, April 3, 1963. G. Allott. U S News 54:95-6 Ap 15 '63
See also
Congressional record
Congressmen
Congresswomen
Contempt of legislative bodies
Government investigations
Legislation—United States
Lobbying
Presidents—United States—Relations with Congress

Anecdotes, facetiae, satire, etc.

They wonder why Congress is so slow. Nat R 16:21-2 Ja 14 '64

Chaplains

Chaplain to the New frontier. R. Massie. il Sat Eve Post 236:70-2 S 21 '63

Committees

Appropriations: the critics of Congress often slight an inner redoubt of the system. J. Walsh. Science 143:548-51 F 7 '64
Big picture: House committee hears views on basic problems of science-government relations. D. S. Greenberg. Science 142:650-3 N 8 '63
Changes on Capitol hill. il U S News 54:20 F 4 '63
Choosing battlefield for GOP; congressional Republicans. il Bsns W p36 S 7 '63
Committee system, key to congressional action. il Sr Schol 82:12-13 F 20 '63
Congress seen key to military space role; Senate and House armed services committees. Aviation W 78:26-7 Mr 4 '63
Easier world credit; Joint economic committee hearings on Brookings study. il Bsns W p 17-18 Ag 3 '63
Fermi prize money: congressional committee takes steps to assume control of annual $50,000 award. D. S. Greenberg. Science 143:1305 Mr 20 '64; Reply. D. O. Walter. 144:796 My 15 '64
How aerospace leaders fared in election. Aviation W 81:26 N 9 '64
Immigration: quotas vs. quality. P. Duke and S. Meisler. il Reporter 32:30-2 Ja 14 '65
Incorrect, illogical, etc; R. McNamara vs Joint committee on atomic energy. il Time 83:31 Ja 3 '64
Kennedy's committees. America 108:736 My 25 '63
Legislators who move school bills in Congress. il NEA J 53:42-3 Ap '64
Now it's the money managers who are under fire. il U S News 54:94-5 Ap 1 '63
Paving the way for Johnson plans, Congress shakes up rules and committees. il U S News 58:33 Ja 18 '65
Pests and poisons; R. Carson before Senate investigative subcommittee. Newsweek 61:86 Je 17 '63
Uproar over stockpiles: a committee's report. U S News 55:10 O 7 '63
Who's stalemated: Congress or the people? C. M. Whelan. America 109:282 S 21 '63

Employees

Congress: hearings on science advisory staff reveals interest, but no strong inside demand. J. Walsh. Science 142:1446 D 13 '63
Congress' helping hands. il Sr Schol 82:36-7 F 20 '63
Scientific advisers for Congress; letter. R. H. Lueck. Science 143:525 F 7 '64; Reply. R. Rossbacher. 144:363 Ap 24 '64
Secretary for the Senate majority: the job, and its power. il U S News 56:43 F 10 '64

Expert advisers

See United States—Congress—Professional staff members

Pages

Congress' helping hands. il Sr Schol 82:36-7 F 20 '63

Powers and duties

Congressional frustration. D. Wolfle. Science 141:865 S 6 '63
Critique of Congress. W. Lippman. il Newsweek 63:18-19 Ja 20 '64
Non rule in America. D. T. Bazelon. bibliog f Commentary 36:438-45 D '63
Speaking out; Congress must reform. R. Drummond. Sat Eve Post 236:8+ F 9 '63
Speaking out; doesn't Congress have ideas of its own? A. Ribicoff. Sat Eve Post 237:6+ Mr 21 '64
Who makes decisions in Washington. B. Hays. il Nations Bsns 53:40-1+ Ja '65

Professional staff members

Congress and science: Daddario study casts doubts on proposals to establish advisory service. D. S. Greenberg. Science 145:904-5 Ag 28 '64
Invisible men who run Congress; congressional staff. R. Evans, jr. il Sat Eve Post 236:13-17 Je 8 '63

Rules and practice

Changes in Congress. New Repub 152:7 Ja 16 '65
Civil-rights tangle: where it is headed. il U S News 56:37-8 My 25 '64
Congress edges toward reform. il Bsns W p28-9 Ap 6 '63
Congress: question of reform of procedures becomes an issue; House committee on rules. J. Walsh. Science 139:201+ Ja 18 '63
Congress: with new sides chosen it appears the next game may be played under some new rules. J. Walsh. Science 146:1280-2 D 4 '64
Do-little Congress talks of more speed; 88th Congress; with editorial comment. Bsns W p25, 204 S 14 '63
Do something Congress? W. V. Shannon. Commonweal 80:464-5 Jl 10 '64
Failure of Congress; with editorial comment. S. Alsop. il Sat Eve Post 236:23-5, 106 D 7 '63
Is Congress its own worst enemy? il Bsns W p 17-19 Ja 4 '64
Legislative reform. D. S. Greenberg. Science 139:1186-7 Mr 22 '63
Lyndon Johnson's stake in reform. E. A. Kolodziej. New Repub 151:14-15 N 21 '64
New kind of national election; excerpts from Congress: the sapless branch. J. S. Clark. Harper 228:72-4+ My '64
Speaking out; Congress must reform. R. Drummond. Sat Eve Post 236:8+ F 9 '63
To move Congress out of its ruts. S. H. Humphrey. il N Y Times Mag p39+ Ap 7 '63

Term of members

See Congressmen—Term

Terminology

Congressional glossary. Sr Schol 82:45 F 20 '63

Voting

Whiplash; liberal Democrats choose Senate whip. Reporter 31:8-10 D 17 '64

84th Congress

Lyndon Johnson talks about Congress and the presidency; excerpts from interview, 1955. L. B. Johnson. U S News 56:25 Ja 6 '64

87th Congress

Democrat margin of victory; with list of all Republican congressmen: their defections to and votes in agreement with Democrats. Nat R 16:960-4 N 3 '64

88th Congress

Ambitious program for the 88th Congress. H. G. Sackett. NEA J 52:32 F '63
Can Johnson get Congress moving? R. Evans and R. Novak. il Sat Eve Post 237:34+ Ap 4 '64
Congress gets a grade of A. Life 57:4 Ag 28 '64
Congress mends its ways. Bsns W p 140 F 15 '64
Democrat margin of victory; with list of all Republican congressmen: their defections to and votes in agreement with Democrats. Nat R 16:961-4 N 3 '64
Easy congressional victories are hard-won. J. N. Eller. America 110:275 F 29 '64
88th Congress. New Repub 151:3-4 O 17 '64
88th Congress: twenty-four key votes; rating the performance of legislators. il New Repub 151:13-20 O 17 '64
Grist for the campaign mills. Bsns W p28-9 O 3 '64
In Congress: the new men begin to chafe. il Bsns W p23-4 F 9 '63
Kennedy's problem: could he get more from Congress? H. Fuller. New Repub 148:12-14 Mr 9 '63
Lethargic 88th vs. L.B.J. Life 55:4 D 13 '63
Wandering paths of a transit bill. V. J. Burke. il Reporter 31:31-3 Jl 16 '64

UNITED STATES—Congress—88th Congress —*Continued*
Washington desk; achievements of the 88th Congress. J. R. Slevin. Duns R 84:5-6 N '64
What the 88th did. K. Crawford. Newsweek 64:46 O 12 '64

88th Congress—1st session

After six months: how JFK is making out with Congress. il U S News 55:32-3 Jl 22 '63
And Congress has work to do. Life 55:4 S 6 '63
As Congress picks up speed . . . il U S News 55:31-3 S 30 '63
As we go to press; congressional scorecard. Recreation 56:211-12 My '63
Atlantic report. Atlan 211:4+ My '63
Book trade and the current session of Congress. R. H. Smith. Pub W 184:38 N 25 '63
Civil rights, then the tax cut? il Newsweek 62:29 O 14 '63
Congress. See issues of Newsweek to January 13, 1964
Congress. See issues of Time to January 3, 1964
Congress and Kennedy, what's coming. V. J. Burke. il Nations Bsns 51:38-9+ Jl '63
Congress confronted with racial issue. Christian Cent 80:821-2 Je 26 '63
Congress isn't always wrong; reaction to the President's proposed tax cut. Nation 197: 169 S 28 '63
Congress: its critics fulminate, but some insiders see chance for most productive session in years. J. Walsh. Science 141:701 Ag 23 '63
Congress settles down for long, slow pull. Bsns W p28 Jl 6 '63
Congress winds up session. Sr Schol 83:16 Ja 10 '64
Congressman looks at Congress. il U S News 55:44 Ag 5 '63
Dog days in Congress. Reporter 29:18+ O 10 '63
Education Congress. il Sr Schol 83:1T Ja 10 '64
Election-year danger signals: why voters criticize the 88th. il Newsweek 63:23 Ja 13 '64
Failure of Congress; with editorial comment. S. Alsop. il Sat Eve Post 236:23-5, 106 D 7 '63
Fishy statesmanship; aquarium for Washington. R. Moley. Newsweek 61:120 Je 24 '63
From Washington straight. Cato. Nat R 15:385 N 5 '63
Heat's on Congress. Bsns W p23-4 Ag 10 '63
Is Congress its own worst enemy? il Bsns W p 17-19 Ja 4 '64
It is the people who face the test; standpattism in Congress. T. Wicker. il N Y Times Mag p 19+ D 8 '63; Reply with rejoinder. E. G. Janosik. p20 Ja 5 '64
Jam in Congress; taxes and civil rights: dead for '63. U S News 55:74 N 18 '63
Kennedy and Congress; with twenty-five days to go. il U S News 55:31-3 N 25 '63
Kennedy's program in trouble; with scoreboard on legislation. Bsns W p28-9 Ap 27 '63
Kicking Congress as a national pastime. J. N. Eller. America 110:70 Ja 18 '64
Letter from Washington; day of the March, August 28, 1963. R. H. Rovere. New Yorker 39:159-66 S 14 '63
Major bills still pending in Congress. Sr Schol 82:20-1 My 15 '63
Members of the 88th Congress. Sr Schol 82: 40-1 F 20 '63
Month in Congress. Cong Digest 42:33-4, 65-6, 97-8, 129-30, 161-2, 257-8, 289-90; 43:1-2, 33-6+ F-Je, N '63-F '64
Progress on the home front; legislative program of President Kennedy. W. V. Shannon. Commonweal 78:294-5 Je 7 '63
Recovering Congress. K. Crawford. Newsweek 62:33 Ag 26 '63
Same Congress. K. Crawford. Newsweek 62: 48 D 9 '63
Sapless branch. K. Crawford. Newsweek 62: 31 Ag 5 '63
Some of the 88th's key figures. il Sr Schol 82: 14-15 F 20 '63
Taxes, treaty, rights: Congress gets busy. il U S News 55:31-2 Ag 26 '63
This month's feature: 88th Congress and higher education. Cong Digest 42:225-56 O '63
Time machine. Reporter 29:16+ N 21 '63
To make it a do-something Congress. S. Zagoria. il N Y Times Mag p26+ S 8 '63
Was it really a do-nothing Congress? il U S News 55:19-21 D 30 '63
What Congress has done so far. il U S News 54:8 Ap 22 '63
Whither Congress? M. McGrory. America 109: 205 Ag 31 '63
Whither the Republicans? R. Evans, jr. Reporter 28:32-4 F 28 '63
Who runs Congress? Reporter 28:14+ Ap 25 '63
Why Congress is balking. il U S News 56: 23-4 Ja 6 '64
Why Congress is deep in trouble. il U S News 55:36-40 Ag 12 '63
Why not abolish representative assemblies? Nat R 16:9-10 Ja 14 '64
Will tax cut be stalled? il U S News 55:33-4 O 28 '63

88th Congress—2d session

Ahead in Congress: when the civil-rights fight is over. U S News 56:34-5 Je 22 '64
Congress. See issues of Newsweek
Congress. See issues of Time to October 9, 1964
Congress: a broad expansion of National defense education act passes relatively unnoticed. J. Walsh. Science 146:383-4 O 16 '64
Congress in the home stretch; what it will do. il U S News 57:30-1 Ag 17 '64
Congress races the Johnson deadline; thirty bills to be passed before recess. Bsns W p32-3 Je 27 '64
Democrats push LBJ's program; pre-convention strategy. Bsns W p 15-16 Ag 1 '64
Do something Congress? W. V. Shannon. Commonweal 80:464-5 Jl 10 '64
88th's challenge to conservation. Am For 70:9 N '64
Grapes of wrath. K. Crawford. Newsweek 63: 32 F 24 '64
Historic 88th adjourns. Sr Schol 85:17 O 21 '64
Letter from Washington. R. H. Rovere. New Yorker 39:133-8 F 15 '64
LBJ and Congress; now a test. il U S News 56:33-4 Ja 13 '64
LBJ and Congress; the next 100 days. il U S News 56:31-2 Mr 30 '64
Month in Congress. Cong Digest 43:65-6, 97-8, 129, 161 Mr-Je '64
No vacation for Congress. America 110:861 Je 27 '64
Now Congress is starting to roll. il U S News 56:37 F 17 '64
Politics of cloture. E. B. Drew. il Reporter 31:19-23 Jl 16 '64
Senate fantasy; debate on Civil rights bill. Reporter 30:12+ Mr 26 '64
Senate; Mr Humphrey's conquering hosts. M. Kempton. New Repub 150:6-8 Ap 4 '64
Smooth sailing for a campaign year. M. McGrory. America 111:61 Jl 18 '64
What Congress did and did not do. il U S News 57:35-7 O 12 '64

89th Congress

And what about the next Congress? il U S News 57:39 O 19 '64
Congress. il Newsweek 64:19-20 D 28 '64; 65:20+ Ja 11; 18-19 Ja 18 '65
Congress. il Time 84:39-40 N 13; 34 N 27; 14-15-D 25 '64; 85:28-9 Ja 1; 16-20 Ja 15; 19 Ja 22 '65
Congress: with new sides chosen it appears the next game may be played under some new rules. J. Walsh. Science 146:1280-2 D 4 '64
House Republicans drop the old guard; Rep. Ford of Michigan replaces Rep. Halleck of Indiana. il Bsns W p22-3 Ja 9 '65
In tune with the leader; Democratic majorities. il Bsns W p 16-17 Ja 2 '65
Johnson Congress; what it will do. il Nations Bsns 52:32-3+ D '64
Johnson's Congress. K. Crawford. Newsweek 64:39 N 9 '64
Mlle's platform: an appeal to the 89th Congress; '64 question. Mlle 58:120-1 Mr '64
Outlook for new lineup in the 89th Congress. il U S News 57:32-3 N 2 '64
President may help elect Congress he won't like. J. Craft. il Nations Bsns 52:23-4 Ap '64
Special check list of major 1965 legislative issues that will affect U.S. business. il Nations Bsns 52:40-1 D '64
Union influence reaches new peak in Congress. il Nations Bsns 52:42 D '64
What I expect; interview. H. H. Humphrey. Nations Bsns 52:33+ D '64
Why it looks like another Democratic Congress. U S News 57:29-30 Ag 31 '64
Will Congress nail together the Great society? R. B. Stolley. il Life 58:36-7 Ja 15 '65

89th Congress—1st session

Can Republicans make a comeback? with statements from congressmen and interview with G. R. Ford. il U S News 58:36-41 Ja 18 '65

UNITED STATES—Congress—89th Congress—1st session—*Continued*
Johnson and the new Congress. il U S News 57:31-2 N 23 '64
Modest reforms. W. V. Shannon. Commonweal 81:533-4 Ja 22 '65
New Congress; it may get out of hand. il U S News 58:23-4 Ja 11 '65
Reforms in Congress. Sr Schol 85:19 Ja 21 '65
What you can expect from the new Congress. il U S News 58:36-7 Ja 4 '65

House of representatives

At last you can see your tax cut; report on bill adopted by House and approved by Senate finance committee; with charts. U S News 56:40-1 F 3 '64
Congressman's view of the problem; excerpts from House out of order. R. Bolling. New Repub 151:13-14 N 21 '64
Consolidating Democratic gains. W. V. Shannon. Commonweal 81:317-18 N 27 '64
Duties and responsibilities of a congressman to the United States. A. C. Powell, jr. Esquire 60:109-12+ S '63
Forge of democracy: the House of representatives, by N. MacNeil. Review
New Repub 148:22-4 My 18 '63. R. D. Novak; Reply. D. I. Wells. 148:31 Je 1 '63
House divided in new way. Life 54:4 Je 7 '63
House: new ball game. il Newsweek 64:38-9 N 9 '64
House rules. M. Kempton. New Repub 150:6-8 Ja 11 '64
House yields to administration on RS-70. Aviation W 79:34-5 Jl 1 '63
Is Congress obsolete? R. Steel. Commentary 38:59-64 S '64
Lower taxes, higher revenue; can LBJ do it? with summary of status in House and Senate finance committee. il U S News 56:84-5 Ja 20 '64
Mr Blatnik plans a purge. D. Rapoport. Reporter 31:32-4 D 3 '64
Reforming the House, a four year term? W. V. Shannon. il N Y Times Mag p22-3+ Ja 10 '65
Republican feud spreads to Congress. U S News 57:33 D 28 '64
'64 election: suppose the South does revolt. il U S News 54:44-5 Je 24 '63
T.R.B. from Washington; power struggle between the Speaker and the House rules committee. New Repub 152:2 Ja 16 '65
Victory for the middle-aged Turks. J. N. Eller. America 112:69 Ja 16 '65
Wanted: a modern house. New Repub 151: 1+ N 21 '64
See also
Apportionment (election law)

House of representatives—Committees

Above inhibition; Appropriations committee. Time 81:28-9 My 17 '63
As civil rights moves ahead: how business may be policed; House judiciary committee. il U S News 55:55 N 11 '63
Cannon to Mahon. Cato. Nat R 16:439 Je 2 '64
Cannon's successor; Appropriations committee. A. Hamilton. New Repub 150:5 My 23 '64
Colonialism in Congress; House interior subcommittee on territorial and insular affairs. Reporter 28:11 Je 20 '63
Committee accepts ICBM reliability. H. M. David. Miss & Roc 14:17-18 Ap 27 '64
Congress: question of reform of procedures becomes an issue; House committee on rules. J. Walsh. Science 139:201+ Ja 18 '63
Cuts for glamor twins; space and research. Bsns W p31 O 12 '63
Daddario unit seeking proper level of R&D aid; interview, ed. by H. M. David. E. Q. Daddario. Miss & Roc 15:26 Ag 10 '64
Date to remember; petition to abolish HUAC. Nation 199:450 D 14 '64
Down to fine print on the tax bill; Ways & means committee's version. il Bsns W p 191-2+ S 14 '63
Elliott committee: final reports issued as fifteen-month investigation of federal research comes to end. D. S. Greenberg. Science 147:131-2 Ja 8 '65
Excise taxes come on the firing line; Ways & means hearings. il Bsns W p 26-7 Je 20 '64
Foreign aid forever. Nat R 16:577 Jl 14 '64
Foundations in business: report; subcommittee of House small business committee. U S News 55:104-5 O 28 '63
From six to twenty; members of Congress against appropriations for HUAC. Nation 196:219 Mr 16 '63
From the House with love; Rights si, prayer no; House judiciary committee. Cato. Nat R 16:144 F 25 '64
From Washington: R and D on Capitol hill. H. Margolis. Bul Atomic Sci 20:33-7 My '64
Guardian of the taxpayers' money; House appropriations subcommittee. U S News 54:19 Je 17 '63
Haggle develops over Ranger failure. H. M. David. Miss & Roc 14:14-15 My 4 '64
He shouldn't be there, and he wasn't; spending of the Education and labor committee. il Time 81:21 Mr 15 '63
House appropriations committee omits provision for LSCA funds. Library J 89:2048 My 15 '64
House armed services committee forms R&D subcommittee to oversee rising research funds. J. Walsh. Science 140:881-2 My 24 '63
House space committee slates Ranger probe. H. M. David. Miss & Roc 14:15 Ap 13 '64
House unit to approve four-year term for JCS; veto threatened. R. G. O'Lone. Aviation W 79:32 O 28 '63
House unit to probe NASA fund shifts. A. P. Alibrando. Aviation W 78:38-9 F 18 '63
House unit to probe rendezvous choice; House space committee. A. P. Alibrando. Aviation W 78:30-1 Ja 28 '63
In taxes: cuts but not much reform. il Bsns W p24-5 F 9 '63
Investigation: mixed motivations led to House decision to probe government support for research; with editorial comment. D. S. Greenberg. Science 141:1245, 1261-4 S 27 '63
Is there really a crisis in U.S. schools? House education subcommittee. il U S News 54:43-5 My 20 '63
Judge Smith moves with deliberate drag; chairman of the House rules committee. D. Oberdorfer. il N Y Times Mag p 13+ Ja 12 '64
Lord of the Flies. M. Kempton. New Repub 148:9-10 Je 22 '63
Maintaining a free society; Un-American activities committee. Christian Cent 81:1515-16 D 9 '64
Management breakdown probably responsible for Ranger problems; with editorial comment. Miss & Roc 14:15, 46 My 11 '64
NASA needs a watchdog; House science and astronautics committee. R. Hotz. Aviation W 78:21 F 18 '63
New look at U.S. reds; interview. E. E. Willis. Nations Bsns 52:58-60+ My '64
New overseers for federal science. J. Walsh. Science 142:210 O 11 '63
Not one word; Education and labor committee. Time 81:26-7 Mr 8 '63
Oh dad, poor dad. M. Kempton. New Repub 149:6-7 S 28 '63
Open season on HUAC. Nation 198:63 Ja 20 '64
Petition House to abolish H.U.A.C. Christian Cent 81:1548 D 16 '64
Public library proposals favorably reported by House subcommittee; House select subcommittee on education. G. Krettek and H. Hubbard. Wilson Lib Bul 37:880 Je '63
Raucous caucus room; House committee on un-American activities hearings on students, rebels, and hangers-on who had journeyed to Castro's Cuba in defiance of State department ban. il Newsweek 62:30+ S 23 '63
Recreation allowance review is sought. G. C. Wilson. Aviation W 81:16-17 Jl 27 '64
Rescue squad; House appropriations committee. New Repub 148:5 Ap 20 '63
Right of petition; HUAC and Women strike for peace. Nation 196:435 My 25 '63
Shape of the cut; House ways and means version of the bill. Time 82:27 S 20 '63
Shuffling off to Buffalo; House committee on un-American activities. Nation 198:497-8 My 18 '64
Slow-down Smith; Rules committee. M. Kempton. New Repub 149:8-9 D 14 '63
Some scandals in the roads program; hearings by a subcommittee of Public works committee. U S News 54:10 My 13 '63
Speaker vs. the hard-liners; House rules committee vacancies. M. Viorst. Reporter 29:43-4 O 24 '63
Stately pace for tax bill. Bsns W p26 My 25 '63
Tax cut comes closer; Ways & means approval of new rate scale, with editorial comment. il Bsns W p23-4, 124 Ag 17 '63
Taxes and confusion: concerning House ways and means committee and new tax bill. Nat R 15:265+ O 8 '63
Testimony that Congress didn't hear; House administration committee. U S News 54: 10 Ap 22 '63

UNITED STATES—Congress—House of representatives—Committees—*Continued*
To the woodshed; House Labor and education committee. Newsweek 61:25-6 Mr 18 '63
Too many and too soon; financial legislation floods Congress. Bsns W p99 O 5 '63
Travel ban defied; investigation of students by House un-American activities committee. il Sr Schol 83:7-8 O 4 '63
Un-American; two women from Women strike for peace indicted at behest of HUAC. New Repub 152:7 Ja 23 '65
U.S. students in Cuba: how far left? role of House committee on un-American activities. W. Schulz. Nat R 15:229 S 24 '63
Up to the Senate. Nation 196:238-9 Mr 23 '63
Ways & means roughs out the new tax bill. Bsns W p78-9 Je 22 '63
What red spy fleet is doing off U.S; implications according to a subcommittee of the House armed services committee. il U S News 55:8 S 9 '63
What to expect now in a civil-rights law; House judiciary committee. il U S News 55:74-5 O 21 '63
What Ways & means is doing: tax reform measures. Bsns W p28 Je 1 '63
Why the H.U.A.C. should go. H. E. Fey; discussion. Christian Cent 80:304-5 Mr 6 '63
Wild time on Capitol hill; investigation of students by House committee on un-American activities. il U S News 55:4 S 23 '63

House of representatives—Speakers

Boy from Bug Tussle. Bsns W p30-1 Mr 23 '63
Speaker vs. the hard-liners; House rules committee vacancies. M. Viorst. Reporter 29:43-4 O 24 '63

Senate

Aerospace leaders to continue in Senate. G. C. Wilson. Aviation W 81:26 S 21 '64
Bubbles, bubbles. M. Kempton. New Repub 149:15-16 Ag 17 '63
Casebook of a southern senator. D. Schoenbrun. il Esquire 60:104-8+ S '63
Congress: the sapless branch, by J. S. Clark. Review
Atlan 214:89-91 S '64. G. W. Johnson
Disestablishmentarianism. W. A. Korns. New Repub 148:6 Mr 16 '63
I am what I am; Mansfield answers critics; excerpts from report. M. Mansfield. U S News 55:20 D 9 '63
Letter from Washington; Senate ratification. R. H. Rovere. New Yorker 39:149-56 O 5 '63
Lib. services and construction act approved by Senate in 89-7 vote. Library J 89:335 Ja 15 '64
Man who leads the southern senators; R. B. Russell. M. Greenfield. Reporter 30:17-21 My 21 '64
Scandal grows and grows in Washington; the Bobby Baker case. K. Wheeler and others. il Life 55:40-40B+ N 22 '63
Senate: a crisis in leadership. il Newsweek 62:29-30 N 18 '63
Senate and the test ban. il Newsweek 62:17-18 Ag 5 '63
Senate elections of '64; where Republicans hope to win. il U S News 54:44-5 Je 10 '63
Senate establishment; concerning Senator Clark's remarkable speech. J. McCartney. Nation 196:219-21 Mr 16 '63
Senate gives advice and consent; ratification of test ban treaty. il Sr Schol 83:17 O 11 '63
Senate journal 1943-45, by A. Drury. Review
Nat R 15:529-30 D 17 '63. L. C. Wilson
Time 82:124+ N 15 '63
Senate races; 1964 election. W. V. Shannon. Commonweal 81:85-6 O 16 '64
Senate roll call on test-ban treaty. U S News 55:12 O 7 '63
Tribute to Barry. Cato. Nat R 16:682 Ag 11 '64
Trip to Moscow and beyond. J. N. Eller. America 109:149 Ag 17 '63
When is a majority a majority? Senate's civil rights debate. il Time 83:22-6 Mr 20 '64
Why the fears over a nuclear-test ban. il U S News 55:39-41 S 23 '63
Wrong priority; cotton-wheat bill ahead of the civil rights bill. Nation 198:253 Mr 16 '64

See also
Senators

Senate—Committees

Advise & consent; F. D. Roosevelt jr. before Senate commerce committee. Time 81:19 Mr 22 '63
Ahead, a tax return as simple as a check? with summary of plan approved by Senate finance committee. il U S News 55:75-6 D 30 '63
As the Baker case inquiry gets going; Senate rules committee. il U S News 55:10 N 11 '63
At last you can see your tax cut; report on bill adopted by House and approved by Senate finance committee; with charts. U S News 56:40-1 F 3 '64
Back to work. Newsweek 61:26 Mr 11 '63
Baker case; concerning testimony before the Senate rules committee. Sr Schol 84:22 F 7 '64
Bobby Baker cover-up. Sat Eve Post 237:88 Ap 25 '64
Bobby Baker revisited; role of Senate rules committee. M. Kempton. New Repub 149:6-7 N 16 '63
Bobby Baker story: Senate unfolds chapter one; hearing of the Senate rules committee. il U S News 55:31 D 30 '63
Clark's bark; committee rigging in the Senate. K. Crawford. Newsweek 61:30 Mr 4 '63
Congress moves, but stays in low gear. il Bsns W p21-2 D 7 '63
Congress: Senator Anderson brings activist record, some definite views, to space committee helm. J. Walsh. Science 139:1036-8 Mr 15 '63
Conversations with the committee; excerpts from hearings before U.S. Senate subcommittee on disarmament, August, 1962. Bul Atomic Sci 19:15-18 Mr '63
Cost. il Time 81:25-6 Mr 8 '63
Crime shows on TV; a federal crackdown coming? excerpts from report. il U S News 57:49-50 N 9 '64
Crucial booster hearings start soon. H. M. David. Miss & Roc 14:13 Je 8 '64
Fast rise of Bobby Baker; with excerpts from testimony before Senate rules committee by D. B. Reynolds, and statement by L. B. Johnson. il U S News 56:55-9 F 3 '64
Frauds against the aged; hearings of Special committee on aging. Consumer Rep 28:131 Mr '63
From Washington straight. Senate internal security subcommittee. Nat R 15:342 O 22 '63
In the bag; O. Otepka and Senate internal security subcommittee. Newsweek 62:36+ N 18 '63
Intelligence gap on Cuba? the Senate gets a report; excerpts from report by the Preparedness investigating subcommittee of the Senate armed services committee. il U S News 54:63-6 My 20 '63
Investigating foreign lobbyists; Senate foreign relations committee. il Bsns W p30-1 F 23 '63
Joyless probe for the Senate; investigation of Bobby Baker. il Bsns W p32-3 N 9 '63
Lower taxes, higher revenue; can LBJ do it? with summary of status in House and Senate finance committee. il U S News 56:84-5 Ja 20 '64
Mr Passman meets his match; foreign-aid program. E. B. Drew. Reporter 31:40-3 N 19 '64
More delay for tax bill; deliberates. Bsns W p32 O 19 '63
Musical chairs; change of chairmanships. New Repub 148:4-5 F 9 '63
Second-act trouble; Valachi hearing by Senate permanent subcommittee on investigations. il Newsweek 62:33-4 O 14 '63
Senate looks at its own housekeeping; Senate rules committee. il U S News 55:71 N 4 '63
Senate unit collects evidence to challenge nuclear test ban. K. Johnsen. Aviation W 79:23 Jl 8 '63
Senate unit to probe separate booster efforts by NASA, DOD. Aviation W 80:37 Je 15 '64
Senators propose instant tax relief; Senate finance committee. Bsns W p25 Ja 25 '64
Something newsy; investigation of Hamilton Wright organization by Senate foreign relations committee. il Newsweek 62:27-8 Jl 22 '63
Speaking out; they can't cover up for Bobby Baker. H. Scott. Sat Eve Post 237:8+ My 9 '64
Staged hearings. Nation 198:42 Ja 13 '64
Strange case of Bobby Baker; investigation by Senate rules committee. il U S News 56:40-2 F 10 '64
TFX board selected Boeing four times; investigation of General dynamics-Grumman contract by Senate investigations subcommittee, with excerpts from hearing. G. C. Wilson. Aviation W 78:22-4 Mr 4 '63
Those pesticides; investigation by a Senate subcommittee. P. Hirsch. New Repub 149:6 Ag 17 '63
Way big crime operates in U.S; concerning testimony before the Rackets subcommittee of the Senate government operations committee. il U S News 55:78-9 O 7 '63

UNITED STATES—Congress—Senate—Committees—*Continued*
What to expect now in a civil-rights law; Senate commerce committee. il U S News 55:74-5 O 21 '63
Who owns the Senate? work of the Democratic steering committee. W. Shannon. New Repub 148:5-6 Mr 2 '63
Why not call McNamara? McClellan subcommittee investigation into the fighter plane (TFX) contract. New Repub 148:6 My 18 '63
With George & Sam on Capitol hill. il Time 82:11-12 Jl 26 '63

Senate—Employees

Bobby was the boy to see. B. H. Bagdikian and D. Oberdorfer. il Sat Eve Post 236: 26-9 D 7 '63

Senate—Rules and practice

Again the filibusteros. il N Y Times Mag p20-1 Mr 1 '64
As the Senate voted. New Repub 150:6 Je 20 '64
Commuters' filibuster. New Repub 148:4 F 23 '63
Eenie, meenie; filibuster, cloture. Cato. Nat R 16:439 Je 2 '64
End for this season; to prevent filibusters. cloture rule. Reporter 28:14+ F 28 '63
Filibuster before the filibuster. il Time 83:26 Ap 3 '64
From Washington straight; demonstrations threatened if filibuster against civil rights bill. Cato. Nat R 15:14 Jl 16 '63
Giving up the battle to win the war. J. N. Eller. America 110:358 Mr 21 '64
Guarding guardians. R. Moley. Newsweek 63: 108 Je 15 '64
Historic vote: seventy-one to twenty-nine; cloture vote. il Newsweek 63:25-6 Je 22 '64
Last filibuster? President Kennedy's civil-rights bill. K. Crawford. Newsweek 62:29 Jl 8 '63
Letter from Washington; government for complete equality for Negro. R. H. Rovere. New Yorker 39:92+ Je 22 '63
Man's step forward in civil rights; cloture vote ending 75-day filibuster. Christian Cent 81:820 Je 24 '64
On its way into law; Senate cloture vote on civil rights bill. il Bsns W p25-8 Je 13 '64
Paradise lost in the Senate. W. V. Shannon. Commonweal 77:528-9 F 15 '63
Russell defends the filibuster. R. B. Russell. il N Y Times Mag p20+ Mr 15 '64
Shame of the Senate. Nation 198:518 My 25 '64
Should the filibuster be abolished? pro and con discussion. Sr Schol 84:12-13 Mr 13 '64
They finally did it: they busted the big filibuster; with report by R. B. Stolley. il Life 56:32-7 Je 19 '64
Vapors of filibustering. Newsweek 62:21 Ag 19 '63
Veteran spokesman for the Old South. Bsns W p28-9 Ap 18 '64
With all deliberate delay; some thoughts on streamlining the Senate. J. S. Clark. New Repub 150:13-15 Ap 18 '64

Constitution

After the Vice President? R. S. Hirschfield. il Nation 198:25-8 Ja 6 '64
American Civil war as a constitutional crisis. A. Bestor. bibliog f Am Hist R 69: 327-52 Ja '64
Better at moralizing than legalizing; Power & the precedent; concerning Title II of civil rights legislative package. Time 82:19-20 Jl 12 '63
Congress and our living Constitution. il Sr Schol 82:6-7 F 20 '63
Conscience and the Constitution. T. Powell. il PTA Mag 58:10-12 N '63
Constitution: hand in hand with the progress of the human mind. il Sr Schol 84:8-9 F 14 '64
Constitution of the United States; text. il Nations Bsns 52:42-52 Ja '64
Deliberate pace in Congress safeguards your rights. F. Morley. il Nations Bsns 51:27-8 Mr '63
Disunited states. New Repub 148:5 My 4 '63
Government's hidden dimension. E. S. Muskie. Sat R 47:18-22 Ap 18 '64
Honest constitutionalism; excerpts from addresses. W. Wilson. U S News 55:96+ Jl 22 '63
How separate should government and God be? address, January 22, 1963. H. C. Wilkinson. Vital Speeches 29:337-40 Mr 15 '63
Ideological heroin. Christian Cent 81:1355-6 N 4 '64
New lamps for old? centralism; address, November 11, 1964. L. Bushnell. Vital Speeches 31:112-14 D 1 '64
Our changing Constitution, by C. Leedham. Review
 Sat R 48:33 Ja 16 '65. I. Dilliard
Our quaint political folkways. J. Ellison. Nation 197:323-5 N 16 '63
Our vanishing Constitution. D. Lawrence. U S News 57:104 Jl 20 '64
Power in Washington, by D. Cater. Review
 Reporter 30:48+ Je 18 '64. A. A. Berle
Reaction's refuge; proposed constitutional amendments. K. Crawford. Newsweek 61: 31 Je 3 '63
Silent amendments. Newsweek 61:35-6 My 20 '63
Succession and business. H. Hazlitt. Newsweek 63:59 Ja 6 '64
Supreme court and the Republic; decisions on reapportionment. F. Morley. Fortune 70: 102+ Ag '64
Symbols, traditions and liberty; address, October 24, 1962. A. G. Rudd. Vital Speeches 29:256 F 1 '63
To reduce uncertainty; death or disability of a president in office. H. Hazlitt. Newsweek 62:86 D 9 '63
U.S. Constitution and the '64 campaign. il Sr Schol 85:6-7 S 23 '64
We hold these truths... C. H. Percy. il PTA Mag 58:4-6 Je '64
What a southern conservative thinks. J. J. Kilpatrick. Sat R 47:15-18 Ap 25 '64; Discussion. 47:27-8 My 16; 24 Je 6 '64
What voting rights does the Constitution guarantee? H. G. Earl. Todays Health 42: 32-3+ S '64
Whose constitution is it? F. Canavan. America 110:867-8 Je 27 '64
 See also
State rights

Amendments

Alabama goes to Court. L. B. Bozell. Nat R 14:445 Je 4 '63
Amending the amendment; Twenty-fourth amendment. Reporter 30:12+ F 13 '64
Assault on the Union. W. Lippmann. Newsweek 61:25 Je 10 '63
Attacks on 14th amendment exposed. Christian Cent 80:732 Je 5 '63
Change the Constitution? Warren urges great debate. U S News 54:19 Je 3 '63
Confederacy revived. America 108:821 Je 8 '63
Constitution, key to freedom. C. B. Motley. Ebony 18:221-2+ S '63
Constitutional right to publish; excerpts from address, May 1, 1963. A. J. Goldberg. U S News 54:120 My 13 '63
Crowd of umbrella heads; states' rights amendments. Reporter 28:10-11 Je 6 '63
God amendment. R. J. Dwyer. Nat R 16:494 Je 16 '64
Government by mob; Fourteenth amendment. D. Lawrence. U S News 55:92 Jl 1 '63
Hobbling the Constitution. W. D. Burnham. Commonweal 78:531-3 S 6 '63
Maybe it's time to look at the antislavery amendment; Thirteenth amendment. A. Avins. il U S News 56:82-4 My 11 '64
More than a symbol; South Dakota approves twenty-fourth amendment. America 110: 179 F 8 '64
Noted jurist says, repeal the Fourteenth amendment. R. N. Wilkin. U S News 57:72-4 Ag 24 '64
Off with the head tax. K. Crawford. Newsweek 61:34 My 6 '63
Only hope. D. Lawrence. U S News 54:112 Je 10 '63
Seventeen states vote to destroy democracy as we know it. T. B. Morgan. il Look 27: 76+ D 3 '63
Stalled at sixteen; states' rights amendments. New Repub 149:6-7 Ag 31 '63
States' rights amendments. il Time 81:22 Je 7 '63
States' rights? proposed amendments. Commonweal 78:269 My 31 '63
Tampering lightly by amendment; famous First's provision on church and state. Christian Cent 80:923-4 Jl 24 '63
To amend, or not to amend, the Constitution. P. A. Freund. il N Y Times Mag p33+ D 13 '64
Tortoise vs. hare; states representation in the House. K. Crawford. Newsweek 61:37 Je 10 '63
Twenty-fourth amendment. Cur Hist 46:240 Ap '64
Twenty-fourth amendment. Newsweek 63:27 F 3 '64
Twenty-fourth amendment. Time 83:19 Ja 31 '64
Twenty-fourth amendment ratified. Christian Cent 81:165 F 5 '64

UNITED STATES—Constitution—Amendments —*Continued*
Uncertain criminal law: rights, wrongs, and doubts. I. R. Kaufman. il Atlan 215:61-7 Ja '65
Undoing a fraud; ratification of the Fourteenth amendment. D. Lawrence. U S News 55:84 Ag 12 '63
Warren again: sit-in cases and Fourteenth amendment. Nat R 14:436 Je 4 '63
See also
Presidents—United States—Succession
Presidents—United States—Term
Woman—Equal rights

Bill of rights

Amending the amendment. America 108:736+ My 25 '63
Anecdote of the young lieutenant. L. H. Pollak. il PTA Mag 58:10-12 Ap '64
Becker amendment. Christian Cent 81:475 Ap 15 '64
Becker amendment would imperil true religion. Christian Cent 81:629 My 13 '64
Becker's golden calf; constitutional amendment. M. E. Marty. Christian Cent 81:726-7 Je 3 '64
Civil liberty and individual responsibility; address. A. Barth. Vital Speeches 31:135-9 D 15 '64
Committing religious suicide; attacks upon the First amendment. Christian Cent 81: 420 Ap 1 '64
Constitutional right to publish; excerpts from address, May 1, 1963. A. J. Goldberg. U S News 54:120 My 13 '63
Cruel and unusual punishments. D. Lawrence. U S News 54:108 Ap 29 '63
Does schoolroom prayer require a new amendment? il Time 83:62+ My 8 '64
Government lawyer looks at the crime problem; Fourth amendment and the administration of criminal justice. il U S News 57:74-6 S 28 '64
How the Constitution was violated; reprint. D. Lawrence. U S News 54:124+ My 6 '63
Intellectual freedom and the federal government; address, May 15, 1963. J. V. Lindsay. Pub W 183:18-21 My 27 '63
Justice Black and the absolute. J. Grossman. Commentary 36:244-8 S '63
Nature's God and the founding fathers; concerning Bill of rights. E. M. Halliday. il Am Heritage 14:102-6 O '63
Nine speak out for the Ten. C. A. Madison. Sat R 46:29 Je 29 '63
Our basic rights: from protest to proclamation; from Boston tea party to Bill of rights. il Sr Schol 83:5 D 13 '63
Our heritage of freedom: The bill of rights. C. Wittke. PTA Mag 58:20-2 S '63
Prayer amendment. America 110:535 Ap 18 '64
Prayer amendments: a Catholic lawyer's view. W. B. Ball. Cath World 199:345-51 S '64
Proceedings of 1963 First amendment conference on meaning of religion in the First amendment. il Cath World 197:280-317 Ag '63
Proposed amendment hit. Sr Schol 84:1T-2T Ap 3 '64
Protecting the right of privacy. P. B. Kurland. il PTA Mag 58:10-12 Mr '64
School prayer referendum point system. Christian Cent 81:591 Ap 29 '64
TV or no TV in court? F. Rodell. il N Y Times Mag p 16+ Ap 12 '64
Wall, not a sieve; separation of church and state. Christian Cent 81:67-8 Ja 15 '64; Discussion. 81:303, 308+ Mr 4 '64

Constitutional convention, 1787

Birth pangs of our Constitution. H. G. Earl. il Todays Health 42:30-1+ Jl '64

Constitutional history

Time to reclaim: the current challenge of American constitutional history. P. L. Murphy. bibliog f Am Hist R 69:64-79 O '63
See also
The federalist
United States—Constitution—Bill of rights

Constitutional law

Equal justice for the poor, too. A. J. Goldberg. il N Y Times Mag p24+ Mr 15 '64
Virtue grounded in principle still prevails at grass roots. F. Morley. Nations Bsns 51: 25-6 Ag '63
See also
United States—Supreme court

Consular and diplomatic service

Moscow embassy: officer named to fill science liaison post. D. S. Greenberg. Science 140:283 Ap 19 '63

Continental Congress

Birth pangs of our Constitution. H. G. Earl. il Todays Health 42:30-1+ Jl '64

Controller general

See United States—General accounting office

Council of economic advisers

Breeze through the corridors; LBJ men begin to move into the agencies. il Newsweek 63:79 My 25 '64
Giving the consumer the what-for. W. H. Peterson. Nat R 14:453-4 Je 4 '63
Government aids to consumers (cont) Consumer Rep 28:80-7 D '63
JFK and the consumer. New Repub 149:5-6 N 2 '63
Kennedy hires one of his critics; J. P. Lewis. Bsns W p78+ My 18 '63
Kennedy's formula for full employment. Bsns W p 110-13 Ja 26 '63
LBJ's brand goes on the economy; CEA report; with editorial comment. il Bsns W p71-4+, 136 Ja 25 '64
Old fire; new council. il Newsweek 61:71-3 Je 3 '63
Old reliable team. il Newsweek 64:84 N 30 '64
Peace, and the price. Commonweal 81:60-1 O 9 '64
Planning to keep the ball rolling. il Bsns W p23-5 N 14 '64
Policy's the same; with editorial comment. il Bsns W p36, 204 N 21 '64
Strikes and the public. H. Malmgren. New Repub 148:6 Ap 20 '63
Trouble after the party. il Time 84:73 Ag 28 '64
Why unemployment stays high; policy-makers debate; with editorial comment. il Bsns W p 133+, 204 N 16 '63
Wiggle watchers. il Time 85:78+ Ja 15 '65

Council of the arts

See United States—National council of the arts

Courts of appeals

Blocking a merger in advance. Bsns W p92+ My 4 '63

Cultural relations

Advisory group submits report on cultural presentations. Dept State Bul 48:46 Ja 14 '63
Appetite for American taste? M. Beloff. Sat R 46:21-2 S 7 '63
Building cultural bridges. M. Marks. il Dance Mag 37:20-1 My '63
Cultural exchange program in Africa: a path to peace; address, December 18, 1962. G. M. Williams. Dept State Bul 48:67-70 Ja 14 '63
Dying, Egypt, dying; U.S. declines contribution to the saving of the Abu Simbel temples. F. Getlein. New Repub 150:26-8 My 30 '64
José Limon reports on Asia tour. D. Duncan. il Dance Mag 38:31-2 F '64
Members named to arts advisory committee and drama panel. Dept State Bul 49:438-9 S 16 '63
Minstrel: American folk songs in Far East. New Yorker 40:22-3 Jl 25 '64
Picture window on the arts. F. Alegria. il Américas 15:27-30 Mr '63
Return of the gentle persuaders; results of reappraising cultural exchange program. il Time 82:36 S 6 '63
Richer by the United States; role of American cultural center, Japan. T. Osada. bibliog il Wilson Lib Bul 39:56-8+ S '64
Roads to international understanding; address, January 15, 1963. C. D. Norrell. Dept State Bul 48:214-17 F 11 '63
Role of music in cultural exchange; address. May 22, 1963. L. D. Battle. Dept State Bul 48:915-17 Je 10 '63
Soviet-American exchanges, tit-for-tat goodwill. S. S. Rosenfeld. Science 143:1413-17 Mr 27 '64
They discover America. C. W. Hall. Read Digest 82:81-6 Je '63
U.S. and Liberia sign agreements on free port and cultural program; joint announcement, May 8, 1964. Dept State Bul 50:829-30 My 25 '64
United States and Malaya sign cultural exchange agreement. Dept State Bul 48:265 F 18 '63
U.S. and Rumania exchange notes on cultural and other exchanges; Department announcement, with text of notes, April 2, 1963. W. A. Crawford; P. Macovei. Dept State Bul 48:661-3 Ap 29 '63
U.S. and U.S.S.R. sign agreement on exchanges for 1964-65; Department statement; with remarks by Ambassador Kohler, February 22, 1964. Dept State Bul 50:451-2 Mr 23 '64

UNITED STATES—Cultural relations—*Cont.*
U.S.-Japan cultural conference to be held at Washington. Dept State Bul 49:582-3 O 14 '63
Who takes care; United States not yet fully developed. R. Stokes. Library J 88:524-5 F 1 '63
Will the swaps keep on? Barghoorn incident. il Bsns W p28-9 N 23 '63
See also
Exchange of persons programs
United States—Information agency
United States—State, Department of—Educational and cultural affairs, Bureau of

Culture, Popular

See United States—Popular culture

Customs

See United States—Social life and customs

Customs, Bureau of

See Customs service—United States

Declaration of Independence

See also
Fourth of July

Signers

They signed away their lives; Declaration of independence. H. Lee. il Todays Health 41:32-5+ Jl '63

Defense, Department of

Achilles heel. W. J. Coughlin. Miss & Roc 12:162 Mr 25 '63
Administration & management stresses better information distribution. Miss & Roc 14:93-5 Mr 30 '64
Amended #137.5 (a) gratuities. il Time 84:102 O 23 '64
And how about the Pentagon now? new era in Washington. M. S. Johnson. il U S News 55:64-5 D 16 '63
Bossing the brass. il Newsweek 61:36+ My 20 '63
Centralization of defense. W. J. Coughlin. Miss & Roc 12:46 F 4 '63
Civilian supremacy. New Repub 148:7 Je 22 '63
Collision in Washington: McNamara vs. the Congress. Newsweek 61:25-6 Mr 25 '63
Congress authorizes $15.3 billion for aircraft, missiles and ships. G. C. Wilson. Aviation W 78:35 My 20 '63
Congressional critics eye DOD civilians. G. C. Wilson. il Aviation W 78:22-3 Je 3 '63
Courage and defense economy. W. J. Coughlin. Miss & Roc 15:46 D 7 '64
Decision due on DOD-Comsat corp. pact. P. J. Klass. Aviation W 80:31-2 Ap 20 '64
Decision making in the Defense department; address, April 20, 1963. R. S. McNamara. Vital Speeches 29:508-12 Je 1 '63
Defense colossus. R. Moley. Newsweek 61:96 Je 17 '63
Defense cutbacks hit professionals. il Bsns W p74-5 F 8 '64
Defense cuts release funds for humanity. Christian Cent 81:164 F 5 '64
Defense dept.'s base curtailments affect fifty-one aerospace installations. Aviation W 81:65+ N 30 '64
Defense economies. Commonweal 81:372 D 11 '64
Department of defense. W. Manchester. il Holiday 33:76-9+ My '63
DOD accepts fund cuts to ease passage. Aviation W 79:20-1 Jl 29 '63
DOD acts to standardize data flow. Miss & Roc 14:14 Mr 23 '64
Department of defense; charts of organization. Miss & Roc 13:153+ Jl 29 '63
DOD claims savings of $1 billion in year. Aviation W 79:33 Jl 15 '63
DOD-Comsat decision sought. J. Trainor. Miss & Roc 14:10 Mr 23 '64
DOD lists biggest research contractors. il Aviation W 80:83-4+ Ja 13 '64
DOD lists major research contractors. Aviation W 81:60-5 D 28 '64
DOD may ease R&D cost-sharing rules. P. J. Klass. Aviation W 81:17 D 28 '64
Department of defense 1963. il Miss & Roc 12:26-121 Mr 25 '63
DOD now favors Comsat channel lease. K. Johnsen. Aviation W 80:19 Mr 23 '64
DOD patent policy tightening. H. Taylor. Miss & Roc 13:14 O 21 '63
DOD research awards total $6.1 billion. il Aviation W 78:83+ F 11 '63
DOD shifts stir ire of Congress, allies. il Aviation W 78:73-5 Mr 11 '63
DOD space position defended. F. G. McGuire. il Miss & Roc 12:12-14 F 4 '63
DOD stresses urgent limited war needs. G. C. Wilson. Aviation W 80:22-4 F 3 '64
DOD to brief firms on long-range plans. Aviation W 80:37 Ja 27 '64
Dr Fubini or: How I learned to stop worrying and love Comsat corp. W. J. Coughlin. Miss & Roc 14:70 Je 1 '64
Down to the dog tags; cost-reduction program. Time 84:24-5 Jl 17 '64
Eulogy to a Dyna-Soar. W. J. Coughlin. Miss & Roc 12:50 Mr 11 '63
FY '65 DOD budget $50 billion. D. C. Breasted. Miss & Roc 14:14 Ja 13 '64
Future of non-profit groups under cloud; facing increased competition and Defense dept. restrictions. K. Johnsen. Aviation W 81:16-17 D 21 '64
Gilpatric explains Defense decision policy. R. L. Gilpatric. Aviaton W 78:32 F 11 '63
Group urged to study application of technology to spur economy. K. Johnsen. Aviation W 79:35 D 16 '63
G&C people and places; key contacts in NASA and military. Miss & Roc 13:73 O 7 '63
Heavy SST financial role seen for DOD. R. H. Cook. Aviation W 80:28-9 Ap 6 '64
House leader cites R&D mismanagement by DOD. Miss & Roc 13:18 N 11 '63
Irreparable loss; civilian authority. R. Moley. Newsweek 62:72 Jl 1 '63
Join the army and feel elite. Time 82:17-18 Jl 26 '63
Joint committee raps DOD, AEC. W. Beller. il Miss & Roc 14:24-5 Mr 2 '64
Lights out; lights-out policy to save electricity. Newsweek 63:23 Ap 13 '64
McNamara and his critics. New Repub 148: 5-6 Mr 30 '63
McNamara-Anderson rifts led to ouster. Aviation W 78:26-7 My 13 '63
McNamara cutback. New Repub 151:5 D 5 '64
McNamara defends decision-making role. Aviation W 78:29 Ap 29 '63
McNamara defines his job. R. S. McNamara. il N Y Times Mag p 13+ Ap 26 '64
McNamara firm on conduct code; with editorial comment. Miss & Roc 15:13, 46 N 2 '64
McNamara: the real story. M. S. Johnson. il U S News 55:56-9 Jl 22 '63
McNamara's band. America 111:734-5 D 5 '64
Major DOD research contractors listed. il Aviation W 80:95+ Ja 20 '64
Management or mediocrity? W. J. Coughlin. Miss & Roc 12:54 Ap 15 '63; Reply. C. K. Simon. 12:7 Ap 29 '63
More DOD centralization urged. Aviation W 79:24 Jl 29 '63
More than a hundred ways to gyp McNamara. J. Ridgeway. New Repub 150:6-7 My 2 '64
National space policy; excerpts from address. E. C. Welsh. Aviation W 80:21 Mr 2 '64
Navy again outgunned. W. J. Coughlin. Miss & Roc 13:52 O 21 '63
New pique; relations between the Pentagon and the press. il Newsweek 63:61 Je 29 '64
New rules on gifts, employment outlined for Pentagon personnel. Aviation W 78:31 Je 3 '63
Non-profit policies face GAO scrutiny. K. Johnsen. Aviation W 81:15 D 28 '64
Pact clarifies NASA, DOD roles at Cape. G. Alexander. Aviation W 78:62 Mr 4 '63
Pendulum may swing back in DOD policy. il Aviation W 80:73-7 Mr 16 '64
Pennies pinched. Newsweek 62:69-70 Jl 22 '63
Pentagon ends probe of top officials over leak. Aviation W 78:27 Ap 8 '63
Pentagon imbalance; address, September 4, 1963. G. W. Anderson. Vital Speeches 29: 743-6 O 1 '63; Summary. U S News 55:24 S 16 '63
Planners for the Pentagon; with editorial comment. il Bsns W p56-8+, 144 Jl 13 '63
Politics in the arms business? with excerpts from Congressional record. il U S News 54: 40-3 My 13 '63
Power at the Pentagon, by J. Raymond. Review
New Repub 150:21-2 Ap 25 '64. R. D. Senter; Reply. J. Raymond. 150:29 My 2 '64
Price of economy. il Newsweek 62:18-19 D 23 '63
Programming's role in defense; excepts from address. C. J. Hitch. Aviation W 81:17 O 12 '64
Project definition technique to be applied to many more programs. J. Trainor. Miss & Roc 14:14-15 Mr 9 '64
Reasonable man. W. J. Coughlin. Miss & Roc 14:46 Mr 2 '64

UNITED STATES—Defense, Department of —*Continued*
Regional foreign policy conference to be held at Los Angeles. Dept State Bul 48:173 F 4 '63
Reorientations hampered ANP program. K. Johnsen. il Aviation W 78:81-7 Ap 1 '63
Revolution: changes in U.S. military policy and military organization. W. J Coughlin. Miss & Roc 14:148 Mr 30; 54 Ap 6; 46 Ap 13 '64
Revolution in the Pentagon. T. H. White. il Look 27:31-44+ Ap 23 '63
Senate approval seen for $47.4-billion DOD budget. H. M. David. il Miss & Roc 13:16-17 S 23 '63
Single defense information office urged. Aviation W 79:36 D 16 '63
Slow-down in the Pentagon. H. W. Baldwin. For Affairs 43:262-80 Ja '65
Solicitous giant. il Time 81:25-6 Ap 26 '63
Speaking out; McNamara monarchy. H. W. Baldwin. Sat Eve Post 236:8+ Mr 9 '63
Subsidized morale. New Repub 151:5 S 26 '64
System will rate contractors. H. Taylor. il Miss & Roc 12:14 F 11 '63
TFX and elements of high tragedy. W. V. Kennedy. America 108:522 Ap 20 '63
Top research contractors listed by DOD. Aviation W 81:87+ D 21 '64
Trimming the fat. R. Hotz. Aviation W 81:11 N 30 '64
USAF, DOD spar over advanced ICBMs. I. Stone. il Aviation W 80:143-5+ Mr 16 '64
U.S. space management in flux. Miss & Roc 13:12 Jl 22 '63
Up in arms; payola prohibition. Newsweek 64:82+ O 26 '64
Value of value. W. J. Coughlin. Miss & Roc 12:62 My 6 '63
Vital factor; civilian v. military control. Newsweek 62:28+ S 16 '63
What can industry do as Pentagon cuts back? il Newsweek 62:87-90 O 7 '63
What's wrong with civil-military relations. T. D. White. Newsweek 61:30 My 27 '63
Who runs America? an examination of a theory that says the answer is a military-industrial complex. D. S. Greenberg; discussion. Science 139:247-8+ Ja 18 '63
Whys have it; three assistants charged with embezzlement. Newsweek 64:23 D 28 '64
X-20 decision may have come earlier. F. G. McGuire. Miss & Roc 12:14 Mr 18 '63
X-22 report is rebuff to DOD civilians. R. G. O'Lone. Aviation W 80:32-3 F 17 '64
See also
Pentagon building, Arlington, Va.
Secretaries of defense (United States)
United States—Defense research and engineering, Director of

Advanced research projects agency

ARPA ending two programs. il Miss & Roc 14:35-6 Mr 30 '64
ARPA taking re-entry launches West. Miss & Roc 12:16 My 6 '63
DOD plans $125-million anti-ICBM effort; ARPA's Project defender. Aviation W 80:31 Ja 20 '64
Fingering nuclear test cheats; detecting and locating underground nuclear blasts. Bsns W p46-7 F 2 '63
Propellant program shift is criticized. Aviation W 80:21 Je 8 '64
Propulsion know-how considered equal to needs of future weapons. il Miss & Roc 14:131-2+ Mr 30 '64
Remote-area conflict research sought. il Aviation W 79:26-7 N 25 '63
Super-power radar nears testing. R. Lindsey. il Miss & Roc 12:28 F 25 '63

Appropriations and expenditures

Pentagon's big cutback of bases. il Newsweek 64:73-4 N 30 '64
Planning for prosperity; concerning reconversion of armament plants. N. Cousins. Sat R 47:32 D 5 '64

Defense intelligence agency

Assignment: global communications. il Miss & Roc 12:109-10+ Mr 25 '63
CIA: battle for secret power. S. Alsop. il Sat Eve Post 236:17-21 Jl 27 '63; Same abr. with title Intelligence business; secret battle for power. Read Digest 83:114-20 O '63
Reflections on the Bob and John show. W. Rogers, jr. New Repub 148:10-11 F 23 '63

Defense science board

Brown wants more ingenuity in DOD research. Miss & Roc 14:31 Mr 30 '64

Defense supply agency

DSA big factor in cost efficiency. il Miss & Roc 12:106-7 Mr 25 '63
Joint panels smooth gaps in interface. il Aviation W 81:21-2 mid-D '64

International security affairs division

Disarmament: an agency in search of a policy. L. W. Martin. il Reporter 29:22-6 Jl 4 '63

Weapons systems evaluation group

Exhaustive planning precedes RFP stage. il Miss & Roc 12:54-6 Mr 25 '63
Military not content with role in WSEG. il Miss & Roc 14:39-40 Mr 30 '64

Defense research and engineering, Director of

Brown oversees all military RDT&E. il Miss & Roc 12:80-1+ Mr 25 '63
Constant reviews yield sharp technical control. Miss & Roc 12:41+ Mr 25 '63
DOD performance system explained; Contractor performance evaluation. C. W. Borklund. il Miss & Roc 13:31-2+ S 16 '63
DDR&E will monitor briefings. Aviation W 79:36 Ag 26 '63
Increasing importance of space acknowledged in new DOD post. Aviation W 79:31 Jl 15 '63
Office overhauls R&D rules; tactical weapons now biggest market. il Miss & Roc 14:28-33 Mr 30 '64
On muddy problems. W. J. Coughlin. Miss & Roc 13:46 D 9 '63
Project definition technique to be applied to many more programs. J. Trainor. Miss & Roc 14:14-15 Mr 9 '64
Services' relationship with directorate is improving steadily. Miss & Roc 14:47-8 Mr 30 '64
Technical information survey aimed at establishing RDT&E data needs. Miss & Roc 14:15 Je 15 '64

Defenses

A-bomb in politics; who's right, who's wrong? il U S News 57:49-50 S 28 '64
Aftermath. W. J. Coughlin. Miss & Roc 15:50 N 9 '64
Again, the gap; nuclear striking power. il Newsweek 64:21 Ag 24 '64
Alice in McNamaraland. W. J. Coughlin. Miss & Roc 15:46 Ag 3 '64
America's invisible arsenal. il U S News 56:68-71 My 18 '64
Arms race: what LBJ faces. il U S News 57:71 N 23 '64
Atlantic relationships and nuclear problems: a French view. F. de Rose. For Affairs 41:479-90 Ap '63
Atomic arsenal; concerning testimony of Secretary McNamara on nuclear test ban treaty before the Senate foreign relations, Senate armed forces and Joint atomic energy committees. il Time 62:11-15 Ag 23 '63; Same abr. with title Our awesome atomic arsenal. Read Digest 83:67-71 N '63
Barry's bomber gap. R. D. Senter. il New Repub 151:9-10 S 12 '64
British report shows big increase in U.S. strategic missile strength. Miss & Roc 15:12 N 23 '64
Case of McNamara and the joint chiefs. J. Alsop. Read Digest 83:102-3 Jl '63
Challenge to military professionalism. R. N. Ginsburgh. bibliog f For Affairs 42:255-68 Ja '64; Excerpts. U S News 56:93 F 17 '64
Chilly future; R. McNamara's exposition of defense policies before the House armed services committee. il Time 81:15-16 F 8 '63
Civil defense in a balanced national security. S. L. Pittman. Bul Atomic Sci 20:24-6 Je '64
Combat vs. computers; testimony before the House defense appropriations subcommittee. C. E. LeMay. Aviation W 80:11 My 4 '64
Command & control reorientation to handle flexible response policy. il Miss & Roc 14:79-80+ Mr 30 '64
Congress considers impact of defense reductions. B. G. Lall. Bul Atomic Sci 20:31-2 F '64
Containing ourselves: some reflections on the enemy within; excerpt. D. Riesman. New Repub 148:14-17 Ap 6 '63
Counting the cost. il Newsweek 61:78+ Mr 25 '63
Cutback in overkill? Newsweek 62:54 Jl 15 '63
Decade of deadly birds. il Time 83:25 My 22 '64
Defending America; as McNamara sees it now; excerpts from news conference. R. S. McNamara. U S News 57:20 N 23 '64
Defense budget stresses tactical needs. Aviation W 82:22-4 Ja 25 '65

UNITED STATES—Defenses—*Continued*
Defense issue. R. Hotz. Aviation W 81:13 S 28 '64
Defense lag; address, August 10, 1964. B. M. Goldwater. Vital Speeches 30:676-8 S 1 '64
Defense message highlights; excerpts. L. B. Johnson. Miss & Roc 16:11 Ja 25 '65
Defense Secretary McNamara says strength now gives U.S. chance to cut arms race costs and perils. D. S. Greenberg. Science 139:472-4 F 8 '63
Defense, space receiving Johnson mark. G. C. Wilson. Aviation W 81:18-19 Ag 31 '64
Defense; the dilemma & the design. il Time 81:22+ F 15 '63
Defense will favor improvements over new weapon developments. Aviation W 81:23-4 N 9 '64
Defensive systems office advances studies of exotic weapons concepts. il Miss & Roc 14:59-60+ Mr 30 '64
Department of defense. W. Manchester. il Holiday 33:76-9+ My '63
DOD has new warhead plan. J. Trainor. Miss & Roc 14:15 Ap 27 '64
DOD shifts stir ire of Congress, allies. il Aviation W 78:73-5 Mr 11 '63
Emergency preparedness functions assigned to Secretary of state; executive order, February 26, 1963. J. F. Kennedy. Dept State Bul 48:629-30 Ap 22 '63
End of overkill? size of the U.S. nuclear arsenal. Sci Am 210:66 F '64
Expert looks at the joint chiefs; pros and cons of military unification. R. L. Gilpatric. il N Y Times Mag p 11+ Mr 29 '64
Eyeball exercise set for detection methods. Aviation W 78:80 My 6 '63
Fortress America; latest in defense ideas. il U S News 54:56-60 Mr 25 '63
From Washington straight. Cato. Nat R 14:189 Mr 12 '63
Future of the navy; address, January 9, 1964. P. H. Nitze. Vital Speeches 30:239-43 F 1 '64
General LeMay's case for new strategic aircraft; excerpts from statement before House defense appropriations subcommittee, February 26, 1964. C. E. LeMay. Aviation W 80:21 Ap 20 '64
Goldwater and the bomb: wrong questions, wrong answers. H. A. Kissinger. Reporter 31:27-8 N 5 '64
Goldwater and the bomber-gap. R. D. Senter. New Repub 150:10-12 Ja 25 '64
Goldwater defense philosophy; excerpts from Where I stand. B. Goldwater. Aviation W 81:11 Ag 31 '64
Goldwater on the gap. New Repub 149:5-6 D 21 '63
Goldwater, Pentagon clash on defense; with editorial comment. J. Trainor. Miss & Roc 15:12, 46 Ag 17 '64
GOP group charges neglect of defense. Aviation W 81:34 O 26 '64
GOP to capitalize on LeMay's charges; with excerpts from testimony before the House defense appropriation subcommittee. G. C. Wilson. Aviation W 80:26-7 Ap 20 '64
Growing political issue; America's atomic strength; excerpts from statements by B. Goldwater and others. il U S News 57:8 Ag 24 '64
Here the U.S. fights the coldest war; with report by C. Mydans. il Life 54:18-27 Mr 1 '63
His chief targets: McNamara and reds; GOP campaign. il Bsns W p 18-19 Ag 1 '64
Improvements in control systems cited. M. J. Yaffee. Aviation W 81:69+ D 14 '64
In the debate over U.S. armed might. U S News 56:6 My 4 '64
Johnson stress on military space seen. Aviation W 79:26-8 D 2 '63
Journals of David E. Lilienthal. Review
New Repub 151:24-5+ O 17 '64. J. W. Finney
Kennedy asks $53.7 billion for defense; with editorial comment. G. C. Wilson. il Aviation W 78:21, 26-8 Ja 21 '63
Khrushchev's losing fight with his marshals. V. Zorza. il Life 57:42-3+ N 6 '64
Last stand of the big bomber; debate between McNamara and LeMay. J. Atwater. il Sat Eve Post 237:13-17 Je 20 '64
Letter from Washington; Cuban crisis. R. H. Rovere. New Yorker 39:125-31 Mr 2 '63
Limits of nuclear war: thinking about the do-able and the un-do-able, by P. Ramsey. Review
Christian Cent 80:1309 O 23 '63. J. H. Smylie
McNamara assesses arms developments; text of testimony before House armed services committee. R. S. McNamara. Aviation W 80:77-9+ F 24 '64
McNamara cites arms lead; sees defense budget leveling. K. Johnsen. Aviation W 79:29 N 25 '63
McNamara claims big strategic edge. Miss & Roc 15:14 Ag 24 '64
McNamara discusses retaliatory forces; text of testimony before House armed services committee. R. S. McNamara. Aviation W 80:74-5+ Mr 2 '64
McNamara outlines nuclear force policy. Aviation W 78:106-9 Ap 22 '63
McNamara vs. Goldwater. W. V. Kennedy. America 111:259 S 12 '64; Reply. J. D. Hayes. 111:394 O 10 '64
McNamara voices some optimism over Nike-X, tells Minuteman plans. H. Taylor. Miss & Roc 14:20-1 F 3 '64
McNamara's doctrine. New Repub 148:4-5 Ap 6 '63
Major aerospace decisions face Johnson. G. C. Wilson. Aviation W 81:22 N 9 '64
Major defense cuts? Commonweal 80:76 Ap 10 '64
Military advice; its use in government; address, February 15, 1964. M. D. Taylor. Vital Speeches 30:336-9 Mr 15 '64
Military defenses of the West; address, November 18, 1963. R. S. McNamara. Vital Speeches 30:114-18 D 1 '63
Military value of missiles in Cuba. R. Hagan and B. Bernstein. il Bul Atomic Sci 19:8-13 F '63
Missile gap. il Time 83:16 Ja 24 '64
Morality of American nuclear policy. W. V. Kennedy. Cath World 199:363-70 S '64
More for less; defense expenditures. Time 85:19B-20 Ja 29 '65
National defense. il Sr Schol 85:4 O 21 '64
National security and the nuclear-test ban. J. B. Wiesner and H. F. York. il Sci Am 211:27-35 bibliog(p 142) O '64; Reply. E. P. Wigner. 211:8+ D '64
National security and world responsibilities; address, June 3, 1964. L. B. Johnson. Dept State Bul 50:950-2 Je 22 '64
National security strategy; address, August 29, 1963. W. F. McKee. Vital Speeches 30:21-4 O 15 '63
National strategy, security, and arms control; address, October 31, 1963. W. C. Foster. Dept State Bul 49:824-9 N 25 '63
Need for automated pushbuttons. W. F. Buckley, jr. Nat R 14:147 F 26 '63
New shape of U.S. defense. il Miss & Roc 12:26-8 Mr 25 '63
New stalemate and new strategy; Secretary McNamara's testimony before the House armed services committee. Bsns W p28 F 2 '63
Nuclear issue; Republican-Democratic dispute; with report by L. Norman. il Newsweek 64:33-4 S 21 '64
Nuclear stockpile: data suggest that in absence of clear policy reserves just growed and growed. E. Langer. Science 144:660-2 My 8 '64
Our defense: a crucial issue for candidates. Life 57:10 S 25 '64
Our defense needs; the long view. R. L. Gilpatric. For Affaris 42:366-78 Ap '64
Overkill budget. Nation 196:434 My 25 '63
Pendulum is swinging too far. T. D. White. il Newsweek 63:22-3 F 24 '64
Pentagon's new stress on tactical C&C systems highlights ISS meeting. M. Getler. Miss & Roc 15:18+ D 7 '64
Planners for the Pentagon; with editorial comment. il Bsns W p56-8+, 144 Jl 13 '63
Power, Senate unit voice test ban fears. K. Johnsen. Aviation W 79:30-1 S 16 '63
Practice of partnership. D. Acheson. For Affairs 41:247-60 Ja '63
Principles of defense management; excerpts from message to Congress, January 18, 1965. L. B. Johnson. Aviation W 82:17 Ja 25 '65
Reason, morality and defense policy. A. C. Enthoven. America 108:461-5, 494-7 Ap 6-13 '63; Correction. 108:597-8 Ap 27 '63
Republican body charges DOD, LBJ with planned weapons obsolescence. H. M. David. Miss & Roc 15:18 Jl 6 '64
Republicans renew Vietnam policy attack; with statements, by President Johnson, and Secretary McNamara. C. Brownlow. Aviation W 81:22-3 Ag 17 '64
$7-billion contract that changed the rules. R. A. Smith. il Fortune 67:96-101+ Mr; 110-11+ Ap '63
Some reflections on civil defense. M. E. Rozen. Bul Atomic Sci 20:21-4 Je '64
Speaking out; strategy and the defense intellectuals. T. D. White. Sat Eve Post 236:10+ My 4 '63

UNITED STATES—Defenses—*Continued*
State of the Union. W. J. Coughlin. Miss & Roc 14:52 Ja 13 '64
Strategy for American security; symposium. il Sat R 46:10-17 My 4 '63
Strength of the United States; address, November 21, 1963. J. F. Kennedy. Vital Speeches 30:101-2 D 1 '63
TFX and elements of high tragedy. W. V. Kennedy. America 108:522 Ap 20 '63
Test: are we the tougher? W. W. Rostow. il N Y Times Mag p21+ Je 7 '64
Test ban treaty; address, July 12, 1963. J. S. Cooper. Vital Speeches 30:201-3 Ja 15 '64
Test ban would not cut defense budget. G. C. Wilson. Aviation W 79:26-7 Ag 19 '63
That visceral feeling. W. J. Coughlin. Miss & Roc 15:46 Ag 31 '64
Tiger will bite. S. Alsop. il Sat Eve Post 236:18 O 19 '63
Trap offered de Gaulle; with reply, by T. W. Stanley. P. M. Gallois. Bul Atomic Sci 19: 24-30 O '63
Two minds. W. J. Coughlin. Miss & Roc 15: 46 Jl 20 '64
USSR can't salvo ICBM's. J. Trainor. Miss & Roc 15:14 Ag 10 '64
U.S. defense policy; address, August 17, 1964. R. S. McNamara. Vital Speeches 30:710-13 S 15 '64; Excerpts. Aviation W 81:17 Ag 24 '64
U.S. destructive power underscored; Polaris singled out. Miss & Roc 16:15 Ja 18 '65
United States military posture today. A. J. Cottrell. bibliog f Cur Hist 47:71-6+ Ag '64
U.S. missile might, can we count on our hole cards? W. Cloud. il Pop Sci 184:70-3+ My '64
U.S, Soviet strengths detailed; with editorial comment. J. Trainor. Miss & Roc 14:14, 46 Ap 20 '64
Unity of the American people; excerpts from address, September 17, 1964. L. B. Johnson. Dept State Bul 51:461-2 O 5 '64
What-was-said gap; Goldwater on capability and control of the U.S. nuclear arsenal. Time 84:15 Ag 21 '64
Where we stand on defense; excerpts from address, November 28, 1963. R. S. McNamara. il Duns R 83:53-4+ F '64; Same. Bul Atomic Sci 20:35-9 Mr '64
Whiz kids vs. military men: who is shaping defense? il U S News 54:46-7 Mr 4 '63
Why LBJ holds the arms line. il Bsns W p28-9 Ja 23 '65
Why McNamara is under fire. U S News 54: 22 Mr 25 '63
Why we are stronger than Russia. R. S. McNamara. il Sat Eve Post 237:15-17 N 7 '64
Will to be strong; address, September 23, 1964. B. M. Goldwater. Vital Speeches 31: 5-7 O 15 '64
Withdrawal from reality. W. J. Coughlin. Miss & Roc 14:46 Je 15 '64; Discussion. 14:7 Je 29 '64
World problems and national security; address, April 25, 1963. B. Goldwater. Vital Speeches 29:482-6 Je 1 '63
Worry over U.S. defense: a Maginot line of missiles? il U S News 56:38-41 Mr 9 '64
See also
Aeronautics, Military—United States
Airplanes, Military—United States
Alaska—Defenses
Atomic warfare—Defenses
Canada-United States ministerial committee on joint defense
Civil defense
Coast defense
Disarmament—United States
Guided missiles
North American air defense command
United States—Air force
United States—Armed forces
United States—Army
United States—Defense, Department of
United States—Navy

Description and travel

America the beautiful: let's not lose it. il Changing T 17:25-9 S '63
American islomania. K. Davis. Mlle 57:122-3+ Je '63
Autoless adventure West. R. Meyer, jr. il Travel 120:38-42 Jl '63
God's own junkyard, by P. Blake. Review Newsweek il 63:50 Ja 13 '64
Guide to family vacations on a budget; symposium. il Redbook 120:87-94 Ap '63
Here be Broadway. R. G. G. Price. Atlan 212: 110-11 S '63
Holiday handbook: United States by bus. K. Simon. il Holiday 34:99-104 Jl '63
Let's travel in autumn. il Mlle 59:181-3 S '64
Letter from Paris; tourists from France. Genêt. New Yorker 40:124-6 My 30 '64
Lost heroes of touring. R. Cantwell. il Sports Illus 20:60-2+ Je 22 '64
Redbook's 1964 guide to family vacations. W. Hartley and E. Hartley. il Redbook 122: 51-8 Ap '64
Report on the Visit U.S.A. program. Holiday 33:138+ F '63
Sikh discovers America. J. S. Rekhi. il Nat Geog Mag 126:558-90 O '64
State guides for summer tourists. il Changing T 17:35-7 Je '63
Teen travel talk; calendar of August events. il Seventeen 23:96 Ag '64
Travels with Charley; condensation. J. Steinbeck. il Read Digest 84:275-8+ Je '64
United States in 1850; from the letters of a Colombian exile. M. Torres. il Américas 16:1-8 F '64
Voyage pittoresque aux Etats-unis de l'Amérique par Paul Svignine; an appreciation. M. B. Davidson. Am Heritage 15:49-51+ F '64
Will you drive to the fair? il Sunset 132:45-6+ Je '64
You don't have to be a hero; automobile camping. M. Rubenstein. il Field & S 68: 40-2+ F '64
See also
Automobile touring—United States
Tourist trade—United States

Diplomatic and consular service

Case against a West Point for diplomats. E. O. Briggs. il N Y Times Mag p20+ My 3 '64
Department closes thirteen posts. Dept State Bul 49:328-9 Ag 26 '63
Diplomatic rapport between Africa and the United States; address, April 10, 1964. G. M. Williams. Dept State Bul 50:698-703 My 4 '64; Same with questions and answers. Ann Am Acad 354:54-64 Jl '64
Education for the new diplomacy; address, March 2, 1963. R. E. Lee. Dept State Bul 48:423-7 Mr 25 '63
Mother doesn't do much; the ambassador's wife in India. C. A. Galbraith. il Atlan 211: 47-52 My '63
Sad state of the Department of state: the hog-tied ambassador. E. Briggs. Esquire 60:100-1+ S '63
United States and Soviet Union sign consular convention; text of convention, with statement by President Johnson. Dept State Bul 50:979-85 Je 22 '64; Excerpts without statement. Cur Hist 47:303-5 N '64
See also
Ambassadors

Economic conditions

Abundance, threat or promise? R. Theobald. Nation 196:387-412 My 11 '63; Discussion. 196:inside cover Je 15 '63
Action in the three-I league. Time 84:103 O 16 '64
Affluence in U.S; the other side of the poverty story. il U S News 57:76-7 D 7 '64
After the landslide, the outlook. il Newsweek 64:73 N 16 '64
American economic republic, by A. A. Berle. Review
Reporter 29:52+ S 12 '63. A. F. Burns
Amidst prosperity, recession warnings. il Newsweek 62:75-6 N 4 '63
Apostle of economic growth; address, November 1, 1963. L. A. Townsend. Vital Speeches 30:111-14 D 1 '63
Are the soaring sixties finally aloft? il Newsweek 63:68-70 Ap 13 '64
Are we flunking economics? address, January 15, 1963. L. H. Hodges. Vital Speeches 29:286-8 F 15 '63
Away from myths. Commonweal 81:83 O 16 '64
Big comeback for the dollar; with editorial comment. Bsns W p98+, 148 Ap 25 '64
Boom surges on to $600 billion economy. il Life 55:34D Jl 5 '63
Bountiful autumn. il Fortune 68:39-40 O '63
Bullish but not boomish. Newsweek 61:85 My 27 '63
Business in 1963. il Time 82:58-61 D 27 '63
Business pulse of the Nation; summary of Economic report. L. B. Johnson. il Newsweek 63:65-8 Ja 27 '64
Business roundup: eighteen month forecast. il Fortune 69:27-8+ Ja '64
Capital spending: a freshening breeze. il Newsweek 61:82-5 Mr 18 '63
Challenge to affluence, by G. Myrdal. Review
Commentary 37:91-2 F '64. B. B. Seligman; Discussion. 37:14-16 Je '64
New Yorker 40:203-4+ Ap 18 '64. N. Bliven
Charting the way to stable growth. il Bsns W p 162+ O 31 '64

UNITED STATES—Economic conditions—*Cont.*
Clouds on the economic horizon; address, October 2, 1964. T. B. Curtis. Vital Speeches 31:29-30 O 15 '64
Consider the horse; or, A study of U.S. capitalism. G. Schwartz. il N Y Times Mag p20+ O 4 '64
Disturbing economics of affluence; excerpts from Hidden face of free enterprise. J. R. Bunting. il Duns R 83:40-1+ Ap '64
Economic arithmetic. New Repub 148:6 Je 15 '63
Economic growth in the West, by A. Maddison. Review
 Sat R 47:30 Ag 8 '64. S. Chase
Economics in the news. il Sr Schol 85:21 S 30; 18 O 14; 16 O 21; 20 N 4; 12 D 2; 11 D 9 '64; 16 Ja 7; 18 Ja 14 '65
Economy: another bumper year. il Newsweek 64:71 S 28 '64
Economy: bouncing back and bullish. Newsweek 61:75 My 13 '63
Economy: moment of uncertainty. il Newsweek 62:73-4 D 2 '63
Economy: vintage year. il Newsweek 62:45-8 D 30 '63
$50 billion worth of good news; survey of U.S. economic prospects for 1964-65. il Life 56:13 Ja 10 '64
Going into next year at a gallop. il Bsns W p27-9 S 19 '64
Going Johnson's way. New Repub 150:3-4 My 9 '64
Golden barrel. H. Hazlitt. Nat R 16:27 Ja 14 '64
Good friend and critic; speaking out on American issues. Bsns W p57-8+ D 14 '63
High gear. Newsweek 64:58 Jl 27 '64
Hitting the target. Time 83:23-4 Ja 10 '64
How much longer? longest peacetime expansion; with editorial comment. il Bsns W p23-5, 158 Mr 28 '64
How they see the work ahead; economists' round table. il Bsns W p26-8 Ja 9 '65
In gauging the boom, watch June; semi-annual meeting of Business council. il Newsweek 64:81 O 26 '64
Income revolution slows up; with charts. Bsns W p 144+ S 28 '63
Inflation as cure-all. H. Hazlitt. Newsweek 61:89 Mr 25 '63
Invisible Americans. B. H. Bagdikian. il Sat Eve Post 236:28-33+ D 21 '63
It's a boom, but nobody has fun. il Bsns W p23-4 N 16 '63
It's just wonderful that it's not too good. il Time 83:99 My 15 '64
Keyserling's case. New Repub 148:2 Mr 2 '63
Labor month in review. See issues of Monthly labor review
Lauding & lamenting: Economic report to Congress. il Time 83:11-12 Ja 24 '64
Life-enriched consumer. il Time 84:79 Ag 7 '64
Look for new records in output, income, profits, jobs. il U S News 56:41-4 Ja 13 '64
Looking up all over. il Time 81:15 My 10 '63
LBJ: hold that line; the price-wage line. Newsweek 63:57-9 F 3 '64
L.B.J.'s great good bear hug. Life 56:4 My 15 '64
Management problems in 1963; interviews with executives. il Harvard Bsns R 41:6-8+ Ja '63
Measuring U.S. growth: report on the soaring sixties; with charts. U S News 55:42-5 N 11 '63
Mr and Mrs Super and U.S. steel. il Newsweek 62:81 O 7 '63
More gains next year, and clear to 1970. il Bsns W p 128+ O 3 '64
More output=more jobs. Time 83:93 My 22 '64
Mythmakers: an essay on power and wealth, by B. D. Nossiter. Review
 Sat R 47:29 Ap 11 '64. D. C. Coyle
New & exuberant. il Time 81:73-7 My 31 '63
New definition of our poor. H. P. Miller. il N Y Times Mag p 11+ Ap 21 '63
New horizons in economics. R. L. Heilbroner. il Sat R 47:31-2+ Ag 29 '64
New strength for dollar. Bsns W p36 Ap 11 '64
Newsweek survey: better business ahead but no boom. il Newsweek 62:66-8 S 2 '63
Next year, a slowdown; economy; jolts on two fronts; interview, ed. by H. Rowen. W. M. Martin. Newsweek 64:93 O 5 '64
1965: good, but not good enough? il Newsweek 65:43-5 Ja 4 '65
No sense raising hell; concerning State of the Union message. New Repub 148:3-4 F 2 '63
Not done with mirrors; President's Economic report. New Repub 150:3-4 F 1 '64
Not enough. Nation 198:1-2 Ja 4 '64
Other side of affluence. Bsns W p 190+ Ap 18 '64
Outlook for '65. H. C. Wallich. Newsweek 65:72 Ja 11 '65
Outlook report: business future for U.S. and Europe. il U S News 56:88-90 Ap 13 '64
Paper economy, by D. T. Bazelon. Review
 Nation 197:183-5 S 28 '63. R. Theobald
Peacetime prosperity. Duns R 83:29 Je '64
President Frei on U.S. capitalism; reprint. E. Frei. America 111:285 S 19 '64
Presidential strategy on recessions. E. T. Folliard. America 109:478 O 26 '63
Prosperity, 1964: it's unprecedented. il Life 57:36-47 O 16 '64
Question of psychology. Time 84:75 D 18 '64
Roots of our most crucial problems. Bsns W p 112 Jl 6 '63
Rosy glow. il Newsweek 63:84+ Ap 27 '64
Security of the United States; address, August 18, 1964. G. Meany. Vital Speeches 30:685-8 S 1 '64
Set for a fifth fat year; with charts. il Bsns W p 11-13 Ja 2 '65
Shock, then recovery; impact of the assassination of Pres. Kennedy, opinions of US economists. il Bsns W p92-3 N 30 '63
Some pinch in the plants. il Time 84:87 S 25 '64
Speaking out; our way of life makes us miserable. E. Fromm. Sat Eve Post 237:8+ Jl 25 '64
Spend, spend, spend. Newsweek 64:68+ S 14 '64
Spring 1964: bloom and boom. il Newsweek 63:15-16 Mr 30 '64
State of business; the long gain. il Time 83:79 Mr 27 '64
State of the economy: concerning President's Economic report to Congress. America 110:156-7 F 1 '64
Still piling up debt, but slower. il Bsns W p75 Ag 22 '64
Still robust in the third. Time 84:97 O 30 '64
Still up, but slowly. il Bsns W p 17-19 Jl 6 '63
Target: $1-trillion a year; Twentieth century fund study. il Bsns W p 102-4 My 2 '64
Tax cut: a dissenting view. P. Dorner. Nation 197:171-3 S 28 '63
Technology's impact on religion; correlation between family income and church membership. C. M. Cook. Christian Cent 81:1083-5 S 2 '64
This problem of bigness; excerpt from Justice for all. B. L. Masse. America 111:128-30 Ag 8 '64
To defend the dollar. H. Hazlitt. Newsweek 61:84 My 20 '63
Too rich, too soft, too surfeited? M. Harper, jr. Sat R 46:68+ Ap 13 '63
Two Americas. Nation 196:237 Mr 23 '63
Two sides of the tape. Fortune 70:95-6 O '64
Understanding the American economy. il Sr Schol 83:6-9 N 15; 16-18 N 22; 22-8+ D 6; 14-16 D 13 '63; 14-15+ Ja 10; 84:10-11+ Ja 31; 16-18 F 7; 14-16 F 21; 13-14+ F 28; 14-15+ Mr 6; 14-15+ Mr 13; 14-15+ Mr 20; 17-18+ Ap 10; 14-16 Ap 17; 14-16 My 1 '64
U.S. economy as two critics see its ultimate aim. il Newsweek 61:82-3 Je 10 '63
Viewing U.S. economy with a Marxist glass; analysis of capitalism's troubles. il Bsns W p67-8+ Ap 13 '63
War on poverty. New Repub 149:3-4 D 28 '63
Well-tempered boom; business upswing accompanied by price stability. il Bsns W p27-9 Je 27 '64
What 1965 holds for business. il U S News 58:22-4 Ja 4 '65
What's become of the affluent society; interview. J. K. Galbraith. U S News 56:66-8 My 4 '64
Where the growth is. il Time 83:84 Je 19 '64
 See also
Business conditions
Cost of living—United States
Debts, Public—United States
Finance—United States
Housing—United States
Immigration and emigration—United States
Minimum wage—United States
Prices—United States
Prosperity
Strikes—United States
Taxation—United States
Unemployment—United States
Wages—United States

UNITED STATES—Economic conditions—*Cont.*

Anecdotes, facetiae, satire, etc.

Drip spoon plate society. S. Wright. il Harper 226:82-4 F '63; Same abr. with title Our drip-spoon-plate economy. Read Digest 83: 207-8 N '63

Economic history

Debts we never paid. R. Wernick. il Am Heritage 16:32-5+ D '64
Enterprising Americans: a business history of the United States, by J. Chamberlain. Review
  Nat R 14:200-1 Mr 12 '63. H. Hazlitt
Nation transformed, ed. by S. Diamond. Review
  New Repub 150:17-18 F 15 '64. E. T. Chase
See also
Banks and banking—United States—Crisis. 1933
Money—United States—History

Economic opportunity, Office of

War on poverty. America 111:771 D 12 '64

Economic policy

After election: President will face these issues. il Nations Bsns 52:40-1+ O '64
American economic republic, by A. Berle. Review
  Fortune 67:94+ Je '63. J. Davenport
  New Repub 148:21-3 Je 22 '63. P. Green
America's great depression, by M. N. Rothbard. Review
  Nat R 16:456-8 Je 2 '64. L. M. Spadaro
America's jobless and Russia's markets. J. Lomax. Nation 196:262-4 Mr 30 '63
Argument heats up on the payments gap; financial men criticize administration policy. il Bsns W p67-8+ Je 8 '63
Atlantic report. Atlan 214:6+ N '64
Balance-of-payments bind. G. Burck. il Fortune 67:112-17 Je '63
Balance of payments, trade expansion, development assistance; excerpts from economic report. L. B. Johnson. Dept State Bul 50:222-3 F 10 '64
Boom ad hoc. il Fortune 70:27-8 D '64
Businessman's prescription for good times; excerpts from address, September 29, 1964. R. C. Tyson. U S News 57:74-6 N 2 '64
Can anyone explain capitalism? R. J. Monsen, jr. Sat R 46:13-15+ D 14 '63
Challenge of prosperity: symposium; presented with the Committee for economic development. il Sat R 48:23-32+ Ja 9 '65
Challenge to affluence, by G. Myrdal. Review
  New Repub 149:23-4 N 2 '63. P. L. Bernstein
  Sat R 47:58-9 Ja 11 '64. H. David
  Sci Am 210:141-2+ Ja '64. L. H. Keyserling
Comeback for inflation? W. V. Shannon. Commonweal 80:354-6 Je 12 '64
Coming: new challenge to U.S. trade. il Nations Bsns 52:54-5+ D '64
Confidence. D. Lawrence. U S News 55:108 S 30 '63
Do fundamental principles really change? reprint with postscript. D. Lawrence. U S News 56:80+ Ja 6 '64
Drift in Washington; where it's heading. il U S News 54:29-30 Ap 1 '63
Drive for economy. Commonweal 79:385 D 27 '63
East-West trade; statement, March 13, 1964. D. Rusk. il Dept State Bul 50:474-84 Mr 30 '64
Economic education of John F. Kennedy. M. J. Rossant. Reporter 28:22-5 F 14 '63; Discussion. 28:10+ Mr 14 '63
Economic goals: view from the White House; address, November 19, 1964. L. B. Johnson. Sat R 48:28-30 Ja 9 '65
Economic growth in the West, by A. Maddison. Review
  Sat R 47:30 Ag 8 '64. S. Chase
Economic impact of defense shifts eyed. K. Johnsen. Aviation W 79:28-9 S 30 '63
Economic issues. H. Hazlitt. Newsweek 64:88 N 2 '64
Economic oracles of the New frontier. R. E. Mooney. il N Y Times Mag p8+ Ag 4 '63
Economic prosperity. il Sr Schol 85:16 S 23 '64
Economic realities: address, January 15, 1964. B. Goldwater. Vital Speeches 30:234-7 F 1 '64
Economic security; address, September 11, 1963. T. B. Curtis. Vital Speeches 30:17-21 O 15 '63
Economy: a case for efficient planning. H. Malmgren. il New Repub 151:41-4+ N 7 '64
Fire from the left. il Time 82:85 N 22 '63
For a guaranteed income. M. D. Reagan. il N Y Times Mag p20+ Je 7 '64
For my father's grandchildren. J. Cogley. Commonweal 77:657-9 Mr 22 '63
Free enterprisers: Kennedy, Johnson & the business establishment, by H. Rowen. Review
  New Repub 151:26-8 S 19 '64. R. L. Strout
Free, growing, full of hope; concerning State of the Union address. Sr Schol 85:21 Ja 14 '65
Goldwater: Republicans will cut taxes, reduce debt; excerpts from address, September 8, 1964. B. M. Goldwater. il U S News 57:117 S 21 '64
Goldwater view of economics. M. Friedman. il N Y Times Mag p35+ O 11 '64
Goldwater's economics; interview. il Bsns W p 176-8+ S 26 '64
Government puts growth policies on trial. il Nations Bsns 51:31-3+ F '63
Government spending, it'll never be cut. il Changing T 17:6-10 Ag '63; Same abr. with title Up, up, up, the relentless rise in government spending. Read Digest 83:231-2+ N '63
Great society: how much to spend. U S News 57:34 D 7 '64
Great society; nation's quest. Commonweal 81:255-8 N 20 '64
Growth mania. H. Hazlitt. Newsweek 61:88 Mr 18 '63
Hard sell. Newsweek 61:22 F 25 '63
Hellerious economics. H. Hazlitt. Newsweek 61:84 Mr 11 '63
Here are Johnson's promises for a Great society: State-of-the-Union message, January 4, 1965. L. B. Johnson. il U S News 58:98-102 Ja 18 '65; Same. Vital Speeches 31:194-8 Ja 15 '65
How planned is our economy? J. Tobin. il N Y Times Mag p 18+ O 13 '63
How to cure poverty. H. Hazlitt. Newsweek 63:75 Ja 27 '64
Impact of foreign aid on the American economy; address, October 23, 1963. D. E. Bell. Dept State Bul 49:830-3 N 25 '63
In the growth game: how can the U.S. reach 'go' again? il Newsweek 61:71 Mr 11 '63
Inflation and statism. H. Hazlitt. Newsweek 63:73 Mr 2 '64
Inflation, danger ahead? G. L. Bach. il Harvard Bsns R 42:49-61 Jl '64
Intellectuals and new deals. A. A. Berle. New Repub 150:21-4 Mr 7 '64
Is economic growth enough? R. Cissell and H. Cissell. il America 111:65-7 Jl 18 '64
Is peace our big danger? L. Lawrence. U S News 57:100 Ag 25 '64
It's time to face the future; excerpts from Challenge to affluence. G. Myrdal. il Look 27:96+ N 19 '63
Johnson's economics; quotations from statements on major economic issues. L. B. Johnson. il Bsns W p47-8+ O 31 '64
Johnson's Eisenhower premise. S. Rousseas. Nation 199:375-9 N 23 '64
Johnson's grand design; concerning State of the Union message; with editorial comment. il Bsns W p 19-21, 108 Ja 9 '65
Kennedy and the liberals. S. E. Harris. New Repub 148:15-16 Je 1 '63
Kennedy's formula for full employment. Bsns W p 110-13 Ja 26 '63
Khrushchev to the rescue. New Repub 148:7 F 23 '63
Let's spend more. H. Rowen. New Repub 148:13-16 My 25 '63
Letter from Washington. R. H. Rovere. New Yorker 38:107-10 F 2 '63
Limits of continuity. New Repub 149:4-6 D 14 '63
LBJ's brand goes on the economy; with editorial comment. il Bsns W p71-4+, 136 Ja 25 '64
LBJ's Great society, what will it be? il U S News 57:33-7 N 23 '64
New defense shifts impact plan based on agricultural program. K. Johnsen. Aviation W 80:21 Je 29 '64
No tightening up, yet; with editorial comment. il Bsns W p33-4, 200 S 26 '64
Not done with mirrors; President's Economic report. New Repub 150:3-4 F 1 '64
Our common cause in world competition; address, November 9, 1964. F. J. Borch. Vital Speeches 31:115-18 D 1 '64
Paper economy, by D. T. Bazelon. Review
  New Repub 148:21-3 My 25 '63. P. Green; Reply with rejoinder. D. J. Ashton. 149:29-30 Jl 13 '63
Pause of conscience. D. Lawrence. U S News 58:116 Ja 25 '65

UNITED STATES—Economic policy—*Cont.*
Perspective on the tasks of the 1960's; address, May 11, 1964. W. W. Rostow. Dept State Bul 50:864-7 Je 1 '64
Planning to keep the ball rolling. il Bsns W p23-5 N 14 '64
President meets with Cabinet; reviews world situation; statement, October 20, 1964. L. B. Johnson. Dept State Bul 51:653 N 9 '64
President outlines position on balance of payments and trade; statements, October 24 and October 28, 1964. L. B. Johnson. Dept State Bul 51:751-2 N 23 '64
President takes office: Johnson-the-inheritor yields to Johnson-on-his own. il Sr Schol 85:6-9 Ja 21 '65
Presidential committee report on fiscal and monetary policy; November 19, 1962. Mo Labor R 86:51 Ja '63
President's calculated risk. M. J. Rossant. Reporter 30:27-9 Ja 30 '64
President's economic report. H. Malmgren. New Repub 148:17-18 F 9 '63
Pressure is on money managers. Bsns W p26 Mr 7 '64
Principle of the Great society. W. Lippmann. Newsweek 65:13 Ja 18 '65
Profitable growth and our world position; address, January 9, 1964. G. W. Ball. Dept State Bul 50:123-8 Ja 27 '64
Right remedy but late and little. Bsns W p 144 Ja 26 '63
Show of confidence. il Time 82:109 D 6 '63
Skeptical Congress; hearings before the Joint congressional committee on the economic report. America 108:219 F 16 '63
Slow growth is no. 1 problem; survey by campus economists. il Bsns W p39-40 D 7 '63
Speaking out; fear threatens our prosperity. W. W. Heller. Sat Eve Post 236:8+ N 9 '63
Spend or save? D. Lawrence. U S News 56: 104 Mr 9 '64
State of the Union. il Newsweek 65:15-19 Ja 11 '65
State of the Union. New Repub 152:4+ Ja 16 '65
Strategy for innovation. M. Michaelis. Bul Bul Atomic Sci 20:19-23 Ap '64
Strengthening the international monetary system; remarks and statements, September 30-October 4, 1963. J. F. Kennedy; C. D. Dillon; G. W. Ball. Dept State Bul 49:610-23 O 21 '63
Tax cut: a dissenting view. P. Dorner. Nation 197:171-3 S 28 '63
Tax trimmers. R. Lekachman. Commentary 35:289-95 Ap '63
Test ban and beyond. N. Cousins. Sat R 46:14+ Ag 10 '63
To stimulate employment. Commonweal 78: 60-1 Ap 12 '63
Top authority's plan to get the economy rolling; statement. A. F. Burns. U S News 54:98-101 F 18 '63
Toward the Great society. Sat Eve Post 237: 84 N 21 '64
U.S. economic problems; address, December 2, 1964. L. B. Johnson. Vital Speeches 31: 130-2 D 15 '64; Excerpts. il U S News 57: 92-3 D 14 '64
U.S. economy, by J. Davenport. Review Time 84:64 N 20 '64
US economy in 1965. New Repub 152:3-4 Ja 2 '65
Vision of LBJ: something for all: concerning State-of-the-Union message. il U S News 58:31-3 Ja 18 '65
Walter Heller's word for 1964: prosperous; interview, ed. by H. Rowen. W. Heller. Newsweek 62:46 D 30 '63
War on poverty. G. Myrdal. New Repub 150: 14-16 F 8 '64
War on want, at home; State of the Union message; with editorial comment. il Bsns W p 19-21, 112 Ja 11 '64
Washington desk. J. R. Slevin. Duns R 84: 5 Ag '64
What the hell do those fellows want? Fortune 67:81-2 F '63; Same abr. with title What those fellows want. Read Digest 82:86-8 Ap '63
What's needed after tax cuts. R. Newcomb. Nations Bsns 52:32-3+ Mr '64
Where America gets its strength; excerpts from World economic problems and policies. T. C. Mann. il Nations Bsns 52:116-17+ N '64
Where both candidates stand on the big issues; with editorial comment. il Bsns W p64-6+, 192 O 10 '64
Where businessmen support Kennedy. Nations Bsns 51:34-5+ F '63
Where do we go from here? il Sr Schol 84: 14-16 My 1 '64
Where Johnson stands on financial issues. il U S News 55:117-19 D 9 '63
Where the poverty program goes next. Bsns W p 144 Ag 22 '64
White House holds conference on export expansion; addresses, September 17, 1963. J. F. Kennedy; D. Rusk; C. A. Herter. Dept State Bul 49:595-605 O 14 '63
White House plan for solving key problems. il U S News 57:39-40 N 9 '64
Whither now, GNP? Nat R 17:10 Ja 12 '65
Why unemployment stays high; policy-makers debate; with editorial comment. il Bsns W p 133+, 204 N 16 '63
Will they believe it? R. Moley. Newsweek 61: 100 F 18 '63
World economic developments; address, November 16, 1964. G. S. Moore. Vital Speeches 31:62-5 Ja 1 '65
Wright Patman: champion of cheap money; interview, ed. by G. R. Rosen. Duns R 83: 59-60+ My '64
Yankee dollar. M. Mayer. Sat Eve Post 237: 28-30 Ja 18 '64

See also
Agricultural administration—United States
Budget—United States
Committee for economic development
Economic assistance, Domestic
Finance—United States
Government spending policy
Income tax—United States
Price regulation by government—United States
Tariff—United States
Taxation—United States
United States—Appropriations and expenditures
United States—Council of economic advisers

Economic relations

Advancing the American national interest without war. A. I. Waskow. Bul Atomic Sci 20:23-5 F '64; Reply with rejoinder. A. Forbes. 20:36-8 Je '64
Cuban embargo myth. P. Geyelin. Reporter 30:18-19 Ap 23 '64
Free enterprise; address, February 21, 1964. W. W. Scranton. Vital Speeches 30:326-8 Mr 15 '64
Government-business team that works; trade missions. A. Fontaine. Read Digest 83:111-14 D '63
Great danger for the world, unless LBJ acts forcefully; German's view. U S News 57:104 D 14 '64
Market price of power. W. Diebold, jr. Sat R 47:40 Mr 28 '64
Pioneers for peace; address, September 26, 1963. J. F. Kennedy. Dept State Bul 49: 631-6 O 21 '63
Profitable growth and our world position; address, January 9, 1964. G. W. Ball. Dept State Bul 50:123-8 Ja 27 '64
Road ahead; address, February 13, 1963. D. Rusk. Dept State Bul 48:311-16 Mr 4 '63
Secretary Rusk interviewed on Voice of America; ed. by R. L. Redeen. D. Rusk. Dept State Bul 50:330-6 Mr 2 '64
Secretary Rusk's news conference of March 6, 1964. D. Rusk. Dept State Bul 50:439-46 Mr 23 '64
Trade and the less developed areas. W. Butler. For Affairs 41:378-83 Ja '63
Trade, investment, and peace; address, October 5, 1964. D. Rusk. Dept State Bul 51:570-5 O 26 '64
Trading with the devil with a shorter spoon. R. Lubar. il Fortune 69:108-12+ Ap '64
U.S. policy in a changing world; address, October 6, 1964. W. W. Rostow. Dept State Bul 51:637-42 N 2 '64
Where democracy ends. Nation 197:81 Ag 24 '63
World trade; address, May 7, 1964. N. A. Rockefeller. Vital Speeches 30:494-7 Je 1 '64

See also
Economic assistance, American
United States—Commerce
United States—Public advisory committee for trade negotiations

Africa

New patterns of African trade; address, April 1, 1964. G. M. Williams. Dept State Bul 50:664-70 Ap 27 '64
Trade developments and trade policy; statement, November 21, 1963. S. Z. Westerfield, jr. Dept State Bul 50:101-4 Ja 20 '64

Brazil

American capital and Brazilian nationalism. W. Baer and M. H. Simonsen. Yale R 53: 192-8 D '63

UNITED STATES—Economic relations—Brazil —*Continued*
Potential in Brazil. J. J. Johnson. Cur Hist 46:1-7 Ja '64
U.S. makes short-term credit available to Brazil. Dept State Bul 48:144 Ja 28 '63

Canada

Climate of world trade and U.S.-Canadian trade relations; address, September 15, 1963. G. G. Johnson. Dept State Bul 49:543-8 O 7 '63
Common market for North America; address, February 20, 1964. L. A. Townsend. Vital Speeches 30:381-4 Ap 1 '64
Interdependence, the basis of U.S.-Canada relations; address, April 25, 1964. G. W. Ball. bibliog f Dept State Bul 50:770-4 My 18 '64
Joint Canadian-United States statement on proposed interest equalization tax, July 21, 1963. Dept State Bul 49:256 Ag 12 '63
United community of North America; address, September 30, 1964. E. Lamb. Vital Speeches 31:46-8 N 1 '64
When Canada looks to its future. il U S News 55:62-5 Ag 5 '63
See also
Joint United States—Canadian committee on trade and economic affairs

Caribbean Region

Intervention and dollar diplomacy in the Caribbean, 1900-1921, by D. G. Munro. Review
Américas 16:38 Jl '64. C. G. Fenwick

China (People's Republic)

Road back to mainland China. C. H. Peake. New Repub 149:10-11 Ag 17 '63; Reply. E. Friedman. 149:39 Ag 31 '63

Communist countries

East-West trade; statement, March 13, 1964. D. Rusk. il Dept State Bul 50:474-84 Mr 30 '64
This month's feature. U.S. trade relations with the red bloc. Cong Digest 43:37-45+ F '64
Trading with the devil with a shorter spoon. R. Lubar. il Fortune 69:108-12+ Ap '64

Cuba

Dramatic flourish, empty gesture; breakdown of U.S. trade embargo on Cuba. il Time 83:23 F 28 '64
Inertia of folly. Nation 198:205 Mr 2 '64
Principles of our policy toward Cuba; address, April 23, 1964. G. W. Ball. Dept State Bul 50:738-44 My 11 '64
U.S. approves amendment to Cuban shipping policy; Department statement, December 16, 1963. Dept State Bul 50:10 Ja 6 '64
United States blocks Cuban assets to counter Communist subversion; press release, July 8, 1963. Dept State Bul 49:160 Jl 29 '63
Wayward buses to Cuba. Life 56:4 Ja 24 '64

Europe, Eastern

Flag follows trade. Time 83:27 My 29 '64

Europe, Western

After Brussels. E. Taylor. Reporter 28:29-32 F 14 '63
Atlantic partners. New Repub 148:3-4 Je 8 '63
Atlantic partnership: a vital force in motion; address, April 28, 1963. G. C. McGhee. Dept State Bul 48:771-5 My 20 '63
Dealing with a new Europe; with editorial comment. il Bsns W p46-54, 88 Jl 4 '64
Europe's boom slows down; where it's heading next. il U S News 57:116-18 O 5 '64
Grain gambit; U.S. grain deal with Great Britain. Newsweek 63:91 Ap 27 '64
Implications for U.S. of breakdown in U.K.-EEC negotiations; text of letter to Senator Paul H. Douglas, February 15, 1963. G. W. Ball. Dept State Bul 48:412-15 Mr 18 '63
International outlook; U.S. relations with EEC. Bsns W p65 Ag 31 '63
Myth about the Common market? E. Griffiths. il Newsweek 62:61-2+ Ag 12 '63
Parallel roles of business and diplomacy in an era of expanding frontiers; address, May 19, 1964. G. C. McGhee. Dept State Bul 51:18-25 Jl 6 '64
Political evolution of Europe; news conference., January 14, 1963. C. de Gaulle. Vital Speeches 29:233-5 F 1 '63
Soviet empire will face new stresses. R. H. Davis. Nations Bsns 51:62-3 D '63
United States and the European economic community; address, June 3, 1963. P. H. Trezise. Dept State Bul 48:971-6 Je 24 '63
Worry shifts to Europe; with editorial comment. il Bsns W p81-2, 156 Je 27 '64

Far East

Trade in the Pacific area; address, February 3, 1964. R. Hilsman. Dept State Bul 50: 293-8 F 24 '64

France

De Gaulle's new Europe: meaning to Britain, U.S. il U S News 54:66-7 F 4 '63

Germany (Democratic Republic)

Synthetic squabble: question of a U.S. chemical-fiber plant in East Germany. Newsweek 65:70-1 Ja 11 '65

Germany (Federal Republic)

Synthetic squabble: question of a U.S. chemical-fiber plant in East Germany. Newsweek 65:70-1 Ja 11 '65

Great Britain

British pound in trouble: what's being done to aid it. U S News 57:92 D 7 '64
Implications for U.S. of breakdown in U.K.-EEC negotiations; text of letter to Senator Paul H. Douglas, February 15, 1963. G. W. Ball. Dept State Bul 48:412-15 Mr 18 '63
U.S. comments on British measures to strengthen economy; statements by Department of state and by Treasury, October 26, 1964. Dept State Bul 51:714-15 N 16 '64

Indonesia

Complete draw. il Fortune 68:79-80+ Ag '63

Israel

U.S. concludes textile agreement with Israel; Department announcement, with text of U.S. note, November 22, 1963, by Walworth Barbour. Dept State Bul 50:51-3 Ja 13 '64

Japan

Joint U.S.-Japan committee concludes third meeting; joint communique, January 28, 1964. Dept State Bul 50:235-8 F 17 '64
Tokyo talks; U.S. delegation in Tokyo. il Newsweek 63:65 F 10 '64
United States and Japan reschedule meeting of Cabinet officials. bibliog f Dept State Bul 50:183-4 F 3 '64
U.S. and Japanese cabinet officers to hold third economic meeting. Dept State Bul 49:833-4 N 25 '63
U.S.-Japan joint communiqué on trade. Cur Hist 46:238-40 Ap '64

Latin America

Doing business with a revolution; address, April 24, 1963. J. T. Connor. Vital Speeches 29:537-40 Je 15 '63
Inter-American economic relations; address, April 2, 1964. F. Herrera. Vital Speeches 30:427-32 My 1 '64
Progress for whom? New Repub 149:3-4 N 30 '63
This month's feature U.S. and the Alliance for progress. Cong Digest 42:67-77+ Mr '63
U.S. business image in Latin America; address, September 23, 1964. D. Rockefeller. Vital Speeches 31:7-10 O 15 '64
See also
Inter-American economic and social council

Mexico

President Johnson and President López Mateos of Mexico hold talks in California; joint communique, February 22, 1964. L. B. Johnson and A. López Mateos. Dept State Bul 50:396-8 Mr 16 '64

Rumania

United States and Rumania agree to broaden mutual relations; announcement of talks, with text of joint communique, June 1, 1964. Dept State Bul 50:924-6 Je 15 '64

Russia

Can we trade with Russia. Duns R 82:39 D '63
How to deal with the Russians. J. Thackray. il Duns R 83:57-8+ My '64
Peace in our time? H. J. Morgenthau. Commentary 37:66-9 Mr '64
Reappraisal of U.S.-U.S.S.R. trade policy; excerpts from address, March 12, 1964. H. J. Berman. Harvard Bsns R 42:139-44+ Jl '64
What it's like to trade with Russia. il Nations Bsns 52:36-7+ Ag '64

United Arab Republic

U.S. concludes textile agreement with U.A.R; Department announcement, with text of U.S. note, December 4, 1963, by John S. Badeau. Dept State Bul 50:54-6 Ja 13 '64

UNITED STATES—Economic relations—*Cont.*

Uruguay

U.S.-Uruguayan trade committee holds talks at Washington. Dept State Bul 51:617 N 2 '64

Viet Nam (Democratic Republic)

Secretary comments on Korean exchange rate system reform; statement, May 3, 1964. D. Rusk. Dept State Bul 50:830 My 25 '64

Yugoslavia

Tito may visit the US. New Repub 149:6 S 14 '63

Education, Office of

Bond sales for higher education: 1962; Office of education survey. W. R. Bokelman and E. C. Deering. il Sch Life 45:20-4 Mr '63
Call me mister. Newsweek 61:88 F 25 '63
Educational leadership. D. Wolfle. Science 143:767 F 21 '64
Educational media center. Sch Life 45:3 Ja '63
First-grade reading under scrutiny; cooperative research program. D. V. Gunderson. Sch Life 47:19-20 O '64
Going up fast; Office of education budget to be doubled. Time 85:50 Ja 15 '65
Project English: a report to the profession. J. Mersand. il Sr Schol 83:15T-16T S 20 '63
Project English; with list of institutions, directors, and subjects. Sch Life 46:6 O '63
Project social studies, a report; curriculum study centers at institutions of higher education. G. R. Smith. Sch Life 45:25-7 Jl '63
Redfaced USOE lists Girlwatcher's manual as programed teaching aid. Library J 88: 4447 N 15 '63
U.S. Dept of education. America 112:97 Ja 23 '65
U.S. office of education: an inside view. S. M. McMurrin. il Sat R 46:78-81 F 16 '63; Reply. J. J. Neumaier. 46:57 Mr 23 '63
USOE Cooperative research. F. A. J. Ianni. Sch Life 46:28-9 O; 15-16 N; 20-1 D '63; 26-7 Mr '64
USOE cooperative research. L. S. Josephs. Sch Life 46:12-13 Je '64

Educational materials laboratory

Educational materials laboratory: Office of education. L. B. Watt. il Sch Life 45:13-15 Je '63

Elementary schools section

Elementary school in the city; a conference report. Sch Life 45:26-34 Je; 16-22 Jl '63

Library services branch

Surveys of school library statistics published by USOE. Library J 89:4614+ N 15 '64
Washington report: from the Library services branch. J. G. Lorenz and H. A. Carl. ALA Bul 57:393-6, 636-8, 1016-17; 58:23-5, 182-4 My, Jl, D '63-Ja, Mr '64
Washington report: from the Library services branch. P. P. Price and H. A. Carl. ALA Bul 58:352-6, 599-602, 986-8 My, Jl, D '64

Employment service

Great manpower grab. F. T. Bow. Read Digest 85:61-7 O '64
How U.S. promotes job-hopping. il Nations Bsns 51:86-8 D '63
Job finding: government cuts in on a private business. il U S News 54:105-7 My 13 '63
Job-finding machine; how to crank it up. E. T. Chase. Harper 229:31-6 Jl '64; Discussion. 229:8+ O '64
Last time we saw you, you were just a little baby! Nat R 15:268 O 8 '63
State-run job agencies woo professionals. il Bsns W p88-9 F 2 '63

Engineer corps

See United States—Army—Corps of engineers

Executive departments

As the federal capital spreads across the Nation; U.S. agencies and programs outside Washington area. il U S News 57:70-1 O 12 '64
Big government: how it spreads; federal government agencies into Maryland and Virginia. il U S News 55:70-5 S 16 '63
Consolidating departments; suggestions for pulling together the government's fragmented resources programs. New Repub 152:5 Ja 2 '65
Executive and independent agencies: ever-spinning wheels of government. il Sr Schol 84:15 F 14 '64
Government grab-bag. Holiday 36:182-3 D '64
Here's the way government grows. il Nations Bsns 52:62-4 Ag '64
How to watch the White House. L. L. Henry. il Nations Bsns 52:34-5+ N '64
President names panel of citizens as consultants on world problems; statement, September 9, 1964. L. B. Johnson. Dept State Bul 51:441 S 28 '64
Sampling of Pentagon alphabet. Miss & Roc 12:118+ Mr 25 '63
White House scouts for top aides. Bsns W p31 D 12 '64
Working man's Washington. J. D. Weaver. Holiday 36:74-5+ D '64

See also

Independent regulatory commissions—United States
Presidents—United States

Fair employment practice, Committee on

Civil-rights message: what was Powell's role? endorsement of fair-employment-practices legislation. U S News 55:19 Jl 8 '63
LBJ on civil rights. Cato. Nat R 16:311 Ap 21 '64
This month's feature: FEPC features of the civil rights bill. Cong Digest 43:67-96 Mr '64

Farmers home administration

FHA plans expanded lending to farmers; interview. H. Bertsch. Suc Farm 61:10+ Mr '63

Federal aviation agency

Accounting office, FAA study utilization of traffic controllers. Aviation W 78:49 Ap 8 '63
Air traffic control blueprint. P. J. Klass. il Aviation W 80:52-4+ Ja 20; 90-1+ Ja 27; 87-91+ F 3 '64
Bringing air safety into the jet age; Project horizon and Project beacon. il Bsns W p70-2 My 4 '63
CAB regional airport plan faces delay. R. H. Cook. Aviation W 80:45 Ap 20 '64
Era of supersonic morality; BONGO experiment to obtain public reaction to sonic boom. J. Lear. Sat R 47:49-50 Je 6 '64; Discussion. 47:46-7 Jl 4 '64
FAA all-weather landing system office urged by pilot's report. Aviation W 78:44 Mr 18 '63
FAA considers lower small field minimums. Aviation W 78:50 Je 24 '63
FAA given funds for new traffic control test, field unit systems. R. G. O'Lone. Aviation W 81:37 S 21 '64
FAA leads search for solution to civil air manpower shortage. J. R. Ashlock. Aviation W 81:35 O 12 '64
FAA selects integrated landing system. P. J. Klass. il Aviation W 79:78-9+ Jl 29 '63
FAA testing extended-range radio link. P. J. Klass. il Aviation W 78:103+ Je 24 '63
FAA using revised light-twin training program for inspectors. il Aviation W 78:102-3 Ap 8 '63
Halaby protests FAA research fund cuts. Aviation W 80:28 Je 1 '64
Jet transport communications. R. L. Conhaim. il Electr World 70:27-30+ N '63
Lone DC-4 plays short-haul role in Island airlines-FAA struggle. Aviation W 79:39 Jl 15 '63
Misunderstanding cited in Electra alarm. J. R. Ashlock. Aviation W 81:28-9 Ag 3 '64
New airline labor fight looms over FAA's proposed crew cut. R. H. Cook. Aviation W 80:35 My 11 '64
Opposition may kill aircraft lighting plan. Aviation W 79:33 S 2 '63
Project longlook. D. B. Kuhn. Flying 75:68 Jl '64
Racing to be first with the fastest; Mach 2, Concorde. il Bsns W p 146+ S 21 '63
Skyway crash preventers. K. Brown. il Pop Mech 120:106-10+ D '63
Sonic boom town; Oklahoma City. R. Burkhardt. New Repub 151:5-6 Ag 22 '64
Subsidy drop is shown in CAB budget; FAA seeks $810 million. L. L. Doty. Aviation W 78:41 Ja 21 '63
Supersonic hot seat. B. Kocivar. il Look 28: 93-5+ My 5 '64
Technicians score FAA on traffic control. Aviation W 79:36-7 Jl 15 '63
Traffic control is focus of FAA budget. R. H. Cook. Aviation W 80:52 Ja 27 '64
U.S.-European common interests create new FAA problem areas. H. J. Coleman. Aviation W 79:173+ O 7 '63
WXCVR; tuning in FAA automatic radio weather broadcasts. H. B. Smith. il Pop Electr 20:63-5+ Ja '64

UNITED STATES—Federal aviation agency —*Continued*

Appropriations and expenditures

FAA funds cut by $64.5 million. Aviation W 79:43 O 14 '63
FAA funds cut threatens ATC research. P. J. Klass. Aviation W 80:45 Je 15 '64

Federal bureau of investigation

At large and most wanted: ten dangerous men. K. Detzer. il Read Digest 84:190-2+ Mr '64
Beginning: agents into Mississippi. Nation 199:21 Jl 27 '64
Big rise in bank robberies and the FBI response. il U S News 54:14 Ap 15 '63
Call in the FBI. R. Moley. Newsweek 65:64 Ja 4 '65
Commission has concluded. . . major recommendations of the Warren commission. il Newsweek 64:63-4 O 5 '64
Cooling the controversy. il Time 84:30 D 11 '64
Crackdown coming on future rioters. il U S News 57:80-1 O 12 '64
Detroit pl combines forces with FBI to solve bizarre document swindle case. Library J 89:825-6 F 15 '64
Enforcing the law: interview with J. Edgar Hoover. J. E. Hoover. il U S News 57:36-40 D 21 '64
Faith of the FBI. R. Moley. Newsweek 61:88 Mr 4 '63
FBI agent as missionary; branch office in Jackson, Miss. W. B. Huie. New Repub 151: 10-11 N 21 '64
FBI and civil rights: J. Edgar Hoover speaks out; excerpts from news conference, with reply by M. L. King. J. E. Hoover. il U S News 57:56-8 N 30 '64
FBI chief speaks up; summary of news conference. J. E. Hoover. Sr Schol 85:21-2 D 2 '64
F.B.I. report; Mr Hoover's recent report on racial disturbance. Commonweal 81:119 O 23 '64
F.B.I. report on racial disturbances during the past summer. America 111:404-5 O 10 '64
Hoover-King meeting. il Newsweek 64:22+ D 14 '64
J. Edgar Hoover and the FBI. il Newsweek 64:21-6 D 7 '64
Jenkins case: unanswered questions. il U S News 57:48 N 2 '64
Jenkins report. Time 84:33-4 O 30 '64
Knives sharpening. Nat R 16:1094 D 15 '64
Last days of Dillinger; excerpt from The Dillinger days. J. Toland. il Look 27:79-80+ F 12 '63
Lessons to be learned; Warren commission's findings. il Time 84:50+ O 2 '64
Mass arrests in civil-rights killings. il U S News 57:11 D 14 '64
Mississippi; gang law. New Repub 151:5-6 Jl 4 '64
Mississippi murders: twenty-one arrests. il Newsweek 64:21-2 D 14 '64
Next: a national police force? with excerpts from television statements by R. Wilkins and FBI analysis of telegram by M. L. King, jr. il U S News 57:44-6+ D 7 '64
Next Mr Hoover. Nation 196:131 F 16 '63
Off the chest & into the fire. il Time 84:31 N 27 '64
Oswald and the FBI. H. Feldman. il Nation 198:86-9 Ja 27 '64
Roll of dishonor; F.B.I.'s list of ten most wanted fugitives. C. Remsberg and B. Remsberg. N Y Times Mag p69 Ja 26 '64
Role of the FBI; excerpts from Warren report. il U S News 57:60-1 O 12 '64
Successor to Mr Hoover, head of the FBI. C. B. Luce. McCalls 91:187-8 My '64
Them are the pictures: Sam Giancana versus J. Edgar Hoover. il Newsweek 62:43-4 Jl 29 '63
Those confidential files. Nation 198:178 F 24 '64
What the FBI found in the Jenkins case: Aftermath: sympathy and job offers for Walter Jenkins. il U S News 57:6 N 2 '64

Federal communications commission

Ambush at Omaha Pass. K. Woodward. il Nation 196:373-5 My 4 '63
American radio today: the listener be damned. D. Smith. il Harper 229:58-63 S '64; Same abr. with title American radio: an insult to the public? Read Digest 85: 115-18 D '64; Discussion. Harper 229:6+ N '64
And now, a brief word from our sponsors. . .; bill prohibiting FCC regulation of broadcast advertising. D. Rapoport. Reporter 30: 26-8 Je 4 '64
Après moi. . . N. N. Minow. Newsweek 61:33 Je 17 '63
Artists and bureaucrats. R. Brustein. New Repub 149:36+ N 2 '63
CBers note! the rules have changed. E. S. Maloney. il Motor B 114:82+ N '64
Chairman Henry on target; FCC's attempt to regulate commerical time standards. R. L. Shayon. Sat R 46:43 O 19 '63
Church looks at television; alleged racial discrimination on television stations in Jackson, Miss. R. L. Shayon. Sat R 47: 36 My 16 '64
Citizens radio rules tightened. Electr World 72:78 O '64
Clearing the air; citizens band violations. il Newsweek 64:78-9 Ag 17 '64
Coincidence or not; opportunities for presentation of viewpoints on any controversial issue. Nat R 15:382-4 N 5 '63
Comments on the new CB rules. L. Buckwalter. Electr World 72:42-3 N '64
Commercials unlimited? New Repub 149:4 N 23 '63
Continuing contract; FCC chairmen. R. L. Shayon. Sat R 46:32 Je 22 '63
Cross talk on what cables should carry; fights between telephone and telegraph companies. il Bsns W p 116+ F 22 '64
Dangerous decision at a desperate time; increase of rates for commercial users of leased telegraph and telephoto services. R. L. Tobin. Sat R 46:49-50 Mr 9 '63
Dial cloud 7 for Paris or Rome; satellite communications system. Bsns W p78 F 22 '64
Does the FCC have AT&T's number? D. Gottlieb and D. Gottlieb. New Repub 148: 17-19 Ap 6 '63
Fairness and the FCC. R. L. Shayon. Sat R 47:21 Ag 22 '64
FCC and 11 meters; a CBer's view. D. T. Geiser. il Pop Electr 20:59-60+ Je '64
FCC establishes fees for radio licenses. Electr World 70:69 Ag '63
FCC gets tougher. Bsns W p38+ Ap 20 '63
FCC on guard. New Repub 150:5 F 8 '64
FCC report. R. E. Tall. See issues of Popular electronics to December 1963
FCC ruling that could aid the Johnsons. U S News 56:8 My 11 '64
FCC's bonanza to tuner makers. il Bsns W p39-40 Jl 6 '63
Fewer commercials. New Repub 148:4-5 Ap 13 '63
$500 million mistake; regulating AT&T the world's biggest business. A. Brynes. New Repub 151:11-14 S 26 '64
Forecast for the FCC. R. L. Shayon. Sat R 47:51 Ja 11 '64
Forty-three cheers; dissenting vote on bill prohibiting the FCC from limiting number and frequency of commercials on the air. R. L. Shayon. Sat R 47:30 Ap 18 '64
Freedom of the air. New Repub 149:6 D 14 '63
From FCC chief, plain talk to broadcasters. U S News 55:30 O 7 '63
Good decision: Pacifica foundation listener-supported FM radio stations. Nation 198: 110 F 3 '64
Green shoot; new chairman. Time 81:72+ My 24 '63
Help quiet commercials. Sci N L 83:118 F 23 '63
How tough are the proposed CB regulations? R. L. Conhaim. Electr World 69:26-8+ My '63
How you can get a license to operate a student experimental radio station. D. T. Geiser. il Pop Electr 19:69-70+ S '63
Important developments in communications; address, April 2, 1963. N. N. Minow. Vital Speeches 29:425-30 My 1 '63
Is pay-TV sneaking to success? community antenna television systems. il Bsns W p32-3 Ap 25 '64
Kennedy's musical chairs; antitrust and FCC get new heads. il Bsns W p28 My 18 '63
LBJ and KTBC; a hot potato for the FCC. il Newsweek 63:83-4 Ap 27 '64
Minow's farewell. New Repub 149:5 Jl 13 '63
Mr Labunski and the Camp Fire girls; concerning FCC local television hearings in Omaha. R. L. Shayon. Sat R 46:41 F 23 '63
Mr Minow's wasteland. W. Sparks. Commonweal 78:7-10 Mr 29 '63
Musical chairs. Newsweek 61:29-30 My 27 '63
New CB regulations. W. A. Stocklin. Electr World 69:8 F '63
New FCC rules now in effect. L. G. Sands. il Electr World 71:30+ My '64
New teeth for the FCC. E. S. Maloney. Motor B 111:165 My '63

UNITED STATES—Federal communications commission—*Continued*
No retreat on the FCC. R. L. Shayon. Sat R 46:34 Je 1 '63
Oaths and silence; investigation of Pacifica foundation. il Newsweek 62:80 N 25 '63
Open channels; scrutiny of the Pacifica foundation. Newsweek 63:75 F 3 '64
Our timid watchdog. Consumer Rep 29:110-11 Mr '64
Pacifica and the FCC: dangerous precedent; with editorial comment. L. B. Frantz. Nation 197:357, 359-61 N 30 '63
Partial insight of Mr Minow. W. F. Buckley jr. Nat R 14:442 Je 4 '63
Proposal to the FCC; a citizens radio technician license. R. L. Conhaim. Electr World 69:48-9 Mr '63
Rating the broadcaster; petition of United church of Christ to deny renewal of the licenses of two television stations in Jackson, Miss. R. L. Shayon. Sat R 47:21 Jl 11 '64
Regulating AT&T. A. Brynes. New Repub 151: 11-14 O 3 '64
Religion and the FCC. M. Cohn. il Reporter 32:32-4 Ja 14 '65
Sad sack agency. Nation 198:2-3 Ja 4 '64
Sell it. Nation 198:385 Ap 20 '64
Sponsor for quality. New Repub 148:3-5 My 4 '63
TV commercials; the government ducks the issue. D. Smith. Nation 198:286-9 Mr 23 '64
TV law that will cost you money. il U S News 56:49 Ap 13 '64
Twenty-two straight commercials. Newsweek 61:87 Ap 15 '63
What is wrong with TV, and with us. C. A. Siepmann. il N Y Times Mag p 13+ Ap 19 '64
What to expect next in television; interview. E. W. Henry. il U S News 57:48-52 Jl 6 '64

Federal council for science and technology

Interest grows in oceanography uses; Interagency committee on oceanography. Miss & Roc 15:71-3 S 21 '64
Where is science taking us? the depths of the sea. il Sat R 46:52-3 N 2 '63

Federal crop insurance corporation

See Federal crop insurance corporation

Federal extension service

What direction for extension? D. Hanson. Suc Farm 62:10 My '64

Federal home loan bank board

Easier borrowing for builders? U S News 56:99 Ja 27 '64
Fight brewing on S&L holding companies. Bsns W p54 Mr 2 '63
Man who makes S&Ls toe the mark. il Bsns W p72-4+ Ja 18 '64
More on savings-loan clampdown. U S News 55:129-31 N 18 '63
New curb for savings-loan firms. U S News 56:86 Ja 20 '64
New U.S. rules for savings and loans; what 1964 will bring. U S News 55:94-5 N 4 '63
S&L watchdogs growl louder; tighter controls over dividend policies. Bsns W p45 O 26 '63

Federal housing administration

As foreclosures rise; bargain counter for houses; role of FHA. il U S News 56:106-7 Mr 16 '64
Costly land for housing projects; roles of General accounting office and Federal housing administration. U S News 55:82-3 D 23 '63
FHA awards recognize architectural merit. il Arch Rec 135:14-15 Ja '64
FHA defaults cause no alarm. U S News 54: 95-6 F 11 '63
FHA honors awards for residential design. il Arch Rec 135:154-62 Ja '64
FHA-insured mortgages; Gruening amendment. Consumer Rep 30:26 Ja '65
FHA joins the tenants' war against noise. il Arch Forum 120:96-7 Mr '64
FHA's winter come-on; modern Florida homes. il Newsweek 63:66 Ja 13 '64
Housing gets another transfusion. Bsns W p 117 S 12 '64
Housing order & its limits. C. Abrams. Commentary 35:10-14 Ja '63
Many ways to finance home remodeling; FHA loans. il Good H 156:170 My '63
You and your home; how to pay for your major remodeling project. House & Gard 123:18-19 Ap '63

Federal maritime commission

Ocean freight rates head into a gale. il Bsns W p96-7 Ag 31 '63

Federal mediation and conciliation service

Automation is for peacemakers, too; federal peacemaking role in labor-management relations. Bsns W p 108 F 22 '64
Big mediator is watching you. H. T. Ludlow. America 110:789-90 Je 6 '64; Reply. L. C. Brown. 111:696-7 N 28 '64
Recent federal and state mediation activity. M. F. Riche. il Mo Labor R 87:786-9 Jl '64
When the rank-and-file balks; demands for job security. Bsns W p68+ O 19 '63
Who will mediate the mediators? E. J. Silberfarb. il Reporter 28:23-6 Mr 14 '63

Federal power commission

Extra-high-voltage at the FPC. il Bsns W p72-4+ S 21 '63
Gassing game. J. Ridgeway. New Repub 150: 4-5 My 9 '64
Power plan for the future; one system to serve whole U.S. il U S News 57:64-5 D 28 '64
Protecting the public: how independent is the FPC? J. Ridgeway. New Repub 149:21-5 S 21 '63
Public be damned. Nation 196:150 F 23 '63
Record rebate. Newsweek 62:82 D 2 '63
Sound and fury. Newsweek 61:68 F 11 '63
Test. Nation 198:566 Je 8 '64
Utility stock options: executive incentive v. public interest. L. Metcalf. il Nation 199: 151-4 S 28 '64

Federal radiation council

Fallout: how much is too much? il Bsns W p27 Je 8 '63
Taking the threat out of milk; removing strontium-90 from milk. Bsns W p58 S 14 '63

Federal reserve board

Administration moves on the payments gap. Bsns W p25 Jl 20 '63
As U.S. moves to protect the dollar; the effect. il U S News 57:89-91 D 7 '64
Cheap-money mania. H. Hazlitt. Newsweek 64:69 D 21 '64
Dampening the fire before it starts; Fed's clampdown on margin requirements. Bsns W p 114 N 9 '63
Danger signals show up in credit. Bsns W p62+ Mr 16 '63
Face of the Fed. Newsweek 62:92-3 N 11 '63
Fed cuts long-term buying; operation nudge. Bsns W p54 My 11 '63
Fed hits back in the Saxon feud; concerning control of national banks. Bsns W p 171-2 S 14 '63
Fed remodels itself; with editorial comment. il Bsns W p64-5+, 180 My 16 '64
Fed tightens credit. Bsns W p28 Je 8 '63
Fed tightens credit just a bit. il Bsns W p94-5 Ja 19 '63
Fed's dilemma. il Fortune 69:27-8 Ap '64
For now, it's just a gentle pull. il Bsns W p72+ N 14 '64
Fourth term on the FRB for Martin. U S News 54:19 F 18 '63
Heroic defense; faltering British pound. il Time 84:99-100 D 4 '64
Kennedy holds the line on money policy; appointments to Federal reserve board. il U S News 55:62 N 11 '63
Money rates face new push. Bsns W p 142 O 26 '63
New face at the Fed; seven governors. Time 82:88 N 8 '63
New look at money management. Bsns W p 148 Jl 11 '64
New touch of caution; with editorial comment. il Bsns W p27-8, 154 N 28 '64
Not in Martin's pocket; Fed's hard money policies. Bsns W p 116 N 9 '63
Now there's a split among men who manage the dollar; Board of governors of Federal reserve system. il U S News 55:60-1 Ag 5 '63
Oddball crusade of Congressman Patman. P. Duke. il Sat Eve Post 237:62-3 Mr 7 '64
Pressure is on money managers. Bsns W p26 Mr 7 '64
Reserve board is target of attack by Democrats. U S News 54:8 Mr 25 '63
Saxon and the Fed cross swords again; concerning corporate savings in national banks. Bsns W p21 Ja 4 '64
Stage set for boost in Fed discount rate. Bsns W p 112 Jl 13 '63
Tightening up. il Time 81:89 Je 14 '63

UNITED STATES—Federal reserve board —*Continued*
Tighter reins on the Fed? Bsns W p68 Jl 4 '64
Too much buying of stocks on credit? il U S News 55:127+ N 18 '63
Treasury due to borrow less. Bsns W p90 Jl 20 '63
View from the street. il Time 82:86 N 22 '63
Wright Patman: champion of cheap money: interview, ed. by G. R. Rosen. Duns R 83: 59-60+ My '64

Federal trade commission

Advertisers and the government missed the boat on the validity of aspirin advertising. Consumer Bul 46:36 My '63
Annals of legislation; background and history of Drug industry antitrust bill. R. Harris. New Yorker 40:48-50+ Mr 14 '64
Back scratching deals raise antitrust ire; reciprocity practices. il Bsns W p45-6 F 9 '63
Can co-op ads survive FTC's broadside? Robinson-Patman act. Bsns W p86+ F 23 '63
Carlton's tar and nicotine. il Consumer Rep 29:114-15 Mr '64
Case of the substituted drug. J. Lear. Sat R 47:62 N 7 '64
Cigarette advertising; testimony presented before FTC. M. E. Brady. il Consumer Rep 29:246-50 My '64
FTC charges "Calories don't count." Pub W 184:34 O 7 '63
FTC guide to pricing; deceptive price advertising. Bsns W p27 Ja 11 '64
FTC kicks some tires; No big breaks for big buyers. Bsns W p34 D 5 '64
FTC presents: the great sandpaper shave; a real-life story of truth in advertising. D. Seligman. il Fortune 70:130-3+ D '64
FTC tries to kick the habit; cigarette ads. il Bsns W p28-9 Ja 25 '64
FTC's new threat is compulsory licensing; makers of tetracycline guilty of price-fixing. Bsns W p27 Ag 17 '63
Frankenstein in ad alley. J. Kaselow. Sat R 47:46-7 Ag 8 '64; Discussion. 47:54 S 12 '64
Growing issue; high cost of justice; with case history. Nations Bsns 51:78-80+ My '63
Initial FTC decision against Crown. Pub W 186:78 Ag 24 '64
Magic of a name: illegal use of term "consumers." Consumer Bul 46:2+ Ap '63
Nightmare for oil marketers; Sun oil case. Bsns W p66 Ja 19 '63
Prentice-Hall consents to FTC order. Pub W 185:70 F 3 '64
Respondents deny FTC'S calories charges. Pub W 185:52 Ja 13 '64
Root of the FTC's confusion. H. B. Meyers. il Fortune 68:114-16+ Ag '63
Still wanted: a definition of high fidelity. Consumer Rep 28:121 Mr '63
To smoke, or not to smoke? il Newsweek 63:70-3 Ja 27 '64
Washington hearings on cigarette labeling. il Time 83:79-80 Mr 27 '64
What one U.S. agency may do about smoking. il U S News 56:39 Ja 27 '64
When is a discount a bargain? F.T.C. guides against deceptive pricing.. Consumer Bul 47:12+ Ja '64
Why you can't call fake fur a fake. Consumer Bul 47:24-5 F '64

Fish and wildlife service

Costly and needless war on predators; condensation of address, November 12, 1962. D. L. Allen. il Audubon Mag 65:85-9+ Mr '63
Gone fishing; oceanographic ships, Albatross IV. il Newsweek 61:60 Je 17 '63
Is our native underwater life worth saving? R. R. Miller. bibliog il Nat Parks Mag 37: 4-9 My '63
War on America's wildlife. A. S. Leopold and others. il Audubon Mag 66:228-33, 306-11 Jl-S '64

Food and drug administration

AMA, the FDA and quacks. J. Ridgeway. New Repub 149:31-3 N 9 '63
Another drug inquiry; FDA's handling of orabilex. Newsweek 63:57 F 24 '64
Antibiotics barred for colds. Sci N L 84: 130 Ag 31 '63
Disillusionment at FDA. Time 81:76 Mr 29 '63
Doctors argue value of new drug laws. Sci N L 84:20 Jl 13 '63
Drug makers launch fight on prominence FDA seeks for generic names on labels. Bsns W p60 S 14 '63
Drug politics: industry seeks Court of appeals to challenge FDA rulings on drug safety. E. Langer. Science 145:139-41 Jl 10 '64; Reply. I. S. Ravdin. 146:12 O 2 '64
Drug safety. Consumer Rep 28:134-7 Mr '63
Drug safety meeting; drug court planned; FDA rules and research discussed. Sci N L 84:21 Jl 13 '63
Drugs; how safe is safe enough? new medical director of the U.S. Food and drug administration. W. R. Young. il Life 57:37-40 Jl 3 '64
FDA: drug agency answers critics by attempting to step up science, but many critical problems remain. E. Langer. Science 142:1280-2 D 6 '63
FDA gets tough. Bsns W p 19 Jl 4 '64
FDA probes popular drug; bonine. Sci N L 84:94 Ag 10 '63
FDA says enovid safe. Sci N L 84:119 Ag 24 '63
FDA: trouble-ridden medical unit gets new director after 2-year search to fill difficult position. E. Langer. Science 143:1018-19 Mr 6 '64
FDA's problem: more work, too few watchdogs. il Bsns W p26-7 My 11 '63
Fracas over fish flour. D. S. Greenberg. il Sat Eve Post 236:34-5 N 23 '63
Freezing to be safe; Great Lakes fishing industry. il Bsns W p36 N 9 '63
Going to seed; hallucinatory drug LSD in morning glory seeds. il Newsweek 62:59 Jl 22 '63
Incredible story behind a cancer cure; krebiozen. S. Blum. il Redbook 123:40-1+ Je '64
Kefauver's last interview. B. H. Frisch. il Sci Digest 54:10-18 N '63
Kraft lays a decholesteroled egg; Miracle egg. Consumer Rep 29:54 F '64
Krebiozen; why it hasn't been tested. Consumer Rep 28:441-3 S '63
Lady cop; chief of the FDA's new investigational drug branch. il Newsweek 61:100 Je 24 '63
Laws alone can't make drugs safe. L. Lessing. il Fortune 67:122-5+ Mr '63
Medical case against krebiozen. il Consumer Rep 29:93-6 F '64
Myths about federal drug policies. H. H. Humphrey. New Repub 150:10-12 My 16 '64
New controls for antibiotics. Consumer Rep 28:463 O '63
New drug threat possible. F. Marley. Sci N L 84:3 Jl 6 '63
New drugs: is government supervision adequate? M. Mintz. il Reporter 28:46-9+ Mr 28 '63; Discussion. 28:11 My 9 '63
New judgment against vitamin quackery. Consumer Rep 29:213 My '64
Nutrition: fad vs. fact; stricter rules for labeling. il Changing T 17:34-6 Jl '63
Psychotoxic drugs: Dodd bill passes Senate, comes to rest in the House: critics are sharpening their knives. J. Walsh. Science 145:1418-20 S 25 '64
Qualms on new drug routine. Bsns W p66 Mr 7 '64
Real voice, by R. Harris. Review
Nation 199:166-8 S 28 '64. E. Langer
Reward. J. Lear. Sat R 46:47 F 2 '63
Safety & effectiveness. Time 83:82 Mr 13 '64
Seek drug-review panels. Sci N L 85:231 Ap 11 '64
Some pills and formulas that are under fire; Congress on medical quackery. U S News 55:10 N 4 '63
Testing. Newsweek 63:52 Mr 9 '64
Total health: address, November 30, 1964. W. H. Chase. Vital Speeches 31:177-81 Ja 1 '65
U.S. food safe from DDT. Sci N L 85:350 My 30 '64
Warning on drugs and driving. Consumer Rep 28:150 Ap '63
When a hazard warning isn't enough: X-33 water repellent. Consumer Rep 29:4-5 Ja '64
Wrinkle lotions; drugs or cosmetics? Consumer Rep 29:319 Jl '64
Writing an Rx on quacks; AMA and FDA national conference on quackery in medicine. il Bsns W p32-3 N 2 '63

Foreign economic policy

See United States—Economic relations

Foreign population

Analysis of the white backlash. W. L. Miller. il N Y Times Mag p27+ Ag 23 '64
Bigotry's shifting patterns. Christian Cent 81: 1196 S 30 '64

See also
Immigration and emigration—United States
also Irish in the United States and similar headings

UNITED STATES—*Continued*

Foreign relations

Acheson's idea: get hardheaded abroad; excerpts from address, December 9, 1964. D. Acheson. U S News 57:14 D 21 '64; Newsweek 64:18 D 21 '64; Time 84:22-3 D 18 '64
Advancing the American national interest without war. A. I. Waskow. Bul Atomic Sci 20:23-5 F '64; Reply with rejoinder. A. Forbes. 20:36-8 Je '64
After election: President will face these issues. il Nations Bsns 52:40-1+ O '64
After the test ban: the US must take the initiative in Europe. Z. Brzezinski. New Repub 149:18-21 Ag 31 '63; Reply. R. Steel. 149:36+ O 5 '63
Agony of success; address, November 14, 1963. H. Cleveland. Dept State Bul 49:845-50 D 2 '63
Ain't it awful? Nation 198:177 F 24 '64
Alliance: whose grand design? il Newsweek 61:17-19 F 11 '63
America gets an unexpected break. H. S. Reuss. Harper 226:37-42 My '63
American commonwealth? A. Buchan. Harper 226:95-101 Je '63
American policy in international affairs; address, February 17, 1964. U. A. Johnson. Dept State Bul 50:364-9 Mr 9 '64
Americans look at the Atlantic future. E. Roper. Sat R 47:26-7 Ja 4 '64
America's efforts toward world order; address, August 12, 1964. L. B. Johnson. Dept State Bul 51:298-301 Ag 31 '64; Same with title Restraint and law. Vital Speeches 30:674-5 S 1 '64
Anatomy of world leadership; address, April 3, 1964. A. E. Stevenson. bibliog f Dept State Bul 50:615-21 Ap 20 '64
And now we look abroad; victory of L. Johnson. M. Ascoli. Reporter 31:24 N 19 '64
And what do our allies think? American involvement in South Vietnam. Newsweek 63:44 My 25 '64
Anti-U.S. riots around the world; why. il U S News 57:11 D 7 '64
Around world: puzzle over U.S; with excerpts from address by President Johnson. il U S News 56:39-41 F 24 '64
As LBJ's honeymoon fades. il U S News 56:35-6 F 17 '64
Atlantic report. Atlan 213:6+ Ja; 6+ Ap; 4+ My; 4+ Je; 214:4+ S '64; 215:12+ Ja '65
Beating a path to Kennedy's door; visiting dignitaries. il U S News 55:46-7 N 4 '63
Beginning. H. Brandon. Sat R 47:6 Mr 7 '64
Beyond the campaign. D. Lawrence. U S News 57:136+ O 19 '64
Big job for U.S. diplomats after the elections. F. B. Stevens. il U S News 57:45-6 N 2 '64
Big problems for the President. il U S News 57:35-8 N 9 '64
Budget of the United States government for the fiscal year ending June 30, 1965; with excerpts from Budget message of the President. il Dept State Bul 50:218-22 F 10 '64
CIA analysis. New Repub 151:3-4 S 12 '64
Challenge of success; address, October 12, 1963. L. B. Johnson. Vital Speeches 30:36-7 N 1 '63
Changing world: '64 a year of peace? F. B. Stevens. U S News 56:54-5 Ja 13 '64
Charter day ceremonies, UCLA; remarks, February 21, 1964. L. B. Johnson. Dept State Bul 50:399-400 Mr 16 '64
Chinks in Fulbright's armor. Christian Cent 81:509 Ap 22 '64
Citizen and foreign policy; address, September 30, 1963. K. Louchheim. Dept State Bul 49:681-4 O 28 '63
Citizen's role in foreign policy legislation; address, April 23, 1964. R. J. Manning. bibliog f Dept State Bul 50:791-7 My 18 '64
Cold war, a look ahead; address, March 28, 1963. W. W. Rostow. Dept State Bul 48:551-7 Ap 15 '63
Cold war strategists predict new moves; analyses from top State department policy-makers. il Nations Bsns 51:60-8+ D '63
Collective insecurity. M. S. Evans. Nat R 15:201-3 S 10 '63
Coming: a subtle shift in dealing with the world. U S News 55:38-9 D 9 '63
Coming great test; trouble abroad, presidential election at home. Christian Cent 81:259-61 F 26 '64
Coming showdown. H. Brandon. Sat R 47:16-17 Ag 15 '64
Containing ourselves: some reflections on the enemy within; excerpt. D. Riesman. New Repub 148:14-17 Ap 6 '63
Count up to ten or even twenty. New Repub 152:5-7 Ja 23 '65
Cracked alliance. L. J. Halle. New Repub 148:17-20 F 23 '63
Crisis diplomacy. H. Cleveland. For Affairs 41:638-49 Jl '63
Crisis thinking. Commonweal 78:125 Ap 26 '63
Critics sharpen President's foreign policy dilemma. P. Lisagor. il Nations Bsns 52:23-4 Je '64
Dangerous failings of our State department. F. J. Lausche. Read Digest 84:54-60 Je '64; Excerpts. U S News 56:22 Je 8 '64
Dangerous game of Let's pretend. A. Drury. il Read Digest 84:37-42 Mr '64
Defeats for U.S. around the world. il U S News 56:46-50 F 10 '64
Defense against Gaullist isolationism. J. P. Warburg. Ann Am Acad 351:24-9 Ja '64
Democratic dialogue; concerning the Fulbright speech. K. Crawford. Newsweek 63:32 Ap 13 '64
Diplomacy of mutual example. Nation 198:41 Ja 13 '64
Diplomat among warriors, by R. Murphy. Review
Nat R 16:827-9 S 22 '64. G. F. Eliot; Reply. D. Keyser. 16:936+ N 3 '64
Diplomat among warriors; excerpt. R. Murphy. il Sat Eve Post 237:32-4+ F 22 '64
Does Johnson have a foreign policy? J. Burnham. Nat R 16:190 Mr 10 '64
Don't tread on whom? H. J. Taylor. Read Digest 85:138-9 Ag '64
Dream world of Goldwater. W. Lippmann. Newsweek 64:13 Ag 3 '64
Drift in Washington; where it's heading. il U S News 54:29-30 Ap 1 '63
East-West relations today; address, February 18, 1964. G. C. McGhee. Dept State Bul 50:488-96 Mr 30 '64
Education for citizenship in the modern world; address, February 16, 1964. D. Rusk. Dept State Bul 50:358-64 Mr 9 '64
Election winner will face historic problems. F. Morley. il Nations Bsns 52:27-8 Mr '64
Entangling alliances: then and now. il Sr Schol 85:7 S 16 '64
First-hand report: new look at how U.S. rates in today's world. M. S. Johnson. il U S News 57:82-4 N 9 '64
Forbidden thoughts. Nation 200:21-2 Ja 11 '65
Foreign affairs debate: are our policies turning obsolete? with editorial comment. Bsns W p28-9, 120 Ap 4 '64
Foreign and other affairs: a view from the radical center, by J. P. Davies, jr. Review
New Repub 151:17-18 O 24 '64. L. J. Halle
Reporter 31:52-3 S 10 '64. C. B. Marshall
Foreign countries, too, mourn first citizen of the world. il U S News 55:48-9 D 2 '63
Foreign interests. R. Steel. Commentary 37:80-2 Mr '64
Foreign policy. il Sr Schol 85:11 O 7 '64
Foreign policy and the American citizen; address, December 10, 1963. D. Rusk. bibliog f Dept State Bul 49:990-6 D 30 '63
Foreign policy and the people's right to know; address, May 5, 1964. R. J. Manning. Dept State Bul 50:868-77 Je 1 '64
Foreign policy and the regulation of international shipping; statement, August 11, 1964. G. G. Johnson. Dept State Bul 51:314-17 Ag 31 '64
Foreign policy: building amid turbulence; address, August 27, 1963. R. J. Manning. Dept State Bul 49:454-60 S 23 '63
Foreign policy issue of this year. Life 57:4 O 2 '64
Foreign policy of the Kennedy administration. J. Burnham. Nat R 15:522 D 17 '63
Foreign policy, old myths and new realities; address, March 25, 1964. J. W. Fulbright. Vital Speeches 30:388-94 Ap 15 '64; Summary. il Time 83:23-4 Ap 3 '64
Foreign policy: same goals, sterner style. Bsns W p31-2 N 30 '63
Four illusions that beset us: U.S. intentions and policy so misunderstood abroad. C. Frankel. il N Y Times Mag p31+ S 22 '63
Four principles of American foreign policy; remarks, September 23, 1964. L. B. Johnson. Dept State Bul 51:543-4 O 19 '64
Fourth dimension of foreign policy: educational and cultural affairs, by P. H. Coombs. Review
Sat R 47:61-2 D 19 '64. W. W. Brickman
Freedom's other face. C. P. Romulo. Sat R 47:16+ D 19 '64
French recipe for folly. E. J. Hughes. Newsweek 62:15 Jl 15 '63
Friction with our fractious friends. Newsweek 63:27 Ja 20 '64
Fulbright and myths. Commonweal 80:101-2 Ap 17 '64

UNITED STATES—Foreign relations—*Cont.*
Fulbright proposal. America 110:500-1 Ap 11 '64
Fulbright's progress. Nation 198:357 Ap 13 '64
Geopolitics and foreign relations. G. E. Pearcy. il Dept State Bul 50:318-30 Mr 2 '64
Giftie gie us; summary of newsletter. F. J. Strauss. Nat R 16:1137 D 29 '64
Goldwater on foreign policy; excerpts from address, September 9, 1964. B. M. Goldwater. U S News 57:118 S 21 '64
Goldwater's foreign policy: let's hear more. il Life 55:4 N 1 '63; Reply. B. M. Goldwater. 56:30B-30D Ja 17 '64
Grand Design revisited: a legacy with life. J. Kraft. Harper 228:104+ F '64
Great deflation. il Time 81:19-20 My 3 '63
Great power and great diversity: the perceptions and policies of President Kennedy; address, December 1, 1963. H. Cleveland. Dept State Bul 49:964-9 D 23 '63
Great society; nation's quest. Commonweal 81:255-8 N 20 '64
Growing foreign-policy row: two top Democrats urge changes. il U S News 56:19 Ap 6 '64
Help wanted by our ambassadors. H. M. Jackson. il N Y Times Mag p36+ O 11 '64
His chief targets: McNamara and reds; GOP campaign. il Bsns W p 18-19 Ag 1 '64
History rocks the boat. New Repub 150:3-4 My 30 '64
Hour of decision: what LBJ faces now. il U S News 57:29-35 D 7 '64
How Europe sees it. J. Burnham. Nat R 14:451 Je 4 '63
How LBJ views the world situation now; excerpts from address, February 21, 1964. L. B. Johnson. il U S News 56:13 Mr 2 '64
How the world sizes up LBJ now. il U S News 57:33-5 D 14 '64
How to take up the slack: President and foreign policy. il Time 83:13 Mr 27 '64
Human rights and foreign policy; excerpts from In pursuit of world order. R. N. Gardner. Sat R 47:23-5+ S 19 '64
Illusion of victory. D. Brandon. Commonweal 78:473-6 Ag 9 '63
Importance of being earnest. Nation 197:21 Jl 13 '63
In an era of self-interest. il Time 83:21-2 Mr 13 '64
In today's world; how successful is U.S. policy? F. B. Stevens. il U S News 55:62-4 Jl 8 '63
Inquiry into the darkness of the cloak, the sharpness of the dagger. J. V. Lindsay. Esquire 61:106-7+ Mr '64
Intellectual underbrush. J. G. Campaigne. Nat R 16:779-80 S 8 '64
Invisible government, by D. Wise and T. B. Ross. Review
  Commonweal 80:639-40+ S 18 '64. W. D. Burnham
Issues as business sees them; symposium. il Nations Bsns 52:84-6 Ap '64
It's one year after JFK: the changes; with interview with J. M. Burns. il U S News 57:60-6 N 23 '64
J.F.K.'s voice fills a hush in the cold war. Life 55:4 Jl 12 '63
Johnson: I intend to submit new proposals to slow arms race; excerpts from address, October 21, 1964. L. B. Johnson. U S News 57:97-8 N 2 '64
Johnson will deal from strength. il Bsns W p 142+ N 7 '64
Johnson's world. New Repub 150:3-4 My 2 '64
Journalism and foreign affairs; address, March 13, 1964. R. J. Manning. Dept State Bul 50:541-9 Ap '64; Same with title Press and the government. Vital Speeches 30:453-7 My 15 '64
Just a minute. il Time 84:21-2 D 4 '64
Kennedy: waiting for the tide. Bsns W p25-6 Mr 16 '63
Kennedy's dilemma; new lineup: where U.S. fits in. F. B. Stevens. U S News 54:36 F 18 '63
Labor: a partner in American foreign policy? J. P. Windmuller. Ann Am Acad 350:104-14 N '63
Lesson from Vietnam. E. J. Hughes. Newsweek 62:17 S 9 '63
Let's make the test pact go for us. Life 55:4 Ag 9 '63
Let's make up our mind. Farm J 88:134 Mr '64
Letter from Washington; American foreign policy; summary of address. J. F. Kennedy. New Yorker 39:96-8 Je 22 '63
Letter from Washington (cont) R. H. Rovere. New Yorker 39:136-8 F 15; 40:149-55 Ap 11 '64
Limits of continuity. New Repub 149:4-6 D 14 '63
McNamara assesses arms developments; text of testimony before House armed services committee. R. S. McNamara. Aviation W 80:77-9+ F 24 '64
Making of foreign policy; television interview, January 11, 1964. D. Rusk; E. F. Goldman. Dept State Bul 50:164-76 F 3 '64
Mandate for change: 1953-1956, by D. D. Eisenhower. Review
  Nat R 15:487-8+ D 3 '63. W. F. Buckley, jr.
  New Yorker 39:235-8 N 16 '63. R. H. Rovere
  Reporter 29:59-60 N 21 '63. D. Cater
Mapping the sore spots. il Time 83:19-20 F 7 '64
Must we be the world's policeman? H. Cleveland. il N Y Times Mag p 14+ My 3 '64
Mysteries of policymaking. E. J. Hughes. Newsweek 65:17 Ja 25 '65
Myths and realities: the debate over U.S. foreign policy; with quotations. Sr Schol 84:8-11 My 8 '64
National interest, 1964; address, June 7, 1964. D. Rusk. Dept State Bul 50:955-8 Je 22 '64
Nationalism, a global headache for Johnson; with editorial comment. il Bsns W p22-3, 76 Ja 4 '64
Negotiation from strength: a study in the politics of power, by C. Bell. Review
  Sat R 46:21+ Ag 3 '63. K. W. Thompson
New aim for America; address, February 4, 1964. P. Howard. Vital Speeches 30:339-43 Mr 15 '64
New diplomatic style. E. J. Hughes. Newsweek 63:15 Ap 6 '64
New frontier and Europe: moment for choice. F. W. Neal. il Nation 197:234-6 O 19 '63
New frontiers without freedom; address, March 16, 1964. E. V. Rickenbacker. Vital Speeches 30:490-4 Je 1 '64
New isolationism. J. Burnham. Nat R 17:60 Ja 26 '65
New isolationism. il Time 85:14 Ja 8 '65
New myths for old; concerning Senator Fulbright's speeches. W. V. Shannon. Commonweal 80:102-3 Ap 17 '64
New perspectives on the United States' world relationships; address, April 29, 1963. C. Bowles. Dept State Bul 48:817-23 My 27 '63
New signal: go slow. New Repub 152:5 Ja 2 '65
No deal on Berlin; hard look at the Berlin situation in the light of the Cuban crisis. D. Brandon. il America 108:192-6 F 9 '63
Non-debate. E. J. Hughes. Newsweek 63:19 Mr 23 '64
Not the first, nor the last; with editorial comment. Bsns W p29-30, 184 O 24 '64
Now for U.S: a tougher line in the world? il U S News 57:47-8 N 23 '64
Nuclear containment. Christian Cent 80:259-60 F 27 '63
Old myths and new realities, by J. W. Fulbright. Review
  Sat R 47:34-6 Ag 15 '64. R. P. Stebbins
On our quarrel with success; address, June 9, 1963. J. K. Galbraith. Dept State Bul 49:52-6 Jl 8 '63
On working with history; address, June 5, 1964. W. W. Rostow. Dept State Bul 50:961-6 Je 22 '64
One-step thinking. W. Lippmann. Newsweek 63:25 Mr 16 '64
One-way to bring on the war that nobody wants. D. Lawrence. U S News 56:108 Ap 6 '64
Openings for diplomacy; Cuba: catalyst of peace. L. Dewart. Nation 196:113-15 F 9 '63
Our foreign policy; address, May 27, 1964. M. O. Hatfield. Vital Speeches 30:533-5 Je 15 '64
Our foreign policy is paralyzed; summaries of statements, ed. by J. R. Moskin. Look 27:25-7 N 19 '63
Our foreign policy; what is it? address, March 3, 1964. N. A. Rockefeller. Vital Speeches 30:402-6 Ap 15 '64; Excerpts. U S News 56:85-7 Mr 16 '64
Our world policy; address, April 20, 1964. L. B. Johnson. Vital Speeches 30:418-22 My 1 '64; Same with title America as a great power. Dept State Bul 50:726-32 My 11 '64
Partisan dialogue. K. Crawford. Newsweek 61:31 F 25 '63
Peace: it's relative. K. Crawford. Newsweek 63:27 Mr 2 '64
Peace offensive. New Repub 150:5 Ja 11 '64
Perfect format; talks with visiting statesmen at U.S. mission building. il Time 82:39 O 4 '63

UNITED STATES—Foreign relations—*Cont.*
Perils of under-simplification. J. Burnham. Nat R 16:766 S 8 '64
Perspective on the tasks of the 1960's; address, May 11, 1964. W. W. Rostow. Dept State Bul 50:864-7 Je 1 '64
Philippines, a new era; address, May 23, 1963. R. Hilsman. Dept State Bul 48:897-900 Je 10 '63
Pioneers for peace; address, September 26, 1963. J. F. Kennedy. Dept State Bul 49:631-6 O 21 '63
Policy and people; address, September 26, 1963. R. J. Manning. Dept State Bul 49:639-44 O 21 '63
Policy makers' size-up: it will be a nervous peace in '65. F. B. Stevens. U S News 58:34 Ja 4 '65
Predictability gap. Time 83:21-2 F 21 '64
Present prospect; address, January 22, 1964. D. Rusk. bibliog f Dept State Bul 50:190-5 F 10 '64; Same with title Our foreign policy. Vital Speeches 30:290-3 Mr 1 '64
President Johnson and Secretary Rusk urge full appropriations for foreign aid; statements, December 12 and December 14, 1963. L. B. Johnson; D. Rusk. Dept State Bul 49:999-1004 D 30 '63
President Johnson and the tides of ideology. F. S. Meyer. Nat R 16:23+ Ja 14 '64
President Johnson discusses the presidency; television interview, March 14, 1964. L. B. Johnson. Dept State Bul 50:523-9 Ap 6 '64
President Johnson receives chiefs of diplomatic missions; remarks with reply, December 13, 1963. L. B. Johnson; G. Sevilla-Sacasa. Dept State Bul 49:996-7 D 30 '63
President Johnson sends message to nonalined nations conference. L. B. Johnson. Dept State Bul 51:581-2 O 26 '64
President meets with Cabinet; reviews world situation; statement, October 20, 1964. L. B. Johnson. Dept State Bul 51:653 N 9 '64
President meets with consultants on foreign affairs; statement, October 21, 1964. L. B. Johnson. Dept State Bul 51:663 N 9 '64
President must now find the answers. Bsns W p29-30 D 5 '64
Prospects for the West, by J. W. Fulbright. Review
Sat R 47:78-9 Ja 4 '64. F. Altschul
Prospectus for the Great society; concerning the State of the Union message. H. Brandon. Sat R 48:14-15 Ja 30 '65
Public diplomacy. M. Ascoli. Reporter 30:10+ Ap 9 '64
Public opinion and national security; address, July 19, 1963. H. M. Jackson. Vital Speeches 29:642-4 Ag 15 '63
Reconsidering our foreign policy. L. J. Halle. New Repub 148:13-15 Mr 23 '63
Report from Washington; watching de Gaulle. H. Brandon. Sat R 47:14 F 22 '64; Reply. J. M. Conlon. 47:43 Ap 11 '64
Responsibilities of a global power; address, September 18, 1964. G. W. Ball. Dept State Bul 51:473-8 O 5 '64
Road ahead; address, February 13, 1963. D. Rusk. Dept State Bul 48:311-16 Mr 4 '63
Rule of law as a foreign policy; address, April 7, 1964. C. S. Rhyne. Vital Speeches 30:467-70 My 15 '64
Rush of changes; where U.S. stands. il U S News 55:41-2 O 21 '63
Russia, China and England; our basic policy remains unchanged; address, October 18, 1964. L. B. Johnson. Vital Speeches 31:34-6 N 1 '64; Same with title President reports on change in Soviet leadership, Chinese nuclear test, and new British government. Dept State Bul 51:610-14 N 2 '64
Screwball insistence. Nation 199:393-4 N 30 '64
Secretary Rusk addresses Advertising council; remarks, March 12, 1963; with questions and answers. D. Rusk. Dept State Bul 48:467-75 Ap 1 '63
Secretary Rusk holds press and radio news briefing:
Houston. Dept State Bul 48:388-93 Mr 18 '63
Los Angeles. Dept State Bul 48:361-8 Mr 11 '63
Secretary Rusk interviewed:
ABC's Issues and answers, July 26, 1964. Dept State Bul 51:231-7 Ag 17 '64
BBC's Encounter program, May 10, 1964. Dept State Bul 50:816-22 My 25 '64
CBS reports program. Dept State Bul 50:4-7 Ja 6 '64
German television. Dept State Bul 51:106-8 Jl 27 '64
GFWC television program, April 13, 1963. Dept State Bul 48:698-703 My 6 '63
Issues and answers program, October 18, 1964. Dept State Bul 51:654-60 N 9 '64
Meet the press, August 30, 1964. Dept State Bul 51:394-400 S 21 '64
NBC's Today program, January 21, 1963. Dept State Bul 48:202-7 F 11 '63
Voice of America. Dept State Bul 50:330-6 Mr 2 '64
Secretary Rusk's news conference:
January 2, 1964. bibliog f Dept State Bul 50:81-9 Ja 20 '64
February 1, 1963. Dept State Bul 48:235-43 F 18 '63
February 7, 1964. Dept State Bul 50:274-84 F 24 '64
February 27, 1964. Dept State Bul 50:403-9 Mr 16 '64
March 6, 1964. Dept State Bul 50:439-46 Mr 23 '64
March 8, 1963. Dept State Bul 48:432-9 Mr 25 '63
March 27, 1964. Dept State Bul 50:570-6 Ap 13 '64
April 3, 1964. Dept State Bul 50:608-14 Ap 20 '64
May 29, 1963. Dept State Bul 48:931-8 Je 17 '63
July 31, 1964. Dept State Bul 51:221-8 Ag 17 '64
August 16, 1963. Dept State Bul 49:356-64 S 2 '63
September 10, 1964. Dept State Bul 51:426-32 S 28 '64
September 14, 1964. Dept State Bul 51:468-72 O 5 '64
October 8, 1964. Dept State Bul 51:575-81 O 26 '64
November 8, 1963. Dept State Bul 49:810-17 N 25 '63
December 23, 1964. Dept State Bul 52:34-41 Ja 11 '65
Senator speaks out; concerning the Fulbright speech. W. Lippman. Newsweek 63:19 Ap 13 '64
Senator's Fulbright's new foreign policy. H. J. Morgenthau. Commentary 37:68-71 My '64
Seven assumptions that beset us. H. M. Jackson. il N Y Times Mag p5+ Ag 4 '63; Same abr. with title Cold war isn't over. Read Digest 83:99-102 N '63; Discussion. N Y Times Mag p6+ Ag 18 '63
Shoo-in fallacy. Nation 198:158-9 F 17 '64
Some proposals to a Goldwater administration concerning foreign affairs. J. Burnham. Nat R 16:589-93 Jl 14 '64
Some reflections on the United States in the United Nations; address, October 23, 1964. P. Talbot. Dept State Bul 51:700-5 N 16 '64
Some thoughts on the conduct of foreign policy; remarks, July 23, 1964. D. Rusk. Dept State Bul 51:185-8 Ag 10 '64
Speaking out; let's stop being foolish about dictators. E. O. Briggs. Sat Eve Post 236:8+ S 14 '63
Speaking out; the CIA is getting out of hand; meddles in foreign policy. E. McCarthy. Sat Eve Post 237:6+ Ja 4 '64
State of the union, address, January 14, 1963. J. F. Kennedy. Vital Speeches 29:226-30 F 1 '63; Same. Cur Hist 44:174-6+ Mr '63; Excerpts. Dept State Bul 48:159-64 F 4 '63
Stop it right away! New Repub 148:3 F 23 '63
Talk with Governor Scranton. H. Brandon. il Sat R 47:12-13 Ap 4 '64
They've got a secret. Nat R 14:97+ F 12 '63
Three cheers; Brazil, Panama, NATO. Time 83:21 Ap 10 '64
Trouble, trouble, trouble, Canada, Cuba, Europe. il Time 81:21 F 15 '63
Ultimate self-interest; growing debate about U.S. foreign policy. il Time 85:14-18 Ja 22 '65
Uncertainty and anxiety abroad; India, Great Britain, Italy. New Repub 149:11-12 D 7 '63
United States foreign policy; address, June 13, 1963. S. Thurmond. Vital Speeches 29:548-51 Jl 1 '63
U.S. foreign policy: problems and challenges for 1963; address, January 11, 1963. R. J. Manning. Dept State Bul 48:138-44 Ja 28 '63
U.S. policy in a changing world; address, October 6, 1964. W. W. Rostow. Dept State Bul 51:637-42 N 2 '64
U.S. policy: old myths, mixed voices. il Newsweek 63:17-18 Ap 6 '64
Unless we lead, all will falter. S. Gruson. il N Y Times Mag p22+ D 8 '63
Unmeasured response. New Repub 151:3-4 Ag 22 '64
Use of power. America 111:229 S 5 '64
View from the seventh floor, by W. W. Rostow. Review
Sat R 47:30-2 Jl 11 '64. L. J. Walinsky
Waging peace. il Time 83:23 Ja 10 '64
Walk through Warsaw. L. J. Halle. New Repub 151:15-18 O 3 '64; Reply. J. Jedruch. 151:38 N 14 '64

UNITED STATES—Foreign relations—*Cont.*
Walter Lippmann, 1964; interview on CBS, ed. by E. Sevareid. New Repub 150:15-18 Ap 25 '64
War on three fronts; new worry for U.S. il U S News 57E:29-30 Ag 24 '64
We and they; Senator Fulbright calls for a reassessment of U.S. policies. New Repub 150:3-4 Ap 18 '64
We face a new kind of world. W. Attwood. il Look 27:25-7 N 5 '63
Week that was will long be with us. Life 57:4 O 30 '64
Well spoken, Mr President. Life 56:4 My 1 '64
West's blacklash. E. J. Hughes. Newsweek 64:13 Ag 10 '64
What have we learned from Panama? N. Cousins. Sat R 47:22 F 1 '64
What Johnson plans now. il U S News 57: 34-7 N 16 '64
What now? Commonweal 77:552 F 22 '63
When skies are grayer. New Repub 150:3-4 F 22 '64
Where our foreign policy goes wrong. Bsns W p 160 Mr 14 '64
Which way with LBJ? J. Chamberlain. Nat R 15:526-7 D 17 '63
Who really makes U.S. foreign policy. il U S News 54:33-5 F 18 '63
Whose myth? whose reality? summary of address. J. W. Fulbright. il Time 83:23-4 Ap 3 '64
Why Russia and China now fear U.S. il U S News 57:66-70 N 30 '64
Why U.S. is in trouble in the world. il U S News 58:48-53 Ja 25 '65
Winds of change, East and West. Newsweek 61:13-15 F 4 '63
Woman writer takes a critical look at America; reprint. M. Craig. U S News 56:78 Mr 2 '64
World challenge to Mr Johnson. L. J. Halle. il N Y Times Mag p 17+ Ap 5 '64
World isn't waiting; international problems and coming campaign. Bsns W p23-5 F 22 '64
World perspectives, 1964. G. Kirk. For Affairs 43:1-13 O '64
World trouble spots facing L.B.J. Sr Schol 85:10-11 Ja 21 '65
Yalta strategy; revival: Soviet-American deal. J. Burnham. Nat R 15:237 S 24 '63
You can't make a policy without breaking eggheads. Nat R 14:141+ F 26 '63

See also
Berlin question, 1945-
Economic assistance, American
Military assistance, American
Monroe doctrine
Secretaries of state (United States)
United Nations—United States
United States—Boundaries
United States—Economic relations
United States—Information agency
United States—State, Department of

Anecdotes, facetiae, satire, etc.

Fine Italian hand; Kennedy administration in Vietnam. Reporter 29:14 O 10 '63
How the West was rapproched; Bertie award. V. Gold. Nat R 16:911 O 20 '64
Unbeatable program for a fiery moderate; excerpts from interview. C. B. Luce. U S News 56:20 F 17 '64

Anti-Communist measures

American policy abroad; address, April 20, 1963. R. M. Nixon. Vital Speeches 29:486-90 Je 1 '63; Excerpts. U S News 54:20 My 6 '63
America's strategy gap; address, December 4, 1962. M. R. Laird. Vital Speeches 29: 245-8 F 1 '63
Bear-baiting. J. Burnham. Nat R 16:718 Ag 25 '64
Brinkmanship is necessary. E. A. Mowrer. Nat R 14:229-31 Mr 26 '63
Call for action against reds in Cuba. U S News 54:6 F 25 '63
Cold war; address, April 5, 1964. J. W. Fulbright. bibliog f Vital Speeches 30:422-7 My 1 '64
Creed for a time of danger; excerpts from address. J. A. Farley. Read Digest 83:49-52 Jl '63
Cuba in Communist world strategy; address, November 15, 1962. L. V. Manrara. Vital Speeches 29:236-40 F 1 '63
East-West trade; statement, March 13, 1964. D. Rusk. il Dept State Bul 50:474-84 Mr 30 '64
Failure of our foreign policy; address, October 21, 1964. B. M. Goldwater. Vital Speeches 31:36-8 N 1 '64; Excerpts. U S News 57:96-7 N 2 '64
Futile crusade: anti-communism as American credo, by S. Lens. Review
Sat R 47:24-5 Jl 4 '64. F. Altschul
Hard line policy pays off; with letter by E. Nuñez Portuondo. U S News 56:6 Ap 13 '64
Independence day 1964; address, July 4, 1964. D. F. Foley. Vital Speeches 30:634-6 Ag 1 '64
Just war in the nuclear age. F. S. Meyer. Nat R 14:105-6+ F 12 '63; Discussion. 14: 207, 296-7, 380 Mr 12, Ap 9, My 7 '63
Let's face up to the truth; address, July 21, 1964. C. L. Gould. Vital Speeches 30:701-4 S 1 '64
Ministers of seven governments meet in Nicaragua; text of final act, April 4, 1963. Dept State Bul 48:719-21 My 6 '63
Money will not make them free. H. Lavine. il Sat R 47:28-9 Ja 25 '64
New world of loosening alliances. Life 56:4 Mr 13 '64
On dealing with the Communist world, by G. F. Kennan. Review
Nat R 16:440 Je 2 '64. J. Burnham
Panama-Sofia-etc. lesson. Nat R 16:52-4 Ja 28 '64
Reshaping policy; concerning Senator Fulbright's speech. Commonweal 80:75-6 Ap 10 '64
Road ahead; address, February 13, 1963. D. Rusk. Dept State Bul 48:311-16 Mr 4 '63
Saving Latin democracies. W. V. Shannon. Commonweal 79:182-4 N 8 '63
Some current issues in U.S. foreign policy; remarks, April 18, 1963; with questions and answers. D. Rusk; G. W. Ball; W. A. Harriman. Dept State Bul 48:679-98 My 6 '63
Statement on U.S. Asian policy; excerpts from address, August 20, 1963. R. Hilsman. Cur Hist 46:112+ F '64
Ungrateful or forgetful? saving our allies from defeat. D. Lawrence. U S News 56: 120 Ap 13 '64
U.S. and Venezuela take firm stand against Communist threats; exchange of greetings; with joint communique. J. F. Kennedy; R. Betancourt. Dept State Bul 48:445-7 Mr 25 '63
U.S. foreign policy: problems and challenges for 1963; address, January 11, 1963. R. J. Manning. Dept State Bul 48:138-44 Ja 28 '63
United States tasks on the world scene: address, November 20, 1963. W. W. Rostow. Dept State Bul 49:921-9 D 16 '63
Vietnam, yes; Cuba, no? D. Lawrence. U S News 57:96 Ag 17 '64
Wanted: a compass. D. Lawrence. U S News 56:108 Je 8 '64
War for U.S. in Asia, pullback in Cuba? il U S News 54:39-42 My 6 '63
Western hemisphere's fight for freedom; address, September 21, 1964. T. C. Mann. Dept State Bul 51:549-52 O 19 '64
What's de Gaulle up to in Asia? il Sr Schol 84:16-20 Mr 6 '64
Where U.S. stands now in cold war. il U S News 56:50-3 My 11 '64
Who gives a whoop? Cuban problem. J. Burnham. Nat R 14:279 Ap 9 '63
Who inherited what from whom? D. Lawrence. U S News 54:108 Mr 11 '63
Why are Americans in Vietnam? an admiral's letter to his sons. W. S. Guest. il U S News 57:132-3 O 19 '64

See also
Propaganda

Bibliography

Congressional documents relating to foreign policy. See issues of Department of state bulletin

History

Speaking out; America the smug. R. Niebuhr. Sat Eve Post 236:12+ N 16 '63

Study and teaching

Not pie-in-the-sky but enlightened self-interest; teaching foreign policy issues today. H. Cleveland. il Sr Schol 83:12T-13T S 27 '63

Afghanistan

King of Afghanistan visits United States; joint communique, September 7, 1963. J. F. Kennedy and Mohammed Zaher. Dept State Bul 49:535 O 7 '63

Africa

American policy in Africa; address, July 7, 1964. J. W. Fredericks. Dept State Bul 51: 197-203 Ag 10 '64
Assistant Secretary Williams visits west and central Africa; statement, May 8, 1964. G. M. Williams. Dept State Bul 50:828-9 My 25 '64

UNITED STATES—Foreign relations—Africa —*Continued*

Basis of U.S. policy in Africa; address, January 25, 1963. G. M. Williams. Dept State Bul 48:251-3 F 18 '63
Diplomatic rapport between Africa and the United States; address, April 10, 1964. G. M. Williams. Dept State Bul 50:698-703 My 4 '64; Same with questions and answers. Ann Am Acad 354:54-64 Jl '64
Emerging nations of Africa; address, March 2, 1963. G. M. Williams. Dept State Bul 48:457-9 Mr 25 '63
Freedom and development; address, September 25, 1964. D. Rusk. Dept State Bul 51:498-503 O 12 '64
Mr Kennedy goes to war. J. Burnham. Nat R 15:59 Jl 30 '63
Momentary eclipse; wave of anti-Americanism. il Newsweek 65:33-4 F 1 '65
Our policy toward Africa; address, July 18, 1963. J. W. Fredericks. Dept State Bul 49:284-90 Ag 19 '63; Same. Vital Speeches 29:699-702 S 1 '63
Special interest; American Negro leadership conference on Africa. New Yorker 40:44-6 O 17 '64
U.S. Negroes' goal: to set Africa policy. il U S News 58:60-1 Ja 11 '65
United States policy and Africa; address, August 18, 1964. W. A. Harriman. Dept State Bul 51:330-3 S 7 '64
U.S. sends message to conference of African leaders at Cairo; message, July 17, 1964. L. B. Johnson. Dept State Bul 51:147 Ag 3 '64
What a senator saw and didn't like on African tour; excerpts from report. il U S News 54:93-4 My 20 '63

Algeria

Communist take-over of Algeria. R. Colby. il U S News 57:52-3 Ag 31 '64

Arab states

Israel's Eshkol: U.S. visit worries Arabs. il U S News 56:22 Je 15 '64

Argentina

U.S. and Argentina reaffirm traditional ties; joint statement, January 24, 1963. D. Rusk and C. M. Muñiz. Dept State Bul 48:211-13 F 11 '63

Asia

From Washington straight. Cato. Nat R 15:432 N 19 '63
Great debate on Asia. E. J. Hughes. Newsweek 65:13 Ja 11 '65
Progress and problems in east Asia: an American viewpoint; address, September 29, 1964. W. P. Bundy. Dept State Bul 51:534-42 O 19 '64
Statement on U.S. Asian policy; excerpts from address, August 20, 1963. R. Hilsman. Cur Hist 46:112+ F '64
United States foreign policy in Asia; address, July 17, 1964. W. Morse. Vital Speeches 30:678-82 S 1 '64
U.S. foreign policy in the Far East; address, June 20, 1963. U. A. Johnson. Dept State Bul 49:78-82 Jl 15 '63
United States policy in southern Asia. W. C. Johnstone. Cur Hist 46:65-70+ F '64
United States policy in the Pacific; address, August 20, 1963. R. Hilsman. Dept State Bul 49:386-93 S 9 '63

Asia, Southeastern

ABC's of southeast Asia. T. D. White. Newsweek 63:31 Je 29 '64
Alternatives. il Time 83:28-9 Je 5 '64
As the war in Asia gets hotter. il U S News 56:12 Je 29 '64
Assistant Secretary Bundy comments on southeast Asia developments in Voice of America interview; ed. by W. McCrory. W. P. Bundy. Dept State Bul 51:334-9 S 7 '64
Attorney General Kennedy completes mission to Far East; interviews and remarks, January 28, 1964. R. F. Kennedy. Dept State Bul 50:239-43 F 17 '64
Back to Geneva. Nation 198:565 Je 8 '64
Back to Geneva? M. Ascoli. Reporter 30:10 Je 4 '64
Bigger war coming in S.E. Asia? with analysis by M. S. Johnson. il U S News 57:27-30 Jl 6 '64
Can U.S. win in Vietnam? an inside report; interview. S. W. Sanders. il U S News 58:50-2 Ja 11 '65
Crumbling line. J. Burnham. Nat R 16:493 Je 16 '64
De Gaulle on Vietnam. R. Steel. Commonweal 80:141-3 Ap 24 '64
Diplomatic poker. New Repub 150:5 Je 6 '64
Doctoring the script. Newsweek 64:41 Jl 13 '64
Facing the Chinese Communist threat. Bsns W p 148 Ag 15 '64
Fire alarm in Asia. New Repub 151:3-5 Jl 4 '64
If it comes to war with Communist China... il U S News 57:42-3 Jl 13 '64
Major crisis for Johnson: southeast Asia falling apart. il U S News 55:42-3 D 23 '63
Mix of fact and myth. J. Gange. Nation 199:63-6 Ag 24 '64
Needed in Vietnam: the will to win. R. M. Nixon. Read Digest 85:37-43 Ag '64
Now: back from the brink of war. il U S News 56:38-9 Je 15 '64
Our stake in southeast Asia. P. Salinger. il Look 28:44+ O 20 '64
Plea for realism in southeast Asia. R. Hilsman. il N Y Times Mag p26+ Ag 23 '64
President outlines basic themes of U.S. policy in southeast Asia; statement, June 2, 1964, with letter by General Eisenhower, written October 25, 1954. L. B. Johnson. Dept State Bul 50:953 Je 22 '64
President signs congressional resolution on southeast Asia; remarks, August 10, 1964. L. B. Johnson. Dept State Bul 51:302-3 Ag 31 '64
Remember the fable of a scorpion and a frog; U.S. policy leaders meet in Honolulu. il Life 56:44-44C Je 12 '64
Salami tactics in southeast Asia; strategy session in Honolulu. il Newsweek 63:41 Je 15 '64
Secretary Rusk discusses Asian situation on NBC program. D. Rusk. Dept State Bul 51:268-70 Ag 24 '64
Secretary Rusk's news conference of July 1, 1964. D. Rusk. Dept State Bul 51:84 Jl 20 '64
Situation in the western Pacific; address, April 25, 1964. D. Rusk. Dept State Bul 50:732-7 My 11 '64
Something happened to the crisis; conference at Hawaii's Camp Smith. Time 83:41 Je 12 '64
Southeast Asian crisis: a proposal; reprint. Nat R 17:48 Ja 26 '65
Time to talk. New Repub 150:4 Je 27 '64
United States and southeast Asia; address, April 8, 1963. U. A. Johnson. Dept State Bul 48:635-41 Ap 29 '63
U.S. calls for frontier patrol to help prevent border incidents between Cambodia and Viet-Nam; statement, May 21, 1964. A. E. Stevenson. bibliog f Dept State Bul 50:907-13 Je 8 '64; Same. Vital Speeches 30:483-7 Je 1 '64
United States takes measures to repel attack against U.S. forces in southeast Asia; U.S. protest to North Viet Nam; with statement, addresses and message to Congress by the President, statements by Secretary Rusk and Secretary McNamara, and text of joint resolution, August 3-7, 1964. bibliog f Dept State Bul 51:258-68 Ag 24 '64
Vietnam: alternative to disaster. D. Grant. il Nation 198:521-3 My 25 '64
War in Asia. il Newsweek 63:24-30+ Je 8 '64
What to expect of new American leaders in Vietnam. il U S News 57:12 Jl 6 '64
What will the United States do in Asia? il Newsweek 63:15-16 Je 1 '64

See also

Vietnamese crisis, 1964

Australia

Shadow and substance of the ANZUS pact. D. Warner. il Reporter 30:21-3 Je 4 '64

Belgium

Vice President's address at Brussels, November 8, 1963. L. B. Johnson. Dept State Bul 49:852-4 D 2 '63

Bolivia

Assistance offered to Bolivia in effort to free U.S. officials; White House statement, December 8, 1963. Dept State Bul 49:998 D 30 '63
President Paz of Bolivia visits United States; text of communique between President Kennedy and President Paz, October 23, 1963. J. F. Kennedy and V. Paz Estenssoro. Dept State Bul 49:787-8 N 18 '63

Brazil

Brazil and Chile. New Repub 150:5-6 Ap 11 '64
Marry in haste... il Newsweek 63:60+ Ap 20 '64
United States and Brazil pledge continued cooperation; exchange of letters, December 13 and December 18, 1963. L. B. Johnson; J. Goulart. Dept State Bul 50:47-9 Ja 13 '64

UNITED STATES—Foreign relations—Brazil
—*Continued*
U.S. regrets misinterpretation of statement on Brazil; statement, March 19, 1963. G. W. Ball. Dept State Bul 48:521 Ap 8 '63
Wishes for what? il Newsweek 63:49 Je 22 '64

Burma

Where reds may take over a key country. il U S News 54:69 Ap 1 '63

Cambodia

Cambodia, China and the U.S. Nation 199:365 N 23 '64; Reply. Norodom Sihanouk. 200: inside cover Ja 25 '65
Cambodia; why the crisis? New Repub 150: 8-10 Ja 4 '64
Chantrea incident; South Vietnamese raid Cambodian border village. il Newsweek 63: 34 Ap 6 '64
Man of sensitivity; Prince Norodom Sihanouk. Newsweek 62:28 D 23 '63
Oriental touch. Newsweek 63:26 Ja 6 '64
Prince & the dragon. il Time 83:32-6 Ap 3 '64
Slumbering prince. il Time 82:24 D 27 '63
There goes Cambodia. D. Warner. il Reporter 30:27-30 Mr 26 '64
U.S. and Cambodia to begin talks on resolving differences. Dept State Bul 51:856 D 14 '64
U.S.-Cambodian talks end without agreement; Department statement, December 17, 1964. Dept State Bul 52:6 Ja 4 '65
U.S. replies to Cambodian charge on chemical operations; letter, August 3, 1964. C. W. Yost. Dept State Bul 51:274 Ag 24 '64

Canada

As Canada heads for showdown at the polls. il U S News 54:48 Ap 8 '63
Atmosphere of trust. il Newsweek 61:57 My 20 '63
Canada, a weakening ally? il U S News 54:41 F 11 '63
Canada explodes over nuclear warheads. il Bsns W p28-9 F 9 '63
Canadian Prime Minister visits Washington; U.S. and Canada agree on Columbia River development and establishment of Campobello Park; joint communique; with joint statements and texts of agreements, January 21-23, 1964. L. B. Johnson; L. B. Pearson. Dept State Bul 50:199-206 F 10 '64
Good neighborhood. L. B. Pearson. For Affairs 43:251-61 Ja '65
How can Canada make her most effective contribution to collective security? address, January 12, 1963. L. B. Pearson. Vital Speeches 29:290-3 Mr 1 '63
Interdependence, the basis of U.S.-Canada relations; address, April 25, 1964. G. W. Ball. bibliog f Dept State Bul 50:770-4 My 18 '64
Letter; question of a forgery. Time 81:27 Je 7 '63
Neighbors agree on nuclear arms. Sr Schol 83:7-8 S 20 '63
North America, the open continent; address, June 16, 1963. W. R. Tyler. Dept State Bul 49:93-7 Jl 15 '63
Now U.S. is the issue in Canada. il U S News 54:31-2 F 18 '63
President Kennedy and Prime Minister Pearson of Canada hold talks; joint communique, May 11, 1963. J. F. Kennedy and L. B. Pearson. Dept State Bul 48:815-17 My 27 '63
Secretary Rusk's news conference of February 1, 1963. D. Rusk. Dept State Bul 48:235-43 F 18 '63
Under Secretary Ball interviewed on Issues and answers; transcript of interview, February 10, 1963. G. W. Ball. Dept State Bul 48:371-3 Mr 11 '63
Washington gives Canada an election and an issue; with statement by U.S. Department of state. W. H. Hessler. Reporter 28:29-31 F 28 '63; Discussion. 28:6+ Mr 28 '63
Weekend at Jack's. il Time 81:32 My 17 '63
What's bothering Canada now about the U.S. il U S News 55:42-3 O 28 '63
When friends fall out. il Time 81:32 F 8 '63
Working together: Columbia River project and Roosevelt International Park, Campobello. il Sr Schol 84:20 F 21 '64
See also
United States—Treaties—Canada

Caribbean Region

Caribbean: our sea of troubles. J. Benitez. Sat R 46:11-13+ Jl 13 '63
Intervention and dollar diplomacy in the Caribbean, 1900-1921, by D. G. Munro. Review
Américas 16:38 Jl '64. C. G. Fenwick

Central America

Castro's neighbors bitter and disillusioned at U.S. il U S News 54:47 Ap 1 '63
Declaration of Central America. il Newsweek 61:40 Ap 1 '63
J.F.K. co-starts in a new Common market: Latinos have a hit; with report by L. Hall. il Life 54:26-35 Mr 29 '63
President to meet chiefs of Central American states and Panama. Dept State Bul 48:213 F 11 '63
Presidents' meeting at San José; statements, addresses and remarks, March 18-21, 1963; with Declaration of Central America. J. F. Kennedy. Dept State Bul 48:511-20 Ap 8 '63
Secretary Rusk interviewed on GFWC television program, April 13, 1963. D. Rusk. Dept State Bul 48:698-703 My 6 '63
Success at San José. il Time 81:14 Mr 29 '63
Theme at Costa Rica: progress. il Sr Schol 82:16 Ap 3 '63
United in spirit and in arms; Rendezvous with destiny; addresses, March 18 and March 21, 1963. J. F. Kennedy. Vital Speeches 29:386-9 Ap 15 '63
Wall over the Caribbean. Nat R 14:267 Ap 9 '63
What JFK is promising to Central Americans. U S News 54:55 Mr 25 '63

China

America's failure in China 1941-50, by Tang Tsou. Review
New Repub 150:28-9 F 15 '64. C. B. Marshall
Reporter bibliog 30:48-9+ Mr 12 '64. R. P. Knapp, jr; Reply with rejoinder. S. L. Falk. 30:6 Ap 23 '64
Sat R il 46:24-5 Jl 13 '63. F. Nossal
Next: large-scale uprisings; interview. C. K. Chiang. il U S News 54:41-4 Mr 4 '63
Wanted: a Taiwan policy. New Repub 149: 5-6 S 14 '63

China (People's Republic)

After 827 talks with red China. il U S News 56:8 My 11 '64
Asia: no rest for U.S. from red pressures. U S News 58:26 Ja 4 '65
Calculations and suggestions. Z. Brzezinski. Newsweek 62:52 N 25 '63
China and the bomb. N. Cousins. Sat R 47: 18+ N 28 '64
China and the United States. O. Gass; discussion. Commentary 35:256-7 Mr '63
China mythology. Nation 197:61 Ag 10 '63
China: new alternatives. C. P. Fitzgerald. Nation 197:155-7 S 21 '63
China prospect. Commonweal 78:523 S 6 '63
Chinese checkers. Christian Cent 82:35-6 Ja 13 '65
Chinese puzzle. R. Hotz. Aviation W 81:11 Ag 10 '64
Chinese puzzle in the U.N. B. Pilkington. Christian Cent 82:50-1 Ja 13 '65
Chou in Africa. Nation 198:21 Ja 6 '64
Communist China and western Europe. O. M. Lee. bibliog f Cur Hist 47:143-8+ S '64
Cuba and the administration; resemblance to problem of China for the Truman administration. W. V. Shannon. Commonweal 77: 585-6 Mr 1 '63
Door into China. New Repub 149:4 D 28 '63
Facing China. New Repub 152:3-4 Ja 9 '65
Fact of China. J. O'Gara. Commonweal 80: 466 Jl 10 '64
Flexing its muscles? il Newsweek 62:30+ Ag 12 '63
Fresh look at our China policy. G. F. Keenan. il N Y Times Mag p27+ N 22 '64
Let's open the door to China. Sat Eve Post 237:84 Jl 25 '64
Living an illusion. il Newsweek 64:38-9 Ag 10 '64
Living with China as a great power. O. E. Clubb. bibliog f Ann Am Acad 351:140-7 Ja '64
Looking at China. Commonweal 81:181 N 6 '64
Mainland China and U.S. security. B. G. Lall. Bul Atomic Sci 20:24-7 Ap '64
Negotiations with China. M. Ascoli. Reporter 32:18 Ja 28 '65
Optimists and the pessimists; shift in power in Russia and explosion of the Chinese nuclear bomb. W. V. Shannon. Commonweal 81:217-18 N 13 '64
Our China policy: a reappraisal. P. K. T. Sih. Cath World 200:84-90 N '64
Recognizing Peking. T. Adams. New Repub 151:36+ N 14 '64
Reviewing a policy. Nation 196:435 My 25 '63

UNITED STATES—Foreign relations—China (People's Republic)—*Continued*
Secretary discusses mainland China in television interview. D. Rusk. Dept State Bul 51:771-2 N 30 '64
To lead or to follow. Nation 198:109 F 3 '64
U.S. China policy and disarmament. F. W. Neal. Bul Atomic Sci 19:5-8 N '63
United States policy toward Communist China; address, December 13, 1963. R. Hilsman. Dept State Bul 50:11-17 Ja 6 '64; Same. Vital Speeches 30:203-7 Ja 15 '64
Waiting for evolution. il Time 84:46-9 N 13 '64
What about mainland China? D. M. Stowe. Christian Cent 82:44-6 Ja 13 '65

Communist countries

Challenge of communism. N. A. Rockefeller. il Look 28:27-9 Je 2 '64
Foreign policy, old myths and new realities; address, March 25, 1964. J. W. Fulbright. Vital Speeches 30:388-94 Ap 15 '64
Hard way to peace, by A. Etzioni. Review Nation 196:271-2 Mr 30 '63. A. Rapoport
Impotence of American power. H. J. Morgenthau. Commentary 36:384-6 N '63; Reply. L. Lipsitz. 37:20-1 Mr '64
Many-hued policy. Time 83:28 Mr 6 '64
Myth of Communist solidarity. V. C. Ferkiss. il Cath World 199:159-66 Je '64
Next steps toward peace: some notes on the two-legged process; address, September 30, 1963. M. Bundy. Dept State Bul 49:625-30 O 21 '63
Our foreign policy; what is it? address, March 3, 1964. N. A. Rockefeller. Vital Speeches 30:402-6 Ap 15 '64
Peace as motion. Commonweal 79:416-17 Ja 10 '64
Peace in our time? H. J. Morgenthau. Commentary 37:66-9 Mr '64
Polycentrism and western policy. G. F. Kennan. For Affairs 42:171-83 Ja '64
Secretary Rusk's news conference of March 27, 1964. D. Rusk. Dept State Bul 50:570-6 Ap 13 '64
Toilsome path to peace; address, March 19, 1964. D. Rusk. Dept State Bul 50:530-5 Ap 6 '64
Toward victory for freedom; address, September 14, 1964. D. Rusk. Dept State Bul 51:463-8 O 5 '64; Same. Vital Speeches 31:2-5 O 15 '64
Two kinds of reds to call on Kennedy. il U S News 55:24 S 23 '63
Where U.S. stands now in cold war. il U S News 56:50-3 My 11 '64
Why we treat different Communist countries differently; address, February 25, 1964. D. Rusk. Dept State Bul 50:390-6 Mr 16 '64; Same. Vital Speeches 30:354-7 Ap 1 '64; Excerpts. U S News 56:55 Mr 9 '64
See also
United States—Commerce—Communist countries
United States—Economic relations—Communist countries

Congo (capital Leopoldville)

As an East-West war heats up in the Congo. il U S News 58:28-9 Ja 4 '65
Congo: another job for U.S. il U S News 57:37 Ag 17 '64
Congo: best bet is Tshombe. Life 57:4 Jl 17 '64
Congo, Congo, who's got the Congo? Nat R 16:757 S 8 '64
Congo: hostages, mercenaries and the CIA. J. Hatch. il Nation 199:452-5 D 14 '64
Congo: new police job for the United States. il U S News 57:60-1 Jl 6 '64
Congo: what was wrong, what is and will be wrong. A. J. Meyers. il U S News 54:59-61 F 4 '63
Left hand, right hand. il Newsweek 63:37 Je 29 '64
Tiptoe to the rescue. il Time 84:20 Ag 21 '64
Tshombe talks about U.S. role in the Congo; interview, ed. by A. J. Meyers. M. Tshombe. il U S News 57:50-1 Ag 3 '64
UN's idiot policy in the Congo. E. Van Den Haag. Nat R 17:61-2 Ja 26 '65
U.S. calls for constructive approach to Congo problem; statements, December 22 and December 24, 1964. A. E. Stevenson. Dept State Bul 52:43-6 Ja 11 '65
United States calls for prompt Congo reunification under U.N. plan; Department statement, January 4, 1963. Dept State Bul 48:91 Ja 21 '63
U.S. cites illegal interference in support of Congo rebellion; statement, December 14, 1964. A. E. Stevenson. Dept State Bul 52:15-24 Ja 4 '65

Cuba

Adopted son in revolt. Newsweek 62:51 S 16 '63
After the Cuban crisis. D. H. Wrong. Commentary 35:28-33 Ja '63
Air will be ours; Cuban fighters tell why they expected air cover; with excerpts from radio messages. M. A. de Varona; G. Herrera. il U S News 54:33-6 F 4 '63
Anatomy of the snafu. T. Flaherty. il Life 54:80-3 My 10 '63; Same abr. with title What we learned from the Bay of Pigs. Read Digest 83:92-4 Jl '63
Another Cuban fiasco? il U S News 54:33-6 Ap 29 '63
As the Cubans see Castro. R. Hudson. Sat R 47:97-9+ O 10 '64
Atlantic report. Atlan 211:6+ My '63
Beware, the mousetrap; Cuba policy. L. B. Bozell. Nat R 14:354 My 7 '63
Boycotting Cuba. New Repub 149:5 D 28 '63
Boycotting Cuba; whose interest does it serve? J. Daniel. New Repub 149:19-22 D 28 '63
Burr under the blanket; Shut up! Cuban situation. Nat R 14:15-6 F 26 '63
Calling for action on Castro. il Bsns W p31-2 F 16 '63
Caribbean, troubled waters; Guantánamo crisis. il Newsweek 63:13-14 F 17 '64
Castro and candor. E. J. Hughes. Newsweek 61:21 My 6 '63
Castro proposal. Commonweal 80:496 Jl 24 '64
Castro's challenge to U.S: the real reasons. il U S News 56:38-9 F 17 '64
Coming: new effort to topple Castro? il U S News 56:39 My 11 '64
Cover story; Bay of Pigs disaster. Reporter 28:16+ F 14 '63
Crack in the door? Nation 196:497 Je 15 '63
Cuba and the administration; resemblance to problem of China for the Truman administration. W. V. Shannon. Commonweal 77:585-6 Mr 1 '63; Discussion. 78:49-51 Ap 5 '63
Cuba, Castro and John F. Kennedy. R. M. Nixon. Read Digest 85:281-4+ N '64
Cuba: how Castro wins and U.S. loses. il U S News 56:66-8 Ap 6 '64
Cuba: how dangerous now; with excerpt from President Kennedy's news conference, February 7, 1963. il U S News 54:58-63 F 18 '63
Cuba in 1964. J. Burnham. Nat R 16:16 Ja 14 '64
Cuba: our cold-shoulder policy. R. A. Falk. il Nation 199:113-17 S 14 '64
Cuba paper. Christian Cent 81:788-9 Je 17 '64
Cuba policy. Commonweal 79:680-1 Mr 6 '64
Cuba revisited. J. A. MacKay. il Christian Cent 81:200-3 F 12 '64; Discussion. 81:402-6, 772 Mr 25, Je 10 '64
Cuba: tragedy in our hemisphere, by M. Zeitlin and R. Scheer. Review
New Repub 150:29-30+ F 15 '64. G. Kolko
Cuba under the lens: no missiles but... il Newsweek 61:19-22 F 18 '63
Cuban build-up. New Repub 148:3-4 F 16 '63
Cuban exiles: the mirage of Havana; Revolutionary recovery movement. A. Burt. Nation 200:76-9 Ja 25 '65
Deal Castro wants with U.S. C. Migdail. U S News 57:47 Ag 10 '64
Debate over Cuba. New Repub 148:5 My 4 '63
Easing off; Guantánamo Bay. il Newsweek 63:34 F 24 '64
For a free Cuba. Nat R 14:483-4 Je 18 '63
Fourth floor, by E. E. T. Smith. Review
Commonweal 77:622-4 Mr 8 '63. D. M. Friedenberg
Freedom house on Cuba. Nation 196:518 Je 22 '63
From Washington straight. Cato. Nat R 14:148 F 26 '63
Fruits of a policy. Commonweal 81:119-20 O 23 '64
Further clarification; concerning interviews with Kennedy and Castro. J. Daniel. New Repub 149:6-7 D 21 '63
Ghosts and reality; U.S. air cover for Bay of Pigs beachhead. il Newsweek 61:15 F 4 '63
Help us fight! cry the angry exiles. H. H. Martin. il Sat Eve Post 236:28-30+ Je 8 '63
How about Donovan? Nation 196:365 My 4 '63
How President Kennedy upset Cuban invasion of April 1961. U S News 54:29-30+ F 4 '63
How Russia is using its Cuban base. U S News 54:45 Mr 4 '63
How to deal with Soviet Cuba short of war. Life 54:4 Mr 8 '63
If flag of surrender is waved before Castro. E. Nuñez Portuondo. U S News 56:6 Ap 13 '64

UNITED STATES—Foreign relations—Cuba —*Continued*

In the works: deal with Castro? U S News 54:65 Je 17 '63
Inevitable questions. S. Alsop. il Sat Eve Post 237:12 Ap 11 '64
Inspection of Cuba. J. G. Patton and others. New Repub 148:38-9 Mr 23 '63
Insurance. Commonweal 77:632 Mr 15 '63
Is Castro an obsession with us? G. S. McGovern. il N Y Times Mag p9+ My 19 '63
Latest facts on Russia's Cuban base; interview. K. B. Keating. il U S News 54:43-5 F 11 '63
Letter from Washington. R. H. Rovere. New Yorker 39:155-62 My 4 '63
Liberation of Cuba; address. P. M. Heilman. Vital Speeches 29:391-4 Ap 15 '63
LBJ and Cuba: what comes next. U S News 55:41 D 23 '63
Measuring the threat. Commonweal 77:551 F 22 '63
Miró and Kennedy: the bitter moment. Newsweek 61:19-20 Ap 29 '63
Mr Eisenhower's paper no. 5. Nat R 16:389-90 My 19 '64
Most critical area in the world. Life 54:4B F 22 '63
New Cuban menace. Nation 196:169 Mr 2 '63
New look at Cuba; exiles resume training. Nation 197:209 O 12 '63
President and his critics. Nation 196:149 F 23 '63
President and his critics. W. A. Williams. Nation 196:226-8+ Mr 16 '63
President Kennedy accepts custody of flag of Cuban brigade; remarks, December 29, 1962. J. F. Kennedy. Dept State Bul 48:88-90 Ja 21 '63
Quandary over Cuba. il Bsns W p26 F 15 '64
Real change in Cuba. R. Hotz. Aviation W 78:17 Mr 4 '63
Real strength of our nation; address, July 15, 1963. W. F. Knowland. Vital Speeches 29:682-6 S 1 '63
Refugee leader blames U.S. for broken promise; excerpts from statement, April 18, 1963. J. Miró Cardona. U S News 54:65-7+ Ap 29 '63
Report from Guantánamo: we're ready for Castro's next step. H. Handleman. il U S News 56:52-3 Mr 2 '64
Rethinking Cuba. Christian Cent 80:1191-2 O 2 '63
Rise and fall of Cuba; address, May 20, 1964. M. L. Simpson. Vital Speeches 30:520-2 Je 15 '64
Road ahead; address, February 13, 1963. D. Rusk. Dept State Bul 48:311-16 Mr 4 '63
Rockets with beards; Castro's complaint of U-2 flights. il Time 83:36 My 1 '64
Second blockade. New Repub 148:3-4 Mr 16 '63
Secretary Rusk holds press and radio news briefing at Los Angeles. D. Rusk. Dept State Bul 48:361-8 Mr 11 '63
Senator and Castroism. Life 56:2 Ap 10 '64
Sense and nonsense on Cuba. New Repub 149:5-6 Jl 13 '63
Shots & a shrimp boat; firing from Soviet-built MIGs out of Cuba. il Time 81:18 Mr 1 '63
Shots heard round the world; firing on shrimp boat, Ala. il Newsweek 61:17-18 Mr 4 '63
Slicing up the Cuban problem. R. Fisher. New Repub 148:13-15 Je 15 '63; Reply. E. F. Betancourt. 149:17-18 Jl 13 '63
Smile of safety; what are we being told about Cuba? C. B. Marshall. New Repub 148:17-18 My 25 '63
Speaking out; let's talk sense about Cuba. J. W. Fulbright. Sat Eve Post 237:8+ My 16 '64
Stop whistling Dixie. Nation 196:109-10 F 9 '63
That month: April's cruelty. il Time 81:21-2 Ap 26 '63
U-2's over Cuba. Commonweal 80:225 My 15 '64
Under Secretary Ball interviewed on Issues and answers; transcript of interview, February 10, 1963. G. W. Ball. Dept State Bul 48:370-1 Mr 11 '63
U.S. asks Cuba for explanation of attack on Floridian; statement, March 28, 1963. Dept State Bul 48:573 Ap 15 '63
United States, Cuba, and Castro, by W. A. Williams. Review
New Repub 148:23-4 Ap 20 '63. S. Shapiro
U.S, Cuba and Guantanamo. il Sr Schol 84:9-11 Mr 13 '64
U.S.-Cuban water battle. il Sr Schol 84:16 F 28 '64
U.S. demands Cuba explain attack on fishing vessel; text of U.S. note. Dept State Bul 48:356 Mr 11 '63
U.S. outlines policy toward Cuban refugees; statement, May 22, 1963. E. M. Martin. Dept State Bul 48:983-90 Je 24 '63
U.S. reaffirms support of OAS decisions on Cuba; Department statement, August 4, 1964. Dept State Bul 51:271 Ag 24 '64
U.S. replies to Cuban charges in U.N. General assembly; statement, December 11, 1964. A. E. Stevenson. Dept State Bul 52:24-6 Ja 4 '65
U.S. sympathizes with Cuban people in aftermath of hurricane Flora; Department statement, October 23, 1963. Dept State Bul 49:741 N 11 '63
US, the USSR, and Cuba. B. Russell. New Repub 150:29 My 23 '64
U.S. warns of Castro declaration of war on hemisphere; text of U.S. note, January 30, 1963. D. S. Morrison. Dept State Bul 48:263-4 F 18 '63
Unofficial envoy: an historic report from two capitals. J. Daniel. New Repub 149:15-20 D 14 '63
Uproar; suggested UN agricultural experimental station in Cuba. Newsweek 61:25 F 25 '63
Variation on a theme; Castro proposes Cuban co-existence with the U.S. il Newsweek 64:49-50 Jl 20 '64
Very well then, we'll be specific; soft policy toward Cuba. Nat R 14:306 Ap 23 '63
War party. Nation 196:189-90 Mr 9 '63
War whoopers. Nation 196:238 Mr 23 '63
We should help the Cuban exiles find a leader. Life 54:4 My 3 '63
We who tried; with report by J. Dille. il Life 54:20-34+ My 10 '63
What's become of Cuba? K. Crawford. Newsweek 62:44 Jl 29 '63
Where America is weakest; interview. A. Burke. il U S News 57:67-9 Jl 13 '64
Who gives a whoop? J. Burnham. Nat R 14:279 Ap 9 '63
See also
Cuba—History—Invasion, 1961

Dahomey

United States recognizes new government of Dahomey; Department statement, January 31, 1964. Dept State Bul 50:239 F 17 '64

Dominican Republic

How Trujillo died. N. Gall. New Repub 148:19-20 Ap 13 '63
Trujillo: the last Caesar, by A. Espaillat. Review
Nat R 15:530-1 D 17 '63. N. Weyl
U.S.-backed reform flops as Bosch gets the bounce. S. Halper. il Life 55:49-50 O 18 '63
U.S. recognizes Dominican and Honduran governments; Department statement, December 14, 1963. Dept State Bul 49:997-8 D 30 '63

Ecuador

U.S. recognizes military junta as government of Ecuador; Department statement, July 31, 1963. Dept State Bul 49:282 Ag 19 '63

Egypt

Double dilemma. Newsweek 62:42+ O 14 '63
Dulles over Suez, by H. Finer. Review
Esquire 62:68+ S '64. M. Muggeridge
Nat R 16:915 O 20 '64. G. F. Eliot
Hoist; Egyptian troops in Yemen. il Newsweek 62:38 Ag 5 '63

Ethiopia

Display of affection. il Time 82:25-6 O 11 '63
Emperor of Ethiopia visits United States; texts of an exchange of toasts between President Kennedy and the Emperor, October 1, 1963, and a joint communique October 2, 1963. J. F. Kennedy; Haile Selassie I, emperor of Ethiopia. Dept State Bul 49:674-5 O 28 '63
Haile Selassie; an old leader with a new role. U.S. News 55:22 O 14 '63

Europe, Eastern

Conditions in eastern Europe; statement, March 10, 1964. W. A. Harriman. Dept State Bul 50:485-7 Mr 30 '64
Eastern Europe: a region in ferment; address, October 13, 1964. G. C. McGhee. Dept State Bul 51:716-21 N 16 '64
United States and a changing Europe; address, March 17, 1964. W. R. Tyler. Dept State Bul 50:587-90 Ap 13 '64
United States and eastern Europe; address, June 14, 1963. E. Anderson. Dept State Bul 49:87-92 Jl 15 '63

Europe, Western

ABC of MLF. A. Fontaine. il Reporter 31:10-14 D 31 '64
America and Europe. New Repub 148:3-4 F 9 '63

UNITED STATES—Foreign relations—Europe, Western—*Continued*
As Europe turns left. il U S News 54:62-4 Ap 29 '63
Atlantic relationships and nuclear problems: a French view. F. de Rose. For Affairs 41: 479-90 Ap '63
Atlantic unity. New Repub 149:3-5 Jl 13 '63
Cities at stake in NATO bargaining. Christian Cent 80:900 Jl 17 '63
Clues to trans-Atlantic distrust. M. Gordey. il N Y Times Mag p25+ Je 9 '63
Coalition diplomacy in a nuclear age. H. A. Kissinger. For Affairs 42:525-45 Jl '64
Collapse of Kennedy's grand design; with editorial comment. S. Alsop. il Sat Eve Post 236:78-82 Ap 6 '63
Common market crisis. C. Emmet. America 108:333-5 Mr 9 '63
Crisis in the western alliance; American and British views. H. J. Morgenthau; G. Hutton. Commentary 35:185-98 Mr '63
Dealing with a new Europe; with editorial comment. il Bsns W p46-54, 88 Jl 4 '64
Demands of power. R. Aron. New Repub 148: 12-13 Mr 30 '63
Europe & the United States; tr. by R. McInerny. R. Aron. Commentary 38:54-60 Ag '64
Europe nervously watches our election. D. W. Brogan. il N Y Times Mag p 15+ O 4 '64
Europe without America. W. Lippmann. Newsweek 61:17 F 18 '63
European integration and American foreign policy; address, February 9, 1963. A. Chayes. Dept State Bul 48:318-22 Mr 4 '63
Evolution of western defense. P. Stehlin. For Affairs 42:70-83 O '63
For a united, nuclear Europe; summary of address. N. A. Rockefeller. Time 81:20 My 3 '63
Gaullism today. W. Lippmann. Newsweek 61: 25 Je 24 '63
Hold fast. P. H. Spaak. For Affairs 41:611-20 Jl '63
In Europe, growing doubts about U.S. il U S News 55:66-7 S 16 '63
International outlook; De Gaulle shakes a big stick at U.S. policies. Bsns W p81-2 F 9 '63
Isolationist Europe; the odds on a turn away from U.S. il U S News 54:56-8 Ap 8 '63
'Ken-ah-dee' abroad: the common cause. il Newsweek 62:31-2+ Jl 8 '63
Letter from Washington. R. H. Rovers. New Yorker 38:103-4+ F 2 '63
Luxury of dissension. Time 81:21-2 F 22 '63
Nassau reconsidered: what can America and Britain do now? A. Buchan. New Repub 148:21-3 Mr 2 '63
New & obscure destination; de Gaulle's veto of Britain's admission to the Common market. il Time 81:22+ F 8 '63; Same abr. with title De Gaulle corners the market. Read Digest 82:65-70 Ap '63
Now the grand redesign; a new kind of crisis. il Newsweek 61:21-2 F 25 '63
Patching up the Atlantic alliance. Bsns W p 132 Ap 27 '63
Practice of partnership. D. Acheson. For Affairs 41:247-60 Ja '63
Problems of success. W. V. Shannon. Commonweal 77:633-4 Mr 15 '63
Putting the squeeze on Germany; policy change on MLF. il Newsweek 64:45 N 23 '64
Revolt of Europe; with editorial comment. E. Griffiths. il Sat Eve Post 236:13-21, 76 Mr 9 '63
Secretary Rusk interviewed on GFWC television program, April 13, 1963. D. Rusk. Dept State Bul 48:698-703 My 6 '63
Size-up of de Gaulle; interview, ed. by A. J. Meyers. R. Aron. il U S News 54:68-72 Ap 22 '63; Same abr. with title Frenchman explains de Gaulle. Read Digest 83:79-82 Jl '63
Strains on the Alliance. H. A. Kissinger. For Affairs 41:261-85 Ja '63
Tensions within the Alliance. R. R. Bowie. For Affairs 42:49-69 O '63
Today's impasse, tomorrow's solution. R. Aron. New Repub 148:13-14 Je 1 '63
U.S. and Europe: the argument over defense. M. S. Johnson. il U S News 54:43 Je 3 '63
U.S. failing in Europe? J. Fromm and F. C. Painton. il U S News 54:48-52 Mr 25 '63
United States in the Atlantic community. L. B. Tennyson. Cur Hist 45:264-70+ N '63
United States of America and the Atlantic partnership; address, November 21, 1963. G. C. McGhee. Dept State Bul 49:954-9 D 23 '63
Unraveling alliances. W. Lippmann. Newsweek 61:21 Mr 18 '63
Vice President Johnson visits northern Europe; addresses, September 4-16, 1963. L. B. Johnson. Dept State Bul 49:583-94 O 14 '63
We too are independent. W. F. Buckley, jr. Nat R 16:526 Je 30 '64
Well, you see, it's this way; Cabot Lodge as special envoy to explain U.S. policy in Vietnam to eight European governments. il Newsweek 64:32 S 14 '64
What do we want in Europe? W. Pfaff; R. Steel. Commonweal 81:411-14 D 18 '64
What NATO needs to stay alive. T. D. White. Newsweek 62:34 D 16 '63
What of the grand design? R. Aron. New Repub 148:8-9 F 16 '63
Who will defend Europe? J. Burnham. Nat R 14:190 Mr 12 '63
Why Kennedy is going to Europe. il U S News 54:41 Je 10 '63
Withdrawal from Europe? an illusion. D. Acheson. il N Y Times Mag p7+ D 15 '63
Wrong Europe. C. Bourdet. Nation 196:191-5 Mr 9 '63

See also
Atlantic community

Far East

Asia: change in the White House. New Repub 149:10-11 D 14 '63
Paris and Peking. E. J. Hughes. Newsweek 63:17 F 10 '64

France

Bonne année, Oncle Charles. W. Dillon. New Repub 150:15-16 Ja 4 '64
Case pro and con de Gaulle. L. Markel. il N Y Times Mag p 19+ Ja 10 '65
Cold slap: France will soon recognize red China. Time 83:23-4 Ja 24 '64
Cursing de Gaulle is not a policy. S. Hoffmann. Reporter 30:38-41 Ja 30 '64
Dangers of hairsplitting; France as a nonsignatory of the test-ban treaty. Nation 199:506 D 28 '64
Dean Acheson speaks out again: target is President de Gaulle; summaries of addresses. D. G. Acheson. U S News 55:15 S 30 '63
De Gaulle: just who he is and what's back of him. il U S News 57:24-6 D 28 '64
De Gaulle: trouble from an ally. U S News 57: 31-2 D 7 '64
France and the U.S: talking again? Newsweek 62:41 O 14 '63
France: the hard facts of nuclear life; with reports by L. Collins and E. Weintal. il Newsweek 61:39-40 Ap 15 '63
Fulbright on de Gaulle. K. Crawford. Newsweek 62:49 N 11 '63
In France, a whispering campaign against U.S; and some shouts. U S News 54:69 F 4 '63
Isolating our allies. N. Orvik. Reporter 29: 32-3 S 12 '63
Letter from Paris; Franco-American rift. Genêt. New Yorker 40:155-8 Mr 21 '64
Meeting of two minds. M. Ascoli. Reporter 28:22-3 F 28 '63
Memories that irk de Gaulle. il U S News 56:57 Mr 30 '64
Nuclear policy and French intransigence. M. W. Hoag. For Affairs 41:286-98 Ja '63
Seeds of discord, by D. S. White. Review
New Repub 150:22-3+ Je 20 '64. M. Viorst
U.S. puzzle: what's de Gaulle up to? U S News 56:36 Je 22 '64
What de Gaulle and JFK have in common. J. Daniel. New Repub 149:5-6 O 19 '63
Why de Gaulle is challenging U.S; interview. M. Couve de Murville. il U S News 56:70-5 Mr 16 '64
Why the French mistrust us. B. B. Fall. il N Y Times Mag p6+ S 6 '64
Words, words, words. Newsweek 61:40 Ap 8 '63

Germany (Democratic Republic)

Department states views on status of East German regime. Dept State Bul 49:355 S 2 '63
U.S. policy on East Germany not affected by test ban treaty; interview. J. F. Kennedy. Dept State Bul 49:354 S 2 '63

Germany (Federal Republic)

Discussions held at Washington with German defense minister; joint statement of the Departments of state and defense, February 27, 1963. Dept State Bul 48:444 Mr 25 '63
Germany gives rise to vast uncertainties. H. J. Morgenthau. il N Y Times Mag p21+ S 8 '63
More talks with the Russians; American and Soviet leaders of public opinion meet in Leningrad. N. Cousins. Sat R 47:30 S 26; 30-1 O 10 '64

UNITED STATES—Foreign relations—Germany (Federal Republic)—*Continued*
On summer agenda: JFK visits allies. Sr Schol 82:19 My 15 '63
President and Chancellor Erhard reaffirm commitment to U.S.-German cooperation within free-world community; joint communique, December 29, 1963; with exchanges of remarks, December 28 and December 29, 1963. L. Erhard; L. B. Johnson. Dept State Bul 50:74-80 Ja 20 '64
President and Secretary Rusk pay tribute to Chancellor Adenauer; letters, October 10 and October 15, 1963. J. F. Kennedy; D. Rusk. Dept State Bul 49:697 N 4 '63
President Kennedy visits Europe; texts of joint communiques released at Bonn, Birch Grove house, Sussex, and Rome, with major addresses and remarks, June 23-July 2, 1963. J. F. Kennedy. Dept State Bul 49:114-28 Jl 22 '63
Some American thoughts on current issues; address, July 16, 1964. G. C. McGhee. Dept State Bul 51:138-44 Ag 3 '64
Will Germany now edge closer to U.S? Kennedy and the Germans. il U S News 54:62-3 Je 24 '63

Ghana

Fighting fantasy. Newsweek 63:54 F 17 '64
From U.S. to Ghana: millions; from Ghana to U.S: insults. il U S News 56:40 F 24 '64
Mobs assail U.S. in Ghana. Sr Schol 84:18 F 21 '64
One party, four walls. Time 83:26+ F 14 '64
Reluctant hero speaks his mind; with letter. il Ebony 18:164 Ap '64

Great Britain

Alliance: time for guidelines. il Newsweek 64:17 D 21 '64
Anglo-American alliance. R. N. Berkes. bibliog f Cur Hist 46:275-81+ My '64
Anglo-American relations; address, May 22, 1963. D. O. Gore. Vital Speeches 29:551-3 Jl 1 '63
Britain and the US. New Repub 151:3-4 D 19 '64
British Prime Minister holds talks with President Johnson; communique, February 13, 1964. L. B. Johnson and A. F. Douglas-Home. Dept State Bul 50:336-7 Mr 2 '64; Same. Cur Hist 46:304-5 My '64
British Prime Minister visits Washington; exchange of greetings, December 7, 1964; with joint communique. H. Wilson; L. B. Johnson. Dept State Bul 51:902-4 D 28 '64
Fox trots no minutes; Mr Johnson's talks with Sir Alec Douglas-Home. il Newsweek 63:21 F 24 '64
New strains on an old alliance. il U S News 56:42 F 24 '64
Relationship of Britain and United States; address, April 1, 1963. H. Wilson. Vital Speeches 29:418-21 My 1 '63
Scrapping of Skybolt. W. S. Just. il Reporter 28:19-21 Ap 11 '63
Speaking out; England's place in the sun. S. Lloyd. Sat Eve Post 236:6+ Mr 2 '63; Excerpts. U S News 54:26 Mr 11 '63
Tory bind; Washington's campaign for a mixed-crew surface force. D. Healey. New Repub 148:14-15 Je 22 '63
U.S. and Britain: LBJ calls the tune. il U S News 57:25-6 D 21 '64
U.S. and U.K. sign agreement on sale of Polaris missiles; announcement, letter from Secretary Rusk, and text of agreement, April 6 and April 9, 1963. Dept State Bul 48:759-64 My 3 '63
What happens to Great Britain now? interview. Earl of Home. il U S News 54:62-5 F 4 '63
Whilst he still lives amongst us; W. Churchill's convictions about Anglo-American friendship. Q. Hogg. il Life 57:49-50+ D 11 '64

Greece

Is U.S. aid to Greece paying off? il U S News 56:6 Mr 16 '64

Guatemala

Damn good sure, overthrow of the leftist government in June 1954. Newsweek 61:19 Mr 4 '63
United States extends recognition to new government of Guatemala; Department statement, April 17, 1963. Dept State Bul 48:703 My 6 '63
Where reds may take over next in Latin America. il U S News 54:48-50 Mr 18 '63

Haiti

Can Haiti be helped? R. L. Mirabeau. Nation 196:416-18 My 18 '63
Haiti; last act of a tragicomedy. B. Rice. Harper 226:65-6+ My '63
How long do we take it? Nation 198:517 My 25 '64
Papa Doc squirms. New Repub 148:10-11 My 11 '63
U.S. and Haiti. Commonweal 81:437 D 25 '64
U.S. pushes drive to oust Haiti's czar. Bsns W p27 My 11 '63
What Papa Doc ordered. Time 81:42 Je 14 '63
Who will shoot Duvalier? New Repub 148:9 My 18 '63

Honduras

Honduras revolt: another blow to U.S. il U S News 55:6 O 14 '63
U.S. recognizes Dominican and Honduran governments; Department statement, December 14, 1963. Dept State Bul 49:997-8 D 30 '63

Hungary

Aid to Hungary. America 112:105+ Ja 23 '65
Decision nears on Hungary. America 109:182 Ag 24 '63
Reluctant cardinal. Newsweek 61:47-8 My 27 '63
U.S.-Hungary accord? America 111:769-70 D 12 '64

India

India, Mideast will strengthen U.S. hand. J. P. Grant. il Nations Bsns 51:68+ D '63
Indian non-alignment and United States policy. P. C. Chakravarti. il Cur Hist 44:129-34+ Mr '63
Seventh fleet: patrolling the Indian Ocean. New Repub 150:8 Ja 11 '64
Troubled India and her neighbors. S. S. Harrison. For Affairs 43:312-30 Ja '65
U.S. and India reaffirm agreement on basic values and objectives; joint communique, June 4, 1963. J. F. Kennedy and S. Radhakrishnan. Dept State Bul 48:969-70 Je 24 '63
Why another ally questions value of its links to U.S; with interview with M. Ayub Khan. il U S News 54:80-3 My 13 '63

Indonesia

In the Far East: still no real peace. il U S News 56:6 F 3 '64
Let's move on Sukarno now. Life 55:4 O 4 '63
Mission to Malaysia. Sr Schol 84:7 F 14 '64
Robert Kennedy's aim: prevent a Sukarno war. il U S News 56:15 Ja 27 '64
Seaweed & soothing words; R. Kennedy's meeting with Sukarno in Tokyo. il Time 83:21 Ja 24 '64
Sukarno the strong. New Repub 151:3 Jl 11 '64
Sukarno's war; will it involve U.S? il U S News 57:63 S 21 '64

Iraq

United State recognizes government of Iraq; Department statement, February 11, 1963. Dept State Bul 48:316 Mr 4 '63

Ireland

On summer agenda: JFK visits allies. Sr Schol 82:19 My 15 '63
President de Valera of Ireland visits United States; texts of exchanges of arrival remarks and toasts and President de Valera's address to Congress, May 28, 1964. L. B. Johnson; E. De Valera. Dept State Bul 50:927-33 Je 15 '64
Prime Minister of Ireland visits the United States; exchange of greetings, October 15, 1963 and text of communique, October 17, 1963. J. F. Kennedy; S. F. Lemass. Dept State Bul 49:737-8 N 11 '63

Israel

Israel's Eshkol: U.S. visit worries Arabs. il U S News 56:22 Je 15 '64
U.S. and Israel exchange views on matters of mutual interest; exchange of greetings, with joint communique, June 2, 1964. L. B. Johnson; L. Eshkol. Dept State Bul 50:958-60 Je 22 '64

Italy

Foreign Minister of Italy holds talks in Washington. J. F. Kennedy and A. Piccioni. Dept State Bul 49:636 O 21 '63

Japan

America encounters Japan, by W. L. Neumann. Review
Nat R il 16:871-2+ O 6 '64. G. Morgenstern
Japan, the United States, and Europe; address, March 28, 1963. U. A. Johnson. Dept State Bul 48:606-12 Ap 22 '63

UNITED STATES—Foreign relations—Japan —*Continued*
Japan, the U.S. and war in South Vietnam; interview, ed. by R. P. Martin. E. Sato. U S News 58:42-3 Ja 11 '65
Japanese security and American policy. G. F. Kennan. For Affairs 43:14-28 O '64
Pilgrim on flight 800. Time 85:24 Ja 15 '65

Jordan

King and President putting on pressure. Newsweek 63:56-7 Ap 20 '64
President Johnson holds talks with King Hussein of Jordan; joint communique, April 15, 1964. Dept State Bul 50:697 My 4 '64

Kenya

Message to Kenya, December 10, 1963. L. B. Johnson. Dept State Bul 50:18 Ja 6 '64

Korea (People's Democratic Republic)

U.S. comments on Communist inspired incidents in Korea; Department statements, July 29 and July 30, 1963. Dept State Bul 49:283 Ag 19 '63

Korea (Republic)

Korea's mendicant mentality? a critique of U.S. policy. P. C. Hahm. For Affairs 43:165-74 O '64
Secretary Rusk holds talks with President of Korea; joint communique, January 29, 1964. D. Rusk and C. H. Park. Dept State Bul 50:238 F 17 '64
United States and Korea ratify consular convention. Dept State Bul 49:905 D 9 '63
United States and Korea reaffirm policy of cooperation; joint statement, October 3, 1964. T. W. Lee; W. P. Bundy. Dept State Bul 51:542 O 19 '64

Laos

Doublecross for the U.S. in Laos. il U S News 54:66-7 Ap 22 '63
King of Laos visits Washington, talks with President Kennedy; joint communique, February 27, 1963. Dept State Bul 48:447-8 Mr 25 '63
Laos: continuing crisis. E. Pace. For Affairs 43:64-74 O '64
Laos; escalation in the air. il Time 83:22-3 Je 19 '64
Laos. Nat R 14:345 My 7 '63
Raising the ante in Laos. il Newsweek 63:39 Je 22 '64
Time to think. Newsweek 63:32+ Je 29 '64
Very fragile structure. New Repub 148:8 My 4 '63

Latin America

Ali, ali, anza free-o! Tiresias. Nat R 14:113-14+ F 12 '63
Ambassadors and AID mission chiefs in Latin America meet. Dept State Bul 50:540 Ap 6 '64
Angry talk & negative action. il Time 82:32 O 11 '63
Are we ignoring Latin America? A. A. Berle. il N Y Times Mag p26+ N 24 '63
Calming a Latin tempest; with editorial comment. il Bsns W p64-8, 96 F 1 '64
Choice for Latin America: Castro threat or Leoni promise. il Newsweek 63:34-6+ Mr 30 '64
Climate of San José. il Time 81:15-16 Mr 22 '63
Cold war drift in Latin America. P. S. Holbo. bibliog f il Cur Hist 44:65-72+ F '63
Crisis of casualness in Latin America. J. P. Davies, jr. Harper 229:12+ Ag '64; Reply. R. R. White. 229:6 O '64
Cuba, Latin America, and communism; address, September 20, 1963. E. M. Martin. Dept State Bul 49:574-82 O 14 '63
Democratic ideal in our policy toward Latin America; address, June 7, 1964. T. C. Mann. Dept State Bul 50:995-1000 Je 29 '64
Firm hand for Latin policy; T. A. Mann, Asst. Secy. for inter-American affairs. Bsns W p 17-18 D 21 '63
Henry Clay: forerunner of Pan-Americanism C. M. Sterling. il Américas 16:1-6 My '64
Incompatibility. Newsweek 63:59 My 18 '64
Latin America: a broad-brush appraisal. P. W. Quigg. For Affairs 42:399-412 Ap '64
Latin America progress report. G. J. Mangone. America 111:10-14 Jl 4 '64
Mann for the job. Time 82:14-15 D 27 '63
Needed: a clear call. America 108:357 Mr 16 '63
New approach to Latin America? W. V. Shannon. Commonweal 80:31-2 Ap 3 '64
New world of Latin America. T. Moscoso. il Sat R 46:23-7+ O 12 '63
Nonrecognition; the diplomatic trap. R. A. Falk. il Nation 198:457-60 My 4 '64
One Mann & twenty problems. il Time 83:15-18 Ja 31 '64
President outlines Latin American policy in letter to Mr Mann. L. B. Johnson. Dept State Bul 50:9-10 Ja 6 '64
President reaffirms pledge to Latin America; address, November 26, 1963. L. B. Johnson. Dept State Bul 49:912-13 D 16 '63
Reflections on San José. Commonweal 78:36 Ap 5 '63
Report to the President on Latin American policy. T. C. Mann. Dept State Bul 51:706-7 N 16 '64
Saving Latin democracies. W. V. Shannon. Commonweal 79:182-4 N 8 '63
U.S. in Latin America. R. M. Schneider. bibliog f Cur Hist 48:1-8+ Ja '65
U.S. policy in Latin America. H. H. Humphrey. For Affairs 42:585-601 Jl '64; Reply. Commonweal 80:439-40 Jl 3 '64
U.S. policy regarding military governments in Latin America; statement, October 6, 1963. E. M. Martin. Dept State Bul 49:698-700 N 4 '63
When they shout, Yanqui, no! A. A. Berle. il N Y Times Mag p9+ Ja 26 '64
Why we are wrong on Latin America. Tiresias. il Nat R 16:225-6+ Mr 24 '64
See also
Latin America and the United States

Latvia

Secretary sends good wishes on Latvia's national day, letter, November 15, 1963. D. Rusk. Dept State Bul 49:932 D 16 '63

Luxembourg

Grand Duchess of Luxembourg meets with President Kennedy. Dept State Bul 48:776 My 20 '63
Vice President Johnson visits Benelux countries; statement, November 4, and addresses, November 7 and 8, 1963. L. B. Johnson. Dept State Bul 49:850-4 D 2 '63

Malagasy

President of Malagasy Republic visits Washington; exchange of greetings, July 27, 1964; with joint communique, July 28, 1964. L. B. Johnson; P. Tsiranana. Dept State Bul 51:229-30 Ag 17 '64

Malaysia

Prime Minister of Malaysia visits Washington; exchange of greetings and toasts; with joint communique, July 22 and July 23, 1964. L. B. Johnson. A. Rahman. Dept State Bul 51:190-3 Ag 10 '64

Malta

President congratulates Malta on independence; letter, September 18, 1964. L. B. Johnson. Dept State Bul 51:503 O 12 '64

Mexico

Along the Mexican border, a new era of friendship. il U S News 57:75-8 N 30 '64
Bright spot in the hemisphere: a close look at Mexico. il U S News 56:95-7 F 24 '64
Community of interest between the U.S. and Mexico; remarks, March 5, 1964. D. Rusk. Dept State Bul 50:449-50 Mr 23 '64
Mexico looks to the North. I. Fabela. Atlan 213:95-8 Mr '64
President Lopez Mateos of Mexico to meet with President Johnson. Dept State Bul 50:89 Ja 20 '64
U.S. betting on Mexico; but there's trouble ahead. il U S News 54:45-7 F 25 '63
U.S.-Mexican relations: new tests for new president. U S News 57:20 D 7 '64

Middle East

American policy in the Near East; address, January 20, 1964. U. A. Johnson. Dept State Bul 50:208-11 F 10 '64
Arabs and the world: Nasser's Arab Nationalist policy, by C. D. Cremeans. Review
Sat R 46:18 Je 1 '63. W. H. Stringer
Countries in search of a character. E. Lengyel. Sat R 47:54 My 9 '64
Diplomatic games. Commonweal 80:353 Je 12 '64
Hussein at bay. New Repub 148:9-10 My 11 '63
India, Mideast will strengthen U.S. hand. J. P. Grant. il Nations Bsns 51:68+ D '63
Middle East misconceptions. C. Leiden. il Nat R 16:67-9 Ja 28 '64
U.S. urges disengagement of foreign forces in Yemen conflict; Department statement, January 3, 1963. Dept State Bul 48:90 Ja 21 '63

UNITED STATES—Foreign relations—*Cont.*

Morocco

King of Morocco exchanges views with President Kennedy; joint communique, March 29, 1963. Dept State Bul 48:601 Ap 22 '63

Netherlands

Vice President's address at Amsterdam, November 7, 1963. L. B. Johnson. Dept State Bul 49:851-2 D 2 '63

Oceania

Reflections on the Pacific community; address, March 28, 1963. H. Cleveland. Dept State Bul 48:613-16 Ap 22 '63

Pakistan

Pakistan-American alliance. M. Ayub Khan. For Affairs 42:195-203 Ja '64
Pakistan: no satisfaction for Mr Ball. il Newsweek 62:37 S 16 '63
Why another ally questions value of its links to U.S; with interview with M. Ayub Khan. il U S News 54:80-3 My 13 '63

Panama

After agreement, what? il Time 83:36+ Mr 6 '64
Another chance. il Newsweek 63:47 F 10 '64
Crisis over the Canal. il Time 83:30+ Ja 17 '64
Crisis with Panama. R. Moley. Newsweek 63:84 F 3 '64
Deadlock in Panama. America 110:178 F 8 '64
Hanging tough. Newsweek 63:42 Mr 9 '64
Inside story of Panama riots. il U S News 56:48-52 Mr 30 '64
Justice and the Canal. W. Sparks. Commonweal 79:564-6 F 7 '64
Let's act our age in Panama. Life 56:4 Ja 24 '64
More than a question of flags. il Newsweek 63:42-3 Ja 20 '64
On toward May. il Time 83:29 Mr 27 '64
Outbreak in Panama. Commonweal 79:472-3 Ja 24 '64
Panama: bluffs, pressures, impasse. il Newsweek 63:45 Ja 27 '64
Panama crisis. R. Niebuhr. New Repub 150:5-6 F 1 '64; Reply. F. H. Wang. 150:38 F 15 '64
Panama: distrust and delay. D. A. Allan and G. Sherman. Reporter 30:28-9 F 27 '64
Panama impasse. K. Crawford. Newsweek 63:21 Mr 30 '64
Panama is first big test; with editorial comment. il Bsns W p23-5. 124 Ja 18 '64
Panama: no U.S. backdown. il U S News 56:29-31 Ja 27 '64
Panama solution. New Repub 150:4 F 15 '64
Panama: the crisis we could have avoided. C. W. Hall. il Read Digest 84:84-9 Ap '64
Panama: the disaster that should have been foreseen; comments concerning Wine is bitter, by Dr M. Eisenhower. Sat Eve Post 237:90 F 22 '64
Panama: the third force. Nation 198:225-6 Mr 9 '64
Panama: why they hate us; more than one torn flag. T. Armbrister. il Sat Eve Post 237:75-9 Mr 7 '64
President restates U.S. position on Panama and Canal Zone; statement, January 23, 1964. L. B. Johnson. Dept State Bul 50:195-6 F 10 '64
Search for a settlement. Newsweek 63:45-6 F 3 '64
Semantics, politics & passion. il Time 83:17 Ja 24 '64
Squeeze is on in Panama. il U S News 56:40 F 17 '64
U.S. and Panama agree on certain procedural matters in Canal Zone; joint communique with U.S. aide memoire, January 10, 1963. J. F. Kennedy and R. F. Chiari. Dept State Bul 48:171-3 F 4 '63
U.S. and Panama announce results of Canal Zone talks; joint communique, July 23, 1963. J. F. Kennedy and R. F. Chiari. Dept State Bul 49:246-7 Ag 12 '63
United States and Panama reestablish diplomatic relations; statement by President Johnson, with OAS announcement, April 3, 1964. L. B. Johnson. Dept State Bul 50:655-6 Ap 27 '64
U.S.-Panamanian accord. il Américas 16:42 My '64
U.S. prepared to review differences with Panama; statement, March 21, 1964. L. B. Johnson. Dept State Bul 50:538-9 Ap 6 '64
What the squabble in Panama is all about; interview. A. I. Selden, jr. il U S News 56:34-7 Ja 27 '64
Who really owns Panama; a source of U.S. trouble. il U S News 56:64-5 Ap 6 '64
Why Panama erupted. il U S News 56:32-3 Ja 20 '64
Will we lose the Canal? E. McDowell. il Nat R 16:107-8 F 11 '64; Discussion. 16:205+ Mr 10 '64

See also
Panama crisis, 1964

Philippines

Dry tinder; question of U.S. military bases. Newsweek 65:35 F 1 '65
Meddling by Sukarno: why Filipinos turn against U.S. il U S News 58:59 Ja 11 '65
New worry for the U.S; trouble with an old ally. il U S News 57:77-9 O 12 '64
President Macapagal of Philippines visits United States; exchange of greetings, October 5, with exchange of toasts at the White House and text of a joint communique, October 6, 1964. L. B. Johnson; D. Macapagal. Dept State Bul 51:628-34 N 2 '64

Poland

Warsaw uprising day; proclamation, July 31, 1964. L. B. Johnson. Dept State Bul 51:271 Ag 24 '64

Portugal

Our about-face on African policy; bases on the Azores. G. M. Houser. Christian Cent 80:675-6 My 22 '63
Price of the Azores; tr. from the Portuguese by G. Rabassa. H. Galvao. Nation 197:432-3 D 21 '63

Rhodesia

United States expresses concern about problem of Rhodesia; Department statement, October 28, 1964. Dept State Bul 51:721-2 N 16 '64

Russia

After test ban: what is next. F. B. Stevens. il U S News 55:58-9 O 7 '63
Are all reds alike? Rusk sees a difference; excerpts from address, February 25, 1964. D. Rusk. U S News 56:55 Mr 9 '64
Back to power politics; nationalism and looser alliances. il Bsns W p27-9 O 19 '63
Change of emphasis. Commonweal 79:63 O 11 '63
Cold war and weapons control. L. W. Martin. Cur Hist 47:1-5+ Jl '64
Cold war is a war. D. Lawrence. U S News 55:124 N 25 '63
Cold war ups and downs. Sr Schol 83:14 N 1 '63
Common action for the control of conflict, by V. P. Rock. Review
U S News il 55:64-6 N 18 '63
Cuba under the lens: no missiles but... il Newsweek 61:1-22 F 18 '63
Defining the cold war. D. Lawrence. U S News 56:128 F 24 '64
Dial K for Khrushchev; direct hot line between Kremlin and White House. Bsns W p36 Ap 13 '63
Easing of the cold war? U S News 54:8 Je 24 '63
East and West enter a new phase. E. Crankshaw. il N Y Times Mag p 16+ Ag 30 '64
East-West thaw. il Bsns W p25-30 S 28 '63
Euphoria. D. Lawrence. U S News 55:132 O 7 '63
First real chance for disarmament. P. M. S. Blackett; discussion. Harper 226:12+ Ja; 8+ Mr '63
Fruits of Castro's plotting; with editorial comment. S. Alsop. il Sat Eve Post 236:75-80 Mr 16 '63
Fulcrum. Nation 199:421-2 D 7 '64
Giving a little; concerning Mr Kennedy's speech at American university. New Repub 149:5 Jl 6 '63
Glance at a decade. E. J. Hughes. Newsweek 62:15 Ag 26 '63
Goldwater and the Soviet Union. W. F. Buckley, jr. Nat R 16:56 Ja 28 '64
Good-by Mr Barghoorn, pleasant journey. il Newsweek 62:37-8 N 25 '63
Harriman: another job to do in Moscow. il U S News 55:14 Jl 22 '63
Hot line to Moscow: how it will work. il U S News 55:8 Jl 1 '63
How far can U.S. trust Gromyko? U S News 55:15 Ag 19 '63
In the cold war: a peace offensive. U S News 56:8 Ja 13 '64
Is a U.S. deal with Russia near? il U S News 55:27-9 Jl 22 '63
Is it to be a truce with Russia? il U S News 56:35-7 My 4 '64
Kennedy-Khrushchev correspondence. E. T. Folliard. America 109:379 O 5 '63
Khrushchev's hidden weakness; captive nations; with editorial comment. R. M. Nixon. il Sat Eve Post 236:23-9, 88 O 12 '63; Same abr. without editorial comment. Read Digest 84:59-64 Ja '64

UNITED STATES—Foreign relations—Russia —*Continued*

Letter from Washington; Senate ratification. R. H. Rovere. New Yorker 39:149-56 O 5 '63

Llewellyn Thompson: JFK's no. 1 Russian expert. L. Bergquist. il Look 27:21-5 F 12 '63

Logic of circumstance. Nation 197:1 Jl 6 '63

Neither dead nor red; Cuban crisis. Earl of Home. Read Digest 82:69-71 F '63

New hopes in the race for peace. Bsns W p26-7 Ja 25 '64

New taste. Newsweek 63:18-19 My 4 '64

Next step: playing it by ear. il Newsweek 62:29-30 O 7 '63

Notes on a 1963 visit with Khrushchev. N. Cousins. il Sat R 47:16-21+ N 7 '64

Now, togetherness with Russia, but three Americans are dead. il U S News 56:4 F 10 '64

Object lesson for optimists. D. L. Flaherty. America 109:148 Ag 17 '63

On dealing with the Communist world, by G. F. Kennan. Review

New Repub 150:25-8 My 16 '64. L. J. Halle

Open wire to Kremlin. il Bsns W p36 Je 29 '63

Our relations with Russia; address, October 19, 1963. J. F. Kennedy. Vital Speeches 30: 34-5 N 1 '63; Excerpts with editorial comment. il U S News 55:126-8 N 11 '63

Playing politics with war. Christian Cent 80:227 F 20 '63

President and Soviet leaders exchange New Year's messages. L. B. Johnson; N. S. Khrushchev and L. Brezhnev. Dept State Bul 50:121 Ja 27 '64

Reaching the Russians; concerning President's speech at American university. New Repub 148:7 Je 22 '63

Real strength of our nation; address, July 15, 1963. W. F. Knowland. Vital Speeches 29:682-6 S 1 '63

Right direction. il Newsweek 62:31 O 14 '63

Russia and China. Commonweal 78:443-4 Jl 26 '63

Russia, China, the U.S. today. F. B. Stevens. U S News 57:59 N 23 '64

Russia in deep trouble; will U.S. give help? interview. G. W. Nutter. il U S News 56: 50-7 Ap 13 '64

Secretary Rusk discusses world developments on Issues and answers, October 18, 1964. D. Rusk. Dept State Bul 51:654-60 N 9 '64

Seven safeguards for dealing with reds. A. Dulles. Nations Bsns 51:66-7+ O '63

Soviet-American relations; address, February 28, 1963. R. F. Starr. bibliog Vital Speeches 29:468-73 My 15 '63

Soviet overflights must stop! Nation 196:257 Mr 30 '63

Speaking out; we can make the Russians disarm. W. P. Reuther. Sat Eve Post 236:10+ D 7 '63

Strange aftermath of the Cuban deal; different cold war from year ago. il U S News 55:51-2 N 11 '63

Strategy of peace; address, June 10, 1963. J. F. Kennedy. Vital Speeches 29:558-61 Jl 1 '63; Same. Dept State Bul 49:2-6 Jl 1 '63; Excerpts. Time 81:18-19 Je 21 '63

Strategy of peace; concerning President Kennedy's speech at the American university in Washington on June 10, 1963. Nation 196:537 Je 29 '63

Strategy of peace: first, a test ban? Newsweek 62:17 Jl 15 '63

Tensions ease under the sign of the moon; President Kennedy addresses the U.N. General assembly. il Newsweek 62:17-18 S 30 '63

Test ban and beyond. N. Cousins. Sat R 46:14+ Ag 10 '63

There's good politics in peace offensive; East-West agreements. Bsns W p22-3 Ja 11 '64

Third round. W. W. Rostow. For Affairs 42: 1-10 O '63

Tiger will bite. S. Alsop. il Sat Eve Post 236:18 O 19 '63

Top Kremlinologist at work: A. Harriman. C. Phillips. il N Y Times Mag p9+ Jl 14 '63

U-2's over Cuba. Commonweal 80:225 My 15 '64

Unfinished business. D. Lawrence. U S News 56:100 Ja 27 '64

Unfinished business; address, September 10, 1963. D. Rusk. Dept State Bul 49:490-6 S 30 '63

U.S.S.R. accepts U.S. proposal for direct communication link; statement, April 5, 1963. Dept State Bul 48:600 Ap 22 '63

U.S. and Soviet Union exchange notes on interference with ships; texts of notes, April 22, August 3, 5 and 18, and September 15, 1964. Dept State Bul 51:482-5 O 5 '64

U.S. and U.S.S.R. sign agreement for direct communications link; White House statement, June 20, 1963, with text of agreement. Dept State Bul 49:50-1 Jl 8 '63

U.S. disclaims responsibility for attacks on Soviet ships; note, April 3, 1963. Dept State Bul 48:599 Ap 22 '63

U.S. protests Soviet planes' violation of Alaskan airspace; note, March 16, 1963. Dept State Bul 48:476 Ap 1 '63

U.S. protests to Soviet Union on incident involving U.S. vessel; Department statement, July 17, 1964. Dept State Bul 51:145 Ag 3 '64

U.S. reaffirms position on NATO multilateral nuclear force; U.S. note to the Soviet Ministry of foreign affairs, August 28, 1964. Dept State Bul 51:367-8 S 14 '64

U.S. rejects Soviet charge on firing on trawler; U.S. note of March 14 and Soviet note of March 12, 1963. Dept State Bul 48:475-6 Ap 1 '63

U.S.-Russian showdown: will it wreck U.N? il U S News 57:39-40 N 30 '64

U.S.-Soviet thaw: a new treaty; provision for exchange of consulates. Newsweek 63:38 Je 8 '64

U.S. tries again to get an A-test ban; new talks set in Moscow. il Bsns W p26-7 Je 15 '63

Unthinkable detente. Nation 198:449 My 4 '64

Ways to peace. Commonweal 79:119-20 O 25 '63

Weighing the advantages; Soviet-American détente. H. Brandon. Sat R 46:16+ N 2 '63

Western powers reject Soviet charges on NATO nuclear defense; exchange of notes between the United States and the Soviet Union, May 18 and April 8, 1963. Dept State Bul 48:860-6 Je 3 '63

What does Kennedy mean? concerning Strategy of peace address, June 10, 1963. F. S. Meyer. Nat R 15:18 Jl 16 '63

Why we must put holes in the iron curtain. Life 55:4B S 13 '63

Will they take Ave? W. F. Buckley, jr. Nat R 15:51 Jl 30 '63

Saudi Arabia

United States assures Saudi Arabia of support and friendship; letter, October 25, 1962. J. F. Kennedy. Dept State Bul 48:144-5 Ja 28 '63

Scandinavia

Touring Vice President LBJ visits Scandinavia. il U S News 55:24 S 16 '63

What Lyndon Johnson found next door to Russia. R. W. Ruth. il U S News 55:73-4 S 23 '63

South Africa

Overthrow of apartheid. P. Duncan. New Repub 148:9-10 Mr 9 '63

South Africa and the world: some maxims and axioms. P. Mason. For Affairs 43:150-64 O '64

Stop South Africa now. New Repub 150:3-4 My 16 '64

Toward a world policy for South Africa. P. Duncan. For Affairs 42:38-48 O '63

Spain

Europita. il Newsweek 61:34+ F 25 '63

Franco, Congress and the Pentagon. C. McWilliams. Christian Cent 80:298-300 Mr 6 '63

Love me, love me not. Newsweek 61:45 My 20 '63

New lover for Franco? New Repub 148:7 F 9 '63

Spain: playing it cool. New Repub 149:5 O 5 '63

Spain's long, hard look at tomorrow. il Sr Schol 82:9-11 Mr 20 '63

Triumph for Franco. Nation 197:251 O 26 '63

United States and Spain renew defense agreement; exchange of notes and letters; with Department announcement and texts of documents. D. Rusk; F. M. Castiella. Dept State Bul 49:686-8 O 28 '63

Syria

U.S. recognizes government of Syrian Arab Republic; Department statement, March 12, 1963. Dept State Bul 48:476 Ap 1 '63

Taiwan

U.S. reaffirms commitments to Taiwan and Viet Nam; statements, April 16, 17 and 20, 1964. D. Rusk. Dept State Bul 50:694-7 My 4 '64

UNITED STATES—Foreign relations—*Cont.*

Tanganyika

President Nyerere of Tanganyika visits Washington; joint communique, July 16, 1963; with announcement of new Peace corps agreement. M. J. K. Nyerere and J. F. Kennedy. Dept State Bul 49:198-9 Ag 5 '63

Togo

U.S. recognizes government of Republic of Togo; statement, June 6, 1963. Dept State Bul 48:969 Je 24 '63

Turkey

President greets Turkish people on anniversary of Republic; message from President Kennedy to Gen. Cemal Gürsel, October 29, 1963. J. F. Kennedy. Dept State Bul 49: 788 N 18 '63
President Johnson expresses hope for end of strife in Cyprus; exchange of messages. C. Gursel; L. B. Johnson. Dept State Bul 50:90 Ja 20 '64
Turkey's internal crisis. S. Lens. Commonweal 80:629-31 S 18 '64

United Arab Republic

Our Yemen policy: pursuit of a mirage. P. Horton. il Reporter 29:28-35 O 24 '63
U.S.A. and U.A.R: crisis in confidence. J. S. Badeau. For Affairs 43:281-96 Ja '65

Venezuela

New Cuban menace. Nation 196:169 Mr 2 '63
Quest of Romulo Betancourt. il Sr Schol 82: 5 Mr 6 '63
U.S. and Venezuela take firm stand against Communist threats; exchange of greetings; with joint communique. J. F. Kennedy; R. Betancourt. Dept State Bul 48:445-7 Mr 25 '63

Viet Nam (Democratic Republic)

Measured & fitting response. il Time 84:11 Ag 14 '64
North Vietnam's bloody nose. Commonweal 80:559 Ag 21 '64
Reunifying Vietnam. New Repub 149:3-5 S 14 '63
Why the torpedo attacks? F. B. Stevens. il U S News 57:24 Ag 17 '64

Viet Nam (Republic)

Agony in Saigon: the lady & the cadaver. D. Warner. Reporter 29:39-42 O 10 '63
American way of death. Nat R 15:424-5 N 19 '63
Any way out? ambassadors, generals, scholars reply. il Newsweek 65:34-6 Ja 18 '65
Asian apocrypha. il Newsweek 63:52 Mr 16 '64
Back of the revolt in South Vietnam. il U S News 55:41 N 11 '63
Behind the denials; coup in South Viet Nam. il Time 82:21 N 8 '63
Blackmail in Vietnam. New Repub 151:4-5 Ag 8 '64
Booby trap. Nation 197:121 S 14 '63
Buddhist revolt; Diem's new opponents deserve US support. E. Wulff. New Repub 149:11-14 Ag 31 '63
Campaign present for Lyndonbird. Nat R 16: 760 S 8 '64
Can Khanh? New Repub 150:3-4 Mr 28 '64
Can the war in Vietnam be won? il Newsweek 63:15-16 Mr 9 '64
Certain painful decisions. Nation 198:129 F 10 '64
Change in personnel. Nation 197:337 N 23 '63
Chips go down on South Vietnam. Bsns W p31-2 Je 27 '64
Chips on Khanh. il Time 83:30 Mr 20 '64
Collision course in Vietnam. U.S. vs. an unruly ally; with excerpts from interview with Mme Nhu. R. P. Martin. il U S News 55:36-8 S 16 '63
Colonel Van and General Harkins. Nation 197:230 O 19 '63
Coup in South Viet Nam. il Sr Schol 83:18 N 15 '63
Darkness on the Mekong. New Repub 150:3-4 F 8 '64
Deadly and perplexing war; Looking for a link. il Newsweek 65:28, 30 Ja 18 '65
Defeat, victory, and pressure on Vietnam. il Newsweek 62:45 N 4 '63
De Gaulle on Vietnam. R. Steel. Commonweal 80:141-3 Ap 24 '64
Diem and the Buddhists. H. G. Fairbanks. Commonweal 78:452-4 Jl 26 '63
Diem from the grave: interview. ed. by C. W. Wiley. Ngo-dinh-Diem. Nat R 15: 426 N 19 '63
Dienbienphu: could it happen again? Time 83:43 My 15 '64
Dilemma of Diem-ocracy. il Sr Schol 83:10-13+ S 20 '63
Diplomacy by television. Time 82:23 S 13 '63
Do we have a chance to win? interview, ed. by R. Carroll. R. Hilsman. Newsweek 64:45 S 21 '64
Double trouble? Sr Schol 85:30 S 23 '64
Edge of chaos. S. Karnow. il Sat Eve Post 236:27-37 S 28 '63
Escalation in Vietnam. New Repub 151:8 N 14 '64
Facing hard facts in Vietnam. H. G. Fairbanks. il Cath World 199:89-95 My '64
Fog over Vietnam. America 110:305-6 Mr 7 '64
Folly in Vietnam. Commonweal 78:364-5 Je 28 '63
Folly in Vietnam. New Repub 149:6-7 S 21 '63
Foreign policy: building amid turbulence; address, August 27, 1963. R. J. Manning. Dept State Bul 49:454-60 S 23 '63
Foreign policy: LBJ's test. Newsweek 63: 19-20 F 10 '64
Four choices in Viet Nam. Time 83:22 F 28 '64
Fresh stir of hope in Vietnam. il Bsns W p36 Mr 21 '64
General Khanh's ailment. Nation 199:101-2 S 14 '64
Get down to cases. Nation 197:169-70 S 28 '63
Getting the story in Vietnam. D. Halberstam. Commentary 39:30-4 Ja '65
Going it alone. Time 84:30 N 20 '64
Governments come, go; but Vietnam war rolls on. il U S News 56:49 F 10 '64
Hard choice for the U.S; get tough or get out. R. P. Martin. il U S News 55:54-7 S 9 '63
Harsh challenge to Johnson: hotter war in Vietnam. il U S News 55:104 D 9 '63
Hold Vietnam. America 112:158-9 Ja 30 '65
Homecoming; H. C. Lodge's defense of administration policy. il Time 84:25 Jl 10 '64
Hopes fade for South Vietnam. Bsns W p29 Ag 29 '64
How to beat the reds in southeast Asia: interview, ed. by S. W. Sanders. Ngo Dinh-Diem. il U S News 54:70-3 F 18 '63
If you wonder how U.S. got involved in Vietnam: questions and answers. il U S News 56:40-1 Je 15 '64
In Asia's hot war: more trouble for U.S. il U S News 55:58 S 2 '63
Inevitable questions. S. Alsop. il Sat Eve Post 237:12 Ap 11 '64
Invitation to depart. Nation 199:449 D 14 '64
Is it a lost war for U.S. in Vietnam? with report by R. P. Martin. il U S News 57:55-7 S 7 '64
Is there a way out for U.S. in Vietnam? il U S News 56:42-4 F 17 '64
Is U.S. changing policy? U S News 57:19 Ag 31 '64
Is Vietnam going the way of Chiang's China? R. P. Martin. il U S News 57:67-9 O 12 '64
Job for the peace movement. Nation 198:253 Mr 16 '64
Lady is for burning; the seven deadly sins of Madame Nhu. C. B. Luce. il Nat R 15: 395-9 N 5 '63
Last Confucian, by D. Warner. Review
New Repub 149:24+ O 19 '63. B. B. Fall
Lesson from Vietnam. E. J. Hughes. Newsweek 62:17 S 9 '63
Letter from Saigon. R. Shaplen. il New Yorker 40:37-8+ Jl 11; 179-86+ S 19 '64
Look at the woodwork. Time 82:31 S 27 '63
Lowdown from the top U.S. command in Saigon; panel discussion with the Life correspondents. M. D. Taylor. il Life 57:46-46B+ N 27 '64
Mac finds out what's gone wrong. il Life 55: 22-7 O 11 '63
Madame Nhu's mission. K. Crawford. Newsweek 62:26 O 28 '63
Manageable mess. il Newsweek 65:34+ Ja 11 '65
Military man sizes up a war U.S. is losing. M. S. Johnson. il U S News 56:40-1 Mr 16 '64
More of the same and hope for the best. il Time 83:20 Mr 27 '64
Needed in Vietnam: the will to win. R. M. Nixon. Read Digest 85:37-43 Ag '64
Negotiate now! Nation 199:82 S 7 '64
New confrontation? il Newsweek 62:28-9 D 30 '63
New coup, old crisis: Maxwell Taylor on the spot; with report by E. Weintal. il Newsweek 64:43-5+ S 21 '64
New faces, more chaos. B. B. Fall. il Nation 197:380-2 D 7 '63
New moves in the war in Vietnam. il U S News 56:14 Mr 9 '64
New policy in Vietnam? H. Brandon. Sat R 47:6 D 12 '64

UNITED STATES—Foreign relations—Viet Nam—*Continued*
New turn in a fifteen-year war: the real story of Vietnam. il U S News 56:50-2 Mr 23 '64
Nhu deal. K. Crawford. Newsweek 62:34 S 16 '63
No extension. Newsweek 64:38 D 14 '64
No-win in Vietnam. New Repub 149:6 O 5 '63
Now it's a war against Americans in Vietnam. il U S News 56:35 Mr 2 '64
On playing God; our relationship with Diem and with these new rulers. Reporter 29: 14+ N 21 '63
Once again: no-win. Nat R 15:467-9 D 3 '63
One of those weeks; McNamara trip to Vietnam. Newsweek 63:42+ My 25 '64
One problem, two solutions. W. Lippmann; J. Alsop. Time 85:48 Ja 1 '65
1,002nd way; efforts to restore a greater measure of civilian government in South Viet Nam. il Time 85:15 Ja 8 '65
Our problem in Vietnam. W. Lippmann. Newsweek 64:23 S 28 '64
Out by 1965. New Repub 149:3 O 19 '63
Paris exiles: Vietnamese political exiles. H. B. Lamb. il Nation 197:65-8 Ag 10 '63
Pause before the din. E. J. Hughes. Newsweek 64:15 Jl 13 '64
President names new ambassador to Saigon, reiterates U.S. policy; statement, June 23, 1964. L. B. Johnson. Dept State Bul 51: 46-7 Jl 13 '64
President pledges continuing support to Republic of Viet Nam; message, December 31, 1963. L. B. Johnson. Dept State Bul 50:121-2 Ja 27 '64
President rearms basic policy in Viet-Nam; White House statement, December 1, 1964. Dept State Bul 51:869-70 D 21 '64
Press the war in Vietnam. Life 55:4 N 22 '63
Pressure on Diem and on the UN. America 109:544 N 9 '63
Problem in Vietnam: what can be saved. il U S News 57:55 S 28 '64
Quandary of Henry Cabot Lodge. S. Karnow. il Sat Eve Post 237:70-3 F 8 '64
Real trouble in Vietnam. il U S News 57:46 D 14 '64
Report from South Vietnam. il U S News 55: 21 O 14 '63
Republicans renew Vietnam policy attack; with statements, by President Johnson, and Secretary McNamara. C. Brownlow. Aviation W 81:22-3 Ag 17 '64
Reunifying Vietnam. New Repub 149:3-5 S 14 '63
Revolt in Vietnam. Commonweal 81:4 S 25 '64
Revolution on the Mekong. J. Burnham. Nat R 15:436 N 19 '63
Saigon coup. America 109:624-5 N 16 '63
Saigon summary. M. Higgins. America 110: 18-21 Ja 4 '64
Secretary Rusk's news conference: December 23, 1964. D. Rusk. Dept State Bul 52:34-41 Ja 11 '65
Secretary Rusk's news conference of March 6, 1964. D. Rusk. Dept State Bul 50:439-46 Mr 23 '64
Secretary Rusk's news conference of November 8, 1963. D. Rusk. Dept State Bul 49:810-17 N 25 '63
Secretary Rusk's news conference of September 10, 1964. D. Rusk. Dept State Bul 51: 426-32 S 28 '64
Showdown in South Vietnam. il U S News 58:35 Ja 4 '65
Situation; possibility of extending the Vietnamese war. Time 84:30-1 D 11 '64
Six months after the coup. T. Molnar. Nat R 16:491 Je 16 '64; Reply with rejoinder. S. Labin. 16:783 S 8 '64
South Vietnam as a campaign issue. S. De Paul. America 111:82 Jl 25 '64
Speaking out; time to end the war. Nation 199:505 D 28 '64
Strange war the U.S. is not winning. R. P. Martin. il U S News 55:48-50 S 30 '63
Tale of two wars. Time 82:35-6 N 1 '63
Tangle in Vietnam. America 109:284 S 21 '63
Time for a change? il Newsweek 64:50 O 12 '64
Time for decision. America 110:788 Je 6 '64
To L.B.J: what is our aim in Vietnam? Life 58:4 Ja 8 '65
To the north. il Time 84:20-1 Jl 31 '64
Truth about the war U.S. is losing; interview. B. B. Fall. il U S News 57:58-62 S 28 '64
Two heads. Reporter 31:12 Jl 16 '64
Ugly Americans of Vietnam; with editorial comment. M. Higgins. il America 111:367, 376-82 O 3 '64
Unclouded judgment. il Time 82:25 O 11 '63
U.S. may pull rug from under Diem. il Bsns W p22 Ag 31 '63
U.S. policy on Viet-Nam; White House statement, October 2, 1963. Dept State Bul 49:624 O 21 '63
U.S. reaffirms commitments to Taiwan and Viet Nam; statements, April 16, 17 and 20, 1964. D. Rusk. Dept State Bul 50:694-7 My 4 '64
U.S. rebuke for Vietnams Mme Nhu. U S News 55:28 O 7 '63
United States recognizes new government of Viet-Nam; Department statement, November 7, 1963. Dept State Bul 49:818 N 25 '63
U.S. re-examines Viet policy. il Sr Schol 83: 18 O 18 '63
U.S. v. the generals. il Time 85:32-3 Ja 1 '65
U.S.-Vietnam politics. K. Crawford. Newsweek 63:46 Ap 20 '64
Unpleasant options. Time 83:17 My 29 '64
Up to November 4. Nation 198:225 Mr 9 '64
Victory in defeat? Newsweek 62:38 S 30 '63
Vietnam: a box for U.S. policy. Bsns W p25-6 S 21 '63
Vietnam, a way out. New Repub 151:5 O 3 '64
Vietnam (again) Commonweal 79:703 Mr 13 '64
Vietnam: crisis of indecision. il Newsweek 62:25-6 S 23 '63
Viet Nam debate. Time 85:21-2 Ja 15 '65
Vietnam dilemma. il Newsweek 64:41 S 28 '64
Viet Nam: do we understand revolution? E. G. Lansdale. For Affairs 43:75-86 O '64
Vietnam: getting to know the Nhus. il Newsweek 62:33-4+ S 9 '63
Vietnam: in the French footsteps. J. Kapstein. il Nation 199:479-82 D 21 '64
Vietnam: miscalculations and alternatives. N. Cousins. Sat R 47:32 D 12 '64
Vietnam: never grimmer. il Newsweek 64:45 D 7 '64
Vietnam, no exit? New Repub 150:3-4 Mr 7 '64
Vietnam: the awful alternative. S. Alsop. Sat Eve Post 237:18 F 22 '64
Vietnam: the roots of the chaos. W. Pfaff. il Commonweal 81:183-90 N 6 '64
Vietnam: the waiting game. S. Alsop. il Sat Eve Post 237:18 O 31 '64
Vietnam: time for reappraisal. Life 56:4 My 29 '64
Vietnam today: a damn shame. il Newsweek 62:36-7 S 2 '63
Vietnam: war and feud get hotter. il U S News 55:4 S 23 '63
Vietnam: wary eye on General Khanh. il Newsweek 64:29 Ag 3 '64
Vietnam: what now? New Repub 151:3-4 D 5 '64
Vietnam: where will it all end? Newsweek 65:11-12 Ja 4 '65
Vietnam, with reason. E. J. Hughes. Newsweek 62:27 N 18 '63
Vietnamese schizophrenia. Nat R 16:186 Mr 10 '64
Vietnam's two wars; with interview with Gen. Dinh. S. Castan. il Look 28:32+ Ja 28 '64
Voyage no. three; U.S. Defense secretary in South Viet Nam. il Time 83:28 Mr 13 '64
War of revolution. America 111:34 Jl 11 '64
War without end. New Repub 148:3-4 Mr 9 '63
Washington's war. Time 82:32-3 O 4 '63
Way out of Vietnam; counter-insurgency warfare. J. Kraft. Harper 229:33-4+ D '64
What chance in Vietnam? J. Burnham. Nat R 15:304 O 8 '63
What happens next to the war in Vietnam. R. P. Martin. il U S News 55:47-9 N 18 '63
What now in Vietnam? Nation 197:425-6 D 21 '63
What now in Vietnam? Nation 200:41 Ja 18 '65
What to do about Vietnam? President Kennedy's condemnation on TV of Diem's regime. il Newsweek 62:23-4 S 16 '63
Where America is weakest; interview. A. Burke. il U S News 57:69-70 Jl 13 '64
Who killed Diem and why? V. L. Borin. il Nat R 16:441-6 Je 2 '64
Why the brush-off? Nation 197:149 S 21 '63
Win with whom? il Newsweek 62:45-6 O 14 '63

See also
Vietnamese crisis, 1964

Yemen

Double dilemma. Newsweek 62:42+ O 14 '63
Gas warfare in Yemen. W. D. Vanrenen. Nat R 15:76-7 Jl 30 '63
Nasser won't play. New Repub 149:5 N 30 '63
Our Yemen policy: pursuit of a mirage. P. Horton. il Reporter 29:28-35 O 24 '63

Yugoslavia

Active coexister visits us. D. Binder. il N Y Times Mag p24+ O 13 '63

UNITED STATES—Foreign relations—Yugoslavia—*Continued*
Man in the middle: Tito. Newsweek 62:67 O 21 '63
President Tito of Yugoslavia visits the Untied States; exchange of greetings, October 17, 1963; with text of communique. J. F. Kennedy; Tito. Dept State Bul 49:738-40 N 11 '63
Talking to Tito; Rusk's courtesy call. Time 81:27-8 My 10 '63
Tito in the United States. M. M. Mestrovic. Commonweal 79:181 N 8 '63
Tito's visit. Commonweal 79:156 N 1 '63
Tito's visit: a worry for U.S. il U S News 55:52 O 28 '63

Zambia

U.S. joins in independence ceremonies in Zambia; message and statement, October 26, 1964. L. B. Johnson; C. W. Engelhard. Dept State Bul 51:722-3 N 16 '64

Zanzibar

Message to Zanzibar, December 9, 1963. L. B. Johnson. Dept State Bul 50:17 Ja 6 '64
United States recognizes the government of Zanzibar; Department statement, February 23, 1964. Dept State Bul 50:424 Mr 16 '64

Foreign service

Bureaucracy abroad. Time 82:22 Jl 5 '63
Case against a West Point for diplomats. E. O. Briggs. il N Y Times Mag p20+ My 3 '64
Education for the new diplomacy; address, March 2, 1963. R. E. Lee. Dept State Bul 48:423-7 Mr 25 '63
Foreign policy needs people, including you; remarks, January 20, 1964. W. J. Crockett. Dept State Bul 50:632 Ap 20 '64
From U.S. officials: a cure for anti-American violence? il U S News 56:61 Mr 30 '64
How to save money: an open letter to Congressman John J. Rooney. H. S. Villard. Harper 228:17+ Ja '64
International trouble-shooter. S. F. Bemis. Sat R 47:52-3 F 22 '64
Marine corps and the foreign service: a working partnership; address, October 16, 1964. D. Rusk. Dept State Bul 51:643-5 N 2 '64
Mrs Louchheim keynote speaker at women's organizations seminar. Dept State Bul 48: 716-17 My 6 '63
Order amended on allowances to certain personnel abroad; executive order, October 18, 1963. J. F. Kennedy. Dept State Bul 49: 802 N 18 '63
Overtime in heaven, by P. Lisagor and M. Higgins. Review
Sat R il 47:33-4 Ag 8 '64. D. Kuhn
Policy and people; address, September 26, 1963. R. J. Manning. Dept State Bul 49:639-44 O 21 '63
Speaking out; waste in the world of diplomacy. E. O. Briggs. Sat Eve Post 236:10+ F 2 '63
USIA foreign service officers to become part of FSO corps; statement, October 3, 1964. L. B. Johnson. Dept State Bul 51:663 N 9 '64
See also
Women as foreign service employees

Forest fire fighters service

Response of man to raw challenge. K. D. Flock. Am For 70:34-5 Jl '64

Forest products laboratory

Woodman, save that tree! K. Detzer. il Am For 70:12-15+ S '64

Forest service

APW: a profit formula. E. P. Cliff. il Am For 69:28-30+ O '63
Bear that almost made me infamous; Smoky Bear's living symbol. K. D. Flock. il Am For 70:20-1+ D '64
Chief's first report. J. Prokop. il Am For 69:4+ S '63
Conservation careers in government. J. H. Caldwell. Nat Parks Mag 37:17-18 N '63
Cool tepee in a hot spot; newest firefighting equipment. il Life 55:41+ N 29 '63
Law and the liability of the public forester. J. W. Giles. Am For 69:31+ Mr '63; Reply. L. F. Marion. 69:2 Je '63
Our loving public. W. W. Huber. il Am For 69:6-7+ Ag '63
Rugged prep school for smoke jumpers. F. A. Tinker. il Pop Mech 119:134-7+ F '63
Sky fire: how science fights it. F. B. Quigg. il Am For 69:12-15+ O '63
South goes scenic. J. K. Vessey. il Am For 70:20-3 Jl '64
Trade winds; visit to Selway Bitterroot wilderness area. J. G. Fuller. Sat R 46:8-9 N 2 '63; Reply. A. Rotonda. 46:32 D 21 '63
Visit to a national grasslands; Cross Timbers grasslands, Tex. D. Beatie. il Nat Parks Mag 38:10-13 O '64
Woodman, save that tree! K. Detzer. il Am For 70:12-15+ S '64

General accounting office

Costly land for housing projects; roles of General accounting office and Federal housing administration. U S News 55:82-3 D 23 '63
GAO charges windfall on helium program. Bsns W p29 Ja 26 '63
GAO praises USAF for savings. Aviation W 79:32 Jl 15 '63
GAO report attacks PHA for design excesses. Arch Rec 136:10 S '64
GAO says air force overstated plug needs. Aviation W 78:64-5 Je 3 '63
Government waste; an official report; summary. U S News 57:10-11 D 28 '64
High price of silence. W. J. Coughlin. Miss & Roc 15:46 N 23 '64
Housing design policies of unconfused accountants. E. Goble. Arch Rec 136:9 O '64
Justice considers GAO pricing claims. K. Johnsen. Aviation W 82:24-5 Ja 11 '65
Non-profit policies face GAO scrutiny. K. Johnsen. Aviation W 81:15 D 28 '64
Reorientations hampered ANP program. K. Johnsen. il Aviation W 78:81-7 Ap 1 '63
Report on wasteland. R. Moley. Newsweek 61:112 Ap 15; 104 Ap 22; 96 Ap 29 '63

General services administration

Karel Yasko of Wisconsin appointed to top federal architecture post. Arch Rec 133:10 Ja '63

Geological survey

Tritium-hydrologic research: some results of the U.S. geological survey research program. C. W. Carlston. bibliog il Science 143: 804-6 F 21 '64

Government

See United States—Politics and government

Government publications

See Government publications

Health, education and welfare, Department of

Health, education and welfare: the first decade. M. B. Folsom. Cur Hist 45:87-91+ Ag '63
Is it everybody's big daddy? il Bsns W p54-8 Ap 4 '64
Water pollution; anti-pollution legislation. New Repub 149:4 D 21 '63

Historic houses, etc.

Great American palaces. J. T. Maher. il Ladies Home J 82:99-103 Ja '65
Herbert Hoover's boyhood home. il Sunset 130:73 Je '63
Homes of America's history. Holiday 34:186-7+ N '63
How much is our heritage worth? House & Gard 125:87 F '64
Landmarks celebration. G. de Zéndegui. Américas 16:inside cover S '64
Life guide; historic homes. il Life 55:19 N 8 '63
Life guide; presidents' houses. il Life 56:9+ F 14 '64
Life guide; springtime tours of houses and gardens. il Life 54:13 Mr 15 '63
Mammon & monuments; excerpt from Independent historical societies. W. M. Whitehill. il Am Heritage 14:38-41+ Ag '63
Our still unspent and yet unexhausted past il Vogue 141:92-9 F 1 '63
Peripatetic reviewer. E. Weeks. Atlan 212: 116+ Ag '63
Robie House saved; Vieux Carré lost? il Arch Forum 118:9 Mr '63
Wrecker, stop that ball. il Newsweek 65:54-5 Ja 25 '65
See also
Literary landmarks
Mount Vernon, Va.
National trust for historic preservation
also subhead Historic houses, etc. under names of states, cities, etc. e.g. New York (city)—Historic houses

History

On history; introduction to American heritage new illustrated history of the United States. J. F. Kennedy. Am Heritage 15:2-4 F '64
Only escape. J. W. Ward. Reporter 29:42+ D 19 '63

UNITED STATES—History—*Continued*
Triumph of conservatism, by G. Kolko. Review
Nation 198:398-400 Ap 20 '64. J. Weinstein
Under the dome of freedom; United States Capitol. L. Aikman. il Nat Geog Mag 125: 4-59 Ja '64
Walk through history with Harry Truman; with editorial comment. J. McCarthy. il Holiday 34:55, 56-61+ N; 96-7+ D '63
We are all descended from grandfathers! grandfathers of the candidates. O. Jensen. il Am Heritage 15:4-13+ Je '64
See also
Education—United States—History
Frontier and pioneer life—United States
Presidents—United States
United States—Church history
United States—Economic history
also subhead History under names of regions, states, etc. e.g. West—History

Bibliography

Articles and other books received; comp. by W. Gray. See issues of American historical review
Recent developments in United States history. J. H. Soltow. bibliog f Ann Am Acad 347:113-28 My '63

Discovery and exploration

See also
America—Discovery and exploration

Historiography

Reconstruction of American history. ed. by J. Highman. Review
Commentary 34:271-3 S '62. S. Lynd; Reply with rejoinder. N. G. Levin, jr. 35:74-5 Ja '63

Study and teaching

Desegregated history. il Time 83:59 Mr 27 '64
How well is history taught? D. W. Robinson. Sat R 47:62-3 D 19 '64
Negro teacher; use of supplementary history booklet in Detroit. T. M. Eubanks. Negro Hist Bul 27:113 F '64
On the road; course on Civil war and the reconstruction at High Point college, N.C. il Newsweek 62:52 Jl 22 '63
So what's new about American studies? H. L. Hurwitz. Sr Schol 84:13T Ap 10 '64
Trouble is teachers. Time 84:90 D 4 '64

Textbooks

American teachers association pushes activity in two vital areas; textbook review commission. Negro Hist Bul 27:149-50 Mr '64
Correcting the image of Negroes in textbooks; address, 1964. C. E. Stewart. Negro Hist Bul 28:29-30+ N '64
Negro teacher; use of supplementary history booklet in Detroit. T. M. Eubanks. Negro Hist Bul 27:113 F '64
Study of Negro blasts racial myths; comments on textbooks. R. P. Alexander. Negro Hist Bul 28:3-6 O '64

Colonial period

Hunt for the regicides. A. Winston. il Am Heritage 16:26-9+ D '64
Shaped in the wilderness: the Americans; excerpts. O. Handlin. Atlan 211:94-106 Je '63
See also
Jamestown, Va.
Pilgrim fathers

Revolution

Enigma of General Howe. T. J. Fleming. il Am Heritage 15:6-11+ F '64
Royal raiders: the Tories of the American revolution, by N. Callahan. Review
Sat R 47:49 F 15 '64. W. C. Kiessel
Work is done, and well done. il Sr Schol 83: 7 O 18 '63
See also
Bunker Hill, Battle of, 1775
Burgoyne's invasion, 1777

Revolution—German mercenaries

Baroness on the battlefield; excerpts from Baroness von Riedesel and the American revolution, ed. and tr. by M. L. Brown. F. C. L. V. Riedesel. il Am Heritage 16: 64-79 D '64

Revolution—History, Military

American historians and the military history of the American revolution. D. Higginbotham. bibliog f Am Hist R 70:18-34 O '64

Revolution—Naval operations

Action off Flamborough Head; excerpt from Great sea battles. O. Warner. il Am Heritage 14:42-9+ Ag '63
Decision at the Chesapeake, by H. A. Larrabee. Review
Sat R 47:27 Ag 1 '64. J. B. Mitchell
Time il 84:86 Ag 21 '64

Revolution—Negroes

Black patriots were heroes at first major battle of Revolution. A. Morrison. il Ebony 19:44-6+ F '64

Revolution—Personal narratives

Baroness on the battlefield; excerpts from Baroness von Riedesel and the American revolution, ed. and tr. by M. L. Brown. F. C. L. V. Riedesel. il Am Heritage 16: 64-79 D '64
Gradele of trobel; battle of Brooklyn Heights. J. Smith. Am Heritage 14:112 Ap '63
Last days and valiant death of Nathan Hale; excerpts from Documentary life of Nathan Hale; ed. by G. D. Seymour. il Am Heritage 15:50-1 Ap '64

Revolution—Strategy

British strategy in war of American independence. P. Mackesy. Yale R 52:539-57 Je '63
Case of the general's dog. il Am Heritage 15:112 Je '64

French and Indian war, 1755-1763

Fantastic adventures of Captain Stobo. R. C. Alberts. il Am Heritage 14:65-77 Ag '63
G. Washington meets a test. T. J. Fleming. il Am Heritage 14:56-9+ F '63

Confederation, 1783-1789

See also
Articles of confederation

1783-1812

Ark of empire, by D. Van Every. Review
Time il 82:110+ O 25 '63
Number 7: Alexander Hamilton's secret attempts to control American foreign policy, by J. Boyd. Review
Sat R 47:22-3 N 28 '64. E. Wright
Voyage pittoresque aux Etats-unis de l'Amérique par Paul Svignine; an appreciation. M. B. Davidson. Am Heritage 15:49-51+ F '64

Constitutional period—1789-1809

Perspective on the founders. V. Miller. il Nat R 14:117-19 F 12 '63
Phantom war of 1804. J. C. Fernández. il Américas 15:23-8 Je '63

Whiskey insurrection, 1794

See Whiskey insurrection, 1794

War of 1812

By heaven, that ship is ours! Constitution vs. Guerrière. L. McKee. il Am Heritage 16:4-11+ D '64
Sailors on wheels. E. S. Allen. Motor B 113:148-51 Mr '64
Victory on Lake Champlain. C. S. Forester. il Am Heritage 15:4-11+ D '63
See also
New Orleans, Battle of, 1815

1815-1861

United States in 1850; from the letters of a Colombian exile. M. Torres. il Américas 16: 1-8 F '64

1849-1877

Man of conscience. R. L. Reynolds. il Am Heritage 14:21-3+ F '63

Civil war

At last Lincoln found a general; excerpt from Centennial history of the Civil war. B. Catton. il N Y Times Mag p34-5+ N 24 '63
How the lost cause was lost. H. S. Commager. il N Y Times Mag p 10-11+ Ag 4 '63
I have been basely murdered. H. H. Peckham. il Am Heritage 14:88-92 Ag '63
Lure of soldiers' letters. P. F. Hoag. Hobbies 68:110-12 My '63
New York's great fire that wasn't. N. Brandt. N Y Times Mag p 109:10+ N 22 '64

UNITED STATES—History—Civil war—*Cont.*
Terrible swift sword: volume II of The centennial history of the Civil war, by B. Catton. Review
Sat R 46:48+ N 16 '63. D. Donald
See also
Confederate States of America
Copperheads (nickname)
Draft riots, 1863
Gettysburg, Battle of, 1863

Civil war—Campaigns and battles

Beat the last drum: the siege of Yorktown, 1781, by T. J. Fleming. Review
Sat R 46:46-7 N 16 '63. E. Thane
Gettysburg and Vicksburg: the battle towns today. R. P. Jordan. il Nat Geog Mag 124:4-57 Jl '63
Old Abe, Wisconsin's Civil war eagle, was there. F. Hallam. il Audubon Mag 65:222-5 Jl '63
Seven days, by C. Dowdey. Review
Am Heritage 15:111-13 Ap '64. B. Catton
Terrible swift sword, by B. Catton. Review
Atlan 212:116+ S '63. E. Weeks
Nat R 15:198+ S 10 '63. G. F. Eliot

Civil war—Causes

American Civil war as a constitutional crisis. A. Bestor. bibliog f Am Hist R 69:327-52 Ja '64
John Brown: God's angry man. L. Bennett, jr. il Ebony 20:96-8+ D '64
Lincoln and the first shot, by R. N. Current. Review
Am Heritage 15:109-10 D '63. B. Catton
Two roads to Sumter, by W. Catton and B. Catton. Review
Sat R 46:47-8 N 16 '63. T. H. Williams
Use of the American Civil war in the debate over Irish home rule. J. M. Hernon, jr. bibliog f Am Hist R 69:1022-6 Jl '64

Civil war—Centennial, 1961-1965

Civil war centennial. B. E. Wheeler. il Hobbies 68:28+ F '64
Just a hundred years ago. C. Sandburg. il Nat Geog Mag 124:1-3 Jl '63

Civil war—Finance, commerce, confiscations, etc.

Was the Secretary of war a traitor? W. A. Swanberg. il Am Heritage 14:34-7+ F '63

Civil war—Medical and sanitary affairs

Surgeons used chloroform; study of Battle of Gettysburg. Sci N L 84:30 Jl 13 '63

Civil war—Naval operations

Du Pont storms Charleston; excerpt from Civil war. S. Foote. il Am Heritage 14:28-34+ Je '63
Last gun of the confederacy: saga of the Shenandoah. C. E. Hinkson. il Read Digest 82:256-8+ Ap '63
Man who stopped the rams. W. W. Wade. il Am Heritage 14:18-23+ Ap '63
Woman who saved the Union navy. G. A. Foster. il Ebony 19:48-50+ Jl '64

Civil war—Negro troops

Negro chaplains in the Civil war. J. W. Blassingame. bibliog Negro Hist Bul 27:24+ O '63

Civil war—Negroes

John Scobell, Union spy in Civil war; excerpts from Eyes and ears of the Civil war. G. A. Foster. il Ebony 19:135-8+ D '63
Northern Negrophobia during the Civil war as reported by the London Times. N. M. Adams. Negro Hist Bul 28:7-8 O '64

Civil war—Personal narratives

Civil, and sometimes uncivil, war: excerpts from manuscripts with sketches by J. E. Taylor, ed. with introd. by B. Catton. E. H. Ripple. Am Heritage 15:50-61 O '64
In search of my son; with editorial comment. S. K. Wightman. il Am Heritage 14:64-78 F '63

Civil war—Prisoners and prisons

Civil, and sometimes uncivil, war; excerpts from manuscripts with sketches by J. E. Taylor, ed. with introd. by B. Catton. E. H. Ripple. Am Heritage 15:50-61 O '64

Civil war—Strategy

—And then Grant took command; excerpt from Centennial history of the Civil war. B. Catton. il N Y Times Mag p26-7+ Ap 26 '64
While we were marching through Georgia; excerpt from Centennial history of the Civil war. B. Catton. il N Y Times Mag p28-9+ N 1 '64

1865-1898

Man of conscience. R. L. Reynolds. il Am Heritage 14:84-91 F '63
President who hurt Negroes most. C. L. Sanders. il Ebony 19:110-12+ My '64
See also
Indians of North America—Wars
Reconstruction (Civil war)

Spanish American war, 1898

Little-known Negro Rough riders. J. R. Phillips. Negro Hist Bul 27:59 D '63

20th century

Can Republicans come back? history shows this. il U S News 57:38-9 N 23 '64
Crossroads: 1913, by P. M. Angle. Review
Am Heritage 14:108-9 O '63. B. Catton

European war, 1914-1918

See European war, 1914-1918—United States

1919-1933

Ordeal of Herbert Hoover. C. N. Degler. Yale R 52:562-83 Je '63

1933-1945

As Byrd sees himself: last of the old New dealers; excerpts from address. H. F. Byrd. U S News 54:20 Ap 15 '63
Cold crusade; the Eisenhower presidency. A. Rosenthal. Nation 196:361-4 Ap 27 '63

World war, 1939-1945

See World war, 1939-1945—United States

1945-

Moments to remember; last four years; address, May 29, 1964. J. L. Golden. Vital Speeches 30:570-2 Jl 1 '64

Korean war, 1950-1953

See Korean war, 1950-1953—American participation

History, Naval

See also
United States—History—Revolution—Naval operations

House of representatives

See United States—Congress—House of representatives

Housing and home finance agency

HHFA honor awards, 1964. il Arch Rec 136:165-74 N '64
Housing design policies of unconfused accountants. E. Goble. Arch Rec 136:9 O '64
Relationship of unemployment to mortgage foreclosures. il Mo Labor R 86:1421-5 D '63
U.S. housing's man with a mission. Bsns W p28-9 O 17 '64

Hydrographic office

See United States—Oceanographic office

Immigration and naturalization service

President praises Immigration and naturalization service; statement, January 17, 1964. L. B. Johnson. Dept State Bul 50:212 F 10 '64

Indian affairs, Bureau of

Educating the American Indian. S. Gifford. il Sch Life 47:10-12 N '64
Indian administration in the United States; address, December 6, 1962. P. Nash. Vital Speeches 29:278-83 F 15 '63
Indian and the poverty war; with editorial comment. T. E. Connolly. America 111:245, 260-1 S 12 '64

Industries

Bargaining focus for 1964-1965. Bsns W p92-3 D 28 '63; p48-9 Ja 2 '65
Energy in the United States. H. A. Meyerhoff. bibliog il Focus 13:1-6 Ap '63
Industry's influentials: the million-dollar companies. il Duns R 83:pt2 125-6 Mr '64
Industry's slide rule is updated by eleven years; new input-output table. il Bsns W p 166-8 N 21 '64
New war between the states: tax subsidies for industry; industrial band programs. il U S News 55:117-18 N 25 '63
Ohio Valley, America's newest industrial empire. D. Reed. il Read Digest 83:193-4+ D '63

UNITED STATES—Industries—*Continued*
Visible strength of U.S. industry; portfolio. Fortune 69:84-93 Ja '64
What can industry do as Pentagon cuts back? il Newsweek 62:87-90 O 7 '63
See also
Building industry
Cattle industry and trade
Disarmament—Economic aspects
Furniture industry and trade
Industrial statistics
Machine industry
Tobacco industry and trade
United States—Economic conditions
also subhead Industries under names of sections, states, cities, e.g. New York (city)—Industries; *also* subhead United States under names of industries, e.g. Steel industry and trade—United States

History

Nation transformed, ed. by S. Diamond. Review
New Repub 150:17-18 F 15 '64. E. T. Chase

Information agency

Can anyone explain capitalism? R. J. Monsen, jr. Sat R 46:26 D 14 '63
Case of the improper imprint; government subsidizes publication of Strategy of deception. D. Dempsey. Sat R 47:26-7 Je 13 '64
Congress cuts off appropriation for IMG. Pub W 186:297 Ag 31 '64
Cover: Carl T. Rowan; top Negro in United States government. Negro Hist Bul 27:138-9 Mr '64
Escape literature; what foreigners think of us. Reporter 28:16 Mr 28 '63
Movies that carry the freight. H. Alpert. il Sat R 47:69-70+ D 12 '64
Murrow legacy. Reporter 30:12+ Mr 12 '64
New look. Newsweek 62:38 N 25 '63
New "Voice" of America. Sr Schol 84:23 Mr 6 '64
Picked to tell the U.S. story abroad. U S News 56:16 F 3 '64
Rowan under fire; excerpts from statements. C. T. Rowan. U S News 56:13 F 10 '64
Same wave length; new director. il Newsweek 63:17 F 3 '64
Senator Javits urges expansion of USIA; summary of address. J. K. Javits. il Pub W 185:25-6 Mr 23 '64
$3.9 million in IMG contracts for fiscal 1965. Pub W 186:88 S 28 '64
To fill the reading gap; Books USA. E. R. Murrow. il Sat R 46:32-3 Ap 27 '63
USIA and the Strategy of deception. Pub W 185:53 Je 29 '64
USIA: building bridges of peace in a changing world; address, December 8, 1964. C. T. Rowan. Dept State Bul 51:906-12 D 28 '64
USIA hit for sponsoring book published in U.S. Pub W 185:31 My 11 '64
USIA launches two new book programs and exhibit of fine bookmaking. Library J 88: 1965 My 15 '63
USIA, Murrow and Rowan. Nation 198:129 F 10 '64
U.S.I.A. offers new jobs for apprentice filmmakers. C. Reynolds. Pop Phot 51:111+ D '62
USIA overseas libraries 1964. C. T. Rowan. il Wilson Lib Bul 39:40-3+ S '64
USIA publishes millionth textbook in translation. Pub W 183:38 My 20 '63
USIA; with editorial comment. E. R. Murrow. Reporter 28:6+ My 9 '63
USIA's expanded Latin America book program. Pub W 186:29-31 Ag 10 '64

Information service

American specialist abroad. E. B. Bohanon. Horn Bk 40:642-5 D '64
Twisted image, by A. Goodfriend. Review
Am Heritage 14:102-3 Je '63
Harper 226:111 Je '63. M. K. Sanders
Sat R 46:29 My 25 '63. B. Smith
USIA foreign service officers to become part of FSO corps; statement, October 3, 1964. L. B. Johnson. Dept State Bul 51:663 N 9 '64

Intellectual life

American culture? qu'est-ceque c'est? L. F. Hannon. il N Y Times Mag p 10+ F 16 '64
Anti-intellectualism in American life, by R. Hofstadter. Review
New Repub 149:19-22 Jl 13 '63. R. Gilman
New Yorker 39:102+ Ja 25 '64. D. Malcolm
Asking the wrong questions. J. F. Fixx. Sat R 47:26 N 7 '64
Backward to normalcy; cultural behavior patterns of the normal American family. J. Shera. Wilson Lib Bul 38:561 Mr '64
Bigger than baseball; the American cultural explosion and the mass media. Mus Am 83:7 Mr '63
Civilization as a process; culture as banal repetition; address, May 27-29, 1963. J. Epstein. ALA Bul 57:664-7 Jl '63
Climate of intellectual freedom; why is it always so bad in California? address, November 6, 1964. E. Castagna. il ALA Bul 59:27-33 Ja '65
Coinskins and culture. Hobbies 67:49 F '63
Culture: getting to be big business. il U S News 54:68-72 Ap 8 '63
Don't knock U.S. culture; adapted from Culture consumers. A. Toffler. il Life 57:96-100+ O 30 '64
Facts, values and libraries; excerpts from address, July 16, 1963. M. W. Gross. ALA Bul 57:829-36 O '63
Not sealed off from life. L. Kronenberger. Vogue 141:136-9 F 1 '63
Out of the golden haze; Pasadena public library. W. Jones. il Library J 89:2298 Je 1 '64
Substance and shadow; visit of British librarians to United States. R. Stokes. Library J 88:3808-9 O 15 '63
See also
American literature
Books and reading
Colleges and universities—United States
Education—United States
United States—Popular culture
also subhead Intellectual life under names of cities, e.g. Chicago—Intellectual life

Interdepartmental committee on nutrition for national defense

What's in a meal? B. Burton. il Américas 15: 4-6 F '63

Interior, Department of

GAO charges windfall on helium program. Bsns W p29 Ja 26 '63
John Muir awards; conservation achievement awards. il Liv Wildn 83:31 Spring '63
Rainbow Bridge: record and requiem. A. W. Smith. Nat Parks Mag 37:2+ My '63
Wedding on the Potomac. P. M. Tilden. Natur Hist 72:64-6 Je '63
See also
United States—Fish and wildlife service
United States—Land management, Bureau of
United States—Outdoor recreation, Bureau of

Internal revenue service

As Congress takes a hand in expense-account rules. U S News 54:112+ Ap 22 '63
Big-brother 7074 is watching you. R. Gannon. il Pop Sci 182:86-8+ Mr '63
Bistros up in arms; vs IRS rules. Bsns W p29 Mr 30 '63
Cold war and the income tax: a protest, by E. Wilson. Review
New Repub 149:25-7 N 30 '63. R. Gilman
Dear diary: $26.73 for . . .: travel and entertainment. Bsns W p 102+ F 23 '63
Expense-account meals: what the rules really are. il U S News 54:96+ Mr 4 '63
Fade out; TV cartoon on tax cheats. il Newsweek 61:48 Ap 1 '63
Foundations as a tax dodge. F. J. Cook. Nation 196:321-5 Ap 20 '63; Reply. J. Williams. 196:inside cover My 18 '63
Great Treasury raid, by P. M. Stern. Review
Sat R 47:30-1 Ap 11 '64. H. S. Taylor
Impact of office automation in the Internal revenue service. R. W. Riche and J. R. Alliston. il Mo Labor R 86:388-93 Ap '63
Is taxpayers revolt brewing? il U S News 54:37-9 Ap 8 '63
Mr Wormser's charter; excerpts from letter to commissioner of the IRS. R. Wormser. Nat R 16:523-4 Je 30 '64
Money men in key spots. Newsweek 65:63 Ja 11 '65
New order to revenue men: make taxpayers happier. il U S News 56:96 My 18 '64
New tax detective: a gimlet-eyed machine. il Bsns W p96-7 F 8 '64
Personal business; deducting travel and entertainment expenses. Bsns W p89 Ap 6 '63
Phantom tax swindlers. K. Wheeler. il Life 54:81-2+ Ap 12 '63
Pulling the tax punch; new regulations. il Bsns W p34 Ap 6 '63
Some deductions. D. T. Bazelon. Commentary 38:67-8 Ag '64
Tax deductions under the new law; with explanation by M. M. Caplin. B. Mills. il Motor B 111:50-1+ Mr '63
Tax men get another earful on expense-account rules. il U S News 54:109-12 My 20 '63
Tax service's numbers game: it's not going so well. U S News 57:79-82 N 2 '64

UNITED STATES—Internal revenue service
—*Continued*
Taxpayers under the microscope. F. J. Cook. il N Y Times Mag p20+ Ap 12 '64
What IRS will look for if they audit your tax return. F. Bailey, jr. Suc Farm 62:39 Ja '64
What new tax law will mean; interview. M. M. Caplin. Nations Bsns 52:38-9+ F '64
Windfall for conspiracy. R. J. Barber. il Nation 199:332-3 N 9 '64
With a business gleam in his eye; IRS rules on expense accounts. il Newsweek 61:67 Ap 8 '63

Interstate commerce commission

Back on the sidetrack again; President's plan. il Time 82:10-11 Ag 2 '63
Freight rates go up piecemeal; on less-than-carload business. Bsns W p32 Mr 30 '63
Green light for piggybacking. Bsns W p95 Ag 31 '63
Green light for rail mergers? Seaboard-Coast line tie-up. il Bsns W p82 D 21 '63
Hope dims for rail settlement; work-rules dispute. Bsns W p24 Ag 3 '63
Merger spooks and spitballs: a look behind the moratorium mirage; address, June 22, 1963. D. P. Loomis. Vital Speeches 29:623-5 Ag 1 '63
Moving rules stymied at least for a time. Consumer Rep 29:412 S '64
New merger plan stuns railroads; Pennsy-Central consolidation opposed. Bsns W p27 O 5 '63
New turn in the battle of the ports; railroad freight rates. U S News 54:11 Je 3 '63
Pennsy takes a gamble; sells holdings in the Norfolk & Western and the Wabash. Bsns W p31 S 19 '64
Rail strike: strategy still is to delay. il Bsns W p22-3 Jl 27 '63
Some new rules of etiquette for moving men. Consumer Rep 29:329 Jl '64
Tough line on line on rail, air mergers; from intergovernmental committee. Bsns W p 140 Mr 16 '63
Until August 29. Newsweek 62:23 Ag 5 '63
Where the rails stand in merger movement. il Bsns W p60-2 Ag 3 '63
Will unions lose rail dispute. il U S News 55:89-91 Ag 5 '63

Job corps

Coming: a crisis for young workers; Labor dept. study. il Bsns W p27 F 16 '63
Forestry's role in youth conservation. W. G. Magnuson. Am For 70:12-14 Ag '64
Here come the boys! J. Prokop. il Am For 70:12-14+ O '64
Hope for Hucklebuck. Time 84:33-4 D 11 '64
If you're male or married; with letter by J. F. Carroll. E. Geller. Library J 89:4952+ D 15 '64
It's D-day for war on poverty. Bsns W p 126 N 28 '64
Poverty war draws business' best; top-level manpower for urban training centers. il Bsns W p23-4 D 19 '64
Putting teens to work; Job corps, President's anti-poverty program. Bsns W p82 Je 6 '64
Surplus youth; a future without jobs. J. S. Coleman. il Nation 196:439-43 My 25 '63
This month's feature: Administration's youth employment bill. Cong Digest 42:291-310 D '63
War on poverty; the first shots. il Newsweek 64:71-4+ D 14 '64
Youth corps bill gets fresh start; new version of New deal's CCC. il Bsns W p79-80 Mr 30 '63
Youth employment act. Nat Parks Mag 37:25 Ap '63

Joint chiefs of staff

Case of McNamara and the joint chiefs. J. Alsop. Read Digest 83:102-3 Jl '63
Expert looks at the joint chiefs; pros and cons of military unification. R. L. Gilpatric. il N Y Times Mag p 11+ Mr 29 '64
House unit to approve four-year term for JCS; veto threatened. R. G. O'Lone. Aviation W 79:32 O 28 '63
JCS shape future weapon concepts. il Miss & Roc 12:91-3 Mr 25 '63
Military chiefs give views on treaty. Aviation W 79:29 Ag 26 '63
Needed: a hot line from military to Congress? M. S. Johnson. il U S News 55:70-1 S 23 '63
Pentagon changes spark an uproar. il U S News 54:21 My 20 '63
Speaking out; strategy and the defense intellectuals. T. D. White. Sat Eve Post 236:10+ My 4 '63
U.S. nuclear team; Joint strategic target planning staff; address, May 14, 1964. T. S. Power. Vital Speeches 30:552-5 Jl 1 '64
Wisdom of test ban: McNamara and the joint chiefs differed. il U S News 55:36 Ag 5 '63

Justice, Department of

Antitrust lunges again at fair trade. Bsns W p20+ Jl 4 '64
As civil rights moves ahead: how business may be policed; Attorney General. il U S News 55:55 N 11 '63
Burke Marshall: quiet fighter for civil rights. S. Booker. il Ebony 19:90-2+ My '64
Crimson in Alabama. Newsweek 62:35 N 25 '63
Department of justice. T. Coffin. il Holiday 33:94-5+ Mr '63
Here we go again; more investigations. W. F. Buckley, jr. Nat R 15:272 O 8 '63
If the Kennedys get the power they ask; role of Attorney General. U S News 55:49-50 Jl 8 '63
Nine young men in charge of integrating America: Attorney General and "general staff." il U S News 55:58-61 Jl 29 '63
Rendezvous of the federal prosecutors. M. Kempton. New Repub 150:6-7 Ap 18 '64
Riot squad for the New frontier. J. Kraft. Harper 227:69-75 Ag '63
Will pension trial bring Hoffa's ouster? Bsns W p53-4 Ap 25 '64

Antitrust division

Antitrust turns tougher. il Bsns W p98-100+ S 12 '64
Humble on its own in West; Tidewater deal off. Bsns W p 28 My 9 '64
Justice gets some sharper teeth; Supreme court decisions reversing mergers approved by regulatory agencies. Bsns W p29-30 Ap 11 '64
Kennedy's musical chairs; antitrust and FCC get new heads. il Bsns W p28 My 18 '63
More power for trustbusters. Time 82:75 S 6 '63
New antitrust chief's goal: more power to police your business; interview. W. H. Orrick, jr. Nations Bsns 51:38-9+ O '63
New crackdown on business? il U S News 56:39-41 My 25 '64
New trust-buster. Newsweek 61:80-1 My 27 '63
Parting the curtains. Newsweek 63:66-7 F 10 '64
Steel gets hit with the big one; Justice dept.'s trustbusters charging producers with price-fixing. il Bsns W p27-8 Ap 11 '64
Steel price increases prompt antitrust probe. Bsns W p25 O 26 '63
What's next in antitrust? interview, ed. by G. R. Rosen. W. H. Orrick, jr. Duns R 83:35-6+ Je '64

Civil rights division

Changing the guard at Justice; appointment of J. Doar. il Time 85:47 Ja 1 '65
Room 5115: Civil rights G.H.Q. il N Y Times Mag p8-9 Jl 7 '63

Labor, Department of

Department of labor. J. D. Weaver. il Holiday 33:78-9+ F '63
Labor department. America 108:289 Mr 2 '63
Labor department marks fifty. il Sr Schol 82:7+ F 27 '63
Learning the needs of youth; Labor dept. summer program to train job counselors. il Bsns W p31 Ag 15 '64
See also
United States—Federal mediation and conciliation service

Anecdotes, facetiae, satire, etc.

One day in the life of James Hoover. J. Hoover. New Yorker 39:76+ Ag 17 '63

Youth opportunity program

Snoops; private lives and public service. J. Ridgeway. New Repub 151:13-17 D 19 '64; Discussion. 152:22 Ja 2; 28-30 Ja 9 '65

Labor policy

Disappointed over Kennedy; AFL-CIO disenchantment. Bsns W p46 Mr 2 '63
Early warning system in labor; Taft-Hartley advisory panel. Bsns W p26-7 Je 1 '63
How union leaders feel about Johnson now. il U S News 56:86-7 Mr 2 '64
Johnson gives labor the word; union chiefs at White House. il Bsns W p25-6 My 9 '64
Labor and the defense economy. Nation 196:518 Je 22 '63
Labor experts urge new policies; interviews. G. D. Reilly; G. Farmer. il Nations Bsns 51:66-8+ Ap '63
Labor monopoly policy reconsidered; excerpt from address. S. Rottenberg. Mo Labor R 86:139 F '63

UNITED STATES—Labor policy—*Continued*

Labor relations; role of government; address, August 27, 1964. C. Donahue. Vital Speeches 30:751-5 O 1 '64

This issue is clear so is the strategy. Nations Bsns 51:96-7 F '63

Union friends dominate federal labor panels. il Nations Bsns 51:56-8+ F '63

U.S. manpower and employment policy. M. S. Gordon. bibliog f Mo Labor R 87:1314-21 N '64

When the time comes. . . Time 83:24 Ap 3 '64

Will the guideposts stick? M. M. Mestrovic. il Duns R 84:41-2+ Jl '64

See also

Labor laws and legislation—United States

United States—National labor relations board

Labor statistics, Bureau of

BLS occupational trend projections: an appraisal; excerpt from address, June 27, 1963. H. Goldstein. Mo Labor R 86:1135-8 O '63

Catching up with our new habits; revision of the CPI. il Bsns W p 112-13+ Mr 7 '64

Competition keeps the price boosts down. Bsns W p29-30 My 4 '63

Scientific and technical personnel in atomic energy. H. S. Liebling and A. Katz. il Mo Labor R 87:633-8 Je '64

What makes workers migrate; Labor dept. study. il Bsns W p61 O 3 '64

Land management, Bureau of

BLM on the move. Am For 70:9 My '64

Forester to head BLM. J. B. Craig. il Am For 69:4-5+ Je '63

Jackrabbit homesteading; retirement site from U.S. Department of the interior, Bureau of land management. S. Cochell. Sr Schol 84:12T F 7 '64

New hope for public land watersheds; Vale project. R. E. Getty. il Am For 70:14-19 D '64

Take a look at the land you own; BLM lands. C. H. Callison. il Audubon Mag 66:302-3 S '64

Library of Congress

Annual report of the librarian of Congress; summary. Wilson Lib Bul 38:815+ Je '64

Automation may rescue library from data flood. Sci N L 85:89 F 8 '64

Automation report made to LC; concerning survey team's report, Automation and the Library of Congress. Wilson Lib Bul 38:523+ Mr '64

Cards-with-books program. J. H. Treyz. il ALA Bul 57:433-4 My '63

Chamber music festival at Library of Congress. il Américas 16:39 O '64

43,000,000 documents that rose from ashes. il Sr Schol 85:5 Ja 21 '65

The Fourth; Jefferson's replacement library for LC. R. Stokes. Library J 88:2648 Jl '63

From the Library of Congress: union catalog of microfilms. E. Hamer and A. McCormick. ALA Bul 57:1017-19 D '63

Librarian of Congress asks for tax break for LC Fired scholar brings suit against Library of Congress. Library J 88:1636+ Ap 15 '63

Library, asylum, platform for uninhibited leaps; address, February 15, 1963. K. Shapiro. il Wilson Lib Bul 37:661-9 Ap '63

Library of Congress. il Library J 90:47-55 Ja 1 '65

LC and ARL announce plans for register of microfilms. Library J 88:4599-600 D 1 '63

LC and automation; concerning survey team's report, Automation and the Library of Congress. M. J. Voigt. il Library J 89:1022-5 Mr 1 '64

Library of Congress and its widening service. C. B. Grannis. Pub W 183:37 Ap 1 '63

Library of Congress: automation urged for bibliographic control but not prescribed as a panacea. J. Walsh. Science 143:452-5 Ja 31 '64

LC creates assistant librarian's post. Library J 88:753 F 15 '63

Library of Congress issues automation conference text. Pub W 186:24 O 26 '64

Library of Congress plans register of microfilms. Pub W 184:26 D 16 '63

Library of Congress report outlines automation possibilities. Library J 89:820+ F 15 '64

LC studies use of perforated tape for reproduction of catalog cards. Library J 89:2303-4 Je 1 '64

LC's space needs become desperate as holdings and services expand. Library J 89:2302 Je 1 '64

Luckless Library of Congress. A. L. Todd. il Sat R 47:24+ Ap 11 '64

National archives of sound recordings? H. Spivacke. il Library J 88:3783-8 O 15 '63

Role of LC. V. Clapp. ALA Bul 58:536 Je '64

Science advice: new division for science policy research set up in LRS to aid Congress. J. Walsh. Science 145:1162-4 S 11 '64

Science policy research division established at Library of Congress. Library J 89:3708 O 1 '64

Toward understanding of the Library of Congress. F. H. Wagman. ALA Bul 57:322-3 Ap '63

Virginia Haviland resigns for permanent post at LC. Library J 89:338 Ja 15 '64

Washington report: from the Library of Congress. E. Hamer. ALA Bul 57:499-500, 638-9, 825-6 Je-Jl, O '63

Washington report: from the Library of Congress. E. E. Hamer and A. McCormick. ALA Bul 57:1017-19; 58:24-5, 97-8, 356-8, 464-6, 602-4, 682-4, 773-4, 988; 59:23 D '63-F, My-O, D '64-Ja '65

Washington report; from the Library of Congress; automation report published. E. Hamer and A. McCormick. ALA Bul 58:184-6 Mr '64

Yung Lo encyclopedia presented to Library of Congress. R. Hilsman; R. D. Rogers. Dept State Bul 49:740 N 11 '63

Appropriations and expenditures

LC returns nearly $4 million to U.S. treasury in 1962. Library J 88:1636 Ap 15 '63

Substantial budget increase approved for Library of Congress. Library J 89:584+ F 1 '64

Catalogs

Manuscript catalog research manual aided by Council on library resources; Library of Congress and the American library association's Library technology project, respectively. Library J 89:829 F 15 '64

Gifts, legacies, etc.

John Secrist collection at the Library of Congress. A. Favia-Artsay. il Hobbies 68:30-2 Je; 30-1+ Jl '63

Library of Congress given 700 rare books; Lessing J. Rosenwald collection. Pub W 186:34 Ag 10 '64

Secrist collection given to Library of Congress. Hobbies 68:124-5 My '63

Manuscript division

Annual report of the manuscripts division of the Library of Congress; excerpts from 1963 Library of Congress journal of current acquisitions; ed. by K. V. Hostick. Hobbies 69:110-11+ S '64

LC expands photocopying program of European manuscripts & archives. Library J 88:1496-8 Ap 1 '63

Union catalog

Program for shared cataloging to be developed by ARL; committee. with Library of Congress. Library J 89:1046 Mr 1 '64

Sharing the cataloging load; planning committee of ARL with LC. Wilson Lib Bul 38:525+ Mr '64

Literary landmarks

See Literary landmarks—United States

Literature

See American literature

Los Alamos scientific laboratory

See United States—Scientific laboratory, Los Alamos, N.Mex.

Manners and customs

See United States—Social life and customs

Maps

Map of the United States (cont) Sr Schol 83:26 O 4 '63; 85:30 O 7 '64

Maps and charts; pressure from private firm may bring rise in government's prices. E. Langer. Science 140:373+ Ap 26 '63

Marine corps

Are the marines really ready to fight? il U S News 57:59-60 N 9 '64

Author says he had plenty to yell about. J. R. McDermott. il Life 55:40+ Ag 16 '63

Beyond the way-out horizon. Time 82:37 O 4 '63

Inconstant marines; case of Capt. Jackson and Lieut. Szili. New Repub 148:3-4 My 11 '63

UNITED STATES—Marine corps—*Continued*
JFK's peace corps. il Newsweek 61:23 F 25 '63
Keep in shape with the marines; women. il McCalls 91:124-5+ O '63
Marine corps and the foreign service: a working partnership; address, October 16, 1964. D. Rusk. Dept State Bul 51:643-5 N 2 '64
Marine justice; Colonel Heinl administratively censured in the case of the killing at Guantanamo. New Repub 148:7 Je 1 '63
Marines landed too; sentimental journey to New Zealand. R. Sherrod. il Sat Eve Post 236:30+ Ap 27 '63
Occurrence at Guantanamo; shooting of Ruben Lopez, an alleged Castro spy. Nation 196:386 My 11 '63; Reply. M. F. Walter. 196: 529 Je 22 '63
These leathernecks had feet to match. R. Wallace. il Life 54:78+ F 22 '63
Top marine with space-age ideas. U S News 55:30 O 7 '63
Toughest marine; with report by D. N. Hamblen. C. S. Wren. il Look 28:36-40 My 5 '64
Violence and silence; case of Rubén Lopez at the U.S. naval base, Guantánamo Bay. Newsweek 61:31-2 My 13 '63
See also
Iwo Jima, Battle of, 1945

Maritime administration

Who shall watch the watchman? Nation 197: 190 O 5 '63

Meteorological applications

Weather computers. R. C. Cowen. il Nation 198:71-3 Ja 20 '64; Same abr. with title Needed, umbrella weather forecasting. Sci Digest 55:25-9 Ap '64

Military air transport service

Big lift completed without major hitch. C. Brownlow. Aviation W 79:58-9+ N 11 '63
Big lift tests army, USAF flexibilities; with editorial comment. Aviation W 79:17, 26-7 O 28 '63
Exercise big lift: opening a 5,700-mile air bridge to Europe; with analysis by M. S. Johnson. M. L. Stone and T. J. O'Halloran. il U S News 55:36-9 N 4 '63
Mercy takes to flight; aeromedical evacuation. J. P. Heffernan. il Todays Health 41:30-4+ Ap '63
Strong MATS influence on airlines noted. L. Booda. Aviation W 79:65+ O 7 '63
Those air lifts. Nation 198:338 Ap 6 '64

Military policy

See United States—Defenses

Mint

Cash in your travels. J. H. Winchester. Travel 123:58-60 Ja '65

Moral conditions

American condition. Nation 197:425 D 21 '63
College morals mirror our society. G. Hechinger and F. M. Hechinger. il N Y Times Mag p22+ Ap 14 '63
Danger from within. D. D. Eisenhower. Read Digest 82:76-82 Mr '63
Ethics in an affluent society; address, October 17, 1963. C. McWilliams. Wilson Lib Bul 38:471-7+ F '64
Face of the future; quotations by Americans aged eighteen to twenty-five. il Look 29:72-4+ Ja 12 '65
False faces for freedom. H. Seifert. Christian Cent 81:1265-7 O 14 '64
Morality USA. J. R. Moskin. il Look 27: 74-8+ S 24 '63; Discussion. 27:15+ N 5 '63; America 109:277-8 S 21 '63
Non-extremism in pursuit of virtue. Nat R 16:1049-50 D 1 '64
Pseudo-ethic, by M. Halsey. Review
Sat R 46:34 O 19 '63. E. Capouya
Rising GMP. Reporter 28:20 Mr 14 '63
Sampler of American scandal! symposium. il Esquire 61:82-95+ Ap '64
Sexuality in crisis. L. J. Averill. Christian Cent 80:1196-9 O 2 '63
Speaking out; hate knows no direction. R. E. McGill. Sat Eve Post 236:8+ D 14 '63
Twisted age. S. Grafton. il Look 28:36-40+ D 15 '64
Vice vs. virtue, a Puritan remembrancer. il Am Heritage 15:72-9 D '63
Woman writer takes a critical look at America; reprint. M. Craig. U S News 56:78 Mr 2 '64
See also
Crime and criminals—United States

Narcotics, Bureau of

Narcotic and drug abuse: report of Advisory commission prescribes for old problems, new dangers. J. Walsh. Science 143:662-6 F 14 '64; Discussion. 144:135-6 Ap 10 '64
New approach; more humane treatment. il Newsweek 61:94 Ap 15 '63

National academy of foreign affairs (proposed)

Department supports bill to establish National academy of foreign affairs; statements, April 4, 1963. G. W. Ball; W. H. Orrick, jr. Dept State Bul 48:619-24 Ap 22 '63
Education for the new diplomacy; address, March 2, 1963. R. E. Lee. Dept State Bul 48:423-7 Mr 25 '63
Memorandum from Secretary Rusk. D. Rusk. Dept State Bul 48:429-31 Mr 25 '63
Panel recommends National academy of foreign affairs. Dept State Bul 48:47 Ja 14 '63
President transmits proposal for Academy of foreign affairs; letter to Lyndon B. Johnson, February 11, 1963. J. F. Kennedy. Dept State Bul 48:427-9 Mr 25 '63

National academy of sciences

See National academy of sciences

National advisory board council for grazing districts

Grazers set policy. il Am For 69:46-7 My '63

National aeronautics and space administration

Access to international brainpower accrues from cooperative projects; NASA-ESRO collaboration. il Miss & Roc 13:149-50 N 25 '63
After moon landing, what next? NASA's dream projects. il Bsns W p 104+ Mr 28 '64
Agreement reached on MOL status, NASA to continue station studies. Aviation W 80:28 Ja 6 '64
AF officers to bolster Apollo management. W. J. Normyle. Aviation W 81:22 Ag 24 '64
Apollo environment attacked. R. Hawkes. Miss & Roc 12:14 My 6 '63
Astronauts, top NASA leadership split over attempting MA-10 shot. il Miss & Roc 12: 16-17 My 27 '63
Boston center finds Capitol critics; with editorial comment by W. J. Coughlin. W. Beller. il Miss & Roc 12:18-19, 50 Ap 22 '63
Buildings for the space program; how NASA deals with architects and engineers. il Arch Rec 133:147-54 Ja '63
Coincidence? opposition to the moon race. Nation 196:433 My 25 '63
Computer pool fought. Sci N L 84:77 Ag 3 '63
Cuts for glamor twins; space and research. Bsns W p31 O 12 '63
Dark clouds in space; fourth national symposium. il Bsns W p 116+ My 9 '64
Directory of key NASA personnel. Miss & Roc 13:235-6+ N 25 '63
Eight vie for Pioneer solar probe. Miss & Roc 12:17 Mr 11 '63
F-1 troubles won't delay Saturn. V. H. Taylor. il Miss & Roc 12:16 Mr 11 '63
Fighting to keep foothold in space. Bsns W p29 Ap 13 '63
Fortunes of NASA; flight of the Mariner IV to Mars. Nation 199:478-9 D 21 '64
Glider may be post-Apollo guinea pig. R. Hawkes. il Miss & Roc 12:26-7 F 11 '63
G&C NASA systems; early programs furnish advanced system fundamentals. il Miss & Roc 13:52-3 O 7 '63
G&C people and places; key contacts in NASA and military. Miss & Roc 13:73 O 7 '63
Hatching our giant space birds; Saturn boosters of Michoud plant. il Bsns W p57-61 Ja 4 '64
Holmes resigns, refuses curb on manned flight authority. A. P. Alibrando. Aviation W 78: 37 Je 17 '63
Hot rocket to nowhere; Project Rover. G. Bylinsky and W. E. Howard. il Sat Eve Post 236:78-81 N 9 '63
House group studies NASA role as Comsat corp. technical adviser. K. Johnsen. Aviation W 80:32 Ap 13 '64
House unit to probe NASA fund shifts. A. P. Alibrando. Aviation W 78:38-9 F 18 '63
How industry can adapt space inventions. il Sci Digest 56:32-3 D '64
Industrial laxness and space waste; Project Mercury report. Sat Eve Post 236:82 N 2 '63

UNITED STATES—National aeronautics and space administration—*Continued*
Is U. S. lagging in the moon race? il U S News 54:60-3 Ap 15 '63
Kennedy plan stirs attack on space funds. A. P. Alibrando. Aviation W 79:29-30 O 7 '63
Large vehicles altar handling concepts. il Aviation W 79:303+ Jl 22 '63
MA-9 boosts hopes for tenth mission. il Miss & Roc 12:10+ My 20 '63
Man for the moon. Newsweek 62:45 Ag 5 '63
Manned Gemini shots top schedule. H. Taylor. il Miss & Roc 15:14 D 21 '64
MOSS planning faces slippage. H. Taylor. Miss & Roc 13:14 Jl 15 '63
Mission growth planned for biosatellite. E. H. Kolcum. il Aviation W 79:20-1 D 30 '63
Moon minus one; resignation of D. B. Holmes. Newsweek 61:68 Je 24 '63
More in '64. Newsweek 63:44 Ja 6 '64
National aeronautics and space administration; charts of organization. Miss & Roc 13:168-70+ Jl 29 '63
NASA. Miss & Roc 13:41-6+ N 25 '63; 15:43-9+ N 30 '64
NASA asks for bids on Biosatellite study. H. M. David. Miss & Roc 12:20 Mr 11 '63
NASA bioscience duties pinpointed. H. M. David. il Miss & Roc 12:32-3 F 4 '63
NASA biotechnology unit meets at Ames. Aviation W 78:103 My 6 '63
NASA, Boeing resuming life-support tests. H. M. David. il Miss & Roc 14:28-9 Ja 27 '64
NASA cites aircraft avionics research. Aviation W 79:121 S 16 '63
NASA Comsat aid opposed in Congress. K. Johnsen. Aviation W 78:30 F 25 '63
NASA confirms delay in Gemini. Aviation W 81:34 S 21 '64
NASA consolidates launch management. Aviation W 82:26 Ja 11 '65
NASA defends oxygen atmosphere for Apollo. Miss & Roc 12:15 My 13 '63
NASA fires a blast; Project Mercury. il Bsns W p30 O 12 '63
NASA flies into rough air. il Bsns W p62-3 Jl 6 '63
NASA focuses on three aircraft areas. E. H. Kolcum. il Aviation W 79:58-60 Ag 5 '63
NASA hopeful on lunar flare feasibility. C. M. Plattner. il Aviation W 81:32-3 D 28 '64
NASA industrial cities. Sci N L 83:98 F 16 '63
NASA laser communications, tracking effort to double in FY '64. M. Getler. il Miss & Roc 13:22-3 N 18 '63
NASA lauds industry performance in Project Mercury production tasks. il Miss & Roc 13:14-16 O 14 '63
NASA may get a military arm. H. M. David. Miss & Roc 13:14 Ag 5 '63
NASA moves to develop ramjet. H. Taylor. Miss & Roc 15:17 N 23 '64
NASA must decide Orion future. W. E. Wilks. il Miss & Roc 15:12-14 D 14 '64
NASA near decision on whether to impact or fly by Mars in '66. H. M. David. il Miss & Roc 14:21 Ja 20 '64
NASA needs a watchdog. R. Hotz. Aviation W 78:21 F 18 '63
NASA outlines Boston center plans. M. Getler. Miss & Roc 12:16-17 Mr 18 '63
NASA planning group approves Apollo X organizational structure. Aviation W 81:14 D 28 '64
NASA planning Mars expedition. W. Burkett. il Miss & Roc 12:34+ My 13 '63
NASA plans for future hinge on three programs. il Miss & Roc 12:43-6+ My 20 '63
NASA plans new technological satellite. E. H. Kolcum. Aviation W 80:26 F 17 '64
NASA plans; special report. il Miss & Roc 12:14-18 F 18 '63
NASA plans variety of Apollo backup systems. Miss & Roc 14:16 Mr 2 '64
NASA reorganization to bring centers under tighter control. Aviation W 79:28 O 14 '63
NASA reshuffles headquarters. H. Taylor. Miss & Roc 13:12 O 14 '63
NASA reveals list of new study projects. Miss & Roc 12:13 F 18 '63
NASA seeking to buy JetStar, expand fleet of aircraft to eighty. il Aviation W 81:18 Jl 20 '64
NASA seeks space station parameters. I. Stone. il Aviation W 78:70-3 Ap 1 '63
NASA seen winning in AMR dispute. Miss & Roc 12:16 My 20 '63
NASA speeds to fill gap in availability of big telescopes. H. Taylor. Miss & Roc 15:17 S 21 '64
NASA starts manned station studies. H. Taylor. il Miss & Roc 12:18-19 Ap 29 '63
NASA studies locomotion, protection. Miss & Roc 14:28 Ap 20 '64
NASA technology utilization scrutiny due. A. P. Alibrando. Aviation W 79:28-9 Ag 5 '63
NASA weighs MA-10 possibility. H. Taylor. il Miss & Roc 12:14 Ap 1 '63
NASA's Lunar logistics system likely to be postponed. H. Taylor. Miss & Roc 12:21 Je 24 '63
National space policy; excerpts from address. E. C. Welsh. Aviation W 80:21 Mr 2 '64
New Houston control facility may direct Gemini sooner than planned; Integrated mission control center. M. Getler. Miss & Roc 13:32-4 Jl 8 '63
New NASA program would fund university satellite development. Aviation W 81:35 O 19 '64
Off target. H. T. Simmons. il Newsweek 62:73 S 23 '63
Off to the moon with a Russian? il U S News 55:60 O 7 '63
On the road to the moon; more spectaculars ahead. il U S News 56:74-6 Ja 13 '64
Outlook better for flight research center. Miss & Roc 13:16 Jl 8 '63
Pact clarifies NASA, DOD roles at Cape. G. Alexander. Aviation W 78:62 Mr 4 '63
Patents; proposal to change NASA regulations. E. Langer. Science 139:1188 Mr 22 '63
Perfect launching; and then a near miss; Syncom into orbit. il Bsns W p61 F 23 '63
Physics of solar flares dissected at symposium. W. Beller. Miss & Roc 13:17 N 4 '63
Pie-in-the-sky; Program plans conference. Newsweek 61:56 F 25 '63
Plan for sharing know-how pressed. Miss & Roc 12:15 Mr 18 '63
Planning ahead. il Newsweek 61:98+ Mr 25 '63
Policy and the scientists. L. A. Dubridge. For Affairs 41:580-1 Ap '63
Probe focuses on NASA-JPL relationship. D. E. Fink. Aviation W 80:29 Ap 27 '64
Profiles; John R. Pierce and Project Echo. C. Tomkins. New Yorker 39:49-50+ S 21 '63
Proposals requested for first study of lunar base systems. Miss & Roc 14:13 Mr 23 '64
Ranger management compromise sought. W. J. Normyle. Aviation W 80:25-6 Je 22 '64
Ranger: oversight subcommittee asks why NASA doesn't prevail on JPL to rigidize projectwise. J. Walsh. Science 144:824-6 My 15 '64
Reasonable man. W. J. Coughlin. Miss & Roc 14:46 Mr 2 '64
Reorganization prompts closer liaison. Miss & Roc 12:59-60 Mr 25 '63
Report on space programs. il Bul Atomic Sci 19:18-25 My '63
Revolution isn't coming, it is already here. J. Dille. il Life 57:94-5+ S 25 '64
Rover slips extra fourteen-sixteen months. F. G. McGuire. il Miss & Roc 12:14-15 Mr 11 '63
Scientists, employes honored by NASA. Aviation W 79:72 O 21 '63
Senate may scrutinize NASA patent waiving. Miss & Roc 16:14 Ja 4 '65
Slow-down in the Pentagon. H. W. Baldwin. For Affairs 43:266-7 Ja '65
Sniping at NASA on space. il Bsns W p92-4+ My 11 '63
Snooping in the park; investigatory techniques. J. Ridgeway. New Repub 152:9-10 Ja 16 '65
Something for Boston; electronics center. W. J. Coughlin. Miss & Roc 13:46 Ag 5 '63
Space agency nears decision on adopting parts qualification list. Miss & Roc 14:17 Ap 20 '64
Space exploration; address, June 7, 1964. J. E. Webb. Vital Speeches 30:620-3 Ag 1 '64
Space isn't for publicity. Bsns W p 168 My 25 '63
Space program: skepticism grows but in context of cold war it is hard for Congress to say no. D. S. Greenberg. Science 139:890-1 Mr 8 '63; Reply with rejoinder. I. S. Menzies. 140:937 My 31 '63
Space science, research effort grows but failures beset lunar missions. A. Alibrando. il Aviation W 78:124-5+ Mr 11 '63
Space slowdown via defective parts? concerning final report on Project Mercury. Sr Schol 83:18 N 15 '63
STL's Mueller replaces Holmes. Aviation W 79:26 Jl 29 '63
Step forward; coordinating space medicine. W. J. Coughlin. Miss & Roc 14:46 Mr 9 '64

UNITED STATES—National aeronautics and space administration—*Continued*
Strike halts Merritt Island work. Aviation W 79:38 S 16 '63
Structure problems of 70s listed. Miss & Roc 13:16-17 S 2 '63
Surveying surveyor. W. J. Coughlin. Miss & Roc 13:46 Ag 12 '63
Syncom II: hovering 22,500 miles up. il Bsns W p26 Ag 3 '63
System will rate contractors. H. Taylor. il Miss & Roc 12:14 F 11 '63
Tighter control over JPL urged in report of House space committee. H. M. David. Miss & Roc 14:15 Je 22 '64
Transforming the Cape into a spaceport. il Bsns W p56-60+ Ap 6 '63
Trouble at the controls. il Newsweek 61:74 Je 3 '63
U.S. alters advanced space plan focus; with editorial comment. D. E. Fink. Aviation W 81:17, 22 S 21 '64
U.S. shifts goals in space. il U S News 55:39-40 N 11 '63
U.S. space management in flux. Miss & Roc 13:12 Jl 22 '63
U.S. to select orbiting lab or lunar base; report of NASA-Industry conference. E. H. Kolcum. Aviation W 78:32-4 F 18 '63
USAF keys space plan to three programs. E. H. Kolcum. il Aviation W 78:26-8 Ja 28 '63
We are moving from preparation to fruition; with editorial comment. J. W. Webb. Miss & Roc 13:37, 262 N 25 '63
White House blocks Apollo slowdown. H. Taylor. Miss & Roc 13:16 D 9 '63
Why the moon race is slowing down. il U S News 55:38-41 O 28 '63
See also
Space flight centers

Ames research center

Ames will need new magnetic field facilities to fulfill role. il Miss & Roc 13:204-9 N 25 '63
New instrument is heart of Ames momentum test. Miss & Roc 13:22-3 S 9 '63
Three-man centrifuge to be new Ames research nucleus. R. Lindsey. il Miss & Roc 12:27 Je 3 '63

Appropriations and expenditures

Action on NASA supplemental delayed. Aviation W 80:20 Mr 9 '64
Aerospace budget. R. Hotz. Aviation W 80:21 Ja 20 '64
Apollo funding stresses fabrication. H. Taylor. il Miss & Roc 12:16-17 F 4 '63
Apollo, Gemini to cost $4 billion yearly. A. P. Alibrando. Aviation W 78:31 Ap 1 '63
Apollo has trouble on earth; lunar landing programs. il Bsns W p54-5 S 14 '63
Apollo in trouble despite increase. il Miss & Roc 14:17 Ja 27 '64
Are we wasting billions in space? S. H. Loory. il Sat Eve Post 236:13-15 S 14 '63
Candidates' records on defense and space bills. il Miss & Roc 15:16 O 19 '64
Communications, tracking to mushroom as electronics tab reaches $60 million. il Miss & Roc 13:42-6+ N 25 '63
Congress may ease NASA budget cuts. A. P. Alibrando. Aviation W 79:322-3 Jl 22 '63
Congressional committees predict quick action on NASA money bill. Aviation W 80:27 F 3 '64
Cut in NASA budget to $5.2 billion is seen; some key congressmen resent warnings. A. P. Alibrando. il Aviation W 80:32-4 Ja 27 '64
Democrats try to ease NASA funds cut. A. P. Alibrando. Aviation W 78:32 Ap 8 '63
DOD ponders new cut in solid funds. H. Taylor. Miss & Roc 13:16-17 Jl 8 '63
FY '65 Apollo funds threatened; with editorial comment. Miss & Roc 13:14, 46 N 4 '63
FY '65 budget; programs at a glance. il Miss & Roc 14:18-19 Ja 27 '64
FY '65 space request is $7.2 billion. Miss & Roc 14:15 Ja 13 '64
$5.445 billion vital to moon goal. H. Taylor. il Miss & Roc 14:14-15 Ja 20 '64
$5.1-billion NASA bill would delay lunar program two to three years. H. M. David. Miss & Roc 13:13 O 14 '63
$5.19 billion voted for NASA. Miss & Roc 13:14 N 18 '63
$5.35-billion NASA budget authorized. A. P. Alibrando. il Aviation W 79:18-19 S 2 '63
Fund-cut threatens plan to ask for $250-million supplemental funding. il Miss & Roc 13:92-3+ N 25 '63
Fund cuts may forfeit moon race. Miss & Roc 12:15 Mr 4 '63
Funding forces one-year Apollo delay. E. H. Kolcum. Aviation W 80:26 Ja 13 '64
Glamour masks waste in space spending. W. Proxmire. il Nations Bsns 51:38-9+ N '63
House considers $5.2 billion for NASA. E. H. Kolcum. Aviation W 79:37 Ag 5 '63
House declines to act on space bill; Senate to set money limit. il Aviation W 80:24 My 25 '64
How haste in space makes waste. J. A. Morris. il Read Digest 85:82-7 Jl '64
Industry to get 3/4 of funds; NASA plans. il Miss & Roc 12:17-18 F 18 '63
JFK at the controls. Newsweek 62:98 O 21 '63
JFK proposal threat to space funds; with editorial comment. H. Taylor. il Miss & Roc 13:25-6, 86 S 30 '63
Kennedy's offer stirs confusion, dismay; with editorial comment. A. P. Alibrando. Aviation W 79:21, 26-7 S 30 '63
Lessons from the Hill. W. J. Coughlin. Miss & Roc 13:50 S 9 '63
Lunik boosts NASA funding hopes. H. Taylor. il Miss & Roc 12:14-15 Ap 8 '63
Manned network gets major push; detailed breakdown of NASA FY '65 R&D budget. Miss & Roc 14:18-19 F 17 '64
Move to slash Apollo funds 10 per cent is narrowly defeated in Senate; with editorial comment. Aviation W 80:11, 25 Je 29 '64
NASA allocations to universities questioned by Senate committee. Aviation W 81:25 Jl 13 '64
NASA and education; fast growth stirs Senate committee to place brakes on new university grants. D. S. Greenberg. Science 142:1042 N 22 '63; Reply. H. L. Dryden. 143:427 Ja 31 '64
NASA asks $800 million for construction. A. P. Alibrando. il Aviation W 78:37-9 F 25 '63
NASA authorization bill peaking near $5.36 billion. H. M. David. il Miss & Roc 13:13 Ag 12 '63
NASA budget little damaged so far. H. M. David. Miss & Roc 14:12 Mr 16 '64
NASA budget may reach $5.3 billion. Aviation W 79:25 O 28 '63
NASA budget of $5.2 billion okayed. H. M. David. Miss & Roc 13:15 Jl 15 '63
NASA construction pace slows. Aviation W 80:139 Mr 16 '64
NASA construction program passes peak. H. Taylor. Miss & Roc 14:18 F 24 '64
NASA cut nearly $500 million; with editorial comment by W. J. Coughlin. H. Taylor. il Miss & Roc 13:16, 50 Jl 1 '63
NASA eyes Apollo follow-on systems; with detailed breakdown of FY '65 R&D budget request. H. Taylor. Miss & Roc 14:18-19 F 10 '64
NASA FY '65 authorization. il Miss & Roc 15:145-9 Jl 27 '64
NASA FY '64 budget authorized by House space committee. Miss & Roc 13:182-4+ Jl 29 '63
NASA fund cuts to slow Saturn 5, LEM. A. P. Alibrando. Aviation W 79:34 D 16 '63
NASA launches fight to restore House fund cuts. H. M. David. Miss & Roc 14:11 Mr 23 '64
NASA lives with a budget cut. Bsns W p61-2 Ja 11 '64
NASA losing ground within Congress. A. P. Alibrando. Aviation W 79:28 S 16 '63
NASA plans to FLOX Atlas. Miss & Roc 13:14 N 11 '63
NASA: rein on budget may stiffen competition for funds between manned program, space sciences. J. Walsh. Science 142:1636-7 D 27 '63
NASA requests budget of $5.7 billion. A. P. Alibrando. il Aviation W 78:29-31 Ja 21 '63
NASA requests $267.9 million for tracking, data net expansion. il Aviation W 80:235-6 Mr 16 '64
NASA says Apollo date hinges on funds, fast budget action. il Aviation W 80:27-8 Ja 20 '64
NASA seeking $5.4 billion; big engine programs to OART. H. Taylor. il Miss & Roc 14:12 Ja 6 '64
NASA still faces budget cuts despite successful MA-9 flight. A. P. Alibrando. Aviation W 78:24 My 27 '63
NASA struggling to hold to 1970 man-on-moon schedule. H. M. David. Miss & Roc 13:15 D 23 '63
NASA subcontracts exceeded $1 billion. Aviation W 80:71 Je 15 '64
NASA: talk of togetherness with Soviets further complicates space politics for the agency. J. Walsh. Science 142:35-8 O 4 '63
NASA voted $5,194 billion. Miss & Roc 14:14 Mr 30 '64

UNITED STATES—National aeronautics and space administration—appropriations and expenditures—*Continued*
NASA warns of risks in House budget slashes. H. M. David. Miss & Roc 13:14 Jl 22 '63
NASA's bumpy budget road. R. Hotz. Aviation W 79:11 Jl 29 '63
NASA's space budget goes under House knife. H. M. David. Miss & Roc 12:18 Je 10 '63
New NASA request cut to $5.2 billion. E. H. Kolcum. Aviation W 80:26-7 Ja 6 '64
Only $5.1 billion for NASA. Miss & Roc 13:13 N 25 '63
Other side of the coin; excerpts from letters. T. J. Rice. Aviation W 79:21 Ag 26 '63
Pork barrel goes into orbit. J. A. Morris. Read Digest 85:87-92 Ag '64
Program breakdown of FY 1964 NASA budget; table. Aviation W 78:31-3 F 25 '63
Prospects for NASA FY '65 fund restoration brighten in Senate. Miss & Roc 14:16 Ap 13 '64
Request set at $5.5-5.6 billion; spending may top that in FY '66; with editorial comment. il Miss & Roc 15:44-6, 218 N 30 '64
Sales to top $8 billion by '70. il Miss & Roc 12:20-2 My 20 '63
Senate approves $5.1 billion for NASA; with editorial comment. Aviation W 79:21, 31 N 25 '63
Senate approves $5.3 billion for NASA. H. M. David. Miss & Roc 15:15 Ag 10 '64
Senate is expected to approve $5.5-billion NASA authorization. A. P. Alibrando. il Aviation W 79:27-8 Ag 12 '63
Senate may restore $60 million for NASA; long delay expected. W. J. Normyle. Aviation W 80:36 Ap 27 '64
Senate restores part of NASA fund cuts. D. E. Fink. Aviation W 79:28 Ag 19 '63
Senate unit restores $52 million to NASA; supplemental vote set. Aviation W 80:24 My 11 '64
Senate unit urges restoration of NASA advanced mission funds. il Aviation W 80:30 Je 15 '64
Senate votes NASA $5.246 billion. H. M. David. il Miss & Roc 14:15 Je 29 '64
Six new NASA flight projects funded. il Miss & Roc 12:16-17 F 11 '63
Some NASA funding restored. Aviation W 79:27 N 18 '63
Soviet lunar plans helping NASA cause; with editorial comment. A. P. Alibrando. Aviation W 79:21, 28-9 O 21 '63
Space age problems. R. Hotz. Aviation W 78:21 Ap 8 '63
Space agency faces possibility of $500-million slash in budget. A. P. Alibrando. Aviation W 78:30 Mr 18 '63
Space budget cut of $490 million urged. A. P. Alibrando. Aviation W 79:26-7 Jl 1 '63
Space funds pass House test; Boston center money survives. D. E. Fink. Aviation W 80:17-18 Mr 30 '64
Space sciences receive budget reprieve. W. J. Normyle. Aviation W 82:23-4 Ja 18 '65
Space science, research effort grows but failures beset lunar missions. A. Alibrando. il Aviation W 78:124-5+ Mr 11 '63
Successful Ranger lunar flight aids NASA budget through Senate. Aviation W 81:24 Ag 10 '64
Surveyor orbiter RFP's expected next month. il Miss & Roc 13:18 S 2 '63
$33 million of NASA FY '65 budget for Apollo backups. Miss & Roc 14:16-17 Ap 6 '64
U.S. space program at funding plateau. il Aviation W 80:107-11 Mr 16 '64
View from Capitol hill. R. Hotz. Aviation W 78:21 Ja 28 '63
Webb protests House unit's cut of $489 million in NASA budget. Aviation W 79:29 Jl 15 '63

Electronics research center

ERC awards to begin shortly. H. Taylor. Miss & Roc 15:10 Ag 17 '64
ERC to let thirty-five to forty contracts. M. Getler. Miss & Roc 15:10-11 N 16 '64
House group to seek further justification of electronics center; with editorial comment. Miss & Roc 14:17, 48 F 17 '64
More for Massachusetts. Nat R 16:224 Mr 24 '64
NASA plans new look at electronics center. Aviation W 79:28 O 28 '63
NASA's superlab in Boston; question that should be asked. Bsns W p65 Mr 7 '64
Proposed research center seen as tonic for electronics effort. il Miss & Roc 13:161-2 N 25 '63
Site of ERC to be announced shortly. Miss & Roc 15:13 Jl 20 '64
Why Boston is puzzled by a federal economy move. il U S News 57:84-6 N 23 '64

Flight research center

Flight research center seeking hypersonic craft for ASP work. il Miss & Roc 13:211-15 N 25 '63

Goddard space flight center

Electronics at NASA's Goddard space flight center; symposium; with editorial comment. il Electr World 71:8, 49-64 Je '64
Goddard aims to build even bigger test facilities. il Miss & Roc 13:193-7 N 25 '63
GEP to alter all astronomy. W. Beller. il Miss & Roc 12:22-3 Mr 4 '63
Goddard management may expand. H. Taylor. Miss & Roc 12:15 Ap 15 '63
Goddard seeks scaling laws to cut cost of environmental testing. W. Beller. il Miss & Roc 15:34-5 Jl 20 '64
Ground station difficulty delays Syncom. G. Alexander. Aviation W 78:64 F 11 '63
Helios to relay more accurate solar data. W. C. Wetmore. il Aviation W 78:48-9+ Mr 4 '63
Large space science satellites get customized test facilities at Goddard. W. Beller. il Miss & Roc 14:33+ My 25 '64
NASA center nears completion of launch-phase simulation facility. W. S. Beller. il Miss & Roc 15:18+ N 2 '64
Nerve center. New Yorker 39:30-2 My 25 '63
New Houston control facility may direct Gemini sooner than planned. M. Getler. Miss & Roc 13:32-4 Jl 8 '63

Jet propulsion laboratory

See Jet propulsion laboratory

Langley research center

Langley explores on the ground while hoping for manned space lab. il Miss & Roc 13:198+ N 25 '63
Langley okays multiple-array concept. il Miss & Roc 14:18 Je 1 '64
Langley simulators perform lunar tasks. D. A. Brown. il Aviation W 80:54-5+ Ap 13 '64

Lewis research center

Lewis will invest half a billion in fiscal '64. il Miss & Roc 13:223-4+ N 25 '63

Manned spacecraft center

Home base for spacemen. il Bsns W p64-7+ My 30 '64
Industry population mushrooms as MSC spawns new markets. Aviation W 81:66-7 N 16 '64
Manned flight center reorganized. Aviation W 79:41 N 11 '63
Manned spacecraft center. il Arch Rec 133:148-51 Ja '63
Manned spacecraft center capable of expanding for future programs. il Aviation W 81:69+ N 23 '64
Manned spacecraft center combines food programs for Apollo, Gemini. Miss & Roc 14:36 Je 8 '64
Manned spacecraft center needs $25 million more in FY '65. il Miss & Roc 13:171-2+ N 25 '63
MSC control center seen ready. R. Pay. il Miss & Roc 16:24-6 Ja 25 '65
MSC seen favoring concentric orbit Gemini-Agena rendezvous. J. Mercer. Miss & Roc 15:30+ O 12 '64
Manned space flight reorganized. il Aviation W 79:37 N 4 '63
Mercury gone, Holmes going; with editorial comment by W. J. Coughlin. Miss & Roc 12:10, 54 Je 17 '63
Mission control begins new space art. il Aviation W 79:274-5+ Jl 22 '63
On a Texas prairie, space city for 200,000. il U S News 54:66-9 F 18 '63
Reorganization at MSC to aid project heads. W. Burkett. il Miss & Roc 13:16 N 11 '63
Shifts at MSC define management areas. Aviation W 78:95 My 27 '63
Some earthier problems. Time 81:21 Je 21 '63
$30-million space test facility to allow Apollo mission simulation. Aviation W 78:65 F 18 '63

Manned space flight, Office of

Mueller succeeds Holmes. Miss & Roc 13:19-20+ Jl 29 '63
Personnel woes plague headquarters. il Miss & Roc 13:157-9 N 25 '63

Marshall space flight center

Campaign charge: blackmail in space program. il U S News 57:8 N 9 '64
Costs and schedules stressed under new Marshall structure. G. Alexander. Aviation W 79:106+ N 18 '63

UNITED STATES—National aeronautics and space administration—Marshall space flight center—*Continued*
Liquid hydrogen test facility bids requested. Aviation W 79:81 Ag 5 '63
Marshall budget near $2 billion. il Miss & Roc 13:164+ N 25 '63
MSFC plans $10 million in studies. Miss & Roc 14:16 Mr 9 '64
Mississippi test operations spending to hit peak in fiscal 1965. il Miss & Roc 13:216+ N 25 '63
S-1C heavy tooling installed at Marshall; center to begin building four stages soon. G. Alexander. il Aviation W 78:50-1+ Mr 25 '63
Studies for Marshall to exceed $7 million. Aviation W 81:61+ Ag 3 '64
Where components must be improved. il Miss & Roc 12:40-1 Je 17 '63

Procurement

Agency renegotiating to incentives. il Miss & Roc 13:103-4+ N 25 '63
Apollo add-on is $500 million. W. Burkett. Miss & Roc 14:14 Je 29 '64
Boeing wins NASA's largest contract. Miss & Roc 12:15 Mr 4 '63
ERC to let thirty-five to forty contracts. M. Getler. Miss & Roc 15:10-11 N 16 '64
Industry studies NASA procurement list. G. Alexander. Aviation W 79:29-31 O 28 '63
JPL: Ranger VI failure increases speculation on jet lab's future links with space agency, Caltech. J. Walsh. Science 143:1014-16 Mr 6 '64
MSFC plans $10 million in studies. Miss & Roc 14:16 Mr 9 '64
NASA explains choice of Boeing over Hughes in Lunar orbiter award. Miss & Roc 14:13 Mr 9 '64
NASA fiscal 1962 procurement doubled. il Aviation W 78:34-5 Ja 28 '63
NASA list of FY 1963 100 top prime contractors. il Miss & Roc 14:18 Ja 20 '64
NASA lists top fiscal '63 contractors. il Aviation W 80:58-60 Mr 30 '64
NASA sets uniform reliability guidelines. Aviation W 79:72+ S 30 '63
NASA tightens Marshall contracts. Aviation W 81:22 D 28 '64
NASA turns to incentives; procurement of the lunar orbiter photo spacecraft. Miss & Roc 13:28 O 7 '63
Space agency consolidating contract administration under national plan. il Miss & Roc 15:47-9 N 30 '64
Space agency procurement up 48 per cent. il Miss & Roc 14:16 Je 8 '64
Space crescent. W. S. Ellis. il Nation 199: 211-16, 239-43, 275-7+ O 12-26 '64

National arboretum

See Washington, D.C.—National arboretum

National archives

Book thieves operate on national levels. Library J 88:4186 N 1 '63
Microfilm defects discussed at National archives meeting; with National bureau of standards and the Eastman-Kodak company. Library J 88:3043 S 1 '63

National board of education (proposed)

Do we need a National board of education? G. W. Angell. Sch & Soc 91:238-9 Sum '63

National cancer institute

Krebiozen case closed. Sci N L 84:258 O 26 '63
Medical case against krebiozen. il Consumer Rep 29:93-6 F '64

National center for environmental sciences

Environmental health center: North Carolina victorious in four-year battle for PHS facility. E. Langer. Science 147:276-7 Ja 15 '65
Pork barrel science; considerations regarding location of new health center. D. S. Greenberg. New Repub 152:22 Ja 23 '65
View from the pork barrel; Congress, PHS, haggle over proposed health center site. E. Langer. Science 140:240+ Ap 12 '63

National council of the arts

To encourage the arts. N. Kent. Am Artist 28:3+ N '64

National cultural center

Party notebook; fund raising for the Kennedy center. P. Mesta. il McCalls 91:20+ Ap '64

National export expansion coordinator

Daniel L. Goldy named national export expansion coordinator. Dept State Bul 50:56 Ja 13 '64

National guard

Another step for efficiency; disbanding of army's organized reserve. il Time 84:26 D 18 '64
Mac the knife; McNamara discloses further defense cuts. Newsweek 64:24+ D 21 '64
McNamara bombshell: merger of reservists. il U S News 57:3 D 21 '64
McNamara's latest reform: why his national guard scheme won't work. S. L. A. Marshall. New Repub 152:13-15 Ja 23 '65
Merge national guard and reserves? McNamara's plan. il U S News 57:61-2 D 14 '64
We've been asked: what happens now to reservists? questions and answers. U S News 57:27 D 28 '64
See also
United States—Air national guard

National historical publications commission

Support for the humanities. D. Wolfle. Science 141:121 Jl 12 '63
$2 million Ford grant to historical papers project. Pub W 186:24 O 26 '64
White House spotlights historical commission plan. Pub W 184:64 Jl 15 '63

National humanities foundation (proposed)

Humanities: proposals to set up national foundation are gathering support in the House and Senate. D. S. Greenberg. Science 147:273-4 Ja 15 '65
National humanities foundation. D. Wolfle. Science 145:449 Jl 31 '64; Discussion. 145: 990 S 4 '64
National humanities foundation. W. S. Moorhead. America 111:597+ N 14 '64
National humanities foundation; summary of report, ed. by C. B. Grannis. F. Burkhardt. Pub W 186:35 D 7 '64

National institute of child health and human development

New institute founded. Sci N L 84:93 Ag 10 '63
New institute to study childhood, age problems. Sci N L 84:329 N 23 '63
Vital new chapter in medical research is being written. J. Raymond. il Parents Mag 38:69+ O '63

National institute of mental health

Housewives in mental health. J. Viorst. il Sci N L 86:234-5 O 10 '64
Mental care program calls on communities. il Bsns W p 104-6 F 9 '63

National institutes of health

Advanced surgery at NIH. il Sci N L 84:194 S 28 '63
Career awards: no more new ones will be made under NIH program. J. Walsh. Science 146:1662 D 25 '64
Changes at NIH: more studies underway; new institute makes researchers, Kennedys, happy. E. Langer. Science 141:414-15 Ag 2 '63
Foreign research: U.S. agencies take steps to limit their support for programs carried out abroad. D. S. Greenberg. Science 141: 138 Jl 12 '63
Health research: honeymoon with Congress is cooling. il U S News 54:98-100 Je 24 '63
Higher education: fourth branch of government? C. K. Arnold. il Sat R 47:60-1+ Ja 18 '64; Reply. L. H. Fountain. 47:62 Mr 21 '64
Money for medical research. il New Repub 149:29-31 N 9 '63
More paper work, less research; betrayal. P. H. Abelson. Science 139:725 F 22 '63; Discussion. 140:721+ My 10 '63
NIH and Fountain; part of problem is that an atmosphere of suspicion has enveloped the relationship. D. S. Greenberg. Science 140:1076-8 Je 7 '63
NIH: budget hits $1-billion mark for first time, but no one seems to be in a mood for celebration. D. S. Greenberg. Science 144:392-3 Ap 24 '64
NIH: House reverses trend, cuts budget request as a new group starts probe into research. D. S. Greenberg. Science 140:467-9 My 3 '63
NIH: moratorium on career awards for researchers called for blend of budgetary and policy reasons. J. Walsh. Science 145:1283-4 S 18 '64
New regulations pertaining to research grants of the Public health service; letter. A. D. Welch. Science 141:1099-100+ S 13 '63
Operating rooms in the round; Clinical center in Bethesda, Md. il Time 82:84 S 13 '63

UNITED STATES—National institutes of health—*Continued*
Problems of NIH: an examination of how other federal agencies handle congressional relations. D. S. Greenberg. Science 140: 1194-5 Je 14 '63; Reply with rejoinder. C. B. Chapman. 141:762-3 Ag 30 '63
Report on fertility research. W. J. Gibbons. Cath World 197:44-50 Ap '63
Surgeons' dream room: new wing at the research hospital of the National institutes of health at Bethesda, Md. il Life 55:93-4+ D 6 '63

National labor relations board

Abridging free speech; decision against General electric. H. Hazlitt. Newsweek 65:49 Ja 4 '65
Agency shop setback; states have power to enforce curbs on unions. Bsns W p 136 D 7 '63
Another setback for employers. U S News 55:85 Jl 15 '63
Beaching the NLRB. Newsweek 61:62 Mr 4 '63
Businessmen's latest worry: the Kennedy labor board. il U S News 54:96+ Ap 8 '63
Coal royalties; small mines win. U S News 57:93 Ag 24 '64
Dissenter praises Labor board; summary of address, December 4, 1963. B. Leedom. U S News 55:108 D 16 '63
Effects of NLRB action on the duty to bargain; excerpt from address, May 27, 1964. F. W. McCulloch. Mo Labor R 87:895-8 Ag '64
If Barry goes to White House: what labor can expect. U S News 57:76-7 Jl 27 '64
Individual and the union. A. W. Blumrosen. Mo Labor R 86:659-65 Je '63
Is Kennedy board rewriting labor law? il U S News 55:91-2 Jl 8 '63
Is labor board rewriting law? U S News 54:107 Ap 22 '63
Key post for Negro; Jenkins gets Labor board job. U S News 55:24 Ag 5 '63
Latest on business's right to close; Darlington manufacturing company case. U S News 55:95 D 2 '63
Many faces of good faith; disputes between General electric and IUE, Kohler and the UAW Nat R 17:12 Ja 12 '65
More freedom to picket; latest from Supreme court; consumer picketing. U S News 56:78 My 4 '64
NLRB authorizes union election at Kingsport. Pub W 185:31 Mr 23 '64
NLRB calls GE unfair; failed to bargain in good faith. Bsns W p 116 D 19 '64
NLRB cracks down on union bias; failure to process a Negro's grievance of Hughes tool co. Houston. Bsns W p50 Jl 11 '64
NLRB job up for grabs; list of candidates for S. Rothman's post. Bsns W p74 Ap 6 '63
NLRB or JFKLB? Newsweek 61:78 F 25 '63
NLRB's new, rough line. M. R. Lefkoe. il Fortune 68:164-6+ N '63
NLRB's thrust for power. R. Moley. Newsweek 61:100 Ap 8 '63
New man at NLRB. Newsweek 61:67 My 6 '63
New speech limit on employers? U S News 54:107-8 Ap 15 '63
1961-62 operations of the National labor relations board; excerpt from annual report. il Mo Labor R 86:1040-4 S '63
1962-63 operations of the National labor relations board; excerpt from twenty-eighth annual report. il Mo Labor R 87:414-18 Ap '64
One for the unions; Kingsport press. Bsns W p 154+ Mr 21 '64
Political picketing by unions? U S News 56:88 Je 8 '64
Role of government in union growth. P. Ross. Ann Am Acad 350:74-85 N '63
Should the U.S. have a labor court? T. R. Brooks. Duns R 83:59-62 Mr '64
Significant decisions in labor cases. See issues of Monthly labor review
Significant decisions in labor cases. See issues of Monthly labor review
Unions get new picketing rights. U S News 55:97 S 30 '63
U.S. vs. the U.S (cont) R. Moley. Newsweek 61:84 F 4 '63
War on business. R. Moley. Newsweek 64:84 Jl 20 '64
Warning on employer rights; excerpts from address, 1964. F. A. O'Connell. U S News 57:87 D 7 '64
What can you tell employees? Leff report. L. L. L. Golden. Sat R 46:50 Ag 10 '63; Reply. B. Liss. 46:49 O 12 '63
When a Negro challenged a union. U S News 57:76 Jl 13 '64
When pickets are used to scare away customers. il U S News 54:74-5 F 4 '63
Where employers are losing more ground to unions. il U S News 57:73-4 D 28 '64
Without due process; National labor relations board against Kohler company. Nat R 15:141 Ag 27 '63

National library of medicine

Medical libraries are in trouble; address, October 1962. S. Adams. bibliog il Library J 88:2615-21 Jl '63
Medical subject headings revised: cross reference guide to the Index medicus. Wilson Lib Bul 39:373 Ja '65
What is MEDLARS? Medical literature analysis and retrieval system. H. Schiller. il Library J 88:949-53 Mr 1 '63

National mediation board

Airline vote halted in fight with NMB. Bsns W p46 My 11 '63
Rail union makes bid for 12,700 at United; 3,000 are ex-members. Aviation W 78:41 F 11 '63

National park service

Conservation or recreation: our swarming national parks. K. Wilson. il Nation 198: 391-5 Ap 20 '64
Guardians not gardeners. Liv Wildn 83:2 Spring '63
High winds blow through the parks. A. W. Smith. Nat Parks Mag 37:2+ D '63
Kind of special breed. M. Frome. il Am For 70:4-5+ Ja '64
Lands we share; address, May 3, 1963. L. C. Binford. Am For 69:16-19+ Jl '63
Man in the middle; G. B. Hartzog, jr. J. Prokop. il Am For 70:34-6+ My '64
National parks research. Recreation 57:193+ Ap '64
On policy and zoning; as natural, historical and recreational. Nat Parks Mag 38:14-15 D '64
Park wilderness in danger? A. W. Smith. Nat Parks Mag 38:2 O '64
Registry for natural history landmarks. Nat Parks Mag 38:16 My '64
Visitor access to the seashores and parks. A. W. Smith. Nat Parks Mag 38:2 N '64
Who'll get Big Muddy campsites? Missouri's development. il Bsns W p30-1 My 4 '63

National parks and reserves

See National parks and reserves—United States

National referral center for science and technology

National referral center at LC begins operations on March 4. Library J 88:1498-9 Ap 1 '63
Referral relationships. J. F. Stearns. Library J 89:1011-14+ Mr 1 '64
Science questions center. W. Davis. Sci N L 86:39 Jl 18 '64

National science foundation

American institute of biological sciences accused of misuse of NSF grant funds. D. S. Greenberg. il Science 139:317-21 Ja 25 '63; Discussion. 142:150+; 143:7-8, 430 O 11 '63, Ja 3, 31 '64
AIBS; bill for 1959-61 less than NSF original estimate. D. S. Greenberg. Science 139: 1039 Mr 15 '63
Biologists' choice. D. Wolfe. Science 139:459 F 8 '63
Centers of excellence: new NSF science development program aims at second twenty universities. J. Walsh. Science 146:1563-6 D 18 '64
Congress and science: NSF hearings provide some illuminating insights on the deteriorating relationship. D. S. Greenberg. Science 142:368-70 O 18 '63
Congress views science; NSF education programs under investigation. Sci N L 84:308 N 16 '63
Emergency meeting of board. D. S. Greenberg. Science 139:392 F 1 '63
First director. D. Wolfle. Science 141:11 Jl 5 '63
Forty first-rate universities. D. Wolfle. Science 144:1413 Je 19 '64; Reply. C. A. MacKenzie. 145:344 Jl 24 '64
How NSF got lost in Mohole. H. Solow. il Fortune 67:138-41+ My '63
Mocked grants backed. W. Wingo. Sci N L 84:37 Jl 20 '63
Morality in science: report on a crisis. J. Lear. il Sat R 46:49-54 Mr 2 '63; Discussion. 46:51-2 My 4; 37-8 Je 1 '63

UNITED STATES—National science foundation—*Continued*
NSF academic year institutes: a review of the program's success. Sch & Soc 92:222 Sum '64
NSF awards grant for project to develop computer cataloging. Library J 88:4182 N 1 '63
NSF grant awarded for expansion of SLA classifications center. Library J 88:4181 N 1 '63
NSF hearings: last year's chill has been replaced by affection and a sizeable budget increase. D. S. Greenberg. Science 144: 979-80 My 22 '64
NSF hopes to double top research centers. Sci N L 84:203 S 28 '63
NSF: new director has ordered small but significant steps aimed at improving operations. D. S. Greenberg. Science 141:1017-18 S 13 '63
NSF: new program aims to speed process for transforming good institutions into excellent ones. D. S. Greenberg. Science 144: 154-5 Ap 10 '64
Policy and the scientists. L. A. DuBridge. For Affairs 41:580-1 Ap '63
Rutgers plans series of seminars on systems for organizing information. Library J 88: 1642+ Ap 15 '63
Science foundation; Leland Haworth of Atomic energy commission named as successor to Alan T. Waterman. D. S. Greenberg. Science 139:1272 Mr 29 '63
Science foundation; new director appoints University of Chicago aide to reactivated deputy post. D. S. Greenberg. Science 140: 960 My 31 '63
Stop! federal expenditures for science. il Newsweek 62:102 O 21 '63
Tomorrow's pioneers. F. L. Phelps. il Américas 15:21-8 F '63

See also
Science curriculum improvement study

National security agency

Playboy sergeant who spied for Russia; Jack Dunlap. D. Oberdorfer. il Sat Eve Post 237: 40+ Mr 7 '64

National security council

National security council; vigilant watchdog or White House pet? il Sr Schol 82:5-7+ F 13 '63

National service corps

See Volunteers in service to America

Naval observatory

New 61-inch astrometric reflector. K. A. Strand. il Sky & Tel 27:204-9+ Ap '64

Naval operations, Office of

Guys who get in their way. il Time 81:28 My 17 '63

Naval research, Office of

Navy studying control of weapons through thinking of them. Miss & Roc 13:20 D 2 '63

Naval research laboratory

Where is science taking us? revision of a paper describing attempt to establish pattern of X-ray emission from the Crab nebula. H. Friedman. il Sat R 47:44-5 Jl 4 '64

Navy

Deep submergence project calls for five-year expenditure of $200 million; Project seabed study of the advanced sea-based deterrent. il Miss & Roc 15:28+ D 21 '64
DOD stalls navy tactical probe. Miss & Roc 14:14 F 10 '64
DASH will be operational in November. L. Booda. Aviation W 79:32-3 Jl 1 '63
Fighting ship still sails the sea. H. W. Baldwin. il N Y Times Mag p 14-15+ Ja 26 '64
Future navy might lack large carriers. Aviation W 78:35 F 11 '63
Future of the navy; address, January 9, 1964. P. H. Nitze. Vital Speeches 30:239-43 F 1 '64
Naval trilogy; coastal minesweeper, U.S.S. Grouse. il Newsweek 62:34-5 O 14 '63
Navy again outgunned. W. J. Coughlin. Miss & Roc 13:52 O 21 '63
Navy at ebb tide. H. W. Baldwin. il Reporter 30:35-8 Ja 30 '64
Navy calls manned aircraft indispensable. G. C. Wilson. Aviation W 78:40-1 F 25 '63
Navy feels defense adequate for now. il Miss & Roc 15:24-6+ S 21 '64
Navy is emerging as major developer of air-launched missiles. M. Yaffee. il Aviation W 80:148-9+ Mr 16 '64
Navy pressed to enlarge anti-submarine capabilities. il Aviation W 80:84-5+ Mr 16 '64
Navy sets December target date for management overhaul. D. C. Breasted. Miss & Roc 13:31 S 30 '63
Navy structure survives reorganization. L. Booda. Aviation W 78:32-3 Je 10 '63
Navy studies deterrent force for 1980s. E. J. Bulban. Aviation W 80:91+ Je 8 '64
Navy told to cut attack carrier force. L. Booda. Aviation W 79:35-6 Ag 19 '63
Navy's role in Cuba, Panama, southeast Asia; interview. D. L. McDonald. il U S News 56:66-70 Mr 2 '64
New four ocean challenge; address, September 18, 1963. J. S. McCain, jr. Vital Speeches 30:57-61 N 1 '63
New navy; condensation. H. W. Baldwin. il Pop Sci 185:65-7+ S '64
Now the whiz kids are tackling the U.S. navy. il U S News 55:59-60 N 25 '63
Ocean-based strategic weapons held neither feasible nor necessary now; Project seabed advanced sea-based deterrent conference. Miss & Roc 15:18 S 7 '64
Policeman of the Pacific; Seventh fleet, photographs. N Y Times Mag p8-9 Ag 16 '64
Sea power selectivity; address, October 10, 1964. D. L. McDonald. Vital Speeches 31: 123-5 D 1 '64
Services delay satellite disclosure. Aviation W 79:25 Jl 29 '63
Seventh fleet: Far East fire brigade. il Newsweek 64:21 Ag 17 '64
Seventh fleet: patrolling the Indian Ocean. New Repub 150:8 Ja 11 '64
Shots in the dark; incidents in the Gulf of Tonkin. Time 84:43B O 2 '64
Silencing the skeptics; U.S.S. Claude V. Ricketts. il Newsweek 64:49 N 9 '64
Stormy days for the navy. il Time 82:37 N 15 '63
Sub rescues, four miles deep. S. D. Pursglove. il Pop Mech 120:69-73+ Ag '63
Two officials under fire; question of Seventh fleet on patrol in Indian Ocean. il U S News 56:13 Ja 6 '64
U.S. fleet: peace keeper in the Mediterranean; Sixth fleet. il U S News 56:42 Mr 16 '64
Western Pacific; area of Seventh fleet; address, May 17, 1963. W. A. Schoech. Vital Speeches 29:584-6 Jl 15 '63

See also
Naval maneuvers
Navy yards and naval stations
United States—Coast guard
World war, 1939-1945—Naval operations

Administration

Martell, Karaberis share management responsibility in separate offices. il Miss & Roc 15:35-7 S 21 '64
Navy reorganization plan faces only grudging acceptance. Miss & Roc 12:36, 39 Je 17 '63

Appropriations and expenditures

ASW budget running at $386.5 million but past approach hampers work. il Miss & Roc 15:40-2 S 21 '64

Boats

See also
Torpedo boats

Education

See also
United States naval academy, Annapolis

History

Bloodshed at dawn; Barron vs. Decatur. C. S. Forester. il Am Heritage 15:40-5+ O '64
Great white fleet. F. Uhlig, jr. il Am Heritage 15:30-43+ F '64

Medical department

These Americans must be gods; U.S. navy doctor in Saigon. S. Karnow. il Sat Eve Post 237:72-3 Ap 25 '64

Naval medical research unit

Worldwide disease busters: the navy medics. A. F. Gonzalez, jr. il Todays Health 42: 36-8+ S '64

Negroes

Guardian of western coastline. il Ebony 20: 40-2+ Ja '65

Officers

Navy's new team. il Time 83:27 Ap 3 '64

Procurement

A-7A contract defines scale of penalties. E. J. Bulban. Aviation W 80:109-10+ Je 15 '64
Chief, navy procurement activities. Miss & Roc 15:40-1 S 21 '64
Navy faces reorganization of forces, procurement structure. il Aviation W 78:80-1+ Mr 11 '63

UNITED STATES—Navy—Procurement—*Cont.*
Navy overhauls R&D, procurement. Miss & Roc 12:17 My 6 '63
Probers told of navy's qualms about bi-service TFX program. Aviation W 79:21-2 Jl 8 '63
Systems integration contract forbids firm from bidding on hardware. Miss & Roc 15:16 N 9 '64

Recreation

Who's going ashore? U.S. sixth fleet in Beirut. il Newsweek 62:79 N 11 '63

Relations with civilians

See United States—Armed forces—Relations with civilians

Navy department

Man in the middle. il Time 81:25 Je 14 '63

Weapons, Bureau of

Navy revising maintenance management. D. E. Fink. il Aviation W 78:92-4 F 4 '63

Yards and docks, Bureau of

Big dish: how haste and secrecy helped navy waste $63 million in race to build huge telescope. D. S. Greenberg. Science 144:1111-12 My 29 '64
New undersea test facility to go operational in December, 1965. Miss & Roc 15:78-9 S 21 '64

Oceanographic office

Maneuvering board and the yachtsman. H. O. Webster. il Motor B 114:38-41 Jl '64

Office of education

See United States—Education, Office of

Officials and employees

See Government employees

Outdoor recreation, Bureau of

Outdoor recreation policies: some differences. R. Agnew. Am For 69:34-5+ Je '63
Planning, a prologue to action; address. F. V. Durand. il Am For 70:26-9+ N '64
Recreation under the microscope. J. F. Shankin. il Am For 69:32-5 Jl '63
Strong mandate; editorial. E. C. Crafts. il Am For 69:10-11 Jl '63

Outdoor recreation resources review commission

Committee for ORRRC report formed in Washington. Nat Parks Mag 37:17 Mr '63
In business! J. B. Craig. il Am For 70:4-5+ S '64
Private outdoor recreation industry; its management. G. W. Cornwell. il Am For 69:36-9+ O '63
Should the outdoors be free? address. W. N. Aspinall. Am For 70:34+ Ap '64
Strong mandate; editorial. E. C. Crafts. il Am For 69:10-11 Jl '63

Patent office

Creativity penalized. B. F. Miessner. Miss & Roc 14:4 My 11 '64; Reply. T. M. Morse. 14:6 Je 8 '64
Crisis in the patent office. S. V. Jones. il Sci Digest 55:65-70 Mr '64
Invention: is it keeping up? interview. D. L. Ladd. il U S News 55:70-3 Jl 15 '63
Searching for patent like needle in haystack; Project HAYSTAQ. Sci N L 84:213 O 5 '63
Top-secret mania. L. A. Stevens. il Nation 197:218-21 O 12 '63
U.S. patent office seeks Negro employees. il Ebony 18:111-12+ O '63
See also
Patents

Peace corps

Ambassadors of good will; the Peace corps; with stories by eight volunteers. S. Shriver. il Nat Geog Mag 126:297-345 S '64
Broad horizons. R. Schumm. il Recreation 56:356-8 O '63
Close look at the Peace corps and its volunteers; interview. R. S. Shriver. il U S News 56:38-41 Ja 6 '64
Colombia: Señor Ron; with report by M. J. Kubic. Newsweek 61:48 Je 3 '63
Doers, not do-gooders, the Peace corps in Nigeria. H. L. Callaway. il Mlle 57:126-9+ Je '63
Eight hundred Americans; Peace corps in the Philippines. J. C. Cort. Commonweal 81:7-10 S 25 '64
Exam; conducted by Civil service commission, New York office. New Yorker 39:22-3 D 21 '63
Forty-four countries call. il Sch Life 45:27 Ap '63
Hundreds of senior citizens wanted. Christian Cent 80:701 My 29 '63
I have the best job in Washington. S. Shriver. il N Y Times Mag p34+ Je 9 '63
Inside the Peace corps. il Seventeen 22:152-3+ My '63
It is almost as good as its intentions. il Time 82:18-22 Jl 5 '63
Kennedy libraries drive collects over 4000 books. Pub W 185:57 Ja 6 '64
My life as a Peace corps girl; ed. by A. St George. J. C. Boegli. il Good H 156:84-5+ Ap '63
New life in a leprosarium. T. Bodman. il Recreation 57:62 F '64
Peace corps after two years. il Sr Schol 82:6-9 Mr 13 '63
Peace corps: agency flourishes as Congress smiles, numbers grow, but full results are not yet in. J. Walsh. Science 140:371-2 Ap 26 '63
Peace corps: frontier for youth S. Shriver. il Parents Mag 38:46-7+ Jl '63
Peace corps in perspective; with reply by S. Shriver and excerpt from report by A. Lage. N. Barron. bibliog il Library J 90:196-201 Ja 15 '65
Peace corps needs librarians for University of Brasilia. Library J 89:209 Ja 15 '64
Peace corps needs more architects. Arch Rec 135:284 Mr '64
Peace corps needs 9,000 in 1964. Library J 88:4448 N 15 '63
Peace corps: no longer an experiment. C. F. Stoerker. Christian Cent 81:1396-8 N 11 '64
Peace corps: nursery for diplomats. I. Sclanders. il Nation 199:31-3 Jl 27 '64
Peace corps placing Kennedy libraries abroad. Pub W 184:22 D 16 '63
Peace corps '64. I. Mothner. il Look 28:70-4+ Je 16 '64
Peace corps training at Ohio university. R. P. Fairfield. Sch & Soc 92:339-41 N 14 '64
PCV an American image. W. Davis. Sci N L 83:165 Mr 16 '63
Peace corps volunteers praise P.E. project. P. Hardberger. il Pop Electr 20: 54-5+ Ja '64
Peace corps volunteer returns; problems of adjustment. D. Pearson. il Sat R 47:54-6+ O 17 '64
Peace corpsmen adjust. Sci N L 87:5 Ja 2 '65
President calls for increase in Peace corps; statement, November 2, 1964. L. B. Johnson. Dept State Bul 51:735-6 N 23 '64
President Nyerere of Tanganyika visits Washington; joint communique, July 16, 1963: with announcement of new Peace corps agreement. M. J. K. Nyerere and J. F. Kennedy. Dept State Bul 49:198-9 Ag 5 '63
President recommends expansion of Peace corps; letter to Lyndon B. Johnson. July 4, 1963. J. F. Kennedy. Dept State Bul 49:170-2 Jl 29 '63
Reporter at large; Peace corps in the Philippines. R. Shaplen. New Yorker 39:50-2+ S 28 '63
Teachers in the Peace corps. M. Edwards. il Sat R 46:42-4+ Jl 20 '63
Teachers wanted. il Sr Schol 82:1T+ Ap 17 '63
Twigs off the branch: sons & daughters in Washington. P. Mesta. il McCalls 92:34+ O '64
Two years of the Peace corps. S. Shriver. For Affairs 41:694-707 Jl '63
Ugly American revisited. E. Burdick and W. Lederer. il Sat Eve Post 236:78-81 My 4 '63
Vogue's eye view of a loving sign. il Vogue 141:91 F 1 '63
Volunteers for progress; Peace corps in Latin America. N. A. Haverstock. il Américas 15:2-10 Jl '63
Wanted: craftsmen for corps. Bsns W p34 Jl 18 '64
When Peace corps teachers return. S. Shriver. il NEA J 52:13-14+ Mr '63
Who is joining the Peace corps? disturbing questions about Catholic participation. J. M. Cronin and T. E. Cronin; discussion. America 108:69, 228-30 Ja 19, F 16 '63
Yankee idealist in Africa. il Life 56:51-4 Mr 20 '64

Appropriations and expenditures

President requests increased appropriation for Peace corps; letter, January 16, 1964. L. B. Johnson. Dept State Bul 50:198 F 10 '64

Politics and government

Affairs of state. S. Alsop. See issues of Saturday evening post

UNITED STATES—Politics and government —*Continued*
After JFK, what? W. D. Burnham. il Commonweal 79:340-3 D 13 '63
After the party truce. R. Moley. Newsweek 62:96 D 16 '63
Aftermath; death of JFK. A. M. Sullivan. Duns R 83:86 Mr '64
American government and administration: recent developments. W. H. Young. Ann Am Acad 348:156-63 Jl '63
American politics: the first half-century. L. W. Koenig. Cur Hist 47:193-8+ O '64
American system; address, August 12, 1964. H. Humphrey. Vital Speeches 30:682-5 S 1 '64
Anarchy. D. Lawrence. U S News 54:96 F 4 '63
Anatomy of a new politics. C. D. Bolton. il Nation 198:529-33 My 25 '64
And crown thy good. . . il Time 82:23-4 D 6 '63
Armies of ignorance. L. J. Halle. New Repub 149:16-17 D 7 '63
Art of politics. G. McGee. il NEA J 52:36-9 F '63
As Johnson really takes over. . . il U S News 56:31-3 Ap 6 '64
As LBJ's honeymoon fades. il U S News 56: 25-6 F 17 '64
As you like it; President's new program. Nat R 14:224-5 Mr 26 '63
Atlantic report. See issues of Atlantic
Back of the change in LBJ. U S News 56: 49 Je 15 '64
Band-aid program? war on poverty. il Newsweek 63:35-6+ F 17 '64
Beyond the campaign. D. Lawrence. U S News 57:136+ O 19 '64
Big, bold plans of Lyndon the Lucky. B. H. Bagdikian. il Sat Eve Post 237:17-19 D 12 '64
Big problems for the President. il U S News 57:35-8 N 9 '64
Bold gamble by the President; concerning State of the Union message. il Newsweek 63:13-14 Ja 20 '64
Byrd's-eye views; address, August 15, 1964. H. F. Byrd. Vital Speeches 30:713-15 S 15 '64
Campaign issues: Goldwater opens his drive; address, September 3, 1964. B. M. Goldwater. il U S News 57:92-5 S 14 '64; Same with title Peace through strength. Vital Speeches 30:743-6 O 1 '64
Candidates spell out the issues. L. B. Johnson; B. M. Goldwater. il N Y Times Mag p23+ N 1 '64
Case for bureaucracy. H. Cleveland. il N Y Times Mag p 19+ O 27 '63
Challenge to military professionalism. R. N. Ginsburgh. bibliog f For Affairs 42:255-68 Ja '64; Excerpts. U S News 56:93 F 17 '64
Changing U.S. electorate. S. Lubell. il Fortune 70:132-5+ Jl '64
Choice. Farm J 88:106 S; 120 O '64 (to be cont)
C-mpr-m-se. Newsweek 61:24+ F 11 '63
Cracking the whip for civil rights. il Newsweek 63:26-8+ Ap 13 '64
Curtain falls and rises. Fortune 70:121-2 N '64
Dangerous mixture: the military and politics. T. D. White. Newsweek 64:33 O 19 '64
Deadlock of democracy, by J. M. Burns. Review
Commentary 35:540-2 Je '63. C. V. Woodward
Nation 197:226-7 O 12 '63. M. Moos
Decline of the East. R. Moley. Newsweek 63:68 Ja 6 '64
Defeating of LBJ. E. J. Hughes. Newsweek 63:17 F 24 '64
Democratic record; address, August 24, 1964. J. O. Pastore. Vital Speeches 30:706-8 S 15 '64
Dialogues in Americanism, ed. by M. Gazzaniga. Review
Nat R 16:1065-6 D 1 '64. J. J. Kilpatrick
Do fundamental principles really change? reprint with postscript. D. Lawrence. U S News 56:80+ Ja 6 '64
Drift in Washington; where it's heading. il U S News 54:29-30 Ap 1 '63
Dual image? reprint. H. Gemmill. U S News 56:96+ F 10 '64
Eisenhower administration: a self-portrait. O. Handlin. il Atlan 212:67-72 N '63; Reply. M. M. Rabb. 213:44 Mr '64
Epistles from the Eisenhower age. M. Kempton. Commentary 35:232-8 Mr '63
Everett Dirksen's newest role. M. Greenfield. il Reporter 30:26-9 Ja 16 '64
Everybody's president. K. Crawford. Newsweek 62:31 D 16 '63
Exclusive interview with the President of the United States; ed. by J. P. Sutherland. L. B. Johnson. il U S News 57:46-7 N 16 '64
Expanding pattern of American law; address, May 2, 1964. J. A. Farley. Vital Speeches 30:497-9 Je 1 '64
Fences against power. S. W. Rousseas. Nation 196:343-6+ Ap 27 '63
From the land of the free to the big PX. I. Kristol. il N Y Times Mag p7+ D 20 '64
From Washington straight (cont) Cato. Nat R 14:104, 148; 16:268, 396 F 12-26 '63, Ap 7, My 19 '64
Golden barrel. H. Hazlitt. Nat R 16:27 Ja 14 '64
Goldwater: next president? il U S News 57: 29-41 Jl 27 '64
Goldwater speaks; quotations, ed. by F. Knebel. B. M. Goldwater. Look 28:81-2+ Ap 21 '64
Goldwater's chances now; what the political experts say. il U S News 57:27-31 Ag 3 '64
Goldwater's opening gun: victory will be ours; address, July 16, 1964. B. M. Goldwater. il U S News 57:92-6 Jl 27 '64; Same with title Republican national convention. Vital Speeches 30:642-4 Ag 15 '64
Good beginning; concerning State of the Union message. M. Ascoli. Reporter 30:26 Ja 30 '64
Great European frustration; world-wide interest in American presidential election. N. Cousins. Sat R 47:14 S 5 '64
Happiness? D. Lawrence. U S News 55:104 Jl 8 '63
Hard-won destiny of Lyndon Johnson. D. Cater. Reporter 29:17-19 D 19 '63
Has Congress a future? W. D. Burnham. il Nation 196:545-8+ Je 29 '63
Here come the conservatives. R. J. Whalen. il Fortune 68:106-9+ D '63
His first tests are coming soon. il Bsns W p 15-16 Ja 4 '64
Hobbling the Constitution. W. D. Burnham. Commonweal 78:531-3 S 6 '63
Hope and reality; President Johnson's inaugural address. K. Crawford. Newsweek 65: 24 F 1 '65
Hour of decision: what LBJ faces now. il U S News 57:29-35 D 7 '64
House of horrors. W. F. Rickenbacker. Nat R 16:323-4 Ap 21 '64
How LBJ is doing his job; interview, ed. by J. Fromm. R. E. Neustadt. il U S News 57:34-7 Ag 3 '64
How the President makes a decision: excerpts from Decision-making in the White House. T. C. Sorensen. Sat R 46:12-15+ Jl 27; 8-12+ Ag 3 '63
How Wallace explains his big vote in Wisconsin; interview. G. C. Wallace. U S News 56:34 Ap 20 '64
If Lyndon Johnson wins big; what the changes will be. il U S News 57:48-50+ O 12 '64
If the Founding Fathers could look at U.S. today. il U S News 54:58-60 My 6 '63
Ike's view: Kennedy regime has sorry record; excerpts from statement, June 13, 1963. D. D. Eisenhower. U S News 54:19 Je 24 '63
Indispensable dissent. R. Moley. Newsweek 64:108 N 16 '64
Inside report: changes LBJ has brought in six months. il U S News 56:46-50+ My 18 '64
Is big government in U.S. getting too big? il U S News 55:46-9 S 9 '63
Is government too big? what Ike and LBJ say; excerpts from addresses, June 8, 1964. L. B. Johnson; D. D. Eisenhower. U S News 56:15-16 Je 22 '64
Is the government ready for the future? R. Drummond. Sat R 47:56+ Ag 29 '64
Is Washington too powerful? R. Kirk; E. F. Goldman. il N Y Times Mag p22+ Mr 1 '64
It's one year after JFK: the changes; interview with J. M. Burns. il U S News 57:60-6 N 23 '64
Johnson sets his course. il U S News 55:35-6 D 16 '63
Johnson's program and its prospects; concerning State-of-the-Union message. il U S News 56:29-31 Ja 20 '64
Die jungen herren der alten erde, by W. S. Schlamm. Review
Nat R 15:400-1 N 5 '63. S. J. Tonsor
Kennedy as target. New Repub 148:3-5 Je 1 '63
Kennedy: waiting for the tide. Bsns W p25-6 Mr 16 '63
Kennedy's problem: could he get more from Congress? H. Fuller. New Repub 148:12-14 Mr 9 '63
Landside view. J. Burnham. il Nat R 16:317-18 Ap 21 '64

UNITED STATES—Politics and government —*Continued*

Letter from Washington. R. H. Rovere. See issues of New Yorker

Liberal: what he is and isn't. E. J. McCarthy. il N Y Times Mag p8+ S 1 '63

LBJ: man in charge. C. W. Bailey, 2d. il Look 28:24-5 Mr 10 '64

Lyndon B. Johnson, the new President; what he stands for. il U S News 55:36-7 D 2 '63

LBJ's campaign opener: we offer a choice; address, August 27, 1964. L. B. Johnson. il U S News 57:66-9 S 7 '64; Same with title Democratic national convention. Vital Speeches 30:708-10 S 15 '64

LBJ's State of the Union. il Sr Schol 84:16 Ja 31 '64

LBJ's way of operating; what makes it different; intimate portrait of Lyndon Johnson. il U S News 56:35-7 Ja 13 '64

Lyndon Johnson, Rex. W. F. Buckley, jr. Nat R 16:438 Je 2 '64

Man of conscience. R. L. Reynolds. il Am Heritage 14:20-3+ F '63

Mandate for change:1953-1956, by D. D. Eisenhower. Review
 Nat R 15:487-8+ D 3 '63. W. F. Buckley, jr.
 New Yorker 39:235-8 N 16 '63. R. H. Rovere
 Reporter 29:59-60 N 21 '63. D. Cater

Mr Kennedy and apathy. Commonweal 78: 267-8 My 31 '63

Move toward immobility. E. Capouya. Sat R 46:36-8+ N 16 '63

Muddled problem of the succession. R. B. Morris. il N Y Times Mag p 11+ D 15 '63

My first eighty years. H. S. Truman. il Sat Eve Post 237:15-19 Je 13 '64

National affairs. See issues of Newsweek

National committees: time to modernize? J. Kraft. Harper 228:107-8+ Je '64

Negro's problem is the white's. E. Ginzberg. il N Y Times Mag p 14+ F 9 '64

Neither an echo nor a choice. M. Ascoli. Reporter 31:22-3 O 8 '64; Discussion. 31:6 N 5 '64

New breed of cat. J. Cogley. Commonweal 77: 609-11 Mr 8 '63

New era in Washington: its meaning. il U S News 55:35-50, 78-83 D 9 '63

New frontier's thrust bogs down in political muddle. M. Smith. Nations Bsns 51:23-4 Mr '63

New frontiers without freedom; address, March 16, 1964. E. V. Rickenbacker. Vital Speeches 30:490-4 Je 1 '64

New G.O.P; interview, ed. by R. Manning. J. V. Lindsay. Atlan 215:39-43 Ja '65

New kind of national election; excerpts from Congress: the sapless branch. J. S. Clark. Harper 228:72-4+ My '64

Nine men who control Congress. C. M. Roberts. il Atlan 213:63-8 Ap '64

Occasions and protests, by J. Dos Passos. Review
 Nat R 17:51-2 Ja 26 '65

On Kennedy and existential politics. N. Mailer. Esquire 60:26+ N '63

Open letter from a military intellectual to a sophisticated liberal leader. R. A. Levine. Bul Atomic Sci 20:24-7 S '64; Discussion. 21:31 Ja '65

Ordeal of power, by E. J. Hughes. Review
 New Yorker 39:195-6+ Mr 16; 119 My 11 '63. R. H. Rovere
 Reporter 28:58+ Mr 28 '63. J. P. Roche

Order of battle, by J. K. Javits. Review
 Commonweal 80:373-4 Je 12 '64. W. D. Burnham

Our government at work (cont) il Sr Schol 84:8-24+ F 14 '64

Our quaint political folkways. J. Ellison. Nation 197:323-5 N 16 '63

Party's responsibility. J. T. Crown. Nation 197:411-13 D 14 '63

Peace: it's relative. K. Crawford. Newsweek 63:27 Mr 2 '64

Philosophy of President Lyndon B. Johnson; excerpts from interview. L. B. Johnson. U S News 55:41 D 2 '63

Political mood of U.S. now; what a nationwide survey shows. il U S News 57:54-63 Ag 24 '64

Political power: USA/USSR, by Z. Brzezinski and S. P. Huntington. Review
 Commonweal 81:46-8 O 2 '64. W. V. O'Brien
 New Repub 150:15-16+ My 23 '64. A. Buchan

Politics becoming a millionaires' game? il U S News 54:58-61 F 25 '63

Politics of the 1920's. W. G. Carleton. Cur Hist 47:210-15+ O '64

Politics of the possible: the American scene. S. Rousseas and J. Farganis. Nation 196: 240-4 Mr 23 '63; Discussion. 197:inside cover, 93 Ag 24 '63

Politics of the space age; excerpt from Space: its impact on man and society, ed. by L. Levy. il Sat Eve Post 237:22-3 F 29 '64

Politics 64, new ball game. Newsweek 62: 24-5 D 9 '63

Polygraph-happy Pentagon. Sat Eve Post 236: 82 My 4 '63

Position papers, 1964. Sat R 47:14-17 F 29; 15-18 Ap 25; 17-20 Je 13; 14-17+ Jl 11; 14-16 Ag 22; 27-9+ S 26; 21-3+ O 17; 21-3 O 31 '64

Poverty package. il Newsweek 63:25-6 Mr 23 '64

Power in Washington, by D. Cater. Review
 New Repub 150:23-4 Ap 11 '64. M. W. Childs
 Newsweek 63:84-6 Mr 9 '64

President and Congress; Mr Johnson's first message; address, November 27, 1963. L. B. Johnson. il U S News 55:102-3 D 9 '63; Same. Vital Speeches 30:130-1 D 15 '63; Dept State Bul 49:910-12 D 16 '63; Cong Digest 43:1-2 Ja '64; Excerpts. Newsweek 62:22 D 9 '63; Summary. Bsns W p23-4 N 30 '63

President Johnson and the tasks ahead; with statements by L. B. Johnson. il Sr Schol 83:6-9 D 13 '63

President Johnson and the tides of ideology. F. S. Meyer. Nat R 16:23+ Ja 14 '64

Presidential papers, by N. Mailer. Review
 Commentary 37:83-5 F '64. M. Decter

Presidential politics in LBJ style. J. Kraft. Harper 228:113-16 Mr '64

Program for a Goldwater administration; symposium. il Nat R 16:585-99 Jl 14 '64

Program of faith; address, July 13, 1964. M. O. Hatfield. Vital Speeches 30:652-4 Ag 15 '64

Questions from a friend; European view. E. J. Hughes. Newsweek 64:15 Ag 24 '64

Real strength of our nation; address, July 15, 1963. W. F. Knowland. Vital Speeches 29:682-6 S 1 '63

Republican success. W. Lippmann. Newsweek 63:13 Mr 30 '64

Schizophrenia in the G.O.P. W. D. Burnham. il Commonweal 79:5-10 S 27 '63

Shadow and substance; essays on the theory and structure of politics, by J. P. Roche. Review
 Nat R 16:1115-18 D 15 '64. S. Parry

Some new views of Senator Goldwater; summary of statements. B. M. Goldwater. il U S News 57:10 Ag 3 '64

South Vietnam as a campaign issue. S. De Paul. America 111:82 Jl 25 '64

State of affairs. H. Brandon. Sat R 47:14 Ap 18 '64

State of affairs. H. Brandon. Sat R 47:14 Ap 18; 9 My 9; 7-8 Jl 4; 6+ Jl 11; 16-17 Ag 15; 18+ S 26; 16+ O 17; 12+ O 31 '64

State of the Union; address, January 8, 1964. L. B. Johnson. Vital Speeches 30:194-7 Ja 15 '64; Same. il U S News 56:66-9 Ja 20 '64; Dept State Bul 50:110-11 Ja 27 '64; Cur Hist 46:176-8 Mr '64

State of the Union; address, January 14, 1963. J. F. Kennedy. Vital Speeches 29:226-30 F 1 '63; Same. Cur Hist 44:174-6+ Mr '63; Excerpts. Dept State Bul 48:159-64 F 4 '63; Summary. il Sr Schol 82:15-17 Ja 30 '63

Stop the world: challenge of the November election. E. Rabinowitch. il Bul Atomic Sci 20:2-5 O '64

Strangelove? Seven days? not likely; U.S. military might vs constitutional government. R. L. Gilpatric. il N Y Times Mag p 15+ My 17 '64

Taking a stand on issues: Goldwater's own words; excerpts from statements and addresses. B. Goldwater. U S News 55:44-6 Jl 15 '63

TR, the strenuous life of a great American; excerpts from T.R: the story of Theodore Roosevelt. N. F. Busch. il Read Digest 83:237-43+ Jl '63

T.R.B. from Washington. See issues of New republic

Tension in U.S. politics. Q. L. Quade. America 110:312-13 Mr 7 '64

This electoral trauma. M. Ascoli. Reporter 31:22 O 22 '64

To make it a do-something Congress. S. Zagoria. il N Y Times Mag p26+ S 8 '63

Trends: Washington mood. See issues of Nation's business

Trouble ahead. R. Hotz. Aviation W 81:11 D 7 '64

UNITED STATES—Politics and government —*Continued*
Truly Republican convention? D. Lawrence. il U S News 57:96 Jl 13 '64
Trying, and gaining; President Johnson's program. il Bsns W p23-5 Ja 23 '65
Two little words. E. J. Hughes. Newsweek 61:19 Ap 8 '63
Union & the world; President Johnson's preparation of State of the Union message. il Time 85:13-14 Ja 8 '65
U.S.-Vietnam politics. K. Crawford. Newsweek 63:46 Ap 20 '64
Wait till next term; Kennedy administration. Reporter 28:16+ Mr 28 '63
Walk through history with Harry Truman; with editorial comment. J. McCarthy. il Holiday 34:55, 56-61+ N; 96-7+ D '63
Walter Lippmann interviewed by Charles Collingwood; excerpts from CBS program. W. Lippmann; C. Collingwood. New Repub 148:15-18 My 18 '63
Walter Lippmann, 1964; interview on CBS, ed. by E. Sevareid. New Repub 150:15-18 Ap 25 '64
Warfare state, by F. J. Cook. Review
Commentary 35:79-81 Ja '63. D. T. Bazelon; Discussion. 35:444 My '63
Washington front. See issues of America
Washington front; church leaders stand up to be counted. J. LaFarge. America 108:897 Je 29 '63
Washington insight; Kennedy and the intellectuals. J. Kraft. Harper 227:112+ N '63
Washington outlook. See issues of Business week
Washington report. W. V. Shannon. See issues of Commonweal
Washington's new set of White House VIPs. il Bsns W p32+ Mr 14 '64
We got rhythm. K. Crawford. Newsweek 61:37 Ap 15 '63
We too are independent. W. F. Buckley, jr. Nat R 16:526 Je 30 '64
Weakened spring of government: a study in nineteenth-century American history. W. D. Farnham. bibliog f Am Hist R 68:662-80 Ap '63
Week of gains for JFK. Bsns W p25-6 My 25 '63
Weighing the campaign. E. Roper. Sat R 47:28 O 31 '64
We're moving deeper into welfare state; interview. V. Bush. Nations Bsns 51:36-7+ Mr '63
What is a liberal? address, October 23, 1964. J. L. Jones. Vital Speeches 31:209-12 Ja 15 '65
What is a liberal? what is a conservative? J. Roddy. Look 28:19-21 Jl 28 '64
What Johnson plans now. il U S News 57:34-7 N 16 '64
What kind of president will Johnson make now? interview. A. Schlesinger, jr. U S News 57:53-5 N 16 '64
What's all this about a power structure in U.S? interview. A. Heard. U S News 55:58-60 Jl 1 '63
What's new in Washington. See issues of Successful farming
What's the mainstream? who is in it? A. Hacker. il N Y Times Mag p5+ S 6 '64
Where did all those Communists come from? F. Canavan. America 108:703 My 18 '63
Where does Goldwater stand? interview. B. Goldwater. il U S News 55:34-41 S 2 '63
Where Nixon stands; interview. R. M. Nixon. il U S News 55:84-91 O 14 '63
Where Rockefeller stands; interview. N. A. Rockefeller. U S News 55:76-83 S 23 '63
Where Romney stands; interview. G. Romney. U S News 56:70-5 Mr 9 '64
Which trend? D. Lawrence. U S News 57:140 S 28 '64
Which way with LBJ? J. Chamberlain. Nat R 15:525-7 D 17 '63
Who inherited what from whom? D. Lawrence. U S News 54:108 Mr 11 '63
Who's running the country? H. J. Morgenthau. Sat R 47:30-1+ Ap 25 '64
Why there's trouble on the New frontier. S. Hyman. il Look 27:30+ Jl 2 '63
Why Wallace withdrew; in the Governor's own words; excerpts from address, July 19, 1964. G. C. Wallace. il U S News 57:56-8 Ag 3 '64
Will it be nine years for LBJ? il U S News 58:37-40 Ja 25 '65
Working man's Washington. J. D. Weaver. Holiday 36:74-5+ D '64

See also
Business—Political aspects
Candidates, Political
Congressmen
Conservatism
Copperheads (nickname)
Democratic party
Elections—United States
Farmers—Political activities
Federal and state relations
Legislation—United States
Lobbying
Local government—United States
Municipal government—United States
Party government
Political campaigns
Political parties—United States
Presidential campaigns
Presidential candidates
Presidents—United States
Primaries
Progressive party
Republican party
Socialism—United States
Suffrage—United States
Trade unions—Political activities
United States—Armed forces—Political activities
United States—Cabinet
United States—Congress
United States—Constitution
United States—Executive departments
Vice-Presidents—United States
also subheads Politics, Politics and government under names of states, cities, etc. e.g. West—Politics; Chicago—Politics and government

Anecdotes, facetiae, satire, etc.

Folk songs for conservatives. N. E. Parmentel, jr. Esquire 60:160-1 D '63
How the West was rapproched; Bertie award. V. Gold. Nat R 16:911 O 20 '64
Instant politics for the busy homemaker. A. Manners. il McCalls 91:58+ Jl '64
King Jack starts a dollar monarchy; excerpts from article in London daily herald. M. Muggeridge. U S News 54:59 F 25 '63
Outsider's newsletter; outsider's newsreal. il Mlle 58:142-3 Mr '64
Unbeatable program for a fiery moderate; excerpts from interview. C. B. Luce. U S News 56:20 F 17 '64
Unthinkables; gangbusters on the New frontier. V. Gold. Nat R 14:278+ Ap 9 '63
What are the magazines saying, dear? il Time 81:37 Mr 1 '63

Bibliography

Let's talk about politics. G. W. Johnson. New Repub 150:17-18+ Mr 14 '64
Paperbacks and the election. S. Arbital. il Sr Schol 85:10T-11T S 30 '64
Political sweepstakes; books with political themes. Time 83:69-70 F 28 '64

Popular culture

After the new frontier; a new lost generation. G. Dickerson. Mlle 59:158-9+ S '64
Anti-intellectualism in American life, by R. Hofstadter. Review
Commentary 36:257-8 S '63. H. B. Parkes
Arts become good business, too. il Bsns W p68-9 Ja 19 '63
Cart and the horse, by L. Kronenberger. Review
Commentary 38:79-81 O '64. R. Langbaum
Christian choice in a changing world; spiritual values vs materialist pressures. J. Voorhis. Christian Cent 81:396-9 Mr 25 '64
Culture consumers, by A. Toffler. Review
Nation 199:466-7 D 14 '64. H. Dienstfrey
Newsweek 64:105A+ N 16 '64
Days and nights in Texas. B. P. Solomon. Harper 227:94-7+ N '63
Disturber of the peace: Paul Goodman; interview, ed. by E. Auchincloss and N. Lynch. P. Goodman. Mlle 58:104-5+ F '64
First new nation, by S. M. Lipset. Review
Harper 227:118+ N '63. P. Pickrel
Have we culture? yes, and no. W. Schuman. il N Y Times Mag p21+ S 22 '63
Mondrian is a paper napkin. V. Goldberg. il Horizon 5:90-1 My '63
Newspapers and the culture beat. J. Tebbel. il Sat R 46:61+ Ap 13 '63; Discussion. 46:54-5 My 11 '63
Public into private and the new boom in unreal estate. A. Gingrich. Esquire 61:4 Ja '64
Race, the dream & the nightmare; excerpts from Waiting for the end. L. A. Fiedler. Commentary 36:297-304 O '63; Reply. J. Pearce. 37:16+ Mr '64
Speaking out; national culture explosion is phony. H. C. Schonberg. Sat Eve Post 236:10+ Jl 13 '63
Squares America needs; reprint. C. H. Brower. il U S News 56:70-2 Ap 6 '64
Weekends, U.S.A: what ever happened to fun? excerpt from The weekenders. M. Gunther. McCalls 91:70-1+ Je '64

UNITED STATES—*Continued*

Population

By 1966 half of us will be under twenty-five. B. Bliven. il N Y Times Mag p47-8+ D 8 '63
How population explosion is changing the U.S; interview. P. M. Hauser. il U S News 57:58-63 Ag 31 '64
How we live; symposium. il Look 28:13-28+ Ja 14 '64
Letting George do it won't do it. W. R. Catton, jr. il Nat Parks Mag 38:4-7 Mr '64
1964 baby. D. Cohen. il Sci Digest 55:12-18 Ja '64
Plant location; where the people are. il Duns R 83:pt2 106-7 Mr '64
U.S. population reaches 192 million. Sci N L 86:25 Jl 11 '64
Way the U.S. is growing, what it means. il U S News 56:82-5 Ja 13 '64
What's ahead in the population boom; interview. R. M. Scammon. il U S News 54:68-71 My 6 '63
See also
Birth rate—United States
Cities and towns—United States
Migration, Internal

Post office department

Artists for stamps; design for special stamp to commemorate founding of the National academy of science. A. Frankfurter. il Art N 62:23+ Sum '63
Change in the Cabinet; emphasis is still on youth. U S News 55:26 S 23 '63
Goodbye, Mr ZIP. Time 82:11-12 Ag 2 '63
Hilarious hunt for the highwaymen; Great Cape Cod mail robbery. E. M. Wylie and R. V. Leary. il Sat Eve Post 236:75-81 Ap 13 '63
Mail: more money or else? Life 54:4 My 10 '63
Mail service; address, September 10, 1964. J. A. Gronouski. Vital Speeches 30:755-7 O 1 '64
Swifter completion of their rounds. A. Shuster. il Sat R 47:17-19+ Mr 21 '64; Discussion. 47:33 Ap 11 '64
What ails the post office? S. E. Cohen. Nation 197:364-7 N 30 '63
See also
Mail handling
Postal censorship
Postal employees
Postal service—United States

President's advisory commission on narcotic and drug abuse

New approach; more humane treatment. il Newsweek 61:94 Ap 15 '63

President's advisory committee on labor-management policy

Easing the stress of job losses. il Bsns W p87-8 My 30 '64
Presidential committee report on fiscal and monetary policy; November 19, 1962. Mo Labor R 86:51 Ja '63

President's advisory committee to strengthen the security of the free world

First meeting held by Advisory committee on aid program. Dept State Bul 48:329 Mr 4 '63
President receives Clay report on AID program; letter, March 22, 1963. J. F. Kennedy. Dept State Bul 48:574 Ap 15 '63
Second meeting held by Advisory committee on aid program. Dept State Bul 48:431 Mr 25 '63
This month's feature: Congress and the foreign aid program. Cong Digest 42:163-92 Je '63

President's commission on heart disease, cancer and stroke

Battle against disease. Sci N L 87:35 Ja 16 '65
Death of Dayton; commission report. il Newsweek 64:70 D 21 '64
Presidential medicine: Johnson panel, lay and medical, to study heart disease, cancer, and strokes. E. Langer. Science 143:1308-9 Mr 20 '64
$3 billion plan. il Time 84:64 D 18 '64
U.S. medicine: LBJ commission on heart disease, cancer and stroke offers sweeping recommendations. E. Langer. Science 146:1662-4 D 25 '64

President's commission on the status of women

Do we undervalue full-time wives? appraisal of report by the President's commission on the status of women. M. Mead. Redbook 122:22+ N '63
Education for the mature woman; excerpts from American women, the report of the President's commission on the status of women. Sat R 46:90 N 16 '63
Progress of the commission on the status of women. K. P. Ellickson. Mo Labor R 86:141-4 F '63
Report of President's commission on the status of women; excerpts from American women. Mo Labor R 86:1166-9 O '63
Status of women. R. Holstein. NEA J 52:68 N '63

President's commission to investigate the assassination of President Kennedy

As others see us; concerning Warren commission report. J. F. Fixx. Sat R 47:35-7 N 7 '64
As Warren inquiry starts: latest on the assassination. il U S News 55:28-30 D 30 '63
Assassination inquiry: slow, careful. il U S News 56:49 Ja 27 '64
Assassination: the trail to a verdict; with report by G. R. Ford. il Life 57:40-50B O 2 '64
Assassination: Warren commission report. il Newsweek 64:32-40+ O 5 '64
Attorney for Oswald. Time 83:47 Mr 6 '64
Back of the secrecy in the assassination probe. il U S News 56:52+ F 24 '64
Between two fires; Mrs Oswald's testimony to Warren commission. il Time 83:16-20 F 14 '64
Book for all to read: Warren report. L. Wainwright. Life 57:35 O 16 '64
Brave little woman; M. Oswald before Warren's investigating commission. il Newsweek 63:17 F 17 '64
Counsel for Oswald. U S News 56:16 Mr 9 '64
Death of a President; told in direct testimony; excerpts. il U S News 57:68-70 D 7 '64
Eye on that window. il Newsweek 63:32+ Je 22 '64
50,000-word leak; testimony of J. Ruby to the Warren commission. Time 84:40 Ag 28 '64
Five publishers issue Warren panel's report. Pub W 186:43-4 O 5 '64
From Washington straight. Nat R 16:311 Ap 21 '64
Heres' what the Warren report will show. il U S News 57:42-3 S 14 '64
History, or hysteria? Trevor-Roper article in London's Sunday times. Newsweek 64:35-6 D 28 '64
History's jury. il Newsweek 62:25-7 D 16 '63
How to read the Warren report. Nat R 16:858 O 6 '64
In the Nation's interest; commission to investigate the assassination of President John F. Kennedy. America 109:789 D 21 '63
JFK's murder: sowers of doubt. il Newsweek 63:22-4 Ap 6 '64
Jumping the gun; premature disclosures. il Newsweek 64:50 Jl 13 '64
Latest on murder of Kennedy: a preview of the Warren report. il U S News 56:43-4 Je 1 '64
Lee Oswald's widow tells her story; summary of testimony. M. Oswald. U S News 56:19 F 17 '64
Oswald; may we have some facts, please? M. Kempton. New Repub 150:13-15 Je 13 '64
Oswald mystery grows deeper and deeper. U S News 56:45 Mr 30 '64
Protecting the President: a job for Superman? il Sr Schol 85:6-9 N 4 '64
Reaction to the Warren commission report. Sr Schol 85:17 O 14 '64
Reporting the report. il Newsweek 64:100-1 O 12 '64
Rush to buy the report on Kennedy assassination. il U S News 57:20 O 12 '64
Sad & solemn duty; commission to investigate the assassination of J. Kennedy. il Time 82:26-7 D 13 '63
Safeguarding the President so it can't occur again. il Bsns W p34+ O 3 '64
Task of the Warren commission. Nation 198:81 Ja 27 '64
Unraveling the mystery of the assassination of John F. Kennedy; the official story. il U S News 57:35-42+ O 5 '64
Untold stories: aftermath of the assassination. il U S News 57:58-62 O 12 '64
Verdict: one man alone. il Sr Schol 85:9-10 O 7 '64
Warren commission. Nation 197:445 D 28 '63
Warren commission. New Repub 150:4 F 29 '64
Warren commission. M. Rosenberg. il Nation 199:110-12 S 14 '64
Warren commission report. il Time 84:45-50 O 2 '64

UNITED STATES—President's commission to investigate the assassination of President Kennedy—*Continued*

Warren commission report; Paraffin test unreliable; Killing still mystery. il Sci N L 86:227, 230 O 10 '64
Warren commission: testimony and evidence. il Time 84:25-7 D 4 '64
Warren findings: some new facts. il U S News 57:44 Jl 6 '64
Warren impeachers. K. Crawford. Newsweek 64:40 O 19 '64
Warren report: a measure of the achievement; with editorial comment. H. L. Packer. il Nation 199:290, 295-9 N 2 '64
Warren report; case for the prosecution. M. Kempton. New Repub 151:13-17 O 10 '64; Reply. S. Rifkin. 151:29 O 24 '64
Warren report; comment. Commonweal 81:59 O 9 '64
Warren report in mass production. D. Dempsey. Sat R 47:25+ N 7 '64
Warren report; paperback editions were produced at record-breaking pace. il Pub W 186:80-2 O 5 '64
Warren's secret. Nat R 16:265-6 Ap 7 '64
Week in the sun; Marguerite Oswald's testimony. il Newsweek 63:29 F 24 '64
What they saw that dreadful day in Dallas; testimony and evidence published. il Newsweek 64:28-30+ D 7 '64
What's your source? premature publication by Journal-American of Ruby's testimony before Warren. il Newsweek 64:68-9 Ag 31 '64

President's committee on equal employment opportunity

Hiring, firing, promoting, unions; policing ahead? EEOC, for Equal employment opportunity commission. U S News 55:107-9 N 11 '63
How new law will police hiring, firing, promoting; role of EEOC. il U S News 56:79-80 Je 29 '64
If rights bill passes: how to hire, fire, promote; role of EEOC, for equal employment opportunity commission. il U S News 56:113-15 F 24 '64
Jobs for Negroes: how much progress in sight? il Newsweek 62:68-70+ Jl 15 '63
Negro drive for jobs; with editorial comment. il Bsns W p52-4+, 124 Ag 17 '63
No Negroes wanted; big construction job at Howard university, Washington. America 108:454 Ap 6 '63
Progress or publicity? Newsweek 61:27 F 25 '63
Union program for eliminating discrimination. Mo Labor R 86:58-9 Ja '63
What happens when government polices your hiring; Motorola case. il U S News 56:87 Mr 30 '64; Same abr. with title Fair to whom? Read Digest 84:129-30 Je '64

President's committee on equal opportunity in the armed forces

Pentagon jumps into the race fight. il U S News 55:49-50 Ag 19 '63

President's council on physical fitness

Top form for teens; physical-fitness pamphlets, vim (for girls) and vigor (for boys) il Newsweek 63:93 My 11 '64

President's foreign intelligence advisory board

Clark Clifford named chairman of Intelligence advisory board. Dept State Bul 48:805 My 20 '63

President's recreation advisory council

New national recreation area system; with excerpts from testimony of Joseph Prendergast. Recreation 56:257-8 Je '63

President's science advisory committee

Education: PSAC panel draws on experience of curriculum reform to point way to wider innovation. J. Walsh. Science 144:394-5 Ap 24 '64
JFK's new science advisor. Sci N L 84:327 N 23 '63
Manpower needs and higher education; summary of report with editoral comment. W. W. Brickman. Sch & Soc 91:110 Mr 9 '63
More pesticide research. Sci N L 83:341-2 Je 1 '63
Nuclear test ban treaty endorsed by Science advisory committee. Dept State Bul 49:430-1 S 16 '63
Pesticide report. Sci Am 209:64 Jl '63
Policy and the scientists. L. A. DuBridge. For Affairs 41:578-80 Ap '63
President's science adviser. P. H. Abelson. Science 142:1025 N 22 '63; Discussion. 142:1257; 143:427-9 D 6 '63; Ja 31 '64
Science information; discussion of report by the President's science advisory committee. C. D. Leake. Science 139:1088 Mr 15 '63

Public advisory committee for trade negotiations

President sets up public advisory committee for trade negotiations. L. B. Johnson. Dept State Bul 50:506 Mr 30 '64

Public buildings

See Public buildings

Public buildings service

Architecture, I'm for it, Yasko says: challenges architects of fifty states to make architecture of U.S. buildings; excerpts from address. K. Yasko. Arch Rec 133:23+ Ap '63

Public health service

Burning question: tobacco and politics. D. S. Greenberg. il Reporter 30:34-5 Ja 30 '64
Chemical controversy; search for cause of dead fish in Mississippi and Missouri Rivers. Time 83:72+ Je 19 '64
Congress plays geography: PHS health center delayed again as Maryland site is firmly excluded. E. Langer. Science 145:1165 S 11 '64
Don't go near the water; use of endrin in Louisiana. New Repub 150:5 Ap 11 '64
Environmental health center: PHS project stalled on several counts; site and scope are still in dispute. E. Langer. Science 141:703-4 Ag 23 '63
Environmental health: Taft center in Cincinnati has been the PHS mainstay in pollution research. J. Walsh. Science 145:31-3 Jl 3 '64
GHQ for pollution fighters; Robert A. Taft sanitary engineering center. il Bsns W p 136+ Ap 25 '64
New tips on fighting some major ills. U S News 54:6 My 6 '63
Oyster stew; problem of water pollution, Great Bay, N.H. P. Hirsch. New Repub 150:7-8 Ja 4 '64
Pesticides: minute quantities linked with massive fish kills; federal policy still uncertain. E. Langer. Science 144:35-7 Ap 3 '64; Discussion. 144:1294 Je 12 '64
Polluted water; timidity in administering the government's control program. New Repub 151:6 Jl 4 '64
Speaking of reorganization. J. Ridgeway. New Repub 151:16 N 21 '64; Reply. J. J. Schrogie. 151:28 D 5 '64
Stimulation of health research. J. H. Cassedy. bibliog Science 145:897-902 Ag 28 '64
Tobacco and health: governmental action seems unlikely until PHS concludes long, two-phase study. D. S. Greenberg. Science 140:1196 Je 14 '63
Tobacco-health issue. F. Marley. il Sci N L 84:373 D 14 '63
Tobacco report: PHS study group, after fourteen month survey, agrees that smoking is indeed harmful. D. S. Greenberg. Science 143:227 Ja 17 '64
View from the pork barrel; Congress, PHS, haggle over proposed health center site. E. Langer. Science 140:240+ Ap 12 '63
Water pollution; anti-pollution legislation. New Repub 149:4 D 21 '63
Water pollution; Merrimack River. New Repub 148:7 Je 29 '63
What killed the fish in the Mississippi River? il U S News 56:52 My 4 '64

See also

United States—Communicable disease center, Atlanta, Ga.
United States—National center for environmental sciences
United States—National institutes of health
United States—Surgeon general's office

Public housing administration

GAO report attacks PHA for design excesses. Arch Rec 136:10 S '64
PHA and design: commissioner outlines aims; excerpts from address, December 5, 1963. M. C. McGuire. Arch Rec 135:23+ Ja '64
Public housing projects receive design awards; low-rent housing projects in Marin City, Calif; Minneapolis, Minn; and Philadelphia, Pa. il Am City 79:82-3 D '64

Public roads, Bureau of

Sign uniformity still lagging. il Am City 79:104 D '64

Race problems

Liberalism and the Negro; symposium. ed. by N. Podhoretz. Commentary 37:25-42 Mr '64

UNITED STATES—Race problems—*Continued*
Negroes & Jews: the new challenge to pluralism. N. Glazer. Commentary 38:29-34 D '64
Race, the dream & the nightmare; excerpts from Waiting for the end. L. A. Fiedler. Commentary 36:297-304 O '63; Reply. J. Pearce. 37:16+ Mr '64
Red Chinese American Negro. W. Worthy. Esquire 62:132+ O '64
Rediscovery of prejudice. Nation 198:337-8 Ap 6 '64
Risks of patriotism. America 109:9 Jl 6 '63
Top judge. A. Morrison. il Ebony 19:111-12+ Mr '64
X factor; effect of white backlash on a presidential election. J. O'Gara. Commonweal 80:628 S 18 '64
See also
Church and race problems
Congress of racial equality
Negroes in the United States

Reclamation, Bureau of

Quiet crisis or lost cause? W. Stegner. Sat R 47:28+ S 19 '64

Relations (diplomatic)
Catholic church

See Catholic church—Relations (diplomatic)—United States

Religious institutions and affairs

Foolish fears; concern over President Johnson's proposed center of prayer. America 110:272 F 29 '64
Fourth American faith, by D. Howlett. Review
Christian Cent 81:1064 Ag 26 '64. T. B. Clark
Interfaith dialogue and church-state issues. B. J. Coughlin. America 108:900-3 Je 29 '63
No more old-time religion. America 108:600 Ap 27 '63
Proceedings of 1963 First amendment conference on meaning of religion in the First amendment. il Cath World 197:280-317 Ag '63
Religion's impact. America 109:227-8 S 7 '63
Religious freedom; the Court expands a concept. T. G. Sanders. Nation 197:25-8 Jl 13 '63
Schoolrooms and prayers. E. J. Hughes. Newsweek 62:15 Jl 1 '63
Second coming. J. Cogley. Commonweal 77:554-5 F 22 '63
Thoughts of a returned expatriate. R. H. Drummond. Christian Cent 81:172-4 F 5 '64
Varieties of unbelief, by M. E. Marty. Review
Commonweal 81:490-1 Ja 8 '65. T. Merton
See also
Association of council secretaries
Baptists in the United States
Catholic church in the United States
Church and state
Churches of Christ
Disciples of Christ
Jews in the United States
Lutheran church in the United States
Methodist church in the United States
Mormons and Mormonism
Negroes in the United States—Religion
Presbyterian church in the United States
Presbyterian church in the United States (South)
Protestant churches—United States
Protestant Episcopal church
United church of Christ
United States—Church history

Renegotiation board

GOP unit seeks renegotiation phase-out. K. Johnsen. Aviation W 80:33-4 Ap 27 '64
Supreme court refuses to hear appeal in Boeing renegotiation. K. Johnsen. Aviation W 80:30 My 11 '64

Reserve forces

See United States—Armed forces—Reserves

Reserve officers training corps

Changes in ROTC: what's ahead. U S News 57:10 S 14 '64
Now, a better deal for students in ROTC. U S News 57:12 O 26 '64
Rot-Cee ranks. il Newsweek 63:84 F 24 '64

Revenue

Enclosed $5, forgive me; government's Conscience fund. Newsweek 63:54+ Je 29 '64
See also
Taxation—United States

Riots

Are the riots planned? Negro riots throughout North. il Bsns W p34 S 5 '64
As race riots spread in North. il U S News 57:34 Ag 17 '64
Civil rights: a movement in search of a direction? with comment on the world's news fronts. il Sr Schol 85:16-20 S 30 '64
Crackdown coming on future rioters. il U S News 57:80-1 O 12 '64
Crisis in race relations; symposium. il U S News 57:23-40 Ag 10 '64
F.B.I. reports on summer riots. Christian Cent 81:1261 O 14 '64
In six states, a week-end of riots. il U S News 57:10 Jl 20 '64
Kill the cops! teenagers riot during Labor day weekend. il Newsweek 64:36+ S 21 '64
Looting: the high cost of race violence. il U S News 57:36-41 S 14 '64
Negro gets the blame; nonviolent demonstrations for civil rights and rioting and looting. Christian Cent 81:1103 S 9 '64
Race riots: Goldwater boon. F. Knebel. il Look 28:34+ S 22 '64
Violent flare-ups. Sr Schol 85:31 S 23 '64
What now? one Negro leader's answer. R. Wilkins. il N Y Times Mag p11+ Ag 16 '64
See also subhead Riots under names of cities, e.g. Rochester, N.Y.—Riots

Rural electrification administration

How a subsidized business thrives; rural electric cooperatives. il Nations Bsns 52:36-7+ O '64
How borrowers make profits on U.S. loans. U S News 55:11 D 16 '63
Power industry vs. rural co-ops: a growing fight. il U S News 54:83-5 Ap 29 '63
REA, a case study of bureaucracy run wild. K. O. Gilmore and E. H. Methvin. il Read Digest 83:81-7 D '63
There's no stopping REA, or is there? H. Kay. il Fortune 67:118-21+ F '63
Unsinkable REA. R. Moley. Newsweek 62:84 Ag 19 '63

School laws and legislation

See School laws and legislation—United States

Science and technology, Office of

Wiesner successor: Donald Hornig, Princeton chemistry head, named to take over top science posts. D. S. Greenberg. Science 142:939 N 15 '63

Scientific laboratory, Los Alamos, N.Mex.

Notes for a gazetteer; Santa Fe's proximity to Los Alamos. P. Hamburger. New Yorker 40:206+ O 17 '64
Phoebus may yield 268-lb. reactor. F. G. McGuire. il Miss & Roc 12:16-17 Ap 8 '63

Scientific research and development, Office of

Policy and the scientists. L. A. DuBridge. For Affairs 41:573-6 Ap '63

Secretary of state

See Secretaries of state (United States)

Securities and exchange commission

Adding up the damage of SEC market study; Funds under fire. il Bsns W p88+ Ag 17 '63
Agree on floor trading rule; SEC and New York exchange. Bsns W p 158 Ap 11 '64
Bank defies SEC on trusts; First national city bank of New York. Bsns W p 136 Ap 13 '63
Big board is under fire; special study of the securities markets. il Bsns W p23-4 Jl 20 '63
Breathing spell on SEC action. Bsns W p 170+ Ap 20 '63
Breeze through the corridors; LBJ men begin to move into the agencies. il Newsweek 63:79 My 25 '64
Career cop; new chairman. il Time 84:74 Jl 17 '64
Choir of approval; proposed changes in U.S. securities laws. Newsweek 61:74 Je 17 '63
Court to rule on scalping; injunction against Capital gains research bureau, inc. U S News 54:84 F 4 '63
Critical examination of SEC proposals. L. Silberman. Harvard Bsns R 42:121-32 N '64
Deadlock on the floor; controversy over floor trading. Newsweek 63:69 Ap 6 '64
Endorsement; report on stock-market operations. Newsweek 62:52 Ag 5 '63
Exchange of heat. il Time 83:89-90 Ap 3 '64
For Wall Street: tighter rules, fewer secrets; special study of securities markets. il Bsns W p23-5 Ap 6 '63

UNITED STATES—Securities and exchange commission—*Continued*
Gaudy façade? Securities and exchange commission report. il Newsweek 63:75-7 My 4 '64
How firms finance outlays now; concerning SEC report. U S News 56:86 My 4 '64
Laws that SEC wants. Bsns W p 116 My 4 '63
LBJ stamp on SEC. Bsns W p26-7 Jl 18 '64
Mr Johnson flunks. Nation 198:613 Je 22 '64
Modernizing the market; concerning SEC report. il Time 82:71-2 Jl 26 '63
Mutual disenchantment; SEC report. il Time 82:65 Ag 16 '63
Neither all bad nor all good; Cohen report on the Nation's securities markets. il Newsweek 62:64-7 Ag 19 '63
New controls for brokers? U S News 54:115-16 My 13 '63
New protection plan on stocks. U S News 54:107 Je 17 '63
No hostility in Securities report. U S News 54:97 Ap 1 '63
On the floor. Newsweek 63:101-2 Ap 20 '64
Out in the open; Securities and exchange commission's report on corporate publicity and public relations. L. L. L. Golden. Sat R 46:52-3 Jl 13 '63
Personal investing; SEC reaches over the counter. il Fortune 67:231-2 My '63
Policeman's lot is not a happy one. il Newsweek 63:63-4 Je 22 '64
P.S. from the SEC. Newsweek 61:76+ F 25 '63
Putting the heat on fund directors. Bsns W p88 Mr 7 '64
Restraint on the floor. il Time 83:104 Ap 17 '64
Ruling on variable annuities. U S News 54:85 F 4 '63
Savings of Americans grow past trillion-dollar mark; summary of report. U S News 56:98 Ap 13 '64
Sears is set to enter the mutual fund race. il Bsns W p 112+ F 15 '64
SEC hands Pru a blow. Bsns W p27-8 Ja 26 '63
SEC head urges: do it yourself; Wall Street rules. Bsns W p 140 D 5 '64
SEC reforms to help, not hamstring. il Newsweek 61:75-6+ Ap 15 '63
SEC vs. Wall Street. R. A. Phalon. il Duns R 81:56-7+ Ap '63
SEC's new cast. il Fortune 70:75 S '64
SEC's swipe at specialists; disorderly market after Kennedy assassination. Bsns W p73 F 1 '64
Showdown on accounting principles. R. N. Anthony. Harvard Bsns R 41:99-106 My '63
Skeptical SEC eye on Wall Street. il Newsweek 62:55-6+ Jl 29 '63
Stock market reform gets a shove. il Bsns W p91-2 F 8 '64
Stock-market study. U S News 55:102 Ag 19 '63
Straight and narrow Wall St; new rules governing the securities industry. Bsns W p 118+ Ag 15 '64
Taking stock; findings of SEC study. il Time 81:91-2 Ap 12 '63
Testing by results. H. Hazlitt. Newsweek 63:70 Je 1 '64
Tightening up on Wall Street. Bsns W p 164 Ap 13 '63
Tighter rules on firms' reports. U S News 54:106 My 27 '63
Uneasy partnership SEC/NYSE. R. I. Robinson and H. R. Bartell, jr. Harvard Bsns R 43:76-88 Ja '65
Urgent questions about the stock market; implications of controversial SEC study. R. F. Murray. bibliog f Harvard Bsns R 42:53-9 S '64
Wall Street can live with the new rules. Bsns W p 120+ O 3 '64
Wall Street musters its defenses; SEC's study of floor trading and stock specialists. il Bsns W p84-6 Jl 27 '63
Wall Street's main event: SEC vs. the specialists. T. A. Wise. il Fortune 69:149-52+ My '64
Watchdog of Wall Street. New Repub 148:7-8 My 25 '63
What Congress is told about the stock market. il U S News 54:67-8 Ap 15 '63
What safeguards are there for today's investors? U S News 55:81-2 D 23 '63
What's wrong in stock exchanges: official study. U S News 55:95 Jl 29 '63

Senate

See United States—Congress—Senate

Small business administration

Agency that helps small business. G. R. Rosen. il Duns R 84:48-9+ N '64
Aiding Negro businessmen; Small business opportunities corp, Phila. Bsns W p 141 Ap 18 '64
Business loans that went sour. il U S News 56:50 Mr 9 '64
Case of the lonesome loan; symposium. il Harvard Bsns R 42:6-8+ N '64
Counseling for small business; Service corps of retired executives (SCORE) advisers. C. B. Grannis. Pub W 186:42 S 21 '64
Government as a banker: easy way to get money. il U S News 57:105-7 O 19 '64
Making of a Negro middle class. H. Lees. il Reporter 31:41-4 O 8 '64
SBA can help small bookshops with operating loans. Pub W 186:48-9 O 12 '64
Where sick companies can turn for advice; Score project. il Bsns W p94+ Ag 15 '64

Social conditions

Abundance for what? by D. Riesman. Review
New Yorker 40:202-5 S 26 '64. N. Bliven
American agenda; evaluation of our society; address, May 1, 1963. J. W. Fulbright. bibliog Vital Speeches 29:520-6 Je 15 '63
Beyond civil rights; lineaments of the integrated society. J. R. Nelson. Christian Cent 81:668-72 My 20 '64
Cold war; address, April 5, 1964. J. W. Fulbright. bibliog f Vital Speeches 30:422-7 My 1 '64
Corrupt society; with foreword by the editors. F. J. Cook. Nation 196:453-96a Je 1 '63; Discussion. 196:inside cover Je 22; inside cover Je 29 '63
Culture against man, by J. Henry. Review
Sat R 46:40 N 23 '63. R. Stein
Sci Am 210:139-40+ My '64. M. D. Sahlins
In the midst of plenty: the poor in America, by B. H. Bagdikian. Review
Christian Cent 81:990 Ag 5 '64. E. Kruuse
Kennedy comes home to trouble. il U S News 55:29-30 Jl 15 '63
Need for spokesmen. Commonweal 78:211 My 17 '63
Our national goals: the hard choices. L. Hazard. Harvard Bsns R 41:22-4+ My '63
Poverty U.S.A. il Newsweek 63:19-20+ F 17 '64; Same abr. with title Poor amid prosperity. Read Digest 84:90-7 Je '64
Return from Russia. W. Ciszek. America 110:408-11 Mr 28 '64
Spiders under the rock. America 109:405 O 12 '63
Thoughts of a returned expatriate. R. H. Drummond. Christian Cent 81:172-4 F 5 '64
World as we want it. G. Hicks. Sat R 47:27-8 Ja 25 '64
See also
Child welfare—United States
Cities and towns—United States
Commercialism
Communication (speech, writing, etc)—Social aspects
Crime and criminals—United States
Divorce—United States
Housing—United States
Lynching
Negroes in the United States
Poor—United States
United States—Population
Women—United States
Youth—United States

Bibliography

Home scene. D. R. Campion. America 108:687-91; 110:651-3 My 11 '63, My 9, '64

History

See United States—Social history

Social history

Abundance for what? by D. Riesman. Review
New Yorker 40:202-5 S 26 '64. N. Bliven
Vanished world, by A. G. Sneller. Review
Newsweek 64:82-3 Jl 20 '64
See also
Negroes in the United States—History

Social life and customs

All around the town; news & notes on our lively, changing cities & suburbs. il Changing T 17:29-30 My '63
Americans in my mind. V. S. Pritchett. il Holiday 34:28-41+ Jl '63
Better never than late. J. K. Lagemann. House & Gard 125:110-11 F '64
Bringing up children: the American vs. the British way. E. Wintour. Harper 229:58-63 Ag '64; Discussion. 229:11-12 O '64

UNITED STATES—Social life and customs—*Continued*
Dime was our passport. H. Golden. il Travel 122:50-2 S '64
Loving Americans. Time 83:75 Mr 6 '64
Neighbours, by H. Bracey. Review
Newsweek il 64:81+ Ag 24 '64
Opinion, please, from London. A. Alvarez. il Mlle 58:92+ Ap '64
Quietmouth American. D. Lloyd. Harper 227: 101-2+ S '63
Saloon. G. Carson. il Am Heritage 14:24-31+ Ap '63
Speaking out; our way of life makes us miserable. E. Fromm. Sat Eve Post 237:8+ Jl 25 '64
They don't make them that way any more. R. P. Smith. il McCalls 90:86-7+ My '63
Thirty years ago; end of prohibition. G. Vincent. il N Y Times Mag p45-6+ D 1 '63
Tormented generation; American students. M. M. Hunt and R. Corman. il Sat Eve Post 236:30, 33-4 O 12 '63
White gloves and ritual curtsies; excerpts from Profession: housewife. P. McGinley. Ladies Home J 80:34+ S '63
Why young couples feel trapped; dissatisfactions of social life after marriage. S. Blum. il Redbook 123:62-3+ S '64

See also
Christmas—United States
Family reunions
Thanksgiving day
also subhead Social life and customs under names of cities, e.g. New York (city) —Social life and customs

Social policy

Free, growing, full of hope; concerning State of the Union address. Sr Schol 85:21 Ja 14 '65
Great society: how much to spend. U S News 57:34 D 7 '64
Here are Johnson's promises for a Great society; State-of-the-Union message, January 4, 1965. L. B. Johnson. il U S News 58:98-102 Ja 18 '65; Same. Vital Speeches 31:194-8 Ja 15 '65
Johnson's grand design; concerning State of the Union message; with editorial comment. il Bsns W p 19-21, 108 Ja 9 '65
LBJ's Great society, what will it be? il U S News 57:33-7 N 23 '64
Modern Utopia; concerning State of the Union message. il Time 85:15-16 Ja 15 '65
No sense raising hell; concerning State of the Union message. New Repub 148:3-4 F 2 '63
President takes office: Johnson-the-inheritor yields to Johnson-on-his own. il Sr Schol 85:6-9 Ja 21 '65
Prospectus for the Great society; concerning the State of the Union message. H. Brandon. Sat R 48:14-15 Ja 30 '65
State of the Union. New Repub 152:4+ Ja 16 '65
State of the Union. il Newsweek 65:15-19 Ja 11 '65
State of the Union; concerning President Johnson's address. America 112:70 Ja 16 '65
Vision of LBJ; something for all; concerning State-of-the-Union message. il U S News 58:31-3 Ja 18 '65

Soil conservation service

Invitation to a fish fry. R. Starnes. Field & S 69:21-2+ O '64
Recreation site finders. L. Fox. il Recreation 56:92-3 F '63

Standards, National bureau of

Bricks without straw bosses. J. Lear. il Sat R 47:45-9 F 1 '64
Frequency & time standards. G. E. Hudson. il Electr World 72:20-3 Ag '64
Microfilm defects discussed at National archives meeting; with National bureau of standards and the Eastman-Kodak company. Library J 88:3043 S 1 '63

Radio propagation laboratory

New NBS facility for better time broadcasts. il(p65) Sci N L 83:75 F 2 '63

State, Department of

Back seat for the liberals. F. Kuh. Nation 196:522-4 Je 22 '63
Beatles of Foggy Bottom. il Life 56:38A Ap 3 '64
Board of foreign scholarships reports on exchange program. Dept State Bul 49:869-70 D 2 '63
Cold war between the Hill and Foggy Bottom. F. G. Dutton. il N Y Times Mag p36+ S 15 '63
Communications satellite program and the Department of state; statement, April 8, 1964. A. Chayes. bibliog f Dept State Bul 50:682-3 Ap 27 '64
Dangerous failings of our State department. F. J. Lausche. Read Digest 84:54-60 Je '64; Excerpts. U. S. News 56:22 Je 8 '64
Department to hold conference for editors and broadcasters. Dept State Bul 50:549 Ap 6 '64
Emergency preparedness functions assigned to Secretary of state; executive order, February 26, 1963. J. F. Kennedy. Dept State Bul 48:629-30 Ap 22 '63
Focus on foreign policy. il N Y Times Mag p8-9 Je 14 '64
Foreign policy conference to be held at Boston. Dept State Bul 49:377 S 2 '63
Foreign policy conference to be held at Cleveland. Dept State Bul 50:899 Je 8 '64
Foreign policy conference to be held at Milwaukee. Dept State Bul 50:424-5 Mr 16 '64
Four up, one out; upper level changes. New Repub 148:6 Mr 30 '63
In the bag; firing of loyalty checker, O. F. Otepka. Newsweek 62:36+ N 18 '63
International orientation for college administrators. L. J. Stiles. Sch & Soc 91:356-8 N 16 '63
McNamara's human problem. Life 55:4 S 20 '63
Making of foreign policy; television interview, January 11, 1964. D. Rusk; E. F. Goldman. Dept State Bul 50:164-76 F 3 '64
Musings from State; D. Rusk on his department and its problems. Time 83:14-15 Ja 24 '64
Name in the game; question of shift in personnel. Time 81:20-1 Mr 15 '63
New top man on Far East. U S News 56: 19 Mr 16 '64
New turmoil over security; Otepka case. il U S News 55:48 N 25 '63
OAU commission on Congo talks with department officers; Department statement, with joint press communique, September 23 and September 30, 1964. Dept State Bul 51: 553 O 19 '64
Publications. See issues of Department of state bulletin
Reorganization prompts closer liaison. Miss & Roc 12:59-60 Mr 25 '63
Sad state of the Department of state: the hog-tied ambassador. E. Briggs. Esquire 60:100-1+ S '63
Security at State; removal of O. F. Otepka. New Repub 149:5 N 23 '63
State's international air role increased. Aviation W 78:38 My 6 '63
Two new members appointed to Advisory committee on arts. Dept State Bul 48:663 Ap 29 '63
Who really makes U.S. foreign policy. il U S News 54:33-5 F 18 '63

See also
Secretaries of state (United States)
United States—Foreign relations
United States—Foreign service

Advisory committee on international business problems

Advisory committee on international business problems established. Dept State Bul 48: 296 F 25 '63

Advisory committee on the arts

First four members appointed to Advisory committee on arts. Dept State Bul 48:448 Mr 25 '63
Members named to arts advisory committee and drama panel. Dept State Bul 49:438-9 S 16 '63

Anecdotes, facetiae, satire, etc.

Sad state of the Department of state: the hog-wild machine. M. Epernay. Esquire 60:102-3+ S '63

Appropriations and expenditures

Department of state budget requests for fiscal 1965; statement, April 28, 1964. D. Rusk. il Dept State Bul 50:836-43 My 25 '64
How to save money; an open letter to Congressman John J. Rooney. H. S. Villard. Harper 228:17+ Ja '64
Secretary Rusk discusses appropriation request before Senate committee; statement, July 16, 1963. D. Rusk. il Dept State Bul 49:260-4 Ag 12 '63

Bulletin

25th anniversary of the Department of state bulletin; statement. D. Rusk. Dept State Bul 51:2 Jl 6 '64

UNITED STATES—State, Department of—*Continued*

Educational and cultural affairs, Bureau of

Need to explore inner space; address, July 2, 1964. L. D. Battle. Dept State Bul 51:110-19 Jl 27 '64
Nickle words for a golden mission. K. Molz. il Wilson Lib Bul 39:44-7 S '64
Roads to international understanding; address, January 15, 1963. C. D. Norrell. Dept State Bul 48:214-17 F 11 '63

History

How the Department of state got its name. R. S. Patterson and H. D. Langley. Dept State Bul 51:370-6 S 14 '64

International scientific affairs, Office of

Science in the State department; Office of international scientific affairs. W. M. Todd. Bul Atomic Sci 20:27-9 D '64

Passport division

Passport barrier; it must come down. H. S. Commager. il N Y Times Mag p 12+ O 20 '63
To travel freely. H. Aptheker. Bul Atomic Sci 20:25 Mr '64

Science adviser, Office of

See United States—State, Department of—International scientific affairs, Office of

Security and consular affairs, Bureau of

From Washington straight; major security scandal expected. Cato. Nat R 15:96 Ag 13 '63

Statistics

Polls and statistics; do they throw light or confusion? il Sr Schol 85:6-8+ O 21 '64
U.S, then and now; statistical portrait. A. Austin. il N Y Times Mag p54+ My 3 '64

Strategic air command

See United States—Air force—Strategic air command

Strategic services, Office of

Deadly gadgets of the OSS; condensation of Of spies & stratagems. S. P. Lovell. il Pop Sci 183:56-9+ Jl '63
Of spies & stratagems, by S. P. Lovell. Review
Newsweek 61:104-5 Mr 18 '63

Strike command

See United States—Armed forces—Strike command

Supreme court

Ashmore seeks to label Court. Christian Cent 80:1458 N 27 '63
Barry fights the Court. A. M. Bickel. New Repub 151:9-11 O 10 '64
Big week for oral arguments. Time 83:48+ Ap 10 '64
Blue & the grey. il Time 82:76 N 8 '63
Center of the storm. il Time 82:52 O 18 '63
Compliments to the Court; refusal to grant certiorari to Court of appeals in Gary, Ind. case. Nat R 16:391 My 19 '64
Court sits, in the center of the storm. N Y Times Mag p30+ N 8 '64
Court to rule on scalping; injunction against Capital gains research bureau, inc. U S News 54:84 F 4 '63
Court will consider religious issues. Christian Cent 81:1293 O 21 '64
Cracks in the closed society; criticism of the United States Supreme court and Mississippi's courts. Time 85:62 Ja 22 '65
Critic of the High court: Louisiana senator speaks out; excerpts from statements. R. B. Long. U S News 56:13 F 10 '64
Device for division; housing integration case, Deerfield, Ill. Time 81:24 Ap 26 '63
Dissenter; Justice Harlan's view of Supreme court's function. Time 84:51+ Jl 3 '64
Either Court or Constitution is wrong on election rules. F. Morley. il Nations Bsns 51:27-8 My '63
Federal judiciary; the usurpation of power; address, July 3, 1964. S. Thurmond. Vital Speeches 30:667-70 Ag 15 '64
For the sake of argument. Reporter 30:12+ Ap 23 '64
Gale winds blow on High court. Bsns W p38 S 26 '64
Inside view of the High court. W. J. Brennan, jr. il N Y Times Mag p35+ O 6 '63
Is the Supreme court reaching for too much power? il U S News 55:64-5 O 7 '63
Job no young lawyer can afford to turn down. il Time 83:66-7 Je 5 '64
Judicial usurpation; address, January 31, 1964. M. Caldwell. Vital Speeches 30:317-20 Mr 1 '64
Justice on trial, by A. L. Todd. Review
New Repub 151:25-6 Ag 8 '64. A. M. Bickel; Correction. A. L. Todd. 151:38 Ag 22 '64
Limits that create liberty & the liberty that creates limits. il Time 84:48-50+ O 9 '64
More bench experience for High-court justices? U S News 54:6 Mr 25 '63
Nation and the nine. I. Dilliard. Sat R 46:39-40 Mr 9 '63
New Court. A. M. Bickel. New Repub 148:15-17 Mr 16 '63
Nine very human men. A. Lewis. il N Y Times Mag p 18+ Ja 17 '65
No advisory opinions. America 108:700 My 18 '63
Our vanishing Constitution. D. Lawrence. U S News 57:104 Jl 20 '64
Pinnacle of the judiciary pyramid. il Sr Schol 84:22-4 F 14 '64
Public accommodations on trial; racial barriers. il Time 84:69 O 16 '64
Relevance of Edmund Burke, ed. by P. J. Stanlis. Review
Nat R 16:1111 D 15 '64. R. Kirk
Sharpening the law on antitrust. il Bsns W p32-4 O 5 '63
Speaking of the split; excerpts from addresses. A. Goldberg; J. M. Harlan. il Time 82:17-18 Ag 23 '63
Supreme court fissures. A. M. Bickel. New Repub 151:15-16 Jl 11 '64
Supreme court on trial, by C. S. Hyneman. Review
Nat R 16:29-31 Ja 14 '64. L. B. Bozell
Nation 199:280 O 26 '64. J. Leavitt
Supreme court opens new term. il Sr Schol 83:19 N 15 '63
Supreme court petitioned to review "Tropic" conviction. Library J 88:1496 Ap 1 '63
Supreme court under fire again. A. T. Mason. Reporter 31:45-8 S 24 '64
TV and the Supreme court. R. Goldfarb. Commonweal 81:150-1 O 30 '64
Thorny issues for High court. Bsns W p 116 O 12 '63
Today High court: younger, less starchy. il Bsns W p30-2 F 2 '63
Tropic of cancer before the Supreme court. Wilson Lib Bul 37:612+ Ap '63
Warren court: fateful decade. il Newsweek 63:24-6+ My 11 '64
What to expect from the Supreme court. il Nations Bsns 52:31-3+ O '64
Will High court O.K. mixed marriages? il U S News 57:10 O 26 '64
Will High court rule on mixed marriages? U S News 56:14 My 11 '64
See also
Judges

Anecdotes, facetiae, satire, etc.

Heisters' day in Court. J. J. Leff. Nat R 16:26 Ja 14 '64

Caricatures and cartoons

Kreuttner festival. J. Kreuttner. Nat R 16:645-8 Jl 28 '64

Decisions

ABC's on prayers in school; questions and answers. il U S News 55:41 Jl 1 '63
After redistricting decision: where states may see changes in taxes, welfare, highways. il U S News 57:34-6 Jl 6 '64
Agency shop setback; states have power to enforce curbs on unions. Bsns W p 136 D 7 '63
All others are invited; Bible-reading case. America 109:34 Jl 13 '63
ALA as amicus curiae: Tropic of Cancer before the U.S. Supreme court; excerpts from brief. bibliog f ALA Bul 58:290-8 Ap '64
Annals of law: Gideon case. A. Lewis. il New Yorker 40:144+ Ap 25; 108+ My 2; 150+ My 9 '64
Another landmark decision. Nation 198:283 Mr 23 '64
Battle over state reapportionment; pro and con discussion. Sr Schol 85:12-13+ O 28 '64
Bedroom issues; interracial marriage in Florida. Newsweek 64:21 D 21 '64
Behind the fight against school prayer; Christian view. H. B. Sissel. il Look 27:25-9 Je 18 '63; Reply. America 108:874 Je 22 '63
Beyond a doubt; right of Negroes to equal access to public accomodations. il Time 84:13-14 D 25 '64
Bible; better in school than in Court. Life 54:4 Mr 15 '63; Discussion. il 54:63-4+ Ap 12 '63

UNITED STATES—Supreme court—Decisions —*Continued*
Bible reading in the public schools. A. W. Steinhilber. bibliog f Sch Life 46:13-16 O '63
Bible reading, prayers, and public schools. W. W. Brickman. Sch & Soc 91:272 O 5 '63
Bigger stick; antitrust laws and banks. Newsweek 62:54 Jl 1 '63
Blow at unions' political power? U S News 54:101 My 27 '63
Brake? school desegregation decision. Newsweek 63:31-2 My 18 '64
Brown decade; Brown v. Board of education. Nat R 16:433-4 Je 2 '64
Call her Miss; ruling on calling Negroes by their first names. Time 83:51 Ap 10 '64
Changing U.S. effects of Supreme court decisions. il U S News 55:70-2 Jl 1 '63
Chaos in the Court; ruling on Tropic of cancer. America 111:83-4 Jl 25 '64
Church and state Bible-reading and recitation of the Lord's prayer in public schools. il Newsweek 62:48 Jl 1 '63
Citizenship & other cases. Time 81:20-1 Mr 1 '63
Civil disobedience: an imprimatur; decision on public accommodations section of Civil rights act. Nat R 16:1134-5 D 29 '64
Civil rights boil-up. A. M. Bickel. New Repub 148:10-14 Je 8 '63
Civil rights decisions; distinction between public and private activity. Commonweal 78:292-3 Je 7 '63
Closing the loophole; jurisdiction over right-to-work issues. Time 82:87 D 13 '63
Coming in out of the rain. Time 82:48+ D 20 '63
Compliment from Mr C; deportation of F. Costello blocked. Time 83:54 F 28 '64
Confusion on church and state. R. L. Gildea. Christian Cent 80:1381-2 N 6 '63
Conscience and religion; case of the United States v. D. A. Seeger. America 111:771 D 12 '64
Conscience and the Constitution. T. Powell. il PTA Mag 58:10-12 N '63
Constitution, key to freedom. C. B. Motley. Ebony 18:221-2+ S '63
Contested cargo; legal battle between expropriated company, C.A.V. and Cuba's Banco nacional. Time 83:71-2 Ap 3 '64
Cool on contempt; Supreme court decision to uphold summary criminal-contempt power. il Time 83:57 Ap 17 '64
Cops v. the courts; standards of police search and seizure. Time 84:59-60 Ag 28 '64
Court backs voter equity. Sr Schol 84:21-2 Mr 6 '64
Court challenges the Congress; Georgia case on apportionment of congressional districts. F. S. Meyer. Nat R 16:233 Mr 24 '64
Court decides wisely; school prayer. Christian Cent 80:851 Jl 3 '63
Court narrows road to corporate growth; hits mergers and joint ventures. Bsns W p30-1 Je 27 '64
Court: 1954-1964. Christian Cent 81:659-60 My 20 '64
Court on prayer. Commonweal 78:388-9 Jl 5 '63
Court says all votes must weigh the same; reapportionment of congressional districts. Bsns W p27 F 22 '64
Court upholds Sabbatarian. Christian Cent 80:854 Jl 3 '63
Courts can't bar seizures; suit by Banco nacional de Cuba against U.S. firm. Sr Schol 84:20+ Ap 10 '64
Crime and reapportionment. A. M. Bickel. New Repub 148:5 Ap 6 '63
Criticism of officials: what new ruling means; libel suit against New York times. U S News 56:15 Mr 23 '64
Crowd of umbrella heads; states' rights amendments. Reporter 28:10-11 Je 6 '63
Decision on the Lord's prayer and Bible reading. J. B. Sheerin. Cath World 197: 276-9 Ag '63
Defense & an explanation; four controversial decisions. Time 83:57-8 Ap 17 '64
Democracy and the Court. W. D. Burnham. il Commonweal 80:499-503 Jl 24 '64
Desegregation decision: Brown v. Board of education, May 17, 1954. H. S. Ashmore. il Sat R 47:68-70+ My 16 '64
Dimensions of democracy in education; address, October 23, 1964. C. A. Thomas. Vital Speeches 31:74-8 N 15 '64
Dirksen breather; opposition to Supreme court decision on reapportionment. Time 84:37 S 18 '64
Dissenter Harlan critical of fellow justices. U S News 55:26 O 28 '63
Equality in representation; congressional districts. Christian Cent 81:291-2 Mr 4 '64
Ex-con overturns the law; with report by M. Durham. il Life 56:83-4+ Je 12 '64
Extending the Fifth: to state courts. Time 83:43 Je 26 '64
Fair challenge to redistricting. Life 57:4 Ag 21 '64
Festivals and judges; two decisions. M. Himmelfarb. Commentary 35:67-70 Ja '63
Five to four score. Newsweek 61:18 Ap 1 '63
Following the returns; Civil rights act test case. R. Moley. Newsweek 64:60 D 28 '64
Freedom of non-speech; Sweeping decision. il Newsweek 63:21-2+ Je 29 '64
Fresh thoughts. Newsweek 63:38-9 Je 15 '64
From the High court: a boost and a setback for unions. il U S News 54:87-8 Je 17 '63
Furor over school prayers: latest in a growing debate; excerpts from testimony, E. H. Tuller; F. J. Sheen. U S News 56:72-4 My 11 '64
Georgia redraws its political map; congressional districts. Bsns W p34 F 29 '64
Gideon's trumpet, by A. Lewis. Review
New Repub 151:21+ Jl 4 '64. H. L. Packer
Sat R 47:28 Je 27 '64. W. B. Butler
Go ahead and say it! boundaries of press freedom advanced by Supreme court. il Time 83:78 Mr 20 '64
God amendment. R. J. Dwyer. Nat R 16: 494 Je 16 '64
God go home. Nat R 14:521 Jl 2 '63
God's little helpers; school prayer issue. R. S. Gallagher. il Reporter 30:24-6 Je 4 '64; Discussion. 31:5 Jl 2 '64
Good behavior of judges who defines it? reprint. D. Lawrence. U S News 57:92+ Jl 6 '64
Government lawyer looks at the crime problem; Fourth amendment and the administration of criminal justice. il U S News 57:74-6 S 28 '64
Government's big stick for enforcing civil rights; with excerpts from statements by T. C. Clark and H. L. Black. il U S News 57:40-2 D 28 '64
High court: its growing impact; with excerpts from majority and dissenting opinions. il U S News 56:34-7 Je 29 '64
High court ruling opens way for showdown in rules dispute; between carriers and operating brotherhoods. Bsns W p 104 Mr 9 '63
How Congress is trying to cut the Supreme court's power; ruling on apportionment. U S News 57:8 Ag 31 '64
How Supreme court is changing U.S; with interviews with C. S. Hyneman and P. B Kurland. il U S News 58:56-62 Ja 18 '65
How Supreme court is reshaping the country. il U S News 57:31-3 Jl 6 '64
How the Constitution was violated; reprint. D. Lawrence. U S News 54:124+ My 6 '63
Illegal Congress? with excerpts of statements by H. L. Black and J. M. Harlan. il U S News 56:31-4 Mr 2 '64
Immunity from criticism; case of advertisement concerning racial conditions in Montgomery, Ala. New Repub 150:7-8 Mr 21 '64
Implications of Supreme court decisions for contemporary church-state problems. W. B. Ball. Cath World 197:296-305 Ag '63
Important victory for a free press, a free nation. R. H. Smith. Pub W 185:33 Mr 16 '64
In God we trust. Nation 197:2 Jl 6 '63
In High court, a blanket rule against segregation? U S News 54:65 Je 3 '63
In High court: when Goldberg says yes, White says no. il U S News 54:65 My 27 '63
In the courts: action for faster integraton. U S News 54:10 Je 10 '63
Interracial cohabitation; case in Florida. New Repub 151:5 D 19 '64
Jury trial barred; Supreme court decision to uphold summary criminal contempt power. Sr Schol 84:15-16 Ap 24 '64
Justice for the poor; the banner of Gideon. R. G. Sherrill. il Nation 198:367-72 Ap 13 '64
Justice gets some sharper teeth; Supreme court decisions reversing mergers approved by regulatory agencies. Bsns W p29-30 Ap 11 '64
Knocking down the pole; Supreme court's ruling on conflict between Sears, Roebuck and Chicago's Stiffel co. over pole lamps. Time 83:86 Mr 20 '64
Landmark I: equal votes. Life 56:4 Je 26 '64
Legal Blue cross? legal-aid plan set up by Brotherhood of railroad trainmen upheld. Time 83:76+ My 1 '64
Letter from Washington; determination of the Negroes for justice. R. H. Rovere. New Yorker 39:101-4+ Je 1 '63
Libel landmark. il Newsweek 63:74 Mr 23 '64

UNITED STATES—Supreme court—Decisions —*Continued*

Loss to make up for; ban on religious observances in schools. il Time 81:13-14 Je 28 '63

Matter of principle; South Carolina case. America 109:127 Ag 10 '63

Meaning of religion in the First amendment; the Torcaso case. M. R. Konvitz. Cath World 197:288-95 Ag '63

Mental urges of the mob. D. Lawrence. U S News 54:112 Je 17 '63

Mergers and monopolies; Lexington bank case. R. J. Barber. New Repub 150:9 Je 13 '64

Moral heritage and the law; prayers and Bible reading in the public schools. Life 54:4 Je 28 '63

More chaos in court. America 111:126-7 Ag 8 '64

More freedom to picket; latest from Supreme court; consumer picketing. U S News 56:78 My 4 '64

More than a quiet concern; public statement by nine clergymen dismayed by Supreme court decisions in obscenity cases. Time 84:22 S 11 '64

Nation chooses sides in fight over prayer. il U S News 56:63-4 My 18 '64

Negro in the Supreme court, 1954-64; address, 1964. R. L. Gill. bibliog Negro Hist Bul 28:51-2+ D '64 (to be cont)

Neighborhood schools win a round in Supreme court. il U S News 56:56 My 18 '64

New charter for state legislatures. il Time 83:22-3 Je 26 '64

New cop on big board beat; not immune from antitrust laws. Bsns W p28 My 25 '63

New dissent to a Robert Kennedy speech. C. Bloch. U S News 55:10 O 28 '63

New limits for an old conflict; reversal of three convictions of one Louisiana civil rights worker. il Time 85:39 Ja 29 '65

New powers for trustbusters. il Time 84:77 Jl 3 '64

New weapons against bigness. S. Marcus. Harvard Bsns R 43:100-8 Ja '65

New York times's vital victory; Alabama libel case. R. L. Tobin. Sat R 47:69-70 Ap 11 '64; Discussion. 47:61 My 9; 52 Je 13 '64

Nightmare for oil marketers; Sun oil case. Bsns W p66 Ja 19 '63

No hostility to God; No place for seditious libel. Time 84:48 D 4 '64

Non-violent revolution; Court's decision involving apportionment in state legislative elections. Nat R 16:519 Je 30 '64

Noted jurist says, repeal the Fourteenth amendment. R. N. Wilkin. U S News 57:72-4 Ag 24 '64

Now, a one-vote margin for Court's liberals? il U S News 54:19 Mr 4 '63

Now 40,000 ex-Americans can be citizens again. U S News 56:13 Je 1 '64

Obliterating the effect; conflict between sit-in convictions and the command of the Civil rights act of 1964. il Time 84:14 D 25 '64

On narrow grounds; defending segregationists of the National states rights party. Time 82:35 D 27 '63

One man, one vote. Commonweal 80:441 Jl 3 '64

One man, one vote: what it means. il U S News 57:62-4 O 19 '64

One man, one vote, yes or no? A. Hacker. il N Y Times Mag p31+ N 8 '64

One voter, one vote. W. D. Burnham. Commonweal 80:12-15 Mr 27 '64

Opening the cockpit doors. il Time 81:24 My 3 '63

Organizing against the Supreme court; prayer and Bible-reading in public schools. R. Kirk. Nat R 16:406 My 19 '64; Discussion. 16:505 Je 16 '64

Paradoxes of freedom, by S. Hook. Review Commentary 35:260-2 Mr '63. L. A. Coser

Passport for Communists; section 6 of the Subversive activities control act of 1950 declared unconstitutional. Time 84:51 Jl 3 '64

Political backlash hits Supreme court; Congress moves to curb Court's power. Bsns W p26 Ag 22 '64

Politics and prayer. K. Crawford. Newsweek 63:36 My 25 '64

Politics of religious equality. F. Canavan. America 108:664-7 My 11 '63

Prayer amendments: a Catholic lawyer's view. W. B. Ball. Cath World 199:345-51 S '64

Prayer and the schools; Bible-reading decision. America 108:898 Je 29 '63

Prayer or pluralism in the schools? J. Carr. Sat R 47:41 Jl 18 '64

Quick test coming for civil rights law. il Bsns W p27-8 O 10 '64

Quiet revolution in state government; reapportionment and redistricting; with chart. Sr Schol 83:13-15+ N 22 '63

Race, sex and the Supreme Court. A. Lewis. il N Y Times Mag p30+ N 22 '64

Reapportionment and the courts. A. M. Bickel. New Repub 150:7 Je 27 '64

Reapportionment, big issue for the 60's. I. Starr. il Sr Schol 85:6T-7T S 30 '64

Reapportionment: rhubarb in the political thicket; with chart. Sr Schol 85:8-11+ O 14 '64

Reapportionment riddle. J. E. Clayton. il Reporter 30:34-7 F 27 '64

Redistricting order; redrawing of Texas congressional district boundaries. Sr Schol 84:18 Mr 20 '64

Reductio ad absurdum; New York prayer case. America 108:282 Mr 2 '63

Religion and public life. W. Herberg. Nat R 15:61 Jl 30 '63

Religion and the Court. J. O'Gara. Commonweal 78:391 Jl 5 '63

Religion in education. W. B. Ball. America 108:528-30+ Ap 20 '63; Discussion. 108:640-3, 818; 109:15 My 4, Je 8, Jl 6 '63

Religion in the schools; Bible-reading cases. America 108:894 Je 29 '63

Religion, orthodoxy, public schools. C. M. Whelan. America 108:640-3 My 4 '63; Reply. T. B. McDonough. 108:818 Je 8 '63

Religious freedom; the Court expands a concept. T. G. Sanders. Nation 197:25-8 Jl 13 '63

Religious instruction: a natural right. R. Kirk. Nat R 16:234 Mr 24 '64; Discussion. 16:374-6 My 5 '64

Religious neutrality. J. J. Regan. America 110:74-6 Ja 18 '64

Religious scholarship and the Court. C. A. Holbrook. Christian Cent 80:1076-8 S 4 '63; Reply. S. E. Mead. 80:1342-3 O 30 '63

R.I. censors' activities ruled unconstitutional; with editorial comment. Pub W 183:42-3, 49 Mr 4 '63

Right to criticize upheld; libel judgment against New York times reversed. Sr Schol 84:30 Ap 3 '64

Right to pray. D. Lawrence. U S News 56:96 Mr 2 '64

Rights bill upheld; decision on public accommodations section. Sr Schol 85:17-18 Ja 7 '65

Role of the courts: conscience of a sovereign people. J. S. Wright. il Reporter 29:27-30 S 26 '63; Reply. N. Thomas. 29:12 O 24 '63

Room for objections & doubts. Time 82:54 O 25 '63

Saving our children from God. L. B. Bozell. Nat R 15:19-22+ Jl 16 '63; Discussion. 15:119 Ag 13 '63

School prayer battle. T. Powell. il Sat R 46:62-4+ Ap 20 '63; Discussion. 46:63 My 18 '63

School prayers and religious warfare. W. Berns. il Nat R 14:315-18 Ap 23 '63; Discussion. 14:421, 473 My 21-Je 4 '63

School prayers decision. Sr Schol 83:9-11 S 13 '63

Schoolrooms and prayers. E. J. Hughes. Newsweek 62:15 Jl 1 '63

Schools react to Court decision. Christian Cent 80:1228 O 9 '63

Science and the race problem; report of the AAAS committee on science in the promotion of human welfare. bibliog Science 142:558-61 N 1 '63; Discussion. 142:1419; 143:306-8, 913-15 D 13 '63, Ja 24, F 28 '64

Second Bible ruling. Sr Schol 83:3T S 13 '63

Secular purpose: Supreme court's decision in the prayer and Bible-reading cases. America 109:127 Ag 10 '63

Sex and the Supreme court; with editorial comment. A. Lewis. Esquire 59:6, 82-3+ Je '63

Shakeup in states; Supreme court decision on apportionment. Sr Schol 85:21+ S 16 '64

Shall we pray? il New Repub 148:4-6 Je 29 '63

Ship of state; Georgia congressional districting case. Nation 198:206 Mr 2 '64

Significant decisions in labor cases. See issues of Monthly labor review

Since the Supreme court spoke; decision on school segregation. A. Lewis. il N Y Times Mag p9+ My 10 '64

Sit-in decisions. Newsweek 64:17-18 Jl 6 '64

Speak up, everybody; decision to reverse libel judgment against the New York times. Nat R 16:222 Mr 24 '64

Speaking out; a liberal calls for aid to church schools. R. M. Hutchins. Sat Eve Post 236:6+ Je 8 '63; Discussion. Christian Cent 80:819-20, 1141 Je 26, S 18 '63

Speaking out; the Supreme court is defying the people. E. M. Dirksen. Sat Eve Post 237:10+ S 12 '64

UNITED STATES—Supreme court—Decisions —*Continued*
States' rights: two-High-court actions. U S News 54:11 Je 24 '63
Storm center of justice. E. Havemann. il Life 56:108-10+ My 22 '64; Same abr. with title Warren court. Read Digest 85:130-5 S '64
Strict caution on miscegenation; case of McLaughlin v. Florida. Time 84:43 D 18 '64
Supreme court and its critics. I. R. Kaufman. Atlan 212:47-53 D '63; Reply. W. S. Anderson. 213:42 Ap '64
Supreme court and public prayer, by C. E. Rice. Review
America 111:49 Jl 11 '64. R. F. Drinan
Nat R 16:775-6 S 8 '64. L. B. Bozell
Supreme court and the consumer. il Consumer Rep 29:424-7 S '64
Supreme court and the Republic; decisions on reapportionment. F. Morley. Fortune 70:102+ Ag '64
Supreme court decision about criminal libel. H. F. Pilpel. Pub W 186:41-2 D 28 '64
Supreme court decision limits censorship. Pub W 186:48-9 Jl 6 '64
Supreme court decision on Bible reading and prayer recitation; with comments by lay and religious leaders. NEA J 52:55-6 S '63
Supreme court draws the line; Wesberry vs. Sanders; Georgia redistricting case. Newsweek 63:15-16 Mr 2 '64
Supreme court hands down major rulings. Sr Schol 82:17 Ap 3 '63
Supreme court, obscenity and censorship. J. J. Regan. Cath World 200:142-8 D '64
Supreme court: rails, stocks, gas. Newsweek 61:62+ Je 3 '63
Supreme court sanctions fair trade in Ohio. Pub W 185:58 Je 15 '64
Supreme court to hear Bible reading cases; Maryland and Pennsylvania. Christian Cent 80:198 F 13 '63
Supreme court vs. corporate mergers. M. Handler and S. D. Robinson. il Fortune 71:164-5+ Ja '65
Supreme court vs. farmer legislatures. Am City 79:7 Jl '64
Ten tragic years. D. Lawrence. U S News 56:120+ My 25 '64
This month's feature: Congress & the apportionment decisions. Cong Digest 44:1-32 Ja '65
This month's feature: Congress & the school prayer decisions. Cong Digest 43:257-88 N '64
Thou shalt not feel inferior! reprint. D. Lawrence. U S News 55:108 S 16 '63
Thunderbolt for bank mergers; ruling in Philadelphia case. Bsns W p80+ Je 22 '63
Time to reclaim: the current challenge of American constitutional history. P. L. Murphy. bibliog f Am Hist R 69:64-79 O '63
To amend, or not to amend, the Constitution. P. A. Freund. il N Y Times Mag p33+ D 13 '64
To prevent hysteria; Lord's prayer and Bible readings in Maryland and Pennsylvania. Christian Cent 80:485-6 Ap 17 '63; Discussion. 80:750 Je 5 '63
Trial without jury; case of Ross R. Barnett and Paul B. Johnson, jr. New Repub 150:5-6 Ap 18 '64
Troubles pile up for most sued union. il Bsns W p 121-2+ Ap 18 '64
Uhuru; redrawing of district lines. Nat R 16:182-3 Mr 10 '64
Unconstitutional prayers; letters to the editor. Nat R 15:163+ Ag 27 '63
Uneven flow. il Time 81:17 Mr 29 '63
Unfinished business: place of religion in public education. America 108:898 Je 29 '63
Union's arbitration demand upheld in merger situation; case arising out of Wiley and Interscience publishers merger. Pub W 185:31-2 Ap 13 '64
US supreme court overrules Rhode Island censors' group. Library J 88:1736 Ap 15 '63
U.S. unions thwarted on foreign-flag ships. Bsns W p 122 F 23 '63
Upheaval in state capitols; how redistricting hits the states. Bsns W p94-6+ Ag 22 '64
Upholding Title II; Civil rights act test case. il Newsweek 64:16+ D 28 '64
Victory for a free press. Sat Eve Post 237:78 Ap 4 '64
Warren again; sit-in cases and Fourteenth amendment. Nat R 14:436 Je 4 '63
Warren court. R. S. Hirschfield. il Nation 198:527-9 My 25 '64
Warren court stands its ground. F. Rodell. il N Y Times Mag p23+ S 27 '64
Watch out for the subverters! apportionment amendment. L. B. Bozell. Nat R 14:398 My 21 '63
We know the man is guilty, but—; murderer James W. Killough and Mallory rule. U S News 57:18 O 19 '64
Welcome home; Section 352 of the 1952 Immigration and nationality act repealed. il Time 83:57 My 29 '64
West's water fight is far from over; Supreme court backs Ariz. over Calif. Bsns W p26 Je 8 '63
What can happen when courts step into state elections; reapportionment in Illinois. il U S News 57:39 S 21 '64
What nine clergymen said about the Supreme court; decisions in obscenity cases. U S News 57:15 S 21 '64
What the courts are ordering states to do; reapportionment of both houses of State legislatures. il U S News 57:40-1 Ag 24 '64
What the Supreme court did to your vote; with editorial comments. C. W. Gifford. Farm J 88:3, 19+, 70 Ag '64
When a former justice speaks out against the Supreme court; excerpts from address. C. E. Whittaker. U S News 57:21 N 9 '64
Where High court put federal standards on state rules. U S News 54:30 Ap 1 '63
Who represents what? R. Moley. Newsweek 63:88 Mr 9 '64
Why clergymen are against school prayer. A. Eisenberg and H. Eisenberg. Redbook 124:38-9+ Ja '65
Why so much crime in the Nation's capital; Mallory rule, interview. R. V. Murray. il U S News 55:92-7 O 21 '63; Reply with rejoinder. 55:92-3 N 4 '63
See also
Dred Scott case

History

March toward equality; excerpt from Portrait of a decade. A. Lewis. Atlan 214:58-64 S '64
Supreme court; ed. by J. A. Garraty. il Am Heritage 14:4-9+ Je; 10-15+ Ag; 38-43+ O; 15:66-71+ D '63; 44-8+ F; 52-5+ Ap '64
This honorable Court; ed. by J. A. Garraty. il Am Heritage 14:4-9+ Je '63
Warren court stands its ground. F. Rodell. il N Y Times Mag p23+ S 27 '64

Surgeon general's office

Boss of the army's medical team. W. R. Vath. il Todays Health 41:24-9 D '63
Smoking and cancer; a verdict; concerning Surgeon general's report. il Sr Schol 84:4-7 F 21 '64

Tariff commission

When steel seeks help from Uncle Sam; steel's case against imports. il Bsns W p80-1 F 15 '64

Tax court

GOP unit seeks renegotiation phase-out. K. Johnsen. Aviation W 80:33-4 Ap 27 '64
Supreme court refuses to hear appeal in Boeing renegotiation. K. Johnsen. Aviation W 80:30 My 11 '64

Temporary national economic committee

Twenty-five years ahead of its time. Duns R 83:52 F '64

Territories and possessions

See also
Guam
Puerto Rico
Trust Territory of the Pacific Islands
Virgin Islands

Trade information committee

Public hearings pertaining to trade agreements: text of regulations of Trade information committee, with notice of public hearing, August 6, 1963. B. Norwood. il Dept State Bul 49:330-2 Ag 26 '63

Trade policy

See United States—Commerce

Travel regulations

See Travel regulations

Travel service

Be my guest: turnpikes, Indians, and bikinis. il Newsweek 61:70 Je 3 '63
Booked for travel: colloquy and pillory: hearings on a new budget for the Travel service. H. Sutton. Sat R 46:44-5+ S 21 '63
Welcome mat for foreign friends. il Am Home 67:4 Ja '64

Treasury department

Financing seven years of deficit; with editorial comment. il Bsns W p 126+, 156 F 23 '63

UNITED STATES—Treasury department—*Continued*
Interest on the debt. New Repub 149:7 O 5 '63
Loan wanted: 11 to 13 billions. U S News 54:108 Je 17 '63
Money men in key spots. Newsweek 65:63 Ja 11 '65
Treasury's Dillon; the conservative power center in Washington. J. Kraft. Harper 226:51-6 Je '63
What kind of monetary men? Time 84:100 D 11 '64
See also
United States—Internal revenue service

Treaties

Treaty information. See issues of Department of state bulletin

Canada

Exchange of notes on Columbia River treaty and downstream power benefits, January 22, 1964; with Annex and attachment relating to terms of sale. P. Martin; D. Rusk. Dept State Bul 50:201-6 F 10 '64
U.S. and Canada hold Columbia River treaty ceremonies; remarks, with exchange of notes, executive order, and Canadian entitlement purchase agreement. L. B. Johnson; L. B. Pearson. Dept State Bul 51:504-16 O 12 '64
U.S. and Canada to tame a river. il U S News 55:44 D 30 '63

Luxembourg

U.S. and Luxembourg exchange ratifications of FEN treaty. Dept State Bul 48:403 Mr 18 '63

Mexico

United States ratifies Chamizal convention. L. B. Johnson; E. M. Martin. Dept State Bul 50:49-51 Ja 13 '64

Panama

Should the Panama Canal treaty be renegotiated at this time? pro and con discussion. il Sr Schol 84:14-16 Ap 10 '64

Urban renewal administration

Cure for sick cities. C. Case. Sat R 46:12-14 F 9 '63
Design goals for urban renewal. W. Slayton. Arch Rec 134:149-52 N '63
Do we need a secretary for urban affairs? pro and con discussion. il Sr Schol 83:10-11 O 11 '63
Mounting scandal of urban renewal. J. Dowdy. Read Digest 84:51-7 Mr '64
Rebuilder of cities; or a new pork barrel? urban renewal program. il Bsns W p64+ D 7 '63
This month's feature: Congress and future of urban renewal. Cong Digest 43:99-128 Ap '64

Veterans administration

Government's most-integrated agency. il Ebony 18:65-6+ Mr '63
Research indemnification: new VA insurance policy offers greater security to researchers. E. Langer. Science 145:798+ Ag 21 '64

Veterans administration hospitals

Rehabilitative recreation in VA hospitals. C. C. Bream, jr. il Recreation 57:224-6 My '64
Socialism in the armed forces. R. Dudman. il New Repub 149:24-6 N 9 '63
Then the bricks came tumbling down; Boston's Veterans administration hospital. Time 83:24 F 7 '64
Veterans hospitals: government medicine in action. R. S. Dillon. Read Digest 82:49-53 Mr '63

Vital statistics

See also
Birth rate—United States

Weather bureau

Aircraft follow hurricane from Genesis; Weather bureau's research flight facility and National hurricane research laboratory. G. Alexander. il Aviation W 81:80-1+ O 19 '64
Bureau buying three Tiros-type satellites. Miss & Roc 14:21 Ja 27 '64
Changing the guard on weather. J. Lear. Sat R 46:35 Ag 3 '63
Forecast: bright. Newsweek 62:89 O 14 '63
Forecasting by computer. A. Ewing. Sci N L 84:87 Ag 10 '63
Gentleman of the guard. J. Lear. il Sat R 46:36-9 Ag 3 '63
How to read a weather map. A. E. Sik. il Motor B 112:48-51+ S '63
New weather discoveries will serve you: interview. R. M. White. il Nations Bsns 52:36-7+ N '64
Radio weathercasts 1963; AM radio stations and their weathercast schedules. il Motor B 111:46-51 Je '63
Riding herd on the twisters; U.S. weather bureau's Severe local storm forecast center (SELS) J. H. Winchester. il Read Digest 85:158-60+ O '64
Weather bureau: partnership of science and government nearly a century old; new chief due. E. Langer. Science 141:508-9 Ag 9 '63
Weather bureau; special report. il Miss & Roc 15:151-4+ N 30 '64
Weather computers. R. C. Cowen. il Nation 198:71-3 Ja 20 '64
World's fair weather watch; Flight advisory weather service. D. L. Coveney. il Flying 74:32+ Ap '64

Yards and docks, Bureau of

See United States—Navy—Yards and docks, Bureau of

Youth conservation corps (proposed)

See United States—Job corps

UNITED STATES (ship) See Ocean liners
UNITED STATES air force academy, Colorado Springs
Air academy chapel: a critical appraisal. A. Temko; discussion. il Arch Forum 118:19 F '63
Air force. il U S Camera 27:40-3+ O '64
Air force academy: a slight gain in altitude. D. Boroff. Harper 226:86-8+ F '63
Air force's egghead factory. M. Mayer. il Sat Eve Post 236:91-5 N 23 '63
Code of honor; air force cadets accused of stealing examination papers. Time 85:20 Ja 29 '65
Duty to pray? compulsory religious service. il Newsweek 63:62-3 F 24 '64
Fall from honor; exam cheating scandal. il Newsweek 65:46 F 1 '65
Protest mandatory chapel. Christian Cent 81:421 Ap 1 '64; Discussion. 81:774, 1178 Je 10, S 23 '64
Revolution at service academies. il U S News 55:74-7 D 2 '63
We are a different breed of cat sir. J. G. Hubbell. il Read Digest 85:225-6+ N '64
UNITED STATES and Bulgaria; United States and Ireland; etc. See Bulgaria and the United States; Ireland and the United States; etc.
UNITED STATES army. Association of. See Association of the United States army
UNITED STATES army language school. See United States—Army—Education
UNITED STATES book exchange, incorporated
International loss for book availability; AID not renewing contract. R. H. Smith. Pub W 185:44 Mr 2 '64
US book exchange employees strike for higher wages. Library J 88:3812 O 15 '63
USBE story. J. Orne. il Library J 89:803-6 F 15 '64
UNITED STATES camera (periodical)
Achievement awards. il U S Camera 27:52-3 Mr '64
Best of the year. il U S Camera 26:57-60 N '63
UNITED STATES-Canadian committee on trade and economic affairs. See Joint United States-Canadian committee on trade and economic affairs
UNITED STATES coast guard academy
Coast guard. E. Scully. il U S Camera 27:48-51+ O '64
UNITED STATES in art
New nation through Russian eyes; reproduction of water colors. P. Svinin. Am Heritage 15:52-63 F '64
See also
Maine in art
West in art
UNITED STATES in literature
Twenty-one great writers on the U.S.A; excerpts from literary works; with introd. comp. by E. Hardwick. Vogue 141:114-15+ F 1 '63
What the Soviets read about America. E. Wasiolek. il Sat R 47:26-7 My 9 '64
See also
New England in literature
South in literature
UNITED STATES industries, incorporated
Our heartless friends, the robots. D. S. Halacy, jr. il Pop Electr 18:39-44+ My '63
UNITED STATES information agency. See United States—Information agency
UNITED STATES information libraries. See American libraries abroad

UNITED STATES Information service. See United States—Information service
UNITED STATES-Japan committee on scientific cooperation. See Joint United States-Japan committee on scientific cooperation
UNITED STATES Junior chamber of commerce
America's ten outstanding young men of 1964. il Look 29:34+ Ja 26 '65
America's ten outstanding young men of 1963. il Look 28:61-3 Ja 28 '64
Good reading for youth show opens in four pilot states. Library J 89:340 Ja 15 '64
Two physicians named outstanding young men. il Todays Health 41:5+ Mr '63
UNITED STATES lawn tennis association
Egg and the net; spectator tennis is sick, participant tennis is flourishing. R. S. Hewlett. il Sports Illus 18:14-17 F 18 '63
Sporting scene. H. W. Wind. il New Yorker 39:126+ S 28 '63; 40:164+ S 26 '64
UNITED STATES libraries of information. See American libraries abroad
UNITED STATES lines
Commodore leaves the sea. I. Taves. il Look 28:38-40+ Ap 21 '64
UNITED STATES marshals
U.S. marshals' 175. il Time 84:56-7 O 23 '64
UNITED STATES merchant marine academy, Kings Point, N.Y.
Merchant marine. M. Orovan. il U S Camera 27:52-5+ O '64
UNITED STATES-Mexican boundary and water commission. See International boundary and water commission (United States and Mexico)
UNITED STATES military academy, West Point
Duty, honor, country; address, May 12,1962. D. MacArthur. il Life 56:36-38A Ap 17 '64; Excerpts. U S News 56:64-5 Ap 20 '64
Revolution at service academies. il U S News 55:74-7 D 2 '63
West Point. E. Bennett. il U S Camera 27: 56-9+ O '64
UNITED STATES national arboretum. See Washington, D.C.—National arboretum
UNITED STATES national commission for UNESCO
Meeting, 1963. Sch & Soc 92:171-2+ Ap 4 '64
UNITED STATES national student association
Beyond make-believe; second annual SR-U.S. national student association magazine contest. S. B. Chickering. Sat R 47:28-9 O 10 '64
Fiasco at Bloomington. W. C. Wooldridge. Nat R 15:303 O 8 '63
Meeting, 1964. E. R. Covert and S. C. Schodde. Sch & Soc 92:387-8 D 12 '64
Meeting, 1963. S. C. Schodde. Sch & Soc 91: 358+ N 16 '63
Meeting, 1962. Sch & Soc 91:146-7 Mr 23 '63
UNITED STATES naval academy, Annapolis
Annapolis. E. Scully. il U S Camera 27:44-7+ O '64
Annapolis: teaching young sea dogs old tricks. D. Boroff; discussion. Harper 226:6 Mr '63
First-class first classmen; Trident scholars. il Time 82:82 N 8 '63
Revolution at service academies. il U S News 55:74-7 D 2 '63
Staubach of navy: humility under pressure. T. Cohane. il Look 28:68-73 S 22 '64
UNITED STATES news and World report (periodical)
Our thirtieth anniversary. D. Lawrence. U S News 54:108 My 27 '63
UNITED STATES of Europe (proposed)
Friend explains de Gaulle. U S News 55:36 Jl 15 '63
UNITED STATES office of education. See United States—Education, Office of
UNITED STATES Olympic basketball committee. See Pan American games
UNITED STATES overseas libraries. See American libraries abroad
UNITED STATES pharmacopoeia. See Pharmacopoeias
UNITED STATES polymeric chemicals, incorporated
Polymeric is a leader in production of prepregs. il Miss & Roc 13:36-7 Ag 12 '63
UNITED STATES post office inspection service. See United States—Post office department
UNITED STATES power squadrons, incorporated
Fifty years for the U.S. power squadrons. C. Schrage. Yachting 115:64+ Ja '64
Free USPS courses start this month. Motor B 114:102-4 S '64
Ladies' auxiliaries. C. Schrage. Yachting 117:58+ Ja '65
Seasoned skipper. il Motor B 113:29-46+ F '64
Under way with the USPS. See issues of Motor boating
USPS free instruction courses. il Motor B 112:80-2 Ag '63
United States power squadrons; fifty years. il Motor B 113:30-46+ F '64
With the power squadrons. C. Schrage. See issues of Yachting
UNITED STATES public health service. See United States—Public health service
UNITED STATES public health service hospital, Carville, La. See Leprosy and lepers
UNITED STATES rubber company
After the battle in U.S. rubber's executive suite. W. J. Miller. il Fortune 70:116-23+ D '64
Antitrust lunges again at fair trade. Bsns W p20+ Jl 4 '64
One name to girdle the globe; UniRoyal trademark for U.S. rubber. il Bsns W p74-5 Ag 1 '64
UNITED STATES savings bonds. See Bonds, Government
UNITED STATES steel corporation
Big steel wants a bigger share. J. McDonald. il Fortune 71:136-9+ Ja '65
Big steel's policy: no pressure on race issue. U S News 55:24 N 11 '63
How steel may save an old market. Bsns W p33 D 5 '64
Innocence of U.S. steel; role of the corporation in the community. C. O. Rice. il Commonweal 80:504-6 Jl 24 '64
Nonstop talks instead of nonstop strikes; steel's Human relations committee. A. H. Raskin. il N Y Times Mag p 12+ Jl 7 '63
Offices share vacation bonus. Bsns W p 117 O 5 '63
Steelmen breathe easier; work of Human relations committee. Bsns W p28 My 11 '63
Streamlining the elephant. Time 82:74 S 27 '63
Thunder in Pittsburgh; reorganization. il Time 83:83-4 Je 19 '64
U.S. steel adopts new corporate look; sales operations centralized. Bsns W p29 S 21 '63
U.S. steel strips for a fight; battle for profits. il Bsns W p 114-16+ S 28 '63
Voice from the dark ages. Fortune 68:102 D '63
What the canmakers really got. Bsns W p31 Mr 9 '63
UNITED STATES testing company
Neither official nor related to CU. Consumer Rep 28:101 Mr '63
Word on rumble; test program by hi fi and USTC. Hi Fi 13:51 My '63
UNITED STATES time corporation
Time bomb for watchmakers. il Bsns W p96+ N 16 '63
Watches for an impulse; Timex. il Time 81:92 Mr 15 '63
UNITED STATES track and field federation
Track's cold war heats up. Sports Illus 18:11 Ap 1 '63
UNITED STATES travel service. See United States—Travel service
UNITED steelworkers of America
Appraisal of Kaiser's sharing plan. C. A. MacIlvaine. Mo Labor R 87:401-4 Ap '64
As steel union gets set for new demands. il U S News 54:93-5 F 25 '63
Battle of Pittsburgh: who to head the USW? il Newsweek 64:81-2 N 23 '64
Bellwether? local nominations for Iorwith Wilbur Abel as new president. Time 85:29 Ja 1 '65
But I love you; President D. McDonald's case for reelection. il Time 84:33-4 N 20 '64
Dry run for steel talks. il Bsns W p92 Ja 19 '63
Extended vacations at Timken. D. G. Rayl. Mo Labor R 87:406 Ap '64
Fight inside union: will it affect steel prices, wages? il U S News 57:80-1 N 23 '64
Fruits of Kaiser plan taste sweet to all; share cost savings. il Bsns W p47-8 S 21 '63
Grassroots militance in steel; model labor pact threatened. Bsns W p 118+ Ag 22 '64
Group incentive; Kaiser plan. T. R. Brooks. Duns R 81:47E-8 Mr '63
How workers benefit when costs are cut; Kaiser steel corporation and Steelworkers union. il U S News 54:91-2 My 6 '63
In steel: no strike, longer vacations, longer contracts. il U S News 54:86 Je 24 '63
Is the lid coming off for bigger pay increases? il U S News 57:95-7 O 19 '64
Issue that stalls steel pact; contracting-out dispute. Bsns W p 104-5 Je 8 '63
Kaiser plan passes first test; savings sharing plan. il Bsns W p48+ My 4 '63
Labor month in review; steel settlement. Mo Labor R 86:III-IV Jl '63

UNITED steelworkers of America—*Continued*
Long range sharing plan for Kaiser steel corp. employees; text of the plan. Mo Labor R 86:154-60 F '63
Long vacations? cool reactions. U S News 55:93 Jl 8 '63
New leader for steelworkers? I. W. Abel vs. D. J. McDonald. U S News 57:104 N 16 '64
New-style contract in steel; meaning for other industries. il U S News 55:77 Jl 1 '63
Next wage test; steel to outdo autos? il U S News 57:92+ O 5 '64
Nonstop talks instead of nonstop strikes; steel's Human relations committee. A. H. Raskin. il N Y Times Mag p 12+ Jl 7 '63
Outsiders keep peace at Kaiser. Bsns W p 105 O 24 '64
Political row perils steel peace. il Bsns W p45-6 N 14 '64
Power struggle alters USW's political course; D. McDonald vs. I. W. Abel. il Bsns W p78+ D 26 '64
Rebellion in steel. R. W. Gibbons. Commonweal 81:540-2 Ja 22 '65
Steel accord near? Bsns W p27 Je 15 '63
Steel reopening uncertain; industry-USW human relations committee. Bsns W p 172 My 18 '63
Steel settles. Bsns W p23 Je 22 '63
Steel talks begin: with round in the wage-price spiral? il U S News 58:70-1 Ja 11 '65
Steel talks start icily. il Bsns W p 116 D 19 '64
Steel-wage talks: industry's position. U S News 57:74-5 D 28 '64
Steel without strikes; with editorial comment. il Bsns W p25-6, 124 Je 29 '63
Steelmen breathe easier; work of Human relations committee. Bsns W p28 My 11 '63
Steel's Abel to raise Cain; imminent collective bargaining sessions between the United steelworkers (USW) and the basic steel industry. H. Kasper. New Repub 152:11-13 Ja 16 '65
Steel's harder face. Bsns W p 102 D 12 '64
Steelworkers talk a tough line. Bsns W p 160 S 26 '64
Unions' latest goal: lifetime jobs. il U S News 58:88+ Ja 25 '65
Union's price for peace in steel. il U S News 57:81-3 D 14 '64
United steelworkers; biennial convention in Atlantic City. H. S. Rosenbloom. Mo Labor R 87:1254-5 N '64
USW nears time of decision. Bsns W p30 Mr 16 '63
USW sees no strike; credit to Human relations committee. il Bsns W p29 F 23 '63
USW simmers as steel talks near. il Bsns W p47-8 N 21 '64
USW vote dims hopes of peace; defeat of McDonald by Abel. Bsns W p81 Ja 9 '65
When workers join in cutting costs; who gains; sharing of savings at Kaiser steel corporation. il U S News 55:113-15 O 21 '63
Where wages are heading in 1963. il U S News 54:93-4 Ap 29 '63
Who has total security? with editorial comment. il Bsns W p45-6, 192 O 17 '64

UNITED student aid funds, incorporated
Financial lever boosts student aid. il Bsns W p 192+ Ap 20 '63
Loans for learning. Time 82:52 S 20 '63

UNITED technology center. See United aircraft corporation

UNITED technology corporation
Ambitious UTC expansion program nearing completion. J. F. Judge. il Miss & Roc 13:30-1 Jl 22 '63
Titan III-C stage zero role revamps UTC structure. R. Lindsey. il Miss & Roc 14:34+ Ja 20 '64
UTC to fire 120-in. Titan III motor. R. Lindsey. il Miss & Roc 12:36-8 F 18 '63

UNITS, Electric. See Electric units

UNIVAC computers. See Calculating machines —Digital computers

UNIVERSAL CITY, Calif.
New kind of king. il Time 85:50-1 Ja 1 '65
Traveler in Flickville. H. Sutton. il Sat R 48:61-2 Ja 9 '65

UNIVERSAL copyright convention. See Copyright

UNIVERSAL decimal classification. See Classification, Decimal

UNIVERSAL declaration of human rights
Fifteen years ago; address, December 10, 1948. J. T. Bodet. UNESCO Courier 16:4-5 D '63
Human rights and foreign policy; excerpts from In pursuit of world order. R. N. Gardner. Sat R 47:23-5+ S 19 '64
Human rights day 1964; messages. A. Quaison-Sackey; Thant. UN Mo Chron 1:i-iii D '64
International promotion of human rights; address, December 8, 1963. R. N. Gardner. Vital Speeches 30:207-9 Ja 15 '64
Text of the Universal declaration of human rights. UNESCO Courier 16:16-17 D '63
UNESCO and human rights for all. il UNESCO Courier 16:6-11 D '63
Universal declaration of human rights. il U N Rev 10:29-32 D '63

UNIVERSAL history. See World history

UNIVERSAL military service. See Military service, Compulsory

UNIVERSAL military training. See Military training

UNIVERSAL pictures company, incorporated
Meanwhile back in Hollywood, efficiency takes over; with report by D. Zeitlin. il Life 55:46-50B D 20 '63

UNIVERSAL time. See Time

UNIVERSE
Can we learn from other planets? excerpt from Of men and galaxies. F. Hoyle. il Sat R 47:63-7 N 7 '64; Discussion. 47:84-6 D 5 '64
Copernicus; a universe revealed. W. Golding. il Holiday 35:56-61+ Ja '64
Exploring the universe; AAAS annual meeting, 26-31 December, 1964, Montreal. D. Wolfle. il Science 146:1190-2 N 27 '64
Galileo Galilei; a new vision of the universe. C. Maccagni. il UNESCO Courier 17:24-5+ My '64
Hugh Downs column; is the universe evaporating? H. Downs. Sci Digest 55:78-9 My '64
Life and death of the universe. il Newsweek 63:63-7 My 25 '64
Prospect for mankind. R. B. Fuller. Sat R 47:26 O 3 '64
Reaching out. il Newsweek 63:82 Ap 13 '64
Scientist in collision: was Velikovsky right? E. Larrabee. Harper 227:48-50+ Ag '63; Discussion. 227:12+ O; 83-7 D '63; 228:12 Ja '64
Size of universe studied. Sci N L 85:340 My 30 '64
See also
Cosmogony
Cosmology
Earth
Life on other planets
Milky way
Solar system

Age

Happy birthday. Newsweek 61:81 My 6 '63

UNIVERSITIES. See Colleges and universities

UNIVERSITY administration. See Colleges and universities—Administration

UNIVERSITY athletics. See College athletics

UNIVERSITY bookstores. See College bookstores

UNIVERSITY degrees. See Degrees, Academic

UNIVERSITY drama. See College and school drama

UNIVERSITY libraries. See College libraries

UNIVERSITY of Giessen. See Colleges and universities—Germany (Federal Republic)

UNIVERSITY of Iowa; University of Texas; etc. See Iowa. University; Texas. University; etc.

UNIVERSITY of the Pacific, Stockton, Calif.
Reform on the coast. il Time 82:71 O 11 '63
Total immersion; first Spanish-speaking college in the U.S. Newsweek 62:60 S 30 '63

UNIVERSITY of the Seven Seas. See Colleges and universities, Traveling

UNIVERSITY of the South, Sewanee, Tenn.
Student, or cipher? il Newsweek 64:52-3 D 28 '64

UNIVERSITY presidents. See College presidents

UNIVERSITY press of Virginia
University press of Virginia formed to serve entire state. Pub W 183:93-4 F 11 '63

UNIVERSITY presses
AAUP; new international moves, internal reorganization; symposium with editorial comment. il Pub W 186:26-47, 66 Jl 6 '64
Big scholar, little gypsy. D. Dempsey. Sat R 47:30-1 My 30 '64
New look in university press advertising. F. Spier. il Pub W 184:22-30 O 7 '63
Progress at the ivy-clad press. B. Perry. Sat R 46:21-2 Je 15 '63
University press started in Montreal. Pub W 183:46 Mr 25 '63
University presses, 1965. E. Schossberger. America 112:45+ Ja 9 '65
When universities become publishers. C. G. Bowen. bibliog Science 140:599-605 My 10 '63

UNIVERSITY presses—*Continued*
Widening concepts in university publishing. C. B. Grannis. Pub W 184:68 Jl 15 '63
See also
Association of American university presses
Cambridge university press
East-West center press
Harvard university press
Johns Hopkins press
Oxford university press
University press of Virginia

Anecdotes, facetiae, satire, etc.
Botany, barometers, and bridgework. H. Frankel. Sat R 47:31+ My 30 '64

Finance
Foundations and subsidies; address. H. S. Bailey, jr. il Pub W 184:43-7 Jl 15 '63

UNIVERSITY professors. See College professors and instructors
UNIVERSITY professors, American association of. See American association of university professors
UNIVERSITY research. See Colleges and universities—Research
UNIVERSITY students. See College students
UNIVERSITY surveys. See Educational surveys
UNLOADING. See Loading and unloading
UNMARRIED man's summer; story. See Gallant, M.
UNMARRIED men. See Bachelors
UNMARRIED mothers. See Mothers, Unmarried
UNMARRIED women. See Single women
UNNA, Warren
Pakistan; friend of our enemies. Atlan 213:79-80+ Mr '64
UNNERSTAD, Edith
Journey to Dalecarlia. Horn Bk 39:580-7 D '63
Why I write for children. Horn Bk 39:110 F '63
UNPOPULARITY. See Popularity
UNRUH, Jesse Marvin
Big Daddy goes to Yale; Chubb fellow. T. G. Harris. il pors Look 27:28-30 F 12 '63
Big Daddy of California. il pors Life 55:47-8+ S 27 '63
Big Daddy's lockup. por Newsweek 62:25 Ag 12 '63
Jesse Unruh: Big Daddy of California. E. Cray. Nation 196:199-207 Mr 9 '63
Shooting at Big Daddy. il por Time 82:18 Ag 23 '63
Unruh bucks the clubs. K. Hendrick. Nation 198:472-4 My 11 '64
UNSINKABLE Molly Brown; musical comedy. See Musical comedies, revues, etc.—Criticisms, plots, etc.
UNSOELD, William F. See Hornbein, T. F. jt. auth.
UNTEL, pseud. See Desbiens, J. P.
UNTERECKER, John
December event; poem. Christian Cent 80:1604 D 25 '63
Fall; poem. Christian Cent 81:1423 N 18 '64
Indian summer midnight; poem. Christian Cent 80:1298 O 23 '63
Midnight geometry; poem. Yale R 54:84 O '64
Songs for a cold month. Christian Cent 80:1576 D 18 '63
Spring bulbs earlier. Flower Grower 50:37+ N '63
UNTERMEYER, Louis
Answering voice. Ladies Home J 81:66+ My '64
Open the door; poem. Good H 157:118 Jl '63
Three notable collections. Poetry 103:382-6 Mr '64
To prayer I go; excerpt from Letters of Robert Frost to Louis Untermeyer; with comment by R. Kahn. Sat Eve Post 236:47-56+ S 14 '63
about
Ever yours, Robert. il por Time 82:102+ S 20 '63
New and selected, and a first volume. D. C. DeJong. Poetry 102:126-7 My '63
UNTIL tomorrow; story. See Mercer, C.
UNTOUCHABLES
Reporter at large. H. R. Isaacs. il New Yorker 40:60-4+ D 12: 75-6+ D 19 '64
Untouchable slaughter. Newsweek 61:42+ F 11 '63
UNTRACHT, Oppi
Untracht on enamels. il por Craft Horiz 23:28-31+ Jl '63
UNUS, Victoria
Giant swing. New Yorker 39:38-9 Ap 20 '63

UNWANTED children. See Children, Unwanted
UPCHURCH, Patricia
How to bring children and books together. Sr Schol 84:17T Mr 6 '64
UPDIKE, John
At a bar in Charlotte Amalie; story. New Yorker 39:26-32 Ja 11 '64
Azores; poem. Harper 228:37 Ja '64
Books (cont) New Yorker 39:90-4+ Ag 24; 203-6+ O 12 '63; 40:176+ Mr 7 '64
Christian roommates; story. New Yorker 40:44-50 Ap 4 '64
Dark; story. New Yorker 40:61-2 O 31 '64
Eclipse. Sat Eve Post 236:92 N 16 '63
Erotic epigrams; poems. Commonweal 78:327 Je 14 '63
Exposé; poem. New Yorker 39:40 My 25 '63
Farewell to the shopping district of Antibes; poem. New Yorker 39:50 Ap 20 '63
Fireworks; poem. New Yorker 40:28 Jl 4 '64
Giving blood; story. New Yorker 39:36-41 Ap 6 '63
Grandmaster Nabokov. New Repub 151:15-18 S 26 '64
Hoeing; poem. New Yorker 39:142 Ap 27 '63
Indian; story. New Yorker 39:24-6 Ag 17 '63
Lamplight; poem. New Repub 150:22 F 29 '64
Leaves; story. New Yorker 40:52-3 N 14 '64
Lucid eye in silver town; story. Sat Eve Post 237:54-5 My 23 '64
Mea culpa. New Yorker 39:137-8+ N 16 '63
Morning; story. New Yorker 40:24-6 Jl 18 '64
Music school; story. New Yorker 40:50-2 D 12 '64
My uncle's death; story. Sat Eve Post 236:48-50 Mr 2 '63
Rescue; story. New Yorker 40:28-31 Ja 2 '65
Sea knell; poem. New Yorker 40:44 Mr 28 '64
Some Frenchmen; poem. New Yorker 39:54 N 9 '63
Twin beds in Rome; story. New Yorker 39:32-5 F 8 '64
Vibration; poem. New Yorker 39:30 F 23 '63
Vow; poem. New Yorker 40:48 My 23 '64
about
Innocence of John Updike. G. La Course. Commonweal 77:512-14 F 8 '63
Updike's fiction: motifs and techniques. P. A. Doyle. por Cath World 199:356-62 S '64
Updike's quest for liturgy. M. Novak. Commonweal 78:192-5 My 10 '63
Youth of an author. R. Gilman. New Repub 148:25-7 Ap 13 '63
UPFIELD, Arthur William
Obituary
Pub W 185:34 Mr 23 '64
UPHAUS, Willard
Crime and punishment. G. W. Johnson. New Repub 148:26+ Je 22 '63
Man of principle. C. M. Cook. Christian Cent 80:1171 S 25 '63
UPHOLSTERED furniture. See Furniture
UPHOLSTERY
Choosing chairs and sofas. Bet Hom & Gard 41:44 My '63
Institute answers your questions on upholstery. Good H 156:163 F '63
Step by step from a fabric to a perfect color scheme. F. Byerly. il Bet Hom & Gard 41:58-63 Ap '63
Upholstered furniture. il Good H 158:146+ Mr '64
UPHOLSTERY, Plastic
Re-upholster your helmsman's seat; vinyl upholstery. N. Meiners. il Motor B 113:30+ Mr '64
UPITS, Andrei
Young Crane; story. McCalls 91:76-7 Ag '64
UPPER atmosphere. See Atmosphere, Upper
UPPER classes
New elegants. il Time 84:54-67 D 4 '64
See also
Debutantes
UPPER Mantle project. See Earth—Internal structure
UPPSALA biochemical laboratory. See Biological laboratories
UPTON, Arthur C.
Radiation hazards. Bul Atomic Sci 19:32-3 Ap '63
UPTON, Don
Stamp act; poem. McCalls 91:115 Ja '64
UPTON, T. Graydon
Economic development in Latin America; address, July 29, 1963. Vital Speeches 29:693-6 S 1 '63
UR
Silver from Ur of ancient Mesopotamia. J. W. Mellichamp and M. Levey. il Science 142:44-5 O 4 '63
URACIL
Partial synchronization of nuclear divisions in root meristems with 5-aminouracil. H. H. Smith and others. il Science 142:595-6 N 1 '63

URACIL—*Continued*
Uracil: failure to restore DNA synthesis while relieving 5-fluorouracil-induced inhibition. M. Reich and H. G. Mandel. bibliog il Science 145:276-7 Jl 17 '64
X-ray diffraction study of a DNA which contains uracil. R. Langridge and J. Marmur. bibliog il Science 143:1450-1 Mr 27 '64
URAL-Altaic languages
Uralic and Altaic: the neglected area. Ann Am Acad 356:86-92 N '64
See also
Altaic languages
URANIUM
Atomic powers bid for civilian market. Bsns W p98+ Jl 13 '63
Copper supply can meet future needs. Sci N L 86:248 O 17 '64
Depleted uranium draws pollutants from exhausts. Sci N L 84:91 Ag 10 '63
Raoult's law study of vanadium pentafluoride in uranium hexafluoride. R. C. Shrewsberry and B. Musulin. bibliog il Science 145:1452-4 S 25 '64
U.S. makes additional quantities of uranium 235 available; statements, July 3, 1963. J. F. Kennedy; G. T. Seaborg. Dept State Bul 49:167-9 Jl 29 '63
See also
Nuclear fuels
Isotopes
Isotopic fractionation of uranium in sandstone. J. N. Rosholt and others. bibliog il Science 139:224-6 Ja 18 '63
URANIUM dioxide. See Uranium oxides
URANIUM mines and mining
United States
Great uranium glut. H. B. Meyers. il Fortune 69:108-11+ F '64
URANIUM oxides
Strain-induced birefringence in fluoride films on uranium dioxide. W. P. Ellis. bibliog il Science 144:1570-2 Je 26 '64
URANIUM prospector; story. See Rudd, H.
URANYL
Uranyl ion coordination. H. T. Evans, jr. bibliog il Science 141:154-8 Jl 12 '63
Uranyl ion coordination. J. O. Edwards and J. A. Stritar. bibliog il Science 142:1651 D 27 '63
URATES. See Uric acid
URBAN, Catherine
Scarecrow's hat; drama. Plays 23:67-72, 95 O '63
URBAN education. See Education, Urban
URBAN growth. See Cities and towns—Growth
URBAN housing. See Housing
URBAN land. See Land
URBAN land institute
Best residential tax havens. Am City 78:140 Mr '63
URBAN league, National. See National urban league
URBAN redevelopment. See City planning; Urban renewal
URBAN redevelopment program. See Urban renewal
URBAN renewal
Are cities obsolete? B. Weissbourd. il Sat R 47:12-15+ D 19 '64; Reply. R. E. Singer. 48:37 Ja 23 '65
Are we committing urban suicide? L. Hazard. Harvard Bsns R 42:152-4+ Jl '64
Big cities try for a comeback. il U S News 57:34-8 D 28 '64
Blow at urban renewal. il Fortune 70:206+ N '64
Cities, the new scale; symposium. il Arch Forum 121:171-209 Ag '64
Construction: public money fuels growth. il Bsns W p118+ Mr 23 '63
Debate: federal participation in urban-renewal projects; discussion at annual lunch of Property owners committee of the Commerce and industry association of New York. New Yorker 40:46-7 D 12 '64
Design goals for urban renewal. W. Slayton. Arch Rec 134:149-52 N '63
Face-lifting; suburbia. Newsweek 63:67-8 F 10 '64
Federal bulldozer, by M. Anderson. Review Nat R 16:1155-6 D 29 '64. H. J. Ullmann
Fiasco of urban renewal. M. Anderson. il Harvard Bsns R 43:6-8+ Ja '65
Five challenges to our cities. P. M. Klutznick. Arch Forum 120:106-8 My '64
For better housing. Bsns W p23 F 1 '64
For U.S. cities: surge of new life. il Bsns W p 11-16 Jl 4 '64
Here's way to rebuild your city; downtown Rochester, N.Y. il Nations Bsns 52:34-5+ My '64
Housing program under fire: President's new cities and urban renewal proposals. il Bsns W p32 F 29 '64
Is this the big industry that can keep U.S. going? il U S News 54:70-4 F 25 '63
Lyndon Johnson's housing program: new cities and suburbs with government calling the signals. U S News 56:6 F 10 '64
Mounting scandal of urban renewal. J. Dowdy. Read Digest 84:51-7 Mr '64
People of the slums. J. Colebrook. New Repub 148:18-22 Je 15; 15-18 Je 29 '63
Planners thriving on renewal. il Bsns W p 134+ Jl 25 '64
Preservation and urban renewal: is coexistence possible? symposium, ed. by B. Snow. il Antiques 84:442-53 O '63
President calls for expanded housing and community programs. Arch Forum 120:5 Mr '64
President's plan for urban America. W. Von Eckardt. New Repub 150:9 F 8 '64
Rebuilder of cities; or a new pork barrel? urban renewal program. il Bsns W p64+ D 7 '63
Renewal gains from Ruberoid contest. il Arch Forum 119:7 S '63
Shame of the cities. T. O'Hanlon. il Duns R 84:58-9+ O '64
Splitsville, U.S.A; urban renewal and racial segregation: Chicago's Negro ghetto. E. Richey. il Reporter 28:35-8 My 23 '63; Discussion. 29:5 Jl 4 '63
Storm warnings fly for urban renewal; concerning Dr Andrew's book, Federal bulldozer. Bsns W p51-2 D 19 '64
Third force in urban renewal. H. Kay. il Fortune 70:130-3+ O '64
This month's feature: Congress and future of urban renewal. Cong Digest 43:99-128 Ap '64
Truth about urban renewal; interview. M. Anderson. Nations Bsns 53:31+ Ja '65
Under the knife, or all for their own good. il Time 84:60-72+ N 6 '64
University studies disclose: this federal program destroys jobs. il Nations Bsns 52:36-7+ Ap '64
Urban program of President Johnson; excerpts from address, January 1964. L. B. Johnson. Am City 79:154+ Mr '64
Urban renewal: a new face on the American city. D. B. Carlson. il Arch Forum 119:80-5 Ag '63
Urban renewal; address, June 25, 1964. W. L. Slayton. Vital Speeches 30:631-4 Ag 1 '64
Urban renewal and the city. W. Von Eckardt. il New Repub 149:15-19 S 14; 17-20 S 21; 16-18 S 28; 21-4 O 5; 14-17 O 19; 16-18 O 26 '63
Urban renewal as creative catalyst. A. Mayer. Arch Rec 135:145-52 My '64
Urban-renewal consultants. R. B. Martin. Am City 79:124+ Ja '64
Urban renewal saves homes; York, Pa. il Am City 78:103 S '63
Urban renewal spark $2 billion private investment. G. A. Christie. il Arch Rec 136:26 D '64
Urban revival: goals and standards; symposium, ed. by R. B. Mitchell. bibliog f il Ann Am Acad 352:1-151 Mr '64
What your city needs to grow. il Nations Bsns 52:31-3+ S '64
See also
Business districts
City planning
URBAN renewal administration. See United States—Urban renewal administration
URBAN sociology. See Sociology, Urban
URBAN training center for Christian mission (proposed)
Training clergy and laity for the inner city. Christian Cent 80:356 Mr 20 '63
URBAN universities. See Colleges and universities, Municipal
URBANISM. See Cities and towns
URBANIZATION. See City and town life
URBANIZED areas. See Metropolitan areas
URBANSKI, Edmund Stephen
Ecuador's socio-political mosaic. bibliog f Cur Hist 46:19-25 Ja '64
Indian in Latin American fiction. Américas 15:20-4 My '63
URBELL, Earl
Let the sea nourish your health. House B 105:122-3+ Je '63
URBEN, Leon J.
Country roads, they're not safe! Suc Farm 61:130 Ap '63

URBINA, Maria Lavalle
Seventeenth session of the Commission on the status of women. por U N Rev 10:40-2 My '63
URCHINS, Sea. See Sea urchins
URDANG, Constance
Editorials; Pastorals; poems. Poetry 102:17-18 Ap '63
To pipe the animals aboard Noah's ark; In the garden; poems. Poetry 104:78-81 My '64
UREA
How to feed urea and cut feed costs. J. Russell. Farm J 88:50 Ap '64
Hydroxyurea; inhibitory effect on DNA metabolism. C. W. Young and S. Hodas. bibliog il Science 146:1172-4 N 27 '64
New look at urea for dairy cows. D. Hillman. il Suc Farm 62:48-9 S '64
Urea: apparent carrier-mediated transport by facilitated diffusion in dogfish erythrocytes. H. V. Murdaugh and others. bibliog il Science 144:52-3 Ap 3 '64
UREA-form
Hydroxyurea: mechanism of action. W. N. Fishbein and P. P. Carbone. bibliog Science 142:1069-70 N 22 '63
Ureotelism of echidna and platypus. D. A. Denton and others. bibliog il Science 139: 1225 Mr 22 '63
UREMIA
New treatments for a fatal kidney ailment. G. G. Greer. Bet Hom & Gard 41:118 O '63
URETHANS
Homograft tolerance in mice: use of urethan and sublethal irradiation. W. E. Davis, jr. and L. J. Cole. bibliog il Science 140:483-4 My 3 '63
Spandex elastic fibers. E. M. Hicks, jr. and others. bibliog il Science 147:373-9 Ja 22 '65
UREY, Harold C.
How much gain from sending men to moon? summary of address, December 30, 1963. U S News 56:10 Ja 13 '64
URIBURU, Ernesto C.
Lobos Island. pors Américas 15:33-7 Je '63
Niña II. Américas 15:2-7 Ap '63
URIC acid
Serum uric acid in young mongoloids. E. T. Mertz and others. bibliog il Science 11:535 Ag 9 '63
Uric acid in the reproductive system of males of the cockroach blattella germanica. L. M. Roth and G. P. Dateo, jr. bibliog il Science 146:782-4 N 6 '64
Uric acid transport system: apparent absence in erythrocytes of the dalmatian coach hound. A. M. Harvey and H. N. Christensen. bibliog il Science 145:826-7 Ag 21 '64
URICASE
Uricase: localization in hepatic microbodies. Z. Hruban and H. Swift. bibliog il Science 146:1316-18 D 4 '64
URIDINE
Incorporation of uridine-H^3 into nuclei of virus-infected tobacco. S. H. Smith and D. E. Schlegel. bibliog il Science 145:1058-9 S 4 '64
See also
Idoxuridine
URINARY organs
Diseases
Drug for urinary infection; NegGram antibacterial drug. F. Marley. Sci N L 85:211 Ap 4 '64
URINE
Crystalline low molecular weight γ-globulin from a human urine. H. F. Deutsch. bibliog il Science 141:435-6 Ag 2 '63
Deoxycytidine in urine of humans after whole-body irradiation. H. K. Berry and others. bibliog il Science 142:396-8 O 18 '63
Excretion of hypertonic urine by a teleost. J. G. Stanley and W. R. Fleming. bibliog il Science 144:63-4 Ap 3 '64
Preparation of retine from human urine. A. Hegyeli and others. il Science 142:1571-2 D 20 '63
Analysis
Inulin and albumin absorption from the proximal tubule in necturus kidney. W. N. Scott and others. bibliog il Science 146:1588-90 D 18 '64
Methylurea and acetamide: active reabsorption by elasmobranch renal tubules. B. Schmidt-Nielsen and L. Rabinowitz. bibliog il Science 146:1587-8 D 18 '64
N-methylmetanephrine: excretion by juvenile psychotics. T. L. Perry. bibliog il Science 139:587-9 F 15 '63
Incontinence
Drug for bedwetters; imipramine. Sci N L 85:307 My 16 '64
Growing up only cure for bed-wetting habit. Sci N L 84:232 O 12 '63
URIQUE RIVER
Lady on a river of rock; Barranca de Cobre, Mexico, ed. by J. O'Reilly, M. E. O'Reilly. il Sports Illus 19:26+ O 21 '63
URIS, Auren
Make your time more productive. Nations Bsns 51:98+ Ap '63
What you can learn from success. Nations Bsns 51:76-8 Jl '63
URIS, Leon
Armageddon; novel; excerpts. Sat Eve Post 236:40-8 Ap 20 '63; 237:38-9 My 30; 34-9 Je 6 '64
URN, Althaea
Uncle Oscar from Enköping; story. Atlan 212:46-53 Jl '63
URQUHART, Brian
Books. New Yorker 40:232-4+ O 31 '64
URSÚA, Pedro de
Ephemeral Amazon kingdom; dark deeds of Lope de Aguirre. R. J. Sender. il Américas 15:28-32 My '63
URUGUAY
See also
Montevideo
Description and travel
At the end of the River Plate. L. Barry. il Pop Phot 52:26+ Je '63
Economic conditions
Looking for customers. New Repub 148:11 Je 1 '63
One day in the life of an Uruguayan. R. Peter. Nat R 15:222 S 24 '63
Wel-fairy tale. il Time 84:46 N 27 '64
Economic relations
U.S.-Uruguayan trade committee holds talks at Washington. Dept State Bul 51:617 N 2 '64
Foreign relations
And then there was one; economic and diplomatic relations with Cuba broken off. Time 84:53 S 18 '64
History
José Artigas: father of Uruguay. H. E. Davis. bibliog il Américas 16:1-5 O '64
Religious institutions and affairs
News of the Christian world. Christian Cent 80:810; 81:1185 Je 19 '63, S 23 '64
URUGUAY science fair. See Science fairs
URUGUAYAN poetry
Six Uruguayan poets; with poems. S. Ibargoyen Islas. il Américas 16:16-21 S '64
URUNDI. See Burundi
USE of time. See Time, Use of
USED automobiles; Used machinery; etc. See Automobiles, Used; Machinery, Used; etc.
USHERWOOD, P. N. R. and Grundfest, H.
Inhibitory postsynaptic potentials in grasshopper muscle. bibliog Science 143:817-18 F 21 '64
USHIJIMA, Richard N. and others
Chromosome complements of two species of primates: cynopithecus niger and presbytis entellus. bibliog Science 146:78-9 O 2 '64
USSERY, Bobby
Shoeshine boy. il pors Time 84:58+ Jl 24 '64
USTINOV, Peter
Peter Ustinov: I like what tempts my eye; interview, ed. by N. Lyon. por Vogue 144: 223-4 O 1 '64
Peter Ustinov speaking; ed. by H. Brandon. Atlan 214:29-33 Jl '64
Ustinov writes of the days when he was a roadster. pors Life 54:56+ Ap 19 '63
about
Photo finish. Criticism
Nation 196:214 Mr 9 '63
New Yorker 39:112 F 23 '63
Newsweek por 61:60 F 25 '63
Sat R 46:30 Mr 2 '63
Theatre Arts il por 47:10-11 Ap '63
Time por 81:75 F 22 '63
UTAH
See also
Booksellers and bookselling—Utah
Bryce Canyon National Park
Education—Utah
Fishing—Utah
Glen Canyon
Green River
Hunting—Utah
Paleontology—Utah
Roads—Utah
Zion National Park

UTAH—*Continued*

Description and travel

Side trip into Utah's past. il Sunset 130:28 My '63

History

Gathering of Zion: the story of the Mormon trail, by W. Stegner. Review
Sat R il 48:31 Ja 16 '65. D. L. Morgan

Politics and government

How it is out there. Time 84:18 Ag 21 '64

UTAH education association
Deliberate slowness. Newsweek 62:52-3 Jl 15 '63
Showdown in Utah. Time 81:62 My 24 '63
Utah key issue at NEA. Sr Schol 83:1T S 13 63; Discussion. 83:8T O 18 '63
Utah: off limits. il Time 83:63 My 29 '64

UTAH. University, Salt Lake City
Changing U of U. Newsweek 64:68-9 D 7 '64
Professor in ballet slippers. N. S. Hey. il Dance Mag 37:48-52 My '63

UTERUS

Surgery

D and C: most common operation on women. G. Naismith. il Todays Health 42:18-19+ Jl '64

UTERUS, Artificial
Lamb experiment may help have human babies; alive in an artificial womb. il Life 57:37-8 Ag 28 '64

UTILITY billing. See Billing

UTILITY rooms. See Rooms

UTILIZATION of land. See Land utilization

UTILIZATION of waste. See Waste, Utilization of

UTLEY, Beatrice
Living with antiques. Antiques 84:165-7 Ag '63

UTOPIAS
From Eden to the nightmare. H. A. Grunwald. il Horizon 5:72-9 Mr '63
Harvard's Skinner, the last of the utopians. S. Klaw. Harper 226:45-51 Ap '63
Utopia and its enemies, by G. Kateb. Review
Commentary 37:77-8+ Ap '64. D. H. Wrong
Nation 197:146-7 S 14 '63. S. Maloff
Utopia and rebellion: the New college experiment; excerpt from Innovation in education. G. Watson. bibliog Sch & Soc 92:72+ F 22 '64
Utopia in the sixties. D. J. Clark. il Cath World 196:357-63 Mr '63
Utopia, limited; excerpt from Vanishing America. W. E. Wilson. il Am Heritage 15: 64-72 O '64

UTT, Daniel
Snakebite ordeal: nineteen terrible hours. por Outdoor Life 135:37-9+ F '65

UTTER, Lawrence W.
Helping our culturally impoverished children. NEA J 52:28-30 N '63

UVACEK, Ed, and Peterson, Chester, Jr
Should you feed common cattle? Suc Farm 62:39 Jl '64

UYEKI, Eugene S. and Cliffe, F. B. Jr
Federal scientist-administrator. bibliog Science 139:1267-70 Mr 29 '63

UYS, Stanley
Experiment in segregation. New Repub 148: 10-11 My 4 '63
I plead not guilty. New Repub 149:12-13 D 28 '63
Protectorates under the gun. New Repub 149: 9-10 S 28 '63
Whither the white belt? New Repub 148:12-14 Je 22 '63

UYSAL, Ahmet. See Walker, B. K. jt. auth.

UZCÁTEGUI, Emilio
Ecuador's novels and novelists. Américas 16: 29-34 My '64

UZMANN, J. R. and Hayduk, S. H.
In vitro culture of the flagellate protozoan hexamita salmonis. bibliog Science 140:290-2 Ap 19 '63

UZZELL, T. M. Jr. See MacGregor, H. C. jt. auth.

V

VA. See United States—Veterans administration

VD. See Venereal diseases

VEA. See Virginia education association

VHF. See Television transmission

VHF television stations. See Television stations

VISTA. See Volunteers in service to America

VITA. See Volunteers for international technical assistance

VOA. See Voice of America (radio program)

VOR (visual omnirange) See Radio aids to aviation

V/STOL (vertical or short take-off and landing) See Airplanes, Vertical take-off and landing

VTA. See Virginia teachers association

VTOL. See Airplanes, Vertical take-off and landing

VTVM (vacuum tube voltmeters) See Voltmeters

VACATION cabins. See Cabins

VACATION camps. See Camps

VACATION houses. See Summer homes

VACATION planning week. See Special days and weeks

VACATION projects
Seed of wonder; Vacation Bible school in the town of Cape May Court House, N.J. il Recreation 56:326-7 S '63
Surprise box. M. L. Weston. Redbook 120: 16 Ap '63
Vacation varieties; teen and pre-teen recreation project. il N Y Times Mag p56 Ag 25 '63
Will their summer be fruitless or fruitful? M. Shearer. il House B 106:136-7+ Je '64
See also
Libraries, Childrens—Projects

VACATION schools. See Summer schools

VACATION villages
Bargain vacations in paradise; Club Méditerranée. J. Stewart-Gordon. il Read Digest 84:217-18+ My '64
Mr Blitz and the total vacation game; Club méditerranée. G. Rogin. il Sports Illus 19: 48-59 Jl 1 '63

VACATIONS
American summer. J. Didion. Vogue 141:117+ My '63
August catastrophe. Time 84:24+ Ag 14 '64
Big boss gets away from it all. il Newsweek 62:57-9 Ag 5 '63
Compatible companions, or How to stay out of trouble when you choose friends for the trip. D. L. McFadden. House B 106:26+ Je '64
Economy vacation. C. B. Colby. Outdoor Life 133:32+ Ap '64
Europe's mad month; August vacations. il Newsweek 64:61 Ag 24 '64
Family and fishing? roll 'em together. T. McNally. il Outdoor Life 131:49-51+ My '63
Family money management. Bet Hom & Gard 41:6+ S '63
Farm vacation. il Travel 122:43-5 Jl '64
Farm vacations; with editorial comment. J. B. Craig. il Am For 70:7, 8-11+ Jl '64
For a heart-of-the-West vacation try: The Tetons, Yellowstone, Salt Lake City. W. R. Wilson. il Suc Farm 61:42-3 Je '63
Give your youngsters a down-on-the-farm vacation. R. Deardorff. il Parents Mag 39: 42-3+ Jl '64
Guide to family vacations on a budget; symposium. il Redbook 120:87-94 Ap '63
Help yourself to one-day holidays. il Am Home 67:32+ Jl '64
Home swapping. Newsweek 63:66 F 17 '64
How to make that family trip: by plane, train, bus, or car? S. A. Mix. il Todays Health 41:30-5+ F '63
I took a vacation at home. A. Z. Chapin. il Suc Farm 62:75+ My '64
If you're thinking about a winter holiday. il U S News 56:42-5 Ja 6 '64
It's time for a little time off. D. Hanson. Suc Farm 61:12 Ag '63
Last search for summer. L. Wainwright. Life 57:31 S 18 '64
Let's travel; College week locales. il Mlle 58:113-14 Ja '64
Letter from Paris: Parisians on summer vacations. Genêt. New Yorker 39:59-60 Ag 17 '63
Life guide; guest farms. il Life 54:12 Ap 26 '63
More for your travel dollar! il Bet Hom & Gard 42:108 Je: 82 S: 12 D '64
Redbook's 1964 guide to family vacations. W. Hartley and E. Hartley. il Redbook 122:51-8 Ap '64
Rise in worker holidays. T. R. Brooks. Duns R 84:46+ D '64
Separate vacations beat none; farm family's split-vacation. M. Scharf. il Farm J 87: 25+ Je '63

VACATIONS—*Continued*
Something special in vacations. J. K. Lagemann. il Read Digest 82:222-3+ Je '63
Swap: New Yorkers with San Francisco visitors to fair. New Yorker 40:19-20 Ag 29 '64
Take a surprise vacation. W. J. Klein. il Redbook 124:28+ D '64
There's fun for everyone when you vacation at home. il Pop Gard 15:28-31 Jl '64
Travel; precious few unspoiled spots. il Time 83:74-5 Je 26 '64
Travel with a purpose; special-interest tours. il Changing T 18:25-9 F '64
Try camping for summer fun. C. Allen. il Ebony 18:127-8+ Je '63
Vacationing? safeguard your home. Good H 156:157 Je '63
Weekends, U.S.A: what ever happened to fun? excerpt from The weekenders. M. Gunther. McCalls 91:70-1+ Je '64
What a second home can do for you. Am Home 67:35 Ap '64
What will your vacation cost? il Changing T 17:43-5 Jl '63
Where to go fishing, vacationing, hunting all over the world (title varies) P. A. Parsons. See issues of Outdoor life
Who needs vacations? C. A. Larson. il Sci Digest 54:77-80 Jl '63
Why we take a dozen vacations a year. E. Pearson. Farm J 87:36B Ag '63
Winter boating vacations. J. A. Emmett. il Outdoor Life 133:80-3 Ja '64
Winter-summer vacation house. il House B 105:86-99+ F '63
Without portfolio; schoolchildrens long summer vacation. C. B. Luce. McCalls 91:144 Je '64
See also
Automobile touring
Camping
Outdoor life

Anecdotes, facetiae, satire, etc.

How not to plan a vacation. B. Ward. Sat R 47:46 D 5 '64

VACATIONS, Employee
EV and camping clubs. D. B. Huyck. il Am For 70:10-11+ Je '64
Offices share vacation bonus; at Big steel. Bsns W p117 O 5 '63
Sweden goes all out for the leisure boom. il Bsns W p32-3 S 7 '63
See also
Leave of absence

VACCARO, Michael J.
Satellites in space. Electr World 71:51-3 Je '64

VACCINATION
Childhood diseases, not licked yet. il Changing T 17:13-15 S '63
Cowpox: man's friendly disease. F. H. Richardson. il Todays Health 42:12+ F '64
Have you kept your immunity up to date? D. A. Dukelow. Todays Health 42:8-9+ Ap '64
Needless agony of smallpox. R. M. Hendrickson. il Todays Health 41:22-3+ Mr '63
Reading, 'riting, 'rithmetic, and revaccination. F. V. Hein. il Todays Health 41:14 S '63
Shots for adults. Changing T 17:11 Mr '63
Spanish doctors in the old Southwest. R. Dunlop. il Todays Health 41:44-7+ F '63
Vaccinations assured for the unprotected. Sci N L 84:329 N 23 '63
Vaccinations children should have. il Good H 157:146 Ag '63
Which shots for your family? G. G. Greer. Bet Hom & Gard 41:18 S '62
See also
Rabies—Immunity

VACCINES
Antipolio substance. F. Marley. Sci N L 85:405 Je 27 '64
Continuously cultured tissue cells and viral vaccines: report of a committee on tissue culture viruses and vaccines; discussion. bibliog Science 140:766+ My 17 '63
Hogs drink new erysipelas vaccine. D. Hagen. Farm J 88:35 Je '64
Pregnant women warned; live virus vaccine hazards. Sci N L 85:308 My 16 '64
Vaccine for cold sores. Time 84:62 S 18 '64
See also
Cancer—Vaccines
Influenza—Vaccines
Rabies vaccine
Tuberculosis—Vaccines
Virus diseases—Vaccines
also subhead Vaccines under names of diseases, e.g. Measles—Vaccines

VACUUM
All-metal diffusion pump practical new route to ultra-high vacuums. W. S. Beller. il Miss & Roc 15:22-3 N 16 '64
Vacuum: measurement techniques and equipment; report on national symposium of the American vacuum society. G. H. Bancroft and others. Science 146:1694-5 D 25 '64
Vacuum: sputtering, desorption, and surface physics; report on annual Sherwood vacuum conference. S. O. Dean. Science 144:1251-2 Je 5 '64

Industrial applications

See Vacuum technology

VACUUM apparatus
Ultrahigh vacuum instrumentation. T. A. Vanderslice. bibiog il Science 142:178-84 O 11 '63

VACUUM cleaners
Extra-large vacuum cleaner, the craftsman Home-n-Shop Vac. il Consumer Bul 48:8-9 F '65
Lightweight upright vacuum cleaners. il Consumer Rep 28:472-5 O '63
Lightweight vacuum cleaners. il Changing T 18:23 Ja '64
New cleaning aid: a vacuum system that is built in. il House B 106:145+ Mr '64
Pitfalls in buying a vacuum cleaner. Consumer Bul 47:2 Ag '64
Shop vacuum for less than $10. J. Copeland. il Pop Sci 186:163-5 Ja '65
Two extremes in vacuum cleaners. il Consumer Rep 29:337-40 Jl '64
Vacuum cleaners. il Consumer Bul 47:6-12 Ag '64
Vacuum cleaners; survey of tank and upright models. il Consumer Rep 29:222-30 My '64
What to look for in a vacuum cleaner. Am Home 67:98-9 O '64
See also
Hoover company

VACUUM cleaning
Built-in cleaning systems. il Consumer Rep 29:339-40 Jl '64

VACUUM filtration. See Sewage disposal—Filtration

VACUUM gages. See Gages

VACUUM in industry. See Vacuum technology

VACUUM pumps
All-metal diffusion pump practical new route to ultra-high vacuums. W. S. Beller. il Miss & Roc 15:22-3 N 16 '64
Electronic pumps: a new approach to vacuum generation. T. C. Sinclair. il Electr World 73:44-5 Ja '65

VACUUM sweepers, Street. See Street cleaning apparatus

VACUUM technology
Scientific instrumentation business thrives independent of program cuts. il Miss & Roc 14:40+ Je 1 '64
Useful void. il Time 83:100 My 15 '64

VACUUM tube amplifiers. See Amplifiers

VACUUM-tube circuits
Handy EP pack. E. G. Louis. il Pop Electr 19:64 N '63

VACUUM tube voltmeters. See Voltmeters

VACUUM tubes
European receiving-tube numbering system. E. L. Elizondo. il Electr World 70:74 N '63
GE working on tunnel-cathode tube. C. D. LaFond. il Miss & Roc 12:22-3 F 11 '63
Innovations in receiving tubes. J. R. Collins. il Electr World 72:54-5+ S '64
Novel electrometer tube. C. E. Atkins. il Electr World 70:44-5 O '63
Sound: tubes or transistors, which should you choose? J. Wesson. U S Camera 27:28+ N '64
Transistors vs tubes for hi-fi. F. L. Mergner. Electr World 71:45+ Ja '64
Transistors vs tubes for hi-fi. R. S. Burwen. Electr World 70:85 D '63
Transistors vs tubes for hi-fi. W. W. Chou. Electr World 71:36+ F '64
Transistors versus tubes for two-way radio. H. H. Rice. il Electr World 72:48-50 N '64
Tube family tree. L. E. Garner, jr. il Pop Electr 18:45-50+ My; 73-8+ Je; 19:51-6+ Ag '63
Understanding burn-out; vacuum tube and pilot lamp filaments. L. Vicens. il Pop Electr 20:69 Mr '64
See also
Cathode ray tubes
Magnetrons
Traveling wave tubes
Vacuum-tube circuits

History

Early vacuum tubes. P. G. Watson. il Electr World 72:42-3+ D '64

VACUUM tubes—History—*Continued*
Secret tube that changed the war. W. I. Orr. il Pop Electr 20:57-9+ Mr '64

Repairing

Octal tube pin repairs. E. G. Louis. il Pop Electr 20:62 Ja '64

VAGABONDS
See also
Tramps

VAGANOVA, Agrippina Yakovlevna
Vaganova; excerpts, tr. by V. Litvinoff. pors Dance Mag 38:40-3 Jl; 42-4+ Ag '64

VAGINA
Vaginal disorders in babies and young children. M. J. E. Senn. McCalls 91:32+ Ja '64

VAGINAL smear test. See Cancer—Diagnosis

VAGINAL trichomoniasis. See Trichomoniasis, Vaginal

VAGRANCY
No right not to work. Time 83:54+ Je 19 '64
See also
Tramps

VAGUS nerves. See Nerves

VAHANIAN, Gabriel
God, man and Marxism. Christian Cent 81:305 Mr 4 '64

VAHANIAN, Tilla
Encourage them to grow. Parents Mag 38:122 O '63

VAHLDIEK, F. W. and others
Tetragonal zirconium oxide prepared under high pressure. bibliog Science 142:1059-60 N 22 '63

VAIL, Betty, and Edwards, Dixon
Jerrie Mock: winner take all. Flying 75:32-3+ Jl '64

VAIL, Thomas Van Husen
Replying in spades. il por Time 81:50 My 31 '63

VAIL, Colo. See Winter resorts

VAIONT DAM, Italy. See Dams—Italy

VAIŠNYS, R. J. See Kirk, R. S. jt. auth.

VALACHI, Joseph
After the TV crime hearings—. il por U S News 55:8 O 14 '63
But listen to his canary. Life 55:4 O 18 '63
Che cosa? means what's that? M. Kempton. New Repub 149:6-7 O 12 '63
Crime syndicate and the way it works. U S News 55:10 Ag 19 '63
Joe Valachi: the killer who told on the mob. P. Maas. il por Sat Eve Post 236:21-3 N 23 '63
Killers in prison; J. Valachi before Arkansas Senator McClellan's permanent investigations subcommittee. il por Time 82:33 O 4 '63
Kiss of death. pors Newsweek 62:34+ O 7 '63
Mafia: the inside story; with editorial comment. P. Maas. il Sat Eve Post 236:19-25, 90 Ag 10 '63
One world; people in current news as television stars. Reporter 29:24+ O 24 '63
Robert Kennedy defines the menace. R. F. Kennedy. il por N Y Times Mag p 15+ O 13 '63
Second-act trouble; Valachi hearing by Senate permanent subcommittee on investigations. il por Newsweek 62:33-4 O 14 '63
Show biz in Washington. Nation 197:229 O 19 '63
Smell of it. Time 82:28 O 11 '63
TV crime story; it's for real. il por Sr Schol 83:17 O 25 '63
Way big crime operates in U.S. il pors U S News 55:78-9 O 7 '63

VALANCES. See Curtains and draperies

VALAORITES, Nanos
(tr) See Seferis, G. Letter to a foreign friend

VALCARCEL, Tomas
New breed in Spain. Cath World 200:155-61 D '64

VALDAGNO, Italy
Miracolo Marzotto. Time 81:94 Mr 8 '63

VALDEZ, R. F.
Noon-duty assistant program. NEA J 53:63 Ap '64

VALE project. See United States—Land management, Bureau of

VALENCIA, Juan I. See Grell, R. F. jt. auth.

VALENCIA (province) Spain
Valencia's tribunal of waters. R. Littell. il Read Digest 83:126-30 D '63

VALENSTEIN, Elliot S. and Valenstein, Thelma
Interaction of positive and negative reinforcing neural systems. bibliog Science 145:1456-8 S 25 '64

VALENSTEIN, Lawrence
Madison avenue: new view, old street. Sat R 46:72-3 Ap 13 '63

VALENSTEIN, Thelma. See Valenstein, E. S. jt. auth.

VALENTE, Caterina
Berlitz Baedeker. Newsweek 63:94 Mr 16 '64

VALENTI, Fernando
Such sweet clawing. il por Time 81:40 Mr 22 '63

VALENTI, Jack
Johnson's men: valuable hunks of humanity. T. Wicker. il por N Y Times Mag p 11+ My 3 '64
Little man who's always there. il por Time 83:25 Ap 3 '64
President's special consultant. por U S News 55:9 D 30 '63

VALENTIN, Curt
Art galleries. R. M. Coates. New Yorker 39:226-8 D 7 '63
Choice's dealer; exhibition. T. B. Hess. il pors Art N 62:26-7+ D '63

VALENTINE, Helen
Young wife's world. See issues of Good housekeeping

VALENTINE, Jean
First love; poem. Atlan 214:58 Ag '64
Miles from home; poem. Yale R 53:552 Je '64

VALENTINE, Raymond C. and Zinder, N. D.
Phenotypic repair of RNA-bacteriophage mutants by streptomycin. bibliog Science 144:1458-9 Je 19 '64

VALENTINE cakes. See Cake

VALENTINE; story. See Jones, J.

VALENTINER, William Reinhold
Merchandising: the big store; W. R. Valentiner memorial exhibition at J. L. Hudson gallery, Detroit. F. Getlein. New Repub 149:24-6 D 21 '63

VALENTINES
Every child's valentine. L. Samuelson. il Sch Arts 62:10 F '63
Old cut-out valentine. il(p 1) Hobbies 67:76 F '63
Old-fashioned valentines. il Sunset 132:90 F '64
Post cards to tell of love. B. Finnegan. il Hobbies 67:118-19 F '63

VALENTINES day

Drama

Straight from the heart. C. Whitman. Plays 23:35-44 F '64

Fiction

Valentine. J. Jones. il Sat Eve Post 236:36-9 F 16 '63

VALENZUELA, Milo
Thinking man's jockey. Sports Illus 18:6 Mr 4 '63

VALERIO, Giorgio
Using his head. Time 82:62 D 27 '63

VALERIY, Ivan, pseud. See Tarsis, V.

VALÉRY, Paul
Career in consciousness. R. Howard. Nation 200:63-4 Ja 18 '65

VALETTA, Malta
Reader's choice. F. R. Smith. Travel 122:7 Jl '64

VALGUARNERA, M.
Listening to the harpsichord; poem. Mlle 59:209 My '64

VÁLI, Ferenc A.
Hungary faces the future. Cur Hist 44:288-93 My '63

VALINE
GUU means valine; first break in genetic code. Sci Am 211:82+ S '64

VALLANDIGHAM, Clement Laird
Most unpopular man in the North. L. W. Koenig. il por Am Heritage 15:12-15+ F '64

VALLDEPERES, Manuel
Books. Américas 15:41-2 D '63; 16:39-40 N '64

VALLEJO, César
Master of pain. H. Gifford. Poetry 105:196-7 D '64

VALLERAND, Jean
Look at music in Quebec. Mus Am 83:18-19 S '63

VALLETTA, Vittorio
Fiat: the big wheel in Italy's traffic. il Newsweek 63:68-70 Ja 20 '64

VALLEY quail shooting. See Quail shooting

VALLEY times today. See San Fernando Valley times

VALTZ, Robert C. K.
Case of the multiplant manufacturer; excerpts from European problems in general management. Harvard Bsns R 42:12-16+ Mr '64

VALUATION
Architecture; appraisal of New York's Seagram building. W. McQuade. Nation 196:448-50 My 25 '63
Beauty and the beast; tax assessment of Seagram building. il Newsweek 61:75 Je 10 '63
How to ban architecture. Arch Forum 118:97 My '63
How to make any city ugly; Seagram building tax assessment. Life 55:4 Ag 16 '63
N.Y. court upholds tax on Seagram tower. il Arch Forum 121:5+ Jl '64
New York courts uphold tax on quality. il Arch Forum 118:5+ My '63
Prestige value; taxing of Seagram building. Time 81:49 Je 7 '63

VALUATION of works of art. See Art—Valuation

VALUE (philosophy) See Worth

VALUE (psychology)
Conflicts in human values. R. N. McMurry. Harvard Bsns R 41:130-6+ My '63
Grouping and human values; excerpt from address. J. W. Gordon. il Sch Life 45:10-15 Jl '63
Life and lasers. R. H. Viguers. Horn Bk 40:343 Ag '64
What are your ultimate objectives? address, September 6, 1963. H. F. Harding. Vital Speeches 29:757-60 O 1 '63

VALUE, Moral. See Worth

VALUE added tax. See Taxation

VALUE analysis
Biggest thing since mass production. L. Stouffer. Read Digest 84:107-10 Ja '64
Value analysis techniques adapted to municipal government; Schenectady, N.Y. P. R. Roan. il Am City 79:101-2 Jl '64
Value engineering progress lacking. W. E. Wilks. Miss & Roc 12:27-8 Ap 8 '63
Value engineers' proper role discussed. D. E. Fink. Aviation W 78:98-9 My 6 '63
Value of value. W. J. Coughlin. Miss & Roc 12:62 My 6 '63
When the Pentagon saves; that's a gang of nickels. il Newsweek 63:63-4+ Mr 9 '64

VALUE of college education. See College education, Value of

VALUE of education. See Education, Value of

VALUE of money; story. See Maxwell, W.

VALVES
How to pick a butterfly valve for waterworks use. il Am City 79:167-8 Ap '64
See also
Automobile engines—Valves

VAMP till ready; story. See McLaughlin, M.

VAN, George E.
Freshest club. Yachting 115:98-100+ Ja '64
Robin wins race from Pt. Huron. Yachting 114:55+ S '63

VAN, John Paul
Colonel Van and General Harkins. Nation 197:230 O 19 '63

VAN ALLEN, James Alfred
James Van Allen tells what space is really like; interview. ed. by W. Cloud. por Pop Sci 182:73-6+ Ap '63
Facts about the 1962 space bomb. J. Lear. il Sat R 46:45-8 Ap 6 '63
Lesson; Starfish test. Nation 196:258 Mr 30 '63

VAN ALLEN, Roach
New approach to reading. bibliog f por Wilson Lib Bul 39:154-9 O '64

VAN ALLEN radiation belts
Charting the earth's radiation belts. il Sky & Tel 28:212-13 O '64
Facts about the 1962 space bomb. J. Lear. il Sat R 46:45-8 Ap 6 '63; Reply with rejoinder. S. F. Singer. 46:50-1 My 4 '63
Forty miles of information every day from space. L. Lessing. il Fortune 69:116-22+ Ja '64
James Van Allen tells what space is really like; interview. ed. by W. Cloud. J. A. Van Allen. il Pop Sci 182:73-6+ Ap '63
Microcircuits survive Van Allen belt. Aviation W 79:101 Ag 19 '63
Planet Jupiter; conference at NASA's Institute for space studies, New York, October 1962. R. Jastrow and N. Panagakos. il Science 139:351-2+ Ja 25 '63
Radiation belts. B. J. O'Brien. il Sci Am 208:84-96 My '63; Reply with rejoinder. S. F. Singer. 209:8+ Jl '63
Radiation belts, natural and artificial. C. E. McIlwain. bibliog il Science 142:355-61 O 18 '63
Recent nuclear blasts boost space radiation hazard. il Sci Digest 53:56-63 Ap '63
Satellite readied to probe radiation belt energetic particles; energetic particles Explorer D. il Miss & Roc 15:15 D 14 '64
Van Allen belts may come from tail of magnetosphere. Miss & Roc 16:28 Ja 18 '65

VAN ALSTINE, Bill
Impact of the Negro on the furniture market. Ebony 18:99-104 Ap '63

VAN ALSTYNE, William W.
Banning the campus speaker. Nation 196:267-8+ Mr 30 '63
Free to join and to meet. PTA Mag 58:10-12 Ja '64

VAN AMEYDEN VAN DUYM, Hidde
Paul Van Ostaijen: an introduction. Poetry 104:177-9 Je '64
(tr) See Ostaijen, P. van. Autobiography
(tr) See Ostaijen, P. van. Gedicht: een schoon gezicht heeft de dagblad-postiche; Avondgeluiden; Berceuse for grown-ups; Gedicht: zon brandt de rozelaar; Oude man

VAN ANDEL, Tjeerd H. and Laborel, Jacques
Recent high relative sea level stand near Recife, Brazil. bibliog Science 145:580-1 Ag 7 '64

VANADIUM
Raoult's law study of vanadium pentafluoride in uranium hexafluoride. R. C. Shrewsberry and S. Musulin. bibliog il Science 145:1452-4 S 25 '64

VAN ARK, Dorothy
Live rich without money. Good H 158:44+ My '64
Mother's daze. Parents Mag 38:62-3+ My '63
My kids won't lift a finger. Parents Mag 38:50-1+ Ag '63
Who says kids want to be understood? Parents Mag 39:40-1+ Jl '64; Same abr. Read Digest 86:39-40+ Ja '65

VAN ARSDALE, Harry, Jr
Labor's welfare state; the New York electrical workers. A. H. Raskin. Atlan 211:37-44 Ap '63

VANARSDEL, Paul P. Jr, and Sells, C. J.
Antigenic histamine release from passively sensitized human leukocytes. bibliog Science 141:1190-1 S 20 '63

VAN BAVEL, C. H. M. and others
Transpiration by sudangrass as an externally controlled process. Science 141:269-70 Jl 19 '63

VAN BEAUMONT, W. and Bullard, R. W.
Sweating: its rapid response to muscular work. bibliog Science 141:643-6 Ag 16 '63

VAN BRAKLE, John
Little girl on a windy day; poem. McCalls 90:157 Ap '63

VAN BREEMEN, Claire
For Jeremy, age one; poem. Christian Cent 81:42 Ja 8 '64

VAN BUREN, Abigail, pseud.
After the honeymoon (cont) por McCalls 90:26+ F '63
How come a nice girl like you isn't married yet? McCalls 90:51+ Jl '63
Mail-order psychology. J. Stanley. il por Mlle 59:94-5+ Je '64

VAN BUREN, Laurie
Long search of Laurie Van Buren. A. Hirshberg. il por Good H 157:64-5+ Jl '63

VAN BUREN, Martin
Martin Van Buren, eighth President 1837-1841. F. Freidel. il por Nat Geog Mag 127:90-3 Ja '65
Speech that toppled a president; excerpts from address, April 14, 1840, ed. with introd. by G. Carson. C. Ogle. por Am Heritage 15:108-11 Ag '64

VAN BUREN, Paul
Linguistic analysis: a way for some to affirm their faith. por Time 84:64 Jl 10 '64
Tillich as apologist. Christian Cent 81:177-9 F 5 '64

VAN BUREN, Ark.
Newspapers
Local touch. il Newsweek 61:56 F 11 '63

VANCE, Ben F.
Gardening in the Midwest (cont of) This month in the Midwest. See issues of Popular gardening

VANCE, Clarice
Six comediennes. J. Walsh. il pors Hobbies 68:32-6+ Ap; 32+ My '63

VANCE, Thomas
Note on Stig Dagerman. Poetry 103:255 Ja '64
(tr) See Dagerman, S. From Birgitta suite

VANCE, Vera
(tr) See Dagerman, S. From Birgitta suite

VAN COTT, Harold J.
Development of a children's zoo. por Recreation 57:402-4 O '64
Three R's of operation. Recreation 56:378-9 O '63

VANCOUVER, British Columbia

Music

[Musical events] Mus Am 84:61 Mr '64

Parks and playgrounds

Heyday in the park. E. Lindsay. il Recreation 57:388-9+ O '64

VANCOUVER ISLAND, British Columbia

Vancouver Island. D. F. Tonkin. il Travel 121:54-6 Ap '64

VANCOUVER music festival. See Music festivals—Canada

VANCOUVER opera association

B. C. Bel Canto. W. Littler. Opera N 28:26 My 2 '64

Canadian classics. W. Littler. Opera N 28: 26 S 28 '63

Sutherland sings Norma. W. Marquis. Mus Am 83:20 N '63

VANDALIA, Ohio

Biggest, loudest show in U.S. sport; Grand American trapshoot. V. Kraft. il Sports Illus 19:26-8+ S 9 '63

VANDALISM

Brooklyn public library branches suffer attacks of vandalism. il Library J 89:1573-4 Ap 1 '64

Creeping junkyard; blighted cities and vanishing wilderness. Life 56:4 Mr 20 '64

God's own junkyard, by P. Blake. Review Arch Forum 120:94-7 Ja '64

Marred masterpieces. il Newsweek 61:62 F 11 '63

Our loving public. W. W. Huber. il Am For 69:6-7+ Ag '63

Phantom of the Uffizi. il Newsweek 65:85 Ja 25 '65

Pray tell, little mermaid, who took your pretty head? il Life 56:28-33 My 8 '64

Reviewing stand; vandalism. A. M. Sullivan. Duns R 81:138 My '63

Spoilers; vacationers in U.S. national parks. il Time 84:66 Jl 3 '64

Square knot; indictment of guests at Fernanda Wanamaker Wetherill's debut. il Newsweek 62:43-4 N 11 '63

Tar is smeared on the cross; Church of the Brethren, Dixon, Ill. Christian Cent 80: 1194 O 2 '63

Tears for a mermaid; decapitation of The little mermaid. il Time 83:34 My 1 '64

Vandalism in Yellowstone Park. R. W. Witzke. il Nat Parks Mag 38:13-15+ F '64

Vandalism: physical & mental. A. M. Sullivan. Duns R 84:92 Jl '64

Vandals in the library. J. C. Furnas. Read Digest 84:175-6+ Ja '64

Wanamaker debut begins and ends up in a rampage; with report by D. Abrahamsen. il Life 55:30-7 S 20 '63

Wanton mutilation in the Uffizi. il Life 58: 72-3 Ja 29 '65

We're losing the war against slobs. R. Starnes. Field & S 69:12-15 Jl '64

VANDANO, Brunello

Coldest place on earth. Life 58:80-3 Ja 22 '65

VAN DE GRAAFF generators. See Electric generators, Electrostatic

VAN DE KAMP, Peter

Barnard's star as an astrometric binary. il Sky & Tel 26:8-9 Jl '63

New planet discovered: Barnard's Star B. A. Ewing. Sci N L 83:261 Ap 27 '63

VANDENBERG, E. J. and Overberger, C. G.

Aromaticity: a key to polymers stable at high temperatures. Science 141:176-7 Jl 12 '63

VAN DEN BERG, Piet

How to shoot down hail. Sci Digest 53:42-5 My '63

VANDENBERG air force base. See Air bases

VAN DEN BERGH, Sidney

Visiting Germany's largest telescope. Sky & Tel 27:268-72 My '64

VANDENBOSCH, Amry

Power balance in Indonesia. Cur Hist 46: 95-100 F '64

Reappraisal in South Africa. Yale R 53:11-25 O '63

VANDENDRIESSCHE, Aurele

Everybody runs to Boston; Boston marathon. W. Bingham. il pors Sports Illus 18:12-17 Ap 29 '63

For glory, & for stew. por Time 83:47 My 1 '64

VAN DEN HAAG, Ernest

Crimes against humanity. Nat R 15:154-7, 367 Ag 27, O 22 '63

Intelligence or prejudice? questions and answers. Nat R 16:1059-63 D 1 '64

Lesson of the Congo. Nat R 16:771-3+ S 8 '64

Motive for intermarriage often neurotic; interview. por U S News 55:86-8 N 18 '63

UN's idiot policy in the Congo. Nat R 17: 61-2 Ja 26 '65

VAN DE POL, W. H.

Is Anglicanism Protestant? excerpt from World Protestantism. Cath World 200:95-9+ N '64

VANDEPUT, Suzanne

Tragedy at Liege; Vandeput's thalidomide baby. J. Gallahue. il por Look 27:72-4+ Mr 12 '63; Discussion. 27:16 Ap 23 '63

VANDERBERG, William

Mountain; poem. Commonweal 79:102 O 18 '63

VANDERBILT, Alfred Gwynne

Third race; Aqueduct. New Yorker 39:32-4 My 11 '63

Vanderbilt vs. racing's establishment. A. Wright. il por Sports Illus 19:18-20+ Ag 12 '63

VANDERBILT, Amy

Gracious living. See issues of McCall's to May 1964

Habit of opera. Opera N 27:8-11 Mr 16 '63

about

Guider. il por Time 81:67 Mr 1 '63

Traveling with children. por Travel 121:42-4 Mr '64

VANDERBILT, Consuelo

Consuelo. por Newsweek 64:55 D 21 '64

VANDERBILT, Harold S.

Another lesson from a master. C. Goren. il Sports Illus 21:72-3 O 12 '64

Ups and downs of a J-boat skipper. por Yachting 116:39-41+ S '64

Voices of two venerable Vanderbilts; ed. by G. Plimpton. por Life 57:64A-64B+ Ag 14 '64

VANDERBILT, Kermit

Publication explosion. Nation 198:219-20 Mr 2 '64

VANDERBILT family

Splendor of a great family; the Vanderbilts; with photographs by T. Frissell. Life 57:50-65 Ag 14 '64

VANDERBILT university, Nashville, Tenn.

For integrated churches; faculty of divinity school. Christian Cent 80:1194 O 2 '63

VANDERBURGH, Charles

Draftee's diary from the Mississippi front. Harper 228:37-45 F '64

VAN DER HAAGEN, Jan K.

Sunlight creates an Egyptian god. Sci Digest 53:48-58 Mr '63

VANDERHOEF, Ray

How can the industry create more bookstores? Pub W 185:36-8 Ja 13 '64

VAN DER HOEVEN, Th. See Woolley, D. W. jt. auth.

VANDERKELEN, Ron

Accomplished but doubting Dutchman. J. Underwood. il por Sports Illus 19:20-2+ Ag 19 '63

VAN DER KLOOT, William G. and Dane, Benjamin

Conduction of the action potential in the frog ventricle. bibliog Science 146:74-5 O 2 '64

VAN DER KROEF, Justus M.

Notes of a new nation. il Nat R 15:390-2 N 5 '63

VAN DER KUIP, Egbert J.

Aruba's one-man resources department. M. Frome. il por Am For 70:24-6+ Jl '64

VAN DER LUBBE, Marinus

Will to believe. M. Kempton. New Repub 150:17-20 Ap 11 '64

VAN DER PLANK, J. E.

Dynamics of epidemics of plant disease. bibliog Science 147:120-4 Ja 8 '65

VAN DER POST, Laurens

Both sides of the wall. Holiday 36:74-7+ O '64

View of all the Russias. Holiday 34:58-70+ O '63

VANDERSLICE, T. A.

Ultrahigh vacuum instrumentation. bibliog Science 142:178-84 O 11 '63

VANDERVOORT, Paul

Art of the mentally retarded on exhibition. Sch Arts 63:10-12 Ja '64

VANDER WERF, Lester S.

Double-purpose plan. Sch & Soc 91:213-14 My 4 '63

VANDERWERF, Rachel

Teach your tots about traffic. Parents Mag 39:64-5+ S '64

VANDERWICKEN, Peter

Commodities: soybeans and salad oil: the greatest scandal in the history of Wall Street is still going on. Esquire 61:91-3+ Ap '64

VANDERZANT, Erma S. and Richardson, C. D.

Ascorbic acid in the nutrition of plant-feeding insects. bibliog Science 140:989-91 My 31 '63

VAN DE STRAETEN, Edgar
Prospects for the Congo. Negro Hist Bul 26:246-7 My '63
VAN DEURS, Kay
Workshop of the children. Parents Mag 38: 52-4 Ag '63
VAN DILLA, M. A. and Fulwyler, M. J.
Radioiodine metabolism in children and adults after the ingestion of very small doses. bibliog Science 144:178-9 Ap 10 '64
VANDIVER, Frank
Uncelebrated soldier. Sat R 46:37 F 9 '63
VAN DOMMELEN, David B.
Art on a sewing machine; Applique decorating with paste and a felt pen; adapted from Decorative wall hangings. il Design 64:113-15+ Ja '63
Decorative wall hangings. il Sch Arts 62:7-9 Ap '63
VAN DOREN, Irita
Irita Van Doren leaves Herald tribune book review. por Pub W 183:122 Je 10 '63
VAN DOREN, Irita, literary award. See Irita Van Doren literary award
VAN DOREN, Mamie
Go, go, GOP. il por Newsweek 62:38 N 11 '63
VAN DOREN, Mark
Born equal; poem. Ladies Home J 80:98 Mr '63
Five poems. Ladies Home J 80:94 Je '63
Statecraft; poem. McCalls 90:190 Ap '63

about

Three notable collections. L. Untermeyer. Poetry 103:382-4 Mr '64
VAN DOREN, Ruth
Our garden is a family affair. por Flower Grower 50:22-5+ S '63
VANDUSEN, Bruce B.
Depressed areas built to order. Nation 200: 79-81 Ja 25 '65
VAN DUSEN, Henry Pitney
Third thoughts on Africa. Christian Cent 81: 855-8 Jl 1 '64

about

Hammarskjöld and holiness; with excerpts from Markings. Christian Cent 81:1596-7 D 23 '64
Successful misunderstanding. por Time 81: 70-1 My 24 '63
Vindication of Pit. Christian Cent 80:847 Je 26 '63
VAN DUYN, Mona
Gardener to his God; Open letter, personal; Time of bees; poems. Poetry 103:173-8 D '63
Garland for Christopher Smart; poem. Poetry 104:4-8 Ap '64
Leaf by leaf. Poetry 102:260-6 Jl '63
VAN DYCK, Stephen A. See Robinson, W. W. 1918-, jt. auth.
VAN DYKE, Dick
America's favorite TV wife. S. Gordon. il pors Look 28:M9-M10+ Ap 21 '64
Dick Van Dyke: TV family man. S. Gordon. il pors Look 27:116-18 N 5 '63
Dick Van Dyke: the star who thinks he isn't. C. R. Jennings. il pors Ladies Home J 80:78-9 O '63
VAN DYKE, Donald C. See Anger, H. O. jt. auth.
VAN DYKE, Jerry
Kid brother. il por Newsweek 61:99 Je 24 '63
VAN DYKE, R. P. and Nusbaum, W. E.
Supervisory controls. Am City 78:97-8 N '63
VANES. See Weather vanes
VANESSA; opera. See Barber, S.
VANE-Tempest-Stewart, Alexander Charles Robert, 9th marquis of Londonderry. See Londonderry, A. C. R. V.-T.-S.
VANE-Tempest-Stewart, Nicolette (Harrison) marchioness of Londonderry. See Londonderry, N. H. V.-T.-S.
VAN FLEET, Clark C.
Invisible death. Atlan 214:53-5 Jl '64
Silent spring on the Pacific slope. Atlan 212: 81-4 Jl '63
VAN GELDER, Richard G.
Reviews. Natur Hist 72:4+ Je '63
Science in action; launching an expedition. Natur Hist 73:64-7 Ap '64
VANGUARD recording society, incorporated
Hardy independent. J. Tebbel. il Hi Fi 14: 46-8 F '64
VANGUARD satellite. See Artificial satellites
VAN GUILDER, Ray
Big grader is best for this small town. Am City 79:97-8 Jl '64
VAN HAVERBEKE, P. Peter
Six quitters. por Esquire 62:102 S '64
VAN HOESEN, Walter H.
Antiques and the tariff. Antiques 85:328+ Mr '64
VANHOOK, Vera
Story of a Hilda Maehling fellow. J. Stocker. NEA J 53:45 O '64
VAN HOOSE, Larry
College football. Sports Illus 21:58-9 O 12 '64
VAN HORN, H. H. See Jacobson, N. L. jt. auth.
VAN HORN, Vicki
Wasn't it great? Seventeen 24:36 Ja '65
VAN HORNE, Harriet
Try letting yourself go! Read Digest 84:48-50 Mr '64
VANILLA
Pears made perfect. C. Claiborne. il N Y Times Mag p64+ Je 9 '63
VAN KEUREN, Dolores
Some day I'll understand you, Mary Ann. Motor B 115:92-3 Ja '65
VAN KRUGEL, E.
Introduction to CPM. Arch Rec 136:337+ S '64
VAN LOON, Gerard Willem
Man with a country; letter. Sat R 48:43 Ja 9 '65
VAN LOON, Hendrik Willem
Man with a country; letter. G. W. Van Loon. Sat R 48:43 Ja 9 '65
VAN LOPIK, Jack R. and Geyer, R. A.
Gravity and magnetic anomalies of the Sierra Madera, Texas, dome. bibliog Science 142: 45-7 O 4 '63
VANN, Gerald
Obituary
Commonweal 78:469 Ag 9 '63
VANN, John Paul
War being lost because an ally won't fight? interview. por U S News 55:39-41 S 16 '63

about

Ugliest American in Vietnam. D. Halberstam. il por Esquire 62:114-17+ N '64
VAN NICE, Robert L.
Structure of St Sophia. Arch Forum 118:131-8+ My '63; 121:45-9 Ag '64
VAN NOPPEN, Otto
Photographer looks at China. il N Y Times Mag p22-3 N 17 '63
VAN NOSTRAND, Jeanne
Seals are about gone. Am Heritage 14:10-17+ Je '63
VANOCUR, Sander
Kennedy's voyage of discovery. Harper 228: 41-5 Ap '64
Requiem for Pope John. Read Digest 83:63 Ag '63
VANOISE NATIONAL PARK. See National parks and reserves—France
VAN OSTEN, Richard
$80,000 saving per case foreseen. Miss & Roc 12:31 F 25 '63
Long future seen for SLV 3B booster. Miss & Roc 12:16-17 Ap 15 '63
VAN OTERLOO, Willem
Musical events; concert performed by The Hague philharmonic at Carnegie Hall. W. Sargeant. New Yorker 39:155-6 My 25 '63
VANOVER, Jo
Designs in day-glo. Design 65:48 N '63
VAN PATTEN, Joyce
Chat with Joyce Van Patten. il pors Theatre Arts 47:16-17+ D '63
VAN POOL, Gerald M.
What's in the wind for student activities? PTA Mag 57:25-7 Ap '63
VAN PRAAG, Alex, Jr
Scuba divers replace missing pipe. Am City 78:84-5 D '63
VAN PRAAGH, Peggy
Year of accomplishment. B. Dean. il por Dance Mag 37:16-17 Ag '63
VAN RENSSELAER, Susan
Harriet Hosmer. Antiques 84:424-8 O '63
VAN RIPER, Robert
Some things that worry me about public relations; address, January 15, 1963. Vital Speeches 29:379-81 Ap 1 '63
VAN RIPER, W. B.
One plant replaces four. Am City 79:110-12 O '64
VAN ROOY, Anton
Kurz, d'Andrade, Santley, Van Rooy, A. Favia-Artsay. por Hobbies 68:30-1 My '63
VAN SICKLE, Kenneth
Make a photograph an etching with a brush. il Pop Phot 52:52-3 F '63
VAN SINDEREN, Adrian
Some views concerning the development of Mount McKinley National Park. Nat Parks Mag 37:19+ S '63
VAN SLYCK, Philip
Where all paths to peace must meet. Sat R 48:28-9 Ja 30 '65
VAN SLYKE, Helen
Boss ladies; symposium, ed. by L. L. Tornabene. por(p 105) Esquire 63:102+ Ja '65

VANSTAN, Ina
Every shred of evidence. Américas 15:30-4 D '63
VAN STRAELEN, V.
Obituary
Nat Parks Mag 38:18 My '64
VAN TIL, William
Genuine educational frontiers. Sat R 47:66-8 Ap 18 '64
How not to make an assignment. NEA J 53: 49-51 O '64
VAN TUYL, Marian
Maps for action. Dance Mag 39:26-7 Ja '65
VAN VECHTEN, Carl
Connoisseur. il por Newsweek 65:62-3 Ja 4 '65
Obituary
Pub W 187:39 Ja 4 '65
VAN VEEN, Frederick
Direct-reading instruments. Electr World 70: 23-7+ Ag '63
Piano tuning, the electronic way. Electr World 72:56-7 S '64
VAN WAGENER, Isabella
Sojourner truth. L. Bennett, jr. il por Ebony 19:62-4+ O '64
VAN WORMER, Joe
Shot with luck. Outdoor Life 131:28-9 Mr '63
They give you the jumps. Outdoor Life 133: 56-9 Mr '64
Tied up by topknots. Outdoor Life 132:62-3+ O '63
VAN WYCK, Susan
Boy meets girl. R. Westbrook. il por Seventeen 23:77+ Ja '64
VANZETTI, Bartolomeo
Last letters home. por Nation 197:86-8 Ag 24 '63
See also
Sacco-Vanzetti case
VANZETTI, Riccardo
Use of infrared testing technique grows. P. J. Klass. il Aviation W 80:82+ My 4 '64
VAPOR baths. See Baths, Vapor
VAPOR pressure
Vapor pressure of ice containing D_2O. S. Matsuo and others. bibliog il Science 145: 1454-5 S 25 '64
VARACTOR diodes. See Diodes
VARELA, Eduardo Mendoza
Vestige of colonial splendor. Américas 15:22-6 Ag '63
VARGA, Robert
Dilemmas of a househusband. Sat R 48:100-3 Ja 2 '65
VARGAS, Getúlio
Most dangerous man in Brazil. J. Dos Passos. il Nat R 15:53-7 Jl 30 '63
VARGAS, Manuela
Flamenco: olé! pors Vogue 144:124-31 O 15 '64
VARIABLE annuities. See Annuities
VARIABLE frequency oscillators. See Oscillators
VARIABLE stars. See Stars, Variable
VARIABLE sweep wings. See Airplane wings
VARIATION (botany) See Mutation (botany)
VARICELLA. See Chicken pox
VARICOSE veins
Varicose vein surgery. Sci N L 83:231 Ap 13 '63
What science has learned about varicose veins. N. D. Fabricant. Todays Health 41: 35+ Ap '63
What we know about varicose veins. G. G. Greer. Bet Hom & Gard 42:36 Mr '64
VARIETY chain stores. See Variety stores
VARIETY stores
Strength in variety. il Time 84:63 N 20 '64
VARILLA, Phillipe Bunau-. See Bunau-Varilla, P.
VARNAY, Astrid
Music to my ears; Varnay's Elektra. I. Kolodin. Sat R 47:31 D 26 '64
Musical events; concert performance of R. Strauss's Elektra with the New York philharmonic. W. Sargeant. New Yorker 40:163 D 19 '64
VARONA, Manuel Antonio de
Air will be ours; Cuban fighters tell why they expected air cover; with excerpts from radio messages. por U S News 54:33-4 F 4 '63
VARSITY shows. See College and school drama
VARTAN, Sylvie
Hooray for the Yé-Yé girls. il pors Life 56: 39-40+ My 29 '64
VARVISO, Silvio
Marathon maestro; interview, ed. by J. W. Freeman. por Opera N 27:15 Mr 30 '63
VASARELY, Victor
Gallery for young people. C. B. Johnson. il Sch Arts 64:50 O '64
Something to blink at. Time 83:75 My 1 '64
VASCONCELOS, José
Odyssey over the border. I. A. Leonard. Sat R 46:37 O 12 '63
VASCULAR diseases
Hypertensive vascular disease produced by homologous renin. G. M. C. Masson and others. bibliog il Science 145:178-80 Jl 10 '64
VASCULAR system
Cardiovascular responses of the chicken to seasonal and induced temperature changes. J. A. Vogel and P. D. Sturkie. bibliog il Science 140:1404-6 Je 28 '63
Seal & man without air: a common defense. il Time 82:74 D 6 '63
VASECTOMY
Male operation. Newsweek 62:84 S 16 '63
VASES
Cockeyed containers! E. Craster. il Bet Hom & Gard 42:70-1 My '64
Fill the glasses. il Bet Hom & Gard 42:128 My '64
See also
Portland vase
VASES, Etruscan
Famous Greeks and mysterious Etruscans. il Art N 63:30-1+ My '64
VASES, Greek
Famous Greeks and mysterious Etruscans. il Art N 63:30-1+ My '64
Pantheon of Greek gods and heroes. il UNESCO Courier 17:24-5 Ap '64
Poetry of vases. il Life 55:56-57A Jl 19 '63
VASIL, I. K. and others
Endive plantlets from freely suspended cells and cell groups grown in vitro. bibliog Science 146:76-7 O 2 '64
VASKA, L.
Oxygen-carrying properties of a simple synthetic system. bibliog Science 140:809-10 My 17 '63
VASOPRESSIN
Slow labor speeded. F. Marley. Sci N L 86:82 Ag 8 '64
VASSALL, William John Christopher
Britain's scandalous spy case. C. Brogan. il Nat R 14:195-6+ Mr 12 '63
Composite portrait of the Soviet spy. H. M. Hyde. il por N Y Times Mag p 14+ F 16 '64
Fact & fancy. Time 81:62 F 8 '63
How a Soviet spy made Britain look slipshod. U S News 54:8 My 6 '63
Letter from London. M. Panter-Downes. New Yorker 39:146-8 My 25 '63
Sin along with Sig. Time 81:31-2 My 3 '63
VASSAR college, Poughkeepsie, N.Y.
Man for Vassar. il Time 81:63 Je 28 '63
Mr Simpson of Vassar. J. Lelyveld. il N Y Times Mag p30-1+ D 13 '64
Oxford to Vassar. Newsweek 62:49 Jl 1 '63
Trade winds; reactions of Vassar graduates to Mary McCarthy's The group. J. G. Fuller. Sat R 46:10-11 O 5 '63
VASSILIKOS, Vassilis
Letter from Athens; tr. by K. Hourmousiades. Poetry 105:60-4 O '64
Poet's novel. A. Decavalles. Poetry 105:65-7 O '64
VASVARY, Louis M.
Questions & answers about dormant sprays. Flower Grower 51:28-9+ F '64
VATH, William R.
Man's oldest fallout problem: baldness. Todays Health 41:46-50 Ag '63; Same abr. with title What men and women should know about baldness. Sci Digest 55:20-5 Mr '64
Nine ways to beat the heat. Read Digest 83: 152-3 Jl '63
VATICAN
New Vatican usage; simplified language. America 109:277 S 21 '63
Spirit of the Vatican; photographs. N Y Times Mag p22-3 Je 9 '63
Uncharted waters. America 108:393-4 Mr 23 '63
Sistine chapel
Glory of the Sistine. il N Y Times Mag p 10-11 Je 16 '63
Michelangelo's magnificent mirror of man. E. O. Hauser. il Read Digest 84:176-80+ My '64
VATICAN CITY
Pope and his realm. il U S News 54:60 Je 24 '63
VATICAN council, 1869-1870
First council of the Vatican: the American experience, by J. J. Hennesey. Review
America 110:23 Ja 4 '64. H. J. Nolan
Commonweal 79:574-6 F 7 '64. J. Ratté

VATICAN council, 2d
Africa and the council. D. E. Hurley. Commonweal 79:10-12 S 27 '63
After the council: back to school? J. V. Gallagher. Cath World 200:28-33 O '64
Arab pressures on the council. America 111:505 O 31 '64
Arabs and the council. America 110:589 My 2 '64
Archbishop Florit and the laity; interview, ed. by W. M. Abbott. E. Florit. America 108:836-7 Je 8 '63
Art and anti-art; concerning drawings of Vatican council II by F. Franck. C. J. McNaspy. America 108:419-20 Mr 23 '63
As the council reconvenes. E. von Kuehnelt-Leddihn. Nat R 14:452 Je 4 '63
Austria's Cardinal at the council; interview, ed. by W. M. Abbott. F. Koenig. America 108:671-2 My 11 '63
Backs council draft on Jews. Christian Cent 81:1078 S 2 '64
Barth's wisdom on Rome. Christian Cent 80:1019 Ag 21 '63
Birth control and the council. G. Baum. Commonweal 81:280+ N 20 '64; Reply with rejoinder. R. W. Crooker. 81:515-17 Ja 15 '65
Bishop denounces council experts. Christian Cent 81:724 Je 3 '64
Bishops differ on conference powers. Christian Cent 80:1457 N 27 '63
Bishops vote rule by divine right. Christian Cent 80:1394 N 13 '63
Bravest schema; no. thirteen, The church in the modern world. il Time 84:74+ O 30 '64
Breaking the walls; curia and the council. il Newsweek 62:80 D 16 '63
Cardinal Bea: an appreciation. G. P. O'Hara. America 108:442-4+ Mr 30 '63
Cardinal Doepfner's views; interview, ed. by W. M. Abbott. J. Doepfner. America 108:714-15 My 18 '63
Cardinal on ecumenism; and the World council. America 110:589 My 2 '64
Cardinals divide. America 110:532 Ap 18 '64
Catholic church battles its old guard. J. T. Elson. il Life 55:114-15+ O 18 '63
Catholics hit Vatican II; conversions decline in Britain. Christian Cent 81:540 Ap 29 '64
Changes in the liturgy; constitution on worship. F. R. McManus. Commonweal 79:594-6+ F 14 '64
Charity the first step. K. Haselden. Christian Cent 80:1539-40 D 11 '63
Church and change. W. H. Lazareth. il Sat R 47:38-9 Jl 18 '64
Church and the council: issues behind the speeches on the nature of the church. J. C. Murray. America 109:451-3 O 19 '63
Civil rights in the church. R. A. Graham. America 109:257-60 S 14 '63
Collegiality: the lid is off. M. E. Marty. Christian Cent 81:1552-3 D 16 '64
Coming reforms in the liturgy. F. R. McManus. Cath World 196:335-42 Mr '63
Communications decree: why the dissent? J. B. Sheerin. Cath World 198:267-71 F '64
Communications schema should be buried. Christian Cent 81:227 F 19 '64
Confrontation in the council. G. Baum. Commonweal 79:311-13 D 6 '63
Conscience at the council. America 109:204 Ag 31 '63
Council and anti-Semitism. Commonweal 80:407 Je 26 '64
Council and the future Commonweal 79:27+ O 4 '63
Council and the Jews. America 110:842-3 Je 20 '64; Discussion. 111:1-2 Jl 4 '64
Council declaration on the Jews. J. L. Lichten. Cath World 199:272-8 Ag '64; Discussion. 200:71 N '64
Council father's charges; changes in text of schema. America 109:699-70 N 30 '63; Reply. L. Binz. 110:42-3 Ja 11 '64
Council jottings. D. R. Campion. America 109:90, 110, 130, 150, 186, 206, 229, 254, 286 Jl 27-S 21 '63
Council jottings. D. R. Campion and D. J. O'Hanlon. America 109:341-3, 377-8, 409-10, 446-7, 479-80, 508-10, 553-5, 626-7, 654-5, 701-2, 765-6, 791 S 28-N 30, D 14-21 '63
Council on anti-Semitism. America 109:224 S 7 '63
Council on anti-Semitism; concerning talk by G. Weigel to National community relations advisory council. America 109:70-1 Jl 20 '63
Council on the move. America 110:396 Mr 28 '64
Council on the move. il Time 82:55 N 8 '63
Council personalities. America 111:368 O 3 '64
Council: planning for the next session. America 109:8 Jl 6 '63
Council politics at dead end. M. E. Marty. Christian Cent 81:1519-20 D 9 '64
Council revisited. J. O'Gara. Commonweal 81:258-9 N 20 '64
Council, right and left. G. D. Kumlien. Commonweal 79:362-3 D 20 '63
Council speeches of Vatican II, ed. by H. Küng and others. Review
Cath World 199:123-4 My '64. J. B. Sheerin
Council still in business. America 110:593 My 2 '64
Council's religious liberty document. J. B. Sheerin. Cath World 199:140-3 Je '64
Council's text on Jews in jeopardy. Christian Cent 81:1548-9 D 16 '64
Crisis in Rome; struggle between the bishops and the Roman curia. Newsweek 62:76 N 25 '63
Cum magno dolore; latest curial maneuver. Time 84:88 O 23 '64
Darkness of Christmas. America 111:791 D 19 '64
Debate on deicide. il Newsweek 64:86 S 28 '64
Deepening the dialogue. A. C. Cochrane. Christian Cent 81:1111 S 9 '64
Dialogue at the top. D. J. O'Hanlon. America 109:231-4 S 7 '63; Reply. D. A. Walsh. 109:441 O 19 '63
La dolce vita ecumenica. K. Bridston. Christian cent 80:679 My 22 '63; Discussion. 80:985-6 Ag 7 '63
Ecumenical council; address, September 14, 1964. Paul VI. Vital Speeches 30:738-41 O 1 '64
Ecumenical next steps; World interchurch service (proposed) Christian Cent 80:483 Ap 17 '63
Ecumenical sadness and hope. M. Novak. Christian Cent 81:1518 D 9 '64
European reaction to the Vatican council. Y. Chabas; F. Luepsen. Christian Cent 80:207-9 F 13 '63
First fruits in Rome; Pope to visit Holy Land. America 109:757 D 14 '63
First fruits of the spirit; Vatican II's newly proclaimed constitution on sacred liturgy. W. J. Leonard. il America 109:798-801 D 21 '63
For the bowl games weekend; special to Sporttrends, Rome, December 4. Christian Cent 81:31 Ja 1 '64
Four views of Rome; books which contradict each other. A. M. Greeley. Reporter 31:64+ S 24 '64
Fresh orientation in the church. R. Rouquette. Cath World 196:343-50 Mr '63
From Döllinger to Vatican II; a century too soon? J. Coulson. Commonweal 79:400-3 D 27 '63
Future role of bishops. W. M. Abbott. America 110:6 Ja 4 '64
Greeks reject another Vatican invitation. Christian Cent 81:956 Jl 29 '64
Head and heart: catechisms with a modern accent. G. E. Carter. America 109:40-3 Jl 13 '63
Highest end; full freedom of conscience. Newsweek 64:102 O 5 '64
Hope for Vatican II action on Jews, religious freedom. Christian Cent 81:628 My 13 '64
How new Pope plans to modernize church. il U S News 55:46-8 O 14 '63
How rules changes affect U.S. Catholics. il U S News 57:16 D 14 '64
How tense are interreligious tensions? J. J. Kane. Cath World 197:351-8 S '63
Impressions from Helsinki, Rome and Montreal. G. A. Lindbeck. Cath World 198:272-80 F '64
Interview with Jean Guitton, the only Catholic layman at the council; ed. by J. Pelissier. J. Guitton. Cath World 196:279-84 F '63
Interview with the Armenian observer at the council; ed. by E. M. Jung. A. K. Sarkissian. Cath World 197:258-63 Jl '63
Intrigue in the council. M. Novak. New Repub 150:10-11 Ja 11 '64
Jews absolved; responsibility for the death of Christ. Sr Schol 85:18 D 9 '64
Johannine council. America 109:345 S 28 '63
Journalists report the council. G. Wills. Nat R 15:572-4 D 31 '63
Laity in Rome. Newsweek 62:92 N 4 '63
Last council? excerpt from Vatican II. R. Caporale. America 111:307-9 S 19 '64
Laymen and the council; concerning chapter IV of the constitution on the church. America 111:795-6 D 19 '64
Layman rediscovered. J. Cogley. Commonweal 79:253-5 N 22 '63
Layman's hopes. J. O'Gara. Commonweal 81:87 O 16 '64

VATICAN council, 2d—*Continued*
Left to mind the store. R. E. Auman. America 109:618 N 16 '63
Letter from the council. D. R. Campion. il America 111:374-5, 406-7, 446-7, 478-9, 512-13, 546-7, 592-3, 654-5, 736-7 O 3-N 21, D 5 '64
Letter from the Pope; Machiavellian intrigue of curia conservatives. Newsweek 64:77 O 26 '64
Letter from Vatican City. X. Rynne. il New Yorker 39:179-86+ S 28; 123-4+ O 26; 144+ N 30 '63; 88+ Ja 18; 40:166+ S 19 '64; 90-103 Ja 9 '65
Letters from Vatican City, by X. Rynne. Review
America 108:906-7 Je 29 '63. G. E. Carter; E. J. Primeau
Cath World 197:324-5 Ag '63. J. B. Sheerin
Commonweal 78:461-2 Jl 26 '63. J. Leo
Liberty and the council. America 108:186 F 9 '63
Liturgical challenge. America 110:135-6 Ja 25 '64
Liturgical changes; concerning the council's Constitution on the sacred liturgy. America 110:753 My 30 '64
Liturgy and the second Vatican council; constitution on the sacred liturgy. H. A. Reinhold. Cath World 198:347-56 Mr '64
Liturgy: barrier or bond? council's constitution on the liturgy. C. J. McNaspy. America 110:278-80 F 29 '64
Mary and the church. America 111:5 Jl 4 '64
Meanwhile, back at home. J. O'Gara. Commonweal 79:216 N 15 '63
Misunderstanding still. America 109:128 Ag 10 '63
Must the council end? Commonweal 80:3-4 Mr 27 '64
Need for criticism. Commonweal 79:243 N 22 '63
Need for reform; constitution on the liturgy. J. B. Mannion. Commonweal 78:495-7 Ag 23 '63
New Catholic image: openness to today's world. J. B. Sheerin. Cath World 198:204-7 Ja '64
New era in the Catholic church. il U S News 55:100 D 16 '63
New image for Catholic church. il U S News 55:112 N 25 '63
No turning back. America 108:852-3 Je 15 '63
On understanding the council; concerning Jean Daniélou's address on the decree on the church. T. L. Sheridan. America 112:122 Ja 23 '65
Open church, by M. Novak. Review
Commonweal 80:582-4 Ag 21 '64. F. R. McManus
Open letter to the American bishops. R. M. Brown. Commonweal 80:411-16 Je 26 '64; Reply. P. J. Hallinan. 80:548 Ag 7 '64
Patriarch Maximos IV and Vatican council II; interview, ed. by E. Inglessis and E. Inglessis. Maximos IV. Cath World 198:372-9 Mr '64
Paul and the curia. il Newsweek 62:62 S 30 '63
Paul VI and the bishops. O. Hastings. il Reporter 29:23-5 D 19 '63
Pope and bishops. G. Baum. Commonweal 79:188-91 N 8 '63
Pope, council and Jews. America 108:427 Mr 30 '63
Pope John's great gift. Read Digest 82:141-6 Ap '63
Pope Paul, firm and realistic. J. B. Sheerin. Cath World 198:75-9 N '63
Pope Paul follows along Pope John's path. R. Neville. il N Y Times Mag p23+ S 22 '63
Pope Paul's address to the curia. M. Novak. Commonweal 79:89-90 O 18 '63
Pope Paul's other dialogue. J. Gremillion. Cath World 198:208-14 Ja '64
Pope runs the church. Time 84:66 N 27 '64
Pope, the bishops, and Edward Gibbon. O. Hastings. il Reporter 31:22-5 D 31 '64
Progress and a cloud. Commonweal 81:117 O 23 '64
Protestant assessment; concerning decree on instruments of social communication. R. M. Brown. Commonweal 79:396-8 D 27 '63
Protestant hopes for the Vatican council. R. M. Brown. il Look 28:21-7 O 6 '64
Protestants on the council. America 108:288-9 Mr 2 '63
Public image of the Catholic church today; symposium. Cath World 199:352-5 S '64
Racism and the council. America 109:507 N 2 '63
Racism and the council; Archbishop O'Boyle of Washington asks for a condemnation of racism. America 111:647 N 21 '64
Reactionaries win second round. Christian Cent 80:1568 D 18 '63
Reformation Sunday in Rome. R. M. Brown. Commonweal 79:280-3 N 29 '63
Report from Rome. D. E. Hurley. America 109:633-4 N 16 '63
Report from Rome. J. O'Gara. Commonweal 79:157-8 N 1 '63
Right to worship according to one's conscience. il Time 84:90 O 2 '64
Road from Trent to Rome. il N Y Times Mag p24-5 N 1 '64
Rome: great battle of ideas. Life 57:4 O 23 '64
Same again please: a layman's hopes of the Vatican council. E. Waugh; discussion. Nat R 13:521; 14:37 D 31 '62-Ja 15 '63; Commonweal 77:487-9 F 1 '63; America 108:440-2 Mr 30 '63
Scripture and tradition in pastoral perspective. G. H. Tavard. Cath World 198:14-20 O '63
Search for freedom. J. Cogley. Commonweal 79:301-4 D 6 '63
Secrecy at the council. F. X. Murphy. America 109:96-7 Jl 27 '63
Shall we wrangle or reason about reforms? J. B. Sheerin. Cath World 199:203-6 Jl '64
Sharing in the council. America 109:227 S 7 '63
Significant correction; norms to regulate interim work. America 108:358-9 Mr 16 '63
Speaking out; ecumenical movement threatens Protestantism. H. A. Buchanan and B. W. Brown. Sat Eve Post 237:10+ O 24 '64; Reply. G. Hinson. Christian Cent 81:1592-5 D 23 '64
Speeding the council. America 109:2 Jl 6 '63
Story of schema seventeen: the church in the present-day world. L. Kaufmann. Cath World 200:8-14 O '64
Table-talk with the Russian observers; failure of the Greek Orthodox to send observers to the first session of the council. E. M. Jung. Cath World 196:273-8 F '63
Taking the council's moving picture. Christian Cent 81:1229 O 7 '64
Test of good will; proposed declaration on anti-Semitism. il Time 84:63+ O 9 '64
Third myth. K. Haselden. Christian Cent 80:1491-3 D 4 '63
This matter of religious freedom. J. C. Murray. America 112:40-3 Ja 9 '65
Three giant steps. E. C. Bianchi; D. R. Campion; C. J. McNaspy. America 111:776-8 D 12 '64
Time to be counted. America 110:178-9 F 8 '64
To be continued. Newsweek 64:91 N 2 '64
Totality of outlook; address, January 24, 1963. B. McEntegart. Vital Speeches 29:299-300 Mr 1 '63
Toward dialogue. America 111:766 D 12 '64
Toward reform. Newsweek 62:101 O 21 '63
Truth first and always: Archbishop of Genoa gives his views; interview, ed. by W. M. Abbott. G. Siri. America 108:434-5 Mr 30 '63
Two bishops speak. G. Young; F. Hengsbach. America 110:14-16 Ja 4 '64
Two council fathers; Cardinal Léger and Cardinal Cushing; interviews, ed. by W. M. Abbott. P. E. Léger; R. Cushing. America 108:862-7 Je 15 '63
Unfinished business. America 112:159 Ja 30 '65
Unfinished council business. Christian Cent 81:1389-90 N 11 '64
Unfinished reformation; report of statement on the need for a reform of the Roman Catholic church. Time 83:66 F 7 '64
Unprecedented changes. America 108:323 Mr 9 '63
Vatican council adopts decree on communications. Pub W 185:60-1 Ja 6 '64
Vatican council progresses. Christian Cent 81:1293 O 21 '64
Vatican council II makes progress. Christian Cent 80:1325 O 30 '63
Vatican council's field of vision. Christian Cent 81:1197 S 30 '64
Vatican dialogue. S. I. Stuber. Christian Cent 81:1405 N 11 '64
Vatican II: a look ahead. D. J. O'Hanlon. America 109:347-9+ S 28 '63
Vatican II and art. C. J. McNaspy. America 110:126-7 Ja 18 '64
Vatican II and Latin America. J. M. Bonino. Christian Cent 81:1616-17 D 30 '64
Vatican II and missions. America 111:444-5 O 17 '64
Vatican II & the Jews. F. E. Cartus. Commentary 39:19-29 Ja '65
Vatican II: early appraisal. F. X. Murphy. America 108:330-2 Mr 9 '63

VATICAN council, 2—*Continued*
Vatican II: legacy of John XXIII. il Sr Schol 83:3+ N 1 '63
Vatican II needs a new approach. F. X. Murphy. Cath World 198:302-7 F '64
Vatican II on music; Constitution on the sacred liturgy. C. J. McNaspy. America 110:55-6 Ja 11 '64
Vatican II re-educates the American bishops. J. Cogley. il N Y Times Mag p35+ N 22 '64
Vatican II: striving for a new spring. E. J. Hughes. il Newsweek 64:55-7 D 14 '64
Vision of a modern church. E. M. Borgese. il Nation 198:46-9 Ja 13 '64
Visit with Cardinal Liénart; interview, ed. by W. M. Abbott. A. Liénart. il America 108:802-3 Je 1 '63
We have a council; with editorial comment. M. E. Marty. Christian Cent 81:1483, 1489-90 D 2 '64
What the Pope said. R. M. Brown. Commonweal 79:165-7 N 1 '63
What went wrong? il Time 82:52+ D 6 '63
When is doctrine pure? excerpt from Open church. M. Novak. Commonweal 80:233-5 My 15 '64
Why not open end Vatican II? Christian Cent 81:132 Ja 29 '64
Winds of change in Rome: the Vatican council moves toward renewal and reform. M. Novak. New Repub 149:11-13 N 16 '63
Women at the council: spectators or collaborators? E. M. Jung. il Cath World 200:277-84 F '65
Word to outsiders. Time 82:64 N 22 '63

Bibliography

Five views of the council; an assessment of new books. D. R. Campion. il America 110:816-19 Je 13 '64
Inside the council. il Newsweek 63:54 Je 22 '64
Journalists report the council. G. Wills. Nat R 15:572-4 D 31 '63; Correction. 16:124 F 11 '64
Vatican II, act II: reportage, speculation and gossip. R. B. Kaiser. Commonweal 80:517-18 Jl 24 '64

1st session

Delegate observers at the first session; Guests of the secretariat. America 109:230 S 7 '63
Ecumenical council; progress report. S. De Gramont. il Sat Eve Post 236:86-91 F 23 '63
Interview with Dr Heiko Oberman; Protestant observer at the first session of the council, ed by J. B. Sheerin. H. Oberman. Cath World 197:100-6 My '63
Interview with Hans Küng; ed. by J. B. Sheerin. H. Küng. Cath World 197:159-63 Je '63
No deadlock: Cardinal Alfrink's views. America 108:729-30 My 25 '63
What has the council accomplished? J. B. Sheerin. Cath World 196:268-72 F '63

2d session

Bishops appraise the council. America 110:141-2 Ja 25 '64
Council's progress. America 109:550 N 9 '63
Efficiency urged in third session; Robert's Rules of order. Christian Cent 81:132-3 Ja 29 '64
End of the deadlock. G. Baum. Commonweal 79:251-3 N 22 '63
End of the session. G. Baum. Commonweal 79:393-6 D 27 '63
Grounds for hope. J. Cogley. Commonweal 79:398-400 D 27 '63
Has the council lost its steam? R. E. Tracy. America 110:162-4 F 1 '64
How is the council going? G. Weigel. America 109:730-2 D 7 '63
Loss and gain. D. R. Campion. il America 110:10-14 Ja 4 '64
New spirit at the council. G. Baum. il Commonweal 79:125-9 O 25 '63
Pope opens second council session. Christian Cent 80:1228 O 9 '63
Readiness for reform; second session's agenda. il Time 82:82 O 4 '63
Roman diary; impressions of the second session. J. Cogley. il America 111:348-51 S 26 '64
Second session. Commonweal 79:383-4 D 27 '63
Second session, by X. Rynne. Review
New Repub 151:28+ Jl 25 '64. F. Gorrell
To the council fathers; concerning Pope Paul VI's discourse to open second session of Vatican II. America 109:412 O 12 '63
Vatican II, scene two. E. J. Hughes. Newsweek 62:27 O 7 '63
Vatican II, session 2. E. Duff. Christian Cent 81:1034-7, 1057-61 Ag 19-26 '64

3d session

Act three. il Newsweek 64:75-6 S 21 '64
Apprehensions about the council. R. M. Brown. Commonweal 81:442-5 D 25 '64; Discussion. 81:530-1+ Ja 22 '65
Bitter end. il Newsweek 64:68-9 N 30 '64
Blossoming of Vatican II. G. Baum. Commonweal 81:130-2 O 23 '64
Church and mankind's future on earth; excerpt from address. E. Schillebeeckx. Cath World 200:218-23 Ja '65
Council adjourns. America 111:734 D 5 '64
Council post-mortem. J. O'Gara. Commonweal 79:569 F 7 '64
Ecumenical council: empire to commonwealth. E. M. Borgese. il Nation 200:51-5 Ja 18 '65
End of session three; constitution de ecclesia. Commonweal 81:339-40 D 4 '64
End of the session. J. O'Gara. Commonweal 81:373-5 D 11 '64
Evangelical simplicity at the council. J. B. Sheerin. Cath World 200:137-41 D '64
Good beginning; third session of the Vatican council. G. Baum. Commonweal 81:66-8 O 9 '64
Mid point in the session. G. Baum. il Commonweal 81:191-4 N 6 '64
Mind of its own; third session. Time 84:75 N 20 '64
Pope Paul's progressive speech; concerning opening address at third session of ecumenical council. J. B. Sheerin. Cath World 200:73-7 N '64
Speedup; third session. il Time 84:70 S 18 '64
Third and last session? America 110:476-7 Ap 4 '64
Third session. D. R. Campion. America 111:252-4 S 12 '64
Triumphs and failures. G. Baum. Commonweal 81:377-81 D 11 '64
Vatican II, act III. M. Novak. New Repub 151:7-8 O 17 '64
Vatican II: part III. Commonweal 81:3-4 S 25 '64
What happened to session three? J. B. Sheerin. Cath World 200:200-4 Ja '65
X. Rynne, gloom, doom and council. Episcopus. America 110:224-5 F 15 '64

VATICAN council, 2d and the press. See Church and the press

VAUDABLE, Maggie
School for wives; L'académie Maxim's. il por Time 81:65 Mr 29 '63

VAUDEVILLE
Blaze Starr in nighttown. T. B. Morgan. il Esquire 62:58-62+ Jl '64
Broadway: season's end; Folies Bergère at Broadway theatre, New York. D. Hering. Dance Mag 38:16-17 Ag '64
Case for naked ladies; Folies Bergère in New York. T. Prideaux. Life 56:17 Je 26 '64
Comediva; All by myself. Time 84:50 Jl 17 '64
Farce de frappe; Folies-Bergère in Manhattan. Time 83:90 Je 12 '64
Folies Bergère. America 111:55 Jl 11 '64
It makes money; Las Vegas's Casino de Paris. il Newsweek 64:90 S 28 '64
Letter from Paris; performance by Le grand music-hall de Moscou at Olympia. Genêt. New Yorker 40:123-4 Je 13 '64
What ever happened to burlesque. L. H. Lapham. il Sat Eve Post 237:72-4 Mr 14 '64
When stripping, look into a man's eyes. S. Loren. il Life 56:56 Ap 10 '64

VAUDOUX. See Voodooism

VAUGHAN, Bill
Who's been grinding your valves, Mac? excerpts from Sorry I stirred it. Read Digest 85:277-8+ N '64
Wily coat hanger; excerpt from Bird thou never wert. Read Digest 85:180A+ S '64

VAUGHAN, Dorothy M.
Strawbery Banke, Portsmouth, N.H. Antiques 86:100-1 Jl '64

VAUGHAN, Malcolm
America's greatest primitive painter. Read Digest 84:126-31 Mr '64

VAUGHAN, Roger
Mad, mad world of the stunt flier. Sat Eve Post 236:26-7 My 18 '63
Motorboat madness. Sat Eve Post 236:34 Ag 24 '63
—See Atwater, J. jt. auth.

VAUGHAN, Stuart
New Rainier; Seattle repertory theater. Time 82:73 N 29 '63

VAUGHN, Esther Gibbons. See Currier, L. G. jt. auth.

VAUGHN, Robert
Last chance; Judith; poems. Poetry 102:90-1 My '63

about

Man inside The man from U.N.C.L.E. il por Time 85:68 Ja 29 '65

VAUGHN, Robert G.
Compressor for less than $10. Pop Sci 184: 152-4 Ap '64
VAUGHN, William Scott
Kodak's new click. il por Time 81:86 Mr 8 '63
William S. Vaughn. pors Duns R 81:35 Je '63
VAULTING (sport)
Alone at the top of the mark. il Sports Illus 19:16-17 S 2 '63
Borrowed pole. il Time 82:52 Ag 16 '63
Exercise in physics. il Time 84:71 Jl 3 '64
Fiber-glass airlift; controversial fiber-glass poles. il Look 27:74-7 My 7 '63
Flying Finn; Pentti Nikula. il Newsweek 61: 85 F 11 '63
How fair is a flip with the flexible pole? il Life 54:36 F 22 '63
Jump up, twist around, set another record. G. S. Brown. il Sports Illus 18:38-9+ F 25 '63
Please be good; new indoor world record. il Time 81:68 F 8 '63
Pole bends, the great Pennel breaks 17-foot barrier. il Life 55:30D-30E S 6 '63
Sixteen extra inches in fiberglas. S. James. il Pop Mech 120:114-15 S '63
Sky's the limit. Newsweek 61:64 My 20 '63
VAULTS
Where they keep the money; portfolio. il Fortune 68:114-17 O '63
See also
Diebold, incorporated
VAUX-le-Vicomte castle. See Castles
VAWTER, Bruce
Beast from the sea. Commonweal 80:253-6 My 22 '64
Debut of the Anchor Bible. Commonweal 81: 396-7 D 11 '64
Reflections on tithing. Commonweal 78:560-3 S 20 '63
VAYDIK, Frank
You can save your elms. Am City 78:110-11 S '63
VAZAKAS, Byron
Poetry chronicle. P. Petrie. Poetry 102:49 Ap '63
VEACH, Lisa
I believe; ed. by A. Armstrong. por Seventeen 22:22 D '63
VEAL
See also
Cookery—Meat
VEAL industry. See Meat industry and trade
VECKLY, John
Big steel; the consumer touch. por Duns R 81:32 Mr '63
VECTOR currents. See Electric currents
VECTRA seamless stockings. See Hosiery
VEDDER, Alan C.
New Mexico Spanish colonial art for Britain. Antiques 83:553-6 My '63
VEECK, Bill
Baseball: another business facing change; interview. pors U S News 55:56-61 Ag 12 '63
Baseball establishment. Esquire 62:45-7+ Ag '64
How I didn't buy a ball club; ed. by E. Linn. por Sat Eve Post 236:78-80 S 7 '63
How I'd build the perfect ball park. por Pop Sci 184:94-5+ Mr '64
Speaking out; ed. by E. Linn. por Sat Eve Post 237:10+ Jl 11 '64
Speaking out. por Sat Eve Post 236:10+ Mr 16 '63
VEENSTRA, John J.
Stormy marriage. por Library J 88:2634-5 Jl '63
VEGETABLE gardening
Easy vegetable gardening. E. S. Henderson. il Horticulture 41:270 My; 310-11 Je '63
Happiness is a thing called vegetable gardening. M. A. Roche. il Flower Grower 51: 40-2+ Ja '64
Harvest secret; pick your vegetables at the peak for best flavor. il Sunset 133:144-5 Ag '64
Kitchen garden. A. C. Jubb. See issues of Flower grower
Kitchen garden (title varies) A. C. Jubb. See issues of Flower grower
Late vegetables. H. E. Barké. il Horticulture 42:14-15+ S '64
Now, the time to plan your vegetable garden. il Good H 158:158-9 Mr '64
Our garden is a family affair. R. Van Doren. il Flower Grower 50:22-5+ S '63
Salad garden at your kitchen door. L. Eisman. Pop Gard 15:16+ Mr '64
Short cuts to better vegetables. il Flower Grower 51:40-1 My '64
Try vegetables that are different. H. Williamson. il Pop Gard 15:12-13+ My '64
Vegetables. A. C. Burrage. il Horticulture 42:22-5+ Ap '64
Vegetables in your garden. E. McClure. il Horticulture 43:34-5+ Ja '65
See also
Herbs
Watering of gardens, lawns, etc.
VEGETABLE handling
Bulk bins for everything. B. Fowler. il Farm J 87:40B-41 O '63
VEGETABLE oils. See Oils and fats, Edible
VEGETABLE salads. See Salads
VEGETABLES
New fruits and vegetables for '65. il Farm J 89:38H Ja '65
New this year. il Horticulture 43:20-3 Ja '65
New vegetables, fruits for '64. il Farm J 88:64G F '64
1963 All-America vegetables. il Sunset 130: 229 Mr '63
Novelty flowers and vegetables for your 1964 garden. il Horticulture 42:20-3 Ja '64
Twenty new fruits and vegetables. L. Donelson. il Farm J 87:64B-64C F '63
See also
Cookery—Vegetables
Greens, Edible
Vegetable gardening
also names of vegetables, e.g. Sweet potatoes

All-America selections

See Plants—All-America selections

Packing

One bad apple can't spoil this pack. il Farm J 88:44F Je '64

Prepackaging

His packaged vegetables lure customers. L. Donelson. Farm J 87:58D Ap '63
VEGETABLES, Canned
See also
Green giant company
VEGETABLES, Frozen
Frozen vegetables. il Consumer Rep 29:304-5 Je '64
VEGETABLES in design. See Design, Decorative—Plant forms
VEHICLES
See also
Ground effect machines
Motor vehicles
Space vehicles
VEINS
See also
Varicose veins

Surgery

See Blood vessels—Surgery
VEJJABUL, Pierra
Bangkok's wonderful Dr Pierra. J. D. Ratcliff. il por Read Digest 85:206-8+ S '64
VELA hotel nuclear detection satellites. See Artificial satellites—Military applications
VELA project. See Atomic bombs—Testing, Detection of
VELA project. See Atomic bombs—Testing, Detection of
VELASCO IBARRA, José María
Ecuador's socio-political mosaic. E. S. Urbanski. bibliog f Cur Hist 46:19-25 Ja '64
VELASCO, Tomás de Torrejón y. See Torrejón y Velasco, T. de
VELÁZQUEZ, Diego Rodríguez de Silva y
Velázquez, a catologue raisonné of his oeuvre, by J. Lopez-Rey. Review
Art N il 62:43 O '63. A. H. Mayor
VELDE, Paul
Hemingway who stayed home. Nation 198:76-7 Ja 20 '64
VELDT; drama. See Bradbury, R.
VELEN, Victor A.
Czech Stalinists die hard. For Affairs 42: 320-8 Ja '64
VELIE, Lester
How Hoffa got Hoffa. Read Digest 85:101-6 D '64
Let's stop mass-producing unemployables! Read Digest 85:59-63 Jl '64
No room at the bottom. Read Digest 84:169-70+ Ap '64
Second chance for George. Read Digest 82: 61-5 Je '63
Stakes in the struggle against Hoffa. Read Digest 84:92-6 Mr '64
Stepping-stones from the slums. Read Digest 83:175-80 O '63
That empty chair by the featherbed. Read Digest 82:97-102 Ap '63
Union that automation built. Read Digest 84:181-2+ Je '64
Where the jobs are. Read Digest 86:102-6 Ja '65
You can't steal a union anymore. Read Digest 83:125-9 Ag '63

VELIKOVSKY, Immanuel
On the recent discoveries concerning Jupiter and Venus. V. Bargmann and L. Motz; reply. P. Anderson. Science 139:670+ F 15 '63
Scientists in collision: was Velikovsky right? E. Larrabee. Harper 227:48-50+ Ag '63; Discussion. 227:12+ O; 83-7 D '63
Velikovsky rides again. H. Margolis. Bul Atomic Sci 20:38-40 Ap '64
VELLORE Christian medical college, India. See Medical colleges
VELLORE Christian medical college and hospital. See Hospitals—India
VELLOSO, Wilson
Progress of the Alliance. Américas 16:10-13 Ja '64
VELOCIMETERS
Velocity measured by laser diffraction. il Aviation W 81:87-9 N 16 '64
VELOCITY of light. See Light—Velocity
VENABLE, Margaret
High school dumping grounds. Sch Arts 63: 32-4 My '64
VENDING machines
Antique vending machines. il Fortune 67:115-17 F '63
Cup that orders its own coffee. S. V. Jones. Sci Digest 54:56 D '63
Get the big bite with your own vender; Fruit-O-Matic. B. Hardy. il Farm J 88:36-7 Ap '64
Little books. New Yorker 40:40 Ap 18 '64
Push-button grocer; vending machines for frozen food. il Bsns W p62 My 4 '63
Push-button sake; new bar in Tokyo. il Newsweek 62:91 N 18 '63
Sales and distribution; vending revitalized. L. Morse. Duns R 83:65 My '64
Supermarket in a vending machine; Swiss invention. il Bsns W p 100, 105 S 14 '63
Ubiquitous salesman. il Time 84:100+ O 23 '64
Vending machines work for food service. H. P. Vermilya. il Arch Rec 133:194-6 My '63
Vending service for readers; stationery supplies; Jero sales co, Drexel Hill, Pa. il Library J 89:3723 O 1 '64
Vendors outgrow machines. il Bsns W p 136+ O 10 '64
VENDOR relations. See Purchasing, Industrial
VENDORS, Street. See Street trades
VENEERS and veneering
Patterns in wood. P. Villiard. il Natur Hist 74:44-5 Ja '65
VENEREAL diseases
Another epidemic of teen-age VD? C. S. Deschin. Ladies Home J 80:30+ Ja '63
Great pox. il Time 85:58 Ja 22 '65
Hideous mien. America 108:215 F 16 '63
NBC turns down a golden chance; program about teenage venereal disease. R. L. Tobin. Sat R 47:61-2 D 12 '64
Needed: a new approach to the VD problem; with study-discussion program, by E. M. Durall. C. S. Deschin. bibliog il PTA Mag 57:25-8, 37 F '63
Spirochete is back. Nation 198:471 My 11 '64
Venereal disease. W. F. Schwartz. NEA J 53:64-5 Mr '64
V.D. menace. M. B. Moore, jr. and M. E. Goodman. Parents Mag 39:143-6 F '64
Venereal disease; social and medical aspects. Consumer Rep 28:496-9 O '63
Youth vs. VD. E. Farnham. PTA Mag 58:37 O '63
See also
Gonorrhea
Syphilis
VENETIAN blinds. See Blinds
VENETIAN rendezvous; story. See Vivante, A.
VENEZIA, Michael
Bug boy rides like an old hand. J. Olsen. il pors Sports Illus 22:26-8+ Ja 25 '65
VENEZUELA
Bomba on the Caroni; diamond discovery il Newsweek 63:78-9 F 24 '64
Most critical area in the world. Life 54:4B F 22 '63
See also
Americans in Venezuela
Communism—Venezuela
Community development—Venezuela
Elections—Venezuela
Iron mines and mining—Venezuela
Land tenure—Venezuela
Margarita Island
Orinoco River
Petroleum industry and trade—Venezuela
Political parties—Venezuela
Presidents—Venezuela
Prisons—Venezuela

Description and travel

Venezuela builds on oil. T. J. Abercrombie. il Nat Geog Mag 123:344-87 Mr '63
Who's gonna take de money and run Venezuela? H. Sutton. il Sat R 46:34-6+ My 11 '63

Economic conditions

First impressions. E. M. von Kuehnelt-Leddihn. Nat R 17:62+ Ja 26 '65
Progressing on its own. Time 83:27 My 22 '64
Rosier than red. Time 82:42 N 1 '63
Si, amigo, ballots beat bullets in Venezuela. il Sr Schol 84:13-15 F 7 '64
Venezuela: the achievement of Don Romulo. A. A. Berle. Reporter 29:33-4 N 7 '63
Where U.S. won and Castro lost in Latin America. D. B. Richardson. il U S News 55:92-4 D 16 '63

Economic policy

Rómulo's successor: doing well. il Time 84: 35 Ag 7 '64

Foreign relations

Cuban intervention in Venezuela; excerpts from report. Américas 16:44 Ap '64
OAS approves Rio treaty measures against Castro regime; with statements, and text of final act, July 22-30, 1964. D. Rusk; L. B. Johnson. bibliog f Dept State Bul 51:174-84 Ag 10 '64
O.A.S. on Venezuela's charges against Cuba; text of act, signed on July 26, 1964. Cur Hist 48:40-4 Ja '65
U.S. and Venezuela take firm stand against Communist threats; exchange of greetings; with joint communique. J. F. Kennedy; R. Betancourt. Dept State Bul 48:445-7 Mr 25 '63
Venezuelan miracle; Cuban attempts at subversion. R. Betancourt. il Reporter 31:37-41 Ag 13 '64

Industries

See also
International basic economy corporation

Native races

See Indians of South America—Venezuela

Politics and government

Atlantic report. Atlan 211:31-2+ My '63
Betancourt's weave. New Repub 149:9 D 14 '63
Choice for Latin America: Castro threat or Leoni promise. il Newsweek 63:34-6+ Mr 30 '64
Counterattack; government reprisal on F.A.L.N. Time 82:33 O 11 '63
Democracia militante, by E. Auvert. Review Américas il 16:39-41 Mr '64. J. Villaverde
Ex-dictator is forced to leave U.S. U S News 55:21 Ag 26 '63
Freedom wins in Venezuela. Life 55:4 D 13 '63
Honduras and Venezuela: electioneering. New Repub 149:7 O 12 '63
Man with a formula to stop Castroism; Venezuela's Betancourt. il Bsns W p64-5 Mr 2 '63
Rebuff to terror. il Newsweek 62:50 D 16 '63
Red pimpernel? guerrilla chief of Armed forces for national liberation (FALN) Newsweek 62:32-3 S 30 '63
Rómulo's last tape. il Time 83:42 Mr 13 '64
Rooster that cannot crow: FALN, the Armed forces of national liberation; with report by M. J. Kubic. il Newsweek 62:40+ Ag 12 '63
Saboteurs on the march. Time 82:24 S 27 '63
Scholar, novelist, and president. L. Dunham. il Américas 16:1-6 D '64
Thwarting subversion. Commonweal 77:608 Mr 8 '63
Time of jubilation. Time 83:29 Mr 20 '64
Venezuela: piracy and violence. il Newsweek 61:48+ F 25 '63
Venezuela: the achievement of Don Romulo. A. A. Berle. Reporter 29:33-4 N 7 '63
Venezuelan miracle. R. Betancourt. il Reporter 31:37-41 Ag 13 '64
Washington welcome to a friend. il Time 81: 22 Mr 1 '63
Yanquis say si, si for Latin in D.C. il Life 54: 30-1 Mr 1 '63
See also
Communism—Venezuela
Elections—Venezuela

Religious institutions and affairs

News of the Christian world (cont) Christian Cent 80:478, 866 Ap 10, Jl 3 '63

VENEZUELA—*Continued*

Social conditions

Big, bad businessmen. E. K. Culhane. America 110:331 Mr 14 '64
First impressions. E. M. von Kuehnelt-Leddihn. Nat R 17:62+ Ja 26 '65
Illegitimate family. Time 81:30 Mr 8 '63

VENEZUELAN pottery. See Pottery, Venezuelan

VENEZUELAN students
Flunking the reds; Central university of Venezuela. Newsweek 63:50 Je 29 '64
Subversion si, study no; strike for right to flunk. Time 83:36 Je 26 '64

VENICE
Winter in Venice; photographs. C. Bavagnoli. Life 56:56-64 F 21 '64

Description

By Venice possessed. J. Morris. Horizon 5:14-16+ Mr '63
Going places, finding things in Venice. K. Bates. il House & Gard 125:40+ Mr '64
Step by step through Venice. R. Deardorff. il Travel 120:53-4+ Ag '63
Stones of Venice. A. Liberman. il Horizon 5:16-24 Mr '63
Venice out of season. W. Marchant. il Holiday 35:52-7+ F '64

Music

Viva Verdi? hecklers of concert performance of Verdi's Il corsaro. Time 82:74 S 13 '63

VENICE biennale. See Art—Exhibitions; Music festivals—Italy

VENICE film festival. See Moving picture festivals

VENING-MEINESZ, Felix Andries
Clock watching genius; reprint. R. Fraser. por Sat R 47:56-7 O 3 '64; Reply. E. Roberts. 47:70 N 7 '64

VENISON
So you don't like venison. F. C. Hibben. il Field & S 68:38-40+ O '63
See also
Cookery—Game

VENN, Grant
Plea for better education. Sci N L 85:372 Je 13 '64

VENOM
Bee venom tolerance in white mice in relation to diet. A. W. Benton and others. bibliog il Science 145:1448-9 S 25 '64
Deadly snakes kill 30,000 people yearly. Sci N L 85:405 Je 27 '64
Disc electrophoresis of hymenoptera venoms and body proteins. R. O'Connor and others. bibliog il Science 145:1320-1 S 18 '64
His dying words: don't blame the snake; it's not it's fault. J. Hicks. il Life 56:38+ F 7 '64
Hymenoptera: pure venom from bees, wasps, and hornets. R. O'Connor and others. il Science 139:420 F 1 '63
Venom and venom apparatus of the bull ant, myrmecia gulosa, fabr. G. W. K. Cavill and others. bibliog il Science 146:79-80 O 2 '64
Venom collection from honey bees. A. W. Benton and others. bibliog il Science 142:228-9 O 11 '63
See also
Poisons
Rattlesnakes

VENTILATION
Cooling your house with free air. G. K. Geerlings. il Pop Sci 183:99-101 Jl '63
Design of ventilating ceilings. il Arch Rec 133:221-2+ Ap '63
Every room can be a breezeway. il House B 106:82-7 Ja '64
How an atrium can increase summer comfort. il House B 105:84-9 Ag '63
How to keep dry in a moist, hot climate. il House B 106:64-9+ Ja '64
This bright and fresh kitchen has its secrets upstairs. il Sunset 131:130-1 O '63
Tricks to speed up the breeze through your house. W. Langewiesche. il House B 105:80-3+ Ag '63
See also
Barns and stables—Heating and ventilation
Tunnels and tunneling—Ventilation

VENTILATORS
Air conditioners and fans. il Consumer Bul 46:33-5 Je '63
How good is your kitchen ventilation? il Bet Hom & Gard 41:22-3 Ag '63

VENTS, Air. See Ventilation

VENTURE capital. See Capital

VENTURES, Joint. See Joint adventures

VENTURI, Ken
After the avalanche. il por Time 83:44 Je 26 '64
Hot finish. il por Newsweek 63:62-3 Je 29 '64
Poor Ken hits it rich again; with editorial comment. A. Wright. il pors Sports Illus 20:6, 12-19 Je 29 '64
Sporting scene. H. W. Wind. il New Yorker 40:78+ Jl 11 '64
Sportsman of the year. A. Wright. il pors Sports Illus 21:32-9 D 21 '64

VENTURI tubes
Venturis offer test stand flexibility. J. F. Judge. il Miss & Roc 14:28+ F 24 '64

VENUS (planet)
Chemistry and petrology of Venus: preliminary deductions. R. F. Mueller. bibliog Science 141:1046-7 S 13 '63; Reply. R. A. Robie. 143:1057 Mr 6 '64
Day on Venus lasts 248 to 258 earth days. Sci N L 86:165 S 12 '64
Giant radio probe is sizing up Venus; Arecibo ionospheric observatory. il Bsns W p48+ Mr 14 '64
Mariner reveals 800F Venus temperature. E H. Kolcum. il Aviation W 78:30-1 Mr 4 '63
Mariner scans a lifeless Venus. F. Sartwell. il Nat Geog Mag 123:732-42 My '63
Mariner-2 microwave observations of Venus. A. H. Barrett and E. Lilley. il Sky & Tel 25:192-5 Ap '63
Mariner II: preliminary reports on measurements of Venus; symposium. bibliog il Science 139:905-11 Mr 8 '63
Medieval astronomers erred in describing Mercury and Venus. S. D. Gossner. il Natur Hist 72:48-9 F '63
Microwave observations of Venus. il Sky & Tel 25:143-4 Mr '63
No life or hydrocarbons likely on planet Venus. Sci N L 86:134 Ag 29 '64
Petrology of Venus: further deductions. L. S. Walter. bibliog Science 143:1161 Mr 13 '64
Photographic record of Venus. G. A. T. Heillegger. il Sky & Tel 25:99 F '63
Radar observations of Venus' rotation. Sky & Tel 28:341 D '64
Venus: a map of its brightness temperature. B. C. Murray and others. bibliog il Science 140:391-2 Ap 26 '63
Venus confirmed. Sci Am 208:80-1 Ap '63
Venus defined. Newsweek 61:62 Mr 11 '63
Venus diameter. il Sky & Tel 26:199 O '63
Venus glows in Mariner portrait. il Life 54:34-5 Mr 22 '63
Venus' inferior conjunction. il Sky & Tel 28:71 Ag '64
Voyage of Mariner II. J. N. James. il Sci Am 209:70-84 bibliog (p 171) Jl '63
Water vapor on Venus. A. Ewing. Sci N L 85:261 Ap 25 '64
With a simple telescope Galileo mapped the true orbit of Venus. T. D. Nicholson. il Natur Hist 73:46-8 My '64

Atmosphere

Cold clouds over Venus. il Sci N L 83:149 Mr 9 '63
Measuring moisture for chances of life. il Time 84:85 D 18 '64
Storm zone on Venus. B. Tufty. Sci N L 83:262 Ap 27 '63
Venus revisited; presence of water vapor. Time 83:117 Ap 17 '64
Venus uncovered; question of Venusian life. il Newsweek 64:53 D 21 '64
Water vapor on Venus. Sky & Tel 27:331+ Je '64

Photographs, maps, etc.

JPL using two radar techniques to prepare map of surface of Venus. R. Pay. Miss & Roc 15:35 D 21 '64

VENUS probe. See Space probes

VENUS'S flytraps
Nature note. Sci N L 86:318 N 14 '64

VERA foundation, incorporated
Bail-bond scandal. D. Oberdorfer. il Sat Eve Post 237:66-7 Je 20 '64
Summons instead of an arrest; Manhattan summons project. G. Samuels. il N Y Times Mag p 16+ Jl 26 '64

VERACRUZ, Mexico
Voladores! dance of the flying pole, by Totonac Indians; photographs. Travel 119:34-7 My '63
Where the union is the boss. il Bsns W p 110-11 Je 13 '64

VERANDAS. See Porches

VERBEEK, Gustave
Upside-downs of Little Lady Lovekins and Old Man Muffaroo; excerpts from Incredible upside-downs of Gustave Verbeek. il Redbook 121:56-7 Je '63

VERBENAS
It likes the sun; Peruvian verbenas. il Sunset 131:254 N '63
See also
Lemon-verbena

VERBIER, Switzerland
Escape to the snow. il Holiday 37:74-7 Ja '65

VERCOE, R. Stephen
Shooting tips. Pop Phot 53:43+ Ag '63

VERDI, Giuseppe
Aida. Criticism
New Yorker 39:177-8 O 26 '63
Opera N 28:24-5 D 7 '63
Opera N 28:33 D 7 '63
Opera N il 28:17-20 D 7 '63
Sat R 48:22 Ja 16 '65
Sat R il(p 1) 46:56 O 26 '63
Collector's Verdi. C. L. Osborne. Hi Fi 13:90+ D '63
Day of the premiere. F. Stevenson. il Opera N 28:13-16 Mr 28 '64
Don Carlo. Criticism
New Yorker 39:74-5 Je 29 '63
New Yorker 39:231-3 N 9 '63
Opera N il 27:25 My 4 '63
Opera N il 28:17-20 Mr 7 '64
Opera N il 28:34 Mr 21 '64
Sat R 46:55+ N 16 '63
I due Foscari. Criticism
Opera N 28:35 Ja 4 '64
Falstaff. Criticism
New Yorker 40:157-8 Mr 14 '64
New Yorker 40:189-90 Ap 4 '64
Newsweek il 63:94 Mr 16 '64
Opera N 29:14-15 Ja 23 '65
Opera N 29:24-5 Ja 23 '65
Opera N 28:24-6 Mr 21 '64
Opera N il 29:17-20 Ja 23 '65
Opera N il 27:32-3 F 2 '63
Opera N il 28:32-3 F 22 '64
Opera N il 28:17-20 Mr 21 '64
Sat R 47:30-1 Mr 21 '64
Sat R 47:61 Ap 11 '64
Time il 83:59 Mr 13 '64
La forza del destino. Criticism
New Yorker 40:199-200 D 5 '64
For Giulini, a triumph; Verdi's Four sacred pieces. J. Diether. Am Rec G 30:676+ Ap '64
Macbeth. Criticism
Opera N il 28:17-20 Ap 4 '64
Sat R 47:38 Ap 4 '64
Man Verdi, by F. Walker. Review
Am Rec G il 29:742-4 My '63. C. J. Luten
Opera N 27:33 Mr 23 '63. R. A. Tuggle
Messa da requiem. il Opera N 28:17-20 Mr 28 '64
Music to my ears. I. Kolodin. Sat R 47:26 My 30 '64
New day for Roncole. M. J. Matz. il Opera N 28:30-1 Ap 4 '64
New kind of event; world premiere of Falstaff, 1892; tr. by M. J. Matz. C. Gatti. Opera N 29:14-15 Ja 23 '65
On DGG's Trovatore, and especially Bergonzi. P. L. Miller. Am Rec G 30:147-8 O '63
On records; Aïda. Opera N 28:34 D 7 '63
On records; Arias. Opera N 28:35 Ap 18 '64
On records; Don Carlo. Opera N 28:35 Mr 7 '64
On records; Falstaff. Opera N 28:35 Mr 21 '64
On records; Falstaff; Highlights only. Opera N 29:34 Ja 23 '65
On records; Macbeth. Opera N 28:35 Ap 4 '64
On records; Messa da requiem. Opera N 28:35 Mr 28 '64
On records; Otello. Opera N 28:35 F 15 '64
On records; Otello. J. W. Freeman. Opera N 27:35 Mr 23 '63
On records; Quattro pezzi sacri. Opera N 29:27 O 17 '64
On records; Requiem mass. Opera N 29:34 Ja 23 '65
On records; Rigoletto. Opera N 28:35 F 22 '64
On records; Rigoletto. il Opera N 29:34 D 12 '64
On records; Simon Boccanegra. Opera N 29:35 Ja 30 '65
On records; Six songs. Opera N 29:34 Ja 23 '65
On records; La Traviata. J. W. Freeman. Opera N 27:37 Mr 16 '63
On records; La Traviata. J. W. Freeman. Opera N 28:34 O 19 '63
On records; La Traviata. Opera N 28:34 Ja 11 '64
On records; Il Trovatore. Opera N 28:35 Ja 18 '64
Otello. Criticism
Mus Am il 84:11-12 F '64
New Yorker 39:76+ Mr 23 '63
New Yorker 40:179 O 10 '64
Opera N 27:33 F 2 '63
Opera N 27:8-11 Mr 23 '63
Opera N 27:17-20 Mr 23 '63
Opera N 27:24-5 Mr 23 '63
Opera N 27:27 My 4 '63
Opera N 29:31 Ja 23 '65
Opera N il 28:17-20 F 15 '64
Sat R il 46:30-1+ Mr 23 '63
Portrait of a master; reprint, tr. by J. W. Freeman. D. Cecchi. il por Opera N 28:6-9 F 15 '64
RCA Victor's Falstaff. P. L. Miller. il Am Rec G 30:564-5+ Mr '64
Rigoletto. Criticism
Opera N 29:17-20 D 12 '64
Opera N il 28:17-20 F 22 '64
Opera N il 28:24-6 F 22 '64
Sacred opera. J. W. Freeman. il Opera N 28:24-6 Mr 28 '64
Simon Boccanegra. Criticism
New Yorker 40:164 D 19 '64
Opera N 29:17-20 Ja 30 '65
Opera N il 29:24-5 Ja 30 '65
La Traviata. Criticism
New Yorker 39:67 D 28 '63
Opera N 27:17-20 Mr 16 '63
Opera N 27:25 Mr 16 '63
Opera N il 28:17-23 Ja 11 '64
Opera N por 28:24-5 Ja 11 '64
La Traviata. P. L. Miller. Am Rec G 30:95 O '63
Il Trovatore. Criticism
New Yorker 39:66 D 21 '63
Opera N il 27:32 F 2 '63
Opera N il 28:17-20 Ja 18 '64
Sat R 46:44+ D 28 '63
Two new Sir Johns help make a Falstaff year. C. L. Osborne. il Hi Fi 14:65-6 Mr '64
Two Rigolettos, with a surprise from Fischer-Dieskau. C. L. Osborne. il Hi Fi 14:75-7 D '64
Unreluctant composers; conversation with Mozart, Verdi and Wagner. L. F. Loveday. il Opera N 28:8-11 Ja 25 '64
Verdi anniversary issue; symposium. il pors Hi Fi 13:10+ O '63
Verdi collaboration. R. Jones. il Am Rec G 30:376-7 Ja '64
Verdi, his music, life and times, by G. Martin. Review
Opera N 28:7 D 7 '63. R. A. Tuggle
Verdi I know; ed. by A. M. Lingg. G. Solti. il Opera N 28:8-11 D 7 '63
Verdi in Italy. P. Elvins. il Opera N 28:31 D 7 '63
Verdi is heard over Wagner's thunder. H. C. Schonberg. il por N Y Times Mag p 14-15+ My 19 '63
Verdi Requiem. il Am Rec G 31:420-1 Ja '65
Verdi-Wagner anniversary; with chronology by M. Bernheimer. H. Weinstock. por Sat R 46:35-7 Jl 27 '63
Vespers and dialogues; performance of I vespri siciliani by, Concert opera association. F. Meklin. Opera N 28:33 F 15 '64
Viva Verdi? hecklers of concert performance of Verdi's Il corsaro. por Time 82:74 S 13 '63

VERDIER, Philippe
Coptic eclectics: the vital mixture. Art N 62:34-9+ S '63
Seventeenth-century French enameled watches in the Walters art gallery. Antiques 84:686-90 D '63

VERDON, Gwen
Fun on TV. pors Dance Mag 38:31 N '64

VERDUN, Battle of, 1916
Open wound at Verdun. il Life 56:54-5 Mr 13 '64
Price of glory: Verdun, 1916, by A. Horne. Review
Am Heritage 14:109-10 Ap '63
Commonweal 78:201-3 My 10 '63. A. E. Mayhew
Nat R 14:161 F 26 '63. G. F. Eliot
Scarred face of Verdun; with photographs by A. Eisenstaedt. Life 56:68-83 Je 5 '64

VERGELIS, Aron
Soviet anti-Semitism: an exchange. Commentary 39:35-6 Ja '65

VERGETTE, Nicholas
Statement on the concept of art. Sch Arts 64:24-6 D '64
about
Nicholas Vergette. il por Sch Arts 64:21-3 D '64

VERITY, M. Anthony, and others
Aortico-pulmonary glomus tissue distribution and blood supply in the adult cat. bibliog Science 145:172-3 Jl 10 '64

VERMICULITE
Montmorillonite-vermiculite interstratification in clays from eocene chalk soils. L. E. DeMumbrum. il Science 140:187-8 Ap 12 '63

VERMILYA, Howard P.
Vending machines work for food service. Arch Rec 133:194-6 My '63
VERMONT
See also
Booksellers and bookselling—Vermont
Fishing—Vermont
Hunting—Vermont
Music festivals—Vermont
Description and travel
Sunday afternoon fox. J. Skow. il Sat Eve Post 237:24-5 D 5 '64
Economic conditions
New sugar in an old state; skiing in Vermont. H. Horn. il Sports Illus 19:30-4 N 18 '63
History
In the name of the great Jehovah and the Continental congress! K. S. Davis. il Am Heritage 14:65-77 O '63
Politics and government
Democrat who took Vermont; first Democrat for governor. R. Tunley. il Sat Eve Post 236:82+ N 23 '63
Flaw. Newsweek 63:22+ Ja 20 '64
Loneliest governor. W. S. Ellis. Reporter 28:45 Ap 25 '63
My poetic career in Vermont politics. W. J. Smith. il Harper 228:54-62 Ja '64; Discussion. 228:6+ Mr '64
VERMONT state forests. See Forests, State
VERMONTERS
Look out, America, here comes Granby. E. Hill. il Sat Eve Post 237:64-5 Ap 4 '64
VERMOUTH. See Wine
VERNE, Jules
Five weeks in a balloon; dramatization. See Olfson, L.
VERNIS Martin. See Lacquer and lacquering
VERNON, Jack. See Suedfeld, P. jt. auth.
VERNON, Raymond
Saints & sinners in foreign investment. Harvard Bsns R 41:146-9+ My '63
VERNON family
Vernon coat-of-arms. H. K. Eilers. il Hobbies 69:126-7 S '64
VERNON, Calif.
This maintenance shop sells service. J. B. Moore. il Am City 78:107-8 Ap '63
VERNON, Okla.
Vernon: an all Negro town in southeastern Oklahoma. J. E. Woodard. Negro Hist Bul 27:115-16 F '64
VEROLME, Cornelis
I did it all. il por Time 81:110 Ap 19 '63
VERONA, Otto Miles
Hi ho, the hierarchy. Esquire 62:74-5 O '64
VERONA, Italy
Music
Tears in Verona. D. A. Mackinnon. il Opera N 28:31 N 16 '63
Verona's magic lands. M. E. Peltz. Opera N 29:27 N 14 '64
VERONICAS. See Speedwells
VEROT, Augustin
Rebel bishop, by M. V. Gannon. Review America 112:82-3 Ja 16 '65. H. J. Nolan
VERRAZANO-NARROWS bridge. See New York (city)—Bridges
VERRETT, Shirley
Quote: unquote; interview, ed. by J. Ardoin. por Mus Am 83:23 N '63
VERRIER, Anthony
British defense policy under Labor. For Affairs 42:282 92 Ja '64
VERS libre. See Free verse
VERSAILLES
Gardens
Versailles; photographic report by M. Perry. Flower Grower 50:46-9 My '63
VERSAILLES, Palace of
Take the train to Versailles. il Sunset 132: 35+ Ja '64
VERSE. See Poetry
VERSIFICATION
Note on prosody. A. R. Ammons. Poetry 102: 202-3 Je '63
VERTANES, Charles A.
Automating the school library: an advanced report. Wilson Lib Bul 37:864-7 Je '63
VERTEBRATES
Immunologic phenomena: cold-blooded vertebrates; report of meeting of the Federation of the American society for experimental microbiology. M. M. Sigel. Science 141:543+ Ag 9 '63
Paleontologic investigations at Big Bone Lick State Park, Kentucky: a preliminary report. C. B. Schultz and others. bibliog il Science 142:1167-9 N 29 '63
Parathion activation by livers of aquatic and terrestrial vertebrates. J. L. Potter and R. D. O'Brien. bibliog il Science 144:55-7 Ap 3 '64
Vertebrate hard tissues; report on special symposium of the section of vertebrate morphology of the American society of zoologists. C. Gans. Science 144:323-4 Ap 17 '64
Virus infections in cold-blooded vertebrates; report on conference. K. Wolf. Science 146: 1603-4 D 18 '64
VERTEBRATES, Fossil
See also
Fishes, Fossil
VERTICAL take-off and landing airplanes. See Airplanes, Vertical take-off and landing
VERTIGO. See Dizziness
VERWOERD, Hendrik Frensch
Black vote. Newsweek 62:36 D 16 '63
Official case for apartheid. H. Muller. il por N Y Times Mag p28+ Je 7 '64
Protectorates under the gun. S. Uys. New Repub 149:9-10 S 28 '63
South African fortnight. W. F. Buckley, jr; discussion. Nat R 14:127 F 12 '63
VERY high frequency television transmission. See Television transmission
VERZÁR, Frederic
Aging of collagen. Sci Am 208:104-8+ bibliog(p200) Ap '63
VESEY, Richard W.
Camcraft Z housing now available. Pop Phot 54:65-7+ Je '64
How to get the most out of Tri-X. il Pop Phot 56:126-7+ Ja '65
VESEY-FITZGERALD, L. D.
Anomalies in Africa. il Natur Hist 73:54-5 D '64
VESPER irises. See Irises
VESSEY, J. K.
South goes scenic. Am For 70:20-3 Jl '64
VESTAL, David
Bent light koans. Pop Phot 55:46+ N '64
Criticism criticized. Pop Phot 55:135+ D '64
Critics at large. Pop Phot 55:22+ Jl; 68-9 Ag '64
First look at a monumental encyclopedia. Pop Phot 54:136-7 My '64
Kodak's new teaching tool. Pop Phot 54:16+ Ap '64
Photographer's eye at modern museum. Pop Phot 55:54+ N '64
Printing papers. Pop Phot 56:138-49+ Ja '65
Recipe for seeing. U S Camera 27:41+ F '64
35-mm spoken here. Pop Phot 55:33+ Ag '64
VESTER, Bertha Spafford
Jerusalem, my home. pors Nat Geog Mag 126: 826-47 D '64
VESTER, John W. and Reino, M. L.
Hepatic glucokinase: a direct effect of insulin. bibliog Science 142:590-1 N 1 '63
VETCH
Finds vetch makes good soil builder. Suc Farm 61:78 S '63
VETERANS. See Service men, Discharged
VETERANS administration. See United States —Veterans administration
VETERANS compensation. See Service mens bonuses
VETERANS organizations. See Service men, Discharged—Organizations
VETERANS pensions. See Pensions, Military
VETERINARY first aid
First aid for dogs. H. G. Tapply. il Field & S 69:86 O '64
VETERINARY medicine
Peticare; veterinary clinics and hospitals. il Newsweek 62:52 D 23 '63
Veterinary helps (title varies) J. W. Bailey. See issues of Successful farming
Veterinary medicine advances human medicine; excerpts from address. W. H. Feldman. Todays Health 41:12+ N '63
What's new in veterinary medicine? il Good H 156:166 Ap '63
See also
Anthelmintics
VETO
See also
United Nations—Voting
VETRA, Vija
Sacred dance at the crossroads. W. Sorell. pors Dance Mag 38:24-5 Ag '64
Vija Vetra, Brooklyn academy of music. J. Maskey. Dance Mag 38:18 D '64
VETROVS, Helen. See Chang, R. S. jt. auth.
VETSERA, Maria, baroness
Mayerling remains a mystery. R. Payne. il por N Y Times Mag p34-5+ Ja 26 '64

VETTER, Eric W.
How to forecast your manpower needs. Nations Bsns 52:102-5+ F '64

VETTER, Robert M.
Herr Biedermeier in Vienna. Antiques 84:698-705 D '63
Pewter collector's progress. Antiques 86:179-83 Ag '64
Ruhmann collection of decorative pewter. Antiques 83:690-3 Je '63

VEZZANI, Cesar
Rococo presents. A. Favia-Artsay. por Hobbies 68:31 Ja '64

VIA della Pergola, Florence. See Opera houses

VIA Veneto. See Rome (city)—Streets

VIANSSON-PONTÉ, Pierre
Waltz of les gaullistes. Esquire 62:104-6+ O '64

about

Brotherhood; inner Gaullist mysteries. Time 82:26+ Jl 5 '63

VIBRATION
Jobs for the jiggle. il Time 82:52-3 Ag 30 '63

Measurement

Vibration instrumentation. S. L. Silver. il Electr World 72:56-8+ N '64

VIBRATO
Soupcon of vibrato. D. Stevens. il Hi Fi 14:53-5+ Ja '64

VIBRATORS
See also
Multivibrators

VIBROTRON pressure transducers. See Transducers

VIBURNUM trilobum. See Cranberry bush

VIBURNUMS
And they smell like gardenias. il Sunset 130:303 Ap '63
Sweet tea viburnum. B. Black. il Pop Gard 16:10+ Ja '65

VICAR; drama. See Hochhuth, R.

VICARS. See Church of England—Clergy

VICE-PRESIDENTIAL candidates
Able and willing Eugene McCarthy. D. S. Broder. New Repub 150:8-9 Je 20 '64
All the way with L.B.J. and who? with report by R. Bendiner. il Life 56:94B-96+ My 8 '64
Among Democrats: who for second place? pors U S News 56:35 Mr 16 '64
Barry's choice: a fighting running mate. il U S News 57:30-1 Jl 27 '64
Big political sprint; L.B.J.'s running mate. T. Wicker. il Sat Eve Post 237:76-7 Ap 25 '64
Bill Millers rev up for November. C. Welles. il Life 57:35-6 Ag 7 '64
Bobby for veep? il Time 83:21-2 Mr 20 '64
Candidates' records on defense and space bills. il Miss & Roc 15:16 O 19 '64
Choice for vice president. J. Kraft. Harper 229:95-8 Ag '64
Cordial affair; Republican vice presidential nomination. il Newsweek 64:27 Jl 20 '64
Dying to tell; who had the veep? pors Time 84:18 Ag 28 '64
Focus on Nov. 3. Nat R 16:634 Jl 28 '64
Goodbye Bobby; President Johnson against Kennedy. il Time 84:18-19 Ag 7 '64
He has a little list; Handicapping: veep sweeps. pors Newsweek 64:24-5 Ag 3 '64
Ike for VP? Nat R 16:573 Jl 14 '64
Ike plan cometh. J. J. Kilpatrick. il Nat R 16:483-6 Je 16 '64; Reply. 16:521+ Je 30 '64
Johnson-Humphrey. New Repub 151:3-4 Ag 8 '64
Lodge, Kennedy top ISO poll. il Sr Schol 84:1T My 8 '64
LBJ's running mate: the man he favors. pors U S News 57:32-3 Ag 3 '64
Making of HHH. il Newsweek 64:18-26 S 7 '64
Man who thought of leaving politics. M. Viorst. New Repub 151:8-9 Ag 8 '64
Mansfield: new possible for LBJ ticket. U S News 57:21 Jl 20 '64
Mlle's platform: an appeal to the 89th Congress; '64 question. Mlle 58:120-1 Mr '64
Mixing it up; H. Humphrey and W. Miller opening campaign. il Time 84:32-3 S 18 '64
1964: who's ahead? H. Brandon. Mlle 58:130-1 Mr '64
No. two man; Democratic Vice Presidential nominee. il Newsweek 63:17-18 Ja 13 '64
Now a Lyndon Johnson party; LBJ and RFK. il Newsweek 64:18-19 Ag 10 '64
On the '64 campaign trail. il Sr Schol 84:17 F 21; 16 Mr 20 '64
People's choice for L.B.J.'s V.P; poll taken by E. Roper analyzed. E. Havemann. il pors Life 57:68-70+ Ag 14 '64
President Humphrey? S. Alsop. Sat Eve Post 237:12 My 2 '64
Running mate. il Time 84:28 Jl 24 '64
Running-mate problem. il U S News 57:33 Jl 20 '64
Student opinions. Sr Schol 84:23 My 8 '64
Thruston Morton, the all-purpose Republican. R. L. Riggs. New Repub 150:8-10 Je 27 '64
Veep. Cato. Nat R 16:682 Ag 11 '64
Vice presidency becoming more attractive goal. P. Lisagor. il Nations Bsns 52:23-4 My '64
Who will get the no. two places? il U S News 56:29-30 Je 22 '64
Why Humphrey gets taken for granted. W. V. Shannon. New Repub 151:10-12 Jl 4 '64; Correction. 151:37 Ag 8 '64
Why the President crossed six men off the list as possible running mates; Johnson-Humphrey ticket, or —? pors U S News 57:14-15 Ag 10 '64
William E. Miller. Newsweek 64:22+ Jl 27 '64
Working list. il Time 84:22-3 Jl 17 '64

VICE-PRESIDENTS

United States

Capsule history of the vice presidency. R. Baker. Holiday 36:48-9 S '64
Choosing a running mate. H. Brandon. Sat R 47:14 Ap 18 '64
Dilemma of succession. J. F. Menez. il Commonweal 79:475-7 Ja 24 '64
Exit Mr Throttlebottom? the vice-president's changing role. Sr Schol 85:12-13+ S 23 '64
Gallery of the vice presidents; with report by H. Graff. il pors Am Heritage 15:78-87 Ag '64
Help wanted: a U.S. vice president. D. M. Allen. il Read Digest 84:73-7 Mr '64
Helping Lyndon. Time 83:22 Ja 10 '64
HHH: we work together. il Newsweek 64:30 N 9 '64
LBJ: who's that? K. Crawford. Newsweek 61:39 F 11 '63
Lyndon Johnson: the man and his record. il U S News 55:38-40 D 2 '63
Official residence for the vice-president? pro and con discussion. il Sr Schol 85:16-17 Ja 21 '65
Picking a vice president. New Repub 150:6 Mr 21 '64
Speaking out; let's stop gambling with the presidency. J. M. Burns. Sat Eve Post 237:12+ Ja 25 '64
Speaking out; we need a vice president now. R. M. Nixon. Sat Eve Post 237:6+ Ja 18 '64
Succession and business. H. Hazlitt. Newsweek 63:59 Ja 6 '64
This month's feature: moves to change presidential succession. Cong Digest 43:130-60 My '64
Triple-H brand on the vice-presidency. D. S. Broder. il N Y Times Mag p30-1+ D 6 '64
Vice presidency. H. Hazlitt. Newsweek 62:86 D 2 '63
Vice presidency: how big a job. il U S News 57:41 S 7 '64
Vice Presidential derby. Nation 198:130 F 10 '64
Vice Presidential skirmish. il Newsweek 63:27-8 Mr 16 '64

Protection

Thirty-five bodyguards for the Vice President? U S News 54:10 Ap 1 '63

VICENS, Luis
Snap-in breadboard. Pop Electr 19:54-5 Jl '63
Understanding burn-out. Pop Electr 20:69 Mr '64

VICK, Albert F. W. jr
Birds will come if there's water. Horticulture 42:22-3 Je '64

VICK chemical company
Battling the common cold. E. M. McCabe. il Parents Mag 38:37+ N '63

VICKERS-Armstrongs, limited
Vickers studying VC.10 tail cone extension as drag reduction move. H. J. Coleman. Aviation W 78:40 Ap 1 '63

VICKERY, Thomas
Olympic sails by computer. Motor B 114:48+ O '64

VICKREY, William
$22 billion to civilian use. Sat R 46:13-14 My 4 '63

VICKSBURG, Miss.
Gettysburg and Vicksburg: the battle towns today. R. P. Jordan. il Nat Geog Mag 124:4-57 Jl '63

Siege, 1863

Prelude to Vicksburg. R. P. Jordan. il Nat Geog Mag 124:42-7 Jl '63

VICOS, Peru
Miracle at Vicos. L. Stowe. il Read Digest 82:222-6+ Ap '63

VICTIM; story. See O'Hara, J.

VICTIMS of duty; drama. See Ionesco, E.

VICTOR, Jack. See Rock, I. jt. auth.

VICTOR, Jon, pseud.
Restraints on American Catholic freedom. bibliog f Harper 227:33-9 D '63

VICTOR, Thelda
Drama the cameras missed; ed. by M. Davidson. por Sat Eve Post 237:24-8+ Jl 11 '64

VICTOR; drama. See Vitrac, R.

VICTOREEN instrument company
Every man for himself; decentralized management. Bsns W p84+ S 19 '64

VICTORIA, queen of Great Britain
King Edward the seventh, by P. Magnus. Review
Atlan il por 213:58-61 Je '64. G. W. Johnson
Queen Victoria, by E. Longford. Review
Life 58:17 Ja 15 '65. C. V. Wedgwood
Sat R il 48:46 Ja 23 '65. R. Fulford

VICTORIA, Australia
See also
Melbourne

VICTORIA, British Columbia

Description

English touch: Victoria. S. Franklin. il Holiday 35:74-5+ Ap '64

VICTORIA and Albert museum, South Kensington
Cellini, Houdon & Others at the V.&A. J. Russell. il Art N 63:30-1+ D '64

VICTORIAN architecture. See Architecture, Victorian

VICTORIAN period
Echoes of the age of Victoria; photographs. A. L. Huxtable. N Y Times Mag p46-7 Ap 7 '63

VICUÑA, Magdalena
Dance in Chile. Américas 15:12-17 D '63

La **VIDA** es sueño; drama. See Calderón de la Barca, P.

VIDAL, Gore
Best man 1968. Esquire 59:59-62+ Mr '63; Excerpts. U S News 54:19 Mr 4 '63
Tarzan revisited. Esquire 60:192-3+ D '63

about

Author. M. K. Harvey. por Sat R 47:32 Je 6 '64
What are the magazines saying, dear? il por Time 81:37 Mr 1 '63

VIDEO tape recorders and recording
Do-it-yourself reruns. il Bsns W p 186+ Ap 18 '64
First home TV tape recorder. D. Scott. il Pop Sci 183:94-6+ O '63
Helical video recorder for television. J. Roizen. il Electr World 72:47-9 O '64
Home television tape recorder for under $200. W. S. Bacon. il Pop Electr 19:60-1 S '63
Leendert Drukker tries Fairchild's video recorder. L. Drukker. il Pop Phot 55:112-13+ Jl '64
Look, ma, I'm on TV! home TV recorder. Telcan. Time 82:52 D 20 '63
Portable TV recorder for student teachers. Sch & Soc 92:330 N 14 '64
Sound advice; Fairchild videotape recorder. R. N. Angus. il Mod Phot 28:50+ Jl '64
Sound advice; home movies on videotape. R. Angus. Mod Phot 27:32-3+ Ag '63
Sound advice; Telcan homevideo system. R. Angus. il Mod Phot 28:48+ Mr '64
Sound for your screen; synchronizing sight and sound. M. A. Matzkin. il Hi Fi 14:51-3+ Ag '64
Spinning head tapes TV at home. il Pop Sci 186:86 Ja '65
Tape up to date. N. Eisenberg. il Hi Fi 14:42-4+ Ag '64
Telcan, TV tape recorder progress report. W. S. Bacon. il Pop Electr 20:69+ F '64
TV tape recorder for home use. M. S. Snitzer. il Electr World 71:26-7 Je '64
Videocorder tapes at low speed. A. Zuckerman. il Pop Sci 185:130-1 O '64
Watch your favorite TV show any time. H. Luckett. il Pop Sci 184:54-5 Je '64
What's newest; television tape recording. Newsweek 62:66+ Jl 22 '63
Will this new U.S. TV tape system be better? Camras system. A. Zuckerman. il Pop Sci 183:96 O '63

VIDICON. See Television cameras

VIDLER, Alexander Roper
Cambridge objectors. por Time 83:78 Mr 6 '64

VIENNA

Art

Vienna: the Athens of central Europe. A. Werner. il Am Artist 28:40-7+ My '64

Description

Booked for travel. H. Sutton. il Sat R 46: 26+ S 7; 48+ S 14 '63
In Vienna. See the world as it used to be. M. Gough. il House B 106:64+ Ag '64

Galleries and museums

Vienna's brave young symbol; Museum des XX jahrhunderts. K. Kuh. il Sat R 46:32-3 Jl 27 '63

Music

Austrian bouts. J. Wechsberg. Opera N 29:31 D 19 '64
[Musical events] (cont) il Mus Am 83:116 D '63; 84:22-3 My; 93-4 D '64
New looks in Vienna. J. Wechsberg. il Opera N 29:21-2 S 26 '64
Notes from our correspondents (cont of) Notes from abroad. See issues of High fidelity
Vienna Kitsch. J. Wechsberg. il Opera N 27:32 Ap 6 '63
Viennese scandal. J. Wechsberg. il Opera N 28:31-2 Mr 21 '64

Spanish riding school

Flight of a white stallion. il Sports Illus 20: 30-2+ Ap 27 '64
White stallions; Lipizzan horses on first extensive North American tour. il Newsweek 63:76 Ap 20 '64
Wonderful white stallions of Vienna. F. Sondern, jr. il Read Digest 82:160-6 Ap '63

Theater

Profiles: H. Qualtinger. J. Wechsberg. New Yorker 39:53-4+ Ap 20 '63

VIENNA opera. See Opera—Austria

VIENNA opera ballet. See Ballet—Austria

VIENNA pawnshop. See Pawnbroking

VIENNA regulator wall clocks. See Clocks

VIENNA state opera. See Opera—Austria

VIENNE, France
Profiles; Mme M. L. Point. J. Wechsberg. New Yorker 39:63+ O 5 '63

VIENNESE cookery. See Cookery, Austrian

VIERECK, Peter
Conscience of the thaw. Sat R 47:38-9 My 16 '64
Wanderers along the Volga. Sat R 47:39 F 1 '64

VIET NAM
See also
Hunting—Viet Nam

VIET NAM (Democratic Republic)
And meanwhile what's happening up north? il Time 83:31-2 My 8 '64
Face of the enemy: Ho and his followers. il Newsweek 63:28-9 Je 8 '64
Fire fight in Tayninh. il Time 84:25 Jl 3 '64
Hanoi: the French view. New Repub 150:5 Mr 14 '64
Lest auld acquaintance: French links. il Newsweek 62:25 S 16 '63
North Vietnam: also in crisis. il Newsweek 63:26-7+ Ja 6 '64
Our options in Vietnam. B. B. Fall. il Reporter 30:17-22 Mr 12 '64
Talk with Ho Chi Minh. B. B. Fall. New Repub 149:19-22 O 12 '63
Two Viet-Nams, by B. B. Fall. Review
Nation 197:421-2 D 14 '63. F. Sully
Vietcong's shadow government in the South. P. Grose. il N Y Times Mag p 10-11+ Ja 24 '65
See also
Food supply—Viet Nam (Democratic Republic)
Guerrillas—Viet Nam (Democratic Republic)
United Nations—Viet Nam (Democratic Republic)

Army

From Vietnam battlefront: while U.S. hesitates, reds carry war south. S. W. Sanders. il U S News 57:38-9 Ag 3 '64
Report on the war. il Time 82:32-3 S 20 '63

Foreign relations

Behind the shooting war: a shift in policy for Ho Chi Minh? U S News 57:12 Ag 17 '64
Why the torpedo attacks? F. B. Stevens. il U S News 57:24 Ag 17 '64

Politics and government

Strategist behind the Vietcong. M. Clos. il N Y Times Mag p7+ Ag 16 '64

VIET NAM (Republic)
AID analysis. New Repub 151:4 S 12 '64
Alert in Vietnam; symposium. il Life 57:30-46B+ N 27 '64
Along the Ho Chi Minh trail. il N Y Times Mag p32-3 N 22 '64
Battle of time and the river. il Newsweek 62:36-8+ Jl 15 '63
Bombs in the ballpark; terrorism directed at Americans. Time 83:38 F 21 '64
CIA analysis. New Repub 151:3-4 S 12 '64
Dead end in Vietnam. J. A. Rose; H. T. Minh; B. B. Fall. New Repub 149:15-22 O 12 '63
Dienbienphu: could it happen again? Time 83:43 My 15 '64
How much time do we have in Vietnam? B. B. Fall. New Repub 150:10-11 F 22 '64
If the war in Vietnam can't be won is neutralization an answer? il Newsweek 63:44-5 F 17 '64
Infiltrators. il Time 84:31-2 Jl 24 '64
Key arena. il Time 84:21 Ag 21 '64
Last Confucian, by D. Warner. Review New Repub 149:24+ O 19 '63. B. B. Fall
Lowdown from the top U.S. command in Saigon; panel discussion with the Life correspondents. M. D. Taylor. il Life 57:46-46B+ N 27 '64
McNamara makes a tour of Vietnam. il Newsweek 62:45 O 7 '63
Misadventure in Vietnam. J. Gange; D. F. Ford. il Nation 199:63-8 Ag 24 '64
More men, more aid. il Time 83:28 My 22 '64
Negotiate now! Nation 199:82 S 7 '64
Of revels & reds. il Time 85:20 Ja 8 '65
Our man in Saigon; with introd. by D. Schoenbrun. G. J. W. Goodman. il Esquire 61:57-60+ Ja '64
Our options in Vietnam. B. B. Fall. il Reporter 30:17-22 Mr 12 '64
Papering it over; continuing political war. il Time 85:26 Ja 15 '65
Paris exiles: Vietnamese political exiles. H. B. Lamb. il Nation 197:65-8 Ag 10 '63
Pause in the war. Time 83:23 Je 19 '64
Saigon exodus. America 111:445 O 17 '64
Search for answers; visit of Secretary McNamara and General Taylor. il Time 82:48 O 4 '63
Secretary McNamara reports on situation in Viet-Nam. R. S. McNamara. Dept State Bul 50:46 Ja 13 '64
Slow train through Viet Nam's war. H. Sochurek. il Nat Geog Mag 126:412-44 S '64
South Viet Nam; new phase. il Time 84:29 S 11 '64
Stake in Viet Nam; address, April 22, 1963; with questions and answers. D. Rusk. Dept State Bul 48:727-35 My 13 '63; Same. Vital Speeches 29:493-7 Je 1 '63
Suggestions, anyone? il Time 84:36+ O 23 '64
Talk with Ho Chi Minh. B. B. Fall. New Repub 149:19-22 O 12 '63
United States assessing reports on conditions in Viet Nam; Department statements, August 21 and August 23, 1963. Dept State Bul 49:398 S 9 '63
Vietnam, basic elements; photographs. N Y Times Mag p 16-17 N 10 '63
Vietnamese speaks out. N. Thai. New Repub 148:14-17 Je 8 '63
Vietnam's story, and our growing role. il N Y Times Mag p 12-13 F 9 '64
War in Vietnam. W. V. Kennedy. America 109:504 N 2 '63
War in Vietnam, Luce version. W. H. Hunter. New Repub 148:15-17 Mr 23 '63
Week that was. il Newsweek 64:31 D 28 '64
When the rains come to Vietnam. N. Sheehan. il N Y Times Mag p 12-13+ Je 14 '64

See also

Aeronautics, Military—Viet Nam (Republic)
Americans in Viet Nam
Catholic church in Viet Nam (Republic)
Catholics in Viet Nam (Republic)
Censorship—Viet Nam (Republic)
Communism—Viet Nam (Republic)
Economic assistance in Viet Nam (Republic)
Forests and forestry—Viet Nam (Republic)
Guerrillas—Viet Nam (Republic)
Hoaimy
Newspapers—Viet Nam (Republic)
Public health—Viet Nam (Republic)
Railroads—Viet Nam (Republic)
Saigon
United Nations—Viet Nam (Republic)
United States—Armed forces—Forces in Viet Nam (Republic)
Vietnamese crisis, 1964
Women—Viet Nam (Republic)

Air force

USAF pushes Vietnamese pilot training. L. Booda. il Aviation W 80:94-5+ Ap 20 '64

Armed forces

Back of the revolt in South Vietnam. il U S News 55:41 N 11 '63
DOD, industry facing Vietnam challenge. L. Booda. il Aviation W 80:93-5+ Ap 13 '64
On top of old Ap Bac. Newsweek 61:48 Ap 15 '63
Setback in Vietnam; defeat at Ap Bac. H. G. Fairbanks. Commonweal 77:593-5 Mr 1 '63
Toward the showdown? il Time 84:23-7 Ag 7 '64
Who is the real enemy in Vietnam? il U S News 56:33-5 Je 1 '64

Army

Changeover in Viet Nam. il Sr Schol 83:20-1 D 6 '63
Close-up of the Vietcong in their jungle. G. Penchenier. il N Y Times Mag p27+ S 13 '64
Elusive Viet Cong. J. A. Rose. New Repub 148:19-26 My 4 '63
End of the glow. il Time 82:32 D 13 '63
Errors in training? teaching culture while reds fight in mud. il U S News 57:59 S 14 '64
Fall of the House of Ngo; with report by Beverly Deepe. il Newsweek 62:27-31 N 11 '63
Is the U.S. better off after Vietnam coup? il Bsns W p31-2 N 9 '63
Letter from Saigon; coup d'etat. R. Shaplen. il New Yorker 39:201-4+ D 14 '63; 40:37-8+ Jl 11 '64
Old question: unwilling or unable to fight? Newsweek 63:32 My 4 '64
Portrait of two soldiers: the Vietnamese; the Vietcong. D. Halberstam. il N Y Times Mag p 11-12 Ja 5 '64
Report on the war. il Time 82:32-3 S 20 '63
Tale of two wars. Time 82:35-6 N 1 '63
Vietnam: what now? New Repub 151:3-4 D 5 '64
Vietnam's two wars; with interview with Gen. Dinh. S. Castan. il Look 28:32+ Ja 28 '64
War being lost because an ally won't fight? interview. J. P. Vann. il U S News 55:39-41 S 16 '63
What happens next to the war in Vietnam. R. P. Martin. il U S News 55:47-9 N 18 '63
Why U.S. is losing in Vietnam, an inside story; interview. S. T. Williams. il U S News 57:62-4+ N 9 '64
With army in charge, war speeds up in Vietnam. R. P. Martin. il U S News 55:51-2 N 25 '63

Boundaries

Security council team to examine Cambodia-Viet-Nam border areas; statement, June 4, 1964; with text of resolution. A. E. Stevenson. Dept State Bul 50:1002-4 Je 29 '64
U.S. calls for frontier patrol to help prevent border incidents between Cambodia and Viet-Nam; statement, May 21, 1964. A. E. Stevenson. bibliog f Dept State Bul 50:907-13 Je 8 '64

Defenses

American special forces in action in Viet Nam. H. Sochurek. il Nat Geog Mag 127:38-65 Ja '65
American tragedy in Vietnam: why GI's die but can't win; with analysis by M. S. Johnson. il U S News 56:40-2 My 11 '64
Atlantic report. Atlan 213:24+ Ap '64
Brief glimmer; Viet Cong launch major assault on Binh Dinh Province. Newsweek 64:41 D 21 '64
Bugle's blare. il Newsweek 62:58+ D 9 '63
Burning fuse. R. Hotz. Aviation W 81:11 Jl 27 '64
Can the war in Vietnam be won? il Newsweek 63:15-16 Mr 9 '64
Can U.S. win in Vietnam? an inside report; interview. S. W. Sanders. il U S News 58:44-7+ Ja 11 '65
Cloud behind the silver lining. F. Sully. il Newsweek 65:34-5 Ja 11 '65
DOD, industry facing Vietnam challenge. L. Booda. il Aviation W 80:93-5+ Ap 13 '64
Drifting toward debacle. il Newsweek 63:44 F 17 '64
Escalating war. R. Hotz. Aviation W 81:11 Jl 20 '64
Eyewitness in South Vietnam; where Americans are fighting: close-up of the shadow war. R. P. Martin. il U S News 56:36-9 Je 1 '64
Faces on the fighting front. il Newsweek 63:30+ Je 8 '64
For better or for worse? Newsweek 63:31-2 Je 29 '64
How much for a million? Operation brushfire. R. K. McCabe. il Newsweek 64:57 N 30 '64

VIET NAM (Republic) —Defenses—*Continued*
I fought in Vietnam; interview. R. L. Moore, jr. il U S News 56:40-7 Je 8 '64
Last chance in the Delta. D. Warner. il Reporter 30:31-4 Ap 9 '64
Let there be light; flare-dropping mission. F. Sully. il Newsweek 64:41 Jl 13 '64
Lions against tigers; battle at Kien Long. Newsweek 63:40 Ap 27 '64
Little Pearl Harbor in Vietnam. il U S News 57:88 N 16 '64
Military man sizes up a war U.S. is losing. M. S. Johnson. il U S News 56:40-1 Mr 16 '64
Minh's move. il Newsweek 63:38+ Ja 27 '64
More of the same; McNamara in Saigon. il Newsweek 63:46+ Mr 23 '64
New turn in a fifteen-year war: the real story of Vietnam. il U S News 56:50-2 Mr 23 '64
No place to hide? il Newsweek 63:39-40 F 3 '64
One man's meat; use of toxic gases. New Repub 148:5 Mr 23 '63
Opening a new front in Vietnam. S. W. Sanders. il U S News 57:26-8 Ag 17 '64
Optimism at Honolulu, problems in Saigon. il Time 82:40 N 29 '63
Our options in Vietnam. B. B. Fall. il Reporter 30:17-22 Mr 12 '64
Over the border. Nation 198:405 Ap 27 '64
Pathet Lao tip the balance. il Newsweek 63:28-30 Je 1 '64
Pressure from the North. Newsweek 64:40-1 Jl 27 '64
South Vietnamese raiders extending war. L. Booda. il Aviation W 80:16-19 Ap 6 '64
Taking the offensive. il Newsweek 64:34 Jl 6 '64
Taylor tries a new start in Vietnam. P. Grose. il N Y Times Mag p 12-13+ Ag 9 '64
Ten miles from town; growing boldness of the Viet Cong. il Newsweek 63:58 Ap 20 '64
This is our enemy; Vietcong guerrilla. S. Karnow. il Sat Eve Post 237:19-25 Ag 22 '64
True story of war in Vietnam. R. L. Moore, jr. il U S News 56:38-41 My 18 '64
Ugliest American in Vietnam. D. Halberstam. il Esquire 62:114-17+ N '64
U.S. bombers are blasted in Vietnam; Bien Hoa airbase. J. Flynn. il Life 57:50-1 N 13 '64
United States policy in Viet-Nam; address, March 26, 1964. R. S. McNamara. Dept State Bul 50:562-70 Ap 13 '64; Same. Vital Speeches 30:394-9 Ap 15 '64
U.S. to increase economic and military aid to Viet-Nam; White House statement, March 17, 1964. Dept State Bul 50:522-3 Ap 6 '64
Vietnam: can the reds be beaten? il Newsweek 63:25 Ja 6 '64
Vietnam: General Taylor faces an all-out war. D. Warner. Reporter 31:50+ Ag 13 '64
Vietnam: go north? S. Alsop. il Sat Eve Post 237:10 Je 20 '64
Vietnam: in the French footsteps. J. Kapstein. il Nation 199:479-82 D 21 '64
Viet-Nam situation; address, August 25, 1963. T. J. C. Heavner. Dept State Bul 49:393-8 S 9 '63
Vietnam: the awful choice. D. Warner. Reporter 30:26-8 F 27 '64
Vietnam victory in three years? U S News 54:16 F 11 '63
Vietnam: will history repeat itself? il Newsweek 63:39+ My 18 '64
War heats up. Time 82:42 D 6 '63
War in Vietnam: real last chance. F. Sully. il Newsweek 63:20 F 10 '64
What Diem thinks about the war in Vietnam. il U S News 55:46-7 Ag 19 '63
Year of the dragon. il Newsweek 63:45-6 F 24 '64

Economic conditions

Vietnam: test case for massive U.S. aid. il Bsns W p82-3+ S 28 '63

Foreign relations

American way of death. Nat R 15:424-5 N 19 '63
Collision course in Vietnam, U.S. vs. an unruly ally; with excerpts from interview with Mme Nhu. R. P. Martin. il U S News 55:36-8 S 16 '63
Madame Nhu's mission. K. Crawford. Newsweek 62:26 O 28 '63
Vietnam: war and feud get hotter. il U S News 55:4 S 23 '63
Wary warmth. il Time 85:22-3 Ja 22 '65
What de Gaulle actually said about Vietnam. B. Fall. Reporter 29:39-41 O 24 '63; Reply with rejoinder. C. Wolf, jr. 29:6+ D 19 '63
What Diem thinks about the war in Vietnam. il U S News 55:46-7 Ag 19 '63
Who killed Diem and why? V. L. Borin. il Nat R 16:441-6 Je 2 '64

History

New faces, more chaos. B. B. Fall. il Nation 197:380-2 D 7 '63
South Viet Nam: birth at Geneva. Time 82:34 S 20 '63
Victory; will it unsnarl the past? il Life 55:40-1 N 15 '63

Politics and government

Agony in Saigon: the lady & the cadaver. D. Warner. Reporter 29:39-42 O 10 '63
Anarchy & agony. il Time 84:33-4 S 4 '64
Atlantic report. Atlan 212:22+ D '63; 213:24+ Ap '64
Back of the revolt in South Vietnam. il U S News 55:41 N 11 '63
Buddhist revolt; Diem's new opponents deserve US support. E. Wulff. New Repub 149:11-14 Ag 31 '63
Buddhist way in Vietnam. J. Langguth. il N Y Times Mag p29+ O 11 '64
Buried report; concerning UN fact-finding mission's investigation. Nat R 16:98 F 11 '64
Can U.S. win in Vietnam? an inside report; interview. S. W. Sanders. il U S News 58:44-7+ Ja 11 '65
Challenge to freedom in Asia; address, June 14, 1963. R. W. Hilsman. Dept State Bul 49:43-50 Jl 8 '63
Changeover in Viet Nam. il Sr Schol 83:20-1 D 6 '63
Collision course in Vietnam, U.S. vs. an unruly ally; with excerpts from interview with Mme Nhu. R. P. Martin. il U S News 55:36-8 S 16 '63
Continued progress; coup against Premier Nguyen Khanh. il Time 84:39 S 18 '64
Coping with Capricorn. il Time 82:19-20 S 6 '63
Coup in South Viet Nam. il Sr Schol 83:18 N 15 '63
Coup no. two. Time 83:31 F 7 '64
Crackdown. il Time 82:18-20 Ag 30 '63
Crazy coup; events of September 13th and 14th. Newsweek 64:41-2 S 28 '64
Death in the delta, intrigue in the cafés. Time 83:46 Ap 17 '64
Deeper and deeper. Nation 199:81-2 S 7 '64
Dictatorial regime; Khanh promoted to president; Buddhists again threaten trouble. il Time 84:26-7 Ag 28 '64
Dilemma of Diem-ocracy. il Sr Schol 83:10-13+ S 20 '63
Dispensable Diem. New Repub 148:3-4 Ap 20 '63
Double trouble? Sr Schol 85:30 S 23 '64
Down, down, down. Time 84:50 N 13 '64
Dragon strikes. Newsweek 63:37-8 Ja 20 '64
Drifting toward debacle. il Newsweek 63:44 F 17 '64
Edge of chaos. S. Karnow. il Sat Eve Post 236:27-37 S 28 '63
End of the play. Nation 199:261 O 26 '64
Endless circles. il Time 84:35 O 9 '64
Fall of the House of Ngo dinh. S. Karnow. il Sat Eve Post 236:75-9 D 21 '63
Fall of the House of Ngo; with report by Beverly Deepe. il Newsweek 62:27-31 N 11 '63
First-half report. il Newsweek 64:37 Ag 10 '64
General Khanh's ailment. Nation 199:101-2 S 14 '64
Government built on sand. R. McCabe and F. Sully. il Newsweek 65:30-2 Ja 18 '65
Governments come, go; but Vietnam war rolls on. il U S News 56:49 F 10 '64
Great emancipator: amnesty for Communist Viet Cong guerrillas. Time 81:30-1 Ap 26 '63
Growing troubles for the Diem regime. il U S News 55:22 Jl 29 '63
Hard choice for the U.S.; get tough or get out. R. P. Martin. il U S News 55:54-7 S 9 '63
Hopes fade for South Vietnam. Bsns W p29 Ag 29 '64
How the world's hottest spot looks to me. H. C. Lodge. il Life 56:38D-38F Ap 17 '64
How to beat the reds in southeast Asia; interview, ed. by S. W. Sanders. Ngo Dinh-Diem. il U S News 54:70-3 F 18 '63
In Asia's hot war: more trouble for U.S. il U S News 55:58 S 2 '63
Intrigue in Saigon. il Newsweek 63:42 Je 15 '64
Is a deal near with Vietnam reds? U S News 58:6 Ja 25 '65

VIET NAM (Republic) —Politics and government—*Continued*
Is it a lost war for U.S. in Vietnam? with report by R. P. Martin. il U S News 57:55-7 S 7 '64
Is the U.S. better off after Vietnam coup? il Bsns W p31-2 N 9 '63
Is there a way out for U.S. in Vietnam? il U S News 56:42-4 F 17 '64
Lady is for burning: the seven deadly sins of Madame Nhu. C. B. Luce. il Nat R 15:395-9 N 5 '63
Laos and Viet-Nam, a prescription for peace; address, May 22, 1964. D. Rusk. Dept State Bul 50:886-91 Je 8 '64; Same, with title International agreements. Vital Speeches 30:546-9 Jl 1 '64
Left hand, right hand. il Newsweek 63:30 Mr 30 '64
Letter from Saigon; coup d'etat. R. Shaplen. il New Yorker 39:201-4+ D 14 '63; 40:37-8+ Jl 11; 179-86+ S 19 '64
Making martyrs; public execution of Viet Cong terrorist, Nguyen Van Troi. il Newsweek 64:60 O 26 '64
National unity and stepped-up war. il Time 83:29 F 14 '64
New coup, old crisis: Maxwell Taylor on the spot; with report by E. Weintal. il Newsweek 64:43-5+ S 21 '64
Ngomanship at home and abroad. il Newsweek 62:39-40 S 23 '63
On paper; projected parliamentary democracy. il Newsweek 64:59 N 2 '64
Once again: no-win. Nat R 15:467-9 D 3 '63
1,002nd way; efforts to restore a greater measure of civilian government in South Viet Nam. il Time 85:15 Ja 8 '65
Out of the frying pan. il Newsweek 65:34+ F 1 '65
Power play. il Newsweek 64:34 Ag 31 '64
President discusses Viet-Nam on CBS and NBC news programs; September 2 and September 9, 1963. J. F. Kennedy. Dept State Bul 49:498-500 S 30 '63
President Johnson holds high-level review of Viet-Nam questions. L. B. Johnson; M. D. Taylor; H. C. Lodge. Dept State Bul 51:432-5 S 28 '64
Problem in Vietnam: what can be saved. il U S News 57:55 S 28 '64
Queen bee. il Time 82:21-5 Ag 9 '63
Quiet but not calm. il Newsweek 64:51-2 O 19 '64
Quiet coup: and now General Khanh. il Newsweek 63:33-4 F 10 '64
Real trouble in Vietnam. il U S News 57:46 D 14 '64
Recent events in South Vietnam; address, November 4, 1963. C. J. Zablocki. Vital Speeches 30:133-4 D 15 '63
Remaking a revolution. Time 84:28 S 25 '64
Reprise from the pagodas. il Time 84:38 D 4 '64
Revolution in the afternoon. il Time 82:28-32 N 8 '63
Road to freedom for South Vietnam. Nat R 15:177-9 S 10 '63
Saigon coup. America 109:624-5 N 16 '63
Saigon: crucial hour? il Newsweek 64:22+ Ag 17 '64
Saigon summary. M. Higgins. America 110:18-21 Ja 4 '64
Saigon 23126 doesn't answer; coup that overthrew and killed President Ngo dinh Diem. il Time 82:41-2 N 15 '63
Saigon's mood is a mixture of euphoria and disquiet. New Repub 149:4 N 16 '63
Second coup. Sr Schol 84:6 F 14 '64
Secretary Rusk's news conference of September 14, 1964. D. Rusk. Dept State Bul 51:468-72 O 5 '64
Seventeen hours that destroyed Diem. il Life 55:34-43 N 15 63
Showdown in South Vietnam. il U S News 58:35 Ja 4 '65
Showdown in Vietnam; all-out fight ahead? il Bsns W p28-9 F 8 '64
Smiles and confusion in Vietnam. il Bsns W p50+ N 23 '63
South Viet Nam: the new regime. il Time 82:40 N 15 '63
Strange war the U.S. is not winning. R. P. Martin. il U S News 55:48-50 S 30 '63
Symbolic suicide; Nguyen Tuong Tam. Newsweek 62:43-4 Jl 22 '63
Tangle in Vietnam. America 109:284 S 21 '63
Tiger by the tail; charges of anti-Buddhist discrimination. America 109:207-8 Ag 31 '63
Time for a change? il Newsweek 64:50 O 12 '64
Time for Diem to mend ways. Life 55:4 Jl 26 '63
Top man in Vietnam: General Khanh grabs power. U S News 56:12 F 10 '64
Tough U.S. envoy moves in on the Vietnamese mess. il Life 55:30B-30C S 6 '63
True story of war in Vietnam. R. L. Moore, jr. il U S News 56:38-41 My 18 '64
Two months' respite; Khanh government's new look. il Newsweek 64:32-3 S 14 '64
Uncertain prospect for Vietnam. Commonweal 79:212 N 15 '63
U.S. and Viet-Nam plan measures to improve situation in Viet-Nam; text of a communique issued by the government of Viet-Nam, December 11, 1964. Dept State Bul 51:904-5 D 28 '64
United States policy in Viet-Nam; address, March 26, 1964. R. S. McNamara. Dept State Bul 50:562-70 Ap 13 '64; Same. Vital Speeches 30:394-9 Ap 15 '64; Excerpts. U S News 56:10 Ap 6 '64
U.S. re-examines Viet policy. il Sr Schol 83:18 O 18 '63
U.S. v. the generals. il Time 85:32-3 Ja 1 '65
Vietnam: a box for U.S. policy. Bsns W p25-6 S 21 '63
Vietnam: a dynasty in disorder. D. Warner. Reporter 29:34+ S 12 '63
Vietnam: descent into desperation. F. Sully. il Newsweek 64:33-4 S 7 '64
Vietnam: getting to know the Nhus. il Newsweek 62:33-4+ S 9 '63
Viet Nam: in double jeopardy? il Sr Schol 85:13-17 D 2 '64
Vietnam: in the French footsteps. J. Kapstein. il Nation 199:479-82 D 21 '64
Vietnam: land without laughter. T. E. Ennis. il Cur Hist 46:101-6 F '64
Vietnam: new star. New Repub 149:3 N 16 '63
Vietnam: odds lengthen. il Newsweek 64:81 O 5 '64
Vietnam repression. Commonweal 78:524-5 S 6 '63
Vietnam, resistance or withdrawal? O. Gass. bibliog f Commentary 37:37-45 My '64; Reply. B. B. Fall. 38:6+ S '64
Viet-Nam situation; address, August 25, 1963. T. J. C. Heavner. Dept State Bul 49:393-8 S 9 '63
Vietnam: the awful choice. D. Warner. Reporter 30:26-8 F 27 '64
Vietnam: wary eye on General Khanh. il Newsweek 64:29 Ag 3 '64
Vietnam: where will it all end? Newsweek 65:11-12 Ja 4 '65
Vietnam's militant Buddhists. D. Warner. il Reporter 31:29-31 D 3 '64
Vietnam's two battles. il N Y Times Mag p8-9 Jl 28 '63
Vietnam's two wars; with interview with Gen. Dinh. S. Castan. il Look 28:32+ Ja 28 '64
War being lost because an ally won't fight? interview. J. P. Vann. il U S News 55:39-41 S 16 '63
War in the pagodas: who is the enemy? il Newsweek 62:35-6+ S 2 '63
What chance in Vietnam? J. Burnham. Nat R 15:304 O 8 '63
What comes next in Vietnam? T. Minh. New Repub 151:7-8 S 12 '64
What Diem thinks about the war in Vietnam. il U S News 55:46-7 Ag 19 '63
What happens next to the war in Vietnam. R. P. Martin. il U S News 55:47-9 N 18 '63
What's really going on in Vietnam. Ngo-dinh-Thuc. il Nat R 15:388-90 N 5 '63
Who killed Diem and why? V. L. Borin. il Nat R 16:441-6 Je 2 '64
Who really runs South Vietnam? U S News 55:13 S 2 '63
Who's at the helm? Newsweek 62:28+ D 23 '63
Who's on top? il Newsweek 64:52+ N 9 '64
Why U.S. is losing in Vietnam, an inside story; interview. S. T. Williams. il U S News 57:62-4+ N 9 '64
With a little bit of luck; provisional constitution. Time 84:40 O 30 '64
Young tigers, and cautious optimism. il Newsweek 62:41-2 N 18 '63

Relief work

To clear & to hold; American AID men in South Viet Nam. E. Pace. il Time 83:21 Mr 27 '64

Religious institutions and affairs

Again, the Buddhists in South Viet Nam. il Time 83:27-8 Je 5 '64
Again Thich Tri Quang. America 110:784 Je 6 '64
Angry Buddhist burns himself alive. il Life 54:24-5 Je 21 '63
Beat them; Buddhist campaign no longer a dispute over religious toleration. il Newsweek 62:46 Ag 19 '63
Behind the Buddhist unrest in southeast Asia. N. F. Busch. Read Digest 83:94-9 D '63
Buddhist crisis. il Time 82:24-6 Jl 26 '63

VIET NAM (Republic) —Religious institutions and affairs—*Continued*
Buddhists fight Diem with sit-downs and suicides. il Life 55:24-5 Ag 2 '63
Buried report; concerning UN fact-finding mission's investigation. Nat R 16:98 F 11 '64
Condemn religious tyranny in South Vietnam. Christian Cent 80:900 Jl 17 '63
Crackdown. il Time 82:18-20 Ag 30 '63
Death v. the family; second Buddhist priest to burn himself to death. Time 82:23 Ag 16 '63
Diem and the Buddhists. H. G. Fairbanks. Commonweal 78:452-4 Jl 26 '63
Diem rebuked; dispute with the nation's Buddhist majority. America 108:895 Je 29 '63
Diem, the mandarin. America 109:111-12 Ag 3 '63
Diem under pressure. il Newsweek 62:48 Jl 29 '63
Diem's other crusade: against Vietnamese Buddhists. New Repub 148:5-6 Je 22 '63
Dilemma of Diem-ocracy. il Sr Schol 83:10-13+ S 20 '63
Execution in Saigon and Vietnam's Catholics. America 110:698+ My 23 '64
Exploding power of the Buddhists. il Life 57:34-41 D 11 '64
Facts, please. America 109:38-9 Jl 13 '63
Fiery protest: self-sacrifice of Thich Quang Duc. il Newsweek 61:63 Je 24 '63
Flames & music. il Time 82:41 O 11 '63
Folly in Vietnam. Commonweal 78:364-5 Je 28 '63
Hard choice for the U.S; get tough or get out. R. P. Martin. il U S News 55:54-7 S 9 '63
Heart of Quang Duc. il Time 82:33 Jl 5 '63
Job on Diem; Buddhist campaign on the issue of religion. America 110:758 My 30 '64
Lady is for burning: the seven deadly sins of Madame Nhu. C. B. Luce. il Nat R 15:395-9 N 5 '63
Letter from Saigon. R. Shaplen. il New Yorker 39:201-4+ D 14 '63
New war in Vietnam; flying of a religious flag. America 108:849 Je 15 '63
Poetic justice in Vietnam? America 110:837 Je 20 '64
Pressure on Diem and on the UN. America 109:544 N 9 '63
Protest in Saigon; archbishop charges harassment of Catholics. America 110:862 Je 27 '64
Queen bee. il Time 82:21-5 Ag 9 '63
Religious crisis. il Time 81:35-6 Je 14 '63
Religious liberty: Buddhist protests and Catholic principles. J. B. Sheerin. Cath World 197:339-40 S '63
Reporting from Saigon; possible political motivation behind the Buddhist anti-government campaign. America 109:152 Ag 17 '63
Road to freedom for South Vietnam. Nat R 15:177-9 S 10 '63
Saigon in perspective. America 109:126 Ag 10 '63
Saigon summary. M. Higgins. America 110:18-21 Ja 4 '64
Same old Diem; anti-Buddhist measures. Nation 196:538 Je 29 '63
17,358 clergymen are half right; Ministers' Vietnam committee. Christian Cent 80:1161-2 S 25 '63; Discussion. 80:1445-6 N 20 '63
Since the Vietnam coup. America 109:695 N 30 '63
South Vietnam: whose funeral pyre? tensions between the Buddhist majority and the Catholic minority. New Repub 148:9 Je 29 '63
Suicide series; South Viet Nam. il Time 82:28 Ag 23 '63
Terror in Vietnam; South Vietnam faces an explosion of religious persecution. America 109:757 D 14 '63
Tiger by the tail; charges of anti-Buddhist discrimination. America 109:207-8 Ag 31 '63
Trial by fire; self-sacrifice of monk, Thich Quang Duc. il Time 81:32 Je 21 '63
Two views of Vietnam. America 109:223 S 7 '63
UN's unfinished business; fact-finding mission on charges of religious persecution in South Vietnam. America 110:136 Ja 25 '64
U.S. may pull rug from under Diem. il Bsns W p22 Ag 31 '63
Vietnam: a dynasty in disorder. D. Warner. Reporter 29:34+ S 12 '63
Vietnam controversy. Commonweal 78:444-5 Jl 26 '63
Vietnam controversy. P. O'Connor. Commonweal 78:537-8 S 6 '63
Vietnam crisis is religious. Christian Cent 80:1093 S 11 '63
Vietnam dilemma. V. S. Kearney; F. J. Buckley. America 109:237-40 S 7 '63
Vietnam: land without laughter. T. E. Ennis. il Cur Hist 46:101-6 F '64
Vietnam repression. Commonweal 78:524-5 S 6 '63
Vietnam's future: all bets are off. il Newsweek 62:35-6 Ag 26 '63
Vietnam's militant Buddhists. D. Warner. il Reporter 31:29-31 D 3 '64
Vietnam's two wars; with interview with Gen. Dinh. S. Castan. il Look 28:32+ Ja 28 '64
War in the pagodas: who is the enemy? il Newsweek 62:35-6+ S 2 '63
What's really going on in Vietnam. Ngo-dinh-Thuc. il Nat R 15:388-90 N 5 '63
When a monk became a human torch; What U.S. has at stake. il U S News 54:8 Je 24 '63
See also
Buddha and Buddhism
Catholic church in Viet Nam

Riots

As Vietnam troops watched: I saw hooligans pillage a town. S. W. Sanders. il U S News 57:57-8 S 7 '64

VIETNAM. See Viet Nam (Republic)

VIETNAMESE
I'm hit! I'm hit! I'm hit! with editorial comment. J. A. Rose. il Sat Eve Post 236:34-47, 84 Mr 23 '63
Miracle at Hoaimy. il Time 83:26 My 1 '64
Smiles and confusion in Vietnam. il Bsns W p50+ N 23 '63
Suicide in many forms. Time 82:32+ Jl 19 '63
Vietcong's shadow government in the South. P. Grose. il N Y Times Mag p 10-11+ Ja 24 '65
When the rains come to Vietnam. N. Sheehan. il N Y Times Mag p 12-13+ Je 14 '64
Who's who in Vietnam? the montagnards. B. B. Fall. il New Repub 151:10-12 O 17 '64

VIETNAMESE crisis, 1964
Aboard the Maddox. B. Wise. il Life 57:21 Ag 14 '64
Action in Tonkin Gulf. il Time 84:11-16 Ag 14 '64
After the show of force: still a losing war in Vietnam; with report by S. W. Sanders. il U S News 57:31-3 Ag 24 '64
Assistant Secretary Bundy comments on southeast Asia developments in Voice of America interview; ed. by W. McCrory. W. P. Bundy. Dept State Bul 51:334-9 S 7 '64
Back to normal. R. K. McCabe. il Newsweek 64:38-9 Ag 24 '64
Bigger war for U.S. in Asia? with reports by Robert P. Martin and others. il U S News 57:21-5 Ag 17 '64
Firm stand in Vietnam. il Bsns W p23-4 Ag 15 '64
Letter from Washington. R. H. Rovere. New Yorker 40:101-7+ Ag 22 '64
New incident off Asia, three versions. il U S News 57:16 O 5 '64
Protracted conflict: note on the Bay of Tonkin. Nat R 16:709 Ag 25 '64
Scary pageant in Peking; anti-U.S. demonstration; with photographs by P. Boulat. N. Liber. il Life 57:54-61 S 4 '64
Shortening the fuse. Nation 199:61 Ag 24 '64
Shots in the dark; incidents in the Gulf of Tonkin. Time 84:43B O 2 '64
Showdown in Asia; U.S. not afraid to fight. il Bsns W p 15-17 Ag 8 '64
Table; between urgent meetings of United Nations security council. New Yorker 40:19-20 Ag 15 '64
Tonkin gulf mystery. Nat R 16:799 S 22 '64
Tonkin Gulf: round II. Nation 199:177 O 5 '64
Under fire: timing of raid announcement. U S News 57:8+ Ag 24 '64
U.S. and Brazil reaffirm commitment to peace; exchange of letters. H. Castelo Branco; L. B. Johnson. Dept State Bul 51:435-6 S 28 '64
United States complaint. UN Mo Chron 1:18-24 Ag '64
United States takes measures to repel attack against U.S. forces in southeast Asia; U.S. protest to North Viet Nam; with statement, addresses and message to Congress by the President, statements by Secretary Rusk and Secretary McNamara, and text of joint resolution, August 3-7, 1964. bibliog f Dept State Bul 51:258-68 Ag 24 '64
Unmeasured response. New Repub 151:3-4 Ag 22 '64
Vanishing margins in Vietnam. C. J. V. Murphy. Fortune 70:110 S '64

VIETNAMESE crisis, 1964—*Continued*
Vietnam. Cato. Nat R 16:716 Ag 25 '64
Vietnam: build-up on a hot border. il Life 57: 26-31 Ag 21 '64
Vietnam: we seek no wider war. il Newsweek 64:17-22 Ag 17 '64
Yep, we were there. Time 84:28-9 O 9 '64
VIETNAMESE soldiers. See Viet Nam (Republic)—Army
VIETNAMESE students in France. See Foreign students in France
VIEW finders
Are RFDR viewfinders accurate? B. Sherman. il Mod Phot 27:70-1+ My '63
Fight against rangefinder parallax. L. A. Mannheim. il Mod Phot 28:98+ My '64
Focusing systems for SLRs. G. Gilbert. il U S Camera 27:42-3+ D '64
It's how you look at it; SLR viewfinders B. Sherman and H. Keppler. il Mod Phot 28:74-5 Mr '64
Rangefinder pro hints and tips. E. Meyers and D. Miller. il Mod Phot 27:72-3 My '63
Twin lens; sportsfinder. F. Henle. il Pop Phot 53:56 N '63
Which viewing system for you? J. Foldes. il U S Camera 27:66-9 F '64
VIEWERS, Infrared
Snooperscope television. il Time 81:75 Ap 19 '63
VIEWPORTS, Space vehicle. See Space vehicles—Viewports
VIGÉE-LEBRUN, Marie Louise Elisabeth
Museum evaluations. A. Frankfurter. il Art N 63:26+ Ja '65
VIGILANCE committees
Still with us. Commonweal 79:495-6 Ja 31 '64
VIGILANTES. See Vigilance committees
VIGUERS, Ruth Hill
Big four speak. por Library J 88:2072-3+ My 15 '63
New children's books. Harper 227:118+ D '63
—and others
Booklist (title varies) See issues of Horn book magazine
VIKING (football club) See Football clubs
VIKING press, Incorporated
Viking press expands children's book department. il Pub W 186:34 O 12 '64
VIKINGS
Columbus wasn't first; Viking ruins L'Anse aux Meadows, Newfoundland. il Sci Digest 55:77-80 F '64
Did Vikings get here first, after all? il U S News 55:10 N 18 '63
Tiny object, big find; soapstone wheel found at L'Anse aux Meadows, Newfoundland. il Sci Digest 56:36 N '64
Viking settlement in America. Sci Am 210:56 Ja '64
Vinland ruins prove Vikings found the New World. H. Ingstad. il Nat Geog Mag 126: 708-34 N '64
VILA, George R.
After the battle in U.S. rubber's executive suite. W. J. Miller. il por Fortune 70:116-23+ D '64
VILCABAMBA, CORDILLERA
By parachute into Peru's lost world; 1963 Vilcabamba expedition. G. B. Baekeland. il Nat Geog Mag 126:268-96 Ag '64
VILCABAMBA, Peru
Lost city. il Time 84:36 Ag 28 '64
VILELLA, Roberto Sánchez. See Sánchez Vilella, R.
VILLA d'Este gardens. See Gardens—Italy
VILLAGE libraries. See Libraries
VILLAGE life
Town no scandal can shake. M. Gellhorn. Vogue 142:144-5+ N 15 '63
Visit to a Russian village. D. Whiteside. il N Y Times Mag p26-7+ D 8 '63
We moved to a small town. B. H. Campbell. il Redbook 122:20+ F '64
VILLAGE voice (newspaper)
Remember their names; Obie awards. Newsweek 63:69 Je 8 '64
VILLAGES
Love and authority; study of Mexican villagers. M. Maccoby. Atlan 213:121-6 Mr '64
Town no scandal can shake. M. Gellhorn. Vogue 142:144-5+ N 15 '63
VILLAGES, Restored
Pioneer village's tenth anniversary, still growing. Hobbies 68:52+ Jl '63
VILLAINS in literature. See Characters in literature
VILLARD, Henry S.
How to save money: an open letter to Congressman John J. Rooney. Harper 228: 17+ Ja '64
VILLAVERDE, Juan
Word with Pedro Calderón. Américas 15:38-9 Jl '63
VILLCHUR, Edgar
High fidelity measurements, science or chaos? Electr World 72:33-5+ Ag '64
Turntable testing at home. Electr World 69: 29-32+ Mr '63
What the consumer should know about record players. Am Rec G 30:4-8+ S '63
VILLEE, Claude A.
Initiation of labor. Science 144:82-4 Ap 3 '64
—See Moore, R. O. jt. auth.
VILLELLA, Edward
Essential instant. por Time 82:64 D 13 '63
Looking at television; appearance of E. Villella. A. Barzel. il por Dance Mag 37:24 Ap '63
VILLIARD, Paul
Multicolored world of caterpillars. il Natur Hist 73:24-31 Ap '64
Patterns in wood. Natur Hist 74:44-5 Ja '65
VILLIERS, Alan
Australia. Nat Geog Mag 124:309-85 S '63
Channel cruise to glorious Devon. il por Nat Geog Mag 124:208-59 Ag '63
Fabled Mount of St Michael. Nat Geog Mag 125:880-98 Je '64
If there were two ships, it was a race. Sports Illus 21:27-9 Jl 20 '64
Ships through the ages; a saga of the sea. il Nat Geog Mag 123:496-545 Ap '63
VILLON, François
Ballade of the ladies of time past, tr. by R. Wilbur. Poetry 105:81-2 N '64
Four poets and two dramatists. W. Fowlie. Poetry 104:187-8 Je '64
VILLON, Marcel Duchamp-. See Duchamp, M.
VILMORIN, Roger de
Squires at large. il por Esquire 62:80 Jl '64
VINAIGRETTE sauce. See Sauces
VINAIGRETTES
Vinaigrettes. E. Ellenbogen. il Antiques 83: 214-17 F '63
VINCENNES-Sèvres porcelain. See Sèvres porcelain
VINCENT, Clark E.
Family in health and illness; some neglected areas. bibliog f Ann Am Acad 346:109-16 Mr '63
Illegitimacy and value dilemmas. Christian Cent 80:801-4 Je 19 '63
VINCENT, G. Robert
Sounds of history; recorded voices of 8,000 celebrities in National voice library. W. B. Furlong. il N Y Times Mag p72+ Mr 22 '64
VINCENT, Geoffrey
Deadly point. N Y Times Mag p62+ Mr 15 '64
Different Africa. N Y Times Mag p90+ S 13 '64
For tidier time. N Y Times Mag p78-80+ Ja 12 '64
Take any number. N Y Times Mag p44+ O 13 '63
Thirty years ago. N Y Times Mag p45-6+ D 1 '63
VINCENT, John
New opera in Buenos Aires. Américas 16:35-8 O '64
VINCENT, Roy, Jr
Here a bear walked. Outdoor Life 132:60-1+ O '63
VINCENT, William S.
Federal aid for parochial and private schools. Sch & Soc 92:355-7 N 28 '64
VINCI, Leonardo da. See Leonardo da Vinci
VINDICATOR, Youngstown. See Youngstown vindicator
VINEGAR
Ways to flavor vinegars. il Sunset 133:131 Ag '64
VINES. See Climbing plants
VINING, Elizabeth Janet (Gray)
Past recaptured; address, November 10, 1962. Library J 88:826-7+ F 15 '63
VINING, Keith
Detroit goes back to the races. Pop Sci 182: 74-6+ F '63
Unsinkable Jonboat. Pop Sci 184:131-3+ F '64
(ed) See Allen, R. American kids can take it!
VINOGRADOV, Aleksandr P. See Rich, A. jt. auth.
VINSON, Carl
Back to Milledgeville. Cato. Nat R 16:762 S 8 '64
Fifty-year man. pors Newsweek 64:20 D 28 '64
Gentleman from Georgia goes home. J. Doolittle. il pors Sat Eve Post 237:26-8 D 5 '64
Georgia's Vinson: battling the Pentagon. por U S News 55:16 S 30 '63
Swamp Fox. por Time 82:18 Jl 26 '63

VINSON, Carlos
All about...ah...brim. por Outdoor Life 131:82-3+ Ap '63
Dirt on chucks. por Outdoor Life 133:46-7+ Je '64

VINSON, S. Bradleigh, and others
Resistance to DDT in the mosquito fish, gambusia affinis. bibliog Science 139:217-18 Ja 18 '63

VINYARD, Dale
Political profile of a university class. Sch & Soc 92:291-3 O 17 '64

VINYL fluoride
Film finish for buildings; Tedlar. Sci N L 83:148 Mr 9 '63

VIOLENCE
Civil rights: a movement in search of a decision? with comment on the world's news fronts. il Sr Schol 85:16-20 S 30 '64
Climate of violence. Nation 197:406-7 D 14 '63
Collective guilt in the U.S.? take a look at the world; with excerpts from address by T. B. Morton. il U S News 55:72-4 D 23 '63
Effects of observing violence. L. Berkowitz. il Sci Am 210:35-41 bibliog(p 152) F '64; Reply with rejoinder. P. Goodman. 210:8 Je '64
Law or violence? J. B. Sheerin. Cath World 199:333-6 S '64; Reply. F. D. Webber. 200:70 N '64
Let's stop scaring our children. M. J. E. Senn. McCalls 92:74+ O '64
Letter from Paris; violence in two great leading republics of the West: United States and France. Genêt. New Yorker 39:155 D 14 '63
Manchurian candidate in Dallas. R. Condon. Nation 197:449-51 D 28 '63
November 22: what did it mean? E. Roper. Sat R 47:28 My 9 '64
Of chaos and courage. J. Ciardi. Sat R 46:25 D 28 '63
Our streets of violence. R. Coles. New Repub 151:19-21 S 5 '64
Picture of violence; effect of filmed violence. il Newsweek 63:91 F 24 '64
Presidential victims. Sr Schol 83:14-15 D 6 '63
Prevalence of violence. J. Cogley. Commonweal 79:481-3 Ja 24 '64
Racial strife: a bloody summer ahead? U S News 56:10 Ap 27 '64
Special effects; violence witnessed on the screen. R. L. Shayon. Sat R 47:22 My 2 '64
Stormy continent: Africa. Sr Schol 84:16-17 Mr 13 '64
Summer of race violence on the way? il U S News 56:34-5 Ap 6 '64
Two faces of TV. Nation 198:43 Ja 13 '64
Unfinished comic crusade. America 109:759 D 14 '63
Uses of violence; outrageous treatment of the American Negro. Nation 197:2-3 Jl 6 '63
Victims. R. Childres. Harper 228:159-62 Ap '64
Violence around us; excerpts from But will it sell? M. Mannes. McCalls 91:74+ F '64
Violence in human behavior; AAAS Philadelphia meeting, December 1962. A. H. Rifkin. il Science 140:904-6 My 24 '63
Violence less rampant. Sci N L 85:307 My 16 '64
Violence pattern in U.S; Check violence threats. Sci N L 84:357 D 7 '63
We're teaching our children that violence is fun; closer look at toys, TV and movies. E. Merriam. Ladies Home J 81:44+ O '64
What are the odds against Castro now? il U S News 55:90-1 D 9 '63
Why murder is contagious; interview. F. Wertham. McCalls 91:136+ F '64
World resounds: Milwaukee; twin assassination in Dallas, Tex. Q. L. Quade. America 109:770 D 14 '63
See also
Mob violence
Terrorism

VIOLET season; story. See Dawkins, C.

VIOLETA; story. See Porter, K. A.

VIOLETS
Virtues of violets as a ground cover. E. L. Sculthorp. il House B 105:220+ S '63

VIOLETT, Ellen
Color of darkness; dramatization of works by J. Purdy. Criticism
New Yorker 39:91-2 O 12 '63
Theatre Arts 47:13 D '63

VIOLIN
Fifteen old violins. Discus. Harper 228:120-1 F '64
Music on a string. C. Marly; reply. K. Leonhardt. il UNESCO Courier 17:33 F '64

Construction

Music on a string. C. Marly; reply. K. Leonhardt. il UNESCO Courier 17:33 F '64

Instruction and study

Fiddling legions; Suzuki's child violinists. il Newsweek 63:73 Mr 23 '64
Warm; Russian violinists. New Yorker 38:25-6 F 2 '63

VIOLIN competitions. See Music—Competitions

VIOLIN making. See Violin—Construction

VIOLIN music
See also
Passacaglias (violin)
Phonograph records—Violin music

VIOLIN playing
Henryk Szeryng; interview, ed. by S. Fleming. H. Szeryng. Hi Fi 13:34+ Ap '63
Roll 'em up, hit 'em up a tune; National old-time fiddlers' contest. il Life 55:89-90 Jl 12 '63
See also
Scordatura
Violin—Instruction and study

VIOLINISTS
Return of the prodigy. il Time 85:49 Ja 15 '65

VIOLONCELLO music
See also
Phonograph records—Violoncello music

VIORST, Judith
Nuclear threat harms children. Sci N L 83:106-7 F 16 '63

VIORST, Milton
Crazy like an uncut excise tax. New Repub 151:10-11 Jl 11 '64
De Gaulle's remembrance of things past. New Repub 150:22-3+ Je 20 '64
GOP: can the moderates come back? Nation 199:217-19 O 12 '64
How medicare was lost this year. New Repub 151:6-7 O 17 '64
Johnson's campaign machinery. New Repub 151:9-10 S 5 '64
Man who thought of leaving politics. New Repub 151:8-9 Ag 8 '64
Political good fortune of medical research. Science 144:267-70 Ap 17 '64
Speaker vs. the hard-liners. Reporter 29:43-4 O 24 '63

VIPERS. See Snakes

VIRACTIN
Prevent common colds; experimental inhalant, viractin. F. Marley. Sci N L 86:355 D 5 '64

VIRAL nucleic acids. See Nucleic acids

VIRDEN, Helen
I recommend rock-sitting. Farm J 88:61 S '64

VIRGIN Mary. See Mary, Virgin

VIRGIN birth. See Mary, Virgin

VIRGIN ISLANDS
Restless Virgins; industrial growth. Time 82:104+ N 15 '63
Virgin Islands charter. B. Robinson. il Yachting 116:41+ N '64
See also
Colleges and universities—Virgin Islands
Fishing—Virgin Islands
St John Island
St Thomas Island

Description and travel

Camera guide to U.S. Virgin Islands. L. Barry. il Pop Phot 53:84-5+ O '63
No organized fun; a private cruise among the Virgin Islands. B. Astor. Vogue 145:114-15+ Ja 15 '65
Sparkling St Thomas. M. M. Davis. il Travel 120:28-31+ D '63
What hath Columbus wrought? B. Laschever. il Sat R 47:67-8+ O 10 '64

VIRGIN ISLANDS, BRITISH. See British Virgin Islands

VIRGINIA
See also
Fishing—Virginia
Gardens—Virginia
Geology—Virginia
Hunting—Virginia
Irrigation—Virginia
Prince Edward County
Roads—Virginia
Shenandoah National Park
Shenandoah Valley

Boundaries

Short time between drinks. Am Heritage 15:94 F '64

Description and travel

Chesapeake country. N. T. Kenney. il Nat Geog Mag 126:370-411 S '64
Leaving on that New River train. J. Walsh. il Hobbies 69:120-4 O '64

VIRGINIA—*Continued*

Historic houses, etc.

Eastern shore of Virginia. R. Pratt. il Ladies Home J 80:74-7 Ap '63
Fresh sense of the lovely past. R. Bailey. il House & Gard 126:176-81+ S '64
History along a U.S. byway; Virginia's Route 5. il Time 84:57-62 Jl 10 '64
Lee's birthplace. il Travel 121:47-9 F '64
Living with antiques; Shirley, Charles City County, Va. B. Snow. il Antiques 83:542-7 My '63
Living with antiques; Toddsbury. G. M. Moore. il Antiques 85:686-9 Je '64
See also
Mount Vernon, Va.

Parks and reserves

How Virginia preserves natural areas. J. J. Shomon. il Audubon Mag 65:106-7 Mr '63

Politics and government

Poor Richard's race; Republican challenge to Senator Harry F. Byrd. Reporter 31:12+ O 22 '64
Virginia comes home. New Repub 151:6 Ag 8 '64

Race problems

Prince Edward County situation. W. V. Heuvel. il NEA J 53:12+ Mr '64
Trip to Virginia. P. Romero. Negro Hist Bul 27:96+ Ja '64

Religious institutions and affairs

News of the Christian world (cont) Christian Cent 80:314+, 938; 81:1150+, 1475-6 Mr 6, Jl 24 '63, S 16, N 25 '64

Social life and customs

Rampart of pedigree. H. Horn. il Sports Illus 18:62-70 F 11 '63

VIRGINIA BEACH, Va.
600 more miles of road in six months. C. Teets. il Am City 79:107 O '64

VIRGINIA CAPES, Battle of the. See United States—History—Revolution—Naval operations

VIRGINIA education association
VEA desegregation move. Sr Schol 85:6T+ D 2 '64

VIRGINIA military institute, Lexington
Dedication of George C. Marshall research library; remarks, May 23, 1964. L. B. Johnson. Dept State Bul 50:922-4 Je 15 '64

VIRGINIA state college, Petersburg

Norfolk division

Second chance for ninety men in Norfolk. J. W. Canan. il Reporter 31:34-6 Jl 16 '64
Some of the problems in fighting poverty. il U S News 56:86-7 Je 8 '64

VIRGINIA teachers association
VEA desegregation move. Sr Schol 85:6T+ D 2 '64

VIRUS, Vaccine. See Vaccines

VIRUS diseases
Goodby to measles! box score on other viruses. il Life 54:85-6+ Ap 19 '63
Niles cluster. il Newsweek 61:88-9 Ap 22 '63
Scientists isolate virus of milker's nodules pox. Sci N L 84:24 Jl 13 '63
Virus diseases of childhood. L. W. Sauer. PTA Mag 58:33-4 My '64
See also
Psittacosis

Vaccines

Quickening war against viruses. M. Pines. Harper 228:90-2+ My '64

VIRUS diseases in animals
Virus infections in cold-blooded vertebrates; report on conference. K. Wolf. Science 146:1603-4 D 18 '64
See also
Cattle—Diseases and pests

VIRUS diseases in plants
See also
Viruses, Plant

VIRUSES
Adenovirus-like particles from cancers induced by adenovirus-12 but free of infectious virus. K. O. Smith and J. L. Melnick. bibliog il Science 145:1190-2 S 11 '64
Algal virus; isolation. R. S. Safferman and M. E. Morris. bibliog il Science 140:679-80 My 10 '63
Bacteria produce viruses. Sci N L 86:6 Jl 4 '64
Base composition of the RNA of a reovirus variant. P. J. Gomatos and I. Tamm. bibliog il Science 140:997-8 My 31 '63
Blue-green algal virus LPP-1: purification and partial characterization. I. R. Schneider and others. bibliog il Science 144:1127-9 My 29 '64
Cerebellar ataxia in hamsters inoculated with rat virus. L. Kilham and G. Margolis. bibliog il Science 143:1047-8 Mr 6 '64
Circulating interferon in mice after intravenous injection of virus. S. Baron and C. E. Buckler. bibliog il Science 141:1061-3 S 13 '63
Complement-fixing antigens in tissue cultures of avian leucosis viruses. D. Armstrong and others. bibliog il Science 144:1584 Je 26 '64
Complex epidemiology of respiratory virus infections. C. H. Andrewes. bibliog Science 146:1274-7 D 4 '64
Effects of polycyclic aromatic carcinogens on viral replication: similarity to actinomycin D. E. De Maeyer and J. De Maeyer-Guignard. bibliog il Science 146:650-1 O 30 '64
Enemies of the unborn. Time 82:100+ S 20 '63
Enzootic Sendai virus infections in mouse breeder colonies within United States. J. C. Parker and others. bibliog il Science 146:936-8 N 13 '64
Epizootic diarrhea of infant mice: identification of the etiologic agent. W. R. Adams and L. M. Kraft. bibliog il Science 141:359-60 Jl 26 '63
Human wart virus: in vitro cultivation. S. Oroszlan and M. A. Rich. bibliog il Science 146:531-3 O 23 '64
Interferon-like viral inhibitor in rabbits after intravenous administration of endotoxin. M. Ho. bibliog il Science 146:1472-4 D 11 '64
Isolation of a viral agent from pseudocowpox disease. C. Moscovici and others. bibliog il Science 141:915-16 S 6 '63; Reply. C. F. Pait. 142:1422+ D 13 '63
Milker's nodules: isolation of a poxvirus from a human case. A. E. Friedman-Kien and others. bibliog il Science 140:1335-6 Je 21 '63
Niles cluster. il Newsweek 61:88-9 Ap 22 '63
Picornaviruses: classification of nine new types. J. L. Melnick and others. bibliog Science 141:153-4 Jl 12 '63
Plant-human virus family; reovirus. Sci Am 209:51 Ag '63
Plaque assay for measurement of cells infected with zoster virus. F. Rapp and M. Benyesh-Melnick. bibliog il Science 141:433-4 Ag 2 '63
Reovirus hemagglutination: inhibition by N-acetyl-D-glucosamine. L. D. Gelb and A. M. Lerner. bibliog il Science 147:404-5 Ja 22 '65
Replicating form of a single-stranded DNA virus: isolation and properties. M. Hayashi and others. bibliog il Science 140:1313-16 Je 21 '63
Rhinoviruses: a description. D. A. J. Tyrrell and R. M. Chanock. bibliog Science 141:152-3 Jl 12 '63
Specific inhibition of replication of animal viruses. I. Tamm and H. J. Eggers. bibliog il Science 142:24-33 O 4 '63; Reply with rejoinder. T. D. Brock. 143:195-6 Ja 17 '64
Synergism between a lactate dehydrogenase-elevating virus and eperythrozoon coccoides. V. Riley. bibliog il Science 146:921-3 N 13 '64
Vaccine for acute colds; adenovirus vaccine. Sci N L 86:404 D 26 '64
Virology; report on fourth Gustav Stern symposium on Perspectives in virology. J. W. Hartley. Science 145:728 Ag 14 '64
Virus involved with degenerative diseases. Sci N L 86:324 N 21 '64
Virus-like particles in blood of two acute leukemia patients. J. D. Almeida and others. bibliog il Science 142:1487-9 D 13 '63
Viruses found expanding before infecting cells. Sci N L 85:25 Ja 11 '64
With the cold season upon us, the mystery of the virus; interview. I. Tamm. il U S News 57:78-80 O 19 '64
See also
Interferon
also names of viruses, e.g. Encephalitis virus

VIRUSES, Plant
Immuno-osmophoresis, a rapid and sensitive method for evaluating viruses. H. W. J. Ragetli and M. Weintraub. bibliog il Science 144:1023-4 My 22 '64
Insect tissue culture: use of blastokinetic stage of leafhopper embryo. H. Hirumi and K. Maramorosch. bibliog il Science 144:1465-7 Je 19 '64

VIRUSES, Plant—*Continued*
Plant-human virus family. Sci Am 209:51 Ag '63
Resistance to erysiphe polygoni of red clover infected with bean yellow mosaic virus. L. N. King and others. bibliog il Science 146:1054-5 N 20 '64
Test-tube grown virus. Sci N L 83:151 Mr 9 '63
Virus as a mutagenic agent in maize. G. F. Sprague and others. bibliog il Science 141: 1052-3 S 13 '63
See also
Corn stunt disease virus
Tobacco mosaic virus
VISCONTI, Luchino
Leopard; interview, ed. by W. Hanson. por Opera N 28:16-18 S 28 '63
Visconti, the leopard man. A. Moravia. il por(p49) Vogue 142:50-1+ Jl '63
VISCOSITY
Cavity formation in thin films of viscous liquids. D. F. Hays and J. B. Feiten. il Science 141:1174-5 S 20 '63
Elasticity of articular cartilage: effect of ions and viscous solutions. L. Sokoloff. bibliog il Science 141:1055-7 S 13 '63
VISES
Small portable vise. il Consumer Bul 46:14 Je '63
Which shop vises do you need? G. Daniels. il Pop Sci 186:152-5+ Ja '65
VISHNEWSKI, Stanley
Spare us, O Lord! America 111:741-2 D 5 '64
VISION. See Sight
VISION (animals) See Sight (animals)
VISIT from the Mahatma; story. See Perera, P.
VISIT; story. See Ridgway, A.
VISIT to Armenia; story. See Shiragian, S.
VISIT to the museum; story. See Nabokov, V.
VISIT to the White House; drama. See Hark, M.
VISITING, Hospital. See Hospitals—Visitors
VISITING housekeepers
Homemaker service: substitute for mothers. V. Block. il Todays Health 43:60-3+ Ja '65
VISITING nurses. See Nurses and nursing, Public health
VISITOR from outer space; drama. See Murray, J.
VISITORS. See Guests; Hospitals—Visitors
VISITORS, Interchange of. See Exchange of persons programs
VISITS of state
Beating a path to Kennedy's door; visiting dignitaries. il U S News 55:46-7 N 4 '63
European leaders to visit U.S. il Sr Schol 83:6 N 8 '63
Profiles; A. B. Duke. New Yorker 40:34-6+ Ag 15 '64
VISLOSKY, Robert
Plaster sculpture. Sch Arts 64:7-9 O '64
VISSCHER, Maurice B.
Animal experiments: regulatory measure in the Senate presents hazards to the public. Science 139:871 Mr 8 '63
VISSER 'T HOOFT, Willem Adolf
Between Constantinople and Rome. Christian Cent 81:1106-8 S 9 '64
Key figure of the World council of churches discusses Christian unity; interview, ed. by E. C. Bianchi. America 109:354-6 S 28 '63
about
On locating Visser 't Hooft. Christian Cent 80:967 Jl 31 '63
VISTA. See Volunteers in service to America
VISUAL aids. See Audio-visual aids
VISUAL deprivation. See Sensory deprivation
VISUAL illusions. See Optical illusions
VISUAL images. See Images and imagery (psychology)
VISUAL instruction. See Audio-visual instruction
VISUAL organs (animals) See Sight (animals)
VISUAL perception. See Perception
VISUAL pigments. See Retina
VISUAL purple
Rhodopsin: an enzyme. D. G. McConnell and D. G. Scarpelli. Science 139:848 Mr 1 '63
VISUAL recognition. See Perception
VISUAL stimulus. See Stimulus and response
VITAL force
Personal power. Newsweek 62:84 Jl 22 '63
VITAL statistics
See also
Infant mortality
Mortality
Suicide

VITALE, John C.
Q tip pointillism. Design 64:158-9 Mr '63
Solids from paper. Sch Arts 64:23-4 S '64
VITAMIN deficiency. See Diet, Deficient
VITAMINS
Polarographic investigation of conjugated fat-soluble vitamins. E. J. Kuta. bibliog il Science 144:1130-1 My 29 '64
See also
Food, Enriched
Vitasafe corporation

Anecdotes, facetiae, satire, etc.

Consultation. B. Roueché. New Yorker 39: 62+ Ag 31 '63

Vitamin A_2

Provitamin A_2 from lutein. P. Budowski and others. bibliog il Science 142:969-71 N 15 '63
Sensitivity of visual receptors of carotenoid-depleted flies: a vitamin A deficiency in an invertebrate. T. H. Goldsmith and others. bibliog il Science 146:65-7 O 2 '64

Vitamin B_1

Thiamine: a novel conversion from thiochrome. G. E. Risinger and P. N. Parker. Science 141:1280-1 S 27 '63

Vitamin B_6

Vitamin B_6; report on International symposium on vitamin B_6. R. H. Bunnell. Science 146:674-7 O 30 '64

Vitamin B_{12}

Four roles found for vitamin B-12 coenzymes. Sci N L 83:360 Je 8 '63
Methylmalonate excretion in vitamin B_{12} deficiency. L. A. Barness and others. bibliog il Science 140:76-7 Ap 5 '63

Vitamin C

Ascorbic acid in the nutrition of plant-feeding insects. E. S. Vanderzant and C. D. Richardson. bibliog il Science 140:989-91 My 31 '63
Microsome fraction of brain: structural changes induced by ascorbic acid. G. K. Aghajanian. bibliog il Science 141:628-30 Ag 16 '63
Packaged potatoes cheat family of vitamin C. Sci N L 83:248 Ap 20 '63

Vitamin D

Vitamin D_3: direct action on the small intestine of the rat. D. Schachter and others. bibliog il Science 143:143-4 Ja 10 '64
Too much of a good thing; Vitamin D poisoning. il Time 84:67 D 11 '64
Vitamin D warning; danger of excessive amounts taken during pregnancy. Newsweek 64:93 D 7 '64

Vitamin E

1-α-tocopheryl acetate: biological activity. H. Weiser and others. bibliog il Science 140:80 Ap 5 '63
Vitamin E oxidation with alkaline ferricyanide. W. A. Skinner and P. Alaupovic. bibliog il Science 140:803-5 My 17 '63

Vitamin K

New form of vitamin K found in spinach study. Sci N L 86:119 Ag 22 '64
Vitamin K compounds in bacteria that are obligate anaerobes. R. J. Gibbons and L. P. Engle. bibliog il Science 146:1307-9 D 4 '64
Vitamin K induced prothrombin formation: antagonism by actinomycin D. R. E. Olson. bibliog il Science 145:926-8 Ag 28 '64; Correction. 147:66 Ja 1 '65
VITASAFE corporation
New judgment against vitamin quackery. Consumer Rep 29:213 My '64
VITICULTURE
Great year? outlook for 1964 vintage in France. Time 84:86 Ag 7 '64
This is the year that will be. il Time 84:74 D 11 '64
Zut! is '64 the year of the century? with report by H. Moffett. il Life 57:107-11 O 30 '64
VITORIA, Francisco de
Father Francisco de Vitoria. il Américas 15: 40-1 N '63
Foundations of modern international law; excerpts from address, October 8, 1963. J. A. Mora. Américas 15:1 N '63
VITRAC, Roger
Victor. Criticism
Vogue 114:112 O 1 '64
VITRY, Raoul de
Who's who in foreign business. por Fortune 70:66 N '64

VITTACHI, Tarzie
Asian English. N Y Times Mag p52+ O 6 '63
VIVALDI, Antonio
Counterpoint/esoteric: a superb product but. . . H. Glass. Am Rec G 30:974 Je '64
On records; Gloria & Credo. Opera N 29:35 D 5 '64
Ricci, a man (with strads) for all seasons. J. Diether. il Am Rec G 31:400-2 Ja '65
VIVANTE, Arturo
Bachelor days; story. New Yorker 39:72 Ja 11 '64
Binoculars; story. New Yorker 40:48-52 S 19 '64
Café filtre; story. New Yorker 40:38-42 Ap 4 '64
Girls of Killini; story. New Yorker 39:47-56 O 5 '63
Nightingale; story. New Yorker 39:136-8 My 18 '63
Prince; story. New Yorker 39:161-4 My 11 '63
Rally; story. New Yorker 39:22-5 Jl 27 '63
Run to the waterfall. New Yorker 40:29 Ag 1 '64
Venetian rendezvous; story. New Yorker 40: 207-8 N 21 '64
Yaddo. Writer 77:28-9 Ag '64
VIVISECTION
Medical progress requires animal research. R. A. Rohweder. Todays Health 41:88 S '63
Resurgent antivivisectionists. Sci Am 208:70-1 Je '63
See also
Laboratory animals
VIZSLAS. See Pointers (dogs)
VIZZARD, James L.
Agricultural revolution; excerpt from New manifesto on rural life. America 111:772-5 D 12 '64
Surpluses and surpluses. Commonweal 79:361-2 D 20 '63
VIZZINI, Calogero
Profiles; the Mafia. N. Lewis. New Yorker 39:42-4+ F 8 '64
VLADIMIROV, Lev
International by definition: Dag Hammarskjöld library; interview, ed. by J. N. Berry, 3d. por Library J 86:4469-72 N 15 '64
VLADY, Marina
Deadly queen. il pors Time 81:54+ Je 14 '63
VLAHA, Richard E.
That's the jet. il por Newsweek 62:94+ N 11 '63
VO-nguyen-Giap
Strategist behind the Vietcong. M. Clos. il por N Y Times Mag p7+ Ag 16 '64
VO, Thanh-Minh
Wanderer. New Yorker 40:39-40 Ap 25 '64
VOCABULARY
Former child objects. V. Schultheis. Wilson Lib Bul 37:552 Mr '63
Jargon in the humanities. J. S. Smith. Harper 228:111-12 Mr '64
See also
Words
VOCABULARY tests
It pays to increase your word power. W. Funk. See issues of Reader's digest
Play on cheeses. M. R. Henry. House & Gard 125:48+ My '64
VOCATION (in religion)
Girl sets out to be a nun; with report by B. Cummiskey. il Life 54:66-79 Mr 15 '63
Let your light shine, sister. M. G. Lacey. America 109:302-5 S 21 '63; Reply. M. Walsh. 109:618 N 16 '63
VOCATIONAL agricultural training. See Agriculture—Study and teaching
VOCATIONAL aptitude tests. See Aptitude tests
VOCATIONAL counselling. See Vocational guidance
VOCATIONAL education
After high school, higher skills. il Sr Schol 85:19 N 11 '64
ACE study: higher education's aloofness from occupational education seems to be thawing. J. Walsh. Science 144:1321-2 Je 12 '64
Are we cheating twenty million students? G. B. Leonard. il Look 27:36-40+ Je 4 '63
Congress: session of reckoning on civil rights affects prospects of new vocational education bill. J. Walsh. Science 140:1196-9 Je 14 '63
Digest of 1961 state reports on vocational education. P. Groom. il Mo Labor R 86:1162-5 O '63
Do our schools neglect the average student? E. H. Hanson. il Parents Mag 38:61+ S '63
Educating youth; the cruel solution. H. Brill. Nation 198:296-7 Mr 23 '64
Five ways to cut unemployment. R. Newcomb. Nations Bsns 52:31-3+ Jl '64
Help wanted, 1964. V. M. Rogers. il NEA J 53:53 F '64
How challenge can be met. il Nations Bsns 51:32-3+ Je '63
How will they make a living? il Time 82: 42 S 6 '63
Increasing enrollments in vocational education. R. M. Walker. il Sch Life 45:15 Jl '63
Jamaica's Youth corps. G. Meek. il Américas 15:13-15 Ap '63
Jobs and jobless. America 108:283 Mr 2 '63
Learning to be unemployable. E. T. Chase. Harper 226:33-40 Ap '63; Discussion. 226: 6+ Je '63
Liberal and the manual arts in education. D. Rucker. Sch & Soc 91:350-2 N 16 '63
Man, education and work, by G. Venn. Review
Sat R 47:69-70 S 19 '64. A. H. Lass
New hope through self-help; Opportunities industrialization center, North Philadelphia. il Ebony 19:27-30+ My '64
Non-collegiate roads to higher education. il Sr Schol 83:18 N 8 '63
Out-of-school youth, February 1963. T. E. Swanstrom. il Mo Labor R 87:1416-24 D '64
Plea for better education. Sci N L 85:372 Je 13 '64
Retraining in South Bend. il Time 83:68+ Je 5 '64
School that just about guarantees a job. D. James. Farm J 87:44H S '63
Schools for your special interests. L. Gravenson. il Holiday 36:139-42 N '64
Studies in success; course for potential high school dropouts, Mount Miguel H.S., San Diego County, Calif. K. Hopkins. il Sr Schol 84:27T Mr 20 '64
Training for those who don't go to college. il Good H 156:148 F '63
Vocation education act of 1963. il Sch Life 46:3-12 Mr '64
Vocational education: in the high school? P. Woodring. Sat R 47:47-8 Ag 15 '64; Reply. A. W. Forbes. 47:53 O 17 '64
What if your youngster doesn't go to college? N. Kuehnl. Bet Hom & Gard 41:40+ My '63
What's happening in education? W. D. Boutwell. PTA Mag 58:23 My '64
Whither vocational education? J. C. Swanson. il NEA J 52:58-60 O '63
Will there be jobs for our children? E. Cohen and S. Fremon. il Parents Mag 38:58-9+ N '63
Young people may not be able to find jobs unless. . . G. J. Hecht. Parents Mag 39: 34 My '64
See also
Agricultural education
Agriculture—Study and teaching
Technical education

Federal aid

See Federal aid to education

Israel

Vocational training in Israel. Mo Labor R 86:1067-9 S '63

United States

See Vocational education

VOCATIONAL guidance
Big job for job hunting. il Sr Schol 85:23-4 N 11 '64
BLS occupational trend projections: an appraisal; excerpt from address, June 27, 1963. H. Goldstein. Mo Labor R 86:1135-8 O '63
Career planning for the age of automation. G. Davenel. il Parents Mag 39:74-6+ S '64
College and career. H. Zuckerman. See issues of Senior scholastic
Decision for Susie Jones. H. L. Howard. il PTA Mag 57:27-9 Je '63
Have a dream. B. Cerf. Seventeen 22:232+ Ag '63
I didn't go to college. il Seventeen 22:146-7+ S '63
Illuminate the whole road; career planning for a young woman. K. Hunter. NEA J 53: 62-3 N '64
Job interview and the follow through. il Sr Schol 83:19+ N 8 '63
Self-help brightens job outlook. il Nations Bsns 51:52-4 Ag '63
Seven steps toward getting a job. J. N. Miller. Read Digest 82:72-5 Mr '63
Should vocational guidance be junked? pro and con discussion. il NEA J 52:30-2 D '63
Training for those who don't go to college. il Good H 156:148 F '63

VOCATIONAL guidance—*Continued*
Vocational counseling in the classroom. S. Cochell. Sr Schol 85:7T O 28 '64
What if your youngster doesn't go to college? N. Kuehnl. Bet Hom & Gard 41:40+ My '63
What will they be when they grow up? with program for discussion group, by M. R. Sherwin. R. Brecher and E. Brecher. il Parents Mag 38:38, 62-3+ F '63
See also
Occupations
Vocational education
VOCATIONAL high school libraries. See High school libraries
VOCATIONAL literature
Career information; yours for the asking. il Sr Schol 83:20-1+ N 8 '63; 85:33-6 N 11 '64
VOCATIONAL rehabilitation
Ready, willing, and able: the handicapped worker. E. C. Holmblad. Todays Health 42:11 D '64
Useful work for disabled; it pays to hire handicapped workers. il Bsns W p48+ My 9 '64
Why penalize firms hiring handicapped workers? H. B. Burr. Harvard Bsns R 41:56-8 Jl '63
VOCATIONAL schools. See Vocational education
VOCATIONAL surveys. See Occupational surveys
VODEHNAL, Andrea
Brief biography. S. Goodman. pors Dance Mag 37:50-1 N '63
VODKA
Russian way and the American way. il Esquire 61:100-1 Ja '64
VOEGELI, Charles Alfred, bp
Episcopal bishop expelled from Haiti. Christian Cent 81:629 My 13 '64
VOELLER, Bruce R.
Gibberellins: their effect on antheridium formation in fern gametophytes. bibliog Science 143:373-5 Ja 24 '64
VOGEL, Albert W.
J. D. Salinger on education. Sch & Soc 91: 240-2 Sum '63
VOGEL, Henry J. See Bryson, V. jt. auth.
VOGEL, James A. and Sturkie, P. D.
Cardiovascular responses of the chicken to seasonal and induced temperature changes. bibliog Science 140:1404-6 Je 28 '63
VOGEL, Sophie B.
French books for children. Library J 88:4428-33 N 15 '63
VOGT, Arnold, and others
Poliovirus type I: neutralization by papain-digested antibodies. bibliog Science 145: 1447-8 S 25 '64
VOGT, William
Reviews. Natur Hist 73:4+ Mr '64
VOGUE (periodical)
What is style? excerpts from World in Vogue, with comments by P. Caulfield. il Mod Phot 27:68-77 N '63
World in Vogue. Review
Mod Phot 27:126 N '63. P. Caulfield
New Repub 150:17+ Ja 11 '64. S. Kauffmann
World in Vogue; excerpts. il Vogue 142:128-33 N 1 '63
VOHRA, H. R.
Kashmir settlement may now be possible. New Repub 150:11-12 Mr 21 '64
VOICE
How pretty do you sound? il Seventeen 22: 112-13+ Mr '63
Sound of beauty. C. Huntley. Seventeen 23: 152+ F '64
Vocal mimicry in tursiops: ability to match numbers and durations of human vocal bursts. J. C. Lilly. bibliog il Science 147: 300-1 Ja 15 '65
Voice detectives go to work on the mystery crash; Pacific air lines 773. D. Nevin. il Life 56:46-46A My 22 '64
VOICE from the woods; story. See Humphrey, W.
VOICE of America (radio program)
Radio marathon broadcasts truth to Cuba! W. I. Orr. il Pop Electr 19:58-9+ Ag '63
Tom Paine, communicator. R. L. Shayon. Sat R 46:51 Ag 10 '63
Who knows? F. D. Elmer, jr. Christian Cent 80:783 Je 12 '63
VOICE of liberty; drama. See Fisher, A.
VOICE-prints. See Voice
VOICES; story. See Taylor, E.
VOIGT, Melvin J.
LC and automation. por Library J 89:1022-5 Mr 1 '64

VOIT, W. J, rubber corporation
Human fish acquires a brighter, tougher skin. C. Phinizy. il Sports Illus 18:62-3 Ap 15 '63
VOLCANIC ash, tuff, etc.
Late twilight glow of the ash stratum from the eruption of Agung volcano. M. P. Meinel and A. B. Meinel. Science 142:582-3 N 1 '63
Volcanic ash from Mount Mazama (Crater Lake) and from Glacier Peak. H. A. Powers and R. E. Wilcox. bibliog il Science 144:1334-6 Je 12 '64
VOLCANIC glass. See Obsidian
VOLCANIC rocks. See Rocks, Igneous
VOLCANIC steam. See Steam, Natural
VOLCANOES
Annals of migration; island of Tristan da Cunha. T. Whiteside. il New Yorker 39:154+ N 9 '63
Ash-covered capital; Irazú's eruption. il Time 83:33 Ja 17 '64
Bali; paradise to inferno, Gunung Agung erupts. il Newsweek 61:36 Ap 1 '63
Basaltic cone suggests constructional origin of some guyots; Mono Lake, Calif. M. N. Christensen and C. M. Gilbert. bibliog il Science 143:240-2 Ja 17 '64
Dead zone; Irazú erupts. il Newsweek 62:65 O 7 '63
Disaster in paradise. W. P. Booth and S. N. Matthews. il Nat Geog Mag 124:436-58 S '63
Dome-shaped volcanic gas vents in Arizona. R. A. Laidley and R. L. DuBois. il Science 145:153-4 Jl 10 '64
Gods of Agung unleash a flow of lava. il Life 54:34-5 Ap 26 '63
Gods speak; Gunung Agung. Time 81:30 Mr 29 '63
Hidden world of volcanoes. H. Tazieff. il UNESCO Courier 16:20-5 O '63
Infrared surveys of Hawaiian volcanoes. W. A. Fischer and others. bibliog il Science 146:733-42 N 6 '64
Lonely wonders of Katmai. E. Gruening. il Nat Geog Mag 123:800-31 Je '63
Mountain of glass: Glass Mountain in Modoc National Forest. R. H. May and W. F. Heald. il Am For 69:32-4 Ag '63
Old volcanoes still erupt. B. Tufty. Sci N L 83:211 Ap 6 '63
Possible lava source. Sci N L 86:5 Jl 4 '64
Sky is falling; Irazú eruption. T. Armbrister. il Sat Eve Post 237:20-5 Ap 11 '64
Spectacular Irazú. C. J. Cordero. il Américas 16:21-7 Ap '64
Twilight phenomena caused by the eruption of Agung volcano. F. E. Volz. bibliog il Science 144:1121-2 My 29 '64
Volcanic squeeze measured in Hawaii. Sci N L 85:200 Mr 28 '64
Volcanic violence over the sea; Iceland's new offshore volcano; photographs. Life 56:36-7 Ap 3 '64
Volcano doctor; Haroun Tazieff's study of Irazú. il Time 83:68+ Ap 24 '64
Volcano on a rampage: the tragedy of Costa Rica; Irazú. il U S News 56:71-3 Je 29 '64
Volcano related to sunset; Indonesian volcano Agung. B. Tufty. Sci N L 84:399 D 21 '63
Volcano spawns a new island; offshore Iceland. il Life 55:36-36A D 13 '63
See also
Kilauea (crater)
Krakatoa (island)
Mauna Kea
Volcanic ash, tuff, etc.
VOLCHOK, Herbert L.
Strontium 90: estimation of worldwide deposition. bibliog Science 145:1451-2 S 25 '64
VOLIO-JIMENEZ, Fernando
International protection of human rights. UN Mo Chron 1:75-81 D '64
VOLK, Harry J.
Portrait of growth: California's startling Union bank. J. Thackray. il por Duns R 84: 44-5+ O '64
VOLK und wissen verlag. See Publishers and publishing—Germany (Democratic Republic)
VOLKER, Adriaan
Peoples of the deltas. UNESCO Courier 17: 44-7 Jl '64
VOLKSWAGEN. See Automobiles, Foreign
VOLKSWAGENWERKE, gmbh. See Automobile industry and trade—Germany (Federal Republic)
VOLLEYBALL
Driven beyond dignity. Nichibo Kaizuka women's volleyball team. E. Whitehead. il Sports Illus 20:16-19 Mr 16 '64

VOLLEYBALL—*Continued*
Games worth the candle. Sports Illus 20:8+ Ja 20 '64
Rough creed: there's no success without suffering; Nichibo women's volleyball team. L. Griggs. il Life 57:42 S 11 '64
VOLLMAN, June R.
Should you rent your home? Am Home 66: 11-13+ My '63
VOLODIN, Alexander
Five evenings. Criticism
America 109:63 Jl 13 '63
New Yorker 39:82+ My 18 '63
VOLPONE; drama. See Jonson, B.
VOLT ohmmeter. See Voltohmmeters
VOLTA, Alessandro
Alessandro Volta. G. De Santillana. il por Sci Am 212:82-91 Ja '65
VOLTAGE
Hi! volts, that is. I. C. Chapel. il Pop Electr 21:82 Ag '64
How big is your volt? R. Jones. il Electr World 71:42+ Je '64
Inexpensive scope and VOM calibrator. H. R. Newhoff. il Pop Electr 21:57-9 O '64
Measuring filament voltage. il Electr World 72:65 Ag '64
Negative-feedback nomogram. A. L. Teubner. il Electr World 70:31 D '63
See also
High voltages
VOLTAGE calibrators. See Calibrators
VOLTAGE divider
Voltage-divider nomogram. D. W. Moffat. il Electr World 71:29+ Mr '64
VOLTAGE regulators
Light-controlled power supply. il Pop Electr 20:53-5+ F; 21:70-2 S '64
Miniature voltage regulators. H. F. Burgess. il Electr World 71:82-3 F '64
Multi-output zener voltage regulator. H. Reed. il Electr World 71:94 F '64
Power supply regulation. A. F. Burr. il Pop Electr 20:63-4 My '64
Transistor voltage regulator. J. R. Gyorki. il Electr World 70:74-5 Jl '63
Voltage regulator design. L. E. Frenzel, jr. il Electr World 71:52-4+ My '64
VOLTAIRE, François Marie Arouet de
They made our world. L. Rosten. por Look 28:94-5 Je 16 '64
Voltaire and the Calas case, by E. Nixon. Review
Commonweal 78:113-16 Ap 19 '63. L. F. X. Mayhew
VOLTMETERS
Auto voltmeter shows you'll go. J. Tartas. il Pop Electr 21:53-5+ D '64
Field-effect transistor voltmeter. J. H. Taylor. il Pop Electr 21:45-8 Jl '64
How big is your volt? R. Jones. il Electr World 71:42+ Je '64
Inside a voltmeter. S. Messin. il Electr World 70:53-6+ N '63
Meter range-extension nomogram. A. L. Teubner. il Electr World 70:37-8 Ag '63
Meterless VTVM. W. J. Millard. il Pop Electr 19:45-8 N '63
Miniature VTVM. R. Wilson. il Pop Electr 22:55-7 Ja '65
Transient evaluator. R. L. Ives. il Electr World 69:45+ My '63
Transistorized VTVM kit. il Pop Electr 19: 63-4 Ag '63
See also
Voltohmmeters
VOLTOHMMETERS
Case of the aluminum ally: low-cost multitester VOM. H. L. Davidson. il Pop Electr 18:46 Mr '63
VOLUME compressor. See Sound—Apparatus
VOLUME expander. See Sound—Apparatus
VOLUMETRIC analysis
See also
Titration
VOLUNTARY foreign aid. See Relief work
VOLUNTARY social agencies. See Social agencies, Voluntary
VOLUNTARY foreign aid. See Relief work
VOLUNTEER service
Australian peace corps helps shed stone age. Sci N L 87:50 Ja 23 '65
Frontier of service; address, June 8, 1964. R. S. Shriver. America 111:14-16 Jl 4 '64
Gringos become amigos; Mexican apostolate for Christian students. America 109:473-4 O 26 '63
Ladies, please come to order! J. Bradford. il Redbook 120:41+ Mr '63
Remarkable story of the dropouts and the college students. A. Fontaine. McCalls 91: 36+ Mr '64
Teen-agers who want to help. J. W. Levin. il N Y Times Mag p53 F 9 '64
Teens work for love, not money. A. Q. Maisel. Parents Mag 38:68+ My '63
Two new ways to curb JD. Life 54:4 Ap 5 '63
Valley of compassion; Valley aid for cancer program. D. Gregory. il Look 27:116-18+ O 22 '63
We will overcome. R. Coles. New Repub 151: 13 Jl 11 '64
What ever happened to the beat generation? Student education corps at Michigan state univ; reprint. J. Reston. il Sr Schol 84:12T Ap 24 '64
What makes them tick? Catholic students volunteer groups. America 108:795-6 Je 1 '63
World outside; excerpts from My favorite things. D. Rodgers. McCalls 92:28+ O '64
See also
Libraries—Volunteer workers
Teachers aides
VOLUNTEER service, International
East works with West. H. T. Bernstein. Bul Atomic Sci 21:37-9 Ja '65
I failed in Puno; Papal volunteer. R. F. Clark. America 112:7 Ja 2 '65; Reply. F. M. Cameron. 112:152 Ja 30 '65
International youth conference in France. il Sch & Soc 92:365-6 N 28 '64
My adventures in Africa: Operation crossroads Africa in Ethiopia. W. Peter. il Seventeen 24:70-1+ Ja '65
Not alms but ACCION. il Time 83:31 Ap 3 '64
Operation crossroads Africa. il Sat R 47:58-9 Ag 15 '64
Peace corps everywhere. il Time 84:43 N 27 '64
Reconciliation in action: volunteer service abroad by young Germans. H. Lehmann. Christian Cent 80:824-6 Je 26 '63
Thought behind ACCION. G. Buckman. il Mlle 60:106-8+ Ja '65
See also
International voluntary workcamps
United States—Peace corps
Volunteers for international technical assistance
VOLUNTEERS for international technical assistance
Technical aid: volunteer group enables scientists, engineers to help underdeveloped nations. D. S. Greenberg. Science 144:1320-1 Je 12 '64
VOLUNTEERS in service to America
Deadliest bullets. R. Dudman. New Repub 148:7 Je 8 '63
Domestic Peace corps? T. R. Brooks. il Commonweal 78:131-3 Ap 26 '63
Esprit de corps. Reporter 28:18-19 F 14 '63
Here come the boys! Job corps and Volunteers in service to America programs. J. Prokop. il Am For 70:12-14+ O '64
If we do get a domestic Peace corps. U S News 55:10 Ag 26 '63
National service corps. R. Hoopes. Seventeen 22:50 Ap '63
National service program; interview. R. W. Boone. NEA J 52:28+ Ap '63
Peace corps in Harlem. il Ebony 18:49-50+ Ag '63
Religion-state conference on civil rights legislation. H. A. Jack. Christian Cent 81: 1566-7+ D 16 '64
Task for a Peace corps; migrant workers. C. Karraker. Christian Cent 80:237-8 F 20 '63
This month's feature: Congress and a domestic Peace corps. Cong Digest 43:3-32 Ja '64
Tryout in Harlem. M. Kempton. New Repub 148:11-13 F 23 '63; Reply. D. L. Hackett. 148:38 Ap 13 '63
We may be dead. Newsweek 62:20 Ag 26 '63
We need a domestic Peace corps. A. S. Flemming. Good H 156:76 My '63
Welfare plum tree. R. Moley. Newsweek 61: 100 F 25 '63
What a Peace corps inside U.S. would do. U S News 54:11 F 4 '63
What about a Peace corps spirit at home? R. F. Kennedy. Sat R 46:20-1 My 25 '63
What you can do for your country. R. Hartley. Seventeen 23:62+ N '64
VOLZ, F. E.
Twilight phenomena caused by the eruption of Agung volcano. bibliog Science 144:1121-2 My 29 '64
VOM calibrators. See Calibrators
VON BÉKESY, Georg
Duplexity theory of taste. bibliog Science 145:834-5 Ag 21 '64

VON BORSTEL, R. C.
Yeast genetics conference. Science 142:1594 D 20 '63
—See Ritossa, F. M. jt. auth.
VON BRAUN, Wernher
Atomic power for rockets. por Pop Sci 185:68-9+ Jl '64
Do the moon photos change our plans? Pop Sci 185:110-13+ N '64
How propellants are fed to liquid-rocket engines. por Pop Sci 185:98-9+ D '64
How spacemen can use laser beams. por Pop Sci 185:128-9+ O '64
Space power from fuel cells. por Pop Sci 185:80-1+ Ag '64
Wernher Von Braun answers your questions (title varies) See issues of Popular science beginning January 1963
What's happening in the race to the moon; interview. por U S News 56:54-7 Je 1 '64
Why and how of the countdown. por Pop Sci 186:66-7+ Ja '65
Why rockets have fins. Pop Sci 185:68-9+ S '64
VONDERHEIDE, Nancy
She started at the top. V. Kraft. il por Sports Illus 19:40-2 Ag 5 '63
VON DREELE, W. H.
Movies. Nat R 16:203-4 Mr 10 '64
Sing along with the liberal Republicans; Smiles; Margie; Stormy weather; I want a girl; M-o-t-h-e-r; 'Til we meet again; poems. Nat R 16:151 F 25 '64
Theater. Nat R 14:291+; 16:34-5 Ap 9 '63, Ja 14 '64
VON ECKARDT, Wolf
Age of anti-architecture. Sat R 48:19-21+ Ja 23 '65
Architecture. New Repub 150:32-4 F 15; 35-6 Je 13; 151:26+ Jl 4 '64
As the Hucksters see us. New Repub 150:14-16 My 30 '64
Aspen summit conference. New Repub 151: 31-2 Jl 25 '64
Changing our unnatural habitat. New Repub 148:20-2 Je 1 '63
Changing the human habitat. New Repub 150:22+ F 1 '64
Community: could this be our town? New Repub 151:17-24 N 7; 38 N 28 '64
Design for culture in Washington. Sat R 47:20-3 My 23 '64
Escape from the automobile. New Repub 152: 18-19 Ja 2 '65
Father and son. New Repub 150:32-4 F 15 '64
Le Corbusier at Harvard. New Repub 149: 27-9 Jl 6 '63
Man who destroyed Paris. Horizon 5:50-75 My '63
President's plan for urban America. New Repub 150:9 F 8 '64
Stalling on the arts. New Repub 150:8 Mr 21 '64
Urban renewal and the city. New Repub 149:15-19 S 14; 17-20 S 21; 16-18 S 28; 21-4 O 5; 14-17 O 19; 16-18 O 26 '63
Washington's chance for splendor. Harper 227:54-64 S '63
Woods move into cities. B. Tufty. Sci N L 85:373 Je 13 '64
VON ERDBERG, Amy
Lines on a picture of Pope John XXIII; poem. Cath World 198:27 O '63
VON FRISCH, Karl
Smell, sex and survival in animals. Sci Digest 53:65-72 F '63
VON HIPPEL, Peter H. and Wong, K. Y.
Neutral salts: the generality of their effects on the stability of macromolecular conformations. bibliog Science 145:577-80 Ag 7 '64
VON HOORN, Richard
Foam rubber fun. Design 66:10-12 S '64
VON HUBEN, H. R. See Watson, G. L. jt. auth.
VON KAMP, Bobby
Boy's trial by fire. J. P. Blank. il Read Digest 83:91-6 N '63
VON KARMAN, Theodore
Military safety, and cooperation with Russian science; interview, ed. by W. Beller and F. G. McGuire. Miss & Roc 12:22-3 F 25 '63

about

Excellent start; first National medal of science. R. Hotz. Aviation W 78:21 F 25 '63
Man from Mars. por Time 81:46+ My 17 '63
Master of the wind. il por Newsweek 61:68 My 20 '63
Other side of space. W. J. Coughlin. Miss & Roc 12:54 My 13 '63
Von Karman wins science medal. il por Miss & Roc 12:22 F 25 '63
Wind's deputy. W. Jonathan. por Sat R 46:48-50 F 2 '63
VON LAUE, Theodore H.
Modern science and the old Adam. Bul Atomic Sci 19:2-5 Ja; 34 Ap; 30 Je '63
VON MIKLOS, Josephine
Smart, personal, and rewarding gifts from the darkroom. il Pop Phot 51:72-5+ D '62
VONNEGUT, Kurt, jr
Lovers anonymous; story. Redbook 121:70-1 O '63
VON PATAKY, Koloman
Rococo presents. A. Favia-Artsay. Hobbies 68:31 Ja '64
VON RECKLINGHAUSEN, D. R. and others
Transistors for hi-fi, panacea or pandemonium? Electr World 70:37-40+ S; 38-40+ O '63
VON SALDERN, Axel
German and Austrian conversation pieces of the nineteenth century. Antiques 86:604-9 N '64
VON STERNBERG, Josef
Von Sternberg principle. Esquire 60:90-7+ O '63
VOODOOISM
Haitian voodoo. il U S News 54:42 My 20 '63
Life in Haiti: voodoo and the church. J. Breda. il Commonweal 78:241-4 My 24 '63
Voodoo and politics. E. Mirel. Sci N L 83:299 My 11 '63
VOORHIS, Jerry
Christian choice in a changing world. Christian Cent 81:396-9 Mr 25 '64
VORBECK, Paul von Lettow-. See Lettow-Vorbeck, P. von
VORHAUS, Louis J.
Speaking out. por Sat Eve Post 236:10+ My 11 '63
VORNHOLT, John
Oklahoma's college of continuing education. Sch & Soc 91:172-3 Ap 6 '63
VORTEX motion
Amateur scientist; vortexes in water and flame. R. A. Singer. il Sci Am 209:133-6+ O '63
Quantized vortex rings in superfluid helium. F. Reif. il Sci Am 211:116-22 bibliog(p 156) D '64
VORTEX rings. See Vortex motion
VOSBURGH, John
Bird songs. Pop Gard 14:26-7+ Mr '63
Our Maine camp. bibliog f Audubon Mag 65: 90-7 Mr '63
60th annual convention. Audubon Mag 67:32-7 Ja '65
VOSKOVEC, George
Reunion. New Yorker 39:20-1 Jl 27 '63
VOSPER, Robert G.
Sermon on an obligation. por ALA Bul 58: 757 O '64

about

Robert G. Vosper, ALA president-elect. A. T. Hamlin. il por ALA Bul 58:698-701 S '64
VOSS, Carl Hermann
John Haynes Holmes: discoverer of Gandhi; excerpt from Rabbi and minister. Christian Cent 81:603-6 My 6 '64
VOSS, George L.
Hunting, anyone? Outdoor Life 131:42-3+ F '63
VOSS, Ray
Moose enough for two. por Outdoor Life 134: 24-7+ Ag '64
VOSS, Robert M.
Sleep-O-Mat. Pop Electr 22:51-3 Ja '65
VOSS, Virginia
College crowd. Mlle 58:77+ Ja '64
Shakespeare is to hear. Mlle 58:122+ F '64
Twelve ways to write for a living. Mlle 56: 140-5+ Mr '63
VOTAPEK, Ralph
Bomb in his lap. Newsweek 65:73 Ja 18 '65
VOTE, Labor. See Trade unions—Political activities
VOTERS. See Suffrage
VOTERS, Registration of
Aim: registration; attempt by Negroes to register in Selma, Ala. il Time 85:20-1 Ja 29 '65
As Negroes seek to vote; Canton, Miss. J. E. Sherman. Christian Cent 81:464 Ap 8 '64
Changing South; voter registration. America 110:272 F 29 '64
Negro registration in the South. P. Watters. New Repub 150:15-17 Ap 4 '64
One more clue to November vote; new Negro voters. il U S News 57:40 O 12 '64
Registration in Alabama. H. Zinn. New Repub 149:11-12 O 26 '63
Shades of Bull Connor; Negroes attempt to register in Selma, Ala. il Newsweek 65:21-2 F 1 '65
Southern Negro drives for the vote. C. Sitton. il N Y Times Mag p28-9 S 29 '63

VOTERS, Registration of—*Continued*
South's war against Negro votes. J. Poppy. Look 27:38+ My 21 '63
That new-fangled thing called voting. J. W. Anderson. New Repub 150:8 Mr 28 '64
Things to come? record-breaking registrations. Newsweek 64:43-4 O 12 '64
Understanding Negro and his right to vote. J. Kenworthy and E. W. Kenworthy. Reporter 30:32-4 Mr 26 '64
Voters on the move. Commonweal 81:180-1 N 6 '64
Who should be qualified to vote? H. Earl. il Todays Health 42:18-21+ Ag '64

VOTING
Across the Nation: the story of the '64 election; with charts. il U S News 57:38-44 N 16 '64
Don't blame the American voter. W. G. Andrews. il N Y Times Mag p42-3+ O 18 '64
Don't vote in the dark; get-out-the vote campaigns. J. Luter. il Todays Health 42: 58-9+ O '64
Factor X for '64: stay-at-homes; with charts. il U S News 57:32-3 Ag 17 '64
How big is the bloc vote? S. M. Lipset. il N Y Times Mag p32-3+ O 25 '64
If people's pocketbooks decide how they vote. il U S News 57:34-5 N 2 '64
Silent vote. Nation 199:261 O 26 '64
TV poll projections: do they interfere with the vote? pro and con discussion. il Sr Schol 85:14-15 S 30 '64
Third force; vote splitting. Nation 199:365-6 N 23 '64
Voting: how you can get people to the polls. A. Balk. Todays Health 42:52-5 Mr '64
What happens to your ballot on Election day? A. Balk. il Todays Health 42:32-5+ N '64
Who votes, who doesn't, and why. il Sr Schol 85:20-1+ S 23 '64
Why don't more Americans vote? A. Balk. il Todays Health 42:28-31+ Ja '64; Correction. 42:84 Mr '64
Why one third of us don't vote; kept away by political and mechanical barriers. R. M. Scammon. il N Y Times Mag p36+ N 17 '63
Your vote counts. M. Hickey. Ladies Home J 81:68 S '64

See also
Elections
Literacy tests (election law)
Suffrage
United Nations—Voting
Voters, Registration of

Literacy tests
See Literacy tests (election law)

VOTING, Fraudulent. See Elections—Corrupt practices

VOTING age. See Suffrage—United States

VOTING machines
Automatic counting updates the election process. il Am City 79:86-8 Ag '64
High cost of voting; less expense by punch-card ballot and Harris votomatic. il Look 28:109-10 D 15 '64
Let's make this an honest election! B. Surface. il Read Digest 85:53-7 S '64

VOTING records, Congressmen. See Congressmen

VOULKOS, Peter H.
Clay movement. il por Time 82:50 Ag 23 '63

VOYAGER probe. See Space probes

VOYAGES
French sailor first in ocean race. il Motor B 114:88-9 Ag '64
Last fling? Bill Willis's Pacific crossings. Newsweek 62:56 N 25 '63
Niña II. E. C. Uriburu. il Américas 15:2-7 Ap '63
One man against the sea. H. Willis. il Sat Eve Post 237:36-8+ Ap 18 '64; Same abr. Read Digest 85:134-9 Jl '64
1,600 miles on a windjammer; Statsraad Lehmkuhl. D. C. Fales. il Pop Sci 185:74-7+ Ag '64
Passagemaker; maiden voyage from Singapore to Greece. R. Beebe. il Yachting 116: 58-60+ O '64
Single-handed passages; across the north Atlantic. F. Chichester. il Yachting 113:43-5+ My '63
Singlehanded to Hawaii. J. S. Letcher, jr. il Yachting 115:87-9+ Ja; 58-60+ F '64
Voyage of pleasure; aboard schooner Moonglow from England to Barbados. C. de Grabowski. il Motor B 113:46-9+ Ap '64
See also
Cruising

VOYAGES around the world
Cruise of a lifetime. J. Hedden. il Yachting 114:54-6+ O '63
Long voyage ends. E. Hiscock. il Yachting 113:48-50+ Mr '63
Twice around in Adios. T. S. Steele. il Yachting 116:34-6+ D '64; 117:98-100+ Ja '65

VOYAGEURS NATIONAL PARK (proposed)
See National parks and reserves—United States

VOYEZ, John
John Voyez, fact and fiction (cont) R. J. Charleston. il Antiques 84:429-33 O '63

VOZNESENSKII, Andrei
Fire in the architectural institute; poem, tr. by S. Kunitz. Atlan 212:103 O '63

about
Beat Voznesensky. R. Creeley. Nation 199: 336-7 N 9 '64
New parabolist. M. Harrington. il Reporter 28:50-2 F 14 '63
On translating Voznesensky. B. Koten. Nation 199:337-8 N 9 '64

VREDEVOE, Donna L. and Hildemann, W. H.
Circulating small lymphocytes: immunologically competent cells with limited reactivities. bibliog Science 141:1272-4 S 27 '63

VREELAND, Diana (Dalziel)
Vreeland Vogue. il por Time 81:53 My 10 '63

VREELAND, Elizabeth
Berlin devours you as you arrive. Vogue 141: 74+ Mr 1 '63

VRON and Willie: story. See Taylor, E.

VUCINICH, Wayne S.
Albanian-Soviet rift. Cur Hist 44:299-304+ My '63

VUILLARD, Edouard
Vuillard close-up. H. L. Farge. Art N 63: 42+ N '64

VULCOON. See Balloons

VULTURES
See also
Condors

VURSELL, H. D.
Madeleine L'Engle. Library J 88:1288-91 Mr 15 '63

W

W particle. See Particles (nuclear physics)

WACB. See World association for Christian broadcasting

WBAI (radio station) See Pacifica foundation

W. C. Bradley memorial library, Columbus, Ga.
Eleven Negroes arrested in Georgia at horizontally integrated library. Library J 88: 2854 Ag '63

WCOTP. See World confederation of organizations of the teaching profession

WEU. See Western European Union

WHHH (radio station) See Radio stations

WHO. See World health organization

WINS (radio station) See Radio stations

WISP (Women's international strike for peace movement) See Women and peace

WMCA (radio station) See Radio stations

WNDT. See Television stations, Educational

WQRS (radio station) See Radio broadcasting—Subscription programs

WQXR (radio station) See Radio stations

W. R. Grace and company. See Grace, W. R. and company

WSP (Women strike for peace movement) See Women and peace

WAAGE, Thomas O.
Great coin shortage; interview. Read Digest 86:31-2+ Ja '65

WABASSO, Fla.
Squeeze play; Hale Indian River orange groves. H. Sutton. Sat R 47:25-6 F 8 '64

WABER, Bernard
You too can lay an egg; excerpt. il Life 54: 113-14+ Ap 5 '63

WACO, Tex.
Switch to slurry seal. C. Hoge. il Am City 79:104-5 Mr '64

WACO Turner open. See Golf—Tournaments

WADDELL, James I.
Last gun of the confederacy; saga of the Shenandoah. C. E. Hinkson. il Read Digest 82:256-8+ Ap '63

WADDINGTON, C. H.
Mobilizing the world's biologists. Bul Atomic Sci 19:39-41 N '63

WADE, Ben F.
One-sided Christology. Christian Cent 80:646-7 My 15 '63
WADE, Henry Menasco
Casus Belli. il Time 83:34+ Mr 27 '64
WADE, James
Alan Hovhaness: pilgrimage to the Orient. Mus Am 83:56 S '63
WADE, Mel
Year-round tennis; ed. by J. C. Bachman. por Recreation 56:174-6 Ap '63
WADE, William W.
Man who stopped the rams. Am Heritage 14:18-23+ Ap '63
WADKINS, Bert V.
It happened in Oklahoma City. NEA J 52: 39-40 N '63
WADSWORTH, Betty G.
Ideas from Parents' magazine's better homemaking center. See issues of Parents' magazine & better homemaking
—and Pierce, Noel
How to choose carpeting with confidence. Parents Mag 38:61+ Ag '63
WADSWORTH, James J.
Most urgent step toward peace. Redbook 121: 54-5+ Ag '63
WAELSCH, Heinrich. See Neidle, A; Purpura, D. P. jt. auths.
WAELSCH, Salome Gluecksohn-. See Gluecksohn-Waelsch, S.
WAFERS
Wafer cookies you bake in an iron. il Sunset 131:116-17 D '63
WAFFLE irons
Three handy appliances. Am Home 67:130 Jl '64
Waffles were never prettier; with recipes. il McCalls 91:128+ Ag '64
WAFFLES
Hawaiian idea, fresh coconut waffles. il Sunset 130:174 Mr '63
Pancakes: waffles. il Suc Farm 61:64+ S '63
Waffles unlimited. il Redbook 121:82-3+ O '63
Waffles were never prettier; with recipes. il McCalls 91:128+ Ag '64
WAGE agreements. See Trade agreements
WAGE bargaining. See Collective bargaining
WAGE differentials
Occupational wage relationships in metropolitan areas, 1961-62. D. J. Blackmore. il Mo Labor R 86:1426-31 D '63
WAGE incentives. See Incentives in industry
WAGE laws. See Labor laws and legislation
WAGE payment plans
Deferred increases due in 1964-1965 and wage escalation G. Ruben. il Mo Labor R86: 1394-7; 87:1381-4 D '63, D '64
Developments under major agreements. G. Ruben. il Mo Labor R 87:1-10 Ja '64
Developments under major agreements. il Mo Labor R 87:1393-400 D '64
Earnings in retail trade, June 1961. H. Schaffer. il Mo Labor R 86:44-51 Ja '63
Pay supplements in finance, insurance, and real estate. V. J. Sheifer. il Mo Labor R 87:305-12 Mr '64
Wage payment plans in metropolitan areas. J. H. Cox. il Mo Labor R 87:794-6 Jl '64
See also
Incentives in industry
Overtime
WAGE policies
Recommendation on Swedish wage policy. Mo Labor R 86:171-2 F '63
WAGE-price policy. See Price regulation by government—United States
WAGENKNECHT, Edward
Spoken word. Hi Fi 14:87-8 F; 84 Je; 72-3 Jl; 90+ Ag; 158+ O '64
WAGES
See also
Bonus system
Income
Labor cost
Non-wage payments
Overtime
Pay days
Profit sharing
Salaries
Tipping
Cost of living adjustments
Deferred increases due in 1965 and wage escalation. G. Ruben. il Mo Labor R 87:1381-4 D '64
Developments under major agreements. G. Ruben. il Mo Labor R 87:1-10 Ja '64
Use of price indexes in escalator contracts. F. S. Cunningham. il Mo Labor R 86:948-52 Ag '63
Economic aspects
Will the guideposts stick? M. M. Mestrovic. il Duns R 84:41-2+ Jl '64
Regulation
Choosing the objectives of national wage-price policy. L. Ulman. Mo Labor R 86:274-5 Mr '63
Lesson of the wage-price record. Bsns W p 120 My 30 '64
Peace, and the price. Commonweal 81:60-1 O 9 '64
Wages, prices and profits. America 110:361 Mr 21 '64
Statistics
Wage chronology: American viscose division, FMC corp; 1959-63. il Mo Labor R 86:1302-6 N '63
See also
Wage differentials
Alaska
White-collar salaries in Hawaii, Puerto Rico, and Alaska. B. B. O'Neal. bibliog f il Mo Labor R 87:301-4 Mr '64
Europe, Western
Unhappy workers. America 108:704-5 My 18 '63
What labor wants, labor gets. il Time 83:98 F 28 '64
France
General and the miners. E. Taylor. il Reporter 28:14-18 Ap 11 '63
Great Britain
In Britain, no to guidelines. U S News 55:94 S 16 '63
Note on the British national incomes commission. H. M. Douty. bibliog f Mo Labor R 86:1015-19 S '63
Hawaii
White-collar salaries in Hawai, Puerto Rico, and Alska. B. B. O'Neal. bibliog f il Mo Labor R 87:301-4 Mr '64
Netherlands
Recent wage control policy in the Netherlands. E. M. Bussey. Mo Labor R 87:517-21 My '64
Puerto Rico
White-collar salaries in Hawaii, Puerto Rico, and Alaska. B. B. O'Neal. bibliog f il Mo Labor R 87:301-4 Mr '64
Russia
Wages not high but they go a long way. il Life 55:62 S 13 '63
Spain
Pressing for change in Spain; government-controlled unions. il Bsns W p94-6 Mr 7 '64
United States
According to color. New Repub 149:5 N 16 '63
Account of American labor in 1964. P. Groom. Mo Labor R 87:1385-92 D '64
Bolstering the boom: record pay and spending. il U S News 58:78-9 Ja 18 '65; Correction. 58:91 Ja 25 '65
Built-in pay raises: what they mean for '64. il U S News 56:65-6 Ja 6 '64
Built-in wage increases; what they will mean in '65. U S News 57:108-9 N 30 '64
Deferred increases due in 1964 and wage escalation. G. Ruben. il Mo Labor R 86: 1394-7 D '63
Developments in manufacturing industries. R. W. Benny. il Mo Labor R 87:11-17 Ja '64
Earnings and hours; tables. See issues of Monthly labor review
Earnings in selected metropolitan areas of the South, June 1961. A. Bauman. il Mo Labor R 86:55-7 Ja '63
Earnings in selected metropolitan areas of the South, June 1962. H. Schaffer. il Mo Labor R 86:940-3 Ag '63
Free vs. the manipulated society; address, November 9, 1964. J. Davenport. Vital Speeches 31:125-8 D 1 '64
Greater wage-price stability ahead. il Nations Bsns 52:36-7+ S '64
How jobs, wages are shifting; with chart. U S News 55:95-6 S 30 '63
How latest raises are running. U S News 55: 70 D 30 '63
Invisible Americans. B. H. Bagdikian. il Sat Eve Post 236:28-33+ D 21 '63
Is labor's wage push more bark than bite? E. K. Faltermayer. il Fortune 69:100-3+ Je '64
Labor's next demand: bigger pay raises. il U S News 55:107-9 N 25 '63
LBJ, Meany at odds on wages. U S News 56: 89 Ap 6 '64

WAGES—United States—*Continued*
Miner is a miner. Nation 199:423 D 7 '64
Real wages: who gets more, who gets less. il U S News 55:94 Jl 8 '63
Restraint on wage raises; Jacobsson's advice. Bsns W p 160 Mr 9 '63
Union plan: after-retirement pay. U S News 56:103 Ap 27 '64
Wage-price policy approaches; excerpt from address. F. C. Pierson. Mo Labor R 86:140 F '63
Wages and jobs. America 108:357-8 Mr 16 '63
Wages in nonmetropolitan areas, Southern and North Central regions. H. Schaffer. il Mo Labor R 86:1033-9 S '63
What is happening to wages in '63. U S News 55:90-1 N 4 '63
Where pay raises are heading in 1964. il U S News 57:61 Ag 3 '64
See also
Equal pay for equal work
Government employees—Salaries, allowances, etc.
Minimum wage—United States
Public officers—Salaries, allowances, etc.
Wages—Regulation
also subhead Wages and hours under names of industries, e.g. Automobile industry and trade—Wages and hours

WAGGONER, William G.
How to make a sliding tool-rest for precision grinding. Pop Sci 185:144-5 Jl '64

WAGMAN, Frederick H.
Academic and research libraries. ALA Bul 58:533 Je '64
Freedom to read; active voice; excerpts from address, 1964. por ALA Bul 58:473-81 Je '64
Game for the thick-skinned; excerpts from address, February 1963. Library J 88:1416 Ap 1 '63
Obligations to the future; address, July 19, 1963. por ALA Bul 57:761-6 S '63
President Wagman on National library week; statement. ALA Bul 58:211 Mr '64
President's report to council. ALA Bul 58: 627-9 Jl '64
President's report to Council. por ALA Bul 58:192-5 Mr '64
Toward understanding of the Library of Congress. ALA Bul 57:322-3 Ap '63
Tribute; to J. F. Kennedy. ALA Bul 57:994 D '63

WAGMAN, Irving H. See Battersby, W. S. jt. auth.

WAGMAN, William
Sodium chloride deprivation: development of sodium chloride as a reinforcement. Science 140:1403-4 Je 28 '63

WAGNER, Constance
House of the Lady Aziza. Reporter 30:35-6 Ja 2 '64

WAGNER, Gary
(comp) Frankly speaking. See issues of McCall's to February 1964

WAGNER, Geoffrey
Mafia. Commonweal 81:22-3 S 25 '64
Movies. Nat R 16:502-3 Je 16 '64
Truth and error. Commonweal 79:757-8 Mr 20 '64

WAGNER, Harvey M.
Practical slants on operations research. bibliog Harvard Bsns R 41:61-71 My '63

WAGNER, Kip
Drowned galleons yield Spanish gold. pors Nat Geog Mag 127:1-37 Ja '65

WAGNER, Leon Lamar
Free-swinging Angel who never fears to tread. R. Creamer. por Sports Illus 19:46+ Ag 12 '63
Has-been who became a star. il pors Ebony 18:102-4+ O '63
Policeman of the outhouse. por Time 81:74+ Je 21 '63

WAGNER, Mary Hagel
Equal opportunity in education. America 111:209 Ag 29 '64

WAGNER, Melinda
Psychiatrist at the drawing board. Todays Health 41:14-17+ Ag '63

WAGNER, O. Walter
Harvest time. Christian Cent 81:990-3 Ag 5 '64

WAGNER, Philip L. See Stone, R. jt. auth.

WAGNER, Richard, 1813-1883
Class of 1813; reflections on Verdi vs. Wagner. P. J. Pirie. il Hi Fi 13:90-2+ O '63
Excerpts from Die Meistersinger, Schorr's Hans Sachs. C. L. Osborne. Hi Fi 14:63-4 Je '64
Flying Dutchman (Der fliegende Holländer) Criticism
Opera N 27:17-20 F 2 '63
Opera N il 27:25-6 F 2 '63
Friedrich Schorr's Hans Sachs. P. L. Miller. Am Rec G 30:976 Je '64
Gift for borrowing. O. Lehmann. il Opera N 28:24-5 F 1 '64
Glitter from the golden age of Wagner singing; Die Walküre. G. Kossodo. Am Rec G 29:426-7 F '63
Götterdämmerung. Criticism
New Yorker 39:148-50 N 23 '63
Opera N il 28:17-20 D 14 '63
Opera N 28:24-5 D 14 '63
Sat R 46:44+ N 30 '63
House that Wagner built. E. Downes. il Hi Fi 14:49-52+ F '64
Jess Thomas as Angel's Lohengrin. G. L. Mayer. Am Rec G 30:494-6+ F '64
Letter from Richard Wagner; imaginary letter to Thomas Scherman. B. Hastings. Opera N 28:4 N 16 '63
Lohengrin. Criticism
Opera N il 28:17-20 F 1 '64
Sat R 47:34 F 15 '64
London's near perfect Siegfried. G. L. Mayer. il Am Rec G 29:686-9 My '63
Die Meistersinger. H. Glass. il Am Rec G 31:26-8+ S '64
Melchior's Siegfried, the greatest then and the greatest still. G. Kossodo. il Am Rec G 30:108-10 O '63
Music to my ears; Rienzi in concert; performance in Philharmonic Hall, New York. I. Kolodin. Sat R 46:27 D 14 '63
Musical events; revival of Rienzi at Lincoln Center, performed by Concert opera association. W. Sargeant. New Yorker 39:199-200 D 7 '63
New look in Valhalla. J. Wechsberg. il Horizon 5:40-5 My '63
On records; Der fliegende Holländer. J. W. Freeman. Opera N 27:35 F 2 '63
On records; Lohengrin. Opera N 28:35 F 1 '64
On records; Die Meistersinger. C. J. Luten. Opera N 29:28 S 26 '64
On records; Siegfried. il Opera N 28:34 D 14 '63
On records; Tristan und Isolde. J. W. Freeman. Opera N 27:35 F 23 '63
Parsifal. Criticism
New Yorker 40:180+ O 10 '64
Opera N il 28:17-20 Mr 28 '64
Opera N il 28:33-4 Ap 18 '64
Records; Wagner's late works. B. Boretz. Nation 198:37-9 Ja 6 '64
Rienzi. Criticism
Opera N 28:4 N 16 '63
Opera N 28:35 Ja 4 '64
Siegfried. Criticism
Hi Fi 13:71-2 Ap '63
Tannhäuser. Criticism
Opera N 27:34-5 Mr 9 '63
Sat R 46:47 F 23 '63
Tristan und Isolde. Criticism
New Yorker 38:150-1 F 16 '63
Opera N il 27:8-12 F 23 '63
Opera N 27:17-20 F 23 '63
Unreluctant composers; conversation with Mozart, Verdi and Wagner. L. F. Loveday. il Opera N 28:8-11 Ja 25 '64
Verdi-Wagner anniversary; with chronology by M. Bernheimer. H. Weinstock. por Sat R 46:35-7 Jl 27 '63
Wagner I know. J. Rosenstock. il Opera N 28:8-11 D 14 '63
Wagner in stereo. H. Kupferberg. il Atlan 212:112+ S '63
Wagner's Ring and its symbols, by R. Donington. Review
New Yorker 39:156-7 S 21 '63. W. Sargeant
Opera N 28:7 D 14 '63. K. Hoover
Die Walküre. Criticism
Opera N 27:32 F 2 '63
See also
Bayreuth festival

Anecdotes, facetiae, satire, etc.

Wagner in travesty. J. W. Stedman. il Opera N 27:24-7 F 23 '63

WAGNER, Robert Ferdinand, 1910-
Lulu of a fight. il por Time 85:21-2 Ja 29 '65
Marriage of necessity. il por Newsweek 64: 28-9 Ag 31 '64
Mayor again is frustrated. por Bsns W p34 Mr 30 '63
Mayor Wagner: a rise in political stock. por U S News 56:21 Je 15 '64
Ordeals of Robert F. Wagner. G. Astor. il pors Look 28:69-70+ Jl 28 '64

WAGNER, Warren H. jr, and Sharp, A. J.
Remarkably reduced vascular plant in the United States. bibliog Science 142:1483-4 D 13 '63

WAGNER, Wieland
New look in Valhalla. J. Wechsberg. il por Horizon 5:40-5 My '63

WAGNER, Wolfgang
Season down under. Mus Am 83:270-1 D '63
WAGNER Lutheran college, Staten Island
Island paradox. R. Hoffman. il Mlle 57:140-2+ O '63
WAGONER, David
Closing time; poem. New Yorker 39:48 Mr 16 '63
Fruit of the tree; poem. New Yorker 40:34 Ag 22 '64
Night of the sad women; poem. New Yorker 40:56 S 19 '64
On seeing an X-ray of my head; Advice to the orchestra; Breathing lesson; poems. Poetry 102:27-30 Ap '63
Water music for the progress of love in a life-raft down the Sammamish slough; Stretching canvases; By the orchard; Words; Leaving something behind; poems. Poetry 104:99-103 My '64
Welcome; poem. New Yorker 40:64 N 7 '64
about
Underestimations. X. J. Kennedy. Poetry 103:332-3 F '64
WAGONER, Ed
Texas forestry association's 50th anniversary; the green gold of Texas. Am For 70:26-9+ S '64
WAGONER, Walter D.
Current situation, and comment thereon. Christian Cent 81:329-30 Mr 11 '64
Frankfurt: the ghost of unity. Christian Cent 81:1089-90 S 2 '64
WAGONS, Circus. See Circus—Equipment
WAGONS-lits. See Railroads—Sleeping cars
WAGSTAFF, Samuel J. jr
Paintings to think about. Art N 62:38+ Ja '64
WAGSTROM, Margaretha
Five day lover. pors Esquire 60:221-3 D '63
WAHBA, I. J. and others
Radiation-induced gelation of dilute aqueous pectin solutions. bibliog Science 139:1297-8 Mr 29 '63
WAHL, Johann Georg
Rhenish cabinet of the eighteenth century. R. C. Smith. il Antiques 87:68-72 Ja '65
WAHL, Paul
Look what's happening to SLRs. Pop Sci 186:142-5+ Ja '65
WAHLEEN, Eric
Deception Pass. il Am For 69:28-9 Je '63
Driftwood fantasies. Am For 69:15 My '63
Tail-end Charlie. il PTA Mag 58:19 Ja '64
Winter motor trip. Travel 120:32-3 D '63
WAHLSTROM, Richard C.
Don't discount oats for growing pigs. Suc Farm 61:69 Ag '63
WAHOO (fish)
Remarkable wahoo. J. Olsen. il Sports Illus 19:80-2+ S 30 '63
WAHOO fishing
Wahoo are sudden. J. Brooks. il Field & S 68:38-9+ N '63
WAIN, John
Further education; story. Ladies Home J 81:84-7 Ap '64
King Caliban; story. Sat Eve Post 236:44-8 Mr 30 '63
New Robert Lowell. New Repub 151:21-3 O 17 '64
Oysters and a novelist's art. New Repub 151:23-4 Ag 8 '64
about
Antidisestablishmentarian. por Time 81:102+ My 24 '63
Merrie England. A. Wilson. Commentary 37:74-5 Je '64
WLB biography. M. L. Holton. por Wilson Lib Bul 37:803 My '63
WAINERDI, Richard E. and DuBeau, N. P.
Nuclear activation analysis. bibliog Science 139:1027-33 Mr 15 '63
—See Guinn, V. P. jt. auth.
WAINWRIGHT, Loudon
Dying girl that no one helped. Life 56:21 Ap 10 '64
Pro turned amateur: Glenn's first hectic days. Life 56:36B Ja 31 '64
View from here. See issues of Life
Visit to the grave. Life 56:15 F 14 '64
about
This is the man you've been asking about. G. P. Hunt. por Life 57:3 O 30 '64
WAISMAN, Harry A. See Gerritsen, T. jt. auth.
WAITE, Helen E.
Listen, my heart; condensation of Make a joyful sound. Read Digest 82:297-308+ Ap '63
WAITE, Morrison Remick
Foot in the door; Munn v. Illinois. C. P. Magrath. il por Am Heritage 15:44-8+ F '64
WAITERS and waitresses
Wages in eating and drinking places, June 1963. G. L. Stelluto. il Mo Labor R 87:544-8 My '64
WAITZ, J. A. and others
Dialysis studies in rats on the long-acting antimalarial CI-501. Science 141:723-5 Ag 23 '63
WAITRESSES. See Waiters and waitresses
WAKAMBA (native race) See Kenya—Native races
WAKE FOREST college, Winston Salem, N.C.
Fight for Wake Forest. il Time 84:73-4 N 27 '64
WAKEFIELD, Dan
Battle plan for integration. Esquire 60:101-4+ O '63
Campus conservatives: where are they now? Mlle 57:292-3+ Ag '63
Dos, which side are you on? Esquire 59:112-14+ Ap '63
In Hazard. Commentary 36:209-17 S '63
Labor shudders at leisure. Nation 196:325-7 Ap 20 '63
Neatest teener. Esquire 59:88-9+ Je '63
Opinion, please. Mlle 60:70+ N '64
WAKEFIELD, Henriette
Memories of Dangeville. H. Doulens. il por Opera N 27:34 F 9 '63
WAKEFIELD, Hugh
Glasswares by Apsley Pellatt. Antiques 87:85-8 Ja '65
WAKEFIELD, Lawrence
Who will get policy baron's fortune? H. Bims. il por Ebony 19:116-18+ O '64
WAKEFIELD, Sherman Day
Amplification: letter to the editor. Christian Cent 80:468 Ap 10 '63
WAKEFULNESS. See Insomnia
WAKELIN, James H. jr
Thresher: lesson and challenge. por Nat Geog Mag 125:759-63 Je '64
WAKEMAN, John
Battle for library books. Parents Mag 38:138-9 Ap '63
British museum bill. Wilson Lib Bul 37:782-5+ My '63
Cultivate their sense of humor. Parents Mag 39:40-1+ Ag '64
WAKES, Ben
Reflections in a well. Read Digest 82:71-2 Ap '63
WAKIN, Edward
Egypt's Christian minority. Christian Cent 81:332-4 Mr 11 '64
How it operates. Sat R 47:68+ F 15 '64
Problem of the Kurds and why. Sat R 47:34 Je 20 '64
Return of Montessori. Sat R 47:61-3 N 21 '64
Visit to a Munich suburb. America 111:235-6 S 5 '64
WAKOSKI, Diane
Winter apples; poem. Nation 197:144 S 14 '63
WAKULLA SPRINGS wildlife sanctuary. See Wildlife sanctuaries
WALAN, Robert
Amateur scientist. Sci Am 210:132-3+ F '64
WALD, George
Receptors of human color vision. bibliog Science 145:1007-16 S 4 '64
—See Brown, P. K. jt. auth.
WALD, Niel, and others
Radiation-induced mouse leukemia: consistent occurrence of an extra and a marker chromosome. bibliog Science 143:810-13 F 21 '64
WALDBAUER, Eugene C.
Build a nature trail. Recreation 57:114 Mr '64
WALDEMAR medical research foundation. See Medical laboratories
WALDEN, Austin T.
If I were young today. por Ebony 18:74 Je '63
WALDEN, Daniel
W. E. B. Du Bois: pioneer reconstruction historian. bibliog f Negro Hist Bul 26:159-60+ F '63
WALDEN, William
Brinker's ratios; poem. New Yorker 40:29 Jl 25 '64
Five poems. New Yorker 40:52 Ap 25 '64
Meanwhile, back at the plot. . . Sat R 48:19-20 Ja 2 '65
Our era in perspective; poem. McCalls 92:154 N '64
WALDENSTROM, Erland
Growing Grangesberg. il por Bsns W p 140+ Mr 21 '64
Who's who in foreign business. por Fortune 69:52 Je '64

WALDMAN, Frederic
Musical events; Dvořák's Requiem mass performed by Musica aeterna. W. Sargeant. New Yorker 40:171-3 Mr 7 '64
WALDMAN, Gary
Boy meets girl. por Seventeen 23:78+ Ja '64
WALDNER, Geoffroy, baronne de
Passion for flowers: Baronne Geoffroy de Waldner and her French garden; with account by V. Lawford. il por Vogue 144:260-9, 275-6+ D '64
WALDO, Mary Jane
Crossing the river of time. Writer 76:7-9 Ap '63
They've closed the Palais royale; story. Good H 157:94-5 N '63
WALDO, Myra
Middle East cook book. House & Gard 123: 131+ F '63
WALDO, Octavia Capuzzi
Egyptian paste jewelry. Sch Arts 62:36-7 Mr '63
WALDRIP, Celle Slack
Time for tears. NEA J 53:63 S '64
WALDRON, Eli
Buffalo Bill's home town. Holiday 34:85-91 Ag '63
Green Bay: the Packers' town. Holiday 34: 68-9+ N '63
Journey down the Mississippi. Holiday 33:80-93+ My '63; Same abr. Read Digest 83:142-51 Jl '63
New American capital of Bohemia. Sat Eve Post 237:98-102 My 23 '64
WALDRON, Ingrid
Courtship sound production in two sympatric sibling drosophila species. bibliog Science 144:191-3 Ap 10 '64
WALDRON, Martin
After dark in St Augustine. Nation 198:648-51 Je 29 '64
WALES
See also
Christmas—Wales
Music—Wales

Description and travel

Wander through Wales. V. Condon. il Travel 120:36-41 Ag '63
WALFORD, Roy L. and others
Serologic typing of human lymphocytes with immune serum obtained after homografting. bibliog Science 144:868-70 My 15 '64
WALINSKY, Adam
Keeping the poor in their place. New Repub 151:15-18 Jl 4 '64
WALINSKY, Louis J.
Five sides to strategy. Sat R 47:30-2 Jl 11 '64
His nation went to prison with him. Sat R 46:44 D 7 '63
New nations in an age of automation. Sat R 47:42+ S 19 '64
WALK in darkness; drama. See Hairston, W.
WALK in the forest; story. See Sterba, M.
WALKER, A. Angus
Renaissance at Rheem. J. B. Weiner. por Duns R 83:35+ Ap '64
WALKER, A. B.
Electrostatic precipitators. Am City 79:148+ S '64
WALKER, Alan
Australia's Life line movement. Christian Cent 81:20-1 Ja 1 '64
South Africa's tragic story. Christian Cent 81:406+ Mr 25 '64

about

Alan Walker in South Africa. H. Henderson. Christian Cent 80:1410+ N 13 '63
Bold mission in South Africa. Christian Cent 80:1070 S 4 '63
Calls for world conference on racial problems. Christian Cent 80:1324 O 30 '63
Throwing out the Life line. il Time 83:34 Ja 24 '64
WALKER, Barbara K. and Uysal, Ahmet
Folk tales in Turkey. Horn Bk 40:42-6 F '64
WALKER, C. Lester
Don't be panic-sold on fire alarms. Read Digest 82:89-92 Ap '63
WALKER, Catherine
Home on the range; poem. McCalls 91:122 Jl '64
WALKER, David
Farmer's son; Homing; poems. Poetry 105: 160-7 N '64
New venture, a new beginning. Writer 77: 9-11+ Ag '64
WALKER, Don
Black bear posse. Outdoor Life 132:40-3+ D '63
—See Guither, H. jt. auth.
WALKER, Donald E.
American dream and crisis; address, August 24, 1964. Vital Speeches 31:78-82 N 15 '64
WALKER, Dora Fogarty
School librarian builds a public image; adaptation of address. por Library J 88: 3258-60 S 15 '63
WALKER, Dorothea
Going places, finding things in the Far East. House & Gard 124:26+ Ag '63
Lovely lesson I learned in Hawaii. House & Gard 126:112-13+ Jl '64
WALKER, Edward A.
How to organize a crew bank. Yachting 115: 220-1 My '64
WALKER, Edwin Anderson
Another assassination attempt by Lee Oswald? por U S News 55:8 D 16 '63
Crusade and collect. il por Newsweek 61:21-2 Ap 1 '63
General v. the cub. il por Time 83:46+ Je 26 '64
Near-miss; attempted assassination. Newsweek 61:34 Ap 22 '63
New clue in attempt to shoot General Walker. U S News 56:10 Ja 13 '64
No indictment in case against Walker. por U S News 54:19 F 4 '63
WALKER, Eric A.
Walker chairman of National science board. Sci N L 85:360 Je 6 '64
WALKER, Estellene P.
South Carolina's program. ALA Bul 58:143-4 F '64
WALKER, Frances
On birthdays; poem. por Seventeen 22:96 Ag '63
WALKER, George Richmond
Art, science, and reality. Bul Atomic Sci 20: 9-12 S '64
WALKER, Gerald
(ed) Christmas I'll never forget. Good H 157: 17-18+ D '63
Englewood and the northern dilemma. Nation 197:7-10 Jl 6 '63
My children's heroes. Good H 156:84-5+ Je '63
Young man, be an executioner. Esquire 60: 62-3 Ag '63
WALKER, Howell
Italian Riviera, land that winter forgot. il Nat Geog Mag 123:743-89 Je '63
WALKER, James
Disillusion; poem. McCalls 90:163 S '63
WALKER, James J.
Man who rode the tiger: the life and times of Judge Samuel Seabury, by H. Mitgang. Review
Sat R 46:43 Mr 30 '63. R. A. Low
WALKER, Jerry L.
New literature for adolescents. Sr Schol 83: 21T Ja 17 '64
WALKER, Jessie
Fireplace wall modernized. Farm J 87:111 Mr '63
Quiet corner for your desk work. Bet Hom & Gard 41:114H Mr '63
WALKER, John H.
We can prevent presidential assassinations. por Look 28:124-6 F 11 '64
WALKER, John S. and others
Water intake of normal children. bibliog Science 140:890-1 My 24 '63
WALKER, Laurence C.
Trees for city deserts. Am For 69:28-30 Mr '63
WALKER, Merle F.
New observations of AE Aquarii. il por Sky & Tel 29:23-5 Ja '65
WALKER, Michael
Thunderstorm, huge dynamo. Sci N L 85: 362-3 Je 6 '64
—See Tufty, B. jt. auth.
WALKER, Mickey
Days of wine and bloody noses; excerpt from Million dollar gate. J. Kearns and O. Fraley. il pors Sports Illus 20:50-4+ Ja 20 '64
WALKER, Norman
Norman Walker and dance company, N.Y. school of printing. J. Maskey. Dance Mag 38:68+ My '64
WALKER, Patrick Gordon. See Gordon Walker, P.
WALKER, Raymond F.
Thermal imaging techniques. Science 140:504-5 My 3 '63
WALKER, Raymond J.
Almanacs. Hobbies 68:122+ Ja '64
WALKER, Richard R. See Smith, R. W. jr, jt. auth.
WALKER, Sir Ronald
Economic and social council in 1963. por U N Rev 10:40-2 Ag '63
Economic and social council in perspective. UN Mo Chron 1:77-80 Ag '64

WALKER, Stan
Record covers: hard sell, soft sell, no sell. Mus Am 83:20-1 Jl '63

WALKER, Ted
Breakwaters; poem. New Yorker 39:32 Je 22 '63
By the saltings; poem. New Yorker 40:25 Jl 11 '64
Carp; poem. New Yorker 39:198 D 7 '63
Estuary; poem. New Yorker 40:46 Ap 11 '64
Five poems: Starlings; Skate fishers; Rook shoot; Burning; By the bridge. New Yorker 40:56-7 O 3 '64
Mushrooms; poem. New Yorker 39:28 Ag 31 '63
Skimmers; poem. New Yorker 39:28 Ja 11 '64

WALKER, Tippy
New faces in a smash new movie; ed. by E. Miller. pors Seventeen 23:132+ Je '64
Merrie and Tippy. New Yorker 40:35-6 My 23 '64

WALKER, Todd
Restless eye of Todd Walker. M. Ornitz. il U S Camera 27:46-9+ Ap '64

WALKER, Valerie E.
Easter eggs in wonderland. Ladies Home J 80:104+ Ap '63

WALKER, Warren S.
Invisible weapons in a secret war. Sat R 47:42 F 1 '64
Spying: the second oldest profession. Sat R 46:30-1+ My 25 '63

WALKER, William
On the steps; interview, ed. by P. Moed. Opera N 27:15 Ap 6 '63

WALKER, William, 1824-1860
One kind of patriot. il por Time 81:29 Ap 26 '63
World and William Walker, by A. Z. Carr. Review
Am Heritage 15:108-9 D '63. B. Catton

WALKER, Zachariah
Summer Sunday; excerpt from Incident in Coatsville; with editorial comment. E. F. Goldman. il Am Heritage 15:50-3+ Je '64

WALKER'S peak; story. See White, R.

WALKIE-talkies. See Radio telephone, Portable

WALKING
American kids can take it! survival hike across Florida, ed. by K. Vining. R. Allen. il Pop Sci 182:106-9+ F '63
Americans can walk. il U S News 54:64 F 25 '63
Bones make the walker. E. Mirel. Sci N L 83:117 F 23 '63
Do you know how to walk? J. H. Hocking. il Recreation 56:219 My '63
Go take a hike. il Changing T 17:45-6 Ag '63
Hit the road, Jack; challenge of marching fifty miles in twenty hours. il Time 81:22 F 22 '63
I've rediscovered walking. C. Fletcher. il Read Digest 82:139-41 Mr '63
JFK's pace corps. il Newsweek 61:23 F 25 '63
Let's take an old-fashioned fifty-mile walk; with account by R. Wallace. il Life 54:72A-78+ F 22 '63
Next: automated people. R. T. Allen. il Sci Digest 53:39-41 My '63
Pedestrian approach. Reporter 28:18+ Mr 14 '63
Shanks' mare. New Yorker 39:23-4 Mr 2 '63
Take a million giant steps; fifty mile hike. Sports Illus 18:8 F 25 '63
Trudging along the blister trail. il Sr Schol 82:16 F 27 '63
Walk, walk, walk. Newsweek 61:74 F 4 '63
Walking; excerpt from Fields of noon. S. Burnford. Atlan 214:66-70 Ag '64
See also
Trails

WALKING in sleep. See Somnambulism

WALKS (paths)
Better approach, and this house looks forty years younger. il House B 105:178-9 S '63
See also
Garden walks

Die **WALKÜRE**; opera. See Wagner, R.

WALL, A. E. P.
Aloha has many meanings. America 111:148 Ag 15 '64

WALL, Carl B.
William Gargan's finest role. Read Digest 83:49-54 S '63

WALL, Michael
Cyprus, island of hate and fear. N Y Times Mag p 13+ Mr 8 '64
Cyprus problem=Makarios problem. N Y Times Mag p38-9+ O 18 '64

WALL clocks. See Clocks

WALL coverings
Fabric covers all. G. O'Brien. il N Y Times Mag pt2 p22-3 S 27 '64
Fake tiling, fake caning. il Vogue 142:136-7+ O 15 '63
Fun and fakery decorate your walls. il Am Home 67:54-5 Ja '64
Wall coverings: what's going on? il Good H 158:108 Ja '64
See also
Wallpaper

WALL hangings
Decorative wall hangings. D. B. Van Dommelen. il Sch Arts 62:7-9 Ap '63
Venice: the biennale. J. Guth and F. Guth. il Craft Horiz 24:48 S '64

WALL-hung toilets. See Water closets

WALL painting. See Mural painting and decoration

WALL paper. See Wallpaper

WALL plaques. See Plaques, plaquettes

WALL shelves. See Shelves

WALL Street Journal
Larceny is good for you; curious ad. il Newsweek 62:54 Jl 1 '63

WALL tennis. See Tennis

WALL-to-wall carpeting. See Rugs and carpets

WALLA WALLA, Wash.
Clean sewers at half the cost. P. H. Meyer. il Am City 78:27 N '63
Truck-mounted chipper-container. V. Tompkins. il Am City 79:18 D '64

WALLACE, Anthony
Exporting the American idea. Sat R 46:54-6 Ap 6 '63

WALLACE, Cecelia
Pacem in terris, Ecclesiam Suam and communism. Cath World 200:231-8 Ja '65

WALLACE, Dorothy
Garden in a window. Am Home 68:26 Ja '65

WALLACE, Dwane L.
Cessna acts to widen twin-engine sales; foresees industry growth; summary of address. Aviation W 78:76+ Mr 18 '63

WALLACE, Forrest
Correct wine for now and 1984. Esquire 61:106-7+ Ja '64

WALLACE, Fred
What stopped the bleeding? il por Time 81:63 Ap 26 '63

WALLACE, George Corley
Before the showdown: Wallace's views; excerpts from statement. por U S News 54:19 Je 17 '63
How Wallace explains his big vote in Wisconsin; interview. por U S News 56:34 Ap 20 '64
Law and order; responsibility of governors. America 108:796 Je 1 '63
U.S. troops in Alabama. por U S News 54:40 My 27 '63
Wallace vote; candidates own story; questions and answers. U S News 56:63 Je 1 '64
Why Wallace withdrew; in the Governor's own words; excerpts from address, July 19, 1964. por U S News 57:56-8 Ag 3 '64

about

Aftermath in Alabama. R. Cleghorn. Reporter 31:34-5 D 3 '64
Alabama's defiant leader Governor Wallace vs. JFK; against racial integration. por U S News 54:23 My 27 '63
Bargain with the devil; Negro applicants at the University of Alabama. il por Newsweek 61:30 Je 10 '63
Boomerang. il por Newsweek 62:24+ S 16 '63
Bounce high the head beams, Governor. V. Gold. Nat R 16:492 Je 16 '64
Counterrevolt? W. F. Buckley, jr. Nat R 16:348 My 5 '64
Gary's rank-and-file reaction. V. Hoffman and J. Strietelmeier. il Reporter 31:28-9 S 10 '64; Reply. D. Radler. 31:6+ O 8 '64
George Wallace shakes up the political scene. H. H. Martin. il pors Sat Eve Post 237:85-9 My 9 '64
Governor Wallace: third-party candidate? U S News 56:33 Je 22 '64
Governor Wallace waits. New Repub 151:5 O 17 '64
Governor Wallace's victories without winning. M. Phelps. America 110:786 Je 6 '64
Huckster for a hot summer. L. Wainwright. Life 56:21 My 8 '64
I was the instrument. Time 84:19 Jl 31 '64
If Wallace stole the dome. P. D. Lagomarcino. New Repub 150:13 My 9 '64
Invader. il por Time 83:18 Mr 27 '64
Judgment on racism. America 110:470 Ap 4 '64
Letter from Washington. R. H. Rovere. New Yorker 40:193-8 My 16 '64

WALLACE, George Corley—about—*Continued*
Letter to a governor. E. J. Hughes. Newsweek 61:19 Je 17 '63
Letting George do it. il Newsweek 62:33-4 S 23 '63
More about the backlash. Time 83:21-2 My 29 '64
More anticlimax than crisis. il Time 82:30 S 20 '63
Next stand. il por Time 81:19 Je 7 '63
Notes and comment. New Yorker 39:19 Je 22 '63
On Wisconsin? Cato. Nat R 16:349 My 5 '64
On, Wisconsin! Reporter 30:14 Ap 23 '64
President vs. a governor: another school showdown. il U S News 55:42-3 S 23 '63
Rattle of eyeteeth. il por Newsweek 63:18-19 Mr 30 '64
Resounding cry. il Time 81:22 My 24 '63
Shaking eyeteeth. il por Newsweek 63:22 My 4 '64
Shameful thing. il por Time 82:26-7 S 13 '63
South's new voice; press opinion. Time 82:65 S 20 '63
Spark in Cambridge. il Newsweek 63:33-4 My 25 '64
State of Maryland. M. Kempton. New Repub 150:6-8 My 23 '64
Stop Wallace. Nat R 16:577 Jl 14 '64
Third man. por Newsweek 64:30+ Jl 20 '64
Two-yacht governors. il Time 81:25 F 22 '63
Uninvited guest. il Time 83:24 My 22 '64
Victorious loser. por Newsweek 63:33 My 18 '64
Wallace and the future of Dixie. R. G. Sherrill. Nation 199:266-72 O 26 '64
Wallace in Alabama. Nation 198:498 My 18 '64
Wallace in Alabama and in Maryland. New Repub 150:4-5 My 16 '64
Wallace in Indiana; with editorial comment. G. Englehart. por Nation 198:449, 451-3 My 4 '64
Wallace in Wisconsin. Nation 198:386 Ap 20 '64
Wallace vs. Goldwater in the South. por U S News 57:16 Jl 27 '64
Wallace vs. Johnson: a problem for Democrats. por U S News 56:20 Mr 23 '64
Wallace victory. America 110:558 Ap 25 '64
Wallace: welcome home you living doll. il por Newsweek 63:18 Je 1 '64
Wallace's Wisconsin, 264,100 votes. il por Newsweek 63:33-4 Ap 20 '64
We want Wallace. T. Coffman. New Repub 151:14 Jl 11 '64
What price Wallace? Newsweek 64:23-4 Ag 3 '64
What Wallace vote proved in North. il por U S News 56:29-32+ Je 1 '64
Where the stars fall. il pors Time 82:17-21 S 27 '63
Who's Wallace? il Time 83:22 Ap 24 '64
Winning without winning. il por Newsweek 63:17+ Je 1 '64
Wisconsin primary. Commonweal 80:133 Ap 24 '64

WALLACE, George J. and Bernard, R. F.
Tests show forty species of birds poisoned by DDT. Audubon Mag 65:198-202 Jl '63

WALLACE, Henry Agard
At seventy-five, Henry Wallace cultivates his garden. C. Phillips. il por N Y Times Mag p47+ O 6 '63

WALLACE, Irving
Irving Wallace bends some rules; interview, ed. by M. Manheim. Writer 78:12-15+ Ja '65

about

Big money writers. R. Schickel. il pors Life 57:58-60+ Jl 31 '64
Rights and permissions. P. Nathan. Pub W 184:45 S 23 '63
Tips: research for next novel. Pub W 184:54 Ag 5 '63

WALLACE, John F.
Girl overboard; story. Ladies Home J 80:54-5 Ja '63

WALLACE, Kevin
Onward and upward with the arts. New Yorker 39:104+ S 7 '63

WALLACE, Mary
Crickets and katydids, long ago. Sat R 46:40-1+ Ap 13 '63

WALLACE, Mike
(ed) See Ngo-dinh-Nhu, Mme. Mike Wallace interviews Madame Nhu

WALLACE, Robert
Fifteen dolphins; poem. Nation 196:106 F 2 '63
Gamble on novices works almost too well. Life 55:100+ O 25 '63
Go, go, Gogolaks! Life 55:127-8 N 8 '63
Kids' books: a happy few amid the junk. Life 57:112-14+ D 11 '64
Kingly glory and ordeal. Life 57:60-5 D 25 '64
Life book review. Life 56:11 Ap 10 '64
Living doll. Harper 228:38-40 Ja '64
National yelp over an earlift. Life 56:34-34A My 8 '64
Non-whiz kid with the quiet gun. Life 55:75-6+ Ag 9 '63
Poet's right to invention. Writer 76:16-18 Mr '63
Recharge at Gettysburg. Life 55:14+ Jl 5 '63
Second impressions; review of paperbacks. See issues of Nation
What kind of place is Dallas? Life 56:67-8+ Ja 31 '64
Where's the party: let's crash it! Life 55:62-4+ Jl 5 '63; Same abr. Read Digest 83:131-5 O '63

WALLACE, Robert (poet)
Forsaken; poem. Atlan 212:60 S '63
Storm; poem. New Yorker 40:197 D 12 '64

WALLACE, Robert Ash
Coin shortage: why it happened; when it will end; interview. por U S News 57:68-70 Jl 27 '64

WALLACE, Sarah L.
Public relations: a three-way definition. Wilson Lib Bul 37:557-61 Mr '63

WALLACE, Walker D.
Alabama boneyard sheds new light on whales. Sci Digest 53:77-80 Ap '63

WALLACE, William A.
Catholics and the science explosion. Cath World 200:109-15 N '64
Radiation and social ethics. America 108:880-3 Je 22 '63

WALLACE, William N.
It's not magic, says Tittle. N Y Times Mag p48+ N 10 '63
Left tackle. N Y Times Mag p 137-41+ N 8 '64
Yale finds a coach. Sat Eve Post 236:74-7 O 12 '63

WALLACE Heaton, limited. See London—Stores

WALLACH, Eli
Talk with the stars. por Newsweek 61:56 F 18 '63
What's with the Wallachs? at home or onstage it's Luv. il pors Life 58:79-81+ Ja 8 '65

WALLACH, Ira
Absence of a cello. Criticism
America 111:497 O 24 '64
Commonweal 81:100-1 O 16 '64
Sat R 47:30 O 24 '64
Time 84:82 O 2 '64

WALLAS, Graham
LBJ's great society. R. Moley. Newsweek 64:102 S 28 '64

WALLBOARD
Hanging things on a gypsum wall. il Sunset 133:124 N '64

WALLEN, Richard W.
Three types of executive personality. Duns R 81:54-6+ F '63

WALLENBERG brothers
Seemly success. il Time 81:98 Je 7 '63

WALLENBERG family
Biggest employer. il Time 82:98 N 29 '63

WALLENDA, Karl
War of nerves on the highwire. B. Ballantine. il pors Sat Eve Post 237:73-7 F 15 '64

WALLENDA family
Death on the high wire. B. Ballantine. il Read Digest 83:53-9 Jl '63
See also
Acrobats and acrobatism

WALLENSTEIN, Aaron, and Albert, L. S.
Plant morphology: its control in proserpinaca by photoperiod, temperature, and gibberellic acid. bibliog Science 140:998-1000 My 31 '63

WALLER, Kim Kurt
Off-camera close-up. Mlle 56:114-15+ F '63
Ski bums: the upland Bohemians. Mlle 58:172-3+ N '63

WALLER, Marion, and others
New serum group, Gm(p) bibliog Science 142:1321-2 D 6 '63

WALLER, William
Justice in Mississippi; notes on the Beckwith trial. J. Herron. Nation 198:179-81 F 24 '64

WALLEYE fishing. See Perch fishing

WALLICH, Henry C.
Berlin's economic future. Atlan 212:130-4 D '63
If creeping inflation begins to run. N Y Times Mag p34+ S 13 '64
Instant tax cut. por Newsweek 65:82 Ja 25 '65
Is recession inevitable? interview, ed. by G. R. Rosen. Duns R 84:30-1+ Ag '64
Outlook for '65. por Newsweek 65:72 Ja 11 '65

WALLING, Ruth
Two stars from Georgia; reflections on the ALA conference in St Louis. E. Moon. il por Library J 89:2919-28 Ag '64
WALLINGFORD, Pa.
See also
Helen Kate Furness free library
WALLMANN, Margherita
Determined lady; interview, ed. by A. M. Lingg. por Opera N 29:14-15 O 17 '64
WALLOONS
Lingua belgica. il Time 81:34 Je 7 '63
WALLOPS ISLAND station. See Proving grounds
WALLOWA MOUNTAINS
Camper's discovery. il Sunset 131:50-5 Jl '63
WALLOWITCH, Edward
Faces of man. il Design 65:200-1 My '64
WALLPAPER
Non-tile tiling. il Vogue 142:134-5 O 15 '63
Shop talk. R. Davidson. il Antiques 83:372+ Ap '63
Wall coverings: what's going on? il Good H 158:108 Ja '64
You can work wonders with problem walls. il Parents Mag 39:61+ Ja '64
WALLS, Josiah Thomas
Know your congressmen. N. L. Milton. Negro Hist Bul 27:17 O '63
WALLS
Bearing walls in Iowa. Arch Forum 118:126-30 My '63
Decorate problem wall with family photo tree. il Parents Mag 38:140 Mr '63
Fireplace wall modernized; photographs. J. Walker. Farm J 87:111 Mr '63
Formwork: time-saver standards. S. Howard. il Arch Rec 136:256 S '64
More Japanese ideas cross the Pacific; multi-ple-panel wall. il Sunset 130:74-5 F '63
Prefabricated flashing for parapet walls. H. Edwards. il Arch Rec 135:209-10 My '64
Preventing cracks in masonry walls. D. Kaminetzky. il Arch Rec 136:210-14 N '64
Unusual structural wall for IBM in Seattle. il Arch Rec 134:104-7 D '63
Wall: glass and clay. il Craft Horiz 23:24-6 My '63
Wall: painted clay. M. Cable. il Craft Horiz 23:27-31+ My '63
You can really scrub vinyl walls. il Sunset 130:168+ My '63
You can work wonders with problem walls. il Parents Mag 39:61+ Ja '64
See also
Garden walls
Panel construction
Paneling
Partitions
Retaining walls
Sea walls
Storage walls
WALLS, Glass
Beach house with vast expanse of glass. A. C. Borg. il Am Home 66:32-3 Je '63
Elegant small house doubles its apparent space by a semi-enclosed court. il Arch Rec 133:122-5 mid-My '63
Frame that lovely view. il House B 106:54+ Ap '64
Glass screen shields glass wall from sun. il Arch Rec 133:210-11 Mr '63
Glass screens this garden and stops the desert wind. il Sunset 132:141 My '64
Green brick front, green woods behind. il House & Gard 123:142-7+ My '63
Leaves through the glass. il Sunset 130:92 F '63
Like a camera it focuses on the view. A. C. Borg. il Am Home 66:24-7 Je '63
Pavilion of glass and concrete trees. il Arch Rec 135:122-3 Ja '64
Playful and colorful. il Sunset 130:102-3 Je '63
Wall: glass and clay. il Craft Horiz 23:24-6 My '63
Wall goes out the garden comes in. il Sunset 133:111 O '64
WALLS, Tile
This is a talking screen. il Sunset 130:144 My '63
Wall: mosaic tiles. K. Sawyer. il Craft Horiz 23:20-3+ My '63
WALNUT CANYON NATIONAL MONUMENT
Walnut Canyon National Monument. I. Smith. il Nat Parks Mag 38:11-13 N '64
WALNUT trees
How to plant an English walnut. J. Krill. il Flower Grower 51:38 Mr '64
Trees of Appalachia. New Repub 150:5 My 2 '64
World run on walnut. G. L'Allemand. il Am For 69:12-15+ Ag '63
See also
Butternut trees
WALPOLE ISLAND group. See Indians of North America—Reservations
WALRUS hunting
Dateline walrus. B. Klineburger. il Field & S 67:23-5 F '63
WALRUSES
Locomotion in pinnipeds. C. Ray. il Natur Hist 72:10-21 Mr '63
WALSER, Martin
Army of words. Holiday 36:24+ O '64
WALSH, Chad
Cadence for our time. Sat R 48:28-30 Ja 2 '65
Early leaf; poem. Christian Cent 80:1166 S 25 '63
Rejoice in the basements of memory; poem. Christian Cent 80:1199 O 2 '63
Return to Galilee. Sat R 47:81 Ja 4 '64
Ropes of nothing; poem. Cath World 197:119 My '63
Scratch any Christ; poem. Christian Cent 80:270 F 27 '63
Vale Virgil, ave Verdi; poem. Sat R 46:29 Mr 9 '63
WALSH, Donald D.
Role of the NDEA. Sat R 46:73-4 F 16 '63
WALSH, Edward
What impetus? Christian Cent 81:1595 D 23 '64
WALSH, George
Wooing of a seven-foot wonder. Sat Eve Post 237:70-1 Mr 14 '64
WALSH, Jim
Favorite & pioneer recording artists. See issues of Hobbies
Leaving on that New River train. Hobbies 69:120-4 O '64
Through the stereoscope. Hobbies 68:24-5+ Ag; 26-7 S; 28 O '63; 69:28-9 Jl; 28 N '64
WALSH, John
Curriculum reform. Science 144:642-6 My 8 '64
WALSH, John S.
Drawing & painting after dark. il Am Artist 27:36-41+ Mr '63
WALSH, John William
In the White House news. P. Wyden. por McCalls 90:36+ Ag '63
WALSH, Michael
Boston beacon. il por Time 81:46+ Ap 26 '63
WALSH, Moira
Films. See issues of America
Movie of the month; a note on two Italian films. Cath World 199:395-6 S '64
Otto Preminger looks at the Catholic church. Cath World 198:365-71 Mr '64
about
Moira and Sister M. America 108:791 Je 1 '63
WALSH, Richard J. Jr
Books, rights and educational broadcasting. Pub W 184:30-3 S 23 '63
WALSH, Thomas F. and Donohue, S. T.
J. Marion Sims, M.D. women's medical emancipator. Todays Health 42:30-1+ Je '64
WALSH, William F.
How Syracuse selected its parking meters. Am City 78:86-8 Ap '63
WALT Disney productions. See Disney, Walt, productions
WALTEMATH, G.
Many moons of Dr Waltemath. J. Ashbrook. bibliog Sky & Tel 28:218 O '64
WALTER, Bruno
Musical record. por Am Rec G 30:374-5 Ja '64
about
Bruno Walter: two views. J. Ardoin; R. Lewenthal. por Mus Am 84:48-9 Mr '64
Education and a joy. J. T. McClure. il pors Hi Fi 14:40-3+ Ja '64
Final release of recordings by the late Bruno Walter. R. Sabin. il por Am Rec G 30:488-91 F '64
Heritage of Bruno Walter; discography. R. C. Marsh. il pors Hi Fi 14:44-8+ Ja '64
Last recordings of Bruno Walter. M. Bernheimer. Sat R 46:58-9 D 28 '63
WALTER, Florence
Bookbinding by Florence Walter. Y. Uchida. il por Craft Horiz 24:28-30 Jl '64
WALTER, Francis E.
Lord of the flies. M. Kempton. New Repub 148:9-10 Je 22 '63
Obituary
Nat R 14:486 Je 18 '63
WALTER, Louis S.
Petrology of Venus: further deductions. bibliog Science 143:1161 Mr 13 '64
WALTER, Nina Willis
Dragon chaser; poem. McCalls 91:219 Ap '64
WALTER, Richard
Street trees. Horticulture 42:18-20+ Jl '64

WALTER Hampden memorial library
Walter Hampden memorial library. L. A. Rachow. il Wilson Lib Bul 38:656-9 Ap '64
WALTERS, Barbara
Jackie Kennedy's perplexing sister. Good H 156:30+ Mr '63
WALTERS, Everett
Course on college teaching. Sch & Soc 91: 286-7 O 5 '63
WALTERS, Gary C. and Rogers, J. V.
Aversive stimulation of the rat: long-term effects on subsequent behavior. bibliog Science 142:70-1 O 4 '63
WALTERS, Herbert S.
New chairman and a new senator. por U S News 55:13 S 2 '63
No crusades. Time 82:17 Ag 30 '63
WALTERS, Jeanne D.
Combinations that click. Flower Grower 50: 42-3+ Ag '63
Feathered jewels. Flower Grower 51:20-1+ Ag '64
Prince for your garden. Flower Grower 50: 20-1+ N '63
Welcome home the bluebird. Flower Grower 50:36-7+ Mr '63
WALTERS art gallery, Baltimore
Seventeenth-century French enameled watches in the Walters art gallery. P. Verdier. il Antiques 84:686-90 D '63
WALTHALL, F. G. See Hedge, C. E. jt. auth.
WALTNER, Elma. See Waltner, W. jt. auth.
WALTNER, Willard, and Waltner, Elma
Bleach-bottle bonanza. Pop Mech 120:146-7 Ag '63
Go fly a kite. Pop Mech 119:160-4 Mr '63
Handsome gift candles. Pop Mech 120:145-7 D '63
Tuned bells for your front door. Pop Sci 185:161 O '64
WALTON, A. See Leo, M. W. M. jt. auth.
WALTON, E. Woodrow
City regains lighting greatness. Am City 79: 131+ Mr '64
WALTON, Eda Lou
I remember Eda Lou. C. Burch. Sat R 46: 14-16 Je 29 '63
WALTON, Harry
Big idea: welding center for casting, too. por Pop Sci 183:100-1 S '63
High-speed ribbon that sands and grinds. Pop Sci 185:136-8 S '64
How to fit fine tools to a case. Pop Sci 185: 130-1+ N '64
How to restore the life of the party. Pop Sci 184:102-5+ Ja; 148-50+ F '64
How to sharpen everything. Pop Sci 185:144-9+ S; 148-53 N; 136-9+ D '64; 186:138-41+ Ja '65
How to succeed in business without an office. Pop Sci 182:64-7 Mr '63
Lightning in your living room. Pop Sci 185: 142-5 N '64
Midget lathe that does mighty jobs. Pop Sci 183:146-9+ O '63
New hand-sized oxy-butane torch. Pop Sci 185:126-8 Ag '64
New robot rainmakers for wall-to-wall lawns. Pop Sci 183:102-5+ Ag '63
Roller rest for precision filing. Pop Sci 184: 140-3 Ap '64
Toolkraft's new high-speed table saw. Pop Sci 185:158-9 N '64
WALTON, Izaak
Truth about Izaak Walton. E. Zern. il Field & S 69:168 O '64
WALTON, John
Education as an academic discipline. Sch & Soc 92:264-5+ O 3 '64
WALTON, Mary V.
In black and white. Reporter 31:40+ Jl 16 '64
WALTON, Robert B.
6-aminopenicillanic acid: inhibition of destruction of cephalosporin C by bacteria. bibliog Science 143:1438-9 Mr 27 '64
WALTON, Sadie G.
Brownsville children's library. Horn Bk 40: 236 Je '64
WALTON, William
Monumental failures and successes. N Y Times Mag p32-3+ Mr 15 '64
Painter plenipotentiary. il por Newsweek 63: 89 Je 8 '64
WALTON, Sir William Turner
Compleat critic. Newsweek 62:54 Ag 19 '63
Facade; entertainment with poems. J. Diether. il Am Rec G 31:304-7 D '64
Shakespeare film scores. J. Diether. il por Am Rec G 30:881-3 My '64
WALWORTH, Arthur
Long, dark days of decline. Sat R 47:25-6 Mr 14 '64
WALWORTH, Dorothy
Bonus notches. pal. Read Digest 85:126-30 D '64

WALZ, Humphrey
Hope for Palestine refugees. Christian Cent 80:306-7 Mr 6 '63
WALZ, Jay
Emperor tries to unite Africa. N Y Times Mag p 18+ Mr 8 '64
Iran's Shah leads a white revolution. N Y Times Mag p23+ O 27 '63
WAN, J. See Bernfeld, P. jt. auth.
WANAMAKER, Sam
As if it were a play. por Opera N 28:8-11 Ja 18 '64
WANAMAKER, Kempton and Southern railroad
Newest train trip just for fun. il Travel 122:49 Jl '64
WAND, Gunter
Exciting and impressive on Everest, Gunter Wand. H. Glass. por Am Rec G 30:510-11 F '64
WANDRUS, Harry
Firearms. See issues of Hobbies to December 1963
Making an oil-cloth floor-covering for Pres. Andrew Johnson's home. Hobbies 68:54+ Jl '63
WANE, Malcolm T.
Strata control and rock mechanics. Science 145:1075 S 4 '64
WANG, Leng-yun
Housewife becomes literate in Communist China; testimony, tr. by D. C. Chu. Sch & Soc 91:379-80 N 30 '63
WANGER, Walter, and Hyams, Joe
Cleopatra. pors Sat Eve Post 236:28-38+ Je 1 '63
WANGOMBE, Mariga T.
African studies our schools. NEA J 52:21-2 F '63
WANKEL engine. See Automobile engines; Gas and oil engines
WAPSHOT scandal; story. See Cheever, J.
WAR
Foretaste of a new kind of war. Sr Schol 84:3 F 21 '64
Hand on the trigger. J. Burnham. Nat R 16: 1013 N 17 '64
Last flower; parable in pictures. J. Thurber. il UNESCO Courier 17:27-8 N '64
1914-1939-1964: is the cycle broken? B. Ward. il N Y Times Mag p5+ D 29 '63
Of arms and the man. J. O'Gara. Commonweal 80:134 Ap 24 '64
Peace in our time. F. L. Greaves. il N Y Times Mag p 16+ Ap 14 '63
Teaching about peace and war; symposium. ed. by H. Taylor. il Sr Schol 83:9T+ N 22 '63; Discussion. 84:6T F 7 '64
Too late for drums? J. Ciardi. Sat R 46:11 Jl 27 '63
War, politics and power, by K. von Clausewitz. Review
Bul Atomic Sci 20:28-9 My '64. P. Tillet
Wasted decades: 1899-1939. F. L. Schuman. bibliog f Cur Hist 46:326-30 Je '64
What price conventional capabilities in Europe? B. Brodie. il Reporter 28:25-9+ My 23 '63
See also
Atomic warfare
European war, 1914-1918
Gases in warfare
Guerrilla warfare
International security
Pacifism
Peace
Preparedness, Military
Strategy

Economic aspects

Disarmament: economic effects. O. Feinstein. bibliog f il Cur Hist 47:81-7 Ag '64

Moral aspects

See also
Atomic warfare—Ethical aspects
War, Ethics of

Psychological aspects

Divergent reactions to the threat of war. P. Ekman and others; reply. E. J. Jay. Science 139:1122 Mr 15 '63
New roads to a world without war. A. I. Waskow. Yale R 54:85-111 O '64

Social aspects

War, violence, and human nature. J. Marmor. Bul Atomic Sci 20:19-22 Mr '64
See also
Atomic warfare—Social aspects
WAR, Accidental. See Atomic weapons—Accidents
WAR, Causes of
One way to bring on the war that nobody wants. D. Lawrence. U S News 56:108 Ap 6 '64

WAR, Causes of—*Continued*
Who really started World war 1? W. S. Bacon. il Pop Electr 20:40-2+ Ap '64; Same abr. with title Computer tells who started World war 1. Sci Digest 56:44-7 Jl '64

WAR, Ethics of
New roads to a world without war. A. I. Waskow. Yale R 54:85-111 O '64

WAR, Prevention of
Away from the brink of war; concerning four recent books. H. H. Ransom. Sat R 47:23-4 Jl 25 '64
Beyond illusion. E. E. Best. Christian Cent 81:40-2 Ja 8 '64
Can a nuclear world war be avoided? N. A. Graebner. Ann Am Acad 351:132-9 Ja '64
Can civilization be assassinated? N. Cousins. Sat R 46:14+ D 21 '63; Reply. C. G. Spiegler. 47:41 Ja 25 '64
Case for international control of weapons. V. Nash. Cur Hist 47:97-102+ Ag '64
Dangerous intersection; value of experiences of Hiroshima and Nagasaki. W. T. Ellis. Sat R 46:31 Ag 24 '63
Demilitarized world and how to get there. W. Millis. Sat R 47:18-22+ S 12 '64
Direction and control of nuclear power; address, September 16, 1964. L. B. Johnson. Dept State Bul 51:458-60 O 5 '64
Disarmament in perspective; symposium. bibliog f Cur Hist 46:321-53+ Je '64
Disarmament picture, 1965. H. A. Jack. Christian Cent 82:104-6 Ja 27 '65
How about some action, now? Nation 198:337 Ap 6 '64
Inquiry into the peace movement. A. Herzog. il N Y Times Mag p 17+ My 19 '63
Making the world safe for diversity; address, June 8, 1964. T. L. Hughes. Dept State Bul 51:6-17 Jl 6 '64
Neither dead nor red; Cuban crisis. Earl of Home. Read Digest 82:69-71 F '63
New roads to a world without war. A. I. Waskow. Yale R 54:85-111 O '64
No finish line for the arms race. R. Hudson. Sat R 46:40 Ag 24 '63
No mission but peace, no enemy but war. A. E. Stevenson. il McCalls 92:112-13+ O '64
Nuclear abolitionism. P. Kecskemeti. Commentary 36:43-8 Jl '63; Reply with rejoinder. A. L. Waskow. 36:394-8 N '63
On the prevention of war, by J. Strachey. Review
Nat R 14:324-5 Ap 23 '63. J. D. Atkinson
One man's war on war. J. Robbins and J. Robbins. il Redbook 123:54-5+ My '64
Orbital bomb. N. Cousins. Sat R 46:24+ My 11 '63
Peace in our time? nuclear weapons as a stabilizer. L. J. Halle. New Repub 149:16-19 D 28 '63
Peace negotiations. Commonweal 79:447 Ja 17 '64
Peace that can be; most commonly advocated means of survival. S. T. Possony. America 112:124-7 Ja 23 '65
Proposal to a foundation: a model World constitutional convention. N. Cousins. Sat R 46:16 Jl 27 '63
Scientists in politics: Council founded by Szilard brings cash and sophistication to lobbying. E. Langer. Science 145:561-3 Ag 7 '64
Search for honorable alternatives to war. T. D. White. Newsweek 62:34 Jl 22 '63
Several sides of defense. F. Altschul. Sat R 46:90 Mr 16 '63
Some major issues before the United Nations; address, March 5, 1963. Thant. Vital Speeches 29:360-4 Ap 1 '63; Same abr. U N Rev 10:16-19 Mr '63; Excerpts. Sat R 46:26 Mr 23 '63
Speaking out; strategy and the defense intellectuals. T. D. White. Sat Eve Post 236:10+ My 4 '63
Speculations during a white night. J. F. Wharton. Sat R 46:15-17 Ap 6 '63
Stopping the war clock. Christian Cent 81:1131-2 S 16 '64
Sure way to prevent nuclear war? interview. T. S. Power. il U S News 58:72-6 Ja 25 '65
Teaching war prevention. S. H. Mendlovitz. Bul Atomic Sci 20:19-22 F '64; Reply. P. Lauter. 20:28 My '64
Thirteenth alarm; address, March 21, 1964. H. Cleveland. Dept State Bul 50:622-6 Ap 20 '64
Toward a new politics. J. Cogley. Commonweal 78:37-8 Ap 5 '63
Toward a warless world. P. A. Schilpp. Christian Cent 81:212-14 F 12 '64
Very real risk, war by accident; technical mistake or fault, and miscalculation or error of judgment. C. N. Barclay. il N Y Times Mag p 17+ My 5 '63
What the U.N. can do, if it will. A. Larson. Sat R 47:20 Je 27 '64

Bibliography

Arms and arms control. Cur Hist 46:354-6 Je '64

WAR, Psychology of. See War—Psychological aspects

WAR and children
Children and the bomb. V. Cadden; reply. B. V. Hyde. Redbook 120:53+ Ap '63
Children and the threat of nuclear war, by Child study association of America. Review
Nation 199:412+ N 30 '64. S. Milgram and A. Milgram
Children's war revisited. E. B. McNeil. Bul Atomic Sci 19:22-4 F '63
I think about him all the time. S. Plapinger. il Ladies Home J 81:55-7+ O '64
Learning to live in a troubled world. B. Spock. Redbook 123:26+ Ag '64
Nuclear threat harms children. J. Viorst. il Sci N L 83:106-7 F 16 '63
Out of darkness. M. Alland. New Yorker 40:178+ Ap 25 '64
Students, teachers, and the bomb. M. Schwebel. NEA J 52:46-8 Mr '63
They thought the war was on. L. Dickert. il McCalls 90:96-7+ Ap '63
Whose children? Nation 198:546 Je 1 '64

WAR and Christianity. See War and religion

WAR and industry. See War—Economic aspects

WAR and peace; drama. See Neumann, A. and others

WAR and religion
Christian and nuclear pacifism. J. E. Dougherty. il Cath World 198:336-46 Mr '64
Christian and war. J. O'Gara. Commonweal 80:171 My 1 '64
Churches and the bomb. J. Albertson. il America 111:692-3 N 28 '64
Ecumenical war games. Nation 199:366-7 N 23 '64
More on the bomb. J. O'Gara. Commonweal 78:66 Ap 12 '63
Pacem in terris: for all humanity; with excerpts. il Newsweek 61:21-2 Ap 22 '63
Preachers again present arms? survey by Fellowship of reconciliation. Christian Cent 80:1162 S 25 '63
Toward peace and justice; Pacem in terris. H. Schomer. Christian Cent 80:703-6 My 29 '63
Urge cease-fire in South Vietnam; religious leaders polled in Washington, D.C. Christian Cent 82:37 Ja 13 '65

WAR and science
Successor to democracy; warning against science. S. A. Coblentz. Christian Cent 81:78-80 Ja 15 '64; Reply. E. S. Scott. 81:341-2 Mr 11 '64
What is left to hope for? M. Born. Bul Atomic Sci 20:2-5 Ap '64
See also
Operations research

WAR and youth
Children's war revisited. E. B. McNeil. Bul Atomic Sci 19:22-4 F '63

WAR casualties
Victims; civilian casualties in Viet Nam (Republic) Nation 198:450 My 4 '64
War casualties in peaceful 1964. U S News 57:22 D 28 '64
Whose children? Nation 198:546 Je 1 '64

WAR crime trials. See Nuremberg trials; World war, 1939-1945—War criminals

WAR crimes
On Juno beach. Newsweek 62:33 Jl 15 '63

WAR criminals. See World war, 1939-1945—War criminals

WAR debts. See Debts, Public

WAR films. See Moving pictures—War films

WAR games
See also
Air maneuvers
Military maneuvers
Naval maneuvers

WAR games, Childrens. See Play

WAR guilt controversy. See European war, 1914-1918—Causes; World war, 1939-1945—Causes

WAR heroes. See Heroes

WAR industries. See Munitions industries

WAR inventions. See Inventions

WAR memorials
See also
Stone Mountain monument

WAR of 1812. See United States—History—War of 1812

WAR pictures
See also
World war, 1939-1945—Photography
World war, 1939-1945—Pictorial works

WAR propaganda
See also
Moving pictures—Propaganda films

WAR surpluses. See Surplus products

WAR veterans. See Service men, Discharged

WARBLERS
Bird worth a forest fire; saving the Kirtland's warbler. L. Line. il Audubon Mag 66:370-5 N '64
Mio, Michigan: strictly for the birds; Huron National Forest Kirtland's warbler management area. J. Calkins. il Am For 69:6+ Je '63
Phylogenetic riddle; olive warbler. W. G. George. il Natur Hist 72:44-7 F '63
Pink-headed warbler. W. Dawn. il Natur Hist 72:28-31 O '63
To save a single songbird; Kirtland's warbler. Audubon Mag 65:211 Jl '63

WARBURG, James P.
Defense against Gaullist isolationism. Ann Am Acad 351:24-9 Ja '64
Today's challenges to diplomacy. Bul Atomic Sci 19:2-4 N '63

WARD, Barbara (Lady Jackson)
City may be as lethal as the bomb. N Y Times Mag p22-3+ Ap 19 '64
Claim against the West. Commonweal 81:219-22 N 13 '64
Foreign aid has succeeded. N Y Times Mag p9+ Jl 12 '64
John Bull X-rays himself. N Y Times Mag p8+ Jl 14 '63
1914-1939-1964: is the cycle broken? N Y Times Mag p5+ D 29 '63
Not of an age but for all time. N Y Times Mag p 17+ Mr 15 '64
Pope of the dialogue. Atlan 212:54-7 S '63
Prelude to independence; address, June 1, 1963. Vital Speeches 29:564-6 Jl 1 '63
Stake: freedom for half of mankind. N Y Times Mag p 19+ Ap 14 '63
Uses of prosperity. Sat R 47:27-9+ Ag 29 '64
We may be rich but they are happy. N Y Times Mag p22-3+ My 5 '63
West debates the great growth issue. N Y Times Mag p22+ O 27 '63

about

Barbara Ward; recipient of Campion award. America 111:682 N 28 '64

WARD, Barbara E.
Surge to the towns. UNESCO Courier 17:5-6 S '64
(ed) Women in the new Asia; excerpts. UNESCO Courier 17:4-27 S '64

WARD, Bill
How not to plan a vacation. Sat R 47:46 D 5 '64

WARD, Brice
Cam-dwell meter for quick, sure auto tuneup. Pop Mech 121:196-8 F '64
SCR automotive ignition system. Electr World 72:44-5+ N '64
Transistor ignition. Pop Electr 20:33-44+ Je '64
ZJ photoflash slave. Pop Electr 18:39-40 Je '63

WARD, Claribel
Appliqué with felt. Sch Arts 62:17 Ap '63

WARD, David
Music to my ears; Khovanshchina at Covent Garden. I. Kolodin. Sat R 46:38 Je 29 '63

WARD, Donovan F.
Four horsemen of quackery: fear, gullibility, deceit, and deadliness. Todays Health 43:10+ Ja '65

WARD, Edmund
Summer on the dales. New Yorker 39:78+ Je 1 '63

WARD, Jack
My first time with an RF. il U S Camera 27:43+ S '64

WARD, John William
Of cogs and machines. Reporter 30:47+ Ja 16 '64
Only escape. Reporter 29:42+ D 19 '63

WARD, Leo R.
Changing opinion on federal aid; excerpt from Federal aid to private schools. Cath World 199:167-74 Je '64

WARD, Lyle Blake
Natural resources; poem. McCalls 92:202 N '64

WARD, Lynd
Artist at work: doing a book in lithography. il Horn Bk 40:34-41 F '64

WARD, Maisie
Maisie Ward's journey. G. N. Shuster. Commonweal 81:123-5 O 23 '64

WARD, Marjory G.
(ed) See Bradley, G. G. Let them go free

WARD, Pete
Boot a few, bat a million. R. Creamer. por Sports Illus 19:48-50 Jl 15 '63

WARD, Richard F. and Werner, S. L.
Analysis of variance of migmatite composition II: comparison of two areas. bibliog Science 143:1032-3 Mr 6 '64
Analysis of variance of the composition of a migmatite. bibliog Science 140:978-9 My 31 '63

WARD, Robert
Crucible. Criticism
Am Rec G il 29:508-9+ Mr '63

WARD, Stephen
As British vice case grew more lurid. U S News 55:8 Ag 5 '63
Case of the sensitive osteopath. il por Time 81:29 Mr 29 '63
Crisis over Christine. E. Behr. il por Sat Eve Post 236:77-85 Jl 13 '63
Dial S for squalor; Regina v. Stephen Thomas Ward. il por Time 82:22+ Ag 2 '63
Doctor Stephen Ward returns. R. West. Esquire 62:138+ S '64
Epitaph: guilty. il por Newsweek 62:34 Ag 12 '63
Ford, Ward, and Graham; civilization vs self-love. W. F. Buckley, jr. Nat R 15:143 Ag 27 '63
I'm all right, Jack. il Newsweek 62:45 Jl 15 '63
Life and times of Dr Stephen Ward. por Newsweek 62:37 Ag 5 '63
Missing model. Newsweek 61:33 Ap 1 '63
Moral post-mortem. il Time 82:20-1 Ag 16 '63
New pornocracy. il por Newsweek 62:35-6 Jl 8 '63
One crowded hour. il por Time 82:26+ Ag 9 '63
Personal report on Britain's biggest scandal. L. Bergquist. il por Look 27:81-6 Jl 30 '63
Price of Christine. il por Time 81:32-3 Je 14 '63
'What the hell. . .' il por Newsweek 61:38+ Je 17 '63
While the prisoner sketched. il por Time 82:25 Jl 5 '63

WARD, W. W.
Never the small stuff. Read Digest 83:23-4 Ag '63

WARD, William
Demon progenitor. Nation 200:14-15 Ja 4 '65
In the ring. Nation 198:660-1 Je 29 '64
Why the students revolt. Nation 200:81-5 Ja 25 '65

WARD-HANNA, Elaine
Feasting afloat. Ladies Home J 80:74-6 Jl '63
Food to please a man. Ladies Home J 80:112-13+ O '63
Millon dollar desserts. Ladies Home J 80:64-6+ S '63
Shortcut cook. Ladies Home J 80:80 My '63

WARDEN, Don
Walk in dignity; address, May 2, 1964. Vital Speeches 30:572-5 Jl 1 '64

WARDLAW, Frank H.
Jaime García Terrés and the *lista negra.* Harper 230:16+ Ja '65
Wardlaw reviews problems and responsibilities. Pub W 184:33-6 Jl 15 '63

WARDROBES. See Closets

WARE, George W.
Marks on German porcelain. Hobbies 69:90-1 Mr '64

WARE, Harlan
My three-hundred-pound ballerina. Writer 76:7-9+ O '63

WARE, Leon
Home is the sailor; story. Good H 156:92-3 My '63

WARE, Martha L.
Higher income for retired teachers. NEA J 53:14 F '64

WARE, Romaine B.
Rugged lilies for all gardeners. Flower Grower 50:36-8 S '63

WARE, W. Porter
Antique sports (cont) Hobbies 68:116-17 Ap '63

WAREHOUSES
AB-SP now operating huge new distribution center. Pub W 185:41 Mr 9 '64
Future of American express. E. K. Faltermayer. Fortune 69:158-9+ Ap '64
Home on the waterfront. G. O'Brien. il N Y Times Mag p 110-11+ N 17 '63
McClurg's new distribution center: speed and service. il Pub W 186:26-9 Ag 10 '64
New nerve centers of distribution. il Duns R 81:pt2 S104-6+ Je '63

WAREHOUSES—*Continued*
Offices and warehouse for a publisher; Oxford university press, Don Mills, Ontario. il Arch Rec 136:160-1 D '64
Offices and warehouse for an industrial park. il Arch Rec 133:196-7 Ap '63
Simplified procedures at Little, Brown's new warehouse. il Pub W 186:31-4 S 7 '64
Substitute warehouse. il Duns R 81:pt2 S106 Je '63
Warehousing and shipping: costs and solutions. P. Wilson; J. T. Beck; R. J. Sweeney. Pub W 184:64-5+ N 4 '63
Warehousing: BMI offers new trade customs. Pub W 184:85-6 O 14 '63
WAREKOIS, E. P. See Mariano, A. N. jt. auth.
WARFARE. See Military art and science
WARFARE, Submarine. See Submarine warfare
WARFIELD, Joe
Compleat virtuosi; *discothèques* of Paris. Time 82:50-1 Jl 5 '63
WARFORD, Joseph
Joseph Warford, silversmith of Albany and Salem, New York. N. S. Rice and J. H. Halpin. il Antiques 85:429-31 Ap '64
WARGNY, Frank O.
Schoolman surveys concept of "the good life" in children's readers; excerpts from article. Library J 88:4832-3 D 15 '63
WARHOL, Andrew
What is pop art? interview; ed. by G. R. Swenson. il Art N 62:26+ N '63
about
Explosion of pop art: exhibition at the Guggenheim museum. A. B. Saarinen. il Vogue 141:86-7+ Ap 15 '63
Saint Andrew. il pors Newsweek 64:100+ D 7 '64
WARIHIO Indians. See Indians of Mexico
WARING, Barbara
Spider; poem. Horn Bk 40:418 Ag '64
WARING, James
James Waring and dance company at Hunter playhouse. M. Marks. Dance Mag 37:58-9+ Mr '63
James Waring and dance company; Judson memorial church. D. Hering. Dance Mag 37:28+ O '63 38:29+ Jl '64
WARING, Penny
Curl up and read. Seventeen 22:60 O '63
WARINNER, Emily V.
Ordeal of the Kanrin Maru. Am Heritage 14:95-7 Ag '63
WARLIKE play. See Play
WARLOCK, Peter, society. See Peter Warlock society
WARM air heating. See Heating
WARMAN, Morris
Portraits by press camera. M. R. Weiss. il por Sat R 47:52-3 Jl 11 '64
WARNE, Colston E.
Board of directors of Consumers union announces. Consumer Rep 28:415 S '63
WARNE, Rob
Young civilian tries to win the fight on the people front. J. Flynn. il pors Life 57:40-5 N 27 '64
WARNECKE, John Carl
Lafayette, he is here. il por Time 82:72 D 13 '63
WARNEKE, Heinz
Zoo puts on a mammoth match-up; elephants carved from a solid block of granite. il por Life 54:40B+ Je 7 '63
WARNEKING, Glenn E.
How's your driver education program? NEA J 53:41 My '64
WARNER, Bob
Canon 35: the case for the defendant. U S Camera 26:64-5+ Jl '63
Fly fishing, cheap and easy. Field & S 68:52-5 Mr '64
Landlocks deluxe. pors Field & S 69:37-9+ My '64
Rio Muy Grande. Field & S 69:27-9+ D '64
River to the Arctic. por Field & S 68:78-80+ Ja '64
WARNER, Denis
After Tahiti, what? Atlan 214:130+ O '64
Agony in Saigon: the lady & the cadaver. Reporter 29:39-42 O 10 '63
Australia: white island in a brown sea. Reporter 28:25-9 My 9 '63
Catastrophic non-war in Laos. Reporter 30:21-4 Je 18 '64
China fans the fires. Reporter 32:16-20 Ja 14 '65
China's new roads: where do they lead? Reporter 29:31-3 S 26 '63
Drawing the line in southeast Asia. Reporter 31:33-6 S 10 '64
Experiment in neutrality. New Repub 148:12-14 F 2 '63
How Sukarno keeps his revolution spinning. Reporter 30:33-6 Ap 23 '64
Land beyond help? Reporter 28:62-4 Mr 28 '63
Last chance in the Delta. Reporter 30:31-4 Ap 9 '64
Legacy of Sarit Thanarat. Reporter 31:42-4 S 24 '64
Malaysia. New Repub 148:11-12 Mr 16 '63
Malaysia: a tempting target. Reporter 31:35-8 N 5 '64
Philippines can't be taken for granted. Reporter 31:30-2 D 17 '64
Shadow and substance of the ANZUS pact. Reporter 30:21-3 Je 4 '64
There goes Cambodia. Reporter 30:27-30 Mr 26 '64
Underground in the Northeast. New Repub 148:8-9 Ap 6 '63
Unfinished business: a neutral zone in southeast Asia? New Repub 149:17-20 D 7 '63
Vietnam: a dynasty in disorder. Reporter 29:34+ S 12 '63
Vietnam: General Taylor faces an all-out war. Reporter 31:50+ Ag 13 '64
Vietnam: the awful choice. Reporter 30:26-8 F 27 '64
Vietnam's militant Buddhists. Reporter 31:29-31 D 3 '64
What we got for pampering Sukarno. Reporter 31:30-2 O 8 '64
WARNER, Dwain W.
Space tracks. Natur Hist 72:8-15 F '63
WARNER, Florence Edwards
Eating up the classics. NEA J 52:24-6 F '63
WARNER, J. C.
National goals and the university. Science 142:462-4 O 25 '63
WARNER, Jack L.
My first hundred years in Hollywood; excerpts, ed. by D. Jennings. por McCalls 91:72-3+ S; 92:128-9+ O; 100-1+ N '64
WARNER, John F.
Quiet revolution. Sat R 47:80-1+ My 16 '64
Will lightning follow the thunder? Sat R 46:54 D 21 '63
WARNER, Ken
Gun that broke the red-tape barrier. Pop Mech 120:108-10+ S '63
Helpful pointers on knives for outdoorsmen. Pop Sci 186:120-3+ Ja '65
Lightest hunting rifle ever made. Pop Sci 185:90+ N '64
Shock-absorbing shotgun, it saves your shoulder. Pop Sci 185:38-9 Jl '64
Swirl-chamber engine runs on what's handy. Pop Mech 119:110-12 Je '63
WARNER, O. Ray
Scholastic ability of school dropouts. bibliog Sch Life 47:21-2 O '64
WARNER, Oliver
Action off Flamborough Head; excerpt from Great sea battles. Am Heritage 14:42-9+ Ag '63
Lepanto. Horizon 5:49-61 Jl '63
WARNER, Rex
Dream of marble, a symphony of light. N Y Times Mag p78-9+ Ap 26 '64
Love of kites and remote places. Life 56:78-80 Ja 17 '64
WARNER, Richard
Verdi is heard over Wagner's thunder. H. C. Schonberg. il por N Y Times Mag p 14-15+ My 19 '63
WARNER Robert
Summer fishing eastern streams. Field & S 68:92-4+ Jl '63
WARNER, Sylvia Ashton-. See Ashton-Warner, S.
WARNER, Sylvia Townsend
Act of reparation; story. New Yorker 40:34-8 F 29 '64
Aging head; story. New Yorker 39:51-4 D 7 '63
Bathrooms remembered. New Yorker 39:33-6 Ja 11 '64
Between two wars; story. New Yorker 40:51-60 O 31 '64
English mosaic; story. New Yorker 39:36-41 F 8 '64
Flying start; story. New Yorker 39:40-1 Ap 20 '63
Long night; story. New Yorker 40:44-51 My 2 '64
Saint (unknown) with two donors; story. New Yorker 40:33-8 Ja 2 '65
Some effects of a hat; story. New Yorker 39:51-8 N 9 '63
Their quiet lives; story. New Yorker 39:40-8 My 11 '63
Three cats; story. New Yorker 40:36-40 My 30 '64

WARNER-Lambert pharmaceutical company
Brothers move on. il Time 83:86 F 21 '64
WARNICK, Donna
It's good to finish something! ed. by M. Longwell. por Farm J 87:47 Ag '63
WARNICK, Dorothy Brant
Mixed-up driving laws can kill you. Travel 121:45-7 Ap '64
Personal business. Travel 122:44-7 S '64
WARNICKE, E. R.
Tips for tired snow fighters. Am City 78:76-7 F '63
WARP, Harold
Pioneer village's tenth anniversary, still growing. Hobbies 68:52+ Jl '63
WARRACK, John
(ed) See Britten, B. Benjamin Britten; musician of the year
WARRANTY
Appliance warranties & service. il Changing T 18:42-5 Ja '64
Consumers sue for defective products. Consumer Bul 47:43+ N '64
Extended warranties and service contracts. il Consumer Bul 46:27-8 Je '63
Guarantee of non-staining properties; Brookpark plastic dishes. il Consumer Bul 46:32 O '63
Guaranteeing more, enjoying it less. Bsns W p46+ Ja 26 '63
How to sweeten a lemon. B. Taylor. il Pop Sci 186:88-91+ Ja '65
Important court decisions favor consumers. Consumer Bul 46:36-7 Mr '63
Long warranties. Consumer Rep 29:165-6 Ap '64
Restatement of warranties. Motor T 16:93 F '64
'64 cars; warranties. il Motor T 15:98-9+ N '63
Warranties: the consumer's rights on paper and in law. il Consumer Rep 28:158-9 Ap '63
WARREN, Charles R.
Surface material of the moon. bibliog Science 140:188-90 Ap 12 '63
WARREN, Dale
Eloquent admirer of simple English primrose. Horticulture 41:74-5 F '63
For the pure joy of it. Horticulture 41:401 Ag '63
Long voyage. Opera N 28:6-7 My 2 '64
WARREN, Earl
Eulogy to John F. Kennedy, November 24, 1963. Vital Speeches 30:99 D 1 '63

about

Changing U.S. effects of Supreme court decisions. il por U S News 55:70-2 Jl 1 '63
Did a justice advise on how to write a bill? U S News 55:9 O 14 '63
Earl Warren goes South. por U S News 54:16 F 25 '63
Hello, Earl. il por Time 81:24 F 22 '63
New look at the Chief Justice. A. Lewis. il pors N Y Times Mag p9+ Ja 19 '64
Provocative pair. Nat R 15:514 D 17 '63
Storm center of justice. E. Havemann. il pors Life 56:108-10+ My 22 '64; Same abr. with title Warren court. Read Digest 85:130-5 S '64
Warren court: fateful decade. il pors Newsweek 63:24-6+ My 11 '64
Warren court stands its ground. F. Rodell. il por N Y Times Mag p23+ S 27 '64
Warren: tolerant toward pickets. il por U S News 55:24 N 11 '63

Caricatures and cartoons

Kreuttner festival. J. Kreuttner. Nat R 16:645-8 Jl 28 '64
WARREN, Elton
Portrait of a TV teacher. il pors Sr Schol 82:24T Mr 13 '63
WARREN, Eva
Earth being so good, would heaven seem best? NEA J 53:8-10+ Mr '64
WARREN, G. F. See Colby, S. R. jt. auth.
WARREN, George T.
Kitchen planning. Arch Rec 135:25+ mid-My '64
WARREN, John Ed
Warren of Cities service. por Fortune 70:67 Jl '64
WARREN, Joyce
Crash; story. New Yorker 40:55-7 O 10 '64
WARREN, Lavinia
Social notes: 100 years ago this month. il Am Heritage 14:112 F '63
WARREN, Mary G.
American landmarks story; Annapolis raiders. Am For 70:36-8+ O '64
WARREN, Phelps
Living with antiques; New York apartment. Antiques 83:326-9 Mr '63
WARREN, Robert Penn
All the king's men: the matrix of experience. Yale R 53:161-7 D '63
Fiddlersburg preacher; story; excerpt from Flood: a romance of our time. por Esquire 60:55-6 Jl '63
Life is from within. Sat R 46:20-1+ Mr 2 '63
Moths against the screen; story; excerpt from novel. Sat Eve Post 237:42-3 Ap 4 '64
World of Daniel Boone. Holiday 34:162+ D '63
WARREN, Roslyn P.
Preference aversion in mice to bitter substance. bibliog Science 140:808-9 My 17 '63
WARREN, Sidney
How to pick a president. Sat R 47:10-13 Jl 4 '64
WARREN, Pa.
Early admission of able children to school. J. W. Birch and others. bibliog Sch Life 46:7-9 Je '64
WARREN commission. See United States—President's commission to investigate the assassination of President Kennedy
WARRIOR dolls. See Toy soldiers
WARSAW, Irene
O.G.I.C. it coming; poem. McCalls 90:190 S '63
WARSAW

City planning

Phoenix cities of Poland. J. M. Fitch. il Horizon 6:52-9 Spr '64

Description

Letter from Warsaw. J. Wechsberg. New Yorker 38:106+ F 9 '63

Music

[Musical events] (cont) Mus Am 83:80 Ja '63

Reconstruction

See Warsaw—City planning

Theater

Theatre. H. Clurman. Nation 197:58-9 Jl 27 '63
WARSAW, pact, 1955
Pro forma; first summit meeting since ouster of Nikita Khrushchev. il Newsweek 65:30 F 1 '65
WARSAW ghetto. See Jews in Poland
WARSAW international festival of contemporary music. See Music festivals—Poland
WARSHIPS
Du Pont storms Charleston; excerpt from Civil war; role of monitors and other ironclads. S. Foote. il Am Heritage 14:28-34+ Je '63
Last gun of the confederacy; saga of the Shenandoah. C. E. Hinkson. il Read Digest 82:256-8+ Ap '63

Sweden

Wasa relics. Hobbies 69:121 N '64

United States

Navy's most hush hush ship. il Sci Digest 55:52-5 Mr '64
Sea Hawk system may appear gradually; anti-submarine destroyer escort system. J. Trainor. Miss & Roc 15:16 Ag 24 '64
Stand-off weapon for Seahawk ships is sole big missile development seen. il Miss & Roc 15:65-9 S 21 '64
See also
Constitution (frigate)
WARSHIPS, Atomic powered
As Polaris ship sails with seven nation crew; destroyer U.S.S. Biddle, demonstration ship for MLF or multilateral force. il U S News 57:48-9 Ag 3 '64
Korth urges all-nuclear line fleet. Aviation W 79:34 N 4 '63
McNamara shifts policy, seeks nuclear power for large ships. Aviation W 78:37 Ap 15 '63
Mixed-manned demonstration ship visits Washington; remarks, October 20, 1964. P. H. Nitze; D. Rusk; D. L. McDonald. Dept State Bul 51:660-3 N 9 '64
Navy votes to go all-nuclear. Bsns W p30 Ap 13 '63
NATO working group supports U.S. plan for mixed nuclear fleet. L. L. Doty. Aviation W 81:25 S 21 '64
Operation sea orbit. Nation 199:129 S 21 '64
Our nuclear navy. G. W. Anderson, jr. il Nat Geog Mag 123:449-50 Mr '63
Polyglot navy; Multilateral force (MLF) Nation 199:21-2 Jl 27 '64
Silencing the skeptics; U.S.S. Claude V. Ricketts. il Newsweek 64:49 N 9 '64
Slow steps toward the atomic fleet; role of MLF in the Atlantic alliance. Bsns W p26-7 D 12 '64

WARSHIPS, Atomic powered—*Continued*
U.S. warship with a seven-nation crew; U.S.S. Claude V. Ricketts. il U S News 57: 12 N 2 '64
WARSHOFSKY, Fred
Vicious chain. Todays Health 41:24-9 Ag '63; Same abr. with title V.D. the vicious chain. Read Digest 83:107-10 D '63
WARSLEY, Albert Edward
After hours. C. M. Wilson. Harper 226:28-32 My '63
WART virus. See Viruses
WARTENBERG, Arlene
Round-the-world dinners. Parents Mag 38:81-4+ S '63
WARTS
Dermatologist talks about warts. W. R. Vath. il Todays Health 41:40-1+ Mr '63
Therapy
What you can do about cattle warts. J. W. Bailey. Suc Farm 62:113 F '64
WARWICK, Dolores
For the feast of the nativity of John the Baptist; poem. Commonweal 78:300 Je 7 '63
WARWICK, James W.
Repeatability of Jupiter's decametric radio emission. bibliog Science 140:814-16 My 17 '63
—and Dulk, G. A.
Faraday rotation on decametric radio emissions from Jupiter. bibliog Science 145: 380-3 Jl 24 '64
WASH, Glenn
Multi-million dollar building boss. il pors Ebony 19:102+ Mr '64
WASH and wear fabrics. See Textile fabrics, Synthetic
WASH drawing
Wash drawing: excerpt from Watson drawing book. E. Watson and A. Watson. il Am Artist 27:18-23+ Mr '63
WASHBURN, Deric
Love nest. Criticism
New Yorker 38:70+ F 2 '63
Theatre Arts 47:65 Mr '63
WASHBURN, O. A.
Beware of timberline bucks. por Field & S 69:50-1+ Je '64
Horn hunters' heaven. Field & S 68:49-51 O '63
WASHBURNE, Norman F.
Match decisions to your problems. Nations Bsns 52:82+ O '64
WASHING compounds. See Cleaning compositions
WASHING machines
Automatic washing machines. il Consumer Bul 46:20-6 Je '63
Britain: how Bloom withered. il Fortune 70: 53-4+ O '64
Compact washing machines. il Consumer Bul 47:6-8 Mr '64
Hotpoint automatic clothes washer. il Consumer Bul 46:21-2 O '63
Is your laundry right for you? R. Charles. il Parents Mag 38:103-5+ O '63
Rising cost of repairs. il Consumer Rep 28: 464-7 O '63
Terrific, timesaving new washers and dryers! Bet Hom & Gard 41:97 O '63
Washing machines. il Consumer Rep 29:416-22 S '64
What to look for in an automatic washer. J. Gillies. il Farm J 88:71 N '64
Control
Thinking washers sensing dryers. N. Craig. il House B 105:152-3+ Mr '63
WASHING of clothes. See Laundry
WASHINGTON, Booker Taliaferro
Let Booker T. Washington speak again! excerpts from address, 1895. U S News 55:88 S 2 '63
New Booker T. casts down his buckets. il pors Ebony 20:66-8+ Ja '65
WASHINGTON, Dinah
Requiem for Queen Dinah. C. L. Sanders. il pors Ebony 19:146-8+ Mr '64
WASHINGTON, Geneva Harrison
Blind leader of the sighted. il pors Ebony 19:60-2+ Mr '64
WASHINGTON, George
To the Roman Catholics in the United States of America. America 111:3 Jl 4 '64
about
Enigma of General Howe. T. J. Fleming. il Am Heritage 15:6-11+ F '64
February: a good month to look at Washington, the man and the city. P. Mesta. por McCalls 91:18+ F '64
George Washington, first President 1789-1797. F. Freidel. il pors Nat Geog Mag 126: 646-57 N '64
G. Washington meets a test. T. J. Fleming. il por Am Heritage 14:56-9+ F '63
James Craik: the first White House physician. J. Luter. il Todays Health 42:46-9+ F '64
Mr Washington and laughter. B. Brooks. Hobbies 68:28 Mr '63
President's day. il Am Heritage 15:106-7 Ag '64
Symbols, traditions and liberty; address, October 24, 1962. A. G. Rudd. Vital Speeches 29:256 F 1 '63
Why Washington stood up in the boat; with reproduction of painting and memoir by W. Whittredge. G. F. Scheer. por Am Heritage 16:17-19 D '64
Drama
American way. A. C. Martens. Plays 23:13-24 F '64
WASHINGTON, George, family
Pater patriae as pater familias. F. Fox. il Am Heritage 14:32-7+ Ap '63
WASHINGTON, D.C.
February: a good month to look at Washington, the man and the city. P. Mesta. McCalls 91:18+ F '64
Hot foot for birds on inaugural route. il Bsns W p34 O 31 '64
Retailers' dream city. il Bsns W p 108-10+ Mr 14 '64
Skyscrapers go home! height limitations. D. Haskell. il Arch Forum 119:132 S '63
Teen scene in Washington, D.C. il Seventeen 23:170-1 S '64
Washington, by C. M. Green. Review
Nation 198:74-5 Ja 20 '64. F. Gutheim
See also
Architecture, Domestic—Washington, D.C.
Booksellers and bookselling—Washington, D.C.
Gardens—Washington, D.C.
Public welfare—Washington, D.C.
White House
Airports
Capitol treatment; Page airways. C. Newlon. il Flying 74:18+ Ap '64
Dulles faces struggle to prove design. R. H. Cook. Aviation W 79:40-1 Ag 26 '63
Dulles international airport. E. Saarinen. il Arch Rec 134:101-10 Jl '63
Funeral influx tests Dulles operations. R. H. Cook. Aviation W 79:29 D 2 '63
Jet-age airport helps its neighbors; Dulles airport. B. A. Roth. il Am City 79:92-3 D '64
Jet-age airport; will it pay its way? Dulles airport. il U S News 55:60-1 S 2 '63
Portico to the jet age; Dulles international airport. il Arch Forum 119:72-83 Jl '63
World's safest airport; Dulles airport. P. Geraci. il Pop Sci 186:110-13 Ja '65
Anecdotes, facetiae, satire, etc.
All unquiet on the Potomac. A. Buchwald. Read Digest 83:185-6+ Jl '63
Architecture
Design for culture in Washington. W. Von Eckardt. il Sat R 47:20-3 My 23 '64
Granite out, glass in; with editorial comment. il Bsns W p30-1, 101-2 Ap 4 '64
Kennedy pro arte et sequitur? A. Frankfurter. il Art N 62:23+ Ja '64
Washington story: fastest-growing skyline in U.S. il U S News 56:102-3 Je 8 '64
See also
Washington, D.C.—Public buildings
Buildings
See Washington, D.C.—Architecture
Churches
Bell tower for the cathedral; with report by R. B. Stolley. il Life 56:53-4+ Je 19 '64
City planning
Airy pavilion for AIA's 1965 D.C. festival. il Arch Forum 119:10 D '63
Architectural league and A.I.A. sponsor program and exhibit on Pennsylvania avenue. Arch Rec 136:128 N '64
Brightening the grand boulevard; Pennsylvania avenue. il Bsns W p32-3 D 12 '64
Cheering up the capital. W. Von Eckardt. New Repub 150:35-6 Je 13 '64
Grand boulevard for Washington; Pennsylvania avenue. A. L. Huxtable. il N Y Times Mag p8-9 My 31 '64
Is this the big industry that can keep U.S. going? il U S News 54:72-3 F 25 '63

WASHINGTON, D. C.—City planning—*Cont.*
Pennsylvania hypotenuse. il Time 83:90 Je 5 '64
Plan prescribes a grand national axis for redevelopment of Pennsylvania avenue. il Arch Rec 136:23+ Jl '64
Washington's chance for splendor. W. Von Eckardt. il Harper 227:54-64 S '63

Clubs

Critics denied re-entry to a Washington club; Cosmos club. U S News 54:10 F 4 '63
Elite meet to form new club; International club of Washington. Bsns W p 128 D 14 '63
Fun in Washington; annual dinner of Gridiron club. Time 81:63 Mr 22 '63
Genesis of men's club; Federal city club. J. H. Doolittle. Esquire 63:115 Ja '65
Science goes to lunch; Cosmos club. E. Langer. il Science 146:1145-9 N 27 '64

Crime

As crime mounts in nation's capital. U S News 57:12 Ag 10 '64
As crime rises in Washington... il U S News 56:10 Je 1 '64
Blight in the Nation's capital. il U S News 54:37-9 F 18 '63
Cause of concern: dark street near Supreme court. il U S News 56:16 F 17 '64
Crime and illiterary in the Nation's capital. U S News 55:8 Jl 22 '63
Crime in Washington. il U S News 54:98-9 F 25 '63
Even more crime in the Nation's capital? U S News 57:10 N 9 '64
Keg with the lit fuse. il Time 81:21 Mr 22 '63
Nation's capital leads the list in murders and assaults. il U S News 55:8 Jl 29 '63
Social tensions in our Nation's capital. M. McGrory. America 108:603 Ap 27 '63
Washington; a city in trouble. B. Davidson. il Sat Eve Post 236:17-23 Jl 13 '63
Washington crime as police chief sees it. U S News 55:20 Jl 15 '63
Washington, D.C. portrait of a sick city. F. Knebel. il Look 27:15-19 Je 4 '63
Why capital's taxi drivers stay home at night. U S News 56:8 F 3 '64
Why so much crime in the Nation's capital; interview. R. V. Murray. il U S News 55: 92-7 O 21 '63; Reply with rejoinder. 55:92-3 N 4 '63

Anecdotes, facetiae, satire, etc.

High cost of living; outrageous terms, inadequate apartments, and murder. M. Greenfield. Reporter 29:50+ N 21 '63; Discussion. 29:8 D 19 '63

Description

Nature's pageantry on the Potomac; with editorial comment. M. Frome. il Am For 69:14-21+ N '63
Washington, D.C. E. Scully. il U S Camera 27:70-4 Ap '64
Washington, the city freedom built. W. Graves. il Nat Geog Mag 126:735-81 D '64
Well traveled camera. D. L. Miller. il Mod Phot 28:34+ Ap '64

Education

Big brothers to troubled children; Whittier school. C. M. Bloomberg and C. H. Troupe. il NEA J 53:22-5 Ja '64
Blight in the Nation's capital. il U S News 54:37-9 F 18 '63
Corporal punishment in D.C. schools? U S News 54:8 Mr 4 '63
D.C. schools: 87.6 per cent Negro now. il U S News 57:10 N 23 '64
Deliberate speed in D.C. S. McBee. New Repub 150:7-8 Je 20 '64
Extraordinary Amidon school. N. Poirier. il Sat Eve Post 237:22-3 D 19 '64
Mandate against hypocrisy? desegregation in in public schools. D. Lawrence. U S News 57:112 N 23 '64
Public education in Washington. A. N. D. Brooks. Negro Hist Bul 26:196-7 Mr '63
Rumblings in D.C. Sr Schol 82:2T-4T Mr 20 '63
School crisis in the Nation's capital; interview. C. F. Hansen. il U S News 54:62-8 Mr 11 '63
Washington's plight. America 108:425 Mr 30 '63

Education, Board of

D.C. Board of educ. confirms library position called temporary since 1962. Library J 89:1839 Ap 15 '64

Galleries and museums

D.A.R. museum depicts Revolutionary war era. il Hobbies 68:52 Ag '63
Jewel case for pre-Columbian gems; Bliss collection in Dumbarton Oaks. K. E. Meyer. il Art N 62:36-9+ F '64
Out of Africa; Museum of African art. F. Getlein. New Repub 150:34+ Je 27 '64
Pop culture; Pop art festival at Washington gallery of modern art. il Time 81:73 My 3 '63
Pre-Columbian art in a post-modern museum; Dumbarton Oaks. il Arch Forum 120:106-11 Mr '64
See also
Corcoran gallery of art
National gallery of art
Smithsonian institution

Gardens

J.F.K.'s new garden. il Life 54:110-12+ My 24 '63
White House; garden treatment. Newsweek 61:26 My 6 '63

Historic houses, etc.

American landmarks celebration seeks to preserve nation's heritage; Cedar Hill, home of Frederick Douglass. C. W. Thomas. il Negro Hist Bul 28:24+ O '64
Beautifully restored homes in the Nation's capital. R. W. Houseman. il Am Home 67: 40-5 Ja '64
Blair House. Mrs A. B. Duke. il House & Gard 127:88-99 Ja '65
Last look at Blair House. il Travel 119:45-7 Je '63
Washington's official hosts. J. Peter. il Look 28:53-9 Ap 21 '64

History

Marching on Washington: an old story to the capital. il U S News 55:29-31 S 2 '63
Washington: capital city, 1879-1960, by C. M. Green. Review
Negro Hist Bul 27:169 Ap '64

Hotels, restaurants, etc.

Personal business. Bsns W p 129 F 16 '63

Housing

Columbia Plaza, and Harbour Square. il Arch Rec 134:200-4 S '63
Other Washington. W. V. Shannon. Commonweal 79:738-9 Mr 20 '64
Tiber Island, and Carrollsburg Square. il Arch Rec 134:196-7 S '63
Washington rent strike. J. Ridgeway. New Repub 150:10 F 8 '64

Anecdotes, facetiae, satire, etc.

High cost of living; outrageous terms, inadequate apartments, and murder. M. Greenfield. Reporter 29:50+ N 21 '63; Discussion. 29:8 D 19 '63

Libraries

Congressman's appraisal; address, April 1964. C. M. Mathias, jr. il Wilson Lib Bul 39:320-2 D '64
See also
Folger Shakespeare library
United States—Library of Congress
Washington, D.C. public library

Lighting

Washington after dark. il U S News 56:64-5 F 17 '64
Washington after dark: the image gets dimmer. il U S News 56:8 Ap 13 '64

Maps

Remapping the Nation's capital. Nat Geog Mag 126:782-3, sup(folded map) D '64

Monuments, statues, etc.

American tradition; four symbols. S. L. Udall. N Y Times Mag p30-1 D 1 '63
FDR memorial: is this it? il U S News 56: 8 Je 1 '64
FDR's tablets. il Newsweek 64:24 Jl 6 '64
Latest turn in the cold war: a battle of statues; Ukrainian poet, T. Shevchenko. il U S News 56:14 Je 29 '64
Reprise: FDR memorial. F. Getlein. New Repub 150:26+ Je 6 '64

Music

[Musical events] (cont) il Mus Am 83:17 F; 16 Mr; 15-16 My; 268-70 D '63; 84:14 F; 18-19 My; 25 Jl; 64 D '64
Potomac potpourri. F. C. Smith. Opera N 28: 32 N 16 '63
See also
National symphony orchestra
Opera society of Washington

WASHINGTON, D. C.—*Continued*

National arboretum

United States national arboretum. C. B. Lees. il Horticulture 42:32-5 My '64

National cultural center

Christmas paintings of Jacqueline Kennedy. il McCalls 91:98-9+ D '63
Memorial to Kennedy. il Life 56:47-8 F 7 '64
Raphael and the spear. W. D. Patterson. Sat R 46:30 O 26 '63
Strike up the bands for culture; U.S. military bands. F. Reynolds. il Am Rec G 29:920-3+ Ag '63
Without portfolio. C. B. Luce. McCalls 91:18+ Je '64

Negroes

Atlantic report. Atlan 211:6+ F '63
Blight in the Nation's capital. il U S News 54:37-9 F 18 '63
Demonstrations or threats? Christian Cent 80:877 Jl 10 '63
Dusk at the mountain, by H. Johnson. Review
Sat R 46:27-8 My 25 '63. J. M. Nabrit, jr
How a race riot happened; high school football game. A. Shuster and B. A. Franklin. il Sat Eve Post 236:15-19 My 4 '63
If nation's capital does rule itself. il U S News 58:42-6 Ja 18 '65
Keg with the lit fuse. il Time 81:21 Mr 22 '63
Nation's worst slum: Washington, D.C. A. E. Meyer. il Atlan 212:89-92 Ag '63
Other Washington; behind the gleaming facade, a squalid sprawl. il Newsweek 62:21-3 Jl 1 '63
School crisis in the Nation's capital; interview. C. F. Hansen. il U S News 54:62-8 Mr 11 '63
Schools and the Negro: integration, then resegregation; Roosevelt high school. il U S News 55:80 N 25 '63
Schools in D.C. now 85.7 per cent Negro. U S News 55:12 N 18 '63
Segregation and suburbia. C. D. Kean. Christian Cent 80:654+ My 15 '63
Slum and gown; Community services project at Howard university. il Newsweek 63:82 My 4 '64
Tale of two cities; white Washington and black Washington. S. Alsop. il Sat Eve Post 236:20 N 16 '63
Washington; a city in trouble. B. Davidson. il Sat Eve Post 236:17-23 Jl 13 '63
Washington: capital city, 1879-1960, by C. M. Green. Review
Negro Hist Bul 27:169 Ap '64
Washington, D.C. portrait of a sick city. F. Knebel. il Look 27:15-19 Je 4 '63
Why so much crime in the Nation's capital; interview. R. V. Murray. il U S News 55:92-7 O 21 '63
Worst race riots in history? excerpts from address, May 5, 1963. A. C. Powell. U S News 54:8 My 13 '63

Newspapers

Dis-establishmentarian; sharp look at the Washington press corps in Esquire. Newsweek 63:46-7 Mr 30 '64
Prosciutto and Mrs Mellon: Washington's society pages. M. Greenfield. il Reporter 30:32-6 Mr 12 '64
Traitor to my class. F. Knebel. il Look 28:32+ Ag 25 '64
See also
Washington star

Parks and playgrounds

Nature's pageantry on the Potomac; with editorial comment. M. Frome. il Am For 69:14-21+ N '63
New JFK memorial playground. il Ebony 20:190-4 N '64

Politics and government

Civil wrongs in the Nation's capital. D. Lawrence. U S News 56:96 F 3 '64
If nation's capital does rule itself. il U S News 58:42-6 Ja 18 '65
No home rule for D.C. J. W. Anderson. New Repub 148:6-7 F 9 '63
Politics as unusual. Reporter 30:11 Je 4 '64
Second Washington. J. H. Doolittle. il Esquire 61:112-14+ My '64
Still no self-rule for nation's capital; here are the reasons. il U S News 56:32-4 Ja 6 '64
That new-fangled thing called voting. J. W. Anderson. New Repub 150:8 Mr 28 '64
Washington's second banana politicians; Administrative assistants to congressmen and senators. L. L. King. il Harper 230:41-7 Ja '65

Public buildings

After twenty years: an end to eyesore tempos in Washington. il U S News 56:16 Ja 13 '64
Capitol clinker; Rayburn House office building. il Time 85:21 Ja 15 '65
Colossal new palace on Capitol hill; Rayburn House office building. J. E. Roper. il Read Digest 86:79-84 Ja '65
Consolation prize for Congress: new offices; Rayburn building. il U S News 56:46-7 Mr 23 '64
Costly new landmark on Capitol hill; Rayburn building. il U S News 54:14 Mr 18 '63
Design for culture in Washington. W. Von Eckardt. il Sat R 47:20-3 My 23 '64
Housewarming on Capitol hill; the Sam Rayburn. il Bsns W p 186 N 14 '64
It isn't fair to Rayburn. W. Von Eckardt. New Repub 151:26+ Jl 4 '64
It's $83 million high; Rayburn House office building. B. Wise. il Life 56:13 Mr 6 '64
Rising living standard for congressmen, too. il U S News 58:44-6 Ja 25 '65
See also
Embassies (buildings)
United States—Capitol

Rapid transit

Nickel buys a ride on the minibus. R. L. Morris. il Am City 79:133-4 Jl '64

Religious institutions and affairs

Church and city; Episcopal church Inner city program. il Newsweek 63:62 F 24 '64
News of the Christian world (cont) Christian Cent 80:188, 316-17, 725-6, 893-4, 1014, 1148-50, 1252-3, 1316+ F 6, Mr 6, My 29, Jl 10, Ag 14, S 18, O 9, 23 '63

Riots

How a race riot happened; high school football game. A. Shuster and B. A. Franklin. il Sat Eve Post 236:15-19 My 4 '63

Social conditions

Other Washington. W. V. Shannon. Commonweal 79:738-9 Mr 20 '64

Social life and customs

Double life of a senator's wife; excerpts from One foot in Washington. E. Proxmire. il Redbook 122:66-74 Ja '64
In the Washington swim. N. H. Dickerson. McCalls 90:46+ Jl '63
Marguerite: hair stylist to Washington's leading ladies. N. H. Dickerson. il McCalls 90:72+ S '63
Party line. il Time 82:21-5 N 22 '63
Pass the salt; Social list of Washington, D.C. Time 82:31 O 11 '63
Perle Mesta's party datebook; New Year's eve parties and New Year's day receptions. P. Mesta. il McCalls 92:24 Ja '65
Perle Mesta's party notebook (cont) P. Mesta. il McCalls 90:134+ My; 14+ Jl '63
Prosciutto and Mrs Mellon: Washington's society pages. M. Greenfield. il Reporter 30:32-6 Mr 12 '64
Washington: the women of the world. il Holiday 35:76-81 Mr '64
See also
White House

Anecdotes, facetiae, satire, etc.

Love in Washington. A. Chamberlin. Esquire 61:69+ Ja '64
Opinion, please, from Washington. R. Baker. il Mlle 58:38+ Mr '64
Washington cocktail. M. Kempton. New Repub 150:7-8 F 22 '64

Stores

Hecht added technical dept: to build volume; Hecht's book department. Pub W 184:84 N 11 '63

Streets

Brightening the grand boulevard; Pennsylvania avenue. il Bsns W p32-3 D 12 '64
Debate on Pennsylvania ave. il Arch Forum 121:10 Jl '64
Grand boulevard for Washington; Pennsylvania avenue. A. L. Huxtable. il N Y Times Mag p8-9 My 31 '64
Grand plan for a Serbonian bog; Pennsylvania avenue plan. Life 56:4 Je 12 '64
New look for the Avenue of the Nation; Pennsylvania avenue. il Sr School 85:14-15+ Ja 21 '65
Pennsylvania avenue. il Arch Forum 121:65-75 Jl '64
Soon: changed look for historic avenue; Pennsylvania avenue project. il U S News 55:11 S 2 '63

WASHINGTON, D. C.—*Continued*

Theater

Rise of rep. il(p60) Time 83:61 F 14 '64

WASHINGTON, D.C. public library
Fallacious formula. H. N. Peterson. il Library J 88:4696-8 D 15 '63

WASHINGTON (state)
Washington ski time. R. Henley. il Travel 123: 36-7 Ja '65

See also
Booksellers and bookselling—Washington (state)
Camping—Washington (state)
Canals—Washington (state)
Cascade Range
Chelan, Lake
Education—Washington (state)
Fishing—Washington (state)
Forests and forestry—Washington (state)
Glacier Peak
Hunting—Washington (state)
Mines and mineral resources—Washington (state)
Olympic National Park
Quinault, Lake
Rainier, Mount
Saint Helens, Mount
Skagit River
Yakima River

Description and travel

Cave walking at Shi Shi Beach. il Sunset 130:52 Ap '63
From Olympia to Capitol State forest. il Sunset 131:44+ N '63
From Tacoma to Olympia, slowly. il Sunset 132:46+ F '64
Scenes on a rockhound's journey. H. D. Brown. il Hobbies 68:123 F '64
Washington state; America's scenic storeroom. B. Fish. il Read Digest 82:151-6 Mr '63
Winter motor trip; Stillaguamish Valley. E. Wahleen. il Travel 120:32-3 D '63

Parks and reserves

Deception Pass. E. Wahleen. il Am For 69:28-9 Je '63
Visit to old Fort Simcoe. il Sunset 130:88 Ap '63

Politics and government

Dan Evans, that's who. il Time 84:40 N 13 '64
Right-wing retreat in Seattle. R. Schear. Reporter 31:35-6 D 3 '64

Religious institutions and affairs

News of the Christian world (cont) Christian Cent 80:624-6, 1183-4, 1250+; 81:1156 My 8, S 25, O 9 '63, S 16 '64

WASHINGTON (state) University, Seattle
Fortress for Seattle. il Arch Forum 121:140-1 Ag '64
New dorms for coeds. il Arch Forum 118:86-7 Mr '63
Teaching reactor in a glass pavilion, University of Washington, Seattle. il Arch Rec 134:182-3 S '63

WASHINGTON, MOUNT
Mt Washington floras. il Natur Hist 72:40-3 F '63
New England's arctic mountain; Mt Washington. J. T. Starr. il Am For 71:22-5+ Ja '65
Summit to be park. Nat Parks Mag 38:17-18 My '64

WASHINGTON correspondents. See Reporters and reporting

WASHINGTON COURT HOUSE, Ohio
From public nuisance to playground. J. M. Whitmer, jr. il Am City 79:117-18 O '64

WASHINGTON crossing the Delaware; painting. See Leutze, E.

WASHINGTON march. See Civil rights demonstrations

WASHINGTON post and Times herald
Good show, Post. il Nat R 14:394 My 21 '63
Their appointed rounds; detention of mail. New Repub 150:6 Mr 14 '64
Tradition: a legacy. il Newsweek 62:30-1 Ag 19 '63

WASHINGTON school of the ballet
With passionate clarity. J. Battey. il Dance Mag 37:44-8 Jl '63

WASHINGTON Senators (baseball) See Baseball clubs

WASHINGTON square, New York. See New York (city)—Washington square

WASHINGTON square outdoor art exhibit, New York. See Art—Exhibitions

WASHINGTON star
Catch a falling Star; new editor. il Time 81:94 Ap 19 '63

WASHINGTON university, St Louis
No streetcar; new intellectual atmosphere. il Newsweek 62:109B-110 O 14 '63

WASHINGTON'S birthday
February: a good month to look at Washington, the man and the city. P. Mesta. McCalls 91:18+ F '64

WASHOUT. See Painting—Technique

WASIOLEK, Edward
What the Soviets read about America. Sat R 47:26-7 My 9 '64

WASKOW, Arthur I.
Advancing the American national interest without war. Bul Atomic Sci 20:23-5 F; 37-8 Je '64
Contradictory initiatives. Bul Atomic Sci 19: 35 Ap '63
How to avoid a race riot. Sat R 46:8-10+ Jl 6 '63
New roads to a world without war. Yale R 54:85-111 O '64
Why I went to jail. por Sat R 46:32-3 Ag 24 '63

WASON, Betty
Gourmets of San Sebastian. Atlan 213:117+ Je '64
Tomato cook book. House & Gard 126:121+ Ag '64

WASP venom. See Venom

WASPS
Clustering wasps, and why they cluster. H. E. Evans. il Audubon Mag 65:236-7 Jl '63
Hot wasp nests; yellow-and-black daubers use radioactive mud. Time 84:35 Ag 14 '64
Inherited male-producing factor in an insect that produces its males from unfertilized eggs. A. Wilkes. bibliog il Science 144:305-7 Ap 17 '64; Reply with rejoinder. S. E. Flanders. 145:726-7 Ag 14 '64
Predatory wasps. H. E. Evans il Sci Am 208:145-50+ Ap '63
Wasp farm, by H. E. Evans. Review
Newsweek il 62:96+ S 23 '63

WASSEF, Ramses Wissa
Experiment in Harrania; revival of Egyptian folk art. P. Davis. il Sch Arts 63:7-10 O '63

WASSERBURG, G. J. and others
Relative contributions of uranium, thorium, and potassium to heat production in the earth. bibliog Science 143:465-7 Ja 31 '64

WASSERMAN, Burt
Random register serigraphs. Sch Arts 64:35-8 O '64

WASSERMAN, Dale
One flew over the cuckoo's nest; dramatization of novel by K. Keasy. Criticism
America 109:753-4 D 7 '63
Commonweal 79:461 Ja 17 '64
New Yorker 39:143 N 23 '63
Newsweek il 62:71 N 25 '63
Sat R 46:24 N 30 '63
Time 82:71 N 22 '63

WASSERMAN, Lew
Meanwhile back in Hollywood, efficiency takes over; with report by D. Zeitlin. il por Life 55:46-50B D 20 '63
New kind of king. il por Time 85:50-1 Ja 1 '65

WASSERMAN, Paul
Management resource; excerpts from address, April 1963. por Library J 89:4280-2 N 1 '64
One of a species; special library, past, present, and future; excerpts from address, April 1963. por Library J 89:797-802 F 15 '64

WASSERMAN, R. H. See Mercer, P. F. jt. auth.

WASSERMANN, Charles
Khrushchev mends some fences. Reporter 29: 36-8 S 26 '63

WASSERSTROM, William
Trade journals of Utopia. Nation 198:98-100 Ja 27 '64

WASSERSUG, Joseph D.
Help for the headache prone. Parents Mag 39:139+ Ap '64
Tetanus: the disease we can prevent but don't. Sci Digest 55:85-9 Ja '64
Weather and how you feel. Sci Digest 54: 62-6 Jl '63
What ever happened to lumbago? Sci Digest 54:64-8 N '63
What every husband should know. Todays Health 42:48-9+ Ap '64

WASSON, Chester R.
Common sense in sampling. Harvard Bsns R 41:109-14 Ja '63

WASSON, Donald
Source material. See issues of Foreign affairs

WASSON, Isabel B.
Bird baths. Audubon Mag 65:179-80 My '63

WASTE, Disposal of. See Refuse and refuse disposal; Sewage disposal

WASTE, Utilization of
Economical plating-waste treatment; cyanide recovery. H. E. P. Barta. il Am City 79: 75-6 Ja '64
Treasures from waste by chemical industries. Sci N L 84:280 N 2 '63
Waste into energy. R. Thomas. il Sci N L 86:282-3 O 31 '64
WASTE baskets
Plastic wastebaskets; versatility unlimited. Good H 156:180f Mr '63
Waste baskets. il Consumer Bul 48:32-4 F '65
WASTE heat
Power company's new rival. il Bsns W p80+ Je 13 '64
Waste into energy. R. Thomas. il Sci N L 86:282-3 O 31 '64
WASTE in government spending. See United States—Appropriations and expenditures
WASTE in industry
See also
Efficiency, Industrial
WASTE paper baskets. See Waste baskets
WASTE products
See also
Bagasse
Trade waste
WASTE water. See Trade waste
WASTING disease. See Animals—Diseases and pests
WATCHES
Chain-drive watches. L. W. Slaughter. il Hobbies 68:51-3 Ja '64
Liverpool watches. L. W. Slaughter. il Hobbies 68:46-7+ Je '63
Men's wrist watches. il Consumer Rep 28: 281-3 Je '63
Musical watches. L. W. Slaughter. il Hobbies 68:46-7+ Ap '63
Railroad watches. L. W. Slaughter. il Hobbies 68:46-7+ My '63
Right care for watches. Good H 158:129 Ja '64
Seventeenth-century French enameled watches in the Walters art gallery. P. Verdier. il Antiques 84:686-90 D '63
Swiss seek to turn their watches ahead; challenge to Bulova's Accutron. il Bsns W p42-4+ Ja 9 '65
Tick-tock stuff. il Vogue 142:146-51+ N 15 '63
Time for a change. il Holiday 35:162 My '64
Timex electric watch. il Consumer Bul 47: 2+ Mr '64
Watch talk. L. W. Slaughter. il Hobbies 67: 46-7 F '63
Watches for an impulse: Timex. Time 81:92 Mr 15 '63
See also
Stop watches
History
Questions of time. L. W. Slaughter. il Hobbies 68:46-7+ O '63
WATER
Amazon's rate of flow; data gathered by United States-Brazilian hydrologic field party. L. C. Davis, jr. il Natur Hist 73:14-19 Je '64
Big drip; questions and answers. J. Daugherty and M. Daugherty. il Sci Digest 55:45-7 F '64
Drops in the hydrologist's bucket. il UNESCO Courier 17:40-1+ Jl '64
Fresh water: temperature of maximum density calculated from compressibility. H. Eklund. bibliog il Science 142:1457-8 D 13 '63
Lateral hypothalamic lesions: effects on drinking elicited by carbachol in preoptic area and posterior hypothalamus. G. Wolf and N. E. Miller. bibliog il Science 143: 585-7 F 7 '64
Radiation damage to artemia cysts: effects of water vapor. W. C. Snipes and W. Gordy. bibliog Science 142:503-4 O 25 '63
Rocks yield water in moon living rehearsal. Sci N L 85:137 F 29 '64
Taste of sodium chloride solutions after adaptation to sodium chloride: implications for the water taste. L. M. Bartoshuk and others. bibliog Science 143:967-8 F 28 '64
Water. E. Janeway. House & Gard 124:146-7 S '63
Water molecule in biological systems; report on conference on forms of water in biologic systems. J. F. Saunders. Science 147:179-81 Ja 8 '65
Water of the world. R. L. Nace. il Natur. Hist 73:10-19 Ja '64
See also
Floods
Hydrologic research
Ocean
Photography of water
Sea water
Analysis
Hydrogen-water vapor mixtures: control of hydrothermal atmospheres by hydrogen osmosis. H. R. Shaw. bibliog il Science 139:1220-2 Mr 22 '63
Hardness
Hard water is best for health. H. A. Schroeder. il Consumer Bul 46:2+ Mr '63
Odor and taste removal
See Water purification
Pollution
See Water pollution
Purification
See Water purification
WATER, Distilled
Now, a drink from the sea. T. Willets. il Motor B 113:90-1+ Ja '64
See also
Sea water—Desalting
WATER, Freezing of. See Freezing
WATER, Irrigation. See Irrigation water
WATER, Saline
Beets and spinach thrive in salt water. Sci N L 86:73 Ag 1 '64
Brackish water becomes fresh; Buckeye, Ariz. W. G. Hamner. il Am City 78:115-16 Mr '63
Passing the salt. il Newsweek 62:56-7 Ag 19 '63
U.S. watering down river; decreasing salt concentration of Colorado River. Sci N L 85:181 Mr 21 '64
See also
Sea water—Desalting
WATER, Underground
Geothermal brine well: mile-deep drill hole may tap ore-bearing magmatic water and rocks undergoing metamorphism. D. E. White and others. bibliog il Science 139: 919-22 Mr 8 '63
Groundwater: flow toward an effluent stream. J. H. Lehr. bibliog il Science 140:1318-20 Je 21 '63
Ground water in North America. H. E. Thomas and L. B. Leopold. bibliog il Science 143:1001-6 Mr 6 '64; Reply with rejoinder. J. D. Hewlett. 144:1407-8 Je 19 '64
Tap volcanic-like water; geothermal well. Sci N L 83:182 Mr 23 '63
Tritium-hydrologic research: some results of the U.S. geological survey research program. C. W. Carlston. bibliog il Science 143:804-6 F 21 '64
Underground water: wasted treasure. V. N. Kunin. il UNESCO Courier 17:14-18+ Jl '64
See also
Artesian wells
Wells
Prospecting
See also
Divining rod
WATER and sewerage technical school, Neosho, Mo.
Water-sewage courses become formal school. C. S. Kramer. il Am City 79:122-3 O '64
WATER birds
Nasal salt gland: independence of salt and water transport. T. Inoue. bibliog il Science 142:1299 D 6 '63
Party; society's annual garden party and visit to Bronx zoo's new aquatic birds house. New Yorker 40:52-3 O 10 '64
Tropical sea birds. A. Sprunt, 4th. il Motor B 112:35+ D '63
See also
Ducks unlimited, incorporated
Shore birds
also names of water birds, e.g. Cormorants
Accidents and hazards
See Birds—Accidents and hazards
WATER closets
Now you can afford a wall-hung toilet; off-the-floor toilet. J. Hand. il Pop Sci 185: 120-2 S '64
WATER color painting
Brush and watercolor; excerpts from Watercolor landscape. R. Brandt. il Design 65: 114-19+ Ja '64
Cézanne: the logical mystery; loan exhibition of watercolors. T. Reff. il Art N 62: 28-31 Ap '63
Figure sketching in watercolor. S. Sutherland. il Am Artist 27:50-3+ O '63
Painting on a world tour. C. Johnson. il Am Artist 27:48-9+ Ap '63

WATER color painting—*Continued*
Rapid watercolors. F. Bates. il Design 65: 158-61 Mr '64
Richard Whorf: painter of Americana. J. Lovoos. il Am Artist 28:32-7+ Ap '64
Turner's pictures of nothing. L. Gowing. il Art N 62:30-3+ O '63
Water color methods. il Design 65:32-6 S '63
Water color page. See issues of American artist

WATER conservation
Conservancy districts: useful tools for water development. H. Mendenhall. il Am For 69: 20-2+ Ag '63
Lament in a dry climate. R. Starnes. Field & S 68:12+ F '64
Soil-use planning for individual and public goals. C. E. Kellogg. Bul Atomic Sci 20:15-18 N '64
Water, a most precious commodity. S. Schuler. il Am Home 67:76-8 Mr '64
When and how to use water meters; Zanesville, Ohio. R. R. Fleming. il Am City 79:110-12 Je '64
See also
National watershed congress

WATER desalting. See Water purification—Desalting; Sea water—Desalting

WATER distribution
Cut water-planning guesswork; Norwalk, Ohio. J. C. Bumstead. il Am City 78:102-4 My '63
Eleven small water systems unite; suburban Detroit. D. A. Keylon. il Am City 78:131+ Ag '63
Intricate Hardy-Cross mazes bow to a computer; water-system design; Waterford Township, Mich. P. M. Hampton. il Am City 79:107-8 S '64
Modern water witching; Troy, Mo. R. S. Miller. il Am City 78:105-6 N '63
Ready to move; Atlanta, Ga. il Am City 78: 116-17 S '63
Togetherness solves a water problem for Glendale, Fox Point and Whitefish Bay, Wis. J. M. Katzban. il Am City 78:86-8 O '63
Water-resources research in the federal government; excerpts from report of the Task group on coordinated water-resources research of the Federal council for science and technology. R. Revelle. bibliog Science 142:1027-33 N 22 '63
See also
Pumping stations
Water pipes
Water tanks

WATER districts
Keep ahead of the water demand; South Huntington, N.Y. water district. O. A. Olsen. il Am City 79:167-8 S '64
Water depletion allowance; High Plains underground water district. New Repub 148: 5 F 9 '63

WATER films. See Surface tension

WATER filters. See Filters and filtration

WATER flow. See Channels

WATER fowl
See also
Water birds

WATER fronts
Cincinnati riverfront redevelopment. H. Weese. il Arch Rec 133:138-9 My '63
Triple-benefit waterfront projects; Suffolk County, N.Y. H. L. Dennison. il Am City 78:110-12 Mr '63

WATER gardens
Add a pool to cool your patio. il Pop Gard 15:48-9 My '64
Falling water in your garden. il Sunset 131: 68-9 Jl '63
For a four-dimensional garden, use water. il House & Gard 125:138-9+ Je '64
How to create your own water garden. il House & Gard 123:216-19 Ap '63
New allure of swimming pools. il House & Gard 123:100-5 Je '63
Salt marsh garden. E. N. Danenberg. il Horticulture 42:46-7 N '64
Water gardens. il House & Gard 123:156-9 Ap '63
See also
Garden pools

WATER heaters
Acceptable faucet water heater; Landam C-1. Consumer Rep 28:263 Je '63
How to avoid those water heater woes. Bet Hom & Gard 42:123 Mr '64
Immersible water heaters: be careful. Consumer Rep 28:227 My '63
Keeps 5,000 bathers in hot water; showers at Clyde Park district's swimming pools, Cicero, Ill. R. W. Holec. Am City 79:29 Ja '64
Water heaters and water softeners. il Bet Hom & Gard 42:114-15 F '64

WATER heating
See also
Hot water supply

WATER hyacinths
Pulchritudinous pest. J. Fix. il Motor B 112: 47+ D '63
World's most exotic nuisance. J. Poling. il Read Digest 85:253-6 O '64

WATER in the body
Milk analysis of the kangaroo rat, dipodomys merriami. G. L. Kooyman. bibliog il Science 142:1467 D 13 '63
Nasal salt excretion and the possible function of the cloaca in water conservation. K. Schmidt-Nielson and others. bibliog Science 142:1300-1 D 6 '63
Sea within us; excerpts from Man and his body. B. F. Miller and R. Goode. Read Digest 82:192C-192D+ Mr '63
Thirst: regulation of body water; report of conference at Florida state university M. J. Wayner, jr and E. M. Sporn. Science 141:740+ Ag 23 '63
Water intake of normal children. J. S. Walker and others. bibliog il Science 140: 890-1 My 24 '63
Water transport across root cell membranes: effect of alkenylsuccinic acids. P. J. C. Kuiper. bibliog il Science 143: 690-1 F 14 '64
Water turnover in cattle. A. L. Black and others. bibliog il Science 144:876-8 My 15 '64

WATER lilies
Care and culture of tropical water lilies in the North. P. W. Stetson. il Horticulture 41:262-3 My '63
Exotic waterlilies, a cool pool of beauty in your garden. T. A. Weston. il Am Home 66: 42-3+ Jl '63
I find enchantment in my water-lily pool. J. Hillstrom. il Flower Grower 51:24-6 Mr '64
Waterlilies. G. Hull. il Pop Gard 14:38-9+ My '63
Waterlilies. P. Nutt. il Horticulture 42:18-21 Je '64

WATER mains. See Water pipes

WATER meters
Case for water meters. il Am City 79:97-9+ D '64
Coin-operated meters prevent water losses; Odessa, Tex. G. T. Morris. il Am City 78: 147-8 Mr '63
Free remote-read registers; Ames, Ia. il Am City 78:145 F '63
Meters save water; Kingston, N.Y. E. T. Cloonan. il Am City 79:147-8 Mr '64
New York city may get water meters. Am City 79:17 F '64
Quarter starts the meter; Township of Vaughan, Ontario, Canada. B. Norris. il Am City 79:116 O '64
What 100 per cent metering did to Philadelphia's water demand. il Am City 79:130+ Ag '64
When and how to use water meters; Zanesville, Ohio. R. R. Fleming. il Am City 79:110-12 Je '64

Repairing

Don't forget the meter shop; Ottumwa, Ia. J. H. Turner. il Am City 80:82-3 Ja '65
Near-perfect meter shop; San Antonio, Tex. H. Riemer. il Am City 78:81-3 N '63

WATER moccasin exercises. See Military maneuvers

WATER ouzels. See Dippers (birds)

WATER pageants. See Aquatic shows

WATER pipes
Growth follows the water mains; Columbia, S.C. C. C. Burnett. il Am City 78:132-3 Je '63
No room for error; blocking transmission line, Grand Rapids, Mich. S. Ferris. il Am City 78:26 Jl '63
Relocation of big mains; Staten Island, N.Y. B. J. Feitelson. il Am City 79:108-10 Mr '64
See also
Pipe joints
Pipe laying
Water distribution

Detection

Easy way to locate non-metallic pipe. G. R. Fisher. il Am City 80:22 Ja '65

Protection

Keep your water pipes from freezing. il Suc Farm 61:94 F '63
Water pipe on the rocks. E. W. Austin. il Pop Sci 183:133 N '63

WATER pipes, Steel
500 feet per day; water line for Wisconsin Rapids, Wis. il Am City 78:88 Jl '63

WATER pollution

Annals of business; soaps and synthetic detergents. T. Whiteside. il New Yorker 40:42-4 D 19 '64
Answer to beach pollution; Milwaukee. il Am City 78:84-5 Ap '63
Anti-pollution program. Nat Parks Mag 38:16 Jl '64
Biggest pesticides disaster to date; Mississippi; with editorial comment. C. H. Callison. Audubon Mag 66:146, 179 My '64
Boat sanitation. E. Robberson. Yachting 116:52-5+ O '64
Can we stop the cancer of river pollution? R. Colas. il UNESCO Courier 17:22-7 Jl '64
Chicago's rivers polluted. Sci N L 85:306 My 16 '64
Contamination of the environment; address, January 28, 1963. P. D. Kilburn. Vital Speeches 29:475-8 My 15 '63
DDT and dieldrin in rivers: a report of the National water quality network. A. W. Breidenbach and J. J. Lichtenberg. bibliog il Science 141:899-901 S '63; Reply with rejoinder. F. J. Wolf. 142:1020-1 N 22 '63
Death in parts per trillion; endrin responsible for death of fish in Mississippi River. Sci Am 210:64 My '64
Death on the Atchafalaya. J. Ridgeway. New Repub 150:13-14 Ap 25 '64
Defenseless America. Nation 196:415 My 18 '63
Detergent-foam bubble about to burst. Am City 79:35 F '64
Detergent mess. B. H. Frisch. il Sci Digest 54:72-8 S '63
Detergent problems. Am City 78:22 My '63
Detergents, deadly hazard to water birds. R. W. Nero. il Audubon Mag 66:26-7 Ja '64
Detergents in water: another view. il U S News 55:76 Ag 19 '63
Don't go near the water; use of endrin in Louisiana. New Repub 150:5 Ap 11 '64
Down by the Styx; Senator Muskie's efforts to strengthen the Nation's program. J. Ridgeway. New Repub 149:8 Ag 31 '63
Endrin in Memphis. New Repub 150:4-5 My 2 '64
Environmental health: Taft center in Cincinnati has been the PHS mainstay in pollution research. J. Walsh. Science 145:31-3 Jl 3 '64
Filth covers the waterfront. B. Tufty and M. Walker. il Sci N L 85:154-5 Mr 7 '64
Fish deaths renew insecticide inquiries. Sci N L 85:242 Ap 18 '64
GHQ for pollution fighters; controversy over fish killed by pesticides. il Bsns W p 136+ Ap 25 '64
Gunboats on the Raritan. J. Ridgeway. New Repub 148:17-19 Je 1 '63
High tide of debris. E. Crimmin. il Motor B 112:24-7+ Jl '63
How to get safer, purer, softer water. D. X. Manners. il House B 106:128-9+ F '64; Same abr. Read Digest 84:121-4 Je '64
Is our environment poisoning us? R. Brecher and E. Brecher. il Parents Mag 38:72-3+ O '63
Just how safe is your drinking water? il U S News 55:74-5 Jl 15 '63
Keeping slime out of the river. il Bsns W p96 Ap 4 '64
Mayfly distribution indicates water quality on the upper Mississippi River. C. R. Fremling. bibliog il Science 146:1164-6 N 27 '64
Multibillion-dollar fight against pollution. il Duns R 81:pt2 S113-14+ Mr '63
Nation's water; how scarce, how polluted? il Sr Schol 83:6-9 D 6 '63
Natural carbon-14 activity of organic substances in streams. A. A. Rosen and M. Rubin. bibliog il Science 143:1163-4 Mr 13 '64
Old mill stream; address, January 30, 1963. il Am For 69:28-30+ Ap '63
Oyster stew; problem of water pollution, Great Bay, N.H. P. Hirsch. New Repub 150:7-8 Ja 4 '64
Patrol boat to fight river pollution; Dade County, Fla. il Am City 79:92 Mr '64
Pesticides washed into seas around Britain. Sci N L 87:41 Ja 16 '65
Poisoned waters; endrin in lower Mississippi. Commonweal 81:556 Ja 29 '65
Polluted water; timidity in administering the government's control program. New Repub 151:6 Jl 4 '64
Pollution boggle. New Repub 151:4 O 17 '64
Pollution; everybody's fight; Pacific Northwest stream pollution. J. C. Hunt. il Am For 70:17-20 S '64
Pollution: it's deadlier than you think. G. Laycock. Field & S 68:10-13 Ja '64
Pollution of U.S. air and water: how serious? interview. L. L. Terry. il U S News 55:98-101 S 16 '63
Pollution report: Bendetsen of Champion. J. B. Craig. il Am For 70:10-11+ O '64
River with a past, and a future; Clark Fork of the Columbia River. J. Brooks. il Field & S 69:12-14+ O '64
St Croix: who owns a river? A. D. Stedman. il Nation 199:490-3 D 21 '64
Sitting on a volcano! J. B. Craig. Am For 70:11 S '64
Solid evidence shows fish die of insecticide. Sci N L 85:226 Ap 11 '64
Taming a troublesome water; Carmi, Ill. J. Keim. il Am City 79:157-8 S '64
To kill a river; Mississippi River. R. Terral. il Bul Atomic Sci 20:35-7 S '64
U.S. requests three IJC studies on water levels and pollution; texts of letters. W. R. Tyler. Dept State Bul 51:598-9 O 26 '64
View from the bridge: politics no picnic on banks of pollution; strong federal agency is likely. E. Langer. Science 142:566-7 N 1 '63
Water pollution bill readied. C. H. Callison. Audubon Mag 67:24 Ja '65
Water pollution; Merrimack River. New Repub 148:7 Je 29 '63
Water pollution report. H. F. Udell. il Motor B 112:92-3+ Ag '63
Water supply and pollution control; report on American medical association congress. J. E. Flanagan, jr. Science 145:840+ Ag 21 '64
Water supply polluted; backflow of sewage from frost-proof toilets. Sci N L 86:70 Ag 1 '64
We must stop contaminating our water; ed. by E. M. Wylie. M. J. E. Senn. Am Home 66:44-5+ Ja '63
What killed the fish in the Mississippi River? il U S News 56:52 My 4 '64
When government is a polluter. C. W. Buchheister. Audubon Mag 65:76 Mr '63
Where is science taking us? detergent waste problem. M. A. Benarde. il Sat R 46:53 Ap 6 '63

See also

Oil pollution of rivers, harbors, etc.
Sea water—Pollution
Sewage disposal

WATER pollution control federation

Engineers honored for water-pollution-control work. il Am City 79:136 N '64

WATER power

Water stretching study underway in Scotland. Sci N L 85:376 Je 13 '64

WATER purification

Activated carbon treatment. D. S. Davies and R. A. Kaplan. il Am City 80:78-81 Ja '65
Back to the river after seventy years; Lowell, Mass. E. J. Tierney and B. Cassidy. il Am City 78:74-6 Ag '63
Big step toward automation; Minneapolis. B. Corlett. il Am City 78:104-5 O '63
Diagnosis was harder than the cure. R. Stone and P. L. Wagner. il Am City 78:177+ S '63
Largest diatomaceous-earth filters; Massena, N.Y. W. K. Neubauer. il Am City 79:76-8 N '64
Most complete waste-water treatment plant in the world; South Tahoe public utility district serving Bijou, Calif.-Lake Tahoe area. W. Priday and others. il Am City 79:123+ S '64
New aspects of waste-water reclamation. E. Weisberg and others. il Am City 79:91-3 Ag '64
Propeller on a platform preserves a pond; Newton, Mass. J. B. Penney. il Am City 79:84-5 Jl '64
Pure water while you wait. E. R. Baumann. il Am City 78:23 D '63
Straining the complaints away; Palisade, Colo. G. A. Nisbet. il Am City 78:98-9 Ap '63
Taming a troublesome water; Carmi, Ill.. J. Keim. il Am City 79:157-8 S '64
Treating troublesome waters; Ottumwa, Ia. H. C. Boeke. il Am City 79:100-2 F '64
Water radiation treated. Sci N L 83:191 Mr 23 '63
Zeta potential cleans a difficult water; Gouveneur, N.Y. il Am City 79:96-8 S '64

See also

Filters and filtration
Swimming pools
Water supply

Desalting

Cheap process tested for desalting water; by natural freezing process. Sci N L 86:216 O 3 '64

WATER purification—Desalting—*Continued*
Passing the salt. il Newsweek 62:56-7 Ag 19 '63
Water desalination in developing countries; summary of report. UN Mo Chron 1:61-2 Ag '64
See also
Sea water—Desalting

WATER purifiers, Domestic
Portable purifier; Pall guard pumpster water purifier. C. Conley. il Field & S 69:133-4 My '64
Water demineralizers. il Consumer Rep 30:19 Ja '65

WATER rates
Modern water rates. il Am City 79:125-6+ N; 97-9+ D '64; 80:95-7+ Ja '65

WATER repellents
Treat gear to shed water. C. B. Colby. Outdoor Life 133:104-5+ F '64
When a hazard warning isn't enough; X-33 water repellent. Consumer Rep 29:4-5 Ja '64

WATER requirements of plants. See Plants—Water requirements

WATER reservoirs. See Reservoirs

WATER resistance. See Hydrodynamics

WATER resources development
Magic of water. M. N. Dana. il Am For 70:8-13+ Mr '64
Water-resources research in the federal government; excerpts from report of the Task group on coordinated water-resources research of the Federal council for science and technology. R. Revelle. bibliog Science 142:1027-33 N 22 '63

WATER scorpions
Cannibal of the pond. S. Radinovsky. il Natur Hist 73:16-25 N '64

WATER shrews. See Shrews

WATER skis and skiing
Advice from an expert: trick skiing. A. Tyll. il Motor B 114:30-3 Jl '64
Babes in a swampland; Cypress gardens. W. B. Furlong. il Sports Illus 19:66-70+ O 21 '63; Same abr. with title Most successful swamp in Ameria. Read Digest 84:164-7+ F '64
Driving for skiing. J. Ostberg. il Yachting 115:115-17+ Ja '64
I ski 106 mph; ed. by J. Speirs. H. Peterson. il Pop Mech 119:126-7+ Mr '63
Look, ma, I'm skiing! J. Hodges. il Motor B 112:32-3+ Jl '63
School for skiers. F. M. Paulson. il Field & S 69:104-9 Je '64
Ski boom for teaching small fry. E. F. Lindsley. il Pop Sci 182:115 Je '63
Superswamp; Cypress gardens. R. Bongartz. il Sat Eve Post 236:78-81 N 23 '63
There's gold in wake of water ski craze. il Bsns W p 110 Jl 20 '63
Who says flying is for the birds? ski-kite. R. Gannon. il Pop Sci 183:52-3 Ag '63

WATER softening
Water heaters and water softeners. il Bet Hom & Gard 42:114-15 F '64
When you want to make hard water soft. Good H 158:126 Ja '64

WATER sports. See Aquatic sports

WATER sprinklers. See Sprinklers

WATER storage
See also
Ponds
Reservoirs
Standpipes
Water tanks

WATER supply
Big atom; solving the water shortage. C. Dreher. il Nation 197:451-4 D 28 '63; Same abr. with title A-power can end the water shortage. Sci Digest 56:57-60 Ag '64
Ground water in North America. H. E. Thomas and L. B. Leopold. bibliog il Science 143:1001-6 Mr 6 '64; Reply with rejoinder. J. D. Hewlett. 144:1407-8 Je 19 '64
Hydrologic decade. Sci Am 209:58 O '63
Water. R. Revelle. il Sci Am 209:92-100+ bibliog(p307) S '63
Water: a common problem. R. L. Nace. Bul Atomic Sci 21:32-4 Ja '65
Water and life; symposium. il UNESCO Courier 17:4-63 Jl '64
Water of the world. R. L. Nace. il Natur Hist 73:10-19 Ja '64
Water supply and treatment. See issues of American city
See also
Airports—Water supply
Artesian wells
Dams
Droughts
Irrigation
Pumping stations
Reservoirs
Water meters
Water pollution
Water rates
Watersheds
Waterworks
Wells

Fluoridation

Biggest toothache; public doubt about fluoridation. Newsweek 62:88-9 D 2 '63
Documenting the case against fluoridation. J. Lear. il Sat R 47:85-92 Ja 4 '64; Same abr. Sci Digest 55:34-9 Ap '64; Discussion. Sat R 47:49-53 F 1; 24-31 F 15; 51-3 Mr 7; 47-9 My 2; 44 Ag 1 '64
Fluoridation fight in N.Y; why the city decided to act; reprint. H. A. Rusk. Sci Digest 55:30-3 Ap '64
Fluoridation raising tempers again on both sides of the border; pro and con discussion. il Sr Schol 82:18-19 F 6 '63
Fluoridation stalemated in Great Britain. C. E. Tiffen. Am City 79:142+ Mr '64
Fluoride and civil liberty. J. Lear. Sat R 48:91 Ja 2 '65
Fluorides for better bites. Time 84:95 N 20 '64
Let's win the fight for fluoridation! A. S. Flemming. Good H 157:10 Jl '63
Politics of fluoridation. H. Margolis. Bul Atomic Sci 20:38-41 Je '64; Reply. S. R. Korf. 20:30 S '64
Real danger in fluoridated water. J. Lear. Sat R 46:77-9 D 7 '63; Discussion. 47:24-31 F 15; 53 Mr 7 '64
Signs promote fluoridated water. il Todays Health 41:64 D '63
Story of fluoridation. G. D. Timmons. Parents Mag 38:139+ N '63
Where is science taking us? effects of fluoride. R. E. Hanford. Sat R 47:54 Mr 7 '64

Statistics

Facts and figures of the Americas. il Américas 16:43 D '64

Tritium content

Tritium distribution in ground water around large underground fusion explosions. F. W. Stead. bibliog il Science 142:1163-5 N 29 '63

Arizona

Battle of the Colorado. il Time 81:31 Je 14 '63
Great thirst. New Repub 149:13-14 Jl 6 '63
Stormy water. il Newsweek 61:26+ Je 17 '63
Too many people, not enough water; coming crisis. il U S News 54:62-4 Je 17 '63
West's water fight is far from over; Supreme court backs Ariz. over Calif. Bsns W p26 Je 8 '63
See also
Central Arizona project (proposed)

Asia, Southeastern

Mekong River plan. G. F. White. il Sci Am 208:49-59 bibliog(p200) Ap '63
Vietnam: the fourth course; international cooperation in science. G. F. White. il Bul Atomic Sci 20:6-10 D '64

California

Diagnosis was harder than the cure. R. Stone and P. L. Wagner. il Am City 78:177+ S '63
Muddy waters; Feather River project. Nat R 14:268 Ap 9 '63
Too many people, not enough water; coming crisis. il U S News 54:62-4 Je 17 '63
West's water fight is far from over; Supreme court backs Ariz. over Calif. Bsns W p26 Je 8 '63

Canada

Quarter starts the meter; Township of Vaughan, Ontario, Canada. B. Norris. il Am City 79:116 O '64

Colorado

Battle of the Colorado. il Time 81:31 Je 14 '63
Great thirst. New Repub 149:13-14 Jl 6 '63
Stormy water. il Newsweek 61:26+ Je 17 '63

Cuba

Rushing a Cuban water cure; Guantanamo. il Bsns W p34-5 Jl 4 '64

Egypt

See also
Nile River

WATER supply—*Continued*

England

Fluoridation stalemated in Great Britain. C. E. Tiffen. Am City 79:142+ Mr '64

Florida

Water problem in Everglades National Park. P. M. Tilden. il Nat Parks Mag 38:4-9 F; 8-11 Mr '64 (to be cont)

Great Lakes Region

When water runs short in the Great Lakes. il U S News 57:98-100 S 28 '64

Honduras

Empty water mains; condensed report. H. Seidel. Am City 78:33 Ap '63

Hong Kong

Drought breaks; pipeline from Communist China's East River. Newsweek 65:34 F 1 '65

Illinois

Industry's view on water and sewerage facilities; survey of Illinois industrialists. il Am City 79:102+ N '64

Israel

Israel's new waterline: will it bring war? O. Schisgall. il Look 27:82+ Ap 9 '63
Israel's water problem. il Sci N L 85:150 Mr 7 '64
Jordan waters; when Israel turns the tap. L. Seligson. il Nation 198:622-4 Je 22 '64
Jordan's troubled waters. W. Mehlman. il Reporter 30:29+ Ja 30 '64
Pumping out the Jordan. New Repub 150:9 Ja 11 '64
Storm over Galilee; initial test tapping in Israeli Jordan waters project. il Time 83:44 My 15 '64
Water war; Syrian-Israeli dispute. Time 84:40 N 27 '64

Japan

How dry they are; Tokyo's reservoirs. il Time 84:24 Ag 21 '64

Los Angeles County, Calif.

Reclaiming used water; Whittier Narrows plant in Los Angeles County. J. D. Parkhurst. il Am City 78:83-5 O '63

Mexico

Colorado water dispute. N. Hundley, jr. For Affairs 42:495-500 Ap '64
Looking for water; moving families from La Laguna to Campeche. Time 81:37 Mr 15 '63
Pinch of salt; Colorado River. il Time 83:42 F 28 '64
U.S. watering down river; decreasing salt concentration of Colorado River. Sci N L 85:181 Mr 21 '64

New York (state)

About: the water we need. F. J. Cook. il N Y Times Mag p90+ N 24 '63

Rhodes (island)

Water for the village; Lindos. J. Martin. il Atlan 212:144+ D '63

South Carolina

More wells weren't the answer; Belton, Honea Path, Anderson County, S.C. J. L. Gassaway. il Am City 79:107-8 Ap '64

Southwestern states

Blueprint for an area short of water. il U S News 55:10 S 9 '63
Bridge Canyon Dam is not necessary; with editorial comment. S. Raushenbush. il Nat Parks Mag 38:2, 4-8 Ap '64
Water challenge of the Pacific Southwest; with editorial comment. S. Raushenbush. il Nat Parks Mag 38:2, 4-7 Je '64
Water for thirsty Southwest. il Bsns W p20-1 Ag 31 '63
Water, water. L. T. King. Commonweal 79:623-6 F 21 '64

Texas

Water depletion allowance; High Plains underground water district. New Repub 148:5 F 9 '63

United States

Check water storage against peak loads. E. A. Farmer. il Am City 78:87-9 My '63
Cities downstream. D. Cort. il Nation 198:95-7 Ja 27 '64
Colorado water dispute. N. Hundley, jr. For Affairs 42:495-500 Ap '64
Here's next round in water fight. Nations Bsns 51:80+ F '63
How to get safer, purer, softer water. D. X. Manners. il House B 106:128-9+ F '64; Same abr. Read Digest 84:121-4 Je '64
Human water needs and water use in America. C. C. Bradley; discussion. Science 139:1105-8+ Mr 15 '63
Lament in a dry climate. R. Starnes. Field & S 68:12+ F '64
Land goes thirsty. il Bsns W p31 N 2 '63
Let the water manager help to bring new industry; Elmira, N.Y. J. G. Copley. il Am City 79:89-90 Je '64
Nation's water crisis. Sci N L 83:363 Je 8 '63
Nation's water; how scarce, how polluted? il Sr Schol 83:6-9 D 6 '63
Need for clean water. R. A. Merritt. Am For 70:2 Mr '64
New sources of water trapped in limestone. Sci N L 86:361 D 5 '64
Our fictitious water famine; excerpt from address, October 22, 1962. J. E. Kinney. il Am City 78:142+ Ap '63; Discussion. 78:18+ My '63
Sprinkling skyrockets hourly peaks. il Am City 79:101-2 Je '64
Water, a most precious commodity. S. Schuler. il Am Home 67:76-8 Mr '64
Water for North America. P. H. Abelson. Science 147:113 Ja 8 '65
Water resources: Congress votes research centers for states; river basin planning bill advances. J. Walsh. Science 145:1022-4 S 4 '64
Water-resources research in the federal government; excerpts from report of the Task group on coordinated water-resources research of the Federal council for science and technology. R. Revelle. bibliog Science 142:1027-33 N 22 '63
Water reuse by design. R. R. Fleming. bibliog il Am City 78:106-8 O '63
Water shortage: famine amidst plenty. il Bsns W p 130-2+ S 26 '64
Water-supply shortage good manpower. Am City 79:7 Je '64
See also subhead Water supply under names of cities, e.g. Oklahoma City—Water supply

Western states

Hydropower dream come true; congressional approval of Pacific Northwest-Southwest intertie. il U S News 57:70 S 7 '64
Magic of water. M. N. Dana. il Am For 70:8-13+ Mr '64
Water, water. L. T. King. Commonweal 79:623-6 F 21 '64

Wisconsin

Togetherness solves a water problem for Glendale, Fox Point and Whitefish Bay, Wis. J. M. Katzban. il Am City 78:86-8 O '63

WATER supply engineering
See also
Water distribution
Waterworks

WATER supply plumbing. See Plumbing

WATER table. See Water, Underground

WATER tanks
Boosters end pressure problems; Central Point, Ore. L. Paull. il Am City 78:133-4 D '63
Bubbles break the ice; in water tank, Kankakee, Ill. il Am City 78:112-13 O '63
Check water storage against peak loads. E. A. Farmer. il Am City 78:87-9 My '63
Don't get caught water-short; Fulton, Mo. J. L. Worley. il Am City 78:133-4 Jl '63
Elevated tank for sailors; Beach Haven, N.J. E. R. Dunphey. il Am City 79:16 D '64
New booster system saves 50 per cent; expanded gravity-water system in Milan, Ill. W. J. Reese. il Am City 79:92-3 Jl '64
New steels save water-works dollars. R. E. Petsinger. il Am City 79:96-7 O '64
See also
Standpipes

WATER-thinned paint. See Paint

WATER training. See Safety education; Swimming—Safety devices and measures

WATER transportation. See Shipping

WATER transportation, Inland. See Inland water transportation

WATER weeds. See Weeds

WATER wells. See Wells

WATER works. See Waterworks

WATERBURY, Conn.

Sanitary affairs

No refuse refused. A. A. Mirto. il Am City 79:117-18 Ap '64

WATERCOLOR painting. See Water color painting
WATERFALLS
See also
Iguassú Falls, Argentina and Brazil
Niagara Falls
WATERFORD glass. See Glassware
WATERFORD TOWNSHIP, Mich.
Intricate Hardy-Cross mazes bow to a computer. P. M. Hampton. il Am City 79:107-8 S '64
WATERFRONT commission of New York harbor
Thieves meet match in waterfront game; G-men fences. il Bsns W p 118 F 23 '63
Waterfront revisited. B. Schulberg. il Sat Eve Post 236:28-32+ S 7 '63
WATERFRONT thieves. See Stealing
WATERFRONTS. See Water fronts
WATERHOUSE, Keith
Ginger man who couldn't. N. Algren. Nation 198:351-2 Ap 6 '64
—and Hall, Willis
Sponge room. Criticism
New Yorker 40:122+ Mr 7 '64
Squat Betty. Criticism
New Yorker 40:122+ Mr 7 '64
WATERING of gardens, lawns, etc.
Have you heard? B. C. Kilvert, jr. il Flower Grower 51:40-1 S '64
How to irrigate your garden. A. Edwards. il Suc Farm 62:62 Jl '64
Time to water. M. R. Beasley. il Pop Gard 14:66-7+ Jl '63
Water; make it work for you. B. Hering. il Pop Gard 15:55-7 My '64
Water to keep green. P. F. Frese. il Pop Gard 15:56 Ap '64
See also
Sprinklers
WATERING of plants
Automation comes to gardening. il Horticulture 42:31 F '64
See also
Plants—Water requirements
WATERLILIES. See Water lilies
WATERLOO, Ont.
Stop surface spalling. D. B. G. Dutton and C. W. Wood. il Am City 79:71-3 N '64
WATERMAN, Alan T.
Changing environment of science; adaptation of address, December 28, 1964. Science 147:13-18 Ja 1 '65
International competition and cooperation; adaptation of statement. Science 145:1261 S 18 '64
Science in the service of man. Bul Atomic Sci 19:3-6 My '63
Scientists and the making of national policy. Science 144:1438-9 Je 19 '64
Scientists and their images. Science 143:311 Ja 24 '64

about

First director. D. Wolfle. Science 141:11 Jl 5 '63
Tomorrow's pioneers. F. L. Phelps. il Américas 15:21-8 F '63
WATERMAN, Robert H. jr. See Welles, J. G. jt. auth.
WATERMELONS
How to eat a watermelon. J. H. Ingersoll. il Pop Gard 15:8 Jl '64
It's watermelon weather. il McCalls 90:116-17 Je '63
WATERMULDER, David B.
Nature of the church. Christian Cent 81:47-9 Ja 8 '64
WATERPROOFING
See also
Dampness in buildings
Water repellents
WATERS, Larry. See Dure, L. jt. auth.
WATERS, Richard
Free space: can public libraries receive it? ALA Bul 58:232-4 Mr '64
WATERS, Walter W.
Bonus march. J. D. Weaver. il por Am Heritage 14:18-23+ Je '63
WATERSHEDS
Conservancy districts; useful tools for water development. H. Mendenhall. il Am For 69:20-2+ Ag '63
New hope for public land watersheds. R. E. Getty. il Am For 79:14-19 D '64
Ravelling watersheds; grazing lands must be restored. C. L. Forsling. il Am For 69:12-14+ F '63
Small watershed projects. H. R. Williams. il Recreation 57:276-8 Je '64
Two views on the Seattle watershed. A. E. Thompson; J. R. Heath. il Am For 69:8-9+ N '63
Use of the dithyramb as a tool in small watershed management. M. K. Goddard. il Am For 69:29 Jl '63
See also
National watershed congress
WATERTON-GLACIER INTERNATIONAL PEACE PARK
Border wilderness. T. S. Choate. il Nat Parks Mag 38:4-7 O '64
By lake launch and open air bus. il Sunset 132:100-5 My '64
WATERTON LAKES NATIONAL PARK
See also
Waterton-Glacier International Peace Park
WATERWAYS
High tide of debris. E. Crimmin. il Motor B 112:24-7+ Jl '63
See also
Rivers

Alaska

Alaska has a new water highway. il Sunset 130:53 Je '63

Canada

See also
St Lawrence Seaway
Welland Ship Canal

Europe

Europe's water arteries. il Fortune 69:51-2+ Ja '64
See also
Danube River

France

Vive les différences! P. Redford. il Motor B 111:38-9+ Ap '63

United States

By barge, river transportation's confluence. Y. Catlin. Ann Am Acad 345:89-94 Ja '63
Okeechobee waterway. J. Emmett. il Yachting 114:132-3 D '63
See also
Florida Ship Canal project
Great Lakes
Intracoastal Waterway
Potomac River
St Lawrence Seaway
WATERWORKS
Airport water works requires more systems; O'Hare international airport, Chicago. M. Callahan. il Am City 79:93-4 Mr '64
Don't forget the meter shop; Ottumwa, Ia. J. H. Turner. il Am City 80:82-3 Ja '65
Hydraulic civilizations. P. Armillas. il UNESCO Courier 17:60-3 Jl '64
Neighborhood showpiece; Haddon Heights, N.J. il Am City 78:153 F '63
No weak spots; Frankfort, Ind. water. J. B. Wilson. il Am City 78:153+ My '63
Our own plant proved better. R. Weidaw and K. Bielert. il Am City 79:102-4 Ag '64
Single-basin flexibility; Wausau, Wis. P. O. Schmidt and L. Tessmer. il Am City 79:88-9 F '64
Supervisory controls. R. P. Van Dyke and W. E. Nusbaum. il Am City 78:97-8 N '63
Supplemental water plant came first; Cape Coral, Fla. R. G. Shanklin, jr. and R. A. Cuevas. il Am City 79:153-5+ O '64
Water on tap for city growth; Grand Rapids, Mich. D. E. Hazelswart. il Am City 78:92-4 S '63
Water supply and treatment. See issues of American city
Water-works corrosion. W. E. Edwards. il Am City 78:86-8 F '63
See also
Filter plants
Pumping stations
Water purification

Meter departments

See Water meters

Public relations

Good water is not enough. E. F. Spitzer. il Am City 78:112-14 My '63
WATKINS, Alexandra Solowij
Silver by Alexandra Watkins. A. Meisel. il Craft Horiz 23:26-7+ N '63
WATKINS, Arthur M.
Come out of household smog. Am Home 66:33 S '63
It's time to slam the door on home-improvement swindlers. Am Home 66:38-9+My '63
Mistaken ideas about heating. Bet Hom & Gard 41:120-1 O '63
St Louis takes the cure. Harper 229:66-70 Ag '64
What you should know about heating your home. Am Home 67:86+ S '64

WATKINS, Arthur M.—*Continued*
Who is blocking building code reforms? Am Home 66:31+ Ja '63
Why new houses cost too much. Sat Eve Post 236:19-25 S 21 '63
WATKINS, C. Malcolm
Smithsonian preview. Antiques 85:86-7 Ja '64
WATKINS, James T. See Travis, M. B. jt. auth.
WATKINS, John L.
Your friend the compass. Motor B 113:44-6+ My '64
WATKINS, Lura Woodside
Byfield stones, our earliest American sculpture? Antiques 84:420-3 O '63
Food warmers and their lamps. Antiques 86:174-8 Ag '64
WATKINS, Vernon
Englyn; poem. Poetry 103:288 F '64
Eyes of an eagle; poem. New Yorker 40:56 D 12 '64
From Ballad of the outer dark; excerpts. Poetry 103:110-23 O '63
Means of protection; poem. New Yorker 40:158 Je 6 '64
Snow curlew; poem. New Yorker 39:40 Mr 30 '63
Sonnet; The prose purveyors of doubt, the dismantlers of. Nation 196:448 My 25 '63
Swan narcissus; poem. New Yorker 39:30 Mr 2 '63
WATKINS, William A.
Science in action. Natur Hist 73:57-9 D '64
WATKINS GLEN, N.Y.
Machine accounting. G. F. Scaptura. il Am City 79:103 Ap '64
Showdown at Watkins Glen; U.S. Grand prix. B. Ottum. Sports Illus 21:91+ O 5 '64
WATLINGTON, Frank
Amateur scientist. Sci Am 210:131-6+ Mr '64
WATSON, A. K.
Common market at the crossroads; address, March 20, 1963. Vital Speeches 29:397-400 Ap 15 '63
WATSON, Albert W.
Mr Blatnik plans a purge. D. Rapoport. Reporter 31:32-4 D 3 '64
WATSON, Aldren. See Watson, E. W. jt. auth.
WATSON, B. J.
Right thing; story. Redbook 121:60-1 S '63
WATSON, Clyde
Storm; poem. Horn Bk 39:94 F '63
WATSON, D. G. and others
Strontium-90 in plants and animals of Arctic Alaska, 1959-61. bibliog Science 144:1005-9 My 22 '64
WATSON, Dori
Sculpture of Merrell Gage. Am Artist 27:60-5+ Je '63
WATSON, Ernest W.
Technique of my color prints. il Am Artist 28:48-53+ O '64
What do you think of modern art? Am Artist 27:3+ F '63
—and Watson, Aldren
Wash drawing; excerpt from Watson drawing book. Am Artist 27:18-23+ Mr '63
(ed) See Ellis, D. Art: sacred & profane
WATSON, G. Leland, and Von Huben, H. R.
Garage full of ideas. Am City 78:71-3 Jl '63
WATSON, Goodwin
Utopia and rebellion: the New college experiment; excerpt from Innovation in education. bibliog Sch & Soc 92:72+ F 22 '64
What do we know about learning? excerpt from what psychology can we trust? NEA J 52:20-2 Mr '63
WATSON, Hugh Seton-. See Seton-Watson, H.
WATSON, Irene. See Sommer, R. jt. auth.
WATSON, Ivan
9.5; a living corpse. Pop Phot 56:166-7+ Ja '65
WATSON, J. A. See Peacock, L. J. jt. auth.
WATSON, J. D.
Involvement of RNA in the synthesis of proteins. bibliog Science 140:17-26 Ap 5 '63
WATSON, John F.
John F. Watson: first historian of American decorative arts. F. Sommer. il por Antiques 83:300-3 Mr '63
WATSON, Kenneth
Myth of the American way. Christian Cent 80:328-30 Mr 13 '63
WATSON, Lily
Spring greeting; poem. Horn Bk 40:211 Ap '64
WATSON, Mark S.
Do we need Guantanamo? New Repub 150:14-15 F 22 '64
Proud hero in war and peace. Sat R 47:42-3 S 26 '64
They were there, Lafayette. Sat R 46:28 Jl 6 '63
Uncle George the general. Sat R 47:36 Jl 11 '64
What three newsmen report about Kennedy news tactics; reprint. U S News 54:42 Ap 15 '63
WATSON, Paul G.
Early vacuum tubes. Electr World 72:42-3+ D '64
WATSON, Robert
Poetry chronicle. M. Swenson. Poetry 102:119-20 My '63
WATSON, Susan
Brief biography. S. Goodman. pors Dance Mag 38:50-1 Mr '64
WATSON, Thomas J. 1914-
Case for balance; liberal arts; address, October 3, 1963. Vital Speeches 30:118-21 D 1 '63
Self-protection; address, June 5, 1964. Vital Speeches 30:598-600 Jl 15 '64
about
Apostle of growth: the unorthodox Mr Watson. J. B. Weiner. por Duns R 84:33-4 N '64
Can IBM keep up the pace? il por Bsns W p92-8 F 2 '63
World of the renaissance executive. il por Newsweek 62:92-4 N 18 '63
WATSON, William
Inventor of the month. S. V. Jones. il por Sci Digest 54:54-5 Ag '63
WATT, Douglas
Concert records (cont) New Yorker 39:163-5 Je 8 '63
Popular records. New Yorker 39:92-4 Je 1 '63
WATT, Lois Belfield
Educational materials laboratory: Office of education. pors Sch Life 45:13-15 Je '63
WATTENBERG, William W.
Guide for parents: your child's mental health. bibliog NEA J 53:35-50 F '64
What students think of teachers. PTA Mag 58:4-6 bibliog(p37) Ja '64
WATTERS, Gail
Azaleas bring new life to retirement years. Pop Gard 15:22-3 Mr '64
WATTERS, Pat
Atlanta: fruits of tokenism. Nation 198:162-5 F 17 '64
It's nearly all white in the South. New Repub 150:11-12 Je 13 '64
Mob behind the marchers. Reporter 30:34-5 Je 18 '64
Negro registration in the South. New Repub 150:15-17 Ap 4 '64
Negro votes beat Barry. New Repub 151:7 N 28 '64
South learns to live with the civil-rights law. Reporter 31:44-6 Ag 13 '64
Spring offensive; Negroes plan the future. Nation 198:117-20 F 3 '64
Their text is a civil rights primer. N Y Times Mag p 10-11+ D 20 '64
Worst yet. New Repub 150:6 Je 27 '64
WATTERS, R. L.
Amateur scientist. Sci Am 208:157-60+ Mr '63
WATTERSON, David G.
Business background is favorable; interview. por U S News 55:46-7 S 16 '63
Profits hit a new high; interview. por U S News 54:44-5 Ap 22 '63
Weakness: credit is more extended now; interview. por(p54) U S News 56:56-7 Mr 2 '64
WATTLE (tree) See Acacias
WATTMETERS
Audio output power meter. K. Berry. il Electr World 70:48-9 O '63
Construct a milliwatt meter. W. L. Blair. il Electr World 71:82-3 Mr '64
R.F. power output measurements. R. L. Conhaim. bibliog il Electr World 70:53-6+ O '63
WATTS, Alan
Gods go West. New Repub 150:24+ Je 27 '64
Who will run your nervous system? New Repub 151:15-16 N 28 '64
WATTS, Andre
What music means to me. por Seventeen 23:22 Ja '64
about
Giant & a prince. por Time 81:60 F 8 '63
High-voltage Mr Watts. R. Kammerer. il por Am Rec G 29:718 My '63
Music to my ears: rising star of A Watts. I. Kolodin. por Sat R 46:53-4 F 16 '63
Prodigies. M. Mayer. por Esquire 61:106-7+ My '64
Real pro. il por Newsweek 61:58 F 11 '63
Teen-ager rocks hall of great music. il pors Life 54:30 F 15 '63
Virtuoso on the rise. il pors Ebony 18:124-6 Ap '63

WATTS, Cecil W.
Watts way. J. Crabbe. il por Am Rec G 31:92-4+ O '64
WATTS, Chester Burleigh
C. B. Watts and the marginal zone of the moon. il por Sky & Tel 27:94-5 F '64
WATTS, Doris Ryder
Library and the teen age (cont of) Public library and the teen age. See issues of Wilson library bulletin to November 1964
Not whether, but how. . . por Sr Schol 82: 9T-10T Mr 13 '63
Public library and the teen-age. See issues of Wilson library bulletin
WATTS, Frances B.
Crimson feather; drama. Plays 22:81-5 Mr '63
Jill-in-the-Box; drama. Plays 23:75-80 D '63
Miss Louisa and the outlaws; drama. Plays 23:55-60 O '63
Runaway genie; drama. Plays 23:43-8 O '63
WATTS, Franklin
One out of four comes back! how costly are returns to the bookseller and the publisher? Pub W 186:51-3 S 7 '64
Role of the publisher's salesman in today's market. Pub W 187:121-4 Ja 18 '65
Should retailers sell to libraries? Pub W 185:120-2 Ja 20 '64
WATTS, Raymond N. Jr
Project Apollo makes progress. Sky & Tel 27:349-51 Je '64
WATUSI. See Burundi—Native races; Uganda —Native races
WAUD, Alfred R.
Creole sketchbook of A. R. Waud. il por Am Heritage 15:33-48 D '63
When Chicago burned; drawings. Am Heritage 14:54-61 Ag '63
WAUER, Roland H.
Hiking in Zion National Park. il Nat Parks Mag 38:8-10 D '64
Unpredictable Nelson bighorn. il Nat Parks Mag 38:10-11 Ag '64
WAUGH, Alec
Spas: goo, golf and games. Sports Illus 20: 88-92+ My 25 '64
about
Books between trains. A. Pippett. por Sat R 46:41-2 N 16 '63
Not unworthy of Evelyn. por Time 82:125 O 4 '63
WAUGH, Auberon
Lord Home got the job; but he won't keep it long. Nat R 15:439 N 19 '63
WAUGH, Coulton
Master path: a study of composition. il por Am Artist 27:48-53+ Je '63
Mixed technique of the old masters. il por Am Artist 28:26-31+ Ap '64
WAUGH, Donna
Heroine. il por Time 82:28 N 1 '63
WAUGH, Evelyn
Alfred Duggan: in memoriam. America 111: 483-5 O 24 '64
Appreciation of Pope John. Sat Eve Post 236:84-5 Jl 27 '63
Basil Seal rides again; story. Esquire 59:74-5 Mr '63
But Barnes laughs. il por Newsweek 64:104+ N 9 '64
Father and son. por Atlan 211:48-51 Mr '63
In which our hero's fortunes fall very low; excerpt from A little learning. Esquire 62: 48-51+ Ag '64
about
Celebration of a happy childhood. J. Gloag. por Sat R 47:36+ N 14 '64
Evelyn Waugh. A. Pryce-Jones. Commonweal 81:343-5 D 4 '64
From imp to blimp. S. Elmerl. Reporter 31: 55-6 D 3 '64
Same always, please. G. W. Casey. Commonweal 77:487-9 F 1 '63; Discussion. por Newsweek 61:57 F 25 '63
Seriousness of Evelyn Waugh. J. Hart. Nat R 16:1152-3 D 29 '64
Suggestion for Mr Waugh. J. Cogley. Commonweal 81:120-2 O 23 '64; Discussion. 81: 352-4 D 4 '64
Thought for the interim; remarks on Vatican II. W. F. Barnett. America 108:440-2 Mr 30 '63
Wall and the jungle: the early novels of Evelyn Waugh. A. B. Kerman. Yale R 53: 199-220 D '63
Waugh is hell, or anyhow, he was once. J. Mitford. Life 57:12+ N 13 '64
Waugh revisited. Christian Cent 80:351 Mr 13 '63
WAUKEGAN, Ill.
New trucks for old. E. E. Smith. il Am City 79:13 Ag '64
WAUSAU, Wis.
Water supply
Single-basin flexibility. P. O. Schmidt and L. Tessmer. il Am City 79:88-9 F '64
WAUSAU, Wis. public library
Wisconsin: a working model; Wausau regional reference system. G. Garrison. il Library J 89:1680-2 Ap 15 '64
WAUWATOSA, Wis.
Sanitary affairs
Incinerator can be attractive. F. D. Kuckuck. il Am City 78:96-8 Mr '63
WAVE motion, Theory of
See also
Interference (light)
WAVERLEY, John Anderson, 1st viscount
Britain after world power; a life across the transition. O. Gass. New Repub 148:18-20 Je 8 '63
John Anderson, Viscount Waverley, by J. W. Wheeler-Bennett. Review
Nat R 14:163 F 26 '63. S. Leslie
WAVES
Highest waves ever seen; reprint. L. Draper. il Sci Digest 56:59-61 N '64
Mystery of the freak sea. G. H. Grant. il Read Digest 83:200-4 O '63
Quakes, winds and great waves. D. Cort. il Nation 198:363-5 Ap 13 '64
See also
Hydrodynamics
Ocean waves
Seiches
WAVES, Brain. See Brain waves
WAX, Richard. See Hanawalt, P. jt. auth.
WAX crayons. See Crayons
WAX figures
How to wax eloquently in California; Movieland wax museum. H. Sutton. il Sat R 48: 37-8 Ja 16 '65
Movie stars made to order; Movieland wax museum, Buena Park. R. R. Olney. il Pop Sci 185:10+ Jl '64
WAX painting. See Encaustic painting
WAXED paper. See Paper, Waxed
WAXES
Don't let polishing floor you. il Consumer Bul 47:6-10 S '64
Self-polishing floor waxes. il Consumer Rep 29:26-8 Ja '64
WAXWINGS
Astaxanthin in the cedar waxwing. A. H. Brush and K. Allen. bibliog il Science 142:47-8 O 4 '63
WAY, David A.
Fifty books and the pursuit of excellence. Pub W 184:92+ S 9 '63
WAY of the cross. See Stations of the cross
WAY-out Cinderella; drama. See Cable, H.
WAY the world runs; story. See Oppenheimer, J. L.
WAY, way down East; drama. See Dias, E. J.
WAYLAND, Ernest
Six speakers for higher fi. Pop Mech 121:192-4 Mr '64
WAYNE, John
God and man in Hollywood. T. B. Morgan. por Esquire 59:74-5+ My '63
WAYNE, Robert
Credit union security. NEA J 52:48 My '63
WAYNE COUNTY, Mich. library
Self-shelving by children; Flat Rock library. W. H. Kaiser. il Library J 89:2146-8+ My 15 '64
Wayne County library establishes resource center for school libraries. Library J 89: 2305-6 Je 1 '64
WAYNE COUNTY jail. See Detroit—Prisons and reformatories
WAYNER, Matthew J. Jr, and Sporn, E. M.
Thirst: regulation of body water. Science 141:740+ Ag 23 '63
WAYS, Max
Era of radical change. Fortune 69:112-15+ My '64
Labor unions are worth the price. Fortune 67:108-13+ My '63
1964: a chance to look at ourselves. Fortune 70:102-5+ O '64
Postwar advance of the five hundred million. Fortune 70:104-9+ Ag '64
Real case for a tax cut. Read Digest 82:105-10 Mr '63
Two Lyndon Johnsons and the U.S. of 1964. Fortune 69:80-3+ Ja '64
WAYS and means committee. See United States—Congress—House of representatives —Committees
WE know that your hearts are heavy; story. See Gerber, M. J.

WE shall overcome (hymn) See Hymns

WEAKFISH fishing
Strategy for specks. G. Heinold. il Outdoor Life 133:14+ F '64

WEALES, Gerald
Beast under the porch. Reporter 31:49-50 O 8 '64
Cradle still rocks. Reporter 30:46+ My 21 '64
Good-bye, Jean. Reporter 31:37+ Jl 2 '64
Kong's kin. Reporter 30:45-6 Je 4 '64
Rittenhouse roundabout. Reporter 29:64-5 O 24 '63
Robert Lowell's memento mori. Reporter 32: 56-7 Ja 28 '65
Star turn. Reporter 31:44+ D 3 '64
Transcendental tax dodge. Reporter 29:63-4 D 5 '63

WEALTH
See also
Capitalists and financiers
Income
Millionaires
Property
Prosperity
Rich, The

WEALTH, Distribution of
Celestial mechanics of unemployment. R. E. Flanders. il Duns R 82:65+ O '63
Disturbing economics of affluence; excerpts from Hidden face of free enterprise. J. R. Bunting. il Duns R 83:40-1+ Ap '64
How to pick a pocket or two; redistribution of income. C. C. Royster. Read Digest 82: 126-7 Je '63
Income revolution slows up; with charts. Bsns W p 144+ S 28 '63
New look at what people own; Fed's study. il Bsns W p 134 Mr 28 '64
Who's getting more money. il U S News 56: 96-7 My 25 '64
Who's rich, who's poor? what's myth, what's fact? excerpts from Rich man, poor man. H. P. Miller. il Changing T 18:19-21 F '64

WEANING of pigs. See Swine—Feeding

WEAPONS
Antiriot weapons. il Time 84:52+ Jl 24 '64
Dilemma of the military. R. D. Senter. il Bul Atomic Sci 19:24-7 D '63
1970 army. J. H. Winchester. il Sci Digest 56:71-5 S '64
Razzle-dazzle in the arsenal; nonnuclear U.S. weapons. il Time 83:71 F 14 '64
Secret race for death ray weapons. il U S News 54:82 F 25 '63
When foul is fair; deadly fake weapons. il Newsweek 64:39 Ag 24 '64
See also
Arrows, Poisoned
Atomic weapons
Firearms
Knives
Munitions
Swords

Control systems

Japan may intensify early warning effort. Aviation W 78:29 Mr 4 '63
Pentagon's new stress on tactical C&C systems highlights ISS meeting. M. Getler. Miss & Roc 15:18+ D 7 '64

History

Weapons gaps through the ages; reprint. il Pop Sci 184:32+ Ja '64

Laws and regulations

Are hatpins enough? case of Arlene Del Fava in New York. il Time 84:62-3 Jl 17 '64
Case of the switchblade; New York's Sullivan law. Newsweek 64:34 Jl 27 '64

Testing

Weapons for bush war; Vietnamese guerrilla war. il Bsns W p 106+ N 16 '63

WEAPONS control. See Disarmament

WEAPONS systems
Anti-satellite weapons tested. J. Trainor. Miss & Roc 15:10-11 S 28 '64
Cancellation scrutiny. W. G. Holder. Aviation W 82:90 Ja 4 '65
Defense will favor improvements over new weapon developments. Aviation W 81:23-4 N 9 '64
Defensive systems office advances studies of exotic weapons concepts. il Miss & Roc 14:59-60+ Mr 30 '64
DOD has new warhead plan. J. Trainor. Miss & Roc 14:15 Ap 27 '64
DOD insists it is developing new weapons systems. Miss & Roc 14:17 Ap 27 '64
Desperate drive to cut defense spending. C. J. V. Murphy. il Fortune 69:94-7+ Ja '64
Doctor J. H. McLean's Peace Makers. Review
Am Heritage il 14:109-12 Je '63. R. M. Ketchum
Improvements in control systems cited. M. L. Yaffee. Aviation W 81:69+ D 14 '64
Israel calls on Bonn to restrict its weapons scientists in Egypt. Aviation W 80:33 My 11 '64
Lonely warrior. R. Hotz. Aviation W 79:21 O 14 '63
Low-cost missile has dual capability. W. S. Beller. il Miss & Roc 15:34-5 D 14 '64
Lower fiscal 1965 defense request seen. L. Booda. Aviation W 79:26-7 O 14 '63
McNamara on research and development; excerpts from testimony before House armed services committee. R. S. McNamara. Aviation W 78:21 F 4 '63
Major national security problems confronting the United States; address, November 18, 1963. R. S. McNamara. Dept State Bul 49:914-21 D 16 '63
Martin-Orlando begins operation of unique armament research facility. il Miss & Roc 15:32-4 D 21 '64
National security and world responsibilities; address, June 3, 1964. L. B. Johnson. Dept State Bul 50:950-2 Je 22 '64
Navy revising maintenance management. D. E. Fink. il Aviation W 78:92-4 F 4 '63
Navy studies deterrent force for 1980s. E. J. Bulban. Aviation W 80:91+ Je 8 '64
Navy studying control of weapons through thinking of them. Miss & Roc 13:20 D 2 '63
Non-nuclear anti-satellite system in making. J. Trainor. Miss & Roc 14:12-13 My 11 '64
Nuclear delivery: theory vs. practice; excerpts from address. T. S. Power. Aviation W 79:21 S 23 '63
Ocean-based strategic weapons held neither feasible nor necessary now; Project seabed advanced sea-based deterrent conference. Miss & Roc 15:18 S 7 '64
Operational satellite killers need non-nuclear destruct device; anti-satellite weapons systems. Miss & Roc 15:10-11 S 28 '64
Our defense needs; the long view. R. L. Gilpatric. For Affairs 42:366-78 Ap '64
Policy and legacy. J. Walsh. Science 142: 1152-3 N 29 '63
Provocation factor of new arms studied. K. Johnsen. Aviation W 80:29 F 10 '64
Research chiefs sophisticating their $1-billion-a-year business. Miss & Roc 14:105-6+ Mr 30 '64
Weapons and technology, 1964. T. C. O'Sullivan. bibliog f Cur Hist 47:6-11+ Jl '64
Weapons development in the United States. R. N. Berkes. bibliog f Cur Hist 47:65-70+ Ag '64
Where defense spending goes from here. il Nations Bsns 51:78-80+ O '63
Where we stand on defense; excerpts from address, November 28, 1963. R. S. McNamara. il Duns R 83:53-4+ F '64; Same. Bul Atomic Sci 20:35-9 Mr '64
Whizziest kid; system analyst Enthoven. il Time 81:18-19 Je 28 '63

WEAPONS systems evaluation group. See United States—Defense, Department of—Weapons systems evaluation group

WEASELS
Measly weasel wears coat of many colors. Sci N L 85:24 Ja 11 '64
Wonderful white weasel. R. Beck. il Outdoor Life 135:48-9+ Ja '65
See also
Ferrets

WEATHER
April weather. Holiday 33:116 Ap '63
Do you know your weather? questions and answers. J. Daugherty and M. Daugherty. il Sci Digest 54:41-3 O '63
Foul weather ahead. J. A. Emmett. il Outdoor Life 132:84-7 Jl '63
Gardener's month. il House & Gard 126:114-15 Jl '64
Ill wind from Hawaii; the Pacific high. il Time 85:56+ Ja 15 '65
Topsy-turvy weather; what it's doing to U.S. il U S News 57:62 Jl 6 '64
We keep our weather eyes open. S. E. Smith. il Parents Mag 39:44-5+ Ag '64
Weather in the garden. R. D. Roe. il Horticulture 41:412-13 Ag '63
What's wrong with the weather. il U S News 54:46-7 Mr 11 '63
Why this freakish weather? L. M. Palmer. il Farm J 87:33 D '63
Word on local weather; Long Island Sound. C. Shields. Yachting 115:140-2 F '64

WEATHER—*Continued*
World-wide temperature and rainfall round-up. il Pop Phot 54:144-5 Ap '64
See also
Cold weather
Droughts
Frost
Meteorological research
Meteorology
Storms
Winds
Winter

Mental and physiological effects

Can you blame it on the weather? W. M. Burnett. il Parents Mag 39:50-1+ N '64
Does climate affect health? il Good H 157:157 S '63
Heat or humidity? how to make your own discomfort index meter. R. M. Benrey. il Pop Sci 183:96-7 Ag '63
Retire by climate. N. D. Ford. il Travel 121: 28-32+ Ja '64
Sleep tendencies: effects of barometric pressure. W. B. Webb and H. Ades. il Science 143:263-4 Ja 17 '64
Under the weather? L. Galton. il Pop Sci 184:88-90+ Ja '64
Weather and how you feel. J. D. Wassersug. Sci Digest 54:62-6 Jl '63
What parents ask about cold-weather ills. M. J. E. Senn. McCalls 92:72 N '64
Winter health, should you go south? B. H. Frisch. Sci Digest 55:57-61 F '64

WEATHER, influence of moon on. See Moon and meteorology

WEATHER and health. See Weather—Mental and physiological effects

WEATHER and plants. See Plants. Effect of climate on

WEATHER bureau (United States) See United States—Weather bureau

WEATHER bureau research flight facility. See United States—Weather bureau

WEATHER control
Bombs in the eye may bring hurricane control. il Life 57:42-3 S 25 '64
Experiment in hurricane modification: preliminary results. R. H. Simpson and J. S. Malkus. il Science 142:498 O 25 '63
How to shoot down hail. P. Van Den Berg. il Sci Digest 53:42-5 My '63
Is man upsetting the weather? il U S News 55:46-9 N 11 '63
Probe planned on changing the weather. Sci N L 86:134 Ag 29 '64
Probing the weather's secrets. il Bsns W p84-6+ My 16 '64
Weather control: use of asphalt coatings to tap solar energy. J. F. Black. il Science 139:226-7 Ja 18 '63
Weather modification: NAS panel report and new program approved by Congress reveal split on policy. J. Walsh. Science 147: 274-6 Ja 15 '65
Weather to order. Newsweek 62:44 Ag 5 '63
See also
Rain making

Laws and regulations

Storm over weather control. il Sr Schol 82:6-8 Mr 20 '63

WEATHER forecasts
Did we guess winter right? il Sci Digest 55: 81-3 Je '64
New weather discoveries will serve you; interview. R. M. White. il Nations Bsns 52: 36-7+ N '64
Toward a world weather bureau. C. Leedham. il N Y Times Mag p29+ S 22 '63
What kind of winter will it be? H. C. Willett. il Sci Digest 54:83-9 N '63
Winds. A. E. Silk. bibliog il Motor B 112:39-41+ O '63
Winter's tale. Newsweek 62:79 N 11 '63
Your weather. See issues of Farm journal
See also
Airplanes in meteorology
Artificial satellites—Meteorological applications
Radar meteorology
Radio broadcasting—Weather forecasts
United States—Weather bureau
Weather lore

WEATHER instruments. See Meteorological instruments

WEATHER lore
Forecasting weather the folklore way. Good H 158:169 Je '64
Weather omens; excerpt from Cornelius Shields on sailing. C. Shields. il Atlan 213: 124 Je '64
Weather rhymes and fishing times. H. G. Tapply and B. Riviere. il Field & S 68:68 Ap '64

WEATHER maps
How to read a weather map. A. E. Silk. il Motor B 112:48-51+ S '63

WEATHER predictions. See Weather forecasts

WEATHER research
Cooperation in outer space. R. N. Gardner. For Affairs 41:350-2 Ja '63
Link abnormal weather to ocean temperature. Sci N L 86:24 Jl 11 '64
Making of weather. J. Lear. Sat R 47:35-8 Ag 1 '64; Correction. 47:65 O 3 '64

WEATHER ships. See Meteorological stations

WEATHER stations. See Meteorological stations

WEATHER stripping
How to weather-strip a door. il Sunset 131: 105-6 S '63
Seal out winter drafts. M. J. Schultz. Am Home 67:87-8 N '64

WEATHER vanes
Vanes; visit to E. G. Washburne & co. New Yorker 40:39-40 S 12 '64

WEATHERFORD, John
Sessional papers: an epilogue. por Library J 88:1630-1 Ap 15 '63

WEATHERLY, Joseph Herbert
Obituary
Motor T por 16:41 Ap '64

WEATHERPROOFING. See Cotton fabrics—Protection

WEATHERS, Barbara
Low-sodium diets can be tasty. Parents Mag 40:66-7+ Ja '65

WEATHERSTRIPPING. See Weather stripping

WEATHERVANES. See Weather vanes

WEATHERWAX, Rudd
Lassie's future. New Yorker 40:36-7 Mr 14 '64

WEAVER, Charles H.
Remarks at talent search. Sci N L 85:164 Mr 14 '64

WEAVER, Ellen C. and Bishop, N. I.
Photosynthetic mutants separate electron paramagnetic resonance signals of Scenedesmus. bibliog Science 140:1095-7 Je 7 '63

WEAVER, Eunice
Angel of the Lazaros. V. Prewett. Read Digest 83:143-4+ D '63

WEAVER, H. E. See Nelson, F. A. jt. auth.

WEAVER, John D.
Bonus march. Am Heritage 14:18-23+ Je '63
Department of labor. Holiday 33:78-9+ F '63
Destry rides again, and again, and again. Holiday 34:77-80+ Ag '63
Instant portrait of the Hollywood starlet. Holiday 33:76-7 Mr '63
Man behind the body. Holiday 36:85-6+ S '64
Political convention: caucus & carnival. Holiday 35:42-5+ Je '64
Selection of a president. Holiday 36:40+ N '64
Working man's Washington. Holiday 36:74-5+ D '64

WEAVER, Kenneth F.
Athens; her golden past still lights the world. Nat Geog Mag 124:100-37 Jl '63
Five worlds of Peru. Nat Geog Mag 125:212-66 F '64

WEAVER, Richard
Richard Weaver, RIP. R. Kirk. Nat R 14:308 Ap 23 '63

WEAVER, Robert
Green Bay may be little, but football is a giant; paintings. Sports Illus 21:44-9 N 2 '64

WEAVER, Robert C.
Background: the urban crisis. PTA Mag 59: 18-20 O '64
Development problems; address, February 27, 1964. Vital Speeches 30:460-3 My 15 '64
Excerpt from testimony before subcommittee on housing, February 19, 1964. Cong Digest 43:110+ Ap '64
Federal housing agencies encouraging good design. Arch Rec 136:103-4 Ag '64
Federal housing chief indorses home-improvement program. por House B 105:31 S '63
Negro as an American; address, June 13, 1963. Vital Speeches 29:625-9 Ag 1 '63
U.S. housing's man with a mission. pors Bsns W p28-9 O 17 '64

WEAVER, Sylvester L.
Why suppress pay-TV? the fight in California. Atlan 214:55-9 O '64; 215:34 Ja '65

about

Battle of Santa Monica. R. L. Shayon. Sat R 47:37 My 9 '64
Battling big odds for pay TV. il pors Bsns W p 139-40+ Je 27 '64
Big play for pay TV's $1.50 splendors. M. Mayer. il por Sat Eve Post 237:71-5 My 2 '64

WEAVER, Sylvester L.—about—*Continued*
Box; will it revolutionize TV? P. O'Neil. il pors Life 57:43-4+ Jl 17 '64
California referendum fifteen. W. F. Buckley, jr. Nat R 16:806 S 22 '64
California's cross-channel battle. il por Newsweek 63:92+ Mr 23 '64
Is pay-TV sneaking to success? il Bsns W p32-3 Ap 25 '64
New emperor of pay. il por Time 84:52 Ag 7 '64
No Pat solutions. Newsweek 63:74-5 Je 22 '64
Pay or free? the coming TV war. D. Smith. Nation 198:504-6 My 18 '64
Pay-TV, set for wake, refuses to lie down. il por Bsns W p34 N 14 '64

WEAVER, Warren
Dreams and responsibilities. Bul Atomic Sci 19:10-11 My '63
Political evolution of Nelson Rockefeller. N Y Times Mag p 11+ F 16 '64
Scientific explanation; adaptation of address, September 24, 1963. Science 143:1297-300 Mr 20 '64

WEAVER, William
Mr Handel slept here too. Hi Fi 14:47-51+ Ap '64
Notes from our correspondents (cont of) Notes from abroad. Hi Fi 13:28+ F; 34 Mr; 18+ My; 10+ O '63; 14:51 O '64; 15:27+ Ja '65
Of poets and poetasters: Verdi and his librettists. Hi Fi 13:109-13+ O '63
(tr) See Moravia, A. Anachronism of Verdi
(ed) See Nilsson, B. Die Nilsson & la Nilsson
(ed) See Zeffirelli, F. Franco Zeffirelli

WEAVERS (folk singers) See Singers

WEAVERVILLE, Calif.
Just for dancing; civil-defense headquarters. Nation 196:415 My 18 '63

WEAVING
Every shred of evidence; rediscovering ancient Peruvian weavers' craft. I. VanStan. il Américas 15:30-4 D '63
Experiment in Harrania; revival of Egyptian folk art. P. Davis. il Sch Arts 63:7-10 O '63
Experimental weaving. M. Schultze. il Sch Arts 63:18-19 S '63
Hella Skowronski. D. Normark. il Craft Horiz 24:18-21+ Ja '64
Looms of progress; Ecuador's Salasacas weave a new life. H. O'Hara. il Américas 17:22-6 Ja '65
Narrow band weaving among the Yoruba of Nigeria. R. Boyer. il Craft Horiz 24:28-9+ N '64
Table top weaving. il House & Gard 125: 118-19 F '64
Woven form; new dimensions in learning. M. Pappas. il Sch Arts 64:34-5 S '64
Woven paintings; experimental weavings fascinate eighth grade artists. J. S. Hart. il Design 65:162-3 Mr '64
See also
Tapestry weaving
Textile design

WEBB, Aileen O.
American craftsmen's council, 1964. Craft Horiz 24:9 My '64
International crafts conference in 1964. Craft Horiz 23:11 Ja '63

WEBB, Beatrice (Potter)
Beatrice Webb's America. S. Bellow. Nation 197:116 S 7 '63
Fabian abroad. S. Kauffmann. New Repub 148:28-30 Je 22 '63

WEBB, Bernice Larson
Vestiges; poem. Horn Bk 39:164 Ap '63

WEBB, Chick
Drum mad and lightning fast. H. Dance. il por Sat R 46:52-3 Je 15 '63

WEBB, Del E, corporation
Reporter at large. C. Trillin. il New Yorker 40:120+ Ap 4 '64

WEBB, Jack
Do-it-yourself homicide. Writer 76:17-20+ O '63

WEBB, James E.
No Apollo slow-down: Webb; interview. por Miss & Roc 12:14-16 Je 3 '63
Saturn V is modern caravel; address, March 2, 1964. Sci N L 85:165-7 Mr 14 '64
Space exploration; address, June 7, 1964. Vital Speeches 30:620-3 Ag 1 '64
We are moving from preparation to fruition. por Miss & Roc 13:37 N 25 '63
Webb looks beyond Apollo. Aviation W 80:11 Mr 23 '64
Year of orderly progression toward our aspirations. por Miss & Roc 15:39 N 30 '64
about
Campaign charge: blackmail in space program. il U S News 57:8 N 9 '64

WEBB, John K. G.
Note about Vellore. Sat R 47:22 O 3 '64

WEBB, Kenneth B.
What can we do with Peter? Recreation 57:103-4 Mr '64

WEBB, Leland
Dissenting opinions of Quentin Whiteside IV; story. Ladies Home J 80:102 Je '63
Point of departure; story. Redbook 122:74-5 Ap '64
Your husband loves me! story. Sat Eve Post 236:50-1 Je 29 '63

WEBB, Paddy
Sidlesham harbor; poem. New Yorker 40:234 N 14 '64

WEBB, Phyllis
Canadian chronicle. Poetry 104:385-92 S '64

WEBB, Thomas D. Jr
How Bobby Baker made some more money; summary of testimony. U S News 56:8 F 17 '64

WEBB, Thomas William, 1807-1885
T. W. Webb, ed. by M. W. Mayall. Review
Sky & Tel por 26:95-6 Ag '63. L. J. Robinson

WEBB, Thompson, jr, and others
Report of visits to scholarly centers in Africa; summary. por Pub W 186:48-50 Jl 20 '64

WEBB, Mrs Vanderbilt
David R. Campbell, 1908-1963. Craft Horiz 23:8-9 My '63

WEBB, W. W. See Hayes, C. E. jt. auth.

WEBB, Wilse B. and Ades, Harlow
Sleep tendencies: effects of barometric pressure. Science 143:263-4 Ja 17 '64

WEBB and Knapp (Canada) limited
Zeckendorf retreats. Time 82:91 Jl 12 '63

WEBB and Knapp, incorporated
Big Bill's troubles; Webb & Knapp's failure. Newsweek 63:83 Je 8 '64
Big deal. E. Rachlis and J. E. Marqusee. il Esquire 59:98-9+ My '63
Cliff-hanging with Bill. Newsweek 64:61-2 Ag 17 '64
He webs but seldom naps. Time 83:100+ Je 12 '64
I'd rather be alive; Zeckendorf facing his biggest troubles yet. il Newsweek 61:83-4 Je 10 '63
In a mood to deal. Newsweek 61:72 F 4 '63
Out on that limb. Time 81:93 My 24 '63
Webb & Knapp lays an egg, but Zeckendorf is still scrambling. Arch Forum 121:8-9 Jl '64
Zeckendorf dickers for help. Bsns W p30 My 4 '63
Zeckendorf finesses for cash again. il Bsns W p 134+ Mr 16 '63
Zeckendorf: going once, going twice. il Arch Forum 119:5+ Ag '63
Zeckendorf pulls in his horns. il Bsns W p34-5 Je 27 '64
Zeckendorf tries auction block. Bsns W p31 Je 1 '63

WEBB institute of naval architecture
Shipmaking tautly taught. il Time 85:57 Ja 1 '65

WEBBER, Howard
Games; story. New Yorker 39:42-6 Mr 30 '63
War stories. New Yorker 39:41-5 Je 8 '63

WEBBER, Milo M.
Antibody suppression by antigen heavily labeled with iodine-131. bibliog Science 143: 132-3 Ja 10 '64

WEBBER, William R. See Freier, P. jt. auth.

WEBENDORFER, John F.
Obituary
Pub W 186:39 S 7 '64

WEBER, Alvin F. and Frommes, S. P.
Nuclear bodies: their prevalence, location, and ultrastructure in the calf. bibliog Science 141:912-13 S 6 '63

WEBER, Darrell J. and Stahmann, M. A.
Ceratocystis infection in sweet potato: its effect on proteins, isozymes, and acquired immunity. bibliog Science 146:929-31 N 13 '64

WEBER, F. N. Jr, and others
Equilibrium sedimentation of uniform rods of tobacco mosaic virus. bibliog Science 140: 1090-2 Je 7 '63
Molecular weight: measurements with gravity cells. bibliog Science 139:837-8 Mr 1 '63

WEBER, George
Enzyme regulation in mammalian tissues. Science 146:1489-92 D 11 '64
—and others
Actinomycin: inhibition of cortisone-induced synthesis of hepatic gluconeogenic enzymes. bibliog Science 142:390-2 O 18 '63

WEBER, Henry M.
Is mourning dove management really management? Am For 69:32-3+ S '63

WEBER, Jean M.
Interference; poem. Christian Cent 80:1462 N 27 '63
WEBER, Jon N.
Oxygen isotope fractionation between coexisting calcite and dolomite. bibliog Science 145:1303-5 S 18 '64
—and La Rocque, A.
Isotope ratios in marine mollusk shells after prolonged contact with flowing fresh water. bibliog Science 142:1666 D 27 '63
WEBER, Karl Maria Friedrich Ernst, freiherr von
Weaver of German opera. R. Eyer. il por Opera N 27:8-13 F 2 '63
WEBER, Lee A.
Managing a branch bookstore: problems and responsibilities. Pub W 186:62-3 O 5 '64
WEBER, Max
Weber's search. il por Time 81:74-5+ Je 14 '63
WEBER, Neal A.
Metric system of measurement; letter. Science 140:1137-8 Je 7 '63
WEBER, Rose
How we manage with eight. Farm J 88:94 My '64
WEBER, William A. See Hendrickson, J. R. jt. auth.
WEBERN, Anton
Life on four records. F. V. Grunfeld. Reporter 31:31-3 Jl 2 '64
WEBS, Spiders. See Spider webs
WEBSTER, Ben
Jazz. W. Balliett. New Yorker 39:138-9 O 5 '63
Jazz concerts; B. Webster and B. Johnson at Philharmonic Hall. W. Balliett. New Yorker 39:82-3 Ag 17 '63
WEBSTER, Daniel
It is . . . a small college . . . yet, there are those who love it. Dartmouth college v. Woodward. R. N. Current. il por Am Heritage 14:10-14+ Ag '63
WEBSTER, Deborah
Meeting-place; poem. Cath World 199:278 Ag '64
WEBSTER, Donald B. jr
Day Jefferson got plastered. Am Heritage 14:24-7 Je '63
WEBSTER, Douglas B.
Ears of dipodomys. Natur Hist 74:26-33 F '65
WEBSTER, Grady L.
Population biology. bibliog Science 139:236+ Ja 18 '63
WEBSTER, Howard O.
Maneuvering board and the yachtsman. Motor B 114:38-41 Jl '64
WEBSTER, Margaret
Off Broadway; Brontës. E. Oliver. New Yorker 39:61-2 Ja '64
WEBSTER, Noah
On the fringe. H. Frankel. Sat R 47:40 Mr 21 '64
WEBSTER, Ron
Spiritual hues; poem. America 109:709 N 30 '63
To you, church bells; poem. America 109:517 N 2 '63
WEBSTER college, Webster Groves, Mo.
One multi-purpose theater-auditorium adapts to every use; Loretto Hilton center. il Arch Rec 136:124-7 D '64
St Joan of Webster Groves. Time 81:59 Je 21 '63
Sister J: secret weapon; with statements by Sister Jacqueline. il Life 57:53-4+ O 23 '64
WEBSTER publishing company
Terms set for acquisition of Webster by McGraw-Hill. Pub W 183:90 F 11 '63
WEBSTERS dictionaries. See English language —Dictionaries
WECHSBERG, Joseph
Baedeker of what not to see. N Y Times Mag p 14+ Je 30 '63
Best cook in the monarchy. Esquire 62:76-7+ Jl '64
Business of music. Holiday 36:64-5+ O '64
Cheers! a votre santé! Common market for drinks. N Y Times Mag p28+ Mr 1 '64
Europe's opera festivals. Theatre Arts 47:59-61+ Ap '63
How to decode a European menu. Sat R 46:44+ Mr 16 '63
Karlsbad. Sat R 48:44-5+ Ja 2 '65
Letter from Belgrade. New Yorker 39:125-6+ S 21 '63
Letter from Berlin (cont) New Yorker 39:41-2+ Ja 18 '64
Letter from Budapest. New Yorker 40:121-2+ Mr 14 '64
Letter from Warsaw. New Yorker 38:106+ F 9 '63
Louvre: halls of greatness. Holiday 35:70-7+ Ja '64
My favorite hotel. Esquire 60:168-9+ D '63
New look in Valhalla. Horizon 5:40-5 My '63
New looks in Vienna. Opera N 29:21-2 S 26 '64
Profiles (cont) New Yorker 39:53-4+ Ap 20; 57-8+ O 5 '63
Prsty of my tailor. Esquire 61:96-7+ Mr '64
Quest for the best hotel in the world. N Y Times Mag p97+ Ap 7 '63
Red cross; a century of dedication. N Y Times Mag p22+ Ag 25 '63
Reporter at large (cont) New Yorker 39:140+ My 18 '63
Room full of takers for any dare. Sat Eve Post 237:30+ My 2 '64
WECHSLER, James
Long journey South. Redbook 122:68-9+ Ap '64
WECKER, Stanley C.
Habitat selection. Sci Am 211:109-16 O '64
WEDDELL seals. See Seals (animals)
WEDDELLITE. See Calcium oxalate
WEDDIGE, Emil
Rebirth for an old art. il por Design 65:171 Mr '64
WEDDING anniversaries
After forty years: a kiss and a cake. il Ebony 19:73-4+ F '64
WEDDING cake. See Cake
WEDDING gifts
Wedding presents; what's in and what's out? J. L. O'Neill. il Am Home 66:17 S '63
WEDDING in Brownsville; story. See Singer, I. B.
WEDDING meals
Do-it-yourself wedding buffet. il Ebony 19:194+ Je '64
WEDDING trips. See Honeymoon
WEDDINGS
Alexandra's wedding. il Newsweek 61:46 My 6 '63
Borrowed for the wedding. K. Denzinger. il Mlle 56:122-4 F '63
Bra', bonny bride and a fortune fair; Princess Alexandra and A. Ogilvy. il Time 81:28 My 3 '63
Etiquette for the wedding guest. Good H 156:162 My '63
Formalities of life; excerpt from Seventeen book of etiquette and entertaining. E. A. Haupt. Seventeen 22:130-1 Je '63
Guide to weddings. A. Vanderbilt. il McCalls 91:70+ Ap '64
In Europe: the splash of grand and royal weddings, 1964. il Vogue 144:76-83 Ag 15 '64
In the high Himalayas an American becomes a royal princess. N. W. Ross. il Sat Eve Post 236:20-5 My 11 '63
Primitive customs live. E. Mirel. Sci N L 83:357 Je 8 '63
Twelve weeks to the wedding. V. Jeffers. il Suc Farm 61:90-1 Mr '63
Wedding of two worlds. L. E. Battaglia. il Nat Geog Mag 124:708-27 N '63
See also
Marriage customs and rites
Photography of weddings
Wedding gifts
Wedding meals

Anecdotes, facetiae, satire, etc.

Here comes the groom. J. Wescott. il Seventeen 23:22 Je '64
Letter from Stan Delaplane. S. Delaplane. Todays Health 41:71 My '63
Mother of the groom. V. T. Klose. Ladies Home J 81:120 My '64
Strange wedding of Widow Ward. N. C. Stevenson and M. Hoyt. Read Digest 82:93-6 Ap '63
WEDDLE, Charles
New flowers by new methods. Horticulture 43:18-19+ Ja '65
WEDEEN, Richard P. and Goldstein, M. H.
Renal tubular localization of chlormerodrin labeled with mercury-203 by autoradiography. bibliog Science 141:438-40 Ag 2 '63
WEDEKIND, Frank
Lulu arrives. G. Martin. il por Opera N 28:8-12 S 28 '63
WEDGWOOD, Cicely Veronica
Great confrontations: Leo the Great and Attila the Hun. Horizon 5:76-80 My '63
King's trial: excerpt from Coffin for King Charles. Horizon 6:32-40 Sum '64
Leith Hill Place, home of Wedgwoods and Darwins. Antiques 83:438-43 Ap '63
Flowered hats and Siamese cats. por Horizon 6:2 Sum '64
WEDGWOOD, Ralph J. See Benditt, E. P. jt. auth.

WEDGWOOD ware
18th century Wedgwood horizons in a Chicago collector's home. il Hobbies 68:28-9 D '63
Heraldry on Wedgwood creamware; with glossary. J. M. Dennis. il Antiques 86:168-73 Ag '64

WEDGEWORTH, Robert
Jazz. por Library J 88:1830-2 My 1 '63

WEEDS
Our glamorous weeds. S. H. Gottscho. il Audubon Mag 65:226-31 Jl '63
Stalking the weed eater. D. L. Goodrich. il Sat Eve Post 237:22-3 Jl 25 '64
Weeds. J. S. Sherwood. Pop Gard 14:99+ My '63

See also
Water hyacinths
Winter cress

Chemical control
Agricultural chemicals, often misused, menace the life of plants, animals, and people. il Consumer Bul 46:27-30 Ap '63
Chemical's effect on quackgrass explained; Atrazine. Sci N L 86:79 Ag 1 '64
Control leafy spurge. Suc Farm 61:75 Ag '63
Corn without plowing. il Farm J 87:44-5+ Ap '63
Farm chemical application. W. G. Lovely. il Suc Farm 61:52-3 My '63
Getting rid of Bermuda in ivy. Sunset 132: 245 Mr '64
Have you heard? B. C. Kilvert, jr. il Flower Grower 50:40 Jl '63
How to get a surer kill on weeds; pre-emergence method. G. W. Wormley. il Farm J 87:40-1+ Ap '63
Late report on chemical fallowing. Suc Farm 61:31 Ag '63
Midtown weed control of redevelopment areas; Philadelphia. il Am City 79:96 Jl '64
New machine spreads weedkiller granules. L. Donelson. il Farm J 87:64E F '63
New machines mix weed killers with soil; trifluralin weed killer. il Farm J 88:38-9+ Mr '64
New weed killers for strawberries. L. Donelson. Farm J 87:58E Ap '63
No plowing or cultivating; new way to grow corn. il Suc Farm 61:27 Ap '63
Now you can control quackgrass. E. Knake and J. J. Feight. Suc Farm 62:61 S '64
Rotate chemical weed killers. Suc Farm 61:6 My '63
Soybean weed killers, they really work. J. Dyer. il Farm J 87:28-9 Je '63
Your 1964 guide to weed-free corn and soybeans. Suc Farm 62:96+ Ap '64
Your 1963 guide to weed-free cornfields. Suc Farm 61:28+ My '63

See also
Herbicides
Ponds—Clearing
2,4-D

Control
Can the manatee save Florida? central and southern Florida flood control district. L. H. Lapham. il Sat Eve Post 237:38-9 Je 27 '64
Trouble-free lawns. P. F. Frese. il Pop Gard 15:54 Ap '64
Use sawdust and enjoy a weed-free garden. B. Brinhart. il Flower Grower 51:42-3 Jl '64
Yellow rocket, best control is make silage. Suc Farm 62:66 Je '64

See also
Cotton goosing
Ponds—Clearing
Weeds—Chemical control

Control by fire
I fight giant foxtail with fire. P. Bates. Suc Farm 62:105 My '64

WEEGEE. See Fellig, A.
WEEK end guests. See Guests
WEEK end houses. See Cottages
WEEKEND diversions. See Leisure
WEEKEND guests. See Guests
WEEKEND in town; story. See Powell, D.
WEEKEND vacations. See Vacations
WEEKLY newspapers. See Newspapers
WEEKLY reader childrens book club. See Book clubs

WEEKS, Allen Alvarez
Talent comes in a bottle. il pors Ebony 19: 44+ Ag '64

WEEKS, Edward
Christmas on twenty-five cents a week; excerpt from Open heart. Read Digest 85:95-6 D '64
Peripatetic reviewer. See issues of Atlantic

WEEKS, James R.
Experimental narcotic addiction; with biographical sketch. Sci Am 210:21, 46-52 Mr '64

WEEKS, John H.
Labor relations aspects of plant relocation. Mo Labor R 86:417-18 Ap '63

WEEKS, Sara
Pup, pup, pup. Atlan 212:117-18 Jl '63

WEEKS, Special. See Special days, weeks and months
WEE-MA-TUK HILLS, Ill. golf course. See Golf courses

WEEMS, David B.
And don't forget the shoe polish. Pop Electr 18:53-6+ Mr '63
Another ceramic tile enclosure. Pop Electr 18:51-5+ Ap '63
For better sound, build the bi-coupler. Pop Electr 21:64-7+ N '64

WEEPING spruce. See Spruce

WEESE, Harry
Current work of Harry Weese. Arch Rec 133: 127-42 My '63
1964 Brunner prize awarded to Harry Weese. por Arch Rec 135:20 Je '64

WEEVILS
See also
Alfalfa weevils

WEGENER, Alfred Lothar
Continental drift. J. T. Wilson. il Sci Am 208:86-100 bibliog(p200) Ap '63

WEGENER, Hertha
(tr) See Roth, E. Forged metal in Germany

WEGENER, Warner S. and Romano, A. H.
Zinc stimulation of RNA and protein synthesis in rhizopus nigricans. bibliog Science 142:1669-70 D 27 '63

WEGNER, Bob
Braving the bulls. por Time 85:60 Ja 29 '65

WEGNER, Grace. See Hanna, J. jt. auth.

WEGST, Audrey V. and others
Detection and quantitation of fallout particles in a human lung. bibliog Science 143:957-9 F 28 '64

WEHNER, George
Otherwordly master; interview, ed. by F. Stevenson. por Opera N 28:22-3 My 2 '64

WEHRAN, Wolf
It started with Steinheil. U S Camera 27:66-7+ N '64

WEIDAW, Robert, and Bielert, Karl
Our own plant proved better. Am City 79: 102-4 Ag '64

WEIDENAAR, Reynold
Printmaker into watercolorist. il por Am Artist 28:36-9+ N '64

WEIDENBAUM, Murray L.
Obstacles to conversion. Bul Atomic Sci 20: 10-14 Ap '64

WEIDLINGER, Paul
Look at the future of structural design; adaptation of address, October 1964. Arch Rec 137:172-4 Ja '65

WEIDMAN, Charles
Charles Weidman: still pioneering. J. Anderson. por Dance Mag 38:32-4 S '64

WEIDMAN, Jerome
How to move a mountain; story. Sat Eve Post 236:46-52 N 30 '63
I remember Barbra. Holiday 34:123-5+ N '63
Party of one. Holiday 33:17-21+ My '63
Raise the banner again for Cozzens. Life 57: 9+ Ag 7 '64

WEIGEL, Gustave
How is the council going? America 109:730-2 D 7 '63
Religious schools and civic harmony. por Cath World 196:351-6 Mr '63

about
Controversy within Catholicism; barring Catholic ecumenists from lecturing. C. D. Kean. Christian Cent 80:358-9 Mr 20 '63
Council on anti-Semitism. America 109:70-1 Jl 20 '63
Ecumenical pioneer. R. M. Brown. Commonweal 79:626-7+ F 21 '64
Father Weigel, pioneer ecumenist. Cath World 198:335 Mr '64
Murray and Weigel: dialogizing duo. Christian Cent 80:599 My 1 '63
Obituary
America 110:67 Ja 18 '64
Christian Cent 81:69-70 Ja 15 '64
Commonweal 79:449 Ja 17 '64
Tributes to Fr. Weigel. America 110:164-6 F 1 '64

WEIGERT, Andrew
Machismo and the priestly vocation. Cath World 199:152-8 Je '64

WEIGHT (physiology)
Food and your health: new guide to the ideal intake. il U S News 56:67 My 18 '64

WEIGHT (physiology)—*Continued*
Our underweight children. L. W. Sauer. il PTA Mag 58:21-2 Mr '64
Taping session; Benné method of weight reducing. Newsweek 63:78 Ja 27 '64
These five cured of overweight. P. Deutsch and R. Deutsch. il Ladies Home J 80:131-2+ Ap '63
Winning the weight battle. F. Marley. il Sci N L 85:230+ Ap 11 '64
You & your diet; wanted! weight for underweights. A. A. Schaal. Good H 156:175-8 Mr '63
See also
Corpulence
Diet
Exercise

WEIGHT lifting
Recreation weight training. R. Cook. il Recreation 57:30-1 Ja '64
Weight training for teenagers. J. Lambrosa. il Recreation 57:516 D '64

WEIGHT reducing preparations
Watch those holiday calories! Consumer Bul 47:17-18 D '64

Anecdotes, facetiae, satire, etc.
Containers don't count. F. E. Decker and others. il Esquire 59:102-3+ Ap '63

WEIGHT throwing
They came out in gale force. J. Underwood. il Sports Illus 20:36+ My 4 '64
See also
Shot putting

WEIGHTLESSNESS
Air force investigating cardiovascular effects of zero-g. H. David. Miss & Roc 14:21 Mr 2 '64
Chickens in high G. Pop Sci 184:19-20+ Ja '64
Defying gravity, in short spurts. il Bsns W p32-3 Je 13 '64
Earth problems for space men. R. A. Pollard. il N Y Times Mag p28+ N 3 '63
Gemini egress-ingress procedures tested during conditions of zero-g. il Aviation W 80:72-3 Je 29 '64
Gemini experiments will explore weightlessness. Miss & Roc 14:41 Je 8 '64
Weightless workshop. R. Gannon. il Pop Sci 182:112-13+ Ap '63
Weightlessness obstacle to space survival: Soviet view. Sci N L 86:103 Ag 15 '64
Weightlessness study program analyzed. H. D. Watkins. il Aviation W 80:52-3+ Mr 2 '64

WEIGHTMAN, J. G.
La vie Bohème. Commentary 38:88-90 S '64
Passion of Scrutiny. Nation 197:393-4 D 7 '63

WEIGHTS and measures
English bronze wool weights. J. P. Hudson. il Antiques 84:691-3 D '63
Foundation of science; reprint. il Sci Digest 56:62-4 S '64
Weights and measures; report on meeting of the International committee of weights and measures. A. V. Astin. Science 143:974+ F 28 '64
See also
Electric standards
Metric system

WEIGLE, Lester J.
Growing problem of executive obsolescence; address. Duns R 83:38-9+ Ap '64

WEIL, Andrew T.
Harvard's Bruner and his yeasty ideas. Harper 229:81-6+ D '64
Strange case of the Harvard drug scandal. Look 27:38+ N 5 '63

WEIL, Gordon L.
Europe moves toward unity. bibliog f Cur Hist 47:321-5+ D '64

WEIL, Max H. See Broder, G. jt. auth.

WEIL, Nicholas A.
Landing men on moon dust. Sci Digest 53:4-11 Mr '63

WEIL, Simone
Simone Weil. J. Ratté. Commonweal 77:669-70 Mr 12 '63
Simone Weil and Edith Stein: modern mystic-martyrs. N. Braybrooke. Christian Cent 81:1461-3 N 25 '64

WEILER, Eberhardt
Immunologically determined and competent cells are affected differentially by actinomycin D. bibliog Science 144:846-9; 145:1074 My 15, S 4 '64

WEILL, Kurt
Herr Huck; television version of Weill's Huckleberry Finn made in Western Germany. il Time 84:42+ Ag 21 '64
Mahagonny. Criticism
Time 83:59 Mr 13 '64
Music to my ears; evening of Kurt Weill at Carnegie Hall. I. Kolodin. Sat R 48:38 Ja 23 '65

WEILL, Raymond H.
Mr Barnard's slip. Time 82:78 O 11 '63

WEINBACH, Eugene C. and Garbus, Joel
Protein as the mitochondrial site for action of uncoupling phenols. bibliog Science 145:824-6 Ag 21 '64

WEINBERG, Alvin M.
Can science offset the population explosion? excerpt from address. Sci Digest 53:17-22 F '63
New estate. Bul Atomic Sci 20:16-19 F '64

WEINBERG, Elliot H.
Laser flash lamps; report on conference. Science 144:432+ Ap 24 '64

WEINBERG, Gerhard L.
Hitler's image of the United States. bibliog f Am Hist R 69:1006-21 Jl '64

WEINBERG, Meyer
School integration, or else. Commonweal 80:106-9 Ap 17 '64

WEINBERGER, Norman M. and Lindsley, D. B.
Behavioral and electroencephalographic arousal to contrasting novel stimulation. bibliog Science 144:1355-7 Je 12 '64

WEINBRECHT, Ruby Y.
What the young librarian thinks of his professional associations. por Library J 88:1417-20 Ap 1 '63

WEINER, Herbert
Christian schools & Israeli children. Commentary 38:39-45 Jl '64; 39:16 Ja '65
Mission to Israel. Commentary 36:108-18 Ag '63

WEINER, Jack B.
Now they're selling quality! Duns R 82:59-60+ O '63
Sales & distribution. Duns R 82:45-6 Ag: 45-6+ S '63
Technology powers ahead. Duns R 82:pt2 155-6+ N '63
What makes a best-managed company? Duns R 82:40-2+ D '63
(ed) See Hoch, L. C. Is it over, over there?
(ed) See Yaseen, L. C. Is it over, over there?

WEINER, Leslie
In the counting house. Criticism
Theatre Arts 47:68 F '63

WEINGARTEN, Irving
Higher and lower. New Yorker 39:46-7 D 7 '63

WEINGARTEN, Violet
Young people and money. Bet Hom & Gard 42:80+ F '64

WEINHARDT, Carl J. jr
Hartford's gallery. New Yorker 40:32-3 Mr 21 '64
Healthy new force. Newsweek 62:89 S 9 '63

WEINHOLD, Albert R.
Rhizomorph production by armillaria mellea induced by ethanol and related compounds. bibliog Science 142:1065-6 N 22 '63
—and Baker, K. F.
System for reporting symposium discussions. Science 144:1474 Je 19 '64

WEINSTEIN, Evelyn
Walk with the wind; poem. Horn Bk 40:530 O '64

WEINSTEIN, Gerald
Do you dig all jive? Sr Schol 85:13T-14T Ja 14 '65
—See Fantini, M. jt. auth.

WEINSTEIN, Harry, and others
Proteinpolysaccharide in connective tissue: inhibition of phase separation. bibliog Science 142:1073-5 N 22 '63

WEINSTEIN, I. Bernard, and others
Reticulocyte protein synthesis: response of ribosome fractions to polyuridylic acid. bibliog Science 140:314-16 Ap 19 '63

WEINSTEIN, James
Pacifier for J. Edgar. Nation 198:658 Je 29 '64
Unreluctant dragons. Nation 198:398-400 Ap 20 '64

WEINSTEIN, Louis. See Chang, T. W. jt. auth.

WEINSTEIN, Rocky
Place that Rocky knows. E. White. il Sports Illus 20:39-40+ My 25 '64

WEINSTOCK, Herbert
Boris from Moscow. Sat R 47:61+ S 26 '64
Donizetti today. Opera N 29:8-12 Ja 9 '65
Handel's Rodelinda. Sat R 47:46 D 26 '64
Long, twisting road. Opera N 28:8-13 F 29 '64
Non-Scala Scala di seta. Sat R 46:65-6 Mr 30 '63
Pastoral tradition. Opera N 27:8-13 Mr 30 '63
Rubinstein's Demon. Sat R 47:69 O 31 '64
Shostakovich in Florence. Sat R 47:65 Je 13 '64
Verdi-Wagner anniversary. Sat R 46:35-7 Jl 27 '63

WEINTRAUB, Michael, and Raymond, Samuel
Antiserums prepared with acrylamide gel used as adjuvant. bibliog Science 142:1677-8 D 27 '63
—See Ragetli, H. W. J. jt. auth.
WEINTRAUB, Sidney
After the U.N. trade conference: lessons and portents. For Affairs 43:37-50 O '64
Theoretical economics. bibliog f Ann Am Acad 352:152-64 Mr '64
WEINTRAUB, Stanley
Accent on his fair lady. Sat R 46:33 Je 8 '63
WEINTRAUB, Sy
Gone are the pals of yesteryear. M. Orshefsky. il Life 54:102 Je 14 '63
WEIR, C. E. See Piermarini, G. J. jt. auth.
WEIR, John
(tr) See Shevchenko, T. By the Aral Sea; If you but knew
(tr) See Shevchenko, T. Encounter on a summer night
WEIR, Walter John
Black oranges; poem. McCalls 90:120 Ag '63
Sonnet; for a grandson given my name. McCalls 91:159 S '64
Spring, now; poem. McCalls 91:215 Ap '64
WEIS, Norman D.
My four years with grizzly bears. il por Outdoor Life 135:52-7+ F '65
WEISBERG, E. and others
New aspects of waste-water reclamation. Am City 79:91-3 Ag '64
WEISBERGER, Bernard A.
Chicago meeting, 1962. Am Hist R 68:880-3 Ap '63
How to get elected. Am Heritage 15:62-77 Ag '64
WEISBORD, Marvin R.
Again the platform builders hammer away. N Y Times Mag p 10+ Jl 5 '64
Bible of the barbershop. Sports Illus 18:54-61 F 18 '63
Do you understand the language of behavior? Parents Mag 39:68-9+ F '64
They all fall down. Parents Mag 38:54-5+ Mr '63
—See Harris, D. B. jt. auth.
WEISER, H. and others
1-α-tocopheryl acetate: biological activity. bibliog Science 140:80 Ap 5 '63
WEISER, Russell S. See Granger, G. A. jt. auth.
WEISGARD, Leonard
Influences and applications. il Horn Bk 40:409-14 Ag '64
WEISINGER, Mort
Outlines and article writing; excerpt from Prose by professionals, ed. by T. Morris. Writer 76:12-15+ Mr '63
WEISKOPF, Herman
Baseball's week. See issues of Sports Illustrated
Now it's alley fights on ice. Sports Illus 19:36-7 D 23 '63
Swimming. Sports Illus 21:58-9 S 14 '64
WEISMAN, Dorothy
Is play obsolete? Sat R 46:77-8 N 16 '63
WEISMILLER, Edward
Fact and fancy. Atlan 212:93-5 O '63
In a sanitarium; Space of time; poems. Poetry 102:306-7 Ag '63
WEISNER, John T.
Make mine amaryllis. Flower Grower 50:22-3+ N '63
WEISS, Bernard
Behavioral pharmacology. Science 144:730-1 My 8 '64
Drugs and behavior. Science 140:1109+ Je 7 '63
WEISS, Boris
Reilly and I. Commentary 35:302-11 Ap '63
WEISS, Carl
Gerald Ferguson: art director of a science magazine. Am Artist 27:42-7+ Je '63
WEISS, E. B.
New rules of personal selling. por Duns R 81:49-51+ F '63
WEISS, Emilio. See Ormsbee, R. A. jt. auth.
WEISS, Leonard
Readjusting United States foreign trade: address, April 5, 1963. Dept State Bul 48:652-60 Ap 29 '63
WEISS, Malcolm P. and Sweet, W. C.
Kope formation (Upper Ordovician): Ohio and Kentucky. bibliog Science 145:1296+ S 18 '64
WEISS, Margaret R.
American landscape. Sat R 46:29-35 S 28 '63
Andre Kertesz, photographer. Sat R 47:28-30 D 26 '64
Baffling black-and-white. Sat R 47:66 S 12 '64
Blumenfeld of UPI. Sat R 47:69-70 My 9 '64
Click transit; SR's annual World travel photo contest. il Sat R 48:64 Ja 2 '65
Communicating a community service. Sat R 46:72-3 S 14 '63
Double exposure. Sat R 47:36-8 S 26 '64
Feininger's eye on the world. Sat R 46:56-8 D 7 '63
Human document. Sat R 47:100-2 O 10 '64
Light is the leitmotif. Sat R 47:30-2 Ja 25 '64
New York, N.Y. Sat R 47:28-31 Mr 28 '64
Photography in the fine arts IV. Sat R 46:39-40 My 18 '63
Pictures of the year make news. Sat R 46:62-3 My 11 '63
Pictures to read by. Sat R 47:40-2 N 21 '64
Portraits by press camera. Sat R 47:52-3 Jl 11 '64
Shooting on site. Sat R 48:28-30 Ja 23 '65
Steichen: a life in photography. Sat R 46:23-5 N 2 '63
Travel in focus. Sat R 47:60-1 Ja 4 '64
Trends in transition. Sat R 47:134-7 Ag 29 '64
U.S. mail: campus for cameras. Sat R 47:58-9 Je 13 '64
War memorial. Sat R 47:34-6 Je 6 '64
[World and its people exhibition at World's fair] Sat R 47:34 Je 27 '64
Your camera keeps flowers in bloom forever. Pop Gard 14:18+ Mr '63
WEISS, Nathan
Cleopatra papers; excerpts. por Esquire 60:33-7+ Ag '63
WEISS, Neil
In the beds; poem. Commonweal 81:234 N 13 '64
WEISS, Paul
Purpose of experiments. Sat R 47:92-4 Ja 4 '64
WEISS, Peter
Persecution and assassination of Marat as performed by the inmates of the asylum of Charenton under the direction of the Marquis de Sade. Criticism
New Yorker 40:204-6 S 19 '64
Vogue 144:94 O 15 '64
WEISS, Theodore
Cater-cousins; poem. New Repub 150:18 My 30 '64
Door in the desert. Poetry 105:134-5 N '64
Latest word; On stuffing a goose; poems. Nation 199:498, 500 D 21 '64
Poetry chronicle. R. Howard. Poetry 102:250-2 Jl '63
Something that might simply be. M. L. Rosenthal. Reporter 29:58 S 12 '63
WEISS, Walter A.
(comp) In quotes. Sat R 46:55 My 18; 50 Je 15 '63
WEISS, William P. and Sokoloff, Louis
Reversal of thyroxine-induced hypermetabolism by puromycin. bibliog Science 140:1324-6 Je 21 '63
WEISSBOURD, Bernard
Are cities obsolete? Sat R 47:12-15+ D 19 '64
WEISSENFELS, Germany
You can't go home to Weissenfels. M. Frankel. il N Y Times Mag p20-1+ Ja 10 '65
WEISSKOPF, Josef
Annals of medicine. B. Roueché. New Yorker 39:174+ O 12 '63
WEISSLITZ, E. F.
Description of a process; Intimation; poems. Nation 199:98 S 7 '64
WEISSMAN, Edward
D.A.'s wrong guess. por Time 84:44 N 6 '64
WEISSMAN, Irving
Guardianship: every child's right. bibliog f Ann Acad 355:134-9 S '64
WEISSMANN, Charles, and Borst, Piet
Double-stranded ribonucleic acid formation in vitro by MS 2 phage-induced RNA synthetase. bibliog Science 142:1188-91 N 29 '63
WEITERSHAUSEN, Marion
Definition; poem. McCalls 91:158 O '63
Frugality; poem. McCalls 90:150 Ag '63
WEITMAN, Morris. See Gruber, H. E. jt. auth.
WEITZMANN, Kurt
Byzantium gloriously re-emerges in Athens. Art N 63:28-31+ Sum '64
Mount Sinai's holy treasures. por Nat Geog Mag 125:107-27 Ja '64
WEIZMANN, Chaim
Science, a force for peace; remarks, February 6, 1964. L. B. Johnson. Dept State Bul 50:285-7 F 24 '64
WELCH, Arnold D.
New regulations pertaining to research grants of the Public health service; letter. Science 141:1099-100+ S 13 '63
WELCH, Edna
Playback puppetry. Design 65:15 S '63
WELCH, G. See Zubek, J. P. jt. auth.
WELCH, H. L.
Loneliness of the outdistanced mouse; story. Esquire 59:111 Je '63

WELCH, Harold W.
Political pawns? Newsweek 63:22+ Mr 30 '64
WELCH, Helen M.
Pitch for placement. por ALA Bul 57:179-85 F '63
WELCH, Leo D.
Men who will run Comsat. por Fortune 67:51 Ap '63
People of the week. por U S News 54:25 Mr 11 '63
Taking a flyer in outer space. il por Newsweek 63:85-8+ Mr 16 '64
WELCH, Lew
From The hermit songs. Poetry 104:228-9 Jl '64
WELCH, Norman A.
What freedom has meant to medicine. Todays Health 42:72 Je '64
WELCH, Paul
Gay world takes to the city streets. Life 56: 68-74 Je 26 '64
Tenting tonight—CCCreatively. Life 55:10 Jl 19 '63
—and others
Corruption uncorked in New York. Life 54: 22-31+ Ap 5 '63
WELCH, Robert Henry Winborne, 1899-
Goldwater and the John Birch society. W. F. Buckley, jr. Nat R 15:430 N 19 '63
Real poop. Time 84:35 D 11 '64
Sick, sick, sick. K. Crawford. Newsweek 64:32 Ag 31 '64
Welch says Communists join Birch society. Christian Cent 80:573 My 1 '63
WELCH, Sam
Bull bass are my hobby. pors Outdoor Life 132:36-9+ Jl '63
WELCHANS, Roger Anthony
Self-probings of a master artist. Commonweal 81:545 Ja 22 '65
WELD, Tuesday
Transformation of Tuesday. il pors Life 55: 47-8+ Jl 26 '63
Tuesday past, Tuesday present. R. W. Lewis. il pors Sat Eve Post 237:28-30+ Ap 11 '64
WELD COUNTY, Colo.
Deerfield a Negro ghost town in Weld County, Colorado; Dearfield colony. A. Harris. Negro Hist Bul 27:38 N '63
WELDERS
Arc welding gun. P. M. Wilson. il Pop Mech 121:171-3 Mr '64
See also
Women as welders
WELDING
Explosive welding with nitroguanidine. L. D. Sadwin. bibliog il Science 143:1164+ Mr 13 '64
Now they're welding with explosives; explosive bonding. J. Joseph. il Pop Mech 121:118-20+ Ap '64
Refractory metal weld developed. il Aviation W 79:85 Jl 8 '63
See also
Brazing
Electric welding
Ultrasonic welding
Equipment
Big idea: welding center for casting, too. H. Walton. il Pop Sci 183:100-4 S '63
WELDING equipment, Electric. See Electric welding equipment
WELDING machines
Microminiature welder wins annual M/R competition for '63. il Miss & Roc 14:39+ My 25 '64
Portable EB welding may get space role. J. F. Judge. il Miss & Roc 14:28+ Je 29 '64
Wilderness welder. E. Rickman. il Hot Rod 16:98 S '63
WELDY, M. L.
How to tackle herd health problems. pors Suc Farm 62:50-1+ N '64
WELENSKY, Sir Roy
United Nations and colonialism in Africa. Ann Am Acad 354:145-52 Jl '64
about
Central Africa; go down, Moses. New Repub 149:13 Jl 20 '63
Crumbling federation. il Time 81:43 Ap 5 '63
Ruination of Royboy. Time 84:35 O 9 '64
Sir Roy's last gasp. New Repub 148:6-7 Mr 23 '63
Sir Roy's last throw. Newsweek 64:56 O 12 '64
WELFARE, Public. See Public welfare
WELFARE, Social. See Social welfare
WELFARE legislation. See Social legislation—United States
WELFARE state. See Social and economic security
WELFARE work. See Public welfare
WELFARE workers. See Social workers
WELL-regulated impulse; story. See Brodkey, H.
WELLAND SHIP CANAL
Canada continues suspension of Welland Canal tolls; exchange of notes, March 31, 1964. P. Martin; I. B. White. Dept State Bul 50:685 Ap 27 '64
U.S. and Canada to reimpose Welland Canal tolls; Department announcement; with exchange of notes. P. Martin; W. W. Butterworth. Dept State Bul 50:68-9 Ja 13 '64
WELLARD, James
Merchandise was human; excerpt from Great Sahara. Horizon 7:110-17 Wint '65
WELLER, L. W.
Cement-stabilized aggregate wins. Am City 78:75-7 N '63
WELLER, R. C.
Last of the hook boats. Yachting 114:126+ Ag '63
Shallow sea cruise. Motor B 111:158-60 Ap '63
WELLES, Chris
Life music review. Life 56:15 Ap 10; 10 My 29; 57:19 Jl 3 '64
No rig, no fix and no quiz. Life 55:133+ O 18 '63
Sheppard case reopened. Life 57:24D Jl 31 '64
WELLES, John G. and Waterman, R. H. jr
Space technology: pay-off from spin-off. bibliog f Harvard Bsns R 42:106-18 Jl '64
WELLES, Orson
Adult prodigy. R. Hatch. il pors Horizon 5: 84-91 Jl '63
Orson Welles and his magic steam engine. D. Macdonald. Esquire 60:14+ Jl '63
WELLINGS, S. R. and Chuinard, R. G.
Epidermal papillomas with virus-like particles in flathead sole, hippoglossoides elassodon. bibliog Science 146:932-4 N 13 '64
WELLINGTON, Jean
Forgive the little children. PTA Mag 58:12-14 Je '64
WELLMAN, Cora
Memorable days with Ludlow Griscom. Audubon Mag 66:247-9 Jl '64
WELLS, Aaron O.
Doctor. Nation 199:515-16 D 28 '64
WELLS, Bernie
One-hour blast. il por Newsweek 64:63 Jl 6 '64
WELLS, Dick
Hot rod magazine championship drag races. Hot Rod 17:52-3+ Je '64
about
Hot rod gets a spark plug. il por Hot Rod 16:24 Jl '63
WELLS, H. G.
Invisible man; dramatization. See Olfson, L.
about
Between education and catastrophe. A. Campbell. New Repub 151:19-20 O 31 '64
Horse's mouth. P. Madow. Nation 199:444-6 D 7 '64
WELLS, Ibert C. See Ryan, W. L. jt. auth.
WELLS, James M.
IPEX: printing and the mind of man. Pub W 184:85-6+ S 9 '63
WELLS, James S.
Plant propagation by grafting. Horticulture 41:80-1 F '63
WELLS, John Barnes
Grace Kerns and John Barnes Wells. J. Walsh. por Hobbies 69:32-5+ My; 32-5+ Je; 32-5 Jl; 34 Ag '64
WELLS, Leon W.
Living ghosts of the concentration camps. N Y Times Mag p 13+ Ja 26 '64
WELLS, Philip V. and Jorgensen, C. D.
Pleistocene wood rat middens and climatic change in Mohave Desert: a record of juniper woodlands. bibliog Science 143:1171-4 Mr 13 '64
WELLS, Reginald
Sketchbook of the great masters. Esquire 59: 104-8 Ap '63
WELLS, Robert W.
And where do you get your ideas? Writer 77:24-5+ Ja '64
German cooking. Sat Eve Post 236:64-6 My 4 '63
Kids should be bored sometimes. Parents Mag 38:64-5+ N '63; Same abr. Read Digest 83: 19+ N '63
Stop the music! story. Redbook 123:40-1 Ag '64

WELLS, Robert W.—*Continued*
To my children, in gratitude. Ladies Home J 81:58+ Ag '64
When Danes want to eat, who cares for calories? Sat Eve Post 236:52-4 Je 8 '63
WELLS, William
World resounds; New York. America 109:767 D 14 '63
WELLS, William D.
Computer simulation of consumer behavior. Harvard Bsns R 41:93-8 My '63
WELLS
Biggest well pays off in tourist coin. C. Hertlein. il Am City 79:28 Ag '64
Don't get caught water-short; Fulton, Mo. J. L. Worley. il Am City 78:133-4 Jl '63
Dry run on wells. E. D. Fales, jr. Am Home 66:42+ S '63
Modern water witching; Troy, Mo. R. S. Miller. il Am City 78:105-6 N '63
Water saved this town; Ladonia, Tex. il Am City 78:107 S '63
Wells replace surface supply; Cadillac, Mich. P. H. Jones. il Am City 78:74-5 Jl '63
See also
Artesian wells
WELLS, Oil. See Oil wells
WELSH, Alexander
Fiction, society and history. New Repub 148: 30-1+ Mr 2 '63
In defense of the public school. New Repub 148:12-13 Je 29 '63
Religion of life insurance. Christian Cent 80: 1541-3, 1574-6 D 11-18 '63
Their brothers' keepers. New Repub 152: 24+ Ja 30 '65
Whiteness of the moon. New Repub 149:12-13 S 28 '63
WELSH, Edward C.
Foundation for space progress; excerpts from address. Aviation W 80:11 Je 22 '64
Future in space; excerpt from address. Aviation W 81:17 N 9 '64
National space policy; excerpts from address. Aviation W 80:21 Mr 2 '64
Welsh sees Soviet try at docking this year; summary of address. Miss & Roc 12:35 Ap 8 '63
Welsh urges civil lunar mission continuation for future benefits. C. M. Plattner. Aviation W 79:27 S 16 '63
WELSH, James
Portrait of a not-so-dark-horse. N Y Times Mag p 12+ Ja 12 '64
WELSH company
Report on Parents' magazine's consumer service bureau activities. E. M. McCabe. il Parents Mag 39:24+ Ja '64
WELSH cookery. See Cookery, Welsh
WELTE, Lou Ann
Those last, late hours of Christmas eve; poem. Horn Bk 40:595 D '64
WELTE vorsetzer. See Musical instruments, Mechanical
WELTNER, Charles Longstreet
Georgia story: two men, two districts. por Newsweek 63:16-17 Mr 2 '64
WELTON, Shirley
Heading off those risky teen marriages. Parents Mag 39:47+ Mr '64
Oh, say, can you ski? Parents Mag 38:66-7+ D '63
Opening school doors to the brain-damaged. Parents Mag 39:78-9+ F '64
WELTS, Anne Quast
New darling of the galleries. R. Lardner. il por Sports Illus 19:14-15 S 2 '63
No reason to stop playing golf now. por Sports Illus 21:56-7 Ag 31 '64
WELTY, Eudora
Where is the voice coming from? story. New Yorker 39:24-5 Jl 6 '63
WEN; drama. See Bellow, S.
WENBERG, Stanley J.
Midwestern interstate co-operation in higher education; address, July 30, 1963. Sch & Soc 92:50-1 F 8 '64
WENDELL, Mitchell
Interstate compact for libraries; address, November 1963. ALA Bul 58:132-4 F '64
WENDLAND, Audrey
Birthday present; story. Redbook 121:22-3 Ag '63
WENDLANDT, Wesley W.
Dynamic reflectance spectroscopy; a new thermal technique. bibliog Science 140: 1085-7 Je 7 '63
WENDLER, Henry G.
Let's bring children into gardens. Horticulture 42:36-7+ My '64
WENDT, Florence Carr
Tips on buying better health insurance coverage. Todays Health 41:44-5 N '63
WENDT, Richard H. and others
Self-maintained visual stimulation in monkeys after long-term visual deprivation. bibliog Science 139:336-8 Ja 25 '63
WENK, Edward, jr
Science advice: new division for science policy research set up in LRS to aid Congress. J. Walsh. por Science 145:1162-4 S 11 '64
Science policy research division established at Library of Congress. Library J 89:3708 O 1 '64
WENK, Eugene J. See Levine, S. jt. auth.
WENKART, Henny
Adventurous ones. il pors Vogue 142:76 Ag 1 '63
Why Jonny can read. Time 81:52 Mr 8 '63
WENNBLOM, Ralph D. and Wormley, G. W. (eds) Crops and soils. See issues of Farm journal
WENNER, Adrian M.
Sound communication in honeybees. Sci Am 210:116-22+ bibliog(p 156) Ap '64
WENNER, Charles E. See DiPaolo, J. A. jt. auth.
WENNERSTRÖM, Stig
Case of the Red Eagle. il por Time 83:30 My 8 '64
Gentleman spy. por Time 82:26 Jl 5 '63
Hell of a nice guy. por Newsweek 62:36-7 Jl 8 '63
Idealist. Time 83:25 Je 19 '64
Include the women. il por Time 84:34 D 11 '64
Master spy who almost got away. I. Ross. Harper 229:47-54 D '64
One solitary flaw. il por Newsweek 63:38 My 11 '64
Red spy's secret: first win the wives. por U S News 57:12 D 7 '64
Spy scandal that concerns the U.S. por U S News 55:8 Jl 8 '63
Swedish spy details Soviet ICBM gamble. G. C. Wilson. Aviation W 81:22-3 D 14 '64
WENNING, Irene Hipp
School gusher. Sr Schol 84:3T My 8 '64
WENSBERG, Erik
Books. Vogue 143:22 Ja 1; 18 F 15; 52 Mr 1; 44 Ap 1; 38 Je; 144:32 Ag 1; 104 S 1 '64
Horse's mouth. Commentary 36:408-10 N '63
WENTORF, R. H. jr
Boron: another form. bibliog Science 147:49-50 Ja 1 '65
—and Kasper, J. S.
Two new forms of silicon. bibliog Science 139: 338-9 Ja 25 '63
WENTWORTH, Vivian
Fulfillment; poem. Farm J 88:78 Ap '64
WENTZ, Richard E.
Disciples and Catholicity. Christian Cent 81:400-1 Mr 25 '64
Splart theology. Christian Cent 80:398-9 Mr 27 '63
WENTZ, W. B.
(ed) See Brandreth, E. J. jr. Record smashing Sabreliner
WENTZEL, Volkmar
Mozambique: land of the good people. il Nat Geog Mag 126:196-231 Ag '64
WENZEL, Evelyn
What is a creative teacher? NEA J 53:8-10 S '64
WERBER, F. X. See Ketley, A. D. jt. auth.
WERBER, Frank
Fourth man makes the trio tick; Kingston trio. il pors Bsns W p56-8 F 23 '63
WERBOFF, Jack
Prenatal irradiation: effects on the development of the central nervous system and postnatal behavior. Science 144:84-6 Ap 3 '64
—and Havlena, Joan
Febrile convulsions in infant rats, and later behavior. bibliog Science 142:684-5 N 8 '63
WERFEL, Alma Maria. See Mahler, A. M. S.
WERICH, Jan
Reunion. New Yorker 39:20-1 Jl 27 '63
WERKMAN, Nick
Master Werkman. H. L. Masin. por Sr Schol 82:24 Mr 6 '63
WERMAN, Robert
Antidromic inhibition accompanied by ventral root positivities. bibliog Science 143:824-5 F 21 '64
WERNECKE, Herbert H.
New perspectives. Christian Cent 80:1242-4 O 9 '63
WERNER, Alfred
Art in a divided city. Am Artist 27:36-41+ Ap '63
Art of Kaethe Kollwitz. Am Artist 27:24-9 N '63
Holbein: master draughtsman. Am Artist 29: 42-7+ F '65
Inspired wood carvers of the Gothic age. Am Artist 27:40-5+ D '63
Leonard Baskin; art for life's sake. Am Artist 28:40-5+ N '64

WERNER, Alfred—*Continued*
Modigliani, master draughtsman. Am Artist 28:18-23+ F '64
Rembrandt's Bible drawings. Am Artist 28: 52-8+ D '64
Twenty-six Israeli artists. Reporter 32:42+ Ja 14 '65
Vienna: the Athens of central Europe. Am Artist 28:40-7+ My '64

WERNER, George, and Crowley, James
Try latest ideas on feeding dairy cows. Suc Farm 62:46-7 Ja '64

WERNER, Georges H. and others
Trachoma; with biographical sketches. Sci Am 210:19, 79-84+ Ja '64

WERNER, M. R.
Horse racing (cont) Sports Illus 19:44 Jl 15 '63

WERNER, Sharon L. See Ward, R. F. jt. auth.

WERNER, Wallace
Graceful prelude to death; with report by M. Smith. il pors Life 56:34-9 Ap 24 '64
Last race. il por Time 83:36 Ap 24 '64
Obituary
Sports Illus 20:15 Ap 20 '64

WERNICK, Robert
Debts we never paid. Am Heritage 16:32-5+ D '64

WERTENBAKER, William
Five minutes before sleep; story. New Yorker 39:28-9 Je 15 '63

WERTH, Alexander
Algerian crisis. Nation 197:341-4 N 23 '63
De Gaulle and the French strikes. Nation 196:239-40 Mr 23 '63
De Gaulle at home with his destiny. Sat R 48:48-9 Ja 9 '65
De Gaulle's bold gambits. Nation 198:339-42 Ap 6 '64
De Gaulle's world view. Nation 198:195-7 F 24 '64
Echoes of Stalinism. Nation 196:308-9 Ap 13 '63
From Napoleon's fall to de Gaulle. Sat R 46:44-5 Je 22 '63
Khrushchev eats his words. Nation 198:64-6 Ja 20 '64
Kremlin votes no confidence. Nation 199:291-5 N 2 '64
Letter from Paris. Nation 196:104-6 F 2 '63
NATO today: the great poker game. Nation 199:399-401 N 30 '64
Recriminations in Moscow. Nation 197:43-6 Jl 27 '63
Red ran the tide of the Volga. Sat R 47:29+ Mr 14 '64
Russia in 1964: report on a two-month visit. Nation 199:183-8 O 5 '64
Russia: the pangs of affluence. Nation 198: 453-6 My 4 '64
Russia's Europe; shifting satellites. Nation 198:644-6 Je 29 '64
Russia's satellites in new orbits. Nation 200: 27-9 Ja 11 '65
Soviet view of World war II. Nation 197:143-5 S 14 '63

WERTHAM, Fredric
Redbook dialogue: Alfred Hitchcock and Dr Fredric Wertham. pors Redbook 120:70-1+ Ap '63
Why murder is contagious; interview. McCalls 91:136+ F '64

WERTHEIM, Gunther K.
Mössbauer effect in chemistry and solid-state physics. bibliog Science 144:253-9 Ap 17 '64

WERTHEIMER, Barbara
Mommy does it hurt to have a baby? Parents Mag 39:110+ N '64

WERTIME, Theodore A.
Man's first encounters with metallurgy. bibliog Science 146:1257-67 D 4 '64

WERTZ, Irma Jackson
Profile. Negro Hist Bul 27:146-7 Mr '64

WESCOE, Clarke
Open door vs. selective admission. Sch & Soc 91:138-40 Mr 23 '63

WESCOTT, Cynthia
H&G's 1964 guide to a durable lawn. House & Gard 125:212 Ap '64
H&G's 1964 guide to plant protection. House & Gard 125:207-11 Ap '64

WESCOTT, Jimmy
From a boy's point of view. See issues of Seventeen
Peanut butter, peanut butter, peanut best! Seventeen 22:140-1+ Mr '63

about

Our point of view of you, Jimmy Wescott; with reply by J. Wescott. J. Ferrell and K. Ferrell. il Seventeen 23:42-3 Ja '64

WESKER, Arnold
Chips with everything; text. Theatre Arts 47:33-57 O '63

about

About the author. por Theatre Arts 47:34-5 O '63
Chips with everything. Criticism
America 109:496 O 26 '63
Commonweal 79:139-41 O 25 '63
Commonweal 79:570-1 F 7 '64
Nation 197:267-8 O 26 '63
New Repub 149:30-1 O 19 '63
Newsweek il 62:72 O 14 '63
Sat R 46:30 O 19 '63
Theatre Arts il 48:10-11 Ja '64
Time il 82:72+ O 11 '63
Vogue 143:62 F 1 '64
Missionary in the theater. J. Beavan. il pors N Y Times Mag p28+ O 13 '63

WESLEY, Charles H.
Crown of gold. Negro Hist Bul 27:194-5 My '64
Emancipation proclamation, a turning point in our history; with biographical sketch. por(p 157) Negro Hist Bul 26:158+ F '63
To us from falling hands... Negro Hist Bul 27:186-7 My '64

WESLEY, John
Aldersgate and 1963. G. Kennedy. Christian Cent 80:677-8 My 22 '63
John Wesley and Aldersgate 1963. P. B. Mather. Christian Cent 80:1581-3 D 18 '63
John Wesley and the Christian ministry, by A. B. Lawson. Review
Christian Cent 81:339 Mr 11 '64. L. M. Starkey, jr
John Wesley: medical missionary in the New World. R. Dunlop. il Todays Health 42:20-3+ D '64

WESLEY, Wallace Ann, and others
What you can do about your pupils' posture. NEA J 52:12-14 N '63

WESLEYAN Methodist church. See Methodist church

WESLEYAN university press
Big scholar, little gypsy. D. Dempsey. Sat R 47:30-1 My 30 '64

WESOLOWSKI, Sigmund A. See Maher, J. F. jt. auth.

WESSEL, Milton R.
Legalized gambling: the dreams and the realities. Nation 200:46-8 Ja 18 '65

WESSEL, Morris A.
Don't rush them out of childhood. Parents Mag 39:48-9+ bibliog(p 22) O '64
Heathly children need doctors, too. Parents Mag 38:70-1+ O '63
When should you see your pediatrician? Todays Health 42:60-1+ N '64
—and Simon, Nissa
Is your baby a sparkler? Parents Mag 38: 68-9+ F '63
Why can't mothers stay in hospitals with their children? Redbook 121:41+ Ag '63

WESSELING, P.
(ed) See Schillebeeckx, E. Procreation and human dignity

WESSELMANN, Tom
What is pop art? interview; ed. by G. R. Swenson. il Art N 62:40-1+ F '64

about

Tom Wesselman. C. B. Johnson. il Sch Arts 63:35 My '64

WESSLING, Frank M.
Is it immature loving? America 110:594-6 My 2 '64

WESSMANN, Lucile Tomlinson
Lady and the funds. por Fortune 68:248 N '63

WESSON, Jerry
Accessories extend the scope, add to the fun of tape recording. U S Camera 26:74-5+ F '63
All recording tapes are not alike. U S Camera 26:74-5+ O '63
Now available in 8mm sound; cartoons, comedies, westerns, sports. U S Camera 26:56-7 Jl '63
On cue! procedure for standardizing film and tape shows. U S Camera 26:76-7 N '63
Sound. See issues of U.S. camera
Tape recorder directory. U S Camera 26:74-5 Mr '63

WEST, Allan M.
Local associations move toward professional negotiation. NEA J 53:26-8 F '64

WEST, Anthony
Advice to a young man. Redbook 123:45+ Jl '64; Same abr. with title When is a young man ready for marriage? Read Digest 85:19+ N '64

WEST, Bill
U.S. is paper world. Sci N L 85:90 F 8 '64
Why a national forest products week? Am For 69:44+ N '63

WEST, Carolyn
Baja California. il Yachting 116:44-7+ O; 58-9+ N '64
Come cruise California! Motor B 111:26-9+ My '63
861 miles: now that's a log race! Motor B 114:50-3+ N '64
Pacific Coast marinas. Motor B 113:78-9+ Ja '64
West Coast skippers stay afloat. Motor B 112:28-9+ D '63
West to northwest. Yachting 115:58-60+ My '64

WEST, Daniel W.
Quiet one. por Newsweek 64:27+ D 21 '64

WEST, E. Gordon
Another Kennedy judge. New Repub 149:6-7 O 5 '63

WEST, Jerry
Best one-two punch in basketball; photographs. Sports Illus 20:36-41 Mr 9 '64

WEST, Jessamyn
For one golden moment; story. Good H 157: 78-9 N '63
Hunting for hoot owls; story. Harper 228: 86-94 Ja '64
In search of a kiss; story. Good H 156:76-7 Je '63
On friendship between women. Holiday 35: 13-17 Mr '64
Prelude to tragedy. Redbook 123:52-3+ Jl '64

WEST, Joan
American coed in Israel. il pors Ebony 18: 105-6+ My '63

WEST, John R.
Logging the Pacific. Yachting 116:66+ Jl '64

WEST, M. L. and Addington, S. K.
Don't compromise on quality. Am City 78:87-8 Mr '63

WEST, Mae
Let me tell you about Mae West. L. H. Lapham. il pors Sat Eve Post 237:76-8 N 14 '64

WEST, Morris Langlo
Author in search of himself; interview, ed. by A. T. Leone. por Cath World 200:172-7 D '64
Builder of bridges for us poor devils. Life 54:84-5 Je 7 '63

WEST, Paul
Spain between the lines. Nation 199:307-8+ N 2 '64

WEST, Rebecca
Doctor Stephen Ward returns. Esquire 62: 138+ S '64
Redbook dialogue: Peter O'Toole & Rebecca West. por Redbook 122:56-7+ Mr '64

WEST, Richard F.
Sad goodbye. por Am For 69:12+ N '63

WEST, Victoria Sackville-. See Sackville-West, V.

WEST
Country living in the West. il Sunset 132: 140+ Ap; 110+ Je '64
Great Rockies. A. B. Guthrie, jr. il Holiday 34:28-41 Ag '63
Take a look at the land you own; BLM lands. C. H. Callison. il Audubon Mag 66: 302-3 S '64
They're closing in on the great open spaces! E. Sevareid. il Read Digest 82:196-8+ F '63
West and its public lands; address, February 6, 1964. S. L. Udall. Vital Speeches 30:297-301 Mr 1 '64
Westward tilt, by N. Morgan. Review
Nation 197:16-17 Jl 6 '63. G. R. Stewart
See also
Agriculture—Western states
American literature—Western states
Cowboys
Fishing—Western states
Frontier and pioneer life—United States
Hunting—Western states
Middle West
Northwest
Roads—Western states
Southwest
Water supply—Western states

Bibliography

Party of one; the Rockies' gifts to American literature. C. Fadiman. il Holiday 34:10+ Ag '63

Description and travel

For a heart-of-the-West vacation try: The Tetons, Yellowstone, Salt Lake City. W. R. Wilson. il Suc Farm 61:42-3 Je '63
[Month] travel in and beyond the West. See issues of Sunset
See also
Pacific Crest Trail system

History

General Sully reports; excerpts from letters, with reproductions of sketches and paintings, ed. by L. Sully. A. Sully. Am Heritage 16:52-63 D '64
Great surveys of the American West, by R. A. Bartlett. Review
Natur Hist 72:4+ Mr '63. N. D. Newell
Trail blazer of the Far West. S. W. Sears. il Am Heritage 14:60-4+ Je '63
West of William H. Ashley, ed. by D. L. Morgan. Review
Am Heritage 15:81-3 Je '64. B. Catton
See also
California—History
Lewis and Clark expedition

Industries

See also
Cattle industry and trade

Politics

In the West, fear is uppermost; Goldwater forces in action. P. R. Wieck. New Repub 151:11-12 Ag 22 '64
It's called Goldwater country; but who's leading? il U S News 57:68-9 O 5 '64
Rocky Mountain politics. P. R. Wieck. il New Repub 150:10-13 Ap 18 '64
Where money from Washington is being turned down. il U S News 56:76-9 Mr 16 '64

WEST AFRICA. See Africa, West

WEST AFRICA, FRENCH. See French West Africa

WEST and East. See East and West

WEST BERLIN. See Berlin (West Berlin)

WEST BERLINERS. See Berliners

WEST CHESTER, Pa.
Old tools learn new tasks. E. Bayliss. il Am City 79:91-3 Ap '64

WEST Coast edition, New York times. See New York times

WEST Coast flood. See Floods—United States

WEST EUROPEAN aerospace industry association. See Eurospace

WEST FRISIAN ISLANDS
Gas battle; world's second largest natural gas deposit. Time 82:110+ N 15 '63

WEST HARTFORD, Conn.
CPM opens a pool ten months early. S. Moses. il Am City 79:78-9 D '64

Community centers

Unified diversity in a whole-family community center; Hartford Jewish community center. il Arch Rec 133:141-6 Je '63

WEST in art
Carl Bodmer's unspoiled West; with portfolio. M. B. Davidson. il Am Heritage 14: 43-65 Ap '63

WEST INDIES
Long way west. M. B. Petersen. il Motor B 111:35-7+ Ap; 38+ My '63
Trade wind world. D. DeFontaine. il Yachting 116:34-6+ N '64
See also
Antigua (island)
Caribbean Region
Dominican Republic
Haiti
Indians of the West Indies
St Martin (island)
Virgin Islands

Climate

Winter weather in the palm belt. W. S. Kals. il Yachting 116:42-3+ N '64

Description and travel

Beneath the Atlantic trades; Windward Islands. il Motor B 112:20-1 Ag '63
Down the Antilles; cruising from the Virgins to Grenada. B. Taylor and A. Taylor. il Yachting 116:49-51+ N '64
Landfalls ahead! West Indies cruise on Cunard liner Franconia. O. R. Cohen. il Travel 123: 48-51 Ja '65
Off-season vacations in the West Indies. il Changing T 17:19-20 Je '63
Overlooked islands. K. Davis. il Mlle 57:106-10 My '63
Well traveled camera; Lesser Antilles. P. Caulfield. il Mod Phot 28:28+ Ja; 18+ Mr '64

Discovery and exploration

Birth of the Antilles. G. de Zénedegui. il Américas 15:17-25 S '63

WEST INDIES, BRITISH
See also
Bahama Islands
Barbados
British Virgin Islands
Trinidad (island)
Trinidad-Tobago
WEST INDIES, FRENCH
De Gaulle's western outpost. il Time 83:29 Mr 20 '64
See also
Martinique
St-Barthélemy (island)
WEST INDIES FEDERATION
Prospects in the Caribbean. P. Sherlock. For Affairs 41:744-56 Jl '63
See also
Sports—West Indies (Federation)
WEST IRIAN
Brother takes over. il Time 81:34 My 10 '63
See also
United Nations—West Irian
WEST NEW GUINEA. See West Irian
WEST PALM BEACH, Fla.
Finance
Trends in municipal finance. J. W. Johnson. il Am City 79:114-15 Ap '64
Parks and playgrounds
Outdoor gym keeps 'em slim. B. York. il Am City 79:29 Ja '64
With a flair for beauty; Flagler park shuffleboard courts. H. W. Kip. il Am City 78:34 O '63
WEST POINT military academy. See United States military academy, West Point
WEST Side urban renewal plan. See New York (city)—Housing
WEST TEXAS rehabilitation center. See Rehabilitation centers
WEST VIRGINIA
See also
Blennerhassett Island
Hunting—West Virginia
Description and travel
Over the Blue Ridge. J. Hay. il Holiday 35:22+ My '64
Economic conditions
Retraining in West Virginia. H. A. Gibbard. Mo Labor R 87:661-2 Je '64
West Virginia: the first front. W. Francois. Reporter 30:21-2 F 13 '64
Mental health, Department of
West Virginia's director of mental health. il Ebony 19:63-8 Ja '64
WEST VIRGINIA gorge. See Potomac River
WESTBROOK, Robert
Boy meets girl. por Seventeen 23:77+ Ja '64
My summer with stars. por Seventeen 23:124-5+ My '64
WESTBY, Barbara
(comp) Commercial cataloging services: a directory. Library J 89:1508-13 Ap 1 '64
WESTCHESTER COUNTY, N.Y.
Our landfill plays favorites. C. E. Pound. il Am City 79:85-6 Ja '64
WESTCHESTER library system
Use of system borrower's cards increases in Westchester County. Library J 89:1706-7 Ap 15 '64
Westchester library system analyzes newspaper coverage. Library J 88:2660-1 Jl '63
WESTCHESTER playhouse. See Theater—United States—History
WESTCOTT, Cynthia
House & garden's 1963 guide to plant protection. il House & Gard 123:222-7 Ap '63
Spray chemicals; are they really dangerous? Am Home 66:12+ Mr '63; Same. Am For 69:15+ Ap '63
War on the insect felons; address. por Am For 70:28+ F '64
WESTCOTT, R. D.
This month in the Southwest (cont of) Things to do this month in the Southwest. See issues of Popular gardening
WESTERFIELD, Samuel Z.
Emancipation centennial address; January 6, 1963; biographical sketch. por(p205) Negro Hist Bul 26:207, 208-9 Ap '63
Trade development and trade policy; statement, November 21, 1963. Dept State Bul 50:101-4 Ja 20 '64
WESTERMAN, R. A.
Somatic inheritance of habituation of responses to light in planarians. bibliog Science 140:676-7 My 10 '63
WESTERN air lines
Western shuns mergers, system growth. Aviation W 78:45 Je 10 '63
Western will focus on 720B, twin-jets. Aviation W 81:48 Ag 24 '64
WESTERN alliance. See Alliances; International relations
WESTERN civilization. See Civilization
WESTERN cookery. See Cookery, American
WESTERN corn rootworms. See Corn rootworms
WESTERN development laboratories. See Philco corporation—Western development laboratories
WESTERN edition, New York times. See New York times
WESTERN electric company
Famous firsts: workers can be a team, too; Hawthorne workers. il Bsns W p49-50 My 25 '63
In-line vacuum ups thin film output; tantalum film. M. Getler. il Miss & Roc 12:35-6 Ap 22 '63
Inventing ways to make things; Engineering research center at Princeton. il Bsns W p 120+ Ap 20 '63
Tomorrow's plant now; Western electric's Kansas City plant. il Bsns W p52-3+ Ag 1 '64
Who is the coronary man? Bsns W p 30-1 F 16 '63
WESTERN electronics show and convention
AF outlines future solid-state R&D. M. Getler and R. Pay. Miss & Roc 15:14-15 Ag 31 '64
WESTERN energy supply and transmission associates
Westward ho! plan for the world's largest electricpower complex. Time 84:111A O 2 '64
WESTERN EUROPE. See Europe, Western
WESTERN European union
No sale; multilateral nuclear force. Newsweek 62:34+ D 16 '63
Yielding a bit; agreement to meeting of Britain and the Common market. Newsweek 62:41-2 Jl 22 '63
WESTERN films. See Moving pictures—Westerns
WESTERN GERMANY. See Germany (Federal Republic)
WESTERN hemisphere
See also
America
Defenses
See also
Inter-American treaty of reciprocal assistance
WESTERN home awards
American institute of architects-Sunset magazine Western home awards. il Sunset 131:82-101 O '63
High daylight indoors. il Sunset 131:102-8 N '63
WESTERN hotels, incorporated
Running hotels with a loose rein. il Bsns W p92+ F 23 '63
WESTERN plays
Tall stranger. E. J. Dias. Plays 22:1-12 Mr '63
WESTERN policy. See International relations
WESTERN ranges. See Stock ranges
WESTERN RESERVE university, Cleveland, Ohio
Cleveland: an early start. philanthropy, and planning built the University circle. J. Walsh. il Science 145:369-71 Jl 24 '64
Center for documentation and communication research
Information retrieval in action. Wilson Lib Bul 37:837 Je '63
WESTERN rite of the Orthodox church. See Orthodox Eastern church in the United States
WESTERN states. See West
WESTERN stories
Destry rides again, and again, and again. J. D. Weaver. il Holiday 34:77-80+ Ag '63
See also
Television broadcasting—Westerns
WESTERN test range. See Proving grounds
WESTERN theatre ballet
Company that refused to be neglected; Western theatre ballet. C. Barnes. il Dance Mag 37:30-4 Jl '63
Dancers at play; Britain's Western theater ballet company's U.S. debut. il Time 82:32 Ag 2 '63
Letter from London; première of Mods and rockers. M. Panter-Downes. New Yorker 39:67+ Ja 25 '64
Western theatre ballet, Jacob's Pillow. D. Hering. il(p28) Dance Mag 37:64-6 S '63
WESTERN union telegraph company
New life in old wires. il Time 84:64 N 20 '64

WESTERN union telegraph company—*Cont.*
Wage chronology; Western union telegraph co; 1954-63. W. Fridie. il Mo Labor R 86: 1307-22 N '63
WESTERN WASHINGTON state college, Bellingham
Students finance an activities center. il Arch Rec 134:132-3 Ag '63
WESTERN wood manufacturing company
There's gold in wake of water ski craze. il Bsns W p 110 Jl 20 '63
WESTERN wood products association
Western lumber plants a new root. il Bsns W p66+ Je 27 '64
WESTERN writers. See Authors, American
WESTERNERS
Rocky Mountain peoples: the three cultures. il Holiday 34:60-5 Ag '63
See also
Texans
WESTHEIMER, F. H. See Kennedy, E. P. jt. auth.
WESTIN, Alan F.
Anti-communism & the corporations. Commentary 36:479-87 D '63; 37:23-4 Ap; 38:6 N '64
WESTING, Arthur H.
Geotropism: its orienting force. bibliog Science 144:1342-4 Je 12 '64
WESTINGHOUSE broadcasting company
Action speaks loudest; conference on Local public service programing. R. L. Shayon. Sat R 46:29 D 21 '63; Reply. W. Shepherd. 47:49 Ja 11 '64
Riches or ruin for theatre? group W's plan for theatre-TV production. G. Eells. Theatre Arts 47:27-32+ N '63
WESTINGHOUSE electric corporation
Breaking a pattern of woes. il Bsns W p90-3 Ag 31 '63
Computer commuter? F. Riley. il Travel 121: 41 Mr '64
Mr Automation. Time 82:73-4 Jl 26 '63
Mk 45 ASTOR now in production at Westinghouse. il Miss & Roc 13:16-17 O 21 '63
New concept in low-cost rapid transit; Transit expressway. il Am City 78:114-15 S '63
New life in an old giant. il Time 84:97-8 O 30 '64
Polaris A-3 launch tube production at Westinghouse: a step-by-step report. il Miss & Roc 15:14-15 D 7 '64
Power reactor makers launch business drive. Bsns W p43-4+ Mr 14 '64
Quiet surprise; new president and chief executive. Newsweek 62:60 Jl 29 '63
Westinghouse now goes all the way. il Bsns W p49-50+ Je 29 '63
Westinghouse outlines design of Gemini radar. Miss & Roc 13:36-7 Ag 19 '63
Westinghouse signs with IUE. Bsns W p53 N 2 '63
White-collar layoffs backfire. Bsns W p 153 Mr 21 '64

Molecular electronics division

New facility is designed for microcircuits. P. J. Klass. il Aviation W 79:114-15+ S 16 '63
WESTINGHOUSE time capsule. See Civilization—Preservation of records
WESTMAN, R. E.
Winter hangover; poem. Am For 70:63 Ja '64
WESTMINSTER college, Fulton, Mo.
Gift for Missouri: bombed-out remains of church of St Mary Aldermanbury, London. il Time 81:35 F 8 '63
WESTMINSTER kennel club show. See Dog shows
WESTMINSTER press
Witness and Westminster. Christian Cent 80:871 Jl 3 '63
WESTMORELAND, William Childs
Inheritor of a wretched war. J. Langguth. il pors N Y Times Mag p27+ N 15 '64
Tough man, tough job. por Time 83:26 My 8 '64
U.S. change in Vietnam new general takes over. il por U S News 56:18 Je 29 '64
WESTON, Edward
Weston's picture is about freedom, yours and mine. R. Hattersley. il Pop Phot 55: 70-1+ S '64
WESTON, Elizabeth
Food forum. McCalls 92:26 O; 46 N; 52 D '64; 28 Ja '65
WESTON, Marybeth Little
Camp double dividend. N Y Times Mag p62+ Ag 18 '63
Fairy-tale wedding, long long ago. N Y Times Mag p66+ Ap 7 '63
Parent and child. N Y Times Mag p96 Ap 21 '63; 109-10+ O 11 '64
Rampant raccoons. N Y Times Mag p29 Jl 21 '63
Surprise box. Redbook 120:16 Ap '63
WESTON, Paul B.
I-factor. Field & S 69:54-8 Ja '65
WESTOVER, Margaret
Side of your child you never see. Parents Mag 38:36-7+ Jl '63
WESTPHAL, Virginia
Teenage novel; a defense. Library J 89:1832-3+ Ap 15 '64
WESTPORT, Conn. public library
Books are her friends; children's room. J. Bunche. il Look 27:54a-54b+ My 7 '63
WET flies. See Fishing lures, flies, etc.
WET storage. See Boats—Storage
WETHERILL mesa. See Mesa Verde National Park
WETHERSFIELD, Conn.
History in towns: Wethersfield, Connecticut, 1634-1964; symposium. il Antiques 86:452-67 O '64
WETMORE, Warren C.
ELDO third-stage model test scheduled. Aviation W 79:73-4+ D 16 '63
WETUMPKA, Ala.
Death of a dump. E. Austin. il Am City 78:29 My '63
WETZEL, Lorraine
Janie found a big idea in the attic. Farm J 87:62 Mr '63
WEVILL, David
Irish hotel; poem. New Yorker 40:164 O 24 '64
WEXFORD festival. See Music festivals—Ireland
WEXLER, Alan
Lonely years of Hamilton Holmes. Ebony 19: 101-2+ N '63
WEXLER, Isadore
Stepping-stones from the slums. L. Velie. il por Read Digest 83:175-80 O '63
WEXLER, Jerome
Insects. il U S Camera 26:62-3+ My '63
WEYERHAEUSER timber company
Sales begin at home. il Bsns W p74+ S 12 '64
Test-tube forests. il Time 81:92 My 10 '63
Weyerhaeuser story. M. Bush. Am For 69: 42+ S '63
WEYHRAUCH, Ernest E.
Automation in the reserved books room. Library J 89:2294-6 Je 1 '64
WEYL, Nathaniel
Broken eggs of the Soviet omelet. Nat R 16: 75-7 Ja 28 '64
Latin America in eruption. Nat R 15:244-5, 453+ S 24, N 19 '63
Profiles in perfidy. Nat R 15:112 Ag 13 '63
Yanqui corruption. Nat R 15:530-1 D 17 '63
WEYR, Thomas
Mindszenty tragedy. Commonweal 79:454-7, 721 Ja 17, Mr 13 '64
WHALEN, Richard E. and Nadler, R. D.
Suppression of the development of female mating behavior by estrogen administered in infancy. Science 141:273-4 Jl 19 '63
—See Feder, H. H. jt. auth.
WHALEN, Richard J.
Banshee, demon, voodoo, phantom, and bingo! Fortune 70:136-9+ N '64
City destroying itself. Fortune 70:114-23+ S '64
Durable threads of J. P. Stevens. Fortune 67:102-9+ Ap '63
Father of the President. Read Digest 83:150-1+ O '63
Founding father; excerpts. Sat Eve Post 237: 26-9+ O 10; 30-2+ O 17 '64
Here come the conservatives. Fortune 68: 106-9+ D '63
Joseph P. Kennedy: a profile in power; excerpt from The founding father: the story of Joseph P. Kennedy. Sat Eve Post 237: 26-9+ O 10 '64
WHALEN, Robert G.
Visit to the three Cape Kennedys. N Y Times Mag p34-5+ D 13 '64
WHALEN, William J. and Fangman, John
Respiration of heart muscle as affected by oxygen tension. bibliog Science 141:274-5 Jl 19 '63
WHALERS. See Boats and boating
WHALES
Barking whales star on TV. il Pop Mech 119: 99 F '63
Discovery of right whales in the Gulf of Mexico. J. C. Moore and E. Clark. bibliog Science 141:269 Jl 19 '63
Giant whale; with photographs by John Dominis. Life 55:38-46 Ag 2 '63
Killer whale! W. J. Cromie. il Read Digest 82:176-80 Mr '63
Lovable killer; captive killer whale, off Vancouver, British Columbia. il Life 57:113-14 N 6 '64

WHALES—*Continued*
Watching the gray whales swim by. il Sunset 134:36+ Ja '65
Whale by the tail; killer whale in captivity. il Newsweek 64:49 Ag 31 '64
Whale of a heart reverberates underseas. Sci N L 84:405 D 28 '63
World's biggest, but for how long? blue whale. C. Ray. il N Y Times Mag p 123-5 D 13 '64

WHALES, Fossil
Alabama boneyard sheds new light on whales; zeuglodon. W. D. Wallace. il Sci Digest 53:77-80 Ap '63

WHALING
Salt spray and sperm whales; Melville whaling room, New Bedford, Mass. free public library. J. S. Healey. il Wilson Lib Bul 37: 565-8 Mr '63
Shore leave a la Russe; Russia's whaling fleet in Melbourne. il Bsns W p30-1 My 23 '64
Whaling off the Golden Gate. K. Lamott. il Holiday 34:148+ D '63
Whaling wife; excerpts from One whaling family, ed. by H. Williams. E. A. Williams. il Am Heritage 15:64-79 Je '64
Ya, ya, ya! big tail! il Newsweek 64:87 O 26 '64

Bibliography
Reviews; history, hunting, and voices of leviathan. R. G. Van Gelder. Natur Hist 72:4+ Je '63

WHALL, Hugh
Boating. Sports Illus 19:48-9 Jl 8; 52-3 Jl 15; 50-1 Ag 12; 52-4 S 16; 70-2 S 30; 66-8 O 14 '63; 20:53-4 F 10; 59 Je 22; 21:52-3 Jl 13; 50+ Jl 27; 70-2 N 16; 92-4 D 7 '64; 22:42+ Ja 25 '65
Over, under and over again. Sports Illus 20:32-3 Je 1 '64
Rowing. Sports Illus 20:72+ Ap 27 '64
Set a sail on a surfboard. Sports Illus 19:34-6+ D 16 '63

WHALLEY, Edward
Hunt for the regicides. A. Winston. il Am Heritage 16:26-9+ D '64

WHAN, Edgar W.
Under wraps. Christian Cent 80:274 F 27 '63

WHARTON, David B.
Walk in the wind. Am For 69:24-5+ Ap '63

WHARTON, Don
America's titanic Christmas package. Read Digest 85:200-2+ D '64
Battle against mail-order pornography. Read Digest 84:147-8+ F '64
Big news in shoes. Read Digest 84:59-62 Mr '64
Great American cookout. Read Digest 82:25-6+ Je '63
Mr Shrink and Stretch. Read Digest 85:39-40+ O '64
Shoplifting: our white-collar scandal. Read Digest 82:73-7 Ap '63
Spectacle that astonished Salonica. Read Digest 83:113-16 S '63
Up in the air with the animal kingdom. Read Digest 85:31-4+ S '64
What's so smart about being late? Read Digest 82:171-4 Ap '63
Who was Cleopatra? Read Digest 83:239-42+ N '63
Year I won the war against cigarettes. Read Digest 86:75-8 Ja '65
Zip goes the hookless wonder. Read Digest 83:168C-168D+ N '63

WHARTON, Edith
Last survivor. por Time 83:101-2+ Je 5 '64

WHARTON, John F.
Is it time for the second step? Sat R 46:8-11+ Ag 17 '63
Speculations during a white night. Sat R 46: 14-17 Ap 6 '63

WHARTON, Joseph
Famous firsts: how business schools began. il Bsns W p 114+ O 19 '63

WHARTON school of finance and commerce. See Pennsylvania. University—Wharton school of finance and commerce

WHAT are you doing in my dreams? story. See Powell, D.

WHAT are you thinking about? story. See Bryan, C. D. B.

WHAT could anybody say? story. See Oppenheimer, M.

WHAT happened; drama. See Stein, G.

WHAT happened on Clutter street; drama. See Fisher, A.

WHAT-ho on the Rialto! story. See Durrell, L.

WHAT I wish (oh, I wish) I had said; story. See Cavanaugh, A.

WHAT is your name? story. See Marx, O.

WHAT makes Sammy run? musical comedy. See Musical comedies, revues, etc.—Criticisms, plots, etc.

WHAT must I say to you? story. See Rosen, N.

WHAT really matters; story. See Wood, M.

WHAT star so humble; story. See Willingham, C.

WHAT we were fighting for; story. See Baker, E.

WHAT women know best; story. See Randall, F. E.

WHATELEY, Donald E.
New light-operated switch. Electr World 70: 47+ N '63

WHATLEY, Linda S. and others
Optical studies at high pressures. bibliog Science 144:968-76 My 22 '64

WHATMOUGH, Joshua
Farewell, groves of academe. por Time 82:81 Jl 12 '63

WHAT'S your problem? story. See Boles, R.

WHEARLEY, Robert L.
Highflying Robert Six. Sat Eve Post 236:82+ F 23 '63

WHEAT
Battle in the furrows; wheat referendum on price supports. il Bsns W p36 My 18 '63
Cerium-144 and cesium-137 measurements in the 1963 United States wheat crop and milling products. D. C. Sutton and K. R. Dwyer. bibliog il Science 145:486-7 Jl 31 '64
Diuron looks good on winter wheat. Suc Farm 62:69 O '64
Farmers slap down wheat plan; secret-ballot referendum. il Bsns W p29 My 25 '63
How much wheat will we plant? Farm J 87: 29+ S '63
New wheat premiums fade during storage. O. Bay. Farm J 87:45 My '63
New wheat program ahead? B. Brantley and F. Bailey, jr. Suc Farm 62:40-1+ F '64
Phytotoxic substance from a species of penicillium. F. A. Norstadt and T. M. McCalla. bibliog il Science 140:410-11 Ap 26 '63
Set your sights on sixty, ninety, or even 120-bushel wheat. K. J. Morrison and L. E. Zeman. il Suc Farm 62:46-7+ S '64
Shorty wheats for the Midwest? Farm J 87: 36 Ag '63
Should you plow back to within allotment? Suc Farm 62:122 Ap '64
Staff of life is sturdy. B. Tufty. Sci N L 85: 387 Je 20 '64
They grow seventy-bushel wheat. L. E. Zeman. il Suc Farm 62:52-3+ F '64
Wheat: a factual survey of what is shaping up for 1964. B. Brantley. il Suc Farm 61: 48-9 O '63
Wheat gibberellins. J. R. Fleming and J. A. Johnson. bibliog il Science 144:1021-2 My 22 '64
Wheat harvest in the Palouse. il Suc Farm 62:30 Jl '64
Wheat shortage ahead? K. Hobson. Farm J 88:16 Ja '64
Which is better for wheat growers? wheat certificate program for 1964; with editorial comment. J. G. Patton; C. B. Shuman. Farm J 87:32-3+, 142 Mr '63
See also
Bulgur

Diseases and pests
Control wheat streak mosaic. Suc Farm 61:87 Ag '63
See also
Rusts (botany)

Grading
Here's what new wheat grades mean. F. Bailey, jr. Suc Farm 62:35 My '64

Hybrids
Fertility restoration and its inheritance in cytoplasmic male-sterile wheat. R. W. Livers. bibliog il Science 144:420 Ap 24 '64
Wheat: reconstitution of the tetraploid component (AABB) of hexaploids. E. R. Kerber. bibliog il Science 143:253-5 Ja 17 '64

Prices
Against the grain? referendum on wheat controls. Newsweek 61:32+ My 20 '63
As a key vote nears on federal controls; wheat plan. U S News 54:11 My 13 '63
Battle in the furrows; wheat referendum on price supports. il Bsns W p36 My 18 '63
Blue eagle, RIP; wheat referendum. Nat R 14:438 Je 4 '63
New worry for politicians; dollar wheat and '64 vote. il U S News 55:86-8 S 16 '63
Two lasting benefits. Farm J 87:90 Jl '63

WHEAT—Prices—*Continued*
What now for wheat? C. W. Gifford. Farm J 87:26-7 Jl '63
Wheat farmers' revolt: the reason and the result; What the growers said. il U S News 54:40-2 Je 3 '63
Wheat problem: back at White House. il U S News 55:39 D 30 '63
Wheat war. il Time 81:30 My 17 '63

Storage

Radiation kills weevil eggs in wheat. Farm J 87:49 O '63

WHEAT certificate program. See Agricultural laws and legislation
WHEAT farmers. See Farmers
WHEAT grades. See Wheat—Grading
WHEAT streak mosaic. See Wheat—Diseases and pests
WHEAT trade
ABC's of American wheat sales to the reds; with statement by J. F. Kennedy. il U S News 55:52-3 O 21 '63
Another October: another Gromyko meeting; Lot of dough from wheat. il Newsweek 62:33-4 O 21 '63
As a boycott hit U.S.-Russia wheat deal. il U S News 56:6 Mr 2 '64
As Russia goes shopping; outlook in the wheat belt. il U S News 55:42-4 O 14 '63
Back on the track; Soviet-American deal. Newsweek 62:95 N 18 '63
Bailing out the Soviet. R. Moley. Newsweek 63:88 Ja 20 '64
Big deal; wheat deal between the U.S. and Russia. Time 83:26 Ja 10 '64
Big grain trader needs more than grain; Cargill, inc. il Bsns W p70-4 Ja 4 '64
Big wheat deal. il Time 82:35 N 15 '63
Bread for Russia; Canadian deal. Time 82:42 S 20 '63
Can we trade with Russia. Duns R 82:39 D '63
Canada gets the ships moving, at a price. Bsns W p51+ N 2 '63
Canada wheat pours into Soviet ships; with editorial comment. il Life 55:4, 30-3 O 11 '63
Continental's coup. il Newsweek 63:65 F 3 '64
Deal in wheat? il Time 82:31 O 4 '63
Deal on wheat; grain sales to the Soviet bloc. New Repub 149:7-8 N 23 '63
Delegation of authority under 1949 Wheat agreement act; executive order, May 22, 1963. J. F. Kennedy. Dept State Bul 48: 914 Je 10 '63
Dialogue? yes; concessions? beware! A. A. Berle, jr. il N Y Times Mag p9+ O 20 '63; Discussion. p26+ N 10 '63; 19-20 Ja 19 '64
Europe, too, can have a farm problem; Kennedy Round of transatlantic tariff cuts. il Sr Schol 85:10-13 Ja 7 '65
Farm boom that red trade built; Canada's grain sales. il U S News 56:98-100 Je 29 '64
Few kernels; US grain sales to Communist countries. Time 82:27 N 1 '63
For and against the grain. Reporter 29:14+ O 10 '63
Global grain dealer and more besides. il Bsns W p56-8+ O 19 '63
Great trade muddle. Sat Eve Post 237:82 Mr 14 '64
Great wheat deal. Time 82:27 O 18 '63
Half-baked; wheat deal between the U.S, Russia and European Communist countries. Time 83:22 Mr 13 '64
How to sell wheat to Russia, now or sometime. Farm J 87:118 N '63
How traders tried to cook wheat deal; U.S. grain merchants met Soviet agents. il Bsns W p28-9 O 5 '63
Impasse on wheat; Soviet offer to buy U.S. wheat. Time 82:30 O 11 '63
Like surfboarding: negotiation for wheat sale to Russia. Newsweek 62:90+ O 7 '63
LBJ's first union showdown; how wheat strike came out. il U S News 56:89-90 Mr 9 '64
Massive wheat sale to U.S.S.R. Sr Schol 83: 8-9 O 4 '63
Mission from Moscow; Soviet foreign trade minister in Washington. il Newsweek 62: 76+ N 4 '63
Next job: moving the wheat; handling Soviet grain. Bsns W p28-9 N 16 '63
Relax trade policies with Communist-bloc nations. Christian Cent 80:1292-3 O 23 '63
Rush to trade with reds: will U.S. join it? il U S News 55:51-2 S 30 '63
Russia's grain is last straw; ILA boycott. il Bsns W p 106-7 F 22 '64
Secretary Rusk's news conference of November 8, 1963. D. Rusk. Dept State Bul 49: 810-17 N 25 '63
Should the U.S. trade with enemies? R. K. Massie. Sat Eve Post 237:19-21 F 1 '64
Soviet-bloc market: so big and yet so far. il Bsns W p53-4 O 19 '63
Soviet-Canadian deal stirs a wheat tempest. Bsns W p28 S 21 '63
Surplus wheat to Russia. B. Tufty. Sci N L 84:245 O 19 '63
Taking the heat off wheat; end of ILA boycott. Bsns W p24-5 F 29 '64
U. S. grain dealers to be allowed to sell wheat to Soviet Union and eastern Europe; statement by President Kennedy, and letter from Attorney General, Octobr 9, 1963. J. F. Kennedy; R. F. Kennedy. Dept State Bul 49:660-7 O 28 '63
U.S. to sell wheat; Communist nations. il Bsns W p29 O 12 '63
U.S. wheat for the Soviets? pro and con discussion. Sr Schol 83:8-9 O 25 '63
Wheat for reds; who's paying? il U S News 56:87-8 F 17 '64
Wheat heat; shortage of U.S. ships to carry wheat to Russia. Newsweek 63:78+ F 17 '64
Wheat jam is broken, at last. Bsns W p27 Ja 11 '64
Wheat leads the way; East-West thaw. il Bsns W p25-8 S 28 '63
Wheat mess. Nat R 15:334 O 22 '63
Wheat sale and the public. E. Roper. il Sat R 46:23 N 16 '63
Wheat to whom? Soviet Union's transshipment to Rumania and possibly Cuba. Cato. Nat R 16:682 Ag 11 '64
Who'll profit from big wheat deal. il U S News 55:50 O 28 '63
Why Freeman's mad; Canada's sale of wheat to Japan. New Repub 149:15 O 26 '63
Why Khrushchev needs to buy wheat. il U S News 55:43 O 14 '63
With the grain. Time 82:102+ O 18 '63
Wrapping up the deal to sell Russia wheat. il Bsns W p30-1 O 19 '63
See also
United States—Commerce—Russia
WHEATON, T. A. See Stewart, I. jt. auth.
WHEATON, Ill.
Not late once in seven years. J. J. Kelly. il Am City 78:84-5 F '63
WHEDON, Julia
Back East; story. Harper 227:84-9 N '63
Special one; story. Seventeen 23:120-1 My '64
WHEEL bugs
Prowess of a wheel bug. il Natur Hist 72:56-7 O '63
WHEEL covers. See Automobiles—Wheels
WHEEL stabilizers. See Automobiles—Stability and stabilizers
WHEELBARROWS
Potting barrow. C. Sinapi. il Pop Mech 120: 148 Jl '63
WHEELER, Bruce E.
Lincolniana in 1962-1963. Hobbies 67:24-5+ F '63; 68:24-5+ F '64
WHEELER, Burton K.
Baron of the Northwest. W. Leuchtenburg. por Sat R 46:87 Mr 16 '63
Tribune of the people. G. Morgenstern. il Nat R 15:66+ Jl 30 '63
WHEELER, E. Todd
Hospital design and function; excerpts. Arch Rec 136:178-80 O '64
WHEELER, Earle Gilmore
Merit will be rewarded. il por Newsweek 64: 19 Jl 6 '64
Three top soldiers. por Time 84:16 Jl 3 '64
WHEELER, Harvey
Challenge of bureaucratized science. Bul Atomic Sci 20:14-17 Ja '64
—and Burdick, Eugene
Politics of destruction. Sat R 46:25-7+ N 9 '63
WHEELER, J. W. and others
Trans-2-dodecenal and 2-methyl-1, 4-quinone produced by a millipede. bibliog Science 144:540-1 My 1 '64
WHEELER, John H.
Banker with a mission. il pors Bsns W p56+ My 16 '64
WHEELER, Joseph L.
Thoughts for the commission. Library J 88: 4170-1 N 1 '63
Words of Wheeler: across the years; quotations. Library J 89:2943 Ag '64
about
Profile: Joseph L. Wheeler; with quotations. D. D. Dennis. il por Library J 89:2941-3 Ag '64
WHEELER, Keith
Big labor hunts for the hard answers. Life 55:73+ Jl 19 '63

WHEELER, Keith—*Continued*
Lurking risks of transfusion. Life 54:70-2+ F 15 '63; Same abr. with title Transfusion: a mixed blessing. Read Digest 84:101-5 Mr '64
Plantom tax swindlers. Life 54:81-2+ Ap 12 '63
XB-70; building the world's weirdest airplane. Life 58:74-80+ Ja 15 '65
—and Lambert, William
Easygoing man behind the image. Life 57: 88-90+ O 23 '64
If the charge is true, Cohn trapped himself by doing something stupid. Life 55:26-31+ O 4 '63
Man who is the President. Life 57:24-9+ Ag 14; 62-6+ Ag 21 '64
—and others
Now see the innards of a fat pig. Life 55: 20-7+ Ag 16 '63
Scandal grows and grows in Washington. Life 55:40-40B+ N 22 '63
WHEELER, Pearl
Pearl Wheeler: a tribute. J. Dougherty. il por Dance Mag 39:52-4 Ja '65
WHEELER, Richard S.
Backlash in California: Proposition 14 gains support. Nat R 16:817 S 22 '64
Berkeley discriminates. Nat R 14:497 Je 18 '63
First flag-raising on Iwo Jima. Am Heritage 15:54-9+ Je '64
WHEELER, Sara H.
Children's libraries. Wilson Lib Bul 39:342 D '64
WHEELER, Thomas C.
Timeless charm of Peggy Lee. Sat Eve Post 237:24-5 O 10 '64
WHEELER, Willis B. and Hollinshead, A. C.
Photosensitizing substance in human serum: effect on HeLa cells. bibliog Science 141: 1279-80 S 27 '63
WHEELER, Willis H.
How to hybridize daffodils. Horticulture 42: 20-1+ Ap '64
WHEELING, W.Va.
Ski or golf at night. E. E. Gaylor. il Am City 80:114 Ja '65

Music

[Musical events] (cont) Mus Am 84:22-3 Ap '64
WHEELING steel corporation
Outsider tries his hand at firing up a lagging steelmaker. il Bsns W p 18-19 D 26 '64
Wheeling tests the water. Bsns W p27 Ap 13 '63
WHEELIS, Allen
Illusionless man & the visionary maid; story. Commentary 37:59-67 My '64
To be a god. Commentary 36:125-34 Ag '63
WHEELOCK, John
It is . . . a small college . . . yet, there are those who love it; Dartmouth college v. Woodward. R. N. Current. il por Am Heritage 14:10-14+ Ag '63
WHEELOCK, John Hall
Dear men and women; poem. New Yorker 39: 22 Jl 13 '63
Earth, take me back; Prayer of the cricket; poems. Poetry 105:83 N '64
Seven sonnets: Garden and a face; So dark, so true; Slow summer twilight; Sea's voice; Cloud-shapes; Bread and wine; In this green nook. New Yorker 40:60 D 5 '64
WHEELS
This walking wheel turns itslef. D. Scott. il Pop Sci 185:44-6 Jl '64
See also
Automobiles—Wheels
Flywheels
WHEELWRIGHT, Vern
Dial indicator. Hot Rod 17:50-1+ Je '64
WHELAN, Charles M.
1963 First amendment conference; statement. por(p306) Cath World 197:310-12 Ag '63
Religion, orthodoxy, public schools. America 108:640-3 My 4 '63
Washington front. America 109:282 S 21 '63
WHELAN, Chris F.
Airline takes the marginal route. il pors Bsns W p 111-12+ Ap 20 '63
WHELAN, Kenneth E.
Benny and his brothers. Harper 228:166-7 Ap '64
WHELAN, Thomas J.
Rise and fall of Jersey City. J. J. Farmer. il Reporter 31:47-9 Ag 13 '64
WHELAN, William P. abp
Archbishop approves apartheid. Christian Cent 81:325 Mr 11 '64
WHELPLEY, Donald A.
Cloud watching can be fun. Sci Digest 54:36-6 Jl '63
WHEN we say good-by; story. See Graison, P.
WHEN you give your heart; story. See Conger, L.
WHERE did it go? story. See Randall, F. E.
WHERE have you been all my life? story. See Lardner, S.
WHERE is the voice coming from? story. See Welty, E.
WHERE the fields are fresh and green; story. See Hudson, L. P.
WHERE'S Annie? story. See Bassing, E.
WHERRY, Don M.
Tape-deck, preamps. Electr World 69:90-1 F '63
WHICH of those two ladies is he married to? story. See O'Brien, E.
WHIELDON, Thomas
Wares of Thomas Whieldon. R. E. Taggart. il Antiques 83:207-11 F '63
WHIFFENPOOFS. See Choral groups and societies
WHIMBEY, Arthur E. See Denenberg, V. H. jt. auth.
WHIPLASH injuries, Automobile. See Traffic accidents
WHIPPER, William
Leader ahead of his times. L. C. Jones. por Am Heritage 14:58-9+ Je '63
WHIPPING. See Corporal punishment
WHIPPLE, Fred I.
Comet belt predicted near farthest planet; summary of address. Sci N L 84:275 N 2 '63
WHIPPLE, George H.
Medical students: source, selection, and training; letter. Science 142:511 N 1 '63
WHIPPLE, Jim
Detroit listening post. See issues of Popular mechanics
WHIRLPOOL corporation
How long a rope for captives? il Bsns W p93-4 Jl 13 '63
Whirlpool; case of noncollectable bad paper. Time 82:78 Jl 5 '63
WHISKERS. See Beards
WHISKEY
About: bourbon. T. Irwin. il N Y Times Mag p75-6 Mr 8 '64
About Scotch whiskey. R. Postgate. il Holiday 33:100-1+ My '63
Distillers co. fights back; Scotch whisky. il Fortune 68:75-6+ O '63
Pouring Scotch whisky into the portfolio. il Bsns W p 170+ N 16 '63
Scotch mist; problem for investors. il Fortune 69:63-4+ Je '64
Scotch whiskies. il Consumer Rep 29:538-41 N '64
Whither whiskies? J. A. Beard. House & Gard 125:122+ Ja '64
See also
Distilling industries
WHISKEY (term)
Department of amplification. A. Reid. New Yorker 40:194-5 N 14 '64
WHISKEY insurrection, 1794
Tax on whiskey? never! G. Carson. il Am Heritage 14:62-4+ Ag '63
WHISKEYTOWN RESERVOIR. See Reservoirs
WHISTLER, James Abbott McNeill
Portraits of three painters. H. Kramer. il Reporter 31:35-6 D 17 '64
WHISTLERS (radio waves) See Radio waves
WHISTLES
Electronic sirens; mobile p.a. and siren systems on public-safety vehicles. J. Kyle. il Electr World 71:32-3 Ap '64
Honk-honk, yip-yip; new police siren. Newsweek 62:65 Jl 1 '63
WHISTLING swans. See Swans
WHISTON, Lionel A. Jr
Complex picture. Christian Cent 80:430 Ap 3 '63
WHITAKER, Annelyne
You can't live there. Negro Hist Bul 26: 223-4 Ap '63
WHITAKER, Arthur P.
Argentina: a fragmented society. Cur Hist 46:15-18+ Ja '64
Argentina: struggle for recovery. Cur Hist 48:16-20+ Ja '65
Left and right extremism in Argentina. Cur Hist 44:84-8+ F '63
WHITAKER, Frederic
Four realists: a review. Am Artist 28:54-61+ O '64
Illustrations of John Moodie. Am Artist 28: 50-5+ Ja '64
Leslie Saalburg, illustrator of mode. Am Artist 27:20-5+ F '63
Magic realism of Gerald Mofchum. Am Artist 27:24-9+ O '63
Millard Sheets; the story of a giant. Am Artist 28:32-7+ D '64

WHITAKER, Frederic—*Continued*
Noél J. Daggett: a determined painter. Am Artist 27:42-7+ Mr '63
Paintings of Maxwell Stewart Simpson. Am Artist 27:32-7+ My '63
Sculpture of Moissaye Marans. Am Artist 28: 44-9+ F '64

WHITAKER, Robert B.
Chevelon Canyon lures backpacking vacationers. Todays Health 42:24-7 F '64

WHITBREAD, Jane
Parent and child. N Y Times Mag p92+ My 19 '63

WHITBREAD, Thomas
Analysis; poem. Harper 228:103 Je '64

WHITBY abbey. See Abbeys

WHITBY school, Greenwich. See Greenwich, Conn.—Education

WHITE, Alexander M.
Museum memo (cont) Natur Hist 73:3 Mr '64

WHITE, Barbara
Myth of Japanese good taste. Craft Horiz 23:21 N '63

WHITE, Bob
River of records. Field & S 68:122-4+ Je '63

WHITE, Byron R.
In High court: when Goldberg says yes, White says no. por U S News 54:65 My 27 '63
New break for criminals? por U S News 56: 16 Je 1 '64

WHITE, C. Langdon
Anglo-America and Latin America; can they become better neighbors? address, August 16, 1963. Vital Speeches 29:746-50 O 1 '63

WHITE, Dolly
Look twice before cutting. Flower Grower 50:45+ Mr '63

WHITE, Donald E. and others
Geothermal brine well: mile-deep drill hole may tap ore-bearing magmatic water and rocks undergoing metamorphism. bibliog Science 139:919-22 Mr 8 '63

WHITE, Doris
Doris White expresses the world around her; with biographical sketch. il por Am Artist 28:38-9+ Ap '64

WHITE, E. B.
Burdens of high office; poem. New Yorker 39:56 O 12 '63
Was lifted by ears as boy, no harm done. New Yorker 40:38 My 9 '64

WHITE, Edmund
Blue boy in black. Criticism
New Yorker 39:88 My 11 '63
Theatre Arts il 47:10-11 Jl '63

WHITE, Edward, 1930-
Been weightless 1,200 times. Life 55:88-9 S 27 '63

WHITE, Edward Douglass
Blue & the grey. il por Time 82:76 N 8 '63

WHITE, Elgin
Where lower is upper. Yachting 114:61-2+ N '63

WHITE, Ellington
Place that Rocky knows. Sports Illus 20: 36+ My 25 '64
Singing rivers and a sea of mud. Sports Illus 19:66-8+ D 16 '63

WHITE, F. Clifton
Men behind Goldwater. R. G. Spivack. il Look 28:45+ N 3 '64
Suite 3505. W. A. Rusher. Nat R 16:683-6 Ag 11 '64

WHITE, Frank
Fishing aplenty for the disabled. Todays Health 42:50-1+ S '64

WHITE, George
(tr) See Gressieker, H. Emperor

WHITE, Gilbert F.
Mekong River plan; with biographical sketch. Sci Am 208:38, 49-59 bibliog(p200) Ap '63
Rivers of international concord. UNESCO Courier 17:32-3+ Jl '64
Vietnam: the fourth course. Bul Atomic Sci 20:6-10 D '64

WHITE, Glenn
Pappy takes over the house. Ladies Home J 80:147-51 Jl '63
Toughest high school in the United States. Ladies Home J 80:69+ Ap '63

WHITE, H. Lee
Is Niarchos heading for port? il Bsns W p 110+ O 24 '64

WHITE, Helen Lyng. See White, J. R. jt. auth.

WHITE, James R. and White, H. L.
Phenethyl alcohol synergism with mitomycin C, porfiromycin, and streptonigrin. bibliog Science 145:1312-13 S 18 '64
Streptomycinoid antibiotics: synergism by puromycin. bibliog Science 146:772-4 N 6 '64

WHITE, Joan
Introduction to Asia; Negligent sea attitudes, poems. Yale R 54:81-2 O '64

WHITE, Joe L. and Burns, A. F.
Infrared spectra of hydronium ion in micaceous minerals. bibliog Science 141:800-1 Ag 30 '63
—See Ledoux, R. L. jt. auth.

WHITE, John F.
New NET programming. por Sr Schol 83:1T O 18 '63

WHITE, K. Owen
Baptist division. por Time 81:84 My 17 '63

WHITE, Laurens P. and Claflin, E. F.
Nitrogen mustard: diminution of toxicity in axenic mice. bibliog Science 140:1400-1 Je 28 '63

WHITE, Margaret Bourke-. See Bourke-White, M.

WHITE, Marion Ross
Reporter at large; dancers in May. L. Ross. il New Yorker 40:35-8+ Jl 18 '64

WHITE, Mike
Player of the week: Cleveland Indians shortstop. por Sports Illus 20:93 Je 8 '64

WHITE, Milton
Boola boola, Babe Ruth, and a jug of whiskey sours; story. Harper 227:70-4 D '63

WHITE, Minor
Bent light koans. D. Vestal. Pop Phot 55:46+ N '64

WHITE, Myrna
Myrna White scores dance success. il pors Ebony 18:59-60+ Ap '63

WHITE, Paul Dudley
Cycling for fitness. Recreation 57:405-6 O '64
How to help your heart. Parents Mag 39:121-5 My '64
Sudden death. Atlan 212:75-8 O '63
—See Todrin, B. jt. auth.

about

Heart doctor talks up walking. R. Wallace. por Life 54:82 F 22 '63
Pedaling to health. il Time 82:42 Ag 2 '63

WHITE, Peter T.
World in New York city. Nat Geog Mag 126: 52-107 Jl '64

WHITE, Philip L.
Food fanatic's four myths of nutrition. por Todays Health 41:72 Je '63
(ed) Let's talk about food. See issues of Today's health

WHITE, Pura Belpre
Bilingual story hour program. por Library J 89:3379-81 S 15 '64

WHITE, Raymond L.
Health checkups for longer life. por Parents Mag 38:163+ S '63
Medicine moves against the environmental threats to health. Todays Health 42:68+ My '64
Pesticides. Science 145:729-30 Ag 14 '64
Ship of hope. Todays Health 41:62-7 Jl '63

WHITE, Robert
Andover bookstore: relocated and thriving. Pub W 185:36-8 Mr 9 '64

WHITE, Robert J. and others
Isolation of the monkey brain: in vitro preparation and maintenance. bibliog Science 141:1060-1 S 13 '63

WHITE, Robert Mayer
New weather discoveries will serve you; interview. por Nations Bsns 52:36-7+ N '64
Scientist's scientist. W. Jonathan. Sat R 47:36-7 Ag 1 '64

WHITE, Robert Michael
Stairway to the stars. por NEA J 52:9-10 Ap '63

about

Sky-high courage. D. Markinko. il pors Ladies Home J 80:62-3+ Ja '63
Writing in the sky. M. E. Jenkins. PTA Mag 57:2-3 Ap '63

WHITE, Robin, 1928-
Battle for understanding. por Sat Eve Post 236:62-4 Je 8 '63
Fiction in India. bibliog Reporter 28:54+ F 14; 14 Mr 14 '63
Gunfight at the Sure Enough; story. Harper 226:95-7 My '63
I'd rather die than say no; story. Mlle 57: 100-1 Je '63
Walker's peak; story. Sat Eve Post 238:48-54 Ja 16 '65
Writing the episodic novel. Writer 77:9-12 My '64
Writing the nonfiction narrative. Writer 76: 10-12 Ag '63

WHITE, Ruth W.
Light in a dark world. bibliog Library J 88:4817-20+ D 15 '63

WHITE, Stanford
Architect's art; exhibition of drawings and watercolors at Manhattan's Davis galleries. il Time 81:90 My 17 '63

WHITE, Stephen
Channels (cont) Horizon 5:113-14 Mr; 112-13 My '62
Upmannship. Horizon 6:104-5 Sum '64
—See Zacharias, J. R. jt. auth.

WHITE, Terence Hanbury
Obituary
Pub W 185:245 Ja 27 '64
Once & future Merlyn. por Time 83:24+ Ja 24 '64

WHITE, Theodore Harold
Backlash. Life 57:100A-100B+ O 16 '64
Each is sure the triumph of the other will wreck the party. Life 56:26-31 My 29 '64
For President Kennedy an epilogue. Life 55:158-9 D 6 '63
Memo to a future historian. Life 57:32-5+ N 13 '64
One wished for a cry, a sob, any human sound. Life 55:32D-32E N 29 '63
Power structure, integration, militancy, freedom now! Life 55:78-80+ N 29 '63
Racial collision in big cities. Life 55:100-2+ N 22 '63
Revolution in the Pentagon. Look 27:31-44+ Ap 23 '63
Squire Scranton bides his time. Life 56:63-8+ F 28 '64

about

Project White. W. F. Buckley. Nat R 16:634-5 Jl 28 '64

WHITE, Thomas Dresser
Air force: getting down to new business. por Newsweek 61:37 My 13 '63
Appraisal of the Secretary of defense. por Newsweek 63:19 Ja 6 '64
Dangerous mixture: the military and politics. por Newsweek 64:33 O 19 '64
French logic vs. computers. por Newsweek 61:24 F 11 '63
From LeMay to McConnell; a change to the new breed. Newsweek 65:16-17 Ja 4 '65
Multilateral force: will it pay its way? por Newsweek 62:52 N 11 '63
Pendulum is swinging too far. por Newsweek 63:22-3 F 24 '64
Policy for Latin America. por Newsweek 61:59 Mr 25 '63
Speaking out. por Sat Eve Post 236:10+ My 4 '63
Test-ban treaty: atomic chess. por Newsweek 62:23 S 9 '63
What NATO needs to stay alive. por Newsweek 62:34 D 16 '63
What's wrong with civil-military relations. por Newsweek 61:30 My 27 '63

WHITE, W. L.
Strike nobody won. Read Digest 83:155-8+ S '63

WHITE, Wallace
Beisbol in Central park; poem. New Yorker 40:46 My 16 '64
Roulette; story. New Yorker 39:42-5 N 2 '63

WHITE, William S.
Meet the Honorable Harry (the rare) Byrd. Read Digest 82:205-7+ Ap '63
Presidents and president-makers. NEA J 53:27 O '64

about

One with connections. por Time 83:69 F 28 '64

WHITE ants. See Termites

WHITE-bellied storks. See Storks

WHITE birch. See Birch

WHITE blood cells. See Blood

WHITE cedar. See Arborvitae

WHITE citizens councils
Fearmongers; with report by B. Bettelheim. il Life 56:71-8+ F 7 '64
Segregationist revival in St Louis; Citizens' council of America. Christian Cent 81:1357 N 4 '64

WHITE collar workers. See Office workers

WHITE dwarf stars. See Stars, Dwarf

WHITE elephants. See Elephants

WHITE footed mice. See Mice, White footed

WHITE House
Ball at the White House; photographs. N Y Times Mag p 12-13 F 23 '64
Biggest reception ever; President Kennedy entertains 1,000 Negroes at White House. il Ebony 18:89-90+ My '63
Bouquet for the White House garden. M. Perry. il Flower Grower 50:17 Jl '63
Caroline's wonderful little White House school. H. Thomas. il Good H 157:84-5+ O '63
Changing hues at White House. il U S News 54:16 F 4 '63
First family has everything but privacy. M. Smith. il Nations Bsns 51:23-4 My '63
For First lady: a big job at the White House. U S News 56:6 Ja 6 '64
How Jackie restyled the White House; paintings, antiques and historic objects. Sat Eve Post 236:42-51 O 26 '63
J.F.K.'s new garden. il Life 54:110-12+ My 24 '63
Johnsons in the White House. il Look 28:15-21 Mr 10 '64
Life visits those White House beagles, Him and Her. il Life 56:68A-68B+ Je 19 '64
A look inside the White House school. il U S News 55:70-2 O 7 '63
No White House interiors, please; restrictions on photography. L. Barry. il Pop Phot 53:26+ D '63
Oh, to be a White House pet! M. Means. McCalls 91:216 N '63
Story of the presidents at Christmas. F. Knebel. il Look 27:16-19 D 31 '63
To keep the White House going. il U S News 56:8 Mr 30 '64
Toward the ideal. il Time 82:60-7 S 6 '63
Weathervane. R. G. Miner. il Flower Grower 50:6 Ag '63
White House garden. M. Perry. il Flower Grower 50:24-33 Ag '63
White House garden: LBJ loves it. il U S News 56:10 My 11 '64
White House: garden treatment. Newsweek 61:26 My 6 '63
White House revisited. N. Cousins. Sat R 47:20 F 8 '64
Why presidents don't like to stay in White House. il U S News 54:48-9 Mr 4 '63
With a new family in the White House. il U S News 55:68-9 D 16 '63

Anecdotes, facetiae, satire, etc.

You should have caught me at the White House. J. Feiffer. il Holiday 33:66-7 Je '63

Caricatures and cartoons

Wits in the White House. T. Wicker. N Y Times Mag p82-3 My 12 '63

History

Camera comes to the White House. R. Butterfield. il Am Heritage 15:33-48 Ag '64
Speech that toppled a president; excerpts from address, April 14, 1840, ed. with introd. by G. Carson. C. Ogle. Am Heritage 15:108-11 Ag '64
Thomas Jefferson, gourmet. J. H. Hazelton. il Am Heritage 15:20-1+ O '64

Libraries

All-American library. Wilson Lib Bul 38:103 O '63
Book list for White House includes architecture. Arch Rec 134:29+ D '63
Books for Americans; White House library. H. Hazlitt. Newsweek 62:80 S 30 '63
Books on education in the White House library. Sat R 46:51 S 21 '63
Educational library for the White House. W W Brickman. Sch & Soc 91:327 N 2 '63
Establishment library. Christian Cent 80:1068 S 4 '63
First ABA Christmas gift of books to White House. Pub W 184:35 D 30 '63
Five-hundred foot shelf. Reporter 29:16+ S 12 '63
For well-read presidents. il Time 82:60 Ag 23 '63
In books. Newsweek 62:70 Ag 26 '63
Mrs Kennedy's library. M. E. Cooley. Library J 88:3560 O 1 '63
New White House library to include 1,780 titles. Library J 88:3180-1 S 15 '63
Two libraries in the White House. C. B. Grannis. Pub W 184:251 Ag 26 '63
2,600 books get White House O.K. il U S News 55:8 Ag 26 '63

WHITE House airplanes. See Airplanes, Government

WHITE House conference on export expansion
Drive to hike exports. il Bsns W p31 S 21 '63

WHITE House conference on narcotic and drug abuse
Addiction: beginnings of wisdom. A. R. Lindesmith; reply. J. S. Williams, jr. Nation 197:inside cover O 26 '63

WHITE House; drama. See Hotchner, A. E.

WHITE House entertaining. See Government entertaining

WHITE House rabbit; drama. See Miller, H. L.

WHITE House receptions. See Government entertaining

WHITE House staff. See Public officers

WHITE memorial foundation, Litchfield, Conn. See Bird sanctuaries

WHITE men in Africa. See Africa—Race problems
WHITE motor company
Heavy-duty, high fear merger; White motor and Cummins engine. Bsns W p94+ O 5 '63
WHITE MOUNTAINS, Calif.
Sky forest of the ancients; Ancient Bristlecone Pine Forest area of Inyo National Forest. W. F. Heald. il Am For 70:34-5+ N '64
WHITE noise generator. See Sound—Apparatus
WHITE perch
Perch that is a bass. W. Davis. il Outdoor Life 134:54-6 Ag '64
WHITE pine. See Pine
WHITE PLAINS, N.Y.

Parks and playgrounds

Zoning for today's needs. J. E. Curtis. Recreation 57:16-17 Ja '64
WHITE rats. See Rats
WHITE SANDS missile range. See Proving grounds
WHITE slave trade. See Prostitution
WHITE Sox (baseball) See Baseball clubs
WHITE tailed deer. See Deer
WHITE tailed deer hunting. See Deer hunting
WHITE-winged doves. See Pigeons
WHITEFIELD, Edwin
Phantom cities in a promised land; with reproductions of paintings. B. L. Heilbron. il Am Heritage 14:52-7 Je '63
WHITEFISH fishing
Whitefish magic. J. Brooks. il Outdoor Life 132:30-1+ Jl '63
WHITEHEAD, Sir Edgar
Will he, won't he, will he, won't he. . ? E. Huxley. Nat R 16:651-2 Jl 28 '64
WHITEHEAD, Eric
Driven beyond dignity. Sports Illus 20:16-19 Mr 16 '64
WHITEHEAD, Matthew J.
Book review. Negro Hist Bul 28:69 D '64
WHITEHEAD, Robert
So they say; interview. por Mlle 57:236-7 Ag '63

about

Inside job. il por Newsweek 64:74-5 D 21 '64
WHITEHEAD, Stanley C. and Goodman, D. A.
Saga of cigarette ads. America 109:387-9 O 5 '63
WHITEHILL, Walter Muir
Mammon & monuments; excerpt from Independent historical societies. Am Heritage 14:38-41+ Ag '63
WHITEHORN, Ethel. See McMahan, I. jt. auth.
WHITEHORN, Katharine
Alexandre the great. Ladies Home J 80:148-53 N '63
How to succeed as a slut. por Time 83:43 Ja 24 '64
WHITEHOUSE, Doris Cheney
Legacy from Mr Ditto. Read Digest 83:201-4 D '63
WHITELAW, John B.
Teacher preparation. por Sch Life 46:11-13 Ja '64
WHITEMAN, P. C. and Koller, D.
Saturation deficit of the mesophyll evaporating surfaces in a desert halophyte. bibliog Science 146:1320-1 D 4 '64
WHITENACK, Carolyn I.
Changing role of the librarian. por Wilson Lib Bul 38:397-400 Ja '64
School libraries. Wilson Lib Bul 39:75+ S '64
WHITESELL, C. D. and Daehler, R. E.
Forests, a natural defense against seismic waves. Am For 70:38-9 N '64
WHITESIDE, Donald
Convict who became a minister. J. Robbins and J. Robbins. il pors Redbook 124:38-9+ D '64
WHITESIDE, Duncan
Visit to a Russian village. il N Y Times Mag p26-7+ D 8 '63
WHITESIDE, Elena
For Soviet women; a thirteen-hour day. N Y Times Mag p28-9+ N 17 '63
WHITESIDE, Thomas
Annals of business. New Yorker 40:42-6+ D 19 '64
Annals of migration. New Yorker 39:154+ N 9 '63
Couple who wouldn't die. Sat Eve Post 236:56-65 Je 22 '63
Reporter at large (cont) New Yorker 39:67-8+ N 30 '63
WHITETAILED deer. See Deer
WHITEY, J. V.
All the prisoners drove away. New Yorker 39:80+ Ja 18 '64
WHITFIELD, Mal
Let's boycott the Olympics. pors Ebony 19:95-6+ Mr '64
WHITFIELD, Mary Ann
You all come to a cookout. Parents Mag 38:61+ Jl '63
WHITFIELD, Robert E.
Steric factors in the chemistry of polypeptides, poly-α-amino acids and proteins. bibliog Science 142:577-9 N 1 '63
WHITING, John
Devils; dramatization of Devils of Loudon, by A. Huxley. Criticism
Commonweal 79:371 D 20 '63
Newsweek 62:77 N 11 '63
Sat R 46:35 N 23 '63
WHITING, Ind.
Whiting doesn't spare the rod. K. Detzer. il Read Digest 82:167-70+ My '63
WHITIS, Margaret Thurston
Credit at the blood bank. Parents Mag 39:58+ D '64
WHITLOCK, J. H. See Evans, J. V. jt. auth.
WHITLOW, Bob
All the marbles? Newsweek 61:93-4 Mr 18 '63
WHITMAN, Ardis
Children of interfaith marriage. Redbook 121:46-7+ Je '63
Problem that plagues the thoughtful woman. Redbook 122:50-1+ F '64
What makes a woman unforgettable? Read Digest 82:72-4 My '63
What young Protestants really believe. Redbook 123:45-7+ Ag '64
WHITMAN, Arthur
Amphibious man. N Y Times Mag p96-7+ My 17 '64
It is no longer like pulling teeth. N Y Times Mag p44+ N 24 '63
K7UGA will get the ham vote. N Y Times Mag p64+ S 13 '64
They jump for joy. N Y Times Mag p93-4+ Ap 5 '64
WHITMAN, Constance
School for jesters; drama. Plays 23:45-52 My '64
Straight from the heart; drama. Plays 23:35-44 F '64
WHITMAN, George B.
Last-minute tax reminders on machinery. Suc Farm 62:36 Ap '64
—and Brantley, Bill
How to get your money's worth out of social security. Suc Farm 61:45-56 F '63
WHITMAN, Howard
Brightening old age in Houston. Todays Health 41:52-3+ S '63
WHITMAN, Marcus
Marcus Whitman: medic, missionary, martyr; excerpt from Doctors on the frontier. R. Dunlop. il Todays Health 42:12-13+ Jl '64
WHITMAN, Roger
First aid for minor household ailments. Am Home 68:76-7 Ja '65
WHITMAN, Ruth
(tr) See Axion esti: This then is I: Six and one regrets for the sky: The sleep of the brave
(tr) See Singer, I. B. Three tales
WHITMAN, Willson
Major Eatherly's high lonesome. Nation 198:440-2 Ap 27 '64
WHITMAN Sampler (candy) See Candy industry and trade
WHITMER, Dana P.
When someone complains. Sr Schol 83:27T Ja 17 '64
WHITMER, J. M. Jr
From public nuisance to playground. Am City 79:117-18 O '64
WHITMORE, Bruce
Hidden power of pictures. U S Camera 26:72+ Ap '63
WHITMORE, F. W. and Zahner, R.
Indoleacetic acid synthesis by polyphenols in the extraction of pinus phloem and cambial tissue. bibliog Science 145:166-7 Jl 10 '64
WHITNEY, Betsey Cushing Roosevelt
Cornucopia life of the Whitneys. A. Talmey. il pors Vogue 145:140-5+ F 1 '65
WHITNEY, C. V.
Pilgrim Mountain buck. Field & S 68:32-4+ F '64
WHITNEY, Dale
Rhine roam. il Travel 120:43-7 S '63
WHITNEY, Edgar A.
Mirror for painting demonstrations. il Am Artist 28:3-5+ N '64
WHITNEY, Frank L.
Architect's expanding role in industrial design. Arch Rec 136:168+ Jl '64
Industrial plant of the future; address, January 29, 1963. Vital Speeches 29:369-72 Ap 1 '63

WHITNEY, John Hay
Advice from a millionaire publisher; address. Sat R 47:71-3 D 12 '64
Newspaper's role; remarks. por Time 84:49 N 20 '64

about

Cornucopia life of the Whitneys. A. Talmey. il pors Vogue 145:140-5+ F 1 '65
Crisis on New York's newspaper row. T. A. Wise. il por Fortune 70:110-13+ O '64
Jock Whitney: unclassified capitalist. T. A. Wise. il por Fortune 70:114-19+ O '64
Trib's Sunday punch; new format. il por Bsns W p34+ S 21 '63

WHITNEY, John Hay, foundation. See John Hay Whitney foundation

WHITNEY, Marion
Trees against the winds. Natur Hist 72:56-9 Je '63

WHITNEY, Phyllis A.
What does a writer expect of an editor? Library J 88:3985-6 O 15 '63
Writing the juvenile mystery. Writer 76:14-18 Ap '63

WHITNEY, Sarah E. U.
Do-it-yourself park; reprint. Recreation 57: 365 S '64

WHITNEY museum of American art, New York
Art galleries; annual exhibition of contemporary American painting (cont) R. M. Coates. New Yorker 39:63-5 Ja 4 '64
Onward and upward. il Newsweek 61:85 Je 17 '63
Tworkov: radical pro. L. Finkelstein. il Art N 63:32-5+ Ap '64
Upside-down museum in Manhattan. il Arch Forum 120:90-3 Ja '64
Whitney record. F. Getlein. New Repub 149: 26+ O 26 '63

WHITSITT, Joyce
Restoration; Beat of freedom: poems. Negro Hist Bul 27:130 F '64

WHITSON, Alexander
Case for individual latitude. Sch Arts 63: 36-8 My '64

WHITT, Robert L.
Man's reach must exceed his grasp; address, March 15, 1963. Vital Speeches 29:439-41 My 1 '63

WHITTAKER, Charles E.
Can integration be forced by federal law? address. por U S News 56:99-101 Mr 23 '64
When a former justice speaks out against the Supreme court; excerpts from address. por U S News 57:21 N 9 '64

WHITTAKER, James Warren
Yankee who conquered Everest. M. Morgan. il por Sat Eve Post 236:40+ Je 29 '63
Yes, I will. il por Time 81:96 My 17 '63

WHITTAKER, R. H.
Dominance and diversity in land plant communities. bibliog Science 147:250-60 Ja 15 '65

WHITTEMORE, Reed
Bad knight; poem. New Repub 149:18 Ag 17 '63
In the woods; poem. New Repub 151:17 Jl 11 '64
Poetry of the assassination. New Repub 151: 17-19 N 21 '64
T. S. Eliot 1888-1965. New Repub 152:28 Ja 16 '65

about

Desperater man than most. R. Sward. Poetry 104:380-1 S '64
Reed Whittemore's mock epics. X. J. Kennedy. Poetry 101:356-7 F '63

WHITTEN, Joan M.
Giant polytene chromosomes in hypodermal cells of developing footpads of dipteran pupae. bibliog Science 143:1437-8 Mr 27 '64
Stretch receptor-like organs in the fly larva: their possible role in growth regulation. bibliog Science 143:260-1 Ja 17 '64

WHITTIER, Bob
Caring for the electrical system. Yachting 113:62-3+ Je '63
Cold weather outboarding. Yachting 116:48-9+ D '64
Installing your outboard steerer. Yachting 113:60-2+ Mr '63
Outboard fuel tanks. Yachting 113:60-2 F '63
Outboard motor and salt water. Yachting 113:56-7+ My '63

WHITTIER, John Greenleaf
Whittier desk at Hartford State House. Hobbies 68:52 O '63

WHITTIER, Calif.
Reclaiming used water. J. D. Parkhurst. il Am City 78:83-5 O '63

WHITTLING. See Wood carving

WHITTON, Charlotte Elizabeth
Mayor is no angel. J. Finan and L. Elliott. por Read Digest 83:154-7 Jl '63

WHITTREDGE, Worthington
Why Washington stood up in the boat; memoir; with reproduction of painting. por Am Heritage 16:18-19 D '64

WHITWORTH, J. W. See Muzik, T. J. jt. auth.

WHO is Rima, what is she? story. See Jaffe, R.

WHO means more to you? story. See Frasier, K.

WHOLE cherry pie; story. See O'Hara, J.

WHOLE wide world; story. See Bittle, C. R.

WHOLESALE food industry. See Food industry and trade

WHOLESALE price index. See Price indexes

WHOLESALE prices. See Prices

WHOLESALE trade
Fourteen important ratios in twenty-one wholesale lines. il Duns R 82:52-4 D '63
Franchising, new scope for an old technique. W. P. Hall. il Harvard Bsns R 42:60-72 Ja '64
Rationale for quantity discounts. J. F. Crowther. il Harvard Bsns R 42:121-7 Mr '64
Ratios of the wholesalers; table. Duns R 84: 62-3 O '64

WHOLESALERS, Book. See Book jobbers

WHOOPING cough
Whooping cough. F. H. Richardson. il Todays Health 42:36-7+ Je '64

WHOOPING cranes. See Cranes (birds)

WHORF, Richard
Richard Whorf: painter of Americana. J. Lovoos. il por Am Artist 28:32-7+ Ap '64

WHO'S afraid of Virginia Woolf? drama. See Albee, E.

WHO'S there? story. See Green, M.

WHO'S who at the zoo; drama. See Miller, H. L.

WHO'S who in America
Who's who updated. R. W. Apple, jr. il N Y Times Mag p94+ My 3 '64

WHY don't you go home? story. See Cuming, C. L.

WHY the sleepy Dormouse; drama. See Fisher, A.

WHYMPER, Edward
They did the impossible, and then. R. Deardorff. il por N Y Times Mag p74-5+ D 6 '64

WHYTE, Dorothy K.
Family quiz game. See issues of Parents' magazine & better homemaking

WHYTE, William F.
Toward an integrated approach for industrial relations research; excerpt from address. Mo Labor R 87:136-9 F '64

WIARDA, Howard J.
Trujilloism without Trujillo. New Repub 151: 5-6 S 19 '64

WIBBERLEY, Leonard
WLB biography. T. Hines. por Wilson Lib Bul 37:882 Je '63

WICHITA, Kan.
Dog census. C. A. Goodrum. il Atlan 211: 82-5 Mr '63
TV and chemical grout. G. Wilton. il Am City 78:78-9 Ag '63
Wichita asks the experts. il Am City 79:161-2+ S '64
Wichita's miracle report. il Am City 78:117-18+ Jl '63

WICHITA, Kan. city library
Free space: can public libraries receive it? report of survey of branch libraries in shopping centers. R. Waters. ALA Bul 58: 232-4 Mr '64

WICHMANN, Barry
Gifted boy finds his way. il pors Life 57:79-80+ D 4 '64

WICK, Deane A. See Keeling, R. O. jr. jt. auth.

WICKE, J. D. and others
Visual evoked potentials as a function of flash luminance and duration. bibliog Science 146:83-5 O 2 '64

WICKER, Tom
Anatomy of the Goldwater boom. N Y Times Mag p7+ Ag 11 '63
Big political sprint. Sat Eve Post 237:76-7 Ap 25 '64
Four tactics in the Johnson campaign. N Y Times Mag p 14+ O 4 '64
Goldwater appeal: not only nuts and kooks. N Y Times Mag p9+ Je 21 '64
It is a zany system, but it works. N Y Times Mag p7+ Jl 19 '64
It is the people who face the test. N Y Times Mag p 19+ D 8 '63; 20 Ja 5 '64
Johnson way with Congress. N Y Times Mag p9+ Mr 8 '64
Johnson's men: valuable hunks of humanity. N Y Times Mag p 11+ My 3 '64
Kennedy without tears. Esquire 61:108-11+ Je '64

WICKER, Tom—*Continued*
LBJ down on the farm. Esquire 62:90-3+ O '64
Name is Smith. N Y Times Mag p 11+ Jl 28 '63
Odds against Goldwater. N Y Times Mag p 18+ N 10 '63
Political pros give the ams a nod. N Y Times Mag p28+ Je 9 '63
Q's and A's about the press conference. N Y Times Mag p24-5 S 8 '63
Reporter must trust his instinct. Sat R 47: 81-2+ Ja 11 '64
WICKER furniture. See Furniture. Wicker
WICKERSHAM, Lucille. See Humphry, J. A. jt. auth.
WICKS, Wesley D. and Kenney, F. T.
RNA synthesis in rat seminal vesicles: stimulation by testosterone. bibliog Science 144: 1346-7 Je 12 '64
WIDE-angle lenses. See Lenses, Photographic
WIDE field photography. See Photography, Wide field
WIDEMAN, John
Astonishing John Wideman. G. Shalit. il pors Look 27:30-6 My 21 '63
WIDER, Stella E.
College. Sch Arts 63:16-17 D '63
WIDICK, B. J.
GM strike: prototype for more conflict. Nation 199:349-52 N 16 '64
Labor ducks the future. Nation 197:389-90 D 7 '63
New round of stalemate. Nation 197:68-70 Ag 10 '63
Studebaker: end of a dream. Nation 198:29-30 Ja 6 '64
WIDING, J. William, Jr, and Diamond, C. G.
Buy by computer. Harvard Bsns R 42:109-20 Mr '64
WIDMAN, Anneliese
Beverly Schmidt and Anneliese Widman at Judson Hall. D. Hering. Dance Mag 37:55-6 F '63
WIDMANN, Art
Shrunken raster: a puzzler. Electr World 70: 92 N '63
WIDNALL, William B.
Excerpt from remarks, January 28, 1964. Cong Digest 43:109+ Ap '64
WIDNER, Ralph R.
Project 70. Am For 70:26-9+ Ja '64
—See Goddard, M. K. jt. auth.
WIDOW; story. See Jhabvala, R. P.
WIDOWHOOD system; story. See Friel, B.
WIDOWS
Echo of heroes. L. Hershey. il McCalls 91: 46+ Jl '64
Widowhood: toward self-understanding. il Changing T 17:17-20 O '63
Widow's troubles studied. Sci N L 85:27 Ja 11 '64
WIECK, Paul R.
In the West, fear is uppermost. New Repub 151:11-12 Ag 22 '64
Rocky Mountain politics. New Repub 150:10-13 Ap 18 '64
Taking care of farmers whoever they are. New Repub 150:9-10 Mr 28 '64
Tight Senate race. New Repub 151:7-8 O 24 '64
WIEDENMAN, Donald
My summer with writers. por Seventeen 23: 124-5+ My '64
WIED-NEUWIED, Maximilian Alexander Philipp, prinz von
Carl Bodmer's unspoiled West; with portfolio. M. B. Davidson. il Am Heritage 14:43-65 Ap '63
WIELAND, Howard
Cold. New Yorker 39:21-2 Je 22 '63
WIELOPOLSKI, Alexander
Futile compromise reconsidered: Wielopolski and Russian policy in the Congress Kingdom, 1861-1863. S. J. Zyzniewski. bibliog f Am Hist R 70:395-412 Ja '65
WIEMAN, Henry Nelson
Empirical theology of Henry Nelson Wieman, ed. by R. W. Bretall. Review
Christian Cent 81:767 Je 10 '64. E. Farley
WIEMAN, John S.
Holly culture on the West coast. Horticulture 41:408 Ag '63
WIENER, Alexander S. and Moor-Jankowski, J.
Blood groups in anthropoid apes and baboons. bibliog Science 142:67-9 O 4 '63
WIENER, Norbert
Machines smarter than men? interview. por U S News 56:84-6 F 24 '64; Same abr. Read Digest 84:121-4 My '64
—See Deutsch, K. W. jt. auth.

about

Cyberneticist. por Newsweek 63:48 Mr 30 '64
Norbert Wiener foresaw new type of medicine. Sci N L 85:215 Ap 4 '64
Obituary
Pub W 185:37 Mr 30 '64
Prodigy who grew up. por Time 83:53 Mr 27 '64
WIENERS, John
In the half light; poem. Nation 198:246 Mr 9 '64
Moon poems. Nation 198:636 Je 22 '64
WIENERS. See Frankfurters
WIER, Ester
Newbery and Caldecott runners-up. il por Library J 89:1381 Mr 15 '64
WIESE, G. M. See Baskin, R. J. jt. auth.
WIESEL, Elie
Postscript to death. I. Halperin. Commonweal 79:713-15 Mr 13 '64
WIESENTHAL, Simon
Sleuth with 6 million clients. C. A. Farnsworth. il por N Y Times Mag p 11+ F 2 '64
WIESNER, Jerome B.
Face-lift for the science curriculum. UNESCO Courier 16:32-6 Jl '63
John F. Kennedy: a remembrance. Science 142:1147-50 N 29 '63
Science in policy, policy in science; excerpt from testimony before the House subcommittee on science, research, and development. Bul Atomic Sci 20:36-40 F '64
Sixteen billions for science; where the money goes; interview. por U S News 56:72-6 F 3 '64
Wiesner report; summary. Am For 69:11 Je '63
—and York, H. F.
National security and the nuclear-test ban; with biographical sketches. Sci Am 211:18, 27-35 bibliog(p 142) O '64

about

Education: Wiesner asks action on pre-college science teaching, offers fairly modest proposals. J. Walsh. Science 140:1292-3 Je 21 '63
New goal for U.S. research? moving away from military. por Bsns W p28 O 26 '63
President's science adviser. P. H. Abelson. Science 142:1025 N 22 '63; Discussion. 143: 427-9 Ja 31 '64
WIFE beating
Wife beater & his wife. il Time 84:81-2 S 25 '64
WIFE game; story. See Turovlin, L.
WIGET, Bud
Wiget's winning year. C. D. Strang. Motor B 111:122-3 F '63
WIGHT, J. B.
Operation mirage. U S Camera 26:66-7+ Jl '63
WIGHTMAN, Edward K.
In search of my son; with editorial comment. S. K. Wightman. il por Am Heritage 14:64-78 F '63
WIGHTMAN, Stillman King
In search of my son. por Am Heritage 14:64-78 F '63
WIGLEY, Roland L.
Pogonophora on the New England continental slope. bibliog Science 141:358-9 Jl 26 '63
WIGNER, Eugene Paul
Events, laws of nature, and invariance principles; address, December 10, 1963. bibliog Science 145:995-9 S 4 '64
Just ask Mrs Mayer. il por Newsweek 62:78+ N 18 '63
WIGRAM, Ralph
Wait now for bombs; Englishman who foresaw the war. V. Lawford. il Atlan 212: 59-69 Jl '63
WIGREN, Harold E.
Educator's viewpoint. por Sr Schol 85:12T-13T+ O 7 '64
WIGS
Art of switchcraft. il Mlle 56:194 Ap '63
Beauty bulletin; do's and don'ts of wig-owning. il Vogue 142:201-2+ S 1 '63
Beauty bulletin; much more hair, many more hairpieces. il Vogue 144:114-17 Ag 15 '64
For windblown ladies. il Motor B 114:68 Jl '64
Look, lady, it's human. J. Ridgeway. New Repub 149:8 O 5 '63
Quick-switch styles; wiglets change casuals to formals. il Ebony 20:158+ N '64
Why women go wig-happy. N. L. Browning. il Sat Eve Post 236:68-70 F 23 '63
Wig and she's an Indian. il Sunset 133:158+ O '64
Wiggery-pokery. il Vogue 142:80+ S 1 '63
WIGTON, C. Benjamin, Jr
Trouble-free industrial concrete floor. Arch Rec 136:193-4 Jl '64

WILBUR, Cornelia B.
Homosexual men and women; interview, ed. by F. R. Schreiber. por Sci Digest 55:55-65 Ap '64
WILBUR, James E.
Ecumenical footnote. America 108:845-6 Je 15 '63
WILBUR, Richard
Complaint; poem. New Yorker 40:36 Ja 23 '65
Proof; poem. Atlan 213:62 Mr '64
Seed leaves; poem. New Yorker 40:42 Ap 4 '64
(tr) See Villon, F. Ballade of the ladies of time past
WILBURN, Theodore
Portsmouth's police chief. il pors Ebony 18: 144+ Ap '63
WILCOX, A. T.
Radiators for frozen skaters. Am City 78:36 Mr '63
WILCOX, Donald L.
Loud-hailer for the telephone. Pop Electr 19:67-9 D '63
WILCOX, Earl. See Alston, A. M. jt. auth.
WILCOX, Frank Nelson
Little-big watercolor of Frank N. Wilcox. N. Kent. il Am Artist 27:31-3+ F '63
WILCOX, Gregor Norman-. See Norman-Wilcox, G.
WILCOX, Helen Merrill
School library reaches out to classroom and curriculum. Library J 88:1104-5 Mr 15 '63
WILCOX, Lee
How to find your own taste in music. House B 105:80+ Ap '63
Listen to the sound of the harp. House B 105:202-3+ O '63
Music can help make Christmas magic for children. House B 105:166-7+ D '63
Stories to read aloud at Christmas time. House B 105:24 D '63
Why not give an opera in the garden? House B 105:112-13+ Je '63
WILCOX, Ray E. See Powers, H. A. jt. auth.
WILCOX, Ted
Prairie drag race. Outdoor Life 131:40-3+ Ja '63
WILCOX, Victor G.
Big little man. Newsweek 64:45 Jl 20 '64
WILCOXSON, Bobby Randell
Good-by to Bobby One-Eye Wilcoxson. B. Clark. pors Read Digest 82:63-8 F '63
WILD, Hans
Notes from our correspondents. Hi Fi 14:28+ Ap '64
WILD animal pets. See Pets
WILD animals. See Animals
WILD animals, Intelligence of. See Animal intelligence
WILD animals in art. See Animals in art
WILD boar hunting
Makers of the sports page. P. Knauth. il Sports Illus 19:41-3 S 16 '63
WILD children. See Children, Wild
WILD ducks. See Ducks, Wild
WILD flower gardens. See Gardens, Wild
WILD flowers
America's wild beauties; excerpts from Odyssey book of American wildflowers; with photographs by F. Grehan. H. W. Rickett. Life 56:60-3 Ap 3 '64
Challenge; New England wild flower preservation society campaigns to preserve the Garden in the woods. B. B. Paine. il Horticulture 42:32-5 O '64
Homes for persecuted wildlings. D. E. Rose. il Horticulture 41:324-5 Je '63
Indian parsnip. D. E. Rose. il Horticulture 41:132 Mr '63
Our glamorous weeds. S. H. Gottscho. il Audubon Mag 65:226-31 Jl '63
Southern wild flowers at their best. E. Lawrence. il Pop Gard 14:37+ Mr '63
Suppose you want hundreds; excerpt from Woodland garden from scratch. J. Hersey. il Horticulture 41:410 Ag '63
These natives love the shade of summer. R. D. Roe. il Flower Grower 51:51-2 My '64
Waves of spring color in Antelope Valley, Calif. il Sunset 132:82-9 Ap '64
Wild flowers. E. F. Steffek. il Horticulture 42:14-17+ My '64
Wildflowers at Stinson Beach. il Sunset 130: 290 My '63
Wildflowers; gardens for people who don't like to garden. il Vogue 141:28 Mr 1 '63
Wild flowers most likely to grow in a garden. Good H 156:141 Mr '63
Wild flowers of New Zealand. C. Wylie. il Horticulture 41:370-1 Jl '63
Wild! wild flowers for your garden. il Am Home 67:50-1+ Ap '64
See also names of wild flowers, e.g. Bloodroot

Bibliography

Flowers afield. M. Bush. Am For 70:39 Ag '64
WILD fowl. See Game birds
WILD fowl decoys. See Decoys (hunting)
WILD gardens. See Gardens, Wild
WILD geese. See Geese, Wild
WILD horses. See Horses
WILD life. See Wildlife
WILD phlox. See Phlox
WILD pig hunting. See Peccary hunting
WILD pinks
Bright perennial rock pink. C. M. Fitch. il Horticulture 41:196 Ap '63
WILD swine. See Woods hogs
WILD West shows. See Rodeos
WILDAVSKYY, Aaron
1,308; who they are, what they do. N Y Times Mag p8+ Jl 12 '64
WILDBRUNN, Helene
Helene Wildbrunn. A. Favia-Artsay. Hobbies 69:30 D '64
WILDCAT hunting. See Bobcat hunting
WILDCATS. See Bobcats
WILDE, Frazar B.
Federal expenditures; address, December 3, 1963. Vital Speeches 30:243-5 F 1 '64
What the tax cut can do. Sat R 47:30-2 Ja 11 '64
Who should get how much? Sat R 48:34 Ja 9 '65
WILDE, James
Letter from the publisher. B. M. Auer. il por Time 83:11 Ja 31 '64
WILDE, Oscar
Books. W. H. Auden. New Yorker 39:155-62+ Mr 9 '63
Bosie, by R. Croft-Cooke. Review
Esquire 62:10+ Ag '64. M. Muggeridge
Breakfast with Oscar. B. Nichols. il Horizon 6:46-7 Autumn '64
Canterville ghost; drama, ed. by W. Hackett. Plays 23:85-94 Mr '64
Degeneracy or decadence? S. Leslie. por Nat R 15:445-6 N 19 '63
Importance of being earnest. Criticism
New Yorker 39:132+ Mr 9 '63
Newsweek 61:86 Mr 11 '63
Theatre Arts il 47:12-13 Ap '63
WILDENSTEIN, Georges
Monsieur Georges; illuminated miniatures from Wildenstein collection at Manhattan's Cloisters. il por Time 81:56-9 Mr 1 '63
Obituary
Art N 62:15 S '63
Pages from an international dealer's private collections. H. La Farge. il Art N 61:45+ F '63
WILDER, Amos N.
Grace confounding; poem. Christian Cent 80: 1607 D 25 '63
WILDER, Billy
Billy the Wild. H. Kurnitz. il por Holiday 35:93-4+ Je '64
Bright Diamond. M. Schumach. il por N Y Times Mag p80-1 My 26 '63
Wilder's dirty-joke film stirs a furor. T. Thompson. il por Life 58:51-2+ Ja 15 '65
WILDER, Stephen
Volvo with v-v-voom! Hot Rod 17:80-3+ D '64
WILDERNESS areas
America's vanishing wilderness. W. O. Douglas. il Ladies Home J 81:37-41+ Jl '64; Same abr. with title To preserve America's glories. Read Digest 86:146-54 Ja '65
Aspinall in the wilderness. New Repub 148:5 F 9 '63
Back packing: family style. H. Kanzler. il Field & S 68:35-7 Je '63
Circle that took us in; Wilderness bill. Am For 70:8-9 Je '64
Coexistence at home; conflict between Agriculture and Interior departments over management of natural resources. A. W. Smith. Nat Parks Mag 37:2+ Ap '63
Congressman Aspinall vs. the people of the United States. P. Brooks. Harper 226:60-3 Mr '63
Conservationist John Muir honored. il Am For 70:46 Je '64
Facts about the Wilderness bill. C. H. Callison. il Liv Wildn 82:11-16 Winter '63
Jewel basin; northwestern Montana. R. F. Cooney. il Liv Wildn 85:7-9 Wint '64
Keeping the wilderness wild; how it will be done. il U S News 57:65-7 Ag 24 '64
Minister delivers sermon calling for enactment of Wilderness bill. Am For 69:6 My '63

WILDERNESS areas—*Continued*
New support for wilderness areas. U S News 57:10 Ag 10 '64
On the carrying capacity of wilderness; excerpt from address, August 26, 1963. S. M. Brandborg. il Liv Wildn 84:28-33 Sum '63
On the trail of the wily special interest. R. Starnes. Field & S 69:14+ My '64
Our fragile wilderness. D. G. Newcomb. il Field & S 68:10-11+ F '64
Pace of wilderness classification; reclassification of primitive areas. M. Nadel. il Liv Wildn 85:16-24 Wint '64
Predators on the Potomac; Wilderness bill in Congress. R. Starnes. Field & S 67: 12+ Mr '63
Prospecting parkland. M. D. Morris. il Recreation 56:190-2 Ap '63
Protecting the Nation's wilderness. il Sr Schol 85:10-12 N 18 '64
S. 4 urged; Wilderness bill. H. M. Albright. Liv Wildn 83:30 Spring '63
Sawtooth wilderness supported; remarks, September 4, 1963. il Liv Wildn 85:37-9 Wint '64
Second look; Wilderness act. S. Donaldson. Liv Wildn 82:2 Winter '62
Selway-Bitterroot wilderness area is created. il Nat Parks Mag 37:19 Mr '63
Selway-Bitterroot wilderness; with editorial comment and with text of decision of the Secretary of agriculture. il Liv Wildn 82: 25-37 Winter '62
Some emerging concepts of natural areas and nature centers. J. J. Shomon. il Audubon Mag 65:176-7 My '63
Trade winds; visit to Selway Bitterroot wilderness area. J. G. Fuller. Sat R 46:8-9 N 2 '63; Reply. A. Rotonda. 46:32 D 21 '63
Transfiguration in wilderness. C. E. Graves. il Liv Wildn 82:9-10 Winter '62
Twelve days under Montana's big sky; Bob Marshall wilderness area. J. Osier. il Liv Wildn 84:22-7 Sum '63
Two new wild areas; Shining Rock wild area and South Warner wild area. Nat Parks Mag 38:18 Ag '64
Two roads lead to conservation; facts about the wilderness bills. Bsns W p32 Ag 15 '64
Visit to a national grasslands; Cross Timbers grasslands, Tex. D. Beatie. il Nat Parks Mag 38:10-13 O '64
Walk in the wind. D. B. Wharton. il Am For 69:24-5+ Ap '63
Why we must save the Allagash. W. O. Douglas. il Field & S 68:24-9+ Jl '63
Wilderness act. P. M. Tilden. Natur Hist 73: 61-2 D '64
Wilderness bill. Nat Parks Mag 38:16 Je '64
Wilderness bill in committee hearing. Liv Wildn 85:30-4 Wint '64
Wilderness bill in the House. Liv Wildn 84: 42-5 Sum '63
Wilderness bill reported. il Liv Wildn 85: 35 Wint '64
Wilderness in Montana, a report. J. J. Craighead. il Liv Wildn 85:25-9 Wint '64
Wilderness plan hits trouble in Kentucky. il U S News 57:68-70 S 21 '64
Wilderness reward. T. Trueblood. il Field & S 67:47-9+ Ap '63
Wilderness trail: summer; Quetico-Superior wilderness country. H. Hoover. il Liv Wildn 83:3-4 Spring '63
Wilderness wins. il Am For 70:8 S '64
Wilderness words for readers. Liv Wildn 83: 29 Spring '63
Wonders of the wilderness. M. Gough. il House B 106:115+ Ag '64
See also
Trail riders of the wilderness

WILDERNESS camping. See Camping

WILDERNESS conference
Eighth biennial wilderness conference. H. Zahniser. il Liv Wildn 84:34-41 Sum '63

WILDERNESS society
Wilderness council in Alaska. M. Nadel. Liv Wildn 84:47 Sum '63
Wilderness council in Wyoming; September 2 to 5, 1962. M. Nadel. il Liv Wildn 82: 38-9 Wint '62

WILDFLOWERS. See Wild flowers

WILDFOWL trust, Slimbridge, England. See Bird sanctuaries

WILDI, Ernst
First complete guide to the art of zooming. Pop Phot 52:118-21+ My '63
Must dimension: motion. Pop Phot 54:110-13+ Je '64
Originals are not for cutting. Pop Phot 54: 118-21 Mr '64

WILDING, John H.
Designing bark cloth. Sch Arts 64:39 S '64

WILDLIFE
Come into my garden; excerpt from The river of life. R. Platt. Read Digest 83: 204C-204D+ S '63
Forests of France and their wildlife. G. Olivier. il Audubon Mag 66:28-31 Ja '64
Reviews; three books on the fauna survival problem. T. D. Carter. il Natur Hist 73: 4+ Ja '64
Silent spring on the Pacific slope; postscript to R. Carson effect on wildlife of use of pesticides. C. C. Van Fleet. Atlan 212:81-4 Jl '63
Strange animals of Australia. D. Fleay. il Nat Geog Mag 124:388-411 S '63
They know the wild in wildlife. I. Petite. il Audubon Mag 66:20-5 Ja '64

Bibliography

Books in review; Wildlife under siege. J. A. Davis, jr. Natur Hist 73:4+ D '64

WILDLIFE conservation
Animals in jeopardy. G. Durrell. il Holiday 34:153-8 N '63
Another Noah's ark for New York; wildlife survival centers. F. Osborn. il N Y Times Mag p24-5+ O 27 '63
Controlling the controllers. Nat Parks Mag 39:20 Ja '65
Early conservation and the golden era of trout fishing; excerpts from This wonderful world of trout. C. K. Fox. il Am For 70: 38-41+ Ja '64
Ebb of winter. J. P. Jackson. il Am For 70: 14-15+ Mr '64
Guardians not gardeners. Liv Wildn 83:2 Spring '63
Key to nature; address, August 1962. R. E. Carlson. il Recreation 56:64-6+ F '63
Natural history chapter. S. L. Udall. Liv Wildn 83:24 Spring '63
Needs for the future; New York state. A. MacBain. il Field & S 68:104+ Jl '63
Or they perish. J. Stuart. il Am For 69: 18-20 D '63
Platform for American conservation. Am For 69:33-44 My; 30-1 Je '63
Preparing for tomorrow; African outlook on the preservation of wildlife. P. M. Olindo. il Natur Hist 73:60-4 Je '64
Rampart Dam: a wildlife catastrophe for nothing? G. H. Gillelan. il Outdoor Life 134:14 15+ D '64
Rocky Mountain animals: paradise replenished. il Holiday 34:42-9 Ag '63
To save wildlife and aid us, too. S. L. Udall. il N Y Times Mag p44-5+ S 15 '63
What good is opossum? W. S. Boardman. Nat Parks Mag 38:19 Je '64
Wildlife headquarters; New York state's small-marsh program. A. MacBain. il Field & S 67:112+ F '63
Wildlife management in the national parks. S. A. Cain and others. il Liv Wildn 83:11-19 Spring '63
Wildlife protective measures. P. M. Tilden. Natur Hist 72:67-8 Je '63
See also
Animals—Protection
Bird sanctuaries
Birds—Protection
Game protection
Wildlife sanctuaries
World wildlife fund

Anecdotes, facetiae, satire, etc.

Asphalt jungle. R. G. G. Price. il Atlan 213: 116+ My '64

WILDLIFE control. See Animal populations—Control

WILDLIFE management. See Game preserves

WILDLIFE photographs. See Animals—Photographs

WILDLIFE photography. See Photography of animals

WILDLIFE populations. See Animal populations

WILDLIFE research. See Zoological research

WILDLIFE sanctuaries
Cat-catching in Topock slough; Havasu Lake national wildlife refuge. il Sunset 132:28 Mr '64
Desert sanctuary: Maricopa County, Ariz. I. Smith. il Nat Parks Mag 37:15-17 S '63
Give-away planned in Hawaii; Hawaiian Islands national wildlife refuge. C. W. Buchheister. Audubon Mag 66:18 Ja '64
Great swamp fights for survival; Morris County, N.J. C. Peet. il Am For 69:24-6+ Mr '63; Same abr. with title They love their swamp. Sci Digest 54:83-6 Ag '63
How the Great Swamp of New Jersey was saved. J. Gale. il Nat Parks Mag 37:10-14 Ag '63

WILDLIFE sanctuaries—*Continued*
Land of mysterious waters; Wakulla Springs wildlife sanctuary. A. D. Cruickshank. il Audubon Mag 65:156-63 My '63
Need for nature study; statement at Patuxent wildlife research center. Sci N L 85:310 My 16 '64
Treasure islands of wildlife; Hawaiian Islands national wildlife refuge. D. B. Marshall. il Audubon Mag 66:160-5 My '64
Unexpected refuge; Adams Unexpected refuge, N.J. H. S. Buyukmihci. il Audubon Mag 65:100-1 Mr '63
We welcome three new sanctuaries; Connecticut, Florida and Wisconsin. C. W. Buchheister. Audubon Mag 66:147 My '64
Wetlands lesson on Long Island; town of Hempstead. C. W. Buchheister. Audubon Mag 65:77 Mr '63
Whooping crane: today and tomorrow. R. C. Clement. il Audubon Mag 66:74-7 Mr '64
Wild swans risk crash landings for corn; whistling swans, Shiawassee national wildlife refuge. P. Innis. il Audubon Mag 66: 304-5 S '64
Wilds at the city's doorstep; Great Swamp wilderness of marshland and forest, Morris County, N.J. il N Y Times Mag p92-4 My 17 '64
See also
Bird sancturaries
Okefenokee national wildlife refuge
WILDLIFE service. See United States—Fish and wildlife service
WILDLIFE survival center. See New York zoological park
WILDMAN, John Hazard
Song before morning. Commonweal 79:370 D 20 '63
Weekly Easter; poem. Cath World 199:215 Jl '64
WILEDEN, A. F.
Family and the community; excerpts from address. por Recreation 58:32 Ja '65
WILENSKY, Ronald
Hi-fi shutoff. Pop Electr 18:50-1+ Je '63
WILENTZ, Elias S.
Myth of the melting pot. Nation 197:186-7 S 28 '63
WILENTZ, Theodore
American bookselling in the 1960's; excerpts from American reading public. por Pub W 183:42-50 Je 17 '63
WILES, Kimball
High school of the future; excerpt from The changing curriculum of the American high school. Sch & Soc 91:32-6 Ja 26 '63
WILEY, Charles W.
(ed) See Ngo-dinh-Diem. Diem from the grave
WILEY, Farida A.
Geological jaunt. New Yorker 40:35 My 9 '64
Miss Wiley reaccompanied. New Yorker 39: 41-3 N 9 '63
WILEY, Marcia
Harborside in California. Yachting 113:62-7 My '63
Waterfront news. See issues of Yachting
(ed) See Adams, H. Yachting interviews
WILEY, Ralph H.
Spondee; a design for predicted log contests. Motor B 111:74+ Ap '63
WILGOSH, L. See Zubek, J. P. jt. auth.
WILHELM, Eugene J. Jr
Sequoia of South America. il Nat Parks Mag 37:8-10 D '63
WILHELMSEN, Frederick D.
Forces at work in today's Spain. America 109:306-14 S 21 '63
Towards a theology of survival. Nat R 17: 17-19 Ja 12 '65
WILKERSON, David
Cross and the switchblade; ed. by J. Sherrill and E. Sherrill. pors Good H 157:49-53+ Jl '63
Preaching the monkey off their backs. il por Time 84:43 Ag 14 '64
WILKES, A.
Inherited male-producing factor in an insect that produces its males from unfertilized eggs. bibliog Science 144:305-7; 145-727 Ap 17, Ag 14 '64
WILKES, Daniel M.
Meet Johnny Foster; reprint. Sci Digest 54: 30-7 S '63
WILKES, Edward T.
Heart murmurs in children. por Parents Mag 39:103+ Ja '64
Tonsillitis. Parents Mag 39:122 My '64
What you should know about anemia. por Parents Mag 38:163-4 S '63
WILKESON, Samuel
Page one news. por Time 82:70 Jl 12 '63
WILKIE, Jane
Loretta Young: the steel butterfly. Good H 156:78-81+ Je '63
WILKIN, Robert N.
Noted jurist says, repeal the Fourteenth amendment. por U S News 57:72-4 Ag 24 '64
WILKINS, Bill
Law of unselfishness. F. Oursler. Read Digest 84:24C F '64
WILKINS, Maurice Hugh Frederick
Molecular configuration of nucleic acids. bibliog Science 140:941-50 My 31 '63
about
He stuck in his thumb and pulled out—DNA! P. Bergstrom. il por Sat R 46:57-8 Mr 2 '63
WILKINS, Roy
After desegregation, what next? por Ebony 18:64-5 S '63
Emphasis on the elections; interview. por U S News 56:61-2+ F 24 '64
Excerpt from testimony. Cong Digest 42:284+ N '63
Negro and the candidates. por Sat R 47: 27-9+ S 26 '64
Negro leader talks tough, target: Harlem hoodlums. por U S News 57:14 Jl 6 '64
Negroes want in. N Y Times Mag p93-4 S 29 '63
Next: a national police force? excerpts from television statements. por U S News 57:44-6 D 7 '64
Two political parties and the Negro vote. McCalls 92:30+ N '64
What now? one Negro leader's answer. por N Y Times Mag p 11+ Ag 16 '64
What the American Negro wants; interview. pors U S News 54:46-52 Ap 29 '63
about
Awful roar. il por Time 82:9-14 Ag 30 '63
Equality is not negotiable. Christian Cent 80:1069 S 4 '63
With new civil-rights law; how Negroes see the future. il por U S News 56:38-9 Je 29 '64
WILKINSON, A. T. S. and others
Toxic residues in soil nine years after treatment with aldrin and heptachlor. Science 143:681-2 F 14 '64
WILKINSON, Bud
Oklahoma-Texas football feud. T. Cohane. il por Look 27:85-7+ O 8 '63
Wails of a winner. il por Time 82:49-50 O 11 '63
WILKINSON, Charles
Basic Bud. il por Time 84:27-8 O 9 '64
WILKINSON, Ernest Leroy
How it is out there. por Time 84:18 Ag 21 '64
WILKINSON, Howard C.
How separate should government and God be? address, January 22, 1963. Vital Speeches 29:337-40 Mr 15 '63
WILKINSON, J. F.
Play-money game that made millions. Sports Illus 19:52-4+ D 2 '63
WILKINSON, Maurice. See Dye, D. L. jt. auth.
WILKINSON, Rupert
Alternative to the city. New Repub 148:22-4 F 2 '63
WILKINSON sword, limited
Blade battle. il Time 85:78 Ja 29 '65
Non-competitive razor blade sets standard; Wilkinson stainless-steel blades. Consumer Bul 46:43 S '63
Now swords are drawn for status. il Bsns W p50-2 F 8 '64
Stainless steel razor blades. il Consumer Rep 28:470-1 O '63
Well fixed for blades. Newsweek 63:67 Je 22 '64
WILKS, Willard E.
Big-solid Saturn hopes discounted. Miss & Roc 14:38 F 10 '64
Martin method cuts silo repair time. Miss & Roc 13:32-3 S 2 '63
WILL, John M.
By ship, the salt of the sea not withstanding. Ann Am Acad 345:81-8 Ja '63
about
Admiral and the opera; sponsorship of the Metropolitan's opening-night Aïda. Q. Eaton. por Opera N 28:16 D 7 '63
WILL
Will in western thought, by V. J. Bourke. Review
Commonweal 80:374 Je 12 '64. J. F. Boler
WILLARD, Charlotte
Alfred Barr: New York forecaster of trends in modern art. Look 27:86-8 Mr 26 '63
WILLARD, Helen D.
Shakespeare in the Harvard Theatre collection. Wilson Lib Bul 38:640-4 Ap '64

WILLARD, Jess
He didn't know the gloves were loaded; excerpt from Million dollar gate; with editorial comment. J. Kearns and O. Fraley. il por Sports Illus 20:4, 48-56 Ja 13 '64
WILLARD, John
Cat and the canary. Criticism
New Yorker 40:94 Ja 23 '65
WILLARD, John C.
Architecture. il Antiques 86:452-6 O '64
WILLE, Wilfred
Legends of a Mexican Plymouth Rock. Américas 16:24-9 N '64
WILLET stained glass studios
Modern-day boom in an Old World art: stained-glass production. il Bsns W p 186-8+ O 17 '64
WILLETS, Tom
Now, a drink from the sea. Motor B 113:90-1+ Ja '64
WILLETT, C. K.
Everything under control in Dixon. Am City 79:112-13 Ap '64
WILLETT, Hurd C.
What kind of winter will it be? por Sci Digest 54:83-9 N '63
Did we guess winter right? il Sci Digest 55:81-3 Je '64
WILLETTE, André Dominic
Christmas rose; poem. America 109:797 D 21 '63
Wartime; poem. America 109:487 O 26 '63
WILLIAM II, German emperor
Emperor's mistakes. H. C. Wolfe. por Sat R 47:65 Ap 11 '64
Kaiser in the Holy Land. T. L. Christie. il pors Sat R 47:42+ Ja 4 '64; Reply. J. Torczyner. 47:41 Ja 25 '64
WILLIAM Carter company. See Carter, William, company
WILLIAM: story. See Burnford, S.
WILLIAMS, Alan Meredith
Carrying on. New Yorker 40:23-4 Jl 4 '64
WILLIAMS, Arthur
Arthur Williams gentleman of leisure. por Recreation 56:305 S '63
WILLIAMS, Barbara C.
Dinners that wait, hurry, warm over or stretch for families on the go. Parents Mag 39:77-9+ S '64
WILLIAMS, Barbara Fischer-. See Fischer-Williams, B.
WILLIAMS, Beth
(ed) Q & Advertising; questions and answers. See issues of McCall's
WILLIAMS, Bret
Rocket ship: poem. Horn Bk 39:96 F '63
WILLIAMS, Byron
Teachers, politics, and politicians. Sr Schol 84:26T Mr 20 '64
WILLIAMS, C. K.
Sleeping over; poem. Poetry 103:364-6 Mr '64
WILLIAMS, Carleton
Constabulary style. Esquire 62:106-7+ N '64
WILLIAMS, Carroll M. See Kafatos, F. C. jt. auth.
WILLIAMS, Charles M.
Senior securities, boon for banks? Harvard Bsns R 41:82-94 Jl '63
WILLIAMS, Cootie
Jazz concerts. W. Balliett. New Yorker 40:100-2 Ap 11 '64
WILLIAMS, D. See Alexander, G. jt. auth.
WILLIAMS, Daniel Day
God's grace and human estrangement. Christian Cent 81:518-19+ Ap 22 '64
Liberal theology reconstructed. Christian Cent 81:1494-6 D 2 '64
WILLIAMS, E. Virginia
What makes a great teacher of classical ballet? Dance Mag 37:20-1 Ag '63
WILLIAMS, Eliza Azelia
Whaling wife; excerpts from One whaling family, ed. by H. Williams. por Am Heritage 15:64-79 Je '64
WILLIAMS, Emlyn
My secret scenes off-stage. por Travel 122:53-5 N '64
WILLIAMS, Ernest W. Jr
Manpower, a prime resource. bibliog f Ann Am Acad 345:122-9 Ja '63
WILLIAMS, Franklin H.
Expanding and protecting human rights throughout the world; statement, July 30, 1964. Dept State Bul 51:418-22 S 21 '64
International human rights year; statement, October 21, 1964. Dept State Bul 51:787-9 N 30 '64
U.N. economic and social council meets at Geneva; statement, July 14 1964. Dept State Bul 51:248-52 Ag 17 '64
U.N. technical assistance program for 1965-66; statement, November 24, 1964. Dept State Bul 51:920-1 D 28 '64
WILLIAMS, George, and Hodges, A. T.
Stretching the street dollar. Am City 78:102-3 O '63
WILLIAMS, Gerhard Mennen
Africa and the world: problems of today and tomorrow; address, August 24, 1963. Dept State Bul 49:432-6 S 16 '63
Africa south of the equator; address, June 18, 1964. Dept State Bul 51:51-4 Jl 13 '64
African issues at the United Nations; address, April 18, 1964. Dept State Bul 50:751-5 My 11 '64
African specter: racial Armageddon. por Nations Bsns 51:72+ D '63
Africa's problems and progress; address, March 1, 1964. Dept State Bul 50:501-6 Mr 30 '64
America's image in Africa; address, November 7, 1964. Dept State Bul 51:730-5 N 23 '64
Assistant Secretary Williams visits west and central Africa; statement, May 8, 1964. Dept State Bul 50:828-9 My 25 '64
Basis of U.S. policy in Africa; address, January 25, 1963. Dept State Bul 48:251-3 F 18 '63
Communism's impact on African nationalism; address, May 13, 1963. Dept State Bul 48:877-81 Je 3 '63
Communist bloc interest in Africa; address, November 18, 1963. Dept State Bul 49:929-32 D 16 '63
Cultural exchange program in Africa: a path to peace; address, December 18, 1962. Dept State Bul 48:67-70 Ja 14 '63
Democracy and the emerging nations of Africa; address, March 14, 1963. Dept State Bul 48:541-5 Ap 8 '63
Developing Africa's human and material resources; address, January 20, 1963. Dept State Bul 48:208-11 F 11 '63
Diplomatic rapport between Africa and the United States; address, April 10, 1964. Dept State Bul 50:698-703 My 4 '64; Same with questions and answers. Ann Am Acad 354:54-64 Jl '64
Emerging nations of Africa; address, March 2, 1963. Dept State Bul 48:457-9 Mr 25 '63
Germany's role in modern Africa; address, May 18, 1963. Dept State Bul 48:901-5 Je 10 '63
New patterns of African trade; address, April 1, 1964. Dept State Bul 50:664-70 Ap 27 '64
Promising trends in Africa; address, February 15, 1964. Dept State Bul 50:370-3 Mr 9 '64
United Nations and the new Africa; address, March 29, 1963. Dept State Bul 48:602-5 Ap 22 '63
Women in the new Africa; address September 24, 1963. Dept State Bul 49:636-9 O 21 '63
WILLIAMS, Greer
Help we need. Atlan 214:112-14 Jl '64
Rockefeller foundation; how it operates. Atlan 213:106-18 Ap '64
WILLIAMS, Hannah
Outdoors in the city's shadow. Natur Hist 72:32-41 My '63
WILLIAMS, Harold L.
If you have trouble getting enough sleep; interview. por U S News 55:76-80 O 28 '63; Same abr. with title Do you have trouble sleeping? Read Digest 84:117-20 Ja '64
WILLIAMS, Harrison A.
Filth we breathe. Sci Digest 53:5-6 My '63
Rapid transit. Nation 196:367-70 My 4 '63
about
People of the week. por U S News 55:15 N 4 '63
WILLIAMS, Harrison A. Jr
Excerpt from debate, August 17, 1964. Cong Digest 44:21+ Ja '65
WILLIAMS, Harry Abbott
Cambridge objectors. il Time 83:78 Mr 6 '64
WILLIAMS, Hollis R.
Small watershed projects. por Recreation 57:276-8 Je '64
WILLIAMS, Hugh, and Williams, Margaret
Irregular verb to love. Criticism
America 109:396 O 5 '63
New Yorker 39:94 S 28 '63
Newsweek 62:60 S 30 '63
Theatre Arts il 47:10-11 D '63
Time il 82:66 S 27 '63
WILLIAMS, J. Paul
Cutting, permissive or controlled. Sch & Soc 91:306-7 O 19 '63
WILLIAMS, Joan
Going ahead; story. Sat Eve Post 237:58-60 D 12 '64
Life book review. Life 56:12 Ap 3 '64
WILLIAMS, Joel
Status report on the Statistics coordinating project. ALA Bul 58:551-3 Je '64

WILLIAMS, John
Music to my ears; William's debut. I. Kolodin. Sat R 46:34 D 21 '63

WILLIAMS, John A.
Literary ghetto. por Sat R 46:21+ Ap 20 '63
Negro in literature today. por Ebony 18:73-6 S '63
This is my country too. por Holiday 36:30-3+ Ag; 58-9+ S; 4+ O '64

WILLIAMS, John Bell
Mr Blatnik plans a purge. D. Rapoport. Reporter 31:32-4 D 3 '64

WILLIAMS, John G.
Freeing flamingos from anklets of death. Nat Geog Mag 124:934-44 D '63

WILLIAMS, John J.
As one good friend to another. .; excerpts from Congressional record. Nat R 14:348 My 7 '63
Crime-hunting senator talks about the mess in Washington; interview. por U S News 55:43-7 N 25 '63
Excerpt from address, January 17, 1963. Cong Digest 42:148+ My '63
More on the case of Adam Clayton Powell; statement. por U S News 54:50 F 18 '63
That lingering aroma. Time 84:21 S 11 '64

about

Favors for Bobby Baker, Jimmy Hoffa's union? por U S News 56:14 Ap 27 '64
Incorruptible John Williams; the conscience of the Senate. J. Daniel. por Read Digest 84:105-10 My '64
Lone-wolf guardian of federal morality. H. B. Meyers. il por Fortune 69:126-9+ Je '64
Senator Williams, public eye. F. W. Collins. il por N Y Times Mag p 18+ F 9 '64

WILLIAMS, John K.
How well-adjusted are you? excerpt from Wisdom of your subconscious mind. Read Digest 85:136-7 S '64

WILLIAMS, Jon L. See Thomas, D. R. jt. auth.

WILLIAMS, Jonathan
Poetry chronicle. R. Howard. Poetry 102:183-4 Je '63

WILLIAMS, Keith
Marrakesh. Atlan 215:112-13+ Ja '65
Real Arabs. Harper 226:64-6+ F '63

WILLIAMS, Lawrence
To Mary with love; story. Good H 158:92-3 F '64

WILLIAMS, Lloyd
On becoming a pro. Pop Phot 52:117+ Ap '63

WILLIAMS, Louis B. See Breyere, E. J. jt. auth.

WILLIAMS, Margaret. See Williams, H. jt. auth.

WILLIAMS, Marion Black
Daisies do tell. Pop Gard 14:42+ Jl '63

WILLIAMS, Martin
Anthology of anthologies. Sat R 47:54 D 26 '64
Armstrong before Dolly. Sat R 47:77+ O 17 '64
Basic LP jazz library. Am Rec G 30:890-1 My '64
Bigger Monk and bigger Duke. Sat R 47:63-4 My 16 '64
Billie Holiday: triumphant decline. Sat R 47:68+ O 31 '64
Bossa from both sides of the border. Sat R 46:57 F 23 '63
Coltrane triumphant. Sat R 48:73-4 Ja 16 '65
Critic as composer. Sat R 47:59 Mr 28 '64
Critics' choice indeed. Sat R 47:64 Je 27 '64
Ella and others. Sat R 47:51 N 28 '64
Ellington era. Sat R 46:59-60 N 16 '63
Gospel at the box office. Sat R 46:41 Ag 31 '63
In praise of Jack Teagarden! Sat R 47:114-15 Mr 14 '64
In the wake of Parker. Sat R 46:71 My 11 '63
Krupa collected. Sat R 47:70 Ja 11 '64
Last trip up the river. Sat R 47:46-7 Je 13 '64
Mid-month recordings. Sat R 46:96 Mr 16 '63
Mostly modernists. Sat R 46:56 Je 15; 78 S 28; 32 D 14 '63; 47:54 F 15; 66-7 Ap 25; 72-3 S 26 '64
Players and popularizers. Sat R 47:45 Ag 22 '64
School of Hawkins. Sat R 47:46-7 Jl 11 '64
Tenacious craft of Horace Silver. Sat R 46:52-3 S 14 '63
Thelonious Monk. Sat R 46:32-3+ Ap 13 '63

—and others
Month's jazz. See issues of American record guide
(ed) See Solal, M. Conversation with Martial Solal

WILLIAMS, Mary Lou
Prayerful one. il pors Time 83:58+ F 21 '64
Profiles. W. Balliett. por New Yorker 40:52-4+ My 2 '64

WILLIAMS, Miller
For J. W. on his marriage in the faith; poem. Poetry 102:376 S '63
For Lucy on the twelfth month; poem. Sat R 46:12 Ag 31 '63
Funeral; poem. Sat R 46:106 O 12 '63
On the death of the veteran; poem. Sat R 46:36 Jl 20 '63
On the slaying of a music student in Philadelphia by teen-agers; poem. Sat R 46:47 Ag 24 '63
To an idealist sitting in; poem. Sat R 46:38 Ag 10 '63

WILLIAMS, Mona
Fresh fresh fresh eye. Writer 76:13-14+ Ag '63

WILLIAMS, Murat W.
Health and social progress in Latin America; address, October 10, 1964. Dept State Bul 51:747-51 N 23 '64

WILLIAMS, Nancy Lace (Quirk)
Africa's uphill struggle for maturity; ed. by A. Eisenberg and H. Eisenberg. pors Ladies Home J 80:38+ O '63

WILLIAMS, Ned
Ned Williams and dance company; Sheridan square playhouse. J. Maskey. Dance Mag 38:28 Ag '64

WILLIAMS, Norman, Jr
Zoning and planning decisions. See issues of American city

WILLIAMS, Paul R.
If I were young today. por Ebony 18:56 Ag '63

WILLIAMS, Percy V.
School dropouts; summary of study. NEA J 52:10-12 F '63

WILLIAMS, Phil
Gas detection aboard boats. Motor B 112:78+ N '63

WILLIAMS, Phyllis
No humdrum vegetables at her house! ed. by R. Behnke. Farm J 88:90-1+ Mr '64

WILLIAMS, Ralph C.
Warm greetings on cold days. Audubon Mag 65:378-80 N '63

WILLIAMS, Raymond
British elections. Nation 199:154-7 S 28 '64

WILLIAMS, Raymond E.
Trustee's role in the new era of library cooperation. ALA Bul 57:559-60 Je '63
Librarian-board relationship to be defined in Minneapolis. Library J 88:2462 Je 15 '63

WILLIAMS, Robert Franklin
Red Chinese American Negro. W. Worthy. Esquire 62:132+ O '64
View from Harlem. A. B. Spellman. Nation 198:656-7 Je 29 '64

WILLIAMS, Robert H.
Sex, Tallahassee. New Repub 150:5 My 23 '64

WILLIAMS, Robley C.
Macromolecules. Science 141:934-5 S 6 '63

WILLIAMS, Roger
Roger Williams Bible. P. W. Schmidtchen. il pors Hobbies 69:106-7 Ja '65

WILLIAMS, Roger J.
Key to health: your heredity; interview. ed. by F. R. Schreiber. por Sci Digest 53:30-9 Ap '63

WILLIAMS, Samuel T.
Why U.S. is losing in Vietnam, an inside story; interview. por U S News 57:62-4+ N 9 '64

WILLIAMS, Simon
Negotiating investment in emerging countries. Harvard Bsns R 43:89-99 Ja '65

WILLIAMS, Stanley M. See Gunn, S. R. jt. auth.

WILLIAMS, T. Harry
Gray and blue grass roots. Sat R 46:47-8 N 16 '63

WILLIAMS, Tennessee
Mama's old stucco house; story. Esquire 63:86-8 Ja '65

about

Glass menagerie. Criticism
Nation 199:60 Ag 10 '64
Innocence of Tennessee Williams. M. Magid. Commentary 35:34-43 Ja '63
Milk train doesn't stop here anymore. Criticism
America 108:449 Mr 30 '63
Commonweal 77:515-17 F 8 '63
Nat R 14:291+ Ap 9 '63
Nation 196:106 F 2 '63
New Repub 148:27 F 2 '63
Newsweek 63:70 Ja 13 '64
Reporter 28:48 Ap 25 '63
Sat R 46:20-1 F 2 '63
Sat R 47:22 Ja 18 '64
Theatre Arts il(p 12) 47:66 F '63
Time 83:52 Ja 10 '64

WILLIAMS, Tennessee—about—*Continued*
No time like the present; excerpts from issues of Time magazine. il pors Esquire 59: 58-9 Ap '63
Tennessee Williams: a new direction? W. R. Mueller. Christian Cent 81:1271-2 O 14 '64
WILLIAMS, Thomas
Another country, another time; story. Sat Eve Post 236:38-41 My 25 '63
Old dancers; story. Sat Eve Post 237:56-8 N 14 '64
Skier's progress; story. New Yorker 38:34-40 F 2 '63
WILLIAMS, Thomas William
Whaling wife; excerpts from One whaling family, ed. by H. Williams. E. A. Williams. il por Am Heritage 15:64-79 Je '64
WILLIAMS, Van Zandt
Optics, an action program. Science 146:1606+ D 18 '64
WILLIAMS, Vaughan
Coates, V. W. and Morton Gould on his mettle. J. Diether. Am Rec G 30:1032 Jl '64
V.W. at his most lovable. J. Diether. por Am Rec G 30:876 My '64
WILLIAMS, Verne O.
Man-made drouth threatens Everglades National Park. il Audubon Mag 65:290-4 S '63
WILLIAMS, Vernon
Just an average lawyer. H. Rezatto. il Read Digest 82:145-8+ My '63
WILLIAMS, W. T.
Computer as a botanist. Sat R 46:44-5 Je 1 '63
WILLIAMS, William Appleman
Cuba: issues and alternatives. Ann Am Acad 351:72-80 Ja '64
President and his critics. Nation 196:226-8+ Mr 16 '63
WILLIAMS, William B.
William B. Williams: the man who runs the Make believe ballroom. il pors Look 27: 78a-78c F 12 '63
WILLIAMS, William Carlos
Cézanne; Moral; poems. Poetry 103:253-4 Ja '64
about
Doctor Williams and tradition. A. Stephens. Poetry 101:360-2 F '63
First and last things. J. Dickey. Poetry 103: 321-4 F '64
He's dead. il por Time 81:47 Mr 15 '63
Legacy of three poets. J. Jacobsen. Commonweal 78:189-92 My 10 '63
Obituary
Nation 196:230 Mr 16 '63
Pub W 183:37 Mr 18 '63
William Carlos Williams. J. E. Slate. Nat R 14:423 My 21 '63
William Carlos Williams as one of us. H. Carruth. New Repub 148:30-2 Ap 13 '63
William Carlos Williams, 1883-1963. J. Ciardi. Sat R 46:18+ Mr 23 '63
William Carlos Williams: in memoriam. H. Kenner. Nat R 14:237 Mr 26 '63
WILLIAMSBURG, Va.
Colonial Christmas. H. W. Dengler. il Am For 70:6-7+ D '64
On the go: shoot history in Virginia. L. Barry. il Pop Phot 52:12+ Ap '63
See also
Colonial Williamsburg garden symposium
WILLIAMSBURG student burgesses. See Forums (discussion and debate)
WILLIAMSON, Alice H.
Herbs on your gift packages. Horticulture 42:30-1 D '64
Win blue ribbons with dried herbs. Horticulture 42:26-7 F '64
WILLIAMSON, Audrey
Albert Finney. Theatre Arts 47:30-2+ O '63
Dramatic accent: singing-actor. Hi Fi 14:53-5+ Mr '64
WILLIAMSON, Isabel K.
Observing the eclipse in Quebec. Sky & Tel 25:204-5 Ap '63
WILLIAMSON, Ruth Lundgren
Companionway (cont of) Out of the galley. See issues of Motor boating
Out of the galley. See issues of Motor boating
WILLIAMSON, Shirley Porter
Light touch. NEA J 52:11 Ap '63
WILLIAMSON, Stanley M. and Koch, C. W.
Xenon tetrafluoride: reaction with aqueous solutions. bibliog Science 139:1046-7 Mr 15 '63
WILLIAMSON, Susan
Girl talk; questions and answers. Seventeen 23:132-3+ My '64
WILLIAMSTON, N.C.
Letter from Williamston. H. Cox. Christian Cent 80:1516-18 D 4 '63
WILLIAMSTOWN, Mass.
See also
Sterling and Francine Clark art institute
WILLIG, John M.
Fifteen letters: most popular game. N Y Times Mag p22+ D 15 '63
Happiness is Mr Lynch's office. N Y Times Mag p50+ O 18 '64
Off-track betting. from the horse's mouth. N Y Times Mag p55+ N 3 '63
WILLINGHAM, Calder
Way it isn't done: notes on the distress of Norman Mailer. Esquire 60:306-8 D '63
What star so humble: story. New Yorker 40: 30-1 Ja 16 '65
WILLIS, Benjamin Coppage
Education the year round: the Dunbar school of Chicago. Atlan 215:83-6 Ja '65
about
Boycotting Ben. Newsweek 62:60 N 4 '63
Chicago close-up: political side of the race issue. il por U S News 55:72-3 N 4 '63
Chicago school chief center of race controversy. por U S News 55:26 O 21 '63
De facto superintendent il por Time 82:56 N 1 '63
Education of Big Ben. il por Time 82:48 Ag 30 '63
Embattled boss of Chicago's schools. W. R. Shelton. il por Sat Eve Post 236:26-7 O 19 '63
Man who said boo. Newsweek 62:94 O 28 '63
Willis resigns in Chicago. por Sr Schol 83: 1T O 25 '63
WILLIS, Edwin E.
New look at U.S. reds; interview. por Nations Bsns 52:58-60+ My '64
WILLIS, J. S.
Potassium and sodium content of tissues of hamsters and ground squirrels during hibernation. bibliog Science 146:546-7 O 23 '64
WILLIS, Jack
Reporter at large. A. J. Liebling. New Yorker 39:95-8+ Ja 11 64
WILLIS, Priscilla D.
Playing the ponies with a pair of experts. Harper 228:48-50 Mr '64; Same abr. Read Digest 84:240-1+ My '64
WILLIS, William
One man against the sea. pors Sat Eve Post 237:36-8+ Ap 18 '64; Same abr. Read Digest 85:134-9 Jl '64
about
Last fling? Newsweek 62:56 N 25 '63
WILLISTON, Samuel
Yankee Socrates. Time 81:65 Mr 1 '63
WILLMARK service system
Willmark is watching; shopping analysts. il Time 81:94 Ap 5 '63
WILLOW
Borer-resistant pussy willows. H. Rohrbach. il Horticulture 41:502-3 O '63
Nature note. Sci N L 85:140 F 29 '64
Three trees with willowy leaves. il Sunset 132:263 Mr '64
WILLOW-leaf pittosporum. See Pittosporum
WILLRICH, Ted L.
Lagoons, where and how to. Suc Farm 61: 38-9+ Jl '63
Terraces for modern farming. Suc Farm 62: 36-7 Jl '64
WILLS, C. H. and company
Special-interest cars: Wills Sainte Claire. K. Caldwell. il Motor T 16:82 N '64
WILLS, Garry
Art of not writing novels. Nat R 16:31-3 Ja 14 '64
Care and feeding of Moloch. Nat R 14:285-7 Ap 9 '63
Eric Hoffer's true beliefs. Nat R 14:502+ Je 18 '63
Journalists report the council. Nat R 15:572-4 D 31 '63
Theater. Nat R 16:458-9 Je 2 '64
What color is God? Nat R 14:408-14+ My 21 '63
Who is imitating whom? Nat R 16:500-2, 696 Je 16, Ag 11 '64
Who will overcome? Nat R 16:818-20 S 22 '64; Correction. 16:881 O 6 '64
about
Catholic freedom and Mr Wills. D. Callahan. Commonweal 80:607-9 S 4 '64; Reply with rejoinder. G. Wills. 81:74 O 9 '64
WILLS, J. B.
Hobbyist writes on Ghent azaleas. Horticulture 41:190 Ap '63
WILLS, J. Walter, sr
Tribute to a business pioneer. il pors Ebony 19:42-4+ Jl '64
WILLS, Jesse E.
Winter feeders in Nashville. Audubon Mag 65:46-7 Ja '63

WILLS, Maurice Morning
World's greatest diamond thief. L. Robinson. il pors Ebony 18:35-6+ My '63

WILLS
Gentle setters sit out their stay of execution; Ida Capers dogs. il Life 54:41 Mr 22 '63
It's a dog's life; will of Miss Ida Capers stipulating that her dogs be put to death. il Time 81:23 Mr 15 '63
Last caprice; excerpts. R. S. Menchin. McCalls 90:126-7+ S '63
Notes and comment; bequests as expressions of interests and personalities of donors. New Yorker 40:19 Jl 11 '64
Personal business. Bsns W p 105 Ja 18 '64
Senate's richest man left an outdated will. U S News 54:11 F 18 '63
What it means to forget about a will; interview. R. A. Wormser. il U S News 54:68-73 Mr 4 '63
What's the simplest way to handle a will? Bet Hom & Gard 41:12+ F '63
Will & two ways; estate of S. K. East. Time 82:64 N 22 '63
Your will: why, what & how. il Changing T 17:25-9 Ap '63
See also
Inheritance

Anecdotes, facetiae, satire, etc.

Heaven had better be good; excerpt from Guess whose hair I'm wearing. H. Dolson. il Harper 226:41-4 Ap '63; Same abr. with title Where there's a will. Read Digest 83: 132-4 S '63
Spirit of conservation; editorial. Am For 69: 11 F '63; Discussion. 69:2 Ap '63

WILLSON, F. M. G.
Rhodesias and Nyasaland. Cur Hist 46:148-55+ Mr '64

WILLYS-Overland motors, incorporated
Special-interest cars; Willys-Knight. D. Laughton. il Motor T 16:83 N '64

WILMER, Harry A.
Odyssey of a psychotherapist. Science 145: 902-3 Ag 28 '64

WILMERDING, John
New look at Robert Salmon. Antiques 87: 89-93 Ja '65

WILMETTE, Ill.
We have no Negro problem; suburb with few Negroes. Christian Cent 82:70 Ja 20 '65

WILMINGTON, Del.
Employee handbook promotes good parking relations. il Am City 79:140 O '64

Lighting

Border-to-border lighting. R. A. Mitchell. il Am City 79:138 Ap '64

WILMORE, Gayraud S. jr
Mood ebony. Christian Cent 82:82 Ja 20 '65
New Negro and the church. Christian Cent 80:168-71 F 6 '63

WILSDORF, Doris Kuhlmann-. See Kuhlmann-Wilsdorf, D.

WILSDORF, Heinz G. F. See Kuhlmann-Wilsdorf, D. jt. auth.

WILSON, Adrian
Adrian Wilson: designer-printer at Tuscany Alley. P. A. Bennett. il por Pub W 185:66-9+ Ap 6 '64

WILSON, Angus
Merrie England. Commentary 37:74-5 Je '64
Party of one. Holiday 35:12+ Je '64

WILSON, Anne
Anne Wilson and company at 92nd street Y. M. Marks. Dance Mag 37:33+ D '63

WILSON, Benjamin J. and Wilson, C. H.
Toxin from aspergillus flavus: production on food materials of a substance causing tremors in mice. bibliog Science 144:177-8 Ap 10 '64

WILSON, Celianna I.
Professional internship: a program and a proposal. bibliog Library J 88:2201-5 Je 1 '63

WILSON, Charles H.
Critics of the schools never die, either. Sat R 47:51-3+ Je 20 '64

WILSON, Charles Morrow
After hours. Harper 226:28-32 My '63
Lamplight inauguration. Am Heritage 15:80-6 D '63

WILSON, Charles R.
Ugly American undergraduate; adaptation of address, December 7, 1963. Sch & Soc 92: 351-4 N 28 '64

WILSON, Christina H. See Wilson, B. J. jt. auth.

WILSON, Doris
We found more than mummies. House B 105: 204-5 My '63

WILSON, Edith (Bolling) Galt
End of a friendship; with memorandum by E. M. House. C. Seymour. il por Am Heritage 14:7-9+ Ag '63
When the cheering stopped. by G. Smith. Review
Time por 83:99-100 Mr 6 '64

WILSON, Edmund
Books (cont) New Yorker 39:139-42+ F 23; 174-80 Mr 23; 165-76+ Ap 20 '63
By dark cocytus' shore; poem. New Yorker 40:70 D 26 '64
Reporter at large. New Yorker 40:63-6+ N 14; 64-6+ N 21; 143-4+ N 28 '64

about

Mr Wilson and the cold war. W. Sheed. Commonweal 79:434-5 Ja 10 '64
People are talking about. . . por Vogue 142: 198-9 S 1 '63
Please Mr Rip Van Winkle, wake up some more. J. Dos Passos. Nat R 16:71-4 Ja 28 '64
Some deductions. D. T. Bazelon. Commentary 38:67-8 Ag '64
To coin a phrase. por Newsweek 61:88 F 25 '63
Wilson. E. Perényi. por Esquire 60:80-5+ Jl '63

WILSON, Edward O.
Pheromones. Sci Am 208:100-6+ My '63

WILSON, Ellen Louise (Axson)
Priceless gift: the love letters of Woodrow Wilson and Eleanor Axson Wilson, ed. by E. W. McAdoo. Review
Nat R 14:203-4 Mr 12 '63. H. Woodward

WILSON, Eugene S.
World look at education. Sat R 47:77-8 Mr 21 '64

WILSON, Francis G.
Some cities are abnormal. Nat R 16:74 Ja 28 '64

WILSON, Frank
What the judge said to Hoffa. U S News 56: 114 Mr 23 '64

WILSON, George MacLean
Say Olympia. il Newsweek 63:74 Mr 9 '64

WILSON, Gill Robb
Airman's world. See issues of Flying

WILSON, Guy C.
To aid hospitalized driver. B. Ruskauff. il por Motor B 111:134-5 F '63

WILSON, H. W, company
Committee on Wilson indexes: how it works. E. B. Colburn. il ALA Bul 59:35-6+ Ja '65
H. W. Wilson foundation renews scholarship program. Library J 89:830+ F 15 '64
Library/USA at the New York world's fair. il Wilson Lib Bul 38:380-1 Ja '64
Lighthouse. See issues of Wilson library bulletin
Results of a scholarship program. J. Ramsey. Wilson Lib Bul 37:571+ Mr '63
Rule, Britannia; visiting British librarians; with list of names. il Wilson Lib Bul 38: 364-6 D '63
Wilson scholarship program renewed. il Wilson Lib Bul 38:521+ Mr '64
See also
Readers' guide to periodical literature

WILSON, Harold
Britain 1965; address, December 16, 1964. Vital Speeches 31:201-8 Ja 15 '65
Britain's policy if labour wins. Atlan 212:61-5 O '63
British Prime Minister visits Washington; exchange of greetings, December 7, 1964. Dept State Bul 51:902-3 D 28 '64
Needs for planned incomes; address, October 26, 1964. Vital Speeches 31:66-7 N 15 '64
New Britain and the Atlantic community; address, March 3, 1964. Vital Speeches 30: 436-9 My 1 '64
Relationship of Britain and United States; address. April 1, 1963. Vital Speeches 29: 418-21 My 1 '63
Wilson defines British socialism. por N Y Times Mag p32+ S 15 '63

about

Alliance: time for guidelines. il por Newsweek 64:17 D 21 '64
And now there's the anti-Establishment. C. Hussey. il N Y Times Mag p42+ My 3 '64
Britain: if labor wins. il por Fortune 69: 51-2+ Je '64
Britain veers left. Nat R 14:267-8 Ap 9 '63
Britain: Wilson's close shave. il por Sr Schol 85:12-16 D 9 '64
Britain's Prime Minister in waiting. por U S News 54:16 F 25 '63
British elections. R. Presthus. Nation 198:480-3 My 11 '64
British election: can Labor win? por Newsweek 64:44+ S 28 '64

WILSON, Harold—about—*Continued*
Choice Britain is making. il por U S News 57:45 O 19 '64
Cruel to lepers; Prime Minister's attack on member for Smethwick. il por Time 84:53 N 13 '64
Elegant anachronism vs. one-man band. S. Gruson. il pors N Y Times Mag p34+ O 11 '64
Great Britain: science and labor's squeakin. V. K. McElheny. Science 146:506-8 O 23 '64
Harold Wilson, on top at last. il por Bsns W p 151 O 24 '64
Harold Wilson's Britain. N. MacKenzie. Harper 228:73-6+ F '64
Harold Wilson's dilemma. A. Lejeune. Nat R 16:970 N 3 '64
Harold Wilson's new look. A. Lejeune. Nat R 14:320 Ap 23 '63
Honorable government. il por Time 84:24-5 N 6 '64
If Britain votes Socialist, Labor's Wilson sets goals. U S News 55:21 O 14 '63
If Wilson wins, Socialist plans for Britain. il por U S News 54:19 Ap 15 '63
Interesting Mr Wilson. S. Alsop. por Sat Eve Post 237:14 D 12 '64
Into battle. por Time 82:30 N 22 '63
Is it to be a little England? il por U S News 57:36-8 D 14 '64
Labor takes action. il Sr Schol 85:9-10 N 11 '64
Labor's love won, by a conservative edge. il por Newsweek 64:56+ O 26 '64
Labour's first few weeks. A. Burnet. New Repub 151:11-12 N 14 '64
Labour's new leader. H. Massingham. New Repub 148:17 Mr 2 '63
Left vs. right in Britain's Labor party. por U S News 54:20 F 18 '63
Letter from London. M. Panter-Downes. New Yorker 39:145 My 25; 40:152-6 O 24; 159-60+ D 12 '64; 60-2 Ja 2 '65
Letter from London; annual conference. M. Panter-Downes. New Yorker 39:208+ O 19 '63
Letter from London; Profumo case. M. Panter-Downes. New Yorker 39:66-9 Je 29 '63
Little Harold knocks at No. ten. T. Green. il pors Life 54:37-8 Ap 12 '63
Lost leader; concerning House of commons debate on the Profumo case. il por Time 81:22-5 Je 28 '63
Next British prime minister? por Sr Schol 82:18 Mr 13 '63
On target; concerning speech at the Labour party's convention. Nation 197:249 O 26 '63
One-man band. E. J. Hughes. por Newsweek 64:59 O 26 '64
Other election. por Sr Schol 85:23 S 30 '64
Other Harold. il por Time 81:29-30 F 22 '63
People matter. Newsweek 63:44+ Mr 16 '64
People of the week. por U S News 54:20 Ap 8 '63; 56:14 Mr 9 '64
Return of the Socialists: shaky course for Britain. il por U S News 57:65-7 O 26 '64
Road to Jerusalem; annual conference. il pors Time 82:34-8 O 11 '63
Score so far. il por Newsweek 64:24+ D 28 '64
Search for an heir. por Newsweek 61:33+ F 4 '63
Sharp left for Britain. A. Lejeune. Nat R 16: 1144 D 29 '64
Socialist who will call the signals in Britain now. il por U S News 57:24 O 26 '64
Strange death of Tory England. J. Mander. Commentary 38:41-5 D '64
Taxicab majority. il por Time 84:32+ O 23 '64
Ten days that shook the Exchequer. C. Brogan. il por Nat R 17:57-8 Ja 26 '65
Under increasing fire: Britain's Wilson. por U S News 57:19 D 7 '64
Unions get new role in Britain. Bsns W p95-6 O 24 '64
U.S. and Britain: LBJ calls the tune. por U S News 57:25-6 D 21 '64
U.S. stake in Britain's election. por U S News 57:55-6 O 12 '64
Weekend in Washington. il por Time 81:32 Ap 12 '63
Wilson: Labor's gray mystery. il pors Newsweek 61:42-4+ Ap 15 '63; Same abr. with title Harold Wilson: Britain's question mark. Read Digest 83:109-13 O '63
Wilson seems shoo-in. por Bsns W p28-9 Je 22 '63
Wilson stirs up a whirlwind. S. Gruson. por(p 1) N Y Times Mag p34+ D 6 '64
Wilson's attempt to export a problem. Life 57:4 N 6 '64
Wilson's problem: staying in control. il Bsns W p 150-2+ O 24 '64
Wooing the middle class. il por Time 81:35 F 15 '63

WILSON, Harriet
Art as education. il Sch Arts 63:30-2 D '63

WILSON, Helen Van Pelt
African violets are sheer delight. Flower Grower 51:22-3 O '64
Beauty and the abstract. Flower Grower 50: 22-4+ D '63
Church gardens. Flower Grower 50:36-9+ Ap '63
I discovered ferns. Flower Grower 50:38-40+ Mr '63
Lights for your garden. Flower Grower 50:8+ N '63
My wide world of house plants. Flower Grower 51:17-19 N '64
Northern pointers. See issues of Flower grower
(ed) Truth & poetry; quotations. See issues of Flower grower
—and Bell, Léonie
Winter fragrance. Flower Grower 51:39+ Ja '64

WILSON, Hugh
Helicopter sightseeing. Travel 121:55-7 My '64
Luxembourg fete. Travel 119:31-3 F '63

WILSON, J. B.
No weak spots. Am City 78:153+ My '63

WILSON, J. Finley
J. Finley Wilson, fraternal orator. M. H. Boulware. bibliog por Negro Hist Bul 27: 67-8 D '63

WILSON, J. Fred
Film trips: excursions unlimited. Sr Schol 85:21T Ja 21 '65

WILSON, James Q.
Exploiting urban decay. Christian Cent 81: 195-7 F 12 '64; Reply. C. C. Ham. 81:774 Je 10 '64

WILSON, James W.
I learned about flying from that. Flying 75: 81 Ag '64

WILSON, Jane
Sunny fragrance; exhibition at Manhattan's Tibor de Nagy gallery. il por Time 81:78 My 24 '63
Where do we go from here? F. Getlein. New Repub 149:34-5 N 2 '63

WILSON, Janet A. See Steinberg, A. G. jt. auth.

WILSON, John A. R
Corporal punishment? NEA J 52:18+ S '63
Your child's intelligence; reprint. Todays Health 41:45 Ag '63

WILSON, John D.
Outlook for business; address, December 5, 1963. Vital Speeches 30:169-72 Ja 1 '64

WILSON, John Gideon
Obituary
Pub W 184:41 S 23 '63

WILSON, John S.
For Bach, a bacchanal in swing. Hi Fi 14: 67-8 Ja '64
Jazz. See issues of High fidelity
Kook from Madagascar. Hi Fi 14:43-5+ My '64
Lighter side. See issues of High fidelity
Major phases of the latest Ellington. Hi Fi 14:114 Ap '64
Peter Nero: an expression of impatience. Hi Fi 13:57-9+ F '63
Real New Orleans sound. Hi Fi 13:59-61+ S '63
Theatre on discs. See issues of Theatre arts

WILSON, John Tuzo
Are the continents drifting? UNESCO Courier 16:4-11 O '63
Continental drift; with biographical sketch. Sci Am 208:38, 86-100 bibliog(p200) Ap '63
On the history of science; excerpts from address. Sat R 47:50-1 My 2 '64
Pattern of uplifted islands in the main ocean basins. bibliog Science 139:592-4 F 15 '63

WILSON, José
Corkscrew; champagne complexes. House & Gard 123:130+ F '63
—and Leaman, Arthur
Going places, finding things in Ireland. House & Gard 125:142-9 Ap '64

WILSON, Kemmons
Single standard for travelers. il Bsns W p 114+ N 16 '63

WILSON, Kirke
Conservation or recreation: our swarming national parks. Nation 198:391-5 Ap 20 '64

WILSON, Lee, and company
Man who has everything, in Wilson, Ark. S. Freedgood. il Fortune 70:143-7+ Ag '64

WILSON, Lyle C.
Hazard of history-by-diary. Nat R 15:529-30 D 17 '63

WILSON, Marilyn
Dream that I couldn't give up. por Redbook 121:6+ O '63

WILSON, Nancy
Greatest pretender. por Time 84:61 Jl 17 '64
Nancy Wilson. L. Robinson. il pors Ebony 19:40-2+ D '63
New Nancy. por Newsweek 64:76 Jl 27 '64
WILSON, Norman H.
Teacher and the quest for peace. Sr Schol 83: 10T N 22 '63
WILSON, O. W.
How the police chief sees it. Harper 228: 140-5 Ap '64
WILSON, Percy
High fidelity newsfronts. N. Eisenberg. il por Hi Fi 13:35+ D '63
Warehousing and shipping: costs and solutions. por Pub W 184:64-5 N 4 '63
WILSON, Peter Cecil
Fastest gavel in the West. il pors Life 55: 60A-60B Jl 12 '63
Lived with: R. Fribourg collection. New Yorker 39:29-30 My 25 '63
WILSON, Peter M.
Marinas in your future. Motor B 115:82-6 Ja '65
Modern marina, from both sides of the gas dock. Motor B 113:75-7+ Ja '64
WILSON, Phillip M.
Arc welding gun. Pop Mech 121:171-3 Mr '64
WILSON, R. B. See French, C. E. jt. auth.
WILSON, Richard
Student speaks. por Mus Am 83:9 Je '63
WILSON, Richard Lawson
Can the GOP survive Goldwater? Look 28: 20-1 Jl 14 '64
Russia's greatest failure. Look 28:88+ F 25 '64
WILSON, Robert E. Lee, 3d
Man who has everything in Wilson, Ark. S. Freedgood. il por Fortune 70:143-7+ Ag '64
WILSON, Robert Erastus
Man with the powerful kick. por Time 84:85 S 11 '64
WILSON, Robert McL.
Another disciple is heard from; concerning The Gospel of Philip. il Time 81:57-8 Mr 8 '63
WILSON, Robert N.
Social structure of a general hospital. bibliog f Ann Am Acad 346:67-76 Mr '63
WILSON, Robert R.
Talking time. Parents Mag 39:79 Jl '64
WILSON, Robley, jr
My son, drawing a picture; poem. Commonweal 81:477 Ja 8 '65
One sort of intimations ode. Reporter 31:40 D 3 '64
WILSON, Rosalind
Shells; story. Ladies Home J 81:84-6 Mr '64
WILSON, Ryder
Build the Multi-Trol. Pop Electr 20:40-2 My '64
Miniature VTVM. Pop Electr 22:55-7 Ja '65
WILSON, Sloan
American way of birth. Harper 229:48-54 Jl '64; Same abr. Read Digest 85:68-72 O '64
WILSON, Steven C.
Focus on Steven C. Wilson. J. Durniak. il por Pop Phot 53:60-3+ O '63
WILSON, Thelma
Miracle for Amanda. McCalls 91:52+ Je '64
WILSON, William E.
Utopia, limited; excerpt from Vanishing America. Am Heritage 15:64-72 O '64
WILSON, William R.
For a heart-of-the-West vacation try: The Tetons, Yellowstone, Salt Lake City. Suc Farm 61:42-3 Je '63
See colorful northeast Iowa. Suc Farm 62:106 O '64
Visit California's glamourland. il Suc Farm 62:58-9+ Mr '64
WILSON, Woodrow
Honest constitutionalism; excerpts from addresses. U S News 55:96+ Jl 22 '63

about

Colonel's folly and the President's distress; with editorial comment. G. T. Grayson. il Am Heritage 15:4-7+ O '64
End of a friendship; with memorandum by E. M. House. il pors Am Heritage 14:4-9+ Ag '63
Give Wilson back to the South! Christian Cent 81:5 Ja 1 '64
Presidential incapacity; letter to the editor. E. D. Toland. Nat R 16:125+ F 11 '64
Priceless gift: the love letters of Woodrow Wilson and Eleanor Axson Wilson. ed. by E. W. McAdoo. Review
Nat R por 14:203-4 Mr 12 '63. H. Woodward
When the cheering stopped, by G. Smith. Review
Sat R 47:25-6 Mr 14 '64. A. Walworth
Time por 83:99-100 Mr 6 '64

WILSON, N.C.

Lighting

Triple-threat lighting program. J. Maynard. il Am City 78:105 Jl '63
WILSON catalog cards. See Catalog cards
WILSON library bulletin
Editorial board. Wilson Lib Bul 39:407 Ja '65
Face to the future and the past. il Wilson Lib Bul 38:391 Ja '64
Lighthouse; redesigned format for WLB; new assistant editor appointed. il Wilson Lib Bul 38:430 Ja '64
September song; letters to the editor. Wilson Lib Bul 38:253 N '63
Wilson bulletin: November 1914. E. M. Phelps. Wilson Lib Bul 39:244 N '64
WLB celebrates 50th anniversary with look at the library's future. Library J 89:4311 N 1 '64
WLB ledger: credit; debit; letters to the editor. Wilson Lib Bul 38:463 F '64
Wilson library bulletin: November 1964. K. Molz. Wilson Lib Bul 39:245 N '64
See also
John Cotton Dana publicity awards
WILSONS disease. See Hepatolenticular degeneration
WILTON, George
TV and chemical grout. Am City 78:78-9 Ag '63
WILTON, Norman
Frosting masterpieces-every easy step! Bet Hom & Gard 41:74-7+ F '63
WILTSE, Kermit T.
Aid to families with dependent children: the basic service. bibliog f Ann Am Acad 355:75-81 S '64
WILTWYCK school for boys, Esopus, N.Y.
Girl who means hope to troubled boys. B. Leavitt. il Look 27:97-100 Je 18 '63
WILWAND, J. Barry
Nightmare ride. por Outdoor Life 134:50-1 Ag '64
WIMBLEDON tennis tournaments. See Tennis
WINAWER, Bonnie P.
Forty knot sailboat. Motor B 112:122-3 S '63
WINCHELL, Donald E.
Compulsory high school attendance? NEA J 53:10-12 F '64
WINCHELL, Walter
What Walter Winchell knows about models. por McCalls 90:110 Jl '63
Winchell v. Sugar Ray. Time 85:48 Ja 1 '65
WINCHESTER, Alice
English conversation pieces from the Mellon collection. Antiques 83:444-8 Ap '63
Living with antiques. Antiques 84:52-6 Jl '63; 86:592-7 N '64
WINCHESTER, James H.
America's top ten targets. Sci Digest 54:54-8 N '63
Canine cavalcade. Travel 121:42-3 F '64
Cash in your travels. Travel 123:58-60 Ja '65
Catalina. Travel 121:24-9 Je '64
Celebration in New Orleans: battle of '65. Travel 122:56-7+ D '64
Chunnel, a new Channel tunnel idea. Sci Digest 55:21-6 Ja '64
Facts about McNamara's folly. Sci Digest 54:14-18 Jl '63
Holland in bloom. Travel 119:28-30 F '63
Holland strikes it rich in natural gas. Read Digest 85:83-6 Ag '64
How we'll answer an SOS from space. Sci Digest 54:81-5 S '63
I came back from a stroke. Read Digest 83:169-74 O '63
Iceland saga. Travel 120:26-31 Ag '63
Is noise driving you crazy? Sci Digest 56:27-31 Ag '64
JFK and Air force one. Read Digest 82:189-90+ F '63
1970 army. Sci Digest 56:71-5 S '64
Report on Canadian science. Sci Digest 56: 75-81 D '64
Riding herd on the twisters. Read Digest 85:158-60+ O '64
SST, aviation's leap in the dark. Sci Digest 55:23-9 F '64
Surprise stopover: Panama. Travel 119:34-7+ Je '63
TV's four days of history. Read Digest 84: 204I-204J+ Ap '64
U.S. horse shows. Travel 120:34-6 S '63
U.S. memorial grounds abroad. Travel 121: 50-4+ My '64
What happens when you shave. Sci Digest 54:22+ O '63
When it's tulip time in Holland. Read Digest 84:146-50 Ap '64
Would you fly in a storm? Sci Digest 55: 85-90 Je '64
WINCHESTER, Jean
Don't fight the baby. Parents Mag 38:38-9+ Jl '63

WINCHESTER-Western division. See Olin Mathieson chemical corporation—Winchester-Western division
WINCKOWSKI, B. F.
Development of an electrical raceway for laboratory application. Arch Rec 134:235-6 S '63
WIND, Edgar
Critique of connoisseurship. bibliog Art N 63:26-9+ Mr '64
Every artist needs a hard-boiled patron; excerpt from Art and anarchy. Harper 228: 98-9+ Mr '64
Long battle between art and the machine; excerpt from Art and anarchy. Harper 228: 65-8+ F '64
WIND, Herbert Warren
Sporting scene (cont) New Yorker 39:128+ F 23; 146+ Mr 23; 117-18+ Ap 20; 58+ Je 15; 44+ Jl 6; 52+ Ag 3; 126+ S 28; 162+ D 14 '63; 87-90+ F 1; 40:133-4+ Ap 11; 178+ My 16; 96+ Je 6; 78+ Jl 11; 164+ S 26; 188+ O 10; 182+ N 7 '64
WIND. See Winds
WIND ensembles
See also
Phonograph records—Wind ensembles
WIND instruments
See also names of wind instruments, e.g. Recorder (musical instrument)
WIND mills. See Windmills
WIND tunnels
Peruvians study rotating-cylinder flap. D. A. Brown. il Aviation W 81:70-1+ D 7 '64
WINDASS, Stanley
Vitality of the United Nations. Yale R 53: 481-96 Je '64
WINDBREAKS
Sun-catching windbreak. D. Huff. il Pop Sci 184:112-13 Je '64
WINDFALL oils and mines, limited
Windfall that fell. il Time 84:64 Ag 14 '64
WINDFALLS
See also
Hurricanes
WINDHAM, Donald
Myopia: story. New Yorker 39:25-9 Jl 13 '63
WINDING
Filament winding; report. il Miss & Roc 13: 22-3+ Ag 12 '63
WINDING machines
Plastic fabrication technique seeks greater share of market. il Miss & Roc 13:22-3+ Ag 12 '63
WINDJAMMER cruises. See Cruising
WINDJAMMERS. See Sailing vessels
WINDLE, William F.
Neuropathology of certain forms of mental retardation; address, February 12, 1963. bibliog Science 140:1186-9 Je 14 '63
Respiratory distress: relation to prematurity and other factors in newborn monkeys. bibliog Science 143:1345-6 Mr 20 '64
—See Munroe, J. S. jt. auth.
WINDMILL theatre. See London—Theater
WINDMILLS
Power from the wind. il UNESCO Courier 17:52-3 Jl '64
Wonderful windmill of Mykonos. il Arch Forum 119:116-17 S '63
WINDMULLER, John P.
Labor: a partner in American foreign policy? Ann Am Acad 350:104-14 N '63
WINDOW blinds. See Blinds
WINDOW boxes. See Flower boxes, planters, etc.
WINDOW cleaning
View from the scaffold. D. Cort. Nation 196: 177-9 Mr 2 '63
WINDOW curtains and draperies. See Curtains and draperies
WINDOW displays. See Show windows
WINDOW dressing. See Show windows
WINDOW full of sky; story. See Yezierska, A.
WINDOW gardening
Catchall or showcase. il Pop Gard 15:69 Jl '64
Garden in a window; growing herbs. D. Wallace. Am Home 68:26 Ja '65
Growing bulbs in pots indoors. K. S. Taylor. il Horticulture 42:24-7+ N '64
Indoor gardening, not by the book. H. B. Grimes. Pop Gard 16:23 Ja '65
Inside story for winter gardeners. S. S. Baker. il Pop Sci 184:107 Ja '64
Servicing the year-round window. J. Fanning. il House & Gard 126:194-5+ D '64
Spring bulbs earlier. J. Unterecker. il Flower Grower 50:37+ N '63
Summer plants for year-round windows. il House & Gard 126:156-9 D '64
Window gardens. D. C. Peattie. Read Digest 83:252C-252D+ N '63
Window gardens are interesting. B. Brinhart. il Horticuture 42:54 Ja '64
WINDOW grilles. See Grilles
WINDOW screens. See Screens (doors, windows, etc)
WINDOW seats
For sitting by the window. il Sunset 133:106 S '64
WINDOW shades
Decorating with a shady approach. R. W. Houseman. il Am Home 66:36-41 Jl '63
For beauty at your windows. House & Gard 123:198 Ap '63
For kitchen glamour add personalized shades and new cabinet faces. il Bet Hom & Gard 41:46 S '63
Have you considered Roman shades? il Sunset 132:186+ My '64
How do your windows go? il Seventeen 23:216-17 My '64
How to decorate window shades. R. S. Miller. il Farm J 87:75 S '63
Shimmering shade pulls to accent your windows. il House & Gard 126:41 S '64
Wonderful ways to wake up your windows. il House & Gard 125:88-97 F '64
WINDOW shelves. See Shelves
WINDOW shields. See Photography—Studios and darkrooms
WINDOWLESS construction
Bell builds cellar in the sky; New York telephone's skycraper. il Bsns W p30-1 F 9 '63
WINDOWS
Arrangements for big windows. il Bet Hom & Gard 42:36 Je '64
Have a problem window? il Bet Hom & Gard 42:116 Je '64
How to choose aluminum storm windows and doors. il Consumer Bul 47:2+ D '64
Ideas for bathroom windows. il Sunset 130: 142 My '63
Now there's a vinyl storm window, too. il Pop Sci 185:150-1 O '64
Picture your winter windows. il House & Gard 124:164-7+ D '63
Pleasant perspectives of windows. il House & Gard 124:22-3 N '63
Roof dormers put lazy attics to work. il Pop Mech 120:164-7+ O '63
Storm and screen combinations. J. Hand. il Pop Mech 120:134-7+ O '63
What to do when you don't like your windows. il Pop Sci 185:112-15 S '64
What you should know about window design. il House & Gard 125:151-3 F '64
Wise ways with windows. R. Charles. il Parents Mag 39:81-4+ F '64
See also
Automobiles—Windows
Curtains and draperies
Glass painting and staining
Lighting
WINDOWS, Space vehicle. See Space vehicles —Viewports
WINDS
Circulation of the upper atmosphere. R. E. Newell. il Sci Am 210:62-72+ bibliog(p 152) Mr '64
How to keep dry in a moist, hot climate. il House B 106:64-9+ Ja '64
Ill wind from Hawaii; the Pacific high. il Time 85:56+ Ja 15 '65
Scissors-like winds affect ionosphere. Sci N L 85:264 Ap 25 '64
Snow eaters of Alberta; chinook thaws. D. Bodington. il Natur Hist 73:60-1 F '64
Wind shear measurement techniques. Aviation W 80:43 Je 8 '64
Winds. A. E. Sik. bibliog il Motor B 112:39-41+ O '63
See also
Hurricanes
Monsoons
Storms
WINDS, Solar. See Solar radiation
WINDSHIELD defrosters. See Automobiles—Windshield defrosters
WINDSHIELDS. See Automobiles—Windshields
WINDSOR, Edward, duke of. See Edward VIII, king of Great Britain
WINDSOR, H. D.
Group leader retires, cum laude. Consumer Rep 29:53-4 F '64
WINDSOR, Wallis (Warfield) duchess of
Duke and Duchess of Windsor in Paris; with photographs by Horst. V. Lawford. Vogue 143:176-87+ Ap 1 '64
WINDWARD ISLANDS. See West Indies
WINE, Sherman
Atheist rabbi. por Time 85:90+ Ja 29 '65
WINE
American ambassador's diplomatic wine wall; California wines presented to Adlai E. Stevenson. il House & Gard 126:244-5 N '64

WINE—*Continued*
California wines; excerpts from Discovering the world of wines. C. Churchill. il Harper 227:50-5 D '63
Corkscrew; the sunny wines of Provence. J. A. Beard. il House & Gard 125:192+ My '64
Correct wine for now and 1984. F. Wallace. il Esquire 61:106-7+ Ja '64
Dessert wines. M. Kaytor. il Look 28:50-1 F 25 '64
Do you know the uniquely American wine Zinfandel? M. A. Amerine. il House B 105:236-7+ N '63
Eleven cooling wine cups to slake summer thirst. E. Kinard. il House B 105:72-5+ Jl '63
Fine wines are symbol of culture. il Ebony 20:100+ Ja '65
Formidable! French wine in cans. Newsweek 64:67 Jl 27 '64
Great grapes; superb 1964 vintage expected in France. il Newsweek 64:96 S 21 '64
In defense of dessert wines. H. Johnson. House & Gard 125:172+ Mr '64
Language of wine. F. Schoonmaker. bibliog il Sat R 47:40-2+ O 24 '64
Lesser wines of Europe. H. Johnson. House & Gard 124:168+ S '63
Luncheon buffet or a picnic with wines. il Sunset 131:128-30+ S '63
Quiz your palate with a wine-tasting party. il House & Gard 123:178+ My '63
She's a big girl; California wine industry. J. Deever. il Sat Eve Post 236:58-61 D 21 '63
Slow night au Relais. P. Redford. il Atlan 212:120+ N '63
Sparkling rose wine punch. il Ebony 18:188+ S '63
Symposium; quarterly dinner of Commanderie de Bordeaux. New Yorker 40:19-20 F 22 '64
Table wines of Spain. T. Prittie. il Atlan 214-108-10 S '64
This is the year that will be. il Time 84:74 D 11 '64
Vermouth for light summer sipping. J. A. Beard. House & Gard 125:140+ Je '64
What wine primers don't tell. L. D. Adams. il Am Home 67:19+ N '64
Why and how to decant wines. J. A. Beard. il House & Gard 124:168+ D '63
Why drink the wines of Italy? F. Schoonmaker. il House B 106:110-11+ F '64
Wine. M. A. Amerine. il Sci Am 211:46-56 bibliog(p 116) Ag '64
Wine & fish. J. A. Beard. House & Gard 123:150+ Mr '63
Wine drinker's tour of Germany. B. Mussey. il House B 106:116-17+ Ag '64
Wine fiesta; a new kind of party for year-end budgets. V. Stanton. il House B 105: 158-9+ D '63
Wine for snobs, friends, and young girls. H. Johnson. Vogue 142:137+ D '63
Wine guide for the triumphant huntsman. J. A. Beard. il House & Gard 126:218+ O '64
Wine tasters' dinner; American chapter of the Confrérie des chevaliers du tastevin. M. Kaytor. il Look 27:52-5 Jl 2 '63
Wines for picnics. H. Johnson. House & Gard 126:120+ Ag '64
Wines of America. H. J. Grossman. il Am Home 66:6+ O '63
Wonderful world of wine. G. Lichine; A. Lichine. il Ladies Home J 81:117-21 S '64
Zut! is '64 the year of the century? with report by H. Moffett. il Life 57:107-11 O 30 '64
See also
Champagne
Cookery—Wine

Advertising

Campaign to create connoisseurs; Americans as wine drinkers. il Bsns W p82-4+ Ag 10 '63

Anecdotes, facetiae, satire, etc.

Shall we, for God's sake, join the ladies? H. F. Ellis. New Yorker 40:142-4 My 23 '64

Prices

Gourmet by the gallon. G. M. Cross. Esquire 61:34+ My '64

Terminology

Wine lovers dictionary. F. Schoonmaker. See occasional issues of House beautiful

WINE cellars
Fine wines are symbol of culture. il Ebony 20:100+ Ja '65

WINE racks
If you serve wine store it attractively in a wine rack. il Am Home 67:20+ N '64

WINE trade
Battle of the Marne. il Newsweek 61:78 F 18 '63
California wines; excerpts from Discovering the world of wines. C. Churchill. il Harper 227:50-5 D '63
Cheers! a votre santé! Common market for drinks. J. Wechsberg. il N Y Times Mag p28+ Mr 1 '64
Pulling the cork. il Newsweek 61:99-101 My 13 '63

WINELAND, Lynn
Honda's Grizzly Cub. il Hot Rod 17:80-1 S '64
Stiff lower lip. Hot Rod 17:94-5 Ag '64

WINEMA NATIONAL FOREST. See National forests

WINER, Richard A.
Big plans for Canaveral. Motor B 114:85 N '64

WINFREE, Robert W.
SCA background-music multiplexer. Electr World 70:42-5 D '63

WING, George A.
National debt. America 111:555-7 N 7 '64

WING, Wayman C.
Walls become columns, and vice versa. Arch Rec 135:202-4 Mr '64

WING, William G.
Beauty part of rowing. Harper 227:26+ S '63

WING shooting. See Quail shooting; Shooting; Skeet (game)

WINGO, Hal
Rescue by copter and bo'sun's chair. Life 58:26-7 Ja 8 '65

WINGO, Lowdon, jr
Recreation and urban development: a policy perspective; excerpts from Trends in American living and outdoor recreation. bibliog f Ann Am Acad 352:129-40 Mr '64

WINGO, Walter
Army looks skyward again. Sci N L 87:26-7 Ja 9 '65
Triplets unlocking code. Sci N L 86:103 Ag 15 '64

WINICK, Arnold
Very irreverent horse trainer. W. Leggett. il por Sports Illus 18:42+ F 4 '63

WINK, Tex.
Sad little story of Wink. R. S. Strother. Read Digest 85:97-100 O '64

WINKLEPLECK, R. L.
Add-on S-meter. Pop Electr 18:48-50 F '63
Emergency household lamp. Pop Electr 18: 55-7 My '63
Revamp your CB for better noise limiting. Pop Electr 20:53-4 Ap '64
Tune away rock-bound CB receiver. Pop Electr 20:47-50 Ap '64
Unusual D.C. to D.C. supply. Electr World 71:62-3 My '64
Wipe out vibrator hash. Pop Electr 19:41-5 D '63

WINKLER, J. Homer
IPEX; new developments in the American printing industry. Pub W 184:78-84+ Ag 5 '63

WINKLER, Richard
Life inside a paper bag. Harper 227:44-5 S '63

WINKLEY, Harvel E.
As the snow flies. Recreation 58:11 Ja '65

WINKS, Robin W.
Essay exam: probing the iceberg; excerpts from address. Sr Schol 85:12T-13T O 21 '64

WINN, Janet
Elegy for an herbalist. New Repub 148:24 Je 22 '63

WINN-Dixie stores, incorporated
Winning in Dixie. il Time 82:90 S 20 '63

WINNER; story. See Ciulla, S. F.

WINNETKA, Ill.

Education

Junior high learning lab; Skokie junior high school. C. D. Thomason. il NEA J 52:15-16 N '63
Senior citizens spark youth to develop talents. J. Beck. il Todays Health 42:60-1+ F '64

WINNETT, Ralph
Siqueiros. New Repub 148:7 Mr 2 '63
Violence in the universities. New Repub 148: 12-13 Ap 13 '63

WINNICK, Pauline
(comp) Libraries and the war on poverty; relevant federal legislative programs. ALA Bul 59:43-8 Ja '65

WINNIPEG, Manitoba
Tux or tackle: Winnipeg. M. Delman. il Travel 119:26-30 My '63

Description

European touch: Winnipeg. J. Ludwig. il Holiday 35:84-5+ Ap '64

WINNIPEG free press
Canada's gadfly; the Winnipeg free press. B. Hutchison. Harper 226:82-6 Ap '63

WINNIPEG symphony orchestra
Victor Feldbrill, conductor Winnipeg symphony, Canada. E. Helm. Mus Am 83:13 My '63

WINNSBORO, Tex.
Crop that never fails us; sixth Autumn trails festival; ed. by J. D. Boyd. C. Spivey. il Farm J 88:36-7+ N '64

WINSLOW, Leon L.
Portraits of Leonard Bahr. Am Artist 28:26-31+ D '64

WINSTED, Conn.
Day there was no money; publicity stunt. W. K. Zinsser. Reporter 29:46-8 S 12 '63

Lighting

Mercury city, U.S.A. A. J. Cannavo. il Am City 78:121 Mr '63

WINSTON, Alexander
Hunt for the regicides. Am Heritage 16:26-9+ D '64
Small candle of Danilo Dolci. Christian Cent 81:1109-10 S 9 '64

WINSTON, Clara
(tr) See Hochhuth, R. Deputy

WINSTON, Harvey D. and Lindzey, Gardner
Albinism and water escape performance in the mouse. bibliog Science 144:189-91; 147:308 Ap 10 '64, Ja 15 '65

WINSTON, Richard
(tr) See Hochhuth, R. Deputy

WINSTON-SALEM, N.C.

Sanitary affairs

Refuse trains bring three-way savings. G. W. Kilday. il Am City 80:88-90 Ja '65

WINTER, Blair
Deeply channeled. Christian Cent 81:1218 S 30 '64

WINTER, Ella
Skimming a life. H. Kramer. Nation 197:283-4 N 2 '63

WINTER, Ethel
Ethel Winter and company, 92nd street Y. J. Maskey. Dance Mag 38:66 Je '64

WINTER, Gibson
Gibson Winter and the great ecclesiastical moving van. Christian Cent 80:663 My 15 '63

WINTER, Harry
Gesture in ecumenism. America 111:614-19 N 14 '64

WINTER, Jack
Family game. New Yorker 39:35-6 Ap 27 '63

WINTER, Otto R.
Little purchases cost lots. Am City 79:150+ Ap '64
Purchasing forum attracts new bidders. Am City 79:97 Ag '64

WINTER, Paul
Trial of Jesus. bibliog f Commentary 38:35-41 S '64

WINTER, Ralph E.
Medicine's next big step, spare parts surgery; reprint. Sci Digest 55:65-9 F '64

WINTER, Sam
Sam Winter retires from old age. J. Shepherd. il pors Look 27:49-52 Ag 13 '63

WINTER
Did we guess winter right? il Sci Digest 55:81-3 Je '64
Even the South is hit hard by winter. il U S News 56:12 Ja 27 '64
Glory of the season, winter. H. H. Graham. il Am For 69:28-9 D '63
Hell's winter howls in. il Life 54:28-39 F 8 '63
In praise of winter; excerpt from Dreamthorp. A. Smith. il Read Digest 85:53-5 D '64
So I go to Walden a-skating; excerpts from Journal, ed. by M. Meltzer. H. D. Thoreau. il N Y Times Mag p 11 D 29 '63
Splendor of winter. B. Tufty. il Sci N L 84:378-9 D 14 '63
What kind of winter will it be? H. C. Willett. il Sci Digest 54:83-9 N '63
When half the world shivers; snow and subzero weather. il Bsns W p32+ F 2 '63
Why winters are getting colder; reprint. W. J. Perkinson. il Sci Digest 56:83-5 D '64
Winter in Bucks County; excerpts from Private line in Bucks County. W. Teller. il Atlan 211:78-81 Mr '63
Winter that was. il Newsweek 61:61 Mr 25 '63

See also
February
January
Snow
Snowstorms

Quotations, maxims, etc.

Winter; comp. by E. F. Murphy. N Y Times Mag p 132 D 13 '64

WINTER aconites
Try winter aconite. P. Goldman. il Horticulture 41:539 O '63

WINTER bouquets. See Flowers, Dried

WINTER camping. See Camping

WINTER carnivals. See Winter sports

WINTER cress
Yellow rocket, best control is make silage. Suc Farm 62:66 Je '64

WINTER driving. See Automobile driving

WINTER fishing. See Fishing, Winter

WINTER garden; drama. See McFarlan, E.

WINTER gardening
Quick and easy tips. il Pop Gard 15:32-3 Ja '64
Winter garden tips. Suc Farm 61:136+ F '63

See also
Greenhouses

WINTER nationals, Pomona, Calif. See Automobile racing

WINTER Olympics. See Olympic games

WINTER Olympics, 1964. See Olympic games, 1964

WINTER pictures. See Photography—Landscapes

WINTER proofing. See Houses—Maintenance and repair

WINTER protection of plants. See Plants, Protection of

WINTER resorts
Gold in the ski hills. D. Cort. Nation 198:120-1 F 3 '64
John Jay's ski chart, leading resorts in the U.S.A. and Canada. Mlle 60:184-7 N '64
Let's travel to ski. Mlle 58:182-7 N '63; 60:190-5 N '64
Life guide; what's down South besides the sun. il Life 56:7 Ja 3 '64
Montana: the big ski country. K. N. Anderson. il Todays Health 43:42-7+ Ja '65
New sugar in an old state; skiing in Vermont. H. Horn. il Sports Illus 19:30-4 N 18 '63
Oh, say, can you ski? S. Welton. il Parents Mag 38:66-7+ D '63
Perfect mountain; Vail, Colo. il Holiday 36:98-103 D '64
Scamp of the ski slope; Mount Snow, Vermont. il Life 54:93-4 F 8 '63
Six square miles of powder; Colorado's Vail becomes full-grown ski resort. F. R. Smith. il Sports Illus 21:52-62 N 23 '64
Ski bums: the upland Bohemians. K. K. Waller. il Mlle 58:172-3+ N '63
Ski incidentals: Colorado; two new resorts in the Colorado Rockies. Vogue 142:164-5 N 15 '63
Skier's West. il Sunset 130:66-73 F '63
Skiing among the angels; Laurentian Mountains. R. Joseph. il Esquire 62:194-7 D '64
Snow at the turn of a switch. J. Hand. il Pop Sci 182:98-101+ Mr '63
Snows of Courchevel. il Holiday 34:98-103 D '63
Some tips for snow dudes; Canada's Laurentian Mountains. L. Barry. il Pop Phot 54:20+ Ja '64
There's more than one way to go to the sun. M. Gough. il House B 106:56+ Ja '64
Travel notes; northern Italy. R. Joseph. Esquire 60:72+ O '63
Velvet Europe; the Continent's winter playgrounds. F. Morton. il Holiday 35:38-53 Ja '64
Wide, wide world at your feet; Swiss resorts. M. Gough. il House B 106:132+ Ap '64

See also
Gstaad, Switzerland
St Moritz, Switzerland
Snoqualmie, Wash.
Sugarbush Valley, Vt.
Sun Valley, Idaho
Zermatt, Switzerland

WINTER sleep. See Hibernation

WINTER sports
Deep River winter carnival. il Recreation 57:63 F '64
Europe's winter wonders. J. Fanelli. il Travel 122:32-8 N '64
Minnesota's winter magic. K. F. Rolvaag. il Travel 122:30-4 D '64
Winter leaves me cold. C. Ford. il Sports Illus 18:E5-8 F 4 '63; Same abr. Read Digest 83:131-3 D '63

See also
Coasting
Curling
Ice boats and ice boating
Skating
Skis and skiing
Snowshoes

WINTER tires. See Tires, Automobile

WINTER vacation houses. See Cabins
WINTER vacations. See Vacations
WINTERBURG, Francis M. See Gedney, G. C. jt. auth.
WINTERICH, John Tracy
Criminal record. See last issue of each month of Saturday review
Harvard's press marks half century of publishing. Pub W 183:14-21 Ap 22 '63
Parnassus Corner: a life of James T. Fields. Pub W 184:26-30 Jl 29 '63
(ed) Your literary I.Q. See issues of Saturday review
WINTERNITZ, Emanuel
In feeble voice, his fabled past. Sat R 46:30-1 Jl 20 '63
WINTERS, Carl S.
Fine art of living. PTA Mag 58:11-12 O '63
WINTERS, Carol
Gone: poem. McCalls 91:153 Mr '64
WINTERS, Helen M.
Cruising in company. Motor B 113:102-3+ F '64
Eating your way south. Motor B 114:30-1+ S '64
WINTERS, Jonathan
What's so funny? J. Hamilton. il pors Look 27:119-22 Je 18 '63
Winging it. pors Newsweek 63:105 My 18 '64
WINTERTHUR museum, Henry Francis Dupont. See Henry Francis Dupont Winterthur museum
WINTOUR, Eleanor
Bringing up children; the American vs. the British way. Harper 229:58-63 Ag '64
Puppy and biscuit. il por Newsweek 63:52 Ja 27 '64
WIRE
See also
Exploding wire phenomena
WIRE explosions, Electric. See Exploding wire phenomena
WIRE sculpture
Coat hanger chandelier. W. Floyd. il Design 65:154 Mr '64
Coat hanger sculpture. F. Major. il Design 65:98-9 Ja '64
Coiled wire menagerie. J. Dukes. il Design 65:190-1 My '64
WIRE tapping
Are they listening in on you? E. D. Fales, jr. il Pop Sci 186:96-9+ Ja '65
Are you being bugged? B. H. Frisch. il Sci Digest 56:38-43 Jl '64
Big brother is listening; telephone taps and hidden microphones. B. H. Bagdikian. il Sat Eve Post 237:68-70 Je 6 '64
Electronic privacy. Nation 199:2 Jl 13 '64
Wiretapping: yes or no? F. E. Imbau; H. Schwartz. Christian Cent 82:75-9 Ja 20 '65
WIRE walking. See Acrobats and acrobatism
WIREHAIRED terriers. See Terriers
WIRELESS earphone. See Earphones
WIRELESS stations. See Radio stations
WIRETAPPING. See Wire tapping
WIREWORMS
Toxic residues in soil nine years after treatment with aldrin and heptachlor. A. T. S. Wilkinson and others. il Science 143:681-2 F 14 '64
WIRGES, Eugene Henry
How to lynch a newspaper. R. Reed. Atlan 214:59-63 N '64
WIRING, Electric. See Electric wire and wiring
WIRKKALA, Tapio
Pair of designing Finns. R. Moss. il por Horizon 5:62-7 Jl '63
WIRTH, Conrad Louis
Parks in your backyard. por Nat Geog Mag 124:647-707 N '63
We must stop destroying our natural riches. por Parents Mag 39:32 Jl '64
about
Conrad Wirth retires. por Recreation 56:481 D '63
Kind of special breed. M. Frome. il pors Am For 70:4-5+ Ja '64
WIRTZ, William Willard
Commonwealth of human responsibility; address, June 15, 1964. Vital Speeches 30:610-12 Ag 1 '64
Excerpt from statement, February 26, 1963. Cong Digest 42:302+ D '63
For the class of '63: job outlook now. por U S News 54:74-5 Ap 29 '63
How to unsettle a dispute; adapted from an address. Sat R 46:28 Mr 9 '63
Labor minister's conference on the Alliance for progress; excerpts from address. Mo Labor R 86:789-93 Jl '63
When junior seeks a job. PTA Mag 57:12-14 bibliog(p37) My '63
Why young people face a shortage of jobs; interview. pors U S News 54:62-7 Ap 1 '63
Worker security in a changing economy: a prefatory note. Mo Labor R 86:612-13 Je '63
about
As rail dispute neared a crisis. U S News 55:69 S 2 '63
Growing worry for U.S: young people out of work. il U S News 54:83-5 F 18 '63
Labor secretary speaks. por Bsns W p48+ O 17 '64
Latest turn in rail dispute; what it all means. por U S News 55:82 Ag 26 '63
Now U.S. is exporting union ideas to Latin America. A. W. Robinson. il por U S News 54:86+ My 20 '63
People of the week. por U S News 55:15 N 4 '63
Why strikes are worrying union leaders. il por U S News 54:86-8 Mr 4 '63
Wirtz emerges from second fiddle job. por Bsns W p78-80 D 21 '63
Wirtz proposal. W. F. Buckley, jr. Nat R 16:267 Ap 7 '64
WISCONSIN
See also
Booksellers and bookselling—Wisconsin
Chippewa River
Courts—Wisconsin
Fishing—Wisconsin
Forests and forestry—Wisconsin
Hunting—Wisconsin
Land—Wisconsin
Libraries—Wisconsin
Music festivals—Wisconsin
Water supply—Wisconsin

Religious institutions and affairs

News of the Christian world (cont) Christian Cent 80:218+, 626-8; 81:1506-8 F 13, My 8 '63, D 2 '64
WISCONSIN library association
Award-winning program for NLW. G. A. Somers. il Wilson Lib Bul 39:472-4 F '65
WISCONSIN state college
Conservatives, too, have tenure. R. Kirk. Nat R 16:729 Ag 25 '64
Whitewash in Whitewater; letter to the editor. S. D. Robertson. Library J 89:2900+ Ag '64
WISCONSIN state college, La Crosse
Recreation majors club. J. Christenson. Recreation 56:101 F '63
WISCONSIN. University, Madison
Cooperative study of educational policy. Sch & Soc 91:300 O 31 '64
Reorganization of Wisconsin's school of education. Sch & Soc 92:330 N 14 '64
Teacher education at Wisconsin. Sch & Soc 92:115+ Mr 21 '64
Wisconsin: Latin America's neighbor. W. P. Glade. il Américas 15:34-7 Jl '63

Library school

Recruiting adult students to library work. Wilson Lib Bul 39:444+ F '65

School of education

Wisconsin vs. NCATE. Sch & Soc 91:236 Sum '63
WISCONSIN university co-op store. See College bookstores
WISE, Bill
Aboard the Maddox. Life 57:21 Ag 14 '64
It's $83 million high. Life 56:13 Mr 6 '64
(ed) See Johnson, L. B. I'm blue-eyed in a brown-eyed family
WISE, David
It will be many years. . . Good H 158:90-1+ F '64
—and Ross, T. B.
Film-maker. New Yorker 39:25-7 F 15 '64
Invisible government; excerpts. Look 28:37+ Je 16; 77-8+ Je 30 '64
WISE, Donald A.
Creating gladiolus. Horticulture 41:430 Ag '63
WISE, Roland
Notes on drawing. il Sch Arts 63:32-5 Je '64
WISE, T. A.
Crisis on New York's newspaper row. Fortune 70:110-13+ O '64
Wall Street's main event: SEC vs. the specialists. Fortune 69:149-52+ My '64
Wherever you look, there's Loeb, Rhoades. Fortune 67:128-31+ Ap '63
Young Ted Etherington's Amex. Fortune 71:166-70+ Ja '65
—See Seligman, D. jt. auth.
WISE woman and the king; opera. See Orff, C.
WISEMAN, Frederick
New producer. New Yorker 39:33-5 S 14 '63

WISEMAN, Robert C.
How to sketch with a camera. U S Camera 27:66-7 S '64
WISER, Thomas Huntington
De-quilling a dog. Field & S 69:94-5 D '64
WISH is for wanting; story. See Brandon, W.
WISHARI, Werner
Our man in Finland. N Y Times Mag p63-4+ N 17 '63
WISHIK, Samuel M.
Influence on the health of our youth. PTA Mag 57:20 F '63
WISHING box; story. See Plath, S.
WISMACH, Kurt
What Ulbricht doesn't know. Atlan 212:114-17 D '63
WISNER, Bill
Cruisingman's guide to a fisherman's boat. Motor B 113:34-5+ My '64
Tackle tells the tale. Motor B 114:46-7+ S '64
WISOTZKY, Joel, and others
Phosphorescence of rat kidneys cooled in liquid nitrogen. Science 140:671-2 My 10 '63
WISPÉ, Lauren G.
Traits of eminent American psychologists. bibliog Science 141:1256-61 S 27 '63
WISTER, Gertrude Smith
Spring; make the most of it with small bulbs. Horticulture 42:14-18 Mr '64
WIT and humor. See Humor
WITCH doctors. See Medicine men
WITCH hazel
Witchery of witch hazel. B. Rivera. il Horticulture 41:181 Mr '63
WITCHCRAFT
Charge: witchcraft; unique petition. Hobbies 69:92 Jl '64
Flight of witches. F. Stevenson. il Opera N 28:24-5 Ja 4 '64
Juju justice: Ivory Coast. il Time 83:35 Ap 24 '64
Prevalence of witches; little revival of black magic in England. il Time 82:53 D 27 '63
Real witches at work; English pagans keep an old cult alive; with report by R. Bone. il Life 57:55-6+ N 13 '64
Sorcerers still practice; Kahuna sorcery. Sci N L 86:359 D 5 '64
Sorcery and society. D. Bess. Nation 199:358-60 N 16 '64
See also
Voodooism
WITCHES of love; story. See McConkey, J.
WITH love from Joe; story. See Deal, B. H.
WITHERS, Samuel
Parent and child. N Y Times Mag p56 Je 16; 45 Je 23; 49 Jl 21; 103 S 29 '63
WITHEY, Robert A.
Gaining new vision for social studies. Sr Schol 85:18T Ja 21 '65
WITHHOLDING tax
Cut your taxes even more. il Changing T 18:17-20 Je '64
Your pay raise: how big? with chart. U S News 56:79 F 24 '64
WITHOUT obligation; story. See Bruce, J.
WITHROW, Hilda
It pays to write confession stories. Writer 77:17-21 F '64
WITNESSES
Dying girl that no one helped. L. Wainwright. Life 56:21 Ap 10 '64
How to tell the truth in court. L. Nizer. il McCalls 90:86-7+ Mr '63
Not getting involved. il Time 83:72+ My 15 '64
Not involved? Sr Schol 84:16 Ap 24 '64
Throwing the bone. Nation 199:262 O 26 '64
What makes an expert? il Time 83:48+ Mr 20 '64
When you take the stand. D. Murray. il Read Digest 82:122-5 F '63
Who cares? L. Gross. il Look 28:17-19 S 8 '64; Same abr. with title Is there a Samaritan in the neighborhood? Read Digest 85:106-10 N '64
See also
Evidence (law)
WITT, Harold V.
Babies; poem. Sat R 46:14 F 9 '63
Divorce; poem. Sat R 47:39 S 26 '64
Fact in the fable; poem. New Yorker 40:148 Ap 18 '64
Rembrandt and Van Gogh; poem. Sat R 46:98 O 12 '63
Right; poem. Sat R 46:30 Ag 31 '63
This smallness; poem. Sat R 47:83 Ja 11 '64
Villanelle of the sinister committee; poem. Nation 197:167 S 21 '63
WITTEN, T. A. and others
Reaction of lymphocytes with purified protein derivative conjugated with fluorescein. bibliog Science 142:596-8 N 1 '63
WITTGENSTEIN, Ludwig
Fly and the fly-bottle: encounters with British intellectuals, by V. Mehta. Review Sat R 46:37-8 Je 22 '63. J. K. Feibleman
WITTKE, Carl
Our heritage of freedom; The bill of rights. PTA Mag 58:20-2 S '63
WITTLINGER, Karl
Do you know the Milky way? text. Theatre Arts 47:37-60 Je '63
about
Do you know the Milky way? Criticism Theatre Arts il(p 15) 47:69 My '63
WITTMANN, Otto
Attraction of Italy for American painters. Antiques 85:552-7 My '64
WITTY, Helen S.
Bean with a difference. il Flower Grower 51:20 My '64
Cold soups for a hot summer. Flower Grower 51:17 Ag '64
Early tomato that's so good. Flower Grower 51:32 Ap '64
Plant now, feast later. Flower Grower 50:53+ My '63
Sweet taste of summer. Flower Grower 51:38 O '64
Vegetables on the grill. Flower Grower 50:46+ Ag '63
We tested our soil. il Flower Grower 51:44-5+ Mr '64
WITTY, Paul
Gifted and the creative student. bibliog f Sch & Soc 92:183-5 Ap 18 '64
Make way for creativity. PTA Mag 57:16-18 bibliog(p35) Mr '63
Surveys of TV, 1949-62. bibliog f Sch & Soc 91:334-6 N 2 '63
What makes children want to learn? PTA Mag 58:21-3 bibliog(p36) N '63
WITZKE, Robert W.
Vandalism in Yellowstone Park. Nat Parks Mag 38:13-15+ F '64
WIVES
After the honeymoon: helpmate or checkmate? A. Van Buren. il McCalls 90:26+ F '63
Close-up of the normal wife. R. Corman. il N Y Times Mag p52+ S 8 '63
Convention wives: help or hindrance? il Newsweek 61:82-3 My 13 '63
Do we undervalue full-time wives? appraisal of report by the President's commission on the status of women. M. Mead. Redbook 122:22+ N '63
Executives, wives, and trouble; President's panel report. W. R. Roberts. il Duns R 85:34-5+ Ja '65
Lonely wife; wife of a traveling man. J. Krantz. il McCalls 91:142-3+ N '63
Privacy vs. secrecy. L. Strong. Am Home 67:38-9 O '64
Why women can't talk to their husbands; Why men don't talk to their wives. M. Holmes. il Todays Health 42:28-33+ Ap '64
Will success spoil your marriage? T. Howard. il McCalls 90:88-9+ Jl '63
Young wife's world. H. Valentine. See issues of Good housekeeping
See also
Ambassadors wives
College presidents wives
Congressmens wives
Housewives
Husbands
Marriage
Physicians wives
Presidents—United States—Wives
Widows
Woman
United States—Wives
WIXOM, Hartt
Rainbows of Flaming Gorge. Field & S 69:100-2+ Jl '64
Trouble-shoot for trout. Outdoor Life 133:48-51+ Mr '64
Wild deer area opens. Outdoor Life 132:38-9+ Ag '63
WIZARD of Oz; drama. See Schwartz, L. S.
WIZNITZER, Louis
Goodby to the biggest sardine. Nation 198:630-2 Je 22 '64
WOAL, S. Theodore
Counselor, yours is a tough assignment. Recreation 57:111 Mr '64
WOBURN abbey. See Country estates—England
WOETZEL, Robert K.
Overview of organized crime: mores versus morality. bibliog f Ann Am Acad 347:1-11 My '63
WOGAMAN, Philip
Focus on the central jurisdiction. Christian Cent 80:1296-8 O 23 '63

WOHLGEMUTH, Donald W.
Annals of business. J. Brooks. New Yorker 39:37-8+ Ja 11 '64
WOHLGEMUTH, Patricia
Portuguese territories and the United Nations. bibliog f Int Concil 545:3-68 N '63
WOHLSCHLAG, Donald E. See DeVries, A. L. jt. auth.
WOHLSTETTER, Albert
Scientists, seers and strategy. bibliog f For Affairs 41:466-78 Ap '63
Technology, prediction, and disorder. Bul Atomic Sci 20:11-15 O '64
WOJCIECHOWSKA, Maia. See Rodman, M. W.
WOJCIKOWSKA, Sonia
Ballet child. N. Sheridan. il pors Dance Mag 37:21-3 Je '63
WOLBARST, John
Big little flash. Mod Phot 28:78-9+ Ja '64
How to be a Polaroid expert. Pop Sci 185: 118-22 D '64
Pictures in a moment. See issues of Modern photography
Polaroid color. Mod Phot 27:60-5+ Mr '63
Polaroid's new pack camera!! Mod Phot 27: 84-5+ O '63
Tankmanship. Mod Phot 27:76-7+ Mr '63
35mm. See issues of Modern photography
WOLD, Finn. See Tsuyuki, H. jt. auth.
WOLF, Arnold Jacob
Anti-Semitism and reunion. Christian Cent 80:709-10 My 29 '63
Reunion and the Jews. H. Küng. Christian Cent 80:829 Je 26 '63
WOLF, Beverly. See Barry, R. E. jt. auth.
WOLF, Bill
Young wizard of computers. R. Bailey. il pors Life 57:107-13+ S 25 '64
WOLF, Edith (Anisfield)
Edith Anisfield Wolf: 1889-1963. H. Bowser. por Sat R 46:23 Ap 13 '63
WOLF, Edwin, 2d
Credo of a library conservative; adaptation of address, October 29, 1963. Library J 89:1903-6 My 1 '64
WOLF, George, and Miller, N. E.
Lateral hypothalamic lesions: effects on drinking elicited by carbachol in preoptic area and posterior hypothalamus. bibliog Science 143:585-7 F 7 '64
WOLF, Harold
Hepatomas in rainbow trout: descriptive and experimental epidemiology. bibliog Science 142:676-8 N 8 '63
WOLF, Henry
How a car works: a primer for your wife. Esquire 62:200-3 D '64
WOLF, Ken
Virus infections in cold-blooded vertebrates. Science 146:1603-4 D 18 '64
—and Quimby, M. C.
Amphibian cell culture: permanent cell line from the bullfrog (rana catesbeiana) bibliog Science 144:1578-80 Je 26 '64
WOLF, Leonard
For the bride; poem. Commonweal 77:641 Mr 15 '63
Gadarenes; poem. Atlan 214:84 S '64
Hunchback; poem. Commonweal 78:139 Ap 26 '63
Persian spring; poem. Commonweal 77:574 F 22 '63
Zero; poem. Atlan 213:116 My '64
WOLF, Marguerite
Meaning of security. Parents Mag 38:64+ D '63
WOLF, Robert E.
Alaska digs out. il Am For 70:10-13+ My '64
WOLF, Willavene, and Wolf, W. C. Jr
Teacher dropouts: still a dilemma. Sch & Soc 92:193-4 Ap 18 '64
WOLF, William
Chartering in the Greek isles. Motor B 113: 50-1+ Ap '64
WOLF, William C. Jr. See Wolf, W. jt. auth.
WOLF children. See Children, Wild
WOLF hunting
Sounds and hounds of a Texas wolf hunt. J. Olsen. il Sports Illus 21:66-72+ S 14 '64
Wild wolf hunt. D. Brown. il Outdoor Life 134:17-19+ D '64
WOLF whistle; story. See Rogin, G.
WOLFE, Alan David, and Hahn, F. E.
Erythromycin: mode of action. bibliog Science 143:1445-6 Mr 27 '64
WOLFE, Barry T. See Hanson, W. jt. auth.
WOLFE, Burton H.
Strange twilight of Harry Bridges. Harper 228:78-80+ Mr '64
WOLFE, Chuck
Great Southwest. Flying 75:34-6+ S '64
Head for The Pass. Flying 75:41-3 S '64
Used aircraft pilot report. Flying 74:48-9+ Ap '64
Used aircraft pilot report; Mooney Mite. por Flying 74:38+ F '64
WOLFE, Deborah Partridge
Pin point portrait of Dr Deborah P. Wolfe. J. H. Roy. Negro Hist Bul 26:176 F '63
WOLFE, Douglas A. and Cornwell, D. G.
Carotenoids of cavernicolous crayfish. bibliog Science 144:1467-9 Je 19 '64
WOLFE, Henia Karmel-. See Karmel-Wolfe, H.
WOLFE, Henry C.
Austrian revival. America 108:297-9 Mr 2 '63
Doom hovered over the Danube. Sat R 47:46 Mr 21 '64
Emperor's mistakes. Sat R 47:65 Ap 11 '64
Europe east of Berlin. Sat R 46:92 Mr 16 '63
Little people. Sat R 47:71 N 7 '64
Memoir of a mission. Sat R 47:21+ Je 13 '64
No sound, only fury. Sat R 46:34 My 4 '63
Where to see practically everybody. Sat R 47:104-6 Mr 14 '64
Zone of quiet desperation. Sat R 47:43 O 10 '64
WOLFE, James E.
Spokesmen for steel and rails see era of labor peace ahead; excerpts from statement. U S News 57:98 O 19 '64

about

Master strategist of the railroad settlement. M. H. Zim. il por Fortune 70:164-6+ Jl '64
Rails close ranks in bargaining. por Bsns W p52+ F 16 '63
WOLFE, Leo
Maurice Sendak. Horn Bk 40:351-4 Ag '64
WOLFE, Raymond
Magnetothermoelectricity; with biographical sketch. Sci Am 210:18, 70-6+ bibliog(p 140) Je '64
WOLFE, Robert A.
Wolfe of Lionel corp. il por Fortune 69:51 Ap '64
WOLFE, Thomas K.
Las Vegas! Esquire 61:97-103+ F '64
Marvelous mouth. Esquire 60:146+ O '63
Public lives: Confidential magazine; reflections in tranquillity by the former owner, Robert Harrison, who managed to get away with it. Esquire 61:87-90+ Ap '64
There goes (varoom! varoom!) that kandy kolored tangerine-flake baby. Esquire 60: 114-18+ N '63
WOLFE, Thomas W.
Shifts in Soviet strategic thought. bibliog f For Affairs 42:475-86 Ap '64
WOLFE, Tom
Wowie! pors Newsweek 65:44-5 F 1 '65
WOLFE, Winifred
Tell me more. Writer 77:17-18 S '64
Yesterday's child; story. Redbook 122:165-96 N '63
WOLFENDEN, Jeremy
What they say as they wait to see Lenin. N Y Times Mag p26-7+ D 13 '64
WOLFERT, Helen
Space; poem. Nation 199:468 D 14 '64
WOLFERT, Ira
Coming: the most marvelous fair ever! Read Digest 84:91-5 Ja '64
Dazzling new shows for sidewalk superintendents. Read Digest 83:134-7 D '63
From farm to supermarket to you. Read Digest 85:124-9 N '64
Hosts to the new travel host. Travel 120:50-2+ S '63; Same abr. with title Around the world with the bedroom builders. Read Digest 83:173-6+ S '63
Most phenomenal athletes in history. Read Digest 85:151-4 O '64
Ocean currents, how the world's bloodstream flows. Pop Sci 183:76-8+ Ag '63
Steel: old giant with new tricks. Read Digest 82:228-30+ F '63
With Ranger VII, to the moon. Read Digest 85:75-80 N '64
WOLFF, Bob
Cry Wolff. H. L. Masin. por Sr Schol 82:24 Ap 24 '63
WOLFF, Fred M.
Light dimmers for home and industry. Electr World 71:25-9+ My '64
WOLFF, Harold
Great GM mystery. bibliog f Harvard Bsns R 42:164-6+ S '64
WOLFF, Karl
Bureaucrat of death. il por Time 84:32 O 9 '64
Bureaucrat of death. por Newsweek 64:57-8 O 12 '64
WOLFF, Kurt
Obituary
Pub W 184:34 O 28 '63

WOLFF, Poppy
Staging strategy for a beautiful party in one room. il pors House & Gard 125:162-5 My '64
WOLFF, Robert Paul
Cold war fiscal policy. Bul Atomic Sci 19:31-3 F '63
WOLFLE, Dael
AAAS council meeting, 1963. Science 143:829-31 F 21 '64
AAAS council meeting, 1962. Science 139:614-16 F 15 '63
WOLFSBURG, Germany
Aalto; Finland's greatest architect. il Arch Forum 118:120-5 Mr '63
WOLFSON, Sir Isaac
Sears of Britain, and more. il por Bsns W p 118-20+ F 8 '64
WOLIN, Meyer J.
Fructose-1,6-diphosphate requirement of streptococcal lactic dehydrogenases. bibliog Science 146:775-7 N 6 '64
WOLLIN, Goesta. See Ericson, D. B. jt. auth.
WOLMAN, Lois
Pink slips and chief executives. Duns R 81:47-8+ F '63
WOLOZIN, Harold
New guides help you plan. Nations Bsns 51:64-7 Ag '63
Why prices stay up. Nations Bsns 51:64-6 F '63
WOLPER, David
Young King David. il por Newsweek 64:111-12 N 23 '64
WOLSELEY, Garnet Joseph Wolseley, viscount
Model major-general, by J. H. Lehmann. Review
Sat R por 47:48 N 21 '64. F. C. Pogue
WOLSTENHOLME, G. E. W.
Obese degeneration of scientific congresses. Science 145:1337-9 S 18 '64
WOLTERECK, Heinze
Nature never fails to astound. il N Y Times Mag p76-7 My 19 '63
WOLTJEN, Harry C.
Delicate art of swimming pool guest control. Pop Gard 15:50 Jl '64
WOLVERINE shoe and tanning corporation
This little pigskin went to market; Hush Puppies, shoes of pigskin. il Bsns W p48+ D 7 '63
WOLVERINES
Sierra wolverine. W. F. Heald. il Nat Parks Mag 38:8-9 O '64
WOLVES
Deer track, wolf track. H. Hoover. il Audubon Mag 66:110-11 Mr '64
Wolf can be a girl's best friend; Faye Ginsburg of Chicago. J. Star. il Look 27:M8+ D 3 '63
Wolf in the family. J. Hellmuth. il Sat Eve Post 236:38-9 O 12 '63
Wolf is virtually gone. C. Callison. il Audubon Mag 66:37 Ja '64
Wolves versus moose on Isle Royale. D. L. Allen and L. D. Mech. il Nat Geog Mag 123:200-19 F '63
See also
Coyotes
WOMACK, David A.
Typewriter as a pulpit. Writer 76:25-6 D '63
WOMAN
Answer to some foolish theories about women. M. M. Hunt. il Redbook 121:66-7+ S '63
Change and challenge for the educated woman. P. Tompkins. Sat R 46:69-70+ My 18 '63
Dangerous sex: the myth of feminine evil, by H. R. Hays. Review
Sat R 47:47-8 D 12 '64. E. Capouya
Feminine mystique, by B. Friedan. Review
Sat R 46:34+ F 23 '63. L. Smith
I don't understand women (and I'm glad of it) O. Nash. Ladies Home J 81:58-9 S '64; Same abr. with title I still don't understand women. Read Digest 85:80-2 D '64
Lady goes round and round; softening of the Catholic attitude toward feminism. America 108:895 Je 29 '63
Mysterious lady. D. Newman and R. Benton. il Mlle 59:8+ Jl '64
New femininity. Time 81:36-7 F 8 '63
On being a woman. J. Brothers. Good H 158:30-3 F; 48-50 Mr; 40+ Ap; 52+ My; 62+ Je '64
Querelle des femmes. N. Eurich. il Sat R 46:64-5+ My 18 '63
Real women. R. Graves. il Ladies Home J 81:151-5 Ja '64
Second sex, etc, etc. W. Sheed. Commonweal 80:15-16 Mr 27 '64; Reply. G. A. Lindbeck. 80:261 My 22 '64
Six clichés in search of a woman: address, October 22, 1964. J. M. Kreps. Vital Speeches 31:147-9 D 15 '64
Today's tensions; women, the problem or the answer; address, November 9, 1963. M. Carpenter. Vital Speeches 30:184-6 Ja 1 '64
Weaker sex? Newsweek 62:47 Jl 1 '63
What Fellini thinks Mastroianni thinks about women. F. Fellini. Vogue 142:50-1+ Ag 15 '63
Will science change marriage? J. Lear. il Sat R 47:75-7 D 5 '64; Discussion. 48:100-2 Ja 2 '65
Word. V. P. McCorry. America 109:615-16 N 9 '63
See also
Beauty, Personal
Education of women
Farm women
Housewives
Matriarchy
Sex differences
Widows
Women and the church
Womens clubs and societies
Young women

Anecdotes, facetiae, satire, etc.

What the books don't know about women. R. Fontaine. Farm J 88:64A F '64

Bibliography

New books; mostly about women. P. Pickrel. il Harper 226:102+ Je '63

Defense

See Self defense for women

Diseases

D and C: most common operation on women. G. Naismith. il Todays Health 42:18-19+ Jl '64
J. Marion Sims, M.D. women's medical emancipator. T. F. Walsh and S. T. Donohue. Todays Health 42:30-1+ Je '64
Twenty-four hours in the life of an obstetrician. E. M. Wylie. il Read Digest 82:52-61 Ap '63
See also
Leucorrhea
Trichomoniasis, Vaginal

Dress

See Clothing and dress

Education

See Education of women

Employment

Arthur J. Goldberg talks to teens. A. J. Goldberg. Seventeen 22:104+ Je '63
Curious quest for womanpower. N. Reeves. Nation 197:89-91 Ag 24 '63
Difference that sex makes. il Time 83:85 Mr 20 '64
For girls only. America 109:473 O 26 '63
How not to waste college on girls; with study-discussion program, by M. Smart. G. Hechinger and F. M. Hechinger. il Parents Mag 39:40, 70-1+ F '64
Job opportunities for women college graduates. S. Swerdloff. bibliog f il Mo Labor R 87:396-400 Ap '64
On the job, women act much like men; Civil service study. il Bsns W p 114-15 O 12 '63
Report of President's commission on the status of women; excerpts from American women. Mo Labor R 86:1166-9 O '63
Special opportunity. P. H. Abelson. Science 145:115 Jl 10 '64; Discussion. 145:1123 S 11 '64
Surprising facts about women, work, marriage. il Sci Digest 54:79-82 O '63
Working women. T. R. Brooks. Duns R 82:62-3 Ag '63
See also
Equal pay for equal work
Household employees
Married women—Employment
Negro women—Employment
Woman—Equal rights
Woman—Occupations

Equal rights

Citizen in a changing world; address, October 12, 1963. K. Louchheim. Dept State Bul 49:704-8 N 4 '63; Same. Vital Speeches 30:93-6 N 15 '63
Convention on political rights of women; text. Dept State Bul 49:327-8 Ag 26 '63
Egalité for Frenchwomen, too. A. Maurois. il N Y Times Mag p62+ Je 7 '64
Equality of women. America 109:473 O 26 '63
Forgive me, but my mind shows; excerpt from Man and civilization: the potential of woman. M. Mannes. Vogue 141:124-7+ My '63

WOMAN—Equal rights—*Continued*
GI bill for women? excerpt from Feminine mystique. B. Friedan. Sat R 46:68 My 18 '63
Mrs Roosevelt's legacy; report on the status of women. E. Peterson. McCalls 91:84+ O '63
Speaking out; women are prisoners of their sex. B. Brophy. Sat Eve Post 236:10+ N 2 '63
Whatever happened to women's rights? P. Foley. Atlan 213:63-5 Mr '64; Same abr. with title Women's rights and what they don't do about them. Read Digest 84:227+ My '64; Discussion. Atlan 214:24+ Jl '64
Women in the new Africa; address, September 24, 1963. G. M. Williams. Dept State Bul 49:636-9 O 21 '63
See also
United Nations—Commission on the status of women

Health and hygiene

Medical facts about douching. Good H 158: 171 Ap '64
See also
Beauty, Personal
Menopause
Menstruation
Pregnancy

Legal status, laws, etc.

Existing law and measures to improve the status of women in the Western hemisphere. G. A. Tillett. Dept State Bul 51: 128-32 Jl 27 '64
Report of President's commission on the status of women; excerpts from American women. Mo Labor R 86:1166-9 O '63

Occupations

Advice to a young woman; interview. M. Divver. Changing T 17:31-4 Ap '63
Art, creativity and the home fires. M. White. il Ladies Home J 81:66-8 Je '64
Careers and women. il Sr Schol 85:22 N 11 '64
Decision for Susie Jones. H. L. Howard. il PTA Mag 57:27-9 Je '63
From scientist to secretary: four medical jobs. il Mlle 57:130-3 S '63
Have job, will travel. M. A. Brice. Mlle 60: 168+ N '64
I didn't go to college. il Seventeen 22:146-7+ S '63
Jobs in the money. S. Auerbach. il Mlle 59: 128-31+ S '64
Jobs that could only happen here; contemporary New York. G. Buckman. il Mlle 58: 152-3+ Ap '64
Problem that plagues the thoughtful woman; marriage-versus-career. A. Whitman. Redbook 122:50-1+ F '64
Twelve ways to write for a living. V. Voss. il Mlle 56:140-5+ Mr '63
Where the jobs are. B. Asbell. Ladies Home J 81:78+ Je '64
Women don't like to look at women. L. Graham. il N Y Times Mag p48+ My 24 '64
See also
Models (persons)
Secretaries
Woman—Employment
Women as authors

Professions

See Woman—Occupations

Psychology

Man talk: the importance of saying no. D. Newman and R. Benton. il Mlle 58:160+ Ap '64
On being a woman. J. Brothers. Good H 158:30-3 F; 48-50 Mr; 40+ Ap; 52+ My; 62+ Je '64
On friendship between women. J. West. Holiday 35:13-17 Mr '64
What makes a woman unforgettable? A. Whitman. Read Digest 82:72-4 My '63
Woman of thirty; with editorial comment. F. Sagan. il Vogue 142:30-5 Jl '63
Women's personalities do not depend on age. Sci N L 84:139 Ag 31 '63
You may be deaf, Ludwig, but I'm not! reactions to music. F. V. Grunfeld. il Reporter 32:51-3 Ja 28 '65

Religious life

See Women and religion

Salaries

See Salaries

Social and moral problems

See also
Alcoholism

Social and moral questions

New look at the oldest difference. G. Marine. il Nation 196:247-9 Mr 23 '63; Same abr. with title Mental differences between the sexes. Sci Digest 53:21-5 Je '63
Speaking out; women are prisoners of their sex. B. Brophy. Sat Eve Post 236:10+ N 2 '63
See also
Prostitution

WOMAN across the street; story. See Dikeman, M.
WOMAN for president. See Women as public officers
WOMAN in literature. See Women in literature
WOMAN suffrage
See also
Women and politics

United States

Our changing Constitution, by C. Leedham. Review
Sat R 48:33 Ja 16 '65. I. Dilliard
Pioneer work in the West: votes for women. il Sr Schol 83:5 D 6 '63

WOMB, Artificial. See Uterus, Artificial

WOMEN

Africa

New kind of African woman. M. Bernheim and E. Bernheim. il N Y Times Mag p 14-15 Jl 7 '63
Women in the new Africa; address September 24, 1963. G. M. Williams. Dept State Bul 49:636-9 O 21 '63

Asia

Women in the new Asia; excerpts, ed. by B. Ward. il UNESCO Courier 17:4-27 S '64

Burma

Burma: family in transition. N. N. Gyi. il UNESCO Courier 17:12-16 S '64

Ceylon

Ceylon: silent victory. S. Siriwardena. il UNESCO Courier 17:7-12 S '64

Congo (capital Leopoldville)

How to appear evolué. il Time 84:33 S 25 '64

Denmark

Danish girls. J. Star. il Look 28:43-6+ Mr 10 '64

France

Egalité for Frenchwomen, too. A. Maurois. il N Y Times Mag p62+ Je 7 '64

Germany (Federal Republic)

Brünnhilde reshaped. il Time 83:28-30 My 8 '64

Great Britain

Chic-ness crosses the channel. J. Laver. il N Y Times Mag p86-7+ N 24 '63

Japan

Gems that grow on command. R. Steinberg. il Sat Eve Post 237:70-3 Je 27 '64
Girls. T. Prideaux. il Life 57:98+ S 11 '64
See also
Geishas

Latin America

Matriarchs of the market. il Time 83:32+ Ja 3 '64
New look; emancipation of Latin American women. il Time 85:24-5 Ja 8 '65

Rome

Silent women of Rome. M. I. Finley. il Horizon 7:56-64 Wint '65

Russia

First in space, but not in femininity. A. R. Topping. il N Y Times Mag p 10-11+ Je 30 '63
For Soviet women: a thirteen-hour day; average Russian wife. E. Whiteside. il N Y Times Mag p28-9+ N 17 '63
Rise of Russian women. T. Gilmore. il Sci Digest 54:8-14 S '63

Sweden

Suffragette nuns. G. D. Kumlien. Commonweal 81:95-7 O 16 '64
Women crash another field; Svenska salpeterverken, Koping, Sweden. Bsns W p 120 Ag 22 '64

Thailand

Thailand: I am no longer the hind legs of an elephant. P. Dickinson. il UNESCO Courier 17:17+ S '64

WOMEN—*Continued*

Turkey

Ataturk & the emancipation of women. A. Afetinan. il UNESCO Courier 16:20-5 D '63

United States

After Nora slammed the door: American women in the 1960s, by E. Merriam. Review
Sat R 47:32-3 Jl 11 '64. M. Mannes
American women are rude; with reply by G. Steinem. M. Bradbury. il N Y Times Mag p48+ Mr 29 '64
American woman: today & tomorrow; summary of report by President's commission on the status of women. il Changing T 18:42-6 F '64
Case of the vanishing spinster. M. K. Sanders. il N Y Times Mag p34+ S 22 '63
Contribution of women in a changing world; address, April 20, 1963. K. Louchheim. Dept State Bul 48:801-5 My 20 '63
Do we undervalue full-time wives? appraisal of report by the President's commission on the status of women. M. Mead. Redbook 122:22+ N '63
End of a legend; five Peace corps girls journey across the Sahara. il Newsweek 63:50 Mr 16 '64
Fairest of the fair; New York girls. il Look 28:106-11 F 11 '64
Female of our species. H. Koningsberger. il Holiday 34:56-67+ Jl '63
Feminine mystique, by B. Friedan. Review
Commonweal 79:100-2 O 18 '63. J. Holzhauer; Reply with rejoinder. Mrs J. S. Arnold. 79:428-30 Ja 10 '64
For girls only. America 109:473 O 26 '63
Individualists; Mlle's annual Merit awards. il Mlle 58:72-6 Ja '64
Inquiry into the feminine mind. N. B. Brown. il N Y Times Mag p 17+ Ap 12 '64
Issues girls, club ladies, camp followers. M. K. Sanders. il N Y Times Mag p38+ D 1 '63
Mlle's annual Merit awards. il Mlle 60:68-71 Ja '65
Speaking out; women don't run the country. J. B. Priestley. Sat Eve Post 237:8+ D 12 '64
Speaking out; women get a dirty deal. T. Caldwell. Sat Eve Post 236:8+ My 25 '63
Trained intelligence: the Nations' greatest weapon; address, June 12, 1963. A. E. Stevenson. Vital Speeches 29:581-4 Jl 15 '63
U.S. women a minority group? Sr Schol 83:6-7 N 8 '63
What makes southern girls different? J. Anderson. il Ladies Home J 80:12+ My '63
Whatever happened to women's rights? P. Foley. Atlan 213:63-5 Mr '64; Same abr. with title Women's rights and what they don't do about them. Read Digest 84:227+ My '64; Discussion. Atlan 214:24+ Jl '64
Why do women have to be so rude? R. Lynes. McCalls 91:71+ Ag '64
Woman's world; report on Marriage and the American woman. Time 81:66 Je 14 '63
Women: emancipation is still to come. B. Bettelheim. il New Repub 151:48-54+ N 7 '64; Discussion. 151:37 N 28; 28-9 D 12 '64
See also
Education of women—United States
Woman—Employment
Woman—Equal rights
Woman suffrage—United States

Viet Nam (Republic)

Viet-Nam: twenty years of change and turmoil. Le-kwang-Kim. il UNESCO Courier 17:22-7 S '64

WOMEN, Famous
Gentle women and the tough. R. Payne. il N Y Times Mag p32-3 S 29 '63
Wicked ladies. L. Paul. il McCalls 90:94-5+ My '63
World of elegant women; photographic portfolio. P. Halsman. McCalls 91:94-9 O '63

WOMEN and international relations
Role of individual women in the world community; address, June 29, 1963. K. Louchheim. Dept State Bul 49:98-9 Jl 15 '63

WOMEN and men
Art of talking to boys; excerpt from Boys and other beasts. B. Lang. McCalls 91:58+ Ag '64
Avoiding the no point system; risking divorce playing bridge with your spouse. L. W. Robinson. il N Y Times Mag p 19+ Ap 19 '64
Ex-bachelor tells girls how to get your man. Ebony 18:158 Ap '63
Forgive me, but my mind shows; excerpt from Man and civilization: the potential of woman. M. Mannes. Vogue 141:124-7+ My '63
Frankly speaking; candid comments on a variety of subjects, comp. by G. Wagner. il McCalls 90:132 Jl '63
GBS and the fair sex; quotations, with introduction by T. C. F. Lowry. il Ladies Home J 81:128+ Ja '64
Ladies' day; one day of gynecocratic rule. il Newsweek 61:36-7 F 4 '63
Man talk: the importance of saying no. D. Newman and R. Benton. il Mlle 58:160+ Ap '64
Power men have over women. M. Mannes. Vogue 143:144-5 Mr 15 '64; Same abr. Read Digest 84:61-3 Je '64; Discussion. 85:71-4 N '64
Real women. R. Graves. il Ladies Home J 81:151-5 Ja '64
Scent of woman, by E. M. Borgese. Review
Reporter 28:46-8 My 9 '63. V. Peterson
Speaking out; women get a dirty deal. T. Caldwell. Sat Eve Post 236:8+ My 25 '63
Visiting Englishmen are no roses. G. Steinem. il N Y Times Mag p63-4 Mr 29 '64
Why men think women talk too much. S. Birmingham. il Redbook 121:43+ Je '63

Anecdotes, facetiae, satire, etc.

Black death on the living-room floor. H. A. Smith. il Sat Eve Post 237:28+ F 1 '64

WOMEN and peace
Arms and the woman. Nation 196:110 F 9 '63
Censorship begins at home; results of letters to the editor on Women strike for peace. M. J. Estren. Nat R 15:209-10 S 10 '63
JFK, the magazines, and peace. J. Tebbel. il Sat R 46:56-7 D 14 '63
JFK: what women can do for peace; interview. J. F. Kennedy. il McCalls 91:102-3+ N '63
Peace ladies. M. Decter. Harper 226:48-53 Mr '63
President Kennedy talks about women and world peace. R. S. Cramer. il Parents Mag 38:57+ N '63
President Kennedy talks about you, your children and peace; ed. by R. Robinson. J. F. Kennedy. il Good H 157:73+ N '63
President Kennedy talks to women about peace; excerpts from interview. J. F. Kennedy. il Redbook 122:51-3+ N '63
Right of petition; HUAC and Women strike for peace. Nation 196:435 My 25 '63
Un-American; two women from Women strike for peace indicted at behest of HUAC. New Repub 152:7 Ja 23 '65
What women can do for peace. J. Fischer. il Harper 226:14+ Ap '63; Same abr. Read Digest 82:55-9 Je '63; Discussion. Harper 226:12+ Je '63

WOMEN and politics
Golda Meir: woman with a cause, by M. Syrkin. Review
Commentary 38:63-4 Jl '64. A. Sherman
Hawaii's top woman politician. il Ebony 18:51-2+ Ap '63
Inquiry into the feminine mind. N. B. Brown. il N Y Times Mag p 17+ Ap 12 '64
Issues girls, club ladies, camp followers. M. K. Sanders. il N Y Times Mag p38+ D 1 '63
Lady, you are in politics! C. May. il Suc Farm 62:73+ N '64
Mayor is no angel. J. Finan and L. Elliott. Read Digest 83:154-7 Jl '63
Mrs Lyndon B. Johnson's challenge to women; excerpt from address, June 24, 1964. C. A. Johnson. il Sat Eve Post 237:88-9 Je 27 '64
Must women be bored with politics? M. Mead. Redbook 123:20+ O '64
New political power of women. Mrs R. J. Stuart. Ladies Home J 81:68+ S '64
Newsweek poll: the women's vote. L. Harris. il Newsweek 64:32 S 21 '64
Now it's wives on the campaign trail. il U S News 57:23 O 12 '64
Politics, a new, wide-open world for women. R. Connable. il Mlle 58:164-7+ Mr '64
Politics without malice; panel discussion, ed. by M. Hickey. il Ladies Home J 81:80+ Ap '64
Togo woman leader. il Ebony 18:44+ Mr '63
Who's been doing your thinking lately? R. B. Sayre. Farm J 88:79+ O '64
Women in the service of community and nation; address, February 3, 1964. K. Louchheim. Dept State Bul 50:347-9 Mr 2 '64
Women, politics, and the future. J. F. Fixx. Sat R 47:22 Je 20 '64
Women's vote; how will it go? survey of political opinion. McCalls 91:70+ Mr '64
See also
Congresswomen
Woman suffrage
Women as public officers

WOMEN and religion
Feminine mystique. Christian Cent 80:759 Je 5 '63
Methodist missions retooled; General conference. B. Thompson. Christian Cent 81:1273 O 14 '64
Pope recognizes women. Christian Cent 81:1165 S 23 '64

WOMEN and the church
Built-in bias. M. Daly. Commonweal 81:508-11 Ja 15 '65
Husband or wall. America 109:404 O 12 '63
Making place for women; Vatican council II. Christian Cent 81:821 Je 24 '64
Suffragette nuns. C. D. Kumlien. Commonweal 81:95-7 O 16 '64
Women and the church. R. Lauer. Commonweal 79:365-8 D 20 '63; Discussion. 79:603-4, 634, 665-6; 80:151 F 14-28, Ap 24 '64
Women at the council: spectators or collaborators? E. M. Jung. il Cath World 200:277-84 F '65
See also
United church women (organization)

WOMEN and the United Nations. See United Nations—Womens participation

WOMEN as air pilots
I flew around the world alone. J. Merriam. il Sat Eve Post 237:77-83 Jl 25 '64
Lady's day in the Comanche 400; ed. by R. Beatty. M. Link. il Flying 75:49-51 S '64
Shades of Amelia; two housewives attempt to circle the globe. il Newsweek 63:20 Mr 30 '64
Sweet explosion in the air; fastest woman flyer. P. Ress. il Sports Illus 19:16-17 Jl 8 '63

Anecdotes, facetiae, satire, etc.

Flight of the Honey bees. B. Haesloop. il Flying 74:48-9+ F '64

WOMEN as artists
Art of Kaethe Kollwitz. A. Werner. il Am Artist 27:24-9 N '63

WOMEN as astronauts
Comely cosmonaut. E. Stevens. il Ladies Home J 80:60+ S '63
Lady goes round and round. America 108:895 Je 29 '63
MA-9 pilot counters skeptics on sightings of small objects. Aviation W 79:31 Jl 1 '63
She orbits over the sex barrier; with report by C. B. Luce. il Life 54:28-33 Je 28 '63
Without portfolio. C. B. Luce. McCalls 90:16+ My '63
Women are different. il Time 81:26+ Je 28 '63
Woman on the moon. Newsweek 63:86 My 11 '64
See also
Tereshkova, V. V.

WOMEN as athletes
At last the girls are ours; women's Olympic track and field team. T. C. Brody. il Sports Illus 21:68-9 Ag 17 '64
Dash of style for track and field. R. Terrell. il Sports Illus 18:12-15 Ja 28 '63
Driven beyond dignity; Nichibo Kaizuka women's volleyball team. E. Whitehead. il Sports Illus 20:16-19 Mr 16 '64
Flamin' Mamie's bouffant belles; Texas track club. G. Rogin. il Sports Illus 20:30-2+ Ap 20 '64
Girl named Sinn. G. Rogin. il Sports Illus 21:58-64 Ag 24 '64
Girls in the Olympics. L. Smith. il Todays Health 42:28-31+ O '64
Lithe envoys to our Latin neighbors; women's U.S. gymnastic team. il Sports Illus 18:28-32 My 6 '63
New upsurge in women's track. il Ebony 18:115-16+ Je '63
Olympic girls. il Life 57:38-47 Jl 31 '64
Rough creed: there's no success without suffering; Nichibo women's volleyball team. L. Griggs. il Life 57:42 S 11 '64
U.S. U.S.S.R. meet. pors Sports Illus 21:12-13 Ag 3 '64
Why can't we beat this girl? photographs of European track stars by N. Leifer. Sports Illus 19:54-7 S 30 '63

WOMEN as authors
Angry young women. E. Moers. il Harper 227:88-92+ D '63
Answering voice. L. Untermeyer. il Ladies Home J 81:66+ My '64
Off the cuff. A. Marple. Writer 76:5-6 Je '63
On women novelists. D. Grumbach. Commonweal 80:198-200 My 8 '64; Discussion. 80:484-5 Jl 10 '64
See also
Women as journalists
Women as poets

WOMEN as automobile drivers. See Automobile drivers

WOMEN as city managers. See City managers

WOMEN as comedians. See Comedians

WOMEN as doctors. See Women as physicians

WOMEN as educators
See also
College professors and instructors

WOMEN as engineers
Let's woo the woman engineer. W. A. Stocklin. Electr World 70:6 Jl '63
Talk of the town. New Yorker 40:22-3 Jl 4 '64
Tenn. state's lady engineer. il Ebony 19:75-6+ Jl '64
Women in science and engineering. D. Wolfle. Science 145:1389 S 25 '64

WOMEN as executives
Boss ladies; symposium, ed. by L. L. Tornabene. pors Esquire 63:102-8+ Ja '65
Three-state store chain's vice-president. il Ebony 19:36-40+ F '64
Upgrading courses for lady brass; UCLA management seminars. Bsns W p 156+ N 16 '63

WOMEN as foreign service employees
Equal employment opportunity; Negro foreign service officers; remarks, March 12, 1964. D. Rusk. Dept State Bul 50:629-31 Ap 20 '64
Women in the service of community and nation; address, February 3, 1964. K. Louchheim. Dept State Bul 50:347-9 Mr 2 '64

WOMEN as gamblers. See Gamblers

WOMEN as humorists. See Humorists

WOMEN as hunters
Hunting, anyone? G. L. Voss. il Outdoor Life 131:42-3+ F '63
Put that rifle down, babe. L. Dietz. il Field & S 69:54-6+ N '64

WOMEN as investors
Ladies and stocks; Bache & co. special investment seminars for women. New Yorker 39:24-6 D 28 '63
Richer sex? Newsweek 61:74 F 11 '63
Women & money; excerpt from Man and civilization: the potential of woman. A. E. Schwabacher, jr. Vogue 141:94-7+ Ap 1 '63

WOMEN as journalists
Journalism of tomorrow. M. A. Guitar. il Mlle 56:162-3+ Mr '63
Twelve ways to write for a living. V. Voss. il Mlle 56:140-5+ Mr '63
See also
Women as reporters

WOMEN as judges
Her Honor takes the bench. pors Time 85:41 Ja 29 '65
People in trouble. A. Schiller. il Harper 228:145-9 Ap '64

WOMEN as jurors
Ladies of the jury. il Sr Schol 83:9 S 20 '63

WOMEN as lawyers
Lady defender; G. T. Root. il Newsweek 63:22 Mr 2 '64
Perils of Portia. il Time 83:47-8 Mr 6 '64

WOMEN as members of Congress. See Congresswomen

WOMEN as ministers
Lady in the pulpit; Barbro Stahl of Stockholm. il Time 81:83 Mr 22 '63
Women in Anglican pulpits? C. Northcott. Christian Cent 80:1360 N 6 '63
See also
Women as priests

WOMEN as musicians
Musical nuns; Diocesan teachers symphony of Pittsburgh; with photographs by B. Spiegel. Look 27:45-8 Mr 12 '63
Two great women pianists. Discus. Harper 228:109-10 Ja '64

WOMEN as novelists. See Women as authors

WOMEN as photographers
Focus on Marilyn Silverstone. L. Barry. il Pop Phot 56:130-5+ Ja '65
What photography did to me! A. Heaney. il U S Camera 26:58-9+ F '63
Women in photojournalism. M. K. Morgan. il Pop Phot 54:41+ F '64

WOMEN as physicians
America's first woman physician; Elizabeth Blackwell. J. Lentz. Todays Health 42:36-7+ Ja '64
Can women take medicine? R. Hoffmann. il Mlle 57:127-9+ S '63
Edith Irby revisited. il Ebony 18:52-4+ Jl '63
New day, new doctor; Negro woman doctor at Arkansas U. med school. il Ebony 19:27-30+ Ap '64
Outstanding women doctors. il pors Ebony 19:68-70+ My '64
Why so few women doctors? M. Fay. il Todays Health 41:46-9+ Je '63
Why there aren't more woman doctors. Sci Digest 53:29 My '63

WOMEN as pianists. See Women as musicians

WOMEN as poets
Poetry of three women. M. Swenson. Nation 196:164-6 F 23 '63
Verse. L. Bogan. New Yorker 39:173-5 Ap 27 '63

WOMEN as priests
Priesthood and women; tr. by W. Kramer. G. Heinzelmann. Commonweal 81:504-8 Ja 15 '65
Woolwich's revolution. C. Northcott. Christian Cent 81:678+ My 20 '64

WOMEN as prisoners. See Prisoners, Women

WOMEN as public officers
Ladies' day; new appointments. il Time 83:22-3 Mr 13 '64
L.B.J.'s hunt for womanpower. P. Lisagor and M. Higgins. il Sat Eve Post 237:86-7 Je 27 '64
More women in top government jobs. il U S News 56:19 Mr 16 '64
Something for the girls; President Johnson appoints women to ten government posts. il Newsweek 63:29-30 Mr 16 '64
Why and why not a woman for president? D. Lawrence. U S News 56:108 F 17 '64
Woman for president? il U S News 56:34-6 F 10 '64

Anecdotes, facetiae, satire, etc.

Thank you, Madam President; dancing at the White House. E. J. Kahn, jr. New Yorker 40:103-4+ My 2 '64

WOMEN as race car drivers. See Automobile drivers

WOMEN as real estate agents
See also
Real estate business

WOMEN as reporters
Prosciutto and Mrs Mellon: Washington's society pages. M. Greenfield. il Reporter 30:32-6 Mr 12 '64

WOMEN as scientists
Need sex desegregation. W. Davis. Sci N L 86:22 Jl 11 '64
New old worlds to conquer; women in marine science. H. Ellsberg. il Mlle 59:106-8+ Je '64
Talk of the town. New Yorker 40:22-3 Jl 4 '64
Will science change marriage? J. Lear. il Sat R 47:75-7 D 5 '64; Discussion. 48:100-2 Ja 2 '65
Women for space study. W. Wingo. Sci N L 84:103 Ag 17 '63
Women in science and engineering. D. Wolfle. Science 145:1389 S 25 '64

WOMEN as spies. See Spies

WOMEN as surgeons
Days are busy for only woman open-heart surgeon. J. G. Harmount. il Todays Health 41:31 Jl '63
What it takes to be wife, mother and heart surgeon. J. L. Block. il Good H 156:34+ My '63

WOMEN as theatrical managers, etc.
Off-Broadway girls. G. Buckman. il Mlle 58:132-3+ N '63

WOMEN as theologians
There are women theologians! list with biographical notes. Christian Cent 80:1053-4 Ag 28 '63

WOMEN as welders
Welder is a lady. il Ebony 18:58+ Ag '63

WOMEN college students. See College students, Women

WOMEN engineers. See Women as engineers

WOMEN golf players. See Golfers

WOMEN in aeronautics. See Women as air pilots

WOMEN in boating
Companionway (cont of) Out of the galley. R. L. Williamson. See issues of Motor boating
Gals take over. L. Miner. il Yachting 114:65-7+ S '63
Lady with a sextant. M. Wiley. Yachting 116:51+ D '64
Out of the galley. R. L. Williamson. See issues of Motor boating
Sailing on the edge. L. Morgan. il Motor B 114:48-9 N '64
Why women make great crews; and we do! J. Gould. il Yachting 116:56-7+ O '64

Anecdotes, facetiae, satire, etc.

Dream boat. H. V. R. Palmer. il Yachting 113:46-7+ Mr '63

WOMEN in literature
Querelle des femmes. N. Eurich. il Sat R 46:64-5+ My 18 '63

WOMEN in politics. See Women and politics

WOMEN lawyers. See Women as lawyers

WOMEN police. See Policewomen

WOMEN prisoners. See Prisoners, Women

WOMEN shoppers. See Shopping and shoppers

WOMEN spies. See Spies

WOMEN strike for peace movement. See Women and peace

WOMEN tennis players. See Tennis players

WOMEN workers. See Woman—Employment

WOMENFOLK (quintet) See Singers

WOMEN'S amateur golf championship. See Golf—Tournaments

WOMENS clothes. See Clothing and dress

WOMENS clubs and societies
Den mother to the clubwomen. B. Fancher. il Sat Eve Post 236:60-1 Mr 9 '63
Don't bug me, Mrs Katydid. il Life 55:109-10+ S 27 '63
Ladies, please come to order! J. Bradford. il Redbook 120:41+ Mr '63
Women's clubs help cities to advance street lighting. J. P. Heck. il Am City 79:114-15 S '64
See also
General federation of women's clubs
Young women's Christian association

WOMENS colleges. See Colleges for women

WOMENS hospital auxiliaries. See Hospitals—Volunteer workers

WOMEN'S national book association
Constance Lindsay Skinner award won by Rachel Carson. Pub W 183:130 F 18 '63
See also
Amy Loveman national award
Constance Lindsay Skinner award

WOMENS pages (in newspapers) See Newspapers—Womens pages

WOMENS pipes. See Tobacco pipes

WOMENS salaries. See Salaries

WOMENS shoes. See Shoes

WOMEN'S wear daily
All the fit that's news to print. G. Greene. il Sat Eve Post 237:77-81 Ap 11 '64

WONACOTT, Wayne A. and others
Elementary school industrial arts in Los Angeles. NEA J 53:31-2 Ja '64

WONDER, Stevie
Wonderful world of Stevie Wonder. il pors Ebony 18:99-100+ Jl '63

WONDER
No wonder! W. E. Sangster. Read Digest 82:126-8 Mr '63

WONDER drugs. See Drugs

WONDER world; musical comedy. See Musical comedies, revues, etc.—Criticisms, plots, etc.

WONDERSTONE
Wonderstone. H. D. Brown. il Hobbies 69:125 Ja '65

WONG, Kwok-ying. See Von Hippel, P. H. jt. auth.

WONNBERGER, Carl
In paperback. Sr Schol 84:18T-19T F 21 '64

WOOD, Abigail
Young living; questions and answers. See issues of Seventeen

WOOD, Alan, steel company
Unions' latest goal: lifetime jobs. il U S News 58:88+ Ja 25 '65

WOOD, C. W.
Plants out-of-the ordinary. See issues of Flower grower

WOOD, Cameron W. See Dutton, D. B. G. jt. auth.

WOOD, Charles
London openings. A. Brien. Theatre Arts 48:32 Ja '64

WOOD, David G.
How businessmen can fight big government and win. Harper 227:77-81 N '63

about

Delayed reaction; attack on business negativism in Harper's. Newsweek 62:91 N 18 '63

WOOD, Eleanor C.
(comp) Old (?) age. N Y Times Mag p 103 Ap 5 '64

WOOD, Elizabeth
Social-welfare planning. Ann Am Acad 352:119-28 Mr '64

WOOD, Evelyn N.
Speed reading. NEA J 52:44+ Ap '63

WOOD, Frederic C.
Sermonizing on sex. por Newsweek 64:45 D 21 '64

WOOD, Garfield A.
Speedboat king: Gar Wood. J. Martenhoff. il por Motor B 114:62+ Jl '64

WOOD, H. Charles
Naval observatory time signals. Electr World 70:30+ Ag '63

WOOD, J. L. and others
Foreign literature of chemistry. Science 140: 610-13 My 10 '63
WOOD, Jim
California Republicans: are the Birchers taking over? Reporter 30:24-6 My 7 '64
WOOD, Joan H.
Family fun with card games. Recreation 56: 400 N '63
WOOD, John A.
Chondrites and chondrules; with biographical sketch. Sci Am 209:20, 64-8+ O '63
WOOD, John F.
Food for peace. Américas 15:1-6 My '63
WOOD, Leonard
When gentlemen prepared for war. F. Russell. il por Am Heritage 15:24-7+ Ap '64
WOOD, Malcolm
Long and short of it; story. Sat Eve Post 236:54-7 Jl 27 '63
Project; story. Sat Eve Post 237:50-3 N 21 '64
What really matters; story. Sat Eve Post 237:56-64 My 16 '64
WOOD, Marion T.
Speaking out. por Sat Eve Post 238:10+ Ja 16 '65
WOOD, Nancy Crawford
Song of the soup kettle. Ladies Home J 80: 78-81+ Mr '63
WOOD, Nancy E.
Identifying speech disorder in the classroom. bibliog por Sch Life 45:6-8 Mr '63
WOOD, Natalie
Born to be a star. il pors Life 55:182-6+ D 20 '63
Boy meets girl. R. Baxter. il por Seventeen 23:76+ Ja '64
Natalie Wood: child of change. G. Zimmermann. il pors Look 27:91-4 Ag 13 '63
WOOD, P. S.
Museum of modern art, growing ever more stately, makes way for the new east wing; poem. New Yorker 39:28 Je 22 '63
WOOD, Robert E.
General who built the world's largest store. J. Reddy. por Read Digest 84:181-5 Ja '64
WOOD, Susan Greenburg
Marchesa Sieuwke Bisleti in Kenya. Vogue 142:64-7 Jl '63
WOOD, Thomas J.
Dade County: unbossed, erratically led. bibliog f Ann Am Acad 353:64-71 My '64
WOOD, William
One of the dead; story. Sat Eve Post 237:42-3 O 31 '64
WOOD, William J.
Confronting the adolescent. Commonweal 79: 409-10 D 27 '63
WOOD, Willis F.
African art gallery fund. Negro Hist Bul 27: 132 F '64
WOOD
Buying furniture? know your wood. il Changing T 17:13-14 Ag '63
Wood; a major structural material for boats. J. W. Plumb. il Motor B 114:34-9 D '64
Wood for eternity. F. Korotkin. il Am For 70:28-9 D '64
Wood you know? questions and answers. J. Daugherty and M. Daugherty. il Sci Digest 56:93-5 D '64
See also
Burls
Driftwood
Plywood

Diseases and pests

Your boat in A.D. 2063; cure for rotted wood. H. A. Calahan. il Motor B 111:26-7+ Mr '63
See also
Termites

Fireproofing

See Fireproofing of wood

Preservation

Your boat in A.D. 2063. H. A. Calahan. il Motor B 111:26-7+ Mr '63

Research

See Wood research
WOOD, Flexible. See Veneers and veneering
WOOD, Laminated
How to make laminated sister ribs. il Motor B 113:28-9+ Mr '64
Some eighteenth-century laminated woodwork. E. H. Pinto. il Antiques 86:197-9 Ag '64
WOOD alcohol. See Methanol
WOOD bending
Bumper jack does the trick in bending plywood. C. L. Hastings. il Pop Mech 119:189 F '63
New twist discovered for bending wood. il Pop Sci 185:70-1 S '64
Now anyone can steam-bend wood. L. C. Miller. il Pop Sci 183:111-13+ D '63
WOOD block prints. See Wood engravings
WOOD carving
Anne Arnold's wood menagerie. E. Dugmore. il Craft Horiz 24:20-3 Jl '64
Carving in native woods. W. D. Sturdevant. il Am Artist 28:59-63+ D '64
Carving wood with power. P. McCafferty. il Pop Sci 182:142-5 Mr '63
Decorative carving made easy with a fly cutter. R. J. DeCristoforo. il Pop Mech 119:194-6 Ap '63
George Lopez; a carver of santos. W. T. Le Viness. il Am Artist 27:25-9+ Ap '63
Images of the infidels; effigies in Kalash cemeteries. P. Graziosi. il Horizon 7:90-3 Wint '65
Inspired wood carvers of the Gothic age. A. Werner. il Am Artist 27:40-5+ D '63
Let's carve a log; fourth grade project in wood sculpture. H. J. McWhinnie. il Sch Arts 63:16-17 F '64
Slow emergence of star sculpture; work of R. Hague. G. Nordland. il Art N 63:30-2+ O '64
Tree sculpture. R. Wrenn. il Design 65:166-7+ Mr '64
Wildlife whittling. J. F. Clark. il Recreation 57:320+ Je '64
Wood. il Craft Horiz 24:92-3 My '64
Wood jewels from ancient Gaul. P. M. Grand. il Art N 63:26-9 My '64
Wood sculpture with a power saw. R. J. De Cristoforo. il Pop Sci 183:141-3 S '63
WOOD chipping machines
That utilizing monster; barker chipper. W. B. Morse. il Am For 71:30-1+ Ja '65
WOOD chips. See Wood waste
WOOD construction
Cedar and the backyard living boom. W. J. Duchaine. il Am For 69:40-3 O '63
WOOD cuts. See Wood engravings
WOOD distillation
See also
Charcoal
WOOD engravings
Portfolio of woodcuts by James Grashow. N. Kent. il Am Artist 28:26-9+ Ja '64
Portraits in wood; exhibition, Baltimore museum of art. il N Y Times Mag p45 N 3 '63
Wizard of the woodcut; A. Frasconi. il Time 82:60-1 D 20 '63
Woodcut illustration. E. Ness. il Horn Bk 40:520-2 O '64
Woodcut portfolio. W. Caxton, jr. il Am Artist 27:50-5+ My '63
WOOD fillers. See Filling materials
WOOD finishing
How to create faux bois. il House & Gard 125:126-7 Ap '64
New way to finish furniture and woodwork in the dark, rich mood. il House B 106: 164-5+ Ap '64
See also
Filling materials
WOOD floors. See Floors, Wood
WOOD ibises. See Wood storks
WOOD lathes. See Lathes
WOOD mouse. See Mice, White footed
WOOD oleoresin. See Terpenes
WOOD paneling. See Paneling
WOOD products industry

Consolidations and mergers

Western lumber plants a new root. il Bsns W p66+ Je 27 '64
WOOD pulp industry
Last chance for Admiralty; island ruined for Japanese-owned pulpwood mill. R. W. Young. il Field & S 69:10-12+ My '64
Timber rush; British Columbia. il Fortune 70:71-2+ N '64
When managerial styles clash; Canada's MacMillan, Bloedel & Powell River, ltd. il Bsns W p65-6+ N 30 '63
See also
Paper making and trade
WOOD pulp paper. See Paper
WOOD research
Woodman, save that tree! K. Detzer. il Am For 70:12-15+ S '64
WOOD roaches. See Cockroaches
WOOD rot. See Wood—Diseases and pests
WOOD storks
Our only native stork, the wood ibis. R. P. Allen. il Nat Geog Mag 125:294-306 F '64
WOOD ticks. See Ticks

WOOD ware. See Woodenware
WOOD waste
Wood chips for poultry litter. il Suc Farm 61:60 D '63
WOOD working. See Woodworking
WOODARD, James E.
Vernon: an all Negro town in southeastern Oklahoma. Negro Hist Bul 27:115-16 F '64
WOODBLOCK printing. See Block printing
WOODBURY, Charles H.
Charles H. Woodbury: Yankee with a paint brush. D. O. Woodbury. il por Am Artist 28:40-5+ D '64
WOODBURY, David O.
Charles H. Woodbury. Am Artist 28:40-5+ D '64
Granpa and the Atlantic Ocean; story. Read Digest 85:59-63 S '64
Please save my son! Read Digest 82:157-8+ F '63
WOODBURY, R. W.
Tree geraniums. Pop Gard 15:16 F '64
WOODBURY, Robert S.
Origins of the lathe. Sci Am 208:132-40+ bibliog(p202) Ap '63
WOODBURY, N.J.
Recreational lakes spring from swamp. J. I. Butzner. il Am City 79:31 S '64
WOODCARVING. See Wood carving
WOODCHUCK hunting
Dirt on chucks. C. Vinson. il Outdoor Life 133:46-7+ Je '64
Far-out chucks. T. Janes. il Outdoor Life 132:50-1+ O '63
Spooking up on chucks. S. L. Simmons. il Outdoor Life 133:64-5+ Mr '64
WOODCOCK, Leonard
New problems for collective bargaining. Mo Labor R 86:271 Mr '63
WOODCOCK shooting
Blackwater paradise. G. B. Evans. il Field & S 69:29-31+ N '64
Pocomoonshine cover. C. Ford. il Field & S 69:6-7+ Ja '65
WOODCRAFT
Know your woodcraft. C. B. Colby. Outdoor Life 131:138-9 My '63
WOODCUTS. See Wood engravings
WOODEN, John
Five midgets and a wink at Nell. J. Underwood. il Sports Illus 20:42+ F 24 '64
Pressure, that's our game: U.C.L.A. il por Time 83:74-5 Ja 17 '64
UCLA's John Wooden. I. R. McVay. il pors Look 27:93-7 Mr 12 '63
WOODEN toys. See Toys
WOODENWARE
Wooden bygones; Pinto collection, England. il Hobbies 68:54 O '63
WOODHULL family
Woodhull coat-of-arms. H. K. Eilers. il Hobbies 69:126-7+ O '64
WOODLAND caribou. See Caribou
WOODLE, Allan S.
Stern drive. Esquire 59:45-6+ My '63
WOODLEY, Richard
Aaron Henry and his friends. New Repub 151:6-7 O 10 '64
It will be a hot summer in Mississippi. Reporter 30:21-4 My 21 '64
Recollection of Michael Schwerner. Reporter 31:23-4 Jl 16 '64
WOODLOTS
AFA's North Carolina land ownership study; new light on small woodlands. J. G. Yoho and R. O. McMahon. il Am For 69:32-4+ N '63
Co-op helps farmers cash in on trees. B. Hardy. Farm J 87:76 Mr '63
Executive sideline: timber; rewards of tree farming. il Duns R 85:39-40+ Ja '65
Maine's farm woodlands. B. Geagan. il Am For 69:34-6 S '63
Small woodlands are a big problem, what can AFA do? K. B. Pomeroy. Am For 70:55 Mr '64
Who's cutting in my woodlot? Am For 70:2+ Ap '64
See also
Forest management
WOODMAN, Lyman L.
Anchorage fights back. Am City 79:118-20 S; 119-21 O '64
Seven severe sickening minutes. Am City 79: 98-9+ My '64
WOODPECKERS
Bird that went into orbit. L. B. Taylor, jr. Read Digest 82:224-5 F '63
Downy woodpecker. J. K. Terres. il Pop Gard 15:4 N '64
Meet the gila woodpecker. il Sunset 130:23 F '63
Summer of the woodpeckers. V. Connor. il Audubon Mag 65:247-8 Jl '63
See also
Flickers
WOODRING, Paul
Editor's bookshelf. See occasional issues of Saturday review
Opportunity is there. Sat R 47:55-6+ Ap 18 '64
Schools educate themselves. Sat R 47:153-5+ Ag 29 '64
—and others
(eds) Education in America. See issues of Saturday review
WOODROW Wilson national fellowship foundation
Fellowships. New Yorker 40:44-6 S 19 '64
WOODS, Damita Jo. See Damita Jo
WOODS, Donald H. See Hayes, S. L. jt. auth.
WOODS, Frank W. and O'Neal, Denny
Tritiated water as a tool for ecological field studies. Science 147:148-9 Ja 8 '65
WOODS, George D.
World bank and affiliates examine pressing problems of economic development. UN Mo Chron 1:59-62 N '64
about
Speeding up Worlds bank's pace. il pors Bsns W p 172+ S 12 '64
WOODS, Gurdon
What's wrong with U.S. art schools? a reply. Art N 62:42+ S '63
WOODS, John
Wheel of Saturday; Scale; Terrible is the child; Too early for dinner at Donald Hall's; Animal; poems. Poetry 103:292-7 F '64
about
Six poets. Poetry 104:108-14 My '64
WOODS, John F. and Nichols, George, jr
Collagenolytic activity in mammalian bone. bibliog Science 142:386-7 O 18 '63
WOODS, John G. See Losi, P. F. jt. auth.
WOODS, K. B. and Leonards, G. A.
Permafrost. Science 143:1060-1 Mr 6 '64
WOODS
Our far-flung correspondents; cabin on Mt Riga, Conn. C. Rand. New Yorker 39:31-2+ Ag 10 '63
Wonderful woods. S. Maas. il Horn Bk 39: 418 Ag '63
See also
Woodcraft
WOODS hogs
Wild pigs' wild ride. il Life 54:51-2 Je 28 '63
Capture
See Animals—Capture
WOODS HOLE, Mass, marine biological laboratory
Visit Woods Hole aquarium. A. G. Melvin. il Hobbies 69:130+ Ag '64
WOODS HOLE, Mass, oceanographic institution
Oceanics, a new wave. il Newsweek 63:70 My 25 '64
WOODSMEN. See Lumberjacks
WOODSON, Carter Godwin
History and significance of Negro history week. M. Jackson. por Negro Hist Bul 27: 72+ D '63
Thought for Christmas. N. L. Milton. Negro Hist Bul 27:68 D '63
WOODSON, W. E. and Freitag, M.
Human factors in electronics. Science 145: 418+ Jl 24 '64
WOODSTOCK, N.Y.
Miracle on a mountain; weird junkpile or a masterpiece? D. L. Goodrich. il Sat Eve Post 237:22-7 S 12 '64
WOODWARD, Bliss
Important letters of prudent boatmen: YSB. Motor B 113:50-1 Mr '64
Plotting tomorrow's course. Motor B 113:37 Je '64
Speak up: there's a decal in the offering. Motor B 111:76+ Mr '63
Under the blue ensign. See issues of Motor boating
WOODWARD, C. Vann
Birth of Jim Crow. Am Heritage 15:52-5+ Ap '64
Checks and imbalances. Commentary 35:540-2 Je '63
Southerner's answer to the Negro question. Reporter 30:39-44 F 27 '64
WOODWARD, David
For those in peril on the sea. UNESCO Courier 16:4-9 My '63
WOODWARD, Dow O. See Bates, W. K. jt. auth.

WOODWARD, Florence
Legacy. Redbook 120:142 Ap '63

WOODWARD, Helen (Rosen)
President Wilson's First lady. Nat R 14:203-4 Mr 12 '63

WOODWARD, Kenneth
Ambush at Omaha Pass. Nation 196:373-5 My 4 '63

WOODWARD, Maria
I believe. por Seventeen 22:168 F; 108 Ag '63

WOODWARD, Robert H.
Classification of authors' cards. Hobbies 69: 116-17+ N '64
College-supported faculty research programs. Sch & Soc 91:109+ Mr 9 '63

WOODWARD, Stanley
Coach. por Newsweek 63:95 F 24 '64

WOODWARD, William H.
It is . . . a small college . . . yet, there are those who love it: Dartmouth college v. Woodward. R. N. Current. il por Am Heritage 14:10-14+ Ag '63

WOODWARE. See Woodenware

WOODWELL, George M.
Ecological effects of radiation; with biographical sketch. Sci Am 208:28, 40-9 Je '63
—and Martin, F. T.
Persistence of DDT in soils of heavily sprayed forest stands. bibliog Science 145:481-3 Jl 31 '64
—and Miller, L. N.
Chronic gamma radiation affects the distribution of radial increment in pinus rigida stems. bibliog Science 139:222-3 Ja 18 '63

WOODWORK
Wood. il Craft Horiz 24:92-3 My '64

WOODWORKING
Men who work with wood. D. Jordan. il Bet Hom & Gard 41:6+ Mr '63
Secret of precision woodwork. J. Burroughs. il Pop Sci 184:121-3+ F '64
Table-saw doodles: could you cut them? R. J. De Cristoforo. il Pop Sci 185:138-40 Jl '64
When a cabinetmaker builds, he makes wood sing. il House B 105:154-5 Ap '63
See also
Joints (carpentry)
Sanding
Wood carving

Projects

Four seasons bowl. J. Burroughs. il Pop Mech 121:152-5 Ja '64
Imagination is the product; Chicago institute of design. C. B. Hicks. il Pop Mech 121:116-20+ Ja '64
Projects you can make in one weekend. il Pop Sci 185:124-7 N '64
Tips for the home shop. R. J. De Cristoforo. il Pop Sci 182:137 F '63
Wordless workshop. R. Doty and others. See issues of Popular science monthly
See also names of projects, e.g. Airplane models

WOODWORKING machinery
See also
Jointers
Routing machines
Sanding machines
Shapers

WOODY, Jack
Two to one in Miami Beach. por Recreation 57:167+ Ap '64

WOODY plants
Woody plant seeds. A. J. Fordham. il Horticulture 42:18-20+ S '64

WOOL

Prices

Sheepmen face rough fight. B. Fowler. Farm J 87:54 Mr '63

WOOLCOCK, Cyril W.
We're not doing right by the gifted. NEA J 52:31-2 N '63

WOOLDRIDGE, Dean E.
How the machine called the brain feels and thinks. N Y Times Mag p24+ O 4 '64
Man's mysterious memory machine. Harper 226:57-63 Je '63

WOOLDRIDGE, William C.
Fiasco at Bloomington. Nat R 15:303 O 8 '63

WOOLEN and worsted fabrics
New woolen fabrics wash without shrinking. Sci N L 85:251 Ap 18 '64

Mothproofing

See Mothproofing

WOOLEN and worsted mills

Wages and hours

Earnings in wool yarn and broadwoven fabric mills, June 1962. C. M. O'Connor. il Mo Labor R 86:533-5 My '63

WOOLES, W. R. and Di Luzio, N. R.
Reticuloendothelial function and the immune response. bibliog Science 142:1078-80 N 22 '63

WOOLEY, Susan O. See Brock, T. D. jt. auth.

WOOLF, Leonard
Evening with Virginia Woolf. E. Irons. New Yorker 39:115-16+ Mr 30 '63
Fine art of self-appraisal. C. Sykes. Nation 199:310-11 N 2 '64
Genius and madness. il por Newsweek 64: 85B-86 S 7 '64
Leonard Woolf's autobiography. A. Mayhew. Commonweal 81:299-302 N 20 '64
Virginia Woolf in her madness. J. M. Edelstein. New Repub 151:15-17 D 5 '64

WOOLF, Virginia
Beginning again, by L. Woolf. Review
Time por 84:122+ S 18 '64
Evening with Virginia Woolf. E. Irons. New Yorker 39:115-16+ Mr 30 '63
Virginia Woolf in her madness. J. M. Edelstein. New Repub 151:15-17 D 5 '64

WOOLLEY, D. W. and Van Der Hoeven, T.
Alteration in learning ability caused by changes in cerebral serotonin and catechol amines. bibliog Science 139:610-11; 145:952 F 15 '63, Ag 28 '64
Prevention of a mental defect of phenylketonuria with serotonin congeners such as melatonin or hydroxytryptophan. bibliog Science 144:1593-4 Je 26 '64
Serotonin deficiency in infancy as one cause of a mental defect in phenylketonuria. bibliog Science 144:883-4 My 15 '64

WOOLLEY, Sir Leonard
Birth of glass; excerpt from History of mankind. UNESCO Courier 16:18-19 Je '63
Commonwealth of medicine; excerpt from History of mankind. UNESCO Courier 16:17 Je '63
First astronomers of China & Babylon; excerpt from History of mankind. UNESCO Courier 16:16-17 Je '63
Schoolboy in Sumer;excerpt from History of mankind. UNESCO Courier 16:14-15 Je '63

WOOLNER, Sidney H.
Federal housing agencies encouraging good design. Arch Rec 136:106+ Ag '64

WOOLSON, Constance Fenimore
Henry James, by L. Edel. Review
New Yorker 39:155-7 S 7 '63. N. Bliven

WOOLSON, Robert
Sidewalk classic. Pop Mech 120:146-51+ N; 128-31 D '63
Twelve MPH scoot-car. Pop Mech 120:138-44+ Ag '63

WOOLVIN, Eleanor K.
Grain in the silo. Writer 76:20-1+ N '63

WOOLWICH, John Arthur Thomas Robinson, bp of. See Robinson, J. A. T.

WOOLWORTH, F. W, and company
Old five-and-ten spreads new wings. il Bsns W p58-60+ N 14 '64

WOOLWORTH, Norman S.
Young blood in a lively old tradition. G. Holland. il por Sports Illus 19:20-2+ Jl 15 '63

WOOMERA missile range. See Proving grounds

WORCESTER, Mass. free public library
Worcester's place of delight. T. Taylor. il Library J 88:4535-7 D 1 '63

WORCESTER foundation for experimental biology
Mecca for the world's biologists. il Bsns W p 140-1+ Ag 15 '64

WORCESTER music festival. See Music festivals—Massachusetts

WORD blindness
Child reads backward? suspect dyslexia. Sci N L 87:61 Ja 23 '65
Reporter at large; research in specific dyslexia at Pediatric language disorder clinic. Babies hospital. C. Tomkins. New Yorker 39:127-8+ S 14 '63

WORD games
Daft fad. il Newsweek 64:104 N 2 '64
I've come back, cried Tom Swiftly. S. Leavitt. il Life 54:19 My 31 '63
Season for Swifties. il Time 81:36 My 31 '63
Soapies. Newsweek 62:75 O 7 '63
Swifty, he said gamely: Tom Swifties. Newsweek 61:81-2 Je 3 '63
Tom Swift carries on gamely. Read Digest 83:44 S '63
Whats-its. Time 83:51 My 29 '64
See also
Crossword puzzles

WORD perception
Visual search. U. Neisser. il Sci Am 210:94-100+ Je '64

WORD tests. See Vocabulary tests

WORDS
Finksville. Newsweek 62:46 Ag 5 '63
Hysteria about words. W. F. Buckley, jr. Nat R 16:100 F 11 '64
Magic and mystery of words; adaptation. J. D. Adams. Sat R 46:8-12 Ag 31 '63
Off the cuff. A. Marple. Writer 76:5 Mr '63
On words, singleness of mind, and the genius loci. M. Benary-Isbert. Horn Bk 40:202-9 Ap '64
Steel and quicksilver. M. Garthwaite. Horn Bk 40:212-14 Ap '64
Word association: common and original response. F. R. Fosmire and H. E. Tryk. bibliog il Science 139:415-16 F 1 '63
Words, words, words; symposium. il Horizon 6:119-20 Wint '64
See also
Anagrams
Dictionaries
English language—Terms and phrases
Slang
Vocabulary

WORDS and thought. See Thought and language

WORDSWORTH country. See Lake District, England

WORK, Henry H.
You have to let your kids go! Parents Mag 39:60-1+ Mr '64

WORK, James C.
Forester's final exam; poem. Am For 69:87 N '63

WORK, Telford H.
Serological evidence of arbovirus infection in the Seminole Indians of southern Florida. bibliog Science 145:270-2 Jl 17 '64

WORK
Labor day, 1964; Social action department statement. America 111:228 S 5 '64
See also
Rest periods
Right to labor

WORK accidents. See Accidents, Industrial

WORK benches
Desk, hobby bench, add legs and it's also a bar. H. M. Burke, jr. il Pop Sci 184:146-8 Ap '64
How to build your own roll-around bench for a radial saw. il Pop Sci 185:140-2 S '64
It's a carpenter's bench. il Sunset 132:136 Ap '64
Knock-down work/op bench. R. W. Jones. il Pop Electr 22:82 Ja '65
Slide-out grinder bench, you sit to work. il Pop Sci 185:130-1 Ag '64
Tested by a handyman; a wonder workbench. il Bet Hom & Gard 41:122 Mr '63
This bench goes together fast. il Bet Hom & Gard 42:16 Mr '64
This work bench will fold away. il Sunset 133:85-6 Ag '64

WORK camps. See Labor camps

WORK camps, International voluntary. See International voluntary workcamps

WORK experience. See Education, Cooperative

WORK holders. See Holding devices (machine work)

WORK measurement
Idle fifth man in the office; office work measurement systems. N. Buckley. il Duns R 82:47-8+ N '63
IBM's study of employee relations and work-measurement standards. T. R. Brooks. Duns R 84:41+ Ag '64

WORK performance standards. See Performance standards

WORK projects administration
See also
Federal art project

WORK rooms, Garden. See Garden houses, shelters, etc.

WORK rules
See also
Railroads—Work rules

WORK schedules. See Schedules

WORK simplification. See Home economics

WORK-study plan. See Education, Cooperative

WORK tables
All-purpose table for portable tools. R. J. De Cristoforo. il Pop Sci 182:146-50 Mr '63
Folding saw table for big panels. A. Lambrecht. il Pop Sci 185:140-1 N '64
Little big saw. il Pop Mech 120:150-1 D '63
Rolling saw table gathers no dust. R. Hoppough. il Pop Sci 183:110 D '63

WORKBENCHES. See Work benches

WORKER priests
Testing the conscience of the church. P. Steinfels. Commonweal 81:244-6 N 13 '64

WORKERS education. See Labor and laboring classes—Education

WORKERS ideas. See Suggestion systems

WORKING day. See Hours of labor

WORKING girls and women
See also
Woman—Employment

WORKING mothers. See Married women—Employment

WORKING week. See Hours of labor

WORKINGMENS leisure. See Leisure

WORKMENS compensation

United States

Workmen's compensation enactments in 1963. N. M. Diamond. il Mo Labor R 86:1432-5 D '63

WORKS of art, Taxation of. See Taxation of works of art

WORKSHOPS
Big ideas for improving your shop and home; symposium. il Pop Sci 183:97-108+ S '63
How to build your own compact storage corner for hand and power tools. il Pop Sci 185:120-4 Jl '64
How to build your own work center for portable power tools. il Pop Sci 184:114-19 Je '64
In-a-wall, home maintenance center. W. C. Lammey. il Pop Mech 119:122-7 Je '63
New ideas for your workshop; New York world's fair. S. M. Gallager. il Pop Sci 184:89-93 My '64
Plan a machinery service center. J. H. Pederson and F. W. Roth. il Suc Farm 62:64-5 Ja '64
Rollaway workshops. W. C. Lammey. il Pop Mech 121:169-73 Ja '64
Science workshops; Community science workshops. il Ebony 18:66-8+ Ag '63
There's space for a shop and the car. il Bet Hom & Gard 42:34 Mr '64
Woman, stay away from my workshop! P. C. King. Am Home 67:103 O '64

Equipment

Big idea: tool turret in a compact shop. S. M. Gallagher. il Pop Sci 183:102-4 S '63
Four homemade accessories for your shop. il Pop Sci 185:128-9 N '64
Let's talk shop. C. Peterson, jr. il Suc Farm 62:36-7 F '64
Popular science buyer's guide to home shop tools. il Pop Sci 183:157+ N; 155-6+ D '63; 184:151-2+ Ja '64
Shop for your chip off the old block. il Bet Hom & Gard 41:106 N '63
See also
Tools

Safety devices and measures

Handyman how-to. il Bet Hom & Gard 41:116-17 Ap '63

WORKSHOPS, Educational. See Educational workshops

WORKSHOPS, Library. See Library institutes and workshops

WORLD. See Earth

WORLD, End of the. See End of the world

WORLD airways, incorporated
Extension of new supplemental charter rights to Pacific asked. L. L. Doty. Aviation W 80:30 Mr 23 '64

WORLD alliance of Reformed churches. See Alliance of Reformed churches throughout the world holding the Presbyterian system

WORLD apart; story. See Heimer, M.

WORLD association for Christian broadcasting
Across the airwaves. E. C. Parker. Christian Cent 80:724-5 My 29 '63

WORLD bank. See International bank for reconstruction and development

WORLD Bible quiz. See Bible study

WORLD book fair. See Book fairs

WORLD calendar plan. See Calendar

WORLD confederation of organizations of the teaching profession
Delegate at Stockholm. M. E. Jenkins. il PTA Mag 57:29-31 F '63
PTA concerns are world concerns. J. Moorhead. il PTA Mag 58:26-8 Ja '64
WCOTP builds a world community of the teaching profession. S. Natarajan. il NEA J 52:30-1 O '63
WCOTP primer. W. G. Carr. il NEA J 53:38-9 O '64

WORLD conference on faith and order
Chats under a hot tin roof. Time 82:40 Ag 2 '63
Creative but unsatisfying; conference at McGill university. M. E. Marty. Christian Cent 80:974-5 Ag 7 '63
Ecumenicity and entomology: new church problem. W. Stringfellow. Christian Cent 81:1239-41 O 7 '64

WORLD conference on faith and order—*Cont.*
Ecumenism in Montreal. I. Beaubien. America 109:16-17 Jl 6 '63
Faith and order conference. D. J. O'Hanlon. America 109:138-41 Ag 10 '63
Hot and ecumenical; conference at McGill university. H. E. Fey. Christian Cent 80:950-1 Jl 31 '63
Montreal: faith and order. G. Baum. Commonweal 78:505-6+ Ag 23 '63
One heart and voice. America 109:66 Jl 20 '63
Outside the gates. B. A. Warkentin. Christian Cent 80:1057 Ag 28 '63
Reflections on Montreal. M. E. Marty. Christian Cent 80:997-9 Ag 14 '63

WORLD conference on national parks. See International union for the conservation of nature and natural resources

WORLD conference on world peace through law
For civilized existence. il Time 82:26-7 Jl 12 '63

WORLD congress of craftsmen
First World congress of craftsmen. il Craft Horiz 24:8-19+ S '64
First World congress of cratsmen. R. Slivka. il Craft Horiz 24:10-11 Ja '64

WORLD cooperation. See International cooperation

WORLD council for peace. See World peace council

WORLD council of churches
Aid to the distressed. G. Murray. Christian Cent 80:756-7 Je 5 '63
Armenian church and ecumenism. C. S. Calian. Christian Cent 81:1007-8 Ag 12 '64
Between Constantinople and Rome. W. A. Visser 't Hooft. Christian Cent 81:1106-8 S 9 '64
Campaign opens on poverty in South. Christian Cent 81:325-6 Mr 11 '64
Cardinal on ecumenism; and the World council. America 110:589 My 2 '64
Cardinal urges prayer for W.C.C. meeting. P. E. Leger. Christian Cent 80:261 F 27 '63
Central committee meets in Enugu. Christian Cent 82:36-7 Ja 13 '65
Charity that got help; fund accounting system. Bsns W p64 O 24 '64
Church and world; meeting of Commission on world mission and evangelism in Mexico city. D. Peerman. Christian Cent 81:104-5 Ja 22 '64
Churchmen hold a peace conference; Geneva. Christian Cent 81:957 Jl 29 '64
Consultation on church growth. W. T. Thomas. Christian Cent 80:1083 S 4 '63
Continental ecumenism; Conference of European churches. G. Murray. Christian Cent 80:278 F 27 '63
Decision at Enugu; Central committee annual meeting. Newsweek 65:71 F 1 '65
Distinguished visitor; Patriarch Alexei, supreme head of the Russian Orthodox church. G. Murray. Christian Cent 81:1411-12 N 11 '64
Ecumenical next steps; World interchurch service (proposed) Christian Cent 80:483 Ap 17 '63
Ecumenicity and entomology: new church problem. W. Stringfellow. Christian Cent 81:239-41 O 7 '64
Geneva to Rome; resolution to establish with the Vatican a joint working committee on interfaith cooperation. il Time 85:89 Ja 29 '65
Home base is everywhere; meeting of Commission on world mission and evangelism, in Mexico city. D. Peerman. Christian Cent 81:70-2 Ja 15 '64
Impressions from Helsinki, Rome and Montreal. G. A. Lindbeck. Cath World 198:272-80 F '64
Is the local church obsolete? H. Moody. Christian Cent 80:1554 D 11 '63
Jar of jam; out went lights; Central committee meetings, Enugu, Nigeria. G. Murray. Christian Cent 82:91 Ja 20 '65
Key figure of the World council of churches discusses Christian unity; interview, ed. by E. C. Bianchi. W. A. Visser 't Hooft. America 109:354-6 S 28 '63
New look at Africa. G. Murray. Christian Cent 81:1540-1 D 9 '64
News of the Christian world. Christian Cent 80:866-7 Jl 3 '63
One body, one table; unresolved differences of eucharistic theology and practice. Christian Cent 80:1159-60 S 25 '63; Discussion. 80:1446 N 20 '63
Pray for Christian unity; week of prayer for Christian unity. Christian Cent 82:5 Ja 6 '65
Protestant ecumenical dilemma. W. D. Wagoner; K. Bridston; W. Nicholls. Christian Cent 81:329-32 Mr 11 '64
Questions at fifteen. Time 82:86 S 13 '63
Questions for the World council. J. R. Nelson. Christian Cent 80:1024-6 Ag 21 '63
Reconciliation in Rochester; work of Central committee. H. E. Fey. Christian Cent 80:1125-7 S 18 '63
Search is pursued; successor to W. A. Visser 't Hooft. G. Murray. Christian Cent 80:1590-2 D 18 '63
Service fosters unity; refugee service in Tanganyika; with editorial comment. G. Murray. Christian Cent 81:261, 278+ F 26 '64
Slow march to unity; Britain's first Faith and order conference. C. Northcott. Christian Cent 81:1231-2 O 7 '64
Successor to Visser 't Hooft. G. Murray. Christian Cent 81:1030 Ag 19 '64; Correction. 81:1148 S 16 '64
Summer flight. G. Murray. Christian Cent 80:1112+ S 11 '63
Thinking the unthinkable; concerning F. Nolde's address at W.C.C. conference, Buck Hill Falls. Christian Cent 81:627-8 My 13 '64
To Ferney from Malagnou. G. Murray. Christian Cent 81:744-5 Je 3 '64
Tremble no more; Pentecostal message to Protestant and Orthodox churches. Christian Cent 80:699 My 29 '63
U.S. conference for the world council. W. T. Thomas. Christian Cent 81:676 My 20 '64
Visser 't Hooft stays. Time 85:60 Ja 22 '65
Voices from Odessa; Christian churches spoke to the world about church unity. America 110:330 Mr 14 '64
Who'll be head man? Time 84:65 S 25 '64
World council. G. Murray. Christian Cent 80:472, 1311 Ap 10, O 23 '63
WCC helps Americans; support for the needy in the Mississippi delta. America 110:695 My 23 '64
W.C.C. sends mission to Mississippi delta. Christian Cent 81:660 My 20 '64

Ecumenical institute
See Ecumenical institute

WORLD court. See International court of justice, The Hague

WORLD economics. See Competition, International; Economic conditions

WORLD fairs. See Exhibitions

WORLD federation of United Nations associations
World federation of United Nations associations meets at United Nations headquarters. il U N Rev 10:31-2 O '63

WORLD festival of youth and students for peace and friendship
Communist international youth and student apparatus, by H. Romerstein. Review
Sr Schol il 84:18-20 My 8 '64. H. Overstreet and B. Overstreet

WORLD flights. See Aviation—World flights

WORLD food congress. See Food and agriculture organization of the United Nations

WORLD food program. See Food supply

WORLD food supply. See Food supply

WORLD fund. See International monetary fund

WORLD government. See International organization

WORLD health. See Public health

WORLD health assembly
World health; the work of the sixteenth assembly. il U N Rev 10:44-5 Je '63

WORLD health day
World health day 1963; message, April 7, 1963. M. G. Candau. il U N Rev 10:15 Ap '63

WORLD health organization
Ills of the world; summary of survey. il U N Rev 10:24-6 Ap '63
Jungle doctor today; American physicians in Malaysia, Cambodia and the new countries of Africa. F. Marley. il Sci N L 86:346-7 N 28 '64
Overseas health aid basic. F. Marley. Sci N L 84:231 O 12 '63
Reproduction study; U.S. grant will create WHO research unit. E. Langer. Science 140:963 My 31 '63
Seventeenth World health assembly meets in Geneva. il U N Rev 11:23-5 Ap '64
See also
World health assembly

WORLD history
And what else happened in 1492? il Sr Schol 83:5 O 11 '63
Before Columbus came. G. Baquero. il Américas 15:35-9 O '63
Eighteen years of challenge and change 1945-63. il Sr Schol 83:12-13 O 4 '63

WOLRD history—*Continued*
Lessons of history; address, Actober 1, 1964. H. G. Heymann. Vital Speeches 31:82-5 N 15 '64
New separate communism course: study in historical context. B. Arveson. il Sr Schol 83:19T O 18 '63
Years of challenge and change 1945-65. Sr Schol 85:42 O 7 '64

Textbooks

Terra incognita; non-western peoples. M. Pines. il Reporter 28:37-9 My 9 '63; Discussion. 28:8 My 23 '63

WORLD inter-church service. See World council of churches

WORLD language. See Language, Universal

WORLD law. See International law

WORLD maps
Map of the world (cont) Sr Schol 83:27-9 O 4 '63; 85:31-3 O 7 '64

WORLD medical association
Invasion fails to fluster World medical assembly. il Todays Health 41:48-9+ F '63

WORLD meteorological organization
Cooperation in outer space. R. N. Gardner. For Affairs 41:351-2 Ja '63
Toward a world weather bureau. C. Leedham. il N Y Times Mag p29+ S 22 '63

WORLD Methodist conference. See Methodist world conference

WORLD of difference; story. See Eclov, S.

WORLD of Ray Bradbury; drama. See Bradbury, R.

WORLD opinion. See Public opinion

WORLD organization. See International organization

WORLD peace council
Doves and stoolpigeons. L. M. Taubinger. il Nat R 16:1103-4 D 15 '64

WORLD police. See International police

WORLD politics
After Cuba: two lessons. E. Rabinowitch. Bul Atomic Sci 19:2-8 F '63
Allies at the funeral. New Repub 149:4-5 D 7 '63
American commonwealth? A. Buchan. Harper 226:95-101 Je '63
Anatomy of world leadership; address, April 3, 1964. A. E. Stevenson. bibliog f Dept State Bul 50:615-21 Ap 20 '64
Appeal to discontent; address, October 15, 1964. G. W. Ball. Dept State Bul 51:622-8 N 2 '64
Atomic age. ed. by M. Grodzins and E. Rabinowitch. Review
New Yorker 40:136-41 Je 13 '64. J. Bernstein
Back to power politics; nationalism and looser alliances. il Bsns W p27-9 O 19 '63
Changing of the guard. W. Lippmann. Newsweek 61:25 My 13 '63
Cold war in perspective. G. Lichtheim. Commentary 37:21-6 Je '64; Reply with rejoinder E. Stillman and W. Pfaff. 38:6+ N '64
Cold war strategists predict new moves; analyses from top State department policy-makers. il Nations Bsns 51:60-8+ D '63
Comment on the world's news fronts; excerpts from the press. See issues of Senior scholastic
Congress for Asia. W. Lippmann. Newsweek 65:9 Ja 4 '65
Cracked alliance. L. J. Halle. New Repub 148:17-20 F 23 '63
Cuba and the nuclear risk. W. Lippmann. Atlan 211:55-8 F '63
Current documents. See issues of Current history
Few peaceful resolutions. E. J. Hughes. Newsweek 63:13 Ja 13 '64
Growth of the world community. E. Luard. Ann Am Acad 351:170-9 Ja '64
International developments; address, August 24, 1963. P. Martin. Vital Speeches 29:752-4 O 1 '63
Japan, the United States, and Europe; address, March 28, 1963. U. A. Johnson. Dept State Bul 48:606-12 Ap 22 '63
Leaders and their mandates; presidential campaign and changes in Britain and the Soviet Union. M. Ascoli. Reporter 31:16 N 5 '64
Must we be the world's policeman? H. Cleveland. il N Y Times Mag p 14+ My 3 '64
New perspectives on the United States' world relationships; address, April 29, 1963. C. Bowles. Dept State Bul 48:817-23 My 27 '63
New world. R. Hotz. Aviation W 81:21 O 26 '64
New world threats: poverty and race; with editorial comment. P. Mason. il Nation 198:63, 68-71 Ja 20 '64
NATO and world responsibilities; address, May 7, 1964. G. W. Ball. Dept State Bul 50:823-8 My 25 '64
Not the first, nor the last; with editorial comment. Bsns W p29-30, 184 O 24 '64
On working with history; address, June 5, 1964. W. W. Rostow. Dept State Bul 50:961-6 Je 22 '64
Opinion, please from New York: predictions on affairs of state for 1965. H. Salisbury. il Mlle 60:13-14 Ja '65
Pax atomica: looking to '64. il Newsweek 63:10-12 Ja 6 '64
Prospects for war and peace; interview. H. Kahn. Nations Bsns 52:34-5+ Jl '64
Prospects for world peace: an overview. H. Kohn. bibliog f Cur Hist 46:321-5+ Je '64
Reflections on the Pacific community; address, March 28, 1963. H. Cleveland. Dept State Bul 48:613-16 Ap 22 '63
Responsibilities of a global power; address, September 18, 1964. G. W. Ball. Dept State Bul 51:473-8 O 5 '64
Results of empire: new problems for old. Newsweek 63:32+ Ja 27 '64
Return to multilateral diplomacy. J. D. Singer. Yale R 53:36-48 O '63
Role of law in political aspects of world affairs; address, December 29, 1962. L. C. Meeker. Dept State Bul 48:83-8 Ja 21 '63
Secretary Rusk discusses the outlook for 1964 over Japanese television; interview, December 24, 1963. D. Rusk. Dept State Bul 50:40-6 Ja 13 '64
Secretary Rusk's news conference of February 7, 1964. D. Rusk. Dept State Bul 50:274-84 F 24 '64
Tomorrow's world; questions and answers. W. Lippmann. Atlan 214:50-5 Ag '64
U.S. and world affairs annual 1963-64. il Sr Schol 83:10-42+ O 4 '63
U.S. and world affairs annual 1964-65; ed. by E. R. Floyd. il Sr Schol 85:12-39+ O 7 '64
U.S. foreign policy: problems and challenges for 1963; address, January 11, 1963. R. J. Manning. Dept State Bul 48:138-44 Ja 28 '63
U.S. policy in a changing world; address, October 6, 1964. W. W. Rostow. Dept State Bul 51:637-42 N 2 '64
Vials of wrath were ready to break. E. Kern. il Life 56:46-61 Ja 3 '64
Walter Lippmann, 1964; interview on CBS, ed. by E. Sevareid. New Repub 150:15-18 Ap 25 '64
Weapons control as seen abroad. C. Quigley. Cur Hist 46:346-53+ Je '64
World order in the sixties. R. Ducci. For Affairs 42:379-90 Ap '64
World stage is set for our President. P. Lisagor. il Nations Bsns 52:23-4 N '64
World summer spotlight. il Sr Schol 84:12-13 My 15 '64
Word view of freedom's hopes and dilemmas; address, August 10, 1964. A. B. Duke. Dept State Bul 51:340-7 S 7 '64; Same. with title Freedom. Vital Speeches 30:696-701 S 1 '64
Worldgram: from the capitals of the world. See issues of U.S. news & World report

See also
Balance of power
Current events
Geopolitics
International relations
League of nations

WORLD population. See Population

WORLD Presbyterian alliance. See Alliance of Reformed churches throughout the world holding the Presbyterian system

WORLD press institute. See Macalester college, St Paul, Minn.

WORLD publishing company
Times Mirror acquires World publishing co. Pub W 184:247 Ag 26 '63

WORLD records
Records unlimited; excerpts from Guinness book of world records. il N Y Times Mag p84 N 24 '63
See also
Aviation records

WORLD recreation congress. See Recreation conferences

WORLD rehabilitation fund, incorporated
U.S. grants aid to Chinese refugees in Hong Kong. Dept State Bul 52:41-2 Ja 11 '65

WORLD rule of law. See Rule of law

WORLD science center (proposed) See New York academy of sciences

WORLD security. See International security

WORLD series. See Baseball

WORLD student Christian federation
Latin American student conference. M. Arias. Christian Cent 81:1188-90 S 23 '64
WORLD tariffs. See Tariff
WORLD tennis (periodical)
Busiest voice in a busy, busy clan. B. La Fontaine. il Sports Illus 20:38-40+ Je 22 '64
WORLD tours
Painting on a world tour. C. Johnson. il Am Artist 27:48-9+ Ap '63
WORLD trade. See Commerce
WORLD trade center. See New York (city)—World trade center (proposed)
WORLD trade week. See Special days, weeks, and months
WORLD travel. See Travel
WORLD union of Catholic teachers
What to do? America 109:223 S 7 '63
WORLD unity. See International organization; International relations; Internationalism
WORLD war, 1914-1918. See European war, 1914-1918
WORLD war, 1939-1945
After twenty-five years. il Newsweek 64:31 S 14 '64
GI's: their war in Europe. R. G. Martin and R. Harrity. il Look 27:72-6 F 26 '63
Omaha Beach, 1944. America 110:787-8 Je 6 '64
Teaching about the great world wars; symposium, ed. by H. L. Hurwitz. il Sr Schol 85:6T-10T+ N 11 '64
Twenty-five years ago: Hitler strikes. H. W. Baldwin. il N Y Times Mag p 11-13+ Ag 30 '64

Aerial operations

Bombing of Germany, by H. Rumpf; tr. by E. Fitzgerald. Review
Commentary 36:323-5 O '63. M. Cunliffe
Combat vs. computers; testimony before the House defense appropriations subcommittee. C. E. LeMay. Aviation W 80:11 My 4 '64
Hiroshima pilot, by W. B. Huie. Review
Nation 198:440-2 Ap 27 '64. W. Whitman
See also
Dresden—Air raids
London—Air raids

Amphibious operations

See also
Dieppe raid, 1942

Art and the war

Out of the cellar; disposition of remainder of personal collections of Hitler and Goering. il Time 85:44 Ja 8 '65
Purloined Pollaiuolo panels. il Time 81:85 Mr 15 '63

Atrocities

Again the issue of German guilt. C. Fitzgibbon. il N Y Times Mag p 17+ Ag 18 '63; Discussion. p4 S 1 '63
Auschwitz comes alive again. il N Y Times Mag p 14-15 Ap 19 '64
Catholic church and Nazi Germany, by G. Lewy. Review
Christian Cent 81:886-8 Jl 8 '64. L. D. Streiker
Cry against a decision of silence; The deputy, by R. Hochhuth. E. Capouya. il Sat R 47:41-2 Mr 21 '64; Reply. Mrs B. Hecht. 47:28 Ap 18 '64
Death haunted their houses. A. Gronowicz. il Sat R 46:37-8 D 28 '63
Destruction of the European Jews, by R. Hilberg. Review
Christian Cent 80:680 My 22 '63. D. Peerman
Haunted Germany; haunted mankind. Sat Eve Post 238:82 Ja 16 '65
Heroes of Warsaw's ghetto; photographs. N Y Times Mag p22-3+ Ap 21 '63
Hochhuth's Representative. C. Barnes. Nation 197:287-8 N 2 '63
Living ghosts of the concentration camps. L. W. Wells. il N Y Times Mag p 13+ Ja 26 '64
Reporter at large; Eichmann trial. H. Arendt. New Yorker 38:40-2+ F 16; 39:40-2+ F 23; 40-2+ Mr 2; 48-50+ Mr 9; 58-60+ Mr 16 '63
Suicide of an ex-Nazi: E. Peters. E. Behr. il Sat Eve Post 237:76-9 Je 13 '64
Tempest over Der stellvertreter. B. Stoop. Christian Cent 80:980-1 Ag 7 '63
See also
Ravensbrueck lapins

Bibliography

New perspectives on the great wars. H. L. Hurwitz. il Sr Schol 85:18T-19T N 11 '64
Soviet view of World war II. A. Werth. Nation 197:143-5 S 14 '63

Campaigns and battles

See also
Ardennes, Battle of the, 1944-1945
Battlefields
Stalingrad, Battle of, 1942-1943

Pacific

Bataan day commemorated; with message from President Kennedy. Dept State Bul 48: 647 Ap 29 '63
MacArthur: the greatest captain of his era. R. E. Dupuy. il U S News 56:78-9 Ap 27 '64
Mastah Freddy's modest miracle. J. Reddy. il Sat Eve Post 238:68+ Ja 30 '65
See also
Guadalcanal, Battle of, 1942-1943
Iwo Jima, Battle of, 1945
Pearl Harbor, Attack on, 1941
Philippine Sea, Battles of the, 1944
World war, 1939-1945—Philippines

Russia

See also
Stalingrad, Battle of, 1942-1943

Western

Books; two accounts, British and American of invasion and campaign of France. A. J. Liebling. New Yorker 39:216-18+ O 19 '63
Brad vs. Monty: an old feud revived; summary of interview. O. N. Bradley. il U S News 58:55 Ja 18 '65
D-day, June 6, 1944; with report by J. L. Ahearn. il Look 28:21-3 Je 16 '64
D-day plus twenty years. C. Fletcher. il Read Digest 84:112-15 Je '64
D-day plus twenty years; re-creation of history for CBS reports. H. Mitgang. il Look 28:78-85 F 25 '64
De Gaulle's D day; Provence invasion. Newsweek 64:36 Ag 24 '64
Ghost of Normandy; twentieth anniversary of D day. Newsweek 63:48+ Je 8 '64
Mamie Eisenhower's longest day, D-day; interview, ed. by P. Mesta. M. Eisenhower. il McCalls 91:69+ Je '64
Pledge to freedom renewed on 20th anniversary of D-day; remarks, June 3, 1964. L. B. Johnson. Dept State Bul 50:954 Je 22 '64
This place is Omaha Beach. il N Y Times Mag p23 My 31 '64
This was it, H hour D day: the view from the beach just twenty years ago. K. Crawford. il Newsweek 63:50-1 Je 8 '64
See also
Dieppe raid, 1942

Catholic church

As The deputy opened. E. C. Parker. Christian Cent 81:349 Mr 11 '64
Cry against a decision of silence; The deputy, by R. Hochhuth. E. Capouya. il Sat R 47:41-2 Mr 21 '64; Reply. Mrs B. Hecht. 47:28 Ap 18 '64
Footnote to The deputy dispute: Jews of Rome, the Nazis and the Vatican. C. Mydans. Life 56:21 My 1 '64
Friar who saved 5,000 Jews. W. I. Fischman. il Look 28:66+ D 1 '64
No letup for Der stellvertreter. E. E. Turner. Christian Cent 80:1269-70 O 16 '63
Open city, silent city. Time 83:65 Ap 3 '64
Pius and the Jews. America 109:70 Jl 20 '63
Pius, Hitler, and the Jews. il Newsweek 63: 78-9 Mr 2 '64
Pius XII & the Jews. il Time 82:85-6 N 1 '63
Play that indicts Pope Pius XII. H. Graef. Cath World 197:380-5 S '63
Play that rocked Europe; The deputy. A. G. Aronowitz. il Sat Eve Post 237:36, 39+ F 29 '64
Der stellvertreter: the play that caused a storm. F. V. Grunfeld. Reporter 30:46+ Ja 30 '64; Discussion. 30:6+ Mr 26 '64

Causes

Hubris remembered. il Time 84:42 S 11 '64
What caused the great world wars? H. L. Hurwitz. il Sr Schol 85:6T-10T N 11 '64

Children and the war

See War and children

Claims

Ethics of lobbying; Philippine war claims. Commonweal 78:236-7 My 24 '63
Philippine war claims. W. V. Shannon. New Repub 148:10-12 My 18 '63

WORLD War, 1939-1945—*Continued*

Confiscation of art treasures, etc.

See World war, 1939-1945—Art and the war

Confiscations and contributions

Deal cuts General aniline knot. Bsns W p29 Mr 9 '63
General aniline goes private. I. Ross. il Fortune 68:127-9+ S '63
General aniline's fate; Justice dept. and Swiss interhandel. Bsns W p38 O 19 '63
What am I bid? Newsweek 61:79 Mr 18 '63

Destruction and pillage

See also
World war, 1939-1945—Aerial operations

Diplomatic history

Diplomat among warriors, by R. Murphy. Review
Nat R 16:827-9 S 22 '64. G. F. Elliot; Reply. D. Keyser. 16:936+ N 3 '64
Diplomat among warriors; excerpt. R. Murphy. il Sat Eve Post 237:32-4+ F 22 '64
When England offered everything to France; excerpt. P. Reynaud. il Sat R 46:26-8 Mr 16 '63
See also
Munich four power agreement, 1938

Fiction

Single works

What we were fighting for. E. Baker. il Sat Eve Post 237:58-60 S 19 '64

Jews

Anne's executioner? Newsweek 61:40+ Ap 29 '63
Appointment with hate. E. Wiesel; discussion. Commentary 35:348-50 Ap '63
Assessing blame. America 108:791-2 Je 1 '63
Bias against man. H. M. Schulweis. Christian Cent 81:361-4 Mr 18 '64
Danish Jews; how their countrymen saved them from the Nazis. R. Tunley. il Sat Eve Post 236:74-5+ F 23 '63
Eichmann in Jerusalem, by H. Arendt. Review
Commentary 36:201-8 S '63. N. Podhoretz; Discussion. 37:6+ F; 16+ My '64
Nat R 15:154-7 Ag 27 '63. E. van den Haag; Discussion. 15:207, 251, 367 S 10-24, O 22 '63
Nat R il 16:1007-12 N 17 '64. M. Geltman; Discussion. 16:1130+ D 29 '64
Newsweek il 61:94-5 Je 17 '63
Time 81:100 My 24 '63
End of the chase; Eichmann's legal expert, E. Rajakowitsch. Time 81:35-6 Ap 26 '63
Friar who saved 5,000 Jews. W. I. Fischman. il Look 28:66+ D 1 '64
Jew against Jew. Time 81:31 Mr 22 '63
Jewish resistance to the Nazis. O. Handlin; discussion. Commentary 35:253-6 Mr '63
New debate over a pope's views on Nazis. U S News 57:12 N 30 '64
Our last days in the Warsaw ghetto. A. Donat. il Commentary 35:378-89 My '63; Reply. S. Dyon. 36:272 O '63
Out of darkness. M. Alland. New Yorker 40:178+ Ap 25 '64
Pius, Hitler, and the Jews. il Newsweek 63:78-9 Mr 2 '64
Pius XII, the Jews, and the German Catholic church. G. Lewy. bibliog Commentary 37: 23-35 F '64
Pius XII, the Jews, and the German Catholic church. G. Lewy. bibliog Commentary 37: 23-35 F '64; Discussion. 37:6+ Je '64
Red bicycle. R. Berczeller. New Yorker 40:151-2+ Mr 7 '64
Reporter at large; Eichmann trial. H. Arendt. New Yorker 38:40-2+ F 16; 39:40-2+ F 23; 40-2+ Mr 2; 48-50+ Mr 9; 58-60+ Mr 16 '63
Requiem; story of performing Verdi's Requiem in Czech ghetto. D. I. Segal. Commonweal 79:262-3 N 22 '63
Rescue in Denmark, by H. Flender. Review
Sat R 46:26+ Je 1 '63. S. Spender
Trip into the blue. R. Berczeller. New Yorker 39:20-1 Ag 24 '63
200,000 persecutions prevented. G. Kent. Read Digest 82:169-70+ Mr '63
Vatican and Auschwitz. America 110:668 My 16 '64

Moral and religious aspects

See also
World war, 1939-1945—Catholic church

Naval operations

Hookie Bell versus Graf Spee. J. Stewart-Gordon. il Read Digest 85:180-2+ D '64
Night before Christmas, by J. Sanders. Review
Newsweek 61:100 Mr 11 '63
Two-ocean war, by S. E. Morrison. Review
Reporter 28:47-8 Je 20 '63. R. P. Knapp, jr
See also
Philippine Sea, Battles of the, 1944

Personal narratives

Brad vs. Monty: an old feud revived; summary of interview. O. N. Bradley. il U S News 58:55 Ja 18 '65
Children of the A-bomb, comp. by A. Osada; tr. by J. Dan and R. Sieben-Morgen. Review
Christian Cent 80:1108-9 S 11 '63. S. Klein
Complete war memoirs of Charles de Gaulle, 1940-1946. Review
Esquire 62:16+ N '64. M. Muggeridge
Giggle of Juan Ramírez. R. Plant. New Yorker 39:162+ N 2 '63
Guadalcanal twenty years after. L. W. Batten, 3d. Yale R 52:418-26 Mr '63
Making history live; students interview relatives and friends to learn what fighting a war really means. B. Follis. il Sr Schol 85:17T N 11 '64
Mamie Eisenhower's longest day, D-day; interview, ed. by P. Mesta. M. Eisenhower. il McCalls 91:69+ Je '64
Mastah Freddy's modest miracle. J. Reddy. il Sat Eve Post 238:68+ Ja 30 '65
Secret mission of Lieutenant Hilsman. J. G. Hubbell. il Read Digest 84:137-8+ F '64
Survivors; widows and children of the chief plotters against Hitler. J. Naar and R. Palm. il Look 28:54+ D 15 '64

Photography

Images of war, by R. Capa. Review
Sat R il 47:34-6 Je 6 '64. M. R. Weiss

Pictorial works

Many faces of war; excerpts from Faces of war. R. Capa. il N Y Times Mag p30-1 Ap 19 '64

Prisoners and prisons

See also
Escapes

Propaganda

See also
Propaganda, German

Radio, radar, etc.

Giggle of Juan Ramírez. R. Plant. New Yorker 39:162+ N 2 '63

Restitution claims

See Restitution claims

Science

See War and science

Secret service

Deadly gadgets of the OSS; condensation of Of spies & stratagems. S. P. Lovell. il Pop Sci 183:56-9+ Jl '63
Room 3603, the story of the British intelligence center in New York during World war II, by H. M. Hyde. Review
Nat R 15:158-60 Ag 27 '63. G. Morgenstern

Strategy

Overlord revisited: an interpretation of American strategy in the European war, 1942-1944. R. M. Leighton. bibliog f Am Hist R 68:919-37 Jl '63
See also
World war, 1939-1949—Aerial operations

Underground movements

Czechoslovakia

Brotherhood of silence, by S. Ilok. Review
Sat R 46:34 My 4 '63. H. C. Wolfe

France

King of the shadows; J. Moulin reburied at the Panthéon. il Time 85:36 Ja 1 '65
When the French lived in darkness; adaptation of address. A. Malraux. il N Y Times Mag p 12-13+ Ja 17 '65

War criminals

Bureaucrat of death; Gen. K. Wolff sentenced. Newsweek 64:57-8 O 12 '64
Crimes and punishment; German war criminals in Breda prison, Netherlands. B. Stoop. Christian Cent 80:564 Ap 24 '63
Exposing the horrors; war crimes trials in Frankfurt. New Repub 150:7-8 F 15 '64
Globke saga. Newsweek 62:41 Jl 22 '63
Haunted Germany; haunted mankind. Sat Eve Post 238:82 Ja 16 '65

WORLD War, 1939-1945—War Criminals—Cont.
Justice since Nuremberg. il Newsweek 61: 52 Je 10 '63
Painful purgative. Time 83:35 Mr 20 '64
Pursuit of guilt; Germany's final roundup of war criminals. G. Brook-Shepherd. Atlan 214:76-80 S '64
Should Nazi criminals receive immunity? Christian Cent 82:69 Ja 20 '65
Sickening past; Auschwitz. il Newsweek 63: 29+ Ja 20 '64
Sleuth with 6 million clients; S. Wiesenthal. C. A. Farnsworth. il N Y Times Mag p 11+ F 2 '64
Time running out. Newsweek 62:54 S 23 '63
When does justice end? il Time 84:22-3 D 25 '64
See also
Nuremberg trials

Denmark

See also
Denmark—History—German occupation, 1940-1945

England

See World war, 1939-1945—Great Britain

France

Books; two accounts, British and American of invasion and campaign of France. A. J. Liebling. New Yorker 39:216-18+ O 19 '63
When England offered everything to France; excerpt. P. Reynaud. il Sat R 46:26-8 Mr 16 '63
See also
France—Army
France—History—German occupation, 1940-1945

Germany

Hitler's image of the United States. G. L. Weinberg. bibliog f Am Hist R 69:1006-21 Jl '64
Ike's view: FDR policy prolonged the war; summary of interview, ed. by E. T. Folliard. D. D. Eisenhower. il U S News 58:12 Ja 4 '65
Plot that almost changed history; July 20, 1944 assassination plot against Hitler. il U S News 57:52-3 Jl 27 '64
See also
Dresden—Air raids
Stalingrad, Battle of, 1942-1943

Great Britain

When England offered everything to France; excerpt. P. Reynaud. il Sat R 46:26-8 Mr 16 '63
See also
London—Air raids

Japan

See also
Pearl Harbor, Attack on, 1941
Philippine Sea, Battles of the, 1944
World war, 1939-1945—Philippines

Pacific

They died hard, those savage men. D. MacArthur. il Life 57:72-4+ Jl 10 '64
Where did Charles Lindbergh go? W. Ross. Esquire 60:152+ O '63
See also
Iwo Jima, Battle of, 1945

Philippines

They died hard, those savage men; excerpt from Reminiscences. D. MacArthur. il Life 57:72-4+ Jl 10 '64
See also
Philippine Sea, Battles of the, 1944

Poland

Living ghosts of the concentration camps. L. W. Wells. il N Y Times Mag p 13+ Ja 26 '64
Out of darkness. M. Alland. New Yorker 40: 178+ Ap 25 '64
See also
Jews in Poland

Russia

Russia at war, 1941-1945, by A. Werth. Review
Nation 199:409-11 N 30 '64. G. G. Kirstein
New Repub 152:20+ Ja 9 '65. H. Koningsberger
Newsweek il 64:102+ N 9 '64
Soviet view of World war II. A. Werth. Nation 197:143-5 S 14 '63
See also
Stalingrad, Battle of, 1942-1943

Switzerland

Spying for peace, by J. Kimche. Review
Nat R 14:534-5 Jl 2 '63. A. Lunn

United States

Hitler's image of the United States. G. L. Weinberg. bibliog f Am Hist R 69:1006-21 Jl '64
See also
Iwo Jima, Battle of, 1945

WORLD wildlife fund
Fending off doomsday. C. Peet. il Am For 70:20-3 Ap '64
Vogue's notebook; Wildlife dinner party, its stars, Joy Adamson and Peter Scott. il Vogue 141:22-3+ F 15 '63
WORLD without end; story. See Fritz, J.
WORLD without war conference, New York. See Peace conferences
WORLD women's congress
Moscow din. il Newsweek 62:38-9 Jl 8 '63
Women's club (Marxist model) il Time 82:24 Jl 5 '63
WORLDS Columbian exposition, 1893. See Chicago—Worlds Columbian exposition, 1893
WORLDS fair, 1939-1940. See New York (city) —Worlds fair, 1939-1940
WORLDS fair, 1964. See New York (city)— Worlds fair, 1964
WORLDS fair, Seattle. See Seattle—Century 21 exposition, 1962
WORLD'S fair corporation
Fair share of trouble; fair's finances. il Time 85:73-4 Ja 29 '65
WORLDS fairs. See Exhibitions
WORLDS of William Shakespeare (dramatic reading) See Dramatic readings
WORLEY, James
Observed near Jericho; poem. Christian Cent 80:1169 S 25 '63
Plea for judgment still; poem. Christian Cent 81:606 My 6 '64
WORLEY, John L.
Don't get caught water-short. Am City 78: 133-4 Jl '63
WORLEY, Joseph F. See Mitchell, J. W. jt. auth.
WORM lizards. See Lizards
WORMAN, Charles G.
American pepperboxes. Hobbies 69:122-3+ Je '64
Blunderbus. Hobbies 69:126-7 Ja '65
Henry Deringer, jr. Hobbies 68:124-5 Ja '64
Krag-Jorgensen. Hobbies 69:125+ Ag '64
Simeon North, pistol maker. Hobbies 69:124-5 O '64
WORMLEY, George W. See Wennblom, R. D. jt. ed.
WORMS
Worm learns. J. Bird. il Sat Eve Post 237: 66-7 Mr 28 '64
See also
Earthworms
Marine worms
Planarians
WORMS, Intestinal and parasitic
Immunize against worms. Sci N L 83:230 Ap 13 '63
New ways to combat parasites in sheep. Suc Farm 61:94 O '63
Preventing heartworm. J. Stetson. il Field & S 68:164+ My '63
What you need to know about beef cattle internal parasites. G. C. Shelton. Suc Farm 62:106 F '64
See also
Cestoda
WORMSER, René A.
Is it time to write a whole new income tax law? por U S News 54:60-4 Mr 18 '63
Mr Wormser's charter; excerpts from letter to commissioner of the IRS. Nat R 16:523-4 Je 30 '64
What it means to forget about a will; interview. por U S News 54:68-73 Mr 4 '63
WORMUTH, Francis D.
Politics of bedlam. Bul Atomic Sci 19:28-30 D '63
WORN-out farms. See Farms, Worn-out
WORRELL, Francis T.
Teachers as scholars. Science 147:358 Ja 22 '65
WORRY
Is this crisis really worthwhile? R. Baker. il Read Digest 84:134-5 My '64
Worry brought me to the edge of breakdown. il Good H 156:10+ My '63
See also
Anxiety
WORSHIP
Celebration of the Gospel, by H. G. Hardin and others. Review
Christian Cent 81:1065 Ag 26 '64. H. G. Davis
How to go to church. R. Matthews. Read Digest 82:60-2 F '63

WORSHIP—*Continued*
Let the earth stand in awe of Him; Christian worship in America. il Sat Eve Post 236: 19-27 D 21 '63
Variety of Catholic attitudes, by T. Westow. Review
Commonweal 79:724 Mr 13 '64. H. A. Reinhold
Way Protestants worship; excerpt from Ecumenical dialogue at Harvard. C. C. Richardson. Cath World 199:175-81 Je '64
Within Protestantism, diversity. M. M. Shideler. Christian Cent 80:295-8 Mr 6 '63; Discussion. 80:498+ Ap 17 '63
See also
Church attendance
Sacraments

WORSTHORNE, Peregrine
Black and white reality; a British observer's view; reprint. U S News 55:62-3 Jl 1 '63
Four weeks of campaigning, or a whole year. N Y Times Mag p29+ S 27 '64
Hailsham again stirs them up. N Y Times Mag p 11+ Ag 11 '63
It's the uncommon Commonwealth. N Y Times Mag p 12+ Mr 8 '64
Price of Profumo: Tories smeared. Life 54: 22-3 Je 21 '63

WORTH, Valerie
Dying willow; poem. Harper 229:130 N '64
Sundial; poem. Harper 227:49 D '63
White geese; poem. Harper 227:43 Jl '63

WORTH
Abacus and the rose; a dialogue after Galileo. J. Bronowski. il Nation 198:4-17 Ja 4 '64
Automation's challenge to education and human values; excerpts from Automation, education, and human values, ed. by William W. Brickman and Stanley Lehrer. bibliog f Sch & Soc 92:303-15 O 31 '64
Christian choice in a changing world; spiritual values vs materialist pressures. J. Voorhis. Christian Cent 81:396-9 Mr 25 '64
Danger beyond smoking. N. Cousins. Sat R 47:22 Ja 25 '64; Same abr. Read Digest 84: 41-2 My '64; Discussion. Sat R 47:31-2 F 15 '64
Need of intellect. R. O. Johann. America 111: 234 S 5 '64
Searching for certitudes. P. Schrag. Commonweal 79:36-40 O 4 '63
Sir, the word is moral! D. R. Kline. Christian Cent 81:455-8 Ap 8 '64
Sir, the world is moral! D. R. Kline. Christian Cent 81:455-8 Ap 8 '64; Discussion. 81:803-4 Je 17 '64
Word. V. P. McCorry. America 110:833-4 Je 13 '64

WORTHAM, Robert
Tenoning jig for fine wood joints. Pop Sci 184: 156-7 Mr '64

WORTHINGTON, Al
Bible in the bullpen. J. Devaney. il pors Sat Eve Post 237:28-9 My 2 '64

WORTHINGTON, Peter
Vietnam: school for U.S. guerrillas. Nation 196:179-80 Mr 2 '63

WORTHINGTON, Robin
How to live with a swing-shift husband. Parents Mag 39:50-1+ O '64

WORTHINGTON, W. Curtis, Jr, and Cathcart, R. S. 3d
Ependymal cilia: distribution and activity in the adult human brain. bibliog Science 139: 221-2 Ja 18 '63

WORTHY, James C.
Church and the businessman. Christian Cent 80:1232-4 O 9 '63

WORTHY, William
Red Chinese American Negro. Esquire 62: 132+ O '64

WORTMAN, Edith Powell
Graduation observation; poem. McCalls 90:123 Je '63
Salvage; poem. McCalls 91:200 N '63

WORTMAN, Leon A.
Christmas lights twinkle to music. Pop Electr 21:45-8 D '64
R.F. coil frequency-finder. Pop Electr 20: 60-1 F '64
These Xmas lights dance to music. Pop Sci 183:129-31 D '63
Twosome. Pop Electr 18:57 F '63

WORTMAN, Max S. Jr
Influences of employer bargaining associations in manufacturing. Mo Labor R 86:272-3 Mr '63

WORTS, George F.
Ready or not, here comes the bride; story. Redbook 120:60-1 F '63

WOUNDS
Burns and other skin lesions; microcirculatory responses in man during healing. J. G. Zimmer and D. J. Demis. bibliog il Science 140:994-6 My 31 '63
Wound-healing process linked to new enzyme. Sci N L 85:79 F 1 '64
See also subhead Wounds and injuries under names of organs and regions of the body, e.g. Brain—Wounds and injuries

WOZZECK; opera. See Berg, A.

WRANGELL, Alaska
Kids in Wrangell. J. K. Davidson. il Reporter 31:38-40 N 5 '64

WRAPPING materials
Food wraps; plastic film. il Consumer Rep 28:423-6 S '63
Glowing gift wraps. il House & Gard 126:170-1+ D '64
Unusual wrapping paper used by Berkeley store; illustrated with famous marks of printers of the 16th century. il Pub W 186: 46 D 7 '64

WRAPPING of packages
Christmas is for giving. il Suc Farm 62:50 D '64
Christmas paper, the long and the short of it. il Consumer Bul 46:27 D '63
For very special delivery; decorated envelopes. il McCalls 91:96-7 D '63
Gift-wrapping guide for people who can't wrap gifts. il Redbook 122:74-8 D '63
Gift wraps; for use after Christmas. il Seventeen 23:112-13+ D '64
Glowing gift wraps. il House & Gard 126: 170-1+ D '64
Herbs on your gift packages. A. H. Williamson. il Horticulture 42:30-1 D '64
If you want to be tidy about it; portable wrapping box. il Sunset 133:81 D '64
Little beauty gifts wrapped in beauty. il Good H 157:102-3+ D '63
Make your own fairyland; using milk cartons for gift wraps! il Seventeen 22:100-1+ D '63
Ornaments that go from package to tree. il House & Gard 124:144-5 D '63
Patchwork packages. il McCalls 92:116-17+ D '64
Royal wrappings. il McCalls 91:92-3 D '63
Special packages for special gifts. il Sunset 131:89 D '63
Wrapping and trimmings (title varies) (cont) New Yorker 39:194-5 D 14 '63
Wrapping it up; Papercraft corporation. New Yorker 40:22 D 26 '64
You wrap first, then decorate. il Sunset 133: 90+ D '64

WREATHS, Christmas. See Christmas decorations

WRECKING
Lipsett brothers: biggest wreckers in the building world. il Arch Forum 120:76-7 Ja '64
Notes and comment; fifteen-story-and-penthouse building on site of Myron C. Taylor mansion. New Yorker 39:15 Ag 24 '63
What goes up must come down. S. Blum. il N Y Times Mag p 10-11+ D 27 '64

WRECKS. See Shipwrecks

WREN, Sir Christopher
Gift for Missouri: bombed-out remains of church of St Mary Aldermanbury, London. il Time 81:35 F 8 '63

WREN houses. See Bird houses

WRENCHES
Things to know about sockets; wrenches. il Pop Sci 185:72-7 Jl '64
Things you never knew about wrenches. il Pop Sci 184:174-6 Ja '64
See also
Torque wrenches

WRENN, Roger
Tree sculpture. Design 65:166-7+ Mr '64

WRESTLING
Coach cracks color barrier. il Ebony 19:77+ Mr '64
Command performance; professional wrestling in Britain. Sports Illus 18:10+ Je 3 '63
Giant bird; Japan's Taiho. il Time 81:69 F 8 '63
It's fun if you get the schwingen of it. C. Essex. il Pop Mech 120:116-17 O '63
Meet Ricki Starr; wrestler with a gimmick. E. Palatsky. il Dance Mag 37:27 My '63
Night the Cyclones met a thunderclap; Iowa state vs Lehigh. il Sports Illus 22:48-9 Ja 25 '65
Snake pit; at Lehigh Valley university. il Newsweek 65:58+ Ja 25 '65
Two guys named Joe jolt Ithaca; wrestling tournament between Oklahoma state and Cornell university, Ithaca, N.Y. M. Kane. il Sports Illus 20:28-9+ Ap 6 '64
See also
Jiu-jitsu

WRIGHT, Alfred
Golf. See issues of Sports illustrated
Hottest man in a furnace. Sports Illus 19: 16-17 Jl 29 '63

WRIGHT, Arthur Frederick
Wright dynasty. por Newsweek 63:103-4 My 25 '64

WRIGHT, Betty Ren
Lady from Blue Rock; story. Redbook 120:52-3 F '63
Outsider; story. Redbook 121:58-9 O '63

WRIGHT, Bruce S.
Grilse of the Upsalquitch. por Field & S 67: 68-9 Ap '63

WRIGHT, Charles David
Dimensions; poem. Harper 230:73 Ja '65
Tongues of men and angels; poem. Sat R 47:30 Je 20 '64

WRIGHT, Charles H.
Negro physician in Detroit. Negro Hist Bul 27:109-10 F '64

WRIGHT, Cora
Are black-and-white films too good? por Pop Phot 52:81 F '63
Bounce flash for color. il Pop Phot 52:46-9+ Ja '63
Confusion about diffusion. por Pop Phot 52: 112-13 Ap '63
Cora Wright's guide through the maze of exposure automation. Pop Phot 54:49-59+ Mr '64
Eye as a meter. por Pop Phot 53:74-5 Jl '63
Fast meter reading. por Pop Phot 52:92-3 Mr '63
First camera with CdS cell. Pop Phot 52:76 F '63
For travel picture insurance, pre-check your equipment. Pop Phot 52:136-7 Ap '63
How to be goof-proof. por Pop Phot 53:75-6 Ag '63
Logetronic's Focatron, an image-sharpness meter. por Pop Phot 52:88-9 My '63

WRIGHT, David
Pastoral; poem. New Yorker 39:56 N 30 '63

WRIGHT, Eric
Blitzkrieg days. New Yorker 40:159-64 Ap 11 '64

WRIGHT, Esmond
Code name and a London contact. Sat R 47: 22-3 N 28 '64
Loyal, but a loser. Sat R 47:37-8+ Jl 11 '64

WRIGHT, Frank Lloyd
Natural houses of Frank Lloyd Wright; photographs. A. L. Huxtable. por N Y Times Mag p78-9 N 17 '63
Wasmuth's great portfolio on Wright reprinted. M. F. Schmertz. il Arch Rec 135: 84+ Ja '64

WRIGHT, George
Garden of good ideas. por Flower Grower 51:22-5 Ag '64

WRIGHT, Guier Scott, jr
Elementary art to develop visual sensitivity. Sch Arts 63:19-20 N '63
Subject matter of art. Sch Arts 62:24 F '63; 64:37-8 D '64

WRIGHT, Guy
Thank you, William Shakespeare! Read Digest 85:82 Ag '64

WRIGHT, H. E. jr. See Zeist, W. van, jt. auth.

WRIGHT, Henry. See Jordy, W. H. jt. auth.

WRIGHT, J. Handly
Tale of two crises; address, November 5, 1963. Vital Speeches 30:122-5 D 1 '63

WRIGHT, J. Skelly
Mentally disabled: stepchildren of the law. New Repub 150:24+ My 9 '64
Role of the courts: conscience of a sovereign people. Reporter 29:27-30 S 26 '63

WRIGHT, James
In memory of a Spanish poet; poem. Nation 196:251 Mr 23 '63
In the open. H. Strickhausen. Poetry 102: 391-2 S '63

WRIGHT, James C.
Highway robbery. por Sat Eve Post 236:19-23 N 30 '63

WRIGHT, Jasper H.
Informal but private. Library J 89:2947-9 Ag '64

WRIGHT, Jess C.
Audio-compression preamplifier. Electr World 72:32-3+ N '64

WRIGHT, Jesse
From the Chinese, a letter from Chu-shin to his son, to be opened after his death; poem. America 111:189 Ag 22 '64
Museum gothics; poem. America 110:487 Ap 4 '64
Perfection; poem. America 111:44 Jl 11 '64

WRIGHT, John K.
Lost world of Cape Canaveral, 1911; excerpt from a student theme. Harper 227:67 N '63

WRIGHT, Leigh. See Brokaw, C. J. jt. auth.

WRIGHT, Leslie S.
Feathering in heavy weather. Yachting 115: 206-7 My '64

WRIGHT, Louis B.
Britain that Shakespeare knew. Nat Geog Mag 125:613-65 My '64
Shakespeare boom: a 400-year success story; interview. por U S News 56:68-71 Ap 27 '64
Shakespeare had an aye for women. NEA J 53:34 N '64

WRIGHT, Marcia
Benjamin Harrison papers; reprint. Hobbies 69:110-11+ Ja '65

WRIGHT, Mary
Wright dynasty. por Newsweek 63:103-4 My 25 '64

WRIGHT, Mary Kathryn
Might makes Wright. por Time 81:74 Je 21 '63

WRIGHT, Phyllis M.
I'm Dr Kildare's doctor. por McCalls 90:70+ S '63

WRIGHT, Quincy
Projected European union and American international prestige. bibliog f Ann Am Acad 348:132-40 Jl '63
Relation of the United Nations to the United States. Science 141:512-13 Ag 9 '63

WRIGHT, Robert B.
East-West trade: the iron curtain eighteen years later; address, November 11, 1964. Dept State Bul 51:815-20 D 7 '64

WRIGHT, Robert H.
Desert arachnids emerge. Natur Hist 74:54-7 F '65

WRIGHT, Robert L.
U.S. patent policy and government research. Bul Atomic Sci 19:9-13 D '63; 20:34 O '64

WRIGHT, Rosco E.
Colorful classroom project: animated films. Sch Arts 64:10-13 O '64

WRIGHT, Sylvia
Do we sit? no, we collapse. N Y Times Mag p26+ Ap 19 '64
Drip spoon plate society. Harper 226:82-4 F '63; Same abr. with title Our drip-spoon-plate economy. Read Digest 83:207-8 N '63
Emergent thing. Mlle 60:124+ D '64
Now the sew-it-yourself boom. N Y Times Mag p 19+ Mr 8 '64
Our disease: compulsive containerism. Life 56:52A F 28 '64

WRIGHT, William C.
Capsule history of opera. Holiday 34:82-3 D '63

WRIGHT, Hamilton, organization, incorporated. See Hamilton Wright organization, incorporated

WRIGHT brothers
How the Wright brothers learned to fly; with quotations from Papers of Wilbur and Orville Wright. G. Soule. il pors Pop Sci 183:51-7 D '63

WRIGHT-Patterson air force museum. See Dayton, Ohio—Galleries and museums

WRIGHTSMAN, Jayne (Larkin)
Connoisseurs. por Vogue 141:117 Mr 1 '63
Fashion pace-setter. H. Markel. il por Good H 156:38-40+ Je '63

WRIGHTSMAN collection. See Art—Private collections

WRIGLEY, Philip Knight
Tragic rebirth of the Chicago Cubs. T. Cohane. il Look 28:60+ Je 16 '64

WRINKLES. See Skin

WRIST watches. See Watches

WRITERS. See Authors

WRITERS colonies. See Authors colonies

WRITERS conferences. See Authors conferences

WRITING
Can you read your own writing? F. Johnson. il Am Artist 27:50-5+ S '63
See also
Authorship
Ciphers
Hieroglyphics
Paleography
Penmanship

History

Art of writing. M. Cohen. il UNESCO Courier 17:4-7+ Mr '64
Echoes from the story of writing; excerpts from L'Ecriture et la psychologie des peuples (Writing and the psychology of peoples) symposium. il UNESCO Courier 17: 22-3 Mr '64
Scripts shrouded in mystery. il UNESCO Courier 17:26-8 Mr '64

Identification

How document detectives catch crooks. J. R. Berry. il Pop Sci 184:120-2+ Ap '64

WRITING (authorship) See Authorship

WRITING (composition) See English language—Composition

WRITING, Asian. See Oriental languages—Writing
WRITING, Chinese. See Chinese language—Writing
WRITING desks. See Desks
WRITING for the press. See Authorship
WRITING paper. See Stationery
WROBLESKI, H. M.
Roulette at the police station. Am City 78:90 Ag '63
WRONG, Dennis H.
After the Cuban crisis. Commentary 35:28-33 Ja '63
Books. Sci Am 208:181-2+ Ap '63
Population myths. Commentary 38:61-4 N '64
Re-imagining society. Commentary 37:77-8+ Ap '64
WROTENBERY, Carl
Island library in the round. Library J 88:4566-8 D 1 '63
WU, Chien-shiung
Nuclear theory verified. Sci N L 83:85 F 9 '63
Queen of physics. por Newsweek 61:92+ My 20 '63
WU, Yuan-li
China's economy and its prospects. bibliog f Cur Hist 47:166-72 S '64
Industrial development in China. bibliog f Cur Hist 45:173-7+ S '63
WUENSCH, Bernhardt J.
Confirmation of the crystal structure of tetrahedrite, $Cu_{12}Sb_4S_{13}$. bibliog Science 141:804-5 Ag 30 '63
—See Buerger, M. J. jt. auth.
WULBERT, Roland
Food of Greenwood. New Repub 149:7 Jl 13 '63
WULF, Louise Sims
Summer of surprises. Recreation 57:168-71 Ap '64
WULFF, Erich
Buddhist revolt. New Repub 149:11-14 Ag 31 '63
WULFF, Lee
Angling's charmed circle. pors Esquire 61:96-7+ My '64
Sermons and buckshot. Esquire 62:109+ N '64

about

Lee Wulff vs. Jock Scott transatlantic salmon challenge match. T. Rogowski. il pors Esquire 59:100-3+ Je '63
WULP, John
Night they all saw, at last, what was happening. Esquire 60:134+ N '63
WUNDERLICH, Bernhard
Solid state of polyethylene. Sci Am 211:80-4+ bibliog(p 154) N '64
WUORINEN, John H.
Scandinavia today. Cur Hist 47:350-4+ D '64
Socialized medicine in Sweden. bibliog f Cur Hist 44:333-8 Je '63
WUORIO, Eva-Lis
Singing silence; story. Sat Eve Post 236:58-60 Mr 23 '63
WURLAN coating process. See Textile fabrics—Coating
WURSTER, Catherine Bauer
Can cities compete with suburbia for family living? Arch Rec 136:149-56 D '64
Obituary
Arch Rec 137:26 Ja '65
WURSTER, William Wilson
Farewell, groves of academe. por Time 82:80-1 Jl 12 '63
Recent work of William Wilson Wurster. il Arch Rec 133:107-18 Ja '63
WURTMAN, Richard J. and others
Melatonin, a pineal substance: effect on the rat ovary. bibliog Science 141:277-8 Jl 19 '63
Melatonin synthesis in the pineal gland: control by light. bibliog Science 142:1071-3 N 22 '63
Melatonin synthesis in the pineal gland: effect of light mediated by the sympathetic nervous system. bibliog Science 143:1328-30 Mr 20 '64
—See Zacharias, L. jt. auth.
WÜRTTEMBERG state opera ballet. See Ballet companies
WUST, Carl J. and others
Actinomycin D: effect on the immune response. bibliog Science 143:1041-3 Mr 6 '64
WUTHERING Heights; drama. See Olfson, L.
WYANT, Ed
Demonstration camp program for retarded. Recreation 57:305 Je '64
WYANT, Rowena
Business failures. See issues of Dun's review and modern industry
WYANT, William K. Jr
Speaking of extremists. New Repub 151:12-16 S 19 '64
WYATT, Colin
Far and near. Natur Hist 72:60-2 N '63
WYATT, Gertrud L.
New town, new school, new problems. Parents Mag 39:68-9+ S '64
WYATT, John
He sends in the smoke for the green goose. M. Kram. por Sports Illus 20:56-8 Je 22 '64
WYATT, Robert H.
Education for responsible freedom. por NEA J 52:41 S '63
Local associations build professional strength. NEA J 53:18-20 F '64
NEA convention, June 28-July 3, 1964. NEA J 53:42-3 My '64
Next steps in federal aid. NEA J 53:35-6 Mr '64
WYATT, Woodrow
Private line from London. V. Cowles. Vogue 145:86-7 F 1 '65
WYCHERLEY, William
Country wife. Criticism
Sat R 47:28 Ag 15 '64
WYCKOFF, Peter
Letter from a broker. Sat R 46:62-3 D 14 '63
WYCKOFF, Ralph W. G. and others
Microradiography of fossilized teeth. Science 140:78-80 Ap 5 '63
WYDEN, Barbara W.
Kids and cops. N Y Times Mag p56-7+ F 23 '64
WYDEN, Peter
In the White House news. McCalls 90:36+ Ag '63
WYETH, Andrew
Andrew Wyeth. E. P. Richardson. il Atlan 213:62-71 Je '64
Andy's world. il pors Time 82:44-52 D 27 '63
Drawings of Andrew Wyeth. A. Mongan. il Am Artist 27:28-33+ S '63
Haunting world of Andrew Wyeth. R. Tunley. il por Read Digest 84:166-70 Ja '64
Wyeth's quiet art. J. Canaday. il por N Y Times Mag p74-5 N 24 '63
WYETH, James
Wyeth the youngest; exhibition at Swarthmore college. il por Time 83:62+ Mr 27 '64
WYETH, Newell Converse
Andy's world. il Time 82:44-52 D 27 '63
WYKAGYL country club course. See Golf courses
WYLIE, Cicely
Rewarding gerberas. Horticulture 41:332 Je '63
Wild flowers of New Zealand. Horticulture 41:370-1 Jl '63
WYLIE, Clifford W.
Confessions of a dirt forester. Am For 70:28-30+ Ap '64
WYLIE, Evan McLeod
Are you giving houseroom to health hazards? Am Home 66:14+ Ap '63
Farewell to the iron bastards; Texas towers await the wreckers. Life 55:7+ Jl 26 '63
Girl who refused to die. Good H 158:92-3+ My '64
One long night in a baby hospital. Good H 158:84-9+ Je '64
Twenty-four hours in the life of an obstetrician. Read Digest 82:52-61 Ap '63
—and Leary, R. V.
Hilarious hunt for the highwaymen. Sat Eve Post 236:75-81 Ap 13 '63
(ed) See Senn, M. J. E. We must stop contaminating our water
WYLIE, I. A. R.
Are you a grievance collector? Read Digest 84:175+ F '64
I enjoy myself most when I'm scared. Read Digest 82:77-80 Je '63
WYLIE, James A.
Can community recreation meet the needs of youth? Recreation 56:406-8 N '63
WYLIE, Janice
And have not love, I am nothing. M. Wylie. il por Ladies Home J 81:76-7+ Mr '64
WYLIE, Max
And have not love, I am nothing. pors Ladies Home J 81:76-7+ Mr '64
Friendly lynch scene, or How to kill a script. Life 57:12 N 6 '64
WYLIE, Philip
Just thinking. Ladies Home J 80:48+ N '63
Triumph; condensation of novel. por Sat Eve Post 236:37-53 F 2 '63
We learned the hard way about fire in the house. Read Digest 84:157-8+ Je '64

WYMAN, Donald
Best forsythias. Horticulture 42:38-9+ Mr '64
Crab apple. Flower Grower 50:40-1+ Ap '63
Fast-growing trees. Am Home 67:100-1 O '64
Groundcovers. Horticulture 43:24-7 Ja '65
Trees of Mount Auburn. Horticulture 42:38-9+ Je '64

WYMAN, Louis C.
Excerpt from address, April 3, 1963. Cong Digest 42:156+ My '63
Why a northerner opposed rights bill; excerpts from statement. por U S News 56:16 F 24 '64

WYMAN, Mark
Chile: revolution of good intentions. Nation 199:320-1+ N 9 '64

WYMAN, William
Haiku & Frost. por Sch Arts 62:25-6 F '63

about

Artistic marriage? William Wyman's homage to Robert Frost. D. P. Shultz. il Sch Arts 62:27 F '63

WYMAN-Gordon company
Androforming process comes of age. J. F. Judge. il Miss & Roc 12:22-3 F 4 '63
Wyman-Gordon set to build world's second biggest forging press. J. F. Judge. il Miss & Roc 16:15-17 Ja 4 '65

WYNDHAM, Francis
Charlie Chaplin at ease. Vogue 144:112-13 N 15 '64
Sophia Loren: the strength of love. Vogue 142:172-3+ O 1 '63

WYNDHAM, George O'Brien, 3d earl of Egremont. See Egremont, G. O. W.

WYNDHAM-QUIN, Windham Thomas, 4th earl of Dunraven. See Dunraven, W. T. W.-Q.

WYNN, Early
Just one more. por Newsweek 62:62-3 Jl 1 '63
Old Indian's last stand. J. Breslin. il pors Life 54:119-20+ Ap 5 '63

WYNN, Nan
Courage vs. cancer. J. Hopkins. por Good H 156:36+ Ap '63

WYNN, Ralph M.
Fetal homeostasis. Science 146:1080+ N 20 '64

WYNNE, Arthur
Fifteen letters; most popular game. J. M. Willig. il N Y Times Mag p22+ D 15 '63

WYNNE, Greville Maynard
Great western spy net. il por Time 81:35 My 17 '63
In from the cold. il por Time 83:33 My 1 '64
Leaks at the top? Newsweek 61:44 My 13 '63
Spies in Moscow: more than meets the eye. pors Newsweek 61:41 My 20 '63
Traders. il por Newsweek 63:40 My 4 '64

WYNNE, Jim
Jim Wynne. J. J. Collins. il pors Motor B 113:27+ Je '64

WYNNE-EDWARDS, V. C.
Population control in animals; with biographical sketch. Sci Am 211:10, 68-74 Ag '64

WYOMING
Turn left at Spring Creek. M. Hagen. il Am For 70:30-1+ S '64

See also

Booksellers and bookselling—Wyoming
Festivals—Wyoming
Fishing—Wyoming
Hunting—Wyoming
Insurance, Unemployment—Wyoming
Jackson Hole Valley
Paleontology—Wyoming

Description and travel

Into Wyoming's wilderness. J. R. Ullman. il Travel 122:54-6+ O '64
Wyoming; wild and wonderful. M. A. Rodgers. il Redbook 120:68-9+ Mr '63
Yellowstone country. B. Ballantine. il Holiday 35:26+ Je '64

WYSE, Lois
Absolute truth about marriage. McCalls 91:58 Je '64

WYSS, Johann
Swiss family Robinson; dramatization. See Olfson, L.

WYSZYŃSKI, Stefan, cardinal
Ask Americans to pray for us; ed. by C. Hotchkiss. por Sat Eve Post 236:58-60 F 2 '63

WYTHE, George
Teacher of statesmen. R. Moley. Newsweek 62:108 D 2 '63

X

XB. See Exploding wire phenomena

X-15 (airplane) See Airplanes, Experimental

X-19 (airplane) See Airplanes, Vertical take-off and landing

X-20 (airplane) See Airplanes, Experimental

X-21 (airplane) See Airplanes, Experimental

XR (extended range) film. See Photography—Films

X RAY analysis. See Crystallography—X ray studies

X RAY diffraction. See X rays—Diffraction

X RAY fluorescence analysis. See Chemistry, Analytic

X RAYS
Crystal structures adopted by black phosphorus at high pressures. J. C. Jamieson. bibliog il Science 139:1291 Mr 29 '63
Two neutron stars seen. A. Ewing. Sci N L 85:291 My 9 '64
Where is science taking us? revision of a paper describing attempt to establish pattern of X-ray emission from the Crab nebula. H. Friedman. il Sat R 47:44-5 Jl 4 '64
X ray. J. Star. il Look 28:30-2+ Je 30 '64
X-ray-induced bulk photovoltaic effect in insulators. S. I. Taimuty and others. il Science 144:173 Ap 10 '64
X-rays and neutron stars. il Sky & Tel 27:215-16 Ap '64

See also

Radiography

Diffraction

X-raying atoms. M. Mann. il Pop Mech 120:112-15 D '63

Industrial applications

See also

Radiation—Industrial applications

Measurement

X-ray astronomy. Sci Am 209:67-8 D '63

Physiological effects

Actinomycin D: suppression of recovery in X-irradiated mammalian cells. M. M. Elkind and others. bibliog il Science 143:1454-7 Mr 27 '64
Allelic mapping in yeast by X-ray-induced mitotic reversion. T. R. Manney and R. K. Mortimer. bibliog il Science 143:581-3 F 7 '64
Cancer; relation of prenatal radiation to development of the disease in childhood. E. J. Sternglass. bibliog il Science 140:1102-4 Je 7 '63; Discussion. 141:1109+; 142:448; 143:994-5 S 13, O 25 '63, Mr 6 '64
Circadian rhythmicity in the sensitivity of two strains of mice to whole-body radiation. D. J. Pizzarello and others. bibliog il Science 145:286-91 Jl 17 '64
Dissociation of homograft response to allogeneic versus xenogeneic skin grafts in irradiated mice. M. L. Tyan and L. J. Cole. bibliog il Science 141:813-14 Ag 30 '63
Electroencephalographic desynchronization in irradiated rats with transected spinal cords. G. P. Cooper and D. J. Kimeldorf. il Science 143:1040-1 Mr 6 '64
Electroencephalographic responses to ionizing radiation. J. Garcia and others. bibliog il Science 140:289-90 Ap 19 '63
Homograft tolerance in mice: use of urethan and sublethal irradiation. W. E. Davis, jr. and L. J. Cole. bibliog il Science 140:483-4 My 3 '63
Homologous disease reactivation by X-radiation. R. S. Schwartz and L. Beldotti. bibliog Science 140:171-2 Ap 12 '63
Low dose radiation of the developing brain. S. P. Hicks and C. J. D'Amato. bibliog il Science 141:903-5 S 6 '63
Motor responses of moths to low-intensity X-ray exposure. J. C. Smith and others. bibliog il Science 140:805-6 My 17 '63
Polyploidy induced by X-rays in Chinese hamster cells in vitro. C. K. Yu and W. K. Sinclair. bibliog il Science 145:508-10 Jl 31 '64
Reduced incidence of persistent chromosome aberrations in mice irradiated at low dose rates. P. C. Nowell and L. J. Cole. bibliog il Science 141:524-6 Ag 9 '63
Sensitivity of the head to X-ray. J. Garcia and others. bibliog il Science 144:1470-2 Je 19 '64
Use X-rays for cancer, not plantar warts. Sci N L 84:344 N 30 '63

X RAYS—Physiological effects—*Continued*
Variations in survival time after whole-body radiation at two times of day. D. J. Pizzarello and others. il Science 139:349 Ja 25 '63
X-ray affects muscles like muscular dystrophy. Sci N L 83:89 F 9 '63
X-ray sensitivity and DNA synthesis in synchronous populations of HeLa cells. T. Terasima and L. J. Tolmach. bibliog il Science 140:490-2 My 3 '63
X rays and the time of day. Sci Am 208:78 Mr '63
X-rays: are there cyclic variations in radiosensitivity? M. Menaker. bibliog Science 143:597 F 7 '64
X-rays: are there cyclic variations in radiosensitivity? R. Rugh and others. bibliog il Science 142:53-6 O 4 '63

Safety devices and measures

X-ray hazard from electron microscopes; letter. V. A. Phillips and J. A. Hugo. Science 143:1120-1 Mr 13 '64; Reply. F. W. Pauli. 144:1178 Je 5 '64

XANTHINE dehydrogenase. See Dehydrogenases

XANTHOPHYLL
Provitamin A_2 from lutein. P. Budowski and others. bibliog il Science 142:969-71 N 15 '63

XAVIER society for the blind
That the blind may read. A. R. McGratty. America 108:792-3 Je 1 '63

XENARIOS, Alexander
Classical approach; Chalcidice mining co. il por Time 81:92 Mr 22 '63

XENON
Bonding in xenon fluorides and halogen fluorides. K. S. Pitzer. bibliog il Science 139:414-15 F 1 '63
Geometry of the perxenate ion. W. C. Hamilton and others. bibliog il Science 141:532-4 Ag 9 '63
Inert gas produces new compound. Sci Digest 53:11 Mr '63
Sodium perxenate hexahydrate. A. Zalkin and others. bibliog il Science 142:501-2 O 25 '63
Thermochemical properties of xenon difluoride and xenon tetrafluoride from mass spectra. H. J. Svec and G. D. Flesch. bibliog il Science 142:954-5 N 15 '63
Xenic acid: reduction at the dropping-mercury electrode. B. Jaselskis. bibliog il Science 143:1324 Mr 20 '64
Xenon difluoride and the nature of the xenon-fluorine bond. P. A. Agron and others. bibliog il Science 139:842-4 Mr 1 '63
Xenon fluorides; fluorine-19 nuclear magnetic resonance spectra. A. C. Rutenberg. bibliog il Science 140:993-4 My 31 '63
Xenon fluorosilicate and related compounds. A. F. Clifford and G. R. Zeilenga. bibliog Science 143:1431 Mr 27 '64
Xenon hexafluoride complexes. H. Selig. bibliog Science 144:537 My 1 '64
Xenon hexafluoride: preparation of pure form and melting point. I. Sheft and others. bibliog Science 145:701-2 Ag 14 '64
Xenon oxyfluoride. D. F. Smith. bibliog il Science 140:899-900 My 24 '63
Xenon tetrafluoride; fluorine-19 high-resolution magnetic resonance spectrum. T. H. Brown and others. bibliog Science 140:178 Ap 12 '63
Xenon tetrafluoride: heat of formation. S. R. Gunn and S. M. Williamson. bibliog Science 140:177-8 Ap 12 '63
Xenon tetrafluoride molecule and its thermal motion: a neutron diffraction study. J. H. Burns and others. bibliog il Science 139:1208-9 Mr 22 '63
Xenon tetroxide: mass spectrum. J. L. Huston and others. il Science 143:1161-2 Mr 13 '64
Xenon tetroxide: preparation and some properties. H. Selig and others. bibliog il Science 143:1322-3 Mr 20 '64

XENON compounds
Barium xenate. A. D. Kirschenbaum and A. V. Grosse. bibliog Science 142:580 N 1 '63
Sodium perxenate and xenon (II) difluoride reduction at the dropping-mercury electrode. B. Jaselskis. bibliog il Science 146:263-4 O 9 '64

XENON flash lamps. See Electric lamps. Flashlight

XENOPHON
On tyranny, by L. Strauss. Review
Commentary 36:412-16 N '63. G. Lichtheim

XEROGRAPHY
Blackout for copiers; red background frustrates Xerox machines. il Bsns W p36 Ja 16 '65
Competition for Xerox. il Newsweek 64:70-2 S 7 '64
Cross-country duplicator sends mail in seconds; long distance xerography. Sci N L 85:392 Je 20 '64
Fortune in facsimile; 914 office copier. il Time 81:92-3 Ap 12 '63
Library copying: xerography. il Library J 88:1858-60 My 1 '63
Photocopying equipment. il Consumer Bul 46:28-32 N '63
Xerox applications; Brown university library. L. G. Vagianos. Library J 88:1792 My 1 '63

XEROX corporation
Birchbark curtain; John Birch society bulletin urging protest against U.N. television specials. R. L. Shayon. Sat R 47:29 O 3 '64
Competition for Xerox. il Newsweek 64:70-2 S 7 '64
Cutting the copier to desk-top size. il Bsns W p60+ S 28 '63
Fortune in facsimile; 914 office copier. il Time 81:92-3 Ap 12 '63
Midtown plaza promotes a Rochester building boom. il Arch Forum 121:8 Jl '64
Strange tactics of extremism, by H. Overstreet and B. Overstreet. Review
Sat R 47:95-6 O 10 '64. R. L. Tobin
They sang along with Mitch; Xerox series of entertainment films based on activities of social agencies of the United Nations. R. L. Shayon. Sat R 47:24 My 30 '64
Warm Scrooge, cold Grudge; Carol for another Christmas, presented on the ABC television network. R. L. Shayon. Sat R 48:39 Ja 16 '64
What's good for U.N. is good for Xerox; six non-commercial 90-minute films on TV concerning UN global activities. Bsns W p80+ Ap 18 '64
Xerox presents the U.N. Christian Cent 81:1484 D 2 '64
Xerox, the U.N. and I.C.Y. C. Soule. il Christian Cent 8:1305-6 O 21 '64

XHOSA language. See Kafir language (Bantu)

XINGUANO INDIANS. See Indians of South America—Brazil

XIRAU, Ramón
Variety and contrast; tr. by J. M. Alonso. Atlan 213:142-5 Mr '64

XOCHIMILCO, Mexico
Chinampas of Mexico. M. D. Coe. il Sci Am 211:90-8 Jl '64

XYLOCOPA. See Carpenter bees

Y

YAF. See Young Americans for freedom (organization)

YASD. See American library association—Young adult services division

YMCA. See Young men's Christian association

YMHA. See Young men's and young women's Hebrew association

YWCA. See Young women's Christian association

YWHA. See Young men's and young women's Hebrew association

YABE, Yoshiro, and others
Oncogenic effect of human adenovirus type 12, in mice. bibliog Science 143:46-7 Ja 3 '64

YABLONSKY, Lewis
Where is science taking us? por Sat R 46:54-6 F 2 '63

YABROFF, Arthur
Treasurer's report; excerpt. ALA Bul 58:631-2 Jl '64
View from the plateau. ALA Bul 57:249 Mr '63

YACHT building
Building a stock fiberglass cruiser. B. Cobb, jr. il Yachting 117:70-2+ Ja '65
Race against the rule; America's cup yacht. B. H. Frisch. il Sci Digest 56:67-73 Jl '64
Visions as the boatman sees them. J. R. Groover. il Motor B 111:48-9 F '63

YACHT clubs
Do-it-yourself yacht club; North Cape yacht club. J. Miner. il Motor B 111:100-1+ Je '63
Freshest club; Bayview yacht club. G. E. Van. il Yachting 115:98-100+ Ja '64
Genial landfall; Royal Bermuda yacht club. R. Joseph. il Esquire 61:68-71 Ap '64
Ideal yacht club; designed by R. Bidwell. A. Zich. il Sports Illus 18:32-6 Ap 22 '63
Juniors of the Royal St Lawrence yacht club. R. C. Craig. il Yachting 114:58-9+ Jl '63

YACHT clubs—*Continued*
Keeping yacht club juniors interested. A. C. Hubert. il Motor B 112:50-1+ D '63
Learning the hard way. E. B. Morris. il Yachting 117:104-5 Ja '65
Rotary yacht squadron of Pennsylvania. F. G. Rogers. Motor B 114:68 D '64
Seattle yacht club opening day. E. Crimmin. il Motor B 113:54+ My '64
Slocum society. B. Robinson. Motor B 111: 52+ Mr '63
Starting a junior sailing program. D. V. Smythe. il Yachting 115:54-6+ My '64
Twenty-one plus, a yacht club's adult sailing program; with photographs. B. D. Barker, 3d. Yachting 115:118-20+ Ja '64
Yacht club's year; Riverside YC. A. Anable. il Yachting 114:46-9+ D '63

YACHT decoration
Dust ruffles on the gas tanks. M. Wiley. il Yachting 115:194 Mr '64

YACHT racing
Agreement to hate; first joint challenge. O. Aisher. il Yachting 116:45+ S '64
Aloha to the Transpac fleet. B. Ruskauff. il Motor B 112:135 Jl '63
American Eagle wings her way toward Newport; America's cup trials on Long Island Sound. H. Whall. il Sports Illus 20:59 Je 22 '64
America's cup. S. Leslie. Nat R 16:918-20 O 20 '64
America's cup course, 1964. il Yachting 116: 67 S '64
America's cup defense; special report. P. Sparkman. il Motor B 113:34-5+ Ap '64
America's cup: racing for glory. L. H. Lapham. il Sat Eve Post 237:26-33 Ag 22 '64
America's cup racing, 1964 style. E. Mosbacher, jr. il Yachting 116:36-8+ S '64
America's cup report; new life in Britain's challenge. E. F. Haylock; M. Davis. il Motor B 113:92-3+ Ja '64
At noon on the Fourth: start of the Trans-Pacific. il Sunset 131:20 Jl '63
Aussies are coming; Australia's challenge for 1967 America's cup races. Newsweek 64:104+ O 5 '64
Battle of the Rhumb line; Bermuda race of 1964. A. F. Loomis. il Yachting 116:43-4+ Ag '64
Beat the bird; second series of America's cup trials. Time 84:58 Jl 24 '64
Bermuda race summaries & awards. Yachting 116:42+ Ag '64
Bermuda 24th. F. Rohr. il Motor B 113:22-3+ Je '64
Big blow and the Blue pig; Bolero and Escapade. A. Zich. il Sports Illus 18:58-60 F 11 '63
Bill Luders has them crying: beat the bird! America's cup race Observation trials. H. Whall. il Sports Illus 21:50+ Jl 27 '64
Blue-water honors to Ondine. R. H. Symonette. il Motor B 111:56+ F '63
Boston girl's long voyage home. A. Zich. il Sports Illus 18:40-2+ Ap 1 '63
Britain's challengers; royal pair prepare for Newport. E. F. Haylock. il Motor B 114: 24-7 Ag '64
Chapman trophy spurs southern speedsters. See issues of Motor boating
Connie to the defense; final America's cup trials. il Time 84:92 S 11 '64
Conquistador conquers the SORC. F. Rohr. il Motor B 113:128-9+ Ap '64
Cornelius Shields on sailing, by C. Shields. Review
Time il 84:68 Ag 14 '64
Cup contenders; America's cup competition. il Newsweek 62:79 N 25 '63
Cup never quivered; Constellation defends America's cup. B. Robinson. il Yachting 116:55-7+ N '64
Cup race: Sovereign challenges the Constellation. il Newsweek 64:50-4 S 14 '64
Destination: Bermuda. A. F. Loomis. il Yachting 115:50-2+ Je '64
Developing a 12-meter crew. E. B. Morris. il Yachting 116:44-6+ Jl '64
Doubloon wins southern title. E. B. Morris. il Yachting 113:50-1+ Ap '63
Down east to Nova Scotia. W. Parks. il Nat Geog Mag 125:852-79 Je '64
Downwind to Diamond Head; goal of the Transpac. B. Robinson. il Yachting 114:38-41+ S '63
England's two-boat try for the cup; Sovereign, and Kurrewa V. C. Mitchell. il Sports Illus 20:46-8 F 17 '64
Fair winds for Hawaii; Four Winds on the Transpac race. F. Rohr. il Motor B 112: 32-5+ O '63
Fastnet race. A. F. Loomis. il Yachting 114: 68+ O '63
Fitting-out time. il Newsweek 63:56+ My 11 '64
For country & for mug; entries for America's Cup. il Time 83:64-5 My 29 '64
Giving them the bird; American Eagle victorious in first week of America's cup trials. il Time 83:46 Je 19 '64
Good luck to Sovereign; America's cup races. Life 57:4 S 18 '64
Guarding against indolence; skipper of America's cup challenger Sovereign. il Time 84:90 S 18 '64
Guinevere first in Miami-Montego Bay race. A. F. Loomis. il Yachting 113:28-9+ Je '63
Heaping cupful of twelves; potential challengers for America's cup. C. Mitchell. il Sports Illus 20:67-8+ My 18 '64
Honolulu preview. R. M. Allan, jr. il Yachting 113:79-81+ Ap '63
How could it have happened again? ed. by J. Gold. A. Boyden. Yachting 116:57+ N '64
How to see the cup races. R. Curley. Yachting 116:166-7 Jl '64
How to see the cup races; America's cup excursion boats. il Motor B 114:44 Ag '64
Importance of starts. A. Knapp, jr. il Yachting 115:106-8+ Ja '64
In a breeze; America's cup 1964 series. il Newsweek 64:84 S 28 '64
In one picture the America's cup story. il Motor B 114:99-101 N '64
Just for fun, three from the northeast. il Flying 75:46-7 Ag '64
Knife & the scow; America's cup races. il Time 84:59 S 25 '64
Lake Michigan's Boat of the year. F. C. Heyes. il Yachting 114:35-7+ D '63
Launching a one-design class. G. Reichert. il Yachting 114:62-3+ Jl '63
Less a race than a ghastly rout; Constellation wins America's cup. C. Mitchell. il Sports Illus 21:30-4+ S 28 '64
Mackinac race. F. C. Heyes. il Motor B 111: 26-7+ Je '63
Mackinacs. F. C. Heyes; G. E. Van. il Yachting 114:54-5+ S '63
Match racing tactics. R. N. Bavier, jr. il Yachting 117:74-6+ Ja '65
Meet the mad Livingstons; campaign to capture the America's cup. C. Phinizy. il Sports Illus 20:70-4+ Mr 16 '64
Methodical Mr Boyden; ed. by J. Lovesey. A. Boyden. Sports Illus 20:72-3 Mr 16 '64
Midwest watch. E. J. Knudsen. il Motor B 112:92 O '63; 113:173 Mr; 124+ Ap; 66+ My; 114:99+ Jl; 116+ S; 126-8 O; 122 N; 78-9 D '64; 115:234 Ja '65
Midwest watch. E. Knudsen. il Motor B 112: 92 O '63; 113:173 Mr; 124+ Ap; 66+ My; 114:99+ Jl '64
Moments that win races; with report by P. Scott. il Sports Illus 21:22-31 Ag 24 '64
Month in yachting. See issues of Yachting
Navigating the Bermuda race. M. H. Farnham. il Yachting 115:41-3+ Je '64
New course; will modernize America's cup racing. P. D. Sparkman. il Motor B 114: 22-3 Ag '64
News of the Olympics. il Yachting 116:25+ Ag; 23+ S; 30-1+ O; 28-30+ D '64
No contest; America's cup. Time 84:80-1 O 2 '64
No stone unturned. J. D. Sleightholme. il Yachting 116:74-5+ S '64
Norpac race. R. S. Carter. il Yachting 116: 35+ O '64
Object is to win the race; H. Long and his yawl, Ondine. A. Zich. il Sports Illus 19: 32-7 Jl 1 '63
Of two better boats, which is more better? England's challengers, yachts Sovereign and Kurrewa V. C. Mitchell. il Sports Illus 20:74+ Je 15 '64
Off to the western races; at Ensenada, Catalina, Hawaii, Long Beach, and up the Colorado. B. Ruskauff. Motor B 111:154-5 My '63
Olympic preview. J. K. Roosevelt. il Yachting 115:41-3 F '64
Olympics: five for Pheidippides. il Motor B 114:108-9 D '64
On the high end of a seesaw; Constellation to defend the America's cup. C. Mitchell. il Sports Illus 21:18-21+ S 14 '64
On the racing circuit. See issues of Motor boating
On the Southern circuit there were divided honors. B. Robinson. il Yachting 115:67-9+ Ap '64
Ondine leads fleet into Hobart; Sydney-Hobart race. A. Salm. il Yachting 113:58-9+ Mr '63
1000 miles without a rudder; Trans-Atlantic race. W. W. Robinson, jr. and S. A. Van Dyck. il Yachting 114:58-60+ S '63

YACHT racing—*Continued*
Only three knew where the wind blew; Annapolis-to-Newport race. H. Whall. il Sports Illus 19:48-9 Jl 8 '63
Other end of the line; America's cup motorboats. C. F. Enloe, jr. il Motor B 114: 39+ Ag '64
Plucking at the Eagle; final trials for next month's America's cup. Time 84:54-5 Ag 28 '64
Princess wins Mazatlan race. A. F. Loomis. il Yachting 113:46-7+ F '63
Race to Hawaii. S. Robertson. il Motor B 111:42+ My '63
Race weeks; Larchmont's 65th; Marblehead's 74th. B. D. Barker, 3d; L. M. Fowle. il Yachting 114:51+ S '63
Racing across the two blue oceans; Islander tops the Transpac. F. Rohr. il Motor B 112: 99+ S '63
Racing across the two blue oceans; Ondine winner in Transatlantic. W. P. Bradley. il Motor B 112:98+ S '63
Remember '63? il Motor B 113:66-74 Ja '64
Rough ride on a sea of troubles; Transatlantic race. N. Hoyt. il Sports Illus 19: 16-17+ Ag 5 '63
Sailing to victory with a needle and thread; 47-foot yawl Robin. H. Whall. il Sports Illus 20:52-4 F 10 '64
Seattle Sixes. R. Saltonstall, jr. il Yachting 115:54-5+ F '64
Secret of the Eagle. il Newsweek 64:69 Jl 27 '64
Silver and bronze medals for a golden team triumph; Olympic races. C. Mitchell. Sports Illus 21:54-6 N 9 '64
'67 challenge; interview. J. Sturrock. Motor B 114:102-3 N '64
Slippery ghost spooks Eagle; Constellation becomes America's cup defender. il Sports Illus 21:36-7 S 7 '64
Smallest winner, biggest fleet; 24th biennial Bermuda race. B. Robinson. il Yachting 116:40-1+ Ag '64
Some of the principles behind the racing rules. F. G. Bemis. Yachting 113:48+ F '63
SORC treasure to Doubloon. F. Rohr. il Motor B 111:164-5+ Ap '63
Southward ho! J. Martenhoff. il Motor B 113: 170+ Mr '64
Spectator craft regulations; America's cup contest. il Motor B 114:45 Ag '64
Story of the America's cup. Sci Digest 56: 69 Jl '64
Target, the America's cup; how to see the 1964 races. il Motor B 114:44-9 Jl '64
Test of heart and mind; America's cup trials. J. Hersey. il Life 57:62-4+ S 4 '64
There's an appeal on that! J. Nash. il Yachting 113:51+ Mr '63
They're here; British challengers for America's cup. il Time 84:74-5 Ag 21 '64
Three nations vie for Transpac honors. B. Ruskauff. Motor B 111:149+ Je '63
3,000 miles of solitude; Single-handed Trans-Atlantic race. D. Lewis. il Yachting 116: 48-50+ O '64
Tiny Burgoo big Bermuda winner. F. Rohr. il Motor B 114:126-8+ Ag '64
To Acapulco with speed. A. Lockabey. il Yachting 115:56-8+ Ap '64
To keep the cup, get a man who knows how. H. Whall. il Sports Illus 20:42-5 Ja 6 '64
Tricks of match racing; excerpt from Cornelius Shields on sailing. C. Shields. il Sports Illus 20:38-47 Je 29 '64
Two hulls are better than one; one-of-a-kind regatta on Biscayne Bay. A. Zich. il Sports Illus 18:12-17 Mr 4 '63
Two seagoing Bearcats beat the odds and the kids. H. Whall. il Sports Illus 21:92-4 D 7 '64
Uneasy way to Acapulco; John B. Kilroy's Kialoa II. C. Mitchell. Sports Illus 20:60-1 Mr 2 '64
Ups and downs of a J-boat skipper. H. S. Vanderbilt. il Yachting 116:39-41+ S '64
Westward ho! B. Ruskauff. Motor B 112:97 O '63; 114:130 O; 118-19 N; 76 D '64; 115: 236-7 Ja '65
Who will win the Honolulu race? R. M. Allan, jr. il Yachting 113:38-9+ Je '63
Why Yankee yachts are so hard to beat; Constellation vs Sovereign. il U S News 57:10 S 28 '64
Will it be Eagle? il Motor B 114:128-30+ S '64
With the racing classes. See issues of Yachting
Year that was. il Motor B 115:62-75 Ja '65
See also
International yacht racing union
Navigation—Competitions
Sailboat racing

Anecdotes, facetiae, satire, etc.
Advanced techniques of losing races. T. Himsworth. il Yachting 115:52-3+ My '64
America's cup races are illegal! H. G. Smith. il Yachting 116:72+ S '64

History
America's cup races; brief history. A. F. Loomis. il Yachting 116:63-6+ S '64
Second hundred years are the hardest; racing for America's cup. S. R. Gookin. il Motor B 113:84-5+ My '64

YACHT safety bureau
Important letters for prudent boatmen: YSB. B. Woodward. il Motor B 113:50-1 Mr '64

YACHTING trophies. See Trophies, Sport

YACHTS
Cup contenders; America's cup competition. il Newsweek 62:79 N 25 '63

Care
Away for the winter; photos and text. Motor B 114:49-51 O '64
Tender loving care of the twelves is the duty of these sturdy craft. W. H. deFontaine. il Yachting 116:62+ S '64

Chartering
Charter in the islands. il Motor B 112:41-4 S '63
Chartering in the Greek isles. W. Wolf. il Motor B 113:50-1+ Ap '64
If you charter instead. B. Robinson. il Yachting 116:56+ Ag '64
North to Antigua; from Martinique. M. P. Ryan. il Motor B 114:42-5 S '64
Planned for chartering. M. Kadey. il Yachting 114:56-7+ N '63
Sound cruising. C. R. Meyer. il Travel 119: 38-40 Je '63
Vive les différences! P. Redford. il Motor B 111:38-9+ Ap '63

Crews
See Seamen

Design
America's cup: tooling up the 12s for another defense; with report by J. R. McDermott. il Life 56:68-74+ Je 12 '64
Bahamian sailing craft. W. R. Johnson, jr. il Yachting 114:49-51+ N '63
Bill Luders has them crying: beat the bird! America's cup race Observation trials. H. Whall. il Sports Illus 21:50+ Jl 27 '64
Boats we meet; North Star. J. Emmett. il Yachting 115:42-3+ Mr '64
Boats we meet; Serenity of Essex, Conn. J. Emmett. il Yachting 116:60-2+ Jl '64
Building a new boat. W. T. Snaith. il Yachting 114:42-5+ Ag; 42-4+ S '63
Chicago YC's new race committee boat. H. T. Van Mell. il Yachting 114:64-5+ Jl '63
Compromise. il Motor B 114:46-7 N '64
Cruiser or a motorsailer. il Yachting 114:66-7+ N '63
Cup boats in construction. P. D. Sparkman. il Motor B 113:114-15+ Je '64
Designer's role. P. L. Rhodes. il Yachting 116:42-4 S '64
Designs. See issues of Yachting
Development of the Twelve. B. Chance, jr. il Motor B 114:36-8+ Ag '64
Express houseboat. il Yachting 113:54+ Mr '63
Fitting-out time. il Newsweek 63:56+ My 11 '64
48-foot masthead cutter. il Motor B 111:64 F '63
42' Herreshoff-designed yawl. il Motor B 112: 58 N '63
Great American sailboats; America Junior. W. H. Koelbel. il Motor B 112:37+ O '63
Great American sailboats; Ingrid. W. H. Koelbel. il Motor B 112:48+ Jl '63
Great American sailboats; Maytime, a cutter for the seven seas. B. Koelbel. il Motor B 113:47+ My '64
Great American sailboats; Meridian, a bluewater yawl. B. Koelbel. il Motor B 114:50+ S '64
Great American sailboats; Sunnie. W. H. Koelbel. il Motor B 112:132-4 S '63
Great American sailboats; Tern, shallow-draft Atkin sloop. B. Koelbel. il Motor B 115:102+ Ja '65
Great American sailboats; Thistle, an ocean-going double-ender. W. H. Koelbel. il Motor B 112:30+ N '63
Matthews 36 convertible sedan. il Yachting 116:63 Jl '64
Motorsailer that really sails. il Yachting 113: 57 F '63
New boat seeks speed through luxury; John B. Kilroy's Kialoa II. H. Whall. il Sports Illus 20:37-9 F 3 '64

YACHTS—Design—*Continued*
New look at the shapes we're in. il Motor B 111:28-37 F '63
Oceanic 49; new ocean racing class. il Yachting 116:60+ N '64
Other man's boat; Fidelia. W. H. DeFontaine. il Yachting 114:50+ D '63
Other man's boat; Libra. il Yachting 115:64-5+ F '64
Other man's boat; Rolling Stone. V. P. L. Ross; D. C. Stone. Yachting 114:72-4+ O '63
Other man's boat; Susan Sage. W. T. Hancourt; K. L. Smith. il Yachting 113:82-3+ Ap '63
Other man's boat; Theme; with photographs. W. H. DeFontaine. Yachting 113:64-6+ F '63
Other man's boat; Tradition. W. H. DeFontaine. il Yachting 116:62-3+ N '64
Pick your plan; cruiser built by Pembroke boats. il Yachting 114:31 D '63
Race against the rule; America's cup yacht. B. H. Frisch. il Sci Digest 56:67-73 Jl '64
Record breaking cruiser; with photographs. M. Crook. Yachting 116:37-9 D '64
Rugged and elegant yacht. il Motor B 111:56 Je '63
Sailorman's cruiser; Elegance in aluminum; 55 feet of twin-diesel luxury. il Motor B 115:106-8 Ja '65
Salamar. il Motor B 114:70-1 S '64
Seagoing diesel yacht. il Motor B 111:66 F '63
Seagoing ketch Jonquil. B. Koelbel. il Motor B 111:152+ Je '63
70's ketch-rigged motorsailer. il Motor B 111:54 Je '63
Shepherd 30. il Yachting 114:34 D '63
Spondee; a design for predicted log contests. R. H. Wiley. il Motor B 111:74+ Ap '63
Taking stock. il Motor B 111:23-5 F '63
Tireless. il Yachting 116:51+ O '64
Toughest babies afloat; tiny sailboats. A. Fontaine. Sports Illus 18:41 Ja 28 '63
Uneasy way to Acapulco; John B. Kilroy's Kialoa II. C. Mitchell. Sports Illus 20:60-1 Mr 2 '64
Yachting interviews: Bill Luders. R. W. Carrick. il Yachting 116:61+ Ag '64

Electric equipment

Small-boat refrigeration: up from the ice age! G. P. Manning. il Motor B 115:76-9+ Ja '65

Electronic equipment

Check-out for your electronics. C. J. Kucyn. il Motor B 112:39+ S '63
Electronics 64-65. il Motor B 113:156-61+ Ja '64; 115:156-61+ Ja '65

Equipment

Do-it-yourself winter windfall. il Motor B 112:50-2+ O '63
Look at Cup boat equipment. B. Robinson. il Yachting 116:69-71+ S '64
Rx for the happy yachtsman. G. P. Manning. il Motor B 112:22-3 O '63
Things to do this winter. G. P. Manning. il Motor B 112:24-6+ O '63
Yachting's boat show. il Yachting 115:127-32+ Ja '64; 117:127-32+ Ja '65

Exhibitions

National boat show '63. il Motor B 111:54-5 Mr '63

Heating and ventilation

Ventilation and stowage. A. W. Moffat. il Yachting 114:46+ Ag '63

Instrument boards

Flying bridge instrument panel. N. Meiners. il Motor B 112:52+ O '63

Interior decoration

See Yacht decoration

Materials

Building a stock fiberglass cruiser. B. Cobb, jr. il Yachting 117:70-2+ Ja '65
New first in fiberglass. il Motor B 113:67 F '64

Purchasing

Bringing that new boat home. B. Clede. il Motor B 113:36-7+ Ap '64
We bought a 55-foot yacht for $500. D. C. Siverts. il Pop Sci 184:4-6+ Ap '64

Renting

Rent yourself a cruise. il Motor B 113:38-41+ My '64

Repairing

Large hole in a small boat. B. Cobb, jr. il Yachting 115:92-4+ Ja; 62-3+ F '64

Storage

All-winter wet storage; recent developments in bubbler systems. D. Lowry. il Yachting 114:68+ N '63
Away for the winter; photos and text. Motor B 14:49-51 O '64
Ice-free wet storage. il Motor B 112:27+ O '63

YACHTS, Ice. See Ice boats and ice boating

YACHTS and yachting
America's cup contenders 1851-1962. il Yachting 116:64-5 S '64
Bringing that new boat home. B. Clede. il Motor B 113:36-7+ Ap '64
Britain's challengers. E. F. Haylock. il Motor B 114:24-7 Ag '64
Calendar of coming events; comp. by R. B. Smith. See issues of Motor boating
Cotton Blossom's racing family; photographs. Motor B 111:126-7 Je '63
Crews of the Henriette. L. Solomon. il Yachting 113:195-7 My '63
Day to measure by. B. Robinson. il Yachting 117:110-11+ Ja '65
England's two-boat try for the cup; Sovereign, and Kurrewa V. C. Mitchell. il Sports Illus 20:46-8 F 17 '64
Families by the boatload; Seattle's boating family of the year. E. Crimmin. il Motor B 111:106+ Ap '63
For country & for mug; entries for America's Cup. il Time 83:64-5 My 29 '64
40-foot fiberglass cruiser. il Motor B 112:58 D '63
Great American sailboats; Captain Cicero; cruising yacht. W. H. Koelbel. il Motor B 113:47+ F '64
Great American sailboats; Maytime, a cutter for the seven seas. B. Koelbel. il Motor B 113:47+ My '64
Great Lakes yachtsman takes a look at the Big Ocean. L. Solomon. il Motor B 111:28+ Je '63
How to rent a yacht on the Riviera. L. R. Hills. il Esquire 59:95-6+ Ap '63
Ides of October. B. Hawkins. il Motor B 114:45+ O '64
Lady of a vanished era; Delphine. B. Ryan. il Yachting 115:186 Mr '64
Launching a one-design class. G. Reichert. il Yachting 114:62-3+ Jl '63
Men and the boats; portfolio. Yachting 116:50-9 S '64
Minimum cruising auxiliaries. B. D. Barker, 3d. il Yachting 115:71-3+ Ja '64
New facilities; new Florida East coast. il Yachting 114:52-3 N '63
Newport notes; the Kennedys and other salts. G. Plimpton. il Harper 226:39-47 Mr '63
News from overseas. Yachting 115:224-5 My '64
News from yachting centers. See issues of Yachting
Northwest gales. E. Crimmin. See issues of Motor boating
Ondine leads fleet into Hobart. A. Salm. il Yachting 113:58-9+ Mr '63
113 years of the 100 Guineas cup; great ships from 1851's America to 1962's Weatherly and Gretel; photographs. Motor B 114:40-3 Ag '64
Over, under and over again; yawl Doubloon battered by gale. H. Whall. il Sports Illus 20:32-3 Je 1 '64
Prospects for the Pacific summer. B. Ruskauff. Motor B 111:149-51 Ap '63
Reaching ahead; special selection of upcoming events, April through October. il Motor B 113:22-3 Mr '64
Remember '63? il Motor B 113:66-74 Ja '64
Sail aboard Gipsy Moth III. J. Parkinson, jr. Yachting 113:45+ My '63
Seasoned skipper. See issues of Motor boating
Shenandoah; stock double cabin cruiser. il Yachting 114:53 Ag '63
Southern yachting; symposium. il Yachting 116:34-54+ N '64
Steam returns to the San Juans. W. Howland. il Yachting 113:40-1+ Mr '63
Switch to power. J. Emmett. il Yachting 113:71-3+ Ap; 50-3+ My '63
Tense sailor for a taut ship; skipper B. Cox of American Eagle. B. Ottum. il Sports Illus 21:46-8 Ag 31 '64
Twelve-meter team. P. D. Sparkman. il Motor B 114:32-5 Ag '64
Two seagoing Bearcats beat the odds and the kids. H. Whall. il Sports Illus 21:92-4 D 7 '64
Under the lee of the longboat. See issues of Yachting
U.S. Twelves. il Motor B 114:28-31+ Ag '64
Wanted badly, a second Cup boat! E. F. Haylock. il Motor B 112:52+ N '63

YACHTS and yachting—*Continued*
Watch the Fords go by; Henry Ford II's Santa Maria. il Newsweek 61:78 Ap 22 '63
What's new when you get there; Florida. R. F. Burnham. il Motor B 112:34-7+ S '63
When cruising the West Indies. T. Coggin and M. Coggin. Yachting 114:121 D '63
Yachtsman's dreamboat; Coastal Queen, remodeled diesel-powered oyster buy-boat. H. Bloomfield. il Yachting 114:57-9+ O '63
Year in yachting. il Yachting 115:79-86+ Ja '64; 117:83-90+ Ja '65
Yo heave ho on a paying guest's chest; skipper makes his hands pay to work. H. Whall. il Sports Illus 21:52-3 Jl 13 '64
Your 1964-1965 boat show. il Motor B 113: 119-84 Ja '64: 115:115-29+ Ja '65
See also
Boats and boating
Catboats
Cookery, Marine
Cruising
Lloyd's register of American yachts
Marinas
Navigation
North American yacht racing union
Schooners
Sloops
Voyages
Women in boating
Yacht racing

Accidents

Bottoms up. G. L. Cochran. il Yachting 115: 144-6 F '64
Twice 360°! Doubloon's double capsize off the South Carolina coast. J. C. Byars. il Yachting 116:64-5+ Jl '64

Anecdotes, facetiae, satire, etc.

How to make a reputation. T. Clement. il Yachting 113:39+ Mr '63
Mr Hardy Lee, his yacht; excerpts with introd. by Alexander C. Brown. Chinks. il Am Heritage 15:24-31 Je '64
100 tons of bronze, son. C. Amory. il Yachting 116:60-1+ S '64
Schizophrenic sailor. W. C. Brewer, jr. il Yachting 115:196-9 Mr '64
Stowaway frog. G. V. Bosenbark. il Yachting 114:124-5 Ag '63

Bibliography

Book reviews. See issues of Yachting
Yachtsman's bookshelf; comp. by J. DeGraff (cont) Yachting 114:162+ N; 122+ D '63

Caricatures and cartoons

Welcome aboard or are you? with cartoons by R. McKie. H. Bergh. Sports Illus 18: 34-41 My 13 '63

Laws and regulations

See Boats and boating—Laws and regulations

YACKULIC, George A.
Found: million-acre cow pasture. Sci Digest 53:79-81 My '63
YACOBUCCI, F. P.
Automation anticipates $165,000 saving on alimony checks. Am City 79:106-7 O '64
YADDO (artists and authors colony) See Authors colonies
YADIN, Yigael
Essenes or zealots? il por Newsweek 63:72 F 10 '64
YAEGER, Peter, and others
College game. Seventeen 23:110-11 Ja '64
YAFFE, James
Dear me, the sky is falling; dramatization. See Spigelgass, L.
YAGI, Kinji, and Bern, H. A.
Electrophysiologic indications of the osmoregulatory role of the teleost urophysis. bibliog Science 142:491-3 O 25 '63
YAHI Indians
Ishi, the last of the Yanas, a primitive Indian between two worlds. A. Métraux. il UNESCO Courier 16:10-13 F '63; Same abr. with title Last stone age man in the U.S. Sci Digest 54:22-7 Jl '63
YAHR, Melvin D. See Allerand, C. D. jt. auth.
YAHRAES, Herbert
Should you try for a better job? Pop Sci 162:110-11+ Ap '63
YAKIMA RIVER
Most underfished river in the U.S. W. W. Hunter. il Outdoor Life 132:24-7+ Ag '63
YALE, Stephen L.
Accepting the possible. Christian Cent 80: 1519-20 D 4 '63
YALE college. See Yale university
YALE conference on the teaching of English
Rock-n-roll prose; summary of address. H. Leavitt. Sr Schol 82:1T-2T+ My 8 '63
YALE Russian chorus. See Choral groups and societies
YALE university
Accelerating. Newsweek 63:52 Ja 27 '64
Architecture and man at Yale. V. Scully. il Sat R 47:26-9 My 23 '64
Big daddy goes to Yale; Chubb fellow. T. G. Harris. il Look 27:28-30 F 12 '63
Building years of a Yale man. W. McQuade. il Arch Forum 118:88-93 Je '63
Death of the gargoyle; new architecture at Yale. il Time 82:80-5 N 15 '63
Double degree at Yale. Time 83:41 Ja 24 '64
Experiment perilous; attempt to discover the nature of blind obedience. Sr Schol 83:2T N 15 '63
New Haven, safe haven; Kingman Brewster, jr. inaugurated as 17th president. il Time 83:73-4 Ap 17 '64
New prexy marches into office at Yale. il Life 56:45 Ap 24 '64
Offered: a short cut to a master's degree. U S News 56:8 Ja 27 '64
Royal blues; Yale corporation. il Time 83:59 Je 26 '64
SOM, Rudolph, and Johnson at Yale. il Arch Forum 119:30-1 N '63
Whiffenpoofs are expensive. R. G. Kaiser. il Esquire 62:134-7+ N '64
Witty reformer; A. W. Griswold. il Time 81: 46 Ap 26 '63
Y of it all. Time 82:51 O 18 '63
Yale finds a coach; J. Pont. W. N. Wallace. il Sat Eve Post 236:74-7 O 12 '63
Yale inauguration. New Yorker 40:42-3 Ap 25 '64
Yale's Catholic professor. Time 82:36 D 27 '63
Yale's new scholarship policy. Sch & Soc 92: 181 Ap 18 '64

Law school

See Yale university—School of law

Libraries

Acquisition from Tibet: Theos Bernard estate. Wilson Lib Bul 39:361+ Ja '65
Beinecke library. il Wilson Lib Bul 38:243 N '63
Contraband collection; gift of unpublished letters of 20th century Russian writers. Wilson Lib Bul 37:822 Je '63
Hot paper; stolen manuscripts from Saragossa cathedral in new Beinecke library, Yale. Newsweek 64:88 N 16 '64
Journal from Magellan's voyage; illuminated manuscript. A. Pigafetta. Wilson Lib Bul 38:714 My '64
Marble to see through; Beinecke rare book and manuscript library. il Newsweek 62: 112 O 21 '63
Rare library at Yale dedicated. il Arch Rec 134:12-13 N '63
Rare Tibetan encyclopedia of Buddhism. Wilson Lib Bul 38:378 Ja '64
Space problem; concerning report: Yale's selective book retirement program. Wilson Lib Bul 38:444-5 F '64
Stolen from Spanish cathedral, rare manuscripts found at Yale; Beinecke library of rare books and manuscripts. Library J 89: 4771-2 D 1 '64
Treasure-house for Yale; new Beinecke rare book and manuscript library. il Library J 88:4579-81 D 1 '63
Yale acquires rare papyrus collection. Pub W 186:35 Ag 10 '64
Yale dedicates new Beinecke library. Pub W 184:30 O 28 '63
Yale's bookshelf: indoor skyscraper; Beinecke rare book and manuscript library. il Life 55:97+ N 15 '63
Yale's iceberg; Beinecke rare book and manuscript library. New Yorker 40:24-5 My 30 '64

School of art and architecture

School for the arts at Yale. il Arch Rec 135:111-20 F '64
Yale's School of art and architecture; symposium. il Arch Forum 120:62-85 F '64

School of law

Case for Yale law school. il Newsweek 61: 100+ Je 10 '63
YALE university press
Mangling a masterpiece; concerning typography of revised edition of Human action by L. von Mises. H. Hazlitt. Nat R 16:366-7 My 5 '64
YALOW, Rosalyn S. See Berson, S. A. jt. auth.
YAMAKAWA, Masao
Talisman; story, tr. by E. Seidensticker. Life 57:94 S 11 '64

YAMAMOTO, Isoroku
Six minutes that changed the world; with editorial comment. S. E. Morison. il Am Heritage 14:50-5+ F '63
YAMAMOTO, Kaoru
Creative writing and school achievement. bibliog f Sch & Soc 91:307-8 O 19 '63
YAMAMOTO, Nobuto
Bacteriophage: an unusual hybrid of serologically unrelated phages P22 and P221. bibliog Science 143:144-5 Ja 10 '64
YAMAMOTO, Yoshihiro. See Fingerman, M. jt. auth.
YAMASAKI, Minoru
Architectural details. Arch Rec 136:169-84 S '64
Good form. il Newsweek 64:98 N 9 '64
Porch for pedestrians. il Time 85:52 Ja 22 '65
Structure plays leading role in latest Yamasaki designs. il Arch Rec 134:103-10 D '63
Yamasaki's first skyscraper; headquarters for Consolidated gas company, Detroit. J. S. Hornbeck. il Arch Rec 133:144-50 My '63
Yamasaki's first tower. D. B. Carlson. il Arch Forum 118:98-113 My '63
YAMEOGO, Maurice
Colored presidents and rulers. G. C. Turner. Negro Hist Bul 27:35 N '63
YAMS. See Sweet potatoes
YANG, Chia-lo
Yung Lo encyclopedia presented to Library of Congress. R. Hilsman; R. D. Rogers. Dept State Bul 49:740 N 11 '63
YANG, Chuan-kwang
Cobra and C. K. Yang. R. Creamer. il pors Sports Illus 19:66-71+ D 23 '63
Please be good. il por Time 81:68 F 8 '63
Yang of China is world's best athlete. T. Maule. il por Sports Illus 18:26-7+ My 6 '63
YANKAUER, Alfred
Maternal and child health problems. bibliog f Ann Am Acad 355:112-20 S '64
YANKEE Doodle (song)
Real Yankee Doodle. T. H. Marsh. il Hobbies 69:30+ Je '64
YANKEE Doodle kitten: drama. See Newman, D.
YANKEES. See New Englanders
YANKEES (baseball) See Baseball clubs
YANKELOVICH, Daniel
New criteria for market segmentation. Harvard Bsns R 42:83-90 Mr '64
YANOFSKY, Charles, and others
Protein structure relationships revealed by mutational analysis. bibliog Science 146:1593-4 D 18 '64
—See Brody, S. jt. auth.
YARBOROUGH, Ralph W.
Excerpt from debate, August 14, 1963. Cong Digest 43:18+ Ja '64
Excerpt from debate, February 2, 1962. Cong Digest 42:52+ F '63
Fair deal for the cold war soldier. Harper 230:82-3 Ja '65
about
Cactus-nasty campaign. il por Time 84:39 O 16 '64
YARDLEY, Jonathan
Adam Clayton Powell's leadership. New Repub 148:30 Ap 20 '63
YARDS. See Home grounds
YARHAM, E. R.
Britain's churchyard yews. Am For 69:36-7+ Je '63
Forests of New Zealand. Am For 70:36-9+ Jl '64
Suomi, land of forests. Am For 69:16-19+ F '63
Tracking the hurricane. UNESCO Courier 16: 24-7 S '63
YARN
Yarns with a Yuletide twist. il Good H 157: 202+ D '63
YARNELL, Jim
Flying photographer. Flying 74:64 Ap; 75:75 S '64
YASEEN, Leonard C.
Is it over, over there? interview, ed. by J. B. Weiner. por Duns R 83:pt2 108-10+ Mr '64
YASKO, Karel H.
Architecture, I'm for it, Yasko says: challenges architects of fifty states to make architecture of U.S. buildings; excerpts from address. Arch Rec 133:23+ Ap '63
Karel Yasko of Wisconsin appointed to top federal architecture post. Arch Rec 133:10 Ja '63
YASTRZEMSKI, Carl
Yaz, Boston's razzmatazz; Boston Red Sox. R. Creamer. il por Sports Illus 18:63-4+ My 20 '63

YATES, Elizabeth
Please answer this. . . Horn Bk 39:162-4 Ap '63
YATES, Peter
Genesis of a music. Hi Fi 13:35-8+ Jl '63
John Cage: builder of new music. Vogue 144:225-9 O 1 '64
YATES, Sidney R.
U.S. expresses continuing concern for future of South-West Africa; statement, October 30, 1963. Dept State Bul 49:946-8 D 16 '63
U.S. restates views on colonialism and Portuguese African territories; statement, March 12, 1963. Dept State Bul 48:581-3 Ap 15 '63
YATSU, L. and Altschul, A. M.
Lipid-protein particles: isloation from seeds of gossypium hirsutum. bibliog Science 142: 1062-4 N 22 '63
YAUCH, John H.
Bar's side of Canon 35. Sat R 46:61-2 Mr 9 '63
YAWL racing. See Yacht racing
YAWNING
What's in a yawn? A. Abarbanel. il Todays Health 42:30-1+ My '64
YDÍGORAS FUENTES, Miguel
Castro problem more serious than ever; statement. por U S News 54:49 Mr 18 '63
about
Frustration of infiltration. D. Kurzman. Sat R 46:25 Jl 20 '63
Where reds may take over next in Latin America. il U S News 54:48-50 Mr 18 '63
YEAKEL, Ralph W. jr
Admixtures for architectural concrete. Arch Rec 133:191-4 F '63
YEAR
See also
Calendar
YEARGIN, Helen
Welder is a lady. il pors Ebony 18:58+ Ag '63
YEARLEY, C. K.
Katanga and the Congo crisis. Commonweal 77:483-6 F 1 '63
YEASTS
Food for the future. E. Hall. il Sci N L 85: 10-11 Ja 4 '64
Fungi and yeasts: chemistry and biochemistry. J. O. Lampen. Science 142:603 N 1 '63
Gene-enzyme relations in histidine biosynthesis in yeast. G. R. Fink. bibliog il Science 146:525-7 O 23 '64
Reductive dechlorination of DDT to DDD by yeast. B. J. Kallman and A. K. Andrews. il Science 141:1050-1 S 13 '63
Toxohormone inhibitory effect on the growth of an unstable strain of yeast. V. Callao and others. bibliog il Science 142:1668-9 D 27 '63
Ultraviolet radiation effects on low molecular weight inorganic phosphates of yeast. E. M. Lieberman and P. A. Swenson. bibliog il Science 142:1315-16 D 6 '63
Yeast genetics conference; report on conference on yeast genetics and related biochemical problems. R. C. Von Borstel. Science 142:1594 D 20 '63
YEATS, Anne
All fresh and wide-eyed. New Yorker 39:40-1 N 2 '63
YEATS, Jack B.
Irishman as hero. Newsweek 65:74 F 1 '65
YEATS, William Butler
All fresh and wide-eyed. New Yorker 39:40-1 N 2 '63
Quarreling with Yeats: a friendly recollection. F. O'Connor. Esquire 62:157+ D '64
YEEND, Frances
Winning soloist; interview, ed. by G. Fitzgerald. por Opera N 27:13 F 23 '63
YEGOROV, Boris
See also
Space flight—Manned flights—Komarov-Yegorov-Feoktistov flight, 1964
YELLIN, Carol Lynn
Year we rediscovered Christmas. Redbook 124:10+ D '64
YELLOW fever
Victory over yellow fever. il Todays Health 42:80 F '64
YELLOW fever mosquitoes. See Mosquitoes
YELLOW rocket. See Winter cress
YELLOWSTONE LAKE
Get the motorboats out of the parks! A. W. Smith. Nat Parks Mag 37:2 Je '63
YELLOWSTONE NATIONAL PARK
Appreciation of Yellowstone National Park. W. F. Heald. il Nat Parks Mag 38:4-7 D '64
Bear facts. J. W. Giles. il Am For 69:26 Jl '63

YELLOWSTONE NATIONAL PARK—*Cont.*
Briton traces the origin of our national park idea. J. Fisher. il Audubon Mag 65:334-41 N '63
Grand old park. il Sunset 130:76-91 Je '63
Heroes and heroism in the Yellowstone country. G. Caesar. Holiday 34:50-1+ Ag '63
Large purposes, large plans; Yellowstone regional plan. A. W. Smith. il Nat Parks Mag 39:2, 4-12 Ja '65
Northern Yellowstone elk reduction goal achieved; with editorial comment. il Nat Parks Mag 37:2, 16 Mr '63
Petrified forests of Yellowstone Park. E. Dorf. il Sci Am 210:106-12+ Ap '64
Too many elk. T. Trueblood. il Field & S 68: 36-9+ Jl '63
Vandalism in Yellowstone Park. R. W. Witzke. il Nat Parks Mag 38:13-15+ F '64

YELLOWTAIL fishing
Yellow streak. B. Beebe. il Outdoor Life 132: 48-9+ Jl '63

YEMEN
Alexandria duet; Feisal and Nasser. Time 84: 28+ S 25 '64
Back to bloodshed. il Time 85:25A Ja 29 '65
Back to normal; second Arab summit conference. il Newsweek 64:41 S 14 '64
Behind the veil of troubled Yemen. T. J. Abercrombie. il Nat Geog Mag 125:402-45 Mr '64
Double dilemma. Newsweek 62:42+ O 14 '63
For Allah & the Imam. il Time 81:38+ Mr 8 '63
Forgotten war. il Time 84:27 Ag 14 '64
Harried are the peacemakers; plan for U.N. truce team. Time 81:30+ Je 21 '63
Hoist; Egyptian troops in Yemen. il Newsweek 62:38 Ag 5 '63
Inside story; Egyptians v. royalists, with report by J. A. Morris, jr. il Newsweek 61:56+ Je 24 '63
Nasser ascendant. il Newsweek 63:46 My 11 '64
Our Yemen policy: pursuit of a mirage. P. Horton. il Reporter 29:28-35 O 24 '63
Puppetmaster; Nasser pulls the strings. Newsweek 65:38+ Ja 18 '65
Stark desert war in Arabia; with report by J. Bonfante. il Life 57:34-43 S 18 '64
Undeclared war. New Repub 149:8 Ag 3 '63; Reply with rejoinder. A. M. Hassan. 149:37 Ag 31 '63
Under the gun. J. A. Morris. il Newsweek 64: 42 D 21 '64
Visit from Nasser. Time 83:30 My 1 '64
See also
United Nations—Yemen

Politics and government

At cross-purposes in the sands of Yemen. D. Holden. il Reporter 28:37+ F 14 '63

YEN, Liang
Growing up with Confucius. Holiday 34:108+ N '63

YENNE, Anne
Feeding the allergic child. Parents Mag 39: 57-8+ My '64

YEOMANS, G. Allan
Speech education, a terrible responsibility. Vital Speeches 30:348-52 Mr 15 '64

YERBY, Lorees
Last minstrel. Criticism
New Yorker 39:82 My 18 '63
Theatre Arts 47:12 Jl '63
Save me a place at Forest Lawn. Criticism
America 108:892 Je 22 '63
Theatre Arts 47:12 Jl '63

YES, but you won't catch me going again; story. See Raphael, F.

YESTERDAY'S child; story. See Wolfe, W.

YEVTUSHENKO, Yevgeny Aleksandrovich. See Evtushenko, E. A.

YEWS
Britain's churchyard yews. E. R. Yarham. il Am For 69:36-7+ Je '63
There's a place in every garden for yews. G. Taloumis. il Pop Gard 14:22-3+ S '63

YÉ-YÉ girls. See Singers

YEYKWANA Indians. See Indians of South America—Venezuela

YEZIERSKA, Anzia
One thousand pages of research. Commentary 36:60-3 Jl '63
Window full of sky; story. Reporter 31:29-31 Jl 2 '64

YGLESIAS, Jose
Poetry of protest. Nation 198:376-7 Ap 13 '64
Spirit of valerian. Nation 198:488-90 My 11 '64

YIDDISH language
Interview; ed. by J. Blocker and R. Elman. I. B. Singer. Commentary 36:364-72 N '63; Reply with rejoinder A. L. Jacobs. 37:18+ Mr '64

YIDDISH literature
Interview; ed. by J. Blocker and R. Elman. I. B. Singer. Commentary 36:364-72 N '63; Reply with rejoinder. A. L. Jacobs. 37:18+ Mr '64

YIDDISH poetry

Translations into English

Spoil; Play without words; By an abandoned house; tr. by J. Hirschman. M. H. Tussman. Poetry 102:381-3 S '63
Three poems: I drew you out of that particular night; Is there a darkness then which was not once light? Since I scarcely know what to do with you; tr. by E. Blum. B. Alquit-Blum. Poetry 104:88-90 My '64

YIDDISH theater. See Theatre—Jews

YIRGOU, Dagnatchew, and Caldwell, R. M.
Stomatal penetration of wheat seedlings by stem and leaf rust: effect of light and carbon dioxide. bibliog Science 141:272-3 Jl 19 '63

YNTEMA, Theodore O.
Businessman looks at today's big issues; excerpts from address, November 5, 1964. por U S News 57:100-4 N 30 '64
Challenge of prosperity. Sat R 48:23-4 Ja 9 '65
National agenda for 1964. Sat R 47:19-20 Ja 11 '64

YOAKUM, Jim
Water-happy wildcats. il Audubon Mag 66: 166-7 My '64

YOB, Gregory
Amateur scientist. Sci Am 211:134-7 D '64

YOCHELSON, Ellis L. See Marek, L. jt. auth.

YODER, Edwin M. Jr
Changing voice of the Dixie vote. Sat R 47:29-30 Ag 1 '64
Dissent in Atlanta. Sat R 46:52+ Ap 20 '63
Dixieland reverie. Sat R 47:39-40 My 30 '64
Motive to greatness. Sat R 47:54-5 F 22 '64
Race was to the racists. Sat R 47:41 O 10 '64

YODER, R. A.
Photography in your school. Sch Arts 64: 19-22 N '64

YOELI, Meir, and others
Plasmodium berghei: cyclical transmissions by experimentally infected anopheles quadrimaculatus. bibliog Science 144:1580-1 Je 26 '64
Tree rat, thamnomys surdaster surdaster, in laboratory research. bibliog Science 142: 1585-6 D 20 '63

YOGA
Heels over head for efficiency. il Life 56: 97-8 F 14 '64
Introducing yoga; interview, ed. by J. Anderson. M. Moya. il Dance Mag 38:40-1+ O '64
Uncoil like a snake, think serpent. P. Benjamin. il N Y Times Mag p35+ Ag 30 '64

YOGURT
Introduction to yogurt. Sunset 130:210-12 My '63
Light dessert with yogurt. il Sunset 131: 138 Ag '63
Making yogurt on your own. Sunset 133:182 N '64

YOHO, James G. and McMahon, R. O.
AFA's North Carolina land ownership study; new light on small woodlands. Am For 69: 32-4+ N '63

YOKOHARI, Ryuichi. See Leon, M. A. jt. auth.

YONKERS, N.Y. public library
Pleasure Island; 1962 summer reading program of Crestwood branch; letter. Mrs D. Schoenfeld. Wilson Lib Bul 37:683-4 Ap '63

YORK, Alvin Cullum
One day's work. il por Time 84:26 S 11 '64; Same abr. with title Taps for a quiet hero. Read Digest 85:131-3 D '64

YORK, Ben
Nation-wide testing program. Recreation 56: 268+ Je '63

YORK, Herbert
San Diego campus. Arch Rec 136:192-4 N '64

YORK, Herbert F. See Wiesner, J. B. jt. auth.

YORK, James H.
How to steal an engineer. Sci Digest 55:27-9 My '64

YORK, Richard
New producer. New Yorker 39:16-18 Ag 10 '63

YORK, Susannah
Enthusiastic actors dig a classic! E. Miller. il pors Seventeen 22:114-15 F '63
Notes and comment. New Yorker 40:31 Je 6 '64
Susannah York: England's offbeat star. J. R. Moskin. il pors Look 27:78-80+ F 26 '63

YORK, Pa.
Urban renewal saves homes. il Am City 78:103 S '63
See also
Martin memorial library

Newspapers

Pride of York County; York (Pa) Gazette and daily winner of Ayer award. il Newsweek 65:56-7 Ja 11 '65
YORKSHIRE pudding. See Cookery, English
YORKSHIRE terriers. See Terriers
YORKTOWN HEIGHTS, N.Y.
Triple-treatment sewage plant. A. Crew. il Am City 79:96-8 Mr '64
YORTY, Samuel
After Sam's scalp. Time 84:15 D 25 '64
Trouble in happyland. J. Phelan. il pors Sat Eve Post 236:78-80+ My 25 '63
YOSEMITE VALLEY
These are the Yosemite walks John Muir said to take. il Sunset 132:60+ My '64
YOSHIHITO, prince of Japan
Japanese Prince meets girl, by go-between. E. Chapin. il por N Y Times Mag p42+ Mr 22 '64
YOSHIMURA, Yuji
Meaning of bonsai. Horticulture 42:16-19+ D '64
YOSHIOKA, Ruby
Fold paper to learn geometry. Sci N L 83: 138-9 Mr 2 '63
YOST, Charles W.
Security council calls for ban on sale of arms to South Africa; statement, August 7, 1963; in explanation of vote. Dept State Bul 49:337-8 Ag 26 '63
Security council continues U.N. force in Cyprus; statement, September 25, 1964. Dept State Bul 51:563-4 O 19 '64
Security council extends mandate of Cyprus peace force; statement, December 18, 1964. Dept State Bul 52:26-7 Ja 4 '65
Security council recommends Malawi for U.N. membership; statement, October 9, 1964. Dept State Bul 51:680 N 9 '64
Security council recommends Malta and Zambia for U.N. membership; statement, October 30, 1964. Dept State Bul 51:759 N 23 '64
Soviet Union vetoes U.S.-U.K. resolution in Security council on Israel and Syrian complaints; statement, September 3, 1963. Dept State Bul 49:522 S 30 '63
U.N. calls on member states to aid in Skopje reconstruction; statement, October 14, 1963. Dept State Bul 49:759-60 N 11 '63
U.S. replies to Cambodian charge on chemical operations; letter, August 3, 1964. Dept State Bul 51:274 Ag 24 '64
United States reserves position on Hungarian credentials at U.N; statement, June 5, 1963. Dept State Bul 49:32 Jl 1 '63
U.S. urges Security council to await OAS action on Haiti; statement, May 9, 1963. Dept State Bul 48:958-9 Je 17 '63
YOU can't run away from Christmas; story. See Streeter, E.
YOU know how it is with women; story. See Stanton, W.
YOULOU, Fulbert
Abbé steps down. por Newsweek 62:37+ Ag 26 '63
Failure of a fetish. il por Time 82:27 Ag 23 '63
YOUNG, A. P. and Schwartz, C. M.
High-pressure synthesis of molybdates with the wolframite structure. bibliog Science 141:348-9 Jl 26 '63
YOUNG, A. S.
How sports helped break the color line. Ebony 18:114-16+ S '63
YOUNG, Allen
Central City festival. Mus Am 83:4-5 Ag '63
Lulu arrives. Mus Am 83:30-1 S '63
Music in the mountains. Mus Am 83:36-7 S '63
YOUNG, Anne
Street of the lace-makers; poem. Commonweal 81:570 Ja 29 '65
YOUNG, Brigham
Here is my home at last! C. Carmer. il por Am Heritage 14:26-33+ F '63
YOUNG, Bruce S.
High commission territories of southern Africa. bibliog Focus 14:1-6 D '63
YOUNG, Catherine
I hear singing Americans; poem. Negro Hist Bul 27:14-16 O '63
YOUNG, Charles W. and Hodas, Sadie
Hydroxyurea: inhibitory effect on DNA metabolism. bibliog Science 146:1172-4 N 27 '64
YOUNG, David, and Auler, Robert
Fresh wind in Illinois. Nat R 14:495 Je 18 '63
YOUNG, Elizabeth
New Canaan book shop: progress report; 1958-1964. Pub W 185:87-91 Ap 27 '64
What do you mean, practical experience? Pub W 185:63-5 My 25 '64
YOUNG, George Allen
Eloquent light. Pop Phot 54:94 Mr '64
YOUNG, Georgia V. See Schneider, R. M. jt. auth.
YOUNG, Guilford
Liturgy; an achievement. America 110:14-15 Ja 4 '64
YOUNG, Howard John Edward
Howie Young: hockey's abominable iceman. D. Anderson. il pors Sat Eve Post 237:30-1 F 22 '64
YOUNG, James Webb
Mister J. Walter Thompson. Sat R 47:71+ Ap 11 '64
YOUNG, Joanne B.
Heritage homes are worth saving. Am Home 67:23-4 My '64
LBJ white house. Am Home 67:5-6 Mr '64
YOUNG, John W.
Outside the ship floating in space. Life 55: 89 S 27 '63
When I came aboard I felt like a rookie. pors Life 56:114+ Je 5 '64
YOUNG, K. E. See Cottrell, W. F. jt. auth.
YOUNG, Kenneth T.
U.S. proposes town-centered planning for Asia; statement, March 4, 1964. Dept State Bul 50:759-61 My 11 '64
YOUNG, Loretta
Loretta Young: the steel butterfly. J. Wilkie. il pors Good H 156:78-81+ Je '63
YOUNG, Margaret B.
Negro mother speaks of her challenging role in a changing world. por Parents Mag 39: 50-1+ Jl '64
YOUNG, Marjorie
Copying good or bad? Sch Arts 62:19-20 Je '63
YOUNG, Otis B.
Real beginning of radio. Sat R 47:48-50 Mr 7 '64
YOUNG, Ralph W.
Last chance for Admiralty. Field & S 69: 10-12+ My '64
YOUNG, Richard David
Drug administration to neonatal rats: effects on later emotionality and learning. bibliog Science 143:1055-7 Mr 6 '64
YOUNG, Richard S. and Ponnamperuma, Cyril
Life: origin and evolution. Science 143:384-5+ Ja 24 '64
YOUNG, Robert F.
Largely about my dog. Writer 76:13-14+ Je '63
YOUNG, Ruth L.
Atlantic lure. Travel 121:62 My '64
YOUNG, Scott
Mayhem on skates. Holiday 35:194+ Ap '64
YOUNG, Stanley
Ask me later. Sat R 47:33 F 22 '64
YOUNG, Stephen M.
Excerpt from address, June 28, 1963. Cong Digest 43:23+ Ja '64
Wasting the taxpayers' money; a senator's report. por U S News 54:14 Mr 4 '63
about
Shooting for the moon. Reporter 30:16+ Ja 30 '64
Taft vs. Young. il por Newsweek 64:36-8 O 26 '64
YOUNG, Tracy
Beginning; story. Seventeen 24:64-5 Ja '65
YOUNG, Virginia Brady
Regeneration; poem. Christian Cent 80:1504 D 4 '63
YOUNG, Virginia G.
Two interpreters: trustee relationships with librarian and staff; excerpt from Library trustee: a practical guide. por Library J 89: 1184-7 Mr 15 '64
YOUNG, Warren R.
Bringing chaos out of order. Life 57:138-40 D 11 '64
Drugs; how safe is safe enough? Life 57:37-40 Jl 3 '64
Runaway train. Life 54:79-80+ Mr 29 '63
Turbulence: hidden giant in the sky. Life 57: 86-8+ D 18 '64
What ever happened to Dr Ivy? Life 57:110-12+ O 9 '64; Same abr. with title Krebiozen, the tragic obsession of Andrew Ivy. Read Digest 86:193-4+ Ja '65
When the doctor examines you. Read Digest 82:89-94 F '63
—and Lambert, William
Marchers' master plan. Life 55:63-4+ Ag 23 '63

YOUNG, Wayland
British labour's arms plan. New Repub 150: 12-14 My 23 '64
Excerpt from address, February 6, 1963. Bul Atomic Sci 19:11 Ap '63
MLF, a West European view. Bul Atomic Sci 20:19-21 N '64
Report from London: the Western alliance. Bul Atomic Sci 19:44+ My '63
YOUNG, Whitney M. jr
Civil rights; discrimination in labor unions; address, May 12, 1964. Vital Speeches 30: 535-7 Je 15 '64
Cry from the dispossessed. Christian Cent 81: 1524-7 D 9 '64
Education, equality and Negro rights; summary of address. por Pub W 185:34-5 My 4 '64
Intermingled revolutions; address, July 20, 1964. Vital Speeches 30:692-4 S 1 '64
Role of the middle-class Negro. Ebony 18: 66-71 S '63
Should there be compensation for Negroes? N Y Times Mag p43+ O 6 '63
We've got to have victories; interview. por U S News 56:56-9 F 24 '64
Whitney M. Young, jr. por(p 1) Negro Hist Bul 27:2 O '63
YOUNG, William C. and others
Hormones and sexual behavior. bibliog Science 143:212-18 Ja 17 '64
YOUNG, William H.
American government and administration: recent developments. Ann Am Acad 348: 156-63 Jl '63
YOUNG, William J. and others
Glucose-6-phosphate dehydrogenase in drosophila: X-linked electrophoretic variants. bibliog Science 143:140-1 Ja 10 '64
YOUNG Americans for freedom (organization)
Angry and old-fashioned. J. Duscha. New Repub 149:6-7 N 30 '63
Campus conservatives: where are they now? D. Wakefield. Mlle 57:292-3+ Ag '63
YOUNG animals. See Animals, Infancy of
YOUNG automobile drivers. See Automobile drivers
YOUNG Crane; story. See Upits, A.
YOUNG men
America's ten outstanding young men of 1963-1964. il Look 28:61-3 Ja 28 '64; 29:34+ Ja 26 '65
Insiders: four young couples who live the life that counts. il Vogue 144:82-91 N 15 '64
YOUNG men's and young women's Hebrew association
92nd street's 90th. il Time 83:76 Ap 10 '64
YOUNG men's Christian association
New look at the Y.M.C.A. P. M. Limbert. Christian Cent 81:760-2 Je 10 '64
Y.M.C.A. for Jews; organization in the Israeli sector of Jerusalem. il Time 85:44 Ja 1 '65
YOUNG people. See Young men; Youth
YOUNG peoples librarians. See Librarians
YOUNG Republicans. See Political clubs and associations
YOUNG women
Charmers, Italian and American. L. Barzini. il Vogue 143:57-8+ Ja 15 '64
Hazards of city courtship. W. K. Zinsser. Read Digest 82:41-2+ Ap '63
Insiders: four young couples who live the life that counts. il Vogue 144:82-91 N 15 '64
See also
College students, Women
YOUNG women's Christian association
Administrative offices and recreation center for YWCA; Pittsburgh, Pa. il Arch Rec 135:159-64 Mr '64
YWCA, international success story. M. F. Rockefeller. il Nat Geog Mag 124:904-33 D '63
YOUNGER, Cal
Illusion of perspective distortion. U S Camera 26:42-9+ N '63
YOUNGER, Joan
(ed) See Stone, A. What wives don't know about sex
YOUNGERT, Eugene
What makes a school good. Atlan 214:72-3 O '64
YOUNGNER, Julius S. and Stinebring, W. R.
Interferon production in chickens injected with brucella abortus. bibliog Science 144: 1022-3 My 22 '64
YOUNGQUIST, Art
Arc welding basics. Pop Mech 121:144-7+ Ja; 173-7+ F '64
Grinding jigs for lathe chisels. Pop Mech 121:182-5+ Mr '64
YOUNGSTOWN, Ohio
Crime
Crime town USA; with editorial comment. J. Kobler. il Sat Eve Post 236:71-6 Mr 9 '63
Newspapers
See also
Youngstown vindicator
YOUNGSTOWN sheet and tube company
Issue that stalls steel pact; contracting-out dispute. Bsns W p 104-5 Je 8 '63
YOUNGSTOWN vindicator
Challenging the strike record. Time 85:44 Ja 22 '65
YOUNT, David
Chronicle of human growth. Sat R 47:65-6 Ag 15 '64
YOUR husband loves me! story. See Webb, L.
YOU'RE too hip, baby; story. See Southern, T.
YOUSSOUPOFF, Felix, prince
Living legends. E. Charles-Roux. il por Vogue 145:130-3+ Ja 1 '65
YOUTH
Holiday cure for bored teen-agers. A. Gillette. il UNESCO Courier 16:24-7 Ap '63
Neatest teener; Miss Teen age America pageant at Dallas. D. Wakefield. il Esquire 59:88-9+ Je '63
New upper class, the kids. M. Mannes. Vogue 142:46-7+ Jl '63
Science looks at Beatlemania. J. A. Osmundsen. il Sci Digest 55:24-6 My '64
Ten delusions of youth; address, February 14, 1963. W. P. Shofstall. Vital Speeches 29:400-3 Ap 15 '63
Why youth riots: the adolescent ghetto; with editorial comment. F. Musgrove. il Nation 199:129, 137-40 S 21 '64
Wild youth: a worldwide program. G. Lucy. Read Digest 85:167-9+ O '64
Youth; address, August 24, 1964. C. T. Rowan. Vital Speeches 30:721-5 S 15 '64
Youth in uniform; photographs. N Y Times Mag p72-3 Je 7 '64
Youth talks about youth. A. Tyler. Vogue 145:85+ F 1 '65
Youthquake. il Vogue 145:112-19 Ja 1 '65
See also
Adolescence
Boys
Church work with youth
Discipline
Girls
Libraries—Work with young people
Negro youth
Puberty
Adjustment
See Adjustment, Social
Employment
America's idle youth. Commonweal 77:583 Mr 1 '63
Are you cheating your child out of a living? M. C. Kohler and A. Fontaine. il Good H 157:76-7+ S '63
Career planning for the age of automation. G. Davenel. il Parents Mag 39:74-6+ S '64
Educating youth; the cruel solution. H. Brill. Nation 198:296-7 Mr 23 '64
Employment of high school graduates and dropouts in 1963. V. C. Perrella. il Mo Labor R 87:522-9 My '64
Employment of high school graduates and dropouts in 1962. J. Schiffman. il Mo Labor R 86:772-9 Jl '63
Employment of school age youth, October 1963. H. R. Hamel. il Mo Labor R 87:767-73 Jl '64
Employment of school-age youth, October 1962. C. Rosenfeld. il Mo Labor R 86:907-13 Ag '63
Few jobs for our youth. W. J. Byron. America 108:801 Je 1 '63
Growing worry for U.S: young people out of work. il U S News 54:83-5 F 18 '63
Job crisis ahead for young people. Changing T 17:6 O '63
Jobs for youth. America 108:795 Je 1 '63
Jobs: key to national unrest? il U S News 54:37-41 Je 24 '63
Labor month in review. Mo Labor R 86:III-IV Mr '63
Life guide: jobs for juniors. il Life 54:19-20 My 3 '63
New core of unemployment. Bsns W p 176 Je 15 '63
Only the beginning. Commonweal 78:340 Je 21 '63
Out-of-school youth, February 1963. T. E. Swanstrom. il Mo Labor R 87:1416-24 D '64
Out-of-school youth, February 1963. V. C. Perrella and F. A. Bogan. il Mo Labor R 87: 1260-8 N '64

YOUTH—Employment—*Continued*
Putting teens to work; Job corps, President's anti-poverty program. Bsns W p82 Je 6 '64
Ski bums: the upland Bohemians. K. K. Waller. il Mlle 58:172-3+ N '63
Surplus youth; a future without jobs. J. S. Coleman. il Nation 196:439-43 My 25 '63
Teen scene at the fair. il Seventeen 23:116-17+ F '64
This month's feature: Administration's youth employment bill. Cong Digest 42:291-310 D '63
Unemployment: accent on youth. Sr Schol 82:16-18 My 15 '63
War on poverty: impact on education. il Sr Schol 85:1T Ja 14 '65
What's happening in education? W. D. Boutwell. PTA Mag 58:23 My '64
When junior seeks a job; with study-discussion program, by E. M. Duvall. W. W. Wirtz. bibliog il PTA Mag 57:12-14, 37 My '63
Why too many farm boys get poor jobs. R. C. Davids. Farm J 88:27+ S '64
Why young people face a shortage of jobs; interview. W. W. Wirtz. il U S News 54:62-7 Ap 1 '63
Will teen-agers make the sixties soar? il U S News 57:102-4 O 26 '64
Will there be jobs for our children? E. Cohen and S. Fremon. il Parents Mag 38:58-9+ N '63
Wirtz proposal. W. F. Buckley, jr. Nat R 16:267 Ap 7 '64
Young people may not be able to find jobs unless. . . G. J. Hecht. Parents Mag 39:34 My '64
Young people without jobs: how real is the problem? il U S News 55:92-4 Ag 19 '63
Your first job. il Changing T 18:31-3 My '64
See also
Labor camps
Student employment
United States—Job corps

Health and hygiene

New teenage medicine. J. Robbins and J. Robbins. il Good H 157:70-1+ Ag '63
Of youth and health. R. P. Goldman and P. W. Goldman. il N Y Times Mag p26 S 6 '64
Stick out your tongue and say ah. il Seventeen 23:130-1 N '64

Political activities

Come on in, politics is fine! C. Pell. Seventeen 23:154+ O '64
Roar, Republicans, roar! witness to political revolution in San Francisco. L. Goldenson. il Seventeen 23:63 O '64
Two open letters to teen-age girls. M. Price; E. M. Peterson. Seventeen 23:232-4 S '64
What you can do this election. Sr Schol 85:36-7 S 23 '64
Your help is wanted in politics; teen-Dems and TARS (Teen-age Republicans) R. Hartley. il Seventeen 23:132-3+ S '64

Reading

See Books and reading

Recreation

See Recreation

Religion

Church for teen-agers; Halepule opio in Aina Haina, Hawaii. il Time 82:57 D 6 '63
Teens talk about religion; symposium. Seventeen 22:132-3+ Mr '63

Africa

See also
African students

China (People's Republic)

Love affair of Comrade Wang; utter denial of personal freedom. J. Marcuse. il N Y Times Mag p40-1+ N 8 '64
Myth who speaks for Mao; Lei Feng. J. Marcuse. il N Y Times Mag p30-1+ N 1 '64
Toughening the next generation. Time 84:48 O 16 '64

England

See Youth—Great Britain

France

Hi pals; Salut les copains. Newsweek 62:65 Jl 29 '63
What's dimming the city of lights? G. Dickerson. Mlle 59:104+ O '64
See also
Youth market

Germany (Democratic Republic)

Young Germans. E. von Hornstein. Atlan 212:122-3+ D '63

Germany (Federal Republic)

Brave buddelers of Berlin. J. O'Donnell. il N Y Times Mag p32-3+ Ap 7 '63
Exclusive Senior scholastic interview. W. Brandt. Sr Schol 83:21 N 15 '63
Germans take lead in economy travel. il Bsns W p30-1 Jl 20 '63
Reconciliation in action; volunteer service abroad by young Germans. H. Lehmann. Christian Cent 80:824-6 Je 26 '63
Young Germans. E. von Hornstein. Atlan 212:122-3+ D '63
Young Germans. N. Ascherson. il Holiday 36:78-83+ O '64
See also
German students

Great Britain

'astings hain't 'ad it so bad since 1066. il Life 57:61-2+ S 18 '64
Battle of the yobs. il Time 83:29 My 29 '64
Clacton giggle; mods and rockers. il Time 83:32-3 Ap 10 '64
Getting a head; fighting Mods and Rockers. il Newsweek 63:34+ Je 1 '64
Most invaluable freedom of them all; Britain and America from viewpoint of higher education. K. Tynan. Seventeen 23:148+ Mr '64
Putting down the queen's teens. P. Gilliatt. Nation 199:227-9 O 12 '64
Rising generation in Britain. R. Kirk. Nat R 17:24 Ja 12 '65
Rocks round the clock; Rockers and Mods at Hastings. il Time 84:24 Ag 14 '64
So young, so cool, so misunderstood; Mods & Rockers. P. Laurie. il Vogue 144:68-9+ Ag 1 '64
What a giggle; teen-age gangs vandalism in Clacton, England. Newsweek 63:46 Ap 13 '64
See also
British students

Ireland

Close-up of Ireland's basic problem. T. Guthrie. il N Y Times Mag p22+ Ja 19 '64

Jamaica

Jamaica's youth corps. G. Meek. il Américas 15:13-15 Ap '63

Japan

Quiet life. Newsweek 64:40+ Jl 20 '64
Yoko is her name. il Seventeen 23:140-1 Ap '64
Young in rebellion. il Life 57:86A-93 S 11 '64

Latin America

Training for future farmers; OAS Inter-American rural youth program. G. Meek. il Américas 16:32-4 O '64

Russia

New men of the Soviet sixties. P. Johnson. il Reporter 28:16-21 My 9 '63
Soviet fathers and sons. G. Feifer. New Repub 148:11-13 Je 1 '63
Tattered banners of Soviet ideology. D. P. Hammer. New Repub 150:13-14 Mr 14 '64
What goes on in those youth cafés. E. Diamond. il McCalls 90:38+ Je '63
What Russian girls are like. G. Frost. il N Y Times Mag p 16-17+ Ja 24 '65
See also
Russian students

United States

Accent on youth at first N.Y. film festival. R. Hemming. Sr Schol 83:25 O 25 '63
Advice to a young woman; interview. M. Diver. Changing T 17:31-4 Ap '63
Affluent child; with study discussion program by the authors. D. Harris and E. Harris. bibliog PTA Mag 58:27-9, 35-6 Mr '64
Allston Wheat's crusade. M. Epernay. Harper 226:53-7 My '63
Art classes. M. W. Brown. il Sch Arts 63:24-8 Je '64
Audition; new teen-age panel. The comers. il New Yorker 40:29-32 Mr 28 '64
Beatles reaction puzzles even psychologists. Sci N L 85:141 F 29 '64
Best of teens, the worst of teens. M. W. Lear. il N Y Times Mag p34+ N 1 '64
Danger! teen-agers. C. Seton. McCalls 92:95+ N '64
Dope invades the suburbs. R. P. Goldman. il Sat Eve Post 237:19-25 Ap 4 '64

YOUTH—United States—*Continued*
Education; acceptance of responsibility; address; July 16, 1964. C. Pell. Vital Speeches 30:725-7 S 15 '64
Eugene Ormandy talks to teens. E. Ormandy. Seventeen 22:98+ Jl '63
Face of the future; quotations by Americans aged eighteen to twenty-five. il Look 29: 72-4+ Ja 12 '65
Glue sniffing. W. C. Burgess. PTA Mag 58: 15-17 Mr '64
Horizons for youth. America 108:283 Mr 2 '63
How many of these things are true about teenagers? W. Peters. il Good H 157:92-3+ N '63
How to keep teens out of trouble; solution in Darien, Conn. R. Carson. il Parents Mag 39:48-9+ Je '64
Kill the cops! teenagers riot during Labor day weekend. il Newsweek 64:36+ S 21 '64
Let's stop kicking the kids around; excerpts from address. W. Hobbs. Read Digest 85: 79-81 Ag '64
Masters of the soft sell. il Am City 79:141+ Ag '64
Message from the President. L. B. Johnson. il Seventeen 23:110-11 S '64
Mice or men in the space age? round-table discussion from 1964 Williamsburg student burgesses. il Sr Schol 84:12-13+ Ap 24 '64
Needed: a national youth policy. C. Pell. NEA J 53:17 D '64
New lost generation: jobless youth. M. Harrington. il N Y Times Mag p 13+ My 24 '64
Paradoxical case of the affluent delinquent. J. Lelyveld. il N Y Times Mag p 13+ O 4 '64
Presidential message on U.S. youth. il Sr Schol 82:7 Mr 6 '63
Southern teen-ager speaks his mind. M. Long. il N Y Times Mag p 15+ N 10 '63
Teen-age manners and make-up; with study-discussion program, by E. M. Duvall. R. H. Loeb, jr. bibliog il PTA Mag 58:30-2, 36 D '63
Teen scene. See issues of Seventeen
Tense generation. S. Grafton. il Look 27:17-23 Ag 27 '63; Same abr. Read Digest 83: 61-6 N '63; Discussion. Look 27:14+ O 8 '63
Those student tours to Europe: what really goes on. G. Bocca. il McCalls 90:92-3+ Jl '63
Today's youth, tomorrow's leaders; round-table discussion from 1963 Williamsburg student burgesses. il Sr Schol 82:16-17 Mr 27 '63
Unemployed youth in our affluent society; address, September 3, 1964. R. F. Male. Vital Speeches 30:734-6 S 15 '64
What industry expects of youth; address, May 25, 1963. L. C. Michelon. Vital Speeches 29:572-6 Jl 1 '63
What the Beatles prove about teenagers; interview. D. Riesman. il U S News 56:88 F 24 '64
What young people are like nowadays. U S News 58:11 Ja 4 '65
When teen-agers start to drink. B. Lang. il N Y Times Mag p47+ Jl 19 '64
Where's the party: let's crash it! R. Wallace. il Life 55:62-4+ Jl 5 '63; Same abr. Read Digest 83:131-5 O '63
Who says teen-agers are soft? C. Edwards. il McCalls 91:40+ O '63
Why young people get into trouble. Farm J 87:82 Ag '63
World wants you: address, June 6, 1963. W. Schrier. Vital Speeches 29:597-600 Jl 15 '63
Would you like to be an adolescent today? with study-discussion program. S. Grafton; L. A. Kirkendall; L. Grayson. bibliog il PTA Mag 58:7-9, 36 My '64
Young rebels with a cause. H. Page. il Parents Mag 39:42-5+ D '64
Youth act. America 108:601 Ap 27 '63
Youth: opportunity to be what? R. Coles. il New Repub 151:59-64 N 7 '64
Youth problems and Kennedy's remedies. U S News 54:9 F 25 '63
See also
College students
Dating
Youth market

YOUTH, Rural. See Rural youth

YOUTH and war. See War and youth

YOUTH associations
See also
Young Americans for freedom (organization)

YOUTH awards. See Rewards, prizes, etc.

YOUTH board. See New York (city)—Youth board

YOUTH centers. See Recreation centers

YOUTH clubs. See Clubs

YOUTH conferences
Middle East youth conference. P. K. Kerns. Christian Cent 81:1066 Ag 26 '64
See also
Baptist world youth conference
Encampment for citizenship
World festival of youth and students for peace and friendship

YOUTH counseling. See Counseling

YOUTH finance. See Budget, Personal

YOUTH forestry camps. See Forestry camps

YOUTH group achievement awards
195 U.S. and Canadian youth groups win! Parents Mag 38:76+ N '63
P/M's tenth annual youth awards. Parents Mag 39:59+ O '64

YOUTH hostels
Family fun the hosteling way. Good H 158: 166 Ap '64
Hosteler's handbook. C. Gmitro. Mlle 59:194-6 My '64
Teen travel talk; hosteling trip. il Seventeen 23:154 My '64
Wonder as you wander. R. E. Carlson. il Recreation 56:272-4 Je '63

YOUTH jury
Jacksonville's jury of juvenile peers. F. Sondern, jr. Parents Mag 38:47+ Ag '63; Same abr. Read Digest 83:82-5 Ag '63
Jury of peers; Terre Haute experiment. il Newsweek 63:22 Ja 20 '64

YOUTH market
Affluent child; with study discussion program by the authors. D. Harris and E. Harris. bibliog PTA Mag 58:27-9, 35-6 Mr '64
Appeal to youth; Ford's concentrating on youth market. il Time 83:74-5 Ja 3 '64
Bring in the kids; they bring the family. il Bsns W p32+ S 5 '64
Drive for the teen-age market; excerpts from The Consumers union report on smoking and the public interest. PTA Mag 58:23-4 O '63
Ford soups up its youth drive; folk-jazz wing dings at colleges. il Bsns W p32-4 Ja 4 '64
Teen-age tide. il Time 84:96+ O 9 '64
Tidy teens; drug store items. Time 82:56 Jl 5 '63
$25 billion-a-year accent on youth. il Newsweek 64:80-2 N 30 '64
Vive les teen-agers! France's youngsters. il Bsns W p48-9 N 23 '63
Will teen-agers make the sixties soar? il U S News 57:102-4 O 26 '64
Younger they are, the more fickle. Bsns W p96 S 21 '63
Youth leads the way. il Bsns W p31 Ja 18 '64

YOUTH movement

Germany

Young Germany 1900-1960, by W. Z. Laqueur.
Review
Commentary 34:178-81 Ag '62. G. L. Mosse; Reply with rejoinder. G. Mayer. 35:75 Ja '63

YOUTH movement, Communist. See World festival of youth and students for peace and friendship

YOUTH opportunity program. See United States—Labor, Department of—Youth opportunity program

YOUTH periodicals. See Periodicals

YOUTH volunteer service. See Volunteer service

YOUTH'S companion (periodical)
Pledge of allegiance. F. Duncan. il Atlan 213:120-1 My '64

YTTERBIUM
Semiconducting region of ytterbium. P. C. Souers and G. Jura. bibliog il Science 140: 481-3 My 3 '63
Ytterbium; effect of pressure and temperature on resistance. R. A. Stager and H. G. Drickamer. bibliog il Science 139:1284 Mr 29 '63

YU, C. K. and Sinclair, W. K.
Polyploidy induced by X-rays in Chinese hamster cells in vitro. bibliog Science 145: 508-10 Jl 31 '64

YU, Chuan-tao, and Zamecnik, P. C.
Effect of bromination on the biological activities of transfer RNA of escherichia coli. bibliog Science 144:856-9 My 15 '64

YU, David
Gloss on glossolalia. Christian Cent 81:1243-4 O 7 '64
Mediating position. Christian Cent 80:713 My 29 '63

YUAN, Luke C. L.
Resonant particles in high-energy physics. Science 140:1430 Je 28 '63

YUASA, Eiko
How to make successful flower arrangements. House B 106:92-113+ Ag '64
Real inside story on sukiyaki. House B 105:156-7+ Ap '63
—See Gordon, E. jt. auth.

YUCATAN
See also
Chichen Itzá
Cozumel Island

Description and travel

Traveling with Mlle: the Yucatán; daiquiris and chacmools. M. Lawrence. Mlle 60:135-6+ D '64

YUCCA
They may grow a foot a day. il Sunset 130:44 My '63

YUDKIN, Samuel
Samuel Yudkin loses National airport concession. Pub W 184:30-1 D 2 '63

YUGOSLAV cookery. See Cookery, Yugoslav

YUGOSLAV literature

Translations into English

Translation of Yugoslav authors urged by visiting publishers. Library J 89:3124 S 1 '64

YUGOSLAV painting. See Painting, Yugoslav

YUGOSLAVIA
Ethnic chauvinism persists. New Repub 149:9 Ag 31 '63
How well can we trust Marshal Tito? R. Sherrod. il Sat Eve Post 236:75-9 Je 22 '63
Secretary-General visits Romania and Yugoslavia. il U N Rev 10:46-7 Je '63
See also
Airlines—Yugoslavia
Architecture—Yugoslavia
Art—Yugoslavia
Belgrade
Churches—Yugoslavia
Communism—Yugoslavia
Communist party (Yugoslavia)
Croatia
Dubrovnik
Earthquakes—Yugoslavia
Economic assistance in Yugoslavia
Libraries—Yugoslavia
Money—Yugoslavia
Music festivals—Yugoslavia
Publishers and publishing—Yugoslavia
Sarajevo
Unemployment—Yugoslavia

Description and travel

Little churches of Ohrid, etc. M. J. Kempner. il Harper 228:28+ Ap '64
Peripatetic reviewer. E. Weeks. Atlan 211:138 Ap '63

Economic conditions

Special road. Y. Blumenfeld. il Newsweek 64:28-9 D 28 '64
See also
Unemployment—Yugoslavia

Economic policy

Return of the baker. Time 81:44 Mr 15 '63

Economic relations

Tito may visit the US. New Repub 149:6 S 14 '63

Foreign relations

Active coexister visits us. D. Binder. il N Y Times Mag p24+ O 13 '63
Advice from the host; winding up of Khrushchev's state visit to Yugoslavia. il Time 82:29 S 6 '63
Billions in U.S. aid and Tito wants to bury capitalism. A. Kucherov. il U S News 55:68-9 S 16 '63
Horse trading; Tito in Leningrad. Newsweek 63:46 Je 22 '64
President Tito of Yugoslavia visits the United States; exchange of greetings, October 17, 1963; with text of communique. J. F. Kennedy; Tito. Dept State Bul 49:738-40 N 11 '63
Social climber; Tito's trips abroad. Reporter 29:18+ N 7 '63
Tito in the United States. M. M. Mestrovic. Commonweal 79:181 N 8 '63
Tito of Yugoslavia: new role for an old rebel? il Sr Schol 83:12-15+ O 11 '63
Titoism in flux. F. W. Neal. Cur Hist 44:294-8+ My '63
Tito's visit: a worry for U.S. il U S News 55:52 O 28 '63
Yugoslavia: after the Partisan generation. A. Rothberg. Yale R 53:221-32 D '63

Industries

Capitalistic comrade. Time 83:94 Ap 3 '64

Politics and government

How to win job security. Time 81:38 Ap 19 '63
Tito for life. Newsweek 61:38+ Ap 22 '63
Tito of Yugoslavia: new role for an old rebel? il Sr Schol 83:12-15+ O 11 '63
Titoism in flux. F. W. Neal. Cur Hist 44:294-8+ My '63
Yugoslavia: after the Partisan generation. A. Rothberg. Yale R 53:221-32 D '63

Relief work

U.N. calls on member states to aid in Skopje reconstruction; statement, October 14, 1963. C. W. Yost. Dept State Bul 49:759-60 N 11 '63

Religious institutions and affairs

See also
Catholic church in Yugoslavia

Social conditions

Jugoslavia: crisis and choice. J. C. Campbell. For Affairs 41:384-97 Ja '63
Tito's visit. New Repub 149:5 O 19 '63

YUGOSLAVIA and the United States
My friend, the Titoist. A. Schalk. Commonweal 80:542-4 Ag 7 '64

YUGOSLAVS
Jugoslavia: crisis and choice. J. C. Campbell. For Affairs 41:384-97 Ja '63

YUKICH, Michael E.
Spin-a-painting. Design 65:30-1+ S '63

YUKON RIVER
Rampart Dam: a wildlife catastrophe for nothing? G. H. Gillelan. il Outdoor Life 134:14-15+ D '64

YULETIDE. See Christmas

YUNGMEYER, Elinor
School libraries. Wilson Lib Bul 38:577 Mr '64

YUNICK, Henry. See Yunick, S.

YUNICK, Smokey
Say, Smokey; questions and answers. See issues of Popular science monthly
Smokey Yunick speaks; ed. by M. Muhleman. por Motor T 15:82 O '63

about

He's all ears for engines. H. McLemore. il pors Pop Sci 184:94-7+ Ja '64

El YUNQUE rain forest. See National forests

YURCHENCO, Henrietta
Antonio and the Ballets de Madrid. Mus Am 84:57 O '64
Blues and banjos. Mus Am 83:21 O '63
Folk (cont) Mus Am 83:131+ Ja; 41 F; 25 Mr; 45 My; 34 O; 49 N; 281 D '63; 84:63 Ja; 52 F; 54 Mr; 56-7 My; 53-4 Jl; 56-7 S; 26+ O; 50-1 N; 270 D '64
Folk music. See issues of American record guide
Folk music around the world a basic library collection. por Library J 88:1838-40 My 1 '63
Folk music in New York (title varies) Mus Am 83:226+ Ja; 34 F; 40 My '63; 84:263 D '64
Music of India. Mus Am 84:26+ O '64
Reviews: folk. Mus Am 83:266 D '63; 84:55 Ja; 43 F; 47 Mr; 49 My '64

YURIKO
Yuriko at 92nd street Y. J. Maskey. Dance Mag 37:28+ Je '63; 39:29+ Ja '65
Yuriko at 92nd street Y. M. Marks. Dance Mag 37:68 Je '63; 38:84 Je '64

Z

ZD (zero defects) See Quality control

ZIP (Zoning improvement plan) See Postal service—United States

ZABAGLIONE. See Desserts

ZABARSKY, Nathan
Case for the slow shutter. il U S Camera 26:72-3 S '63
Small aperture long exposure for fall color. H. Keppler. il Mod Phot 28:80-1 N '64

ZABEL, William D.
What's in the package? lessons in practical detective work for supermarket shoppers. Harper 227:12+ Ag '63

ZABLOCKI, Clement J.
Recent events in South Vietnam; address, November 4, 1963. Vital Speeches 30:133-4 D 15 '63

ZABRISKIE, George. See Holmes, D. A. jt. auth.

ZACCHINI, Madeline
Notes and comment; mother of human cannonballs. New Yorker 39:19 Ag 17 '63
ZACHARIAS, Jerrold R. and White, Stephen
Requirements for major curriculum revision; excerpt from New curricula. Sch & Soc 92:66-72 F 22 '64
ZACHARIAS, Leona, and Wurtman, R. J.
Blindness: its relation to age of menarche. bibliog Science 144:1154-5 My 29 '64
ZACHARY, Frank
Fair that was. New Yorker 40:122+ Ap 11 '64
ZACKAY, Victor F.
Strength of steel. Sci Am 209:72-82 bibliog(p 140) Ag '63
ZADIG, Alfred T. K.
Few raps for the rapprochement. Christian Cent 81:801-3 Je 17 '64
ZAFRULLA KHAN, Sir Muhammad
Almost at threshold of universal freedom; excerpt from address, December 26, 1962. U N Rev 10:7-8 Ja '63
ZAGOREN, Ruby
We took our children to Europe. House B 106:10+ Jl '64
ZAGORIA, Donald S.
(ed) Communist China and the Soviet bloc. bibliog f Ann Am Acad 349:1-162 S '63
Communist China is a paper dragon. N Y Times Mag p40-1+ O 18 '64
Widening gulf between Mao and Khrushchev. Reporter 28:38-40 Ap 25 '63
ZAGORIA, Sam
To make it a do-something Congress. N Y Times Mag p26+ S 8 '63
ZAGORIN, Perez
English history, 1558-1640: a bibliographical survey. bibliog f Am Hist R 68:364-84 Ja '63
ZAGREB, Yugoslavia
Music
Notes from abroad. K. Blaukopf. Hi Fi 13: 26+ D '63
ZAGREB biennale. See Music festivals—Yugoslavia
ZAGRI, Sidney
Hoffa's voice on Capitol hill. il pors Bsns W p45-6+ S 14 '63
ZAHL, Harold A.
Secret tube that changed the war. W. I. Orr. il por Pop Electr 20:57-9+ Mr '64
ZAHL, Paul A.
Finding the Mt Everest of all living things. il pors Nat Geog Mag 126:10-51 Jl '64
Fluorescent gems from Davy Jone's locker. il Nat Geog Mag 124:260-71 Ag '63
Malaysia's giant flowers and insect-trapping plants. il Nat Geog Mag 125:680-701 My '64
Mystery of the monarch butterfly. il Nat Geog Mag 123:588-98 Ap '63
ZAHN, Gordon C.
Church under Hitler. Commonweal 80:445-8 Jl 3 '64
ZAHN, Walter G.
Optimist books for boys. Sr Schol 82:23T Mr 13 '63
ZAHNER, R. See Whitmore, F. W. jt. auth.
ZAHNISER, Howard
Eighth biennial wilderness conference. Liv Wildn 84:34-41 Sum '63
Lake Solitude sermon; reprint. Liv Wildn 85:2 Wint '64
Poem: When midway in the living wilderness. Liv Wildn 84:14 Sum '63
Wilderness bill in committee hearing. Liv Wildn 85:30-4 Wint '64
about
Circle that took us in. Am For 70:8-9 Je '64
Howard Clinton Zahniser, 1906-64; with tributes from newspapers. il por Liv Wildn 85:3-6 Wint '64
Obituary
Nat Parks Mag 38:17 Je '64
ZAITLIN, Milton, and Ferris, W. R.
Unusual aggregation of a nonfunctional tobacco mosaic virus protein. bibliog Science 143:1451-2 Mr 27 '64
ZAITSEV, Vïacheslav Mikhailovich
Young designer changes things. il pors Life 55:113-14 S 13 '63
ZAK, Radovan. See Gordon, P. jt. auth.
ZAKIA, Richard D.
Film-speed trap. Pop Phot 55:68-9 S '64
—See Todd, H. N. jt. auth.
ZAKON, David L.
Thoughts on drying flowers in silica. Horticulture 41:470-1 S '63
ZALAMEA, Luis
Farmer, city founder, and poet. Américas 15:35-9 N '63
Green thumb that paid off. Américas 15:29-33 F '63
ZALE jewelry company
Diamonds for the masses. J. McDonald. il Fortune 70:134-7+ D '64
ZALEZNIK, Abraham
Human dilemmas of leadership. Harvard Bsns R 41:49-55 Jl '63
ZALKIN, Allan, and others
Crystal and molecular structure of ferrichrome A. bibliog Science 146:261-3 O 9 '64
Sodium perxenate hexahydrate. bibliog Science 142:501-2 O 25 '63
ZALKIND, David
Curl up and read. Seventeen 23:80 Mr '64
ZALTZMAN-NIRENBERG, P. See Udenfriend, S. jt. auth.
ZAMBIA
Born to riches. il Newsweek 64:65-6 O 26 '64
Horsemanship; statue of Rhodes returned to British South Africa co. Time 84:33 D 18 '64
Kaunda of Zambia. C. Northcott. Christian Cent 81:238-9 F 19 '64
Rhodesias and Nyasaland. F. M. G. Wilson. Cur Hist 46:148-55+ Mr '64
Tomorrow the moon; independence day. il Time 84:43-4 O 30 '64
Zambia: new nation in Africa. T. P. Melady. Cath World 200:91-4 N '64
See also
United Nations—Zambia
ZAMCHICK, David
Arts and humanities. Sr Schol 83:32T Ja 17 '64
Arts and humanities. Sr Schol 85:23T D 2 '64
ZAMECNIK, Paul C. See Yu, C. T. jt. auth.
ZAMOYTA, Vincent C.
Layman teaches theology. Cath World 199: 22-7 Ap '64
ZAMPONI, Linda
Vienna swoons over Nureyev and swans. Dance Mag 38:28+ D '64
ZANDONAI, Riccardo
On records; Conchita (excerpts) P. Elvins. Opera N 29:33-4 Ja 16 '65
ZANGRANDO, Robert L.
Direction of the March. bibliog Negro Hist Bul 27:60-4 D '63
ZANGWILL, Israel
Zangwill in retrospect. J. Gross. Commentary 38:54-7 D '64
ZANKER, Alfred
Now on the road to prosperity, Spain. U S News 57:54-6 Jl 27 '64
ZANTZINGER, William Devereux
Spinsters' ball. il por Time 81:26 F 22 '63
ZANUCK, Darryl Francis
Boss makes $150,000, employe 2.4 million. U S News 54:10 Je 3 '63
Darryl Zanuck: last of the movie moguls. E. Havemann. por McCalls 91:134-5+ O '63
ZANUTTO, James M.
Year's best glamor book. Pop Phot 52:70-5 Ap '63
ZANZIBAR
African Cuba? Time 83:45 Ap 17 '64
An African Cuba? with account by J. Nugent. il Newsweek 63:34-5 Ja 27 '64
Aspects of Zanzibar. A. Conner. il Reporter 28:44-5 Mr 28 '63
But which is the tail? Tanganyika. Newsweek 63:40 My 4 '64
Calming down. Newsweek 63:40 Mr 9 '64
Cuckoo coup. il Time 83:20-1 Ja 24 '64
Good-by to all that. il Newsweek 63:54 Ap 27 '64
Long way from Utopia. Time 82:21 D 20 '63
Losing a good crisis. Commonweal 80:225 My 15 '64
No future in cloves. New Repub 149:8 Ag 3 '63
Odd man out. il Time 83:37 Mr 20 '64
Tanganyika: the tribulations of a good man. C. Sterling. il Reporter 30:21-5 Ap 9 '64
Tangibar; United Republic of Tanganyika and Zanzibar. il Time 83:30 My 1 '64
Threats & protests. Time 83:24 Ja 31 '64
Three-legged race; Communist penetration. Newsweek 64:33-4 Jl 6 '64
See also
Communism—Zanzibar
Elections—Zanzibar
Tanzania
United Nations—Zanzibar
ZAPALSKI, Art
Spin-a-painting. M. E. Yukich. il Design 65: 30-1+ S '63
ZAPATA, Celia
Cultural haven in the California pines. Américas 16:22-6 Je '64
ZAPF, Hermann
Hermann Zapf: calligrapher, type designer, master of the book arts. P. A. Bennett. il pors Pub W 187:72-4+ Ja 4 '65

ZAPF, Herman—*Continued*
Hermann Zapf's letters. F. Johnson. il Am Artist 28:42-7+ O '64
ZAR und zimmerman; opera. See Lortzing, A.
ZAROMB, Solomon
Peace levy approach. Bul Atomic Sci 20:33-4 Ap '64
ZARTMAN, I. William
Sahara: bridge or barrier? bibliog Int Concil 541:3-62 Ja '63
ZARTMAN, R. E. and others
Ancient granite gneiss in the Black Hills, South Dakota. bibliog Science 145:479-81 Jl 31 '64
ZARUR, Alziro
Man from above. il por Time 82:29-30 D 27 '63
ZAVADA, Mary
Hochhuth in London; a drama critic looks at Der stellvertreter. America 110:139-40 Ja 25 '64
My old ladies. Reporter 29:35-6 D 5 '63
Play's the thing. America 109:511-12 N 2 '63
ZAVALA, Albert. See Leonard, D. J. jt. auth.
ZAVALETA, Carlos E.
Machu Picchu in danger; letter. Américas 16:48 O '64
ZEARFOSS, Robert N.
Lenten reading. Christian Cent 80:274 F 27 '63
ZECKENDORF, William
Big Bill on Broadway: too many kibitzers. il por Newsweek 62:65 Jl 22 '63
Big Bill's troubles. por Newsweek 63:83 Je 8 '64
Big deal. E. Rachlis and J. E. Marqusee. il por Esquire 59:98-9+ My '63
Cliff-hanging with Bill. por Newsweek 64:61-2 Ag 17 '64
He webs but seldom naps. por Time 83:100+ Je 12 '64
I'd rather be alive; Zeckendorf facing his biggest troubles yet. por Newsweek 61:83-4 Je 10 '63
In a mood to deal. por Newsweek 61:72 F 4 '63
Out on that limb. Time 81:93 My 24 '63
Zeckendorf dickers for help. Bsns W p30 My 4 '63
Zeckendorf finesses for cash again. il por Bsns W p 134+ Mr 16 '63
Zeckendorf: going once, going twice. il pors Arch Forum 119:5+ Ag '63
Zeckendorf pulls in his horns. il Bsns W p34-5 Je 27 '64
Zeckendorf retreats. Time 82:91 Jl 12 '63
Zeckendorf wheels, deals and survives. por Arch Forum 119:7 Jl '63
ZEEB; story. See Rode, A.
ZEFFIRELLI, Franco
Franco Zeffirelli; interview, ed. by W. Weaver. por Hi Fi 14:30+ Mr '64
about
Crusade against boredom; new production of Verdi's Falstaff at the Met. il por Time 83:59 Mr 13 '64
Final fugue. il por Newsweek 63:94 Mr 16 '64
High order of talent. M. Mayer. il pors Opera N 28:6-15 Mr 21 '64
Revised standard Dane. il Time 82:38 D 27 '63
ZEIGERMAN, Gerald
Dame Sybil and Dame Edith; story. Mlle 58:70-1 D '63
ZEIGLER, John M. and others
Direct readout of sediment analyses by settling tube for computer processing. Science 145:51 Jl 3 '64
ZEIK, Michael D.
Age of prophets. Commonweal 78:67-70 Ap 12 '63
Sociological perspectives an anti-Semitism. Commonweal 81:19 S 25 '64
Zen Catholicism. Commonweal 78:324-5 Je 14 '63
ZEILENGA, G. R. See Clifford, A. F. jt. auth.
ZEIST, Willem van, and Wright, H. E. jr
Preliminary pollen studies at Lake Zeribar, Zagros mountains, southwestern Iran. bibliog Science 140:65-7 Ap 5 '63
Die ZEIT. See Newspapers—Germany (Federal Republic)
ZEITLIN, Arnold
Ghana's young theatre. Theatre Arts 47:65-7+ N '63
ZEITLIN, David
At last Hollywood discovers the toast of Broadway: Julie. Life 57:117-18+ N 13 '64
Life movie review. Life 56:21 Je 12 '64
Seen any good titles lately? Life 56:103-4 F 7 '64
Skydiving chute-em-up. Life 54:91-3 Ap 12 '63
Super snooper to rate TV: a watch truck is watching you. Life 57:57+ S 25 '64
What wounded the industry now helps it. Life 55:50B D 20 '63
ZEITLIN, Harry, and others
Solid-solid interaction studies by spectral reflectance. bibliog Science 141:423-4 Ag 2 '63
ZEITZ, L. and Lee, R. M.
Bromine analysis in 5-bromouracil-labeled DNA by X-ray fluorescence. bibliog Science 142:1670-3 D 27 '63
ZELENKA, Johann Dismas
Discoveries from the past. H. Kupferberg. il Atlan 214:139-40 D '64
ZELEZNICK, L. D. and others
Biosynthesis of streptococcal cell walls; a rhamnose polysaccharide. bibliog Science 140:400-1 Ap 26 '63
ZELITCH, Israel
Reduction of transpiration of leaves through stomatal closure induced by alkenylsuccinic acids. bibliog Science 143:692-3 F 14 '64
ZELKO, Harold P.
Make your meetings more worth while. Nations Bsns 52:92-4+ S '64
ZELKOVA serrata
Wineglass-shaped tree seen as elm substitute. Sci N L 85:57 Ja 25 '64
ZELMAN, Norman
Improved foils, multiple-station presses, widen use of roll leaf. por Pub W 185:90+ Mr 2 '64
ZEMAN, Henry F.
Hit and miss. Outdoor Life 133:50-1+ F '64
New ice-fishing ideas. Outdoor Life 135:48-9+ F '65
Picture yourself. il por Outdoor Life 132:44-7+ Ag '63
ZEN Buddhism
Zen Catholicism, by A. Graham. Review
America 108:752-4 My 25 '63. T. Merton; Reply. M. W. Hess. 108:893 Je 29 '63
Cath World 197:389-90 S '63. G. MacEoin
Commonweal 78:324-5 Je 14 '63. M. D. Zeik
ZÉNDEGUI, Guillermo de
Birth of the Antilles. Américas 15:17-25 S '63
Day for rededication. Américas 15:1 Ap '63
Martí in Mexico. Américas 15:12-16 Je '63
Oldest city in the United States. Américas 16:7-14 My '64
Temple of the Spanish language. Américas 16:4-9 Ja '64
Today's art in yesterday's city. Américas 15:23-6 Mr '63
When the British captured Havana. Américas 16:21-8 Mr '64
ZENER diodes. See Diodes
ZEOLITES
Chinoptilolite: a new occurrence in North Carolina phosphorite. T. P. Rooney and P. F. Kerr. il Science 144:1453 Je 19 '64
Zeolite ZK-5: a new molecular sieve. G. T. Kerr. il Science 140:1412 Je 28 '63
ZEPHYR lilies
Atamasco lily. I. D. Jolly. il Horticulture 41:409 Ag '63
Little witches and the rain lilies. il Sunset 131:154+ Ag '63
ZEPHYRANTHES. See Zephyr lilies
ZEPP, Ira G. jr
Church-state confrontation in Maryland. Christian Cent 82:84+ Ja 20 '65
ZERMATT, Switzerland
Epidemic in the Alps; typhoid-fever. il Newsweek 61:86 Ap 8 '63
First came rumors, fears, then the ugly truth: typhoid! C. McCarry. il Sat Eve Post 236:84-7 My 25 '63
Sickness on the slopes; typhoid fever. il Time 81:34 Ap 5 '63
Wide, wide world at your feet. M. Gough. il House B 106:207-8 Ap '64
ZERN, Ed
Exit, laughing. See issues of Field & stream
Planes vs. fair chase. Field & S 68:10-11+ Ag '63
about
How to hide the truth. T. Trueblood. il por Field & S 67:26+ Ap '63
ZERO defects. See Quality control
ZERO; story. See O'Hara, J.
ZETTERBERG, Hans L.
Bookkeeping as a barometer. Wilson Lib Bul 38:541-4 Mr '64
ZEUGLODON. See Whales, Fossil
ZEUS project. See Guided missiles—Defenses
ZEVI, Tullia
Art. New Repub 151:32-4 S 19 '64

ZEYA, H. I. and Spitznagel, J. K.
Antibacterial and enzymic basic proteins from leukocyte lysosomes: separation and identification. bibliog Science 142:1085-7 N 22 '63

ZGLENICKI, Charles. See McKaig, H. L. jr, jt. auth.

ZICH, Arthur
Boating (cont) Sports Illus 18:58-60 F 11; 43-4+ Ap 22 '63
Boston girl's long voyage home. Sports Illus 18:40-2+ Ap 1 '63
Ideal yacht club. Sports Illus 18:32-6 Ap 22 '63
Object is to win the race. Sports Illus 19: 32-7 Jl 1 '63
Ruffled race across a mirror. Sports Illus 18:22-5 My 6 '63
Two hulls are better than one. Sports Illus 18:12-17 Mr 4 '63

about

Patient madmen of Sheepshead Bay. Sports Illus 18:18-23 F 4 '63

ZICH, Patricia
Flags for space. Sch Arts 63:43 N '63

ZIDE, Larry
How to buy tape recorders. Mod Phot 28:147+ D '64
Sound advice. Mod Phot 28:56+ S; 42+ O '64; 29:26+ Ja '65
Sound ideas. See issues of American record guide
Tape transports: inside out. Mod Phot 28: 95+ O '64
—See Furst, R. E. jt. auth.

ZIDE, Rochelle
Rochelle Zide. S. Goodman. pors Dance Mag 37:52-3 Ap '63

ZIEGFELD, Edwin
Paradox & prospect. Sch Arts 62:36-7 F '63

ZIEGFELD, Florenz
Ziegfelds' girl; excerpts. P. Ziegfeld. il pors Ladies Home J 81:62-4+ Jl; 107-11 Ag '64

ZIEGFELD, Patricia
Ziegfelds' girl; excerpts. pors Ladies Home J 81:62-4+ Jl; 107-11 Ag '64

ZIEGLER, Earle F.
Have you a recreation philosophy? por Recreation 56:399-400 N '63

ZIEGLER, Esther E. See Brydon, M. W. jt. auth.

ZIELINSKI, Tadeusz
Latest styles; Warsaw international festival of contemporary music. Mus Am 84:27+ Ja '64
Question of style. Mus Am 84:19-21 Mr '64

ZIELINSKI, Vickie
Strange case of Edgar Smith. D. G. M. Coxe. il Nat R 15:273-8 O 8 '63

ZIETZ, Isidore
Mystery of earthquakes; where, when, what to do; interview. por U S News 56:37-9 Ap 13 '64

ZIGROSSER, Carl
Prints of Edward Hopper. Am Artist 27:38-43+ N '63

ZIGZAG sewing machines. See Sewing machines

ZIHUATANEJO, Mexico
Beachcombing at Zihuatanejo. il Sunset 133: 43+ O '64
Reader's choice. D. E. W. Tisdale. Travel 120:8 Ag '63

ZILKHA and sons, incorporated
Brothers Zilkha: a new world. il Bsns W p80-2+ My 9 '64

ZILL, Jo Ahern
Sporting look. Sports Illus 18:40-6 Mr 4; 48-50 My 6 '63

ZILSEL, Paul R.
Mass production of knowledge. Bul Atomic Sci 20:28-9 Ap '64

ZIM, Marvin Hugo
Master strategist of the railroad settlement. Fortune 70:164-6+ Jl '64

ZIM Israel navigation company, limited
Success at sea. Time 83:98 Mr 13 '64

ZIMBEL, Elaine
When a community votes no. Sat R 48:54-5 Ja 16 '65

ZIMMER, Gale Koschmann
Saving the Atlantic green turtle: a biological experiment. por Nat Parks Mag 38:11-13 D '64

ZIMMER, James G. and Demis, D. J.
Burns and other skin lesions; microcirculatory responses in man during healing. bibliog Science 140:994-6 My 31 '63

ZIMMER, Jill Schary
With a cast of thousands. McCalls 91:130-3+ N '63

ZIMMERMAN, Eleanor Halbrook
All that I asked of April; poem. Ladies Home J 80:102 Ap '63
First love; poem. McCalls 92:51 Ja '65

ZIMMERMAN, Irene
Focus on Brazil. Library J 88:3030-1 S 1 '63

ZIMMERMAN, Isidore
Wrong man behind the bars. J. Howard. il pors Life 56:57-8+ My 15 '64

ZIMMERMAN, John
Earthly delights in Paradise. il Sat Eve Post 236:62-5 Ap 27 '63
Great fair. il Sat Eve Post 237:26-35 My 23 '64
Rage to ski. il Sat Eve Post 236:24-9 F 9 '63

about

Focus on Zimmerman. J. Durniak. il por Pop Phot 52:82-91+ Ap '63
View from the bridge. il U S Camera 27:52-3 Ap '64

ZIMMERMAN, Joseph
Technique for substaining behavior with conditioned reinforcement. bibliog Science 142: 682-4 N 8 '63

ZIMMERMAN, Joseph Francis
Worcester rezones. Am City 79:99-100 Je '64

ZIMMERMANN, Egon
Fight for life by the home team; downhill ski race. P. Ress. il pors Sports Illus 20: 32-9 Ja 27 '64

ZIMMERMANN, Martin H.
How sap moves in trees. Sci Am 208:132-8+ bibliog(p 192) Mr '63

ZIMO, Betty
Roads make history. Sch Arts 63:18-20 Mr '64

ZIMPEL, Lloyd
Showdown in California. Commonweal 81: 153-5 O 30 '64
Voices from the place of snakes. Nation 198:537-8 My 25 '64

ZINC in the body
Zinc activation of a coordinated response in hydra. H. M. Lenhoff and J. R. Zwisler. bibliog il Science 142:1666-8 D 27 '63

ZINC paint. See Paint

ZINC sulfate
Zinc stimulation of RNA and protein synthesis in rhizopus nigricans. W. S. Wegener and A. H. Romano. bibliog il Science 142: 1669-70 D 27 '63

ZINDER, Norton D. See Valentine, R. C. jt. auth.

ZINFANDEL wine. See Wine

ZINJANTHROPUS. See Man, Prehistoric

ZINK, John
Whopping baron of the prairie. J. D. Brown. il pors Sports Illus 19:60-2+ N 4 '63

ZINKHAM, William H. and others
Lactate dehydrogenase in pigeon testes: genetic control by three loci. bibliog Science 144:1353-4 Je 12 '64
Lactate dehydrogenase in tests: dissociation and recombination of subunits. bibliog Science 142:1303-4 D 6 '63
—See Blanco, A. jt. auth.

ZINN, Howard
Battle-scarred youngsters. Nation 197:193-7 O 5 '63
Incident in Hattiesburg. Nation 198:501-4 My 18 '64
Mississippi idea. Nation 199:371-5 N 23 '64
Registration in Alabama. New Repub 149: 11-12 O 26 '63

ZINNEMANN, Fred
Zinnemann pictures a modern dilemma. W. Johnson. por Sr Schol 85:28 S 30 '64

ZINNIAS
Zinnias for brilliance all summer. R. D. Roe. il Horticulture 41:214 Ap '63

ZINSSER, William K.
Barbie is a million-dollar doll. Sat Eve Post 237:72-3 D 12 '64
Bright new comic clowns toward success: Woody Allen. Sat Eve Post 236:26-7 S 21 '63
But where will I keep my movie magazines? Sat Eve Post 238:74+ Ja 16 '65
Day there was no money. Reporter 29:46-8 S 12 '63
Dear Haircurl: help! Life 55:25+ O 18 '63
Far out on Long Island. Horizon 5:4-27 My '63
Goodbye Burma-Shave. Sat Eve Post 237:65-6 S 5 '64
Hazards of city courtship. Read Digest 82: 41-2+ Ap '63
Necklines make you nervous? Sat Eve Post 237:26-9 F 22 '64
Pipe this. Sat Eve Post 237:58-9 My 30 '64
Weekend guests from "we're so glad you could come" to "we're so sorry you have to go" and vice versa; excerpts. McCalls 90:92-3+ Ag '63

ZIO Tom; opera. See Trecate, L. F.

ZIOLKOWSKI, Korczak
World's biggest one-man job. J. M. Liston. il pors Pop Sci 184:68-71 Je '64

ZION NATIONAL PARK
Hiking in Zion National Park. R. H. Wauer. il Nat Parks Mag 38:8-10 D '64
ZIONISM
Israel and Zionism. A. Segal. il Nation 197: 293-6 N 9 '63
Jewish & other nationalisms. H. R. Trevor-Roper. Commentary 35:15-21 Ja '63
Judaism for all seasons. L. R. Sussman. Christian Cent 80:427-9 Ap 3 '63
Zionism and Judaism. C. E. Schulman. Christian Cent 80:858-60 Jl 3 '63
See also
Israel
Jewish-Arab relations
ZIPKIN, Herbert
Rover's conversion. pors Field & S 68:156-8 Ap '64
ZIPPERS
Fifty years of zip. S. V. Jones. il N Y Times Mag p 108-9 Ap 28 '63
Gap in zippers? il Consumer Rep 28:317-18 Jl '63
U.S. and Japan agree on exports of zipper chain from Japan; Department announcement, exchange of letters between Ambassador Ryuji Takeuchi and Assistant secretary of state for economic affairs G. Griffith Johnson, and attachment. Dept State Bul 49:449 S 16 '63
Zip goes the hookless wonder. D. Wharton. Read Digest 83:168C-168D+ N '63
Zipper that hides itself; Zipaway. Consumer Rep 29:156 Ap '64
ZIRCON
Meteoritic zircon. U. B. Marvin and C. Klein, jr. bibliog il Science 146:919-20 N 13 '64
ZIRCONIUM
Phase transformation at high temperatures in hafnia and zirconia. W. L. Baun. bibliog il Science 140:1330-1 Je 21 '63
Zirconium and hafnium in stone meteorites. W. D. Ehmann and J. L. Setser. bibliog il Science 139:594-5 F 15 '63
ZIRCONIUM oxides
Tetragonal zirconium oxide prepared under high pressure. F. W. Vahldiek and others. bibliog il Science 142:1059-60 N 22 '63
ZISCH, William E.
Still propelling itself into the space age. il pors Bsns W p86-8+ Jl 11 '64
ZISKIND, Sylvia
Pre-college library. Wilson Lib Bul 37:856-8 Je '63
ZISTEL, Era
Playing possums; excerpt from Gentle people. il por Audubon Mag 66:290-3 S '64
ZITÁCUARO, Mexico
Mexican waterworks. H. Sutton. il Sat R 47:28 Mr 21 '64
ZITHER
Ancient magic of the zither. A. Delman. il House B 105:94-5+ Jl '63
ZIZI; revue. See Musical comedies, revues, etc.—Criticisms, plots, etc.
ZIZYPHUS jujuba. See Jujubes
ZODIAC
Warning to Mao, it's the year of the dragon. R. Hughes. il N Y Times Mag p24-5+ Mr 1 '64
ZODIACAL light
Getting acquainted with astronomy. il Sky & Tel 28:140-1 S '64
Twilight phenomena caused by the eruption of Agung volcano. F. E. Volz. bibliog il Science 144:1121-2 My 29 '64
ZOGBAUM, Wilfred M.
Zogbaum makes a sculpture. M. N. Tabak. il pors Art N 63:42-5+ D '64
ZOLA, Joan
Adventures of a test taker. Nat R 17:21-3 Ja 12 '65
ZOLBERG, Aristide R.
French-speaking West Africa. bibliog f Cur Hist 45:347-54 D '63
ZOLOTOW, Maurice
Spoofmaster. Sat Eve Post 236:26-7 Ap 20 '63
Stage-struck: the romance of Alfred Lunt & Lynn Fontanne; excerpts. Look 28:92-9+ D 15 '64
ZONDAG, H. A.
Lactate dehydrogenase isozymes: lability at low temperature. bibliog Science 142:965-7 N 15 '63
ZONE plates. See Diffraction
ZONED heat. See Heating
ZONING
Cluster zoning: one step toward a better suburbia. G. D. Lloyd. il Am Home 67: 46-7 Je '64
How zoning can bring beauty; Clayton, Mo. C. W. O'Key. il Am City 78:100-1 Ap '63
Man's caboose is not his castle; zoning suit in Florida's Dade County. il Time 83:67 Je 12 '64
One site saved; Merrywood. New Repub 149: 6 N 30 '63
Worcester rezones. J. F. Zimmerman. il Am City 79:99-100 Je '64
Zoning and planning decisions; ed. by N. Williams, jr. See issues of American city
Zoning for today's needs; White Plains, N.Y. J. E. Curtis. Recreation 57:16-17 Ja '64
Zoning is in trouble; report on 30th annual conference of the American society of planning. Am City 79:36-7 Je '64
ZONING improvement plan. See Postal service—United States
ZONING law
See also
Building laws and regulations
ZOO story; drama. See Albee, E.
ZOOFLAGELLATES. See Flagellates
ZOOK, Mary
Don't feed the bears. Nat Parks Mag 37: 7-9 Je '63
Treasury treasures. Travel 121:46-7 Je '64
ZOOLOGICAL gardens
Birthday parties at the zoo; Swope park zoological gardens, Kansas City, Mo. G. K. Clarke. il Am City 78:101-2 Mr '63
Development of a children's zoo; Turtle Back zoo, West Orange, N.J. H. J. Van Cott. il Recreation 57:402-4 O '64
Duluth's most controversial citizen: Mr Magoo. H. Montgomery. il Am For 69:8+ O '63
Dumb friends. Holiday 35:160-1 Je '64
Multi-level zoo; Los Angeles. il Recreation 57:279 Je '64
News in zoos. il Time 83:54 My 22 '64
Party of one; confessions of a zoo-lover. A. Wilson. il Holiday 35:12+ Je '64
Reporter at large; meeting of American association of zoological parks and aquariums. E. Hahn. New Yorker 40:131-2+ S 19 '64
Survival centers for rare wild animals; with report by P. Hunt. il Life 57:46-52+ Ag 21 '64
What's new at the zoo; Turtle Back zoo, West Orange, N.J. H. J. Van Cott. il Am City 79:33 My '64
Zoo's who; with photographs by J. Cooke. Sat Eve Post 236:28-31 Ag 10 '63
See also
Menageries
also names of zoological gardens, e.g. St Louis zoological garden

Buildings

Two wings for the big cats: Denver, Colo. il Am City 80:24 Ja '65
ZOOLOGICAL models
Day of the dinosaur: Sinclair refining's exhibit at World's fair. il Bsns W p34-5 O 19 '63
Getting there is half the fun: dinosaur models for Sinclair's New York world's fair exhibit. H. B. Comstock. il Pop Sci 183:50-3 S '63
Monsters arrive for the World's fair: the dinosaurs invade. il Life 55:87-8+ D 6 '63
Return of the dinosaur; fiber-glass models for the World's fair. il Newsweek 62:76 S 16 '63
Take-apart trout; visible trout by Renwal products inc. C. Conley. il Field & S 69:97 N '64
World's fair dinosaurs; life-size for the Sinclair oil corp. exhibit. il Sci Digest 54: 48-9 Ag '63
ZOOLOGICAL research
Of toads and half-truths; zoology in the U.S. J. Speicher. Reporter 29:50+ O 10 '63
See also
Entomological research
Fishery research
ZOOLOGICAL society, New York. See New York zoological society
ZOOLOGICAL society of London
Letter from London. M. Panter-Downes. New Yorker 39:100+ Je 15 '63
ZOOLOGY
Zoology: Sixteenth international congress. G. B. Moment. Science 143:164-6 Ja 10 '64
See also
Animals
International congress of zoology
Ornithology

Classification

Molar size sequences and fossil taxonomy. S. M. Garn and others. bibliog il Science 142:1060 N 22 '63
Phylogenetic riddle; olive warbler. W. G. George. il Natur Hist 72:44-7 F '63

ZOOLOGY—*Continued*

Ecology

Habitat selection. S. C. Wecker. il Sci Am 211:109-16 O '64
See also
Animal populations

Africa

Jambo gasbag safari in Africa. A. Smith. il Sat Eve Post 236:40-7 N 9 '63
My life among wild chimpanzees. J. Goodall. il Nat Geog Mag 124:272-308 Ag '63

Africa, Central

Safari armed with microscopes; Unesco mission to the Congo. J. Balogh. il UNESCO Courier 17:24-7 O '64

Africa, East

To protect an African that was; Serengeti National Park and Ngorongoro conservation area. il N Y Times Mag p42-3 Ja 10 '65

Alaska

Kodiak bear war. J. Rearden. il Outdoor Life 134:17-19+ Ag '64

Antarctic Regions

Antarctic micrometazoa; fresh-water species in the McMurdo Sound area. E. C. Dougherty and L. G. Harris. bibliog il Science 140:497-8 My 3 '63

Arctic Regions

See also
Musk oxen

Australia

Tie me kangaroo, down. il Time 83:35 Mr 6 '64

Canada

See also
Zoology—Saskatchewan

Florida

Spring on a Florida river; photographs by S. Grossman; with account by M. L. Grossman. Sports Illus 20:38-44+ Mr 30 '64

Galápagos Islands

In Darwin's footsteps. il Newsweek 63:52 Ja 20 '64
Unusual Galápagos. B. Tufty. il Sci N L 85: 151 Mr 7 '64

Great Britain

Introduced menace: American gray squirrel threat to British woodlands. M. Shorten. il Natur Hist 73:42-9 bibliog(p67) D '64

Hawaii

Hawaiian monk seal; Leeward Islands. D. W. Rice. il Natur Hist 73:48-55 F '64

Malagasy

Madagascar lemurs: isolated primates. J. J. Petter. il Natur Hist 72:22-7 Mr '63

Nevada

Mystery ram of Dead Mountain; Nevada. C. E. Gillham. il Field & S 67:14+ Ap '63

New Zealand

Flightless birds face extinction. A. Scholes. il Sci N L 85:26 Ja 11 '64

Saskatchewan

Cycle of living. W. O. Pruitt, jr. il Holiday 33:32+ F '63

Surinam

Beastly place for a hunt. J. Olsen. il Sports Illus 21:62-6+ N 9 '64

Tanganyika

Anomalies in Africa: albino giraffe, and spotted zebra; photographs. L. D. Vesey-Fitzgerald. Natur Hist 73:54-5 D '64
Serengeti National Park; with editorial comment. E. Huxley. il Nat Parks Mag 38:2, 10-14 My '64

Texas

Biological visit to McKittrick Canyon. F. R. Gehlbach. il Nat Parks Mag 37:4-7 Mr '63

Tibet

Mystery ram of Dead Mountain; Nevada. C. E. Gillham. il Field & S 67:14+ Ap '63

United States

Top trophy of North America? G. Fitz. il Outdoor Life 133:17-21+ F '64

ZOOLOGY, Marine. See Marine fauna
ZOOM cameras. See Moving picture cameras
ZOOM lenses. See Lenses, Photographic
ZOONOSES. See Communicable diseases in animals
ZOOPLANKTON. See Plankton
ZOOS. See Zoological gardens
ZOOSPORES
Zoospores in scenedesmus obliquus. F. R. Trainor. bibliog il Science 142:1673-4 D 27 '63
ZOOXANTHELLA
Mass expulsion of zooxanthellae from Jamaican reef communities after hurricane Flora. T. F. Goreau. bibliog il Science 145: 383-6 Jl 24 '64
ZORGNIOTTI, Adrian W.
Death of a seamstress. Opera N 28:24-5 Mr 14 '64
ZORITCH, George
George Zoritch today. W. Como. il pors Dance Mag 38:48-51+ S '64
ZORK, Don
Big and old and just right for us. Am Home 67:38-41 Je '64
ZORNES, Milford
Watercolor page; with biographical sketch. il por Am Artist 27:36-7 N '63
ZORZA, Victor
How we can profit from the China-Soviet break. Look 27:49-50 N 19 '63
Khrushchev's losing fight with his marshals. Life 57:42-3+ N 6 '64
ZOYSIA. See Grasses
ZOYSIA Japonica. See Grasses
ZSEBOEK, Zoltan Balint
New aristocracy. il por Newsweek 64:39-40 Jl 27 '64
ZUBAY, Geoffrey
Molecular model for protein synthesis. bibliog Science 140:1092-5 Je 7 '63
ZUBEK, John P.
Counteracting effects of physical exercises performed during prolonged perceptual deprivation. bibliog Science 142:504-6 O 25 '63
—and Welch, G.
Electroencephalographic changes after prolonged sensory and perceptual deprivation. bibliog Science 139:1209-10 Mr 22 '63
—and Wilgosh, L.
Prolonged immobilization of the body: changes in performance and in the electroencephalogram. bibliog Science 140:306-8 Ap 19 '63
—and others
Cutaneous sensitivity after prolonged visual deprivation. bibliog Science 144:1591-3 Je 26 '64
Electroencephalographic changes during and after fourteen days of perceptual deprivation. bibliog Science 139:490-2 F 8 '63
ZUCK, Robert K.
Botanical field meeting. Science 145:1216 S 11 '64
ZUCKER, Isabel
Children grow in gardens. Pop Gard 15:34-5 Jl '64
ZUCKERMAN, Art
How to buy a tape recorder. por Pop Sci 185:98-102 Jl '64
Learn animation from the pros. Pop Phot 55:170-1+ N '64
Norelco 150 carry-corder. Pop Phot 55:58+ N '64
Sound track your home movies. Pop Mech 120:196-8 O '63
Sound with your pictures. Pop Phot 53:18+ Jl '63
Think small, it's bigger than you think! Pop Phot 55:107+ O '64
ZUCKERMAN, Harold
College and career. See issues of Senior scholastic
ZUCKERT, Eugene M.
Military space program; excerpts from address. Aviation W 78:17 Mr 25 '63
Zuckert discusses TFX, follow-on aircraft. Aviation W 79:18 S 2 '63
Zuckert gives views on aerospace issues; interview. por Aviation W 80:72-3 Mr 2 '64
about
Zuckert attacks AFA on test ban stand. Aviation W 79:31 S 16 '63
Zuckert defends F-111 winner selection. G. C. Wilson. Aviation W 78:301 Mr 11 '63
ZUKOFSKY, Celia, and Zukofsky, Louis
Versions of Catullus; poem. Poetry 105:155-60 D '64
ZUKOFSKY, Louis
A-17, a coronal; poem. Poetry 103:124-37 O '63

ZUKOFSKY, Louis—*Continued*
Old poet moves to a new apartment fourteen times: poem. Poetry 101:373-82 Mr '63
—See Zukofsky, C. jt. auth.

about

Beyond the heirlooms of tradition. A. Rich. Poetry 105:128-9 N '64
Touching sacred objects. W. Stafford. Poetry 102:117 My '63

ZUMBO, Jim
Nothing like it. Outdoor Life 134:28-31+ D '64

ZUMBRUN, Alvin J. T.
Maryland; a law-enforcement dilemma. bibliog f Ann Am Acad 347:58-66 My '63

ZURBARÁN, Francisco de
Zurbarán's claims to fame. J. M. Brown. il Art N 63:31-3+ Ja '65

ZURICH, Switzerland

Description

Public ugliness is not necessary. A. Klingler. il House B 106:96-9+ Jl '64
Step by step through Zurich. R. Deardorff. il Travel 120:33-4+ Jl '63

Music

Americans in Zurich. E. V. Epstein. il Opera N 28:32 Ap 18 '64

Stores

Alpine view of U.S.A; American fair at Jelmoli department store. il Bsns W p30-1 Mr 7 '64
There's more than one reason for going to Zurich. E. Gordon. House B 106:99+ Jl '64

ZURICH festival. See Music festivals—Switzerland

ZWEIFACH, Benjamin W. See Janoff, A. jt. auth.

ZWICK, Daan
All about grain. Pop Phot 52:56-63+ Ap '63

ZWICKY, Fritz
Chief watchman. W. Jonathan. por Sat R 47:43 Jl 4 '64

ZWINGLI, Ulrich
Third man. il por Time 84:56-7 Jl 17 '64

ZWIRZ, Bob
Miracle marabous. Field & S 67:54-5 Ap '63

ZWISLER, John R. See Lenhoff, H. M. jt. auth.

ZWOLAK, Vic
Nobody can help; dual meets and championship meets, cross country running. Newsweek 62:94 D 2 '63

ZYGMUND, George
How far have we gone? Mod Phot 27:48+ O; 100+ N '63

ZYGOTES
Control of growth in plant cells. F. C. Steward. il Sci Am 209:104-13 O '63

ZYLA, Nan
Jewels of the sea. Design 65:10-11+ S '63

ZYZNIEWSKI, Stanley J.
Futile compromise reconsidered: Wielopolski and Russian policy in the Congress Kingdom, 1861-1863. bibliog f Am Hist R 70:395-412 Ja '65

Gary Library [redacted]
0 0038 00004725

MONT [illegible] COLLEGE
MONTPELIER, VT.

WITHDRAWN